W9-AUR-284

Title section: lists the drug's commonly used brand names in both the United States and Canada.

Precautions: tells you what to avoid or be careful of when using the drug, and when medical supervision is required.

Proper use of this medicine: tells how to store and use the drug, including usual doses and information such as what to do if you miss a dose.

Additional Information: when necessary, gives details about other uses that are not shown in the product labeling.

Abacavir (Systemic)—Introductory Version   1

ABACAVIR Systemic— INTRODUCTORY VERSION

Commonly used brand name(s):

In the U.S.—
Ziagen

Description

Abacavir (a-BAK-a-veer) is used, in combination with other medicines, in the treatment of the infection caused by the human immunodeficiency virus (HIV). HIV is the virus that causes acquired immunodeficiency syndrome (AIDS).

Abacavir will not cure or prevent HIV infection or AIDS; however, it helps keep HIV from reproducing and appears to slow down the destruction of the immune system. This may help delay the development of problems usually related to AIDS or HIV disease. Abacavir will not keep you from spreading HIV to other people. People who receive this medicine may continue to have other problems usually related to AIDS or HIV disease.

This medicine is available only with your doctor's prescription, in the following dosage forms:

Oral
- Oral solution (U.S.)
- Tablets (U.S.)

Before Using This Medicine

In deciding to use a medicine, the risks of taking the medicine must be weighed against the good it will do. This is a decision you and your doctor will make. For abacavir, the following should be considered:

Allergies—Tell your doctor if you have ever had any unusual or allergic reaction to abacavir. *This medicine should not be taken if you have ever had an allergic reaction to it, because it could cause another severe reaction that may result in death.* Also tell your health care professional if you are allergic to any other substances, such as foods, preservatives, or dyes.

Pregnancy—Abacavir has not been studied in pregnant women. However, it has been found to cause birth defects and other problems in animals at doses many times the human dose. Before taking this medicine, make sure your doctor knows if you are pregnant or if you may become pregnant.

Breast-feeding—It is not known whether abacavir passes into breast milk. However, because of the possibility that this medicine could cause unwanted effects in nursing babies and the risk of passing HIV on to the infant, breast-feeding is usually not recommended.

Children—This medicine has been tested in children 3 months of age and older and, in effective doses, has not been shown to cause different side effects or problems than it does in adults.

Older adults—Many medicines have not been studied specifically in older people. Therefore, it may not be known whether they work exactly the same way they do in younger adults or if they cause different side effects or problems in older people. There is no specific information comparing use of abacavir in the elderly with use in other age groups.

Other medicines—Although certain medicines should not be used together at all, in other cases two different medicines may be used together even if an interaction might occur. In these cases, your doctor may want to change the dose, or other precautions may be necessary. Tell your health care professional if you are taking any other prescription or nonprescription (over-the-counter [OTC]) medicine.

Proper Use of This Medicine

Take this medicine exactly as directed by your doctor. Do not take it more often, and do not take it for a longer time than your doctor ordered.

Dosing—The dose of abacavir will be different for different patients. *Follow your doctor's orders or the directions on the label.* The following information includes only the average doses of abacavir. *If your dose is different, do not change it unless your doctor tells you to do so.*

- For *oral* dosage form (oral solution or tablets):
  —For HIV infection:
  - Adults and adolescents 16 years of age and older—300 milligrams (mg) two times a day.
  - Children 3 months to 16 years of age—Dose is based on body weight and must be determined by your doctor. The usual dose is 8 mg per kilogram (kg) (3.6 mg per pound) of body weight two times a day.

Missed dose—If you miss a dose of this medicine, take it as soon as you remember. However, if it is almost time for the next dose, skip the missed dose and go back to your regular dosing schedule. Do not double doses.

Storage—To store this medicine:
- Keep out of the reach of children.
- Store away from heat and direct light.
- Do not store in the bathroom, near the kitchen sink, or in other damp places. Heat or moisture may cause the medicine to break down.
- Keep the oral solution from freezing.
- Do not keep outdated medicine or medicine no longer needed. Be sure that any discarded medicine is out of the reach of children.

Precautions While Using This Medicine

This medicine may cause a severe allergic reaction in some patients. This reaction usually occurs within 6 weeks after the medicine is started but may occur at any time. If untreated, it can lead to severe low blood pressure and even death. *Stop taking this medicine and check with your doctor immediately if you notice sudden fever, skin rash, diarrhea, nausea, stomach pain, vomiting, or a feeling of unusual tiredness or illness, cough, shortness of breath, or sore throat.*

When you begin taking this medicine, you will be given a warning card which describes symptoms of severe allergic reactions that may be caused by abacavir. The warning card also provides information about how to treat these allergic reactions. For your safety, you should carry the warning card with you at all times.

Side Effects of This Medicine

Along with its needed effects, a medicine may cause some unwanted effects. Although not all of these side effects may occur, if they do occur they may need medical attention.

---

2   Acarbose (Systemic)—Introductory Version

Stop taking this medicine and get emergency help immediately if any of the following side effects occur:
  Less common
    Abdominal or stomach pain; cough; diarrhea; difficult or labored breathing; fever; headache; joint or muscle pain; nausea; numbness or tingling of hands, feet, or face; redness and soreness of eyes; shortness of breath; skin rash; sore throat; sores in mouth; swelling of feet or lower legs; vomiting; unusual feeling of discomfort or illness; unusual tiredness

Check with your doctor as soon as possible if any of the following side effects occur:
  Rare
    Abdominal swelling; decreased appetite; fast, shallow breathing; sleepiness

Other side effects may occur that usually do not need medical attention. These side effects may go away during treatment as your body adjusts to the medicine. However, check with your doctor if any of the following side effects continue or are bothersome:
  More common
    Headache
  Less common
    Trouble in sleeping

Other side effects not listed above may also occur in some patients. If you notice any other effects, check with your doctor.

Developed: 06/14/1999
Revised: 09/28/2000

ACARBOSE Systemic— INTRODUCTORY VERSION

Commonly used brand name(s):

In the U.S.—
Precose

Description

Acarbose (AY-car-bose) is used to treat a type of diabetes mellitus (sugar diabetes) called type 2 diabetes. Normally, your pancreas releases insulin into the blood stream after you eat. Insulin is used by all the cells in your body to help turn the food you eat into energy. This is done by using glucose (sugar) in the blood as quick energy. When you have type 2 diabetes, insulin is still produced by your pancreas, but the amount of insulin produced may not be enough or your body may not be using it properly and you may still need more. Because of this, the insulin is not able to lower your blood sugar properly and you will have too much sugar in your blood. Acarbose lowers your blood sugar by preventing the breakdown of starch into sugar. It may be used alone or in combination with another type of oral diabetes medicine called a sulfonylurea.

This medicine is available only with your doctor's prescription, in the following dosage form:

Oral
- Tablets (U.S.)

Before Using This Medicine

In deciding to use a medicine, the risks of taking the medicine must be weighed against the good it will do. This is a decision you and your doctor will make. For acarbose, the following should be considered:

Allergies—Tell your doctor if you have ever had any unusual or allergic reaction to acarbose. Also tell your health care professional if you are allergic to any other substances, such as foods, preservatives, or dyes.

Pregnancy—Acarbose has not been studied in pregnant women. However, it is easier during pregnancy to control your blood sugar by using injections of insulin rather than by taking acarbose. Close control of your blood sugar can reduce the chance of your baby gaining too much weight, having birth defects, or having high blood sugar before birth. Be sure to tell your doctor if you plan to become pregnant or you think you are pregnant.

Breast-feeding—It is not known whether acarbose passes into breast milk. However, acarbose is not recommended during breast-feeding.

Children—Studies on this medicine have been done only in adult patients, and there is no specific information comparing use of acarbose in children with use in other age groups.

Older adults—This medicine has been tested in a limited number of elderly people and has not been shown to cause different side effects or problems in older people than it does in younger adults.

Other medicines—Although certain medicines should not be used together at all, in other cases two different medicines may be used together even if an interaction might occur. In these cases, your doctor may want to change the dose, or other precautions may be necessary. When you are taking acarbose, it is especially important that your health care professional know if you are taking any of the following:
- Activated charcoal or
- Medicine for digestion that contains amylase or pancreatin (e.g., Creon)—Use of these medicines with acarbose may prevent acarbose from working properly

Other medical problems—The presence of other medical problems may affect the use of acarbose. Make sure you tell your doctor if you have any other medical problems, especially:
- Diabetic ketoacidosis or
- Fever or
- Infection or
- Surgery or
- Trauma—Insulin is needed to control these conditions
- Digestion problems or
- Inflammatory bowel disease or
- Intestinal blockage or
- Other intestinal problems—Acarbose should not be used
- Kidney disease (severe)—Higher blood levels of acarbose may occur; acarbose should not be used
- Liver disease—Acarbose may make this condition worse

Proper Use of This Medicine

Follow carefully the special meal plan your doctor gave you. This is the most important part of controlling your con-

---

Before using this medicine: explains what you and your health care professional should consider in advance, such as allergies and special diet restrictions.

Side effects: lists both common and rare side effects of the drug and whether they require medical attention.

Description: tells how to pronounce the drug's name, what the drug is used for, what dosage forms are available, and if a doctor must prescribe the drug.

Index
Guide

Index

The following excerpts are examples of the information included in the Index, which starts on page I1.

Brand name – manufacturer brand name is identified by *italics*.

- *Lanoxin*—Digoxin—*See* Digitalis Medicines (Systemic), 556, MC-8

Combination Listing – Includes a series of ingredients that act together.

Propoxyphene, Aspirin, and Caffeine —*See* Narcotic Analgesics and Aspirin (Systemic), 1069

Drug Effect – Identifies the drug's effect on the body. It is identified by parenthesis (e.g., topical, otic, nasal, systemic). A systemic effect would affect the entire body, topical - the skin, otic - the ears, nasal - the nose, ophthalmic - the eyes, etc.

Mometasone–*See* Corticosteroids–Medium to Very High Potency (Topical), 486; *See also* Corticosteroids (Nasal), 469

Mometasone (Nasal), 1032

Family Monograph Title – Groups multiple drugs into a common grouping. A reference to a family monograph typically appears in bold.

Bumetanide, 3265—*See Diuretics* (Systemic), 588, MC-4

Calcium Channel Blocking Agents (Systemic), 3265

Generic or common name – Identified by bold.

- **Fexofenadine (Systemic), 697, MC-11**

AZT—See Zidovudine (Systemic), 1563

Page number - Identifies the location of the drug entry in the first page of a drug entry, and/or the Additional Products and Uses appendix. If an image of a drug is included in the Medicine Chart, the page number will be preceded by "MC".

- *Relafen*—Nabumetone—*See* Anti-inflammatory Drugs, Nonsteroidal (Systemic), 171, MC-17

Pound sign – Identifies a drug not published in the printed version of the USP DI. Exclusions can be accessed on the USP DI Updates Online website. See the back cover of book for details on accessing the site.

Talc (Intrapleural-Local), #

'See' reference – Indicates that more information on a drug can be found in a single or family drug entry.

Monistat 7 Vaginal Suppositories—Miconazole— *See* Antifungals, Azole (Vaginal), 137

Single Entry Title - Includes one drug; each drug may have multiple brand names and common names but only one generic name.

- **Celecoxib (Systemic), 358, MC-6**

Square symbol – Precedes drug name and identifies a drug included in the Medicine Chart.

- **Sildenafil (Systemic), 1359, MC-21**

CONSUMER DRUG REFERENCE

2002 Edition

MICROMEDEX Thomson Healthcare and US Pharmacopeia

Consumer Reports
A Division of Consumers Union
Yonkers, New York

Library of Congress Catalog Card Number: 81-640842
ISBN: 0-89043-961-3

First Printing, November 2001

Manufactured in the United States of America

Published simultaneously by MICROMEDEX under the title USP DI. Volume II (Advice for the Patient)®,
Twenty-second Edition, 2002. Previous editions of this book appeared under the title United States
Pharmacopeia Drug Information for the Consumer.

The Consumer Drug Reference 2002, is published by Consumer Reports, a division of Consumers Union
of U.S., Inc. Consumers Union is an independent, nonprofit testing organization serving only
consumers. Since 1936, it has been a comprehensive source for unbiased reporting about products and
services, personal finance, health and nutrition, and other consumer concerns. It is chartered under the
Not-For-Profit Corporation Law of the State of New York. Consumers Union derives its income mainly from
the sale of Consumer Reports magazine and other publications and services, such as Consumer Reports
Online, Consumer Reports on Health, Consumer Reports Travel Letter, and annual publications like this.
Income is also derived from nonrestrictive, noncommercial contributions, grants, and fees.

Consumers Union accepts no advertising or product samples and is not beholden in any way to any
commercial or governmental interest. Its Ratings and reports are solely for the use of the readers of its
publications. Neither the Ratings nor the reports nor any Consumers Reports publication, including this
book, may be used in advertising or for any commercial purpose. Consumers Union will take all steps
available to it to prevent such uses of its material, its name, or the name of Consumer Reports.

NOTICE AND WARNING

Concerning U. S. Patent or Trademark Rights

The inclusion in Consumer Drug Reference of entry on any drug in respect to which patent or trademark
rights may exist shall not be deemed, and is not intended as, a grant of, or authority to exercise, any right
or privilege protected by such patent or trademark. All such rights and privileges are vested in the patent or
trademark owner, and no other person may exercise the same without express permission, authority, or
license secured from such patent or trademark owner.

The listing of selected brand names is intended only for ease of reference. The inclusion of a brand name
does not mean MICROMEDEX, the USPC, or Consumers Union has any particular knowledge that the
brand listed has properties different from other brands of the same drug, nor should it be interpreted as an
endorsement by MICROMEDEX, the USPC, or by Consumers Union. Similarly, the fact that a particular
brand has not been included does not indicate that the product has been judged to be unsatisfactory or
unacceptable.

Check the Index first. It's on page I-1.

Contents

Consumer Drug Reference

Foreword to the Consumer Reports Edition

Medicines that are safe, effective, and even lifesaving may also, ironically, become a source of serious trouble. In fact, harmful or adverse reactions to medications are one of the nation's leading killers—and are especially common among people who take multiple medications.

Some adverse reactions are unexpected, but most are well documented in the medical literature. Before taking any new medicine or combination of medicines, it's a good idea to question your doctor and/or pharmacist about the product. And it's also important for you to learn the key facts about any medication you are taking from an up-to-date, objective source, such as the Consumer Drug Reference 2002.

This volume is designed to make it easy for you to find the information you need about both prescription and over-the-counter medications. It comes from organizations with years of experience in bringing you health information. MICROMEDEX, a worldwide leader in health and safety databases, has developed this information in conjunction with the United States Pharmacopeia (USP), a not-for-profit organization that for many decades has set official standards for medical products in the United States. And Consumer Reports—in its own pages and in the pages of Consumer Reports on Health and other publications—has set the standard for authoritative, reliable, and unbiased reporting on health issues, along with product testing and buying guidance.

This reference work lists almost every medicine—prescription and nonprescription—available in the United States and Canada. It provides consumers with the most up-to-date information about drug usage and potential side effects. Organized alphabetically by generic or family name, each profile of a specific drug—more than 11,000 different brand and generic entries in all—lists indications, proper usage, precautions, side effects, different dosage forms, and common brand names. This book is thoroughly indexed according to both generic and brand names, making it easy to look up any medication. You'll find information on prescription drugs, like beta-blockers, over-the-counter remedies, such as calamine lotion, as well as nutritional supplements like vitamins and minerals.

Most important, unlike the information in other such books available to the consumer—notably the Physicians' Desk Reference—the information presented in this guide is not a mere replication of the drug manufacturers' package inserts. The Consumer Drug Reference 2002 has been assembled by consensus of many experts—physicians, pharmacists, pharmacologists, dentists, nurses, chemists, microbiologists, and other individuals particularly qualified to judge drugs—and is supported by 35 USP advisory panels representing differing medical specialties, health professionals, and consumers. The guide is constantly in revision, which allows it to contain the latest information on a particular drug, sometimes even before the information is readily available elsewhere.

Consumers can help in that review, too. Even the exacting approval process undertaken by the U.S. Food and Drug Administration cannot possibly predict all the side effects of drugs on the market. It's important that patients report any side effects of drugs to their physicians and those physicians relay the information to the FDA. That information, in turn, will find its way into future editions of the Consumer Drug Reference.

The Consumer Drug Reference 2002 is the most comprehensive drug-information book available to the public, and we are proud to present it to our readers.

To The Reader

When purchasing a medicine, whether over-the-counter (nonprescription) or with a doctor's prescription, you may have questions about its usefulness to you, the best way to take it, possible side effects, and precautions to take to avoid complications. For instance, some medicines should be taken with meals, others between meals. Some may make you drowsy while others may tend to keep you awake. Alcoholic or other beverages, other medicines, certain foods, or smoking may affect the way your medicine works. As for side effects, some are merely bothersome and may go away while others may require medical attention.

Consumer Drug Reference 2002 contains information that may provide general answers to some of your questions as well as suggestions for the correct use of your medicine. It is important to remember, however, that the human body is very complex and medicines may act differently on different people—and even in the same person at different times. If you want additional information about your medicine or its possible side effects, ask your doctor, nurse, pharmacist, or other health care provider. They are there to help you.

Notice:

The information about the drugs contained herein is general in nature and is intended to be used in consultation with your health care providers. It is not intended to replace specific instructions or directions or warnings given to you by your physician or other prescriber or accompanying a particular product. The information is selective and it is not claimed that it includes all known precautions, contraindications, effects, or interactions possibly related to the use of a drug. The information may differ from that contained in the product labeling which is required by law. The information is not sufficient to make an evaluation as to the risks and benefits of taking a particular drug in a particular case and is not medical advice for individual problems and should not alone be relied upon for these purposes. Since the inclusion or exclusion of particular information about a drug is judgmental in nature and since opinion as to drug usage may differ, you may wish to consult additional sources. Should you desire additional information or if you have any questions as to how this information may relate to you in particular, ask your doctor, nurse, pharmacist, or other health care provider.

Since new drugs are constantly being marketed and since previously unreported side effects, newly recognized precautions, or other new information for any given drug may come to light at any time, continuously updated drug information sources should be consulted as necessary. The Food and Drug Administration (FDA) maintains a web site of very recent FDA-approved labeling changes that the Consumer Drug Reference 2002 may not contain. The address for the FDA's website is www.fda.gov/medwatch/safety.htm.

There are many brands of drugs on the market. The listing of selected brand names is intended only for ease of reference. The inclusion of a brand name does not mean the authors have any particular knowledge that the brand listed has properties different from other brands of the same drug, nor should it be interpreted as an endorsement. Similarly, the fact that a brand name has not been included does not indicate that that particular brand has been judged to be unsatisfactory or unacceptable.

If any of the information in this book causes you special concern, do not decide against taking any medicine prescribed for you without first checking with your doctor.

How To Use This Book

Consumer Drug Reference 2002 contains a section of general information about the appropriate use of any medicine, as well as individual discussions of a wide variety of commonly and not so commonly used medicines. You should read both the general information and the information specific to the medicine you are taking. See page G-1 for this general information.

Each medicine has a generic name that all manufacturers who make that medicine must use. Some manufacturers also create a brand name to put on the label and to use in advertising. Look in the index for the generic name or the brand name of the medicine about which you have questions. We have put the generic names and common brand names in the same index, so you do not have to know whether the name you have is a generic name or a brand name. However, it is a good idea for you to learn both the generic and the brand names of the medicines you are using and to write them down and keep them for future use.

Although the informational entries generally appear in alphabetical order by generic name, there are numerous occasions when closely related medicines are grouped under a family name. Therefore, the surest way to quickly find the page number of the information about each medicine is to look in the index first.

The information for each medicine is presented according to the area of the body that is affected. As a general rule, information for one type of use will not be the same as for other types of use. For example, if you take tetracycline capsules by mouth for their systemic effect in treating an infection, the information will not be the same as for tetracycline ointment, which is applied directly to the skin for its topical effects. And both of these will be different from the information for tetracyclines used in the eye. The common divisions used in this publication are:
- BUCCAL—For general effects throughout the body when a medicine is placed in the cheek pocket, allowed to dissolve, and slowly absorbed.
- DENTAL—For local effects when applied to the teeth or gums.
- INHALATION—For local, and in some cases systemic, effects when inhaled into the lungs.

- INTRA-AMNIOTIC—For local effects when a medicine is injected into the sac that contains the fetus and amniotic fluid.
- INTRACAVERNOSAL—For local effects in the penis when a medicine is given by injection.
- LINGUAL—For general effects throughout the body when a medicine is absorbed through the lining of the mouth.
- MUCOSAL—For local effects when applied directly to mucous membranes (for example, the inside of the mouth).
- NASAL—For local effects when used in the nose.
- OPHTHALMIC—For local effects when applied directly to the eyes.
- ORAL-LOCAL—For local effects in the gastrointestinal tract when taken by mouth (i.e., not absorbed into the body).
- OTIC—For local effects when used in the ear.
- PARENTERAL-LOCAL—For local effects in a specific area of the body when given by injection.
- RECTAL—For local, and in some cases systemic, effects when used in the rectum.
- SUBLINGUAL—For general effects throughout the body when a medicine is placed under the tongue, allowed to dissolve, and slowly absorbed.
- SYSTEMIC—For general effects throughout the body; applies to most medicines when taken by mouth or given by injection or transdermal patch.
- TOPICAL—For local effects when applied directly to the skin.
- VAGINAL—For local, and in some cases systemic, effects when used in the vagina.

About USP

The United States Pharmacopeia (USP) is an independent, not-for-profit organization that sets the official standards of strength, quality, purity, packaging, and labeling for medical products used in the United States. Membership is composed of delegates from accredited colleges of medicine and pharmacy in the U.S.; state medical and pharmaceutical associations; many national associations concerned with medicines, such as the American Medical Association, the American Nurses Association, the American Dental Association, the National Community Pharmacists Association, and the American Pharmaceutical Association; and various departments of the federal government, including the Food and Drug Administration. Other members represent the public. USP was established 181 years ago, and is the only national body that represents the professions of both pharmacy and medicine.

The first convention came into being on January 1, 1820, and within the year published the first national drug formulary of the United States. The U.S. Pharmacopeia of 1820 contained 217 drug names, divided into two groups according to the level of general acceptance and usage.

Since 1974, MICROMEDEX, headquartered south of Denver, Colorado, has been the leading provider of clinical information and decision support tools within the healthcare community. Today, in over 9,000 facilities and more than 90 countries, MICROMEDEX knowledge bases are relied upon to provide current, comprehensive information on drugs, diseases, toxicology, alternative medicine, and patient education.

Together, USP and MICROMEDEX have the opportunity to expand the impact of authoritative USP DI® information by building on the strong MICROMEDEX foundation that exists throughout healthcare markets in the U.S. and internationally.

About USP DI

Consumer Drug Reference 2002 is Volume II of USP DI. Volume I contains drug use information in technical language for the physician, dentist, pharmacist, nurse, or other health care provider, and Volume II is its lay language counterpart for use by consumers. Volume III provides information on approved drug products and legal requirements. Together, the volumes form the foundation of a coordinated approach to drug-use education.

USP DI was first published in 1980. It is continuously reviewed and revised and is intended for use by prescribers, dispensers, and consumers of medications. The information represents the consensus of the USP Committee of Revision and its Advisory Panels and anyone, including users of medicines, may contribute through review and comment on drafts of the monographs when public availability is announced in USP DI Review.

Introductory Version monographs are included in this publication in order to provide information on newly approved medicines. These monographs are based primarily on the manufacturers' package inserts and have not gone through the full USP DI development process. They are meant to fill the immediate need for information on a temporary basis until a full monograph can be developed.

For further information about USP DI or to comment on how the information published in this volume might better meet your information needs, please contact: MICROMEDEX, 6200 S. Syracuse Way, Suite 300, Greenwood Village, CO 80111; telephone (303) 486-6400; telefax (303) 486-6464; Email: uspdi@mdx.com There are drugs for which monographs are not included in this published version of the USP DI database due to space constraints. Copies of the monographs are available on the MICROMEDEX website. See the inside back cover of this book for details on how to access the site.

Index

Brand names are in *italics*. There are many brands of drugs and the listing of selected American and Canadian brand names in this index are intended only for ease of reference. There are additional brands that have not been included in the book. The inclusion of a brand name does not mean the authors have any particular knowledge that the brand listed has properties different from other brands of the same drug, nor should it be interpreted as an endorsement. Similarly, the fact that a particular brand has not been included does not indicate that the product has been judged to be unsatisfactory or unacceptable. The page numbers MC-1 to MC-24 refer to the product identification photographs in The Medicine Chart.

— Drugs for which monographs are not included in this published version of the *USP DI* database due to space constraints. Copies of the monographs are available on the MICROMEDEX *USP DI* Updates Online website. See the back cover of this book for details on how to access the site.

A

Abacavir (Systemic), 1
Abacavir, Lamivudine, and Zidovudine (Systemic), 1629
Abbokinase— See Thrombolytic Agents (Systemic), 1501
Abbokinase Open-Cath— See Thrombolytic Agents (Systemic), 1501
ABELCET— See Amphotericin B Lipid Complex (Systemic), 59
Abenol— See Acetaminophen (Systemic), 4
Abitrate— See Clofibrate (Systemic), 459
Abreva— See Docosanol (Topical), 648
Acarbose (Systemic), 2, MC-1
A.C.&C.— See Narcotic Analgesics and Aspirin (Systemic), 1142
Accolate— See Zafirlukast (Systemic), 1589, MC-24
Accupep HPF— See Enteral Nutrition Formulas (Systemic), #
Accupril— See Angiotensin-converting Enzyme (ACE) Inhibitors (Systemic), 90, MC-20
Accuretic— See Angiotensin-converting Enzyme (ACE) Inhibitors and Hydrochlorothiazide (Systemic), 94
Accutane— See Isotretinoin (Systemic), 944, MC-12
Accutane Roche— See Isotretinoin (Systemic), 944
Acebutolol— See Beta-adrenergic Blocking Agents (Systemic), 272
ACE Inhibitors— See Angiotensin-converting Enzyme (ACE) Inhibitors (Systemic), 90
ACE Inhibitors and Hydrochlorothiazide— See Angiotensin-converting Enzyme (ACE) Inhibitors and Hydrochlorothiazide (Systemic), 94
Acel-Imune— See Diphtheria and Tetanus Toxoids and Pertussis Vaccine Adsorbed (Systemic), 619
Acellular DTP— See Diphtheria and Tetanus Toxoids and Pertussis Vaccine Adsorbed (Systemic), 619
Acenocoumarol— See Anticoagulants (Systemic), 112
Aceon— See Angiotensin-converting Enzyme (ACE) Inhibitors (Systemic), 90
Acet-2— See Narcotic Analgesics and Acetaminophen (Systemic), 1138
Acet-3— See Narcotic Analgesics and Acetaminophen (Systemic), 1138
Aceta Elixir— See Acetaminophen (Systemic), 4
Acetaminophen (Systemic), 4, MC-1

Acetaminophen, Aspirin, and Caffeine— See Acetaminophen and Salicylates (Systemic), 6
Acetaminophen, Aspirin, and Caffeine, Buffered— See Acetaminophen and Salicylates (Systemic), 6
Acetaminophen, Aspirin, Salicylamide, and Caffeine— See Acetaminophen and Salicylates (Systemic), 6
Acetaminophen and Caffeine— See Acetaminophen (Systemic), 4
Acetaminophen and Codeine— See Narcotic Analgesics and Acetaminophen (Systemic), 1138, MC-1
Acetaminophen, Codeine, and Caffeine— See Narcotic Analgesics and Acetaminophen (Systemic), 1138
Acetaminophen, Salicylamide, and Caffeine— See Acetaminophen and Salicylates (Systemic), 6
Acetaminophen and Salicylates (Systemic), 6
Acetaminophen, Sodium Bicarbonate, and Citric Acid (Systemic), 11
Acetaminophen Uniserts— See Acetaminophen (Systemic), 4
Aceta Tablets— See Acetaminophen (Systemic), 4
Acetazolam— See Carbonic Anhydrase Inhibitors (Systemic), 373
Acetazolamide— See Carbonic Anhydrase Inhibitors (Systemic), 373
Acet Codeine 30— See Narcotic Analgesics and Acetaminophen (Systemic), 1138
Acet Codeine 60— See Narcotic Analgesics and Acetaminophen (Systemic), 1138
Acetocot— See Corticosteroids—Glucocorticoid Effects (Systemic), 513
Acetohexamide— See Antidiabetic Agents, Sulfonylurea (Systemic), 131
Acetoxyl 2.5 Gel— See Benzoyl Peroxide (Topical), 265
Acetoxyl 5 Gel— See Benzoyl Peroxide (Topical), 265
Acetoxyl 10 Gel— See Benzoyl Peroxide (Topical), 265
Acetoxyl 20 Gel— See Benzoyl Peroxide (Topical), 265
Acetylcysteine (Inhalation), 14
Acetylsalicylic acid— See Salicylates (Systemic), 1394
Achromycin— See Tetracyclines (Topical), #
Achromycin V— See Tetracyclines (Systemic), 1487
Aciclovir— See Acyclovir (Systemic), 18; See Acyclovir (Topical), 20
Acilac— See Laxatives (Oral), 964
AcipHex— See Rabeprazole (Systemic), 1346, MC-20

Acitretin (Systemic), 15
Aclophen— See Antihistamines, Decongestants, and Analgesics (Systemic), 164
Aclovate— See Corticosteroids—Low Potency (Topical), 518
Acne-Aid Aqua Gel— See Benzoyl Peroxide (Topical), 265
Acne Aid 10 Cream— See Benzoyl Peroxide (Topical), 265
Acne-Aid Gel— See Resorcinol and Sulfur (Topical), #
Acne-Aid Vanishing Cream— See Benzoyl Peroxide (Topical), 265
Acne Lotion 10— See Alcohol and Sulfur (Topical), #
Acnomel Acne Cream— See Resorcinol and Sulfur (Topical), #
Acnomel B.P. 5 Lotion— See Benzoyl Peroxide (Topical), 265
Acnomel Cake— See Resorcinol and Sulfur (Topical), #
Acnomel Cream— See Resorcinol and Sulfur (Topical), #
Acnomel Vanishing Cream— See Resorcinol and Sulfur (Topical), #
Acridynil anisidide— See Amsacrine (Systemic), 64
Acrivastine and Pseudoephedrine— See Antihistamines and Decongestants (Systemic), 159
Act— See Histamine H₂-receptor Antagonists (Systemic), 863
Actagen— See Antihistamines and Decongestants (Systemic), 159
Actagen-C Cough— See Cough/Cold Combinations (Systemic), 522
Actamin— See Acetaminophen (Systemic), 4
Actamin Extra— See Acetaminophen (Systemic), 4
Actamin Super— See Acetaminophen (Systemic), 4
Act-Hib— See Haemophilus b Conjugate Vaccine (Systemic), 848
Actibine— See Yohimbine (Systemic), 1588
Acticin Cream— See Permethrin (Topical), 1266
Acticort 100— See Corticosteroids—Low Potency (Topical), 518
Actidose-Aqua— See Charcoal, Activated (Oral), 395
Actidose with Sorbitol— See Charcoal, Activated (Oral), 395
Actifed— See Antihistamines and Decongestants (Systemic), 159
Actifed Allergy Nighttime Caplets— See Antihistamines and Decongestants (Systemic), 159
Actifed with Codeine Cough— See Cough/Cold Combinations (Systemic), 522

Aminophylline— *See* Bronchodilators, Theophylline (Systemic), 314

Aminosalicylate Sodium (Systemic), #

5-aminosalicylic acid— *See* Mesalamine (Oral), 1056; *See* Mesalamine (Rectal), #

Amiodarone (Systemic), 48, MC-1

Ami Rax— *See* Theophylline, Ephedrine, and Hydroxyzine (Systemic), #

Ami-Tex— *See* Cough/Cold Combinations (Systemic), 522

Ami-Tex LA— *See* Cough/Cold Combinations (Systemic), 522

Amitone— *See* Antacids (Oral), 98; *See* Calcium Supplements (Systemic), 353

Amitriptyline— *See* Antidepressants, Tricyclic (Systemic), 126, MC-1, MC-2

Amlexanox (Mucosal-Local), 49

Amlodipine (Systemic), 50, MC-2

Amlodipine and Benazepril (Systemic), 52, MC-2

Ammonia N 13— *See* Radiopharmaceuticals (Diagnostic), 1347

Ammonia Spirit, Aromatic (Inhalation), #

Ammoniated Mercury (Topical), #

Ammonium Molybdate— *See* Molybdenum Supplements (Systemic), #

Amobarbital— *See* Barbiturates (Systemic), 239

Amoxapine— *See* Antidepressants, Tricyclic (Systemic), 126

Amoxicillin— *See* Penicillins (Systemic), 1251, MC-2

Amoxicillin and Clavulanate— *See* Penicillins and Beta-lactamase Inhibitors (Systemic), 1258, MC-2

Amoxil— *See* Penicillins (Systemic), 1251, MC-2

Amphetamine— *See* Amphetamines (Systemic), 54

Amphetamine and Dextroamphetamine— *See* Amphetamines (Systemic), 54, MC-2

Amphetamines (Systemic), 54

Amphocin— *See* Amphotericin B (Systemic), 57

Amphojel— *See* Antacids (Oral), 98

Amphojel 500— *See* Antacids (Oral), 98

Amphojel Plus— *See* Antacids (Oral), 98

Amphotec— *See* Amphotericin B Cholesteryl Complex (Systemic), 58

Amphotericin B (Systemic), 57

Amphotericin B (Topical), #

Amphotericin B Cholesteryl Complex (Systemic), 58

Amphotericin B Lipid Complex (Systemic), 59

Amphotericin B Liposomal Complex (Systemic), 61

Ampicillin— *See* Penicillins (Systemic), 1251, MC-2

Ampicillin and Sulbactam— *See* Penicillins and Beta-lactamase Inhibitors (Systemic), 1258

Ampicin— *See* Penicillins (Systemic), 1251

Amprenavir (Systemic), 62

Amsacrine (Systemic), 64

Amsa P-D— *See* Amsacrine (Systemic), 64

Amyl Nitrite (Systemic), #

Amytal— *See* Barbiturates (Systemic), 239

Anabolic Steroids (Systemic), 66

Anacin— *See* Salicylates (Systemic), 1394

Anacin-3— *See* Acetaminophen (Systemic), 4

Anacin Caplets— *See* Salicylates (Systemic), 1394

Anacin with Codeine— *See* Narcotic Analgesics and Aspirin (Systemic), 1142

Anacin Extra Strength— *See* Salicylates (Systemic), 1394

Anacin-3 Extra Strength— *See* Acetaminophen (Systemic), 4

Anacin Maximum Strength— *See* Salicylates (Systemic), 1394

Anacin Tablets— *See* Salicylates (Systemic), 1394

Anacobin— *See* Vitamin B_{12} (Systemic), 1575

Anadrol-50— *See* Anabolic Steroids (Systemic), 66

Anaflex 750— *See* Salicylates (Systemic), 1394

Anafranil— *See* Antidepressants, Tricyclic (Systemic), 126

Anagrelide (Systemic), 69

Ana-Guard— *See* Bronchodilators, Adrenergic (Oral/Injection), 310

Analgesic Otic— *See* Antipyrine and Benzocaine (Otic), 192

Anamine— *See* Antihistamines and Decongestants (Systemic), 159

Anamine HD— *See* Cough/Cold Combinations (Systemic), 522

Anamine T.D.— *See* Antihistamines and Decongestants (Systemic), 159

Anandron— *See* Antiandrogens, Nonsteroidal (Systemic), 104

Anaplex HD— *See* Cough/Cold Combinations (Systemic), 522

Anapolon 50— *See* Anabolic Steroids (Systemic), 66

Anaprox— *See* Anti-inflammatory Drugs, Nonsteroidal (Systemic), 179

Anaprox DS— *See* Anti-inflammatory Drugs, Nonsteroidal (Systemic), 179

Anaspaz— *See* Anticholinergics/Antispasmodics (Systemic), 106

Anastrozole (Systemic), 70

Anatuss— *See* Cough/Cold Combinations (Systemic), 522

Anatuss with Codeine— *See* Cough/Cold Combinations (Systemic), 522

Anatuss DM— *See* Cough/Cold Combinations (Systemic), 522

Anatuss LA— *See* Cough/Cold Combinations (Systemic), 522

Anbesol, Baby— *See* Anesthetics (Dental), 80

Anbesol Baby Jel— *See* Anesthetics (Dental), 80

Anbesol Gel— *See* Anesthetics (Dental), 80

Anbesol Liquid— *See* Anesthetics (Dental), 80

Anbesol Maximum Strength Gel— *See* Anesthetics (Dental), 80

Anbesol Maximum Strength Liquid— *See* Anesthetics (Dental), 80

Anbesol Regular Strength Gel— *See* Anesthetics (Dental), 80

Anbesol Regular Strength Liquid— *See* Anesthetics (Dental), 80

Ancalixir— *See* Barbiturates (Systemic), 239

Ancef— *See* Cephalosporins (Systemic), 387

Ancobon— *See* Flucytosine (Systemic), 771

Ancotil— *See* Flucytosine (Systemic), 771

Andec— *See* Antihistamines and Decongestants (Systemic), 159

Andec-TR— *See* Antihistamines and Decongestants (Systemic), 159

Andrest 90-4— *See* Androgens and Estrogens (Systemic), 76

Andriol— *See* Androgens (Systemic), 71

Androcur— *See* Cyproterone (Systemic), 556

Androderm— *See* Androgens (Systemic), 71

Andro-Estro 90-4— *See* Androgens and Estrogens (Systemic), 76

AndroGel 1%— *See* Androgens (Systemic), 71

Androgens (Systemic), 71

Androgens and Estrogens (Systemic), 76

Androgyn L.A.— *See* Androgens and Estrogens (Systemic), 76

Android— *See* Androgens (Systemic), 71

Android-F— *See* Androgens (Systemic), 71

Andro L.A. 200— *See* Androgens (Systemic), 71

Andronate 100— *See* Androgens (Systemic), 71

Andronate 200— *See* Androgens (Systemic), 71

Andropository 200— *See* Androgens (Systemic), 71

Andryl 200— *See* Androgens (Systemic), 71

Anergan 25— *See* Antihistamines, Phenothiazine-derivative (Systemic), 173

Anergan 50— *See* Antihistamines, Phenothiazine-derivative (Systemic), 173

Anesthetics (Dental), 80

Anesthetics (Ophthalmic), #

Anesthetics (Parenteral-Local), 83

Anesthetics (Rectal), 85

Anesthetics (Topical), 88

Anesthetics, General (Systemic), #

Anexsia 5/500— *See* Narcotic Analgesics and Acetaminophen (Systemic), 1138

Anexsia 7.5/650— *See* Narcotic Analgesics and Acetaminophen (Systemic), 1138

Angiotensin-converting Enzyme (ACE) Inhibitors (Systemic), 90

Angiotensin-converting Enzyme (ACE) Inhibitors and Hydrochlorothiazide (Systemic), 94

Anileridine— *See* Narcotic Analgesics— For Pain Relief (Systemic), 1147

Aniline violet— *See* Methylene Blue (Systemic), 1077

Anisindione— *See* Anticoagulants (Systemic), 112

Anisotropine— *See* Anticholinergics/Antispasmodics (Systemic), 106

Anisoylated plasminogen-streptokinase activator complex— *See* Thrombolytic Agents (Systemic), 1501

Anistreplase— *See* Thrombolytic Agents (Systemic), 1501

Anolor-300— *See* Butalbital and Acetaminophen (Systemic), 324

Anolor DH 5— *See* Narcotic Analgesics and Acetaminophen (Systemic), 1138

Anoquan— *See* Butalbital and Acetaminophen (Systemic), 324

Benazepril and Hydrochlorothiazide— *See* Angiotensin-converting Enzyme (ACE) Inhibitors and Hydrochlorothiazide (Systemic), 94, MC-3

Bendroflumethiazide— *See* Diuretics, Thiazide (Systemic), 642

Benefix— See Factor IX (Systemic), 751

Benemid— See Probenecid (Systemic), 1311

Benoxyl 5 Lotion— See Benzoyl Peroxide (Topical), 265

Benoxyl 10 Lotion— See Benzoyl Peroxide (Topical), 265

Benoxyl 20 Lotion— See Benzoyl Peroxide (Topical), 265

Bensulfoid Cream— See Resorcinol and Sulfur (Topical), #

Bentiromide (Diagnostic), 255

Bentoquatam (Topical), 256

Bentyl— See Anticholinergics/Antispasmodics (Systemic), 106

Bentylol— See Anticholinergics/Antispasmodics (Systemic), 106

Benuryl— See Probenecid (Systemic), 1311

Benxyl 5 Lotion— See Benzoyl Peroxide (Topical), 265

Benxyl 10 Lotion— See Benzoyl Peroxide (Topical), 265

Benxyl 20 Lotion— See Benzoyl Peroxide (Topical), 265

Benylin Adult Formula Cough Suppressant— See Dextromethorphan (Systemic), 592

Benylin Codeine D-E— See Cough/Cold Combinations (Systemic), 522

Benylin Decongestant— See Pseudoephedrine (Systemic), 1334

Benylin DM— See Dextromethorphan (Systemic), 592

Benylin DM for children— See Dextromethorphan (Systemic), 592

Benylin DM for Children 12 Hour— See Dextromethorphan (Systemic), 592

Benylin DM-D— See Cough/Cold Combinations (Systemic), 522

Benylin DM-D for Children— See Cough/Cold Combinations (Systemic), 522

Benylin DM-D-E— See Cough/Cold Combinations (Systemic), 522

Benylin DM-D-E Extra Strength— See Cough/Cold Combinations (Systemic), 522

Benylin DM-E— See Cough/Cold Combinations (Systemic), 522

Benylin DM-E Extra Strength— See Cough/Cold Combinations (Systemic), 522

Benylin DM 12 Hour— See Dextromethorphan (Systemic), 592

Benylin-E— See Guaifenesin (Systemic), 844

Benylin Expectorant— See Cough/Cold Combinations (Systemic), 522

Benylin 4 Flu— See Cough/Cold Combinations (Systemic), 522

Benylin Multi-Symptom— See Cough/Cold Combinations (Systemic), 522

Benylin Pediatric Cough Suppressant— See Dextromethorphan (Systemic), 592

Benzac AC 2½ Gel— See Benzoyl Peroxide (Topical), 265

Benzac AC 5 Gel— See Benzoyl Peroxide (Topical), 265

Benzac AC 10 Gel— See Benzoyl Peroxide (Topical), 265

Benzac AC Wash 10— See Benzoyl Peroxide (Topical), 265

Benzac AC Wash 2½ Gel— See Benzoyl Peroxide (Topical), 265

Benzac 5 Gel— See Benzoyl Peroxide (Topical), 265

Benzac 10 Gel— See Benzoyl Peroxide (Topical), 265

Benzacot— See Trimethobenzamide (Systemic), #

Benzac W 2½ Gel— See Benzoyl Peroxide (Topical), 265

Benzac W 5 Gel— See Benzoyl Peroxide (Topical), 265

Benzac W 10 Gel— See Benzoyl Peroxide (Topical), 265

Benzac W Wash 5— See Benzoyl Peroxide (Topical), 265

Benzac W Wash 10— See Benzoyl Peroxide (Topical), 265

5 Benzagel— See Benzoyl Peroxide (Topical), 265

10 Benzagel— See Benzoyl Peroxide (Topical), 265

2½ Benzagel Acne Gel— See Benzoyl Peroxide (Topical), 265

5 Benzagel Acne Gel— See Benzoyl Peroxide (Topical), 265

10 Benzagel Acne Gel— See Benzoyl Peroxide (Topical), 265

2½ Benzagel Acne Lotion— See Benzoyl Peroxide (Topical), 265

5 Benzagel Acne Lotion— See Benzoyl Peroxide (Topical), 265

5 Benzagel Acne Wash— See Benzoyl Peroxide (Topical), 265

5 Benzagel Liquid Acne Soap— See Benzoyl Peroxide (Topical), 265

Benzalkonium Chloride— *See* Spermicides (Vaginal), 1428

Benzamycin— See Erythromycin and Benzoyl Peroxide (Topical), 708

Benzatropine— *See* Antidyskinetics (Systemic), 137

Benzfetamine— *See* Appetite Suppressants, Sympathomimetic (Systemic), 197

Benzhexol— *See* Antidyskinetics (Systemic), 137

Benznidazole (Systemic), #

Benzocaine— *See* Anesthetics (Dental), 80; *See* Anesthetics (Rectal), 85; *See* Anesthetics (Topical), 88

Benzocaine and Menthol— *See* Anesthetics (Dental), 80; *See* Anesthetics (Topical), 88

Benzocaine and Phenol— *See* Anesthetics (Dental), 80

Benzodent— See Anesthetics (Dental), 80

Benzodiazepines (Systemic), 257

Benzonatate (Systemic), 264, MC-3

Benzoporphyrin Derivative— *See* Verteporfin (Parenteral-Local), 1560

Benzoyl Peroxide (Topical), 265

Benzphetamine— *See* Appetite Suppressants, Sympathomimetic (Systemic), 197

Benztropine— *See* Antidyskinetics (Systemic), 137, MC-3

Benzyl Benzoate (Topical), 268

Bepridil— *See* Calcium Channel Blocking Agents (Systemic), 349

Berlin blue— See Prussian Blue (Oral), #

Berotec— See Bronchodilators, Adrenergic (Inhalation), 304

Beta-2— See Bronchodilators, Adrenergic (Inhalation), 304

Beta-adrenergic Blocking Agents (Ophthalmic), 270

Beta-adrenergic Blocking Agents (Systemic), 272

Beta-adrenergic Blocking Agents and Thiazide Diuretics (Systemic), 278

Beta-carotene (Systemic), 282

Betacort Scalp Lotion— See Corticosteroids—Medium to Very High Potency (Topical), 520

Betaderm— See Corticosteroids—Medium to Very High Potency (Topical), 520

Betaderm Scalp Lotion— See Corticosteroids—Medium to Very High Potency (Topical), 520

Betagan— See Beta-adrenergic Blocking Agents (Ophthalmic), 270

Beta-HC— See Corticosteroids—Low Potency (Topical), 518

Betaine (Systemic), 284

Betaloc— See Beta-adrenergic Blocking Agents (Systemic), 272

Betaloc Durules— See Beta-adrenergic Blocking Agents (Systemic), 272

Betamethasone— *See* Corticosteroids (Ophthalmic), 505; *See* Corticosteroids (Otic), 507; *See* Corticosteroids (Rectal), 509; *See* Corticosteroids—Glucocorticoid Effects (Systemic), 513; *See* Corticosteroids—Medium to Very High Potency (Topical), 520

Betapace— See Beta-adrenergic Blocking Agents (Systemic), 272, MC-21

Betapen-VK— See Penicillins (Systemic), 1251

Betaseron— See Interferon Beta-1b (Injection), 918

Betatrex— See Corticosteroids—Medium to Very High Potency (Topical), 520

Beta-Val— See Corticosteroids—Medium to Very High Potency (Topical), 520

Betaxin— See Thiamine (Vitamin B₁) (Systemic), 1494

Betaxolol— *See* Beta-adrenergic Blocking Agents (Ophthalmic), 270; *See* Beta-adrenergic Blocking Agents (Systemic), 272

Betaxon— See Beta-adrenergic Blocking Agents (Ophthalmic), 270

Betaxon— See Levobetaxolol (Ophthalmic), 982

Bethanechol (Systemic), 285

Betimol— See Beta-adrenergic Blocking Agents (Ophthalmic), 270

Betnesol— See Corticosteroids (Ophthalmic), 505; *See* Corticosteroids (Otic), 507; *See* Corticosteroids—Glucocorticoid Effects (Systemic), 513

Betnetsol— See Corticosteroids (Rectal), 509

Betnovate— See Corticosteroids—Medium to Very High Potency (Topical), 520

Betnovate-½— See Corticosteroids—Medium to Very High Potency (Topical), 520

Betoptic— See Beta-adrenergic Blocking Agents (Ophthalmic), 270

Betoptic S— See Beta-adrenergic Blocking Agents (Ophthalmic), 270

Bewon— See Thiamine (Vitamin B₁) (Systemic), 1494

Bexarotene (Systemic), 286

Biamine— *See* Thiamine (Vitamin B₁) (Systemic), 1494

BIAVAX II— *See* Rubella and Mumps Virus Vaccine Live (Systemic), #

Biaxin— *See* Clarithromycin (Systemic), 447, MC-6

Bicalutamide— *See* Antiandrogens, Nonsteroidal (Systemic), 104

Bicholate Lilas— *See* Laxatives (Oral), 964

Bicillin L-A— *See* Penicillins (Systemic), 1251

Bicitra— *See* Citrates (Systemic), 443

BiCNU— *See* Carmustine (Systemic), 380

Bifenabid— *See* Probucol (Systemic), 1316

Bilagog— *See* Laxatives (Oral), 964

Bilax— *See* Laxatives (Oral), 964

Bilivist— *See* Cholecystographic Agents, Oral (Diagnostic), 421

Bilopaque— *See* Cholecystographic Agents, Oral (Diagnostic), 421

Biloptin— *See* Cholecystographic Agents, Oral (Diagnostic), 421

Biltricide— *See* Praziquantel (Systemic), #

Bimatoprost (Ophthalmic), 1629

BioCal— *See* Calcium Supplements (Systemic), 353

Bioclate— *See* Antihemophilic Factor (Systemic), 151

Biohisdex DM— *See* Cough/Cold Combinations (Systemic), 522

Biohisdine DM— *See* Cough/Cold Combinations (Systemic), 522

Biohist-LA— *See* Antihistamines and Decongestants (Systemic), 159

Bion Tears— *See* Hydroxypropyl Methylcellulose (Ophthalmic), 880

Bio-Syn— *See* Corticosteroids—Medium to Very High Potency (Topical), 520

Biotin (Systemic), 289

Biotirmone— *See* Dextrothyroxine (Systemic), 594

Bio-Well— *See* Lindane (Topical), 993

Biperiden— *See* Antidyskinetics (Systemic), 137

Biphetane DC Cough— *See* Cough/Cold Combinations (Systemic), 522

Biquin Durules— *See* Quinidine (Systemic), 1341

Bisac-Evac— *See* Laxatives (Oral), 964

Bisacodyl— *See* Laxatives (Oral), 964; *See* Laxatives (Rectal), 970

Bisacodyl and Docusate— *See* Laxatives (Oral), 964

Bisacolax— *See* Laxatives (Oral), 964; *See* Laxatives (Rectal), 970

Bisco-Lax— *See* Laxatives (Rectal), 970

Bismatrol— *See* Bismuth Subsalicylate (Oral), 290

Bismatrol Extra Strength— *See* Bismuth Subsalicylate (Oral), 290

Bismed— *See* Bismuth Subsalicylate (Oral), 290

Bismuth Subsalicylate (Oral), 290

Bismuth Subsalicylate, Metronidazole, and Tetracycline—For *H. pylori* (Systemic), 292

Bisoprolol— *See* Beta-adrenergic Blocking Agents (Systemic), 272, MC-3

Bisoprolol and Hydrochlorothiazide— *See* Beta-adrenergic Blocking Agents and Thiazide Diuretics (Systemic), 278, MC-3

Bitolterol— *See* Bronchodilators, Adrenergic (Inhalation), 304

Black-Draught— *See* Laxatives (Oral), 964

Black-Draught Lax-Senna— *See* Laxatives (Oral), 964

Blenoxane— *See* Bleomycin (Systemic), 295

Bleomycin (Systemic), 295

Bleph-10— *See* Sulfonamides (Ophthalmic), 1445

Blistex Daily Conditioning Treatment for Lips— *See* Sunscreen Agents (Topical), #

Blistex Medicated Lip Conditioner— *See* Sunscreen Agents (Topical), #

Blistex Medicated Lip Conditioner with Sunscreen— *See* Sunscreen Agents (Topical), #

Blistex Regular— *See* Sunscreen Agents (Topical), #

Blistex Sunblock— *See* Sunscreen Agents (Topical), #

Blistex Ultraprotection— *See* Sunscreen Agents (Topical), #

Blocadren— *See* Beta-adrenergic Blocking Agents (Systemic), 272

Blue— *See* Pyrethrins and Piperonyl Butoxide (Topical), 1336

Bonamine— *See* Meclizine/Buclizine/Cyclizine (Systemic), 1038

Bonefos— *See* Clodronate (Systemic), 456

Bonine— *See* Meclizine/Buclizine/Cyclizine (Systemic), 1038

Bontril PDM— *See* Appetite Suppressants, Sympathomimetic (Systemic), 197

Bontril Slow-Release— *See* Appetite Suppressants, Sympathomimetic (Systemic), 197

Botox— *See* Botulinum Toxin Type A (Parenteral-Local), 296

Botulinum Toxin Type A (Parenteral-Local), 296

Botulinum Toxin Type B (Parenteral-Local), 298

BQ Cold— *See* Antihistamines, Decongestants, and Analgesics (Systemic), 164

Breonesin— *See* Guaifenesin (Systemic), 844

Brethaire— *See* Bronchodilators, Adrenergic (Inhalation), 304

Brethine— *See* Bronchodilators, Adrenergic (Oral/Injection), 310, MC-22

Brevicon— *See* Estrogens and Progestins (Oral Contraceptives) (Systemic), 729

Brevicon 0.5/35— *See* Estrogens and Progestins (Oral Contraceptives) (Systemic), 729

Brevicon 1/35— *See* Estrogens and Progestins (Oral Contraceptives) (Systemic), 729

Brevital— *See* Anesthetics, General (Systemic), #

Brevoxl-4-Cleansing Lotion— *See* Benzoyl Peroxide (Topical), 265

Brevoxl-8-Cleansing Lotion— *See* Benzoyl Peroxide (Topical), 265

Brevoxl-4-Gel— *See* Benzoyl Peroxide (Topical), 265

Brevoxl-8-Gel— *See* Benzoyl Peroxide (Topical), 265

Brexin-L.A.— *See* Antihistamines and Decongestants (Systemic), 159

Bricanyl— *See* Bronchodilators, Adrenergic (Oral/Injection), 310

Bricanyl Turbuhaler— *See* Bronchodilators, Adrenergic (Inhalation), 304

Brietal— *See* Anesthetics, General (Systemic), #

Brimonidine (Ophthalmic), 299

Brinzolamide (Ophthalmic), 300

Brofed Liquid— *See* Antihistamines and Decongestants (Systemic), 159

Bromadrine PD— *See* Antihistamines and Decongestants (Systemic), 159

Bromadrine TR— *See* Antihistamines and Decongestants (Systemic), 159

Bromaline— *See* Antihistamines and Decongestants (Systemic), 159

Bromanate— *See* Antihistamines and Decongestants (Systemic), 159

Bromanate DC Cough— *See* Cough/Cold Combinations (Systemic), 522

Bromanyl— *See* Cough/Cold Combinations (Systemic), 522

Bromarest DX Cough— *See* Cough/Cold Combinations (Systemic), 522

Bromatane DX Cough— *See* Cough/Cold Combinations (Systemic), 522

Bromatapp— *See* Antihistamines and Decongestants (Systemic), 159

Bromazepam— *See* Benzodiazepines (Systemic), 257

Bromfed— *See* Antihistamines and Decongestants (Systemic), 159

Bromfed-DM— *See* Cough/Cold Combinations (Systemic), 522

Bromfed-PD— *See* Antihistamines and Decongestants (Systemic), 159

Bromfenex— *See* Antihistamines and Decongestants (Systemic), 159

Bromfenex PD— *See* Antihistamines and Decongestants (Systemic), 159

Bromocriptine (Systemic), 301

Bromodiphenhydramine and Codeine— *See* Cough/Cold Combinations (Systemic), 522

Bromodiphenhydramine, Diphenhydramine, Codeine, Ammonium Chloride, and Potassium Guaiacolsulfonate— *See* Cough/Cold Combinations (Systemic), 522

Bromophen T.D.— *See* Antihistamines and Decongestants (Systemic), 159

Bromo-Seltzer— *See* Acetaminophen, Sodium Bicarbonate, and Citric Acid (Systemic), 11

Bromotuss with Codeine— *See* Cough/Cold Combinations (Systemic), 522

Bromphen— *See* Antihistamines (Systemic), 153

Bromphen DC with Codeine Cough— *See* Cough/Cold Combinations (Systemic), 522

Bromphen DX Cough— *See* Cough/Cold Combinations (Systemic), 522

Brompheniramine— *See* Antihistamines (Systemic), 153

Brompheniramine and Phenylephrine— *See* Antihistamines and Decongestants (Systemic), 159

Brompheniramine, Phenylephrine, and Phenylpropanolamine— *See* Antihistamines and Decongestants (Systemic), 159

Brompheniramine, Phenylephrine, Phenylpropanolamine, and Codeine— *See* Cough/Cold Combinations (Systemic), 522

Brompheniramine, Phenylephrine, Phenylpropanolamine, Codeine, and Guaifenesin— *See* Cough/Cold Combinations (Systemic), 522

Brompheniramine, Phenylephrine, Phenylpropanolamine, and Dextromethorphan— *See* Cough/Cold Combinations (Systemic), 522

Brompheniramine, Phenylephrine, Phenylpropanolamine, and Guaifenesin— *See* Cough/Cold Combinations (Systemic), 522

Brompheniramine, Phenylephrine, Phenylpropanolamine, Hydrocodone, and Guaifenesin— *See* Cough/Cold Combinations (Systemic), 522

Brompheniramine and Phenylpropanolamine— *See* Antihistamines and Decongestants (Systemic), 159

Brompheniramine, Phenylpropanolamine, and Acetaminophen— *See* Antihistamines, Decongestants, and Analgesics (Systemic), 164

Brompheniramine, Phenylpropanolamine, and Codeine— *See* Cough/Cold Combinations (Systemic), 522

Brompheniramine, Phenylpropanolamine, and Dextromethorpan— *See* Cough/Cold Combinations (Systemic), 522

Brompheniramine and Pseudoephedrine— *See* Antihistamines and Decongestants (Systemic), 159

Brompheniramine, Pseudoephedrine, and Acetaminophen— *See* Antihistamines, Decongestants, and Analgesics (Systemic), 164

Brompheniramine, Pseudoephedrine, and Dextromethorphan— *See* Cough/Cold Combinations (Systemic), 522

Brompheril— *See* Antihistamines and Decongestants (Systemic), 159

Bronalide— *See* Corticosteroids (Inhalation), 496

Bronchial— *See* Theophylline and Guaifenesin (Systemic), #

Bronchodilators, Adrenergic (Inhalation), 304

Bronchodilators, Adrenergic (Oral/Injection), 310

Bronchodilators, Theophylline (Systemic), 314

Broncho-Grippol-DM— *See* Dextromethorphan (Systemic), 592

Broncholate— *See* Cough/Cold Combinations (Systemic), 522

Broncomar-GG— *See* Theophylline and Guaifenesin (Systemic), #

Brondelate— *See* Oxtriphylline and Guaifenesin (Systemic), #

Bronkaid Mist— *See* Bronchodilators, Adrenergic (Inhalation), 304

Bronkaid Mistometer— *See* Bronchodilators, Adrenergic (Inhalation), 304

Bronkaid Suspension Mist— *See* Bronchodilators, Adrenergic (Inhalation), 304

Bronkometer— *See* Bronchodilators, Adrenergic (Inhalation), 304

Bronkosol— *See* Bronchodilators, Adrenergic (Inhalation), 304

Bronkotuss Expectorant— *See* Cough/Cold Combinations (Systemic), 522

Brontex— *See* Cough/Cold Combinations (Systemic), 522

Brotane DX Cough— *See* Cough/Cold Combinations (Systemic), 522

Bucet— *See* Butalbital and Acetaminophen (Systemic), 324

Buckley's DM— *See* Cough/Cold Combinations (Systemic), 522

Buclizine— *See* Meclizine/Buclizine/Cyclizine (Systemic), 1038

Budesonide— *See* Corticosteroids (Inhalation), 496; *See* Corticosteroids (Nasal), 502; *See* Corticosteroids (Rectal), 509; *See* Corticosteroids—Glucocorticoid Effects (Systemic), 513

Buffered Aspirin— *See* Salicylates (Systemic), 1394

Buffered Aspirin and Caffeine— *See* Salicylates (Systemic), 1394

Bufferin Caplets— *See* Salicylates (Systemic), 1394

Bufferin Extra Strength Caplets— *See* Salicylates (Systemic), 1394

Bufferin Tablets— *See* Salicylates (Systemic), 1394

Buffets II— *See* Acetaminophen and Salicylates (Systemic), 6

Buffex— *See* Salicylates (Systemic), 1394

Buffinol— *See* Salicylates (Systemic), 1394

Buffinol Extra— *See* Salicylates (Systemic), 1394

Buf-Puf Acne Cleansing Bar with Vitamin E— *See* Salicylic Acid (Topical), #

Bullfrog Body— *See* Sunscreen Agents (Topical), #

Bullfrog Extra Moisturizing— *See* Sunscreen Agents (Topical), #

Bullfrog For Kids— *See* Sunscreen Agents (Topical), #

Bullfrog Original Concentrated— *See* Sunscreen Agents (Topical), #

Bullfrog Sport— *See* Sunscreen Agents (Topical), #

Bullfrog Sunblock— *See* Sunscreen Agents (Topical), #

Bumetanide— *See* Diuretics, Loop (Systemic), 633, MC-3

Bumex— *See* Diuretics, Loop (Systemic), 633

Buphenyl— *See* Sodium Phenylbutyrate (Systemic), #

Bupivacaine— *See* Anesthetics (Parenteral-Local), 83

Buprenex— *See* Narcotic Analgesics—For Pain Relief (Systemic), 1147; *See* Narcotic Analgesics—For Surgery and Obstetrics (Systemic), 1154

Buprenorphine— *See* Narcotic Analgesics—For Pain Relief (Systemic), 1147; *See* Narcotic Analgesics—For Surgery and Obstetrics (Systemic), 1154

Bupropion (Systemic), 317, MC-3

Buscopan— *See* Anticholinergics/Antispasmodics (Systemic), 106

Buserelin (Systemic), 319

Busodium— *See* Barbiturates (Systemic), 239

BuSpar— *See* Buspirone (Systemic), 320, MC-4

BuSpar DIVIDOSE— *See* Buspirone (Systemic), 320

Buspirone (Systemic), 320, MC-4

Bustab— *See* Buspirone (Systemic), 320

Busulfan (Systemic), 322

Busulfex— *See* Busulfan (Systemic), 322

Butabarbital— *See* Barbiturates (Systemic), 239

Butace— *See* Butalbital and Acetaminophen (Systemic), 324

Butalan— *See* Barbiturates (Systemic), 239

Butalbital-AC— *See* Butalbital and Aspirin (Systemic), 327

Butalbital and Acetaminophen (Systemic), 324

Butalbital, Acetaminophen, and Caffeine— *See* Butalbital and Acetaminophen (Systemic), 324, MC-4

Butalbital, Acetaminophen, Caffeine, and Codeine— *See* Barbiturates, Aspirin, and Codeine (Systemic), 245

Butalbital, Acetaminophen, Caffeine, and Codeine (Systemic), 331

Butalbital and Aspirin (Systemic), 327

Butalbital, Aspirin, and Caffeine— *See* Butalbital and Aspirin (Systemic), 327, MC-4

Butalbital, Aspirin, Caffeine, and Codeine— *See* Barbiturates, Aspirin, and Codeine (Systemic), 245

Butalbital compound— *See* Butalbital and Aspirin (Systemic), 327

Butalbital Compound with Codeine— *See* Barbiturates, Aspirin, and Codeine (Systemic), 245

Butalgen— *See* Butalbital and Aspirin (Systemic), 327

Butamben— *See* Anesthetics (Topical), 88

Butazolidin— *See* Anti-inflammatory Drugs, Nonsteroidal (Systemic), 179

Butenafine (Topical), 334

Butesin Picrate— *See* Anesthetics (Topical), 88

Butibel— *See* Belladonna Alkaloids and Barbiturates (Systemic), 252

Butinal with Codeine No.3— *See* Barbiturates, Aspirin, and Codeine (Systemic), 245

Butisol— *See* Barbiturates (Systemic), 239

Butoconazole— *See* Antifungals, Azole (Vaginal), 145

Butorphanol— *See* Narcotic Analgesics—For Pain Relief (Systemic), 1147; *See* Narcotic Analgesics—For Surgery and Obstetrics (Systemic), 1154

Butorphanol (Nasal-Systemic), 336

Butyl aminobenzoate— *See* Anesthetics (Topical), 88

C

C2— *See* Salicylates (Systemic), 1394

cA2— *See* Infliximab (Systemic), 900

Cabergoline (Systemic), 338

Cafcit— *See* Caffeine (Systemic), 339

Cafergot-PB— *See* Headache Medicines, Ergot Derivative–containing (Systemic), 853

Cafertine— *See* Headache Medicines, Ergot Derivative–containing (Systemic), 853

Capozide— See Angiotensin-converting Enzyme (ACE) Inhibitors and Hydrochlorothiazide (Systemic), 94

Capreomycin (Systemic), 362

Capsaicin (Topical), 363

Captimer— See Tiopronin (Systemic), #

Captopril— *See* Angiotensin-converting Enzyme (ACE) Inhibitors (Systemic), 90, MC-4

Captopril and Hydrochlorothiazide— *See* Angiotensin-converting Enzyme (ACE) Inhibitors and Hydrochlorothiazide (Systemic), 94

Carafate— See Sucralfate (Oral), 1438, MC-22

Carbachol (Ophthalmic), 365

Carbacot— See Skeletal Muscle Relaxants (Systemic), 1420

Carbamazepine (Systemic), 366, MC-4

Carbamide; *See* Urea (Intra-amniotic), #

Carbamylcholine— *See* Carbachol (Ophthalmic), 365

Carbastat— See Carbachol (Ophthalmic), 365

Carbatrol— See Carbamazepine (Systemic), 366

Carbenicillin— *See* Penicillins (Systemic), 1251

Carbetapentane, Chlorpheniramine, and Phenylephrine (Systemic), MC-4

Carbetocin (Systemic), 370

Carbex— See Selegiline (Systemic), 1403

Carbidopa and Levodopa— *See* Levodopa (Systemic), 985, MC-4

Carbinoxamine— *See* Antihistamines (Systemic), 153

Carbinoxamine Compound— See Cough/Cold Combinations (Systemic), 522

Carbinoxamine Compound-Drops— See Cough/Cold Combinations (Systemic), 522

Carbinoxamine and Pseudoephedrine— *See* Antihistamines and Decongestants (Systemic), 159

Carbinoxamine, Pseudoephedrine, and Dextromethorphan— *See* Cough/Cold Combinations (Systemic), 522

Carbiset— See Antihistamines and Decongestants (Systemic), 159

Carbiset-TR— See Antihistamines and Decongestants (Systemic), 159

Carbocaine— See Anesthetics (Parenteral-Local), 83

Carbocaine with Neo-Cobefrin— See Anesthetics (Parenteral-Local), 83

Carbodec— See Antihistamines and Decongestants (Systemic), 159

Carbodec DM— See Cough/Cold Combinations (Systemic), 522

Carbodec DM Drops— See Cough/Cold Combinations (Systemic), 522

Carbodec TR— See Antihistamines and Decongestants (Systemic), 159

Carbohydrates and Electrolytes (Systemic), 370

Carbol-Fuchsin (Topical), 372

Carbolith— See Lithium (Systemic), 996

Carbonic Anhydrase Inhibitors (Systemic), 373

Carbon, medicinal— *See* Charcoal, Activated (Oral), 272

Carboplatin (Systemic), 376

Carboprost (Systemic), 378

Carboptic— See Carbachol (Ophthalmic), 365

Cardec— See Antihistamines and Decongestants (Systemic), 159

Cardec DM— See Cough/Cold Combinations (Systemic), 522

Cardec DM Drops— See Cough/Cold Combinations (Systemic), 522

Cardec DM Pediatric— See Cough/Cold Combinations (Systemic), 522

Cardec-S— See Antihistamines and Decongestants (Systemic), 159

Cardene— See Calcium Channel Blocking Agents (Systemic), 349

Cardioquin— See Quinidine (Systemic), 1341

Cardizem CD— See Calcium Channel Blocking Agents (Systemic), 349, MC-7

Cardizem SR— See Calcium Channel Blocking Agents (Systemic), 349

Cardura— See Doxazosin (Systemic), 660, MC-8

Cardura-1— See Doxazosin (Systemic), 660

Cardura-2— See Doxazosin (Systemic), 660

Cardura-4— See Doxazosin (Systemic), 660

Carisoprodol— See Skeletal Muscle Relaxants (Systemic), 1420, MC-4

Cari-Tab— See Vitamins and Fluoride (Systemic), 1586

Carmol-HC— See Corticosteroids—Low Potency (Topical), 518

Carmustine (Implantation-Local), 379

Carmustine (Systemic), 380

Carnation Follow-Up Formula— See Infant Formulas (Systemic), #

Carnation Good Start— See Infant Formulas (Systemic), #

Carnation Instant Breakfast— See Enteral Nutrition Formulas (Systemic), #

Carnation Instant Breakfast No Sugar Added— See Enteral Nutrition Formulas (Systemic), #

Carnitor— See Levocarnitine (Systemic), #

Caroid— See Laxatives (Oral), 964

Carteolol— *See* Beta-adrenergic Blocking Agents (Ophthalmic), 270; *See* Beta-adrenergic Blocking Agents (Systemic), 272

Carter's Little Pills— See Laxatives (Oral), 964

Cartia XT— See Diltiazem (Systemic), MC-7

Carticel— See Chondrocytes, Autologous Cultured (Implantation-Local), 424

Cartrol— See Beta-adrenergic Blocking Agents (Systemic), 272

Carvedilol (Systemic), 382, MC-4

Casanthranol— *See* Laxatives (Oral), 964

Casanthranol and Docusate— *See* Laxatives (Oral), 964

Cascara Sagrada— *See* Laxatives (Oral), 964

Cascara Sagrada and Aloe— *See* Laxatives (Oral), 964

Cascara Sagrada and Phenolphthalein— *See* Laxatives (Oral), 964

Casec— See Enteral Nutrition Formulas (Systemic), #

Casodex— See Antiandrogens, Nonsteroidal (Systemic), 104

Caspofungin (Systemic), 384

Castellani Paint— *See* Carbol-Fuchsin (Topical), 372

Castellani Paint Modified (Color)— See Carbol-Fuchsin (Topical), 372

Castor Oil— *See* Laxatives (Oral), 964

Cataflam— See Anti-inflammatory Drugs, Nonsteroidal (Systemic), 179

Catapres— See Clonidine (Systemic), 464

Catapres-TTS-1— See Clonidine (Systemic), 464

Catapres-TTS-2— See Clonidine (Systemic), 464

Catapres-TTS-3— See Clonidine (Systemic), 464

Catrix Correction— See Sunscreen Agents (Topical), #

Catrix LipSaver— See Sunscreen Agents (Topical), #

Caverject— See Alprostadil (Local), 33

C2 Buffered— See Salicylates (Systemic), 1394

C2 Buffered with Codeine— See Narcotic Analgesics and Aspirin (Systemic), 1142

CCK— *See* Cholecystokinin (Diagnostic), #

CCNU— *See* Lomustine (Systemic), 999

C2 with Codeine— See Narcotic Analgesics and Aspirin (Systemic), 1142

2-CdA— *See* Cladribine (Systemic), 445

Cebid Timecelles— See Ascorbic Acid (Vitamin C) (Systemic), 205

Ceclor— See Cephalosporins (Systemic), 387

Ceclor CD— See Cephalosporins (Systemic), 387, MC-5

Cecon— See Ascorbic Acid (Vitamin C) (Systemic), 205

Cecore 500— See Ascorbic Acid (Vitamin C) (Systemic), 205

Cedax— See Cephalosporins (Systemic), 387

Cedocard-SR— See Nitrates—Oral (Systemic), 1188

Cee-202047— See Ascorbic Acid (Vitamin C) (Systemic), 205

CeeNU— See Lomustine (Systemic), 999

Cefaclor— See Cephalosporins (Systemic), 387, MC-4, MC-5

Cefadroxil— *See* Cephalosporins (Systemic), 387, MC-5

Cefadyl— See Cephalosporins (Systemic), 387

Cefamandole— *See* Cephalosporins (Systemic), 387

Cefazolin— *See* Cephalosporins (Systemic), 387

Cefdinir— *See* Cephalosporins (Systemic), 387

Cefepime— *See* Cephalosporins (Systemic), 387

Cefixime— *See* Cephalosporins (Systemic), 387, MC-5

Cefobid— See Cephalosporins (Systemic), 387

Cefonicid— *See* Cephalosporins (Systemic), 387

Cefoperazone— *See* Cephalosporins (Systemic), 387

Cefotan— See Cephalosporins (Systemic), 387

Cefotaxime— *See* Cephalosporins (Systemic), 387

Cefotetan— *See* Cephalosporins (Systemic), 387

Cefoxitin— See Cephalosporins (Systemic), 387

Cefpodoxime— *See* Cephalosporins (Systemic), 387, MC-5

Cefprozil— *See* Cephalosporins (Systemic), 387, MC-5

Ceftazidime— *See* Cephalosporins (Systemic), 387

Ceftibuten (Systemic); *See* Cephalosporins (Systemic), 387

Ceftin— See Cephalosporins (Systemic), 387, MC-5

Ceftizoxime— *See* Cephalosporins (Systemic), 387

Ceftriaxone— *See* Cephalosporins (Systemic), 387

Cefuroxime— *See* Cephalosporins (Systemic), 387, MC-5

Cefzil— See Cephalosporins (Systemic), 387, MC-5

Celebrex— See Celecoxib (Systemic), 385, MC-5

Celecoxib (Systemic), 385, MC-5

Celestoderm-V— See Corticosteroids—Medium to Very High Potency (Topical), 520

Celestoderm-V/2— See Corticosteroids—Medium to Very High Potency (Topical), 520

Celestone— See Corticosteroids—Glucocorticoid Effects (Systemic), 513

Celestone Phosphate— See Corticosteroids—Glucocorticoid Effects (Systemic), 513

Celestone Soluspan— See Corticosteroids—Glucocorticoid Effects (Systemic), 513

Celexa— See Citalopram (Systemic), 441, MC-6

CellCept— See Mycophenolate (Systemic), 1128

Cellulose Sodium Phosphate (Systemic), #

Celontin— See Anticonvulsants, Succinimide (Systemic), 121

Cemill— See Ascorbic Acid (Vitamin C) (Systemic), 205

Cenafed— See Pseudoephedrine (Systemic), 1334

Cenafed Plus— See Antihistamines and Decongestants (Systemic), 159

Cena-K— See Potassium Supplements (Systemic), 1300

Cenocort A-40— See Corticosteroids—Glucocorticoid Effects (Systemic), 513

Cenocort Forte— See Corticosteroids—Glucocorticoid Effects (Systemic), 513

Cenolate— See Ascorbic Acid (Vitamin C) (Systemic), 205

Ceo-Two— See Laxatives (Rectal), 970

Cephalexin— *See* Cephalosporins (Systemic), 387, MC-5

Cephalosporins (Systemic), 387

Cephalothin— *See* Cephalosporins (Systemic), 387

Cephapirin— *See* Cephalosporins (Systemic), 387

Cephradine— *See* Cephalosporins (Systemic), 387

Ceporacin— See Cephalosporins (Systemic), 387

Ceptaz— See Cephalosporins (Systemic), 387

Cerebyx— See Anticonvulsants, Hydantoin (Systemic), 117

Ceredase— See Alglucerase (Systemic), #

Cerespan— See Papaverine (Systemic), #

Cerezyme— See Imiglucerase (Systemic), 892

Cerivastatin— *See* HMG-CoA Reductase Inhibitors (Systemic), 869, 1629, MC-5

Cerivastatin (Systemic), #, 1629, MC-5

Cerose-DM— See Cough/Cold Combinations (Systemic), 522

Certiva— See Diphtheria and Tetanus Toxoids and Pertussis Vaccine Adsorbed (Systemic), 619

Cerubidine— See Daunorubicin (Systemic), 577

Cervidil— See Dinoprostone (Cervical/Vaginal), 613

C.E.S.— See Estrogens (Systemic), 718

Cesamet— See Nabilone (Systemic), 1129

Cetacort— See Corticosteroids—Low Potency (Topical), 518

Cetamide— See Sulfonamides (Ophthalmic), 1445

Cetane— See Ascorbic Acid (Vitamin C) (Systemic), 205

Cetaphen with Codeine— See Narcotic Analgesics and Acetaminophen (Systemic), 1138

Cetaphen Extra-Strength with Codeine— See Narcotic Analgesics and Acetaminophen (Systemic), 1138

Cetirizine— *See* Antihistamines (Systemic), 153, MC-5

Cetrorelix (Systemic), 392

Cetrotide— See Cetrorelix (Systemic), 392

Cevi-Bid— See Ascorbic Acid (Vitamin C) (Systemic), 205

Cevimeline (Systemic), 393

Chap-et Sun Ban Lip Conditioner— See Sunscreen Agents (Topical), #

Chap Stick— See Sunscreen Agents (Topical), #

Chap Stick Sunblock— See Sunscreen Agents (Topical), #

Chap Stick Sunblock Petroleum Jelly Plus— See Sunscreen Agents (Topical), #

CharcoAid— See Charcoal, Activated (Oral), 395

CharcoAid 2000— See Charcoal, Activated (Oral), 395

CharcoAid G— See Charcoal, Activated (Oral), 395

Charcoal, Activated (Oral), 395

Charcoal, Activated, and Sorbitol— *See* Charcoal, Activated (Oral), 395

Charcodote— See Charcoal, Activated (Oral), 395

Charcodote TFS-25— See Charcoal, Activated (Oral), 395

Charcodote TFS-50— See Charcoal, Activated (Oral), 395

Chemdec— See Antihistamines and Decongestants (Systemic), 159

Chemet— See Succimer (Systemic), 1437

Chenodeoxycholic acid— *See* Chenodiol (Systemic), 397

Chenodiol (Systemic), 397

Cheracol— See Cough/Cold Combinations (Systemic), 522

Cheracol D Cough— See Cough/Cold Combinations (Systemic), 522

Cheracol Plus— See Cough/Cold Combinations (Systemic), 522

Cherapas— See Reserpine, Hydralazine, and Hydrochlorothiazide (Systemic), #

Chibroxin— See Norfloxacin (Ophthalmic), 1198

Children's Formula Cough— See Cough/Cold Combinations (Systemic), 522

Children's Nasalcrom— See Cromolyn (Nasal), 541

Children's Tylenol Cold Multi-Symptom— See Antihistamines, Decongestants, and Analgesics (Systemic), 164

Children's Tylenol Cold Plus Cough Multi Symptom— See Cough/Cold Combinations (Systemic), 522

Children's Vicks NyQuil Cold/Cough Relief— See Cough/Cold Combinations (Systemic), 522

Chirocaine— See Anesthetics (Parenteral-Local), 83

C-Hist-SR— See Antihistamines and Decongestants (Systemic), 159

Chlo-Amine— See Antihistamines (Systemic), 153

Chlophedianol (Systemic), #

Chloracol Ophthalmic Solution— See Chloramphenicol (Ophthalmic), 403

Chlorafed— See Antihistamines and Decongestants (Systemic), 159

Chlorafed H.S. Timecelles— See Antihistamines and Decongestants (Systemic), 159

Chlorafed Timecelles— See Antihistamines and Decongestants (Systemic), 159

Chloral Hydrate (Systemic), 398

Chlorambucil (Systemic), 401

Chloramphenicol (Ophthalmic), 403

Chloramphenicol (Otic), 405

Chloramphenicol (Systemic), 406

Chloraseptic Lozenges— See Anesthetics (Dental), 80

Chloraseptic Lozenges Cherry Flavor— See Anesthetics (Dental), 80

Chloraseptic Lozenges, Children's— See Anesthetics (Dental), 80

Chlorate— See Antihistamines (Systemic), 153

Chlordiazepoxide— *See* Benzodiazepines (Systemic), 257, MC-5

Chlordiazepoxide and Amitriptyline (Systemic), 408

Chlordiazepoxide and Clindinium (Systemic), 411, MC-5

Chlordrine S.R.— See Antihistamines and Decongestants (Systemic), 159

Chlorfed— See Antihistamines and Decongestants (Systemic), 159

Chlorfed II— See Antihistamines and Decongestants (Systemic), 159

Chlorgest-HD— See Cough/Cold Combinations (Systemic), 522

Chlorhexidine (Dental), 413

Chlorhexidine (Implantation-Dental), 414

Chlormethine— *See* Mechlorethamine (Systemic), 1036; *See* Mechlorethamine (Topical), #

2-Chlorodeoxyadenosine— *See* Cladribine (Systemic), 445

Chlorofair Ophthalmic Ointment— See Chloramphenicol (Ophthalmic), 403

Chlorofair Ophthalmic Solution— See Chloramphenicol (Ophthalmic), 403

Chloromag— See Magnesium Supplements (Systemic), 1017

Chloromycetin— See Chloramphenicol (Otic), 405; *See* Chloramphenicol (Systemic), 406

Chloromycetin Ophthalmic Ointment— See Chloramphenicol (Ophthalmic), 403

Chloromycetin for Ophthalmic Solution— See Chloramphenicol (Ophthalmic), 403

Chloroprocaine— *See* Anesthetics (Parenteral-Local), 83

Chloroptic Ophthalmic Solution— See Chloramphenicol (Ophthalmic), 403

Chloroptic S.O.P.— See Chloramphenicol (Ophthalmic), 403

Chloroquine (Systemic), 415

Chlorothiazide— *See* Diuretics, Thiazide (Systemic), 642

Chloroxine (Topical), 418

Chlorphedrine SR— See Antihistamines and Decongestants (Systemic), 159

Chlorphenamine— *See* Antihistamines (Systemic), 153

Chlorphenesin— *See* Skeletal Muscle Relaxants (Systemic), 1420

Chlorpheniramine— *See* Antihistamines (Systemic), 153

Chlorpheniramine and Codeine— *See* Cough/Cold Combinations (Systemic), 522

Chlorpheniramine and Dextromethorphan— *See* Cough/Cold Combinations (Systemic), 522

Chlorpheniramine, Dextromethorphan, and Acetaminophen— *See* Cough/Cold Combinations (Systemic), 522

Chlorpheniramine, Ephedrine, and Guaifenesin— *See* Cough/Cold Combinations (Systemic), 522

Chlorpheniramine, Ephedrine, Phenylephrine, and Carbetapentane— *See* Cough/Cold Combinations (Systemic), 522

Chlorpheniramine, Ephedrine, Phenylephrine, Dextromethorphan, Ammonium Chloride, and Ipecac— *See* Cough/Cold Combinations (Systemic), 522

Chlorpheniramine and Hydrocodone— *See* Cough/Cold Combinations (Systemic), 522

Chlorpheniramine, Phenindamine, Phenylephrine, Dextromethorphan, Acetaminophen, Salicylamide, Caffeine, and Ascorbic Acid— *See* Cough/Cold Combinations (Systemic), 522

Chlorpheniramine, Phenindamine, and Phenylpropanolamine— *See* Antihistamines and Decongestants (Systemic), 159

Chlorpheniramine, Pheniramine, Pyrilamine, Phenylephrine, Hydrocodone, Salicylamide, Caffeine, and Ascorbic Acid— *See* Cough/Cold Combinations (Systemic), 522

Chlorpheniramine and Phenylephrine— *See* Antihistamines and Decongestants (Systemic), 159

Chlorpheniramine, Phenylephrine, and Acetaminophen— *See* Antihistamines, Decongestants, and Analgesics (Systemic), 164

Chlorpheniramine, Phenylephrine, Codeine, and Ammonium Chloride— *See* Cough/Cold Combinations (Systemic), 522

Chlorpheniramine, Phenylephrine, Codeine, and Potassium Iodide— *See* Cough/Cold Combinations (Systemic), 522

Chlorpheniramine, Phenylephrine, and Dextromethorphan— *See* Cough/Cold Combinations (Systemic), 522

Chlorpheniramine, Phenylephrine, Dextromethorphan, Acetaminophen, and Salicylamide— *See* Cough/Cold Combinations (Systemic), 522

Chlorpheniramine, Phenylephrine, Dextromethorphan, and Guaifenesin— *See* Cough/Cold Combinations (Systemic), 522

Chlorpheniramine, Phenylephrine, Dextromethorphan, Guaifenesin, and Ammonium Chloride— *See* Cough/Cold Combinations (Systemic), 522

Chlorpheniramine, Phenylephrine, and Guaifenesin— *See* Cough/Cold Combinations (Systemic), 522

Chlorpheniramine, Phenylephrine, and Hydrocodone— *See* Cough/Cold Combinations (Systemic), 522

Chlorpheniramine, Phenylephrine, Hydrocodone, Acetaminophen, and Caffeine— *See* Cough/Cold Combinations (Systemic), 522

Chlorpheniramine, Phenylephrine, and Methscopolamine— *See* Antihistamines, Decongestants, and Anticholinergics (Systemic), 170

Chlorpheniramine, Phenylephrine, and Phenylpropanolamine— *See* Antihistamines and Decongestants (Systemic), 159

Chlorpheniramine, Phenylephrine, Phenylpropanolamine, Atropine, Hyoscyamine, and Scopolamine— *See* Antihistamines, Decongestants, and Anticholinergics (Systemic), 170

Chlorpheniramine, Phenylephrine, Phenylpropanolamine, Carbetapentane, and Potassium Guaiacolsulfonate— *See* Cough/Cold Combinations (Systemic), 522

Chlorpheniramine, Phenylephrine, Phenylpropanolamine, and Codeine— *See* Cough/Cold Combinations (Systemic), 522

Chlorpheniramine, Phenylephrine, Phenylpropanolamine, Dextromethorphan, Potassium Guaiacolsulfonate, and Ipecac— *See* Cough/Cold Combinations (Systemic), 522

Chlorpheniramine, Phenylephrine, Phenylpropanolamine, and Dihydrocodeine— *See* Cough/Cold Combinations (Systemic), 522

Chlorpheniramine and Phenylpropanolamine— *See* Antihistamines and Decongestants (Systemic), 159

Chlorpheniramine, Phenylpropanolamine, and Acetaminophen— *See* Antihistamines, Decongestants, and Analgesics (Systemic), 164

Chlorpheniramine, Phenylpropanolamine, Acetaminophen, and Caffeine— *See* Antihistamines, Decongestants, and Analgesics (Systemic), 164

Chlorpheniramine, Phenylpropanolamine, and Aspirin— *See* Antihistamines, Decongestants, and Analgesics (Systemic), 164

Chlorpheniramine, Phenylpropanolamine, and Caramiphen— *See* Cough/Cold Combinations (Systemic), 522

Chlorpheniramine, Phenylpropanolamine, Codeine, Guaifenesin, and Acetaminophen— *See* Cough/Cold Combinations (Systemic), 522

Chlorpheniramine, Phenylpropanolamine, and Dextromethorphan— *See* Cough/Cold Combinations (Systemic), 522

Chlorpheniramine, Phenylpropanolamine, Dextromethorphan, and Acetaminophen— *See* Cough/Cold Combinations (Systemic), 522

Chlorpheniramine, Phenylpropanolamine, Dextromethorphan, and Ammonium Chloride— *See* Cough/Cold Combinations (Systemic), 522

Chlorpheniramine, Phenylpropanolamine, Dextromethorphan, and Aspirin— *See* Cough/Cold Combinations (Systemic), 522

Chlorpheniramine, Phenylpropanolamine, and Guaifenesin— *See* Cough/Cold Combinations (Systemic), 522

Chlorpheniramine, Phenylpropanolamine, Guaifenesin, and Acetaminophen— *See* Cough/Cold Combinations (Systemic), 522

Chlorpheniramine, Phenylpropanolamine, Guaifenesin, Sodium Citrate, and Citric Acid— *See* Cough/Cold Combinations (Systemic), 522

Chlorpheniramine, Phenylpropanolamine, and Methscopolamine— *See* Antihistamines, Decongestants, and Anticholinergics (Systemic), 170

Chlorpheniramine, Phenyltoloxamine, Ephedrine, Codeine, and Guaiacol Carbonate— *See* Cough/Cold Combinations (Systemic), 522

Chlorpheniramine, Phenyltoloxamine, and Phenylephrine— *See* Antihistamines and Decongestants (Systemic), 159

Chlorpheniramine, Phenyltoloxamine, Phenylephrine, and Phenylpropanolamine— *See* Antihistamines and Decongestants (Systemic), 159

Chlorpheniramine, Phenyltoloxamine, Phenylpropanolamine, and Acetaminophen— *See* Antihistamines, Decongestants, and Analgesics (Systemic), 164

Chlorpheniramine and Pseudoephedrine— *See* Antihistamines and Decongestants (Systemic), 159

Chlorpheniramine, Pseudoephedrine, and Acetaminophen— *See* Antihistamines, Decongestants, and Analgesics (Systemic), 164

Chlorpheniramine, Pseudoephedrine, and Codeine— *See* Cough/Cold Combinations (Systemic), 522

Contac Severe Cold Formula Night Strength— *See* Cough/Cold Combinations (Systemic), 522

Conten— *See* Butalbital and Acetaminophen (Systemic), 324

Control— *See* Phenylpropanolamine (Systemic), 1280

Contuss— *See* Cough/Cold Combinations (Systemic), 522

Co-oxycodAPAP— *See* Narcotic Analgesics and Acetaminophen (Systemic), 1138

Copaxone— *See* Glatiramer Acetate (Systemic), 824

Cope— *See* Salicylates (Systemic), 1394

Cophene-B— *See* Antihistamines (Systemic), 153

Cophene No. 2— *See* Antihistamines and Decongestants (Systemic), 159

Cophene-S— *See* Cough/Cold Combinations (Systemic), 522

Cophene-X— *See* Cough/Cold Combinations (Systemic), 522

Cophene XP— *See* Cough/Cold Combinations (Systemic), 522

Cophene-XP— *See* Cough/Cold Combinations (Systemic), 522

Copolymer-1— *See* Glatiramer Acetate (Systemic), 824

Copper Gluconate— *See* Copper Supplements (Systemic), 493

Copper Supplements (Systemic), 493

Coppertone All Day Protection— *See* Sunscreen Agents (Topical), #

Coppertone Dark Tanning— *See* Sunscreen Agents (Topical), #

Coppertone Kids Sunblock— *See* Sunscreen Agents (Topical), #

Coppertone Lipkote— *See* Sunscreen Agents (Topical), #

Coppertone Moisturizing Sunscreen— *See* Sunscreen Agents (Topical), #

Coppertone Moisturizing Suntan— *See* Sunscreen Agents (Topical), #

Coppertone Sport— *See* Sunscreen Agents (Topical), #

Coppertone Sport Ultra Sweatproof— *See* Sunscreen Agents (Topical), #

Coppertone Tan Magnifier— *See* Sunscreen Agents (Topical), #

Coppertone Waterbabies Sunblock— *See* Sunscreen Agents (Topical), #

Coppertone Waterproof Sunblock— *See* Sunscreen Agents (Topical), #

Co-proxAPAP— *See* Narcotic Analgesics and Acetaminophen (Systemic), 1138

Coptin— *See* Sulfonamides and Trimethoprim (Systemic), 1454

Coptin 1— *See* Sulfonamides and Trimethoprim (Systemic), 1454

Co-Pyronil 2— *See* Antihistamines and Decongestants (Systemic), 159

Coradur— *See* Nitrates—Oral (Systemic), 1188

Cordarone— *See* Amiodarone (Systemic), 48, MC-1

Cordarone Intravenous— *See* Amiodarone (Systemic), 48

Cordarone I.V.— *See* Amiodarone (Systemic), 48

Cordol— *See* Corticosteroids—Glucocorticoid Effects (Systemic), 513

Cordran— *See* Corticosteroids—Medium to Very High Potency (Topical), 520

Cordran SP— *See* Corticosteroids—Medium to Very High Potency (Topical), 520

Coreg— *See* Carvedilol (Systemic), 382, MC-4

Corgard— *See* Beta-adrenergic Blocking Agents (Systemic), 272

Coricidin D— *See* Antihistamines, Decongestants, and Analgesics (Systemic), 164

Coricidin D Long Acting— *See* Antihistamines and Decongestants (Systemic), 159

Coricidin Non-Drowsy Sinus Formula— *See* Decongestants and Analgesics (Systemic), 581

Coristex-DH— *See* Cough/Cold Combinations (Systemic), 522

Coristine-DH— *See* Cough/Cold Combinations (Systemic), 522

Corium— *See* Chlordiazepoxide and Clidinium (Systemic), 411

Cormax— *See* Corticosteroids—Medium to Very High Potency (Topical), 520

Coronex— *See* Nitrates—Oral (Systemic), 1188; *See* Nitrates—Sublingual, Chewable, or Buccal (Systemic), 1190

Correctol— *See* Laxatives (Oral), 964

Correctol Caplets— *See* Laxatives (Oral), 964

Correctol Herbal Tea— *See* Laxatives (Oral), 964

Correctol Stool Softener Soft Gels— *See* Laxatives (Oral), 964

Corsym— *See* Antihistamines and Decongestants (Systemic), 159

Cortacet— *See* Corticosteroids—Low Potency (Topical), 518

Cortaid— *See* Corticosteroids—Low Potency (Topical), 518

Cortamed— *See* Corticosteroids (Ophthalmic), 505

Cortastat— *See* Corticosteroids—Glucocorticoid Effects (Systemic), 513

Cortastat 10— *See* Corticosteroids—Glucocorticoid Effects (Systemic), 513

Cortastat LA— *See* Corticosteroids—Glucocorticoid Effects (Systemic), 513

Cortate— *See* Corticosteroids—Low Potency (Topical), 518

Cortatrigen Ear— *See* Neomycin, Polymyxin B, and Hydrocortisone (Otic), 1172

Cortatrigen Modified Ear Drops— *See* Neomycin, Polymyxin B, and Hydrocortisone (Otic), 1172

Cort-Biotic— *See* Neomycin, Polymyxin B, and Hydrocortisone (Otic), 1172

Cort-Dome— *See* Corticosteroids (Rectal), 509; *See* Corticosteroids—Low Potency (Topical), 518

Cortef— *See* Corticosteroids—Glucocorticoid Effects (Systemic), 513; *See* Corticosteroids—Low Potency (Topical), 518

Cortef Feminine Itch— *See* Corticosteroids—Low Potency (Topical), 518

Cortenema— *See* Corticosteroids (Rectal), 509

Corticaine— *See* Corticosteroids—Low Potency (Topical), 518

Corticosteroids (Dental), 495

Corticosteroids (Inhalation), 496

Corticosteroids (Nasal), 502

Corticosteroids (Ophthalmic), 505

Corticosteroids (Otic), 507

Corticosteroids (Rectal), 509

Corticosteroids and Acetic Acid (Otic), 511

Corticosteroids—Glucocorticoid Effects (Systemic), 513

Corticosteroids—Low Potency (Topical), 518

Corticosteroids—Medium to Very High Potency (Topical), 520

Corticreme— *See* Corticosteroids—Low Potency (Topical), 518

Cortifair— *See* Corticosteroids—Low Potency (Topical), 518

Cortifoam— *See* Corticosteroids (Rectal), 509

Cortiment-10— *See* Corticosteroids (Rectal), 509

Cortiment-40— *See* Corticosteroids (Rectal), 509

Cortisol— *See* Corticosteroids (Ophthalmic), 505; *See* Corticosteroids (Rectal), 509; *See* Corticosteroids and Acetic Acid (Otic), 511; *See* Corticosteroids—Glucocorticoid Effects (Systemic), 513; *See* Corticosteroids—Low Potency (Topical), 518

Cortisone— *See* Corticosteroids—Glucocorticoid Effects (Systemic), 513

Cortisporin— *See* Neomycin, Polymyxin B, and Hydrocortisone (Otic), 1172

Cortisporin Eye/Ear Suspension— *See* Neomycin, Polymyxin B, and Hydrocortisone (Ophthalmic), 1170

Cortisporin Ophthalmic Suspension— *See* Neomycin, Polymyxin B, and Hydrocortisone (Ophthalmic), 1170

Cortoderm— *See* Corticosteroids—Low Potency (Topical), 518

Cortomycin— *See* Neomycin, Polymyxin B, and Hydrocortisone (Otic), 1172

Cortone— *See* Corticosteroids—Glucocorticoid Effects (Systemic), 513

Cortone Acetate— *See* Corticosteroids—Glucocorticoid Effects (Systemic), 513

Cortone Acetate-ICN— *See* Corticosteroids—Glucocorticoid Effects (Systemic), 513

Cortril— *See* Corticosteroids—Low Potency (Topical), 518

Coryphen— *See* Salicylates (Systemic), 1394

Corzide— *See* Beta-adrenergic Blocking Agents and Thiazide Diuretics (Systemic), 278

Cosmegen— *See* Dactinomycin (Systemic), 565

Cosopt— *See* Dorzolamide and Timolol (Ophthalmic), 658

CoSudafed— *See* Cough/Cold Combinations (Systemic), 522

CoSudafed Cough Tablets with Decongestant— *See* Cough/Cold Combinations (Systemic), 522

CoSudafed Expectorant— *See* Cough/Cold Combinations (Systemic), 522

Cotabs— *See* Narcotic Analgesics and Acetaminophen (Systemic), 1138

Cotanal-65— *See* Narcotic Analgesics—For Pain Relief (Systemic), 1147

Cotazym— *See* Pancrelipase (Systemic), 1239

Cotazym-65 B— *See* Pancrelipase (Systemic), 1239

Cotazym E.C.S. 8— *See* Pancrelipase (Systemic), 1239

Cotazym E.C.S. 20— *See* Pancrelipase (Systemic), 1239

Cotazym-S— *See* Pancrelipase (Systemic), 1239

Cotolone— *See* Corticosteroids—Glucocorticoid Effects (Systemic), 513

Co-triamterzide— *See* Diuretics, Potassium-sparing and Hydrochlorothiazide (Systemic), 639

Cotridin— *See* Cough/Cold Combinations (Systemic), 522

Cotridin Expectorant— *See* Cough/Cold Combinations (Systemic), 522

Cotrim— *See* Sulfonamides and Trimethoprim (Systemic), 1454

Cotrimazine— *See* Sulfonamides and Trimethoprim (Systemic), 1454

Cotrim DS— *See* Sulfonamides and Trimethoprim (Systemic), 1454

Cotrimoxazole— *See* Sulfonamides and Trimethoprim (Systemic), 1454

Cotrim Pediatric— *See* Sulfonamides and Trimethoprim (Systemic), 1454

Co-Tuss V— *See* Cough/Cold Combinations (Systemic), 522

Cotylbutazone— *See* Anti-inflammatory Drugs, Nonsteroidal (Systemic), 179

CoTylenol Cold Medication— *See* Cough/Cold Combinations (Systemic), 522

Cough/Cold Combinations (Systemic), 522

Cough-X— *See* Dextromethorphan (Systemic), 592

Coumadin— *See* Anticoagulants (Systemic), 112, MC-24

Covangesic— *See* Antihistamines, Decongestants, and Analgesics (Systemic), 164

Covera-HS— *See* Verapamil (Systemic), MC-24

Coversyl— *See* Angiotensin-converting Enzyme (ACE) Inhibitors (Systemic), 90

Cozaar— *See* Losartan (Systemic), 1007, MC-14

CP Oral— *See* Antihistamines and Decongestants (Systemic), 159

CPT-11— *See* Irinotecan (Systemic), 933

Cramp End— *See* Anti-inflammatory Drugs, Nonsteroidal (Systemic), 179

Creon 5— *See* Pancrelipase (Systemic), 1239

Creon 10— *See* Pancrelipase (Systemic), 1239

Creon 20— *See* Pancrelipase (Systemic), 1239

Creo-Terpin— *See* Dextromethorphan (Systemic), 592

Crinone— *See* Progestins—For Noncontraceptive Use (Systemic), 1328

Criticare HN— *See* Enteral Nutrition Formulas (Systemic), #

Crixivan— *See* Indinavir (Systemic), 898

Crolom— *See* Cromolyn (Ophthalmic), 542

Cromoglicic acid— *See* Cromolyn (Inhalation), 537; *See* Cromolyn (Ophthalmic), 542

Cromoglycic acid— *See* Cromolyn (Inhalation), 537; *See* Cromolyn (Ophthalmic), 542

Cromolyn (Inhalation), 537

Cromolyn (Nasal), 541

Cromolyn (Ophthalmic), 542

Cromolyn (Oral), 543

Cromolyn Nasal Solution— *See* Cromolyn (Nasal), 541

Crotamiton (Topical), #

Crucial— *See* Enteral Nutrition Formulas (Systemic), #

Cruex Aerosol Powder— *See* Undecylenic Acid, Compound (Topical), #

Cruex Antifungal Cream— *See* Undecylenic Acid, Compound (Topical), #

Cruex Antifungal Powder— *See* Undecylenic Acid, Compound (Topical), #

Cruex Antifungal Spray Powder— *See* Undecylenic Acid, Compound (Topical), #

Cruex Cream— *See* Undecylenic Acid, Compound (Topical), #

Cruex Powder— *See* Undecylenic Acid, Compound (Topical), #

Crystamine— *See* Vitamin B_{12} (Systemic), 1575

Crysti-12— *See* Vitamin B_{12} (Systemic), 1575

Crysticillin 300 A.S.— *See* Penicillins (Systemic), 1251

C-Tussin Expectorant— *See* Cough/Cold Combinations (Systemic), 522

Cuplex Gel— *See* Salicylic Acid (Topical), #

Cupric Sulfate— *See* Copper Supplements (Systemic), 493

Cuprimine— *See* Penicillamine (Systemic), #

Cupri-Pak— *See* Copper Supplements (Systemic), 493

Curel Everyday Sun Protection— *See* Sunscreen Agents (Topical), #

Curretab— *See* Progestins—For Noncontraceptive Use (Systemic), 1328

Cutacura Acne 5 Cream— *See* Benzoyl Peroxide (Topical), 265

Cutar Water Dispersible Emollient Tar— *See* Coal Tar (Topical), 478

Cuticura Acne 5 Cream— *See* Benzoyl Peroxide (Topical), 265

Cuticura Ointment— *See* Sulfur (Topical), #

Cutivate— *See* Corticosteroids—Medium to Very High Potency (Topical), 520

Cutter Pleasant Protection— *See* Diethyltoluamide (Topical), #

Cyanide Antidote Package— *See* Sodium Thiosulfate (Systemic), #

Cyanocobalamin— *See* Vitamin B_{12} (Systemic), 1575

Cyanocobalamin Co 57— *See* Radiopharmaceuticals (Diagnostic), 1347

Cyanoject— *See* Vitamin B_{12} (Systemic), 1575

Cyclandelate (Systemic), 545

Cyclen— *See* Estrogens and Progestins (Oral Contraceptives) (Systemic), 729

Cyclizine— *See* Meclizine/Buclizine/Cyclizine (Systemic), 1038

Cyclobenzaprine (Systemic), 546, MC-6

Cyclocort— *See* Corticosteroids—Medium to Very High Potency (Topical), 520

Cyclogyl— *See* Cyclopentolate (Ophthalmic), 548

Cyclomen— *See* Danazol (Systemic), 570

Cyclopentolate (Ophthalmic), 548

Cyclophosphamide (Systemic), 549

Cycloserine (Systemic), 552

Cyclospasmol— *See* Cyclandelate (Systemic), 545

Cyclosporin A— *See* Cyclosporine (Systemic), 553

Cyclosporine (Systemic), 553, MC-6

Cycrin— *See* Progestins—For Noncontraceptive Use (Systemic), 1328, MC-14

Cyklokapron— *See* Antifibrinolytic Agents (Systemic), 140

Cylert— *See* Pemoline (Systemic), 1248, MC-18

Cylert Chewable— *See* Pemoline (Systemic), 1248

Cyomin— *See* Vitamin B_{12} (Systemic), 1575

Cyproheptadine— *See* Antihistamines (Systemic), 153, MC-6

Cyproterone (Systemic), 556

Cystadane— *See* Betaine (Systemic), 284

Cytadren— *See* Aminoglutethimide (Systemic), 42

Cystagon— *See* Cysteamine (Systemic), 558

Cysteamine (Systemic), 558

Cystospaz— *See* Anticholinergics/Antispasmodics (Systemic), 106

Cystospaz-M— *See* Anticholinergics/Antispasmodics (Systemic), 106

Cytadren— *See* Aminoglutethimide (Systemic), 42

Cytarabine (Systemic), 559

Cytarabine, Liposomal (Intrathecal), 561

Cytomel— *See* Thyroid Hormones (Systemic), 1503

Cytosar— *See* Cytarabine (Systemic), 559

Cytosar-U— *See* Cytarabine (Systemic), 559

Cytosine arabinoside— *See* Cytarabine (Systemic), 559

Cytotec— *See* Misoprostol (Systemic), 1108, MC-15

Cytovene— *See* Ganciclovir (Systemic), 813

Cytovene-IV— *See* Ganciclovir (Systemic), 813

Cytoxan— *See* Cyclophosphamide (Systemic), 549

D

Dacarbazine (Systemic), 562

D.A. Chewable— *See* Antihistamines, Decongestants, and Anticholinergics (Systemic), 170

Dacliximab— *See* Daclizumab (Systemic), 564

Daclizumab (Systemic), 564

Dacodyl— *See* Laxatives (Oral), 964; *See* Laxatives (Rectal), 970

Dactinomycin (Systemic), 565

Dagenan— *See* Sulfapyridine (Systemic), 1439

Dalacin— *See* Clindamycin (Vaginal), 452

Dalacin C— *See* Clindamycin (Systemic), 449

Dalacin C Flavored Granules— *See* Clindamycin (Systemic), 449

Dalacin C Phosphate— *See* Clindamycin (Systemic), 449

Dalacin T Topical Solution— *See* Clindamycin (Topical), 451

Dalalone— *See* Corticosteroids—Glucocorticoid Effects (Systemic), 513

Dalalone D.P.— *See* Corticosteroids—Glucocorticoid Effects (Systemic), 513

Dexacorten-LA— *See* Corticosteroids— Glucocorticoid Effects (Systemic), 513

Dexacort Turbinaire— *See* Corticosteroids (Nasal), 502

Dexafed Cough— *See* Cough/Cold Combinations (Systemic), 522

Dexair— *See* Corticosteroids (Ophthalmic), 505

Dexamethasone— *See* Corticosteroids (Inhalation), 496; *See* Corticosteroids (Nasal), 502; *See* Corticosteroids (Ophthalmic), 505; *See* Corticosteroids (Otic), 507; *See* Corticosteroids—Glucocorticoid Effects (Systemic), 513, MC-6; *See* Corticosteroids—Low Potency (Topical), 518

Dexamethasone Intensol— *See* Corticosteroids—Glucocorticoid Effects (Systemic), 513

Dexamfetamine— *See* Amphetamines (Systemic), 54

Dexaphen SA— *See* Antihistamines and Decongestants (Systemic), 159

Dexasone— *See* Corticosteroids—Glucocorticoid Effects (Systemic), 513

Dexasone L.A.— *See* Corticosteroids—Glucocorticoid Effects (Systemic), 513

Dexatrim Maximum Strength Caplets— *See* Phenylpropanolamine (Systemic), 1280

Dexatrim Maximum Strength Capsules— *See* Phenylpropanolamine (Systemic), 1280

Dexatrim Maximum Strength Tablets— *See* Phenylpropanolamine (Systemic), 1280

Dexbrompheniramine and Pseudoephedrine— *See* Antihistamines and Decongestants (Systemic), 159

Dexbrompheniramine, Pseudoephedrine, and Acetaminophen— *See* Antihistamines, Decongestants, and Analgesics (Systemic), 164

Dexchlor— *See* Antihistamines (Systemic), 153

Dexchlorpheniramine— *See* Antihistamines (Systemic), 153

Dexchlorpheniramine, Pseudoephedrine, and Guaifenesin— *See* Cough/Cold Combinations (Systemic), 522

Dexedrine— *See* Amphetamines (Systemic), 54

Dexedrine Spansule— *See* Amphetamines (Systemic), 54, MC-7

DexFerrum— *See* Iron Supplements (Systemic), 936

DexIron— *See* Iron Supplements (Systemic), 936

Dexitac Stay Alert Stimulant— *See* Caffeine (Systemic), 339

Dexone— *See* Corticosteroids—Glucocorticoid Effects (Systemic), 513

Dexone 0.75— *See* Corticosteroids—Glucocorticoid Effects (Systemic), 513

Dexone 1.5— *See* Corticosteroids—Glucocorticoid Effects (Systemic), 513

Dexone 4— *See* Corticosteroids—Glucocorticoid Effects (Systemic), 513

Dexone LA— *See* Corticosteroids—Glucocorticoid Effects (Systemic), 513

Dexophed— *See* Antihistamines and Decongestants (Systemic), 159

Dexotic— *See* Corticosteroids (Ophthalmic), 505

Dexrazoxane (Systemic), 591

Dextroamphetamine— *See* Amphetamines (Systemic), 54, MC-7

Dextromethorphan (Systemic), 592

Dextromethorphan and Acetaminophen— *See* Cough/Cold Combinations (Systemic), 522

Dextromethorphan and Guaifenesin— *See* Cough/Cold Combinations (Systemic), 522

Dextromethorphan and Iodinated Glycerol— *See* Cough/Cold Combinations (Systemic), 522

Dextropropoxyphene— *See* Narcotic Analgesics—For Pain Relief (Systemic), 1147

Dextrose and Electrolytes— *See* Carbohydrates and Electrolytes (Systemic), 370

DextroStat— *See* Amphetamines (Systemic), 54

Dextrothyroxine (Systemic), 594

Dey-Lute Isoetharine S/F— *See* Bronchodilators, Adrenergic (Inhalation), 304

Dey-Lute Metaproterenol— *See* Bronchodilators, Adrenergic (Inhalation), 304

Dezocine (Systemic), 595

DFMO— *See* Eflornithine (Systemic), #

DFP— *See* Antiglaucoma Agents, Cholinergic, Long-acting (Ophthalmic), 148

DHCplus— *See* Narcotic Analgesics and Acetaminophen (Systemic), 1138

D.H.E. 45— *See* Headache Medicines, Ergot Derivative–containing (Systemic), 853

DHPG— *See* Ganciclovir (Systemic), 813

DHS Tar Gel Shampoo— *See* Coal Tar (Topical), 478

DHS Tar Shampoo— *See* Coal Tar (Topical), 478

DHS Zinc— *See* Pyrithione (Topical), #

DHT— *See* Vitamin D and Related Compounds (Systemic), 1577

DHT Intensol— *See* Vitamin D and Related Compounds (Systemic), 1577

DiaBeta— *See* Antidiabetic Agents, Sulfonylurea (Systemic), 131

Diabetic Tussin DM— *See* Cough/Cold Combinations (Systemic), 522

Diabetic Tussin EX— *See* Guaifenesin (Systemic), 844

DiabetiSource— *See* Enteral Nutrition Formulas (Systemic), #

Diabe-TUSS DM— *See* Dextromethorphan (Systemic), 592

Diabinese— *See* Antidiabetic Agents, Sulfonylurea (Systemic), 131

Dialose— *See* Laxatives (Oral), 964

Dialose Plus— *See* Laxatives (Oral), 964

Dialume— *See* Antacids (Oral), 98

Diamicron— *See* Antidiabetic Agents, Sulfonylurea (Systemic), 131

Diamox— *See* Carbonic Anhydrase Inhibitors (Systemic), 373

Diamox Sequels— *See* Carbonic Anhydrase Inhibitors (Systemic), 373

Diaper Rash Ointment— *See* Calamine (Topical), 342

Diapid— *See* Lypressin (Systemic), 1014

Diar-Aid— *See* Attapulgite (Oral), 222

Diarrest— *See* Attapulgite (Oral), 222

Diarr-Eze— *See* Loperamide (Oral), 1001

Diasorb— *See* Attapulgite (Oral), 222

Diastat— *See* Benzodiazepines (Systemic), 257

Diatrizoate and Iodipamide— *See* Radiopaque Agents (Diagnostic, Local), #

Diatrizoates— *See* Radiopaque Agents (Diagnostic), #; *See* Radiopaque Agents (Diagnostic, Local), #

Diatrol— *See* Attapulgite (Oral), 222

Diazemuls— *See* Benzodiazepines (Systemic), 257

Diazepam— *See* Benzodiazepines (Systemic), 257, MC-7

Diazepam Intensol— *See* Benzodiazepines (Systemic), 257

Diazoxide (Oral), 597

Dibent— *See* Anticholinergics/Antispasmodics (Systemic), 106

Dibenzyline— *See* Phenoxybenzamine (Systemic), 1277

Dibucaine— *See* Anesthetics (Rectal), 85; *See* Anesthetics (Topical), 88

Dicarbosil— *See* Antacids (Oral), 98; *See* Calcium Supplements (Systemic), 353

Dichlorphenamide— *See* Carbonic Anhydrase Inhibitors (Systemic), 373

Diclofenac— *See* Anti-inflammatory Drugs, Nonsteroidal (Ophthalmic), 177; *See* Anti-inflammatory Drugs, Nonsteroidal (Systemic), 179, MC-7

Diclofenac (Topical), 599

Diclofenac and Misoprostol (Systemic), 601, MC-7

Diclofenamide— *See* Carbonic Anhydrase Inhibitors (Systemic), 373

Dicloxacillin— *See* Penicillins (Systemic), 1251

Dicoumarol— *See* Anticoagulants (Systemic), 112

Dicumarol— *See* Anticoagulants (Systemic), 112

Dicyclomine— *See* Anticholinergics/Antispasmodics (Systemic), 106, MC-7

Dicycloverine— *See* Anticholinergics/Antispasmodics (Systemic), 106

Didanosine (Systemic), 603

2,3-dideoxyinosine— *See* Didanosine (Systemic), 603

Didrex— *See* Appetite Suppressants, Sympathomimetic (Systemic), 197

Didronel— *See* Etidronate (Systemic), 743

Dienestrol— *See* Estrogens (Vaginal), 724

Diet-Aid Maximum Strength— *See* Phenylpropanolamine (Systemic), 1280

Diethylcarbamazine (Systemic), #

Diethylpropion— *See* Appetite Suppressants, Sympathomimetic (Systemic), 197

Diethylstilbestrol— *See* Estrogens (Systemic), 718

Diethylstilbestrol and Methyltestosterone— *See* Androgens and Estrogens (Systemic), 76

Diethyltoluamide (Topical), #

Difenidol— *See* Diphenidol (Systemic), 614

Difenoxin and Atropine (Systemic), 606

Differin— *See* Adapalene (Topical), 22

Diflorasone— *See* Corticosteroids—Medium to Very High Potency (Topical), 520

Diflucan— *See* Antifungals, Azole (Systemic), 142, MC-9

Diflucan-150— *See* Antifungals, Azole (Systemic), 142, MC-9

Diflucortolone— *See* Corticosteroids—Medium to Very High Potency (Topical), 520

Diflunisal— *See* Anti-inflammatory Drugs, Nonsteroidal (Systemic), 179

Difluorophate— *See* Antiglaucoma Agents, Cholinergic, Long-acting (Ophthalmic), 148

Difluphyl— *See* Antiglaucoma Agents, Cholinergic, Long-acting (Ophthalmic), 148

Diflupyl— *See* Antiglaucoma Agents, Cholinergic, Long-acting (Ophthalmic), 148

Di-Gel— *See* Antacids (Oral), 98

Digitaline— *See* Digitalis Medicines (Systemic), 608

Digitalis Medicines (Systemic), 608

Digitek— *See* Digoxin (Systemic), MC-7

Digitoxin— *See* Digitalis Medicines (Systemic), 608

Digoxin— *See* Digitalis Medicines (Systemic), 608, MC-7

Dihistine DH— *See* Cough/Cold Combinations (Systemic), 522

Dihistine Expectorant— *See* Cough/Cold Combinations (Systemic), 522

Dihydrocodeine, Acetaminophen, and Caffeine— *See* Narcotic Analgesics and Acetaminophen (Systemic), 1138

Dihydrocodeine compound— *See* Narcotic Analgesics and Aspirin (Systemic), 1142

Dihydroergotamine— *See* Headache Medicines, Ergot Derivative–containing (Systemic), 853

Dihydroergotamine (Nasal-Systemic), 610

Dihydroergotamine mesilate— *See* Dihydroergotamine (Nasal-Systemic), 610

Dihydroergotamine-Sandoz— *See* Headache Medicines, Ergot Derivative–containing (Systemic), 853

Dihydromorphinone— *See* Narcotic Analgesics—For Pain Relief (Systemic), 1147

Dihydrotachysterol— *See* Vitamin D and Related Compounds (Systemic), 1577

Diiodohydroxyquin— *See* Iodoquinol (Oral), #

Diiodohydroxyquinoline— *See* Iodoquinol (Oral), #

Dilacor-XR— *See* Calcium Channel Blocking Agents (Systemic), 349

Dilantin— *See* Anticonvulsants, Hydantoin (Systemic), 117

Dilantin-30— *See* Anticonvulsants, Hydantoin (Systemic), 117

Dilantin-125— *See* Anticonvulsants, Hydantoin (Systemic), 117

Dilantin Infatabs— *See* Anticonvulsants, Hydantoin (Systemic), 117, MC-19

Dilantin Kapseals— *See* Anticonvulsants, Hydantoin (Systemic), 117, MC-19

Dilatair— *See* Phenylephrine (Ophthalmic), #

Dilatrate-SR— *See* Nitrates—Oral (Systemic), 1188

Dilaudid— *See* Narcotic Analgesics—For Pain Relief (Systemic), 1147

Dilaudid-5— *See* Narcotic Analgesics—For Pain Relief (Systemic), 1147

Dilaudid Cough— *See* Cough/Cold Combinations (Systemic), 522

Dilaudid-HP— *See* Narcotic Analgesics—For Pain Relief (Systemic), 1147

Dilocaine— *See* Anesthetics (Parenteral-Local), 83

Dilor— *See* Dyphylline (Systemic), 674

Dilor-202037— *See* Dyphylline (Systemic), 674

Dilotab— *See* Decongestants and Analgesics (Systemic), 581

Diloxanide (Systemic), #

Diltiazem— *See* Calcium Channel Blocking Agents (Systemic), 349, MC-7

Dimacol Caplets— *See* Cough/Cold Combinations (Systemic), 522

Dimaphen— *See* Antihistamines and Decongestants (Systemic), 159

Dimaphen S.A.— *See* Antihistamines and Decongestants (Systemic), 159

Dimelor— *See* Antidiabetic Agents, Sulfonylurea (Systemic), 131

Dimenhydrinate— *See* Antihistamines (Systemic), 153

dimercaptosuccinic acid— *See* Succimer (Systemic), 1437

Dimetane— *See* Antihistamines (Systemic), 153

Dimetane-DC Cough— *See* Cough/Cold Combinations (Systemic), 522

Dimetane Decongestant— *See* Antihistamines and Decongestants (Systemic), 159

Dimetane Decongestant Caplets— *See* Antihistamines and Decongestants (Systemic), 159

Dimetane-DX Cough— *See* Cough/Cold Combinations (Systemic), 522

Dimetane Expectorant— *See* Cough/Cold Combinations (Systemic), 522

Dimetane Expectorant-C— *See* Cough/Cold Combinations (Systemic), 522

Dimetane Expectorant-DC— *See* Cough/Cold Combinations (Systemic), 522

Dimetapp— *See* Antihistamines and Decongestants (Systemic), 159

Dimetapp Allergy Liqui-Gels— *See* Antihistamines (Systemic), 153

Dimetapp Allergy Sinus Caplets— *See* Antihistamines, Decongestants, and Analgesics (Systemic), 164

Dimetapp-A Sinus— *See* Decongestants and Analgesics (Systemic), 581

Dimetapp-C— *See* Cough/Cold Combinations (Systemic), 522

Dimetapp Chewables— *See* Antihistamines and Decongestants (Systemic), 159

Dimetapp Clear— *See* Antihistamines and Decongestants (Systemic), 159

Dimetapp Cold and Allergy— *See* Antihistamines and Decongestants (Systemic), 159

Dimetapp Cold & Allergy Quick Dissolve— *See* Antihistamines and Decongestants (Systemic), 159

Dimetapp Cold & Fever Suspension— *See* Antihistamines, Decongestants, and Analgesics (Systemic), 164

Dimetapp DM— *See* Cough/Cold Combinations (Systemic), 522

Dimetapp-DM— *See* Cough/Cold Combinations (Systemic), 522

Dimetapp DM Cold & Cough— *See* Cough/Cold Combinations (Systemic), 522

Dimetapp Extentabs— *See* Antihistamines and Decongestants (Systemic), 159

Dimetapp 4-Hour— *See* Antihistamines and Decongestants (Systemic), 159

Dimetapp Liqui-Fills— *See* Antihistamines and Decongestants (Systemic), 159

Dimetapp Maximum Strength Cold & Cough Liqui-Gels— *See* Cough/Cold Combinations (Systemic), 522

Dimetapp Oral Infant Drops— *See* Antihistamines and Decongestants (Systemic), 159

Dimetapp Sinus Caplets— *See* Decongestants and Analgesics (Systemic), 581

Dimethyl Sulfoxide (Mucosal), 612

D(Rh$_o$) immune globulin— *See* Rh$_o$(D) Immune Globulin (Systemic), 1360

Dinate— *See* Antihistamines (Systemic), 153

Dinoprost (Intra-amniotic), #

Dinoprostone (Cervical/Vaginal), 613

Diocaine— *See* Anesthetics (Ophthalmic), #

Diocto— *See* Laxatives (Oral), 964

Diocto-C— *See* Laxatives (Oral), 964

Diocto-K— *See* Laxatives (Oral), 964

Diocto-K Plus— *See* Laxatives (Oral), 964

Dioctolose Plus— *See* Laxatives (Oral), 964

Diodex— *See* Corticosteroids (Ophthalmic), 505

Diodoquin— *See* Iodoquinol (Oral), #

Dioeze— *See* Laxatives (Oral), 964

Dioneofrine— *See* Phenylephrine (Ophthalmic), #

Diosuccin— *See* Laxatives (Oral), 964

Dioval 40— *See* Estrogens (Systemic), 718

Dioval XX— *See* Estrogens (Systemic), 718

Diovan— *See* Valsartan (Systemic), 1553, MC-24

Diovan HCT— *See* Valsartan and Hydrochlorothiazide (Systemic), 1555, MC-24

Diovol— *See* Antacids (Oral), 98

Diovol Caplets— *See* Antacids (Oral), 98

Diovol Ex— *See* Antacids (Oral), 98

Diovol Extra Strength— *See* Antacids (Oral), 98

Diovol Plus— *See* Antacids (Oral), 98

Diovol Plus AF— *See* Antacids (Oral), 98

Dioxybenzone, Oxybenzone, and Padimate O— *See* Sunscreen Agents (Topical), #

Dipentum— *See* Olsalazine (Oral), 1211

Diphen Cough— *See* Antihistamines (Systemic), 153

Diphenhist— *See* Antihistamines (Systemic), 153

Diphenhist Captabs— *See* Antihistamines (Systemic), 153

Diphenhydramine— *See* Antihistamines (Systemic), 153

Diphenhydramine, Codeine, and Ammonium Chloride— *See* Cough/Cold Combinations (Systemic), 522

Diphenhydramine, Dextromethorphan, and Ammonium Chloride— *See* Cough/Cold Combinations (Systemic), 522

Diphenhydramine, Phenylpropanolamine, and Aspirin— *See* Antihistamines, Decongestants, and Analgesics (Systemic), 164

Diphenhydramine and Pseudoephedrine— *See* Antihistamines and Decongestants (Systemic), 159

Diphenhydramine, Pseudoephedrine, and Acetaminophen— *See* Antihistamines, Decongestants, and Analgesics (Systemic), 164

Diphenidol (Systemic), 614

Diphenoxylate and Atropine (Systemic), 615, MC-3

Diphenpyraline, Phenylephrine, and Dextromethorphan— *See* Cough/Cold Combinations (Systemic), 522

Diphenylhydantoin— *See* Anticonvulsants, Hydantoin (Systemic), 117

Diphenylpyraline, Phenylpropanolamine, Acetaminophen, and Caffeine— *See* Antihistamines, Decongestants, and Analgesics (Systemic), 164

Diphtheria Antitoxin (Systemic), #

Diphtheria and Tetanus Toxoids (Systemic), 618

Diphtheria and Tetanus Toxoids for Pediatric Use— *See* Diphtheria and Tetanus Toxoids (Systemic), 618

Diphtheria and Tetanus Toxoids and Pertussis Vaccine Adsorbed (Systemic), 619

Diphtheria and Tetanus Toxoids and Pertussis Vaccine Adsorbed and Haemophilus b Conjugate Vaccine (Systemic), 621

Dipivefrin (Ophthalmic), 622

Dipivefrine— *See* Dipivefrin (Ophthalmic), 622

Diprivan— *See* Anesthetics, General (Systemic), #

Diprolene— *See* Corticosteroids—Medium to Very High Potency (Topical), 520

Diprolene AF— *See* Corticosteroids—Medium to Very High Potency (Topical), 520

Diprophylline— *See* Dyphylline (Systemic), 674

Diprosone— *See* Corticosteroids—Medium to Very High Potency (Topical), 520

Dipyridamole and Aspirin (Systemic), 623

Dipyridamole—Diagnostic (Systemic), 625

Dipyridamole—Therapeutic (Systemic), 626, MC-7

Diquinol— *See* Iodoquinol (Oral), #

Dirithromycin (Systemic), 628

Disalcid— *See* Salicylates (Systemic), 1394

Disipal— *See* Orphenadrine (Systemic), 1220

Disobrom— *See* Antihistamines and Decongestants (Systemic), 159

Disodium clodronate— *See* Clodronate (Systemic), 456

Disophrol Chronotabs— *See* Antihistamines and Decongestants (Systemic), 159

Disopyramide (Systemic), 629

Di-Sosul— *See* Laxatives (Oral), 964

Di-Sosul Forte— *See* Laxatives (Oral), 964

Di-Spaz— *See* Anticholinergics/Antispasmodics (Systemic), 106

Disulfiram (Systemic), 631

Dithranol— *See* Anthralin (Topical), 102

Ditropan— *See* Oxybutynin (Systemic), 1230

Ditropan XL— *See* Oxybutynin (Systemic), MC-18

Diucardin— *See* Diuretics, Thiazide (Systemic), 642

Diuchlor H— *See* Diuretics, Thiazide (Systemic), 642

Diulo— *See* Diuretics, Thiazide (Systemic), 642

Diupres— *See* Rauwolfia Alkaloids and Thiazide Diuretics (Systemic), #

Diuretics, Loop (Systemic), 633

Diuretics, Potassium-sparing (Systemic), 636

Diuretics, Potassium-sparing, and Hydrochlorothiazide (Systemic), 639

Diuretics, Thiazide (Systemic), 642

Diurigen with Reserpine— *See* Rauwolfia Alkaloids and Thiazide Diuretics (Systemic), #

Diuril— *See* Diuretics, Thiazide (Systemic), 642

Diutensen-R— *See* Rauwolfia Alkaloids and Thiazide Diuretics (Systemic), #

Divalproex— *See* Valproic Acid (Systemic), 1549, MC-8

Dixarit— *See* Clonidine (Systemic), 464

Dizac— *See* Benzodiazepines (Systemic), 257

dl-Methionine— *See* Racemethionine (Systemic), #

DML Facial Moisturizer— *See* Sunscreen Agents (Topical), #

DMSA— *See* Succimer (Systemic), 1437

DMSO— *See* Dimethyl Sulfoxide (Mucosal), 612

DNase I— *See* Dornase Alfa (Inhalation), 654

Doak Oil— *See* Coal Tar (Topical), 478

Doak Oil Forte— *See* Coal Tar (Topical), 478

Doak Oil Forte Therapeutic Bath Treatment— *See* Coal Tar (Topical), 478

Doak Oil Therapeutic Bath Treatment For All-Over Body Care— *See* Coal Tar (Topical), 478

Doak Tar Lotion— *See* Coal Tar (Topical), 478

Doak Tar Shampoo— *See* Coal Tar (Topical), 478

Doan's Backache Pills— *See* Salicylates (Systemic), 1394

Doan's Regular Strength Tablets— *See* Salicylates (Systemic), 1394

Docetaxel (Systemic), 646

Docosanol (Topical), 648

Doctar Hair & Scalp Shampoo and Conditioner— *See* Coal Tar (Topical), 478

Doctar Shampoo— *See* Coal Tar (Topical), 478

Docucal-P— *See* Laxatives (Oral), 964

Docu-K Plus— *See* Laxatives (Oral), 964

Docusate— *See* Laxatives (Oral), 964; *See* Laxatives (Rectal), 970

Dodd's Extra Strength— *See* Salicylates (Systemic), 1394

Dodd's Pills— *See* Salicylates (Systemic), 1394

Dofetilide (Systemic), 649

DOK— *See* Laxatives (Oral), 964

DOK Softgels— *See* Laxatives (Oral), 964

Doktors— *See* Phenylephrine (Nasal), 1278

Dolacet— *See* Narcotic Analgesics and Acetaminophen (Systemic), 1138

Dolagesic— *See* Narcotic Analgesics and Acetaminophen (Systemic), 1138

Dolasetron (Systemic), 650

Dolgesic— *See* Anti-inflammatory Drugs, Nonsteroidal (Systemic), 179

Dolmar— *See* Butalbital and Acetaminophen (Systemic), 324

Dolobid— *See* Anti-inflammatory Drugs, Nonsteroidal (Systemic), 179

Dolomine— *See* Salicylates (Systemic), 1394

Dolophine— *See* Narcotic Analgesics—For Pain Relief (Systemic), 1147

Dolotic— *See* Antipyrine and Benzocaine (Otic), 192

Dolsed— *See* Atropine, Hyoscyamine, Methenamine, Methylene Blue, Phenyl Salicylate, and Benzoic Acid (Systemic), 218

Domperidone (Systemic), 652

Dom-Valproic— *See* Valproic Acid (Systemic), 1549

Donatussin— *See* Cough/Cold Combinations (Systemic), 522

Donatussin DC— *See* Cough/Cold Combinations (Systemic), 522

Donatussin Drops— *See* Cough/Cold Combinations (Systemic), 522

Dondril— *See* Cough/Cold Combinations (Systemic), 522

Donepezil (Systemic), 653, MC-8

Donnagel— *See* Attapulgite (Oral), 222; *See* Kaolin, Pectin, and Belladonna Alkaloids (Systemic), #

Donnagel-MB— *See* Kaolin and Pectin (Oral), 946

Donnagel-PG— *See* Kaolin, Pectin, and Paregoric (Systemic), #

Donnamor— *See* Belladonna Alkaloids and Barbiturates (Systemic), 252

Donnapine— *See* Belladonna Alkaloids and Barbiturates (Systemic), 252

Donnatal— *See* Belladonna Alkaloids and Barbiturates (Systemic), 252

Donnatal Extentabs— *See* Belladonna Alkaloids and Barbiturates (Systemic), 252

Donnatal No. 2— *See* Belladonna Alkaloids and Barbiturates (Systemic), 252

Donphen— *See* Belladonna Alkaloids and Barbiturates (Systemic), 252

Dopamet— *See* Methyldopa (Systemic), 1072

Doral— *See* Benzodiazepines (Systemic), 257

Dorcol Children's Cold Formula— *See* Antihistamines and Decongestants (Systemic), 159

Dorcol Children's Cough— *See* Cough/Cold Combinations (Systemic), 522

Dorcol Children's Decongestant Liquid— *See* Pseudoephedrine (Systemic), 1334

Dorcol DM— *See* Cough/Cold Combinations (Systemic), 522

Dormanex 2— *See* Antihistamines (Systemic), 153

Dormarex 2— *See* Antihistamines (Systemic), 153

Dornase Alfa (Inhalation), 654, 1629

Doryx— *See* Tetracyclines (Systemic), 1487

Dorzolamide (Ophthalmic), 656

Dorzolamide and Timolol (Ophthalmic), 658

Dosaflex— *See* Laxatives (Oral), 964

Doss— *See* Laxatives (Oral), 964

D.O.S. Softgels— *See* Laxatives (Oral), 964

Dostinex— *See* Cabergoline (Systemic), 338

Dovonex— *See* Calcipotriene (Topical), 343

Doxazosin (Systemic), 660, MC-8

Doxepin— *See* Antidepressants, Tricyclic (Systemic), 126, MC-8

Doxepin (Topical), 662

Doxidan— *See* Laxatives (Oral), 964

Emo-Cort— See Corticosteroids—Low Potency (Topical), 518

Emo-Cort Scalp Solution— See Corticosteroids—Low Potency (Topical), 518

Empirin— See Salicylates (Systemic), 1394

Empirin with Codeine No.3— See Narcotic Analgesics and Aspirin (Systemic), 1142

Empirin with Codeine No.4— See Narcotic Analgesics and Aspirin (Systemic), 1142

Empracet-30— See Narcotic Analgesics and Acetaminophen (Systemic), 1138

Empracet-60— See Narcotic Analgesics and Acetaminophen (Systemic), 1138

Emtec-30— See Narcotic Analgesics and Acetaminophen (Systemic), 1138

Emulsoil— See Laxatives (Oral), 964

E-Mycin— See Erythromycins (Systemic), 712

ENA 713— *See* Rivastigmine (Systemic), 1385

Enalapril— See Angiotensin-converting Enzyme (ACE) Inhibitors (Systemic), 90, MC-8

Enalaprilat— *See* Angiotensin-converting Enzyme (ACE) Inhibitors (Systemic), 90

Enalapril and Diltiazem (Systemic), 681

Enalapril and Felodipine (Systemic), 683

Enalapril and Hydrochlorothiazide— *See* Angiotensin-converting Enzyme (ACE) Inhibitors and Hydrochlorothiazide (Systemic), 94, MC-8

Enbrel— See Etanercept (Systemic), 734

Encainide (Systemic), 685

Encare— See Spermicides (Vaginal), 1428

Endafed— See Antihistamines and Decongestants (Systemic), 159

Endagen-HD— See Cough/Cold Combinations (Systemic), 522

Endal— See Cough/Cold Combinations (Systemic), 522

Endal Expectorant— See Cough/Cold Combinations (Systemic), 522

Endal-HD— See Cough/Cold Combinations (Systemic), 522

Endal-HD Plus— See Cough/Cold Combinations (Systemic), 522

Endantadine— See Amantadine (Systemic), 38

Endep— See Antidepressants, Tricyclic (Systemic), 126

Endocaine— See Anesthetics (Topical), 88

Endocet— See Narcotic Analgesics and Acetaminophen (Systemic), 1138, MC-18

Endolor— See Butalbital and Acetaminophen (Systemic), 324

Endur-Acin— See Niacin (Vitamin B$_3$) (Systemic), 1175; *See* Niacin—For High Cholesterol (Systemic), 1177

Enduron— See Diuretics, Thiazide (Systemic), 642

Enduronyl— See Rauwolfia Alkaloids and Thiazide Diuretics (Systemic), #

Enduronyl Forte— See Rauwolfia Alkaloids and Thiazide Diuretics (Systemic), #

Enemol— See Laxatives (Rectal), 970

Enercal— See Enteral Nutrition Formulas (Systemic), #

Enerjets— See Caffeine (Systemic), 339

Enfamil— See Infant Formulas (Systemic), #

Enfamil Human Milk Fortifier— See Infant Formulas (Systemic), #

Enfamil with Iron— See Infant Formulas (Systemic), #

Enfamil Premature Formula— See Infant Formulas (Systemic), #

Enfamil Premature Formula with Iron— See Infant Formulas (Systemic), #

Enflurane— *See* Anesthetics, General (Systemic), #

Engerix-B— See Hepatitis B Vaccine Recombinant (Systemic), 861

Enkaid— See Encainide (Systemic), 685

Enomine— See Cough/Cold Combinations (Systemic), 522

Enoxacin— *See* Fluoroquinolones (Systemic), 776

Enoxaparin (Systemic), 686

Ensure— See Enteral Nutrition Formulas (Systemic), #

Ensure with Fiber— See Enteral Nutrition Formulas (Systemic), #

Ensure High Protein— See Enteral Nutrition Formulas (Systemic), #

Ensure HN— See Enteral Nutrition Formulas (Systemic), #

Ensure Plus— See Enteral Nutrition Formulas (Systemic), #

Ensure Plus HN— See Enteral Nutrition Formulas (Systemic), #

E.N.T.— See Antihistamines and Decongestants (Systemic), 159

Entacapone (Systemic), 688

Entacyl— See Piperazine (Systemic), #

Entamide— See Diloxanide (Systemic), #

Enteral Nutrition Formula, Blenderized— *See* Enteral Nutrition Formulas (Systemic), #

Enteral Nutrition Formula, Disease-specific— *See* Enteral Nutrition Formulas (Systemic), #

Enteral Nutrition Formula, Fiber-containing— *See* Enteral Nutrition Formulas (Systemic), #

Enteral Nutrition Formula, Milk-based— *See* Enteral Nutrition Formulas (Systemic), #

Enteral Nutrition Formula, Modular— *See* Enteral Nutrition Formulas (Systemic), #

Enteral Nutrition Formula, Monomeric (Elemental)— *See* Enteral Nutrition Formulas (Systemic), #

Enteral Nutrition Formula, Polymeric— *See* Enteral Nutrition Formulas (Systemic), #

Enteral Nutrition Formulas (Systemic), #

Entex— See Cough/Cold Combinations (Systemic), 522

Entex LA— See Cough/Cold Combinations (Systemic), 522

Entex Liquid— See Cough/Cold Combinations (Systemic), 522

Entex PSE— See Cough/Cold Combinations (Systemic), 522

Entocort— See Corticosteroids (Rectal), 509; *See* Corticosteroids—Glucocorticoid Effects (Systemic), 513

Entrition Half-Strength— See Enteral Nutrition Formulas (Systemic), #

Entrition HN— See Enteral Nutrition Formulas (Systemic), #

Entrophen Caplets— See Salicylates (Systemic), 1394

Entrophen Extra Strength— See Salicylates (Systemic), 1394

Entrophen 15 Maximum Strength Tablets— See Salicylates (Systemic), 1394

Entrophen 10 Super Strength Caplets— See Salicylates (Systemic), 1394

Entrophen Tablets— See Salicylates (Systemic), 1394

Entuss-D— See Cough/Cold Combinations (Systemic), 522

Entuss-D Jr.— See Cough/Cold Combinations (Systemic), 522

Entuss Expectorant— See Cough/Cold Combinations (Systemic), 522

Enulose— See Laxatives (Oral), 964

Enzymase-16— See Pancrelipase (Systemic), 1239

Epatiol— See Tiopronin (Systemic), #

Ephedrine— *See* Bronchodilators, Adrenergic (Oral/Injection), 310

Ephedrine, Carbetapentane, and Guaifenesin— *See* Cough/Cold Combinations (Systemic), 522

Ephedrine and Guaifenesin— *See* Cough/Cold Combinations (Systemic), 522

Ephedrine and Potassium Iodide— *See* Cough/Cold Combinations (Systemic), 522

Epiclase— See Phenacemide (Systemic), #

Epifoam— See Corticosteroids—Low Potency (Topical), 518

Epifrin— See Epinephrine (Ophthalmic), 689

Epimorph— See Narcotic Analgesics—For Pain Relief (Systemic), 1147; *See* Narcotic Analgesics—For Surgery and Obstetrics (Systemic), 1154

Epinal— See Epinephrine (Ophthalmic), 689

Epinephrine— *See* Bronchodilators, Adrenergic (Inhalation), 304; *See* Bronchodilators, Adrenergic (Oral/Injection), 310

Epinephrine (Ophthalmic), 689

Epinephryl Borate— *See* Epinephrine (Ophthalmic), 689

EpiPen Auto-Injector— See Bronchodilators, Adrenergic (Oral/Injection), 310

EpiPen Jr. Auto-Injector— See Bronchodilators, Adrenergic (Oral/Injection), 310

Epirubicin (Systemic), 690

Epistatin— *See* HMG-CoA Reductase Inhibitors (Systemic), 869

Epitol— See Carbamazepine (Systemic), 366

Epival— See Valproic Acid (Systemic), 1549

Epivir— See Lamivudine (Systemic), 955, 1629, MC-13

Epivir-HBV— See Lamivudine (Systemic), 955, MC-13

EPO— *See* Epoetin (Systemic), 693

Epoetin (Systemic), 693

Epogen— See Epoetin (Systemic), 693

Epoprostenol (Systemic), 695

Eppy/N— See Epinephrine (Ophthalmic), 689

Eprex— See Epoetin (Systemic), 693

Epromate-M— See Meprobamate and Aspirin (Systemic), 1048

Eprosartan (Systemic), 698

Epsom salts— *See* Laxatives (Oral), 964

Eptastatin— *See* HMG-CoA Reductase Inhibitors (Systemic), 869

Equagesic— See Meprobamate and Aspirin (Systemic), 1048

Equalactin— See Laxatives (Oral), 964

Equanil— *See* Meprobamate (Systemic), #

Equibron G— *See* Theophylline and Guaifenesin (Systemic), #

Equilet— *See* Antacids (Oral), 98

Ercaf— *See* Headache Medicines, Ergot Derivative–containing (Systemic), 853

Ergamisol— *See* Levamisole (Systemic), 980

Ergo-Caff— *See* Headache Medicines, Ergot Derivative–containing (Systemic), 853

Ergocalciferol— *See* Vitamin D and Related Compounds (Systemic), 1577

Ergodryl— *See* Headache Medicines, Ergot Derivative–containing (Systemic), 853

Ergoloid Mesylates (Systemic), 699

Ergomar— *See* Headache Medicines, Ergot Derivative–containing (Systemic), 853

Ergometrine— *See* Ergonovine/Methylergonovine (Systemic), 700

Ergonovine— *See* Ergonovine/Methylergonovine (Systemic), 700

Ergonovine/Methylergonovine (Systemic), 700

Ergostat— *See* Headache Medicines, Ergot Derivative–containing (Systemic), 853

Ergot alkaloids, dihydrogenated— *See* Ergoloid Mesylates (Systemic), 699

Ergotamine— *See* Headache Medicines, Ergot Derivative–containing (Systemic), 853

Ergotamine, Belladonna Alkaloids, and Phenobarbital (Systemic), 702

Ergotamine and Caffeine— *See* Headache Medicines, Ergot Derivative–containing (Systemic), 853

Ergotamine, Caffeine, and Belladonna Alkaloids— *See* Headache Medicines, Ergot Derivative–containing (Systemic), 853

Ergotamine, Caffeine, Belladonna Alkaloids, and Pentobarbital— *See* Headache Medicines, Ergot Derivative–containing (Systemic), 853

Ergotamine, Caffeine, and Cyclizine— *See* Headache Medicines, Ergot Derivative–containing (Systemic), 853

Ergotamine, Caffeine, and Dimenhydrinate— *See* Headache Medicines, Ergot Derivative–containing (Systemic), 853

Ergotamine, Caffeine, and Diphenhydramine— *See* Headache Medicines, Ergot Derivative–containing (Systemic), 853

Ergotrate— *See* Ergonovine/Methylergonovine (Systemic), 700

Ergotrate Maleate— *See* Ergonovine/Methylergonovine (Systemic), 700

Eridium— *See* Phenazopyridine (Systemic), 1267

Erybid— *See* Erythromycins (Systemic), 712

Eryc— *See* Erythromycins (Systemic), 712

ERYC-250— *See* Erythromycins (Systemic), 712

ERYC-333— *See* Erythromycins (Systemic), 712

Erycette— *See* Erythromycin (Topical), 706

EryDerm— *See* Erythromycin (Topical), 706

Erygel— *See* Erythromycin (Topical), 706

Erymax— *See* Erythromycin (Topical), 706

EryPed— *See* Erythromycins (Systemic), 712

Ery-Sol— *See* Erythromycin (Topical), 706

Ery-Tab— *See* Erythromycins (Systemic), 712, MC-8

Erythra-Derm— *See* Erythromycin (Topical), 706

Erythro— *See* Erythromycins (Systemic), 712

Erythrocin— *See* Erythromycins (Systemic), 712

Erythrocot— *See* Erythromycins (Systemic), 712

Erythromid— *See* Erythromycins (Systemic), 712

Erythromycin (Ophthalmic), 705

Erythromycin (Topical), 706

Erythromycin Base— *See* Erythromycins (Systemic), 712

Erythromycin and Benzoyl Peroxide (Topical), 708

Erythromycin Estolate— *See* Erythromycins (Systemic), 712

Erythromycin Ethylsuccinate— *See* Erythromycins (Systemic), 712, MC-8

Erythromycin Gluceptate— *See* Erythromycins (Systemic), 712

Erythromycin Lactobionate— *See* Erythromycins (Systemic), 712

Erythromycins (Systemic), 712, MC-8

Erythromycin Stearate— *See* Erythromycins (Systemic), 712, MC-8

Erythromycin Stearate Filmtab— *See* Erythromycins (Systemic), 712, MC-8

Erythromycin and Sulfisoxazole (Systemic), 709

Erythropoietin, recombinant, human— *See* Epoetin (Systemic), 693

Eryzole— *See* Erythromycin and Sulfisoxazole (Systemic), 709

Eserine Salicylate— *See* Physostigmine (Ophthalmic), 1286

Eserine Sulfate— *See* Physostigmine (Ophthalmic), 1286

Esgic— *See* Butalbital and Acetaminophen (Systemic), 324

Esgic-Plus— *See* Butalbital and Acetaminophen (Systemic), 324

Esidrix— *See* Diuretics, Thiazide (Systemic), 642

Eskalith— *See* Lithium (Systemic), 996

Eskalith CR— *See* Lithium (Systemic), 996

Eskazole— *See* Albendazole (Systemic), 23

Esomeprazole (Systemic), 715

Essential Care Creamy Dandruff Shampoo— *See* Salicylic Acid and Sulfur (Topical), #

Essential Care Maximum Strength Dandruff Shampoo— *See* Salicylic Acid and Sulfur (Topical), #

Essential Care Medicated Shampoo Wash— *See* Salicylic Acid and Sulfur (Topical), #

Estar— *See* Coal Tar (Topical), 478

Estazolam— *See* Benzodiazepines (Systemic), 257

Esterified Estrogens— *See* Estrogens (Systemic), 718

Esterified Estrogens and Methyltestosterone— *See* Androgens and Estrogens (Systemic), 76, MC-9

Estinyl— *See* Estrogens (Systemic), 718

Estivin II— *See* Naphazoline (Ophthalmic), 1135

Estrace— *See* Estrogens (Systemic), 718, MC-8; *See* Estrogens (Vaginal), 724

Estracyt— *See* Estramustine (Systemic), 717

Estraderm— *See* Estrogens (Systemic), 718

Estradiol— *See* Estrogens (Systemic), 718, MC-8; *See* Estrogens (Vaginal), 724

Estragyn 5— *See* Estrogens (Systemic), 718

Estragyn LA 5— *See* Estrogens (Systemic), 718

Estra-L 40— *See* Estrogens (Systemic), 718

Estramustine (Systemic), 717

Estratab— *See* Estrogens (Systemic), 718, MC-9

Estratest— *See* Androgens and Estrogens (Systemic), 76, MC-9

Estratest H.S.— *See* Androgens and Estrogens (Systemic), 76, MC-9

Estro-A— *See* Estrogens (Systemic), 718

Estro-Cyp— *See* Estrogens (Systemic), 718

Estrofem— *See* Estrogens (Systemic), 718

Estrogens (Systemic), 718

Estrogens (Vaginal), 724

Estrogens, Conjugated— *See* Estrogens (Systemic), 718, MC-8; *See* Estrogens (Vaginal), 724

Estrogens, Conjugated, and Estrogens,Conjugated and Medroxyprogesterone— *See* Conjugated Estrogens and Medroxyprogesterone for Ovarian Hormone Therapy (OHT) (Systemic), 491, MC-8, MC-9

Estrogens, Conjugated, and Methyltestosterone— *See* Androgens and Estrogens (Systemic), 76

Estrogens, Esterified— *See* Estrogens (Systemic), 718, MC-9

Estrogens, Esterified and Methyltestosterone— *See* Androgens and Estrogens (Systemic), 76, MC-9

Estrogens and Progestins (Oral Contraceptives) (Systemic), 729

Estrogens and Progestins (Ovarian Hormone Therapy) (Systemic), 727

Estro-L.A.— *See* Estrogens (Systemic), 718

Estrone— *See* Estrogens (Systemic), 718; *See* Estrogens (Vaginal), 724

Estrone '5'— *See* Estrogens (Systemic), 718

Estropipate— *See* Estrogens (Systemic), 718, MC-9; *See* Estrogens (Vaginal), 724

Estro-Span— *See* Estrogens (Systemic), 718

Estrostep— *See* Estrogens and Progestins (Oral Contraceptives) (Systemic), 729

Estrostep Fe— *See* Estrogens and Progestins (Oral Contraceptives) (Systemic), 729, MC-17

Etacrynic acid— *See* Diuretics, Loop (Systemic), 633

Etanercept (Systemic), 734

Ethacrynic Acid— *See* Diuretics, Loop (Systemic), 633

Ethambutol (Systemic), 735

Ethambutol and Isoniazid (Systemic), 737

Ethchlorvynol (Systemic), 739

Ethinamate (Systemic), 740

Ethinyl Estradiol— *See* Estrogens (Systemic), 718

Ethionamide (Systemic), 741

Ethmozine— *See* Moricizine (Systemic), 1124

Ethopropazine— *See* Antidyskinetics (Systemic), 137

Femiron— *See* Iron Supplements (Systemic), 936

Femizole-7— *See* Antifungals, Azole (Vaginal), 145

Femizol-M— *See* Antifungals, Azole (Vaginal), 145

Femogex— *See* Estrogens (Systemic), 718

FemPatch— *See* Estrogens (Systemic), 718

Femstat 3— *See* Antifungals, Azole (Vaginal), 145

Fendol— *See* Cough/Cold Combinations (Systemic), 522

Fenesin— *See* Guaifenesin (Systemic), 844

Fenesin DM— *See* Cough/Cold Combinations (Systemic), 522

Fenicol Ophthalmic Ointment— *See* Chloramphenicol (Ophthalmic), 403

Fenofibrate (Systemic), 756, MC-9

Fenoprofen— *See* Anti-inflammatory Drugs, Nonsteroidal (Systemic), 179

Fenoterol— *See* Bronchodilators, Adrenergic (Inhalation), 304

Fentanyl— *See* Narcotic Analgesics—For Surgery and Obstetrics (Systemic), 1154

Fentanyl (Systemic), 758

Fentanyl (Transdermal-Systemic), 760

Feosol— *See* Iron Supplements (Systemic), 936

Feostat— *See* Iron Supplements (Systemic), 936

Feostat Drops— *See* Iron Supplements (Systemic), 936

Feratab— *See* Iron Supplements (Systemic), 936

Fer-gen-sol— *See* Iron Supplements (Systemic), 936

Fergon— *See* Iron Supplements (Systemic), 936

Fer-In-Sol Capsules— *See* Iron Supplements (Systemic), 936

Fer-In-Sol Drops— *See* Iron Supplements (Systemic), 936

Fer-In-Sol Syrup— *See* Iron Supplements (Systemic), 936

Fer-Iron Drops— *See* Iron Supplements (Systemic), 936

Fero-Grad— *See* Iron Supplements (Systemic), 936

Fero-Gradumet— *See* Iron Supplements (Systemic), 936

Ferospace— *See* Iron Supplements (Systemic), 936

Ferralet— *See* Iron Supplements (Systemic), 936

Ferralet Slow Release— *See* Iron Supplements (Systemic), 936

Ferralyn Lanacaps— *See* Iron Supplements (Systemic), 936

Ferra-TD— *See* Iron Supplements (Systemic), 936

Ferretts— *See* Iron Supplements (Systemic), 936

Ferric ferrocyanide— *See* Prussian Blue (Oral), #

Ferric (III) hexacyanoferrate (II)— *See* Prussian Blue (Oral), #

Ferrlecit— *See* Iron Supplements (Systemic), 936

Ferrous Citrate Fe 59— *See* Radiopharmaceuticals (Diagnostic), 1347

Ferrous Fumarate— *See* Iron Supplements (Systemic), 936

Ferrous Gluconate— *See* Iron Supplements (Systemic), 936

Ferrous Sulfate— *See* Iron Supplements (Systemic), 936

Fertinex— *See* Urofollitropin (Systemic), #

Fertinic— *See* Iron Supplements (Systemic), 936

Fertinorm HP— *See* Urofollitropin (Systemic), #

Ferumoxides— *See* MRI Contrast Agents, Iron-containing (Diagnostic), 1020

Feverall, Children's— *See* Acetaminophen (Systemic), 4

Feverall, Infants'— *See* Acetaminophen (Systemic), 4

Feverall Junior Strength— *See* Acetaminophen (Systemic), 4

Feverall Sprinkle Caps, Children's— *See* Acetaminophen (Systemic), 4

Feverall Sprinkle Caps Junior Strength— *See* Acetaminophen (Systemic), 4

Fexofenadine (Systemic), 763, MC-9

Fexofenadine and Pseudoephedrine (Systemic), 764, MC-9

Fiberall— *See* Laxatives (Oral), 964

Fiberlan— *See* Enteral Nutrition Formulas (Systemic), #

Fiber-Lax— *See* Laxatives (Oral), 964

FiberNorm— *See* Laxatives (Oral), 964

Fibersource— *See* Enteral Nutrition Formulas (Systemic), #

Fibersource HN— *See* Enteral Nutrition Formulas (Systemic), #

Fibrepur— *See* Laxatives (Oral), 964

Filgrastim— *See* Colony Stimulating Factors (Systemic), 489

Finac— *See* Sulfur (Topical), #

Finasteride (Systemic), 766, MC-9

Fiorgen— *See* Butalbital and Aspirin (Systemic), 327

Fioricet— *See* Butalbital and Acetaminophen (Systemic), 324, MC-4

Fioricet with Codeine— *See* Barbiturates, Aspirin, and Codeine (Systemic), 331; *See* Butalbital and Acetaminophen (Systemic), 324; *See* Butalbital, Acetaminophen, Caffeine, and Codeine (Systemic), 331

Fiorinal— *See* Butalbital and Aspirin (Systemic), 327

Fiorinal-C ½— *See* Barbiturates, Aspirin, and Codeine (Systemic), 245

Fiorinal-C ½— *See* Barbiturates, Aspirin, and Codeine (Systemic), 245

Fiorinal with Codeine No.3— *See* Barbiturates, Aspirin, and Codeine (Systemic), 245

Fiormor— *See* Butalbital and Aspirin (Systemic), 327

FK 506— *See* Tacrolimus (Systemic), 1461

Flagyl— *See* Metronidazole (Systemic), 1086; *See* Metronidazole (Vaginal), 1089

Flagyl I.V.— *See* Metronidazole (Systemic), 1086

Flagyl I.V. RTU— *See* Metronidazole (Systemic), 1086

Flamazine— *See* Silver Sulfadiazine (Topical), 1415

Flarex— *See* Corticosteroids (Ophthalmic), 505

Flatulex— *See* Simethicone (Oral), 1417

Flavorcee— *See* Ascorbic Acid (Vitamin C) (Systemic), 205

Flavored Alka-Seltzer Effervescent Pain Reliever and Antacid— *See* Aspirin, Sodium Bicarbonate, and Citric Acid (Systemic), 210

Flavoxate (Systemic), 767

Flecainide (Systemic), 768

Fleet Babylax— *See* Laxatives (Rectal), 970

Fleet Bisacodyl— *See* Laxatives (Rectal), 970

Fleet Enema— *See* Laxatives (Rectal), 970

Fleet Enema for Children— *See* Laxatives (Rectal), 970

Fleet Enema Mineral Oil— *See* Laxatives (Rectal), 970

Fleet Glycerin Laxative— *See* Laxatives (Rectal), 970

Fleet Laxative— *See* Laxatives (Oral), 964; *See* Laxatives (Rectal), 970

Fleet Mineral Oil— *See* Laxatives (Oral), 964

Fleet Pediatric Enema— *See* Laxatives (Rectal), 970

Fleet Phospho-Soda— *See* Laxatives (Oral), 964

Fleet Relief— *See* Anesthetics (Rectal), 85

Fleet Soflax Gelcaps— *See* Laxatives (Oral), 964

Fleet Soflax Overnight Gelcaps— *See* Laxatives (Oral), 964

Fletcher's Castoria— *See* Laxatives (Oral), 964

Flexeril— *See* Cyclobenzaprine (Systemic), 546, MC-6

Flexoject— *See* Orphenadrine (Systemic), 1220

Floctafenine— *See* Anti-inflammatory Drugs, Nonsteroidal (Systemic), 179

Flolan— *See* Epoprostenol (Systemic), 695

Flomax— *See* Tamsulosin (Systemic), 1467, MC-22

Flonase— *See* Corticosteroids (Nasal), 502; *See* Fluticasone (Nasal), #

Florinef— *See* Fludrocortisone (Systemic), 774

Florone— *See* Corticosteroids—Medium to Very High Potency (Topical), 520

Florone E— *See* Corticosteroids—Medium to Very High Potency (Topical), 520

Flovent— *See* Fluticasone (Inhalation-Local), 786

Flovent Diskus— *See* Fluticasone (Inhalation-Local), 786

Flovent Rotadisk— *See* Fluticasone (Inhalation-Local), 786

Floxin— *See* Fluoroquinolones (Systemic), 776, MC-17

Floxin I.V.— *See* Fluoroquinolones (Systemic), 776

Floxin Otic— *See* Ofloxacin (Otic), 1207

Floxuridine (Systemic), 770

Flozenges— *See* Sodium Fluoride (Systemic), 1425

Fluanxol— *See* Thioxanthenes (Systemic), 1498

Fluanxol Depot— *See* Thioxanthenes (Systemic), 1498

Fluclox— *See* Penicillins (Systemic), 1251

Flucloxacillin— *See* Penicillins (Systemic), 1251

Fumasorb— See Iron Supplements (Systemic), 936

Fumerin— See Iron Supplements (Systemic), 936

Fungizone— See Amphotericin B (Topical), #

Fungizone Intravenous— See Amphotericin B (Systemic), 57

Furacin Soluble Dressing— See Nitrofurazone (Topical), 1197

Furacin Topical Cream— See Nitrofurazone (Topical), 1197

Furacin Topical Solution— See Nitrofurazone (Topical), 1197

Furadantin— See Nitrofurantoin (Systemic), 1195

Furamide— See Diloxanide (Systemic), #

Furazolidone (Oral), #

Furosemide— *See* Diuretics, Loop (Systemic), 633, MC-10

Furoside— See Diuretics, Loop (Systemic), 633

Furoxone— See Furazolidone (Oral), #

Furoxone Liquid— See Furazolidone (Oral), #

Fusidic Acid (Systemic), 807

Fusidin Leo— See Fusidic Acid, 807

G

Gabapentin (Systemic), 808, MC-10

Gabitril— See Tiagabine (Systemic), 1505

Gadodiamide (Diagnostic)— *See* Magnetic Resonance Imaging Contrast Agents (Diagnostic), 1019

Gadopentetate (Diagnostic)— *See* Magnetic Resonance Imaging Contrast Agents (Diagnostic), 1019

Gadoteridol (Diagnostic)— *See* Magnetic Resonance Imaging Contrast Agents (Diagnostic), 1019

Gadoversetamide (Diagnostic)— *See* Magnetic Resonance Imaging Contrast Agents (Diagnostic), 1019

Galantamine (Systemic), 810

Gallium Citrate Ga 67— *See* Radiopharmaceuticals (Diagnostic), 1347

Gallium Nitrate (Systemic), #

Gamimune N 5%— See Immune Globulin Intravenous (Human) (Systemic), 896

Gamimune N 10%— See Immune Globulin Intravenous (Human) (Systemic), 896

Gamimune N 5% S/D— See Immune Globulin Intravenous (Human) (Systemic), 896

Gamimune N 10% S/D— See Immune Globulin Intravenous (Human) (Systemic), 896

Gamma benzene hexachloride— *See* Lindane (Topical), 993

Gammagard S/D— See Immune Globulin Intravenous (Human) (Systemic), 896

Gammagard S/D 0.5 g— See Immune Globulin Intravenous (Human) (Systemic), 896

Gammar-P IV— See Immune Globulin Intravenous (Human) (Systemic), 896

Gamulin Rh— See Rh₀(D) Immune Globulin (Systemic), 1360

Ganciclovir (Implantation-Ophthalmic), 812

Ganciclovir (Systemic), 813

Ganirelix (Systemic), 815

Ganite— See Gallium Nitrate (Systemic), #

Gantanol— See Sulfonamides (Systemic), 1446

Gantrisin— See Sulfonamides (Ophthalmic), 1445; *See* Sulfonamides (Systemic), 1446

Garamycin— See Aminoglycosides (Systemic), 44; *See* Gentamicin (Ophthalmic), 821; *See* Gentamicin (Topical), #

Garamycin Otic Solution— See Gentamicin (Otic), 822

Gas-Ban— See Antacids (Oral), 98

Gasmas— See Antacids (Oral), 98

Gas Relief— See Simethicone (Oral), 1417

Gastrocote— See Antacids (Oral), 98

Gastrocrom— See Cromolyn (Oral), 543

Gastrolyte— See Carbohydrates and Electrolytes (Systemic), 370

Gastrosed— See Anticholinergics/Antispasmodics (Systemic), 106

Gastrozepin— See Anticholinergics/Antispasmodics (Systemic), 106

Gas-X— See Simethicone (Oral), 1417

Gatifloxacin (Systemic); *See* Fluoroquinolones (Systemic), 776, MC-10

Gaviscon— See Antacids (Oral), 98

Gaviscon-2— See Antacids (Oral), 98

Gaviscon Acid Plus Gas Relief— See Antacids (Oral), 98

Gaviscon Acid Relief— See Antacids (Oral), 98

Gaviscon Extra Strength Acid Relief— See Antacids (Oral), 98

Gaviscon Extra Strength Relief Formula— See Antacids (Oral), 98

Gaviscon Heartburn Relief— See Antacids (Oral), 98

Gaviscon Heartburn Relief Extra Strength— See Antacids (Oral), 98

Gax-X Extra Strength— See Simethicone (Oral), 1417

GBH— See Lindane (Topical), 993

GBP— See Gabapentin (Systemic), 808

G-CSF— See Colony Stimulating Factors (Systemic), 489

Gee-Gee— See Guaifenesin (Systemic), 844

Gelpirin— See Acetaminophen and Salicylates (Systemic), 6

Gelpirin-CCF— See Cough/Cold Combinations (Systemic), 522

Gelusil— See Antacids (Oral), 98

Gelusil Extra Strength— See Antacids (Oral), 98

Gemcitabine (Systemic), 816

Gemfibrozil (Systemic), 818, MC-10

Gemonil— See Barbiturates (Systemic), 239

Gemtuzumab Ozogamicin (Systemic), 819, 1629

Gemzar— See Gemcitabine (Systemic), 816

Genabid— See Papaverine (Systemic), #

Genac— See Antihistamines and Decongestants (Systemic), 159

Genahist— See Antihistamines (Systemic), 153

Gen-Allerate— See Antihistamines (Systemic), 153

Gen-Alprazolam— See Benzodiazepines (Systemic), 257

Gen-Amantadine— See Amantadine (Systemic), 38

Genamin— See Antihistamines and Decongestants (Systemic), 159

Genapap Children's Elixir— See Acetaminophen (Systemic), 4

Genapap Children's Tablets— See Acetaminophen (Systemic), 4

Genapap Extra Strength Caplets— See Acetaminophen (Systemic), 4

Genapap Extra Strength Tablets— See Acetaminophen (Systemic), 4

Genapap, Infants'— See Acetaminophen (Systemic), 4

Genapap Regular Strength Tablets— See Acetaminophen (Systemic), 4

Genaphed— See Pseudoephedrine (Systemic), 1334

Genasal Nasal Spray Up to 12 Hour Relief— See Oxymetazoline (Nasal), 1231

Genasoft Plus Softgels— See Laxatives (Oral), 964

Genaspore Cream— See Tolnaftate (Topical), #

Genasyme— See Simethicone (Oral), 1417

Genatap— See Antihistamines and Decongestants (Systemic), 159

Genaton— See Antacids (Oral), 98

Genaton Extra Strength— See Antacids (Oral), 98

Genatuss— See Guaifenesin (Systemic), 844

Genatuss DM— See Cough/Cold Combinations (Systemic), 522

Gen-Bromazepam— See Benzodiazepines (Systemic), 257

Gencalc 600— See Calcium Supplements (Systemic), 353

Gen-Cimetidine— See Histamine H₂-receptor Antagonists (Systemic), 863

Gen-Clonazepam— See Benzodiazepines (Systemic), 257

Gencold— See Antihistamines and Decongestants (Systemic), 159

Gen-Cromoglycate— See Cromolyn (Nasal), 541

Gendecon— See Antihistamines, Decongestants, and Analgesics (Systemic), 164

Genebs Extra Strength Caplets— See Acetaminophen (Systemic), 4

Genebs Regular Strength Tablets— See Acetaminophen (Systemic), 4

Genebs X-Tra— See Acetaminophen (Systemic), 4

Gen-Famotidine— See Histamine H₂-receptor Antagonists (Systemic), 863

Gen-Fibro— See Gemfibrozil (Systemic), 818

Gen-Glybe— See Antidiabetic Agents, Sulfonylurea (Systemic), 131

Gen-Indapamide— See Indapamide (Systemic), 897

Genite— See Cough/Cold Combinations (Systemic), 522

Gen-K— See Potassium Supplements (Systemic), 1300

Gen-Medroxy— See Progestins—For Noncontraceptive Use (Systemic), 1328

Gen-Metformin— See Metformin (Systemic), 1057

Gen-Minocycline— See Tetracyclines (Systemic), 1487

Gen-Minoxidil— See Minoxidil (Topical), 1104

Gravol L/A— See Antihistamines (Systemic), 153

Gravol Liquid— See Antihistamines (Systemic), 153

Great Shake— See Enteral Nutrition Formulas (Systemic), #

Great Shake Jr.— See Enteral Nutrition Formulas (Systemic), #

Grifulvin V— See Griseofulvin (Systemic), 841, MC-11

Grisactin— See Griseofulvin (Systemic), 841

Grisactin Ultra— See Griseofulvin (Systemic), 841

Griseofulvin (Systemic), 841, MC-11

Gris-PEG— See Griseofulvin (Systemic), 841

Growth Hormone (Systemic), 843

GT31-104— See Colesevelam (Oral-Local), 485

GT31-2020014HB— See Colesevelam (Oral-Local), 485

Guaifed— See Cough/Cold Combinations (Systemic), 522

Guaifed-PD— See Cough/Cold Combinations (Systemic), 522

Guaifenesin (Systemic), 844, MC-11

Guaifenex G— See Guaifenesin (Systemic), MC-11

Guaifenex PPA 75— See Cough/Cold Combinations (Systemic), 522

Guaifenex PSE 60— See Cough/Cold Combinations (Systemic), 522, MC-20

Guaifenex PSE 120— See Cough/Cold Combinations (Systemic), 522, MC-20

GuaiMAX-D— See Cough/Cold Combinations (Systemic), 522

Guaipax— See Cough/Cold Combinations (Systemic), 522

Guaitab— See Cough/Cold Combinations (Systemic), 522

Guaivent— See Cough/Cold Combinations (Systemic), 522

Guaivent PD— See Cough/Cold Combinations (Systemic), 522

Guai-Vent/PSE— See Cough/Cold Combinations (Systemic), 522

Guanabenz (Systemic), 846

Guanadrel (Systemic), #

Guanethidine (Systemic), #

Guanfacine (Systemic), #, MC-11

GuiaCough CF— See Cough/Cold Combinations (Systemic), 522

GuiaCough PE— See Cough/Cold Combinations (Systemic), 522

Guiamid D.M. Liquid— See Cough/Cold Combinations (Systemic), 522

Guiatuss— See Guaifenesin (Systemic), 844

Guiatuss A.C.— See Cough/Cold Combinations (Systemic), 522

Guiatuss CF— See Cough/Cold Combinations (Systemic), 522

Guiatuss DAC— See Cough/Cold Combinations (Systemic), 522

Guiatuss-DM— See Cough/Cold Combinations (Systemic), 522

Guiatussin with Codeine Liquid— See Cough/Cold Combinations (Systemic), 522

Guiatussin DAC— See Cough/Cold Combinations (Systemic), 522

Guiatussin w/Dextromethorphan— See Cough/Cold Combinations (Systemic), 522

Guiatuss PE— See Cough/Cold Combinations (Systemic), 522

G-well— See Lindane (Topical), 993

Gynecort— See Corticosteroids—Low Potency (Topical), 518

Gynecort 10— See Corticosteroids—Low Potency (Topical), 518

GyneCure— See Antifungals, Azole (Vaginal), 145

GyneCure Ovules— See Antifungals, Azole (Vaginal), 145

GyneCure Vaginal Ointment Tandempak— See Antifungals, Azole (Vaginal), 145

GyneCure Vaginal Ovules Tandempak— See Antifungals, Azole (Vaginal), 145

Gyne-Lotrimin— See Antifungals, Azole (Vaginal), 145

Gyne-Lotrimin 3— See Antifungals, Azole (Vaginal), 145

Gyne-Lotrimin Combination Pack— See Antifungals, Azole (Vaginal), 145

Gyne-Lotrimin 3 Combination Pack— See Antifungals, Azole (Vaginal), 145

Gynergen— See Headache Medicines, Ergot Derivative–containing (Systemic), 853

Gynogen L.A. 20— See Estrogens (Systemic), 718

Gynogen L.A. 40— See Estrogens (Systemic), 718

Gynol II Extra Strength Contraceptive Jelly— See Spermicides (Vaginal), 1428

Gynol II Original Formula Contraceptive Jelly— See Spermicides (Vaginal), 1428

H

Habitrol— See Nicotine (Systemic), 1182

Haemophilus b Conjugate Vaccine (HbOC—Diphtheria CRM$_{197}$ Protein Conjugate)— See Haemophilus b Conjugate Vaccine (Systemic), 848

Haemophilus b Conjugate Vaccine (PRP-D—Diphtheria Toxoid Conjugate)— See Haemophilus b Conjugate Vaccine (Systemic), 848

Haemophilus b Conjugate Vaccine (PRP-OMP—Meningococcal Protein Conjugate)— See Haemophilus b Conjugate Vaccine (Systemic), 848

Haemophilus b Conjugate Vaccine (PRP-T—Tetanus Protein Conjugate)— See Haemophilus b Conjugate Vaccine (Systemic), 848

Haemophilus b Conjugate Vaccine (Systemic), 848

Haemophilus b Polysaccharide Vaccine (Systemic), 849

Haemophilus influenzae type b polysaccharide vaccine— See Haemophilus b Polysaccharide Vaccine (Systemic), 849

Halazepam— See Benzodiazepines (Systemic), 257

Halcinonide— See Corticosteroids—Medium to Very High Potency (Topical), 520

Halcion— See Benzodiazepines (Systemic), 257

Haldol— See Haloperidol (Systemic), 850

Haldol Decanoate— See Haloperidol (Systemic), 850

Haldol LA— See Haloperidol (Systemic), 850

Haley's M-O— See Laxatives (Oral), 964

Halfan— See Halofantrine (Systemic), #

Halfprin— See Salicylates (Systemic), 1394

Halobetasol— See Corticosteroids—Medium to Very High Potency (Topical), 520

Halodrin— See Androgens and Estrogens (Systemic), 76

Halofantrine (Systemic), #

Halofed— See Pseudoephedrine (Systemic), 1334

Halofed Adult Strength— See Pseudoephedrine (Systemic), 1334

Halog— See Corticosteroids—Medium to Very High Potency (Topical), 520

Halog-E— See Corticosteroids—Medium to Very High Potency (Topical), 520

Haloperidol (Systemic), 850, MC-11

Halotestin— See Androgens (Systemic), 71

Halothane— See Anesthetics, General (Systemic), #

Halotussin— See Guaifenesin (Systemic), 844

Halotussin-DM— See Cough/Cold Combinations (Systemic), 522

Haltran— See Anti-inflammatory Drugs, Nonsteroidal (Systemic), 179

Harmonyl— See Rauwolfia Alkaloids (Systemic), 1354

Havrix— See Hepatitis A Vaccine Inactivated (Systemic), 860

Hawaiian Baby Faces Sunblock— See Sunscreen Agents (Topical), #

Hawaiian Tropic Baby Faces— See Sunscreen Agents (Topical), #

Hawaiian Tropic Baby Faces Sunblock— See Sunscreen Agents (Topical), #

Hawaiian Tropic Dark Tanning— See Sunscreen Agents (Topical), #

Hawaiian Tropic Dark Tanning with Sunscreen— See Sunscreen Agents (Topical), #

Hawaiian Tropic Just For Kids— See Sunscreen Agents (Topical), #

Hawaiian Tropic Land Sport— See Sunscreen Agents (Topical), #

Hawaiian Tropic Plus— See Sunscreen Agents (Topical), #

Hawaiian Tropic Plus Sunblock— See Sunscreen Agents (Topical), #

Hawaiian Tropic Protective Tanning— See Sunscreen Agents (Topical), #

Hawaiian Tropic Protective Tanning Dry— See Sunscreen Agents (Topical), #

Hawaiian Tropic Self-tanning Sunblock— See Sunscreen Agents (Topical), #

Hawaiian Tropic Sport Sunblock— See Sunscreen Agents (Topical), #

Hawaiian Tropic Sunblock— See Sunscreen Agents (Topical), #

Hawaiian Tropic Water Sport— See Sunscreen Agents (Topical), #

Hayfebrol— See Antihistamines and Decongestants (Systemic), 159

HbPV— See Haemophilus b Polysaccharide Vaccine (Systemic), 849

HB vaccine— See Hepatitis B Vaccine Recombinant (Systemic), 861

hCG— See Chorionic Gonadotropin (Systemic), 426

HDCV— *See* Rabies Vaccine (Systemic), #
Headache Medicines, Ergot Derivative–containing (Systemic), 853
Headache Tablet— See Salicylates (Systemic), 1394
Head & Shoulders Dandruff Shampoo (Fine or Oily) Hair— See Pyrithione (Topical), #
Head & Shoulders Dandruff Shampoo (Normal) Hair— See Pyrithione (Topical), #
Head & Shoulders Dandruff Shampoo Plus Conditioner 2 in 1 (Fine or Oily Hair)— See Pyrithione (Topical), #
Head & Shoulders Dry Scalp (Normal or Dry Hair)— See Pyrithione (Topical), #
Head & Shoulders Intensive Treatment Conditioning Formula Dandruff Lotion Shampoo— See Selenium Sulfide (Topical), #
Head & Shoulders Intensive Treatment 2 in 1 (Persistent Dandruff Shampoo plus Conditioner in One) Formula Dandruff Lotion Shampoo— See Selenium Sulfide (Topical), #
Head & Shoulders Intensive Treatment Regular Formula Dandruff Lotion Shampoo— See Selenium Sulfide (Topical), #
Healthprin Adult Low Strength— See Salicylates (Systemic), 1394
Healthprin Full Strength— See Salicylates (Systemic), 1394
Healthprin Half-Dose— See Salicylates (Systemic), 1394
Helidac— See Bismuth Subsalicylate, Metronidazole, and Tetracycline—For *H. pylori* (Systemic), 292
Helixate— See Antihemophilic Factor (Systemic), 151
Hemabate— See Carboprost (Systemic), 378
Hemocyte— See Iron Supplements (Systemic), 936
Hemofil M— See Antihemophilic Factor (Systemic), 151
Hemophilus b polysaccharide vaccine— *See* Haemophilus b Polysaccharide Vaccine (Systemic), 849
Hemorrhoidal HC— See Corticosteroids (Rectal), 509
Hemril-HC Uniserts— See Corticosteroids (Rectal), 509
Hepahydrin— See Laxatives (Oral), 964
Hepalean— See Heparin (Systemic), 858
Heparin (Systemic), 858
Heparin Leo— See Heparin (Systemic), 858
Hepatic-Aid II— See Enteral Nutrition Formulas (Systemic), #
Hepatitis A Vaccine Inactivated (Systemic), 860
Hepatitis B Vaccine Recombinant (Systemic), 861
Heptalac— See Laxatives (Oral), 964
Heptogesic— See Meprobamate and Aspirin (Systemic), 1048
Heptovir— See Lamivudine (Systemic), 955
Herbal Laxative— See Laxatives (Oral), 964
Herbopyrine— See Salicylates (Systemic), 1394
Herceptin— See Trastuzumab (Systemic), 1530
Herpecin-L Cold Sore— See Sunscreen Agents (Topical), #
Herplex Liquifilm— See Idoxuridine (Ophthalmic), 887

Hetrazan— See Diethylcarbamazine (Systemic), #
Hexadrol— See Corticosteroids—Glucocorticoid Effects (Systemic), 513
Hexadrol Phosphate— See Corticosteroids—Glucocorticoid Effects (Systemic), 513
Hexalen— See Altretamine (Systemic), 37
Hexalol— See Atropine, Hyoscyamine, Methenamine, Methylene Blue, Phenyl Salicylate, and Benzoic Acid (Systemic), 218
Hexamethylmelamine— *See* Altretamine (Systemic), 37
Hexit— See Lindane (Topical), 993
Hib CPS— *See* Haemophilus b Polysaccharide Vaccine (Systemic), 849
Hib polysaccharide vaccine— *See* Haemophilus b Polysaccharide Vaccine (Systemic), 849
Hibtiter— See Haemophilus b Conjugate Vaccine (Systemic), 848
Hi-Cor 1.0— See Corticosteroids—Low Potency (Topical), 518
Hi-Cor 2.5— See Corticosteroids—Low Potency (Topical), 518
Hiprex— See Methenamine (Systemic), 1061
Hip-Rex— See Methenamine (Systemic), 1061
Hismanal— See Antihistamines (Systemic), 153
Histafed C— See Cough/Cold Combinations (Systemic), 522
Histagesic Modified— See Antihistamines, Decongestants, and Analgesics (Systemic), 164
Histalet— See Antihistamines and Decongestants (Systemic), 159
Histalet Forte— See Antihistamines and Decongestants (Systemic), 159
Histamine (Diagnostic), #
Histamine H₂-receptor Antagonists (Systemic), 863
Histantil— See Antihistamines, Phenothiazine-derivative (Systemic), 173
Histatab Plus— See Antihistamines and Decongestants (Systemic), 159
Histatan— See Antihistamines and Decongestants (Systemic), 159
Histatuss Pediatric— See Cough/Cold Combinations (Systemic), 522
Hista-Vadrin— See Antihistamines and Decongestants (Systemic), 159
Histenol— See Cough/Cold Combinations (Systemic), 522
Histinex DM— See Cough/Cold Combinations (Systemic), 522
Histinex HC— See Cough/Cold Combinations (Systemic), 522
Histinex PV— See Cough/Cold Combinations (Systemic), 522
Histor-D— See Antihistamines and Decongestants (Systemic), 159
Histosal— See Antihistamines, Decongestants, and Analgesics (Systemic), 164
Histrelin (Systemic), 867
Histussin HC— See Cough/Cold Combinations (Systemic), 522
HIVID— See Zalcitabine (Systemic), 1590
hMG— *See* Menotropins (Systemic), 1047
HMG-CoA Reductase Inhibitors (Systemic), 869

HMS Liquifilm— See Corticosteroids (Ophthalmic), 505
HOE 901— *See* Insulin Glargine (Systemic), 911
HOE 71GT— *See* Insulin Glargine (Systemic), 911
Hold DM— See Dextromethorphan (Systemic), 592
Homapin— See Anticholinergics/Antispasmodics (Systemic), 106
Homatropine— See Anticholinergics/Antispasmodics (Systemic), 106; *See* Atropine/Homatropine/Scopolamine (Ophthalmic), 220
Homosalate— *See* Sunscreen Agents (Topical), #
Homosalate, Menthyl Anthranilate, and Octyl Methoxycinnamate— *See* Sunscreen Agents (Topical), #
Homosalate, Menthyl Anthranilate, Octyl Methoxycinnamate, Octyl Salicylate, and Oxybenzone— *See* Sunscreen Agents (Topical), #
Homosalate, Octocrylene, Octyl Methoxycinnamate, and Oxybenzone— *See* Sunscreen Agents (Topical), #
Homosalate, Octyl Methoxycinnamate, Octyl Salicylate, and Oxybenzone— *See* Sunscreen Agents (Topical), #
Homosalate, Octyl Methoxycinnamate, and Oxybenzone— *See* Sunscreen Agents (Topical), #
Homosalate and Oxybenzone— *See* Sunscreen Agents (Topical), #
Honvol— See Estrogens (Systemic), 718
H₂Oxyl 2.5 Gel— See Benzoyl Peroxide (Topical), 265
H₂Oxyl 5 Gel— See Benzoyl Peroxide (Topical), 265
H₂Oxyl 10 Gel— See Benzoyl Peroxide (Topical), 265
H₂Oxyl 20 Gel— See Benzoyl Peroxide (Topical), 265
HRIG— *See* Rabies Immune Globulin (Systemic), #
Humalog— See Insulin Lispro (Systemic), 913
Human chorionic gonadotropin— *See* Chorionic Gonadotropin (Systemic), 426
Human deoxyribonuclease I, recombinant— *See* Dornase Alfa (Inhalation), 654
Human gonadotropins— *See* Menotropins (Systemic), 1047
Human growth hormone— *See* Growth Hormone (Systemic), 843
Human menopausal gonadotropins— *See* Menotropins (Systemic), 1047
Humate-P— See Antihemophilic Factor (Systemic), 151
Humatrope— See Growth Hormone (Systemic), 843
Humegon— See Menotropins (Systemic), 1047
Humibid DM— See Cough/Cold Combinations (Systemic), 522
Humibid DM Pediatric— See Cough/Cold Combinations (Systemic), 522
Humibid Guaifenesin Plus— See Cough/Cold Combinations (Systemic), 522
Humibid L.A.— See Guaifenesin (Systemic), 844

Humibid Sprinkle— *See* Guaifenesin (Systemic), 844

Humorsol— *See* Antiglaucoma Agents, Cholinergic, Long-acting (Ophthalmic), 148

Humulin 10/90— *See* Insulin (Systemic), 902

Humulin 20/80— *See* Insulin (Systemic), 902

Humulin 30/70— *See* Insulin (Systemic), 902

Humulin 40/60— *See* Insulin (Systemic), 902

Humulin 50/50— *See* Insulin (Systemic), 902

Humulin 70/30— *See* Insulin (Systemic), 902

Humulin 70/30 Pen— *See* Insulin (Systemic), 902

Humulin L— *See* Insulin (Systemic), 902

Humulin-L— *See* Insulin (Systemic), 902

Humulin N— *See* Insulin (Systemic), 902

Humulin N Pen— *See* Insulin (Systemic), 902

Humulin-N— *See* Insulin (Systemic), 902

Humulin-R— *See* Insulin (Systemic), 902

Humulin-R— *See* Insulin (Systemic), 902

Humulin R, Regular (Concentrated), U-202047— *See* Insulin (Systemic), 902

Humulin U— *See* Insulin (Systemic), 902

Humulin-U— *See* Insulin (Systemic), 902

Hurricaine— *See* Anesthetics (Dental), 80

Hyalgan— *See* Hyaluronate Sodium (Systemic), 871

Hyaluronate Sodium (Systemic), 871

Hyaluronate Sodium Derivative (Systemic), 872

Hyaluronic acid— *See* Hyaluronate Sodium (Systemic), 871

Hyaluronidase (Systemic), 1629

Hyate:C— *See* Antihemophilic Factor (Systemic), 151

Hybolin Decanoate— *See* Anabolic Steroids (Systemic), 66

Hybolin-Improved— *See* Anabolic Steroids (Systemic), 66

Hycamtin— *See* Topotecan (Systemic), 1521

HycoClear Tuss— *See* Cough/Cold Combinations (Systemic), 522

Hycodan— *See* Narcotic Analgesics—For Pain Relief (Systemic), 1147

Hycomed— *See* Narcotic Analgesics and Acetaminophen (Systemic), 1138

Hycomine— *See* Cough/Cold Combinations (Systemic), 522

Hycomine Compound— *See* Cough/Cold Combinations (Systemic), 522

Hycomine Pediatric— *See* Cough/Cold Combinations (Systemic), 522

Hycomine-S Pediatric— *See* Cough/Cold Combinations (Systemic), 522

Hyco-Pap— *See* Narcotic Analgesics and Acetaminophen (Systemic), 1138

Hycotuss Expectorant— *See* Cough/Cold Combinations (Systemic), 522

Hydergine— *See* Ergoloid Mesylates (Systemic), 699

Hydergine LC— *See* Ergoloid Mesylates (Systemic), 699

Hyderm— *See* Corticosteroids—Low Potency (Topical), 518

Hydralazine (Systemic), 873, MC-11

Hydralazine and Hydrochlorothiazide (Systemic), #

Hydrate— *See* Antihistamines (Systemic), 153

Hydrea— *See* Hydroxyurea (Systemic), 882, 1629

Hydrisalic— *See* Salicylic Acid (Topical), #

Hydrobexan— *See* Vitamin B_{12} (Systemic), 1575

Hydrocet— *See* Narcotic Analgesics and Acetaminophen (Systemic), 1138

Hydro-chlor— *See* Diuretics, Thiazide (Systemic), 642

Hydrochlorothiazide— *See* Diuretics, Thiazide (Systemic), 642, MC-11

Hydrocil Instant— *See* Laxatives (Oral), 964

Hydro-Cobex— *See* Vitamin B_{12} (Systemic), 1575

Hydrocodone— *See* Narcotic Analgesics—For Pain Relief (Systemic), 1147

Hydrocodone and Acetaminophen— *See* Narcotic Analgesics and Acetaminophen (Systemic), 1138, MC-11

Hydrocodone with APAP— *See* Narcotic Analgesics and Acetaminophen (Systemic), 1138

Hydrocodone and Aspirin— *See* Narcotic Analgesics and Aspirin (Systemic), 1142

Hydrocodone and Guaifenesin— *See* Cough/Cold Combinations (Systemic), 522

Hydrocodone and Homatropine— *See* Cough/Cold Combinations (Systemic), 522

Hydrocodone and Ibuprofen (Systemic), 875, MC-11

Hydrocodone and Potassium Guaiacolsulfonate— *See* Cough/Cold Combinations (Systemic), 522

Hydrocort— *See* Corticosteroids (Rectal), 509

Hydrocortisone— *See* Corticosteroids (Dental), 495; *See* Corticosteroids (Ophthalmic), 505; *See* Corticosteroids (Rectal), 509; *See* Corticosteroids—Glucocorticoid Effects (Systemic), 513; *See* Corticosteroids—Low Potency (Topical), 518

Hydrocortisone Acetate— *See* Corticosteroids—Low Potency (Topical), 518

Hydrocortisone and Acetic Acid— *See* Corticosteroids and Acetic Acid (Otic), 511

Hydrocortisone Butyrate— *See* Corticosteroids—Medium to Very High Potency (Topical), 520

Hydrocortisone Probutate— *See* Corticosteroids—Medium to Very High Potency (Topical), 520

Hydrocortisone Valerate— *See* Corticosteroids—Medium to Very High Potency (Topical), 520

Hydrocortone— *See* Corticosteroids—Glucocorticoid Effects (Systemic), 513

Hydrocortone Acetate— *See* Corticosteroids—Glucocorticoid Effects (Systemic), 513

Hydrocortone Phosphate— *See* Corticosteroids—Glucocorticoid Effects (Systemic), 513

Hydro-Crysti-12— *See* Vitamin B_{12} (Systemic), 1575

Hydro-D— *See* Diuretics, Thiazide (Systemic), 642

HydroDIURIL— *See* Diuretics, Thiazide (Systemic), 642

Hydroflumethiazide— *See* Diuretics, Thiazide (Systemic), 642

Hydrogesic— *See* Narcotic Analgesics and Acetaminophen (Systemic), 1138

Hydromet— *See* Cough/Cold Combinations (Systemic), 522

Hydromine— *See* Cough/Cold Combinations (Systemic), 522

Hydromine Pediatric— *See* Cough/Cold Combinations (Systemic), 522

Hydromorphone— *See* Narcotic Analgesics—For Pain Relief (Systemic), 1147

Hydromorphone and Guaifenesin— *See* Cough/Cold Combinations (Systemic), 522

Hydromox— *See* Diuretics, Thiazide (Systemic), 642

Hydropane— *See* Cough/Cold Combinations (Systemic), 522

Hydrophed— *See* Theophylline, Ephedrine, and Hydroxyzine (Systemic), #

Hydrophen— *See* Cough/Cold Combinations (Systemic), 522

Hydropine— *See* Rauwolfia Alkaloids and Thiazide Diuretics (Systemic), #

Hydropine H.P.— *See* Rauwolfia Alkaloids and Thiazide Diuretics (Systemic), #

Hydropres— *See* Rauwolfia Alkaloids and Thiazide Diuretics (Systemic), #

Hydrosine— *See* Rauwolfia Alkaloids and Thiazide Diuretics (Systemic), #

Hydrostat IR— *See* Narcotic Analgesics—For Pain Relief (Systemic), 1147

Hydrotensin— *See* Rauwolfia Alkaloids and Thiazide Diuretics (Systemic), #

Hydro-Tex— *See* Corticosteroids—Low Potency (Topical), 518

Hydroxocobalamin— *See* Vitamin B_{12} (Systemic), 1575, 1629

Hydroxychloroquine (Systemic), 877, MC-11

Hydroxy-Cobal— *See* Vitamin B_{12} (Systemic), 1575

Hydroxyprogesterone— *See* Progestins—For Noncontraceptive Use (Systemic), 1328

Hydroxypropyl Cellulose (Ophthalmic), 879

Hydroxypropyl Methylcellulose (Ophthalmic), 880

Hydroxypropyl Methylcellulose (Parenteral-Local), 881

Hydroxyurea (Systemic), 882, 1629

Hydroxyzine— *See* Antihistamines (Systemic), 153, MC-11

Hy/Gestrone— *See* Progestins—For Noncontraceptive Use (Systemic), 1328

Hygroton— *See* Diuretics, Thiazide (Systemic), 642

Hylan G-F 20— *See* Hyaluronate Sodium Derivative (Systemic), 872

Hylorel— *See* Guanadrel (Systemic), #

Hylutin— *See* Progestins—For Noncontraceptive Use (Systemic), 1328

Hyoscine— *See* Atropine/Homatropine/Scopolamine (Ophthalmic), 220

Hyoscine hydrobromide— *See* Anticholinergics/Antispasmodics (Systemic), 106

Insta-Char Pediatric with Cherry Flavor in a Sorbitol Base— See Charcoal, Activated (Oral), 395

Instantine— See Salicylates (Systemic), 1394

Insulin, (R)— See Insulin (Systemic), 902

Insulin (Systemic), 902

Insulin Aspart, 909

Insulin Glargine (Systemic), 911

Insulin Human, (R)— See Insulin (Systemic), 902

Insulin Human, Buffered, (R)— See Insulin (Systemic), 902

Insulin, Isophane, (NPH)— See Insulin (Systemic), 902

Insulin, Isophane, Human, (NPH)— See Insulin (Systemic), 902

Insulin, Isophane, Human, and Insulin Human, (NPH and R)— See Insulin (Systemic), 902

Insulin Lispro (Systemic), 913

Insulin Zinc, (L)— See Insulin (Systemic), 902

Insulin Zinc, Extended, (U)— See Insulin (Systemic), 902

Insulin Zinc, Extended, Human, (U)— See Insulin (Systemic), 902

Insulin Zinc, Human, (L)— See Insulin (Systemic), 902

Insulin Zinc, Prompt, (S)— See Insulin (Systemic), 902

Intal— See Cromolyn (Inhalation), 537

Intal Inhaler— See Cromolyn (Inhalation), 537

Intal Syncroner— See Cromolyn (Inhalation), 537

Intercon 0.5/35— See Estrogens and Progestins (Oral Contraceptives) (Systemic), 729

Intercon 1/35— See Estrogens and Progestins (Oral Contraceptives) (Systemic), 729

Intercon 1/50— See Estrogens and Progestins (Oral Contraceptives) (Systemic), 729

Interferon Alfa-2a, Recombinant— See Interferons, Alpha (Systemic), 921

Interferon Alfa-2b, Recombinant— See Interferons, Alpha (Systemic), 921

Interferon Alfacon-1 (Systemic), 915

Interferon Alfa-n1 (Ins)— See Interferons, Alpha (Systemic), 921

Interferon Alfa-n3— See Interferons, Alpha (Systemic), 921

Interferon Beta-1a (Systemic), 916

Interferon Beta-1b (Systemic), 918

Interferon, Gamma (Systemic), 920

Interferons, Alpha (Systemic), 921

Interleukin-2— See Aldesleukin (Systemic), 26

Interleukin-11, Recombinant— See Oprelvekin (Systemic), 1218

Intralipid— See Fat Emulsions (Systemic), #

Introlan— See Enteral Nutrition Formulas (Systemic), #

Introlite— See Enteral Nutrition Formulas (Systemic), #

Intron A— See Interferons, Alpha (Systemic), 921

Inulin (Diagnostic), #

Inversine— See Mecamylamine (Systemic), 1034

Invirase— See Saquinavir (Systemic), 1401

Iobenguane, Radioiodinated— See Radiopharmaceuticals (Diagnostic), 1347

Iobenguane, Radioiodinated (Therapeutic), #

Iobid DM— See Cough/Cold Combinations (Systemic), 522

Iocetamic Acid— See Cholecystographic Agents, Oral (Diagnostic), 421

Iodal HD— See Cough/Cold Combinations (Systemic), 522

Iodine (Topical), 923

Iodine, Strong (Systemic), #

Iodine tincture— See Iodine (Topical), 923

Iodipamide— See Radiopaque Agents (Diagnostic), #

Iodochlorhydroxyquin— See Clioquinol (Topical), 454

Iodochlorhydroxyquin and hydrocortisone— See Clioquinol and Hydrocortisone (Topical), 455

Iodohippurate Sodium I 123— See Radiopharmaceuticals (Diagnostic), 1347

Iodohippurate Sodium I 131— See Radiopharmaceuticals (Diagnostic), 1347

Iodopen— See Sodium Iodide (Systemic), #

Iodoquinol (Oral), #

Iofed— See Antihistamines and Decongestants (Systemic), 159

Iofed PD— See Antihistamines and Decongestants (Systemic), 159

Iofetamine I 123— See Radiopharmaceuticals (Diagnostic), 1347

Iohexol— See Radiopaque Agents (Diagnostic), #; See Radiopaque Agents (Diagnostic, Local), #

Iohist-D— See Antihistamines and Decongestants (Systemic), 159

Iohist DM— See Cough/Cold Combinations (Systemic), 522

Ionamin— See Appetite Suppressants, Sympathomimetic (Systemic), 197

Ionax Astringent Skin Cleanser Topical Solution— See Salicylic Acid (Topical), #

Ionil Plus Shampoo— See Salicylic Acid (Topical), #

Ionil Shampoo— See Salicylic Acid (Topical), #

Ionil T Plus— See Coal Tar (Topical), 478

Iopamidol— See Radiopaque Agents (Diagnostic), #

Iopanoic Acid— See Cholecystographic Agents, Oral (Diagnostic), 421

Iophen-C Liquid— See Cough/Cold Combinations (Systemic), 522

Iophen DM— See Cough/Cold Combinations (Systemic), 522

Iopidine— See Apraclonidine (Ophthalmic), 200

Iosal II— See Cough/Cold Combinations (Systemic), 522

Iosopan— See Antacids (Oral), 98

Iosopan Plus— See Antacids (Oral), 98

Iothalamate— See Radiopaque Agents (Diagnostic), #; See Radiopaque Agents (Diagnostic, Local), #

Iothalamate Sodium I 125— See Radiopharmaceuticals (Diagnostic), 1347

Iotussin HC— See Cough/Cold Combinations (Systemic), 522

Ioversol— See Radiopaque Agents (Diagnostic), #

Ioxaglate— See Radiopaque Agents (Diagnostic), #; See Radiopaque Agents (Diagnostic, Local), #

Ipecac (Oral), 925

I-Pentolate— See Cyclopentolate (Ophthalmic), 548

I-Phrine— See Phenylephrine (Ophthalmic), #

I-Picamide— See Tropicamide (Ophthalmic), #

Ipodate— See Cholecystographic Agents, Oral (Diagnostic), 421

Ipol— See Poliovirus Vaccine (Systemic), #

Ipratropium (Inhalation), 926

Ipratropium (Nasal), 929

Ipratropium and Albuterol (Inhalation-Local), 931, 1629

I-Pred— See Corticosteroids (Ophthalmic), 505

Ipsatol Cough Formula for Children and Adults— See Cough/Cold Combinations (Systemic), 522

IPV— See Poliovirus Vaccine (Systemic), #

Irbesartan (Systemic), 932, MC-12

Ircon— See Iron Supplements (Systemic), 936

Irinotecan (Systemic), 933

Iron blue— See Prussian Blue (Oral), #

Iron Dextran— See Iron Supplements (Systemic), 936

Iron-Polysaccharide— See Iron Supplements (Systemic), 936

Iron Sorbitol— See Iron Supplements (Systemic), 936

Iron Supplements (Systemic), 936

ISDN— See Nitrates—Oral (Systemic), 1188

Ismelin— See Guanethidine (Systemic), #

ISMO— See Nitrates—Oral (Systemic), 1188

Iso-Acetazone— See Isometheptene, Dichloralphenazone, and Acetaminophen (Systemic), 939

Isobutal— See Butalbital and Aspirin (Systemic), 327

Isobutyl— See Butalbital and Aspirin (Systemic), 327

Isocaine— See Anesthetics (Parenteral-Local), 83

Isocaine 2%— See Anesthetics (Parenteral-Local), 83

Isocaine 3%— See Anesthetics (Parenteral-Local), 83

Isocal— See Enteral Nutrition Formulas (Systemic), #

Isocal HN— See Enteral Nutrition Formulas (Systemic), #

Isocarboxazid— See Antidepressants, Monoamine Oxidase (MAO) Inhibitor (Systemic), 123

Isocet— See Butalbital and Acetaminophen (Systemic), 324

Isocom— See Isometheptene, Dichloralphenazone, and Acetaminophen (Systemic), 939

Isoetharine— See Bronchodilators, Adrenergic (Inhalation), 304

Isoetretin— See Acitretin (Systemic), 15

Isoflurane— See Anesthetics, General (Systemic), #

Isoflurophate— See Antiglaucoma Agents, Cholinergic, Long-acting (Ophthalmic), 148

Isolan— See Enteral Nutrition Formulas (Systemic), #

Isolin— See Butalbital and Aspirin (Systemic), 327

Isollyl— See Butalbital and Aspirin (Systemic), 327

Isollyl with Codeine— See Barbiturates, Aspirin, and Codeine (Systemic), 245

Isometheptene, Dichloralphenazone, and Acetaminophen (Systemic), 939

Isomil— See Infant Formulas (Systemic), #

Isomil SF— See Infant Formulas (Systemic), #

Isoniazid (Systemic), 941

Isoniazid and Thiacetazone (Systemic), #

Isopap— See Butalbital and Acetaminophen (Systemic), 324

Isoproterenol— *See* Bronchodilators, Adrenergic (Inhalation), 304; *See* Bronchodilators, Adrenergic (Oral/Injection), 310

Isoptin— See Calcium Channel Blocking Agents (Systemic), 349

Isoptin SR— See Calcium Channel Blocking Agents (Systemic), 349

Isopto— See Carbachol (Ophthalmic), 365

Isopto Alkaline— See Hydroxypropyl Methylcellulose (Ophthalmic), 880

Isopto Atropine— See Atropine/Homatropine/Scopolamine (Ophthalmic), 220

Isopto Carpine— See Pilocarpine (Ophthalmic), 1287

Isopto-Cetamide— See Sulfonamides (Ophthalmic), 1445

Isopto Eserine— See Physostigmine (Ophthalmic), 1286

Isopto Frin— See Phenylephrine (Ophthalmic), #

Isopto Homatropine— See Atropine/Homatropine/Scopolamine (Ophthalmic), 220

Isopto Hyoscine— See Atropine/Homatropine/Scopolamine (Ophthalmic), 220

Isopto Plain— See Hydroxypropyl Methylcellulose (Ophthalmic), 880

Isopto Tears— See Hydroxypropyl Methylcellulose (Ophthalmic), 880

Isorbid— See Nitrates—Sublingual, Chewable, or Buccal (Systemic), 1190

Isordil— See Nitrates—Sublingual, Chewable, or Buccal (Systemic), 1190

Isordil Tembids— See Nitrates—Oral (Systemic), 1188

Isordil Titradose— See Nitrates—Oral (Systemic), 1188

Isosorbide Dinitrate— *See* Nitrates—Oral (Systemic), 1190, MC-12; *See* Nitrates—Sublingual, Chewable, or Buccal (Systemic), 1190, MC-12

Isosorbide Mononitrate— *See* Nitrates—Oral (Systemic), 1188, MC-12

Isosource— See Enteral Nutrition Formulas (Systemic), #

Isosource HN— See Enteral Nutrition Formulas (Systemic), #

IsoSource VHN— See Enteral Nutrition Formulas (Systemic), #

Isotamine— See Isoniazid (Systemic), 941

Isotein HN— See Enteral Nutrition Formulas (Systemic), #

Isotretinoin (Systemic), 944, MC-12

Isoxsuprine (Systemic), #

Isradipine— *See* Calcium Channel Blocking Agents (Systemic), 349

I-Sulfacet— See Sulfonamides (Ophthalmic), 1445

Isuprel— See Bronchodilators, Adrenergic (Inhalation), 304; *See* Bronchodilators, Adrenergic (Oral/Injection), 310

Isuprel Mistometer— See Bronchodilators, Adrenergic (Inhalation), 304

Itraconazole— *See* Antifungals, Azole (Systemic), 142, MC-12

I-Tropine— See Atropine/Homatropine/Scopolamine (Ophthalmic), 220

Iveegam— See Immune Globulin Intravenous (Human) (Systemic), 896

Ivermectin (Systemic), #

IVIG— *See* Immune Globulin Intravenous (Human) (Systemic), 896

IvyBlock— See Bentoquatam (Topical), 256

J

Japanese Encephalitis Virus Vaccine (Systemic), #

Jectofer— See Iron Supplements (Systemic), 936

Jenamicin— See Aminoglycosides (Systemic), 44

Jenest— See Estrogens and Progestins (Oral Contraceptives) (Systemic), 729

Je-Vax— See Japanese Encephalitis Virus Vaccine (Systemic), #

Jevity— See Enteral Nutrition Formulas (Systemic), #

Johnson's Baby Sunblock— See Sunscreen Agents (Topical), #

Johnson's Baby Sunblock Extra Protection— See Sunscreen Agents (Topical), #

Johnson's No More Tears Baby Sunblock— See Sunscreen Agents (Topical), #

Jopanonsyre— See Cholecystographic Agents, Oral (Diagnostic), 421

Just Tears— See Hydroxypropyl Methylcellulose (Ophthalmic), 880

K

K-8— See Potassium Supplements (Systemic), 1300

K+ 10— See Potassium Supplements (Systemic), 1300

K-10— See Potassium Supplements (Systemic), 1300

Kabolin— See Anabolic Steroids (Systemic), 66

Kadian— See Narcotic Analgesics—For Pain Relief (Systemic), 1147

Kaletra— See Lopinavir and Ritonavir (Systemic), 1003, 1629

Kalium Durules— See Potassium Supplements (Systemic), 1300

Kalmex— See Salicylates (Systemic), 1394

Kanamycin— *See* Aminoglycosides (Systemic), 44

Kanamycin (Oral), #

Kantrex— See Aminoglycosides (Systemic), 44; *See* Kanamycin (Oral), #

Kaochlor 10%— See Potassium Supplements (Systemic), 1300

Kaochlor-10— See Potassium Supplements (Systemic), 1300

Kaochlor-20— See Potassium Supplements (Systemic), 1300

Kaochlor S-F 10%— See Potassium Supplements (Systemic), 1300

Kao Lectrolyte— See Carbohydrates and Electrolytes (Systemic), 370

Kaolin and Pectin (Oral), 946

Kaolin, Pectin, and Belladonna Alkaloids (Systemic), #

Kaolin, Pectin, and Paregoric (Systemic), #

Kaon— See Potassium Supplements (Systemic), 1300

Kaon-Cl— See Potassium Supplements (Systemic), 1300

Kaon-Cl-10— See Potassium Supplements (Systemic), 1300

Kaon-Cl 20% Liquid— See Potassium Supplements (Systemic), 1300

Kaopectate— See Attapulgite (Oral), 222

Kaopectate Advanced Formula— See Attapulgite (Oral), 222

Kaopectate II— See Loperamide (Oral), 1001

Kaopectate Maximum Strength— See Attapulgite (Oral), 222

Kaopek— See Attapulgite (Oral), 222

Kao-Spen— See Kaolin and Pectin (Oral), 946

Kapectolin— See Kaolin and Pectin (Oral), 946

Karacil— See Laxatives (Oral), 964

Karidium— See Sodium Fluoride (Systemic), 1425

Kasof— See Laxatives (Oral), 964

Kato— See Potassium Supplements (Systemic), 1300

Kay Ciel— See Potassium Supplements (Systemic), 1300

Kaylixir— See Potassium Supplements (Systemic), 1300

K+ Care— See Potassium Supplements (Systemic), 1300

K+ Care ET— See Potassium Supplements (Systemic), 1300

KCL 5%— See Potassium Supplements (Systemic), 1300

K-Dur— See Potassium Supplements (Systemic), 1300, MC-19

Keep Alert— See Caffeine (Systemic), 339

Keflex— See Cephalosporins (Systemic), 387

Keflin— See Cephalosporins (Systemic), 387

Keftab— See Cephalosporins (Systemic), 387

Kefurox— See Cephalosporins (Systemic), 387

Kefzol— See Cephalosporins (Systemic), 387

K-Electrolyte— See Potassium Supplements (Systemic), 1300

Kellogg's Castor Oil— See Laxatives (Oral), 964

Kemadrin— See Antidyskinetics (Systemic), 137

Kenac— See Corticosteroids—Medium to Very High Potency (Topical), 520

Kenacort— See Corticosteroids—Glucocorticoid Effects (Systemic), 513

Kenacort Diacetate— See Corticosteroids— Glucocorticoid Effects (Systemic), 513

Kenaject-40— See Corticosteroids—Glucocorticoid Effects (Systemic), 513

Kenalog— See Corticosteroids—Medium to Very High Potency (Topical), 520

Kenalog-10— See Corticosteroids—Glucocorticoid Effects (Systemic), 513

Kenalog-40— See Corticosteroids—Glucocorticoid Effects (Systemic), 513

Kenalog-H— See Corticosteroids—Medium to Very High Potency (Topical), 520

Kenalog in Orabase— See Corticosteroids (Dental), 495

Kendral-Ipratropium— See Ipratropium (Inhalation), 926

Ken-Jec 40— See Corticosteroids—Glucocorticoid Effects (Systemic), 513

Kenonel— See Corticosteroids—Medium to Very High Potency (Topical), 520

Keoxifene hydrochloride— See Raloxifene (Systemic), 1349

Keppra— See Levetiracetam (Systemic), 981

Keralyt— See Salicylic Acid (Topical), #

Keratex Gel— See Salicylic Acid (Topical), #

Kerlone— See Beta-adrenergic Blocking Agents (Systemic), 272

Kestrone-5— See Estrogens (Systemic), 718

Ketalar— See Anesthetics, General (Systemic), #

Ketamine— See Anesthetics, General (Systemic), #

Ketazolam— See Benzodiazepines (Systemic), 257

Ketoconazole— See Antifungals, Azole (Systemic), 142, MC-12

Ketoconazole (Topical), 947

Ketoprofen— See Anti-inflammatory Drugs, Nonsteroidal (Systemic), 179, MC-12

Ketorolac (Ophthalmic), 949

Ketorolac (Systemic), 950, MC-12

Ketotifen (Ophthalmic), 952

Ketotifen (Systemic), 954

Key-Pred— See Corticosteroids—Glucocorticoid Effects (Systemic), 513

Key-Pred SP— See Corticosteroids—Glucocorticoid Effects (Systemic), 513

K-G Elixir— See Potassium Supplements (Systemic), 1300

KI— See Potassium Iodide (Systemic), #

Kiddy Koff— See Cough/Cold Combinations (Systemic), 522

K-Ide— See Potassium Supplements (Systemic), 1300

Kidrolase— See Asparaginase (Systemic), 208

KIE— See Cough/Cold Combinations (Systemic), 522

Kildane— See Lindane (Topical), 993

Kindercal— See Enteral Nutrition Formulas (Systemic), #

Kinesed— See Belladonna Alkaloids and Barbiturates (Systemic), 252

Kinevac— See Sincalide (Diagnostic), #

Klean-Prep— See Polyethylene Glycol and Electrolytes (Local), 1299

K-Lease— See Potassium Supplements (Systemic), 1300

Klerist-D— See Antihistamines and Decongestants (Systemic), 159

K-Long— See Potassium Supplements (Systemic), 1300

Klonopin— See Benzodiazepines (Systemic), 257, MC-6

K-Lor— See Potassium Supplements (Systemic), 1300

Klor-Con 8— See Potassium Supplements (Systemic), 1300, MC-19

Klor-Con 10— See Potassium Supplements (Systemic), 1300, MC-19

Klor-Con/EF— See Potassium Supplements (Systemic), 1300

Klor-Con Powder— See Potassium Supplements (Systemic), 1300

Klor-Con/25 Powder— See Potassium Supplements (Systemic), 1300

Klorvess— See Potassium Supplements (Systemic), 1300

Klorvess Effervescent Granules— See Potassium Supplements (Systemic), 1300

Klorvess 10% Liquid— See Potassium Supplements (Systemic), 1300

Klotrix— See Potassium Supplements (Systemic), 1300

K-Lyte— See Potassium Supplements (Systemic), 1300

K-Lyte/Cl— See Potassium Supplements (Systemic), 1300

K-Lyte/Cl 50— See Potassium Supplements (Systemic), 1300

K-Lyte/Cl Powder— See Potassium Supplements (Systemic), 1300

K-Lyte DS— See Potassium Supplements (Systemic), 1300

K-Med 900— See Potassium Supplements (Systemic), 1300

K-Norm— See Potassium Supplements (Systemic), 1300

Koate-HP— See Antihemophilic Factor (Systemic), 151

Koffex DM— See Dextromethorphan (Systemic), 592

Kogenate— See Antihemophilic Factor (Systemic), 151

Kolephrin Caplets— See Antihistamines, Decongestants, and Analgesics (Systemic), 164

Kolephrin/DM Cough and Cold Medication— See Cough/Cold Combinations (Systemic), 522

Kolephrin GG/DM— See Cough/Cold Combinations (Systemic), 522

Kolephrin NN Liquid— See Cough/Cold Combinations (Systemic), 522

Kolyum— See Potassium Supplements (Systemic), 1300

Kondremul— See Laxatives (Oral), 964

Kondremul Plain— See Laxatives (Oral), 964

Konsyl— See Laxatives (Oral), 964

Konsyl-D— See Laxatives (Oral), 964

Konsyl Easy Mix— See Laxatives (Oral), 964

Konsyl-Orange— See Laxatives (Oral), 964

Konsyl-Orange Sugar Free— See Laxatives (Oral), 964

Konyne 80— See Factor IX (Systemic), 751

Kophane— See Cough/Cold Combinations (Systemic), 522

Kophane Cough and Cold Formula— See Cough/Cold Combinations (Systemic), 522

Koromex Cream— See Spermicides (Vaginal), 1428

Koromex Crystal Clear Gel— See Spermicides (Vaginal), 1428

Koromex Foam— See Spermicides (Vaginal), 1428

Koromex Jelly— See Spermicides (Vaginal), 1428

K-P— See Kaolin and Pectin (Oral), 946

KPAB— See Aminobenzoate Potassium (Systemic), #

K-Pek— See Attapulgite (Oral), 222

K-Phos M. F.— See Phosphates (Systemic), 1282

K-Phos Neutral— See Phosphates (Systemic), 1282

K-Phos No. 2— See Phosphates (Systemic), 1282

K-Phos Original— See Phosphates (Systemic), 1282

Kronofed-A Jr. Kronocaps— See Antihistamines and Decongestants (Systemic), 159

Kronofed-A Kronocaps— See Antihistamines and Decongestants (Systemic), 159

Krypton Kr 81m— See Radiopharmaceuticals (Diagnostic), 1347

K-Sol— See Potassium Supplements (Systemic), 1300

K-Tab— See Potassium Supplements (Systemic), 1300

Kudrox Double Strength— See Antacids (Oral), 98

Ku-Zyme HP— See Pancrelipase (Systemic), 1239

K-Vescent— See Potassium Supplements (Systemic), 1300

Kwelcof Liquid— See Cough/Cold Combinations (Systemic), 522

Kwell— See Lindane (Topical), 993

Kwellada— See Lindane (Topical), 993

Kwildane— See Lindane (Topical), 993

Kytril— See Granisetron (Systemic), 840

L

LA-12— See Vitamin B$_{12}$ (Systemic), 1575

LAAM— See Levomethadyl (Systemic), #

Labetalol— See Beta-adrenergic Blocking Agents (Systemic), 272, MC-13

Lacril— See Hydroxypropyl Methylcellulose (Ophthalmic), 880

Lacrisert— See Hydroxypropyl Cellulose (Ophthalmic), 879

LactiCare-HC— See Corticosteroids—Low Potency (Topical), 518

Lactisol— See Salicylic Acid (Topical), #

Lactofree— See Infant Formulas (Systemic), #

Lactulax— See Laxatives (Oral), 964

Lactulose— See Laxatives (Oral), 964

Lagol— See Anesthetics (Topical), 88

LAM— See Levomethadyl (Systemic), #

Lamictal— See Lamotrigine (Systemic), 958, MC-13

Lamictal CD— See Lamotrigine (Systemic), MC-13

Lamisil— See Terbinafine (Systemic), 1478, 1630, MC-22; See Terbinafine (Topical), 1480

Life Antacid Plus— *See* Antacids (Oral), 98

Lignocaine— *See* Anesthetics (Dental), 80; *See* Anesthetics (Parenteral-Local), 83; *See* Anesthetics (Topical), 88; *See* Lidocaine (Topical), 991

Limbitrol— *See* Chlordiazepoxide and Amitriptyline (Systemic), 408

Limbitrol DS— *See* Chlordiazepoxide and Amitriptyline (Systemic), 408

Lincocin— *See* Lincomycin (Systemic), #

Lincomycin (Systemic), #

Lincorex— *See* Lincomycin (Systemic), #

Lindane (Topical), 993

Linezolid (Systemic), 994

Linhist-L.A.— *See* Antihistamines and Decongestants (Systemic), 159

Lioresal— *See* Baclofen (Systemic), 236

Lioresal Intrathecal— *See* Baclofen (Intrathecal-Systemic), 235

Liothyronine— *See* Thyroid Hormones (Systemic), 1503

Liotrix— *See* Thyroid Hormones (Systemic), 1503

Lipancreatin— *See* Pancrelipase (Systemic), 1239

Lipisorb— *See* Enteral Nutrition Formulas (Systemic), #

Lipitor— *See* Atorvastatin (Systemic), 213, MC-3

Lipitor— *See* HMG-CoA Reductase Inhibitors (Systemic), 869, MC-3

Liposyn II— *See* Fat Emulsions (Systemic), #

Liposyn III— *See* Fat Emulsions (Systemic), #

Liquaemin— *See* Heparin (Systemic), 858

Liqui-Char— *See* Charcoal, Activated (Oral), 395

Liqui-Char with Sorbitol— *See* Charcoal, Activated (Oral), 395

Liquid Cal— *See* Calcium Supplements (Systemic), 353

Liquid Cal-202057— *See* Calcium Supplements (Systemic), 353

Liqui-Doss— *See* Laxatives (Oral), 964

Liquid Pred— *See* Corticosteroids—Glucocorticoid Effects (Systemic), 513

Liqui-E— *See* Vitamin E (Systemic), 1582

Liqui-Histine-D— *See* Antihistamines and Decongestants (Systemic), 159

Liqui-Histine DM— *See* Cough/Cold Combinations (Systemic), 522

Liquimat Light— *See* Alcohol and Sulfur (Topical), #

Liquimat Medium— *See* Alcohol and Sulfur (Topical), #

Liqui-Minic Infant Drops— *See* Antihistamines and Decongestants (Systemic), 159

Liquiprin Children's Elixir— *See* Acetaminophen (Systemic), 4

Liquiprin Infants' Drops— *See* Acetaminophen (Systemic), 4

Liquor Carbonis Detergens— *See* Coal Tar (Topical), 478

Lisadimate, Oxybenzone, and Padimate O— *See* Sunscreen Agents (Topical), #

Lisadimate and Padimate O— *See* Sunscreen Agents (Topical), #

Lisinopril— *See* Angiotensin-converting Enzyme (ACE) Inhibitors (Systemic), 90, MC-13

Lisinopril and Hydrochlorothiazide— *See* Angiotensin-converting Enzyme (ACE) Inhibitors and Hydrochlorothiazide (Systemic), 94, MC-13

Lisolipin— *See* Dextrothyroxine (Systemic), 594

Listerex Golden Scrub Lotion— *See* Salicylic Acid (Topical), #

Listerex Herbal Scrub Lotion— *See* Salicylic Acid (Topical), #

Lite Pred— *See* Corticosteroids (Ophthalmic), 505

Lithane— *See* Lithium (Systemic), 996

Lithium (Systemic), 996, MC-13

Lithizine— *See* Lithium (Systemic), 996

Lithobid— *See* Lithium (Systemic), 996

Lithonate— *See* Lithium (Systemic), 996

Lithotabs— *See* Lithium (Systemic), 996

Livostin— *See* Levocabastine (Ophthalmic), 984

Locacorten— *See* Corticosteroids—Low Potency (Topical), 518

Locoid— *See* Corticosteroids—Medium to Very High Potency (Topical), 520

Lodine— *See* Anti-inflammatory Drugs, Nonsteroidal (Systemic), 179

Lodine XL— *See* Anti-inflammatory Drugs, Nonsteroidal (Systemic), 179, MC-9

Lodoxamide (Ophthalmic), 998

Lodoxamide trometamol— *See* Lodoxamide (Ophthalmic), 998

Lodrane LD— *See* Antihistamines and Decongestants (Systemic), 159

Lodrane Liquid— *See* Antihistamines and Decongestants (Systemic), 159

Loestrin 1/20— *See* Estrogens and Progestins (Oral Contraceptives) (Systemic), 729

Loestrin 1.5/30— *See* Estrogens and Progestins (Oral Contraceptives) (Systemic), 729

Loestrin Fe— *See* Estrogens and Progestins (Oral Contraceptives) (Systemic), 729

Loestrin Fe 1.5/30— *See* Estrogens and Progestins (Oral Contraceptives) (Systemic), 729, MC-17

Loestrin Fe 1/20— *See* Norethindrone, Iron, and Ethinyl Estradiol (Systemic), MC-17

Lofene— *See* Diphenoxylate and Atropine (Systemic), 615

Logen— *See* Diphenoxylate and Atropine (Systemic), 615

Lomefloxacin— *See* Fluoroquinolones (Systemic), 776

Lomine— *See* Anticholinergics/Antispasmodics (Systemic), 106

Lomocot— *See* Diphenoxylate and Atropine (Systemic), 615

Lomotil— *See* Diphenoxylate and Atropine (Systemic), 615

Lomustine (Systemic), 999

Loniten— *See* Minoxidil (Systemic), 1103

Lonox— *See* Diphenoxylate and Atropine (Systemic), 615, MC-3

Lo/Ovral— *See* Estrogens and Progestins (Oral Contraceptives) (Systemic), 729, MC-17

Loperacap— *See* Loperamide (Oral), 1001

Loperamide (Oral), 1001

Lopid— *See* Gemfibrozil (Systemic), 818

Lopinavir and Ritonavir (Systemic), 1003, 1629

Lopresor— *See* Beta-adrenergic Blocking Agents (Systemic), 272

Lopresor SR— *See* Beta-adrenergic Blocking Agents (Systemic), 272

Lopressor— *See* Beta-adrenergic Blocking Agents (Systemic), 272, MC-15

Lopressor HCT— *See* Beta-adrenergic Blocking Agents and Thiazide Diuretics (Systemic), 278

Loprox— *See* Ciclopirox (Topical), 429

Lopurin— *See* Allopurinol (Systemic), 30

Lorabid— *See* Loracarbef (Systemic), 1005, MC-14

Loracarbef (Systemic), 1005, MC-14

Loratadine— *See* Antihistamines (Systemic), 153, MC-14

Loratadine and Pseudoephedrine— *See* Antihistamines and Decongestants (Systemic), 159, MC-14

Lorazepam— *See* Benzodiazepines (Systemic), 257, MC-14

Lorazepam Intensol— *See* Benzodiazepines (Systemic), 257

Lorcet 10/650— *See* Narcotic Analgesics and Acetaminophen (Systemic), 1138

Lorcet-HD— *See* Narcotic Analgesics and Acetaminophen (Systemic), 1138

Lorcet Plus— *See* Narcotic Analgesics and Acetaminophen (Systemic), 1138

Lorelco— *See* Probucol (Systemic), 1316

Loroxide 5 Lotion— *See* Benzoyl Peroxide (Topical), 265

Loroxide 5.5 Lotion— *See* Benzoyl Peroxide (Topical), 265

Lortab— *See* Narcotic Analgesics and Acetaminophen (Systemic), 1138

Lortab ASA— *See* Narcotic Analgesics and Aspirin (Systemic), 1142

Lortab 2.5/500— *See* Narcotic Analgesics and Acetaminophen (Systemic), 1138

Lortab 5/500— *See* Narcotic Analgesics and Acetaminophen (Systemic), 1138

Lortab 7.5/500— *See* Narcotic Analgesics and Acetaminophen (Systemic), 1138

Lortab 10/500— *See* Narcotic Analgesics and Acetaminophen (Systemic), 1138

Losartan (Systemic), 1007, MC-14

Losartan and Hydrochlorothiazide (Systemic), #, MC-14

Losec— *See* Omeprazole (Systemic), 1212

Losopan— *See* Antacids (Oral), 98

Losopan Plus— *See* Antacids (Oral), 98

Lotemax— *See* Loteprednol (Ophthalmic), 1008

Lotensin— *See* Angiotensin-converting Enzyme (ACE) Inhibitors (Systemic), 90; *See* Benazepril (Systemic), MC-3

Lotensin HCT— *See* Angiotensin-converting Enzyme (ACE) Inhibitors and Hydrochlorothiazide (Systemic), 94; *See* Benazepril and Hydrochlorothiazide (Systemic), MC-3

Loteprednol (Ophthalmic), 1008

Lotio Alsulfa— *See* Sulfur (Topical), #

Lotrel— *See* Amlodipine and Benazepril (Systemic), 52, MC-2

Lotriderm— *See* Clotrimazole and Betamethasone (Topical), 473

Lotrimin AF Cream— *See* Clotrimazole (Topical), 472

M

Methotrimeprazine— *See* Phenothiazines (Systemic), 1268

Methoxsalen (Extracorporeal-Systemic), 1067

Methoxsalen (Systemic), 1069

Methoxsalen (Topical), 1071

Methoxyflurane— *See* Anesthetics, General (Systemic), #

Methscopolamine— *See* Anticholinergics/Antispasmodics (Systemic), 106

Methsuximide— *See* Anticonvulsants, Succinimide (Systemic), 121

Methyclothiazide— *See* Diuretics, Thiazide (Systemic), 642

Methylcellulose— *See* Laxatives (Oral), 964

Methylcotolone— *See* Corticosteroids—Glucocorticoid Effects (Systemic), 513

Methyldopa (Systemic), 1072, MC-15

Methyldopa and Chlorothiazide— *See* Methyldopa and Thiazide Diuretics (Systemic), 1074

Methyldopa and Hydrochlorothiazide— *See* Methyldopa and Thiazide Diuretics (Systemic), 1074

Methyldopa and Thiazide Diuretics (Systemic), 1074

Methylene Blue (Systemic), 1077

Methylergometrine— *See* Ergonovine/Methylergonovine (Systemic), 700

Methylergonovine— *See* Ergonovine/Methylergonovine (Systemic), 700

Methylin— *See* Methylphenidate (Systemic), MC-15

Methylphenidate (Systemic), 1078, MC-15

Methylprednisolone— *See* Corticosteroids—Glucocorticoid Effects (Systemic), 353, MC-15

Methyltestosterone— *See* Androgens (Systemic), 71

Methylthionine chloride— *See* Methylene Blue (Systemic), 1077

Methyprylon (Systemic), 1080

Methysergide (Systemic), 1082

Meticorten— *See* Corticosteroids—Glucocorticoid Effects (Systemic), 513

Metipranolol— *See* Beta-adrenergic Blocking Agents (Ophthalmic), 270

Metoclopramide (Systemic), 1083, MC-15

Metoclopramide Intensol— *See* Metoclopramide (Systemic), 1083

Metolazone— *See* Diuretics, Thiazide (Systemic), 642, MC-15

Metopirone— *See* Metyrapone (Systemic), #

Metoprolol— *See* Beta-adrenergic Blocking Agents (Systemic), 272, MC-15

Metoprolol and Hydrochlorothiazide— *See* Beta-adrenergic Blocking Agents and Thiazide Diuretics (Systemic), 278

Metric 21— *See* Metronidazole (Systemic), 1086

Metrizamide— *See* Radiopaque Agents (Diagnostic), #

MetroCream— *See* Metronidazole (Topical), 1088

Metrodin— *See* Urofollitropin (Systemic), #

MetroGel— *See* Metronidazole (Topical), 1088

MetroGel-Vaginal— *See* Metronidazole (Vaginal), 1089

Metro I.V.— *See* Metronidazole (Systemic), 1086

MetroLotion— *See* Metronidazole (Topical), 1088

Metronidazole (Systemic), 1086, MC-15

Metronidazole (Topical), 1088

Metronidazole (Vaginal), 1089

Metyrapone (Systemic), #

Metyrosine (Systemic), 1091

Mevacor— *See* HMG-CoA Reductase Inhibitors (Systemic), 869, MC-14

Mevinolin— *See* HMG-CoA Reductase Inhibitors (Systemic), 869

Mexiletine (Systemic), 1093

Mexitil— *See* Mexiletine (Systemic), 1093

Mezlin— *See* Penicillins (Systemic), 1251

Mezlocillin— *See* Penicillins (Systemic), 1251

MGP— *See* Magnesium Supplements (Systemic), 1017

M-Hist— *See* Antihistamines and Decongestants (Systemic), 159

Miacalcin— *See* Calcitonin (Nasal-Systemic), 344; *See* Calcitonin (Systemic), 346

Mi-Acid— *See* Antacids (Oral), 98

Mi-Acid Double Strength— *See* Antacids (Oral), 98

Mibefradil (Systemic), 1094

mIBG— *See* Iobenguane, Radioiodinated (Therapeutic), #

Micanol— *See* Anthralin (Topical), 102

Micardis— *See* Telmisartan (Systemic), 1470

Micatin— *See* Miconazole (Topical), 1096

Miconazole— *See* Antifungals, Azole (Vaginal), 145

Miconazole-7— *See* Antifungals, Azole (Vaginal), 145

Miconazole (Topical), 1096

Micozole— *See* Antifungals, Azole (Vaginal), 145

Micrainin— *See* Meprobamate and Aspirin (Systemic), 1048

MICRhoGAM— *See* Rh₀(D) Immune Globulin (Systemic), 1360

Micro-K— *See* Potassium Supplements (Systemic), 1300

Micro-K 10— *See* Potassium Supplements (Systemic), 1300

Micro-K LS— *See* Potassium Supplements (Systemic), 1300

Microlipid— *See* Enteral Nutrition Formulas (Systemic), #

Micronase— *See* Antidiabetic Agents, Sulfonylurea (Systemic), 131

microNefrin— *See* Bronchodilators, Adrenergic (Inhalation), 304

Micronor— *See* Progestins—For Contraceptive Use (Systemic), 1324, MC-17

Midahist DH— *See* Cough/Cold Combinations (Systemic), 522

Midamor— *See* Diuretics, Potassium-sparing (Systemic), 636

Midazolam (Systemic), 1097, 1629

Midchlor— *See* Isometheptene, Dichloralphenazone, and Acetaminophen (Systemic), 939

Midodrine (Systemic), 1098

Midol IB— *See* Anti-inflammatory Drugs, Nonsteroidal (Systemic), 179

Midrin— *See* Isometheptene, Dichloralphenazone, and Acetaminophen (Systemic), 939

Mifeprex— *See* Mifepristone (Systemic), 1100

Mifepristone (Systemic), 1100

Migergot— *See* Headache Medicines, Ergot Derivative–containing (Systemic), 853

Miglitol (Systemic), 1101

Migquin— *See* Isometheptene, Dichloralphenazone, and Acetaminophen (Systemic), 939

Migranal— *See* Dihydroergotamine (Nasal-Systemic), 610

Migrapap— *See* Isometheptene, Dichloralphenazone, and Acetaminophen (Systemic), 939

Migratine— *See* Isometheptene, Dichloralphenazone, and Acetaminophen (Systemic), 939

Migrazone— *See* Isometheptene, Dichloralphenazone, and Acetaminophen (Systemic), 939

Migrend— *See* Isometheptene, Dichloralphenazone, and Acetaminophen (Systemic), 939

Migrex— *See* Isometheptene, Dichloralphenazone, and Acetaminophen (Systemic), 939

Milkinol— *See* Laxatives (Oral), 964

Milophene— *See* Clomiphene (Systemic), 461

Miltown— *See* Meprobamate (Systemic), #

'Miltown'-200— *See* Meprobamate (Systemic), #

'Miltown'-202037— *See* Meprobamate (Systemic), #

'Miltown'-202057— *See* Meprobamate (Systemic), #

Mineral Oil— *See* Laxatives (Oral), 964; *See* Laxatives (Rectal), 970

Mineral Oil and Glycerin— *See* Laxatives (Oral), 964

Mineral Oil, Glycerin, and Phenolphthalein— *See* Laxatives (Oral), 964

Mineral Oil and Phenolphthalein— *See* Laxatives (Oral), 964

Minestrin 1/20— *See* Estrogens and Progestins (Oral Contraceptives) (Systemic), 729

Mini-Gamulin Rh— *See* Rh₀(D) Immune Globulin (Systemic), 1360

Minims Atropine— *See* Atropine/Homatropine/Scopolamine (Ophthalmic), 220

Minims Cyclopentolate— *See* Cyclopentolate (Ophthalmic), 548

Minims Homatropine— *See* Atropine/Homatropine/Scopolamine (Ophthalmic), 220

Minims Phenylephrine— *See* Phenylephrine (Ophthalmic), #

Minims Pilocarpine— *See* Pilocarpine (Ophthalmic), 1287

Minims Tetracaine— *See* Anesthetics (Ophthalmic), #

Minims Tropicamide— *See* Tropicamide (Ophthalmic), #

Minipress— *See* Prazosin (Systemic), 1306

Minizide— *See* Prazosin and Polythiazide (Systemic), #

Minocin— *See* Tetracyclines (Systemic), 1487

Minocycline— *See* Tetracyclines (Systemic), 1487, MC-15

Minocycline (Dental), 1630

Min-Ovral— See Estrogens and Progestins (Oral Contraceptives) (Systemic), 729

Minoxidil (Systemic), 1103

Minoxidil (Topical), 1104

Minoxigaine— See Minoxidil (Topical), 1104

Mintezol— See Thiabendazole (Systemic), 1492, 1630

Mintox— See Antacids (Oral), 98

Mintox Extra Strength— See Antacids (Oral), 98

Minums Phenylephrine— See Phenylephrine (Ophthalmic), #

Miocarpine— See Pilocarpine (Ophthalmic), 1287

Mio-Rel— See Orphenadrine (Systemic), 1220

Miostat— See Carbachol (Ophthalmic), 365

Miradon— See Anticoagulants (Systemic), 112

Mirapex— See Pramipexole (Systemic), 1305, MC-19

Mircette— See Estrogens and Progestins (Oral Contraceptives) (Systemic), 729, MC-6

Mirtazapine (Systemic), 1106, MC-15

Misoprostol (Systemic), 1108, MC-15

Mithracin— See Plicamycin (Systemic), 1293

Mithramycin— See Plicamycin (Systemic), 1293

Mitomycin (Systemic), 1109

Mitomycin-C— See Mitomycin (Systemic), 1109

Mitotane (Systemic), 1111

Mitoxantrone (Systemic), 1112

Mitride— See Isometheptene, Dichloralphenazone, and Acetaminophen (Systemic), 939

Mitrolan— See Laxatives (Oral), 964

MK594— See Losartan (Systemic), 1007

MK790— See Levomethadyl (Systemic), #

M-M-R II— See Measles, Mumps, and Rubella Virus Vaccine Live (Systemic), 1030

Moban— See Molindone (Systemic), 1118

Moban Concentrate— See Molindone (Systemic), 1118

Mobic— See Anti-inflammatory Drugs, Nonsteroidal (Systemic), 179; *See* Meloxicam (Systemic), 1043

Mobidin— See Salicylates (Systemic), 1394

Moclobemide (Systemic), 1114

Moctanin— See Monoctanoin (Local), 1122

Modafinil (Systemic), 1116

Modane— See Laxatives (Oral), 964

Modane Bulk— See Laxatives (Oral), 964

Modane Plus— See Laxatives (Oral), 964

Modane Soft— See Laxatives (Oral), 964

Modecate— See Phenothiazines (Systemic), 1268

Modecate Concentrate— See Phenothiazines (Systemic), 1268

ModiCon— See Estrogens and Progestins (Oral Contraceptives) (Systemic), 729

Modified Shohl's solution— See Citrates (Systemic), 443

Moditen Enanthate— See Phenothiazines (Systemic), 1268

Moditen HCl— See Phenothiazines (Systemic), 1268

Moducal— See Enteral Nutrition Formulas (Systemic), #

Moduret— See Diuretics, Potassium-sparing and Hydrochlorothiazide (Systemic), 639

Moduretic— See Diuretics, Potassium-sparing and Hydrochlorothiazide (Systemic), 639

Moexipril— See Angiotensin-converting Enzyme (ACE) Inhibitors (Systemic), 90, MC-15

Moexipril and Hydrochlorothiazide— See Angiotensin-converting Enzyme (ACE) Inhibitors and Hydrochlorothiazide (Systemic), 94

Mogadon— See Benzodiazepines (Systemic), 257

Moisture Drops— See Hydroxypropyl Methylcellulose (Ophthalmic), 880

Molatoc— See Laxatives (Oral), 964

Molatoc-CST— See Laxatives (Oral), 964

Molindone (Systemic), 1118

Mol-Iron— See Iron Supplements (Systemic), 936

Molybdenum Supplements (Systemic), 1120

Molypen— See Molybdenum Supplements (Systemic), 1120

Mometasone— See Corticosteroids (Nasal), 502; *See* Corticosteroids—Medium to Very High Potency (Topical), 520

Mometasone (Nasal), #

Monazole— See Antifungals, Azole (Vaginal), 145

Monistat 3— See Antifungals, Azole (Vaginal), 145

Monistat 3 Combination Pack— See Antifungals, Azole (Vaginal), 145

Monistat 3 Dual-Pak— See Antifungals, Azole (Vaginal), 145

Monistat 7— See Antifungals, Azole (Vaginal), 145

Monistat 7 Combination Pack— See Antifungals, Azole (Vaginal), 145

Monistat 7 Dual-Pak— See Antifungals, Azole (Vaginal), 145

Monistat-Derm— See Miconazole (Topical), 1096

Monistat 5 Tampon— See Antifungals, Azole (Vaginal), 145

Monistat 3 Vaginal Ovules— See Antifungals, Azole (Vaginal), 145

Monistat 7 Vaginal Suppositories— See Antifungals, Azole (Vaginal), 145

Monitan— See Beta-adrenergic Blocking Agents (Systemic), 272

Monocid— See Cephalosporins (Systemic), 387

Monoclate-P— See Antihemophilic Factor (Systemic), 151

Monoctanoin (Local), 1122

Monodox— See Tetracyclines (Systemic), 1487

Mono-Gesic— See Salicylates (Systemic), 1394

Monoket— See Nitrates—Oral (Systemic), 1188

Mononine— See Factor IX (Systemic), 751

Monooctanoin— See Monoctanoin (Local), 1122

Monopril— See Angiotensin-converting Enzyme (ACE) Inhibitors (Systemic), 90, MC-10

Montelukast (Systemic), 1123, MC-16

Monurol— See Fosfomycin (Systemic), 804

Mooredec— See Antihistamines and Decongestants (Systemic), 159

8-MOP— See Methoxsalen (Systemic), 1069

Moracizine— See Moricizine (Systemic), 1124

Moranyl— See Suramin (Systemic), #

Moricizine (Systemic), 1124

Morphine— See Narcotic Analgesics—For Pain Relief (Systemic), 1147, MC-16; *See* Narcotic Analgesics—For Surgery and Obstetrics (Systemic), 1154, MC-16

Morphine Extra-Forte— See Narcotic Analgesics—For Pain Relief (Systemic), 1147

Morphine Forte— See Narcotic Analgesics—For Pain Relief (Systemic), 1147

Morphine H.P.— See Narcotic Analgesics—For Pain Relief (Systemic), 1147

Morphitec— See Narcotic Analgesics—For Pain Relief (Systemic), 1147

M.O.S.— See Narcotic Analgesics—For Pain Relief (Systemic), 1147

M.O.S.-S.R.— See Narcotic Analgesics—For Pain Relief (Systemic), 1147

Motilium— See Domperidone (Systemic), 652

Motofen— See Difenoxin and Atropine (Systemic), 606

Motrin— See Anti-inflammatory Drugs, Nonsteroidal (Systemic), 179, MC-12

Motrin Chewables— See Anti-inflammatory Drugs, Nonsteroidal (Systemic), 179

Motrin, Children's— See Anti-inflammatory Drugs, Nonsteroidal (Systemic), 179

Motrin, Children's Oral Drops— See Anti-inflammatory Drugs, Nonsteroidal (Systemic), 179

Motrin-IB— See Anti-inflammatory Drugs, Nonsteroidal (Systemic), 179

Motrin-IB Caplets— See Anti-inflammatory Drugs, Nonsteroidal (Systemic), 179

Motrin, Junior Strength Caplets— See Anti-inflammatory Drugs, Nonsteroidal (Systemic), 179

Motrin IB Sinus— See Decongestants and Analgesics (Systemic), 581

Motrin IB Sinus Caplets— See Decongestants and Analgesics (Systemic), 581

6-MP— See Mercaptopurine (Systemic), 1053

MRI Contrast Agents, Iron-containing (Diagnostic), 1020

M-R-VAX II— See Measles and Rubella Virus Vaccine Live (Systemic), 1028

M S Contin— See Narcotic Analgesics—For Pain Relief (Systemic), 1147, MC-16

MSIR— See Narcotic Analgesics—For Pain Relief (Systemic), 1147

MS•IR— See Narcotic Analgesics—For Pain Relief (Systemic), 1147

MS/L— See Narcotic Analgesics—For Pain Relief (Systemic), 1147

MS/L Concentrate— See Narcotic Analgesics—For Pain Relief (Systemic), 1147

MS/S— See Narcotic Analgesics—For Pain Relief (Systemic), 1147

Mucinum— See Laxatives (Oral), 964

Muco-Fen DM— See Cough/Cold Combinations (Systemic), 522

Mucolysin— See Tiopronin (Systemic), #

Mucomyst— See Acetylcysteine (Inhalation), 14

Mucomyst-10— See Acetylcysteine (Inhalation), 14

Mucosil-10— See Acetylcysteine (Inhalation), 14

Mudrane GG-2— See Theophylline and Guaifenesin (Systemic), #

Multipax— See Antihistamines (Systemic), 153

Multiple Vitamins and Fluoride— *See* Vitamins and Fluoride (Systemic), 1586, MC-21

Mulvidren-F— See Vitamins and Fluoride (Systemic), 1586

Mumpsvax— See Mumps Virus Vaccine Live (Systemic), #

Mumps Virus Vaccine Live (Systemic), #
Mupirocin (Nasal), #
Mupirocin (Topical), 1125
Muromonab-CD3 (Systemic), 1126

Muro's Opcon— See Naphazoline (Ophthalmic), 1135

Muse— See Alprostadil (Local), 33

Muskol— See Diethyltoluamide (Topical), #

Mustargen— See Mechlorethamine (Systemic), 1036

Mutamycin— See Mitomycin (Systemic), 1109

Myambutol— See Ethambutol (Systemic), 735

My Baby Gas Relief Drops— See Simethicone (Oral), 1417

Mycelex-7— See Antifungals, Azole (Vaginal), 145

Mycelex Cream— See Clotrimazole (Topical), 472

Mycelex-G— See Antifungals, Azole (Vaginal), 145

Mycelex Solution— See Clotrimazole (Topical), 472

Mycelex Troches— See Clotrimazole (Oral), 471

Mycelex Twin Pack— See Antifungals, Azole (Vaginal), 145

Mycifradin— See Neomycin (Oral), #

Myciguent— See Neomycin (Topical), 1165

Mycitracin— See Neomycin, Polymyxin B, and Bacitracin (Topical), 1168

Myclo Cream— See Clotrimazole (Topical), 472

Myclo-Gyne— See Antifungals, Azole (Vaginal), 145

Myclo Solution— See Clotrimazole (Topical), 472

Myclo Spray Solution— See Clotrimazole (Topical), 472

Myco II— See Nystatin and Triamcinolone (Topical), #

Mycobiotic II— See Nystatin and Triamcinolone (Topical), #

Mycobutin— See Rifabutin (Systemic), 1365

Mycogen II— See Nystatin and Triamcinolone (Topical), #

Mycolog II— See Nystatin and Triamcinolone (Topical), #

Mycophenolate (Systemic), 1128

My Cort— See Corticosteroids—Low Potency (Topical), 518

Mycostatin— See Nystatin (Oral), 1200; *See* Nystatin (Topical), 1202; *See* Nystatin (Vaginal), 1203

Myco-Triacet II— See Nystatin and Triamcinolone (Topical), #

Mycotussin— See Cough/Cold Combinations (Systemic), 522

Mydfrin— See Phenylephrine (Ophthalmic), #

Mydriacyl— See Tropicamide (Ophthalmic), #

Mydriafair— See Tropicamide (Ophthalmic), #

My-E— See Erythromycins (Systemic), 712

Myfedrine— See Pseudoephedrine (Systemic), 1334

Mygel— See Antacids (Oral), 98

Mygel II— See Antacids (Oral), 98

Myhistine DH— See Cough/Cold Combinations (Systemic), 522

Myhistine Expectorant— See Cough/Cold Combinations (Systemic), 522

Myhydromine— See Cough/Cold Combinations (Systemic), 522

Myhydromine Pediatric— See Cough/Cold Combinations (Systemic), 522

Myidone— See Primidone (Systemic), 1310

Mykacet— See Nystatin and Triamcinolone (Topical), #

Mykacet II— See Nystatin and Triamcinolone (Topical), #

Mykrox— See Diuretics, Thiazide (Systemic), 642

Mylagen— See Antacids (Oral), 98

Mylagen II— See Antacids (Oral), 98

Mylagen Gelcaps— See Antacids (Oral), 98

Mylanta— See Antacids (Oral), 98

Mylanta-AR Acid Reducer— See Histamine H_2-receptor Antagonists (Systemic), 863

Mylanta Calcium-Rich— See Antacids (Oral), 98

Mylanta Calcium-Rich Double Strength— See Antacids (Oral), 98

Mylanta Double Strength— See Antacids (Oral), 98

Mylanta Double Strength Plain— See Antacids (Oral), 98

Mylanta Extra Strength— See Antacids (Oral), 98

Mylanta Gas— See Simethicone (Oral), 1417

Mylanta Gas Relief— See Simethicone (Oral), 1417

Mylanta Gelcaps— See Antacids (Oral), 98

Mylanta Natural Fiber Supplement— See Laxatives (Oral), 964

Mylanta Sugar Free Natural Fiber Supplement— See Laxatives (Oral), 964

Myleran— See Busulfan (Systemic), 322

Mylicon Drops— See Simethicone (Oral), 1417

Mylotarg— See Gemtuzumab Ozogamicin (Systemic), 819, 1629

Mymethasone— See Corticosteroids—Glucocorticoid Effects (Systemic), 513

Myminic Expectorant— See Cough/Cold Combinations (Systemic), 522

Myminicol— See Cough/Cold Combinations (Systemic), 522

Myobloc— See Botulinum Toxin Type B (Parenteral-Local), 298

Myochrysine— See Gold Compounds (Systemic), 834

Myolin— See Orphenadrine (Systemic), 1220

Myotrol— See Orphenadrine (Systemic), 1220

Myoview— See Radiopharmaceuticals (Diagnostic), 1347

Myphetane DC Cough— See Cough/Cold Combinations (Systemic), 522

Myphetane DX Cough— See Cough/Cold Combinations (Systemic), 522

Myphetapp— See Antihistamines and Decongestants (Systemic), 159

Myrosemide— See Diuretics, Loop (Systemic), 633

Mysoline— See Primidone (Systemic), 1310

Mytelase Caplets— See Antimyasthenics (Systemic), 190

Mytrex— See Nystatin and Triamcinolone (Topical), #

Mytussin AC— See Cough/Cold Combinations (Systemic), 522

Mytussin DAC— See Cough/Cold Combinations (Systemic), 522

Mytussin DM— See Cough/Cold Combinations (Systemic), 522

MZM— See Carbonic Anhydrase Inhibitors (Systemic), 373

N

9-1-1— See Corticosteroids—Low Potency (Topical), 518

Nabilone (Systemic), 1129

Nabumetone— *See* Anti-inflammatory Drugs, Nonsteroidal (Systemic), 179, MC-16

Nadolol— *See* Beta-adrenergic Blocking Agents (Systemic), 272, MC-16

Nadolol and Bendroflumethiazide— *See* Beta-adrenergic Blocking Agents and Thiazide Diuretics (Systemic), 278

Nadopen-V— See Penicillins (Systemic), 1251

Nadopen-V 200— See Penicillins (Systemic), 1251

Nadopen-V 400— See Penicillins (Systemic), 1251

Nadostine— See Nystatin (Oral), 1200; *See* Nystatin (Topical), 1202; *See* Nystatin (Vaginal), 1203

Nadroparin (Systemic), 1131

Nadrothyron-D— See Dextrothyroxine (Systemic), 594

Nafarelin (Systemic), 1133

Nafazair— See Naphazoline (Ophthalmic), 1135

Nafcil— See Penicillins (Systemic), 1251

Nafcillin— *See* Penicillins (Systemic), 1251

Naftifine (Topical), #

Naftin— See Naftifine (Topical), #

Naganin— See Suramin (Systemic), #

Naganol— See Suramin (Systemic), #

Nalbuphine— *See* Narcotic Analgesics—For Pain Relief (Systemic), 1147; *See* Narcotic Analgesics—For Surgery and Obstetrics (Systemic), 1154

Nalcrom— See Cromolyn (Oral), 543

Nalda-Relief Pediatric Drops— See Antihistamines and Decongestants (Systemic), 159

Naldecon— See Antihistamines and Decongestants (Systemic), 159

Naldecon-CX Adult Liquid— See Cough/Cold Combinations (Systemic), 522

Naldecon-DX Adult Liquid— See Cough/Cold Combinations (Systemic), 522

Naldecon-DX Children's Syrup— See Cough/Cold Combinations (Systemic), 522

Novagest Expectorant w/Codeine— See Cough/Cold Combinations (Systemic), 522

Novahistex— See Antihistamines and Decongestants (Systemic), 159

Novahistex C— See Cough/Cold Combinations (Systemic), 522

Novahistex DH— See Cough/Cold Combinations (Systemic), 522

Novahistex DH Expectorant— See Cough/Cold Combinations (Systemic), 522

Novahistex DM— See Dextromethorphan (Systemic), 592

Novahistex DM w/Decongestant— See Cough/Cold Combinations (Systemic), 522

Novahistex DM Expectorant w/Decongestant— See Cough/Cold Combinations (Systemic), 522

Novahistex Expectorant w/Decongestant— See Cough/Cold Combinations (Systemic), 522

Novahistine— See Antihistamines and Decongestants (Systemic), 159

Novahistine DH— See Cough/Cold Combinations (Systemic), 522

Novahistine DH Liquid— See Cough/Cold Combinations (Systemic), 522

Novahistine DM— See Dextromethorphan (Systemic), 592

Novahistine DM Expectorant w/Decongestant— See Cough/Cold Combinations (Systemic), 522

Novahistine DM w/Decongestant— See Cough/Cold Combinations (Systemic), 522

Novahistine DMX Liquid— See Cough/Cold Combinations (Systemic), 522

Novahistine Expectorant— See Cough/Cold Combinations (Systemic), 522

Novamoxin— See Penicillins (Systemic), 1251

Novantrone— See Mitoxantrone (Systemic), 1112

Nova Rectal— See Barbiturates (Systemic), 239

Novasen— See Salicylates (Systemic), 1394

Novasen Sp.C— See Salicylates (Systemic), 1394

Novo-AC and C— See Narcotic Analgesics and Aspirin (Systemic), 1142

Novo-Alprazol— See Benzodiazepines (Systemic), 257

Novo-Ampicillin— See Penicillins (Systemic), 1251

Novo-Atenol— See Beta-adrenergic Blocking Agents (Systemic), 272

Novo-AZT— See Zidovudine (Systemic), 1595

Novo-Baclofen— See Baclofen (Systemic), 236

Novobetamet— See Corticosteroids—Medium to Very High Potency (Topical), 520

Novo-Butamide— See Antidiabetic Agents, Sulfonylurea (Systemic), 131

Novocain— See Anesthetics (Parenteral-Local), 83

Novo-Carbamaz— See Carbamazepine (Systemic), 366

Novo-Chlorhydrate— See Chloral Hydrate (Systemic), 398

Novochlorocap— See Chloramphenicol (Systemic), 406

Novo-Chlorpromazine— See Phenothiazines (Systemic), 1268

Novo-Cimetine— See Histamine H_2-receptor Antagonists (Systemic), 863

Novo-Clopate— See Benzodiazepines (Systemic), 257

Novo-Cloxin— See Penicillins (Systemic), 1251

Novo-cromolyn— See Cromolyn (Inhalation), 537

Novo-Difenac— See Anti-inflammatory Drugs, Nonsteroidal (Systemic), 179

Novo-Difenac SR— See Anti-inflammatory Drugs, Nonsteroidal (Systemic), 179

Novo-Diflunisal— See Anti-inflammatory Drugs, Nonsteroidal (Systemic), 179

Novo-Digoxin— See Digitalis Medicines (Systemic), 608

Novo-Diltazem— See Calcium Channel Blocking Agents (Systemic), 349

Novo-Dipam— See Benzodiazepines (Systemic), 257

Novo-Dipiradol— See Dipyridamole—Diagnostic (Systemic), 625; See Dipyridamole—Therapeutic (Systemic), 626

Novodoparil— See Methyldopa and Thiazide Diuretics (Systemic), 1074

Novo-Doxepin— See Antidepressants, Tricyclic (Systemic), 126

Novo-Doxylin— See Tetracyclines (Systemic), 1487

Novo-Famotidine— See Histamine H_2-receptor Antagonists (Systemic), 863

Novoferrogluc— See Iron Supplements (Systemic), 936

Novoferrosulfa— See Iron Supplements (Systemic), 936

Novofibrate— See Clofibrate (Systemic), 459

Novo-Flupam— See Benzodiazepines (Systemic), 257

Novo-Flurprofen— See Anti-inflammatory Drugs, Nonsteroidal (Systemic), 179

Novo-Folacid— See Folic Acid (Vitamin B_9) (Systemic), 794

Novofumar— See Iron Supplements (Systemic), 936

Novo-Furantoin— See Nitrofurantoin (Systemic), 1195

Novo-Gemfibrozil— See Gemfibrozil (Systemic), 818

Novo-Gesic C8— See Narcotic Analgesics and Acetaminophen (Systemic), 1138

Novo-Gesic C15— See Narcotic Analgesics and Acetaminophen (Systemic), 1138

Novo-Gesic C30— See Narcotic Analgesics and Acetaminophen (Systemic), 1138

Novo-Glyburide— See Antidiabetic Agents, Sulfonylurea (Systemic), 131

Novo-Hydrazide— See Diuretics, Thiazide (Systemic), 642

Novohydrocort— See Corticosteroids—Low Potency (Topical), 518

Novo-Hydroxyzin— See Antihistamines (Systemic), 153

Novo-Hylazin— See Hydralazine (Systemic), 873

Novo-Indapamide— See Indapamide (Systemic), 897

Novo-Keto-EC— See Anti-inflammatory Drugs, Nonsteroidal (Systemic), 179

Novo-Ketotifen— See Ketotifen (Systemic), 954

Novo-Levobunolol— See Beta-adrenergic Blocking Agents (Ophthalmic), 270

Novo-Lexin— See Cephalosporins (Systemic), 387

Novolin 70/30— See Insulin (Systemic), 902

Novolin ge 30/70— See Insulin (Systemic), 902

Novolin ge Lente— See Insulin (Systemic), 902

Novolin ge NPH— See Insulin (Systemic), 902

Novolin ge NPH Penfill— See Insulin (Systemic), 902

Novolin ge 10/90 Penfill— See Insulin (Systemic), 902

Novolin ge 20/80 Penfill— See Insulin (Systemic), 902

Novolin ge 30/70 Penfill— See Insulin (Systemic), 902

Novolin ge 40/60 Penfill— See Insulin (Systemic), 902

Novolin ge 50/50 Penfill— See Insulin (Systemic), 902

Novolin ge Toronto— See Insulin (Systemic), 902

Novolin ge Toronto Penfill— See Insulin (Systemic), 902

Novolin ge Ultralente— See Insulin (Systemic), 902

Novolin L— See Insulin (Systemic), 902

Novolin N— See Insulin (Systemic), 902

Novolin N PenFill— See Insulin (Systemic), 902

Novolin N Prefilled— See Insulin (Systemic), 902

Novolin 70/30 PenFill— See Insulin (Systemic), 902

Novolin 70/30 Prefilled— See Insulin (Systemic), 902

Novolin R— See Insulin (Systemic), 902

Novolin R PenFill— See Insulin (Systemic), 902

Novolin R Prefilled— See Insulin (Systemic), 902

NovoLog— See Insulin Aspart, 909

Novo-Lorazem— See Benzodiazepines (Systemic), 257

Novomedopa— See Methyldopa (Systemic), 1072

Novo-Medrone— See Progestins—For Noncontraceptive Use (Systemic), 1328

Novo-Metformin— See Metformin (Systemic), 1057

Novo-Methacin— See Anti-inflammatory Drugs, Nonsteroidal (Systemic), 179

Novometoprol— See Beta-adrenergic Blocking Agents (Systemic), 272

Novo-Miconazole Vaginal Ovules— See Antifungals, Azole (Vaginal), 145

Novo-Minocycline— See Tetracyclines (Systemic), 1487

Novo-Naprox— See Anti-inflammatory Drugs, Nonsteroidal (Systemic), 179

Novo-Naprox Sodium— See Anti-inflammatory Drugs, Nonsteroidal (Systemic), 179

Novo-Naprox Sodium DS— See Anti-inflammatory Drugs, Nonsteroidal (Systemic), 179

Novo-Niacin— See Niacin (Vitamin B_3) (Systemic), 1175; See Niacin—For High Cholesterol (Systemic), 1177

Novonidazol— *See* Metronidazole (Systemic), 1086

Novo-Nifedin— *See* Calcium Channel Blocking Agents (Systemic), 349

Novopentobarb— *See* Barbiturates (Systemic), 239

Novo-Pen-VK— *See* Penicillins (Systemic), 1251

Novo-Peridol— *See* Haloperidol (Systemic), 850

Novo-Pheniram— *See* Antihistamines (Systemic), 153

Novo-Pindol— *See* Beta-adrenergic Blocking Agents (Systemic), 272

Novo-Pirocam— *See* Anti-inflammatory Drugs, Nonsteroidal (Systemic), 179

Novo-Poxide— *See* Benzodiazepines (Systemic), 257

Novopramine— *See* Antidepressants, Tricyclic (Systemic), 126

Novopranol— *See* Beta-adrenergic Blocking Agents (Systemic), 272

Novo-Profen— *See* Anti-inflammatory Drugs, Nonsteroidal (Systemic), 179

Novo-Propamide— *See* Antidiabetic Agents, Sulfonylurea (Systemic), 131

Novopyrazone— *See* Sulfinpyrazone (Systemic), #

Novoquinidin— *See* Quinidine (Systemic), 1341

Novo-Ranitidine— *See* Histamine H_2-receptor Antagonists (Systemic), 863

Novoreserpine— *See* Rauwolfia Alkaloids (Systemic), 1354

Novo-Ridazine— *See* Phenothiazines (Systemic), 1268

Novo-Rythro— *See* Erythromycins (Systemic), 712

Novo-rythro— *See* Erythromycins (Systemic), 712

Novo-rythro Encap— *See* Erythromycins (Systemic), 712

Novo-Salmol— *See* Bronchodilators, Adrenergic (Inhalation), 304; *See* Bronchodilators, Adrenergic (Oral/Injection), 310

Novosecobarb— *See* Barbiturates (Systemic), 239

Novo-Selegiline— *See* Selegiline (Systemic), 1403

Novosemide— *See* Diuretics, Loop (Systemic), 633

NovoSeven— *See* Factor VIIa (Systemic), 752

Novo-Soxazole— *See* Sulfonamides (Systemic), 1446

Novospiroton— *See* Diuretics, Potassium-sparing (Systemic), 636

Novo-Spirozine— *See* Diuretics, Potassium-sparing and Hydrochlorothiazide (Systemic), 639

Novo-Sundac— *See* Anti-inflammatory Drugs, Nonsteroidal (Systemic), 179

Novo-Tamoxifen— *See* Tamoxifen (Systemic), 1465

Novo-Temazepam— *See* Benzodiazepines (Systemic), 257

Novo-Tenoxicam— *See* Anti-inflammatory Drugs, Nonsteroidal (Systemic), 179

Novo-Tetra— *See* Tetracyclines (Systemic), 1487

Novo-Thalidone— *See* Diuretics, Thiazide (Systemic), 642

Novo-Timol— *See* Beta-adrenergic Blocking Agents (Systemic), 272

Novo-Tolmetin— *See* Anti-inflammatory Drugs, Nonsteroidal (Systemic), 179

Novo-Triamzide— *See* Diuretics, Potassium-sparing and Hydrochlorothiazide (Systemic), 639

Novo-Trifluzine— *See* Phenothiazines (Systemic), 1268

Novo-Trimel— *See* Sulfonamides and Trimethoprim (Systemic), 1454

Novo-Trimel D.S.— *See* Sulfonamides and Trimethoprim (Systemic), 1454

Novo-Triolam— *See* Benzodiazepines (Systemic), 257

Novo-Tripramine— *See* Antidepressants, Tricyclic (Systemic), 126

Novotriptyn— *See* Antidepressants, Tricyclic (Systemic), 126

Novo-Valproic— *See* Valproic Acid (Systemic), 1549

Novo-Veramil— *See* Calcium Channel Blocking Agents (Systemic), 349

Novoxapam— *See* Benzodiazepines (Systemic), 257

Noxzema Anti-Acne Gel— *See* Salicylic Acid (Topical), #

Noxzema Anti-Acne Pads Maximum Strength— *See* Salicylic Acid (Topical), #

Noxzema Anti-Acne Pads Regular Strength— *See* Salicylic Acid (Topical), #

Noxzema Clear-ups Maximum Strength 10 Lotion— *See* Benzoyl Peroxide (Topical), 265

Noxzema Clear-ups On-The-Spot 10 Lotion— *See* Benzoyl Peroxide (Topical), 265

Noxzema Moisturizer— *See* Sunscreen Agents (Topical), #

Nozinan— *See* Phenothiazines (Systemic), 1268

Nozinan Liquid— *See* Phenothiazines (Systemic), 1268

Nozinan Oral Drops— *See* Phenothiazines (Systemic), 1268

NP-27 Cream— *See* Tolnaftate (Topical), #

NPH Iletin— *See* Insulin (Systemic), 902

NPH Iletin II— *See* Insulin (Systemic), 902

NPH insulin, NPH— *See* Insulin (Systemic), 902

NPH Purified Insulin— *See* Insulin (Systemic), 902

NP-27 Powder— *See* Tolnaftate (Topical), #

NP-27 Solution— *See* Tolnaftate (Topical), #

NP-27 Spray Powder— *See* Tolnaftate (Topical), #

Nu-Alpraz— *See* Benzodiazepines (Systemic), 257

Nu-Amoxi— *See* Penicillins (Systemic), 1251

Nu-Ampi— *See* Penicillins (Systemic), 1251

Nu-Baclofen— *See* Baclofen (Systemic), 236

Nubain— *See* Narcotic Analgesics—For Pain Relief (Systemic), 1147; *See* Narcotic Analgesics—For Surgery and Obstetrics (Systemic), 1154

NuBasics— *See* Enteral Nutrition Formulas (Systemic), #

NuBasics with Fiber— *See* Enteral Nutrition Formulas (Systemic), #

NuBasics Plus— *See* Enteral Nutrition Formulas (Systemic), #

NuBasics VHP— *See* Enteral Nutrition Formulas (Systemic), #

Nu-Cal— *See* Calcium Supplements (Systemic), 353

Nu-Carbamazepine— *See* Carbamazepine (Systemic), 366

Nu-Cephalex— *See* Cephalosporins (Systemic), 387

Nu-Cimet— *See* Histamine H_2-receptor Antagonists (Systemic), 863

Nu-Cloxi— *See* Penicillins (Systemic), 1251

Nucochem— *See* Cough/Cold Combinations (Systemic), 522

Nucochem Expectorant— *See* Cough/Cold Combinations (Systemic), 522

Nucochem Pediatric Expectorant— *See* Cough/Cold Combinations (Systemic), 522

Nucofed— *See* Cough/Cold Combinations (Systemic), 522

Nucofed Expectorant— *See* Cough/Cold Combinations (Systemic), 522

Nucofed Pediatric Expectorant— *See* Cough/Cold Combinations (Systemic), 522

Nu-Cotrimox— *See* Sulfonamides and Trimethoprim (Systemic), 1454

Nu-Cotrimox DS— *See* Sulfonamides and Trimethoprim (Systemic), 1454

Nucotuss Expectorant— *See* Cough/Cold Combinations (Systemic), 522

Nucotuss Pediatric Expectorant— *See* Cough/Cold Combinations (Systemic), 522

Nu-Diclo— *See* Anti-inflammatory Drugs, Nonsteroidal (Systemic), 179

Nu-Diltiaz— *See* Calcium Channel Blocking Agents (Systemic), 349

Nu-Doxycycline— *See* Tetracyclines (Systemic), 1487

Nu-Famotidine— *See* Histamine H_2-receptor Antagonists (Systemic), 863

Nu-Flurbiprofen— *See* Anti-inflammatory Drugs, Nonsteroidal (Systemic), 179

Nu-Gemfibrozil— *See* Gemfibrozil (Systemic), 818

Nu-Glyburide— *See* Antidiabetic Agents, Sulfonylurea (Systemic), 131

Nu-Ibuprofen— *See* Anti-inflammatory Drugs, Nonsteroidal (Systemic), 179

Nu-Indapamide— *See* Indapamide (Systemic), 897

Nu-Indo— *See* Anti-inflammatory Drugs, Nonsteroidal (Systemic), 179

Nu-Iron— *See* Iron Supplements (Systemic), 936

Nu-Iron 150— *See* Iron Supplements (Systemic), 936

Nujol— *See* Laxatives (Oral), 964

Nu-Levocarb— *See* Levodopa (Systemic), 985

Nu-Loperamide— *See* Loperamide (Oral), 1001

Nu-Loraz— *See* Benzodiazepines (Systemic), 257

NuLYTELY— *See* Polyethylene Glycol and Electrolytes (Local), 1299

NuLYTELY, Cherry Flavor— *See* Polyethylene Glycol and Electrolytes (Local), 1299

Nu-Medopa— *See* Methyldopa (Systemic), 1072

Nu-Metformin—See Metformin (Systemic), 1057

Nu-Metop—See Beta-adrenergic Blocking Agents (Systemic), 272

Numorphan—See Narcotic Analgesics—For Pain Relief (Systemic), 1147

Numzident—See Anesthetics (Dental), 80

Num-Zit Gel—See Anesthetics (Dental), 80

Num-Zit Lotion—See Anesthetics (Dental), 80

Nu-Naprox—See Anti-inflammatory Drugs, Nonsteroidal (Systemic), 179

Nu-Nifed—See Calcium Channel Blocking Agents (Systemic), 349

Nu-Pen-VK—See Penicillins (Systemic), 1251

Nupercainal—See Anesthetics (Rectal), 85

Nupercainal Cream—See Anesthetics (Topical), 88

Nupercainal Ointment—See Anesthetics (Topical), 88

Nu-Pirox—See Anti-inflammatory Drugs, Nonsteroidal (Systemic), 179

Nuprin—See Anti-inflammatory Drugs, Nonsteroidal (Systemic), 179

Nuprin Caplets—See Anti-inflammatory Drugs, Nonsteroidal (Systemic), 179

Nu-Prochlor—See Phenothiazines (Systemic), 1268

Nu-Ranit—See Histamine H$_2$-receptor Antagonists (Systemic), 863

Nursoy—See Infant Formulas (Systemic), #

Nu-Selegiline—See Selegiline (Systemic), 1403

Nu-Tetra—See Tetracyclines (Systemic), 1487

Nutracort—See Corticosteroids—Low Potency (Topical), 518

Nutramigen—See Infant Formulas (Systemic), #

Nutren 1.0—See Enteral Nutrition Formulas (Systemic), #

Nutren 1.5—See Enteral Nutrition Formulas (Systemic), #

Nutren 2.0—See Enteral Nutrition Formulas (Systemic), #

Nutren 1.0 with Fiber—See Enteral Nutrition Formulas (Systemic), #

NutriHep—See Enteral Nutrition Formulas (Systemic), #

Nutrilan—See Enteral Nutrition Formulas (Systemic), #

NutriSource—See Enteral Nutrition Formulas (Systemic), #

NutriSource HN—See Enteral Nutrition Formulas (Systemic), #

NutriVent—See Enteral Nutrition Formulas (Systemic), #

Nutropin—See Growth Hormone (Systemic), 843

Nutropin AQ—See Growth Hormone (Systemic), 843

Nu-Valproic—See Valproic Acid (Systemic), 1549

Nu-Verap—See Calcium Channel Blocking Agents (Systemic), 349

Nyaderm—See Nystatin (Topical), 1202; *See* Nystatin (Vaginal), 1203

Nydrazid—See Isoniazid (Systemic), 941

Nylidrin (Systemic), 1199

Nystatin (Oral), 1200

Nystatin (Topical), 1202

Nystatin (Vaginal), 1203

Nystatin and Triamcinolone (Topical), #

Nystex—See Nystatin (Oral), 1200; *See* Nystatin (Topical), 1202

Nystop—See Nystatin (Topical), 1202

Nytcold Medicine—See Cough/Cold Combinations (Systemic), 522

Nytilax—See Laxatives (Oral), 964

Nytime Cold Medicine Liquid—See Cough/Cold Combinations (Systemic), 522

Nytol QuickCaps—See Antihistamines (Systemic), 153

Nytol QuickGels—See Antihistamines (Systemic), 153

O

OB—See Androgens and Estrogens (Systemic), 76

Obenix—See Appetite Suppressants, Sympathomimetic (Systemic), 197

Obezine—See Appetite Suppressants, Sympathomimetic (Systemic), 197

Occlusal-HP Topical Solution—See Salicylic Acid (Topical), #

Occlusal Topical Solution—See Salicylic Acid (Topical), #

Occulcort—See Corticosteroids—Medium to Very High Potency (Topical), 520

OCL—See Polyethylene Glycol and Electrolytes (Local), 1299

Octamide—See Metoclopramide (Systemic), 1083

Octatropine—*See* Anticholinergics/Antispasmodics (Systemic), 106

Octicair—See Neomycin, Polymyxin B, and Hydrocortisone (Otic), 1172

Octigen—See Neomycin, Polymyxin B, and Hydrocortisone (Otic), 1172

Octocaine—See Anesthetics (Parenteral-Local), 83

Octocaine-50—See Anesthetics (Parenteral-Local), 83

Octocaine-100—See Anesthetics (Parenteral-Local), 83

Octocrylene and Octyl Methoxycinnamate—*See* Sunscreen Agents (Topical), #

Octocrylene, Octyl Methoxycinnamate, Octyl Salicylate, and Oxybenzone—*See* Sunscreen Agents (Topical), #

Octocrylene, Octyl Methoxycinnamate, Octyl Salicylate, Oxybenzone, and Titanium Dioxide—*See* Sunscreen Agents (Topical), #

Octocrylene, Octyl Methoxycinnamate, and Oxybenzone—*See* Sunscreen Agents (Topical), #

Octocrylene, Octyl Methoxycinnamate, Oxybenzone, and Titanium Dioxide—*See* Sunscreen Agents (Topical), #

Octocrylene, Octyl Methoxycinnamate, and Titanium Dioxide—*See* Sunscreen Agents (Topical), #

Octostim—See Desmopressin (Systemic), 589

Octoxinol—*See* Spermicides (Vaginal), 1428

Octoxynol 9—*See* Spermicides (Vaginal), 1428

Octreotide (Systemic), 1204

Octyl Methoxycinnamate—*See* Sunscreen Agents (Topical), #

Octyl Methoxycinnamate and Octyl Salicylate—*See* Sunscreen Agents (Topical), #

Octyl Methoxycinnamate, Octyl Salicylate, and Oxybenzone—*See* Sunscreen Agents (Topical), #

Octyl Methoxycinnamate, Octyl Salicylate, Oxybenzone, and Padimate O—*See* Sunscreen Agents (Topical), #

Octyl Methoxycinnamate, Octyl Salicylate, Oxybenzone, Padimate O, and Titanium Dioxide—*See* Sunscreen Agents (Topical), #

Octyl Methoxycinnamate, Octyl Salicylate, Oxybenzone, Phenylbenzimidazole, and Titanium Dioxide—*See* Sunscreen Agents (Topical), #

Octyl Methoxycinnamate, Octyl Salicylate, Oxybenzone, and Titanium Dioxide—*See* Sunscreen Agents (Topical), #

Octyl Methoxycinnamate, Octyl Salicylate, Phenylbenzimidazole, and Titanium Dioxide—*See* Sunscreen Agents (Topical), #

Octyl Methoxycinnamate, Octyl Salicylate, and Titanium Dioxide—*See* Sunscreen Agents (Topical), #

Octyl Methoxycinnamate and Oxybenzone—*See* Sunscreen Agents (Topical), #

Octyl Methoxycinnamate, Oxybenzone, and Padimate O—*See* Sunscreen Agents (Topical), #

Octyl Methoxycinnamate, Oxybenzone, Padimate O, and Titanium Dioxide—*See* Sunscreen Agents (Topical), #

Octyl Methoxycinnamate, Oxybenzone, and Titanium Dioxide—*See* Sunscreen Agents (Topical), #

Octyl Methoxycinnamate and Padimate O—*See* Sunscreen Agents (Topical), #

Octyl Methoxycinnamate and Phenylbenzimidazole—*See* Sunscreen Agents (Topical), #

Octyl Salicylate—*See* Sunscreen Agents (Topical), #

Octyl Salicylate and Padimate O—*See* Sunscreen Agents (Topical), #

Ocu-Caine—See Anesthetics (Ophthalmic), #

Ocu-Carpine—See Pilocarpine (Ophthalmic), 1287

Ocu-Chlor Ophthalmic Ointment—See Chloramphenicol (Ophthalmic), 403

Ocu-Chlor Ophthalmic Solution—See Chloramphenicol (Ophthalmic), 403

OcuClear—See Oxymetazoline (Ophthalmic), 1233

Ocucoat—See Hydroxypropyl Methylcellulose (Ophthalmic), 880; *See* Hydroxypropyl Methylcellulose (Parenteral-Local), 881

Ocucoat PF—See Hydroxypropyl Methylcellulose (Ophthalmic), 880

Ocu-Dex—See Corticosteroids (Ophthalmic), 505

Ocufen—See Anti-inflammatory Drugs, Nonsteroidal (Ophthalmic), 177

Ocuflox—See Ofloxacin (Ophthalmic), 1206

Oreticyl— See Rauwolfia Alkaloids and Thiazide Diuretics (Systemic), #

Oreticyl Forte— See Rauwolfia Alkaloids and Thiazide Diuretics (Systemic), #

ORETON Methyl— See Androgens (Systemic), 71

Orfro— See Orphenadrine (Systemic), 1220

ORG 10172— *See* Danaparoid (Systemic), 569

Organidin NR— See Guaifenesin (Systemic), 844

Orgaran— See Danaparoid (Systemic), 569

Orimune— See Poliovirus Vaccine (Systemic), #; *See* Poliovirus Vaccine Live Oral (Systemic), #

Orinase— See Antidiabetic Agents, Sulfonylurea (Systemic), 131

Orlaam— See Levomethadyl (Systemic), #, 1629

Orlistat (Oral-Local), 1219, MC-18

Ornade— See Antihistamines and Decongestants (Systemic), 159

Ornade-A.F.— See Antihistamines and Decongestants (Systemic), 159

Ornade-DM 10— See Cough/Cold Combinations (Systemic), 522

Ornade-DM 15— See Cough/Cold Combinations (Systemic), 522

Ornade-DM 30— See Cough/Cold Combinations (Systemic), 522

Ornade Expectorant— See Cough/Cold Combinations (Systemic), 522

Ornade Spansules— See Antihistamines and Decongestants (Systemic), 159

Ornex Maximum Strength Caplets— See Decongestants and Analgesics (Systemic), 581

Ornex No Drowsiness Caplets— See Decongestants and Analgesics (Systemic), 581

Ornex Severe Cold No Drowsiness Caplets— See Cough/Cold Combinations (Systemic), 522

Ornidyl— See Eflornithine (Systemic), #

Oro-Clense— See Chlorhexidine (Dental), 413

Orphenadrine (Systemic), 1220, MC-18

Orphenadrine and Aspirin (Systemic), 1222

Orphenadrine, Aspirin, and Caffeine— *See* Orphenadrine and Aspirin (Systemic), 1222

Orphenagesic— See Orphenadrine and Aspirin (Systemic), 1222

Orphenagesic Forte— See Orphenadrine and Aspirin (Systemic), 1222

Orphenate— See Orphenadrine (Systemic), 1220

ORS-bicarbonate— *See* Carbohydrates and Electrolytes (Systemic), 370

ORS-bicarbonate— See Carbohydrates and Electrolytes (Systemic), 370

ORS-citrate— *See* Carbohydrates and Electrolytes (Systemic), 370

ORS-citrate— See Carbohydrates and Electrolytes (Systemic), 370

Ortho 0.5/35— See Estrogens and Progestins (Oral Contraceptives) (Systemic), 729

Ortho 1/35— See Estrogens and Progestins (Oral Contraceptives) (Systemic), 729

Ortho 7/7/7— See Estrogens and Progestins (Oral Contraceptives) (Systemic), 729

Ortho 10/11— See Estrogens and Progestins (Oral Contraceptives) (Systemic), 729

Ortho-Cept— See Estrogens and Progestins (Oral Contraceptives) (Systemic), 729, MC-6

Orthoclone OKT3— See Muromonab-CD3 (Systemic), 1126

Ortho-Creme— See Spermicides (Vaginal), 1428

Ortho/CS— See Ascorbic Acid (Vitamin C) (Systemic), 205

Ortho-Cyclen— See Estrogens and Progestins (Oral Contraceptives) (Systemic), 729, MC-17

Ortho Dienestrol— See Estrogens (Vaginal), 724

Ortho-Est— See Estrogens (Systemic), 718

Ortho-Gynol— See Spermicides (Vaginal), 1428

Ortho-Novum 1/35— See Estrogens and Progestins (Oral Contraceptives) (Systemic), 729, MC-17

Ortho-Novum 1/50— See Estrogens and Progestins (Oral Contraceptives) (Systemic), 729

Ortho-Novum 7/7/7— See Estrogens and Progestins (Oral Contraceptives) (Systemic), 729, MC-17

Ortho-Novum 10/11— See Estrogens and Progestins (Oral Contraceptives) (Systemic), 729

Ortho-Prefest— See Estrogens and Progestins (Ovarian Hormone Therapy) (Systemic), 727

Ortho Tri-Cyclen— See Estrogens and Progestins (Oral Contraceptives) (Systemic), 729, MC-17

Orthoxicol Cough— See Cough/Cold Combinations (Systemic), 522

Or-Tyl— See Anticholinergics/Antispasmodics (Systemic), 106

Orudis— See Anti-inflammatory Drugs, Nonsteroidal (Systemic), 179

Orudis-E— See Anti-inflammatory Drugs, Nonsteroidal (Systemic), 179

Orudis KT— See Anti-inflammatory Drugs, Nonsteroidal (Systemic), 179

Orudis-SR— See Anti-inflammatory Drugs, Nonsteroidal (Systemic), 179

Oruvail— See Anti-inflammatory Drugs, Nonsteroidal (Systemic), 179

Os-Cal— See Calcium Supplements (Systemic), 353

Os-Cal 500— See Calcium Supplements (Systemic), 353

Os-Cal Chewable— See Calcium Supplements (Systemic), 353

Os-Cal 500 Chewable— See Calcium Supplements (Systemic), 353

Oseltamivir (Systemic), 1225

Osmoglyn— See Glycerin (Systemic), 832

Osmolite— See Enteral Nutrition Formulas (Systemic), #

Osmolite HN— See Enteral Nutrition Formulas (Systemic), #

Ostoforte— See Vitamin D and Related Compounds (Systemic), 1577

Otic-Care— See Neomycin, Polymyxin B, and Hydrocortisone (Otic), 1172

Otic-Care Ear— See Neomycin, Polymyxin B, and Hydrocortisone (Otic), 1172

Otimar— See Neomycin, Polymyxin B, and Hydrocortisone (Otic), 1172

Otisan— See Neomycin, Polymyxin B, and Hydrocortisone (Otic), 1172

Otocalm— See Antipyrine and Benzocaine (Otic), 192

Otocidin— See Neomycin, Polymyxin B, and Hydrocortisone (Otic), 1172

Otocort— See Neomycin, Polymyxin B, and Hydrocortisone (Otic), 1172

Otrivin Measured Dose Pump with Moisturizers— See Xylometazoline (Nasal), #

Otrivin Nasal Drops— See Xylometazoline (Nasal), #

Otrivin Nasal Spray— See Xylometazoline (Nasal), #

Otrivin Nasal Spray with Eucalyptol— See Xylometazoline (Nasal), #

Otrivin Nasal Spray with Moisturizers— See Xylometazoline (Nasal), #

Otrivin Pediatric Nasal Drops— See Xylometazoline (Nasal), #

Otrivin Pediatric Nasal Spray— See Xylometazoline (Nasal), #

Otrivin With Measured-Dose Pump— See Xylometazoline (Nasal), #

Ovcon-35— See Estrogens and Progestins (Oral Contraceptives) (Systemic), 729

Ovcon-50— See Estrogens and Progestins (Oral Contraceptives) (Systemic), 729

Ovide— See Malathion (Topical), 1021

Ovidrel— See Choriogonadotripin Alfa (Systemic), 425

Ovol— See Simethicone (Oral), 1417

Ovol-40— See Simethicone (Oral), 1417

Ovol-80— See Simethicone (Oral), 1417

Ovol-160— See Simethicone (Oral), 1417

Ovral— See Estrogens and Progestins (Oral Contraceptives) (Systemic), 729

Ovrette— See Progestins—For Contraceptive Use (Systemic), 1324

Oxacillin— See Penicillins (Systemic), 1251

Oxamniquine (Systemic), 1226

Oxandrin— See Anabolic Steroids (Systemic), 66

Oxandrolone— See Anabolic Steroids (Systemic), 66

Oxaprozin— See Anti-inflammatory Drugs, Nonsteroidal (Systemic), 179, MC-18

Oxazepam— See Benzodiazepines (Systemic), 257, MC-18

Oxcarbazepine (Systemic), 1228

Oxeze— See Formoterol (Inhalation-Local), 801

Oxeze Turbuhaler— See Bronchodilators, Adrenergic (Inhalation), 304

Oxiconazole (Topical), #

Oxistat— See Oxiconazole (Topical), #

Oxizole— See Oxiconazole (Topical), #

Oxprenolol— *See* Beta-adrenergic Blocking Agents (Systemic), 272

Oxsoralen— See Methoxsalen (Systemic), 1069

Oxsoralen Lotion— See Methoxsalen (Topical), 1071

Oxsoralen-Ultra— See Methoxsalen (Systemic), 1069

Oxtriphylline— See Bronchodilators, Theophylline (Systemic), 314

Oxtriphylline and Guaifenesin (Systemic), #

Oxy Balance Deep Action Night Formula Lotion—See Benzoyl Peroxide (Topical), 265

Oxy 10 Balance Emergency Spot Treatment Cover-Up Formula Gel—See Benzoyl Peroxide (Topical), 265

Oxy 10 Balance Emergency Spot Treatment Invisible Formula Gel—See Benzoyl Peroxide (Topical), 265

Oxy 10 Balance Maximum Medicated Face Wash—See Benzoyl Peroxide (Topical), 265

Oxybenzone and Padimate O—*See* Sunscreen Agents (Topical), #

Oxybenzone and Roxadimate—*See* Sunscreen Agents (Topical), #

Oxybutynin (Systemic), 1230, MC-18

Oxy Clean Extra Strength Cleanser Topical Solution—See Salicylic Acid (Topical), #

Oxy Clean Medicated Cleanser—See Salicylic Acid (Topical), #

Oxy Clean Medicated Pads—See Salicylic Acid (Topical), #

Oxy Clean Medicated Pads Maximum Strength—See Salicylic Acid (Topical), #

Oxy Clean Medicated Pads Regular Strength—See Salicylic Acid (Topical), #

Oxy Clean Medicated Pads Sensitive Skin—See Salicylic Acid (Topical), #

Oxy Clean Medicated Soap—See Salicylic Acid (Topical), #

Oxy Clean Regular Strength Medicated Cleanser Topical Solution—See Salicylic Acid (Topical), #

Oxy Clean Regular Strength Medicated Pads—See Salicylic Acid (Topical), #

Oxy Clean Sensitive Skin Cleanser Topical Solution—See Salicylic Acid (Topical), #

Oxy Clean Sensitive Skin Pads—See Salicylic Acid (Topical), #

Oxycocet—See Narcotic Analgesics and Acetaminophen (Systemic), 1138

Oxycodan—See Narcotic Analgesics and Aspirin (Systemic), 1142

Oxycodone—*See* Narcotic Analgesics—For Pain Relief (Systemic), 1147, MC-18

Oxycodone and Acetaminophen—*See* Narcotic Analgesics and Acetaminophen (Systemic), 1138, MC-18

Oxycodone with APAP—*See* Narcotic Analgesics and Acetaminophen (Systemic), 1138

Oxycodone and Aspirin—*See* Narcotic Analgesics and Aspirin (Systemic), 1142

OxyContin—See Narcotic Analgesics—For Pain Relief (Systemic), 1147, MC-18

OxyContin SR—See Narcotic Analgesics—For Pain Relief (Systemic), 1147

Oxyderm 5 Lotion—See Benzoyl Peroxide (Topical), 265

Oxyderm 10 Lotion—See Benzoyl Peroxide (Topical), 265

Oxyderm 20 Lotion—See Benzoyl Peroxide (Topical), 265

Oxymetazoline (Nasal), 1231

Oxymetazoline (Ophthalmic), 1233

Oxymethalone—See Anabolic Steroids (Systemic), 66

Oxymetholone—*See* Anabolic Steroids (Systemic), 66

Oxymorphone—*See* Narcotic Analgesics—For Pain Relief (Systemic), 1147

Oxy Night Watch Maximum Strength Lotion—See Salicylic Acid (Topical), #

Oxy Night Watch Night Time Acne Medication Extra Strength Lotion—See Salicylic Acid (Topical), #

Oxy Night Watch Night Time Acne Medication Regular Strength Lotion—See Salicylic Acid (Topical), #

Oxy Night Watch Sensitive Skin Lotion—See Salicylic Acid (Topical), #

Oxypentifylline—*See* Pentoxifylline (Systemic), 1263

Oxy 5 Regular Strength Cover-Up Cream—See Benzoyl Peroxide (Topical), 265

Oxy 5 Regular Strength Vanishing Lotion—See Benzoyl Peroxide (Topical), 265

Oxy Sensitive Skin Vanishing Formula Lotion—See Salicylic Acid (Topical), #

Oxy 5 Sensitive Skin Vanishing Lotion—See Benzoyl Peroxide (Topical), 265

Oxytetracycline—*See* Tetracyclines (Systemic), 1487

Oxytocin (Systemic), 1234

Oysco—See Calcium Supplements (Systemic), 353

Oysco 500 Chewable—See Calcium Supplements (Systemic), 353

Oyst-Cal 500—See Calcium Supplements (Systemic), 353

Oystercal 500—See Calcium Supplements (Systemic), 353

P

Pacaps—See Butalbital and Acetaminophen (Systemic), 324

Pacerone—See Amiodarone (Systemic), MC-1

PACIS—See Bacillus Calmette-Guérin (BCG) Live—for Cancer (Mucosal-Local), 234

Paclitaxel (Systemic), 1235

P-A-C Revised Formula—See Salicylates (Systemic), 1394

Padimate O—*See* Sunscreen Agents (Topical), #

Pain Aid—See Salicylates (Systemic), 1394

Palafer—See Iron Supplements (Systemic), 936

Palivizumab (Systemic), 1237

Paludrine—See Proguanil (Systemic), #

2-PAM—*See* Pralidoxime (Systemic), #

2-PAM chloride—*See* Pralidoxime (Systemic), #

Pamelor—See Antidepressants, Tricyclic (Systemic), 126

Pamidronate (Systemic), 1238

Pamine—See Anticholinergics/Antispasmodics (Systemic), 106

P-aminoclonidine—*See* Apraclonidine (Ophthalmic), 200

Pamprin-IB—See Anti-inflammatory Drugs, Nonsteroidal (Systemic), 179

Panacet 5/500—See Narcotic Analgesics and Acetaminophen (Systemic), 1138

Panadol—See Acetaminophen (Systemic), 4

Panadol, Children's—See Acetaminophen (Systemic), 4

Panadol Extra Strength—See Acetaminophen (Systemic), 4

Panadol, Infants'—See Acetaminophen (Systemic), 4

Panadol Junior Strength Caplets—See Acetaminophen (Systemic), 4

Panadol Maximum Strength Caplets—See Acetaminophen (Systemic), 4

Panadol Maximum Strength Tablets—See Acetaminophen (Systemic), 4

Panasal 5/500—See Narcotic Analgesics and Aspirin (Systemic), 1142

Pancoate—See Pancrelipase (Systemic), 1239

Pancrease—See Pancrelipase (Systemic), 1239

Pancrease MT 4—See Pancrelipase (Systemic), 1239

Pancrease MT 10—See Pancrelipase (Systemic), 1239

Pancrease MT 16—See Pancrelipase (Systemic), 1239

Pancrease MT 20—See Pancrelipase (Systemic), 1239

Pancrelipase (Systemic), 1239

Pancreozyme—*See* Cholecystokinin (Diagnostic), #

Pandel—See Corticosteroids—Medium to Very High Potency (Topical), 520

Panectyl—See Antihistamines, Phenothiazine-derivative (Systemic), 173

Panesclerina—See Probucol (Systemic), 1316

Panlor—See Narcotic Analgesics and Acetaminophen (Systemic), 1138

Pannaz—See Antihistamines, Decongestants, and Anticholinergics (Systemic), 170

Panokase—See Pancrelipase (Systemic), 1239

PanOxyl AQ 2½ Gel—See Benzoyl Peroxide (Topical), 265

PanOxyl AQ 5 Gel—See Benzoyl Peroxide (Topical), 265

PanOxyl AQ 10 Gel—See Benzoyl Peroxide (Topical), 265

PanOxyl Aquagel 2.5—See Benzoyl Peroxide (Topical), 265

PanOxyl Aquagel 5—See Benzoyl Peroxide (Topical), 265

PanOxyl Aquagel 10—See Benzoyl Peroxide (Topical), 265

PanOxyl Aquagel 20—See Benzoyl Peroxide (Topical), 265

PanOxyl 5 Bar—See Benzoyl Peroxide (Topical), 265

PanOxyl 10 Bar—See Benzoyl Peroxide (Topical), 265

PanOxyl 5 Gel—See Benzoyl Peroxide (Topical), 265

PanOxyl 10 Gel—See Benzoyl Peroxide (Topical), 265

PanOxyl 15 Gel—See Benzoyl Peroxide (Topical), 265

PanOxyl 20 Gel—See Benzoyl Peroxide (Topical), 265

PanOxyl 5 Wash—See Benzoyl Peroxide (Topical), 265

PanOxyl 10 Wash—See Benzoyl Peroxide (Topical), 265

Panretin—See Alitretinoin (Topical), 29

Pantoloc—See Pantoprazole (Systemic), 1241

Pantopon— *See* Narcotic Analgesics—For Pain Relief (Systemic), 1147
Pantoprazole (Systemic), 1241, 1630
Pantothenic Acid (Vitamin B₅) (Systemic), #
Papaveretum— *See* Narcotic Analgesics—For Pain Relief (Systemic), 1147
Papaverine (Intracavernosal), #
Papaverine (Systemic), #
Paplex— *See* Salicylic Acid (Topical), #
Paplex Ultra— *See* Salicylic Acid (Topical), #
Paracetamol— *See* Acetaminophen (Systemic), 4
Paraflex— *See* Skeletal Muscle Relaxants (Systemic), 1420
Parafon Forte— *See* Chlorzoxazone and Acetaminophen (Systemic), 419
Parafon Forte DSC— *See* Skeletal Muscle Relaxants (Systemic), 1420
Para-Hist HD— *See* Cough/Cold Combinations (Systemic), 522
Paral— *See* Paraldehyde (Systemic), #
Paraldehyde (Systemic), #
Paramethadione— *See* Anticonvulsants, Dione (Systemic), 115
Paraplatin— *See* Carboplatin (Systemic), 376
Paraplatin-AQ— *See* Carboplatin (Systemic), 376
Paregoric— *See* Opium Preparations (Systemic), 1216
Parepectolin— *See* Attapulgite (Oral), 222
Paricalcitol— *See* Vitamin D and Related Compounds (Systemic), 1577
Parlodel— *See* Bromocriptine (Systemic), 301
Parlodel SnapTabs— *See* Bromocriptine (Systemic), 301
Parnate— *See* Antidepressants, Monoamine Oxidase (MAO) Inhibitor (Systemic), 123
Paroxetine (Systemic), 1242, MC-18
Parsidol— *See* Antidyskinetics (Systemic), 137
Parsitan— *See* Antidyskinetics (Systemic), 137
Partuss LA— *See* Cough/Cold Combinations (Systemic), 522
PAS— *See* Aminosalicylate Sodium (Systemic), #
Patanol— *See* Olopatadine (Ophthalmic), 1210
Pathocil— *See* Penicillins (Systemic), 1251
Pavabid— *See* Papaverine (Systemic), #
Pavabid HP— *See* Papaverine (Systemic), #
Pavacels— *See* Papaverine (Systemic), #
Pavacot— *See* Papaverine (Systemic), #
Pavagen— *See* Papaverine (Systemic), #
Pavarine— *See* Papaverine (Systemic), #
Pavased— *See* Papaverine (Systemic), #
Pavatine— *See* Papaverine (Systemic), #
Pavatym— *See* Papaverine (Systemic), #
Paveral— *See* Narcotic Analgesics—For Pain Relief (Systemic), 1147
Paverolan— *See* Papaverine (Systemic), #
Paxil— *See* Paroxetine (Systemic), 1242, MC-18
Paxipam— *See* Benzodiazepines (Systemic), 257
PBZ— *See* Antihistamines (Systemic), 153

PBZ-SR— *See* Antihistamines (Systemic), 153
PC-Cap— *See* Narcotic Analgesics and Aspirin (Systemic), 1142
PCE— *See* Erythromycins (Systemic), 712
PDF— *See* Sodium Fluoride (Systemic), 1425
Pedameth— *See* Racemethionine (Systemic), #
PediaCare Allergy Formula— *See* Antihistamines (Systemic), 153
PediaCare Children's Cough-Cold— *See* Cough/Cold Combinations (Systemic), 522
PediaCare Cold-Allergy— *See* Antihistamines and Decongestants (Systemic), 159
PediaCare Cold Formula— *See* Antihistamines and Decongestants (Systemic), 159
PediaCare Cough-Cold— *See* Cough/Cold Combinations (Systemic), 522
PediaCare Infants' Oral Decongestant Drops— *See* Pseudoephedrine (Systemic), 1334
PediaCare Night Rest Cough-Cold Liquid— *See* Cough/Cold Combinations (Systemic), 522
Pediacof Cough— *See* Cough/Cold Combinations (Systemic), 522
Pediacare 50— *See* Corticosteroids—Glucocorticoid Effects (Systemic), 513
Pediaflor— *See* Sodium Fluoride (Systemic), 1425
Pedialyte— *See* Carbohydrates and Electrolytes (Systemic), 370
Pedialyte Freezer Pops— *See* Carbohydrates and Electrolytes (Systemic), 370
Pediapred— *See* Corticosteroids—Glucocorticoid Effects (Systemic), 513
PediaPressin Pediatric Drops— *See* Cough/Cold Combinations (Systemic), 522
Pediasure— *See* Enteral Nutrition Formulas (Systemic), #
Pediasure with Fiber— *See* Enteral Nutrition Formulas (Systemic), #
Pediatric Charcodote— *See* Charcoal, Activated (Oral), 395
Pediazole— *See* Erythromycin and Sulfisoxazole (Systemic), 709
Pedi-Dent— *See* Sodium Fluoride (Systemic), 1425
Pedi-Dri— *See* Nystatin (Topical), 1202
Pediotic— *See* Neomycin, Polymyxin B, and Hydrocortisone (Otic), 1172
Pedituss Cough— *See* Cough/Cold Combinations (Systemic), 522
Pedvaxhib— *See* Haemophilus b Conjugate Vaccine (Systemic), 848
PEG-ADA— *See* Pegademase (Systemic), #
Pegademase (Systemic), #
PEG-adenosine Deaminase— *See* Pegademase (Systemic), #
Peganone— *See* Anticonvulsants, Hydantoin (Systemic), 117
Pegasparagase (Systemic), 1245
PEG-3550 & Electrolytes— *See* Polyethylene Glycol and Electrolytes (Local), 1299
Peginterferon Alfa-2b (Parenteral), #, 1630
PEG-Intron— *See* Peginterferon Alfa-2b (Parenteral), 1630; **Peginterferon Alfa-2b (Parenteral), #**

PEG-L-asparaginase— *See* Pegasparagase (Systemic), 1245
Peglyte— *See* Polyethylene Glycol and Electrolytes (Local), 1299
Pelamine— *See* Antihistamines (Systemic), 153
Pemirolast (Ophthalmic), 1247
Pemoline (Systemic), 1248, MC-18
Penbritin— *See* Penicillins (Systemic), 1251
Penbutolol— *See* Beta-adrenergic Blocking Agents (Systemic), 272
Penciclovir (Topical), 1250
Penecort— *See* Corticosteroids—Low Potency (Topical), 518
Penetrex— *See* Fluoroquinolones (Systemic), 776
Penglobe— *See* Penicillins (Systemic), 1251
Penicillamine (Systemic), #
Penicillin G— *See* Penicillins (Systemic), 1251
Penicillins (Systemic), 1251
Penicillins and Beta-lactamase Inhibitors (Systemic), 1258
Penicillin V— *See* Penicillins (Systemic), 1251, MC-18
Penlac Nail Laquer— *See* Ciclopirox (Topical), 429
Pentacarinat— *See* Pentamidine (Inhalation), #; *See* Pentamidine (Systemic), 1261
Pentacort— *See* Corticosteroids—Low Potency (Topical), 518
Pentagastrin (Diagnostic), #
Pentam 300— *See* Pentamidine (Systemic), 1261
Pentamidine (Inhalation), #
Pentamidine (Systemic), 1261
Pentamycetin Ophthalmic Ointment— *See* Chloramphenicol (Ophthalmic), 403
Pentamycetin Ophthalmic Solution— *See* Chloramphenicol (Ophthalmic), 403
Pentasa— *See* Mesalamine (Oral), 1056
Penta-Valproic— *See* Valproic Acid (Systemic), 1549
Pentavlon— *See* Pentagastrin (Diagnostic), #
Pentazine— *See* Antihistamines, Phenothiazine-derivative (Systemic), 173
Pentazine VC w/Codeine— *See* Cough/Cold Combinations (Systemic), 522
Pentazocine— *See* Narcotic Analgesics—For Pain Relief (Systemic), 1147
Pentazocine and Acetaminophen— *See* Narcotic Analgesics and Acetaminophen (Systemic), 1138
Pentazocine and Aspirin— *See* Narcotic Analgesics and Aspirin (Systemic), 1142
Penthrane— *See* Anesthetics, General (Systemic), #
Pentids— *See* Penicillins (Systemic), 1251
Pentobarbital— *See* Barbiturates (Systemic), 239
Pentolair— *See* Cyclopentolate (Ophthalmic), 548
Pentosan (Systemic), #
Pentostatin (Systemic), #
Pentothal— *See* Anesthetics, General (Systemic), #
Pentoxifylline (Systemic), 1263, MC-18
Pentrax Anti-Dandruff Tar Shampoo— *See* Coal Tar (Topical), 478

Phendiet-105— *See* Appetite Suppressants, Sympathomimetic (Systemic), 197

Phendimetrazine— *See* Appetite Suppressants, Sympathomimetic (Systemic), 197

Phenelzine— *See* Antidepressants, Monoamine Oxidase (MAO) Inhibitor (Systemic), 123

Phenergan— *See* Antihistamines, Phenothiazine-derivative (Systemic), 173, MC-20

Phenergan with Codeine— *See* Cough/Cold Combinations (Systemic), 522

Phenergan with Dextromethorphan— *See* Cough/Cold Combinations (Systemic), 522

Phenergan Expectorant— *See* Cough/Cold Combinations (Systemic), 522

Phenergan Expectorant w/Codeine— *See* Cough/Cold Combinations (Systemic), 522

Phenergan Fortis— *See* Antihistamines, Phenothiazine-derivative (Systemic), 173

Phenergan Plain— *See* Antihistamines, Phenothiazine-derivative (Systemic), 173

Phenergan VC— *See* Antihistamines and Decongestants (Systemic), 159

Phenergan VC with Codeine— *See* Cough/Cold Combinations (Systemic), 522

Phenergan VC Expectorant— *See* Cough/Cold Combinations (Systemic), 522

Phenergan VC Expectorant w/Codeine— *See* Cough/Cold Combinations (Systemic), 522

Phenerzine— *See* Antihistamines, Phenothiazine-derivative (Systemic), 173

Phenetron— *See* Antihistamines (Systemic), 153

Phenhist DH w/Codeine— *See* Cough/Cold Combinations (Systemic), 522

Phenhist Expectorant— *See* Cough/Cold Combinations (Systemic), 522

Phenindamine— *See* Antihistamines (Systemic), 153

Pheniramine, Codeine, and Guaifenesin— *See* Cough/Cold Combinations (Systemic), 522

Pheniramine and Phenylephrine— *See* Antihistamines and Decongestants (Systemic), 159

Pheniramine, Phenylephrine, and Acetaminophen— *See* Antihistamines, Decongestants, and Analgesics (Systemic), 164

Pheniramine, Phenylephrine, Codeine, Sodium Citrate, Sodium Salicylate, and Caffeine— *See* Cough/Cold Combinations (Systemic), 522

Pheniramine, Phenylephrine, and Dextromethorphan— *See* Cough/Cold Combinations (Systemic), 522

Pheniramine, Phenylephrine, Phenylpropanolamine, Hydrocodone, and Guaifenesin— *See* Cough/Cold Combinations (Systemic), 522

Pheniramine, Phenylephrine, Sodium Salicylate, and Caffeine— *See* Antihistamines, Decongestants, and Analgesics (Systemic), 164

Pheniramine, Phenyltoloxamine, Pyrilamine, and Phenylpropanolamine— *See* Antihistamines and Decongestants (Systemic), 159

Pheniramine, Pyrilamine, Hydrocodone, Potassium Citrate, andAscorbic Acid— *See* Cough/Cold Combinations (Systemic), 522

Pheniramine, Pyrilamine, Phenylephrine, Phenylpropanolamine, and Hydrocodone— *See* Cough/Cold Combinations (Systemic), 522

Pheniramine, Pyrilamine, and Phenylpropanolamine— *See* Antihistamines and Decongestants (Systemic), 159

Pheniramine , Pyrilamine, Phenylpropanolamine, Acetaminophen, and Caffeine— *See* Antihistamines, Decongestants, and Analgesics (Systemic), 164

Pheniramine, Pyrilamine, Phenylpropanolamine, and Codeine— *See* Cough/Cold Combinations (Systemic), 522

Pheniramine, Pyrilamine, Phenylpropanolamine, Codeine, Acetaminophen, and Caffeine— *See* Cough/Cold Combinations (Systemic), 522

Pheniramine, Pyrilamine, Phenylpropanolamine, and Dextromethorphan— *See* Cough/Cold Combinations (Systemic), 522

Pheniramine, Pyrilamine, Phenylpropanolamine, Dextromethorphan, and Ammonium Chloride— *See* Cough/Cold Combinations (Systemic), 522

Pheniramine, Pyrilamine, Phenylpropanolamine, Dextromethorphan, and Guaifenesin— *See* Cough/Cold Combinations (Systemic), 522

Pheniramine, Pyrilamine, Phenylpropanolamine, and Guaifenesin— *See* Cough/Cold Combinations (Systemic), 522

Pheniramine, Pyrilamine, Phenylpropanolamine, and Hydrocodone— *See* Cough/Cold Combinations (Systemic), 522

Pheniramine, Pyrilamine, Phenylpropanolamine, Hydrocodone, and Guaifenesin— *See* Cough/Cold Combinations (Systemic), 522

Phenobarbital— *See* Barbiturates (Systemic), 239, MC-19

Phenobarbital, Aspirin, and Codeine— *See* Barbiturates, Aspirin, and Codeine (Systemic), 245

Phenoject-50— *See* Antihistamines, Phenothiazine-derivative (Systemic), 173

Phenolphthalein— *See* Laxatives (Oral), 964

Phenolphthalein and Docusate— *See* Laxatives (Oral), 964

Phenolphthalein Petrogalar— *See* Laxatives (Oral), 964

Phenolphthalein and Senna— *See* Laxatives (Oral), 964

Phenol red— *See* Phenolsulfonphthalein (Diagnostic), #

Phenolsulfonphthalein (Diagnostic), #

Phenoptic— *See* Phenylephrine (Ophthalmic), #

Phenothiazines (Systemic), 1268

Phenoxybenzamine (Systemic), 1277

Phentercot— *See* Appetite Suppressants, Sympathomimetic (Systemic), 197

Phentermine— *See* Appetite Suppressants, Sympathomimetic (Systemic), 197, MC-19

Phentolamine and Papaverine (Intracavernosal), #

Phentride— *See* Appetite Suppressants, Sympathomimetic (Systemic), 197

Phenylalanine mustard— *See* Melphalan (Systemic), 1045

Phenylbenzimidazole— *See* Sunscreen Agents (Topical), #

Phenylbenzimidazole and Sulisobenzone— *See* Sunscreen Agents (Topical), #

Phenylbutazone— *See* Anti-inflammatory Drugs, Nonsteroidal (Systemic), 179

Phenyldrine— *See* Phenylpropanolamine (Systemic), 1280

Phenylephrine (Nasal), 1278

Phenylephrine (Ophthalmic), #

Phenylephrine and Acetaminophen— *See* Decongestants and Analgesics (Systemic), 581

Phenylephrine and Codeine— *See* Cough/Cold Combinations (Systemic), 522

Phenylephrine, Dextromethorphan, and Guaifenesin— *See* Cough/Cold Combinations (Systemic), 522

Phenylephrine and Guaifenesin— *See* Cough/Cold Combinations (Systemic), 522

Phenylephrine, Guaifenesin, Acetaminophen, Salicylamide, and Caffeine— *See* Cough/Cold Combinations (Systemic), 522

Phenylephrine and Hydrocodone— *See* Cough/Cold Combinations (Systemic), 522

Phenylephrine, Hydrocodone, and Guaifenesin— *See* Cough/Cold Combinations (Systemic), 522

Phenylephrine, Phenylpropanolamine, and Acetaminophen— *See* Decongestants and Analgesics (Systemic), 581

Phenylephrine, Phenylpropanolamine, Carbetapentane, and Potassium Guaiacolsulfonate— *See* Cough/Cold Combinations (Systemic), 522

Phenylephrine, Phenylpropanolamine, and Guaifenesin— *See* Cough/Cold Combinations (Systemic), 522

Phenylfenesin L.A.— *See* Cough/Cold Combinations (Systemic), 522

Phenylpropanolamine (Systemic), 1280

Phenylpropanolamine and Acetaminophen— *See* Decongestants and Analgesics (Systemic), 581

Phenylpropanolamine, Acetaminophen, and Aspirin— *See* Decongestants and Analgesics (Systemic), 581

Phenylpropanolamine, Acetaminophen, and Caffeine— *See* Decongestants and Analgesics (Systemic), 581

Phenylpropanolamine, Acetaminophen, Salicylamide, and Caffeine— *See* Decongestants and Analgesics (Systemic), 581

Phenylpropanolamine and Aspirin— *See* Decongestants and Analgesics (Systemic), 581

Phenylpropanolamine and Caramiphen— *See* Cough/Cold Combinations (Systemic), 522

PMS Egozinc—See Zinc Supplements (Systemic), 1599

PMS-Ferrous Sulfate—See Iron Supplements (Systemic), 936

PMS-Fluphenazine—See Phenothiazines (Systemic), 1268

PMS Haloperidol—See Haloperidol (Systemic), 850

PMS-Hydromorphone—See Narcotic Analgesics—For Pain Relief (Systemic), 1147

PMS-Hydromorphone Syrup—See Narcotic Analgesics—For Pain Relief (Systemic), 1147

PMS Isoniazid—See Isoniazid (Systemic), 941

PMS-Lactulose—See Laxatives (Oral), 964

PMS Levazine—See Perphenazine and Amitriptyline (Systemic), #

PMS-Levothyroxine Sodium—See Thyroid Hormones (Systemic), 1503

PMS Lindane—See Lindane (Topical), 993

PMS-Loperamide Hydrochloride—See Loperamide (Oral), 1001

PMS-Methylphenidate—See Methylphenidate (Systemic), 1078

PMS-Metoclopramide—See Metoclopramide (Systemic), 1083

PMS Nylidrin—See Nylidrin (Systemic), 1199

PMS Nystatin—See Nystatin (Oral), 1200

PMS-Oxtriphylline—See Bronchodilators, Theophylline (Systemic), 314

PMS Perphenazine—See Phenothiazines (Systemic), 1268

PMS-Phosphates—See Laxatives (Oral), 964

PMS-Piroxicam—See Anti-inflammatory Drugs, Nonsteroidal (Systemic), 179

PMS Primidone—See Primidone (Systemic), 1310

PMS Prochlorperazine—See Phenothiazines (Systemic), 1268

PMS Procyclidine—See Antidyskinetics (Systemic), 137

PMS-Progesterone—See Progestins—For Noncontraceptive Use (Systemic), 1328

pms Propranolol—See Beta-adrenergic Blocking Agents (Systemic), 272

pms-Pyrazinamide—See Pyrazinamide (Systemic), #

PMS-Sennosides—See Laxatives (Oral), 964

PMS-Sodium cromoglycate—See Cromolyn (Inhalation), 537

PMS-Sulfasalazine—See Sulfasalazine (Systemic), 1442

PMS-Sulfasalazine E.C.—See Sulfasalazine (Systemic), 1442

PMS-Theophylline—See Bronchodilators, Theophylline (Systemic), 314

PMS Thioridazine—See Phenothiazines (Systemic), 1268

PMS Trifluoperazine—See Phenothiazines (Systemic), 1268

PMS Trihexyphenidyl—See Antidyskinetics (Systemic), 137

pms-Valproic Acid—See Valproic Acid (Systemic), 1549

pms-Valproic Acid E.C.—See Valproic Acid (Systemic), 1549

PMS-Yohimbine—See Yohimbine (Systemic), 1588

Pneumococcal Conjugate Vaccine (Systemic), 1295

Pneumococcal Vaccine Polyvalent (Systemic), 1296

Pneumomist—See Guaifenesin (Systemic), 844

Pneumopent—See Pentamidine (Inhalation), #

Pneumotussin HC—See Cough/Cold Combinations (Systemic), 522

Pneumovax 23—See Pneumococcal Vaccine Polyvalent (Systemic), 1296

P.N. Ophthalmic—See Neomycin, Polymyxin B, and Gramicidin (Ophthalmic), 1169

Pnu-Imune 23—See Pneumococcal Vaccine Polyvalent (Systemic), 1296

Podocon-25—See Podophyllum (Topical), #

Podofilox (Topical), 1297

Podofin—See Podophyllum (Topical), #

Podophyllotoxin—See Podofilox (Topical), 1297

Podophyllum (Topical), #

Polaramine—See Antihistamines (Systemic), 153

Polaramine Expectorant—See Cough/Cold Combinations (Systemic), 522

Polaramine Repetabs—See Antihistamines (Systemic), 153

Poliovirus Vaccine (Systemic), #

Poliovirus Vaccine Inactivated— *See* Poliovirus Vaccine (Systemic), #

Poliovirus Vaccine Inactivated Enhanced Potency— *See* Poliovirus Vaccine (Systemic), #

Poliovirus Vaccine Live Oral— *See* Poliovirus Vaccine (Systemic), #

Poliovirus Vaccine Live Oral (Systemic), #

Polocaine—See Anesthetics (Parenteral-Local), 83

Polocaine-MPF—See Anesthetics (Parenteral-Local), 83

Poloxamer 188— *See* Laxatives (Oral), 964

Polycarbophil— *See* Laxatives (Oral), 964

Polycillin—See Penicillins (Systemic), 1251

Polycillin-N—See Penicillins (Systemic), 1251

Polycitra-K—See Citrates (Systemic), 443

Polycitra-K Crystals—See Citrates (Systemic), 443

Polycitra-LC—See Citrates (Systemic), 443

Polycitra Syrup—See Citrates (Systemic), 443

Polycose—See Enteral Nutrition Formulas (Systemic), #

Poly-D—See Antihistamines and Decongestants (Systemic), 159

Poly D—See Antihistamines and Decongestants (Systemic), 159

Polydimethylsiloxane— *See* Silicone Oil 5000 Centistokes (Parenteral-Local), #

Polyethylene Glycol 3550— *See* Laxatives (Oral), 964

Polyethylene Glycol and Electrolytes (Local), 1299

Polygam S/D—See Immune Globulin Intravenous (Human) (Systemic), 896

Polygesic—See Narcotic Analgesics and Acetaminophen (Systemic), 1138

Poly Hist Forte—See Antihistamines and Decongestants (Systemic), 159

Poly-Histine-CS—See Cough/Cold Combinations (Systemic), 522

Poly-Histine-D—See Antihistamines and Decongestants (Systemic), 159

Poly-Histine-DM—See Cough/Cold Combinations (Systemic), 522

Poly-Histine-D Ped—See Antihistamines and Decongestants (Systemic), 159

Polymox—See Penicillins (Systemic), 1251

Polythiazide—See Diuretics, Thiazide (Systemic), 642

Poly-Vi-Flor—See Vitamins and Fluoride (Systemic), 1586, MC-21

Pondocillin—See Penicillins (Systemic), 1251

Pond's Daily Replenishing Moisturizer— See Sunscreen Agents (Topical), #

Ponstan—See Anti-inflammatory Drugs, Nonsteroidal (Systemic), 179

Ponstel—See Anti-inflammatory Drugs, Nonsteroidal (Systemic), 179

Pontocaine—See Anesthetics (Ophthalmic), #; *See* Anesthetics (Parenteral-Local), 83

Pontocaine Cream—See Anesthetics (Rectal), 85; *See* Anesthetics (Topical), 88

Pontocaine Ointment—See Anesthetics (Rectal), 85; *See* Anesthetics (Topical), 88

Porfimer (Systemic), #

Portalac—See Laxatives (Oral), 964

Postacne—See Alcohol and Sulfur (Topical), #

Posture—See Calcium Supplements (Systemic), 353

Potaba—See Aminobenzoate Potassium (Systemic), #

Potaba Envules—See Aminobenzoate Potassium (Systemic), #

Potaba Powder—See Aminobenzoate Potassium (Systemic), #

Potasalan—See Potassium Supplements (Systemic), 1300

Potassium Acetate—See Potassium Supplements (Systemic), 1300

Potassium aminobenzoate—See Aminobenzoate Potassium (Systemic), #

Potassium Bicarbonate—See Potassium Supplements (Systemic), 1300

Potassium Bicarbonate and Potassium Chloride—See Potassium Supplements (Systemic), 1300

Potassium Bicarbonate and Potassium Citrate—See Potassium Supplements (Systemic), 1300

Potassium Bitartrate and Sodium Bicarbonate—See Laxatives (Oral), 964; *See* Laxatives (Rectal), 970

Potassium Chloride—See Potassium Supplements (Systemic), 1300, MC-19

Potassium Citrate—See Citrates (Systemic), 443

Potassium Citrate and Citric Acid—See Citrates (Systemic), 443

Potassium Citrate and Sodium Citrate— *See* Citrates (Systemic), 443

Potassium citrate, sodium citrate, and citric acid—See Citrates (Systemic), 443

Potassium Gluconate—See Potassium Supplements (Systemic), 1300

Probucol (Systemic), 1316

Procainamide (Systemic), 1317

Procaine— See Anesthetics (Parenteral-Local), 83

Pro-Cal-Sof— See Laxatives (Oral), 964

Procan SR— See Procainamide (Systemic), 1317

Procarbazine (Systemic), 1319

Procardia— See Calcium Channel Blocking Agents (Systemic), 349

Procardia XL— See Calcium Channel Blocking Agents (Systemic), 349, MC-17

Procaterol— See Bronchodilators, Adrenergic (Inhalation), 304

Prochlorperazine— See Phenothiazines (Systemic), 1268, MC-19

Proconvertin— See Factor VIIa (Systemic), 752

Procrit— See Epoetin (Systemic), 693

Proctocort— See Corticosteroids (Rectal), 509

ProctoFoam/non-steroid— See Anesthetics (Rectal), 85

Proctosol-HC— See Corticosteroids (Rectal), 509

Procyclid— See Antidyskinetics (Systemic), 137

Procyclidine— See Antidyskinetics (Systemic), 137

Procytox— See Cyclophosphamide (Systemic), 549

Prodiem Plain— See Laxatives (Oral), 964

Prodiem Plus— See Laxatives (Oral), 964

Prodrox— See Progestins—For Noncontraceptive Use (Systemic), 1328

Profasi— See Chorionic Gonadotropin (Systemic), 426

Profasi HP— See Chorionic Gonadotropin (Systemic), 426

Pro-Fast— See Appetite Suppressants, Sympathomimetic (Systemic), 197

Profenal— See Anti-inflammatory Drugs, Nonsteroidal (Ophthalmic), 177

Profenamine— See Antidyskinetics (Systemic), 137

Profen II— See Cough/Cold Combinations (Systemic), 522

Profen-LA— See Cough/Cold Combinations (Systemic), 522

Profiber— See Enteral Nutrition Formulas (Systemic), #

Profilnine SD— See Factor IX (Systemic), 751

Progestasert— See Progesterone Intrauterine Device (IUD), 1322

Progesterone— See Progestins—For Noncontraceptive Use (Systemic), 1328, MC-19

Progesterone Intrauterine Device (IUD), 1322

Progestins—For Contraceptive Use (Systemic), 1324

Progestins—For Noncontraceptive Use (Systemic), 1328

Proglycem— See Diazoxide (Oral), 597

Prograf— See Tacrolimus (Systemic), 1461

Proguanil (Systemic), #

Prohibit— See Haemophilus b Conjugate Vaccine (Systemic), 848

Prohim— See Yohimbine (Systemic), 1588

Prolamine— See Phenylpropanolamine (Systemic), 1280

Prolastin— See Alpha₁-proteinase Inhibitor, Human (Systemic), #

Pro-Lax— See Laxatives (Oral), 964

Proleukin— See Aldesleukin (Systemic), 26

Prolixin— See Phenothiazines (Systemic), 1268

Prolixin Concentrate— See Phenothiazines (Systemic), 1268

Prolixin Decanoate— See Phenothiazines (Systemic), 1268

Prolixin Enanthate— See Phenothiazines (Systemic), 1268

Prolopa 50-25— See Levodopa and Benserazide (Systemic), 988

Prolopa 100-25— See Levodopa and Benserazide (Systemic), 988

Prolopa 200-50— See Levodopa and Benserazide (Systemic), 988

Proloprim— See Trimethoprim (Systemic), #

Promacot— See Antihistamines, Phenothiazine-derivative (Systemic), 173

Promatussin DM— See Cough/Cold Combinations (Systemic), 522

Promatussin DM Children's Syrup— See Cough/Cold Combinations (Systemic), 522

Promazine— See Phenothiazines (Systemic), 1268

Pro-Med 50— See Antihistamines, Phenothiazine-derivative (Systemic), 173

Promet— See Antihistamines, Phenothiazine-derivative (Systemic), 173

Promethazine— See Antihistamines, Phenothiazine-derivative (Systemic), 173, MC-20

Promethazine and Codeine— See Cough/Cold Combinations (Systemic), 522

Promethazine, Codeine, and Potassium Guaiacolsulfonate— See Cough/Cold Combinations (Systemic), 522

Promethazine and Dextromethorphan— See Cough/Cold Combinations (Systemic), 522

Promethazine DM— See Cough/Cold Combinations (Systemic), 522

Promethazine and Phenylephrine— See Antihistamines and Decongestants (Systemic), 159

Promethazine, Phenylephrine, and Codeine— See Cough/Cold Combinations (Systemic), 522

Promethazine, Phenylephrine, Codeine, and Potassium Guaiacolsulfonate— See Cough/Cold Combinations (Systemic), 522

Promethazine, Phenylephrine, and Potassium Guaiacolsulfonate— See Cough/Cold Combinations (Systemic), 522

Promethazine and Potassium Guaiacolsulfonate— See Cough/Cold Combinations (Systemic), 522

Promethazine, Pseudoephedrine, and Dextromethorphan— See Cough/Cold Combinations (Systemic), 522

Promethazine VC— See Antihistamines and Decongestants (Systemic), 159

Promethazine VC w/Codeine— See Cough/Cold Combinations (Systemic), 522

Prometh w/Dextromethorphan— See Cough/Cold Combinations (Systemic), 522

Promethist w/Codeine— See Cough/Cold Combinations (Systemic), 522

Prometh VC with Codeine— See Cough/Cold Combinations (Systemic), 522

Prometh VC Plain— See Antihistamines and Decongestants (Systemic), 159

Prometrium— See Progestins—For Noncontraceptive Use (Systemic), 1328, MC-19

Promine— See Procainamide (Systemic), 1317

Prominic Expectorant— See Cough/Cold Combinations (Systemic), 522

Prominicol Cough— See Cough/Cold Combinations (Systemic), 522

Promist HD Liquid— See Cough/Cold Combinations (Systemic), 522

ProMod— See Enteral Nutrition Formulas (Systemic), #

Promote— See Enteral Nutrition Formulas (Systemic), #

Promote with Fiber— See Enteral Nutrition Formulas (Systemic), #

Prompt— See Laxatives (Oral), 964

Pronestyl— See Procainamide (Systemic), 1317

Pronestyl-SR— See Procainamide (Systemic), 1317

Pronto Lice Killing Shampoo Kit— See Pyrethrins and Piperonyl Butoxide (Topical), 1336

Propacet 100— See Narcotic Analgesics and Acetaminophen (Systemic), 1138

Propac Plus— See Enteral Nutrition Formulas (Systemic), #

Propaderm— See Corticosteroids—Medium to Very High Potency (Topical), 520

Propafenone (Systemic), 1332

Propagest— See Phenylpropanolamine (Systemic), 1280

Prop-a-Hist— See Antihistamines and Decongestants (Systemic), 159

Propanthel— See Anticholinergics/Antispasmodics, 106

Propantheline— See Anticholinergics/Antispasmodics (Systemic), 106

Propa pH Medicated Acne Cream Maximum Strength— See Salicylic Acid (Topical), #

Propa pH Medicated Cleansing Pads Maximum Strength— See Salicylic Acid (Topical), #

Propa pH Medicated Cleansing Pads Sensitive Skin— See Salicylic Acid (Topical), #

Propa pH Perfectly Clear Skin Cleanser Topical Solution Normal/Combination Skin— See Salicylic Acid (Topical), #

Propa pH Perfectly Clear Skin Cleanser Topical Solution Oily Skin— See Salicylic Acid (Topical), #

Propa pH Perfectly Clear Skin Cleanser Topical Solution Sensitive Skin Formula— See Salicylic Acid (Topical), #

Proparacaine— See Anesthetics (Ophthalmic), #

Propecia— See Finasteride (Systemic), 766, MC-9

Propericiazine— See Phenothiazines (Systemic), 1268

Propine— See Dipivefrin (Ophthalmic), 622

Propine C Cap B.I.D.— See Dipivefrin (Ophthalmic), 622

Propiomazine (Systemic), #

Q

R

Recombinant coagulation factor VIIa— *See* Factor VIIa (Systemic), 752

Recombinant factor VIIa— *See* Factor VIIa (Systemic), 752

Recombinate— See Antihemophilic Factor (Systemic), 151

Recombivax HB— See Hepatitis B Vaccine Recombinant (Systemic), 861

Recombivax HB Dialysis Formulation— See Hepatitis B Vaccine Recombinant (Systemic), 861

Rectocort— See Corticosteroids (Rectal), 509

Rectosol-HC— See Corticosteroids (Rectal), 509

Rectovalone— See Corticosteroids (Rectal), 509

Rederm— See Corticosteroids—Low Potency (Topical), 518

Redutemp— See Acetaminophen (Systemic), 4

Reese's Pinworm Caplets— See Pyrantel (Oral), #

Reese's Pinworm Medicine— See Pyrantel (Oral), #

Regitine— See Phentolamine and Papaverine (Intracavernosal), #

Reglan— See Metoclopramide (Systemic), 1083

Regonol— See Antimyasthenics (Systemic), 190

Regranex— See Becaplermin (Topical), 251

Regroton— See Rauwolfia Alkaloids and Thiazide Diuretics (Systemic), #

Regulace— See Laxatives (Oral), 964

Regular Iletin II— See Insulin (Systemic), 902

Regular (Concentrated) Iletin II, U-202047— See Insulin (Systemic), 902

Regular Insulin— See Insulin (Systemic), 902

Regular insulin, R— *See* Insulin (Systemic), 902

Regular Strength Ascriptin— See Salicylates (Systemic), 1394

Regulax SS— See Laxatives (Oral), 964

Regulex— See Laxatives (Oral), 964

Regulex-D— See Laxatives (Oral), 964

Reguloid Natural— See Laxatives (Oral), 964

Reguloid Natural Sugar Free— See Laxatives (Oral), 964

Reguloid Orange— See Laxatives (Oral), 964

Reguloid Orange Sugar Free— See Laxatives (Oral), 964

Rehydralyte— See Carbohydrates and Electrolytes (Systemic), 370

Relafen— See Anti-inflammatory Drugs, Nonsteroidal (Systemic), 179, MC-16

Relaxadon— See Belladonna Alkaloids and Barbiturates (Systemic), 252

Relaxazone— See Skeletal Muscle Relaxants (Systemic), 1420

Relefact TRH— See Protirelin (Diagnostic), #

Relenza— See Zanamivir (Inhalation-Systemic), 1594

Relief Eye Drops for Red Eyes— See Phenylephrine (Ophthalmic), #

Relisorm— See Gonadorelin (Systemic), 836

Remcol-C— See Cough/Cold Combinations (Systemic), 522

Remeron— See Mirtazapine (Systemic), 1106, MC-15

Remeron SolTab— See Mirtazapine (Systemic), 1106

Remicade— See Infliximab (Systemic), 900

Remifentanil— *See* Narcotic Analgesics— For Surgery and Obstetrics (Systemic), 1154

Reminyl— See Galantamine (Systemic), 810

Remular— See Skeletal Muscle Relaxants (Systemic), 1420

Remular-S— See Skeletal Muscle Relaxants (Systemic), 1420

Renagel— See Sevelamer (Oral), 1410

Renedil— See Calcium Channel Blocking Agents (Systemic), 349

Renese— See Diuretics, Thiazide (Systemic), 642

Renova— See Tretinoin (Topical), 1535

Rentamine Pediatric— See Cough/Cold Combinations (Systemic), 522

Repaglinide (Systemic), 1356, MC-21

Repan— See Butalbital and Acetaminophen (Systemic), 324

Replete— See Enteral Nutrition Formulas (Systemic), #

Replete with Fiber— See Enteral Nutrition Formulas (Systemic), #

Requip— See Ropinirole (Systemic), 1390

Resaid S.R.— See Antihistamines and Decongestants (Systemic), 159

Rescaps-D S.R.— See Cough/Cold Combinations (Systemic), 522

Rescon— See Antihistamines and Decongestants (Systemic), 159

Rescon-DM— See Cough/Cold Combinations (Systemic), 522

Rescon-ED— See Antihistamines and Decongestants (Systemic), 159

Rescon-GG— See Cough/Cold Combinations (Systemic), 522

Rescon JR— See Antihistamines and Decongestants (Systemic), 159

Rescriptor— See Delavirdine (Systemic), 587

Rescudose— See Narcotic Analgesics— For Pain Relief (Systemic), 1147

Rescula— See Unoprostone (Ophthalmic), 1547

Reserfia— See Rauwolfia Alkaloids (Systemic), 1354

Reserpine— *See* Rauwolfia Alkaloids (Systemic), 1354

Reserpine and Chlorothiazide— *See* Rauwolfia Alkaloids and Thiazide Diuretics (Systemic), #

Reserpine and Chlorthalidone— *See* Rauwolfia Alkaloids and Thiazide Diuretics (Systemic), #

Reserpine, Hydralazine, and Hydrochlorothiazide (Systemic), #

Reserpine and Hydrochlorothiazide— *See* Rauwolfia Alkaloids and Thiazide Diuretics (Systemic), #

Reserpine and Hydroflumethiazide— *See* Rauwolfia Alkaloids and Thiazide Diuretics (Systemic), #

Reserpine and Methyclothiazide— *See* Rauwolfia Alkaloids and Thiazide Diuretics (Systemic), #

Resol— See Carbohydrates and Electrolytes (Systemic), 370

Resorcinol (Topical), #

Resorcinol and Sulfur (Topical), #

Resource— See Enteral Nutrition Formulas (Systemic), #

Resource Plus— See Enteral Nutrition Formulas (Systemic), #

Respa-1st— See Cough/Cold Combinations (Systemic), 522

Respa-DM— See Cough/Cold Combinations (Systemic), 522

Respahist— See Antihistamines and Decongestants (Systemic), 159

Respaire-60 SR— See Cough/Cold Combinations (Systemic), 522

Respaire-120 SR— See Cough/Cold Combinations (Systemic), 522

Respalor— See Enteral Nutrition Formulas (Systemic), #

Respbid— See Bronchodilators, Theophylline (Systemic), 314

RespiGam— See Respiratory Syncytial Virus Immune Globulin Intravenous (Systemic), 1359

Respiratory Syncytial Virus Immune Globulin Intravenous (Systemic), 1359

Restoril— See Benzodiazepines (Systemic), 257, MC-22

Resyl— See Guaifenesin (Systemic), 844

Retavase— See Thrombolytic Agents (Systemic), 1501

Reteplase, Recombinant— *See* Thrombolytic Agents (Systemic), 1501

Retin-A— See Tretinoin (Topical), 1535

Retin-A MICRO— See Tretinoin (Topical), 1535

Retin-A Regimen Kit— See Tretinoin (Topical), 1535

Retinoic acid— *See* Tretinoin (Topical), 1535

Retinol— *See* Vitamin A (Systemic), 1572

Retisol-A— See Tretinoin (Topical), 1535

Retrovir— See Zidovudine (Systemic), 1630

Rev-Eyes— See Dapiprazole (Ophthalmic), 574

ReVia— See Naltrexone (Systemic), #

Rezamid Acne Treatment— See Resorcinol and Sulfur (Topical), #

Rezamid Lotion— See Resorcinol and Sulfur (Topical), #

rFVIIa— *See* Factor VIIa (Systemic), 752

RhD immune globulin— *See* Rh$_o$(D) Immune Globulin (Systemic), 1360

rhDNase— *See* Dornase Alfa (Inhalation), 654

Rheaban— See Attapulgite (Oral), 222

Rheumatrex— See Methotrexate—For Noncancerous Conditions (Systemic), 1065

Rh-IG— *See* Rh$_o$(D) Immune Globulin (Systemic), 1360

Rh immune globulin— *See* Rh$_o$(D) Immune Globulin (Systemic), 1360

Rhinalar— See Corticosteroids (Nasal), 502

Rhinall— See Phenylephrine (Nasal), 1278

Rhinall-10 Children's Flavored Nose Drops— See Phenylephrine (Nasal), 1278

Rhinatate— See Antihistamines and Decongestants (Systemic), 159

Rhinocaps— See Decongestants and Analgesics (Systemic), 581

Rhinocort— See Corticosteroids (Nasal), 502

Rhinocort Aqua— See Corticosteroids (Nasal), 502

Rhinocort Turbuhaler— *See* Corticosteroids (Nasal), 502

Rhinolar-EX— *See* Antihistamines and Decongestants (Systemic), 159

Rhinolar-EX 12— *See* Antihistamines and Decongestants (Systemic), 159

Rhinosyn— *See* Antihistamines and Decongestants (Systemic), 159

Rhinosyn-DM— *See* Cough/Cold Combinations (Systemic), 522

Rhinosyn-DMX Expectorant— *See* Cough/ Cold Combinations (Systemic), 522

Rhinosyn-PD— *See* Antihistamines and Decongestants (Systemic), 159

Rhinosyn-X— *See* Cough/Cold Combinations (Systemic), 522

Rhodis— *See* Anti-inflammatory Drugs, Nonsteroidal (Systemic), 179

Rhodis-EC— *See* Anti-inflammatory Drugs, Nonsteroidal (Systemic), 179

RhoGAM— *See* Rh$_o$(D) Immune Globulin (Systemic), 1360

Rh$_o$(D) Immune Globulin (Systemic), 1360

Rh$_o$(D) immune human globulin— *See* Rh$_o$(D) Immune Globulin (Systemic), 1360

Rho-Loperamide— *See* Loperamide (Oral), 1001

Rhotrimine— *See* Antidepressants, Tricyclic (Systemic), 126

r-HuEPO— *See* Epoetin (Systemic), 693

Rhulicort— *See* Corticosteroids—Low Potency (Topical), 518

Ribavirin (Systemic), 1361

Ribavirin and Interferon Alfa-2b, Recombinant (Systemic), 1362

Riboflavin (Vitamin B$_2$) (Systemic), 1363

Rice Syrup Solids and Electrolytes— *See* Carbohydrates and Electrolytes (Systemic), 370

Ricobid— *See* Antihistamines and Decongestants (Systemic), 159

Ricobid Pediatric— *See* Antihistamines and Decongestants (Systemic), 159

Rid— *See* Pyrethrins and Piperonyl Butoxide (Topical), 1336

Rid-A-Pain— *See* Anesthetics (Dental), 80

Rid-A-Pain Compound— *See* Acetaminophen and Salicylates (Systemic), 6

Ridaura— *See* Gold Compounds (Systemic), 834

Rifabutin (Systemic), 1365

Rifadin— *See* Rifampin (Systemic), 1367

Rifadin IV— *See* Rifampin (Systemic), 1367

Rifamate— *See* Rifampin and Isoniazid (Systemic), 1369

Rifampicin— *See* Rifampin (Systemic), 1367

Rifampicin and isoniazid— *See* Rifampin and Isoniazid (Systemic), 1369

Rifampin (Systemic), 1367

Rifampin and Isoniazid (Systemic), 1369

Rifampin, Isoniazid, and Pyrazinamide (Systemic), #

Rifapentine (Systemic), 1372

Rifater— *See* Rifampin, Isoniazid, and Pyrazinamide (Systemic), #

RIG— *See* Rabies Immune Globulin (Systemic), #

rIL-11— *See* Oprelvekin (Systemic), 1218

Rilutek— *See* Riluzole (Systemic), 1373

Riluzole (Systemic), 1373

Rimactane— *See* Rifampin (Systemic), 1367

Rimantadine (Systemic), 1375, MC-21

Rimexolone (Ophthalmic), 1376

Rimso-50— *See* Dimethyl Sulfoxide (Mucosal), 612

Rinade B.I.D.— *See* Antihistamines and Decongestants (Systemic), 159

Riopan— *See* Antacids (Oral), 98

Riopan Extra Strength— *See* Antacids (Oral), 98

Riopan Plus— *See* Antacids (Oral), 98

Riopan Plus Double Strength— *See* Antacids (Oral), 98

Riopan Plus Extra Strength— *See* Antacids (Oral), 98

Riphenidate— *See* Methylphenidate (Systemic), 1078

Risedronate (Systemic), 1377

Risperdal— *See* Risperidone (Systemic), 1378, MC-21

Risperidone (Systemic), 1378, MC-21

Ritalin— *See* Methylphenidate (Systemic), 1078, MC-15

Ritalin SR— *See* Methylphenidate (Systemic), 1078

Ritalin-SR— *See* Methylphenidate (Systemic), 1078, MC-15

Ritodrine (Systemic), 1381

Ritonavir (Systemic), 1382

Rituxan— *See* Rituximab (Systemic), 1384

Rituximab (Systemic), 1384

Rivastigmine (Systemic), 1385

Rivotril— *See* Benzodiazepines (Systemic), 257

Rizatriptan (Systemic), 1386

RMS Uniserts— *See* Narcotic Analgesics— For Pain Relief (Systemic), 1147

Ro7-1051— *See* Benznidazole (Systemic), #

RO 11-1163— *See* Moclobemide (Systemic), 1114

Robafen AC Cough— *See* Cough/Cold Combinations (Systemic), 522

Robafen CF— *See* Cough/Cold Combinations (Systemic), 522

Robafen DAC— *See* Cough/Cold Combinations (Systemic), 522

Robafen DM— *See* Cough/Cold Combinations (Systemic), 522

Robalog— *See* Corticosteroids—Glucocorticoid Effects (Systemic), 513

Robaxin— *See* Skeletal Muscle Relaxants (Systemic), 1420

Robaxin-750— *See* Skeletal Muscle Relaxants (Systemic), 1420

Robidone— *See* Narcotic Analgesics—For Pain Relief (Systemic), 1147

Robidrine— *See* Pseudoephedrine (Systemic), 1334

Robigesic— *See* Acetaminophen (Systemic), 4

Robinul— *See* Anticholinergics/Antispasmodics (Systemic), 106

Robinul Forte— *See* Anticholinergics/Antispasmodics (Systemic), 106

Robitussin— *See* Guaifenesin (Systemic), 844

Robitussin A-C— *See* Cough/Cold Combinations (Systemic), 522

Robitussin-CF— *See* Cough/Cold Combinations (Systemic), 522

Robitussin with Codeine— *See* Cough/Cold Combinations (Systemic), 522

Robitussin Cold, Cough & Flu Liqui-Gels— *See* Cough/Cold Combinations (Systemic), 522

Robitussin Cold and Cough Liqui-Gels— *See* Cough/Cold Combinations (Systemic), 522

Robitussin Cough & Cold— *See* Cough/ Cold Combinations (Systemic), 522

Robitussin Cough & Cold Liqui-Fills— *See* Cough/Cold Combinations (Systemic), 522

Robitussin-DAC— *See* Cough/Cold Combinations (Systemic), 522

Robitussin-DM— *See* Cough/Cold Combinations (Systemic), 522

Robitussin Maximum Strength Cough and Cold— *See* Cough/Cold Combinations (Systemic), 522

Robitussin Maximum Strength Cough Suppressant— *See* Dextromethorphan (Systemic), 592

Robitussin Night Relief— *See* Cough/Cold Combinations (Systemic), 522

Robitussin Night-Time Cold Formula— *See* Cough/Cold Combinations (Systemic), 522

Robitussin-PE— *See* Cough/Cold Combinations (Systemic), 522

Robitussin Pediatric— *See* Dextromethorphan (Systemic), 592

Robitussin Pediatric Cough & Cold— *See* Cough/Cold Combinations (Systemic), 522

Robitussin Pediatric Cough Suppressant— *See* Dextromethorphan (Systemic), 592

Robitussin Severe Congestion Liqui-Gels— *See* Cough/Cold Combinations (Systemic), 522

Rocaltrol— *See* Vitamin D and Related Compounds (Systemic), 1577

Rocephin— *See* Cephalosporins (Systemic), 387

Rochagan— *See* Benznidazole (Systemic), #

Rodex— *See* Pyridoxine (Vitamin B$_6$) (Systemic), 1337

R.O.-Dexasone— *See* Corticosteroids (Ophthalmic), 505

Rofact— *See* Rifampin (Systemic), 1367

Rofecoxib (Systemic), 1388, MC-21

Roferon-A— *See* Interferons, Alpha (Systemic), 921

Rogaine— *See See* Minoxidil (Topical), 1104

Rogaine Extra Strength For Men— *See* Minoxidil (Topical), 1104

Rogaine For Men— *See* Minoxidil (Topical), 1104

Rogaine For Women— *See* Minoxidil (Topical), 1104

Rogitine— *See* Phentolamine and Papaverine (Intracavernosal), #

Rolaids— *See* Antacids (Oral), 98

Rolaids Calcium Rich— *See* Calcium Supplements (Systemic), 353

Rolaids Extra Strength— *See* Antacids (Oral), 98

Rolatuss Expectorant— *See* Cough/Cold Combinations (Systemic), 522

Rolatuss w/Hydrocodone— *See* Cough/ Cold Combinations (Systemic), 522

Salutensin— *See* Rauwolfia Alkaloids and Thiazide Diuretics (Systemic), #

Salutensin-Demi— *See* Rauwolfia Alkaloids and Thiazide Diuretics (Systemic), #

Samarium Sm 153 Lexidronam (Therapeutic), #

Sandimmune— *See* Cyclosporine (Systemic), 553

Sandoglobulin— *See* Immune Globulin Intravenous (Human) (Systemic), 896

SandoSource Peptide— *See* Enteral Nutrition Formulas (Systemic), #

Sandostatin— *See* Octreotide (Systemic), 1204

Sandostatin LAR Depot— *See* Octreotide (Systemic), 1204

SangCya— *See* Cyclosporine (Systemic), 553

Sani-Supp— *See* Laxatives (Rectal), 970

Sanorex— *See* Appetite Suppressants, Sympathomimetic (Systemic), 197

Sans-Acne— *See* Erythromycin (Topical), 706

Sansert— *See* Methysergide (Systemic), 1082

Saquinavir (Systemic), 1401, 1630

Sarafem— *See* Fluoxetine (Systemic), 783, MC-10

Sargramostim— *See* Colony Stimulating Factors (Systemic), 489

Sarisol No. 2— *See* Barbiturates (Systemic), 239

Sarna HC 1.0%— *See* Corticosteroids— Low Potency (Topical), 518

S.A.S.-500— *See* Sulfasalazine (Systemic), 1442

S.A.S. Enteric-500— *See* Sulfasalazine (Systemic), 1442

SAStid Soap— *See* Salicylic Acid and Sulfur (Topical), #

Scabene— *See* Lindane (Topical), 993

Scheinpharm Testone-Cyp— *See* Androgens (Systemic), 71

Scheinpharm Triamcine-A— *See* Corticosteroids—Glucocorticoid Effects (Systemic), 513

Sclerosol— *See* Talc (Intrapleural-Local), #

Scopolamine— *See* Anticholinergics/Antispasmodics (Systemic), 106; *See* Atropine/Homatropine/Scopolamine (Ophthalmic), 220

Scot-Tussin DM— *See* Cough/Cold Combinations (Systemic), 522

Scot-tussin Expectorant— *See* Guaifenesin (Systemic), 844

Scot-Tussin Original 5-Action Cold Medicine— *See* Antihistamines, Decongestants, and Analgesics (Systemic), 164

Scot-Tussin Senior Clear— *See* Cough/Cold Combinations (Systemic), 522

SD Deprenyl— *See* Selegiline (Systemic), 1403

SDZ-212713— *See* Rivastigmine (Systemic), 1385

SDZ ENA 713— *See* Rivastigmine (Systemic), 1385

Sea wasp antivenon— *See* Antivenin, Box Jellyfish (Systemic), #

Seba-Nil Liquid Cleanser— *See* Alcohol and Acetone (Topical), #

Sebex-T Tar Shampoo— *See* Salicylic Acid, Sulfur, and Coal Tar (Topical), #

Sebucare— *See* Salicylic Acid (Topical), #

Sebulex (with Conditioners)— *See* Salicylic Acid and Sulfur (Topical), #

Sebulex (Regular)— *See* Salicylic Acid and Sulfur (Topical), #

Sebulon— *See* Pyrithione (Topical), #

Sebutone— *See* Salicylic Acid, Sulfur, and Coal Tar (Topical), #

Secobarbital— *See* Barbiturates (Systemic), 239

Secobarbital and Amobarbital— *See* Barbiturates (Systemic), 239

Seconal— *See* Barbiturates (Systemic), 239

Sectral— *See* Beta-adrenergic Blocking Agents (Systemic), 272

Sedapap— *See* Butalbital and Acetaminophen (Systemic), 324

Seldane— *See* Antihistamines (Systemic), 153

Seldane-D— *See* Antihistamines and Decongestants (Systemic), 159

Select 1/35— *See* Estrogens and Progestins (Oral Contraceptives) (Systemic), 729

Selegiline-5— *See* Selegiline (Systemic), 1403

Selegiline (Systemic), 1403

Selenious Acid— *See* Selenium Supplements (Systemic), 1405

Selenium— *See* Selenium Supplements (Systemic), 1405

Selenium Sulfide (Topical), #

Selenium Supplements (Systemic), 1405

Sele-Pak— *See* Selenium Supplements (Systemic), 1405

Selepen— *See* Selenium Supplements (Systemic), 1405

Selestoject— *See* Corticosteroids—Glucocorticoid Effects (Systemic), 513

Selexid— *See* Penicillins (Systemic), 1251

Selsun— *See* Selenium Sulfide (Topical), #

Selsun Blue— *See* Selenium Sulfide (Topical), #

Selsun Blue Dry Formula— *See* Selenium Sulfide (Topical), #

Selsun Blue Extra Conditioning Formula— *See* Selenium Sulfide (Topical), #

Selsun Blue Extra Medicated Formula— *See* Selenium Sulfide (Topical), #

Selsun Blue Oily Formula— *See* Selenium Sulfide (Topical), #

Selsun Blue Regular Formula— *See* Selenium Sulfide (Topical), #

Semicid— *See* Spermicides (Vaginal), 1428

Semilente insulin, S— *See* Insulin (Systemic), 902

Semprex-D— *See* Antihistamines and Decongestants (Systemic), 159

Senexon— *See* Laxatives (Oral), 964

Senna— *See* Laxatives (Oral), 964; *See* Laxatives (Rectal), 970

Senna-Gen— *See* Laxatives (Oral), 964

Sennosides— *See* Laxatives (Oral), 964

Sennosides and Docusate— *See* Laxatives (Oral), 964

Senokot— *See* Laxatives (Oral), 964; *See* Laxatives (Rectal), 970

Senokot Children's Syrup— *See* Laxatives (Oral), 964

Senokot EXTRA— *See* Laxatives (Oral), 964

Senokot-S— *See* Laxatives (Oral), 964

Senokot XTRA— *See* Laxatives (Oral), 964

Senolax— *See* Laxatives (Oral), 964

SensoGARD Canker Sore Relief— *See* Anesthetics (Dental), 80

Sensorcaine— *See* Anesthetics (Parenteral-Local), 83

Sensorcaine-MPF— *See* Anesthetics (Parenteral-Local), 83

Sensorcaine-MPF Spinal— *See* Anesthetics (Parenteral-Local), 83

Sential— *See* Corticosteroids—Low Potency (Topical), 518

Septocaine— *See* Anesthetics (Parenteral-Local), 83

Septra— *See* Sulfonamides and Trimethoprim (Systemic), 1454

Septra DS— *See* Sulfonamides and Trimethoprim (Systemic), 1454

Septra Grape Suspension— *See* Sulfonamides and Trimethoprim (Systemic), 1454

Septra I.V.— *See* Sulfonamides and Trimethoprim (Systemic), 1454

Septra Suspension— *See* Sulfonamides and Trimethoprim (Systemic), 1454

Ser-A-Gen— *See* Reserpine, Hydralazine, and Hydrochlorothiazide (Systemic), #

Seralazide— *See* Reserpine, Hydralazine and Hydrochlorothiazide (Systemic), #

Ser-Ap-Es— *See* Reserpine, Hydralazine, and Hydrochlorothiazide (Systemic), #

Serax— *See* Benzodiazepines (Systemic), 257

Serentil— *See* Phenothiazines (Systemic), 1268, 1629

Serentil Concentrate— *See* Phenothiazines (Systemic), 1268

Serevent— *See* Bronchodilators, Adrenergic (Inhalation), 304

Serevent Diskhaler— *See* Bronchodilators, Adrenergic (Inhalation), 304

Serevent Diskus— *See* Bronchodilators, Adrenergic (Inhalation), 304

Sermorelin (Systemic), 1406

Sero-Gesic— *See* Salicylates (Systemic), 1394

Seromycin— *See* Cycloserine (Systemic), 552

Serophene— *See* Clomiphene (Systemic), 461

Seroquel— *See* Quetiapine (Systemic), 1339, MC-20

Serostim— *See* Growth Hormone (Systemic), 843

Serpalan— *See* Rauwolfia Alkaloids (Systemic), 1354

Serpasil— *See* Rauwolfia Alkaloids (Systemic), 1354

Serpazide— *See* Reserpine, Hydralazine, and Hydrochlorothiazide (Systemic), #

Sertan— *See* Primidone (Systemic), 1310

Sertraline (Systemic), 1407, MC-21

Serutan— *See* Laxatives (Oral), 964

Serutan Toasted Granules— *See* Laxatives (Oral), 964

Serzone— *See* Nefazodone (Systemic), 1162, 1630, MC-16

Sevelamer (Oral), 1410

Sevoflurane (Inhalation-Systemic), #

Sevorane— *See* Sevoflurane (Inhalation-Systemic), #

Shade Oil-Free— *See* Sunscreen Agents (Topical), #

Shade Sunblock— *See* Sunscreen Agents (Topical), #

SMA 13— *See* Infant Formulas (Systemic), #

SMA 20— *See* Infant Formulas (Systemic), #

SMA 24— *See* Infant Formulas (Systemic), #

SMA 27— *See* Infant Formulas (Systemic), #

SMA Lo-Iron 13— *See* Infant Formulas (Systemic), #

SMA Lo-Iron 20— *See* Infant Formulas (Systemic), #

SMA Lo-Iron 24— *See* Infant Formulas (Systemic), #

Sm 153-EDTMP— *See* Samarium Sm 153 Lexidronam (Systemic), #

Smelling salts— *See* Ammonia Spirit, Aromatic (Inhalation), #

Sm 153 ethylenediaminetetramethylene phosphonic acid— *See* Samarium Sm 153 Lexidronam (Systemic), #

SMZ-TMP— *See* Sulfonamides and Trimethoprim (Systemic), 1454

Snaplets-DM— *See* Cough/Cold Combinations (Systemic), 522

Snaplets-EX— *See* Cough/Cold Combinations (Systemic), 522

Snaplets-FR— *See* Acetaminophen (Systemic), 4

Snaplets-Multi— *See* Cough/Cold Combinations (Systemic), 522

Soda Mint— *See* Sodium Bicarbonate (Systemic), 1423

Sodium Ascorbate— *See* Ascorbic Acid (Vitamin C) (Systemic), 205

Sodium aurothiomalate— *See* Gold Compounds (Systemic), 834

Sodium azodisalicylate— *See* Olsalazine (Oral), 1211

Sodium Benzoate and Sodium Phenylacetate (Systemic), #

Sodium Bicarbonate (Systemic), 1423

Sodium Chloride (Intra-amniotic), #

Sodium Chromate Cr 51— *See* Radiopharmaceuticals (Diagnostic), 1347

Sodium Citrate and Citric Acid— *See* Citrates (Systemic), 443

Sodium cromoglycate— *See* Cromolyn (Inhalation), 537; *See* Cromolyn (Nasal), 541; *See* Cromolyn (Ophthalmic), 542; *See* Cromolyn (Oral), 543

Sodium Ferric Gluconate— *See* Iron Supplements (Systemic), 936

Sodium Fluoride (Systemic), 1425, MC-21

Sodium Fluoride F 18— *See* Radiopharmaceuticals (Diagnostic), 1347

Sodium Iodide (Systemic), #

Sodium Iodide I 123— *See* Radiopharmaceuticals (Diagnostic), 1347

Sodium Iodide I 131— *See* Radiopharmaceuticals (Diagnostic), 1347

Sodium Iodide I 131 (Therapeutic), #

Sodium Pertechnetate Tc 99m— *See* Radiopharmaceuticals (Diagnostic), 1347

Sodium Phenylbutyrate (Systemic), #

Sodium Phosphate— *See* Laxatives (Oral), 964

Sodium Phosphate P 32 (Therapeutic), #

Sodium Phosphates; *See* Laxatives (Oral), 964

Sodium Phosphates— *See* Laxatives (Rectal), 970; *See* Phosphates (Systemic), 1282

Sodium Salicylate— *See* Salicylates (Systemic), 1394

Sodium Sulamyd— *See* Sulfonamides (Ophthalmic), 1445

Sodium Thiosulfate (Systemic), #

Sodium Tyropanoate— *See* Cholecystographic Agents, Oral (Diagnostic), 421

Soflax— *See* Laxatives (Oral), 964

Soframycin Ophthalmic— *See* Framycetin (Ophthalmic), 805

Softsense Skin Essential Everyday UV Protectant— *See* Sunscreen Agents (Topical), #

Solagé— *See* Mequinol and Tretinoin (Topical), 1051

Solaraze— *See* Diclofenac (Topical), 599

Solbar— *See* Sunscreen Agents (Topical), #

Solbar Liquid— *See* Sunscreen Agents (Topical), #

Solbar PF— *See* Sunscreen Agents (Topical), #

Solbar PF Liquid— *See* Sunscreen Agents (Topical), #

Solbar PF Ultra— *See* Sunscreen Agents (Topical), #

Solbar Plus— *See* Sunscreen Agents (Topical), #

Solbar Shield— *See* Sunscreen Agents (Topical), #

Solex A15 Clear— *See* Sunscreen Agents (Topical), #

Solfoton— *See* Barbiturates (Systemic), 239

Solganal— *See* Gold Compounds (Systemic), 834

Solu-Cortef— *See* Corticosteroids—Glucocorticoid Effects (Systemic), 513

Solu-Flur— *See* Sodium Fluoride (Systemic), 1425

Solugel 4— *See* Benzoyl Peroxide (Topical), 265

Solugel 8— *See* Benzoyl Peroxide (Topical), 265

Solu-Medrol— *See* Corticosteroids—Glucocorticoid Effects (Systemic), 513

Solurex— *See* Corticosteroids—Glucocorticoid Effects (Systemic), 513

Solurex-LA— *See* Corticosteroids—Glucocorticoid Effects (Systemic), 513

Soma— *See* Skeletal Muscle Relaxants (Systemic), 1420

Somatrem— *See* Growth Hormone (Systemic), 843

Somatropin, Recombinant— *See* Growth Hormone (Systemic), 843

Sominex— *See* Antihistamines (Systemic), 153

Somnol— *See* Benzodiazepines (Systemic), 257

Sonata— *See* Zaleplon (Systemic), 1592, MC-24

Sopamycetin Ophthalmic Ointment— *See* Chloramphenicol (Ophthalmic), 403

Sopamycetin Ophthalmic Solution— *See* Chloramphenicol (Ophthalmic), 403

Sorbitrate— *See* Nitrates—Oral (Systemic), 1188; *See* Nitrates—Sublingual, Chewable, or Buccal (Systemic), 1190

Soriatane— *See* Acitretin (Systemic), 15

Sotacor— *See* Beta-adrenergic Blocking Agents (Systemic), 272

Sotalol— *See* Beta-adrenergic Blocking Agents (Systemic), 272, MC-21

Soyalac— *See* Infant Formulas (Systemic), #

Span-FF— *See* Iron Supplements (Systemic), 936

Sparfloxacin— *See* Fluoroquinolones (Systemic), 776

Sparfloxacin (Systemic), #

Spaslin— *See* Belladonna Alkaloids and Barbiturates (Systemic), 252

Spasmoban— *See* Anticholinergics/Antispasmodics (Systemic), 106

Spasmoject— *See* Anticholinergics/Antispasmodics (Systemic), 106

Spasmolin— *See* Belladonna Alkaloids and Barbiturates (Systemic), 252

Spasmophen— *See* Belladonna Alkaloids and Barbiturates (Systemic), 252

Spasquid— *See* Belladonna Alkaloids and Barbiturates (Systemic), 252

Spectazole— *See* Econazole (Topical), 675

Spectinomycin (Systemic), 1427

Spectrobid— *See* Penicillins (Systemic), 1251

Spectro-Caine— *See* Anesthetics (Ophthalmic), #

Spectro-Chlor Ophthalmic Ointment— *See* Chloramphenicol (Ophthalmic), 403

Spectro-Chlor Ophthalmic Solution— *See* Chloramphenicol (Ophthalmic), 403

Spectro-Cyl— *See* Tropicamide (Ophthalmic), #

Spectro-Genta— *See* Gentamicin (Ophthalmic), 821

Spectro-Homatropine— *See* Atropine/Homatropine/Scopolamine (Ophthalmic), 220

Spectro-Pentolate— *See* Cyclopentolate (Ophthalmic), 548

Spectro-Sporin— *See* Neomycin, Polymyxin B, and Bacitracin (Ophthalmic), 1167

Spectro-Sulf— *See* Sulfonamides (Ophthalmic), 1445

Spec-T Sore Throat Anesthetic— *See* Anesthetics (Dental), 80

Spermicides (Vaginal), 1428

Spersacarpine— *See* Pilocarpine (Ophthalmic), 1287

Spersadex— *See* Corticosteroids (Ophthalmic), 505

Spersaphrine— *See* Phenylephrine (Ophthalmic), #

Spiramycin (Systemic), 1432

Spiramycine Coquelusédal— *See* Spiramycin (Systemic), 1432

Spironolactone— *See* Diuretics, Potassium-sparing (Systemic), 636, MC-21

Spironolactone and Hydrochlorothiazide— *See* Diuretics, Potassium-sparing and Hydrochlorothiazide (Systemic), 639

Spirozide— *See* Diuretics, Potassium-sparing and Hydrochlorothiazide (Systemic), 639

Sporanox— *See* Antifungals, Azole (Systemic), 142, MC-12

SRC Expectorant— *See* Cough/Cold Combinations (Systemic), 522

SSD— *See* Silver Sulfadiazine (Topical), 1415

SSD AF— *See* Silver Sulfadiazine (Topical), 1415

Sulfanilamide— *See* Sulfonamides (Vaginal), 1449
Sulfapyridine (Systemic), 1439
Sulfasalazine (Systemic), 1442, MC-22
Sulfathiazole, sulfacetamide, and sulfabenzamide— *See* Sulfonamides (Vaginal), 1449
Sulfatrim— *See* Sulfonamides and Trimethoprim (Systemic), 1454
Sulfatrim DS— *See* Sulfonamides and Trimethoprim (Systemic), 1454
Sulfatrim Pediatric— *See* Sulfonamides and Trimethoprim (Systemic), 1454
Sulfatrim S/S— *See* Sulfonamides and Trimethoprim (Systemic), 1454
Sulfatrim Suspension— *See* Sulfonamides and Trimethoprim (Systemic), 1454
Sulfex— *See* Sulfonamides (Ophthalmic), 1445
Sulfinpyrazone (Systemic), #
Sulfisoxazole— *See* Sulfonamides (Ophthalmic), 1445; *See* Sulfonamides (Systemic), 1446
Sulfisoxazole and Phenazopyridine— *See* Sulfonamides and Phenazopyridine (Systemic), 1451
Sulfizole— *See* Sulfonamides (Systemic), 1446
Sulfolax— *See* Laxatives (Oral), 964
Sulfonamides (Ophthalmic), 1445
Sulfonamides (Systemic), 1446
Sulfonamides (Vaginal), 1449
Sulfonamides and Phenazopyridine (Systemic), 1451
Sulfonamides and Trimethoprim (Systemic), 1454
Sulforcin— *See* Resorcinol and Sulfur (Topical), #
Sulfur (Topical), #
Sulindac— *See* Anti-inflammatory Drugs, Nonsteroidal (Systemic), 179, MC-22
Sulphacetamide— *See* Sulfonamides (Ophthalmic), 1445
Sulphafurazole— *See* Sulfonamides (Ophthalmic), 1445
Sulphasalazine— *See* Sulfasalazine (Systemic), 1442
Sulpho-Lac— *See* Sulfur (Topical), #
Sulten-10— *See* Sulfonamides (Ophthalmic), 1445
Sultrin— *See* Sulfonamides (Vaginal), 1449
Sumacal— *See* Enteral Nutrition Formulas (Systemic), #
Sumatriptan (Systemic), 1457, MC-22
Sumycin— *See* Tetracyclines (Systemic), MC-22
Sundown— *See* Sunscreen Agents (Topical), #
Sundown Broad Spectrum Sunblock— *See* Sunscreen Agents (Topical), #
Sundown Sport Sunblock— *See* Sunscreen Agents (Topical), #
Sundown Sunblock— *See* Sunscreen Agents (Topical), #
Sundown Sunscreen— *See* Sunscreen Agents (Topical), #
Sunkist— *See* Ascorbic Acid (Vitamin C) (Systemic), 205
Sunscreen Agents (Topical), #, #
Supac— *See* Acetaminophen and Salicylates (Systemic), 6
Supartz— *See* Hyaluronidase (Systemic), 1629

Superlipid— *See* Probucol (Systemic), 1316
Supeudol— *See* Narcotic Analgesics—For Pain Relief (Systemic), 1147
Suplena— *See* Enteral Nutrition Formulas (Systemic), #
Suppap-120— *See* Acetaminophen (Systemic), 4
Suppap-325— *See* Acetaminophen (Systemic), 4
Suppap-202063— *See* Acetaminophen (Systemic), 4
Supprelin— *See* Histrelin (Systemic), 867
Suppressin DM— *See* Cough/Cold Combinations (Systemic), 522
Suppressin DM Caplets— *See* Cough/Cold Combinations (Systemic), 522
Suppressin DM Plus— *See* Cough/Cold Combinations (Systemic), 522
Suprane— *See* Desflurane (Inhalation-Systemic), #
Suprax— *See* Cephalosporins (Systemic), 387, MC-5
Suprefact— *See* Buserelin (Systemic), 319
Supres— *See* Methyldopa and Thiazide Diuretics (Systemic), 1074
Suprofen— *See* Anti-inflammatory Drugs, Nonsteroidal (Ophthalmic), 177
Suramin (Systemic), #
Surfak— *See* Laxatives (Oral), 964
Surgam— *See* Anti-inflammatory Drugs, Nonsteroidal (Systemic), 179
Surgam SR— *See* Anti-inflammatory Drugs, Nonsteroidal (Systemic), 179
Surmontil— *See* Antidepressants, Tricyclic (Systemic), 126
Susano— *See* Belladonna Alkaloids and Barbiturates (Systemic), 252
Sustacal— *See* Enteral Nutrition Formulas (Systemic), #
Sustacal Basic— *See* Enteral Nutrition Formulas (Systemic), #
Sustacal with Fiber— *See* Enteral Nutrition Formulas (Systemic), #
Sustacal Plus— *See* Enteral Nutrition Formulas (Systemic), #
Sustagen— *See* Enteral Nutrition Formulas (Systemic), #
Sustiva— *See* Efavirenz (Systemic), 677
Sutilan— *See* Tiopronin (Systemic), #
Syllact— *See* Laxatives (Oral), 964
Syllamalt— *See* Laxatives (Oral), 964
Symmetrel— *See* Amantadine (Systemic), 38
Synacort— *See* Corticosteroids—Low Potency (Topical), 518
Synagis— *See* Palivizumab (Systemic), 1237
Synalar— *See* Corticosteroids—Medium to Very High Potency (Topical), 520
Synalar-HP— *See* Corticosteroids—Medium to Very High Potency (Topical), 520
Synalgos-DC— *See* Narcotic Analgesics and Aspirin (Systemic), 1142
Synamol— *See* Corticosteroids—Medium to Very High Potency (Topical), 520
Synarel— *See* Nafarelin (Systemic), 1133
Syn-Diltiazem— *See* Calcium Channel Blocking Agents (Systemic), 349
Synemol— *See* Corticosteroids—Medium to Very High Potency (Topical), 520
Synercid— *See* Quinupristin and Dalfopristin (Systemic), 1345

Synflex— *See* Anti-inflammatory Drugs, Nonsteroidal (Systemic), 179
Synflex DS— *See* Anti-inflammatory Drugs, Nonsteroidal (Systemic), 179
Syn-Nadolol— *See* Beta-adrenergic Blocking Agents (Systemic), 272
Synophylate-GG— *See* Theophylline and Guaifenesin (Systemic), #
Synphasic— *See* Estrogens and Progestins (Oral Contraceptives) (Systemic), 729
Syn-Pindolol— *See* Beta-adrenergic Blocking Agents (Systemic), 272
SYN-Rx AM Treatment— *See* Cough/Cold Combinations (Systemic), 522
Synthroid— *See* Thyroid Hormones (Systemic), 1503, MC-13
Syntocinon— *See* Oxytocin (Systemic), 1234
Synvinolin— *See* HMG-CoA Reductase Inhibitors (Systemic), 869
Synvisc— *See* Hyaluronate Sodium Derivative (Systemic), 872
Syprine— *See* Trientine (Systemic), #
Syracol CF— *See* Cough/Cold Combinations (Systemic), 522

T

206 Shake— *See* Enteral Nutrition Formulas (Systemic), #
217— *See* Salicylates (Systemic), 1394
217 Strong— *See* Salicylates (Systemic), 1394
222— *See* Narcotic Analgesics and Aspirin (Systemic), 1142
282— *See* Narcotic Analgesics and Aspirin (Systemic), 1142
292— *See* Narcotic Analgesics and Aspirin (Systemic), 1142
309-F— *See* Suramin (Systemic), #
Tac-3— *See* Corticosteroids—Glucocorticoid Effects (Systemic), 513
Tacaryl— *See* Antihistamines, Phenothiazine-derivative (Systemic), 173
Tacrine (Systemic), 1460
Tacrolimus (Systemic), 1461
Tacrolimus (Topical), 1464
Tagamet— *See* Histamine H_2-receptor Antagonists (Systemic), 863
Tagamet HB— *See* Histamine H_2-receptor Antagonists (Systemic), 863
Talacen— *See* Narcotic Analgesics and Acetaminophen (Systemic), 1138
Talc (Intrapleural-Local), #
Talwin— *See* Narcotic Analgesics—For Pain Relief (Systemic), 1147
Talwin Compound— *See* Narcotic Analgesics and Aspirin (Systemic), 1142
Talwin-Nx— *See* Narcotic Analgesics—For Pain Relief (Systemic), 1147
Tambocor— *See* Flecainide (Systemic), 768
Tamiflu— *See* Oseltamivir (Systemic), 1225
Tamine S.R.— *See* Antihistamines and Decongestants (Systemic), 159
Tamofen— *See* Tamoxifen (Systemic), 1465
Tamone— *See* Tamoxifen (Systemic), 1465
Tamoxifen (Systemic), 1465, MC-22
Tamsulosin (Systemic), 1467, MC-22
Tanafed— *See* Antihistamines and Decongestants (Systemic), 159

Tenuate— See Appetite Suppressants, Sympathomimetic (Systemic), 197

Tenuate Dospan— See Appetite Suppressants, Sympathomimetic (Systemic), 197

Tepanil Ten-Tab— See Appetite Suppressants, Sympathomimetic (Systemic), 197

Tequin— See Fluoroquinolones (Systemic), 776, MC-10

Teramine— See Appetite Suppressants, Sympathomimetic (Systemic), 197

Terazol 3— See Antifungals, Azole (Vaginal), 145

Terazol 7— See Antifungals, Azole (Vaginal), 145

Terazol 3 Dual-Pak— See Antifungals, Azole (Vaginal), 145

Terazol 3 Vaginal Ovules— See Antifungals, Azole (Vaginal), 145

Terazosin (Systemic), 1477, MC-22

Terbinafine (Systemic), 1478, 1630

Terbinafine (Topical), 1480

Terbutaline— *See* Bronchodilators, Adrenergic (Inhalation), 304; *See* Bronchodilators, Adrenergic (Oral/Injection), 310, MC-22

Terconazole— *See* Antifungals, Azole (Vaginal), 145

Terfenadine— *See* Antihistamines (Systemic), 153

Terfenadine and Pseudoephedrine— *See* Antihistamines and Decongestants (Systemic), 159

Teriparatide (Systemic), 1482

Terramycin— See Tetracyclines (Systemic), 1487

Tersac Cleansing Gel— See Salicylic Acid (Topical), #

Tersa-Tar Mild Therapeutic Shampoo with Protein and Conditioner— See Coal Tar (Topical), 478

Tersa-Tar Soapless Tar Shampoo— See Coal Tar (Topical), 478

Tersa-Tar Therapeutic Shampoo— See Coal Tar (Topical), 478

Tes Est Cyp— See Androgens and Estrogens (Systemic), 76

Teslac— See Testolactone (Systemic), #

Teslascan— See Mangafodipir (Systemic), 1023

Tessalon— See Benzonatate (Systemic), 264

Testamone 100— See Androgens (Systemic), 71

Testaqua— See Androgens (Systemic), 71

Test-Estro Cypionate— See Androgens and Estrogens (Systemic), 76

Testex— See Androgens (Systemic), 71

Testoderm— See Androgens (Systemic), 71

Testoderm with Adhesives— See Androgens (Systemic), 71

Testoderm TTS— See Androgens (Systemic), 71

Testolactone (Systemic), #

Testopel Pellets— See Androgens (Systemic), 71

Testosterone— *See* Androgens (Systemic), 71

Testosterone and Estradiol— *See* Androgens and Estrogens (Systemic), 76

Testred— See Androgens (Systemic), 71

Testred Cypionate 200— See Androgens (Systemic), 71

Testrin-P.A.— See Androgens (Systemic), 71

Tetanus Antitoxin (Systemic), #

Tetanus Immune Globulin (Systemic), 1483

Tetanus Toxoid (Systemic), 1484

Tetanus and Diphtheria Toxoids for Adult Use— *See* Diphtheria and Tetanus Toxoids (Systemic), 618

Tetracaine— *See* Anesthetics (Ophthalmic), #; *See* Anesthetics (Parenteral-Local), 83; *See* Anesthetics (Rectal), 85; *See* Anesthetics (Topical), 88

Tetracaine and Menthol— *See* Anesthetics (Rectal), 85; *See* Anesthetics (Topical), 88

Tetracycline— *See* Tetracyclines (Ophthalmic), 1486; *See* Tetracyclines (Systemic), 1487, MC-22; *See* Tetracyclines (Topical), #

Tetracycline Periodontal Fibers (Dental), 1485

Tetracyclines (Ophthalmic), 1486

Tetracyclines (Systemic), 1487, MC-22

Tetracyclines (Topical), #

Tetrahydroaminoacridine— *See* Tacrine (Systemic), 1460

Tetramethylthionine chloride— *See* Methylene Blue (Systemic), 1077

Tetramune; See Diphtheria and Tetanus Toxoids and Pertussis Vaccine Adsorbed and Haemophilus b Conjugate Vaccine (Systemic), 621

Teveten— See Eprosartan (Systemic), 698

Texacort— See Corticosteroids—Low Potency (Topical), 518

T-Gel— See Coal Tar (Topical), 478

T/Gel Therapeutic Conditioner— See Coal Tar (Topical), 478

T/Gel Therapeutic Shampoo— See Coal Tar (Topical), 478

T-Gesic— See Narcotic Analgesics and Acetaminophen (Systemic), 1138

THA— *See* Tacrine (Systemic), 1460

Thalidomide (Systemic), 1490

Thalitone— See Diuretics, Thiazide (Systemic), 642

Thallous Chloride TI 201— *See* Radiopharmaceuticals (Diagnostic), 1347

THALOMID— See Thalidomide (Systemic), 1490

Theo-24— See Bronchodilators, Theophylline (Systemic), 314

Theobid Duracaps— See Bronchodilators, Theophylline (Systemic), 314

Theochron— See Bronchodilators, Theophylline (Systemic), 314

Theocon— See Theophylline and Guaifenesin (Systemic), #

Theo-Dur— See Bronchodilators, Theophylline (Systemic), 314, MC-23

Theolair— See Bronchodilators, Theophylline (Systemic), 314

Theolair-SR— See Bronchodilators, Theophylline (Systemic), 314

Theolate— See Theophylline and Guaifenesin (Systemic), #

Theomax DF— See Theophylline, Ephedrine, and Hydroxyzine (Systemic), #

Theophylline— *See* Bronchodilators, Theophylline (Systemic), 314, MC-23

Theophylline, Ephedrine, Guaifenesin, and Phenobarbital (Systemic), #

Theophylline, Ephedrine, and Hydroxyzine (Systemic), #

Theophylline, Ephedrine, and Phenobarbital (Systemic), #

Theophylline and glyceryl guaiacolate— *See* Theophylline and Guaifenesin (Systemic), #

Theophylline and Guaifenesin (Systemic), #

Theo-SR— See Bronchodilators, Theophylline (Systemic), 314

Theo-Time— See Bronchodilators, Theophylline (Systemic), 314

Theovent Long-Acting— See Bronchodilators, Theophylline (Systemic), 314

Theo-X— See Bronchodilators, Theophylline (Systemic), 314

TheraCys— See Bacillus Calmette-Guérin (BCG) Live—For Cancer (Mucosal-Local), 234

TheraFlu Flu, Cold & Cough Medicine— See Cough/Cold Combinations (Systemic), 522

TheraFlu/Flu and Cold Medicine— See Antihistamines, Decongestants, and Analgesics (Systemic), 164

TheraFlu/Flu and Cold Medicine for Sore Throat— See Antihistamines, Decongestants, and Analgesics (Systemic), 164

TheraFlu Maximum Strength Non-Drowsy Formula Flu, Cold & Cough Medicine— See Cough/Cold Combinations (Systemic), 522

TheraFlu Maximum Strength Non-Drowsy Formula Flu, Cold & Cough Medicine Caplets— See Cough/Cold Combinations (Systemic), 522

TheraFlu Nighttime Maximum Strength Flu, Cold & Cough— See Cough/Cold Combinations (Systemic), 522

TheraFlu Sinus Maximum Strength Caplets— See Decongestants and Analgesics (Systemic), 581

Theralax— See Laxatives (Rectal), 970

Theramycin Z— See Erythromycin (Topical), 706

Theraplex T Shampoo— See Coal Tar (Topical), 478

Therevac Plus— See Laxatives (Rectal), 970

Therevac-SB— See Laxatives (Rectal), 970

Thermazene— See Silver Sulfadiazine (Topical), 1415

Thiabendazole (Systemic), 1492, 1630

Thiabendazole (Topical), #

Thiamazole— *See* Antithyroid Agents (Systemic), 194

Thiamine (Vitamin B₁) (Systemic), 1494

Thiazina— See Isoniazid and Thiacetazone (Systemic), #

Thiethylperazine (Systemic), #

Thioguanine (Systemic), #

Thiola— See Tiopronin (Systemic), #

Thionex— See Lindane (Topical), 993

Thiopental— *See* Anesthetics, General (Systemic), #

Thiopentone— *See* Anesthetics, General (Systemic), #

Thioplex— See Thiotepa (Systemic), 1496

Thioproperazine— *See* Phenothiazines (Systemic), 1268

Thioridazine— *See* Phenothiazines (Systemic), 1268, MC-23

Thiosol— See Tiopronin (Systemic), #

Topotecan (Systemic), 1521
Toprol-XL— *See* Beta-adrenergic Blocking Agents (Systemic), 272, MC-15
Topsyn— *See* Corticosteroids—Medium to Very High Potency (Topical), 520
TOPV— *See* Poliovirus Vaccine (Systemic), #
Toradol— *See* Ketorolac (Systemic), 950
Torecan— *See* Thiethylperazine (Systemic), #
Toremifene (Systemic), 1523
Tornalate— *See* Bronchodilators, Adrenergic (Inhalation), 304
Torsemide (Systemic), 1524, MC-23
Totacillin— *See* Penicillins (Systemic), 1251
Totacillin-N— *See* Penicillins (Systemic), 1251
Total Eclipse Moisturizing Skin— *See* Sunscreen Agents (Topical), #
Total Eclipse Oily and Acne Prone Skin Sunscreen— *See* Sunscreen Agents (Topical), #
Touro A&H— *See* Antihistamines and Decongestants (Systemic), 159
Touro EX— *See* Guaifenesin (Systemic), 844
Touro LA Caplets— *See* Cough/Cold Combinations (Systemic), 522
t-PA— *See* Thrombolytic Agents (Systemic), 1501
2-PAM— *See* Pralidoxime (Systemic), #
2-PAM chloride— *See* Pralidoxime (Systemic), #
T-Phyl— *See* Bronchodilators, Theophylline (Systemic), 314
Trac Tabs 2X— *See* Atropine, Hyoscyamine, Methenamine, Methylene Blue, Phenyl Salicylate, and Benzoic Acid (Systemic), 218
Tramacort-D— *See* Corticosteroids—Glucocorticoid Effects (Systemic), 513
Tramadol (Systemic), 1527, MC-23
Trancot— *See* Meprobamate (Systemic), #
Trandate— *See* Beta-adrenergic Blocking Agents (Systemic), 272
Trandolapril— *See* Angiotensin-converting Enzyme (ACE) Inhibitors (Systemic), 90, MC-23
Trandolapril and Verapamil (Systemic), 1528
Tranexamic Acid— *See* Antifibrinolytic Agents (Systemic), 140
Transderm-Nitro— *See* Nitrates—Topical (Systemic), 1193
Transderm-Scōp— *See* Anticholinergics/Antispasmodics (Systemic), 106
Transderm-V— *See* Anticholinergics/Antispasmodics (Systemic), 106
Trans-Plantar— *See* Salicylic Acid (Topical), #
Trans-Ver-Sal— *See* Salicylic Acid (Topical), #
Tranxene-SD— *See* Benzodiazepines (Systemic), 257
Tranxene-SD Half Strength— *See* Benzodiazepines (Systemic), 257
Tranxene T-Tab— *See* Benzodiazepines (Systemic), 257
Tranylcypromine— *See* Antidepressants, Monoamine Oxidase (MAO) Inhibitor (Systemic), 123
Trasicor— *See* Beta-adrenergic Blocking Agents (Systemic), 272

Trastuzumab (Systemic), 1530
TraumaCal— *See* Enteral Nutrition Formulas (Systemic), #
Traum-Aid HBC— *See* Enteral Nutrition Formulas (Systemic), #
Travasorb HN— *See* Enteral Nutrition Formulas (Systemic), #
Travasorb Renal Diet— *See* Enteral Nutrition Formulas (Systemic), #
Travasorb STD— *See* Enteral Nutrition Formulas (Systemic), #
Travatan— *See* Travoprost (Ophthalmic), 1630
Traveltabs— *See* Antihistamines (Systemic), 153
Travoprost (Ophthalmic), 1630
Trazodone (Systemic), 1531, MC-23
Trecator-SC— *See* Ethionamide (Systemic), 741
Trelstar Depot— *See* Triptorelin (Systemic), 1541
Trendar— *See* Anti-inflammatory Drugs, Nonsteroidal (Systemic), 179
Trental— *See* Pentoxifylline (Systemic), 1263, MC-18
Tretinoin (Systemic), 1533
Tretinoin (Topical), 1535
Triacet— *See* Corticosteroids—Medium to Very High Potency (Topical), 520
Triacin C Cough— *See* Cough/Cold Combinations (Systemic), 522
Triad— *See* Butalbital and Acetaminophen (Systemic), 324
Triadapin— *See* Antidepressants, Tricyclic (Systemic), 126
Triaderm— *See* Corticosteroids—Medium to Very High Potency (Topical), 520
Triafed w/Codeine— *See* Cough/Cold Combinations (Systemic), 522
Trial— *See* Antacids (Oral), 98
Trialodine— *See* Trazodone (Systemic), 1531
Triam-A— *See* Corticosteroids—Glucocorticoid Effects (Systemic), 513
Triamcinolone— *See* Corticosteroids (Dental), 495; *See* Corticosteroids (Inhalation), 496; *See* Corticosteroids (Nasal), 502; *See* Corticosteroids—Glucocorticoid Effects (Systemic), 513; *See* Corticosteroids—Medium to Very High Potency (Topical), 520
Triam-Forte— *See* Corticosteroids—Glucocorticoid Effects (Systemic), 513
Triaminic— *See* Antihistamines and Decongestants (Systemic), 159
Triaminic-12— *See* Antihistamines and Decongestants (Systemic), 159
Triaminic Allergy— *See* Antihistamines and Decongestants (Systemic), 159
Triaminic AM Non-Drowsy Cough and Decongestant— *See* Cough/Cold Combinations (Systemic), 522
Triaminic Chewables— *See* Antihistamines and Decongestants (Systemic), 159
Triaminic Cold— *See* Antihistamines and Decongestants (Systemic), 159
Triaminic-DM Cough Relief— *See* Cough/Cold Combinations (Systemic), 522
Triaminic DM Day Time for Children— *See* Cough/Cold Combinations (Systemic), 522
Triaminic-DM Expectorant— *See* Cough/Cold Combinations (Systemic), 522

Triaminic DM Long Lasting for Children— *See* Dextromethorphan (Systemic), 592
Triaminic DM NightTime for Children— *See* Cough/Cold Combinations (Systemic), 522
Triaminic Expectorant— *See* Cough/Cold Combinations (Systemic), 522
Triaminic Expectorant with Codeine— *See* Cough/Cold Combinations (Systemic), 522
Triaminic Expectorant DH— *See* Cough/Cold Combinations (Systemic), 522
Triaminicin— *See* Antihistamines, Decongestants, and Analgesics (Systemic), 164
Triaminicin with Codeine— *See* Cough/Cold Combinations (Systemic), 522
Triaminicin Cold, Allergy, Sinus— *See* Antihistamines, Decongestants, and Analgesics (Systemic), 164
Triaminic Night Time— *See* Cough/Cold Combinations (Systemic), 522
Triaminicol DM— *See* Cough/Cold Combinations (Systemic), 522
Triaminicol Multi-Symptom Cold and Cough Medicine— *See* Cough/Cold Combinations (Systemic), 522
Triaminicol Multi-Symptom Relief Colds with Coughs— *See* Cough/Cold Combinations (Systemic), 522
Triaminic Oral Infant Drops— *See* Antihistamines and Decongestants (Systemic), 159
Triaminic Sore Throat Formula— *See* Cough/Cold Combinations (Systemic), 522
Triaminic TR— *See* Antihistamines and Decongestants (Systemic), 159
Triaminic Triaminicol— *See* Cough/Cold Combinations (Systemic), 522
Triamolone 40— *See* Corticosteroids—Glucocorticoid Effects (Systemic), 513
Triamonide 40— *See* Corticosteroids—Glucocorticoid Effects (Systemic), 513
Triamterene— *See* Diuretics, Potassium-sparing (Systemic), 636
Triamterene and Hydrochlorothiazide— *See* Diuretics, Potassium-sparing and Hydrochlorothiazide (Systemic), 639, MC-23
Trianide Mild— *See* Corticosteroids—Medium to Very High Potency (Topical), 520
Trianide Regular— *See* Corticosteroids—Medium to Very High Potency (Topical), 520
Triaprin— *See* Butalbital and Acetaminophen (Systemic), 324
Triatec-8— *See* Narcotic Analgesics and Acetaminophen (Systemic), 1138
Triatec-30— *See* Narcotic Analgesics and Acetaminophen (Systemic), 1138
Triatec-8 Strong— *See* Narcotic Analgesics and Acetaminophen (Systemic), 1138
Triavil— *See* Perphenazine and Amitriptyline (Systemic), #
Triaz— *See* Benzoyl Peroxide (Topical), 265
Triaz Cleanser— *See* Benzoyl Peroxide (Topical), 265
Triazolam— *See* Benzodiazepines (Systemic), 257, MC-23
Tribavirin— *See* Ribavirin (Systemic), 1361
Tribenzagan— *See* Trimethobenzamide (Systemic), #

Tropical Blend Dry Oil— See Sunscreen Agents (Topical), #

Tropical Blend Waterproof— See Sunscreen Agents (Topical), #

Tropicamide (Ophthalmic), #

Trosyd AF— See Tioconazole (Topical), 1512

Trosyd J— See Tioconazole (Topical), 1512

Trovafloxacin (Systemic), 1544, MC-24

Trovan— See Trovafloxacin (Systemic), 1544, MC-24

Troxidone— *See* Anticonvulsants, Dione (Systemic), 115

Truphylline— See Bronchodilators, Theophylline (Systemic), 314

Trusopt— See Dorzolamide (Ophthalmic), 656

Truxophyllin— See Bronchodilators, Theophylline (Systemic), 314

Tryptophan— *See* L-Tryptophan (Systemic), 1012

L-Tryptophan (Systemic), 1012

Trysul— See Sulfonamides (Vaginal), 1449

T-Stat— See Erythromycin (Topical), 706

Tubasal— See Aminosalicylate Sodium (Systemic), #

Tuberculin PPD TINE TEST— See Tuberculin, Purified Protein Derivative (PPD) (Injection), #

Tuberculin, Purified Protein Derivative (PPD) (Injection), #

Tubersol— See Tuberculin, Purified Protein Derivative (PPD) (Injection), #

Tuinal— See Barbiturates (Systemic), 239

Tums— See Antacids (Oral), 98; *See* Calcium Supplements (Systemic), 353

Tums 500— See Calcium Supplements (Systemic), 353

Tums Anti-gas/Antacid— See Antacids (Oral), 98

Tums E-X— See Antacids (Oral), 98; *See* Calcium Supplements (Systemic), 353

Tums Extra Strength— See Antacids (Oral), 98; *See* Calcium Supplements (Systemic), 353

Tums Regular Strength— See Calcium Supplements (Systemic), 353

Tums Ultra— See Antacids (Oral), 98

Tusquelin— See Cough/Cold Combinations (Systemic), 522

Tuss-Ade— See Cough/Cold Combinations (Systemic), 522

Tussafed— See Cough/Cold Combinations (Systemic), 522

Tussafed Drops— See Cough/Cold Combinations (Systemic), 522

Tussafin Expectorant— See Cough/Cold Combinations (Systemic), 522

Tuss Allergine Modified T.D.— See Cough/Cold Combinations (Systemic), 522

Tussaminic C Forte— See Cough/Cold Combinations (Systemic), 522

Tussaminic C Pediatric— See Cough/Cold Combinations (Systemic), 522

Tussaminic DH Forte— See Cough/Cold Combinations (Systemic), 522

Tussaminic DH Pediatric— See Cough/Cold Combinations (Systemic), 522

Tussanil DH— See Cough/Cold Combinations (Systemic), 522

Tussar-2— See Cough/Cold Combinations (Systemic), 522

Tussar DM— See Cough/Cold Combinations (Systemic), 522

Tussar SF— See Cough/Cold Combinations (Systemic), 522

Tuss-DA— See Cough/Cold Combinations (Systemic), 522

Tuss Delay— See Antihistamines, Decongestants, and Anticholinergics (Systemic), 170

Tuss-DM— See Cough/Cold Combinations (Systemic), 522

Tussex Cough— See Cough/Cold Combinations (Systemic), 522

Tussgen— See Cough/Cold Combinations (Systemic), 522

Tuss-Genade Modified— See Cough/Cold Combinations (Systemic), 522

Tussi-12— See Carbetapentane, Chlorpheniramine, and Phenylephrine (Systemic), MC-4

Tussigon— See Cough/Cold Combinations (Systemic), 522

Tussilyn DM— See Cough/Cold Combinations (Systemic), 522

Tussionex— See Cough/Cold Combinations (Systemic), 522

Tussionex Pennkinetic— See Cough/Cold Combinations (Systemic), 522

Tussi-Organidin DM NR Liquid— See Cough/Cold Combinations (Systemic), 522

Tussi-Organidin DM-S NR Liquid— See Cough/Cold Combinations (Systemic), 522

Tussi-Organidin NR Liquid— See Cough/Cold Combinations (Systemic), 522

Tussi-Organidin-S NR Liquid— See Cough/Cold Combinations (Systemic), 522

Tussirex— See Cough/Cold Combinations (Systemic), 522

Tuss-LA— See Cough/Cold Combinations (Systemic), 522

Tusso-DM— See Cough/Cold Combinations (Systemic), 522

Tussogest— See Cough/Cold Combinations (Systemic), 522

Tuss-Ornade Spansules— See Cough/Cold Combinations (Systemic), 522

Twice-A-Day Extra Moisturizing 12-Hour Nasal Spray— See Oxymetazoline (Nasal), 1231

Twice-A-Day Soothing 12-Hour Nasal Spray— See Oxymetazoline (Nasal), 1231

Twilite Caplets— See Antihistamines (Systemic), 153

Twin-K— See Potassium Supplements (Systemic), 1300

TwoCal HN— See Enteral Nutrition Formulas (Systemic), #

2,3-dideoxyinosine— *See* Didanosine (Systemic), 603

Two-Dyne— See Butalbital and Acetaminophen (Systemic), 324

Ty-Cold Cold Formula— See Cough/Cold Combinations (Systemic), 522

Tylenol Allergy Sinus Medication Extra Strength Caplets— See Antihistamines, Decongestants, and Analgesics (Systemic), 164

Tylenol Allergy Sinus Medication Maximum Strength Caplets— See Antihistamines, Decongestants, and Analgesics (Systemic), 164

Tylenol Allergy Sinus Medication Maximum Strength Gelcaps— See Antihistamines, Decongestants, and Analgesics (Systemic), 164

Tylenol Allergy Sinus Medication Maximum Strength Geltabs— See Antihistamines, Decongestants, and Analgesics (Systemic), 164

Tylenol Allergy Sinus Night Time Medicine Maximum Strength Caplets— See Cough/Cold Combinations (Systemic), 164

Tylenol Arthritis Extended Release— See Acetaminophen (Systemic), 4

Tylenol Caplets— See Acetaminophen (Systemic), 4

Tylenol Children's Chewable Tablets— See Acetaminophen (Systemic), 4

Tylenol Children's Cold DM Medication— See Cough/Cold Combinations (Systemic), 522

Tylenol Children's Elixir— See Acetaminophen (Systemic), 4

Tylenol Children's Suspension Liquid— See Acetaminophen (Systemic), 4

Tylenol with Codeine— See Acetaminophen and Codeine (Systemic), MC-1

Tylenol with Codeine Elixir— See Narcotic Analgesics and Acetaminophen (Systemic), 1138

Tylenol with Codeine No.1— See Narcotic Analgesics and Acetaminophen (Systemic), 1138

Tylenol with Codeine No.2— See Narcotic Analgesics and Acetaminophen (Systemic), 1138

Tylenol with Codeine No.3— See Narcotic Analgesics and Acetaminophen (Systemic), 1138

Tylenol with Codeine No.4— See Narcotic Analgesics and Acetaminophen (Systemic), 1138

Tylenol with Codeine No.1 Forte— See Narcotic Analgesics and Acetaminophen (Systemic), 1138

Tylenol Cold and Flu— See Cough/Cold Combinations (Systemic), 522

Tylenol Cold and Flu No Drowsiness Powder— See Cough/Cold Combinations (Systemic), 522

Tylenol Cold Medication— See Cough/Cold Combinations (Systemic), 522

Tylenol Cold Medication Caplets— See Cough/Cold Combinations (Systemic), 522

Tylenol Cold Medication Children's— See Antihistamines, Decongestants, and Analgesics (Systemic), 164

Tylenol Cold Medication Extra Strength Daytime Caplets— See Cough/Cold Combinations (Systemic), 522

Tylenol Cold Medication Extra Strength Nighttime Caplets— See Cough/Cold Combinations (Systemic), 522

Tylenol Cold Medication, Non-Drowsy Caplets— See Cough/Cold Combinations (Systemic), 522

Tylenol Cold Medication, Non-Drowsy Gelcaps— See Cough/Cold Combinations (Systemic), 522

U

VasoClear A— See Naphazoline (Ophthalmic), 1135

Vasocon— See Naphazoline (Ophthalmic), 1135

Vasocon Regular— See Naphazoline (Ophthalmic), 1135

Vasodilan— See Isoxsuprine (Systemic), #

Vasofrinic— See Antihistamines and Decongestants (Systemic), 159

Vasopressin (Systemic), #

Vasotec— See Angiotensin-converting Enzyme (ACE) Inhibitors (Systemic), 90, MC-8

VCF— See Spermicides (Vaginal), 1428

V-Cillin K— See Penicillins (Systemic), 1251

V-Dec-M— See Cough/Cold Combinations (Systemic), 522

Veetids— See Penicillins (Systemic), 1251, MC-18

Velban— See Vinblastine (Systemic), 1564

Velbe— See Vinblastine (Systemic), 1564

Velosef— See Cephalosporins (Systemic), 387

Velosulin BR— See Insulin (Systemic), 902

Velosulin Human— See Insulin (Systemic), 902

Vendone— See Narcotic Analgesics and Acetaminophen (Systemic), 1138

Venlafaxine (Systemic), 1558, MC-24

Venoglobulin-I— See Immune Globulin Intravenous (Human) (Systemic), 896

Venoglobulin-S— See Immune Globulin Intravenous (Human) (Systemic), 896

Ventodisk— See Bronchodilators, Adrenergic (Inhalation), 304

Ventolin— See Bronchodilators, Adrenergic (Inhalation), 304; *See* Bronchodilators, Adrenergic (Oral/Injection), 310

Ventolin Nebules— See Bronchodilators, Adrenergic (Inhalation), 304

Ventolin Nebules P.F.— See Bronchodilators, Adrenergic (Inhalation), 304

Ventolin Rotacaps— See Bronchodilators, Adrenergic (Inhalation), 304

VePesid— See Etoposide (Systemic), 745

Veracolate— See Laxatives (Oral), 964

Verapamil— *See* Calcium Channel Blocking Agents (Systemic), 349, MC-24

Verazinc— See Zinc Supplements (Systemic), 1599

Verelan— See Calcium Channel Blocking Agents (Systemic), 349, MC-24

Verelan PM— See Verapamil (Systemic), MC-24

Vermox— See Mebendazole (Systemic), 1032

Versacaps— See Cough/Cold Combinations (Systemic), 522

Versed— See Midazolam (Systemic), 1097, 1629

Versel Lotion— See Selenium Sulfide (Topical), #

Verteporfin (Parenteral-Local), 1560

Verukan-HP Topical Solution— See Salicylic Acid (Topical), #

Verukan Topical Solution— See Salicylic Acid (Topical), #

Vesanoid— See Tretinoin (Systemic), 1533

Vesprin— See Phenothiazines (Systemic), 1268

Vexol— See Rimexolone (Ophthalmic), 1376

V-Gan-25— See Antihistamines, Phenothiazine-derivative (Systemic), 173

V-Gan-50— See Antihistamines, Phenothiazine-derivative (Systemic), 173

Viadur— See Leuprolide (Systemic), 976

Viagra— See Sildenafil (Systemic), 1413, MC-21

Vi-Atro— See Diphenoxylate and Atropine (Systemic), 615

Vibal— See Vitamin B$_{12}$ (Systemic), 1575

Vibal LA— See Vitamin B$_{12}$ (Systemic), 1575

Vibramycin— See Tetracyclines (Systemic), 1487

Vibra-Tabs— See Tetracyclines (Systemic), 1487

Vibra-Tabs C-Pak— See Tetracyclines (Systemic), 1487

Vibutal— See Butalbital and Aspirin (Systemic), 327

Vicks Children's DayQuil Allergy Relief— See Antihistamines and Decongestants (Systemic), 159

Vicks Children's NyQuil— See Cough/Cold Combinations (Systemic), 522

Vicks Children's NyQuil Cold/Cough Relief— See Cough/Cold Combinations (Systemic), 522

Vicks 44 Cough and Cold Relief Liqui-Caps— See Cough/Cold Combinations (Systemic), 522

Vicks 44 Cough and Cold Relief Non-Drowsy Liqui-Caps— See Cough/Cold Combinations (Systemic), 522

Vicks 44 Cough Relief— See Dextromethorphan (Systemic), 592

Vicks Cough Syrup— See Cough/Cold Combinations (Systemic), 522

Vicks DayQuil 4 Hour Allergy Relief— See Antihistamines and Decongestants (Systemic), 159

Vicks DayQuil 12 Hour Allergy Relief— See Antihistamines and Decongestants (Systemic), 159

Vicks DayQuil Liquicaps— See Cough/Cold Combinations (Systemic), 522

Vicks DayQuil Multi-Symptom Cold/Flu Liquicaps— See Cough/Cold Combinations (Systemic), 522

Vicks DayQuil Multi-Symptom Cold/Flu Relief— See Cough/Cold Combinations (Systemic), 522

Vicks DayQuil Non-Drowsy Cold/Flu— See Cough/Cold Combinations (Systemic), 522

Vicks DayQuil Sinus Pressure and Congestion Relief Caplets— See Cough/Cold Combinations (Systemic), 522

Vicks DayQuil Sinus Pressure & Pain Relief Caplets— See Decongestants and Analgesics (Systemic), 581

Vicks 44D Cough and Head Congestion— See Cough/Cold Combinations (Systemic), 522

Vicks 44D Dry Hacking Cough and Head Congestion— See Cough/Cold Combinations (Systemic), 522

Vicks 44E Cough & Chest Congestion— See Cough/Cold Combinations (Systemic), 522

Vicks Formula 44-D— See Cough/Cold Combinations (Systemic), 522

Vicks Formula 44-d Pediatric— See Cough/Cold Combinations (Systemic), 522

Vicks Formula 44E— See Cough/Cold Combinations (Systemic), 522

Vicks Formula 44e Pediatric— See Cough/Cold Combinations (Systemic), 522

Vicks Formula 44M— See Cough/Cold Combinations (Systemic), 522

Vick Sinex 12-Hour Nasal Spray— See Oxymetazoline (Nasal), 1231

Vick Sinex 12-Hour Ultra Fine Mist for Sinus Relief— See Oxymetazoline (Nasal), 1231

Vicks 44M Cough, Cold and Flu Relief— See Cough/Cold Combinations (Systemic), 522

Vicks 44M Cough, Cold and Flu Relief LiquiCaps— See Cough/Cold Combinations (Systemic), 522

Vicks NyQuil— See Cough/Cold Combinations (Systemic), 522

Vicks NyQuil Hot Therapy— See Cough/Cold Combinations (Systemic), 522

Vicks NyQuil Liqui-Caps— See Cough/Cold Combinations (Systemic), 522

Vicks NyQuil Multi-Symptom Cold/Flu LiquiCaps— See Cough/Cold Combinations (Systemic), 522

Vicks NyQuil Multi-Symptom Cold/Flu Relief— See Cough/Cold Combinations (Systemic), 522

Vicks Pediatric 44D Cough & Head Decongestion— See Cough/Cold Combinations (Systemic), 522

Vicks Pediatric 44E— See Cough/Cold Combinations (Systemic), 522

Vicks Pediatric 44M Multi-Symptom Cough & Cold— See Cough/Cold Combinations (Systemic), 522

Vicks Sinex— See Phenylephrine (Nasal), 1278

Vicodin— See Narcotic Analgesics and Acetaminophen (Systemic), 1138, MC-11

Vicodin ES— See Narcotic Analgesics and Acetaminophen (Systemic), 1138, MC-11

Vicodin Tuss— See Cough/Cold Combinations (Systemic), 522

Vicoprofen— See Hydrocodone and Ibuprofen (Systemic), 875, MC-11

Vidarabine (Ophthalmic), 1562

Vi-Daylin/F— See Vitamins and Fluoride (Systemic), 1586

Videx— See Didanosine (Systemic), 603

Vigabatrin (Systemic), 1563

Vinblastine (Systemic), 1564

Vincaleukoblastine— *See* Vindesine (Systemic), 1568

Vincasar PFS— See Vincristine (Systemic), 1566

Vincol— See Tiopronin (Systemic), #

Vincrex— See Vincristine (Systemic), 1566

Vincristine (Systemic), 1566

Vindesine (Systemic), 1568

Vinorelbine (Systemic), 1570

Vioform— See Clioquinol (Topical), 454

Vioform-Hydrocortisone Cream— See Clioquinol and Hydrocortisone (Topical), 455

Vioform-Hydrocortisone Lotion— See Clioquinol and Hydrocortisone (Topical), 455

Vioform-Hydrocortisone Mild Cream— See Clioquinol and Hydrocortisone (Topical), 455

Vioform-Hydrocortisone Mild Ointment—See Clioquinol and Hydrocortisone (Topical), 455

Vioform-Hydrocortisone Ointment—See Clioquinol and Hydrocortisone (Topical), 455

Viokase—See Pancrelipase (Systemic), 1239

Vioxx—See Rofecoxib (Systemic), 1388, MC-21

Viprynium—*See* Pyrvinium (Oral), #

Vira-A—See Vidarabine (Ophthalmic), 1562

Viracept—See Nelfinavir (Systemic), 1163

Viramune—See Nevirapine (Systemic), 1173

Viranol—See Salicylic Acid (Topical), #

Viranol Ultra—See Salicylic Acid (Topical), #

Virazid—See Ribavirin (Systemic), 1361

Virazole—See Ribavirin (Systemic), 1361

Viridium—See Phenazopyridine (Systemic), 1267

Virilon—See Androgens (Systemic), 71

Virilon IM—See Androgens (Systemic), 71

Viroptic—See Trifluridine (Ophthalmic), 1537

Visine L.R.—See Oxymetazoline (Ophthalmic), 1233

Viskazide—See Beta-adrenergic Blocking Agents and Thiazide Diuretics (Systemic), 278

Visken—See Beta-adrenergic Blocking Agents (Systemic), 272

Vistacrom—See Cromolyn (Ophthalmic), 542

Vistaril—See Antihistamines (Systemic), 153

Vistide—See Cidofovir (Systemic), 431

Visudyne—See Verteporfin (Parenteral-Local), 1560

Vitabee 6—See Pyridoxine (Vitamin B$_6$) (Systemic), 1337

Vitabee 12—See Vitamin B$_{12}$ (Systemic), 1575

Vitalax Super Smooth Sugar Free Orange Flavor—See Laxatives (Oral), 964

Vitalax Unflavored—See Laxatives (Oral), 964

Vital High Nitrogen—See Enteral Nutrition Formulas (Systemic), #

Vitamin A (Systemic), 1572

Vitamin A acid—See Tretinoin (Topical), 1535

Vitamin A Acid—See Tretinoin (Topical), 1535

Vitamin B$_1$—*See* Thiamine (Vitamin B$_1$) (Systemic), 1494

Vitamin B$_2$—*See* Riboflavin (Vitamin B$_2$) (Systemic), 1363

Vitamin B$_3$—*See* Niacin (Vitamin B$_3$) (Systemic), 1175

Vitamin B$_3$—*See* Niacin (Vitamin B$_3$) (Systemic), 1175

Vitamin B$_3$—*See* Niacin—For High Cholesterol (Systemic), 1177

Vitamin B$_5$—*See* Pantothenic Acid (Vitamin B$_5$) (Systemic), #

Vitamin B$_9$—*See* Folic Acid (Vitamin B$_9$) (Systemic), 794

Vitamin B$_{12}$ (Systemic), 1575

Vitamin B w—*See* Biotin (Systemic), 289

Vitamin C—*See* Ascorbic Acid (Vitamin C) (Systemic), 205

Vitamin D—See Vitamin D and Related Compounds (Systemic), 1577

Vitamin D and Related Compounds (Systemic), 1577

Vitamin E (Systemic), 1582

Vitamin H—*See* Biotin (Systemic), 289

Vitamin K$_1$—*See* Vitamin K (Systemic), 1584

Vitamin K$_4$—*See* Vitamin K (Systemic), 1584

Vitamin K (Systemic), 1584

Vitamins A, D, and C and Fluoride—*See* Vitamins and Fluoride (Systemic), 1586

Vitamins and Fluoride (Systemic), 1586

Vitamins, Prenatal (Systemic), MC-24

Vitaneed—See Enteral Nutrition Formulas (Systemic), #

Vita Plus E—See Vitamin E (Systemic), 1582

Vitinoin—See Tretinoin (Topical), 1535

Vitrasert—See Ganciclovir (Implantation-Ophthalmic), 812

Vitravene—See Fomivirsen (Parenteral-Local), 800

Vivactil—See Antidepressants, Tricyclic (Systemic), 126

Vivarin—See Caffeine (Systemic), 339

Vivelle—See Estrogens (Systemic), 718

Vivol—See Benzodiazepines (Systemic), 257

Vivonex Pediatric—See Enteral Nutrition Formulas (Systemic), #

Vivonex Plus—See Enteral Nutrition Formulas (Systemic), #

Vivonex T.E.N.—See Enteral Nutrition Formulas (Systemic), #

Vivotif Berna—See Typhoid Vaccine Live Oral (Systemic), #

V-Lax—See Laxatives (Oral), 964

VM-26—*See* Teniposide (Systemic), 1475

Volmax—See Bronchodilators, Adrenergic (Oral/Injection), 310, MC-1

Voltaren—See Anti-inflammatory Drugs, Nonsteroidal (Ophthalmic), 177

Voltaren—See Anti-inflammatory Drugs, Nonsteroidal (Systemic), 179

Voltaren Ophtha—See Anti-inflammatory Drugs, Nonsteroidal (Ophthalmic), 177

Voltaren Ophthalmic—See Anti-inflammatory Drugs, Nonsteroidal (Ophthalmic), 177

Voltaren Rapide—See Anti-inflammatory Drugs, Nonsteroidal (Systemic), 179

Voltaren SR—See Anti-inflammatory Drugs, Nonsteroidal (Systemic), 179

VōSol HC—See Corticosteroids and Acetic Acid (Otic), 511

VP-16—*See* Etoposide (Systemic), 745

Vumon—See Teniposide (Systemic), 1475

W

Wake-Up—See Caffeine (Systemic), 339

Warfarin—*See* Anticoagulants (Systemic), 112, MC-24

Warfilone—See Anticoagulants (Systemic), 112

Wart-Off Topical Solution—See Salicylic Acid (Topical), #

Waterbabies Little Licks—See Sunscreen Agents (Topical), #

Waterbabies Sunblock—See Sunscreen Agents (Topical), #

Water O 15—*See* Radiopharmaceuticals (Diagnostic), 1347

4-Way 12-Hour Nasal Spray—See Oxymetazoline (Nasal), 1231

Webber Vitamin E—See Vitamin E (Systemic), 1582

Wehgen—See Estrogens (Systemic), 718

Welchol—See Colesevelam (Oral-Local), 485

Wellbutrin—See Bupropion (Systemic), 317, MC-3

Wellbutrin SR—See Bupropion (Systemic), 317, MC-3

Wellcovorin—See Leucovorin (Systemic), 974

Wellferon—See Interferons, Alpha (Systemic), 921

Westcort—See Corticosteroids—Medium to Very High Potency (Topical), 520

West-Decon—See Antihistamines and Decongestants (Systemic), 159

Westhroid—See Thyroid Hormones (Systemic), 1503

Whole-cell DTP—*See* Diphtheria and Tetanus Toxoids and Pertussis Vaccine Adsorbed (Systemic), 619

Wigraine—See Headache Medicines, Ergot Derivative–containing (Systemic), 853

Winpred—See Corticosteroids—Glucocorticoid Effects (Systemic), 513

WinRho SD—See Rh$_o$(D) Immune Globulin (Systemic), 1360

Winstrol—See Anabolic Steroids (Systemic), 66

Wintrocin—See Erythromycins (Systemic), 712

Wolfina—See Rauwolfia Alkaloids (Systemic), 1354

Wycillin—See Penicillins (Systemic), 1251

Wygesic—See Narcotic Analgesics and Acetaminophen (Systemic), 1138

Wymox—See Penicillins (Systemic), 1251

Wytensin—See Guanabenz (Systemic), 846

X

Xalatan—See Latanoprost (Ophthalmic), 962

Xanax—See Benzodiazepines (Systemic), 257, MC-1

Xanax TS—See Benzodiazepines (Systemic), 257

Xeloda—See Capecitabine (Systemic), 360, 1629

Xenical—See Orlistat (Oral-Local), 1219, MC-18

Xenon Xe 127—*See* Radiopharmaceuticals (Diagnostic), 1347

Xenon Xe 133—*See* Radiopharmaceuticals (Diagnostic), 1347

Xerac BP 5—See Benzoyl Peroxide (Topical), 265

Xopenex—See Levalbuterol (Inhalation-Local), 978

X-Prep Liquid—See Laxatives (Oral), 964

X-Seb—See Salicylic Acid (Topical), #

The Medicine Chart

The Medicine Chart presents photographs of the most frequently prescribed medicines in the United States. In general, commonly used brand name products and a representative sampling of generic products have been included. The pictorial listing is not intended to be inclusive and does not represent all products on the market. Only selected solid oral dosage forms (capsules and tablets) have been included. The inclusion of a product does not mean the authors have any particular knowledge that the product included has properties different from other products, nor should it be interpreted as an endorsement. Similarly, the fact that a particular product has not been included does not indicate that the product has been judged to be unsatisfactory or unacceptable.

The drug products in *The Medicine Chart* are listed alphabetically by generic name of active ingredient(s). Brand names are in **bold.**

The size and color of the products shown are intended to match the actual product as closely as possible; however, there may be some differences due to variations caused by the photographic process. Also, manufacturers may occasionally change the color, imprinting, or shape of their products, and for a period of time both the "old" and the newly changed dosage forms may be on the market. Such changes may not occur uniformly throughout the different dosages of the product. When applicable these types of changes will be incorporated in the subsequent versions of *The Medicine Chart* as they are brought to our attention.

To locate a particular drug in *The Medicine Chart* please refer to the index.

Use of this chart is limited to serving as an initial guide in identifying drug products. The identity of a product should be verified further before any action is taken.

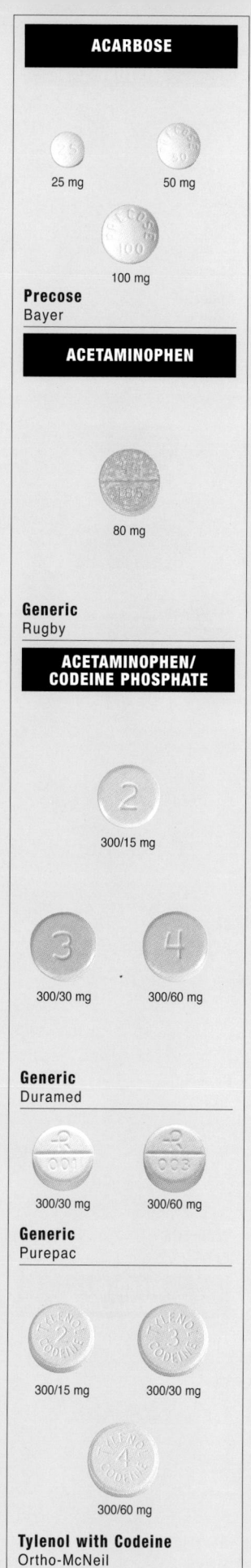

ACARBOSE

25 mg   50 mg

100 mg

Precose
Bayer

ACETAMINOPHEN

80 mg

Generic
Rugby

ACETAMINOPHEN/ CODEINE PHOSPHATE

2
300/15 mg

3   4
300/30 mg   300/60 mg

Generic
Duramed

300/30 mg   300/60 mg

Generic
Purepac

300/15 mg   300/30 mg

300/60 mg

Tylenol with Codeine
Ortho-McNeil

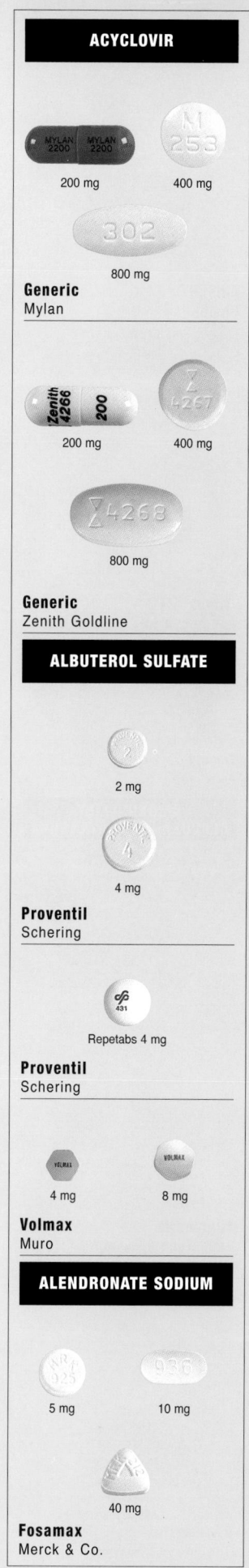

ACYCLOVIR

200 mg   400 mg

302
800 mg

Generic
Mylan

200 mg   400 mg

4268
800 mg

Generic
Zenith Goldline

ALBUTEROL SULFATE

2 mg

4 mg

Proventil
Schering

Repetabs 4 mg

Proventil
Schering

4 mg   8 mg

Volmax
Muro

ALENDRONATE SODIUM

5 mg   10 mg

40 mg

Fosamax
Merck & Co.

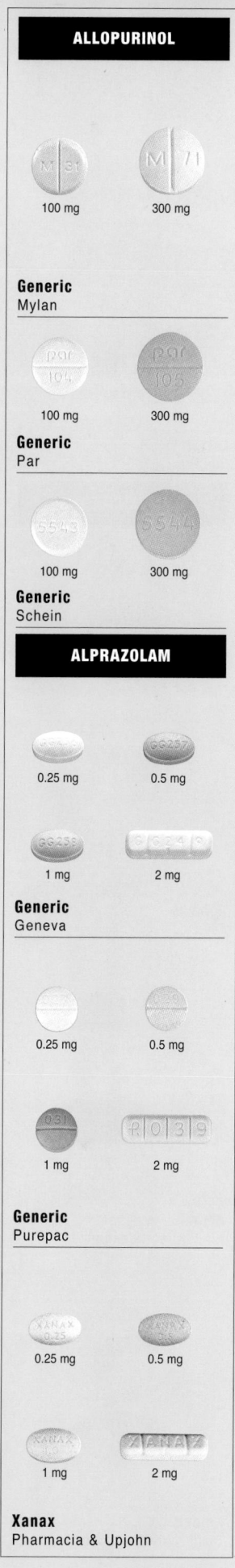

ALLOPURINOL

100 mg   300 mg

Generic
Mylan

100 mg   300 mg

Generic
Par

100 mg   300 mg

Generic
Schein

ALPRAZOLAM

0.25 mg   0.5 mg

1 mg   2 mg

Generic
Geneva

0.25 mg   0.5 mg

1 mg   2 mg

Generic
Purepac

0.25 mg   0.5 mg

1 mg   2 mg

Xanax
Pharmacia & Upjohn

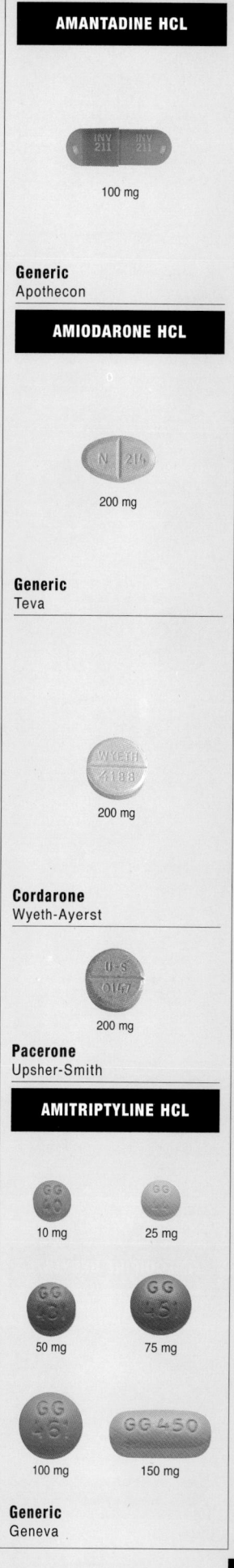

AMANTADINE HCL

100 mg

Generic
Apothecon

AMIODARONE HCL

200 mg

Generic
Teva

200 mg

Cordarone
Wyeth-Ayerst

200 mg

Pacerone
Upsher-Smith

AMITRIPTYLINE HCL

10 mg   25 mg

50 mg   75 mg

100 mg   150 mg

Generic
Geneva

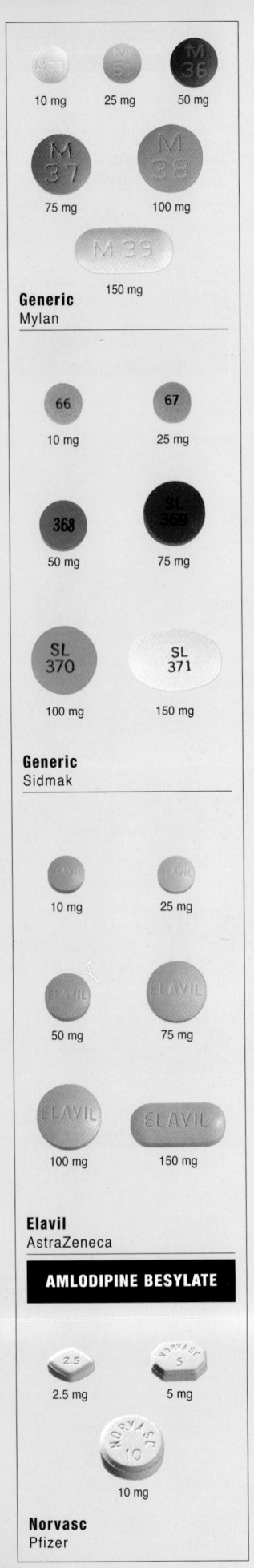

10 mg   25 mg   50 mg

M 37 — 75 mg   M 38 — 100 mg

M 39 — 150 mg

Generic
Mylan

66 — 10 mg   67 — 25 mg

368 — 50 mg   SL 369 — 75 mg

SL 370 — 100 mg   SL 371 — 150 mg

Generic
Sidmak

10 mg   25 mg

50 mg   75 mg

100 mg   150 mg

Elavil
AstraZeneca

AMLODIPINE BESYLATE

2.5 mg   5 mg

10 mg

Norvasc
Pfizer

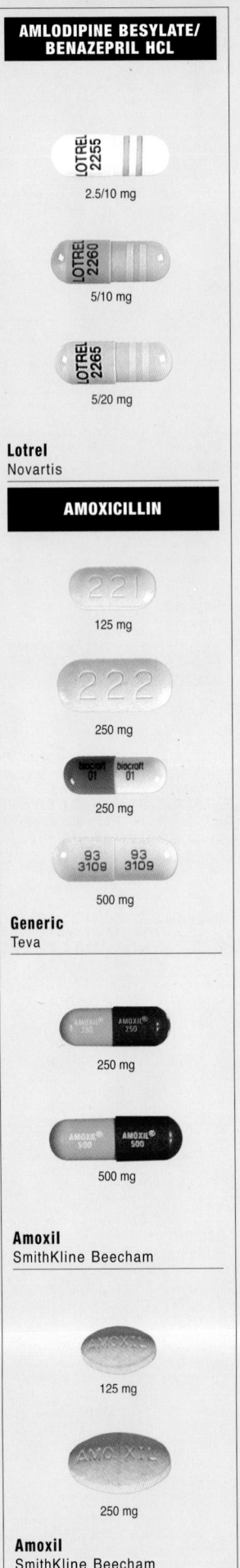

AMLODIPINE BESYLATE/ BENAZEPRIL HCL

LOTREL 2255 — 2.5/10 mg

LOTREL 2260 — 5/10 mg

LOTREL 2265 — 5/20 mg

Lotrel
Novartis

AMOXICILLIN

221 — 125 mg

222 — 250 mg

biocraft 01 / biocraft 01 — 250 mg

93 3109 / 93 3109 — 500 mg

Generic
Teva

AMOXIL 250 / AMOXIL 250 — 250 mg

AMOXIL 500 / AMOXIL 500 — 500 mg

Amoxil
SmithKline Beecham

AMOXIL — 125 mg

AMOXIL — 250 mg

Amoxil
SmithKline Beecham

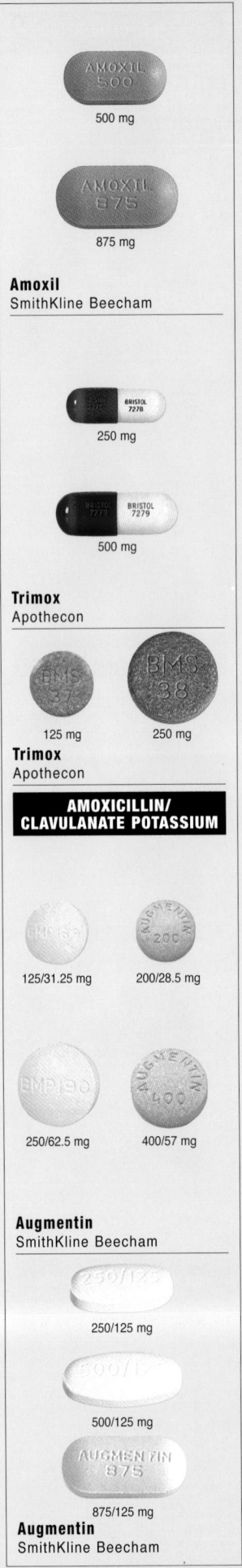

AMOXIL 500 — 500 mg

AMOXIL 875 — 875 mg

Amoxil
SmithKline Beecham

BRISTOL 7278 — 250 mg

BRISTOL 7279 — 500 mg

Trimox
Apothecon

BMS 37 — 125 mg   BMS 38 — 250 mg

Trimox
Apothecon

AMOXICILLIN/ CLAVULANATE POTASSIUM

AUGMENTIN 125 — 125/31.25 mg   AUGMENTIN 200 — 200/28.5 mg

AMP 190 — 250/62.5 mg   AUGMENTIN 400 — 400/57 mg

Augmentin
SmithKline Beecham

250/125 — 250/125 mg

500/125 — 500/125 mg

AUGMENTIN 875 — 875/125 mg

Augmentin
SmithKline Beecham

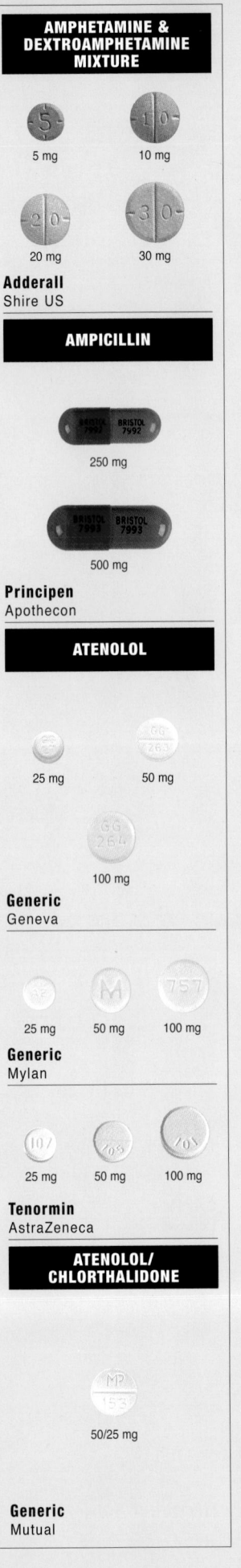

AMPHETAMINE & DEXTROAMPHETAMINE MIXTURE

5 — 5 mg   10 — 10 mg

20 — 20 mg   30 — 30 mg

Adderall
Shire US

AMPICILLIN

BRISTOL 7992 / BRISTOL 7992 — 250 mg

BRISTOL 7993 / BRISTOL 7993 — 500 mg

Principen
Apothecon

ATENOLOL

25 mg   GG 263 — 50 mg

GG 264 — 100 mg

Generic
Geneva

RE 25 mg   M 50 mg   757 100 mg

Generic
Mylan

107 25 mg   268 50 mg   705 100 mg

Tenormin
AstraZeneca

ATENOLOL/ CHLORTHALIDONE

MP 153 — 50/25 mg

Generic
Mutual

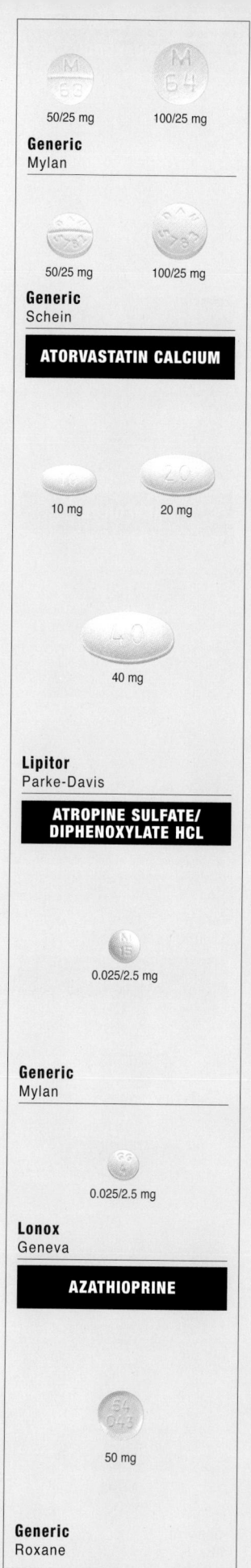

50/25 mg   **100/25 mg**

Generic
Mylan

50/25 mg   **100/25 mg**

Generic
Schein

ATORVASTATIN CALCIUM

10 mg   **20 mg**

40 mg

Lipitor
Parke-Davis

ATROPINE SULFATE/ DIPHENOXYLATE HCL

0.025/2.5 mg

Generic
Mylan

0.025/2.5 mg

Lonox
Geneva

AZATHIOPRINE

50 mg

Generic
Roxane

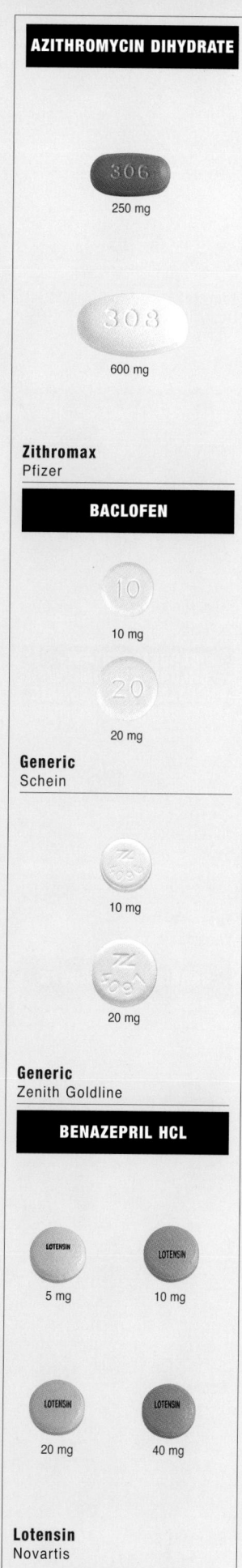

AZITHROMYCIN DIHYDRATE

250 mg

600 mg

Zithromax
Pfizer

BACLOFEN

10 mg

20 mg

Generic
Schein

10 mg

20 mg

Generic
Zenith Goldline

BENAZEPRIL HCL

5 mg   **10 mg**

20 mg   **40 mg**

Lotensin
Novartis

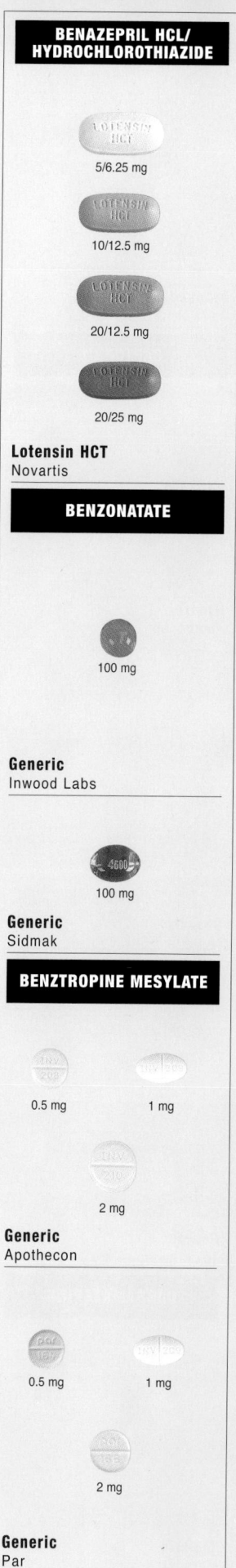

BENAZEPRIL HCL/ HYDROCHLOROTHIAZIDE

5/6.25 mg

10/12.5 mg

20/12.5 mg

20/25 mg

Lotensin HCT
Novartis

BENZONATATE

100 mg

Generic
Inwood Labs

100 mg

Generic
Sidmak

BENZTROPINE MESYLATE

0.5 mg   **1 mg**

2 mg

Generic
Apothecon

0.5 mg   **1 mg**

2 mg

Generic
Par

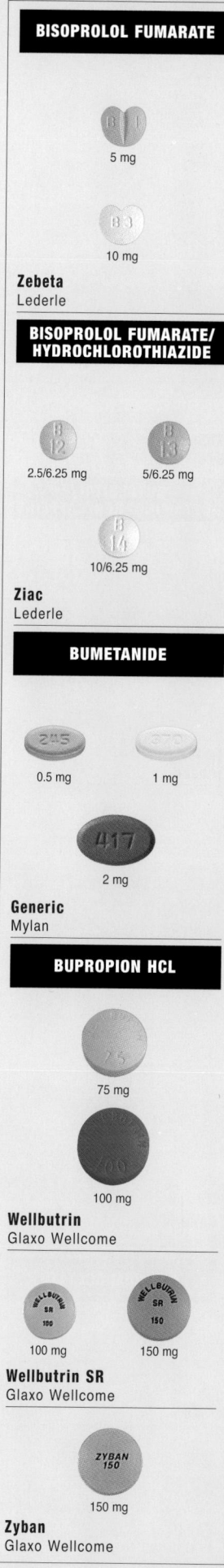

BISOPROLOL FUMARATE

5 mg

10 mg

Zebeta
Lederle

BISOPROLOL FUMARATE/ HYDROCHLOROTHIAZIDE

2.5/6.25 mg   **5/6.25 mg**

10/6.25 mg

Ziac
Lederle

BUMETANIDE

0.5 mg   **1 mg**

2 mg

Generic
Mylan

BUPROPION HCL

75 mg

100 mg

Wellbutrin
Glaxo Wellcome

100 mg   **150 mg**

Wellbutrin SR
Glaxo Wellcome

150 mg

Zyban
Glaxo Wellcome

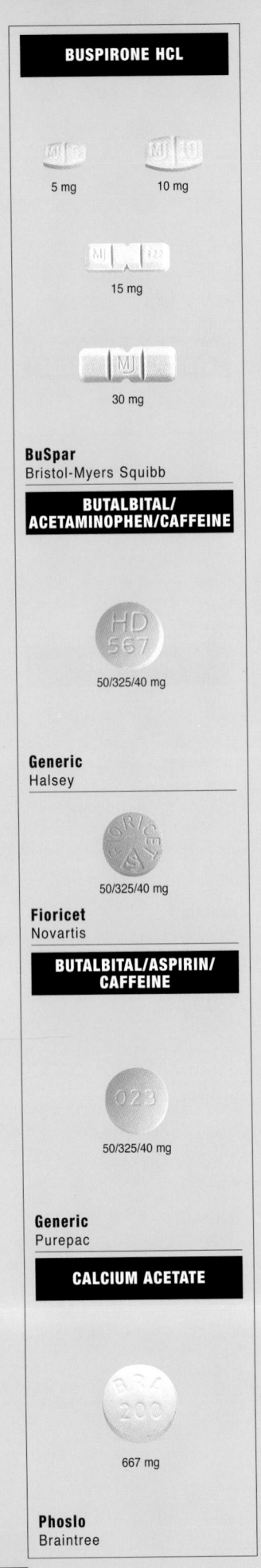
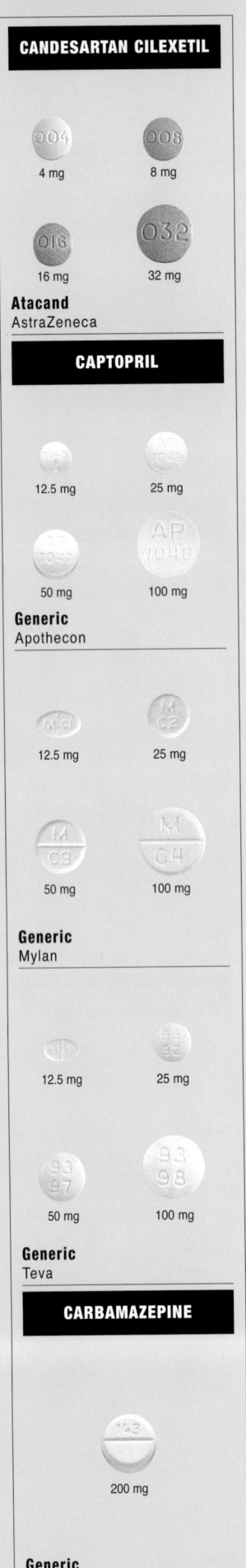
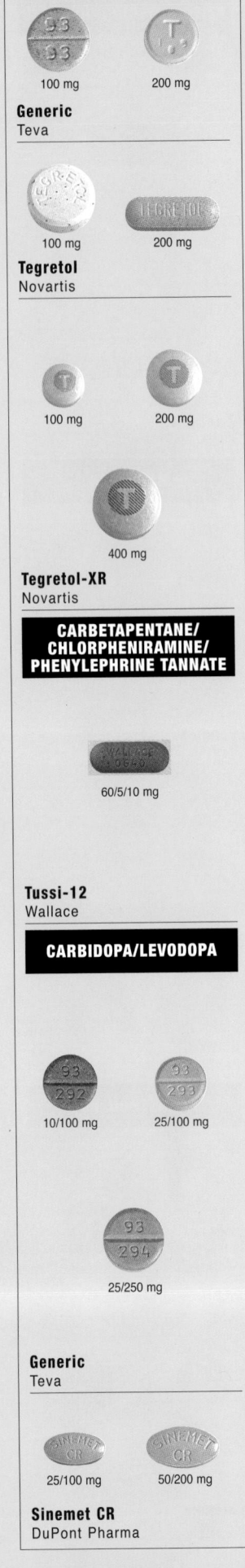
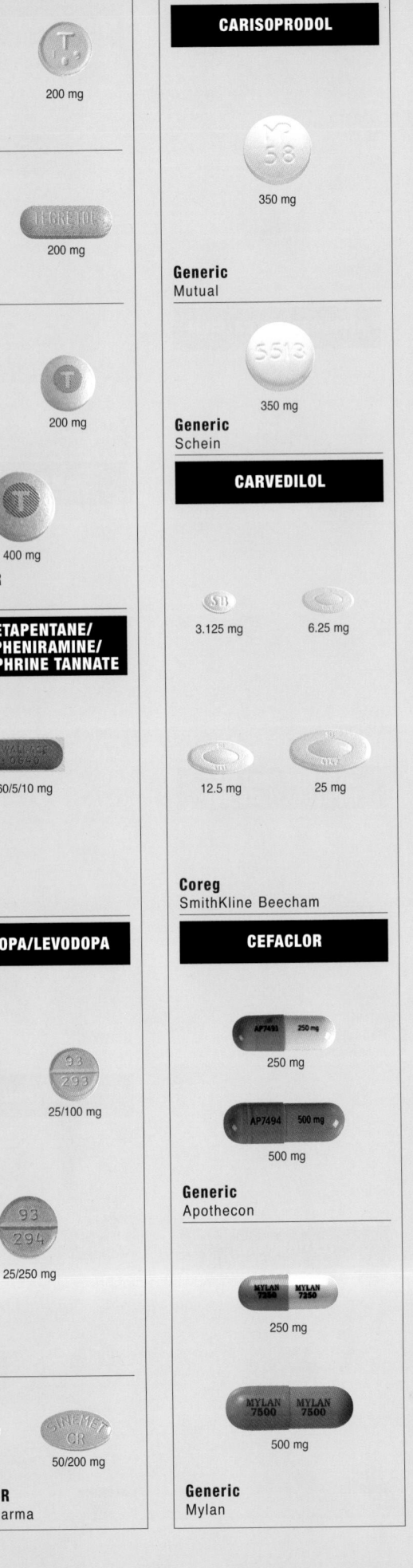

BUSPIRONE HCL

5 mg   10 mg

15 mg

30 mg

BuSpar
Bristol-Myers Squibb

BUTALBITAL/ ACETAMINOPHEN/CAFFEINE

HD 567

50/325/40 mg

Generic
Halsey

50/325/40 mg

Fioricet
Novartis

BUTALBITAL/ASPIRIN/ CAFFEINE

023

50/325/40 mg

Generic
Purepac

CALCIUM ACETATE

B.R.A 200

667 mg

Phoslo
Braintree

CANDESARTAN CILEXETIL

004   008
4 mg   8 mg

016   032
16 mg   32 mg

Atacand
AstraZeneca

CAPTOPRIL

12.5 mg   25 mg

50 mg   AP 7048
100 mg

Generic
Apothecon

M C1   M C2
12.5 mg   25 mg

M C3   M C4
50 mg   100 mg

Generic
Mylan

12.5 mg   25 mg

93 97   93 98
50 mg   100 mg

Generic
Teva

CARBAMAZEPINE

143

200 mg

Generic
Purepac

93 93   T
100 mg   200 mg

Generic
Teva

TEGRETOL   TEGRETOL
100 mg   200 mg

Tegretol
Novartis

T   T
100 mg   200 mg

T

400 mg

Tegretol-XR
Novartis

CARBETAPENTANE/ CHLORPHENIRAMINE/ PHENYLEPHRINE TANNATE

60/5/10 mg

Tussi-12
Wallace

CARBIDOPA/LEVODOPA

93 292   93 293
10/100 mg   25/100 mg

93 294

25/250 mg

Generic
Teva

SINEMET CR   SINEMET CR
25/100 mg   50/200 mg

Sinemet CR
DuPont Pharma

CARISOPRODOL

MC 58

350 mg

Generic
Mutual

5513

350 mg

Generic
Schein

CARVEDILOL

SB
3.125 mg   6.25 mg

12.5 mg   25 mg

Coreg
SmithKline Beecham

CEFACLOR

AP7491 250 mg

250 mg

AP7494 500 mg

500 mg

Generic
Apothecon

MYLAN 7250   MYLAN 7250

250 mg

MYLAN 7500   MYLAN 7500

500 mg

Generic
Mylan

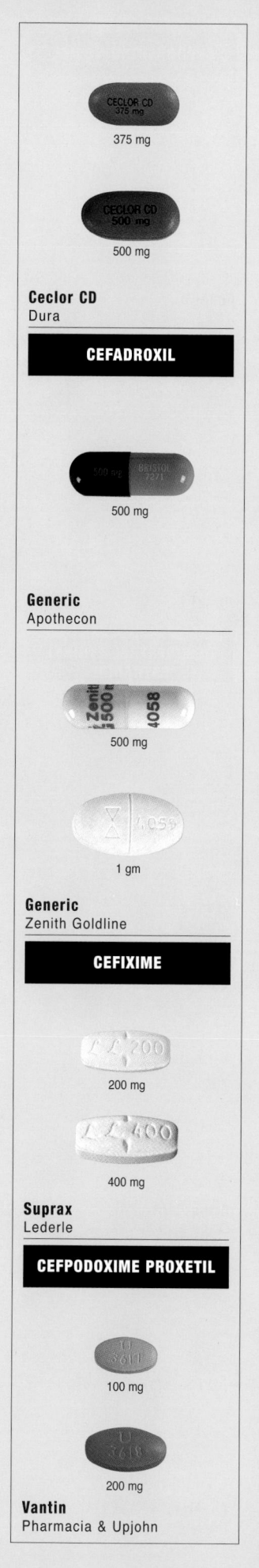
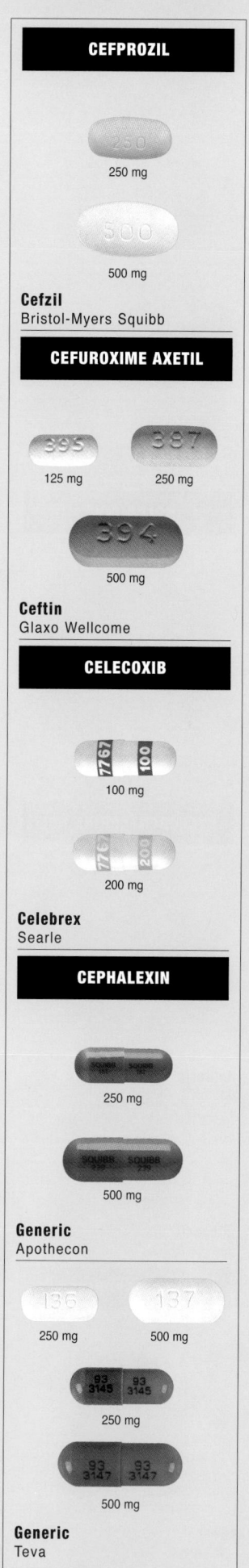
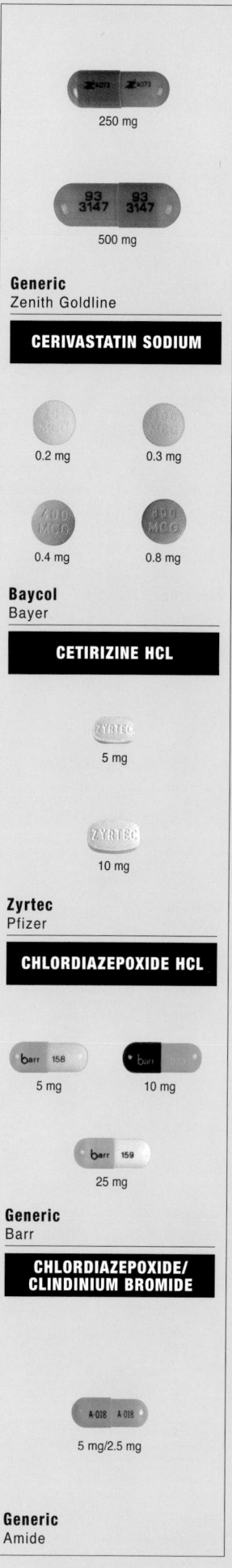
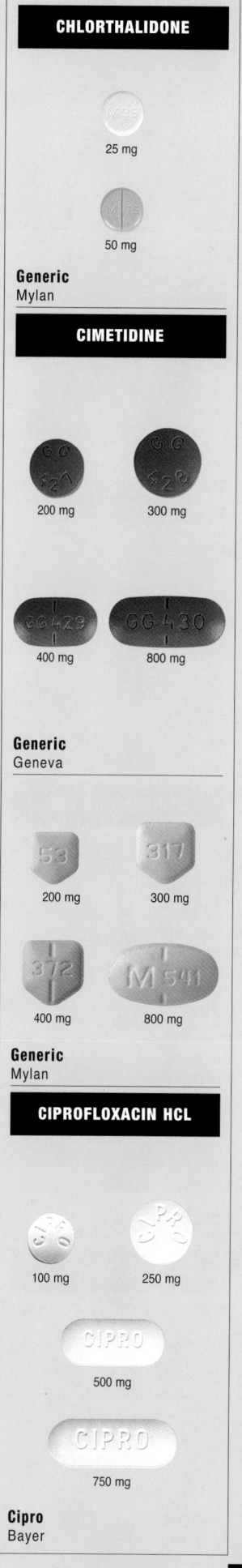

Column 1

375 mg

500 mg

Ceclor CD
Dura

CEFADROXIL

500 mg

Generic
Apothecon

500 mg

4058

1 gm

Generic
Zenith Goldline

CEFIXIME

200 mg

400 mg

Suprax
Lederle

CEFPODOXIME PROXETIL

100 mg

200 mg

Vantin
Pharmacia & Upjohn

Column 2

CEFPROZIL

250 mg

500 mg

Cefzil
Bristol-Myers Squibb

CEFUROXIME AXETIL

125 mg

250 mg

394

500 mg

Ceftin
Glaxo Wellcome

CELECOXIB

100 mg

200 mg

Celebrex
Searle

CEPHALEXIN

250 mg

500 mg

Generic
Apothecon

136   250 mg

137   500 mg

250 mg

500 mg

Generic
Teva

Column 3

250 mg

500 mg

Generic
Zenith Goldline

CERIVASTATIN SODIUM

0.2 mg

0.3 mg

0.4 mg

0.8 mg

Baycol
Bayer

CETIRIZINE HCL

5 mg

10 mg

Zyrtec
Pfizer

CHLORDIAZEPOXIDE HCL

5 mg

10 mg

25 mg

Generic
Barr

CHLORDIAZEPOXIDE/
CLINDINIUM BROMIDE

5 mg/2.5 mg

Generic
Amide

Column 4

CHLORTHALIDONE

25 mg

50 mg

Generic
Mylan

CIMETIDINE

200 mg

300 mg

400 mg

800 mg

Generic
Geneva

200 mg

300 mg

400 mg

800 mg

Generic
Mylan

CIPROFLOXACIN HCL

100 mg

250 mg

500 mg

750 mg

Cipro
Bayer

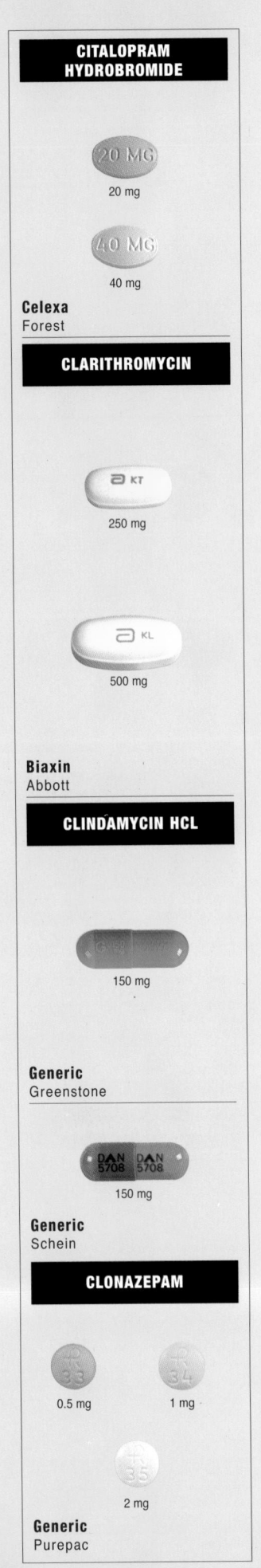

CITALOPRAM HYDROBROMIDE

20 mg

40 mg

Celexa
Forest

CLARITHROMYCIN

250 mg

500 mg

Biaxin
Abbott

CLINDAMYCIN HCL

150 mg

Generic
Greenstone

150 mg

Generic
Schein

CLONAZEPAM

0.5 mg   1 mg

2 mg

Generic
Purepac

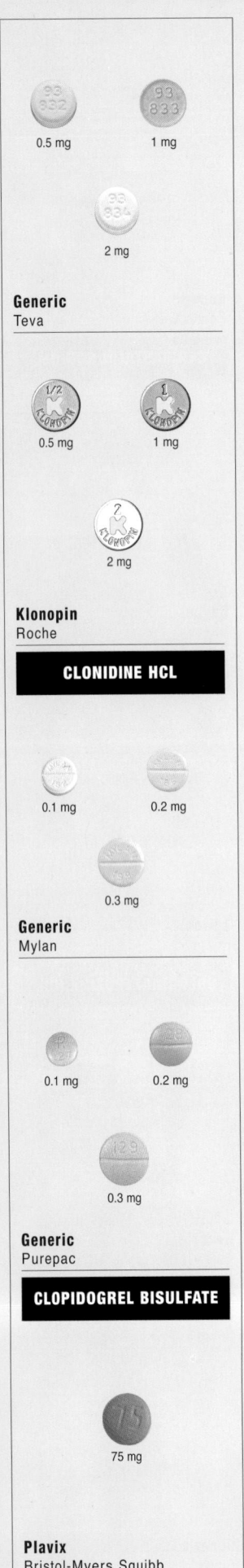

0.5 mg   1 mg

2 mg

Generic
Teva

0.5 mg   1 mg

2 mg

Klonopin
Roche

CLONIDINE HCL

0.1 mg   0.2 mg

0.3 mg

Generic
Mylan

0.1 mg   0.2 mg

0.3 mg

Generic
Purepac

CLOPIDOGREL BISULFATE

75 mg

Plavix
Bristol-Myers Squibb

CLORAZEPATE DIPOTASSIUM

3.75 mg   7.5 mg

15 mg

Generic
Mylan

COLCHICINE

0.6 mg

Generic
Schein

CYCLOBENZAPRINE HCL

10 mg

Generic
Mylan

10 mg

Flexeril
Merck & Co.

CYCLOSPORINE

25 mg

100 mg

Neoral
Novartis

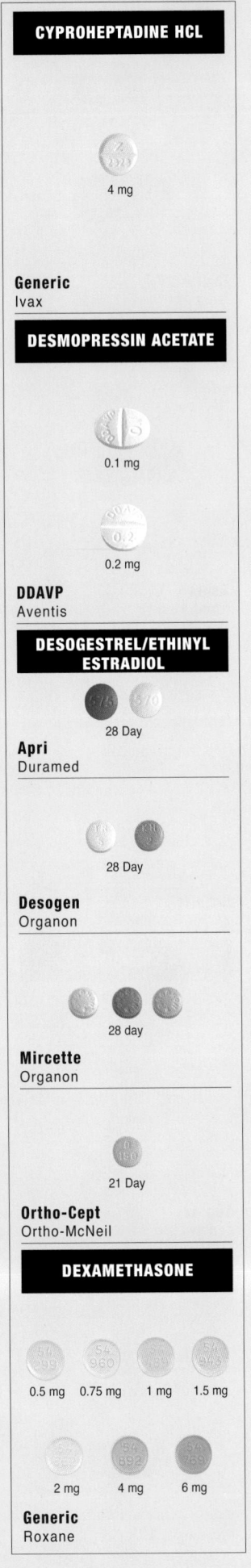

CYPROHEPTADINE HCL

4 mg

Generic
Ivax

DESMOPRESSIN ACETATE

0.1 mg

0.2 mg

DDAVP
Aventis

DESOGESTREL/ETHINYL ESTRADIOL

28 Day

Apri
Duramed

28 Day

Desogen
Organon

28 day

Mircette
Organon

21 Day

Ortho-Cept
Ortho-McNeil

DEXAMETHASONE

0.5 mg   0.75 mg   1 mg   1.5 mg

2 mg   4 mg   6 mg

Generic
Roxane

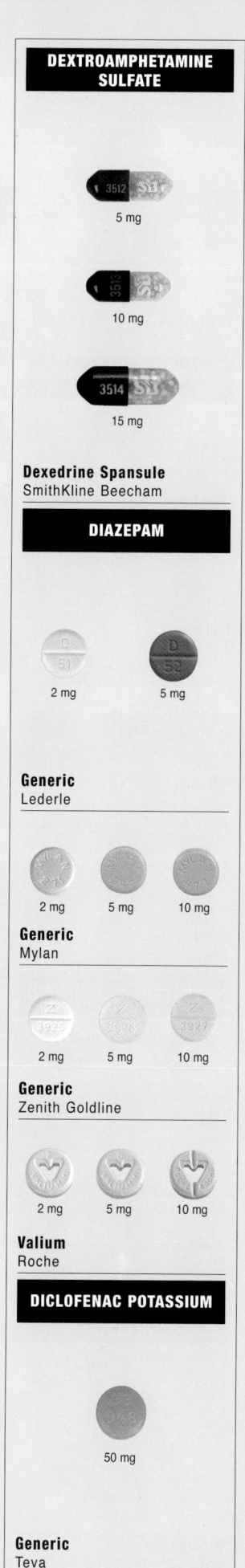

DEXTROAMPHETAMINE SULFATE

5 mg

10 mg

15 mg

Dexedrine Spansule
SmithKline Beecham

DIAZEPAM

2 mg — 5 mg

Generic
Lederle

2 mg — 5 mg — 10 mg

Generic
Mylan

2 mg — 5 mg — 10 mg

Generic
Zenith Goldline

2 mg — 5 mg — 10 mg

Valium
Roche

DICLOFENAC POTASSIUM

50 mg

Generic
Teva

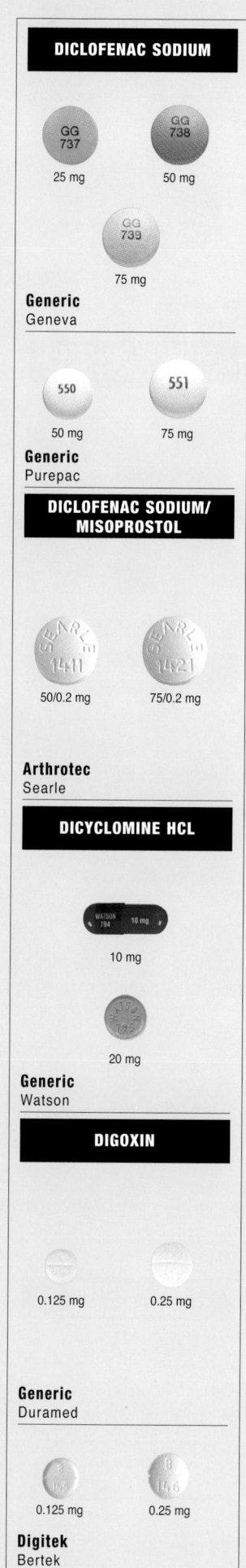

DICLOFENAC SODIUM

GG 737 — 25 mg

GG 738 — 50 mg

GG 739 — 75 mg

Generic
Geneva

550 — 50 mg

551 — 75 mg

Generic
Purepac

DICLOFENAC SODIUM/ MISOPROSTOL

SEARLE 1411 — 50/0.2 mg

SEARLE 1421 — 75/0.2 mg

Arthrotec
Searle

DICYCLOMINE HCL

WATSON 794 — 10 mg

WATSON 795 — 20 mg

Generic
Watson

DIGOXIN

0.125 mg — 0.25 mg

Generic
Duramed

0.125 mg — 0.25 mg

Digitek
Bertek

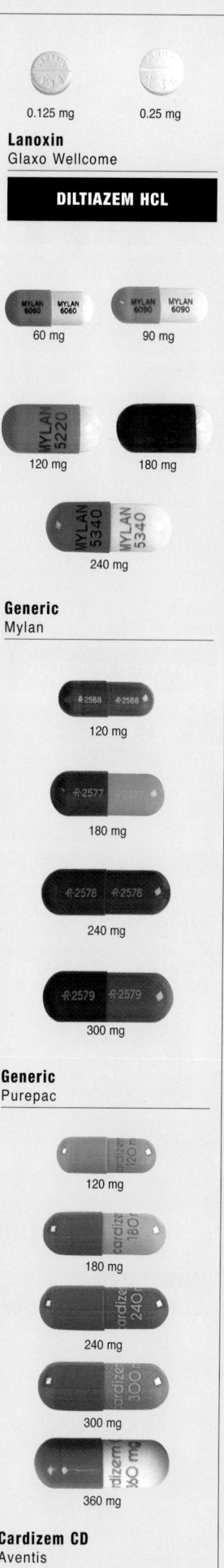

0.125 mg — 0.25 mg

Lanoxin
Glaxo Wellcome

DILTIAZEM HCL

MYLAN 6060 — 60 mg

MYLAN 6090 — 90 mg

MYLAN 5220 — 120 mg

180 mg

MYLAN 5340 — 240 mg

Generic
Mylan

R-2588 — 120 mg

R-2577 — 180 mg

R-2578 — 240 mg

R-2579 — 300 mg

Generic
Purepac

120 mg

180 mg

240 mg

300 mg

360 mg

Cardizem CD
Aventis

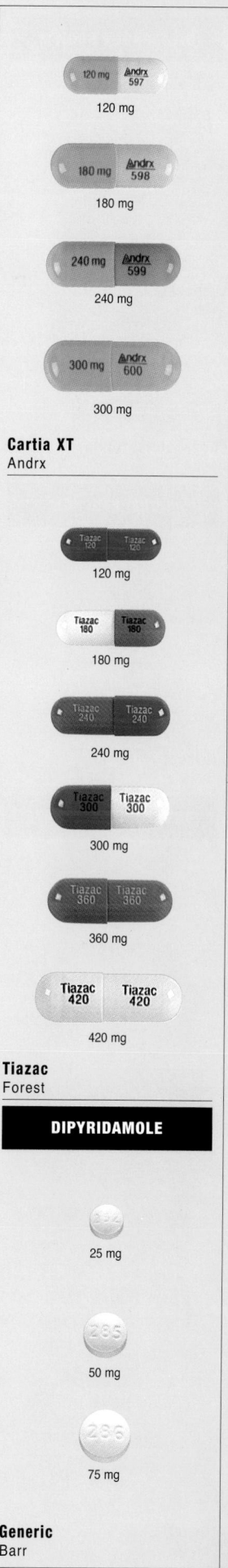

120 mg — Andrx 597

180 mg — Andrx 598

240 mg — Andrx 599

300 mg — Andrx 600

Cartia XT
Andrx

Tiazac 120 — 120 mg

Tiazac 180 — 180 mg

Tiazac 240 — 240 mg

Tiazac 300 — 300 mg

Tiazac 360 — 360 mg

Tiazac 420 — 420 mg

Tiazac
Forest

DIPYRIDAMOLE

25 mg

50 mg

75 mg

Generic
Barr

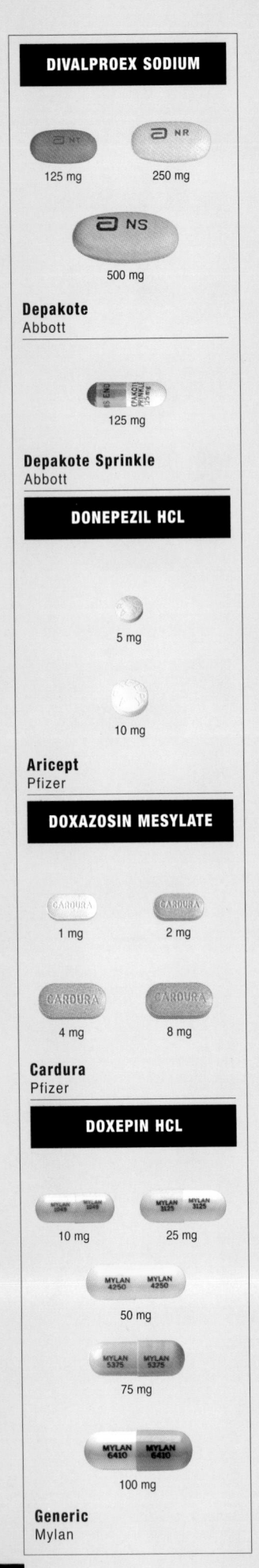

DIVALPROEX SODIUM

125 mg   250 mg

500 mg

Depakote
Abbott

125 mg

Depakote Sprinkle
Abbott

DONEPEZIL HCL

5 mg

10 mg

Aricept
Pfizer

DOXAZOSIN MESYLATE

1 mg   2 mg

4 mg   8 mg

Cardura
Pfizer

DOXEPIN HCL

10 mg   25 mg

50 mg

75 mg

100 mg

Generic
Mylan

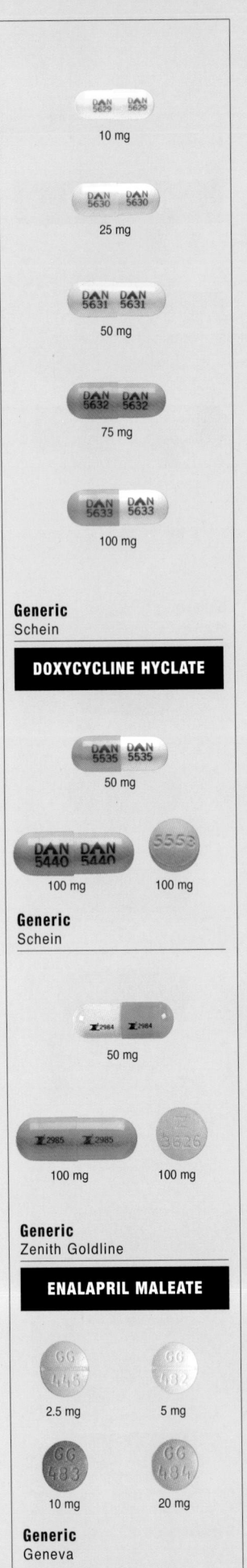

10 mg

25 mg

50 mg

75 mg

100 mg

Generic
Schein

DOXYCYCLINE HYCLATE

50 mg

100 mg   100 mg

Generic
Schein

50 mg

100 mg   100 mg

Generic
Zenith Goldline

ENALAPRIL MALEATE

2.5 mg   5 mg

10 mg   20 mg

Generic
Geneva

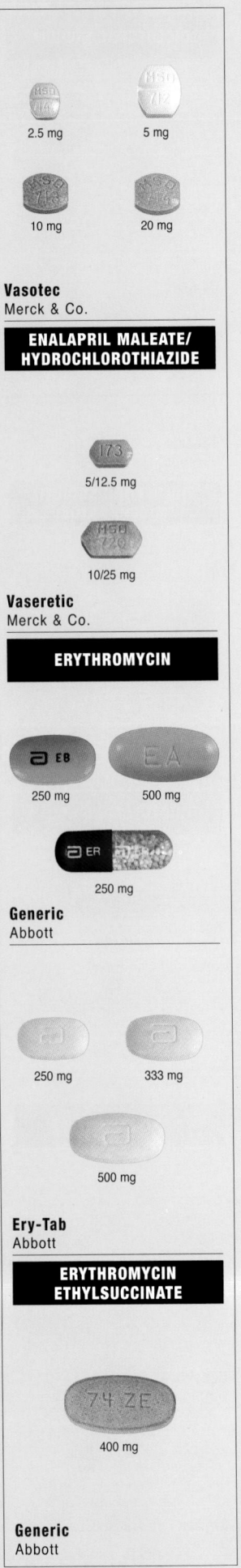

2.5 mg   5 mg

10 mg   20 mg

Vasotec
Merck & Co.

ENALAPRIL MALEATE/ HYDROCHLOROTHIAZIDE

5/12.5 mg

10/25 mg

Vaseretic
Merck & Co.

ERYTHROMYCIN

250 mg   500 mg

250 mg

Generic
Abbott

250 mg   333 mg

500 mg

Ery-Tab
Abbott

ERYTHROMYCIN ETHYLSUCCINATE

400 mg

Generic
Abbott

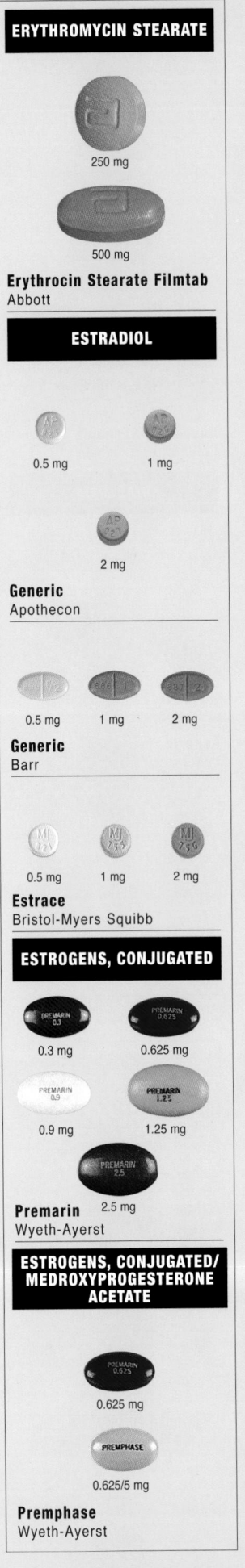

ERYTHROMYCIN STEARATE

250 mg

500 mg

Erythrocin Stearate Filmtab
Abbott

ESTRADIOL

0.5 mg   1 mg

2 mg

Generic
Apothecon

0.5 mg   1 mg   2 mg

Generic
Barr

0.5 mg   1 mg   2 mg

Estrace
Bristol-Myers Squibb

ESTROGENS, CONJUGATED

0.3 mg   0.625 mg

0.9 mg   1.25 mg

2.5 mg

Premarin
Wyeth-Ayerst

ESTROGENS, CONJUGATED/ MEDROXYPROGESTERONE ACETATE

0.625 mg

0.625/5 mg

Premphase
Wyeth-Ayerst

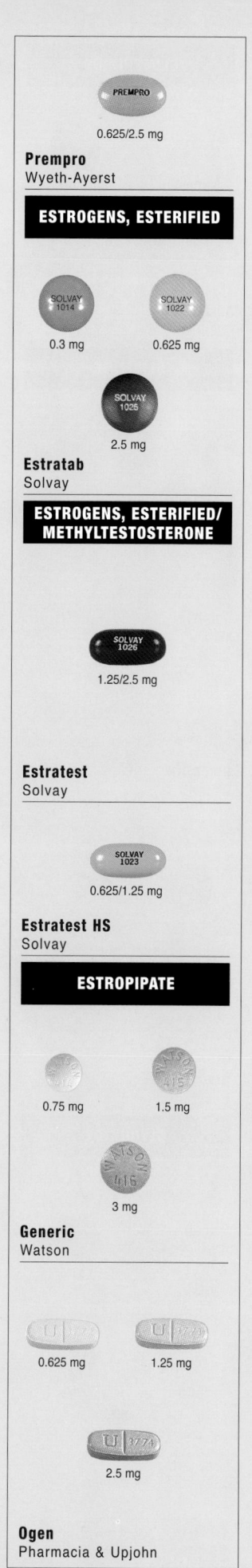

Prempro
Wyeth-Ayerst

ESTROGENS, ESTERIFIED

0.3 mg 0.625 mg

2.5 mg

Estratab
Solvay

ESTROGENS, ESTERIFIED/ METHYLTESTOSTERONE

1.25/2.5 mg

Estratest
Solvay

0.625/1.25 mg

Estratest HS
Solvay

ESTROPIPATE

0.75 mg 1.5 mg

3 mg

Generic
Watson

0.625 mg 1.25 mg

2.5 mg

Ogen
Pharmacia & Upjohn

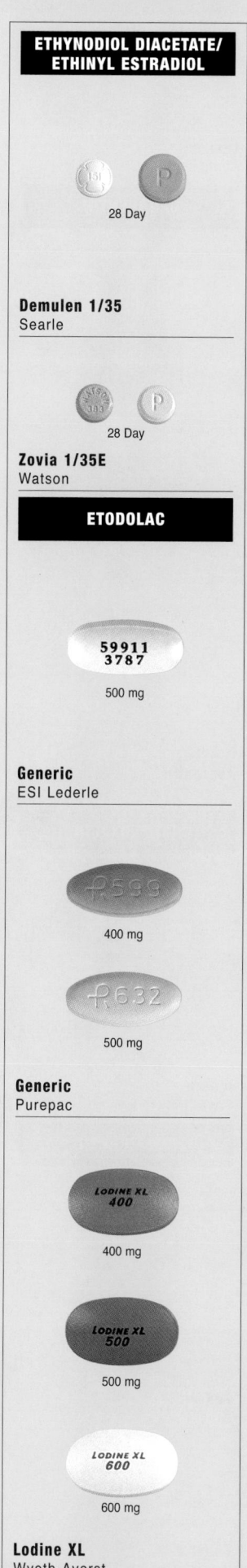

ETHYNODIOL DIACETATE/ ETHINYL ESTRADIOL

28 Day

Demulen 1/35
Searle

28 Day

Zovia 1/35E
Watson

ETODOLAC

500 mg

Generic
ESI Lederle

400 mg

500 mg

Generic
Purepac

LODINE XL 400 400 mg

LODINE XL 500 500 mg

LODINE XL 600 600 mg

Lodine XL
Wyeth-Ayerst

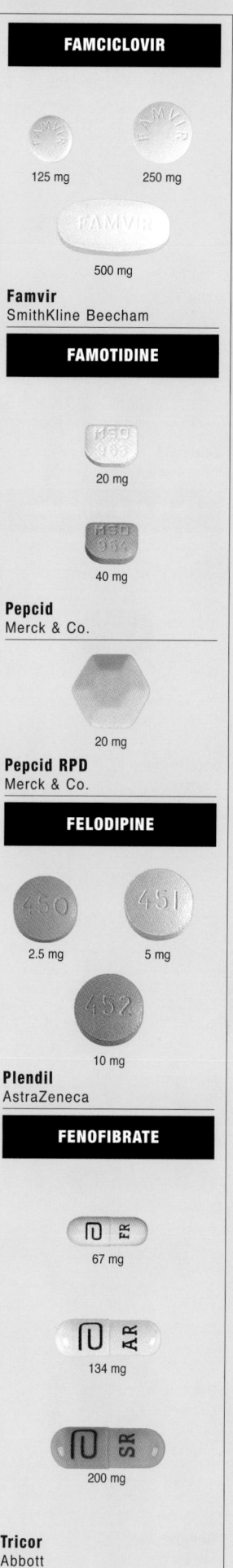

FAMCICLOVIR

125 mg 250 mg

FAMVIR 500 mg

Famvir
SmithKline Beecham

FAMOTIDINE

20 mg

40 mg

Pepcid
Merck & Co.

20 mg

Pepcid RPD
Merck & Co.

FELODIPINE

2.5 mg 5 mg

452 10 mg

Plendil
AstraZeneca

FENOFIBRATE

67 mg

134 mg

200 mg

Tricor
Abbott

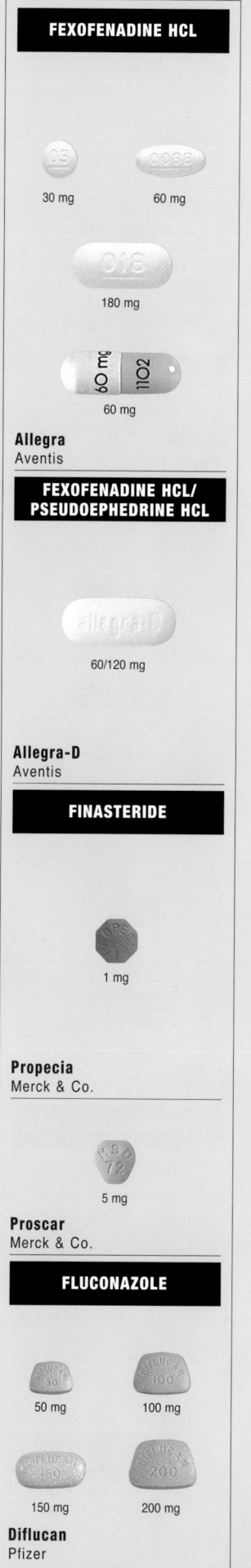

FEXOFENADINE HCL

30 mg 60 mg

180 mg

60 mg

Allegra
Aventis

FEXOFENADINE HCL/ PSEUDOEPHEDRINE HCL

60/120 mg

Allegra-D
Aventis

FINASTERIDE

1 mg

Propecia
Merck & Co.

5 mg

Proscar
Merck & Co.

FLUCONAZOLE

50 mg 100 mg

150 mg 200 mg

Diflucan
Pfizer

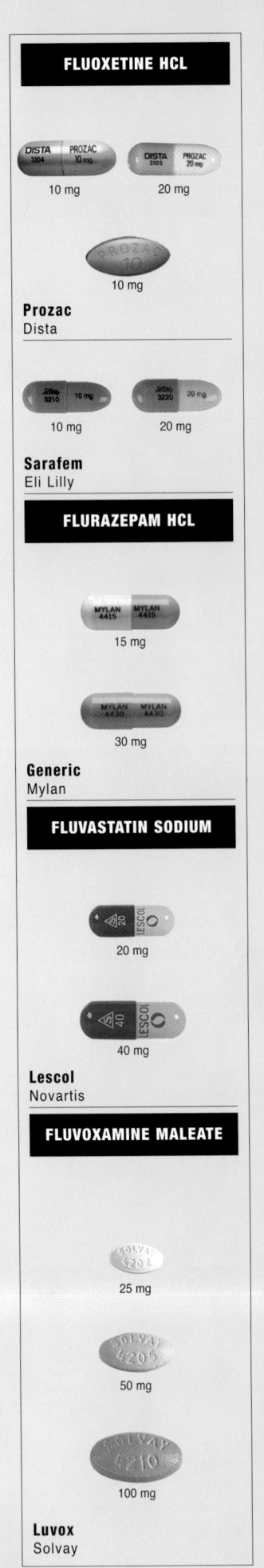

FLUOXETINE HCL

10 mg   20 mg

10 mg

Prozac
Dista

10 mg   20 mg

Sarafem
Eli Lilly

FLURAZEPAM HCL

15 mg

30 mg

Generic
Mylan

FLUVASTATIN SODIUM

20 mg

40 mg

Lescol
Novartis

FLUVOXAMINE MALEATE

25 mg

50 mg

100 mg

Luvox
Solvay

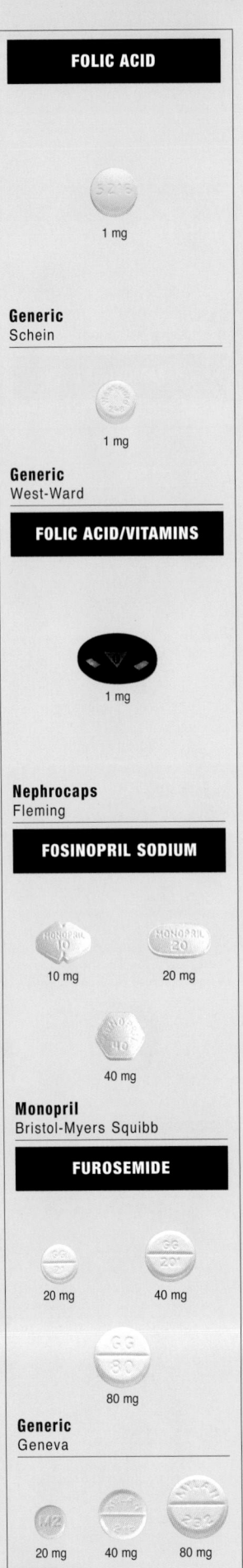

FOLIC ACID

1 mg

Generic
Schein

1 mg

Generic
West-Ward

FOLIC ACID/VITAMINS

1 mg

Nephrocaps
Fleming

FOSINOPRIL SODIUM

10 mg   20 mg

40 mg

Monopril
Bristol-Myers Squibb

FUROSEMIDE

20 mg   40 mg

80 mg

Generic
Geneva

20 mg   40 mg   80 mg

Generic
Mylan

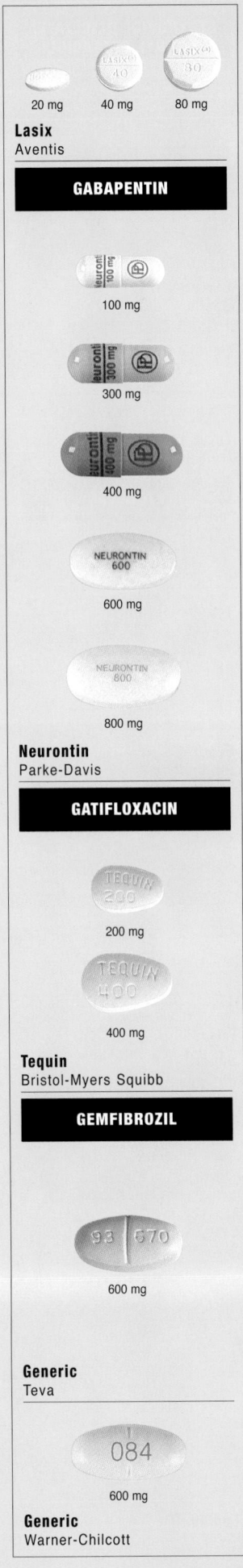

20 mg   40 mg   80 mg

Lasix
Aventis

GABAPENTIN

100 mg

300 mg

400 mg

600 mg

800 mg

Neurontin
Parke-Davis

GATIFLOXACIN

200 mg

400 mg

Tequin
Bristol-Myers Squibb

GEMFIBROZIL

600 mg

Generic
Teva

600 mg

Generic
Warner-Chilcott

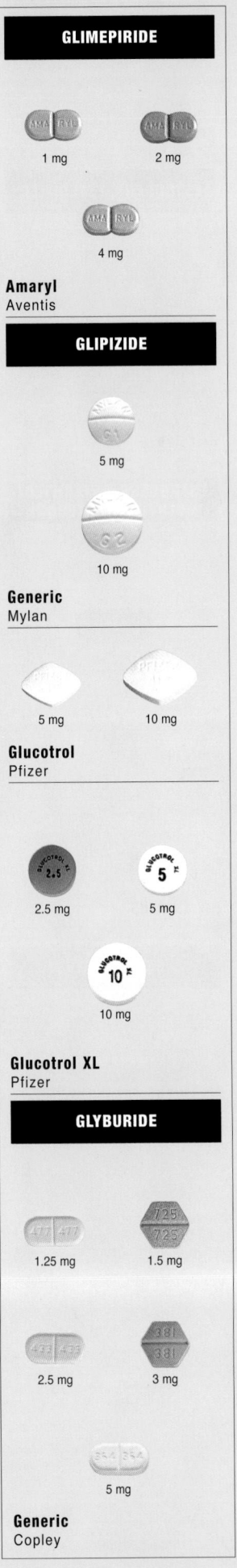

GLIMEPIRIDE

1 mg   2 mg

4 mg

Amaryl
Aventis

GLIPIZIDE

5 mg

10 mg

Generic
Mylan

5 mg   10 mg

Glucotrol
Pfizer

2.5 mg   5 mg

10 mg

Glucotrol XL
Pfizer

GLYBURIDE

1.25 mg   1.5 mg

2.5 mg   3 mg

5 mg

Generic
Copley

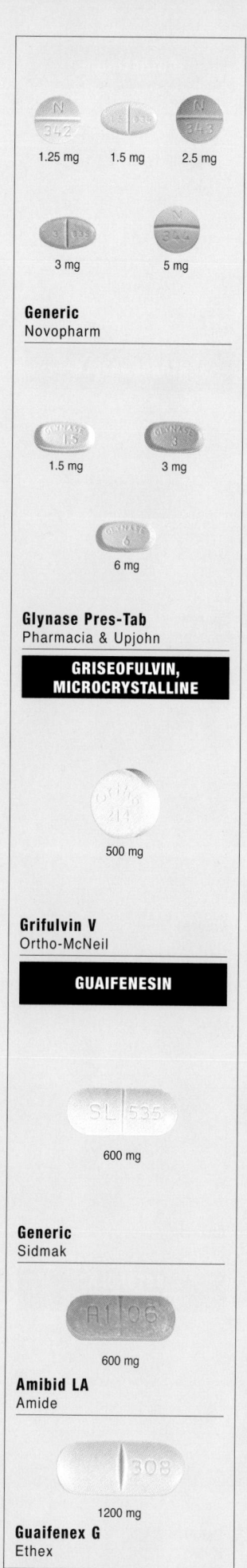

1.25 mg | **1.5 mg** | **2.5 mg**

3 mg | **5 mg**

Generic
Novopharm

1.5 mg | **3 mg**

6 mg

Glynase Pres-Tab
Pharmacia & Upjohn

GRISEOFULVIN, MICROCRYSTALLINE

500 mg

Grifulvin V
Ortho-McNeil

GUAIFENESIN

600 mg

Generic
Sidmak

600 mg

Amibid LA
Amide

1200 mg

Guaifenex G
Ethex

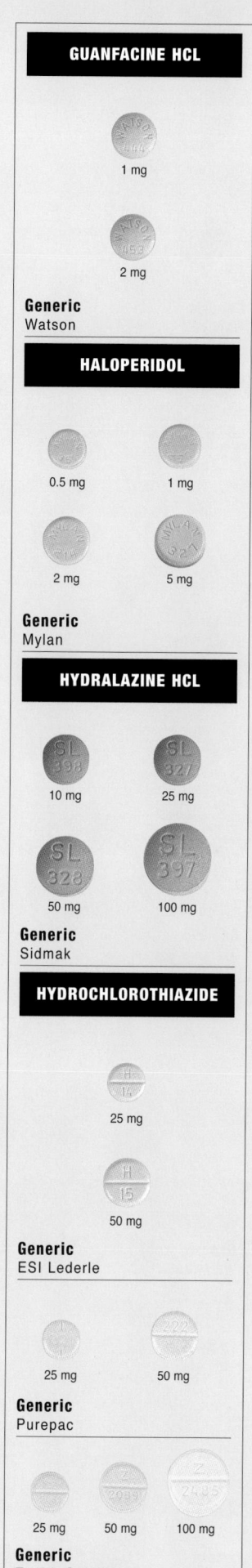

GUANFACINE HCL

1 mg

2 mg

Generic
Watson

HALOPERIDOL

0.5 mg | **1 mg**

2 mg | **5 mg**

Generic
Mylan

HYDRALAZINE HCL

10 mg | **25 mg**

50 mg | **100 mg**

Generic
Sidmak

HYDROCHLOROTHIAZIDE

25 mg

50 mg

Generic
ESI Lederle

25 mg | **50 mg**

Generic
Purepac

25 mg | **50 mg** | **100 mg**

Generic
Zenith Goldline

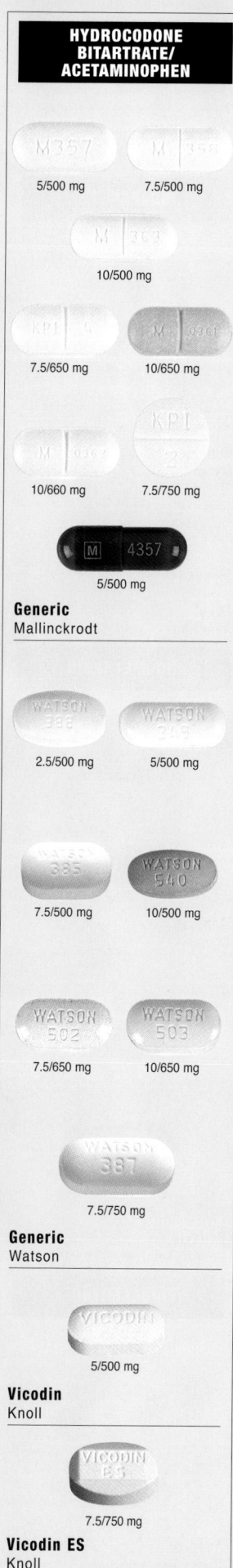

HYDROCODONE BITARTRATE/ ACETAMINOPHEN

5/500 mg | **7.5/500 mg**

10/500 mg

7.5/650 mg | **10/650 mg**

10/660 mg | **7.5/750 mg**

5/500 mg

Generic
Mallinckrodt

2.5/500 mg | **5/500 mg**

7.5/500 mg | **10/500 mg**

7.5/650 mg | **10/650 mg**

7.5/750 mg

Generic
Watson

5/500 mg

Vicodin
Knoll

7.5/750 mg

Vicodin ES
Knoll

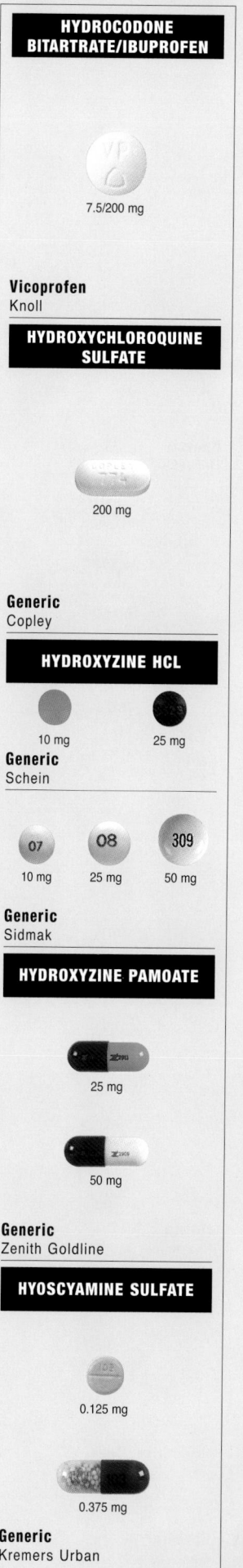

HYDROCODONE BITARTRATE/IBUPROFEN

7.5/200 mg

Vicoprofen
Knoll

HYDROXYCHLOROQUINE SULFATE

200 mg

Generic
Copley

HYDROXYZINE HCL

10 mg | **25 mg**

Generic
Schein

10 mg | **25 mg** | **50 mg**

Generic
Sidmak

HYDROXYZINE PAMOATE

25 mg

50 mg

Generic
Zenith Goldline

HYOSCYAMINE SULFATE

0.125 mg

0.375 mg

Generic
Kremers Urban

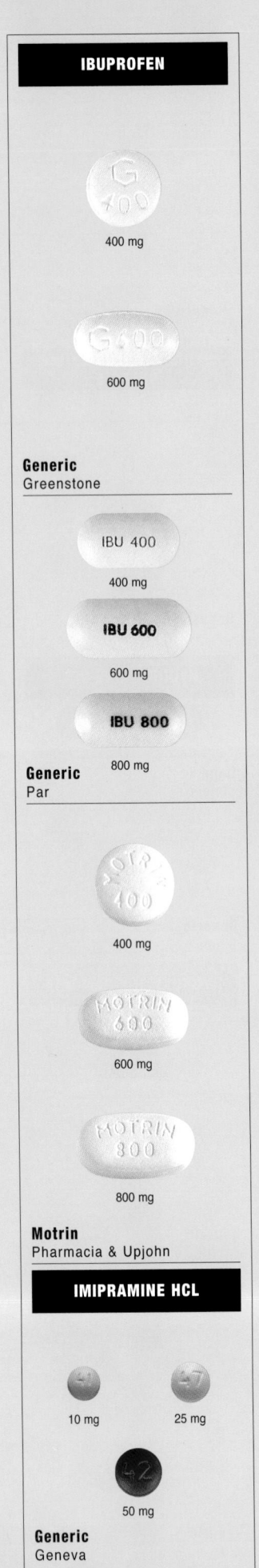

IBUPROFEN

400 mg

600 mg

Generic
Greenstone

IBU 400
400 mg

IBU 600
600 mg

IBU 800
800 mg

Generic
Par

MOTRIN 400
400 mg

MOTRIN 600
600 mg

MOTRIN 800
800 mg

Motrin
Pharmacia & Upjohn

IMIPRAMINE HCL

10 mg   25 mg

50 mg

Generic
Geneva

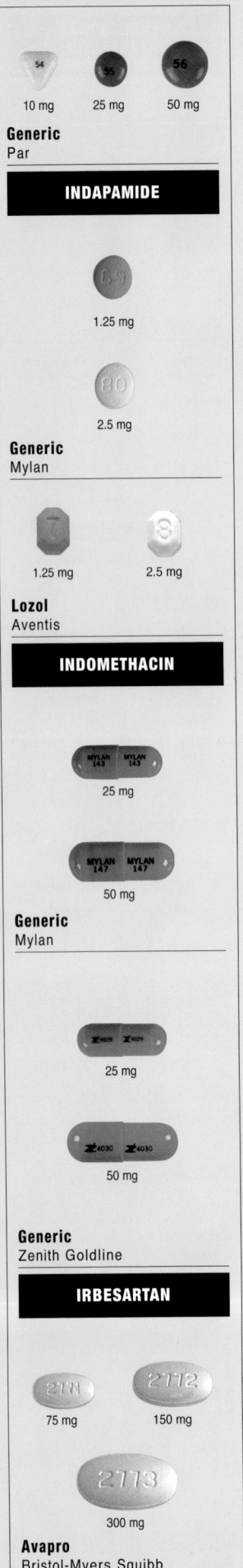

54 10 mg   55 25 mg   56 50 mg

Generic
Par

INDAPAMIDE

1.25 mg

2.5 mg

Generic
Mylan

1.25 mg   2.5 mg

Lozol
Aventis

INDOMETHACIN

MYLAN 143 MYLAN 143
25 mg

MYLAN 147 MYLAN 147
50 mg

Generic
Mylan

25 mg

50 mg

Generic
Zenith Goldline

IRBESARTAN

2871 75 mg   2772 150 mg

2773 300 mg

Avapro
Bristol-Myers Squibb

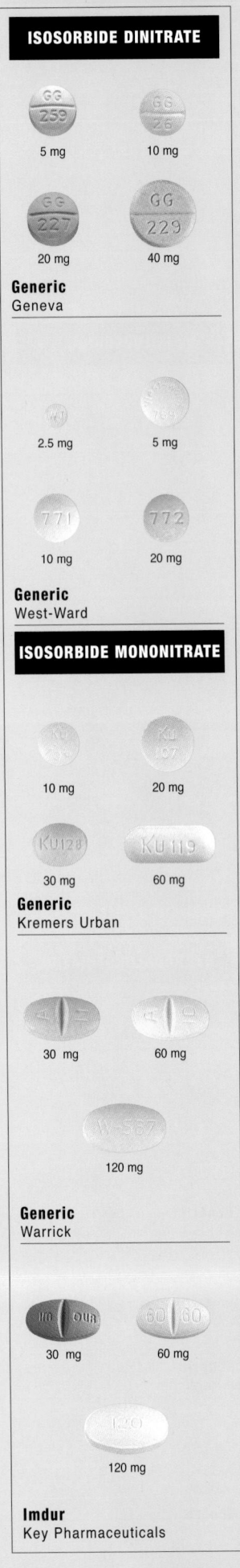

ISOSORBIDE DINITRATE

GG 259 5 mg   GG 26 10 mg

GG 227 20 mg   GG 229 40 mg

Generic
Geneva

2.5 mg   5 mg

771 10 mg   772 20 mg

Generic
West-Ward

ISOSORBIDE MONONITRATE

KU 10 mg   KU 107 20 mg

KU128 30 mg   KU119 60 mg

Generic
Kremers Urban

30 mg   60 mg

N-567
120 mg

Generic
Warrick

IM OUR 30 mg   60 60 60 mg

120
120 mg

Imdur
Key Pharmaceuticals

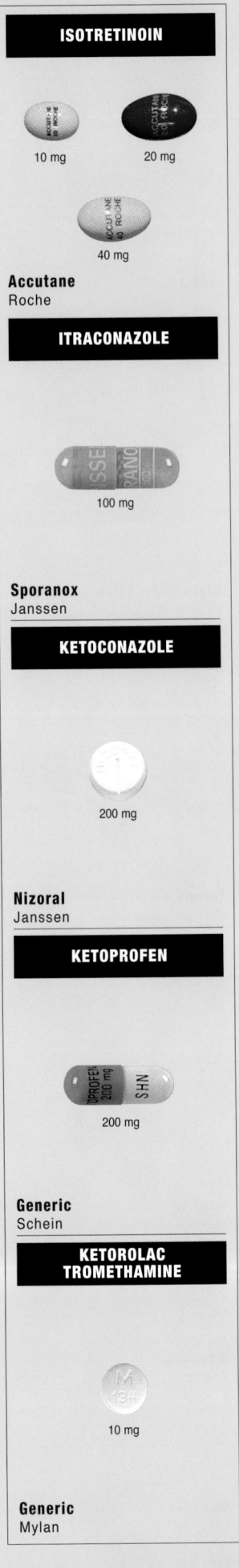

ISOTRETINOIN

10 mg   20 mg

40 mg

Accutane
Roche

ITRACONAZOLE

ISSE PANO
100 mg

Sporanox
Janssen

KETOCONAZOLE

200 mg

Nizoral
Janssen

KETOPROFEN

OPROFEN 200 mg SHN
200 mg

Generic
Schein

KETOROLAC TROMETHAMINE

M 134
10 mg

Generic
Mylan

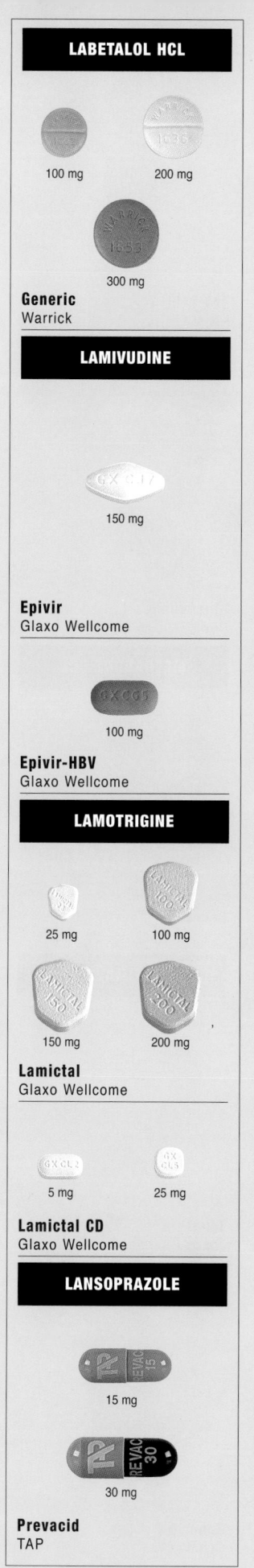

LABETALOL HCL

100 mg   200 mg

300 mg

Generic
Warrick

LAMIVUDINE

150 mg

Epivir
Glaxo Wellcome

100 mg

Epivir-HBV
Glaxo Wellcome

LAMOTRIGINE

25 mg   100 mg

150 mg   200 mg

Lamictal
Glaxo Wellcome

5 mg   25 mg

Lamictal CD
Glaxo Wellcome

LANSOPRAZOLE

15 mg

30 mg

Prevacid
TAP

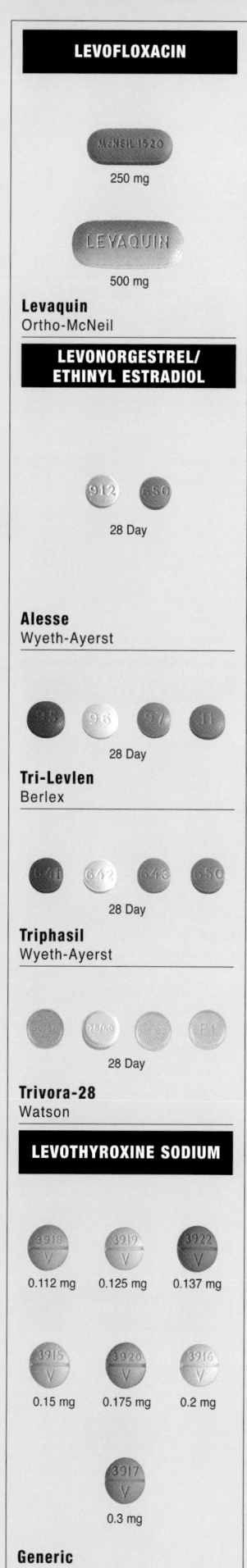

LEVOFLOXACIN

250 mg

500 mg

Levaquin
Ortho-McNeil

LEVONORGESTREL/ ETHINYL ESTRADIOL

28 Day

Alesse
Wyeth-Ayerst

28 Day

Tri-Levlen
Berlex

28 Day

Triphasil
Wyeth-Ayerst

28 Day

Trivora-28
Watson

LEVOTHYROXINE SODIUM

0.112 mg   0.125 mg   0.137 mg

0.15 mg   0.175 mg   0.2 mg

0.3 mg

Generic
Qualitest

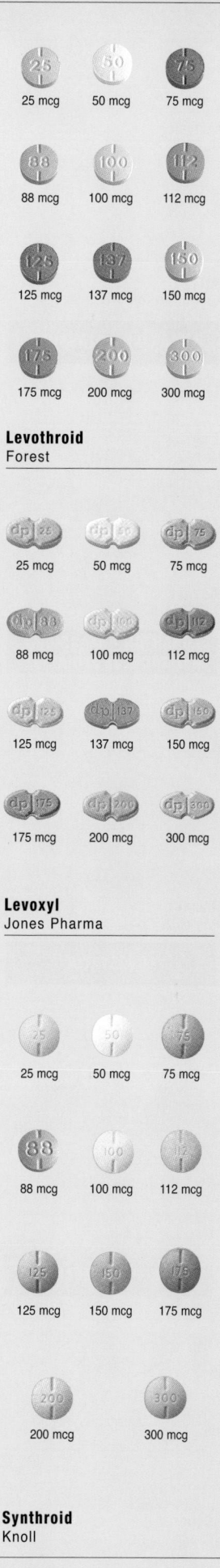

25 mcg   50 mcg   75 mcg

88 mcg   100 mcg   112 mcg

125 mcg   137 mcg   150 mcg

175 mcg   200 mcg   300 mcg

Levothroid
Forest

25 mcg   50 mcg   75 mcg

88 mcg   100 mcg   112 mcg

125 mcg   137 mcg   150 mcg

175 mcg   200 mcg   300 mcg

Levoxyl
Jones Pharma

25 mcg   50 mcg   75 mcg

88 mcg   100 mcg   112 mcg

125 mcg   150 mcg   175 mcg

200 mcg   300 mcg

Synthroid
Knoll

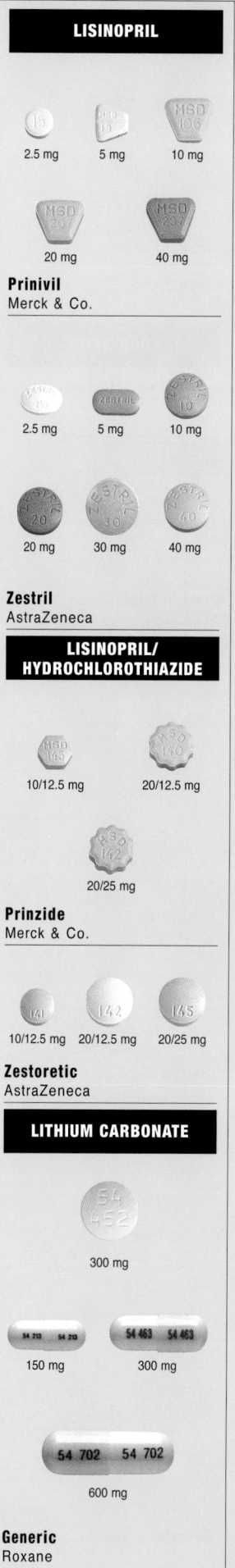

LISINOPRIL

2.5 mg   5 mg   10 mg

20 mg   40 mg

Prinivil
Merck & Co.

2.5 mg   5 mg   10 mg

20 mg   30 mg   40 mg

Zestril
AstraZeneca

LISINOPRIL/ HYDROCHLOROTHIAZIDE

10/12.5 mg   20/12.5 mg

20/25 mg

Prinzide
Merck & Co.

10/12.5 mg   20/12.5 mg   20/25 mg

Zestoretic
AstraZeneca

LITHIUM CARBONATE

300 mg

150 mg   300 mg

600 mg

Generic
Roxane

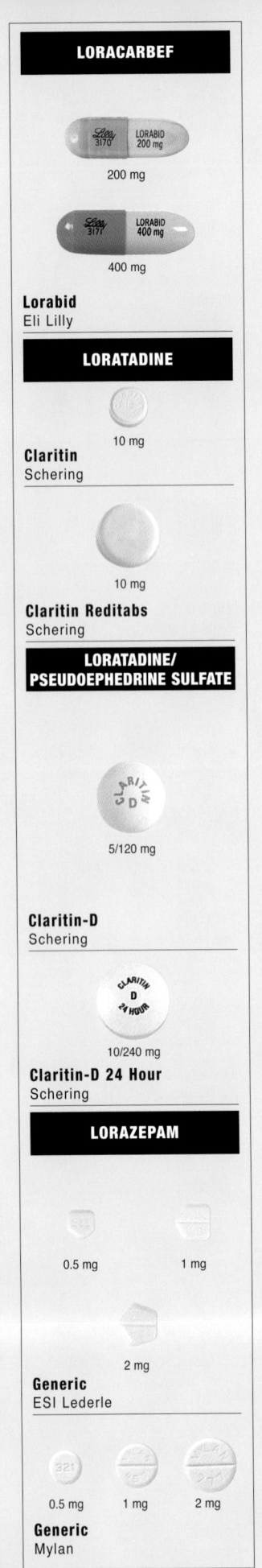

LORACARBEF

200 mg

400 mg

Lorabid
Eli Lilly

LORATADINE

10 mg

Claritin
Schering

10 mg

Claritin Reditabs
Schering

LORATADINE/ PSEUDOEPHEDRINE SULFATE

5/120 mg

Claritin-D
Schering

10/240 mg

Claritin-D 24 Hour
Schering

LORAZEPAM

0.5 mg   1 mg

2 mg

Generic
ESI Lederle

0.5 mg   1 mg   2 mg

Generic
Mylan

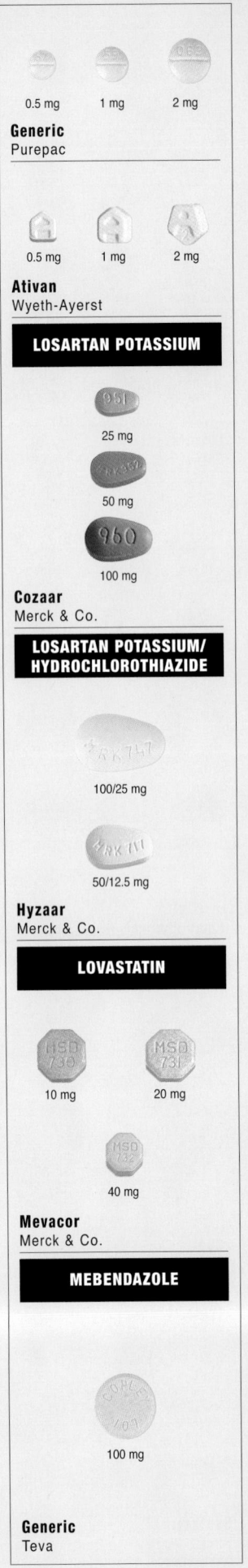

0.5 mg   1 mg   2 mg

Generic
Purepac

0.5 mg   1 mg   2 mg

Ativan
Wyeth-Ayerst

LOSARTAN POTASSIUM

25 mg

50 mg

100 mg

Cozaar
Merck & Co.

LOSARTAN POTASSIUM/ HYDROCHLOROTHIAZIDE

100/25 mg

50/12.5 mg

Hyzaar
Merck & Co.

LOVASTATIN

10 mg   20 mg

40 mg

Mevacor
Merck & Co.

MEBENDAZOLE

100 mg

Generic
Teva

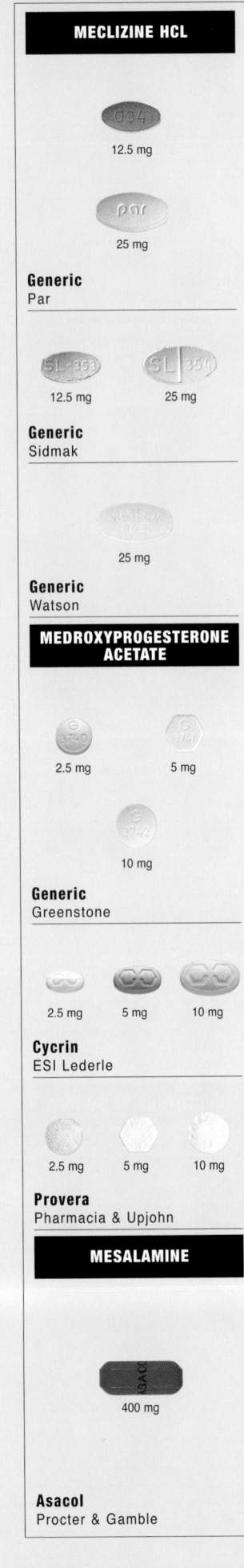

MECLIZINE HCL

12.5 mg

25 mg

Generic
Par

12.5 mg   25 mg

Generic
Sidmak

25 mg

Generic
Watson

MEDROXYPROGESTERONE ACETATE

2.5 mg   5 mg

10 mg

Generic
Greenstone

2.5 mg   5 mg   10 mg

Cycrin
ESI Lederle

2.5 mg   5 mg   10 mg

Provera
Pharmacia & Upjohn

MESALAMINE

400 mg

Asacol
Procter & Gamble

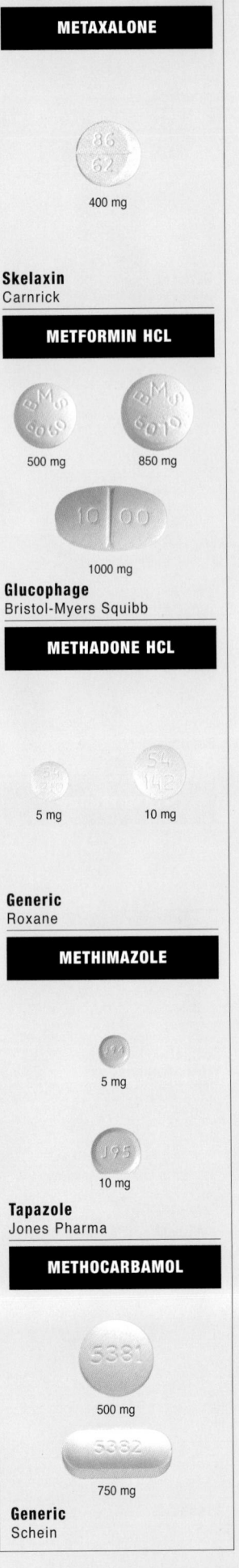

METAXALONE

400 mg

Skelaxin
Carnrick

METFORMIN HCL

500 mg   850 mg

1000 mg

Glucophage
Bristol-Myers Squibb

METHADONE HCL

5 mg   10 mg

Generic
Roxane

METHIMAZOLE

5 mg

10 mg

Tapazole
Jones Pharma

METHOCARBAMOL

500 mg

750 mg

Generic
Schein

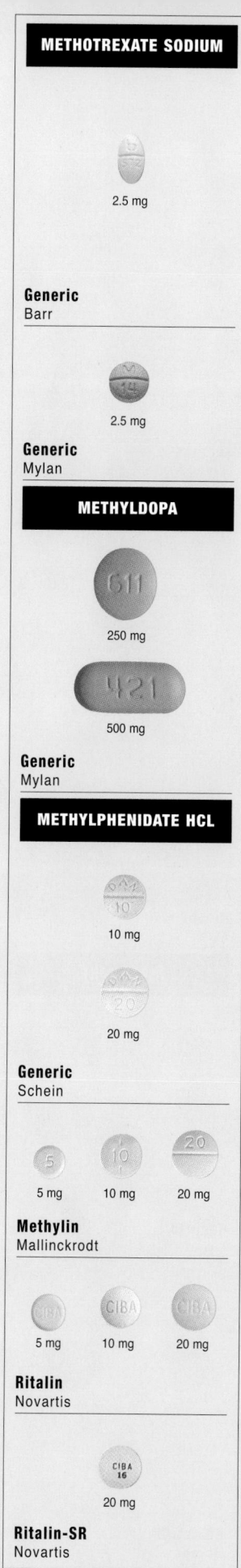
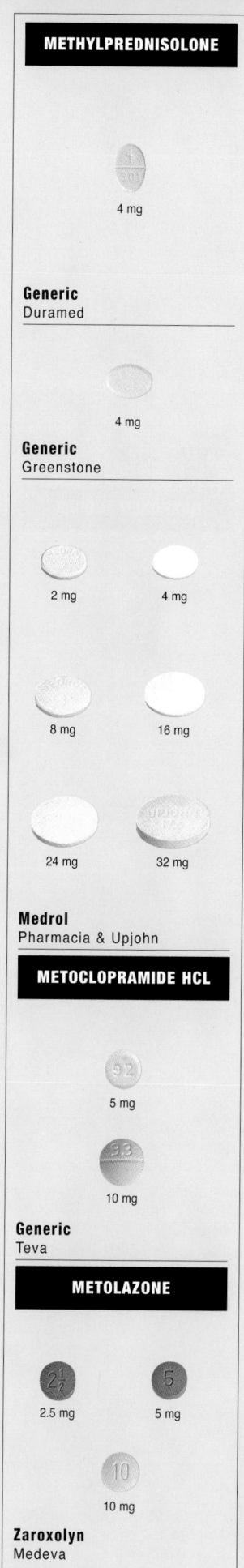
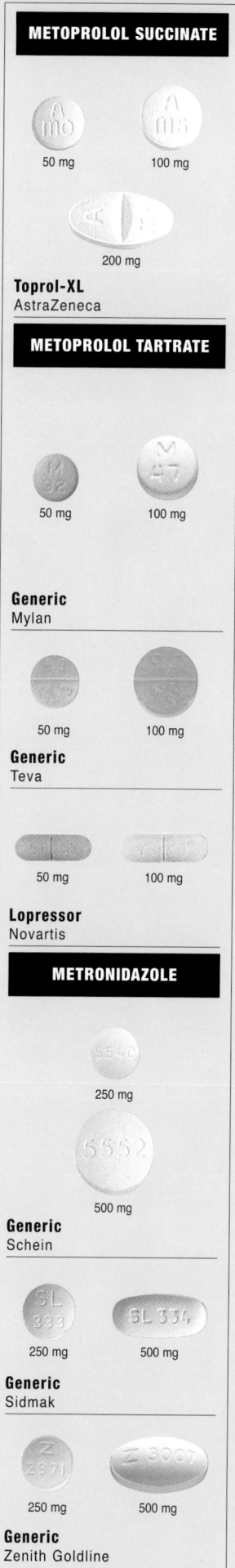
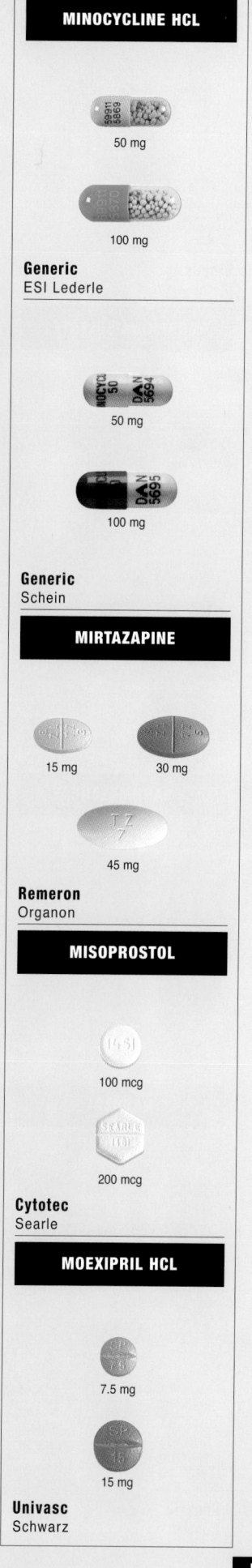

METHOTREXATE SODIUM

2.5 mg

Generic
Barr

2.5 mg

Generic
Mylan

METHYLDOPA

250 mg

500 mg

Generic
Mylan

METHYLPHENIDATE HCL

10 mg

20 mg

Generic
Schein

5 mg | 10 mg | 20 mg

Methylin
Mallinckrodt

5 mg | 10 mg | 20 mg

Ritalin
Novartis

20 mg

Ritalin-SR
Novartis

METHYLPREDNISOLONE

4 mg

Generic
Duramed

4 mg

Generic
Greenstone

2 mg | 4 mg

8 mg | 16 mg

24 mg | 32 mg

Medrol
Pharmacia & Upjohn

METOCLOPRAMIDE HCL

5 mg

10 mg

Generic
Teva

METOLAZONE

2½ mg | 5 mg

10 mg

Zaroxolyn
Medeva

METOPROLOL SUCCINATE

50 mg | 100 mg

200 mg

Toprol-XL
AstraZeneca

METOPROLOL TARTRATE

50 mg | 100 mg

Generic
Mylan

50 mg | 100 mg

Generic
Teva

50 mg | 100 mg

Lopressor
Novartis

METRONIDAZOLE

250 mg

500 mg

Generic
Schein

250 mg | 500 mg

Generic
Sidmak

250 mg | 500 mg

Generic
Zenith Goldline

MINOCYCLINE HCL

50 mg

100 mg

Generic
ESI Lederle

50 mg

100 mg

Generic
Schein

MIRTAZAPINE

15 mg | 30 mg

45 mg

Remeron
Organon

MISOPROSTOL

100 mcg

200 mcg

Cytotec
Searle

MOEXIPRIL HCL

7.5 mg

15 mg

Univasc
Schwarz

MC 15

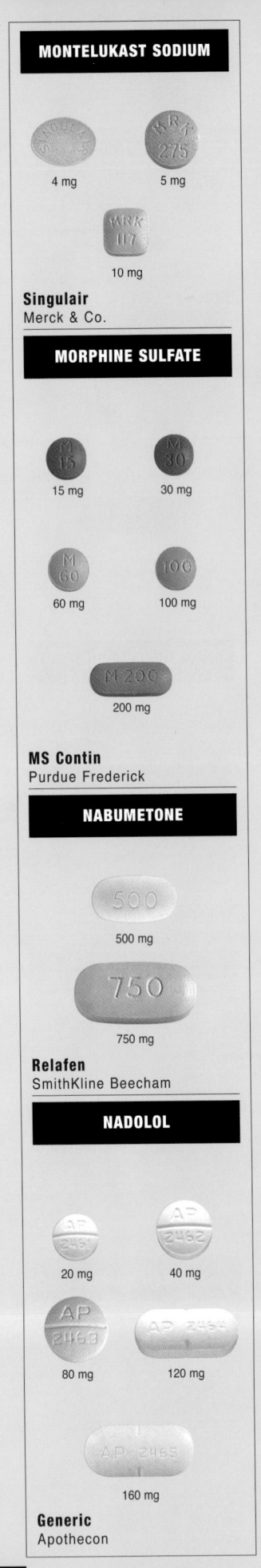

MONTELUKAST SODIUM

4 mg   5 mg

10 mg

Singulair
Merck & Co.

MORPHINE SULFATE

15 mg   30 mg

60 mg   100 mg

200 mg

MS Contin
Purdue Frederick

NABUMETONE

500 mg

750 mg

Relafen
SmithKline Beecham

NADOLOL

20 mg   40 mg

80 mg   120 mg

160 mg

Generic
Apothecon

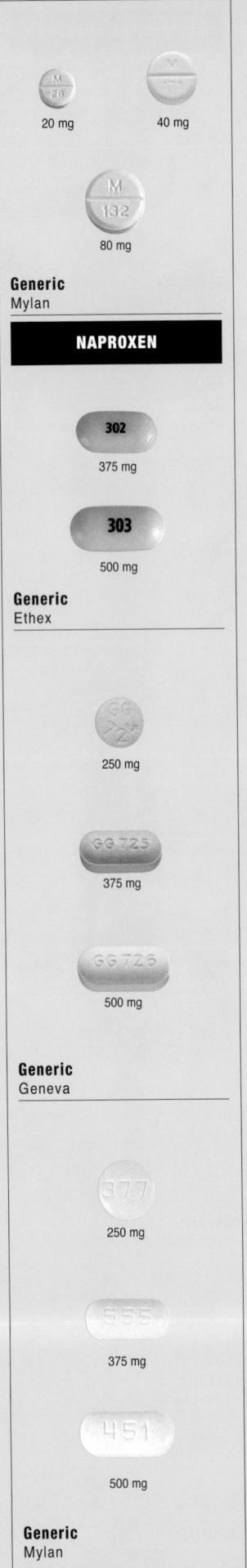

20 mg   40 mg

80 mg

Generic
Mylan

NAPROXEN

375 mg

500 mg

Generic
Ethex

250 mg

375 mg

500 mg

Generic
Geneva

250 mg

375 mg

500 mg

Generic
Mylan

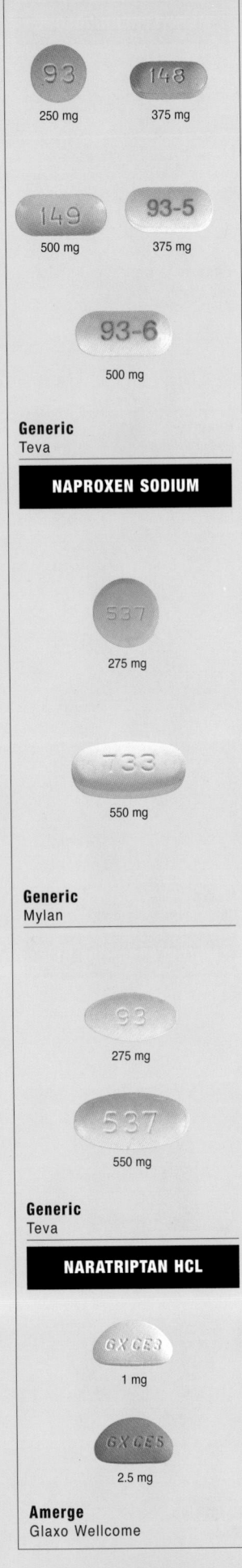

250 mg   375 mg

500 mg   375 mg

500 mg

Generic
Teva

NAPROXEN SODIUM

275 mg

550 mg

Generic
Mylan

275 mg

550 mg

Generic
Teva

NARATRIPTAN HCL

1 mg

2.5 mg

Amerge
Glaxo Wellcome

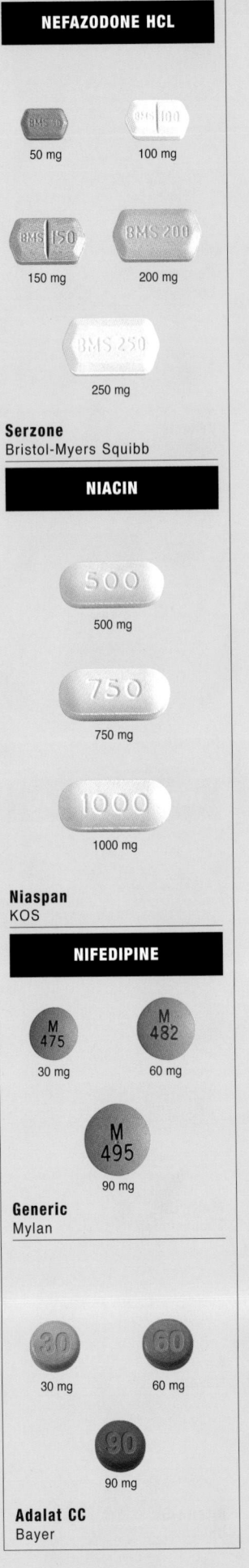

NEFAZODONE HCL

50 mg   100 mg

150 mg   200 mg

250 mg

Serzone
Bristol-Myers Squibb

NIACIN

500 mg

750 mg

1000 mg

Niaspan
KOS

NIFEDIPINE

30 mg   60 mg

90 mg

Generic
Mylan

30 mg   60 mg

90 mg

Adalat CC
Bayer

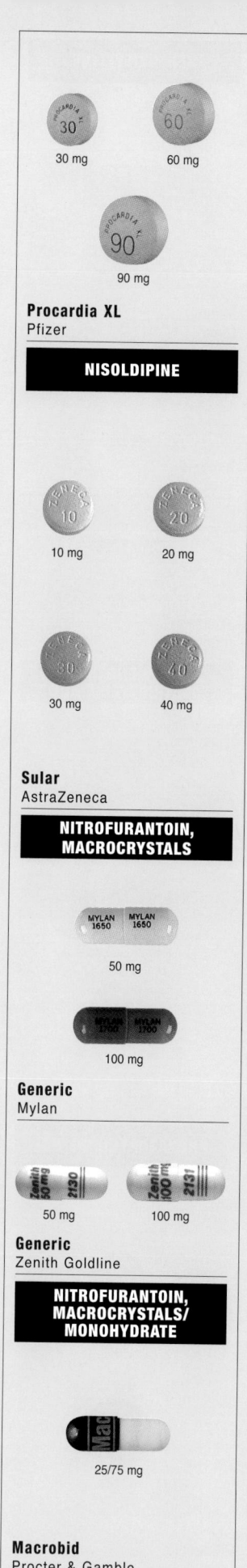

Procardia XL
Pfizer

NISOLDIPINE

Sular
AstraZeneca

NITROFURANTOIN, MACROCRYSTALS

Generic
Mylan

Generic
Zenith Goldline

NITROFURANTOIN, MACROCRYSTALS/ MONOHYDRATE

Macrobid
Procter & Gamble

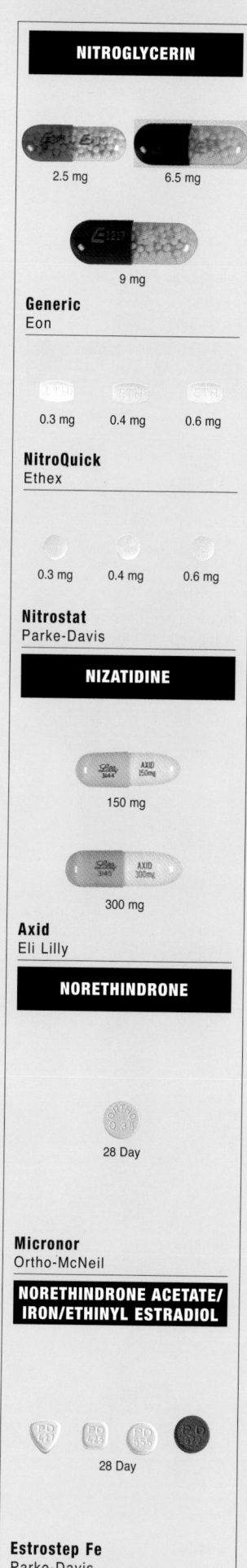

NITROGLYCERIN

Generic
Eon

NitroQuick
Ethex

Nitrostat
Parke-Davis

NIZATIDINE

Axid
Eli Lilly

NORETHINDRONE

Micronor
Ortho-McNeil

NORETHINDRONE ACETATE/ IRON/ETHINYL ESTRADIOL

Estrostep Fe
Parke-Davis

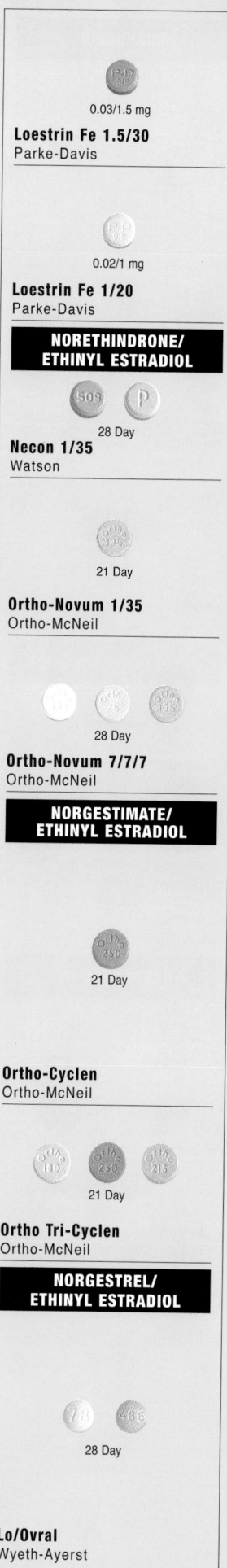

Loestrin Fe 1.5/30
Parke-Davis

Loestrin Fe 1/20
Parke-Davis

NORETHINDRONE/ ETHINYL ESTRADIOL

Necon 1/35
Watson

Ortho-Novum 1/35
Ortho-McNeil

Ortho-Novum 7/7/7
Ortho-McNeil

NORGESTIMATE/ ETHINYL ESTRADIOL

Ortho-Cyclen
Ortho-McNeil

Ortho Tri-Cyclen
Ortho-McNeil

NORGESTREL/ ETHINYL ESTRADIOL

Lo/Ovral
Wyeth-Ayerst

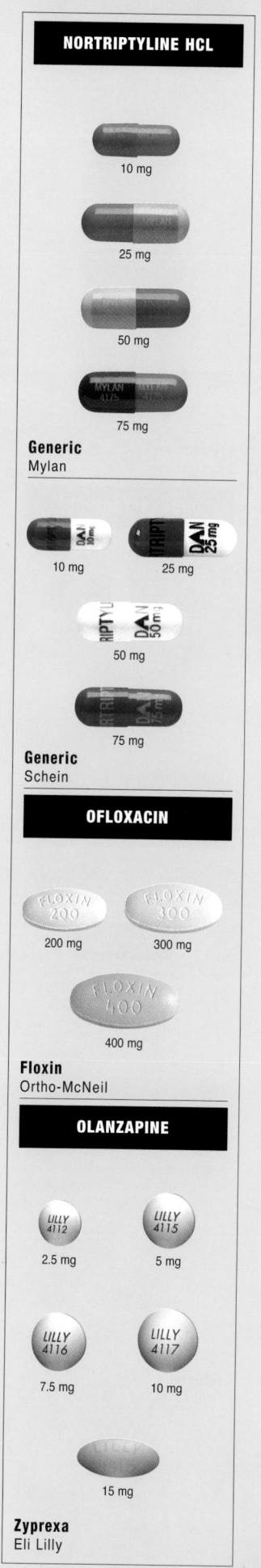

NORTRIPTYLINE HCL

Generic
Mylan

Generic
Schein

OFLOXACIN

Floxin
Ortho-McNeil

OLANZAPINE

Zyprexa
Eli Lilly

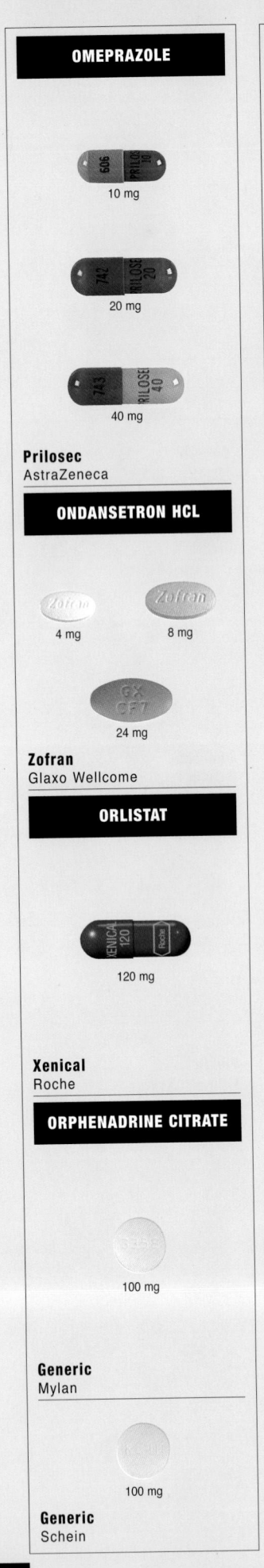

OMEPRAZOLE

10 mg

20 mg

40 mg

Prilosec
AstraZeneca

ONDANSETRON HCL

4 mg

8 mg

24 mg

Zofran
Glaxo Wellcome

ORLISTAT

120 mg

Xenical
Roche

ORPHENADRINE CITRATE

100 mg

Generic
Mylan

100 mg

Generic
Schein

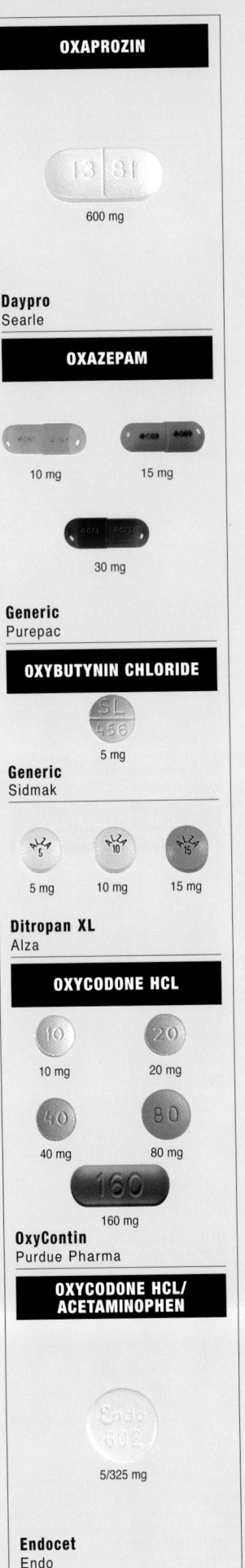

OXAPROZIN

600 mg

Daypro
Searle

OXAZEPAM

10 mg

15 mg

30 mg

Generic
Purepac

OXYBUTYNIN CHLORIDE

5 mg

Generic
Sidmak

5 mg

10 mg

15 mg

Ditropan XL
Alza

OXYCODONE HCL

10 mg

20 mg

40 mg

80 mg

160 mg

OxyContin
Purdue Pharma

OXYCODONE HCL/ ACETAMINOPHEN

5/325 mg

Endocet
Endo

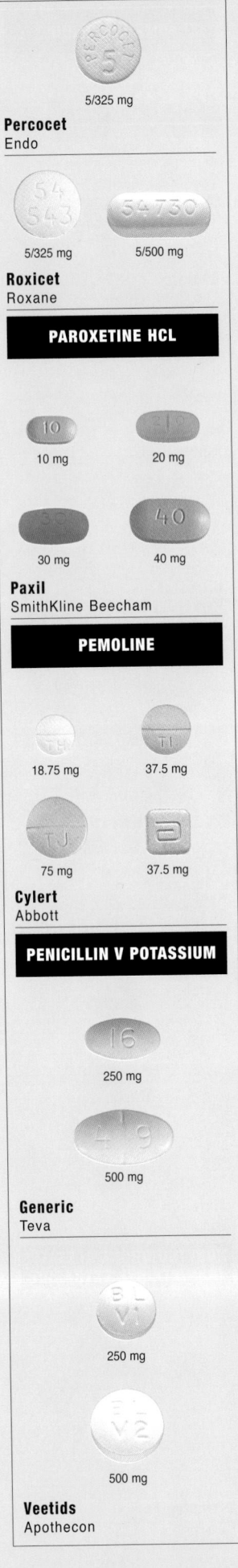

5/325 mg

Percocet
Endo

5/325 mg

5/500 mg

Roxicet
Roxane

PAROXETINE HCL

10 mg

20 mg

30 mg

40 mg

Paxil
SmithKline Beecham

PEMOLINE

18.75 mg

37.5 mg

75 mg

37.5 mg

Cylert
Abbott

PENICILLIN V POTASSIUM

250 mg

500 mg

Generic
Teva

250 mg

500 mg

Veetids
Apothecon

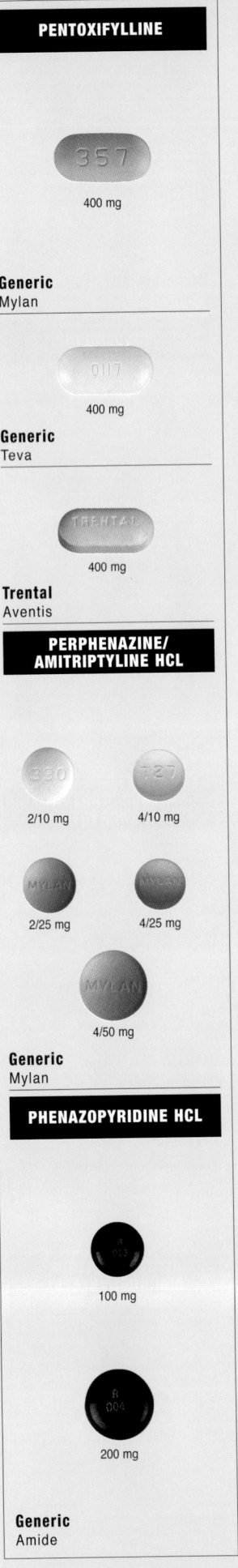

PENTOXIFYLLINE

400 mg

Generic
Mylan

400 mg

Generic
Teva

400 mg

Trental
Aventis

PERPHENAZINE/ AMITRIPTYLINE HCL

2/10 mg

4/10 mg

2/25 mg

4/25 mg

4/50 mg

Generic
Mylan

PHENAZOPYRIDINE HCL

100 mg

200 mg

Generic
Amide

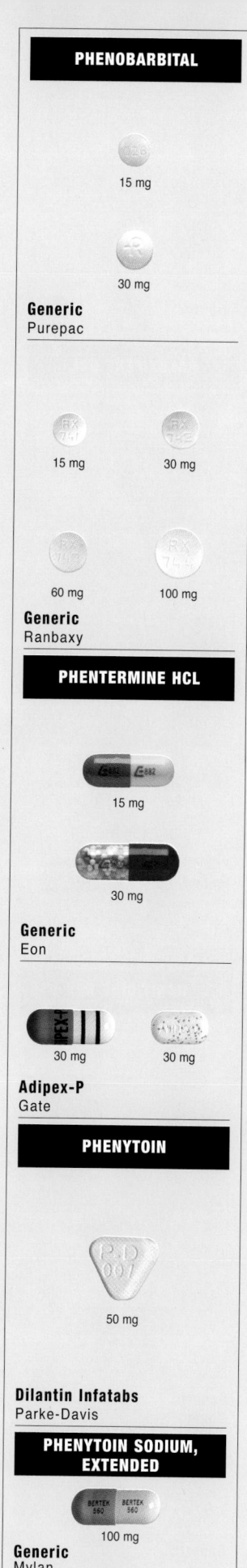

PHENOBARBITAL

15 mg

30 mg

Generic
Purepac

15 mg　　　30 mg

60 mg　　　100 mg

Generic
Ranbaxy

PHENTERMINE HCL

15 mg

30 mg

Generic
Eon

30 mg　　　30 mg

Adipex-P
Gate

PHENYTOIN

50 mg

Dilantin Infatabs
Parke-Davis

PHENYTOIN SODIUM, EXTENDED

100 mg

Generic
Mylan

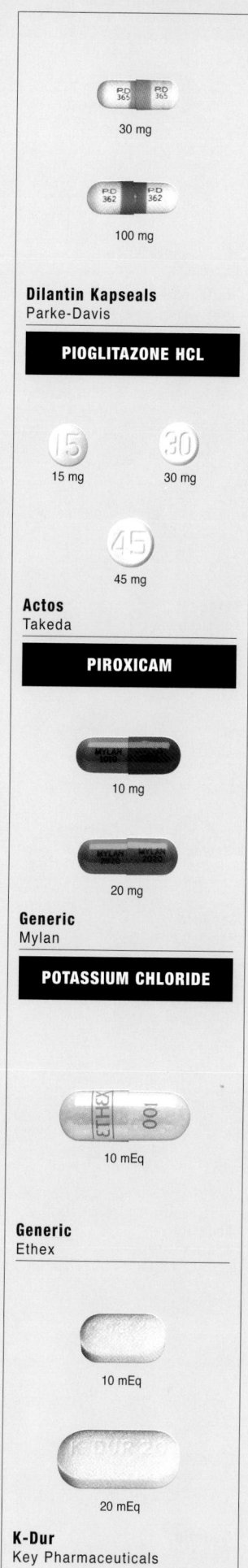

30 mg

100 mg

Dilantin Kapseals
Parke-Davis

PIOGLITAZONE HCL

15 mg　　　30 mg

45 mg

Actos
Takeda

PIROXICAM

10 mg

20 mg

Generic
Mylan

POTASSIUM CHLORIDE

10 mEq

Generic
Ethex

10 mEq

20 mEq

K-Dur
Key Pharmaceuticals

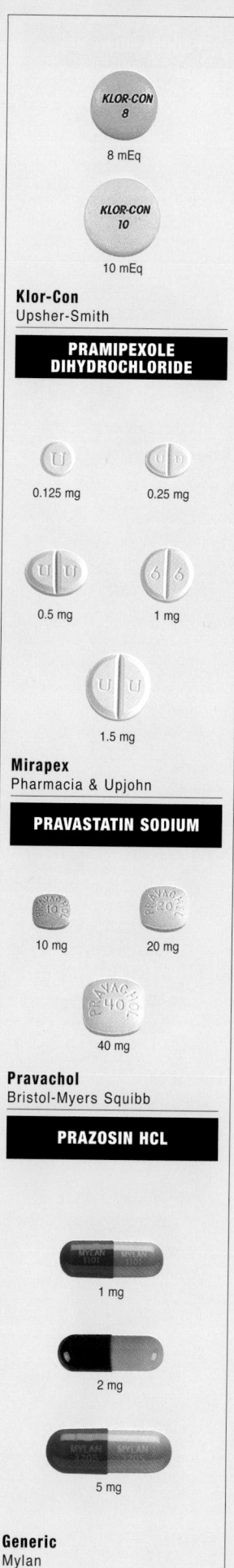

8 mEq

10 mEq

Klor-Con
Upsher-Smith

PRAMIPEXOLE DIHYDROCHLORIDE

0.125 mg　　　0.25 mg

0.5 mg　　　1 mg

1.5 mg

Mirapex
Pharmacia & Upjohn

PRAVASTATIN SODIUM

10 mg　　　20 mg

40 mg

Pravachol
Bristol-Myers Squibb

PRAZOSIN HCL

1 mg

2 mg

5 mg

Generic
Mylan

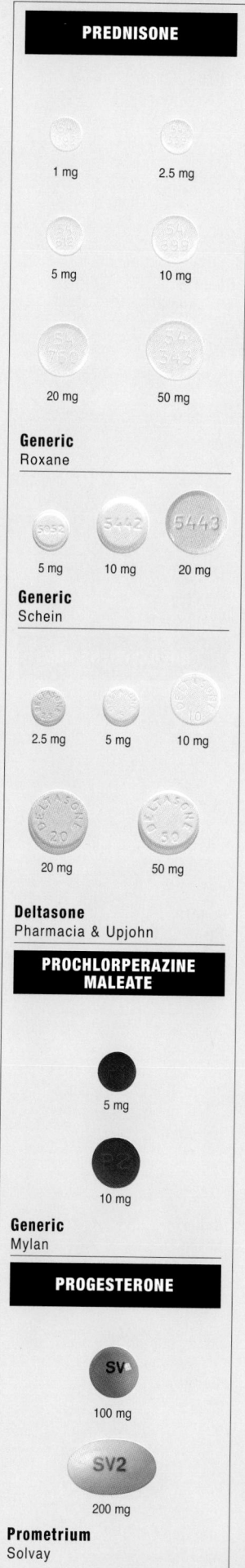

PREDNISONE

1 mg　　　2.5 mg

5 mg　　　10 mg

20 mg　　　50 mg

Generic
Roxane

5 mg　　　10 mg　　　20 mg

Generic
Schein

2.5 mg　　　5 mg　　　10 mg

20 mg　　　50 mg

Deltasone
Pharmacia & Upjohn

PROCHLORPERAZINE MALEATE

5 mg

10 mg

Generic
Mylan

PROGESTERONE

100 mg

200 mg

Prometrium
Solvay

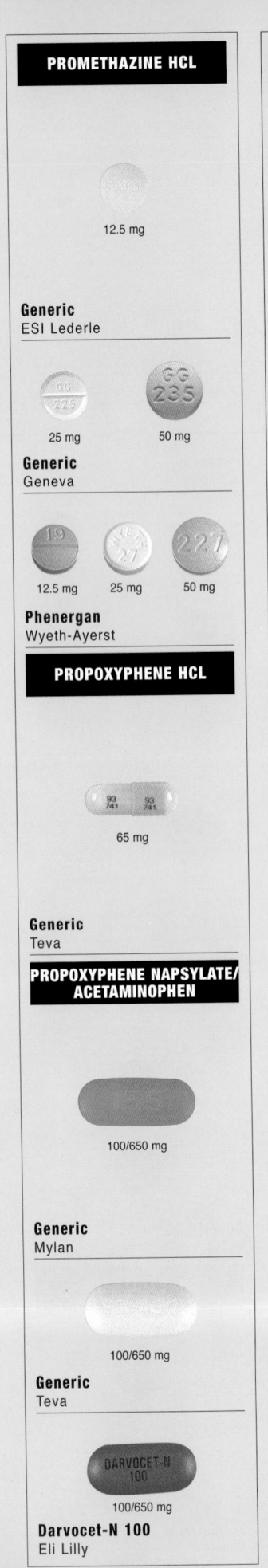

PROMETHAZINE HCL

12.5 mg

Generic
ESI Lederle

25 mg 50 mg

Generic
Geneva

12.5 mg 25 mg 50 mg

Phenergan
Wyeth-Ayerst

PROPOXYPHENE HCL

65 mg

Generic
Teva

PROPOXYPHENE NAPSYLATE/ ACETAMINOPHEN

100/650 mg

Generic
Mylan

100/650 mg

Generic
Teva

100/650 mg

Darvocet-N 100
Eli Lilly

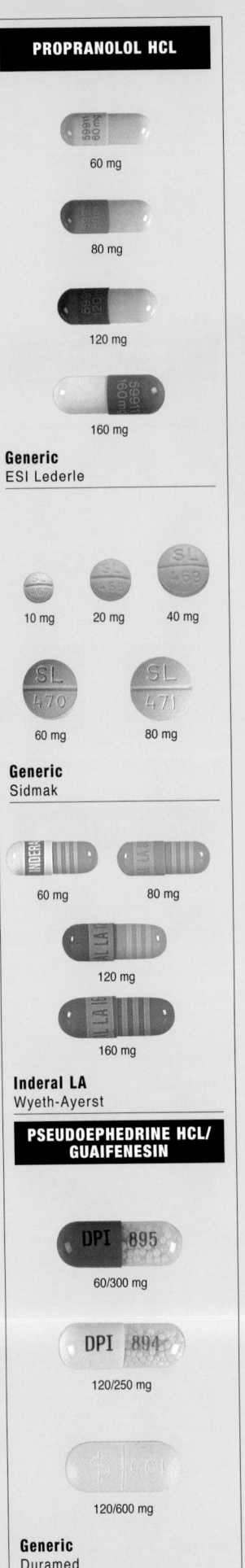

PROPRANOLOL HCL

60 mg

80 mg

120 mg

160 mg

Generic
ESI Lederle

10 mg 20 mg 40 mg

60 mg 80 mg

Generic
Sidmak

60 mg 80 mg

120 mg

160 mg

Inderal LA
Wyeth-Ayerst

PSEUDOEPHEDRINE HCL/ GUAIFENESIN

DPI 895

60/300 mg

DPI 894

120/250 mg

120/600 mg

Generic
Duramed

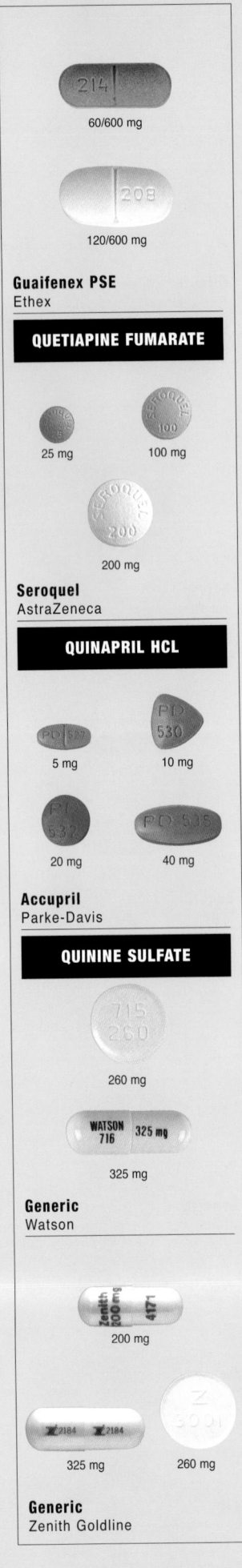

60/600 mg

120/600 mg

Guaifenex PSE
Ethex

QUETIAPINE FUMARATE

25 mg 100 mg

200 mg

Seroquel
AstraZeneca

QUINAPRIL HCL

PD 527 PD 530
5 mg 10 mg

PD 532 PD 535
20 mg 40 mg

Accupril
Parke-Davis

QUININE SULFATE

260 mg

WATSON 716 325 mg

325 mg

Generic
Watson

Zenith 200 mg 4171

200 mg

2184 2184
325 mg

Z 3001
260 mg

Generic
Zenith Goldline

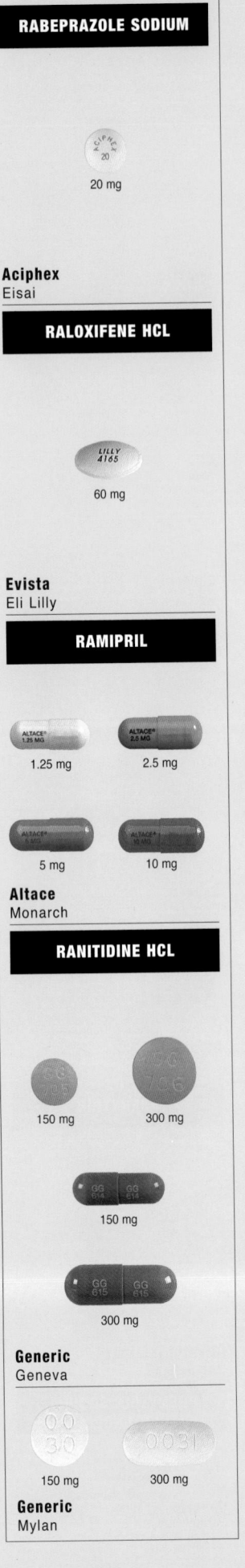

RABEPRAZOLE SODIUM

20 mg

Aciphex
Eisai

RALOXIFENE HCL

LILLY 4165
60 mg

Evista
Eli Lilly

RAMIPRIL

ALTACE 1.25 MG ALTACE 2.5 MG
1.25 mg 2.5 mg

ALTACE 5 MG ALTACE 10 MG
5 mg 10 mg

Altace
Monarch

RANITIDINE HCL

150 mg 300 mg

GG 614 GG 614
150 mg

GG 615 GG 615
300 mg

Generic
Geneva

0030 0031
150 mg 300 mg

Generic
Mylan

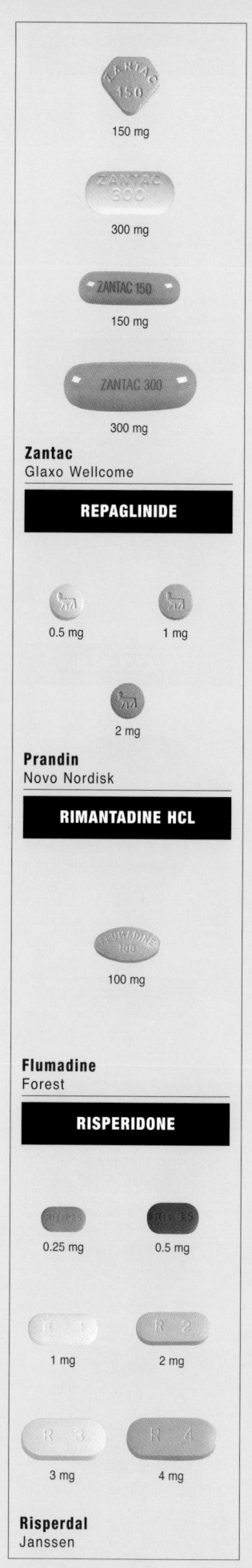

150 mg

300 mg

150 mg

300 mg

Zantac
Glaxo Wellcome

REPAGLINIDE

0.5 mg **1 mg**

2 mg

Prandin
Novo Nordisk

RIMANTADINE HCL

100 mg

Flumadine
Forest

RISPERIDONE

0.25 mg **0.5 mg**

1 mg **2 mg**

3 mg **4 mg**

Risperdal
Janssen

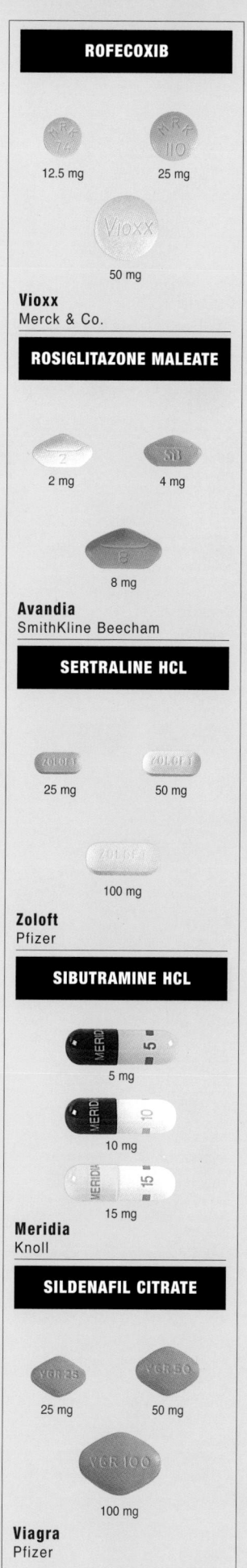

ROFECOXIB

12.5 mg **25 mg**

50 mg

Vioxx
Merck & Co.

ROSIGLITAZONE MALEATE

2 mg **4 mg**

8 mg

Avandia
SmithKline Beecham

SERTRALINE HCL

25 mg **50 mg**

100 mg

Zoloft
Pfizer

SIBUTRAMINE HCL

5 mg

10 mg

15 mg

Meridia
Knoll

SILDENAFIL CITRATE

25 mg **50 mg**

100 mg

Viagra
Pfizer

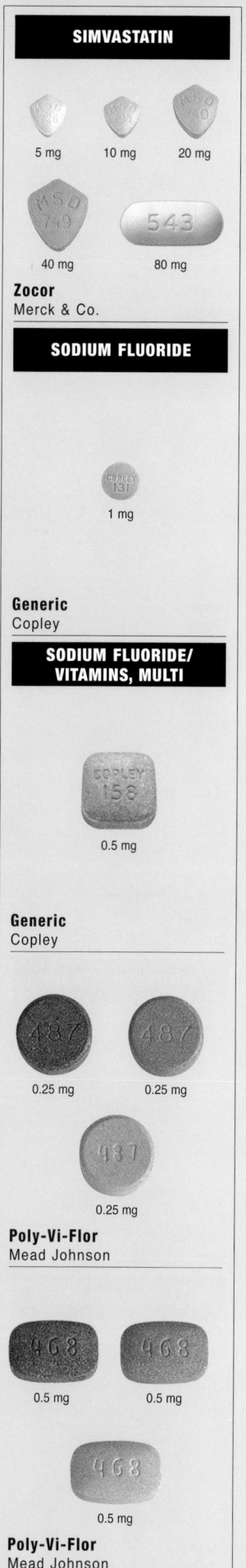

SIMVASTATIN

5 mg **10 mg** **20 mg**

40 mg **80 mg**

Zocor
Merck & Co.

SODIUM FLUORIDE

1 mg

Generic
Copley

SODIUM FLUORIDE/ VITAMINS, MULTI

0.5 mg

Generic
Copley

0.25 mg **0.25 mg**

0.25 mg

Poly-Vi-Flor
Mead Johnson

0.5 mg **0.5 mg**

0.5 mg

Poly-Vi-Flor
Mead Johnson

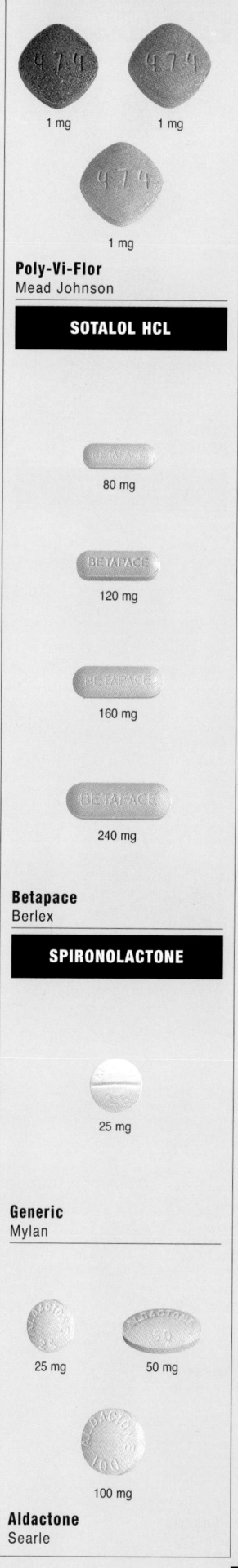

1 mg **1 mg**

1 mg

Poly-Vi-Flor
Mead Johnson

SOTALOL HCL

80 mg

120 mg

160 mg

240 mg

Betapace
Berlex

SPIRONOLACTONE

25 mg

Generic
Mylan

25 mg **50 mg**

100 mg

Aldactone
Searle

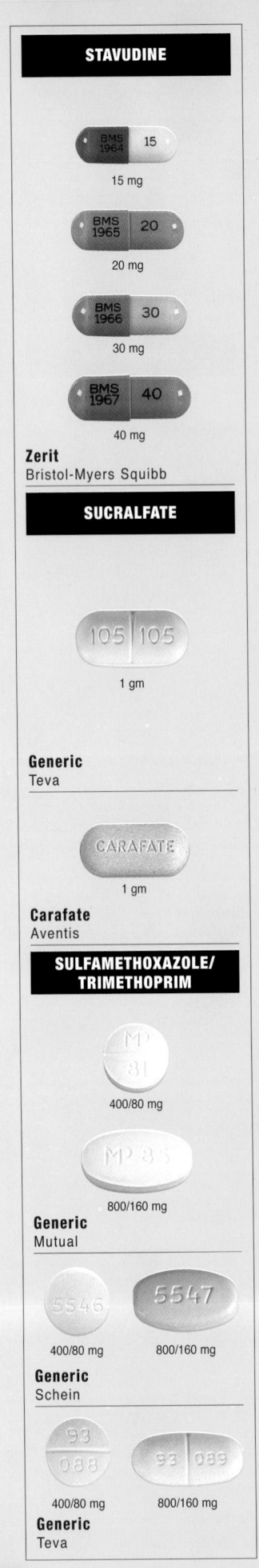

STAVUDINE

BMS 1964 15 — 15 mg

BMS 1965 20 — 20 mg

BMS 1966 30 — 30 mg

BMS 1967 40 — 40 mg

Zerit
Bristol-Myers Squibb

SUCRALFATE

105 | 105 — 1 gm

Generic
Teva

CARAFATE — 1 gm

Carafate
Aventis

SULFAMETHOXAZOLE/ TRIMETHOPRIM

MP 81 — 400/80 mg

MP 85 — 800/160 mg

Generic
Mutual

5546 — 400/80 mg   **5547** — 800/160 mg

Generic
Schein

93 088 — 400/80 mg   **93 089** — 800/160 mg

Generic
Teva

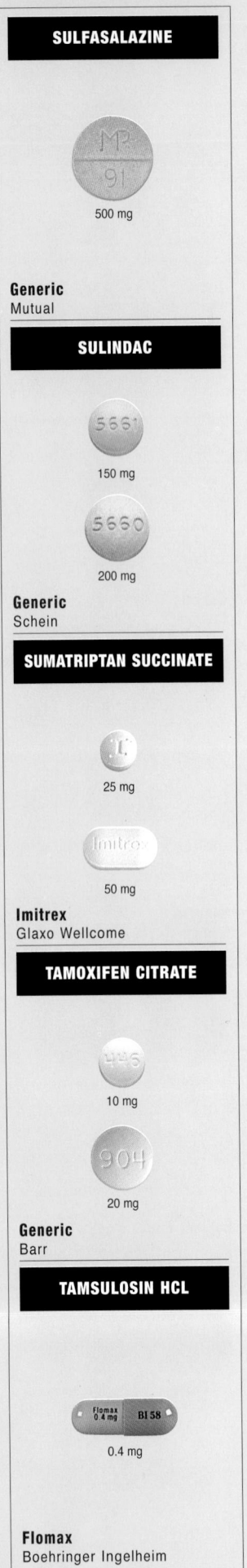

SULFASALAZINE

MP 91 — 500 mg

Generic
Mutual

SULINDAC

5661 — 150 mg

5660 — 200 mg

Generic
Schein

SUMATRIPTAN SUCCINATE

L — 25 mg

Imitrex — 50 mg

Imitrex
Glaxo Wellcome

TAMOXIFEN CITRATE

446 — 10 mg

904 — 20 mg

Generic
Barr

TAMSULOSIN HCL

Flomax 0.4 mg | BI 58 — 0.4 mg

Flomax
Boehringer Ingelheim

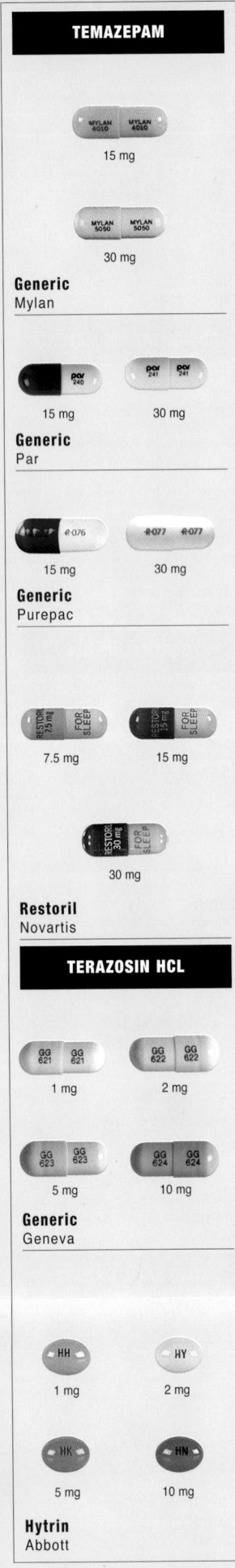

TEMAZEPAM

MYLAN 4010 | MYLAN 4010 — 15 mg

MYLAN 5050 | MYLAN 5050 — 30 mg

Generic
Mylan

par 240 — 15 mg   **par 241 | par 241** — 30 mg

Generic
Par

R-076 — 15 mg   **R-077 | R-077** — 30 mg

Generic
Purepac

RESTORIL 7.5 mg | FOR SLEEP — 7.5 mg   **RESTORIL 15 mg | FOR SLEEP** — 15 mg

RESTORIL 30 mg | FOR SLEEP — 30 mg

Restoril
Novartis

TERAZOSIN HCL

GG 621 | GG 621 — 1 mg   **GG 622 | GG 622** — 2 mg

GG 623 | GG 623 — 5 mg   **GG 624 | GG 624** — 10 mg

Generic
Geneva

HH — 1 mg   **HY** — 2 mg

HK — 5 mg   **HN** — 10 mg

Hytrin
Abbott

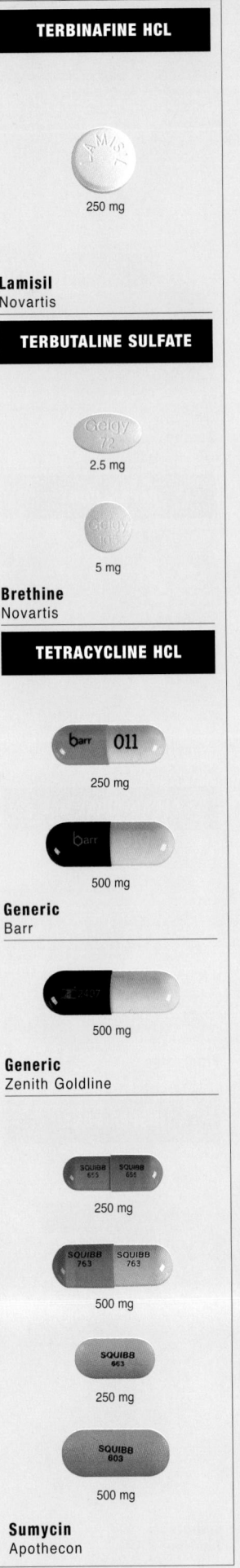

TERBINAFINE HCL

LAMISIL — 250 mg

Lamisil
Novartis

TERBUTALINE SULFATE

Geigy 72 — 2.5 mg

Geigy 105 — 5 mg

Brethine
Novartis

TETRACYCLINE HCL

barr 011 — 250 mg

barr — 500 mg

Generic
Barr

Z 2407 — 500 mg

Generic
Zenith Goldline

SQUIBB 655 | SQUIBB 655 — 250 mg

SQUIBB 763 | SQUIBB 763 — 500 mg

SQUIBB 663 — 250 mg

SQUIBB 603 — 500 mg

Sumycin
Apothecon

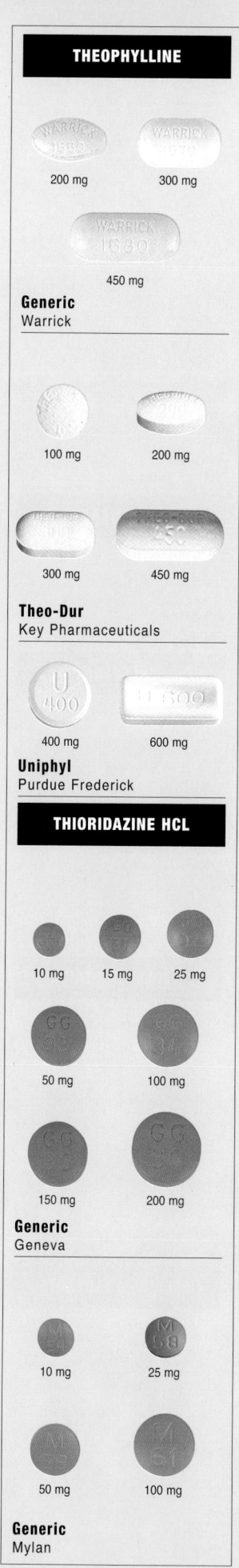

THEOPHYLLINE

WARRICK 1680 — 200 mg
WARRICK 1670 — 300 mg
WARRICK 1680 — 450 mg

Generic
Warrick

100 mg
200 mg
300 mg
450 mg

Theo-Dur
Key Pharmaceuticals

U 400 — 400 mg
U 600 — 600 mg

Uniphyl
Purdue Frederick

THIORIDAZINE HCL

10 mg
15 mg
25 mg

GG — 50 mg
GG — 100 mg

GG — 150 mg
GG — 200 mg

Generic
Geneva

M — 10 mg
M 58 — 25 mg
M — 50 mg
M 51 — 100 mg

Generic
Mylan

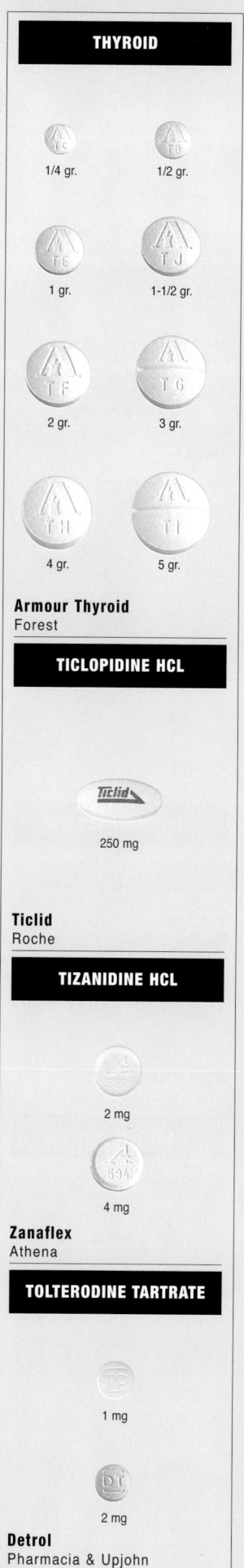

THYROID

A TC — 1/4 gr.
A TD — 1/2 gr.
A TE — 1 gr.
A TJ — 1-1/2 gr.
A TF — 2 gr.
A TG — 3 gr.
A TH — 4 gr.
A TI — 5 gr.

Armour Thyroid
Forest

TICLOPIDINE HCL

Ticlid — 250 mg

Ticlid
Roche

TIZANIDINE HCL

4 597 — 2 mg
4 594 — 4 mg

Zanaflex
Athena

TOLTERODINE TARTRATE

TC — 1 mg
DT — 2 mg

Detrol
Pharmacia & Upjohn

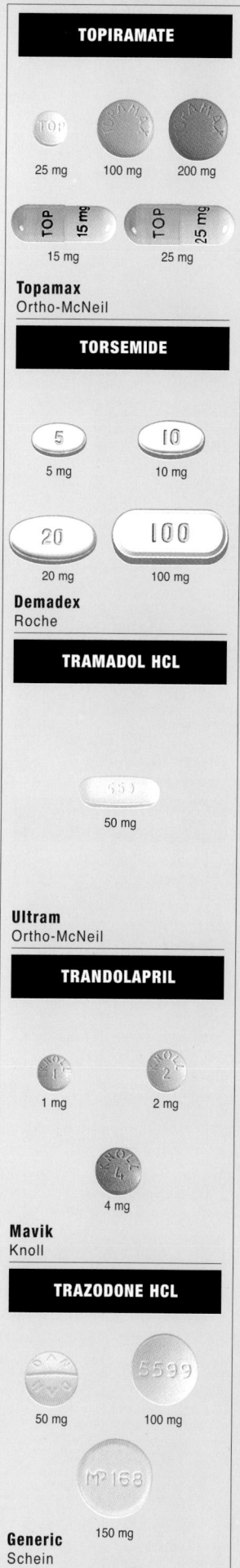

TOPIRAMATE

TOP — 25 mg
TOPAMAX — 100 mg
TOPAMAX — 200 mg
TOP 15 mg — 15 mg
TOP 25 mg — 25 mg

Topamax
Ortho-McNeil

TORSEMIDE

5 — 5 mg
10 — 10 mg
20 — 20 mg
100 — 100 mg

Demadex
Roche

TRAMADOL HCL

651 — 50 mg

Ultram
Ortho-McNeil

TRANDOLAPRIL

KNOLL 1 — 1 mg
KNOLL 2 — 2 mg
KNOLL 4 — 4 mg

Mavik
Knoll

TRAZODONE HCL

50 mg
5599 — 100 mg
MP 168 — 150 mg

Generic
Schein

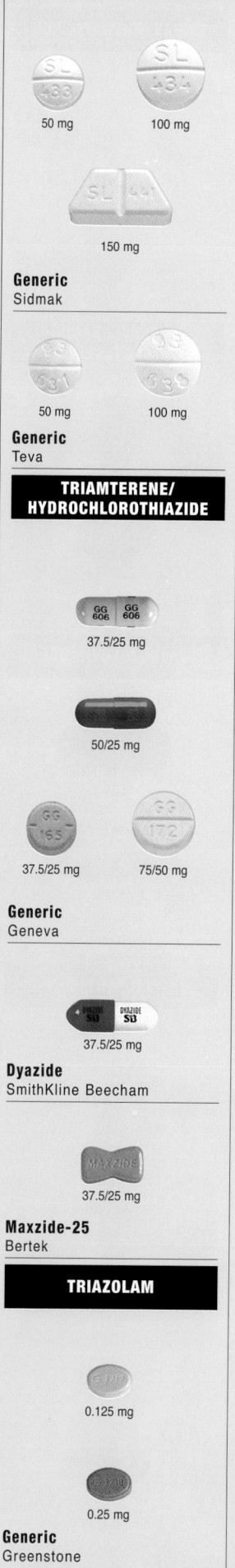

SL 433 — 50 mg
SL 434 — 100 mg
SL 441 — 150 mg

Generic
Sidmak

93 531 — 50 mg
93 638 — 100 mg

Generic
Teva

TRIAMTERENE/ HYDROCHLOROTHIAZIDE

GG 606 GG 606 — 37.5/25 mg
50/25 mg
GG 165 — 37.5/25 mg
GG 172 — 75/50 mg

Generic
Geneva

DYAZIDE SB DYAZIDE SB — 37.5/25 mg

Dyazide
SmithKline Beecham

MAXZIDE — 37.5/25 mg

Maxzide-25
Bertek

TRIAZOLAM

0.125 mg
0.25 mg

Generic
Greenstone

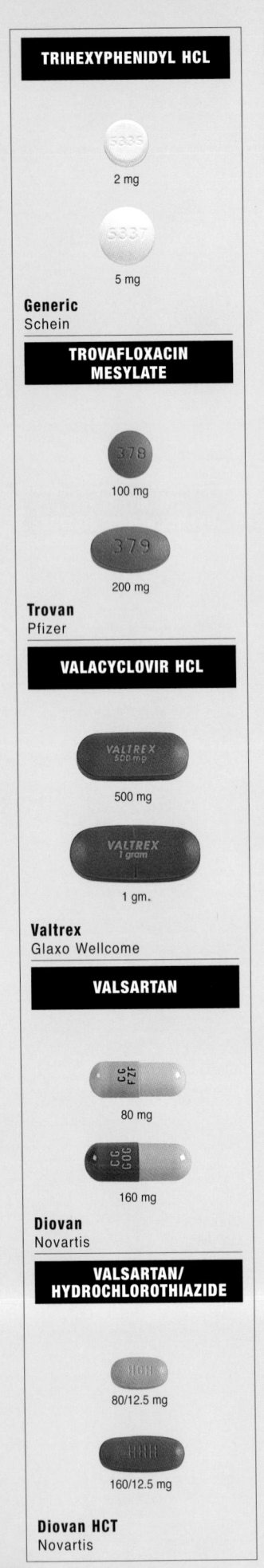

TRIHEXYPHENIDYL HCL

5335 — 2 mg

5337 — 5 mg

Generic
Schein

TROVAFLOXACIN MESYLATE

378 — 100 mg

379 — 200 mg

Trovan
Pfizer

VALACYCLOVIR HCL

VALTREX 500 mg — 500 mg

VALTREX 1 gram — 1 gm.

Valtrex
Glaxo Wellcome

VALSARTAN

CG FZF — 80 mg

CG GOG — 160 mg

Diovan
Novartis

VALSARTAN/ HYDROCHLOROTHIAZIDE

HGH — 80/12.5 mg

160/12.5 mg

Diovan HCT
Novartis

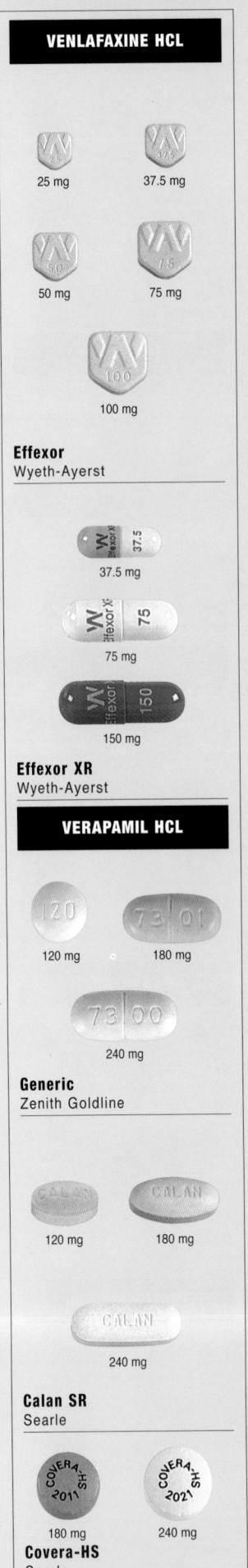

VENLAFAXINE HCL

25 mg   37.5 mg

50 mg   75 mg

100 mg

Effexor
Wyeth-Ayerst

Effexor XR 37.5 — 37.5 mg

Effexor XR 75 — 75 mg

Effexor XR 150 — 150 mg

Effexor XR
Wyeth-Ayerst

VERAPAMIL HCL

120 — 120 mg   73 01 — 180 mg

73 00 — 240 mg

Generic
Zenith Goldline

CALAN — 120 mg   CALAN — 180 mg

CALAN — 240 mg

Calan SR
Searle

COVERA-HS 2011 — 180 mg   COVERA-HS 2021 — 240 mg

Covera-HS
Searle

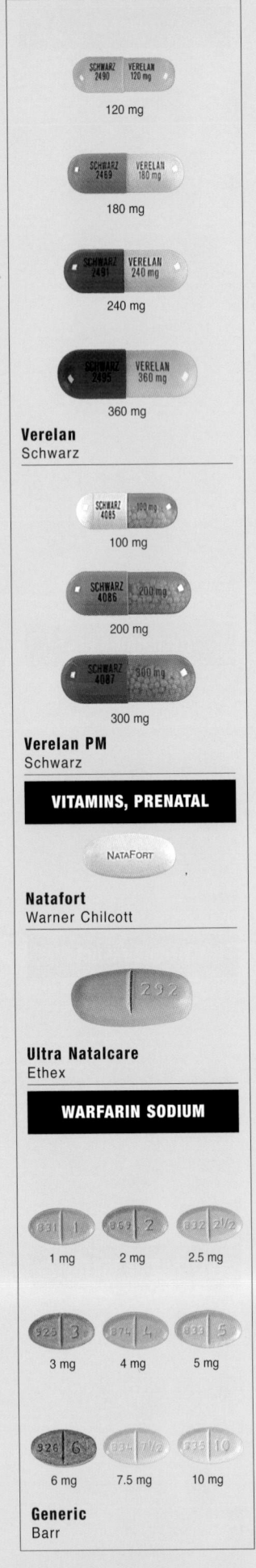

SCHWARZ 2490 VERELAN 120 mg — 120 mg

SCHWARZ 2469 VERELAN 180 mg — 180 mg

SCHWARZ 2491 VERELAN 240 mg — 240 mg

SCHWARZ 2495 VERELAN 360 mg — 360 mg

Verelan
Schwarz

SCHWARZ 4085 100 mg — 100 mg

SCHWARZ 4086 200 mg — 200 mg

SCHWARZ 4087 300 mg — 300 mg

Verelan PM
Schwarz

VITAMINS, PRENATAL

NATAFORT

Natafort
Warner Chilcott

292

Ultra Natalcare
Ethex

WARFARIN SODIUM

831 1 — 1 mg   832 2 — 2 mg   832 2½ — 2.5 mg

925 3 — 3 mg   874 4 — 4 mg   833 5 — 5 mg

926 6 — 6 mg   834 7½ — 7.5 mg   835 10 — 10 mg

Generic
Barr

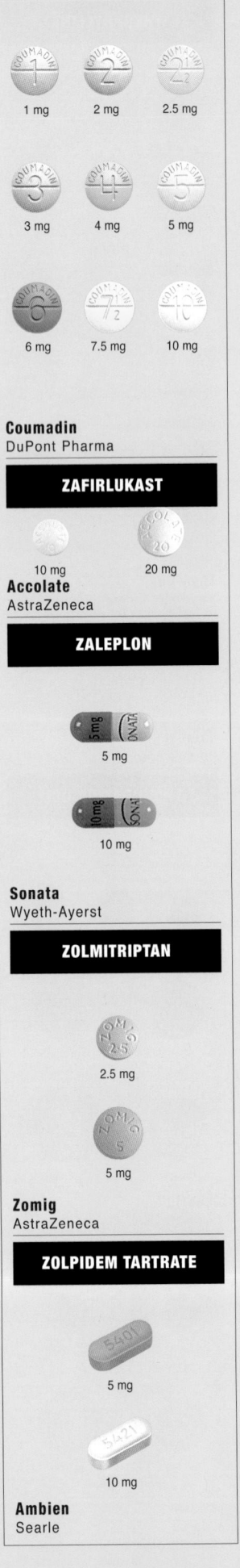

COUMADIN 1 — 1 mg   COUMADIN 2 — 2 mg   COUMADIN 2½ — 2.5 mg

COUMADIN 3 — 3 mg   COUMADIN 4 — 4 mg   COUMADIN 5 — 5 mg

COUMADIN 6 — 6 mg   COUMADIN 7½ — 7.5 mg   COUMADIN 10 — 10 mg

Coumadin
DuPont Pharma

ZAFIRLUKAST

10 mg   ACCOLATE 20 — 20 mg

Accolate
AstraZeneca

ZALEPLON

5 mg SONATA — 5 mg

10 mg SONATA — 10 mg

Sonata
Wyeth-Ayerst

ZOLMITRIPTAN

ZOMIG 2.5 — 2.5 mg

ZOMIG 5 — 5 mg

Zomig
AstraZeneca

ZOLPIDEM TARTRATE

5401 — 5 mg

5421 — 10 mg

Ambien
Searle

General Information

GENERAL INFORMATION ABOUT USE OF MEDICINES

There are two kinds of information about the proper use of medicines. One type applies to a certain medicine or group of medicines only. The other type is more general and applies to the use of any medicine.

The information that follows is general in nature. For your own safety, health, and well being, however, it is important that you learn about the proper use of your specific medicines as well. You can get this information from your health care professional, or find it in the individual listings of this book.

Before Using Your Medicine

Before you use any medicine, tell your health care professional:

— if you have ever had an allergic or unusual reaction to any medicine, food, or other substance, such as yellow dye or sulfites.

— if you are on a low-salt, low-sugar, or any other special diet. Most medicines contain more than their active ingredient, and many liquid medicines contain alcohol.

— *if you are pregnant or if you plan to become pregnant.* Certain medicines may cause birth defects or other problems in the unborn child. For other medicines, safe use during pregnancy has not been established. *The use of any medicine during pregnancy must be carefully considered* and should be discussed with a health care professional.

— *if you are breast-feeding.* Some medicines may pass into the breast milk and cause unwanted effects in the baby.

— *if you are now taking or have taken any medicines or dietary supplements in the recent past.* Do not forget over-the-counter (nonprescription) medicines such as pain relievers, laxatives, and antacids or dietary supplements.

— *if you have any medical problems* other than the one(s) for which your medicine was prescribed.

— *if you have difficulty remembering things or reading labels.*

Storage of Your Medicine

It is important to store your medicines properly. Guidelines for proper storage include:

• *Keep out of the reach of children.*
• Keep medicines in their original containers.
• Store away from heat and direct light.
• Do not store capsules or tablets in the bathroom, near the kitchen sink, or in other damp places. Heat or moisture may cause the medicine to break down. Also, do not leave the cotton plug in a medicine container that has been opened, since it may draw moisture into the container.
• Keep liquid medicines from freezing.

• Do not store medicines in the refrigerator unless directed to do so.
• Do not leave your medicines in an automobile for long periods of time.
• Do not keep outdated medicine or medicine that is no longer needed. Be sure that any discarded medicine is out of the reach of children.

Proper Use of Your Medicine

Take medicine only as directed, at the right time, and for the full length of your prescribed treatment. If you are using an over-the-counter (nonprescription) medicine, follow the directions on the label unless otherwise directed by your health care professional. If you feel that your medicine is not working for you, check with your health care professional.

Unless your pharmacist has packaged different medicines together in a "bubble-pack," different medicines should never be mixed in one container. It is best to keep your medicines tightly capped in their original containers when not in use. Do not remove the label since directions for use and other important information may appear on it.

To avoid mistakes, do not take medicine in the dark. Always read the label before taking, especially noting the expiration date and any directions for use.

For oral (by mouth) medicines:

• In general, it is best to take oral medicines with a full glass of water. However, follow your health care professional's directions. Some medicines should be taken with food, while others should be taken on an empty stomach.
• When taking most long-acting forms of a medicine, each dose should be swallowed whole. Do not break, crush, or chew before swallowing unless you have been specifically told that it is all right to do so.
• If you are taking liquid medicines, you should use a specially marked measuring spoon or other device to measure each dose accurately. Ask your pharmacist about these devices. The average household teaspoon may not hold the right amount of medicine.
• Oral medicine may come in a number of different dosage forms, such as tablets, capsules, and liquids. If you have trouble swallowing the dosage form prescribed for you, check with your health care professional. Another dosage form that you can swallow more easily may be available.
• Child-resistant caps on medicine containers have decreased greatly the number of accidental poisonings that occur each year. Use of these caps is required by law. However, if you find it hard to open such caps, you may ask your pharmacist for a regular, easier-to-open cap. He or she can provide you with a regular cap if you request it. However, you must make this request each time you get a prescription filled.

For skin patches:

- Apply the patch to a clean, dry skin area that has little or no hair and is free of scars, cuts, or irritation. Remove the previous patch before applying a new one.
- Apply a new patch if the first one becomes loose or falls off.
- Apply each patch to a different area of skin to prevent skin irritation or other problems.
- Do not try to trim or cut the adhesive patch to adjust the dosage. Check with your health care professional if you think the medicine is not working as it should.

For inhalers:

- Medicines that come in inhalers usually come with patient directions. Read the directions carefully before using the medicine. If you do not understand the directions, or if you are not sure how to use the inhaler, check with your health care professional.
- Since different types of inhalers may be used in different ways, it is very important to follow carefully the directions given to you.

For ophthalmic (eye) drops:

- To prevent contamination, do not let the tip of the eye drop applicator touch any surface (including the eye) and keep the container tightly closed.
- The bottle may not be full; this is to provide proper drop control.
- How to apply: First, wash your hands. Tilt your head back and, with the index finger, pull the lower eyelid away from the eye to form a pouch. Drop the medicine into the pouch and gently close your eyes. Do not blink. Keep your eyes closed for 1 to 2 minutes.
- If your medicine is for glaucoma or inflammation of the eye: Follow the directions for application that are listed above. However, immediately after placing the drops in your eye, apply pressure to the inside corner of the eye with your middle finger. Continue to apply pressure for 1 to 2 minutes after the medicine has been placed in the eye. This will help prevent the medicine from being absorbed into the body and causing side effects.
- After applying the eye drops, wash your hands to remove any medicine.

For ophthalmic (eye) ointments:

- To prevent contamination of the eye ointment, do not let the tip of the applicator touch any surface (including the eye). After using, wipe the tip of the ointment tube with a clean tissue and keep the tube tightly closed.
- How to apply: First, wash your hands. Pull the lower eyelid away from the eye to form a pouch. Squeeze a thin strip of ointment into the pouch. A l-cm (approximately 1/3-inch) strip of ointment is usually enough unless otherwise directed. Gently close your eyes and keep them closed for 1 to 2 minutes.
- After applying the eye ointment, wash your hands to remove any medicine.

For nasal (nose) drops:

- How to use: Blow your nose gently. Tilt your head back while standing or sitting up, or lie down on your back on a bed and hang your head over the side. Place the drops into each nostril and keep your head tilted back for a few minutes to allow the medicine to spread throughout the nose.
- Rinse the dropper with hot water and dry with a clean tissue. Replace the cap right after use. To avoid the spread of infection, do not use the container for more than one person.

For nasal (nose) spray:

- How to use: Blow your nose gently. With your head upright, spray the medicine into each nostril. Sniff briskly while squeezing the bottle quickly and firmly.
- Rinse the tip of the spray bottle with hot water, taking care not to suck water into the bottle, and dry with a clean tissue. Replace the cap right after cleaning. To avoid the spread of infection, do not use the container for more than one person.

For otic (ear) drops:

- To prevent contamination of the ear drops, do not touch the applicator tip to any surface (including the ear).
- The bottle may not be full; this is to provide proper drop control.
- How to apply: Lie down or tilt the head so the ear needing treatment faces up. For adults, gently pull the earlobe up and back (pull down and back for children). Drop the medicine into the ear canal. Keep the ear facing up for about 5 minutes so the medicine can run to the bottom of the ear canal (For young children and other patients who cannot stay still for 5 minutes, try to keep the ear facing up for at least 1 or 2 minutes.)
- Do not rinse the dropper after use. Wipe the tip of the dropper with a clean tissue and keep the container tightly closed.

For rectal suppositories:

- How to insert suppository: First, wash your hands. Remove the foil wrapper and moisten the suppository with water. Lie down on your side. Push the suppository well up into the rectum with your finger. If the suppository is too soft to insert, chill it in the refrigerator for 30 minutes or run cold water over it before removing the foil wrapper.
- Wash your hands after you have inserted the suppository.

For rectal cream or ointment:

- Clean and dry the rectal area. Apply a small amount of cream or ointment and rub it in gently.
- If your health care professional wants you to insert the medicine into the rectum: First, attach the plastic applicator tip onto the opened tube. Insert the applicator tip into the rectum and gently squeeze the tube to deliver the cream. Remove the applicator tip from the tube and wash with hot, soapy water. Replace the cap of the tube after use.
- Wash your hands after you have inserted the medicine.

For vaginal medicines:
- How to insert the medicine: First, wash your hands. Use the special applicator. Follow any special directions that are provided by the manufacturer. If you are pregnant, however, check with your health care professional before using the applicator to insert the medicine.
- Lie on your back, with your knees drawn up. Using the applicator, insert the medicine into the vagina as far as you can without using force or causing discomfort. Release the medicine by pushing on the plunger. Wait several minutes before getting up.
- Wash the applicator and your hands with soap and warm water.

Precautions While Using Your Medicine

Never give your medicine to anyone else. It has been prescribed for your personal medical problem or condition and may be harmful to another person.

Many medicines should not be taken with other medicines or with alcoholic beverages. Follow your health care professional's directions to help avoid problems.

Before having any kind of surgery (including dental surgery) or emergency treatment, tell the physician or dentist about any medicine you are taking.

If you think you have taken an overdose of any medicine or if a child has taken a medicine by accident: Call your poison control center or your health care professional at once. Keep those telephone numbers handy. Also, keep a bottle of Ipecac Syrup safely stored in your home in case you are told to cause vomiting. Read the directions on the label of Ipecac Syrup before using.

Side Effects of Your Medicine

Along with its intended effects, a medicine may cause some unwanted effects. Some of these side effects may need medical attention, while others may not. It is important for you to know what side effects may occur and what you should do if you notice signs of them. Check with your health care professional about the possible side effects of the medicines you are taking, or if you notice any unusual reactions or side effects.

Additional Information

It is a good idea for you to learn both the generic and brand names of your medicine and even to write them down for future use.

Many prescriptions may not be refilled until your pharmacist checks with your health care professional. *To save time, do not wait until you have run out of medicine before requesting a refill.* This is especially important if you must take your medicine every day.

When traveling:
- Carry your medicine with you rather than putting it in your checked luggage. Checked luggage may get lost or stored in very cold or very hot areas.
- Make sure a source of medicine is available where you are traveling, or take a large enough supply to last during your visit. It is also a good idea to take a copy of your written prescription with you.

If you want more information about your medicines, ask your health care professional. *Do not be embarrassed to ask questions* about any medicine you are taking. To help you remember, it may be useful to write down any questions and bring them with you on your next visit to your health care professional.

AVOIDING MEDICINE MISHAPS

Tips Against Tampering

Over-the-counter (OTC) or nonprescription medicines are now packaged so that it will be easier to notice signs of tampering. A tamper-evident package is required either to be unique so that it cannot be copied easily, or to have a barrier or indicator (with an identifying characteristic, such as a pattern, picture, or logo) that will be easily noticed if broken. For two-piece, unsealed, hard gelatin capsules, two tamper-evident features are required. Improved packaging also includes using special wrappers, seals, or caps on the outer and/or inner containers, or sealing each dose in its own pouch.

Even with such packaging, however, no system is completely safe. It is important that you do your part by checking for signs of tampering whenever you buy or use a medicine.

The following information may help you detect possible signs of tampering.

Protecting yourself

General common sense suggestions include the following:
- When buying a drug product, *consider* the dosage form (for example, capsules, tablets, syrup), the type of packaging, and the tamper-evident features. Ask yourself: Would it be easy for someone to tamper with this product? Will I be able to determine whether or not this product has been tampered with?
- *Look very carefully* at the outer packaging of the drug product before you buy it. After you buy it, also check the inner packaging as soon as possible.
- If the medicine has a protective packaging feature, it should be described in the labeling. This description is required to be placed so that it will not be affected if the feature is broken or missing. If the feature is broken or missing, *do not buy or use* the product. If you have already purchased the product, return it to the store. Always be sure to tell someone in charge about any problems.
- *Do not take* medicines that show even the slightest signs of tampering or do not seem quite right.
- Never take medicines in the dark or in poor lighting. *Read* the label and check each dose of medicine before you take it.

What to look for

Packaging

- Are there breaks, cracks, or holes in the outer or inner wrapping or protective cover or seal?
- Does the outer or inner covering appear to have been disturbed, unwrapped, or replaced?
- Does a plastic or other shrink band (tight-fitting wrap) around the top of the bottle appear distorted or stretched, as though it had been rolled down and then put back into place? Is the band missing? Has the band been slit and retaped?
- Is the bottom of the container intact?
- Does the container appear to be too full or not full enough?
- Is the cap on tight?
- Are there bits of paper or glue stuck on the rim of the container (does it seem like the container once had a bottle seal)?
- Is the cotton plug or filler in the bottle torn, sticky, or stained, or does it appear to have been taken out and put back?
- Do eye drops have a protective seal? All eye drops must be sealed when they are made, in order to keep them germ-free. Do not use if there is any sign of a broken or removed seal.
- Check the bottom as well as the top of a tube. Is the tube properly sealed? Metal tubes crimped up from the bottom like a tube of toothpaste should be firmly sealed.
- Are the expiration date, lot number, and other information the same on both the container and its outer wrapping or box?

Liquids

- Is the medicine the usual color? Thickness?
- Is a normally clear liquid cloudy or colored?
- Are there particles (small pieces) in the bottom of the bottle or floating in the solution? For some liquids, called suspensions, floating particles are normal.
- Does the medicine have a strange or different taste or odor (for example, bleach, acid, gasoline-like, or other pungent or sharp odor)? Do not taste the medicine if it has a strange odor.

Tablets

- Do the tablets look different than they usually do? Do they have unusual spots or markings? If they normally are shiny and smooth, are some dull or rough? Is there anything unusual about the color?
- Are the tablets all the same size and thickness?
- If there is printing on the tablets, do they all have the same imprint? Is the imprint missing from any?
- Do the tablets have a strange or different odor or taste?
- Are any of the tablets broken?

Capsules

- Do the capsules look different than they usually do? Are any cracked or dented? Are they all the same size and color?
- Do they have their normal shiny appearance or are some dull? Do some have fingerprints on them as though they have been handled?
- Are the capsules all the same length?
- If there is printing on the capsules, do they all have the same imprint? Is the imprint missing from any? Do the imprints all line up the same way?
- Do the capsules have an unexpected or unusual odor or taste?

Tubes and jars (ointments, creams, pastes, etc.)

- Does the product or container look different than usual?
- Are ointments and creams smooth and non-gritty? Have they separated?

Be a wise consumer. Look for signs of tampering before you buy a medicine and again each time you take a dose. Also, pay attention to the daily news in order to learn about any reported tampering.

It is important to understand that a change in the appearance or condition of a product may not mean that the package has been tampered with. The manufacturer may have changed the color of a medicine or its packaging. Also, the product may be breaking down with age or it may have had rough or unusual handling in shipping. In addition, some minor product variations may be normal.

Whenever you suspect that something is unusual about a medicine or its packaging, take it to your pharmacist. He or she is familiar with most products and their packaging. If there are serious concerns or problems, your pharmacist should report it to the USP Practitioners' Reporting Network[SM] (USP PRN®) at 1-800-487-7776, or other appropriate authorities.

Unintentional Poisoning

According to information provided by the American Association of Poison Control Centers, over one million children 6 years of age and under were unintentionally poisoned in 1998.

Adults also may be unintentionally poisoned. This happens most often through carelessness or lack of information. For example, people can be poisoned by taking medicines in the dark and getting the wrong one, or taking medicine prescribed for a friend to treat "the same symptoms."

Drug poisoning from an unintentional overdose is one type of accidental poisoning contributing to these figures. Other causes include household chemical poisoning from unintentional ingestion or contact, and inhaled poisoning—for example, carbon monoxide from a car.

Children are ready victims

The natural curiosity of children makes them ready victims of poisoning. Children explore everywhere and investigate their environment. What they find frequently goes into their mouths. They do not understand the danger and possibly cannot read warning labels.

Accidental poisoning from medicine is especially dangerous in small children because a medicine's strength is usually based on its use in adults. Even a small quantity of an adult dose can sometimes poison a child.

Preventing poisoning from medicines

- Store medicines out of the sight and reach of children, preferably in a locked cabinet—not in the bathroom medicine cabinet or in a food cabinet. Always store your medicines in a secure place.
- If you have children living with you or as occasional guests, you should have child-resistant caps on your medicine containers. These will help ensure that an accidental poisoning does not occur in your home. (Adults who have difficulty opening child-resistant closures may request traditional, easy-to-open packaging for their medicines.)
- If you are called to the telephone or to answer the door while you are taking a medicine, take the container with you or put the medicine out of the reach of small children. Children act quickly—usually when no one is watching.
- Always replace lids and return medicines to their storage place after use, even if you will be using them again soon.
- Date medicines when purchased and clean out your medicines periodically. Discard prescription medicines that are past their expiration or "beyond use" date. As medicines grow old, the chemicals in them may change. In general, medicines that do not have an expiration date should not be kept for more than 1 year. Carefully dis- card any medicines so children cannot get them. Rinse containers well before discarding in the trash.
- Take only those medicines prescribed for you and give medicines only to those for whom they are prescribed. A medicine that worked well for one person may harm another.
- It is best to keep all medicines in their original containers with their labels intact. The label contains valuable information for taking the medicine properly. Also, in case of accidental poisoning, it is important to know the ingredients in a drug product and any emergency instructions from the manufacturer. While prescription medicines usually do not list ingredients, information on the label makes it possible for your pharmacist to identify the contents.
- Ask your pharmacist to include on the label the number of tablets or capsules that he or she put in the container. In case of poisoning, it may be important to know roughly how many tablets or capsules were taken.
- Do not trust your memory—read the label before using the medicine, and take it as directed.
- If a medicine container has no label or the label has been defaced so you are not absolutely sure what it says, do not use it.
- Turn on a light when taking or giving medicines at night or in a dark room.
- Label medicine containers with poison symbols, especially if you have children, individuals with poor vision, or other persons in your home who cannot read well.

- Teach children that medicine is not candy by calling each medicine by its proper name.
- Do not take medicines in front of children. They may wish to imitate you.
- Communicate these safety rules to any babysitters you have and remember them if you babysit or are visiting a house with children. Children are naturally curious and can get into a pocketbook, briefcase, or overnight bag that contains medicines.

What to do if a poisoning happens

Remember:

- There may be no immediate, significant symptoms or warning signs, particularly in a child.
- Nothing you can give will work equally well in all cases of poisoning. In fact, one "antidote" may counteract the effects of another.
- Many poisons act quickly, leaving little time for treatment.

Therefore:

- If you think someone has swallowed medicine or a household product, and the person is unconscious, having seizures (convulsions), or is not breathing, immediately call for an ambulance. Otherwise, do not wait to see what effect the poison will have or if symptoms of overdose develop; immediately call a poison control center (listed in the white pages of your telephone book under "Poison Control" or inside the front cover with other emergency numbers). These numbers should be posted beside every telephone in the house, as should those of your pharmacist, the police, the fire department, and ambulance services. (Some poison control centers have TTY capability for the deaf. Check with your local center if you or someone in your family requires this service.)
- Have the container with you when you call so you can read the label on the product for ingredients.
- Describe what, when, and how much was taken and the age and condition of the person poisoned—for example, if the person is vomiting, choking, drowsy, shows a change in color or temperature of skin, is conscious or unconscious, or is convulsing.
- *Do not induce vomiting* unless instructed by medical personnel. *Do not induce vomiting or force liquids* into a person who is convulsing, unconscious, or very drowsy.
- Stay calm and in control of the situation.

Keep a bottle of Ipecac Syrup stored in a secure place in your home for emergency use. It is available at pharmacies in 1 ounce bottles without prescription. Ipecac Syrup is often recommended to induce vomiting in cases of poisoning.

Activated Charcoal also is sometimes recommended in certain types of poisoning and you may wish to add a supply to your emergency medicines. It is available without a pre-

GETTING THE MOST OUT OF YOUR MEDICINES

scription. Before using this medicine for poisoning, however, call a poison control center for advice.

To get the most out of your medicines, there are certain things that you must do. Your health care professionals will be working with you, but you also have a responsibility for your own health.

Communicating With Your Health Care Provider

Communication between you and your health care professional is central to good medical care. Your health care professional needs to know about you, your medical history, and your current problems. In turn, you need to understand the recommendations he or she is making and what you will need to do to follow the treatment. You will have to ask questions—and answer some too. Communication is a two-way process.

Giving information

Your health care professional needs to know some details about your past and present medical history. In discussing these details, you should always be completely open and honest. Your health professional's diagnosis and treatment will be based in part on the information that you provide. A complete list of the details that should be included in a full medical history is provided below.

"Medical history" checklist

A "medical history" checklist covers the following information:

- All the serious illnesses you have ever had and the approximate dates.
- Your current symptoms, if any.
- **All** the medicines and dietary supplements you are taking or have taken in the recent past. This includes prescription and nonprescription medicines (such as pain relievers, antacids, laxatives, and cold medicines, etc.) and herbal medicines and home remedies. This is especially important if you are seeing more than one health care professional; if you are having surgery, including dental or emergency treat-ment; or if you get your medicines from more than one source.
- **Any** allergies or sensitivities to medicines, foods, or other substances.
- Your smoking, drinking, and exercise habits.
- Any recent changes in your lifestyle or personal habits. New job? Retired? Change of residence? Death in family? Married? Divorced? Other?
- Any special diet you are on—low-sugar, low-sodium, low-fat, or a diet to lose or gain weight.
- If you are pregnant, plan to become pregnant, or if you are breast-feeding.
- All the vaccinations and vaccination boosters you have had, with dates if possible.
- Any operations you have had, including dental and those performed on an outpatient basis, and any accidents that have required hospitalization.
- Illnesses or conditions that run in your family.
- Cause of death of closest relatives.

Remember, be sure to tell your health care professional at each visit if there have been any changes since your last visit.

Medical history forms

Many health care professionals have a standard "medical history" form they will ask you to fill out when they see you for the first time. Some may ask the questions and write down the answers for you. If you will be visiting a health care professional for the first time, prepare yourself before you go by thinking about the questions that might be asked and jotting down the answers—including dates—so that you will not forget an important detail. Once your "medical history" is in the files, subsequent visits will take less time.

You will have to supply each health care provider you see—every time you see one—with complete information about what happened since your last visit. It is important that your records are updated so he or she can make sound recommendations for your continued treatment, or treatment of any new problems.

Medical history file

It will simplify things if you develop a "medical history" file at home for yourself and each family member for whom you are responsible. Setting up the file will take time. However, once it is established, you need only to keep it up-to-date and remember to take it with you when you see a health care professional. This will be easier than having to repeat the information each time and running the risk of confusing or forgetting details.

It is also a good idea to carry in your wallet a card that summarizes your chronic medical conditions, the medicines you are taking, and your allergies and drug sensitivities. You should keep this card as up-to-date as possible. Many pharmacists provide these cards as a service.

Getting information

In order to benefit from your health care professional's advice you must understand completely everything that he or she tells you. Do not be embarrassed to ask questions, or to ask him or her to explain again any instruction or detail that you do not understand. Then it is up to you to carry out those instructions precisely. If there is a failure in any part of this system, you will pay an even higher price—physically and financially—for your health care.

Your health care professional may provide instructions to you in written form. If he or she does not, you may want to write them down or ask the health care professional to write them down for you. If you do not have time to jot down everything while you are still with your health care professional, sit down in the waiting room before you leave and write down the information while it is still fresh in your mind and you can still ask questions. If you have been given a prescription, ask for written information about the drug and how to take it. Your pharmacist can also answer questions when you have your prescription filled.

What you need to know about your medicines

There are a number of things that you should know about each medicine you are taking. These include:

- The medicine's generic and brand name.
- How the medicine will help you and the expected results. How it makes you feel. How long it takes to begin working.
- How much to take at one time.
- How often to take the medicine.
- How long it will be necessary to take the medicine.
- When to take it. Before, during, after meals? At bedtime? At any other special times?
- How to take it. With water? With fruit juice? With food?
- What to do if you forget to take it (miss a dose).
- Foods, drinks, or other medicines that you should not take while taking the medicine.
- Restrictions on activities while taking the medicine, such as driving a car or operating other motor vehicles.
- Possible side effects. What to do if they appear. How to minimize the side effects. How soon they will go away.
- When to seek help if there are problems.
- How long to wait before reporting no change in your symptoms.
- How to store the medicine.
- The expiration date.
- The cost of the medicine.
- How to have your prescription refilled, if necessary.

Other information

Following are some other issues and information that you may want to consider:

- Ask your health care professional about the ingredients in the medicines (both prescription and over-the-counter [OTC]) you are taking and whether there may be a conflict with other medicines. Your health care professional can help you avoid dangerous combinations or drug products that contain ingredients to which you are allergic or sensitive.
- Ask your health care professional for help in developing a system for taking your medicines properly, particularly if you are taking a number of them on a daily basis. When you are a patient in a hospital, ask for instructions before you are discharged. Do not hesitate or be embarrassed to ask questions or ask for help.
- If you are over 60 years of age, ask your health care professional if the dose of the medicine is right for you. Some medicines should be given in lower doses to certain older individuals.
- If you are taking several different medicines, ask your health care professional if all of them are necessary for you. You should take only those medicines that you need.
- Medicines should be kept in the container they came in. If this is not possible when you are at work or away from home, ask your pharmacist to provide or recommend a container to transport your medicines safely. The use of "pill boxes" can also cause some problems, such as broken or chipped tablets, mistaking one medicine for another, and even interactions between the medicine and the metal of these boxes.

- Some people have trouble taking tablets or capsules. Your health care professional will know if another dosage form is available, and if tablet or capsule contents can be taken in a liquid. If this is an ongoing problem, ask your prescriber to write the prescription for the dosage form you can take most comfortably.
- To protect children from accidental poisoning, child-resistant caps are required by law on most oral prescription medicines. These containers are designed so children will have difficulty opening them. Since many adults also find these containers hard to open, the law allows consumers to request traditional, easy-to-open packaging for their drugs. If you do not use child-resistant packaging, make sure that your medicines are stored where small children cannot see or reach them. If you use child-resistant containers, ask your pharmacist to show you how to open them.

Consumer education is one of your health care professional's most important responsibilities. To supplement what you learn during your visit, ask if there is any written information about your medicines that you can take home with you. Your health care professional may also have available various reference books or computerized drug information that you can consult for details about precautions, side effects, and proper use of your medicines.

Your Health Care Team

Your health care team will be made up of several different health care professionals. Each of these individuals will play an important part in the overall provision of your health care. It is important that you understand the roles of each of these providers and what you should be able to expect from each of them.

Your dentist

In addition to providing care and maintenance of your mouth, teeth, and gums, your dentist is also an essential member of your overall health care team since your oral health and general health often affect one another.

In providing dental treatment, your dentist should base his or her decisions upon an extensive knowledge of your current condition and past medical and dental history. Because the dentist is a prescriber of medications, it is very important that he or she is aware of your **full** medical and dental history. A complete medical and dental history should include the information that is listed in the "Medical history checklist" section above. Even if you do not consider this information important, you should inform your dentist as fully as possible.

In the treatment of any dental/oral problem your dentist should make every effort to inform you as fully as possible about the nature of the problem. He or she should explain why this problem has occurred, the advantages and disadvantages of available treatments (including no treatment), and what types of preventive measures can be employed to avoid future problems. These measures may include periodic visits to the dentist, and a general awareness of the manner in which dental and overall health may affect one another. In any type of treatment, your dentist should always allow you to ask questions, and should be willing to answer them to your satisfaction. In selecting a dentist, it is important to keep in mind the role of the dentist as a member of the health care team, and the extent of the information that he or she should be asking for and providing. There are also several practical issues that you should consider, such as:

- Is the dentist a specialist or general practitioner?
- What are the office hours?
- Is the dentist or his/her associates available after office hours by phone? In emergencies, will you be able to contact a dentist?
- What is the office policy on cancellations?
- What types of payment are accepted at the office?
- What is the office policy on x-ray procedures?
- Is the dentist willing to work with other medical and/or dental specialists that you may be seeing?

Your dentist should be an integral part of your health care team. In treating problems and providing general maintenance of your oral health, your dentist should base decisions upon a full dental and medical history. He or she should also be willing to answer any questions that you have regarding your oral health, any medications prescribed, and preventive measures to avoid future problems.

Your nurse

Depending upon the setting, type of therapy being administered, and state regulations, the role of the nurse in your health care team may vary. Registered nurses practice in diverse health care settings, such as hospitals, outpatient clinics or physicians' offices, schools, workplaces, homes, and long-term care facilities like nursing homes and retirement centers. Some nurses, including certified nurse practitioners and midwives, hold a master's degree in nursing and may assume the role of primary health care professional, either in practice by themselves or in joint practices with physicians. In most states, nurse practitioners may prescribe selected medications. Clinical nurse specialists also have a master's degree in nursing and specialize in a particular area of health care. In some hospitals, long-term care facilities, and out-patient care settings, licensed practical nurses (LPNs) have certain responsibilities in administering medication to patients. LPNs usually work under the supervision of a RN or physician. Nursing aides assist RNs and LPNs with different kinds of patient care activities. In most places where people receive health care, RNs may be the primary source of information for drug therapies and other medical treatments. It is important that you be aware of the roles and responsibilities of the nurses participating in your health care.

Professional nurses participate with other health professionals to ensure that your medication therapy is safe and effective and to monitor any effects (both desired and negative) from the medication. You may be admitted to the hospital so that nurses can administer medications and monitor your response to therapy. In hospitals or long-term care facilities, nurses are responsible for administering your medications in their proper dosage form and dose, and at correct time intervals, as well as monitoring your response to these medica-

tions. At home or in outpatient settings, nurses should ensure that you have the proper information and support of others, if needed, to get the medication and take it as prescribed. When nurses administer medication, they should explain why you are receiving this medication, how it works, any possible side effects, special precautions or actions that you must take while using the medication, and any potential interactions with other medications.

If you experience any side effects or symptoms from a medication, you should always tell your health care provider. It is important that these reactions be detected before they become serious or permanent. You can seek advice about possible ways to minimize these side effects from your nurse. Your health care professional should also be made aware of any additional medical problems or conditions (such as pregnancy) that you may have, since these can also affect the safety and effectiveness of a medication.

The professional nurse is someone who can help to clarify drug information. In most health care settings, nurses are accessible and can answer your questions or direct you to others who can assist you. Professional nurses are skilled in the process of patient teaching. To make sure that patients learn important inforrnation about their health problem and its treatment, RNs often use a combination of teaching methods, such as verbal instruction, written materials, demonstration, and audio-visual instructions. Above all, professional nurses should teach at a pace and level that are appropriate for you. RNs can also help you design a medication schedule that fits your lifestyle and may be less likely to cause unwanted side effects.

Your pharmacist

Your pharmacist is an important member of your health care team. In addition to performing traditional services, such as dispensing medications, your pharmacist can help you understand your medications and how to take them safely and effectively. By keeping accurate and up-to-date records and monitoring your use of medications, your pharmacist can help to protect you from improper medication therapy, unwanted side effects, and dangerous drug interactions. Because your pharmacist can play a vital role in protecting and improving your health, you should seek a pharmacist who will provide these services.

To provide you with the best possible care, your pharmacist should be informed about your current condition and medication history. Your personal medication history should include the information that is listed in the "Medical history checklist" section above. Your pharmacist should also be aware of any special packaging needs that you may have (such as child-resistant or easy-to-open containers). Your pharmacist should keep accurate and up-to-date records that contain this information. If you visit a new pharmacy that does not have access to your medication records, it is important that you inform that pharmacist as fully as possible about your medical history or provide him or her with a copy of your medication records from your previous pharmacy. In general, in order to get the most out of your pharmacy services, it is best to get all of your medications (including OTCs) from the same pharmacy. Your pharmacist should be a knowledgeable and approachable source of information about your medications. Some of the information that your pharmacist should explain is listed in the "What you need to know about your medicines" section above. Ideally, this information should also be provided in written form, so that you may refer to it later if you have any questions or problems. The pharmacist should always be willing to answer any questions that you have regarding your medications, and should also be willing to contact your physician or other health care professionals (dentist, nurses, etc.) on your behalf if necessary.

Your pharmacist can also help you with information on the costs of your medicines. Many medicines are available from more than one company. They may have equal effects but different costs. Your insurance company, HMO, or other third-party payment group may reimburse you for only some of these medications or only for part of their costs. Your pharmacist will be able to tell you which of these medications are covered by your payment plan or which cost less.

In selecting a pharmacist, it is important that you understand the role of the pharmacist as a member of your health care team and the extent of information that he or she should be asking for and providing. Because pharmacies can offer different types of services and have different policies regarding patient information, some of the issues that you should consider in selecting a pharmacist also relate to the pharmacy where that person practices. There are several issues regarding the pharmacist and pharmacy that you should consider, such as:

- Does the pharmacy offer written information that you can take home? Home delivery?
- Are you able to talk to your pharmacist without other people hearing you?
- Can the pharmacist be reached easily by phone? In an emergency, is a pharmacist available twenty-four hours (including weekends and holidays) by phone?
- What types of payment are accepted in the pharmacy?
- Does the pharmacy accept your HMO or third-party payment plan?
- Does the pharmacy offer any specialized services, such as diabetes education?

You should select your pharmacist and pharmacy as carefully as you select your physician, and stay with the same pharmacy so that all of your medication records are in the same place. This will help to ensure that your records are accurate and up-to-date and will allow you to develop a beneficial relationship with your pharmacist.

Your physician

One of the most important health care decisions that you will make is your choice of a personal physician. The physician is central to your health care team, and is responsible for helping you maintain your overall health. In addition to detecting and treating ailments or adverse conditions, your physician and his or her coworkers should also serve as primary sources of health care information. Because the physi-

cian plays such an important role in your overall health care, it is important that you understand the full range of the physician's role as health care and information provider.

In providing any type of treatment or counseling, your physician should base his or her decisions upon an extensive knowledge of your current condition and past medical history. A complete medical history should include the information that is listed in the "Medical history checklist" section above. Your physician should keep accurate and comprehensive medical records containing this information. Because your treatment (and your health) is dependent upon a full disclosure of your medical history, as well as any factors that may currently be affecting your health (i.e., stress, smoking, drug use, etc.), it is important that you inform your physician as fully as possible, even if you might not consider this information important.

It is important that you inform your personal physician of any other physicians (such as specialists or subspecialists), dentists, or other health care professionals that you are seeing. You should also inform your physician of the pharmacy that you use or intend to use, so that he or she can contact the pharmacist if necessary.

In treating any health problem, your physician should make every effort to help you understand completely the nature of the problem and its treatment. He or she should take the time to explain the problem, why it may have occurred, and what preventive measures (if any) can be taken to avoid it in the future. Your physician should explain fully the reasons for any prescribed treatment. He or she should also be willing to discuss alternative therapies, especially if you are uncomfortable with the one that has been prescribed. Your physician should always be willing to answer all of your questions to your satisfaction.

In selecting a physician, you should look for one who will provide a full range of services. You may also want to consider your physician's medical credentials. Your local medical society should be able to provide specific facts about your physician's traning, experience, and membership in professional societies.

Cost and payment are two of the most important issues in contemporary health care. Your physician should be sensitive to the costs of your treatment and the manner in which you intend to pay for this and related medications. If you belong to an HMO or third-party payment plan, be sure that your physician is aware of your involvement in the plan. You should also be aware of the different types of payment that are accepted at the physician's office.

In prescribing medications, your physician should take into account the manner in which you intend to pay for your drugs, and should be aware of any specific concerns regarding the costs of your treatment and medication. He or she should also explain why brand or generic medication may be preferable in certain situations.

In selecting a physician, there are also several practical issues and matters of convenience that you should consider, such as:

- Is the office convenient to your home or work?
- What are the office hours?
- Is your physician or his/her associates or partners available (twenty-four hours) by phone? In emergencies, will you be able to contact a physician?
- Are you able to arrange appointments to fit your schedule? What is the office policy on cancellations?
- Is the physician well regarded in the community? Does he or she have a reputation for listening to patients and answering questions?
- Does the physician have admitting privileges at a hospital of your preference?
- Does he/she participate in your health plan?

In addition to the considerations already mentioned, your physician should be sensitive to the special concerns of treating the elderly. Older patients can present disease processes differently from younger adults, can react differently to certain drugs and dosages, and may have preexisting conditions that require special treatments to be prescribed.

There are also several special issues to consider in your selection of a pediatrician or family physician. If your child is not old enough to understand all instructions and information, it is important that your child's physician explain to you any information about a problem and all instructions for treatment. When your child is of school age, the physician should speak directly to the child as well, asking and answering questions, and providing information about cause and prevention of medical problems and the use of medications. He or she should choose a dosage form and dose that is appropriate for your child's age and explain what to do if the child has certain symptoms, such as fever, vomiting, etc. (including the amount and type of medicine to give, if any, and when to call him or her for advice).

Your physician should be a primary source of information about your health and any medications that you are taking. In providing treatment for medical problems or conditions, the physician should base decisions on a full medical history and be willing to answer any questions that you have regarding your health, treatment, and medications.

Managing Your Medicines

To get the full benefit and reduce risks in taking your medicines, it is important to follow instructions exactly. This means taking the right medicine and dose, at correct time intervals, for the length of time prescribed. Bad effects can result from taking too much or too little of a medicine, or taking it too often or not often enough.

Establishing a system

Whether you are taking one or several medicines, you should develop a system for taking them. It can be just as difficult to remember whether you took your once-a-day medicine as it can be to keep track of a number of medicines that need to be taken several times a day. Many medicines also have special instructions that can further complicate proper use.

Establish a way of knowing whether you took your medicines properly, then make that a part of your daily routine. If you take one or two medicines a day, you may only need to take them at the same time that you perform some other regular task, such as brushing your teeth or getting dressed.

For most people, a check-off record can also be a handy way of managing multiple medicines. Keep your medicine record in a handy, visible place next to where you take your medicines. Check off each dose as you take it. If you miss a dose, make a note about what happened and what you did on the back of the record or the bottom of the sheet.

Be sure to note any unwanted effects or anything unusual that you think may be connected with your medicines. Also note if a medicine does not do what you expect, but remember that some medicines take a while before having a noticeable effect.

If you keep a check-off record faithfully, you will know for sure whether or not you took your medicine. You will also have a complete record for your health care professionals to review when you visit them again. This information can help them determine if the medicine is working properly or causing unwanted side effects, or whether adjustments should be made in your medicines and/or doses.

If your medicines or the instructions for taking them are changed, correct your record or make a new one. Keep the old record until you are sure this information is no longer needed.

You might want to color code your medicine containers to help tell them apart. If you are having trouble reading labels or if you are color-blind, codes that can be recognized by touch (rubber bands, a cotton ball, or a piece of emery board, for instance) can be attached to the container. If you code your medicines, be sure these identifications are included on any medicine record you use. If necessary, ask your pharmacist to type medicine labels in large letters for easier reading.

A check-off list is not the only method for recording medicine use. If this system does not work for you, ask your health care professional for help in developing an alternative. Be sure he or she knows all the medicines prescribed for you and any nonprescription medicines you take regularly, the hours you usually eat your meals, and any special diet you are following.

Informed management

Your medicines have been prescribed for you and your condition. Ask your health care professional what benefits to expect, what side effects may occur, and when to report any side effects. If your symptoms go away, do not decide you are well and stop taking your medicine. If you stop too soon, the symptoms may come back. Finish all of the medicine if you have been told to do so. However, if you develop diarrhea or other unpleasant side effects, do not continue with the medicine; call your health care professional and report these effects. A change in dose or in the kind of medicine you are taking may be necessary.

When you are given a prescription for a medicine, ask the person who wrote it to explain it to you. For example, does "four times a day" mean one in the morning, one at noon, one in the evening, and one at bedtime; or does it mean every six hours around the clock? When a prescription says "take as needed," ask how close together the doses can be taken and what the maximum number of doses you can take in one day should be. Does "take with liquids" mean with water, milk, or something else? Are there some liquids that should avoided? What does "take with food" mean? At every mealtime (some people must eat six meals a day), or with a snack? Do not trust your memory—have the instructions written down. You must understand exactly what the pre-scriber wants you to do in order to "take as directed."

When the pharmacist dispenses your medicine, you have another opportunity to clarify information or to ask other questions. Before you leave, check the label on your med-icine to be sure it matches the prescription and your under-standing of what you are to do. If it does not, ask more questions.

The key to getting the most from your prescribed treatments is following instructions accurately and intelligently. If you have questions or doubts about the prescribed treatment, do not decide to stop taking the medicine or fail to follow the prescribed regimen. Discuss your questions and doubts with your health care professional.

The time and effort put into setting up a system to manage your medicines and establishing a routine for taking them will pay off by relieving anxiety and helping you get the most from your prescribed treatment.

Taking Your Medicine

To take medicines safely and get the greatest benefit from them, it is important to establish regular habits so you are less likely to make mistakes.

Before taking any medicine, read the label and any accom-panying information. You can also consult books to learn more about the medicine. If you have unanswered ques-tions, check with your health care professional.

The label on the container of a prescription medicine should bear your first and last name; the name of the prescriber; the pharmacy address and telephone number; the prescription number; the date of dispensing; and directions for use. Some states or provinces may have additional require-ments. If the name of the drug product is not on the label, ask the pharmacist to include the brand (if any) and generic names. An expiration date may also appear. All of this infor-mation is important in identifying your medicines and using them properly. The labels on containers should never be removed and all medicines should be kept in their original containers.

Some tips for taking medicines safely and accurately include the following:

- Read the label of each medicine container three times:
—before you remove it from its storage place,
—before you take the lid off the container to remove the dose, and

—before you replace the container in its storage place.
- Never take medicines in the dark, even if you think you know exactly where to find them.
- Use standard measuring devices to take your medi-cines (household teaspoons, cups, or glasses vary widely in the amount they hold). Ask your pharmacist for help with measuring.
- Set bottles and boxes of medicines on a clear area, well back from the edge of the surface to prevent con-tainers and/or caps from being knocked to the floor.
- When pouring liquid medicines, pick up the container with the label against the palm of your hand to protect it from being stained by dripping medicine.
- Wipe off the top and neck of bottles of liquid medicines to keep labels from being obscured, and to make it less likely that the lid will stick.
- Shake all liquid suspensions of drug products before pouring so that ingredients are mixed thoroughly.
- If you are taking medicine with water, use a full, 8 ounce glassful, not just enough to get it down. Too little liquid with some medicines can prevent the medicine from working properly, and can cause throat irritation if the medicine does not get completely to the stomach.
- To avoid accidental confusion of lids, labels, and med-icines, replace the lid on one container before opening another.
- When you are interrupted while taking your medicine, take the container with you or put the medicine out of the reach of small children. It only takes a second for them to take an overdose. When you return, check the label of the medicine to be sure you have the right one.
- Crush tablets or open capsules to take with food or beverages if your health care professional has told you that this will not affect the way the medicine works. If you have difficulty swallowing a tablet or capsule, check with your health care professional about the availability of a different dosage form.
- Follow any diet instructions or other treatment mea-sures prescribed by your health care professional.
- If at any point you realize you have taken the wrong medicine or the wrong amount, call your health care professional immediately. In an emergency, call your local emergency number.

When you have finished taking your medicines, mark it down immediately on your medication calendar to avoid "double dosing." Also make note of any unusual changes in your body, including change in weight, color or amount of urine, perspiration, or coughed-up matter; as well as your pulse, temperature, or any other items you may have been instructed to observe for your condition or your medicine.

Try to take your medicines on time, but a half-hour early or late will usually not upset your schedule. If you are more than several hours late and are getting close to your next scheduled dose, check any instructions that were given to you by your health care professional. If you did not receive instructions about missed doses, check with your health care professional. You may also find missed dose informa-tion in the entries included in this book.

When your medicines are being managed by someone else (for example, when you are a patient in a hospital or nursing home), question what is happening to you and communicate what you know about your previous drug therapy or any other treatments. If you know you always take one, not two, of a certain tablet, say so and ask that your record be checked before you take the medicine. If you think you are receiving the wrong treatment or medication, do not hesitate to say so. You should always remain involved in your own therapy.

Many hospitals and nursing homes now offer counseling in medicine management as part of their discharge planning for patients. If you or a family member are getting ready to come home, ask your health care professional if you can be part of such instruction.

The "Expiration Date" on Medicine Labels

To assure that a drug product meets applicable standards of identity, strength, quality, and purity at the time of use, an "expiration date" is added by the manufacturer to the label of most prescription and nonprescription drug products.

The expiration date on a drug product is valid only as long as the product is stored in the original, unopened container under the storage conditions specified by the manufacturer. Among other things, humidity, temperature, light, and even air can effect drugs. A medicine taken after the expiration date may have changed in potency or may have formed harmful material as it deteriorates. Contamination with germs can also occur. The safest rule is not to use any medicine beyond the expiration date.

Preventing deterioration

A drug begins to deteriorate the minute it is made. The manufacturer in calculating the expiration date factors in this rate of deterioration. Keeping the drug product in the container supplied by the pharmacist helps slow down deterioration. Storing the drug in a proper manner—for example, in a light-resistant container or in a cool, dry place (not the bathroom medicine cabinet)—also helps. The need for medicines to be kept in their containers and stored properly cannot be overstressed.

Patients sometimes ask their health care professionals to prescribe a large quantity of a particular medicine in order to "economize." Although this may be all right in some cases, this practice may backfire. If you have a large supply of your medicine and it deteriorates before you can use it all, or if your doctor changes your medicine, you may lose out.

Sometimes deterioration can be recognized by physical changes in the drug, such as a change in odor or appearance. For example, aspirin tablets develop a vinegar odor when they break down. These changes are not true of all drugs, however, and the absence of physical changes should not be assumed to mean that no deterioration has occurred.

Some liquid medicines mixed at the pharmacy will have a "beyond use" date on the label. This is an expiration date that is calculated from the date of preparation in the pharmacy. This is a definite date, after which you should throw away any remaining medicine.

If your prescription medicines do not bear an "expiration" or "beyond use" date, your dispensing pharmacist is the best person to advise you about how long they can be safely used.

ABOUT THE MEDICINES YOU ARE TAKING

New Drugs–From Idea to Marketplace

To be sold legitimately in the United States, new drugs must pass through a rigorous system of approval specified in the Food, Drug, and Cosmetic Act and supervised by the Food and Drug Administration (FDA). Except for certain drugs subject to other regulatory provisions, no new drug for human use may be marketed in this country unless FDA has approved a "New Drug Application" (NDA) for it.

The idea

The creation of a new drug usually starts with an idea. Most likely that idea results from the study of a disease or group of symptoms. Ideas can also come from observations of clinical research. This may involve many years of study, or the idea may occur from an accidental discovery in a research laboratory. Some may be coincidental discoveries, as in the case of penicillin.

Idea development takes place most often in the laboratory of a pharmaceutical company, but may also happen in laboratories at research institutions like the National Institutes of Health, at medical centers and universities, or in the laboratory of a chemical company.

Animal testing

A new drug is first tested on animals to help determine how toxic the substance may be. Most drugs interfere in some way with normal body functions. These animal studies are designed to discover the degree of that interference and the extent of the toxic effects.

After successful animal testing, perhaps over several years, the sponsors of the new drug apply to the FDA for an Investigational New Drug (IND) application. This status allows the drug to be tested in humans. As part of their request, the sponsoring manufacturer must submit the results of the animal studies, plus a detailed outline of the proposed human testing and information about the researchers that will be involved.

Human testing

Drug testing in humans usually consists of three consecutive phases. "Informed consent" must be secured from all volunteers participating in this testing.

Phase I testing is most often done on young, healthy adults. This testing is done on a relatively small number of subjects, generally between 20 and 80. Its purpose is to learn more about the biochemistry of the drug: how it acts on the body and how the body reacts to it. The procedure differs for some drugs, however. For example, Phase I testing of cancer drugs involves actual cancer patients from the beginning of testing.

During Phase II, small controlled clinical studies are designed to test the effectiveness and relative safety of the drug. These are done on closely monitored patients who have the disease for which the drug is being tested. Their numbers seldom go beyond 100 to 200 patients. Some volunteers for Phase II testing who have severely complicated conditions may be excluded.

A "control" group of people of comparable physical and disease types is used in double-blind, controlled experiments for most drugs. These experiments are conducted by medical investigators thoroughly familiar with the disease and this type of research. In a double-blind experiment, the patient, the health professional, and other personnel do not know whether the patient is receiving the drug being tested, another active drug, or no medicine at all (a placebo or "sugar pill"). This helps eliminate bias and assures the accuracy of results. The findings of these tests are statistically analyzed to determine whether they are "significant" or due to chance alone.

Phase III consists of larger studies. This testing is performed after effectiveness of the drug has been established and is intended to gather additional evidence of effectiveness for specific uses of the drug. These studies also help discover adverse drug reactions that may occur with the drug. Phase III studies involve a few hundred to several thousand patients who have the disease the drug is intended to treat.

Patients with additional diseases or those receiving other therapy may be included in later Phase II and Phase III studies. They would be expected to be representative of certain segments of the population who would receive the drug following approval for marketing.

Final approval

When a sponsor believes the investigational studies on a drug have shown it to be safe and effective in treating specific conditions, a New Drug Application (NDA) is submitted to FDA. This application is accompanied by all the documentation from the company's research, including complete records of all the animal and human testing. This documentation can run to many thousands of pages.

The NDA and its documentation must then be reviewed by FDA physicians, pharmacologists, chemists, statisticians, and other professionals experienced in evaluating new drugs. Proposed labeling information for the physician and pharmacist is also screened for accuracy, completeness, and conformity to FDA-approved wording.

Regulations call for the FDA to review an NDA within 180 days. This period may be extended if additional data is required and, in some cases, may take several years. When all research phases are considered, the actual time it takes from idea to marketplace may be 8 to 10 years or even longer. However, for drugs representing major therapeutic advances, FDA may "fast-track" the approval process to try to get those drugs to patients who need them as soon as possible.

After approval

After a drug is marketed, the manufacturer must inform the FDA of any unexpected side effects or toxicity that comes to its attention. Consumers and health care professionals have an important role in helping to identify any previously unre-

ported effects. If new evidence indicates that the drug may present an "imminent hazard," the FDA can withdraw approval for marketing or add new information to the drug's labeling at any time.

Generic drugs

After a new drug is approved for marketing, a patent will generally protect the financial interests of the drug's developer for a number of years. The traditional protection period is for 17 years. In reality, however, the period is much less due to the extended period of time needed to gain approval before marketing can begin. Recognizing that a considerable part of a drug's patent life may be tied up in the approval process, in 1984 the U.S. Congress passed a law providing patent extension for drugs whose commercial sale may have been unduly delayed by the approval process.

Any manufacturer can apply for permission to produce and market a drug after the patent for the drug has expired. Following a procedure called an Abbreviated New Drug Application (ANDA), the applicant must show that its product has a comparable potency and effect to the original product. Although the extensive clinical testing completed by the originator during the drug's development does not have to be repeated, comparative testing between the products must be done.

Drug Names

Every drug must have a nonproprietary name, a name that is available for each manufacturer to use. These names are commonly called generic names.

The FDA requires the generic name of a drug product to be placed on its labeling. However, manufacturers often use brand names in promoting their products. In general, brand names are shorter and easier to use than the corresponding generic name. The manufacturer then emphasizes its brand name (which cannot be used by anyone else) in advertising and other promotions. Often, the consumer may not realize that a brand name drug is also available under other brand names or by generic name. Ask your pharmacist if you have any questions about the names of your medicines.

Drug Quality

After an NDA or an ANDA has been approved for a product, the manufacturer must then meet all requirements relating to production. These include the FDA's current Good Manufacturing Practice regulations and any applicable standards relating to strength, quality, purity, packaging, and labeling that are established by the United States Pharmacopeia (USP).

Routine product testing by the manufacturer is required by the Good Manufacturing Practice regulations of the FDA (the FDA itself does not routinely test all products, except in cases where there is a suspicion that something may be wrong). In addition to governmental requirements, drug products must meet public standards of strength, quality, and purity that are developed by USP. In order to market their products, all manufacturers in the United States must meet USP-established standards unless they specifically choose not to meet the standards for a particular product. In this case, that product's label must state that it is "not USP" and how it differs from USP standards (this occurs very rarely).

Differences in Drug Products

Although standards to ensure strength, quality, purity, and bioequivalence (comparable potency and effect) exist, the standards allow for variations in certain factors that may produce other differences from product to product. These product variations may be important to some patients, since not all patients are "equivalent." For example, the size, shape, and coating may vary and, therefore, be harder or easier for some patients to swallow; an oral liquid will taste good to some patients and bad to others; one manufacturer may use lactose as an inactive ingredient in its product, while another product may contain a different inactive ingredient; one product may contain sugar or alcohol while another product does not.

In deciding to use one therapeutically equivalent product over another, consumers should keep the following in mind:

- Consider convenience factors of drug products (for example, ease of taking a particular dosage form).
- Don't overlook the convenience of the package. The package must protect the drug in accordance with USP requirements, but packages can be quite different in their ease of carrying, storing, opening, and measuring.
- If you have an allergy or any type of dietary restriction, you need to be aware of the "inactive" ingredients that may be present in different medicines. These inactive ingredients may vary from product to product.
- Price is always a consideration. The price difference between products (e.g., different brands, or brands versus generics) may be a major factor in the overall price of a prescription. Talk to your pharmacist about price considerations. Some states require that the pharmacist dispense exactly what is prescribed. However, other states allow the pharmacist to dispense less expensive medicines when appropriate.

Aside from differences in the drug product, there are many other factors that may influence the effectiveness of a medicine. For example, your diet, body chemistry, medical conditions, or other drugs you are taking may affect how much of a dose of a particular medicine gets into the body.

For the majority of drugs, slight differences in the amount of drug made available to the body will not make any therapeutic difference. For other drugs, the precise amount that gets into the body is more critical. For example, some heart or epilepsy medicines may create problems for the patient if the dose delivered to the body varies for some reason.

For those drugs in the critical category, it is a good idea to stay on the specific product you started on. Changes should only be made after a consultation with the health care professional who prescribed the medicine. If you feel that a certain batch of your medicine is more potent or does not work as well as other batches, or if you have other questions, check with your health care professional.

ABACAVIR   Systemic

Commonly used brand name(s):

In the U.S.—
   Ziagen

Description

Abacavir (a-BAK-a-veer) is used, in combination with other medicines, in the treatment of the infection caused by the human immunodeficiency virus (HIV). HIV is the virus that causes acquired immunodeficiency syndrome (AIDS).

Abacavir will not cure or prevent HIV infection or AIDS; however, it helps keep HIV from reproducing and appears to slow down the destruction of the immune system. This may help delay the development of problems usually related to AIDS or HIV disease. Abacavir will not keep you from spreading HIV to other people. People who receive this medicine may continue to have other problems usually related to AIDS or HIV disease.

This medicine is available only with your doctor's prescription, in the following dosage forms:

   Oral
     • Oral solution (U.S.)
     • Tablets (U.S.)

Before Using This Medicine

In deciding to use a medicine, the risks of taking the medicine must be weighed against the good it will do. This is a decision you and your doctor will make. For abacavir, the following should be considered:

Allergies—Tell your doctor if you have ever had any unusual or allergic reaction to abacavir. *This medicine should not be taken if you have ever had an allergic reaction to it, because it could cause another severe reaction that may result in death.* Also tell your health care professional if you are allergic to any other substances, such as foods, preservatives, or dyes.

Pregnancy—Abacavir has not been studied in pregnant women. However, it has been found to cause birth defects and other problems in animals at doses many times the human dose. Before taking this medicine, make sure your doctor knows if you are pregnant or if you may become pregnant.

Breast-feeding—It is not known whether abacavir passes into breast milk. However, because of the possibility that this medicine could cause unwanted effects in nursing babies and the risk of passing HIV on to the infant, breast-feeding is usually not recommended.

Children—This medicine has been tested in children 3 months of age and older and, in effective doses, has not been shown to cause different side effects or problems than it does in adults.

Older adults—Many medicines have not been studied specifically in older people. Therefore, it may not be known whether they work exactly the same way they do in younger adults or if they cause different side effects or problems in older people. There is no specific information comparing use of abacavir in the elderly with use in other age groups.

Other medicines—Although certain medicines should not be used together at all, in other cases two different medicines may be used together even if an interaction might occur. In these cases, your doctor may want to change the dose, or other precautions may be necessary. Tell your health care professional if you are taking any other prescription or nonprescription (over-the-counter [OTC]) medicine.

Proper Use of This Medicine

Take this medicine exactly as directed by your doctor. Do not take it more often, and do not take it for a longer time than your doctor ordered.

Dosing—The dose of abacavir will be different for different patients. *Follow your doctor's orders or the directions on the label.* The following information includes only the average doses of abacavir. *If your dose is different, do not change it* unless your doctor tells you to do so.

   • For *oral* dosage form (oral solution or tablets):
    —For HIV infection:
     • Adults and adolescents 16 years of age and older—300 milligrams (mg) two times a day.
     • Children 3 months to 16 years of age—Dose is based on body weight and must be determined by your doctor. The usual dose is 8 mg per kilogram (kg) (3.6 mg per pound) of body weight two times a day.

Missed dose—If you miss a dose of this medicine, take it as soon as you remember. However, if it is almost time for the next dose, skip the missed dose and go back to your regular dosing schedule. Do not double doses.

Storage—To store this medicine:
   • Keep out of the reach of children.
   • Store away from heat and direct light.
   • Do not store in the bathroom, near the kitchen sink, or in other damp places. Heat or moisture may cause the medicine to break down.
   • Keep the oral solution from freezing.
   • Do not keep outdated medicine or medicine no longer needed. Be sure that any discarded medicine is out of the reach of children.

Precautions While Using This Medicine

This medicine may cause a severe allergic reaction in some patients. This reaction usually occurs within 6 weeks after the medicine is started but may occur at any time. If untreated, it can lead to severe low blood pressure and even death. *Stop taking this medicine and check with your doctor immediately if you notice sudden fever, skin rash, diarrhea, nausea, stomach pain, vomiting, or a feeling of unusual tiredness or illness, cough, shortness of breath, or sore throat.*

When you begin taking this medicine, you will be given a warning card which describes symptoms of severe allergic reactions that may be caused by abacavir. The warning card also provides information about how to treat these allergic reactions. For your safety, you should carry the warning card with you at all times.

Side Effects of This Medicine

Along with its needed effects, a medicine may cause some unwanted effects. Although not all of these side effects may occur, if they do occur they may need medical attention.

Stop taking this medicine and get emergency help immediately if any of the following side effects occur:

Less common
> Abdominal or stomach pain; cough; diarrhea; difficult or labored breathing; fever; headache; joint or muscle pain; nausea; numbness or tingling of hands, feet, or face; redness and soreness of eyes; shortness of breath; skin rash; sore throat; sores in mouth; swelling of feet or lower legs; vomiting; unusual feeling of discomfort or illness; unusual tiredness

Check with your doctor as soon as possible if any of the following side effects occur:

Rare
> Abdominal swelling; decreased appetite; fast, shallow breathing; sleepiness

Other side effects may occur that usually do not need medical attention. These side effects may go away during treatment as your body adjusts to the medicine. However, check with your doctor if any of the following side effects continue or are bothersome:

More common
> Headache

Less common
> Trouble in sleeping

Other side effects not listed above may also occur in some patients. If you notice any other effects, check with your doctor.

Developed: 06/14/1999
Revised: 6/1/2001

ACARBOSE   Systemic

Commonly used brand name(s):

In the U.S.—
> Precose

Description

Acarbose (AY-car-bose) is used to treat a type of diabetes mellitus (sugar diabetes) called type 2 diabetes. Normally, your pancreas releases insulin into the blood stream after you eat. Insulin is used by all the cells in your body to help turn the food you eat into energy. This is done by using glucose (sugar) in the blood as quick energy. When you have type 2 diabetes, insulin is still produced by your pancreas, but the amount of insulin produced may not be enough or your body may not be using it properly and you may still need more. Because of this, the insulin is not able to lower your blood sugar properly and you will have too much sugar in your blood. Acarbose lowers your blood sugar by preventing the breakdown of starch into sugar. It may be used alone or in combination with another type of oral diabetes medicine called a sulfonylurea.

This medicine is available only with your doctor's prescription, in the following dosage form:

Oral
> • Tablets (U.S.)

Before Using This Medicine

In deciding to use a medicine, the risks of taking the medicine must be weighed against the good it will do. This is a decision you and your doctor will make. For acarbose, the following should be considered:

Allergies—Tell your doctor if you have ever had any unusual or allergic reaction to acarbose. Also tell your health care professional if you are allergic to any other substances, such as foods, preservatives, or dyes.

Pregnancy—Acarbose has not been studied in pregnant women. However, it is easier during pregnancy to control your blood sugar by using injections of insulin rather than by taking acarbose. Close control of your blood sugar can reduce the chance of your baby gaining too much weight, having birth defects, or having high blood sugar before birth. Be sure to tell your doctor if you plan to become pregnant or you think you are pregnant.

Breast-feeding—It is not known whether acarbose passes into breast milk. However, acarbose is not recommended during breast-feeding.

Children—Studies on this medicine have been done only in adult patients, and there is no specific information comparing use of acarbose in children with use in other age groups.

Older adults—This medicine has been tested in a limited number of elderly people and has not been shown to cause different side effects or problems in older people than it does in younger adults.

Other medicines—Although certain medicines should not be used together at all, in other cases two different medicines may be used together even if an interaction might occur. In these cases, your doctor may want to change the dose, or other precautions may be necessary. When you are taking acarbose, it is especially important that your health care professional know if you are taking any of the following:

> • Activated charcoal or
> • Medicine for digestion that contains amylase or pancreatin (e.g., Creon)—Use of these medicines with acarbose may prevent acarbose from working properly

Other medical problems—The presence of other medical problems may affect the use of acarbose. Make sure you tell your doctor if you have any other medical problems, especially:

> • Diabetic ketoacidosis or
> • Fever or
> • Infection or
> • Surgery or
> • Trauma—Insulin is needed to control these conditions

> • Digestion problems or
> • Inflammatory bowel disease or
> • Intestinal blockage or
> • Other intestinal problems—Acarbose should not be used

> • Kidney disease (severe)—Higher blood levels of acarbose may occur; acarbose should not be used

> • Liver disease—Acarbose may make this condition worse

Proper Use of This Medicine

Follow carefully the special meal plan your doctor gave you. This is the most important part of controlling your condition, and is necessary if the medicine is to work properly. Also, exercise regularly and test for sugar in your blood or urine as directed.

For this medicine to work properly it must be taken at the beginning of each main meal.

Dosing—The dose of acarbose will be different for different patients. *Follow your doctor's orders or the directions on the label.* The following information includes only the average doses of acarbose. *If your dose is different, do not change it* unless your doctor tells you to do so.

- For *oral* dosage form (tablets):
  - For type 2 diabetes:
    - Adults—At first the dose is 25 milligrams (mg) three times a day, at the start of each main meal. Your dose may then be adjusted by your doctor.
    - Children—Use and dose must be determined by your doctor.

Missed dose—*It is important that you do not miss any doses.* However, if you finish a meal and you have forgotten to take the medicine, do not take the missed dose. Instead, take the next dose at the beginning of your next meal, as scheduled. *Do not double doses.*

Storage—To store this medicine:

- Keep out of the reach of children.
- Store away from heat and direct light.
- Do not store in the bathroom, near the kitchen sink, or in other damp places. Heat or moisture may cause the medicine to break down.
- Do not keep outdated medicine or medicine no longer needed. Be sure that any discarded medicine is out of the reach of children.

Precautions While Using This Medicine

Your doctor will want to check your progress at regular visits, especially during the first few weeks you take this medicine.

It is very important to follow carefully any instructions from your health care team about:

- Alcohol—Drinking alcohol may cause severe low blood sugar. Discuss this with your health care team.
- Other medicines—Do not take other medicines during the time you are taking acarbose unless they have been discussed with your doctor. This especially includes nonprescription medicines such as aspirin, and medicines for appetite control, asthma, colds, cough, hay fever, or sinus problems.
- Counseling—Other family members need to learn how to prevent side effects or help with side effects if they occur. Also, patients with diabetes may need special counseling about diabetes medicine dosing changes that might occur because of lifestyle changes, such as changes in exercise and diet. Furthermore, counseling on contraception and pregnancy may be needed because of the problems that can occur in patients with diabetes during pregnancy.
- Travel—Keep a recent prescription and your medical history with you. Be prepared for an emergency as you would normally. Make allowances for changing time zones and keep your meal times as close as possible to your usual meal times.

In case of emergency—There may be a time when you need emergency help for a problem caused by your diabetes. You need to be prepared for these emergencies. It is a good idea to wear a medical identification (ID) bracelet or neck chain at all times. Also, carry an ID card in your wallet or purse that says that you have diabetes and a list of all of your medicines.

Acarbose does not cause hypoglycemia (low blood sugar). However, low blood sugar can occur if you take acarbose with another type of diabetes medicine, delay or miss a meal or snack, exercise more than usual, drink alcohol, or cannot eat because of nausea or vomiting. *Symptoms of low blood sugar must be treated before they lead to unconsciousness (passing out).* Different people may feel different symptoms of low blood sugar. *It is important that you learn which symptoms of low blood sugar you usually have so that you can treat it quickly.*

Symptoms of low blood sugar include anxiety; behavior change similar to being drunk; blurred vision; cold sweats; confusion; cool, pale skin; difficulty in thinking; drowsiness; excessive hunger; fast heartbeat; headache (continuing); nausea; nervousness; nightmares; restless sleep; shakiness; slurred speech; or unusual tiredness or weakness.

If symptoms of low blood sugar occur, *eat glucose tablets or gel or honey, or drink fruit juice to relieve the symptoms. Table sugar (sucrose) or regular (nondiet) soft drinks will not work.* Also, check your blood for low blood sugar. *Glucagon is used in emergency situations when severe symptoms such as seizures (convulsions) or unconsciousness occur.* Have a glucagon kit available, along with a syringe and needle, and know how to use it. Members of your household also should know how to use it.

Hyperglycemia (high blood sugar) may occur if you do not take enough or skip a dose of your antidiabetic medicine, overeat or do not follow your meal plan, have a fever or infection, or do not exercise as much as usual.

Symptoms of high blood sugar include blurred vision; drowsiness; dry mouth; flushed, dry skin; fruit-like breath odor; increased urination; ketones in urine; loss of appetite; stomachache, nausea, or vomiting; tiredness; troubled breathing (rapid and deep); unconsciousness; or unusual thirst.

If symptoms of high blood sugar occur, *check your blood sugar level and then call your doctor for instructions.*

Side Effects of This Medicine

Along with its needed effects, a medicine may cause some unwanted effects. Although not all of these side effects may occur, if they do occur they may need medical attention.

Check with your doctor as soon as possible if any of the following side effects occur:

Rare

Yellow eyes or skin

Other side effects may occur that usually do not need medical attention. These side effects may go away during treatment as your body adjusts to the medicine. However, check with your doctor if any of the following side effects continue or are bothersome:

More common

Abdominal or stomach pain; bloated feeling or passing of gas; diarrhea

Other side effects not listed above may also occur in some patients. If you notice any other effects, check with your doctor.

Developed: 07/31/98

ACETAMINOPHEN   Systemic

Commonly used brand name(s):

In the U.S.—
Aceta Elixir[1]
Aceta Tablets[1]
Acetaminophen Uniserts[1]
Actamin[1]
Actamin Extra[1]
Actamin Super[2]
Aminofen[1]
Aminofen Max[1]
Apacet Capsules[1]
Apacet Elixir[1]
Apacet Extra Strength Caplets[1]
Apacet Extra Strength Tablets[1]
Apacet, Infants'[1]
Apacet Regular Strength
  Tablets[1]
Aspirin Free Anacin Maximum
  Strength Caplets[1]
Aspirin Free Anacin Maximum
  Strength Gel Caplets[1]
Aspirin Free Anacin Maximum
  Strength Tablets[1]
Aspirin-Free Excedrin Caplets[2]
Banesin[1]
Bayer Select Maximum
  Strength Headache Pain
  Relief Formula[2]
Dapa[1]
Dapa X-S[1]
Datril Extra-Strength[1]
Feverall, Children's[1]
Feverall, Infants'[1]
Feverall Junior Strength[1]
Feverall Sprinkle Caps,
  Children's[1]
Feverall Sprinkle Caps Junior
  Strength[1]
Genapap Children's Elixir[1]
Genapap Children's Tablets[1]
Genapap Extra Strength
  Caplets[1]
Genapap Extra Strength
  Tablets[1]
Genapap, Infants'[1]
Genapap Regular Strength
  Tablets[1]
Genebs Extra Strength
  Caplets[1]
Genebs Regular Strength
  Tablets[1]
Genebs X-Tra[1]
Liquiprin Children's Elixir[1]
Liquiprin Infants' Drops[1]
Neopap[1]

Oraphen-PD[1]
Panadol, Children's[1]
Panadol, Infants'[1]
Panadol Junior Strength
  Caplets[1]
Panadol Maximum Strength
  Caplets[1]
Panadol Maximum Strength
  Tablets[1]
Phenaphen Caplets[1]
Redutemp[1]
Snaplets-FR[1]
St. Joseph Aspirin-Free Fever
  Reducer for Children[1]
Suppap-120[1]
Suppap-325[1]
Suppap-650[1]
Tapanol Extra Strength
  Caplets[1]
Tapanol Extra Strength
  Tablets[1]
Tempra[1]
Tempra D.S[1]
Tempra, Infants'[1]
Tempra Syrup[1]
Tylenol Arthritis Extended
  Relief
Tylenol Children's Chewable
  Tablets[1]
Tylenol Children's Elixir[1]
Tylenol Children's Suspension
  Liquid[1]
Tylenol Extra-Strength Adult
  Liquid Pain Reliever[1]
Tylenol Extra Strength
  Caplets[1]
Tylenol Extra Strength
  Gelcaps[1]
Tylenol Extra Strength Tablets[1]
Tylenol Infants' Drops[1]
Tylenol Infants' Suspension
  Drops[1]
Tylenol Junior Strength
  Caplets[1]
Tylenol Junior Strength
  Chewable Tablets[1]
Tylenol Regular Strength
  Caplets[1]
Tylenol Regular Strength
  Tablets[1]
Valorin[1]
Valorin Extra[1]

Commonly used brand name(s):

In Canada—
Abenol[1]
Actimol Chewable Tablets[1]
Actimol Children's Suspension[1]
Actimol Infants' Suspension[1]
Actimol Junior Strength
  Caplets[1]
Anacin-3[1]
Anacin-3 Extra Strength[1]
Apo-Acetaminophen[1]
Atasol Caplets[1]
Atasol Drops[1]
Atasol Forte Caplets[1]

Atasol Forte Tablets[1]
Atasol Oral Solution[1]
Atasol Tablets[1]
Excedrin Caplets[2]
Excedrin Extra Strength
  Caplets[2]
Exdol[1]
Exdol Strong[1]
Panadol[1]
Panadol Extra Strength[1]
Robigesic[1]
Rounox[1]

Tempra Caplets[1]
Tempra Chewable Tablets[1]
Tempra Drops[1]
Tempra Syrup[1]
Tylenol Caplets[1]
Tylenol Children's Chewable
  Tablets[1]

Tylenol Drops[1]
Tylenol Elixir[1]
Tylenol Gelcaps[1]
Tylenol Junior Strength
  Caplets[1]
Tylenol Tablets[1]

Other commonly used names are APAP[1] and paracetamol[1].

This information applies to the following medicines:
1. Acetaminophen (a-seat-a-MIN-oh-fen)‡§
2. Acetaminophen and Caffeine (a-seat-a-MIN-oh-fen and kaf-EEN)

Description

Acetaminophen is used to relieve pain and reduce fever. Unlike aspirin, it does not relieve the redness, stiffness, or swelling caused by rheumatoid arthritis. However, it may relieve the pain caused by mild forms of arthritis.

This medicine is available without a prescription; however, your medical doctor or dentist may have special instructions on the proper dose of acetaminophen for your medical condition.

Acetaminophen is available in the following dosage forms:

Oral
  Acetaminophen
  - Capsules (U.S.)
  - Oral granules (in packets) (U.S.)
  - Oral liquid (drops) for babies (U.S. and Canada)
  - Oral liquid for children (U.S. and Canada)
  - Oral liquid for adults (U.S.)
  - Oral powders (in capsules) (U.S.)
  - Oral suspension (drops) for babies (U.S. and Canada)
  - Oral suspension (liquid) for children (U.S. and Canada)
  - Tablets (U.S. and Canada)
  - Chewable tablets (U.S. and Canada)
  Acetaminophen and Caffeine
  - Tablets (U.S. and Canada)

Rectal
  Acetaminophen
  - Suppositories (U.S. and Canada)

Before Using This Medicine

If you are taking this medicine without a prescription, carefully read and follow any precautions on the label. For acetaminophen, the following should be considered:

Allergies—Tell your doctor if you have ever had any unusual or allergic reaction to acetaminophen or aspirin. Also tell your health care professional if you are allergic to any other substances, such as foods, preservatives, or dyes.

Pregnancy—Although studies have not been done in pregnant women, acetaminophen has not been reported to cause birth defects or other problems.

Breast-feeding—Although acetaminophen passes into the breast milk in small amounts, it has not been reported to cause problems in nursing babies.

Children—This medicine has been tested in children and has not been shown to cause different side effects or problems than it does in adults. However, some children's products containing acetaminophen also contain aspartame, which may be dangerous if it is given to children with phenylketonuria.

Older adults—Acetaminophen has been tested and has not been shown to cause different side effects or problems in older people than it does in younger adults.

Other medicines—Although certain medicines should not be used together at all, in other cases two different medicines may be used together even if an interaction might occur. In these cases, your doctor may want to change the dose, or other precautions may be necessary. Tell your health care professional if you are taking any other prescription or nonprescription (over-the-counter [OTC]) medicine.

Other medical problems—The presence of other medical problems may affect the use of acetaminophen. Make sure you tell your doctor if you have any other medical problems, especially:

- Alcohol abuse or
- Kidney disease (severe) or
- Hepatitis or other liver disease—The chance of serious side effects may be increased

- Phenylketonuria—Some brands of acetaminophen contain aspartame, which can make your condition worse

Proper Use of This Medicine

Unless otherwise directed by your medical doctor or dentist:

- *Do not take more of this medicine than is recommended on the package label.* If too much is taken, liver and kidney damage may occur.
- *Children up to 12 years of age should not take this medicine more than 5 times a day.*

To use *acetaminophen oral granules* (e.g., Snaplets-FR):

- Just before the medicine is to be taken, open the number of packets needed for one dose. Mix the granules inside of the packets with a small amount of soft food, such as applesauce, ice cream, or jam. Eat the acetaminophen granules along with the food.

To use *acetaminophen oral powders* (e.g., Feverall Sprinkle Caps [Children's or Junior Strength]):

- These capsules are not intended to be swallowed whole. Instead, just before the medicine is to be taken, open the number of capsules needed for one dose. Empty the powder from each capsule into 1 teaspoonful of water or other liquid. Drink the medicine along with the liquid. You may drink more liquid after taking the medicine. You may also mix the powder with a small amount of soft food, such as applesauce, ice cream, or jam. Eat the acetaminophen powder along with the food.

For patients using *acetaminophen suppositories:*

- If the suppository is too soft to insert, chill it in the refrigerator for 30 minutes or run cold water over it before removing the foil wrapper.
- To insert the suppository:
  —First remove the foil wrapper and moisten the suppository with cold water. Lie down on your side and use your finger to push the suppository well up into the rectum.

Dosing—The dose of acetaminophen will be different for different patients. *Follow your doctor's orders or the directions on the label.* The following information includes only the average doses of acetaminophen. *If your dose is different, do not change it* unless your doctor tells you to do so.

The number of capsules, tablets, teaspoonfuls of oral solution or suspension that you take, the amount of oral granules or powders that you take, or the number of suppositories that you use, depends on the strength of the medicine. Also, the number of doses you use each day and the time allowed between doses depend on the strength of the medicine.

- For *oral* dosage forms (capsules, granules, powders, solution, suspension, or tablets) and *rectal* dosage forms (suppositories):
  —For pain or fever:
  - Adults and teenagers—325 or 500 milligrams (mg) every three or four hours, 650 mg every four to six hours, or 1000 mg every six hours as needed. For short-term treatment (up to ten days), the total dose should not be more than 4000 mg (for example, eight 500-mg tablets) a day. For long-term treatment, the total dose should not be more than 2600 mg (for example, eight 325-mg tablets) a day.
  - Children—Acetaminophen dose is based on the child's age.
    —Infants up to 3 months of age: 40 mg every four hours as needed.
    —Infants 4 to 12 months of age: 80 mg every four hours as needed.
    —Children 1 to 2 years of age: 120 mg every four hours as needed.
    —Children 2 to 4 years of age: 160 mg every four hours as needed.
    —Children 4 to 6 years of age: 240 mg every four hours as needed.
    —Children 6 to 9 years of age: 320 mg every four hours as needed.
    —Children 9 to 11 years of age: 320 to 400 mg every four hours as needed.
    —Children 11 to 12 years of age: 320 to 480 mg every four hours as needed.

Storage—To store this medicine:

- Keep out of the reach of children.
- Store away from heat and direct light.
- Do not store acetaminophen tablets (including caplets and gelcaps), capsules, or granules in the bathroom, near the kitchen sink, or in other damp places. Heat or moisture may cause the medicine to break down.
- Keep the liquid and suppository forms of this medicine from freezing.
- Do not keep outdated medicine or medicine no longer needed. Be sure that any discarded medicine is out of the reach of children.

Precautions While Using This Medicine

If you will be taking this medicine for a long time, especially in high doses (more than eight 325-mg or five 500-mg doses a day), your doctor should check your progress at regular visits.

Check with your medical doctor or dentist:

- If you are taking this medicine to relieve pain, including arthritis pain, and the pain lasts for more than 10 days for adults or 5 days for children or if the pain gets worse, new symptoms occur, or the painful area is red or swollen. These could be signs of a serious condition that needs medical or dental treatment.
- If you are taking this medicine to bring down a fever, and the fever lasts for more than 3 days or returns, the fever

gets worse, new symptoms occur, or redness or swelling is present. These could be signs of a serious condition that needs treatment.
- If you are taking this medicine for a sore throat, and the sore throat is very painful, lasts for more than 2 days, or occurs together with or is followed by fever, headache, skin rash, nausea, or vomiting.

Check the labels of all prescription and nonprescription (over-the-counter [OTC]) medicines you now take. If any contain acetaminophen, check with your health care professional. Taking them together with this medicine may cause an overdose.

If you will be taking more than an occasional 1 or 2 doses of acetaminophen, *do not drink alcoholic beverages.* To do so may increase the chance of liver damage, especially if you drink large amounts of alcoholic beverages regularly, if you take more acetaminophen than is recommended on the package label, or if you take it regularly for a long time.

Taking certain other medicines together with acetaminophen may increase the chance of unwanted effects. The risk will depend on how much of each medicine you take every day, and on how long you take the medicines together. If your medical doctor or dentist directs you to take these medicines together on a regular basis, follow his or her directions carefully. However, *do not take any of the following medicines together with acetaminophen for more than a few days unless your doctor has directed you to do so and is following your progress:*

Aspirin or other salicylates
Diclofenac (e.g., Voltaren)
Diflunisal (e.g., Dolobid)
Etodolac (e.g., Lodine)
Fenoprofen (e.g., Nalfon)
Floctafenine (e.g., Idarac)
Flurbiprofen, oral (e.g., Ansaid)
Ibuprofen (e.g., Motrin)
Indomethacin (e.g., Indocin)
Ketoprofen (e.g., Orudis)
Ketorolac (e.g., Toradol)
Meclofenamate (e.g., Meclomen)
Mefenamic acid (e.g., Ponstel)
Nabumetone (e.g., Relafen)
Naproxen (e.g., Naprosyn)
Oxaprozin (e.g., Daypro)
Phenylbutazone (e.g., Butazolidin)
Piroxicam (e.g., Feldene)
Sulindac (e.g., Clinoril)
Tenoxicam (e.g., Apo-Tenoxicam)
Tiaprofenic acid (e.g., Surgam)
Tolmetin (e.g., Tolectin)

Acetaminophen may interfere with the results of some medical tests. Before you have any medical tests, tell the person in charge if you have taken acetaminophen within the past 3 or 4 days. If possible, it is best to call the laboratory where the test will be done about 4 days ahead of time, to find out whether this medicine may be taken during the 3 or 4 days before the test.

For *diabetic patients:*
- Acetaminophen may cause false results with some blood glucose (sugar) tests. If you notice any change in your test results, or if you have any questions about this possible problem, check with your health care professional. This is especially important if your diabetes is not well-controlled.

For patients taking one of the products that contain *caffeine* in addition to acetaminophen:
- Caffeine may interfere with the results of a test that uses adenosine (e.g., Adenocard) or dipyridamole (e.g., Persantine) to help find out how well your blood is flowing through certain blood vessels. Therefore, you should not have any caffeine for 8 to 12 hours before the test.

If you think that you or anyone else may have taken an overdose of acetaminophen, get emergency help at once, even if there are no signs of poisoning. Signs of severe poisoning may not appear for 2 to 4 days after the overdose is taken, but treatment to prevent liver damage or death must be started as soon as possible. Treatment started more than 24 hours after the overdose is taken may not be effective.

Side Effects of This Medicine

Along with its needed effects, a medicine may cause some unwanted effects. Although not all of these side effects may occur, if they do occur they may need medical attention.

Check with your doctor immediately if any of the following side effects occur:
Rare
Yellow eyes or skin
Symptoms of overdose
Diarrhea; increased sweating; loss of appetite; nausea or vomiting; stomach cramps or pain; swelling, pain, or tenderness in the upper abdomen or stomach area

Also, check with your doctor as soon as possible if any of the following side effects occur:
Rare
Bloody or black, tarry stools; bloody or cloudy urine; fever with or without chills (not present before treatment and not caused by the condition being treated); pain in lower back and/or side (severe and/or sharp); pinpoint red spots on skin; skin rash, hives, or itching; sores, ulcers, or white spots on lips or in mouth; sore throat (not present before treatment and not caused by the condition being treated); sudden decrease in amount of urine; unusual bleeding or bruising; unusual tiredness or weakness

Other side effects not listed above may also occur in some patients. If you notice any other effects, check with your doctor.

Revised: 08/17/2000

ACETAMINOPHEN AND SALICYLATES Systemic

Commonly used brand name(s):

In the U.S.—

Buffets II[2]	Goody's Extra Strength
Excedrin Extra-Strength	Tablets[1]
Caplets[1]	Goody's Headache Powders[1]
Excedrin Extra-Strength	Rid-A-Pain Compound[4]
Tablets[1]	Saleto[3]
Excedrin Migraine[1]	Supac[2]
Gelpirin[2]	Vanquish Caplets[2]

Note: In Canada, Excedrin contains acetaminophen and caffeine, but no aspirin.

This information applies to the following medicines:
1. Acetaminophen, Aspirin, and Caffeine (a-seat-a-MIN-oh-fen AS-pir-in and kaf-EEN)†
2. Acetaminophen, Aspirin, and Caffeine, Buffered (a-seat-a-MIN-oh-fen AS-pir-in and kaf-EEN, BUF-fered)†
3. Acetaminophen, Aspirin, Salicylamide, and Caffeine (a-seat-a-MIN-oh-fen AS-pir-in sal-i-SILL-a-mide and kaf-EEN)†
4. Acetaminophen, Salicylamide, and Caffeine (a-seat-a-MIN-oh-fen sal-i-SILL-a-mide and kaf-EEN)†

†Not commercially available in Canada.

Description

Acetaminophen and salicylate combination medicines relieve pain and reduce fever. They may be used to relieve occasional pain caused by mild inflammation or arthritis (rheumatism). The acetaminophen, aspirin, and caffeine combination also may be used to relieve pain associated with migraine headaches.

Neither acetaminophen nor salicylamide is as effective as aspirin for treating chronic or severe pain, or other symptoms, caused by inflammation or arthritis. Some of these combination medicines do not contain any aspirin. Even those that do contain aspirin may not contain enough to be effective in treating these conditions.

A few reports have suggested that acetaminophen and salicylates used together may cause kidney damage or cancer of the kidney or urinary bladder. This may occur if large amounts of both medicines are taken together for a very long time. However, taking usual amounts of these combination medicines for a short time has not been shown to cause these unwanted effects. Also, these effects are not likely to occur with either acetaminophen or a salicylate used alone, even if large amounts have been taken for a long time. Therefore, for long-term use, it may be best to use either acetaminophen or a salicylate, but not both, unless you are under a doctor's care.

Before giving any of these combination medicines to a child, check the package label very carefully. Some of these medicines are too strong for use in children. If you are not certain whether a specific product can be given to a child, or if you have any questions about the amount to give, check with your health care professional.

These medicines are available without a prescription. However, your doctor may have special instructions on the proper dose of these medicines for your medical condition.

These medicines are available in the following dosage forms:

Oral

Acetaminophen, Aspirin, and Caffeine
- Oral powders (U.S.)
- Tablets (U.S.)

Acetaminophen, Aspirin, and Caffeine, Buffered
- Tablets (U.S.)

Acetaminophen, Aspirin, Salicylamide, and Caffeine
- Tablets (U.S.)

Acetaminophen, Salicylamide, and Caffeine
- Capsules (U.S.)

Before Using This Medicine

If you are taking this medicine without a prescription, carefully read and follow any precautions on the label. For acetami-nophen and salicylate combinations, the following should be considered:

Allergies—Tell your doctor if you have ever had any unusual or allergic reaction to acetaminophen, aspirin or other salicylates including methyl salicylate (oil of wintergreen), or to any of the following medicines:

Diclofenac (e.g., Voltaren)
Diflunisal (e.g., Dolobid)
Etodolac (e.g., Lodine)
Fenoprofen (e.g., Nalfon)
Floctafenine (e.g., Idarac)
Flurbiprofen, oral (e.g., Ansaid)
Ibuprofen (e.g., Motrin)
Indomethacin (e.g., Indocin)
Ketoprofen (e.g., Orudis)
Ketorolac (e.g., Toradol)
Meclofenamate (e.g., Meclomen)
Mefenamic acid (e.g., Ponstel)
Nabumetone (e.g., Relafen)
Naproxen (e.g., Naprosyn)
Oxaprozin (e.g., Daypro)
Phenylbutazone (e.g., Butazolidin)
Piroxicam (e.g., Feldene)
Sulindac (e.g., Clinoril)
Tenoxicam (e.g., Mobiflex)
Tiaprofenic acid (e.g., Surgam)
Tolmetin (e.g., Tolectin)

Also tell your health care professional if you are allergic to any other substances, such as foods, preservatives, or dyes.

Pregnancy—
- *For acetaminophen:* Studies on birth defects have not been done in humans. However, acetaminophen has not been reported to cause birth defects or other problems.
- *For aspirin:* Studies in humans have not shown that aspirin causes birth defects. However, aspirin has been shown to cause birth defects in animals. *Do not take aspirin during the last 3 months of pregnancy unless it has been ordered by your doctor.* Some reports have suggested that too much use of aspirin late in pregnancy may cause a decrease in the newborn's weight and possible death of the fetus or newborn infant. However, the mothers in these reports had been taking much larger amounts of aspirin than are usually recommended. Studies of mothers taking aspirin in the doses that are usually recommended did not show these unwanted effects. However, there is a chance that regular use of aspirin late in pregnancy may cause unwanted effects on the heart or blood flow in the fetus or newborn infant. Use of aspirin during the last 2 weeks of pregnancy may cause bleeding problems in the fetus before or during delivery, or in the newborn infant. Also, too much use of aspirin during the last 3 months of pregnancy may increase the length of pregnancy, prolong labor, cause other problems during delivery, or cause severe bleeding in the mother before, during, or after delivery.
- *For salicylamide:* Studies on birth defects have not been done in humans.
- *For caffeine:* Studies in humans have not shown that caffeine causes birth defects. However, use of large amounts of caffeine by the mother during pregnancy may cause problems with the heart rhythm of the fetus and may affect the growth of the fetus. Studies in animals have shown that caffeine causes birth defects

when given in very large doses (amounts equal to the amount of caffeine in 12 to 24 cups of coffee a day).

Breast-feeding—

* *For acetaminophen and for aspirin:* Acetaminophen and aspirin pass into breast milk; however, they have not been reported to cause problems in nursing babies.
* *For caffeine:* Caffeine (contained in some of these combination medicines) passes into breast milk in small amounts. Taking caffeine in the amounts present in these medicines has not been reported to cause problems in nusing babies. However, studies have shown that babies may appear jittery and have trouble in sleeping when their mothers drink large amounts of caffeine-containing beverages. Therefore, breast-feeding mothers who use these medicines probably should limit the amount of caffeine they take in from other medicines or from beverages.

Children—

* *For acetaminophen:* Acetaminophen has been tested in children and, in effective doses, has not been shown to cause different side effects or problems than it does in adults.
* *For aspirin and for salicylamide: Do not give a medicine containing aspirin or salicylamide to a child with symptoms of a virus infection, especially flu or chickenpox, without first discussing its use with your child's doctor.* This is very important because aspirin may cause a serious illness called Reye's syndrome in children with fever caused by a virus infection, especially flu or chickenpox. Children who do not have a virus infection may also be more sensitive to the effects of aspirin, especially if they have a fever or have lost large amounts of body fluid because of vomiting, diarrhea, or sweating. This may increase the chance of side effects during treatment.
* *For caffeine:* There is no specific information comparing use of caffeine in children younger than 12 years of age with use in other age groups. However, caffeine is not expected to cause different side effects or problems in children than it does in adults.

Teenagers—*Teenagers with fever or other symptoms of a virus infection, especially flu or chickenpox, should check with a doctor before taking a medicine containing aspirin or salicylamide.* Aspirin and salicylamide may cause a serious illness called Reye's syndrome in teenagers with fever caused by a virus infection, especially flu or chickenpox.

Older adults—Elderly people may be more likely than younger adults to develop serious kidney problems if they take large amounts of these combination medicines for a long time. Therefore, it is best that elderly people not take this medicine for more than 5 days in a row unless they are under a doctor's care.

* *For acetaminophen:* Acetaminophen has been tested and, in effective doses, has not been shown to cause different side effects or problems in older people than it does in younger adults.
* *For aspirin:* People 60 years of age and older are especially sensitive to the effects of aspirin. This may increase the chance of side effects during treatment.
* *For caffeine:* Many medicines have not been studied specifically in older people. Therefore, it may not be known whether they work exactly the same way they do in younger adults or if they cause different side effects or problems in older people. There is no specific infor-

mation comparing use of caffeine in the elderly with use in other age groups.

Other medicines—Although certain medicines should not be used together at all, in other cases two different medicines may be used together even if an interaction might occur. In these cases, your doctor may want to change the dose, or other precautions may be necessary. When you are taking an acetaminophen and salicylate combination, it is especially important that your health care professional know if you are taking any of the following:

* Anticoagulants (blood thinners) or
* Carbenicillin by injection (e.g., Geopen) or
* Cefamandole (e.g., Mandol) or
* Cefoperazone (e.g., Cefobid) or
* Cefotetan (e.g., Cefotan) or
* Dipyridamole (e.g., Persantine) or
* Divalproex (e.g., Depakote) or
* Heparin or
* Inflammation or pain medicine, except narcotics, or
* Pentoxifylline (e.g., Trental) or
* Plicamycin (e.g., Mithracin) or
* Ticarcillin (e.g., Ticar) or
* Valproic acid (e.g., Depakene)—Taking these medicines together with aspirin (present in some of these combination medicines) may increase the chance of serious bleeding

* Antidiabetics, oral (diabetes medicine you take by mouth)—Aspirin (present in some of these combination medicines) may increase the effects of the antidiabetic medicine; a change in dose may be needed if aspirin is taken regularly

* Ciprofloxacin (e.g., Cipro) or
* Enoxacin (e.g., Penetrex) or
* Itraconazole (e.g., Sporanox) or
* Ketoconazole (e.g., Nizoral) or
* Lomefloxacin (e.g., Maxaquin) or
* Norfloxacin (e.g., Noroxin) or
* Ofloxacin (e.g., Floxin) or
* Tetracyclines (medicine for infection), taken by mouth—Antacids (present in buffered forms of acetaminophen and salicylate combination medicines) can keep these other medicines from working properly if the medicines are taken too closely together

* Methotrexate (e.g., Mexate)—Taking aspirin (present in some of these combination medicines) together with methotrexate may increase the chance of serious side effects

* Probenecid (e.g., Benemid)—Aspirin (present in some of these combination medicines) can keep probenecid from working properly for treating gout

* Sulfinpyrazone (e.g., Anturane)—Aspirin (present in some of these combination medicines) can keep sulfinpyrazone from working properly for treating gout; also, taking aspirin together with sulfinpyrazone may increase the chance of bleeding

* Urinary alkalizers (medicine that makes the urine less acid, such as acetazolamide [e.g., Diamox], calcium- and/or magnesium-containing antacids, dichlorphenamide [e.g., Daranide], methazolamide [e.g., Neptazane], potassium or sodium citrate and/or citric acid, sodium bicarbonate [baking soda])—These medicines may make aspirin (present in some of these combination

medicines) less effective by causing it to be removed from the body more quickly

Other medical problems— The presence of other medical problems may affect the use of acetaminophen and salicylate combinations. Make sure you tell your doctor if you have any other medical problems, especially:

- Alcohol abuse or
- Asthma, allergies, and nasal polyps (history of) or
- Hepatitis or other liver disease or
- Kidney disease—The chance of serious side effects may be increased

- Anemia or
- Stomach ulcer or other stomach problems—Aspirin (present in some of these combination medicines) may make these conditions worse

- Gout—Aspirin (present in some of these combination medicines) can make this condition worse and can also lessen the effects of some medicines used to treat gout

- Heart disease—Caffeine (present in some of these combination medicines) can make your condition worse

- Hemophilia or other bleeding problems—Aspirin (present in some of these combination medicines) increases the chance of serious bleeding

Proper Use of This Medicine

Take this medicine with food or a full glass (8 ounces) of water to lessen the chance of stomach upset.

Unless otherwise directed by your doctor:

- *Do not take more of this medicine than directed on the package label.* Taking too much acetaminophen may cause liver damage or lead to other medical problems because of an overdose. Also, taking too much aspirin can cause stomach problems or lead to other medical problems because of an overdose.
- *Children up to 12 years of age should not take this medicine more often than five times a day.*

Check with your doctor before taking one of these combination medicines to treat severe or chronic inflammation or arthritis (rheumatism). These combination medicines may not relieve the severe pain, redness, swelling, or stiffness caused by these conditions unless very large amounts are taken for a long time. *It is best not to take acetaminophen and salicylate combination medicines in large amounts for a long time* unless you are under a doctor's care.

If a combination medicine containing aspirin has a strong vinegar-like odor, do not use it. This odor means the medicine is breaking down. If you have any questions about this, check with your pharmacist.

Dosing— The dose of acetaminophen and salicylate combination medicines will be different for different patients. *Follow your doctor's orders or the directions on the label.* The following information includes only the average doses of these combination medicines. *If your dose is different, do not change it* unless your doctor tells you to do so.

The number of capsules, tablets (including caplets), or packets of oral powders that you take depends on the total amount of acetaminophen and salicylate (aspirin and/or salicylamide) in one capsule, tablet, or packet of oral powder. Also, the number of doses you take each day and the time

allowed between doses depend on the strength of the medicine.

- For *oral (capsules or tablets [including caplets])* dosage forms:
  —For pain, fever, or mild arthritis symptoms:
    - Adults and teenagers—The usual dose is 1 or 2 capsules or tablets every three, four, or six hours, depending on the strength of the product. Do not take any of these combination medicines for more than ten days, unless otherwise directed by your doctor.
    - Children—Use and dose must be determined by your doctor.
  —For migraine headaches:
    - Adults and teenagers—The usual dose is 2 tablets (250 mg acetaminophen, and 250 mg of aspirin, and 65 mg of caffeine in combination) every six hours as necessary for relief from migraine headaches. Do not take for relief of migraine headache for more than two days, unless otherwise directed by your doctor.
    - Children—Use and dose must be determined by your doctor.
- For *oral (powder)* dosage form:
  —For pain, fever, or mild arthritis symptoms:
    - Adults and teenagers—This medicine is very strong. Each packet of powder contains 260 mg of acetaminophen and 520 mg of aspirin (a total of 780 mg of both medicines). The usual dose is one packet of powder every four to six hours. Do not take this medicine for more than ten days, unless otherwise directed by your doctor.
    - Children—The oral powder dosage form is too strong to use in children 12 years of age or younger.

Storage— To store this medicine:

- Keep out of the reach of children. Overdose of the salicylates in these combination medicines is very dangerous in young children.
- Store away from heat and direct light.
- Do not store tablets (including caplets), capsules, or powders in the bathroom, near the kitchen sink, or in other damp places. Heat or moisture may cause the medicine to break down.
- Do not keep outdated medicine or medicine no longer needed. Be sure that any discarded medicine is out of the reach of children.

Precautions While Using This Medicine

If you will be taking this medicine for a long time, or in high doses, *your doctor should check your progress at regular visits.* This is especially important for elderly people, who may be more likely than younger adults to develop serious kidney problems if they take large amounts of this medicine for a long time.

Check with your doctor:

- If you are taking this medicine to relieve pain and the pain lasts for more than 10 days (5 days for children), if the pain gets worse, if new symptoms occur, or if the painful area is red or swollen. These could be signs of a serious condition that needs treatment.
- If you are taking this medicine to bring down a fever, and the fever lasts for more than 3 days or returns, if your fever gets worse, if new symptoms occur, or if redness

or swelling is present. These could be signs of a serious condition that needs treatment.
- If you are taking this medicine for a sore throat, and the sore throat is very painful, lasts for more than 2 days, or occurs together with or is followed by fever, headache, skin rash, nausea, or vomiting.

Do not take any of the combination medicines containing aspirin for 5 days before any surgery, including dental surgery, unless otherwise directed by your medical doctor or dentist. Taking aspirin during this time may cause bleeding problems.

Check the label of all over-the-counter (OTC), nonprescription, and prescription medicines you now take. If any of them contain acetaminophen, aspirin, other salicylates such as bismuth subsalicylate (e.g., Pepto Bismol) or magnesium salicylate (e.g., Nuprin Backache Caplets), or salicylic acid (present in some shampoos and skin products), *check with your health care professional. Using any of them together with this medicine may cause an overdose.*

Stomach problems may be more likely to occur if you drink three or more alcoholic beverages while you are taking aspirin. Also, liver damage may be more likely to occur if you drink three or more alcoholic beverages while you are taking acetaminophen.

Taking certain other medicines together with acetaminophen and salicylates may increase the chance of unwanted effects. The risk will depend on how much of each medicine you take every day, and on how long you take the medicines together. If your medical doctor or dentist directs you to take these medicines together on a regular basis, follow his or her directions carefully. However, *do not take any of the following medicines together with any of these combination medicines for more than a few days unless your doctor has directed you to do so and is following your progress:*

    Diclofenac (e.g., Voltaren)
    Diflunisal (e.g., Dolobid)
    Etodolac (e.g., Lodine)
    Fenoprofen (e.g., Nalfon)
    Floctafenine (e.g., Idarac)
    Flurbiprofen, oral (e.g., Ansaid)
    Ibuprofen (e.g., Motrin)
    Indomethacin (e.g., Indocin)
    Ketoprofen (e.g., Orudis)
    Ketorolac (e.g., Toradol)
    Meclofenamate (e.g., Meclomen)
    Mefenamic acid (e.g., Ponstel)
    Nabumetone (e.g., Relafen)
    Naproxen (e.g., Naprosyn)
    Oxaprozin (e.g., Daypro)
    Phenylbutazone (e.g., Butazolidin)
    Piroxicam (e.g., Feldene)
    Sulindac (e.g., Clinoril)
    Tenoxicam (e.g., Mobiflex)
    Tiaprofenic acid (e.g., Surgam)
    Tolmetin (e.g., Tolectin)

The antacid present in buffered forms of these combination medicines can keep other medicines from working properly. If you need to take a buffered form of this medicine, and you are also taking one of the following medicines, *be sure to take the buffered acetaminophen and salicylate combination medicine:*
- *At least 6 hours before or 2 hours after taking ciprofloxacin (e.g., Cipro) or lomefloxacin (e.g., Maxaquin).*

- *At least 8 hours before or 2 hours after taking enoxacin (e.g., Penetrex).*
- *At least 2 hours after taking itraconazole (e.g., Sporanox).*
- *At least 3 hours before or after taking ketoconazole (e.g., Nizoral).*
- *At least 2 hours before or after taking norfloxacin (e.g., Noroxin) or ofloxacin (e.g., Floxin).*
- *At least 3 or 4 hours before or after taking a tetracycline antibiotic by mouth.*
- *At least 1 or 2 hours before or after taking any other medicine by mouth.*

If you are taking a laxative containing cellulose, do not take it within 2 hours of taking this medicine. Taking the laxative and this medicine close together may make this medicine less effective by preventing the salicylate in it from being absorbed by your body.

Acetaminophen and salicylate combinations may interfere with the results of some medical tests. Before you have any medical tests, tell the person in charge if you have taken any of these combination medicines within the past 3 or 4 days. If possible, it is best to call the laboratory where the test will be done about 4 days ahead of time to find out whether the medicine may be taken during the 3 or 4 days before the test.

For patients with diabetes:
- Acetaminophen and salicylate combinations may cause false results with some blood and urine glucose (sugar) tests. If you notice any change in your test results, or if you have any questions about this possible problem, check with your health care professional. This is especially important if your diabetes is not well-controlled.

For patients taking one of the products that contain *caffeine:*
- Caffeine may interfere with the results of a test that uses adenosine (e.g., Adenocard) or dipyridamole (e.g., Persantine) to help find out how well your blood is flowing through certain blood vessels. Therefore, you should not have any caffeine for 8 to 12 hours before the test.

If you think that you or anyone else may have taken an overdose of this medicine, get emergency help at once. Taking an overdose of a salicylate may cause unconsciousness or death. The first symptom of an aspirin overdose may be ringing or buzzing in the ears. Other signs include convulsions (seizures), hearing loss, confusion, severe drowsiness or tiredness, severe excitement or nervousness, and unusually fast or deep breathing. Signs of severe acetaminophen overdose may not appear until 2 to 4 days after the overdose is taken, but treatment to prevent liver damage or death must be started within 24 hours or less after the overdose is taken.

Side Effects of This Medicine

Along with its needed effects, a medicine may cause some unwanted effects. Although not all of these side effects may occur, if they do occur they may need medical attention.

Check with your doctor immediately if any of the following side effects occur:
    Less common or rare
        Coughing; difficulty in swallowing; dizziness, lightheadedness, or feeling faint (severe); flushing, redness, or other change in skin color; shortness of breath, troubled breathing, tightness in chest, or wheezing; sudden decrease in amount of urine; swelling of eyelids, face, or lips

Signs and symptoms of overdose

Agitation, anxiety, excitement, irritability, nervousness, or restlessness; any loss of hearing; bloody urine; confusion or delirium; convulsions (seizures); diarrhea (severe or continuing); dizziness or lightheadedness; drowsiness (severe); fast or deep breathing; fast or irregular heartbeat (for medicines containing caffeine); fever; frequent urination (for medicines containing caffeine); hallucinations (seeing, hearing, or feeling things that are not there); headache (severe or continuing); increased sensitivity to touch or pain (for medicines containing caffeine); increased sweating; increased thirst; loss of appetite; muscle trembling or twitching (for medicines containing caffeine); nausea or vomiting (continuing, sometimes with blood); ringing or buzzing in ears (continuing); seeing flashes of "zig-zag" lights (for medicines containing caffeine); stomach cramps or pain (severe or continuing); swelling, pain, or tenderness in the upper abdomen or stomach area; trouble in sleeping (for medicines containing caffeine); uncontrollable flapping movements of the hands, especially in elderly patients; unexplained fever; vision problems

Signs of overdose in children

Changes in behavior; drowsiness or tiredness (severe); fast or deep breathing

Also, check with your doctor as soon as possible if any of the following side effects occur:

Less common or rare

Bloody or black, tarry stools; bloody or cloudy urine; fever with or without chills (not present before treatment and not caused by the condition being treated); pain in lower back and/or side (severe and/or sharp); pinpoint red spots on skin; skin rash, hives, or itching; sores, ulcers, or white spots on lips or in mouth; sore throat (not present before treatment and not caused by the condition being treated); stuffy nose; swelling of face, fingers, feet, or lower legs; unusual bleeding or bruising; unusual tiredness or weakness; vomiting of blood or material that looks like coffee grounds; weight gain; yellow eyes or skin

Other side effects may occur that usually do not need medical attention. These side effects may go away during treatment as your body adjusts to the medicine. However, check with your doctor if any of the following side effects continue or are bothersome:

More common

Heartburn or indigestion (for medicines containing aspirin); nausea, vomiting, or stomach pain (for medicines containing aspirin)

Less common

Drowsiness (for medicines containing salicylamide); trouble in sleeping, nervousness, or jitters (for medicines containing caffeine)

Some side effects may occur after you have stopped taking these combination medicines, especially if you have taken large amounts of them for a long time. *Check with your doctor immediately* if any of these side effects occur after you have stopped taking these medicines:

Rare

Bloody or cloudy urine; decreased urination; swelling of face, fingers, feet, or lower legs; weight gain

Other side effects not listed above may also occur in some patients. If you notice any other effects, check with your doctor.

Revised: 07/12/94
Interim revision: 03/11/99

ACETAMINOPHEN, SODIUM BICARBONATE, AND CITRIC ACID
Systemic†

Commonly used brand name(s):

In the U.S.—
Bromo-Seltzer

†Not commercially available in Canada.

Description

Acetaminophen, sodium bicarbonate, and citric acid (a-seat-a-MIN-oh-fen, SOE-dee-um bi-KAR-boe-nate, and SI-trik AS-id) combination is used to relieve pain occurring together with heartburn, sour stomach, or acid indigestion. The acetaminophen in this combination medicine is the pain reliever. The sodium bicarbonate in this medicine is an antacid. It neutralizes stomach acid by combining with it to form a new substance that is not an acid.

This medicine is available without a prescription; however, your doctor may have special instructions on the proper dose for your medical condition.

Acetaminophen, sodium bicarbonate, and citric acid combination is available in the following dosage form:

Oral
• Effervescent granules (U.S.)

Before Using This Medicine

If you are taking this medicine without a prescription, carefully read and follow any precautions on the label. For acetaminophen, sodium bicarbonate, and citric acid combination, the following should be considered:

Allergies—Tell your doctor if you have ever had any unusual or allergic reaction to acetaminophen or aspirin, or to sodium bicarbonate. Also tell your health care professional if you are allergic to any other substances, such as foods, preservatives, or dyes.

Diet—Make certain your health care professional knows if you are on a low-sodium, low-sugar, or any other special diet. This medicine contains a large amount of sodium (more than 750 mg for each 325 mg of acetaminophen).

Pregnancy—Although studies on birth defects have not been done in humans, the ingredients in this combination medicine have not been reported to cause birth defects in humans. However, you should avoid this medicine if you tend to retain (keep) body water because the sodium in it can cause the body to hold water. This can result in swelling and weight gain.

Breast-feeding—Acetaminophen passes into the breast milk in small amounts. However, acetaminophen, sodium bicarbonate, and citric acid have not been reported to cause problems in nursing babies.

Children—Acetaminophen has been tested in children and has not been shown to cause different side effects or problems than it does in adults. However, sodium bicarbonate should not be given to young children (under 6 years of age) unless ordered by their doctor. Small children with stomach problems usually cannot describe their symptoms very well. They should be checked by a doctor, because they may have a condition that needs other treatment.

Older adults—Acetaminophen has been tested and has not been shown to cause different side effects or problems in older people than it does in younger adults. However, the large amount of sodium in this combination medicine can be harmful to some elderly people. Therefore, it is best that older people not use this medicine for more than 5 days in a row, unless otherwise directed by their doctor.

Other medicines—Although certain medicines should not be used together at all, in other cases two different medicines may be used together even if an interaction might occur. In these cases, your doctor may want to change the dose, or other precautions may be necessary. When you are taking this combination medicine, it is especially important that your health care professional know if you are taking any of the following:

- Alcohol—The chance of liver damage may be increased

- Ciprofloxacin (e.g., Cipro) or
- Enoxacin (e.g., Penetrex) or
- Itraconazole (e.g., Sporanox) or
- Ketoconazole (e.g., Nizoral) or
- Lomefloxacin (e.g., Maxaquin) or
- Methenamine (e.g., Mandelamine) or
- Norfloxacin (e.g., Noroxin) or
- Ofloxacin (e.g., Floxin) or
- Tetracyclines (medicine for infection), taken by mouth— Sodium bicarbonate can keep these medicines from working properly

- Mecamylamine (e.g., Inversine)—Sodium bicarbonate can increase the risk of unwanted effects by causing mecamylamine to stay in your body longer than usual

Other medical problems—The presence of other medical problems may affect the use of acetaminophen, sodium bicarbonate, and citric acid combination. Make sure you tell your doctor if you have any other medical problems, especially:

- Alcohol abuse or
- Hepatitis or other liver disease—The chance of serious side effects, including liver damage, may be increased
- Appendicitis (symptoms of, such as stomach or lower abdominal pain, cramping, bloating, soreness, nausea, or vomiting)—Sodium bicarbonate can make your condition worse; also, people who may have appendicitis need medical attention and should not try to treat themselves
- Edema (swelling of face, fingers, feet, or lower legs caused by too much water in the body) or
- Heart disease or
- High blood pressure or
- Toxemia of pregnancy—The sodium in this combination medicine can make these conditions worse
- Kidney disease—The chance of serious side effects may be increased

Proper Use of This Medicine

Unless otherwise directed by your doctor, do not take more of this medicine than is recommended on the package label. If too much is taken, liver damage or other serious side effects may occur.

To use this medicine:

- This medicine must be taken in the form of a liquid that is made from the effervescent granules. Do not swallow the granules themselves.
- To make the liquid, pour the amount of effervescent granules directed on the package into a glass. Then add ½ glass (4 ounces) of cool water.
- Drink all of the liquid. You may drink the liquid while it is still fizzing or after the fizzing stops.
- Add a little more water to the glass and drink that, to make sure that you get the full amount of the medicine.

Dosing—The dose of this combination medicine will be different for different people. *Follow your doctor's orders or the directions on the label.* The following information includes only the average doses of the acetaminophen in this combination medicine. *If your dose is different, do not change it* unless your doctor tells you to do so.

- For *oral* dosage form (effervescent granules):
  —For pain and upset stomach:
  - Adults and teenagers—325 to 650 milligrams (mg) of acetaminophen, dissolved in water, every four hours as needed. The bottle cap can be used to measure the dose. There are 325 mg of acetaminophen in three-fourths of a capful.
  - Children—Use and dose must be determined by your doctor.

Missed dose—If your doctor has directed you to take this medicine according to a regular schedule and you miss a dose, take it as soon as you remember. However, if it is almost time for your next dose, skip the missed dose and go back to your regular dosing schedule. Do not double doses.

Storage—To store this medicine:

- Keep out of the reach of children.
- Store away from heat and direct light.
- Do not store this medicine in the bathroom, near the kitchen sink, or in other damp places. Heat or moisture may cause the medicine to break down.
- Do not keep outdated medicine or medicine no longer needed. Be sure that any discarded medicine is out of the reach of children.

Precautions While Using This Medicine

If you will be taking this medicine for a long time (more than 10 days in a row), your doctor should check your progress at regular visits.

Check with your doctor if your pain and/or upset stomach last for more than 10 days or if they get worse, if new symptoms occur, or if the painful area is red or swollen. These could be signs of a serious condition that needs medical treatment.

The sodium bicarbonate in this combination medicine can keep other medicines from working properly if the 2 medicines are taken too close together. *Always take this medicine:*

- *At least 6 hours before or 2 hours after taking ciprofloxacin (e.g., Cipro) or lomefloxacin (e.g., Maxaquin).*

- *At least 8 hours before or 2 hours after taking enoxacin (e.g., Penetrex).*
- *At least 2 hours after taking itraconazole (e.g., Sporanox).*
- *At least 3 hours before or after taking ketoconazole (e.g., Nizoral).*
- *At least 2 hours before or after taking norfloxacin (e.g., Noroxin) or ofloxacin (e.g., Floxin).*
- *At least 3 or 4 hours before or after taking a tetracycline antibiotic by mouth.*
- *At least 1 or 2 hours before or after taking any other medicine by mouth.*

Check the labels of all nonprescription (over-the-counter [OTC]) and prescription medicines you now take. If any contain acetaminophen or sodium, check with your health care professional. Taking them together with this medicine may cause an overdose.

Taking certain other medicines together with acetaminophen may increase the chance of unwanted effects. The risk will depend on how much of each medicine you take every day, and on how long you take the medicines together. If your medical doctor or dentist directs you to take these medicines together on a regular basis, follow his or her directions carefully. However, *do not take any of the following medicines together with acetaminophen for more than a few days, unless your doctor has directed you to do so and is following your progress:*

    Aspirin or other salicylates
    Diclofenac (e.g., Voltaren)
    Diflunisal (e.g., Dolobid)
    Etodolac (e.g., Lodine)
    Fenoprofen (e.g., Nalfon)
    Floctafenine (e.g., Idarac)
    Flurbiprofen, oral (e.g., Ansaid)
    Ibuprofen (e.g., Motrin)
    Indomethacin (e.g., Indocin)
    Ketoprofen (e.g., Orudis)
    Ketorolac (e.g., Toradol)
    Meclofenamate (e.g., Meclomen)
    Mefenamic acid (e.g., Ponstel)
    Nabumetone (e.g., Relafen)
    Naproxen (e.g., Naprosyn)
    Oxaprozin (e.g., Daypro)
    Phenylbutazone (e.g., Butazolidin)
    Piroxicam (e.g., Feldene)
    Sulindac (e.g., Clinoril)
    Tenoxicam (e.g., Mobiflex)
    Tiaprofenic acid (e.g., Surgam)
    Tolmetin (e.g., Tolectin)

If you will be taking more than an occasional 1 or 2 doses of this medicine:

- *Do not drink alcoholic beverages.* Drinking alcoholic beverages while you are taking acetaminophen may increase the chance of liver damage, especially if you drink large amounts of alcoholic beverages regularly, if you take more acetaminophen than is recommended on the package label, or if you take it regularly for a long time.
- *Do not also drink a lot of milk or eat a lot of milk products.* To do so may increase the chance of side effects.
- To prevent side effects caused by too much sodium in the body, you may need to limit the amount of sodium

in the foods you eat. Some foods that contain large amounts of sodium are canned soup, canned vegetables, pickles, ketchup, green and ripe (black) olives, relish, frankfurters and other sausage-type meats, soy sauce, and carbonated beverages. If you have any questions about this, check with your health care professional.

Acetaminophen may interfere with the results of some medical tests. Before you have any medical tests, tell the person in charge if you have taken acetaminophen within the past 3 or 4 days. If possible, it is best to call the laboratory where the test will be done about 4 days ahead of time, to find out whether this medicine may be taken during the 3 or 4 days before the test.

For diabetic patients:

- Acetaminophen may cause false results with some blood glucose (sugar) tests. If you notice any change in your test results, or if you have any questions about this possible problem, check with your health care professional. This is especially important if your diabetes is not well-controlled.

If you think that you or anyone else may have taken an overdose of this medicine, get emergency help at once, even if there are no signs of poisoning. Signs of severe acetaminophen poisoning may not appear for 2 to 4 days after the overdose is taken, but treatment to prevent liver damage or death must be started as soon as possible. Treatment started more than 24 hours after the overdose is taken may not be effective.

Side Effects of This Medicine

Along with its needed effects, a medicine may cause some unwanted effects. Although the following side effects occur very rarely when 1 or 2 doses of this combination medicine is taken occasionally, they may be more likely to occur if:

- too much medicine is taken
- the medicine is taken several times a day
- the medicine is taken for more than a few days in a row

Check with your doctor immediately if any of the following side effects occur:

Rare
    Yellow eyes or skin

Symptoms of overdose
    Diarrhea; increased sweating; loss of appetite; nausea or vomiting; stomach cramps or pain; swelling, pain, or tenderness in the upper abdomen or stomach area

Also, check with your doctor as soon as possible if any of the following side effects occur:

Less common or rare
    Bloody or black, tarry stools; bloody or cloudy urine, frequent urge to urinate, or sudden decrease in amount of urine; fever with or without chills (not present before treatment and not caused by the condition being treated); headache (continuing); increased blood pressure; mood or mental changes; muscle pain or twitching; nervousness or restlessness; pain (severe and/or sharp) in lower back and/or side; skin rash, hives, or itching; slow breathing; sores, ulcers, or white spots on lips or in mouth; sore throat (not present before treatment and not caused by the condition being treated); swelling of face, fingers, ankles, feet, or lower legs; unpleasant taste;

unusual bleeding or bruising; unusual tiredness or weakness; weight gain

Other side effects may occur that usually do not need medical attention. These side effects may go away during treatment as your body adjusts to the medicine. However, check with your doctor if any of the following side effects continue or are bothersome:

Less common
   Increased thirst

Other side effects not listed above may also occur in some patients. If you notice any other effects, check with your doctor.

Revised: 07/12/94

ACETYLCYSTEINE   Inhalation

Commonly used brand name(s):

In the U.S.—
   Mucomyst
   Mucomyst-10
   Mucosil
   Generic name product may be available.

In Canada—
   Mucomyst

Another commonly used name is *N*-acetylcysteine.

Description

Acetylcysteine (a-se-teel-SIS-teen) is a mucolytic (medicine that destroys or dissolves mucus). It is usually given by inhalation but may be given in other ways in a hospital.

Acetylcysteine is used for certain lung conditions when increased amounts of mucus make breathing difficult. Acetylcysteine liquefies (thins) or dissolves mucus so that it may be coughed up. Sometimes the mucus may have to be removed by suction.

This medicine is available only with your doctor's prescription, in the following dosage form:

Inhalation
   • Solution (U.S. and Canada)

Before Using This Medicine

In deciding to use a medicine, the risks of taking the medicine must be weighed against the good it will do. This is a decision you and your doctor will make. For acetylcysteine, the following should be considered:

Allergies—Tell your doctor if you have ever had any unusual or allergic reaction to acetylcysteine. Also tell your health care professional if you are allergic to any other substances, such as foods, preservatives, or dyes.

Pregnancy—Acetylcysteine has not been studied in pregnant women. However, acetylcysteine has not been shown to cause birth defects or other problems in animal studies when given in doses larger than the recommended human dose.

Breast-feeding—It is not known whether acetylcysteine passes into the breast milk. Although most medicines pass into breast milk in small amounts, many of them may be used

safely while breast-feeding. Mothers who are taking this medicine and who wish to breast-feed should discuss this with their doctor.

Children—Although there is no specific information comparing use of acetylcysteine in children with use in other age groups, this medicine is not expected to cause different side effects or problems in children than it does in adults.

Older adults—Many medicines have not been studied specifically in older people. Therefore, it may not be known whether they work exactly the same way they do in younger adults or if they cause different side effects or problems in older people. There is no specific information comparing use of acetylcysteine in the elderly with use in other age groups.

Other medical problems—The presence of other medical problems may affect the use of acetylcysteine. Make sure you tell your doctor if you have any other medical problems, especially:

   • Asthma—Acetylcysteine may make the condition worse

   • Decreased ability to cough—The mucus may have to be removed by suctioning

Proper Use of This Medicine

Use acetylcysteine only as directed. Do not use more of it and do not use it more often than your doctor ordered. To do so may increase the chance of side effects.

If you are using this medicine at home, make sure you understand exactly how to use it. If you have any questions about this, check with your doctor.

After using acetylcysteine, try to cough up the loosened or thinned mucus. If this does not work, it may have to be suctioned out. This will prevent too much mucus from building up in the lungs. If you have any questions about this, check with your doctor.

Dosing—The dose of acetylcysteine will be different for different patients. *Follow your doctor's orders or the directions on the label.* The following information includes only the average doses of acetylcysteine. *If your dose is different, do not change it* unless your doctor tells you to do so.

The amount of solution that you use depends on the strength of the medicine and the method of inhalation used. Also, *the number of doses you use each day, the time allowed between doses, and the length of time you use the medicine depend on the medical problem for which you are using acetylcysteine.*

   • For *inhalation* dosage form (solution):
      —To thin or dissolve mucus in lung diseases:
      • Adults and children—
         —3 to 5 milliliters (mL) of a 20% solution or 6 to 10 mL of a 10% solution used in a nebulizer three or four times a day. The medicine is inhaled through a face mask, mouthpiece, or tracheostomy.
         —The 10 or 20% solution may be used for inhalation as a heavy mist in a tent or croupette.
         —Sometimes the 10 or 20% solution is placed directly into the trachea or through a catheter into the trachea for certain conditions.
      —For use in tests to diagnose lung problems:
      • Adults and children—1 to 2 mL of a 20% solution or 2 to 4 mL of a 10% solution used for inhalation or placed directly into the trachea two or three times before the test.

Missed dose—If you miss a dose of this medicine, use it as soon as possible. Then use any remaining doses for that day at regularly spaced intervals.

Storage—To store this medicine:

- Keep out of the reach of children.
- Before the container is opened, store it away from heat and direct light.
- After the container is opened, store it in the refrigerator. However, keep the medicine from freezing. The opened container should be discarded after 4 days.
- Do not keep outdated medicine or medicine no longer needed. Be sure that any discarded medicine is out of the reach of children.

Precautions While Using This Medicine

If your condition does not improve or if it becomes worse, check with your doctor.

Side Effects of This Medicine

Along with its needed effects, a medicine may cause some unwanted effects. Although not all of these side effects may occur, if they do occur they may need medical attention.

Check with your doctor as soon as possible if any of the following side effects occur:

Less common
Wheezing, tightness in chest, or difficulty in breathing (especially in asthma patients)

Rare
Skin rash or other irritation

Other side effects may occur that usually do not need medical attention. These side effects may go away during treatment as your body adjusts to the medicine. However, check with your doctor if any of the following side effects continue or are bothersome:

Less common
Clammy skin; fever; increase in amount of mucus in lungs; irritation or soreness of mouth, throat, or lungs; nausea or vomiting; runny nose

For patients using a face mask for inhalation of acetylcysteine:

- The mask may leave a stickiness on your face. This can be removed with water.

When you use acetylcysteine, you may notice that the medicine has an unpleasant odor at first. However, this smell will go away soon after you use the medicine.

Other side effects not listed above may also occur in some patients. If you notice any other effects, check with your doctor.

Revised: 05/14/97

ACITRETIN   Systemic

Commonly used brand name(s):

In the U.S.—
Soriatane

Commonly used brand name(s):

In Canada—
Soriatane

Other commonly used names are 13-cis acitretin, etretin, and isoetretin.

Description

Acitretin (a-si-TRE-tin) is used to help relieve and control severe skin disorders, such as severe psoriasis. It works by allowing normal growth and development of the skin. Acitretin may continue to work after you stop taking it, but usually after a time, the skin condition returns and you may need to begin taking it again.

Acitretin must not be used to treat women who are able to bear children unless other forms of treatment have been tried first and failed. Acitretin must not be taken during pregnancy because it causes birth defects in humans. If you are able to bear children, it is very important that you read, understand, and follow the pregnancy warnings for acitretin.

You must take important precautions while taking acitretin and continue with them for a period of time after you stop taking the medicine. The precautions are:

- *Women should not become pregnant* and should use two methods of very effective birth control. The birth control methods should begin 1 month before starting the medicine and continue for *at least 2 or 3 years* after discontinuing the medicine or as directed by your doctor.
- *Men and women should not donate blood* for transfusion purposes during treatment and *for 2 or 3 years* after discontinuing the medicine or as directed by your doctor.
- *Men and women should not drink alcohol* during treatment and for 2 months after discontinuing the medicine.

If you do not think these precautions are reasonable, you should discuss this with your doctor *before* starting to take this medicine.

This medicine is available only with your doctor's prescription, in the following dosage form(s):

Oral
- Tablets (U.S. and Canada)

Before Using This Medicine

In deciding to use a medicine, the risks of taking the medicine must be weighed against the good it will do. This is a decision you and your doctor will make. For acitretin, the following should be considered:

Allergies—Tell your doctor if you have ever had any unusual reaction to acitretin, etretinate, isotretinoin, tretinoin, or vitamin A–like preparations, including vitamin A supplements. Also tell your health care professional if you are allergic to any other substances, such as foods, preservatives, or dyes.

Diet—Make certain your health care provider knows if you are on any special diet, such as a low-sodium, low-cholesterol, or low-sugar diet. Discuss with your doctor how often you drink alcohol, even if it is only an occasional drink.

Pregnancy—*Acitretin must not be taken during pregnancy. It has been shown to cause serious birth defects and other problems in humans.*

Before taking this medicine, make sure your doctor knows if you are pregnant or if you may become pregnant. *Beginning at least 1 month before you start to take acitretin, you should plan on using two effective forms of birth control to prevent pregnancy.* In addition, since it is not known how long pregnancy should be avoided after treatment stops, you should *plan not to become pregnant for at least 2 or 3 years after you stop taking acitretin* or as directed by your doctor. *If you become pregnant, stop taking the medicine and tell your doctor.*

Breast-feeding—It is not known whether acitretin passes into the breast milk. However, use of *acitretin is not recommended during breast-feeding* because it may cause unwanted effects in nursing babies. *You also should plan not to breast-feed for at least 2 or 3 years after you stop taking acitretin.*

Children—This medicine has been tested in some children and has been shown not to cause different side effects or problems in children than it does in adults. However, children may be more sensitive to some of the medicine's effect on bones, which may prevent normal bone growth during puberty. This can cause them to grow up to be shorter adults than expected. Therefore, it is especially important that you discuss with the child's doctor the good that this medicine may do as well as the risks of using it.

Older adults—This medicine has been tested and has not been shown to cause different side effects or problems in older people than it does in younger adults. However, some older patients may have higher levels of the medicine in the blood stream as compared to younger adults, and they may be more sensitive to its effects. This may increase their chance of developing side effects during treatment.

Other medicines—Although certain medicines should not be used together at all, in other cases two different medicines may be used together, even if an interaction might occur. In these cases, your doctor may want to change the dose, or other precautions may be necessary. When you are taking acitretin, it is especially important that your health care professional know if you are taking any of the following:

- Alcoholic beverages—Drinking alcohol may convert acitretin to a much longer-acting product that can stay in the body 60 times longer than acitretin does. This may result in a greater chance of developing side effects for months or years, depending on how much and how often one drinks. This unusual effect can occur even after you stop taking acitretin, especially for the first 2 months after you stop taking this medicine

- Cyclosporine (e.g., Sandimmune or Neoral) or
- Hydantoins, such as phenytoin (e.g., Dilantin)—Acitretin may increase the effects of these medicines

- Etretinate (e.g., Tegison) or
- Isotretinoin (e.g., Accutane) or
- Tretinoin (oral) (e.g., Vesanoid) or
- Tretinoin (topical) (e.g., Avita, Renova, or Retin A) or
- Vitamin A, including vitamin supplements—Etretinate, isotretinoin, and tretinoin are not used together with acitretin; problems in skin, vision, and bone may be more likely to occur when they are used at the same time. If vitamin A is taken with acitretin, the dose of vitamin A should not exceed the *minimum* recommended daily allowance (RDA)

- Methotrexate—Acitretin may increase the chance of causing liver problems if used with methotrexate

- Oral contraceptives, progestin-only (e.g., Micronor)—Acitretin may prevent progestin-only oral contraceptives from working properly and may result in an unplanned pregnancy. This does not occur with oral contraceptives containing both estrogens and progestins

- Tetracyclines—Using acitretin at the same time that tetracyclines are used may increase the chance of severe pressure occurring in the brain

Other medical problems—The presence of other medical problems may affect the use of acitretin. Make sure you tell your doctor if you have any other medical problems, especially:

- Diabetes mellitus (sugar diabetes) or
- High cholesterol or triglycerides, uncontrollable (or history of) or
- Inflammation of pancreas (or history of)—Acitretin may make these conditions worse or increase cholesterol or triglyceride problems

- Hypervitaminosis A (or history of)—If you have past or current problems with toxic symptoms from vitamin A, acitretin may increase the chance that they will occur again

- Kidney disease, severe or
- Liver disease, severe—May cause acitretin to stay in the body for a longer period of time and increase the chance of side effects

---

Proper Use of This Medicine

Patient information is usually provided with acitretin. Read it carefully before using this medicine.

Take acitretin with a main meal or with a glass of milk.

For women— *This medicine may cause birth defects.* To make sure you are not pregnant before beginning treatment, your doctor will ask you to:

- *Use two effective forms of birth control (contraception) for at least 1 month before beginning treatment.*
- *Report when your menstrual periods are normal.*
- *Take a pregnancy test within 1 week before beginning the treatment to make sure you are not pregnant.*
- *Begin your acitretin treatment on Day 2 or Day 3 of your next menstrual period.*
- *Sign a paper to show that you understand the importance of not becoming pregnant for at least 2 to 3 years after you stop taking this medicine, according to the advice of your doctor.*

Using two effective forms of birth control for *at least* 2 or 3 years after you stop taking acitretin, according to the advice of your doctor, is very important to help prevent an unplanned pregnancy. *If you do not think this is reasonable, you should discuss this with your doctor before you start taking this medicine.*

Dosing—The dose of acitretin will be different for different patients. *Follow your doctor's orders or the directions on the label.* The following information includes only the average doses of acitretin. *If your dose is different, do not change it* unless your doctor tells you to do so.

The number of tablets that you take depends on the strength of the medicine. Also, *the number of doses you take each day, the time allowed between doses, and the length of time you take the medicine depend on the medical problem for which you are taking acitretin.*

- For *oral* dosage form (tablets):
  —For severe psoriasis:
  - Adults—25 or 50 milligrams (mg) a day as a single dose. After four weeks, a dose of 25 to 75 mg a day is used.
  - Children—Use and dose must be determined by your doctor.
  —For other severe skin disorders (such as bullous or nonbullous erythroderma, lamellar ichthyoses, and keratosis follicularis):
  - Adults—25 milligrams (mg) a day. After four weeks, a dose of 10 to 75 mg a day is used.
  - Children—Use and dose must be determined by your doctor.

Missed dose—Take the missed dose as soon as possible. However, if you do not remember the missed dose until the next day, skip the missed dose and go back to your regular dosing schedule. Do not double doses. If you have any questions about this, check with your doctor.

Storage—To store this medicine:
- Keep out of the reach of children.
- Store away from heat and direct light.
- Do not store in the bathroom, near the kitchen sink, or in other damp places. Heat or moisture may cause the medicine to break down.
- Do not keep outdated medicine or medicine no longer needed. Be sure that any discarded medicine is out of the reach of children.

Precautions While Using This Medicine

It is important that your doctor check your progress at regular visits while you are taking this medicine. *If your condition has improved and you are no longer taking acitretin, your progress must still be checked.* This is especially important for children or elderly patients, who may be more sensitive to the effects of this medicine, and for women who want to become pregnant after they stop taking the medicine.

Your skin condition may improve or get worse during the first 3 weeks of treatment and you also may notice some skin irritation from the medicine. With continued use, the expected skin irritation will lessen after a few weeks. *Check with your health care professional any time skin irritation becomes severe or if your skin condition does not improve within 8 to 12 weeks.*

Do not drink alcohol while taking this medicine or for at least 2 months after discontinuing treatment.
- Drinking alcohol can change the medicine in the body to a product that stays in your body for an extended period of time. This can increase your chance of developing side effects for a longer period of time than if you hadn't consumed alcohol.
- If a woman consumes alcohol during acitretin treatment, she should consider delaying a pregnancy for longer than 2 or 3 years or as directed by her doctor.

Do not donate blood during treatment with acitretin, for 2 or 3 years following treatment, or as otherwise directed by your doctor. Although problems resulting from a blood transfusion are not likely, this precaution prevents the possibility that your blood would be used in pregnant women.

Acitretin can cause dryness of the eyes, blur your vision, or cause other vision problems. Be aware that while using acitretin *you may see a sudden decrease in your night vision* (ability to see before the sun rises or after the sun goes down). Also, acitretin may cause your eyes to be more sensitive to light, including sunlight, than they are normally. *These effects can make certain activities dangerous, such as driving or operating machines.*

Check with your doctor if you experience any vision or eye problem. Wearing contact lenses may become uncomfortable. Your doctor may suggest using artificial tears to keep your eyes from getting too dry.

Acitretin may cause dryness of the mouth, nose, and throat. For temporary relief of mouth dryness, use sugarless candy or gum, melt bits of ice in your mouth, or use a saliva substitute. However, if your mouth continues to feel dry for more than 2 weeks, check with your medical doctor or dentist. Continuing dryness of the mouth may increase the chance of developing dental disease, including tooth decay, gum disease, and fungus infections.

Avoid overexposing your skin to wind, cold weather, and sunlight, even on cloudy days. Your skin will be more prone to sunburn, dryness, or irritation, especially during the first 2 or 3 weeks. However, you should not stop taking this medicine, unless the skin irritation becomes too severe. For best results:
- Wear sunglasses that can block ultraviolet (UV) light. Ordinary sunglasses may not protect your eyes.
- Regularly use sunscreen or sunblocking lotions with a sun protection factor (SPF) of at least 15.
- Wear protective clothing and hats and stay out of direct sunlight, especially between the hours of 10 a.m. and 3 p.m.
- Apply creams, lotions, or moisturizers often. Your health care professional can help you choose the right skin products for you to reduce skin dryness and irritation.
- Do not use an artificial light, such as a sunlamp, unless directed otherwise by your doctor.

Unless your doctor tells you otherwise, it is especially important to avoid using the following skin products:
- Any topical acne product or skin product containing a peeling agent (such as benzoyl peroxide, resorcinol, salicylic acid, or sulfur).
- Hair products that are irritating, such as permanents or hair removal products.
- Skin products that cause sensitivity to the sun, such as those containing spices or limes.
- Skin products containing a large amount of alcohol, such as astringents, shaving creams, or after-shave lotions.
- Skin products that are too drying or abrasive, such as some cosmetics, soaps, or skin cleansers.

Using these products when taking acitretin may cause mild to severe irritation of the skin.

Do not take doses of vitamin A or any vitamin supplement containing vitamin A that exceeds the minimum recommended allowance (RDA) while you are taking this medicine. To do so may increase the chance of developing side effects.

Side Effects of This Medicine

Along with its needed effects, a medicine may cause some unwanted effects. Although not all of these side effects may occur, if they do occur they may need medical attention.

Check with your doctor immediately if any of the following side effects occur:
  More common
    Headache (severe and continuing); nausea or vomiting (severe and continuing)

Less common
> Blurred vision; eye pain

Rare
> Abdominal or stomach pain; double vision or other problems in seeing, including decreased night vision after sunset and before sunrise; darkened urine; yellowing of the skin or eyes

Check with your doctor as soon as possible if any of the following side effects occur:

More common
> Back pain; bone or joint pain; difficulty in moving or walking; headache; stiff, painful muscles

Less common
> Eye problems, such as loss of eyebrows or eyelashes, redness or swelling of the eyelid, redness of the eyes, sensitivity of eyes to light, or watery eyes; loosening of the fingernails; redness or soreness around fingernails

Rare
> Coughing, hoarseness, trouble in speaking, or influenza-like symptoms; itchy or painful ears; skin problems, such as abnormal sensation of burning or stinging of skin, cracking of skin, redness of skin, skin irritation or rash (including a rash that looks like psoriasis), skin infection, skin ulcers, skin odor (unusual), or small red spots in skin; sore on the edge of the eyelid (stye); thick, white, curd-like vaginal discharge; vaginal itching or irritation

Symptoms of overdose
> Drowsiness; headache (severe and continuing); irritability; itchy skin; nausea or vomiting (severe and continuing)

Other side effects may occur that usually do not need medical attention. These side effects may go away during treatment as your body adjusts to the medicine. However, check with your doctor if any of the following side effects continue or are bothersome:

More common
> Chapped, red, or swollen lips; difficulty in wearing contact lenses; dryness of eyes; dry or runny nose; increased ability to sunburn; increased amount of ear wax (unusual); itchy skin; nosebleeds; irritation in mouth or swollen gums; loss of hair (usually reversible); scaling and peeling of eyelids, fingertips, palms, and soles of feet; sticky skin; unusual thirst

Less common
> Constipation; diarrhea; fatigue; increased sweating

Other side effects not listed above may also occur in some patients. If you notice any other effects, check with your doctor.

Developed: 4/24/98

ACYCLOVIR   Systemic

Commonly used brand name(s):

In the U.S.—
> Zovirax

In Canada—

Alti-Acyclovir	Zovirax Wellstat Pac
Avirax	Zovirax Zostab Pac
Zovirax	

Another commonly used name is aciclovir.

Description

Acyclovir (ay-SYE-kloe-veer) belongs to the family of medicines called antivirals, which are used to treat infections caused by viruses. Usually these medicines work for only one kind or group of virus infections.

Acyclovir is used to treat the symptoms of chickenpox, shingles, herpes virus infections of the genitals (sex organs), the skin, the brain, and mucous membranes (lips and mouth), and widespread herpes virus infections in newborns. Acyclovir is also used to prevent recurrent genital herpes infections. Although acyclovir will not cure herpes, it does help relieve the pain and discomfort and helps the sores (if any) heal faster.

Acyclovir may also be used for other virus infections as determined by your doctor. However, it does not work in treating certain virus infections, such as the common cold.

Acyclovir is available only with your doctor's prescription, in the following dosage forms:

Oral
- Capsules (U.S. and Canada)
- Oral suspension (U.S. and Canada)
- Tablets (U.S. and Canada)

Parenteral
- Injection (U.S. and Canada)

Before Using This Medicine

In deciding to use a medicine, the risks of taking the medicine must be weighed against the good it will do. This is a decision you and your doctor will make. For acyclovir, the following should be considered:

Allergies—Tell your doctor if you have ever had any unusual or allergic reaction to acyclovir, ganciclovir, or valacyclovir. Also tell your health care professional if you are allergic to any other substances, such as foods, sulfites or other preservatives, or dyes.

Pregnancy—Acyclovir has been used in pregnant women and has not been reported to cause birth defects or other problems. However, studies have not been done in humans. Studies in rabbits have shown that acyclovir given by injection may keep the fetus from becoming attached to the lining of the uterus (womb). However, acyclovir has not been shown to cause birth defects or other problems in mice given many times the usual human dose, or in rats or rabbits given several times the usual human dose.

Breast-feeding—Acyclovir passes into breast milk. However, it has not been reported to cause problems in nursing babies.

Children—A limited number of studies have been done using oral acyclovir in children, and it has not caused different effects or problems in children than it does in adults.

Older adults—Acyclovir has been used in the elderly and has not been shown to cause different side effects or problems in older people than it does in younger adults. However, some of the side effects involving the central nervous system, for example, agitation, confusion, dizziness, and drowsiness, may be more severe in older adults.

Other medicines—Although certain medicines should not be used together at all, in many cases two different medicines may be used together even if an interaction might occur. In these cases, changes in dose or other precautions may be necessary. If you are taking acyclovir it is especially important that your health care professional know if you are taking any of the following:

- Carmustine (e.g., BiCNU) or
- Cisplatin (e.g., Platinol) or
- Combination pain medicine containing acetaminophen and aspirin (e.g., Excedrin) or other salicylates or
- Cyclosporine (e.g., Sandimmune) or
- Deferoxamine (e.g., Desferal) (with long-term use) or
- Gold salts (medicine for arthritis) or
- Inflammation or pain medicine, except narcotics, or
- Lithium (e.g., Lithane) or
- Methotrexate (Mexate) or
- Other medicine for infection or
- Penicillamine (e.g., Cuprimine) or
- Plicamycin (e.g., Mithracin) or
- Streptozocin (e.g., Zanosar) or
- Tiopronin (Thiola)—Concurrent use of these medicines with acyclovir may increase the chance for side effects, especially when kidney disease is present

Other medical problems—The presence of other medical problems may affect the use of acyclovir. Make sure you tell your doctor if you have any other medical problems, especially:

- Dehydration or
- Kidney disease—Dehydration or kidney disease may increase blood levels of acyclovir, increasing the chance of side effects
- Nerve disease—Acyclovir by injection may increase the chance for nervous system side effects

Proper Use of This Medicine

Patient information about the treatment of herpes, chickenpox, or shingles is available with this medicine. Read it carefully before using this medicine.

Acyclovir is best used as soon as possible after the symptoms of herpes infection or shingles (for example, pain, burning, blisters) *begin to appear.*

If you are taking acyclovir for the *treatment of chickenpox*, it is best to *start taking acyclovir as soon as possible after the first sign of the chickenpox rash*, usually within one day.

Acyclovir capsules, tablets, and oral suspension may be taken with meals or on an empty stomach.

If you are using *acyclovir oral suspension*, use a specially marked measuring spoon or other device to measure each dose accurately. The average household teaspoon may not hold the right amount of liquid.

Acyclovir is best taken with a full glass (8 ounces) of water.

To help clear up your herpes infection, chickenpox, or shingles, *keep taking acyclovir for the full time of treatment*, even if your symptoms begin to clear up after a few days. *Do not miss any doses.* However, *do not use this medicine more often or for a longer time than your doctor ordered.*

Dosing—The dose of acyclovir will be different for different patients. *Follow your doctor's orders or the directions on the label.* The following information includes only the average doses of acyclovir. Your dose may be different if you have kidney disease. *If your dose is different, do not change it* unless your doctor tells you to do so.

The number of capsules or tablets or teaspoonfuls of suspension that you take depends on the strength of the medicine. Also, *the number of doses you take each day, the time allowed between doses, and the length of time you take the medicine depend on the medical problem for which you are taking acyclovir.*

- For *oral* dosage forms (capsules, oral suspension, or tablets):
  —For treatment of genital herpes:
  - Adults and children 12 years of age and older—200 milligrams (mg) five times a day for ten days.
  - Children up to 12 years of age—Use and dose must be determined by the doctor.
  —For prevention of recurrent outbreaks of genital herpes infections:
  - Adults and children 12 years of age and older—200 to 400 mg two to five times a day for five days or up to twelve months, depending on how often your outbreaks of infection occur.
  - Children up to 12 years of age—Use and dose must be determined by the doctor.
  —For treatment of chickenpox:
  - Adults and children who weigh over 88 pounds (40 kilograms)—800 mg four times a day for five days.
  - Children 2 years of age and older and weighing 88 pounds (40 kilograms) or less—Dose is based on body weight and must be determined by the doctor. The usual dose is 20 mg per kilogram (kg) of body weight, up to 800 mg, four times a day for five days.
  - Children up to 2 years of age—Use and dose must be determined by the doctor.
  —For treatment of shingles:
  - Adults and children 12 years of age and older—800 mg five times a day for seven to ten days.
  - Children up to 12 years of age—Use and dose must be determined by the doctor.
- For *injection* dosage form:
  —For treatment of herpes of the brain, genitals, or mucous membranes, or for the treatment of shingles:
  - Adults and children 12 years of age and older—Dose is based on body weight and must be determined by the doctor. The usual dose is 5 to 10 mg of acyclovir per kg (2.3 to 4.5 mg per pound) of body weight, injected slowly into a vein over at least a one-hour period, and repeated every eight hours for five to ten days.
  - Children up to 12 years of age—Dose is based on body weight and must be determined by the doctor. The usual dose is 10 mg to 20 mg of acyclovir per kg (4.5 mg to 9.1 mg per pound) of body weight, injected slowly into a vein over at least a one-hour period and repeated every eight hours for seven to ten days.
  —For treatment of widespread herpes virus infection in newborns:
  Infants from birth to 3 months of age—Dose is based on body weight and must be determined by the doctor. The usual dose is 10 mg of acyclovir per kg (4.5 mg per pound) of body weight, injected slowly into a vein over at least a one-hour period and repeated every eight hours for ten days.

Missed dose—If you do miss a dose of this medicine, take it as soon as possible. However, if it is almost time for

your next dose, skip the missed dose and go back to your regular dosing schedule. Do not double doses.

Storage— To store this medicine:

- Keep out of the reach of children.
- Store away from heat and direct light.
- Do not store the capsule or tablet form of this medicine in the bathroom, near the kitchen sink, or in other damp places. Heat or moisture may cause the medicine to break down.
- Do not keep outdated medicine or medicine no longer needed. Be sure that any discarded medicine is out of the reach of children.

Precautions While Using This Medicine

If your symptoms do not improve within a few days, or if they become worse, check with your doctor.

The areas affected by herpes, chickenpox, or shingles should be kept as clean and dry as possible. Also, wear loose-fitting clothing to avoid irritating the sores (blisters).

It is important to remember that acyclovir will not keep you from spreading herpes to others.

Herpes infection of the genitals can be caught from or spread to your partner during any sexual activity. Even though you may get herpes if your partner has no symptoms, the infection is more likely to be spread if sores are present. This is true until the sores are completely healed and the scabs have fallen off. *Therefore, it is best to avoid any sexual activity if either you or your sexual partner has any symptoms of herpes*. The use of a latex condom ("rubber") may help prevent the spread of herpes. However, spermicidal (sperm-killing) jelly or a diaphragm will probably not help.

Side Effects of This Medicine

Along with its needed effects, a medicine may cause some unwanted effects. Although not all of these side effects may occur, if they do occur they may need medical attention.

Check with your doctor immediately if any of the following side effects occur:

More common—For acyclovir injection only
> Pain, swelling, or redness at place of injection

Less common—For acyclovir injection only; more common with rapid injection
> Abdominal or stomach pain; decreased frequency of urination or amount of urine; increased thirst; loss of appetite; nausea or vomiting; unusual tiredness or weakness

Rare—For acyclovir injection only
> Black, tarry stools; blood in urine or stools; chills, fever, or sore throat; confusion; convulsions (seizures); hallucinations (seeing, hearing, or feeling things that are not there); hives; pinpoint red spots on skin; trembling; unusual bleeding or bruising

Frequency not determined
> *For acyclovir injection only*
>> Bluish coloring, especially of the hands and feet; bruising at the injection site; delirium; faintness or lightheadedness; mood or mental changes; persistent bleeding or oozing from puncture sites or mucous membranes (bowel, mouth, nose, or urinary bladder)
> *For both oral acyclovir and acyclovir injection*
>> blistering, peeling, or loosening of skin; changes in facial skin color; changes in vision; confusion;

convulsions (seizures); coughing; difficulty in breathing or swallowing; dizziness or feeling faint; severe; fast heartbeat; muscle cramps, pain, or weakness; nausea or vomiting; red or irritated eyes; seeing, hearing, or feeling things that are not there; sense of agitation or uneasiness; skin rash, itching, or hives; sore throat, fever, or chills; sores, ulcers, or white spots in mouth or on lips; swelling of eyelids, face, feet, hands, lower legs or lips; swollen, painful, or tender lymph nodes (glands) in neck, armpit, or groin

Other side effects may occur that usually do not need medical attention. These side effects may go away during treatment as your body adjusts to the medicine. However, check with your doctor if any of the following side effects continue or are bothersome:

More common—For oral acyclovir only; especially with high doses
> General feeling of discomfort or illness

Less common—For oral acyclovir only; especially seen with long-term use or high doses
> Diarrhea; headache

Frequency not determined
> Agitation; loss of hair; burning, prickling, or tingling sensations; drowsiness

Other side effects not listed above may also occur in some patients. If you notice any other effects, check with your doctor.

Additional Information

Once a medicine has been approved for marketing for a certain use, experience may show that it is also useful for other medical problems. Although not specifically included in product labeling, acyclovir by injection is used in certain patients with the following medical conditions:

- Herpes simplex (for prevention of repeated infections) in people with a weak immune system
- Herpes zoster infections of the eye
- Shingles (for prevention of repeated infections) in people with a weak immune system

Other than the above information, there is no additional information relating to proper use, precautions, or side effects for these uses.

Revised: 06/08/99

ACYCLOVIR   Topical

Commonly used brand name(s):

In the U.S.—
> Zovirax

In Canada—
> Zovirax

Other commonly used names are aciclovir and acycloguanosine.

Description

Acyclovir (ay-SYE-kloe-veer) belongs to the family of medicines called antivirals. Antivirals are used to treat infections caused by viruses. Usually they work for only one kind or group of virus infections.

Topical acyclovir is used to treat the symptoms of herpes simplex virus infections of the skin, mucous membranes, and genitals (sex organs). Although topical acyclovir will not cure herpes simplex, it may help relieve the pain and discomfort and may help the sores (if any) heal faster. Topical acyclovir may also be used for other conditions as determined by your doctor.

Acyclovir is available only with your doctor's prescription, in the following dosage forms:

Topical
- Cream (Canada)
- Ointment (U.S. and Canada)

Before Using This Medicine

In deciding to use a medicine, the risks of using the medicine must be weighed against the good it will do. This is a decision you and your doctor will make. For acyclovir, the following should be considered:

Allergies—Tell your doctor if you have ever had any unusual or allergic reaction to acyclovir. Also tell your health care professional if you are allergic to any other substances, such as preservatives or dyes.

Pregnancy—Topical acyclovir has not been studied in pregnant women. However, this medicine has not been shown to cause birth defects or other problems in animal studies using mice, rats, or rabbits, except when given in very high doses in a study using rats.

Breast-feeding—It is not known whether topical acyclovir passes into the breast milk. However, acyclovir ointment has not been reported to cause problems in nursing babies, even though small amounts of topical acyclovir are absorbed through the mother's skin and mucous membranes. Although most medicines pass into breast milk in small amounts, many of them may be used safely while breast-feeding. Mothers who are taking this medicine and who wish to breast-feed should discuss this with their doctor.

Children—Studies on this medicine have been done only in adult patients, and there is no specific information comparing use of topical acyclovir in children with use in other age groups.

Older adults—Many medicines have not been studied specifically in older people. Therefore, it may not be known whether they work exactly the same way they do in younger adults. Although there is no specific information comparing the use of topical acyclovir in the elderly with use in other age groups, this medicine is not expected to cause different side effects or problems in older people than it does in younger adults.

Other medicines—Although certain medicines should not be used together at all, in other cases two different medicines may be used together even if an interaction might occur. In these cases, your doctor may want to change the dose, or other precautions may be necessary. Tell your health care professional if you are using any other topical prescription or nonprescription (over-the-counter [OTC]) medicine that is to be applied to the same area of the skin.

Proper Use of This Medicine

Acyclovir may come with patient information about herpes simplex infections. Read this information carefully. If you have any questions, check with your health care professional.

Do not use this medicine in the eyes.

Acyclovir is best used as soon as possible after the signs and symptoms of herpes infection (for example, pain, burning, or blisters) begin to appear.

Use a finger cot or rubber glove when applying this medicine. This will help keep you from spreading the infection to other areas of your body and will prevent the transmission of the infection to other persons. Apply enough medicine to completely cover all the sores (blisters). A 1.25-centimeter (approximately ½-inch) strip of ointment applied to each area of the affected skin measuring 5 × 5 centimeters (approximately 2 × 2 inches) is usually enough, unless otherwise directed by your doctor.

To help clear up your herpes infection, *continue using acyclovir for the full time of treatment*, even if your symptoms begin to clear up after a few days. *Do not miss any doses.* However, *do not use this medicine more often or for a longer time than your doctor ordered.*

Dosing—The dose of topical acyclovir will be different for different patients. *Follow your doctor's orders or the directions on the label.* The following information includes only the average dose of topical acyclovir. *If your dose is different, do not change it* unless your doctor tells you to do so.

- For *topical* dosage form (cream):
  —For herpes simplex infection:
    - Adults—Apply to the affected area(s), four to six times a day, for up to ten days.
    - Children—Use and dose must be determined by your doctor.

- For *topical* dosage form (ointment):
  —For herpes simplex infection:
  In the U.S.
    - Adults—Apply to the affected area(s), every three hours, for a total of six times a day, for seven days.
    - Children—Use and dose must be determined by your doctor.
  In Canada
    - Adults—Apply to the affected area(s), four to six times a day, for up to ten days.
    - Children—Use and dose must be determined by your doctor.

Missed dose—If you miss a dose of this medicine, apply it as soon as possible. However, if it is almost time for your next dose, skip the missed dose and go back to your regular dosing schedule.

Storage—To store this medicine:
- Keep out of the reach of children.
- Store away from heat and direct light.
- Keep the medicine from freezing.
- Do not keep outdated medicine or medicine no longer needed. Be sure that any discarded medicine is out of the reach of children.

Precautions While Using This Medicine

Women with genital herpes may be more likely to get cancer of the cervix (opening to the womb). Therefore, it is very important that Pap tests be taken at least once a year to check for cancer. Cervical cancer can be cured if found and treated early.

If your symptoms do not improve within 1 week, or if they become worse, check with your doctor.

The areas affected by herpes should be kept as clean and dry as possible. Also, wear loose-fitting clothing to avoid irritating the sores (blisters).

Herpes infection of the genitals can be caught from or spread to your partner during any sexual activity. Although you may get herpes even though your sexual partner has no symptoms, the infection is more likely to be spread if sores are present. This is true until the sores are completely healed and the scabs have fallen off. The use of a condom (prophylactic) may help prevent the spread of herpes. However, spermicidal (sperm-killing) jelly or a diaphragm will not help prevent the spread of herpes. *Therefore, it is best to avoid any sexual activity if either you or your partner has any symptoms of herpes. It is also important to remember that acyclovir will not keep you from spreading herpes to others.*

Side Effects of This Medicine

Along with its needed effects, a medicine may cause some unwanted effects. The following side effects may go away during treatment as your body adjusts to the medicine. However, check with your doctor if any of these effects continue or are bothersome:

More common
 Mild pain, burning, or stinging

Less common
 Itching

Rare
 Itching, stinging, or redness of the genital area; skin rash

Other side effects not listed above may also occur in some patients. If you notice any other effects, check with your doctor.

Revised: 06/15/99

ADAPALENE   Topical

Commonly used brand name(s):

In the U.S.—
 Differin

In Canada—
 Differin

Description

Adapalene (a-DAP-a-leen) is used to treat acne. It works partly by keeping skin pores clear.

Adapalene is available only with your doctor's prescription, in the following dosage form:

Topical
 • Gel (U.S. and Canada)

Before Using This Medicine

In deciding to use a medicine, the risks of applying the medicine must be weighed against the good it will do. This is a decision you and your doctor will make. For adapalene, the following should be considered:

Allergies—Tell your doctor if you have ever had any unusual or allergic reaction to adapalene. Also tell your health care professional if you are allergic to any other substances, such as foods, preservatives, or dyes.

Pregnancy—Adapalene has not been studied in pregnant women. It is not recommended for use during pregnancy. Adapalene in large doses has been shown to cause some bone problems in the fetuses of some animals. Before using this medicine, make sure your doctor knows if you are pregnant or if you are trying to become pregnant.

Breast-feeding—It is not known if adapalene passes into breast milk.

Children—Studies of this medicine have been done only in adult patients, and there is no specific information comparing use of adapalene in children up to 12 years of age with use in other age groups. In teenagers, adapalene is not expected to cause different side effects or problems than it does in adults.

Older adults—Many medicines have not been studied specifically in older people. Therefore, it may not be known whether they work exactly the same way they do in younger adults or if they cause different side effects or problems in older people. There is no specific information comparing use of adapalene in the elderly with use in other age groups. Older adults are not likely to develop acne.

Other medicines—Although certain medicines should not be used together at all, in other cases two different medicines may be used together even if an interaction might occur. In these cases, your doctor may want to change the dose, or other precautions may be necessary. Tell your doctor and pharmacist if you are using any other topical prescription or nonprescription (over-the-counter [OTC]) medicine that is to be applied to the same area of the skin.

Other medical problems—The presence of other medical problems may affect the use of adapalene. Make sure you tell your doctor if you have any other medical problems, especially:

 • Eczema or
 • Seborrheic dermatitis—Use of this medicine may cause or increase the irritation associated with eczema or seborrheic dermatitis

Proper Use of This Medicine

It is very important that you use this medicine only as directed. Do not use more of it, do not use it more often, and do not use it for a longer time than your doctor ordered. To do so may cause irritation of the skin.

Do not apply this medicine to windburned or sunburned skin or on open wounds.

Do not use this medicine in or around the eyes, lips, or inside of the nose. Spread the medicine away from these areas when applying. If the medicine accidently gets on these areas, wash with water at once.

Apply the medicine to clean, dry areas of the skin affected by acne. Rub in gently and well. Wash your hands afterwards to remove any medicine that may remain on them.

To help clear up your acne completely, *it is very important that you keep using this medicine for the full time of treatment,* even if your symptoms begin to clear up after a short time. If you stop using this medicine too soon, your acne may return or get worse.

Dosing—*Follow your doctor's orders or the directions on the label*. The following information includes only the average doses of adapalene. *If your dose is different, do not change it* unless your doctor tells you to do so.

- For *topical* dosage form (gel):
  —For acne:
    - Adults and teenagers—Apply a small amount as a thin film once a day, at least one hour before bedtime. Apply the medicine to dry, clean areas affected by acne. Rub in gently and well.
    - Children—Use and dose must be determined by your doctor.

Missed dose—If you miss a dose of this medicine, skip the missed dose and go back to your regular dosing schedule. Do not double doses.

Storage—To store this medicine:
- Keep out of the reach of children.
- Do not keep outdated medicine or medicine no longer needed. Be sure that any discarded medicine is out of the reach of children.

Precautions While Using This Medicine

During the first 3 weeks you are using adapalene, your acne may seem to get worse before it gets better. Full improvement should be seen within 12 weeks, especially if you use the medicine every day. You should not stop using adapalene if your acne seems worse at first, unless irritation or other symptoms become severe. Check with your doctor if your acne does not improve within 8 to 12 weeks.

Do not apply any topical product to the same area where you are using adapalene, unless otherwise directed by your doctor. If applied to the same area treated with adapalene, the following products may cause mild to severe irritation of the skin:

- Hair products that irritate the skin, such as permanents or hair removal products
- Skin products for acne (such as clindamycin or erythromycin) or other skin products containing a peeling agent (such as benzoyl peroxide, resorcinol, salicylic acid, or sulfur)
- Skin products that cause one to be more sensitive to the sun, such as those containing spices or lime
- Skin products that are too drying or that contain a large amount of alcohol, such as astringents, cosmetics, shaving creams, or after-shave lotions
- Skin products that are abrasive, such as some soaps or skin cleansers

Your doctor may ask you to use other topical products, such as benzoyl peroxide, clindamycin, or erythromycin, during your treatment with adapalene. Applying the products at different times of the day will lessen the chance of causing skin irritation.

If your skin becomes too dry or red at any time, discuss with your doctor whether you should continue using adapalene. Applying creams, lotions, or moisturizers as needed helps lessen these skin problems.

During treatment with this medicine, avoid getting too much sun on treated areas and do not use sunlamps. Since your skin may be more prone to sunburn or skin irritation, use sunscreen or sunblocking lotions regularly with a sun protection factor (SPF) of 15 or more. Wear protective clothing against sun, wind, and cold weather.

Side Effects of This Medicine

Along with its needed effects, a medicine may cause some unwanted effects. Although not all of these side effects may occur, if they do occur, they may need medical attention.

Check with your doctor as soon as possible if any of the following side effects occur:
> *More common*—especially during the first month of use
> Burning sensation or stinging of skin; dryness and peeling of skin; itching of skin; redness of skin

Other side effects may occur that usually do not need medical attention. These side effects may go away during treatment as your body adjusts to the medicine. However, check with your doctor if the following side effect continues or is bothersome:
> *Rare*—more common during the first month of use
> Worsening of acne

Other side effects not listed above may also occur in some patients. If you notice any other effects, check with your doctor.

Developed: 06/02/97

ALBENDAZOLE   Systemic†

Commonly used brand name(s):

In the U.S.—
Albenza

the United Kingdom—
Eskazole
Zentel

†Not commercially available in Canada.

Description

Albendazole (al-BEN-da-zole) is used to treat infections caused by worms. Albendazole works by keeping the worm from absorbing sugar (glucose), so that the worm loses energy and dies.

Albendazole is used to treat:
- Hydatid disease (echinococcosis);
- Infection of the nervous system caused by pork tapeworms (neurocysticercosis).

Albendazole is available only with your doctor's prescription, in the following dosage forms:
Oral
- Oral suspension (United Kingdom)
- Tablets (U.S. and United Kingdom)

Before Using This Medicine

In deciding to use a medicine, the risks of taking the medicine must be weighed against the good it will do. This is a decision you and your doctor will make. For albendazole, the following should be considered:

Allergies—Tell your doctor if you have ever had any unusual or allergic reaction to albendazole. Also tell your health care professional if you are allergic to any other substances, such as foods, preservatives, or dyes.

Pregnancy—Albendazole has not been studied in pregnant women. However, studies in animals have shown that albendazole can cause birth defects or other problems. Before taking this medicine, make sure your doctor knows if you are pregnant or if you may become pregnant. Women of child-bearing age should take the medicine within 7 days after the start of their period (menstrual cycle). After a negative pregnancy test, birth control must be used during treatment and for 1 month after stopping treatment with albendazole.

Breast-feeding—Albendazole passes into animal milk. It is not known whether albendazole passes into human breast milk. Although most medicines pass into breast milk in small amounts, many of them may be used safely while breast-feeding. Mothers who are taking this medicine and who wish to breast-feed should discuss this with their doctor.

Children—Although there is very little specific information comparing use of albendazole in children with use in other age groups, this medicine is not expected to cause different side effects or problems in children than it does in adults.

Older adults—Many medicines have not been studied specifically in older people. Therefore, it may not be known whether they work exactly the same way they do in younger adults or if they cause different side effects or problems in older people. There is no specific information comparing use of albendazole in the elderly with use in other age groups.

Other medicines—Although certain medicines should not be used together at all, in other cases two different medicines may be used together even if an interaction might occur. In these cases, your doctor may want to change the dose, or other precautions may be necessary. When you are taking albendazole, it is especially important that your health care professional know if you are taking any of the following:

- Cimetidine (e.g., Tagamet, Tagamet HB) or
- Corticosteroids (cortisone-like medicines) or
- Praziquantel (e.g., Biltricide)—Use of these medicines with albendazole has been shown to increase the effects of albendazole

Other medical problems—The presence of other medical problems may affect the use of albendazole. Make sure you tell your doctor if you have any other medical problems, especially:

- Cysticercosis involving the eye—Patients who are being treated with albendazole for pork tapeworms of the nervous system (neurocysticercosis) should be examined for lesions in the eye; use of albendazole may increase the chance of side effects involving the eye
- Liver disease—Patients with liver disease may have an increased chance of side effects

Proper Use of This Medicine

No special preparations (fasting, laxatives, or enemas) or other steps are necessary before, during, or immediately after treatment with albendazole.

Albendazole is best *taken with meals, especially with food containing fat*, to help your body absorb the medicine better.

For patients taking the *tablet form* of albendazole:

- Tablets should be swallowed whole with a small amount of liquid.

To help clear up your infection completely, *take this medicine exactly as directed by your doctor for the full time of treatment*. In some infections, additional treatments with this medicine may be needed at 2-week intervals to clear up the infection completely. *Do not miss any doses.*

Dosing—The dose of albendazole will be different for different patients. *Follow your doctor's orders or the directions on the label*. The following information includes only the average doses of albendazole. *If your dose is different, do not change it* unless your doctor tells you to do so.

The number of doses you take each day, the time allowed between doses, and the length of time you take the medicine depend on the medical problem for which you are taking albendazole.

- For *oral* dosage form (tablets):
  —For hydatid disease:
    - Adults, teenagers, and children weighing 60 kilograms (132 pounds) and over—400 milligrams (mg) two times a day for twenty-eight days. Treatment may need to be repeated in fourteen days.
    - Adults, teenagers, and children weighing less than 60 kilograms (132 pounds)—15 mg per kilogram (6.8 milligrams per pound) of body weight per day divided into two doses and taken for twenty-eight days. Treatment may need to be repeated in fourteen days.
  —For infections of the nervous system caused by pork tapeworm (neurocysticercosis):
    - Adults, teenagers, and children weighing 60 kilograms (132 pounds) and over—400 milligrams (mg) two times a day for eight to thirty days.
    - For adults, teenagers, and children weighing less than 60 kilograms (132 pounds)—15 mg per kilogram (6.8 mg per pound) of body weight per day divided into two doses and taken for eight to thirty days.

Missed dose—If you miss a dose of this medicine, take it as soon as possible. However, if it is almost time for your next dose, skip the missed dose and go back to your regular dosing schedule. Do not double doses.

Storage—To store this medicine:

- Keep out of the reach of children.
- Store away from heat and direct light.
- Do not store in the bathroom, near the kitchen sink, or in other damp places. Heat or moisture may cause the medicine to break down.
- Keep the suspension form of this medicine from freezing.
- Do not keep outdated medicine or medicine no longer needed. Be sure that any discarded medicine is out of the reach of children.

Precautions While Using This Medicine

It is important that your doctor check your progress after treatment. This is to make sure that the infection is cleared up completely, and to allow your doctor to check for any unwanted effects.

If your symptoms do not improve after you have taken this medicine for the full course of treatment, or if they become worse, check with your doctor.

For women of childbearing age, it is important that you use birth control while taking albendazole since this medicine can cause birth defects or other problems.

Side Effects of This Medicine

Along with its needed effects, a medicine may cause some unwanted effects. Although not all of these side effects may occur, if they do occur they may need medical attention.

Check with your doctor as soon as possible if any of the following side effects occur:

Rare
> Fever; skin rash or itching; sore throat; unusual tiredness and weakness

Other side effects may occur that usually do not need medical attention. These side effects may go away during treatment as your body adjusts to the medicine. However, check with your doctor if any of the following side effects continue or are bothersome:

Less common
> Abdominal pain; diarrhea; dizziness; headache; nausea; vomiting

Rare
> Thinning or loss of hair

Other side effects not listed above may also occur in some patients. If you notice any other effects, check with your doctor.

Additional Information

Once a medicine has been approved for marketing for a certain use, experience may show that it is also useful for other medical problems. Although these uses are not included in product labeling in the U.S., albendazole is used in certain patients with the following infections:

- Capillariasis;
- Cutaneous larva migrans;
- Common roundworms (ascariasis);
- Hookworms (ancylostomiasis and necatoriasis);
- Pinworms (enterobiasis or oxyuriasis);
- Strongyloidiasis;
- Tapeworms (taeniasis);
- Trichostrongyliasis;
- Whipworms (trichuriasis).

For patients taking albendazole for *hookworms:*

- In hookworm infections, anemia may occur. Therefore, your doctor may want you to take iron supplements. If so, it is important to take iron every day while you are being treated for hookworm infection. Do not miss any doses. Your doctor may also want you to keep taking iron supplements for at least 3 to 6 months after you stop taking albendazole. If you have any questions about this, check with your doctor.

For patients taking albendazole for *pinworms:*

- In some patients, pinworms may return after treatment with albendazole. Wear pajamas and underwear to sleep, take a bath every day, and wash (not shake) all bedding and nightclothes (pajamas) after treatment to help prevent reinfection. Treatment may be repeated after 3 weeks.
- Pinworms may be easily passed from one person to another, especially among persons in the same household. Therefore, all household members may have to be treated at the same time to prevent their infection or reinfection.

Other than the above information, there is no additional information relating to proper use, precautions, or side effects for these uses.

Revised: 6/3/99

ALBUMIN MICROSPHERES SONICATED   Systemic

Commonly used brand name(s):

In the U.S.—
> Optison

Description

The albumin microspheres sonicated (al-BYOO-min mye-kroe-SFEERS SON-i-kay-ted) preparation is an ultrasound contrast agent. Ultrasound contrast agents are used to help provide a clear picture during ultrasound. Ultrasound is a special kind of diagnostic procedure. It uses high-frequency sound waves to create images or "pictures" of certain areas inside the body. The sound waves produced by the ultrasound equipment can be reflected (bounced off) by different parts of the body, like for example, the heart. As the sound waves return they are electronically converted into images on a television screen. Unlike x-rays, ultrasound does not involve ionizing radiation.

The albumin microspheres sonicated preparation contains very small gas-filled albumin microspheres that reflect the sound waves and help create a better picture. The albumin microspheres sonicated preparation is given by injection into a vein before ultrasound to help diagnose problems of the heart.

The albumin microspheres sonicated preparation is to be given only by or under the direct supervision of a doctor with specialized training in ultrasound procedures. It is available in the following dosage form:

Parenteral
- Injection (U.S.)

Before Having This Test

In deciding to use a diagnostic agent, any risks of the test must be weighed against the good it will do. This is a decision you and your doctor will make. Also, test results may be affected by other things. For the albumin microspheres sonicated preparation, the following should be considered:

Allergies—Tell your doctor if you have ever had any unusual or allergic reaction to products containing human serum albumin or blood products. Also tell your doctor if you are allergic to any other substances, such as foods, preservatives, or dyes.

Pregnancy—Studies on this agent have not been done in pregnant women. However, in animal studies, the albumin microspheres sonicated preparation caused birth defects and other problems (such as decreased weight). Be sure you have discussed this with your doctor.

Breast-feeding—It is not known whether albumin microspheres sonicated pass into breast milk. However, your doctor may want you to stop breast-feeding for some time after you receive this preparation. Be sure you have discussed this with your doctor.

Children—Studies on this agent have been done only in adult patients, and there is no specific information comparing use of albumin microspheres sonicated in children with use in other age groups.

Older adults—Many medicines have not been studied specifically in older people. Therefore, it may not be known whether they work exactly the same way they do in younger adults. There is no specific information comparing use of albumin microspheres sonicated in the elderly with use in other age groups.

Other medical problems—The presence of other medical problems may affect the use of albumin microspheres sonicated. Make sure you tell your doctor if you have any other medical problems, especially:

- Congenital heart defects or
- Heart shunt or
- Liver problems—Use of the albumin microspheres sonicated preparation is not recommended because its effect when these conditions are present is not known

Preparation for This Test

Your doctor may have special instructions for you in preparation for your test. If you do not understand the instructions you receive or if you have not received such instructions, check with your doctor in advance.

Precautions After Having This Test

There are no special precautions to observe after having this test.

Side Effects of This Medicine

Along with its needed effects, a medicine may cause some unwanted effects. Although not all of these side effects may occur, if they do occur they many need medical attention.

Check with your doctor immediately if any of the following side effects occur:

Less common or rare
Chest pain; difficulty breathing or shortness of breath; itching; skin rash

Other side effects may occur that usually do not need medical attention. These side effects may go away after treatment as your body adjusts to the medicine. Check with your doctor if any of the following side effects continue or are bothersome:

More common
Dizziness; flushing of skin or sensation of warmth; headache; nausea and/or vomiting

Less common
Changes in taste; dryness of mouth; fatigue; pain at injection site; weakness

Other side effects not listed above may also occur in some patients. If you notice any other effects, check with your doctor.

Developed: 12/07/1998

ALDESLEUKIN   Systemic†

Commonly used brand name(s):

In the U.S.—
Proleukin
Other commonly used names are interleukin-2 and IL-2.

†Not commercially available in Canada.

Description

Aldesleukin (al-des-LOO-kin) is a synthetic (man-made) version of a substance called interleukin-2. Interleukins are produced naturally by cells in the body to help white blood cells work. Aldesleukin is used to treat cancer of the kidney and skin cancer that has spread to other parts of the body.

Aldesleukin causes some other very serious effects in addition to its helpful effects. Some effects can be fatal. For that reason, aldesleukin is given only in the hospital. If severe side effects occur, which is common, treatment in an intensive care unit (ICU) may be necessary. Other effects may not be serious but may cause concern. Before you begin treatment with aldesleukin, you and your doctor should talk about the good this medicine will do as well as the risks of using it.

Aldesleukin is to be administered only by or under the immediate supervision of your doctor. It is available in the following dosage form:

Parenteral
- Injection (U.S.)

Before Using This Medicine

In deciding to use a medicine, the risks of taking the medicine must be weighed against the good it will do. This is a decision you and your doctor will make. For aldesleukin, the following should be considered:

Allergies—Tell your doctor if you have ever had any unusual or allergic reaction to aldesleukin.

Pregnancy—Aldesleukin has not been studied in humans or in animals. However, because this medicine may cause serious side effects, use during pregnancy is usually not recommended.

Be sure that you have discussed this with your doctor before receiving this medicine.

Breast-feeding—It is not known whether aldesleukin passes into breast milk.

Children—There is no specific information comparing use of aldesleukin in children with use in other age groups.

Older adults—Many medicines have not been studied specifically in older people. Therefore, it may not be known whether they work exactly the same way they do in younger adults. There is no specific information comparing use of aldesleukin in the elderly with use in other age groups.

Other medicines—Although certain medicines should not be used together at all, in other cases two different medicines may be used together even if an interaction might occur. In these cases, your doctor may want to change the dose, or other precautions may be necessary. Tell your health care professional if you are taking *any* other medicine.

Other medical problems—The presence of other medical problems may affect the use of aldesleukin. Make sure you tell your doctor if you have any other medical problems, especially:

- Chickenpox (including recent exposure) or
- Herpes zoster (shingles)—Risk of severe disease affecting other parts of the body
- Heart disease or
- Immune system problems or
- Liver disease or
- Lung disease or
- Psoriasis or

- Underactive thyroid—May be worsened by aldesleukin
- Infection—Aldesleukin may decrease your body's ability to fight infection
- Kidney disease—Effects of aldesleukin may be increased because of slower removal from the body
- Mental problems—Aldesleukin may make them worse
- Seizures (history of)—Aldesleukin can cause seizures

Proper Use of This Medicine

Dosing—The dose of aldesleukin will be different for different patients. The dose that is used may depend on a number of things, including what the medicine is being used for, the patient's weight, and whether or not other medicines are also being taken. Because this medicine can cause very serious side effects, your doctor will be watching your dose very carefully and may change it as needed. If you have any questions about the proper dose of aldesleukin, ask your doctor.

Precautions While Using This Medicine

Aldesleukin can temporarily affect the white blood cells in your blood, increasing the chance of getting an infection. It can also lower the number of platelets, which are necessary for proper blood clotting. If this occurs, there are certain precautions you can take, especially when your blood count is low, to reduce the risk of infection or bleeding:

- If you can, avoid people with infections. *Check with your doctor immediately* if you think you are getting an infection or if you get a fever or chills, cough or hoarseness, lower back or side pain, or painful or difficult urination.
- *Check with your doctor immediately* if you notice any unusual bleeding or bruising; black, tarry stools; blood in urine or stools; or pinpoint red spots on your skin.
- Be careful when using a regular toothbrush, dental floss, or toothpick. Your medical doctor, dentist, or nurse may recommend other ways to clean your teeth and gums. Check with your medical doctor before having any dental work done.
- Do not touch your eyes or the inside of your nose unless you have just washed your hands and have not touched anything else in the meantime.
- Be careful not to cut yourself when you are using sharp objects such as a safety razor or fingernail or toenail cutters.
- Avoid contact sports or other situations where bruising or injury could occur.

Side Effects of This Medicine

Along with its needed effects, a medicine may cause some unwanted effects. Some side effects will have signs or symptoms that you can see or feel. Your doctor may watch for others by doing certain tests.

Check with your doctor or nurse immediately if any of the following side effects occur:

More common
　Fever or chills; shortness of breath

Less common
　Black, tarry stools; blisters on skin; blood in urine; bloody vomit; chest pain; cough or hoarseness; lower back or side pain; painful or difficult urination; pinpoint red spots on skin; stomach pain (severe); unusual bleeding or bruising

Check with your health care professional as soon as possible if any of the following side effects occur:

More common
　Agitation; confusion; diarrhea; dizziness; drowsiness; mental depression; nausea and vomiting; sores in mouth and on lips; tingling of hands or feet; unusual decrease in urination; unusual tiredness; weight gain of 5 to 10 pounds or more

Less common
　Bloating and stomach pain; blurred or double vision; faintness; fast or irregular heartbeat; loss of taste; rapid breathing; redness, swelling, and soreness of tongue; trouble in speaking; yellow eyes and skin

Rare
　Changes in menstrual periods; clumsiness; coldness; convulsions (seizures); listlessness; muscle aches; pain or redness at site of injection; sudden inability to move; swelling in the front of the neck; swelling of feet or lower legs; weakness

This medicine may also cause the following side effects that your doctor will watch for:

More common
　Anemia; heart problems; kidney problems; liver problems; low blood pressure; low platelet counts in blood; low white blood cell counts; other blood problems; underactive thyroid

Other side effects may occur that usually do not need medical attention. These side effects may go away during treatment as your body adjusts to the medicine. Also, your health care professional may be able to tell you about ways to prevent or reduce some of these side effects. Check with your health care professional if any of the following side effects continue or are bothersome or if you have any questions about them:

More common
　Dry skin; loss of appetite; skin rash or redness with burning or itching, followed by peeling; unusual feeling of discomfort or illness

Less common
　Constipation; headache; joint pain; muscle pain

Other side effects not listed above may also occur in some patients. If you notice any other effects, check with your doctor.

Developed: 09/15/93
Interim revision: 06/17/98

ALENDRONATE　Systemic

Commonly used brand name(s):

In the U.S.—
　Fosamax

In Canada—
　Fosamax

Description

Alendronate (a-LEN-dro-nate) is used to prevent or treat osteoporosis (thinning of the bone) in women after menopause and to treat osteoporosis in men. It may also be used to treat Paget's disease of bone and osteoporosis (thinning of the bone) caused by glucocorticoid treatment.

Alendronate is available only with your doctor's prescription, in the following dosage form:

Oral
- Tablets (U.S. and Canada)

Before Using This Medicine

In deciding to use a medicine, the risks of taking the medicine must be weighed against the good it will do. This is a decision you and your doctor will make. For alendronate, the following should be considered:

Allergies—Tell your doctor if you have ever had any unusual or allergic reaction to alendronate. Also tell your health care professional if you are allergic to any other substances, such as foods, preservatives, or dyes.

Diet—Make certain your health care professional knows if you are on any special diet, such as a low-sodium or low-sugar diet. Your doctor may recommend that you eat a balanced diet with an adequate amount of calcium and vitamin D (found in milk or other dairy products).

Pregnancy—Alendronate has not been studied in pregnant women. However, studies in animals have shown that alendronate causes birth defects and other pregnancy problems. Before taking this medicine, make sure your doctor knows if you are pregnant or if you may become pregnant.

Breast-feeding—It is not known whether alendronate passes into breast milk. However, this medicine has been reported to pass into the milk of lactating rats.

Children—Studies on this medicine have been done only in adult patients and there is no specific information comparing use of alendronate in children with use in other age groups.

Older adults—This medicine has been tested and has not been shown to cause different side effects or problems in older people than it does in younger adults.

Other medicines—Although certain medicines should not be used together at all, in other cases two different medicines may be used together even if an interaction might occur. In these cases, your doctor may want to change the dose, or other precautions may be necessary. When you are taking alendronate, it is especially important that your health care professional know if you are taking the following:

- Aspirin or products that contain aspirin—Use with alendronate may cause or make esophagus, intestine, or stomach problems worse

Other medical problems—The presence of other medical problems may affect the use of alendronate. Make sure you tell your doctor if you have any other medical problems, especially:

- Digestion problems—Taking alendronate may be harmful to the esophagus, intestine, or stomach

- Esophagus problems or
- Intestine problems or
- Stomach problems—Alendronate may make these conditions worse

- Kidney problems—The effects of alendronate may be increased

Proper Use of This Medicine

Take alendronate with a full glass (6 to 8 ounces) of plain water on an empty stomach. It should be taken in the morning at least 30 minutes before any food, beverage, or other medicines. Food and beverages, such as mineral water, coffee, tea, or juice, will decrease the amount of alendronate absorbed by the body. Waiting longer than 30 minutes will allow more of the drug to be absorbed. Medicines such as antacids or calcium or vitamin supplements will also decrease the absorption of alendronate.

Do not lie down for 30 minutes after taking alendronate. This will help alendronate reach your stomach faster. It will also help prevent irritation to your esophagus.

Your doctor may recommend that you eat a balanced diet with an adequate amount of calcium and vitamin D (found in milk or other dairy products). However, do not take any food, beverages, or calcium or vitamin supplements within 30 minutes or longer of taking alendronate. To do so may keep this medicine from working properly.

Dosing—The dose of alendronate will be different for different patients. *Follow your doctor's orders or the directions on the label.* The following information includes only the average doses of alendronate. *If your dose is different, do not change it* unless your doctor tells you to do so.

For treatment of Paget's disease of bone:
- Adults—40 milligrams (mg) once a day in the morning, taken at least thirty minutes before the first food, beverage, or medication. You should take alendronate with six to eight ounces of plain water. Your treatment may continue for six months. Your doctor may repeat the treatment.
- Children—Use and dose must be determined by your doctor.

For treatment of osteoporosis in men (thinning of bone):
- Adults—10 mg once a day in the morning, taken at least thirty minutes before the first food, beverage, or medication. You should take alendronate with six to eight ounces of plain water.

For treatment of postmenopausal osteoporosis (thinning of bone):
- Adults—10 mg once a day in the morning or 70 mg once a week, taken at least thirty minutes before the first food, beverage, or medication. You should take alendronate with six to eight ounces of plain water.

For prevention of postmenopausal osteoporosis (thinning of bone):
- Adults—5 mg once a day in the morning or 35 mg once a week, taken at least thirty minutes before the first food, beverage, or medication. You should take alendronate with six to eight ounces of plain water.

For treatment of osteoporosis (thinning of bone) caused by glucocorticoid treatment:
- Adults—5 mg once a day in the morning, taken at least thirty minutes before the first food, beverage, or medication. In postmenopausal women not receiving estrogen, the dose is 10 mg once a day in the morning, taken at least thirty minutes before the first food, beverage, or medication. You should take alendronate with six to eight ounces of plain water.

Missed dose—If you miss a dose of this medicine, do not take it later in the day. Resume your usual schedule the next morning. Do not double doses.

Storage—To store this medicine:
- Keep out of the reach of children.
- Store away from heat and direct light.
- Do not store in the bathroom, near the kitchen sink, or in other damp places. Heat or moisture may cause the medicine to break down.
- Keep the medicine from freezing. Do not refrigerate.
- Do not keep outdated medicine or medicine no longer needed. Be sure that any discarded medicine is out of the reach of children.

Side Effects of This Medicine

Along with its needed effects, a medicine may cause some unwanted effects. Although not all of these side effects may occur, if they do occur they may need medical attention.

Check with your doctor as soon as possible if any of the following side effects occur:
More common
    Abdominal pain
Less common
    Difficulty in swallowing; heartburn; irritation or pain of the esophagus; muscle pain
Rare
    Skin rash

Other side effects may occur that usually do not need medical attention. These side effects may go away during treatment as your body adjusts to the medicine. However, check with your doctor if any of the following side effects continue or are bothersome:
Less common
    Constipation; diarrhea; full or bloated feeling; gas; headache; nausea

Other side effects not listed above may also occur in some patients. If you notice any other effects, check with your doctor.

Developed: 01/06/97
Revised: 01/10/2001

ALITRETINOIN   Topical†

Commonly used brand name(s):

In the U.S.—
    Panretin Gel

†Not commercially available in Canada.

Description

Alitretinoin (al-i-TRET-i-no-in) is used as a topical treatment for cutaneous AIDS-related Kaposi's sarcoma in cases when there is no need for oral or intravenous medication.

This medicine is available only with your doctor's prescription, in the following dosage form:

Topical
- Gel (U.S.)

Before Using This Medicine

In deciding to use a medicine, the risks of taking the medicine must be weighed against the good it will do. This is a decision you and your doctor will make. For alitretinoin, the following should be considered:

Allergies—Tell your doctor if you have ever had any unusual or allergic reaction to a retinoid (vitamin A) drug product.

Pregnancy—Alitretinoin has not been studied in pregnant women. Alitretinoin has been shown to cause birth defects in animals. However, this medicine may be needed in serious diseases or other situations that threaten the mother's life. Be sure you have discussed this with your doctor. Discuss these possible effects with your doctor.

Breast-feeding—It is not known whether this medicine passes into breast milk. However, alitretinoin is not recommended during breast-feeding, because it may cause unwanted effects in nursing babies.

Children—Studies of this medicine have been done only in adult patients, and there is no specific information comparing the use of alitretinoin in children with use in other age groups.

Older adults—Many medicines have not been studied specifically in older people. Therefore, it may not be known whether they work exactly the same way they do in younger adults or if they cause different side effects or problems in older people. There is no specific information comparing the use of alitretinoin in the elderly with use in other age groups.

Other medicines—Although certain medicines should not be used together at all, in other cases two different medicines may be used together even if an interaction might occur. In these cases, your doctor may want to change the dose or other precautions may be necessary. When you are taking alitretinoin, it is especially important that your doctor and pharmacist know if you are using the following:

- DEET-containing insect repellants—Concurrent use with products containing DEET may increase DEET side effects

Other medical problems—The presence of other medical problems may affect the use of alitretinoin. Make sure to tell your doctor if you have any other medical problems, especially

- Cutaneous T-cell lymphoma—May be more likely to experience side effects of alitretinoin gel.

Proper Use of This Medicine

Avoid the use of occlusive dressings

Dosing—*Follow your doctor's orders or the directions on the label*. The following information includes only the average doses of alitretinoin. *If your dose is different, do not change it* unless your doctor tells you to do so.

- For *topical* dosage form (gel):
    —For cutaneous Kaposi's sarcoma:
    - Adults—Apply a generous amount to the affected area of the skin two times day, or as directed by your doctor, and allow to dry for three to five minutes before covering with clothing.
    - Children—Use and dose must be determined by your doctor.

Missed dose—If you miss a dose of this medicine, use it as soon as possible. However, if it is almost time for your next dose, skip the missed dose and go back to your regular dosing schedule. Do not double doses.

Storage—To store this medicine:

• Keep out of the reach of children.
• Store away from heat.
• Do not keep outdated medicine or medicine no longer needed. Ask your health care professional how you should dispose of any medicine you do not use. Be sure that any discarded medicine is out of the reach of children.

Precautions While Using This Medicine

It is very important that your doctor check your progress at regular visits to make sure that this medicine is working properly and to check for unwanted effects.

This medicine increases the sensitivity of the treated areas of your skin to sunlight or sun lamps. Therefore, *exposure to the sun, even through window glass or on a cloudy day, could cause a serious burn.*

Avoid application of the gel to normal skin surrounding the lesions or to mucous membranes

Side Effects of This Medicine

Along with its needed effects, a medicine may cause some unwanted effects. Although not all of these side effects may occur, if they do occur they may need medical attention.

Check with your doctor as soon as possible if any of the following side effects occur:

More common
Abrasion of skin; blisters on skin; burning pain; cracking, crusting, drainage, or oozing of the skin; groove in the skin; peeling of skin; severe rash; skin redness; sloughing of skin; swelling at the site of application

Less common
Stinging or tingling of skin

Other side effects may occur that usually do not need medical attention. These side effects may go away during treatment as your body adjusts to the medicine. However, check with your doctor if any of the following side effects continue or are bothersome:

More common
Itching; rash

Less common
Increased sensitivity to the sun

Other side effects not listed above may also occur in some patients. If you notice any other effects, check with your doctor.

Revised: 12/2/99

ALLOPURINOL   Systemic

Commonly used brand name(s):

In the U.S.—
Aloprim
Zyloprim
Generic name product may be available.

In Canada—
Apo-Allopurinol
Purinol
Zyloprim

Description

Allopurinol (al-oh-PURE-i-nole) is used to treat chronic gout (gouty arthritis). This condition is caused by too much uric acid in the blood.

This medicine works by causing less uric acid to be produced by the body. Allopurinol will not relieve a gout attack that has already started. Also, it does not cure gout, but it will help prevent gout attacks. However, it works only after you have been taking it regularly for a few months. Allopurinol will help prevent gout attacks only as long as you continue to take it.

Allopurinol is also used to prevent or treat other medical problems that may occur if too much uric acid is present in the body. These include certain kinds of kidney stones or other kidney problems.

Certain medicines or medical treatments can greatly increase the amount of uric acid in the body. This can cause gout or kidney problems in some people. Allopurinol is also used to prevent these problems, and can be given as either a tablet or an injection if necessary

Allopurinol is available only with your doctor's prescription in the following dosage form:

Oral
• Tablets (U.S. and Canada)
Parenteral
• Injection (U.S.)

Before Using This Medicine

In deciding to use a medicine, the risks of taking the medicine must be weighed against the good it will do. This is a decision you and your doctor will make. For allopurinol, the following should be considered:

Allergies—Tell your doctor if you have ever had any unusual or allergic reaction to allopurinol. Also tell your health care professional if you are allergic to any other substances, such as foods, preservatives, or dyes.

Pregnancy—Although studies on birth defects have not been done in pregnant women, allopurinol has not been reported to cause problems in humans. In one study in mice, large amounts of allopurinol caused birth defects and other unwanted effects. However, allopurinol did not cause birth defects or other problems in rats or rabbits given doses up to 20 times the amount usually given to humans.

Breast-feeding—Allopurinol passes into the breast milk. Mothers who are taking this medicine and who wish to breast-feed should discuss this with their doctor.

Children—This medicine has been tested in children and, in effective doses, has not been shown to cause different side effects or problems than it does in adults.

Older adults—Many medicines have not been studied specifically in older people. Therefore, it may not be known whether they work exactly the same way they do in younger adults or if they cause different side effects or problems in older people. There is no specific information comparing use of allopurinol in the elderly with use in other age groups.

Other medicines—Although certain medicines should not be used together at all, in other cases two different medicines may be used together even if an interaction might occur. In these cases, your doctor may want to change the dose, or other precautions may be necessary. When you are taking allopurinol, it is especially important that your doctor and pharmacist know if you are taking any of the following:

- Anticoagulants (blood thinners)—Allopurinol may increase the chance of bleeding; changes in the dose of the anticoagulant may be needed, depending on blood test results

- Azathioprine (e.g., Imuran) or
- Mercaptopurine (e.g., Purinethol)—Allopurinol may cause higher blood levels of azathioprine or mercaptopurine, leading to an increased chance of serious side effects

Other medical problems— The presence of other medical problems may affect the use of allopurinol. Make sure you tell your doctor if you have any other medical problems, especially:

- Congestive heart disease or
- Diabetes mellitus (sugar diabetes) or
- High blood pressure or
- Kidney disease—There is an increased risk of severe allergic reactions or other serious effects; a change in the dose of allopurinol may be needed

Proper Use of This Medicine

If this medicine upsets your stomach, it may be taken after meals. If stomach upset (indigestion, nausea, vomiting, diarrhea, or stomach pain) continues, check with your doctor.

In order for this medicine to help you, it must be taken regularly as ordered by your doctor.

To help prevent kidney stones while taking allopurinol, adults should drink at least 10 to 12 full glasses (8 ounces each) of fluids each day unless otherwise directed by their doctor. Check with the doctor about the amount of fluids that children should drink each day while receiving this medicine. Also, your doctor may want you to take another medicine to make your urine less acidic. It is important that you follow your doctor's instructions very carefully.

For patients taking allopurinol for *chronic gout:*

- After you begin to take allopurinol, gout attacks may continue to occur for a while. However, if you take this medicine regularly as directed by your doctor, the attacks will gradually become less frequent and less painful. After you have been taking allopurinol regularly for several months, the attacks may stop completely.
- Allopurinol is used to help prevent gout attacks. It will not relieve an attack that has already started. *Even if you take another medicine for gout attacks, continue to take this medicine also.*

Dosing— The dose of allopurinol will be different for different patients. *Follow your doctor's orders or the directions on the label.* The following information includes only the average doses of allopurinol. *If your dose is different, do not change it* unless your doctor tells you to do so.

The number of tablets that you take each day and the number of times that you take the medicine every day depend on the strength of the medicine, on the dose that you need, and on the reason you are taking allopurinol. Up to 300 milligrams (mg) of allopurinol can be taken at one time. Doses larger than 300 mg a day should be divided into smaller amounts that are taken two, three, or even four times a day.

- For the *oral* dosage form (tablets):
  —For gout:
    - Adults—At first, most people will take 100 mg a day. After about a week, your doctor will probably increase the dose gradually until the amount of uric acid in your blood has been lowered to normal levels. The total amount of allopurinol is usually not more than 800 mg a day. After the uric acid has remained at normal levels for a while, your doctor may lower your dose gradually until you are taking the smallest amount of medicine that will keep the uric acid from increasing again.
    - Children and teenagers—Use and dose must be determined by the doctor.
  —For kidney stones:
    - Adults—100 to 800 mg a day, depending on the kind of kidney stones.
    - Children and teenagers—Use and dose must be determined by the doctor.
  —For preventing or treating medical problems that may occur if certain treatments increase the amount of uric acid in the blood:
    - Adults—600 to 800 mg a day, starting one to three days before the treatment.
    - Children—The dose depends on the child's age
      —Children up to 6 years of age: 50 mg (one-half of a 100-mg tablet) three times a day.
      —Children 6 to 10 years of age: One 100-mg tablet three times a day or one 300-mg tablet a day.
      —Children 11 years of age and older: The dose may be the same as for adults.

- For the *parenteral* dosage form (injection):
  —For preventing or treating medical problems that may occur if certain treatments increase the amount of uric acid in the blood:
    - Adults—200 to 400 mg per square meter of body surface area (mg/m^2) a day, injected into a vein. Starting one to two days before treatment, this dose may be given as a single dose or divided into smaller doses as determined by your doctor. Your doctor will check your uric acid level and may change your dose based on the level. However, the dose is usually not more than 600 mg per day.
    - Children—At first, 200 mg per square meter of body surface area (mg/m^2) per day, injected into a vein. Starting one to two days before treatment, this dose may be given as a single dose or divided into smaller doses as determined by your doctor. Your doctor will check your uric acid level and may change your dose based on the level.

Missed dose— If you miss a dose of this medicine, take it as soon as possible. However, if it is almost time for your next dose, skip the missed dose and go back to your regular dosing schedule. Do not double doses.

Storage— To store this medicine:
- Keep out of the reach of children.
- Store away from heat and direct light.
- Do not store this medicine in the bathroom, near the kitchen sink, or in other damp places. Heat or moisture may cause the medicine to break down.
- Do not keep outdated medicine or medicine no longer needed. Be sure that any discarded medicine is out of the reach of children.

Precautions While Using This Medicine

Your doctor should check your progress at regular visits. Blood tests may be needed to make sure that this medicine is working properly and is not causing unwanted effects.

Drinking too much alcohol may increase the amount of uric acid in the blood and lessen the effects of allopurinol. Therefore, people with gout and other people with too much uric acid in the body should be careful to limit the amount of alcohol they drink.

Taking too much vitamin C may make the urine more acidic and increase the possibility of kidney stones forming while you are taking allopurinol. Therefore, check with your doctor before you take vitamin C while taking this medicine.

Check with your doctor immediately:
- *If you notice a skin rash, hives, or itching while you are taking allopurinol.*
- *If chills, fever, joint pain, muscle aches or pains, sore throat, or nausea or vomiting occur, especially if they occur together with or shortly after a skin rash.*

Very rarely, these effects may be the first signs of a serious reaction to the medicine.

Allopurinol may cause some people to become drowsy or less alert than they are normally. *Make sure you know how you react to this medicine before you drive, use machines, or do anything else that could be dangerous if you are not alert.*

Side Effects of This Medicine

Along with its needed effects, a medicine may cause some unwanted effects. Although not all of these side effects may occur, if they do occur they may need medical attention.

Stop taking this medicine and check with your doctor immediately if any of the following side effects occur:
  More common
    Skin rash or sores, hives, or itching
  Rare
    Black, tarry stools; bleeding sores on lips; blood in urine or stools; chills, fever, muscle aches or pains, nausea, or vomiting—especially if occurring with or shortly after a skin rash; difficult or painful urination; pinpoint red spots on skin; redness, tenderness, burning, or peeling of skin; red and/or irritated eyes; red, thickened, or scaly skin; shortness of breath, troubled breathing, tightness in chest, or wheezing; sores, ulcers, or white spots in mouth or on lips; sore throat and fever; sudden decrease in amount of urine; swelling in upper abdominal (stomach) area; swelling of face, fingers, feet, or lower legs; swollen and/or painful glands; unusual bleeding or bruising; unusual tiredness or weakness; weight gain (rapid); yellow eyes or skin

Also, check with your doctor as soon as possible if any of the following side effects occur:
  Rare
    Loosening of fingernails; numbness, tingling, pain, or weakness in hands or feet; pain in lower back or side; unexplained nosebleeds

Other side effects may occur that usually do not need medical attention. These side effects may go away during treatment as your body adjusts to the medicine. However, check with your doctor if any of the following side effects continue or are bothersome:
  Less common or rare
    Diarrhea; drowsiness; headache; indigestion; nausea or vomiting occurring without a skin rash or other side effects; stomach pain occurring without other side effects; unusual hair loss

Other side effects not listed above may also occur in some patients. If you notice any other effects, check with your doctor.

Revised: 03/30/00

ALOSETRON   Systemic*†

Commonly used brand name(s):

In the U.S.—
Lotronex

*†Not commercially available in the U.S. and Canada.

Description

Alosetron (a-LOE-se-tron) is a medicine used to treat irritable bowel syndrome (IBS) in women who have diarrhea as their main symptom. IBS has been called by many names, including irritable colon and spastic colon. IBS is a medical condition causing cramping abdominal pain, abdominal discomfort, urgency (a sudden need to have a bowel movement), and irregular bowel habits, such as diarrhea and constipation. It is not clear why some people develop IBS. It may be caused by your body's overreaction to a body chemical called serotonin. This overreaction may cause your intestinal system to be overactive. Alosetron works by blocking the action of serotonin on the intestinal system. This reduces the cramping abdominal pain, abdominal discomfort, urgency, and diarrhea caused by IBS.

Alosetron was withdrawn from the U.S. market by Glaxo-Wellcome on request of the Food and Drug Administration in November 2000.

Before Using This Medicine

In deciding to use a medicine, the risks of taking the medicine must be weighed against the good it will do. This is a decision you and your doctor will make. For alosetron, the following should be considered:

Allergies—Tell your doctor if you have ever had any unusual or allergic reaction to alosetron. Also, tell your health care professional if you are allergic to any other substances, such as foods, preservatives, or dyes.

Pregnancy—Alosetron has not been studied in pregnant women. However, alosetron has not been shown to cause birth defects or other problems in animal studies.

Breast-feeding—It is not known whether alosetron passes into human breast milk. Although most medicines pass into breast milk in small amounts, many of them may be used safely while breast-feeding. Mothers who are taking this medicine and who wish to breast-feed should discuss this with their doctor.

Children—Studies on this medicine have been done only in adult patients, and there is no specific information comparing use of alosetron in children with use in other age groups.

Older adults—This medicine has been tested and has not been shown to cause different side effects or problems in older people than it does in younger adults.

Other medical problems—The presence of other medical problems may affect the use of this medicine. Make sure you tell your doctor if you have any other medical problems, especially constipation, Crohn's disease, diverticulitis, intestinal adhesions, obstructions or strictures, ischemic colitis, ulcerative colitis, or toxic megacolon.

Proper Use of This Medicine

This medicine may be taken with or without food.

Constipation occurring during therapy with alosetron may be treated with laxatives, fiber, or a brief interruption in therapy. Your doctor will help you with constipation that may occur during therapy.

Dosing—The dose of alosetron may be different for different patients. *Follow your doctor's orders or the directions on the label.* The following information includes only the average doses of alosetron. *If your dose is different, do not change it* unless your doctor tells you to do so.

The number of doses you take each day, the time allowed between doses, and the length of time you take the medicine depend on the medical problem for which you are taking alosetron.

- For *oral* dosage form (tablets):
  —For irritable bowel syndrome associated with diarrhea:
    - Adults—1 mg twice daily
    - Children—Use and dose must be determined by your doctor.

Missed dose—If you miss a dose of this medicine, take it as soon as possible. However, if it is almost time for your next dose, skip the missed dose and go back to your regular dosing schedule. Do not double doses.

Storage—To store this medicine:
- Keep out of the reach of children.
- Do not store in the bathroom, near the kitchen sink, or in other damp places. Heat or moisture may cause the medicine to break down.
- Keep the medicine from freezing. Do not refrigerate.
- Do not keep outdated medicine or medicine no longer needed. Ask your health care professional how you should dispose of any medicine you do not use. Be sure that any discarded medicine is out of the reach of children.

Precautions While Using This Medicine

If you will be taking this medicine for a long time, *it is very important that your doctor check you at regular visits.*

Side Effects of This Medicine

Along with its needed effects, a medicine may cause some unwanted effects. Although not all of these side effects may occur, if they do occur they may need medical attention.

Check with your doctor immediately if any of the following side effects occur:
Less Common
  Constipation, severe
Rare
  Abdominal tenderness, pain; fever; rectal bleeding; stomach cramps; watery or bloody diarrhea

Get emergency help immediately if any of the following symptoms of overdose occur:
Symptoms of Overdose
  Convulsions (seizures); clumsiness, unsteadiness, trembling, or other problems with muscle control or coordination; difficulty breathing; shakiness and unsteady walk; withdrawn or socially detached behavior

Other side effects may occur that usually do not need medical attention. These side effects may go away during treatment as your body adjusts to the medicine. However, check with your doctor if any of the following side effects continue or are bothersome:
More Common
  Constipation, mild or moderate

Other side effects not listed above may also occur in some patients. If you notice any other effects, check with your doctor.

Developed: 04/18/2000
Revised: 12/19/2000

ALPROSTADIL Local

Commonly used brand name(s):
In the U.S.—
Caverject
Edex
Muse
Prostin VR Pediatric

In Canada—
Caverject
Prostin VR

Other commonly used names are PGE$_1$ and prostaglandin E$_1$.

Description

Alprostadil (al-PROS-ta-dil) belongs to a group of medicines called vasodilators that can increase blood flow by expanding blood vessels. Alprostadil is used to produce erections in some men who need treatment for erectile dysfunction (sexual impotence). This medicine causes an erection because it increases the blood flow to the penis.

Alprostadil injection should not be used as a sexual aid by men who do not have erectile dysfunction. If the medicine is not used properly, permanent damage to the penis and loss of the ability to have erections could result.

Alprostadil is used alone or with medical tests to help diagnose erectile dysfunction that may be caused by nerve or blood vessel problems in the penis.

Alprostadil is available only with your doctor's prescription, in the following dosage forms:
Intraurethral
- Suppositories (U.S.)

Parenteral
- Injection (U.S. and Canada)

Before Using This Medicine

In deciding to use a medicine, the risks of using the medicine must be weighed against the good it will do. This is a decision you and your doctor will make. For alprostadil, the following should be considered:

Allergies—Tell your doctor if you have ever had any unusual or allergic reaction to alprostadil. Also tell your health care professional if you are allergic to any other substances, such as foods, preservatives, or dyes.

Older adults—This medicine has been tested and has not been shown to cause different side effects or problems in older people than it does in younger adults.

Other medicines—Although certain medicines should not be used together at all, in other cases two different medicines may be used together even if an interaction might occur. In these cases, your doctor may want to change the dose, or other precautions may be necessary. Tell your health care professional if you are taking any other prescription or nonprescription (over-the-counter [OTC]) medicine.

Other medical problems—The presence of other medical problems may affect the use of alprostadil. Make sure you tell your doctor if you have any other medical problems, especially:

- Abnormal penis, including curved penis and birth defects of the penis—Chance of problems occurring may be increased
- Bleeding problems—Chance of bleeding at the place of injection may be increased
- Infection of penis or
- Red or itchy (inflamed) penis—Conditions may worsen with the use of alprostadil suppositories. Also, local skin problems and minor bleeding from inserting the suppository may occur
- Conditions causing thickened blood or slower blood flow, including leukemia; multiple myeloma (tumors of the bone marrow); polycythemia, sickle cell disease, or thrombocythemia (blood problems) or
- Priapism (history of)—Patients with these conditions have an increased risk of priapism (erection lasting longer than 6 hours) while using alprostadil

Proper Use of This Medicine

Special patient directions come with the suppositories and some of the injection medicines. *Read the directions carefully before using the medicine.*

For the injections—There are several alprostadil products that can be injected. Although the injection method is the same, the mixing procedures are different. *Be sure you know which of these products you will be using and the proper way to mix the injection.*

- One product called Alprostadil for Injection (brand names *Caverject* and *Edex*) is available as a powder in an injection bottle (vial). *Caverject* must be mixed with a solution called Bacteriostatic Water for Injection USP. *Edex* must be mixed with a solution called Sodium Chloride Injection USP. The solution for mixing comes with your product and may be already loaded into a syringe or contained in another injection bottle (vial).

- Another product is called Alprostadil Injection (brand names *Prostin VR Pediatric* and *Prostin VR*). Although the medicine is already in solution, it is much too strong to be injected into the penis. The solution must be mixed (diluted) with another liquid that is sold as a separate prescription, called 0.9% Sodium Chloride Injection USP. In most cases, a pharmacist will make this solution for you, giving you the proper strength that you need. Check with your doctor or pharmacist to make sure the solution has been diluted before using it.

It is important to follow several steps to prepare your alprostadil injection correctly. Before drawing up the medicine into the syringe:

- Wash your hands with soap and water.
- Set the bottles on a clean surface. Wipe the top of the injection bottles with an alcohol swab. *Do not wipe the needle.* Throw away the alcohol swab.
- You may need to attach the needle to the syringe. Do not take the cap off yet.

How to mix Caverject:

- If the syringe already contains the Bacteriostatic Water for Injection USP, then you need only add the plunger to the syringe. To do this:
  - Pick up the rod-like plunger and place it within the barrel of the syringe until it touches the rubber piece. Gently screw the plunger into the rubber piece until it seems secure. Do not use a lot of force.
  - Hold the syringe by the barrel (not the plunger) and take the cap off the needle.
  - You are now ready to mix the water and the powder. Skip to the directions under the title, *"To mix the water and powder."*
- If the syringe does not already contain the Bacteriostatic Water for Injection USP, you must withdraw 1 milliliter (mL) of it from the bottle provided. To do this:
  - Pick up the syringe and take the cap off the needle.
  - Pull the plunger back to the 1-mL mark on the syringe. This pulls air into the syringe. Insert the needle into rubber top of the bottle while it is upright and inject the 1 mL of air into the bottle.
  - Turn the bottle upside down using one hand. Be sure the tip of the needle is covered by solution.
  - With your other hand, pull the plunger back slowly to withdraw 1 mL of solution into the syringe. Remove the needle and skip to the directions under the title, *"To mix the water and powder."*
- *To mix the water and powder:*
  - Insert the needle into the bottle of alprostadil and inject 1 milliliter of Bacteriostatic Water for Injection USP from your syringe into the bottle of alprostadil.
  - Remove the needle from the bottle, holding the barrel of the syringe.
  - Gently swirl the bottle to mix the powder into the solution, turning it upside down to wet all the powder in the bottle.
  - Follow the directions below, *"How to draw your dose into the syringe."*

How to mix Edex:

- The syringe already contains the Sodium Chloride Injection USP. You need only attach the needle to the syringe and add the plunger. To do this:
  - Remove the needle from its package. Do not remove the needle cap. Gently screw the needle into place on the syringe tip.

—Pick up the rod-like plunger and place it within the barrel of the syringe until it touches the rubber piece. Gently screw the plunger into the rubber piece until it seems secure. Do not use a lot of force.

—Hold the syringe by the barrel (not the plunger) and take the cap off the needle.

—You are now ready to mix the Sodium Chloride Injection USP and the powder.

—Insert the needle into the bottle of alprostadil and inject 1.2 milliliters of the Sodium Chloride Injection USP from your syringe into the bottle of alprostadil.

—Remove the needle from the bottle, holding the barrel of the syringe.

—Gently swirl the bottle to mix the powder into the solution, turning it upside down to wet all the powder in the bottle.

—Follow the directions below, *"How to draw your dose into the syringe."*

How to mix Prostin VR or Prostin VR Pediatric:

• You will need to get exact mixing instructions from your doctor or pharmacist if you are given two solutions to be mixed. Follow them carefully, asking the pharmacist or doctor any questions that you might have before injecting the medicine.

• After you or the pharmacist has mixed these solutions, follow the directions below, *"How to draw your dose into the syringe."*

How to draw your dose into the syringe (for all injection products):

• Check the solution to make sure it is clear. *Do not use the mixture if you can see anything solid in the solution or if the solution is cloudy or colored.*

• After the alprostadil solution is mixed and the needle is inserted into the alprostadil bottle, turn the bottle with the syringe as a unit upside down in one hand. Be sure the tip of the needle is covered by the solution. With your other hand, pull the plunger back slowly to draw the correct dose of the medicine into the syringe.

• Hold the syringe with the measuring scale at eye level to see that the proper dose is withdrawn and to check for air bubbles. To remove air bubbles, tap gently on the measuring scale of the syringe to move any bubbles to the top of the syringe near the needle.

• If your dose measures too low in the syringe, withdraw more solution from the bottle. If there is too much medicine in the syringe, put some back into the bottle. Then check your dose again.

• Remove the needle from the bottle, holding the barrel of the syringe, not the plunger.

• Place the cover back on the needle. You are now ready to inject your dose. Follow the directions below, *"How to give the alprostadil injection."*

How to give the alprostadil injection:

• Choose a spot on your penis as directed by your doctor where you will give the injection.

• Clean the injection site with alcohol. Sitting upright or slightly reclined, hold your penis against the side of your thigh so that it cannot move.

• Remove the cover from the needle and hold the needle at a 90-degree angle to the place of injection.

• Insert the needle until almost all of the metal part of the needle is inserted into the penis.

• Do not inject the medicine just under the surface of the skin, at the top or head of the penis, or at the base of the penis near the scrotum or testes. Avoid injecting the medicine into blood vessels that you can see.

• Press the plunger down slowly, taking 5 to 10 seconds to release the dose into the penis.

• The injection is usually not painful. If the injection is very painful or if you notice bruising or swelling at the place of injection, that means you are injecting the medicine under the skin. Stop, withdraw the needle, and reposition it properly before continuing with the injection.

• Remove the needle and recap it.

• After you have completed the injection, put pressure on the place of injection for about 5 minutes or until any bleeding stops. This will prevent bruising. Then massage your penis as instructed by your doctor. This helps the medicine spread to all parts of the penis, so that the medicine will work better.

Choose a different place of injection each time you use the medicine to prevent skin problems. This includes switching the place of injection from the right side of the penis for one injection to the left side for the next injection.

After a single-use injection is mixed, the medicine must be used immediately. Throw away any unused mixture in the syringe. It cannot be stored for a later injection.

Do not reuse your needles.

How to throw away the syringes and bottles safely:

Dispose of your materials properly. *Caverject* comes in a plastic case that can be permanently locked with the red locking device that is included with the packaging. When the case label is removed, you can see a hole in the center of the case. The red locking device can be inserted and, by firmly pressing it down with your thumb, you will permanently lock the case. The locked case is safe to be thrown away.

If you do not have the plastic case or are using *Prostin VR* or *Prostin VR Pediatric* injection, unscrew the needle from the barrel of the syringe. Then bend, break, or cut the needle into two pieces with wire cutters. The pieces can be placed in a heavy plastic container, such as a bleach container, and thrown away. Or you may give them to a health care professional to throw away. If you have any questions about disposing of the syringe and needles, ask your health care professional.

For suppositories—*Before inserting the suppository, you should urinate.* The small amount of urine normally left in your urethra will help dissolve the suppository after it is inserted.

How to insert suppositories:

• Remove the delivery device containing the suppository from the foil. Remove the cap from the applicator stem.

• Stretch your penis upward to extend its length, pressing your penis top and bottom. Gently insert the delivery stem up to its collar into your urethra (located at the top of the penis). *If you have pain or a pulling feeling in the penis, withdraw the device and start again.*

• Press the button down slowly as far as it will go. This releases the suppository into the urethra. After holding the delivery device within your penis still for 5 seconds, carefully rock the penis and delivery device as a unit from side to side. This helps remove the suppository from the device.

• Remove the delivery device while your penis is upright. Look at the device to make sure that the suppository was completely released.

- Repeat the process if a part of the suppository remains in the device.
- After the suppository is completely released, roll your penis between your hands for 10 seconds. This helps to dissolve the suppository. If you feel any stinging, continue this motion to help stop it.
- Sitting, standing, or walking for 10 minutes while an erection is developing helps increase the blood flow to your penis to gain a proper erection.

How to throw away the suppository delivery device safely:

- Replace the cap on the delivery device. After storing it in the foil, fold and throw away.

For injections or suppositories—This medicine usually begins to work in about 5 to 10 minutes. You should attempt intercourse within 10 to 30 minutes after using the medicine. An erection may continue after ejaculation.

Dosing—The dose of alprostadil will be different for different patients. *Follow your doctor's orders or the directions on the label.* The following information includes only the average doses of alprostadil. *If your dose is different, do not change it* unless your doctor tells you to do so.

- For the treatment of erectile dysfunction:
  —For *injection* dosage form:
  - Adults—1.25 to 60 micrograms (mcg) as a single dose once a day. Your exact dose will be determined by your doctor. Inject this medicine very slowly into your penis as shown to you by your doctor ten to thirty minutes before intercourse. Allow five to ten seconds to completely inject the dose. Do not inject more than one dose within twenty-four hours. Also, do not use this medicine for more than two days in a row or more than three times a week.
  —For *suppository* dosage form:
  - Adults—125, 250, 500, or 1000 mcg as a single dose once a day. Your exact dose will be determined by your doctor. Insert this medicine into the urethra of your penis as shown to you by your doctor ten to thirty minutes before intercourse. Do not insert more than two doses within twenty-four hours.

Storage—To store this medicine:

- Keep out of the reach of children.
- Refrigerate Alprostadil Injection USP. Keep the medicine from freezing.
- Alprostadil for Injection while in the powder form can be stored at room temperature (between 15 and 25 °C or 59 and 77 °F) for 3 months. After it is mixed, the solution must be used immediately.
- Refrigerate alprostadil suppositories. Keep from freezing. They may be stored at room temperature for 14 days.
- Do not keep outdated medicine or medicine no longer needed. Be sure that any discarded medicine is out of the reach of children.

Precautions While Using This Medicine

Do not use alprostadil if you have a penile implant unless advised by doctor.

If using the alprostadil suppository, use a condom when having sexual intercourse with a pregnant female. Although harm to the fetus is unlikely, using a condom will protect the fetus from exposure to this medicine. *If a woman can become pregnant, use of contraceptive methods is recommended* because the effects of this medicine on early pregnancy are not known.

Use alprostadil exactly as directed by your doctor. Do not use more of it and do not use it more often than your doctor ordered. If too much is used, the erection lasts too long and does not reverse when it should. This condition is called priapism. If the erection is not reversed, the blood supply to the penis may be cut off and permanent damage may occur.

Contact your doctor immediately if the erection lasts longer than 4 hours or if it becomes painful. This may be a sign of priapism and must be treated right away to prevent permanent damage.

If you notice bleeding at the place where you injected the medicine, put pressure on the spot until the bleeding stops. If it doesn't stop within 10 minutes, check with your doctor.

Side Effects of This Medicine

Along with its needed effects, a medicine may cause some unwanted effects. Although not all of these side effects may occur, if they do occur they may need medical attention.

Check with your doctor immediately if the following side effects occur:
  Rare
    Curving of penis with pain during erection; erection continuing for 4 to 6 hours; erection continuing longer than 6 hours with severe and continuing pain of the penis; swelling in or pain of the testes

  Symptoms of too much medicine being absorbed into the body
    Dizziness; faintness; pelvic pain; flu-like symptoms

Other side effects may occur that usually do not need medical attention. These side effects may go away during treatment as your body adjusts to the medicine. However, check with your doctor if any of the following side effects continue or are bothersome:
  More common
    Bleeding at place of injection, short-term; mild bleeding or spotting from urethra (suppository only); pain at place of injection; painful erection; stinging of urethra (suppository only)

  Rare
    Bruising or clotted blood in penis at place of injection, usually caused by an incorrect injection

    Female partners may experience itching or stinging of vagina when you first begin using the alprostadil suppository. These side effects may not be caused from the medicine but may result if female partner has not had frequent or recent sexual intercourse.

Other side effects not listed above may also occur in some patients. If you notice any other effects, check with your doctor.

Revised: 08/19/97

ALTRETAMINE   Systemic

Commonly used brand name(s):

In the U.S.—
   Hexalen

In Canada—
   Hexalen

Another commonly used name is hexamethylmelamine.

Description

Altretamine (al-TRET-a-meen) belongs to the group of medicines called antineoplastics. It is used to treat cancer of the ovaries. It may also be used to treat other kinds of cancer, as determined by your doctor.

Altretamine interferes with the growth of cancer cells, which are eventually destroyed. Since the growth of normal body cells may also be affected by altretamine, other effects will also occur. Some of these may be serious and must be reported to your doctor. Other effects may not be serious but may cause concern. Some effects may not occur for months or years after the medicine is used.

Before you begin treatment with altretamine, you and your doctor should talk about the good this medicine will do as well as the risks of using it.

Altretamine is available only with your doctor's prescription in the following dosage form:

   Oral
   • Capsules (U.S. and Canada)

Before Using This Medicine

In deciding to use a medicine, the risks of taking the medicine must be weighed against the good it will do. This is a decision you and your doctor will make. For altretamine, the following should be considered:

Allergies—Tell your doctor if you have ever had any unusual or allergic reaction to altretamine.

Pregnancy—There is a chance that this medicine may cause birth defects if either the male or female is taking it at the time of conception or if it is taken during pregnancy. In addition, many cancer medicines may cause sterility that could be permanent. Although sterility has not been reported with this medicine, it does occur in animals and the possibility should be kept in mind.

Be sure that you have discussed this with your doctor before taking this medicine. It is best to use some kind of birth control while you are taking altretamine. Tell your doctor right away if you think you have become pregnant while taking altretamine.

Breast-feeding—Because altretamine may cause serious side effects, breast-feeding is generally not recommended while you are taking it.

Children—There is no specific information comparing use of altretamine in children with use in other age groups.

Older adults—Many medicines have not been studied specifically in older people. Therefore, it may not be known whether they work exactly the same way they do in younger adults. Although there is no specific information comparing use of altretamine in the elderly with use in other age groups, this medicine is not expected to cause different side effects or problems in older people than it does in younger adults.

Other medicines—Although certain medicines should not be used together at all, in other cases two different medicines may be used together even if an interaction might occur. In these cases, your doctor may want to change the dose, or other precautions may be necessary. When you are taking altretamine, it is especially important that your health care professional know if you are taking any of the following:

   • Amphotericin B by injection (e.g., Fungizone) or
   • Antithyroid agents (medicine for overactive thyroid) or
   • Azathioprine (e.g., Imuran) or
   • Chloramphenicol (e.g., Chloromycetin) or
   • Colchicine or
   • Flucytosine (e.g., Ancobon) or
   • Ganciclovir (e.g., Cytovene) or
   • Interferon (e.g., Intron A, Roferon-A) or
   • Plicamycin (e.g., Mithracin) or
   • Zidovudine (e.g., AZT, Retrovir) or
   • If you have ever been treated with radiation or cancer medicines—Altretamine may increase the effects of these medicines or radiation therapy on the blood
   • Monoamine oxidase (MAO) inhibitors (furazolidone [e.g., Furoxone], phenelzine [e.g., Nardil], procarbazine [e.g., Matulane], selegiline [e.g., Eldepryl], tranylcypromine [e.g., Parnate])—Taking altretamine while you are taking MAO inhibitors may cause a severe drop in blood pressure

Other medical problems—The presence of other medical problems may affect the use of altretamine. Make sure you tell your doctor if you have any other medical problems, especially:

   • Chickenpox (including recent exposure) or
   • Herpes zoster (shingles)—Risk of severe disease affecting other parts of the body
   • Nervous system problems—May be worsened by altretamine
   • Infection—Altretamine may decrease your body's ability to fight infection
   • Kidney disease—Effects of altretamine may be increased because of slower removal from the body
   • Liver disease—Effects may be changed because altretamine is activated and cleared from the body by the liver

Proper Use of This Medicine

This medicine often causes nausea and vomiting. However, it is very important that you continue to receive the medicine even if you begin to feel ill. Taking this medicine after meals will lessen stomach upset. Ask your health care professional for other ways to lessen these effects.

Dosing—The dose of altretamine will be different for different patients. The dose that is used may depend on a number of things, including what the medicine is being used for, the patient's size, and whether or not other medicines are also being taken. *If you are taking altretamine at home, follow your doctor's orders or the directions on the label.* If you have any questions about the proper dose of altretamine, ask your doctor.

Missed dose—If you miss a dose of this medicine, take it as soon as possible. However, if it is almost time for your next dose, skip the missed dose and go back to your regular dosing schedule. Do not double doses.

Storage—To store this medicine:
   • Keep out of the reach of children.

- Store away from heat and direct light.
- Do not store in the bathroom, near the kitchen sink, or in other damp places. Heat or moisture may cause the medicine to break down.
- Do not keep outdated medicine or medicine no longer needed. Be sure that any discarded medicine is out of the reach of children.

Precautions While Using This Medicine

It is very important that your doctor check your progress at regular visits to make sure that this medicine is working properly and to check for unwanted effects.

While you are being treated with altretamine, and after you stop treatment with it, *do not have any immunizations (vaccinations) without your doctor's approval.* Altretamine may lower your body's resistance and there is a chance you might get the infection the immunization is meant to prevent. In addition, other persons living in your household should not take oral polio vaccine since there is a chance they could pass the polio virus on to you. Also, avoid persons who have taken oral polio vaccine within the last several months. Do not get close to them and do not stay in the same room with them for very long. If you cannot take these precautions, you should consider wearing a protective face mask that covers the nose and mouth.

Altretamine can temporarily lower the number of white blood cells in your blood, increasing the chance of getting an infection. It can also lower the number of platelets, which are necessary for proper blood clotting. If this occurs, there are certain precautions you can take, especially when your blood count is low, to reduce the risk of infection or bleeding:

- If you can, avoid people with infections. *Check with your doctor immediately* if you think you are getting an infection or if you get a fever or chills, cough or hoarseness, lower back or side pain, or painful or difficult urination.
- *Check with your doctor immediately* if you notice any unusual bleeding or bruising; black, tarry stools; blood in urine or stools; or pinpoint red spots on your skin.
- Be careful when using a regular toothbrush, dental floss, or toothpick. Your medical doctor, dentist, or nurse may recommend other ways to clean your teeth and gums. Check with your medical doctor before having any dental work done.
- Do not touch your eyes or the inside of your nose unless you have just washed your hands and have not touched anything else in the meantime.
- Be careful not to cut yourself when you are using sharp objects such as a safety razor or fingernail or toenail cutters.
- Avoid contact sports or other situations where bruising or injury could occur.

Side Effects of This Medicine

Along with its needed effects, a medicine may cause some unwanted effects. Although not all of these side effects may occur, if they do occur they may need medical attention.

Also, because of the way these medicines act on the body, there is a chance that they might cause other unwanted effects that may not occur until months or years after the medicine is used. These delayed effects may include certain types of cancer, such as leukemia. Discuss these possible effects with your doctor.

Check with your doctor or nurse immediately if any of the following side effects occur:
Less common or rare
Black, tarry stools; blood in urine or stools; cough or hoarseness, accompanied by fever or chills; fever or chills; lower back or side pain, accompanied by fever or chills; painful or difficult urination, accompanied by fever or chills; pinpoint red spots on skin; unusual bleeding or bruising; unusual tiredness

Check with your doctor as soon as possible if any of the following side effects occur:
More common
Anxiety; clumsiness; confusion; convulsions (seizures); dizziness; mental depression; numbness in arms or legs; weakness

Rare
Skin rash or itching

Other side effects may occur that usually do not need medical attention. These side effects may go away during treatment as your body adjusts to the medicine. Also, your health care professional may be able to tell you about ways to prevent or reduce some of these side effects. Check with your doctor if any of the following side effects continue or are bothersome or if you have any questions about them:
More common
Nausea and vomiting

Less common
Diarrhea; loss of appetite; stomach cramps

Other side effects not listed above may also occur in some patients. If you notice any other effects, check with your doctor.

Additional Information

Once a medicine has been approved for marketing for a certain use, experience may show that it is also useful for other medical problems. Although this use is not included in product labeling, altretamine is used in certain patients with the following medical condition:

- Cancer of the lung

Other than the above information, there is no additional information relating to proper use, precautions, or side effects for this use.

Revised: 01/29/1999

AMANTADINE   Systemic

Commonly used brand name(s):

In the U.S.—
Symmetrel
Generic name product may be available.

In Canada—
Endantadine
Gen-Amantadine
Symmetrel
Generic name product may be available.

Description

Amantadine (a-MAN-ta-deen) is an antiviral. It is used to prevent or treat certain influenza (flu) infections (type A). It may be given alone or along with flu shots. Amantadine will not work for colds, other types of flu, or other virus infections.

Amantadine also is an antidyskinetic. It is used to treat Parkinson's disease, sometimes called paralysis agitans or shaking palsy. It may be given alone or with other medicines for Parkinson's disease. By improving muscle control and reducing stiffness, this medicine allows more normal movements of the body as the disease symptoms are reduced. Amantadine is also used to treat stiffness and shaking caused by certain medicines used to treat nervous, mental, and emotional conditions.

Amantadine may be used for other conditions as determined by your doctor.

Amantadine is available only with your doctor's prescription, in the following dosage forms:

Oral
- Capsules (U.S. and Canada)
- Syrup (U.S. and Canada)
- Tablets (U.S.)

Before Using This Medicine

In deciding to use a medicine, the risks of taking the medicine must be weighed against the good it will do. This is a decision you and your doctor will make. For amantadine, the following should be considered:

Allergies—Tell your doctor if you have ever had any unusual or allergic reaction to amantadine. Also tell your health care professional if you are allergic to any other substances, such as foods, preservatives, or dyes.

Pregnancy—Studies have not been done in humans. However, there have been reports of birth defects, including birth defects of the heart, when women took amantadine during the first trimester of pregnancy. Also, a malformation involving the lower leg occurred in one infant. In addition, studies in some animals have shown that amantadine is harmful to the fetus and causes birth defects. Before taking this medicine, make sure your doctor knows if you are pregnant or if you may become pregnant.

Breast-feeding—Amantadine passes into breast milk. However, the effects of amantadine in newborn babies and infants are not known. It may be necessary for you to take another medicine or to stop breast-feeding during treatment. Be sure you have discussed the risks and benefits of the medicine with your doctor.

Children—This medicine has been tested in children over 1 year of age and has not been shown to cause different side effects or problems in these children than it does in adults. There is no specific information comparing the use of amantadine in children under 1 year of age with use in other age groups.

Older adults—Elderly people are especially sensitive to the effects of amantadine. Confusion, difficult urination, blurred vision, constipation, and dry mouth, nose, and throat may be especially likely to occur.

Other medicines—Although certain medicines should not be used together at all, in other cases two different medicines may be used together even if an interaction might occur. In these cases, your doctor may want to change the dose, or other precautions may be necessary. When you are taking amantadine, it is especially important that your health care professional know if you are taking any of the following:

- Amphetamines or
- Appetite suppressants (diet pills), except fenfluramine (e.g., Pondimin), or
- Caffeine (e.g., NoDoz) or
- Chlophedianol (e.g., Ulone) or
- Cocaine or
- Medicine for asthma or other breathing problems or
- Medicine for colds, sinus problems, or hay fever or other allergies (including nose drops or sprays) or
- Methylphenidate (e.g., Ritalin) or
- Nabilone (e.g., Cesamet) or
- Pemoline (e.g., Cylert)—The use of amantadine with these medicines may increase the chance of unwanted effects such as nervousness, irritability, trouble in sleeping, and possibly seizures or irregular heartbeat
- Anticholinergics (medicine for abdominal or stomach spasms or cramps)—The use of amantadine with these medicines may increase the chance of unwanted effects such as blurred vision, dryness of the mouth, confusion, hallucinations, and nightmares
- Quinidine (e.g., Quinaglute Dura-tabs, Quinidex Extentabs) or
- Quinine or
- Trimethoprim and sulfamethoxazole (e.g., Bactrim, Septra)—These medicines may increase the amount of amantadine in the blood and increase the chance for side effects

Other medical problems—The presence of other medical problems may affect the use of amantadine. Make sure you tell your doctor if you have any other medical problems, especially:

- Eczema (recurring)—Amantadine may cause or worsen eczema

- Epilepsy or other seizure disorder (history of)—Amantadine may increase the frequency of convulsions (seizures) in patients with a seizure disorder

- Heart disease or other circulation problems or
- Swelling of feet and ankles—Amantadine may increase the chance of swelling of the feet and ankles, and may worsen heart disease or circulation problems

- Kidney disease—Amantadine is removed from the body by the kidneys; patients with kidney disease will need to receive a lower dose of amantadine

- Mental or emotional illness—Higher doses of amantadine may cause confusion, hallucinations, and nightmares

- Substance abuse (drug or alcohol abuse), history of—The chance of side effects from this medicine may be increased

Proper Use of This Medicine

For patients *taking amantadine to prevent or treat flu infections:*
- Talk to your doctor about the possibility of getting a flu shot if you have not had one yet.
- This medicine is *best taken before exposure, or as soon as possible after exposure*, to people who have the flu.

- To help keep yourself from getting the flu, *keep taking this medicine for the full time of treatment*. Or if you already have the flu, continue taking this medicine for the full time of treatment even if you begin to feel better after a few days. This will help to clear up your infection completely. If you stop taking this medicine too soon, your symptoms may return. This medicine should be taken for at least 2 days after all your flu symptoms have disappeared.
- This medicine works best when there is a constant amount in the blood. *To help keep the amount constant, do not miss any doses. Also, it is best to take the doses at evenly spaced times day and night.* For example, if you are to take two doses a day, the doses should be spaced about 12 hours apart. If this interferes with your sleep or other daily activities, or if you need help in planning the best times to take your medicine, check with your health care professional.
- If you are using the oral liquid form of amantadine, use a specially marked measuring spoon or other device to measure each dose accurately. The average household teaspoon may not hold the right amount of liquid.

For patients *taking amantadine for Parkinson's disease or movement problems* caused by certain medicines used to treat nervous, mental, and emotional conditions:

- *Take this medicine exactly as directed by your doctor.* Do not miss any doses and do not take more medicine than your doctor ordered.
- Improvement in the symptoms of Parkinson's disease usually occurs in about 2 days. However, in some patients this medicine must be taken for up to 2 weeks before full benefit is seen.

Dosing—The dose of amantadine will be different for different patients. *Follow your doctor's orders or the directions on the label.* The following information includes only the average doses of amantadine. Your dose may be different if you have kidney disease. *If your dose is different, do not change it* unless your doctor tells you to do so. The number of capsules, tablets, or teaspoonfuls of suspension that you take depends on the strength of the medicine. Also, *the number of doses you take each day, the time allowed between doses, and the length of time you take the medicine depend on the medical problem for which you are taking amantadine*.

- For *oral* dosage forms (capsules, syrup, and tablets):
  —For the *treatment or prevention of flu:*
  - Older adults—100 milligrams once a day.
  - Adults and children 12 years of age and older—200 milligrams once a day, or 100 milligrams two times a day.
  - Children 9 to 12 years of age—100 milligrams two times a day.
  - Children 1 to 9 years of age—Dose is based on body weight and must be determined by the doctor.
  - Children up to 1 year of age—Use and dose must be determined by your doctor
  —For the *treatment of Parkinson's disease or movement problems:*
  - Older adults—100 milligrams once a day to start. The dose may be increased slowly over time, if needed.
  - Adults—100 milligrams one or two times a day. Your doctor may increase this dose, if needed.

- Children—Dose has not been determined.

Missed dose—If you miss a dose of this medicine, take it as soon as possible. This will help to keep a constant amount of medicine in the blood. However, if it is almost time for your next dose, skip the missed dose and go back to your regular dosing schedule. Do not double doses.

Storage—To store this medicine:
- Keep out of the reach of children.
- Store away from heat and direct light.
- Do not store the capsule form of this medicine in the bathroom, near the kitchen sink, or in other damp places. Heat or moisture may cause the medicine to break down.
- Keep the oral liquid form of this medicine from freezing.
- Do not keep outdated medicine or medicine no longer needed. Be sure that any discarded medicine is out of the reach of children.

Precautions While Using This Medicine

Drinking alcoholic beverages while taking this medicine may cause increased side effects such as circulation problems, dizziness, lightheadedness, fainting, or confusion. Therefore, *do not drink alcoholic beverages while you are taking this medicine*.

This medicine may cause some people to become dizzy, confused, or lightheaded, or to have blurred vision or trouble concentrating. *Make sure you know how you react to this medicine before you drive, use machines, or do anything else that could be dangerous if you are dizzy or are not alert or able to see well.* If these reactions are especially bothersome, check with your doctor.

Getting up suddenly from a lying or sitting position also may be a problem because of the dizziness, lightheadedness, or fainting that may be caused by this medicine. Getting up slowly may help. If this problem continues or gets worse, check with your doctor.

If amantadine causes you to feel very depressed or to have thoughts of suicide, check with your doctor immediately.

Amantadine may cause dryness of the mouth, nose, and throat. For temporary relief of mouth dryness, use sugarless candy or gum, melt bits of ice in your mouth, or use a saliva substitute. However, if your mouth continues to feel dry for more than 2 weeks, check with your doctor or dentist. Continuing dryness of the mouth may increase the chance of dental disease, including tooth decay, gum disease, and fungus infections.

This medicine may cause purplish red, net-like, blotchy spots on the skin. This problem occurs more often in females and usually occurs on the legs and/or feet after this medicine has been taken regularly for a month or more. Although the blotchy spots may remain as long as you are taking this medicine, they usually go away gradually within 2 to 12 weeks after you stop taking the medicine. If you have any questions about this, check with your doctor.

For patients *taking amantadine to prevent or treat flu infections:*

- If your symptoms do not improve within a few days, if they become worse, or you develop new symptoms, check with your doctor.

For patients *taking amantadine for Parkinson's disease or movement problems* caused by certain medicines used to treat nervous, mental, and emotional conditions:

- *Patients with Parkinson's disease must be careful not to overdo physical activities as their condition improves and body movements become easier* since injuries resulting from falls may occur. Such activities must be gradually increased to give your body time to adjust to changing balance, circulation, and coordination.
- Some patients may notice that this medicine gradually loses its effect while they are taking it regularly for a few months. If you notice this, check with your doctor. Your doctor may want to adjust the dose or stop the medicine for a while and then restart it to restore its effect.
- *Do not suddenly stop taking this medicine without first checking with your doctor* since your Parkinson's disease may get worse very quickly. Your doctor may want you to reduce your dose gradually before stopping the medicine completely.

Side Effects of This Medicine

Along with its needed effects, a medicine may cause some unwanted effects. Although not all of these side effects may occur, if they do occur they may need medical attention.

Check with your doctor immediately if any of the following side effects occur:

Less common
Blurred vision; confusion (especially in elderly patients); difficult urination (especially in elderly patients); fainting; hallucinations (seeing, hearing, or feeling things that are not there); swelling of hands, feet, or lower legs

Rare
Convulsions (seizures); decreased vision or any change in vision; difficulty in coordination; fever, chills, or sore throat; increased blood pressure; increase in body movements; irritation and swelling of the eye; loss of memory; mental depression; severe mood or mental changes; skin rash; slurred speech; thoughts of suicide or attempts at suicide; unexplained shortness of breath

Other side effects may occur that usually do not need medical attention. These side effects may go away during treatment as your body adjusts to the medicine. However, check with your doctor if any of the following side effects continue or are bothersome:

More common
Agitation, anxiety, or nervousness; difficulty concentrating; dizziness or lightheadedness; headache; irritability; loss of appetite; nausea; purplish red, net-like, blotchy spots on skin; trouble in sleeping or nightmares

Less common or rare
Constipation; decrease in sexual desire; diarrhea; drowsiness; dryness of the mouth, nose, and throat; false sense of well-being; headache; vomiting; unusual tiredness or weakness

Other side effects not listed above may also occur in some patients. If you notice any other effects, check with your doctor.

Additional Information

Once a medicine has been approved for marketing for a certain use, experience may show that it is also useful for other medical problems. Although this use is not included in product labeling, amantadine is used in certain patients with the following medical condition:

- Unusual tiredness or weakness associated with multiple sclerosis

Other than the above information, there is no additional information relating to proper use, precautions, or side effects for this use.

Revised: 05/21/2001

AMIFOSTINE   Systemic

Commonly used brand name(s):

In the U.S.—
Ethyol

In Canada—
Ethyol

Description

Amifostine (am-i-FOS-teen) is used to help prevent or lessen some side effects caused by other medicines or radiation therapy that are used to treat cancer.

This medicine is available only with your doctor's prescription, in the following dosage form(s):

Parenteral
- Injection (U.S. and Canada)

Before Using This Medicine

In deciding to use a medicine, the risks of using the medicine must be weighed against the good it will do. This is a decision you and your doctor will make. For amifostine, the following should be considered:

Allergies—Tell your doctor if you have ever had any unusual or allergic reaction to amifostine.

Pregnancy—Amifostine has not been studied in pregnant women. However, in animal studies, large doses caused toxic or harmful effects in the fetus.

Because amifostine is used together with other medicines that can cause birth defects or other harmful effects in the fetus, it is usually recommended that women being treated for cancer use birth control.

Breast-feeding—It is not known whether amifostine passes into the breast milk. However, because amifostine is used together with other medicines that may cause serious side effects in nursing infants, breast-feeding is generally not recommended during treatment.

Children—Although this medicine has been given to a limited number of children, there is no specific information comparing use of amifostine in children with use in other age groups.

Older adults—Many medicines have not been studied specifically in older people. Therefore, it may not be known whether they work exactly the same way they do in younger adults or if they cause different side effects or problems in older people. Although amifostine has been given to a limited number of elderly people, there is no specific information comparing use of amifostine in the elderly with use in other age groups.

Other medicines—Although certain medicines should not be used together at all, in other cases two different medicines may be used together even if an interaction might occur. In these cases, your doctor may want to change the dose, or other precautions may be necessary. When you are receiving amifostine, it is especially important that your health care professional know if you are taking any of the following:

- Amantidine (e.g., Symmetrel) or
- Antidepressants (medicine for depression) or
- Antihypertensives (medicine for high blood pressure) or
- Antipsychotics (medicine for mental illness) or
- Beta-adrenergic blocking agents used in the eye, such as betaxolol (e.g., Betoptic), carteolol (e.g., Ocupress), levobunolol (e.g., Betagan), metipranolol (e.g., Opti-Pranolol), and timolol (e.g., Timoptic), or
- Bromocriptine (e.g., Parlodel) or
- Deferoxamine (e.g., Desferal) or
- Diuretics (water pills) or
- Levodopa (e.g., Dopar) or
- Medicine for heart disease or
- Nabilone (e.g., Cesamet) (with high doses) or
- Narcotic pain medicine or
- Nimodipine (e.g., Nimotop) or
- Pentamidine (e.g., Pentam) or
- Pimozide (e.g., Orap) or
- Promethazine (e.g., Phenergan) or
- Trimeprazine (e.g., Temaril)—Amifostine sometimes causes low blood pressure while it is being injected. These other medicines may add to this effect and increase the chance of a severe lowering of your blood pressure during treatment. You may have to stop taking the other medicine for a while before amifostine is given, but *do not stop taking it on your own*. Instead, the doctor who is treating your cancer should plan the best way to avoid this problem together with the doctor who ordered the other medicine for you.

Other medical problems—The presence of other medical problems may affect the use of amifostine. Make sure you tell your doctor if you have any other medical problems, especially:

- Heart or blood vessel disease or
- Low blood pressure or
- Stroke (history of) or
- Transient ischemic attacks (sometimes called TIAs or "ministrokes"), history of—Some of amifostine's side effects can cause harm to patients with these conditions

- Kidney disease—The chance of low blood calcium may be increased in people with some forms of kidney disease

Proper Use of This Medicine

Dosing—The dose of amifostine will be different for different patients. It depends on the patient's size. The medicine will be given by, or under the immediate supervision of, the doctor treating you for cancer.

- For *parenteral* dosage form (injection):
  —For preventing or lessening side effects caused by medicines used to treat cancer:
  - Adults—910 milligrams (mg) for each square meter of body surface area, injected into a vein starting 30 minutes before the cancer medicine.
  - Children—Use and dose will have to be determined by the doctor.
  —For preventing or lessening side effects caused by radiation therapy used to treat cancer:
  - Adults—200 milligrams (mg) for each square meter of body surface area, injected into a vein starting 15 to 30 minutes before the radiation treatment.
  - Children—Use and dose will have to be determined by the doctor.

Side Effects of This Medicine

Along with its needed effects, a medicine may cause some unwanted effects. Although not all of these side effects may occur, if they do occur they may need medical attention.

Tell the doctor or the person giving you the injection right away if you feel dizzy or faint while the injection is being given. Also, check with your doctor as soon as possible if any of the following side effects occur later on:
  Rare
    Burning or tingling sensation; muscle cramps

Other side effects may occur that usually do not need medical attention. These side effects may go away during treatment as your body adjusts to the medicine. However, check with your doctor if any of the following side effects continue or are bothersome:
  More common
    Nausea and vomiting
  Less common or rare
    Chills; skin rash; sleepiness (severe); sneezing

Other side effects that sometimes occur are harmless and will go away without treatment. These are:
  Less common or rare
    Feeling unusually warm or cold; flushing or redness of face or neck; hiccups

Other side effects not listed above may also occur in some patients. If you notice any other effects, check with your doctor.

Developed: 06/29/1998
Revised: 10/30/2000

AMINOGLUTETHIMIDE Systemic

Commonly used brand name(s):

In the U.S.—
  Cytadren

In Canada—
  Cytadren

Description

Aminoglutethimide (a-mee-noe-gloo-TETH-i-mide) acts on a part of the body called the adrenal cortex. It affects production of steroids and also has some other effects. Aminoglutethimide is used to treat some kinds of tumors that affect the adrenal cortex. Also, it is sometimes used when the adrenal cortex is overactive without being cancerous.

In addition, aminoglutethimide is sometimes used to treat certain other conditions as determined by your doctor.

Aminoglutethimide is available only with your doctor's prescription, in the following dosage form:

Oral
- Tablets (U.S. and Canada)

Before Using This Medicine

In deciding to use a medicine, the risks of taking the medicine must be weighed against the good it will do. This is a decision you and your doctor will make. For aminoglutethimide, the following should be considered:

Allergies—Tell your doctor if you have ever had any unusual or allergic reaction to glutethimide or aminoglutethimide. Also tell your health care professional if you are allergic to any other substances, such as foods, preservatives, or dyes.

Pregnancy—Aminoglutethimide has been shown to cause birth defects in humans and animals. However, this medicine may be needed in serious diseases or in other situations that threaten the mother's life. In addition, aminoglutethimide has been shown to cause fertility problems in animals. Be sure you have discussed this with your doctor before taking this medicine.

Breast-feeding—It is not known whether aminoglutethimide passes into breast milk. However, this medicine has not been reported to cause problems in nursing babies.

Children—Aminoglutethimide has been tested in a limited number of children. However, the effects of aminoglutethimide in children were difficult to determine because it was given in combination with other medicines.

Older adults—Lack of energy is more likely to occur in the elderly, who are usually more sensitive to the effects of aminoglutethimide.

Other medicines—Although certain medicines should not be used together at all, in other cases two different medicines may be used together even if an interaction might occur. In these cases, your doctor may want to change the dose, or other precautions may be necessary. When you are taking aminoglutethimide it is especially important that your health care professional know if you are taking any of the following:

- Dexamethasone (e.g., Decadron)—Aminoglutethimide increases the rate at which dexamethasone is removed from the body

Other medical problems—The presence of other medical problems may affect the use of aminoglutethimide. Make sure you tell your doctor if you have any other medical problems, especially:

- Chickenpox (including recent exposure) or
- Herpes zoster (shingles)—Risk of severe disease affecting other parts of the body
- Infection—May affect the adrenal cortex. If a steroid supplement is being used, a change in dose may be needed
- Kidney disease or

- Liver disease—Effects of aminoglutethimide may be increased because of slower removal from the body
- Underactive thyroid—Aminoglutethimide can cause underactive thyroid

Proper Use of This Medicine

Take this medicine only as directed by your doctor. Do not take more or less of it, and do not take it more often than your doctor ordered.

This medicine sometimes causes nausea and vomiting. This effect usually goes away or lessens after you have taken the medicine for a while. It is very important that you continue to use this medicine even if you begin to feel ill. Ask your health care provider for ways to lessen these effects. *Do not stop taking this medicine without first checking with your doctor.*

If you vomit shortly after taking a dose of aminoglutethimide, check with your doctor. You will be told whether to take the dose again or to wait until the next scheduled dose.

Dosing—The dose of aminoglutethimide will be different for different patients. The dose that is used may depend on a number of things, including what the medicine is being used for, the patient's weight, and whether or not other medicines are also being taken. *If you are taking aminoglutethimide at home, follow your doctor's orders or the directions on the label.* If you have any questions about the proper dose of aminoglutethimide, ask your doctor.

Missed dose—If you miss a dose of this medicine and remember within 2 to 4 hours of the missed dose, take it as soon as possible. Then go back to your regular dosing schedule. However, if it is almost time for your next dose, skip the missed dose and go back to your regular dosing schedule. Do not double doses.

Storage—To store this medicine:
- Keep out of the reach of children.
- Store away from heat and direct light.
- Do not store in the bathroom, near the kitchen sink, or in other damp places. Heat or moisture may cause the medicine to break down.
- Do not keep outdated medicine or medicine no longer needed. Be sure that any discarded medicine is out of the reach of children.

Precautions While Using This Medicine

It is very important that your doctor check your progress at regular visits to make sure that the medicine is working properly and does not cause unwanted effects.

Your doctor may want you to carry a medical identification card or wear a bracelet stating that you are taking this medicine.

Before you have any kind of surgery (including dental surgery) or emergency treatment, tell the medical doctor or dentist in charge that you are taking this medicine. Because this medicine affects the adrenal gland, extra steroids may be needed.

Check with your doctor right away if you get an injury, infection, or illness of any kind. This medicine may weaken your body's defenses against infection or inflammation.

This medicine may cause some people to become dizzy, drowsy, or less alert than they are normally. *Make sure you know how you react to this medicine before you drive, use machines, or do anything else that could be dangerous if you are dizzy or are not alert.*

Side Effects of This Medicine

Along with its needed effects, a medicine may cause some unwanted effects. Some side effects will have signs or symptoms that you can see or feel. Your doctor may watch for others by doing certain tests. Some of the unwanted effects that may be caused by aminoglutethimide are listed below. Although not all of these side effects may occur, if they do occur they may need medical attention.

Check with your doctor immediately if any of the following side effects occur:
Rare
   Black, tarry stools; blood in urine or stools; cough or hoarseness, accompanied by fever or chills; fever or chills; lower back or side pain, accompanied by fever or chills; painful or difficult urination, accompanied by fever or chills; pinpoint red spots on skin; shortness of breath; unusual bleeding or bruising; yellow eyes or skin

Check with your doctor as soon as possible if the following side effects occur:
More common
   Drowsiness; measles-like skin rash or itching on face and/or palms of hands
Less common
   Clumsiness; dizziness or lightheadedness (especially when getting up from a lying or sitting position); fast heartbeat; mental depression; shakiness; slurred speech; uncontrolled eye movements; unusual tiredness or weakness
Rare
   Neck tenderness or swelling

This medicine may also cause the following side effects that your doctor will watch for:
More common
   Low red blood cell count; low white blood cell count

Other side effects may occur that usually do not need medical attention. These side effects may go away during treatment as your body adjusts to the medicine. However, check with your health care professional if any of the following side effects continue or are bothersome:
More common
   Loss of appetite; nausea
Less common or rare
   Deepening of voice in females; headache; increased hair growth in females; irregular menstrual periods; muscle pain; vomiting

Other side effects not listed above may also occur in some patients. If you notice any other effects, check with your doctor.

Additional Information

Once a medicine has been approved for marketing for a certain use, experience may show that it is also useful for other medical problems. Although these uses are not included in product labeling, aminoglutethimide is used in certain patients with the following medical conditions:
- Breast cancer
- Prostate cancer

Other than the above information, there is no additional information relating to proper use, precautions, or side effects for these uses.

Revised: 04/09/93
Interim revision: 04/29/94; 08/14/98

AMINOGLYCOSIDES   Systemic

Commonly used brand name(s):

In the U.S.—
Amikin[1]   Kantrex[3]
Garamycin[2]   Nebcin[7]
G-Mycin[2]   Netromycin[5]
Jenamicin[2]

In Canada—
Amikin[1]   Nebcin[7]
Cidomycin[2]   Netromycin[5]
Garamycin[2]

Note: For quick reference, the following aminoglycosides are numbered to match the corresponding brand names.

This information applies to the following medicines:
1. Amikacin (am-i-KAY-sin)‡
2. Gentamicin (jen-ta-MYE-sin)‡
3. Kanamycin (kan-a-MYE-sin)†‡
4. Neomycin (nee-oh-MYE-sin)†‡
5. Netilmicin (ne-til-MYE-sin)
6. Streptomycin (strep-toe-MYE-sin)‡§
7. Tobramycin (toe-bra-MYE-sin)‡

†Not commercially available in Canada.
‡Generic name product may be available in the U.S.
§Generic name product may be available in Canada.

Description

Aminoglycosides (a-mee-noe-GLYE-koe-sides) are used to treat serious bacterial infections. They work by killing bacteria or preventing their growth.

Aminoglycosides are given by injection to treat serious bacterial infections in many different parts of the body. In addition, some aminoglycosides may be given by irrigation (applying a solution of the medicine to the skin or mucous membranes or washing out a body cavity) or by inhalation into the lungs. Streptomycin may also be given for tuberculosis (TB). These medicines may be given with 1 or more other medicines for bacterial infections, or they may be given alone. Aminoglycosides may also be used for other conditions as determined by your doctor. However, aminoglycosides will not work for colds, flu, or other virus infections.

Aminoglycosides given by injection are usually used for serious bacterial infections for which other medicines may not work. However, aminoglycosides may also cause some serious side effects, including damage to your hearing, sense of balance, and kidneys. These side effects may be more likely to occur in elderly patients and newborn infants. *You and your doctor should talk about the good these medicines may do as well as the risks of receiving them.*

Aminoglycosides are to be administered only by or under the immediate supervision of your doctor. They are available in the following dosage forms:
Inhalation
Amikacin
   • Inhalation solution (U.S.)

Gentamicin
  • Inhalation solution (U.S.)
Kanamycin
  • Inhalation solution (U.S.)
Tobramycin
  • Inhalation solution (U.S.)

Irrigation
Kanamycin
  • Irrigation solution (U.S.)

Parenteral
Amikacin
  • Injection (U.S. and Canada)
Gentamicin
  • Injection (U.S. and Canada)
Kanamycin
  • Injection (U.S.)
Neomycin
  • Injection (U.S.)
Netilmicin
  • Injection (U.S. and Canada)
Streptomycin
  • Injection (U.S. and Canada)
Tobramycin
  • Injection (U.S. and Canada)

Before Receiving This Medicine

In deciding to use a medicine, the risks of taking the medicine must be weighed against the good it will do. This is a decision you and your doctor will make. For aminoglycosides, the following should be considered:

Allergies—Tell your doctor if you have ever had any unusual or allergic reaction to any of the aminoglycosides. Also tell your health care professional if you are allergic to any other substances, such as foods, sulfites, or other preservatives.

Pregnancy—Studies on most of the aminoglycosides have not been done in pregnant women. Some reports have shown that aminoglycosides, especially streptomycin and tobramycin, may cause damage to the infant's hearing, sense of balance, and kidneys if the mother was receiving the medicine during pregnancy. However, this medicine may be needed in serious diseases or other situations that threaten the mother's life. Be sure you have discussed this with your doctor.

Breast-feeding—Aminoglycosides pass into breast milk in small amounts. However, they are not absorbed very much when taken by mouth. To date, aminoglycosides have not been reported to cause problems in nursing babies.

Children—Children are especially sensitive to the effects of aminoglycosides. Damage to hearing, sense of balance, and kidneys is more likely to occur in premature infants and neonates.

Older adults—Elderly people are especially sensitive to the effects of aminoglycosides. Serious side effects, such as damage to hearing, sense of balance, and kidneys may occur in elderly patients.

Other medicines—Although certain medicines should not be used together at all, in other cases two different medicines may be used together even if an interaction might occur. In these cases, your doctor may want to change the dose, or other precautions may be necessary. When you are receiving aminoglycosides it is especially important that your health care professional knows if you are taking any of the following:

• Aminoglycosides, used on the skin or mucous membranes and by injection at the same time; or more than one aminoglycoside at a time or
• Anti-infectives by mouth or by injection (medicine for infection) or
• Capreomycin (e.g., Capastat) or
• Carmustine (e.g., BiCNU) or
• Chloroquine (e.g., Aralen) or
• Cisplatin (e.g., Platinol) or
• Combination pain medicine containing acetaminophen and aspirin (e.g., Excedrin) or other salicylates (with large amounts taken regularly) or
• Cyclosporine (e.g., Sandimmune) or
• Deferoxamine (e.g., Desferal) (with long-term use) or
• Gold salts (medicine for arthritis) or
• Hydroxychloroquine (e.g., Plaquenil) or
• Inflammation or pain medicine, except narcotics, or
• Lithium (e.g., Lithane) or
• Methotrexate (e.g., Mexate) or
• Penicillamine (e.g., Cuprimine) or
• Plicamycin (e.g., Mithracin) or
• Quinine (e.g., Quinamm) or
• Streptozocin (e.g., Zanosar) or
• Tiopronin (e.g., Thiola)—Use of any of these medicines with aminoglycosides may increase the chance of hearing, balance, or kidney side effects.

Other medical problems—The presence of other medical problems may affect the use of the aminoglycosides. Make sure you tell your doctor if you have any other medical problems, especially:

• Kidney disease—Patients with kidney disease may have increased aminoglycoside blood levels and increased chance of side effects

• Loss of hearing and/or balance (eighth-cranial-nerve disease)—High aminoglycoside blood levels may cause hearing loss or balance disturbances

• Myasthenia gravis or
• Parkinson's disease—Aminoglycosides may cause muscular problems, resulting in further muscle weakness

Proper Use of This Medicine

To help clear up your infection completely, *aminoglycosides must be given for the full time of treatment*, even if you begin to feel better after a few days. Also, this medicine works best when there is a certain amount in the blood or urine. To help keep the correct level, aminoglycosides must be given on a regular schedule.

Dosing—The dose of aminoglycosides will be different for different patients. *Follow your doctor's orders or the directions on the label.* The following information includes only the average doses of aminoglycosides. Your dose may be different if you have kidney disease. *If your dose is different, do not change it* unless your doctor tells you to do so.

The dose of most aminoglycosides is based on body weight and must be determined by your doctor. The medicine is injected into a muscle or vein. Depending on the aminoglycoside prescribed, doses are given at different times and for different lengths of time. These times are as follows:

For amikacin
- For *all* dosage forms:
  —Adults and children: The dose is given every eight or twelve hours for seven to ten days.
  —Newborn babies: The dose is given every twelve hours for seven to ten days.
  —Premature babies: The dose is given every eighteen to twenty-four hours for seven to ten days.

For gentamicin
- For *all* dosage forms:
  —Adults and children: The dose is given every eight hours for seven to ten days or more.
  —Infants: The dose is given every eight to sixteen hours for seven to ten days or more.
  —Premature and full-term newborn babies: The dose is given every twelve to twenty-four hours for seven to ten days or more.

For kanamicin
- For *all* dosage forms:
  —Adults and children: The dose is given every eight or twelve hours for seven to ten days.

For netilmicin
- For *all* dosage forms:
  —Adults and children: The dose is given every eight or twelve hours for seven to fourteen days.

For tobramycin
- For *all* dosage forms:
  —Adults and adolescents: The dose is given every six to eight hours for seven to ten days or more.
  —Older infants and children: The dose is given every six to sixteen hours.
  —Premature and full-term newborn babies: The dose is given every twelve to twenty-four hours.

For streptomycin
- For *all* dosage forms—The dose of streptomycin is often not based on body weight and the amount given depends on the disease being treated.
  —*Treatment of tuberculosis (TB):*
    - Adults and adolescents: 1 gram injected into a muscle once a day. This will be reduced to two or three times a week, if possible. This medicine must be given with other medicines for tuberculosis (TB).
    - Children: Dose is based on body weight and must be determined by your doctor. This dose is injected into a muscle once a day. This medicine must be given with other medicines for tuberculosis (TB).
  —*Treatment of bacterial infections:*
    - Adults and adolescents: 1 to 2 grams of streptomycin is injected into a muscle every six to twelve hours.
    - Children: Dose is based on body weight and must be determined by your doctor. This dose is injected into a muscle every six to twelve hours.

Side Effects of This Medicine

Along with its needed effects, a medicine may cause some unwanted effects. Although not all of these side effects may occur, if they do occur they may need medical attention.

Check with your health care professional immediately if any of the following side effects occur:
  More common
    Any loss of hearing; clumsiness or unsteadiness; dizziness; greatly increased or decreased frequency of urination or amount of urine; increased thirst; loss of appetite; nausea or vomiting; numbness, tingling, or burning of face or mouth (streptomycin only); muscle twitching, or convulsions (seizures); ringing or buzzing or a feeling of fullness in the ears
  Less common
    Any loss of vision (streptomycin only); skin rash, itching, redness, or swelling
  Rare—Once-daily or "high dose" gentamicin only-
    Shaking; chills; fever
  All aminoglycosides-
    Difficulty in breathing; drowsiness; weakness

In addition, leg cramps, skin rash, fever, and convulsions (seizures) may occur when gentamicin is given by injection into the muscle or a vein, and into the spinal fluid.

For up to several weeks after you stop receiving this medicine, it may still cause some side effects that need medical attention. Check with your doctor if you notice any of the following side effects or if they get worse:
    Any loss of hearing; clumsiness or unsteadiness; dizziness; greatly increased or decreased frequency of urination or amount of urine ; increased thirst; loss of appetite; nausea or vomiting; ringing or buzzing or a feeling of fullness in the ears

Other side effects not listed above may also occur in some patients. If you notice any other effects, check with your doctor.

Revised: 10/25/99
Interim revision: 10/25/99

AMINOLEVULINIC ACID   Topical

Commonly used brand name(s):

In the U.S.—
  Levulan Kerastick

Description

Aminolevulinic acid (a-mee-noh–LEV–U–lin–ik AS–id) application followed by exposure to a certain type of light (blue light using the BLU–U Blue Light Photodynamic Therapy Illuminator) treats the skin condition called actinic keratoses.

This medicine is available only with your doctor's prescription, in the following dosage form:

Topical
- Solution (U.S.)

Before Using This Medicine

In deciding to use a medicine, the risks of using the medicine must be weighed against the good it will do. This is a decision

you and your doctor will make. For aminolevulinic acid the following should be considered:

Allergies—Tell your doctor if you have ever had any unusual or allergic reaction to aminolevulinic acid or porphyrins.

Pregnancy—Studies on effects in pregnancy have not been done in either humans or animals.

Breast-feeding—It is not known whether aminolevulinic acid passes into breast milk. Although most medicines pass into breast milk in small amounts, many of them may be used safely while breast–feeding. Mothers who are taking this medicine and who wish to breast–feed should discuss this with their doctor.

Children—Studies on this medicine have been done only in adult patients, and there is no specific information comparing use of aminolevulinic acid in children with use in other age groups.

Older adults—Many medicines have not been studied specifically in older people. Therefore, it may not be known whether they work exactly the same way they do in younger adults or if they cause different side effects or problems in older people. There is no specific information comparing use of aminolevulinic acid in the elderly with use in other age groups.

Other medicines—Although certain medicines should not be used together at all, in other cases two different medicines may be used together even if an interaction might occur. In these cases, your doctor may want to change the dose, or other precautions may be necessary. When you are taking aminolevulinic acid, it is especially important that your doctor and pharmacist know if you are taking any of the following:

- Antidiabetics, oral (diabetes medicine you take by mouth) or
- Antipsychotics (medicine for mental illness) or
- Griseofulvin (eg, Fulvicin U/F, Grifulvin V) or
- Sulfonamides (sulfa medicine) or
- Tetracyclines (medicine for infection) or
- Thiazide diuretics (water pills)—May increase your skin's sensitivity to sunlight or bright indoor lights

Other medical problems—The presence of other medical problems may affect the use of aminolevulinic acid. Make sure you tell your doctor if you have any other medical problems, especially:

- Skin sensitivity to light or
- Porphyria—May be worsened by aminolevulinic acid

Proper Use of This Medicine

Dosing— Aminolevulinic acid is applied to your skin in your doctor's office. *Blue light illumination treatment must be followed with* BLU–U Blue Light Photodynamic Therapy Illuminator *in your doctor's office 14 to 18 hours after the application.* The blue light treatment lasts approximately 17 minutes. Your doctor may want to re-treat you after 8 weeks if your skin condition did not completely resolve.

Call your doctor if you cannot return for the blue light illumination treatment after the aminolevulinic acid application. You should then protect the treated skin from sunlight and prolonged or intense light for at least 40 hours.

Precautions While Using This Medicine

After aminolevulinic acid application you should avoid exposure to sunlight or bright indoor light (e.g., from examination lamps, operating room lamps, tanning beds, or being close to lights) up until the time of the blue light treatment. Wide-brimmed hats or similar head covering can help protect you from sunlight or sources of light.

Sunscreens will not protect you from sunlight or sources of light.

Reduce your exposure to light if you experience stinging or burning on the treated areas before blue light treatment.

Do not wash the treated areas before the blue light treatment.

You and the doctor will wear eye protection during the blue light treatment.

During the blue light treatment you will experience sensations of tingling, stinging, prickling or burning of the treated skin. These feelings of discomfort should improve at the end of the light treatment.

Following treatment, the actinic keratoses and possibly the surrounding skin will redden and swelling and scaling may also occur. These changes are temporary and should completely resolve by 4 weeks after treatment.

Side Effects of This Medicine

Along with its needed effects, a medicine may cause some unwanted effects. Although not all of these side effects may occur, if they do occur they may need medical attention.

Check with your doctor immediately if any of the following side effects occur:
  Less common
    Bleeding

Other side effects may occur that usually do not need medical attention. These side effects may go away during treatment as your body adjusts to the medicine. However, check with your doctor if any of the following side effects continue or are bothersome.
  More Common
    Burning, crawling, itching, numbness, prickling, "pins and needles," stinging, or tingling feelings; darkening of treated skin; lightening of treated skin; scaling or crusting; skin sore; small red raised itchy bumps; swelling of skin

  Less common
    Blister; oozing; open sore on skin; pain; pus filled blister or pimple; raw skin; scabbing; tenderness.

Other side effects not listed above may also occur in some patients. If you notice any other effects, check with your doctor.

Developed: 04/07/00

AMIODARONE   Systemic

Commonly used brand name(s):

In the U.S.—
Cordarone
Cordarone I.V.

In Canada—
Cordarone
Cordarone Intravenous
pms-Amiodarone

Description

Amiodarone (am-ee-OH-da-rone) belongs to the group of medicines known as antiarrhythmics. It is used to correct irregular heartbeats to a normal rhythm.

Amiodarone produces its helpful effects by slowing nerve impulses in the heart and acting directly on the heart tissues.

This medicine is available only with your doctor's prescription, in the following dosage forms:

Oral
  • Tablets (U.S. and Canada)

Parenteral
  • Injection (U.S. and Canada)

Before Using This Medicine

In deciding to use a medicine, the risks of taking the medicine must be weighed against the good it will do. This is a decision you and your doctor will make. For amiodarone, the following should be considered:

Allergies—Tell your doctor if you have ever had any unusual or allergic reaction to amiodarone. Also tell your health care professional if you are allergic to any other substances, such as foods, preservatives, or dyes.

Pregnancy—Amiodarone has been shown to cause thyroid problems in babies whose mothers took amiodarone when pregnant. In addition, there is concern that amiodarone could cause slow heartbeat in the newborn. However, this medicine may be needed in serious situations that threaten the mother's life. Be sure you have discussed this with your doctor before taking this medicine.

Breast-feeding—Although amiodarone passes into breast milk, it has not been shown to cause problems in nursing babies. However, amiodarone has been shown to cause growth problems in rats. It may be necessary for you to stop breast-feeding during treatment. Be sure you have discussed the risks and benefits of the medicine with your doctor.

Children—Amiodarone can cause serious side effects in any patient. Therefore, it is especially important that you discuss with the child's doctor the good that this medicine may do as well as the risks of using it.

Older adults—Elderly patients may be more likely to get thyroid problems with this medicine. Also, difficulty in walking and numbness, tingling, trembling, or weakness in hands or feet are more likely to occur in the elderly.

Other medicines—Although certain medicines should not be used together at all, in other cases two different medicines may be used together even if an interaction might occur. In these cases, your doctor may want to change the dose, or other precautions may be necessary. When you are taking amiodarone, it is especially important that your health care professional know if you are taking any of the following:

  • Anticoagulants (blood thinners) or
  • Other heart medicine or
  • Phenytoin (e.g., Dilantin)—Effects of phenytoin may be increased

Other medical problems—The presence of other medical problems may affect the use of amiodarone. Make sure you tell your doctor if you have any other medical problems, especially:

  • Hepatitis, acute— Risk of adverse effects is increased.
  • Liver disease—Effects of amiodarone may be increased because of slower removal from the body
  • Thyroid problems—Risk of overactive or underactive thyroid is increased

Proper Use of This Medicine

Take amiodarone exactly as directed by your doctor even though you may feel well. Do not take more medicine than ordered and do not miss any doses.

Dosing—The dose of amiodarone will be different for different patients. *Follow your doctor's orders or the directions on the label.* The following information includes only the average doses of amiodarone. *If your dose is different, do not change it* unless your doctor tells you to do so:

  • For *oral* dosage form (tablets):
    —For treatment of *ventricular arrhythmias:*
      • Adults—At first, 800 to 1600 milligrams (mg) per day taken in divided doses. Then, 600 to 800 mg per day for one month. Then, 400 mg per day.
      • Children—Dose is based on body weight and must be determined by your doctor. The dose for the first ten days is usually 10 mg per kilogram (4.55 mg per pound) of body weight per day. Then, the dose is decreased to 5 mg per kilogram (2.27 mg per pound) of body weight per day. After several weeks, the dose is then decreased to 2.5 mg per kilogram (1.14 mg per pound) of body weight per day.

  • For *injection* dosage form:
    —For treatment of *ventricular arrhythmias*
      • Adults—At first, the dose is 150 mg injected into a vein for ten minutes, followed by a dose of 360 mg injected into a vein for six hours, followed by a dose of 540 mg injected into a vein for eighteen hours. After the first twenty-four hours of therapy, the dose is 720 mg injected into a vein every twenty-four hours; this dose may be continued for as long as three weeks.
      • Children—Use is not recommended.

Missed dose—If you miss a dose of this medicine, do not take the missed dose at all and do not double the next one. Instead, go back to your regular dosing schedule. If you miss two or more doses in a row, check with your doctor.

Storage—To store this medicine:
  • Keep out of the reach of children.
  • Store away from heat and direct light.
  • Do not store in the bathroom, near the kitchen sink, or in other damp places. Heat or moisture may cause the medicine to break down.
  • Do not keep outdated medicine or medicine no longer needed. Be sure that any discarded medicine is out of the reach of children.

Precautions While Using This Medicine

It is important that your doctor check your progress at regular visits to make sure the medicine is working properly. This will allow for changes to be made in the amount of medicine you are taking, if necessary.

Your doctor may want you to carry a medical identification card or bracelet stating that you are taking this medicine.

Before having any kind of surgery (including dental surgery) or emergency treatment, tell the medical doctor or dentist in charge that you are taking this medicine.

Amiodarone increases the sensitivity of your skin to sunlight; too much exposure could cause a serious sunburn. Your skin may continue to be sensitive to sunlight for several months after treatment when this medicine is stopped. A sunburn can occur even through window glass or thin cotton clothing. If you must go out in the sunlight, *cover your skin and wear a wide-brimmed hat. A product applied to the skin to prevent sunburn should also be used. In case of a severe sunburn, check with your doctor.*

After you have taken this medicine for a long time, it may cause a blue-gray color to appear on your skin, especially in areas exposed to the sun, such as your face, neck, and arms. This color will usually fade after treatment with amiodarone has ended, although it may take several months. However, check with your doctor if this effect occurs.

Check with your doctor if you notice any changes in your vision, such as a decrease in peripheral vision or a decrease in the clarity of the objects that you see.

Side Effects of This Medicine

Along with its needed effects, a medicine may cause some unwanted effects. Although not all of these side effects may occur, if they do occur they may need medical attention. Also, some side effects may not appear until several weeks or months, or even years, after you start taking amiodarone.

Check with your doctor immediately if any of the following side effects occur:

More common
Cough; painful breathing; shortness of breath

Check with your doctor as soon as possible if any of the following side effects occur:

More common
Dizziness, lightheadedness, or fainting; fever (slight); numbness or tingling in fingers or toes; sensitivity of skin to sunlight; trembling or shaking of hands; trouble in walking; unusual and uncontrolled movements of the body; weakness of arms or legs

Less common
Blue-gray coloring of skin on face, neck, and arms; blurred vision or blue-green halos seen around objects; coldness; dry eyes; dry, puffy skin; fast or irregular heartbeat; nervousness; pain and swelling in scrotum; sensitivity of eyes to light; sensitivity to heat; slow heartbeat; sweating; swelling of feet or lower legs; trouble in sleeping; unusual tiredness; weight gain or loss

Rare
Skin rash; yellow eyes or skin

Other side effects may occur that usually do not need medical attention. These side effects may go away during treatment as your body adjusts to the medicine. However, check with your doctor if any of the following side effects continue or are bothersome:

More common
Constipation; headache; loss of appetite; nausea and vomiting

Less common
Bitter or metallic taste; decreased sexual ability in males; decrease in sexual interest; dizziness; flushing of face

After you stop using this medicine, your body may need time to adjust. The length of time this takes depends on the amount of medicine you were using and how long you used it. During this period of time check with your doctor if you notice any of the following side effects:
Cough; fever (slight); painful breathing; shortness of breath

Other side effects not listed above may also occur in some patients. If you notice any other effects, check with your doctor.

Revised: 06/13/2001

AMLEXANOX   Mucosal-Local

Commonly used brand name(s):

In the U.S.—
Aphthasol

Description

Amlexanox (am-LEX-an-ox) is used as a paste in the mouth to treat aphthous ulcers (canker sores).

This medicine is available only with your doctor's prescription, in the following dosage form:

Mucosal-Local
• Oral paste (U.S.)

Before Using This Medicine

In deciding to use a medicine, the risks of using the medicine must be weighed against the good it will do. This is a decision you and your doctor will make. For amlexanox, the following should be considered:

Allergies—Tell your doctor if you have ever had any unusual or allergic reaction to amlexanox. Also tell your health care professional if you are allergic to any other substances, such as preservatives or dyes.

Pregnancy—Amlexanox has not been studied in humans. However, studies in animals have not found that it causes any birth defects or other problems.

Breast-feeding—It is not known whether amlexanox passes into breast milk in humans. However, it does pass into the milk in lactating animals. Although most medicines pass into human breast milk in small amounts, many of them may be used safely while breast-feeding. Mothers who are taking this medicine and who wish to breast-feed should discuss this with their doctor.

Children—There is no specific information comparing use of amlexanox in children with use in other age groups.

Older adults—Many medicines have not been studied specifically in older people. Therefore, it may not be known whether they work exactly the same way they do in younger adults. There is no specific information comparing use of amlexanox in the elderly with use in other age groups.

Other medicines—Although certain medicines should not be used together at all, in other cases two different medicines may be used together even if an interaction might occur. In these cases, your doctor may want to change the dose, or other precautions may be necessary. Tell your health care professional if you are using any other prescription or nonprescription (over-the-counter [OTC]) medicine.

Other medical problems—The presence of other medical problems may affect the use of amlexanox. Make sure you tell your doctor if you have any other medical problems, especially:

- Immune system problems—It is not known if this medicine will work properly in patients with these problems

Proper Use of This Medicine

How to use this medicine:

- Apply this medicine to the canker sore as soon as you notice it.
- Squeeze a small amount of the paste (about 1/4 inch) onto your fingertip. Using gentle pressure, dab the paste onto each sore in your mouth.
- Wash your hands immediately after using amlexanox paste.
- Keep using the medicine until the sore is healed. However, if it is not healed after 10 days, check with your doctor.
- Do not get any of the paste in your eyes. If any gets in your eyes, wash them out with water right away.

Dosing—The dose of amlexanox paste may be different for different patients. *Follow your doctor's orders or the directions on the label.* The following information includes only the average doses of amlexanox. *If your dose is different, do not change it* unless your doctor tells you to do so.

- For *mucosal-local* dosage form (oral paste):
  —For treatment of canker sores:
    - Adults—Apply to each canker sore in the mouth four times a day, after you brush your teeth after breakfast, lunch, dinner, and at bedtime.
    - Children—Use and dose must be determined by your doctor.

Missed dose—If you miss a dose of this medicine, apply it as soon as possible. However, if it is almost time for the next dose, skip the missed dose and go back to your regular dosing schedule.

Storage—To store this medicine:

- Keep out of the reach of children.
- Store away from heat and direct light.
- Do not store in the bathroom, near the kitchen sink, or in other damp places. Heat or moisture may cause the medicine to break down.
- Do not keep outdated medicine or medicine no longer needed. Be sure that any discarded medicine is out of the reach of children.

Side Effects of This Medicine

Along with its needed effects, a medicine may cause some unwanted effects. The following side effects may go away during treatment as your body adjusts to the medicine. However, check with your doctor if any of these effects continue or are bothersome:

> *Less common or rare*
> Burning, stinging, or pain at place medicine is applied; inflammation of mucous membranes; diarrhea; nausea

Other side effects not listed above also may occur in some patients. If you notice any other effects, check with your doctor.

Developed: 08/07/98

AMLODIPINE   Systemic

Commonly used brand name(s):

In the U.S.—
Norvasc

In Canada—
Norvasc

Description

Amlodipine (am-LOE-di-peen) is a calcium channel blocker used to treat angina (chest pain) and high blood pressure. Amlodipine affects the movement of calcium into the cells of the heart and blood vessels. As a result, amlodipine relaxes blood vessels and increases the supply of blood and oxygen to the heart while reducing its workload.

High blood pressure adds to the workload of the heart and arteries. If it continues for a long time, the heart and arteries may not function properly. This can damage the blood vessels of the brain, heart, and kidneys, resulting in a stroke, heart failure, or kidney failure. High blood pressure may also increase the risk of heart attacks. These problems may be less likely to occur if blood pressure is controlled.

This medicine is available only with your doctor's prescription, in the following dosage form:

> *Oral*
> - Tablets (U.S.and Canada)

Before Using This Medicine

In deciding to use a medicine, the risks of taking the medicine must be weighed against the good it will do. This is a decision you and your doctor will make. For amlodipine, the following should be considered:

Allergies—Tell your doctor if you have ever had any unusual or allergic reaction to amlodipine. Also tell your health care professional if you are allergic to any other substances, such as foods, preservatives, or dyes.

Pregnancy—Amlodipine has not been studied in pregnant women. However, studies in animals have shown that, at very high doses, amlodipine may cause fetal death. Before taking this medicine, make sure your doctor knows if you are pregnant or if you may become pregnant.

Breast-feeding—It is not known whether amlodipine passes into breast milk. Although most medicines pass into breast milk in small amounts, many of them may be used safely while breast-feeding. Mothers who are taking this medicine and who wish to breast-feed should discuss this with their doctor.

Children—Studies on this medicine have been done only in adult patients, and there is no specific information comparing use of amlodipine in children with use in other age groups.

Older adults—Elderly people may be especially sensitive to the effects of amlodipine. This may increase the chance of side effects during treatment.

Other medicines—Although certain medicines should not be used together at all, in other cases two different medicines may be used together even if an interaction might occur. In these cases, your doctor may want to change the dose, or other precautions may be necessary. Tell your health care professional if you are using any other prescription or nonprescription (over-the-counter [OTC]) medicine.

Other medical problems—The presence of other medical problems may affect the use of amlodipine. Make sure you tell your doctor if you have any other medical problems, especially:

- Congestive heart failure—There is a small chance that amlodipine may make this condition worse
- Liver disease—Higher blood levels of amlodipine may result and a smaller dose may be needed
- Very low blood pressure—Amlodipine may make this condition worse

Proper Use of This Medicine

Take this medicine exactly as directed even if you feel well and do not notice any chest pain. Do not take more of this medicine and do not take it more often than your doctor ordered. Do not miss any doses.

For patients taking this medicine *for high blood pressure:*

- In addition to the use of the medicine your doctor has prescribed, treatment for your high blood pressure may include weight control and care in the types of food you eat, especially foods high in sodium (salt). Your doctor will tell you which of these are most important for you. You should check with your doctor before changing your diet.
- Many patients who have high blood pressure will not notice any signs of the problem. In fact, many may feel normal. It is very important that you *take your medicine exactly as directed* and that you keep your appointments with your doctor even if you feel well.
- Remember that this medicine will not cure your high blood pressure but it does help control it. Therefore, you must continue to take it as directed if you expect to lower your blood pressure and keep it down. *You may have to take high blood pressure medicine for the rest of your life.* If high blood pressure is not treated, it can cause serious problems such as heart failure, blood vessel disease, stroke, or kidney disease.

Dosing—The dose of amlodipine will be different for different patients. *Follow your doctor's orders or the directions on the label.* The following information includes only the average doses of amlodipine. *If your dose is different, do not change it* unless your doctor tells you to do so.

The number of tablets that you take depends on the strength of the medicine.

- For *oral* dosage form (tablets):
  - For angina (chest pain):
    - Adults—5 to 10 milligrams (mg) once a day.
    - Children—Use must be determined by your doctor.
  - For high blood pressure:
    - Adults—2.5 to 10 mg once a day.
    - Children—Use must be determined by your doctor.

Missed dose—If you miss a dose of this medicine, take it as soon as possible. However, if it is almost time for your next dose, skip the missed dose and go back to your regular dosing schedule. Do not double doses.

Storage—To store this medicine:

- Keep out of the reach of children.
- Store away from heat and direct light.
- Do not store in the bathroom, near the kitchen sink, or in other damp places. Heat or moisture may cause the medicine to break down.
- Keep the medicine from freezing. Do not refrigerate.
- Do not keep outdated medicine or medicine no longer needed. Be sure that any discarded medicine is out of the reach of children.

Precautions While Using This Medicine

It is important that your doctor check your progress at regular visits. This will allow your doctor to make sure the medicine is working properly and to change the dosage if needed.

If you have been using this medicine regularly for several weeks, do not suddenly stop using it. Stopping suddenly may cause your chest pain or high blood pressure to come back or get worse. Check with your doctor for the best way to reduce gradually the amount you are taking before stopping completely.

Chest pain resulting from exercise or physical exertion usually is reduced or prevented by this medicine. This may tempt you to be too active. *Make sure you discuss with your doctor a safe amount of exercise for your medical problem.*

After taking a dose of this medicine you may get a headache that lasts for a short time. This should become less noticeable after you have taken this medicine for a while. If this effect continues, or if the headaches are severe, check with your doctor.

In some patients, tenderness, swelling, or bleeding of the gums may appear soon after treatment with this medicine is started. Brushing and flossing your teeth carefully and regularly and massaging your gums may help prevent this. *See your dentist regularly* to have your teeth cleaned. Check with your medical doctor or dentist if you have any questions about how to take care of your teeth and gums, or if you notice any tenderness, swelling, or bleeding of your gums.

For patients taking this medicine *for high blood pressure:*

- *Do not take other medicines unless they have been discussed with your doctor.* This especially includes over-the-counter (nonprescription) medicines for appetite control, asthma, colds, cough, hay fever, or sinus problems, since they may tend to increase your blood pressure.

Side Effects of This Medicine

Along with its needed effects, a medicine may cause some unwanted effects. Although not all of these side effects may occur, if they do occur they may need medical attention.

Check with your doctor as soon as possible if any of the following side effects occur:
More common
Swelling of ankles or feet

Less common
   Dizziness; pounding heartbeat

Rare
   Chest pain; dark yellow urine; dizziness or lightheadedness when getting up from a lying or sitting position; slow heartbeat; yellow eyes or skin

Other side effects may occur that usually do not need medical attention. These side effects may go away during treatment as your body adjusts to the medicine. However, check with your doctor if any of the following side effects continue or are bothersome:

More common
   Abdominal pain; flushing; headache; sleepiness or unusual drowsiness

Less common
   Nausea; unusual tiredness or weakness

Other side effects not listed above may also occur in some patients. If you notice any other effects, check with your doctor.

Revised: 05/12/2000

AMLODIPINE AND BENAZEPRIL
Systemic†

Commonly used brand name(s):

In the U.S.—
   Lotrel

†Not commercially available in Canada.

Description

Amlodipine (am-LOH-di-peen) and benazepril (ben-AY-ze-pril) combination belongs to the class of medicines called high blood pressure medicines (antihypertensives). It is used to treat high blood pressure (hypertension).

High blood pressure adds to the workload of the heart and arteries. If it continues for a long time, the heart and arteries may not function properly. This can damage the blood vessels of the brain, heart, and kidneys, resulting in a stroke, heart failure, or kidney failure. High blood pressure may also increase the risk of heart attacks. These problems may be less likely to occur if blood pressure is controlled.

The exact way in which this medicine works is not known. Amlodipine is a type of medicine known as a calcium channel blocker. Calcium channel blocking agents affect the movement of calcium into the cells of the heart and blood vessels. Benazepril is a type of medicine known as an angiotensin-converting enzyme (ACE) inhibitor. It blocks an enzyme in the body that is necessary in producing a substance that causes blood vessels to tighten. The action of both medicines together is to relax blood vessels, lower blood pressure, and increase the supply of blood and oxygen to the heart.

This medicine is available only with your doctor's prescription, in the following dosage form:

Oral
   • Capsules (U.S.)

Before Using This Medicine

In deciding to use a medicine, the risks of taking the medicine must be weighed against the good it will do. This is a decision you and your doctor will make. For amlodipine and benazepril combination, the following should be considered:

Allergies—Tell your doctor if you have ever had any unusual or allergic reaction to amlodipine or benazepril, as well as to any other ACE inhibitor (captopril, enalapril, fosinopril, lisinopril, moexipril, quinapril, ramipril, or trandolapril). Also tell your health care professional if you are allergic to any other substances, such as foods, preservatives, or dyes.

Pregnancy—Studies with this combination medicine have not been done in pregnant women. However, use of any of the ACE inhibitors during pregnancy, especially in the second and third trimesters (after the first 3 months) can cause low blood pressure, kidney failure, an underdeveloped skull, or even death in newborns. *Therefore, it is important that you check with your doctor immediately if you think that you may be pregnant.* Be sure that you have discussed this with your doctor before taking this combination medicine.

Breast-feeding—Benazepril passes into breast milk. Use of this combination medicine is not recommended in women who are breast-feeding.

Children—Studies on this medicine have been done only in adult patients, and there is no specific information comparing use of amlodipine and benazepril combination in children with use in other age groups.

Older adults—This medicine has been tested in patients 65 years of age or older and has not been shown to cause different side effects or problems in older people than it does in younger adults. However, blood levels of amlodipine may be increased in the elderly and elderly people may be more sensitive to the effects of this medicine.

Racial differences—Black patients may be less sensitive to the blood pressure–lowering effects of this medicine. In addition, the risk of a serious allergic reaction involving swelling of the face, mouth, hands, or feet may be increased.

Other medicines—Although certain medicines should not be used together at all, in other cases two different medicines may be used together even if an interaction might occur. In these cases, your doctor may want to change the dose, or other precautions may be necessary. When you are taking this medicine, it is especially important that your health care professional know if you are taking any of the following:
   • Diuretics (water pills)—Effects on blood pressure may be increased
   • Potassium-containing medicines or supplements or
   • Salt substitutes that contain potassium—Use of these substances with ACE inhibitors may result in an unusually high potassium level in the blood, which can lead to irregular heart rhythm and other problems

Other medical problems—The presence of other medical problems may affect the use of this medicine. Make sure you tell your doctor if you have any other medical problems, especially:
   • Bee-sting allergy treatments or
   • Dialysis—Increased risk of serious allergic reaction occurring
   • Dehydration—Lowering effects on blood pressure may be increased

- Diabetes mellitus (sugar diabetes)—Increased risk of potassium levels in the body becoming too high
- Heart or blood vessel disease—Lowering blood pressure may make problems resulting from these conditions worse
- Kidney disease or
- Liver disease—Effects may be increased because of slower removal of this medicine from the body
- Scleroderma or
- Systemic lupus erythematosus (SLE) (or history of)—Increased risk of blood problems caused by ACE inhibitors

Proper Use of This Medicine

Take this medicine exactly as directed by your doctor, at the same time each day. Do not take more of it and do not take it more often than directed.

Dosing—The dose of this medicine will be different for different patients. *Follow your doctor's orders or the directions on the label.* The following information includes only the average doses of this medicine. *If your dose is different, do not change it* unless your doctor tells you to do so.

The number of tablets that you take depends on the strength of the medicine. Also, *the number of doses you take each day, the time allowed between doses, and the length of time you take the medicine depend on the medical problem for which you are taking it.*

- For *oral* dosage form (capsules):
  —For high blood pressure:
  - Adults—1 capsule a day. Your doctor may increase your dose if needed.
  - Children—Use and dose must be determined by your doctor.

Missed dose—If you miss a dose of this medicine, take it as soon as possible. However, if it is almost time for your next dose, skip the missed dose and go back to your regular dosing schedule. Do not double doses.

Storage—To store this medicine:
- Keep out of the reach of children.
- Store away from heat and direct light.
- Do not store in the bathroom, near the kitchen sink, or in other damp places. Heat or moisture may cause the medicine to break down.
- Do not keep outdated medicine or medicine no longer needed. Be sure that any discarded medicine is out of the reach of children.

Precautions While Using This Medicine

It is very important that your doctor check your progress at regular visits. This will allow your doctor to make sure the medicine is working properly, to check for unwanted effects, and to change the dosage if needed.

If you think that you may have become pregnant, check with your doctor immediately. Use of this medicine, especially during the second and third trimesters (after the first 3 months) of pregnancy, may cause serious injury or even death to the unborn child.

Do not take any other medicines, especially potassium supplements, or salt substitutes that contain potassium unless approved or prescribed by your doctor.

Dizziness, lightheadedness, or fainting may occur after the first dose, especially if you have been taking a diuretic (water pill). Make sure you know how you react to the medicine before you drive, use machines, or do other things that could be dangerous if you experience these effects.

Check with your doctor if you notice any signs of fever, sore throat, or chills. These could be symptoms of an infection resulting from low white blood cell counts.

Check with your doctor if you notice difficult breathing or swelling of the face, arms, or legs. These could be symptoms of a serious allergic reaction.

Check with your doctor if you become sick while taking this medicine, especially with severe or continuing vomiting or diarrhea. These conditions may cause you to lose too much water, possibly resulting in low blood pressure.

Dizziness, lightheadedness, or fainting may also occur if you exercise or if the weather is hot. Heavy sweating can cause loss of too much water and result in low blood pressure. Use extra care during exercise or hot weather.

In some patients, tenderness, swelling, or bleeding of the gums may appear soon after treatment with this medicine is started. Brushing and flossing your teeth carefully and regularly and massaging your gums may help prevent this. *See your dentist regularly* to have your teeth cleaned. Check with your medical doctor or dentist if you have any questions about how to take care of your teeth and gums, or if you notice any tenderness, swelling, or bleeding of your gums.

Before having any kind of surgery (including dental surgery) or emergency treatment, tell the medical doctor or dentist in charge that you are taking this medicine.

Side Effects of This Medicine

Along with its needed effects, a medicine may cause some unwanted effects. Although not all of these side effects may occur, if they do occur they may need medical attention.

Check with your doctor immediately if any of the following side effects occur:
Rare
Swelling of face, mouth, hands, or feet; trouble in swallowing or breathing (sudden) and/or hoarseness

Check with your doctor as soon as possible if any of the following side effects occur:
Less common
Dizziness, lightheadedness, or fainting; swelling of ankles, feet, or lower legs
Signs and symptoms of too much potassium in the body
Confusion; irregular heartbeat; nervousness; numbness or tingling in hands, feet, or lips; shortness of breath; weakness or heaviness of legs
Rare
Bleeding gums, fatigue, nosebleeds, and/or pale skin; blisters in mouth spreading to trunk, scalp, or other areas; chills, fever, or sore throat; nausea or vomiting; sores in mouth, or on arms, feet, hands, legs, or lips (sudden); stomach pain or bloating with fever, nausea, or vomiting; unusual bleeding or bruising; yellow eyes or skin

Other side effects may occur that usually do not need medical attention. These side effects may go away during treatment as your body adjusts to the medicine. However, check with

your doctor if any of the following side effects continue or are bothersome:

Less common
 Awareness of heartbeat; cough (dry, continuing); flushing; sleepiness

Other side effects not listed above may also occur in some patients. If you notice any other effects, check with your doctor.

Developed: 08/10/98
Revised: 04/20/00

AMPHETAMINES Systemic

Commonly used brand name(s):

In the U.S.—
Adderall[3]	Dexedrine[2]
Desoxyn[4]	Dexedrine Spansule[2]
Desoxyn Gradumet[4]	DextroStat[2]

In Canada—
Dexedrine[2]
Dexedrine Spansule[2]

Note: For quick reference, the following amphetamines are numbered to match the corresponding brand names.

This information applies to the following medicines:
1. Amphetamine (am-FET-a-meen)†‡
2. Dextroamphetamine (dex-troe-am-FET-a-meen)‡
3. Dextroamphetamine and amphetamine (dex-troe-am-FET-a-meen and am-FET-a-meen)†‡
4. Methamphetamine (meth-am-FET-a-meen)†

†Not commercially available in Canada.
‡Generic name product may be available in the U.S.

Description

Amphetamines (am-FET-a-meens) belong to the group of medicines called central nervous system (CNS) stimulants. They are used to treat attention-deficit hyperactivity disorder (ADHD). Amphetamines increase attention and decrease restlessness in patients who are overactive, unable to concentrate for very long or are easily distracted, and have unstable emotions. These medicines are used as part of a total treatment program that also includes social, educational, and psychological treatment.

Amphetamine and dextroamphetamine are also used in the treatment of narcolepsy (uncontrollable desire for sleep or sudden attacks of deep sleep).

Amphetamines should not be used for weight loss or weight control or to combat unusual tiredness or weakness or replace rest. When used for these purposes, they may be dangerous to your health.

Amphetamines may also be used for other conditions as determined by your doctor.

These medicines are available only with a doctor's prescription. Prescriptions cannot be refilled. A new prescription must be obtained from your doctor each time you or your child needs this medicine.

Amphetamines are available in the following dosage forms:

Oral
 Amphetamine
  • Tablets (U.S.)

Amphetamine and dextroamphetamine
 • Tablets (U.S.)
Dextroamphetamine
 • Extended-release capsules (U.S. and Canada)
 • Tablets (U.S. and Canada)
Methamphetamine
 • Tablets (U.S.)
 • Extended-release tablets (U.S.)

Before Using This Medicine

In deciding to use a medicine, the risks of taking the medicine must be weighed against the good it will do. This is a decision you and your doctor will make. For amphetamines, the following should be considered:

Allergies—Tell your doctor if you have ever had any unusual or allergic reaction to amphetamine, dextroamphetamine, ephedrine, epinephrine, isoproterenol, metaproterenol, methamphetamine, norepinephrine, phenylephrine, phenylpropanolamine, pseudoephedrine, or terbutaline. Also tell your health care professional if you are allergic to any other substances, such as foods, preservatives, or dyes.

Pregnancy—Studies have not been done in humans. However, animal studies have shown that amphetamines may increase the chance of birth defects if taken during the early months of pregnancy.

In addition, overuse of amphetamines during pregnancy may increase the chances of a premature delivery and of having a baby with a low birth weight. Also, the baby may become dependent on amphetamines and experience withdrawal effects such as agitation and drowsiness.

Breast-feeding—Amphetamines pass into breast milk. Although this medicine has not been reported to cause problems in nursing babies, it is best not to breast-feed while you are taking an amphetamine. Be sure you have discussed this with your doctor.

Children—When amphetamines are used for long periods of time in children, they may cause unwanted effects on behavior and growth. Before these medicines are given to a child, you should discuss their use with your child's doctor.

Older adults—Many medicines have not been studied specifically in older people. Therefore, it may not be known whether they work exactly the same way they do in younger adults or if they cause different side effects or problems in older people. There is no specific information comparing use of amphetamines in the elderly with use in other age groups.

Other medicines—Although certain medicines should not be used together at all, in many cases two different medicines may be used together even if an interaction might occur. In these cases, changes in dose or other precautions may be necessary. When you are taking amphetamines, it is especially important that your health care professional know if you are taking any of the following:

• Amantadine (e.g., Symmetrel) or
• Caffeine (e.g., NoDoz) or
• Chlophedianol (e.g., Ulone) or
• Methylphenidate (e.g., Ritalin) or
• Nabilone (e.g., Cesamet) or
• Pemoline (e.g., Cylert)—Use of these medicines may increase the CNS stimulation effects of amphetamines and cause unwanted effects such as nervousness, irritability, trouble in sleeping, and possibly convulsions (seizures)
• Appetite suppressants (diet pills) or

- Medicine for asthma or other breathing problems or
- Medicine for colds, sinus problems, or hay fever or other allergies (including nose drops or sprays)—Use of these medicines may increase the CNS stimulation effects of amphetamines and cause unwanted effects such as nervousness, irritability, trouble in sleeping, or convulsions (seizures), as well as unwanted effects on the heart and blood vessels

- Beta-adrenergic blocking agents (acebutolol [e.g., Sectral], atenolol [e.g., Tenormin], betaxolol [e.g., Kerlone], carteolol [e.g., Cartrol], labetalol [e.g., Normodyne], metoprolol [e.g., Lopressor], nadolol [e.g., Corgard], oxprenolol [e.g., Trasicor], penbutolol [e.g., Levatol], pindolol [e.g., Visken], propranolol [e.g., Inderal], sotalol [e.g., Sotacor], timolol [e.g., Blocadren])—Use of amphetamines with beta-blocking agents may increase the chance of high blood pressure and heart problems

- Cocaine—Use by persons taking amphetamines may cause a severe increase in blood pressure and other unwanted effects, including nervousness, irritability, trouble in sleeping, or convulsions (seizures)

- Digitalis glycosides (heart medicine)—Amphetamines may cause additive effects, resulting in irregular heartbeat

- Meperidine—Use of meperidine by persons taking amphetamines is not recommended because the chance of serious side effects (such as high fever, convulsions, or coma) may be increased

- Monoamine oxidase (MAO) inhibitors (furazolidone [e.g., Furoxone], phenelzine [e.g., Nardil], procarbazine [e.g., Matulane], selegiline [e.g., Eldepryl], tranylcypromine [e.g., Parnate])—Taking amphetamines while you are taking or within 2 weeks of taking monoamine oxidase (MAO) inhibitors may increase the chance of serious side effects such as sudden and severe high blood pressure or fever

- Thyroid hormones—The effects of either these medicines or amphetamines may be increased; unwanted effects may occur in patients with heart or blood vessel disease

- Tricyclic antidepressants (amitriptyline [e.g., Elavil], amoxapine [e.g., Asendin], clomipramine [e.g., Anafranil], desipramine [e.g., Pertofrane], doxepin [e.g., Sinequan], imipramine [e.g., Tofranil], nortriptyline [e.g., Aventyl], protriptyline [e.g., Vivactil], trimipramine [e.g., Surmontil])—Although tricyclic antidepressants may be used with amphetamines to help make them work better, using the two medicines together may increase the chance of fast or irregular heartbeat, severe high blood pressure, or high fever

Other medical problems—The presence of other medical problems may affect the use of amphetamines. Make sure you tell your doctor if you have any other medical problems, especially:

- Anxiety or tension (severe) or
- Drug abuse or dependence (history of) or
- Glaucoma or
- Heart or blood vessel disease or
- High blood pressure or
- Mental illness (severe), especially in children, or
- Overactive thyroid or
- Tourette's syndrome (history of) or other tics—Amphetamines may make the condition worse

Proper Use of This Medicine

Take this medicine only as directed by your doctor. Do not take more or less of it, do not take it more often, and do not take it for a longer time than your doctor ordered. If too much is taken, it may become habit-forming (causing mental or physical dependence).

If you think this medicine is not working properly after you have taken it for several weeks, *do not increase the dose.* Instead, check with your doctor.

For patients taking *the short-acting form* of this medicine:
- Take the last dose for each day at least 6 hours before bedtime to help prevent trouble in sleeping.

For patients taking *the long-acting form* of this medicine:
- Take the daily dose about 10 to 14 hours before bedtime to help prevent trouble in sleeping.
- These capsules or tablets should be swallowed whole. Do not break, crush, or chew them before swallowing.

Amphetamines may be taken with or without food or on a full or empty stomach. However, if your doctor tells you to take the medicine a certain way, take it exactly as directed.

Dosing—The dose of amphetamines will be different for different patients. *Follow your doctor's orders or the directions on the label.* The following information includes only the average doses of amphetamines. *If your dose is different, do not change it* unless your doctor tells you to do so.

The number of capsules or tablets that you take depends on the strength of the medicine. Also, *the number of doses you take each day, the time allowed between doses, and the length of time you take the medicine depend on the medical problem for which you are taking amphetamines.*

For amphetamine
- For *oral* dosage form (tablets):
  —For attention-deficit hyperactivity disorder:
    - Adults—At first, 5 milligrams (mg) one to three times a day. Your doctor may increase your dose if needed.
    - Children 6 years of age and older—At first, 5 mg one or two times a day. Your doctor may increase your dose if needed.
    - Children 3 to 6 years of age—At first, 2.5 mg once a day. Your doctor may increase your dose if needed.
    - Children younger than 3 years of age—Use is not recommended.
  —For narcolepsy:
    - Adults—At first, 5 mg one to three times a day. Your doctor may increase your dose if needed.
    - Children 12 years of age and older—At first, 5 mg two times a day. Your doctor may increase your dose if needed.
    - Children 6 to 12 years of age—At first, 2.5 mg two times a day. Your doctor may increase your dose if needed.
    - Children younger than 6 years of age—Dose must be determined by your doctor.

For amphetamine and dextroamphetamine
- For *oral* dosage form (tablets):
  —For attention-deficit hyperactivity disorder:
    - Children 6 years of age and older—At first, 5 milligrams (mg) one or two times a day. Your doctor may increase your dose if needed.

- Children 3 to 6 years of age—At first, 2.5 mg once a day. Your doctor may increase your dose if needed.
- Children younger than 3 years of age—Use is not recommended.
—For narcolepsy:
- Adults—Usually 5 to 60 mg a day, divided into two or three smaller doses.
- Children 12 years of age and older—At first, 10 mg a day. Your doctor may increase your dose if needed.
- Children 6 to 12 years of age—At first, 5 mg a day. Your doctor may increase your dose if needed.
- Children younger than 6 years of age—Dose must be determined by your doctor.

For dextroamphetamine
- For *oral extended-release capsule* dosage form:
  —For attention-deficit hyperactivity disorder:
  - Adults—5 to 60 milligrams (mg) a day.
  - Children 6 years of age and older—At first, 5 mg one or two times a day. Your doctor may increase your dose if needed.
  - Children 3 to 6 years of age—At first, 2.5 mg a day. Your doctor may increase your dose if needed.
  - Children younger than 3 years of age—Use is not recommended.
  —For narcolepsy:
  - Adults—5 to 60 mg a day.
  - Children 12 years of age and older—At first, 10 mg a day. Your doctor may increase your dose if needed.
  - Children 6 to 12 years of age—At first, 5 mg a day. Your doctor may increase your dose if needed.
  - Children 3 to 6 years of age—Dose must be determined by your doctor.
  - Children younger than 3 years of age—Use is not recommended.
- For *oral tablet* dosage form:
  —For attention-deficit hyperactivity disorder:
  - Adults—5 to 60 mg a day.
  - Children 6 years of age and older—At first, 5 mg one or two times a day. Your doctor may increase your dose if needed.
  - Children 3 to 6 years of age—At first, 2.5 mg a day. Your doctor may increase your dose if needed.
  - Children younger than 3 years of age—Use is not recommended.
  —For narcolepsy:
  - Adults—5 to 60 mg a day.
  - Children 12 years of age and older—At first, 10 mg a day. Your doctor may increase your dose if needed.
  - Children 6 to 12 years of age—At first, 5 mg a day. Your doctor may increase your dose if needed.
  - Children younger than 6 years of age—Dose must be determined by your doctor.

For methamphetamine
- For *oral tablet* dosage form:
  —For attention-deficit hyperactivity disorder:
  - Children 6 years of age and older—At first, 5 milligrams (mg) one or two times a day. Your doctor may increase your dose if needed.
  - Children younger than 6 years of age—Use is not recommended.

- For *oral extended-release tablet* dosage form:
  —For attention-deficit hyperactivity disorder:
  - Children 6 years of age and older—20 to 25 mg a day.
  - Children younger than 6 years of age—Use is not recommended.

Missed dose—If you miss a dose of this medicine and your dosing schedule is:

- One dose a day—Take the missed dose as soon as possible, but not later than stated above, to prevent trouble in sleeping. However, if you do not remember the missed dose until the next day, skip it and go back to your regular dosing schedule. Do not double doses.
- Two or three doses a day—If you remember within an hour or so of the missed dose, take the dose right away. However, if you do not remember until later, skip it and go back to your regular dosing schedule. Do not double doses.

Storage—To store this medicine:

- Keep out of the reach of children.
- Store away from heat and direct light.
- Do not store the capsule or tablet form of this medicine in the bathroom, near the kitchen sink, or in other damp places. Heat or moisture may cause the medicine to break down.
- Do not keep outdated medicine or medicine no longer needed. Be sure that any discarded medicine is out of the reach of children.

Precautions While Using This Medicine

Your doctor should check your progress at regular visits to make sure that this medicine does not cause unwanted effects.

If you will be taking this medicine in large doses for a long time, *do not stop taking it without first checking with your doctor*. Your doctor may want you to reduce gradually the amount you are taking before stopping completely.

This medicine may cause some people to feel a false sense of well-being or to become dizzy, lightheaded, or less alert than they are normally. *Make sure you know how you react to this medicine before you drive, use machines, or do anything else that could be dangerous if you are dizzy or are not alert.*

Before you have any medical tests, tell the medical doctor in charge that you are taking this medicine. The results of the metyrapone test may be affected by this medicine.

If you have been using this medicine for a long time and you think you may have become mentally or physically dependent on it, check with your doctor. Some signs of dependence on amphetamines are:

- A strong desire or need to continue taking the medicine.
- A need to increase the dose to receive the effects of the medicine.
- Withdrawal effects (for example, mental depression, nausea or vomiting, stomach cramps or pain, trembling, unusual tiredness or weakness) occurring after the medicine is stopped.

Side Effects of This Medicine

Along with its needed effects, a medicine may cause some unwanted effects. Although not all of these side effects may occur, if they do occur they may need medical attention.

Check with your doctor as soon as possible if any of the following side effects occur:

More common
   Irregular heartbeat

Rare
   Chest pain; fever, unusually high; skin rash or hives; uncontrolled movements of head, neck, arms, and legs

With long-term use or high doses
   Difficulty in breathing; dizziness or feeling faint; increased blood pressure; mood or mental changes; pounding heartbeat; unusual tiredness or weakness

Other side effects may occur that usually do not need medical attention. These side effects may go away during treatment as your body adjusts to the medicine. However, check with your doctor if any of the following side effects continue or are bothersome:

More common
   False sense of well-being; irritability; nervousness; restlessness; trouble in sleeping

   Note: After these stimulant effects have worn off, drowsiness, trembling, unusual tiredness or weakness, or mental depression may occur.

Less common
   Blurred vision; changes in sexual desire or decreased sexual ability; constipation; diarrhea; dizziness or lightheadedness; dryness of mouth or unpleasant taste; fast or pounding heartbeat; headache; increased sweating; loss of appetite; nausea or vomiting; stomach cramps or pain; weight loss

After you stop using this medicine, your body may need time to adjust. The length of time this takes depends on the amount of medicine you were using and how long you used it. During this period of time check with your doctor if you notice any of the following side effects:

   Mental depression; nausea or vomiting; stomach cramps or pain; trembling; unusual tiredness or weakness

Other side effects not listed above may occur also in some patients. If you notice any other effects check with your doctor.

Revised: 08/18/94
Interim revision: 08/13/98

AMPHOTERICIN B   Systemic

Commonly used brand name(s):

In the U.S.—
   Amphocin
   Fungizone Intravenous
   Generic name product may be available.

In Canada—
   Fungizone Intravenous

Description

Amphotericin B (am-foe-TER-i-sin Bee) is an antifungal. It is used to help the body overcome serious fungus infections. It may also be used for other problems as determined by your doctor.

Amphotericin B is available only with your doctor's prescription. It is available in the following dosage form:

Parenteral
   • Injection (U.S. and Canada)

Before Receiving This Medicine

In deciding to use a medicine, the risks of taking the medicine must be weighed against the good it will do. This is a decision you and your doctor will make. For amphotericin B, the following should be considered:

Allergies—Tell your doctor if you have ever had any unusual or allergic reaction to amphotericin B. Also tell your health care professional if you are allergic to any other substances, such as foods, preservatives, or dyes.

Pregnancy—Amphotericin B has not been reported to cause birth defects or other problems in humans.

Breast-feeding—Amphotericin B has not been reported to cause problems in nursing babies.

Children—Although there is no specific information comparing use of amphotericin B in children with use in other age groups, this medicine is not expected to cause different side effects or problems in children than it does in adults.

Older adults—Many medicines have not been studied specifically in older people. Therefore, it may not be known whether they work exactly the same way they do in younger adults or if they cause different side effects or problems in older people. There is no specific information comparing use of amphotericin B in the elderly with use in other age groups.

Other medicines—Although certain medicines should not be used together at all, in other cases two different medicines may be used together even if an interaction might occur. In these cases, your doctor may want to change the dose, or other precautions may be necessary. When you are taking amphotericin B, it is especially important that your health care professional knows if you are taking any of the following:

   • Antineoplastics (cancer medicine) or
   • Antithyroid agents (medicine for overactive thyroid) or
   • Azathioprine (e.g., Imuran) or
   • Chloramphenicol (e.g., Chloromycetin) or
   • Colchicine or
   • Cyclophosphamide (e.g., Cytoxan) or
   • Flucytosine (e.g., Ancobon) or
   • Ganciclovir (e.g., Cytovene) or
   • Interferon (e.g., Intron A, Roferon-A) or
   • Mercaptopurine (e.g., Purinethol) or
   • Zidovudine (e.g., AZT, Retrovir) or
   • X-ray treatment—Use of amphotericin B with any of these medicines or x-ray treatment may increase the chance of side effects affecting the blood

   • Bumetanide (e.g., Bumex) or
   • Carmustine (e.g., BiCNU) or
   • Cisplatin (e.g., Platinol) or
   • Combination pain medicine containing acetaminophen and aspirin (e.g., Excedrin) or other salicylates (with large amounts taken regularly) or
   • Cyclosporine (e.g., Sandimmune) or
   • Deferoxamine (e.g., Desferal) (with long-term use) or
   • Diuretics (water pills) or
   • Ethacrynic acid (e.g., Edecrin) or
   • Furosemide (e.g., Lasix) or
   • Gold salts (medicine for arthritis) or
   • Indapamide (e.g., Lozol) or
   • Inflammation or pain medicine, except narcotics, or

- Lithium (e.g., Lithane) or
- Other medicine for infection or
- Plicamycin (e.g., Mithracin) or
- Streptozocin (e.g., Zanosar) or
- Tacrolimus (e.g., Prograf) or
- Tiopronin (e.g., Thiola)—Using these medicines with amphotericin B may increase the risk of side effects affecting the kidneys

- Corticosteroids (cortisone-like medicine) or
- Corticotropin (ACTH)—Use of amphotericin B with these medicines may cause changes in the blood that may increase the chance for heart problems

- Digitalis glycosides (heart medicine)—Use of amphotericin B with digitalis medicines (such as digoxin) may cause changes in the blood that may increase the chance of heart problems

- Methotrexate (e.g., Mexate) or
- Penicillamine (e.g., Cuprimine)—Using these medicines with amphotericin B may increase the risk of side effects affecting the blood and the kidneys

Other medical problems—The presence of other medical problems may affect the use of amphotericin B. Make sure you tell your doctor if you have any other medical problems, especially:
- Kidney disease—Amphotericin B may cause side effects affecting the kidneys

Proper Use of This Medicine

Dosing—The dose of amphotericin B will be different for different patients. The following information includes only the average doses of amphotericin B. Your dose may be different if you have kidney disease.

- For the *injection* dosage form:
  - Adults and children: A small test dose is usually given first to see how you react to the medicine. The dose is then increased, depending on what your infection is and how well you tolerate the medicine. The dose must be determined by your doctor.

Side Effects of This Medicine

Along with its needed effects, a medicine may cause some unwanted effects. Although not all of these side effects may occur, if they do occur they may need medical attention.

Check with your health care professional immediately if any of the following side effects occur:
More common
  With intravenous injection
    Fever and chills; headache; increased or decreased urination; irregular heartbeat; muscle cramps or pain; nausea; pain at the place of injection; unusual tiredness or weakness; vomiting

Less common or rare
  With intravenous injection
    Blurred or double vision; convulsions (seizures); numbness, tingling, pain, or weakness in hands or feet; shortness of breath, troubled breathing, wheezing, or tightness in chest; skin rash or itching; sore throat and fever; unusual bleeding or bruising

With spinal injection
    Blurred vision or any change in vision; difficult urination; numbness, tingling, pain, or weakness

Other side effects may occur that usually do not need medical attention. These side effects may go away during treatment as your body adjusts to the medicine. However, check with your doctor if any of the following side effects continue or are bothersome:
More common
  With intravenous injection
    Diarrhea; headache; indigestion; loss of appetite; nausea or vomiting; stomach pain

Less common
  With spinal injection
    Back, leg, or neck pain; dizziness or lightheadedness; headache; nausea or vomiting

Other side effects not listed above may also occur in some patients. If you notice any other effects, check with your doctor.

Revised: 06/08/99

AMPHOTERICIN B CHOLESTERYL COMPLEX   Systemic

Commonly used brand name(s):

In the U.S.—
Amphotec

Description

Amphotericin (am-foe-TER-i-sin) B cholesteryl complex is an antifungal medicine. It is used to help the body overcome serious infections, such as aspergillosis, that are caused by fungus.

This medicine is available only with your doctor's prescription, in the following dosage form:

Parenteral
  - Injection (U.S.)

Before Using This Medicine

In deciding to use a medicine, the risks of using the medicine must be weighed against the good it will do. This is a decision you and your doctor will make. For amphotericin B cholesteryl complex, the following should be considered:

Allergies—Tell your doctor if you have ever had any unusual or allergic reaction to amphotericin B cholesteryl complex. Also tell your health care professional if you are allergic to any other substances, such as foods, preservatives, or dyes.

Pregnancy—Amphotericin B cholesteryl complex has not been studied in pregnant women. However, amphotericin B cholesteryl complex has not been shown to cause birth defects or other problems in animal studies. Before taking this medicine, make sure your doctor knows if you are pregnant or if you may become pregnant.

Breast-feeding—It is not known whether amphotericin B cholesteryl complex passes into breast milk. However, amphotericin B cholesteryl complex is not recommended during breast-feeding because it may cause unwanted effects in nursing infants.

Children—This medicine has been tested in children and, in effective doses, has not been shown to cause different side effects or problems than it does in adults.

Older adults—This medicine has been tested in a limited number of patients 65 years of age or older and has not been shown to cause different side effects or problems in older people than it does in younger adults.

Other medicines—Although certain medicines should not be used together at all, in other cases two different medicines may be used together even if an interaction might occur. In these cases, your doctor may want to change the dose, or other precautions may be necessary. When you are using amphotericin B cholesteryl complex, it is especially important that your health care professional know if you are taking any of the following:

- Aminoglycosides (amikacin [e.g., Amikin], gentamicin [e.g., Garamycin], kanamycin [e.g., Kantrex], neomycin [e.g., Mycifradin], netilmicin [e.g., Netromycin], streptomycin, tobramycin [e.g., Nebcin]) or
- Cyclosporine (e.g., Sandimmune) or
- Pentamidine (e.g., NebuPent, Pentam 300) or
- Tacrolimus (e.g., Prograf)—Use of these medicines with amphotericin B cholesteryl complex may increase the risk of side effects affecting the kidneys

- Antineoplastic agents (cancer medicine)—Use of cancer medicines with amphotericin B cholesteryl complex may increase the risk of side effects affecting the blood, kidneys, and lungs

- Atracurium (e.g., Tracrium) or
- Gallamine (e.g., Flaxedil) or
- Metocurine (e.g., Metubine Iodide) or
- Pancuronium (e.g., Pavulon) or
- Tubocurarine or
- Vecuronium (e.g., Norcuron)—Use of these medicines with amphotericin B cholesteryl complex may increase the effects of these medicines

- Corticosteroids (cortisone-like medicine) or
- Corticotropin (ACTH) or
- Digitalis glycosides (heart medicine)—Use of amphotericin B cholesteryl complex with corticosteroids, corticotropin, or digitalis medicines (such as digoxin) may cause changes in the blood that may increase the chance of heart problems

Other medical problems—The presence of other medical problems may affect the use of amphotericin B cholesteryl complex. Make sure you tell your doctor if you have any other medical problems.

Proper Use of This Medicine

Dosing—The dose of amphotericin B cholesteryl complex will be different for different patients. The following information includes only the average doses of amphotericin B cholesteryl complex.

- For *injection* dosage form:
  - For treatment of aspergillosis:
    - Adults and children—3 to 4 milligrams per kilogram (1.36 to 1.81 mg per pound) of body weight, injected slowly into a vein, once a day.

Side Effects of This Medicine

Along with its needed effects, a medicine may cause some unwanted effects. Although not all of these side effects may occur, if they do occur they may need medical attention.

Check with your doctor as soon as possible if any of the following side effects occur:

More common
Chills; fever; headache; nausea

Less common
Difficulty in breathing; dizziness or fainting; increased heartbeat; unusual bleeding or bruising

Rare
Difficulty in swallowing; hives; itching, especially of feet or hands; reddening of skin, especially around ears; swelling of eyes, face, or inside of nose; unusual tiredness or weakness (sudden and severe)

Other side effects may occur that usually do not need medical attention. These side effects may go away during treatment as your body adjusts to the medicine. However, check with your doctor if any of the following side effects continue or are bothersome:

Less common
Vomiting

Other side effects not listed above may also occur in some patients. If you notice any other effects, check with your doctor.

Developed: 04/28/98

AMPHOTERICIN B LIPID COMPLEX
Systemic

Commonly used brand name(s):

In the U.S.—
Abelcet

Description

Amphotericin (am-foe-TER-i-sin) B lipid complex is an antifungal medicine. It is used to help the body overcome serious infections caused by fungus.

This medicine is available only with your doctor's prescription, in the following dosage form:

Parenteral
- Injection (U.S.)

Before Using This Medicine

In deciding to use a medicine, the risks of using the medicine must be weighed against the good it will do. This is a decision you and your doctor will make. For amphotericin B lipid complex, the following should be considered:

Allergies—Tell your doctor if you have ever had any unusual or allergic reaction to amphotericin B lipid complex. Also tell your health care professional if you are allergic to any other substances, such as foods, preservatives, or dyes.

Pregnancy—Amphotericin B lipid complex has not been studied in pregnant women. Before taking this medicine, make sure your doctor knows if you are pregnant or if you may become pregnant.

Breast-feeding—It is not known whether amphotericin B lipid complex passes into breast milk. However, amphotericin B lipid complex is not recommended during breast-feeding, because it may cause unwanted effects in nursing infants.

Children—This medicine has been tested in children and, in effective doses, has not been shown to cause different side effects or problems than it does in adults.

Older adults—This medicine has been tested in a limited number of patients 65 years of age or older and has not been shown to cause different side effects or problems in older people than it does in younger adults.

Other medicines—Although certain medicines should not be used together at all, in other cases two different medicines may be used together even if an interaction might occur. In these cases, your doctor may want to change the dose, or other precautions may be necessary. When you are using amphotericin B lipid complex, it is especially important that your health care professional know if you are taking any of the following:

- Acyclovir by injection (e.g., Zovirax) or
- Aminoglycosides (amikacin [e.g., Amikin], gentamicin [e.g., Garamycin], kanamycin [e.g., Kantrex], neomycin [e.g., Mycifradin], netilmicin [e.g., Netromycin], streptomycin, tobramycin [e.g., Nebcin]) or
- Anticonvulsants (medicine for seizures) or
- Bacitracin by injection or
- Capreomycin (e.g., Capastat) or
- Cidofovir (e.g., Vistide) or
- Ciprofloxacin (e.g., Cipro) or
- Cyclosporine (e.g., Sandimmune) or
- Deferoxamine (e.g., Desferal) or
- Demeclocycline (e.g., Declomycin) or
- Foscarnet (e.g., Foscavir) or
- Gold salts (medicine for arthritis) or
- Inflammation or pain medicine or
- Lithium or
- Oxytetracycline (e.g., Terramycin) or
- Pamidronate (e.g., Aredia) or
- Penicillamine (e.g., Cuprimine, Depen) or
- Pentamidine (e.g., NebuPent, Pentam 300) or
- Polymyxins by injection or
- Rifampin (e.g., Rifadin, Rimactane) or
- Sulfamethoxazole and trimethoprim combination (e.g., Bactrim, Cotrim, Septra, Sulfatrim) or
- Sulfonamides (e.g., sulfadiazine, sulfamethizole [e.g., Thiosulfil Forte], sulfamethoxazole [e.g., Gantanol, Urobak], sulfisoxazole [e.g., Gantrisin]) or
- Tacrolimus (e.g., Prograf) or
- Tetracycline (e.g., Achromycin, Sumycin) or
- Tiopronin (e.g., Thiola) or
- Vancomycin by injection (e.g., Vancocin)—Use of these medicines with amphotericin B lipid complex may increase the risk of side effects affecting the kidneys
- Corticosteroids (cortisone-like medicine) or
- Corticotropin (ACTH) or
- Digitalis glycosides (heart medicine)—Use of amphotericin B lipid complex with corticosteroids, corticotropin, or digitalis medicines (such as digoxin) may cause changes in the blood that may increase the chance of heart problems
- Antineoplastic agents (cancer medicine) or
- Chloramphenicol (e.g., Chloromycetin) or

- Clozapine (e.g., Clozaril) or
- Colchicine or
- Didanosine (e.g., Videx) or
- Eflornithine (e.g., Ornidyl) or
- Flucytosine (e.g., Ancobon) or
- Ganciclovir (e.g., Cytovene) or
- Interferon (e.g., Intron A, Roferon-A) or
- Uracil mustard or
- X-ray treatment or
- Zidovudine (e.g., AZT, Retrovir)—Use of these medicines or x-ray treatment with amphotericin B lipid complex may increase the risk of side effects affecting the blood, kidneys, and lungs

Other medical problems—The presence of other medical problems may affect the use of amphotericin B lipid complex. Make sure you tell your doctor if you have any other medical problems, especially:

- Blood transfusion—Amphotericin B lipid complex may cause side effects affecting the lungs

- Kidney disease—Amphotericin B lipid complex may make your kidney problems worse

Proper Use of This Medicine

Dosing—The dose of amphotericin B lipid complex will be different for different patients. The following information includes only the average doses of amphotericin B lipid complex.

- For *injection* dosage form:
  —For treatment of serious infection caused by fungus:
    - Adults and children—5 milligrams per kilogram (2.27 mg per pound) of body weight per day, injected slowly into a vein.

Side Effects of This Medicine

Along with its needed effects, a medicine may cause some unwanted effects. Although not all of these side effects may occur, if they do occur they may need medical attention.

Check with your doctor as soon as possible if any of the following side effects occur:

More common
   Chills and fever; headache; nausea and vomiting

Less common
   Difficulty in breathing; sore throat and fever; unusual bleeding or bruising; unusual tiredness and weakness

Rare
   Increased or decreased urination

Other side effects may occur that usually do not need medical attention. These side effects may go away during treatment as your body adjusts to the medicine. However, check with your doctor if any of the following side effects continue or are bothersome:

More common
   Diarrhea; loss of appetite; stomach pain

Other side effects not listed above may also occur in some patients. If you notice any other effects, check with your doctor.

Developed: 04/17/98

AMPHOTERICIN B LIPOSOMAL COMPLEX Systemic

Commonly used brand name(s):

In the U.S.—
AmBisome

Description

Amphotericin B (am-foe-TER-i-sin) liposomal complex is an antifungal and an antiprotozoal medicine. It is used to help the body overcome serious infections caused by fungus or protozoa.

This medicine is available only with your doctor's prescription, in the following dosage form:

Parenteral
  • Injection (U.S.)

Before Using This Medicine

In deciding to use a medicine, the risks of using the medicine must be weighed against the good it will do. This is a decision you and your doctor will make. For amphotericin B liposomal complex, the following should be considered:

Allergies—Tell your doctor if you have ever had any unusual or allergic reaction to amphotericin B liposomal complex. Also tell your health care professional if you are allergic to any other substances, such as foods, preservatives, or dyes.

Pregnancy—Amphotericin B liposomal complex has not been reported to cause birth defects or other problems in humans. However, studies in animals have shown that amphotericin B liposomal complex causes the fetus to abort and other problems. Before taking this medicine, make sure your doctor knows if you are pregnant or if you may become pregnant.

Breast-feeding—It is not known whether amphotericin B liposomal complex passes into breast milk. However, amphotericin B liposomal complex is not recommended during breast-feeding, because it may cause unwanted effects in nursing babies.

Children—Appropriate studies performed to date have not demonstrated pediatrics-specific problems that would limit the usefulness of amphotericin B liposomal complex in children.

Older adults—Many medicines have not been studied specifically in older people. Therefore, it may not be known whether they work exactly the same way they do in younger adults. Although there is no specific information comparing use of amphotericin B liposomal complex in the elderly with use in other age groups, this medicine is not expected to cause different side effects or problems in older people than it does in younger adults.

Other medicines—Although certain medicines should not be used together at all, in other cases two different medicines may be used together even if an interaction might occur. In these cases, your doctor may want to change the dose, or other precautions may be necessary. When you are receiving amphotericin B liposomal complex, it is especially important that your health care professional know if you are taking any of the following:

  • Aminoglycosides (amikacin [e.g., Amikin], gentamicin [e.g., Garamycin], kanamycin [e.g., Kantrex], neomycin [e.g., Mycifradin], netilmicin [e.g., Netromycin], streptomycin, tobramycin [e.g., Nebcin]) or
  • Cyclosporine (e.g., Sandimmune) or
  • Pentamidine (e.g., NebuPent, Pentam 300) or
  • Tacrolimus (e.g., Prograf)—Use of these medicines with amphotericin B liposomal complex may increase the risk of side effects affecting the kidneys
  • Antineoplastic agents (cancer medicine)—Use of cancer medicines with amphotericin B liposomal complex may increase the risk of side effects affecting the blood, kidneys, and lungs
  • Atracurium (e.g., Tracrium) or
  • Gallamine (e.g., Flaxedil) or
  • Metocurine (e.g., Metubine Iodide) or
  • Pancuronium (e.g., Pavulon) or
  • Tubocurarine or
  • Vecuronium (e.g., Norcuron)—Use of these medicines with amphotericin B liposomal complex may increase the effects of these medicines
  • Corticosteroids (cortisone-like medicine) or
  • Corticotropin (ACTH) or
  • Digitalis glycosides (heart medicine)—Use of amphotericin B liposomal complex with corticosteroids, corticotropin, or digitalis medicines (such as digoxin) may cause changes in the blood that may increase the chance of heart problems

Other medical problems—The presence of other medical problems may affect the use of amphotericin B liposomal complex. Make sure you tell your doctor if you have any other medical problems, especially:

  • Blood transfusion—Amphotericin B liposomal complex may cause side effects affecting the lungs
  • Kidney disease—Amphotericin B liposomal complex may make your kidney problems worse

Proper Use of This Medicine

Dosing—The dose of amphotericin B liposomal complex will be different for different patients. The following information includes only the average doses of amphotericin B liposomal complex.

  • For the treatment of infection caused by fungus or protozoa
    —For *injection* dosage form:
      • Adults and children: 3 to 6 milligrams (mg) per kilogram (1.36 to 2.73 mg per pound) of body weight once a day, injected slowly into a vein. The number of days that you receive this treatment depends on the medical problem for which you are receiving amphotericin B liposomal complex.

Side Effects of This Medicine

Along with its needed effects, a medicine may cause some unwanted effects. Although not all of these side effects may occur, if they do occur they may need medical attention.

Check with your doctor as soon as possible if any of the following side effects occur:
More common
    Chills; fever; irregular heartbeat; muscle cramps or pain; unusual tiredness or weakness
Less common
    Back pain; chest pain; dark urine; difficulty in breathing; headache; yellowing of eyes or skin

Rare

Difficulty in swallowing; hives; itching, especially of feet or hands; reddening of skin, especially around ears; swelling of eyes, face, or inside of nose; unusual tiredness or weakness (sudden and severe)

Other side effects may occur that usually do not need medical attention. These side effects may go away during treatment as your body adjusts to the medicine. However, check with your doctor if any of the following side effects continue or are bothersome:

More common

Abdominal pain; cough; diarrhea; dizziness; nausea; vomiting

Less common

Skin rash

Other side effects not listed above may also occur in some patients. If you notice any other effects, check with your doctor.

Developed: 03/26/98
Revised: 11/22/00

AMPRENAVIR   Systemic

Commonly used brand name(s):

In the U.S.—
Agenerase

Description

Amprenavir (Am-PREN-a-veer) is a protease inhibitor. It is used in combination with other medicines to treat patients who are infected with the human immunodeficiency virus (HIV).

HIV is the virus that causes acquired immune deficiency syndrome (AIDS). Amprenavir may slow down the destruction of the immune system caused by HIV. This may help delay the development of problems usually related to AIDS or HIV disease. However, this medicine will not cure or prevent HIV infection, and it will not keep you from spreading the virus to other people. Patients who are taking this medicine may continue to have the problems usually related to AIDS or HIV disease.

This medicine is available only with your doctor's prescription, in the following dosage forms:

Oral
- Capsules (U.S.)
- Oral solution (U.S.)

Before Using This Medicine

In deciding to use a medicine, the risks of taking the medicine must be weighed against the good it will do. This is a decision you and your doctor will make. For amprenavir, the following should be considered:

Allergies—Tell your doctor if you have ever had any unusual or allergic reaction to amprenavir or sulfa medicines. Also tell your health care professional if you are allergic to any other substances, such as foods, preservatives, or dyes.

Pregnancy—Amprenavir has not been studied in pregnant women. However, studies in animals have shown that amprenavir causes birth defects and other problems. Before taking this medicine, make sure your doctor knows if you are pregnant or if you may become pregnant.

Breast-feeding—It is not known whether amprenavir passes into breast milk. However, breast-feeding is not recommended in patients with HIV-infection because of the risk of passing the HIV virus on to the nursing infant.

Children—This medicine has been tested in children 4 years of age and older. In effective doses, the medicine has not been shown to cause different side effects or problems than it does in adults.

Older adults—Many medicines have not been studied specifically in older people. Therefore, it may not be known whether they work exactly the same way they do in younger adults or if they cause different side effects or problems in older people. There is no specific information comparing use of amprenavir in the elderly with use in other age groups.

Other medicines—Although certain medicines should not be used together at all, in other cases two different medicines may be used together even if an interaction might occur. In these cases, your doctor may want to change the dose, or other precautions may be necessary. When you are taking amprenavir, it is especially important that your health care professional know if you are taking any other medicines (prescription or over-the-counter [OTC]), especially the following:

- Amiodarone (e.g., Cordarone) or
- Astemizole (e.g., Hismanal) or
- Bepridil (e.g., Vascor) or
- Cisapride (e.g., Propulsid) or
- Clozapine (e.g., Clozaril) or
- Dihydroergotamine (e.g., D.H.E. 45) or
- Ergotamine (e.g., Cafergot) or
- HMG-CoA reductase inhibitors (atorvastatin [e.g., Lipitor], cerivastatin [e.g., Baycol], lovastatin [e.g., Mevacor], pravastatin [e.g., Pravachol], simvastatin [e.g., Zocor]) or
- Midazolam (e.g., Versed) or
- Quinidine (e.g., Quinaglute, Cardioquin, or Quinidex) or
- Triazolam (e.g., Halcion) or
- Tricyclic antidepressants (amitriptyline [e.g., Elavil], amoxapine [e.g., Asendin], clomipramine [e.g., Anafranil], desipramine [e.g., Norpramin], doxepin [e.g., Sinequan], imipramine [e.g., Tofranil], nortriptyline [e.g., Aventyl, Pamelor], protriptyline [e.g., Vivactil], trimipramine [e.g., Surmontil]) or
- Warfarin (e.g., Coumadin)—There is a possibility that amprenavir may interfere with the removal of these medicines from the body, which could lead to serious side effects
- Antacids or
- Didanosine (e.g., Videx)—Use of antacids or didanosine with amprenavir may keep amprenavir from working properly if taken close together; antacids and didanosine should be taken at least one hour before or after amprenavir
- Carbamazepine (e.g., Tegretol) or
- Rifabutin (e.g., Mycobutin)—Use of carbamazepine or rifabutin with amprenavir may increase the amount of carbamazepine or rifabutin and decrease the amount of amprenavir in the body
- Disulfiram (e.g., Antabuse) or
- Metronidazole (e.g., Flagyl)—The oral solution form of amprenavir should not be taken with these medicines because serious side effects may occur

- Oral contraceptives—Amprenavir may cause these medicines to be less effective

- Phenobarbital or
- Phenytoin (e.g., Dilantin) or
- Rifampin (e.g., Rifadin, Rifamate, Rifater, Rimactane) or
- St. John's Wort—Use of these medicines with amprenavir may decrease the amount of amprenavir in the body and may keep amprenavir from working properly

- Sildenafil (e.g., Viagra)—Use of this medicine with amprenavir may increase the amount of sildenafil in the body and may increase the chance for side effects, such as low blood pressure, changes in vision, and erection of the penis lasting more than 4 hours

Other medical problems—The presence of other medical problems may affect the use of amprenavir. Make sure you tell your doctor if you have any other medical problems, especially:

- Diabetes mellitus or
- Hemophilia—Amprenavir may make these conditions worse

- Kidney failure or
- Liver failure—Amprenavir oral solution should not be used because serious side effects may occur

- Liver disease—Effects of amprenavir may be increased because of slower removal of amprenavir from the body

- Vitamin K deficiency—The high amounts of vitamin E in amprenavir dosage forms may increase the chance of bleeding problems in patients who are deficient in vitamin K

Proper Use of This Medicine

Amprenavir may be taken with or without food. *However, it should not be taken with a high-fat meal.* Taking amprenavir with a high-fat meal may decrease the amount of amprenavir that is absorbed by the body and prevent the medicine from working properly.

You should not drink alcoholic beverages while you are taking the oral solution form of this medicine.

It is important to take amprenavir as part of a combination treatment. *Be sure to take all the medicines your doctor has prescribed for you, including amprenavir.*

Take this medicine exactly as directed by your doctor. Do not take more of it, do not take it more often, and do not take it for a longer time than your doctor ordered. Also, do not stop taking this medicine without checking with your doctor first.

Keep taking amprenavir for the full time of treatment, even if you begin to feel better.

This medicine works best when there is a constant amount in the blood. *To help keep the amount constant, do not miss any doses. Also, it is best to take the doses at evenly spaced times, day and night.* For example, if you are to take two doses a day, the doses should be spaced about 12 hours apart. If you need help in planning the best times to take your medicine, check with your health care professional.

Only take medicine that your doctor has prescribed especially for you. Do not share your medicine with others.

Dosing—The dose of amprenavir will be different for different patients. *Follow your doctor's orders or the directions on the label.* The following information includes only the average doses of amprenavir. *If your dose is different, do not change it* unless your doctor tells you to do so.

The number of capsules or teaspoonfuls of solution that you take depends on the strength of the medicine.

- For *oral* dosage form (capsules):
  —For treatment of HIV infection:
  - Adults, adolescents 17 years of age and older, and adolescents 13 through 16 years of age who weigh 50 kilograms (kg) (110 pounds) or more—1200 milligrams (mg) (eight 150-mg capsules) two times a day.
  - Children 4 to 13 years of age and adolescents 13 through 16 years of age who weigh less than 50 kg (110 pounds)—Dose is based on body weight and must be determined by your doctor. The usual dose is 20 mg per kg (9.1 mg per pound) of body weight two times a day or 15 mg per kg (6.8 mg per pound) of body weight three times a day, up to a maximum dose of 2400 mg per day.
  - Children up to 4 years of age—Use and dose must be determined by your doctor.

- For *oral* dosage form (oral solution):
  —For treatment of HIV infection:
  - Adults, adolescents 17 years of age and older, and adolescents 13 through 16 years of age who weigh 50 kg (110 pounds) or more— 1400 mg two times a day.
  - Children 4 to 12 years of age and adolescents 13 through 16 years of age who weigh less that 50 kg (110 pounds)—Dose is based on body weight and must be determined by your doctor. The usual dose is 22.5 mg per kg (10.2 mg per pound) of body weight two times a day or 17 mg per kg (7.7 mg per pound) of body weight three times a day, up to a maximum dose of 2800 mg per day.
  - Children up to 4 years of age—Use and dose must be determined by your doctor.

Missed dose—If you are taking amprenavir capsules and you miss a dose, take it as soon as possible. However, if it is almost time for your next dose, skip the missed dose and go back to your regular dosing schedule. Do not double doses.

If you are taking amprenavir oral solution and you miss a dose, if it has been less than 4 hours since the dose was missed, take it immediately and then go back to your regular dosing schedule. If it has been more than 4 hours since the dose was missed, skip it and go back to your regular dosing schedule.

Storage—To store this medicine:

- Keep out of the reach of children.
- Store away from heat and direct light.
- Do not store in the bathroom, near the kitchen sink, or in other damp places. Heat or moisture may cause the medicine to break down.
- Keep the medicine from freezing. Do not refrigerate.
- Do not keep outdated medicine or medicine no longer needed. Be sure that any discarded medicine is out of the reach of children.

Precautions While Using This Medicine

Do not take any other medicines without checking with your doctor first. This includes prescription and nonprescription medicines. This also includes food supplements, herbs and vitamins. To do so may increase the chance of side effects from amprenavir or other medicines.

This medicine may decrease the effects of some oral contraceptives (birth control pills). *To avoid unwanted pregnancy, it is a good idea to use some additional contraceptive measures while being treated with amprenavir.*

For patients with diabetes: Amprenavir may affect blood sugar levels. If you notice a change in the results of your blood or urine sugar tests or if you have any questions, check with your doctor.

Do not take vitamin E supplements while you are taking amprenavir. At recommended dosages, amprenavir supplies more than the Reference Daily Intake of vitamin E for adults and children.

It is very important that your doctor check your progress at regular visits to make sure this medicine is working properly and to check for unwanted effects, especially increases in blood sugar.

Amprenavir does not decrease the risk of transmitting the HIV infection to others through sexual contact or by contamination through blood. HIV may be acquired from or spread to others through infected body fluids, including blood, vaginal fluid, or semen. *If you are infected, it is best to avoid any sexual activity involving an exchange of body fluids with other people. If you do have sex, always wear (or have your partner wear) a condom ("rubber"). Only* use condoms made of latex, and *use them every time you have vaginal, anal, or oral sex.* The use of a spermicide (such as nonoxynol-9) may also help prevent the spread of HIV if it is not irritating to the vagina, rectum, or mouth. Spermicides have been shown to kill HIV in lab tests. Do not use oil-based jelly, cold cream, baby oil, or shortening as a lubricant—these products can cause the condom to break. Lubricants without oil, such as *K-Y Jelly,* are recommended. Women may wish to carry their own condoms. Birth control pills and diaphragms will help protect against pregnancy, but they will not prevent someone from giving or getting the AIDS virus. *If you inject drugs,* get help to stop. *Do not share needles or equipment with anyone.* In some cities, more than half of the drug users are infected, and sharing even 1 needle or syringe can spread the virus. If you have any questions about this, check with your health care professional.

Side Effects of This Medicine

Along with its needed effects, a medicine may cause some unwanted effects. Although not all of these side effects may occur, if they do occur they may need medical attention.

Check with your doctor as soon as possible if any of the following side effects occur:
More common
    Dry or itchy skin; fatigue; increased hunger; increased thirst; increased urination; skin rash
Less common
    Burning or prickling sensation in arms or legs; depression; mood or mental changes
Rare
    Blistering, peeling, or loosening of skin and mucous membranes; buffalo hump; fever; general feeling of discomfort or illness; unexplained weight loss

Other side effects may occur that usually do not need medical attention. These side effects may go away during treatment as your body adjusts to the medicine. However, check with your doctor if any of the following side effects continue or are bothersome:
More common
    Abdominal pain; burning or prickling sensation around the mouth; diarrhea; nausea; vomiting

Less common or rare
    Change in sense of taste

Other side effects not listed above may also occur in some patients. If you notice any other effects, check with your doctor.

It is possible that the fat on your body may distribute itself differently or you may accumulate more body fat while you are taking this medicine. If you have concerns about this, check with your doctor.

Developed: 06/14/99
Revised: 04/17/2001

AMSACRINE   Systemic*

Commonly used brand name(s):

In Canada—
    AMSA P-D

Other commonly used names are acridinyl anisidide and m-AMSA.

*Not commercially available in the U.S.

Description

Amsacrine (AM-sah-kreen) belongs to the general group of medicines known as antineoplastics. It is used to treat acute adult leukemia.

Amsacrine interferes with the growth of cancer cells, which are then eventually destroyed by the body. Since the growth of normal body cells may also be affected by amsacrine, other effects will also occur. Some of these may be serious and must be reported to your doctor. Other effects, like hair loss, may not be serious but may cause concern. Some effects may not occur until months or years after the medicine is used.

Before you begin treatment with amsacrine, you and your doctor should talk about the good this medicine will do as well as the risks of using it.

Amsacrine is to be administered only by or under the supervision of your doctor. It is available in the following dosage form:
Parenteral
    • Injection (Canada)

Before Using This Medicine

In deciding to use a medicine, the risks of taking the medicine must be weighed against the good it will do. This is a decision you and your doctor will make. For amsacrine, the following should be considered:

Allergies—Tell your doctor if you have ever had any unusual or allergic reaction to amsacrine.

Pregnancy—Studies on effects in pregnancy have not been done in either humans or animals.

Before receiving amsacrine make sure your doctor knows if you are pregnant or if you may become pregnant. It is best to use some kind of birth control while you are receiving amsacrine. Tell your doctor right away if you think you have become pregnant while receiving amsacrine.

Breast-feeding—Amsacrine is not recommended during breast-feeding, because it may cause unwanted effects in nursing babies.

Children—Studies on this medicine have been done only in adult patients, and there is no specific information comparing use of amsacrine in children with use in other age groups.

Older adults—Many medicines have not been studied specifically in older people. Therefore, it may not be known whether they work exactly the same way they do in younger adults or if they cause different side effects or problems in older people. There is no specific information comparing use of amsacrine in the elderly with use in other age groups.

Other medicines—Although certain medicines should not be used together at all, in other cases two different medicines may be used together even if an interaction might occur. In these cases, your doctor may want to change the dose, or other precautions may be necessary. When you are receiving amsacrine, it is especially important that your health care professional know if you are taking any of the following:

- Acyclovir (e.g., Zovirax) or
- Anticonvulsants (seizure medicine) or
- Antidiabetics, oral (diabetes medicine taken by mouth) or
- Anti-infectives by mouth or by injection (medicine for infection) or
- Antipsychotics (medicine for mental illness) or
- Captopril (e.g., Capoten) or
- Enalapril (e.g., Vasotec) or
- Flecainide (e.g., Tambocor) or
- Gold salts (medicine for arthritis) or
- Imipenem or
- Inflammation or pain medicine, except narcotics or
- Lisinopril (e.g., Prinivil, Zestril) or
- Maprotiline (e.g., Ludiomil) or
- Penicillamine (e.g., Cuprimine) or
- Pimozide (e.g., Orap) or
- Procainamide (e.g., Pronestyl) or
- Promethazine (e.g., Phenergan) or
- Ramipril (e.g., Altace) or
- Sulfasalazine (e.g., Azulfidine) or
- Tiopronin (e.g., Thiola) or
- Tocainide (e.g., Tonocard) or
- Tricyclic antidepressants (medicine for depression) or
- Trimeprazine (e.g., Temaril)—Concurrent use of these agents with amsacrine may cause blood disorders

- Alpha interferons (e.g., Intron A, Roferon-A) or
- Amphotericin B by injection (e.g., Fungizone) or
- Antineoplastics, other (cancer medicine) or
- Antithyroid agents (medicine for overactive thyroid) or
- Azathioprine (e.g., Imuran) or
- Chloramphenicol (e.g., Chloromycetin) or
- Colchicine or
- Cyclophosphamide (e.g. Cytoxan) or
- Flucytosine (e.g. Ancoban) or
- Ganciclovir (e.g., Cytovene) or
- Zidovudine (e.g., AZT, Retrovir)—Concurrent use of these agents with amsacrine increases the risk of infection
- If you have ever been treated with radiation or cancer medicines—Amsacrine may increase the effects of these medicines or radiation therapy on the blood

Other medical problems—The presence of other medical problems may affect the use of amsacrine. Make sure you tell your doctor if you have any other medical problems, especially:

- Bone marrow depression or

- Infection—There may be an increased risk of infections or worsening infections because of the body's reduced ability to fight them
- Chickenpox (including recent exposure) or
- Herpes zoster (shingles)—Risk of severe disease affecting other parts of the body
- Heart rhythm problems—Patients who have problems with heart rhythms may have increased problems while taking amsacrine
- Kidney disease or
- Liver disease—Effects of amsacrine may be increased because of its slower removal from the body

Proper Use of This Medicine

Amsacrine often causes nausea and vomiting. However, it is very important that you continue to receive the medication, even if you begin to feel ill. Ask your health care professional for ways to lessen these effects.

Dosing—The dose of amsacrine will be different for different patients. The dose that is used may depend on a number of things, including what the medicine is being used for, the patient's body size, and whether or not other medicines are also being taken. *If you are taking or receiving amsacrine at home, follow your doctor's orders or the directions on the label.* If you have any questions about the proper dose of amsacrine, ask your doctor.

Precautions While Using This Medicine

It is very important that your doctor check your progress at regular visits to make sure that this medicine is working properly and to check for unwanted effects.

While you are being treated with amsacrine, and after you stop treatment with it, *do not have any immunizations (vaccinations) without your doctor's approval.* Amsacrine may lower your body's resistance, and there is a chance you might get the infection the immunization is meant to prevent. In addition, other persons living in your household should not take oral polio vaccine, since there is a chance they could pass the polio virus on to you. Also, avoid persons who have taken oral polio vaccine within the last several months. Do not get close to them, and do not stay in the same room with them for very long. If you cannot take these precautions, you should consider wearing a protective face mask that covers the nose and mouth.

Amsacrine can temporarily lower the number of white blood cells in your blood, increasing the chance of getting an infection. It can also lower the number of platelets, which are necessary for proper blood clotting. If this occurs, there are certain precautions you can take, especially when your blood count is low, to reduce the risk of infection or bleeding:

- If you can, avoid people with infections. *Check with your doctor immediately* if you think you are getting an infection or if you get a fever or chills, cough or hoarseness, lower back or side pain, or painful or difficult urination.
- *Check with your doctor immediately* if you notice any unusual bleeding or bruising; black, tarry stools; blood in urine or stools; or pinpoint red spots on your skin.
- Be careful when using a regular toothbrush, dental floss, or toothpick. Your medical doctor, dentist, or nurse may recommend other ways to clean your teeth and gums. Check with your medical doctor before having any dental work done.

- Do not touch your eyes or the inside of your nose unless you have just washed your hands and have not touched anything else in the meantime.
- Be careful not to cut yourself when you are using sharp objects such as a safety razor or fingernail or toenail cutters.
- Avoid contact sports or other situations where bruising or injury could occur.

If amsacrine accidentally leaks out of the vein into which it is injected, it may damage some tissues and cause scarring. *Tell the doctor or nurse right away if you notice redness, pain, or swelling at the place of injection.*

Side Effects of This Medicine

Along with its needed effects, a medicine may cause some unwanted effects. Although not all of these side effects may occur, if they do occur they may need medical attention.

Check with your doctor or nurse immediately if any of the following side effects occur:

More common
> Accumulation of pus or swollen, red, tender area of infection around the rectum; Black tarry stools; blood in urine or stools; cough or hoarseness; fever or chills; lower back or side pain; painful or difficult urination; pinpoint red spots on skin; sores, ulcers, or white spots on lips, tongue, or inside mouth; unusual bleeding or bruising; unusual tiredness or weakness

Less common
> Abdominal pain or tenderness; blurred vision; confusion; dark urine; diarrhea; dizziness, faintness, or light-headedness; fast, pounding, or irregular heartbeat or pulse; fever; itching; nausea; palpitations; convulsions (seizures); vomiting or vomiting of blood or material that looks like coffee grounds; yellow eyes or skin

Other side effects may occur that usually do not need medical attention. These side effects may go away during treatment as your body adjusts to the medicine. However, check with your doctor if any of the following side effects continue or are bothersome.

More Common
> Burning, crawling, numbness, prickling, "pins and needles", or tingling feelings; headache

Less common
> Bleeding gums; difficulty swallowing; hives; loss of appetite; loss of strength or energy; muscle or bone pain; pain or redness at site of injection; rash; redness and swelling of gums

This medicine often causes a temporary loss of hair. After treatment with amsacrine has ended, normal hair growth should return.

Other side effects not listed above may also occur in some patients. If you notice any other effects, check with your doctor.

Developed: 04/24/00

ANABOLIC STEROIDS   Systemic

Commonly used brand name(s):

In the U.S.—

Anadrol-50[3]	Hybolin-Improved[1]
Deca-Durabolin[1]	Kabolin[1]
Durabolin[1]	Oxandrin[2]
Durabolin-50[1]	Winstrol[4]
Hybolin Decanoate[1]	

In Canada—
Anapolon 50[3]
Deca-Durabolin[1]

Note: For quick reference, the following anabolic steroids are numbered to match the corresponding brand names.

This information applies to the following medicines:
1. Nandrolone (NAN-droe-lone)‡
2. Oxandrolone (ox-AN-droe-lone)†
3. Oxymetholone (ox-i-METH-oh-lone)
4. Stanozolol (stan-OH-zoe-lole)†

†Not commercially available in Canada.
‡Generic name product may be available in the U.S.

Description

This medicine belongs to the group of medicines known as anabolic (an-a-BOL-ik) steroids. They are related to testosterone, a male sex hormone. Anabolic steroids help to rebuild tissues that have become weak because of serious injury or illness. A diet high in proteins and calories is necessary with anabolic steroid treatment.

Anabolic steroids are used for several reasons:

- to help patients gain weight after a severe illness, injury, or continuing infection. They also are used when patients fail to gain or maintain normal weight because of unexplained medical reasons.
- to treat certain types of anemia.
- to treat certain kinds of breast cancer in some women.
- to treat hereditary angioedema, which causes swelling of the face, arms, legs, throat, windpipe, bowels, or sexual organs.

Anabolic steroids may also be used for other conditions as determined by your doctor.

Anabolic steroids are available only with your doctor's prescription, in the following dosage forms:

Oral
> Oxandrolone
> - Tablets (U.S.)
> Oxymetholone
> - Tablets (U.S. and Canada)
> Stanozolol
> - Tablets (U.S.)

Parenteral
> Nandrolone
> - Injection (U.S. and Canada)

Before Using This Medicine

In deciding to use a medicine, the risks of taking the medicine must be weighed against the good it will do. This is a decision

you and your doctor will make. For anabolic steroids, the following should be considered:

Allergies—Tell your doctor if you have ever had any unusual or allergic reaction to anabolic steroids or androgens (male sex hormones). Also tell your health care professional if you are allergic to any other substances, such as foods, preservatives, or dyes.

Pregnancy—Anabolic steroids are not recommended during pregnancy. They may cause the development of male features in the female fetus and premature growth and development of male features in the male fetus. Be sure you have discussed this with your doctor.

Breast-feeding—It is not known whether anabolic steroids can cause problems in nursing babies. There is very little experience with their use in mothers who are breast-feeding.

Children—Anabolic steroids may cause children to stop growing. In addition, they may make male children develop too fast sexually and may cause male-like changes in female children.

Older adults—When elderly male patients are treated with anabolic steroids, they may have an increased risk of enlarged prostate or cancer of the prostate.

Other medicines—Although certain medicines should not be used together at all, in other cases two different medicines may be used together even if an interaction might occur. In these cases, your doctor may want to change the dose, or other precautions may be necessary. When you are taking anabolic steroids, it is especially important that your health care professional know if you are taking any of the following:

- Acetaminophen (e.g., Tylenol) (with long-term, high-dose use) or
- Amiodarone (e.g., Cordarone) or
- Androgens (male hormones) or
- Anti-infectives by mouth or by injection (medicine for infection) or
- Antithyroid agents (medicine for overactive thyroid) or
- Carbamazepine (e.g., Tegretol) or
- Carmustine (e.g., BiCNU) or
- Chloroquine (e.g., Aralen) or
- Dantrolene (e.g., Dantrium) or
- Daunorubicin (e.g., Cerubidine) or
- Disulfiram (e.g., Antabuse) or
- Divalproex (e.g., Depakote) or
- Estrogens (female hormones) or
- Etretinate (e.g., Tegison) or
- Gold salts (medicine for arthritis) or
- Hydroxychloroquine (e.g., Plaquenil) or
- Mercaptopurine (e.g., Purinethol) or
- Methotrexate (e.g., Mexate) or
- Methyldopa (e.g., Aldomet) or
- Naltrexone (e.g., Trexan) (with long-term, high-dose use) or
- Oral contraceptives (birth control pills) containing estrogen or
- Phenothiazines (acetophenazine [e.g., Tindal], chlorpromazine [e.g., Thorazine], fluphenazine [e.g., Prolixin], mesoridazine [e.g., Serentil], perphenazine [e.g., Trilafon], prochlorperazine [e.g., Compazine], promazine [e.g., Sparine], promethazine [e.g., Phenergan], thioridazine [e.g., Mellaril], trifluoperazine [e.g., Stelazine], triflupromazine [e.g., Vesprin], trimeprazine [e.g., Temaril]) or

- Phenytoin (e.g., Dilantin) or
- Plicamycin (e.g., Mithracin) or
- Valproic acid (e.g., Depakene)—Taking anabolic steroids with any of these medicines may increase the chances of liver damage. Your doctor may want you to have extra blood tests to check for this if you must take both medicines

- Anticoagulants, oral (blood thinners you take by mouth)—Anabolic steroids can increase the effect of these medicines and possibly cause excessive bleeding

Other medical problems—The presence of other medical problems may affect the use of anabolic steroids. Make sure you tell your doctor if you have any other medical problems, especially:

- Breast cancer (in males and some females)
- Diabetes mellitus (sugar diabetes)—Anabolic steroids can decrease blood sugar levels
- Enlarged prostate or
- Prostate cancer—Anabolic steroids may make these conditions worse by causing more enlargement of the prostate or more growth of a tumor
- Heart or blood vessel disease—Anabolic steroids can worsen these conditions by increasing blood cholesterol levels
- Kidney disease
- Liver disease
- Too much calcium in the blood (or history of) (in females)—Anabolic steroids may worsen this condition by raising the amount of calcium in the blood even more

Proper Use of This Medicine

Take this medicine only as directed. Do not take more of it and do not take it more often than your doctor ordered. To do so may increase the chance of side effects.

In order for this medicine to work properly, it is important that you follow a diet high in proteins and calories. If you have any questions about this, check with your health care professional.

Dosing—The dose of these medicines will be different for different patients. *Follow your doctor's orders or the directions on the label.* The following information includes only the average doses of these medicines. *If your dose is different, do not change it* unless your doctor tells you to do so.

The number of tablets that you take depends on the strength of the medicine. Also, *the number of doses you take each day, the time allowed between doses, and the length of time you take the medicine depend on the medical problem for which you are taking the anabolic steroid.*

For nandrolone decanoate
- For *injection* dosage form:
  —For treatment of certain types of anemia:
    - Women and girls 14 years of age and older—50 to 100 milligrams (mg) injected into a muscle every one to four weeks.
    - Men and boys 14 years of age and older—50 to 200 mg injected into a muscle every one to four weeks. Your doctor may want to continue treatment for up to twelve weeks. After a four-week rest

period without receiving this medicine, your doctor may want you to repeat the cycle.
- Children up to 2 years of age—Dose must be determined by your doctor.
- Children 2 to 13 years of age—25 to 50 mg injected into a muscle every three to four weeks.

For nandrolone phenpropionate
- For *injection* dosage form:
  —For treatment of certain breast cancers in women:
    - Adults—25 to 100 milligrams (mg) injected into a muscle once a week for up to twelve weeks. After a four-week rest period without receiving this medicine, your doctor may want you to repeat the cycle.
    - Children—Dose must be determined by your doctor.

For oxandrolone
- For *oral* dosage form (tablets):
  —For treatment in rebuilding tissue after a serious illness or injury:
    - Adults and teenagers—2.5 milligrams (mg) two to four times a day for up to four weeks. Your doctor may increase your dose up to 20 mg a day.
    - Children—Dose is based on body weight and must be determined by your doctor. The usual dose is 0.25 mg per kilogram (kg) (0.11 mg per pound) of body weight a day.

For oxymetholone
- For *oral* dosage form (tablets):
  —For treatment of certain types of anemia:
    - Adults, teenagers, children, and older infants—Dose is based on body weight and must be determined by your doctor. The usual dose is 1 to 5 milligrams (mg) per kilogram (kg) (0.45 to 2.3 mg per pound) of body weight a day.
    - Premature and newborn infants—Dose is based on body weight or size and must be determined by your doctor. The usual dose is 0.175 mg per kg (0.08 mg per pound) of body weight once a day.

For stanozolol
- For *oral* dosage form (tablets):
  —To prevent hereditary angioedema, which causes swelling of the face, arms, legs, throat, windpipe, bowels, or sexual organs:
    - Adults and teenagers—At first, 2 milligrams (mg) three times a day to 4 mg four times a day for five days. Then, your doctor may slowly lower the dose to 2 mg once a day or once every other day.

Missed dose—If you miss a dose of this medicine and your dosing schedule is:
- One dose a day—Take the missed dose as soon as possible. However, if you do not remember it until the next day, skip the missed dose and go back to your regular dosing schedule. Do not double doses.
- More than one dose a day—Take the missed dose as soon as possible. However, if it is almost time for your next dose, skip the missed dose and go back to your regular dosing schedule. Do not double doses.

If you have any questions about this, check with your doctor.

Storage—To store this medicine:
- Keep out of the reach of children.
- Store away from heat and direct light.

- Do not store the tablet form of this medicine in the bathroom, near the kitchen sink, or in other damp places. Heat or moisture may cause the medicine to break down.
- Keep the liquid form of this medicine from freezing.
- Do not keep outdated medicine or medicine no longer needed. Be sure that any discarded medicine is out of the reach of children.

Precautions While Using This Medicine

Your doctor should check your progress at regular visits to make sure that this medicine does not cause unwanted effects.

For diabetic patients:
- This medicine may affect blood sugar levels. If you notice a change in the results of your blood or urine sugar tests or if you have any questions, check with your doctor.

Side Effects of This Medicine

Tumors of the liver, liver cancer, or peliosis hepatis, a form of liver disease, have occurred during long-term, high-dose therapy with anabolic steroids. Although these effects are rare, they can be very serious and may cause death. Discuss these possible effects with your doctor.

Along with its needed effects, a medicine may cause some unwanted effects. Although not all of these side effects may occur, if they do occur they may need medical attention.

Check with your doctor immediately if any of the following side effects occur:
  For both females and males
    Less common
      Yellow eyes or skin
    Rare (with long-term use)
      Black, tarry, or light-colored stools; dark-colored urine; purple- or red-colored spots on body or inside the mouth or nose; sore throat and/or fever; vomiting of blood

Also, check with your doctor as soon as possible if any of the following side effects occur:
  For both females and males
    Less common
      Bone pain; nausea or vomiting; sore tongue; swelling of feet or lower legs; unusual bleeding; unusual weight gain
    Rare (with long-term use)
      Abdominal or stomach pain; feeling of discomfort (continuing); headache (continuing); hives; loss of appetite (continuing); unexplained weight loss; unpleasant breath odor (continuing)

  For females only
    More common
      Acne or oily skin; enlarging clitoris; hoarseness or deepening of voice; irregular menstrual periods; unnatural hair growth; unusual hair loss
    Less common
      Mental depression; unusual tiredness

  For young males (boys) only
    More common
      Acne; enlarging penis; increased frequency of erections; unnatural hair growth

Less common
Unexplained darkening of skin

For sexually mature males only
More common
Enlargement of breasts or breast soreness; frequent or continuing erections; frequent urge to urinate

For elderly males only
Less common
Difficult or frequent urination

Other side effects may occur that usually do not need medical attention. These side effects may go away during treatment as your body adjusts to the medicine. However, check with your doctor if any of the following side effects continue or are bothersome:

For both females and males
Less common
Chills; diarrhea; feeling of abdominal or stomach fullness; muscle cramps; trouble in sleeping; unusual decrease or increase in sexual desire

For males only
More common
Acne
Less common
Decreased sexual ability

Other side effects not listed above may also occur in some patients. If you notice any other effects, check with your doctor.

Additional Information

Once a medicine has been approved for marketing for a certain use, experience may show that it is also useful for other medical problems. Although these uses are not included in product labeling, anabolic steroids may be used in certain patients with the following medical conditions:

- Certain blood clotting diseases
- Growth failure
- Turner's syndrome

Other than the above information, there is no additional information relating to proper use, precautions, or side effects for these uses.

Revised: 06/20/92
Interim revision: 06/08/94; 06/23/97; 06/22/98

ANAGRELIDE   Systemic

Commonly used brand name(s):

In the U.S.—
Agrylin

In Canada—
Agrylin

Description

Anagrelide (an-AG-re-lide) is used to decrease the risk of blood clots in patients who have too many platelet cells in their blood.

This medicine is available only with your doctor's prescription, in the following dosage form:

Oral
- Capsules (U.S. and Canada)

Before Using This Medicine

In deciding to use a medicine, the risks of taking the medicine must be weighed against the good it will do. This is a decision you and your doctor will make. For anagrelide, the following should be considered:

Allergies—Tell your doctor if you have ever had any unusual or allergic reaction to anagrelide. Also tell your health care professional if you are allergic to any other substances, such as foods, preservatives, or dyes.

Pregnancy—Anagrelide has not been studied in pregnant women. This medicine has been found to cause toxic or harmful effects in animals, but was not found to cause birth defects.

It is best to use some kind of birth control while you are taking anagrelide. Tell your doctor right away if you think you have become pregnant while taking anagrelide.

Breast-feeding—It is not known whether anagrelide passes into breast milk. Although most medicines pass into breast milk in small amounts, many of them may be used safely while breast-feeding. Mothers who are taking this medicine and who wish to breast-feed should discuss this with their doctor.

Children—Studies on this medicine have been done only on adult patients, and there is no specific information comparing use of anagrelide in children with use in other age groups.

Teenagers—Studies on this medicine have been done only on adult patients, and there is no specific information comparing use of anagrelide in teenagers with use in other age groups.

Other medical problems—The presence of other medical problems may affect the use of anagrelide. Make sure you tell your doctor if you have any other medical problems, especially:

- Heart disease (known or suspected)—Anagrelide can cause unwanted effects on the heart
- Kidney disease—Anagrelide rarely causes unwanted effects on the kidney
- Liver disease—Blood levels of anagrelide may be increased, possibly increasing the chance of side effects. Also, this medicine sometimes causes unwanted effects on the liver

---

Proper Use of This Medicine

Dosing—The dose of anagrelide will be different for different patients. *Follow your doctor's orders or the directions on the label*. The following information includes only the average doses of anagrelide. *If your dose is different, do not change it* unless your doctor tells you to do so.

The number of capsules that you take depends on the strength of the medicine.

- For *oral* dosage form (capsules):
  - For too many platelets in the blood:
    - Adults—0.5 milligrams (mg) four times a day, or 1 mg two times a day, for at least one week. After

that, the dose is adjusted to the dose that keeps the number of platelets normal.
- Children—Use and dose must be determined by your doctor.

Storage—To store this medicine:
- Keep out of the reach of children.
- Store away from heat and direct light.
- Do not store in the bathroom, near the kitchen sink, or in other damp places. Heat or moisture may cause the medicine to break down.
- Do not keep outdated medicine or medicine no longer needed. Be sure that any discarded medicine is out of the reach of children.

Precautions While Using This Medicine

It is very important that your doctor check your progress at regular visits to make sure that this medicine is working properly and to check for unwanted effects.

Anagrelide can cause unwanted effects on the heart, including a heart attack. *Check with your doctor and/or get emergency help immediately if you experience any signs or symptoms of a heart attack.*

Side Effects of This Medicine

Along with its needed effects, a medicine may cause some unwanted effects. Although not all of these side effects may occur, if they do occur they may need medical attention.

Check with your doctor and/or get emergency help immediately if any of the following side effects occur:

Less common
> Sudden severe headache or weakness; symptoms of a heart attack, which may include anxiety, cold sweating, increased heart rate, nausea or vomiting, severe pain or pressure in the chest and/or the jaw, neck, back, or arms, and shortness of breath

Check with your doctor as soon as possible if any of the following side effects occur:

More common
> Abdominal or stomach pain; dizziness; irregular heartbeat; weakness

Less common
> Blood in urine; blurred or double vision; difficulty in breathing; faintness; flushing; numbness or tingling in hands or feet; painful or difficult urination; swelling of feet or lower legs; unusual bleeding or bruising; unusual tiredness

Other side effects may occur that usually do not need medical attention. These side effects may go away during treatment as your body adjusts to the medicine. However, check with your doctor if any of the following side effects continue or are bothersome:

More common
> Diarrhea; gas or bloating of stomach; headache; heartburn; pain

Less common or rare
> Back pain; canker sore; confusion; constipation; fever or chills; general feeling of discomfort or illness; joint pain; leg cramps; loss of appetite; mental depression; muscle pain; nervousness; ringing in the ears; skin rash or itching; sleepiness; stuffy or runny nose; trouble in sleeping; unusual sensitivity to light

Anagrelide may cause a temporary loss of hair in some people.

Other side effects not listed above may also occur in some patients. If you notice any other effects, check with your doctor.

Developed: 03/26/1998
Revised: 02/05/2001

ANASTROZOLE   Systemic

Commonly used brand name(s):

In the U.S.—
> Arimidex

In Canada—
> Arimidex

Description

Anastrozole (an-ASS-troh-zole) is a medicine that is used to treat breast cancer.

Many breast cancer tumors grow in response to estrogen. This medicine interferes with the production of estrogen in the body. As a result, the amount of estrogen that the tumor is exposed to is reduced, limiting the growth of the tumor.

This medicine is available only with your doctor's prescription, in the following dosage form(s):

Oral
- Tablets (U.S. and Canada)

Before Using This Medicine

In deciding to use a medicine, the risks of taking the medicine must be weighed against the good it will do. This is a decision you and your doctor will make. For anastrozole, the following should be considered:

Allergies—Tell your doctor if you have ever had any unusual or allergic reaction to anastrozole. Also tell your health care professional if you are allergic to any other substances, such as foods, preservatives, or dyes.

Pregnancy—Anastrozole has not been studied in pregnant women. However, studies in animals have shown that anastrozole causes miscarriages, decreased weight or death of the fetus, and problems with bone formation. Be sure that you have discussed this with your doctor before taking this medicine. Tell your doctor right away if you think you have become pregnant while taking anastrozole.

Breast-feeding—It is not known whether anastrozole passes into the breast milk. However, anastrozole is not recommended during breast-feeding because it may cause unwanted effects in nursing babies.

Children—Studies on this medicine have been done only in adult patients, and there is no specific information comparing use of anastrozole in children with use in other age groups.

Older adults—This medicine has been tested in a limited number of patients 65 years of age or older and has not been shown to cause different side effects or problems in older people than it does in younger adults.

Other medicines—Although certain medicines should not be used together at all, in other cases two different medicines may be used together even if an interaction might occur. In these cases, your doctor may want to change the dose, or other precautions may be necessary. Tell your health care professional if you are taking any other prescription or nonprescription (over-the-counter [OTC]) medicine.

Other medical problems—The presence of other medical problems may affect the use of anastrozole. Make sure you tell your doctor if you have any other medical problems.

Proper Use of This Medicine

Take this medicine only as directed by your doctor. Do not use more or less of it, and do not use it more often than your doctor ordered.

Anastrozole sometimes causes nausea, vomiting, and diarrhea. However, it is very important that you continue to use the medicine, even if you begin to feel ill. Ask your doctor, nurse, or pharmacist for ways to lessen these effects.

Dosing—The dose of anastrozole will be different for different patients. *Follow your doctor's orders or the directions on the label.* The following information includes only the average doses of anastrozole. *If your dose is different, do not change it* unless your doctor tells you to do so.

- For *oral* dosage form (tablets):
  —For breast cancer:
  - Adults—1 mg once a day.
  - Children—Use and dose must be determined by your doctor.

Missed dose—If you do miss a dose of this medicine, do not take the missed dose at all and do not double the next one. Instead, go back to your regular dosing schedule and check with your doctor.

Storage—To store this medicine:
- Keep out of the reach of children.
- Store away from heat and direct light.
- Do not store in the bathroom, near the kitchen sink, or in other damp places. Heat or moisture may cause the medicine to break down.
- Keep the medicine from freezing. Do not refrigerate.
- Do not keep outdated medicine or medicine no longer needed. Be sure that any discarded medicine is out of the reach of children.

Precautions While Using This Medicine

It is important that your doctor check your progress at regular visits to make sure this medicine is working properly and to check for unwanted effects.

Side Effects of This Medicine

Along with its needed effects, a medicine may cause some unwanted effects. Although not all of these side effects may occur, if they do occur they may need medical attention.

Check with your doctor immediately if any of the following side effects occur:
  More common
    Chest pain; shortness of breath; swelling of feet or lower legs

Check with your doctor as soon as possible if any of the following side effects occur:
  Less common
    Cough or hoarseness; difficult or painful urination; dizziness, severe; fever or chills; headache, continuing; increased blood pressure; lower back or side pain; pain, tenderness, bluish color, or swelling of foot or leg; sore throat; sudden shortness of breath; unusual tiredness or weakness; vaginal bleeding (unexpected and heavy)

Other side effects may occur that usually do not need medical attention. These side effects may go away during treatment as your body adjusts to the medicine. However, check with your doctor if any of the following side effects continue or are bothersome:
  More common
    Back pain; body aches or pain; bone pain; congestion; constipation; cough; diarrhea; dizziness; dry mouth; dryness or soreness of throat; feeling of warmth; fever; flushing or redness of skin, especially on face and neck; headache; hoarseness; hot flashes; increased appetite; loss of appetite and weight loss; mood or mental changes; nausea or vomiting; pain, general; pelvic pain; runny nose; skin rash; stomach pain; sweating; tender, swollen glands in neck; trouble in swallowing; voice changes; weakness

  Less common
    Anxiety and confusion; breast pain; chills; cough or a cough producing mucus; diarrhea; difficulty breathing; fever; general feeling of discomfort or illness; headache; itching of skin; joint pain; loss of appetite; loss of hair; muscle pain; nausea; nervousness; numbness or tingling of hands or feet; shivering; shortness of breath; sleepiness or unusual drowsiness; sore throat; stuffy or runny nose; sweating; tightness in chest; trouble sleeping or sleeplessness; unusual tiredness or weakness; vaginal dryness; vomiting; weight gain; wheezing

Other side effects not listed above may also occur in some patients. If you notice any other effects, check with your health care professional.

Developed: 08/13/1998
Revised: 12/07/2000

ANDROGENS   Systemic

Commonly used brand name(s):

In the U.S.—

Androderm[3]	Depo-Testosterone[3]
AndroGel 1%[3]	Everone 200[3]
Android[2]	Halotestin[1]
Android-F[1]	ORETON Methyl[2]
Andro L.A. 200[3]	T-Cypionate[3]
Andronate 100[3]	Testamone 100[3]
Andronate 200[3]	Testaqua[3]
Andropository 200[3]	Testex[3]
Andryl 200[3]	Testoderm[3]
Delatest[3]	Testoderm with Adhesives[3]
Delatestryl[3]	Testoderm TTS[3]
Depotest[3]	Testopel Pellets[3]

Testred[2]   Virilon[2]
Testred Cypionate 200[3]   Virilon IM[3]
Testrin-P.A.[3]

In Canada—
  Andriol[3]   Malogen in Oil[3]
  Delatestryl[3]   Metandren[2]
  Depo-TestosteroneCypionate[3]   Scheinpharm Testone-Cyp[3]
  Halotestin[1]

Note: For quick reference, the following androgens are numbered to
      match the corresponding brand names.

This information applies to the following medicines
  1. Fluoxymesterone (floo-ox-i-MES-te-rone)‡
  2. Methyltestosterone (meth-il-tes-TOS-te-rone)‡
  3. Testosterone (tes-TOS-te-rone)‡

‡Generic name product may be available in the U.S.

Description

Androgens (AN-droe-jens) are male hormones. Some androgens are naturally produced in the body and are necessary
for the normal sexual development of males.

Androgens are used for several reasons, such as:
  • to replace the hormone when the body is unable to pro-
    duce enough on its own.
  • to stimulate the beginning of puberty in certain boys who
    are late starting puberty naturally.
  • to treat certain types of breast cancer in females.

In addition, some of these medicines may be used for other
conditions as determined by your doctor.

Androgens are available only with your doctor's prescription,
in the following dosage forms:

Oral
  Fluoxymesterone
    • Tablets (U.S. and Canada)
  Methyltestosterone
    • Capsules (U.S.)
    • Tablets (U.S. and Canada)
  Testosterone
    • Capsules (Canada)

Parenteral
  Testosterone
    • Injection (U.S. and Canada)

Subcutaneous
  Testosterone
    • Implants (Pellets) (U.S.)

Topical
  Testosterone
    • Gel
    • Ointment
    • Transdermal systems (skin patches) (U.S.)

Before Using This Medicine

In deciding to use a medicine, the risks of taking the medicine
must be weighed against the good it will do. This is a decision
you and your doctor will make. For androgens, the following
should be considered:

Allergies—Tell your doctor if you have ever had any unusual or allergic reaction to androgens. Also tell your health
care professional if you are allergic to any other substances,
such as foods, preservatives, or dyes.

Pregnancy—Androgens are not recommended during
pregnancy. When given to pregnant women, the medicine
has caused male features to develop in female babies.

Breast-feeding—Use is not recommended in nursing
mothers, since androgens may pass into the breast milk and
may cause unwanted effects in the nursing baby, such as
premature (too early) sexual development in males and development of male features in female babies.

Children—Androgens may cause children to stop
growing. In addition, androgens may make male children develop too fast sexually and may cause male-like changes in
female children.

Older adults—When older male patients are treated with
androgens, they may have an increased risk of enlarged
prostate (a male gland) or their existing prostate cancer may
get worse. For these reasons, a prostate examination and a
blood test to check for prostate cancer is often done before
androgens are prescribed for men over 50 years of age.
These examinations may be repeated during treatment.

Other medicines—Although certain medicines should
not be used together at all, in other cases two different medicines may be used together even if an interaction might
occur. In these cases, your doctor may want to change the
dose, or other precautions may be necessary. When you are
taking androgens, it is especially important that your health
care professional know if you are taking any of the following:
  • Acetaminophen (e.g., Tylenol) (with long-term, high-
    dose use) or
  • Amiodarone (e.g., Cordarone) or
  • Anabolic steroids (nandrolone [e.g., Anabolin], oxandro-
    lone [e.g., Anavar], oxymetholone [e.g., Anadrol], stan-
    ozolol [e.g., Winstrol]) or
  • Anti-infectives by mouth or by injection (medicines for
    infection) or
  • Antithyroid agents (medicines for overactive thyroid) or
  • Carbamazepine (e.g., Tegretol) or
  • Carmustine (e.g., BiCNU) or
  • Chloroquine (e.g., Aralen) or
  • Dantrolene (e.g., Dantrium) or
  • Daunorubicin (e.g., Cerubidine) or
  • Disulfiram (e.g., Antabuse) or
  • Divalproex (e.g., Depakote) or
  • Estrogens (female hormones) or
  • Etretinate (e.g., Tegison) or
  • Gold salts (medicines for arthritis) or
  • Hydroxychloroquine (e.g., Plaquenil) or
  • Mercaptopurine (e.g., Purinethol) or
  • Methotrexate (e.g., Mexate) or
  • Methyldopa (e.g., Aldomet) or
  • Naltrexone (e.g., Trexan) (with long-term, high-dose
    use) or
  • Oral contraceptives (birth control pills) containing es-
    trogen or
  • Phenothiazines (acetophenazine [e.g., Tindal], chlor-
    promazine [e.g., Thorazine], fluphenazine [e.g., Pro-
    lixin], mesoridazine [e.g., Serentil], perphenazine [e.g.,
    Trilafon], prochlorperazine [e.g., Compazine], proma-
    zine [e.g., Sparine], promethazine [e.g., Phenergan],
    thioridazine [e.g., Mellaril], trifluoperazine [e.g., Stela-
    zine], triflupromazine [e.g., Vesprin], trimeprazine [e.g.,
    Temaril]) or
  • Phenytoin (e.g., Dilantin) or
  • Plicamycin (e.g., Mithracin) or
  • Valproic acid (e.g., Depakene)—Use of these medicines
    with androgens may increase the chance of liver prob-
    lems. Your doctor may want you to have extra blood
    tests that check your liver while you are taking any of
    these medicines with an androgen

- Anticoagulants (blood thinners)—Androgens can increase the effect of these medicines and possibly cause excessive bleeding

Other medical problems— The presence of other medical problems may affect the use of androgens. Make sure you tell your doctor if you have any other medical problems, especially:

- Breast cancer (in males) or
- Prostate cancer—Androgens can cause growth of these tumors
- Breast cancer (in females)—Androgens may cause high calcium levels in the blood to become worse
- Diabetes mellitus (sugar diabetes)—Androgens can increase or decrease blood sugar levels. Careful monitoring of blood glucose should be done
- Edema (swelling of face, hands, feet, or lower legs) or
- Kidney disease or
- Liver disease—These conditions can be worsened by the fluid retention (keeping too much water in the body) that can be caused by androgens. Also, liver disease can prevent the body from removing the medicine from the bloodstream as fast as it normally would. This could increase the chance of side effects occurring
- Enlarged prostate—Androgens can cause further enlargement of the prostate
- Heart or blood vessel disease—Androgens can make these conditions worse because androgens may increase blood cholesterol levels. Also, androgens can cause fluid retention (keeping too much water in the body), which also can worsen heart or blood vessel disease

Proper Use of This Medicine

Take this medicine only as directed. Do not take more of it and do not take it more often than your doctor ordered. Doing so may increase the chance of side effects.

There are two types of testosterone skin patches. The matrix-type is applied to skin of the scrotum. The reservoir-type is never applied to the skin of the scrotum. It is applied to other parts of the body. Be sure you know which type you are using so that you will apply it properly. These skin patches come with patient directions. Read them carefully before using the patch.

For patients taking *fluoxymesterone* or *methyltestosterone:*
- Take this medicine with food to lessen possible stomach upset, unless otherwise directed by your doctor.

For patients using the *matrix-type skin patch of testosterone (Testoderm or Testoderm with Adhesives):*
- You must apply the patch to the scrotum because the medicine easily passes into your body at this area. Other areas of your skin are too thick for the medicine to work properly.
- Wash and dry your hands thoroughly before and after handling the patch.
    —Before applying the patch:
    - Clean and dry your scrotum.
    - You should also dry-shave this area once a week by using a shaver only (no soap or water). To dry-shave, stretch the skin of your scrotum with your fingers. Use short gentle strokes with no pressure on the razor to remove the hair. Do not use shaving cream or hair-removing creams (e.g., Nair).

- You may sit with your legs apart or stand while applying the patch.
—To apply the patch:
    - Open the wrapper containing the patch at the point shown on the package.
    - Carefully remove the patch from its protective plastic liner by peeling the patch from the liner starting at the corner.
    - Warm your scrotum for a few seconds before applying the patch to achieve the best results. Stretch the skin of your scrotum gently to remove the folds by pulling the penis up and to the side. Another way is to pull your scrotum down. Use your first and middle fingers to stretch the skin of your scrotum.
    - Place the shiny side of the patch onto the warm stretched skin of your scrotum.
    - Press the shiny side of the patch firmly in place with the palm of your hand for about 10 seconds. Make sure there is good contact, especially around the edges. The patch should stick to your scrotum and show the natural wrinkles of your scrotum.
    - Put on comfortable, close-fitting briefs (underwear) after applying the patch.
    - If a patch becomes loose or falls off, you may reapply it or discard it and apply a new patch.
—To remove the skin patch:
    - Gently peel the patch from the skin.
    - You may reuse the patch after removing it for swimming, bathing, showering, or sexual activity. First, remove the patch and place the shiny (sticky) side up on a counter. Before you reapply the patch, be sure the skin on your scrotum is dry. Then, follow the directions to reapply the patch.
    - When the wearing period is over, fold the patch in half with the sticky sides together. Place the folded, used patch in its protective pouch or in aluminum foil. Be sure to throw it away out of the reach of children and pets.

For patients using the *reservoir-type skin patch of testosterone (Androderm or Testoderm TTS):*
- Apply the patch called *Androderm* to the abdomen, back, thighs, or arms. Apply the patch called *Testoderm TTS* to the back, arms, or upper buttocks. *Do not apply these patches to the scrotum.*
- Do not apply the patch to areas of the body that seem bony, such as the top of the shoulders or near the elbows, or to areas that may have to support your body while sleeping or sitting, such as the hips or shoulder blades. Apply each new patch to a different place. Do not reapply a patch to the same area of skin for 7 days.
- Wash and dry your hands thoroughly before and after handling the patch.
    —Before applying the patch, clean and dry the application site.
    —To apply the patch:
    - Open the wrapper containing the patch at the point shown on the package.
    - Carefully remove the patch from its protective plastic liner by peeling the patch from the liner, starting at the corner.
    - Place the shiny side of the patch onto the skin.
    - Press the shiny side of the patch firmly in place with the palm of your hand for about 10 seconds.

© 2002 MICROMEDEX Thomson Healthcare

Be sure there is good contact, especially around the edges.
- If a patch becomes loose or falls off, you may reapply it or discard it and apply a new patch.

—To remove the skin patch:
- Gently peel the patch from the skin.
- You do not need to remove this patch for swimming, bathing, showering, or sexual activity.
- When the wearing period is over, fold the patch in half with the sticky sides together. Place the folded, used patch in its protective pouch or in aluminum foil. Be sure to throw it away out of the reach of children and pets.

Dosing—The dose of these medicines will be different for different patients. *Follow your doctor's orders or the directions on the label.* The following information includes only the average doses of these medicines. *If your dose is different, do not change it* unless your doctor tells you to do so.

The number of capsules or tablets that you take depends on the strength of the medicine. Also, *the number of doses you take each day, the time between doses, and the length of time you take the medicine depend on the medical problem for which you are taking the androgen.*

For fluoxymesterone
- For *oral* dosage form (tablets):
  —For androgen hormone replacement in men:
  - Adults—5 milligrams (mg) one to four times a day.
  —For treatment of breast cancer in women:
  - Adults—10 to 40 mg a day in divided doses.
  —For treatment of delayed sexual development in boys:
  - Children—2.5 to 10 mg a day for four to six months.

For methyltestosterone
- For *oral* dosage forms (capsules or tablets):
  —For androgen hormone replacement in men:
  - Adults—10 to 50 milligrams (mg) a day.
  —For treatment of breast cancer in women:
  - Adults—50 mg one to four times a day. Your doctor may decrease your dose to 50 mg two times a day after two to four weeks.
  —For treatment of delayed sexual development in boys:
  - Children—5 to 25 mg a day for four to six months.

For testosterone
- For *injection* dosage form:
  —For androgen hormone replacement in men:
  - Adults—25 to 50 milligrams (mg) injected into a muscle two or three times a week.
  —For treatment of breast cancer in women:
  - Adults—50 to 100 mg injected into a muscle three times a week.
  —For treatment of delayed sexual development in boys:
  - Children—Up to 100 mg injected into a muscle once a month for four to six months.
- For *subcutaneous* dosage form (implants):
  —For androgen hormone replacement in men:
  - Adults—150 to 450 milligram (mg) (two to six implants) inserted into the skin every three to six months.

—For treatment of delayed sexual development in boys:
- Children—Use and dose must be determined by your doctor.
- For *topical* dosage forms:
  —For androgen hormone replacement in men:

When using the brand name AndroGel 1% testosterone gel
- The recommended starting dose is one 5 gram packet applied once daily (preferably in the morning) to clean, dry, intact skin of the shoulders and upper arms and/or abdomen. Allow the application sites to dry prior to dressing and wash hands with soap and water after application.

When using the brand name Testoderm or Testoderm with Adhesives patches (matrix-type)
- Adults—4 or 6 mg (one patch) applied to your scrotum once a day at about 8 a.m. The patch should be worn at least twenty-two of the twenty-four hours in a day.
- Children—Use and dose must be determined by your doctor.

When using the brand name Androderm patches (reservoir-type)
- Adults and teenagers 15 years of age and older—2.5 to 7.5 mg (one to three patches) applied to the abdomen, back, thighs, or upper arms once a day at about 10 p.m. The patch(es) should be worn for twenty-four hours a day.
- Children up to 15 years of age—Use and dose must be determined by your doctor.

When using the brand name Testoderm TTS patches (reservoir-type)
- Adults—5 mg (one patch) applied to the back, arms, or upper buttocks once a day at about 8 a.m. Your doctor may increase your dose if necessary. The patch should be worn at least twenty-two of the twenty-four hours in a day.
- Children up to 18 years of age—Use and dose must be determined by your doctor.

For testosterone cypionate or testosterone enanthate
- For *injection* dosage form:
  —For androgen hormone replacement in men:
  - Adults—50 to 400 milligrams (mg) injected into a muscle every two to four weeks.
  —For treatment of breast cancer in women:
  - Adults—200 to 400 mg injected into a muscle every two to four weeks.
  —For treatment of delayed sexual development in boys:
  - Children—Up to 100 mg injected into a muscle once a month for four to six months.

For testosterone propionate
- For *injection* dosage form:
  —For androgen hormone replacement in men:
  - Adults—25 to 50 milligrams (mg) injected into a muscle two or three times a week.
  —For treatment of breast cancer in women:
  - Adults—50 to 100 mg injected into a muscle three times a week.
  —For treatment of delayed sexual development in boys:
  - Children—Up to 100 milligrams injected into a muscle once a month for four to six months.

For testosterone undecanoate
- For *oral* dosage form (capsules):
  - —For androgen hormone replacement in men:
    - Adults—120 to 160 milligrams (mg) divided into two doses a day taken with meals for two to three weeks. Then dose is reduced to 40 to 120 mg a day, taken with meals, and divided into 2 doses a day when possible.

Missed dose—For oral dosage forms: If you miss a dose of this medicine and your dosing schedule is:
- One dose a day—Take the missed dose as soon as possible. However, if you do not remember it until the next day, skip the missed dose and go back to your regular dosing schedule. Do not double doses.
- More than one dose a day—Take the missed dose as soon as possible. However, if it is almost time for your next dose, skip the missed dose and go back to your regular dosing schedule. Do not double doses.

For topical dosage forms (patches): If you miss a dose of this medicine or your patch falls off within 12 hours after applying it and cannot be reapplied, skip the rest of the dose and go back to your regular dosing schedule. Do not double doses.

If you have any questions about this, check with your doctor.

Storage—To store this medicine:
- Keep out of the reach of children.
- Store away from heat and direct light.
- Do not store in the bathroom, near the kitchen sink, or in other damp places. Heat or moisture may cause the medicine to break down.
- Keep the injection form of this medicine from freezing.
- Do not keep outdated medicine or medicine no longer needed. Be sure that any discarded medicine is out of the reach of children.

Precautions While Using This Medicine

Your doctor should check your progress at regular visits to make sure this medicine does not cause unwanted effects.

For patients with diabetes mellitus (sugar diabetes):
- This medicine may affect blood sugar levels. If you notice a change in the results of your blood or urine sugar tests or if you have any questions, check with your doctor.

For patients using the brand name Testoderm patches (matrix-type):
- In some cases, this medicine can pass from you to your sexual partner. Tell your doctor if your female sex partner has a great increase in acne. Also, tell your doctor if her hair begins to grow in odd places like her upper lip, chest, or back. This will not occur if you are using the reservoir-type skin patch because it is not applied to the scrotum and because it has a protective liner.

Side Effects of This Medicine

Discuss these possible effects with your doctor:
- Tumors of the liver, liver cancer, or peliosis hepatis (a form of liver disease) have occurred during long-term, high-dose therapy with androgens. Although these effects are rare, they can be very serious and may cause death.
- Androgens can stimulate existing prostate cancer in men who already have it but have not yet been diagnosed. Also, the prostate (a male gland) may become

enlarged. Enlargement of the prostate does not mean that cancer will develop. If enlargement occurs and you have difficulty in urinating, it is a good idea to be checked by your doctor.
- When androgens are used in women, especially in high doses, male-like changes may occur, such as hoarseness or deepening of the voice, unnatural hair growth, or unusual hair loss. Most of these changes will go away if the medicine is stopped as soon as the changes are noticed. However, some changes, such as voice changes or enlarged clitoris, may not go away.
- When androgens are used in high doses in males, they interfere with the production of sperm. This effect is usually temporary and only happens during the time you are taking the medicine. However, discuss this possible effect with your doctor if you are planning on having children.

Along with its needed effects, a medicine may cause some unwanted effects. Although not all of these side effects appear very often, when they do occur they may require medical attention. Check with your doctor as soon as possible if any of the following side effects occur:

More common
  For females only
  Acne or oily skin; decreased breast size; irregular menstrual cycles; hoarseness or deepening of voice; increase in size of female genitals; increase in unnatural hair growth or male pattern baldness
  Note: These symptoms may occur in females whose male sexual partner uses a scrotal patch.

  For males only
  Blistering of skin under patch (especially when the nonscrotal patch is applied to bony areas of the skin); breast soreness or enlargement; frequent or continuing erection of penis lasting up to 4 hours or painful penile erections lasting longer than 4 hours; frequent urge to urinate; itching or redness of skin under patch (less likely with nonscrotal patch) or at site of implants, mild to severe

  For prepubertal boys only
  Acne; early growth of pubic hair; enlargement of penis; frequent or continuing erections

Less common
  For males or females
  Dizziness; frequent or continuing headache; lack or loss of strength; nausea; overall body flushing, redness, or itching of skin; rapid weight gain; rapidly changing moods, such as depersonalization, dysphoria, euphoria, depression, paranoia, and quick to react or overreact emotionally; swelling of feet or lower legs; unusual bleeding; unusual tiredness; vomiting; yellow skin or eyes (occurring with fluoxymesterone or methyltestosterone more often than with testosterone)

For females with breast cancer or bedridden males or females—in addition to the side effects listed above
  Confusion or mental depression; constipation; increased thirst; increased urge to urinate or increased amount of urine

For males only
  Black, tarry stools; burning sensation or hardening

or thickening of skin under patch; chills; continuing pain at site of implants; difficulty in urinating; itching, skin redness, or rash under patch, severe (less likely with nonscrotal patch); pain in scrotum or groin; vomiting of blood or material that looks like coffee grounds

Rare
For males or females—more likely with oral androgens or long-term or high doses of androgens
Abdominal or stomach pain, continuing; bad breath odor, continuing; black, tarry or light-colored stools or dark urine; fever; hives; loss of appetite, continuing; mood or mental changes; purple or red spots on body or inside the mouth or nose; sore throat; swelling, pain, or tenderness of abdomen; vomiting of blood

Other side effects may occur that usually do not need medical attention. These side effects may go away during treatment as your body adjusts to the medicine. However, check with your doctor if any of the following side effects continue or are bothersome:

Less common
For males and females
Acne, mild; diarrhea; hair loss or thinning of hair; increase in pubic hair growth; infection, pain, redness, or other irritation at site of injection; decrease or increase in sexual desire or drive; nervousness; stomach pain; trouble in sleeping

For males only
Decrease in testicle size; infection, pain, redness, swelling, sores, or other skin irritation underneath patch

Other side effects not listed above may also occur in some patients. If you notice any other effects, check with your doctor.

Additional Information

Once a medicine has been approved for marketing for a certain use, experience may show that it is also useful for other medical problems. Although these uses are not included in product labeling, androgens are used in certain patients with the following medical conditions:

- Anemias (blood problems)
- Delayed growth spurt
- Development of male features in transsexuals
- Microphallus (underdevelopment of the penis)
- Lichen sclerosus (a skin problem of the vulva)

Other than the above information, there is no additional information relating to proper use, precautions, or side effects for these uses.

Revised: 01/25/2001

ANDROGENS AND ESTROGENS
Systemic

Commonly used brand name(s):

In the U.S.—
Andrest 90-4[5]
Andro-Estro 90-4[5]
Androgyn L.A.[5]
De-Comberol[5]

Deladumone[5]
Delatestadiol[5]
depAndrogyn[5]
Depo-Testadiol[5]
Depotestogen[5]
Duo-Cyp[5]
Duo-Gen L.A.[5]
Dura-Dumone 90/4[5]
Duratestin[5]
Estratest[3]
Estratest H.S.[3]
Halodrin[4]
Menoject-L.A.[5]
OB[5]
Premarin with Methyltestosterone[2]
Teev[5]
Tes Est Cyp[5]
Test-Estro Cypionate[5]
Tylosterone[1]
Valertest No. 1[5]
Valertest No. 2[5]

In Canada—
Climacteron[5]
Duogex L.A.[5]
Neo-Pause[5]
Premarin with Methyltestosterone[2]

Another commonly used name for diethylstilbestrol is DES.

Note: For quick reference, the following androgens and estrogens are numbered to match the corresponding brand names.

This information applies to the following medicines:
1. Diethylstilbestrol and Methyltestosterone (dye-eth-il-stil-BESS-trole and meth-il-tes-TOSS-ter-one)
2. Estrogens, Conjugated, and Methyltestosterone (ESS-troe-jenz, CON-ju-gate-ed, and meth-il-tes-TOSS-ter-one)
3. Estrogens, Esterified, and Methyltestosterone (ESS-troe-jenz, ess-TAIR-i-fyed, and meth-il-tes-TOSS-ter-one)
4. Fluoxymesterone and Ethinyl Estradiol (floo-ox-e-MESS-ter-own and ETH-in-il ess-tra-DYE-ole)
5. Testosterone and Estradiol (tess-TOSS-ter-own and ess-tra-DYE-ole)‡

‡Generic name product may be available in the U.S.

Description

Androgens and estrogens (AN-droe-jens and ESS-troe-jens) are hormones. Estrogens are produced by the body in greater amounts in females. They are necessary for normal sexual development of the female and for regulation of the menstrual cycle during the childbearing years. Androgens are produced by the body in greater amounts in males. However, androgens are also present in females in small amounts.

The ovaries and adrenal glands begin to produce less of these hormones after menopause. This combination product is prescribed to make up for this lower production of hormones. This may relieve signs of menopause, such as hot flashes and unusual sweating, chills, faintness, or dizziness.

Androgens and estrogens may also be used for other conditions as determined by your doctor.

There is no medical evidence to support the belief that the use of estrogens (contained in this combination medicine) will keep the patient feeling young, keep the skin soft, or delay the appearance of wrinkles. Nor has it been proven that the use of estrogens during the menopause will relieve emotional and nervous symptoms, unless these symptoms are caused by other menopausal symptoms, such as hot flashes.

A paper called "Information for the Patient" should be given to you with your prescription. Read this carefully. Also, before you use an androgen and estrogen product, you and your doctor should discuss the good that it will do as well as the risks of using it.

This medicine is available only with your doctor's prescription, in the following dosage forms:

Oral
Diethylstilbestrol and Methyltestosterone
- Tablets (U.S.)

Estrogens, Conjugated, and Methyltestosterone
  • Tablets (U.S. and Canada)
Estrogens, Esterified, and Methyltestosterone
  • Tablets (U.S.)
Fluoxymesterone and Ethinyl Estradiol
  • Tablets (U.S.)

Parenteral
  Testosterone and Estradiol
    • Injection (U.S. and Canada)

Before Using This Medicine

In deciding to use a medicine, the risks of taking the medicine must be weighed against the good it will do. This is a decision you and your doctor will make. For androgen and estrogen combination products, the following should be considered:

Allergies—Tell your doctor if you have ever had any unusual or allergic reaction to androgens, anabolic steroids, or estrogens. Also tell your health care professional if you are allergic to any other substances, such as foods, preservatives, or dyes.

Pregnancy—Estrogens (contained in this combination medicine) are not recommended for use during pregnancy, since some estrogens have been shown to cause serious birth defects in humans. Some daughters of women who took diethylstilbestrol (DES) during pregnancy have developed reproductive (genital) tract problems and, rarely, cancer of the vagina and/or uterine cervix when they reached childbearing age. Some sons of women who took DES during pregnancy have developed urinary-genital tract problems.

Androgens (contained in this combination medicine) should not be used during pregnancy because they may cause male-like changes in a female baby.

Breast-feeding—Use of this medicine is not recommended in nursing mothers. Estrogens pass into the breast milk and their possible effect on the baby is not known. It is not known if androgens pass into breast milk. However, androgens may cause unwanted effects in nursing babies such as too early sexual development in males or male-like changes in females.

Older adults—This medicine has been tested and has not been shown to cause different side effects or problems in older women than it does in younger females.

Other medicines—Although certain medicines should not be used together at all, in other cases two different medicines may be used together even if an interaction might occur. In these cases, your doctor may want to change the dose, or other precautions may be necessary. When you are taking an androgen and estrogen combination product, it is especially important that your health care professional know if you are taking any of the following:

  • Acetaminophen (e.g., Tylenol) (with long-term, high-dose use) or
  • Amiodarone (e.g., Cordarone) or
  • Anabolic steroids (nandrolone [e.g., Anabolin], oxandrolone [e.g., Anavar], oxymetholone [e.g., Anadrol], stanozolol [e.g., Winstrol]) or
  • Anti-infectives by mouth or by injection (medicine for infection) or
  • Antithyroid agents (medicine for overactive thyroid) or
  • Carbamazepine (e.g., Tegretol) or
  • Carmustine (e.g., BiCNU) or
  • Chloroquine (e.g., Aralen) or
  • Dantrolene (e.g., Dantrium) or
  • Daunorubicin (e.g., Cerubidine) or

  • Disulfiram (e.g., Antabuse) or
  • Divalproex (e.g., Depakote) or
  • Etretinate (e.g., Tegison) or
  • Gold salts (medicine for arthritis) or
  • Hydroxychloroquine (e.g., Plaquenil) or
  • Mercaptopurine (e.g., Purinethol) or
  • Methotrexate (e.g., Mexate) or
  • Methyldopa (e.g., Aldomet) or
  • Naltrexone (e.g., Trexan) (with long-term, high-dose use) or
  • Phenothiazines (acetophenazine [e.g., Tindal], chlorpromazine [e.g., Thorazine], fluphenazine [e.g., Prolixin], mesoridazine [e.g., Serentil], perphenazine [e.g., Trilafon], prochlorperazine [e.g., Compazine], promazine [e.g., Sparine], promethazine [e.g., Phenergan], thioridazine [e.g., Mellaril], trifluoperazine [e.g., Stelazine], triflupromazine [e.g., Vesprin], trimeprazine [e.g., Temaril]) or
  • Phenytoin (e.g., Dilantin) or
  • Plicamycin (e.g., Mithracin) or
  • Valproic acid (e.g., Depakene)—Androgens, estrogens, and all of these medicines can cause liver damage. Your doctor may want you to have extra blood tests that tell about your liver, while you are taking any of these medicines with an androgen and estrogen combination product.

  • Anticoagulants (blood thinners)—Androgens can cause an increased effect of blood thinners, which could lead to uncontrolled or excessive bleeding

  • Cyclosporine (e.g., Sandimmune)—Estrogens can increase the chances of toxic effects to the kidney or liver from cyclosporine because estrogens can interfere with the body's ability to get the cyclosporine out of the bloodstream as it normally would

Other medical problems—The presence of other medical problems may affect the use of androgen and estrogen combination products. Make sure you tell your doctor if you have any other medical problems, especially:

  • Blood clots (or history of during previous estrogen therapy)—Estrogens may worsen blood clots or cause new clots to form

  • Breast cancer (active or suspected)—Estrogens may cause growth of the tumor

  • Changes in vaginal bleeding of unknown causes—Some irregular vaginal bleeding is a sign that the lining of the uterus is growing too much or is a sign of cancer of the uterus lining; estrogens may make these conditions worse

  • Diabetes mellitus (sugar diabetes)—Androgens can decrease blood sugar levels

  • Edema (swelling of feet or lower legs caused by retaining [keeping] too much body water) or
  • Heart or circulation disease or
  • Kidney disease or
  • Liver disease—Androgens can worsen these conditions because androgens cause the body to retain extra fluid (keep too much body water). Also, heart or circulation disease can be worsened by androgens because androgens may increase blood cholesterol levels

  • Endometriosis—Estrogens may worsen endometriosis by causing growth of endometriosis implants

  • Fibroid tumors of the uterus—Estrogens may cause fibroid tumors to increase in size

- Gallbladder disease or gallstones (or history of)—There is no clear evidence as to whether estrogens increase the risk of gallbladder disease or gallstones

- Jaundice (or history of during pregnancy)—Estrogens use may worsen or cause jaundice in these patients

- Liver disease—Toxic drug effects may occur in patients with liver disease because the body is not able to get this medicine out of the bloodstream as it normally would

- Porphyria—Estrogens can worsen porphyria

Proper Use of This Medicine

For patients taking any of the androgen and estrogen products by mouth:
- *Take this medicine only as directed by your doctor. Do not take more of it and do not take it for a longer time than your doctor ordered.*
- Try to take the medicine at the same time each day to reduce the possibility of side effects and to allow it to work better.
- Nausea may occur during the first few weeks after you start taking estrogens. This effect usually disappears with continued use. If the nausea is bothersome, it can usually be prevented or reduced by taking each dose with food or immediately after food.

Dosing—The dose of these medicines will be different for different patients. *Follow your doctor's orders or the directions on the label.* The following information includes only the average doses of these medicines. *If your dose is different, do not change it* unless your doctor tells you to do so.

The number of tablets that you take depends on the strength of the medicine. Also, *the number of doses you take each day, the time allowed between doses, and the length of time you take the medicine depend on the medical problem for which you are taking combinations of androgen and estrogen.*

For diethylstilbestrol and methyltestosterone
- For *oral* dosage form (tablets):
  —For treatment of certain signs of menopause, such as hot flashes and unusual sweating, chills, faintness, or dizziness:
    - Adults—0.25 milligrams (mg) of diethylstilbestrol and 5 mg of methyltestosterone once a day for twenty-one days. Stop the medicine for seven days, then repeat the twenty-one day cycle. After a while, your doctor may decrease your dose to 0.125 mg of diethylstilbestrol and 2.5 mg of methyltestosterone once a day for twenty-one days. Again, after stopping for seven days, you will then repeat the cycle.

For conjugated estrogens and methyltestosterone
- For *oral* dosage form (tablets):
  —For treatment of certain signs of menopause, such as hot flashes and unusual sweating, chills, faintness, or dizziness:
    - Adults—1.25 milligrams (mg) of conjugated estrogens and 10 mg of methyltestosterone once a day for twenty-one days. Stop the medicine for seven days, then repeat the twenty-one day cycle.

For esterified estrogens and methyltestosterone
- For *oral* dosage form (tablets):
  —For treatment of certain signs of menopause, such as hot flashes and unusual sweating, chills, faintness, or dizziness:
    - Adults—0.625 to 2.5 milligrams of esterified estrogens and 1.25 to 5 mg of methyltestosterone once a day for twenty-one days. Stop the medicine for seven days, then repeat the twenty-one day cycle.

For fluoxymesterone and ethinyl estradiol
- For *oral* dosage form (tablets):
  —For treatment of certain signs of menopause, such as hot flashes and unusual sweating, chills, faintness, or dizziness:
    - Adults—1 to 2 milligrams (mg) of fluoxymesterone and 0.02 to 0.04 mg of ethinyl estradiol two times a day for twenty-one days. Stop the medicine for seven days, then repeat the twenty-one day cycle.

For testosterone cypionate and estradiol cypionate
- For *injection* dosage form:
  —For treatment of certain signs of menopause, such as hot flashes and unusual sweating, chills, faintness, or dizziness:
    - Adults—50 milligrams (mg) of testosterone cypionate and 2 mg of estradiol cypionate injected into a muscle once every four weeks.

For testosterone enanthate and estradiol valerate
- For *injection* dosage form:
  —For treatment of certain signs of menopause, such as hot flashes and unusual sweating, chills, faintness, or dizziness:
    - Adults—90 milligrams (mg) of testosterone enanthate and 4 mg of estradiol valerate injected into a muscle once every four weeks.

For testosterone enanthate benzilic acid hydrazone, estradiol dienanthate, and estradiol benzoate
- For *injection* dosage form:
  —For treatment of bone loss (osteoporosis) or certain signs of menopause, such as hot flashes and unusual sweating, chills, faintness, or dizziness:
    - Adults—150 milligrams (mg) of testosterone enanthate benzilic acid hydrazone, 7.5 mg of estradiol dienanthate, and 1 mg of estradiol benzoate injected into a muscle once every four to eight weeks or less.

Missed dose—If you miss a dose of this medicine and your dosing schedule is:
- One dose a day—Take the missed dose as soon as possible. However, if you do not remember it until the next day, skip the missed dose and go back to your regular dosing schedule. Do not double doses.
- More than one dose a day—Take the missed dose as soon as possible. However, if it is almost time for your next dose, skip the missed dose and go back to your regular dosing schedule. Do not double doses.

If you have any questions about this, check with your doctor.

Storage—To store this medicine:
- Keep out of the reach of children.
- Store away from heat and direct light.
- Do not store in the bathroom medicine cabinet because the heat or moisture may cause the medicine to break down.
- Keep the injectable form of this medicine from freezing.

• Do not keep outdated medicine or medicine no longer needed. Be sure that any discarded medicine is out of the reach of children.

Precautions While Using This Medicine

It is very important that your doctor check your progress at regular visits to make sure this medicine does not cause unwanted effects. These visits will usually be every 6 to 12 months, but many doctors require them more often.

It is not yet known whether the use of estrogen increases the risk of breast cancer in women. Therefore, it is very important that you regularly check your breasts for any unusual lumps or discharge. You should also have a mammogram (x-ray picture of the breasts) done if your doctor recommends it.

In some patients using estrogens, tenderness, swelling, or bleeding of the gums may occur. Brushing and flossing your teeth carefully and regularly and massaging your gums may help prevent this. See your dentist regularly to have your teeth cleaned. Check with your medical doctor or dentist if you have any questions about how to take care of your teeth and gums, or if you notice any tenderness, swelling, or bleeding of your gums.

For diabetic patients:

• This medicine may affect blood sugar levels. If you notice a change in the results of your blood or urine sugar tests or if you have any questions, check with your doctor.

If you think that you may have become pregnant, check with your doctor immediately. Continued use of this medicine during pregnancy may cause birth defects or future health problems in the child.

In studies with oral contraceptives (birth control pills) containing estrogens, cigarette smoking during the use of estrogens was shown to cause an increased risk of serious side effects affecting the heart or blood circulation, such as dangerous blood clots, heart attack, or stroke. The risk increased as the amount of smoking and the age of the smoker increased. Women aged 35 and over were at greatest risk when they smoked while using oral contraceptives containing estrogens. It is not known if this risk exists with the use of androgens and estrogens for symptoms of menopause. However, smoking may make estrogens less effective.

Do not give this medicine to anyone else. Your doctor has prescribed it specifically for you after studying your health record and the results of your physical examination. Androgens and estrogens may be dangerous for some people because of differences in their health and body chemistry.

Side Effects of This Medicine

Discuss these possible effects with your doctor:

• Tumors of the liver, liver cancer, and peliosis hepatis (a form of liver disease) have occurred during long-term, high-dose therapy with androgens. Although these effects are rare, they can be very serious and may cause death.
• When androgens are used in women, especially in high doses, male-like changes may occur, such as hoarseness or deepening of the voice, unnatural hair growth, or unusual hair loss. Most of these changes will go away if the medicine is stopped as soon as the changes are noticed. However, some changes, such as voice changes, may not go away.

• The prolonged use of estrogens has been reported to increase the risk of endometrial cancer (cancer of the uterus lining) in women after menopause. The risk seems to increase as the dose and the length of use increase. When estrogens are used in low doses for less than one year, there is less risk. The risk is also reduced if a progestin (another female hormone) is added to, or replaces part of, your estrogen dose. If the uterus has been removed by surgery (total hysterectomy), there is no risk of endometrial cancer.
• It is not yet known whether the use of estrogens increases the risk of breast cancer in women. Although some large studies show an increased risk, most studies and information gathered to date do not support this idea.

Along with its needed effects, a medicine may cause some unwanted effects. Although not all of these side effects may occur, if they do occur they may need medical attention.

Check with your doctor immediately if any of the following side effects occur:
Less common
   Yellow eyes or skin
Rare
   Uncontrolled jerky muscle movements; vomiting of blood (with long-term use or high doses)

Also, check with your doctor as soon as possible if any of the following side effects occur:
More common
   Acne or oily skin (severe); breast pain or tenderness; changes in vaginal bleeding (spotting, breakthrough bleeding, prolonged or heavier bleeding, or complete stoppage of bleeding); enlarged clitoris; enlargement or decrease in size of breasts; hoarseness or deepening of voice; swelling of feet or lower legs; unnatural hair growth; unusual hair loss; weight gain (rapid)
Less common or rare
   Confusion; dizziness; flushing or redness of skin; headaches (frequent or continuing); hives (especially at place of injection); shortness of breath (unexplained); skin rash, hives, or itching; unusual bleeding; unusual tiredness or drowsiness
With long-term use or high doses
   Black, tarry, or light-colored stools; dark-colored urine; general feeling of discomfort or illness (continuing); hives (frequent or continuing); loss of appetite (continuing); lump in, or discharge from breast; nausea (severe); pain, swelling, or tenderness in stomach or upper abdomen (continuing); purple- or red-colored spots on body or inside the mouth or nose; sore throat or fever (continuing); unpleasant breath odor (continuing); vomiting (severe)

Other side effects may occur that usually do not need medical attention. These side effects may go away during treatment as your body adjusts to the medicine. However, check with your doctor if any of the following side effects continue or are bothersome:
More common
   Bloating of abdomen or stomach; cramps of abdomen or stomach; loss of appetite (temporary); nausea (mild); stomach pain (mild); unusual increase in sexual desire; vomiting (mild)

Less common
> Constipation; diarrhea (mild); dizziness (mild); headaches (mild); infection, redness, pain, or other irritation at place of injection; migraine headaches; problems in wearing contact lenses; trouble in sleeping

Also, many women who are taking a progestin (another type of female hormone) with this medicine will begin to have monthly vaginal bleeding again, similar to menstrual periods. This effect will continue for as long as this medicine is used. However, monthly bleeding will not occur in women who have had the uterus removed by surgery (total hysterectomy).

Other side effects not listed above may also occur in some patients. If you notice any other effects, check with your doctor.

Revised: 06/30/92
Interim revision: 06/21/94

ANESTHETICS   Dental

Commonly used brand name(s):

In the U.S.—

Anbesol, Baby[1]	Orabase, Baby[1]
Anbesol Maximum Strength Gel[1]	Orabase-B with Benzocaine[1]
Anbesol Maximum Strength Liquid[1]	Orajel, Baby[1]
Anbesol Regular Strength Gel[3]	Orajel Maximum Strength[1]
Anbesol Regular Strength Liquid[3]	Orajel Nighttime Formula, Baby[1]
Benzodent[1]	Oratect Gel[1]
Chloraseptic Lozenges[2]	Rid-A-Pain[1]
Chloraseptic Lozenges, Children's[1]	SensoGARD Canker Sore Relief[1]
Dentapaine[1]	Spec-T Sore Throat Anesthetic[1]
Dent-Zel-Ite[1]	Sucrets, Children's[4]
Hurricaine[1]	Sucrets Maximum Strength[4]
Numzident[1]	Sucrets Regular Strength[4]
Num-Zit Gel[1]	Xylocaine[5]
Num-Zit Lotion[1]	Xylocaine Viscous[5]
	Zilactin-L[5]

In Canada—

Anbesol Baby Jel[1]	Dentocaine[1]
Anbesol Gel[3]	Orajel, Baby[1]
Anbesol Liquid[3]	Orajel Extra Strength[1]
Anbesol Maximum Strength Liquid[3]	Orajel Liquid[1]
	Topicaine[1]
Chloraseptic Lozenges Cherry Flavor[2]	Xylocaine[5]
	Xylocaine Viscous[5]

Other commonly used names are: dyclocaine[4] ethyl aminobenzoate[1] lignocaine[5].

Note: For quick reference, the following anesthetics are numbered to match the corresponding brand names.

This information applies to the following medicines:
1. Benzocaine (BEN-zoe-kane)
2. Benzocaine and Menthol (BEN-zoe-kane and MEN-thole)
3. Benzocaine and Phenol (BEN-zoe-kane and FEE-nole)
4. Dyclonine (DYE-kloe-neen)
5. Lidocaine (LYE-doe-kane)‡

‡Generic name product may be available in the U.S.

Description

Dental anesthetics (an-ess-THET-iks) are used in the mouth to relieve pain or irritation caused by many conditions. Examples include toothache, teething, and sores in or around the mouth, such as cold sores, canker sores, and fever blisters. Also, some of these medicines are used to relieve pain or irritation caused by dentures or other dental appliances, including braces. However, if you have an infection or a lot of large sores in your mouth, check with your medical doctor or dentist before using a dental anesthetic because other kinds of treatment may be needed. Also, the chance of side effects is increased.

One form of lidocaine is also used to relieve pain caused by certain throat conditions. Some forms of benzocaine, benzocaine and menthol combination, and dyclonine are also used to relieve sore throat pain.

Some of these medicines are available only with your medical doctor's or dentist's prescription. Others are available without a prescription; however, your medical doctor or dentist may have special instructions on the proper use and dose for your medical problem. Some nonprescription (over-the-counter [OTC]) aerosols, gels, liquids, or ointments that contain a local anesthetic are not meant to be used in or around the mouth. If you have any questions about which product to use, check with your pharmacist.

These medicines are available in the following dosage forms:

Dental
  Benzocaine
  • Aerosol spray (U.S.)
  • Dental paste (U.S.)
  • Film-forming gel (U.S.)
  • Gel (U.S. and Canada)
  • Lozenges (U.S.)
  • Ointment (U.S. and Canada)
  • Solution (liquid) (U.S. and Canada)
  Benzocaine and Menthol
  • Lozenges (U.S. and Canada)
  Benzocaine and Phenol
  • Gel (U.S. and Canada)
  • Solution (liquid) (U.S. and Canada)
  Dyclonine
  • Lozenges (U.S.)
  Lidocaine
  • Aerosol spray (U.S. and Canada)
  • Ointment (U.S. and Canada)
  • Solution (U.S. and Canada)
  • Viscous (very thick) solution (U.S. and Canada)

Before Using This Medicine

If you are taking this medicine without a prescription, carefully read and follow any precautions on the label. For dental anesthetics, the following should be considered:

Allergies—Tell your doctor if you have ever had any unusual or allergic reaction to a local anesthetic, especially one that was applied to any part of the body as a liquid, cream, ointment, or spray. Also tell your health care professional if you are allergic to any other substances, such as foods, preservatives, or dyes.

Pregnancy—Dental anesthetics have not been reported to cause birth defects or other problems in humans.

Breast-feeding—Dental anesthetics have not been reported to cause problems in nursing babies.

Children—Children may be especially sensitive to the effects of dental anesthetics. This may increase the chance of unwanted effects, some of which can be serious, during treatment. When using a dental anesthetic for a child, be very careful not to use more of the medicine than directed on the label, unless otherwise directed by your health care professional. Teething medicines that contain benzocaine may be used in babies 4 months of age and older. One product that contains benzocaine (Orabase-B with Benzocaine) may be used in children 6 years of age and older. Most of the other nonprescription (over-the-counter [OTC]) medicines that contain a dental anesthetic may be used in children 2 years of age and older. However, these other nonprescription products should not be used in infants or children younger than 2 years of age unless prescribed by a health care professional.

Older adults—Elderly people are especially sensitive to the effects of many local anesthetics. This may increase the chance of side effects during treatment, especially with lidocaine. Nonprescription (over-the-counter [OTC]) products containing local anesthetics are not likely to cause problems. However, elderly people should be especially careful not to use more medicine than directed on the package label, unless otherwise directed by a medical doctor or a dentist.

Other medicines—Although certain medicines should not be used together at all, in other cases two different medicines may be used together even if an interaction might occur. In these cases, your doctor may want to change the dose, or other precautions may be necessary. Before you use a dental anesthetic, check with your medical doctor, dentist, or pharmacist if you are taking any other prescription or nonprescription (over-the-counter [OTC]) medicine.

Proper Use of This Medicine

For safe and effective use of this medicine:
- Follow your medical doctor's or dentist's instructions if this medicine was prescribed.
- Follow the manufacturer's package directions if you are treating yourself.
- *Do not use more of this medicine, do not use it more often, and do not use it for a longer time than directed.* To do so may increase the chance of absorption into the body and the risk of side effects. This is particularly important for young children and elderly patients, especially with lidocaine.
- Dental anesthetics should be used only for conditions being treated by your medical doctor or dentist or for problems listed in the package directions. *Do not use any of them for other problems without first checking with your medical doctor or dentist.* These medicines should not be used if certain kinds of infections are present.

To use *the viscous (very thick) liquid form of lidocaine* (e.g., Xylocaine Viscous):
- This medicine may cause serious side effects if too much of it is swallowed. Be certain that you understand exactly how you are to use this medicine, and whether or not you are to swallow it. Follow your medical doctor's or dentist's directions very carefully. Also, *be very careful to measure the exact amount of medicine that you are to use.* Use a special measuring spoon to measure the amount; regular household teaspoons or soup spoons that you use at the table may not measure the amount correctly. These measures are especially important when this medicine is used for young children, who are especially sensitive to its effects.
- If you are using this medicine for a problem in the mouth, you may apply it to the sore places with a cotton-tipped applicator. Or, you may swish the measured amount of medicine around in your mouth until you are certain that it has reached all of the sore places. *Do not swallow*

the medicine unless your medical doctor or dentist has told you to do so.
- If you are using this medicine for a problem in the throat, gargle with the measured amount of medicine as directed by your doctor. *Do not swallow the medicine unless your doctor has told you to do so.*

To use *benzocaine film-forming gel* (e.g., Oratect Gel):
- Children may find it difficult to apply this medicine correctly. They should be helped by an adult.
- First, dry the area where the medicine is needed, using a swab included in the package.
- Apply the gel to a second swab. Then roll the swab over the dried area.
- Keep your mouth open and dry for about 30 to 60 seconds after applying the medicine. A film will form where you placed the medicine.
- Do not remove the film. It will slowly disappear and should be gone about 6 hours after the medicine was applied.

To use *other gel or liquid forms of a dental anesthetic:*
- Apply the medicine to the sore places with a clean finger, a cotton-tipped applicator, or a piece of gauze.
- When relieving pain caused by dentures or other dental appliances, *do not apply this medicine directly to the appliance, and do not place the appliance in your mouth while the medicine is there,* unless directed to do so by your dentist. Instead, apply the medicine to the sore areas in your mouth and wait until the pain is relieved. Then rinse your mouth with water before replacing the appliance.

To use *benzocaine dental paste* (e.g., Orabase-B with Benzocaine):
- Use a cotton-tipped applicator to dab small amounts of the medicine onto the sore places. Do not rub or try to spread the medicine with your finger while you are applying it, because the medicine will become crumbly and gritty.

To use *aerosol or spray forms of a dental anesthetic:*
- To help prevent unwanted effects, be very careful not to inhale (breathe in) the medicine. Also, do not spray the back of your mouth or throat with it unless your medical doctor or dentist directs you to do so.

To use *lozenge forms of benzocaine, benzocaine and menthol, or dyclonine:*
- These lozenges should be dissolved slowly in the mouth. Do not bite or chew them or swallow them whole. Before giving a lozenge to a young child, be sure that the child understands these directions and will follow them.

Dosing—The dose of these medicines will be different for different patients. *Follow your health care professional's orders or the directions on the label.* The following information includes only the average doses of these medicines. *If your dose is different, do not change it* unless your medical doctor or dentist tells you to do so.

For benzocaine
- For *dental paste* dosage form:
  —For sores in and around the mouth, sore gums, or pain caused by dental appliances:
  - Adults, teenagers, and children 6 years of age and older—Apply a small amount of the medicine to the painful areas.
  - Children up to 6 years of age—Use and dose must be determined by your health care professional.

- For *film-forming gel, liquid, and ointment* dosage forms:
  —For sores in and around the mouth, toothache, sore gums, or pain caused by dental appliances:
  - Adults, teenagers, and children 2 years of age and older—Apply a small amount of medicine to the painful areas up to four times a day.
  - Children up to 2 years of age—Use and dose must be determined by your health care professional.

- For *gel* dosage form:
  —For sores in and around the mouth, toothache, sore gums, or pain caused by dental appliances:
  - Adults, teenagers, and children 2 years of age and older—Apply a small amount of medicine to the painful areas up to four times a day.
  - Children up to 2 years of age—Use and dose must be determined by your health care professional.
  —For teething pain:
  - Infants up to 4 months of age—Use and dose must be determined by your health care professional.
  - Infants and children 4 months to 2 years of age—Apply a small amount of the 7.5% or 10% benzocaine gel to sore gums up to four times a day.
  - Children 2 years of age and older—Apply any strength of benzocaine gel to sore gums up to four times a day.

- For *lozenge* dosage form:
  —For pain in the mouth or throat:
  - Adults and teenagers—One lozenge, dissolved slowly in the mouth every two hours as needed.
  - Children up to 2 years of age—Use and dose must be determined by your health care professional.
  - Children 2 years of age and older—One children's strength (5-milligram [mg]) lozenge, dissolved slowly in the mouth every two hours as needed.

- For *aerosol spray* dosage form:
  —For pain in the mouth:
  - Adults and teenagers—One or 2 sprays, pointed at the sore places. Each spray should last about one second.
  - Children—Use and dose must be determined by your dentist.

For benzocaine and menthol combination
- For *lozenge* dosage form:
  —For pain in the mouth or throat:
  - Adults, teenagers, and children 2 years of age and older—One lozenge, dissolved slowly in the mouth every two hours as needed.
  - Children up to 2 years of age—Use and dose must be determined by your health care professional.

For benzocaine and phenol combination
- For *gel* dosage form:
  —For sores in and around the mouth, teething, toothache, sore gums, or pain caused by dental appliances:
  - Adults, teenagers, and children 2 years of age and older—Apply a small amount of medicine to the painful areas up to four times a day.

- Children up to 2 years of age—Use and dose must be determined by your health care professional.

- For *liquid* dosage form:
  —For sores in and around the mouth, toothache, sore gums, or pain caused by dental appliances:
  - Adults, teenagers, and children 2 years of age and older—Apply a small amount of medicine to the painful areas up to four times a day.
  - Children up to 2 years of age—Use and dose must be determined by your health care professional.

For dyclonine
- For *lozenge* dosage form:
  —For pain in the mouth or throat:
  - Adults and teenagers—One 2-milligram (mg) or 3-mg lozenge, dissolved slowly in the mouth every two hours as needed.
  - Children up to 2 years of age—Use and dose must be determined by your health care professional.
  - Children 2 years of age and older—One children's strength (1.2-mg) lozenge, dissolved slowly in the mouth every two hours as needed.

For lidocaine
- For *dental liquid* dosage form (e.g., Zilactin-L):
  —For sores on the lips and around the mouth:
  - Adults and teenagers—Apply to sores every one or two hours for the first three days. Then apply as needed.
  - Children—Dose must be determined by your health care professional.

- For *dental ointment* dosage form:
  —For gum pain:
  - Adults—Apply a small amount of medicine to the sore places. Do not apply the ointment directly to dentures, braces, or other dental appliances, unless your dentist has directed you to do so.
  - Children—Use and dose must be determined by your health care professional.

- For *aerosol spray* dosage form:
  —For pain in the mouth:
  - Adults and teenagers—Two sprays, pointed at the sore places. Do not use more than twenty sprays a day.
  - Children—Use and dose must be determined by your health care professional.

- For *viscous (very thick) solution* dosage form (e.g., Xylocaine Viscous):
  —For pain in the mouth:
  - Adults and teenagers—One tablespoonful of medicine (or less), swished around in the mouth, then spit out. Or, apply a total of 1 tablespoonful (or less) to the sore places with a cotton-tipped applicator. This medicine should not be used more often than every three hours.
  - Infants and children up to 3 years of age—Apply a total of one-fourth of a teaspoonful (or less) to the sore places with a cotton-tipped applicator. This medicine should not be used more often than every three hours.
  - Children 3 years of age and older—Apply a small amount of medicine to the sore places with a cotton-tipped applicator. The largest amount that

can be used must be determined by your health care professional.

—For sore throat pain:
- Adults and teenagers—One tablespoonful, used as a gargle. Swallow after gargling only if directed to do so by your doctor. Otherwise, spit out the medicine after gargling with it.
- Children—Dose must be determined by your doctor.

Missed dose—If your health care professional has directed you to use this medicine on a regular schedule, and you miss a dose, use it as soon as possible. However, if it is almost time for your next dose, skip the missed dose and go back to your regular dosing schedule. Do not double doses.

Storage—To store this medicine:
- Keep out of the reach of children.
- Store away from heat and direct light.
- Do not store throat lozenge forms of benzocaine, benzocaine and menthol combination, or dyclonine in the bathroom, near the kitchen sink, or in other damp places. Heat or moisture may cause the medicine to break down.
- Keep the medicine from freezing.
- Do not puncture, break, or burn aerosol containers, even when they are empty.
- Do not keep outdated medicine or medicine no longer needed. Be sure that any discarded medicine is out of the reach of children.

Precautions While Using This Medicine

Check with your medical doctor:
- If you are using this medicine for a sore throat and your sore throat is severe or lasts for more than 2 days.
- If other symptoms, such as fever, headache, skin rash, swelling, nausea, or vomiting, are also present.

You may have a condition that needs other treatment.

Check with your health care professional:
- If you are using this medicine for pain or sores in or around the mouth and your condition does not get better within 7 days or gets worse.
- If you notice other symptoms, such as swelling, rash, or fever.

You may have a condition that needs other treatment.

Check with your dentist:
- If you are using this medicine for a toothache. This medicine should not be used for a long time. It is meant to relieve toothache pain temporarily, until the problem causing the toothache can be corrected. Arrange for treatment as soon as possible.
- If you are using this medicine to relieve pain caused by new dentures or other dental appliances, an adjustment to your appliance may be needed to prevent more soreness. Also, if your dentist has ordered you to apply this medicine to the appliance before inserting it or to keep the appliance in your mouth while using the medicine, he or she will want to make sure that the medicine is not causing any unwanted effects.

False test results may occur if benzocaine or lidocaine is present in your body when a certain laboratory test is done. This test uses a medicine called bentiromide (e.g., Chymex) to show how well your pancreas is working. You should not use any products containing benzocaine or lidocaine for about 72 hours (3 days) before this test is done.

If you are using this medicine in the back of the mouth, or in the throat, *do not eat or drink anything for one hour after using it.* When this medicine is applied to these areas, it may interfere with swallowing and cause choking.

Do not chew gum or food while your mouth or throat feels numb after you use this medicine. To do so may cause an injury. You may accidentally bite your tongue or the inside of your cheeks.

Side Effects of This Medicine

Along with its needed effects, a medicine may cause some unwanted effects. Although not all of these side effects may occur, if they do occur they may need medical attention.

Stop using this medicine and check with your medical doctor or dentist immediately if any of the following side effects occur:

Less common
 Large swellings that look like hives on skin or in mouth or throat

Signs and symptoms of too much medicine being absorbed by the body
 Blurred or double vision; confusion; convulsions (seizures); dizziness or lightheadedness; drowsiness; feeling hot, cold, or numb; headache; increased sweating; ringing or buzzing in the ears; shivering or trembling; slow or irregular heartbeat; troubled breathing; unusual anxiety, excitement, nervousness, or restlessness; unusual paleness; unusual tiredness or weakness

Also, check with your health care professional as soon as possible if any of the following side effects occur:

Less common
 Burning, stinging, swelling, or tenderness not present before treatment; skin rash, redness, itching, or hives in or around the mouth

Other side effects not listed above may also occur in some patients. If you notice any other effects, check with your medical doctor or dentist.

Revised: 06/13/00

ANESTHETICS   Parenteral-Local

Commonly used brand name(s):

In the U.S.—

Carbocaine[7]	Nesacaine[3]
Carbocaine with Neo-Cobefrin[7]	Nesacaine-MPF[3]
Chirocaine[5]	Novocain[9]
Citanest Forte[8]	Octocaine[6]
Citanest Plain[8]	Polocaine[7]
Dalcaine[6]	Polocaine-MPF[7]
Dilocaine[6]	Pontocaine[10]
Duranest[4]	Sensorcaine[2]
Duranest-MPF[4]	Sensorcaine-MPF[2]
Isocaine[7]	Sensorcaine-MPF Spinal[2]
L-Caine[6]	Septocaine[1]
Lidoject-1[6]	Xylocaine[6]
Lidoject-2[6]	Xylocaine-MPF[6]
Marcaine[2]	Xylocaine-MPF with Glucose[6]
Marcaine Spinal[2]	

In Canada—

Astracaine 4%[1]	Octocaine-100[6]
Astracaine 4% Forte[1]	Polocaine[7]
Carbocaine[7]	Pontocaine[10]
Citanest Forte[8]	Sensorcaine[2]
Citanest Plain[8]	Sensorcaine Forte[2]
Isocaine 2%[7]	Ultracaine D-S[1]
Isocaine 3%[7]	Ultracaine D-S Forte[1]
Marcaine[2]	Xylocaine[6]
Nesacaine-CE[3]	Xylocaine Test Dose[6]
Novocain[9]	Xylocaine 5% Spinal[6]
Octocaine-50[6]	

Another commonly used name for lidocaine is lignocaine.

Note: For quick reference, the following anesthetics are numbered to match the corresponding brand names.

This information applies to the following medicines:

1. Articaine (AR-ti-kane)
2. Bupivacaine (byoo-PIV-a-kane)‡
3. Chloroprocaine (klor-oh-PROE-kane)‡
4. Etidocaine (e-TI-doe-kane)†
5. Levobupivacaine (Lee-voe-byoo-PIV-a-kane)†
6. Lidocaine (LYE-doe-kane)‡§
7. Mepivacaine (me-PIV-a-kane)‡
8. Prilocaine (PRIL-oh-kane)§
9. Procaine (PROE-kane)‡
10. Tetracaine (TET-ra-kane)

†Not commercially available in Canada.
‡Generic name product may be available in the U.S.
§Generic name product may be available in Canada.

Description

Parenteral-local anesthetics (an-ess-THET-iks) are given by injection to cause loss of feeling before and during surgery, dental procedures (including dental surgery), or labor and delivery. These medicines do not cause loss of consciousness.

These medicines are given only by or under the immediate supervision of a medical doctor or dentist, or by a specially trained nurse, in the doctor's office or in a hospital.

These medicines are available in the following dosage forms:

Parenteral

Articaine
  • Injection (U.S. and Canada)
Bupivacaine
  • Injection (U.S. and Canada)
Chloroprocaine
  • Injection (U.S. and Canada)
Etidocaine
  • Injection (U.S.)
Levobupivacaine
  • Injection (U.S.)
Lidocaine
  • Injection (U.S. and Canada)
Mepivacaine
  • Injection (U.S. and Canada)
Prilocaine
  • Injection (U.S. and Canada)
Procaine
  • Injection (U.S. and Canada)
Tetracaine
  • Injection (U.S. and Canada)

Before Receiving This Medicine

In deciding to use a medicine, the risks of using the medicine must be weighed against the good it will do. This is a decision you and your medical doctor, dentist, or nurse will make. For local anesthetics, the following should be considered:

Allergies—Tell your medical doctor, dentist, or nurse if you have ever had any unusual or allergic reaction to a local anesthetic or to epinephrine (e.g., Adrenalin). Also tell your medical doctor, dentist, nurse, or pharmacist if you are allergic to any other substances, such as sulfites or other preservatives, especially aminobenzoic acid (also called para-aminobenzoic acid [PABA]).

Pregnancy—Local anesthetics have not been reported to cause birth defects in humans.

Use of a local anesthetic during labor and delivery may rarely cause unwanted effects. These medicines may increase the length of labor by making it more difficult for the mother to bear down (push). They may also cause unwanted effects in the fetus or newborn baby, especially if certain medical problems are present at the time of delivery. Before receiving a local anesthetic for labor and delivery, you should discuss with your doctor the good that this medicine will do as well as the risks of receiving it.

Breast-feeding—It is not known whether local anesthetics pass into breast milk. However, these medicines have not been reported to cause problems in nursing babies.

Children—Children may be especially sensitive to the effects of parenteral-local anesthetics. This may increase the chance of side effects.

Older adults—Elderly people are especially sensitive to the effects of parenteral-local anesthetics. This may increase the chance of side effects.

Other medicines—Although certain medicines should not be used together at all, in other cases two different medicines may be used together even if an interaction might occur. In these cases, your medical doctor, dentist, or nurse may want to change the dose, or other precautions may be necessary. It is very important that you tell the person in charge if you are taking:

• Beta-adrenergic blocking agents (carteolol [e.g., Cartrol], carvedilol [e.g., Coreg], labetolol [e.g., Normodyne], nadolol [e.g., Corgard], oxprenolol [e.g., Trasicor], penbutolol [e.g., Levatol], pindolol [e.g., Visken], propranolol [e.g., Inderal], sotalol [e.g., Sotacor], timolol [e.g., Blocadren]) or
• Carteolol (ophthalmic) (e.g., Ocupress) or
• Levobunolol (ophthalmic) (e.g., Betagan) or
• Metipranolol (ophthalmic) (e.g., OptiPranolol) or
• Timolol (ophthalmic) (e.g., Timoptic)—Use of some local anesthetics with these medicines may increase the risk of high blood pressure or a slow heart rate
• Central nervous system (CNS) depressants (medicines that cause drowsiness)—Use of local anesthetics with these medicines may increase the risk that drowsiness will occur
• Digoxin (e.g., Lanoxin)—Use of some local anesthetics with this medicine may increase the risk of irregular heartbeats
• Haloperidol (e.g., Haldol) or
• Phenothiazines (e.g., Phenergan)—Use of these medicines may reduce the effectiveness of the local anesthetic
• Tricyclic antidepressants (amitriptyline [e.g., Elavil], amoxapine [e.g., Asendin], clomipramine [e.g., Anafranil], desipramine [e.g., Norpramin], doxepin [e.g., Sinequan], imipramine [e.g., Tofranil], nortriptyline [e.g.,

Aventyl], protriptyline [e.g., Vivactil], trimipramine [e.g., Surmontil]) or

- Maprotiline (e.g., Ludiomil)—Use of some local anesthetics with these medicines may increase the chance of some problems, including high blood pressure and irregular heartbeats

- Any other medicine, prescription or nonprescription (over-the-counter [OTC]), or
- "Street" drugs, such as amphetamines ("uppers"), barbiturates ("downers"), cocaine (including "crack"), marijuana, phencyclidine (PCP, "angel dust"), and heroin or other narcotics—Serious side effects may occur if anyone gives you a local anesthetic without knowing that you have taken another medicine

Other medical problems—The presence of other medical problems may affect the use of local anesthetics. Make sure you tell your medical doctor, dentist, or nurse if you have *any* other medical problems, especially:

- Asthma—Increased chance of allergic-like reactions with use of some local anesthetics

- Brain infection or tumor or
- Blood clotting disorders—Increased chance of bleeding with injection of local anesthetics

- Diabetes mellitus (sugar diabetes)—Use of local anesthetics can cause stress on your heart if you have diabetes mellitus

- Heart disease—Use of local anesthetics can worsen some kinds of heart disease

- History of migraine headaches—Use of local anesthetics can worsen headaches

- Hypertension (high blood pressure) or
- Hypotension (low blood pressure)—Use of local anesthetics can cause hypotension or hypertension

- Hyperthyroidism—Use of some local anesthetics can cause stress on your heart if you have hyperthyroidism

- Kidney disease or
- Liver disease—Increased chance of side effects

- Methemoglobinemia—Prilocaine may make this condition worse

- Peripheral vascular disease—Use of some local anesthetics can make this condition worse or can cause your blood pressure to increase

- Skin infection or inflammation—Your physician may not want to inject the local anesthetic into infected or inflamed skin because the local anesthetic may not work as well

Proper Use of This Medicine

Dosing—The dose of a local anesthetic will be different for different patients. Your health care professional will decide on the right amount for you, depending on:

- Your age;
- Your general physical condition;
- The reason the local anesthetic is being given; and
- Other medicines you are taking or will receive before or after the local anesthetic is given.

Precautions After Receiving This Medicine

For patients going home before the numbness or loss of feeling caused by a local anesthetic wears off:

- During the time that the injected area feels numb, serious injury can occur without your knowing about it. Be especially careful to avoid injury until the anesthetic wears off or feeling returns to the area.
- If you have received a local anesthetic injection in your mouth, do not chew gum or food while your mouth feels numb. You may injure yourself by biting your tongue or the inside of your cheeks.

Side Effects of This Medicine

Along with its needed effects, a medicine may cause some unwanted effects. Although not all of these side effects may occur, if they do occur they may need medical attention. While you are in the hospital or your medical doctor's or dentist's office, your medical doctor, dentist, or nurse will carefully follow the effects of any medicine you have received. However, some effects may not be noticed until later.

Check with your dentist or medical doctor immediately if any of the following side effects occur:
  Less common or rare
    Bluish lips and fingernails; breathing problems; chest pain; convulsions (seizures); dizziness; drowsiness; fatigue; fever; headache; irregular heartbeat; itching; nausea and/or vomiting; pale skin, troubled breathing, exertional, unusual bleeding or bruising, unusual tiredness or weakness; raised red swellings on the skin, lips, tongue, or in the throat; rapid heart rate; restlessness; unusual tiredness or weakness

Check with your dentist or medical doctor as soon as possible if any of the following side effects occur:
  Less common or rare
    Back pain; constipation; difficulty in opening the mouth; inability to hold bowel movement and/or urine; loss of sexual function; paralysis of legs; persistent numbness; prolonged numbness or tingling of lips and mouth; shivering; skin rash; tingling or "pins and needles" sensation

Other side effects not listed above may also occur in some patients. If you notice any other effects, check with your medical doctor or dentist.

Revised: 09/06/2000

ANESTHETICS   Rectal

Commonly used brand name(s):

In the U.S.—

Americaine Hemorrhoidal[1]	Pontocaine Ointment[5]
Nupercainal[2]	ProctoFoam/non-steroid[3]
Fleet Relief[3]	Tronolane[3]
Pontocaine Cream†[4]	Tronothane[3]

In Canada—
  Nupercainal[2]
  Tronothane[3]

Other commonly used names are: amethocaine[4], cinchocaine[2], ethyl aminobenzoate[1], pramocaine[3].

Note: For quick reference, the following anesthetics are numbered to match the corresponding brand names.

This information applies to the following medicines:
1. Benzocaine (BEN-zoe-kane)
2. Dibucaine (DYE-byoo-kane)‡
3. Pramoxine (pra-MOX-een)
4. Tetracaine (TET-ra-kane)
5. Tetracaine and Menthol (TET-ra-kane and MEN-thol)

---

‡Generic name product may be available in the U.S.
†Not commercially available in Canada.

Description

Rectal anesthetics (an-ess-THET-iks) are used to relieve the pain and itching of hemorrhoids (piles) and other problems in the rectal area. However, if you have hemorrhoids that bleed, especially after a bowel movement, check with your doctor before using this medicine. Bleeding may mean that you have a condition that needs other treatment.

These medicines are available without a prescription; however, your doctor may have special instructions on the proper use and dose for your medical problem.

These medicines are available in the following dosage forms:

Rectal
Benzocaine
  • Ointment (U.S.)
Dibucaine
  • Ointment (U.S. and Canada)
Pramoxine
  • Aerosol foam (U.S.)
  • Cream (U.S. and Canada)
  • Ointment (U.S.)
Tetracaine
  • Cream (U.S.)
Tetracaine and Menthol
  • Ointment (U.S.)

Before Using This Medicine

If you are using this medicine without a prescription, carefully read and follow any precautions on the label. For rectal anesthetics, the following should be considered:

Allergies—Tell your doctor if you have ever had any unusual or allergic reaction to a local anesthetic, especially one that was applied to any part of the body as a liquid, cream, ointment, or spray. Also tell your health care professional if you are allergic to any other substances, such as foods, preservatives, or dyes.

Pregnancy—Rectal anesthetics have not been reported to cause birth defects or other problems in humans.

Breast-feeding—Rectal anesthetics have not been reported to cause problems in nursing babies.

Children—Children may be especially sensitive to the effects of local anesthetics. This may increase the chance of side effects during treatment.

Older adults—Elderly people are especially sensitive to the effects of local anesthetics. This may increase the chance of side effects during treatment.

Other medicines—Although certain medicines should not be used together at all, in other cases two different medicines may be used together even if an interaction might occur. In these cases, your doctor may want to change the dose, or other precautions may be necessary. Before you use a rectal anesthetic, check with your health care professional if you are taking any other prescription or nonprescription (over-the-counter [OTC]) medicine.

Other medical problems—The presence of other medical problems may affect the use of rectal anesthetics. Make sure you tell your doctor if you have any other medical problems, especially:

  • Infection at or near place of treatment or
  • Large sores, broken skin, or severe injury at or near place of treatment—The chance of unwanted effects may be increased

---

Proper Use of This Medicine

For safe and effective use of this medicine:

  • Rectal anesthetics usually come with patient directions. Read them carefully before using the medicine, even if it was prescribed by your doctor. Check with your pharmacist if you have any questions about how to use the product.
  • Follow your doctor's instructions if this medicine was prescribed.
  • Follow the manufacturer's package directions if you are treating yourself.
  • *Do not use more of this medicine, do not use it more often, and do not use it for a longer time than directed.* To do so may increase the chance of absorption into the body and the chance of unwanted effects.

This medicine should be used only for conditions being treated by your doctor or for problems listed on the package label. *Do not use it for other problems without first checking with your doctor.* This medicine should not be used if certain kinds of infections are present.

For *applying a rectal anesthetic to the area around the rectum:*

  • First, clean the area, using mild soap and water or a cleansing wipe. Rinse the area carefully and dry it gently with a soft towel or toilet paper.
  • Apply a small amount of medicine to the sore area, using a piece of gauze, a tissue, or a "finger cot."

For *inserting a rectal cream or ointment inside the rectum:*

  • Use only products that come packaged in pre-filled applicators or that come packaged with a special inserter called a rectal tube.
  • If you are using a product that has an inserter (rectal tube) packaged separately from the tube of cream or ointment:
    —Remove the cap from the tube of cream or ointment. Attach the inserter to the top of the tube. Squeeze the tube until a little cream or ointment comes out on the inserter. Then spread the cream or ointment over the inserter.
    —Place the inserter into your rectum and squeeze the tube until a small amount of medicine comes out. Then remove the inserter from your body.
    —Remove the inserter from the tube and replace the cap. Then wash the applicator carefully.
  • If you are using the product that comes in pre-filled applicators:
    —Follow the manufacturer's directions for using the applicator and inserting the medicine. Each applicator is meant to be used only once. Throw the applicator away after using it.

© 2002 MICROMEDEX Thomson Healthcare

For *inserting the rectal aerosol foam (e.g., Proctofoam/nonsteroid) into the rectum:*
- Do not insert the container itself into your rectum. Use the applicator provided.
- To fill the container—First, shake the container hard for several seconds. Then, holding the container upright, insert it into the applicator. Press the cap of the container until the foam reaches the fill line of the applicator. Remove the applicator from the container.
- To use the medicine—Place a small amount of foam on the tip of the applicator. Insert the applicator into your rectum, then push the plunger as far as possible. Remove the applicator. Then take it apart and wash it carefully.

Dosing—The dose of rectal anesthetics will be different for different patients. *Follow your doctor's orders or the directions on the label.* The following information includes only the average doses of these medicines. *If your dose is different, do not change it* unless your doctor tells you to do so.

For benzocaine
- For pain and itching of hemorrhoids or other problems in the rectal area:
  - —For *rectal ointment* dosage form:
    - Adults—Apply a small amount of ointment to the area around the rectum up to six times a day.
    - Children—Use and dose must be determined by the doctor.

For dibucaine
- For pain and itching of hemorrhoids or other problems in the rectal area:
  - —For *rectal ointment* dosage form:
    - Adults—Insert a small amount of ointment into the rectum three or four times a day, in the morning, in the evening, and after bowel movements. Or, apply a small amount of ointment to the area around the rectum three or four times a day.
    - Children—Use and dose must be determined by the doctor.

For pramoxine
- For pain and itching of hemorrhoids or other problems in the rectal area:
  - —For *rectal cream* dosage form:
    - Adults—Apply a small amount to the area around the rectum up to five times a day, in the morning, in the evening, and after bowel movements.
    - Children—Use and dose must be determined by the doctor.
  - —For *rectal ointment* dosage form:
    - Adults—Insert a small amount of ointment into the rectum up to five times a day, in the morning, in the evening, and after bowel movements. Or, apply a small amount to the area around the rectum up to five times a day, in the morning, in the evening, and after bowel movements.
  - —For the *rectal aerosol foam* dosage form:
    - Adults—Insert 1 applicatorful into the rectum two or three times a day. Or, apply a small amount to the area around the rectum three or four times a day.
    - Children—Use and dose must be determined by the doctor.

For tetracaine and for tetracaine and menthol
- For pain and itching of hemorrhoids or other problems in the rectal area:

—For the *rectal cream* or *rectal ointment* dosage form:
- Adults—Insert a small amount into the rectum up to six times a day. Or, apply a small amount to the area around the rectum up to six times a day.
- Children—Use and dose must be determined by the doctor.

Missed dose—If your doctor has directed you to use this medicine on a regular schedule and you miss a dose, use it as soon as possible. However, if it is almost time for your next dose, skip the missed dose and go back to your regular dosing schedule.

Storage—To store this medicine:
- Keep out of the reach of children.
- Store away from heat and direct light.
- Keep the medicine from freezing.
- Do not puncture, break, or burn the pramoxine aerosol foam container, even after it is empty.
- Do not keep outdated medicine or medicine no longer needed. Be sure that any discarded medicine is out of the reach of children.

Precautions While Using This Medicine

Check with your doctor:
- If your condition does not improve after you have been using this medicine regularly for 7 days, or if it becomes worse.
- If any bleeding from the rectum occurs.
- If you notice any rash, redness, or irritation that was not present before you started using this medicine.

False test results may occur if benzocaine or tetracaine is present in your body when a certain laboratory test is done. This test uses a medicine called bentiromide (e.g., Chymex) to show how well your pancreas is working. You should not use any products containing benzocaine or tetracaine for about 72 hours (3 days) before this test is done.

Side Effects of This Medicine

Along with its needed effects, a medicine may cause some unwanted effects. Although not all of these side effects may occur, if they do occur they may need medical attention.

Stop using this medicine and check with your doctor immediately if any of the following side effects occur:
Signs and symptoms of too much medicine being absorbed by the body
Blurred or double vision; confusion; convulsions (seizures); dizziness or lightheadedness; drowsiness; feeling hot, cold, or numb; increased sweating; ringing or buzzing in ears; shivering or trembling; slow or irregular heartbeat; unusual anxiety, excitement, nervousness, or restlessness; unusual paleness

Also, check with your doctor as soon as possible if any of the following side effects occur:
Less common
Burning, stinging, swelling, or tenderness not present before treatment; skin rash, redness, itching, or hives at or near place of application

Other side effects not listed above may also occur in some patients. If you notice any other effects, check with your doctor.

Revised: 09/01/94

ANESTHETICS   Topical

Commonly used brand name(s):

In the U.S.—

Almay Anti-itch Lotion[7]
Americaine Topical Anesthetic
    First Aid Ointment[1]
Americaine Topical Anesthetic
    Spray[1]
Butesin Picrate[3]
Dermoplast[2]
Lagol[1]

Nupercainal Cream[4]
Nupercainal Ointment[4]
Pontocaine Cream[8]
Pontocaine Ointment[9]
Pramegel[7]
Prax[6]
Tronothane[6]
Xylocaine[5]

In Canada—

After Burn Double Strength
    Gel[5]
After Burn Double Strength
    Spray[5]
After Burn Gel[5]
After Burn Spray[5]
Alphacaine[5]
Dermoplast[2]

Endocaine[1]
Norwood Sunburn Spray[5]
Nupercainal Ointment[4]
Pramegel[7]
Shield Burnasept Spray[1]
Tronothane[6]
Xylocaine[5]

Other commonly used names are: Amethocaine[8], Butyl aminobenzoate[3], Cinchocaine[4], Ethyl aminobenzoate[1], Lignocaine[5], Pramocaine[6].

Note: For quick reference, the following anesthetics are numbered to match the corresponding brand names.

This information applies to the following medicines:
1. Benzocaine (BEN-zoe-kane)‡
2. Benzocaine and Menthol (BEN-zoe-kane and MEN-thol)
3. Butamben (byoo-TAM-ben)
4. Dibucaine (DYE-byoo-kane)‡
5. Lidocaine (LYE-doe-kane)‡
6. Pramoxine (pra-MOX-een)
7. Pramoxine and Menthol (pra-MOX-een and MEN-thol)
8. Tetracaine (TET-ra-kane)
9. Tetracaine and Menthol (TET-ra-kane and MEN-thol)†

†Not commercially available in Canada.
‡Generic name product may be available in the U.S.

Description

This medicine belongs to a group of medicines known as topical local anesthetics (an-ess-THET-iks). Topical anesthetics are used to relieve pain and itching caused by conditions such as sunburn or other minor burns, insect bites or stings, poison ivy, poison oak, poison sumac, and minor cuts and scratches.

Topical anesthetics deaden the nerve endings in the skin. They do not cause unconsciousness as do general anesthetics used for surgery.

Most topical anesthetics are available without a prescription; however, your doctor may have special instructions on the proper use and dose for your medical problem.

These medicines are available in the following dosage forms:

Topical
Benzocaine
  • Cream (U.S.)
  • Ointment (U.S.)
  • Topical aerosol (U.S.)
  • Topical spray solution (Canada)
Benzocaine and Menthol
  • Lotion (U.S.)
  • Topical aerosol solution (U.S. and Canada)
Butamben
  • Ointment (U.S.)

Dibucaine
  • Cream (U.S.)
  • Ointment (U.S. and Canada)
Lidocaine
  • Film-forming gel (U.S.)
  • Jelly (Canada)
  • Ointment (U.S. and Canada)
  • Topical aerosol (Canada)
  • Topical spray solution (Canada)
Pramoxine
  • Cream (U.S. and Canada)
  • Lotion (U.S.)
Pramoxine and Menthol
  • Gel (U.S. and Canada)
  • Lotion (U.S.)
Tetracaine
  • Cream (U.S.)
Tetracaine and Menthol
  • Ointment (U.S.)

Before Using This Medicine

If you are using this medicine without a prescription, carefully read and follow any precautions on the label. For topical anesthetics, the following should be considered:

Allergies—Tell your doctor if you have ever had any unusual or allergic reaction to a local anesthetic, especially when applied to the skin or other areas of the body. Also tell your health care professional if you are allergic to any other substances, such as foods, preservatives, or dyes, especially aminobenzoic acid (also called para-aminobenzoic acid [PABA]), to parabens (preservatives in many foods and medicines), or to paraphenylenediamine (a hair dye).

Pregnancy—Although studies on effects in pregnancy have not been done in humans, topical anesthetics have not been reported to cause problems in humans. Lidocaine has not been shown to cause birth defects or other problems in animal studies. Other topical anesthetics have not been studied in animals.

Breast-feeding—Topical anesthetics have not been reported to cause problems in nursing babies.

Children—Benzocaine may be absorbed through the skin of young children and cause unwanted effects. There is no specific information comparing use of other topical anesthetics in children with use in other age groups, but it is possible that they may also cause unwanted effects in young children. Check with your doctor before using any product that contains a topical anesthetic for a child younger than 2 years of age.

Older adults—Many medicines have not been studied specifically in older people. Therefore, it may not be known whether they work exactly the same way they do in younger adults or if they cause different side effects or problems in older people. There is no specific information comparing use of topical anesthetics in the elderly with use in other age groups.

Other medicines—Although certain medicines should not be used together at all, in other cases two different medicines may be used together even if an interaction might occur. In these cases, your doctor may want to change the dose, or other precautions may be necessary. Tell your health care professional if you are taking any other prescription or nonprescription (over-the-counter [OTC]) medicine.

Other medical problems—The presence of other medical problems may affect the use of topical anesthetics. Before using a topical anesthetic, check with your health care professional if you have any other medical problems, especially:

- Infection at or near the place of application or
- Large sores, broken skin, or severe injury at the area of application—The chance of side effects may be increased

---

Proper Use of This Medicine

For safe and effective use of this medicine:

- Follow your doctor's instructions if this medicine was prescribed.
- Follow the manufacturer's package directions if you are treating yourself.
- Unless otherwise directed by your doctor, *do not use this medicine on large areas, especially if the skin is broken or scraped. Also, do not use it more often than directed on the package label, or for more than a few days at a time.* To do so may increase the chance of absorption through the skin and the chance of unwanted effects. This is especially important when benzocaine is used for children younger than 2 years of age.

This medicine should be used only for problems being treated by your doctor or conditions listed in the package directions. *Check with your doctor before using it for other problems, especially if you think that an infection may be present.* This medicine should not be used to treat certain kinds of skin infections or serious problems, such as severe burns.

Read the package label very carefully to see if the product contains any alcohol. Alcohol is flammable and can catch on fire. *Do not use any product containing alcohol near a fire or open flame, or while smoking. Also, do not smoke after applying one of these products until it has completely dried.*

If you are using this medicine on your face, *be very careful not to get it in your eyes, mouth, or nose.* If you are using an aerosol or spray form of this medicine, do not spray it directly on your face. Instead, use your hand or an applicator (for example, a sterile gauze pad or a cotton swab) to apply the medicine.

For patients using *butamben:*

- Butamben may stain clothing and discolor hair. It may not be possible to remove the stains. To avoid this, do not touch your clothing or your hair while applying the medicine. Also, cover the treated area with a loose bandage after applying butamben, to protect your clothes.

Dosing—The dose of a topical anesthetic will be different for different patients. *Follow your doctor's orders or the directions on the label.* The following information includes only the average doses of these medicines. *If your dose is different, do not change it* unless your doctor tells you to do so.

For benzocaine and for benzocaine and menthol combination
- For *topical* dosage forms (aerosol solution, cream, lotion, ointment, and spray solution):
  —For pain and itching caused by minor skin conditions:
    - Adults and children 2 years of age and older—Apply to the affected area three or four times a day as needed.
    - Children younger than 2 years of age—Dose must be determined by your doctor.

For butamben
- For *topical* dosage form (ointment):
  —For pain and itching caused by minor skin conditions:
    - Adults—Apply to the affected area three or four times a day as needed.
    - Children—Dose must be determined by your doctor.

For dibucaine
- For *topical cream* dosage form:
  —For pain and itching caused by minor skin conditions:
    - Adults and children 2 years of age and older—Apply to the affected area three or four times a day as needed.
    - Children up to 2 years of age—Dose must be determined by your doctor.

- For *topical ointment* dosage form:
  —For pain and itching caused by minor skin conditions:
    - Adults—Apply to the affected area three or four times a day as needed. The largest amount that may be used in a twenty-four-hour period is 30 grams, but much smaller amounts are usually enough.
    - Children 2 years of age and older—Apply to the affected area three or four times a day as needed. Do not use more than 7.5 grams in a twenty-four-hour period.
    - Children up to 2 years of age—Dose must be determined by your doctor.

For lidocaine
- For *topical* dosage forms (aerosol solution, jelly, ointment, and spray solution):
  —For pain and itching caused by minor skin conditions:
    - Adults—Apply to the affected area three or four times a day as needed.
    - Children—Dose must be determined by your doctor.

For pramoxine and for pramoxine and menthol combination
- For *topical* dosage forms (cream, gel, and lotion):
  —For pain and itching caused by minor skin conditions:
    - Adults and children 2 years of age and older—Apply to the affected area three or four times a day as needed.
    - Children younger than 2 years of age—Dose must be determined by your doctor.

For tetracaine and for tetracaine and menthol combination
- For *topical* dosage forms (cream and ointment):
  —For pain and itching caused by minor skin conditions:
    - Adults and teenagers—Apply to the affected area three or four times a day as needed. The largest amount that may be used in a twenty-four-hour period is 30 grams (a whole tube of the medicine), but much smaller amounts are usually enough.

- Children 2 years of age and older—Apply to the affected area three or four times a day as needed. Do not use more than 7 grams (about one-fourth of a tube of the medicine) in a twenty-four-hour period.
- Children younger than 2 years of age—Dose must be determined by your doctor.

Missed dose—If your doctor has ordered you to use this medicine according to a regular schedule and you miss a dose, use it as soon as possible. However, if it is almost time for your next dose, skip the missed dose and use your next dose at the regularly scheduled time.

Storage—To store this medicine:

- Keep out of the reach of children.
- Store away from heat and direct light.
- Keep the medicine from freezing.
- Do not puncture, break, or burn aerosol containers, even when they are empty.
- Do not keep outdated medicine or medicine no longer needed. Be sure that any discarded medicine is out of the reach of children.

Precautions While Using This Medicine

After applying this medicine to the skin of a child, *watch the child carefully to make sure that he or she does not get any of the medicine into his or her mouth.* Topical anesthetics can cause serious side effects, especially in children, if any of the medicine gets into the mouth or is swallowed.

Stop using this medicine and check with your doctor:
- *If your condition does not improve within 7 days, or if it gets worse.*
- *If the area you are treating becomes infected.*
- *If you notice a skin rash, burning, stinging, swelling, or any other sign of irritation that was not present when you began using this medicine.*
- *If you swallow any of the medicine.*

Side Effects of This Medicine

Along with its needed effects, a medicine may cause some unwanted effects. Although not all of these side effects may occur, if they do occur they may need medical attention.

Check with your doctor immediately if any of the following side effects occur:

Less common
   Large swellings that look like hives on the skin or in the mouth or throat

Symptoms of too much medicine being absorbed by the body—very rare
   Blurred or double vision; confusion; convulsions (seizures); dizziness or lightheadedness; drowsiness; feeling hot, cold, or numb; headache; increased sweating; ringing or buzzing in the ears; shivering or trembling; slow or irregular heartbeat; troubled breathing; unusual anxiety, excitement, nervousness, or restlessness; unusual paleness; unusual tiredness or weakness

Also, check with your doctor as soon as possible if any of the following side effects occur:
   Burning, stinging, or tenderness not present before treatment; skin rash, redness, itching, or hives

Other side effects not listed above may also occur in some patients. If you notice any other effects, check with your doctor.

Revised: 08/29/94

ANGIOTENSIN-CONVERTING ENZYME (ACE) INHIBITORS
Systemic

Commonly used brand name(s):

In the U.S.—

Accupril[10]	Monopril[6]
Aceon[9]	Prinivil[7]
Altace[11]	Univasc[8]
Capoten[2]	Vasotec[4,5]
Lotensin[1]	Zestril[7]
Mavik[12]	

In Canada—

Accupril[10]	Mavik[12]
Altace[11]	Monopril[6]
Capoten[2]	Prinivil[7]
Coversyl[9]	Vasotec[4,5]
Inhibace[3]	Zestril[7]
Lotensin[1]	

Note: For quick reference, the following angiotensin-converting enzyme (ACE) inhibitors are numbered to match the corresponding brand names.

This information applies to the following medicines:
1. Benazepril (ben-AY-ze-pril)
2. Captopril (KAP-toe-pril)
3. Cilazapril (sye-LAY-za-pril)*
4. Enalapril (e-NAL-a-pril)
5. Enalaprilat (e-NAL-a-pril-at)
6. Fosinopril (foe-SIN-oh-pril)
7. Lisinopril (lyse-IN-oh-pril)
8. Moexipril (moe-EX-i-pril)†
9. Perindopril (per-IN-doe-pril)
10. Quinapril (KWIN-a-pril)
11. Ramipril (ra-MI-pril)
12. Trandolapril (tran-DOE-la-pril)

---

*Not commercially available in the U.S.
†Not commercially available in Canada.

Description

ACE inhibitors belong to the class of medicines called high blood pressure medicines (antihypertensives). They are used to treat high blood pressure (hypertension).

High blood pressure adds to the workload of the heart and arteries. If it continues for a long time, the heart and arteries may not function properly. This can damage the blood vessels of the brain, heart, and kidneys, resulting in a stroke, heart failure, or kidney failure. High blood pressure may also increase the risk of heart attacks. These problems may be less likely to occur if blood pressure is controlled.

Lisinopril, captopril, ramipril, and trandolapril are used in some patients after a heart attack. After a heart attack, some of the heart muscle is damaged and weakened. The heart muscle may continue to weaken as time goes by. This makes it more difficult for the heart to pump blood. Lisinopril use may be started within 24 hours after a heart attack to increase survival rate. Captopril, ramipril, and trandolapril help slow down the further weakening of the heart.

Captopril is also used to treat kidney problems in some diabetic patients who use insulin to control their diabetes. Over time, these kidney problems may get worse. Captopril may help slow down the further worsening of kidney problems.

In addition, some ACE inhibitors are used to treat congestive heart failure or may be used for other conditions as determined by your doctor.

The exact way that these medicines work is not known. They block an enzyme in the body that is necessary to produce a substance that causes blood vessels to tighten. As a result, they relax blood vessels. This lowers blood pressure and increases the supply of blood and oxygen to the heart.

These medicines are available only with your doctor's prescription, in the following dosage forms:

Oral
   Benazepril
     • Tablets (U.S. and Canada)
   Captopril
     • Tablets (U.S. and Canada)
   Cilazapril
     • Tablets (Canada)
   Enalapril
     • Tablets (U.S. and Canada)
   Fosinopril
     • Tablets (U.S. and Canada)
   Lisinopril
     • Tablets (U.S. and Canada)
   Moexipril
     • Tablets (U.S.)
   Perindopril
     • Tablets (U.S. and Canada)
   Quinapril
     • Tablets (U.S. and Canada)
   Ramipril
     • Capsules (U.S. and Canada)
   Trandolapril
     • Tablets (U.S. and Canada)

Parenteral
   Enalaprilat
     • Injection (U.S. and Canada)

Before Using This Medicine

In deciding to use a medicine, the risks of taking the medicine must be weighed against the good it will do. This is a decision you and your doctor will make. For the angiotensin-converting enzyme (ACE) inhibitors, the following should be considered:

Allergies—Tell your doctor if you have ever had any unusual or allergic reaction to benazepril, captopril, cilazapril, enalapril, fosinopril, lisinopril, moexipril, perindopril, quinapril, ramipril, or trandolapril. Also tell your health care professional if you are allergic to any other substances, such as foods, preservatives, or dyes.

Pregnancy—Use of ACE inhibitors during pregnancy, especially in the second and third trimesters (after the first three months) can cause low blood pressure, severe kidney failure, too much potassium, or even death in the newborn. *Therefore, it is important that you check with your doctor immediately if you think that you may be pregnant.* Be sure

that you have discussed this with your doctor before taking this medicine. In addition, if you are taking:

• *Benazepril*—Benazepril has not been shown to cause birth defects in rats when given in doses more than 300 times the highest recommended human dose.
• *Captopril*—Studies in rabbits and rats at doses up to 400 times the recommended human dose have shown that captopril causes an increase in deaths of the fetus and newborn. Also, captopril has caused deformed skulls in the offspring of rabbits given doses 2 to 70 times the recommended human dose.
• *Enalapril*—Studies in rats at doses many times the recommended human dose have shown that use of enalapril causes the fetus to be smaller than normal. Studies in rabbits have shown that enalapril causes an increase in fetal death. Enalapril has not been shown to cause birth defects in rats or rabbits.
• *Fosinopril*—Studies in rats have shown that fosinopril causes the fetus to be smaller than normal. Studies in rabbits have shown that fosinopril causes fetal death, probably due to extremely low blood pressure. In rats, birth defects such as skeletal and facial deformities were seen. However, it is not clear that the deformities were related to fosinopril. Birth defects were not seen in rabbits.
• *Lisinopril*—Studies in mice and rats at doses many times the recommended human dose have shown that use of lisinopril causes a decrease in successful pregnancies, a decrease in the weight of infants, and an increase in infant deaths. It has also caused a decrease in successful pregnancies and abnormal bone growth in rabbits. Lisinopril has not been shown to cause birth defects in mice, rats, or rabbits.
• *Moexipril*—Studies in rats given up to 90 times the recommended human dose, and studies in rabbits given up to 0.7 times the recommended human dose, did not show that moexipril causes birth defects in animals.
• *Perindopril*—Studies in rabbits given up to 50 times the recommended human dose, and monkeys given up to 17 times the recommended human dose, did not show that perindopril causes birth defects in animals.
• *Quinapril*—Studies in rats have shown that quinapril causes lower birth weights and changes in kidney structure of the fetus. However, birth defects were not seen in rabbits given quinapril.
• *Ramipril*—Studies in animals have shown that ramipril causes lower birth weights.
• *Trandolapril*—Studies in rabbits, rats, and monkeys did not show that trandolapril causes any birth defects in animals.

Breast-feeding—
• *Benazepril, captopril, enalapril, enalaprilat, and fosinopril*—These medicines pass into breast milk.
• *Cilazapril, lisinopril, moexipril, perindopril, quinapril, ramipril, and trandolapril*—It is not known whether these medicines pass into breast milk. However, these medicines have not been reported to cause problems in nursing babies.

Children—Children may be especially sensitive to the blood pressure–lowering effect of ACE inhibitors. This may increase the chance of side effects or other problems during treatment. Therefore, it is especially important that you discuss with the child's doctor the good that this medicine may do as well as the risks of using it.

Older adults—This medicine has been tested in a limited number of patients 65 years of age or older and has not been shown to cause different side effects or problems in older people than it does in younger adults.

Other medicines—Although certain medicines should not be used together at all, in other cases two different medicines may be used together even if an interaction might occur. In these cases, your doctor may want to change the dose, or other precautions may be necessary. When you are taking or receiving ACE inhibitors it is especially important that your health care professional know if you are taking any of the following:

- Alcohol or
- Diuretics (water pills)—Effects on blood pressure may be increased. In addition, some diuretics make the increase in potassium in the blood caused by ACE inhibitors even greater

- Potassium-containing medicines or supplements or
- Salt substitutes or
- Low-salt milk—Use of these substances with ACE inhibitors may result in an unusually high potassium level in the blood, which can lead to heart rhythm and other problems

Other medical problems—The presence of other medical problems may affect the use of the ACE inhibitors. Make sure you tell your doctor if you have any other medical problems, especially:

- Diabetes mellitus (sugar diabetes)—Increased risk of potassium levels in the body becoming too high, or increased effect of insulin on control of blood sugar

- Heart or blood vessel disease or
- Low sodium diet—Lowering blood pressure may make problems resulting from these conditions worse

- Kidney disease or
- Liver disease—ACE inhibitors' effects may be increased because of slower removal of medicine from the body

- Kidney transplant—Increased risk of kidney disease caused by ACE inhibitors

- Systemic lupus erythematosus (SLE)—Increased risk of blood problems caused by ACE inhibitors

- Previous reaction to any ACE inhibitor or previous occurrence involving hoarseness; swelling of face, mouth, hands, or feet; or sudden trouble in breathing—Reaction is more likely to occur again

Proper Use of This Medicine

To help you remember to take your medicine, try to get into the habit of taking it at the same time each day.

For patients taking *captopril or moexipril:*
- These medicines are best taken on an empty stomach 1 hour before meals, unless you are otherwise directed by your doctor.

For patients taking this medicine *for high blood pressure:*
- In addition to the use of the medicine your doctor has prescribed, treatment for your high blood pressure may include weight control and care in the types of foods you eat, especially foods high in sodium. Your doctor will tell you which of these are most important for you. You should check with your doctor before changing your diet.

- Many patients who have high blood pressure will not notice any signs of the problem. In fact, many may feel normal. It is very important that you *take your medicine exactly as directed* and that you keep your appointments with your doctor even if you feel well.

- Remember that this medicine will not cure your high blood pressure but it does help control it. Therefore, you must continue to take it as directed if you expect to lower your blood pressure and keep it down. *You may have to take high blood pressure medicine for the rest of your life.* If high blood pressure is not treated, it can cause serious problems such as heart failure, blood vessel disease, stroke, or kidney disease.

Dosing—The dose of the ACE inhibitor will be different for different patients. *Follow your doctor's orders or the directions on the label.* The following information includes only the average doses. *If your dose is different, do not change it* unless your doctor tells you to do so.

The number of capsules or tablets that you take depends on the strength of the medicine. Also, *the number of doses you take each day, the time allowed between doses, and the length of time you take the medicine depend on the medical problem for which you are taking the ACE inhibitor.*

For benazepril
- For *oral* dosage form (tablets):
  —For high blood pressure:
  - Adults—10 milligrams (mg) once a day at first. Then, your doctor may increase your dose to 20 to 40 mg a day taken as a single dose or divided into two doses.
  - Children—Use and dose must be determined by your doctor.

For captopril
- For *oral* dosage form (tablets):
  —For congestive heart failure:
  - Adults—25 to 100 mg two or three times a day.
  - Children—Dose must be determined by your doctor.
  —For high blood pressure:
  - Adults—25 to 50 mg two or three times a day.
  - Children—Dose must be determined by your doctor.
  —For kidney problems related to diabetes:
  - Adults—25 mg three times a day.
  —For treatment after a heart attack:
  - Adults—12.5 to 50 mg three times a day.

For cilazapril
- For *oral* dosage form (tablets):
  —For congestive heart failure:
  - Adults—0.5 mg once a day at first. Then your doctor may increase your dosage up to 5 mg once a day.
  - Children—Use and dose must be determined by your doctor.
  —For high blood pressure:
  - Adults—2.5 to 10 mg once a day.
  - Children—Use and dose must be determined by your doctor.

For enalapril
- For *oral* dosage form (tablets):
  —For congestive heart failure:
  - Adults—2.5 mg once a day or two times a day at first. Your doctor may increase your dose to 5 to

40 mg a day taken as a single dose or divided into two doses.
- Children—Use and dose must be determined by your doctor.
—For high blood pressure:
- Adults—5 mg once a day at first. Then, your doctor may increase your dose to 10 to 40 mg a day taken as a single dose or divided into two doses.
- Children—Use and dose must be determined by your doctor.
—For treating weakened heart muscle:
- Adults—2.5 mg two times a day at first. Then, your doctor may increase your dose up to 20 mg a day taken in divided doses.

- For *injection* dosage form:
—For high blood pressure:
- Adults—1.25 mg every six hours injected into a vein.
- Children—Use and dose must be determined by your doctor.

For fosinopril
- For *oral* dosage form (tablets):
—For congestive heart failure:
- Adults—10 mg once a day at first. Then your doctor may increase your dose to 20 to 40 mg once a day.
—For high blood pressure:
- Adults—10 to 40 mg once a day.
- Children—Use and dose must be determined by your doctor.

For lisinopril
- For *oral* dosage form (tablets):
—For congestive heart failure:
- Adults—5 to 20 mg once a day.
- Children—Use and dose must be determined by your doctor.
—For high blood pressure:
- Adults—10 to 40 mg once a day.
- Children—Use and dose must be determined by your doctor.
—For immediate treatment after a heart attack:
- Adults—5 mg once a day at first. Your doctor may increase the dose to 10 mg once a day.
- Children—Use and dose must be determined by your doctor.

For moexipril
- For *oral* dosage form (tablets):
—For high blood pressure:
- Adults—7.5 mg once a day. Then, your doctor may increase your dose up to 30 mg a day taken as a single dose or divided into two doses.
- Children—Use and dose must be determined by your doctor.

For perindopril
- For *oral* dosage form (tablets):
—For high blood pressure:
- Adults—4 mg once a day. Then, your doctor may increase your dosage up to 16 mg a day taken as a single dose or divided into two doses.
- Children—Use and dose must be determined by your doctor.

For quinapril
- For *oral* dosage form (tablets):
—For high blood pressure:
- Adults—10 to 20 mg once a day at first. Then, your doctor may increase your dosage up to 80 mg a day taken as a single dose or divided into two doses.
- Children—Use and dose must be determined by your doctor.
—For congestive heart failure:
- Adults—5 mg twice a day at first. Then, your doctor may increase your dose to 20 to 40 mg a day taken in two divided doses.

For ramipril
- For *oral* dosage form (capsules):
—For high blood pressure:
- Adults—2.5 mg once a day at first. Then, your doctor may increase your dosage up to 20 mg a day taken as a single dose or divided into two doses.
- Children—Use and dose must be determined by your doctor.
—For congestive heart failure after a heart attack:
- Adults—2.5 to 5 mg twice a day.
—For reducing risk of heart attack, stroke or death from cardiovascular causes
- Adults—2.5 mg once a day for one week. For the next three weeks the dose is 5 mg a day, and then increased as needed to 10 mg a day. The dose may be divided if needed.

Note: For use in people aged 55 and older.

For trandolapril
- For *oral* dosage form (tablets):
—For high blood pressure:
- Adults—1 to 2 mg once a day at first. Then, your doctor may increase your dose to 2 to 4 mg a day taken as a single or divided into two doses.
- Children—Use and dose must be determined by your doctor.
—For treatment after a heart attack:
- Adults—1 mg once a day at first. Then, your doctor may increase your dose up to 4 mg a day taken as a single or divided into two doses.

Missed dose—If you miss a dose of this medicine, take it as soon as possible. However, if it is almost time for your next dose, skip the missed dose and go back to your regular dosing schedule. Do not double doses.

Storage—To store this medicine:
- Keep out of the reach of children.
- Store away from heat and direct light.
- Do not store in the bathroom, near the kitchen sink, or in other damp places. Heat or moisture may cause the medicine to break down.
- Do not keep outdated medicine or medicine no longer needed. Be sure that any discarded medicine is out of the reach of children.

Precautions While Using This Medicine

It is important that your doctor check your progress at regular visits to make sure that this medicine is working properly and to check for unwanted effects.

For patients taking this medicine *for high blood pressure:*
- *Do not take other medicines unless they have been discussed with your doctor.* This especially includes over-the-counter (nonprescription) medicines for appetite control, asthma, colds, cough, hay fever, or sinus problems, since they may tend to increase your blood pressure.

Dizziness or light-headedness may occur after the first dose of this medicine, especially if you have been taking a diuretic (water pill). Make sure you know how you react to this medicine before you drive, use machines, or do anything else that could be dangerous if you are dizzy.

Check with your doctor right away if you become sick while taking this medicine, especially with severe or continuing nausea and vomiting or diarrhea. These conditions may cause you to lose too much water and lead to low blood pressure.

Notify your doctor immediately if you are or become pregnant while taking this medicine.

Check with your doctor if you have any signs of infection such as chills, fever, or sore throat, because these may be signs of neutropenia.

Dizziness, light-headedness, or fainting also may occur if you exercise or if the weather is hot. Heavy sweating can cause loss of too much water and low blood pressure. Use extra care during exercise or hot weather.

Avoid alcoholic beverages until you have discussed their use with your doctor. Alcohol may make the low blood pressure effect worse and/or increase the possibility of dizziness or fainting.

Before having any kind of surgery (including dental surgery) or emergency treatment, tell the medical doctor or dentist in charge that you are taking this medicine.

For patients taking *captopril or fosinopril:*
- Before you have any medical tests, tell the doctor in charge that you are taking this medicine. The results of some tests may be affected by this medicine.

Side Effects of This Medicine

Along with its needed effects, a medicine may cause some unwanted effects. Although not all of these side effects may occur, if they do occur they may need medical attention.

Check with your doctor immediately if any of the following side effects occur:
Rare
Fever and chills; hoarseness; swelling of face, mouth, hands, or feet; trouble in swallowing or breathing (sudden); stomach pain, itching of skin, or yellow eyes or skin

Check with your doctor as soon as possible if any of the following side effects occur:
Less common
Dizziness, light-headedness, or fainting; skin rash, with or without itching, fever, or joint pain
Rare
Abdominal pain, abdominal distention, fever, nausea, or vomiting; chest pain
Signs and symptoms of too much potassium in the body
Confusion; irregular heartbeat; nervousness; numbness or tingling in hands, feet, or lips; shortness of breath or difficulty breathing; weakness or heaviness of legs

Other side effects may occur that usually do not need medical attention. These side effects may go away during treatment as your body adjusts to the medicine. However, check with your doctor if any of the following side effects continue or are bothersome:
More common
Cough (dry, persistent); headache
Less common
Diarrhea; loss of taste; nausea; unusual tiredness

Other side effects not listed above may also occur in some patients. If you notice any other effects, check with your doctor.

Additional Information

Once a medicine has been approved for marketing for a certain use, experience may show that it is also useful for other medical problems. Although these uses are not included in product labeling, ACE inhibitors are used in certain patients with the following medical conditions:
- Hypertension in scleroderma (high blood pressure in patients with hardening and thickening of the skin)
- Renal crisis in scleroderma (kidney problems in patients with hardening and thickening of the skin)

Other than the above information, there is no additional information relating to proper use, precautions, or side effects for these uses.

Revised: 04/02/2001

ANGIOTENSIN-CONVERTING ENZYME (ACE) INHIBITORS AND HYDROCHLOROTHIAZIDE
Systemic†

Commonly used brand name(s):

In the U.S.—

Accuretic[6]	Uniretic[5]
Capozide[2]	Vaseretic[3]
Lotensin HCT[1]	Zestoretic[4]
Prinzide[4]	

In Canada—

Accuretic[6]	Vaseretic[3]
Prinzide[4]	Zestoretic[4]

Note: For quick reference, the following medicines are numbered to match the corresponding brand names.

This information applies to the following medicines:
1. Benazepril and Hydrochlorothiazide (ben-AY-ze-pril and hye-droe-klor-oh-THYE-a-zide)†
2. Captopril and Hydrochlorothiazide (KAP-toe-pril)†‡
3. Enalapril and Hydrochlorothiazide (e-NAL-a-pril)
4. Lisinopril and Hydrochlorothiazide (lyse-IN-oh-pril)
5. Moexipril and Hydrochlorothiazide (moe-EX-i-pril)†
6. Quinapril and Hydrochlorothiazide (KWIN-a-pril)

†Not commercially available in Canada.
‡Generic name product may be available in the U.S.

Description

This combination belongs to the class of medicines called high blood pressure medicines (antihypertensives). It is used to treat high blood pressure (hypertension).

High blood pressure adds to the workload of the heart and arteries. If it continues for a long time, the heart and arteries may not function properly. This can damage the blood vessels of the brain, heart, and kidneys, resulting in a stroke, heart failure, or kidney failure. High blood pressure may also increase the risk of heart attacks. These problems may be less likely to occur if blood pressure is controlled.

The exact way in which benazepril, captopril, enalapril, lisinopril, moexipril, and quinapril work is not known. They block an enzyme in the body that is necessary to produce a substance that causes blood vessels to tighten. As a result, they relax blood vessels. This lowers blood pressure and increases the supply of blood and oxygen to the heart. Hydrochlorothiazide helps reduce the amount of salt and water in the body by acting on the kidneys to increase the flow of urine; this also helps to lower blood pressure.

This combination may also be used for other conditions as determined by your doctor.

This medicine is available only with doctor's prescription, in the following dosage forms:

Oral
Benazepril and Hydrochlorothiazide
- Tablets (U.S.)
Captopril and Hydrochlorothiazide
- Tablets (U.S.)
Enalapril and Hydrochlorothiazide
- Tablets (U.S. and Canada)
Lisinopril and Hydrochlorothiazide
- Tablets (U.S. and Canada)
Moexipril and Hydrochlorothiazide
- Tablets (U.S.)
Quinapril and Hydrochlorothiazide
- Tablets (U.S. and Canada)

Before Using This Medicine

In deciding to use a medicine, the risks of taking the medicine must be weighed against the good it will do. This is a decision you and your doctor will make. For the angiotensin-converting enzyme (ACE) inhibitors and hydrochlorothiazide, the following should be considered:

Allergies—Tell your doctor if you have ever had any unusual or allergic reaction to benazepril, enalapril, captopril, lisinopril, moexipril, quinapril, sulfonamides (sulfa drugs), bumetanide, furosemide, acetazolamide, dichlorphenamide, or methazolamide or to hydrochlorothiazide or any of the other thiazide diuretics (water pills). Also tell your health care professional if you are allergic to any other substances, such as foods, sulfites or other preservatives, or dyes.

Pregnancy—Studies with this combination medicine have not been done in pregnant women. However, use of any of the ACE inhibitors during pregnancy, especially in the second and third trimesters (after the first three months), can cause low blood pressure, kidney failure, too much potassium, or even death in newborns. *Therefore, it is important that you check with your doctor immediately if you think that you may be pregnant.* Be sure that you have discussed this with your doctor before taking this medicine. In addition, if your medicine contains:

- *Benazepril*—Studies in rats, mice and rabbits at doses up to 300 times the recommended human dose showed no evidence of birth defects.
- *Captopril*—Studies in rabbits and rats at doses up to 400 times the recommended human dose have shown that captopril causes an increase in death of the fetus and newborn. Also, captopril has caused deformed skulls in the offspring of rabbits given doses 2 to 70 times the recommended human dose.
- *Enalapril*—Studies in rats at doses many times the recommended human dose have shown that use of enalapril causes the fetus to be smaller than normal. Studies in rabbits have shown that enalapril causes an increase in fetal death. Enalapril has not been shown to cause birth defects in rats or rabbits.
- *Lisinopril*—Studies in mice and rats at doses many times the recommended human dose have shown that use of lisinopril causes a decrease in successful pregnancies, a decrease in the weight of infants, and an increase in infant deaths. It has also caused a decrease in successful pregnancies and abnormal bone growth in rabbits. Lisinopril has not been shown to cause birth defects in mice, rats, or rabbits.
- *Moexipril*—Studies in rats and rabbits did not show moexipril to cause birth defects.
- *Quinapril*—Studies in rats showed quinapril caused reduced body weights but did not show it to cause birth defects in either rats or rabbits.
- *Hydrochlorothiazide*—Hydrochlorothiazide has not been shown to cause birth defects or other problems in animal studies. However, when hydrochlorothiazide is used during pregnancy, it may cause side effects including jaundice, blood problems, and low potassium in the newborn baby.

Breast-feeding—
- *Benazepril*—Passes into breast milk. However, this medicine has not been reported to cause problems in nursing babies.
- *Captopril*—Passes into breast milk. However, this medicine has not been reported to cause problems in nursing babies.
- *Enalapril*—Passes into breast milk. However, this medicine has not been reported to cause problems in nursing babies.
- *Lisinopril*—It is not known whether lisinopril passes into breast milk. However, this medicine has not been reported to cause problems in nursing babies.
- *Moexipril*—It is not known whether moexipril passes into breast milk. However, this medicine has not been reported to cause problems in nursing babies.
- *Quinapril*—Passes into breast milk. However, this medicine has not been reported to cause problems in nursing babies.
- *Hydrochlorothiazide*—Passes into breast milk. However, this medicine has not been reported to cause problems in nursing babies.

Children—Children may be especially sensitive to the blood pressure–lowering effect of ACE inhibitors. This may increase the chance of side effects or other problems during treatment. Extra caution may be necessary when using hydrochlorothiazide in infants with jaundice because it can make this condition worse. Therefore, it is especially important that you discuss with the child's doctor the good that this medicine may do as well as the risks of using it.

Older adults—Dizziness or lightheadedness and symptoms of too much potassium loss may be more likely to occur in the elderly, who may be more sensitive to the effects of this medicine.

Other medicines—Although certain medicines should not be used together at all, in other cases two different medicines may be used together even if an interaction might occur. In these cases, your doctor may want to change the dose, or other precautions may be necessary. When taking ACE inhibitors and hydrochlorothiazide it is especially important that your health care professional know if you are taking any of the following:

- Cholestyramine or
- Colestipol—Use with thiazide diuretics may prevent the diuretic from working properly; the diuretic should be taken at least 1 hour before or 4 hours after cholestyramine or colestipol
- Diabetes medication (insulin or tablets)—Blood sugar levels may change; extra care in self monitoring is necessary
- Digitalis glycosides (heart medicine)—If potassium levels in the body are decreased, symptoms of digitalis toxicity may occur
- Diuretics (water pills)—Effects on blood pressure may be increased
- Lithium (e.g., Lithane)—Risk of lithium overdose, even at low doses, may be increased
- Potassium-containing medicines or supplements or
- Salt substitutes or
- Low-salt milk—Use of these substances with ACE inhibitors may result in an unusually high potassium level in the blood, which can lead to heart rhythm and other problems
- Tetracycline—Use with quinapril will decrease the effects of tetracycline

Other medical problems—The presence of other medical problems may affect the use of the ACE inhibitors. Make sure you tell your doctor if you have any other medical problems, especially:

- Diabetes mellitus (sugar diabetes)—Increased risk of potassium levels in the body becoming too high
- Gout (or history of)—Hydrochlorothiazide may increase the amount of uric acid in the body, which can lead to gout
- Heart or blood vessel disease or
- Heart attack or stroke (recent)—Lowering blood pressure may make problems resulting from these conditions worse
- Kidney disease or
- Liver disease—Effects may be increased because of slower removal from the body
- Kidney transplant—Increased risk of kidney disease caused by ACE inhibitors
- Pancreatitis (inflammation of the pancreas)—Hydrochlorothiazide can make this condition worse
- Systemic lupus erythematosus (SLE) (or history of)—Hydrochlorothiazide may worsen the condition, and there is an increased risk of blood problems caused by ACE inhibitors

- Previous reaction to benazepril, captopril, enalapril, lisinopril, moexipril, or quinapril involving hoarseness; swelling of face, mouth, hands, or feet; or sudden trouble in breathing—Reaction is more likely to occur again

Proper Use of This Medicine

To help you remember to take your medicine, try to get into the habit of taking it at the same time each day.

For patients taking *captopril and hydrochlorothiazide* or *moexipril and hydrochlorothiazide:*

- This medicine is best taken on an empty stomach 1 hour before meals, unless you are otherwise directed by your doctor.

For patients taking this medicine *for high blood pressure:*

- In addition to the use of the medicine your doctor has prescribed, treatment for your high blood pressure may include weight control and care in the types of foods you eat, especially foods high in sodium. Your doctor will tell you which of these are most important for you. You should check with your doctor before changing your diet.
- Many patients who have high blood pressure will not notice any signs of the problem. In fact, many may feel normal. It is very important that you *take your medicine exactly as directed* and that you keep your appointments with your doctor even if you feel well.
- Remember that this medicine will not cure your high blood pressure but it does help control it. Therefore, you must continue to take it as directed if you expect to lower your blood pressure and keep it down. *You may have to take high blood pressure medicine for the rest of your life.* If high blood pressure is not treated, it can cause serious problems such as heart failure, blood vessel disease, stroke, or kidney disease.

This medicine may cause you to have an unusual feeling of tiredness when you begin to take it. You may also notice an increase in the amount of urine or in your frequency of urination. After you have taken the medicine for a while, these effects should lessen. In general, to keep the increase in urine from affecting your sleep:

- If you are to take a single dose a day, take it in the morning after breakfast.
- If you are to take more than one dose a day, take the last dose no later than 6 p.m., unless otherwise directed by your doctor.

However, it is best to plan your dose or doses according to a schedule that will least affect your personal activities and sleep. Ask your health care professional to help you plan the best time to take this medicine.

Dosing—The dose of these medicines will be different for different patients. *Follow your doctor's orders or the directions on the label.* The following information includes only the average doses of these medicines. *If your dose is different, do not change it* unless your doctor tells you to do so.

The number of tablets that you take depends on the strength of the medicine.

For benazepril and hydrochlorothiazide combination
- For *oral* dosage form (tablets):
   —For high blood pressure:
      - Adults—1 tablet once a day.
      - Children—Use and dose must be determined by your doctor.

For captopril and hydrochlorothiazide combination
- For *oral* dosage form (tablets):
  —For high blood pressure:
  - Adults—1 tablet two or three times a day.
  - Children—Dose is based on body weight and must be determined by your doctor.

For enalapril and hydrochlorothiazide combination
- For *oral* dosage form (tablets):
  —For high blood pressure:
  - Adults—1 tablet once or twice a day.
  - Children—Dose is based on body weight and must be determined by your doctor.

For lisinopril and hydrochlorothiazide combination
- For *oral* dosage form (tablets):
  —For high blood pressure:
  - Adults—1 or 2 tablets once a day.
  - Children—Dose must be determined by your doctor.

For moexipril and hydrochlorothiazide combination
- For *oral* dosage form (tablets):
  —For high blood pressure:
  - Adults—1 or 2 tablets once a day.
  - Children—Use and dose must be determined by your doctor.

For quinapril and hydrochlorothiazide combination
- For *oral* dosage form (tablets):
  —For high blood pressure:
  - Adults—1 tablet once or twice a day.
  - Children—Use and dose must be determined by your doctor.

Missed dose—If you miss a dose of this medicine, take it as soon as possible. However, if it is almost time for your next dose, skip the missed dose and go back to your regular dosing schedule. Do not double doses.

Storage—To store this medicine:
- Keep out of the reach of children.
- Store away from heat and direct light.
- Do not store in the bathroom, near the kitchen sink, or in other damp places. Heat or moisture may cause the medicine to break down.
- Do not keep outdated medicine or medicine no longer needed. Be sure that any discarded medicine is out of the reach of children.

Precautions While Using This Medicine

It is important that your doctor check your progress at regular visits to make sure that this medicine is working properly and to check for unwanted effects.

Dizziness or lightheadedness may occur, especially after the first dose of this medicine. Make sure you know how you react to the medicine before you drive, use machines, or do anything else that could be dangerous if you are dizzy.

Check with your doctor right away if you become sick while taking this medicine, especially with severe or continuing nausea and vomiting or diarrhea. These conditions may cause you to lose too much water and lead to low blood pressure.

Check with your doctor if you have signs of infection, such as sore throat, fever, and/or chills. Infections may be a sign of low white blood cell count (neutropenia).

Dizziness, lightheadedness, or fainting may also occur if you exercise or if the weather is hot. Heavy sweating can cause loss of too much water and low blood pressure. Use extra care during exercise or hot weather.

Avoid alcoholic beverages until you have discussed their use with your doctor. Alcohol may make the low blood pressure effect worse and/or increase the possibility of dizziness or fainting.

Before having any kind of surgery (including dental surgery) or emergency treatment, tell the medical doctor or dentist in charge that you are taking this medicine.

For patients taking *captopril and hydrochlorothiazide:*
- Before you have any medical tests, tell the doctor in charge that you are taking this medicine. The results of some tests may be affected by this medicine.

For patients taking this medicine *for high blood pressure:*
- *Do not take other medicines unless they have been discussed with your doctor.* This especially includes over-the-counter (nonprescription) medicines for appetite control, asthma, colds, cough, hay fever, or sinus problems, since they may tend to increase your blood pressure.

For *diabetic patients:*
- Hydrochlorothiazide (contained in this combination medicine) may raise blood sugar levels. While you are taking this medicine, be especially careful in testing for sugar in your urine.

Hydrochlorothiazide (contained in this combination medicine) may cause your skin to be more sensitive to sunlight than it is normally. Exposure to sunlight, even for brief periods of time, may cause a skin rash, itching, redness or other discoloration of the skin, or a severe sunburn. When you first begin taking this medicine:
- Stay out of direct sunlight, especially between the hours of 10:00 a.m. and 3:00 p.m., if possible.
- Wear protective clothing, including a hat. Also, wear sunglasses.
- Apply a sun block product that has a skin protection factor (SPF) of at least 15. Some patients may require a product with a higher SPF number, especially if they have a fair complexion. If you have any questions about this, check with your health care professional.
- Apply a sun block lipstick that has an SPF of at least 15 to protect your lips.
- Do not use a sunlamp or tanning bed or booth.

If you have a severe reaction from the sun, check with your doctor.

Before you have any medical tests, tell the doctor in charge that you are taking this medicine. The results of some tests may be affected by this medicine.

Side Effects of This Medicine

Along with its needed effects, a medicine may cause some unwanted effects. Although not all of these side effects may occur, if they do occur you may need medical attention.

Seek medical attention immediately or call your doctor if any of the following side effects occur:
  Rare
    Swelling of face, mouth, hands, or feet; trouble in swallowing or breathing (sudden); hoarseness; fever and chills

Check with your doctor as soon as possible if any of the following side effects occur:

Less common
  Dizziness, lightheadedness, or fainting; skin rash, with or without itching, fever, or joint pain

Rare
  Chest pain; joint pain; lower back or side pain; stomach pain (severe) with nausea and vomiting; unusual bleeding or bruising; yellow eyes or skin

Signs and symptoms of too much or too little potassium in the body
  Dryness of mouth; increased thirst; irregular heartbeat; mood or mental changes; muscle cramps or pain; numbness or tingling in hands, feet, or lips; weakness or heaviness of legs; weak pulse

Other side effects may occur that usually do not need medical attention. These side effects may go away during treatment as your body adjusts to the medicine. However, check with your doctor if any of the following side effects continue or are bothersome:

More common
  Cough (dry, persistent)

Less common
  Diarrhea; headache; increased sensitivity of skin to sunlight (skin rash, itching, redness or other discoloration of skin or severe sunburn after exposure to sunlight); loss of appetite; loss of taste; stomach upset; unusual tiredness

Other side effects not listed above may also occur in some patients. If you notice any other effects, check with your doctor.

Additional Information

Once a medicine has been approved for marketing for a certain use, experience may show that it is also useful for other medical problems. Although this use is not included in product labeling, ACE inhibitors and hydrochlorothiazide are used in certain patients with the following medical condition:

- Congestive heart failure

Other than the above information, there is no additional information relating to proper use, precautions, or side effects for this use.

Revised: 5/20/2000

ANTACIDS   Oral

Commonly used brand name(s):

In the U.S.—

Advanced Formula Di-Gel[29]	Aludrox[9]
Alamag[2]	Alu-Tab[25]
Alamag Plus[9]	Amitone[27]
Alenic Alka[15]	Amphojel[25]
Alenic Alka Extra Strength[18]	Antacid Gelcaps[31]
Alka-Mints[27]	Antacid Liquid[9]
Alkets[27]	Antacid Liquid Double
Alkets Extra Strength[27]	Strength[9]
Almacone[9]	Basaljel[23]
Almacone II[9]	Calglycine[27]
AlternaGEL[21]	Chooz[27]
Alu-Cap[25]	Dicarbosil[27]

Di-Gel[29]	Mintox Extra Strength[9]
Equilet[27]	Mygel[9]
Foamicon[19]	Mygel II[9]
Gaviscon[15]	Mylanta[11]
Gaviscon-2[20]	Mylanta Double Strength[12]
Gaviscon Extra Strength	Mylanta Gelcaps[28]
Relief Formula[17]	Nephrox[25]
Gelusil[9]	Phillips'[35]
Genaton[15]	Phillips' Chewable[35]
Genaton Extra Strength[18]	Phillips' Concentrated Double
Kudrox Double Strength[9]	Strength[35]
Losopan[32]	Riopan[32]
Losopan Plus[33]	Riopan Plus[33]
Lowsium Plus[33]	Riopan Plus Double Strength[33]
Maalox[2]	Rolaids[28]
Maalox Antacid Caplets[31]	Rulox[2]
Maalox Heartburn Relief	Rulox No. 1[2]
Formula[14]	Rulox No. 2[2]
Maalox Plus[9]	Rulox Plus[9]
Maalox Plus, Extra Strength[9]	Simaal Gel[9]
Maalox TC[2]	Simaal 2 Gel[9]
Magnalox[9]	Tempo[4]
Magnalox Plus[9]	Titralac[27]
Mag-Ox 400[36]	Titralac Extra Strength[27]
Mallamint[27]	Titralac Plus[30]
Maox 420[36]	Tums[27]
Marblen[31]	Tums Anti-gas/Antacid[30]
Mi-Acid[10]	Tums E-X[27]
Mi-Acid Double Strength[9]	Tums Ultra[27]
Mintox[2]	Uro-Mag[36]

In Canada—

Almagel 200[2]	Maalox Antacid Caplets[31]
Alugel[25]	Maalox HRF[13]
Alu-Tab[25]	Maalox Plus[9]
Amphojel[25]	Maalox Plus, Extra Strength[9]
Amphojel 500[2]	Maalox TC[2]
Amphojel Plus[8]	Mylanta[9]
Basaljel[25]	Mylanta Double Strength[9]
Diovol[6]	Mylanta Double Strength Plain[2]
Diovol Caplets[2]	Mylanta Extra Strength[9]
Diovol Ex[2]	Neutralca-S[2]
Diovol Plus[8]	Phillips'[35]
Diovol Plus AF[29]	PMS Alumina, Magnesia, and
Gasmas[7]	Simethicone[9]
Gaviscon Acid Plus Gas	Rafton[3]
Relief[29]	Riopan[32]
Gaviscon Acid Relief[28]	Riopan Extra Strength[32]
Gaviscon Extra Strength Acid	Riopan Plus[33]
Relief[28]	Riopan Plus Extra Strength[33]
Gaviscon Heartburn Relief[13]	Rolaids[28]
Gaviscon Heartburn Relief	Rolaids Extra Strength[28]
Extra Strength[13]	Trial[27]
Gelusil[2]	Tums[27]
Gelusil Extra Strength[2]	Tums Extra Strength[27]
Life Antacid[2]	Tums Ultra[27]
Life Antacid Plus[9]	Univol[2]
Maalox[2]	

Note: For quick reference the following antacids are numbered to match the corresponding brand names.

This information applies to the following medicines:

1. Alumina, Calcium Carbonate, and Sodium Bicarbonate (a-LOO-mi-na, KAL-see-um KAR-bon-ate, and SOE-dee-um bi-KAR-bon-ate)*†‡
2. Alumina and Magnesia (a-LOO-mi-na and mag-NEE-zha)‡§
3. Alumina, Calcium Carbonate, and Sodium Bicarbonate or Alumina, Magnesium Trisilicate, and Sodium Bicarbonate (a-LOO-mi-na, KAL-see-um KAR-bon-ate, and SOE-dee-um bi-KAR-bon-ate or a-LOO-mi-na, mag-NEE-zhum trye-SILL-i-kate, and SOE-dee-um bi-KAR-bon-ate)*†‡
4. Alumina, Magnesia, Calcium Carbonate, and Simethicone (a-LOO-mi-na, mag-NEE-zha, KAL-see-um KAR-bon-ate, and Si-METH-i-kone)

5. Alumina, Magnesia, and Magnesium Carbonate (a-LOO-mi-na, mag-NEE-zha, and mag-NEE-zhum KAR-bon-ate)
6. Alumina, Magnesia, and Magnesium Carbonate or Alumina, Magnesia, and Simethicone (a-LOO-mi-na, mag-NEE-zha, and mag-NEE-zhum KAR-bon-ate or a-LOO-mi-na, mag-NEE-zha, and Si-METH-i-kone)
7. Alumina, Magnesia, Magnesium Carbonate, and Simethicone (a-LOO-mi-na, mag-NEE-zha, mag-NEE-zhum KAR-bon-ate, and Si-METH-i-kone)
8. Alumina, Magnesia, Magnesium Carbonate, and Simethicone or Alumina, Magnesia, and Simethicone (a-LOO-mi-na, mag-NEE-zha, mag-NEE-zhum KAR-bon-ate, and Si-METH-i-kone or a-LOO-mi-na, mag-NEE-zha, and Si-METH-i-kone)
9. Alumina, Magnesia, and Simethicone (a-LOO-mi-na, mag-NEE-zha, and Si-METH-i-kone)‡§
10. Alumina, Magnesia, and Simethicone or Calcium and Magnesium Carbonates (a-LOO-mi-na, mag-NEE-zha, and Si-METH-i-kone or KAL-see-um and mag-NEE-zhum KAR-bon-ates)‡§
11. Alumina, Magnesia, and Simethicone or Calcium Carbonate or Calcium Carbonate and Magnesia (a-LOO-mi-na, mag-NEE-zha, and Si-METH-i-kone or KAL-see-um KAR-bon-ate or KAL-see-um KAR-bon-ate and mag-NEE-zha,)‡§
12. Alumina, Magnesia, and Simethicone or Calcium Carbonate and Magnesia (a-LOO-mi-na, mag-NEE-zha, and Si-METH-i-kone or KAL-see-um KAR-bon-ate and mag-NEE-zha,)‡§
13. Alumina, Magnesium Alginate, and Magnesium Carbonate (a-LOO-mi-na, mag-NEE-zhum al-JI-nate, and mag-NEE-zhum KAR-bon-ate)
14. Alumina and Magnesium Carbonate (a-LOO-mi-na and mag-NEE-zhum KAR-bon-ate)
15. Alumina and Magnesium Carbonate or Alumina, Magnesium Trisilicate, and Sodium Bicarbonate (a-LOO-mi-na and mag-NEE-zhum KAR-bon-ate or a-LOO-mi-na, mag-NEE-zhum trye-SILL-i-kate, and SOE-dee-um bi-KAR-bon-ate)
16. Alumina, Magnesium Carbonate, and Simethicone (a-LOO-mi-na, mag-NEE-zhum KAR-bon-ate, and Si-METH-i-kone)
17. Alumina, Magnesium Carbonate, and Simethicone or Alumina, Magnesium Carbonate, and Sodium Bicarbonate (a-LOO-mi-na, mag-NEE-zhum KAR-bon-ate, and Si-METH-i-kone or a-LOO-mi-na, mag-NEE-zhum KAR-bon-ate, and SOE-dee-um bi-KAR-bon-ate)
18. Alumina, Magnesium Carbonate, and Sodium Bicarbonate (a-LOO-mi-na, mag-NEE-zhum KAR-bon-ate, and SOE-dee-um bi-KAR-bon-ate)
19. Alumina and Magnesium Trisilicate (a-LOO-mi-na and mag-NEE-zhum trye-SILL-i-kate)
20. Alumina, Magnesium Trisilicate, and Sodium Bicarbonate (a-LOO-mi-na, mag-NEE-zhum trye-SILL-i-kate, and SOE-dee-um bi-KAR-bon-ate)
21. Alumina and Simethicone (a-LOO-mi-na and Si-METH-i-kone)
22. Alumina and Sodium Bicarbonate (a-LOO-mi-na and SOE-dee-um bi-KAR-bon-ate)
23. Aluminum Carbonate, Basic (a-LOO-mi-num KAR-bon-ate, BA-sic)
24. Aluminum Carbonate, Basic, and Simethicone (a-LOO-mi-num KAR-bon-ate, BA-sic, and Si-METH-i-kone)
25. Aluminum Hydroxide (a-LOO-mi-num hye-DROX-ide)‡§
26. Aluminum Hydroxide, Magnesium Carbonate, and Sodium Bicarbonate (a-LOO-mi-num hye-DROX-ide, mag-NEE-zhum KAR-bon-ate, and SOE-dee-um bi-KAR-bon-ate)‡§
27. Calcium Carbonate (KAL-see-um KAR-bon-ate)‡
28. Calcium Carbonate and Magnesia (KAL-see-um KAR-bon-ate and mag-NEE-zha,)
29. Calcium Carbonate, Magnesia, and Simethicone (KAL-see-um KAR-bon-ate, mag-NEE-zha, and Si-METH-i-kone)
30. Calcium Carbonate and Simethicone (KAL-see-um KAR-bon-ate and Si-METH-i-kone)
31. Calcium and Magnesium Carbonates (KAL-see-um and mag-NEE-zhum KAR-bon-ates)
32. Magaldrate (MAG-al-drate)‡

33. Magaldrate and Simethicone (MAG-al-drate and Si-METH-i-kone)‡
34. Magnesium Carbonate and Sodium Bicarbonate (mag-NEE-zhum KAR-bon-ate and SOE-dee-um bi-KAR-bon-ate)
35. Magnesium Hydroxide (mag-NEE-zhum hye-DROX-ide)‡§
36. Magnesium Oxide (mag-NEE-zhum OX-ide)

*Not commercially available in the U.S.
†Not commercially available in Canada.
‡Generic name product may be available in the U.S.
§Generic name product may be available in Canada.

Description

Antacids are taken by mouth to relieve heartburn, sour stomach, or acid indigestion. They work by neutralizing excess stomach acid. Some antacid combinations also contain simethicone, which may relieve the symptoms of excess gas. Antacids alone or in combination with simethicone may also be used to treat the symptoms of stomach or duodenal ulcers.

With larger doses than those used for the antacid effect, magnesium hydroxide (magnesia) and magnesium oxide antacids produce a laxative effect. The information that follows applies only to their use as an antacid.

Some antacids, like aluminum carbonate and aluminum hydroxide, may be prescribed with a low-phosphate diet to treat hyperphosphatemia (too much phosphate in the blood). Aluminum carbonate and aluminum hydroxide may also be used with a low-phosphate diet to prevent the formation of some kinds of kidney stones. Aluminum hydroxide may also be used for other conditions as determined by your doctor.

These medicines are available without a prescription. However, your doctor may have special instructions on the proper use and dose of these medicines for your medical problem. They are available in the following dosage forms:

Oral
Alumina, Calcium Carbonate, and Sodium Bicarbonate
• Oral suspension (Canada)
Alumina and Magnesia
• Oral suspension (U.S. and Canada)
• Tablets (Canada)
• Chewable tablets (U.S. and Canada)
Alumina, Magnesia, Calcium Carbonate, and Simethicone
• Chewable tablets (U.S.)
Alumina, Magnesia, and Magnesium Carbonate
• Chewable tablets (Canada)
Alumina, Magnesia, Magnesium Carbonate, and Simethicone
• Chewable tablets (Canada)
Alumina, Magnesia, and Simethicone
• Oral suspension (U.S. and Canada)
• Chewable tablets (U.S. and Canada)
Alumina, Magnesium Alginate, and Magnesium Carbonate
• Oral suspension (Canada)
• Chewable tablets (Canada)
Alumina and Magnesium Carbonate
• Oral suspension (U.S.)
• Chewable tablets (U.S.)
Alumina, Magnesium Carbonate, and Simethicone
• Oral suspension (U.S.)
Alumina, Magnesium Carbonate, and Sodium Bicarbonate
• Chewable tablets (U.S.)

Alumina and Magnesium Trisilicate
- Chewable tablets (U.S.)

Alumina, Magnesium Trisilicate, and Sodium Bicarbonate
- Chewable tablets (U.S.)

Alumina and Simethicone
- Gel (U.S.)

Alumina and Sodium Bicarbonate
- Chewable tablets (Canada)

Aluminum Carbonate, Basic
- Capsules (U.S.)
- Tablets (U.S.)

Aluminum Carbonate, Basic, and Simethicone
- Oral suspension (U.S.)

Aluminum Hydroxide
- Capsules (U.S. and Canada)
- Oral suspension (U.S. and Canada)
- Gel (U.S. and Canada)
- Tablets (U.S. and Canada)
- Chewable tablets (Canada)

Calcium Carbonate
- Chewing gum (U.S.)
- Lozenges (U.S.)
- Oral suspension (U.S.)
- Tablets (U.S.)
- Chewable tablets (U.S. and Canada)

Calcium Carbonate and Magnesia
- Oral suspension (Canada)
- Tablets (U.S.)
- Chewable tablets (U.S. and Canada)

Calcium Carbonate, Magnesia, and Simethicone
- Oral suspension (Canada)
- Chewable tablets (U.S. and Canada)

Calcium Carbonate and Simethicone
- Oral suspension (U.S.)
- Chewable tablets (U.S.)

Calcium and Magnesium Carbonates
- Oral suspension (U.S.)
- Tablets (U.S. and Canada)

Magaldrate
- Oral suspension (U.S. and Canada)
- Chewable tablets (Canada)

Magaldrate and Simethicone
- Oral suspension (U.S. and Canada)
- Chewable tablets (U.S. and Canada)

Magnesium Carbonate and Sodium Bicarbonate
- Chewable tablets (Canada)

Magnesium Hydroxide
- Milk of magnesia (U.S. and Canada)
- Chewable tablets (U.S. and Canada)

Magnesium Oxide
- Capsules (U.S.)
- Tablets (U.S.)

Before Using This Medicine

If you are taking this medicine without a prescription, carefully read and follow any precautions on the label. For antacids, the following should be considered:

Allergies—Tell your health care professional if you have ever had any unusual or allergic reaction to aluminum-, calcium-, magnesium-, simethicone-, or sodium bicarbonate–containing medicines. Also, tell your health care professional if you are allergic to any other substances, such as foods, preservatives, or dyes.

Diet—Make certain your health care professional knows if you are on a low-sodium diet. Some antacids contain large amounts of sodium.

Pregnancy—Studies on effects in pregnancy have not been done in either humans or animals. However, there have been reports of antacids causing side effects in babies whose mothers took antacids for a long time, especially in high doses during pregnancy. Also, sodium-containing medicines should be avoided if you tend to retain (keep) body water.

Breast-feeding—Some aluminum-, calcium-, or magnesium-containing antacids may pass into breast milk. However, these medicines have not been reported to cause problems in nursing babies.

Children—Antacids should not be given to young children (under 6 years of age) unless ordered by their doctor. Since children cannot usually describe their symptoms very well, a doctor should first check the child. The child may have a condition that needs other treatment. If so, antacids will not help and may even cause unwanted effects or make the condition worse. In addition, aluminum- or magnesium-containing medicines should not be given to premature or very young children because they may cause serious side effects, especially when given to children who have kidney disease or who are dehydrated.

Older adults—Aluminum-containing antacids should not be used by elderly persons with bone problems or with Alzheimer's disease. The aluminum may cause their condition to get worse.

Other medicines—Although certain medicines should not be used together at all, in other cases two different medicines may be used together even if an interaction might occur. In these cases, your doctor may want to change the dose, or other precautions may be necessary. When you are taking antacids, it is especially important that your health care professional know if you are taking any of the following:

- Cellulose sodium phosphate (e.g., Calcibind)—Calcium-containing antacids may decrease the effects of cellulose sodium phosphate; use with magnesium-containing antacids may prevent either medicine from working properly; antacids should not be taken within 1 hour of cellulose sodium phosphate

- Fluoroquinolones (medicine for infection)—Antacids may decrease the effects of these medicines

- Isoniazid taken by mouth (e.g., INH)—Aluminum-containing antacids may decrease the effects of isoniazid; isoniazid should be taken at least 1 hour before or after the antacid

- Ketoconazole (e.g., Nizoral) or
- Methenamine (e.g., Mandelamine)—Antacids may decrease the effects of ketoconazole or methenamine; these medicines should be taken 3 hours before the antacid

- Mecamylamine (e.g., Inversine)—Antacids may increase the effects and possibly the side effects of mecamylamine

- Sodium polystyrene sulfonate resin (SPSR) (e.g., Kayexalate)—This medicine may decrease the effects of antacids

- Tetracyclines (medicine for infection) taken by mouth—Use with antacids may decrease the effects of both medicines; antacids should not be taken within 3 to 4 hours of tetracyclines

Other medical problems—The presence of other medical problems may affect the use of antacids. Make sure you tell your doctor if you have any other medical problems, especially:

- Alzheimer's disease (for aluminum-containing antacids only) or
- Appendicitis (or signs of) or
- Bone fractures or
- Colitis or
- Constipation (severe and continuing) or
- Hemorrhoids or
- Intestinal blockage or
- Intestinal or rectal bleeding—Antacids may make these conditions worse
- Colostomy or
- Ileostomy or
- Inflamed bowel—Use of antacids may cause the body to retain (keep) water and electrolytes such as sodium and/or potassium
- Diarrhea (continuing)—Aluminum-containing antacids may cause the body to lose too much phosphorus; magnesium-containing antacids may make diarrhea worse
- Edema (swelling of feet or lower legs) or
- Heart disease or
- Liver disease or
- Toxemia of pregnancy—Use of sodium-containing antacids may cause the body to retain (keep) water
- Kidney disease—Antacids may cause higher blood levels of aluminum, calcium, or magnesium, which may increase the risk of serious side effects
- Sarcoidosis—Use of calcium-containing antacids may cause kidney problems or too much calcium in the blood
- Underactive parathyroid glands—Use with calcium-containing antacids may cause too much calcium in the blood

Proper Use of This Medicine

For patients taking the *chewable tablet form* of this medicine:

- Chew the tablets well before swallowing. This is to allow the medicine to work faster and be more effective.

For patients taking this medicine for a *stomach or duodenal ulcer:*

- *Take it exactly as directed and for the full time of treatment as ordered by your doctor,* to obtain maximum relief of your symptoms.
- Take it 1 and 3 hours after meals and at bedtime for best results, unless otherwise directed by your doctor.

For patients taking *aluminum carbonate* or *aluminum hydroxide* to *prevent kidney stones:*

- Drink plenty of fluids for best results, unless otherwise directed by your doctor.

For patients taking *aluminum carbonate* or *aluminum hydroxide* for *hyperphosphatemia* (too much phosphate in the blood):

- Your doctor may want you to follow a low-phosphate diet. If you have any questions about this, check with your doctor.

Dosing—The dose of an antacid will be different for different patients. *Follow your doctor's orders or the directions on the label.*

Missed dose—If your doctor has told you to take this medicine on a regular schedule and you miss a dose, take it as soon as possible. However, if it is almost time for your next dose, skip the missed dose and go back to your regular dosing schedule. Do not double doses.

Storage—To store this medicine:

- Keep out of the reach of children.
- Store away from heat and direct light.
- Do not store the capsule, tablet, or lozenge form of this medicine in the bathroom, near the kitchen sink, or in other damp places. Heat or moisture may cause the medicine to break down.
- Keep the liquid or gel form of this medicine from freezing.
- Do not keep outdated medicine or medicine no longer needed. Be sure that any discarded medicine is out of the reach of children.

Precautions While Using This Medicine

If this medicine has been ordered by your doctor and you will be taking it in large doses, or for a long time, your doctor should check your progress at regular visits. This is to make sure the medicine does not cause unwanted effects.

Some tests may be affected by this medicine. Tell the doctor in charge that you are taking this medicine before you have any tests to determine how much acid your stomach produces.

Do not take this medicine:

- *if you have any signs of appendicitis or inflamed bowel* (such as stomach or lower abdominal pain, cramping, bloating, soreness, nausea, or vomiting). Instead, check with your doctor as soon as possible.
- *within 1 to 2 hours or more of taking other medicine by mouth.* To do so may keep the other medicine from working properly.

For patients on a *sodium-restricted diet:*

- Some antacids (especially those containing sodium bicarbonate) contain a large amount of sodium. If you have any questions about this, check with your health care professional.

For patients taking this medicine for increased stomach acid:

- *Do not take it for more than 2 weeks unless otherwise directed by your doctor.* Antacids should be used only for occasional relief.
- If your stomach problem is not helped by the antacid or if it keeps coming back, check with your doctor.
- Using magnesium- or sodium bicarbonate–containing antacids too often, or in high doses, may produce a laxative effect. This happens fairly often and depends on the individual's sensitivity to the medicine.

For patients taking *aluminum-containing antacids* (including magaldrate):

- Before you have any test in which a radiopharmaceutical will be used, tell the doctor in charge that you are taking this medicine. The results of the test may be affected by aluminum-containing antacids.

For patients taking *calcium-* or *sodium bicarbonate–containing antacids:*

- *Do not take the antacid with large amounts of milk or milk products.* To do so may increase the chance of side effects.

Side Effects of This Medicine

Along with its needed effects, a medicine may cause some unwanted effects. Although the following side effects occur very rarely when this medicine is taken as recommended, they may be more likely to occur if:

- too much medicine is taken
- it is taken in large doses
- it is taken for a long time
- it is taken by patients with kidney disease

Check with your doctor as soon as possible if any of the following side effects (which may be signs of overdose) occur:

For aluminum-containing antacids (including magaldrate)

Bone pain; constipation (severe and continuing); feeling of discomfort (continuing); loss of appetite (continuing); mood or mental changes; muscle weakness; swelling of wrists or ankles; weight loss (unusual)

For calcium-containing antacids

Constipation (severe and continuing); difficult or painful urination; frequent urge to urinate; headache (continuing); loss of appetite (continuing); mood or mental changes; muscle pain or twitching; nausea or vomiting; nervousness or restlessness; slow breathing; unpleasant taste; unusual tiredness or weakness

For magnesium-containing antacids (including magaldrate)

Difficult or painful urination (with magnesium trisilicate); dizziness or lightheadedness; feeling of discomfort (continuing); irregular heartbeat; loss of appetite (continuing); mood or mental changes; muscle weakness; unusual tiredness or weakness; weight loss (unusual)

For sodium bicarbonate–containing antacids

Frequent urge to urinate; headache (continuing); loss of appetite (continuing); mood or mental changes; muscle pain or twitching; nausea or vomiting; nervousness or restlessness; slow breathing; swelling of feet or lower legs; unpleasant taste; unusual tiredness or weakness

Other side effects may occur that usually do not need medical attention. These side effects may go away during treatment as your body adjusts to the medicine. However, check with your doctor if any of the following side effects continue or are bothersome:

More common

Chalky taste

Less common

Constipation (mild); diarrhea or laxative effect; increased thirst; speckling or whitish discoloration of stools; stomach cramps

Other side effects not listed above may also occur in some patients. If you notice any other effects, check with your doctor.

Revised: 07/18/1996

ANTHRALIN   Topical

Commonly used brand name(s):

In the U.S.—

Drithocreme	Dritho-Scalp
Drithocreme HP	Micanol

In Canada—

Anthraforte 1	Anthranol 0.2
Anthraforte 2	Anthranol 0.4
Anthranol 0.1	Anthrascalp

Another commonly used name is dithranol.

Description

Anthralin (AN-thra-lin) is used to treat psoriasis. It may also be used to treat other skin conditions as determined by your doctor.

In the U.S., this medicine is available only with your doctor's prescription. In Canada, this medicine should be used only on the advice of your doctor.

This medicine is available in the following dosage forms:

Topical
- Cream (U.S. and Canada)
- Ointment (Canada)

Before Using This Medicine

In deciding to use a medicine, the risks of using the medicine must be weighed against the good it will do. This is a decision you and your doctor will make. For anthralin, the following should be considered:

Allergies—Tell your doctor if you have ever had any unusual or allergic reactions to anthralin, parabens, or salicylic acid. Also tell your health care professional if you are allergic to any other substances, such as foods, preservatives, or dyes.

Pregnancy—Anthralin may be absorbed through the skin. However, studies on effects in pregnancy have not been done in either humans or animals.

Breast-feeding—Anthralin may be absorbed through the mother's skin. However, it is not known whether anthralin passes into the breast milk. Although most medicines pass into breast milk in small amounts, many of them may be used safely while breast-feeding. Mothers who are using this medicine and who wish to breast-feed should discuss this with their doctor.

Children—Studies on this medicine have been done only in adult patients, and there is no specific information comparing use of anthralin in children with use in other age groups.

Older adults—Many medicines have not been studied specifically in older people. Therefore, it may not be known whether they work exactly the same way they do in younger adults or if they cause different side effects or problems in older people. There is no specific information comparing use of anthralin in the elderly with use in other age groups.

Other medicines—Although certain medicines should not be used together at all, in other cases two different medicines may be used together even if an interaction might occur. In these cases, your doctor may want to change the dose, or other precautions may be necessary. Tell your health care professional if you are using any other topical prescription or nonprescription (over-the-counter [OTC]) medicine that is to be applied to the same area of the skin.

Other medical problems—The presence of other medical problems may affect the use of anthralin. Make sure you tell your doctor if you have any other medical problems, especially:

- Skin diseases or problems (other)—Anthralin may make the condition worse

Proper Use of This Medicine

Keep this medicine away from the eyes and mucous membranes, such as the mouth and the inside of the nose.

Do not apply this medicine to blistered, raw, or oozing areas of the skin or scalp.

Do not use this medicine on your face or sex organs or in the folds and creases of your skin. If you have any questions about this, check with your doctor.

Use this medicine only as directed. Do not use more of it, do not use it more often, and do not use it for a longer time than your doctor ordered. To do so may increase the chance of side effects.

Anthralin may be used in different ways. In some cases, it is applied at night and allowed to remain on the affected areas overnight, then washed off the next morning or before the next application. In other cases, it may be applied and allowed to remain on the affected areas for a short period of time (usually 10 to 30 minutes), then washed off. (This is called short contact treatment.) Make sure you understand exactly how you are to use this medicine. If you have any questions about this, check with your doctor.

Anthralin may cause irritation of normal skin. If it does, petrolatum may be applied to the skin or scalp around the affected areas for protection.

Apply a thin layer of anthralin to only the affected area of the skin or scalp and rub in gently and well.

Immediately after applying this medicine, wash your hands to remove any medicine that may be on them.

For patients using *anthralin for short contact* (usually 10 to 30 minutes) treatment:

- After applying anthralin, allow the medicine to remain on the affected area for 10 to 30 minutes or as directed by your doctor. Then remove the medicine by bathing, if the anthralin was applied to the skin, or by shampooing, if it was applied to the scalp.

For patients using the *cream form* of anthralin for overnight treatment:

- If anthralin cream is applied to the skin, any medicine remaining on the affected areas the next morning should be removed by bathing.
- If anthralin cream is applied to the scalp, shampoo to remove the scales and any medicine remaining on the affected areas from the previous application. Dry the hair and, after parting, rub the cream into the affected areas. Check with your doctor to see when the cream should be removed.

For patients using the *ointment form* of anthralin for overnight treatment:

- If anthralin ointment is applied to the skin at night, any ointment remaining on the affected areas the next morning should be removed with warm liquid petrolatum followed by bathing.
- If anthralin ointment is applied to the scalp at night, shampoo the next morning to clean the scalp.

Dosing—The dose of anthralin will be different for different patients. *Follow your doctor's orders or the directions on the label.* The following information includes only the average doses of anthralin. *If your dose is different, do not change it* unless your doctor tells you to do so.

- For psoriasis:
  —For *cream* dosage form:
  - Adults—Apply to the dry, affected area(s) of the skin once a day, preferably at night, or as directed by your doctor. Wash medicine off skin at the proper time.
  - Children—Use and dose must be determined by your doctor.
  —For *ointment* dosage form:
  - Adults—Apply to the dry, affected area(s) of the skin once a day or as directed by your doctor. Wash medicine off skin at the proper time.
  - Children—Use and dose must be determined by your doctor.

Missed dose—If you miss a dose of this medicine, apply it as soon as possible. However, if it is almost time for your next dose, skip the missed dose and go back to your regular dosing schedule. Do not double doses.

Storage—To store this medicine:

- Keep out of the reach of children.
- Store away from heat and direct light.
- Keep the medicine from freezing.
- Keep tube tightly capped.
- Do not keep outdated medicine or medicine no longer needed. Be sure that any discarded medicine is out of the reach of children.

Precautions While Using This Medicine

Anthralin may stain the skin, hair, fingernails, clothing, bed linens, or bathtub or shower. The stain on the skin or hair will wear off in several weeks after you stop using this medicine. Some ways to prevent or lessen anthralin staining include:

- Wear plastic gloves when you apply this medicine.
- Avoid getting the medicine on your clothing or on bed linens. Ask your doctor if you can wear a plastic cap while sleeping if you apply your medicine to your scalp at bedtime.
- Remove any medicine on the surface of the bathtub or shower stall by immediately rinsing it with hot water after bathing or showering. Afterwards wash the bathtub or shower stall with a household cleanser to remove any remaining deposits.

Side Effects of This Medicine

Anthralin has been shown to cause tumors in animals. However, there have been no reports of anthralin causing tumors in humans.

Along with its needed effects, a medicine may cause some unwanted effects. Although not all of these side effects may occur, if they do occur you may need medical attention.

Check with your doctor as soon as possible if any of the following side effects occur:

More common
> Redness or other skin irritation of treated or uninvolved skin not present before use of this medicine

Rare
> Skin rash

Other side effects not listed above may also occur in some patients. If you notice any other effects, check with your doctor.

Additional Information

Once a medicine has been approved for marketing for a certain use, experience may show that it is also useful for other medical problems. Although this use is not included in product labeling, anthralin is used in certain patients with the following medical condition:

- Alopecia areata (patchy hair loss)

Other than the above information, there is no additional information relating to proper use, precautions, or side effects for this use.

Revised: 06/30/98

ANTIANDROGENS, NONSTEROIDAL   Systemic

Commonly used brand name(s):

In the U.S.—
> Casodex[1]
> Eulexin[2]
> Nilandron[3]

In Canada—
> Anandron[3]
> Casodex[1]
> Euflex[2]

This information applies to the following medicines:
1. Bicalutamide (bye-ka-LOO-ta-mide)
2. Flutamide (FLOO-ta-mide)
3. Nilutamide (nye-LOO-ta-mide)

Description

Nonsteroidal antiandrogens are used to treat cancer of the prostate gland. The prostate gland is present only in males; therefore, females do not get prostate cancer.

Nonsteroidal antiandrogens block the effect of the male hormone testosterone in the body. Giving a nonsteroidal antiandrogen together with another treatment that decreases the amount of testosterone produced in the body is one way of treating this type of cancer.

These medicines are available only with your doctor's prescription, in the following dosage form(s):

Oral
> Bicalutamide
> - Tablets (U.S. and Canada)
> Flutamide
> - Capsules (U.S.)
> - Tablets (Canada)

> Nilutamide
> - Tablets (U.S. and Canada)

Before Using This Medicine

In deciding to use a medicine, the risks of taking the medicine must be weighed against the good it will do. This is a decision you and your doctor will make. For the nonsteroidal antiandrogens, the following should be considered:

Allergies—Tell your doctor if you have ever had any unusual or allergic reaction to any of the nonsteroidal antiandrogens. Also tell your health care professional if you are allergic to any other substances, such as foods, preservatives, or dyes.

Fertility—Nonsteroidal antiandrogens, and other treatments for prostate cancer that are used together with these medicines, may cause low sperm counts or otherwise decrease a man's ability to father a child. In some cases, these effects may be permanent. Men who wish to have children should discuss this with their doctors before starting treatment.

Pregnancy—Nonsteroidal antiandrogens are usually given to men. However, if one of these medicines is needed by a woman, it is very important that an effective method of avoiding pregnancy be used during treatment. Because these medicines block the effect of the male hormone, testosterone, they may interfere with the normal development of a male fetus.

Breast-feeding—Nonsteroidal antiandrogens are usually given to men, and it is not known whether any of these medicines passes into breast milk. However, nonsteroidal antiandrogens can cause serious side effects. Therefore, if a woman needs one of these medicines, she should not breast-feed during treatment.

Children—Studies with the nonsteroidal antiandrogens have been done only in adults, and there is no specific information comparing the use of these medicines in children with use in other age groups. There is a chance that a nonsteroidal antiandrogen could interfere with the development of boys. However, cancer of the prostate gland usually occurs in middle-aged or older men, so it is very unlikely that a child would need these medicines.

Older adults—Nonsteroidal antiandrogens have been tested in elderly people and have not been shown to cause different side effects or problems than they do in younger adults.

Race—A serious side effect of nilutamide that affects the lungs may be more likely to occur in Asian patients than in Caucasian patients.

Other medicines—Although certain medicines should not be used together at all, in other cases two different medicines may be used together even if an interaction might occur. In these cases, your doctor may want to change the dose, or other precautions may be necessary. When you are taking a nonsteroidal antiandrogen, it is especially important that your health care professional know if you are taking any of the following:

- Anticoagulants such as warfarin (e.g., Coumadin)—Flutamide or nilutamide may increase the effects of the anticoagulant. Your doctor may recommend having your blood tested more often so that the dose of anticoagulant can be changed if necessary

- Phenytoin (e.g., Dilantin) or
- Theophylline (e.g., Theo-Dur; Theolair)—Nilutamide may increase the blood levels of these medicines in your body, which can increase the risk of serious side effects

Also tell your doctor if you smoke tobacco. Tobacco smoking may increase the risk of a rare side effect of flutamide.

Other medical problems—The presence of other medical problems may affect the use of nonsteroidal antiandrogens. Make sure you tell your doctor if you have any other medical problems, especially:

- Certain blood deficiencies or disorders or
- Tobacco smoking—Increased risk of anemia, other blood disorders, and jaundice
- Liver disease—The chance of serious side effects may be increased
- Lung disease or other breathing problems—One side effect of nilutamide can make your condition worse; your doctor may want to select a different antiandrogen

---

Proper Use of This Medicine

Take this medicine exactly as directed by your doctor. Do not take more or less of it, and do not take it more often than your doctor ordered. The exact amount of medicine you need has been carefully worked out. Taking too much may increase the chance of side effects, while taking too little may not improve your condition.

It is best to take this medicine at the same time each day. If you have been directed to take the medicine once a day, you may take it either in the morning or in the evening.

Bicalutamide and nilutamide may be taken with food or on an empty stomach.

A nonsteroidal antiandrogen is often used together with another medicine, which is given by injection. *It is very important that the two medicines be used as directed. Follow your doctor's instructions very carefully about when to use these medicines.*

Unwanted effects, including hot flashes and decreased sexual ability, may occur during treatment for prostate cancer. Also, symptoms that often occur in men with prostate cancer, including difficult or painful urination, bloody urine, and urinary tract infections, may occur or continue to occur for a while, until your condition starts to improve. *It is very important that you continue to take the medicine, even if it causes side effects or if you start to feel better. Do not stop taking this medicine without first checking with your doctor.*

If you vomit shortly after taking a dose of this medicine, check with your doctor. You will be told whether to take the dose again or to wait until the next scheduled dose.

Dosing—The doses of these medicines will be different for different patients. *Follow your doctor's orders or the directions on the label.* The following information includes only the average doses of these medicines. *If your dose is different, do not change it* unless your doctor tells you to do so.

The number of capsules or tablets that you take depends on the strength of the medicine. Also, *the number of doses you take each day, the time allowed between doses, and the length of time you take the medicine depend on which of these medicines you are taking.*

For bicalutamide
- For the *oral* dosage form (tablets):
  —For prostate cancer:
  - Adults—50 milligrams (mg) (one tablet) once a day.
  - Children—It is unlikely that bicalutamide would be needed to treat cancer of the prostate in a child. If a child needs this medicine, the dose would have to be determined by the doctor.

For flutamide
- For *oral* dosage forms (capsules or tablets):
  —For prostate cancer:
  - Adults—250 milligrams (mg) (two 125-mg capsules or one 250-mg tablet) every eight hours.
  - Children—It is unlikely that flutamide would be needed to treat cancer of the prostate in a child. If a child needs this medicine, the dose would have to be determined by the doctor.

For nilutamide
- For the *oral* dosage form (tablets):
  —For prostate cancer:
  - Adults—300 milligrams (mg) (six 50-mg tablets) once a day for the first thirty days, then 150 mg (three 50-mg tablets) once a day.
  - Children—It is unlikely that nilutamide would be needed to treat cancer of the prostate in a child. If a child needs this medicine, the dose would have to be determined by the doctor.

Missed dose—If you miss a dose of this medicine, take it as soon as possible.

For bicalutamide or nilutamide: If you do not remember your missed dose until the next day, skip the missed dose and go back to your regular dosing schedule. Do not double doses.

For flutamide: If it is almost time for your next dose, skip the missed dose and go back to your regular dosing schedule. Do not double doses.

Storage—To store this medicine:
- Keep out of the reach of children.
- Store away from heat and direct light.
- Do not store in the bathroom, near the kitchen sink, or in other damp places. Heat or moisture may cause the medicine to break down.
- Do not keep outdated medicine or medicine no longer needed. Be sure that any discarded medicine is out of the reach of children.

Precautions While Using This Medicine

It is very important that your doctor check your progress at regular visits to make sure that this medicine is working properly and to check for unwanted effects.

Nonsteroidal antiandrogens rarely cause liver problems during treatment. The most important signs of this side effect are pain or tenderness in the upper right side of the abdomen (stomach) and yellow eyes or skin. *Check with your doctor immediately if either of these occurs. Also, check with your doctor as soon as possible* if itching occurs or your urine appears unusually dark. Other possible symptoms, such as loss of appetite, nausea or vomiting, and "flu-like" symptoms (headache, muscle or joint pain, or tiredness), can occur during treatment even if you are not having any liver problems. These symptoms usually do not need medical attention. However, if two or more of them occur at the same time, and they last for more than a few days, check with your doctor even if you do not have any of the other symptoms mentioned earlier.

For patients taking *nilutamide:*

- *Check with your doctor right away* if shortness of breath or difficult breathing occurs or gets worse during treatment.
- *Be very careful while driving, especially when you drive into or out of tunnels.* Nilutamide can temporarily change the way your eyes react to light. You may not be able to see as well as usual for up to several minutes after going from bright light to darkness or from dark to lighted areas. Also, nilutamide can cause your eyes to be more sensitive to light than they are normally. Wearing eyeglasses with tinted lenses or sunglasses may help reduce these effects.
- Drinking alcoholic beverages while taking nilutamide may cause unwanted effects in some people. Possible effects include feeling dizzy, lightheaded, or faint; flushing of the face; or a general feeling of illness. *If you notice any of these effects, do not drink any more alcoholic beverages while you are being treated with this medicine.*

Side Effects of This Medicine

Along with its needed effects, a medicine may cause some unwanted effects. Although not all of these side effects may occur, if they do occur they may need medical attention.

Check with your doctor immediately if any of the following side effects occur:

Less common
    Chest pain; shortness of breath or difficult or troubled breathing

Rare
    Pain or tenderness in the upper right side of the abdomen (stomach); yellow eyes or skin

Also, check with your doctor as soon as possible if any of the following side effects occur:

More common
    Cough or hoarseness; fever; runny nose; sneezing; sore throat; tightness in chest or wheezing

Less common
    Bloody or black, tarry stools; chills (flutamide only); itching; lower back or side pain (flutamide only); mental depression; numbness, tingling, pain, or muscle weakness in hands, arms, feet, or legs; skin rash; swelling of face, fingers, feet, or lower legs; unusual tiredness or weakness

Rare
    Bluish-colored lips, fingernails, or palms of hands (flutamide only); dark urine; dizziness (severe) or fainting (flutamide only); feeling of severe pressure in head (flutamide only); pinpoint red spots on skin; unusual bleeding or bruising

Other side effects may occur that usually do not need medical attention. These side effects may go away during treatment as your body adjusts to the medicine. However, check with your doctor if any of the following side effects continue or are bothersome:

More common
    Constipation; decrease in or loss of appetite; diarrhea; dizziness; headache; impotence or decrease in

sexual desire; nausea; swelling of breasts with pain or tenderness; trouble in sleeping

Less common
    Bloated feeling, gas, or indigestion; change in color vision (nilutamide only); confusion; drowsiness; dryness of mouth; "flu-like" symptoms, such as headache, muscle or joint pain, or tiredness (occurring together); nervousness; vomiting

Although not all of the side effects listed above have been reported for all of these medicines, they have been reported for at least one of them. However, because all nonsteroidal antiandrogens are very similar, it is possible that any of the above side effects may occur with any of these medicines.

In addition to the effects listed above, hot flashes (flushing, sudden sweating, and feeling of warmth) often occur during treatment with these medicines. Also, flutamide may cause your urine to have an amber or a yellow-green color. These effects are harmless and do not need medical attention.

Other side effects not listed above may also occur in some patients. If you notice any other effects, check with your doctor.

Developed: 06/22/98
Revised: 1/13/2000

ANTICHOLINERGICS/ ANTISPASMODICS   Systemic

Commonly used brand name(s):

In the U.S.—

Anaspaz[8]	Levbid[8]
A-Spas S/L[8]	Levsin[8]
Banthine[10]	Levsinex Timecaps[8]
Bentyl[5]	Levsin/SL[8]
Cantil[9]	Pro-Banthine[13]
Cystospaz[8]	Quarzan[4]
Cystospaz-M[8]	Robinul[6]
Donnamar[8]	Robinul Forte[6]
ED-SPAZ[8]	Symax SL[8]
Gastrosed[8]	Transderm-Scōp[14]
Homapin[7]	

In Canada—

Bentylol[5]	Propanthel[13]
Buscopan[14]	Robinul[6]
Formulex[5]	Robinul Forte[6]
Gastrozepin[12]	Spasmoban[5]
Levsin[8]	Transderm-V[14]
Pro-Banthine[13]	

Other commonly used names are: dicycloverine[5], glycopyrronium bromide[6], hyoscine hydrobromide[14], hyoscine methobromide[11], methanthelinium[10], and octatropine[1].

Note: For quick reference, the following anticholinergics/antispasmodics are numbered to match the corresponding brand names.

This information applies to the following medicines:
1. Anisotropine (an-iss-oh-TROE-peen)†‡
2. Atropine (A-troe-peen)‡§
3. Belladonna (bell-a-DON-a)†‡
4. Clidinium (kli-DI-nee-um)†
5. Dicyclomine (dye-SYE-kloe-meen)‡
6. Glycopyrrolate (glye-koe-PYE-roe-late)‡
7. Homatropine (hoe-MA-troe-peen)†
8. Hyoscyamine (hye-oh-SYE-a-meen)‡

9. Mepenzolate (me-PEN-zoe-late)†
10. Methantheline (meth-AN-tha-leen)†
11. Methscopolamine (meth-skoe-POL-a-meen)*†
12. Pirenzepine (peer-EN-ze-peen)*
13. Propantheline (proe-PAN-the-leen)‡
14. Scopolamine (scoe-POL-a-meen)‡

---

*Not commercially available in the U.S.
†Not commercially available in Canada.
‡Generic name product may be available in the U.S.
§Generic name product may be available in Canada.

Description

The anticholinergics/antispasmodics are a group of medicines that include the natural belladonna alkaloids (atropine, belladonna, hyoscyamine, and scopolamine) and related products.

The anticholinergics/antispasmodics are used to relieve cramps or spasms of the stomach, intestines, and bladder. Some are used together with antacids or other medicine in the treatment of peptic ulcer. Others are used to prevent nausea, vomiting, and motion sickness.

Anticholinergics/antispasmodics are also used in certain surgical and emergency procedures. In surgery, some are given by injection before anesthesia to help relax you and to decrease secretions, such as saliva. During anesthesia and surgery, atropine, glycopyrrolate, hyoscyamine, and scopolamine are used to help keep the heartbeat normal. Atropine is also given by injection to help relax the stomach and intestines for certain types of examinations. Some anticholinergics are also used to treat poisoning caused by medicines such as neostigmine and physostigmine, certain types of mushrooms, and poisoning by "nerve" gases or organic phosphorous pesticides (for example, demeton [Systox], diazinon, malathion, parathion, and ronnel [Trolene]). Also, anticholinergics can be used for painful menstruation, runny nose, and to prevent urination during sleep.

These medicines may also be used for other conditions as determined by your doctor.

The anticholinergics/antispasmodics are available only with your doctor's prescription in the following dosage forms:

Oral
Anisotropine
 • Tablets (U.S.)
Atropine
 • Tablets (U.S.)
 • Soluble tablets (U.S.)
Belladonna
 • Tincture (U.S.)
Clidinium
 • Capsules (U.S.)
Dicyclomine
 • Capsules (U.S. and Canada)
 • Syrup (U.S. and Canada)
 • Tablets (U.S. and Canada)
Glycopyrrolate
 • Tablets (U.S. and Canada)
Homatropine
 • Tablets (U.S.)
Hyoscyamine
 • Extended-release capsules (U.S.)
 • Extended-release tablets (U.S.)
 • Elixir (U.S.)
 • Oral solution (U.S. and Canada)
 • Tablets (U.S. and Canada)

Mepenzolate
 • Tablets (U.S.)
Methantheline
 • Tablets (U.S.)
Methscopolamine
 • Capsule (U.S.)
 • Extended-release tablets (U.S.)
 • Syrup (U.S.)
 • Tablets (U.S.)
Pirenzepine
 • Tablets (Canada)
Propantheline
 • Tablets (U.S. and Canada)
Scopolamine
 • Tablets (Canada)
Parenteral
Atropine
 • Injection (U.S. and Canada)
Dicyclomine
 • Injection (U.S.)
Glycopyrrolate
 • Injection (U.S. and Canada)
Hyoscyamine
 • Injection (U.S.)
Scopolamine
 • Injection (U.S. and Canada)
Rectal
Scopolamine
 • Suppositories (Canada)
Transdermal
Scopolamine
 • Transdermal disk (U.S. and Canada)

Before Using This Medicine

In deciding to use a medicine, the risks of taking the medicine must be weighed against the good it will do. This is a decision you and your doctor will make. For anticholinergics/antispasmodics the following should be considered:

Allergies—Tell your doctor if you have ever had any unusual or allergic reaction to any of the natural belladonna alkaloids (atropine, belladonna, hyoscyamine, and scopolamine), or any related products. Also, tell your health care professional if you are allergic to any other substances, such as foods, preservatives, or dyes.

Pregnancy—If you are pregnant or if you may become pregnant, make sure your doctor knows if your medicine contains any of the following:
 • *Atropine*—Atropine has not been shown to cause birth defects or other problems in animals. However, when injected into humans during pregnancy, atropine has been reported to increase the heartbeat of the fetus.
 • *Belladonna*—Studies on effects in pregnancy have not been done in either humans or animals.
 • *Clidinium*—Clidinium has not been studied in pregnant women. However, clidinium has not been shown to cause birth defects or other problems in animal studies.
 • *Dicyclomine*—Dicyclomine has been associated with a few cases of human birth defects but dicyclomine has not been confirmed as the cause.
 • *Glycopyrrolate*—Glycopyrrolate has not been studied in pregnant women. However, glycopyrrolate did not cause birth defects in animal studies, but did decrease the chance of becoming pregnant and the newborn's chance of surviving after weaning.

• *Hyoscyamine*—Studies on effects in pregnancy have not been done in either humans or animals. However, when injected into humans during pregnancy, hyoscyamine has been reported to increase the heartbeat of the fetus.
• *Mepenzolate*—Mepenzolate has not been studied in pregnant women. However, studies in animals have not shown that mepenzolate causes birth defects or other problems.
• *Propantheline*—Studies on effects in pregnancy have not been done in either humans or animals.
• *Scopolamine*—Studies on effects in pregnancy have not been done in either humans or animals.

Breast-feeding—Although these medicines may pass into the breast milk, they have not been reported to cause problems in nursing babies. However, the flow of breast milk may be reduced in some patients. The use of dicyclomine in nursing mothers has been reported to cause breathing problems in infants.

Children—Unusual excitement, nervousness, restlessness, or irritability and unusual warmth, dryness, and flushing of skin are more likely to occur in children, who are usually more sensitive to the effects of anticholinergics. Also, when anticholinergics are given to children during hot weather, a rapid increase in body temperature may occur. In infants and children, especially those with spastic paralysis or brain damage, this medicine may be more likely to cause severe side effects. Shortness of breath or difficulty in breathing has occurred in children taking dicyclomine.

Older adults—Confusion or memory loss; constipation; difficult urination; drowsiness; dryness of mouth, nose, throat, or skin; and unusual excitement, nervousness, restlessness, or irritability may be more likely to occur in the elderly, who are usually more sensitive than younger adults to the effects of anticholinergics. Also, eye pain may occur, which may be a sign of glaucoma.

Other medicines—Although certain medicines should not be used together at all, in other cases two different medicines may be used together even if an interaction might occur. In these cases, your doctor may want to change the dose, or other precautions may be necessary. When you are taking anticholinergics/antispasmodics, it is especially important that your health care professional know if you are taking any of the following:

• Antacids or
• Diarrhea medicine containing kaolin or attapulgite or
• Ketoconazole (e.g., Nizoral)—Using these medicines with an anticholinergic may lessen the effects of the anticholinergic

• Central nervous system (CNS) depressants (medicines that cause drowsiness)—Taking scopolamine with CNS depressants may increase the effects of either medicine

• Other anticholinergics (medicine for abdominal or stomach spasms or cramps) or
• Tricyclic antidepressants (amitriptyline [e.g., Elavil], amoxapine [e.g., Asendin], clomipramine [e.g., Anafranil], desipramine [e.g., Pertofrane], doxepin [e.g., Sinequan], imipramine [e.g., Tofranil], nortriptyline [e.g., Aventyl], protriptyline [e.g., Vivactil], trimipramine [e.g., Surmontil])—Taking anticholinergics with tricyclic antidepressants or other anticholinergics may cause an increase in the effects of the anticholinergic

• Potassium chloride (e.g., Kay Ciel)—Using this medicine with an anticholinergic may make gastrointestinal problems caused by potassium worse

Other medical problems—The presence of other medical problems may affect the use of anticholinergics/antispasmodics. Make sure you tell your doctor if you have any other medical problems, especially:

• Bleeding problems (severe)—These medicines may increase heart rate, which would make bleeding problems worse

• Brain damage (in children)—May increase the CNS effects of this medicine

• Colitis (severe) or
• Dryness of mouth (severe and continuing) or
• Enlarged prostate or
• Fever or
• Glaucoma or
• Heart disease or
• Hernia (hiatal) or
• High blood pressure (hypertension) or
• Intestinal blockage or other intestinal problems or
• Lung disease (chronic) or
• Myasthenia gravis or
• Toxemia of pregnancy or
• Urinary tract blockage or difficult urination—These medicines may make these conditions worse

• Down's syndrome—These medicines may cause an increase in pupil dilation and heart rate

• Kidney disease or
• Liver disease—Higher blood levels may occur and cause an increase in side effects

• Overactive thyroid—These medicines may further increase heart rate

• Spastic paralysis (in children)—This condition may increase the effects of the anticholinergic

Proper Use of This Medicine

Take this medicine only as directed. Do not take more of it, do not take it more often, and do not take it for a longer time than your doctor ordered. To do so may increase the chance of side effects.

Dosing—The dose of the anticholinergic/antispasmodic will be different for different patients. *Follow your doctor's orders or the directions on the label.* The following information includes only the average doses of your medicine. *If your dose is different, do not change it* unless your doctor tells you to do so.

The number of capsules or tablets or teaspoonfuls of solution or syrup that you take depends on the strength of the medicine. Also, *the number of doses you take each day, the time allowed between doses, and the length of time you take the medicine depends on the medical problem for which you are taking this medicine.*

For anisotropine
• For *oral* dosage forms (tablets):
  —To treat duodenal or stomach ulcers:
    • Older adults, adults, and teenagers—50 milligrams (mg) three times a day. Your doctor may change the dose if needed.
    • Children—Dose must be determined by your doctor.

For atropine
- For *oral* dosage form (tablets):
  —To treat duodenal or stomach ulcers, intestine problems, or urinary problems:
    - Older adults, adults, and teenagers—300 to 1200 micrograms (mcg) every four to six hours.
    - Children—Dose is based on body weight. The usual dose is 10 mcg per kilogram (kg) (4.5 mcg per pound) of body weight every four to six hours. However, the dose will not be more than 400 mcg every four to six hours.

- For *injectable* dosage form:
  —To treat duodenal or stomach ulcers or intestine problems:
    - Older adults, adults, and teenagers—400 to 600 mcg injected into a muscle, vein, or under the skin every four to six hours.
    - Children—The dose is based on body weight. The usual dose is 10 mcg per kilogram (kg) (4.5 mcg per pound) of body weight injected under the skin every four to six hours. However, the dose will not be more than 400 mcg every four to six hours.
  —To treat heart problems:
    - Older adults, adults, and teenagers—400 to 1000 mcg injected into a vein every one to two hours as needed. The total dose will not be more than 2 mg.
    - Children—The dose is based on body weight. The usual dose is 10 to 30 mcg per kilogram (kg) (4.5 to 13.6 mcg per pound) of body weight injected under the skin.

For belladonna
- For *oral* dosage form (oral solution):
  —To treat duodenal or stomach ulcers or intestine problems:
    - Older adults, adults, and teenagers—180 to 300 micrograms (mcg) three or four times a day. The dose should be taken 30 to 60 minutes before meals and at bedtime. Your doctor may change the dose if needed.
    - Children—The dose is based on body weight. The usual dose is 9 mcg per kilogram (kg) (4 mcg per pound) of body weight three or four times a day.

For clidinium
- For *oral* dosage form (capsules):
  —To treat duodenal or stomach ulcers:
    - Older adults, adults, and teenagers—2.5 to 5 milligrams (mg) three or four times a day. The dose should be taken before meals and at bedtime. Your doctor may change the dose if needed.
    - Children—Dose must be determined by your doctor.

For dicyclomine
- For *oral* dosage forms (capsules, extended-release tablets, syrup, tablets):
  —To treat intestine problems:
    - Older adults, adults, and teenagers—10 to 20 milligrams (mg) three or four times a day. Some people may take 30 mg two times a day. Your doctor may change the dose if needed. Your dose will not be more than 160 mg a day.
    - Children 2 years of age and older—5 to 10 mg three or four times a day. Your doctor may change the dose if needed.

- Children 6 months to 2 years of age—5 to 10 mg of the syrup three or four times a day. Your doctor may change the dose if needed.
- Children up to 6 months of age—Use is not recommended.

- For *injectable* dosage form:
  —To treat intestine problems:
    - Older adults, adults, and teenagers—20 mg injected into a muscle every four to six hours. Your doctor may change the dose if needed.
    - Children—Dose must be determined by your doctor.

For glycopyrrolate
- For *oral* dosage form (tablets):
  —To treat duodenal or stomach ulcers:
    - Older adults, adults, and teenagers—To start, 1 to 2 milligrams (mg) two or three times a day. Some people may also take 2 mg at bedtime. Your doctor may change the dose if needed. However, your dose will not be more than 8 mg a day.
    - Children—Dose must be determined by your doctor.

- For *injectable* dosage form:
  —To treat duodenal or stomach ulcers:
    - Older adults, adults, and teenagers—100 to 200 micrograms (mcg) injected into a muscle or vein. The dose may be repeated every four hours up to four times a day.
    - Children—Dose must be determined by your doctor.

For homatropine
- For *oral* dosage form:
  —To treat duodenal or stomach ulcers:
    - Older adults, adults, and teenagers—5 to 10 milligrams (mg) three or four times a day. Your doctor may change the dose if needed.
    - Children—Dose must be determined by your doctor.

For hyoscyamine
- For *oral* dosage forms (capsules, elixir, oral solution, tablets):
  —To treat duodenal or stomach ulcers, intestine problems, or urinary problems:
    - Older adults, adults, and teenagers—125 to 500 micrograms (mcg) four to six times a day. Some people may take 375 mcg two times a day. The tablets should be taken 30 to 60 minutes before meals. Your doctor may change the dose if needed.
    - Children—Dose is based on body weight. The usual dose is 12.5 to 187 mcg every four hours if needed.

- For *injectable* dosage form:
  —To treat duodenal or stomach ulcers or intestine problems:
    - Older adults, adults, and teenagers—250 to 500 mcg injected into a muscle, vein, or under the skin every four to six hours.
    - Children—Dose must be determined by your doctor.

For mepenzolate
- For *oral* dosage form (tablets):
  —To treat duodenal or stomach ulcers or intestine problems:
  - Older adults, adults, and teenagers—25 to 50 milligrams (mg) four times a day, with meals and at bedtime. Your doctor may change the dose if needed.
  - Children—Dose must be determined by your doctor.

For methantheline
- For *oral* dosage form (tablets):
  —To treat intestine or stomach ulcers, intestine problems, or urinary problems:
  - Older adults, adults, and teenagers—50 to 100 milligrams (mg) every six hours. Your doctor may change the dose if needed.
  - Children 1 year of age and older—12.5 to 50 mg four times a day. Your doctor may change the dose if needed.
  - Children 1 month to 1 year of age—12.5 mg four times a day. Your doctor may change the dose if needed.
  - Children up to 1 month of age—12.5 mg two times a day. Your doctor may change the dose if needed.

For methscopolamine
- For *oral* dosage form (tablets):
  —To treat duodenal or stomach ulcers or intestine problems:
  - Older adults, adults, and teenagers—2.5 to 5 milligrams (mg) four times a day, one-half hour before meals and at bedtime. Your doctor may change the dose if needed.
  - Children—Dose is based on body weight. The usual dose is 200 micrograms (mcg) per kilogram (kg) (90.9 mcg per pound) of body weight four times a day. The dose should be taken before meals and at bedtime.

For pirenzepine
- For *oral* dosage form (tablets):
  —To treat duodenal or stomach ulcers or intestine problems:
  - Older adults, adults, and teenagers—50 milligrams (mg) two times a day, in the morning and at bedtime. Your doctor may change the dose if needed.
  - Children—Dose must be determined by your doctor.

For propantheline
- For *oral* dosage form (tablets):
  —To treat duodenal or stomach ulcers:
  - Older adults, adults, and teenagers—7.5 to 15 milligrams (mg) three times a day, one-half hour before meals, and 30 mg at bedtime. Your doctor may change the dose if needed.
  - Children—Dose is based on body weight. The usual dose is 375 micrograms (mcg) per kilogram (kg) (170 mcg per pound) of body weight four times a day. Your doctor may change the dose if needed.

For scopolamine
- For *oral* dosage form (tablets):
  —To treat urinary problems or intestine problems or painful menstruation:
  - Older adults, adults, and teenagers—10 to 20 milligrams (mg) three or four times a day. Your doctor may change the dose if needed.
  - Children—Dose must be determined by your doctor.
- For *injectable* dosage form:
  —To treat urinary problems or intestine problems:
  - Older adults, adults, and teenagers—10 to 20 mg three or four times a day. Your doctor may change the dose if needed.
  - Children—Dose must be determined by your doctor.
- For *rectal* dosage form (suppository):
  —To treat urinary problems or intestine problems or painful menstruation:
  - Older adults, adults, and teenagers—Insert one 10 mg suppository rectally three or four times a day. Your doctor may change the dose if needed.
  - Children—Dose must be determined by your doctor.
- For *transdermal* dosage form (patch):
  —To treat motion sickness:
  - Older adults, adults, and teenagers—Apply one 500 to 1000 microgram (mcg) patch behind ear at least four to twelve hours (depending on the product) before antinausea effect is needed.
  - Children—Use is not recommended.

Missed dose—If you miss a dose of this medicine, take it as soon as possible. However, if it is almost time for your next dose, skip the missed dose and go back to your regular dosing schedule. Do not double doses.

For patients *taking any of these medicines by mouth:*
- Take this medicine 30 minutes to 1 hour before meals unless otherwise directed by your doctor.

To use the *rectal suppository* form of *scopolamine:*
- If the suppository is too soft to insert, chill it in the refrigerator for 30 minutes or run cold water over it before removing the foil wrapper.
- To insert the suppository: First remove the foil wrapper and moisten the suppository with cold water. Lie down on your side and use your finger to push the suppository well up into the rectum.

To use the *transdermal disk* form of *scopolamine:*
- This medicine usually comes with patient directions. Read them carefully before using this medicine.
- Wash and dry your hands thoroughly before and after handling.
- Apply the disk to the hairless area of skin behind the ear. Do not place over any cuts or irritations.

Storage—To store this medicine:
- Keep out of the reach of children. Overdose is especially dangerous in young children.
- Store away from heat and direct light.
- Do not store the capsule or tablet form of this medicine in the bathroom, near the kitchen sink, or in other damp places. Heat or moisture may cause the medicine to break down.

- Keep the liquid form of this medicine tightly closed and keep it from freezing. Do not refrigerate the syrup form of this medicine.
- Do not keep outdated medicine or medicine no longer needed. Be sure that any discarded medicine is out of the reach of children.

Precautions While Using This Medicine

If you think you or someone else may have taken an overdose, get emergency help at once. Taking an overdose of any of the belladonna alkaloids or taking scopolamine with alcohol or other CNS depressants may lead to unconsciousness and possibly death. Some signs of overdose are clumsiness or unsteadiness; dizziness; severe drowsiness; fever; hallucinations (seeing, hearing, or feeling things that are not there); confusion; shortness of breath or troubled breathing; slurred speech; unusual excitement, nervousness, restlessness, or irritability; fast heartbeat; and unusual warmth, dryness, and flushing of skin.

These medicines may make you sweat less, causing your body temperature to increase. *Use extra care not to become overheated during exercise or hot weather while you are taking this medicine,* since overheating may result in heat stroke. Also, hot baths or saunas may make you dizzy or faint while you are taking this medicine.

Check with your doctor before you stop using this medicine. Your doctor may want you to reduce gradually the amount you are using before stopping completely. Stopping this medicine may cause withdrawal side effects such as vomiting, sweating, and dizziness.

Anticholinergics may cause some people to have blurred vision. *Make sure your vision is clear before you drive or do anything else that could be dangerous if you are not able to see well.* These medicines may also cause your eyes to become more sensitive to light than they are normally. Wearing sunglasses may help lessen the discomfort from bright light.

These medicines, especially in high doses, may cause some people to become dizzy or drowsy. *Make sure you know how you react to this medicine before you drive, use machines, or do anything else that could be dangerous if you are dizzy or are not alert.*

Dizziness, lightheadedness, or fainting may occur, especially when you get up from a lying or sitting position. Getting up slowly may help lessen this problem.

These medicines may cause dryness of the mouth, nose, and throat. For temporary relief of mouth dryness, use sugarless candy or gum, melt bits of ice in your mouth, or use a saliva substitute. However, if your mouth continues to feel dry for more than 2 weeks, check with your medical doctor or dentist. Continuing dryness of the mouth may increase the chance of dental disease, including tooth decay, gum disease, and fungus infections.

For patients taking *scopolamine:*
- This medicine will add to the effects of alcohol and other CNS depressants (medicines that slow down the nervous system, possibly causing drowsiness). Some examples of CNS depressants are antihistamines or medicine for hay fever, other allergies, or colds; sedatives, tranquilizers, or sleeping medicine; prescription pain medicine or narcotics; barbiturates; medicine for seizures; muscle relaxants; or anesthetics, including some dental anesthetics. *Check with your doctor before taking any of the above while you are using this medicine.*

For patients *taking any of these medicines by mouth:*
- Do not take this medicine within 2 or 3 hours of taking antacids or medicine for diarrhea. Taking antacids or antidiarrhea medicines and this medicine too close together may prevent this medicine from working properly.

Side Effects of This Medicine

Along with its needed effects, a medicine may cause some unwanted effects. Although not all of these side effects may occur, if they do occur they may need medical attention.

Check with your doctor as soon as possible if any of the following side effects occur:

Rare
Confusion (especially in the elderly); dizziness, lightheadedness (continuing), or fainting; eye pain; skin rash or hives

Symptoms of overdose
Blurred vision (continuing) or changes in near vision; clumsiness or unsteadiness; confusion; convulsions (seizures); difficulty in breathing, muscle weakness (severe), or tiredness (severe); dizziness; drowsiness (severe); dryness of mouth, nose, or throat (severe); fast heartbeat; fever; hallucinations (seeing, hearing, or feeling things that are not there); slurred speech; unusual excitement, nervousness, restlessness, or irritability; unusual warmth, dryness, and flushing of skin

Other side effects may occur that usually do not need medical attention. These side effects may go away during treatment as your body adjusts to the medicine. However, check with your doctor if any of the following side effects continue or are bothersome:

More common
Constipation (less common with hyoscyamine); decreased sweating; dryness of mouth, nose, throat, or skin

Less common or rare
Bloated feeling; blurred vision; decreased flow of breast milk; difficult urination; difficulty in swallowing; drowsiness (more common with high doses of any of these medicines and with usual doses of scopolamine when given by mouth or by injection); false sense of well-being (for scopolamine only); headache; increased sensitivity of eyes to light; lightheadedness (with injection); loss of memory; nausea or vomiting; redness or other signs of irritation at place of injection; trouble in sleeping (for scopolamine only); unusual tiredness or weakness

For patients using *scopolamine:*
- After you stop using scopolamine, your body may need time to adjust. The length of time this takes depends on the amount of scopolamine you were using and how long you used it. During this period of time check with your doctor if you notice any of the following side effects:
Anxiety; irritability; nightmares; trouble in sleeping

For patients using the *transdermal disk* of *scopolamine:*
- While using the disk or even after removing it, your eyes may become more sensitive to light than usual. You may

also notice the pupil in one eye is larger than the other. Check with your doctor if this side effect continues or is bothersome

Other side effects not listed above may also occur in some patients. If you notice any other effects, check with your doctor.

Additional Information

Once a medicine has been approved for marketing for a certain use, experience may show that it is also useful for other medical problems. Although these uses are not included in product labeling, anticholinergics/antispasmodics are used in certain patients with the following medical conditions:

- Diarrhea
- Excessive watering of mouth
- Asthma treatment (atropine)

Other than the above information, there is no additional information relating to proper use, precautions, or side effects for these uses.

Revised: 02/27/2001

ANTICOAGULANTS　Systemic

Commonly used brand name(s):

In the U.S.—
　Coumadin[4]
　Miradon[2]

In Canada—
　Coumadin[4]
　Sintrom[1]
　Warfilone[4]

Other commonly used names are nicoumalone[4] and dicoumarol[2].

Note: For quick reference, the following anticoagulants are numbered to match the corresponding brand names.

This information applies to the following medicines:
1. Acenocoumarol (a-see-no-COOM-a-rol)*
2. Anisindione (an-iss-in-DYE-one)†
3. Dicumarol (dye-KOO-ma-role)†‡
4. Warfarin (WAR-far-in)‡

This information does *not* apply to ardeparin, dalteparin, danaparoid, enoxaparin, or heparin.

*Not commercially available in the U.S.
†Not commercially available in Canada.
‡Generic name product may be available in the U.S.

Description

Anticoagulants decrease the clotting ability of the blood and therefore help to prevent harmful clots from forming in the blood vessels. These medicines are sometimes called blood thinners, although they do not actually thin the blood. They also will not dissolve clots that already have formed, but they may prevent the clots from becoming larger and causing more serious problems. They are often used as treatment for certain blood vessel, heart, and lung conditions.

In order for an anticoagulant to help you without causing serious bleeding, it must be used properly and all of the precautions concerning its use must be followed exactly. Be sure that you have discussed the use of this medicine with your doctor. It is very important that you understand all of your doctor's orders and that you are willing and able to follow them exactly.

Anticoagulants are available only with your doctor's prescription, in the following dosage forms:

Oral
　Acenocoumarol
　　• Tablets (Canada)
　Anisindione
　　• Tablets (U.S.)
　Dicumarol
　　• Tablets (U.S.)
　Warfarin
　　• Tablets (U.S. and Canada)

Parenteral
　Warfarin
　　• Injection (U.S. and Canada)

Before Using This Medicine

In deciding to use a medicine, the risks of taking the medicine must be weighed against the good it will do. This is a decision you and your doctor will make. For anticoagulants, the following should be considered:

Allergies—Tell your doctor if you have ever had any unusual or allergic reaction to an anticoagulant. Also tell your health care professional if you are allergic to any other substances, such as foods, preservatives, or dyes.

Pregnancy—Anticoagulants may cause birth defects. They may also cause other problems affecting the physical or mental growth of the fetus or newborn baby. In addition, use of this medicine during the last 6 months of pregnancy may increase the chance of severe, possibly fatal, bleeding in the fetus. If taken during the last few weeks of pregnancy, anticoagulants may cause severe bleeding in both the fetus and the mother before or during delivery and in the newborn infant.

Do not begin taking this medicine during pregnancy, and do not become pregnant while taking it, unless you have first discussed the possible effects of this medicine with your doctor. Also, if you suspect that you may be pregnant and you are already taking an anticoagulant, check with your doctor at once. Your doctor may suggest that you take a different anticoagulant that is less likely to harm the fetus or the newborn infant during all or part of your pregnancy. Anticoagulants may also cause severe bleeding in the mother if taken soon after the baby is born.

Breast-feeding—Warfarin is not likely to cause problems in nursing babies. Other anticoagulants may pass into the breast milk. A blood test can be done to see if unwanted effects are occurring in the nursing baby. If necessary, another medicine that will overcome any unwanted effects of the anticoagulant can be given to the baby.

Children—Very young babies may be especially sensitive to the effects of anticoagulants. This may increase the chance of bleeding during treatment.

Older adults—Elderly people are especially sensitive to the effects of anticoagulants. This may increase the chance of bleeding during treatment.

Other medicines—Although certain medicines should not be used together at all, in other cases two different medicines may be used together even if an interaction might occur. In these cases, your doctor may want to change the dose, or other precautions may be necessary. *Many dif-*

ferent medicines can affect the way anticoagulants work in your body. Therefore, it is very important that your health care professional knows if you are taking *any* other prescription or nonprescription (over-the-counter [OTC]) medicine, especially:

- Amiodarone (e.g., Cordarone) or
- Cimetidine (e.g., Tagamet) or
- Metronidazole (e.g., Flagyl) or
- Omeprazole (e.g., Prilosec) or
- Zafirlukast (e.g., Accolate)—Effects of anticoagulants may be increased because of slower removal from the body

- Anabolic steroids (nandrolone [e.g., Anabolin], oxandrolone [e.g., Anavar], oxymetholone [e.g., Anadrol], stanozolol [e.g., Winstrol]) or
- Androgens (male hormones) or
- Antifungals, azole (e.g., Diflucan) or
- Antithyroid agents (medicine for overactive thyroid) or
- Aspirin or other salicylates, including bismuth subsalicylate (e.g., Pepto-Bismol) or
- Cephalosporins (medicine for infection) or
- Cinchophen or
- Clofibrate (e.g., Abitrate, Atromid-S) or
- Danazol (e.g., Danocrine) or
- Dextrothyroxine or
- Diflunisal or
- Disulfiram (e.g., Antabuse) or
- Fluvoxamine (e.g., Luvox) or
- Inflammation or pain medicine (except narcotics) or
- Lepirudin (e.g., Refludan) or
- Medications causing low platelet count or
- Paroxetine (e.g., Paxil) or
- Propafenone (e.g., Rythmol) or
- Quinidine (e.g., Quinidex) or
- Sertraline (e.g., Zoloft) or
- Sulfapyridine or
- Sulfasalazine (e.g., Azulfidine) or
- Thyroid hormones or
- Ticlopidine (e.g., Ticlid) or
- Zileuton (e.g., Zyflo)—These medications may increase the effects of anticoagulants and may increase the chance of bleeding

- Carbenicillin by injection (e.g., Geopen) or
- Dipyridamole (e.g., Persantine) or
- Divalproex (e.g., Depakote) or
- Moxalactam (e.g., Moxam) or
- Pentoxifylline (e.g., Trental) or
- Plicamycin (e.g., Mithracin) or
- Sulfinpyrazone (e.g., Anturane) or
- Thrombolytic agents (medicine for blood clots) or
- Ticarcillin (e.g., Ticar) or
- Valproic acid (e.g., Depakene)—Using any of these medicines together with anticoagulants may increase the chance of bleeding

- Alcohol (with chronic use) or
- Barbiturates or
- Carbamazepine (e.g., Tegretol) or
- Corticosteroids (cortisone-like medicine) or
- Glutethimide (e.g., Doriden) or
- Griseofulvin (e.g., Fulvicin) or
- Phenylbutazone (e.g., Butazolidin) or
- Phenytoin (e.g., Dilantin) or
- Primidone (e.g., Mysoline) or
- Rifampin (e.g., Rifadin)—Effects of anticoagulants may be decreased because of faster removal from the body

- Vitamin K (e.g., AquaMEPHYTON)—Vitamin K helps produce some important blood clotting factors and may decrease the effects of anticoagulants if used at the same time

Other medical problems—The presence of other medical problems may affect the use of anticoagulants. *Many medical problems and treatments will affect the way your body responds to this medicine*. Make sure you tell your doctor if you have *any* other medical problems, or if you have recently had any of the following conditions or medical procedures, especially:

- Aneurysm (swelling in a blood vessel) especially in the head or chest or
- Bleeding in the brain or
- Blood disorders or diseases, especially thrombocytopenia (low platelet count), polycythemia (high red blood cell count), or leukemia or
- Bruising, excessive or
- Cancer of the internal organs, especially of the abdomen or
- Childbirth, recent or
- Diabetes mellitus (sugar diabetes) or
- Diverticulitis or
- Falls or blows to the body or head or
- Heart infection or
- Hemophilia or other bleeding problems or
- Hypertension (high blood pressure) or
- Inflammation of blood vessels or
- Intestinal problems, especially conditions that may affect the absorption of food or vitamins or
- Liver disease or
- Pregnancy, terminated or
- Spinal anesthetics or spinal puncture or
- Surgery, major, especially of the head or eye, or dental surgery or
- Toxemia of pregnancy or
- Ulcers, active, of the stomach, lung, or urinary tract or
- Vitamin K deficiency or
- Wounds, open, surgical or from an ulcer—These conditions may increase the chance of bleeding

In addition, it is important that you tell your doctor if you are now being treated by any other medical doctor or dentist.

Proper Use of This Medicine

Take this medicine only as directed by your doctor. Do not take more or less of it, do not take it more often, and do not take it for a longer time than your doctor ordered. This is especially important for elderly patients, who are especially sensitive to the effects of anticoagulants. Also, it is best if you take this medicine at the same time each day.

Your doctor or health care professional should check your progress at regular visits. A blood test must be taken regularly to see how fast your blood is clotting. This will help your doctor decide on the proper amount of anticoagulant you should be taking each day. Some patients may be able to test their blood at home; discuss with your doctor whether or not this is possible for you.

Dosing—The dose of these medicines will be different for different patients. *Follow your doctor's orders or the directions on the label*. The following information includes only the average doses of these medicines. *If your dose is different, do not change it* unless your doctor tells you to do so.

For acenocoumarol
- For *oral* dosage form (tablets):
  —For preventing or treating harmful blood clots:
    - Adults—The usual dose is 1 to 10 milligrams (mg) per day, adjusted according to blood tests.
    - Children—Dose must be determined by your doctor.

For anisindione
- For *oral* dosage form (tablets):
  —For preventing or treating harmful blood clots:
    - Adults—The usual dose is 25 to 250 milligrams (mg) per day, adjusted according to blood tests.
    - Children—Dose must be determined by your doctor.

For dicumarol
- For *oral* dosage form (tablets):
  —For preventing or treating harmful blood clots:
    - Adults—The usual dose is 25 to 200 milligrams (mg) per day, adjusted according to blood tests.
    - Children—Dose must be determined by your doctor.

For warfarin
- For *oral* dosage form (tablets):
  —For preventing or treating harmful blood clots:
    - Adults—The starting dose is usually 2 to 5 milligrams (mg) per day for two to four days. Then, your dose may be adjusted, depending on your condition and results of routine blood tests.
    - Children—Dose must be determined by your doctor.
- For *injection* dosage form:
  —For preventing or treating harmful blood clots:
    - Adults—The starting dose is usually 2 to 5 milligrams (mg) per day for two to four days. Then, your dose may be adjusted, depending on your condition and results of routine blood tests.
    - Children—Dose must be determined by your doctor.

Missed dose—If you miss a dose of this medicine, take it as soon as possible. Then go back to your regular dosing schedule. If you do not remember until the next day, do not take the missed dose at all and do not double the next one. *Doubling the dose may cause bleeding.* Instead, go back to your regular dosing schedule. It is recommended that you keep a record of each dose as you take it to avoid mistakes. Also, be sure to give your doctor a record of any doses you miss. If you have any questions about this, check with your doctor.

Storage—To store this medicine:
- Keep out of the reach of children.
- Store away from heat and direct light.
- Do not store this medicine in the bathroom, near the kitchen sink, or in other damp places. Heat or moisture may cause the medicine to break down.
- Do not keep outdated medicine or medicine no longer needed. Be sure that any discarded medicine is out of the reach of children.

Precautions While Using This Medicine

Tell all medical doctors, dentists, and pharmacists you go to that you are taking this medicine.

Check with your doctor right away if you notice any unusual bleeding or bruising.

Check with your health care professional before you start or stop taking any other medicine, or change the amount you are taking. This includes any nonprescription (over-the-counter [OTC]) medicine, even aspirin or acetaminophen. Many medicines change the way this medicine affects your body. You may not be able to take the other medicine, or the dose of your anticoagulant may need to be changed.

It is important that you carry identification stating that you are using this medicine. If you have any questions about what kind of identification to carry, check with your health care professional.

While you are taking this medicine, it is very important that you avoid sports and activities that may cause you to be injured. Report to your doctor any falls, blows to the body or head, or other injuries, since serious internal bleeding may occur without your knowing about it.

Be careful to avoid cutting yourself. This includes taking special care in brushing your teeth and in shaving. Use a soft toothbrush and floss gently. Also, it is best to use an electric shaver rather than a blade.

Drinking too much alcohol may change the way this anticoagulant affects your body. You should not drink regularly on a daily basis or take more than 1 or 2 drinks at any time. If you have any questions about this, check with your doctor.

The foods that you eat may also affect the way this medicine affects your body. Eat a normal, balanced diet while you are taking this medicine. *Do not go on a reducing diet, make other changes in your eating habits, start taking vitamins, or begin using other nutrition supplements unless you have first checked with your health care professional.* Also, check with your doctor if you are unable to eat for several days or if you have continuing stomach upset, diarrhea, or fever. These precautions are important because the effects of the anticoagulant depend on the amount of vitamin K in your body. Therefore, it is best to have the same amount of vitamin K in your body every day. Some multiple vitamins and some nutrition supplements contain vitamin K. Vitamin K is also present in green, leafy vegetables (such as broccoli, cabbage, collard greens, kale, lettuce, and spinach) and some vegetable oils. It is especially important that you do not make large changes in the amounts of these foods that you eat every day while you are taking an anticoagulant.

Check with your doctor if you are unable to eat for several days or if you have continuing stomach upset, diarrhea, or fever. This could decrease the amount of vitamin K that gets into your body and could affect this medicine.

Be careful if the weather is very hot for several days. This could increase the effects of the medicine.

After you stop taking this medicine, your body will need time to recover before your blood clotting ability returns to normal. Your health care professional can tell you how long this will take depending on which anticoagulant you were taking. *Use the same caution during this period of time as you did while you were taking the anticoagulant.*

Side Effects of This Medicine

Along with its needed effects, a medicine may cause some unwanted effects. Although not all of these side effects may occur, if they do occur they may need medical attention.

Since many things can affect the way your body reacts to this medicine, you should always watch for signs of unusual bleeding. Unusual bleeding may mean that your body is getting more medicine than it needs. *Check with your doctor immediately if any of the following signs of bleeding or overdose occur:*

Bleeding from gums when brushing teeth; blood in urine; nosebleeds; pinpoint red spots on skin; unusual bleeding or bruising; unusually heavy bleeding or oozing from cuts or wounds; unusually heavy or unexpected menstrual bleeding

Signs and symptoms of bleeding inside the body— dose-related

Abdominal or stomach pain or swelling; back pain or backaches; black, tarry stools; bleeding in eye; blood in stools; blood in vomit or vomit that looks like coffee grounds; blood in urine; blurred vision; chest pain; confusion; constipation; coughing up blood; diarrhea (sudden and severe); dizziness or fainting; headache (continuing or severe); joint pain, stiffness, or swelling; loss of appetite; nausea and vomiting (severe); nervousness; numbness or tingling of hands, feet, or face; paralysis; shortness of breath; weakness (sudden)

Also, check with your doctor as soon as possible if any of the following side effects occur:

Less common

Cough or hoarseness; fever or chills; lower back or side pain; painful or difficult urination; skin rash, hives, or itching

Rare

Blisters or itching on skin; blue or purple toes; dark urine; pain in toes; painful red sores on skin, especially on thighs, breasts, penis, or buttocks; sores, ulcers, or white spots in mouth or throat; sudden increase or decrease in amount of urine; swelling of face, feet, and/or lower legs; trouble in breathing; yellow eyes or skin

Other side effects may occur that usually do not need medical attention. These side effects may go away during treatment as your body adjusts to the medicine. However, check with your doctor if any of the following side effects continue or are bothersome:

Less common or rare

Bloated stomach or gas (with dicumarol); cold intolerance; diarrhea (more common with dicumarol); loss of appetite; nausea or vomiting (more common with dicumarol); stomach cramps or pain

These medicines sometimes cause temporary loss of hair on the scalp.

Depending on your diet, *anisindione* may cause your urine to turn orange. Since it may be hard to tell the difference between blood in the urine and this normal color change, check with your doctor if you notice any color change in your urine.

Other side effects not listed above may also occur in some patients. If you notice any other effects, check with your doctor.

Revised: 5/18/99

ANTICONVULSANTS, DIONE
Systemic

Other commonly used names for trimethadione are TMO, trimethadionum, trimethinum, and troxidone.

This information applies to the following medicines:
Paramethadione (par-a-meth-a-DYE-one)*†
Trimethadione (trye-meth-a-DYE-one)*†

*Not commercially available in the U.S.
†Not commercially available in Canada.

Description

Dione anticonvulsants are used to control certain types of seizures in the treatment of epilepsy. They act on the central nervous system (CNS) to reduce the number of seizures. These medicines cannot cure epilepsy and will only work to control seizures for as long as you continue to take them.

Before Using This Medicine

In deciding to use a medicine, the risks of taking the medicine must be weighed against the good it will do. This is a decision you and your doctor will make. For dione anticonvulsants, the following should be considered:

Allergies—Tell your doctor if you have ever had any unusual or allergic reaction to anticonvulsant medicines. Also tell your health care professional if you are allergic to any other substances, such as foods, preservatives, or dyes.

Pregnancy—There have been reports of increased birth defects when dione anticonvulsants were used during pregnancy. The use of an effective method of birth control is recommended during treatment with dione anticonvulsants. Be sure you have discussed this with your doctor before taking this medicine. Dione anticonvulsants may also cause a bleeding problem in the mother during delivery and in the newborn. Doctors can help prevent this by giving vitamin K to the mother before and during delivery, and to the baby immediately after birth.

Breast-feeding—It is not known whether this medicine passes into breast milk. However, dione anticonvulsants may have serious unwanted effects, and breast-feeding is not recommended.

Children—Although there is no specific information comparing use of dione anticonvulsants in children with use in other age groups, these medicines are not expected to cause different side effects or problems in children than they do in adults.

Older adults—This medicine has been tested in a very small number of older people. Dione anticonvulsants are removed from the body more slowly in older people than in younger people. Higher blood levels of the medicine may occur, which may increase the chance of unwanted effects. Your doctor may give you a different dose than a younger person would receive.

Other medicines—Although certain medicines should not be used together at all, in other cases 2 different medicines may be used together even if an interaction might occur. In these cases, your doctor may want to change the dose, or other precautions may be necessary. When you are taking dione anticonvulsants, it is especially important that your health care professional know if you are taking any of the following:

- Central nervous system (CNS) depressants (medicine that causes drowsiness) or
- Tricyclic antidepressants (medicine for depression)—Using these medicines together may increase the CNS depressant effects

Other medical problems—The presence of other medical problems may affect the use of the dione anticonvulsants. Make sure you tell your doctor if you have any other medical problems, especially:

- Blood disease or
- Diseases of the eye or optic nerve or
- Kidney disease or
- Liver disease—Dione anticonvulsants may make the condition worse. Liver disease may cause higher blood levels of this medicine, which may increase the chance of side effects
- Porphyria—Trimethadione may make the condition worse

Proper Use of This Medicine

For patients taking *paramethadione capsules:*

- Swallow the capsules whole. Do not crush, chew, or break them before swallowing.

For patients taking *trimethadione solution:*

- Use a specially marked measuring spoon, a plastic syringe, or a small marked measuring cup to measure each dose accurately. The average household teaspoon may not hold the right amount of liquid.

For patients taking *trimethadione chewable tablets:*

- The tablets should be crushed and dissolved in a small amount of water or chewed before they are swallowed.

If this medicine upsets your stomach, take it with a small amount of food or milk unless otherwise directed by your doctor.

Take this medicine only as directed by your doctor, to benefit your condition as much as possible. Do not take more or less of it and do not take it more or less often than your doctor ordered.

Dosing—The dose of dione anticonvulsants will be different for different patients. *Follow your doctor's orders or the directions on the label.* The following information includes only the average doses of paramethadione and trimethadione. *If your dose is different, do not change it unless your doctor tells you to do so.*

The number of tablets or capsules or teaspoonfuls of solution that you take depends on the strength of the medicine.

For paramethadione

- For *oral* dosage forms (capsules):
  —Adults and teenagers: To start, 300 milligrams (mg) three times a day. Your doctor may increase your dose by 300 mg every week until seizures are controlled or side effects appear. However, the dose is usually not more than 2400 mg a day, taken in three or four smaller doses.
  —Children 6 years of age and over: 300 mg three times a day.
  —Children 2 to 6 years of age: 200 mg three times a day.

—Children up to 2 years of age: 100 mg three times a day.

For trimethadione

- For *oral* dosage forms (capsules, solution, tablets):
  —Adults and teenagers: To start, 300 milligrams (mg) three times a day. Your doctor may increase your dose by 300 mg every week until seizures are controlled or side effects appear. However, the dose is usually not more than 2400 mg a day, taken in three or four smaller doses.
  —Children 6 years of age and over: 300 mg three or four times a day.
  —Children 2 to 6 years of age: 200 mg three times a day.
  —Children up to 2 years of age: 100 mg three times a day.

Missed dose—If you miss a dose of this medicine, take it as soon as possible. However, if it is almost time for your next dose, skip the missed dose and go back to your regular dosing schedule. If only one dose is missed, it may be taken at bedtime.

Storage—To store this medicine:

- Keep out of the reach of children.
- Store away from heat and direct light.
- Do not store the capsule form of this medicine in the bathroom, near the kitchen sink, or in other damp places. Heat or moisture may cause the medicine to break down.
- Store trimethadione chewable tablets in the refrigerator.
- Keep the liquid form of this medicine from freezing.
- Do not keep outdated medicine or medicine no longer needed. Be sure that any discarded medicine is out of the reach of children.

Precautions While Using This Medicine

It is very important that your doctor check your progress at regular visits. This is necessary to allow dose adjustments and to test for serious unwanted effects.

Tell your doctor as soon as possible if you have a sore throat, fever, or general feeling of tiredness, or if you notice any unusual bleeding or bruising, such as red or purple spots on the skin, nosebleed, or bleeding gums.

Dione anticonvulsants may cause your eyes to become more sensitive to bright light than they are normally, making it difficult for you to see well. Wearing sunglasses and avoiding too much exposure to bright light may help lessen the discomfort. You may also have difficulty seeing in light that changes in brightness. If you notice this effect, be especially careful when driving at night.

This medicine will add to the effects of alcohol and other CNS depressants (medicines that slow down the nervous system, possibly causing drowsiness). Some examples of CNS depressants are antihistamines or medicine for hay fever, other allergies, or colds; sedatives, tranquilizers, or sleeping medicine; prescription pain medicine or narcotics; barbiturates; medicine for seizures; muscle relaxants; or anesthetics, including some dental anesthetics. *Check with your doctor before taking any of the above while you are using this medicine.*

Dione anticonvulsants may cause some people to become drowsy or less alert than they are normally. *Make sure you know how you react to this medicine before you drive, use machines, or do anything else that could be dangerous if you are not alert.* After you have taken this medicine for a while, this effect may not be so bothersome.

Before having any kind of surgery, dental treatment, or emergency treatment, tell the medical doctor or dentist in charge that you are taking this medicine. Taking dione anticonvulsants together with medicines that are used during surgery or dental or emergency treatments may increase the CNS depressant effects.

Check with your doctor as soon as possible if you suspect you have become pregnant.

Do not stop taking dione anticonvulsant medicines without first checking with your doctor. Your doctor may want to reduce your dose gradually. Stopping this medicine suddenly may cause seizures.

Side Effects of This Medicine

Along with its needed effects, a medicine may cause some unwanted effects. Although not all of these side effects may occur, if they do occur they may need medical attention.

Check with your doctor as soon as possible if any of the following side effects occur:
More common
Changes in vision, especially night blindness, glare or snowy image caused by bright light, or double vision
Rare
Confusion; convulsions (seizures); dark or cloudy urine; dizziness; fever; loss of appetite or weight; muscle weakness (severe), especially drooping eyelids, or difficulty in chewing, swallowing, talking, or breathing; nausea or vomiting; pain in abdomen, chest, muscles or joints; shortness of breath; skin rash or itching; sore throat and fever; swelling of face, hands, legs, and feet; swollen lymph nodes; unusual bleeding or bruising, such as recurring nosebleeds, bleeding gums, or vaginal bleeding, or red or purple spots on skin; unusual tiredness or weakness; yellow eyes or skin
Symptoms of overdose
Clumsiness or unsteadiness; coma; dizziness (severe); drowsiness (severe); nausea (severe); problems with vision

Other side effects may occur that usually do not need medical attention. These side effects may go away during treatment as your body adjusts to the medicine. However, check with your doctor if any of the following side effects continue or are bothersome:
More common
Dizziness; drowsiness; headache; increased sensitivity of eyes to light; irritability
Less common
Behavior or mood changes; blood pressure changes; hair loss; hiccups; loss of appetite; stomach pain, nausea, or vomiting; tingling, burning, or prickly sensations; trouble in sleeping; unusual weight loss

Other side effects not listed above may also occur in some patients. If you notice any other effects, check with your doctor.

Revised: 12/4/95

ANTICONVULSANTS, HYDANTOIN
Systemic

Commonly used brand name(s):

In the U.S.—

Cerebyx[2]	Dilantin Kapseals[4]
Dilantin[4]	Mesantoin[3]
Dilantin-125[4]	Peganone[1]
Dilantin Infatabs[4]	Phenytex[4]

In Canada—

Cerebyx[2]	Dilantin-125[4]
Dilantin[4]	Dilantin Infatabs[4]
Dilantin-30[4]	

Another commonly used name for phenytoin is diphenylhydantoin.

Note: For quick reference, the following hydantoin anticonvulsants are numbered to match the corresponding brand names.

This information applies to the following medicines:
1. Ethotoin (ETH-oh-toyn)†
2. Fosphenytoin (fos-FEN-i-toyn)
3. Mephenytoin (me-FEN-i-toyn)†
4. Phenytoin (FEN-i-toyn)‡

---

†Not commercially available in Canada.
‡Generic name product may be available in the U.S.

Description

Hydantoin anticonvulsants (hye-DAN-toyn an-tye-kon-VUL-sants) are used most often to control certain convulsions or seizures in the treatment of epilepsy. Phenytoin also may be used for other conditions as determined by your doctor.

In seizure disorders, these medicines act on the central nervous system (CNS) to reduce the number and severity of seizures. Hydantoin anticonvulsants may also produce some unwanted effects. These depend on the patient's individual condition, the amount of medicine taken, and how long it has been taken. It is important that you know what the side effects are and when to call your doctor if they occur.

Hydantoin anticonvulsants are available only with your doctor's prescription, in the following dosage forms:
Oral
Ethotoin
- Tablets (U.S.)

Mephenytoin
- Tablets (U.S.)

Phenytoin
- Extended capsules (U.S. and Canada)
- Prompt capsules (U.S.)
- Oral suspension (U.S. and Canada)
- Chewable tablets (U.S. and Canada)

Parenteral
Fosphenytoin
- Injection (U.S. and Canada)

Phenytoin
- Injection (U.S. and Canada)

Note: Because fosphenytoin is converted to phenytoin in your body, it has the same effects as those listed for phenytoin in the following sections.

Before Using This Medicine

In deciding to use a medicine, the risks of taking the medicine must be weighed against the good it will do. This is a decision

---

you and your doctor will make. For hydantoin anticonvulsants, the following should be considered:

Allergies—Tell your doctor if you have ever had any unusual or allergic reaction to any hydantoin anticonvulsant medicine. Also tell your health care professional if you are allergic to any other substance, such as foods, preservatives, or dyes.

Pregnancy—Although most mothers who take medicine for seizure control deliver normal babies, there have been reports of increased birth defects when these medicines were used during pregnancy. It is not definitely known if any of these medicines are the cause of such problems.

Also, pregnancy may cause a change in the way hydantoin anticonvulsants are absorbed in your body. You may have more seizures, even though you are taking your medicine regularly. Your doctor may need to increase the anticonvulsant dose during your pregnancy.

In addition, when taken during pregnancy, this medicine may cause a bleeding problem in the mother during delivery and in the newborn. This may be prevented by giving vitamin K to the mother during delivery, and to the baby immediately after birth.

Breast-feeding—Ethotoin and phenytoin pass into the breast milk in small amounts. It is not known whether mephenytoin passes into breast milk. Be sure you have discussed the risks and benefits of the medicine with your doctor.

Children—Some side effects, especially bleeding, tender, or enlarged gums and enlarged facial features, are more likely to occur in children and young adults. Also, unusual and excessive hair growth may occur, which is more noticeable in young girls. In addition, some children may not do as well in school after using high doses of this medicine for a long time.

Older adults—Some medicines may affect older patients differently than they do younger patients. Overdose is more likely to occur in elderly patients and in patients with liver disease.

Other medicines—Although certain medicines should not be used together at all, in other cases two different medicines may be used together even if an interaction might occur. In these cases, your doctor may want to change the dose, or other precautions may be necessary. When you are taking or receiving hydantoin anticonvulsants, it is especially important that your health care professional know if you are taking any of the following:

- Alcohol or
- Central nervous system (CNS) depressants (medicine that causes drowsiness)—Long-term use of alcohol may decrease the blood levels of hydantoin anticonvulsants, resulting in decreased effects; use of hydantoin anticonvulsants in cases where a large amount of alcohol is consumed may increase the blood levels of the hydantoin, resulting in an increased risk of side effects
- Amiodarone (e.g., Cordarone)—Use with phenytoin and possibly with other hydantoin anticonvulsants may increase blood levels of the hydantoin, resulting in an increase in serious side effects
- Antacids or
- Medicine containing calcium—Use of antacids or calcium supplements may decrease the absorption of phenytoin; doses of antacids and phenytoin or calcium sup-

plements and phenytoin should be taken 2 to 3 hours apart

- Anticoagulants (blood thinners) or
- Chloramphenicol (e.g., Chloromycetin) or
- Cimetidine (e.g., Tagamet) or
- Disulfiram (e.g., Antabuse) (medicine for alcoholism) or
- Isoniazid (INH) (e.g., Nydrazid) or
- Fluconazole (e.g., Diflucan) or
- Fluoxetine (e.g., Prozac) or
- Itraconazole (e.g., Sporanox) or
- Ketoconazole (e.g., Nizoral) or
- Miconazole (e.g., Monistat) or
- Phenylbutazone (e.g., Butazolidin) or
- Sulfonamides (sulfa drugs)—Blood levels of hydantoin anticonvulsants may be increased, increasing the risk of serious side effects; hydantoin anticonvulsants may increase the effects of the anticoagulants at first, but with continued use may decrease the effects of these medicines
- Corticosteroids (cortisone-like medicines) or
- Estrogens (female hormones) or
- Oral contraceptives (birth-control pills) containing estrogens or progestins or
- Progestin injection contraceptives (e.g., Depo-Provera) or
- Progestin implant contraceptives (e.g., Norplant)—Hydantoin anticonvulsants may decrease the effects of these medicines; use of hydantoin anticonvulsants with estrogen- or progestin-containing contraceptives may result in breakthrough bleeding and contraceptive failure; additional birth control measures may be needed to decrease the risk of pregnancy
- Diazoxide (e.g., Proglycem)—Use with hydantoin anticonvulsants may decrease the effects of both medicines; therefore, these medicines should not be taken together
- Felbamate (e.g., Felbatrol)—Blood levels of hydantoin anticonvulsants may be increased, and blood levels of felbamate may be decreased. Your doctor may need to adjust your dosage
- Lidocaine—Risk of slow heartbeat may be increased. Other effects of lidocaine may be decreased because hydantoin anticonvulsants may cause it to be removed from the body more quickly
- Methadone (e.g., Dolophine, Methadose)—Long-term use of phenytoin may bring on withdrawal symptoms in patients being treated for drug dependence
- Phenacemide (e.g., Phenurone)—Use with hydantoin anticonvulsants may increase the risk of serious side effects
- Rifampin (e.g., Rifadin)—Use with phenytoin may decrease the effects of phenytoin; your doctor may need to adjust your dosage
- Streptozocin (e.g., Zanosar)—Phenytoin may decrease the effects of streptozocin; therefore, these medicines should not be used together
- Sucralfate (e.g., Carafate)—Use of sucralfate may decrease the absorption of hydantoin anticonvulsants
- Theophylline (e.g., Theo-Dur)—Hydantoin anticonvulsants may make this medicine less effective

• Valproic acid (e.g., Depakene, Depakote)—Use with phenytoin, and possibly other hydantoin anticonvulsants, may increase seizure frequency and increase the risk of serious side effects affecting the liver, especially in infants

Other medical problems—The presence of other medical problems may affect the use of hydantoin anticonvulsants. Make sure you tell your doctor if you have any other medical problems, especially:

• Alcohol abuse—Blood levels of phenytoin may be decreased, decreasing its effects
• Blood disease—Risk of serious infections rarely may be increased by hydantoin anticonvulsants
• Diabetes mellitus (sugar diabetes) or
• Porphyria or
• Systemic lupus erythematosus—Hydantoin anticonvulsants may make the condition worse
• Fever above 101 °F for longer than 24 hours—Blood levels of hydantoin anticonvulsants may be decreased, decreasing the medicine's effects
• Heart disease—Administration of phenytoin by injection may change the rhythm of the heart
• Kidney disease or
• Liver disease—Blood levels of hydantoin anticonvulsants may be increased, leading to an increase in serious side effects
• Thyroid disease—Blood levels of thyroid hormones may be decreased

---

Proper Use of This Medicine

For patients taking the *liquid form* of this medicine:
• Shake the bottle well before using.
• Use a specially marked measuring spoon, a plastic syringe, or a small measuring cup to measure each dose accurately. The average household teaspoon may not hold the right amount of liquid.

For patients taking the *chewable tablet form* of this medicine:
• Tablets may be chewed or crushed before they are swallowed, or may be swallowed whole.

For patients taking the *capsule form* of this medicine:
• Swallow the capsule whole.

If this medicine upsets your stomach, take it with food, unless otherwise directed by your doctor. The medicine should always be taken at the same time in relation to meals to make sure that it is absorbed in the same way.

To control your medical problem, *take this medicine every day* exactly as ordered by your doctor. Do not take more or less of it than your doctor ordered. To help you remember to take the medicine at the correct times, try to get into the habit of taking it at the same time each day.

Dosing—The dose of hydantoin anticonvulsants will be different for different patients. *Follow your doctor's orders or the directions on the label.* The following information includes only the average doses of ethotoin, fosphenytoin, mephenytoin, and phenytoin. *If your dose is different, do not change it* unless your doctor tells you to do so.

The number of capsules or tablets or teaspoonfuls of suspension that you take or the number of injections you receive depends on the strength of the medicine. Also, *the number of doses you take each day, the time allowed between doses, and the length of time you take the medicine depend on the medical problem for which you are using a hydantoin anticonvulsant.*

For ethotoin
• For *oral* dosage form (tablets):
—As an anticonvulsant:
• Adults and teenagers—To start, 125 to 250 milligrams (mg) four to six times a day. Your doctor may increase your dose gradually over several days if needed. However, the dose is usually not more than 3000 mg a day.
• Children—To start, up to 750 mg a day, based on the age and weight of the child. The doctor may increase the dose gradually if needed.

For fosphenytoin
• For *injection* dosage form:
—As an anticonvulsant:
• Adults and children—Dose is based on the illness being treated, and the body weight or size of the patient. The medicine is injected into a vein or muscle.

For mephenytoin
• For *oral* dosage form (tablets):
—As an anticonvulsant:
• Adults and teenagers—To start, 50 to 100 milligrams (mg) once a day. Your doctor may increase your dose by 50 to 100 mg a day at weekly intervals if needed. However, the dose is usually not more than 1200 mg a day.
• Children—To start, 25 to 50 mg once a day. The doctor may increase the dose by 25 to 50 mg a day at weekly intervals if needed. However, the dose is usually not more than 400 mg a day.

For phenytoin
• For *oral* dosage forms (capsules, chewable tablets, or suspension):
—As an anticonvulsant:
• Adults and teenagers—To start, 100 to 125 milligrams (mg) three times a day. Your doctor may adjust your dose at intervals of seven to ten days if needed.
• Children—Dose is based on body weight or body surface area. The usual dose is 5 mg of phenytoin per kilogram (kg) (2.3 mg per pound) of body weight to start. The doctor may adjust the dose if needed.
• Older adults—Dose is based on body weight. The usual dose is 3 mg per kg (1.4 mg per pound) of body weight. The doctor may need to adjust the dose based on your response to the medicine.
• For *injection* dosage form:
—As an anticonvulsant:
• Adults and children—Dose is based on the illness being treated, and the body weight or size of the patient. The medicine is usually injected into a vein.

Missed dose—*If you miss a dose of this medicine* and your dosing schedule is:
• One dose a day—Take the missed dose as soon as possible. However, if you do not remember the missed dose until the next day, skip it and go back to your regular dosing schedule. Do not double doses.

- More than one dose a day—Take the missed dose as soon as possible. However, if it is within 4 hours of your next dose, skip the missed dose and go back to your regular dosing schedule. Do not double doses.

If you miss doses for 2 or more days in a row, check with your doctor.

Storage—To store this medicine:

- Keep out of the reach of children.
- Store away from heat and direct light.
- Do not store in the bathroom, near the kitchen sink, or in other damp places. Heat or moisture may cause the medicine to break down.
- Keep the liquid form of this medicine from freezing. Do not refrigerate.
- Do not keep outdated medicine or medicine no longer needed. Be sure any discarded medicine is out of the reach of children.

Precautions While Using This Medicine

Your doctor should check your progress at regular visits, especially during the first few months of treatment with this medicine. During this time the amount of medicine you are taking may have to be changed often to meet your individual needs.

Do not start or stop taking any other medicine without your doctor's advice. Other medicines may affect the way this medicine works.

This medicine will add to the effects of alcohol and other CNS depressants (medicines that may make you drowsy or less alert). Some examples of CNS depressants are antihistamines or medicine for hay fever, other allergies, or colds; sedatives, tranquilizers, or sleeping medicine; prescription pain medicine or narcotics; barbiturates; other medicine for seizures; muscle relaxants; or anesthetics, including some dental anesthetics. *Check with your doctor before taking any of the above while you are using this medicine.*

Do not take this medicine within 2 to 3 hours of taking antacids or medicine for diarrhea. Taking these medicines and hydantoin anticonvulsants too close together may make the hydantoins less effective.

Do not change brands or dosage forms of phenytoin without first checking with your doctor. Different products may not work the same way. If you refill your medicine and it looks different, check with your pharmacist.

If you have been taking this medicine regularly for several weeks or more, do not suddenly stop taking it. Your doctor may want you to reduce gradually the amount you are taking before stopping completely.

Your doctor may want you to carry a medical identification card or bracelet stating that you are taking this medicine.

For diabetic patients:

- This medicine may affect blood sugar levels. If you notice a change in the results of your blood or urine sugar tests or if you have any questions, check with your doctor.

Before you have any medical tests, tell the doctor in charge that you are taking this medicine. The results of some tests (including the dexamethasone, metyrapone, or Schilling tests, and certain thyroid function tests) may be affected by this medicine.

Before having any kind of surgery, dental treatment, or emergency treatment, tell the medical doctor or dentist in charge that you are taking this medicine. Taking hydantoin anticonvulsants together with medicines that are used during surgery or dental or emergency treatments may cause increased side effects.

This medicine may cause some people to become dizzy, lightheaded, drowsy, or less alert than they are normally. After you have taken this medicine for a while, this effect may not be so bothersome. However, *make sure you know how you react to this medicine before you drive, use machines, or do anything else that could be dangerous if you are dizzy or are not alert.*

Oral contraceptives (birth control pills) containing estrogen or progestin, contraceptive progestin injections (e.g., Depo-Provera), and implant contraceptive forms of progestin (e.g., Norplant) may not work properly if you take them while you are taking hydantoin anticonvulsants. Unplanned pregnancies may occur. You should use a different or additional means of birth control while you are taking hydantoin anticonvulsants. If you have any questions about this, check with your health care professional.

For patients taking *phenytoin* or *mephenytoin:*

- In some patients (usually younger patients), tenderness, swelling, or bleeding of the gums (gingival hyperplasia) may appear soon after phenytoin or mephenytoin treatment is started. To help prevent this, brush and floss your teeth carefully and regularly and massage your gums. Also, *see your dentist every 3 months to have your teeth cleaned. If you have any questions about how to take care of your teeth and gums, or if you notice any tenderness, swelling, or bleeding of your gums, check with your doctor or dentist.*

Side Effects of This Medicine

Along with its needed effects, a medicine may cause some unwanted effects. Although not all of these side effects may occur, if they do occur they may need medical attention.

Check with your doctor as soon as possible if any of the following side effects or signs of overdose occur:

More common

Bleeding, tender, or enlarged gums (rare with ethotoin); burning, tingling, pain, or itching, especially in the groin—following fosphenytoin injection; clumsiness or unsteadiness; confusion; continuous, uncontrolled back-and-forth and/or rolling eye movements—may be sign of overdose; swollen glands in neck or underarms; fever; muscle pain; skin rash or itching; slurred speech or stuttering—may be sign of overdose; sore throat; trembling—may be sign of overdose; unusual excitement, nervousness, or irritability

Rare

Bone malformations; burning pain at place of injection; chest discomfort; chills and fever; dark urine; dizziness; frequent breaking of bones; headache; joint pain; learning difficulties—in children taking high doses for a long time; light gray–colored stools; loss of appetite; nausea or vomiting; pain of penis on erection; restlessness or agitation; slowed growth; stomach pain (severe); troubled or quick, shallow breathing; uncontrolled jerking or twisting movements of hands, arms, or legs; uncontrolled movements of lips, tongue, or cheeks; unusual bleeding (such as nosebleeds) or bruising; unusual tiredness or weakness; weight loss (unusual); yellow eyes or skin

Rare (with long-term use of phenytoin)
Numbness, tingling, or pain in hands or feet

Symptoms of overdose
Blurred or double vision; clumsiness or unsteadiness (severe); confusion (severe); dizziness or drowsiness (severe); seizures; staggering walk; stuttering or slurred speech

Other side effects may occur that usually do not need medical attention. These side effects may go away during treatment as your body adjusts to the medicine. However, check with your doctor if any of the following side effects continue or are bothersome:

More common
Constipation; dizziness (mild); drowsiness (mild)

Less common
Diarrhea (with ethotoin); enlargement of jaw; muscle twitching; swelling of breasts—in males; thickening of lips; trouble in sleeping; unusual and excessive hair growth on body and face (more common with phenytoin); widening of nose tip

Other side effects not listed above may also occur in some patients. If you notice any other effects, check with your doctor.

Additional Information

Once a medicine has been approved for marketing for a certain use, experience may show that it is also useful for other medical problems. Although these uses are not included in product labeling, phenytoin is used in certain patients with the following medical conditions:

- Cardiac arrhythmias (changes in your heart rhythm) caused by digitalis medicine
- Myotonia congenita or
- Myotonic muscular dystrophy or
- Neuromyotonia (certain muscle disorders)
- Paroxysmal choreoathetosis (certain movement disorders)
- Tricyclic antidepressant poisoning
- Trigeminal neuralgia (tic douloureux)

Other than the above information, there is no additional information relating to proper use, precautions, or side effects for these uses.

Revised: 05/01/00

ANTICONVULSANTS, SUCCINIMIDE
Systemic

Commonly used brand name(s):

In the U.S.—
Celontin[2]
Zarontin[1]

In Canada—
Celontin[2]
Zarontin[1]

Note: For quick reference, the following succinimide anticonvulsants are numbered to match the corresponding brand names.

This information applies to the following medicines:
1. Ethosuximide (eth-oh-SUX-i-mide)‡
2. Methsuximide (meth-SUX-i-mide)

‡Generic name product may be available in the U.S.

Description

Succinimide anticonvulsants are used to control certain seizures in the treatment of epilepsy. These medicines act on the central nervous system (CNS) to reduce the number and severity of seizures.

This medicine is available only with your doctor's prescription, in the following dosage forms:

Oral
Ethosuximide
- Capsules (U.S. and Canada)
- Syrup (U.S. and Canada)
Methsuximide
- Capsules (U.S. and Canada)

Before Using This Medicine

In deciding to use a medicine, the risks of taking the medicine must be weighed against the good it will do. This is a decision you and your doctor will make. For succinimide anticonvulsants, the following should be considered:

Allergies—Tell your doctor if you have ever had any unusual or allergic reaction to anticonvulsant medicines. Also tell your health care professional if you are allergic to any other substances, such as foods, preservatives, or dyes.

Pregnancy—Although succinimide anticonvulsants have not been shown to cause problems in humans, there have been unproven reports of increased birth defects associated with the use of other anticonvulsant medicines.

Breast-feeding—Ethosuximide passes into breast milk. It is not known whether methsuximide passes into breast milk. However, these medicines have not been reported to cause problems in nursing babies.

Children—Succinimide anticonvulsants are not expected to cause different side effects or problems in children than they do in adults.

Older adults—Many medicines have not been studied specifically in older people. Therefore, it may not be known whether they work exactly the same way they do in younger adults. Although there is no specific information comparing use of succinimide anticonvulsants in the elderly to use in other age groups, they are not expected to cause different side effects or problems in older people than they do in younger adults.

Other medicines—Although certain medicines should not be used together at all, in other cases two different medicines may be used together even if an interaction might occur. In these cases, your doctor may want to change the dose, or other precautions may be necessary. When you are taking succinimide anticonvulsants, it is especially important that your health care professional know if you are taking any of the following:

- Central nervous system (CNS) depressants (medicines that cause drowsiness)—Using these medicines together may increase CNS depressant effects
- Haloperidol (e.g., Haldol)—A change in the pattern and/or the frequency of seizures may occur; the dose of either medicine may need to be changed

Other medical problems—The presence of other medical problems may affect the use of succinimide anticonvulsants. Make sure you tell your doctor if you have any other medical problems, especially:

- Blood disease or
- Intermittent porphyria or
- Kidney disease (severe) or
- Liver disease—Succinimide anticonvulsants may make the condition worse

Proper Use of This Medicine

This medicine must be taken every day in regularly spaced doses as ordered by your doctor. Do not take more or less of it than your doctor ordered.

If this medicine upsets your stomach, take it with food or milk unless otherwise directed by your doctor.

Dosing—The dose of succinimide anticonvulsants will be different for different patients. *Follow your doctor's orders or the directions on the label.* The following information includes only the average doses of ethosuximide and methsuximide. *If your dose is different, do not change it* unless your doctor tells you to do so.

The number of capsules or teaspoonfuls of syrup that you take depends on the strength of the medicine. Also, *the number of doses you take each day, the time allowed between doses, and the length of time you take the medicine depend on the medical problem for which you are taking a succinimide anticonvulsant.*

For ethosuximide
- For *oral* dosage form (capsules or syrup):
  —As an anticonvulsant:
  - Adults and children 6 years of age and over—To start, 250 milligrams (mg) twice a day. Your doctor may increase your dose gradually if needed. However, the dose is usually not more than 1500 mg a day.
  - Children up to 6 years of age—To start, 250 mg once a day. Your doctor may increase your dose gradually if needed. However, the dose is usually not more than 1000 mg a day.

For methsuximide
- For *oral* dosage form (capsules):
  —As an anticonvulsant:
  - Adults, teenagers, and children—To start, 300 milligrams (mg) once a day. Your doctor may increase your dose gradually if needed. However, the dose is usually not more than 1200 mg a day.

Missed dose—If you miss a dose of this medicine, take it as soon as possible. However, if it is within 4 hours of your next dose, skip the missed dose and go back to your regular dosing schedule. Do not double doses.

Storage—To store this medicine:
- Keep out of the reach of children.
- Store away from heat and direct light.
- Do not store the capsule form of this medicine in the bathroom, near the kitchen sink, or in other damp places. Heat or moisture may cause the medicine to break down.
- Keep the liquid form of this medicine from freezing. Do not refrigerate.
- Do not keep outdated medicine or medicine that is no longer needed. Be sure any discarded medicine is out of the reach of children.

Precautions While Using This Medicine

Your doctor should check your progress at regular visits, especially during the first few months of treatment with this medicine. During this time the amount of medicine you are taking may have to be changed often to meet your individual needs.

If you have been taking a succinimide anticonvulsant regularly, do not stop taking it without first checking with your doctor. Your doctor may want you to reduce gradually the amount you are taking before stopping completely. Stopping this medicine suddenly may cause seizures.

Do not start or stop taking any other medicine without your doctor's advice. Other medicines may affect the way this medicine works.

This medicine will add to the effects of alcohol and other CNS depressants (medicines that slow down the nervous system, possibly causing drowsiness). Some examples of CNS depressants are antihistamines or medicine for hay fever, other allergies, or colds; sedatives, tranquilizers, or sleeping medicine; prescription pain medicine or narcotics; barbiturates; medicine for seizures; muscle relaxants; or anesthetics, including some dental anesthetics. *Check with your doctor before taking any of the above while you are using this medicine.*

This medicine may cause some people to become drowsy or less alert than they are normally. *Make sure you know how you react to this medicine before you drive, use machines, or do anything else that could be dangerous if you are not alert.* After you have taken this medicine for a while, this effect may lessen.

Before having any kind of surgery, dental treatment, or emergency treatment, tell the medical doctor or dentist in charge that you are taking this medicine. Taking succinimide anticonvulsants together with medicines that are used during surgery or dental or emergency treatments may increase the CNS depressant effects.

Your doctor may want you to carry a medical identification card or bracelet stating that you are taking this medicine.

For patients taking *methsuximide:*
- Do not use capsules that are not full or in which the contents have melted, because they may not work properly.

Side Effects of This Medicine

Along with its needed effects, a medicine may cause some unwanted effects. Although not all of these side effects may occur, if they do occur they may need medical attention.

Check with your doctor as soon as possible if any of the following side effects occur:
More common
  Muscle pain; skin rash and itching; swollen glands; sore throat and fever

Less common
> Aggressiveness; difficulty in concentration; mental depression; nightmares

Rare
> Chills; increased chance of certain types of seizures; mood or mental changes; nosebleeds or other unusual bleeding or bruising; shortness of breath; sores, ulcers, or white spots on lips or in mouth; unusual tiredness or weakness; wheezing, tightness in chest, or troubled breathing

Symptoms of overdose
> Drowsiness (severe); nausea and vomiting (severe); troubled breathing

Other side effects may occur that usually do not need medical attention. These side effects may go away during treatment as your body adjusts to the medicine. However, check with your doctor if any of the following side effects continue or are bothersome:

More common
> Clumsiness or unsteadiness; dizziness; drowsiness; headache; hiccups; loss of appetite; nausea or vomiting; stomach cramps

Less common
> Irritability

Other side effects not listed above may also occur in some patients. If you notice any other effects, check with your doctor.

Revised: 02/05/2001

ANTIDEPRESSANTS, MONOAMINE OXIDASE (MAO) INHIBITOR
Systemic

Commonly used brand name(s):

In the U.S.—
Nardil[2]
Parnate[3]
Marplan[1]

In Canada—
Nardil[2]
Parnate[3]

Note: For quick reference, the following antidepressants are numbered to match the corresponding brand names.

This information applies to the following medicines:
1. Isocarboxazid (eye-so-car-BOX-a-zid)†
2. Phenelzine (FEN-el-zeen)
3. Tranylcypromine (tran-ill-SIP-roe-meen)

Note: This information does *not* apply to furazolidone, procarbazine, or selegiline.

†Not commercially available in Canada.

Description

Monoamine oxidase (MAO) inhibitors are used to relieve certain types of mental depression. They work by blocking the action of a chemical substance known as monoamine oxidase (MAO) in the nervous system.

Although these medicines are very effective for certain patients, they may also cause some unwanted reactions if not taken in the right way. It is very important to avoid certain foods, beverages, and medicines while you are being treated with an MAO inhibitor. Your health care professional will help you obtain a list to carry in your wallet or purse as a reminder of which products you should avoid.

MAO inhibitors are available only with your doctor's prescription, in the following dosage forms:

Oral
> Isocarboxazid
> • Tablets (U.S.)
> Phenelzine
> • Tablets (U.S. and Canada)
> Tranylcypromine
> • Tablets (U.S. and Canada)

Before Using This Medicine

In deciding to use a medicine, the risks of taking the medicine must be weighed against the good it will do. This is a decision you and your doctor will make. For monoamine oxidase (MAO) inhibitors, the following should be considered:

Allergies—Tell your doctor if you have ever had any unusual or allergic reaction to any MAO inhibitor. Also tell your health care professional if you are allergic to any other substances, such as foods, preservatives, or dyes.

Diet—Dangerous reactions such as sudden high blood pressure may result when MAO inhibitors are taken with certain foods or drinks. The following foods should be avoided:

• Foods that have a high tyramine content (most common in foods that are aged or fermented to increase their flavor), such as cheeses; fava or broad bean pods; yeast or meat extracts; smoked or pickled meat, poultry, or fish; fermented sausage (bologna, pepperoni, salami, summer sausage) or other fermented meat; sauerkraut; or any overripe fruit. If a list of these foods and beverages is not given to you, ask your health care professional to provide one.

• Alcoholic beverages or alcohol-free or reduced-alcohol beer and wine.

• Large amounts of caffeine-containing food or beverages such as coffee, tea, cola, or chocolate.

Pregnancy—A limited study in pregnant women showed an increased risk of birth defects when these medicines were taken during the first 3 months of pregnancy. In animal studies, MAO inhibitors caused a slowing of growth and increased excitability in the newborn when very large doses were given to the mother during pregnancy.

Breast-feeding—Tranylcypromine passes into the breast milk; it is not known whether isocarboxazid or phenelzine passes into breast milk. Problems in nursing babies have not been reported.

Children—Studies on these medicines have been done only in adult patients, and there is no specific information comparing use of MAO inhibitors in children with use in other age groups. However, animal studies have shown that these medicines may slow growth in the young. Therefore, be sure to discuss with your doctor the use of these medicines in children.

Older adults—Dizziness or lightheadedness may be especially likely to occur in elderly patients, who are usually more sensitive than younger adults to these effects of MAO inhibitors.

Other medicines—Although certain medicines should not be used together at all, in other cases two different medicines may be used together even if an interaction might occur. In these cases, your doctor may want to change the dose, or other precautions may be necessary. When you are taking MAO inhibitors, it is especially important that your health care professional know if you are taking any of the following:

- Amphetamines or
- Antihypertensives (high blood pressure medicine) or
- Appetite suppressants (diet pills) or
- Cyclobenzaprine (e.g., Flexeril) or
- Fluoxetine (e.g., Prozac) or
- Levodopa (e.g., Dopar, Larodopa) or
- Maprotiline (e.g., Ludiomil) or
- Medicine for asthma or other breathing problems or
- Medicines for colds, sinus problems, or hay fever or other allergies (including nose drops or sprays) or
- Meperidine (e.g., Demerol) or
- Methylphenidate (e.g., Ritalin) or
- Monoamine oxidase (MAO) inhibitors, other, including furazolidone (e.g., Furoxone), procarbazine (e.g., Matulane), or selegiline (e.g., Eldepryl), or
- Paroxetine (e.g., Paxil), or
- Sertraline (e.g., Zoloft), or
- Tricyclic antidepressants (amitriptyline [e.g., Elavil], amoxapine [e.g., Asendin], clomipramine [e.g., Anafranil], desipramine [e.g., Pertofrane], doxepin [e.g., Sinequan], imipramine [e.g., Tofranil], nortriptyline [e.g., Aventyl], protriptyline [e.g., Vivactil], trimipramine [e.g., Surmontil])—Using these medicines while you are taking or within 2 weeks of taking MAO inhibitors may cause serious side effects such as sudden rise in body temperature, extremely high blood pressure, severe convulsions, and death; however, sometimes certain of these medicines may be used with MAO inhibitors under close supervision by your doctor
- Antidiabetics, oral (diabetes medicine you take by mouth) or
- Insulin—MAO inhibitors may change the amount of antidiabetic medicine you need to take
- Bupropion (e.g., Wellbutrin)—Using bupropion while you are taking or within 2 weeks of taking MAO inhibitors may cause serious side effects such as seizures
- Buspirone (e.g., BuSpar)—Use with MAO inhibitors may cause high blood pressure
- Carbamazepine (e.g., Tegretol)—Use with MAO inhibitors may increase seizures
- Central nervous system (CNS) depressants (medicines that cause drowsiness)—Using these medicines with MAO inhibitors may increase the CNS and other depressant effects
- Cocaine—Cocaine use by persons taking MAO inhibitors, including furazolidone and procarbazine, may cause a severe increase in blood pressure
- Dextromethorphan—Use with MAO inhibitors may cause excitement, high blood pressure, and fever
- Trazodone or
- Tryptophan used as a food supplement or a sleep aid— Use of these medicines by persons taking MAO inhibitors, including furazolidone and procarbazine, may

cause mental confusion, excitement, shivering, trouble in breathing, or fever

Other medical problems—The presence of other medical problems may affect the use of MAO inhibitors. Make sure you tell your doctor if you have any other medical problems, especially:

- Alcohol abuse—Drinking alcohol while you are taking an MAO inhibitor may cause serious side effects
- Angina (chest pain) or
- Headaches (severe or frequent)—These conditions may interfere with warning signs of serious side effects of MAO inhibitors
- Asthma or bronchitis—Some medicines used to treat these conditions may cause serious side effects when used while you are taking an MAO inhibitor
- Diabetes mellitus (sugar diabetes)—These medicines may change the amount of insulin or oral antidiabetic medication that you need
- Epilepsy—Seizures may occur more often
- Heart or blood vessel disease or
- Liver disease or
- Mental illness (or history of) or
- Parkinson's disease or
- Recent heart attack or stroke—MAO inhibitors may make the condition worse
- High blood pressure—Condition may be affected by these medicines
- Kidney disease—Higher blood levels of MAO inhibitors may occur, which increases the chance of side effects
- Overactive thyroid or
- Pheochromocytoma (PCC)—Serious side effects may occur

Proper Use of This Medicine

Sometimes this medicine must be taken for several weeks before you begin to feel better. Your doctor should check your progress at regular visits, especially during the first few months of treatment, to make sure that this medicine is working properly and to check for unwanted effects.

Take this medicine only as directed by your doctor. Do not take more of it, do not take it more often, and do not take it for a longer time than your doctor ordered.

MAO inhibitors may be taken with or without food or on a full or empty stomach. However, if your doctor tells you to take the medicine a certain way, take it exactly as directed.

Dosing—The dose of MAO inhibitors will be different for different patients. *Follow your doctor's orders or the directions on the label.* The following information includes only the average doses of phenelzine and tranylcypromine. *If your dose is different, do not change it* unless your doctor tells you to do so.

The number of tablets that you take depends on the strength of the medicine. Also, *the number of doses you take each day, the time allowed between doses, and the length of time you take the medicine depend on the medical problem for which you are using an MAO inhibitor.*

For isocarboxazid
- For *oral* dosage form (tablets):
  —For treatment of depression:
    - Adults—To start, 10 milligrams (mg) twice a day. Your doctor may increase your dose gradually as

needed. However, the dose usually is not more than 60 mg a day.
- Children younger than 16 years of age—Use and dose must be determined by the doctor.

For phenelzine
- For *oral* dosage form (tablets):
  —For treatment of depression:
    - Adults—Dose is based on your body weight. To start, the usual dose is 1 milligram (mg) per kilogram (kg) of body weight (0.45 mg per pound) a day. Your doctor may decrease or increase your dose as needed. However, the dose usually is not more than 90 mg a day.
    - Children younger than 16 years of age—Use and dose must be determined by the doctor.
    - Older adults—To start, 15 mg in the morning. Your doctor may increase your dose gradually as needed. However, the dose usually is not more than 60 mg a day.

For tranylcypromine
- For *oral* dosage form (tablets):
  —For treatment of depression:
    - Adults—To start, 30 milligrams (mg) a day. Your doctor may increase your dose gradually as needed. However, the dose usually is not more than 60 mg a day.
    - Children younger than 16 years of age—Use and dose must be determined by the doctor.
    - Older adults—To start, 2.5 to 5 mg a day. The doctor may increase your dose as needed. However, the dose usually is not more than 45 mg a day.

Missed dose—If you miss a dose of this medicine, take it as soon as possible. However, if it is within 2 hours of your next dose, skip the missed dose and go back to your regular dosing schedule. Do not double doses.

Storage—To store this medicine:
- Keep out of the reach of children.
- Store away from heat and direct light.
- Do not store in the bathroom, near the kitchen sink, or in other damp places. Heat or moisture may cause the medicine to break down.
- Do not keep outdated medicine or medicine no longer needed. Be sure that any discarded medicine is out of the reach of children.

Precautions While Using This Medicine

When taken with certain foods, drinks, or other medicines, MAO inhibitors can cause very dangerous reactions such as sudden high blood pressure (also called hypertensive crisis). To avoid such reactions, *obey the following rules of caution:*

- Do not eat foods that have a high tyramine content (most common in foods that are aged or fermented to increase their flavor), such as cheeses; fava or broad bean pods; yeast or meat extracts; smoked or pickled meat, poultry, or fish; fermented sausage (bologna, pepperoni, salami, and summer sausage) or other fermented meat; sauerkraut; or any overripe fruit. If a list of these foods is not given to you, ask your health care professional to provide one.
- Do not drink alcoholic beverages or alcohol-free or reduced-alcohol beer and wine.

- Do not eat or drink large amounts of caffeine-containing food or beverages such as coffee, tea, cola, or chocolate.
- Do not take any other medicine unless approved or prescribed by your doctor. This especially includes nonprescription (over-the-counter [OTC]) medicine, such as that for colds (including nose drops or sprays), cough, asthma, hay fever, and appetite control; "keep awake" products; or products that make you sleepy.

This medicine will add to the effects of alcohol and other CNS depressants (medicines that slow down the nervous system, possibly causing drowsiness). Some examples of CNS depressants are antihistamines or medicine for hay fever, other allergies, or colds; sedatives, tranquilizers, or sleeping medicine; prescription pain medicine or narcotics; barbiturates; medicine for seizures; muscle relaxants; or anesthetics, including some dental anesthetics. *Check with your doctor before taking any of the above while you are using this medicine.*

Check with your doctor or hospital emergency room immediately if severe headache, stiff neck, chest pains, fast heartbeat, or nausea and vomiting occur while you are taking this medicine. These may be symptoms of a serious side effect that should have a doctor's attention.

Do not stop taking this medicine without first checking with your doctor. Your doctor may want you to reduce gradually the amount you are using before stopping completely.

Dizziness, lightheadedness, or fainting may occur, especially when you get up from a lying or sitting position. *Getting up slowly may help.* When you get up from lying down, sit on the edge of the bed with your feet dangling for 1 or 2 minutes. Then stand up slowly. If the problem continues or gets worse, check with your doctor.

This medicine may cause blurred vision or make some people drowsy or less alert than they are normally. *Make sure you know how you react to this medicine before you drive, use machines, or do anything else that could be dangerous if you are unable to see well or are not alert.*

Before having any kind of surgery, dental treatment, or emergency treatment, tell the medical doctor or dentist in charge that you are using this medicine or have used it within the past 2 weeks. Taking MAO inhibitors together with medicines that are used during surgery or dental or emergency treatments may increase the risk of serious side effects.

Your doctor may want you to carry an identification card stating that you are using this medicine.

For patients with *angina* (chest pain):
- This medicine may cause you to have an unusual feeling of good health and energy. However, *do not suddenly increase the amount of exercise you get without discussing it with your doctor.* Too much activity could bring on an attack of angina.

For *diabetic* patients:
- This medicine may affect blood sugar levels. While you are using this medicine, be especially careful in testing for sugar in your blood or urine. If you have any questions about this, check with your doctor.

After you stop using this medicine, you must continue to obey the rules of caution for at least 2 weeks concerning food, drink, and other medicine, since these things may continue to react with MAO inhibitors.

Side Effects of This Medicine

Along with its needed effects, a medicine may cause some unwanted effects. Although not all of these side effects may occur, if they do occur they may need medical attention.

Stop taking this medicine and get emergency help immediately if any of the following side effects occur:
Symptoms of unusually high blood pressure (hypertensive crisis)
Chest pain (severe); enlarged pupils; fast or slow heartbeat; headache (severe); increased sensitivity of eyes to light; increased sweating (possibly with fever or cold, clammy skin); nausea and vomiting; stiff or sore neck

Check with your doctor as soon as possible if any of the following side effects occur:
More common
Dizziness or lightheadedness (severe), especially when getting up from a lying or sitting position
Less common
Diarrhea; fast or pounding heartbeat; swelling of feet or lower legs; unusual excitement or nervousness
Rare
Dark urine; fever; skin rash; slurred speech; sore throat; staggering walk; yellow eyes or skin
Symptoms of overdose
Anxiety (severe); confusion; convulsions (seizures); cool, clammy skin; dizziness (severe); drowsiness (severe); fast and irregular pulse; fever; hallucinations (seeing, hearing, or feeling things that are not there); headache (severe); high or low blood pressure; muscle stiffness; sweating; troubled breathing; trouble in sleeping (severe); unusual irritability

Other side effects may occur that usually do not need medical attention. These side effects may go away during treatment as your body adjusts to the medicine. However, check with your doctor if any of the following side effects continue or are bothersome:
More common
Blurred vision; decreased amount of urine; decreased sexual ability; dizziness or lightheadedness (mild), especially when getting up from a lying or sitting position; drowsiness; headache (mild); increased appetite (especially for sweets) or weight gain; increased sweating; muscle twitching during sleep; nausea; restlessness; shakiness or trembling; tiredness and weakness; trouble in sleeping
Less common or rare
Chills; constipation; decreased appetite; dryness of mouth

Other side effects not listed above may also occur in some patients. If you notice any other effects, check with your doctor.

Additional Information

Once a medicine has been approved for marketing for a certain use, experience may show that it is also useful for other medical problems. Although these uses are not included in product labeling, phenelzine and tranylcypromine are used in certain patients with the following medical conditions:
• Headache
• Panic disorder

Other than the above information, there is no additional information relating to proper use, precautions, or side effects for these uses.

Revised: 06/16/00

ANTIDEPRESSANTS, TRICYCLIC
Systemic

Commonly used brand name(s):

In the U.S.—

Anafranil[3]	Pamelor[7]
Asendin[2]	Sinequan[5]
Aventyl[7]	Surmontil[9]
Elavil[1]	Tipramine[6]
Endep[1]	Tofranil[6]
Norfranil[6]	Tofranil-PM[6]
Norpramin[4]	Vivactil[8]

In Canada—

Anafranil[3]	Novopramine[6]
Apo-Amitriptyline[1]	Novo-Tripramine[9]
Apo-Imipramine[6]	Novotriptyn[1]
Apo-Trimip[9]	Pertofrane[4]
Asendin[2]	Rhotrimine[9]
Aventyl[7]	Sinequan[5]
Elavil[1]	Surmontil[9]
Impril[6]	Tofranil[6]
Levate[1]	Triadapin[5]
Norpramin[4]	Triptil[8]
Novo-Doxepin[5]	

Note: For quick reference, the following tricyclic antidepressants are numbered to match the corresponding brand names.

This information applies to the following medicines:
1. Amitriptyline (a-mee-TRIP-ti-leen)‡§
2. Amoxapine (a-MOX-a-peen)‡
3. Clomipramine (cloe-MIP-ra-meen)‡
4. Desipramine (dess-IP-ra-meen)‡§
5. Doxepin (DOX-e-pin)‡
6. Imipramine (im-IP-ra-meen)‡
7. Nortriptyline (nor-TRIP-ti-leen)‡
8. Protriptyline (proe-TRIP-ti-leen)‡
9. Trimipramine (trye-MIP-ra-meen)‡

‡Generic name product may be available in the U.S.
§Generic name product may be available in Canada.

Description

Tricyclic antidepressants are used to relieve mental depression.

One form of this medicine (imipramine) is also used to treat enuresis (bedwetting) in children. Another form (clomipramine) is used to treat obsessive-compulsive disorders. Tricyclic antidepressants may be used for other conditions as determined by your doctor.

These medicines are available only with your doctor's prescription, in the following dosage forms:
Oral
Amitriptyline
• Syrup (Canada)
• Tablets (U.S. and Canada)
Amoxapine
• Tablets (U.S. and Canada)

Clomipramine
- Capsules (U.S.)
- Tablets (Canada)

Desipramine
- Tablets (U.S. and Canada)

Doxepin
- Capsules (U.S. and Canada)
- Oral solution (U.S.)

Imipramine
- Capsules (U.S.)
- Tablets (U.S. and Canada)

Nortriptyline
- Capsules (U.S. and Canada)
- Oral solution (U.S.)

Protriptyline
- Tablets (U.S. and Canada)

Trimipramine
- Capsules (U.S. and Canada)
- Tablets (Canada)

Parenteral

Amitriptyline
- Injection (U.S.)

Imipramine
- Injection (U.S.)

Before Using This Medicine

In deciding to use a medicine, the risks of taking the medicine must be weighed against the good it will do. This is a decision you and your doctor will make. For tricyclic antidepressants, the following should be considered:

Allergies—Tell your doctor if you have ever had any unusual or allergic reaction to any tricyclic antidepressant or to carbamazepine, maprotiline, or trazodone. Also tell your health care professional if you are allergic to any other substances, such as foods, preservatives, or dyes.

Pregnancy—Studies have not been done in pregnant women. However, there have been reports of newborns suffering from muscle spasms and heart, breathing, and urinary problems when their mothers had taken tricyclic antidepressants immediately before delivery. Also, studies in animals have shown that some tricyclic antidepressants may cause unwanted effects in the fetus.

Breast-feeding—Tricyclic antidepressants pass into the breast milk. Doxepin has been reported to cause drowsiness in the nursing baby.

Children—Children are especially sensitive to the effects of this medicine. This may increase the chance of side effects during treatment. However, side effects in children taking this medicine for bedwetting usually disappear upon continued use. The most common of these are nervousness, sleeping problems, tiredness, and mild stomach upset. If these side effects continue or are bothersome, check with your doctor.

Older adults—Drowsiness, dizziness, confusion, vision problems, dryness of mouth, constipation, and problems in urinating are more likely to occur in elderly patients, who are usually more sensitive than younger adults to the effects of tricyclic antidepressants.

Other medicines—Although certain medicines should not be used together at all, in other cases 2 different medicines may be used together even if an interaction might occur. In these cases, your doctor may want to change the dose, or other precautions may be necessary. When you are taking a tricyclic antidepressant, it is especially important that your health care professional know if you are taking any of the following:

- Amphetamines or
- Appetite suppressants (diet pills) or
- Ephedrine or
- Epinephrine (e.g., Adrenalin) or
- Isoproterenol (e.g., Isuprel) or
- Medicine for asthma or other breathing problems or
- Medicine for colds, sinus problems, or hay fever or other allergies or
- Phenylephrine (e.g., Neo-Synephrine)—Using these medicines with tricyclic antidepressants may increase the risk of serious effects on the heart

- Antipsychotics (medicine for mental illness) or
- Clonidine (e.g., Catapres)—Using these medicines with tricyclic antidepressants may increase the CNS depressant effects and increase the chance of serious side effects

- Antithyroid agents (medicine for overactive thyroid) or
- Cimetidine (e.g., Tagamet)—Using these medicines with tricyclic antidepressants may increase the chance of serious side effects

- Central nervous system (CNS) depressants (medicine that causes drowsiness)—Using these medicines with tricyclic antidepressants may increase the CNS depressant effects

- Guanadrel (e.g., Hylorel) or
- Guanethidine (e.g., Ismelin)—Tricyclic antidepressants may keep these medicines from working as well

- Methyldopa (e.g., Aldomet) or
- Metoclopramide (e.g., Reglan) or
- Metyrosine (e.g., Demser) or
- Pemoline (e.g., Cylert) or
- Pimozide (e.g., Orap) or
- Promethazine (e.g., Phenergan) or
- Rauwolfia alkaloids (alseroxylon [e.g., Rauwiloid], deserpidine [e.g., Harmonyl], rauwolfia serpentina [e.g., Raudixin], reserpine [e.g., Serpasil]) or
- Trimeprazine (e.g., Temaril)—Tricyclic antidepressants may cause certain side effects to be more severe and occur more often

- Metrizamide—The risk of seizures may be increased

- Monoamine oxidase (MAO) inhibitors (furazolidone [e.g., Furoxone], isocarboxazid [e.g., Marplan], phenelzine [e.g., Nardil], procarbazine [e.g., Matulane], selegiline [e.g., Eldepryl], tranylcypromine [e.g., Parnate])—Taking tricyclic antidepressants while you are taking or within 2 weeks of taking MAO inhibitors may cause sudden high body temperature, extremely high blood pressure, severe convulsions, and death; however, sometimes certain of these medicines may be used together under close supervision by your doctor

Other medical problems—The presence of other medical problems may affect the use of tricyclic antidepressants. Make sure you tell your doctor if you have any other medical problems, especially:

- Alcohol abuse (or history of)—Drinking alcohol may cause increased CNS depressant effects

- Asthma or
- Bipolar disorder (manic-depressive illness) or
- Blood disorders or
- Convulsions (seizures) or
- Difficult urination or

- Enlarged prostate or
- Glaucoma or increased eye pressure or
- Heart disease or
- High blood pressure (hypertension) or
- Schizophrenia—Tricyclic antidepressants may make the condition worse
- Kidney disease or
- Liver disease—Higher blood levels of tricyclic antidepressants may result, increasing the chance of side effects
- Overactive thyroid or
- Stomach or intestinal problems—Tricyclic antidepressants may cause an increased chance of serious side effects

Proper Use of This Medicine

To lessen stomach upset, take this medicine with food, even for a daily bedtime dose, unless your doctor has told you to take it on an empty stomach.

Take this medicine only as directed by your doctor, to benefit your condition as much as possible. Do not take more of it, do not take it more often, and do not take it for a longer time than your doctor ordered.

Sometimes this medicine must be taken for several weeks before you begin to feel better. Your doctor should check your progress at regular visits.

To use *doxepin oral solution:*
- This medicine is to be taken by mouth even though it comes in a dropper bottle. The amount you should take should be measured with the dropper provided with your prescription and diluted just before you take each dose. Dilute each dose with about one-half glass (4 ounces) of water, milk, citrus fruit juice, tomato juice, or prune juice. Do not mix this medicine with grape juice or carbonated beverages since these may decrease the medicine's effectiveness.
- Doxepin oral solution must be mixed immediately before you take it. Do not prepare it ahead of time.

Dosing—The dose of tricyclic antidepressants will be different for different patients. *Follow your doctor's orders or the directions on the label*. The following information includes only the average doses of tricyclic antidepressants. *If your dose is different, do not change it* unless your doctor tells you to do so.

The number of capsules or tablets, or the amount of solution or syrup that you take depends on the strength of the medicine. Also, *the number of doses you take each day, the time allowed between doses, and the length of time you take the medicine depend on the medical problem for which you are taking tricyclic antidepressants.*

For amitriptyline
- For *tablet* dosage form:
  —For depression:
    - Adults—At first, 25 milligrams (mg) two to four times a day. Your doctor may increase your dose gradually as needed. However, the dose is usually not more than 150 mg a day, unless you are in the hospital. Some hospitalized patients may need higher doses.
    - Teenagers—At first, 10 mg three times a day, and 20 mg at bedtime. Your doctor may increase your dose gradually as needed. However, the dose is usually not more than 100 mg a day.

- Children 6 to 12 years of age—10 to 30 mg a day.
- Children up to 6 years of age—Use and dose must be determined by your doctor.
- Older adults— At first, 25 mg at bedtime. Your doctor may increase your dose gradually as needed. However, the dose is usually not more than 100 mg a day.

- For *syrup* dosage form:
  —For depression:
    - Adults—At first, 25 mg two to four times a day. Your doctor may increase your dose gradually as needed.
    - Teenagers—At first, 10 mg three times a day, and 20 mg at bedtime. Your doctor may increase your dose gradually as needed. However, the dose is usually not more than 100 mg a day.
    - Children 6 to 12 years of age—10 to 30 mg a day.
    - Children up to 6 years of age—Use and dose must be determined by your doctor.
    - Older adults—At first, 10 mg three times a day, and 20 mg at bedtime. Your doctor may increase your dose gradually as needed. However, the dose is usually not more than 100 mg a day.

- For *injection* dosage form:
  —For depression:
    - Adults—20 to 30 mg four times a day, injected into a muscle.
    - Children up to 12 years of age—Use and dose must be determined by your doctor.

For amoxapine
- For *tablet* dosage form:
  —For depression:
    - Adults—At first, 50 milligrams (mg) two to three times a day. Your doctor may increase your dose gradually as needed.
    - Children up to 16 years of age—Use and dose must be determined by your doctor.
    - Older adults—At first, 25 mg two to three times a day. Your doctor may increase your dose gradually as needed.

For clomipramine
- For *capsule or tablet* dosage forms:
  —For obsessive-compulsive disorders:
    - Adults—At first, 25 milligrams (mg) once a day. Your doctor may increase your dose gradually as needed. However, the dose is usually not more than 250 mg a day, unless you are in the hospital. Some hospitalized patients may need higher doses.
    - Teenagers and children 10 years of age and over—At first, 25 mg once a day. Your doctor may increase your dose gradually as needed. However, the dose is usually not more than 200 mg a day.
    - Children up to 10 years of age—Use and dose must be determined by your doctor.
    - Older adults—At first, 20 to 30 mg a day. Your doctor may increase your dose gradually as needed.

For desipramine
- For *tablet* dosage form:
  —For depression:
    - Adults—100 to 200 milligrams (mg) a day. Your doctor may increase your dose gradually as

needed. However, the dose is usually not more than 300 mg a day.
- Teenagers—25 to 50 mg a day. Your doctor may increase your dose gradually as needed. However, the dose is usually not more than 100 mg a day.
- Children 6 to 12 years of age—10 to 30 mg a day.
- Older adults—25 to 50 mg a day. Your doctor may increase your dose gradually as needed. However, the dose is usually not more than 150 mg a day.

For doxepin
- For *capsule or solution* dosage forms:
  —For depression:
    - Adults—At first, 25 milligrams (mg) three times a day. Your doctor may increase your dose gradually as needed. However, the dose is usually not more than 150 mg a day, unless you are in the hospital. Some hospitalized patients may need higher doses.
    - Children up to 12 years of age—Use and dose must be determined by your doctor.
    - Older adults—At first, 25 to 50 mg a day. Your doctor may increase your dose gradually as needed.

For imipramine
- For *tablet* dosage form:
  —For depression:
    - Adults—25 to 50 milligrams (mg) three to four times a day. Your doctor may increase your dose gradually as needed. However, the dose is usually not more than 200 mg a day, unless you are in the hospital. Some hospitalized patients may need higher doses.
    - Adolescents—25 to 50 mg a day. Your doctor may increase your dose gradually as needed. However, the dose is usually not more than 100 mg a day.
    - Children 6 to 12 years of age—10 to 30 mg a day.
    - Children up to 6 years of age—Use and dose must be determined by your doctor.
    - Older adults—At first, 25 mg at bedtime. Your doctor may increase your dose gradually as needed. However, the dose is usually not more than 100 mg a day.
  —For bedwetting:
    - Children—25 mg once a day, taken one hour before bedtime. Your doctor may increase the dose as needed, based on the child's age.
- For *capsule* dosage form:
  —For depression:
    - Adults—At first, 75 mg a day taken at bedtime. Your doctor may increase your dose gradually as needed. However, the dose is usually not more than 200 mg a day, unless you are in the hospital. Some hospitalized patients may need higher doses.
    - Children up to 12 years of age—Use and dose must be determined by your doctor.
- For *injection* dosage form:
  —For depression:
    - Adults—Dose must be determined by your doctor. It is injected into a muscle. The dose is usually not more than 300 mg a day.

- Children up to 12 years of age—Use and dose must be determined by your doctor.

For nortriptyline
- For *capsule or solution* dosage forms:
  —For depression:
    - Adults—25 milligrams (mg) three to four times a day. Your doctor may increase your dose gradually as needed. However, the dose is usually not more than 150 mg a day.
    - Teenagers—25 to 50 mg a day. Your doctor may increase your dose gradually as needed.
    - Children 6 to 12 years of age—10 to 20 mg a day.
    - Older adults—30 to 50 mg a day. Your doctor may increase your dose gradually as needed.

For protriptyline
- For *tablet* dosage form:
  —For depression:
    - Adults—At first, 5 to 10 milligrams (mg) three to four times a day. Your doctor may increase your dose gradually as needed. However, the dose is usually not more than 60 mg a day.
    - Teenagers—At first, 5 mg three times a day. Your doctor may increase your dose gradually as needed.
    - Children up to 12 years of age—Use and dose must be determined by your doctor.
    - Older adults—At first, 5 mg three times a day. Your doctor may increase your dose gradually as needed.

For trimipramine
- For *capsule or tablet* dosage forms:
  —For depression:
    - Adults—At first, 75 milligrams (mg) a day. Your doctor may increase your dose as needed. However, the dose is usually not more than 200 mg a day, unless you are hospitalized. Some hospitalized patients may need higher doses.
    - Teenagers—At first, 50 mg a day. Your doctor may increase your dose gradually as needed. However, the dose is usually not more than 100 mg a day.
    - Children up to 12 years of age—Use and dose must be determined by your doctor.
    - Older adults—At first, 50 mg a day. Your doctor may increase your dose gradually as needed. However, the dose is usually not more than 100 mg a day.

Missed dose—If you miss a dose of this medicine and your dosing schedule is:
- One dose a day at bedtime—Do not take the missed dose in the morning since it may cause disturbing side effects during waking hours. Instead, check with your doctor.
- More than one dose a day—Take the missed dose as soon as possible. However, if it is almost time for your next dose, skip the missed dose, and go back to your regular dosing schedule. Do not double doses.

If you have any questions about this, check with your doctor.

Storage—To store this medicine:
- Keep out of the reach of children. Overdose of this medicine is very dangerous in young children.
- Store away from heat and direct light.
- Do not store the tablet or capsule form of this medicine in the bathroom, near the kitchen sink, or in other damp

places. Heat or moisture may cause the medicine to break down.
- Keep the liquid form of this medicine from freezing.
- Do not keep outdated medicine or medicine no longer needed. Be sure that any discarded medicine is out of the reach of children.

Precautions While Using This Medicine

It is very important that your doctor check your progress at regular visits to allow dosage adjustments and to help reduce side effects.

This medicine will add to the effects of alcohol and other CNS depressants (medicines that make you drowsy or less alert). Some examples of CNS depressants are antihistamines or medicine for hay fever, other allergies, or colds; sedatives, tranquilizers, or sleeping medicine; prescription pain medicine or narcotics; barbiturates; medicine for seizures; muscle relaxants; or anesthetics, including some dental anesthetics. *Check with your medical doctor or dentist before taking any of the above while you are taking this medicine.*

This medicine may cause some people to become drowsy. *If this occurs, do not drive, use machines, or do anything else that could be dangerous if you are not alert.*

Dizziness, lightheadedness, or fainting may occur, especially when you get up from a lying or sitting position. Getting up slowly may help. If this problem continues or gets worse, check with your doctor.

This medicine may cause dryness of the mouth. For temporary relief, use sugarless gum or candy, melt bits of ice in your mouth, or use a saliva substitute. However, if your mouth continues to feel dry for more than 2 weeks, check with your medical doctor or dentist. Continuing dryness of the mouth may increase the chance of dental disease, including tooth decay, gum disease, and fungus infections.

Tricyclic antidepressants may cause your skin to be more sensitive to sunlight than it is normally. Exposure to sunlight, even for brief periods of time, may cause a skin rash, itching, redness or other discoloration of the skin, or a severe sunburn. When you begin taking this medicine:
- Stay out of direct sunlight, especially between the hours of 10:00 a.m. and 3:00 p.m., if possible.
- Wear protective clothing, including a hat. Also, wear sunglasses.
- Apply a sun block product that has a skin protection factor (SPF) of at least 15. Some patients may require a product with a higher SPF number, especially if they have a fair complexion. If you have any questions about this, check with your health care professional.
- Apply a sun block lipstick that has an SPF of at least 15 to protect your lips.
- Do not use a sunlamp or tanning bed or booth.

If you have a severe reaction from the sun, check with your doctor.

Before you have any medical tests, tell the medical doctor in charge that you are taking this medicine. The results of the metyrapone test may be affected by this medicine.

Before having any kind of surgery, dental treatment, or emergency treatment, tell the medical doctor or dentist in charge that you are using this medicine. Taking tricyclic antidepressants together with medicines used during surgery or dental or emergency treatments may increase the risk of side effects.

For diabetic patients:
- This medicine may affect blood sugar levels. If you notice a change in the results of your blood or urine sugar tests or if you have any questions, check with your doctor.

Do not stop taking this medicine without first checking with your doctor. Your doctor may want you to reduce gradually the amount you are using before stopping completely. This may help prevent a possible worsening of your condition and reduce the possibility of withdrawal symptoms such as headache, nausea, and/or an overall feeling of discomfort.

The effects of this medicine may last for 3 to 7 days after you have stopped taking it. Therefore, all the precautions stated here must be observed during this time.

For patients taking protriptyline:
- If taken late in the day, protriptyline may interfere with nighttime sleep.

Side Effects of This Medicine

Along with its needed effects, a medicine may cause some unwanted effects. Although not all of these side effects may occur, if they do occur they may need medical attention.

Stop taking this medicine and get emergency help immediately if any of the following side effects occur:
> *Reported for amoxapine only*—rare
>> Convulsions (seizures); difficult or fast breathing; fever with increased sweating; high or low (irregular) blood pressure; loss of bladder control; muscle stiffness (severe); pale skin; unusual tiredness or weakness

Check with your doctor as soon as possible if any of the following side effects occur:
> *Less common*
>> Blurred vision; confusion or delirium; constipation (especially in the elderly); decreased sexual ability (more common with amoxapine and clomipramine); difficulty in speaking or swallowing; eye pain; fainting; fast or irregular heartbeat (pounding, racing, skipping); hallucinations; loss of balance control; mask-like face; nervousness or restlessness; problems in urinating; shakiness or trembling; shuffling walk; slowed movements; stiffness of arms and legs

> *Reported for amoxapine only (in addition to the above)*—less common
>> Lip smacking or puckering; puffing of cheeks; rapid or worm-like movements of tongue; uncontrolled chewing movements; uncontrolled movements of hands, arms, or legs

> *Rare*
>> Anxiety; breast enlargement in both males and females; hair loss; inappropriate secretion of milk—in females; increased sensitivity to sunlight; irritability; muscle twitching; red or brownish spots on skin; ringing, buzzing, or other unexplained sounds in the ears; seizures (more common with clomipramine); skin rash and itching; sore throat and fever; swelling of face and tongue; swelling of testicles (more common with amoxapine); trouble with teeth or

gums (more common with clomipramine); weakness; yellow eyes or skin

Symptoms of acute overdose

Confusion; convulsions (seizures); disturbed concentration; drowsiness (severe); enlarged pupils; fast, slow, or irregular heartbeat; fever; hallucinations (seeing, hearing, or feeling things that are not there); restlessness and agitation; shortness of breath or troubled breathing; unusual tiredness or weakness (severe); vomiting

Other side effects may occur that usually do not need medical attention. These side effects may go away during treatment as your body adjusts to the medicine. However, check with your doctor if any of the following side effects continue or are bothersome:

More common

Dizziness; drowsiness; dryness of mouth; headache; increased appetite (may include craving for sweets); nausea; tiredness or weakness (mild); unpleasant taste; weight gain

Less common

Diarrhea; heartburn; increased sweating; trouble in sleeping (more common with protriptyline, especially when taken late in the day); vomiting

Certain side effects of this medicine may occur after you have stopped taking it. Check with your doctor if you notice any of the following effects:

Headache; irritability; nausea, vomiting, or diarrhea; restlessness; trouble in sleeping, with vivid dreams; unusual excitement

Reported for amoxapine only (in addition to the above)

Lip smacking or puckering; puffing of cheeks; rapid or worm-like movements of the tongue; uncontrolled chewing movements; uncontrolled movements of arms or legs

Other side effects not listed above also may occur in some patients. If you notice any other effects, check with your doctor.

Additional Information

Once a medicine has been approved for marketing for a certain use, experience may show that it is also useful for other medical problems. Although these uses are not included in product labeling, tricyclic antidepressants are used in certain patients with the following medical conditions:

- Attention deficit hyperactivity disorder (hyperactivity in children) (desipramine, imipramine, and protriptyline)
- Bulimia (uncontrolled eating, followed by vomiting) (amitriptyline, clomipramine, desipramine, and imipramine)
- Cocaine withdrawal (desipramine and imipramine)
- Headache prevention (for certain types of frequent or continuing headaches) (most tricyclic antidepressants)
- Itching with hives due to cold temperature exposure (doxepin)
- Narcolepsy (extreme tendency to fall asleep suddenly) (clomipramine, desipramine, imipramine, and protriptyline)
- Neurogenic pain (a type of continuing pain) (amitriptyline, clomipramine, desipramine, doxepin, imipramine, nortriptyline, and trimipramine)
- Panic disorder (clomipramine, desipramine, doxepin, nortriptyline, and trimipramine)

- Stomach ulcer (amitriptyline, doxepin, and trimipramine)
- Urinary incontinence (imipramine)

Other than the above information, there is no additional information relating to proper use, precautions, or side effects for these uses.

Revised: 05/22/92
Interim revision: 06/1/92; 03/01/93; 04/29/94; 08/08/97

ANTIDIABETIC AGENTS, SULFONYLUREA Systemic

Commonly used brand name(s):

In the U.S.—

Amaryl[4]	Glucotrol XL[5]
DiaBeta[6]	Glynase PresTab[6]
Diabinese[2]	Micronase[6]
Dymelor[1]	Orinase[8]
Glucotrol[5]	Tolinase[7]

In Canada—

Albert Glyburide[6]	Euglucon[6]
Apo-Chlorpropamide[2]	Gen-Glybe[6]
Apo-Glyburide[6]	Medi-Glybe[6]
Apo-Tolbutamide[8]	Novo-Butamide[8]
DiaBeta[6]	Novo-Glyburide[6]
Diabinese[2]	Novo-Propamide[2]
Diamicron[3]	Nu-Glyburide[6]
Dimelor[1]	Orinase[8]

Another commonly used name for glyburide is glibenclamide.

Note: For quick reference, the following sulfonylurea antidiabetic agents are numbered to match the corresponding brand names.

This information applies to the following medicines:

1. Acetohexamide (a-set-oh-HEX-a-mide)‡
2. Chlorpropamide (klor-PROE-pa-mide)‡§
3. Gliclazide (GLIK-la-zide)*
4. Glimepiride (GLYE-me-pye-ride)†
5. Glipizide (GLIP-i-zide)†
6. Glyburide (GLYE-byoo-ride)‡
7. Tolazamide (tole-AZ-a-mide)†‡
8. Tolbutamide (tole-BYOO-ta-mide)‡§

*Not commercially available in the U.S.
†Not commercially available in Canada.
‡Generic name product may be available in the U.S.
§Generic name product may be available in Canada.

Description

Sulfonylurea antidiabetic agents (also known as sulfonylureas) are used to treat a certain type of diabetes mellitus (sugar diabetes) called type 2 diabetes. When you have type 2 diabetes, insulin is still being produced by your pancreas. Sometimes the amount of insulin you produce may not be enough or your body may not be using it properly and you may still need more. Sulfonylureas work by causing your pancreas to release more insulin into the blood stream. All of the cells in your body need insulin to help turn the food you eat into energy. This is done by using sugar (or glucose) in the blood as quick energy. Or the sugar may be stored in the form of fats, sugars, and proteins for use later, such as for energy between meals.

Sometimes insulin that is being produced by the body is not able to help sugar get inside the body's cells. Sulfonylureas help insulin get into the cells where it can work properly to lower blood sugar. In this way, sulfonylureas will help lower blood sugar and help restore the way you use food to make energy.

Many people with type 2 diabetes can control their blood sugar level with diet or diet and exercise alone. Following a diabetes diet plan and exercising will always be important with any type of diabetes. To work properly, the amount of sulfonylurea you use must be balanced against the amount and type of food you eat and the amount of exercise you do. If you change your diet, your exercise, or both, you will want to test your blood sugar level so that it does not drop too low (hypoglycemia) or rise too high (hyperglycemia). Your health care professional will teach you what to do if this happens.

Sometimes patients with type 2 diabetes might need to change to treatment with insulin for a short period of time during pregnancy or for a serious medical condition, such as diabetic coma; ketoacidosis; severe injury, burn, or infection; or major surgery. In these conditions, insulin and blood sugar can change fast and blood sugar can be best controlled with insulin instead of a sulfonylurea.

At some point, a sulfonylurea may stop working as well and your blood sugar level will go up. You will need to know if this happens and what to do. Instead of taking more of this medicine, your doctor may change you to another sulfonylurea. Or your doctor may have you inject small doses of insulin or take another oral antidiabetic medicine called metformin along with your sulfonylurea to help the insulin you make work better. If that does not bring down the amount of sugar in your blood, your doctor may have you stop taking the oral antidiabetic agents and begin receiving only insulin injections.

Chlorpropamide may also be used for other conditions as determined by your doctor.

Oral antidiabetic medicines do not help diabetic patients who have type 1 diabetes because these patients cannot produce or release insulin from their pancreas gland. Their blood sugar is best controlled by insulin injections.

Sulfonylureas are available only with your doctor's prescription, in the following dosage forms:

Oral
Acetohexamide
• Tablets (U.S. and Canada)
Chlorpropamide
• Tablets (U.S. and Canada)
Gliclazide
• Tablets (Canada)
Glimepiride
• Tablets (U.S.)
Glipizide
• Tablets (U.S.)
• Extended-release Tablets (U.S.)
Glyburide
• Tablets (U.S. and Canada)
• Micronized Tablets (U.S.)
Tolazamide
• Tablets (U.S.)
Tolbutamide
• Tablets (U.S. and Canada)

Before Using This Medicine

In deciding to use a medicine, the risks of taking the medicine must be weighed against the good it will do. This is a decision you and your doctor will make. For sulfonylurea medicines, the following should be considered:

Allergies—Tell your doctor if you have ever had any unusual or allergic reaction to sulfonylureas, or to sulfonamide-type (sulfa) medicines, including thiazide diuretics (a certain type of water pill). Also tell your health care professional if you are allergic to any other substances, such as foods, preservatives, or dyes.

Pregnancy—Sulfonylureas are rarely used during pregnancy. The amount of insulin you need changes during and after pregnancy. For this reason, it is easier to control your blood sugar using injections of insulin, rather than with the use of sulfonylureas. Close control of your blood sugar can reduce your chance of having high blood sugar during the pregnancy and of your baby gaining too much weight, or having birth defects. Be sure to tell your doctor if you plan to become pregnant or if you think you are pregnant. If insulin is not available or cannot be used and sulfonylureas are used during pregnancy, they should be stopped at least 2 weeks before the delivery date (one month before for chlorpropamide and glipizide). Lowering of blood sugar can occur as a rebound effect at delivery and for several days following birth and will be watched closely by your health care professionals.

Breast-feeding—Chlorpropamide and tolbutamide pass into human breast milk and glimepiride passes into the milk of rats. Chlorpropamide and glimepiride are not recommended in nursing mothers but, in some cases, tolbutamide has been used. It is not known if other sulfonylureas pass into breast milk. Check with your doctor if you are thinking about breast-feeding.

Children—There is little information about the use of sulfonylureas in children. Type 2 diabetes is unusual in this age group.

Older adults—Some elderly patients may be more sensitive than younger adults to the effects of sulfonylureas, especially when more than one antidiabetic medicine is being taken or if other medicines that affect blood sugar are also being taken. This may increase your chance of developing low blood sugar during treatment. Furthermore, the first signs of low or high blood sugar are not easily seen or do not occur at all in older patients. This may increase the chance of low blood sugar developing during treatment.

Also, elderly patients who take chlorpropamide are more likely to hold too much body water.

Other medicines—Although certain medicines should not be used together at all, in other cases two different medicines may be used together even if an interaction might occur. In these cases, your doctor may want to change the dose, or other precautions may be necessary. *Do not take any other medicine, unless prescribed or approved by your doctor.* When you are taking sulfonylurea antidiabetic drugs, it is especially important that your health care professional know if you are taking any of the following:
• Alcohol—When low blood sugar occurs, it may last longer than usual if more than a small amount of alcohol is taken, especially on an empty stomach. Small amounts of alcohol at mealtime usually do not cause problems with your blood sugar but may cause a redness (called flushing) in the face, arms, and neck that

can be uncomfortable. This can occur with most of the sulfonylureas but is most likely to occur with chlorpropamide and has occurred up to 12 hours after alcohol was taken during chlorpropamide use

- Anticoagulants (blood thinners)—The effect of either the blood thinner or the antidiabetic medicine may be increased or decreased if the two medicines are used together

- Aspirin or other salicylates or
- Azole antifungals (miconazole [e.g., Monistat I.V.], fluconazole [e.g., Diflucan]) or
- Chloramphenicol (e.g., Chloromycetin) or
- Cimetidine (e.g., Tagamet) or
- Fluouroquinolones (ciprofloxacin [e.g., Cipro], enoxacin [e.g., Penetrex], lomefloxacin [e.g., Maxaquin], norfloxacin [e.g., Noroxin], ofloxacin [e.g., Floxin]) or
- Quinidine (e.g., Quinidex) or
- Quinine or
- Ranitidine (e.g., Zantac)—These medicines may increase the chances of low blood sugar

- Asparaginase (e.g., Elspar) or
- Corticosteroids (cortisone-like medicine) or
- Lithium (e.g., Lithonate) or
- Thiazide diuretics (e.g., Dyazide)—These medicines may increase the chances of high blood sugar

- Asthma medicines or
- Cough or cold medicines or
- Hay fever or allergy medicines—Many medicines (including nonprescription [over-the-counter] products) can affect the control of your blood sugar

- Beta-adrenergic blocking agents (acebutolol [e.g., Sectral], atenolol [e.g., Tenormin], betaxolol [e.g., Kerlone], bisoprolol [e.g., Zebeta], carteolol [e.g., Cartrol], labetalol [e.g., Normodyne], metoprolol [e.g., Lopressor], nadolol [e.g., Corgard], oxprenolol [e.g., Trasicor], penbutolol [e.g., Levatol], pindolol [e.g., Visken], propranolol [e.g., Inderal], sotalol [e.g., Betapace], timolol [e.g., Blocadren])—Beta-adrenergic blocking agents may increase the chance that high or low blood sugar can occur. Also, they can hide symptoms of low blood sugar (such as fast heartbeat). Because of this, a person with diabetes might not recognize that he or she has low blood sugar and might not take immediate steps to treat it. Beta-adrenergic blocking agents can also cause low blood sugar to last longer than usual

- Cyclosporine [e.g., Sandimmune]—Sulfonylureas can increase the effects of cyclosporine

- Guanethidine (e.g., Ismelin) or
- Monoamine oxidase (MAO) inhibitors (furazolidone [e.g., Furoxone], isocarboxazid [e.g., Marplan], phenelzine [e.g., Nardil], procarbazine [e.g., Matulane], selegiline [e.g., Eldepryl], or tranylcypromine [e.g., Parnate])—Taking a sulfonylurea while you are taking (or within 2 weeks of taking) these medicines may increase the chances of low blood sugar occurring

- Octreotide (e.g., Sandostatin) or
- Pentamidine (e.g., Pentam)—Use of these medicines with sulfonylureas may increase the chance of either high or low blood sugar occurring

Other medical problems—The presence of other medical problems may affect the use of the sulfonylurea antidiabetic medicines. Make sure you tell your doctor if you have any other medical problems, especially:

- Acid in the blood (acidosis) or
- Burns (severe) or
- Diabetic coma or
- Fever, high or
- Injury, severe or
- Ketones in the blood (diabetic ketoacidosis) or
- Surgery, major or
- Any other condition in which insulin needs change rapidly—Insulin may be needed temporarily to control diabetes in patients with these conditions because changes in blood sugar may occur rapidly and without much warning; also, your blood sugar may need to be tested more often

- Diarrhea, continuing or
- Female hormone changes for some women (e.g., during puberty, pregnancy, or menstruation) or
- Infection, severe or
- Mental stress, severe or
- Overactive adrenal gland, not properly controlled or
- Problems with intestines, severe or
- Slow stomach emptying or
- Vomiting, continuing or
- Any other condition that causes severe blood sugar changes—Insulin may be needed temporarily to control diabetes mellitus in patients with these conditions because changes in blood sugar may occur rapidly and without much warning; also, your blood sugar may need to be tested more often

- Heart disease—Chlorpropamide or tolbutamide causes some patients to retain (keep) more body water than usual. Heart disease may be worsened by this extra body water

- Kidney disease or
- Liver disease—Your blood sugar may be increased or decreased, partly because of slower removal of sulfonylurea from the body; this may change the amount of sulfonylurea you need

- Overactive thyroid, not properly controlled or
- Underactive thyroid, not properly controlled—Your blood sugar may be increased or decreased, partly because the medicine may be removed from the body too fast or too slow. Until your thyroid condition is controlled, the amount of sulfonylurea you need may change. Also, your blood sugar may need to be tested more often

- Underactive adrenal gland, not properly controlled or
- Underactive pituitary gland, not properly controlled or
- Undernourished condition or
- Weakened physical condition or
- Any other condition that causes low blood sugar—Patients with these conditions may be more likely to develop low blood sugar while taking sulfonylureas

Proper Use of This Medicine

Use this medicine only as directed even if you feel well and do not notice any signs of high blood sugar. Do not take more of this medicine and do not take it more often than your doctor ordered. To do so may increase the chance of serious side effects. Remember that this medicine will not cure your diabetes but it does help control it. Therefore, you must continue to take it as directed if you expect to lower your blood sugar and keep it low. *You may have to take an antidiabetic medicine for the rest of your life.* If high blood sugar is not treated, it can cause serious problems, such as heart failure, blood vessel disease, eye disease, or kidney disease.

Your doctor will give you instructions about diet, exercise, how to test your blood sugar levels, and how to adjust your dose when you are sick.

- Diet—The daily number of calories in the meal plan should be adjusted by your doctor or a registered dietitian to help you reach and maintain a healthy body weight. In addition, regular meals and snacks are arranged to meet the energy needs of your body at different times of the day. *It is very important that you follow your meal plan carefully.*
- Exercise—Ask your doctor what kind of exercise to do, the best time to do it, and how much you should do each day.
- Blood tests—This is the best way to tell whether your diabetes is being controlled properly. Blood sugar testing helps you and your health care team adjust the dose of your medicine, meal plan, or exercise schedule.
- On sick days—When you become sick with a cold, fever, or the flu, you need to take your usual dose of sulfonylurea, even if you feel too ill to eat. This is especially true if you have nausea, vomiting, or diarrhea. Infection usually increases your need to produce more insulin. Sometimes you may need to be switched from your sulfonylurea to insulin for a short period of time while you are sick to properly control blood sugar. Call your doctor for specific instructions. Continue taking your sulfonylurea and try to stay on your regular meal plan. If you have trouble eating solid food, drink fruit juices, nondiet soft drinks, or clear soups, or eat small amounts of bland foods. A dietitian or your health care professional can give you a list of foods and the amounts to use for sick days. Test your blood sugar level at least every 4 hours while you are awake and check your urine for ketones. If ketones are present, call your doctor at once. If you have severe or prolonged vomiting, check with your doctor. Even when you start feeling better, let your doctor know how you are doing.

For patients taking *glipizide extended-release tablets:*

- Swallow the tablet whole, without breaking, crushing, or chewing it.
- You may sometimes notice what looks like a tablet in your stool. Do not worry. After you swallow the tablet, the medicine in the tablet is absorbed inside your body. Then the tablet passes into your stool without changing its shape. The medicine has entered your body and will work properly.

Dosing—The dose of these medicines will be different for different patients. *Follow your doctor's orders or the directions on the label.* The following information includes only the average doses of these medicines. *If your dose is different, do not change it* unless your doctor tells you to do so.

The number of tablets that you take depends on the strength of the medicine. Also, *the number of doses you take each day, the time allowed between doses, and the length of time you take the medicine depend on the amount of sugar in your blood or urine.*

For acetohexamide
- For *oral* dosage form (tablets):
  —For treating type 2 diabetes:
    - Adults—At first, 250 milligrams (mg) once a day. Some elderly people may need a lower dose at first. Then, your doctor may change your dose a little at a time if needed. The dose is usually not more than 1.5 grams a day. If your dose is 1 gram or more, the dose is usually divided into two doses. These doses are taken before the morning and evening meals.
    - Children—The type of diabetes treated with this medicine is rare in children. However, if a child needs this medicine, the dose would have to be determined by the doctor.

For chlorpropamide
- For *oral* dosage form (tablets):
  —For treating type 2 diabetes:
    - Adults—At first, 250 milligrams (mg) once a day. Some elderly people may need a lower dose of 100 to 125 mg a day at first. Then, your doctor may change your dose a little at a time if needed. The dose is usually not more than 750 mg a day.
    - Children—The type of diabetes treated with this medicine is rare in children. However, if a child needs this medicine, the dose would have to be determined by the doctor.

For gliclazide
- For *oral* dosage form (tablets):
  —For treating type 2 diabetes:
    - Adults—80 milligrams (mg) a day with a meal as a single dose or 160 to 320 mg divided into two doses taken with the morning and evening meals.
    - Children—The type of diabetes treated with this medicine is rare in children. However, if a child needs this medicine, the dose would have to be determined by the doctor.

For glimepiride
- For *oral* dosage form (tablets):
  —For treating type 2 diabetes:
    - Adults:
      —Glimepiride alone: At first, 1 to 2 milligrams (mg) once a day with breakfast or the first main meal. The dose then may be increased by your doctor based on your blood sugar level.
      —Glimepiride with metformin: The usual dose is 8 mg once a day with breakfast or the first main meal.
      —Glimepiride with insulin: The usual dose is 8 mg once a day with breakfast or the first main meal.
    - Children—The type of diabetes treated with this medicine is rare in children. However, if a child needs this medicine, the dose would have to be determined by the doctor.

For glipizide
- For *oral* dosage form (tablets):
  —For treating type 2 diabetes:
    - Adults—At first, 5 milligrams (mg) once a day. Some elderly people may need a lower dose of 2.5 mg a day at first. Then, your doctor may change your dose a little at a time if needed. The

dose is usually not more than 40 mg a day. If your dose is 15 mg or more, the dose is usually divided into two doses. These doses are taken thirty minutes before the morning and evening meals.

- Children—The type of diabetes treated with this medicine is rare in children. However, if a child needs this medicine, the dose would have to be determined by the doctor.
- For *oral* dosage form (extended-release tablets):
  —For treating type 2 diabetes:
  - Adults—At first, 5 mg once a day with breakfast. Then, your doctor may change your dose a little at a time if needed. The dose is usually not more than 20 mg a day.
  - Children—The type of diabetes treated with this medicine is rare in children. However, if a child needs this medicine, the dose would have to be determined by the doctor.

For glyburide
- For *oral* dosage form (nonmicronized tablets):
  —For treating type 2 diabetes:
  - Adults—At first, 2.5 to 5 milligrams (mg) once a day. Some elderly people may need a lower dose of 1.25 to 2.5 mg a day at first. Then, your doctor may change your dose a little at a time if needed. The dose is usually not more than 20 mg a day. If your dose is 10 mg or more, the dose usually is divided into two doses. These doses are taken with the morning and evening meals.
  - Children—The type of diabetes treated with this medicine is rare in children. However, if a child needs this medicine, the dose would have to be determined by the doctor.
- For *oral* dosage form (micronized tablets):
  —For treating type 2 diabetes:
  - Adults—At first, 1.5 to 3 mg a day. Some elderly people may need a low dose of 0.75 to 3 mg a day at first. Then, your doctor may change your dose a little at a time if needed. The dose is usually not more than 12 mg a day. If your dose is 6 mg or more, the dose is usually divided into two doses. These doses are taken with the morning and evening meals. A single dose is taken with breakfast or with the first meal.
  - Children—The type of diabetes treated with this medicine is rare in children. However, if a child needs this medicine, the dose would have to be determined by the doctor.

For tolazamide
- For *oral* dosage form (tablets):
  —For treating type 2 diabetes:
  - Adults—At first, 100 to 250 milligrams (mg) once a day in the morning. Then, your doctor may change your dose a little at a time if needed. The dose is usually not more than 1 gram a day. If your dose is 500 mg or more, the dose is usually divided into two doses. These doses are taken with the morning and evening meals.
  - Children—The type of diabetes treated with this medicine is rare in children. However, if a child needs this medicine, the dose would have to be determined by the doctor.

For tolbutamide
- For *oral* dosage form (tablets):
  —For treating type 2 diabetes:
  - Adults—At first, 1000 to 2000 milligrams (mg) a day. Some elderly people may need lower doses to start. The dose is usually divided into two doses. These doses are taken before the morning and evening meals. Your doctor may change your dose a little at a time if needed. The dose is usually not more than 3000 mg a day.
  - Children—The type of diabetes treated with this medicine is rare in children. However, if a child needs this medicine, the dose would have to be determined by the doctor.

Missed dose—If you miss a dose of this medicine, take it as soon as possible. However, if it is almost time for your next dose, skip the missed dose and go back to your regular dosing schedule. Do not double doses.

Storage—To store this medicine:
- Keep out of the reach of children.
- Store away from heat and direct light.
- Do not store in the bathroom, near the kitchen sink, or in other damp places. Heat or moisture may cause the medicine to break down.
- Do not keep outdated medicine or medicine no longer needed. Be sure that any discarded medicine is out of the reach of children.

Precautions While Using This Medicine

Your doctor will want to check your progress at regular visits, especially during the first few weeks that you take this medicine.

It is very important to follow carefully any instructions from your health care team about:
- Alcohol—Drinking alcohol may cause severe low blood sugar. Discuss this with your health care team.
- Tobacco—If you have been smoking for a long time and suddenly stop, your dosage of sulfonylurea may need to be reduced. If you decide to quit, tell your doctor first.
- Other medicines—Do not take other medicines unless they have been discussed with your doctor. This especially includes nonprescription medicines, such as aspirin, and medicines for appetite control, asthma, colds, cough, hay fever, or sinus problems.
- Counseling—Other family members need to learn how to prevent side effects or help with side effects in the patient if they occur. Also, patients with diabetes, especially teenagers, may need special counseling about sulfonylurea or insulin dosing changes that might occur because of lifestyle changes, such as changes in exercise and diet. Furthermore, counseling on contraception and pregnancy may be needed because of the problems that can occur in women with diabetes who become pregnant.
- Travel—Carry a recent prescription and your medical history. Be prepared for an emergency as you would normally. Make allowances for changing time zones, and keep your meal times as close as possible to your usual meal times.
- Protecting skin from sunlight—Sulfonylureas can make you more sensitive to the sun. Use of sunblock products that have a skin protection factor (SPF) of at least 15 on

your skin and lips can help to prevent sunburn. Do not use a sunlamp or tanning bed or booth.

In case of emergency —There may be a time when you need emergency help for a problem caused by your diabetes. You need to be prepared for these emergencies. It is a good idea to:

- Wear a medical identification (I.D.) bracelet or neck chain at all times. Also, carry an I.D. card in your wallet or purse that says that you have diabetes and a list of all of your medicines.
- Keep some kind of quick-acting sugar handy to treat low blood sugar.
- Have a glucagon kit and a syringe and needle available in case severe low blood sugar occurs. Check and re-place any expired kits regularly.

Too much of a sulfonylurea can cause low blood sugar (also called hypoglycemia). *Symptoms of low blood sugar must be treated before they lead to unconsciousness (passing out).* Different people may feel different symptoms of low blood sugar. *It is important that you learn which symptoms of low blood sugar you usually have so that you can treat it quickly.*

- Symptoms of low blood sugar can include: anxious feeling, behavior change similar to being drunk, blurred vision, cold sweats, confusion, cool pale skin, difficulty in concentrating, drowsiness, excessive hunger, fast heartbeat, headache, nausea, nervousness, night-mares, restless sleep, shakiness, slurred speech, and unusual tiredness or weakness.
- The symptoms of low blood sugar may develop quickly and may result from:
  —delaying or missing a scheduled meal or snack.
  —exercising more than usual.
  —drinking a significant amount of alcohol.
  —taking certain medicines.
  —taking too high a dose of sulfonylurea.
  —if using insulin, using too much insulin.
  —sickness (especially with vomiting or diarrhea).
- Know what to do if symptoms of low blood sugar occur. Eating some form of quick-acting sugar when symptoms of low blood sugar first appear will usually prevent them from getting worse. Good sources of sugar include:
  —Glucose tablets or gel, fruit juice or nondiet soft drink (4 to 6 ounces [one-half cup]), corn syrup or honey (1 tablespoon), sugar cubes (6 one-half-inch sized), or table sugar (dissolved in water).
    - Do not use chocolate because its fat slows down the sugar entering the bloodstream.
    - If a snack is not scheduled for an hour or more you should also eat a light snack, such as crackers or a half sandwich, or drink an 8-ounce glass of milk.
  —Glucagon is used in emergency situations such as unconsciousness. Have a glucagon kit available, along with a syringe and needle, and know how to prepare and use it. Members of your household also should know how and when to use it.

High blood sugar (hyperglycemia) is another problem related to uncontrolled diabetes. *If you have any symptoms of high blood sugar, contact your health care team right away.* If high blood sugar is not treated, severe hyperglycemia can occur, leading to ketoacidosis (diabetic coma) and death.

- Symptoms of high blood sugar appear more slowly than those of low blood sugar. Symptoms can include: blurred vision; drowsiness; dry mouth; flushed and dry skin; fruit-like breath odor; increased urination; loss of appetite; stomachache, nausea, or vomiting; tiredness; troubled breathing (rapid and deep); and unusual thirst.
- Symptoms of severe high blood sugar (called ketoaci-dosis or diabetic coma) that need immediate hospitaliza-tion include: flushed dry skin, fruit-like breath odor, ke-tones in urine, passing out, troubled breathing (rapid and deep).
- High blood sugar symptoms may occur if you:
  —have a fever, diarrhea, or an infection.
  —if using insulin, do not take enough insulin or skip a dose of insulin.
  —do not exercise as much as usual.
  —overeat or do not follow your meal plan.
- Know what to do if high blood sugar occurs. Your doctor may recommend changes in your sulfonylurea dose or meal plan to avoid high blood sugar. Symptoms of high blood sugar must be corrected before they progress to more serious conditions. Check with your doctor often to make sure you are controlling your blood sugar, *but do not change the dose of your medicine without checking with your doctor.* Your doctor might discuss the following with you:
  —Decreasing your dose for a short time for special needs, such as when you cannot exercise as you normally do.
  —Increasing your dose when you plan to eat an un-usually large dinner, such as on holidays. This type of increase is called an anticipatory dose.
  —Delaying a meal if your blood sugar is over 200 mg/dL to allow time for your blood sugar to go down. An extra dose or an injection of insulin may be needed if your blood sugar does not come down shortly.
  —Not exercising if your blood sugar is over 240 mg/dL and reporting this to your doctor immediately.
  —Being hospitalized if ketoacidosis or diabetic coma occurs with a possible change of treatment.

Side Effects of This Medicine

The use of sulfonylurea antidiabetic agents has been re-ported, but not proven in all studies, to increase the risk of death from heart and blood vessel disease. Patients with di-abetes are already more likely to have these problems if they do not control their blood sugar. Some sulfonylureas, such as glyburide and gliclazide, can have a positive effect on heart and blood vessel disease. It is important to know that prob-lems can occur, but it is also not known if other sulfonylureas, particularly tolbutamide, help to cause these problems. It is known that if blood sugar is not controlled, such problems can occur.

Along with their needed effects, sulfonylureas may cause some unwanted effects. Although not all of these side effects may occur, if they do occur they may need medical attention.

Check with your doctor immediately if any of the following side effects occur:
  Less common
    Convulsions (seizures); unconsciousness

Also, check with your doctor as soon as possible if any of the following side effects occur:
  More common
    Low blood sugar, including anxious feeling, behavior change similar to being drunk, blurred vision, cold sweats, confusion, cool pale skin, difficulty in con-centrating, drowsiness, excessive hunger, fast

heartbeat, headache, nausea, nervousness, night-mares, restless sleep, shakiness, slurred speech, unusual tiredness or weakness; unusual weight gain

Less common
Peeling of skin; skin redness, itching, or rash

Rare
Chest pain; chills; coughing up blood; dark urine; fever; fluid-filled skin blisters; general feeling of illness; increased amounts of sputum (phlegm); increased sweating; light-colored stools; pale skin; sensitivity to the sun; shortness of breath; sore throat; thinning of the skin; unusual bleeding or bruising; unusual tiredness or weakness; yellow eyes or skin

Other side effects may occur that usually do not need medical attention. These side effects may go away during treatment as your body adjusts to the medicine. However, check with your doctor if any of the following side effects continue or are bothersome:

More common
Changes in sense of taste; constipation; diarrhea; dizziness; increased amount of urine or more frequent urination; heartburn; increased or decreased appetite; passing of gas; stomach pain, fullness, or discomfort; vomiting

Less common or rare
Difficulty in focusing the eyes; increased sensitivity of skin to sun

For patients taking chlorpropamide or tolbutamide:
• Rarely, some patients who take chlorpropamide may retain (keep) more body water than usual. This happens even less often with tolbutamide. Check with your doctor as soon as possible if any of the following signs occur:
Depression; swelling or puffiness of face, ankles, or hands

Other side effects not listed above may also occur in some patients. If you notice any other effects, check with your doctor.

Additional Information

Once a medicine has been approved for marketing for a certain use, experience may show that it is also useful for other medical problems. Although this use is not included in product labeling, chlorpropamide is used in certain patients with the following medical condition:
• Diabetes insipidus (water diabetes)

If you are taking this medicine for water diabetes, the advice listed above that relates to diet for patients with *sugar* diabetes *does not apply to you*. However, the advice about hypoglycemia (low blood sugar) *does* apply to you. Call your doctor right away if you feel any of the symptoms described.

Other than the above information, there is no additional information relating to its proper use, precautions, or side effects for this use.

Revised: 12/29/99

ANTIDYSKINETICS   Systemic

Commonly used brand name(s):

In the U.S.—

Akineton[2]	Kemadrin[4]
Artane[5]	Parsidol[3]
Artane Sequels[5]	Trihexane[5]
Cogentin[1]	Trihexy[5]

In Canada—

Akineton[2]	Kemadrin[4]
Apo-Benztropine[1]	Parsitan[3]
Apo-Trihex[5]	PMS Benztropine[1]
Artane[5]	PMS Procyclidine[4]
Artane Sequels[5]	PMS Trihexyphenidyl[5]
Cogentin[1]	Procyclid[4]

Other commonly used names are: Benzatropine[1], Profenamine[3].

Note: For quick reference, the following antidyskinetics are numbered to match the corresponding brand names.

This information applies to the following medicines:
1. Benztropine (BENZ-troe-peen)‡§
2. Biperiden (bye-PER-i-den)
3. Ethopropazine (eth-oh-PROE-pa-zeen)
4. Procyclidine (proe-SYE-kli-deen)
5. Trihexyphenidyl (trye-hex-ee-FEN-i-dill)‡

Note: This information does *not* apply to Amantadine, Carbidopa and Levodopa, Diphenhydramine, Haloperidol, and Levodopa.

---

‡Generic name product may be available in the U.S.
§Generic name product may be available in Canada.

Description

Antidyskinetics are used to treat Parkinson's disease, sometimes referred to as "shaking palsy." By improving muscle control and reducing stiffness, this medicine allows more normal movements of the body as the disease symptoms are reduced. It is also used to control severe reactions to certain medicines such as reserpine (e.g., Serpasil) (medicine to control high blood pressure) or phenothiazines, chlorprothixene (e.g., Taractan), thiothixene (e.g., Navane), loxapine (e.g., Loxitane), and haloperidol (e.g., Haldol) (medicines for nervous, mental, and emotional conditions).

Antidyskinetics may also be used for other conditions as determined by your doctor.

These medicines are available only with your doctor's prescription in the following dosage forms:

Oral
Benztropine
• Tablets (U.S. and Canada)
Biperiden
• Tablets (U.S. and Canada)
Ethopropazine
• Tablets (U.S. and Canada)
Procyclidine
• Elixir (Canada)
• Tablets (U.S. and Canada)
Trihexyphenidyl
• Extended-release capsules (U.S. and Canada)
• Elixir (U.S. and Canada)
• Tablets (U.S. and Canada)

Parenteral
Benztropine
• Injection (U.S. and Canada)
Biperiden
• Injection (U.S.)

Before Using This Medicine

In deciding to use a medicine, the risks of taking the medicine must be weighed against the good it will do. This is a decision you and your doctor will make. For antidyskinetics, the following should be considered:

Allergies—Tell your doctor if you have ever had any unusual or allergic reaction to antidyskinetics. Also tell your health care professional if you are allergic to any other substances, such as foods, preservatives, or dyes.

Pregnancy—Studies on effects in pregnancy have not been done in either humans or animals. However, antidyskinetics have not been shown to cause problems in humans.

Breast-feeding—It is not known if antidyskinetics pass into breast milk. Although most medicines pass into breast milk in small amounts, many of them may be used safely while breast-feeding. Mothers who are taking these medicines and who wish to breast-feed should discuss this with their doctor.

Since antidyskinetics tend to decrease the secretions of the body, it is possible that the flow of breast milk may be reduced in some patients.

Children—Children may be especially sensitive to the effects of antidyskinetics. This may increase the chance of side effects during treatment.

Older adults—Agitation, confusion, disorientation, hallucinations, memory loss, and mental changes are more likely to occur in elderly patients, who are usually more sensitive to the effects of antidyskinetics.

Other medicines—Although certain medicines should not be used together at all, in other cases 2 different medicines may be used together even if an interaction might occur. In these cases, your doctor may want to change the dose, or other precautions may be necessary. When you are taking an antidyskinetic, it is especially important that your health care professional know if you are taking any of the following:

- Anticholinergics (medicine for abdominal or stomach spasms or cramps) or
- Central nervous system (CNS) depressants (medicine that causes drowsiness) or
- Tricyclic antidepressants (medicine for depression)—Using these medicines together with antidyskinetics may result in additive effects, increasing the chance of unwanted effects

Other medical problems—The presence of other medical problems may affect the use of antidyskinetics. Make sure you tell your doctor if you have any other medical problems, especially:

- Difficult urination or
- Enlarged prostate or
- Glaucoma or
- Heart or blood vessel disease or
- High blood pressure or
- Intestinal blockage or
- Myasthenia gravis or
- Uncontrolled movements of hands, mouth, or tongue—Antidyskinetics may make the condition worse
- Kidney disease or
- Liver disease—Higher blood levels of the antidyskinetics may result, increasing the chance of side effects

Proper Use of This Medicine

Take this medicine only as directed by your doctor. Do not take more of it, do not take it more often, and do not take it for a longer period of time than your doctor ordered. To do so may increase the chance of side effects.

To lessen stomach upset, take this medicine with meals or immediately after meals, unless otherwise directed by your doctor.

Dosing—The dose of antidyskinetics will be different for different patients. *Follow your doctor's orders or the directions on the label*. The following information includes only the average doses of benztropine, biperiden, ethopropazine, procyclidine, and trihexyphenidyl. *If your dose is different, do not change it* unless your doctor tells you to do so.

The number of capsules, tablets, or teaspoonfuls of elixir that you take depends on the strength of the medicine. Also, *the number of doses you take each day, the time allowed between doses, and the length of time you take the medicine depend on the medical problem for which you are taking antidyskinetics.*

For benztropine
- For *oral* dosage forms (tablets):
  —For Parkinson's disease or certain severe side effects caused by some other medicines:
    - Adults—To start, 0.5 to 4 milligrams (mg) a day, depending on your condition. Your doctor will adjust your dose as needed; however, the dose is usually not more than 6 mg a day.
    - Children—Use and dose must be determined by your doctor.

- For *injection* dosage form:
  —For Parkinson's disease or certain severe side effects caused by some other medicines:
    - Adults—1 to 4 mg a day, depending on your condition. Your doctor will adjust your dose as needed; however, the dose is usually not more than 6 mg a day.
    - Children—Use and dose must be determined by your doctor.

For biperiden
- For *oral* dosage forms (tablets):
  —For Parkinson's disease or certain severe side effects caused by some other medicines:
    - Adults—2 mg up to four times a day. Your doctor will adjust your dose, depending on your condition; however, the dose is usually not more than 16 mg a day.
    - Children—Use and dose must be determined by your doctor.

- For *injection* dosage form:
  —For Parkinson's disease or certain severe side effects caused by some other medicines:
    - Adults—2 mg, injected into a muscle or vein. The dose may be repeated if needed; however, the dose is usually not given more than four times a day.
    - Children—Use and dose is based on body weight and must be determined by your doctor.

For ethopropazine
- For *oral* dosage forms (tablets):
  - —For Parkinson's disease or certain severe side effects caused by some other medicines:
    - Adults—50 mg one or two times a day. Your doctor will adjust your dose as needed; however, the dose is usually not more than 600 mg a day.
    - Children—Use and dose must be determined by your doctor.

For procyclidine
- For *oral* dosage forms (elixir or tablets):
  - —For Parkinson's disease or certain severe side effects caused by some other medicines:
    - Adults—To start, 2.5 mg three times a day after meals. Your doctor may need to adjust your dose, depending on your condition.
    - Children—Use and dose must be determined by your doctor.

For trihexyphenidyl
- For *extended-release oral* dosage forms (extended-release capsules):
  - —For Parkinson's disease or certain severe side effects caused by some other medicines:
    - Adults—5 mg after breakfast. Your doctor may add another 5 mg dose to be taken twelve hours later, depending on your condition.
    - Children: Use and dose must be determined by your doctor.
- For other *oral* dosage forms (elixir or tablets):
  - —For Parkinson's disease or certain severe side effects caused by some other medicines:
    - Adults—To start, 1 to 2 mg a day. Your doctor may adjust your dose as needed; however, the dose is usually not more than 15 mg a day.
    - Children—Use and dose must be determined by your doctor.

Missed dose—If you miss a dose of this medicine, take it as soon as possible. However, if it is within 2 hours of your next dose, skip the missed dose and go back to your regular dosing schedule. Do not double doses.

Storage—To store this medicine:
- Keep out of the reach of children.
- Store away from heat and direct light.
- Do not store the capsule or tablet form of this medicine in the bathroom, near the kitchen sink, or in other damp places. Heat or moisture may cause the medicine to break down.
- Keep the liquid form of this medicine from freezing.
- Do not keep outdated medicine or medicine no longer needed. Be sure that any discarded medicine is out of the reach of children.

Precautions While Using This Medicine

Your doctor should check your progress at regular visits, especially for the first few months you take this medicine. This will allow your dosage to be changed as necessary to meet your needs.

Your doctor may want you to have your eyes examined by an ophthalmologist (eye doctor) before and also sometime later during treatment.

Do not stop taking this medicine without first checking with your doctor. Your doctor may want you to reduce gradually the amount you are taking before stopping completely, to prevent side effects or the worsening of your condition.

This medicine will add to the effects of alcohol and other CNS depressants (medicines that slow down the nervous system, possibly causing drowsiness). Some examples of CNS depressants are antihistamines or medicine for hay fever, other allergies, or colds; sedatives, tranquilizers, or sleeping medicine; prescription pain medicine or narcotics; barbiturates; medicine for seizures; muscle relaxants; or anesthetics, including some dental anesthetics. *Check with your doctor before taking any of the above while you are using this medicine.*

Do not take this medicine within 1 hour of taking medicine for diarrhea. Taking these medicines too close together will make this medicine less effective.

If you think you or anyone else has taken an overdose of this medicine, get emergency help at once. Taking an overdose of this medicine may lead to unconsciousness. Some signs of an overdose are clumsiness or unsteadiness; seizures; severe drowsiness; severe dryness of mouth, nose and throat; fast heartbeat; hallucinations (seeing, hearing, or feeling things that are not there); mood or mental changes; shortness of breath or troubled breathing; trouble in sleeping; and unusual warmth, dryness, and flushing of skin.

This medicine may cause your eyes to become more sensitive to light than they are normally. Wearing sunglasses and avoiding too much exposure to bright light may help lessen the discomfort.

This medicine may cause some people to have blurred vision or to become drowsy, dizzy, or less alert than they are normally. *Make sure you know how you react to this medicine before you drive, use machines, or do anything else that could be dangerous if you are dizzy or are not alert or able to see well.*

Dizziness, lightheadedness, or fainting may occur, especially when you get up from lying or sitting. Getting up slowly may help. If the problem continues or gets worse, check with your doctor.

This medicine may make you sweat less, causing your body temperature to increase. *Use extra care to avoid becoming overheated during exercise or hot weather while you are taking this medicine, since overheating may result in heat stroke.* Also, hot baths or saunas may make you feel dizzy or faint while you are taking this medicine.

This medicine may cause dryness of the mouth. For temporary relief, use sugarless candy or gum, melt bits of ice in your mouth, or use a saliva substitute. However, if your mouth continues to feel dry for more than 2 weeks, check with your medical doctor or dentist. Continuing dryness of the mouth may increase the chance of dental disease, including tooth decay, gum disease, and fungus infections.

Side Effects of This Medicine

Along with its needed effects, a medicine may cause some unwanted effects. Although not all of these side effects may occur, if they do occur they may need medical attention.

Check with your doctor as soon as possible if any of the following side effects occur:
- *Rare*
  - Confusion (more common in the elderly or with high doses); eye pain; skin rash

Symptoms of overdose

Clumsiness or unsteadiness; drowsiness (severe); dryness of mouth, nose, or throat (severe); fast heartbeat; hallucinations (seeing, hearing, or feeling things that are not there); mood or mental changes; seizures; shortness of breath or troubled breathing; trouble in sleeping; warmth, dryness, and flushing of skin

Other side effects may occur that usually do not need medical attention. These side effects may go away during treatment as your body adjusts to the medicine. However, check with your doctor if any of the following side effects continue or are bothersome:

More common

Blurred vision; constipation; decreased sweating; difficult or painful urination (especially in older men); drowsiness; dryness of mouth, nose, or throat; increased sensitivity of eyes to light; nausea or vomiting

Less common or rare

Dizziness or lightheadedness when getting up from a lying or sitting position; false sense of well-being (especially in the elderly or with high doses); headache; loss of memory (especially in the elderly); muscle cramps; nervousness; numbness or weakness in hands or feet; soreness of mouth and tongue; stomach upset or pain; unusual excitement (more common with large doses of trihexyphenidyl)

After you stop using this medicine, your body may need time to adjust. The length of time this takes depends on the amount of medicine you were using and how long you used it. During this period of time check with your doctor if you notice any of the following side effects:

Anxiety; difficulty in speaking or swallowing; dizziness or lightheadedness when getting up from a lying or sitting position; fast heartbeat; loss of balance control; mask-like face; muscle spasms, especially of face, neck, and back; restlessness or desire to keep moving; shuffling walk; stiffness of arms or legs; trembling and shaking of hands and fingers; trouble in sleeping; twisting movements of body

Other side effects not listed above may also occur in some patients. If you notice any other effects, check with your doctor.

Revised: 05/11/93

ANTIFIBRINOLYTIC AGENTS
Systemic

Commonly used brand name(s):

In the U.S.—
Amicar[1]
Cyklokapron[2]

In Canada—
Amicar[1]
Cyklokapron[2]

Another commonly used name for aminocaproic acid is epsilon-aminocaproic acid[1].

This information applies to the following medicines:
1. Aminocaproic Acid (a-mee-noe-ka-PROE-ik ASS-id)‡
2. Tranexamic Acid (tran-ex-AM-ik ASS-id)

‡Generic name product may be available in the U.S.

Description

Antifibrinolytic (an-tee-fye-bri-noh-LIT-ik) agents are used to treat serious bleeding, especially when the bleeding occurs after dental surgery (particularly in patients with hemophilia) or certain other kinds of surgery. These medicines are also sometimes given before an operation to prevent serious bleeding in patients with medical problems that increase the chance of serious bleeding.

Antifibrinolytic agents may also be used for other conditions as determined by your doctor.

Antifibrinolytic agents are available only with your doctor's prescription, in the following dosage forms:

Oral
Aminocaproic acid
 • Syrup (U.S. and Canada)
 • Tablets (U.S. and Canada)
Tranexamic acid
 • Tablets (U.S. and Canada)

Parenteral
Aminocaproic acid
 • Injection (U.S. and Canada)
Tranexamic acid
 • Injection (U.S. and Canada)

Before Using This Medicine

In deciding to use a medicine, the risks of taking the medicine must be weighed against the good it will do. This is a decision you and your doctor will make. For antifibrinolytic agents, the following should be considered:

Allergies—Tell your doctor if you have ever had any unusual or allergic reaction to aminocaproic acid or tranexamic acid. Also tell your health care professional if you are allergic to any other substances, such as foods, preservatives, or dyes.

Pregnancy—Studies on birth defects have not been done in humans. However, these medicines have been given to pregnant women without causing birth defects or other problems.

Studies on effects of aminocaproic acid in pregnancy have not been done in animals. Tranexamic acid has not been shown to cause birth defects or other problems in animal studies.

Breast-feeding—These medicines have not been reported to cause problems in nursing babies. However, small amounts of tranexamic acid pass into the breast milk.

Children—Although there is no specific information comparing use of aminocaproic acid or tranexamic acid in children with use in other age groups, these medicines are not expected to cause different side effects or problems in children than they do in adults.

Older adults—
 • *For aminocaproic acid:* Although there is no specific information comparing use of aminocaproic acid in the elderly with use in other age groups, this medicine is not expected to cause different side effects or problems in older people than it does in younger adults.

• *For tranexamic acid:* Tranexamic acid has been tested and has not been shown to cause different side effects or problems in older people than it does in younger adults.

Other medicines—Although certain medicines should not be used together at all, in other cases two different medicines may be used together even if an interaction might occur. In these cases, your doctor may want to change the dose, or other precautions may be necessary. Tell your health care professional if you are taking any other prescription or nonprescription (over-the-counter [OTC]) medicine.

Other medical problems—The presence of other medical problems may affect the use of antifibrinolytic agents. Make sure you tell your doctor if you have any other medical problems, especially:

• Blood clots or a history of medical problems caused by blood clots or
• Blood in the urine or
• Color vision problems or
• Heart disease or
• Kidney disease or
• Liver disease—The chance of side effects may be increased

Proper Use of This Medicine

Take this medicine only as directed by your doctor. Do not take more or less of it, do not take it more often, and do not take it for a longer time than your doctor ordered. To do so may increase the chance of unwanted effects.

Dosing—The dose of these medicines will be different for different patients. *Follow your doctor's orders or the directions on the label.* The following information includes only the average doses of these medicines. *If your dose is different, do not change it* unless your doctor tells you to do so.

For aminocaproic acid
• To prevent or treat serious bleeding:
  —For *oral* dosage forms (syrup or tablets):
    • Adults—For the first hour, the dose is 5 grams. Then the dose is 1 or 1.25 grams per hour for eight hours.
    • Children—Dose is based on body weight or size and must be determined by your doctor. For the first hour, the dose is usually 100 milligrams (mg) per kilogram (kg) (45.4 mg per pound) of body weight. Then the dose is 33.3 mg per kg (15.1 mg per pound) of body weight per hour.
  —For *injection* dosage form:
    • Adults—At first, the dose is 4 to 5 grams injected into a vein, over a period of one hour. Then the dose is 1 gram per hour, injected into a vein over a period of eight hours.
    • Children—Dose is based on body weight or size and must be determined by your doctor. At first, the dose is usually 100 mg per kg (45.4 mg per pound) of body weight, injected into a vein over a period of one hour. Then the dose is 33.3 mg per kg (15.1 mg per pound) of body weight per hour, injected into a vein.

For tranexamic acid
• To prevent or treat serious bleeding after dental surgery:
  —For *oral* dosage form (tablets):
    • Adults and children—Dose is based on body weight and must be determined by your doctor.

The dose is usually 25 milligrams (mg) per kilogram (kg) (11.4 mg per pound) of body weight every six to eight hours, beginning one day before surgery. After surgery, the dose is usually 25 mg per kg (11.4 mg per pound) of body weight every six to eight hours for two to ten days.
  —For *injection* dosage form:
    • Adults and children—Dose is based on body weight and must be determined by your doctor. The dose is usually 10 mg per kg (4.5 mg per pound) of body weight, injected into a vein just before surgery. After surgery, the dose is usually 10 mg per kg (4.5 mg per pound) of body weight, injected into a vein every six to eight hours for two to ten days.

Missed dose—
• *For aminocaproic acid* (e.g., Amicar): If you miss a dose, take it as soon as possible. However, if you do not remember until it is almost time for your next dose, double the next dose. Then go back to your regular dosing schedule.
• *For tranexamic acid* (e.g., Cyklokapron): If you miss a dose, take it as soon as possible. Then take any remaining doses for the day at regularly spaced times. Do not double doses. If you have any questions about this, check with your doctor.

Storage—To store this medicine:
• Keep out of the reach of children.
• Store away from heat and direct light.
• Do not store the tablet form of this medicine in the bathroom, near the kitchen sink, or in other damp places. Heat or moisture may cause the medicine to break down.
• Do not keep outdated medicine or medicine no longer needed. Be sure that any discarded medicine is out of the reach of children.

Precautions While Using This Medicine

If you will be taking tranexamic acid for longer than several days, your doctor may want you to have your eyes checked regularly by an ophthalmologist (eye doctor). This will allow your doctor to check for unwanted effects that may be caused by this medicine.

If you are using aminocaproic acid syrup as a mouth rinse to control oral bleeding, and you are in the first or second trimester of pregnancy, you should spit out the syrup after rinsing without swallowing it.

Side Effects of This Medicine

Along with its needed effects, a medicine may cause some unwanted effects. Although not all of these side effects may occur, if they do occur they may need medical attention.

The same effect that makes aminocaproic acid or tranexamic acid help prevent or stop bleeding also may cause blood clots that could be dangerous. Check with your doctor immediately if any of the following possible signs and symptoms of blood clots occur:

Less common or rare
  Headache (severe and sudden); loss of coordination (sudden); pains in chest, groin, or legs, especially the calves; shortness of breath (sudden); slurred speech (sudden); vision changes (sudden); weakness or numbness in arm or leg

Also, check with your doctor as soon as possible if any of the following side effects occur:

Less common or rare
  For aminocaproic acid
    Dizziness; headache; muscle pain or weakness (severe and continuing); ringing or buzzing in ears; skin rash; slow or irregular heartbeat—with the injection only; stomach cramps or pain; stuffy nose; sudden decrease in amount of urine; swelling of face, feet, or lower legs; unusual tiredness or weakness; weight gain (rapid)

  For tranexamic acid
    Blurred vision or other changes in vision; dizziness or lightheadedness; unusual tiredness or weakness

Other side effects may occur that usually do not need medical attention. These side effects may go away during treatment as your body adjusts to the medicine. However, check with your doctor if any of the following side effects continue or are bothersome:

  Diarrhea; dry ejaculation; nausea or vomiting; unusual menstrual discomfort; watery eyes

Other side effects not listed above may also occur in some patients. If you notice any other effects, check with your doctor.

Revised: 08/13/97

ANTIFUNGALS, AZOLE Systemic

Commonly used brand name(s):

In the U.S.—
Diflucan[1]
Nizoral[3]
Sporanox[2]

In Canada—
Diflucan[1]   Nizoral[3]
Diflucan-150[1]   Sporanox[2]

Note: For quick reference, the following antifungals are numbered to match the corresponding brand names.

This information applies to the following medicines:
  1. Fluconazole (floo-KOE-na-zole)
  2. Itraconazole (i-tra-KOE-na-zole)
  3. Ketoconazole (kee-toe-ko-NA-zole)

Description

Azole antifungals are used to treat serious fungus infections that may occur in different parts of the body. These medicines may also be used for other problems as determined by your doctor.

Azole antifungals are available only with your doctor's prescription, in the following dosage forms:

Oral
Fluconazole
  • Capsules (Canada)
  • Oral suspension (U.S. and Canada)
  • Tablets (U.S. and Canada)
Itraconazole
  • Capsules (U.S. and Canada)
  • Oral solution (U.S.)

Ketoconazole
  • Oral suspension (Canada)
  • Tablets (U.S. and Canada)
Parenteral
Fluconazole
  • Injection (U.S. and Canada)
Itraconazole
  • Injection (U.S.)

Before Using This Medicine

In deciding to use a medicine, the risks of taking the medicine must be weighed against the good it will do. This is a decision you and your doctor will make. For the azole antifungals, the following should be considered:

Allergies—Tell your doctor if you have ever had any unusual or allergic reaction to any of the azole antifungals. Also tell your health care professional if you are allergic to any other substances, such as foods, preservatives, or dyes.

Pregnancy—Studies have not been done in pregnant women. However, studies in some animals have shown that azole antifungals, taken in high doses, may cause harm to the mother and the fetus. They have caused birth defects in animals. Before taking these medicines, make sure your doctor knows if you are pregnant or if you may become pregnant.

Breast-feeding—Azole antifungals pass into breast milk. Mothers who are taking these medicines and who wish to breast-feed should discuss this with their doctors.

Children—A small number of children have been safely treated with azole antifungals. Be sure to discuss with your child's doctor the use of these medicines in children.

Older adults—Many medicines have not been studied specifically in older people. Therefore, it may not be known whether they work exactly the same way they do in younger adults or if they cause different side effects or problems in older people. There is no specific information comparing use of azole antifungals in the elderly with use in other age groups.

Other medicines—Although certain medicines should not be used together at all, in other cases two different medicines may be used together even if an interaction might occur. In these cases, your doctor may want to change the dose, or other precautions may be necessary. When you are taking azole antifungals, it is especially important that your health care professional know if you are taking any of the following:

  • Acetaminophen (e.g., Tylenol) (with long-term, high-dose use) or
  • Amiodarone (e.g., Cordarone) or
  • Anabolic steroids (nandrolone [e.g., Anabolin], oxandrolone [e.g., Anavar], oxymetholone [e.g., Anadrol], stanozolol [e.g., Winstrol]) or
  • Androgens (male hormones) or
  • Antithyroid agents (medicine for overactive thyroid) or
  • Carmustine (e.g., BiCNU) or
  • Chloroquine (e.g., Aralen) or
  • Dantrolene (e.g., Dantrium) or
  • Daunorubicin (e.g., Cerubidine) or
  • Disulfiram (e.g., Antabuse) or
  • Divalproex (e.g., Depakote) or
  • Estrogens (female hormones) or
  • Etretinate (e.g., Tegison) or
  • Gold salts (medicine for arthritis) or

- Hydroxychloroquine (e.g., Plaquenil) or
- Mercaptopurine (e.g., Purinethol) or
- Methotrexate (e.g., Mexate) or
- Methyldopa (e.g., Aldomet) or
- Naltrexone (e.g., Trexan) (with long-term, high-dose use) or
- Oral contraceptives (birth control pills) containing estrogen or
- Other anti-infectives by mouth or by injection (medicine for infection) or
- Phenothiazines (acetophenazine [e.g., Tindal], chlorpromazine [e.g., Thorazine], fluphenazine [e.g., Prolixin], mesoridazine [e.g., Serentil], perphenazine [e.g., Trilafon], prochlorperazine [e.g., Compazine], promazine [e.g., Sparine], promethazine [e.g., Phenergan], thioridazine [e.g., Mellaril], trifluoperazine [e.g., Stelazine], triflupromazine [e.g., Vesprin], trimeprazine [e.g., Temaril]) or
- Plicamycin (e.g., Mithracin) or
- Valproic acid (e.g., Depakene)—Use of these medicines with azole antifungals may increase the chance of side effects affecting the liver

- Amantadine (e.g., Symmetrel) or
- Antacids or
- Anticholinergics (medicine for abdominal or stomach spasms or cramps) or
- Antidepressants (medicine for depression) or
- Antidyskinetics (medicine for Parkinson's disease or other conditions affecting control of muscles) or
- Antihistamines or
- Antipsychotics (medicine for mental illness) or
- Buclizine (e.g., Bucladin) or
- Cimetidine (e.g., Tagamet) or
- Cyclizine (e.g., Marezine) or
- Cyclobenzaprine (e.g., Flexeril) or
- Disopyramide (e.g., Norpace) or
- Famotidine (e.g., Pepcid) or
- Flavoxate (e.g., Urispas) or
- Ipratropium (e.g., Atrovent) or
- Meclizine (e.g., Antivert) or
- Methylphenidate (e.g., Ritalin) or
- Nizatidine (e.g., Axid) or
- Omeprazole (e.g., Prilosec) or
- Orphenadrine (e.g., Norflex) or
- Oxybutynin (e.g., Ditropan) or
- Procainamide (e.g., Pronestyl) or
- Promethazine (e.g., Phenergan) or
- Quinidine (e.g., Quinidex) or
- Ranitidine (e.g., Zantac) or
- Sucralfate (e.g., Carafate) or
- Trimeprazine (e.g., Temaril)—Use of these medicines may decrease the effects of itraconazole and ketoconazole; these medicines should be taken at least 2 hours after itraconazole or ketoconazole

- Antidiabetic agents, oral (chlorpropamide [e.g., Diabinese], glipizide [e.g., Glucotrol], glyburide [e.g., DiaBeta, Micronase], tolbutamide [e.g., Orinase]) or
- Cyclosporine (e.g., Sandimmune) or
- Digoxin (e.g., Lanoxin) or
- Warfarin (e.g., Coumadin)—Azole antifungals may increase the effects of these medicines, which may increase the chance of side effects

- Astemizole (e.g., Hismanal) or
- Terfenadine (e.g., Seldane)—These medicines should not be taken with fluconazole, itraconazole, or ketoconazole; these azole antifungals may increase the chance of serious side effects of astemizole or terfenadine

- Carbamazepine (e.g., Tegretol) or
- Isoniazid or
- Rifampin (e.g., Rifadin)—These medicines may decrease the effects of azole antifungals
- Cisapride (e.g., Propulsid)—Cisapride should not be taken with itraconazole or oral ketoconazole; these azole antifungals may increase the chance of serious side effects of cisapride
- Didanosine (e.g., ddI, Videx)—Use of didanosine with itraconazole or ketoconazole may decrease the effects of itraconazole or ketoconazole, as well as of didanosine. Itraconazole and ketoconazole should be taken at least 2 hours before or 2 hours after didanosine is given
- Indinavir (e.g., Crixivan)—Use of indinavir with ketoconazole may increase the effects of indinavir
- Lovastatin (e.g., Mevacor) or
- Simvastatin (e.g., Zocor)—Use of these medicines with itraconazole may increase the effects of lovastatin or simvastatin
- Midazolam (e.g., Versed) or
- Triazolam (e.g., Halcion)—Use of these medicines with itraconazole or ketoconazole may increase the effects of midazolam or triazolam
- Phenytoin (e.g., Dilantin)—Use of phenytoin with azole antifungals may increase the effects of the azole antifungals, increase side effects of azole antifungals affecting the liver, and increase the chance of phenytoin side effects
- Pimozide (e.g.,Orap) or
- Quinidine (e.g., Quinaglute, Cardioquin, Quinidex) —Pimozide or quinidine should not be taken with itraconazole; itraconazole may increase the chance of serious side effects of pimozide or quinidine

Other medical problems—The presence of other medical problems may affect the use of azole antifungals. Make sure you tell your doctor if you have any other medical problems, especially:

- Achlorhydria (absence of stomach acid) or
- Hypochlorhydria (decreased amount of stomach acid)—Itraconazole and ketoconazole may not be absorbed from the stomach as well in patients who have low levels of or no stomach acid

- Alcohol abuse (or history of) or
- Liver disease—Alcohol abuse or liver disease may increase the chance of side effects caused by azole antifungals

- Kidney disease—The effects of fluconazole may be increased in patients with kidney disease

Proper Use of This Medicine

Ketoconazole and the *capsule form of itraconazole* should be taken with a meal or a snack. The *oral solution form of itraconazole* should be taken on an empty stomach. If you have any questions about the antifungal medicine you are taking, check with your health care professional.

For patients taking the *oral liquid form of fluconazole, itraconazole, or ketoconazole:*

- Use a specially marked measuring spoon or other device to measure each dose accurately. The average household teaspoon may not hold the right amount of liquid.

If you have achlorhydria (absence of stomach acid) or hypochlorhydria (decreased amount of stomach acid), and you are taking itraconazole or ketoconazole, your doctor may want you to take your medicine with an acidic drink. You may dissolve your medicine in cola or seltzer water and drink the solution, or your may take your medicine with a glass of cola or seltzer water. Your doctor may suggest that you dissolve each capsule or tablet in a teaspoonful of weak hydrochloric acid solution to help you absorb the medicine better. Your health care professional can prepare the solution for you. After you dissolve the tablet in the acid solution, add this mixture to a small amount (1 or 2 teaspoonfuls) of water in a glass. Drink the mixture through a plastic or glass drinking straw. Place the straw behind your teeth, as far back in your mouth as you can. This will keep the acid from harming your teeth. Be sure to drink all the liquid to get the full dose of medicine. Next, swish around in your mouth about one-half glass of water and then swallow it. This will help wash away any acid that may remain in your mouth or on your teeth.

To help clear up your infection completely, *it is very important that you keep taking this medicine for the full time of treatment,* even if your symptoms begin to clear up or you begin to feel better after a few days. Since fungus infections may be very slow to clear up, you may have to continue taking this medicine every day for as long as 6 months to a year or more. Some fungus infections never clear up completely and require continuous treatment. If you stop taking this medicine too soon, your symptoms may return.

This medicine works best when there is a constant amount in the blood. *To help keep the amount constant, do not miss any doses. Also, it is best to take each dose at the same time every day.* If you need help in planning the best time to take your medicine, check with your health care professional.

Dosing—The dose of azole antifungals may be different for different patients. *Follow your doctor's orders or the directions on the label.* The following information includes only the average doses of azole antifungals. Your dose of fluconazole may be different if you have kidney disease. *If your dose is different, do not change it* unless your doctor tells you to do so.

The number of capsules or tablets, or the amount of oral suspension or injection that you take depends on the strength of the medicine. Also, *the number of doses you take each day, the time allowed between doses, and the length of time you take the medicine depend on the medical problem for which you are taking azole antifungals.*

For fluconazole
- For fungus infections:
  —For *capsule* dosage form:
  - Adults—150 milligrams (mg) as a single dose to treat vaginal yeast infections.
  - Children up to 18 years of age—Dose must be determined by your doctor.
  —For *oral suspension* and *tablet* dosage forms:
  - Adults and teenagers—200 to 400 mg on the first day, then 100 to 400 mg once a day for weeks or months, depending on the medical problem being treated. A vaginal yeast infection is treated with a single dose of 150 mg.
  - Children 6 months of age and older—6 to 12 mg per kilogram (mg/kg) (2.7 to 5.4 mg per pound) of body weight on the first day, then 3 to 12 mg/kg (1.35 to 5.4 mg per pound) of body weight once a day for weeks or months, depending on the medical problem being treated.
  - Infants and children up to 6 months of age—Dose must be determined by your doctor.
  —For *injection* dosage form:
  - Adults and teenagers—200 to 400 mg on the first day, then 100 to 400 mg once a day, injected into a vein, for weeks or months, depending on the medical problem being treated.
  - Children 6 months of age and older—6 to 12 mg per kilogram (mg/kg) (2.7 to 5.4 mg per pound) of body weight on the first day, then 3 to 12 mg/kg (1.35 to 5.4 mg per pound) of body weight once a day, injected into a vein, for weeks or months, depending on the medical problem being treated.
  - Infants and children up to 6 months of age—Dose must be determined by your doctor.

For itraconazole
- For fungus infections:
  —For *capsule* dosage form:
  - Adults and teenagers—200 milligrams (mg) once a day, which may be increased up to 400 mg once a day for weeks or months, depending on the medical problem being treated. Fingernail and toenail infections are treated with 200 mg one or two times a day for weeks or months.
  - Children up to 16 years of age—Dose must be determined by your doctor.
  —For *injection* dosage form:
  - Adults—200 milligrams (mg) twice a day for 4 doses, then 200 mg once a day.
  - Children—Dose must be determined by your doctor.
  —For *oral solution* dosage form:
  - Adults and teenagers—100 to 200 mg once a day for days or weeks, depending on the medical problem being treated.
  - Children up to 12 years of age—Dose must be determined by your doctor.

For ketoconazole
- For fungus infections:
  —For *oral* dosage form (oral suspension and tablets):
  - Adults and teenagers—200 to 400 milligrams (mg) once a day for days or weeks, depending on the medical problem being treated.
  - Children over 2 years of age—3.3 to 6.6 mg per kilogram (1.5 to 3 mg per pound) of body weight once a day for days or weeks, depending on the medical problem being treated.
  - Infants and children up to 2 years of age—Dose must be determined by your doctor.

Missed dose—If you miss a dose of this medicine, take it as soon as possible. This will help to keep a constant amount of medicine in the blood. However, if it is almost time for your next dose, skip the missed dose and go back to your regular dosing schedule. Do not double doses.

Storage—To store this medicine:
- Keep out of the reach of children.
- Store away from heat and direct light.
- Do not store the capsule or tablet form of this medicine in the bathroom, near the kitchen sink, or in other damp places. Heat or moisture may cause the medicine to break down.
- Keep the oral liquid form of this medicine from freezing.

- Do not keep outdated medicine or medicine no longer needed. Be sure that any discarded medicine is out of the reach of children.

Precautions While Using This Medicine

It is important that your doctor check your progress at regular visits. This will allow your doctor to check for any unwanted effects.

If your symptoms do not improve within a few weeks (or months for some infections), or if they become worse, check with your doctor.

These medicines should not be taken with astemizole (e.g., Hismanal), cisapride (e.g., Propulsid), or terfenadine (e.g., Seldane). Doing so may increase the risk of serious side effects affecting the heart.

Liver problems may be more likely to occur if you drink alcoholic beverages while you are taking ketoconazole. Alcoholic beverages may also cause stomach pain, nausea, vomiting, headache, or flushing or redness of the face. Other alcohol-containing preparations (for example, elixirs, cough syrups, tonics) may also cause problems. These problems may occur for at least a day after you stop taking ketoconazole. Therefore, *you should not drink alcoholic beverages or use alcohol-containing preparations while you are taking this medicine and for at least a day after you stop taking it.*

If you are taking antacids, cimetidine (e.g., Tagamet), famotidine (e.g., Pepcid), nizatidine (e.g., Axid), omeprazole (e.g., Prilosec), or ranitidine (e.g., Zantac) while you are taking itraconazole or ketoconazole, take the other medicine at least 2 hours after you take itraconazole or ketoconazole. If you take these medicines at the same time that you take itraconazole or ketoconazole, they will keep your antifungal medicine from working properly.

Ketoconazole may cause your eyes to become more sensitive to light than they are normally. Wearing sunglasses and avoiding too much exposure to bright light may help lessen the discomfort.

Side Effects of This Medicine

Along with its needed effects, a medicine may cause some unwanted effects. Although not all of these effects may occur, if they do occur they may need medical attention.

Check with your doctor immediately if any of the following side effects occur:
  Less common
    Fever and chills; skin rash or itching
  Rare
    Dark or amber urine; fever and sore throat; loss of appetite; pale stools; reddening, blistering, peeling, or loosening of skin and mucous membranes; stomach pain; unusual bleeding or bruising; unusual tiredness or weakness; yellow eyes or skin

Other side effects may occur that usually do not need medical attention. These side effects may go away during treatment as your body adjusts to the medicine. However, check with your doctor if any of the following side effects continue or are bothersome:
  Less common
    Constipation; diarrhea; dizziness; drowsiness; headache; nausea; vomiting

Rare—for ketoconazole
    Decreased sexual ability in males; enlargement of the breasts in males; increased sensitivity of the eyes to light; menstrual irregularities

Other side effects not listed above may also occur in some patients. If you notice any other effects, check with your doctor.

Additional Information

Once a medicine has been approved for marketing for a certain use, experience may show that it is also useful for other medical problems. Although these uses are not included in product labeling, azole antifungals are used in certain patients with the following medical conditions:

- Cryptococcosis
- Cushing's syndrome
- Febrile neutropenia
- Fungus infections in newborns
- Hirsutism
- Histoplasmosis
- Paronychia (infection of the tissue surrounding the nail)
- *Penicillium marneffei* infection
- Pneumonia caused by fungus
- Prostate cancer
- Ringworm of the beard, hand, or scalp
- Septicemia (infection of the blood) caused by fungus
- Skin infection (including leishmaniasis and sporotrichosis)

Other than the above information, there is no additional information relating to proper use, precautions, or side effects for these uses.

Developed: 11/14/1994
Revised: 02/07/2001

ANTIFUNGALS, AZOLE   Vaginal

Commonly used brand name(s):

In the U.S.—

FemCare[2]	Monistat 3[4]
Femizol-M[4]	Monistat 3 Combination Pack[4]
Femstat 3[1]	Monistat 5 Tampon[4]
Gyne-Lotrimin[2]	Monistat 7[4]
Gyne-Lotrimin Combination Pack[2]	Monistat 7 Combination Pack[4]
Gyne-Lotrimin3[2]	Mycelex-7[2]
Gyne-Lotrimin3 Combination Pack[2]	Mycelex-G[2]
Miconazole-7[4]	Mycelex Twin Pack[2]
Monistat 1[6]	Terazol 3[5]
	Terazol 7[5]
	Vagistat-1[6]

In Canada—

Canesten Combi-Pak 1-Day Therapy[2]	GyneCure[6]
Canesten Combi-Pak 3-Day Therapy[2]	GyneCure Ovules[6]
Canesten 1-Day Cream Combi-Pak[2]	GyneCure Vaginal Ointment Tandempak[6]
Canesten 1-Day Therapy[2]	GyneCure Vaginal Ovules Tandempak[6]
Canesten 3-Day Therapy[2]	Micozole[4]
Canesten 6-Day Therapy[2]	Monazole 7[4]
Clotrimaderm[2]	Monistat 3 Dual-Pak[4]
Ecostatin Vaginal Ovules[3]	Monistat 3 Vaginal Ovules[4]
	Monistat 7[4]

Monistat 7 Dual-Pak[4]
Monistat 7 Vaginal
  Suppositories[4]
Myclo-Gyne[2]
Novo-Miconazole Vaginal
  Ovules[4]

Terazol 3[5]
Terazol 3 Dual Pak[5]
Terazol 3 Vaginal Ovules[5]
Terazol 7[5]

Note: For quick reference, the following azole antifungals are numbered to match the corresponding brand names.

This information applies to the following medicines
1. Butoconazole (byoo-toe-KON-a-zole)†
2. Clotrimazole (kloe-TRIM-a-zole)‡
3. Econazole (e-KON-a-zole)*
4. Miconazole (mi-KON-a-zole)‡
5. Terconazole (ter-KON-a-zole)
6. Tioconazole (tye-oh-KON-a-zole)

*Not commercially available in the U.S.
†Not commercially available in Canada.
‡Generic name product may be available in the U.S.

Description

Vaginal azoles (A-zoles) are used to treat yeast (fungus) infections of the vagina.

For first-time users, make sure your doctor has checked and confirmed that you have a vaginal yeast infection before you use the vaginal azole antifungal medicines that do not require a prescription. Vaginal yeast infections can reoccur over time and, when the same symptoms occur again, self-treating with these medicines is recommended. However, you should see your doctor if the symptoms occur again within 2 months.

Some vaginal azoles are available only with your doctor's prescription. Most are available without a prescription; however, your doctor may have special instructions on the proper use of this medicine.

Vaginal azoles are available in the following dosage forms:

Vaginal
  Butoconazole
    • Cream (U.S.)
  Clotrimazole
    • Cream (U.S. and Canada)
    • Tablets (U.S. and Canada)
  Econazole
    • Suppositories (Canada)
  Miconazole
    • Cream (U.S. and Canada)
    • Suppositories (U.S. and Canada)
    • Tampons (U.S.—California only)
  Terconazole
    • Cream (U.S. and Canada)
    • Suppositories (U.S. and Canada)
  Tioconazole
    • Ointment (U.S. and Canada)
    • Suppositories (Canada)

Before Using This Medicine

In deciding to use a medicine, the risks of using the medicine must be weighed against the good it will do. This is a decision you and your doctor will make. For vaginal azoles, the following should be considered:

Allergies—Tell your doctor if you have ever had any unusual or allergic reaction to any of the azoles. Also tell your health care professional if you are allergic to any other substances, such as foods, preservatives, or dyes.

Pregnancy—Studies have not been done in humans for use of all azole antifungals during the first trimester of pregnancy. These medicines are safe and effective when used for at least 7 days during the second and third trimesters of pregnancy. However, check with your doctor before using this medicine during the first trimester of pregnancy. Also, use of 1- and 3-day treatments may not be effective during pregnancy.

Breast-feeding—It is not known whether vaginal azoles pass into the breast milk. However, these medicines have not been shown to cause problems in nursing babies.

Children—Studies on these medicines have been done only in adult patients, and there is no specific information comparing use of vaginal azoles in children with use in other age groups. It is recommended that these medicines not be used in children up to 12 years of age.

Older adults—Many medicines have not been studied specifically in older people. Therefore, it may not be known whether they work exactly the same way they do in younger adults. Although there is no specific information comparing use of vaginal azoles in the elderly with use in other age groups, they are not expected to cause different side effects or problems in older people than they do in younger adults.

Other medicines—Although certain medicines should not be used together at all, in other cases two different medicines may be used together even if an interaction might occur. In these cases, your doctor may want to change the dose, or other precautions may be necessary. Tell your health care professional if you are using any other vaginal prescription or nonprescription (over-the-counter [OTC]) medicine. When you are taking miconazole, it is especially important that your health care professional know if you are taking any of the following:

• Warfarin (e.g., Coumadin; Warfilone)—Using with warfarin may cause bleeding and/or bruising

Proper Use of This Medicine

Vaginal azoles usually come with patient directions. Read them carefully before using this medicine.

Use this medicine at bedtime, unless otherwise directed by your doctor. The vaginal tampon form of miconazole should be left in the vagina overnight and removed the next morning.

This medicine is usually inserted into the vagina with an applicator. However, if you are pregnant, check with your doctor before using the applicator.

Some of the vaginal suppositories or tablets come packaged with a small tube of cream. This cream can be applied outside of the vagina in the genital area to treat itching. The packages are called combination, dual, or twin packs.

To help clear up your infection completely, *it is very important that you keep using this medicine for the full time of treatment*, even if your symptoms begin to clear up after a few days. If you stop using this medicine too soon, your symptoms may return. *Do not miss any doses. Also, do not stop using this medicine if your menstrual period starts during the time of treatment.*

Dosing—The dose of these medicines will be different for different patients. *Follow your doctor's orders or the directions on the label.* The following information includes only the average doses of these medicines. *If your dose is different, do not change it* unless your doctor tells you to do so.

For butoconazole
- For yeast infection:
  —For *vaginal cream* dosage form:
    • Adults and teenagers:
      —Women who are not pregnant: 100 milligrams (mg) (one full applicator) of 2% cream inserted into the vagina at bedtime for three nights in a row.
      —Pregnant women, after the third month: 100 mg (one full applicator) of 2% cream inserted into the vagina at bedtime for six nights in a row.
    • Children up to 12 years of age—Use and dose must be determined by your doctor.
  —For *vaginal suppository* dosage form:
    • Adults and teenagers:
      —Women who are not pregnant: 100 mg (one suppository) inserted into the vagina at bedtime for three nights in a row.
      —Children up to 12 years of age—Use and dose must be determined by your doctor.

For clotrimazole
- For yeast infection:
  —For *vaginal cream* dosage form:
    • Adults and teenagers—The dose depends on the strength of the cream.
      —1% cream: 50 milligrams (mg) (one full applicator) inserted into the vagina at bedtime for six to fourteen nights in a row.
      —2% cream: 100 mg (one full applicator) inserted into the vagina at bedtime for three nights in a row.
      —10% cream: 500 mg (one full applicator) inserted into the vagina at bedtime for one night only.
    • Children up to 12 years of age—Use and dose must be determined by your doctor.
  —For *vaginal tablet* dosage form:
    • Adults and teenagers—The dose depends on the strength of the vaginal tablet.
      —Women who are not pregnant:
        • 100-mg tablet: Insert one tablet into the vagina at bedtime for six or seven nights in a row.
        • 200-mg tablet: Insert one tablet into the vagina at bedtime for three nights in a row.
        • 500-mg tablet: Insert one tablet into the vagina at bedtime for one night only.
      —Pregnant women: 100 mg (one vaginal tablet) inserted into the vagina at bedtime for seven nights in a row.
    • Children up to 12 years of age—Use and dose must be determined by your doctor.

For econazole
- For yeast infection:
  —For *vaginal suppository* dosage form:
    • Adults and teenagers—150 milligrams (mg) (one vaginal suppository) inserted into the vagina at bedtime for three nights in a row.
    • Children up to 12 years of age—Use and dose must be determined by your doctor.

For miconazole
- For yeast infection:
  —For *vaginal cream* dosage form:
    • Adults and teenagers—200 milligrams (one full applicator) inserted into the vagina at bedtime for seven nights in a row. Treatment may be repeated if needed.
    • Children up to 12 years of age—Use and dose must be determined by your doctor.
  —For *vaginal suppository* dosage form:
    • Adults and teenagers—The dose depends on the strength of the suppository.
      —100-milligrams (mg) suppository: Insert one vaginal suppository into the vagina at bedtime for seven nights in a row. Treatment may be repeated if needed.
      —200-mg suppository or
      —400-mg suppository: Insert one vaginal suppository into the vagina at bedtime for three nights in a row. Treatment may be repeated if needed.
    • Children up to 12 years of age—Use and dose must be determined by your doctor.
  —For *tampon* dosage form:
    • Adults and teenagers—100 mg (one tampon) inserted into the vagina at bedtime and then removed the next morning. This is repeated every night for five nights in a row.
    • Children up to 12 years of age—Use and dose must be determined by your doctor.

For terconazole
- For yeast infection:
  —For *vaginal cream* dosage form:
    • Adults and teenagers—The dose depends on the strength of the cream.
      —0.4% cream: 20 milligrams (mg) (one full applicator) inserted into the vagina at bedtime for seven nights in a row.
      —0.8% cream: 40 mg (one full applicator) inserted into the vagina at bedtime for three nights in a row.
    • Children up to 12 years of age—Use and dose must be determined by your doctor.
  —For *vaginal suppository* dosage form:
    • Adults and teenagers—80 mg (one vaginal suppository) inserted into the vagina at bedtime for three nights in a row.
    • Children up to 12 years of age—Use and dose must be determined by your doctor.

For tioconazole
- For yeast infection:
  —For *vaginal ointment* dosage form:
    • Adults and teenagers—300 milligrams (mg) (one full applicator) of 6.5% ointment inserted into the vagina at bedtime for one night only.
    • Children up to 12 years of age—Use and dose must be determined by your doctor.
  —For *vaginal suppository* dosage form:
    • Adults and teenagers—300 mg (one vaginal suppository) inserted into the vagina at bedtime for one night only.
    • Children up to 12 years of age—Use and dose must be determined by your doctor.

Missed dose—If you miss a dose of this medicine, insert it as soon as possible. However, if it is almost time for your next dose, skip the missed dose and go back to your regular dosing schedule.

Storage—To store this medicine:
- Keep out of the reach of children.
- Store away from heat and direct light.

- Do not store the vaginal suppository or vaginal tablet form of this medicine in the bathroom, near the kitchen sink, or in other damp places. Heat or moisture may cause the medicine to break down.
- Keep the vaginal cream, ointment, and suppository forms of this medicine from freezing.
- Do not keep outdated medicine or medicine no longer needed. Be sure that any discarded medicine is out of the reach of children.

Precautions While Using This Medicine

If your symptoms do not improve within 3 days or have not disappeared in 7 days, or if they become worse, check with your doctor. The 1- or 3-day treatments may take up to 7 days to completely clear up your infection. However, not all vaginal infections are caused by yeast. If symptoms occur again within 2 months, check with your doctor.

Vaginal medicines usually will come out of the vagina during treatment. To keep the medicine from getting on your clothing, wear a minipad or sanitary napkin. The use of non-medicated tampons (like those used for menstrual periods) is not recommended since they may soak up the medicine.

To help clear up your infection completely and to help make sure it does not return, good health habits are also required.

- Wear cotton panties (or panties or pantyhose with cotton crotches) instead of synthetic (for example, nylon or rayon) panties.
- Wear only clean panties.

If you have any questions about this, check with your health care professional.

Vaginal yeast infections are not usually spread by having sex and your sex partner does not need to be treated. However, if the sex partner has symptoms of local itching or skin irritation of the penis, he may benefit by being treated also.

If you use latex or rubber birth control devices (condoms, diaphragms, or cervical caps), you should wait 3 days after treatment with azole antifungal agents before using them again. Many brands of vaginal azoles contain oils in the product that can weaken these devices. This increases the chances of a condom breaking during sexual intercourse. The rubber in cervical caps or diaphragms may break down faster and wear out sooner. Check with your health care professional to make sure the vaginal azole product you are using can be used with latex rubber birth control devices.

Check with your doctor before douching to obtain advice about whether you may douche and, if allowed, the proper method.

Side Effects of This Medicine

Along with its needed effects, a medicine may cause some unwanted effects. Although not all of these side effects may occur, if they do occur they may need medical attention.

Check with your doctor as soon as possible if any of the following side effects occur:
Less common
Vaginal burning, itching, discharge, or other irritation not present before use of this medicine

Rare
Skin rash or hives

Other side effects may occur that usually do not need medical attention. These side effects may go away during treatment as your body adjusts to the medicine. However, check with your doctor if any of the following side effects continue or are bothersome:
Less common or rare
Abdominal or stomach cramps or pain; burning or irritation of penis of sexual partner; headache

Other side effects not listed above may also occur in some patients. If you notice any other effects, check with your doctor.

Revised: 03/16/2001

ANTIGLAUCOMA AGENTS, CHOLINERGIC, LONG-ACTING
Ophthalmic

Commonly used brand name(s):

In the U.S.—
Humorsol[1]
Phospholine Iodide[2]

In Canada—
Phospholine Iodide[2]

France—
Diflupyl[3]

Other commonly used names are: DFP[3], difluorophate[3], dyflos[3], and ecothiopate[2].

Note: For quick reference, the following medicines are numbered to match the corresponding brand names.

This information applies to the following medicines:
1. Demecarium (dem-e-KARE-ee-um)†
2. Echothiophate (ek-oh-THYE-oh-fate)
3. Isoflurophate (eye-soe-FLURE-oh-fate)*†

*Not commercially available in the U.S.
†Not commercially available in Canada.

Description

Demecarium, echothiophate, and isoflurophate are used in the eye to treat certain types of glaucoma and other eye conditions, such as accommodative esotropia. They may also be used in the diagnosis of certain eye conditions, such as accommodative esotropia.

These medicines are available only with your doctor's prescription, in the following dosage forms:

Ophthalmic
Demecarium
- Ophthalmic solution (eye drops) (U.S.)
Echothiophate
- Ophthalmic solution (eye drops) (U.S. and Canada)
Isoflurophate
- Ophthalmic ointment (eye ointment) (France)

Before Using This Medicine

In deciding to use a medicine, the risks of using the medicine must be weighed against the good it will do. This is a decision

you and your doctor will make. For demecarium, echothiophate, or isoflurophate, the following should be considered:

Allergies—Tell your doctor if you have ever had any unusual or allergic reaction to demecarium, echothiophate, or isoflurophate. Also tell your health care professional if you are allergic to any other substances, such as preservatives.

Pregnancy—Because of the toxicity of these medicines in general, demecarium, echothiophate, and isoflurophate are not recommended during pregnancy.

Breast-feeding—Demecarium, echothiophate, and isoflurophate may be absorbed into the body. These medicines are not recommended during breast-feeding, because they may cause unwanted effects in nursing babies. It may be necessary for you to use another medicine or to stop breast-feeding during treatment. Be sure you have discussed the risks and benefits of the medicine with your doctor.

Children—Demecarium, echothiophate, or isoflurophate can cause serious side effects in any patient. When this medicine is used for a long time, eye cysts may occur. These eye cysts occur more often in children than in adults. Therefore, it is especially important that you discuss with the child's doctor the good that this medicine may do as well as the risks of using it.

Older adults—Many medicines have not been studied specifically in older people. Therefore, it may not be known whether they work exactly the same way they do in younger adults or if they cause different side effects or problems in older people. There is no specific information comparing use of these medicines in the elderly with use in other age groups. However, demecarium, echothiophate, or isoflurophate can cause serious side effects in any patient.

Other medicines—Although certain medicines should not be used together at all, in other cases two different medicines may be used together even if an interaction might occur. In these cases, your doctor may want to change the dose, or other precautions may be necessary. When you are taking demecarium, echothiophate, or isoflurophate, it is especially important that your health care professional know if you are taking any of the following:

- Amantadine (e.g., Symmetrel) or
- Anticholinergics (medicine for abdominal or stomach spasms or cramps) or
- Antidepressants (medicine for depression) or
- Antidyskinetics (medicine for Parkinson's disease or other conditions affecting control of muscles) or
- Antihistamines or
- Antimyasthenics (ambenonium [e.g., Mytelase], neostigmine [e.g., Prostigmin], pyridostigmine [e.g., Mestinon]) or
- Antipsychotics (medicine for mental illness) or
- Buclizine (e.g., Bucladin) or
- Carbamazepine (e.g., Tegretol) or
- Cyclizine (e.g., Marezine) or
- Cyclobenzaprine (e.g., Flexeril) or
- Disopyramide (e.g., Norpace) or
- Flavoxate (e.g., Urispas) or
- Ipratropium (e.g., Atrovent) or
- Meclizine (e.g., Antivert) or
- Methylphenidate (e.g., Ritalin) or
- Orphenadrine (e.g., Norflex) or
- Oxybutynin (e.g., Ditropen) or
- Procainamide (e.g., Pronestyl) or
- Promethazine (e.g., Phenergan) or
- Quinidine (e.g., Quinidex) or

- Trimeprazine (e.g., Temaril)—May increase the possibility of side effects or toxic effects; use of these medicines with demecarium, echothiophate, or isoflurophate is not recommended except under close supervision by your doctor
- Malathion (topical) (e.g., Prioderm)—May increase the possibility of side effects or toxic effects, especially if large amounts of malathion are used

Pesticides or insecticides—Make sure you tell your doctor if you have been exposed recently to pesticides or insecticides.

Other medical problems—The presence of other medical problems may affect the use of demecarium, echothiophate, or isoflurophate. Make sure you tell your doctor if you have any other medical problems, especially:

- Asthma or
- Epilepsy or
- Heart disease or
- High or low blood pressure (severe) or
- Myasthenia gravis or
- Overactive thyroid or
- Parkinsonism or
- Stomach ulcer or other stomach problems or
- Urinary tract blockage—If this medicine is absorbed into the body, it may make the condition worse
- Down's syndrome (mongolism)—This medicine may cause these children to become hyperactive
- Eye disease or problems (other)—May increase absorption of this medicine into the body or this medicine may make the condition worse

Proper Use of This Medicine

To use the *ophthalmic solution (eye drops) form* of this medicine:
- First, wash your hands. Tilt the head back and, pressing your finger gently on the skin just beneath the lower eyelid, pull the lower eyelid away from the eye to make a space. Drop the medicine into this space. Let go of the eyelid and gently close the eyes. Do not blink. Keep the eyes closed and apply pressure to the inner corner of the eye with your finger for 1 or 2 minutes to allow the medicine to be absorbed by the eye.
- Remove any excess solution around the eye with a clean tissue, being careful not to touch the eye.
- Immediately after using the eye drops, wash your hands to remove any medicine that may be on them.
- To keep the medicine as germ-free as possible, do not touch the applicator tip to any surface (including the eye). Also, keep the container tightly closed.
- The preservative in the eye drops containing the medicine, demecarium, may be absorbed by soft contact lenses. If you wear soft contact lenses, and your doctor has informed you that you can wear them while taking this medication, you should wait at least 15 minutes after applying the eye drops before inserting your lenses.

To use the *ophthalmic ointment (eye ointment) form* of this medicine:
- First, wash your hands. Tilt the head back and, pressing your finger gently on the skin just beneath the lower eyelid, pull the lower eyelid away from the eye to make a space. Squeeze a thin strip of ointment into this space. A ½-cm (approximately ¼-inch) strip of ointment is usually enough, unless you have been told by your doctor

to use a different amount. Let go of the eyelid and gently close the eyes. Keep the eyes closed for 1 to 2 minutes to allow the medicine to be absorbed by the eye.

- Immediately after using the eye ointment, wash your hands to remove any medicine that may be on them.
- Since isoflurophate loses its effectiveness when exposed to moisture, do not wash the tip of the ointment tube or allow it to touch any moist surface (including the eye).
- To keep the medicine as germ-free as possible, do not touch the applicator tip to any surface (including the eye). After using this eye ointment, wipe the tip of the ointment tube with a clean tissue and keep the tube tightly closed.

It is very important that you use this medicine only as directed. Do not use more of it and do not use it more often than your doctor ordered. To do so may increase the chance of too much medicine being absorbed into the body and the chance of side effects.

If the applicator tip touches any surface (including the eye), it may become contaminated with bacteria, which may increase the chance of developing an eye infection. If you think the applicator has become contaminated, notify your doctor immediately.

Eye ointment usually causes blurred vision for a short time after you use it, and eye drops containing these medicines may affect your vision for several hours after you use them. Therefore, ask your doctor if the dose (or one of the doses if you use more than 1 dose a day) can be used at bedtime.

Dosing—The doses of these medicines will be different for different patients. *Follow your doctor's orders or the directions on the label.* The following information includes only the average doses of these medicines. *If your dose is different, do not change it* unless your doctor tells you to do so.

For demecarium
- For *ophthalmic solution (eye drops)* dosage form:
  —For glaucoma:
  - Adults and older children—Use one drop in the eye one or two times a day.
  - Infants and young children—Use and dose must be determined by your doctor.
  —For treatment of accommodative esotropia:
  - Adults and older children—Use one drop in the eye once a day for two to three weeks, then one drop in the eye once every two days for three to four weeks, then use as determined by the doctor.
  - Infants and young children—Use and dose must be determined by your doctor.
  —For diagnosis of accommodative esotropia:
  - Adults and older children—Use one drop in the eye once a day for two weeks, then one drop in the eye once every two days for two to three weeks.
  - Infants and young children—Use and dose must be determined by your doctor.

For echothiophate
- For *ophthalmic solution (eye drops)* dosage form:
  —For glaucoma:
  - Adults and older children—Use one drop in the eye one or two times a day.
  - Infants and younger children—Use and dose must be determined by your doctor.

  —For treatment of accommodative esotropia:
  - Adults and older children—Use one drop in the eye once a day or one drop in the eye once every two days.
  - Infants and young children—Use and dose must be determined by your doctor.
  —For diagnosis of accommodative esotropia:
  - Adults and older children—Use one drop in the eye once a day at bedtime for two to three weeks.
  - Infants and young children—Use and dose must be determined by your doctor.

For isoflurophate
- For *ophthalmic ointment* dosage form:
  —For glaucoma:
  - Adults and older children—Use the ointment in the eyes once every three days or as often as three times a day as directed by the doctor.
  - Infants and young children—Use and dose must be determined by your doctor.
  —For treatment of accommodative esotropia:
  - Adults and older children—Use the ointment in the eyes once a day at bedtime for two weeks, then once a week or as often as once every two days as directed by the doctor.
  - Infants and young children—Use and dose must be determined by your doctor.
  —For diagnosis of accommodative esotropia:
  - Adults and older children—Use the ointment in the eyes once a day at bedtime for two weeks.
  - Infants and young children—Use and dose must be determined by your doctor.

Missed dose—If you miss a dose of this medicine and your dosing schedule is:
- One dose every other day—Use the missed dose as soon as possible if you remember it on the day it should be used. However, if you do not remember the missed dose until the next day, use it at that time. Then skip a day and start your dosing schedule again. Do not double doses.
- One dose a day—Use the missed dose as soon as possible. However, if you do not remember the missed dose until the next day, skip the missed dose and go back to your regular dosing schedule. Do not double doses.
- More than one dose a day—Use the missed dose as soon as possible. However, if it is almost time for your next dose, skip the missed dose and go back to your regular dosing schedule. Do not double doses.

If your dosing schedule is different from all of the above and you miss a dose of this medicine, or if you have any questions about this, check with your doctor.

Storage—To store this medicine:
- Keep out of the reach of children. Overdose of demecarium, echothiophate, or isoflurophate is very dangerous in young children.
- Store away from heat and direct light.
- Keep this medicine from freezing.
- Do not keep outdated medicine or medicine no longer needed. Be sure that any discarded medicine is out of the reach of children.

Precautions While Using This Medicine

If you are using this medicine for glaucoma, your doctor should check your eye pressure at regular visits to make sure the medicine is working.

If you will be using this medicine for a long time, your doctor should examine your eyes at regular visits to make sure this medicine does not cause unwanted effects.

Before you have any kind of surgery (including eye surgery), dental treatment, or emergency treatment, tell the medical doctor or dentist in charge and the anesthesiologist or anesthetist (the person who puts you to sleep) that you are using this medicine or have used it within the past month.

These medicines should not be used if an eye infection is present, or if the eye is wounded or injured. If redness, pain, or discharge develops, or if a foreign object becomes lodged in one or both eyes, or if you suffer a blow to the eye or eye area, notify your doctor immediately.

Avoid breathing in even small amounts of carbamate- or organophosphate-type insecticides or pesticides (for example, carbaryl [Sevin], demeton [Systox], diazinon, malathion, parathion, ronnel [Trolene], or TEPP). They may add to the effects of this medicine. Farmers, gardeners, residents of communities undergoing insecticide or pesticide spraying or dusting, workers in plants manufacturing such products, or other persons exposed to such poisons should protect themselves by wearing a mask over the nose and mouth, changing clothes frequently, and washing hands often.

Make sure your vision is clear before you drive, use machines, or do anything else that could be dangerous if you are not able to see well. This is because:

- After you apply this medicine to your eyes, your pupils may become unusually small. This may cause you to see less well at night or in dim light.
- After you begin using this medicine, your vision may be blurred or there may be a change in your near or distance vision.
- The eye ointment form of this medicine usually causes blurred vision for a short time after you apply it.

Side Effects of This Medicine

Along with its needed effects, a medicine may cause some unwanted effects. Although not all of these side effects may occur, if they do occur they may need medical attention.

Check with your doctor immediately if any of the following side effects occur:
Rare
　Burning, redness, stinging, or other eye irritation; eye pain; veil or curtain appearing across part of vision

Symptoms of too much medicine being absorbed into the body
　Increased sweating; loss of bladder control; muscle weakness; nausea, vomiting, diarrhea, or stomach cramps or pain; shortness of breath, tightness in chest, or wheezing; slow or irregular heartbeat; unusual tiredness or weakness; watering of mouth

　Note: The most common of these symptoms, especially in children, are *nausea, vomiting, diarrhea, and stomach cramps or pain.* Your doctor may tell you to stop taking the medicine if any of these side effects occur.

　　　Too much medicine being absorbed is rare with the eye ointment form of this medicine.

Other side effects may occur that usually do not need medical attention. These side effects may go away during treatment as your body adjusts to the medicine. However, check with

your doctor if any of the following side effects continue or are bothersome:
　Blurred vision or change in near or distance vision; difficulty in seeing at night or in dim light; headache or browache; twitching of eyelids; watering of eyes

Other side effects not listed above may also occur in some patients. If you notice any other effects, check with your doctor.

Revised: 06/15/99

ANTIHEMOPHILIC FACTOR
Systemic

Commonly used brand name(s):

In the U.S.—

Alphanate	Koate-HP
Bioclate	Kogenate
Helixate	Kogenate FS
Hemofil M	Monarc-M
Humate-P	Monoclate-P
Hyate:C	Recombinate

Generic name product may be available.

In Canada—

Hemofil M	Kogenate
Hyate:C	Recombinate
Koate-HP	

Other commonly used names are AHF and factor VIII.

Description

Antihemophilic (an-tee-hee-moe-FIL-ik) factor (AHF) is a protein produced naturally in the body. It helps the blood form clots to stop bleeding.

Hemophilia A, also called classical hemophilia, is a condition in which the body does not make enough AHF. If you do not have enough AHF and you become injured, your blood will not form clots as it should, and you may bleed into and damage your muscles and joints. One type of AHF is used to treat another condition called von Willebrand disease, in which there is a risk of bleeding. AHF also may be used for other conditions as determined by your doctor.

The AHF that your doctor will give you is obtained naturally from human or pig blood or artificially by a man-made process.

AHF obtained from human blood has been treated. It is not likely to contain harmful viruses such as hepatitis B virus; hepatitis C virus (non-A, non-B hepatitis); or human immunodeficiency virus (HIV), the virus that causes acquired immunodeficiency syndrome (AIDS). The man-made and pork AHF products do not contain these viruses.

AHF is available only with your doctor's prescription, in the following dosage form:

Parenteral
- Injection (U.S. and Canada)

Before Using This Medicine

In deciding to use a medicine, the risks of taking the medicine must be weighed against the good it will do. This is a decision

you and your doctor will make. For antihemophilic factor (AHF), the following should be considered:

Allergies—Tell your doctor if you have ever had any unusual or allergic reaction to AHF. Also tell your health care professional if you are allergic to any other substances, such as foods, preservatives, or dyes.

Pregnancy—Studies on effects in pregnancy have not been done in either humans or animals.

Breast-feeding—It is not known whether AHF passes into breast milk. Although most medicines pass into breast milk in small amounts, many of them may be used safely while breast-feeding. Mothers who are using this medicine and who wish to breast-feed should discuss this with their doctor.

Children—This medicine has been tested in children and, in effective doses, has not been shown to cause different side effects or problems than it does in adults.

Older adults—This medicine has been tested and has not been shown to cause different side effects or problems in older people than it does in younger adults.

Other medicines—Although certain medicines should not be used together at all, in other cases two different medicines may be used together even if an interaction might occur. In these cases, your doctor may want to change the dose, or other precautions may be necessary. Tell your health care professional if you are using any other prescription or nonprescription (over-the-counter [OTC]) medicine.

Other medical problems—The presence of other medical problems may affect the use of AHF. Make sure you tell your doctor if you have any other medical problems.

Proper Use of This Medicine

Some medicines given by injection may sometimes be given at home to patients who do not need to be in the hospital. If you are using this medicine at home, your health care professional will teach you how to prepare and inject the medicine. You will have a chance to practice preparing and injecting it. *Be certain that you understand exactly how the medicine is to be prepared and injected.*

To prepare this medicine:

- Take the dry medicine and the liquid (diluent) out of the refrigerator or freezer and bring them to room temperature, as directed by your doctor.
- Wipe rubber surface of bottles with alcohol swab and allow to dry.
- When injecting the liquid (diluent) into the dry medicine, *aim the stream of liquid (diluent) against the wall of the container of dry medicine* to prevent foaming.
- *Swirl the container gently to dissolve the medicine. Do not shake the container.*
- Check the solution to make sure it is clear. Do not use medicine if you can see anything solid in the solution or if the solution is cloudy

Use this medicine right away. It should not be kept longer than 3 hours after it has been prepared, as directed on the package or by your doctor.

A plastic disposable syringe and filter needle must be used with this medicine. The medicine may stick to the inside of a glass syringe, and you may not receive a full dose.

Do not reuse syringes and needles. Put used syringes and needles in a puncture-resistant disposable container, or dispose of them as directed by your health care professional.

Dosing—The dose of antihemophilic factor (AHF) will be different for different patients. The dose you receive will be based on:

- Your body weight.
- The amount of AHF your body is able to make.
- How much, how often, and where in your body you are bleeding.
- Whether or not your body has built up a defense (antibody) against this medicine.

Your dose of this medicine may even be different at different times. It is important that you *follow your doctor's orders.*

Missed dose—If you miss a dose of this medicine, check with your doctor as soon as possible for instructions. If you cannot reach your doctor, use your usual dose as soon as you remember.

Storage—To store this medicine:

- Keep out of the reach of children.
- Some AHF products must be stored in the refrigerator and some in the freezer. However, some of them may be kept at room temperature for short periods of time. Store this medicine as directed by your doctor or by the manufacturer.
- Do not keep outdated medicine or medicine no longer needed. Be sure that any discarded medicine is out of the reach of children.

Precautions While Using This Medicine

If you were recently diagnosed with hemophilia A, you should receive hepatitis A and hepatitis B vaccines to reduce even further your risk of getting hepatitis A or B from antihemophilic factor.

It is recommended that you carry identification stating that you have hemophilia A, and what medicine you are using. If you have any questions about what kind of identification to carry, check with your health care professional.

After a while, your body may build up a defense (antibody) against this medicine. *Tell your doctor if this medicine seems to be less effective than usual.*

Side Effects of This Medicine

Along with its needed effects, a medicine may cause some unwanted effects. Some side effects will have signs or symptoms that you can see or feel. Your doctor may watch for others by doing certain tests.

Check with your doctor immediately if any of the following side effects occur, because they may mean that you are having a serious allergic reaction to the medicine:

Less common or rare

Changes in facial skin color; fast or irregular breathing; puffiness or swelling of the eyelids or around the eyes; shortness of breath, troubled breathing, tightness in chest, and/or wheezing; skin rash, hives, and/or itching

Also, check with your doctor as soon as possible if any of the following occur:

Less common or rare

Chills; fever; nausea; tenderness, pain, swelling, warmth, skin discoloration, and noticeable veins over affected area; sensation of burning, warmth, heat, numbness, tightness, or tingling; unusual bleeding or bruising; unusual tiredness or weakness

Other side effects may occur that usually do not need medical attention. These side effects may go away during treatment as your body adjusts to the medicine. However, check with your doctor if any of the following side effects continue or are bothersome:

Less common
> Burning, stinging, or swelling at place of injection; dizziness or lightheadedness; dry mouth or bad taste in mouth; headache; nosebleed; redness of face; vomiting

Other side effects not listed above may also occur in some patients. If you notice any other effects, check with your doctor.

Developed: 07/30/93
Revised: 9/22/99

ANTIHISTAMINES   Systemic

Commonly used brand name(s):

In the U.S.—

Aller-Chlor[5]	Hyrexin[10]
AllerMax Caplets[10]	Hyzine-50[12]
Aller-med[10]	Nasahist B[3]
Atarax[12]	Nervine Nighttime Sleep-Aid[10]
Banophen[10]	Nolahist[14]
Banophen Caplets[10]	Nytol QuickCaps[10]
Benadryl[10]	Nytol QuickGels[10]
Benadryl Allergy[10]	Optimine[2]
Bromphen[3]	PBZ[16]
Calm X[9]	PBZ-SR[16]
Chlo-Amine[5]	PediaCare Allergy Formula[5]
Chlorate[5]	Pelamine[16]
Chlor-Trimeton[5]	Periactin[7]
Chlor-Trimeton Allergy[5]	Phenetron[5]
Chlor-Trimeton Repetabs[5]	Polaramine[8]
Claritin[13]	Polaramine Repetabs[8]
Claritin Reditabs[13]	Siladryl[10]
Compoz[10]	Sleep-Eze D[10]
Contac 12 Hour Allergy[6]	Sleep-Eze D Extra Strength[10]
Cophene-B[3]	Sominex[10]
Dexchlor[8]	Tavist[6]
Dimetapp Allergy Liqui-Gels[3]	Tavist-1[6]
Dinate[9]	Telachlor[5]
Diphen Cough[10]	Teldrin[5]
Diphenhist[10]	Triptone Caplets[9]
Diphenhist Captabs[10]	Twilite Caplets[10]
Dormarex 2[10]	Unisom Nighttime Sleep Aid[11]
Dramamine[9]	Unisom Sleep Gels Maximum Strength[10]
Dramanate[9]	
Genahist[10]	Vistaril[12]
Gen-Allerate[5]	Zyrtec[4]
Hydrate[9]	

Note: Seldane was withdrawn from the U.S. market by the U.S. Food and Drug Administration in February 1998. Hismanal was withdrawn from the U.S. market by the manufacturer in June, 1999.

In Canada—

Allerdryl[10]	Dimetane[3]
Apo-Dimenhydrinate[9]	Gravol[9]
Apo-Hydroxyzine[12]	Gravol Filmkote[9]
Atarax[12]	Gravol Filmkote (Junior Strength)[9]
Benadryl[10]	
Chlor-Tripolon[5]	Gravol I/M[9]
Claritin[13]	Gravol I/V[9]

Gravol L/A[9]	PMS-Cyproheptadine[7]
Gravol Liquid[9]	PMS-Dimenhydrinate[9]
Multipax[12]	Polaramine[8]
Novo-Hydroxyzin[12]	Polaramine Repetabs[8]
Novo-Pheniram[5]	Reactine[4]
Novo-Terfenadine[15]	Tavist[6]
Optimine[2]	Traveltabs[9]
Periactin[7]	Zyrtec[4]

Note: Hismanal and Seldane have been removed from the Canadian market.

Note: For quick reference, the following antihistamines are numbered to match the corresponding brand names.

This information applies to the following medicines:
1. Astemizole (a-STEM-mi-zole)*†
2. Azatadine (a-ZA-ta-deen)
3. Brompheniramine (brome-fen-EER-a-meen)‡
4. Cetirizine (se-TI-ra-zeen)
5. Chlorpheniramine (klor-fen-EER-a-meen)‡
6. Clemastine (KLEM-as-teen)‡
7. Cyproheptadine (si-proe-HEP-ta-deen)‡
8. Dexchlorpheniramine (dex-klor-fen-EER-a-meen)‡
9. Dimenhydrinate (dye-men-HYE-dri-nate)‡§
10. Diphenhydramine (dye-fen-HYE-dra-meen)‡§
11. Doxylamine (dox-ILL-a-meen)†
12. Hydroxyzine (hye-DROX-i-zeen)‡§
13. Loratadine (lor-AT-a-deen)
14. Phenindamine (fen-IN-da-meen)†
15. Terfenadine (ter-FEN-a-deen)*†
16. Tripelennamine (tri-pel-ENN-a-meen)‡

---

*Not commercially available in the U.S.
†Not commercially available in Canada.
‡Generic name product may be available in the U.S.
§Generic name product may be available in Canada.

Description

Antihistamines are used to relieve or prevent the symptoms of hay fever and other types of allergy. They work by preventing the effects of a substance called histamine, which is produced by the body. Histamine can cause itching, sneezing, runny nose, and watery eyes. Also, in some persons histamine can close up the bronchial tubes (air passages of the lungs) and make breathing difficult.

Some of the antihistamines are also used to prevent motion sickness, nausea, vomiting, and dizziness. In patients with Parkinson's disease, diphenhydramine may be used to decrease stiffness and tremors. Also, the syrup form of diphenhydramine is used to relieve the cough due to colds or hay fever. In addition, since antihistamines may cause drowsiness as a side effect, some of them may be used to help people go to sleep.

Hydroxyzine is used in the treatment of nervous and emotional conditions to help control anxiety. It can also be used to help control anxiety and produce sleep before surgery.

Antihistamines may also be used for other conditions as determined by your doctor.

Some antihistamine preparations are available only with your doctor's prescription. Others are available without a prescription. However, your doctor may have special instructions on the proper dose of the medicine for your medical condition.

These medicines are available in the following dosage forms:

Oral
Astemizole
• Oral suspension (Germany and United Kingdom)
• Tablets (Germany and United Kingdom)

Azatadine
- Tablets (U.S. and Canada)

Brompheniramine
- Capsules (U.S.)
- Elixir (U.S. and Canada)
- Tablets (Canada)

Cetirizine
- Syrup (U.S.)
- Tablets (U.S. and Canada)

Chlorpheniramine
- Extended-release capsules (U.S.)
- Syrup (U.S. and Canada)
- Tablets (U.S. and Canada)
- Chewable tablets (U.S.)
- Extended-release tablets (U.S. and Canada)

Clemastine
- Syrup (U.S. and Canada)
- Tablets (U.S. and Canada)

Cyproheptadine
- Syrup (Canada)
- Tablets (U.S. and Canada)

Dexchlorpheniramine
- Syrup (U.S. and Canada)
- Tablets (U.S. and Canada)
- Extended-release tablets (U.S. and Canada)

Dimenhydrinate
- Extended-release capsules (Canada)
- Oral Solution (U.S. and Canada)
- Syrup (U.S. and Canada)
- Tablets (U.S. and Canada)
- Chewable tablets (U.S. and Canada)

Diphenhydramine
- Capsules (U.S. and Canada)
- Elixir (U.S. and Canada)
- Tablets (U.S.)

Doxylamine
- Tablets (U.S.)

Hydroxyzine
- Capsules (U.S. and Canada)
- Oral suspension (U.S.)
- Syrup (U.S. and Canada)
- Tablets (U.S.)

Loratadine
- Syrup (U.S. and Canada)
- Tablets (U.S. and Canada)

Phenindamine
- Tablets (U.S.)

Terfenadine
- Oral suspension (Australia and United Kingdom)
- Tablets (Australia and United Kingdom)

Tripelennamine
- Elixir (U.S.)
- Tablets (U.S. and Canada)
- Extended-release tablets (U.S.)

Parenteral

Brompheniramine
- Injection (U.S.)

Chlorpheniramine
- Injection (U.S. and Canada)

Dimenhydrinate
- Injection (U.S. and Canada)

Diphenhydramine
- Injection (U.S. and Canada)

Hydroxyzine
- Injection (U.S. and Canada)

Rectal

Dimenhydrinate
- Suppositories (Canada)

Before Using This Medicine

In deciding to use a medicine, the risks of taking the medicine must be weighed against the good it will do. This is a decision you and your doctor will make. For antihistamines, the following should be considered:

Allergies—Tell your doctor if you have ever had any unusual or allergic reaction to antihistamines. Also tell your health care professional if you are allergic to any other substances, such as foods, preservatives, or dyes.

Diet—Make certain your health care professional knows if you are on a low-sodium, low-sugar, or any other special diet. Most medicines contain more than their active ingredient, and many liquid medicines contain alcohol.

It is very important that you do not take astemizole (e.g., Hismanal) or terfenadine (e.g., Seldane) with grapefruit juice. Studies have shown that taking astemizole or terfenadine and grapefruit juice may cause heart rhythm problems.

Pregnancy—Hydroxyzine is not recommended for use in the first months of pregnancy since it has been shown to cause birth defects in animal studies when given in doses many times higher than the usual human dose. Be sure you have discussed this with your doctor.

Astemizole and terfenadine have not been studied in pregnant women. However, studies in animals have shown that these medicines cause birth defects or other problems when given in doses higher than the usual human dose. Before taking this medicine, make sure your doctor knows if you are pregnant or if you may become pregnant.

Azatadine, brompheniramine, cetirizine, chlorpheniramine, clemastine, cyproheptadine, dexchlorpheniramine, dimenhydrinate, diphenhydramine, doxylamine, loratadine, and tripelennamine have not been studied in pregnant women. However, these medicines have not been shown to cause birth defects or other problems in animal studies.

Breast-feeding—Small amounts of antihistamines pass into the breast milk. Use is not recommended since babies are more susceptible to the side effects of antihistamines, such as unusual excitement or irritability. Also, since these medicines tend to decrease the secretions of the body, it is possible that the flow of breast milk may be reduced in some patients. It is not known yet whether astemizole, cetirizine, loratadine, or terfenadine cause these same side effects.

Children—Serious side effects, such as convulsions (seizures), are more likely to occur in younger patients and would be of greater risk to infants than to older children or adults. In general, children are more sensitive to the effects of antihistamines. Also, nightmares or unusual excitement, nervousness, restlessness, or irritability may be more likely to occur in children.

Older adults—Elderly patients are usually more sensitive to the effects of antihistamines. Confusion; difficult or painful urination; dizziness; drowsiness; feeling faint; or dryness of mouth, nose, or throat may be more likely to occur in elderly patients. Also, nightmares or unusual excitement, nervousness, restlessness, or irritability may be more likely to occur in elderly patients.

Other medicines—Although certain medicines should not be used together at all, in other cases different medicines may be used together even if an interaction might occur. In these cases, your doctor may want to change the dose, or other precautions may be necessary. When you are taking antihistamines it is especially important that your health care professional knows if you are taking any of the following:

- Anticholinergics (medicine for abdominal or stomach spasms or cramps)—Side effects, such as dryness of mouth, of antihistamines or anticholinergics may be more likely to occur

- Clarithromycin (e.g., Biaxin) or
- Erythromycin (e.g., E-Mycin) or
- Itraconazole (e.g., Sporanox) or
- Ketoconazole (e.g., Nizoral) or
- Troleandomycin—Use of these medicines with astemizole or terfenadine may cause heart problems, such as an irregular heartbeat; these medicines should not be used together

- Bepridil (e.g., Vascor) or
- Disopyramide (e.g., Norpace) or
- Maprotiline (e.g., Ludiomil) or
- Phenothiazines (acetophenazine [e.g., Tindal], chlorpromazine [e.g., Thorazine], fluphenazine [e.g., Prolixin], mesoridazine [e.g., Serentil], perphenazine [e.g., Trilafon], prochlorperazine [e.g., Compazine], promazine [e.g., Sparine], promethazine [e.g., Phenergan], thioridazine [e.g. Mellaril], trifluoperazine [e.g., Stelazine], triflupromazine [e.g., Vesprin], trimeprazine [e.g., Temaril]) or
- Pimozide (e.g., Orap) or
- Procainamide (e.g., Pronestyl) or
- Quinidine (e.g., Quinaglute Dura-tabs) or
- Tricyclic antidepressants (amitriptyline [e.g., Elavil], amoxapine [e.g., Asendin], clomipramine [e.g., Anafranil], desipramine [e.g., Pertofrane], doxepin [e.g., Sinequan], imipramine [e.g., Tofranil], nortriptyline [e.g., Aventyl], protriptyline [e.g., Vivactil], trimipramine [e.g., Surmontil])—Use of these medicines with astemizole or terfenadine may increase the risk of heart rhythm problems

- Central nervous system (CNS) depressants (medicines that cause drowsiness)—Effects, such as drowsiness, of CNS depressants or antihistamines may be worsened; also, taking maprotiline or tricyclic antidepressants may cause some side effects of either of these medicines, such as dryness of mouth, to become more severe

- Cisapride (e.g., Propulsid) or
- HIV-protease inhibitors (indinavir [e.g., Crixivan], nelfinavir [e.g., Viracept], ritonavir [e.g., Norvir], saquinavir [e.g., Fortovase, Invirase]) or
- Mibefradil (e.g., Posicor) or
- Serotonin reuptake inhibitors (fluoxetine [e.g., Prozac], fluvoxamine [e.g., Luvox], nefazodone [e.g., Serzone], paroxetine [e.g., Paxil], sertraline [e.g., Zoloft]) or
- Sparfloxacin (e.g., Zagam) or
- Zileuton (e.g., Zyflo)—Use of these medicines with astemizole or terfenadine may cause heart problems; these medicines should not be used with astemizole or terfenadine

- Monoamine oxidase (MAO) inhibitors (furazolidone [e.g., Furoxone], isocarboxazid [e.g., Marplan], phenelzine [e.g., Nardil], procarbazine [e.g., Matulane], selegiline [e.g., Eldepryl], tranylcypromine [e.g., Parnate])—If you are now taking, or have taken within the past 2 weeks, any of the MAO inhibitors, the side effects of the antihistamines, such as drowsiness and dryness of mouth, may become more severe; these medicines should not be used together

- Quinine—Use of this medicine with astemizole may cause heart problems, such as irregular heartbeat; these medicines should not be used together

Other medical problems—The presence of other medical problems may affect the use of antihistamines. Make sure you tell your doctor if you have any other medical problems, especially:

- Enlarged prostate or
- Urinary tract blockage or difficult urination—Antihistamines may make urinary problems worse

- Glaucoma—These medicines may cause a slight increase in inner eye pressure that may make the condition worse

- Heart rhythm problems (history of) or
- Intestinal obstruction
- Low potassium blood levels—Use of astemizole or terfenadine can cause serious heart rhythm problems

- Liver disease—Higher blood levels of astemizole or terfenadine may result, which may increase the chance of heart problems

- Stomach ulcer

Proper Use of This Medicine

Antihistamines are used to relieve or prevent the symptoms of your medical problem. Take them only as directed. Do not take more of them and do not take them more often than recommended on the label, unless otherwise directed by your doctor. To do so may increase the chance of side effects.

Dosing—The dose of an antihistamine will be different for different patients. *Follow your doctor's orders or the directions on the label.* The following information includes only the average doses of antihistamines. *If your dose is different, do not change it* unless your doctor tells you to do so.

The number of capsules or tablets or teaspoonfuls of liquid that you take or the number of suppositories you use depends on the strength of the medicine. Also, *the number of doses you take each day and the time between doses depends on whether you are taking a short-acting or long-acting form of antihistamine.*

- For use as an antihistamine:
    For astemizole
    - For *oral* dosage forms (tablets or liquid):
        —Adults and teenagers: 10 milligrams (mg) once a day.
        —Children younger than 6 years of age: 0.2 mg per kilogram (kg) (0.1 mg per pound) of body weight once a day.
        —Children 6 to 12 years of age: 5 mg once a day.

    For azatadine
    - For *oral* dosage form (tablets):
        —Adults: 1 to 2 milligrams (mg) every eight to twelve hours as needed.
        —Children younger than 12 years of age: Use and dose must be determined by your doctor.

—Children 12 years of age and older: 0.5 mg to 1 mg two times a day as needed.

For brompheniramine
- For *regular (short-acting) oral* dosage forms (capsules, tablets, or liquid):
  —Adults and teenagers: 4 milligrams (mg) every four to six hours as needed.
  —Children 2 to 6 years of age: 1 mg every four to six hours as needed.
  —Children 6 to 12 years of age: 2 mg every four to six hours as needed.
- For *injection* dosage form:
  —Adults and teenagers: 10 milligrams (mg) injected into a muscle, under the skin, or into a vein every eight to twelve hours.
  —Children younger than 12 years of age: 0.125 mg per kilogram (0.06 mg per pound) of body weight injected into a muscle, under the skin, or into a vein three or four times a day as needed.

For cetirizine
- For *oral* dosage forms (syrup and tablets):
  —Adults: 5 to 10 milligrams (mg) once a day.
  —Children younger than 2 years of age: Use and dose must be determined by your doctor.
  —Children 2 to 6 years of age: 2.5 mg once a day, up to a maximum of 5 mg once a day or 2.5 mg twice a day.
  —Children 6 years of age and older: 5 to 10 mg once a day.

For chlorpheniramine
- For *regular (short-acting) oral* dosage forms (tablets or liquid):
  —Adults and teenagers: 4 milligrams (mg) every four to six hours as needed.
  —Children younger than 6 years of age: Use and dose must be determined by your doctor.
  —Children 6 to 12 years of age: 2 mg three or four times a day as needed.
- For *long-acting oral* dosage forms (capsules or tablets):
  —Adults: 8 or 12 milligrams (mg) every eight to twelve hours as needed.
  —Children younger than 12 years of age: Use and dose must be determined by your doctor.
  —Children 12 years of age and older: 8 mg every twelve hours as needed.
- For *injection* dosage form:
  —Adults: 5 to 40 milligrams (mg) injected into a muscle, into a vein, or under the skin.
  —Children: 0.0875 mg per kilogram (0.04 mg per pound) of body weight injected under the skin every six hours as needed.

For clemastine
- For *oral* dosage forms (tablets or liquid):
  —Adults and teenagers: 1.34 milligrams (mg) two times a day or 2.68 mg one to three times a day as needed.
  —Children younger than 6 years of age: Use and dose must be determined by your doctor.
  —Children 6 to 12 years of age: 0.67 to 1.34 mg two times a day.

For cyproheptadine
- For *oral* dosage forms (tablets or liquid):
  —Adults and children 14 years of age and older: 4 milligrams (mg) every eight hours. The doctor may increase the dose if needed.
  —Children 2 to 6 years of age: 2 mg every eight to twelve hours as needed.
  —Children 6 to 14 years of age: 4 mg every eight to twelve hours as needed.

For dexchlorpheniramine
- For *regular (short-acting) oral* dosage forms (tablets or liquid):
  —Adults and teenagers: 2 milligrams (mg) every four to six hours as needed.
  —Children 2 to 5 years of age: 0.5 mg every four to six hours as needed.
  —Children 5 to 12 years of age: 1 mg every four to six hours as needed.
- For *long-acting oral* dosage form (tablets):
  —Adults: 4 or 6 milligrams (mg) every eight to twelve hours as needed.
  —Children: Use and dose must be determined by your doctor.

For diphenhydramine
- For *oral* dosage forms (capsules, tablets, or liquid):
  —Adults and teenagers: 25 to 50 milligrams (mg) every four to six hours as needed.
  —Children younger than 6 years of age: 6.25 to 12.5 mg every four to six hours.
  —Children 6 to 12 years of age: 12.5 to 25 mg every four to six hours.
- For *injection* dosage form:
  —Adults: 10 to 50 milligrams (mg) injected into a muscle or into a vein.
  —Children: 1.25 mg per kg (0.6 mg per pound) of body weight injected into a muscle four times a day.

For doxylamine
- For *oral* dosage form (tablets):
  —Adults and teenagers: 12.5 to 25 milligrams (mg) every four to six hours as needed.
  —Children younger than 6 years of age: Use and dose must be determined by your doctor.
  —Children 6 to 12 years of age: 6.25 to 12.5 mg every four to six hours as needed.

For hydroxyzine
- For *oral* dosage forms (capsules, tablets, or liquid):
  —Adults and teenagers: 25 to 100 milligrams (mg) three or four times a day as needed.
  —Children younger than 12 years of age: 0.5 mg per kg (0.2 mg per pound) of body weight every six hours as needed.

For loratadine
- For *oral* dosage forms (tablets or liquid):
  —Adults and children 6 years of age and older: 10 milligrams (mg) once a day.
  —Children 2 to 5 years of age: 5 mg once a day.

For phenindamine
- For *oral* dosage form (tablets):
  —Adults and teenagers: 25 milligrams (mg) every four to six hours as needed.

—Children younger than 6 years of age: Use and dose must be determined by your doctor.
—Children 6 to 12 years of age: 12.5 mg every four to six hours as needed.

For terfenadine
- For *oral* dosage forms (tablets or liquid):
  —Adults and teenagers: 60 milligrams (mg) every twelve hours.
  —Children 3 to 6 years of age: 15 mg every twelve hours as needed.
  —Children 7 to 12 years of age: 30 mg every twelve hours as needed.

For tripelennamine
- For *regular (short-acting) oral* dosage forms (tablets or liquid):
  —Adults: 25 to 50 milligrams (mg) every four to six hours as needed.
  —Children: 1.25 mg per kilogram (kg) (0.6 mg per pound) of body weight every six hours as needed.
- For *long-acting oral* dosage form (tablets):
  —Adults: 100 milligrams (mg) every eight to twelve hours as needed.
  —Children: Use and dose must be determined by your doctor.

- For nausea, vomiting, and vertigo (only dimenhydrinate and diphenhydramine are used for vertigo):

  For dimenhydrinate
  - For *regular (short-acting) oral* dosage forms (tablets or liquid):
    —Adults and teenagers: 50 to 100 milligrams (mg) every four to six hours as needed.
    —Children 2 to 6 years of age: 12.5 to 25 mg every six to eight hours as needed.
    —Children 6 to 12 years of age: 25 to 50 mg every six to eight hours as needed.
  - For *long-acting oral* dosage form (capsules):
    —Adults: 1 capsule (contains 25 milligrams [mg] for immediate action and 50 mg for long action) every twelve hours.
    —Children: Use and dose must be determined by your doctor.
  - For *injection* dosage form:
    —Adults: 50 milligrams (mg) injected into a muscle or into a vein every four hours as needed.
    —Children: 1.25 mg per kg (0.6 mg per pound) of body weight injected into a muscle or into a vein every six hours as needed.
  - For *suppository* dosage form:
    —Adults: 50 to 100 milligrams (mg) inserted into the rectum every six to eight hours as needed.
    —Children younger than 6 years of age: Use and dose must be determined by your doctor.
    —Children 6 to 8 years of age: 12.5 to 25 mg inserted into the rectum every eight to twelve hours as needed.
    —Children 8 to 12 years of age: 25 to 50 mg inserted into the rectum every eight to twelve hours as needed.
    —Children 12 years of age and older: 50 mg inserted into the rectum every eight to twelve hours as needed.

For diphenhydramine
- For *oral* dosage forms (capsules, tablets, or liquid):
  —Adults: 25 to 50 milligrams (mg) every four to six hours as needed.
  —Children: 1 to 1.5 mg per kg (0.45 to 0.7 mg per pound) of body weight every four to six hours as needed.
- For *injection* dosage form:
  —Adults: 10 milligrams (mg) injected into a muscle or into a vein. Dose may be increased to 25 to 50 mg every two to three hours.
  —Children: 1 to 1.5 mg per kg (0.45 to 0.68 mg per pound) of body weight injected into a muscle every six hours.

For hydroxyzine
- For *oral* dosage forms (capsules, tablets, or liquid):
  —Adults: 25 to 100 milligrams (mg) three or four times a day as needed.
  —Children younger than 6 years of age: 12.5 mg every six hours as needed.
  —Children 6 years of age and older: 12.5 to 25 mg every six hours as needed.
  For *injection* dosage form:
  —Adults: 25 to 100 milligrams (mg) injected into a muscle.
  —Children: 1 mg per kg (0.45 mg per pound) of body weight injected into a muscle.

- For Parkinson's disease:
  For diphenhydramine
  - For *oral* dosage forms (capsules, tablets, or liquid):
    —Adults: 25 milligrams (mg) three times a day when starting treatment. Your doctor may increase the dose gradually later if needed.
  - For *injection* dosage form:
    —Adults: 10 to 50 milligrams (mg) injected into a muscle or into a vein.
    —Children: 1.25 mg per kg (0.6 mg per pound) of body weight four times a day injected into a muscle.

- For use as a sedative (to help sleep):
  For diphenhydramine
  - For *oral* dosage forms (capsules, tablets, or liquid):
    —Adults: 50 milligrams (mg) twenty to thirty minutes before bedtime if needed.

  For doxylamine
  - For *oral* dosage form (tablets):
    —Adults: 25 milligrams (mg) thirty minutes before bedtime if needed.
    —Children: Use and dose must be determined by your doctor.

  For hydroxyzine
  - For *oral* dosage forms (capsules, tablets, or liquid):
    —Adults: 50 to 100 milligrams (mg).
    —Children: 0.6 mg per kg (0.3 mg per pound) of body weight.
  - For *injection* dosage form:
    —Adults: 50 milligrams (mg) injected into a muscle.

• For anxiety:

For hydroxyzine

• For *oral* dosage forms (capsules, tablets, or liquid):

—Adults: 50 to 100 milligrams (mg).

—Children: 0.6 mg per kilogram (0.3 mg per pound) of body weight.

• For *injection* dosage form:

—Adults: 50 to 100 milligrams (mg) injected into a muscle every four to six hours as needed.

—Children: 1 mg per kilogram (0.45 mg per pound) of body weight injected into a muscle.

Missed dose—If you are taking this medicine regularly and you miss a dose, take it as soon as possible. However, if it is almost time for your next dose, skip the missed dose and go back to your regular dosing schedule. Do not double doses.

For patients *taking this medicine by mouth:*

• Antihistamines can be taken with food or a glass of water or milk to lessen stomach irritation if necessary. However, food may change the amount of astemizole that is absorbed. For this reason, astemizole should be taken on an empty stomach.

• If you are taking the extended-release tablet form of this medicine, swallow the tablets whole. Do not break, crush, or chew before swallowing.

For patients taking *dimenhydrinate or diphenhydramine for motion sickness:*

• Take this medicine at least 30 minutes or, even better, 1 to 2 hours before you begin to travel.

For patients using the *suppository form of this medicine:*

• To insert suppository: First remove the foil wrapper and moisten the suppository with cold water. Lie down on your side and use your finger to push the suppository well up into the rectum. If the suppository is too soft to insert, chill the suppository in the refrigerator for 30 minutes or run cold water over it before removing the foil wrapper.

For patients using the *injection form of this medicine:*

• If you will be giving yourself the injections, make sure you understand exactly how to give them. If you have any questions about this, check with your health care professional.

Storage—To store this medicine:

• Keep out of the reach of children, since overdose may be very dangerous in children.

• Store away from heat and direct light.

• Do not store the capsule or tablet form of this medicine in the bathroom medicine cabinet, near the kitchen sink, or in other damp places. Heat or moisture may cause the medicine to break down.

• Keep the liquid form of this medicine from freezing.

• Do not keep outdated medicine or medicine no longer needed. Be sure that any discarded medicine is out of the reach of children.

Precautions While Using This Medicine

Before you have any skin tests for allergies, tell the doctor in charge that you are taking this medicine. The results of the test may be affected by this medicine.

When taking antihistamines on a regular basis, make sure your doctor knows if you are taking large amounts of aspirin at the same time (as for arthritis or rheumatism). Effects of too much aspirin, such as ringing in the ears, may be covered up by the antihistamine.

*Astemizole and terfenadine should **not** be taken with clarithromycin (e.g., Biaxin), erythromycin (e.g., E-Mycin), itraconazole (e.g., Sporanox), ketoconazole (e.g., Nizoral), mibefradil (e.g., Posicor), or troleandomycin.* Using these medicines together may increase the risk of serious side effects affecting the heart.

Antihistamines will add to the effects of alcohol and other CNS depressants (medicines that slow down the nervous system, possibly causing drowsiness). Some examples of CNS depressants are sedatives, tranquilizers, or sleeping medicine; prescription pain medicine or narcotics; barbiturates; medicine for seizures; muscle relaxants; or anesthetics, including some dental anesthetics. *Check with your doctor before taking any of the above while you are using this medicine.*

This medicine may cause some people to become drowsy or less alert than they are normally. Even if taken at bedtime, it may cause some people to feel drowsy or less alert on arising. Some antihistamines are more likely to cause drowsiness than others. Drowsiness is less likely with cetirizine, and rare with astemizole, loratadine, and terfenadine. *Make sure you know how you react to the antihistamine you are taking before you drive, use machines, or do anything else that could be dangerous if you are not alert.*

Antihistamines may cause dryness of the mouth, nose, and throat. Some antihistamines are more likely to cause dryness of the mouth than others (astemizole and terfenadine, for example, more commonly produce this effect). For temporary relief of mouth dryness, use sugarless candy or gum, melt bits of ice in your mouth, or use a saliva substitute. However, if your mouth continues to feel dry for more than 2 weeks, check with your medical doctor or dentist. Continuing dryness of the mouth may increase the chance of dental disease, including tooth decay, gum disease, and fungus infections.

For patients using *dimenhydrinate, diphenhydramine, or hydroxyzine:*

• This medicine controls nausea and vomiting. For this reason, it may cover up the signs of overdose caused by other medicines or the symptoms of appendicitis. This will make it difficult for your doctor to diagnose these conditions. Make sure your doctor knows that you are taking this medicine if you have other symptoms of appendicitis such as stomach or lower abdominal pain, cramping, or soreness. Also, if you think you may have taken an overdose of any medicine, tell your doctor that you are taking this medicine.

For patients using *diphenhydramine or doxylamine as a sleeping aid:*

• If you are already taking a sedative or tranquilizer, do not take this medicine without consulting your doctor first.

Side Effects of This Medicine

Along with its needed effects, a medicine may cause some unwanted effects. Although not all of these side effects may occur, if they do occur they may need medical attention.

Check with your doctor immediately if the following side effects occur:

Less common or rare with high doses of astemizole or terfenadine;—less frequent or rare with azatadine, cetirizine, clemastine, cyproheptadine, dexchlorpheniramine, diphenhydramine, or loratadine

Fast or irregular heartbeat; fever; abdominal or stomach pain; burning; chills; clay-colored stools or dark urine; cough; diarrhea; difficulty swallowing; dizziness; fast heartbeat; fever; headache; hives; itching; prickly sensations; puffiness or swelling of the eyelids or around the eyes, face, lips or tongue; seizures; shortness of breath; skin rash; tightness in chest; tingling; unusual tiredness or weakness; wheezing

Also, check with your doctor as soon as possible if any of the following side effects occur:

Less common or rare

Sore throat; unusual bleeding or bruising; unusual tiredness or weakness

Symptoms of overdose

Clumsiness or unsteadiness; convulsions (seizures); drowsiness (severe); dryness of mouth, nose, or throat (severe); feeling faint; flushing or redness of face; hallucinations (seeing, hearing, or feeling things that are not there); shortness of breath or troubled breathing; trouble in sleeping

Other side effects may occur that usually do not need medical attention. These side effects may go away during treatment as your body adjusts to the medicine. However, check with your health care professional if any of the following side effects continue or are bothersome:

More common

Drowsiness; dry mouth, nose, or throat; gastrointestinal upset, stomach pain, or nausea; increased appetite and weight gain; thickening of mucus

Less common or rare

Blurred vision or any change in vision; clumsiness or unsteadiness; confusion (not with diphenhydramine); constipation; diarrhea; difficult or painful urination; dizziness (not with brompheniramine, hydroxyzine, or tripelennamine); drowsiness (with high doses of astemizole, loratadine, and terfenadine; dryness of mouth, nose, or throat; early menstruation; fast heartbeat; fatigue; gastrointestinal upset, stomach pain or nausea; increased appetite and weight gain; increased sensitivity of skin to sun; increased sweating; loss of appetite; nightmares (not with azatadine, chlorpheniramine, cyproheptadine, hydroxyzine, or loratadine); ringing or buzzing in ears; skin rash; thickening of mucus; tremor; unusual excitement, nervousness, restlessness, or irritability; vomiting

Other side effects not listed above may also occur in some patients. If you notice any other effects, check with your health care professional.

Additional Information

Once a medicine has been approved for marketing for a certain use, experience may show that it is also useful for other medical problems. Although this use is not included in product labeling, astemizole, cetirizine, loratadine, and terfenadine are used in certain patients with asthma together with asthma medicines. The antihistamine is used before and during exposure to substances that cause reactions, to prevent or reduce bronchospasm (wheezing or difficulty in breathing).

Cyproheptadine is used as an appetite stimulant, in adults and children

Cyproheptadine is used for treatment of vascular headaches.

Other than the above information, there is no additional information relating to proper use, precautions, or side effects for this use.

Revised: 11/10/2000

ANTIHISTAMINES AND DECONGESTANTS Systemic

Commonly used brand name(s):

In the U.S.—

Actagen[28]	Carbodec TR[8]	Dimaphen[5]
Actifed[28]	Cardec[8]	Dimaphen S.A.[5]
Actifed Allergy Nighttime Caplets[20]	Cardec-S[8]	Dimetane Decongestant[3]
	Cenafed Plus[28]	
	Chemdec[8]	Dimetane Decongestant Caplets[3]
Alcomed[5]	C-Hist-SR[13]	
Alcomed 2-60[19]	Chlorafed[15]	Dimetapp[5]
Allent[7]	Chlorafed H.S. Timecelles[15]	Dimetapp Cold and Allergy[5]
Allercon[28]		
Allerest Maximum Strength[15]	Chlorafed Timecelles[15]	Dimetapp Cold & Allergy Quick Dissolve[5]
Allerfrim[28]	Chlordrine S.R.[15]	
Allerphed[28]	Chlorfed[15]	Dimetapp Extentabs[5]
Amilon[9]	Chlorfed II[15]	
Anamine[15]	Chlorphedrine SR[15]	Dimetapp 4-Hour[5]
Anamine T.D.[15]	Chlor-Rest[12]	Disobrom[19]
Andec[8]	Chlortox[13]	Disophrol Chronotabs[19]
Andec-TR[8]	Chlor-Trimeton 4 Hour Relief[15]	
Aprodrine[28]		Dorcol Children's Cold Formula[15]
A.R.M. Maximum Strength Caplets[12]	Chlor-Trimeton 12 Hour Relief[15]	
		Drixomed[19]
	Chlor-Trimeton Allergy-D 12 Hour[15]	Drixoral Cold and Allergy[19]
Atrofed[28]		
Atrohist Pediatric[15]		Drize[15]
Atrohist Pediatric Suspension Dye Free[16]	Claritin-D 12 Hour[21]	Duralex[15]
	Claritin-D 24 Hour[21]	Dura-Tap PD[15]
	Cold and Allergy[5]	Dura-Vent/A[12]
Banophen[20]	Cold-Gest Cold[12]	Ed A-Hist[10]
Benadryl Allergy Decongestant Liquid Medication[20]	Colfed-A[15]	Endafed[7]
	Comhist[13]	E.N.T.[5]
	Comhist LA[13]	Genac[28]
	Contac 12-Hour[12]	Genamin[12]
Biohist-LA[8]	Contac Maximum Strength 12-Hour Caplets[12]	Genatap[5]
Brexin L.A.[15]		Gencold[12]
Brofed Liquid[7]		Hayfebrol[15]
Bromadrine PD[7]	Cophene No. 2[15]	Histalet[15]
Bromadrine TR[7]	Co-Pyronil 2[15]	Histalet Forte[17]
Bromaline[5]	CP Oral[8]	Histatab Plus[10]
Bromanate[5]	Dallergy Jr[7]	Histatan[16]
Bromatapp[5]	Deconamine[15]	Hista-Vadrin[11]
Bromfed[7]	Deconamine SR[15]	Histor-D[10]
Bromfed-PD[7]	Decongestabs[14]	Iofed[7]
Bromfenex[7]	Deconomed SR[15]	Iofed PD[7]
Bromfenex PD[7]	Delhistine D[23]	Iohist-D[23]
Bromophen T.D.[4]	Demazin[12]	Klerist-D[15]
Brompheril[19]	Demazin Repetabs[12]	Kronofed-A Jr. Kronocaps[15]
Carbiset[8]		
Carbiset-TR[8]	Dexaphen SA[19]	
Carbodec[8]	Dexophed[19]	

Kronofed-A
 Kronocaps[15]
Linhist-L.A.[13]
Liqui-Histine-D[23]
Liqui-Minic Infant
 Drops[24]
Lodrane LD[7]
Lodrane Liquid[7]
Med-Hist[15]
Metahistine D[23]
M-Hist[7]
Mooredec[8]
Myphetapp[5]
Nalda-Relief
 Pediatric Drops[14]
Naldecon[14]
Naldecon Pediatric
 Drops[14]
Naldecon Pediatric
 Syrup[14]
Naldelate[14]
Naldelate Pediatric
 Drops[14]
Naldelate Pediatric
 Syrup[14]
Nalex-A[13]
Nalfed[7]
Nalfed-PD[7]
Nalgest[14]
Nalgest Pediatric[14]
Nalphen[14]
Nalphen Pediatric[14]
ND Clear T.D.[15]
Nolamine[9]
Novafed A[15]
Novahistine[10]
Ornade
 Spansules[12]
PediaCare Cold-
 Allergy[15]
PediaCare Cold
 Formula[15]
Phenergan VC[25]
Pherazine VC[25]
Poly D[23]
Poly Hist Forte[17]
Poly-Histine-D[23]
Poly-Histine-D
 Ped[23]
Promethazine VC[25]
Prometh VC Plain[25]
Prop-a-Hist[14]

Pseudo-Chlor[15]
Pseudo-gest Plus[15]
Q-Hist LA[13]
Resaid S.R.[12]
Rescon[15]
Rescon-ED[15]
Rescon JR[15]
Respahist[7]
Rhinatate[16]
Rhinolar-EX[12]
Rhinolar-EX 12[12]
Rhinosyn[15]
Rhinosyn-PD[15]
Ricobid[10]
Ricobid Pediatric[10]
Rinade B.I.D.[15]
Rolatuss Plain[10]
Rondamine[8]
Rondec[8]
Rondec Chewable[7]
Rondec Drops[8]
Rondec-TR[8]
R-Tannamine[16]
R-Tannamine
 Pediatric[16]
R-Tannate[16]
R-Tannate
 Pediatric[16]
Ru-Tuss[10]
Ryna[15]
Rynatan[16]
Rynatan Pediatric[16]
Rynatan-S
 Pediatric[16]
Seldane-D[27]
Semprex-D[1]
Shellcap[7]
Shellcap PD[7]
Silafed[28]
Silaminic[12]
Sinucon[14]
Sinucon Pediatric
 Drops[14]
Sudafed Plus[15]
Tamine S.R.[4]
Tanafed[15]
Tanoral[16]
Tavist-D[18]
Teldrin 12 Hour
 Allergy Relief[12]
Temazin Cold[12]
Touro A&H[7]

Triaminic[12]
Triaminic-12[12]
Triaminic Allergy[12]
Triaminic
 Chewables[12]
Triaminic Cold[12]
Triaminic Oral
 Infant Drops[24]
Triaminic TR[24]
Trihist-D[23]
Trinalin Repetabs[2]
Tri-Nefrin Extra
 Strength[12]
Triofed[28]
Triotann[16]
Triotann Pediatric[16]
Triotann-S
 Pediatric[16]
Tri-Phen-Chlor[14]
Tri-Phen-Chlor
 Pediatric[14]
Tri-Phen-Chlor
 T.R.[14]
Tri-Phen-Mine
 Pediatric Drops[14]
Tri-Phen-Mine
 Pediatric Syrup[14]
Tri-Phen-Mine
 S.R.[14]
Triphenyl[12]
Triposed[28]
Tritan[16]
Tri-Tannate[16]
Tri-Tannate
 Pediatric[16]
ULTRAbrom[7]
ULTRAbrom PD[7]
Uni-Decon[14]
Uni-Multihist D[23]
Vanex Forte
 Caplets[17]
Vicks Children's
 DayQuil Allergy
 Relief[15]
Vicks DayQuil 4
 Hour Allergy
 Relief[5]
Vicks DayQuil 12
 Hour Allergy
 Relief[5]
West-Decon[14]

In Canada—

Actifed[28]
Chlor-Tripolon
 Decongestant[12]
Chlor-Tripolon
 N.D.[21]
Claritin Extra[21]
Coricidin D Long
 Acting[12]
Corsym[12]
Dimetapp[4]

Dimetapp
 Chewables[5]
Dimetapp Clear[5]
Dimetapp
 Extentabs[4]
Dimetapp Liqui-
 Fills[5]
Dimetapp Oral
 Infant Drops[4]
Drixoral[19]

Drixoral Night[19]
Drixtab[19]
Neo Citran A[22]
Novahistex[15]
Ornade[12]
Ornade-A.F.[12]
Ornade
 Spansules[12]
Triaminic[12]
Trinalin Repetabs[2]
Vasofrinic[15]

Note: Seldane-D (terfenadine and pseudoephedrine) was withdrawn from the U.S. market by the Food and Drug Administration in February 1998.

Note: In November 2000, the Food and Drug Administration (FDA) issued a public health warning regarding phenylpropanolamine (PPA) due to the risk of hemorrhagic stroke. The FDA, supported by results of a research program, requested that manufacturers voluntarily discontinue marketing products that contain PPA and that consumers work with their healthcare providers to select alternative products.

Note: For quick reference the following antihistamine and decongestant combinations are numbered to match the corresponding brand names.

This information applies to the following medicines:

1. Acrivastine and Pseudoephedrine (AK-ri-vas-teen and soo-doe-e-FED-rin)†
2. Azatadine and Pseudoephedrine (a-ZA-ta-deen and soo-doe-e-FED-rin)
3. Brompheniramine and Phenylephrine (brome-fen-EER-a-meen and fen-ill-EF-rin)†
4. Brompheniramine, Phenylephrine, and Phenylpropanolamine (brome-fen-EER-a-meen fen-ill-EF-rin and fen-ill-proe-pa-NOLE-a-meen)
5. Brompheniramine and Phenylpropanolamine (brome-fen-EER-a-meen and fen-ill-proe-pa-NOLE-a-meen)‡
6. No product available
7. Brompheniramine and Pseudoephedrine (brome-fen-EER-a-meen and soo-doe-e-FED-rin)†‡
8. Carbinoxamine and Pseudoephedrine (kar-bi-NOX-a-meen and soo-doe-e-FED-rin)†
9. Chlorpheniramine, Phenindamine, and Phenylpropanolamine (klor-fen-EER-a-meen fen-IN-da-meen and fen-ill-proe-pa-NOLE-a-meen)†
10. Chlorpheniramine and Phenylephrine (klor-fen-EER-a-meen and fen-ill-EF-rin)†
11. Chlorpheniramine, Phenylephrine, and Phenylpropanolamine (klor-fen-EER-a-meen fen-ill-EF-rin and fen-ill-proe-pa-NOLE-a-meen)†
12. Chlorpheniramine and Phenylpropanolamine (klor-fen-EER-a-meen and fen-ill-proe-pa-NOLE-a-meen)‡
13. Chlorpheniramine, Phenyltoloxamine, and Phenylephrine (klor-fen-EER-a-meen fen-ill-toe-LOX-a-meen and fen-ill-EF-rin)†
14. Chlorpheniramine, Phenyltoloxamine, Phenylephrine, and Phenylpropanolamine (klor-fen-EER-a-meen fen-ill-toe-LOX-a-meen fen-ill-EF-rin and fen-ill-proe-pa-NOLE-a-meen)†
15. Chlorpheniramine and Pseudoephedrine (klor-fen-EER-a-meen and soo-doe-e-FED-rin)‡
16. Chlorpheniramine, Pyrilamine, and Phenylephrine (klor-fen-EER-a-meen peer-ILL-a-meen and fen-ill-EF-rin)†
17. Chlorpheniramine, Pyrilamine, Phenylephrine, and Phenylpropanolamine (klor-fen-EER-a-meen peer-ILL-a-meen fen-ill-EF-rin and fen-ill-proe-pa-NOLE-a-meen)†
18. Clemastine and Phenylpropanolamine (KLEM-as-teen and fen-ill-proe-pa-NOLE-a-meen)†
19. Dexbrompheniramine and Pseudoephedrine (dex-brom-fen-EER-a-meen and soo-doe-e-FED-rin)
20. Diphenhydramine and Pseudoephedrine (dye-fen-HYE-dra-meen and soo-doe-e-FED-rin)
21. Loratadine and Pseudoephedrine (lor-AT-a-deen and soo-doe-e-FED-rin)
22. Pheniramine and Phenylephrine (fen-EER-a-meen and fen-ill-EF-rin)*
23. Pheniramine, Phenyltoloxamine, Pyrilamine, and Phenylpropanolamine (fen-EER-a-meen fen-ill-toe-LOX-a-meen peer-ILL-a-meen and fen-ill-proe-pa-NOLE-a-meen)†
24. Pheniramine, Pyrilamine, and Phenylpropanolamine (fen-EER-a-meen peer-ILL-a-meen and fen-ill-proe-pa-NOLE-a-meen)
25. Promethazine and Phenylephrine (proe-METH-a-zeen and fen-ill-EF-rin)†‡
26. No product available
27. Terfenadine and Pseudoephedrine (ter-FEN-a-deen and soo-doe-e-FED-rin)*†
28. Triprolidine and Pseudoephedrine (trye-PROE-li-deen and soo-doe-e-FED-rin)‡

---

*Not commercially available in the U.S.
†Not commercially available in Canada.
‡Generic name product may be available in the U.S.

Description

Antihistamine and decongestant combinations are used to treat the nasal congestion (stuffy nose), sneezing, and runny nose caused by colds and hay fever.

Antihistamines work by preventing the effects of a substance called histamine, which is produced by the body. Histamine can cause itching, sneezing, runny nose, and watery eyes. Antihistamines contained in these combinations are:

acrivastine, azatadine, brompheniramine, carbinoxamine, chlorpheniramine, clemastine, dexbrompheniramine, diphenhydramine, loratadine, pheniramine, phenyltoloxamine, promethazine, pyrilamine, terfenadine, and triprolidine.

The decongestants, such as phenylephrine, phenylpropanolamine (also known as PPA), and pseudoephedrine, produce a narrowing of blood vessels. This leads to clearing of nasal congestion, but it may also cause an increase in blood pressure in patients who have high blood pressure.

Some of these combinations are available only with your doctor's prescription. Others are available without a prescription; however, your doctor may have special instructions on the proper dose of the medicine for your medical condition. They are available in the following dosage forms:

Oral
Acrivastine and Pseudoephedrine
- Capsules (U.S.)

Azatadine and Pseudoephedrine
- Extended-release tablets (U.S. and Canada)

Brompheniramine and Phenylephrine
- Elixir (U.S.)
- Tablets (U.S.)

Brompheniramine, Phenylephrine, and Phenylpropanolamine
- Elixir (U.S. and Canada)
- Oral solution (Canada)
- Tablets (Canada)
- Extended-release tablets (U.S. and Canada)

Brompheniramine and Phenylpropanolamine
- Capsules (Canada)
- Elixir (U.S.)
- Oral solution (U.S. and Canada)
- Tablets (U.S.)
- Chewable tablets (U.S. and Canada)
- Extended-release tablets (U.S.)

Brompheniramine and Pseudoephedrine
- Extended-release capsules (U.S.)
- Oral solution (U.S.)
- Syrup (U.S.)
- Tablets (U.S.)
- Chewable tablets (U.S.)

Carbinoxamine and Pseudoephedrine
- Oral solution (U.S.)
- Syrup (U.S.)
- Tablets (U.S.)
- Extended-release tablets (U.S.)

Chlorpheniramine, Phenindamine, and Phenylpropanolamine
- Extended-release tablets (U.S.)

Chlorpheniramine and Phenylephrine
- Elixir (U.S.)
- Oral solution (U.S.)
- Oral suspension (U.S.)
- Syrup (U.S.)
- Tablets (U.S.)
- Extended-release tablets (U.S.)

Chlorpheniramine, Phenylephrine, and Phenylpropanolamine
- Tablets (U.S.)

Chlorpheniramine and Phenylpropanolamine
- Extended-release capsules (U.S. and Canada)
- Oral solution (U.S. and Canada)
- Extended-release oral suspension (Canada)
- Syrup (U.S. and Canada)
- Tablets (U.S.)
- Extended-release tablets (U.S. and Canada)

Chlorpheniramine, Phenyltoloxamine, and Phenylephrine
- Extended-release capsules (U.S.)
- Tablets (U.S.)
- Extended-release tablets (U.S.)

Chlorpheniramine, Phenyltoloxamine, Phenylephrine, and Phenylpropanolamine
- Oral solution (U.S.)
- Syrup (U.S.)
- Extended-release tablets (U.S.)

Chlorpheniramine and Pseudoephedrine
- Capsules (U.S.)
- Extended-release capsules (U.S. and Canada)
- Oral solution (U.S. and Canada)
- Oral suspension (U.S.)
- Syrup (U.S.)
- Tablets (U.S.)
- Chewable tablets (U.S.)
- Extended-release tablets (U.S.)

Chlorpheniramine, Pyrilamine, and Phenylephrine
- Oral suspension (U.S.)
- Tablets (U.S.)

Chlorpheniramine, Pyrilamine, Phenylephrine, and Phenylpropanolamine
- Tablets (U.S.)
- Extended-release tablets (U.S.)

Clemastine and Phenylpropanolamine
- Extended-release tablets (U.S. and Canada)

Dexbrompheniramine and Pseudoephedrine
- Tablets (U.S. and Canada)
- Extended-release tablets (U.S. and Canada)

Diphenhydramine and Pseudoephedrine
- Capsules (U.S.)
- Oral solution (U.S.)
- Tablets (U.S. and Canada)

Loratadine and Pseudoephedrine
- Extended-release tablets (U.S. and Canada)

Pheniramine and Phenylephrine
- for Oral solution (Canada)

Pheniramine, Phenyltoloxamine, Pyrilamine, and Phenylpropanolamine
- Extended-release capsules (U.S.)
- Elixir (U.S.)

Pheniramine, Pyrilamine, and Phenylpropanolamine
- Oral solution (U.S.)
- Extended-release tablets (U.S. and Canada)

Promethazine and Phenylephrine
- Syrup (U.S.)

Terfenadine and Pseudoephedrine
- Withdrawn from the U.S. market by the Food and Drug Administration in February 1998

Triprolidine and Pseudoephedrine
- Syrup (U.S. and Canada)
- Tablets (U.S. and Canada)

Before Using This Medicine

If you are taking this medicine without a prescription, carefully read and follow any precautions on the label. For antihistamine and decongestant combinations, the following should be considered:

Allergies—Tell your doctor if you have ever had any unusual or allergic reaction to antihistamines or to amphetamine, dextroamphetamine (e.g., Dexedrine), ephedrine (e.g., Ephed II), epinephrine (e.g., Adrenalin), isoproterenol (e.g., Isuprel), metaproterenol (e.g., Alupent), methamphetamine (e.g., Desoxyn), norepinephrine (e.g., Levophed), phenylephrine (e.g., Neo-Synephrine), pseudoephedrine (e.g., Sudafed), PPA (e.g., Dexatrim), or terbutaline (e.g., Brethine).

Diet—It is very important that you do not take terfenadine-containing medicines (e.g., Seldane-D) with grapefruit juice. Studies have shown that taking terfenadine and grapefruit juice may cause heart rhythm problems.

Pregnancy—The occasional use of antihistamine and decongestant combinations is not likely to cause problems in the fetus or in the newborn baby. However, when these medicines are used at higher doses and/or for a long time, the chance that problems might occur may increase. For the individual ingredients of these combinations, the following apply:

- *Alcohol*—Some of these combination medicines contain alcohol. Too much use of alcohol during pregnancy may cause birth defects.
- *Antihistamines*—Antihistamines have not been shown to cause problems in humans.
- *Phenylephrine*—Studies on birth defects have not been done in either humans or animals with phenylephrine.
- *Phenylpropanolamine*—Studies on birth defects have not been done in either humans or animals with phenylpropanolamine. However, it seems that women who take phenylpropanolamine in the weeks following delivery are more likely to suffer mental or mood changes.
- *Promethazine*—Phenothiazines, such as promethazine (contained in some of these combination medicines [e.g., Phenergan-D]), have been shown to cause jaundice and muscle tremors in a few newborn infants whose mothers received phenothiazines during pregnancy. Also, the newborn baby may have blood clotting problems if promethazine is taken by the mother within 2 weeks before delivery.
- *Pseudoephedrine*—Studies on birth defects with pseudoephedrine have not been done in humans. In animal studies pseudoephedrine did not cause birth defects but did cause a decrease in average weight, length, and rate of bone formation in the animal fetus when administered in high doses.

Breast-feeding—Small amounts of antihistamines and decongestants pass into the breast milk. Use is not recommended since the chances are greater for this medicine to cause side effects, such as unusual excitement or irritability, in the nursing baby. Also, since antihistamines tend to decrease the secretions of the body, it is possible that the flow of breast milk may be reduced in some patients. It is not known yet whether loratadine or terfenadine causes these same side effects.

Children—Very young children are usually more sensitive to the effects of this medicine. Increases in blood pressure, nightmares or unusual excitement, nervousness, restlessness, or irritability may be more likely to occur in children. Also, mental changes may be more likely to occur in young children taking combination medicines that contain phenylpropanolamine. *Before giving any of these combination medicines to a child, check the package label very carefully. Some of these medicines are too strong for use in children.* If you are not certain whether a specific product can be given to a child, or if you have any questions about the amount to give, check with your health care professional.

Older adults—Confusion, difficult and painful urination, dizziness, drowsiness, dryness of mouth, or convulsions (seizures) may be more likely to occur in the elderly, who are usually more sensitive to the effects of this medicine. Also, nightmares or unusual excitement, nervousness, restlessness, or irritability may be more likely to occur in elderly patients.

Other medicines—Although certain medicines should not be used together at all, in other cases different medicines may be used together even if an interaction might occur. In these cases, your doctor may want to change the dose, or other precautions may be necessary. When you are taking antihistamines it is especially important that your health care professional know if you are taking any of the following:

- Anticholinergics (medicine for abdominal or stomach spasms or cramps)—Side effects, such as dryness of mouth, of antihistamines or anticholinergics may be more likely to occur

- Azithromycin (e.g., Zithromax) or
- Clarithromycin (e.g., Biaxin) or
- Erythromycin (e.g., E-Mycin) or
- Itraconazole (e.g., Sporanox) or
- Ketoconazole (e.g., Nizoral)—Use of these medicines with the terfenadine-containing combination may cause heart problems, such as an irregular heartbeat; these medicines should not be used together

- Central nervous system (CNS) depressants—Effects, such as drowsiness, of CNS depressants or antihistamines may be worsened

- Cisapride (e.g., Propulsid) or
- HIV protease inhibitors (indinavir [e.g., Crixivan], nelfinavir [e.g., Viracept], ritonavir [e.g., Norvir], saquinavir [e.g., Invirase]) or
- Mibefradil (e.g., Posicor) or
- Serotonin reuptake inhibitors (fluvoxamine [e.g., Luvox], nefazodone [e.g., Serzone], sertraline [e.g., Zoloft]) or
- Sparfloxacin (e.g., Zagam) or
- Zileuton (e.g., Zyflo)—Use of these medicines with terfenadine may cause heart problems; these medicines should not be used with terfenadine

- Maprotiline (e.g., Ludiomil) or
- Tricyclic antidepressants (amitriptyline [e.g., Elavil], amoxapine [e.g., Asendin], clomipramine [e.g., Anafranil], desipramine [e.g., Pertofrane], doxepin [e.g., Sinequan], imipramine [e.g., Tofranil], nortriptyline [e.g., Aventyl], protriptyline [e.g., Vivactil], trimipramine [e.g., Surmontil])—Effects, such as drowsiness, of CNS depressants or antihistamines may be worsened; also, taking these medicines together may cause some of their side effects, such as dryness of mouth, to become more severe

- Monoamine oxidase (MAO) inhibitors (furazolidone [e.g., Furoxone], isocarboxazid [e.g., Marplan], phenelzine [e.g., Nardil], procarbazine [e.g., Matulane], selegiline [e.g., Eldepryl], tranylcypromine [e.g., Parnate])—If you are now taking, or have taken within the past 2 weeks, any of the MAO inhibitors, the side effects of the antihistamines may become more severe; these medicines should not be used together

- Rauwolfia alkaloids (alseroxylon [e.g., Rauwiloid], deserpidine [e.g., Harmonyl], rauwolfia serpentina [e.g., Raudixin], reserpine [e.g., Serpasil])—These medicines may increase or decrease the effect of the decongestant

Also, if you are taking one of the combinations containing phenylpropanolamine or pseudoephedrine and are also taking:

- Amantadine (e.g., Symmetrel) or
- Amphetamines or
- Appetite suppressants (diet pills), except fenfluramine (e.g., Pondimin) or
- Caffeine (e.g., NoDoz) or
- Chlophedianol (e.g., Ulone) or
- Medicine for asthma or other breathing problems or
- Medicine for colds, sinus problems, or hay fever or other allergies (including nose drops or sprays) or
- Methylphenidate (e.g., Ritalin) or
- Nabilone (e.g., Cesamet) or
- Pemoline (e.g., Cylert)—Using any of these medicines together with an antihistamine and decongestant combination may cause excessive stimulant side effects, such as difficulty in sleeping, heart rate problems, nervousness, and irritability

- Beta-adrenergic blocking agents (acebutolol [e.g., Sectral], atenolol [e.g., Tenormin], betaxolol [e.g., Kerlone], bisoprolol [e.g., Zebeta], carteolol [e.g., Cartrol], labetalol [e.g., Normodyne], metoprolol [e.g., Lopressor], nadolol [e.g., Corgard], oxprenolol [e.g., Trasicor], penbutolol [e.g., Levatol], pindolol [e.g., Visken], propanolol [e.g., Inderal], sotalol [e.g., Sotacor], timolol [e.g., Blocadren])—Using any of these medicines together with an antihistamine and decongestant combination may cause high blood pressure and heart problems (e.g., unusually slow heartbeat)

Other medical problems—The presence of other medical problems may affect the use of antihistamine and decongestant combinations. Make sure you tell your doctor if you have any other medical problems, especially:

- Diabetes mellitus (sugar diabetes)—The decongestant in this medicine may put diabetic patients at a greater risk of having heart or blood vessel disease

- Enlarged prostate or
- Urinary tract blockage or difficult urination—Some of the effects of antihistamines may make urinary problems worse

- Glaucoma—A slight increase in inner eye pressure may occur

- Heart or blood vessel disease or
- High blood pressure—The decongestant in this medicine may cause the blood pressure to increase and may also speed up the heart rate

- Kidney disease—Higher blood levels of loratadine may result, which may increase the chance of side effects. The dosage of loratadine-containing combination may need to be reduced

- Liver disease—Higher blood levels of terfenadine may result, which may increase the chance of heart problems (for terfenadine-containing combination only; higher blood levels of loratadine may result, which may increase the chance of side effects)

- Overactive thyroid—If the overactive thyroid has caused a fast heart rate, the decongestant in this medicine may cause the heart rate to speed up further

Proper Use of This Medicine

Take this medicine only as directed. Do not take more of it and do not take it more often than recommended on the label, unless otherwise directed by your doctor. To do so may increase the chance of side effects.

If this medicine irritates your stomach, you may take it with food or a glass of water or milk, to lessen the irritation.

For patients *taking the extended-release capsule or tablet form of this medicine:*

- Swallow it whole.
- Do not crush, break, or chew before swallowing.
- If the capsule is too large to swallow, you may mix the contents of the capsule with applesauce, jelly, honey, or syrup and swallow without chewing.

Dosing—There is a large variety of antihistamine and decongestant combination products on the market. Some products are for use in adults only, while others may be used in children. If you have any questions about this, check with your health care professional.

The dose of antihistamines and decongestants will be different for different products. The number of capsules or tablets or teaspoonfuls of liquid or granules that you take depends on the strengths of the medicines. Also, *the number of doses you take each day and the time between doses depend on whether you are taking a short-acting or long-acting form of antihistamine and decongestant. Follow your doctor's orders if this medicine was prescribed. Or, follow the directions on the box if you are buying this medicine without a prescription.*

Missed dose—If you are taking this medicine regularly and you miss a dose, take it as soon as possible. However, if it is almost time for your next dose, skip the missed dose and go back to your regular dosing schedule. Do not double doses.

Storage—To store this medicine:
- Keep out of the reach of children.
- Store away from heat and direct light.
- Do not store in the bathroom, near the kitchen sink, or in other damp places. Heat or moisture may cause the medicine to break down.
- Keep the liquid form of this medicine from freezing.
- Do not keep outdated medicine or medicine no longer needed. Be sure that any discarded medicine is out of the reach of children.

Precautions While Using This Medicine

Before you have any skin tests for allergies, tell the doctor in charge that you are taking this medicine. The results of the test may be affected by the antihistamine in this medicine.

When taking antihistamines (contained in this combination medicine) on a regular basis, make sure your doctor knows if you are taking large amounts of aspirin at the same time (as for arthritis or rheumatism). Effects of too much aspirin, such as ringing in the ears, may be covered up by the antihistamine.

*Terfenadine-containing combination should **not** be taken with clarithromycin (e.g., Biaxin), erythromycin (e.g., E-Mycin), itraconazole (e.g., Sporanox), ketoconazole (e.g., Nizoral), or mibefradil (e.g., Posicor).* Using these medicines together may increase the risk of serious side effects affecting the heart.

The antihistamine in this medicine will add to the effects of alcohol and other CNS depressants (medicines that slow down the nervous system, possibly causing drowsiness). Some examples of CNS depressants are other antihistamines or medicine for hay fever, other allergies, or colds; sedatives, tranquilizers, or sleeping medicine; prescription pain medicine or narcotics; barbiturates; medicine for seizures; muscle relaxants; or anesthetics, including some dental anesthetics. *Check with your doctor before taking any of the above while you are taking this medicine.*

The antihistamine in this medicine may cause some people to become drowsy, dizzy, or less alert than they are normally. *Some antihistamines are more likely to cause drowsiness than others (loratadine and terfenadine, for example, rarely produce this effect). Make sure you know how you react before you drive, use machines, or do anything else that could be dangerous if you are dizzy or are not alert.*

The decongestant in this medicine may add to the central nervous system (CNS) stimulant and other effects of phenylpropanolamine (PPA)-containing diet aids. *Do not use medicines for diet or appetite control while taking this medicine unless you have checked with your doctor.*

The decongestant in this medicine may cause some people to be nervous or restless or to have trouble in sleeping. If you have trouble in sleeping, *take the last dose of this medicine for each day a few hours before bedtime.* If you have any questions about this, check with your doctor.

Antihistamines may cause dryness of the mouth, nose, and throat. Some antihistamines are more likely to cause dryness of the mouth than others (loratadine and terfenadine, for example, rarely produce this effect). For temporary relief, use sugarless candy or gum, melt bits of ice in your mouth, or use a saliva substitute. However, if your mouth continues to feel dry for more than 2 weeks, check with your dentist. Continuing dryness of the mouth may increase the chance of dental disease, including tooth decay, gum disease, and fungus infections.

For patients *using promethazine-containing medicine:*

- This medicine controls nausea and vomiting. For this reason, it may cover up the signs of overdose caused by other medicines or the symptoms of intestinal blockage. This will make it difficult for your doctor to diagnose these conditions. Make sure your doctor knows that you are taking this medicine if you have other symptoms such as stomach or lower abdominal pain, cramping, or soreness. Also, if you think you may have taken an overdose of any medicine, tell your doctor that you are taking this medicine.

Side Effects of This Medicine

Along with its needed effects, a medicine may cause some unwanted effects. Although serious side effects occur rarely when this medicine is taken as recommended, they may be more likely to occur if:

- too much medicine is taken
- it is taken in large doses
- it is taken for a long period of time

Get emergency help immediately if any of the following symptoms of overdose occur:

Clumsiness or unsteadiness; convulsions (seizures); drowsiness (severe); dryness of mouth, nose, or throat (severe); flushing or redness of face; hallucinations (seeing, hearing, or feeling things that are not there); headache (continuing); shortness of breath or troubled breathing; slow, fast, or irregular heartbeat; trouble in sleeping

For promethazine only

Muscle spasms (especially of neck and back); restlessness; shuffling walk; tic-like (jerky) movements of head and face; trembling and shaking of hands

Also, check with your doctor as soon as possible if any of the following side effects occur:

Rare

Mood or mental changes; sore throat and fever; tightness in chest; unusual bleeding or bruising; unusual tiredness or weakness

Other side effects may occur that usually do not need medical attention. These side effects may go away during treatment as your body adjusts to the medicine. However, check with your health care professional if any of the following side effects continue or are bothersome:

More common—rare with loratadine- or terfenadine–containing combination

Drowsiness; thickening of the bronchial secretions

Less common—more common with high doses

Blurred vision; confusion; difficult or painful urination; dizziness; dryness of mouth, nose, or throat; headache; loss of appetite; nightmares; pounding heartbeat; ringing or buzzing in ears; skin rash; stomach upset or pain (more common with pyrilamine and tripelennamine); unusual excitement, nervousness, restlessness, or irritability

Other side effects not listed above may also occur in some patients. If you notice any other effects, check with your doctor.

Revised: 12/18/2000

ANTIHISTAMINES, DECONGESTANTS, AND ANALGESICS   Systemic

Commonly used brand name(s):

In the U.S.—

Aclophen[5]	Alumadrine[8]
Actifed Cold & Sinus[26]	BC Multi Symptom Cold
Actifed Cold & Sinus Caplets[26]	Powder[10]
Actifed Sinus Nighttime[18]	Benadryl Allergy/Cold[18]
Actifed Sinus Nighttime Caplets[18]	Benadryl Allergy/Sinus Headache Caplets[18]
Alka-Seltzer Plus Allergy Medicine Liqui-Gels[13]	BQ Cold[8]
Alka-Seltzer Plus Cold Medicine[10]	Children's Tylenol Cold Multi-Symptom[13]
Alka-Seltzer Plus Cold Medicine Liqui-Gels[13]	Chlor-Trimeton Allergy-Sinus Caplets[8]
Allerest Sinus Pain Formula Caplets[13]	Codimal[13]
	Co-Hist[13]
	Comtrex Allergy-Sinus[13]

Comtrex Allergy-Sinus Caplets[13]
Congestant D[8]
Contac Allergy/Sinus Night Caplets[18]
Contac Cold/Flu Night Caplets[18]
Coridicin D[8]
Covangesic[15]
Dapacin Cold[8]
Dimetapp Allergy Sinus Caplets[2]
Dimetapp Cold & Fever Suspension[4]
Dristan Cold Maximum Strength Caplets[4]
Dristan Cold Multi-Symptom Formula[5]
Drixoral Allergy-Sinus[16]
Drixoral Cold and Flu[16]
Duadacin[8]
Gendecon[5]
Histagesic Modified[5]
Histosal[25]
Kolephrin Caplets[13]
ND-Gesic[14]
Night-Time Effervescent Cold[17]
Norel Plus[12]
Phenate T.D.[8]
Pyrroxate Caplets[8]
Scot-Tussin Original 5-Action Cold Formula[21]
Simplet[13]
Sinapils[9]
Sinarest[13]

Sinarest Extra Strength Caplets[13]
Sine-Off Sinus Medicine Caplets[13]
Singlet for Adults[13]
Sinulin[8]
Sinus Headache & Congestion[13]
Sinutab Sinus Allergy Maximum Strength[13]
Sinutab Sinus Allergy Maximum Strength Caplets[13]
TheraFlu/Flu and Cold Medicine[13]
TheraFlu/Flu and Cold Medicine for Sore Throat[13]
Triaminicin Cold, Allergy, Sinus[8]
Tylenol Allergy Sinus Medication Maximum Strength Caplets[13]
Tylenol Allergy Sinus Medication Maximum Strength Gelcaps[13]
Tylenol Allergy Sinus Medication Maximum Strength Geltabs[13]
Tylenol Allergy Sinus Night Time Medicine Maximum Strength Caplets[18]
Tylenol Flu NightTime Hot Medication Maximum Strength[18]
Tylenol Flu NightTime Medication Maximum Strength Gelcaps[18]

In Canada—

Actifed Plus Extra Strength Caplets[26]
Alka-Seltzer Plus Cold Medicine[10]
Coricidin D[10]
Dristan[5]
Dristan Extra Strength Caplets[5]
Dristan Formula P[24]
Neo Citran Colds and Flu[20]
Neo Citran Colds and Flu Calorie Reduced[20]
Neo Citran Extra Strength Colds and Flu[20]

Oradrine-2[19]
Sinutab Extra Strength Caplets[13]
Sinutab Regular Caplets[13]
Sinutab SA[23]
Triaminicin[22]
Tylenol Allergy Sinus Medication Extra Strength Caplets[13]
Tylenol Cold Medication Children's[13]
Tylenol Flu Medication Extra Strength Gelcaps[18]

Note: In November 2000, the Food and Drug Administration(FDA) issued a public health warning regarding phenylpropanolamine (PPA) due to the risk of hemorrhagic stroke. The FDA, supported by results of a research program, requested that manufacturers voluntarily discontinue marketing products that contain PPA and that consumers work with their healthcare providers to select alternative products.

Note: For quick reference, the following antihistamines, decongestants, and analgesics are numbered to match the corresponding brand names.

This information applies to the following medicines:
1. No product available
2. Brompheniramine, Phenylpropanolamine, and Acetaminophen (brome-fen-IR-a-meen fen-ill-proe-pa-NOLE-a-meen and a-set-a-MIN-oh-fen)†
3. No product available
4. Brompheniramine, Pseudoephedrine, and Acetaminophen (brome-fen-IR-a-meen soo-doe-e-FED-rin and a-set-a-MIN-oh-fen)†
5. Chlorpheniramine, Phenylephrine, and Acetaminophen (klor-fen-EER-a-meen fen-il-EF-rin and a-set-a-MIN-oh-fen)
6. No product available

7. No product available
8. Chlorpheniramine, Phenylpropanolamine, and Acetaminophen (klor-fen-EER-a-meen fen-ill-proe-pa-NOLE-a-meen and a-set-a-MIN-oh-fen)
9. Chlorpheniramine, Phenylpropanolamine, Acetaminophen, and Caffeine (klor-fen-EER-a-meen fen-ill-proe-pa-NOLE-a-meen a-set-a-MIN-oh-fen and kaf-EEN)†
10. Chlorpheniramine, Phenylpropanolamine, and Aspirin (klor-fen-EER-a-meenfen-ill-proe-pa-NOLE-a-meen and AS-pir-in)
11. No product available
12. Chlorpheniramine, Phenyltoloxamine, Phenylpropanolamine, and Acetaminophen (klor-fen-EER-a-meen fen-ill-tole-OX-a-meen fen-ill-proe-pa-NOLE-a-meen and a-set-a-MIN-oh-fen)†
13. Chlorpheniramine, Pseudoephedrine, and Acetaminophen (klor-fen-EER-a-meen soo-doe-e-FED-rin and a-set-a-MIN-oh-fen)
14. Chlorpheniramine, Pyrilamine, Phenylephrine, and-Acetaminophen (klor-fen-EER-a-meen peer-ILL-a-meen fen-il-EF-rin and a-set-a-MIN-oh-fen)†
15. Chlorpheniramine, Pyrilamine, Phenylephrine, Phenylpropanolamine, and Acetaminophen (klor-fen-EER-a-meen peer-ILL-a-meen fen-il-EF-rin fen-ill-proe-pa-NOLE-a-meen and a-set-a-MIN-oh-fen)†
16. Dexbrompheniramine, Pseudoephedrine, and Acetaminophen (dex-brome-fen-EER-a-meen soo-doe-e-FED-rin and a-set-a-MIN-oh-fen)†
17. Diphenhydramine, Phenylpropanolamine, and Aspirin (dye-fen-HYE-dra-meen fen-ill-proe-pa-NOLE-a-meen and AS-pir-in)†
18. Diphenhydramine, Pseudoephedrine, and Acetaminophen (dye-fen-HYE-dra-meen soo-doe-e-FED-rin and a-set-a-MIN-oh-fen)†
19. Diphenylpyraline, Phenylpropanolamine, Acetaminophen, and Caffeine (dye-fen-il-PEER-a-leen fen-ill-proe-pa-NOLE-a-meen a-set-a-MIN-oh-fen and kaf-EEN)*
20. Pheniramine, Phenylephrine, and Acetaminophen (fen-EER-a-meen fen-il-EF-rin and a-set-a-MIN-oh-fen)*
21. Pheniramine, Phenylephrine, Sodium Salicylate, and Caffeine (fen-EER-a-meen fen-il-EF-rin SOE-dee-um sa-LI-si-lateand kaf-EEN)†
22. Pheniramine, Pyrilamine, Phenylpropanolamine, Acetaminophen, and Caffeine (fen-EER-a-meen peer-ILL-a-meen fen-ill-proe-pa-NOLE-a-meen a-set-a-MIN-oh-fen and kaf-EEN)*
23. Phenyltoloxamine, Phenylpropanolamine, and Acetaminophen (fen-ill-tole-OX-a-meen fen-ill-proe-pa-NOLE-a-meen and a-set-a-MIN-oh-fen)*
24. Pyrilamine, Phenylephrine, Aspirin, and Caffeine (peer-ILL-a-meen fen-il-EF-rin AS-pir-in and kaf-EEN)*
25. Pyrilamine, Phenylpropanolamine, Acetaminophen, and Caffeine (peer-ILL-a-meen fen-ill-proe-pa-NOLE-a-meen a-set-a-MIN-oh-fen and kaf-EEN)†
26. Triprolidine, Pseudoephedrine, and Acetaminophen (trye-PROE-li-deen soo-doe-e-FED-rin and a-set-a-MIN-oh-fen)

*Not commercially available in the U.S.
†Not commercially available in Canada.

Description

Antihistamine, decongestant, and analgesic combinations are taken by mouth to relieve the sneezing, runny nose, sinus and nasal congestion (stuffy nose), fever, headache, and aches and pain of colds, influenza, and hay fever. These combinations do not contain any ingredient to relieve coughs.

Antihistamines are used to relieve or prevent the symptoms of hay fever and other types of allergy. They may also help relieve some symptoms of the common cold, such as sneezing and runny nose. They work by preventing the effects of a substance called histamine, which is produced by the body. Antihistamines contained in these combinations are:

brompheniramine, chlorpheniramine, dexbrompheniramine, diphenhydramine, pheniramine, phenyltoloxamine, pyrilamine, and triprolidine.

Decongestants, such as phenylephrine, phenylpropanolamine (also known as PPA), and pseudoephedrine, produce a narrowing of blood vessels. This leads to clearing of nasal congestion, but it may also cause an increase in blood pressure in patients who have high blood pressure.

Analgesics, such as acetaminophen and salicylates (e.g., aspirin, sodium salicylate), are used in these combination medicines to help relieve fever, headache, aches, and pain.

Some of these medicines are available without a prescription. However, your doctor may have special instructions on the proper dose of these medicines for your medical condition. These medicines are available in the following dosage forms:

Oral

Brompheniramine, Phenylpropanolamine, and Acetaminophen
- Tablets (U.S.)

Brompheniramine, Pseudoephedrine, and Acetaminophen
- Oral suspension (U.S.)
- Tablets (U.S.)

Chlorpheniramine, Phenylephrine, and Acetaminophen
- Capsules (Canada)
- Tablets (U.S. and Canada)
- Extended-release tablets (U.S.)

Chlorpheniramine, Phenylpropanolamine, and Acetaminophen
- Capsules (U.S.)
- Tablets (U.S.)
- Extended-release tablets (U.S.)

Chlorpheniramine, Phenylpropanolamine, Acetaminophen, and Caffeine
- Tablets (U.S.)

Chlorpheniramine, Phenylpropanolamine, and Aspirin
- Effervescent tablets (U.S. and Canada)
- For oral solution (U.S.)
- Tablets (Canada)

Chlorpheniramine, Phenyltoloxamine, Phenylpropanolamine, and Acetaminophen
- Capsules (U.S.)

Chlorpheniramine, Pseudoephedrine, and Acetaminophen
- Capsules (U.S. and Canada)
- For oral solution (U.S.)
- Oral solution (U.S. and Canada)
- Tablets (U.S. and Canada)
- Chewable tablets (U.S. and Canada)

Chlorpheniramine, Pyrilamine, Phenylephrine, and Acetaminophen
- Tablets (U.S.)

Chlorpheniramine, Pyrilamine, Phenylephrine, Phenylpropanolamine, and Acetaminophen
- Tablets (U.S.)

Dexbrompheniramine, Pseudoephedrine, and Acetaminophen
- Extended-release tablets (U.S.)

Diphenhydramine, Phenylpropanolamine, and Aspirin
- Effervescent tablets (U.S.)

Diphenhydramine, Pseudoephedrine, and Acetaminophen
- For oral solution (U.S.)
- Tablets (U.S. and Canada)

Diphenylpyraline, Phenylpropanolamine, Acetaminophen, and Caffeine
- Tablets (Canada)

Pheniramine, Phenylephrine, and Acetaminophen
- For oral solution (Canada)

Pheniramine, Phenylephrine, Sodium Salicylate, and Caffeine
- Oral solution (U.S.)

Pheniramine, Pyrilamine, Phenylpropanolamine, Acetaminophen, and Caffeine
- Tablets (Canada)

Phenyltoloxamine, Phenylpropanolamine, and Acetaminophen
- Extended-release tablets (Canada)

Pyrilamine, Phenylephrine, Aspirin, and Caffeine
- Tablets (Canada)

Pyrilamine, Phenylpropanolamine, Acetaminophen, and Caffeine
- Tablets (U.S.)

Triprolidine, Pseudoephedrine, and Acetaminophen
- Tablets (U.S. and Canada)

Before Using This Medicine

If you are taking this medicine without a prescription, carefully read and follow any precautions on the label. For antihistamine, decongestant, and analgesic combinations, the following should be considered:

Allergies—Tell your doctor if you have ever had any unusual or allergic reaction to any of the ingredients contained in this medicine. If this medicine contains *aspirin* or *another salicylate*, before taking it, check with your doctor if you have ever had any unusual or allergic reaction to any of the following medicines:

Diclofenac (e.g., Voltaren)
Diflunisal (e.g., Dolobid)
Etodolac (e.g., Lodine)
Fenoprofen (e.g., Nalfon)
Floctafenine
Flurbiprofen, by mouth (e.g., Ansaid)
Ibuprofen (e.g., Motrin)
Indomethacin (e.g., Indocin)
Ketoprofen (e.g., Orudis)
Meclofenamate (e.g., Meclomen)
Mefenamic acid (e.g., Ponstel)
Methyl salicylate (oil of wintergreen)
Nabumetone (e.g., Relafen)
Naproxen (e.g., Naprosyn)
Oxaprozin (e.g., Daypro)
Oxyphenbutazone (e.g., Tandearil)
Phenylbutazone (e.g., Butazolidin)
Piroxicam (e.g., Feldene)
Sulindac (e.g., Clinoril)
Suprofen (e.g., Suprol)
Tenoxicam (e.g., Mobiflex)
Tiaprofenic acid (e.g., Surgam)
Tolmetin (e.g., Tolectin)
Zomepirac (e.g., Zomax)

Also tell your health care professional if you are allergic to any other substances, such as foods, preservatives, or dyes.

Pregnancy—The occasional use of antihistamine, decongestant, and analgesic combinations is not likely to cause problems in the fetus or in the newborn baby. However, when these medicines are used at higher doses and/or for a long time, the chance that problems might occur may increase.

For the individual ingredients of these combinations, the following apply:

- *Acetaminophen*—Acetaminophen has not been shown to cause birth defects or other problems in humans. However, studies on birth defects have not been done in humans.
- *Alcohol*—Some of these combination medicines contain large amounts of alcohol. Too much use of alcohol during pregnancy may cause birth defects.
- *Antihistamines*—Antihistamines have not been shown to cause problems in humans.
- *Caffeine*—Studies in humans have not shown that caffeine causes birth defects. However, studies in animals have shown that caffeine causes birth defects when given in very large doses (amounts equal to the amount of caffeine contained in 12 to 24 cups of coffee a day).
- *Phenylephrine*—Studies on birth defects have not been done in either humans or animals with phenylephrine.
- *Phenylpropanolamine*—Studies on birth defects have not been done in either humans or animals with phenylpropanolamine. However, it seems that women who take phenylpropanolamine in the weeks following delivery are more likely to suffer mental or mood changes.
- *Pseudoephedrine*—Studies on birth defects with pseudoephedrine have not been done in humans. In animal studies pseudoephedrine did not cause birth defects but did cause a decrease in average weight, length, and rate of bone formation in the animal fetus when administered in high doses.
- *Salicylates (e.g., aspirin)*—Salicylates have not been shown to cause birth defects in humans. Studies on birth defects in humans have been done with aspirin. However, salicylates have been shown to cause birth defects in animals. Regular use of salicylates late in pregnancy may cause unwanted effects on the heart or blood flow in the fetus or newborn baby. Use of salicylates during the last 2 weeks of pregnancy may cause bleeding problems in the fetus before or during delivery, or in the newborn baby. Also, too much use of salicylates during the last 3 months of pregnancy may increase the length of pregnancy, prolong labor, cause other problems during delivery, or cause severe bleeding in the mother before, during, or after delivery. *Do not take aspirin during the last 3 months of pregnancy unless it has been ordered by your doctor.*

Breast-feeding—If you are breast-feeding the chance that problems might occur depends on the ingredients of the combination. For the individual ingredients of these combinations, the following apply:

- *Acetaminophen*—Acetaminophen passes into the breast milk. However, it has not been shown to cause problems in nursing babies.
- *Alcohol*—Alcohol passes into the breast milk. However, the amount of alcohol in recommended doses of this medicine does not usually cause problems in nursing babies.
- *Antihistamines*—Use is not recommended since the chances are greater for this medicine to cause side effects, such as unusual excitement or irritability, in the nursing baby. Also, since antihistamines tend to decrease the secretions of the body, it is possible that the flow of breast milk may be reduced in some women.
- *Caffeine*—Small amounts of caffeine pass into the breast milk and may build up in the nursing baby. However, the amount of caffeine in recommended doses of this medicine does not usually cause problems in nursing babies.
- *Decongestants (e.g., phenylephrine, phenylpropanolamine, pseudoephedrine)*—Decongestants may pass into the breast milk and may cause unwanted effects in nursing babies of mothers taking this medicine.
- *Salicylates (e.g., aspirin, sodium salicylate)*—Salicylates pass into the breast milk. Although salicylates have not been reported to cause problems in nursing babies, it is possible that problems may occur if large amounts are taken regularly.

Children—Very young children are usually more sensitive to the effects of this medicine. Increases in blood pressure, nightmares, unusual excitement, nervousness, restlessness, or irritability may be more likely to occur in children. Also, mental changes may be more likely to occur in young children taking these combination medicines.

Before giving any of these combination medicines to a child, check the package label very carefully. Some of these medicines are too strong for use in children. If you are not certain whether a specific product can be given to a child, or if you have any questions about the amount to give, check with your health care professional.

Do not give aspirin or other salicylates to a child with a fever or other symptoms of a virus infection, especially flu or chickenpox, without first discussing their use with your child's doctor. This is very important because salicylates may cause a serious illness called Reye's syndrome in children with fever caused by a virus infection, especially flu or chickenpox. Also, children may be more sensitive to the aspirin or other salicylates contained in some of these medicines, especially if they have a fever or have lost large amounts of body fluid because of vomiting, diarrhea, or sweating.

Teenagers—*Do not give aspirin or other salicylates to a teenager with a fever or other symptoms of a virus infection, especially flu or chickenpox, without first discussing their use with your child's doctor.* This is very important because salicylates may cause a serious illness called Reye's syndrome in teenagers with fever caused by a virus infection, especially flu or chickenpox.

Older adults—The elderly are usually more sensitive to the effects of this medicine. Confusion, difficult or painful urination, dizziness, drowsiness, feeling faint, or dryness of mouth, nose, or throat may be more likely to occur in elderly patients. Also, nightmares or unusual excitement, nervousness, restlessness, or irritability may be more likely to occur in the elderly.

Other medicines—Although certain medicines should not be used together at all, in other cases two different medicines may be used together even if an interaction might occur. In these cases, your doctor may want to change the dose, or other precautions may be necessary. When you are taking antihistamine, decongestant, and analgesic combinations it is especially important that your health care professional know if you are taking *any* other prescription or nonprescription (over-the-counter [OTC]) medicine, for example, aspirin or other medicine for allergies. Some medicines may change the way this medicine affects your body. Also, the effect of other medicines may be increased or reduced by some of the ingredients in this medicine.

Other medical problems—The presence of other medical problems may affect the use of antihistamine, decongestant, and analgesic combinations. Make sure you tell your doctor if you have any other medical problems, especially:

- Alcohol abuse—Acetaminophen-containing medicines increase the chance of liver damage
- Anemia—Taking a salicylate-containing medicine may make the anemia worse
- Asthma, allergies, and nasal polyps, history of, or
- Asthma attacks—Taking a salicylate-containing medicine may cause an allergic reaction in which breathing becomes difficult; also, although antihistamines open tightened bronchial passages, other effects of the antihistamines may cause secretions to become thick so that during an asthma attack it might be difficult to cough them up
- Diabetes mellitus (sugar diabetes)—The decongestant in this medicine may put the patient with diabetes at a greater risk of having heart or blood vessel disease
- Enlarged prostate or
- Urinary tract blockage or difficult urination—Some of the effects of antihistamines may cause urinary problems to get worse
- Glaucoma—A slight increase in inner eye pressure may occur
- Gout—Aspirin- or sodium salicylate-containing medicine may make the gout worse and reduce the benefit of the medicines used for gout
- Hemophilia or other bleeding problems—Aspirin- or sodium salicylate-containing medicine increases the chance of bleeding
- Hepatitis or other liver disease—There is a greater chance of side effects because the medicine is not broken down and may build up in the body; also, if liver disease is severe there is a greater chance that aspirin-containing medicine may cause bleeding
- Heart or blood vessel disease or
- High blood pressure—The decongestant in this medicine may cause the blood pressure to increase and may also speed up the heart rate; also, caffeine-containing medicine, if taken in large amounts, may have a similar effect on the heart
- Kidney disease (severe)—The kidneys may be affected, especially if too much of this medicine is taken for a long time
- Overactive thyroid—If the overactive thyroid has caused a fast heart rate, the decongestant in this medicine may cause the heart rate to speed up further
- Stomach ulcer or other stomach problems—Salicylate-containing medicine may make the ulcer worse or cause bleeding of the stomach

Proper Use of This Medicine

Take this medicine only as directed. Do not take more of it and do not take it more often than recommended on the label, unless otherwise directed by your doctor. To do so may increase the chance of side effects.

If this medicine irritates your stomach, you may take it with food or a glass of water or milk, to lessen the irritation.

For patients taking the extended-release tablet form of this medicine:

- Swallow the tablets whole.
- Do not crush, break, or chew before swallowing.

If a combination medicine containing aspirin has a strong vinegar-like odor, do not use it. This odor means the medicine is breaking down. If you have any questions about this, check with your pharmacist.

Dosing—The dose of these combination medicines will be different for different products. *Follow the directions on the box if you are taking this medicine without a prescription. Or, follow your doctor's orders if this medicine was prescribed.* The following information includes only the average doses for these combinations.

The number of capsules or tablets or teaspoonfuls of liquid that you take depends on the strength of the medicine.

There is a large variety of antihistamine, decongestant, and analgesic combination products on the market. Some products are for use in adults only, while others may be used in children. If you have any questions about this, check with your health care professional.

For cold symptoms and sinus pain and congestion:

- For *regular (short-acting) oral* dosage forms (chewable tablets, capsules, liquid, or tablets):
  —Adults and children 12 years of age and older: Usually the dose is 1 to 2 capsules or tablets, or 1 teaspoonful of liquid, every four to six hours.
  —Children 6 to 12 years of age: Usually the dose is 1 tablet, 4 chewable tablets, or 1 to 2 teaspoonfuls of liquid every four hours.
  —Children up to 6 years of age: Use and dose must be determined by your doctor.
- For *oral* dosage forms that *must be dissolved* (effervescent tablets or powder):
  —Adults and children 12 years of age and older: Usually the dose is 2 effervescent tablets or the contents of 1 packet of powder dissolved as directed on the package.
  —Children up to 12 years of age: Use and dose must be determined by your doctor.
- For *long-acting oral* dosage form (tablets):
  —Adults and children 12 years of age and older: Usually the dose is 1 to 2 tablets every 12 hours.
  —Children up to 12 years of age: Use and dose must be determined by your doctor.

Missed dose—If you must take this medicine regularly and you miss a dose, take it as soon as possible. However, if it is almost time for your next dose, skip the missed dose and go back to your regular dosing schedule. Do not double doses.

Storage—To store this medicine:

- Keep this medicine out of the reach of children. Overdose is very dangerous in young children.
- Store away from heat and direct light.
- Do not store the capsule or tablet form of this medicine in the bathroom, near the kitchen sink, or in other damp places. Heat or moisture may cause the medicine to break down.
- Keep the liquid form of this medicine from freezing.
- Do not keep outdated medicine or medicine no longer needed. Be sure that any discarded medicine is out of the reach of children.

Precautions While Using This Medicine

Before you have any skin tests for allergies, tell the doctor in charge that you are taking this medicine. The results of the test may be affected by the antihistamine in this medicine.

Check with your doctor if your symptoms do not improve or become worse, or if you have a high fever.

The antihistamine in this medicine will add to the effects of alcohol and other central nervous system (CNS) depressants (medicines that slow down the nervous system, possibly causing drowsiness). Some examples of CNS depressants are other antihistamines or medicine for hay fever, other allergies, or colds; sedatives, tranquilizers, or sleeping medicine; prescription pain medicine or narcotics; barbiturates; medicine for seizures; muscle relaxants; or anesthetics, including some dental anesthetics. *Check with your doctor before taking any of the above while you are taking this medicine.*

Also, stomach problems may be more likely to occur if you drink alcoholic beverages while taking a medicine that contains aspirin. In addition, drinking large amounts of alcoholic beverages while taking a medicine that contains acetaminophen may cause liver damage.

The antihistamine in this medicine may cause some people to become drowsy, dizzy, or less alert than they are normally. *Make sure you know how you react to this medicine before you drive, use machines, or do anything else that could be dangerous if you are dizzy or are not alert.*

The decongestant in this medicine may cause some people to become nervous or restless or to have trouble sleeping. If you have trouble sleeping, *take the last dose of this medicine for each day a few hours before bedtime.* If you have any questions about this, check with your doctor.

Also, this medicine may add to the CNS stimulant and other effects of phenylpropanolamine (PPA)-containing diet aids. *Do not use medicines for diet or appetite control while taking this medicine unless you have checked with your doctor.*

Before having any kind of surgery (including dental surgery) or emergency treatment, tell the medical doctor or dentist in charge that you are taking this medicine.

Antihistamines may cause dryness of the mouth, nose, and throat. For temporary relief of mouth dryness, use sugarless candy or gum, melt bits of ice in your mouth, or use a saliva substitute. However, if your mouth continues to feel dry for more than 2 weeks, check with your dentist. Continuing dryness of the mouth may increase the chance of dental disease, including tooth decay, gum disease, and fungus infections.

Check the label of all over-the-counter (OTC), nonprescription, and prescription medicines you now take. If any contain acetaminophen or aspirin or other salicylates, including diflunisal or bismuth subsalicylate (e.g., Pepto-Bismol), be especially careful. This combination medicine contains acetaminophen and/or a salicylate. Therefore, taking it while taking any other medicine that contains these drugs may lead to overdose. If you have any questions about this, check with your health care professional.

For patients taking *aspirin-containing medicine:*

- Do not take aspirin-containing medicine within 5 days before any surgery, including dental surgery, unless otherwise directed by your medical doctor or dentist.

Taking aspirin during this time may cause bleeding problems.

For diabetic patients taking *salicylate-containing medicine,* false urine sugar test results may occur:

- If you take 8 or more 325-mg (5-grain) doses of aspirin every day for several days in a row.
- If you take 8 or more 325-mg (5-grain), or 4 or more 500-mg (10-grain), doses of sodium salicylate a day.

Smaller doses or occasional use usually will not affect urine sugar tests. If you have any questions about this, check with your health care professional, especially if your diabetes is not well controlled.

Side Effects of This Medicine

Along with its needed effects, a medicine may cause some unwanted effects. Although serious side effects occur rarely when this medicine is taken as recommended, they may be more likely to occur if:

- too much medicine is taken
- it is taken in large doses
- it is taken for a long time

Get emergency help immediately if any of the following symptoms of overdose occur:

For all combinations

Clumsiness or unsteadiness; convulsions (seizures); drowsiness (severe); dryness of mouth, nose, or throat (severe); fast heartbeat; flushing or redness of face; hallucinations (seeing, hearing, or feeling things that are not there); headache (continuing and/or severe); increased sweating; nausea or vomiting (severe or continuing); shortness of breath or troubled breathing; stomach cramps or pain (severe or continuing); trouble sleeping

For acetaminophen-containing only

Diarrhea; loss of appetite; swelling or tenderness in the upper abdomen or stomach area

Note: Signs of severe acetaminophen overdose may not appear until 2 to 4 days after the overdose is taken, but treatment to prevent liver damage or death must be started within 24 hours or less after the overdose is taken.

For salicylate-containing only

Any loss of hearing; bloody urine; changes in behavior (in children); confusion; diarrhea (severe or continuing); drowsiness or tiredness (severe, especially in children); fast or deep breathing (especially in children); fever; ringing or buzzing in ears (continuing); uncontrollable flapping movements of the hands (especially in elderly patients); unusual thirst; vision problems

Also, check with your doctor as soon as possible if any of the following side effects occur:

More common

Nausea or vomiting; stomach pain (mild)

Less common or rare

Bloody or black tarry stools; changes in urine or problems with urination; skin rash, hives, or itching; sore throat and fever; swelling of face, feet, or lower legs; tightness in chest; unusual bleeding or bruising; unusual tiredness or weakness; vomiting of blood or material that looks like coffee grounds; weight gain (unusual); yellow eyes or skin

6

Other side effects may occur that usually do not need medical attention. These side effects may go away during treatment as your body adjusts to the medicine. However, check with your doctor if any of the following side effects continue or are bothersome:

More common

Drowsiness; heartburn or indigestion (for salicylate-containing medicines); thickening of mucus

Less common—more common with high doses

Blurred vision; confusion; difficult or painful urination; dizziness; dryness of mouth, nose, or throat; headache; loss of appetite; nightmares; pounding heartbeat; ringing or buzzing in ears; skin rash; stomach upset or stomach pain; unusual excitement, nervousness, restlessness, or irritability

Not all of the side effects listed above have been reported for each of these medicines, but they have been reported for at least one of them. There are some similarities among these combination medicines, so many of the above side effects may occur with any of these medicines.

Other side effects not listed above may also occur in some patients. If you notice any other effects, check with your doctor.

Revised: 12/18/2000

ANTIHISTAMINES, DECONGESTANTS, AND ANTICHOLINERGICS   Systemic †

Commonly used brand name(s):

In the U.S.—

AH-chew[1]	Pannaz[3]
Atrohist Plus[2]	Phenahist-TR[2]
D.A. Chewable[1]	Phenchlor S.H.A.[2]
Dallergy[1]	Pre-Hist-D[1]
Dallergy Caplets[1]	Pro-Tuss[2]
Deconhist[2]	Q-Tuss[2]
Dura-Vent/DA[1]	Rolatuss SR[2]
Extendryl[1]	Ru-Tab[2]
Extendryl JR[1]	Ru-Tuss[2]
Extendryl SR[1]	Stahist[2]
Mescolor[4]	Tuss Delay[2]
OMNIhist L.A.[1]	

Note: In November 2000, the Food and Drug Administration (FDA) issued a public health warning regarding phenylpropanolamine (PPA) due to the risk of hemorrhagic stroke. The FDA, supported by results of a research program, requested that manufacturers voluntarily discontinue marketing products that contain PPA and that consumers work with their healthcare providers to select alternative products.

Note: For quick reference the following antihistamine, decongestant, and anticholinergic combinations are numbered to match the corresponding brand names.

This information applies to the following medicines:
1. Chlorpheniramine, Phenylephrine, and Methscopolamine (klor-fen-EER-a-meen fen-ill-EF-rin and meth-skoe-POL-a-meen)†
2. Chlorpheniramine, Phenylephrine, Phenylpropanolamine, Atropine, Hyoscyamine, and Scopolamine (klor-fen-EER-a-meen fen-ill-EF-rin fen-ill-proe-pa-NOLE-a-meen A-troe-peen hye-oh-SYE-a-meen and skoe-POL-a-meen)†
3. Chlorpheniramine, Phenylpropanolamine, and Methscopolamine (klor-fen-EER-a-meen fen-ill-proe-pa-NOLE-a-meen and meth-skoe-POL-a-meen)†
4. Chlorpheniramine, Pseudoephedrine, and Methscopolamine (klor-fen-EER-a-meen soo-doe-e-FED-rin and meth-skoe-POL-a-meen)†

†Not commercially available in Canada.

Description

Antihistamine, decongestant, and anticholinergic combinations are used to treat the nasal congestion (stuffy nose) and runny nose caused by allergies.

Antihistamines work by preventing the effects of a substance called histamine, which is produced by the body. Histamine can cause itching, sneezing, runny nose, and watery eyes. The antihistamine contained in these combinations is chlorpheniramine.

The decongestants in these combinations, phenylephrine, phenylpropanolamine (also known as PPA), and pseudoephedrine produce a narrowing of blood vessels. This leads to clearing of nasal congestion, but it may also cause an increase in blood pressure in patients who have high blood pressure.

Anticholinergics, such as atropine, hyoscyamine, methscopolamine, and scopolamine may help produce a drying effect in the nose and chest.

These combinations are available only with your doctor's prescription in the following dosage forms:

Chlorpheniramine, Phenylephrine, and Methscopolamine
- Extended-release capsules (U.S.)
- Syrup (U.S.)
- Tablets (U.S.)
- Chewable tablets (U.S.)
- Extended-release tablets (U.S.)

Chlorpheniramine, Phenylephrine, Phenylpropanolamine, Atropine, Hyoscyamine, and Scopolamine
- Extended-release tablets (U.S.)

Chlorpheniramine, Phenylpropanolamine, and Methscopolamine
- Extended-release tablets (U.S.)

Chlorpheniramine, Pseudoephedrine, and Methscopolamine
- Extended-release tablets (U.S.)

Before Using This Medicine

In deciding to use a medicine, the risks of taking the medicine must be weighed against the good it will do. This is a decision you and your doctor will make. For antihistamine, decongestant, and anticholinergic combinations, the following should be considered:

Allergies—Tell your doctor if you have ever had any unusual or allergic reactions to antihistamines or anticholinergics, or to amphetamine, dextroamphetamine (e.g., Dexedrine), ephedrine (e.g., Ephed II), epinephrine (e.g., Adrenalin), isoproterenol (e.g., Isuprel), metaproterenol (e.g., Alupent), methamphetamine (e.g., Desoxyn), norepinephrine (e.g., Levophed), phenylephrine (e.g., Neo-Synephrine), phenylpropanolamine [PPA] (e.g., Dexatrim), pseudoephedrine (e.g., Sudafed), or terbutaline (e.g., Brethine). Also, tell your health care professional if you are allergic to any other substances, such as foods, preservatives, or dyes.

Pregnancy—For the individual ingredients of these combinations, the following apply:
- *Antihistamines*—Antihistamines have not been shown to cause problems in humans.
- *Atropine*—Studies on effects in pregnancy have not been done in humans. Atropine has not been shown to cause birth defects or other problems in animals.
- *Hyoscyamine*—Studies on effects in pregnancy have not been done in either humans or animals.
- *Methscopolamine*—Studies on effects in pregnancy have not been done in either humans or animals.
- *Phenylephrine*—Studies on birth defects have not been done in either humans or animals.
- *Phenylpropanolamine*—Studies on birth defects have not been done in either humans or animals. However, it seems that some women who take phenylpropanolamine in the weeks following delivery are more likely to suffer mental or mood changes.
- *Pseudoephedrine*—Studies on birth defects have not been done in humans. Pseudoephedrine has not been shown to cause birth defects in animal studies. However, studies in animals have shown that pseudoephedrine causes a reduction in average weight, length, and rate of bone formation in the animal fetus.
- *Scopolamine*—Studies on effects in pregnancy have not been done in pregnant women. However, studies in animals at doses many times the human dose have shown that scopolamine causes a small increase in the number of fetal deaths.

Breast-feeding—Small amounts of antihistamines, decongestants, and anticholinergics may pass into the breast milk. Use is not recommended since this medicine may cause side effects, such as unusual excitement or irritability, in the nursing baby. Also, since this medicine tends to decrease the secretions of the body, it is possible that the flow of breast milk may be reduced in some women.

Children—Very young children are usually more sensitive than adults to the effects of this medicine. Increases in blood pressure, nightmares or unusual excitement, nervousness, restlessness, or irritability may be more likely to occur in children. Also, mental changes may be more likely to occur in young children taking combination medicines that contain phenylpropanolamine. Also, when anticholinergics are given to children during hot weather, a rapid increase in body temperature may occur, which may lead to heat stroke. In infants and children, especially those with spastic paralysis or brain damage, this medicine may be especially likely to cause severe side effects.

Older adults—Confusion or memory loss, difficult and painful urination, dizziness, drowsiness, dryness of mouth, or convulsions (seizures) may be more likely to occur in the elderly, who are usually more sensitive than younger adults to the effects of this medicine. Also, nightmares or unusual excitement, nervousness, restlessness, or irritability may be more likely to occur in elderly patients. In addition, eye pain may occur, which may be a sign of glaucoma.

Other medicines—Although certain medicines should not be used together at all, in other cases different medicines may be used together even if an interaction might occur. In these cases, your doctor may want to change the dose, or other precautions may be necessary. When you are taking this medicine it is especially important that your health care professional know if you are taking any of the following:
- Amantadine (e.g., Symmetrel) or

- Amphetamines or
- Appetite suppressants (diet pills), except fenfluramine (e.g., Pondimin), or
- Beta-adrenergic blocking agents (acebutolol [e.g., Sectral], atenolol [e.g., Tenormin], betaxolol [e.g., Kerlone], bisoprolol [e.g., Zebeta], carteolol [e.g., Cartrol], labetalol [e.g., Normodyne], metoprolol [e.g., Lopressor], nadolol [e.g., Corgard], oxprenolol [e.g., Trasicor], penbutolol [e.g., Levatol], pindolol [e.g., Visken], propranolol [e.g., Inderal], sotalol [e.g., Sotacor], timolol [e.g., Blocadren]) or
- Caffeine (e.g., NoDoz) or
- Chlophedianol (e.g., Ulone) or
- Cocaine or
- Digitalis medicine (heart medicine) or
- Medicine for asthma or other breathing problems or
- Medicine for colds, sinus problems, or hay fever or other allergies (including nose drops or sprays) or
- Methylphenidate (e.g., Ritalin) or
- Nabilone (e.g., Cesamet) or
- Pemoline (e.g., Cylert)—Using any of these medicines together with a decongestant-containing combination may cause excessive stimulant side effects, such as difficulty in sleeping, heart rate problems, nervousness, and irritability
- Central nervous system (CNS) depressants—Using these combinations with CNS depressants may worsen the effects (e.g., drowsiness) of CNS depressants or antihistamines
- Monoamine oxidase (MAO) inhibitors (furazolidone [e.g., Furoxone], isocarboxazid [e.g., Marplan], phenelzine [e.g., Nardil], procarbazine [e.g., Matulane], selegiline [e.g., Eldepryl], tranylcypromine [e.g., Parnate])—Taking an antihistamine, decongestant, and anticholinergic combination while you are taking or within 2 weeks of taking MAO inhibitors, may make the side effects of the antihistamines, decongestants, and anticholinergics more severe; these medicines should not be used together
- Other anticholinergics (medicine for abdominal or stomach spasms or cramps)—Side effects of antihistamines or anticholinergics, such as dryness of mouth, may be more likely to occur
- Potassium chloride (e.g., Kay Ciel)—Using this medicine with an anticholinergic-containing medicine may make gastrointestinal problems caused by potassium worse
- Rauwolfia alkaloids (alseroxylon [e.g., Rauwiloid], deserpidine [e.g., Harmonyl], rauwolfia serpentina [e.g., Raudixin], reserpine [e.g., Serpasil])—These medicines may increase or decrease the effect of the decongestant in this medicine
- Tricyclic antidepressants (amitriptyline [e.g., Elavil], amoxapine [e.g., Asendin], clomipramine [e.g., Anafranil], desipramine [e.g., Pertofrane], doxepin [e.g., Sinequan], imipramine [e.g., Tofranil], nortriptyline [e.g., Aventyl], protriptyline [e.g., Vivactil], trimipramine [e.g., Surmontil])—Effects, such as drowsiness, may be worsened; also, taking these medicines together may make some of the anticholinergic side effects, such as dryness of mouth, more severe

Other medical problems—The presence of other medical problems may affect the use of antihistamine, decongestant, and anticholinergic combinations. Make sure you tell your doctor if you have any other medical problems, especially:

- Brain damage in children or
- Down syndrome or
- Dryness of mouth (severe and continuing) or
- Enlarged prostate or
- Fever or
- Glaucoma or
- Intestinal blockage or other intestinal problems or
- Kidney disease or
- Liver disease or
- Lung disease or
- Mental or emotional problems or
- Myasthenia gravis or
- Toxemia of pregnancy or
- Urinary tract blockage or difficult urination—These medicines may make these conditions worse
- Diabetes mellitus (sugar diabetes)—The decongestant in this medicine may put diabetic patients at greater risk of having heart or blood vessel disease
- Heart or blood vessel disease or
- High blood pressure—The decongestant and anticholinergic in this medicine may cause the blood pressure to increase and may also speed up the heart rate
- Overactive thyroid—If the overactive thyroid has caused a fast heartbeat, the decongestant and anticholinergic in this medicine may cause the heart rate to speed up further

Proper Use of This Medicine

Take this medicine only as directed. Do not take more of it and do not take it more often than recommended on the label, unless otherwise directed by your doctor. To do so may increase the chance of side effects.

If this medicine irritates your stomach, you may take it with food or a glass of water or milk, to lessen the irritation.

For patients *taking the extended-release capsule or extended-release tablet form of this medicine:*

- Swallow the capsule or tablet whole.
- Do not crush, break, or chew before swallowing.
- If the capsule is too large to swallow, you may mix the contents of the capsule with applesauce, jelly, honey, or syrup and swallow without chewing.

Dosing—The dose of these combination medicines will be different for different patients. *Follow your doctor's orders or the directions on the label.* The following information includes only the average doses for these combinations. *If your dose is different, do not change it* unless your doctor tells you to do so.

The number of capsules or tablets or teaspoonfuls of syrup that you take depends on the strength of the medicine. Also, the number of doses you take each day and the time between doses depend on whether you are taking a short-acting or a long-acting form of this medicine.

- For *regular (short-acting)* dosage forms (syrup, tablets, or chewable tablets):
  - —For allergy and cold symptoms:
    - Adults and children 12 years of age and older—1 or 2 tablets or chewable tablets, or 1 to 2 teaspoonfuls of syrup every four to six hours.

- Children up to 6 years of age—Use and dose must be determined by your doctor.
    - Children 6 to 12 years of age—1 chewable tablet or 1 teaspoonful of syrup every four hours.
- For *long-acting* dosage forms (extended-release capsules or tablets):
  - —For allergy and cold symptoms:
    - Adults and children 12 years of age and older—1 capsule or tablet every twelve hours.
    - Children up to 12 years of age—Use and dose must be determined by your doctor.

Missed dose—If you miss a dose of this medicine, take it as soon as possible. However, if it is almost time for your next dose, skip the missed dose and go back to your regular dosing schedule. Do not double doses.

Storage—To store this medicine:

- Keep out of the reach of children.
- Store away from heat and direct light.
- Do not store in the bathroom, near the kitchen sink, or in other damp places. Heat or moisture may cause the medicine to break down.
- Keep the liquid form of this medicine from freezing.
- Do not keep outdated medicine or medicine no longer needed. Be sure that any discarded medicine is out of the reach of children.

Precautions While Using This Medicine

Check with your doctor if your symptoms do not improve or become worse, or if you have a high fever.

Before you have any skin tests for allergies, tell the doctor in charge that you are taking this medicine. The results of the test may be affected by the antihistamine in this medicine.

These medicines may make you sweat less, causing your body temperature to increase. *Use extra care not to become overheated during exercise or hot weather while you are taking this medicine,* since overheating may result in heat stroke. Also hot baths or saunas may make you dizzy or faint while you are taking this medicine.

The anticholinergic contained in this medicine may cause some people to have blurred vision. *Make sure your vision is clear before you drive or do anything else that could be dangerous if you are not able to see well.* These medicines may also cause your eyes to become more sensitive to light than they are normally. Wearing sunglasses may help lessen the discomfort from bright light.

These medicines may cause some people to become dizzy or drowsy. *Make sure you know how you react to this medicine before you drive, use machines, or do anything else that could be dangerous if you are dizzy or are not alert.*

The decongestant in this medicine may cause some people to be nervous or restless or to have trouble in sleeping. If you have trouble in sleeping, *take the last dose of this medicine for each day a few hours before bedtime.* If you have any questions about this, check with your doctor.

The decongestant in this medicine may add to the central nervous system (CNS) stimulant and other effects of phenylpropanolamine (PPA)-containing diet aids. *Do not use medicines for diet or appetite control while taking this medicine unless you have checked with your doctor.*

Before having any kind of surgery (including dental surgery) or emergency treatment, tell the medical doctor or dentist in charge that you are taking this medicine.

This medicine may cause dryness of the mouth, nose, and throat. For temporary relief, use sugarless candy or gum, melt bits of ice in your mouth, or use a saliva substitute. However, if your mouth continues to feel dry for more than 2 weeks, check with your dentist. Continuing dryness of the mouth may increase the chance of dental disease, including tooth decay, gum disease, and fungus infections.

If you think you or someone else may have taken an overdose, get emergency help at once. Taking an overdose of this medicine or taking this medicine with alcohol or other CNS depressants may lead to unconsciousness and possibly death.

Side Effects of This Medicine

Along with its needed effects, a medicine may cause some unwanted effects. Although not all of these side effects may occur, if they do occur they may need medical attention.

Get emergency help immediately if any of the following symptoms of overdose occur:
> Clumsiness or unsteadiness; convulsions (seizures); drowsiness (severe); dryness of mouth, nose, or throat (severe); fast heartbeat; flushing or redness of face; hallucinations (seeing, hearing, or feeling things that are not there); headache (continuing); shortness of breath or troubled breathing; trouble in sleeping

> *For pseudoephedrine only*
> Unusual nervousness, restlessness, or excitement

Also, check with your doctor as soon as possible if any of the following side effects occur:
> *Rare*
> Irregular or slow heartbeat; mood or mental changes; skin rash, hives, or itching; sore throat and fever; tightness in chest; unusual bleeding or bruising; unusual tiredness or weakness

Other side effects may occur that usually do not need medical attention. These side effects may go away during treatment as your body adjusts to the medicine. However, check with your health care professional if any of the following side effects continue or are bothersome:
> *More common*
> Drowsiness; nervousness; restlessness; thickening of mucus; trouble in sleeping

> *Less common*—more common with high doses
> Blurred vision; confusion; difficult or painful urination; dizziness; dryness of mouth, nose, or throat; fast or pounding heartbeat; headache; increased sweating; loss of appetite; nausea or vomiting; nightmares; ringing or buzzing in ears; trembling; unusual excitement, nervousness, restlessness, or irritability; unusual paleness; weakness

Other side effects not listed above may also occur in some patients. If you notice any other effects, check with your doctor.

Revised: 12/18/2000

ANTIHISTAMINES, PHENOTHIAZINE-DERIVATIVE
Systemic

Commonly used brand name(s):

In the U.S.—

Anergan 25[2]	Promacot[2]
Anergan 50[2]	Pro-Med 50[2]
Antinaus 50[2]	Promet[2]
Pentazine[2]	Prorex-25[2]
Phenazine 25[2]	Prorex-50[2]
Phenazine 50[2]	Prothazine[2]
Phencen-50[2]	Prothazine Plain[2]
Phenergan[2]	Shogan[2]
Phenergan Fortis[2]	Tacaryl[1]
Phenergan Plain[2]	Temaril[3]
Phenerzine[2]	V-Gan-25[2]
Phenoject-50[2]	V-Gan-50[2]
Pro-50[2]	

In Canada—
> Histantil[2]
> Panectyl[3]
> Phenergan[2]

Another commonly used name for trimeprazine is alimemazine[3].

Note: For quick reference, the following antihistamines, are numbered to match the corresponding brand names.

This information applies to the following medicines:
1. Methdilazine (meth-DILL-a-zeen)[†]
2. Promethazine (proe-METH-a-zeen)[‡§]
3. Trimeprazine (trye-MEP-ra-zeen)[‡]

[†]Not commercially available in Canada.
[‡]Generic name product may be available in the U.S.
[§]Generic name product may be available in Canada.

Description

Phenothiazine (FEE-noe-THYE-a-zeen)-derivative antihistamines are used to relieve or prevent the symptoms of hay fever and other types of allergy. They work by preventing the effects of a substance called histamine, which is produced by the body. Histamine can cause itching, sneezing, runny nose, and watery eyes. Also, in some persons histamine can close up the bronchial tubes (air passages of the lungs) and make breathing difficult.

Some of these antihistamines are also used to prevent motion sickness, nausea, vomiting, and dizziness. In addition, some of them may be used to help people go to sleep and control their anxiety before or after surgery.

Phenothiazine-derivative antihistamines may also be used for other conditions as determined by your doctor.

In the U.S. these antihistamines are available only with your doctor's prescription. In Canada some are available without a prescription. However, your doctor may have special instructions on the proper dose of the medicine for your medical condition.

These medicines are available in the following dosage forms:
> *Oral*
> Methdilazine
> • Syrup (U.S.)
> • Tablets (U.S.)
> • Chewable tablets (U.S.)

Promethazine
* Syrup (U.S. and Canada)
* Tablets (U.S. and Canada)

Trimeprazine
* Extended-release capsules (U.S.)
* Syrup (U.S. and Canada)
* Tablets (U.S. and Canada)

Parenteral

Promethazine
* Injection (U.S. and Canada)

Rectal

Promethazine
* Suppositories (U.S.)

Before Using This Medicine

In deciding to use a medicine, the risks of taking the medicine must be weighed against the good it will do. This is a decision you and your doctor will make. For phenothiazine-derivative antihistamines, the following should be considered:

Allergies—Tell your doctor if you have ever had any unusual or allergic reaction to these medicines or to phenothiazines. Also tell your health care professional if you are allergic to any other substances, such as foods, preservatives, or dyes.

Pregnancy—Methdilazine, promethazine, and trimeprazine have not been studied in pregnant women. In animal studies, promethazine has not been shown to cause birth defects. However, other phenothiazine medicines caused jaundice and muscle tremors in a few newborn babies whose mothers received these medicines during pregnancy. Also, the newborn baby may have blood clotting problems if promethazine is taken by the mother within 2 weeks before delivery.

Breast-feeding—Small amounts of antihistamines pass into the breast milk. Use by nursing mothers is not recommended since babies are more sensitive to the side effects of antihistamines, such as unusual excitement or irritability. Also, with the use of phenothiazine-derivative antihistamines there is the chance that the nursing baby may be more at risk of having difficulty in breathing while sleeping or of the sudden infant death syndrome (SIDS). However, more studies are needed to confirm this.

In addition, since these medicines tend to decrease the secretions of the body, it is possible that the flow of breast milk may be reduced in some patients.

Children—Serious side effects, such as convulsions (seizures), are more likely to occur in younger patients and would be of greater risk to infants than to older children or adults. In general, children are more sensitive to the effects of antihistamines. Also, nightmares or unusual excitement, nervousness, restlessness, or irritability may be more likely to occur in children. *The use of phenothiazine-derivative antihistamines is not recommended in children who have a history of difficulty in breathing while sleeping, or a family history of sudden infant death syndrome (SIDS).*

Children who show signs of Reye's syndrome should not be given phenothiazine-derivative antihistamines, especially by injection. Uncontrolled movements that may occur with phenothiazine-derivative antihistamines may be mistakenly confused with symptoms of Reye's syndrome.

Teenagers—Adolescents who show signs of Reye's syndrome should not be given phenothiazine-derivative antihistamines, especially by injection. Uncontrolled movements that may occur with phenothiazine-derivative antihistamines may be mistakenly confused with symptoms of Reye's syndrome.

Older adults—Elderly patients are especially sensitive to the effects of antihistamines. Confusion; difficult or painful urination; dizziness; drowsiness; feeling faint; or dryness of the mouth, nose, or throat may be more likely to occur in elderly patients. Also, nightmares or unusual excitement, nervousness, restlessness, or irritability may be more likely to occur in elderly patients. In addition, uncontrolled movements may be more likely to occur in elderly patients taking phenothiazine-derivative antihistamines.

Other medicines—Although certain medicines should not be used together at all, in other cases two different medicines may be used together even if an interaction might occur. In these cases, your doctor may want to change the dose, or other precautions may be necessary. When taking phenothiazine-derivative antihistamines, it is especially important that your health care professional know if you are taking/receiving any of the following:

* Amoxapine (e.g., Asendin) or
* Antipsychotics (medicine for mental illness) or
* Methyldopa (e.g., Aldomet) or
* Metoclopramide (e.g., Reglan) or
* Metyrosine (e.g., Demser) or
* Pemoline (e.g., Cylert) or
* Pimozide (e.g., Orap) or
* Rauwolfia alkaloids (alseroxylon [e.g., Rauwiloid], deserpidine [e.g., Harmonyl], rauwolfia serpentina [e.g., Raudixin], reserpine [e.g., Serpasil])—Side effects of these medicines, such as uncontrolled body movements, may become more severe and frequent if they are used together with phenothiazine-derivative antihistamines

* Anticholinergics (medicine for abdominal or stomach spasms or cramps)—Side effects of phenothiazine-derivative antihistamines or anticholinergics, such as dryness of mouth, may be more likely to occur

* Central nervous system (CNS) depressants (medicines that cause drowsiness) or
* Maprotiline or
* Tricyclic antidepressants (medicine for depression)—Effects of CNS depressants or antihistamines, such as drowsiness, may become more severe; also, taking maprotiline or tricyclic antidepressants may cause some side effects of antihistamines, such as dryness of mouth, to become more severe

* Contrast agent, injected into spinal canal—If you are having an x-ray test of the head, spinal canal, or nervous system for which you are going to receive an injection into the spinal canal, phenothiazine-derivative antihistamines may increase the chance of seizures; stop taking any phenothiazine-derivative antihistamine 48 hours before the test and do not start taking it until 24 hours after the test

* Levodopa—When used together with phenothiazine-derivative antihistamines, the levodopa may not work as it should

* Monoamine oxidase (MAO) inhibitors (furazolidone [e.g., Furoxone], isocarboxazid [e.g., Marplan], phenelzine [e.g., Nardil], procarbazine [e.g., Matulane], selgiline [e.g., Eldepryl], tranylcypromine [e.g., Parnate])—If

you are now taking or have taken within the past 2 weeks any of the MAO inhibitors, the side effects of the phenothiazine-derivative antihistamines may become more severe; these medicines should not be used together

Other medical problems—The presence of other medical problems may affect the use of antihistamines. Make sure you tell your doctor if you have any other medical problems, especially:

- Blood disease or
- Heart or blood vessel disease—These medicines may cause more serious conditions to develop

- Enlarged prostate or
- Urinary tract blockage or difficult urination—Phenothiazine-derivative antihistamines may cause urinary problems to become worse

- Epilepsy—Phenothiazine-derivative antihistamines, especially promethazine given by injection, may increase the chance of seizures

- Glaucoma—These medicines may cause a slight increase in inner eye pressure that may worsen the condition

- Jaundice—Phenothiazine-derivative antihistamines may make the condition worse

- Liver disease—Phenothiazine-derivative antihistamines may build up in the body, which may increase the chance of side effects such as muscle spasms

- Reye's syndrome—Phenothiazine-derivative antihistamines, especially promethazine given by injection, may increase the chance of uncontrolled movements

Proper Use of This Medicine

Antihistamines are used to relieve or prevent the symptoms of your medical problem. Take them only as directed. Do not take more of them and do not take them more often than recommended on the label, unless otherwise directed by your doctor. To do so may increase the chance of side effects.

For patients *taking this medicine by mouth:*

- Antihistamines can be taken with food or a glass of water or milk to lessen stomach irritation if necessary.
- If you are taking the *extended-release capsule* form of this medicine, swallow it whole. Do not break, crush, or chew before swallowing.

For patients taking *promethazine for motion sickness:*

- Take this medicine 30 minutes to 1 hour before you begin to travel.

For patients using the *suppository form of this medicine:*

- To insert suppository: First remove the foil wrapper and moisten the suppository with cold water. Lie down on your side and use your finger to push the suppository well up into the rectum. If the suppository is too soft to insert, chill the suppository in the refrigerator for 30 minutes or run cold water over it before removing the foil wrapper.

For patients using the *injection form of this medicine:*

- If you will be giving yourself the injections, make sure you understand exactly how to give them. If you have any questions about this, check with your health care professional.

Dosing—The dose of an antihistamine will be different for different patients. *Follow your doctor's orders or the di-*

rections on the label. The following information includes only the average doses of antihistamines. *If your dose is different, do not change it* unless your doctor tells you to do so.

The number of capsules or tablets or teaspoonfuls of liquid that you take depends on the strength of the medicine. Also, *the number of doses you take each day and the time between doses depends on whether you are taking a short-acting or long-acting form of antihistamine.*

For methdilazine

- For *regular (short-acting) oral* dosage forms (tablets or liquid):
  —For allergy symptoms:
  - Adults and teenagers—8 milligrams (mg) every six to twelve hours as needed.
  - Children younger than 3 years of age—Use and dose must be determined by your doctor.
  - Children 3 to 12 years of age—4 mg every six to twelve hours as needed.

For promethazine

- For *regular (short-acting) oral* dosage forms (tablets or liquid):
  —For allergy symptoms:
  - Adults and teenagers—10 to 12.5 mg four times a day before meals and at bedtime; or 25 mg at bedtime as needed.
  - Children younger than 2 years of age—Use and dose must be determined by your doctor.
  - Children 2 years of age and older—Your doctor will determine dose based on the weight and/or size of the child. Children usually are given 5 to 12.5 mg three times a day or 25 mg at bedtime as needed.
  —For nausea and vomiting:
  - Adults and teenagers—25 mg for the first dose, then 10 to 25 mg every four to six hours if needed.
  - Children younger than 2 years of age—Use and dose must be determined by your doctor.
  - Children 2 years of age and older—Your doctor will determine dose based on the weight and/or size of the child. Children usually are given 10 to 25 mg every four to six hours as needed.
  —For prevention of motion sickness:
  - Adults and teenagers—25 mg taken one-half to one hour before traveling. The dose may be repeated eight to twelve hours later if needed.
  - Children younger than 2 years of age—Use and dose must be determined by your doctor.
  - Children 2 years of age and older—Your doctor will determine dose based on the weight and/or size of the child. Children usually are given 10 to 25 mg one-half to one hour before traveling. The dose may be repeated eight to twelve hours later if needed.
  —For vertigo (dizziness):
  - Adults and teenagers—25 mg two times a day as needed.
  - Children younger than 2 years of age—Use and dose must be determined by your doctor.
  - Children 2 years of age and older—Your doctor will determine dose based on the weight and/or size of the child. Children usually are given 10 to 25 mg two times a day as needed.
  —For use as a sedative:
  - Adults and teenagers—25 to 50 mg.

- Children younger than 2 years of age—Use and dose must be determined by your doctor.
- Children 2 years of age and older—Your doctor will determine dose based on the weight and/or size of the child. Children usually are given 10 to 25 mg.
- For *injection* dosage form:
  —For allergy symptoms:
    - Adults and teenagers—25 mg injected into a muscle or into a vein.
    - Children younger than 2 years of age—Use and dose must be determined by your doctor.
    - Children 2 years of age and older—Your doctor will determine dose based on the weight and/or size of the child. Children usually are given 6.25 to 12.5 mg injected into a muscle three times a day or 25 mg at bedtime as needed.
  —For nausea and vomiting:
    - Adults and teenagers—12.5 to 25 mg injected into a muscle or into a vein every four hours as needed.
    - Children younger than 2 years of age—Use and dose must be determined by your doctor.
    - Children 2 years of age and older—Your doctor will determine dose based on the weight and/or size of the child. Children usually are given 12.5 to 25 mg injected into a muscle every four to six hours as needed.
  —For use as a sedative:
    - Adults and teenagers—25 to 50 mg injected into a muscle or into a vein.
    - Children younger than 2 years of age—Use and dose must be determined by your doctor.
    - Children 2 years of age and older—Your doctor will determine dose based on the weight and/or size of the child. Children usually are given 12.5 to 25 mg injected into a muscle.
- For *suppository* dosage form:
  —For allergy symptoms:
    - Adults and teenagers—25 mg inserted in rectum. Another 25-mg suppository may be inserted two hours later if needed.
    - Children younger than 2 years of age—Use and dose must be determined by your doctor.
    - Children 2 years of age and older—Your doctor will determine dose based on the weight and/or size of the child. Children usually are given 6.25 to 12.5 mg inserted into the rectum three times a day or 25 mg at bedtime as needed.
  —For nausea and vomiting:
    - Adults and teenagers—25 mg inserted into the rectum for the first dose, then 12.5 to 25 mg every four to six hours if needed.
    - Children younger than 2 years of age—Use and dose must be determined by your doctor.
    - Children 2 years of age and older—Your doctor will determine dose based on the weight and/or size of the child. Children usually are given 12.5 to 25 mg inserted into the rectum every four to six hours as needed.
  —For vertigo (dizziness):
    - Adults and teenagers—25 mg inserted into the rectum, two times a day as needed.
    - Children younger than 2 years of age—Use and dose must be determined by your doctor.

- Children 2 years of age and older—Your doctor will determine dose based on the weight and/or size of the child. Children usually are given 12.5 to 25 mg inserted into the rectum two times a day as needed.
  —For use as a sedative:
    - Adults and teenagers—25 to 50 mg inserted into the rectum.
    - Children younger than 2 years of age—Use and dose must be determined by your doctor.
    - Children 2 years of age and older—Your doctor will determine dose based on the weight and/or size of the child. Children usually are given 12.5 to 25 mg inserted into the rectum.

For trimeprazine
- For *regular (short-acting) oral* dosage forms (tablets or liquid):
  —For allergy symptoms:
    - Adults and teenagers—2.5 mg four times a day as needed.
    - Children younger than 2 years of age—Use and dose must be determined by your doctor.
    - Children 2 to 3 years of age—1.25 mg at bedtime or three times a day as needed.
    - Children 3 to 12 years of age—2.5 mg at bedtime or three times a day as needed.
- For *long-acting oral* dosage forms (extended-release capsules):
  —For allergy symptoms:
    - Adults and teenagers—5 mg every twelve hours as needed.
    - Children younger than 6 years of age—Use and dose must be determined by your doctor.
    - Children 6 to 12 years of age—5 mg once a day as needed.

Missed dose—If you are taking this medicine regularly and you miss a dose, take it as soon as possible. However, if it is almost time for your next dose, skip the missed dose and go back to your regular dosing schedule. Do not double doses.

Storage—To store this medicine:
- Keep out of the reach of children, since overdose may be very dangerous in children.
- Store away from heat and direct light.
- Do not store the capsule or tablet form of this medicine in the bathroom medicine cabinet, near the kitchen sink, or in other damp places. Heat or moisture may cause the medicine to break down.
- Keep the liquid form of this medicine from freezing.
- Do not keep outdated medicine or medicine no longer needed. Be sure that any discarded medicine is out of the reach of children.

Precautions While Using This Medicine

Tell the doctor in charge that you are taking this medicine before you have any skin tests for allergies. The results of the tests may be affected by this medicine.

When taking phenothiazine-derivative antihistamines on a regular basis, make sure your doctor knows if you are taking large amounts of aspirin at the same time (as for arthritis or rheumatism). Effects of too much aspirin, such as ringing in the ears, may be covered up by the antihistamine.

Phenothiazine-derivative antihistamines will add to the effects of alcohol and other CNS depressants (medicines that slow down the nervous system, possibly causing drowsiness). Some examples of CNS depressants are sedatives, tranquilizers, or sleeping medicine; prescription pain medicine or narcotics; barbiturates; medicine for seizures; muscle relaxants; or anesthetics, including some dental anesthetics. *Check with your doctor before taking any of the above while you are using this medicine.*

This medicine may cause some people to become drowsy or less alert than they are normally. Even if taken at bedtime, it may cause some people to feel drowsy or less alert on arising. *Make sure you know how you react to the phenothiazine-derivative antihistamine you are taking before you drive, use machines, or do anything else that could be dangerous if you are not alert.*

Phenothiazine-derivative antihistamines may cause dryness of the mouth, nose, and throat. For temporary relief of mouth dryness, use sugarless candy or gum, melt bits of ice in your mouth, or use a saliva substitute. However, if your mouth continues to feel dry for more than 2 weeks, check with your medical doctor or dentist. Continuing dryness of the mouth may increase the chance of dental disease, including tooth decay, gum disease, and fungus infections.

This medicine controls nausea and vomiting. For this reason, it may cover up some of the signs of overdose caused by other medicines or the symptoms of appendicitis. This will make it difficult for your doctor to diagnose these conditions. Make sure your doctor knows that you are taking this medicine if you have other symptoms of appendicitis such as stomach or lower abdominal pain, cramping, or soreness. Also, if you think you may have taken an overdose of any medicine, tell your doctor that you are taking this medicine.

Side Effects of This Medicine

Along with its needed effects, a medicine may cause some unwanted effects. Although not all of these side effects may occur, if they do occur they may need medical attention.

Check with your doctor as soon as possible if any of the following side effects occur:
Less common or rare
Sore throat and fever; unusual bleeding or bruising; unusual tiredness or weakness

Symptoms of overdose
Clumsiness or unsteadiness; convulsions (seizures); drowsiness (severe); dryness of mouth, nose, or throat (severe); feeling faint; flushing or redness of face; hallucinations (seeing, hearing, or feeling things that are not there); muscle spasms (especially of neck and back); restlessness; shortness of breath or troubled breathing; shuffling walk; tic-like (jerky) movements of head and face; trembling and shaking of hands; trouble in sleeping

Other side effects may occur that usually do not need medical attention. These side effects may go away during treatment as your body adjusts to the medicine. However, check with your health care professional if any of the following side effects continue or are bothersome:
More common
Drowsiness (less common with methdilazine); thickening of mucus
Less common or rare
Blurred vision or any change in vision; burning or

stinging of rectum (with rectal suppository); confusion; difficult or painful urination; dizziness; dryness of mouth, nose, or throat; fast heartbeat; feeling faint; increased sensitivity of skin to sun; increased sweating; loss of appetite; nightmares; ringing or buzzing in ears; skin rash; unusual excitement, nervousness, restlessness, or irritability

Other side effects not listed above may also occur in some patients. If you notice any other effects, check with your health care professional.

Revised: 07/26/94

ANTI-INFLAMMATORY DRUGS, NONSTEROIDAL   Ophthalmic

Commonly used brand name(s):

In the U.S.—
Ocufen[2]
Profenal[4]
Voltaren Ophthalmic[1]

In Canada—
Indocid[3]
Ocufen[2]
Voltaren Ophtha[1]

Another commonly used name for indomethacin is indometacin[3].

Note: For quick reference, the following nonsteroidal anti-inflammatory drugs are numbered to match the corresponding brand names.

This information applies to the following medicines:
1. Diclofenac (dye-KLOE-fen-ak)
2. Flurbiprofen (flure-BI-proe-fen)‡
3. Indomethacin (in-doe-METH-a-sin)*
4. Suprofen (soo-PROE-fen)†

*Not commercially available in the U.S.
†Not commercially available in Canada.
‡Generic name product may be available in the U.S.

Description

Ophthalmic anti-inflammatory medicines are used in the eye to lessen problems that can occur during or after some kinds of eye surgery. Sometimes, the pupil of the eye gets smaller during an operation. This makes it more difficult for the surgeon to reach some areas of the eye. Some of these medicines are used to help prevent this. Also, some of them are used after eye surgery, to relieve effects such as inflammation or edema (too much fluid in the eye).

These medicines may also be used for other conditions, as determined by your ophthalmologist (eye doctor).

These medicines are available only with your doctor's prescription, in the following dosage forms:
Ophthalmic
Diclofenac
• Ophthalmic solution (U.S. and Canada)
Flurbiprofen
• Ophthalmic solution (U.S. and Canada)
Indomethacin
• Ophthalmic suspension (Canada)
Suprofen
• Ophthalmic solution (U.S.)

Before Using This Medicine

In deciding to use a medicine, the risks of taking the medicine must be weighed against the good it will do. This is a decision you and your doctor will make. For ophthalmic anti-inflammatory medicines, the following should be considered:

Allergies—Tell your doctor if you have ever had any unusual or allergic reaction to one of the ophthalmic anti-inflammatory medicines or other serious reactions, especially asthma or wheezing, runny nose, or hives, to any of the following medicines:

Aspirin or other salicylates
Diclofenac (e.g., Voltaren)
Diflunisal (e.g., Dolobid)
Etodolac (e.g., Lodine)
Fenoprofen (e.g., Nalfon)
Floctafenine (e.g., Idarac)
Flurbiprofen, oral (e.g., Ansaid)
Ibuprofen (e.g., Motrin)
Indomethacin (e.g., Indocin)
Ketoprofen (e.g., Orudis)
Ketorolac (e.g., Toradol)
Meclofenamate (e.g., Meclomen)
Mefenamic acid (e.g., Ponstel)
Nabumetone (e.g., Relafen)
Naproxen (e.g., Naprosyn)
Oxyphenbutazone (e.g., Tandearil)
Phenylbutazone (e.g., Butazolidin)
Piroxicam (e.g., Feldene)
Sulindac (e.g., Clinoril)
Suprofen (e.g., Suprol)
Tenoxicam (e.g., Mobiflex)
Tiaprofenic acid (e.g., Surgam)
Tolmetin (e.g., Tolectin)
Zomepirac (e.g., Zomax)

Also tell your health care professional if you are allergic to any other substances, such as foods, preservatives, or dyes.

Pregnancy—Although studies on birth defects have not been done in pregnant women after use of these medicines in the eye, ophthalmic anti-inflammatory medicines have not been reported to cause birth defects or other problems. Studies have been done in animals receiving anti-inflammatory medicines by mouth in amounts that are much greater than the amounts used in the eye. These medicines did not cause birth defects in these studies. However, they decreased the weight or slowed the growth of the fetus and caused other, more serious, harmful effects on the fetus when they were given in amounts that were large enough to cause harmful effects in the mother. Also, when these medicines were given to animals late in pregnancy, they increased the length of pregnancy or prolonged labor.

Breast-feeding—It is not known whether any of these medicines pass into the breast milk after they are placed in the eye. Diclofenac, indomethacin, and suprofen pass into the breast milk when they are are taken by mouth. It is not known whether flurbiprofen passes into the breast milk when it is taken by mouth. However, these medicines have not been shown to cause problems in nursing babies.

Children—These medicines have been studied only in adults, and there is no specific information about their use in children.

Older adults—These medicines have been tested and have not been shown to cause different side effects or problems in older people than they do in younger adults.

Other medicines—Although certain medicines should not be used together at all, in other cases two different medicines may be used together even if an interaction might occur. In these cases, your doctor may want to change the dose, or other precautions may be necessary. Tell your health care professional if you are using any other prescription or nonprescription (over-the-counter [OTC]) medicine.

Other medical problems—The presence of other medical problems may affect the use of these medicines. Make sure you tell your doctor if you have any other medical problems, especially:

- Hemophilia or other bleeding problems—The possibility of bleeding may be increased
- Viral eye infection (epithelial herpes simplex keratitis), or a history of having a viral eye infection—It is possible that a current infection could be made worse or an old infection could return
- Use of soft contact lenses—Eye irritation, such as redness and burning of the eyes, may occur

Proper Use of This Medicine

To use:
- First, wash your hands. Tilt the head back and, pressing your finger gently on the skin just beneath the lower eyelid, pull the lower eyelid away from the eye to make a space. Drop the medicine into this space. Let go of the eyelid and gently close the eyes. Do not blink. Keep the eyes closed and apply pressure to the inner corner of the eye with your finger for 1 or 2 minutes to allow the medicine to be absorbed by the eye.
- Immediately after using the eye drops, wash your hands to remove any medicine that may be on them.
- To keep the medicine as germ-free as possible, do not touch the applicator tip to any surface (including the eye). Also, always keep the container tightly closed.

Do not use this medicine more often or for a longer time than your doctor ordered. To do so may increase the chance of side effects.

Do not use any leftover medicine for future eye problems without first checking with your doctor. If certain kinds of infection are present, using this medicine may make the infection worse and possibly lead to eye damage.

Dosing—The dose of these medicines will be different for different patients. *Follow your doctor's orders or the directions on the label.* The following information includes only the average doses of these medicines. *If your dose is different, do not change it* unless your doctor tells you to do so.

For diclofenac
- Adults:
  —To treat photophobia (sensitivity to light) which may occur after incisional refractive surgery: Your health care professional will probably give you the medicine before the operation, starting with 1 drop in the eye within one hour of surgery, then 1 drop fifteen minutes after surgery, then 1 drop four times a day beginning four to six hours after surgery and continuing for up to three days as needed.
  —To relieve inflammation in the eye following cataract surgery: 1 drop in the eye four times a day beginning twenty-four hours after cataract surgery and throughout the first two weeks following the operation.

- Children: Use and dose must be determined by the doctor.

For flurbiprofen
- Adults:
  —For use before an eye operation: Your health care professional will probably give you the medicine before your operation.
  —To relieve inflammation: Use and dose must be determined by the doctor.
- Children: Use and dose must be determined by the doctor.

For indomethacin
- Adults:
  —For use before an eye operation: Your health care professional will probably give you the medicine before your operation.
  —To relieve inflammation or edema in the eye: 1 drop in the eye four times a day.
- Children: Use and dose must be determined by the doctor.

For suprofen
- Adults:
  —For use before an eye operation: Your health care professional will probably give you the medicine before your operation.
- Children: Use and dose must be determined by the doctor.

Missed dose—If you miss a dose of this medicine, apply it as soon as possible. But if it is almost time for your next dose, skip the missed dose and go back to your regular dosing schedule.

Storage—To store this medicine:
- Keep out of the reach of children.
- Store away from heat and direct light.
- Keep the medicine from freezing.
- Do not keep outdated medicine or medicine no longer needed. Be sure that any discarded medicine is out of the reach of children.

Precautions While Using This Medicine

Wearing soft (hydrogel) contact lenses during treatment with diclofenac has caused severe irritation (redness and itching) in some people. Therefore, *do not wear soft contact lenses during the time that you are being treated with diclofenac.*

Side Effects of This Medicine

Along with its needed effects, a medicine may cause some unwanted effects. Check with your doctor as soon as possible if any of the following side effects occur:

Less common or rare
Bleeding in the eye or redness or swelling of the eye or the eyelid (not present before you started using this medicine or becoming worse while you are using this medicine); blurred vision or other change in vision; fever or chills; itching or tearing; nausea or vomiting; pain; sensitivity to light; shortness of breath; sticky or matted eyelashes; swelling of face; throbbing pain; tightness in chest; troubled breathing; wheezing

Other side effects may occur that usually do not need medical attention. The following side effects usually do not need med-

ical attention. However, check with your doctor if they continue or are bothersome.

More common
Burning, stinging, or mild discomfort after application; dry eyes

Less common or rare
Bigger or smaller pupils (black part of eye); headache; trouble in sleeping; runny or stuffy nose; unusual weakness

Other side effects not listed above may also occur in some patients. If you notice any other effects, check with your doctor.

Revised: 08/13/98
Interim revision: 09/10/98

ANTI-INFLAMMATORY DRUGS, NONSTEROIDAL   Systemic

Commonly used brand name(s):

In the U.S.—

Actron[9]	Indocin SR[8]
Advil[7]	Lodine[3]
Advil Caplets[7]	Lodine XL[3]
Advil, Children's[7]	Meclomen[10]
Aleve[14]	Medipren[7]
Anaprox[14]	Medipren Caplets[7]
Anaprox DS[14]	Midol IB[7]
Ansaid[6]	Mobic[12]
Bayer Select Ibuprofen Pain	Motrin[7]
Relief Formula Caplets [7]	Motrin Chewables[7]
Cataflam[1]	Motrin, Children's[7]
Clinoril[18]	Motrin, Children's Oral Drops[7]
Cotylbutazone[16]	Motrin-IB[7]
Cramp End[7]	Motrin-IB Caplets[7]
Daypro[15]	Motrin, Junior Strength
Dolgesic[7]	Caplets[7]
Dolobid[2]	Nalfon[4]
EC-Naprosyn[14]	Nalfon 200[4]
Excedrin IB[7]	Naprelan[14]
Excedrin IB Caplets[7]	Naprosyn[14]
Feldene[17]	Nuprin[7]
Genpril[7]	Nuprin Caplets[7]
Genpril Caplets[7]	Orudis[9]
Haltran[7]	Orudis KT[9]
Ibifon 600 Caplets[7]	Oruvail[9]
Ibren[7]	Pamprin-IB[7]
Ibu[7]	Ponstel[11]
Ibu-200[7]	Q-Profen[7]
Ibu-4[7]	Relafen[13]
Ibu-6[7]	Rufen[7]
Ibu-8[7]	Tolectin 200[21]
Ibuprin[7]	Tolectin 600[21]
Ibuprohm[7]	Tolectin DS[21]
Ibuprohm Caplets[7]	Trendar[7]
Ibu-Tab[7]	Voltaren[1]
Indocin[8]	

In Canada—

Actiprofen Caplets[7]	Ansaid[6]
Advil[7]	Apo-Diclo[1]
Advil Caplets[7]	Apo-Diflunisal[2]
Albert Tiafen[20]	Apo-Flurbiprofen[6]
Alka Butazolidin[16]	Apo-Ibuprofen[7]
Anaprox[14]	Apo-Indomethacin[8]
Anaprox DS[14]	Apo-Keto[9]

Apo-Keto-E[9]
Apo-Napro-Na[14]
Apo-Napro-Na DS[14]
Apo-Naproxen[14]
Apo-Phenylbutazone[16]
Apo-Piroxicam[17]
Apo-Sulin[18]
Apo-Tenoxicam[19]
Butazolidin[16]
Clinoril[18]
Daypro[15]
Dolobid[2]
Feldene[17]
Froben[6]
Froben SR[6]
Idarac[5]
Indocid[8]
Indocid SR[8]
Medipren Caplets[7]
Mobiflex[19]
Motrin[7]
Motrin-IB[7]
Nalfon[4]
Naprosyn[14]
Naprosyn-E[14]
Naprosyn-SR[14]
Naxen[14]
Novo-Difenac[1]
Novo-Difenac SR[1]
Novo-Diflunisal[2]
Novo-Flurprofen[6]
Novo-Keto-EC[9]
Novo-Methacin[8]

Novo-Naprox[14]
Novo-Naprox Sodium[14]
Novo-Naprox Sodium DS[14]
Novo-Pirocam[17]
Novo-Profen[7]
Novo-Sundac[18]
Novo-Tenoxicam[19]
Novo-Tolmetin[21]
Nu-Diclo[1]
Nu-Flurbiprofen[6]
Nu-Ibuprofen[7]
Nu-Indo[8]
Nu-Naprox[14]
Nu-Pirox[17]
Orudis[9]
Orudis-E[9]
Orudis-SR[9]
Oruvail[9]
PMS-Piroxicam[17]
Ponstan[11]
Relafen[13]
Rhodis[9]
Rhodis-EC[9]
Surgam[20]
Surgam SR[20]
Synflex[14]
Synflex DS[14]
Tolectin 200[21]
Tolectin 400[21]
Tolectin 600[21]
Voltaren[1]
Voltaren Rapide[1]
Voltaren SR[1]

Other commonly used names are: Etodolic acid[3] Indometacin[8] Meclofenamic acid[10].

Note: For quick reference, the following nonsteroidal anti-inflammatory drugs are numbered to match the corresponding brand names.

This information applies to the following medicines:

1. Diclofenac (dye-KLOE-fen-ak)
2. Diflunisal (dye-FLOO-ni-sal)‡
3. Etodolac (ee-TOE-doe-lak)†
4. Fenoprofen (fen-oh-PROE-fen)‡
5. Floctafenine (flok-ta-FEN-een)*
6. Flurbiprofen (flure-BI-proe-fen)‡§
7. Ibuprofen (eye-byoo-PROE-fen)‡§
8. Indomethacin (in-doe-METH-a-sin)‡
9. Ketoprofen (kee-toe-PROE-fen)‡
10. Meclofenamate (me-kloe-FEN-am-ate)†‡
11. Mefenamic Acid (me-fe-NAM-ik)
12. Meloxicam (mel-OX-i-cam)‡
13. Nabumetone (na-BYOO-me-tone)
14. Naproxen (na-PROX-en)‡
15. Oxaprozin (ox-a-PROE-zin)
16. Phenylbutazone (fen-ill-BYOO-ta-zone)‡
17. Piroxicam (peer-OX-i-kam)‡
18. Sulindac (sul-IN-dak)‡
19. Tenoxicam (ten-OX-i-kam)*
20. Tiaprofenic Acid (tie-a-pro-FEN-ik)*
21. Tolmetin (TOLE-met-in)‡

This information does *not* apply to aspirin or other salicylates or to ketorolac (e.g., Toradol).

---

*Not commercially available in the U.S.
†Not commercially available in Canada.
‡Generic name product may be available in the U.S.
§Generic name product may be available in Canada.

Description

Nonsteroidal anti-inflammatory drugs (also called NSAIDs) are used to relieve some symptoms caused by arthritis (rheu-matism), such as inflammation, swelling, stiffness, and joint pain. However, this medicine does not cure arthritis and will help you only as long as you continue to take it.

Some of these medicines are also used to relieve other kinds of pain or to treat other painful conditions, such as:

- gout attacks;
- bursitis;
- tendinitis;
- sprains, strains, or other injuries; or
- menstrual cramps.

Ibuprofen and naproxen are also used to reduce fever.

Meclofenamate is also used to reduce the amount of bleeding in some women who have very heavy menstrual periods.

Nonsteroidal anti-inflammatory drugs may also be used to treat other conditions as determined by your doctor.

Any nonsteroidal anti-inflammatory drug can cause side effects, especially when it is used for a long time or in large doses. Some of the side effects are painful or uncomfortable. Others can be more serious, resulting in the need for medical care and sometimes even death. If you will be taking this medicine for more than one or two months or in large amounts, you should discuss with your doctor the good that it can do as well as the risks of taking it. Also, it is a good idea to ask your doctor about other forms of treatment that might help to reduce the amount of this medicine that you take and/or the length of treatment.

One of the nonsteroidal anti-inflammatory drugs, phenylbu-tazone, is especially likely to cause very serious side effects. These serious side effects are more likely to occur in patients 40 years of age or older than in younger adults, and the risk becomes greater as the patient's age increases. Before you take phenylbutazone, be sure that you have discussed its use with your doctor. *Also, do not use phenylbutazone to treat any painful condition other than the one for which it was prescribed by your doctor.*

Although ibuprofen and naproxen may be used instead of aspirin to treat many of the same medical problems, they must not be used by people who are allergic to aspirin.

The 200-mg strength of ibuprofen and the 220-mg strength of naproxen are available without a prescription. However, your health care professional may have special instructions on the proper dose of these medicines for your medical condition.

Other nonsteroidal anti-inflammatory drugs and other strengths of ibuprofen and naproxen are available only with your medical doctor's or dentist's prescription. These medicines are available in the following dosage forms:

Oral
Diclofenac
- Tablets (U.S. and Canada)
- Delayed-release tablets (U.S. and Canada)
- Extended-release tablets (Canada)
Diflunisal
- Tablets (U.S. and Canada)
Etodolac
- Capsules (U.S.)
- Tablets (U.S.)
- Extended-release tablets (U.S.)
Fenoprofen
- Capsules (U.S. and Canada)
- Tablets (U.S. and Canada)
Floctafenine
- Tablets (Canada)

Flurbiprofen
- Extended-release capsules (Canada)
- Tablets (U.S. and Canada)

Ibuprofen
- Oral suspension (U.S.)
- Tablets (U.S. and Canada)
- Chewable tablets (U.S.)

Indomethacin
- Capsules (U.S. and Canada)
- Extended-release capsules (U.S. and Canada)
- Oral suspension (U.S.)

Ketoprofen
- Capsules (U.S. and Canada)
- Extended-release capsules (U.S. and Canada)
- Tablets (U.S.)
- Delayed-release tablets (Canada)
- Extended-release tablets (Canada)

Meclofenamate
- Capsules (U.S.)

Mefenamic Acid
- Capsules (U.S. and Canada)

Meloxicam
- Tablets (U.S.)

Nabumetone
- Tablets (U.S. and Canada)

Naproxen
- Oral suspension (U.S. and Canada)
- Tablets (U.S. and Canada)
- Delayed-release tablets (U.S. and Canada)
- Extended-release tablets (U.S. and Canada)

Oxaprozin
- Tablets (U.S. and Canada)

Phenylbutazone
- Capsules (U.S.)
- Tablets (U.S. and Canada)
- Buffered tablets (Canada)

Piroxicam
- Capsules (U.S. and Canada)

Sulindac
- Tablets (U.S. and Canada)

Tenoxicam
- Tablets (Canada)

Tiaprofenic Acid
- Extended-release capsules (Canada)
- Tablets (Canada)

Tolmetin
- Capsules (U.S. and Canada)
- Tablets (U.S. and Canada)

Rectal

Diclofenac
- Suppositories (Canada)

Indomethacin
- Suppositories (U.S. and Canada)

Ketoprofen
- Suppositories (Canada)

Naproxen
- Suppositories (Canada)

Piroxicam
- Suppositories (Canada)

Before Using This Medicine

In deciding to use a medicine, the risks of taking the medicine must be weighed against the good it will do. This is a decision you and your health care professional will make. For the non-

steroidal anti-inflammatory drugs, the following should be considered:

Allergies—Tell your health care professional if you have ever had any unusual or allergic reaction to any of the non-steroidal anti-inflammatory drugs, or to any of the following medicines:
- Aspirin or other salicylates
- Ketorolac (e.g., Toradol)
- Oxyphenbutazone (e.g., Oxalid, Tandearil)
- Suprofen (e.g., Suprol)
- Zomepirac (e.g., Zomax)

Also tell your health care professional if you are allergic to any other substances, such as foods, preservatives, or dyes.

Diet—Make certain your health care professional knows if you are on any special diet, such as a low-sodium or low-sugar diet. Some of these medicines contain sodium or sugar.

Pregnancy—Studies on birth defects with these medicines have not been done in humans. However, there is a chance that these medicines may cause unwanted effects on the heart or blood flow of the fetus or newborn baby if they are taken regularly during the last few months of pregnancy. Also, studies in animals have shown that these medicines, if taken late in pregnancy, may increase the length of pregnancy, prolong labor, or cause other problems during delivery. If you are pregnant, do not take any of these medicines, including nonprescription (over-the-counter [OTC]) ibuprofen or naproxen, without first discussing its use with your doctor.

Studies in animals have not shown that fenoprofen, floctafenine, flurbiprofen, ibuprofen, ketoprofen, nabumetone, naproxen, phenylbutazone, piroxicam, tiaprofenic acid, or tolmetin causes birth defects. Diflunisal caused birth defects of the spine and ribs in rabbits, but not in mice or rats. Diclofenac and meclofenamate caused unwanted effects on the formation of bones in animals. Etodolac and oxaprozin caused birth defects in animals. Indomethacin caused slower development of bones and damage to nerves in animals. In some animal studies, sulindac caused unwanted effects on the development of bones and organs. Studies on birth defects with mefenamic acid have not been done in animals.

Even though most of these medicines did not cause birth defects in animals, many of them did cause other harmful or toxic effects on the fetus, usually when they were given in such large amounts that the pregnant animals became sick.

Breast-feeding—
- *For indomethacin:* Indomethacin passes into the breast milk and has been reported to cause unwanted effects in nursing babies.
- *For meclofenamate:* Use of meclofenamate by nursing mothers is not recommended, because in animal studies it caused unwanted effects on the newborn's development.
- *For phenylbutazone:* Phenylbutazone passes into the breast milk and may cause unwanted effects, such as blood problems, in nursing babies.
- *For piroxicam:* Studies in animals have shown that piroxicam may decrease the amount of milk.

Although other anti-inflammatory analgesics have not been reported to cause problems in nursing babies, diclofenac, diflunisal, fenoprofen, flurbiprofen, meclofenamate, mefenamic acid, naproxen, piroxicam, and tolmetin pass into the breast milk. It is not known whether etodolac, floctafenine, ibuprofen, ketoprofen, nabumetone, oxaprozin, sulindac, or tiaprofenic acid passes into human breast milk.

Children—

- *For ibuprofen:* Ibuprofen has been tested in children 6 months of age and older. It has not been shown to cause different side effects or problems than it does in adults.
- *For indomethacin and for tolmetin:* Indomethacin and tolmetin have been tested in children 2 years of age and older and have not been shown to cause different side effects or problems than they do in adults.
- *For naproxen:* Studies with naproxen in children 2 years of age and older have shown that skin rash may be more likely to occur.
- *For oxaprozin:* Oxaprozin has been used in children with arthritis. However, there is no specific information comparing use of this medicine in children with use in other age groups.
- *For phenylbutazone:* Use of phenylbutazone in children up to 15 years of age is not recommended.
- *For other anti-inflammatory analgesics:* There is no specific information on the use of other anti-inflammatory analgesics in children.

Most of these medicines, especially indomethacin and phenylbutazone, can cause serious side effects in any patient. Therefore, it is especially important that you discuss with the child's doctor the good that this medicine may do as well as the risks of using it.

Older adults—Certain side effects, such as confusion, swelling of the face, feet, or lower legs, or sudden decrease in the amount of urine, may be especially likely to occur in elderly patients, who are usually more sensitive than younger adults to the effects of nonsteroidal anti-inflammatory drugs. Also, elderly people are more likely than younger adults to get very sick if these medicines cause stomach problems. With phenylbutazone, blood problems may also be more likely to occur in the elderly.

Other medicines—Although certain medicines should not be used together at all, in other cases two different medicines may be used together even if an interaction might occur. In these cases, your doctor may want to change the dose, or other precautions may be necessary. When you are taking a nonsteroidal anti-inflammatory drug, it is especially important that your health care professional know if you are taking any of the following:

- Anticoagulants (blood thinners) or
- Cefamandole (e.g., Mandol) or
- Cefoperazone (e.g., Cefobid) or
- Cefotetan (e.g., Cefotan) or
- Heparin or
- Plicamycin (e.g., Mithracin) or
- Valproic acid—The chance of bleeding may be increased

- Aspirin—The chance of serious side effects may be increased if aspirin is used together with a nonsteroidal anti-inflammatory drug on a regular basis

- Ciprofloxacin (e.g., Cipro) or
- Enoxacin (e.g., Penetrex) or
- Itraconazole (e.g., Sporanox) or
- Ketoconazole (e.g., Nizoral) or
- Lomefloxacin (e.g., Maxaquin) or
- Norfloxacin (e.g., Noroxin) or
- Ofloxacin (e.g., Floxin) or
- Tetracyclines, oral—The buffered form of phenylbutazone (e.g., Alka Butazolidin) may keep these medicines from working properly if the 2 medicines are taken too close together

- Cyclosporine (e.g., Sandimmune) or

- Digitalis glycosides (heart medicine) or
- Lithium (e.g., Lithane) or
- Methotrexate (e.g., Mexate) or
- Phenytoin (e.g., Dilantin)—Higher blood levels of these medicines and an increased chance of side effects may occur
- Penicillamine (e.g., Cuprimine)—The chance of serious side effects may be increased, especially with phenylbutazone (e.g., Cotylbutazone)
- Probenecid (e.g., Benemid)—Higher blood levels of the nonsteroidal anti-inflammatory drug and an increased chance of side effects may occur
- Triamterene (e.g., Dyrenium)—The chance of kidney problems may be increased, especially with indomethacin
- Zidovudine (e.g., AZT, Retrovir)—The chance of serious side effects may be increased, especially with indomethacin

Other medical problems—The presence of other medical problems may affect the use of nonsteroidal anti-inflammatory drugs. Make sure you tell your doctor if you have any other medical problems, especially:

- Alcohol abuse or
- Bleeding problems or
- Colitis, Crohn's disease, diverticulitis, stomach ulcer, or other stomach or intestinal problems or
- Diabetes mellitus (sugar diabetes) or
- Hemorrhoids or
- Hepatitis or other liver disease or
- Kidney disease (or history of) or
- Rectal irritation or bleeding, recent, or
- Systemic lupus erythematosus (SLE) or
- Tobacco use (or recent history of)—The chance of side effects may be increased

- Anemia or
- Asthma or
- Epilepsy or
- Fluid retention (swelling of feet or lower legs) or
- Heart disease or
- High blood pressure or
- Kidney stones (or history of) or
- Low platelet count or
- Low white blood cell count or
- Mental illness or
- Parkinson's disease or
- Polymyalgia rheumatica or
- Porphyria or
- Temporal arteritis—Some nonsteroidal anti-inflammatory drugs may make these conditions worse

- Ulcers, sores, or white spots in mouth—Ulcers, sores, or white spots in the mouth sometimes mean that the medicine is causing serious side effects; if these sores or spots are already present before you start taking the medicine, it will be harder for you and your doctor to recognize that these side effects might be occurring

---

Proper Use of This Medicine

For patients taking *a capsule, tablet (including caplet), or liquid form* of this medicine:

- *Take tablet or capsule forms of these medicines with a full glass (8 ounces) of water.* Also, do not lie down for about 15 to 30 minutes after taking the medicine. This helps to prevent irritation that may lead to trouble in swallowing.

- To lessen stomach upset, these medicines should be taken with food or an antacid. This is especially important when you are taking indomethacin, mefenamic acid, phenylbutazone, or piroxicam, which should always be taken with food or an antacid. Taking the extended-release tablet dosage form of flurbiprofen or naproxen and taking nabumetone with food may also help the medicine be absorbed into your body more quickly. However, your doctor may want you to take the first 1 or 2 doses of other nonsteroidal anti-inflammatory drugs 30 minutes before meals or 2 hours after meals. This helps the medicine start working a little faster when you first begin to take it. However, after the first few doses, take the medicine with food or an antacid.
- It is not necessary to take delayed-release (enteric-coated) tablets with food or an antacid, because the enteric coating helps protect your stomach from the irritating effects of the medicine. Also, it is not necessary to take ketoprofen extended-release capsules (e.g., Oruvail) with food or an antacid, because the medicine inside the capsules is enteric coated.
- If you will be taking your medicine together with an antacid, one that contains magnesium and aluminum hydroxides (e.g., Maalox) may be the best kind of antacid to use, unless your doctor has directed you to use another antacid. However, do not mix the liquid form of ibuprofen, indomethacin, or naproxen together with an antacid, or any other liquid, before taking it. To do so may cause the medicine to break down. If stomach upset (indigestion, nausea, vomiting, stomach pain, or diarrhea) continues or if you have any questions about how you should be taking this medicine, check with your health care professional.
- Some of these medicines must be swallowed whole. Tablets should not be crushed, chewed, or broken, and capsules should not be emptied out, before you take the medicine. These include delayed-release (enteric-coated) or extended-release tablets or capsules, diflunisal tablets (e.g., Dolobid), and phenylbutazone tablets (e.g., Butazolidin). If you are not sure whether you are taking a delayed-release or extended-release form of your medicine, check with your pharmacist.

For patients using *a suppository form* of this medicine:
- If the suppository is too soft to insert, chill it in the refrigerator for 30 minutes or run cold water over it before removing the foil wrapper.
- To insert the suppository: First remove the foil wrapper and moisten the suppository with cold water. Lie down on your side and use your finger to push the suppository well up into the rectum.
- Indomethacin suppositories should be kept inside the rectum for at least one hour so that all of the medicine can be absorbed by your body. This helps the medicine work better.

For patients taking *nonprescription (over-the-counter [OTC]) ibuprofen or naproxen:*
- This medicine comes with a patient information sheet. Read it carefully. If you have any questions about this information, check with your health care professional.

For safe and effective use of this medicine, do not take more of it, do not take it more often, and do not take it for a longer time than ordered by your health care professional or directed on the nonprescription (over-the-counter [OTC]) package label. Taking too much of any of these medicines may increase the chance of unwanted effects, especially in elderly patients.

When used for severe or continuing arthritis, a nonsteroidal anti-inflammatory drug must be taken regularly as ordered by your doctor in order for it to help you. These medicines usually begin to work within one week, but in severe cases up to two weeks or even longer may pass before you begin to feel better. Also, several weeks may pass before you feel the full effects of the medicine.

For patients taking *mefenamic acid:*
- *Always take mefenamic acid with food or antacids.*
- *Do not take mefenamic acid for more than 7 days at a time* unless otherwise directed by your doctor. To do so may increase the chance of side effects, especially in elderly patients.

For patients taking *phenylbutazone:*
- Phenylbutazone is intended to treat your current medical problem only. *Do not take it for any other aches or pains.* Also, phenylbutazone should be used for the shortest time possible because of the chance of serious side effects, especially in patients who are 40 years of age or older.

Dosing—The dose of these medicines will be different for different patients. *Follow your doctor's orders or the directions on the label.* The following information includes only the average doses of these medicines. *If your dose is different, do not change it* unless your doctor tells you to do so.

The number of capsules or tablets or teaspoonfuls of suspension that you take, or the number of suppositories that you use, depends on the strength of the medicine. Also, *the number of doses you take each day, the time allowed between doses, and the length of time you take the medicine depend on the medical problem for which you are taking the medicine.*

People with arthritis usually need to take more of a nonsteroidal anti-inflammatory drug during a flare-up than they do between flare-ups of arthritis symptoms. Therefore, your dose may need to be increased or decreased as your condition changes.

For diclofenac
- For *tablet* dosage form:
  —For relieving pain or menstrual cramps:
  - Adults—50 milligrams (mg) three times a day as needed. Your doctor may direct you to take 100 mg for the first dose only.
  - Children—Use and dose must be determined by your doctor.
  —For rheumatoid arthritis:
  - Adults—At first, 50 mg three or four times a day. Your doctor may increase the dose, if necessary, up to a total of 225 mg a day. After your condition improves your doctor may direct you to take a lower dose.
  - Children—Use and dose must be determined by your doctor.
  —For osteoarthritis:
  - Adults—At first, 50 mg two or three times a day. Usually, no more than a total of 150 mg a day should be taken. After your condition improves your doctor may direct you to take a lower dose.
  - Children—Use and dose must be determined by your doctor.
  —For spondylitis (lower back pain):
  - Adults—At first, 25 mg four or five times a day. After your condition improves your doctor may direct you to take a lower dose.

- Children—Use and dose must be determined by your doctor.
- For *delayed-release tablet* dosage form:
  —For rheumatoid arthritis:
  - Adults—At first, 50 mg three or four times a day. Your doctor may increase the dose, if necessary, up to a total of 225 mg a day. After your condition improves your doctor may direct you to take a lower dose.
  - Children—Use and dose must be determined by your doctor.
  —For osteoarthritis:
  - Adults—At first, 50 mg two or three times a day. Usually, no more than a total of 150 mg a day should be taken. After your condition improves your doctor may direct you to take a lower dose.
  - Children—Use and dose must be determined by your doctor.
  —For spondylitis (lower back pain):
  - Adults—At first, 25 mg four or five times a day. After your condition improves your doctor may direct you to take a lower dose.
  - Children—Use and dose must be determined by your doctor.
- For *extended-release tablet* dosage form:
  —For rheumatoid arthritis, osteoarthritis, or spondylitis:
  - Adults—Usually 75 or 100 mg once a day, in the morning or evening. Some people may need 75 mg twice a day, in the morning and evening. Take the medicine at the same time every day.
  - Children—Use and dose must be determined by your doctor.
- For *rectal* dosage form (suppositories):
  —For rheumatoid arthritis, osteoarthritis, or spondylitis:
  - Adults—One 50-mg or 100-mg suppository, inserted into the rectum. The suppository is usually used only at night by people who take tablets during the day. Usually, no more than a total of 150 mg of diclofenac should be used in a day from all dosage forms combined.
  - Children—Use and dose must be determined by your doctor.

For *diflunisal*

- For *oral* dosage form (tablets):
  —For pain:
  - Adults—1000 milligrams (mg) for the first dose, then 500 mg every eight to twelve hours as needed. Some people may need only 500 mg for the first dose, then 250 mg every eight to twelve hours as needed. Usually, no more than a total of 1500 mg a day should be taken.
  - Children—Dose must be determined by your doctor.
  —For rheumatoid arthritis or osteoarthritis:
  - Adults—At first, 250 or 500 mg twice a day. Your doctor may increase the dose, if necessary, up to a total of 1500 mg a day. After your condition improves your doctor may direct you to take a lower dose.
  - Children—Dose must be determined by your doctor.

For *etodolac*

- For *oral* dosage forms (capsules or tablets):
  —For pain:
  - Adults—400 milligrams (mg) for the first dose, then 200 to 400 mg every six to eight hours as needed. Usually, no more than a total of 1200 mg a day should be taken.
  - Children—Use and dose must be determined by your doctor.
  —For osteoarthritis:
  - Adults—At first, 400 mg two or three times a day or 300 mg three or four times a day. Usually, no more than a total of 1200 mg a day should be taken. After your condition improves your doctor may direct you to take a lower dose.
  - Children—Use and dose must be determined by your doctor.
- For *extended-release tablet* dosage form:
  —For rheumatoid arthritis, osteoarthritis, or spondylitis:
  - Adults—Usually 400 to 1000 mg once a day. Take the medicine at the same time every day.
  - Children—Use and dose must be determined by your doctor.

For *fenoprofen*

- For *oral* dosage forms (capsules or tablets):
  —For pain:
  - Adults—200 milligrams (mg) every four to six hours as needed.
  - Children—Use and dose must be determined by your doctor.
  —For arthritis:
  - Adults—At first, 300 to 600 mg three or four times a day. Your doctor may increase the dose, if necessary, up to a total of 3200 mg a day. After your condition improves your doctor may direct you to take a lower dose.
  - Children—Use and dose must be determined by your doctor.

For *floctafenine*

- For *oral* dosage form (tablets):
  —For pain:
  - Adults—200 to 400 milligrams (mg) every six to eight hours, as needed. Usually, no more than 1200 mg a day should be taken.
  - Children—Use is not recommended.

For *flurbiprofen*

- For *oral tablet* dosage form:
  —For menstrual cramps:
  - Adults—50 milligrams (mg) four times a day.
  - Children—Use and dose must be determined by your doctor.
  —For bursitis, tendinitis, or athletic injuries:
  - Adults—50 mg every four to six hours as needed.
  - Children—Use and dose must be determined by your doctor.
  —For rheumatoid arthritis or osteoarthritis:
  - Adults—At first, 200 to 300 mg a day, divided into smaller amounts that are taken two to four times a day. Usually, no more than a total of 300 mg a day should be taken. After your condition improves your doctor may direct you to take a lower dose.
  - Children—Use and dose must be determined by your doctor.
  —For spondylitis (lower back pain):
  - Adults—At first, 50 mg four times a day. Your doctor may increase the dose, if necessary, up to a total of 300 mg a day. After your condition improves your doctor may direct you to take a lower dose.

- Children—Use and dose must be determined by your doctor.
- For *extended-release capsule* dosage form:
  —For arthritis:
    - Adults—200 mg once a day, in the evening. Take the medicine at the same time every day.
    - Children—Use and dose must be determined by your doctor.

For ibuprofen
- For *oral* dosage forms (oral suspension, tablets, chewable tablets):
  —For pain or menstrual cramps:
    - Adults and teenagers—200 to 400 milligrams (mg) every four to six hours as needed. If you are taking the medicine without a prescription from your health care professional, do not take more than a total of 1200 mg (six 200-mg tablets) a day.
    - Children up to 12 years of age—Use and dose must be determined by your doctor.
  —For fever:
    - Adults and teenagers—200 to 400 mg every four to six hours as needed. If you are taking the medicine without a prescription from your health care professional, do not take more than a total of 1200 mg (six 200-mg tablets) a day.
    - Children 6 months to 12 years of age—The medicine should be used only with a prescription from your doctor. The dose is based on body weight and on the body temperature. For fevers lower than 102.5 °F (39.2 °C) the dose is 5 mg per kilogram (kg) (about 2.2 mg per pound) of body weight. For higher fevers the dose is 10 mg per kg (about 4.5 mg per pound) of body weight.
    - Infants younger than 6 months of age—Use and dose must be determined by your doctor.
  —For arthritis:
    - Adults and teenagers—At first, a total of 1200 to 3200 mg a day, divided into smaller amounts that are taken three or four times a day. After your condition improves your doctor may direct you to take a lower dose.
    - Children 6 months to 12 years of age—The dose is based on body weight. At first, a total of 30 to 40 mg per kg (about 13.6 to 18 mg per pound) of body weight a day, divided into smaller amounts that are taken three or four times a day. Your doctor may increase the dose, if necessary, up to a total of 50 mg per kg (about 21 mg per pound) of body weight a day. After your condition improves your doctor may direct you to take a lower dose.
    - Infants younger than 6 months of age—Use and dose must be determined by your doctor.

For indomethacin
- For *capsule or oral suspension* dosage forms:
  —For arthritis:
    - Adults—At first, 25 or 50 milligrams (mg) two to four times a day. Your doctor may increase the dose, if necessary, up to a total of 200 mg a day. After your condition improves your doctor may direct you to take a lower dose.
    - Children—The dose is based on body weight. At first, 1.5 to 2.5 mg per kilogram (kg) (about 0.7 to 1.1 mg per pound) of body weight a day, divided into smaller amounts that are taken three or four times a day. Your doctor may increase the dose,

if necessary, up to a total of 4 mg per kg (about 1.8 mg per pound) of body weight or 200 mg a day, whichever is less. After your condition improves your doctor may direct you to take a lower dose.
  —For gout:
    - Adults—100 mg for the first dose, then 50 mg three times a day. After the pain is relieved, your doctor may direct you to take a lower dose for a while before stopping treatment completely.
    - Children—Use and dose must be determined by your doctor.
  —For bursitis or tendinitis:
    - Adults—25 mg three or four times a day or 50 mg three times a day.
    - Children—Use and dose must be determined by your doctor.
- For *extended-release capsule* dosage form:
  —For arthritis:
    - Adults—75 mg once a day, in the morning or evening. Some people may need to take 75 mg twice a day, in the morning and evening. Take the medicine at the same time each day.
    - Children—Dose must be determined by your doctor.
- For *rectal suppository* dosage form:
  —For arthritis, bursitis, tendinitis, or gout:
    - Adults—One 50-mg suppository, inserted into the rectum up to four times a day.
    - Children—One 50-mg suppository, inserted into the rectum up to four times a day. The suppository dosage form is too strong for small children. However, the suppositories may be used for large or heavy children if they need doses as large as 50 mg.

For ketoprofen
- For *capsule, tablet, or delayed-release tablet* dosage forms:
  —For pain or menstrual cramps:
    - Adults—25 to 50 milligrams (mg) every six to eight hours as needed. Some people may need to take as much as 75 mg every six to eight hours. Doses larger than 75 mg are not likely to give better relief.
    - Over-the-counter medication—12.5 mg every 4 to 6 hours.
    - Children—Use and dose must be determined by your doctor.
  —For arthritis:
    - Adults—At first, 50 mg four times a day or 75 mg three times a day. Your doctor may increase the dose, if necessary, up to a total of 300 mg a day. After your condition improves your doctor may direct you to take a lower dose.
    - Children—Use and dose must be determined by your doctor.
- For *extended-release capsule or extended-release tablet* dosage forms:
  —For arthritis:
    - Adults—150 or 200 mg once a day, in the morning or evening. Take the medicine at the same time every day.
    - Children—Use and dose must be determined by your doctor.

- For *rectal suppository* dosage form:
  —For arthritis:
    - Adults—50 or 100 mg twice a day, inserted into the rectum, in the morning and evening. Sometimes, the suppository is used only at night by people who take an oral dosage form (capsules or delayed-release tablets) during the day. Usually, no more than a total of 300 mg of ketoprofen should be used in a day from all dosage forms combined.
    - Children—Use and dose must be determined by your doctor.

For meclofenamate
- For *oral* dosage form (capsules):
  —For arthritis:
    - Adults and teenagers 14 years of age and older—At first, 50 milligrams (mg) four times a day. Your doctor may increase the dose, if necessary, up to a total of 400 mg a day. After your condition improves your doctor may direct you to take a lower dose.
    - Children up to 14 years of age—Use and dose must be determined by your doctor.
  —For pain:
    - Adults and teenagers 14 years of age and older—50 mg every four to six hours. Some people may need as much as 100 mg every four to six hours.
    - Children up to 14 years of age—Use and dose must be determined by your doctor.
  —For menstrual cramps and heavy menstrual bleeding:
    - Adults and teenagers 14 years of age and older—100 mg three times a day for up to six days.
    - Children up to 14 years of age—Use and dose must be determined by your doctor.

For mefenamic acid
- For *oral* dosage form (capsules):
  —For pain and for menstrual cramps:
    - Adults and teenagers 14 years of age and older—500 milligrams (mg) for the first dose, then 250 mg every six hours as needed for up to seven days.
    - Children up to 14 years of age—Use and dose must be determined by your doctor.

For meloxicam
- For *oral* dosage form (tablets):
  —For osteoarthritis:
    - Adults—7.5 milligrams (mg) daily in a single dose.

For nabumetone
- For *oral* dosage form (tablets):
  —For arthritis:
    - Adults—At first, 1000 milligrams (mg) once a day, in the morning or evening, or 500 mg twice a day, in the morning and evening. Your doctor may increase the dose, if necessary, up to a total of 2000 mg a day. After your condition improves your doctor may direct you to take a lower dose.
    - Children—Use and dose must be determined by your doctor.

For naproxen
- For *naproxen (e.g., Naprosyn) tablet, oral suspension, and delayed-release tablet* dosage forms:
  —For arthritis:
    - Adults—At first, 250, 375, or 500 milligrams (mg) two times a day, in the morning and evening. Your

doctor may increase the dose, if necessary, up to a total of 1500 mg a day. After your condition improves your doctor may direct you to take a lower dose.
    - Children—The dose is based on body weight. At first, 5 mg per kilogram (kg) (about 2.25 mg per pound) of body weight twice a day. After your condition improves your doctor may direct you to take a lower dose.
  —For bursitis, tendinitis, menstrual cramps, and other kinds of pain:
    - Adults—500 mg for the first dose, then 250 mg every six to eight hours as needed.
    - Children—Use and dose must be determined by your doctor.
  —For gout:
    - Adults—750 mg for the first dose, then 250 mg every eight hours until the attack is relieved.
    - Children—Use and dose must be determined by your doctor.
- For *naproxen extended-release tablet (e.g., Naprelan)* dosage form:
  —For arthritis and pain:
    - Adults—750 to 1000 mg once a day, in the morning or evening.
    - Children—The extended-release tablets are too strong for use in children.
- For *naproxen (e.g., Naprosyn) rectal suppository* dosage form:
  —For arthritis:
    - Adults—One 500-mg suppository, inserted into the rectum at bedtime. The suppository is usually used only at night by people who take an oral dosage form (tablets, oral suspension, or delayed-release tablets) during the day. Usually, no more than a total of 1500 mg of naproxen should be used in a day from all dosage forms combined.
    - Children—The suppositories are too strong for use in children.
- For *naproxen sodium (e.g., Aleve, Anaprox) tablet* dosage form:
  —For arthritis:
    - Adults—At first, 275 or 550 mg two times a day, in the morning and evening, or 275 mg in the morning and 550 mg in the evening. Your doctor may increase the dose, if necessary, up to a total of 1650 mg a day. After your condition improves your doctor may direct you to take a lower dose.
    - Children—Naproxen sodium tablets are too strong for most children. Naproxen (e.g., Naprosyn) tablets or oral suspension are usually used for children.
  —For bursitis and tendinitis:
    - Adults—550 mg for the first dose, then 275 mg every six to eight hours as needed.
    - Children—Use and dose must be determined by your doctor. Naproxen sodium tablets are too strong for most children.
  —For gout:
    - Adults—825 mg for the first dose, then 275 mg every eight hours until the attack is relieved.
    - Children—Use and dose must be determined by your doctor. Naproxen sodium tablets are too strong for most children.

—For pain, fever, and menstrual cramps:
- Adults and children 12 years of age or older—For nonprescription (over-the-counter [OTC]) use: 220 mg (one tablet) every eight to twelve hours as needed. Some people may get better relief if they take 440 mg (two tablets) for the first dose, then 220 mg twelve hours later on the first day only. If you are taking this medicine without a prescription from your health care professional, do not take more than three 220-mg tablets a day. If you are older than 65 years of age, do not take more than two 220-mg tablets a day. Your health care professional may direct you to take larger doses.
- Children up to 12 years of age—Use and dose must be determined by your doctor.

For oxaprozin
- For *oral* dosage form (tablets):
  —For arthritis:
  - Adults—At first, 600 milligrams (mg) once or twice a day, or 1200 mg once a day. Some people may need a larger amount for the first dose only. Your doctor may increase the dose, if necessary, up to 1800 mg a day. This large dose should always be divided into smaller amounts that are taken two or three times a day. After your condition improves your doctor may direct you to take a lower dose.
  - Children—Use and dose must be determined by your doctor.

For phenylbutazone
- For *oral* dosage forms (capsules, tablets, and buffered tablets):
  —For severe arthritis:
  - Adults and teenagers 15 years of age and older—At first, 100 milligrams (mg) three or four times a day. Some people may need a higher dose of 200 mg three times a day. After your condition improves your doctor may direct you to take a lower dose for a while before stopping treatment completely. This medicine should not be taken for longer than a few weeks.
  - Children up to 15 years of age—Use is not recommended.
  —For gout:
  - Adults—400 mg for the first dose, then 100 mg every four hours for one week or less.
  - Children up to 15 years of age—Use is not recommended.

For piroxicam
- For *oral* dosage form (capsules):
  —For arthritis:
  - Adults—20 milligrams (mg) once a day or 10 mg twice a day.
  - Children—Dose must be determined by your doctor.
  —For menstrual cramps:
  - Adults—40 mg once a day for one day only, then 20 mg once a day if needed.
  - Children—Dose must be determined by your doctor.
- For *rectal* dosage form (suppositories):
  —For arthritis:
  - Adults—20 mg once a day or 10 mg twice a day.
  - Children—Dose must be determined by your doctor.

For sulindac
- For *oral* dosage form (tablets):
  —For arthritis:
  - Adults—At first, 150 or 200 milligrams (mg) twice a day. After your condition improves, your doctor may direct you to take a lower dose.
  - Children—Use and dose must be determined by your doctor.
  —For gout, bursitis, or tendinitis:
  - Adults—At first, 200 mg twice a day. After the pain is relieved, your doctor may direct you to take a lower dose for a while before treatment is stopped completely.
  - Children—Use and dose must be determined by your doctor.

For tenoxicam
- For *oral* dosage form (tablets):
  —For arthritis:
  - Adults and teenagers 16 years of age and older—At first, 20 milligrams (mg) once a day, at the same time each day. For some people, a smaller dose of 10 mg (one-half tablet) a day may be enough.
  - Children and teenagers up to 16 years of age—Dose must be determined by your doctor.

For tiaprofenic acid
- For *oral tablet* dosage form:
  —For arthritis:
  - Adults—At first, 200 milligrams (mg) three times a day or 300 mg twice a day. After your condition improves, your doctor may direct you to take a lower dose.
  - Children—Use and dose must be determined by your doctor.
- For *extended-release capsule* dosage form:
  —For arthritis:
  - Adults—600 mg (two capsules) once a day, at the same time each day.
  - Children—Use and dose must be determined by your doctor.

For tolmetin
- For *oral* dosage forms (capsules or tablets):
  —For arthritis:
  - Adults—At first, 400 milligrams (mg) three times a day. Your doctor may increase the dose, if necessary, up to a total of 1800 mg a day. After your condition improves, your doctor may direct you to take a lower dose.
  - Children 2 years of age and older—The dose is based on body weight. At first, 20 mg per kilogram (kg) (about 9 mg per pound) of body weight a day, divided into smaller amounts that are taken three or four times a day. Your doctor may increase the dose, if necessary, up to 30 mg per kg (about 13.5 mg per pound) of body weight a day. After your condition improves, your doctor may direct you to take a lower dose.
  - Children up to 2 years of age—Dose must be determined by your doctor.

Missed dose—If your health care professional has ordered you to take this medicine according to a regular schedule, and you miss a dose, take it as soon as you remember. However, if it is almost time for your next dose, skip the missed dose and go back to your regular dosing schedule. (For long-acting medicines or extended-release dosage forms that are only taken once or twice a day, take the missed dose only if you remember within an hour or two after the dose should have been taken. If you do not remember until later, skip the missed dose and go back to your regular dosing schedule.) Do not double doses.

Storage—To store this medicine:

- Keep out of the reach of children.
- Store away from heat and direct light.
- Do not store tablets or capsules in the bathroom, near the kitchen sink, or in other damp places. Heat or moisture may cause the medicine to break down.
- Keep liquid and suppository forms of this medicine from freezing.
- Do not keep outdated medicine or medicine no longer needed. Be sure that any discarded medicine is out of the reach of children.

Precautions While Using This Medicine

If you will be taking this medicine for a long time, as for arthritis (rheumatism), your doctor should check your progress at regular visits. Your doctor may want to do certain tests to find out if unwanted effects are occurring, especially if you are taking phenylbutazone. The tests are very important because serious side effects, including ulcers, bleeding, or blood problems, can occur without any warning.

Stomach problems may be more likely to occur if you drink alcoholic beverages while being treated with this medicine. Also, alcohol may add to the depressant side effects of phenylbutazone.

If you consume 3 or more alcoholic beverages per day, check with your doctor before taking this medicine.

Taking two or more of the nonsteroidal anti-inflammatory drugs together on a regular basis may increase the chance of unwanted effects. Also, taking acetaminophen, aspirin or other salicylates, or ketorolac (e.g., Toradol) regularly while you are taking a nonsteroidal anti-inflammatory drug may increase the chance of unwanted effects. The risk will depend on how much of each medicine you take every day, and on how long you take the medicines together. If your health care professional directs you to take these medicines together on a regular basis, follow his or her directions carefully. However, *do not take acetaminophen or aspirin or other salicylates together with this medicine for more than a few days, and do not take any ketorolac (e.g., Toradol) while you are taking this medicine, unless your doctor has directed you to do so and is following your progress.*

Before having any kind of surgery (including dental surgery), tell the medical doctor or dentist in charge that you are taking this medicine. If possible, this should be done when your surgery is first being planned. Some of the nonsteroidal anti-inflammatory drugs can increase the chance of bleeding during and after surgery. It may be necessary for you to stop treatment for a while, or to change to a different nonsteroidal anti-inflammatory drug that is less likely to cause bleeding.

This medicine may cause some people to become confused, drowsy, dizzy, lightheaded, or less alert than they are normally. It may also cause blurred vision or other vision problems in some people. *Make sure you know how you react to this medicine before you drive, use machines, or do anything else that could be dangerous if you are confused, dizzy, or drowsy, or if you are not alert and able to see well.* If these reactions are especially bothersome, check with your doctor.

For patients taking *the buffered form of phenylbutazone (e.g., Alka-Butazolidin):*

- This medicine contains antacids that can keep other medicines from working properly if the 2 medicines are taken too close together. *Always take this medicine:*
  —*At least 6 hours before or 2 hours after taking ciprofloxacin (e.g., Cipro) or lomefloxacin (e.g., Maxaquin).*
  —*At least 8 hours before or 2 hours after taking enoxacin (e.g., Penetrex).*
  —*At least 2 hours after taking itraconazole (e.g., Sporanox).*
  —*At least 3 hours before or after taking ketoconazole (e.g., Nizoral).*
  —*At least 2 hours before or after taking norfloxacin (e.g., Noroxin) or ofloxacin (e.g., Floxin).*
  —*At least 1 to 3 hours before or after taking a tetracycline antibiotic by mouth.*
  —*At least 1 or 2 hours before or after taking any other medicine by mouth.*

For patients taking *mefenamic acid:*

- If diarrhea occurs while you are using this medicine, *stop taking it and check with your doctor immediately. Do not take it again without first checking with your doctor*, because severe diarrhea may occur each time you take it.

Some people who take nonsteroidal anti-inflammatory drugs may become more sensitive to sunlight than they are normally. Exposure to sunlight, even for brief periods of time, may cause severe sunburn; blisters on the skin; skin rash, redness, itching, or discoloration; or vision changes. When you begin taking this medicine:

- Stay out of direct sunlight, especially between the hours of 10:00 a.m. and 3:00 p.m., if possible.
- Wear protective clothing, including a hat and sunglasses.
- Apply a sun block product that has a skin protection factor (SPF) of at least 15. Some patients may require a product with a higher SPF number, especially if they have a fair complexion. If you have any questions about this, check with your health care professional.
- Do not use a sunlamp or tanning bed or booth.

If you have a severe reaction from the sun, check with your doctor.

Serious side effects, including ulcers or bleeding, can occur during treatment with this medicine. Sometimes serious side effects can occur without any warning. However, possible warning signs often occur, including severe abdominal or stomach cramps, pain, or burning; black, tarry stools; severe, continuing nausea, heartburn, or indigestion; and/or vomiting of blood or material that looks like coffee grounds. *Stop taking this medicine and check with your doctor immediately if you notice any of these warning signs.*

Check with your doctor immediately if chills, fever, muscle aches or pains, or other influenza-like symptoms occur, especially if they occur shortly before, or together with, a skin rash. Very rarely, these effects may be the first signs of a serious reaction to this medicine.

Nonsteroidal anti-inflammatory drugs may cause a serious type of allergic reaction called anaphylaxis. Although this is rare, it may occur more often in patients who are allergic to aspirin or to any of the nonsteroidal anti-inflammatory drugs. *Anaphylaxis requires immediate medical attention.* The most serious signs of this reaction are very fast or irregular breathing, gasping for breath, wheezing, or fainting. Other signs may include changes in color of the skin of the face; very fast but irregular heartbeat or pulse; hive-like swellings on the skin; and puffiness or swellings of the eyelids or around the eyes. If these effects occur, get emergency help at once. Ask someone to drive you to the nearest hospital emergency room. If this is not possible, do not try to drive yourself. Call an ambulance, lie down, cover yourself to keep warm, and prop your feet higher than your head. Stay in that position until help arrives.

For patients taking *ibuprofen* or *naproxen* without a prescription:

* Check with your medical doctor or dentist:
    —if your symptoms do not improve or if they get worse.
    —if you are using this medicine to bring down a fever and the fever lasts more than 3 days or returns.
    —if the painful area is red or swollen.

Side Effects of This Medicine

Along with its needed effects, a medicine may cause some unwanted effects. Although not all of these side effects may occur, if they do occur they may need medical attention.

Stop taking this medicine and get emergency help right away if any of the following side effects occur:
Rare—For all nonsteroidal anti-inflammatory drugs
    Fainting; fast or irregular breathing; fast, irregular heartbeat or pulse; hive-like swellings (large) on face, eyelids, mouth, lips, or tongue; puffiness or swelling of the eyelids or around the eyes; shortness of breath, troubled breathing, wheezing, or tightness in chest

Also, stop taking this medicine and check with your doctor immediately if any of the following side effects occur:
More common—for mefenamic acid only
    Diarrhea

More common—for phenylbutazone only
    Swelling of face, hands, feet, or lower legs; weight gain (rapid)

Symptoms of phenylbutazone overdose
    Bluish color of fingernails, lips, or skin; headache (severe and continuing)

Rare—for all nonsteroidal anti-inflammatory drugs
    Abdominal or stomach pain, cramping, or burning (severe); bloody or black, tarry stools; chest pain; convulsions (seizures); fever with or without chills; nausea, heartburn, and/or indigestion (severe and continuing); pinpoint red spots on skin; sores, ulcers, or white spots on lips or in mouth; spitting up blood; unexplained nosebleeds; unusual bleeding or bruising; vomiting of blood or material that looks like coffee grounds

Also, check with your doctor as soon as possible if any of the following side effects occur:
More common
    Bleeding from rectum (with suppositories); headache (severe), especially in the morning (for indomethacin only); skin rash

Less common or rare
    Bladder pain; bleeding from cuts or scratches that lasts longer than usual; bleeding or crusting sores on lips; bloody or cloudy urine or any problem with urination,

such as difficult, burning, or painful urination; change in urine color or odor; frequent urge to urinate; sudden, large increase or decrease in the amount of urine; or loss of bladder control; blurred vision or any change in vision; burning feeling in throat, chest, or stomach; confusion, forgetfulness, mental depression, or other mood or mental changes; cough or hoarseness; decreased hearing, any other change in hearing, or ringing or buzzing in ears; difficulty in swallowing; eye pain, irritation, dryness, redness, and/or swelling; hallucinations (seeing, hearing, or feeling things that are not there); headache (severe), throbbing, or with stiff neck or back; hives, itching of skin, or any other skin problem, such as blisters, redness or other color change, tenderness, burning, peeling, thickening, or scaliness; increased blood pressure; irritated tongue; light-colored stools; loosening or splitting of fingernails; muscle cramps, pain, or weakness; numbness, tingling, pain, or weakness in hands or feet; pain in lower back and/or side (severe); swelling and/or tenderness in upper abdominal or stomach area; swelling of face, feet, or lower legs (if taking phenylbutazone, stop taking it and check with your doctor immediately); swelling of lips or tongue; swollen and/or painful glands (especially in the neck or throat area); thirst (continuing); trouble in speaking; unexplained runny nose or sneezing; unexplained, unexpected, or unusually heavy vaginal bleeding; unusual tiredness or weakness; weight gain (rapid) (if taking phenylbutazone, stop taking it and check with your doctor immediately); yellow eyes or skin

Other side effects may occur that usually do not need medical attention. These side effects may go away during treatment as your body adjusts to the medicine. However, check with your doctor if any of the following side effects continue or are bothersome:
More common
    Abdominal or stomach cramps, pain, or discomfort (mild to moderate); diarrhea (if taking mefenamic acid, stop taking it and check with your doctor immediately); dizziness, drowsiness, or lightheadedness; headache (mild to moderate); heartburn, indigestion, nausea, or vomiting

Less common or rare
    Bitter taste or other taste change; bloated feeling, gas, or constipation; decreased appetite or loss of appetite; fast or pounding heartbeat; flushing or hot flashes; general feeling of discomfort or illness; increased sensitivity of eyes to light; increased sensitivity of skin to sunlight; increased sweating; irritation, dryness, or soreness of mouth; nervousness, anxiety, irritability, trembling, or twitching; rectal irritation (with suppositories); trouble in sleeping; unexplained weight loss; unusual tiredness or weakness without any other symptoms

Although not all of the side effects listed above have been reported for all of these medicines, they have been reported for at least one of them. However, since all anti-inflammatory analgesics are very similar, it is possible that any of the above side effects may occur with any of these medicines.

Some side effects may occur many days or weeks after you have stopped using phenylbutazone. During this time *check with your doctor immediately* if you notice any of the following side effects:

> Sore throat and fever; ulcers, sores, or white spots in mouth; unusual bleeding or bruising; unusual tiredness or weakness

Other side effects not listed above may also occur in some patients. If you notice any other effects, check with your doctor.

Revised: 02/06/2001

ANTIMYASTHENICS   Systemic

Commonly used brand name(s):

In the U.S.—

Mestinon[3]	Prostigmin[2]
Mestinon Timespans[3]	Regonol[3]
Mytelase Caplets[1]	

In Canada—

Mestinon[3]	Prostigmin[2]
Mestinon-SR[3]	Regonol[3]

Note: For quick reference, the following antimyasthenics are numbered to match the corresponding brand names.

This information applies to the following medicines:
1. Ambenonium (am-be-NOE-nee-um)†
2. Neostigmine (nee-oh-STIG-meen)‡
3. Pyridostigmine (peer-id-oh-STIG-meen)

†Not commercially available in Canada.
‡Generic name product may be available in the U.S.

Description

Antimyasthenics are given by mouth or by injection to treat myasthenia gravis. Neostigmine may also be given by injection as a test for myasthenia gravis. Sometimes neostigmine is given by injection to prevent or treat certain urinary tract or intestinal disorders. In addition, neostigmine or pyridostigmine may be given by injection as an antidote to certain types of muscle relaxants used in surgery.

These medicines are available only with your doctor's prescription in the following dosage forms:

Oral
Ambenonium
  • Tablets (U.S.)
Neostigmine
  • Tablets (U.S. and Canada)
Pyridostigmine
  • Syrup (U.S.)
  • Tablets (U.S. and Canada)
  • Extended-release tablets (U.S. and Canada)

Parenteral
Neostigmine
  • Injection (U.S. and Canada)
Pyridostigmine
  • Injection (U.S. and Canada)

Before Using This Medicine

In deciding to use a medicine, the risks of taking the medicine must be weighed against the good it will do. This is a decision you and your doctor will make. For the antimyasthenics, the following should be considered:

Allergies—Tell your doctor if you have ever had any unusual or allergic reaction to ambenonium, bromides, neostigmine, or pyridostigmine. Also tell your health care professional if you are allergic to any other substances, such as foods, preservatives, or dyes.

Pregnancy—Antimyasthenics have not been reported to cause birth defects; however, muscle weakness has occurred temporarily in some newborn babies whose mothers took antimyasthenics during pregnancy.

Breast-feeding—Antimyasthenics have not been reported to cause problems in nursing babies.

Children—Although there is no specific information comparing use of antimyasthenics in children with use in other age groups, these medicines are not expected to cause different side effects or problems in children than they do in adults.

Older adults—Many medicines have not been studied specifically in older people. Therefore, it may not be known whether they work exactly the same way they do in younger adults. Although there is not much information comparing use of antimyasthenics in the elderly with use in other age groups, these medicines are not expected to cause different side effects or problems in older people than they do in younger adults.

Other medicines—Although certain medicines should not be used together at all, in other cases 2 different medicines may be used together even if an interaction might occur. In these cases, your doctor may want to change the dose, or other precautions may be necessary. When you are taking an antimyasthenic, it is especially important that your health care professional knows if you are using any of the following:

• Demecarium (e.g., Humorsol) or
• Echothiophate (e.g., Phospholine Iodide) or
• Isoflurophate (e.g., Floropryl) or
• Malathion (e.g., Prioderm)—Using these medicines with antimyasthenics may result in serious side effects

• Guanadrel (e.g., Hylorel) or
• Guanethidine (e.g., Ismelin) or
• Mecamylamine (e.g., Inversine) or
• Procainamide (e.g., Pronestyl) or
• Trimethaphan (e.g., Arfonad)—The effects of these medicines may interfere with the actions of the antimyasthenics

Other medical problems—The presence of other medical problems may affect the use of the antimyasthenics. Make sure you tell your doctor if you have any other medical problems, especially:

• Intestinal blockage or
• Urinary tract blockage or
• Urinary tract infection—These medicines may make the condition worse

Proper Use of This Medicine

Your doctor may want you to take this medicine with food or milk to help lessen the chance of side effects. If you have any questions about how you should be taking this medicine, check with your doctor.

Take this medicine only as directed. Do not take more of it, do not take it more often, and do not take it for a longer time than your doctor ordered. To do so may increase the chance of side effects.

If you are taking this medicine *for myasthenia gravis:*
- When you first begin taking this medicine, your doctor may want you to keep a daily record of:
  —the time you take each dose.
  —how long you feel better after taking each dose.
  —how long you feel worse.
  —any side effects that occur.

This is to help your doctor decide whether the dose of this medicine should be increased or decreased and how often the medicine should be taken in order for it to be most effective in your condition.

Dosing—The dose of these medicines will be different for different patients. *Follow your doctor's orders or the directions on the label.* The following information includes only the average doses of these medicines. *If your dose is different, do not change it* unless your doctor tells you to do so.

The number of tablets or teaspoonfuls of syrup that you take depends on the strength of the medicine. Also, *the number of doses you take each day, the time allowed between doses, and the length of time you take the medicine depend on the medical problem for which you are taking these medicines.*

For ambenonium
- For *oral* dosage form (tablets):
  —For myasthenia gravis:
    - Adults and teenagers—At first, the dose is 5 milligrams (mg) three or four times per day. Then, if needed, the dose will be adjusted by your doctor.
    - Children—The dose is based on body weight or size and must be determined by your doctor. The total daily dose is usually 300 micrograms (mcg) per kilogram (kg) (136 mcg per pound) of body weight or 10 mg per square meter of body surface area. This dose may be divided into three or four smaller doses. If needed, the total daily dose will be increased to 1.5 mg per kg (0.68 mg per pound) of body weight or 50 mg per square meter of body surface area. This dose may be divided into three or four smaller doses.

For neostigmine
- For *oral* dosage form (tablets):
  —For myasthenia gravis:
    - Adults and teenagers—At first, the dose is 15 milligrams (mg) every three or four hours. Then, the dose is 150 mg taken over a twenty-four-hour period.
    - Children—The dose is based on body weight or size and must be determined by your doctor. The total daily dose is usually 2 mg per kilogram (kg) (0.91 mg per pound) of body weight or 60 mg per square meter of body surface area. This dose may be divided into six to eight smaller doses.
- For *injection* dosage form:
  —For myasthenia gravis:
    - Adults and teenagers—The usual dose is 500 micrograms (mcg) injected into a muscle or under the skin.
    - Children—The dose is based on body weight and must be determined by your doctor. It is usually 10 to 40 mcg per kg (4.5 to 18.2 mcg per pound)

of body weight, injected into a muscle or under the skin, every two or three hours.
  —For urinary tract or intestinal disorders:
    - Adults and teenagers—The usual dose is 250 to 500 mcg, injected into a muscle or under the skin, as needed.
    - Children—Use and dose must be determined by your doctor.

For pyridostigmine
- For *oral* dosage forms (syrup and tablets):
  —For myasthenia gravis:
    - Adults and teenagers—At first, the dose is 30 to 60 milligrams (mg) every three or four hours. Then, the dose is 60 mg to 1.5 grams (usually 600 mg) per day.
    - Children—The dose is based on body weight or size and must be determined by your doctor. The total daily dose is usually 7 mg per kilogram (kg) (3.2 mg per pound) of body weight or 200 mg per square meter of body surface area. This dose may be divided into five or six smaller doses.
- For *long-acting oral* dosage form (extended-release tablets):
  —For myasthenia gravis:
    - Adults and teenagers—The usual dose is 180 to 540 mg one or two times per day.
    - Children—Dose must be determined by your doctor.
- For *injection* dosage form:
  —For myasthenia gravis:
    - Adults and teenagers—The usual dose is 2 mg, injected into a muscle or vein, every two or three hours.
    - Children—The dose is based on body weight and must be determined by your doctor. It is usually 50 to 150 micrograms (mcg) per kg (22.7 to 68.1 mcg per pound) of body weight, injected into a muscle every four to six hours.

Missed dose—If you miss a dose of this medicine, take it as soon as you remember. However, if it is almost time for your next dose, skip the missed dose and go back to your regular dosing schedule. Do not double doses.

Storage—To store this medicine:
- Keep out of the reach of children.
- Store away from heat and direct light.
- Do not store the tablet form of this medicine in the bathroom, near the kitchen sink, or in other damp places. Heat or moisture may cause the medicine to break down.
- Keep the syrup form of pyridostigmine from freezing.
- Do not keep outdated medicine or medicine no longer needed. Be sure that any discarded medicine is out of the reach of children.

Side Effects of This Medicine

Along with its needed effects, a medicine may cause some unwanted effects. Although not all of these side effects may occur, if they do occur they may need medical attention.

Check with your doctor immediately if any of the following side effects occur:
Symptoms of overdose
  Blurred vision; clumsiness or unsteadiness; confusion; convulsions (seizures); diarrhea (severe); increase

in bronchial secretions or watering of mouth (excessive); increasing muscle weakness (especially in the arms, neck, shoulders, and tongue); muscle cramps or twitching; nausea or vomiting (severe); shortness of breath, troubled breathing, wheezing, or tightness in chest; slow heartbeat; slurred speech; stomach cramps or pain (severe); unusual irritability, nervousness, restlessness, or fear; unusual tiredness or weakness

Also, check with your doctor as soon as possible if any of the following side effects occur:

Rare

Redness, swelling, or pain at place of injection (for pyridostigmine injection only); skin rash (does not apply to ambenonium)

Other side effects may occur that usually do not need medical attention. These side effects may go away during treatment as your body adjusts to the medicine. However, check with your doctor if any of the following side effects continue or are bothersome:

More common

Diarrhea; increased sweating; increased watering of mouth; nausea or vomiting; stomach cramps or pain

Less common

Frequent urge to urinate; increase in bronchial secretions; unusually small pupils; unusual watering of eyes

Other side effects not listed above may also occur in some patients. If you notice any other effects, check with your doctor.

Revised: 09/30/91
Interim revision: 07/18/94

ANTIPYRINE AND BENZOCAINE
Otic

Commonly used brand name(s):

In the U.S.—

A/B Otic	Aurodex
Allergen	Auroto
Analgesic Otic	Dolotic
Antiben	Ear Drops
Auralgan	Otocalm

Generic name product may be available.

In Canada—
Auralgan
Earache Drops

Another commonly used name for antipyrine is phenazone. Another commonly used name for benzocaine is ethyl aminobenzoate.

Description

Antipyrine and benzocaine (an-tee-PYE-reen and BEN-zoe-kane) combination is used in the ear to help relieve the pain, swelling, and congestion of some ear infections. It will not cure the infection itself. An antibiotic will be needed to treat the infection. This medicine is also used to soften earwax so that the earwax can be washed away more easily.

In the U.S., this medicine is available only with your doctor's prescription. In Canada, this medicine is available without a prescription. However, your doctor may have special instructions on the proper dose for your ear problem. This medicine is available in the following dosage form:

Otic
- Otic solution (ear drops) (U.S. and Canada)

Before Using This Medicine

In deciding to use a medicine, the risks of using the medicine must be weighed against the good it will do. This is a decision you and your doctor will make. For antipyrine and benzocaine combination, the following should be considered:

Allergies—Tell your doctor if you have ever had any unusual or allergic reaction to antipyrine or benzocaine or other local anesthetics. Also tell your health care professional if you are allergic to any other substances, such as foods, preservatives, or dyes.

Pregnancy—Although studies on effects in pregnancy have not been done in either humans or animals, this medicine has not been reported to cause problems in humans.

Breast-feeding—It is not known whether this medicine passes into the breast milk. Although most medicines pass into breast milk in small amounts, many of them may be used safely while breast-feeding. Mothers who are using this medicine and who wish to breast-feed should discuss this with their doctor.

Children—Infants, especially infants up to 3 months of age, may be especially sensitive to the effects of the benzocaine in this combination medicine. This may increase the chance of side effects. However, this medicine is not expected to cause different side effects or problems in older children than it does in adults.

Older adults—Many medicines have not been studied specifically in older people. Therefore, it may not be known whether they work exactly the same way they do in younger adults. Although there is no specific information comparing use of antipyrine and benzocaine in the elderly with use in other age groups, this medicine is not expected to cause different side effects or problems in older people than it does in younger adults.

Other medical problems—The presence of other medical problems may affect the use of antipyrine and benzocaine combination. Make sure you tell your doctor if:
- Your ear is draining—The chance of unwanted effects may be increased

Proper Use of This Medicine

You may warm the ear drops to body temperature (37 °C or 98.6 °F) by holding the bottle in your hand for a few minutes before applying the drops.

To use:
- Lie down or tilt the head so that the affected ear faces up. Gently pull the earlobe up and back for adults (down and back for children) to straighten the ear canal. Drop the medicine into the ear canal. Keep the ear facing up for about 5 minutes to allow the medicine to coat the ear canal. (For young children and other patients who cannot stay still for 5 minutes, try to keep the ear facing up for at least 1 or 2 minutes.) A sterile cotton plug may be moistened with a few drops of this medicine and gently placed at the ear opening for no longer than 5 to 10 minutes to help keep the medicine from leaking out.

Anti-thymocyte Globulin (Rabbit) (Systemic)   193

If you have any questions about this, check with your doctor.
- To keep the medicine as germ-free as possible, do not touch the dropper to any surface (including the ear).
- *Do not rinse the dropper after use.* Wipe the tip of the dropper with a clean tissue and keep the container tightly closed.

If you are using this medicine to help remove earwax, the ear should be flushed with warm water after you have used this medicine for 2 or 3 days. This is usually done by your doctor. If you have been directed to flush the ear out yourself, make sure that you have learned how to do it correctly. Follow the instructions carefully.

Dosing—The dose of this medicine will be different for different patients. *Follow your doctor's orders or the directions on the label.* The following information includes only the average amounts of this medicine. *If your dose is different, do not change it* unless your doctor tells you to do so.
- For *otic* dosage form (ear drops):
  —Adults and children:
    - For ear pain caused by an infection—Use enough medicine to fill the entire ear canal every one or two hours until the pain is relieved.
    - For softening earwax before removal—Use enough medicine to fill the entire ear canal three times a day for two or three days.

Missed dose—If you miss a dose of this medicine, use it as soon as you remember. However, if it is almost time for your next dose, skip the missed dose and go back to your regular dosing schedule.

Storage—To store this medicine:
- Keep out of the reach of children.
- Store away from heat and direct light.
- Keep the medicine from freezing.
- Do not keep outdated medicine or medicine no longer needed. Be sure that any discarded medicine is out of the reach of children.

Side Effects of This Medicine

Along with its needed effects, a medicine may cause some unwanted effects. The following side effects may mean that you are having an allergic reaction to the medicine. Stop using the medicine right away if any of them occur. Check with your doctor if any of the following effects continue or are bothersome:

Itching, burning, redness, or oozing sores in the ear

Other side effects not listed above may also occur in some patients. If you notice any other effects, check with your doctor.

Revised: 07/14/95

ANTI-THYMOCYTE GLOBULIN (RABBIT) Systemic†

Commonly used brand name(s):

In the U.S.—
Thymoglobulin

Other commonly used names are.
Anti-thymocyte immunoglobulin

†Not commercially available in Canada.

Description

Anti-thymocyte globulin (rabbit) (an-tee-THI-mo-cite) is an immunosuppressant. It is used to reduce the body's natural immunity in patients who receive kidney transplants.

When a patient receives an organ transplant, the body's white blood cells will try to get rid of (reject) the transplanted organ. Anti-thymocyte globulin (rabbit) works by preventing the white blood cells from doing this.

The effect of anti-thymocyte globulin (rabbit) on the white blood cells may also reduce the body's ability to fight infections. Before you begin treatment, you and your doctor should talk about the good this medicine will do as well as the risks of using it.

Anti-thymocyte globulin (rabbit) is to be administered only by or under the immediate supervision of your doctor. It is available in the following dosage form:

Parenteral
- Injection (U.S.)

Before Using This Medicine

In deciding to use a medicine, the risks of taking the medicine must be weighed against the good it will do. This is a decision you and your doctor will make. For anti-thymocyte globulin (rabbit), the following should be considered:

Allergies—Tell your doctor if you have ever had any unusual or allergic reaction to anti-thymocyte globulin (rabbit) or to rabbits. Anti-thymocyte globulin came from rabbit cells. Also tell your doctor and pharmacist if you are allergic to any other substances, such as preservatives.

Pregnancy—Studies on effects in pregnancy have not been done in either humans or animals. It is not known whether anti-thymocyte globulin (rabbit) causes harmful effects on the fetus. Before receiving this medicine, make sure your doctor knows if you are pregnant or if you may become pregnant.

Breast-feeding—It is not known whether anti-thymocyte globulin (rabbit) passes into breast milk. Anti-thymocyte globulin (rabbit) has not been reported to cause problems in nursing babies. However, it may be necessary for you to stop breast-feeding during treatment. Be sure you have discussed the risks and benefits of the medicine with your doctor.

Children—Although there is no specific information comparing use of anti-thymocyte globulin (rabbit) in children with use in other age groups, this medicine is not expected to cause different side effects or problems in children than it does in adults.

Older adults—Many medicines have not been studied specifically in older people. Therefore, it may not be known whether they work exactly the same way they do in younger adults or if they cause different side effects or problems in older people. There is no specific information comparing use of anti-thymocyte globulin (rabbit) in the elderly with use in other age groups.

Other medicines—Although certain medicines should not be used together at all, in other cases two different medicines may be used together even if an interaction might occur. In these cases, your doctor may want to change the

dose, or other precautions may be necessary. When you are receiving anti-thymocyte globulin (rabbit), it is especially important that your doctor and pharmacist know if you are taking any of the following: Immunosuppressants—There may be an increased risk of infection and development of cancer because anti-thymocyte globulin (rabbit) reduces the body's ability to fight them. Your doctor may need to change your dose.

Other medical problems—The presence of other medical problems may affect the use of anti-thymocyte globulin (rabbit). Make sure you tell your doctor if you have any other medical problems, especially:

- Allergic to rabbit protein (history of)—Risk of serious allergic reaction, bleeding, and infection.
- Infection—Anti-thymocyte globulin (rabbit) decreases your body's ability to fight infection.

Proper Use of This Medicine

Dosing—The dose of anti-thymocyte globulin (rabbit) may be different for different patients. Anti-thymocyte globulin (rabbit) is usually given by a doctor or nurse in the hospital. The following information includes only the average doses of anti-thymocyte globulin (rabbit):

- For *injection* dosage form:
  —To treat kidney transplant rejection:
  - Adults—1.5 milligrams for every kilogram (2.2 pounds) of your body weight injected into a vein every day for 7 to 14 days.
  - Children—Use and dose must be determined by your doctor.

Precautions While Using This Medicine

Treatment with anti-thymocyte globulin (rabbit) may also increase the chance of getting other infections. If you can, avoid people with colds or other infections. If you think you are getting a cold or other infection, check with your doctor.

This medicine commonly causes fever and chills within a few hours after the first dose. These effects should be less after the second dose. However, *check with your doctor or nurse immediately* if you have chest pain, rapid or irregular heartbeat, shortness of breath or wheezing, or swelling of the face or throat after any dose.

Side Effects of This Medicine

Along with its needed effects, a medicine may cause some unwanted effects.

Because of the way that anti-thymocyte globulin (rabbit) acts on the body, there is a chance that it may cause effects that may not occur until years after the medicine is used. These delayed effects may include certain types of cancer, such as lymphomas and skin cancers. Discuss these possible effects with your doctor.

Although not all of these side effects may occur, if they do occur they may need medical attention.

Check with your doctor as soon as possible if any of the following side effects occur:

More common
  Black, tarry stools; bladder pain; chest pain; chills; cloudy or bloody urine; cold; confusion; cough or hoarseness; fast heartbeat; fever; flu-like symptoms; frequent urge to urinate; high blood pressure; irregular or slow heartbeat; lower back or side pain; numbness or tingling around lips hands, or feet;

painful or difficult urination; shortness of breath or troubled breathing; sore throat; sores, ulcers, or white spots on lips or in mouth; swollen glands; tiredness or weakness; unexplained anxiety; unusual bleeding or bruising; weakness or heaviness of legs

Less common
  Burning or stinging of skin; painful cold sores or blisters on lips, nose, eyes, or genitals

Other side effects may occur that usually do not need medical attention. These side effects may go away during treatment as your body adjusts to the medicine. However, check with your doctor if any of the following side effects continue or are bothersome.

More common
  Abdominal pain; diarrhea; difficult or labored breathing; dizziness; general feeling of discomfort or illness; headache; loss of strength or energy; muscle pain or weakness; nausea; pain; swelling of ankles, feet, and fingers; tightness in chest; unusual weak feeling; wheezing

Less common
  White patches on mouth, tongue, or throat

Other side effects not listed above may also occur in some patients. If you notice any other effects, check with your doctor.

Developed: 04/20/00

ANTITHYROID AGENTS   Systemic

Commonly used brand name(s):

In the U.S.—
  Tapazole[1]

In Canada—
  Propyl-Thyracil[2]
  Tapazole[1]

Another commonly used name for methimazole is thiamazole[1].

Note: For quick reference, the following antithyroid agents are numbered to match the corresponding brand names.

This information applies to the following medicines:
  1. Methimazole (meth-IM-a-zole)
  2. Propylthiouracil (proe-pill-thye-oh-YOOR-a-sill)‡

‡Generic name product may be available in the U.S.

Description

Methimazole and propylthiouracil are used to treat conditions in which the thyroid gland produces too much thyroid hormone.

These medicines work by making it harder for the body to use iodine to make thyroid hormone. They do not block the effects of thyroid hormone that was made by the body before their use was begun.

Methimazole and propylthiouracil are available only with your doctor's prescription, in the following dosage forms:

Oral
  Methimazole
  • Tablets (U.S. and Canada)
  Propylthiouracil
  • Tablets (U.S. and Canada)

Before Using This Medicine

In deciding to use a medicine, the risks of taking the medicine must be weighed against the good it will do. This is a decision you and your doctor will make. For antithyroid agents, the following should be considered:

Allergies—Tell your doctor if you have ever had any unusual or allergic reaction to methimazole or propylthiouracil. Also tell your health care professional if you are allergic to any other substances, such as foods, preservatives, or dyes.

Pregnancy—Use of too large a dose during pregnancy may cause problems in the fetus. However, use of the proper dose, with careful monitoring by the doctor, is not likely to cause problems.

Breast-feeding—These medicines pass into breast milk. (Methimazole passes into breast milk more freely and in higher amounts than propylthiouracil.) However, your doctor may allow you to continue to breast-feed, if your dose is low and the infant gets frequent check-ups. If you are taking a large dose, it may be necessary for you to stop breast-feeding during treatment.

Children—This medicine has been used in children and, in effective doses, has not been shown to cause different side effects or problems in children than it does in adults.

Teenagers—This medicine has been used in teenagers and, in effective doses, has not been shown to cause different side effects or problems in teenagers than it does in adults.

Older adults—Elderly people may have an increased chance of certain side effects during treatment. Your doctor may need to take special precautions while you are taking this medicine.

Other medicines—Although certain medicines should not be used together at all, in other cases two different medicines may be used together even if an interaction might occur. In these cases, your doctor may want to change the dose, or other precautions may be necessary. When you are taking antithyroid agents, it is especially important that your health care professional know if you are taking any of the following:

- Amiodarone or
- Iodinated glycerol or
- Potassium iodide (e.g., Pima)—The use of these medicines may change the effect of antithyroid agents
- Anticoagulants (blood thinners)—The use of antithyroid agents may affect the way anticoagulants work in your body
- Digitalis glycosides—The use of antithyroid agents may affect the amount of digitalis glycosides in the bloodstream

Other medical problems—The presence of other medical problems may affect the use of antithyroid agents. Make sure you tell your doctor if you have any other medical problems, especially:

- Liver disease—The body may not get this medicine out of the bloodstream at the usual rate, which may increase the chance of side effects

Proper Use of This Medicine

Use this medicine only as directed by your doctor. Do not use more or less of it and do not use it more often or for a longer time than your doctor ordered. To do so may increase the chance of side effects.

This medicine works best when there is a constant amount in the blood. *To help keep the amount constant, do not miss any doses. Also, if you are taking more than one dose a day, it is best to take the doses at evenly spaced times day and night.* For example, if you are to take 3 doses a day, the doses should be spaced about 8 hours apart. If this interferes with your sleep or other daily activities, or if you need help in planning the best times to take your medicine, check with your health care professional.

Food in your stomach may change the amount of methimazole that is able to enter the bloodstream. To make sure that you always get the same effects, try to take methimazole at the same time in relation to meals every day. That is, always take it with meals or always take it on an empty stomach.

Dosing—The dose of these medicines will be different for different patients. *Follow your doctor's orders or the directions on the label.* The following information includes only the average doses of these medicines. *If your dose is different, do not change it* unless your doctor tells you to do so.

The number of tablets that you take or the number of suppositories that you use depends on the strength of the medicine. Also, *the number of doses you take each day, the time allowed between doses, and the length of time you take the medicine depend on the medical problem for which you are taking antithyroid agents.*

For methimazole
- For *oral* dosage form (tablets):
  —For treatment of hyperthyroidism (overactive thyroid):
  - Adults and teenagers—At first, 15 to 60 milligrams (mg) a day for up to six to eight weeks. Later, your doctor may want to lower your dose to 5 to 30 mg a day. This may be taken once a day or it may be divided into two doses a day.
  - Children—Dose is based on body weight and must be determined by your doctor. The usual dose is 0.4 mg per kilogram (kg) (0.18 mg per pound) of body weight a day. Later, your doctor may want to lower the dose to 0.2 mg per kg (0.09 mg per pound) of body weight a day. The dose may be taken once a day or it may be divided into two doses a day.
  —For treatment of thyrotoxicosis (a thyroid emergency):
  - Adults and teenagers—15 to 20 mg every four hours.
- For *rectal* dosage form (suppositories):
  —For treatment of thyrotoxicosis (a thyroid emergency):
  - Adults and teenagers—15 to 20 mg inserted into the rectum every four hours. Your doctor may change your dose as needed.
  - Children—The dose is based on body weight and must be determined by your doctor. The usual dose is 0.4 mg per kg (0.18 mg per pound) of body weight inserted into the rectum a day. This may be used as a single dose or or it may be divided into two doses a day.

For propylthiouracil
- For *oral* dosage form (tablets):
  —For treatment of hyperthyroidism (overactive thyroid):
  - Adults and teenagers—At first, 300 to 900 milligrams (mg) a day. Some people may need up to

1200 mg a day. This may be taken as a single dose or it may be divided into two to four doses in a day. Later, your doctor may lower your dose to 50 to 600 mg a day.

- Children 6 to 10 years of age—At first, 50 to 150 mg a day. This may be taken as a single dose or it may be divided into two to four doses in a day. Later, your doctor may change your dose as needed.
- Children 10 years of age and older—At first, 50 to 300 mg a day. This may be taken as a single dose or it may be divided into two to four doses in a day. Then, your doctor may change your dose as needed.

—For treatment of thyrotoxicosis (a thyroid emergency):

- Adults and teenagers—200 to 400 mg every four hours. Your doctor will lower your dose as needed.
- Newborn infants—Dose is based on body weight and must be determined by your doctor. The usual dose is 10 mg per kilogram (kg) (4.5 mg per pound) of body weight a day. This is usually divided into more than one dose a day.

• For *rectal* dosage forms (enemas or suppositories):

—For treatment of thyrotoxicosis (a thyroid emergency):

- Adults and teenagers—200 to 400 mg inserted into the rectum every four hours. Your doctor may change your dose as needed.
- Children 6 to 10 years of age—50 to 150 mg inserted into the rectum a day. This dose may be used as a single dose or it may be divided into two to four doses in a day. Your doctor may change your dose as needed.
- Children 10 years of age and older—50 to 300 mg inserted into the rectum a day. This dose may be used as a single dose or it may be divided into two to four doses in a day. Your doctor may change your dose as needed.
- Newborn infants—Dose is based on body weight and must be determined by your doctor. The usual dose is 10 mg per kg (4.5 mg per pound) of body weight inserted into the rectum. This is usually divided into more than one dose a day. Your doctor may change your dose as needed.

Missed dose—If you miss a dose of this medicine, take it as soon as possible. If it is almost time for your next dose, take both doses together. Then go back to your regular dosing schedule. If you miss more than one dose or if you have any questions about this, check with your doctor.

Storage—To store this medicine:
- Keep out of the reach of children.
- Store away from heat and direct light.
- Do not store in the bathroom, near the kitchen sink, or in other high-moisture areas. Heat or moisture may cause the medicine to break down.
- Do not keep outdated medicine or medicine no longer needed. Be sure that any discarded medicine is out of the reach of children.

Precautions While Using This Medicine

It is very important that your doctor check your progress at regular visits to make sure that this medicine is working properly and to check for unwanted effects.

It may take several days or weeks for this medicine to work. However, *do not stop taking this medicine without first checking with your doctor*. Some medical problems may require several years of continuous treatment.

Before having any kind of surgery (including dental surgery) or emergency treatment, *tell the medical doctor or dentist in charge that you are taking this medicine.*

Check with your doctor right away if you get an injury, infection, or illness of any kind. Your doctor may want you to stop taking this medicine or change the amount you are taking.

While you are being treated with antithyroid agents, and after you stop treatment with it, *do not have any immunizations (vaccinations) without your doctor's approval*. Antithyroid agents may lower your body's resistance and there is a chance you might get the infection the immunization is meant to prevent. In addition, other persons living in your household should not take or have recently taken oral polio vaccine since there is a chance they could pass the polio virus on to you. Also, avoid other persons who have taken oral polio vaccine. Do not get close to them, and do not stay in the same room with them for very long. If you cannot take these precautions, you should consider wearing a protective face mask that covers the nose and mouth.

Before you have any medical tests, tell the doctor in charge that you are taking this medicine. The results of some tests may be affected by this medicine.

Side Effects of This Medicine

Along with its needed effects, a medicine may cause some unwanted effects. Although not all of these side effects may occur, if they do occur they may need medical attention.

Check with your doctor immediately if any of the following side effects occur:

Less common
Cough; fever or chills (continuing or severe); general feeling of discomfort, illness or weakness; hoarseness; mouth sores; pain, swelling, or redness in joints; throat infection

Rare
Yellow eyes or skin

Check with your doctor as soon as possible if any of the following side effects occur:

More common
Fever (mild and temporary); skin rash or itching

Rare
Backache; black, tarry stools; blood in urine or stools; shortness of breath; increase in bleeding or bruising; increase or decrease in urination; numbness or tingling of fingers, toes, or face; pinpoint red spots on skin; swelling of feet or lower legs; swollen lymph nodes; swollen salivary glands

Symptoms of overdose
Changes in menstrual periods; coldness; constipation; dry, puffy skin; headache; listlessness or sleepiness; muscle aches; swelling in the front of the neck; unusual tiredness or weakness; weight gain (unusual)

Other side effects may occur that usually do not need medical attention. These side effects may go away during treatment as your body adjusts to the medicine. However, check with

your doctor if any of the following side effects continue or are bothersome:

Less common

Dizziness; loss of taste (for methimazole); nausea; stomach pain; vomiting

Other side effects not listed above may also occur in some patients. If you notice any other effects, check with your doctor.

Revised: 04/21/92
Interim revision: 06/03/94

APPETITE SUPPRESSANTS, SYMPATHOMIMETIC Systemic

Commonly used brand name(s):

In the U.S.—

Adipex-P[5]	Phentercot[5]
Adipost[4]	Phentride[5]
Bontril PDM[4]	Plegine[4]
Bontril Slow-Release[4]	Prelu-2[4]
Didrex[1]	Pro-Fast[5]
Fastin[5]	PT 105[4]
Ionamin[5]	Sanorex[3]
Mazanor[3]	Tenuate[2]
Melfiat[4]	Tenuate Dospan[2]
Obenix[5]	Tepanil Ten-Tab[2]
Obezine[4]	Teramine[5]
Phendiet[4]	Zantryl[5]
Phendiet-105[4]	

In Canada—

Ionamin[5]	Tenuate[2]
Sanorex[3]	Tenuate Dospan[2]

Other commonly used names are:

Amfepramone
Benzfetamine

Note: For quick reference, the following appetite suppressants are numbered to match the corresponding brand names.

This information applies to the following medicines:

1. Benzphetamine (benz-FET-a-meen)†
2. Diethylpropion (dye-eth-il-PROE-pee-on)‡
3. Mazindol (MAY-zin-dole)
4. Phendimetrazine (fen-dye-MET-ra-zeen)†‡
5. Phentermine (FEN-ter-meen)‡

Note: This information does *not* apply to phenylpropanolamine.

†Not commercially available in Canada.
‡Generic name product may be available in the U.S.

Description

Sympathomimetic appetite suppressants are used in the short-term treatment of obesity. Their appetite-reducing effect tends to decrease after a few weeks. Because of this, these medicines are useful only during the first few weeks of a weight-loss program. The sympathomimetic appetite suppressants can help you to lose weight while you are learning new ways to eat and to exercise. Changes in eating habits and activity level must be developed and continued long-term in order for you to continue losing weight and to keep the lost weight from returning.

These medicines are available only with your doctor's prescription, in the following dosage forms:

Oral

Benzphetamine
• Tablets (U.S.)
Diethylpropion
• Tablets (U.S. and Canada)
• Extended-release tablets (U.S. and Canada)
Mazindol
• Tablets (U.S. and Canada)
Phendimetrazine
• Extended-release capsules (U.S.)
• Tablets (U.S.)
Phentermine
• Capsules (U.S.)
• Resin capsules (U.S. and Canada)
• Tablets (U.S.)

Before Using This Medicine

In deciding to use a medicine, the risks of taking the medicine must be weighed against the good it may do. This is a decision you and your doctor will make. For sympathomimetic appetite suppressants, the following should be considered:

Allergies—Tell your doctor if you have ever had any unusual or allergic reaction to this medicine or amphetamine, dextroamphetamine, ephedrine, epinephrine, isoproterenol, metaproterenol, methamphetamine, norepinephrine, phenylephrine, phenylpropanolamine, pseudoephedrine, terbutaline, or other appetite suppressants. Also tell your health care professional if you are allergic to any other substances, such as foods, preservatives, or dyes.

Diet—You must follow a reduced-calorie diet while using an appetite suppressant in order to lose weight. Also, in order to keep the lost weight from returning, changes in diet and exercise must be continued after the weight has been lost.

Pregnancy—If a pregnant woman takes this medicine in high doses or more often than the doctor has directed, it may cause withdrawal symptoms in the newborn baby. Also, medicines similar to sympathomimetic appetite suppressants can cause birth defects in the newborn baby if a pregnant woman takes them in high doses. Before taking this medicine, make sure your doctor knows if you are pregnant or if you may become pregnant.

Breast-feeding—Diethylpropion and benzphetamine pass into breast milk. It is not known if other sympathomimetic appetite suppressants pass into breast milk. However, use of sympathomimetic appetite suppressants during breast-feeding is not recommended, because it may cause unwanted effects in nursing babies.

Children—Studies on these medicines have been done only in adult patients, and there is no specific information comparing use of sympathomimetic appetite suppressants in children with use in other age groups. The use of these medicines by children younger than 16 years of age is not recommended.

Older adults—Many medicines have not been studied specifically in older people. Therefore, it may not be known whether they work exactly the same way they do in younger adults or if they cause different side effects or problems in older people. There is no specific information comparing use of appetite suppressants in the elderly with use in other age groups.

Other medicines—Although certain medicines should not be used together at all, in other cases two different medicines may be used together even if an interaction might occur. In these cases, your doctor may want to change the dose, or other precautions may be necessary. When you are taking appetite suppressants, it is especially important that your health care professional know if you are taking any of the following:

- Amantadine (e.g., Symmetrel) or
- Amphetamines or
- Caffeine (e.g., NoDoz) or
- Chlophedianol (e.g., Ulone) or
- Cocaine or
- Medicine for asthma or other breathing problems or
- Medicine for colds, sinus problems, or hay fever or other allergies (including nose drops or sprays) or
- Methylphenidate (e.g., Ritalin) or
- Nabilone (e.g., Cesamet) or
- Pemoline (e.g., Cylert)—Using these medicines with sympathomimetic appetite suppressants may increase the central nervous system (CNS) stimulant effects, such as irritability, nervousness, trembling or shaking, or trouble in sleeping
- Appetite suppressants (diet pills), other or
- Selective serotonin reuptake inhibitors (citalopram [e.g., Celexa], fluoxetine [e.g., Prozac], fluvoxamine [e.g., Luvox], paroxetine [e.g., Paxil], sertraline [e.g., Zoloft])—It is not known whether using two different appetite suppressants together or using a sympathomimetic appetite suppressant with a selective serotonin reuptake inhibitor is safe and effective. There have been some serious unwanted effects on the hearts of people who used two different appetite suppressants together
- Monoamine oxidase (MAO) inhibitors (furazolidone [e.g., Furoxone], isocarboxazid [e.g., Marplan], phenelzine [e.g., Nardil], procarbazine [e.g., Matulane], selegiline [e.g., Eldepryl], tranylcypromine [e.g., Parnate])—*Do not take an appetite suppressant while you are taking or less than 14 days after taking a monoamine oxidase (MAO) inhibitor*. If you do, you may develop sudden extremely high blood pressure
- Tricyclic antidepressants (amitriptyline [e.g., Elavil], amoxapine [e.g., Asendin], clomipramine [e.g., Anafranil], desipramine [e.g., Pertofrane], doxepin [e.g., Sinequan], imipramine [e.g., Tofranil], nortriptyline [e.g., Aventyl], protriptyline [e.g., Vivactil], trimipramine [e.g., Surmontil])—Using these medicines with sympathomimetic appetite suppressants may cause high blood pressure or irregular heartbeat

Other medical problems—The presence of other medical problems may affect the use of appetite suppressants. Make sure you tell your doctor if you have any other medical problems, especially:

- Alcohol abuse (or history of) or
- Drug abuse or dependence (or history of)—Dependence on appetite suppressants may be more likely to develop
- Diabetes mellitus (sugar diabetes)—The amount of insulin or oral antidiabetic medicine that you need to take may change
- Epilepsy—Diethylpropion may increase the risk of having seizures
- Family history of mental illness—Mental depression or other mental illness may be more likely to occur
- Glaucoma or
- Heart or blood vessel disease or
- High blood pressure or
- Mental illness or
- Overactive thyroid—Appetite suppressants may make the condition worse
- Kidney disease—Higher blood levels of the appetite suppressant may occur, increasing the chance of serious side effects

Proper Use of This Medicine

In order to prevent trouble in sleeping, if you are taking:

- One dose of this medicine a day, take it about 10 to 14 hours before bedtime.
- More than one dose of this medicine a day, take the last dose of the day about 4 to 6 hours before bedtime.

For patients taking a *long-acting form* of this medicine:

- Swallow these capsules or tablets whole. Do not break, crush, or chew before swallowing.

For patients taking *mazindol:*

- This medicine may be taken with food, if needed, to prevent stomach upset.

Take this medicine only as directed by your doctor. Do not take more of it, do not take it more often, and do not take it for a longer time than your doctor ordered. If too much is taken, it may cause unwanted effects or become habit-forming.

If you think this medicine is not working properly after you have taken it for a few weeks, *do not increase the dose*. Instead, check with your doctor.

Dosing—The dose of appetite suppressants will be different for different patients. *Follow your doctor's orders or the directions on the label*. The following information includes only the average doses of appetite suppressants. *If your dose is different, do not change it* unless your doctor tells you to do so.

For benzphetamine

- For *oral* dosage form (tablets):
  - For appetite suppression:
    - Adults—At first, 25 to 50 milligrams (mg) once a day, taken in midmorning or midafternoon. Your doctor may need to adjust your dose.
    - Children up to 16 years of age—Use is not recommended.

For diethylpropion

- For *oral* dosage form (tablets):
  - For appetite suppression:
    - Adults—25 milligrams (mg) three times a day, taken one hour before meals.
    - Children up to 16 years of age—Use is not recommended.
- For *long-acting oral* dosage form (extended-release tablets):
  - For appetite suppression:
    - Adults—75 mg once a day, taken in midmorning.
    - Children up to 16 years of age—Use is not recommended.

For mazindol

- For *oral* dosage form (tablets):
  - For appetite suppression:
    - Adults—At first, 1 milligram (mg) once a day. Your doctor may need to adjust your dose.

- Children up to 16 years of age—Use is not recommended.

For phendimetrazine
- For *long-acting oral* dosage form (extended-release capsules):
  —For appetite suppression:
  - Adults—105 mg once a day, taken thirty to sixty minutes before the morning meal.
  - Children up to 16 years of age—Use is not recommended.
- For *oral* dosage form (tablets):
  —For appetite suppression:
  - Adults—17.5 to 35 mg two or three times a day, taken one hour before meals.
  - Children up to 16 years of age—Use is not recommended.

For phentermine
- For *oral* dosage form (capsules):
  —For appetite suppression:
  - Adults—15 to 37.5 milligrams (mg) once a day, taken before breakfast or one to two hours after breakfast.
  - Children up to 16 years of age—Use is not recommended.
- For *oral* dosage form (tablets):
  —For appetite suppression:
  - Adults—15 to 37.5 mg once a day, taken before breakfast or one to two hours after breakfast. Instead of taking it once a day, your doctor may tell you to take smaller doses thirty minutes before meals.
  - Children up to 16 years of age—Use is not recommended.
- For *oral resin* dosage form (capsules):
  —For appetite suppression:
  - Adults—15 to 30 mg once a day, taken before breakfast.
  - Children up to 16 years of age—Use is not recommended.

Missed dose—If you miss a dose of this medicine, skip the missed dose and continue with your regular dosing schedule. Do not double doses.

Storage—To store this medicine:
- Keep out of the reach of children.
- Store away from heat and direct light.
- Do not store in the bathroom, near the kitchen sink, or in other damp places. Heat or moisture may cause the medicine to break down.
- Do not keep outdated medicine or medicine no longer needed. Be sure that any discarded medicine is out of the reach of children.

Precautions While Using This Medicine

Your doctor should check your progress at regular visits to make sure that this medicine does not cause unwanted effects.

If you think this medicine is not working properly after you have taken it for a few weeks, *do not increase the dose.* Instead, check with your doctor.

Do not take an appetite suppressant with or less than 14 days after taking a monoamine oxidase (MAO) inhibitor. If you do, you may very suddenly develop extremely high blood pressure.

Taking a sympathomimetic appetite suppressant may cause a positive result in urine screening tests for amphetamines.

Sympathomimetic appetite suppressants may cause dryness of the mouth. For temporary relief, use sugarless candy or gum, melt bits of ice in your mouth, or use a saliva substitute. However, if your mouth continues to feel dry for more than 2 weeks, check with your medical doctor or dentist. Continuing dryness of the mouth may increase the chance of developing dental disease, including tooth decay, gum disease, and fungus infections.

This medicine may cause some people to feel a false sense of well-being or to become dizzy, lightheaded, drowsy, or less alert than they are normally. *Make sure you know how you react to this medicine before you drive, use machines, or do anything else that could be dangerous if you are dizzy or are not alert.*

Before having any kind of surgery, dental treatment, or emergency treatment, tell the medical doctor or dentist in charge that you are using this medicine. Taking appetite suppressants together with medicines that are used during surgery or dental or emergency treatments may cause serious side effects.

Check with your doctor immediately if you notice a decrease in your ability to exercise, if you faint, or if you have chest pain, swelling of your feet or lower legs, or trouble in breathing. These may be symptoms of very serious heart or lung problems.

If you have been taking this medicine for a long time or in large doses and *you think you may have become mentally or physically dependent on it, check with your doctor.*
- Some signs of dependence on appetite suppressants are:
  —a strong desire or need to continue taking the medicine.
  —a need to increase the dose to receive the effects of the medicine.
  —withdrawal side effects (for example, mental depression, nausea or vomiting, stomach cramps or pain, trembling, unusual tiredness or weakness) when you stop taking the medicine.

For *patients with diabetes:*
- This medicine may affect blood sugar levels. If you notice a change in the results of your urine or blood sugar test or if you have any questions, check with your doctor.

If you have been taking this medicine in large doses or for a long time, *do not stop taking it without first checking with your doctor.* Your doctor may want you to reduce gradually the amount you are taking before stopping completely. This will help prevent withdrawal side effects.

Side Effects of This Medicine

Appetite suppressants may cause some serious side effects, including heart and lung problems. *You and your doctor should discuss the good this medicine may do as well as the risks of taking it.*

Along with its needed effects, a medicine may cause some unwanted effects. Although not all of these side effects may occur, if they do occur they may need medical attention.

Check with your doctor immediately if any of the following side effects occur:
Rare
  Chest pain; decreased ability to exercise; fainting; swelling of feet or lower legs; trouble in breathing

Check with your doctor as soon as possible if any of the following side effects occur:

More common
   Increased blood pressure

Less common or rare
   Difficult or painful urination; fast or irregular heartbeat; feeling that others can hear your thoughts; feeling that others are watching you or controlling your behavior; hallucinations (feeling, seeing, or hearing things that are not there); headache (severe); mental depression; numbness, especially on one side of the face or body; skin rash or hives; sore throat and fever (with diethylpropion); talking, feeling, and acting with excitement and activity you cannot control; unusual bleeding or bruising (with diethylpropion)

Symptoms of overdose
   Abdominal or stomach cramps; coma; confusion; convulsions (seizures); diarrhea (severe); dizziness, lightheadedness, or fainting; fast breathing; feeling of panic; fever; hallucinations (seeing, hearing or feeling things that are not there); high or low blood pressure; hostility with urge to attack; irregular heartbeat; nausea or vomiting (severe); overactive reflexes; restlessness; trembling or shaking; tiredness, weakness, and mental depression following effects of excitement

Abuse of a sympathomimetic appetite suppressant (taking the medicine in larger doses or taking it more frequently or for a longer time than the doctor ordered) can cause the following side effects:

   Changes in personality; excessive, excited activity; irritability (severe); mental illness (severe), similar to schizophrenia; skin disease; trouble in sleeping (severe)

Other side effects may occur that usually do not need medical attention. These side effects may go away during treatment as your body adjusts to the medicine. However, check with your doctor if any of the following side effects continue or are bothersome:

More common
   Constipation; dizziness or lightheadedness; dryness of mouth; false sense of well-being; headache; irritability; nausea or vomiting; nervousness or restlessness; stomach cramps or pain; trembling or shaking; trouble in sleeping

   Note: After the stimulant effects have worn off, drowsiness, unusual tiredness or weakness, or mental depression may occur.

Less common or rare
   Blurred vision; changes in sexual desire or decreased sexual ability; diarrhea; drowsiness; frequent urge to urinate or increased urination; increased sweating; unpleasant taste

Although not all of the side effects listed above have been reported for all of these medicines, they have been reported for at least one of them. However, since all of the sympathomimetic appetite suppressants are similar, any of the above side effects may occur with any of these medicines.

After you stop using this medicine, your body may need time to adjust. The length of time this takes depends on the amount of medicine you were using and how long you used

it. During this time check with your doctor if you notice any of the following side effects:

   Extreme tiredness or weakness; mental depression; nausea or vomiting; stomach cramps or pain; trembling; trouble in sleeping or nightmares

Other side effects not listed above may also occur in some patients. If you notice any other effects, check with your doctor.

Revised: 04/26/99

APRACLONIDINE   Ophthalmic

Commonly used brand name(s):

In the U.S.—
   Iopidine

In Canada—
   Iopidine

Other commonly used names are aplonidine and p-aminoclonidine.

Description

Apraclonidine (a-pra-KLON-i-deen) 0.5% is used to treat glaucoma when the medications you have been using for glaucoma do not reduce your eye pressure enough.

Apraclonidine 1% is used just before and after certain types of eye surgery (argon laser trabeculoplasty, argon laser iridotomy, and Nd:YAG laser posterior capsulotomy). The medicine is used to control or prevent a rise in pressure within the eye (ocular hypertension) that can occur after this type of surgery.

Apraclonidine 0.5% is available only with your doctor's prescription. Apraclonidine 1% is given in the hospital at the time of the surgery. This medicine is available in the following dosage form:

Ophthalmic
   • Ophthalmic solution (eye drops) (U.S. and Canada)

Before Using This Medicine

In deciding to use a medicine, the risks of using the medicine must be weighed against the good it will do. This is a decision you and your doctor will make. For apraclonidine, the following should be considered:

Allergies—Tell your doctor if you have ever had any unusual or allergic reaction to apraclonidine or clonidine. Also tell your health care professional if you are allergic to any other substances, such as preservatives.

Pregnancy—Apraclonidine has not been studied in pregnant women. However, apraclonidine has been shown to cause death of the fetus when given by mouth to pregnant rabbits in doses that are many times larger than the human dose. Before using this medicine, make sure your doctor knows if you are pregnant or if you may become pregnant.

Breast-feeding—It is not known whether apraclonidine passes into the breast milk. Although most medicines pass into breast milk in small amounts, many of them may be used safely while breast-feeding. Mothers who are using 0.5% apraclonidine and who wish to breast-feed should discuss this with their doctor. For mothers who are to be treated with

1% apraclonidine during eye surgery, your doctor may want you to stop breast-feeding during the day of your surgery.

Children—Studies on this medicine have been done only in adult patients, and there is no specific information comparing use of apraclonidine in children with use in other age groups.

Older adults—Many medicines have not been studied specifically in older people. Therefore, it may not be known whether they work exactly the same way they do in younger adults or if they cause different side effects or problems in older people. There is no specific information comparing use of apraclonidine in the elderly with use in other age groups.

Other medicines—Although certain medicines should not be used together at all, in other cases two different medicines may be used together even if an interaction might occur. In these cases, your doctor may want to change the dose, or other precautions may be necessary. Tell your health care professional if you are using any other prescription or nonprescription (over-the-counter [OTC]) medicine.

Other medical problems—The presence of other medical problems may affect the use of apraclonidine. Make sure you tell your doctor if you have any other medical problems, especially:

- Depression or
- Heart or blood vessel disease or
- High blood pressure—Apraclonidine may make the condition worse

- Kidney disease or
- Liver disease—Higher blood levels of apraclonidine may result, which may lead to increased side effects

- Unusual reaction to a medicine that reduces the pressure within the eye—Apraclonidine is a strong reducer of eye pressure and could also cause this reaction

- Vasovagal attack (history of)—The signs and symptoms are paleness, nausea, sweating, slow heartbeat, sudden and severe tiredness or weakness, and possibly fainting, usually brought on by emotional stress caused by fear or pain. Apraclonidine may cause this reaction to happen again

---

Proper Use of This Medicine

If your doctor ordered two different eye drops to be used together, wait at least 10 minutes between the times you apply the medicines. This will help to keep the second medicine from "washing out" the first one.

To use the *eye drops:*

- First, wash your hands. Tilt the head back and, pressing your finger gently on the skin just beneath the lower eyelid, pull the lower eyelid away from the eye to make a space. Drop the medicine into this space. Let go of the eyelid and gently close the eyes. Do not blink. Keep the eyes closed and apply pressure to the inner corner of the eye with your finger for 1 or 2 minutes to allow the medicine to be absorbed by the eye.
- If you think you did not get the drop of medicine into your eye properly, use another drop.
- To keep the medicine as germ-free as possible, do not touch the applicator tip to any surface (including the eye). Also, keep the container tightly closed.

Use this medicine only as directed. Do not use more of it and do not use it more often than your doctor ordered. To do

so may increase the chance of too much medicine being absorbed into the body and the chance of side effects.

It is important that your doctor check your progress at regular visits. This is to make sure the medicine is working properly.

Dosing—The dose of ophthalmic apraclonidine will be different for different patients. *Follow the doctor's orders or the directions on the label.* The following information includes only the average doses of ophthalmic apraclonidine. *If your dose is different, do not change it* unless your doctor tells you to do so.

- For *ophthalmic solution (eye drops)* dosage form:
  —For glaucoma (0.5% apraclonidine):
  - Adults—Use one drop in each eye two or three times a day.
  - Children—Use and dose must be determined by your doctor.
  —For preventing ocular hypertension before and after eye surgery (1% apraclonidine):
  - Adults—One drop is placed in the affected eye one hour before surgery, then one drop in the same eye immediately after surgery.
  - Children—Use and dose must be determined by your doctor.

Missed dose—If you are using this medicine regularly and you miss a dose, use it as soon as possible. However, if it is almost time for your next dose, skip the missed dose and go back to your regular dosing schedule. Do not double doses.

Storage—To store this medicine:

- Keep out of the reach of children.
- Store away from heat and direct light.
- The 0.5% eye drops may be stored in the refrigerator. However, keep the medicine from freezing.
- Do not keep outdated medicine or medicine no longer needed. Be sure that any discarded medicine is out of the reach of children.

Precautions While Using This Medicine

This medicine may cause some people to become dizzy, drowsy, or less alert than they are normally. *Make sure you know how you react to this medicine before you drive, use machines, or do anything else that could be dangerous if you are not alert.*

Apraclonidine may cause your eyes to become more sensitive to light than they are normally. Wearing sunglasses and avoiding too much exposure to bright light may help lessen the discomfort.

Side Effects of This Medicine

Along with its needed effects, a medicine may cause some unwanted effects. Although not all of these side effects may occur, if they do occur they may need medical attention.

Check with your doctor or nurse as soon as possible if the following side effects occur:

For 0.5% apraclonidine
More common
Allergic reaction (redness, itching, tearing of eye)
Less common or rare
Blurred vision or change in vision; chest pain; clumsiness or unsteadiness; depression; dizziness; eye discharge, irritation, or pain; irregular heart-

beat; numbness or tingling in fingers or toes; raising of upper eyelid; rash around eyes; redness of eyelid, or inner lining of eyelid; swelling of eye, eyelid, or inner lining of eyelid; swelling of face, hands, or feet; wheezing or troubled breathing

For 1% apraclonidine
Less common or rare
Allergic reaction (redness of eye or inner lining of eyelid, swelling of eyelid, watering of eye); irregular heartbeat

Other side effects may occur that usually do not need medical attention. These side effects may go away during treatment as your body adjusts to the medicine. However, check with your doctor or nurse if any of the following side effects continue or are bothersome:

For 0.5% apraclonidine
More common
Dryness of mouth; eye discomfort

Less common or rare
Change in taste or smell; constipation; crusting or scales on eyelid or corner of eye; discoloration of white part of eye; drowsiness or sleepiness; dry nose or eyes; general feeling of discomfort or illness; headache; increased sensitivity of eyes to light; muscle aches; nausea; nervousness; paleness of eye or inner lining of eyelid; runny nose; sore throat; tiredness or weakness; trouble in sleeping

For 1% apraclonidine
More common
Increase in size of pupil of eye; paleness of eye or inner lining of eyelid; raising of upper eyelid

Less common or rare
Runny nose

Other side effects not listed above may also occur in some patients. If you notice any other effects, check with your doctor or nurse.

Revised: 06/21/94
Interim revision: 07/03/95

ARDEPARIN Systemic

Commonly used brand name(s):

In the U.S.—
Normiflo

Description

Ardeparin (ar-dee-PA-rin) is used to prevent deep venous thrombosis, a condition in which harmful blood clots form in the blood vessels of the legs. These blood clots can travel to the lungs and can become lodged in the blood vessels of the lungs, causing a condition called pulmonary embolism. Ardeparin is used for several days after knee replacement surgery, while you are unable to walk. It is during this time that blood clots are most likely to form. Ardeparin also may be used for other conditions as determined by your doctor.

Ardeparin is available only with your doctor's prescription, in the following dosage form:

Parenteral
• Injection (U.S.)

Before Using This Medicine

In deciding to use a medicine, the risks of using the medicine must be weighed against the good it will do. This is a decision you and your doctor will make. For ardeparin, the following should be considered:

Allergies—Tell your doctor if you have ever had any unusual or allergic reaction to ardeparin or heparin. Also tell your health care professional if you are allergic to any other substances, such as foods, especially pork or pork products, preservatives, or dyes.

Pregnancy—Ardeparin has not been studied in pregnant women. However, it has been found to cause birth defects in animals. Discuss these possible effects with your doctor.

Breast-feeding—It is not known whether this medicine passes into breast milk. Although most medicines pass into breast milk in small amounts, many of them may be used safely while breast-feeding. Mothers who are using this medicine and who wish to breast-feed should discuss this with their doctor.

Children—Studies on this medicine have been done only in adult patients, and there is no specific information comparing use of ardeparin in children with use in other age groups.

Older adults—This medicine has been tested and has not been shown to cause different side effects or problems in older people than it does in younger adults.

Other medicines—Although certain medicines should not be used together at all, in other cases two different medicines may be used together even if an interaction might occur. In these cases, your doctor may want to change the dose, or other precautions may be necessary. Tell your health care professional if you are using any other prescription or nonprescription (over-the-counter [OTC]) medicine.

Other medical problems—The presence of other medical problems may affect the use of ardeparin. Make sure you tell your doctor if you have any other medical problems, especially:
• Bleeding problems or
• Eye problems caused by diabetes or high blood pressure or
• Heart infection or
• High blood pressure (hypertension) or
• Kidney disease or
• Liver disease or
• Stomach or intestinal ulcer (active) or
• Stroke—The risk of bleeding may be increased

Also, tell your doctor if you have received ardeparin or heparin before and had a reaction to either of them called thrombocytopenia (a low platelet count in the blood), or if new blood clots formed while you were receiving the medicine.

In addition, *tell your doctor if you have recently had medical surgery*. This may increase the risk of serious bleeding when you are taking ardeparin.

Proper Use of This Medicine

If you are using ardeparin at home, your health care professional will teach you how to inject yourself with the medicine. *Be sure to follow the directions carefully. Check with your health care professional if you have any problems using the medicine.*

Put used syringes in a puncture-resistant, disposable container, or dispose of them as directed by your health care professional.

Dosing—The dose of ardeparin will be different for different patients. *Follow your doctor's orders or the directions on the label.* The following information includes only the average doses of ardeparin. *If your dose is different, do not change it* unless your doctor tells you to do so. The dose you receive will be based on your body weight.

- For *injection* dosage form:
  —For prevention of deep venous thrombosis (leg clots) and pulmonary embolism (lung clots):
    - Adults—The dose is given every twelve hours for up to fourteen days after surgery.
    - Children—Use and dose must be determined by your doctor.

Missed dose—If you miss a dose of this medicine, use it as soon as possible. However, if it is almost time for your next dose, skip the missed dose and go back to your regular dosing schedule. Do not double doses.

Storage—To store this medicine:
- Keep out of the reach of children.
- Store away from heat and direct light.
- Keep the medicine from freezing. Do not refrigerate.
- Do not keep outdated medicine or medicine no longer needed. Be sure that any discarded medicine is out of the reach of children.

Precautions While Using This Medicine

Tell all your medical doctors and dentists that you are using this medicine.

Check with your doctor immediately if you notice any of the following side effects:
- Bruising or bleeding, especially bleeding that is hard to stop. Bleeding inside the body sometimes appears as bloody or black, tarry stools, or faintness.
- Back pain; burning, pricking, tickling, or tingling sensation; leg weakness; numbness; paralysis; or problems with bowel or bladder function.

Side Effects of This Medicine

Along with its needed effects, a medicine may cause some unwanted effects. Although not all of these side effects may occur, if they do occur they may need medical attention.

Stop using this medicine and check with your doctor immediately if any of the following side effects occur:

Less common
  Bleeding gums; coughing up blood; deep, dark purple bruise, pain, or swelling at place of injection; difficulty in breathing or swallowing; dizziness; headache; increased menstrual flow or vaginal bleeding; nosebleeds; paralysis; prolonged bleeding from cuts; red or dark brown urine; red or black, tarry stools; shortness of breath; unexplained pain, swelling, or discomfort, especially in the chest, abdomen, joints, or muscles; unusual bruising; vomiting of blood or coffee ground-like material; weakness

Rare
  Back pain; burning, pricking, tickling, or tingling sensation; leg weakness; numbness; problems with bowel or bladder function; rash consisting of pinpoint, purple-red spots, often beginning on the legs

Also, check with your doctor as soon as possible if any of the following side effects occur:

Less common
  Fever

Rare
  Skin rash, hives, or itching

Other side effects may occur that usually do not need medical attention. These side effects may go away during treatment as your body adjusts to the medicine. However, check with your doctor if any of the following side effects continue or are bothersome:

Less common
  Nausea; pain at injection site; vomiting

Other side effects not listed above may also occur in some patients. If you notice any other effects, check with your doctor.

Developed: 03/26/98
Interim revision: 07/10/98

ARSENIC TRIOXIDE   Systemic — INTRODUCTORY VERSION

Commonly used brand name(s):

In the U.S.—
  Trisenox

Description

Arsenic trioxide (AR-sen-ik try-OX-ide) belongs to the general group of medicines called antineoplastics. It is used to treat leukemia in patients who have not responded to other medication regimens. It may also be used to treat other kinds of cancer, as determined by your doctor.

Arsenic trioxide seems to interfere with the growth of cancer cells, which are then eventually destroyed by the body. Since the growth of normal body cells may also be affected by arsenic trioxide, other effects will also occur. Some of these may be serious and must be reported to your doctor.

This medicine is available only with your doctor's prescription, in the following dosage forms:

Parenteral
- Injection (U.S.)

Before Using This Medicine

In deciding to use a medicine, the risks of taking the medicine must be weighed against the good it will do. This is a decision

you and your doctor will make. For arsenic trioxide, the following should be considered:

Allergies — Tell your doctor if you have ever had any unusual or allergic reaction to arsenic.

Pregnancy — There is a chance that this medicine may cause birth defects if it is taken at time of conception or if it is taken by the mother during pregnancy. Studies in rats and mice have shown that arsenic trioxide causes birth defects in the fetus and other problems (including miscarriage). Studies on the effects in pregnancy have not been done in humans.

Be sure that you have discussed these possible effects with your doctor before receiving this medicine. Before receiving arsenic trioxide make sure your doctor knows if you are pregnant or if you may become pregnant. It is best to use some kind of birth control while you are receiving arsenic trioxide. Tell your doctor right away if you think you have become pregnant while receiving arsenic trioxide.

Breast-feeding — Arsenic is distributed into human breast milk. Arsenic trioxide is not recommended during breast-feeding, because it may cause unwanted effects in nursing babies.

Children — Studies on this medicine have been done only in a limited number of patients over the age of 5 years, and there is no specific information comparing use of arsenic trioxide in children under the age of 5 with use in other age groups.

Older adults — Many medicines have not been studied specifically in older people. Therefore, it may not be known whether they work exactly the same way they do in younger adults or if they cause different side effects or problems in older people. There is no specific information comparing use of arsenic trioxide in the elderly with use in other age groups.

Other medicines — Although certain medicines should not be used together at all, in other cases two different medicines may be used together even if an interaction might occur. In these cases, your doctor may want to change the dose, or other precautions may be necessary. When you are taking arsenic trioxide, it is especially important that your health care provider know if you are taking any of the following:

- Amphotericin B by injection (e.g., Fungizone) or
- Antiarrhythmics (acebutolol [e.g., Sectral], adenosine [e.g., Adenocard], amiodarone [e.g., Cordarone], atenolol [e.g., Tenormin], digoxin [e.g., Lanoxin], digitoxin [e.g., Crystodigin], diltiazem [e.g., Cardizem], disopyramide [e.g., Norpace], encainide [e.g., Enkaid], esmolol [e.g., Brevibloc], flecainide [e.g., Tambocor], metoprolol [e.g., Lopressor], mexilitine [e.g., Mexitil], moricizine [e.g., Ethmozine], nadolol [e.g., Corgard], oxprenolol [e.g., Trasicor], phenytoin [e.g., Dilantin], procainamide [e.g., Procan], propafenone [e.g., Rythmol], propranolol [e.g., Inderal], quinidine [e.g., Quinaglute], sotalol [e.g., Betapace], timolol [e.g., Blocadren], tocainide [e.g., Tonocard], verapamil [e.g., Isoptin]) or
- Antifungals, azole (fluconazole [e.g., Diflucan], itraconazole [e.g., Sporanox], ketoconazole [e.g., Nizoral]) or
- Antihistamines or
- Fluoroquinolones (ciprofloxacin [e.g., Cipro], enoxacin [e.g., Penetrex], grepafloxacin [e.g., Raxar], levofloxacin [e.g., Levaquin], lomefloxacin [e.g., Maxaquin], norfloxacin [e.g., Noroxin], ofloxacin [e.g., Floxin], sparfloxacin [e.g., Zagam]) or

- Diuretics, potassium-depleting (bumetanide [e.g., Bumex], ethacrynic acid [e.g., Edecrin], furosemide [e.g., Lasix], indapamide [e.g., Lozol], thiazide diuretics [water pills]) or
- Tricyclic antidepressants (amitriptyline [e.g., Elavil], amoxapine [e.g., Asendin], clomipramine [e.g., Anafranil], desipramine [e.g., Norpramin], doxepin [e.g., Sinequan], imipramine [e.g., Tofranil], nortriptyline [e.g., Pamelor], protriptyline [e.g., Vivactil], trimipramine [e.g., Surmontil])—These medicines may increase the risk of experiencing a life threatening heart rhythm problem while taking arsenic trioxide and concurrent use of these agents with arsenic trioxide may cause blood disorders or
- Thioridazine (e.g., Mellaril)—These medicines may increase the risk of experiencing a life threatening heart rhythm problem while taking arsenic trioxide.

Other medical problems — The presence of other medical problems may affect the use of arsenic trioxide. Make sure you tell your doctor if you have any other medical problems, especially:

- Abnormal heart rhythms or
- Congestive heart failure or
- Low magnesium levels in the blood or
- Low potassium levels in the blood—These medical problems may increase the risk of experiencing a life threatening heart rhythm problem while taking arsenic trioxide.

- Kidney problems—Arsenic trioxide is removed from the body by the kidneys; kidney problems may cause the drug to build up.

Proper Use of This Medicine

Dosing — The dose of arsenic trioxide will be different for different patients. The dose that is used may depend on a number of things, including the patient's body size, and whether or not other medicines are also being taken. If you have any questions about the proper dose of arsenic trioxide, ask your doctor.

- For *injectable* dosage form:
  —For acute promyelocytic leukemia:
    - Adults and children 5 years of age and older— Induction, 0.15 milligram (mg) per kilogram (kg) of body weight daily until bone marrow remission occurs (up to 60 doses). Consolidation, 0.15 mg per kg of body weight daily for 25 doses over a period of up to 5 weeks.
    - Children under 5 years of age—Use and dose must be determined by your doctor.

Precautions While Using This Medicine

It is very important that your doctor check your progress at regular visits to make sure that this medicine is working properly and to check for unwanted effects.

Acute promyelocytic leukemia (APL) can temporarily lower the number of white blood cells in your blood, increasing the chance of getting an infection. It can also lower the number of platelets, which are necessary for proper blood clotting. APL may also interact with medications which cause blood problems. Arsenic trioxide therapy may improve these conditions. If this occurs, there are certain precautions you can take, especially when your blood count is low, to reduce the risk of infection or bleeding:

- If you can, avoid people with infections. *Check with your doctor immediately* if you think you are getting an infection or if you get a fever or chills, cough or hoarseness, lower back or side pain, or painful or difficult urination.
- *Check with your doctor immediately* if you notice any unusual bleeding or bruising; black, tarry stools; blood in urine or stools; or pinpoint red spots on your skin.
- Be careful when using a regular toothbrush, dental floss, or toothpick. Your medical doctor, dentist, or nurse may recommend other ways to clean your teeth and gums. Check with your medical doctor before having any dental work done.
- Do not touch your eyes or the inside of your nose unless you have just washed your hands and have not touched anything else in the meantime.
- Be careful not to cut yourself when you are using sharp objects such as a safety razor or fingernail or toenail cutters.
- Avoid contact sports or other situations where bruising or injury could occur.

Side Effects of This Medicine

Along with its needed effects, a medicine may cause some unwanted effects. Although not all of these side effects may occur, if they do occur they may need medical attention.

Check with your doctor immediately if any of the following side effects occur:

More common (>50%)

Chills; convulsions (seizures); cough; decreased urine output; dry mouth; eye pain; general feeling of illness; headache; increased thirst; irregular heartbeat; loss of appetite; mood changes; muscle pain or cramps; nausea or vomiting; numbness or tingling in hands, feet, or lips; shortness of breath or trouble breathing; sore throat; unusual tiredness or weakness

Symptoms of Overdose

Get emergency help immediately if any of the following symptoms of overdose occur

Confusion; convulsions (seizures); muscle weakness, severe

Less common (10–50%)

Abdominal cramps; black, tarry stools; bluish lips or skin; blurred vision; chest pain; dizziness or lightheadedness; fever; flushed, dry skin; fruit-like breath odor; high or low blood pressure; increased hunger; increased urine output; irregular or pounding heartbeat or pulse; painful or difficult urination; sores, ulcers, or white spots on lips or in mouth; stomachache; sweating; swollen glands; unusual bleeding or bruising; unexplained weight loss; unusual weight gain; wheezing

Rare (<10%)

Anxiety; behavior changes similar to drunkenness; bleeding; blood in urine or stools; bluish fingernails, palms, or nailbeds; bruising; cloudy urine; cold sweats; cool pale skin; drowsiness; headache; large hives; persistent bleeding or oozing from puncture sites, mouth, or nose; rash; severe nausea; shakiness; sore mouth or tongue; swelling of eyelids, lips,

or face; vomiting of blood or material that looks like coffee grounds; white patches in mouth and/or on tongue

Other side effects may occur that usually do not need medical attention. These side effects may go away during treatment as your body adjusts to the medicine. However, check with your doctor if any of the following side effects continue or are bothersome.

More common (>50%)

Diarrhea

Less common (10–50%)

Acid or sour stomach; back pain; belching; bloating or swelling of face, hands, lower legs, and/or feet; bone pain; constipation; flushing; heartburn; heavy nonmenstrual vaginal bleeding; indigestion; itchy, red skin; injection site pain, redness, or swelling; itching; joint or muscle pain; limb pain; loss of appetite; mental depression; neck pain; nosebleeds; pale skin; shivering chills; trouble sleeping or getting to sleep; weight gain

Rare (<10%)

Agitation; blisters inside the mouth; coughing or spitting up blood; earache; eye dryness, redness, or pain; loss of bowel or bladder control; night sweats; rapid, shallow breathing; ringing in the ears; small red or purple spots on skin; swelling of abdominal or stomach area; swelling or puffiness of face or eyelids; swollen, painful, or tender lymph glands in neck, armpit, or groin

Other side effects not listed above may also occur in some patients. If you notice any other effects, check with your doctor.

Developed: 12/01/2000
Revised: 04/10/2001

ASCORBIC ACID (VITAMIN C)
Systemic

Commonly used brand name(s):

In the U.S.—

Ascorbicap	Cetane
Cebid Timecelles	Cevi-Bid
Cecon	Flavorcee
Cecore 500	Mega-C/A Plus
Cee-500	Ortho/CS
Cemill	Sunkist
Cenolate	

Generic name product may be available.

In Canada—
Apo-C

Description

Vitamins (VYE-ta-mins) are compounds that you *must* have for growth and health. They are needed in small amounts only and are usually available in the foods that you eat. Ascorbic (a-SKOR-bik) acid, also known as vitamin C, is necessary for wound healing. It is needed for many functions in the body, including helping the body use carbohydrates, fats, and protein. Vitamin C also strengthens blood vessel walls.

Lack of vitamin C can lead to a condition called scurvy, which causes muscle weakness, swollen and bleeding gums, loss of teeth, and bleeding under the skin, as well as tiredness and depression. Wounds also do not heal easily. Your health care professional may treat scurvy by prescribing vitamin C for you.

Some conditions may increase your need for vitamin C. These include:
- AIDS (acquired immune deficiency syndrome)
- Alcoholism
- Burns
- Cancer
- Diarrhea (prolonged)
- Fever (prolonged)
- Infection (prolonged)
- Intestinal diseases
- Overactive thyroid (hyperthyroidism)
- Stomach ulcer
- Stress (continuing)
- Surgical removal of stomach
- Tuberculosis

Also, the following groups of people may have a deficiency of vitamin C:
- Infants receiving unfortified formulas
- Smokers
- Patients using an artificial kidney (on hemodialysis)
- Patients who undergo surgery
- Individuals who are exposed to long periods of cold temperatures

Increased need for vitamin C should be determined by your health care professional.

Vitamin C may be used for other conditions as determined by your health care professional.

Claims that vitamin C is effective for preventing senility and the common cold, and for treating asthma, some mental problems, cancer, hardening of the arteries, allergies, eye ulcers, blood clots, gum disease, and pressure sores have not been proven. Although vitamin C is being used to reduce the risk of cardiovascular disease and certain types of cancer, there is not enough information to show that these uses are effective.

Injectable vitamin C is given by or under the supervision of a health care professional. Other forms of vitamin C are available without a prescription.

Vitamin C is available in the following dosage forms:

Oral
- Extended-release capsules (U.S.)
- Oral solution (U.S.)
- Syrup (U.S.)
- Tablets (U.S. and Canada)
- Chewable tablets (U.S. and Canada)
- Effervescent tablets (U.S.)
- Extended-release tablets (U.S. and Canada)

Parenteral
- Injection (U.S.)

Importance of Diet

For good health, it is important that you eat a balanced and varied diet. Follow carefully any diet program your health care professional may recommend. For your specific dietary vi-

tamin and/or mineral needs, ask your health care professional for a list of appropriate foods. If you think that you are not getting enough vitamins and/or minerals in your diet, you may choose to take a dietary supplement.

Vitamin C is found in various foods, including citrus fruits (oranges, lemons, grapefruit), green vegetables (peppers, broccoli, cabbage), tomatoes, and potatoes. It is best to eat fresh fruits and vegetables whenever possible since they contain the most vitamins. Food processing may destroy some of the vitamins. For example, exposure to air, drying, salting, or cooking (especially in copper pots), mincing of fresh vegetables, or mashing potatoes may reduce the amount of vitamin C in foods. Freezing does not usually cause loss of vitamin C unless foods are stored for a very long time.

Vitamins alone will not take the place of a good diet and will not provide energy. Your body also needs other substances found in food such as protein, minerals, carbohydrates, and fat. Vitamins themselves often cannot work without the presence of other foods.

The daily amount of vitamin C needed is defined in several different ways.

For U.S.—
- Recommended Dietary Allowances (RDAs) are the amount of vitamins and minerals needed to provide for adequate nutrition in most healthy persons. RDAs for a given nutrient may vary depending on a person's age, sex, and physical condition (e.g., pregnancy).
- Daily Values (DVs) are used on food and dietary supplement labels to indicate the percent of the recommended daily amount of each nutrient that a serving provides. DV replaces the previous designation of United States Recommended Daily Allowances (US-RDAs).

For Canada—
- Recommended Nutrient Intakes (RNIs) are used to determine the amounts of vitamins, minerals, and protein needed to provide adequate nutrition and lessen the risk of chronic disease.

Normal daily recommended intakes for vitamin C are generally defined as follows:

Persons	U.S. (mg)	Canada (mg)
Infants and children		
Birth to 3 years of age	30–40	20
4 to 6 years of age	45	25
7 to 10 years of age	45	25
Adolescent and adult males	50–60	25–40
Adolescent and adult females	50–60	25–30
Pregnant females	70	30–40
Breast-feeding females	90–95	55
Smokers	100	45–60

Before Using This Dietary Supplement

If you are taking this dietary supplement without a prescription, carefully read and follow any precautions on the label. For vitamin C, the following should be considered:

Allergies—Tell your health care professional if you have ever had any unusual or allergic reaction to ascorbic acid. Also, tell your health care professional if you are allergic to any other substances, such as foods, sulfites or other preservatives, or dyes.

Pregnancy—It is especially important that you are receiving enough vitamins when you become pregnant and that you continue to receive the right amount of vitamins throughout your pregnancy. Healthy fetal growth and development depend on a steady supply of nutrients from mother to fetus.

However, taking too much vitamin C daily throughout pregnancy may harm the fetus.

Breast-feeding—It is especially important that you receive the right amounts of vitamins so that your baby will also get the vitamins needed to grow properly. You should also check with your doctor if you are giving your baby an unfortified formula. In that case, the baby must get the vitamins needed some other way. However, taking large amounts of a dietary supplement while breast-feeding may be harmful to the mother and/or baby and should be avoided.

Children—Problems in children have not been reported with intake of normal daily recommended amounts.

Older adults—Problems in older adults have not been reported with intake of normal daily recommended amounts.

Medicines or other dietary supplements—Although certain medicines or dietary supplements should not be used together at all, in other cases they may be used together even if an interaction might occur. In these cases, your health care professional may want to change the dose, or other precautions may be necessary. Tell your health care professional if you are taking any other dietary supplement or any prescription or nonprescription (over-the-counter [OTC]) medicine.

Other medical problems—The presence of other medical problems may affect the use of vitamin C. Make sure you tell your health care professional if you have any other medical problems, especially:

- Blood problems—High doses of vitamin C may cause certain blood problems

- Diabetes mellitus (sugar diabetes)—Very high doses of vitamin C may interfere with tests for sugar in the urine

- Glucose-6-phosphate dehydrogenase (G6PD) deficiency—High doses of vitamin C may cause hemolytic anemia

- Kidney stones (history of)—High doses of vitamin C may increase risk of kidney stones in the urinary tract

Proper Use of This Dietary Supplement

Dosing—The amount of vitamin C needed to meet normal daily recommended intakes will be different for different individuals. The following information includes only the average amounts of vitamin C.

- For *oral* dosage form (capsules, tablets, oral solution, syrup):
  —To prevent deficiency, the amount taken by mouth is based on normal daily recommended intakes:
  For the U.S.
    - Adult and teenage males—50 to 60 milligrams (mg) per day.
    - Adult and teenage females—50 to 60 mg per day.
    - Pregnant females—70 mg per day.
    - Breast-feeding females—90 to 95 mg per day.
    - Smokers—100 mg per day.
    - Children 4 to 10 years of age—45 mg per day.
    - Children birth to 3 years of age—30 to 40 mg per day.

For Canada
    - Adult and teenage males—25 to 40 mg per day.
    - Adult and teenage females—25 to 30 mg per day.
    - Pregnant females—30 to 40 mg per day.
    - Breast-feeding females—55 mg per day.
    - Smokers—45 to 60 mg per day.
    - Children 4 to 10 years of age—25 mg per day.
    - Children birth to 3 years of age—20 mg per day.
  —To treat deficiency:
    - Adults and teenagers—Treatment dose is determined by prescriber for each individual based on the severity of deficiency. The following dose has been determined for scurvy: 500 mg a day for at least 2 weeks.
    - Children—Treatment dose is determined by prescriber for each individual based on the severity of deficiency. The following dose has been determined for scurvy: 100 to 300 mg a day for at least 2 weeks.

For those individuals taking the *oral liquid form* of vitamin C:

- This preparation is to be taken by mouth even though it comes in a dropper bottle.
- This dietary supplement may be dropped directly into the mouth or mixed with cereal, fruit juice, or other food.

Missed dose—If you miss taking a vitamin for one or more days there is no cause for concern, since it takes some time for your body to become seriously low in vitamins. However, if your health care professional has recommended that you take this vitamin, try to remember to take it as directed every day.

Storage—To store this dietary supplement:

- Keep out of the reach of children.
- Store away from heat and direct light.
- Do not store in the bathroom, near the kitchen sink, or in other damp places. Heat or moisture may cause the dietary supplement to break down.
- Keep the oral liquid form of this dietary supplement from freezing.
- Do not keep outdated dietary supplements or those no longer needed. Be sure that any discarded dietary supplement is out of the reach of children.

Precautions While Using This Dietary Supplement

Vitamin C is not stored in the body. If you take more than you need, the extra vitamin C will pass into your urine. Very large doses may also interfere with tests for sugar in diabetics and with tests for blood in the stool.

Side Effects of This Dietary Supplement

Along with its needed effects, a dietary supplement may cause some unwanted effects. Although not all of these side effects may occur, if they do occur, they may need medical attention.

Check with your health care professional as soon as possible if the following side effect occurs:

Less common or rare—with high doses
Side or lower back pain

Other side effects may occur that usually do not need medical attention. These side effects may go away during treatment as your body adjusts to the dietary supplement. However, check with your health care professional as soon as possible if any of the following side effects continue or are bothersome:

Less common or rare—with high doses

Diarrhea; dizziness or faintness (with the injection only); flushing or redness of skin; headache; increase in urination (mild); nausea or vomiting; stomach cramps

Other side effects not listed above may also occur in some individuals. If you notice any other effects, check with your health care professional.

Additional Information

Once a medicine or dietary supplement has been approved for marketing for a certain use, experience may show that it is also useful for other medical problems. Although these uses are not included in product labeling, vitamin C is used in certain patients with the following medical conditions:

- Overdose of iron (to help another drug in decreasing iron levels in the body)
- Methemoglobinemia (a blood disease)

Other than the above information, there is no additional information relating to proper use, precautions, or side effects for these uses.

Revised: 05/01/95

ASPARAGINASE   Systemic

Commonly used brand name(s):

In the U.S.—
Elspar

In Canada—
Kidrolase

Another commonly used name is colaspase.

Description

Asparaginase (a-SPARE-a-gi-nase) belongs to the group of medicines known as enzymes. It is used to treat some kinds of cancer of the blood. It may also be used to treat other kinds of cancer, as determined by your doctor.

All cells need a chemical called asparagine to stay alive. Normal cells can make this chemical for themselves, while cancer cells cannot. Asparaginase breaks down asparagine in the body. Since the cancer cells cannot make more asparagine, they die.

Before you begin treatment with asparaginase, you and your doctor should talk about the good this medicine will do as well as the risks of using it.

Asparaginase is to be administered only by or under the supervision of your doctor. It is available in the following dosage form:

Parenteral
- Injection (U.S. and Canada)

Before Using This Medicine

In deciding to use a medicine, the risks of taking the medicine must be weighed against the good it will do. This is a decision you and your doctor will make. For asparaginase, the following should be considered:

Allergies—Tell your doctor if you have ever had any unusual or allergic reaction to asparaginase.

Pregnancy—Asparaginase has not been studied in pregnant women. However, studies in mice and rats have shown that asparaginase slows the weight gain of infants and may also increase the risk of birth defects or cause a decrease in successful pregnancies. In addition, asparaginase has caused birth defects in rabbits.

It is best to use some kind of birth control while you are receiving asparaginase. Tell your doctor right away if you think you have become pregnant while receiving asparaginase.

Breast-feeding—It is not known whether asparaginase passes into breast milk. However, because asparaginase may cause serious side effects, breast-feeding is generally not recommended while you are receiving it.

Children—This medicine has been tested in children and has not been shown to cause different side effects or problems than it does in adults. In fact, the side effects of this medicine seem to be less severe in children than in adults.

Older adults—Many medicines have not been studied specifically in older people. Therefore, it may not be known whether they work exactly the same way they do in younger adults or if they cause different side effects or problems in older people. There is no specific information comparing use of asparaginase in the elderly with use in other age groups.

Other medicines—Although certain medicines should not be used together at all, in other cases two different medicines may be used together even if an interaction might occur. In these cases, your doctor may want to change the dose, or other precautions may be necessary. When you are receiving asparaginase it is especially important that your health care professional know if you are taking any of the following:

- Probenecid (e.g., Benemid) or
- Sulfinpyrazone (e.g., Anturane)—Asparaginase may raise the concentration of uric acid in the blood. Since these medicines are used to lower uric acid levels, they may not work as well in patients receiving asparaginase

- If you have ever been treated with radiation or cancer medicines—Asparaginase may increase the total effects of these medications and radiation therapy

Other medical problems—The presence of other medical problems may affect the use of asparaginase. Make sure you tell your doctor if you have any other medical problems, especially:

- Chickenpox (including recent exposure) or
- Herpes zoster (shingles)—Risk of severe disease affecting other parts of the body

- Diabetes mellitus (sugar diabetes)—Asparaginase may increase glucose (sugar) in the blood

- Gout or
- Kidney stones—Asparaginase may increase levels of uric acid in the body, which can cause gout or kidney stones

- Infection—Asparaginase can reduce your body's ability to fight infection

- Liver disease—Asparaginase may worsen the condition

• Pancreatitis (inflammation of the pancreas)—Asparaginase may cause pancreatitis

Proper Use of This Medicine

This medicine is usually given together with certain other medicines. If you are using a combination of medicines, it is important that you receive each one at the proper time. If you are taking some of these medicines by mouth, ask your health care professional to help you plan a way to remember to take them at the right times.

While you are using this medicine, your doctor may want you to drink extra fluids so that you will pass more urine. This will help prevent kidney problems and keep your kidneys working well.

This medicine often causes nausea, vomiting, and loss of appetite. However, it is very important that you continue to receive the medicine, even if you begin to feel ill. After several doses, your stomach upset should lessen. Ask your health care professional for ways to lessen these effects.

Dosing—The dose of asparaginase will be different for different patients. The dose that is used may depend on a number of things, including what the medicine is being used for, the patient's weight, and whether or not other medicines are also being taken. *If you are receiving asparaginase at home, follow your doctor's orders or the directions on the label.* If you have any questions about the proper dose of asparaginase, ask your doctor.

Precautions While Using This Medicine

It is very important that your doctor check your progress at regular visits to make sure that this medicine is working properly and to check for unwanted effects.

While you are being treated with asparaginase, and after you stop treatment with it, *do not have any immunizations (vaccinations) without your doctor's approval.* Asparaginase may lower your body's resistance and there is a chance you might get the infection the immunization is meant to prevent. In addition, other persons living in your household should not take oral polio vaccine since there is a chance they could pass the polio virus on to you. Also, avoid persons who have taken oral polio vaccine within the last several months. Do not get close to them, and do not stay in the same room with them for very long. If you cannot take these precautions, you should consider wearing a protective face mask that covers the nose and mouth.

Before you have any medical tests, tell the medical doctor in charge that you are receiving this medicine. The results of thyroid tests may be affected by this medicine.

Side Effects of This Medicine

Along with its needed effects, a medicine may cause some unwanted effects. Some side effects will have signs or symptoms that you can see or feel. Your doctor may watch for others by doing certain tests. Some of the unwanted effects that may be caused by asparaginase are listed below. Although not all of these effects may occur, if they do occur, they may need medical attention.

Also, because of the way these medicines act on the body, there is a chance that they might cause other unwanted effects that may not occur until months or years after the medicine is used. These delayed effects may include certain types of cancer, such as leukemia. Discuss these possible effects with your doctor.

Check with your doctor or nurse immediately if any of the following side effects occur:
More common
Joint pain; puffy face; skin rash or itching; stomach pain (severe) with nausea and vomiting; trouble in breathing
Less common
Frequent urination; swelling of feet or lower legs; unusual thirst
Rare
Fever or chills; headache (severe); inability to move arm or leg; infection; pain in lower legs; unusual bleeding or bruising

Check with your health care professional as soon as possible if any of the following side effects occur:
Less common
Confusion; drowsiness; hallucinations (seeing, hearing, or feeling things that are not there); lower back or side pain; mental depression; nervousness; sores in mouth or on lips; unusual tiredness

This medicine may also cause the following side effect that your doctor will watch for:
More common
Bleeding problems; liver problems

Other side effects may occur that usually do not need medical attention. These side effects may go away during treatment as your body adjusts to the medicine. Also, your health care professional may be able to tell you about ways to prevent or reduce some of these side effects. Check with your health care professional if any of the following side effects continue or are bothersome or if you have any questions about them:
More common
Headache (mild); loss of appetite; nausea or vomiting; stomach cramps; weight loss

After you stop receiving asparaginase, it may still produce some side effects that need attention. During this period of time, *check with your doctor or nurse immediately* if any of the following side effects occur:
Headache (severe); inability to move arm or leg; stomach pain (severe) with nausea and vomiting

Other side effects not listed above may also occur in some patients. If you notice any other effects, check with your health care professional.

Additional Information

Once a medicine has been approved for marketing for a certain use, experience may show that it is also useful for other medical problems. Although these uses are not included in product labeling, asparaginase is used in certain patients with the following condition:

• Cancer of the lymph system (certain types)

Other than the above information, there is no additional information relating to proper use, precautions, or side effects for this use.

Revised: 04/09/93
Interim revision: 04/29/94; 08/14/98

ASPIRIN, SODIUM BICARBONATE, AND CITRIC ACID   Systemic

Commonly used brand name(s):

In the U.S.—
Alka-Seltzer Effervescent Pain Reliever and Antacid

Flavored Alka-Seltzer Effervescent Pain Reliever and Antacid

In Canada—
Alka-Seltzer Effervescent Pain Reliever and Antacid

Flavored Alka-Seltzer Effervescent Pain Reliever and Antacid

Other commonly used names for aspirin are acetylsalicylic acid and ASA. Because Aspirin is a brand name in Canada, ASA is the term that commonly appears on Canadian product labels.

Description

Aspirin, sodium bicarbonate, and citric acid (AS-pir-in, SOE-dee-um bye-KAR-boe-nate, and SI-trik AS-id) combination is used to relieve pain occurring together with heartburn, sour stomach, or acid indigestion.

The aspirin in this combination is the pain reliever. Aspirin belongs to the group of medicines known as salicylates (sa-LISS-ih-lates) and to the group of medicines known as anti-inflammatory analgesics. The sodium bicarbonate in this medicine is an antacid. It neutralizes stomach acid by combining with it to form a new substance that is not an acid.

Aspirin, sodium bicarbonate, and citric acid combination may also be used to lessen the chance of heart attack, stroke, or other problems that may occur when a blood vessel is blocked by blood clots. The aspirin in this medicine helps prevent dangerous blood clots from forming. However, this effect of aspirin may increase the chance of serious bleeding in some people. Therefore, aspirin should be used for this purpose only when your doctor decides, after studying your medical condition and history, that the danger of blood clots is greater than the risk of bleeding. *Do not take aspirin to prevent blood clots or a heart attack unless it has been ordered by your doctor.*

This combination medicine is available without a prescription. However, your doctor may have special instructions on the proper dose for your medical condition.

Aspirin, sodium bicarbonate, and citric acid combination is available in the following dosage form:

Oral
- Effervescent tablets (U.S. and Canada)

Before Using This Medicine

If you are taking this medicine without a prescription, carefully read and follow any precautions on the label. For aspirin, sodium bicarbonate, and citric acid combination, the following should be considered:

Allergies—Tell your doctor if you have ever had any unusual or allergic reaction to aspirin or other salicylates, including methyl salicylate (oil of wintergreen), or to any of the following medicines:

Diclofenac (e.g., Voltaren)
Diflunisal (e.g., Dolobid)
Etodolac (e.g., Lodine)
Fenoprofen (e.g., Nalfon)
Floctafenine (e.g., Idarac)
Flurbiprofen, oral (e.g., Ansaid)

Ibuprofen (e.g., Motrin)
Indomethacin (e.g., Indocin)
Ketoprofen (e.g., Orudis)
Ketorolac (e.g., Toradol)
Meclofenamate (e.g., Meclomen)
Mefenamic acid (e.g., Ponstel)
Nabumetone (e.g., Relafen)
Naproxen (e.g., Naprosyn)
Oxaprozin (e.g., Daypro)
Oxyphenbutazone (e.g., Tandearil)
Phenylbutazone (e.g., Butazolidin)
Piroxicam (e.g., Feldene)
Sulindac (e.g., Clinoril)
Suprofen (e.g., Suprol)
Tenoxicam (e.g., Mobiflex)
Tiaprofenic acid (e.g., Surgam)
Tolmetin (e.g., Tolectin)
Zomepirac (e.g., Zomax)

Also tell your health care professional if you are allergic to any other substances, such as foods, preservatives, or dyes.

Diet—Make certain your health care professional knows if you are on any special diet, such as a low-sodium or low-sugar diet. This medicine contains a large amount of sodium (more than 500 mg in each tablet).

Pregnancy—Studies in humans have not shown that aspirin causes birth defects in humans. However, it has been shown to cause birth defects in animal studies.

Do not take aspirin during the last 3 months of pregnancy unless it has been ordered by your doctor. Some reports have suggested that too much use of aspirin late in pregnancy may cause a decrease in the newborn's weight and possible death of the fetus or newborn infant. However, the mothers in these reports had been taking much larger amounts of aspirin than are usually recommended. Studies of mothers taking aspirin in the doses that are usually recommended did not show these unwanted effects. However, there is a chance that regular use of aspirin late in pregnancy may cause unwanted effects on the heart or blood flow in the fetus or in the newborn infant.

Use of aspirin during the last 2 weeks of pregnancy may cause bleeding problems in the fetus before or during delivery or in the newborn infant. Also, too much use of aspirin during the last 3 months of pregnancy may increase the length of pregnancy, prolong labor, cause other problems during delivery, or cause severe bleeding in the mother before, during, or after delivery.

The sodium in this combination medicine can cause your body to hold water. This may result in swelling and weight gain. Therefore, you should not use this combination medicine if you tend to hold body water.

Breast-feeding—Aspirin passes into the breast milk. However, aspirin (in the amounts used to relieve pain or prevent blood clots), sodium bicarbonate, and citric acid have not been reported to cause problems in nursing babies.

Children—*Do not give any medicine containing aspirin to a child with fever or other symptoms of a virus infection, especially flu or chickenpox, without first discussing its use with your child's doctor.* This is very important because aspirin may cause a serious illness called Reye's syndrome in children with fever caused by a virus infection, especially flu or chickenpox. Children who do not have a virus infection may also be more sensitive to the effects of aspirin, especially if they have a fever or have lost large amounts of body fluid because of vomiting, diarrhea, or sweating. This may increase the chance of side effects during treatment.

Teenagers—*Teenagers with fever or other symptoms of a virus infection, especially flu or chickenpox, should check with a doctor before taking this medicine.* The aspirin in this combination medicine may cause a serious illness called Reye's syndrome in teenagers with fever caused by a virus infection, especially flu or chickenpox.

Older adults—People 60 years of age and older are especially sensitive to the effects of aspirin. This may increase the chance of side effects during treatment. Also, the sodium in this combination medicine can be harmful to some elderly people, especially if large amounts of the medicine are taken regularly. Therefore, it is best that older people not use this medicine for more than 5 days in a row, unless otherwise directed by their doctor.

Other medicines—Although certain medicines should not be used together at all, in other cases two different medicines may be used together even if an interaction might occur. In these cases, your doctor may want to change the dose, or other precautions may be necessary. When you are taking this combination medicine, it is especially important that your health care professional know if you are taking any of the following:

- Anticoagulants (blood thinners) or
- Carbenicillin by injection (e.g., Geopen) or
- Cefamandole (e.g., Mandol) or
- Cefoperazone (e.g., Cefobid) or
- Cefotetan (e.g., Cefotan) or
- Dipyridamole (e.g., Persantine) or
- Divalproex (e.g., Depakote) or
- Heparin or
- Pentoxifylline (e.g., Trental) or
- Plicamycin (e.g., Mithracin) or
- Ticarcillin (e.g., Ticar) or
- Valproic acid (e.g., Depakene)—Use of these medicines together with aspirin may increase the chance of bleeding

- Antidiabetics, oral (diabetes medicine you take by mouth)—Aspirin may increase the effects of these medicines; a change in dose may be needed

- Ciprofloxacin (e.g., Cipro) or
- Enoxacin (e.g., Penetrex) or
- Itraconazole (e.g., Sporanox) or
- Ketoconazole (e.g., Nizoral) or
- Lomefloxacin (e.g., Maxaquin) or
- Methenamine (e.g., Mandelamine) or
- Norfloxacin (e.g., Noroxin) or
- Ofloxacin (e.g., Floxin) or
- Tetracyclines (medicine for infection), taken by mouth—Sodium bicarbonate can keep these medicines from working properly

- Mecamylamine (e.g., Inversine)—Sodium bicarbonate may increase the chance of unwanted effects by causing mecamylamine to stay in your body longer than usual

- Medicine for pain and/or inflammation (except narcotics) or
- Methotrexate (e.g., Mexate) or
- Vancomycin (e.g., Vancocin)—The chance of serious side effects may be increased

- Probenecid (e.g., Benemid) or

- Sulfinpyrazone (e.g., Anturane)—Aspirin can keep these medicines from working properly when they are used to treat gout

Other medical problems—The presence of other medical problems may affect the use of this combination medicine. Make sure you tell your doctor if you have any other medical problems, especially:

- Anemia or
- Stomach ulcer or other stomach problems—Aspirin can make these conditions worse

- Appendicitis (symptoms of, such as stomach or lower abdominal pain, cramping, bloating, soreness, nausea, or vomiting)—Sodium bicarbonate can make your condition worse; also, people who may have appendicitis need medical attention and should not try to treat themselves

- Asthma, allergies, and nasal polyps (history of) or
- Kidney disease or
- Liver disease—The chance of serious side effects may be increased

- Edema (swelling of face, fingers, feet, or lower legs caused by too much water in the body) or
- Heart disease or
- High blood pressure or
- Toxemia of pregnancy—The sodium in this combination medicine can make these conditions worse

- Gout—Aspirin can make this condition worse and can also keep some medicines used to treat gout from working properly

- Hemophilia or other bleeding problems—Aspirin increases the chance of serious bleeding

Proper Use of This Medicine

Unless otherwise directed by your doctor, do not take more of this medicine than is recommended on the package label. If too much is taken, serious side effects may occur.

Do not take this medicine if it has a strong vinegar-like odor. This odor means the aspirin in it is breaking down. If you have any questions about this, check with your health care professional.

To use this medicine:
- The tablets must be dissolved in water before taking. Do not swallow the tablets or any pieces of the tablets.
- Place the number of tablets needed for one dose (1 or 2 tablets) into a glass. Then add ½ glass (4 ounces) of cool water.
- Check to be sure that the tablets have disappeared completely. This shows that all of the medicine is in the liquid. Then drink all of the liquid. You may drink the liquid while it is still fizzing or after the fizzing stops.
- Add a little more water to the glass and drink that, to make sure that you get the full amount of the medicine.

Dosing—The dose of this combination medicine will be different for different people. *Follow your doctor's orders or the directions on the label.* The following information includes only the average doses of this combination medicine. *If your dose is different, do not change it* unless your doctor tells you to do so.

- For *oral* dosage forms (effervescent tablets):
  —For pain and upset stomach:
    - Adults and teenagers—One or two regular-strength (325-milligram [mg]) tablets every four to six hours as needed, one extra-strength (500-mg) tablet every four to six hours as needed, or two extra-strength (500-mg) tablets every six hours as needed, dissolved in water. Elderly people should not take more than four regular-strength or extra-strength tablets a day. Other adults and teenagers should not take more than 6 regular-strength flavored tablets, 8 regular-strength unflavored tablets, or 7 extra-strength tablets a day.
    - Children—The dose depends on the child's age.
      —Children younger than 3 years of age: Use and dose must be determined by your doctor.
      —Children 3 to 5 years of age: One-half of a regular-strength (325-mg) tablet, dissolved in water, every four to six hours as needed.
      —Children 6 to 12 years of age: One regular-strength (325-mg) tablet, dissolved in water, every four to six hours as needed.
  —For reducing the chance of heart attack, stroke, or other problems that may occur when a blood vessel is blocked by blood clots:
    - Adults—One regular-strength (325-mg) tablet a day, dissolved in water.
    - Children and teenagers—Use and dose must be determined by your doctor.

Missed dose—If your doctor has ordered you to take this medicine according to a regular schedule and you miss a dose, take it as soon as you remember. However, if it is almost time for your next dose, skip the missed dose and go back to your regular dosing schedule. Do not double doses.

Storage—To store this medicine:
- Keep out of the reach of children. Overdose is very dangerous in young children.
- Store away from heat and direct light.
- Do not store in the bathroom, near the kitchen sink, or in other damp places. Heat or moisture may cause the medicine to break down.
- Do not keep outdated medicine or medicine no longer needed. Be sure that any discarded medicine is out of the reach of children.

Precautions While Using This Medicine

If you will be taking this medicine for a long time (more than 5 days in a row for children or 10 days in a row for adults), your doctor should check your progress at regular visits.

Check with your doctor if your pain and/or upset stomach last for more than 10 days for adults or 5 days for children or if they get worse, if new symptoms occur, or if the painful area is red or swollen. These could be signs of a serious condition that needs medical treatment.

The sodium bicarbonate in this combination medicine can keep other medicines from working properly if the 2 medicines are taken too close together. *Always take this medicine:*
- *At least 6 hours before or 2 hours after taking ciprofloxacin (e.g., Cipro) or lomefloxacin (e.g., Maxaquin).*
- *At least 8 hours before or 2 hours after taking enoxacin (e.g., Penetrex).*
- *At least 2 hours after taking itraconazole (e.g., Sporanox).*
- *At least 3 hours before or after taking ketoconazole (e.g., Nizoral).*
- *At least 2 hours before or after taking norfloxacin (e.g., Noroxin) or ofloxacin (e.g., Floxin).*
- *At least 3 or 4 hours before or after taking a tetracycline antibiotic by mouth.*
- *At least 1 or 2 hours before or after taking any other medicine by mouth.*

If you are also taking a laxative that contains cellulose, take this combination medicine at least 2 hours before or after you take the laxative. Taking the medicines too close together may lessen the effects of aspirin.

Check the labels of all nonprescription (over-the-counter [OTC]) and prescription medicines you now take. If any contain aspirin or other salicylates, including bismuth subsalicylate (e.g., Pepto-Bismol), magnesium salicylate (e.g., Nuprin Backache Caplets), or salsalate (e.g., Disalcid); if any contain salicylic acid (present in some shampoos or medicines for your skin); or if any contain sodium, *check with your health care professional.* Taking other salicylate-containing or other sodium-containing products together with this medicine may cause an overdose.

Do not take aspirin for 5 days before any surgery, including dental surgery, unless otherwise directed by your medical doctor or dentist. Taking aspirin during this time may cause bleeding problems.

For patients taking this medicine to lessen the chance of a heart attack, stroke, or other problems caused by blood clots:
- *Take only the amount of aspirin ordered by your doctor.* If you need a medicine to relieve pain, a fever, or arthritis, your doctor may not want you to take extra aspirin. It is a good idea to discuss this with your doctor, so that you will know ahead of time what medicine to take.
- *Do not stop taking this medicine for any reason without first checking with the doctor who directed you to take it.*

Taking certain other medicines together with a salicylate may increase the chance of unwanted effects. The risk will depend on how much of each medicine you take every day, and on how long you take the medicines together. If your doctor directs you to take these medicines together on a regular basis, follow his or her directions carefully. However, *do not take any of the following medicines together with a salicylate for more than a few days, unless your doctor has directed you to do so and is following your progress:*

Acetaminophen (e.g., Tylenol)
Diclofenac (e.g., Voltaren)
Diflunisal (e.g., Dolobid)
Etodolac (e.g., Lodine)
Fenoprofen (e.g., Nalfon)
Floctafenine (e.g., Idarac)
Flurbiprofen, oral (e.g., Ansaid)
Ibuprofen (e.g., Motrin)
Indomethacin (e.g., Indocin)
Ketoprofen (e.g., Orudis)
Ketorolac (e.g., Toradol)
Meclofenamate (e.g., Meclomen)
Mefenamic acid (e.g., Ponstel)
Nabumetone (e.g., Relafen)
Naproxen (e.g., Naprosyn)
Oxaprozin (e.g., Daypro)

Phenylbutazone (e.g., Butazolidin)
Piroxicam (e.g., Feldene)
Sulindac (e.g., Clinoril)
Tenoxicam (e.g., Mobiflex)
Tiaprofenic acid (e.g., Surgam)
Tolmetin (e.g., Tolectin)

If you will be taking more than an occasional 1 or 2 doses of this medicine:

- *Do not drink alcoholic beverages.* Drinking alcoholic beverages while you are taking aspirin, especially if you take aspirin regularly or in large amounts, may increase the chance of stomach problems.
- *Do not drink a lot of milk or eat a lot of milk products.* To do so may increase the chance of side effects.
- To prevent side effects caused by too much sodium in the body, you may need to limit the amount of sodium in the foods you eat. Some foods that contain large amounts of sodium are canned soup, canned vegetables, pickles, ketchup, green and ripe (black) olives, relish, frankfurters and other sausage-type meats, soy sauce, and carbonated beverages. If you have any questions about this, check with your health care professional.

Before you have any medical tests, tell the person in charge that you are taking this medicine. The results of some tests may be affected by the aspirin in this combination medicine.

For *diabetic patients:*

- Aspirin can cause false urine glucose (sugar) test results if you regularly take 8 or more 324-mg, or 4 or more 500-mg (extra-strength), tablets a day. Smaller amounts or occasional use of aspirin usually will not affect the test results. However, check with your health care professional if you notice any change in your urine glucose test results. This is especially important if your diabetes is not well-controlled.

If you think that you or anyone else may have taken an overdose, get emergency help at once. Taking an overdose of aspirin may cause unconsciousness or death, especially in young children. Signs of overdose include convulsions (seizures), hearing loss, confusion, ringing or buzzing in the ears, severe drowsiness or tiredness, severe excitement or nervousness, and fast or deep breathing.

Side Effects of This Medicine

Along with its needed effects, a medicine may cause some unwanted effects. Although the following side effects occur very rarely when 1 or 2 doses of this combination medicine is taken occasionally, they may be more likely to occur if:

- too much medicine is taken.
- the medicine is taken several times a day.
- the medicine is taken for more than a few days in a row.

Get emergency help immediately if any of the following side effects occur:

Any loss of hearing; bloody urine; confusion; convulsions (seizures); diarrhea (severe or continuing); difficulty in swallowing; dizziness, lightheadedness, or feeling faint (severe); drowsiness (severe); excitement or nervousness (severe); fast or deep breathing; flushing, redness, or other change in skin color; hallucinations (seeing, hearing, or feeling things that are not there); nausea or vomiting (severe or continuing); shortness of breath, troubled breathing, tightness in chest, or wheezing; stomach pain (severe or continuing);

swelling of eyelids, face, or lips; unexplained fever; uncontrollable flapping movements of the hands (especially in elderly patients); vision problems

Signs of overdose in children

Changes in behavior; drowsiness or tiredness (severe); fast or deep breathing

Also, check with your doctor as soon as possible if any of the following side effects occur:

Less common or rare

Bloody or black, tarry stools; frequent urge to urinate; headache (severe or continuing); increased blood pressure; loss of appetite (continuing); mood or mental changes; muscle pain or twitching; ringing or buzzing in ears (continuing); skin rash, hives, or itching; slow breathing; swelling of face, fingers, ankles, feet, or lower legs; unpleasant taste; unusual tiredness or weakness; vomiting of blood or material that looks like coffee grounds; weight gain (unusual)

Other side effects may occur that usually do not need medical attention. These side effects may go away during treatment as your body adjusts to the medicine. However, check with your health care professional if any of the following side effects continue or are bothersome:

Heartburn or indigestion; increased thirst; nausea or vomiting; stomach pain (mild)

Other side effects not listed above may also occur in some patients. If you notice any other effects, check with your doctor.

Revised: 08/29/94

ATORVASTATIN   Systemic

Commonly used brand name(s):

In the U.S.—
Lipitor
Generic name product may be available.

Description

Atorvastatin (a-TOR-va-stat-in) is used to lower cholesterol and triglyceride (fat-like substances) levels in the blood. Using this medicine may help prevent medical problems caused by such substances clogging the blood vessels.

Atorvastatin belongs to the group of medicines called 3-hydroxy-3-methylglutaryl coenzyme A (HMG-CoA) reductase inhibitors. It works by blocking an enzyme that is needed by the body to make cholesterol, thereby reducing the amount of cholesterol in the blood.

Atorvastatin is available only with your doctor's prescription, in the following dosage form:

Oral

- Tablets (U.S.)

Before Using This Medicine

In addition to its helpful effects in treating your medical problem, this type of medicine may have some harmful effects.

In deciding to use a medicine, the risks of taking the medicine must be weighed against the good it will do. This is a decision you and your doctor will make. For atorvastatin, the following should be considered:

Allergies—Tell your doctor if you have ever had any unusual or allergic reaction to atorvastatin. Also tell your health care professional if you are allergic to any other substances, such as foods, preservatives, or dyes.

Diet—Before prescribing medicine for your condition, your doctor will probably try to control your condition by prescribing a personal diet for you. Such a diet may be low in fats, sugars, and/or cholesterol. Many people are able to control their condition by carefully following their doctor's orders for proper diet and exercise. *Medicine is prescribed only when additional help is needed* and is effective only when a schedule of diet and exercise is properly followed.

Also, this medicine is less effective if you are greatly overweight. It may be very important for you to go on a weight-reducing diet. However, check with your doctor before going on any diet.

Pregnancy—Atorvastatin should not be used during pregnancy or by women who plan to become pregnant in the near future. This medicine blocks formation of cholesterol, which is necessary for the fetus to develop properly. Atorvastatin may cause birth defects or other problems in the baby if taken during pregnancy. An effective form of birth control should be used during treatment with these medicines. *Check with your doctor immediately if you think you have become pregnant while taking this medicine.* Be sure you have discussed this with your doctor.

Breast-feeding—It is not known if atorvastatin passes into breast milk. However, it should not be used during breast-feeding because it may cause serious unwanted effects in nursing babies.

Children—Studies on atorvastatin have been done only in adult patients and there is no specific information comparing use of atorvastatin in children with use in other age groups.

Older adults—This medicine has been tested in a limited number of patients 65 years of age or older and has not been shown to cause different problems in older people than it does in younger adults. However, blood levels of atorvastatin tend to be higher in older people than they do in younger adults.

Other medicines—Although certain medicines should not be used together at all, in other cases two different medicines may be used together even if an interaction might occur. In these cases, your doctor may want to change the dose, or other precautions may be necessary. When you are taking atorvastatin it is especially important that your health care professional know if you are taking any of the following medications:

- Antifungals, azole (e.g., Diflucan) or
- Erythromycin (e.g., Erythrocin) or
- Gemfibrozil (e.g., Lopid) or
- Immunosuppressants, especially cyclosporine (e.g., Sandimmune) or
- Niacin (nicotinic acid)—Use of these medicines with atorvastatin may increase the risk of developing muscle problems (causing the release of muscle pigment into the urine) that may lead to kidney failure

Other medical problems—The presence of other medical problems may affect the use of atorvastatin. Make sure you tell your doctor if you have any other medical problems, especially:

- Alcohol abuse (or history of) or

- Liver disease (or history of) or
- Liver enzymes, persistently high levels—Use of this medicine may make liver problems worse

- Convulsions (seizures), not well-controlled, or
- Electrolyte or metabolic enzyme deficiencies or disorders or
- Infection, severe or
- Low blood pressure or
- Major surgery or trauma, recent—Patients with these conditions may be at risk of developing muscle problems (causing the release of muscle pigment into the urine) that may lead to kidney failure

Proper Use of This Medicine

Use this medicine only as directed by your doctor. Do not use more or less of it, and do not use it more often or for a longer time than your doctor ordered. Also, this medicine works best if there is a constant amount in the blood. To help keep this amount constant, do not miss any doses and take the medicine at the same time each day.

Remember that this medicine will not cure your condition but it does help control it. Therefore, you must continue to take it as directed if you expect to keep your cholesterol levels down.

Follow carefully the special diet your doctor gave you. This is the most important part of controlling your condition and is necessary if the medicine is to work properly.

Atorvastatin should not be taken with large amounts of grapefruit juice or other grapefruit products because these may increase the concentrations of atorvastatin in the body

Dosing—The dose of atorvastatin will be different for different patients. *Follow your doctor's orders or the directions on the label.* The following information includes only the average doses of atorvastatin. *If your dose is different, do not change it* unless your doctor tells you to do so:

- For *oral* dosage form (tablets):
  —Adults: 10 milligrams (mg) once daily. Your doctor may increase your dose if needed.
  —Children: Use and dose must be determined by your doctor.

Missed dose—If you miss a dose of this medicine, take it as soon as possible. However, if it is almost time for your next dose, skip the missed dose and go back to your regular dosing schedule. Do not double doses.

Storage—To store this medicine:
- Keep out of the reach of children.
- Store away from heat and direct light.
- Do not store in the bathroom, near the kitchen sink, or in other damp places. Heat or moisture may cause the medicine to break down.
- Do not keep outdated medicine or medicine no longer needed. Be sure that any discarded medicine is out of the reach of children.

Precautions While Using This Medicine

It is very important that your doctor check your progress at regular visits. This will allow your doctor to see if the medicine is working properly to lower your cholesterol and triglyceride levels and to decide if you should continue to take it.

Check with your doctor immediately if you think that you may be pregnant. HMG-CoA reductase inhibitors may cause birth defects or other problems in the baby if taken during pregnancy.

All rights reserved

Before having any kind of surgery (including dental surgery) or emergency treatment, tell the medical doctor or dentist in charge that you are taking this medicine.

Do not take over-the-counter (OTC) niacin preparations without consulting your doctor. Niacin may increase atorvastatin's adverse effects on muscle, which can lead to serious kidney problems.

Do not use excessive amounts of alcohol while taking atorvastatin because it can worsen the adverse effects of this medicine on the liver.

Check with your doctor immediately if you experience unexplained muscle pain, tenderness, or weakness, especially if it is accompanied by unusual tiredness or fever, because the medicine's adverse effects on muscle can lead to serious kidney problems.

Side Effects of This Medicine

Along with its needed effects, a medicine may cause some unwanted effects. Although not all of these side effects may occur, if they do occur they may need medical attention.

Check with your doctor immediately if any of the following side effects occur:

Less common or rare
> Muscle cramps, pain, stiffness, swelling, or weakness, especially if accompanied by unusual tiredness or fever

Other side effects may occur that usually do not need medical attention. These side effects may go away during treatment as your body adjusts to the medicine. However, check with your doctor if any of the following side effects continue or are bothersome:

Less common
> Abdominal pain; belching or excessive gas; constipation; diarrhea; heartburn, indigestion, or stomach discomfort; skin rash

Other side effects not listed above may also occur in some patients. If you notice any other effects, check with your doctor.

Developed: 08/13/1998
Revised: 08/07/2000

ATOVAQUONE   Systemic

Commonly used brand name(s):

In the U.S.—
> Mepron

In Canada—
> Mepron

Description

Atovaquone (a-TOE-va-kwone) is used to treat and to prevent *Pneumocystis carinii* (noo-moe-SISS-tis) pneumonia (PCP), a very serious kind of pneumonia. This particular kind of pneumonia occurs commonly in patients whose immune systems are not working normally, such as cancer patients, transplant patients, and patients with acquired immune deficiency syndrome (AIDS).

This medicine is available only with your doctor's prescription, in the following dosage form:

Oral
- Oral suspension (U.S.)
- Tablets (Canada)

Before Receiving This Medicine

In deciding to use a medicine, the risks of taking the medicine must be weighed against the good it will do. This is a decision you and your doctor will make. For atovaquone, the following should be considered:

Allergies— Tell your doctor if you have ever had any unusual or allergic reaction to atovaquone. Also tell your health care professional if you are allergic to any other substances, such as foods, preservatives, or dyes.

Diet—Make certain your health care professional knows if you are on any special diet. This medicine must be taken with balanced meals so that it can work properly.

Pregnancy—Atovaquone has not been studied in pregnant women. However, studies in rabbits have shown an increase in miscarriages and other harmful effects in the mother and fetus. Before taking this medicine, make sure your doctor knows if you are pregnant or if you may become pregnant.

Breast-feeding—It is not known whether atovaquone passes into human breast milk. However, it was found in the milk of rats. Be sure you have discussed the risks and benefits of atovaquone with your doctor.

Children—Atovaquone has been tested in a limited number of children 1 month of age to 13 years old. It is not known if this medicine causes different side effects or problems in children than it does in adults.

Older adults—Many medicines have not been studied specifically in older people. Therefore, it may not be known whether they work exactly the same way they do in younger adults or if they cause different side effects or problems in older people. There is no specific information comparing use of atovaquone in the elderly with use in other age groups.

Other medicines—Although certain medicines should not be used together at all, in other cases two different medicines may be used together even if an interaction might occur. In these cases, your doctor may want to change the dose, or other precautions may be necessary. When you are taking atovaquone, it is especially important that your health care professional know if you are taking any of the following:

- Rifampin (e.g., Rifadin)—Use of rifampin with atovaquone may decrease the amount of atovaquone in the blood and keep it from working properly

Other medical problems—The presence of other medical problems may affect the use of atovaquone. Make sure you tell your doctor if you have any other medical problems, especially:

- Stomach or intestinal disorders—Atovaquone may not work properly in patients with some kinds of stomach or intestinal problems

Proper Use of This Medicine

It is *important that you take atovaquone with a balanced meal*. This is to make sure the medicine is fully absorbed into the body and will work properly.

Atovaquone tablets may be crushed if necessary to make it easier to swallow the tablets.

Because atovaquone tablets and oral suspension do not produce the same amount of medicine in the blood, the *tablets and the suspension cannot be switched and used in place of each other*.

For patients taking the *oral liquid* form of this medicine:

- This medicine is to be taken by mouth. Use a specially marked measuring spoon or other device to measure each dose accurately. The average household teaspoon may not hold the right amount of liquid.
- Do not use after the expiration date on the label since the medicine may not work properly after that date. Check with your pharmacist if you have any questions about this.

To help clear up your infection completely, *keep taking your medicine for the full time of treatment*, even if you begin to feel better after a few days. If you stop taking this medicine too soon, your symptoms may return.

Atovaquone works best when there is a constant amount in the blood. *To help keep the amount constant, do not miss any doses.*

Dosing—The dose of atovaquone may be different for different patients. *Follow your doctor's orders or the directions on the label*. The following information includes only the average doses of atovaquone. *If your dose is different, do not change it* unless your doctor tells you to do so.

- For treatment of *Pneumocystis carinii* pneumonia (PCP):
  - —For *oral suspension* dosage form:
    - Adults and teenagers—750 milligrams (mg) taken with a meal two times a day for twenty-one days.
    - Children—Use and dose must be determined by your doctor.
  - —For *tablet* dosage form:
    - Adults and teenagers—750 mg taken with a meal three times a day for twenty-one days.
    - Children—Use and dose must be determined by your doctor.
- For prevention of *Pneumocystis carinii* pneumonia (PCP):
  - —For *oral suspension* dosage form:
    - Adults and teenagers—1500 milligrams (mg) once a day with a meal.
    - Children—Use and dose must be determined by your doctor.

Missed dose—If you miss a dose of this medicine, take it as soon as possible. This will help to keep a constant amount of medicine in the blood. However, if it is almost time for your next dose, skip the missed dose and go back to your regular dosing schedule. Do not double doses.

Storage—To store this medicine:

- Keep out of the reach of children.
- Store away from heat and direct light.
- Do not store in the bathroom, near the kitchen sink, or in other damp places. Heat or moisture may cause the medicine to break down.
- Do not keep outdated medicine or medicine no longer needed. Be sure that any discarded medicine is out of the reach of children.
- Do not freeze.

Precautions While Using This Medicine

If your symptoms do not improve within a few days, or if they become worse, check with your doctor.

Side Effects of This Medicine

Along with its needed effects, a medicine may cause some unwanted effects. Although not all of these side effects may occur, if they do occur they may need medical attention.

Check with your doctor immediately if any of the following side effects occur:

More common
  Fever; skin rash

Other side effects may occur that usually do not need medical attention. These side effects may go away during treatment as your body adjusts to the medicine. However, check with your doctor if any of the following side effects continue or are bothersome:

More common
  Cough; diarrhea; headache; nausea; trouble in sleeping; vomiting

Other side effects not listed above may also occur in some patients. If you notice any other effects, check with your doctor.

Revised: 10/31/99

ATOVAQUONE AND PROGUANIL
Systemic—INTRODUCTORY VERSION

Commonly used brand name(s):

In the U.S.—
  Malarone

Description

Antiprotozoals (AN-ti-pro-to-ZO-uls) are medicines that are used to prevent and treat malaria, a red blood cell infection transmitted by the bite of a mosquito. This medicine is a combination of two medicines, atovaquone (a-TOE-va-kwone) and proguanil (pro-GWAN-il).

This medicine is available only with your doctor's prescription, in the following dosage form:

Oral
  - Tablets (U.S.)

Before Using This Medicine

In deciding to use a medicine, the risks of taking the medicine must be weighed against the good it will do. This is a decision you and your doctor will make. For atovaquone and proguanil, the following should be considered:

Allergies—Tell your doctor if you have ever had any unusual or allergic reaction to atovaquone or proguanil hydrochloride. Also tell your health care professional if you are allergic to any other substances, such as preservatives or dyes.

Pregnancy—Atovaquone and proguanil combination has not been studied in pregnant women. However, this medicine has not been shown to cause birth defects or other problems in animal studies. Before taking this medicine, make sure your doctor knows if you are pregnant or if you may become pregnant It is advisable for pregnant women to avoid traveling to areas where there is a chance of getting malaria.

Breast-feeding—It is not known if atovaquone passes into human breast milk, but it was found in the milk of rats.

Proguanil passes into breast milk, but in small quantities. Be sure you have discussed the risks and benefits of this medicine with your doctor.

Children— Studies on this medicine have been done only in patients who weigh more than 25 pounds (11 kilograms [kg]) and there is no specific information comparing use of atovaquone and proguanil combination in patients of lesser weight.

Older adults—Many medicines have not been studied specifically in older people. Therefore, it may not be known whether they work exactly the same way they do in younger adults or if they cause different side effects or problems in older people. There is no specific information comparing use of atovaquone and proguanil in the elderly with use in other age groups.

Other medicines— Although certain medicines should not be used together at all, in other cases two different medicines may be used together even if an interaction might occur. In these cases, your doctor may want to change the dose, or other precautions may be necessary. When you are taking atovaquone and proguanil, it is especially important that your health care professional know if you are taking any of the following:

- Rifampin (e.g., Rifadin)—Use of rifampin may decrease the amount of atovaquone in the blood and keep it from working properly

- Metoclopramide (e.g., Reglan)—Use of metoclopramide with atovaquone and proguanil may lessen the amount of atovaquone your body absorbs

- Tetracycline (e.g., Sumycin)—Use of tetracycline lowers the amount of atovaquone in your blood.

Other medical problems—The presence of other medical problems may affect the use of atovaquone and proguanil. Make sure you tell your doctor if you have any other medical problems, especially:

- Diarrhea or vomiting—The amount of atovaquone and proguanil the body can absorb may be decreased.

- Kidney disease or failure—The amount of atovaquone and proguanil the body can eliminate may be decreased.

- Return of previously treated malaria—Atovaquone and proguanil may not work in treating the malaria again; your doctor may need to give you another type of medicine.

Proper Use of This Medicine

Be sure to take this medicine at the same time each day.

Take this medicine with food or with a milky drink. This will help your body absorb the maximal amount of medicine.

If you vomit within 1 hour of taking this medicine, take the entire dose again as soon as your stomach can tolerate it.

Dosing—The dose of atovaquone and proguanil will be different for different patients. *Follow your doctor's orders or the directions on the label.* The following information includes only the average doses of atovaquone and proguanil. *If your dose is different, do not change it* unless your doctor tells you to do so.

The number of tablets that you take depends on the strength of the medicine. Also, *the number of doses you take each day, the time allowed between doses, and the length of time you take the medicine depend on the medical problem for which you are taking atovaquone and proguanil.*

- For *oral* dosage form (tablets):
  - —For malaria prevention:
    - Adults—250 milligrams (mg) of atovaquone and 100 mg proguanil (1 adult strength tablet) per day, starting 1–2 days before entering malarial area and continuing for 7 days following return.
    - Children weighing 25 pounds (11 kilograms [kg]) or more—Dosage is according to weight and will be determined by your doctor.
    - Children weighing less than 25 pounds (11 kg)— Use and dose must be determined by your doctor.
  - —For malaria treatment:
    - Adults—1 gram of atovaquone and 400 mg of proguanil (4 adult strength tablets) once daily as a single dose taken three days in a row.
    - Children weighing 25 pounds (11 kg) or more— Dosage is based on body weight and must be determined by your doctor.
    - Children weighing less than 25 pounds (11 kg)— Use and dose must be determined by your doctor.

Missed dose—If you miss a dose of this medicine, take it as soon as possible. Contact your doctor as soon as possible for additional instructions since you may need additional protective measures.

Storage—To store this medicine:

- Keep out of the reach of children.
- Store at room temperature.
- Do not store in the bathroom, near the kitchen sink, or in other damp places. Heat or moisture may cause the medicine to break down.
- Do not keep outdated medicine or medicine no longer needed. Ask your health care professional how you should dispose of any medicine you do not use. Be sure that any discarded medicine is out of the reach of children.

Precautions While Using This Medicine

Malaria is spread by the bites of certain kinds of infected female mosquitoes. If you are living in, or will be traveling to, an area where there is a chance of getting malaria, the following mosquito-control measures will help to prevent infection:

- Remain in air-conditioned or well-screened rooms to reduce contact with mosquitoes.
- If possible, sleep under mosquito netting, preferably netting coated or soaked with permethrin, to avoid being bitten by malaria-carrying mosquitoes.
- Wear long-sleeved shirts or blouses and long trousers to protect your arms and legs, especially from dusk through dawn when mosquitoes are out.
- Apply mosquito repellent, preferably one containing DEET, to uncovered areas of the skin from dusk through dawn when mosquitoes are out.
- Use a pyrethrum-containing flying insect spray to kill mosquitoes in living and sleeping quarters during evening and nighttime hours.

Side Effects of This Medicine

Along with its needed effects, a medicine may cause some unwanted effects. Side effects may occur that usually do not need medical attention. These side effects may go away during treatment as your body adjusts to the medicine. However, check with your health care professional if any of the following side effects continue or are bothersome:

More common

Abdominal pain; back pain; coughing; diarrhea; fever; headache; itching skin (pediatrics only); lack of or loss of strength; nausea; muscle pain; sore throat; sneezing; vomiting

Less common

Acid or sour stomach; belching; dizziness; flu-like symptoms; heartburn; indigestion; loss of appetite; stomach discomfort, upset or pain; weight loss

Other side effects not listed above may also occur in some patients. If you notice any other effects, check with your doctor.

Developed: 11/03/2000

ATROPINE, HYOSCYAMINE, METHENAMINE, METHYLENE BLUE, PHENYL SALICYLATE, AND BENZOIC ACID Systemic†

Commonly used brand name(s):

In the U.S.—

Atrosept	Urimed
Dolsed	Urinary Antiseptic No. 2
Hexalol	Urised
Prosed/DS	Uriseptic
Trac Tabs 2X	Uritab
UAA	Uritin
Uridon Modified	Uro-Ves

†Not commercially available in Canada.

Description

Atropine (A-troe-peen), hyoscyamine (hye-oh-SYE-a-meen), methenamine (meth-EN-a-meen), methylene (METH-i-leen) blue, phenyl salicylate (FEN-ill sa-LI-si-late), and benzoic acid (ben-ZOE-ik AS-id) combination medicine is an anticholinergic, anti-infective, and analgesic. It is given by mouth to help relieve the discomfort caused by urinary tract infections; however, it will not cure the infection itself. This combination medicine may also be used for other conditions as determined by your doctor.

This medicine is available only with your doctor's prescription in the following dosage form:

Oral

• Tablets (U.S.)

Before Using This Medicine

In deciding to use a medicine, the risks of taking the medicine must be weighed against the good it will do. This is a decision you and your doctor will make. For this combination medicine, the following should be considered:

Allergies—Tell your doctor if you have ever had any unusual or allergic reaction to any of the belladonna alkaloids such as atropine, hyoscyamine, and scopolamine, or to aspirin or other salicylates. Also tell your health care professional if you are allergic to any other substances, such as foods, preservatives, or dyes.

Diet—While you are taking this combination medicine, it is important for your urine to be acidic. To do this, your doctor may recommend that you eat more protein and such foods as cranberries (especially cranberry juice with vitamin C added), plums, or prunes. You should avoid foods that make the urine more alkaline, such as most fruits (especially citrus fruits and juices), milk, and other dairy products.

Pregnancy—Studies have not been done in either humans or animals.

Breast-feeding—Although methenamine and very small amounts of atropine and hyoscyamine (contained in this combination medicine) pass into the breast milk, this medicine has not been reported to cause problems in nursing babies.

Children—Unusual excitement, nervousness, restlessness or irritability, and unusual warmth, dryness, and flushing of skin are more likely to occur in children, who are usually more sensitive to the effects of atropine and hyoscyamine (contained in this combination medicine). Also, when atropine and hyoscyamine are given to children during hot weather, a rapid increase in body temperature may occur. In infants and children, especially those with spastic paralysis or brain damage, this medicine may be more likely to cause severe side effects.

Older adults—Confusion or memory loss, constipation, difficult urination, excitement, agitation, drowsiness, or dryness of mouth may be more likely to occur in elderly patients, who are usually more sensitive than younger adults to the effects of atropine and hyoscyamine. Also, this combination medicine may cause eye pain in patients who have untreated glaucoma.

Other medicines—Although certain medicines should not be used together at all, in other cases two different medicines may be used together even if an interaction might occur. In these cases, your doctor may want to change the dose, or other precautions may be necessary. When you are taking this combination medicine, it is especially important that your health care professional know if you are taking any of the following:

• Antacids or
• Diarrhea medicine containing kaolin or attapulgite or
• Thiazide diuretics (water pills) or
• Urinary alkalizers (medicine that makes the urine less acid, such as acetazolamide [e.g., Diamox], calcium- and/or magnesium-containing antacids, dichlorphenamide [e.g., Daranide], methazolamide [e.g., Neptazone], potassium or sodium citrate and/or citric acid, sodium bicarbonate [baking soda])—Use with these medicines may decrease the effects of this combination medicine

• Ketoconazole (e.g., Nizoral)—Use with this combination medicine may reduce the effects of ketoconazole

• Other anticholinergics (medicine for abdominal or stomach spasms or cramps)—Use with these medicines may increase the effects of atropine and hyoscyamine

• Potassium chloride (e.g., Slow K or K-Dur)—May worsen or cause an increase in lesions (sores) of the stomach or intestine

• Sulfonamides (sulfa medicine)—Use with this combination medicine may increase the risk of crystals forming in the urine

Other medical problems—The presence of other medical problems may affect the use of this combination medicine. Make sure you tell your doctor if you have any other medical problems, especially:

- Bleeding problems (severe)—This combination medicine may increase heart rate, which would make bleeding problems worse

- Brain damage (in children)—May increase the central nervous system (CNS) effects of this combination medicine

- Colitis (severe) or
- Dryness of mouth (severe or continuing) or
- Enlarged prostate or
- Fever or
- Glaucoma or
- Heart disease or
- Hernia (hiatal) or
- High blood pressure or
- Intestinal blockage or other intestinal or stomach problems or
- Lung disease or
- Myasthenia gravis or
- Toxemia of pregnancy or
- Urinary tract blockage or difficult urination—This combination medicine may make these conditions worse

- Dehydration or
- Kidney disease or
- Liver disease—Higher levels of medicine may result and increase the risk of side effects

- Overactive thyroid—May increase the heart rate

Proper Use of This Medicine

Take this medicine only as directed. Do not take more of it, do not take it more often, and do not take it for a longer time than your doctor ordered. To do so may increase the chance of side effects.

Each dose should be taken with a full glass (8 ounces) of water or other liquid (except citrus juices and milk). Drink plenty of water or other liquids every day, unless otherwise directed by your doctor. Drinking enough liquids will help your kidneys work better and lessen your discomfort.

To help clear up your infection completely, *keep taking this medicine for the full time of treatment* even if you begin to feel better after a few days. *Do not miss any doses.*

In order for this medicine to work well, your urine must be acid (pH 5.5 or below). To make sure that your urine is acid:

- Before you start taking this medicine, check your urine with phenaphthazine paper or another test to see if it is acid. If you have any questions about this, check with your health care professional.
- You may need to change your diet; however, check with your doctor first if you are on a special diet (for example, for diabetes). To help make your urine more acid you should avoid most fruits (especially citrus fruits and juices), milk and other dairy products, and other foods which make the urine more alkaline. Eating more protein and foods such as cranberries (especially cranberry juice with vitamin C added), plums, or prunes may also help. If your urine is still not acid enough, check with your doctor.

Dosing—The dose of this combination medicine will be different for different patients. *Follow your doctor's orders or the direction on the label.* The following information includes only the average doses of this combination medicine.

If your dose is different, do not change it unless your doctor tells you to do so.

- For *oral* dosage form (tablets):
  - —For relief of urinary tract symptoms:
    - Adults and children 12 years of age and older—1 to 2 tablets four times a day.
    - Children 6 to 12 years of age—Dose must be determined by the doctor.
    - Children up to 6 years of age—Use is not recommended.

Missed dose—If you miss a dose of this medicine, take it as soon as possible. However, if it is almost time for your next dose, skip the missed dose and go back to your regular dosing schedule. Do not double doses.

Storage—To store this medicine:

- Keep out of the reach of children.
- Store away from heat and direct light.
- Do not store this medicine in the bathroom, near the kitchen sink, or in other damp places. Heat or moisture may cause the medicine to break down.
- Do not keep outdated medicine or medicine no longer needed. Be sure that any discarded medicine is out of the reach of children.

Precautions While Using This Medicine

If your symptoms do not improve within a few days or if they become worse, check with your doctor.

These medicines may make you sweat less, causing your body temperature to increase. *Use extra care not to become overheated during exercise or hot weather while you are taking this medicine,* since overheating may result in heat stroke. Also, hot baths or saunas may make you dizzy or faint while you are taking this medicine.

This medicine may cause some people to have blurred vision. *Make sure you know how you react to this medicine before you drive, use machines, or do anything else that could be dangerous if you are not able to see well. If your vision continues to be blurred, check with your doctor.*

This medicine may cause dryness of the mouth. For temporary relief, use sugarless candy or gum, melt bits of ice in your mouth, or use a saliva substitute. However, if your mouth continues to feel dry for more than 2 weeks, check with your dentist. Continuing dryness of the mouth may increase the chance of dental disease, including tooth decay, gum disease, and fungus infections.

Do not take this medicine within 2 or 3 hours of taking antacids or medicine for diarrhea. Taking antacids or antidiarrhea medicines and this medicine too close together may prevent this medicine from working properly.

Side Effects of This Medicine

Along with its needed effects, a medicine may cause some unwanted effects. Although not all of these side effects may occur, if they do occur they may need medical attention.

Check with your doctor as soon as possible if any of the following side effects occur:

Less common or rare
Blurred vision; eye pain; skin rash or hives

Symptoms of overdose
Blood in urine and/or stools; diarrhea; dizziness; drowsiness (severe); fast heartbeat; flushing or redness of face; headache (severe or continuing); lower back pain; pain or burning while urinating; ringing or

buzzing in the ears; shortness of breath or troubled breathing; sweating; unusual tiredness or weakness

Other side effects may occur that usually do not need medical attention. These side effects may go away during treatment as your body adjusts to the medicine. However, check with your doctor if any of the following side effects continue or are bothersome:

Less common

Difficult urination (more common with large doses taken over a prolonged period of time); dryness of mouth, nose, or throat; nausea or vomiting; stomach upset or pain (more common with large doses taken over a prolonged period of time)

This medicine may cause your urine and/or stools to turn blue or blue-green. This is to be expected while you are taking this medicine.

Other side effects not listed above may also occur in some patients. If you notice any other effects, check with your doctor.

Revised: 05/11/93

ATROPINE/HOMATROPINE/ SCOPOLAMINE   Ophthalmic

Commonly used brand name(s):

In the U.S.—

AK-Homatropine[2]	Isopto Atropine[1]
Atropair[1]	Isopto Homatropine[2]
Atropine Care[1]	Isopto Hyoscine[3]
Atropine Sulfate S.O.P.[1]	I-Tropine[1]
Atropisol[1]	Ocu-Tropine[1]
Atrosulf[1]	Spectro-Homatropine[2]
I-Homatrine[2]	

In Canada—

Atropisol[1]	Minims Atropine[1]
Isopto Atropine[1]	Minims Homatropine[2]
Isopto Homatropine[2]	

Another commonly used name for scopolamine is hyoscine.

Note: For quick reference, the following medicines are numbered to match the corresponding brand names.

This information applies to the following medicines:
1. Atropine (A-troe-peen)‡§
2. Homatropine (hoe-MA-troe-peen)‡§
3. Scopolamine (skoe-POL-a-meen)†

†Not commercially available in Canada.
‡Generic name product may be available in the U.S.
§Generic name product may be available in Canada.

Description

Ophthalmic atropine, homatropine, and scopolamine are used to dilate (enlarge) the pupil of the eye. They are used before eye examinations, before and after eye surgery, and to treat certain eye conditions, such as uveitis or posterior synechiae.

These medicines are available only with your doctor's prescription, in the following dosage forms:

Ophthalmic
Atropine
• Ophthalmic ointment (U.S. and Canada)
• Ophthalmic solution (eye drops) (U.S. and Canada)
Homatropine
• Ophthalmic solution (eye drops) (U.S. and Canada)
Scopolamine
• Ophthalmic solution (eye drops) (U.S.)

Before Using This Medicine

In deciding to use a medicine, the risks of using the medicine must be weighed against the good it will do. This is a decision you and your doctor will make. For ophthalmic atropine, homatropine, and scopolamine, the following should be considered:

Allergies—Tell your doctor if you have ever had any unusual or allergic reaction to atropine, homatropine, or scopolamine. Also tell your health care professional if you are allergic to any other substances, such as certain preservatives.

Pregnancy—Studies on effects in pregnancy have not been done in either humans or animals. However, these medicines may be absorbed into the body.

Breast-feeding—These medicines may be absorbed into the body. Atropine passes into the breast milk in very small amounts and may cause side effects, such as fast pulse, fever, or dry skin, in babies of nursing mothers using ophthalmic atropine. It is not known whether homatropine or scopolamine passes into breast milk. Although most medicines pass into breast milk in small amounts, many of them may be used safely while breast-feeding. Mothers who are using one of these medicines and who wish to breast-feed should discuss this with their doctor.

Children—Infants and young children and children with blond hair or blue eyes may be especially sensitive to the effects of atropine, homatropine, or scopolamine. This may increase the chance of side effects during treatment. Children should use a lower strength of this medicine.

Older adults—Elderly people are especially sensitive to the effects of atropine, homatropine, or scopolamine. This may increase the chance of side effects during treatment.

Other medicines—Although certain medicines should not be used together at all, in other cases two different medicines may be used together even if an interaction might occur. In these cases, your doctor may want to change the dose, or other precautions may be necessary. Tell your health care professional if you are using any other prescription or nonprescription (over-the-counter [OTC]) medicine.

Other medical problems—The presence of other medical problems may affect the use of ophthalmic atropine, homatropine, or scopolamine. Make sure you tell your doctor if you have any other medical problems, especially:
• Brain damage (in children) or
• Down's syndrome (mongolism) (in children and adults) or
• Glaucoma or
• Other eye diseases or problems or
• Spastic paralysis (in children)—Use of ophthalmic atropine, homatropine, or scopolamine may make the condition worse

Proper Use of This Medicine

To use the ophthalmic solution *(eye drops) form* of this medicine:

- First, wash your hands. Tilt the head back and, pressing your finger gently on the skin just beneath the lower eyelid, pull the lower eyelid away from the eye to make a space. Drop the medicine into this space. Let go of the eyelid and gently close the eyes. Do not blink. Keep the eyes closed and apply pressure to the inner corner of the eye with your finger for 2 or 3 minutes to allow the medicine to be absorbed by the eye.
- Immediately after using the eye drops, wash your hands to remove any medicine that may be on them. If you are using the eye drops for an infant or child, be sure to wash his or her hands immediately afterwards also, and do not let any of the medicine get in his or her mouth. In addition, wipe off any medicine that may have accidentally gotten on the infant or child, including his or her face or eyelids.
- To keep the medicine as germ-free as possible, do not touch the applicator tip to any surface (including the eye). Also, keep the container tightly closed.

To use the *ointment form* of this medicine:

- First, wash your hands. Tilt the head back and, pressing your finger gently on the skin just beneath the lower eyelid, pull the lower eyelid away from the eye to make a space. Squeeze a thin strip of ointment into this space. A ⅓- to ½-cm (approximately ⅛-inch in infants and young children and ¼-inch in older children and adults) strip of ointment is usually enough, unless you have been told by your doctor to use a different amount. Let go of the eyelid and gently close the eyes. Keep the eyes closed for 1 or 2 minutes to allow the medicine to be absorbed by the eye.
- Immediately after using the eye ointment, wash your hands to remove any medicine that may be on them. If you are using the eye ointment for an infant or child, be sure to wash his or her hands immediately afterwards also, and do not let any of the medicine get in his or her mouth. In addition, wipe off any medicine that may have accidentally gotten on the infant or child, including his or her face or eyelids.
- To keep the medicine as germ-free as possible, do not touch the applicator tip to any surface (including the eye). After using the eye ointment, wipe the tip of the ointment tube with a clean tissue and keep the tube tightly closed.

Use this medicine only as directed. Do not use more of it and do not use it more often than your doctor ordered. To do so may increase the chance of too much medicine being absorbed into the body and the chance of side effects. *This is especially important when this medicine is used in infants and children, since overdose is very dangerous in infants and children.*

Dosing—The doses of these medicines will be different for different patients. *Follow your doctor's orders or the directions on the label.* The following information includes only the average doses of these medicines. *If your dose is different, do not change it* unless your doctor tells you to do so.

The number of doses you use each day, the time allowed between doses, and the length of time you use the medicine depend on the medical problem for which you are using atropine, homatropine, or scopolamine.

For atropine
- For *ophthalmic ointment* dosage form:
  —For uveitis:
  - Adults—Use a thin strip of the ointment in the eye one or two times a day.
  - Children—Use a thin strip of the ointment in the eye one to three times a day.
  —For eye examinations:
  - Adults—Use and dose must be determined by your doctor.
  - Children—Use a thin strip of the ointment in the eye three times a day for one to three days before the examination.
- For *ophthalmic solution (eye drops)* dosage form:
  —For uveitis:
  - Adults—Use one drop in the eye one or two times a day.
  - Children—Use one drop in the eye one to three times a day.
  —For eye examinations:
  - Adults—Use and dose must be determined by your doctor.
  - Children—Use one drop in the eye two times a day for one to three days before the examination.

For homatropine
- For *ophthalmic solution (eye drops)* dosage form:
  —For uveitis:
  - Adults and children—Use 1 or 2 drops in the eye two or three times a day.
  —For eye examinations:
  - Adults—Use 1 or 2 drops in the eye. May be repeated every five to ten minutes for two or three doses.
  - Children—Use 1 or 2 drops in the eye every ten minutes for two or three doses.

For scopolamine
- For *ophthalmic solution (eye drops)* dosage form:
  —For uveitis:
  - Adults and children—Use one drop in the eye up to four times a day.
  —For eye examinations:
  - Adults—Use one drop in the eye one hour before the examination.
  - Children—Use one drop in the eye two times a day for two days before the examination.
  —For posterior synechiae:
  - Adults—Use one drop in the eye every ten minutes for three doses.
  - Children—Use and dose must be determined by your doctor.
  —For use before and after surgery:
  - Adults and children—Use one drop in the eye one to four times a day.

Missed dose—If you miss a dose of this medicine and your dosing schedule is:

- One dose a day—Apply the missed dose as soon as possible. However, if you do not remember the missed dose until the next day, skip the missed dose and go back to your regular dosing schedule. Do not double doses.
- More than one dose a day—Apply the missed dose as soon as possible. However, if it is almost time for your

next dose, skip the missed dose and go back to your regular dosing schedule. Do not double doses.

Storage—To store this medicine:

- Keep out of the reach of children. Overdose of this medicine is very dangerous for infants and children.
- Store away from heat and direct light.
- Keep this medicine from freezing.
- Do not keep outdated medicine or medicine no longer needed. Be sure that any discarded medicine is out of the reach of children.

Precautions While Using This Medicine

After you apply this medicine to your eyes:

- Your pupils will become unusually large and you will have blurring of vision, especially for close objects. *Make sure your vision is clear before you drive, use machines, or do anything else that could be dangerous if you are not able to see well.*
- Your eyes will become more sensitive to light than they are normally. *Wear sunglasses to protect your eyes from sunlight and other bright lights.*

These effects may continue for several days after you stop using this medicine. However, check with your doctor if they continue longer than:

- 14 days if you are using atropine.
- 3 days if you are using homatropine.
- 7 days if you are using scopolamine.

Side Effects of This Medicine

Along with its needed effects, a medicine may cause some unwanted effects. Although not all of these side effects may occur, if they do occur they may need medical attention.

Check with your doctor immediately if any of the following side effects occur:

Symptoms of too much medicine being absorbed into the body

Clumsiness or unsteadiness; confusion or unusual behavior; dryness of skin; fast or irregular heartbeat; fever; flushing or redness of face; seeing, hearing, or feeling things that are not there; skin rash; slurred speech; swollen stomach in infants; thirst or unusual dryness of mouth; unusual drowsiness, tiredness, or weakness

Other side effects may occur that usually do not need medical attention. These side effects may go away during treatment as your body adjusts to the medicine. However, check with your doctor if any of the following side effects continue or are bothersome:

Blurred vision; brief burning or stinging of the eyes; eye irritation not present before use of this medicine; increased sensitivity of eyes to light; swelling of the eyelids

Other side effects not listed above may also occur in some patients. If you notice any other effects, check with your doctor.

Revised: 03/03/00

ATTAPULGITE   Oral

Commonly used brand name(s):

In the U.S.—

Diar-Aid	Kaopectate Maximum
Diarrest	Strength
Diasorb	Kaopek
Diatrol	K-Pek
Donnagel	Parepectolin
Kaopectate	Rheaban
Kaopectate Advanced	
Formula	

In Canada—
Fowler's
Kaopectate

Description

Attapulgite (at-a-PULL-gite) is taken by mouth to treat diarrhea. Attapulgite is a clay-like powder believed to work by adsorbing the bacteria or germ that may be causing the diarrhea.

This medicine is available without a prescription; however, the product's directions and warnings should be carefully followed. In addition, your doctor may have special instructions on the proper dose or use of attapulgite medicine for your medical condition.

Attapulgite is available in the following dosage forms:

Oral
Attapulgite
- Oral suspension (U.S. and Canada)
- Tablets (U.S. and Canada)
- Chewable tablets (U.S. and Canada)

Before Using This Medicine

If you are taking this medicine without a prescription, carefully read and follow any precautions on the label. For attapulgite, the following should be considered:

Pregnancy—This medicine is not absorbed into the body and is not likely to cause problems.

Breast-feeding—This medicine is not absorbed into the body and is not likely to cause problems.

Children—The fluid loss caused by diarrhea may result in a severe condition. For this reason, antidiarrheals must not be given to young children (under 3 years of age) without first checking with their doctor. In older children with diarrhea, antidiarrheals may be used, but it is also very important that a sufficient amount of liquids be given to replace the fluid lost by the body. If you have any questions about this, check with your health care professional.

Older adults—The fluid loss caused by diarrhea may result in a severe condition. For this reason, elderly persons with diarrhea, in addition to using an antidiarrheal, must receive a sufficient amount of liquids to replace the fluid lost by the body. If you have any questions about this, check with your health care professional.

Other medicines—Although certain medicines should not be used together at all, in other cases two different medicines may be used together even if an interaction might occur. In these cases, your doctor may want to change the dose, or other precautions may be necessary. *If you are taking any other medicine, do not take it within 2 to 3 hours of attapulgite.* Taking the medicines at the same time may prevent the other medicine from being absorbed by your body. If you have any questions about this, check with your health care professional.

Other medical problems—The presence of other medical problems may affect the use of attapulgite. Make sure you tell your doctor if you have any other medical problems, especially:

- Dysentery—This condition may get worse; a different kind of treatment may be needed

---

Proper Use of This Medicine

Do not use attapulgite to treat your diarrhea if you have a fever or if there is blood or mucus in your stools. Contact your doctor.

Take this medicine after each loose bowel movement following the directions in the product package, unless otherwise directed by your doctor.

Importance of diet and fluid intake while treating diarrhea:

- *In addition to using medicine for diarrhea, it is very important that you replace the fluid lost by the body and follow a proper diet.* For the first 24 hours you should eat gelatin and drink plenty of clear liquids, such as ginger ale, decaffeinated cola, decaffeinated tea, and broth. During the next 24 hours you may eat bland foods, such as cooked cereals, bread, crackers, and applesauce. Fruits, vegetables, fried or spicy foods, bran, candy, and caffeine and alcoholic beverages may make the condition worse.
- If too much fluid has been lost by the body due to the diarrhea a serious condition may develop. Check with your doctor as soon as possible if any of the following occurs:
  Decreased urination
  Dizziness and lightheadedness
  Dryness of mouth
  Increased thirst
  Wrinkled skin

Dosing—The dose of attapulgite will be different for different patients. *Follow your doctor's orders or the directions on the label.* The following information includes only the average doses of attapulgite.

The number of tablets or teaspoonfuls of suspension that you take depends on the strength of the medicine.

- For diarrhea:
  —For *oral* dosage form (suspension):
    - Adults and children 12 years of age and older— The usual dose is 1200 to 1500 milligrams (mg) taken after each loose bowel movement. No more than 9000 mg should be taken in twenty-four hours.
    - Children 6 to 12 years of age—The usual dose is 600 mg taken after each loose bowel movement. No more than 4200 mg should be taken in twenty-four hours.
    - Children 3 to 6 years of age—The usual dose is 300 mg taken after each loose bowel movement. No more than 2100 mg should be taken in twenty-four hours.
    - Children up to 3 years of age—Use and dose must be determined by your doctor.

  —For *oral* dosage form (tablets):
    - Adults and children 12 years of age and older— The usual dose is 1200 to 1500 mg taken after each loose bowel movement. No more than 9000 mg should be taken in twenty-four hours.
    - Children 6 to 12 years of age—The usual dose is 750 mg taken after each loose bowel movement. No more than 4500 mg should be taken in twenty-four hours.
    - Children 3 to 6 years of age—The oral suspension dosage form should be used in this age group.

  —For *oral* dosage form (chewable tablets):
    - Adults and children 12 years of age and older— The usual dose is 1200 mg taken after each loose bowel movement. No more than 8400 mg should be taken in twenty-four hours.
    - Children 6 to 12 years of age—The usual dose is 600 mg taken after each loose bowel movement. No more than 4200 mg should be taken in twenty-four hours.
    - Children 3 to 6 years of age—The usual dose is 300 mg taken after each loose bowel movement. No more than 2100 mg should be taken in twenty-four hours.
    - Children up to 3 years of age—Use and dose must be determined by your doctor.

Storage—To store this medicine:

- Keep out of the reach of children.
- Store away from heat and direct light.
- Keep the liquid form of this medicine from freezing.
- Do not keep outdated medicine or medicine no longer needed. Be sure that any discarded medicine is out of the reach of children.

Precautions While Using This Medicine

Check with your doctor if your diarrhea does not stop after 1 or 2 days or if you develop a fever.

Side Effects of This Medicine

Along with its needed effects, a medicine may cause some unwanted effects. No serious side effects have been reported for this medicine. However, constipation may occur in some patients, especially if they take a lot of it. Check with your doctor as soon as possible if constipation continues or is bothersome.

Other side effects not listed above may also occur in some patients. If you notice any other effects, check with your doctor.

Revised: 08/12/94
Interim revision: 04/27/95

AZATHIOPRINE   Systemic

Commonly used brand name(s):

In the U.S.—
　Imuran
　Generic name product may be available.

In Canada—
　Imuran

Description

Azathioprine (ay-za-THYE-oh-preen) belongs to the group of medicines known as immunosuppressive agents. It is used to reduce the body's natural immunity in patients who receive organ transplants. It is also used to treat rheumatoid arthritis. Azathioprine may also be used for other conditions as determined by your doctor.

Azathioprine is a very strong medicine. You and your doctor should talk about the need for this medicine and its risks. Even though azathioprine may cause side effects that could be very serious, remember that it may be required to treat your medical problem.

Azathioprine is available only with your doctor's prescription, in the following dosage forms:

Oral
- Tablets (U.S. and Canada)

Parenteral
- Injection (U.S. and Canada)

Before Using This Medicine

In deciding to use a medicine, the risks of taking the medicine must be weighed against the good it will do. This is a decision you and your doctor will make. For azathioprine, the following should be considered:

Allergies—Tell your doctor if you have ever had any unusual or allergic reaction to azathioprine. Also tell your health care professional if you are allergic to any other substances, such as foods, preservatives, or dyes.

Pregnancy—Use of azathioprine is not recommended during pregnancy. It may cause birth defects if either the male or the female is using it at the time of conception. The use of birth control methods is recommended. If you have any questions about this, check with your doctor.

Breast-feeding—Azathioprine passes into breast milk. Because this medicine may cause serious side effects, breast-feeding is generally not recommended while you are using it.

Children—This medicine has been tested in children and, in effective doses, has not been shown to cause different side effects or problems than it does in adults.

Older adults—Many medicines have not been studied specifically in older people. Therefore, it may not be known whether they work exactly the same way they do in younger adults. Although there is no specific information comparing use of azathioprine in the elderly with use in other age groups, this medicine is not expected to cause different side effects or problems in older people than it does in younger adults.

Dental—The effects of azathioprine may cause increased infections and delayed healing. Dental work, whenever possible, should be completed prior to beginning this medicine.

Other medicines—Although certain medicines should not be used together at all, in other cases two different medicines may be used together even if an interaction might occur. In these cases, your doctor may want to change the dose, or other precautions may be necessary. When you are taking or receiving azathioprine it is especially important that your health care professional know if you are taking any of the following:

- Allopurinol (e.g., Zyloprim)—May interfere with removal of azathioprine from the body; effects of azathioprine (including toxicity) may be increased

- Chlorambucil (e.g., Leukeran) or
- Corticosteroids (cortisone-like medicine) or
- Cyclophosphamide (e.g., Cytoxan) or
- Cyclosporine (e.g., Sandimmune) or
- Mercaptopurine (e.g., Purinethol) or
- Muromonab-CD3 (monoclonal antibody) (e.g., Orthoclone OKT3)—There may be an increased risk of infection and cancer because azathioprine reduces the body's ability to fight them

Other medical problems—The presence of other medical problems may affect the use of azathioprine. Make sure you tell your doctor if you have any other medical problems, especially:

- Chickenpox (including recent exposure) or
- Herpes zoster (shingles)—Risk of severe disease affecting other parts of the body
- Gout—Allopurinol (used to treat gout) may increase wanted and unwanted effects of azathioprine
- Infection—Azathioprine decreases your body's ability to fight infection
- Kidney disease or
- Liver disease—Effects of azathioprine may be increased because of slower removal from the body
- Pancreatitis (inflammation of the pancreas)—Azathioprine can cause pancreatitis

Proper Use of This Medicine

Use this medicine only as directed by your doctor. Do not use more or less of it, and do not use it more often than your doctor ordered. The exact amount of medicine you need has been carefully worked out. Taking too much may increase the chance of side effects, while taking too little may not properly treat your condition.

This medicine is sometimes given together with certain other medicines. If you are using a combination of medicines, make sure that you take each one at the proper time and do not mix them up. Ask your health care professional to help you plan a way to remember to take your medicines at the right times.

Do not stop taking this medicine without first checking with your doctor.

Azathioprine sometimes causes nausea or vomiting. Taking this medicine after meals or at bedtime may lessen stomach upset. Ask your health care professional for other ways to lessen these effects.

If you vomit shortly after taking a dose of azathioprine, check with your doctor. You will be told whether to take the dose again or to wait until the next scheduled dose.

Dosing—The dose of azathioprine will be different for different patients. Follow your doctor's orders or the directions on the label. The following information includes only the average doses of azathioprine. *If your dose is different, do not change it* unless your doctor tells you to do so.

The number of doses you take each day, the time allowed between doses, and the length of time you take the medicine depend on the medical problem for which you are taking azathioprine.

- For *oral* dosage form (tablets):
  - For transplant rejection:
    - Adults, teenagers, and children: Dose is based on body weight or size. The usual beginning dose is 3 to 5 milligrams (mg) per kilogram (kg) (1.5 to 2 mg per pound) of body weight a day. As time

goes on, your doctor may lower your dose to 1 to 3 mg per kg (0.5 to 1.5 mg per pound) of body weight a day.

—For rheumatoid arthritis:

- Adults, teenagers, and children: Dose is based on body weight or size. The usual beginning dose is 1 mg per kg (0.5 mg per pound) of body weight a day. Your doctor will increase this dose as needed. The highest dose is usually not more than 2.5 mg per kg (1 mg per pound) of body weight a day. Your doctor may then lower your dose as needed.

- For *injection* dosage form:
  —For transplant rejection:
  - Adults, teenagers, and children: Dose is based on body weight or size. The usual beginning dose is 3 to 5 milligrams (mg) per kilogram (kg) (1.5 to 2 mg per pound) of body weight a day. As time goes on, your doctor may lower your dose to 1 to 3 mg per kg (0.5 to 1.5 mg per pound) of body weight a day.

Missed dose—If you miss a dose of this medicine and your dosing schedule is:

- One dose a day—Do not take the missed dose at all and do not double the next one. Instead, go back to your regular dosing schedule and check with your doctor.
- More than one dose a day—Take the missed dose as soon as you remember it. If it is time for your next dose, take both doses together, then go back to your regular dosing schedule. If you miss more than one dose, check with your doctor.

Storage—To store this medicine:

- Keep out of the reach of children.
- Store away from heat and direct light.
- Do not store in the bathroom, near the kitchen sink, or in other damp places. Heat or moisture may cause the medicine to break down.
- Do not keep outdated medicine or medicine no longer needed. Be sure that any discarded medicine is out of the reach of children.

Precautions While Using This Medicine

It is very important that your doctor check your progress at regular visits to make sure that this medicine is working properly and to check for unwanted effects.

While you are being treated with azathioprine, and after you stop treatment with it, *it is important to see your doctor about the immunizations (vaccinations) you should receive. Do not get any immunizations without your doctor's approval.* Azathioprine lowers your body's resistance to infections. For some immunizations, there is a chance you might get the infection the immunization is meant to prevent. For other immunizations, it may be especially important to receive the immunization to prevent a disease. In addition, other persons living in your household should not take oral polio vaccine since there is a chance they could pass the polio virus on to you. Also, avoid persons who have recently taken oral polio vaccine. Do not get close to them, and do not stay in the same room with them for very long. If you cannot take these precautions, you should consider wearing a protective face mask that covers the nose and mouth.

Azathioprine can temporarily lower the number of white blood cells in your blood, increasing the chance of getting an infec-tion. It can also lower the number of platelets, which are necessary for proper blood clotting. If this occurs, there are certain precautions you can take, especially when your blood count is low, to reduce the risk of infection or bleeding:

- If you can, avoid people with infections. Check with your doctor as soon as possible if you think you are getting an infection or if you get a fever or chills, cough or hoarseness, lower back or side pain, or painful or difficult urination.
- Check with your doctor as soon as possible if you notice any unusual bleeding or bruising; black, tarry stools; blood in urine or stools; or pinpoint red spots on your skin.
- Be careful when using a regular toothbrush, dental floss, or toothpick. Your medical doctor, dentist, or nurse may recommend other ways to clean your teeth and gums. Check with your health care professional before having any dental work done.
- Do not touch your eyes or the inside of your nose unless you have just washed your hands and have not touched anything else in the meantime.
- Be careful not to cut yourself when you are using sharp objects such as a safety razor or fingernail or toenail cutters.
- Avoid contact sports or other situations where bruising or injury could occur.

Side Effects of This Medicine

Along with its needed effects, a medicine may cause some unwanted effects. Some side effects will have signs or symptoms that you can see or feel. Your doctor will watch for others by doing certain tests.

Also, because of the way this medicine acts on the body, there is a chance that it might cause other unwanted effects that may not occur until months or years after the medicine is used. These delayed effects may include certain types of cancer, such as leukemia, lymphoma, or skin cancer. However, the risk of cancer seems to be lower in people taking azathioprine for arthritis. Discuss these possible effects with your doctor.

Check with your doctor as soon as possible if any of the following side effects occur:

More common
Cough or hoarseness; fever or chills; lower back or side pain; painful or difficult urination; unusual tiredness or weakness

Less common
Black, tarry stools; blood in urine or stools; pinpoint red spots on skin; unusual bleeding or bruising

Rare
Fast heartbeat; fever (sudden); muscle or joint pain; nausea, vomiting, and diarrhea (severe); redness or blisters on skin; shortness of breath; sores in mouth and on lips; stomach pain; swelling of feet or lower legs; unusual feeling of discomfort or illness (sudden)

This medicine may also cause the following side effect that your doctor will watch for:
Less common
Liver problems

For patients taking this medicine for *rheumatoid arthritis:*

- Signs and symptoms of blood problems (black, tarry stools; blood in urine or stools; cough or hoarseness; fever or chills; lower back or side pain; painful or difficult urination; pinpoint red spots on skin; unusual tiredness or weakness; or unusual bleeding or bruising) are less likely to occur in patients taking azathioprine for rheumatoid arthritis than in patients taking azathioprine for transplant rejection. This is because lower doses are often used.

Other side effects may occur that usually do not need medical attention. These side effects may go away during treatment as your body adjusts to the medicine. However, check with your doctor if any of the following side effects continue or are bothersome:

More common
    Loss of appetite; nausea or vomiting

Less common
    Skin rash

After you stop using this medicine, it may still produce some side effects that need attention. During this period of time check with your doctor as soon as possible if you notice any of the following:

    Black, tarry stools; blood in urine; cough or hoarseness; fever or chills; lower back or side pain; painful or difficult urination; pinpoint red spots on skin; unusual bleeding or bruising

Other side effects not listed above may also occur in some patients. If you notice any other effects, check with your doctor.

Additional Information

Once a medicine has been approved for marketing for a certain use, experience may show that it is also useful for other medical problems. Although these uses are not included in product labeling, azathioprine is used in certain patients with the following medical conditions:

- Bowel disease, inflammatory
- Cirrhosis, biliary
- Dermatomyositis, systemic
- Glomerulonephritis
- Hepatitis, chronic active
- Lupus erythematosus, systemic
- Myasthenia gravis
- Myopathy, inflammatory
- Nephrotic syndrome
- Pemphigoid
- Pemphigus

Other than the above information, there is no additional information relating to proper use, precautions, or side effects for these uses.

Revised: 12/03/98

AZELAIC ACID   Topical†

Commonly used brand name(s):

In the U.S.—
    Azelex

†Not commercially available in Canada.

Description

Azelaic acid (ay-ze-LAY-ik AS-id) is used to treat mild to moderate acne. It works in part by stopping the growth of skin bacteria that can help cause acne. Azelaic acid also helps to lessen acne by keeping skin pores (tiny openings on the skin's surface) clear.

It may also be used to treat other conditions as determined by your doctor.

Azelaic acid is available only with your doctor's prescription, in the following dosage form:

Topical
    • Cream (U.S.)

Before Using This Medicine

In deciding to use a medicine, the risks of taking the medicine must be weighed against the good it will do. This is a decision you and your doctor will make. For azelaic acid, the following should be considered:

Allergies—Tell your doctor if you have ever had any unusual or allergic reaction to azelaic acid. Also tell your health care professional if you are allergic to any other substances, such as foods, preservatives, or dyes.

Pregnancy—Azelaic acid has not been studied in pregnant women.

Breast-feeding—Small amounts of azelaic acid are absorbed through the skin into the bloodstream. It is possible that tiny amounts of the medicine may pass into the breast milk. However, this medicine has not been reported to cause problems in nursing babies.

Children—Studies of this medicine have been done only in adult patients, and there is no specific information comparing use of azelaic acid in children with use in other age groups.

Older adults—Many medicines have not been studied specifically in older people. Therefore, it may not be known whether they work exactly the same way they do in younger adults or if they cause different side effects or problems in older people. There is no specific information comparing use of azelaic acid in the elderly with use in other age groups.

Other medicines—Although certain medicines should not be used together at all, in other cases two different medicines may be used together even if an interaction might occur. In these cases, your doctor may want to change the dose, or other precautions may be necessary. Tell your doctor and pharmacist if you are using any other topical prescription or nonprescription (over-the-counter [OTC]) medicine that is to be applied to the same area of the skin.

Proper Use of This Medicine

When applying the cream, use only a small amount of medicine and apply a thin film to clean, dry skin that is affected by acne. It is important to rub it in gently but well.

After applying azelaic acid cream, wash your hands well to remove any medicine that may remain on them.

Keep this medicine away from the eyes, other mucous membranes, such as the mouth, lips, and inside of the nose, and sensitive areas of the neck. If the medicine accidentally gets on these areas, wash with water at once.

To help clear up your acne completely, *it is very important that you keep using this medicine for the full time of treat-*

ment, even if your symptoms begin to clear up after a short time. If you stop using this medicine too soon, your acne may return or get worse.

Dosing—The dose of azelaic acid will be different for different patients. *Follow your doctor's orders or the directions on the label.* The following information includes only the average doses of azelaic acid. *If your dose is different, do not change it* unless your doctor tells you to do so.

- For *topical* dosage form (cream):
  —For acne:
  - Adults and teenagers—Apply a small amount two times a day, usually in the morning and the evening, to areas affected by acne. Rub in gently but well. When you are just beginning to use the medicine, your doctor may want you to apply the medicine only one time a day for a few days, to reduce the chance of skin irritation.
  - Children—Use and dose must be determined by your doctor.

Missed dose—If you miss a dose of this medicine, use it as soon as possible. However, if it is almost time for your next dose, skip the missed dose and go back to your regular dosing schedule. Do not double doses.

Storage—To store this medicine:

- Keep out of the reach of children.
- Store away from heat and direct light.
- Keep the medicine from freezing. Do not refrigerate.
- Do not keep outdated medicine or medicine no longer needed. Be sure that any discarded medicine is out of the reach of children.

Precautions While Using This Medicine

If your acne does not improve within 4 weeks, or if it becomes worse, check with your health care professional. However, it may take longer than 4 weeks before you notice full improvement in your acne even if you use the medicine every day.

If this medicine causes too much redness, peeling, or dryness of your skin, check with your doctor. It may be necessary for you to reduce the number of times a day that you use the medicine or to stop using the medicine for a short time until your skin is less irritated.

If your doctor has ordered another medicine to be applied to the skin along with this medicine, it is best to apply them at different times. This may help keep your skin from becoming too irritated. Also, if the medicines are used at or near the same time, they may not work properly.

You may continue to use cosmetics (make-up) while you are using this medicine for acne. However, it is best to use only water-base cosmetics. Also, it is best not to use cosmetics too heavily or too often. They may make your acne worse. If you have any questions about this, check with your doctor.

Side Effects of This Medicine

Along with its needed effects, a medicine may cause some unwanted effects. Although not all of these side effects may occur, if they do occur, they may need medical attention.

Check with your doctor as soon as possible if any of the following side effects occur:

Rare

White spots or lightening of treated areas of dark skin—in patients with dark complexions, although usually not lightened beyond normal skin color

Other side effects may occur that usually do not need medical attention. These side effects may go away during treatment as your body adjusts to the medicine. However, check with your doctor if any of the following side effects continue or are bothersome:

More common

Burning, stinging, or tingling of skin, mild; dryness of skin; itching of skin; peeling of skin; redness of skin

Other side effects not listed above may also occur in some patients. If you notice any other effects, check with your doctor.

Additional Information

Once a medicine has been approved for marketing for a certain use, experience may show that it is also useful for other medical problems. Although this use is not included in product labeling, azelaic acid is used in certain patients with the following medical condition:

- Melasma

Other than the above information, there is no additional information relating to proper use, precautions, or side effects for this use.

Developed: 06/27/96

AZELASTINE   Nasal

Commonly used brand name(s):

In the U.S.—
Astelin

Description

Azelastine (a-ZEL-as-teen) nasal solution is used to help treat the symptoms (runny nose, sneezing, itching) of seasonal (short-term) allergic rhinitis and vasomotor rhinitis.

This medicine works by blocking the effect of histamine on certain cells.

This medicine is available only with your doctor's prescription, in the following dosage form(s):

Nasal
- Nasal solution (U.S.)

Before Using This Medicine

In deciding to use a medicine, the risks of using the medicine must be weighed against the good it will do. This is a decision you and your doctor will make. For nasal azelastine, the following should be considered:

Allergies—Tell your doctor if you have ever had any unusual or allergic reaction to azelastine. Also tell your health care professional if you are allergic to any other substances, such as foods, preservatives, or dyes.

Pregnancy—Azelastine has not been studied in pregnant women. However, studies in animals have found that very large doses of azelastine cause birth defects and other problems. Before using this medicine, make sure your doctor knows if you are pregnant or if you may become pregnant.

Breast-feeding—It is not known whether azelastine passes into breast milk. Although most medicines pass into breast milk in small amounts, many of them may be used safely while breast-feeding. Mothers who are using this medicine and who wish to breast-feed should discuss this with their doctor.

Children—This medicine has been tested in children and, in effective doses, has not been shown to cause different side effects or problems in children, older than 5 years of age, than it does in adults.

Older adults—Many medicines have not been studied specifically in older people. Therefore, it may not be known whether they work exactly the same way they do in younger adults. Although there is no specific information comparing use of nasal azelastine in the elderly with use in other age groups, this medicine has been used in a small number of older patients and is not expected to cause different side effects or problems in older people than it does in younger adults.

Other medicines—Although certain medicines should not be used together at all, in other cases two different medicines may be used together even if an interaction might occur. In these cases, your doctor may want to change the dose, or other precautions may be necessary. When you are taking azelastine, it is especially important that your health care professional know if you are taking any of the following:

- Alcohol or
- Central nervous system (CNS) depressants (medicine that causes drowsiness) or
- Tricyclic antidepressants (amitriptyline [e.g., Elavil], amoxapine [e.g., Asendin], clomipramine [e.g., Anafranil], desipramine [e.g., Pertofrane], doxepin [e.g., Sinequan], imipramine [e.g., Tofranil], nortriptyline [e.g., Aventyl], protriptyline [e.g., Vivactil], trimipramine [e.g., Surmontil])—Use of these medicines with azelastine may increase the risk of drowsiness
- Cimetidine—May cause an increase in the blood levels of azelastine, which may result in increased effects

Other medical problems—The presence of other medical problems may affect the use of azelastine. Make sure you tell your doctor if you have any other medical problems, especially:

- Kidney disease—Blood levels of azelastine may be increased, leading to increased effects

Proper Use of This Medicine

This medicine usually comes with patient directions. Read them carefully before using the medicine.

Before using this medicine, clear the nasal passages by blowing your nose.

To prepare this medicine:

- Before you use a new bottle of azelastine spray, the spray pump will need to be primed (started). If your pharmacist assembled the unit for you, check to see if it has already been primed by pumping the unit once. If a full spray comes out, the unit has already been primed; if not you must prime the pump.
- To prime a new bottle, hold the bottle upright and away from you, then pump it four times or until you see a fine spray.
- If you have not used the spray for 3 or more days, pump it two times or until you see a fine spray.

To keep the applicator clean, wipe the nosepiece with a clean tissue and replace the dust cap after each use.

Use this medicine only as directed. Do not use more of it and do not use it more often than your doctor ordered. To do so may increase the chance of side effects.

Dosing—The dose of azelastine will be different for different patients. *Follow your doctor's orders or the directions on the label.* The following information includes only the average doses of azelastine. *If your dose is different, do not change it* unless your doctor tells you to do so.

- For *nasal* dosage form (nose spray):
  —For treatment of seasonal allergic rhinitis:
    - Adults and teenagers—Use 2 sprays in each nostril two times a day.
    - Children 5 to 11 years of age—Use 1 spray in each nostril two times a day.
    - Children younger than 5 years of age—Use and dose must be determined by your doctor.
  —For treatment of vasomotor rhinitis:
    - Adults and teenagers—Use 2 sprays in each nostril two times a day.
    - Children younger than 12 years of age—Use and dose must be determined by your doctor

Missed dose—If you miss a dose of this medicine, use it as soon as possible. However, if it is almost time for your next dose, skip the missed dose and go back to your regular dosing schedule. Do not double doses.

Storage—To store this medicine:

- Keep out of the reach of children.
- Store away from heat and direct light.
- Store the bottle upright at room temperature, with the pump tightly closed.
- Do not store in the bathroom, near the kitchen sink, or in other damp places. Heat or moisture may cause the medicine to break down.
- Do not keep outdated medicine or medicine no longer needed. Be sure that any discarded medicine is out of the reach of children.

Precautions While Using This Medicine

This medicine will add to the effects of alcohol and other CNS depressants (medicines that slow down the nervous system, possibly causing drowsiness). Some examples of CNS depressants are antihistamines or medicine for hay fever, other allergies, or colds; sedatives, tranquilizers, or sleeping medicine; prescription pain medicine or narcotics; medicine for seizures; muscle relaxants; or anesthetics, including some dental anesthetics. *Check with your doctor before taking any of the above while you are using this medicine.*

This medicine may cause some people to become dizzy, drowsy, or less alert than they are normally. Even if used at bedtime, it may cause some people to feel drowsy or less alert on arising. *Make sure you know how you react to this medicine before you drive, use machines, or do anything else that could be dangerous if you are not alert.*

Keep the spray away from the eyes because this medicine may cause irritation or blurred vision. Closing your eyes while you are using this medicine may help keep it out of your eyes.

Side Effects of This Medicine

Along with its needed effects, a medicine may cause some unwanted effects. Although not all of these side effects may occur, if they do occur they may need medical attention.

Check with your doctor as soon as possible if any of the following side effects occur:

Rare

Blood in urine; cough; eye pain or redness or blurred vision or other change in vision; rapid heartbeat; shortness of breath, tightness in chest, troubled breathing, or wheezing; skin rash, hives, or itching; sores in mouth or on lips

Other side effects may occur that usually do not need medical attention. These side effects may go away during treatment as your body adjusts to the medicine. However, check with your doctor if any of the following side effects continue or are bothersome:

More common

Bitter taste in mouth; drowsiness or sleepiness

Less common

Bloody mucus or unexplained nosebleeds; burning inside the nose; dizziness; dryness of mouth; headache; muscle aches or pain; nausea; sore throat; sudden outbursts of sneezing; unusual tiredness or weakness; weight gain

Other side effects not listed above may also occur in some patients. If you notice any other effects, check with your doctor.

Developed: 07/14/1998
Revised: 01/17/2001

AZELASTINE Ophthalmic— INTRODUCTORY VERSION

Commonly used brand name(s):

In the U.S.—
Optivar

Description

Azelastine (a-ZEL-as-teen) ophthalmic (eye) solution is used to treat itching of the eye caused by a condition known as allergic conjunctivitis. It works by preventing the effects of certain inflammatory substances, which are produced by cells in your eyes and sometimes cause allergic reactions.

This medicine is available only with your doctor's prescription, in the following dosage form:

Ophthalmic
• Solution (eye drops) (U.S.)

Before Using This Medicine

In deciding to use a medicine, the risks of using the medicine must be weighed against the good it will do. This is a decision you and your doctor will make. For azelastine, the following should be considered:

Allergies—Tell your doctor if you have ever had any unusual or allergic reaction to azelastine. Also tell your health care professional if you are allergic to any other substances, such as preservatives.

Pregnancy—Azelastine has not been studied in pregnant women. However, studies in animals have found that azelastine, given in high doses, causes harmful effects on the fetus.

Before taking this medicine, make sure your doctor knows if you are pregnant or if you may become pregnant.

Breast-feeding—It is not known whether azelastine passes into human breast milk after being used in the eye. Although most medicines pass into breast milk in small amounts, many of them may be used safely while breast-feeding. Mothers who are taking this medicine and who wish to breast-feed should discuss this with their doctor.

Children—Studies on this medicine have been done only in adult patients, and there is no specific information comparing use of azelastine in children under the age of 3 years with use in other age groups.

Older adults—This medicine has been tested and has not been shown to cause different side effects or problems in older people than it does in younger adults.

Other medicines—Although certain medicines should not be used together at all, in other cases two different medicines may be used together even if an interaction might occur. In these cases, your doctor may want to change the dose, or other precautions may be necessary. Tell your health care professional if you are using any other prescription or nonprescription (over-the-counter [OTC]) medicine.

Proper Use of This Medicine

Do not wear contact lenses if your eyes are red. If your eyes are not red, contact lenses should be removed before you use this medicine. Also, you should wait at least 10 minutes after using this medicine before putting the contact lenses back in.

To use:

• The bottle is only partially full to provide proper drop control.
• First, wash your hands. Tilt the head back and, pressing your finger gently on the skin just beneath the lower eyelid, pull the lower eyelid away from the eye to make a space. Drop the medicine into this space. Let go of the eyelid and gently close the eyes. Do not blink. Keep the eyes closed for 1 to 2 minutes to allow the medicine to be absorbed by the eye.
• If you think you did not get the drop of medicine into your eye properly, use another drop.
• Immediately after using the eye drops, wash your hands to remove any medicine that may be on them.

To keep the medicine as germ-free as possible, do not touch the applicator tip to any surface (including the eye). Also, keep the container tightly closed. Serious damage to the eye and possible loss of vision may result from using contaminated eye drops.

Dosing—The dose of azelastine will be different for different patients. *Follow your doctor's orders or the directions on the label*. The following information includes only the average doses of azelastine. *If your dose is different, do not change it* unless your doctor tells you to do so.

• For *ophthalmic* dosage form (eye drops):
—For eye allergy:
• Adults and children 3 years of age and older— Use one drop in the affected eye twice a day.
• Children younger than 3 years of age—Use and dose must be determined by your doctor.

Missed dose—If you miss a dose of this medicine, use it as soon as possible. However, if it is almost time for your next dose, skip the missed dose and go back to your regular dosing schedule. Do not double doses.

Storage—To store this medicine:

- Keep bottle in an upright position.
- Keep out of the reach of children.
- Keep the medicine from freezing. Store the medicine at room temperature.
- Do not keep outdated medicine or medicine no longer needed. Ask your health care professional how you should dispose of any medicine you do not use. Be sure that any discarded medicine is out of the reach of children.

Precautions While Using This Medicine

If your symptoms do not improve within a few days or if they become worse, check with your doctor.

Side Effects of This Medicine

Along with its needed effects, a medicine may cause some unwanted effects. Although not all of these side effects may occur, if they do occur they may need medical attention.

Check with your doctor immediately if any of the following side effects occur:

Less common
Cough; difficulty breathing; noisy breathing; shortness of breath; tightness in chest; wheezing

Other side effects may occur that usually do not need medical attention. These side effects may go away during treatment as your body adjusts to the medicine. However, check with your doctor if any of the following side effects continue or are bothersome:

More common
Bitter taste in mouth; headaches; temporary eye burning or stinging

Less common
Burning, dry or itching eyes; blurred vision, temporary; chills; diarrhea; eye discharge or excessive tearing; fever; general feeling of discomfort or illness; hoarseness or other voice changes; itching skin; joint pain; loss of appetite; muscle aches and pains; nausea; redness, pain, swelling of eye, eyelid, or inner lining of eyelid; runny nose; shivering; sneezing; sore throat; stuffy nose; sweating; tender, swollen glands in neck; trouble in swallowing; trouble sleeping; unusual tiredness or weakness; vomiting

Other side effects not listed above may also occur in some patients. If you notice any other effects, check with your doctor.

Developed: 10/27/2000
Revised: 01/03/2001

AZITHROMYCIN   Systemic

Commonly used brand name(s):

In the U.S.—
Zithromax

In Canada—
Zithromax

Description

Azithromycin (az-ith-roe-MYE-sin) is used to treat bacterial infections in many different parts of the body. It is also used to prevent *Mycobacterium avium* complex (MAC) disease in patients infected with the human immunodeficiency virus (HIV). It works by killing bacteria or preventing their growth. However, this medicine will not work for colds, flu, or other viral infections. Azithromycin may be used for other problems as determined by your doctor.

Azithromycin is available only with your doctor's prescription, in the following dosage forms:

Oral
- Capsules (U.S. and Canada)
- Oral suspension (U.S. and Canada)
- Tablets (U.S. and Canada)

Parenteral
- Injection (U.S.)

Before Using This Medicine

In deciding to use a medicine, the risks of taking the medicine must be weighed against the good it will do. This is a decision you and your doctor will make. For azithromycin, the following should be considered:

Allergies—Tell your doctor if you have ever had any unusual or allergic reaction to azithromycin or to any related medicines such as erythromycin. Also tell your health care professional if you are allergic to any other substances, such as foods, preservatives, or dyes.

Pregnancy—Azithromycin has not been studied in pregnant women. However, azithromycin has not been shown to cause birth defects or other problems in animal studies.

Breast-feeding—It is not known whether azithromycin passes into breast milk. Although most medicines pass into breast milk in small amounts, many of them may be used safely while breast-feeding. Mothers who are taking this medicine and who wish to breast-feed should discuss this with their doctor.

Children—This medicine has been tested in a limited number of children up to the age of 16. In effective doses, the medicine has not been shown to cause different side effects or problems than it does in adults.

Older adults—This medicine has been tested in a limited number of elderly patients and has not been shown to cause different side effects or problems in older people than it does in younger adults.

Other medicines—Although certain medicines should not be used together at all, in other cases two different medicines may be used together even if an interaction might occur. In these cases, your doctor may want to change the dose, or other precautions may be necessary. When you are taking azithromycin, it is especially important that your health care professional know if you are taking any of the following:

- Antacids, aluminum- and magnesium-containing—Antacids may decrease the amount of azithromycin in the blood, which may decrease its effects. To avoid problems, azithromycin should be taken at least 1 hour before or at least 2 hours after antacids

Other medical problems—The presence of other medical problems may affect the use of azithromycin. Make sure

you tell your doctor if you have any other medical problems, especially:

- Liver disease—Patients with severe liver disease may have an increased chance of side effects

Proper Use of This Medicine

Azithromycin capsules and pediatric oral suspension should be taken at least 1 hour before or at least 2 hours after meals. Azithromycin tablets and adult single dose oral suspension may be taken with or without food.

To help clear up your infection completely, *keep taking azithromycin for the full time of treatment*, even if you begin to feel better after a few days. If you stop taking this medicine too soon, your symptoms may return.

Dosing—The dose of azithromycin will be different for different patients. *Follow your doctor's orders or the directions on the label.* The following information includes only the average doses of azithromycin. *If your dose is different, do not change it* unless your doctor tells you to do so.

The number of capsules or tablets or the amount of suspension that you take depends on the medical problem for which you are taking azithromycin.

- For the *capsule* dosage form:
  —For bronchitis, strep throat, pneumonia, and skin infections:
    - Adults and adolescents 16 years of age and older—500 milligrams (mg) on the first day, then 250 mg once a day on days two through five.
    - Children up to 16 years of age—Use and dose must be determined by your doctor.
  —For chlamydia infections:
    - Adults and adolescents 16 years of age and older—1000 mg taken once as a single dose.
    - Children up to 16 years of age—Use and dose must be determined by your doctor.
- For the *oral suspension* dosage form:
  —For chancroid in men and chlamydia infections:
    - Adults and adolescents—1 gram taken once as a single dose.
    - Children 6 months to 12 years of age—Use and dose must be determined by your doctor.
  —For gonococcal infections:
    - Adults and adolescents—2 grams taken once as a single dose.
    - Children 6 months to 12 years of age—Use and dose must be determined by your doctor.
  —For otitis media and pneumonia:
    - Children 6 months to 12 years of age—10 milligrams (mg) per kilogram (kg) (4.5 mg per pound) of body weight once a day on the first day, then 5 mg per kg (2.2 mg per pound) of body weight once a day on days two through five.
  —For strep throat:
    - Adults and adolescents—The oral suspension is usually not used. Refer to azithromycin capsules or tablets.
    - Children 2 to 12 years of age—12 mg per kg (5.4 mg per pound) of body weight once a day for five days.
    - Children up to 2 years of age—Use and dose must be determined by your doctor.

- For the *tablet* dosage form:
  —For bronchitis, strep throat, pneumonia, and skin infections:
    - Adults and adolescents 16 years of age and older—500 milligrams (mg) on the first day, then 250 mg once a day on days two through five.
    - Children up to 16 years of age—Use and dose must be determined by your doctor.
  —For chlamydia infections:
    - Adults and adolescents 16 years of age and older—1000 mg taken once as a single dose.
    - Children up to 16 years of age—Use and dose must be determined by your doctor.
  —For prevention of *Mycobacterium avium* complex (MAC) disease:
    - Adults and adolescents 16 years of age and older—1200 mg once a week.
    - Children up to 16 years of age—Use and dose must be determined by your doctor.
- For *injection* dosage form:
  —For pelvic inflammatory disease:
    - Adults and adolescents 16 years of age and older—500 milligrams (mg) once a day for one or two days, injected into a vein.
    - Children up to 16 years of age—Use and dose must be determined by your doctor.
  —For pneumonia:
    Adults and adolescents 16 years of age and older—500 mg once a day for at least two days, injected into a vein.
    Children up to 16 years of age—Use and dose must be determined by your doctor.

Missed dose—If you miss a dose of this medicine, take it as soon as possible. However, if it is almost time for your next dose, skip the missed dose and go back to your regular dosing schedule. Do not double doses.

Storage—To store this medicine:
- Keep out of the reach of children.
- Store away from heat and direct light.
- Store the pediatric suspension form of azithromycin in the refrigerator.
- Do not store in the bathroom, near the kitchen sink, or in other damp places. Heat or moisture may cause the medicine to break down.
- Do not keep outdated medicine or medicine no longer needed. Be sure that any discarded medicine is out of the reach of children.

Precautions While Using This Medicine

If your symptoms do not improve within a few days, or if they become worse, check with your doctor.

Side Effects of This Medicine

Along with its needed effects, a medicine may cause some unwanted effects. Although not all of these side effects may occur, if they do occur they may need medical attention.

Stop taking this medicine and get emergency help immediately if any of the following side effects occur:
  More common (for injection form only)
    Pain, redness, and swelling at site of injection
  Rare
    Abdominal or stomach cramps or pain (severe); abdominal tenderness; diarrhea (watery and severe,

which may be bloody); difficulty in breathing; fever; joint pain; skin rash; swelling of face, mouth, neck, hands, and feet

Other side effects may occur that usually do not need medical attention. These side effects may go away during treatment as your body adjusts to the medicine. However, check with your doctor if any of the following side effects continue or are bothersome:

Less common
Diarrhea (mild); nausea; stomach pain or discomfoom-iting

Rare
Dizziness; headache

Other side effects not listed above may also occur in some patients. If you notice any other effects, check with your doctor.

Additional Information

Once a medicine has been approved for marketing for a certain use, experience may show that it is also useful for other medical problems. Although these uses are not included in product labeling, azithromycin is used in certain patients with the following medical condition:

- Trachoma (treatment)

Other than the above information, there is no additional information relating to proper use, precautions, or side effects for this use.

Revised: 08/08/2000

AZTREONAM   Systemic†

Commonly used brand name(s):

In the U.S.—
Azactam

†Not commercially available in Canada.

Description

Aztreonam (AZ-tree-oh-nam) is an antibiotic that is used to treat infections caused by bacteria. It works by killing bacteria or preventing their growth.

Aztreonam is used to treat bacterial infections in many different parts of the body. It is sometimes given with other antibiotics. This medicine will not work for colds, flu, or other viral infections.

This medicine is available only with your doctor's prescription. It is available in the following dosage form:

Parenteral
- Injection (U.S.)

Before Receiving This Medicine

In deciding to use a medicine, the risks of taking the medicine must be weighed against the good it will do. This is a decision you and your doctor will make. For aztreonam, the following should be considered:

Allergies—Tell your doctor if you have ever had any unusual or allergic reaction to aztreonam. Also tell your health care professional if you are allergic to any other substances, such as foods, preservatives, or dyes.

Pregnancy—Studies have not been done in humans. However, aztreonam has not been shown to cause birth defects or other problems in studies in rabbits and rats given up to 15 times the highest human daily dose.

Breast-feeding—Aztreonam passes into the breast milk in small amounts. However, this medicine is not absorbed when taken by mouth, and problems have not been seen in nursing babies.

Children—Studies have been done in children and have shown that aztreonam is effective in treating certain bacterial infections and that side effects in children are similar to those experienced by adults. Elevations of liver enzymes and reductions in white blood cell counts were seen in children who were given high doses of this medicine or who had more serious infections.

Older adults—Aztreonam has been tested in a limited number of patients 65 years of age or older and has not been shown to cause different side effects or problems in older people than it does in younger adults.

Other medicines—Although certain medicines should not be used together at all, in other cases two different medicines may be used together even if an interaction might occur. In these cases, your doctor may want to change the dose, or other precautions may be necessary. Tell your health care professional if you are taking any other prescription or nonprescription (over-the-counter [OTC]) medicine.

Other medical problems—The presence of other medical problems may affect the use of aztreonam. Make sure you tell your doctor if you have any other medical problems, especially:

- Liver disease—Patients receiving high doses of aztreonam for a long time, who also have severe liver disease, may have an increased chance of side effects
- Kidney disease—Patients with kidney disease may have an increased chance of side effects

Proper Use of This Medicine

To help clear up your infection completely, *aztreonam must be given for the full time of treatment*, even if you begin to feel better after a few days. Also, this medicine works best when there is a constant amount in the blood or urine. To help keep the amount constant, aztreonam must be given on a regular schedule.

Dosing—The dose of aztreonam will be different for different patients. *Follow your doctor's orders or the directions on the label*. The following information includes only the average doses of aztreonam. Your dose may be different if you have kidney disease. *If your dose is different, do not change it* unless your doctor tells you to do so.

- For *injection* dosage form:
  —Adults and children 16 years of age and older: 1 to 2 grams injected slowly into a vein over a twenty- to sixty-minute period. This is repeated every six to twelve hours.
  —Children up to 16 years of age: Dosage is based on body weight and must be determined by your doctor.

Side Effects of This Medicine

Along with its needed effects, a medicine may cause some unwanted effects. Although not all of these side effects may occur, if they do occur they may need medical attention.

Check with your doctor immediately if any of the following side effects occur:

Less common or rare

Black, tarry stools; blood in urine or stools; burning or itching of vagina; chest pain; chills; confusion; convulsions (seizures); cough; dark urine; diarrhea; difficulty in breathing; discharge from vagina; discomfort, inflammation, or swelling at the injection site; dizziness; eye pain; fever; flu-like symptoms; general feeling of illness; headache; hives; light gray-colored stools; loss of appetite; numbness of tongue; pinpoint red spots on skin; seeing double; skin rash, redness, or itching; sore throat; unusual bleeding or bruising; unusual tiredness or weakness; yellow skin or eyes

Other side effects may occur that usually do not need medical attention. These side effects may go away during treatment as your body adjusts to the medicine. However, check with your doctor if any of the following side effects continue or are bothersome:

Less common or rare

Abdominal or stomach cramps; altered sense of taste; bad breath; breast tenderness; burning or prickling feeling of skin; flushing; increased sweating; mouth ulcers; muscular aches; nasal congestion; nausea or vomiting; ringing, buzzing, or noise in ear; small, nonraised, round, purplish or red spots on skin; sneezing; trouble in sleeping

Other side effects not listed above may also occur in some patients. If you notice any other effects, check with your doctor.

Revised: 03/23/99

BACILLUS CALMETTE-GUÉRIN (BCG) LIVE   Systemic

Commonly used brand name(s):

In the U.S.—
TICE BCG

Description

Bacillus Calmette-Guérin (Ba-SIL'es Kal-met Geh-rin) (BCG) vaccine is given by injection to help prevent tuberculosis (TB). TB is a serious disease that can cause severe illness. It is spread by close contact with people who already have TB, such as people living in the same house. Some infected people do not appear to be sick, but they can still spread TB to others. BCG vaccine does not provide 100% protection. Therefore it is important to avoid people with TB, even if you have received the vaccine.

BCG vaccine is to be administered only by or under the direct supervision of a doctor. It is available in the following dosage forms:

Parenteral
• Multiple-puncture device (U.S.)
• Injection (Canada)

Before Receiving This Vaccine

In deciding to use a medicine, the risks of taking the medicine must be weighed against the good it will do. This is a decision you and your doctor will make. For BCG vaccine, the following should be considered:

Allergies—Tell your doctor if you have ever had any unusual or allergic reaction to BCG vaccine. Also tell your health care professional if you are allergic to any other substances, such as foods, preservatives, or dyes.

Pregnancy—Studies on effects in pregnancy have not been done in either humans or animals. Before you receive BCG vaccine, make sure your doctor knows if you are pregnant or if you may become pregnant.

Breast-feeding—It is not known whether BCG vaccine passes into the breast milk. Although most medicines pass into breast milk in small amounts, many of them may be used safely while breast-feeding. Mothers who will receive or have received BCG vaccine and who wish to breast-feed should discuss this with their doctor.

Children—BCG vaccine has been used widely in children, and it has not been reported to cause different side effects or problems in children than it does in adults.

Older adults—Many medicines have not been studied specifically in older people. Therefore, it may not be known whether they work exactly the same way they do in younger adults or if they cause different side effects or problems in older people. There is no specific information comparing use of BCG vaccine in the elderly with use in other age groups.

Other medicines—Although certain medicines should not be used together at all, in other cases two different medicines may be used together even if an interaction might occur. In these cases, your doctor may want to change the dose, or other precautions may be necessary. When you are going to receive BCG vaccine, it is especially important that your health care professional know if you are taking any of the following:

• Antituberculosis medicines (rifampin [e.g., Rifadin], isoniazid [e.g., Nydrazid])—These medicines may prevent BCG vaccine from working properly

• Corticosteroids (e.g., cortisone-like medicine)—Concurrent administration may result in increased risk of systemic infection

• Immunosuppressants (e.g., Sandimmune, Imuran)—Because these medicines reduce the body's natural immunity, they may prevent BCG from working properly. Also, the risk of infection may be increased

• Virus vaccines (e.g., Poliovax)—Concurrent administration with BCG is not recommended

Other medical problems—The presence of other medical problems may affect the use of BCG vaccine. Make sure you tell your doctor if you have any other medical problems, especially:

• Fever—If an infection is present, the chance of side effects from BCG vaccine may be increased

• Immunity problems—BCG vaccine may not work properly in persons with decreased natural immunity; also, the risk of side effects from BCG vaccine may be increased.

• Widespread skin infections

Proper Use of This Vaccine

Dosing—The dose of BCG vaccine may be different for different patients.

Side Effects of This Vaccine

Along with its needed effects, a medicine may cause some unwanted effects. Although not all of these side effects may occur, if they do occur they may need medical attention.

More common
Accumulation of pus; peeling or scaling of the skin; sores at place of injection; sores at different sites of the skin; swollen lymph glands

Rare
Cough; fever; increase in bone pain; skin rash

Other side effects not listed above may also occur in some patients. If you notice any other effects, check with your doctor.

Developed: 07/20/95

BACILLUS CALMETTE-GUÉRIN (BCG) LIVE— for Cancer Mucosal-Local

Commonly used brand name(s):

In the U.S.—
Pacis
TheraCys
TICE BCG

In Canada—
ImmuCyst
Pacis

Description

Bacillus Calmette-Guérin (Ba-SIL-es Kal-met Geh-rin) (BCG) is used as a solution that is run through a tube (instilled through a catheter) into the bladder to treat bladder cancer. The exact way it works against cancer is not known, but it may work by stimulating the body's immune system.

BCG is to be administered only by or under the immediate supervision of your doctor. It is available in the following dosage form:

Mucosal-Local
• Bladder instillation (U.S. and Canada)

Before Receiving This Medicine

In deciding to use a medicine, the risks of taking the medicine must be weighed against the good it will do. This is a decision you and your doctor will make. For BCG, the following should be considered:

Allergies—Tell your doctor if you have ever had any unusual or allergic reaction to BCG.

Pregnancy—BCG has not been studied in pregnant women or animals. Make sure your doctor knows if you are pregnant or if you may become pregnant before receiving BCG.

Breast-feeding—It is not known whether BCG passes into the breast milk.

Children—There is no specific information comparing use of BCG for treatment of cancer in children with use in other age groups.

Older adults—This medicine has been tested and has not been shown to cause different side effects or problems in older people than it does in younger adults.

Other medicines—Although certain medicines should not be used together at all, in other cases two different medicines may be used together even if an interaction might occur. In these cases, your doctor may want to change the dose, or other precautions may be necessary. When receiving BCG it is especially important that your health care professional know if you are taking any of the following:

• Amphotericin B by injection (e.g., Fungizone) or
• Antineoplastics (cancer medicine) or
• Antithyroid agents (medicine for overactive thyroid) or
• Azathioprine (e.g., Imuran) or
• Chlorambucil (e.g., Leukeran) or
• Chloramphenicol (e.g., Chloromycetin) or
• Colchicine or
• Corticosteroids (cortisone-like medicine) or
• Cyclophosphamide (e.g., Cytoxan) or
• Cyclosporine (e.g., Sandimmune) or
• Flucytosine (e.g., Ancobon) or
• Ganciclovir (e.g., Cytovene) or
• Interferon (e.g., Intron A, Roferon-A) or
• Mercaptopurine (e.g., Purinethol) or
• Methotrexate (e.g., Mexate) or
• Muromonab-CD3 (e.g., Orthoclone OKT3) or
• Plicamycin (e.g., Mithracin) or
• Zidovudine (e.g., AZT, Retrovir)—Because these medicines reduce the body's natural immunity, they may prevent BCG from stimulating the immune system and will cause it to be less effective. In addition, the risk of infection may be increased

Other medical problems—The presence of other medical problems may affect the use of BCG. Make sure you tell your doctor if you have any other medical problems, especially:

• Fever—Infection may be present and could cause problems

• Immunity problems—BCG treatment is less effective and there is a risk of infection

• Urinary tract infection—Infection and irritation of the bladder may occur

Proper Use of This Medicine

Your doctor will ask you to empty your bladder completely before the solution is instilled into it.

Follow your doctor's instructions carefully about how long to hold the solution in your bladder:
• The solution should be held in your bladder for 2 hours. If you think you cannot hold it, tell your health care professional.
• During the first hour, your doctor may have you lie for 15 minutes each on your stomach, back, and each side.
• When you do empty your bladder, you should be sitting down.

It is important that you drink extra fluids for several hours after each treatment with BCG so that you will pass more urine. Also, empty your bladder frequently. This will help prevent bladder problems.

BCG is a live product. In other words, it contains active bacteria that can cause infection. Some bacteria will be present for several hours in urine that you pass after each treatment with BCG. Any urine that you pass during the first 6 hours after each treatment should be disinfected with an equal amount (usually about 1 cup) of undiluted household bleach. After the bleach is added to the urine, it should be allowed to sit for 15 minutes before it is flushed. If you have any questions about this, check with your doctor.

Dosing—The dose of BCG will be different for different patients. The dose that is used may depend on a number of things. *If you are receiving BCG at home, follow your doctor's orders or the directions on the label.* If you have any questions about the proper dose of BCG, ask your doctor.

Precautions While Using This Medicine

While you are being treated with BCG, and for 6 to 12 weeks after you stop treatment with it, avoid contact with people who have tuberculosis. If you think you have been exposed to someone with tuberculosis, tell your doctor.

While you are being treated with BCG and for a few weeks after you stop treatment with it, do not have any immunizations (vaccinations) without your doctor's approval.

Side Effects of This Medicine

Along with its needed effects, a medicine may cause some unwanted effects. Although not all of these side effects may occur, if they do occur they may need medical attention.

Check with your doctor as soon as possible if any of the following side effects occur:
  More common
    Blood in urine; fever and chills; frequent urge to urinate; increased frequency of urination; joint pain; nausea and vomiting; painful urination (severe or continuing)

  Rare
    Cough; skin rash

Other side effects may occur that usually do not need medical attention. These side effects may go away during treatment as your body adjusts to the medicine. However, check with your doctor if any of the following side effects continue or are bothersome or if you have any questions about them:
  More common
    Burning during first urination after treatment

After you stop using this medicine, your body may need time to adjust. The length of time this takes depends on the amount of medicine you were using and how long you used it. During this period of time (up to 6 months after treatment with BCG) check with your doctor if you notice any of the following side effects:
    Cough; fever

Other side effects not listed above may also occur in some patients. If you notice any other effects, check with your doctor.

Revised: 08/17/2000

BACLOFEN   Intrathecal-Systemic

Commonly used brand name(s):

In the U.S.—
  Lioresal Intrathecal

In Canada—
  Lioresal Intrathecal

Description

Intrathecal baclofen (In-trah-THE-kal BAK-loe-fen) is used to help relax certain muscles in your body. It relieves the spasms, cramping, and tightness of muscles caused by medical problems such as multiple sclerosis, cerebral palsy, or certain injuries to the spine. Intrathecal baclofen does not cure these problems, but it may allow other treatment, such as physical therapy, to be more helpful in improving your condition.

Intrathecal baclofen acts on the central nervous system (CNS) to produce its muscle relaxant effects. Its actions on the CNS may also cause some of the medicine's side effects.

This medicine is delivered by a drug pump directly into the spinal fluid of your back. A doctor will surgically place the pump and monitor the dose of the medication that is delivered by the pump. The dose of intrathecal baclofen will be different for different patients and will depend on the type of muscle tightness that you have.

Intrathecal baclofen is given only by or under the direct supervision of a doctor. It is available in the following dosage form:
  Intrathecal
  • Injection (U.S. and Canada)

Before Using This Medicine

In deciding to use a medicine, the risks of using the medicine must be weighed against the good it will do. This is a decision you and your doctor will make. For intrathecal baclofen, the following should be considered:

Allergies—Tell your doctor if you have ever had any unusual or allergic reaction to intrathecal or oral baclofen. Also tell your health care professional if you are allergic to any other substances, such as foods, preservatives, or dyes.

Pregnancy—This medicine has not been studied in pregnant women. However, studies in animals have shown that baclofen causes birth defects and other problems during pregnancy. Before taking this medicine make sure your doctor knows if you are pregnant or if you may become pregnant.

Breast-feeding—Oral baclofen passes into the breast milk. However, it is not known whether intrathecal baclofen passes into breast milk. This medicine has not been reported to cause problems in nursing babies.

Children—This medicine has been tested in children 4 years of age and older. Effective doses have not been shown to cause different side effects or problems in children than it does in adults. However, this medicine may not be safe for children younger than 4 years of age.

Older adults—Side effects such as hallucinations, confusion or mental depression, other mood or mental changes, and severe drowsiness may be especially likely to occur in elderly patients, who may be more sensitive than younger adults to the effects of intrathecal baclofen.

Other medicines—Although certain medicines should not be used together at all, in other cases two different medicines may be used together even if an interaction might occur. In these cases, your doctor may want to change the dose, or other precautions may be necessary. When you are using intrathecal baclofen, it is especially important that your health care professional know if you are using any of the following:

- Alcohol or
- Central nervous system (CNS) depressants (medicines that may make you drowsy)—The chance of side effects may be increased

Other medical problems—The presence of other medical problems may affect the use of intrathecal baclofen. Make sure you tell your doctor if you have any other medical problems, especially:

- Epilepsy or
- Kidney disease or
- Mental or emotional problems or
- Spinal lesions—The chance of side effects may be increased

Precautions While Using This Medicine

Your doctor should check your progress at regular visits, especially during the first few weeks of treatment with this medicine. During this time, the amount of medicine you are using may have to be changed often to meet your individual needs. Make sure to keep all appointments to refill the pump. If the pump is not refilled on time, you may experience return of your muscle tightness and withdrawal symptoms including hallucinations and convulsions (seizures).

Intrathecal baclofen will add to the effects of alcohol and other CNS depressants (medicines that may make you drowsy or less alert). Some examples of CNS depressants are antihistamines or medicine for hay fever, other allergies, or colds; sedatives, tranquilizers, or sleeping medicine; prescription pain medicine or narcotics; barbiturates; medicine for seizures; other muscle relaxants; and anesthetics, including some dental anesthetics. *Check with your doctor before taking any of the above while you are using intrathecal baclofen.*

Intrathecal baclofen may cause dizziness, drowsiness, false sense of well-being, lightheadedness, vision problems, or clumsiness or unsteadiness in some people. *Make sure you know how you react to this medicine before you drive, use machines, or do anything else that could be dangerous if you are not alert, well-coordinated, and able to see well.*

Intrathecal baclofen may cause dryness of the mouth. For temporary relief, use sugarless candy or gum, melt bits of ice in your mouth, or use a saliva substitute. However, if dry mouth continues for more than 2 weeks, check with your medical doctor or dentist. Continuing dryness of the mouth may increase the chance of dental disease, including tooth decay, gum disease, and fungus infections.

Dizziness, lightheadedness, or fainting may occur when you get up suddenly from a lying or sitting position. Getting up slowly may help lessen this problem.

Side Effects of This Medicine

Along with its needed effects, a medicine may cause some unwanted effects. Although not all of these side effects may occur, if they do occur they may need medical attention.

Check with your doctor as soon as possible if any of the following side effects occur:

More common
    Convulsions (seizures)

Less common or rare
    Blurred vision or double vision; fainting; mental depression; muscle weakness; ringing or buzzing in ears; seeing, hearing, or feeling things that are not there; shortness of breath or troubled breathing

Symptoms of overdose
    Convulsions (seizures); dizziness, drowsiness, or lightheadedness; increased watering of the mouth; mental confusion; muscle weakness; nausea and/or vomiting; shortness of breath or troubled breathing

Other side effects may occur that usually do not need medical attention. These side effects may go away during treatment as your body adjusts to the medicine. However, check with your doctor if any of the following side effects continue or are bothersome:

More common
    Constipation; difficult urination; dizziness; headache; nausea and/or vomiting; numbness or tingling in hands or feet; sleepiness

Less common
    Clumsiness, unsteadiness, trembling, or other problems with muscle control; diarrhea; difficulty sleeping; dizziness or lightheadedness, especially when getting up from a lying or sitting position; dry mouth; frequent urge to urinate; irritation of the skin at the site where the pump is located; itching of the skin; sexual problems; slurred speech or other speech problems; swelling of ankles, feet, or lower legs; trembling or shaking

Some side effects may occur after you have stopped using this medicine. *Check with your doctor immediately* if any of the following effects occur:
    Convulsions (seizures); facial flushing, headache, increased sweating, or slow heartbeat; increased muscle spasms; seeing, hearing, or feeling things that are not there

Other side effects not listed above may also occur in some patients. If you notice any other effects, check with your doctor.

Developed: 07/08/98

BACLOFEN   Systemic

Commonly used brand name(s):

In the U.S.—
    Lioresal
    Generic name product may be available.

In Canada—

Lioresal	Nu-Baclofen
Apo-Baclofen	PMS-Baclofen
Novo-Baclofen	

Description

Baclofen (BAK-loe-fen) is used to help relax certain muscles in your body. It relieves the spasms, cramping, and tightness of muscles caused by medical problems such as multiple sclerosis or certain injuries to the spine. Baclofen does not cure these problems, but it may allow other treatment, such as physical therapy, to be more helpful in improving your condition.

Baclofen acts on the central nervous system (CNS) to produce its muscle relaxant effects. Its actions on the CNS may also cause some of the medicine's side effects. Baclofen may also be used to relieve other conditions as determined by your doctor.

This medicine is available only with your doctor's prescription, in the following dosage form:

Oral
- Tablets (U.S. and Canada)

Before Using This Medicine

In deciding to use a medicine, the risks of taking the medicine must be weighed against the good it will do. This is a decision you and your doctor will make. For baclofen, the following should be considered:

Allergies—Tell your doctor if you have ever had any unusual or allergic reaction to baclofen. Also tell your health care professional if you are allergic to any other substances, such as foods, preservatives, or dyes.

Pregnancy—Studies on birth defects with baclofen have not been done in humans. However, studies in animals have shown that baclofen, when given in doses several times the human dose, increases the chance of hernias and incomplete or slow development of bones in the fetus, and of lower birth weight.

Breast-feeding—Baclofen passes into the breast milk. However, this medicine has not been reported to cause problems in nursing babies.

Children—Studies on this medicine have been done only in adult patients, and there is no specific information comparing use of baclofen in children with use in other age groups.

Older adults—Side effects such as hallucinations, confusion or mental depression, other mood or mental changes, and severe drowsiness may be especially likely to occur in elderly patients, who are usually more sensitive than younger adults to the effects of baclofen.

Other medicines—Although certain medicines should not be used together at all, in other cases two different medicines may be used together even if an interaction might occur. In these cases, your doctor may want to change the dose, or other precautions may be necessary. When you are taking baclofen, it is especially important that your health care professional know if you are taking any of the following:
- Antidepressants, tricyclic (amitriptyline [e.g., Elavil]), amoxapine [e.g., Asendin], clomipramine [e.g., Anafranil], desipramine [e.g., Pertofrane], doxepin [e.g., Sinequan], imipramine [e.g., Tofranil], nortriptyline [e.g., Aventyl], protriptyline [e.g., Vivactil], trimipramine [e.g., Surmontil]) or
- Central nervous system (CNS) depressants (medicines that causes drowsiness)—The chance of side effects may be increased

Other medical problems—The presence of other medical problems may affect the use of baclofen. Make sure you tell your doctor if you have any other medical problems, especially:
- Diabetes mellitus (sugar diabetes)—Baclofen may raise blood sugar levels

- Epilepsy or
- Kidney disease or
- Mental or emotional problems or
- Stroke or other brain disease—The chance of side effects may be increased

Proper Use of This Medicine

Dosing—The dose of baclofen will be different for different patients. *Follow your doctor's orders or the directions on the label.* The following information includes only the average doses of baclofen. *If your dose is different, do not change it* unless your doctor tells you to do so.
- For *oral* dosage form (tablets):
  —For muscle relaxation:
  - Adults and teenagers—At first, the dose is 5 milligrams (mg) three times a day. Then, each dose may be increased by 5 mg every three days until the desired response is reached. No more than 80 mg should be taken within a twenty-four-hour period.
  - Children—Use and dose must be determined by your doctor.

Missed dose—If you miss a dose of this medicine, and you remember within an hour or so of the missed dose, take it as soon as you remember. However, if you do not remember until later, skip the missed dose and go back to your regular dosing schedule. Do not double doses.

Storage—To store this medicine:
- Keep out of the reach of children.
- Store away from heat and direct light.
- Do not store in the bathroom, near the kitchen sink, or in other damp places. Heat or moisture may cause the medicine to break down.
- Do not keep outdated medicine or medicine no longer needed. Be sure that any discarded medicine is out of the reach of children.

Precautions While Using This Medicine

Do not suddenly stop taking this medicine. Unwanted effects may occur if the medicine is stopped suddenly. Check with your doctor for the best way to reduce gradually the amount you are taking before stopping completely.

This medicine will add to the effects of alcohol and other CNS depressants (medicines that slow down the nervous system, possibly causing drowsiness). Some examples of CNS depressants are antihistamines or medicine for hay fever, other allergies, or colds; sedatives, tranquilizers, or sleeping medicine; prescription pain medicine or narcotics; barbiturates; medicine for seizures; other muscle relaxants; or anesthetics, including some dental anesthetics. *Check with your doctor before taking any of the above while you are using baclofen.*

This medicine may cause drowsiness, dizziness, vision problems, or clumsiness or unsteadiness in some people. *Make sure you know how you react to this medicine before you drive, use machines, or do anything else that could be dangerous if you are not alert, well-coordinated, and able to see well.*

For *diabetic patients:*
- This medicine may cause your blood sugar levels to rise. If you notice a change in the results of your blood or urine sugar test or if you have any questions about this, check with your doctor.

Side Effects of This Medicine

Along with its needed effects, a medicine may cause some unwanted effects. Although not all of these side effects may occur, if they do occur they may need medical attention.

Check with your doctor as soon as possible if any of the following side effects occur:

Less common or rare
Bloody or dark urine; chest pain; fainting; hallucinations (seeing or hearing things that are not there); mental depression or other mood changes; ringing or buzzing in the ears; skin rash or itching

Symptoms of overdose
Blurred or double vision; convulsions (seizures); muscle weakness (severe); shortness of breath or unusually slow or troubled breathing; vomiting

Other side effects may occur that usually do not need medical attention. These side effects may go away during treatment as your body adjusts to the medicine. However, check with your doctor if any of the following side effects continue or are bothersome:

More common
Confusion; dizziness or lightheadedness; drowsiness; nausea; unusual weakness, especially muscle weakness

Less common or rare
Abdominal or stomach pain or discomfort; clumsiness, unsteadiness, trembling, or other problems with muscle control; constipation; diarrhea; difficult or painful urination or decrease in amount of urine; false sense of well-being; frequent urge to urinate or uncontrolled urination; headache; loss of appetite; low blood pressure; muscle or joint pain; numbness or tingling in hands or feet; pounding heartbeat; sexual problems in males; slurred speech or other speech problems; stuffy nose; swelling of ankles; trouble in sleeping; unexplained muscle stiffness; unusual excitement; unusual tiredness; weight gain

Some side effects may occur after you have stopped taking this medicine, especially if you stop taking it suddenly. *Check with your doctor immediately* if any of the following effects occur:
Convulsions (seizures); hallucinations (seeing or hearing things that are not there); increase in muscle spasm, cramping, or tightness; mood or mental changes; unusual nervousness or restlessness

Other side effects not listed above may also occur in some patients. If you notice any other effects, check with your doctor.

Additional Information

Once a medicine has been approved for marketing for a certain use, experience may show that it is also useful for other medical problems. Although this use is not included in product labeling, baclofen is used in certain patients with trigeminal neuralgia (severe burning or stabbing pain along the nerves in the face); also called "tic douloureux."

There is no additional information relating to proper use, precautions, or side effects for this use of baclofen.

Revised: 05/19/99

BALSALAZIDE   Systemic— INTRODUCTORY VERSION

Commonly used brand name(s):

In the U.S.—
Colazal

Description

Balsalazide (bal–SAL–a–zide) helps to decrease inflammation in the colon by blocking the production of certain chemicals that cause the bowel to become overactive.

This medicine is available only with your doctor's prescription, in the following dosage form:

Oral
• Capsules (U.S.)

Before Using This Medicine

In deciding to use a medicine, the risks of taking the medicine must be weighed against the good it will do. This is a decision you and your doctor will make. For balsalazide, the following should be considered:

Allergies—Tell your doctor if you have ever had any unusual or allergic reaction to salicylates or balsalazide or mesalamine. Also tell your health care professional if you are allergic to any other substances, such as foods, preservatives, or dyes.

Pregnancy—Balsalazide has not been studied in pregnant women. However, balsalazide has not been shown to cause birth defects or other problems in animal studies.

Breast-feeding—It is not known if balsalazide passes into breast milk. Although most medicines pass into breast milk in small amounts, many of them may be used safely while breast-feeding. Mothers who are taking this medicine and who wish to breast-feed should discuss this with their doctor.

Children—Studies on this medicine have been done only in adult patients, and there is no specific information comparing the use of balsalazide in children with use in other age groups.

Older adults—Many medicines have not been studied specifically in older people. Therefore, it may not be known whether they work exactly the same way they do in younger adults or if they cause different side effects or problems in older people. There is no specific information comparing the use of balsalazide in the elderly with use in other age groups.

Other medicines—Although certain medicines should not be used together at all, in other cases two different medicines may be used together even if an interaction might occur. In these cases, your doctor may want to change the dose, or other precautions may be necessary. Tell your health care professional if you are taking any other prescription or nonprescription (over-the-counter [OTC]) medicine.

Other medical problems—The presence of other medical problems may affect the use of balsalazide. Make sure you tell your doctor if you have any other medical problems, especially:
• Pyloric stenosis—Balsalazide capsules may take longer to reach the colon.
• Kidney problems—Balsalazide should be used with caution.

Proper Use of This Medicine

Dosing—The dose of balsalazide will be different for different patients. *Follow your doctor's orders or the directions on the label.* The following information includes only the average dose of balsalazide. *If your dose is different, do not change it* unless your doctor tells you to do so.

- For *oral* dosage form (capsules):
  —For treatment of ulcerative colitis
    - Adults—Three 750-milligram (mg) balsalazide capsules three times a day for a total daily dose of 6.75 grams for eight weeks. You may need to take the medicine for up to twelve weeks as ordered by your doctor.
    - Children—Use and dosage must be determined by your doctor.

Missed dose— If you miss a dose of this medicine, take it as soon as possible. However, if it is almost time for your next dose, skip the missed dose and go back to your regular dosing schedule. Do not double doses.

Storage—To store this medicine:

- Keep out of the reach of children.
- Keep the medicine from freezing. Do not refrigerate.
- Do not store in the bathroom, near the kitchen sink, or in other damp places. Heat or moisture may cause the medicine to break down.
- Do not keep outdated medicine or medicine no longer needed. Ask your health care professional how you should dispose of any medicine you do not use. Be sure that any discarded medicine is out of the reach of children.

Precautions While Using This Medicine

It is important that your doctor check your progress at regular visits. This will allow your doctor to check for any unwanted effects.

If your symptoms become worse, check with your doctor.

Side Effects of This Medicine

Side effects may occur that usually do not need medical attention. These side effects may go away during treatment as your body adjusts to the medicine. However, check with your doctor if any of the following side effects continue or are bothersome.

More Common
  Diarrhea; stomach pain

Less common
  Blood in urine; constipation; coughing; cramps; dry mouth; fever; flu-like symptoms; passing of gas; heart burn or upset stomach; joint pain; loss of appetite; lower back pain; muscle pain; pain or burning while urinating; stuffy nose; trouble sleeping or getting to sleep; unusual tiredness or weakness; yellowish skin

Other side effects not listed above may also occur in some patients. If you notice any other effects, check with your doctor.

Developed: 11/09/2000

BARBITURATES Systemic

Commonly used brand name(s):

In the U.S.—

Alurate[2]	Mebaral[4]
Amytal[1]	Nembutal[6]
Barbita[7]	Sarisol No. 2[3]
Busodium[3]	Seconal[8]
Butalan[3]	Solfoton[7]
Butisol[3]	Tuinal[9]
Luminal[7]	

In Canada—

Amytal[1]	Nova Rectal[6]
Ancalixir[7]	Novopentobarb[6]
Butisol[3]	Novosecobarb[8]
Mebaral[4]	Seconal[8]
Nembutal[6]	Tuinal[9]

In other countries—
  Gemonil[5]

Note: For quick reference, the following barbiturates are numbered to match the corresponding brand names.

This information applies to the following medicines:
1. Amobarbital (am-oh-BAR-bi-tal)‡
2. Aprobarbital (a-proe-BAR-bi-tal)†
3. Butabarbital (byoo-ta-BAR-bi-tal)‡
4. Mephobarbital (me-foe-BAR-bi-tal)
5. Metharbital (meth-AR-bi-tal)*†
6. Pentobarbital (pen-toe-BAR-bi-tal)‡
7. Phenobarbital (fee-noe-BAR-bi-tal)‡§
8. Secobarbital (see-koe-BAR-bi-tal)‡
9. Secobarbital and Amobarbital (see-koe-BAR-bi-tal and am-oh-BAR-bi-tal)

*Not commercially available in the U.S.
†Not commercially available in Canada.
‡Generic name product may be available in the U.S.
§Generic name product may be available in Canada.

Description

Barbiturates (bar-BI-tyoo-rates) belong to the group of medicines called central nervous system (CNS) depressants (medicines that cause drowsiness). They act on the brain and CNS to produce effects that may be helpful or harmful. This depends on the individual patient's condition and response and the amount of medicine taken.

Some of the barbiturates may be used before surgery to relieve anxiety or tension. In addition, some of the barbiturates are used as anticonvulsants to help control seizures in certain disorders or diseases, such as epilepsy. Barbiturates may also be used for other conditions as determined by your doctor.

The barbiturates have been used to treat insomnia (trouble in sleeping); but if they are used regularly (for example, every day) for insomnia, they are usually not effective for longer than 2 weeks. The barbiturates have also been used to relieve nervousness or restlessness during the daytime. However, the barbiturates have generally been replaced by safer medicines for the treatment of insomnia and daytime nervousness or tension.

If too much of a barbiturate is used, it may become habit-forming.

Barbiturates should not be used for anxiety or tension caused by the stress of everyday life.

These medicines are available only with your doctor's prescription, in the following dosage forms:

Oral
Amobarbital
- Capsules (U.S. and Canada)
- Tablets (U.S. and Canada)

Aprobarbital
- Elixir (U.S.)

Butabarbital
- Capsules (U.S.)
- Elixir (U.S.)
- Tablets (U.S. and Canada)

Mephobarbital
- Tablets (U.S. and Canada)

Metharbital
- Tablets (Other countries)

Pentobarbital
- Capsules (U.S. and Canada)
- Elixir (U.S.)

Phenobarbital
- Capsules (U.S.)
- Elixir (U.S. and Canada)
- Tablets (U.S. and Canada)

Secobarbital
- Capsules (U.S. and Canada)

Secobarbital and Amobarbital
- Capsules (U.S. and Canada)

Parenteral
Amobarbital
- Injection (U.S. and Canada)

Pentobarbital
- Injection (U.S. and Canada)

Phenobarbital
- Injection (U.S. and Canada)

Secobarbital
- Injection (U.S.)

Rectal
Pentobarbital
- Suppositories (U.S. and Canada)

Before Using This Medicine

In deciding to use a medicine, the risks of taking the medicine must be weighed against the good it will do. This is a decision you and your doctor will make. For barbiturates, the following should be considered:

Allergies—Tell your doctor if you have ever had any unusual or allergic reaction to barbiturates. Also tell your health care professional if you are allergic to any other substances, such as foods, preservatives, or dyes.

Pregnancy—Barbiturates have been shown to increase the chance of birth defects in humans. However, this medicine may be needed in serious diseases or other situations that threaten the mother's life. Be sure you have discussed this and the following information with your doctor:

- Taking barbiturates regularly during pregnancy may cause bleeding problems in the newborn infant. In addition, taking barbiturates regularly during the last 3 months of pregnancy may cause the baby to become dependent on the medicine. This may lead to withdrawal side effects in the baby after birth.
- One study in humans has suggested that barbiturates taken during pregnancy may increase the chance of brain tumors in the baby.

- Barbiturates taken for anesthesia during labor and delivery may reduce the force and frequency of contractions of the uterus; this may prolong labor and delay delivery.
- Use of barbiturates during labor may cause breathing problems in the newborn infant.

Breast-feeding—Barbiturates pass into the breast milk and may cause drowsiness, slow heartbeat, shortness of breath, or troubled breathing in babies of nursing mothers taking this medicine.

Children—Unusual excitement may be more likely to occur in children, who are usually more sensitive than adults to the effects of barbiturates.

Older adults—Confusion, mental depression, and unusual excitement may be more likely to occur in the elderly, who are usually more sensitive than younger adults to the effects of barbiturates.

Other medicines—Although certain medicines should not be used together at all, in other cases 2 different medicines may be used together even if an interaction might occur. In these cases, your doctor may want to change the dose, or other precautions may be necessary. When you are taking a barbiturate, it is especially important that your health care professional know if you are taking any of the following:

- Adrenocorticoids (cortisone-like medicine) or
- Anticoagulants (blood thinners) or
- Carbamazepine or
- Corticotropin (ACTH)—Barbiturates may decrease the effects of these medicines

- Central nervous system (CNS) depressants (medicines that cause drowsiness)—Using these medicines with barbiturates may result in increased CNS depressant effects

- Divalproex sodium or
- Valproic acid—Using these medicines with barbiturates may change the amount of either medicine that you need to take

- Oral contraceptives (birth control pills) containing estrogens—Barbiturates may decrease the effectiveness of these oral contraceptives, and you may need to change to a different type of birth control

Other medical problems—The presence of other medical problems may affect the use of barbiturates. Make sure you tell your doctor if you have any other medical problems, especially:

- Alcohol abuse (or history of) or
- Drug abuse or dependence (or history of)—Dependence on barbiturates may develop

- Anemia (severe) or
- Asthma (history of), emphysema, or other chronic lung disease or
- Diabetes mellitus (sugar diabetes) or
- Hyperactivity (in children) or
- Mental depression or
- Overactive thyroid or
- Porphyria (or history of)—Barbiturates may make the condition worse

- Kidney disease or
- Liver disease—Higher blood levels of barbiturates may result, increasing the chance of side effects

- Pain—Barbiturates may cause unexpected excitement or mask important symptoms of more serious problems

- Underactive adrenal gland—Barbiturates may interfere with the effects of other medicines needed for this condition

---

Proper Use of This Medicine

For patients taking the *extended-release capsule or tablet form* of this medicine:

- These capsules or tablets are to be swallowed whole. Do not break, crush, or chew before swallowing.

For patients using the *rectal suppository form* of this medicine:

- To insert the suppository: First remove the foil wrapper and moisten the suppository with cold water. Lie down on your side and use your finger to push the suppository well up into the rectum.
- Wash your hands with soap and water.

Use this medicine only as directed by your doctor. Do not use more of it, do not use it more often, and do not use it for a longer time than your doctor ordered. If too much is used, it may become habit-forming (causing mental or physical dependence).

If you think this medicine is not working properly after you have taken it for a few weeks, *do not increase the dose.* To do so may increase the chance of your becoming dependent on the medicine. Instead, check with your doctor.

If you are taking this medicine for epilepsy, it must be taken every day in regularly spaced doses as ordered by your doctor in order for it to control your seizures. This is necessary to keep a constant amount of medicine in the blood. To help keep the amount constant, do not miss any doses.

Dosing—The dose of barbiturates will be different for different patients. *Follow your doctor's orders or the directions on the label.* The following information includes only the average doses of barbiturates. *If your dose is different, do not change it* unless your doctor tells you to do so.

The number of capsules, tablets, or teaspoonfuls of elixir that you take, the number of suppositories you use, or the number of injections you receive depends on the strength of the medicine. Also, *the number of doses you take each day, the time allowed between doses, and the length of time you take the medicine depend on the medical problem for which you are taking barbiturates.*

For amobarbital
- For *oral* dosage form (tablets or capsules):
  —For trouble in sleeping:
  - Adults—65 to 200 milligrams (mg) at bedtime.
  - Children—Dose must be determined by your doctor.
  —For daytime sedation:
  - Adults—50 to 300 mg, taken in smaller doses during the day.
  - Children—Dose is based on body weight or size and must be determined by your doctor. The usual dose is 2 mg per kilogram (kg) (0.9 mg per pound) of body weight taken three times a day.
  —For sedation before surgery:
  - Adults—200 mg taken one to two hours before surgery.
  - Children—Dose is based on body weight and must be determined by your doctor. The usual dose is 2 to 6 mg per kg (0.9 to 2.7 mg per pound)

of body weight, taken before surgery. However, the dose is usually not more than 100 mg.
  —For sedation during labor:
  - Adults—200 to 400 mg every one to three hours if needed. However, the total dose is usually not more than 1000 mg.
- For *injection* dosage form:
  —For trouble in sleeping:
  - Adults—65 to 200 mg, injected into a muscle or vein.
  - Children up to 6 years of age—Dose is based on body weight and must be determined by your doctor. The usual dose is 2 to 3 mg per kg (0.9 to 1.4 mg per pound) of body weight, injected into a muscle.
  - Children 6 years of age and over—Dose is based on body weight and must be determined by your doctor. The usual dose is 2 to 3 mg per kg (0.9 to 1.4 mg per pound) of body weight, injected into a muscle, or 65 to 500 mg injected into a vein.
  —For daytime sedation:
  - Adults—30 to 50 mg two or three times a day, injected into a muscle or vein.
  —For sedation before surgery:
  - Children—Dose is based on body weight and must be determined by your doctor. The usual dose is 3 to 5 mg per kg (1.4 to 2.3 mg per pound) of body weight or 65 to 500 mg per dose, injected into a vein.
  —For control of seizures:
  - Adults and children 6 years of age and over—65 to 500 mg per dose, injected into a vein.
  - Children up to 6 years of age—Dose is based on body weight or size and must be determined by your doctor. The usual dose is 3 to 5 mg per kg (1.4 to 2.3 mg per pound) of body weight, injected into a muscle or vein.

For aprobarbital
- For *oral* dosage form (elixir):
  —For trouble in sleeping:
  - Adults—40 to 160 milligrams (mg) at bedtime.
  - Children—Dose must be determined by your doctor.
  —For daytime sedation:
  - Adults—40 mg three times a day.
  - Children—Dose must be determined by your doctor.

For butabarbital
- For *oral* dosage form (elixir or tablets):
  —For trouble in sleeping:
  - Adults—50 to 100 milligrams (mg) at bedtime.
  - Children—Dose must be determined by your doctor.
  —For daytime sedation:
  - Adults—15 to 30 mg three or four times a day.
  - Children—Dose is based on body weight or size and must be determined by your doctor. The usual dose is 2 mg per kilogram (kg) (0.9 mg per pound) of body weight three times a day.
  —For sedation before surgery:
  - Adults—50 to 100 mg sixty to ninety minutes before surgery.
  - Children—Dose is based on body weight and must be determined by your doctor. The usual dose is 2 to 6 mg per kg (0.9 to 2.7 mg per pound)

of body weight. However, the dose is usually not more than 100 mg.

For mephobarbital
- For *oral* dosage form (tablets):
  —For daytime sedation:
    - Adults—32 to 100 milligrams (mg) three or four times a day.
    - Children—16 to 32 mg three or four times a day.
  —For control of seizures:
    - Adults—200 to 600 mg a day, taken in smaller doses during the day.
    - Children up to 5 years of age—16 to 32 mg three or four times a day.
    - Children 5 years of age and over—32 to 64 mg three or four times a day.

For metharbital
- For *oral* dosage form (tablets):
  —For control of seizures:
    - Adults—At first, 100 milligrams (mg) one to three times a day. Your doctor may increase your dose if needed. However, the dose is usually not more than 800 mg a day.
    - Children—50 mg one to three times a day.

For pentobarbital
- For *oral* dosage form (elixir or capsules):
  —For trouble in sleeping:
    - Adults—100 milligrams (mg) at bedtime.
    - Children—Dose must be determined by your doctor.
  —For daytime sedation:
    - Adults—20 mg three or four times a day.
    - Children—Dose is based on body weight and must be determined by your doctor. The usual dose is 2 to 6 mg per kilogram (kg) (0.9 to 2.7 mg per pound) of body weight per day.
  —For sedation before surgery:
    - Adults—100 mg before surgery.
    - Children—Dose is based on body weight and must be determined by your doctor. The usual dose is 2 to 6 mg per kilogram (0.9 to 2.7 mg per pound) of body weight, taken before surgery. However, the dose is usually not more than 100 mg.
- For *injection* dosage form:
  —For trouble in sleeping:
    - Adults—150 to 200 mg, injected into a muscle. Or, 100 mg injected into a vein, with additional small doses given if needed. However, the dose is usually not more than 500 mg.
    - Children—Dose is based on body weight and must be determined by your doctor. The usual dose is 2 to 6 mg per kg (0.9 to 2.7 mg per pound) of body weight, injected into a muscle. Or, 50 mg injected into a vein, with additional small doses given if needed.
  —For sedation before surgery:
    - Adults—150 to 200 mg, injected into a muscle.
    - Children—Dose is based on body weight and must be determined by your doctor. The usual dose is 2 to 6 mg per kg (0.9 to 2.7 mg per pound) of body weight, injected into a muscle. However, the dose is usually not more than 100 mg.

—For control of seizures:
  - Adults—At first, 100 mg injected into a vein. Additional small doses may be given if needed. However, the dose is usually not more than 500 mg.
  - Children—At first, 50 mg injected into a muscle or vein. Additional small doses may be given if needed.
- For *rectal* dosage form (suppositories):
  —For trouble in sleeping:
    - Adults—120 to 200 mg inserted into the rectum at bedtime.
    - Children up to 2 months of age—Dose must be determined by your doctor.
    - Children 2 months to 1 year of age—30 mg inserted into the rectum at bedtime.
    - Children 1 to 4 years of age—30 or 60 mg inserted into the rectum at bedtime.
    - Children 5 to 12 years of age—60 mg inserted into the rectum at bedtime.
    - Children 12 to 14 years of age—60 or 120 mg inserted into the rectum at bedtime.
  —For daytime sedation:
    - Adults—30 mg inserted into the rectum two to four times a day.
    - Children—Dose is based on body weight or size and must be determined by your doctor. The usual dose is 2 mg per kg (0.9 mg per pound) of body weight, inserted into the rectum three times a day.
  —For sedation before surgery:
    - Children up to 2 months of age—Dose must be determined by your doctor.
    - Children 2 months to 1 year of age—30 mg inserted into the rectum.
    - Children 1 to 4 years of age—30 or 60 mg inserted into the rectum.
    - Children 5 to 12 years of age—60 mg inserted into the rectum.
    - Children 12 to 14 years of age—60 or 120 mg inserted into the rectum.

For phenobarbital
- For *oral* dosage form (elixir, capsules, or tablets):
  —For trouble in sleeping:
    - Adults—100 to 320 milligrams (mg) at bedtime.
    - Children—Dose must be determined by your doctor.
  —For daytime sedation:
    - Adults—30 to 120 mg a day, taken in smaller doses two or three times during the day.
    - Children—Dose is based on body weight or size and must be determined by your doctor. The usual dose is 2 mg per kilogram (kg) (0.9 mg per pound) of body weight three times a day.
  —For sedation before surgery:
    - Children—Dose is based on body weight and must be determined by your doctor. The usual dose is 1 to 3 mg per kg (0.45 to 1.4 mg per pound) of body weight.
  —For control of seizures:
    - Adults—60 to 250 mg a day.
    - Children—Dose is based on body weight and must be determined by your doctor. The usual dose is 1 to 6 mg per kg (0.45 to 2.7 mg per pound) of body weight a day.

- For *injection* dosage form:
  - —For trouble in sleeping:
    - Adults—100 to 325 mg, injected into a muscle or vein, or under the skin.
    - Children—Dose must be determined by your doctor.
  - —For daytime sedation:
    - Adults—30 to 120 mg a day, injected into a muscle or a vein, or under the skin, in smaller doses two or three times during the day,
    - Children—Dose must be determined by your doctor.
  - —For sedation before surgery:
    - Adults—130 to 200 mg, injected into a muscle sixty to ninety minutes before surgery.
    - Children—Dose is based on body weight and must be determined by your doctor. The usual dose is 1 to 3 mg per kg (0.45 to 1.4 mg per pound) of body weight, injected into a muscle or vein sixty to ninety minutes before surgery.
  - —For control of seizures:
    - Adults—100 to 320 mg injected into a vein. The dose may be repeated if needed, but is usually not more than 600 mg a day. However, higher doses may be needed for certain types of continuing seizures.
    - Children—Dose is based on body weight and must be determined by your doctor. At first, the usual dose is 10 to 20 mg per kg (4.5 to 9 mg per pound) of body weight, injected into a vein. Later, 1 to 6 mg per kg (0.45 to 2.7 mg per pound) of body weight a day, injected into a vein. Higher doses may be needed for certain types of continuing seizures.

For secobarbital

- For *oral* dosage form (capsules):
  - —For trouble in sleeping:
    - Adults—100 milligrams (mg) at bedtime.
    - Children—Dose must be determined by your doctor.
  - —For daytime sedation:
    - Adults—30 to 50 mg three or four times a day.
    - Children—Dose is based on body weight or size and must be determined by your doctor. The usual dose is 2 mg per kilogram (kg) (0.9 mg per pound) of body weight three times a day.
  - —For sedation before surgery:
    - Adults—200 to 300 mg one or two hours before surgery.
    - Children—Dose is based on body weight and must be determined by your doctor. The usual dose is 2 to 6 mg per kg (0.9 to 2.7 mg per pound) of body weight one or two hours before surgery. However, the dose is usually not more than 100 mg.
- For *injection* dosage form:
  - —For trouble in sleeping:
    - Adults—100 to 200 mg injected into a muscle, or 50 to 250 mg injected into a vein.
    - Children—Dose is based on body weight or size and must be determined by your doctor. The usual dose is 3 to 5 mg per kg (1.4 to 2.3 mg per pound) of body weight, injected into a muscle. However, the dose is usually not more than 100 mg.

- —For sedation before dental procedures:
  - Adults—Dose is based on body weight and must be determined by your doctor. The usual dose is 1.1 to 2.2 mg per kg (0.5 to 1 mg per pound) of body weight, injected into a muscle ten to fifteen minutes before the procedure.
  - Children—Dose must be determined by your dentist.
- —For sedation before a nerve block:
  - Adults—100 to 150 mg, injected into a vein.
- —For sedation before surgery:
  - Children—Dose is based on body weight and must be determined by your doctor. The usual dose is 4 to 5 mg per kg (1.8 to 2.3 mg per pound) of body weight, injected into a muscle.
- —For seizures from tetanus:
  - Adults—Dose is based on body weight and must be determined by your doctor. The usual dose is 5.5 mg per kg (2.5 mg per pound) of body weight, injected into a muscle or vein. Dose may be repeated every three to four hours if needed.
  - Children—Dose is based on body weight and must be determined by your doctor. The usual dose is 3 to 5 mg per kg (1.4 to 2.3 mg per pound) of body weight, injected into a muscle or vein.

For secobarbital and amobarbital combination

- For *oral* dosage form (capsules):
  - —For trouble in sleeping:
    - Adults—1 capsule at bedtime.
    - Children—Dose must be determined by your doctor.
  - —For sedation before surgery:
    - Adults—1 capsule taken one hour before surgery.
    - Children—Dose must be determined by your doctor.

Missed dose—If you are taking this medicine regularly (for example, every day as in epilepsy) and you do miss a dose, take it as soon as possible. However, if it is almost time for your next dose, skip the missed dose and go back to your regular dosing schedule. Do not double doses.

Storage—To store this medicine:

- Keep out of the reach of children since overdose is especially dangerous in children.
- Store away from heat and direct light.
- Do not store the capsule or tablet form of this medicine in the bathroom, near the kitchen sink, or in other damp places. Heat or moisture may cause the medicine to break down.
- Keep the liquid form of this medicine from freezing.
- Store the suppository form of this medicine in the refrigerator.
- Do not keep outdated medicine or medicine no longer needed. Be sure that any discarded medicine is out of the reach of children.

Precautions While Using This Medicine

If you will be using this medicine regularly for a long time:

- Your doctor should check your progress at regular visits.
- Do not stop using it without first checking with your doctor. Your doctor may want you to reduce gradually the amount you are using before stopping completely.

This medicine will add to the effects of alcohol and other CNS depressants (medicines that slow down the nervous system, possibly causing drowsiness). Some examples of CNS depressants are antihistamines or medicine for hay fever, other allergies, or colds; sedatives, tranquilizers, or sleeping medicine; prescription pain medicine or narcotics; medicine for seizures; muscle relaxants; or anesthetics, including some dental anesthetics. *Check with your doctor before taking any of the above while you are using this medicine.*

Before you have any medical tests, tell the medical doctor in charge that you are taking this medicine. The results of the metyrapone test may be affected by this medicine.

If you have been using this medicine for a long time and you think that you may have become mentally or physically dependent on it, check with your doctor. Some signs of mental or physical dependence on barbiturates are:

- a strong desire or need to continue taking the medicine.
- a need to increase the dose to receive the effects of the medicine.
- withdrawal side effects (for example, anxiety or restlessness, convulsions [seizures], feeling faint, nausea or vomiting, trembling of hands, trouble in sleeping) occurring after the medicine is stopped.

If you think you or someone else may have taken an overdose of this medicine, get emergency help at once. Taking an overdose of a barbiturate or taking alcohol or other CNS depressants with the barbiturate may lead to unconsciousness and possibly death. Some signs of an overdose are severe drowsiness, severe confusion, severe weakness, shortness of breath or slow or troubled breathing, slurred speech, staggering, and slow heartbeat.

This medicine may cause some people to become dizzy, lightheaded, drowsy, or less alert than they are normally. Even if taken at bedtime, it may cause some people to feel drowsy or less alert on arising. *Make sure you know how you react to this medicine before you drive, use machines, or do anything else that could be dangerous if you are dizzy or are not alert.*

Oral contraceptives (birth control pills) containing estrogen may not work properly if you take them while you are taking barbiturates. Unplanned pregnancies may occur. You should use a different or additional means of birth control while you are taking barbiturates. If you have any questions about this, check with your health care professional.

Side Effects of This Medicine

Along with its needed effects, a medicine may cause some unwanted effects. Although not all of these side effects may occur, if they do occur they may need medical attention.

Check with your doctor immediately if any of the following side effects occur:
Rare
Bleeding sores on lips; chest pain; fever; muscle or joint pain; red, thickened, or scaly skin; skin rash or hives; sores, ulcers, or white spots in mouth (painful); sore throat and/or fever; swelling of eyelids, face, or lips; wheezing or tightness in chest

Also, check with your doctor as soon as possible if any of the following side effects occur:
Less common
Confusion; mental depression; unusual excitement

Rare
Hallucinations (seeing, hearing, or feeling things that are not there); unusual bleeding or bruising; unusual tiredness or weakness
With long-term or chronic use
Bone pain, tenderness, or aching; loss of appetite; muscle weakness; weight loss (unusual); yellow eyes or skin
Symptoms of overdose
Confusion (severe); decrease in or loss of reflexes; drowsiness (severe); fever; irritability (continuing); low body temperature; poor judgment; shortness of breath or slow or troubled breathing; slow heartbeat; slurred speech; staggering; trouble in sleeping; unusual movements of the eyes; weakness (severe)

Other side effects may occur that usually do not need medical attention. These side effects may go away during treatment as your body adjusts to the medicine. However, check with your doctor if any of the following side effects continue or are bothersome:
More common
Clumsiness or unsteadiness; dizziness or lightheadedness; drowsiness; "hangover" effect

Less common
Anxiety or nervousness; constipation; feeling faint; headache; irritability; nausea or vomiting; nightmares or trouble in sleeping

For very ill patients:
- Confusion, mental depression, and unusual excitement may be more likely to occur in very ill patients

After you stop using this medicine, your body may need time to adjust. If you took this medicine in high doses or for a long time, this may take up to about 15 days. During this period of time check with your doctor if any of the following side effects occur (usually occur within 8 to 16 hours after medicine is stopped):
Anxiety or restlessness; convulsions (seizures); dizziness or lightheadedness; feeling faint; hallucinations (seeing, hearing, or feeling things that are not there); muscle twitching; nausea or vomiting; trembling of hands; trouble in sleeping, increased dreaming, or nightmares; vision problems; weakness

Other side effects not listed above may also occur in some patients. If you notice any other effects, check with your doctor.

Additional Information

Once a medicine has been approved for marketing for a certain use, experience may show that it is also useful for other medical problems. Although this use is not included in product labeling, phenobarbital is used in certain patients with the following medical condition:

- Hyperbilirubinemia (high amount of bile pigments in the blood that may lead to jaundice)

Other than the above information, there is no additional information relating to proper use, precautions, or side effects for these uses.

Revised: 01/27/92
Interim revision: 08/29/94

BARBITURATES, ASPIRIN, AND CODEINE Systemic

Commonly used brand name(s):

In the U.S.—

Ascomp with Codeine No.3[1]
Butalbital Compound with Codeine[1]
Butinal with Codeine No.3[1]

Fiorinal with Codeine No.3[1]
Idenal with Codeine[1]
Isollyl with Codeine[1]

In Canada—

Fiorinal-C ¼[1]
Fiorinal-C ½[1]
Phenaphen with Codeine No.2[2]
Phenaphen with Codeine No.3[2]

Phenaphen with Codeine No.4[2]
Tecnal-C ¼[1]
Tecnal-C ½[1]

Note: For quick reference, the following combination medicines are numbered to match the corresponding brand names.

This information applies to the following medicines:
1. Butalbital, Aspirin, and Codeine‡ (byoo-TAL-bi-tal AS-pir-in and KOE-deen)
2. Phenobarbital, Aspirin, and Codeine‡ (fee-noe-BAR-bi-tal AS-pir-in and KOE-deen)*

---

*Not commercially available in the U.S.
‡In Canada, *Aspirin* is a brand name. Acetylsalicylic acid is the generic name in Canada. ASA, a synonym for acetylsalicylic acid, is the term that commonly appears on Canadian product labels.

Description

Barbiturate (bar-BI-tyoo-rate), aspirin, and codeine combinations are used to relieve headaches and other kinds of pain. These combination medicines may provide better pain relief than either aspirin or codeine used alone. In some cases, relief of pain may come at lower doses of each medicine.

Codeine is a narcotic analgesic (nar-KOT-ik an-al-JEE-zik) that acts in the central nervous system (CNS) to relieve pain. Many of its side effects are also caused by actions in the CNS. Butalbital and phenobarbital belong to the group of medicines called barbiturates. Barbiturates also act in the CNS to produce their effects.

When you use a barbiturate or codeine for a long time, your body may get used to the medicine so that larger amounts are needed to produce the same effects. This is called tolerance to the medicine. Also, barbiturates and codeine may become habit-forming (causing mental or physical dependence) when they are used for a long time or in large doses. Physical dependence may lead to withdrawal symptoms when you stop taking the medicine. In patients who get headaches, the first symptom of withdrawal may be new (rebound) headaches.

The butalbital, aspirin, and codeine combination also contains caffeine (kaf-EEN). Caffeine may help to relieve headaches. However, caffeine can also cause physical dependence when it is used for a long time. This may lead to withdrawal (rebound) headaches when you stop taking it.

Aspirin is not a narcotic and does not cause physical dependence. However, it may cause other unwanted effects if too much is taken.

These combination medicines are available only with your doctor's prescription, in the following dosage forms:

Oral
Butalbital, Aspirin, Caffeine, and Codeine
• Capsules (U.S. and Canada)
• Tablets (U.S.)
Phenobarbital, Aspirin, and Codeine
• Capsules (Canada)

Before Using This Medicine

In deciding to use a medicine, the risks of taking the medicine must be weighed against the good it will do. This is a decision you and your doctor will make. For barbiturate, aspirin, and codeine combinations, the following should be considered:

Allergies—Tell your doctor if you have ever had any unusual or allergic reaction to aspirin or other salicylates including methyl salicylate (oil of wintergreen); butalbital, phenobarbital, or other barbiturates; caffeine; codeine; or any of the following medicines:

Diclofenac (e.g., Voltaren)
Diflunisal (e.g., Dolobid)
Etodolac (e.g., Lodine)
Fenoprofen (e.g., Nalfon)
Floctafenine (e.g., Idarac)
Flurbiprofen, oral (e.g., Ansaid)
Ibuprofen (e.g., Motrin)
Indomethacin (e.g., Indocin)
Ketoprofen (e.g., Orudis)
Ketorolac (e.g., Toradol)
Meclofenamate (e.g., Meclomen)
Mefenamic acid (e.g., Ponstel)
Nabumetone (e.g., Relafen)
Naproxen (e.g., Naprosyn)
Oxaprozin (e.g., Daypro)
Oxyphenbutazone (e.g., Tandearil)
Phenylbutazone (e.g., Butazolidin)
Piroxicam (e.g., Feldene)
Sulindac (e.g., Clinoril)
Suprofen (e.g., Suprol)
Tenoxicam (e.g., Mobiflex)
Tiaprofenic acid (e.g., Surgam)
Tolmetin (e.g., Tolectin)
Zomepirac (e.g., Zomax)

Also tell your health care professional if you are allergic to any other substances, such as foods, preservatives, or dyes.

Pregnancy—
• *For butalbital or phenobarbital:* Barbiturates have been shown to increase the chance of birth defects in humans. Also, one study in humans has suggested that barbiturates taken during pregnancy may increase the chance of brain tumors in the baby. Barbiturates may cause breathing problems in the newborn baby if taken just before or during delivery.
• *For aspirin:* Although studies in humans have not shown that aspirin causes birth defects, aspirin has caused birth defects in animal studies. *Do not take aspirin during the last 3 months of pregnancy unless it has been ordered by your doctor.* Some reports have suggested that use of aspirin late in pregnancy may cause a decrease in the newborn's weight and possible death of the fetus or newborn baby. However, the mothers in these reports had been taking much larger amounts of aspirin than are usually recommended. Studies of mothers taking aspirin in the doses that are usually recommended did not show these unwanted effects. There is a chance that regular use of aspirin late

---

in pregnancy may cause unwanted effects on the heart or blood flow in the fetus or in the newborn baby. Also, use of aspirin during the last 2 weeks of pregnancy may cause bleeding problems in the fetus before or during delivery or in the newborn baby. In addition, too much use of aspirin during the last 3 months of pregnancy may increase the length of pregnancy, prolong labor, cause other problems during delivery, or cause severe bleeding in the mother before, during, or after delivery.

- *For codeine:* Although studies on birth defects with codeine have not been done in pregnant women, it has not been reported to cause birth defects. However, it may cause breathing problems in the newborn baby if taken just before or during delivery. Codeine did not cause birth defects in animal studies, but it caused slower development of bones and other harmful effects in the fetus.
- *For caffeine:* Studies in humans have not shown that caffeine causes birth defects. However, use of large amounts of caffeine during pregnancy may cause problems with the heart rhythm and the growth of the fetus. Also, studies in animals have shown that caffeine causes birth defects when given in very large doses (amounts equal to those in 12 to 24 cups of coffee a day).

Breast-feeding—Although this combination medicine has not been reported to cause problems, the chance always exists, especially if the medicine is taken for a long time or in large amounts.

- *For butalbital or phenobarbital:* Barbiturates pass into the breast milk and may cause drowsiness, unusually slow heartbeat, shortness of breath, or troubled breathing in nursing babies.
- *For aspirin:* Aspirin passes into the breast milk. However, taking aspirin in the amount present in these combination medicines has not been reported to cause problems in nursing babies.
- *For codeine:* Codeine passes into the breast milk in small amounts. However, it has not been reported to cause problems in nursing babies.
- *For caffeine:* The caffeine in the butalbital, aspirin, and codeine combination medicine passes into the breast milk in small amounts. Taking caffeine in the amounts present in this combination medicine has not been reported to cause problems in nursing babies. However, studies have shown that nursing babies may appear jittery when their mothers drink large amounts of caffeine-containing beverages. Therefore, breast-feeding mothers who use caffeine-containing medicines should probably limit the amount of caffeine they take in from other medicines or from beverages.

Children—

- *For butalbital or phenobarbital:* Although barbiturates often cause drowsiness, some children become excited after taking them.
- *For aspirin: Do not give a medicine containing aspirin to a child with fever or other symptoms of a virus infection, especially flu or chickenpox, without first discussing its use with your child's doctor.* This is very important because aspirin may cause a serious illness called Reye's syndrome in children with fever caused by a virus infection, especially flu or chickenpox. Children who do not have a virus infection may also be more sensitive to the effects of aspirin, especially if they have a fever or have lost large amounts of body fluid

because of vomiting, diarrhea, or sweating. This may increase the chance of side effects during treatment.

- *For caffeine:* There is no specific information comparing use of caffeine in children up to 12 years of age with use in other age groups. However, caffeine is not expected to cause different side effects or problems in children than it does in adults.

Teenagers—*Teenagers with fever or other symptoms of a virus infection, especially flu or chickenpox, should check with a doctor before taking this medicine.* The aspirin in this combination medicine may cause a serious illness called Reye's syndrome in teenagers with fever caused by a virus infection, especially flu or chickenpox.

Older adults—

- *For butalbital or phenobarbital:* Confusion, depression, or excitement may be especially likely to occur in elderly patients, who are usually more sensitive than younger adults to the effects of barbiturates.
- *For aspirin:* Elderly patients are more sensitive than younger adults to the effects of aspirin. This may increase the chance of side effects during treatment.
- *For codeine:* Breathing problems may be especially likely to occur in elderly patients, who are usually more sensitive than younger adults to the effects of codeine.
- *For caffeine:* Many medicines have not been studied specifically in older people.Therefore, it may not be known whether they work exactly the same way they do in younger adults or if they cause different side effects or problems in older people. There is no specific information comparing use of caffeine in the elderly with use in other age groups.

Other medicines—Although certain medicines should not be used together at all, in other cases two different medicines may be used together even if an interaction might occur. In these cases, your doctor may want to change the dose, or other precautions may be necessary. When you are taking this combination medicine, it is especially important that your health care professional know if you are taking any of the following:

- Antacids, large amounts taken regularly, especially calcium- and/or magnesium-containing antacids or sodium bicarbonate (baking soda), or
- Urinary alkalizers (medicine that makes the urine less acid, such as acetazolamide [e.g., Diamox], dichlorphenamide [e.g., Daranide], methazolamide [e.g., Neptazane], potassium or sodium citrate and/or citric acid)—These medicines may cause aspirin to be removed from the body faster than usual, which may shorten the length of time that aspirin is effective; acetazolamide, dichlorphenamide, and methazolamide may also increase the chance of side effects when taken together with aspirin

- Anticoagulants (blood thinners) or
- Heparin—Use of these medicines together with aspirin may increase the chance of bleeding; also, barbiturates, especially phenobarbital, may decrease the effects of anticoagulants

- Antidepressants, tricyclic (amitriptyline [e.g., Elavil], amoxapine [e.g., Asendin], clomipramine [e.g., Anafranil], desipramine [e.g., Pertofrane], doxepin [e.g., Sinequan], imipramine [e.g., Tofranil], nortriptyline [e.g., Aventyl], protriptyline [e.g., Vivactil], trimipramine [e.g., Surmontil]) or
- Central nervous system (CNS) depressants (medicines that often cause drowsiness)—These medicines may

add to the effects of barbiturates and codeine and increase the chance of drowsiness or other side effects

- Carbamazepine or
- Contraceptives, oral (birth control pills) containing estrogens or
- Corticosteroids (cortisone-like medicines) or
- Corticotropin (ACTH)—Barbiturates, especially phenobarbital, may make these medicines less effective

- Divalproex (e.g., Depakote) or
- Methotrexate (e.g., Mexate) or
- Valproic acid (e.g., Depakene) or
- Vancomycin (e.g., Vancocin)—The chance of serious side effects may be increased

- Naltrexone (e.g., Trexan)—Naltrexone blocks the pain-relieving effect of codeine

- Probenecid (e.g., Benemid) or
- Sulfinpyrazone (e.g., Anturane)—Aspirin can keep these medicines from working properly for treating gout

Other medical problems—The presence of other medical problems may affect the use of butalbital, aspirin, and codeine combination. Make sure you tell your doctor if you have any other medical problems, especially:
- Alcohol abuse (or history of) or
- Drug abuse or dependence (or history of)—Dependence on barbiturates and/or codeine may develop

- Asthma, especially if occurring together with other allergies and nasal polyps (history of), or
- Brain disease or head injury or
- Colitis or
- Convulsions (seizures) (history of) or
- Emphysema or other chronic lung disease or
- Enlarged prostate or problems with urination or
- Gallbladder disease or gallstones or
- Hyperactivity (in children) or
- Kidney disease or
- Liver disease—The chance of serious side effects may be increased

- Diabetes mellitus (sugar diabetes) or
- Mental depression or
- Overactive thyroid or
- Porphyria (or history of)—Barbiturates can make these conditions worse

- Gout—Aspirin can make this condition worse and can also lessen the effects of some medicines used to treat gout

- Heart disease (severe)—The caffeine in the butalbital, aspirin, and codeine combination can make some kinds of heart disease worse

- Hemophilia or other bleeding problems or
- Vitamin K deficiency—Aspirin increases the chance of serious bleeding

- Stomach ulcer, especially with a history of bleeding, or other stomach problems—Aspirin can make your condition worse

Proper Use of This Medicine

Take this medicine with food or a full glass (8 ounces) of water to lessen stomach irritation.

Do not take this medicine if it has a strong vinegar-like odor. This odor means the aspirin in it is breaking down. If you have any questions about this, check with your health care professional.

Take this medicine only as directed by your doctor. Do not take more of it, do not take it more often, and do not take it for a longer time than your doctor ordered. If a barbiturate or codeine is taken regularly (for example, every day), it may become habit-forming (causing mental or physical dependence). Regular use of caffeine can also cause physical dependence. Dependence is especially likely to occur in people who take these medicines to relieve frequent headaches. Also, taking too much of this combination medicine may cause stomach problems or other medical problems.

This medicine will relieve a headache best if you *take it as soon as the headache begins.* If you get warning signs of a migraine, take this medicine as soon as you are sure that the migraine is coming. This may even stop the headache pain from occurring. *Lying down in a quiet, dark room for a while after taking the medicine also helps to relieve headaches.*

People who get a lot of headaches may need to take a different medicine to help prevent headaches. *It is important that you follow your doctor's directions about taking the other medicine, even if your headaches continue to occur.* Headache-preventing medicines may take several weeks to start working. Even after they do start working, your headaches may not go away completely. However, your headaches should occur less often, and they should be less severe and easier to relieve than before. This will reduce the amount of headache relievers that you need. If you do not notice any improvement after several weeks of headache-preventing treatment, check with your doctor.

Dosing—The dose of these medicines will be different for different patients. *Follow your doctor's orders or the directions on the label.* The following information includes only the average doses of these medicines. *If your dose is different, do not change it* unless your doctor tells you to do so.

The number of capsules or tablets that you take depends on the strength of the medicine.

For Butalbital, Aspirin, and Codeine combination
- For *oral* dosage forms (capsules and tablets):
  —For relieving pain:
  - Adults—One or 2 capsules or tablets every four hours as needed. You should not take more than six capsules or tablets a day.
  - Children—Dose must be determined by your doctor.

For Phenobarbital, Aspirin, and Codeine combination
- For *oral* dosage form (capsules):
  —For relieving pain:
  - Adults—One or 2 capsules every three or four hours as needed.
  - Children—Dose must be determined by your doctor.

Missed dose—If your doctor has ordered you to take this medicine according to a regular schedule and you miss a dose, take it as soon as you remember. However, if it is almost time for your next dose, skip the missed dose and go back to your regular dosing schedule. Do not double doses.

Storage—To store this medicine:
- Keep out of the reach of children. Overdose is especially dangerous in young children.
- Store away from heat and direct light.

- Do not store this medicine in the bathroom, near the kitchen sink, or in other damp places. Heat or moisture may cause the medicine to break down.
- Do not keep outdated medicine or medicine no longer needed. Be sure that any discarded medicine is out of the reach of children.

Precautions While Using This Medicine

Check with your doctor:
- If the medicine stops working as well as it did when you first started using it. This may mean that you are in danger of becoming dependent on the medicine. *Do not try to get better pain relief by increasing the dose.*
- *If you are having headaches more often than you did before you started using this medicine.* This is especially important if a new headache occurs within 1 day after you took your last dose of headache medicine, headaches begin to occur every day, or a headache continues for several days in a row. This may mean that you are dependent on the headache medicine. *Continuing to take this medicine will cause even more headaches later on.* Your doctor can give you advice on how to relieve the headaches.

Check the labels of all nonprescription (over-the-counter [OTC]) and prescription medicines you now take. If any contain a narcotic, a barbiturate, aspirin, or other salicylates, including diflunisal, check with your doctor or pharmacist. Taking them together with this medicine may cause an overdose.

The barbiturate and the codeine in this medicine will add to the effects of alcohol and other CNS depressants (medicines that slow down the nervous system, possibly causing drowsiness). Some examples of CNS depressants are antihistamines or medicine for hay fever, other allergies, or colds; sedatives, tranquilizers, or sleeping medicine; other prescription pain medicine or narcotics; other barbiturates; medicine for seizures; muscle relaxants; or anesthetics, including some dental anesthetics. Also, stomach problems may be more likely to occur if you drink alcoholic beverages while you are taking aspirin. Therefore, *do not drink alcoholic beverages, and check with your doctor before taking any of the medicines listed above, while you are using this medicine.*

This medicine may cause some people to become drowsy, dizzy, or lightheaded, or to feel a false sense of well-being. *Make sure you know how you react to this medicine before you drive, use machines, or do anything else that could be dangerous if you are dizzy or are not alert and clearheaded.*

Dizziness, lightheadedness, or fainting may occur, especially when you get up suddenly from a lying or sitting position. Getting up slowly may help lessen this problem. Lying down for a while may relieve these effects.

Nausea or vomiting may occur, especially after the first couple of doses. This effect may go away if you lie down for a while. However, if nausea or vomiting continues, check with your doctor.

Before having any kind of surgery (including dental surgery) or emergency treatment, tell the medical doctor or dentist in charge that you are taking this medicine. Serious side effects can occur if your medical doctor or dentist gives you certain medicines without knowing that you have taken a barbiturate or codeine.

Do not take this medicine for 5 days before any planned surgery, including dental surgery, unless otherwise directed by your medical doctor or dentist. Taking aspirin during this time may cause bleeding problems.

Before you have any medical tests, tell the person in charge that you are taking this medicine. The caffeine in the butalbital, aspirin, and codeine combination interferes with the results of certain tests that use dipyridamole (e.g., Persantine) to help show how well blood is flowing to your heart. Caffeine should not be taken for 8 to 12 hours before the test. The results of some other tests may also be affected by this medicine.

If you have been taking large amounts of this medicine, or if you have been taking it regularly for several weeks or more, *do not suddenly stop using it without first checking with your doctor.* Your doctor may want you to reduce gradually the amount you are taking before stopping completely, to lessen the chance of withdrawal side effects.

If you think you or anyone else may have taken an overdose of this medicine, get emergency help at once. Taking an overdose of this medicine or taking alcohol or CNS depressants with this medicine may lead to unconsciousness or death. Signs of overdose of this medicine include convulsions (seizures); hearing loss; confusion; ringing or buzzing in the ears; severe excitement, nervousness, or restlessness; severe dizziness; severe drowsiness; unusually slow or troubled breathing; and severe weakness.

Side Effects of This Medicine

Along with its needed effects, a medicine may cause some unwanted effects. Although not all of these side effects may occur, if they do occur they may need medical attention.

The following side effects may mean that a serious allergic reaction is occurring. Check with your doctor or get emergency help immediately if they occur, especially if several of them occur at the same time.
   Less common or rare
      Bluish discoloration or flushing or redness of skin (occurring together with other effects listed in this section); coughing, shortness of breath, troubled breathing, tightness in chest, or wheezing; difficulty in swallowing; dizziness or feeling faint (severe); hive-like swellings (large) on eyelids, face, lips, or tongue; skin rash, itching, or hives; stuffy nose (occurring together with other effects listed in this section)

Also check with your doctor immediately if any of the following side effects occur, especially if several of them occur together:
   Rare
      Bleeding or crusting sores on lips; chest pain; fever with or without chills; red, thickened, or scaly skin; sores, ulcers, or white spots in mouth (painful); sore throat (unexplained); tenderness, burning, or peeling of skin
   Symptoms of overdose
      Anxiety, confusion, excitement, irritability, nervousness, restlessness, or trouble in sleeping (severe, especially with products containing caffeine); cold, clammy skin; convulsions (seizures); diarrhea (severe or continuing); dizziness, lightheadedness, drowsiness, or weakness (severe); frequent urina-

tion (for products containing caffeine); hallucinations (seeing, hearing, or feeling things that are not there); increased sensitivity to touch or pain (for products containing caffeine); increased thirst; low blood pressure; muscle trembling or twitching (for products containing caffeine); nausea or vomiting (severe or continuing), sometimes with blood; pinpoint pupils of eyes; ringing or buzzing in ears (continuing) or hearing loss; seeing flashes of "zig-zag" lights (for products containing caffeine); slow, fast, or irregular heartbeat; slow, fast, irregular, or troubled breathing; slurred speech; staggering; stomach pain (severe); uncontrollable flapping movements of the hands (especially in elderly patients); unusual movements of the eyes; vision problems

Also, check with your doctor as soon as possible if any of the following side effects occur:

> *Less common or rare*
>> Bloody or black, tarry stools; bloody urine; confusion or mental depression; pinpoint red spots on skin; skin rash, hives, or itching (without other signs of an allergic reaction to aspirin listed above); sore throat and fever; stomach pain (severe); swollen or painful glands; trembling or uncontrolled muscle movements; unusual bleeding or bruising; unusual excitement (mild); unusual tiredness or weakness (mild)

Other side effects may occur that usually do not need medical attention. These side effects may go away during treatment as your body adjusts to the medicine. However, check with your doctor if any of the following side effects continue or are bothersome:

> *More common*
>> Bloated or "gassy" feeling; dizziness, lightheadedness, or drowsiness (mild); heartburn or indigestion; nausea, vomiting, or stomach pain (occurring without other symptoms of overdose)

Other side effects not listed above may also occur in some patients. If you notice any other effects, check with your doctor.

Revised: 07/14/92
Interim revision: 07/19/94

BARIUM SULFATE   Diagnostic

Description

Barium sulfate is a radiopaque agent. Radiopaque agents are used to help diagnose certain medical problems. Since radiopaque agents are opaque to (block) x-rays, the areas of the body in which they are localized will appear white on the x-ray film. This creates the needed distinction, or contrast, between one organ and other tissues. The contrast will help the doctor see any special conditions that may exist in that organ or part of the body.

Barium sulfate is taken by mouth or given rectally by enema. If taken by mouth, it makes the esophagus, the stomach, and/or the small intestine opaque to the x-rays so that they can be "photographed." If it is given by enema, the colon and/or the small intestine can be seen and photographed by x-rays.

The dose of barium sulfate will be different for different patients and depends on the type of test. The strength of the suspension and tablet is determined by how much barium they contain. Different tests will require a different strength and amount of suspension (some may require the tablet form), depending on the age of the patient, the contrast needed, and the x-ray equipment used.

Barium sulfate is to be used only by or under the direct supervision of a doctor.

Before Having This Test

In deciding to use a diagnostic test, any risks of the test must be weighed against the good it will do. This is a decision you and your doctor will make. Also, test results may be affected by other things. For barium sulfate, the following should be considered:

Allergies—Tell your doctor if you have ever had any unusual or allergic reaction to barium sulfate. Also, tell your doctor if you are allergic to any other substances, such as foods, preservatives, or dyes.

Pregnancy—X-rays of the abdomen are usually not recommended during pregnancy. This is to avoid exposing the fetus to radiation. Be sure you have discussed this with your doctor.

Breast-feeding—Barium sulfate does not pass into the breast milk. This medicine has not been reported to cause problems in nursing babies.

Children—Although there is no specific information comparing use of barium sulfate in children with use in other age groups, this agent is not expected to cause different side effects or problems in children than it does in adults.

Older adults—This contrast agent has been used in older people and has not been shown to cause different side effects or problems in them than it does in younger adults.

Other medical problems—The presence of other medical problems may affect the use of barium sulfate. Make sure you tell your doctor if you have any other medical problems, especially:

- Asthma, hay fever, or other allergies (history of)—If you have a history of these conditions, the risk of having a reaction, such as an allergic reaction to the additives in the barium sulfate preparation, is greater

- Cystic fibrosis—The risk of blockage in the small bowel is greater

- Dehydration—Barium sulfate may cause severe constipation

- Intestinal blockage or perforation—Barium sulfate may make this condition worse

Preparation for This Test

Your doctor may have special instructions for you in preparation for your test. If you have not received such instructions or if you do not understand them, check with your doctor in advance.

For some tests your doctor may tell you not to eat after 8 the evening before the test. You may be allowed to drink small amounts of clear liquids until midnight; however, check first with your doctor. For other tests you may need to eat meals free of fiber and bulk the day before the test. You may also need to use a laxative.

Precautions After Having This Test

Make sure to drink plenty of liquids after the test. Otherwise, barium sulfate may cause severe constipation.

Side Effects of This Medicine

Along with its needed effects, a radiopaque agent may cause some unwanted effects. Although not all of these side effects may occur, if they do occur they may need medical attention.

Check with your doctor immediately if any of the following side effects occur:

Rare
   Bloating; constipation (severe, continuing); cramping (severe); nausea or vomiting; stomach or lower abdominal pain; tightness in chest or troubled breathing; wheezing

Other side effects may occur that usually do not need medical attention. These side effects may go away as your body adjusts to this agent. However, check with your doctor if any of the following side effects continue or are bothersome:

More common
   Constipation or diarrhea; cramping

Other side effects not listed above may also occur in some patients. If you notice any other effects, check with your doctor.

Revised: 07/26/94

BASILIXIMAB   Systemic

Commonly used brand name(s):

In the U.S.—
   Simulect

Description

Basiliximab (ba-sil-IK-si-mab) belongs to a group of medicines known as immunosuppressive agents. It is used to lower the body's natural immunity in patients who receive kidney transplants.

When a patient receives a kidney transplant, the body's white blood cells will try to get rid of (reject) the transplanted kidney. Basiliximab works by preventing the white blood cells from getting rid of the transplanted kidney. The effect of basiliximab on the white blood cells may also reduce the body's ability to fight infections.

Basiliximab is to be administered only by or under the immediate supervision of your doctor. It is available in the following dosage form:

Parenteral
   • Injection (U.S.)

Before Receiving This Medicine

In deciding to use a medicine, the risks of receiving the medicine must be weighed against the good it will do. This is a decision you and your doctor will make. For basiliximab, the following should be considered:

Allergies—Tell your doctor if you have ever had any unusual or allergic reaction to proteins. Also tell your health care professional if you are allergic to any other substances.

Pregnancy—Basiliximab crosses the placenta. However, basiliximab has not been studied in pregnant women. Women of childbearing age are advised to use contraception before receiving basiliximab. Use of the contraception should continue until 2 months after treatment with basiliximab is completed.

Breast-feeding—It is not known if basiliximab passes into breast milk. Patients receiving basiliximab should not breast-feed their babies.

Children—Studies on the use of basiliximab in children have not been completed. Preliminary information on the use of basiliximab in children suggests children have the same side effects from receiving basiliximab as those experienced by adult patients, and basiliximab works as well to prevent rejection of the transplanted kidney in children as it does in adult patients.

Older adults—Many medicines have not been studied specifically in older people. Therefore, it may not be known whether they work exactly the same way as they do in younger adults or if they cause different side effects or problems in older people. There is no specific information comparing use of basiliximab in the elderly with use in other age groups.

Other medicines—Tell your health care professional if you are using any other prescription or nonprescription (over-the-counter [OTC]) medicine.

Other medical problems—The presence of other medical problems may affect the use of basiliximab. Make sure you tell your doctor if you have any other medical problems, especially:

   • Cancer—Basiliximab may make this condition worse

   • Infection—Basiliximab may decrease the body's ability to fight infection

Proper Use of This Medicine

Dosing—The dose of basiliximab may be different for different patients. Your doctor will decide what dose should be used for you. The following information includes only the usual doses of basiliximab.

   • For *injection* dosage form:
      —To prevent kidney transplant rejection:
      • Adults—20 milligrams (mg).
      • Children—12 mg per square meter of body surface area (mg/m^2).

Most patients receive one dose before and one dose after surgery.

Precautions While Receiving This Medicine

If you are continuing your course of therapy with basiliximab after you are discharged from the hospital, *it is very important that your doctor check your progress at regular visits.* Your doctor will want to do laboratory tests to make sure basiliximab is working properly.

It is important to maintain good dental hygiene and see a dentist regularly for teeth cleaning.

If you are a woman of childbearing age, you should use effective contraception while receiving this medicine and for 2 months after treatment with basiliximab is completed.

Side Effects of This Medicine

Along with its needed effects, a medicine may cause some unwanted effects. Although not all of these side effects may occur, if they do occur they may need medical attention.

Check with your doctor as soon as possible if any of the following side effects occur:

More common
Abdominal pain; back pain; coughing; dizziness; fever or chills; loss of energy or weakness; painful urination; shortness of breath; sore throat; swelling of the ankles, body, face, feet or lower legs; trembling or shaking of the hands or feet; vomiting; white patches in the mouth or throat or on the tongue

Less common
Abnormal vision; agitation; anxiety; bleeding, tender, or enlarged gums; blood in the stool; bruising; chest pain; depression; difficulty in urinating; fatigue; itching; numbness or pain in the legs; skin rash; sores in the mouth; "stocking and gloves" sensation of the hands or feet; tingling

Other side effects may occur that usually do not need medical attention. These side effects may go away during treatment as your body adjusts to the medicine. However, check with your doctor if any of the following side effects continue or are bothersome:

More common
Acne; constipation; diarrhea; headache; heartburn; nausea; trouble in sleeping; weight gain

Less common
Excessive hair growth; joint pain; muscle pain

Other side effects not listed above may also occur in some patients. If you notice any other effects, check with your doctor.

Developed: 07/09/98

BECAPLERMIN   Topical

Commonly used brand name(s):

In the U.S.—
Regranex

Description

Becaplermin (be-KAP-ler-min) is used to treat skin ulcers, usually on the lower leg, in patients with diabetes mellitus (sugar diabetes). It works by locally stimulating the wound to heal. It is important to use other methods for good skin ulcer care when using becaplermin.

Becaplermin is available only with your doctor's prescription, in the following dosage form(s):

Topical
• Gel (U.S.)

Before Using This Medicine

In deciding to use a medicine, the risks of using the medicine must be weighed against the good it will do. This is a decision you and your doctor will make. For becaplermin, the following should be considered:

Allergies—Tell your doctor if you have ever had any unusual or allergic reaction to becaplermin, parabens, or metacresol. Also tell your health care professional if you are allergic to any other substances, such as foods, preservatives, or dyes.

Pregnancy—Studies on effects in pregnancy have not been done in either humans or animals.

Breast-feeding—It is not known whether becaplermin passes into the breast milk. However, this medicine has not been reported to cause problems in nursing babies.

Children—Although there is no specific information comparing use of becaplermin in children 16 years of age or older with use in other age groups, this medicine is not expected to cause different side effects or problems in children than it does in adults. This medicine has not been studied in children up to 16 years of age.

Older adults—Many medicines have not been studied specifically in older people. Therefore, it may not be known whether they work exactly the same way they do in younger adults or if they cause different side effects or problems in older people. There is no specific information comparing use of becaplermin in the elderly with use in other age groups.

Other medicines—Although certain medicines should not be used together at all, in other cases two different medicines may be used together even if an interaction might occur. In these cases, your doctor may want to change the dose, or other precautions may be necessary. Tell your doctor and pharmacist if you are using any other topical prescription or nonprescription (over-the-counter [OTC]) medicine that is to be applied to the same area of the skin.

Other medical problems—The presence of other medical problems may affect the use of becaplermin. Make sure you tell your doctor if you have any other medical problems, especially:

• Skin cancer or tumors at the site of the ulcer—Use of becaplermin is not recommended because its effect on these conditions is not known
• Wounds that show exposed joints, tendons, ligaments, or bone—Use of becaplermin is not recommended because it is not known if it would work for these conditions
• Wounds that are closed manually by your health care professional—Use of becaplermin is not recommended because these wounds require a sterile product

Proper Use of This Medicine

To make using becaplermin as safe and reliable as possible, you should understand how and when to use this medicine and what effects may be expected. A paper with information for the patient will be given to you with your filled prescription and will provide many details concerning the use of becaplermin. *Read this paper carefully* and ask your health care professional for any additional information or explanation.

It is important to prevent the tip of the tube from touching the skin ulcer or any other object to keep the medicine from becoming impure and a possible source of infection.

There are several *important steps that will help you apply your medicine properly.*

- Wash your hands before preparing your dose.
- The proper amount to measure depends on the size of the tube you are using and the size of the skin ulcer. You should expect the dose to change each week or every other week, depending on the rate your skin ulcer changes in size.
- Measure the proper amount carefully onto a clean surface such as wax paper. Then, transfer the medicine to your skin ulcer by using an applicator aid, such as a cotton swab or tongue depressor.
- Spread the medicine on your skin ulcer as a thin (about 1/16th of an inch), even, continuous film.
- After wetting a gauze pad with 0.9% Sodium Chloride Irrigation USP, apply it on top of your medicated skin ulcer.
- After 12 hours, remove the medicine left on the skin ulcer with 0.9% Sodium Chloride Irrigation USP or water.
- Keep the ulcer from becoming too dry. When changing the dressing, the existing bandage may need to be wetted with 0.9% Sodium Chloride Irrigation USP to help remove the bandage and prevent injury to the healing ulcer.
- Wet a new gauze pad with 0.9% Sodium Chloride Irrigation USP. Apply it on top of your skin ulcer that no longer has the medicine on it and wait 12 hours before applying the medicine again. Therefore, the medicine is reapplied every 24 hours, with a change in the wound dressing in between applications.

Dosing—The dose of becaplermin will be different for different patients. *Follow your doctor's orders or the directions on the label.* The following information includes only the average dose of becaplermin. *If your dose is different, do not change it* unless your doctor tells you to do so.

- For *topical* dosage form (gel):
  —For skin ulcers caused by diabetes mellitus (sugar diabetes):
    - Adults and children 16 years of age and over—Apply an amount of gel once a day and leave it on for twelve hours. The amount applied will change each week or every other week, depending on the changing size of the skin ulcer.
    - Children up to 16 years of age—Use and dose must be determined by the doctor.

Missed dose—If you miss a dose of this medicine, use it as soon as possible. However, if it is almost time for your next dose, skip the missed dose and go back to your regular dosing schedule. Do not double doses. If you have any questions about this, check with your doctor.

Storage—To store this medicine:
- Keep out of the reach of children.
- Store in the refrigerator. However, keep the medicine from freezing.
- Do not keep outdated medicine or medicine no longer needed. Be sure that any discarded medicine is out of the reach of children.

Precautions While Using This Medicine

Your doctor should *check your progress at regular visits* to make sure that this medicine does not cause unwanted effects. As your skin ulcer changes in size, *your doctor may change your dose weekly or every other week.*

Becaplermin works best when used with other methods for good skin ulcer care, such as not bearing weight on the leg that has the skin ulcer. Your doctor will discuss these methods with you.

Discuss with your doctor whether you should continue the medicine if your skin ulcer is not reduced by 30% in 10 weeks or your skin ulcer does not improve after 20 weeks. If your skin ulcer does improve, your doctor may keep you on the medicine until your skin ulcer is completely healed.

It is important to use the proper amount and not to use more than prescribed.

Check the expiration date before using becaplermin and do not use it if it is out of date. The expiration date is located stamped on the crimped portion at the bottom of the tube.

Side Effects of This Medicine

Along with its needed effects, a medicine may cause some unwanted effects. Although not all of these side effects may occur, if they do occur they may need medical attention.

Check with your doctor as soon as possible if the following side effect occurs:
Less common
    Reddened skin near ulcer; skin rash near ulcer

Other side effects not listed above may also occur in some patients. If you notice any other effects, check with your doctor.

Developed: 3/30/98

BELLADONNA ALKALOIDS AND BARBITURATES   Systemic

Commonly used brand name(s):

In the U.S.—

Antrocol[2]	Donphen[1]
Barbidonna[1]	Hyosophen[1]
Barbidonna No. 2[1]	Kinesed[1]
Barophen[1]	Malatal[1]
Bellalphen[1]	Relaxadon[1]
Butibel[3]	Spaslin[1]
Donnamor[1]	Spasmolin[1]
Donnapine[1]	Spasmophen[1]
Donnatal[1]	Spasquid[1]
Donnatal Extentabs[1]	Susano[1]
Donnatal No. 2[1]	

In Canada—
Donnatal[1]
Donnatal Extentabs[1]

Note: For quick reference, the following beladonna alkaloids and barbiturates are numbered to match the corresponding brand names.

This information applies to the following medicines:
1. Atropine, Hyoscyamine, Scopolamine, and Phenobarbital (A-troe-peen, hye-oh-SYE-a-meen, skoe-POL-a-meen, and fee-noe-BAR-bi-tal)†
2. Atropine and Phenobarbital (A-troe-peen and fee-noe-BAR-bi-tal)†
3. Belladonna and Butabarbital (Bell-a-don-a and byoo-ta-BAR-bi-tal)†

---

†Not commercially available in Canada.

Description

Belladonna alkaloids and barbiturates are combination medicines taken to relieve cramping and spasms of the stomach and intestines. They are used also to decrease the amount of acid formed in the stomach.

These medicines are available only with your doctor's prescription in the following dosage forms:

Oral

Atropine, Hyoscyamine, Scopolamine, and Phenobarbital
- Capsules (U.S.)
- Elixir (U.S. and Canada)
- Tablets (U.S. and Canada)
- Chewable tablets (U.S.)
- Extended-release tablets (U.S. and Canada)

Atropine and Phenobarbital
- Capsules (U.S.)
- Elixir (U.S.)
- Tablets (U.S.)

Belladonna and Butabarbital
- Elixir (U.S.)
- Tablets (U.S.)

Before Using This Medicine

In deciding to use a medicine, the risks of taking the medicine must be weighed against the good it will do. This is a decision you and your doctor will make. For belladona alkaloids and barbiturates, the following should be considered:

Allergies—Tell your doctor if you have ever had any unusual or allergic reaction to belladonna alkaloids (atropine, belladonna, hyoscyamine, and scopolamine) or to barbiturates (butabarbital, phenobarbital). Also, tell your health care professional if you are allergic to any other substances, such as foods, preservatives, or dyes.

Pregnancy—Belladonna alkaloids have not been shown to cause problems in humans. However, barbiturates (contained in this medicine) have been shown to increase the chance of birth defects in humans. Also, when taken during pregnancy, barbiturates may cause bleeding problems in the newborn baby. Be sure that you have discussed this with your doctor before taking this medicine.

Breast-feeding—Belladonna alkaloids or barbiturates have not been shown to cause problems in nursing babies. However, traces of the belladonna alkaloids and barbiturates pass into the breast milk. Also, because the belladonna alkaloids tend to decrease the secretions of the body, it is possible that the flow of breast milk may be reduced in some patients.

Children—Severe side effects may be more likely to occur in infants and children, especially those with spastic paralysis or brain damage. Unusual excitement, nervousness, restlessness, or irritability and unusual warmth, dryness, and flushing of skin are more likely to occur in children, who are usually more sensitive to the effects of belladonna alkaloids. Also, when belladonna alkaloids are given to children during hot weather, a rapid increase in body temperature may occur. In addition, the barbiturate in this medicine could cause some children to become hyperactive.

Older adults—Confusion or memory loss; constipation; difficult urination; drowsiness; dryness of mouth, nose, throat, or skin; and unusual excitement, nervousness, restlessness, or irritability may be more likely to occur in the elderly, who are usually more sensitive than younger adults to the effects of belladonna alkaloids and barbiturates. Also, eye pain may occur, which may be a sign of glaucoma.

Other medicines—Although certain medicines should not be used together at all, in other cases two different medicines may be used together even if an interaction might occur. In these cases, your doctor may want to change the dose, or other precautions may be necessary. When you are taking belladonna alkaloids and barbiturates, it is especially important that your health care professional know if you are taking any of the following:

- Adrenocorticoids (cortisone-like medicine) or
- Corticotropin (ACTH)—Belladonna alkaloids and barbiturates may decrease the response to these medicines

- Antacids or
- Diarrhea medicine containing kaolin or attapulgite—These medications may decrease the response to belladonna alkaloids

- Anticholinergics (medicine for abdominal or stomach spasms or cramps)—Belladonna alkaloids and barbiturates may increase the response to anticholinergics

- Anticoagulants (blood thinners)—Belladonna alkaloids and barbiturates may decrease the effect of this medicine

- Central nervous system (CNS) depressants (medicines that cause drowsiness)—The CNS effects of either medicine could be increased

- Ketoconazole (e.g., Nizoral)—Using ketoconazole with this combination medicine may lessen the effects of ketoconazole and barbiturates

- Monoamine oxidase (MAO) inhibitors (furazolidone [e.g., Furoxone], isocarboxazid [e.g., Marplan], phenelzine [e.g., Nardil], procarbazine [e.g., Matulane], selegiline [Eldepryl]; tranylcypromine [e.g., Parnate])—Taking belladonna alkaloids and barbiturates while you are taking or within 2 weeks of taking monoamine oxidase inhibitors may increase the effects of the barbiturates

- Potassium chloride (e.g., Slow K or K-Dur)—May cause an increase in lesions (sores) of the stomach or intestine

Other medical problems—The presence of other medical problems may affect the use of belladonna alkaloids and barbiturates. Make sure you tell your doctor if you have any other medical problems, especially:

- Asthma, emphysema, or other chronic lung disease or
- Dryness of mouth (severe and continuing) or
- Enlarged prostate or
- Glaucoma or
- Heart disease or
- Hyperactivity (in children) or
- Intestinal blockage or other intestinal problems or
- Urinary tract blockage or difficult urination—Belladonna alkaloids and barbiturates may make these conditions worse

- Brain damage (in children) or
- Spastic paralysis (in children)—These conditions may increase the effects of the medicine

- Down's syndrome (mongolism)—This condition may increase the side effects of the medicine

- Kidney disease or

- Liver disease—Higher levels of the belladonna alkaloid and barbiturate may result, possibly leading to increased side effects

Proper Use of This Medicine

Take this medicine about ½ to 1 hour before meals, unless otherwise directed by your doctor.

Take this medicine only as directed. Do not take more or less of it, do not take it more often, and do not take it for a longer time than your doctor ordered. To do so may increase the chance of side effects.

Dosing—The dose of belladonna alkaloids and barbiturates combination will be different for different patients. *Follow your doctor's orders or the directions on the label.* The following information includes only the average doses of these combination medicines. *If your dose is different, do not change it* unless your doctor tells you to do so.

The number of capsules or tablets or the amount of solution you take depends on the strength of the medicine. Also, *the number of doses you take each day, the time allowed between doses, and the length of time you take the medicine depend on the medical problem for which you are taking these combination products.*

For atropine, hyoscyamine, scopolamine, and phenobarbital combination
- For stomach or intestine problems:
  —For *oral* dosage form (capsules or tablets):
    - Older adults, adults, and teenagers—1 or 2 capsules two to four times a day. Your doctor may change the dose if needed.
    - Children—Dose must be determined by your doctor.
  —For *oral* dosage form (solution):
    - Adults and teenagers—The usual dose is 1 to 2 teaspoonfuls (5 to 10 milliliters [mL]) three or four times a day. Your doctor may change the dose if needed.
    - Children—Dose is based on body weight and must be determined by your doctor. The usual dose is 0.5 to 7.5 mL every four to six hours. Your doctor may change the dose if needed.
  —For *oral* dosage form (chewable tablets):
    - Older adults, adults, and teenagers—Chew 1 or 2 tablets three or four times a day. Your doctor may change the dose if needed.
    - Children up to 2 years of age—Use is not recommended.
    - Children 2 to 12 years of age—½ to 1 tablet three or four times a day. Your doctor may change the dose if needed.
  —For *oral* dosage form (extended-release tablets):
    - Older adults, adults, and teenagers—1 tablet every eight to twelve hours. Your doctor may change the dose if needed.
    - Children—Use is not recommended.

For atropine and phenobarbital
- For stomach or intestine problems:
  —For *oral* dosage form (capsules or tablets):
    - Older adults, adults, and teenagers—1 or 2 capsules or tablets two to four times a day. Your doctor may change the dose if needed.
    - Children—Dose must be determined by your doctor.

  —For *oral* dosage form (solution):
    - Older adults, adults, and teenagers—1 to 2 teaspoonfuls (5 to 10 milliliters [mL]) three or four times a day. Your doctor may change the dose if needed.
    - Children—Dose is based on body weight and must be determined by your doctor. The usual dose is 0.5 to 3 mL every four to six hours. Your doctor may change the dose if needed.

For belladonna and butabarbital
- For stomach or intestine problems:
  —For *oral* dosage form (solution):
    - Older adults, adults and teenagers—1 to 2 teaspoonfuls (5 to 10 milliliters [mL]) three or four times a day. Your doctor may change the dose if needed.
    - Children up to 6 years of age—1.25 to 2.5 mL three or four times a day. Your doctor may change the dose if needed.
    - Children 6 to 12 years of age—2.5 to 5 mL three or four times a day. Your doctor may change the dose if needed.
  —For *oral* dosage form (tablets):
    - Older adults, adults, and teenagers—1 or 2 tablets three or four times a day. Your doctor may change the dose if needed.
    - Children—Dose must be determined by your doctor.

Missed dose—If you miss a dose of this medicine, take it as soon as possible. However, if it is almost time for your next dose, skip the missed dose and go back to your regular dosing schedule. Do not double doses.

Storage—To store this medicine:
- Keep this medicine out of the reach of children. Overdose of belladonna alkaloids and barbiturates is especially dangerous in young children.
- Store away from heat and direct light.
- Do not store the capsule or tablet form of this medicine in the bathroom, near the kitchen sink, or in other damp places. Heat or moisture may cause the medicine to break down.
- Keep the liquid form of this medicine from freezing.
- Do not keep outdated medicine or medicine no longer needed. Be sure that any discarded medicine is out of the reach of children.

Precautions While Using This Medicine

This medicine will add to the effects of alcohol and other CNS depressants (medicines that slow down the nervous system, possibly causing drowsiness). Some examples of CNS depressants are antihistamines or medicine for hay fever, other allergies, or colds; sedatives, tranquilizers, or sleeping medicine; prescription pain medicine or narcotics; barbiturates; medicine for seizures; muscle relaxants; or anesthetics, including some dental anesthetics. *Check with your doctor before taking any of the above while you are taking this medicine.*

Do not take this medicine within 1 hour of taking antacids or medicine for diarrhea. Taking them too close together will make the belladonna alkaloids less effective.

Belladonna alkaloids will often make you sweat less, causing your body temperature to increase. *Use extra care not to become overheated during exercise or hot weather while you are taking this medicine,* as overheating could possibly result in heat stroke. This is especially important in children taking belladonna alkaloids.

This medicine may cause your eyes to become more sensitive to light than they are normally. Wearing sunglasses and avoiding too much exposure to bright light may help lessen the discomfort.

This medicine may cause some people to have blurred vision or to become drowsy, dizzy, or less alert than they are normally. *Make sure you know how you react to this medicine before you drive, use machines, or do anything else that could be dangerous if you are not alert or able to see well.*

This medicine may cause dryness of the mouth, nose, and throat. For temporary relief of mouth dryness, use sugarless candy or gum, melt bits of ice in your mouth, or use a saliva substitute. However, if your mouth continues to feel dry for more than 2 weeks, check with your dentist. Continuing dryness of the mouth may increase the chance of dental disease, including tooth decay, gum disease, and fungus infections.

Side Effects of This Medicine

Along with its needed effects, a medicine may cause some unwanted effects. Although not all of these side effects may occur, if they do occur they may need medical attention.

Check with your doctor as soon as possible if any of the following side effects occur:
Rare
> Eye pain; skin rash or hives; sore throat and fever; unusual bleeding or bruising; yellow eyes or skin

Symptoms of overdose
> Blurred vision (continuing) or changes in near vision; clumsiness or unsteadiness; confusion; convulsions (seizures); dizziness (continuing); drowsiness (severe); dryness of mouth, nose, or throat (severe); fast heartbeat; fever; hallucinations (seeing, hearing, or feeling things that are not there); shortness of breath or troubled breathing; slurred speech; unusual excitement, nervousness, restlessness, or irritability; unusual warmth, dryness, and flushing of skin

Other side effects may occur that usually do not need medical attention. These side effects may go away during treatment as your body adjusts to the medicine. However, check with your doctor if any of the following side effects continue or are bothersome:
More common
> Constipation; decreased sweating; dizziness; drowsiness; dryness of mouth, nose, throat, or skin

Less common or rare
> Bloated feeling; blurred vision; decreased flow of breast milk; difficult urination; difficulty in swallowing; headache; increased sensitivity of eyes to sunlight; loss of memory; nausea or vomiting; unusual tiredness or weakness

Other side effects not listed above may also occur in some patients. If you notice any other effects, check with your doctor.

Revised: 08/09/2000

BENTIROMIDE   Diagnostic†

†Not commercially available in Canada.

Description

Bentiromide (ben-TEER-oh-mide) is used to help find out if the pancreas is working the way it should. The pancreas helps break down the bentiromide almost the same way it helps to break down food.

After bentiromide is broken down, a part of it appears in the urine. By measuring how much appears in the urine, your doctor can tell how well your pancreas is working.

How the test is done: Bentiromide is given by mouth as a single dose. After you take bentiromide, all of your urine is collected for the next six hours. The total amount is measured and a small sample is saved and examined. Your doctor may repeat the test after seven days.

This medicine was withdrawn from the U.S. market in October 1996.

Before Having This Test

In deciding to use a diagnostic test, any risks of the test must be weighed against the good it will do. This is a decision you and your doctor will make. Also, test results may be affected by other things. For the test using bentiromide, the following should be considered:

Allergies—Tell your doctor if you have ever had any unusual or allergic reaction to bentiromide. Also tell your doctor if you are allergic to any other substances, such as foods, preservatives, or dyes.

Diet—Eating prunes or cranberries shortly before the bentiromide test period starts will affect test results. Avoid these foods for 3 days before the test.

Pregnancy—Studies with bentiromide have not been done in pregnant women. However, in animal studies bentiromide has not been shown to cause birth defects or other problems.

Breast-feeding—It is not known whether bentiromide passes into the breast milk. However, this medicine has not been reported to cause problems in nursing babies.

Children—Studies on this medicine have been done only in older children and adult patients, and there is no specific information comparing use of bentiromide in children up to 6 years of age with use in other age groups.

Older adults—Many medicines have not been studied specifically in older people. Therefore, it may not be known whether they work exactly the same way they do in younger adults or if they cause different side effects or problems in older people. There is no specific information comparing use of bentiromide in the elderly with use in other age groups.

Other medicines—Although certain medicines should not be used together at all, in other cases two different medicines may be used together even if an interaction might occur. In these cases, your doctor may want to change the dose, or other precautions may be necessary. When you are taking bentiromide it is especially important that your doctor know if you are taking or using any of the following:
• Acetaminophen (e.g., Tylenol) or

- Chloramphenicol (e.g., Chloromycetin) or
- Local anesthetics (e.g., benzocaine and lidocaine) or
- Para-aminobenzoic acid (PABA)-containing preparations (e.g., sunscreens and some multivitamins) or
- Procainamide (e.g., Pronestyl) or
- Sulfonamides (sulfa medicines) or
- Thiazide diuretics (water pills)—Use of these medicines during the test period will affect the test results

- Pancreatic supplements (e.g., pancrelipase)—Use of pancreatic supplements may give false test results

Other medical problems—The presence of other medical problems may affect the results of the test. Make sure you tell your doctor if you have any other medical problems, especially:

- Disease of the stomach and intestines or
- Kidney disease or
- Liver disease (severe)—These medical problems may cause false test results

Preparation for This Test

Your doctor may ask you to avoid certain medicines or foods for at least 72 hours before this test is done. *Follow your doctor's instructions carefully.* Otherwise, this test may not work and may have to be done again.

Unless otherwise directed by your doctor:

- Do not eat anything after midnight the night before the test. Some foods may affect the results of the test.
- Urinate before taking bentiromide. You should have an empty bladder when you take the test.
- After taking bentiromide, drink a large glass of water (at least 8 ounces). Drink another large glass of water in 2 hours and then 2 more glasses of water in the next 4 hours. This will help increase the amount of urine, which is needed for testing.

Side Effects of This Medicine

Along with its needed effects, a medicine may cause some unwanted effects. Although not all of these side effects may occur, if they do occur they may need medical attention.

Check with your health care professional immediately if either of the following side effects occurs:
   Rare
      Shortness of breath or troubled breathing

Other side effects may occur that usually do not need medical attention. These side effects should go away as the effects of the medicine wear off. However, check with your doctor if any of the following side effects continue or are bothersome:
   More common
      Diarrhea; headache

   Less common or rare
      Gas; nausea and vomiting; weakness

Other side effects not listed above may also occur in some patients. If you notice any other effects, check with your doctor.

Revised: 10/16/2000

BENTOQUATAM   Topical†

Commonly used brand name(s):

In the U.S.—
   IvyBlock

†Not commercially available in Canada.

Description

Bentoquatam (BEN-toe-kwa-tam) protects the skin like a shield against poison ivy, poison oak, and poison sumac by physically blocking skin contact with their resin. The best protection against getting these conditions is to avoid contact with these plants. This medicine does not dry oozing and weeping caused by the rash of poison ivy, poison oak, or poison sumac.

Bentoquatam is available without prescription in the following dosage form:

   Topical
   • Lotion (U.S.)

Before Using This Medicine

If you are using this medicine without a prescription, carefully read and follow any precautions on the label. For bentoquatam, the following should be considered:

Allergies—Tell your doctor if you have ever had any unusual or allergic reaction to bentoquatam. Also tell your health care professional if you are allergic to any other substances, such as foods, preservatives, or dyes.

Pregnancy—Studies on effects in pregnancy have not been done in humans.

Breast-feeding—Bentoquatam has not been reported to cause problems in nursing babies.

Children—Although there is no specific information comparing use of bentoquatam in children 6 years of age or older with use in other age groups, this medicine is not expected to cause different side effects or problems in these children than it does in adults. Use is not recommended for children up to 6 years of age.

Older adults—Many medicines have not been studied specifically in older people. Therefore, it may not be known whether they work exactly the same way they do in younger adults. Although there is no specific information comparing use of bentoquatam in the elderly with use in other age groups, this medicine is not expected to cause different side effects or problems in older people than it does in younger adults.

Other medicines—Although certain medicines should not be used together at all, in other cases two different medicines may be used together even if an interaction might occur. In these cases, your doctor may want to change the dose, or other precautions may be necessary. Tell your health care professional if you are using any other topical prescription or nonprescription (over-the-counter [OTC]) medicine that is to be applied to the same area of the skin.

Other medical problems—The presence of other medical problems may affect the use of bentoquatam. Make sure

you tell your doctor if you have any other medical problems, especially:

- Contact dermatitis, allergic, due to poison ivy, poison oak, or poison sumac—Bentoquatam should not be applied to the rash of poison ivy, poison oak, or poison sumac and should be discontinued if such a rash develops

Proper Use of This Medicine

Although this medicine provides some protection, avoiding contact with poison ivy, poison oak, or poison sumac is best.

Do not use this medicine in or near the eyes. If this medicine does get into your eyes, wash them out immediately for 20 minutes with large amounts of cool tap water. If your eyes still burn or are painful, check with your doctor.

To use *bentoquatam lotion:*

- Shake the lotion well before using.
- Rub on enough lotion to leave a smooth wet film on skin.
- Allow the medicine to dry on the skin at least 15 minutes before being exposed to poison ivy, poison oak, or poison sumac.
- Maximum protection lasts for 4 hours but lotion must be reapplied whenever the dried film on the skin cannot be seen.
- Remove medicine with soap and water when it is no longer needed.

Dosing—*Follow your doctor's orders or the directions on the label.* The following information includes only the average dose of bentoquatam. *If your dose is different, do not change it* unless your doctor tells you to do so.

- For prevention of skin irritation from poison ivy, poison oak, or poison sumac (allergic contact dermatitis):
  —For *topical* dosage form (lotion):
    - Adults and children six years of age and older—Apply to the area(s) of skin that may be affected at least fifteen minutes before exposure. Reapply whenever dry film is not seen or every four hours as needed.
    - Children up to six years of age—Use must be determined by the doctor.

Storage—To store this medicine:

- Keep out of the reach of children.
- Store away from heat and direct light.
- Keep the medicine from freezing. Do not refrigerate.
- Do not keep outdated medicine or medicine no longer needed. Be sure that any discarded medicine is out of the reach of children.

Precautions While Using This Medicine

If a rash or irritation occurs, stop using bentoquatam and check with your health care professional.

Side Effects of This Medicine

Along with its needed effects, a medicine may cause some unwanted effects. Although not all of these side effects may occur, if they do occur they may need medical attention.

Check with your doctor as soon as possible if any of the following side effects occur:
  Rare
    Mild redness of skin

Other side effects not listed above may also occur in some patients. If you notice any other effects, check with your doctor.

Developed: 05/07/97

BENZODIAZEPINES Systemic

Commonly used brand name(s):

In the U.S.—

Alprazolam Intensol[1]	Lorazepam Intensol[12]
Ativan[12]	Paxipam[10]
Dalmane[9]	ProSom[8]
Diastat[7]	Restoril[17]
Diazepam Intensol[7]	Serax[14]
Dizac[7]	Tranxene-SD[6]
Doral[16]	Tranxene-SD Half Strength[6]
Halcion[18]	Tranxene T-Tab[6]
Klonopin[5]	Valium[7]
Librium[3]	Xanax[1]

In Canada—

Alti-Alprazolam[1]	Novo-Alprazol[1]
Alti-Bromazepam[2]	Novo-Clopate[6]
Alti-Clonazepam[5]	Novo-Dipam[7]
Alti-Triazolam[18]	Novo-Flupam[9]
Apo-Alpraz[1]	Novo-Lorazem[12]
Apo-Chlordiazepoxide[3]	Novo-Poxide[3]
Apo-Clonazepam[5]	Novo-Temazepam[17]
Apo-Clorazepate[6]	Novo-Triolam[18]
Apo-Diazepam[7]	Novoxapam[14]
Apo-Flurazepam[9]	Nu-Alpraz[1]
Apo-Lorazepam[12]	Nu-Loraz[12]
Apo-Oxazepam[14]	PMS-Clonazepam[5]
Apo-Temazepam[17]	PMS-Diazepam[7]
Apo-Triazo[18]	Restoril[17]
Ativan[12]	Rivotril[5]
Clonapam[5]	Serax[14]
Dalmane[9]	Somnol[9]
Diazemuls[7]	Tranxene[6]
Frisium[4]	Valium[7]
Gen-Alprazolam[1]	Vivol[7]
Gen-Bromazepam[2]	Xanax[1]
Gen-Clonazepam[5]	Xanax TS[1]
Gen-Triazolam[18]	
Halcion[18]	
Lectopam[2]	
Mogadon[13]	

Note: For quick reference, the following benzodiazepines are numbered to match the corresponding brand names.

This information applies to the following medicines:

1. Alprazolam (al-PRAZ-oh-lam)‡§
2. Bromazepam (broe-MA-ze-pam)*
3. Chlordiazepoxide (klor-dye-az-e-POX-ide)‡
4. Clobazam (KLOE-ba-zam)*
5. Clonazepam (kloe-NA-ze-pam)‡
6. Clorazepate (klor-AZ-e-pate)‡
7. Diazepam (dye-AZ-e-pam)‡
8. Estazolam (ess-TA-zoe-lam)†‡
9. Flurazepam (flure-AZ-e-pam)‡
10. Halazepam (hal-AZ-e-pam)†
11. Ketazolam (kee-TAY-zoe-lam)*†
12. Lorazepam (lor-AZ-e-pam)‡
13. Nitrazepam (nye-TRA-ze-pam)*
14. Oxazepam (ox-AZ-e-pam)‡
15. Prazepam (PRAZ-e-pam)*†
16. Quazepam (KWA-ze-pam)†

17. Temazepam (tem-AZ-e-pam)‡
18. Triazolam (trye-AY-zoe-lam)‡§

---

*Not commercially available in the U.S.
†Not commercially available in Canada.
‡Generic name product may be available in the U.S.
§Generic name product may be available in Canada.

Description

Benzodiazepines (ben-zoe-dye-AZ-e-peens) belong to the group of medicines called central nervous system (CNS) depressants (medicines that slow down the nervous system).

Some benzodiazepines are used to relieve anxiety. However, benzodiazepines should not be used to relieve nervousness or tension caused by the stress of everyday life.

Some benzodiazepines are used to treat insomnia (trouble in sleeping). However, if used regularly (for example, every day) for insomnia, they usually are not effective for more than a few weeks.

Many of the benzodiazepines are used in the treatment of other conditions, also. Diazepam is used to help relax muscles or relieve muscle spasm. Diazepam injection is used before some medical procedures to relieve anxiety and to reduce memory of the procedure. Chlordiazepoxide, clorazepate, diazepam, and oxazepam are used to treat the symptoms of alcohol withdrawal. Alprazolam and clonazepam are used in the treatment of panic disorder. Clobazam, clonazepam, clorazepate, diazepam, and lorazepam are used in the treatment of certain convulsive (seizure) disorders, such as epilepsy. The benzodiazepines may also be used for other conditions as determined by your doctor.

Benzodiazepines may be habit-forming (causing mental or physical dependence), especially when taken for a long time or in high doses.

These medicines are available only with your doctor's prescription, in the following dosage forms:

Oral
Alprazolam
  • Oral solution (U.S.)
  • Tablets (U.S. and Canada)
Bromazepam
  • Tablets (Canada)
Chlordiazepoxide
  • Capsules (U.S. and Canada)
Clobazam
  • Tablets (Canada)
Clonazepam
  • Tablets (U.S. and Canada)
Clorazepate
  • Capsules (Canada)
  • Tablets (U.S.)
  • Extended-release tablets (U.S.)
Diazepam
  • Oral solution (U.S. and Canada)
  • Tablets (U.S. and Canada)
Estazolam
  • Tablets (U.S.)
Flurazepam
  • Capsules (U.S. and Canada)
  • Tablets (Canada)
Halazepam
  • Tablets (U.S.)
Lorazepam
  • Oral concentrate (U.S.)
  • Tablets (U.S. and Canada)
  • Sublingual tablets (Canada)
Nitrazepam
  • Tablets (Canada)
Oxazepam
  • Capsules (U.S.)
  • Tablets (U.S. and Canada)
Quazepam
  • Tablets (U.S.)
Temazepam
  • Capsules (U.S. and Canada)
Triazolam
  • Tablets (U.S. and Canada)

Parenteral
Chlordiazepoxide
  • Injection (U.S.)
Diazepam
  • Injection (U.S. and Canada)
Lorazepam
  • Injection (U.S. and Canada)

Rectal
Diazepam
  • For rectal solution (may be prepared in U.S. and Canada from diazepam injection)
  • Rectal gel (U.S.)

Before Using This Medicine

In deciding to use a medicine, the risks of taking the medicine must be weighed against the good it will do. This is a decision you and your doctor will make. For benzodiazepines, the following should be considered:

Allergies—Tell your doctor if you have ever had any unusual or allergic reaction to benzodiazepines. Also tell your health care professional if you are allergic to any other substances, such as foods, preservatives, or dyes. Certain benzodiazepine products may contain lactose, parabens, or soybean oil.

Pregnancy—Chlordiazepoxide and diazepam have been reported to increase the chance of birth defects when used during the first 3 months of pregnancy. Although similar problems have not been reported with the other benzodiazepines, the chance always exists since all of the benzodiazepines are related.

Studies in animals have shown that clonazepam, lorazepam, and temazepam cause birth defects or other problems, including death of the animal fetus.

Too much use of a benzodiazepine during pregnancy may cause the baby to become dependent on the medicine. This may lead to withdrawal side effects after birth. Also, use of benzodiazepines during pregnancy, especially during the last weeks, may cause body temperature problems, breathing problems, difficulty in feeding, drowsiness, or muscle weakness in the newborn infant.

Benzodiazepines given just before or during labor may cause weakness in the newborn infant. When diazepam is given in high doses (especially by injection) within 15 hours before delivery, it may cause breathing problems, muscle weakness, difficulty in feeding, and body temperature problems in the newborn infant.

Breast-feeding—Benzodiazepines may pass into the breast milk and cause drowsiness, difficulty in feeding, and weight loss in nursing babies of mothers taking these medicines.

Children—Most of the side effects of these medicines are more likely to occur in children, especially the very young. These patients are usually more sensitive than adults to the effects of benzodiazepines.

It is possible that using clonazepam for long periods of time may cause unwanted effects on physical and mental growth in children. If such effects do occur, they may not be noticed until many years later. Before this medicine is given to children for long periods of time, you should discuss its use with your child's doctor.

Older adults—Most of the side effects of these medicines are more likely to occur in the elderly, who are usually more sensitive to the effects of benzodiazepines.

Taking benzodiazepines for trouble in sleeping may cause more daytime drowsiness in elderly patients than in younger adults. In addition, falls and related injuries are more likely to occur in elderly patients taking benzodiazepines.

Other medicines—Although certain medicines should not be used together at all, in other cases two different medicines may be used together even if an interaction might occur. In these cases, your doctor may want to change the dose, or other precautions may be necessary. When you are taking or receiving benzodiazepines it is especially important that your health care professional know if you are taking any of the following:

- Central nervous system (CNS) depressants (medicines that cause drowsiness)—The CNS depressant effects of either these medicines or benzodiazepines may be increased; your doctor may want to change the dose of either or both medicines

- Fluvoxamine (e.g., Luvox) or
- Itraconazole (e.g., Sporanox) or
- Ketoconazole (e.g., Nizoral) or
- Nefazodone (e.g., Serzone)—Higher blood levels of benzodiazepines may occur, increasing the chance that side effects will occur; your doctor may want to change the dose of either or both medicines, or give you a different medicine

Other medical problems—The presence of other medical problems may affect the use of benzodiazepines. Make sure you tell your doctor if you have any other medical problems, especially:

- Alcohol abuse (or history of) or
- Drug abuse or dependence (or history of)—Dependence on benzodiazepines may be more likely to develop
- Brain disease—CNS depression and other side effects of benzodiazepines may be more likely to occur
- Difficulty in swallowing (in children) or
- Emphysema, asthma, bronchitis, or other chronic lung disease or
- Glaucoma or
- Hyperactivity or
- Mental depression or
- Mental illness (severe) or
- Myasthenia gravis or
- Porphyria or
- Sleep apnea (temporary stopping of breathing during sleep)—Benzodiazepines may make these conditions worse

- Epilepsy or history of seizures—Although some benzodiazepines are used in treating epilepsy, starting or suddenly stopping treatment with these medicines may increase seizures
- Kidney or liver disease—Higher blood levels of benzodiazepines may result, increasing the chance that side effects will occur

---

Proper Use of This Medicine

For caregivers administering *diazepam rectal gel:*
- Discuss with the patient's medical doctor exactly when and how to use diazepam rectal gel.
- Discuss with the patient's medical doctor when you should call for emergency help.
- Read the instructions that you received with the medicine before you need to use it.
- Stay with the patient after administering diazepam rectal gel to check his or her condition as instructed by the doctor.

For patients taking *clorazepate extended-release tablets:*
- Swallow tablets whole.
- Do not crush, break, or chew before swallowing.

For patients taking *alprazolam, diazepam, or lorazepam concentrated oral solution:*
- Measure each dose carefully using the dropper provided with the medicine.
- It is recommended that each dose be mixed with water, soda or soda-like beverages, or semisolid food such as applesauce or pudding, just before it is taken.
- Take the entire mixture right away. It should not be saved to be used later.

For patients taking *lorazepam sublingual tablets:*
- Do not chew or swallow the tablet. This medicine is meant to be absorbed through the lining of the mouth. Place the tablet under your tongue (sublingual) and let it slowly dissolve there. Do not swallow for at least 2 minutes.

Take this medicine only as directed by your doctor. Do not take more of it, do not take it more often, and do not take it for a longer time than your doctor ordered. If too much is taken, it may become habit-forming (causing mental or physical dependence).

If you think this medicine is not working properly after you have taken it for a few weeks, *do not increase the dose*. Instead, check with your doctor.

For patients taking this medicine on a regular schedule *for epilepsy or other seizure disorder:*
- *In order for this medicine to control your seizures, it must be taken every day in regularly spaced doses as ordered by your doctor.* This is necessary to keep a constant amount of the medicine in the blood. To help keep the amount constant, do not miss any doses.

For patients taking this medicine *for insomnia:*
- *Do not take this medicine when your schedule does not permit you to get a full night's sleep (7 to 8 hours).* If you must wake up before this, you may continue to feel drowsy and may experience memory problems, because the effects of the medicine have not had time to wear off.

For patients taking *flurazepam:*
- *When you begin to take this medicine, your sleeping problem will improve somewhat the first night. How-*

ever, 2 or 3 nights may pass before you receive the full effects of this medicine.

Dosing— The dose of benzodiazepines will be different for different patients. *Follow your doctor's orders or the directions on the label.* The following information includes only the average doses of benzodiazepines. *If your dose is different, do not change it* unless your doctor tells you to do so.

The number of capsules or tablets, or the amount of solution that you take, or the number of injections you receive, depends on the strength of the medicine. Also, *the number of doses you take each day, the time allowed between doses, and the length of time you take the medicine depend on the medical problem for which you are taking benzodiazepines.*

For alprazolam
- For *oral* dosage form (solution or tablets):
  —For anxiety:
    - Adults—At first, 0.25 to 0.5 milligram (mg) three times a day. Your doctor may increase your dose if needed. However, the dose usually is not more than 4 mg a day.
    - Children younger than 18 years of age—Use and dose must be determined by your doctor.
    - Older adults—At first, 0.25 mg two or three times a day. Your doctor may increase your dose if needed.
  —For panic disorder:
    - Adults—At first, 0.5 mg three times a day. Your doctor may increase your dose if needed. However, the dose usually is not more than 10 mg a day.
    - Children younger than 18 years of age—Use and dose must be determined by your doctor.

For bromazepam
- For *oral* dosage form (tablets):
  —For anxiety:
    - Adults—6 to 30 milligrams (mg) a day, taken in smaller doses during the day.
    - Children younger than 18 years of age—Use and dose must be determined by your doctor.
    - Older adults—At first, up to 3 mg a day. Your doctor may change your dose if needed.

For chlordiazepoxide
- For *oral* dosage form (capsules):
  —For anxiety:
    - Adults—5 to 25 milligrams (mg) three or four times a day.
    - Children 6 years of age and older—5 mg two to four times a day. Your doctor may increase your dose if needed.
    - Children younger than 6 years of age—Use and dose must be determined by your doctor.
    - Older adults—At first, 5 mg two to four times a day. Your doctor may increase your dose if needed.
  —For sedation during withdrawal from alcohol:
    - Adults—At first, 50 to 100 mg, repeated if needed. However, the dose usually is not more than 300 mg a day.
    - Children—Use and dose must be determined by your doctor.

- For *injection* dosage form:
  —For anxiety:
    - Adults—At first, 50 to 100 mg, injected into a muscle or vein. Then, if needed, 25 to 50 mg three or four times a day.
    - Teenagers—25 to 50 mg, injected into a muscle or vein.
    - Children younger than 12 years of age—Use and dose must be determined by your doctor.
    - Older adults—25 to 50 mg, injected into a muscle or vein.
  —For sedation during withdrawal from alcohol:
    - Adults—At first, 50 to 100 mg, injected into a muscle or vein. If needed, the dose may be repeated in two to four hours.
    - Children—Use and dose must be determined by your doctor.

For clobazam
- For *oral* dosage form (tablets):
  —For control of seizures:
    - Adults—At first, 5 to 15 milligrams (mg) a day. Your doctor may increase your dose if needed. However, the dose usually is not more than 80 mg a day.
    - Children 2 to 16 years of age—At first, 5 mg a day. Your doctor may increase your dose if needed. However, the dose usually is not more than 40 mg a day.
    - Children younger than 2 years of age—Dose is based on body weight and must be determined by your doctor.

For clonazepam
- For *oral* dosage form (tablets):
  —For control of seizures:
    - Adults—At first, 0.5 milligram (mg) three times a day. Your doctor may increase your dose if needed. However, the dose usually is not more than 20 mg a day.
    - Infants and children younger than 10 years of age—Dose is based on body weight and must be determined by your doctor.
  —For panic disorder:
    - Adults—At first, 0.25 mg two times a day. Your doctor may increase your dose if needed. However, the dose usually is not more than 4 mg a day.
    - Children—Use and dose must be determined by your doctor.

For clorazepate
- For *oral* dosage form (capsules or tablets):
  —For anxiety:
    - Adults and teenagers—7.5 to 15 mg two to four times a day. Or your doctor may want you to start by taking 15 mg at bedtime.
    - Children younger than 12 years of age—Use and dose must be determined by your doctor.
    - Older adults—At first, 3.75 to 15 mg a day. Your doctor may increase your dose if needed.
  —For sedation during withdrawal from alcohol:
    - Adults and teenagers—At first, 30 mg. Your doctor will set up a schedule that will gradually reduce your dose.
    - Children younger than 12 years of age—Use and dose must be determined by your doctor.

—For control of seizures:
- Adults and teenagers—At first, up to 7.5 mg taken three times a day. Your doctor may increase your dose if needed. However, the dose usually is not more than 90 mg a day.
- Children 9 to 12 years of age—At first, up to 7.5 mg two times a day. Your doctor may increase your dose if needed. However, the dose usually is not more than 60 mg a day.
- Children younger than 9 years of age—Use and dose must be determined by your doctor.

• For *oral* dosage form (extended-release tablets):
—For anxiety:
- Adults and teenagers—Your doctor may change your dosage form to the extended-release tablet if you are already taking 3.75 or 7.5 milligrams (mg) of clorazepate three times a day. The extended-release tablet is taken one time each day.
- Children younger than 12 years of age—Use and dose must be determined by your doctor.
—For control of seizures:
- Adults, teenagers, and children 9 to 12 years of age—Your doctor may change your dosage form to the extended-release tablet if you are already taking 3.75 or 7.5 milligrams (mg) of clorazepate three times a day. The extended-release tablet is taken one time each day.
- Children younger than 9 years of age—Use and dose must be determined by your doctor.

For diazepam
• For *oral* dosage form (solution or tablets):
—For anxiety:
- Adults—2 to 10 mg two to four times a day.
- Children 6 months of age and older—Dose is based on body weight or size and must be determined by your doctor.
- Children younger than 6 months of age—Use is not recommended.
- Older adults—2 to 2.5 mg one or two times a day. Your doctor may increase your dose if needed.
—For sedation during withdrawal from alcohol:
- Adults—At first, 10 mg three or four times a day. Your doctor will set up a schedule that will gradually decrease your dose.
- Children—Use and dose must be determined by your doctor.
—For control of seizures:
- Adults—2 to 10 mg two to four times a day.
- Children 6 months of age and older—Dose is based on body weight or size and must be determined by your doctor.
- Children younger than 6 months of age—Use is not recommended.
- Older adults—2 to 2.5 mg one or two times a day. Your doctor may increase your dose if needed.
—For relaxing muscles:
- Adults—2 to 10 mg three or four times a day.
- Children 6 months of age and older—Dose is based on body weight or size and must be determined by your doctor.
- Children younger than 6 months of age—Use is not recommended.
- Older adults—2 to 2.5 mg one or two times a day. Your doctor may increase your dose if needed.

• For *injection* dosage form:
—For anxiety:
- Adults—2 to 10 mg, injected into a muscle or vein.
- Children—Use and dose must be determined by your doctor.
- For older adults—2 to 5 mg, injected into a muscle or vein.
—For sedation during withdrawal from alcohol:
- Adults—At first, 10 mg injected into a muscle or vein. If needed, 5 to 10 mg may be given three or four hours later.
- Children—Use and dose must be determined by your doctor.
—For sedation before surgery or other procedures:
- Adults—5 to 20 mg, injected into a muscle or vein.
- Children—Use and dose must be determined by your doctor.
- Older adults—2 to 5 mg, injected into a muscle or vein.
—For control of seizures:
- Adults—At first, 5 to 10 mg, usually injected into a vein every ten to fifteen minutes, stopping if the total dose reaches 30 mg. If needed, this treatment may be repeated in two to four hours.
- Children 5 years of age and older—At first, 1 mg, usually injected into a vein every two to five minutes, stopping if the total dose reaches 10 mg. This treatment may be repeated in two to four hours.
- Infants older than 30 days of age and children younger than 5 years of age—At first, 0.2 to 0.5 mg, usually injected into a vein every two to five minutes, stopping if the total dose reaches 5 mg. This treatment may be repeated in two to four hours.
- Newborns and infants 30 days of age and younger—Use and dose must be determined by your doctor.
- Older adults—2 to 5 mg, injected into a muscle or vein.
—For relaxing muscle spasms:
- Adults—At first, 5 to 10 mg injected into a muscle or vein. The dose may be repeated in three or four hours.
- Children—Use and dose must be determined by your doctor.
- Older adults—2 to 5 mg, injected into a muscle or vein.
—For relaxing muscles in tetanus:
- Adults—At first, 5 to 10 mg injected into a muscle or vein. Your doctor may increase your dose if needed.
- Children 5 years of age and older—5 to 10 mg, injected into a muscle or vein. The dose may be repeated every three to four hours if needed.
- Infants older than 30 days of age and children younger than 5 years of age—1 to 2 mg, injected into a muscle or vein. The dose may be repeated every three to four hours if needed.
- Newborns and infants 30 days of age and younger—Use and dose must be determined by your doctor.

• For *rectal* dosage form (gel or solution):
—For control of seizures:
- Adults and teenagers—Dose is based on body weight and must be determined by your doctor.

- Children—Dose is based on body weight and must be determined by your doctor.

For estazolam
- For *oral* dosage form (tablets):
  —For trouble in sleeping:
    - Adults—1 milligram (mg) at bedtime. Your doctor may increase your dose if needed. However, the dose usually is not more than 2 mg.
    - Children younger than 18 years of age—Use and dose must be determined by your doctor.

For flurazepam
- For *oral* dosage form (capsules or tablets):
  —For trouble in sleeping:
    - Adults—15 or 30 milligrams (mg) at bedtime.
    - Children younger than 15 years of age—Use and dose must be determined by your doctor.
    - Older adults—At first, 15 mg at bedtime. Your doctor may increase your dose if needed.

For halazepam
- For *oral* dosage form (tablets):
  —For anxiety:
    - Adults—20 to 40 milligrams (mg) three or four times a day.
    - Children younger than 18 years of age—Use and dose must be determined by your doctor.
    - Older adults—20 mg one or two times a day.

For lorazepam
- For *oral* dosage form (concentrate or tablets):
  —For anxiety:
    - Adults and teenagers—1 to 3 milligrams (mg) two or three times a day.
    - Children younger than 12 years of age—Use and dose must be determined by your doctor.
    - Older adults—0.5 to 2 mg a day, taken in smaller doses during the day.
  —For trouble in sleeping:
    - Adults and teenagers—2 to 4 mg taken at bedtime.
    - Children younger than 12 years of age—Use and dose must be determined by your doctor.
- For *sublingual tablet* dosage form:
  —For anxiety:
    - Adults—2 to 3 mg a day, in smaller doses placed under the tongue during the day. Your doctor may increase your dose if needed. However, the dose usually is not more than 6 mg a day.
    - Children younger than 18 years of age—Use and dose must be determined by your doctor.
    - Older adults—At first, 0.5 mg a day. Your doctor may increase your dose if needed.
  —For sedation before surgery:
    - Adults—Dose is based on body weight and will be determined by your doctor. However, the dose usually is not more than 4 mg, placed under the tongue, one to two hours before surgery.
    - Children—Use and dose must be determined by your doctor.
- For *injection* dosage form:
  —For sedation before surgery or other procedures:
    - Adults—Dose is based on body weight and will be determined by your doctor. However, the dose usually is not more than 4 mg, injected into a muscle or vein.

- Children younger than 18 years of age—Use and dose must be determined by your doctor.
  —For control of seizures:
    - Adults—At first, 4 mg slowly injected into a vein. The dose may be repeated after ten to fifteen minutes if needed.
    - Children younger than 18 years of age—Use and dose must be determined by your doctor.

For nitrazepam
- For *oral* dosage form (tablets):
  —For trouble in sleeping:
    - Adults—5 to 10 milligrams (mg) at bedtime.
    - Children—Use and dose must be determined by your doctor.
    - Older adults—At first, 2.5 mg taken at bedtime. Your doctor may increase your dose if needed.
  —For control of seizures:
    - Children less than 30 kilograms (66 pounds) of body weight—Dose is based on body weight and will be determined by your doctor.

For oxazepam
- For *oral* dosage form (capsules or tablets):
  —For anxiety:
    - Adults—10 to 30 milligrams (mg) three or four times a day.
    - Children younger than 12 years of age—Use and dose must be determined by your doctor.
    - Older adults—At first, 5 mg one or two times a day or 10 mg three times a day. Your doctor may increase your dose if needed. However, the dose usually is not more than 15 mg four times a day.
  —For sedation during withdrawal from alcohol:
    - Adults—15 to 30 mg three or four times a day.
    - Children younger than 12 years of age—Use and dose must be determined by your doctor.

For quazepam
- For *oral* dosage form (tablets):
  —For trouble in sleeping:
    - Adults—7.5 to 15 milligrams (mg) at bedtime.
    - Children younger than 18 years of age—Use and dose must be determined by your doctor.

For temazepam
- For *oral* dosage form (capsules):
  —For trouble in sleeping:
    - Adults—15 milligrams (mg) at bedtime. Your doctor may change your dose if needed.
    - Children younger than 18 years of age—Use and dose must be determined by your doctor.
    - Older adults—At first, 7.5 mg at bedtime. Your doctor may increase your dose if needed.

For triazolam
- For *oral* dosage form (tablets):
  —For trouble in sleeping:
    - Adults—0.125 to 0.25 milligram (mg) at bedtime.
    - Children younger than 18 years of age—Use and dose must be determined by your doctor.
    - Older adults—At first, 0.125 mg at bedtime. Your doctor may increase your dose if needed.

Missed dose—If you are taking this medicine regularly (for example, every day as for epilepsy) and you miss a dose, take it right away if you remember within an hour or so of the missed dose. However, if you do not remember until later, skip the missed dose and go back to your regular dosing schedule. Do not double doses.

Storage—To store this medicine:

- Keep out of the reach of children. Overdose of benzodiazepines may be especially dangerous in children.
- Store away from heat and direct light.
- Do not store the capsule or tablet form of this medicine in the bathroom, near the kitchen sink, or in other damp places. Heat or moisture may cause the medicine to break down.
- Keep the liquid form of this medicine from freezing.
- Do not keep outdated medicine or medicine no longer needed. Be sure that any discarded medicine is out of the reach of children.

Precautions While Using This Medicine

If you will be *taking a benzodiazepine regularly for a long time:*

- Your doctor should check your progress at regular visits to make sure that this medicine does not cause unwanted effects. If you are taking a benzodiazepine for convulsions (seizures), this is also important during the first few months of treatment.
- Check with your doctor at regular visits to see if you need to continue taking this medicine.

If you are taking a benzodiazepine for *epilepsy or another seizure disorder:*

- Your doctor may want you to carry a medical identification card or bracelet stating that you are taking this medicine.

If you are taking a benzodiazepine for *insomnia* (trouble in sleeping):

- If you think you need this medicine for more than 7 to 10 days, be sure to discuss it with your doctor. Insomnia that lasts longer than this may be a sign of another medical problem.
- You may have difficulty sleeping (rebound insomnia) for the first few nights after you stop taking this medicine.

Benzodiazepines may be habit-forming (causing mental or physical dependence), especially when taken for a long time or in high doses. Some signs of dependence on benzodiazepines are:

- A strong desire or need to continue taking the medicine.
- A need to increase the dose to receive the effects of the medicine.
- Withdrawal effects (for example, irritability, nervousness, trouble in sleeping, abdominal or stomach cramps, trembling or shaking) occurring after the medicine is stopped.

If you think you may have become mentally or physically dependent on this medicine, check with your doctor. Do not stop taking it suddenly.

If you have been taking this medicine in large doses or for a long time, do not stop taking it without first checking with your doctor. Your doctor may want you to reduce gradually the amount you are taking before stopping completely. Stopping this medicine suddenly may cause withdrawal side effects, including seizures. Stopping this medicine suddenly is most likely to cause seizures if you have been taking it for epilepsy or another seizure disorder.

This medicine will add to the effects of alcohol and other central nervous system (CNS) depressants (medicines that slow down the nervous system, possibly causing drowsiness).

Some examples of CNS depressants are antihistamines or medicine for hay fever, other allergies, or colds; sedatives, tranquilizers, or sleeping medicine; prescription pain medicine or narcotics; barbiturates; medicine for seizures; muscle relaxants; or anesthetics, including some dental anesthetics. This effect may last for a few days after you stop taking this medicine. *Check with your doctor before taking any of the above while you are taking this medicine.*

If you think you or someone else may have taken an overdose of this medicine, get emergency help at once. Taking an overdose of a benzodiazepine or taking alcohol or other CNS depressants with the benzodiazepine may lead to unconsciousness and possibly death. Some signs of an overdose are continuing slurred speech or confusion, severe drowsiness, severe weakness, and staggering.

Before you have any medical tests, tell the medical doctor in charge that you are taking this medicine. The results of the metyrapone test may be affected by chlordiazepoxide.

If you develop any unusual and strange thoughts or behavior while you are taking this medicine, be sure to discuss it with your doctor. Some changes that have occurred in people taking this medicine are like those seen in people who drink alcohol and then act in a manner that is not normal. Other changes may be more unusual and extreme, such as confusion, agitation, and hallucinations (seeing, hearing, or feeling things that are not there).

This medicine may cause some people, especially older persons, to become drowsy, dizzy, lightheaded, clumsy or unsteady, or less alert than they are normally. Even if taken at bedtime, it may cause some people to feel drowsy or less alert on arising. *Make sure you know how you react to this medicine before you drive, use machines, or do anything else that could be dangerous if you are dizzy or are not alert.*

Side Effects of This Medicine

Along with its needed effects, a medicine may cause some unwanted effects. Although not all of these side effects may occur, if they do occur they may need medical attention.

Check with your doctor as soon as possible if any of the following side effects occur:

Less common

Anxiety; confusion (may be more common in the elderly); fast, pounding, or irregular heartbeat; lack of memory of events taking place after benzodiazepine is taken (may be more common with triazolam); mental depression

Rare

Abnormal thinking, including disorientation, delusions (holding false beliefs that cannot be changed by facts), or loss of sense of reality; agitation; behavior changes, including aggressive behavior, bizarre behavior, decreased inhibition, or outbursts of anger; convulsions (seizures); hallucinations (seeing, hearing, or feeling things that are not there); hypotension (low blood pressure); muscle weakness; skin rash or itching; sore throat, fever, and chills; trouble in sleeping; ulcers or sores in mouth or throat (continuing); uncontrolled movements of body, including the eyes; unusual bleeding or bruising; unusual excitement, nervousness, or irritability; unusual tiredness or weakness (severe); yellow eyes or skin

Symptoms of overdose

Confusion (continuing); convulsions (seizures); drowsiness (severe) or coma; shakiness; slow heartbeat; slow reflexes; slurred speech (continuing); staggering; troubled breathing; weakness (severe)

For patients having *chlordiazepoxide, diazepam, or lorazepam injected:*

• Check with your doctor if there is redness, swelling, or pain at the place of injection.

Other side effects may occur that usually do not need medical attention. These side effects may go away during treatment as your body adjusts to the medicine. However, check with your doctor if any of the following side effects continue or are bothersome:

More common

Clumsiness or unsteadiness; dizziness or lightheadedness; drowsiness; slurred speech

Less common or rare

Abdominal or stomach cramps or pain; blurred vision or other changes in vision; changes in sexual desire or ability; constipation; diarrhea; dryness of mouth or increased thirst; false sense of well-being; headache; increased bronchial secretions or watering of mouth; muscle spasm; nausea or vomiting; problems with urination; trembling or shaking; unusual tiredness or weakness

Not all of the side effects listed above have been reported for each of these medicines, but they have been reported for at least one of them. All of the benzodiazepines are similar, so any of the above side effects may occur with any of these medicines.

After you stop using this medicine, your body may need time to adjust. During this time, check with your doctor if you notice any of the following side effects:

More common

Irritability; nervousness; trouble in sleeping

Less common

Abdominal or stomach cramps; confusion; fast or pounding heartbeat; increased sense of hearing; increased sensitivity to touch and pain; increased sweating; loss of sense of reality; mental depression; muscle cramps; nausea or vomiting; sensitivity of eyes to light; tingling, burning, or prickly sensations; trembling or shaking

Rare

Confusion as to time, place, or person; convulsions (seizures); feelings of suspicion or distrust; hallucinations (seeing, hearing, or feeling things that are not there)

Other side effects not listed above may also occur in some patients. If you notice any other effects, check with your doctor.

Additional Information

Once a medicine has been approved for marketing for a certain use, experience may show that it is also useful for other medical problems. Although these uses are not included in product labeling, some of the benzodiazepines are used in certain patients with the following medical conditions:

• Nausea and vomiting caused by cancer chemotherapy
• Tension headache
• Tremors

Other than the above information, there is no additional information relating to proper use, precautions, or side effects for these uses.

Revised: 04/05/2001

BENZONATATE   Systemic

Commonly used brand name(s):

In the U.S.—
Tessalon
Generic name product may be available.

In Canada—
Tessalon

Description

Benzonatate (ben-ZOE-na-tate) is used to relieve coughs due to colds or influenza (flu). It is not to be used for chronic cough that occurs with smoking, asthma, or emphysema or when there is an unusually large amount of mucus or phlegm (pronounced flem) with the cough.

Benzonatate relieves cough by acting directly on the lungs and the breathing passages. It may also act on the cough center in the brain.

This medicine is available only with your doctor's prescription, in the following dosage form:

Oral
• Capsules (U.S. and Canada)

Before Using This Medicine

In deciding to use a medicine, the risks of taking the medicine must be weighed against the good it will do. This is a decision you and your doctor will make. For benzonatate, the following should be considered:

Allergies—Tell your doctor if you have ever had any unusual or allergic reaction to benzonatate or to tetracaine or other local anesthetics. Also tell your health care professional if you are allergic to any other substances, such as foods, preservatives, or dyes.

Pregnancy—Studies on effects in pregnancy have not been done in either humans or animals.

Breast-feeding—It is not known whether benzonatate passes into breast milk. Although most medicines pass into breast milk in small amounts, many of them may be used safely while breast-feeding. Mothers who are taking this medicine and who wish to breast-feed should discuss this with their doctor.

Children—*It is very important that children do not chew or suck on the capsule before swallowing it.* If the benzonatate contained in the capsules comes in contact with the mouth, it may cause the mouth and throat to become numb (loss of feeling) and choking may occur.

Older adults—Many medicines have not been studied specifically in older people. Therefore, it may not be known whether they work exactly the same way they do in younger adults or if they cause different side effects or problems in older people. There is no specific information comparing use of benzonatate in the elderly with use in other age groups.

Other medicines—Although certain medicines should not be used together at all, in other cases 2 different medicines may be used together even if an interaction might occur. In these cases, your doctor may want to change the dose, or other precautions may be necessary. Tell your health care professional if you are taking any other prescription or non-prescription (over-the-counter [OTC]) medicine.

Other medical problems—The presence of other medical problems may affect the use of benzonatate. Make sure you tell your doctor if you have any other medical problems, especially:

- Mucus or phlegm with cough—Since benzonatate decreases coughing, it makes it difficult to get rid of the mucus that may collect in the lungs and airways with some diseases

Proper Use of This Medicine

It is very important that you do not chew or suck on the capsule before swallowing it. If the benzonatate contained in the capsules comes in contact with the mouth, it may cause the mouth and throat to become numb (loss of feeling) and choking may occur.

Dosing—The dose of benzonatate will be different for different patients. *Follow your doctor's orders or the directions on the label.* The following information includes only the average doses of benzonatate. *If your dose is different, do not change it* unless your doctor tells you to do so.

- For *oral* dosage form (capsules):
  —For cough:
  - Adults—100 milligrams (mg) three times a day as needed.
  - Children—
    Up to 10 years of age: Use and dose must be determined by your doctor.
    10 years of age and older: 100 mg three times a day as needed.

Missed dose—If you must take this medicine regularly and you miss a dose, take it as soon as possible. However, if it is almost time for your next dose, skip the missed dose and go back to your regular dosing schedule. Do not double doses.

Storage—To store this medicine:

- Store away from heat and direct light.
- Keep out of the reach of children.
- Do not store this medicine in the bathroom, near the kitchen sink, or in other damp places. Heat or moisture may cause the medicine to break down.
- Do not keep outdated medicine or medicine no longer needed. Be sure that any discarded medicine is out of the reach of children.

Precautions While Using This Medicine

If your cough has not become better after 7 days or if you have a high fever, skin rash, or continuing headache with the cough, check with your doctor. These signs may mean that you have other medical problems.

Side Effects of This Medicine

Along with its needed effects, a medicine may cause some unwanted effects. Although not all of these side effects may occur, if they do occur they may need medical attention.

Check with your doctor as soon as possible if any of the following side effects occur:
Rare
  Confusion; signs of hypersensitivity reactions, such as bronchospasm (shortness of breath, difficulty in breathing, tightness in chest, and/or wheezing) or laryngospasm (difficulty in speaking or breathing); visual hallucinations (seeing things that are not there)

Symptoms of overdose
  Convulsions (seizures); restlessness; trembling

Other side effects may occur that usually do not need medical attention. These side effects may go away during treatment as your body adjusts to the medicine. However, check with your health care professional if any of the following side effects continue or are bothersome:
Less common or rare
  Burning sensation in the eyes; constipation; dizziness (mild); drowsiness (mild); headache; itching; nausea or vomiting; skin rash; stuffy nose

Other side effects not listed above may also occur in some patients. If you notice any other effects, check with your doctor.

Revised: 08/13/98

BENZOYL PEROXIDE Topical

Commonly used brand name(s):

In the U.S.—

Acne-Aid Vanishing Cream	Clearasil Maximum Strength
Acne-Aid Aqua Gel	Medicated Anti-Acne 10
Ambi 10 Acne Medication	Vanishing Lotion
Benoxyl 5 Lotion	Clear By Design 2.5 Gel
Benoxyl 10 Lotion	Clearplex 5
Benzac AC 2½ Gel	Clearplex 10
Benzac AC 5 Gel	Cuticura Acne 5 Cream
Benzac AC 10 Gel	Del-Aqua-5 Gel
Benzac AC Wash 2½	Del-Aqua-10 Gel
Benzac AC Wash 5	Desquam-E 2.5 Gel
Benzac AC Wash 10	Desquam-E 5 Gel
Benzac 5 Gel	Desquam-E 10 Gel
Benzac 10 Gel	Desquam-X 10 Bar
Benzac W 2½ Gel	Desquam-X 2.5 Gel
Benzac W 5 Gel	Desquam-X 5 Gel
Benzac W 10 Gel	Desquam-X 10 Gel
Benzac W Wash 5	Desquam-X 5 Wash
Benzac W Wash 10	Desquam-X 10 Wash
5 Benzagel	Exact 5 Tinted Cream
10 Benzagel	Exact 5 Vanishing Cream
BenzaShave 5 Cream	Fostex 10 Bar
BenzaShave 10 Cream	Fostex 10 Cream
Brevoxyl-4 Gel	Fostex 5 Gel
Brevoxyl-8 Gel	Fostex 10 BPO Gel
Brevoxyl-4 Cleansing Lotion	Fostex 10 Wash
Brevoxyl-8 Cleansing Lotion	Loroxide 5.5 Lotion
Clean & Clear Persagel 5	Neutrogena Acne Mask 5
Clean & Clear Persagel 10	Noxzema Clear-ups Maximum
Clearasil Maximum Strength	Strength 10 Lotion
Medicated Anti-Acne 10	Noxzema Clear-ups On-The-
Tinted Cream	Spot 10 Lotion
Clearasil Maximum Strength	Oxy Balance Deep Action
Medicated Anti-Acne 10	Night Formula Lotion
Vanishing Cream	

Oxy 10 Balance Emergency
   Spot Treatment Cover-Up
   Formula Gel
Oxy 10 Balance Emergency
   Spot Treatment Invisible
   Formula Gel
Oxy Balance Emergency Spot
   Treatment Invisible Formula
   Gel
Oxy 10 Balance Maximum
   Medicated Face Wash

PanOxyl AQ 2½ Gel
PanOxyl AQ 5 Gel
PanOxyl AQ 10 Gel
PanOxyl 5 Bar
PanOxyl 10 Bar
PanOxyl 5 Gel
PanOxyl 10 Gel
Student's Choice Acne
   Medication
Triaz
Triaz Cleanser

Generic name product may be available.

In Canada—

Acetoxyl 2.5 Gel
Acetoxyl 5 Gel
Acetoxyl 10 Gel
Acetoxyl 20 Gel
Acnomel B.P. 5 Lotion
Benoxyl 5 Lotion
Benoxyl 10 Lotion
Benoxyl 20 Lotion
Benzac AC 5 Gel
Benzac AC 10 Gel
Benzac W 5 Gel
Benzac W 10 Gel
Benzac W Wash 5
Benzac W Wash 10
2.5 Benzagel Acne Gel
5 Benzagel Acne Gel
10 Benzagel Acne Gel
2.5 Benzagel Acne Lotion
5 Benzagel Acne Lotion
5 Benzagel Acne Wash
5 Benzagel Liquid Acne Soap
Clearasil BP Plus 5 Lotion
Clearasil BP Plus Skin Tone
   Cream
Dermacne
Dermoxyl Aqua 5 Gel
Dermoxyl 5 Gel
Dermoxyl 10 Gel
Dermoxyl 20 Gel
Desquam-X 5 Gel
Desquam-X 10 Gel

Desquam-X 5 Wash
Desquam-X 10 Wash
H_2 Oxyl 2.5 Gel
H_2 Oxyl 5 Gel
H_2 Oxyl 10 Gel
H_2 Oxyl 20 Gel
Loroxide 5 Lotion
Oxyderm 5 Lotion
Oxyderm 10 Lotion
Oxyderm 20 Lotion
Oxy 5 Regular Strength
   Cover-Up Cream
Oxy 5 Regular Strength
   Vanishing Lotion
Oxy 5 Sensitive Skin
   Vanishing Lotion
PanOxyl Aquagel 2.5
PanOxyl Aquagel 5
PanOxyl Aquagel 10
PanOxyl Aquagel 20
PanOxyl 5 Bar
PanOxyl 10 Bar
PanOxyl 5 Gel
PanOxyl 10 Gel
PanOxyl 15 Gel
PanOxyl 20 Gel
PanOxyl 5 Wash
PanOxyl 10 Wash
Solugel 4
Solugel 8
Xerac BP 5

Description

Benzoyl peroxide (BEN-zoe-ill per-OX-ide) is used to treat acne.

It may also be used for other conditions as determined by your doctor.

Some of these preparations are available only with your doctor's prescription. Others are available without a prescription; however, your doctor may have special instructions on the proper use of benzoyl peroxide for your medical condition.

Benzoyl peroxide is available in the following dosage forms:

Topical
- Cleansing bar (U.S. and Canada)
- Cream (U.S. and Canada)
- Gel (U.S. and Canada)
- Lotion (U.S. and Canada)
- Cleansing lotion (U.S. and Canada)
- Facial mask (U.S.)
- Stick

Before Using This Medicine

If you are using this medicine without a prescription, carefully read and follow any precautions on the label. For benzoyl peroxide, the following should be considered:

Allergies—Tell your doctor if you have ever had any unusual or allergic reaction to benzoyl peroxide. Also tell your health care professional if you are allergic to any other substances, such as preservatives or dyes.

Pregnancy—Studies on effects in pregnancy have not been done in either humans or animals. However, benzoyl peroxide may be absorbed through the skin.

Breast-feeding—Benzoyl peroxide may be absorbed through the mother's skin. It is not known whether it passes into the breast milk. However, this medicine has not been reported to cause problems in nursing babies.

Children—For children up to 12 years of age: Studies on this medicine have been done only in adult patients, and there is no specific information comparing use of benzoyl peroxide with use in other age groups. For children 12 years of age and older: Although there is no specific information comparing use of benzoyl peroxide in children with use in other age groups, this medicine is not expected to cause different side effects or problems in children 12 years of age and older than it does in adults.

Older adults—Many medicines have not been studied specifically in older people. Therefore, it may not be known whether they work exactly the same way they do in younger adults. Although there is no specific information comparing use of benzoyl peroxide in the elderly with use in other age groups, this medicine is not expected to cause different side effects or problems in older people than it does in younger adults.

Other medicines—Although certain medicines should not be used together at all, in other cases two different medicines may be used together even if an interaction might occur. In these cases, your doctor may want to change the dose, or other precautions may be necessary. Tell your health care professional if you are using any other topical prescription or nonprescription (over-the-counter [OTC]) medicine that is to be applied to the same area of the skin.

Other medical problems—The presence of other medical problems may affect the use of benzoyl peroxide. Make sure you tell your doctor if you have any other medical problems, especially:
- Dermatitis, seborrheic or
- Eczema or
- Red or raw skin, including sunburned skin—Irritation will occur if benzoyl peroxide is used with these conditions

Proper Use of This Medicine

It is very important that you use this medicine only as directed. Do not use more of it and do not use it more often than recommended on the label, unless otherwise directed by your doctor. To do so may cause irritation of the skin.

Do not use this medicine in or around the eyes or lips, or inside the nose, or on sensitive areas of the neck. Spread the medicine away from these areas when applying. If the medicine gets on these areas, wash with water at once.

Do not apply this medicine to windburned or sunburned skin or on open wounds, unless otherwise directed by your doctor.

This medicine usually comes with patient directions. Read them carefully before using the medicine.

To use the *cream, gel, lotion, or stick form* of benzoyl peroxide:

- Before applying, wash the affected area with nonmedicated soap and water or with a mild cleanser and then gently pat dry with a towel.
- Apply enough medicine to cover the affected areas, and rub in gently.

To use the *shave cream form* of benzoyl peroxide:

- Wet the area to be shaved.
- Apply a small amount of the shave cream and gently rub over entire area.
- Shave.
- Rinse the area and pat dry.
- After-shave lotions or other drying face products should not be used without checking with your doctor first.

To use the *cleansing bar, cleansing lotion, or soap form* of benzoyl peroxide:

- Use to wash the affected areas as directed.

To use the *facial mask form* of benzoyl peroxide:

- Before applying, wash the affected area with a nonmedicated cleanser. Then rinse and pat dry.
- Using a circular motion, apply a thin layer of the mask evenly over the affected area.
- Allow the mask to dry for 15 to 25 minutes.
- Then rinse thoroughly with warm water and pat dry.

After applying the medicine, wash your hands to remove any medicine that might remain on them.

Dosing—The dose of benzoyl peroxide will be different for different patients. *Follow your doctor's orders or the directions on the label.* The following information includes only the average doses of benzoyl peroxide. *If your dose is different, do not change it* unless your doctor tells you to do so.

- For acne:
  —For *cleansing bar* dosage form:
  - Adults and children 12 years of age and over— Use two or three times a day, or as directed by your doctor.
  - Children up to 12 years of age—Use and dose must be determined by your doctor.
  —For *cleansing lotion, cream,* or *gel* dosage forms:
  - Adults and children 12 years of age and over— Use on the affected area(s) of the skin one or two times a day.
  - Children up to 12 years of age—Use and dose must be determined by your doctor.
  —For *lotion* dosage form:
  - Adults and children 12 years of age and over— Use on the affected area(s) of the skin one to four times a day.
  - Children up to 12 years of age—Use and dose must be determined by your doctor.
  —For *facial mask* dosage form:
  - Adults and children 12 years of age and over— Use one time a week or as directed by your doctor.
  - Children up to 12 years of age—Use and dose must be determined by your doctor.

—For *stick* dosage form:
- Adults and children 12 years of age and over— Use on the affected area(s) of the skin one to three times a day.
- Children up to 12 years of age—Use and dose must be determined by your doctor.

Missed dose—If you miss a dose of this medicine, apply or use it as soon as possible. Then go back to your regular dosing schedule.

Storage—To store this medicine:
- Keep out of the reach of children.
- Store away from heat and direct light.
- Keep the cream, gel, or liquid form of this medicine from freezing.
- Do not keep outdated medicine or medicine no longer needed. Be sure that any discarded medicine is out of the reach of children.

Precautions While Using This Medicine

During the first 3 weeks you are using benzoyl peroxide, your skin may become irritated. Also, your acne may seem to get worse before it gets better. If your skin problem has not improved within 4 to 6 weeks, check with your health care professional.

You should not wash the areas of the skin treated with benzoyl peroxide for at least 1 hour after application.

Avoid using any other topical medicine on the same area within 1 hour before or after using benzoyl peroxide. Otherwise, benzoyl peroxide may not work properly.

Unless your doctor tells you otherwise, it is especially important to avoid using the following skin products on the same area as benzoyl peroxide:

Any other topical acne product or skin product containing a peeling agent (such as resorcinol, salicylic acid, sulfur, or tretinoin);

Hair products that are irritating, such as permanents or hair removal products;

Skin products that cause sensitivity to the sun, such as those containing lime or spices;

Skin products containing a large amount of alcohol, such as astringents, shaving creams, or after-shave lotions; or

Skin products that are too drying or abrasive, such as some cosmetics, soaps, or skin cleansers.

Using these products along with benzoyl peroxide may cause mild to severe irritation of the skin. Although skin irritation can occur, some doctors sometimes allow benzoyl peroxide to be used with tretinoin to treat acne. Usually tretinoin is applied at night so that it doesn't cause a problem with any other topical products that you might use during the day. Check with your doctor before using any other topical medicines with benzoyl peroxide.

This medicine may bleach hair or colored fabrics.

Check with your doctor at any time your skin becomes too dry or irritated. Your health care professional can help you choose the right skin products for you to reduce skin dryness and irritation.

Side Effects of This Medicine

Along with its needed effects, a medicine may cause some unwanted effects. Although not all of these side effects may occur, if they do occur they may need medical attention.

Check with your doctor as soon as possible if any of the following side effects occur:

Less common or rare
Painful irritation of skin, including burning, blistering, crusting, itching, severe redness, or swelling; skin rash

Symptoms of overdose
Burning, itching, scaling, redness, or swelling of skin (severe)

Other side effects may occur that usually do not need medical attention. These side effects may go away during treatment as your body adjusts to the medicine. However, check with your health care professional if any of the following side effects continue or are bothersome:

Less common
Dryness or peeling of skin (may occur after a few days); feeling of warmth, mild stinging, and redness of skin

Other side effects not listed above may also occur in some patients. If you notice any other effects, check with your health care professional.

Additional Information

Once a medicine has been approved for marketing for a certain use, experience may show that it is also useful for other medical problems. Although these uses are not included in product labeling, benzoyl peroxide is used in certain patients with the following medical conditions:

- Decubital ulcer (bed sores)
- Stasis ulcer (a certain type of ulcer)

Other than the above information, there is no additional information relating to proper use, precautions, or side effects for these uses.

Revised: 07/29/98

BENZYL BENZOATE   Topical†

In the U.S.—
Ascarosan Moist

†Not commercially available in Canada.

Description

Benzyl benzoate (ben-ZILL ben-ZOE-ate) is used to treat lice and scabies infestations. This medicine is believed to be absorbed by the lice and mites and to destroy them by acting on their nervous system.

This medicine is available without a prescription; however, your doctor may have special instructions on the proper use of this medicine for your medical condition.

Benzyl benzoate is available in the following dosage form:

Topical
- Emulsion (United Kingdom)

Before Using This Medicine

If you are using this medicine without a prescription, carefully read and follow any precautions on the label. For topical benzyl benzoate, the following should be considered:

Allergies—Tell your doctor if you have ever had any unusual or allergic reaction to benzyl benzoate.

Pregnancy—Benzyl benzoate has not been reported to cause birth defects or other problems in humans. However, the manufacturer recommends that this medicine should be used by pregnant women only if it is necessary. Before taking this medicine, make sure your doctor knows if you are pregnant or if you may become pregnant.

Breast-feeding—Benzyl benzoate has not been reported to cause problems in nursing babies. However, the manufacturer recommends that breast-feeding be suspended during treatment.

Children—Although there is no specific information comparing use of benzyl benzoate in children with use in other age groups, this medicine is not expected to cause different side effects or problems in children than it does in adults.

Older adults—Many medicines have not been studied specifically in older people. Therefore, it may not be known whether they work exactly the same way they do in younger adults or if they cause different side effects or problems in older people. There is no specific information comparing use of benzyl benzoate in the elderly with use in other age groups. However, older people may have dry skin and the medicine may make the condition worse.

Other medical problems—The presence of other medical problems may affect the use of benzyl benzoate. Make sure you tell your doctor if you have any other medical problems, especially:

- Inflammation of the skin (severe)—Use of benzyl benzoate may make the condition worse

Proper Use of This Medicine

Benzyl benzoate usually comes with patient directions. Read them carefully before using this medicine.

Use this medicine only as directed. Do not use more of it and do not use it more often than recommended on the label. To do so may increase the chance of absorption through the skin and the chance of side effects.

Keep this medicine away from the eyes and other mucous membranes, such as the inside of the nose, because it may cause irritation. If you accidentally get some in your eyes, flush them thoroughly with water at once.

Do not use benzyl benzoate on open wounds, such as cuts or sores on the skin or scalp. To do so may increase the amount of absorption, which may increase the chance of side effects.

Your sexual partner or partners, especially, and all members of your household may need to be treated also, since the infestation may spread to persons in close contact. If these persons have not been examined for infestation or if you have any questions about this, check with your doctor.

To use this medicine for *lice:*

- If your hair has any cream, lotion, ointment, or oil-based product on it, shampoo, rinse, and dry your hair and scalp well before applying benzyl benzoate.
- Apply enough medicine to thoroughly wet the dry hair and scalp or skin.
- Allow the medicine to remain on the affected areas for 24 hours.
- Then, thoroughly wash the affected areas with warm water and soap or regular shampoo.
- Rinse thoroughly and dry with a clean towel.
- After rinsing and drying, use a fine-toothed comb (less than 0.3 mm between the teeth) to remove any remaining nits (eggs) or nit shells from your hair, or, if you have fine hair, you may use a tweezer or your fingernails to pick nits out.

To use this medicine for *scabies:*

- If your skin has any cream, lotion, ointment, or oil on it, wash, rinse, and dry your skin well before applying benzyl benzoate.
- If you take a bath or shower before using benzyl benzoate, dry the skin well before applying the medicine.
- Apply enough medicine to cover the entire skin surface from the neck down, including the soles of your feet, and rub in well.
- Allow the medicine to remain on the body for 24 hours.
- Then, thoroughly wash the body with warm water and soap.
- Rinse thoroughly and dry with a clean towel.

Immediately after using benzyl benzoate, wash your hands to remove any medicine that may be on them.

Treatment may need to be repeated for severe infestation.

Dosing—The dose of benzyl benzoate will be different for different patients. *Follow your doctor's orders or the directions on the label.* The following information includes only the average doses of benzyl benzoate. *If your dose is different, do not change it* unless your doctor tells you to do so.

The number of doses that you use each day, the time allowed between doses, and the length of time you use the medicine depend on the medical problem for which you are using benzyl benzoate.

- For *topical* dosage form (emulsion):
  - For lice infestation:
    - Adults—Use just one time. For severe cases, treatment may be repeated two or three times after twenty-four hours.
    - Children—
      For infants: Use mixed with three parts of water, just one time.
      For older children: Use mixed with an equal quantity of water, just one time.
  - For scabies infestation:
    - Adults—Use just one time. For severe cases, treatment may be repeated after twenty-four hours one time anytime within five days.
    - Children—
      For infants: Use mixed with three parts of water, just one time.

For older children: Use mixed with an equal quantity of water, just one time.

Storage—To store this medicine:

- Keep out of the reach of children.
- Store away from heat and direct light.
- Keep the medicine from freezing. Do not refrigerate.
- Do not keep outdated medicine or medicine no longer needed. Be sure that any discarded medicine is out of the reach of children.

Precautions While Using This Medicine

To prevent reinfection or spreading of the infection to other people, good health habits are required. These include the following:

- For *lice infestation:*
  - Disinfecting or washing combs, curlers, and brushes in very hot water (65 °C or 150 °F) for about 10 minutes immediately after using.
  - Washing in very hot water all recently worn clothing and used bed linens and towels, and drying them in a hot dryer for at least 20 minutes. Articles that cannot be washed may be dry-cleaned, pressed with a hot iron, or just placed in a hot dryer.
  - Sealing stuffed toys and other non-washable articles in a plastic bag for 2 weeks, or placing these items in the freezer (in sealed plastic bags) for 12 to 24 hours.
  - Vacuuming all rugs, mattresses, pillows, furniture, and car seats to get rid of fallen hairs with lice.
- For *scabies infestation:* Washing all recently worn clothing such as underwear and pajamas, and used sheets, pillowcases, and towels in very hot water or dry-cleaning.

Side Effects of This Medicine

Along with its needed effects, a medicine may cause some unwanted effects. Although not all of these side effects may occur, if they do occur they may need medical attention.

Check with your doctor as soon as possible if any of the following side effects occur:
Symptoms of overdose
Blister formation, crusting, itching, oozing, reddening, or scaling of skin; difficulty in urinating (dribbling); jerking movements; sudden loss of consciousness

Other side effects may occur that usually do not need medical attention. These side effects may go away during treatment as your body adjusts to the medicine. However, check with your doctor if any of the following side effects continue or are bothersome:
Less common or rare
Burning or itching of skin

Other side effects not listed above may also occur in some patients. If you notice any other effects, check with your doctor.

Developed: 01/21/94

BETA-ADRENERGIC BLOCKING AGENTS Ophthalmic

Commonly used brand name(s):

In the U.S.—

AKBeta[4]	Ocupress[2]
Betagan[4]	OptiPranolol[5]
Betaxon[3]	Timoptic[6]
Betimol[6]	Timoptic in Ocudose[6]
Betoptic[1]	Timoptic-XE[6]
Betoptic S[1]	

In Canada—

Apo-Timop[6]	Ophtho-Bunolol[4]
Betagan[4]	Tim-AK[6]
Betoptic S[1]	Timoptic[6]
Novo-Levobunolol[4]	Timoptic-XE[6]
Novo-Timol[6]	

Note: For quick reference, the following beta-adrenergic blocking agents are numbered to match the corresponding brand names.

This information applies to the following medicines:
1. Betaxolol (be-TAX-oh-lol)
2. Carteolol (KAR-tee-oh-lole)†
3. Levobetaxolol (lee-voh-be-TAX-oh-lol)†
4. Levobunolol (lee-voe-BYOO-noe-lole)‡
5. Metipranolol (met-i-PRAN-oh-lol)†
6. Timolol (TYE-moe-lole)‡§

†Not commercially available in Canada.
‡Generic name product may be available in the U.S.
§Generic name product may be available in Canada.

Description

Betaxolol, carteolol, levobetaxolol, levobunolol, metipranolol, and timolol are used to treat certain types of glaucoma. They appear to work by reducing the production of fluid in the eye. This lowers the pressure in the eye.

These medicines are available only with your doctor's prescription, in the following dosage forms:

Ophthalmic
 Betaxolol
 • Ophthalmic solution (eye drops) (U.S.)
 • Ophthalmic suspension (eye drops) (U.S. and Canada)
 Carteolol
 • Ophthalmic solution (eye drops) (U.S.)
 Levobetaxolol
 • Ophthalmic suspension (eye drops) (U.S.)
 Levobunolol
 • Ophthalmic solution (eye drops) (U.S. and Canada)
 Metipranolol
 • Ophthalmic solution (eye drops) (U.S.)
 Timolol
 • Extended-release ophthalmic solution (eye drops) (U.S. and Canada)
 • Ophthalmic solution (eye drops) (U.S. and Canada)

Before Using This Medicine

In deciding to use a medicine, the risks of taking the medicine must be weighed against the good it will do. This is a decision you and your doctor will make. For ophthalmic beta-adrenergic blocking agents, the following should be considered:

Allergies—Tell your doctor if you have ever had any unusual or allergic reaction to any of the beta-adrenergic blocking agents, either ophthalmic or systemic, such as acebutolol, atenolol, betaxolol, bisoprolol, carteolol, labetalol,levobetaxolol, levobunolol, metipranolol, metoprolol, nadolol, oxprenolol, penbutolol, pindolol, propranolol, sotalol, or timolol. Also tell your health care professional if you are allergic to any other substances, such as sulfites or preservatives.

Pregnancy—Ophthalmic beta-adrenergic blocking agents may be absorbed into the body. These medicines have not been studied in pregnant women. Studies in animals have not shown that betaxolol, levobunolol, metipranolol, or timolol causes birth defects. However, high doses of levobetaxolol given by mouth to pregnant rabbits have been shown to cause birth defects in rabbit babies, and very large doses of carteolol given by mouth to pregnant rats have been shown to cause wavy ribs in rat babies. In addition, some studies in animals have shown that beta-adrenergic blocking agents increase the chance of death in the animal fetus. Before using ophthalmic beta-adrenergic blocking agents, make sure your doctor knows if you are pregnant or if you may become pregnant.

Breast-feeding—Betaxolol and timolol, and maybe other beta-adrenergic blocking agents, when taken by mouth, may pass into the breast milk. Since ophthalmic beta-adrenergic blocking agents may be absorbed into the body, they, too, may pass into the breast milk. However, it is not known whether ophthalmic beta-adrenergic blocking agents pass into the breast milk, and these medicines have not been reported to cause problems in nursing babies.

Children—Infants may be especially sensitive to the effects of ophthalmic beta-adrenergic blocking agents. This may increase the chance of side effects during treatment.

Older adults—Elderly people are especially sensitive to the effects of ophthalmic beta-adrenergic blocking agents. If too much medicine is absorbed into the body, the chance of side effects during treatment may be increased.

Other medicines—Although certain medicines should not be used together at all, in other cases two different medicines may be used together even if an interaction might occur. In these cases, your doctor may want to change the dose, or other precautions may be necessary. Tell your health care professional if you are using any other prescription or nonprescription (over-the-counter [OTC]) medicine.

Other medical problems—The presence of other medical problems may affect the use of ophthalmic beta-adrenergic blocking agents. Make sure you tell your doctor if you have any other medical problems, especially:
 • Allergic reactions, severe (history of)—Use of an ophthalmic beta-adrenergic blocking agent may reduce the effectiveness of the medicine (epinephrine) used to treat severe allergic reactions
 • Asthma (or history of), chronic bronchitis, emphysema, or other lung disease—Severe breathing problems, including death due to bronchospasm (spasm of the bronchial tubes), have been reported in patients with asthma following use of some ophthalmic beta-adrenergic blocking agents (carteolol, levobunolol, metipranolol, and timolol). Although most often not a problem, the pos-

sibility of wheezing or troubled breathing also exists with betaxolol and levobetaxolol

- Diabetes mellitus (sugar diabetes) or
- Hypoglycemia (low blood sugar)—Ophthalmic beta-adrenergic blocking agents may cover up some signs and symptoms of hypoglycemia (low blood sugar), such as fast heartbeat and trembling, although they do not cover up other signs, such as dizziness or sweating
- Heart or blood vessel disease—Ophthalmic beta-adrenergic blocking agents may decrease heart activity
- Myasthenic conditions—Ophthalmic beta-adrenergic blocking agents may worsen muscle weakness caused by diseases such as myasthenia gravis.
- Overactive thyroid—Ophthalmic beta-adrenergic blocking agents may cover up certain signs and symptoms of hyperthyroidism (overactive thyroid). Suddenly stopping the use of ophthalmic beta-adrenergic blocking agents may cause a sudden and dangerous increase in thyroid symptoms

Proper Use of This Medicine

To use:
- First, wash your hands. With the middle finger, apply pressure to the inside corner of the eye (and continue to apply pressure for 1 or 2 minutes after the medicine has been placed in the eye). *This is especially important if the ophthalmic beta-adrenergic blocking agent is used to treat infants and children.* Tilt the head back and with the index finger of the same hand, pull the lower eyelid away from the eye to form a pouch. Drop the medicine into the pouch and gently close the eyes. Do not blink. Keep the eyes closed for 1 or 2 minutes to allow the medicine to be absorbed.
- Immediately after using the eye drops, wash your hands to remove any medicine that may be on them.
- To keep the medicine as germ-free as possible, do not touch the applicator tip to any surface (including the eye). Also, keep the container tightly closed.
- If you are using levobunolol with the compliance cap (C Cap):
  —Before using the eye drops for the first time, make sure the number 1 or the correct day of the week appears in the window on the cap.
  —Remove the cap and use the eye drops as directed.
  —Replace the cap. Holding the cap between your thumb and forefinger, rotate the bottle until the cap clicks to the next position. This will tell you the time of your next dose.
  —After every dose, rotate the bottle until the cap clicks to the position that tells you the time of your next dose.
- If you are using the gel-forming timolol solution:
  —Before using the eye drops each time, turn the closed bottle upside-down and shake once.
  —If you use other eye drops in addition to the gel-forming solution, the other eye drops should be used first, then wait at least ten minutes before using this medicine.
- If you wear soft contact lenses and your eye drops contain benzalkonium chloride:
  —Remove your contacts before you use your eye drops. Wait for fifteen minutes after using the eye drops before putting your contacts in your eyes.

Use this medicine only as directed. Do not use more of it and do not use it more often than your doctor ordered. To do so may increase the chance of too much medicine being absorbed into the body and the chance of side effects.

Dosing—The dose of betaxolol, carteolol, levobetaxolol, levobunolol, metipranolol, or timolol will be different for different patients. *Follow your doctor's orders or the directions on the label.* The following information includes only the average doses. *If your dose is different, do not change it* unless your doctor tells you to do so.

The number of doses of medicine that you use also depends on the strength of the medicine.

For betaxolol, carteolol, or metipranolol
- For *ophthalmic drops* dosage forms:
  —For glaucoma:
    - Adults and older children—Topical, to the conjunctiva, 1 drop two times a day.
    - Infants and younger children—Dose must be determined by the doctor.

For levobetaxolol
- For *ophthalmic drops* dosage form:
  —For glaucoma:
    - Adults—Topical, to the conjunctiva, 1 drop two times a day.
    - Children—Use and dose must be determined by the doctor.

For levobunolol or timolol
- For *ophthalmic drops* dosage forms:
  —For glaucoma:
    - Adults and older children—Topical, to the conjunctiva, 1 drop one or two times a day.
    - Infants and younger children—Dose must be determined by the doctor.

Missed dose—If you miss a dose of this medicine and your dosing schedule is:
- One dose a day—Use the missed dose as soon as possible. However, if you do not remember the missed dose until the next day, skip the missed dose and go back to your regular dosing schedule. Do not double doses.
- More than one dose a day—Use the missed dose as soon as possible. However, if it is almost time for your next dose, skip the missed dose and go back to your regular dosing schedule. Do not double doses.

If you have any questions about this, check with your doctor.

Storage—To store this medicine:
- Keep out of the reach of children.
- Store away from heat and direct light.
- Store levobetaxolol in an upright position.
- Keep this medicine from freezing.
- Do not keep outdated medicine or medicine no longer needed. Be sure that any discarded medicine is out of the reach of children.

Precautions While Using This Medicine

Your doctor should check your eye pressure at regular visits to make certain that your glaucoma is being controlled.

Contact your physician immediately if you are having eye surgery, you experience trauma to your eye, or you develop an eye infection to determine if you should continue to use your present container of eye drops.

For a short time after you use this medicine, your vision may be blurred. Make sure your vision is clear before you drive, use machines, or do anything else that could be dangerous if you are not able to see well.

Before you have any kind of surgery, dental treatment, or emergency treatment, tell the medical doctor or dentist in charge that you are using this medicine. Using an ophthalmic beta-adrenergic blocking agent during this time may cause an increased risk of side effects.

For diabetic patients:

• *Ophthalmic beta-adrenergic blocking agents may affect blood sugar levels. They may also cover up some signs of hypoglycemia (low blood sugar),* such as trembling or increase in pulse rate or blood pressure. However, other signs of low blood sugar, such as dizziness or sweating, are not affected. If you notice a change in the results of your blood or urine sugar tests or if you have any questions, check with your doctor.

Some ophthalmic beta-adrenergic blocking agents (betaxolol, carteolol, and metipranolol) may cause your eyes to become more sensitive to light than they are normally. Wearing sunglasses and avoiding too much exposure to bright light may help lessen the discomfort.

Side Effects of This Medicine

Along with its needed effects, a medicine may cause some unwanted effects. Although not all of these side effects may occur, if they do occur they may need medical attention.

Check with your doctor as soon as possible if any of the following side effects occur:

More common
Redness of eyes or inside of eyelids

Less common or rare
Blurred vision or other change in vision; different size pupils of the eyes; discoloration of the eyeball; droopy upper eyelid; eye pain; redness or irritation of the tongue; seeing double; swelling, irritation or inflammation of eye or eyelid

Symptoms of too much medicine being absorbed into the body
Ankle, knee, or great toe joint pain; ankle, knee, or great toe joint swelling; anxiety or nervousness; bloody or cloudy urine; breast pain; burning or prickling feeling on body; change in taste; chest pain; chills; clumsiness or unsteadiness; confusion or mental depression; coughing, wheezing, or troubled breathing; decreased sexual ability; diarrhea; difficult, burning, or painful urination; dizziness or feeling faint; drowsiness; dryness or soreness of throat; ear pain; feeling of constant movement; fever; hair loss; hallucinations (seeing, hearing, or feeling things that are not there); headache; hoarseness; irregular, fast, slow, or pounding heartbeat; lightheadedness; lower back or side pain; muscle or joint aches or pain; muscle tightness or stiffness; nausea or vomiting; raw, red, blistering, scaly, or crusted areas of the skin; ringing or buzzing in the ears; runny, stuffy, or bleeding nose; skin rash, hives, or itching; swelling of feet, ankles, or lower legs; trouble in sleeping; unusual tiredness or weakness

Other side effects may occur that usually do not need medical attention. These side effects may go away during treatment as your body adjusts to the medicine. However, check with your doctor if any of the following side effects continue or are bothersome:

More common
Blurred vision, temporary; decreased night vision; stinging of eye or other eye irritation (when medicine is applied)

The side effect of blurred vision is associated primarily with levobetaxolol and the timolol gel-forming solution and usually lasts from thirty seconds to five minutes.

Less common or rare
Acid or sour stomach; belching; browache; constipation; crusting of eyelashes; dryness of eye; dry skin; feeling of something in the eye; heartburn; increased sensitivity of eye to light; indigestion; itching, stinging, burning, or watering of eye or other eye irritation; pain, redness, warmth, or swelling of muscles

Other side effects not listed above may also occur in some patients. If you notice any other effects, check with your doctor.

Revised: 05/25/00

BETA-ADRENERGIC BLOCKING AGENTS   Systemic

Commonly used brand name(s):

In the U.S.—

Betapace[13]	Lopressor[7]
Blocadren[14]	Normodyne[6]
Cartrol[5]	Sectral[1]
Corgard[8]	Tenormin[2]
Inderal[12]	Toprol-XL[7]
Inderal LA[12]	Trandate[6]
Kerlone[3]	Visken[11]
Levatol[10]	Zebeta[4]

In Canada—

Apo-Atenolol[2]	Novometoprol[7]
Apo-Metoprolol[7]	Novo-Pindol[11]
Apo-Metoprolol (Type L)[7]	Novo-Timol[14]
Apo-Propranolol[12]	Novopranol[12]
Apo-Timol[14]	Nu-Metop[7]
Betaloc[7]	pms Propranolol[12]
Betaloc Durules[7]	Sectral[1]
Blocadren[14]	Slow-Trasicor[9]
Corgard[8]	Sotacor[13]
Detensol[12]	Syn-Nadolol[8]
Inderal[12]	Syn-Pindolol[11]
Inderal LA[12]	Tenormin[2]
Lopresor[7]	Trandate[6]
Lopresor SR[7]	Trasicor[9]
Monitan[1]	Visken[11]
Novo-Atenol[2]	

Note: For quick reference, the following beta-adrenergic blocking agents are numbered to match the corresponding brand names.

This information applies to the following medicines:
1. Acebutolol (a-se-BYOO-toe-lole)‡
2. Atenolol (a-TEN-oh-lole)‡§
3. Betaxolol (be-TAX-oh-lol)†
4. Bisoprolol (bis-OH-proe-lol)†
5. Carteolol (KAR-tee-oh-lole)†
6. Labetalol (la-BET-a-lole)
7. Metoprolol (met-oh-PROE-lol)‡§

8. Nadolol (nay-DOE-lole)‡§
9. Oxprenolol (ox-PREN-oh-lole)*
10. Penbutolol (pen-BYOO-toe-lole)†
11. Pindolol (PIN-doe-lole)‡§
12. Propranolol (proe-PRAN-oh-lole)‡§
13. Sotalol (SOE-ta-lole)
14. Timolol (TYE-moe-lole)‡§

*Not commercially available in the U.S.
†Not commercially available in Canada.
‡Generic name product may be available in the U.S.
§Generic name product may be available in Canada.

Description

This group of medicines is known as beta-adrenergic blocking agents, beta-blocking agents, or, more commonly, beta-blockers. Beta-blockers are used in the treatment of high blood pressure (hypertension). Some beta-blockers are also used to relieve angina (chest pain) and in heart attack patients to help prevent additional heart attacks. Beta-blockers are also used to correct irregular heartbeat, prevent migraine headaches, and treat tremors. They may also be used for other conditions as determined by your doctor.

Beta-blockers work by affecting the response to some nerve impulses in certain parts of the body. As a result, they decrease the heart's need for blood and oxygen by reducing its workload. They also help the heart to beat more regularly.

Beta-adrenergic blocking agents are available only with your doctor's prescription, in the following dosage forms:

Oral
Acebutolol
  • Capsules (U.S.)
  • Tablets (Canada)
Atenolol
  • Tablets (U.S. and Canada)
Betaxolol
  • Tablets (U.S.)
Bisoprolol
  • Tablets (U.S.)
Carteolol
  • Tablets (U.S.)
Labetalol
  • Tablets (U.S. and Canada)
Metoprolol
  • Tablets (U.S. and Canada)
  • Extended-release tablets (U.S. and Canada)
Nadolol
  • Tablets (U.S. and Canada)
Oxprenolol
  • Tablets (Canada)
  • Extended-release tablets (Canada)
Penbutolol
  • Tablets (U.S.)
Pindolol
  • Tablets (U.S. and Canada)
Propranolol
  • Extended-release capsules (U.S. and Canada)
  • Oral solution (U.S.)
  • Tablets (U.S. and Canada)
Sotalol
  • Tablets (U.S. and Canada)
Timolol
  • Tablets (U.S. and Canada)

Parenteral
Atenolol
  • Injection (U.S.)
Labetalol
  • Injection (U.S. and Canada)
Metoprolol
  • Injection (U.S. and Canada)
Propranolol
  • Injection (U.S. and Canada)

Before Using This Medicine

In deciding to use a medicine, the risks of taking the medicine must be weighed against the good it will do. This is a decision you and your doctor will make. For the beta-blockers, the following should be considered:

Allergies—Tell your doctor if you have ever had any unusual or allergic reaction to the beta-blocker medicine prescribed. Also tell your health care professional if you are allergic to any other substances, such as foods, preservatives, or dyes.

Pregnancy—Use of some beta-blockers during pregnancy has been associated with low blood sugar, breathing problems, a lower heart rate, and low blood pressure in the newborn infant. Other reports have not shown unwanted effects on the newborn infant. Animal studies have shown some beta-blockers to cause problems in pregnancy when used in doses many times the usual human dose. Before taking any of these medicines, make sure your doctor knows if you are pregnant or if you may become pregnant.

Breast-feeding—It is not known whether bisoprolol, carteolol, or penbutolol passes into breast milk. All other beta-blockers pass into breast milk. Problems such as slow heartbeat, low blood pressure, and trouble in breathing have been reported in nursing babies. Mothers who are taking beta-blockers and who wish to breast-feed should discuss this with their doctor.

Children—Some of these medicines have been used in children and, in effective doses, have not been shown to cause different side effects or problems in children than they do in adults.

Older adults—Some side effects are more likely to occur in the elderly, who are usually more sensitive to the effects of beta-blockers. Also, beta-blockers may reduce tolerance to cold temperatures in elderly patients.

Other medicines—Although certain medicines should not be used together at all, in other cases two different medicines may be used together even if an interaction might occur. In these cases, your doctor may want to change the dose, or other precautions may be necessary. When you are taking or receiving a beta-blocker it is especially important that your health care professional know if you are taking any of the following:

  • Allergen immunotherapy (allergy shots) or
  • Allergen extracts for skin testing—Beta-blockers may increase the risk of serious allergic reaction to these medicines
  • Aminophylline (e.g., Somophyllin) or
  • Caffeine (e.g., NoDoz) or
  • Dyphylline (e.g., Lufyllin) or
  • Oxtriphylline (e.g., Choledyl) or
  • Theophylline (e.g., Somophyllin-T)—The effects of both these medicines and beta-blockers may be blocked; in

addition, theophylline levels in the body may be increased, especially in patients who smoke
- Antidiabetics, oral (diabetes medicine you take by mouth) or
- Insulin—There is an increased risk of hyperglycemia (high blood sugar); beta-blockers may cover up certain symptoms of hypoglycemia (low blood sugar) such as increases in pulse rate and blood pressure, and may make the hypoglycemia last longer
- Calcium channel blockers (bepridil [e.g., Bepadin], diltiazem [e.g., Cardizem], felodipine [e.g., Plendil], flunarizine [e.g., Sibelium], isradipine [e.g., DynaCirc], nicardipine [e.g., Cardene], nifedipine [e.g., Procardia], nimodipine [e.g., Nimotop], verapamil [e.g., Calan]) or
- Clonidine (e.g., Catapres) or
- Guanabenz (e.g., Wytensin)—Effects on blood pressure may be increased. In addition, unwanted effects may occur if clonidine, guanabenz, or a beta-blocker is stopped suddenly after use together. Unwanted effects on the heart may occur when beta-blockers are used with calcium channel blockers
- Cocaine—Cocaine may block the effects of beta-blockers; in addition, there is an increased risk of high blood pressure, fast heartbeat, and possibly heart problems if you use cocaine while taking a beta-blocker
- Monoamine oxidase (MAO) inhibitors (furazolidone [e.g., Furoxone], isocarboxazid [e.g., Marplan], phenelzine [e.g., Nardil], procarbazine [e.g., Matulane], selegiline [e.g., Eldepryl], tranylcypromine [e.g., Parnate])—Taking beta-blockers while you are taking or within 2 weeks of taking monoamine oxidase (MAO) inhibitors may cause severe high blood pressure

Other medical problems—The presence of other medical problems may affect the use of the beta blockers. Make sure you tell your doctor if you have any other medical problems, especially:
- Allergy, history of (asthma, eczema, hay fever, hives), or
- Bronchitis or
- Emphysema—Severity and duration of allergic reactions to other substances may be increased; in addition, beta-blockers can increase trouble in breathing
- Bradycardia (unusually slow heartbeat) or
- Heart or blood vessel disease—There is a risk of further decreased heart function; also, if treatment is stopped suddenly, unwanted effects may occur
- Diabetes mellitus (sugar diabetes)—Beta-blockers may cause hyperglycemia (high blood sugar) and circulation problems; in addition, if your diabetes medicine causes your blood sugar to be too low, beta-blockers may cover up some of the symptoms (fast heartbeat), although they will not cover up other symptoms such as dizziness or sweating
- Kidney disease or
- Liver disease—Effects of beta-blockers may be increased because of slower removal from the body
- Mental depression (or history of)—May be increased by beta-blockers
- Myasthenia gravis or
- Psoriasis—Beta-blockers may make these conditions worse

- Overactive thyroid—Stopping beta-blockers suddenly may increase symptoms; beta-blockers may cover up fast heartbeat, which is a sign of overactive thyroid

Proper Use of This Medicine

For patients taking the *extended-release capsule or tablet* form of this medicine:
- Swallow the capsule or tablet whole.
- Do not crush, break (except metoprolol succinate extended-release tablets, which may be broken in half), or chew before swallowing.

For patients taking the *concentrated oral solution* form of *propranolol:*
- This medicine is to be taken by mouth even though it comes in a dropper bottle. The amount you should take is to be measured only with the specially marked dropper.
- Mix the medicine with some water, juice, or a carbonated drink. After drinking all the liquid containing the medicine, rinse the glass with a little more liquid and drink that also, to make sure you get all the medicine. If you prefer, you may mix this medicine with applesauce or pudding instead.
- Mix the medicine immediately before you are going to take it. Throw away any mixed medicine that you do not take immediately. Do not save medicine that has been mixed.

Ask your doctor about checking your pulse rate before and after taking beta-blocking agents. If your doctor tells you to check your pulse regularly while you are taking this medicine, and it is much slower than the rate your doctor has designated, check with your doctor. A pulse rate that is too slow may cause circulation problems.

To help you remember to take your medicine, try to get into the habit of taking it at the same time each day.

For patients taking this medicine *for high blood pressure:*
- In addition to the use of the medicine your doctor has prescribed, treatment for your high blood pressure may include weight control and care in the types of foods you eat, especially foods high in sodium. Your doctor will tell you which of these are most important for you. You should check with your doctor before changing your diet.
- Many patients who have high blood pressure will not notice any signs of the problem. In fact, many may feel normal. However, if high blood pressure is not treated, it can cause serious problems such as heart failure, blood vessel disease, stroke, or kidney disease.
- Remember that this medicine will not cure your high blood pressure but it does help control it. It is very important that you *take your medicine exactly as directed*, even if you feel well. You must continue to take it as directed if you expect to lower your blood pressure and keep it down. *You may have to take high blood pressure medicine for the rest of your life.* Also, it is very important to keep your appointments with your doctor, even if you feel well.

Dosing—The dose of beta-blocker will be different for different patients. *Follow your doctor's orders or the directions on the label.* The following information includes only the average doses. *If your dose is different, do not change it* unless your doctor tells you to do so.

The number of capsules or tablets or teaspoonfuls of solution that you take depends on the strength of the medicine. Also, *the number of doses you take each day, the time allowed between doses, and the length of time you take the medicine depend on the medical problem for which you are taking the beta-blocker.*

For acebutolol
- For *oral* dosage forms (capsules and tablets):
  —For angina (chest pain) or irregular heartbeat:
    • Adults—200 milligrams (mg) two times a day. The dose may be increased up to a total of 1200 mg a day.
    • Children—Dose must be determined by your doctor.
  —For high blood pressure:
    • Adults—200 to 800 mg a day as a single dose or divided into two daily doses.
    • Children—Dose must be determined by your doctor.

For atenolol
- For *oral* dosage form (tablets):
  —For angina (chest pain):
    • Adults—50 to 100 mg once a day.
  —For high blood pressure:
    • Adults—25 to 100 mg once a day.
    • Children—Dose must be determined by your doctor.
  —For treatment after a heart attack:
    • Adults—50 mg ten minutes after the last intravenous dose, followed by another 50 mg twelve hours later. Then 100 mg once a day or 50 mg two times a day for six to nine days or until discharge from hospital.
- For *injection* dosage form:
  —For treatment of heart attacks:
    • Adults—5 mg given over 5 minutes. The dose is repeated ten minutes later.

For betaxolol
- For *oral* dosage form (tablets):
  —For high blood pressure:
    • Adults—10 mg once a day. Your doctor may double your dose after seven to fourteen days.
    • Children—Dose must be determined by your doctor.

For bisoprolol
- For *oral* dosage form (tablets):
  —For high blood pressure:
    • Adults—5 to 10 mg once a day.
    • Children—Dose must be determined by your doctor.

For carteolol
- For *oral* dosage form (tablets):
  —For high blood pressure:
    • Adults—2.5 to 10 mg once a day.
    • Children—Dose must be determined by your doctor.

For labetalol
- For *oral* dosage form (tablets):
  —For high blood pressure:
    • Adults—100 to 400 mg two times a day.
    • Children—Dose must be determined by your doctor.

- For *injection* dosage form:
  —For high blood pressure:
    • Adults—20 mg injected slowly over two minutes with additional injections of 40 and 80 mg given every ten minutes if needed, up to a total of 300 mg; may be given instead as an infusion at a rate of 2 mg per minute to a total dose of 50 to 300 mg.
    • Children—Dose must be determined by your doctor.

For metoprolol
- For *regular (short-acting) oral* dosage form (tablets):
  —For high blood pressure or angina (chest pain):
    • Adults—100 to 450 mg a day, taken as a single dose or in divided doses.
    • Children—Dose must be determined by your doctor.
  —For treatment after a heart attack:
    • Adults—50 mg every six hours starting fifteen minutes after last intravenous dose. Then 100 mg two times a day for three months to 1 to 3 years.
- For *long-acting oral* dosage forms (extended-release tablets):
  —For high blood pressure or angina (chest pain):
    • Adults—Up to 400 mg once a day.
    • Children—Dose must be determined by your doctor.
- For *injection* dosage form:
  —For treatment of a heart attack:
    • Adults—5 mg every two minutes for three doses.

For nadolol
- For *oral* dosage form (tablets):
  —For angina (chest pain):
    • Adults—40 to 240 mg once a day.
  —For high blood pressure:
    • Adults—40 to 320 mg once a day.
    • Children—Dose must be determined by your doctor.

For oxprenolol
- For *regular (short-acting) oral* dosage form (tablets):
  —For high blood pressure:
    • Adults—20 mg three times a day. Your doctor may increase your dose up to 480 mg a day.
    • Children—Dose must be determined by your doctor.
- For *long-acting oral* dosage form (extended-release tablets):
  —For high blood pressure:
    • Adults—120 to 320 mg once a day.
    • Children—Dose must be determined by your doctor.

For penbutolol
- For *oral* dosage form (tablets):
  —For high blood pressure:
    • Adults—20 mg once a day.
    • Children—Dose must be determined by your doctor.

For pindolol
- For *oral* dosage form (tablets):
  —For high blood pressure:
    • Adults—5 mg two times a day. Your doctor may increase your dose up to 60 mg a day.

- Children—Dose must be determined by your doctor.

For propranolol
- For *regular (short-acting) oral* dosage forms (tablets and oral solution):
  —For angina (chest pain):
  - Adults—80 to 320 mg a day taken in two, three, or four divided doses.
  —For irregular heartbeat:
  - Adults—10 to 30 mg three or four times a day.
  - Children—500 micrograms (0.5 mg) to 4 mg per kilogram of body weight a day taken in divided doses.
  —For high blood pressure:
  - Adults—40 mg two times a day. Your doctor may increase your dose up to 640 mg a day.
  - Children—500 micrograms (0.5 mg) to 4 mg per kilogram of body weight a day taken in divided doses.
  —For diseased heart muscle (cardiomyopathy):
  - Adults—20 to 40 mg three or four times a day.
  —For treatment after a heart attack:
  - Adults—180 to 240 mg a day taken in divided doses.
  —For treating pheochromocytoma:
  - Adults—30 to 160 mg a day taken in divided doses.
  —For preventing migraine headaches:
  - Adults—20 mg four times a day. Your doctor may increase your dose up to 240 mg a day.
  —For trembling:
  - Adults—40 mg two times a day. Your doctor may increase your dose up to 320 mg a day.
- For *long-acting oral* dosage form (extended-release capsules):
  —For high blood pressure:
  - Adults—80 to 160 mg once a day. Doses up to 640 mg once a day may be needed in some patients.
  —For angina (chest pain):
  - Adults—80 to 320 mg once a day.
  —For preventing migraine headaches:
  - Adults—80 to 240 mg once a day.
- For *injection* dosage form:
  —For irregular heartbeat:
  - Adults—1 to 3 mg given at a rate not greater than 1 mg per minute. Dose may be repeated after two minutes and again after four hours if needed.
  - Children—10 to 100 micrograms (0.01 to 0.1 mg) per kilogram of body weight given intravenously every six to eight hours.

For sotalol
- For *oral* dosage form (tablets):
  —For irregular heartbeat:
  - Adults—80 mg two times a day. Your doctor may increase your dose up to 320 mg per day taken in two or three divided doses.
  - Children—Dose must be determined by your doctor.

For timolol
- For *oral* dosage form (tablets):
  —For high blood pressure:
  - Adults—10 mg two times a day. Your doctor may increase your dose up 60 mg per day taken as a single dose or in divided doses.

- Children—Dose must be determined by your doctor.
  —For treatment after a heart attack:
  - Adults—10 mg two times a day.
  —For preventing migraine headaches:
  - Adults—10 mg two times a day. Your doctor may increase your dose up to 30 mg once a day or in divided doses.

Missed dose—Do not miss any doses. This is especially important when you are taking only one dose per day. Some conditions may become worse if this medicine is not taken regularly.

If you do miss a dose of this medicine, take it as soon as possible. However, if it is within 4 hours of your next dose (8 hours when using atenolol, betaxolol, bisoprolol, carteolol, labetalol, nadolol, penbutolol, sotalol, or extended-release [long-acting] metoprolol, oxprenolol, or propranolol), skip the missed dose and go back to your regular dosing schedule. Do not double doses.

Storage—To store this medicine:
- Keep out of the reach of children.
- Store away from heat and direct light.
- Do not store in the bathroom, near the kitchen sink, or in other damp places. Heat or moisture may cause the medicine to break down.
- Do not keep outdated medicine or medicine no longer needed. Be sure that any discarded medicine is out of the reach of children.

Precautions While Using This Medicine

It is important that your doctor check your progress at regular visits. This is to make sure the medicine is working for you and to allow the dosage to be changed if needed.

Do not stop taking this medicine without first checking with your doctor. Your doctor may want you to reduce gradually the amount you are taking before stopping completely. Some conditions may become worse when the medicine is stopped suddenly, and the danger of heart attack is increased in some patients.

Make sure that you have enough medicine on hand to last through weekends, holidays, or vacations. You may want to carry an extra written prescription in your billfold or purse in case of an emergency. You can then have it filled if you run out of medicine while you are away from home.

Your doctor may want you to carry medical identification stating that you are taking this medicine.

Before having any kind of surgery (including dental surgery) or emergency treatment, tell the medical doctor or dentist in charge that you are taking this medicine.

For *diabetic patients:*
- *This medicine may cause your blood sugar levels to rise.* Also, *this medicine may cover up signs of hypoglycemia (low blood sugar),* such as change in pulse rate.

This medicine may cause some people to become dizzy, drowsy, or lightheaded. *Make sure you know how you react to this medicine before you drive, use machines, or do anything else that could be dangerous if you are dizzy or are not alert.* If the problem continues or gets worse, check with your doctor.

Beta-blockers may make you more sensitive to cold temperatures, especially if you have blood circulation problems.

Beta-blockers tend to decrease blood circulation in the skin, fingers, and toes. Dress warmly during cold weather and be careful during prolonged exposure to cold, such as in winter sports.

Chest pain resulting from exercise or physical exertion is usually reduced or prevented by this medicine. This may tempt a patient to be overly active. *Make sure you discuss with your doctor a safe amount of exercise for your medical problem.*

Before you have any medical tests, tell the doctor in charge that you are taking this medicine. The results of some tests may be affected by this medicine.

Before you have any allergy shots, tell the doctor in charge that you are taking a beta-blocker. Beta-blockers may cause you to have a serious reaction to the allergy shot.

For patients with *allergies to foods, medicines, or insect stings:*

- There is a chance that this medicine will cause allergic reactions to be worse and harder to treat. If you have a severe allergic reaction while you are being treated with this medicine, check with a doctor right away so that it can be treated. Be sure to tell the doctor that you are taking a beta-blocker.

For patients taking this medicine *for high blood pressure:*

- *Do not take other medicines unless they have been discussed with your doctor.* This especially includes over-the-counter (nonprescription) medicines for appetite control, asthma, colds, cough, hay fever, or sinus problems since they may tend to increase your blood pressure.

For patients taking *labetalol by mouth:*

- *Dizziness, lightheadedness, or fainting may occur, especially when you get up from a lying or sitting position.* This is more likely to occur when you first start taking labetalol or when the dose is increased. *Getting up slowly may help.* When you get up from lying down, sit on the edge of the bed with your feet dangling for 1 to 2 minutes. Then stand up slowly. If the problem continues or gets worse, check with your doctor.
- The dizziness, lightheadedness, or fainting is also more likely to occur if you drink alcohol, stand for long periods of time, or exercise, or if the weather is hot. *While you are taking this medicine, be careful to limit the amount of alcohol you drink. Also, use extra care during exercise or hot weather or if you must stand for long periods of time.*

For patients receiving *labetalol by injection:*

- It is very important that you lie down flat while receiving labetalol and for up to 3 hours afterward. If you try to get up too soon, you may become dizzy or faint. *Do not try to sit or stand until your doctor or nurse tells you to do so.*

Side Effects of This Medicine

Along with its needed effects, a medicine may cause some unwanted effects. Although not all of these side effects may occur, if they do occur they may need medical attention.

Check with your doctor as soon as possible if any of the following side effects occur:

Less common
> Breathing difficulty and/or wheezing; cold hands and feet; mental depression; shortness of breath; slow heartbeat (especially less than 50 beats per minute); swelling of ankles, feet, and/or lower legs

Rare
> Back pain or joint pain; chest pain; confusion (especially in elderly patients); dark urine—for acebutolol, bisoprolol, or labetalol; dizziness or lightheadedness when getting up from a lying or sitting position; fever and sore throat; hallucinations (seeing, hearing, or feeling things that are not there); irregular heartbeat; red, scaling, or crusted skin; skin rash; unusual bleeding and bruising; yellow eyes or skin—for acebutolol, bisoprolol, or labetalol

Signs and symptoms of overdose (in the order in which they may occur)
> Slow heartbeat; dizziness (severe) or fainting; fast or irregular heartbeat; difficulty in breathing; bluish-colored fingernails or palms of hands; convulsions (seizures)

Other side effects may occur that usually do not need medical attention. These side effects may go away during treatment as your body adjusts to the medicine. However, check with your doctor if any of the following side effects continue or are bothersome:

More common
> Decreased sexual ability; dizziness or lightheadedness; drowsiness (slight); trouble in sleeping; unusual tiredness or weakness

Less common or rare
> Anxiety and/or nervousness; changes in taste—for labetalol only; constipation; diarrhea; dry, sore eyes; frequent urination—for acebutolol and carteolol only; itching of skin; nausea or vomiting; nightmares and vivid dreams; numbness and/or tingling of fingers and/or toes; numbness and/or tingling of skin, especially on scalp—for labetalol only; stomach discomfort; stuffy nose

Although not all of the side effects listed above have been reported for all of these medicines, they have been reported for at least one of them. Since all of the beta-adrenergic blocking agents are very similar, any of the above side effects may occur with any of these medicines. However, they may be more or less common with some agents than with others.

After you have been taking a beta-blocker for a while, it may cause unpleasant or even harmful effects if you stop taking it too suddenly. After you stop taking this medicine or while you are gradually reducing the amount you are taking, check with your doctor right away if any of the following occur:
> Chest pain; fast or irregular heartbeat; general feeling of discomfort or illness or weakness; headache; shortness of breath (sudden); sweating; trembling

For patients taking *labetalol:*

- You may notice a tingling feeling on your scalp when you first begin to take labetalol. This is to be expected and usually goes away after you have been taking labetalol for a while.

Other side effects not listed above may also occur in some patients. If you notice any other effects, check with your doctor.

Additional Information

Once a medicine has been approved for marketing for a certain use, experience may show that it is also useful for other

medical problems. Although these uses are not included in product labeling, some beta-blockers are used in certain patients with the following medical conditions:

- Glaucoma
- Neuroleptic-induced akathisia (restlessness or the need to keep moving caused by some medicines used to treat nervousness or mental and emotional disorders)

Other than the above information, there is no additional information relating to proper use, precautions, or side effects for these uses.

Revised: 05/13/93
Interim revision: 08/18/97; 08/13/98

BETA-ADRENERGIC BLOCKING AGENTS AND THIAZIDE DIURETICS Systemic

Commonly used brand name(s):

In the U.S.—

Corzide 40/5[4]	Tenoretic 50[1]
Corzide 80/5[4]	Tenoretic 100[1]
Inderide[6]	Timolide 10-25[7]
Inderide LA[6]	Ziac[2]
Lopressor HCT[3]	

In Canada—

Corzide[4]	Timolide[7]
Inderide[6]	Viskazide[5]
Tenoretic[1]	

Note: For quick reference, the following beta-adrenergic blocking agents and thiazide diuretics are numbered to match the corresponding brand names.

This information applies to the following medicines:

1. Atenolol and Chlorthalidone (a-TEN-oh-lole and klor-THAL-i-doan)‡
2. Bisoprolol and Hydrochlorothiazide (bis-OH-proe-lol and hye-droe-klor-oh-THYE-a-zide)†
3. Metoprolol and Hydrochlorothiazide (me-TOE-proe-lole and hye-droe-klor-oh-THYE-a-zide)†
4. Nadolol and Bendroflumethiazide (NAY-doe-lole and ben-droe-floo-meth-EYE-a-zide)
5. Pindolol and Hydrochlorothiazide (PIN-doe-lole and hye-droe-klor-oh-THYE-a-zide)*
6. Propranolol and Hydrochlorothiazide (proe-PRAN-oh-lole and hye-droe-klor-oh-THYE-a-zide)‡
7. Timolol and Hydrochlorothiazide (TIM-oh-lole and hye-droe-klor-oh-THYE-a-zide)

*Not commercially available in the U.S.
†Not commercially available in Canada.
‡Generic name product may be available in the U.S.

Description

Beta-adrenergic blocking agent (more commonly, beta-blockers) and thiazide diuretic combinations belong to the group of medicines known as antihypertensives (high blood pressure medicine). Both ingredients of the combination control high blood pressure, but they work in different ways. Beta-blockers (atenolol, bisoprolol, metoprolol, nadolol, pindolol, propranolol, and timolol) reduce the work load on the heart as well as having other effects. Thiazide diuretics (bendroflumethiazide, chlorthalidone, and hydrochlorothiazide) reduce the amount of fluid pressure in the body by increasing the flow of urine.

High blood pressure adds to the work load of the heart and arteries. If it continues for a long time, the heart and arteries may not function properly. This can damage the blood vessels of the brain, heart, and kidneys, resulting in a stroke, heart failure, or kidney failure. High blood pressure may also increase the risk of heart attacks. These problems may be less likely to occur if blood pressure is controlled.

Beta-blocker and thiazide diuretic combinations are available only with your doctor's prescription, in the following dosage forms:

Oral
Atenolol and chlorthalidone
- Tablets (U.S. and Canada)
Bisoprolol and hydrochlorothiazide
- Tablets (U.S.)
Metoprolol and hydrochlorothiazide
- Tablets (U.S.)
Nadolol and bendroflumethiazide
- Tablets (U.S. and Canada)
Pindolol and hydrochlorothiazide
- Tablets (Canada)
Propranolol and hydrochlorothiazide
- Extended-release capsules (U.S.)
- Tablets (U.S. and Canada)
Timolol and hydrochlorothiazide
- Tablets (U.S. and Canada)

Before Using This Medicine

In deciding to use a medicine, the risks of taking the medicine must be weighed against the good it will do. This is a decision you and your doctor will make. For the beta-blocker and thiazide diuretic combinations, the following should be considered:

Allergies—Tell your doctor if you have ever had any unusual or allergic reaction to beta-blockers, sulfonamides (sulfa drugs), bumetanide, furosemide, acetazolamide, dichlorphenamide, methazolamide, or any of the thiazide diuretics. Also tell your health care professional if you are allergic to any other substances, such as foods, preservatives, or dyes.

Pregnancy—Use of some beta-blockers during pregnancy has been associated with low blood sugar, breathing problems, a slower heart rate, and low blood pressure in the newborn infant. Other reports have not shown unwanted effects in the newborn infant. Animal studies have shown some beta-blockers to cause problems in pregnancy when used in doses many times the usual human dose.

Studies with thiazide diuretics have not been done in pregnant women. However, use of thiazide diuretics during pregnancy may cause side effects such as jaundice, blood problems, and low potassium in the newborn infant. Animal studies have not shown thiazide diuretic medicines to cause birth defects even when used in doses several times the usual human dose.

Before taking a beta-blocker and thiazide diuretic combination, make sure your doctor knows if you are pregnant or if you may become pregnant.

Breast-feeding—Atenolol, metoprolol, nadolol, propranolol, pindolol, timolol, and thiazide diuretics pass into breast milk. It is not known whether bisoprolol passes into breast milk. Thiazide diuretics may decrease the flow of breast milk.

Children—Although there is no specific information comparing use of this combination medicine in children with use in other age groups, this medicine is not expected to cause different side effects or problems in children than it does in adults. However, extra caution may be necessary in infants with jaundice, because these medicines can make the condition worse.

Older adults—Some side effects, especially dizziness or lightheadedness and signs and symptoms of too much potassium loss, may be more likely to occur in the elderly, who are usually more sensitive to the effects of this medicine. Also, beta-blockers may reduce tolerance to cold temperatures in elderly patients.

Other medicines—Although certain medicines should not be used together at all, in other cases 2 different medicines may be used together even if an interaction might occur. In these cases, your doctor may want to change the dose, or other precautions may be necessary. When you are taking beta-blocker and thiazide diuretic combinations, it is especially important that your health care professional know if you are taking any of the following:

- Allergy shots or
- Allergy skin tests—The beta-blocker contained in this medicine may increase the risk of a serious allergic reaction to these medicines

- Aminophylline (e.g., Somophyllin) or
- Caffeine (e.g., NoDoz) or
- Dyphylline (e.g., Lufylline) or
- Oxtriphylline (e.g., Choledyl) or
- Theophylline (e.g., Somophyllin-T)—The effects of these medicines and beta-blockers may be blocked; in addition, theophylline levels in the body may be increased, especially in patients who smoke

- Antidiabetics, oral (diabetes medicine you take by mouth) or
- Insulin—There is an increased risk of hyperglycemia (high blood sugar); the beta-blocker contained in this medicine may also cover up certain symptoms of hypoglycemia (low blood sugar), such as increases in pulse rate and blood pressure, and may make the hypoglycemia last longer

- Calcium channel blockers (amlodipine [e.g., Norvasc], bepridil [e.g., Bepadin], diltiazem [e.g., Cardizem], felodipine [e.g., Plendil], flunarizine [e.g., Sibelium], isradipine [e.g., DynaCirc], nicardipine [e.g., Cardene], nifedipine [e.g., Procardia], nimodipine [e.g., Nimotop], verapamil [e.g., Calan]) or
- Clonidine (e.g., Catapres) or
- Guanabenz (e.g., Wytensin)—Effects on blood pressure may be increased. In addition, unwanted effects may occur if clonidine, guanabenz, or a beta-blocker are stopped suddenly after use together. Unwanted effects on the heart may occur when beta-blocker and thiazide diuretic combinations are used with calcium channel blockers

- Cocaine—Cocaine may block the effects of beta-blockers; in addition, there is an increased risk of high blood pressure, fast heartbeat, and possibly heart problems if you use cocaine while taking a beta-blocker and thiazide diuretic combination

- Digitalis glycosides (heart medicine)—Use with beta-blocker and thiazide diuretic combinations may cause high blood levels of digoxin, which may increase the chance of side effects

- Lithium—The thiazide diuretic contained in this combination may cause high blood levels of lithium, which may increase the chance of side effects

- Monoamine oxidase (MAO) inhibitors (furazolidone [e.g., Furoxone], isocarboxazid [e.g., Marplan], phenelzine [e.g., Nardil], procarbazine [e.g., Matulane], selegiline [e.g., Eldepryl], tranylcypromine [e.g., Parnate])—Taking a beta-blocker and thiazide diuretic combination while you are taking or within 2 weeks of taking monoamine oxidase (MAO) inhibitors may cause severe high blood pressure

Other medical problems—The presence of other medical problems may affect the use of the beta-blockers and thiazide diuretics. Make sure you tell your doctor if you have any other medical problems, especially:

- Allergy, history of (asthma, eczema, hay fever, hives), or
- Bronchitis or
- Emphysema—This combination medicine may make allergic reactions to other substances more severe or make the reaction last longer; in addition, the beta-blocker contained in this combination can increase trouble in breathing

- Bradycardia (unusually slow heartbeat) or
- Heart or blood vessel disease—This combination medicine may make these heart problems worse; also, if treatment is stopped suddenly, unwanted effects may occur

- Diabetes mellitus (sugar diabetes)—The beta-blocker contained in this medicine may cause hyperglycemia (high blood sugar) and circulation problems; in addition, if your diabetes medicine causes your blood sugar to be too low, beta-blockers may cover up some of the symptoms (fast heartbeat), although they will not cover up other symptoms such as dizziness or sweating; the thiazide diuretic contained in this medicine may increase the amount of sugar in the blood

- Gout (history of) or
- Lupus erythematosus (history of) or
- Pancreatitis (inflammation of the pancreas)—The thiazide diuretic contained in this medicine may make these conditions worse

- Kidney disease or
- Liver disease—Effects of this medicine may be increased because of slower removal from the body

- Mental depression (or history of) or
- Myasthenia gravis or
- Pheochromocytoma or
- Psoriasis or
- Raynaud's syndrome—The beta-blocker contained in this medicine may make these conditions worse

- Overactive thyroid—Stopping this medicine suddenly may increase symptoms of overactive thyroid; the beta-blocker contained in this medicine may cover up fast heartbeat, which is a sign of overactive thyroid

Proper Use of This Medicine

In addition to the use of the medicine your doctor has prescribed, treatment for your high blood pressure may include weight control and care in the types of foods you eat, especially foods high in sodium. Your doctor will tell you which of these are most important for you. You should check with your doctor before changing your diet.

Many patients who have high blood pressure will not notice any signs of the problem. In fact, many may feel normal. It is very important that you *take your medicine exactly as di-*

rected and that you keep your appointments with your doctor even if you feel well.

Remember that this medicine will not cure your high blood pressure but it does help control it. Therefore, you must continue to take it as directed if you expect to lower your blood pressure and keep it down. *You may have to take high blood pressure medicine for the rest of your life.* If high blood pressure is not treated, it can cause serious problems such as heart failure, blood vessel disease, stroke, or kidney disease.

For patients taking the *extended-release tablet* form of this medicine:

- Swallow the tablet whole.
- Do not crush, break, or chew before swallowing.

To help you remember to take your medicine, try to get into the habit of taking it at the same time each day.

Ask your doctor about checking your pulse rate before and after taking beta-blocking agents. Then, while you are taking this medicine, check your pulse regularly. If it is much slower than your usual rate (or less than 50 beats per minute), check with your doctor. A pulse rate that is too slow may cause circulation problems.

The thiazide diuretic (e.g., bendroflumethiazide, chlorthalidone, or hydrochlorothiazide) contained in this combination medicine may cause you to have an unusual feeling of tiredness when you begin to take it. You may also notice an increase in the amount of urine or in your frequency of urination. After you take the medicine for a while, these effects should lessen. To keep the increase in urine from affecting your sleep:

- If you are to take a single dose a day, take it in the morning after breakfast.
- If you are to take more than one dose a day, take the last dose no later than 6 p.m., unless otherwise directed by your doctor.

However, it is best to plan your dose or doses according to a schedule that will least affect your personal activities and sleep. Ask your health care professional to help you plan the best time to take this medicine.

Do not miss any doses. This is especially important when you are taking only one dose per day. Some conditions may become worse when this medicine is not taken regularly.

Dosing—The dose of beta-blocker and thiazide diuretic combinations will be different for different patients. *Follow your doctor's orders or the directions on the label.* The following information includes only the average doses of beta-blocker and thiazide diuretic combinations. *If your dose is different, do not change it* unless your doctor tells you to do so.

The number of capsules or tablets that you take depends on the strength of the medicine.

For atenolol and chlorthalidone combination
- For *oral* dosage form (tablets):
  —For high blood pressure:
    - Adults—1 or 2 tablets once a day.
    - Children—Dose must be determined by your doctor.

For bisoprolol and hydrochlorothiazide combination
- For *oral* dosage form (tablets):
  —For high blood pressure:
    - Adults—1 or 2 tablets once a day.
    - Children—Dose must be determined by your doctor.

For metoprolol and hydrochlorothiazide combination
- For *oral* dosage form (tablets):
  —For high blood pressure:
    - Adults—1 or 2 tablets a day.
    - Children—Dose must be determined by your doctor.

For nadolol and bendroflumethiazide combination
- For *oral* dosage form (tablets):
  —For high blood pressure:
    - Adults—1 tablet once a day.
    - Children—Dose must be determined by your doctor.

For pindolol and hydrochlorothiazide combination
- For *oral* dosage form (tablets):
  —For high blood pressure:
    - Adults—1 or 2 tablets once a day.
    - Children—Dose must be determined by your doctor.

For propranolol and hydrochlorothiazide combination
- For *regular (short-acting) oral* dosage form (tablets):
  —For high blood pressure:
    - Adults—1 or 2 tablets two times a day.
    - Children—Dose must be determined by your doctor.
- For *long-acting oral* dosage form (capsules):
  —For high blood pressure:
    - Adults—1 capsule a day.
    - Children—Dose must be determined by your doctor.

For timolol and hydrochlorothiazide combination
- For *oral* dosage form (tablets):
  —For high blood pressure:
    - Adults—1 tablet two times a day or 2 tablets once a day.
    - Children—Dose must be determined by your doctor.

Missed dose—If you miss a dose of this medicine, take it as soon as possible. However, if it is within 4 hours of your next dose (8 hours if you are using atenolol and chlorthalidone, bisoprolol and hydrochlorothiazide, nadolol and bendroflumethiazide, or extended-release propranolol and hydrochlorothiazide), skip the missed dose and go back to your regular dosing schedule. Do not double doses.

Storage—To store this medicine:
- Keep out of the reach of children.
- Store away from heat and direct light.
- Do not store in the bathroom, near the kitchen sink, or in other damp places. Heat or moisture may cause the medicine to break down.
- Do not keep outdated medicine or medicine no longer needed. Be sure that any discarded medicine is out of the reach of children.

Precautions While Using This Medicine

It is important that your doctor check your progress at regular visits. This is to make sure the medicine is properly controlling your blood pressure and to allow the dosage to be changed if needed.

Do not stop taking this medicine without first checking with your doctor. Your doctor may want you to reduce gradually the amount you are taking before stopping completely. Some conditions may become worse when the medicine is stopped suddenly, and the risk of heart attack is increased in some patients.

Make sure that you have enough medicine on hand to last through weekends, holidays, or vacations. You may want to carry an extra written prescription in your billfold or purse in case of an emergency. You can then have it filled if you run out of medicine while you are away from home.

Your doctor may want you to carry medical identification stating that you are taking this medicine.

Do not take other medicines unless they have been discussed with your doctor. This especially includes over-the-counter (nonprescription) medicines for appetite control, asthma, colds, cough, hay fever, or sinus problems since they may increase your blood pressure.

Before having any kind of surgery (including dental surgery) or emergency treatment, tell the medical doctor or dentist in charge that you are taking this medicine.

For *diabetic patients:*

- *This medicine may increase your blood sugar levels. Also, this medicine may cover up signs of hypoglycemia (low blood sugar), such as change in pulse rate.* While you are taking this medicine, be especially careful in testing for sugar in your urine. If you have any questions about this, check with your doctor.

The thiazide diuretic contained in this medicine may cause a loss of potassium from your body.

- To help prevent this, your doctor may want you to:
  —eat or drink foods that have a high potassium content (for example, orange or other citrus fruit juices), or
  —take a potassium supplement, or
  —take another medicine to help prevent the loss of the potassium in the first place.
- It is very important to follow these directions. Also, it is important not to change your diet on your own. This is more important if you are already on a special diet (as for diabetes), or if you are taking a potassium supplement or a medicine to reduce potassium loss. Extra potassium may not be necessary and, in some cases, too much potassium could be harmful.

Check with your doctor if you become sick and have severe or continuing vomiting or diarrhea. These problems may cause you to lose additional water and potassium.

This medicine may cause some people to become dizzy, drowsy, lightheaded, or less alert than they are normally. *Make sure you know how you react to this medicine before you drive, use machines, or do anything else that could be dangerous if you are dizzy or are not alert.* If the problem continues or gets worse, check with your doctor.

The beta-blocker (atenolol, bisoprolol, metoprolol, nadolol, pindolol, propranolol, or timolol) contained in this medicine may make you more sensitive to cold temperatures, especially if you have blood circulation problems. Beta-blockers tend to decrease blood circulation in the skin, fingers, and toes. Dress warmly during cold weather and be careful during prolonged exposure to cold, such as in winter sports.

This medicine may cause your skin to be more sensitive to sunlight than it is normally. Exposure to sunlight, even for brief periods of time, may cause a skin rash, itching, redness or other discoloration of the skin, or a severe sunburn. When you begin taking this medicine:

- Stay out of direct sunlight, especially between the hours of 10:00 a.m. and 3:00 p.m., if possible.

- Wear protective clothing, including a hat. Also, wear sunglasses.
- Apply a sun block product that has a skin protection factor (SPF) of at least 15. Some patients may require a product with a higher SPF number, especially if they have a fair complexion. If you have any questions about this, check with your health care professional.
- Apply a sun block lipstick that has an SPF of at least 15 to protect your lips.
- Do not use a sunlamp or tanning bed or booth.

If you have a severe reaction from the sun, check with your doctor.

Before you have any medical tests, tell the doctor in charge that you are taking this medicine. The results of some tests may be affected by this medicine.

For patients with allergies to foods, medicines, or insect stings:

- There is a chance that this medicine will make allergic reactions worse and harder to treat. If you have a severe allergic reaction while you are being treated with this medicine, check with a doctor right away so that it can be treated.

Side Effects of This Medicine

Along with its needed effects, a medicine may cause some unwanted effects. Although not all of these side effects may occur, if they do occur they may need medical attention.

Check with your doctor as soon as possible if any of the following side effects occur:

Less common

Breathing difficulty and/or wheezing; cold hands and feet; mental depression; slow heartbeat (especially less than 50 beats per minute); swelling of ankles, feet, and/or lower legs

Rare

Black, tarry stools; blood in urine or stools; chest pain; dark urine; fever, chills, cough, or sore throat; hallucinations (seeing, hearing, or feeling things that are not there); joint pain; lower back or side pain; pinpoint red spots on skin; red, scaling, or crusted skin; skin rash or hives; stomach pain (severe) with nausea and vomiting; unusual bleeding or bruising; or yellow eyes or skin

Signs and symptoms of too much potassium or sodium loss

Confusion; convulsions (seizures); dryness of mouth; increased thirst; irregular heartbeats; irritability, mood or mental changes; muscle cramps or pain; nausea or vomiting, unusual tiredness or weakness; weak pulse

Signs and symptoms of overdose (in the order in which they may occur)

Slow heartbeat; dizziness (severe) or fainting; difficulty in breathing; bluish-colored fingernails or palms of hands; convulsions (seizures)

Other side effects may occur that usually do not need medical attention. These side effects may go away during treatment as your body adjusts to the medicine. However, check with your doctor if any of the following side effects continue or are bothersome:

More common

Decreased sexual ability; dizziness or lightheadedness; drowsiness (mild); trouble in sleeping

Less common
> Anxiety or nervousness; constipation; diarrhea; increased sensitivity of skin to sunlight (skin rash, itching, redness or other discoloration of skin, or severe sunburn); loss of appetite; numbness or tingling of fingers and toes; stomach discomfort or upset; stuffy nose

Rare
> Changes in taste; dry, sore eyes; itching of skin; nightmares and vivid dreams

Although not all of the above side effects have been reported for all of these medicines, they have been reported for at least one of the beta-blockers or thiazide diuretics. Since all of the beta-blockers are very similar and the thiazide diuretics are also very similar, any of the above side effects may occur with any of these medicines. However, they may be more common with some combinations than with others.

After you have been taking this medicine for a while, it may cause unpleasant or even harmful effects if you stop taking it too suddenly. After you stop taking this medicine or while you are gradually reducing the amount you are taking, check with your doctor right away if any of the following occur:
> Chest pain; fast or irregular heartbeat; general feeling of discomfort, illness, or weakness; headache; shortness of breath (sudden); sweating; trembling

Other side effects not listed above may also occur in some patients. If you notice any other effects, check with your doctor.

Revised: 08/23/94

BETA-CAROTENE   Systemic

Commonly used brand name(s):

In the U.S.—
Lumitene
Max-Caro
Generic name product may be available.

Description

Vitamins (VYE-ta-mins) are compounds that you *must* have for growth and health. They are needed in small amounts only and are usually available in the foods that you eat. Beta-carotene (bay-ta-KARE-oh-teen) is converted in the body to vitamin A, which is necessary for healthy eyes and skin.

A lack of vitamin A may cause a rare condition called night blindness (problems seeing in the dark). It may also cause dry eyes, eye infections, skin problems, and slowed growth. Your health care professional may treat these problems by prescribing either beta-carotene, which your body can change into vitamin A, or vitamin A for you.

Some conditions may increase your need for vitamin A. These include:
- Cystic fibrosis
- Diarrhea, continuing
- Illness, long-term
- Injury, serious
- Liver disease
- Malabsorption problems
- Pancreas disease

Increased need for vitamin A should be determined by your health care professional.

Claims that beta-carotene is effective as a sunscreen have not been proven. Although beta-carotene supplements are being studied for their ability to reduce the risk of certain types of cancer and possibly heart disease, there is not enough information to show that this is effective.

Beta-carotene may be used to treat other conditions as determined by your doctor.

Beta-carotene is available without a prescription in the following dosage forms:

Oral
- Capsules (U.S. and Canada)
- Tablets (U.S. and Canada)
- Chewable tablets (Canada)

Importance of Diet

For good health, it is important that you eat a balanced and varied diet. Follow carefully any diet program your health care professional may recommend. For your specific dietary vitamin and/or mineral needs, ask your health care professional for a list of appropriate foods. If you think that you are not getting enough vitamins and/or minerals in your diet, you may choose to take a dietary supplement.

It is documented that people who consume diets high in fruits and vegetables have a reduced risk of heart disease and certain cancers. Fruits and vegetables are rich in beta-carotene and other nutrients that may be beneficial.

Beta-carotene is found in carrots; dark-green leafy vegetables, such as spinach and green leaf lettuce; sweet potatoes; broccoli; cantaloupe; and winter squash. The body converts beta-carotene into vitamin A. Ordinary cooking does not destroy beta-carotene.

Vitamins alone will not take the place of a good diet and will not provide energy. Your body needs other substances found in food, such as protein, minerals, carbohydrates, and fat. Vitamins themselves often cannot work without the presence of other foods. For example, some fat is needed so that beta-carotene can be absorbed into the body.

Before Using This Dietary Supplement

If you are taking this dietary supplement without a prescription, carefully read and follow any precautions on the label. For beta-carotene, the following should be considered:

Allergies—Tell your health care professional if you have ever had any unusual or allergic reaction to beta-carotene. Also tell your health care professional if you are allergic to any other substances, such as foods, preservatives, or dyes.

Pregnancy—It is especially important that you are receiving enough vitamins when you become pregnant and that you continue to receive the right amount of vitamins throughout your pregnancy. The healthy growth and development of the fetus depend on a steady supply of nutrients from the mother.

Beta-carotene has not been studied in pregnant women. However, no problems with fertility or pregnancy have been reported in women taking up to 30 milligrams (mg) of beta-carotene a day. The effects of taking more than 30 mg a day are not known.

Breast-feeding—It is especially important that you receive the right amounts of vitamins so that your baby will also get the vitamins needed to grow properly. However, taking large amounts of a dietary supplement while breast-feeding may be harmful to the mother and/or baby and should be avoided.

Children—Problems in children have not been documented with intake of normal daily recommended amounts.

Older adults—Problems in older adults have not been documented with intake of normal daily recommended amounts.

Medicines or other dietary supplements—Although certain medicines or dietary supplements should not be used together at all, in other cases they may be used together even if an interaction might occur. In these cases, your health care professional may want to change the dose, or other precautions may be necessary. Tell your health care professional if you are taking any other dietary supplement or any prescription or nonprescription (over-the-counter [OTC]) medicine.

Other medical problems—The presence of other medical problems may affect the use of beta-carotene. Make sure you tell your health care professional if you have any other medical problems, especially:

- Eating disorders or
- Kidney disease or
- Liver disease—These conditions may cause high blood levels of beta-carotene, which may increase the chance of side effects

Proper Use of This Dietary Supplement

Dosing—For use as a dietary supplement:

- For *oral* dosage forms (capsules or chewable tablets):
  —Adults and teenagers: 6 to 15 milligrams (mg) of beta-carotene (the equivalent of 10,000 to 25,000 Units of vitamin A activity) per day.
  —Children: 3 to 6 mg of beta-carotene (the equivalent of 5,000 to 10,000 Units of vitamin A activity) per day.

If you have high blood levels of vitamin A, your body will convert less beta-carotene to vitamin A.

Missed dose—If you miss taking a vitamin for one or more days there is no cause for concern, since it takes some time for your body to become seriously low in vitamins. However, if your health care professional has recommended that you take this vitamin, try to remember to take it as directed every day.

Storage—To store this dietary supplement:

- Keep out of the reach of children.
- Store away from heat and direct light.
- Do not store in the bathroom, near the kitchen sink, or in other damp places. Heat or moisture may cause the dietary supplement to break down.
- Keep the dietary supplement from freezing. Do not refrigerate.
- Do not keep outdated dietary supplements or those no longer needed. Be sure that any discarded dietary supplement is out of the reach of children.

Precautions While Using This Dietary Supplement

Use of beta-carotene has been associated with an increased risk of lung cancer in people who smoke or who have been exposed to asbestos. One study of 29,000 male smokers found an 18% increase in lung cancer in the group receiving 20 mg of beta-carotene a day for 5 to 8 years. Another study of 18,000 people found 28% more lung cancers in people with a history of smoking and/or asbestos exposure. These people took 30 mg of beta-carotene in addition to 25,000 Units of retinol (a form of vitamin A) a day for 4 years. However, one study of 22,000 male physicians, some of them smokers or former smokers, found no increase in lung cancer. These people took 50 mg of beta-carotene every other day for 12 years. If you smoke or have a history of smoking or asbestos exposure, you should not take large amounts of beta-carotene supplements for long periods of time. However, foods that are rich in beta-carotene are considered safe and appear to lower the risk of some types of cancer and possibly heart disease.

Side Effects of This Dietary Supplement

Along with its needed effects, a dietary supplement may cause some unwanted effects. The following side effects may go away during treatment as your body adjusts to the dietary supplement. However, check with your health care professional if any of the following side effects continue or are bothersome:

More common
Yellowing of palms, hands, or soles of feet, and to a lesser extent the face (this may be a sign that your dose of beta-carotene as a nutritional supplement is too high)

Rare
Diarrhea; dizziness; joint pain; unusual bleeding or bruising

Other side effects not listed above may also occur in some individuals. If you notice any other effects, check with your health care professional.

Additional Information

Once a product has been approved for marketing for a certain use, experience may show that it is also useful for other medical problems. Although this use is not included in product labeling, beta-carotene is used in certain patients with the following medical conditions:

- Polymorphous light eruption (a type of reaction to sun)
- Erythropoietic protoporphyria photosensitivity reaction (a type of reaction to sun)

Breast-feeding—Beta-carotene has not been reported to cause problems in nursing babies.

Children—This medicine has been tested in children and, in effective doses, has not been shown to cause different side effects or problems in children than it does in adults.

Older Adults—Many medicines have not been studied specifically in older people. Therefore, it may not be known whether they work exactly the same way they do in younger adults. Although there is no specific information comparing use of beta-carotene in the elderly with use in other age groups, it is not expected to cause different side effects or problems in older people than it does in younger adults.

Dosing—The dose of beta-carotene will be different for different patients. *Follow your doctor's orders or the directions on the label.* The following information includes only the average doses of beta-carotene. *If your dose is dif-*

ferent, do not change it unless your doctor tells you to do so.

- For *oral* dosage forms (capsules or tablets):
  - —To treat or prevent a reaction to sun in patients with erythropoietic protoporphyria:
    - Adults and teenagers—30 to 300 milligrams (mg) of beta-carotene (the equivalent of 50,000 to 500,000 Units of vitamin A activity) a day.
    - Children—30 to 150 mg of beta-carotene (the equivalent of 50,000 to 250,000 Units of vitamin A activity) a day.
  - —To treat or prevent a reaction to sun in patients with polymorphous light eruption:
    - Adults and teenagers—75 to 180 mg of beta-carotene (the equivalent of 125,000 to 300,000 Units of vitamin A activity) a day.
    - Children—30 to 150 mg of beta-carotene (the equivalent of 50,000 to 250,000 Units of vitamin A activity) a day.

Missed dose—If you miss a dose of this medicine, take it as soon as possible. However, if it is almost time for your next dose, skip the missed dose and go back to your regular dosing schedule. Do not double doses.

Other than the above information, there is no additional information relating to proper use, precautions, or side effects for these uses.

Revised: 07/09/97

BETAINE   Systemic†

Commonly used brand name(s):

In the U.S.—
Cystadane

†Not commercially available in Canada.

Description

Betaine (BAY-ta-een) is used to treat a lack of or defect in certain enzymes that causes too much homocysteine in the blood and urine. This medicine removes the extra homocysteine from the body.

This medicine is available only with your doctor's prescription, in the following dosage form:

Oral
- Powder for solution (U.S.)

Before Using This Medicine

In deciding to use a medicine, the risks of taking the medicine must be weighed against the good it will do. This is a decision you and your doctor will make. For betaine, the following should be considered:

Allergies—Tell your doctor if you have ever had any unusual or allergic reaction to betaine. Also tell your health care professional if you are allergic to any other substances, such as foods, preservatives, or dyes.

Pregnancy—Studies on effects in pregnancy have not been done in either humans or animals.

Breast-feeding—It is not known whether betaine passes into breast milk. Although most medicines pass into breast milk in small amounts, many of them may be used safely while breast-feeding. Mothers who are using this medicine and who wish to breast-feed should discuss this with their doctor.

Children—This medicine has been tested in children and, in effective doses, has not been shown to cause different side effects or problems than it does in adults. However, children may require more frequent changes in their dose than adults.

Older adults—Many medicines have not been studied specifically in older people. Therefore, it may not be known whether they work exactly the same way they do in younger adults or if they cause different side effects or problems in older people. There is no specific information comparing the use of betaine in the elderly with use in other age groups.

Proper Use of This Medicine

Betaine powder should be mixed with 4 to 6 ounces of juice, milk, or water until completely dissolved. The solution should be used immediately after mixing.

Do not use if the powder does not dissolve completely or gives a colored solution.

Betaine should be taken with meals.

It is important that you follow any special instructions from your doctor, such as taking folic acid, pyridoxine (vitamin B_6), and vitamin B_{12} supplements. If you have any questions about this, check with your doctor.

Dosing—The dose of betaine will be different for different patients. *Follow your doctor's orders or the directions on the label.* The following information includes only the average doses of betaine. *If your dose is different, do not change it* unless your doctor tells you to do so.

- For *oral* dosage form (powder for solution):
  - —To prevent buildup of homocysteine:
    - Adults, teenagers, and children 3 years of age and older—The starting dose is usually 3 grams taken two times a day with meals. Your doctor may adjust your dose as needed.
    - Children younger than 3 years of age—The dose is based on body weight and must be determined by your doctor. Betaine should be taken with meals.

Missed dose—If you miss a dose of this medicine, take it as soon as possible. However, if it is almost time for your next dose, skip the missed dose and go back to your regular dosing schedule. Do not double doses.

Storage—To store this medicine:
- Keep out of the reach of children.
- Store away from heat and direct light.
- Do not store in the bathroom, near the kitchen sink, or in other damp places. Heat or moisture may cause the medicine to break down.
- Keep the medicine from freezing. Do not refrigerate.
- Do not keep outdated medicine or medicine no longer needed. Be sure that any discarded medicine is out of the reach of children.

Precautions While Using This Medicine

Your doctor should check your progress at regular visits to make sure that this medicine is working properly.

Side Effects of This Medicine

Along with its needed effects, a medicine may cause some unwanted effects. Some side effects may occur that usually do not need medical attention. These side effects may go away during treatment as your body adjusts to the medicine. However, check with your doctor if any of the following side effects continue or are bothersome:

Less common
    Diarrhea; nausea; stomach upset

Betaine may cause a body odor. Other side effects not listed above may also occur in some patients. If you notice any other effects, check with your doctor.

Developed: 01/23/98

BETHANECHOL Systemic

Commonly used brand name(s):

In the U.S.—
    Duvoid
    Urabeth
    Urecholine
    Generic name product may be available.

In Canada—
    Duvoid
    Urecholine

Description

Bethanechol (be-THAN-e-kole) is taken to treat certain disorders of the urinary tract or bladder. It helps to cause urination and emptying of the bladder. Bethanechol may also be used for other conditions as determined by your doctor.

Bethanechol is available only with your doctor's prescription in the following dosage forms:

Oral
    • Tablets (U.S. and Canada)
Parenteral
    • Injection (U.S. and Canada)

Before Using This Medicine

In deciding to use a medicine, the risks of taking the medicine must be weighed against the good it will do. This is a decision you and your doctor will make. For bethanechol, the following should be considered:

Allergies—Tell your doctor if you have ever had any unusual or allergic reaction to bethanechol. Also tell your health care professional if you are allergic to any other substances, such as foods, preservatives, or dyes.

Pregnancy—Studies on effects in pregnancy have not been done in either humans or animals.

Breast-feeding—It is not known whether bethanechol passes into the breast milk.

Children—Although there is no specific information comparing use of bethanechol in children with use in other age groups, this medicine is not expected to cause different side effects or problems in children than it does in adults.

Older adults—Many medicines have not been studied specifically in older people. Therefore, it may not be known whether they work exactly the same way they do in younger adults. Although there is no specific information comparing use of bethanechol in the elderly with use in other age groups, it is not expected to cause different side effects or problems in older people than it does in younger adults.

Other medicines—Although certain medicines should not be used together at all, in other cases two different medicines may be used together even if an interaction might occur. In these cases, your doctor may want to change the dose, or other precautions may be necessary. Tell your health care professional if you are taking any other prescription or nonprescription (over-the-counter [OTC]) medicine.

Other medical problems—The presence of other medical problems may affect the use of bethanechol. Make sure you tell your doctor if you have any other medical problems, especially:

• Asthma or
• Epilepsy or
• Heart or blood vessel disease or
• Intestinal blockage or
• Low blood pressure or
• Parkinson's disease or
• Recent bladder or intestinal surgery or
• Stomach ulcer or other stomach problems or
• Urinary tract blockage or difficult urination—Bethanechol may make these conditions worse

• High blood pressure—Bethanechol may cause a rapid fall in blood pressure

• Overactive thyroid—Bethanechol may further increase the chance of heart problems

Proper Use of This Medicine

Take this medicine on an empty stomach (either 1 hour before or 2 hours after meals) to lessen the possibility of nausea and vomiting, unless otherwise directed by your doctor.

Take this medicine only as directed. Do not take more of it, do not take it more often, and do not take it for a longer time than your doctor ordered. To do so may increase the chance of side effects.

Dosing—The dose of bethanechol will be different for different patients. *Follow your doctor's orders or the directions on the label.* The following information includes only the average doses of bethanechol. *If your dose is different, do not change it* unless your doctor tells you to do so.

• To empty the bladder:
    —For *oral* dosage form (tablets):
        • Adults—25 to 50 milligrams (mg) three or four times a day.
        • Children—Dose is based on body weight and must be determined by your doctor. The usual dose is 0.6 mg per kilogram (kg) (0.27 mg per pound) of body weight a day. This dose is divided into smaller doses and taken three or four times a day.
    —For *injection* dosage form:
        • Adults—5 mg injected under the skin three or four times a day.
        • Children—Dose is based on body weight and must be determined by your doctor. The usual dose is 0.2 mg per kg (0.09 mg per pound) of body

weight a day. This dose is divided into smaller doses, which are injected under the skin three or four times a day.

Missed dose—If you miss a dose of this medicine and you remember within an hour or so of the missed dose, take it right away. However, if you do not remember until 2 or more hours after, skip the missed dose and go back to your regular dosing schedule. Do not double doses.

Storage—To store this medicine:
- Keep out of the reach of children.
- Store away from heat and direct light.
- Do not store the tablet form of this medicine in the bathroom, near the kitchen sink, or in other damp places. Heat or moisture may cause the medicine to break down.
- Do not keep outdated medicine or medicine no longer needed. Be sure that any discarded medicine is out of the reach of children.

Precautions While Using This Medicine

Dizziness, lightheadedness, or fainting may occur, especially when you get up from a lying or sitting position. Getting up slowly may help lessen this problem.

Side Effects of This Medicine

Along with its needed effects, a medicine may cause some unwanted effects. Although not all of these side effects may occur, if they do occur they may need medical attention.

Check with your doctor as soon as possible if any of the following side effects occur:
Rare—more common with the injection
Shortness of breath, wheezing, or tightness in chest

Other side effects may occur that usually do not need medical attention. These side effects may go away during treatment as your body adjusts to the medicine. However, check with your doctor if any of the following side effects continue or are bothersome:
Less common or rare—more common with the injection
Belching; blurred vision or change in near or distance vision; diarrhea; dizziness or lightheadedness; feeling faint; frequent urge to urinate; headache; increased watering of mouth or sweating; nausea or vomiting; redness or flushing of skin or feeling of warmth; seizures; sleeplessness, nervousness, or jitters; stomach discomfort or pain

Other side effects not listed above may also occur in some patients. If you notice any other effects, check with your doctor.

Additional Information

Once a medicine has been approved for marketing for a certain use, experience may show that it is also useful for other medical problems. Although these uses are not included in product labeling, bethanechol is used in certain patients with the following medical conditions:
- Certain stomach problems
- Gastroesophageal reflux (caused by acid in the stomach washing back up into the esophagus)
- Megacolon (an abnormally large or dilated colon)

Other than the above information, there is no additional information relating to proper use, precautions, or side effects for these uses.

Revised: 05/12/93
Interim revision: 06/27/94

BEXAROTENE   Systemic†

Commonly used brand name(s):

In the U.S.—
Targretin

†Not commercially available in Canada.

Description

Bexarotene (beks-AIR-oh-teen) belongs to the group of medicines known as retinoids (RET-i-noyds). It is used to treat a certain type of cancer called cutaneous T-cell lymphoma. It works by interfering with the growth of the cancerous cells.

This medicine is available only with your doctor's prescription, in the following dosage form:
Oral
- Capsule (U.S.)

Before Using This Medicine

In deciding to use a medicine, the risks of taking the medicine must be weighed against the good it will do. This is a decision you and your doctor will make. For bexarotene, the following should be considered:

Allergies—Tell your doctor if you have ever had any unusual or allergic reaction to bexarotene or other retinoid (vitamin A) preparations. Also tell your health care professional if you are allergic to any other substances, such as foods, preservatives, or dyes.

Pregnancy—*Bexarotene must not be taken during pregnancy because of the possible risks to the infant. In addition, bexarotene must not be taken if there is a chance that you may become pregnant 1 month before treatment, during treatment, and within 1 month after treatment is ended.* Women who are able to have children must have a pregnancy test done within 1 week before starting bexarotene, to make sure they are not pregnant. The pregnancy test must be repeated once a month during treatment. For 1 month before treatment with bexarotene, during treatment, and for 1 month after treatment is over, you must use two effective forms of birth control at the same time. Male patients with sexual partners who are pregnant, possibly pregnant, or who could become pregnant must use condoms during sexual intercourse while taking bexarotene and for at least 1 month after taking the last dose. Be sure you have discussed this information with your doctor.

Breast-feeding—It is not known whether this medicine passes into breast milk. However, bexarotene is not recommended during breast-feeding, because it may cause unwanted effects in nursing babies.

Children—Studies of this medicine have been done only in adult patients, and there is no specific information comparing the use of bexarotene in children with use in other age groups.

Older adults—This medicine has been tested in a patients 60 years of age or older and has not been shown to cause different side effects or problems in older people than it does in younger adults. However, elderly patients may be more sensitive to the effects of bexarotene.

Other medicines—Although certain medicines should not be used together at all, in other cases two different medicines may be used together even if an interaction might occur. In these cases, your doctor may want to change the dose or other precautions may be necessary. When you are taking bexarotene, it is especially important that your health care professional know if you are using any of the following:

- Acyclovir (e.g., Zovirax) or
- Anticonvulsants (seizure medicine) or
- Antidiabetics, oral (diabetes medicine taken by mouth) or
- Anti-infectives by mouth or by injection (medicine for infection) or
- Antipsychotics (medicine for mental illness) or
- Captopril (e.g., Capoten) or
- Enalapril (e.g., Vasotec) or
- Flecainide (e.g., Tambocor) or
- Gold salts (medicine for arthritis) or
- Imipenem or
- Inflammation or pain medicine, except narcotics or
- Lisinopril (e.g., Prinivil, Zestril) or
- Maprotiline (e.g., Ludiomil) or
- Penicillamine (e.g., Cuprimine) or
- Pimozide (e.g., Orap) or
- Procainamide (e.g., Pronestyl) or
- Promethazine (e.g., Phenergan) or
- Ramipril (e.g., Altace) or
- Sulfasalazine (e.g., Azulfidine) or
- Tiopronin (e.g., Thiola) or
- Tocainide (e.g., Tonocard) or
- Tricyclic antidepressants (medicine for depression) or
- Trimeprazine (e.g., Temaril)—Concurrent use of these agents with bexarotene may cause blood disorders

- Alpha interferons (e.g., Intron A, Roferon-A) or
- Amphotericin B by injection (e.g., Fungizone) or
- Antineoplastics, other (cancer medicine) or
- Antithyroid agents (medicine for overactive thyroid) or
- Azathioprine (e.g., Imuran) or
- Chloramphenicol (e.g., Chloromycetin) or
- Colchicine or
- Cyclophosphamide (e.g., Cytoxan) or
- Flucytosine (e.g., Ancobon) or
- Ganciclovir (e.g., Cytovene) or
- Zidovudine (e.g., AZT, Retrovir)—Concurrent use of these agents with bexarotene increases the risk of infection

- If you have ever been treated with radiation or cancer medicines—Bexarotene may increase the effects that these medicines or radiation therapy may have on the blood

- Phenobarbital or
- Phenytoin (e.g., Dilantin) or
- Rifampin (e.g., Rifadin, Rimactane) or

- Erythromycin (e.g., E-Mycin, Ery-Tab, Ilotycin) or
- Grapefruit juice or
- Itraconazole (e.g., Sporanox) or
- Ketoconazole (e.g., Nizoral)—These medicines may increase or decrease the metabolism (breakdown) of bexarotene, leading to higher-than-usual or lower-than-usual amounts of bexarotene in the body

- Gemfibrozil (e.g., Lopid)—This medicine may lead to higher-than-usual amounts of bexarotene in the body
- Insulin (e.g., Humulin, Novolin) or
- Medications that make your body more sensitive to insulin, such as:
  Pioglitazone (e.g., Actos) or
  Rosiglitazone (e.g., Avandia)
- Medications that help your body to secrete more insulin, such as:
  Acetohexamide (e.g., Dymelor) or
  Chlorpropamide (e.g., Diabinese) or
  Glimepiride (e.g., Amaryl) or
  Glipizide (e.g., Glucotrol) or
  Glyburide (e.g., DiaBeta) or
  Tolazamide (e.g., Tolinase) or
  Tolbutamide (e.g., Orinase)—Use of bexarotene may increase the effects of these medicines, which may cause low blood sugar (hypoglycemia)

- Vitamin A supplements (e.g., Aquasol A)—May increase the chance of side effects

Other medical problems—The presence of other medical problems may affect the use of bexarotene. Make sure to tell your doctor if you have any other medical problems, especially

- Bone marrow depression, existing or
- Infection—There may be an increased risk of infections or worsening of infections because of the body's reduced ability to fight them
- Cataracts—May cause new cataracts or worsen previous cataracts
- Chickenpox (including recent exposure) or
- Herpes zoster (shingles)—Risk of severe disease affecting other parts of the body
- Diabetes mellitus—May be more likely to experience low blood sugar (hypoglycemia).
- High cholesterol—Bexarotene can cause an increase in cholesterol levels.
- Kidney disease—May increase the chance of side effects
- Liver disease—Effects of bexarotene may be increased because of slower removal from the body.

- Pancreatitis or
- Risk factors for pancreatitis, such as:
  Drinking large quantities of alcohol or
  Problems with your gallbladder or biliary tract or
  Diabetes mellitus (sugar diabetes) that is not well-controlled or
  High cholesterol that is not well-controlled or
  Taking medicines that cause high levels of triglycerides (fat-like substances) or
  Taking medicines that are toxic to the pancreas or
  Prior pancreatitis—Bexarotene can cause an increase in triglyceride levels which can cause inflammation of the pancreas.
- Photosensitivity—Bexarotene may cause increased sensitivity of the skin to sunlight

Proper Use of This Medicine

Use this medicine exactly as directed by your doctor. Do not use more or less of it, and do not use it more often than your doctor ordered. The exact amount of medicine you need has been carefully worked out. Using too much will increase the risk of side effects, while using too little may not improve your condition.

Dosing—The dose of bexarotene will be different for different patients. *Follow your doctor's orders or the directions on the label.* The following information includes only the average doses of bexarotene. *If your dose is different, do not change it* unless your doctor tells you to do so.

- For *oral* dosage form (capsule):
  —For cutaneous T-cell lymphoma:
  - Adults—Dose is based on body size and must be determined by your doctor. The usual dose is 300 milligrams (mg) for each square meter of body surface area taken once a day with a meal. Your dose may then be adjusted by your doctor.
  - Children—Use and dose must be determined by your doctor.

Missed dose—If you miss a dose of this medicine, take it as soon as possible. However, if it is almost time for your next dose, skip the missed dose and go back to your regular dosing schedule. Do not double doses.

Storage—To store this medicine:

- Keep out of the reach of children.
- Do not store in the bathroom, near the kitchen sink, or in other damp places. Heat or moisture may cause the medicine to break down.
- Do not keep outdated medicine or medicine no longer needed. Ask your health care professional how you should dispose of any medicine you do not use. Be sure that any discarded medicine is out of the reach of children.

Precautions While Using This Medicine

It is very important that your doctor check your progress at regular visits to make sure that this medicine is working properly and to check for unwanted effects.

While you are being treated with bexarotene, and after you stop treatment with it, *do not have any immunizations (vaccinations) without your doctor's approval.* Bexarotene may lower your body's resistance, and there is a chance you might get the infection that the immunization is meant to prevent. In addition, other persons living in your household should not take oral polio vaccine, since there is a chance they could pass the polio virus on to you. Also, avoid persons who have taken oral polio vaccine within the last several months. Do not get close to them, and do not stay in the room with them for very long. If you cannot take these precautions, you should consider wearing a protective face mask that covers the nose and mouth.

Bexarotene can temporarily lower the number of white blood cells in your blood, increasing the chance of getting an infection. It can also lower the number of platelets, which are necessary for proper blood clotting. If this occurs, there are certain precautions you can take, especially when your blood count is low, to reduce the risk of infection or bleeding:

- If you can, avoid people with infections. *Check with your doctor immediately* if you think you are getting an infection or if you get a fever or chills, cough or hoarseness, lower back or side pain, or painful or difficult urination.
- *Check with your doctor immediately* if you notice any unusual bleeding or bruising; black, tarry stools; blood in urine or stools; or pinpoint red spots on your skin.
- Be careful when using a regular toothbrush, dental floss, or toothpick. Your medical doctor, dentist, or nurse may recommend other ways to clean your teeth and gums. Check with your medical doctor before having any dental work done.

- Do not touch your eyes or the inside of your nose unless you have just washed your hands and have not touched anything else in the meantime.
- Be careful not to cut yourself when you are using sharp objects such as a safety razor or fingernail or toenail cutters.
- Avoid contact sports or other situations where bruising or injury could occur.

Bexarotene may cause your skin to be more sensitive to sunlight than it is normally. Exposure to sunlight, even for brief periods of time, may cause a skin rash, itching, redness or other discoloration of the skin, or a severe sunburn. When you begin taking this medicine:

- Stay out of direct sunlight, especially between the hours of 10:00 a.m. and 3:00 p.m., if possible.
- Wear protective clothing, including a hat. Also, wear sunglasses.
- Apply a sun block product that has a skin protection factor (SPF) of at least 15. Some patients may require a product with a higher SPF number, especially if they have a fair complexion. If you have any questions about this, check with your health care professional.
- Apply a sun block lipstick that has an SPF of at least 15 to protect your lips.
- Do not use a sunlamp or tanning bed or booth.

Side Effects of This Medicine

Along with its needed effects, a medicine may cause some unwanted effects. Although not all of these side effects may occur, if they do occur they may need medical attention.

Since this medication is given in varying doses, the actual frequency of side effects may vary. In general, side effects are less common with lower doses than with higher doses.

Check with your doctor as soon as possible if any of the following side effects occur:

More common

Unusual tiredness or weakness; skin rash or other skin and mucous membrane lesions; fever; increase in lipid or cholesterol levels; coldness, dry, puffy skin or weight gain; chills, cough, hoarseness, lower back or side pain or painful or difficult urination; swelling of the arms, feet, hands, or legs

Less Common

Severe stomach pain with nausea or vomiting; shortness of breath; yellow eyes or skin

Other side effects may occur that usually do not need medical attention. These side effects may go away during treatment as your body adjusts to the medicine. However, check with your doctor if any of the following side effects continue or are bothersome:

More common

Abdominal pain; hair loss; loss of appetite; loss of strength or energy, tiredness or weakness; back pain; diarrhea; dry skin; general feeling of discomfort or illness; trouble in sleeping; headache; nausea or vomiting

Other side effects not listed above may also occur in some patients. If you notice any other effects, check with your doctor.

Developed: 03/30/00
Revised: 05/12/00

BIOTIN   Systemic

Other commonly used names are vitamin H, coenzyme R, or vitamin Bw.

Description

Biotin (BYE-oh-tin) supplements are used to prevent or treat biotin deficiency.

Vitamins (VYE-ta-mins) are compounds that you must have for growth and health. They are needed in only small amounts and are usually available in the foods that you eat. Biotin is necessary for formation of fatty acids and glucose, which are used as fuels by the body. It is also important for the metabolism of amino acids and carbohydrates.

A lack of biotin is rare. However, if it occurs it may lead to skin rash, loss of hair, high blood levels of cholesterol, and heart problems.

Some conditions may increase your need for biotin. These include:

- Genetic disorder of biotin deficiency
- Seborrheic determatitis in infants
- Surgical removal of the stomach

Increased need for biotin should be determined by your health care professional.

Claims that biotin supplements are effective in the treatment of acne, eczema (a type of skin disorder), or hair loss have not been proven.

Biotin supplements are available without a prescription in the following dosage forms:

Oral
- Capsules (U.S.)
- Tablets (U.S. and Canada)

Importance of Diet

For good health, it is important that you eat a balanced and varied diet. Follow carefully any diet program your health care professional may recommend. For your specific vitamin and/or mineral needs, ask your health care professional for a list of appropriate foods. If you think that you are not getting enough vitamins and/or minerals in your diet, you may choose to take a dietary supplement.

Biotin is found in various foods, including liver, cauliflower, salmon, carrots, bananas, soy flour, cereals, and yeast. Biotin content of food is reduced by cooking and preserving.

Vitamins alone will not take the place of a good diet and will not provide energy. Your body needs other substances found in food, such as protein, minerals, carbohydrates, and fat. Vitamins themselves cannot work without the presence of other foods.

The daily amount of biotin needed is defined in several different ways.

For U.S.—
- Recommended Dietary Allowances (RDAs) are the amount of vitamins and minerals needed to provide for adequate nutrition in most healthy persons. RDAs for a given nutrient may vary depending on a person's age, sex, and physical condition (e.g., pregnancy).
- Daily Values (DVs) are used on food and dietary supplement labels to indicate the percent of the recommended daily amount of each nutrient that a serving provides. DVs replace the previous designation of United States Recommended Daily Allowances (US-RDAs).

For Canada—
- Recommended Nutrient Intakes (RNIs) are used to determine the amounts of vitamins, minerals, and protein needed to provide adequate nutrition and lessen the risk of chronic disease.

Because lack of biotin is rare, there is no RDA or RNI for it. Normal daily recommended intakes for biotin are generally defined as follows:

Infants and children—
　　Birth to 3 years of age: 10 to 20 micrograms (mcg).
　　4 to 6 years of age: 25 mcg.
　　7 to 10 years of age: 30 mcg.
Adolescents and adults—
　　30 to 100 mcg.

Before Using This Dietary Supplement

If you are taking this dietary supplement without a prescription, carefully read and follow any precautions on the label. For biotin, the following should be considered:

Allergies—Tell your health care professional if you have ever had any unusual or allergic reaction to biotin. Also tell your health care professional if you are allergic to any other substances, such as foods, preservatives, or dyes.

Pregnancy—It is especially important that you are receiving enough vitamins and minerals when you become pregnant and that you continue to receive the right amount of vitamins and minerals throughout your pregnancy. The healthy growth and development of the fetus depend on a steady supply of nutrients from the mother. However, taking large amounts of a dietary supplement in pregnancy may be harmful to the mother and/or fetus and should be avoided.

Breast-feeding—It is especially important that you receive the right amounts of vitamins so that your baby will also get the vitamins needed to grow properly. However, taking large amounts of a dietary supplement while breast-feeding may be harmful to the mother and/or baby and should be avoided.

Children—Problems in children have not been reported with intake of normal daily recommended amounts.

Older adults—Problems in older adults have not been reported with intake of normal daily recommended amounts.

Proper Use of This Dietary Supplement

Dosing—The amount of biotin to meet normal daily recommended intakes will be different for different individuals. The following information includes only the average amounts of biotin.

- For *oral* dosage form (capsules or tablets):
　—To prevent deficiency, the amount taken by mouth is based on normal daily recommended intakes:
　　- Adults and teenagers—30 to 100 micrograms (mcg) per day.
　　- Children 7 to 10 years of age—30 mcg per day.
　　- Children 4 to 6 years of age—25 mcg per day.
　　- Children birth to 3 years of age—10 to 20 mcg per day.
　—To treat deficiency:
　　- Adults, teenagers, and children—Treatment dose is determined by prescriber for each individual based on severity of deficiency.

Missed dose—If you miss taking biotin supplements for one or more days there is no cause for concern, since it takes some time for your body to become seriously low in biotin. However, if your health care professional has recommended that you take biotin, try to remember to take it as directed every day.

Storage—To store this dietary supplement:
- Keep out of the reach of children.
- Store away from heat and direct light.
- Do not store in the bathroom, near the kitchen sink, or in other damp places. Heat or moisture may cause the dietary supplement to break down.
- Keep the dietary supplement from freezing. Do not re-frigerate.
- Do not keep outdated dietary supplements or those no longer needed. Be sure that any discarded dietary sup-plement is out of the reach of children.

Side Effects of This Dietary Supplement

No side effects have been reported for biotin in amounts up to 10 milligrams a day. However, check with your health care professional if you notice any unusual effects while you are taking it.

Revised: 09/26/91
Interim revision: 06/02/92; 04/25/95

BISMUTH SUBSALICYLATE   Oral

Commonly used brand name(s):

In the U.S.—

Bismatrol	Pepto-Bismol Easy-to-
Bismatrol Extra Strength	Swallow Caplets
Pepto-Bismol	Pepto-Bismol Maximum
	Strength

Generic name product may be available.

In Canada—
Bismed
Pepto-Bismol
PMS-Bismuth Subsalicylate

Description

Bismuth subsalicylate (BIS-muth sub-sa-LIS-a-late) is used to treat diarrhea. It is also used to relieve the symptoms of an upset stomach, such as heartburn, indigestion, and nausea.

This medicine is available without a prescription; however, your doctor may have special instructions on the proper use and dose for your medical problem. Bismuth subsalicylate is available in the following dosage forms:

Oral
- Oral suspension (U.S. and Canada)
- Tablets (U.S.)
- Chewable tablets (U.S. and Canada)

Before Using This Medicine

If you are taking this medicine without a prescription, carefully read and follow any precautions on the label. For bismuth subsalicylate, the following should be considered:

Allergies—Tell your doctor if you have ever had any un-usual or allergic reaction to bismuth subsalicylate or to other

salicylates, such as aspirin, including methyl salicylate (oil of wintergreen), or to any of the following medicines:
- Carprofen (e.g., Rimadyl)
- Diclofenac (e.g., Voltaren)
- Diflunisal (e.g., Dolobid)
- Fenoprofen (e.g., Nalfon)
- Floctafenine (e.g., Idarac)
- Flurbiprofen taken by mouth (e.g., Ansaid)
- Ibuprofen (e.g., Motrin)
- Indomethacin (e.g., Indocin)
- Ketoprofen (e.g., Orudis)
- Ketorolac (e.g., Toradol)
- Meclofenamate (e.g., Meclomen)
- Mefenamic acid (e.g., Ponstel)
- Naproxen (e.g., Naprosyn)
- Oxyphenbutazone (e.g., Tandearil)
- Phenylbutazone (e.g., Butazolidin)
- Piroxicam (e.g., Feldene)
- Sulindac (e.g., Clinoril)
- Suprofen (e.g., Suprol)
- Tiaprofenic acid (e.g., Surgam)
- Tolmetin (e.g., Tolectin)
- Zomepirac (e.g., Zomax)

Also tell your health care professional if you are allergic to any other substances, such as certain foods, sulfites or other preservatives, or dyes.

Diet—Make certain your health care professional knows if you are on any special diet, such as a low-sodium or low-sugar diet.

Pregnancy—The occasional use of bismuth subsalicylate is not likely to cause problems in the fetus or in the newborn baby. However, based on what is known about the use of other salicylates, especially at high doses and for long pe-riods of time, the following information may also apply for bis-muth subsalicylate.

Salicylates have not been shown to cause birth defects in humans. However, studies in animals have shown that salic-ylates may cause birth defects.

There is a chance that regular use of salicylates late in preg-nancy may cause unwanted effects on the heart or blood flow in the fetus or in the newborn infant.

Use of salicylates during the last 2 weeks of pregnancy may cause bleeding problems in the fetus before or during delivery or in the newborn infant. Also, too much use of salicylates during the last 3 months of pregnancy may increase the length of pregnancy, prolong labor, cause other problems during delivery, or cause severe bleeding in the mother be-fore, during, or after delivery.

Breast-feeding—Salicylates pass into the breast milk. Al-though they have not been shown to cause problems in nursing babies, it is possible that problems may occur if large amounts of salicylates are taken regularly.

Children—The fluid loss caused by diarrhea may result in a severe condition. For this reason, medicine for diarrhea must not be given to young children (under 3 years of age) without first checking with their doctor. In older children with diarrhea, medicine for diarrhea may be used, but it is also very important that a sufficient amount of liquids be given to replace the fluid lost by the body. If you have any questions about this, check with your health care professional.

Also, children are usually more sensitive to the effects of sa-licylates, especially if they have a fever or have lost large amounts of body fluid because of vomiting, diarrhea, or sweating.

The bismuth in this medicine may cause severe constipation in children.

In addition, do not use this medicine to treat nausea or vomiting in children or teenagers who have or are recovering from the flu or chickenpox. If nausea or vomiting is present, check with the child's doctor because this could be an early sign of Reye's syndrome.

Older adults—The fluid loss caused by diarrhea may result in a severe condition. For this reason, elderly persons with diarrhea should not take this medicine without first checking with their doctor. It is also very important that a sufficient amount of liquids be taken to replace the fluid lost by the body. If you have any questions about this, check with your health care professional.

Also, the elderly may be more sensitive to the effects of salicylates. This may increase the chance of side effects during treatment. In addition, the bismuth in this medicine may cause severe constipation in the elderly.

Other medicines—Although certain medicines should not be used together at all, in other cases two different medicines may be used together even if an interaction might occur. In these cases, your doctor may want to change the dose, or other precautions may be necessary. When taking bismuth subsalicylate it is especially important that your health care professional know if you are taking any of the following:

- Anticoagulants (blood thinners) or
- Heparin—The salicylate in this medicine may increase the chance of bleeding

- Antidiabetics, oral (diabetes medicine you take by mouth)—This medicine may make the levels of sugar in the blood become too low

- Medicine for pain and/or inflammation (except narcotics)—If these medicines contain salicylates, use of bismuth subsalicylate (which also contains salicylate) may lead to increased side effects and overdose

- Probenecid (e.g., Benemid) or
- Sulfinpyrazone (e.g., Anturane)—Bismuth subsalicylate may make these medicines less effective for treating gout

- Tetracyclines by mouth (medicine for infection)—The tablet form of bismuth subsalicylate should be taken at least 1 to 3 hours before or after tetracyclines; otherwise it may decrease the effectiveness of the tetracycline

Other medical problems—The presence of other medical problems may affect the use of bismuth subsalicylate. Make sure you tell your doctor if you have any other medical problems, especially:

- Dysentery—This condition may get worse; a different kind of treatment may be needed

- Gout—The salicylate in this medicine may worsen the gout and make the medicines taken for gout less effective

- Hemophilia or other bleeding problems—The salicylate in this medicine may increase the chance of bleeding

- Kidney disease—There is a greater chance of side effects because the body may be unable to get rid of the bismuth subsalicylate

- Stomach ulcer—Use of this medicine may make the ulcer worse

Proper Use of This Medicine

For safe and effective use of this medicine:

- Follow your doctor's instructions if this medicine was prescribed.
- Follow the manufacturer's package directions if you are treating yourself.

For patients using this medicine to treat diarrhea:

- *It is very important that the fluid lost by the body be replaced and that a proper diet be followed.* For the first 24 hours you should drink plenty of clear liquids, such as ginger ale, decaffeinated cola, decaffeinated tea, broth, and gelatin. During the next 24 hours you may eat bland foods, such as cooked cereals, bread, crackers, and applesauce. Fruits, vegetables, fried or spicy foods, bran, candy, and caffeine and alcoholic beverages may make the diarrhea worse.

- If too much fluid has been lost by the body due to the diarrhea a serious condition may develop. Check with your doctor as soon as possible if any of the following signs of too much fluid loss occur:
  Decreased urination
  Dizziness and lightheadedness
  Dryness of mouth
  Increased thirst
  Wrinkled skin

Dosing—The dose of bismuth subsalicylate will be different for different patients. *Follow your doctor's orders or the directions on the label.* The following information includes only the average doses of bismuth subsalicylate. *If your dose is different, do not change it* unless your doctor tells you to do so.

The number of tablets or tablespoonfuls or teaspoonfuls of suspension that you take depends on the strength of the medicine.

- For *oral* dosage form (suspension):
  —For diarrhea or upset stomach:
  - Adults and teenagers—The usual dose is 2 tablespoonfuls every half-hour to one hour if needed. You should not take more than 16 tablespoonfuls of the regular-strength suspension or 8 tablespoonfuls of the concentrate in twenty-four hours.
  - Children 9 to 12 years of age—The usual dose is 1 tablespoonful every half-hour to one hour. You should not take more than 8 tablespoonfuls of the regular-strength suspension or 4 tablespoonfuls of the concentrate in twenty-four hours.
  - Children 6 to 9 years of age—The usual dose is 2 teaspoonfuls every half-hour to one hour. You should not take more than 16 teaspoonfuls of the regular-strength suspension or 8 teaspoonfuls of the concentrate in twenty-four hours.
  - Children 3 to 6 years of age—The usual dose is 1 teaspoonful every half-hour to one hour. You should not take more than 8 teaspoonfuls of the regular-strength suspension or 4 teaspoonfuls of the concentrate in twenty-four hours.
  - Children up to 3 years of age—Dose is based on body weight:
    —For children weighing 6.4 to 13 kilograms (kg) (14 to 28 pounds): The usual dose is ½ tea-

spoonful of the regular-strength suspension or ¼ teaspoonful of the concentrate.
—For children weighing over 13 kg (29 pounds): The usual dose is 1 teaspoonful of the regular-strength suspension or ½ teaspoonful of the concentrate.

- For *oral* dosage forms (tablets or chewable tablets):
  —For diarrhea or upset stomach:
    - Adults and teenagers—The usual dose is 2 tablets every half-hour to one hour. You should not take more than 16 tablets in twenty-four hours.
    - Children 9 to 12 years of age—The usual dose is 1 tablet every half-hour to one hour. You should not take more than 8 tablets in twenty-four hours.
    - Children up to 9 years of age—The oral suspension is the preferred dosage form for this age group.

Missed dose—If your doctor has ordered you to take this medicine according to a regular schedule and you miss a dose, take it as soon as you remember. However, if it is almost time for your next dose, skip the missed dose and go back to your regular dosing schedule. Do not double doses.

Storage—To store this medicine:
- Keep out of the reach of children. Overdose is very dangerous in young children.
- Store away from heat and direct light.
- Do not store the tablet form of this medicine in the bathroom, near the kitchen sink, or in other damp places. Heat or moisture may cause the medicine to break down.
- Keep the liquid form of this medicine from freezing.
- Do not keep outdated medicine or medicine no longer needed. Be sure that any discarded medicine is out of the reach of children.

Precautions While Using This Medicine

Check the labels of all over-the-counter (OTC), nonprescription, and prescription medicines you now take. If any contain aspirin or other salicylates, be especially careful. Using other salicylate-containing products while taking this medicine may lead to overdose. If you have any questions about this, check with your health care professional.

For diabetic patients:
- False urine sugar test results may occur if you are regularly taking large amounts of bismuth subsalicylate or other salicylates.
- Smaller doses or occasional use of bismuth subsalicylate usually will not affect urine sugar tests. However, check with your health care professional (especially if your diabetes is not well-controlled) if:
  —you are not sure how much salicylate you are taking every day.
  —you notice any change in your urine sugar test results.
  —you have any other questions about this possible problem.

If you think that you or anyone else may have taken an overdose, get emergency help at once. Taking an overdose of this medicine may cause unconsciousness or death. Signs of overdose include convulsions (seizures), hearing loss, confusion, ringing or buzzing in the ears, severe drowsiness or tiredness, severe excitement or nervousness, and fast or deep breathing.

If you are taking this medicine for diarrhea, check with your doctor:
- if your symptoms do not improve within 2 days or if they become worse.
- if you also have a high fever.

Side Effects of This Medicine

Along with its needed effects, a medicine may cause some unwanted effects. Although not all of these side effects may occur, if they do occur they may need medical attention.

When this medicine is used occasionally or for short periods of time at low doses, side effects usually are rare. However, check with your doctor immediately if any of the following side effects occur, since they may indicate that too much medicine is being taken:

Anxiety; any loss of hearing; confusion; constipation (severe); diarrhea (severe or continuing); difficulty in speaking or slurred speech; dizziness or lightheadedness; drowsiness (severe); fast or deep breathing; headache (severe or continuing); increased sweating; increased thirst; mental depression; muscle spasms (especially of face, neck, and back); muscle weakness; nausea or vomiting (severe or continuing); ringing or buzzing in ears (continuing); stomach pain (severe or continuing); trembling; uncontrollable flapping movements of the hands (especially in elderly patients) or other uncontrolled body movements; vision problems

In some patients bismuth subsalicylate may cause dark tongue and/or grayish black stools. This is only temporary and will go away when you stop taking this medicine.

Other side effects not listed above may also occur in some patients. If you notice any other effects, check with your doctor.

Revised: 02/03/92
Interim revision: 09/01/94

BISMUTH SUBSALICYLATE, METRONIDAZOLE, AND TETRACYCLINE—FOR *H. PYLORI*
Systemic

Commonly used brand name(s):

In the U.S.—
Helidac

Description

Bismuth subsalicylate (BIS-muth sub-sa-LIS-a-late), metronidazole (me-troe-NI-da-zole), and tetracycline (tet-ra-SYE-kleen) are taken together with a histamine H_2-receptor antagonist to treat ulcers related to infection with the *H. pylori* bacteria (germ).

This package contains a combination of three different medicines. The individual medicines contained in this package should not be used alone or for other purposes than to treat ulcers related to infection with *H. pylori*.

This combination of medicines is available only with your doctor's prescription, in the following dosage forms:

Oral
- Blister card containing chewable tablets, tablets, and capsules (U.S.)

Before Using This Medicine

In deciding to use a medicine, the risks of taking this combination of medicines must be weighed against the good it will do. This is a decision you and your doctor will make. For this combination of medicines (bismuth subsalicylate, metronidazole, and tetracycline), the following should be considered:

Allergies—Tell your doctor if you have ever had any unusual or allergic reaction to bismuth subsalicylate, aspirin or other salicylates, metronidazole, or tetracycline. Also tell your health care professional if you are allergic to any other substances, such as foods, preservatives, or dyes.

Pregnancy—The use of this combination of medicines in pregnant women is not recommended. Tetracycline may have toxic effects on the fetus during the early stages of pregnancy. Also, use of tetracycline in the last half of pregnancy may cause the unborn infant's teeth to become permanently discolored.

Breast-feeding—Use of this combination of medicines is not recommended since metronidazole amd tetracycline pass into breast milk and may cause serious unwanted effects in nursing babies.

Children—Infants and children up to 8 years of age should not take this combination of medicines unless directed by the child's doctor. Tetracycline may cause permanent discoloration of the teeth.

Children or teenagers who have or who are recovering from chickenpox or influenza should not use this combination of medicines unless directed by the child's doctor. If nausea or vomiting occurs after taking this combination of medicines, check with the child's doctor. Nausea or vomiting could be early signs of Reye's syndrome, a rare but serious illness.

Older adults—Many medicines have not been studied specifically in older people. Therefore, it may not be known whether they work exactly the same way they do in younger adults or if they cause different side effects or problems in older people. There is no specific information comparing the use of this combination of medicines (bismuth subsalicylate, metronidazole, and tetracycline) in the elderly with its use in other age groups.

Other medicines—Although certain medicines should not be used together at all, in other cases different medicines may be used together even if an interaction might occur. In these cases, your doctor may want to change the dose, or other precautions may be necessary. When you are taking this combination of medicines (bismuth subsalicylate, metronidazole, and tetracycline), it is especially important that your health care professional know if you are taking any of the following:
- Alcohol—Consuming alcohol during treatment or for at least 1 day after treatment with metronidazole in this combination of medicines may cause stomach pain, nausea, vomiting, headaches, and flushing or redness of the face

- Antacids or
- Iron-containing medicine or
- Sodium bicarbonate or
- Zinc—Use of these medicines with tetracycline in this combination of medicines may decrease the effect of tetracycline
- Anticoagulants (blood thinners)—This combination of medicines may change the bleeding times in patients taking anticoagulants
- Antidiabetic medicines (diabetes medicine you take by mouth) or
- Insulin—The bismuth subsalicylate in this combination of medicines may make the levels of sugar in the blood become too low
- Aspirin or
- Other salicylates—The bismuth subsalicylate in this combination of medicines may add to the effects of aspirin or other salicylates, increasing the risk of toxicity
- Barbiturates, especially phenobarbital or
- Carbamazepine (e.g., Tegretol) or
- Glutethimide (e.g., Doriglute) or
- Phenylbutazone (e.g., Butazolidin) or
- Phenytoin (e.g., Dilantin) or
- Primidone (e.g., Mysoline) or
- Rifampin (e.g., Rifadin)—Taking any of these medicines with metronidazole in this combination of medicines may decrease the effects of metronidazole
- Disulfiram (e.g., Antabuse)—Patients taking disulfiram with metronidazole in this combination of medicines may have an increased risk of side effects
- Oral contraceptives (birth control pills)—Use of birth control pills with tetracycline in this combination of medicines may decrease the effect of the birth control pills and increase the chance of unwanted pregnancy
- Penicillin—Use of penicillin with tetracycline in this combination of medicines may decrease the effects of penicillin

Other medical problems—The presence of other medical problems may affect the use of this combination of medicines (bismuth subsalicylate, metronidazole, and tetracycline). Make sure you tell your doctor if you have any other medical problems, especially:
- Kidney disease or
- Liver disease—Higher blood levels of metronidazole and tetracycline in this combination of medicines may occur, resulting in an increased risk of side effects

Proper Use of This Medicine

This combination of medicines (bismuth subsalicylate, metronidazole, and tetracycline) comes with instructions for the patient included in the package. Make sure you read and understand the instructions, or ask your health care professional if you need additional information or explanation. It is important that you understand and follow the instructions exactly.

Also, it is important that you complete the full course of therapy with this combination of medicines to help clear up the infection from *H. pylori* related to your ulcer.

Dosing—Each day's therapy is packaged on a blister card that contains eight chewable tablets (each containing 262.4 milligrams [mg] of bismuth subsalicylate), four tablets (each containing 250 mg of metronidazole), and four capsules (each containing 500 mg of tetracycline).

- For *oral* dosage forms (blister card containing chewable tablets, tablets, and capsules):
  - For the treatment of ulcers related to infection with *H. pylori*:
    - Adults—For each dose of this combination of medicines:
      - Chew and swallow two tablets of bismuth subsalicylate (525 mg)
      - Swallow one tablet of metronidazole (250 mg)
      - Swallow one capsule of tetracycline (500 mg)
      Be sure to swallow the tablet of metronidazole and the capsule of tetracycline with a full glass (eight ounces) of water. This will help prevent irritation of the esophagus (tube between the throat and stomach) or stomach.
      Each dose of this combination of medicines (bismuth subsalicylate, metronidazole, and tetracycline) is taken four times a day, with meals and at bedtime, for fourteen days. Your doctor will also prescribe for you another medicine, a histamine H$_2$-receptor antagonist, which will come with its own directions and must be taken along with this combination of medicines
    - Children—Use and dose must be determined by your doctor.

Missed dose—If you miss a dose of this combination of medicines, skip the missed dose and go back to your regular dosing schedule. Do not double doses. If you miss more than four doses of this combination of medicines, check with your doctor.

Storage—To store this combination of medicines:
- Keep out of the reach of children.
- Store away from heat and direct light.
- Do not store in the bathroom, near the kitchen sink, or in other damp places. Heat or moisture may cause these medicines to break down.
- Keep these medicines from freezing. Do not refrigerate.
- Do not keep outdated medicine or medicine no longer needed. Be sure that any discarded medicine is out of the reach of children.

Precautions While Using This Medicine

Check the labels of all over-the-counter (OTC), nonprescription, and prescription medicines you now take. If any contain aspirin or other salicylates, be especially careful. Using other salicylate-containing products while taking bismuth subsalicylate in this combination of medicines may lead to overdose. If you have any questions about this, check with your health care professional.

Do not take milk, milk formulas, or other dairy products within 1 to 2 hours of the time you take tetracycline in this combination of medicines. Milk and other dairy products may keep tetracycline from working properly.

Do not take antacids or sodium bicarbonate within 1 to 2 hours of the time you take tetracycline in this combination of medicines. Also, *do not take iron preparations* (including vitamin preparations that contain iron) within 2 to 3 hours of the time you take tetracycline in this combination of medicines. To do so may keep tetracycline from working properly.

Drinking alcoholic beverages while taking metronidazole in this combination of medicines may cause stomach pain, nausea, vomiting, headache, or flushing or redness of the face. Other alcohol-containing preparations (for example, elixirs, cough syrups, tonics) may also cause problems. These problems may last for at least a day after you stop taking metronidazole. Also, metronidazole may cause alcoholic beverages to taste different. Therefore, *you should not drink alcoholic beverages or take other alcohol-containing preparations while you are taking metronidazole in this combination of medicines and for at least a day after stopping it.*

The metronidazole in this combination of medicines may cause some people to become dizzy or lightheaded. *Make sure you know how you react to this combination of medicines before you drive, use machines, or do anything else that could be dangerous if you are dizzy or are not alert.*

Oral contraceptives (birth control pills) may not work properly if you take them while you are taking tetracycline in this combination of medicines. Unplanned pregnancies may occur. You should use a different or additional means of birth control while you are taking tetracycline in this combination of medicines. If you have any questions about this, check with your health care professional.

The tetracycline in this combination of medicines may cause your skin to be more sensitive to sunlight than it is normally. Exposure to sunlight, even for brief periods of time, may cause a skin rash, itching, redness or other discoloration of the skin, or a severe sunburn. When you begin taking the tetracycline in this combination of medicines:
- Stay out of direct sunlight, especially between the hours of 10:00 a.m. and 3:00 p.m., if possible.
- Wear protective clothing, including a hat. Also, wear sunglasses.
- Apply a sun block product that has a skin protection factor (SPF) of at least 15. Some patients may require a product with a higher SPF number, especially if they have a fair complexion. If you have any questions about this, check with your health care professional.
- Apply a sun block lipstick that has an SPF of at least 15 to protect your lips.
- Do not use a sunlamp or tanning bed or booth.

You may still be more sensitive to sunlight or sunlamps for 2 weeks to several months or more after stopping tetracycline in this combination of medicines. *If you have a severe reaction, check with your doctor.*

Before having surgery (including dental surgery) with a general anesthetic, tell the medical doctor or dentist in charge that you are taking tetracycline in this combination of medicines.

Side Effects of This Medicine

Along with its needed effects, a medicine may cause some unwanted effects. Although not all of these side effects may occur, if they do occur they may need medical attention.

Check with your doctor as soon as possible if any of the following side effects occur:

More common
  Abdominal pain; bloody or black, tarry stools; diarrhea; nausea

Less common
  Burning, prickling, or tingling sensations; dizziness; vomiting

Rare
  Bloody vomit; convulsions (seizures); fainting; heart at-

tack; high blood pressure; irritation of the mouth; irritation of the tongue; joint pain and swelling; pain; sensitivity of skin to sunlight; skin rash; trouble in swallowing

Symptoms of overdose
> Clumsiness or unsteadiness; confusion; continuing ringing or buzzing in ears; convulsions; diarrhea; fast heartbeat; fast or deep breathing; fever; nausea; pain, numbness, or tingling in arms, legs, hands, or feet; unusual tiredness; vomiting

Other side effects may occur that usually do not need medical attention. These side effects may go away during treatment as your body adjusts to the medicine. However, check with your doctor if any of the following side effects continue or are bothersome:

Less common or rare
> Burning or itching around anus; constipation; general feeling of discomfort or illness; loss of appetite; nervousness; trouble in sleeping; unusual tiredness or weakness

In some patients, bismuth subsalicylate in this combination of medicines may cause dark tongue and/or grayish black stools. This is only temporary and will go away when you stop taking bismuth subsalicylate.

Other side effects not listed above may also occur in some patients. If you notice any other effects, check with your doctor.

Developed: 07/28/98

BLEOMYCIN Systemic

Commonly used brand name(s):

In the U.S.—
Blenoxane

In Canada—
Blenoxane

Description

Bleomycin (blee-oh-MYE-sin) belongs to the general group of medicines called antineoplastics. It is used to treat several types of cancer, including cervix and uterus cancer, head and neck cancer, testicle and penile cancer, and certain types of lymphoma. Bleomycin also may used for other conditions, as determined by your doctor.

Bleomycin seems to act by interfering with the growth of cancer cells, which are eventually destroyed. Since the growth of normal body cells may also be affected by bleomycin, other effects will also occur. Some of these may be serious and must be reported to your doctor. Other effects, like darkening of skin or hair loss, may not be serious but may cause concern. Some effects may not occur for months or years after the medicine is used.

Before you begin treatment with bleomycin, you and your doctor should talk about the good this medicine will do as well as the risks of using it.

Bleomycin is to be administered only by or under the immediate supervision of your doctor. It is available in the following dosage form:

Parenteral
> • Injection (U.S. and Canada)

Before Using This Medicine

In deciding to use a medicine, the risks of taking the medicine must be weighed against the good it will do. This is a decision you and your doctor will make. For bleomycin, the following should be considered:

Allergies—Tell your doctor if you have ever had any unusual or allergic reaction to bleomycin.

Pregnancy—Studies have not been done in pregnant women. However, there is a chance that this medicine may cause birth defects if either the male or female is receiving it at the time of conception or if it is used during pregnancy. Studies in mice given large doses of bleomycin have shown that it causes birth defects. In addition, many cancer medicines may cause sterility which could be permanent. Although sterility has not been reported with this medicine, the possibility should be kept in mind.

Be sure that you have discussed this with your doctor before receiving this medicine. It is best to use some kind of birth control while you are receiving bleomycin. Tell your doctor right away if you think you have become pregnant while receiving bleomycin.

Breast-feeding—Because bleomycin may cause serious side effects, breast-feeding is generally not recommended while you are receiving it.

Children—Although there is no specific information comparing use of bleomycin in children with use in other age groups, this medicine is not expected to cause different side effects or problems in children than it does in adults.

Older adults—Lung problems are more likely to occur in elderly patients (over 70 years of age), who are usually more sensitive to the effects of bleomycin.

Other medical problems—The presence of other medical problems may affect the use of bleomycin. Make sure you tell your doctor if you have any other medical problems, especially:

> • Kidney disease—Effects of bleomycin may be increased because of slower removal from the body
>
> • Liver disease—Bleomycin can cause liver problems
>
> • Lung disease—Bleomycin may worsen the condition

Smoking—Tell your doctor if you smoke. The risk of lung problems is increased in people who smoke.

Proper Use of This Medicine

Bleomycin is sometimes given together with certain other medicines. If you are using a combination of medicines, it is important that you receive each medicine at the proper time. If you are taking some of these medicines by mouth, ask your health care professional to help you plan a way to take them at the right times.

Bleomycin often causes nausea, vomiting, and loss of appetite. However, it is very important that you continue to receive the medicine, even if you begin to feel ill. Ask your health care professional for ways to lessen these effects.

Dosing—The dose of bleomycin will be different for different patients. The dose that is used may depend on a number of things, including what the medicine is being used for, the patient's weight, and whether or not other medicines are also being taken. *If you are receiving bleomycin at home, follow your doctor's orders or the directions on the label.* If you have any questions about the proper dose of bleomycin, ask your doctor.

Precautions While Using This Medicine

It is very important that your doctor check your progress at regular visits to make sure that this medicine is working properly and to check for unwanted effects.

Before having any kind of surgery (including dental surgery) or emergency treatment, *tell the medical doctor or dentist in charge that you are receiving or have received this medicine.*

Side Effects of This Medicine

Along with its needed effects, a medicine may cause some unwanted effects. Although not all of these side effects may occur, if they do occur they may need medical attention.

Also, because of the way these medicines act on the body, there is a chance that they might cause other unwanted effects that may not occur until months or years after the medicine is used. These delayed effects may include certain types of cancer, such as leukemia. Discuss these possible effects with your doctor.

Check with your doctor or nurse immediately if the following side effects occur:

More common
  Fever and chills (occurring within 3 to 6 hours after a dose)

Less common
  Confusion; faintness; wheezing

Rare
  Chest pain (sudden severe); weakness in arms or legs (sudden)

Check with your health care professional as soon as possible if any of the following side effects occur:

More common
  Cough; shortness of breath; sores in mouth and on lips

Other side effects may occur that usually do not need medical attention. These side effects may go away during treatment as your body adjusts to the medicine. Also, your health care professional may be able to tell you about ways to prevent or reduce some of these side effects. Check with your health care professional if any of the following side effects continue or are bothersome or if you have any questions about them:

More common
  Darkening or thickening of skin; dark stripes on skin; itching of skin; skin rash or colored bumps on fingertips, elbows, or palms; skin redness or tenderness; swelling of fingers; vomiting and loss of appetite

Less common
  Changes in fingernails or toenails; weight loss

Bleomycin may cause a temporary loss of hair in some people. After treatment has ended, normal hair growth should return, although it may take several months.

Side effects that affect your lungs (for example, cough and shortness of breath) may be more likely to occur if you smoke.

After you stop receiving bleomycin, it may still produce some side effects that need attention. During this period of time, check with your health care professional *immediately* if you notice either of the following:
  Cough; shortness of breath

Other side effects not listed above may also occur in some patients. If you notice any other effects, check with your health care professional.

Additional Information

Once a medicine has been approved for marketing for a certain use, experience may show that it is also useful for other medical problems. Although this use is not included in product labeling, bleomycin is used in certain patients with the following medical conditions:

• Bone cancer
• Kaposi's sarcoma
• Malignant melanoma
• Mycosis fungoides (a type of lymphoma)
• Skin cancer
• Thyroid cancer
• Verruca vulgaris (warts)

For patients being treated with bleomycin for warts:
• Bleomycin is used to treat severe cases of warts when other treatments have not worked.
• Before using bleomycin, tell your doctor if you have problems with circulation. Bleomycin can cause paleness or coldness in fingers treated for warts.
• Bleomycin is injected directly into the wart. Because it is not absorbed into the body, it does not cause loss of hair, lung problems, or other unwanted effects described above. However, it may cause burning or pain at the place of injection. Skin rash or itching, nail loss, and pain or coldness in the finger where bleomycin was injected have also been reported.

Other than the above information, there is no additional information relating to proper use, precautions, or side effects for these uses.

Revised: 06/24/98

BOTULINUM TOXIN TYPE A
Parenteral-Local

Commonly used brand name(s):

In the U.S.—
  Botox

In Canada—
  Botox

Description

Botulinum toxin type A (BOT-yoo-lye-num) is used to treat certain eye conditions, such as:
• Blepharospasm—A condition in which the eyelid will not stay open, because of a spasm of a muscle of the eye.

• Strabismus—A condition in which the eyes do not line up properly.

Botulinum toxin type A is injected into the surrounding muscle or tissue of the eye, but not into the eye itself. Depending on your condition, more than one treatment may be required.

This medicine is to be administered only by, or under the immediate supervision of, your doctor. It is available in the following dosage form:

Parenteral-Local
• Injection (U.S. and Canada)

Before Receiving This Medicine

In deciding to receive a medicine, the risks of receiving the medicine must be weighed against the good it will do. This is a decision you and your doctor will make. For botulinum toxin type A, the following should be considered:

Allergies—Tell your doctor if you have ever had any unusual or allergic reaction to botulinum toxin type A. Also tell your health care professional if you are allergic to any other substances.

Pregnancy—Studies on effects in pregnancy have not been done in either humans or animals.

Breast-feeding—It is not known whether botulinum toxin type A passes into the breast milk. However, this medicine has not been reported to cause problems in nursing babies.

Children—Studies on this medicine have been done only in adult patients, and there is no specific information comparing use of botulinum toxin type A in children up to 12 years of age with use in other age groups.

Older adults—Many medicines have not been studied specifically in older people. Therefore, it may not be known whether they work exactly the same way they do in younger adults. Although there is no specific information comparing use of botulinum toxin type A in the elderly with use in other age groups, this medicine is not expected to cause different side effects or problems in older people than it does in younger adults.

Other medicines—Although certain medicines should not be used together at all, in other cases two different medicines may be used together even if an interaction might occur. In these cases, your doctor may want to change the dose, or other precautions may be necessary. Tell your health care professional if you are using any other ophthalmic prescription or nonprescription (over-the-counter [OTC]) medicine.

Other medical problems—The presence of other medical problems may affect the use of botulinum toxin type A. Make sure you tell your doctor if you have any other medical problems, especially:

• Heart problems or other medical conditions that may worsen with rapidly increasing activity—Treatment with botulinum toxin type A may give you better vision and the desire to become more active in your daily life; this may put a strain on your heart and body

• Infection with *Clostridium botulinum* toxin (botulism poisoning), history of—Persons with a history of infection with *Clostridium botulinum* toxin (botulism poisoning) may have produced antibodies that may interfere with botulinum toxin type A therapy and make it less effective

Proper Use of This Medicine

Dosing—The dose of botulinum toxin type A will be different for different patients. The following information includes only the average doses of botulinum toxin type A.

• For *injection* dosage form:
—For certain eye conditions:
• Adults and children 12 years of age and older—One or more injections into the muscles around the eyes one or more times, depending on the condition being treated.
• Children up to 12 years of age—Use and dose must be determined by your doctor.

Precautions After Receiving This Medicine

After you have received this medicine and your vision is better, you may find that you are a lot more active than you were before. You should increase your activities slowly and carefully to allow your heart and body time to get stronger. Also, before you start any exercise program, check with your doctor.

Side Effects of This Medicine

Along with its needed effects, a medicine may cause some unwanted effects. Although not all of these side effects may occur, if they do occur they may need medical attention.

Check with your doctor as soon as possible if any of the following side effects occur:
More common—For blepharospasm
Dryness of the eye; inability to close the eyelid completely
Less common or rare—For blepharospasm
Decreased blinking; irritation of the cornea (colored portion) of the eye; turning outward or inward of the edge of the eyelid

Other side effects may occur that usually do not need medical attention. These side effects may go away as your body adjusts to the medicine. However, check with your doctor if any of the following side effects continue or are bothersome:
More common—For blepharospasm
Blue or purplish bruise on eyelid; drooping of the upper eyelid; irritation or watering of the eye; sensitivity of the eye to light
More common—For horizontal strabismus
Drooping of the upper eyelid; eye pointing upward or downward instead of straight ahead
Less common or rare—For blepharospasm or strabismus
Skin rash; swelling of the eyelid skin
Less common or rare—For horizontal strabismus
Difficulty finding the location of objects; double vision

Other side effects not listed above may also occur in some patients. If you notice any other effects, check with your doctor.

Additional Information

Once a medicine has been approved for marketing for a certain use, experience may show that it is also useful for other medical problems. Although these uses are not included in product labeling, botulinum toxin type A is used in certain patients with the following medical conditions:

- Deep facial lines or wrinkles
- Frey's syndrome (gustatory sweating) (red area and sweating on the cheek while eating)
- Hyperhidrosis (severe sweating of the palms and armpits)
- Spasms of the arms, feet, hands, or legs caused by brain injury, multiple sclerosis, spinal cord injury, or stroke
- Spasms of the arms and legs in children with cerebral palsy
- Spasms of the face
- Spasms of the hand, including writer's cramp and musician's cramp
- Spasms of the neck
- Spasms of the vocal cords

Revised: 01/24/2001

BOTULINUM TOXIN TYPE B
Parenteral-Local—INTRODUCTORY VERSION

Commonly used brand name(s):

In the U.S.—
Myobloc

Description

Botulinum toxin type B (BOT-yoo-lye-num) is used to treat abnormal head position and neck pain that is a result of cervical dystonia.

Botulinum toxin type B is injected into the muscles that are affected. Depending on your condition, more than one treatment may be required.

This medicine is to be administered only by, or under the immediate supervision of, your doctor. It is available in the following dosage form:

Parenteral
- Injection (U.S.)

Before Using This Medicine

In deciding to use a medicine, the risks of receiving the medicine must be weighed against the good it will do. This is a decision you and your doctor will make. For botulinum toxin type B, the following should be considered:

Allergies—Tell your doctor if you have ever had any unusual or allergic reaction to botulinum toxin type B or any other type of botulinum toxin. Also tell your health care professional if you are allergic to any other substances, such as foods, preservatives, or dyes.

Pregnancy—Studies on effects in pregnancy have not been done in either humans or animals.

Breast-feeding—It is not known whether botulinum toxin type B passes into the breast milk. Although most medicines pass into breast milk in small amounts, many of them may be used safely while breast-feeding. Mothers who are taking this medicine and who wish to breast-feed should discuss this with their doctor.

Children—Studies on this medicine have been done only in adult patients, and there is no specific information comparing use of botulinum toxin type B in children with use in other age groups.

Older adults—Many medicines have not been studied specifically in older people. Therefore, it may not be known whether they work exactly the same way they do in younger adults. Although there is no specific information comparing use of botulinum toxin type B in the elderly with use in other age groups, this medicine is not expected to cause different side effects or problems in older people than it does in younger adults.

Other medicines—Although certain medicines should not be used together at all, in other cases two different medicines may be used together even if an interaction might occur. In these cases, your doctor may want to change the dose, or other precautions may be necessary. Tell your health care professional if you are using any other prescription or nonprescription (over-the-counter [OTC]) medicine.

Proper Use of This Medicine

Dosing—The dose of botulinum toxin type B will be different for different patients. The following information includes only the average doses of botulinum toxin type B.

- For *injection* dosage form:
  —For abnormal head position and neck pain
    - Adults—One or more injections into the affected muscles for a total of 2500 to 5000 units of botulinum toxin type B.
    - Children—Use and dose must be determined by your doctor.

Side Effects of This Medicine

Along with its needed effects, a medicine may cause some unwanted effects. Although not all of these side effects may occur, if they do occur they may need medical attention.

Check with your doctor as soon as possible if any of the following side effects occur:
More common
    Difficulty swallowing; infection

Other side effects may occur that usually do not need medical attention. These side effects may go away during treatment as your body adjusts to the medicine. However, check with your doctor if any of the following side effects continue or are bothersome:
More common
    Acid or sour stomach; back pain; belching; cough; difficulty in moving; dizziness; dry mouth; flu-like syndrome; headache; heartburn or indigestion; injection site pain; lack or loss of strength or energy; muscle pain, stiffness, or weakness; nausea; neck pain; pain, swelling, or redness in joints; stomach discomfort, upset, or pain

Other side effects not listed above may also occur in some patients. If you notice any other effects, check with your doctor.

Developed: 02/20/2001

BRIMONIDINE   Ophthalmic

Commonly used brand name(s):

In the U.S.—
Alphagan

Description

Brimonidine (bri-MOE-ni-deen) is used to treat glaucoma or another condition in which pressure in the eye is too high (ocular hypertension).

This medicine is available only with your doctor's prescription, in the following dosage form:

Ophthalmic
- Ophthalmic solution (eye drops) (U.S.)

Before Using This Medicine

In deciding to use a medicine, the risks of using the medicine must be weighed against the good it will do. This is a decision you and your doctor will make. For ophthalmic brimonidine, the following should be considered:

Allergies—Tell your doctor if you have ever had any unusual or allergic reaction to brimonidine. Also tell your health care professional if you are allergic to any other substances, such as preservatives.

Pregnancy—Brimonidine has not been studied in pregnant women. Studies in animals have shown that brimonidine crosses the placenta, but very high doses have not been shown to cause harmful effects in the fetus.

Breast-feeding—It is not known whether brimonidine passes into human breast milk. However, it has been shown to pass into the milk of nursing animals.

Children—Studies on this medicine have been done only in adult patients. There is no specific information comparing use of brimonidine in children with use in other age groups.

Older adults—Many medicines have not been studied specifically in older people. Therefore, it may not be known whether they work exactly the same way they do in younger adults or if they cause different side effects or problems in older people. There is no specific information comparing use of brimonidine in the elderly with use in other age groups.

Other medicines—Although certain medicines should not be used together at all, in other cases two different medicines may be used together even if an interaction might occur. In these cases, your doctor may want to change the dose, or other precautions may be necessary. When you are using brimonidine, it is especially important that your health care professional know if you are taking any of the following:

- Monoamine oxidase (MAO) inhibitors (furazolidone [e.g., Furoxone], isocarboxazid [e.g., Marplan], phenelzine [e.g., Nardil], procarbazine [e.g., Matulane], selegiline [e.g., Eldepryl], tranylcypromine [e.g., Parnate])— Brimonidine should not be taken while you are taking or within two weeks of taking monoamine oxidase (MAO) inhibitors

Other medical problems—The presence of other medical problems may affect the use of brimonidine. Make sure you tell your doctor if you have any other medical problems, especially:

- Heart or blood vessel disease or

- Low blood pressure—Although very little ophthalmic brimonidine is absorbed into the body, there is a possibility that it could affect blood pressure
- Kidney disease or
- Liver disease—Higher blood levels of brimonidine may result
- Mental depression—Use of brimonidine may make this condition worse

Proper Use of This Medicine

If your doctor ordered two different eye drops to be used together, wait at least 10 minutes between the times you apply the medicines. This will help to keep the second medicine from "washing out" the first one.

To use the *eye drops:*
- First, wash your hands. Tilt your head back and, pressing your finger gently on the skin just beneath the lower eyelid, pull the lower eyelid away from the eye to make a space. Drop the medicine into this space. Let go of the eyelid and gently close the eyes. Do not blink. Keep the eyes closed and apply pressure to the inner corner of the eye with your finger for 1 or 2 minutes to allow the medicine to be absorbed by the eye.
- If you think you did not get the drop of medicine into your eye properly, use another drop.
- To keep the medicine as germ-free as possible, do not touch the applicator tip to any surface (including the eye). Also, keep the container tightly closed.

Use this medicine only as directed. Do not use more of it and do not use it more often than your doctor ordered. To do so may increase the chance of too much medicine being absorbed into the body and the chance of side effects.

Dosing—The dose of ophthalmic brimonidine will be different for different patients. *Follow your doctor's orders or the directions on the label.* The following information includes only the average doses of ophthalmic brimonidine. *If your dose is different, do not change it* unless your doctor tells you to do so.

- For *ophthalmic* dosage form (eye drops):
  —For glaucoma or ocular hypertension:
    - Adults—Use one drop in the affected eye or eyes three times a day.
    - Children—Use and dose must be determined by your doctor.

Missed dose—If you miss a dose of this medicine, use it as soon as possible. However, if it is almost time for the next dose, skip the missed dose and go back to your regular dosing schedule. Do not double doses.

Storage—To store this medicine:
- Keep out of the reach of children.
- Store away from heat and direct light.
- Do not store in the bathroom, near the kitchen sink, or in other damp places. Heat or moisture may cause the medicine to break down.
- Do not keep outdated medicine or medicine no longer needed. Be sure that any discarded medicine is out of the reach of children.

Precautions While Using This Medicine

It is very important that your doctor check your progress at regular visits to make sure that this medicine is working properly and to check for unwanted effects.

This medicine may cause some people to become dizzy, drowsy, tired, or less alert than they are normally. *Make sure you know how you react to this medicine before you drive, use machines, or do anything else that could be dangerous if you are not alert.*

Check with your doctor right away if you experience fainting.

If you wear soft contact lenses: These eye drops contain a preservative that could be absorbed by soft lenses. *Wait at least 15 minutes after putting these eye drops in before you put in your soft contact lenses.*

Brimonidine may cause your eyes to become more sensitive to light than they are normally. Wearing sunglasses and avoiding too much exposure to bright light may help lessen the discomfort.

Side Effects of This Medicine

Along with its needed effects, a medicine may cause some unwanted effects. Although not all of these side effects may occur, if they do occur they may need medical attention.

Check with your doctor as soon as possible if any of the following side effects occur:

More common
   Headache; itching of eye; redness of eye or inner lining of eyelid; swelling of eyelid; tearing of eye

Less common
   Ache or pain in eye; bloody eye; blurred vision or other change in vision; dizziness; fainting; feeling of something in the eye; increased blood pressure; mental depression; muscle pain; nausea or vomiting; oozing in eye; redness, swelling, and/or itching of eyelid; runny or stuffy nose; sneezing; swelling of eye

Other side effects may occur that usually do not need medical attention. These side effects may go away during treatment as your body adjusts to the medicine. However, check with your doctor if any of the following side effects continue or are bothersome:

More common
   Burning, stinging, or tearing of eye; drowsiness or tiredness; dryness of mouth

Less common
   Anxiety; crusting on eyelid or corner of eye; discoloration of white part of eye; dryness of eye; increased sensitivity of eye to light; muscle weakness; paleness of eye or inner lining of eyelid; pounding heartbeat; taste changes; trouble in sleeping

Other side effects not listed above may also occur in some patients. If you notice any other effects, check with your doctor.

Developed: 07/14/98

BRINZOLAMIDE   Ophthalmic

Commonly used brand name(s):

In the U.S.—
   Azopt

Description

Brinzolamide (brin-ZOH-la-mide) is a carbonic anhydrase inhibitor that is used in the eye. It is used to treat increased pressure in the eye caused by open-angle glaucoma. It is also used to treat a condition called hypertension of the eye.

This medicine is available only with your doctor's prescription, in the following dosage form:

Ophthalmic
   • Ophthalmic suspension (eye drops) (U.S.)

Before Using This Medicine

In deciding to use a medicine, the risks of using the medicine must be weighed against the good it will do. This is a decision you and your doctor will make. For ophthalmic brinzolamide, the following should be considered:

Allergies—Tell your doctor if you have ever had any unusual or allergic reaction to brinzolamide or to any of the sulfonamides (sulfa medicines). Also tell your health care professional if you are allergic to any other substances, such as benzalkonium chloride or other preservatives.

Pregnancy—Ophthalmic brinzolamide has not been studied in pregnant women. However, in animals given very high doses by mouth it caused decreased weight gain and some harmful effects in both the mothers and offspring. Before using this medicine, make sure your doctor knows if you are pregnant or if you may become pregnant.

Breast-feeding—It is not known whether ophthalmic brinzolamide passes into breast milk. However, it has been found to pass into breast milk in animals and the breast-fed offspring gained less weight than normal. Discuss with your doctor whether or not to breast-feed during treatment with this medicine.

Children—Studies on this medicine have been done only in adult patients and there is no specific information comparing use of brinzolamide in children with use in other age groups.

Other medicines—Although certain medicines should not be used together at all, in other cases two different medicines may be used together even if an interaction might occur. In these cases, your doctor may want to change the dose, or other precautions may be necessary. When you are taking brinzolamide, it is especially important that your health care professional know if you are taking any of the following:

   • Carbonic anhydrase inhibitor–type glaucoma medicine you take by mouth (for example, acetazolamide [e.g., Diamox], dichlorphenamide [e.g., Daranide], or methazolamide [e.g., Neptazane])—Effects of these medicines and brinzolamide on the body may be increased

Other medical problems—The presence of other medical problems may affect the use of brinzolamide. Make sure you tell your doctor if you have any other medical problems, especially:

   • Kidney disease, severe or
   • Liver disease—Effects of ophthalmic brinzolamide may be increased because of slower removal from the body

Proper Use of This Medicine

This medicine should be shaken before each use.

To use: First, wash your hands. Tilt the head back and, pressing your finger gently on the skin just beneath the lower eyelid, pull the lower eyelid away from the eye to make a space. Drop the medicine into this space. Let go of the eyelid and gently close the eyes. Do not blink. Keep the eyes closed and apply pressure to the inner corner of the eye with your finger for 1 or 2 minutes to allow the medicine to be absorbed by the eye. Immediately after using the eye drops, wash your hands to remove any medicine that may be on them. To keep the medicine as germ-free as possible, do not touch the applicator tip to any surface (including the eye). Also, keep the container tightly closed.

Use this medicine only as directed by your doctor. Do not use more of it and do not use it more often than your doctor ordered. To do so may increase the chance of too much medicine being absorbed into the body and the chance of side effects.

If your doctor ordered two different eye drops to be used together, wait at least 10 minutes between the times you apply the medicines. This will help to keep the second medicine from "washing out" the first one.

Dosing—The dose of ophthalmic brinzolamide will be different for different patients. *Follow your doctor's orders or the directions on the label.* The following information includes only the average doses of brinzolamide. *If your dose is different, do not change it* unless your doctor tells you to do so.

- For *ophthalmic* dosage form (eye drops):
  —For glaucoma or hypertension of the eye:
    • Adults—Use 1 drop in the eye three times a day.
    • Children—Use and dose must be determined by your doctor.

Missed dose—If you miss a dose of this medicine, use it as soon as you remember. However, if it is almost time for the next dose, skip the missed dose and go back to your regular dosing schedule. Do not double doses.

Storage—To store this medicine:
- Keep out of the reach of children.
- Store away from heat and direct light.
- Keep the medicine from freezing.
- Do not keep outdated medicine or medicine no longer needed. Be sure that any discarded medicine is out of the reach of children.

Precautions While Using This Medicine

It is important that your doctor check your progress at regular visits to make sure that this medicine is working properly and is not causing unwanted effects.

If itching, redness, swelling, or other signs of eye or eyelid irritation occur, check with your doctor. These signs may mean that you are allergic to ophthalmic brinzolamide.

The preservative used in these eye drops may be absorbed by soft contact lenses and cause irritation of your eyes. Soft contact lenses should be taken out before you use brinzolamide eye drops. Lenses may be put back in the eyes 15 minutes after you have used the medicine.

Check with your doctor if you get an injury or infection in your eye or if you are scheduled to have eye surgery. Your doctor may want you to use a fresh bottle of brinzolamide eye drops in case the present bottle of eye drops has become contaminated during use.

This medicine may cause some people to have blurred vision for a short time after each use. *Make sure you know how you react to this medicine before you drive, use machines, or do anything else that could be dangerous if you cannot see properly.*

Side Effects of This Medicine

Along with its needed effects, a medicine may cause some unwanted effects. Although not all of these side effects may occur, if they do occur they may need medical attention.

Check with your doctor as soon as possible if any of the following side effects occur:
Less common
Discharge from the eye; feeling of something in the eye; headache; redness, soreness, irritation, or pain of eye or eyelid; skin rash

Rare
Chest pain; dizziness; excessive muscle tone; hair loss; hives; kidney pain; itching, swelling, or other signs of eye or eyelid irritation; seeing double; shortness of breath; sore throat

Other side effects may occur that usually do not need medical attention. These side effects may go away during treatment as your body adjusts to the medicine. However, check with your doctor if any of the following side effects continue or are bothersome:
More common
Bitter, sour, or other unusual taste; blurred vision for a short time after use of medicine

Less common
Burning, stinging, or discomfort when medicine is applied; dry eye; runny nose

Other side effects not listed above may also occur in some patients. If you notice any other effects, check with your doctor.

Developed: 08/06/98

BROMOCRIPTINE Systemic

Commonly used brand name(s):

In the U.S.—
Parlodel
Parlodel SnapTabs
Generic name product may be available.

In Canada—
Alti-Bromocriptine
Apo-Bromocriptine
Parlodel

Description

Bromocriptine (broe-moe-KRIP-teen) belongs to the group of medicines known as ergot alkaloids. Bromocriptine blocks release of a hormone called prolactin from the pituitary gland. Prolactin affects the menstrual cycle and milk production. Bromocriptine is used to treat certain menstrual problems or to stop milk production in some women or men who have abnormal milk leakage. It is also used to treat infertility in both men and women that occurs because the body made too much prolactin.

Bromocriptine is also used to treat some people who have Parkinson's disease. It works by stimulating certain parts of the brain and nervous system that are involved in this disease.

Bromocriptine is also used to treat acromegaly (overproduction of growth hormone) and pituitary prolactinomas (tumors of the pituitary gland).

Bromocriptine may also be used for other conditions as determined by your doctor.

Bromocriptine is available only with your doctor's prescription, in the following dosage forms:

Oral
- Capsules (U.S. and Canada)
- Tablets (U.S. and Canada)

Before Using This Medicine

In deciding to use a medicine, the risks of taking the medicine must be weighed against the good it will do. This is a decision you and your doctor will make. For bromocriptine, the following should be considered:

Allergies—Tell your doctor if you have ever had any unusual or allergic reaction to bromocriptine or other ergot medicines such as ergotamine. Also tell your health care professional if you are allergic to any other substances, such as foods, preservatives, or dyes.

Pregnancy—Bromocriptine is not generally recommended for use during pregnancy. However, bromocriptine can be used during pregnancy in certain patients who are closely monitored by their doctor.

Breast-feeding—This medicine stops milk from being produced.

Children—Studies of this medicine have been done only in teenagers over 15 years of age and adult patients. There is no specific information comparing use of bromocriptine in children with use in other age groups.

Teenagers—This medicine has been tested in a limited number of teenagers 15 years of age and older. In effective doses, the medicine has not been shown to cause different side effects or problems than it does in adults. Appropriate studies have not been done in teenagers younger than 15 years of age, and there is no specific information comparing use of bromocriptine in these teenagers with use in other age groups.

Older adults—Confusion, hallucinations, or uncontrolled body movements may be more likely to occur in elderly patients, who are usually more sensitive than younger adults to the effects of bromocriptine.

Other medicines—Although certain medicines should not be used together at all, in other cases two different medicines may be used together even if an interaction might occur. In these cases, your doctor may want to change the dose, or other precautions may be necessary. When you are taking bromocriptine, it is especially important that your health care professional know if you are taking any of the following:
- Ergot alkaloids (dihydroergotamine [e.g., D.H.E. 45], ergoloid mesylates [e.g., Hydergine], ergonovine [e.g., Ergotrate], ergotamine [e.g., Gynergen], methylergonovine [e.g., Methergine], methysergide [e.g., Sansert])—Severe cases of high blood pressure have occurred with the use of bromocriptine. This may be made worse with the use of ergot alkaloids
- Erythromycin (e.g., E.E.S. or Erytab) or

- Risperidone (e.g., Risperdal) or
- Ritonavir (e.g., Norvir)—Use of these medications with bromocriptine may greatly increase the effects of bromocriptine

Other medical problems—The presence of other medical problems may affect the use of bromocriptine. Make sure you tell your doctor if you have any other medical problems, especially:
- High blood pressure (or history of) or
- Pregnancy-induced high blood pressure (history of)—Rarely, bromocriptine can make the high blood pressure worse

- Liver disease—Toxic effects of bromocriptine may occur in patients with liver disease because the body is not able to remove bromocriptine from the bloodstream as it normally would

- Mental problems (history of)—Bromocriptine may make certain mental problems worse

Proper Use of This Medicine

If bromocriptine upsets your stomach, it may be taken with meals or milk. Also, taking the dose at bedtime may help to lessen nausea if it occurs. If stomach upset continues, check with your doctor. Your doctor may recommend that you take the first doses vaginally.

Dosing—The dose of bromocriptine will be different for different patients. *Follow your doctor's orders or the directions on the label*. The following information includes only the average doses of bromocriptine. *If your dose is different, do not change it* unless your doctor tells you to do so.

The number of capsules or tablets that you take depends on the strength of the medicine. Also, *the number of doses you take each day, the time allowed between doses, and the length of time you take the medicine depend on the medical problem for which you are taking bromocriptine.*
- For *oral* dosage forms (capsules and tablets):
  —For infertility, male hormone problem (male hypogonadism), starting the menstrual cycle (amenorrhea), or stopping abnormal milk secretion from nipples (galactorrhea):
  - Adults and teenagers 15 years of age or older— At first, 1.25 to 2.5 milligrams (mg) once a day taken at bedtime with a snack. Then your doctor may change your dose by 2.5 mg every three to seven days as needed. Doses greater than 5 mg a day are taken in divided doses with meals or at bedtime with a snack.
  - Teenagers less than 15 years of age and children—Use and dose must be determined by your doctor.
  —For lowering growth hormone (acromegaly):
  - Adults and teenagers 15 years of age or older— At first, 1.25 to 2.5 milligrams (mg) once a day taken at bedtime with a snack for three days. Then your doctor may change your dose by 1.25 or 2.5 mg every three to seven days as needed. Doses greater than 5 mg are divided into smaller doses and taken with meals or at bedtime with a snack.
  - Teenagers less than 15 years of age and children—Use and dose must be determined by your doctor.

—For Parkinson's disease:
- Adults and teenagers 15 years of age or older—At first, 1.25 milligrams (mg) one or two times a day taken with meals or at bedtime with a snack. Then your doctor may change your dose over several weeks as needed.
- Teenagers less than 15 years of age and children—Use and dose must be determined by your doctor.

—For pituitary tumors:
- Adults and teenagers 15 years of age or older—At first, 1.25 milligrams (mg) two or three times a day taken with meals. Then your doctor may change your dose over several weeks as needed.
- Teenagers less than 15 years of age and children—Use and dose must be determined by your doctor.

Missed dose—If you miss a dose of this medicine and remember it within 4 hours, take the missed dose when you remember it. However, if a longer time has passed, skip the missed dose and go back to your regular dosing schedule. Do not double doses.

Storage—To store this medicine:
- Keep out of the reach of children.
- Store away from heat and direct light.
- Do not store in the bathroom, near the kitchen sink, or in other damp places. Heat or moisture may cause the medicine to break down.
- Do not keep outdated medicine or medicine no longer needed. Be sure that any discarded medicine is out of the reach of children.

Precautions While Using This Medicine

It is important that your doctor check your progress at regular visits, to make sure that this medicine is working properly and to check for unwanted effects.

This medicine may cause some people to become drowsy, dizzy, or less alert than they are normally. *Make sure you know how you react to this medicine before you drive, use machines, or do anything else that could be dangerous if you are dizzy or are not alert.*

Dizziness is more likely to occur after the first dose of bromocriptine. Taking the first dose at bedtime or when you are able to lie down may lessen problems. It may also be helpful if you get up slowly from a lying or sitting position. Your doctor may also recommend that you take the first dose vaginally.

Bromocriptine may cause dryness of the mouth. For temporary relief, use sugarless candy or gum, melt bits of ice in your mouth, or use a saliva substitute. However, *if dry mouth continues for more than 2 weeks, check with your medical doctor or dentist.* Continuing dryness of the mouth may increase the chance of dental disease, including tooth decay, gum disease, and fungus infections.

It may take several weeks for bromocriptine to work. Do not stop taking this medicine or reduce the amount you are taking without first checking with your doctor.

Drinking alcohol while you are taking bromocriptine may cause you to have a certain reaction. *Avoid alcoholic beverages until you have discussed this with your doctor.* Some of the symptoms you may have if you drink any alcohol while you are taking this medicine are blurred vision, chest pain, confusion, fast or pounding heartbeat, flushing or redness of face, nausea, severe weakness, sweating, throbbing headache, or vomiting.

For females who are able to bear children and who are *taking this medicine for menstrual or infertility problems, to stop milk production, or to treat acromegaly or pituitary tumors:*
- It is best to use some type of birth control while you are taking bromocriptine. However, do not use oral contraceptives ("the Pill") since they may prevent this medicine from working. For women using bromocriptine for infertility, tell your doctor when your normal menstrual cycle returns. If you wish to become pregnant, you and your doctor should decide on the best time for you to stop using birth control. Tell your doctor right away if you think you have become pregnant while taking this medicine. You and your doctor should discuss whether or not you should continue to take bromocriptine during pregnancy.
- *Check with your doctor right away* if you develop blurred vision, a sudden headache, or severe nausea and vomiting.

Side Effects of This Medicine

Along with its needed effects, a medicine may cause some unwanted effects. Although not all of these side effects may occur, if they do occur they may need medical attention.

Some serious side effects have occurred during the use of bromocriptine to stop milk flow after pregnancy or abortion. These side effects have included strokes, seizures (convulsions), and heart attacks. Some deaths have also occurred. You should discuss with your doctor the good that this medicine will do as well as the risks of using it.

Check with your doctor immediately if any of the following side effects occur:
Rare
Black, tarry stools; bloody vomit; chest pain (severe); convulsions (seizures); fainting; fast heartbeat; headache (unusual); increased sweating; nausea and vomiting (continuing or severe); nervousness; shortness of breath (unexplained); vision changes (such as blurred vision or temporary blindness); weakness (sudden)

Check with your doctor as soon as possible if any of the following side effects occur:
Less common—reported more often in patients with Parkinson's disease
Confusion; hallucinations (seeing, hearing, or feeling things that are not there); uncontrolled movements of the body, such as the face, tongue, arms, hands, head, and upper body
Rare—reported more often in patients taking large doses
Abdominal or stomach pain (continuing or severe); increased frequency of urination; loss of appetite (continuing); lower back pain; runny nose (continuing); weakness

Other side effects may occur that usually do not need medical attention. These side effects may go away during treatment as your body adjusts to the medicine. However, check with your doctor if any of the following side effects continue or are bothersome:
More common
Dizziness or lightheadedness, especially when getting up from a lying or sitting position; nausea
Less common
Constipation; diarrhea; drowsiness or tiredness; dry mouth; leg cramps at night; loss of appetite; mental

depression; stomach pain; stuffy nose; tingling or pain in fingers and toes when exposed to cold; vomiting

Some side effects may be more likely to occur in patients who are taking bromocriptine for Parkinson's disease, acromegaly, or pituitary tumors since they may be taking larger doses.

Other side effects not listed above may also occur in some patients. If you notice any other effects, check with your doctor.

Additional Information

Once a medicine has been approved for marketing for a certain use, experience may show that it is also useful for other medical problems. Although these uses are not included in product labeling, bromocriptine is used in certain patients with the following medical conditions:

- To stop milk production after an abortion or miscarriage or in women after a delivery who should not breast-feed for medical reasons
- Neuroleptic malignant syndrome

Other than the above information, there is no additional information relating to proper use, precautions, or side effects for these uses.

Revised: 08/09/95
Interim revision: 08/20/97

BRONCHODILATORS, ADRENERGIC   Inhalation

Commonly used brand name(s):

In the U.S.—

Adrenalin Chloride[3]	Maxair[9]
Airet[1]	Maxair Autohaler[9]
Alupent[8]	Medihaler-Iso[7]
Arm-a-Med Isoetharine[6]	microNefrin[3]
Arm-a-Med Metaproterenol[8]	Nephron[3]
Asthmahaler Mist[3]	Primatene Mist[3]
AsthmaNefrin[3]	Proventil[1]
Beta-2[6]	Proventil HFA[1]
Brethaire[12]	S-2[3]
Bronkaid Mist[3]	Serevent[11]
Bronkaid Suspension Mist[3]	Serevent Diskus[11]
Bronkometer[6]	Tornalate[2]
Bronkosol[6]	Vaponefrin[3]
Dey-Lute Isoetharine[6]	Ventolin[1]
Dey-Lute Metaproterenol[8]	Ventolin Nebules[1]
Isuprel[7]	Ventolin Rotacaps[1]
Isuprel Mistometer[7]	

In Canada—

Alupent[8]	Novo-Salmol[1]
Apo-Salvent[1]	Oxeze Turbuhaler[5]
Berotec[4]	Pro-Air[10]
Bricanyl Turbuhaler[12]	Serevent[11]
Bronkaid Mistometer[3]	Serevent Diskhaler[11]
Foradil[5]	Serevent Diskus[11]
Gen-Salbutamol Sterinebs P.F.[1]	Vaponefrin[3]
	Ventodisk[1]
Isuprel[7]	Ventolin[1]
Isuprel Mistometer[7]	Ventolin Nebules P.F.[1]
Maxair[9]	Ventolin Rotacaps[1]

Other commonly used names are:
Adrenaline[3]
Orciprenaline[7]
Salbutamol[1]

Note: For quick reference, the following adrenergic bronchodilators are numbered to match the corresponding brand names.

This information applies to the following medicines:
1. Albuterol (al-BYOO-ter-ole)‡§
2. Bitolterol (bye-TOLE-ter-ole)†
3. Epinephrine (ep-i-NEF-rin)‡
4. Fenoterol (fen-OH-ter-ole)*
5. Formoterol (for-MOH-ter-ol)*§
6. Isoetharine (eye-soe-ETH-a-reen)†‡
7. Isoproterenol (eye-soe-proe-TER-e-nole)‡
8. Metaproterenol (met-a-proe-TER-e-nole)‡
9. Pirbuterol (peer-BYOO-ter-ole)
10. Procaterol (proe-KAY-ter-ole)*
11. Salmeterol (sal-ME-te-role)
12. Terbutaline (ter-BYOO-ta-leen)

*Not commercially available in the U.S.
†Not commercially available in Canada.
‡Generic name product may be available in the U.S.
§Generic name product may be available in Canada.

Description

Adrenergic bronchodilators are medicines that are breathed in through the mouth to open up the bronchial tubes (air passages) of the lungs. Some of these medicines are used to treat the symptoms of asthma, chronic bronchitis, emphysema, and other lung diseases, while others are used to prevent the symptoms.

Salmeterol is a long-acting bronchodilator that is used with anti-inflammatory medication to prevent asthma attacks. *Salmeterol is different from the other adrenergic bronchodilators because it does not act quickly enough to relieve an asthma attack that has already started.*

Some of these medicines are also breathed in through the mouth to prevent bronchospasm (wheezing or difficulty in breathing) caused by exercise. Also, epinephrine may be used in the treatment of croup.

All of these medicines, except some epinephrine preparations, are available only with your doctor's prescription. Although some of the epinephrine preparations are available without a prescription, your doctor may have special instructions on the proper dose of epinephrine for your medical condition.

These medicines are available in the following dosage forms:

Inhalation
Albuterol
- Inhalation aerosol (U.S. and Canada)
- Inhalation solution (U.S. and Canada)
- Powder for inhalation (U.S. and Canada)
Bitolterol
- Inhalation aerosol (U.S.)
- Inhalation solution (U.S.)
Epinephrine
- Inhalation aerosol (U.S. and Canada)
- Inhalation solution (U.S. and Canada)
Fenoterol
- Inhalation aerosol (Canada)
- Inhalation solution (Canada)
Formoterol
- Powder for inhalation (Canada)

Isoetharine
- Inhalation aerosol (U.S.)
- Inhalation solution (U.S.)

Isoproterenol
- Inhalation aerosol (U.S. and Canada)
- Inhalation solution (U.S. and Canada)

Metaproterenol
- Inhalation aerosol (U.S. and Canada)
- Inhalation solution (U.S. and Canada)

Pirbuterol
- Inhalation aerosol (U.S. and Canada)

Procaterol
- Inhalation aerosol (Canada)

Salmeterol
- Inhalation aerosol (U.S. and Canada)
- Powder for inhalation (U.S. and Canada)

Terbutaline
- Inhalation aerosol (U.S. and Canada)

Before Using This Medicine

In deciding to use a medicine, the risks of taking the medicine must be weighed against the good it will do. This is a decision you and your doctor will make. For inhalation adrenergic bronchodilators, the following should be considered:

Allergies—Tell your doctor if you have ever had any unusual or allergic reaction to albuterol, bitolterol, epinephrine, fenoterol, formoterol, isoetharine, isoproterenol, metaproterenol, pirbuterol, procaterol, salmeterol, terbutaline, or other inhalation medicines. Also tell your health care professional if you are allergic to sulfites, which may be used as a preservative in some of these medicines or to lactose, contained in powders for inhalation.

Pregnancy—
- *For albuterol, bitolterol, formoterol, metaproterenol, and salmeterol:* These medicines are used to treat asthma in pregnant women. Although there are no studies on birth defects in humans, problems have not been reported. Some studies in animals have shown that they cause birth defects when given in doses many times higher than the human dose.
- *For epinephrine:* Women given epinephrine subcutaneously (under the skin) during pregnancy have been studied. The babies of these women had more birth defects than expected, although the severity of the mother's asthma may have contributed to this result.
- *For fenoterol, isoproterenol, pirbuterol, procaterol, and terbutaline:* These medicines are used to treat asthma in pregnant women. Although there are no studies on birth defects in humans, problems have not been reported. These medicines have not been shown to cause birth defects in animal studies when given in doses many times higher than the human dose.
- *For isoetharine:* Studies on birth defects have not been done in either humans or animals.

Breast-feeding—
- —It is not known whether these medicines pass into the breast milk. Although most medicines pass into breast milk in small amounts, many of them may be used safely while breast-feeding. Mothers who are using these medicines and who wish to breast-feed should discuss this with their doctor.

Children—Appropriate studies performed to date have not demonstrated pediatrics-specific problems that would limit the usefulness of these medicines in children. However, isoetharine is not recommended for use in children.

Older adults—
- *For albuterol, bitolterol, epinephrine, fenoterol, isoetharine, isoproterenol, metaproterenol, pirbuterol, procaterol, and terbutaline:* These medicines have not been studied specifically in older people. Therefore, it may not be known whether they work exactly the same way they do in younger adults or if they cause different side effects or problems in older people. There is no specific information comparing use of inhalation adrenergic bronchodilators in the elderly with use in other age groups.
- *For salmeterol:* This medicine has been tested in a limited number of patients 65 years of age or older. It has not been shown to cause different side effects or problems in older people than it does in younger adults.

Other medicines—Although certain medicines should not be used together at all, in other cases two different medicines may be used together even if an interaction might occur. In these cases, your doctor may want to change the dose, or other precautions may be necessary. When you are using inhalation adrenergic bronchodilators, it is especially important that your health care professional know if you are taking any of the following:
- Beta-adrenergic blocking agents (acebutolol [e.g., Sectral], atenolol [e.g., Tenormin], betaxolol [e.g., Kerlone], carteolol [e.g., Cartrol], labetalol [e.g., Normodyne], metoprolol [e.g., Lopressor], nadolol [e.g., Corgard], oxprenolol [e.g., Trasicor], penbutolol [e.g., Levatol], pindolol [e.g., Visken], propranolol [e.g., Inderal], sotalol [e.g., Sotacor], timolol [e.g., Blocadren])—These medicines may make your condition worse and prevent the adrenergic bronchodilators from working properly
- Disopyramide,
- Quinidine,
- Phenothiazines, or
- Procainamide—These medicines may increase the risk of heart problems

Other medical problems—The presence of other medical problems may affect the use of inhalation adrenergic bronchodilators. Make sure you tell your doctor if you have any other medical problems, especially:
- Heart or blood vessel disease—These medicines may make these conditions worse
- High blood pressure, not well controlled—Epinephrine may make this condition worse
- Overactive thyroid or
- Pheochromocytoma, diagnosed or suspected—The chance of side effects may be increased

Proper Use of This Medicine

These medicines come with patient directions. Read them carefully before using the medicine. If you do not understand the directions or if you are not sure how to use the medicine, ask your health care professional to show you what to do. Also, ask your health care professional to check regularly how you use the medicine to make sure you are using it properly.

Use this medicine only as directed. Do not use more of it and do not use it more often than recommended on the label, unless otherwise directed by your doctor. Using the medicine more often may increase the chance of serious unwanted effects. Deaths have occurred when too much inhalation bronchodilator medicine was used.

Keep the spray away from your eyes because it may cause irritation.

Salmeterol and formoterol are used to prevent asthma attacks. They are not used to relieve an attack that has already started. For relief of an asthma attack that has already started, you should use another medicine (not formoterol) that starts working faster than salmeterol does. *If you do not have another medicine to use for an attack or if you have any questions about this, check with your doctor.* Because the effects of salmeterol and formoterol usually last about 12 hours, doses should never be taken more than two times a day or less than 12 hours apart.

Some *epinephrine* preparations are available without a doctor's prescription. However, *do not use this medicine unless you are seeing a doctor about asthma. Do not use this medicine* if you have been hospitalized for asthma treatment or if you are taking a prescription medicine for asthma, unless you have been told to do so by a doctor.

When you use the inhaler for the first time, or if you have not used it in a while, the inhaler may not deliver the right amount of medicine with the first puff. Therefore, before using the inhaler, you may have to test or prime it.

- *To test or prime most inhalers:*
  —Insert the medicine container (canister) firmly into the clean mouthpiece according to the manufacturer's directions. Check to make sure it is placed properly into the mouthpiece.
  —Take the cap off the mouthpiece and shake the inhaler three or four times.
  —Hold the inhaler well away from you at arm's length and press the top of the canister, spraying the medicine into the air *two* times. The inhaler will now be ready to provide the right amount of medicine when you use it.
- *To use most inhalers:*
  —Using your thumb and one or two fingers, hold the inhaler upright, with the mouthpiece end down and pointing toward you.
  —Take the cap off the mouthpiece. Check the mouthpiece to make sure it is clear. Then, gently shake the inhaler three or four times.
  —Breathe out slowly to the end of a normal breath.
  —Use the inhalation method recommended by your doctor:
    - Open-mouth method—Place the mouthpiece about 1 to 2 inches (2 fingerwidths) in front of your widely opened mouth. Make sure the inhaler is aimed into your mouth so the spray does not hit the roof of your mouth or your tongue.
    - Closed-mouth method—Place the mouthpiece in your mouth between your teeth and over your tongue with your lips closed tightly around it. Make sure your tongue or teeth are not blocking the opening.
  —Start to breathe in slowly through your mouth. At the same time, press the top of the canister one time to get 1 puff of medicine. Continue to breathe in slowly for 3 to 5 seconds. Count the seconds while breathing in. It is important to press the canister and breathe in slowly at the same time so the medicine gets into your lungs. This step may be difficult at first. If you are using the closed-mouth method and

you see a fine mist coming from your mouth or nose, the inhaler is not being used correctly.
  —Hold your breath as long as you can up to 10 seconds. This gives the medicine time to settle into your airways and lungs.
  —Take the mouthpiece away from your mouth and breathe out slowly.
  —If your doctor has told you to inhale more than 1 puff of medicine at each dose, gently shake the inhaler again and take the next puff following exactly the same steps you used for the first puff. Press the canister one time for each puff of medicine.
  —When you are done, wipe off the mouthpiece and replace the cap.

Your doctor, nurse, or pharmacist may want you to use a spacer or holding chamber with the inhaler. A spacer helps get the medicine into the lungs and reduces the amount of medicine that stays in your mouth and throat.

To use a spacer with the inhaler:

- Attach the spacer to the inhaler according to the manufacturer's directions. There are different types of spacers available, but the method of breathing is the same with most spacers.
- Gently shake the inhaler and spacer three or four times.
- Hold the mouthpiece of the spacer away from your mouth and breathe out slowly to the end of a normal breath.
- Place the mouthpiece into your mouth between your teeth and over your tongue with your lips closed around it.
- Press down on the canister top one time to release 1 puff of medicine into the spacer. Within one or two seconds, begin to breathe in slowly through your mouth for three to five seconds. Do not breathe in through your nose. Count the seconds while inhaling.
- Hold your breath as long as you can up to ten seconds (count slowly to ten).
- Breathe out slowly. Do not remove the mouthpiece from your mouth. Breathe in and out slowly two or three times to make sure the spacer is emptied.
- If your doctor has told you to take more than 1 puff of medicine at each dose, gently shake the inhaler and spacer again, and take the next puff, following exactly the same steps you used for the first puff. Do not put more than 1 puff of medicine into the spacer at a time.
- If you rinse your mouth with water after you have finished, be sure to spit out the rinse water. Do not swallow it.
- When you are finished, remove the spacer from the inhaler. Wipe off the mouthpiece and replace the cap.
- Clean the inhaler and mouthpiece at least once a week.
  —*To clean the inhaler:*
    - Remove the canister from the inhaler and set the canister aside.
    - Wash the mouthpiece and cap with warm, soapy water. Then, rinse well with warm, running water.
    - Shake off the excess water and let the inhaler parts air dry completely before putting the inhaler back together.
- Save your inhaler. Refill units may be available.

For patients using the powder for inhalation dosage form:

- These medicines are used with a special device. If you do not understand the directions that come with the inhaler or if you are not sure how to use the inhaler, ask your health care professional to show you how to use it. Also, ask your health care professional to check regularly how you use the inhaler to make sure you are using it properly.

For patients using the inhalation solution dosage form:
- If you are using this medicine in a nebulizer, make sure you understand exactly how to use it. If you have any questions about this, check with your health care professional.
- Do not use if solution turns pinkish to brownish in color or if it becomes cloudy.
- Do not mix another inhalation medicine with an adrenergic bronchodilator medicine in the nebulizer unless told to do so by your health care professional.

Dosing—The dose of these medicines will be different for different patients. *Follow your doctor's orders or the directions on the label.* The following information includes only the average doses of these medicines. *If your dose is different, do not change it* unless your doctor tells you to do so.

The number of inhalations or the amount of medicine that you use depends on the strength of the medicine. Also, *the number of doses you take each day, the time allowed between doses, and the length of time you take the medicine depend on the medical problem for which you are taking the adrenergic bronchodilator.*

For albuterol
- For *inhalation aerosol* dosage form:
  —For preventing or treating bronchospasm:
  - Adults and children 4 years of age and older—2 inhalations (puffs) every four to six hours.
  - Children up to 4 years of age—Dose must be determined by your doctor.
  —For preventing bronchospasm caused by exercise:
  - Adults and children 4 years of age and older—2 inhalations (puffs) taken fifteen minutes before you start to exercise.
  - Children up to 4 years of age—Dose must be determined by your doctor.
- For *inhalation solution* dosage form:
  —For preventing or treating bronchospasm:
  - Adults and children 12 years of age and older—This medicine is used in a nebulizer and is taken by inhalation over five to fifteen minutes. The usual dose is 2.5 milligrams (mg) of albuterol taken every four to six hours if needed.
  - Children up to 12 years of age—This medicine is used in a nebulizer and is taken by inhalation over five to fifteen minutes. The usual dose is 1.25 to 2.5 milligrams (mg) of albuterol taken every four to six hours if needed.
- For *capsules (powder) for inhalation* dosage form:
  —For preventing or treating bronchospasm:
  - Adults and children 4 years of age and older—200 or 400 mcg taken by inhalation every four to six hours.
  - Children up to 4 years of age—Dose must be determined by your doctor.
  —For preventing bronchospasm caused by exercise:
  - Adults and children 4 years of age and older—200 mcg taken by inhalation fifteen minutes before you start to exercise.

- Children up to 4 years of age—Dose must be determined by your doctor.

For albuterol sulfate
- For *inhalation aerosol* dosage form:
  —For treating bronchospasm:
  - Adults and children 12 years of age and older—2 inhalations (puffs) every four to six hours.
  - Children up to 12 years of age—Dose must be determined by your doctor.

For bitolterol
- For *inhalation aerosol* dosage form:
  —For preventing or treating bronchospasm:
  - Adults and children 12 years of age and older—2 inhalations (puffs) every eight hours or 2 inhalations (puffs) at first, allowing one to three minutes between each puff. This dose may be followed by another puff, if needed. However, the dose taken each day should not be more than 2 puffs every four hours or 3 puffs every six hours.
  - Children up to 12 years of age—Dose must be determined by your doctor.
  —For preventing bronchospasm caused by exercise:
  - Adults and teenagers—2 inhalations (puffs) taken five minutes before you start to exercise.
  - Children—1 or 2 inhalations (puffs) taken five minutes before you start to exercise.
- For *inhalation solution* dosage form:
  —For preventing or treating bronchospasm:
  - Adults and children 12 years of age and older—This medicine is used in a nebulizer and is taken by inhalation over ten to fifteen minutes. The usual dose is 1 to 2.5 milligrams (mg) of bitolterol taken three or four times a day. Doses should be taken at least four hours apart.
  - Children up to 12 years of age—Dose must be determined by your doctor.

For epinephrine
- For treating bronchospasm:
  —For *inhalation aerosol* dosage form:
  - Adults and children 4 years of age and older—1 inhalation (puff). The dose may be repeated after at least one minute, if needed. Doses should be taken at least three hours apart.
  - Children up to 4 years of age—Dose must be determined by your doctor.
  —For *inhalation solution* dosage form:
  - Adults and children 4 years of age and older—This medicine should be used in a hand-bulb nebulizer. The usual dose is 1 to 3 inhalations (puffs) of a 1% solution. Doses should be taken at least three hours apart.
  - Children up to 4 years of age—Dose must be determined by your doctor.

For fenoterol
- For *inhalation aerosol* dosage form:
  —For preventing or treating bronchospasm:
  - Adults and children 12 years of age and older—100 or 200 micrograms (mcg), repeated three or four times a day if needed. This medicine should not be taken more often than every four hours. The total dose should not be more than 8 puffs a day of the 100 mcg per spray product or 6 puffs of the 200 mcg per spray product.

- Children up to 12 years of age—Dose must be determined by your doctor.
- For *inhalation solution* dosage form:
  —For preventing or treating bronchospasm:
    - Adults and children 12 years of age and older—This medicine is used in a nebulizer and is taken by inhalation over ten to fifteen minutes. The usual dose is 0.5 to 1 milligram (mg) of fenoterol taken every six hours if needed.
    - Children up to 12 years of age—Dose must be determined by your doctor.

For formoterol
- For *powder for inhalation* dosage form:
  —For preventing bronchospasm:
    - Adults and children 12 years of age and older—6 or 12 mcg taken by oral inhalation twice daily
    - Children under 12 years of age—Use and dose must be determined by your doctor.

For isoetharine
- For *inhalation solution* dosage form:
  —For treating bronchospasm:
    - Adults—This medicine is used in a nebulizer and is taken by inhalation over fifteen to twenty minutes. The amount of medicine you use and whether it requires dilution depends on the product ordered by your doctor. The usual dose is 2.5 to 10 milligrams (mg). This medicine usually should not be used more often than every four hours.
    - Children—Use is not recommended.
- For *inhalation aerosol* dosage form:
  —For treating bronchospasm:
    - Adults and teenagers—1 or 2 inhalations (puffs). This dose may be repeated every four hours as necessary.
    - Children—Use is not recommended.

For isoproterenol
- For *inhalation solution* dosage form:
  —For treating bronchospasm:
    - Adults and teenagers—This medicine is used in a nebulizer and is taken by inhalation over ten to twenty minutes. The usual dose is 2.5 milligrams (mg). This medicine usually should not be used more often than every four hours.
    - Children—This medicine is used in a nebulizer and is taken by inhalation over ten to twenty minutes. The usual dose is 0.05 to 0.1 milligram (mg) per kilogram (kg) of body weight, up to 1.25 mg, diluted. The dose may be repeated every four hours, if needed.

For isoproterenol hydrochloride
- For *inhalation aerosol* dosage form:
  —For treating bronchospasm:
    - Adults and children 12 years of age and older—1 inhalation (puff), repeated after two to five minutes if needed. This dose is taken every three to four hours.
    - Children up to 12 years of age—Use is not recommended.

For isoproterenol sulfate
- For *inhalation aerosol* dosage form:
  —For treating bronchospasm:
    - Adults and children 12 years of age and older—1 inhalation (puff), repeated after two to five minutes

if needed. This dose is taken every four to six hours.
    - Children up to 12 years of age—Dose must be determined by your doctor.

For metaproterenol
- For *inhalation aerosol* dosage form:
  —For preventing and treating bronchospasm:
    - Adults and children 12 years of age and older—2 or 3 inhalations (puffs) every three to four hours. The total dose should not be more than 12 puffs a day.
    - Children up to 12 years of age—1 to 3 inhalations (puffs) every three to four hours. The total dose should not be more than 12 puffs a day.
- For *inhalation solution* dosage form:
  —For preventing or treating bronchospasm:
    - Adults and children 6 years of age and older—This medicine is used in a nebulizer and is taken by inhalation. The amount of medicine you use and whether it requires dilution depends on the product ordered by your doctor. The usual dose is 10 to 15 milligrams (mg) taken three or four times a day. Doses should be taken at least four hours apart.
    - Children up to 6 years of age—This medicine is used in a nebulizer and is taken by inhalation. The amount of medicine you use and whether it requires dilution depends on the product ordered by your doctor. The usual dose is 5 to 15 milligrams (mg) taken three or four times a day, at least four hours apart.

For pirbuterol
- For *inhalation aerosol* dosage form:
  —For preventing and treating bronchospasm:
    - Adults and children—1 or 2 inhalations (puffs) every four to six hours. The total dose should not be more than 12 puffs a day.
  —For preventing bronchospasm caused by exercise:
    - Adults and children—2 inhalations (puffs) taken five minutes before you start to exercise.

For procaterol
- For *inhalation aerosol* dosage form:
  —For preventing and treating bronchospasm:
    - Adults and children 12 years of age and older—1 or 2 inhalations (puffs) three times a day.
    - Children up to 12 years of age—Dose must be determined by your doctor.
  —For preventing bronchospasm caused by exercise:
    - Adults and children 12 years of age and older—1 or 2 inhalations (puffs) taken at least fifteen minutes before you start to exercise.

For salmeterol
- For the *inhalation aerosol* dosage form:
  —For preventing bronchospasm:
    - Adults and children 12 years of age and older—2 inhalations (puffs) two times a day, in the morning and evening. Doses should be taken about twelve hours apart.
    - Children up to 12 years of age—Dose must be determined by your doctor.

  Note: Canadian manufacturer states that use in children ages 4 years and older is 2 inhalations twice daily.

—For preventing bronchospasm caused by exercise:

- Adults and children 12 years of age and older—2 inhalations (puffs) taken at least thirty to sixty minutes before you start to exercise. If you are already using salmeterol two times a day to treat your asthma, you do not need to use additional salmeterol before you exercise.
- Children up to 12 years of age—Dose must be determined by your doctor.

- For the *powder for inhalation* dosage form:
  —For preventing bronchospasm:
  - Adults and children 4 years of age and older—1 inhalation (the contents of one blister) two times a day, in the morning and evening. Doses should be taken about twelve hours apart.
  - Children up to 4 years of age—Use and dose must be determined by your doctor.
  —For preventing bronchospasm caused by exercise:
  - Adults and children 4 years of age and older—1 inhalation (the contents of one blister) at least 30 minutes before exercise
  - Children up to 4 years of age—Use and dose must be determined by your doctor.

For terbutaline

- For *inhalation aerosol* dosage form:
  —For preventing or treating bronchospasm:
  - Adults and children—
    —For the 200 microgram (mcg) per metered spray product: 2 inhalations (puffs) every four to six hours.
    —For the 500 mcg per metered spray product: 1 inhalation (puff), repeated after five minutes if needed. The total dose should not be more than 6 puffs a day.
  —For preventing bronchospasm caused by exercise:
  - Adults and children—
    —For the 200 microgram (mcg) per metered spray product: 2 inhalations (puffs) taken five to fifteen minutes before you start to exercise.

Missed dose—

- *For fomoterol:* If you miss a regularly scheduled dose of formoterol and it has been less than 6 hours since the scheduled time, take the dose as soon as possible and then go back to your regular dosing schedule. If it has been longer than 6 hours, skip the dose and take the next dose at the regularly scheduled time. Do not double doses.
- *For salmeterol:* If you use salmeterol inhalation regularly and you miss a dose of this medicine, use it as soon as possible. Then go back to your regular schedule. Do not double doses. If you have wheezing or breathlessness before the next dose is due, you should use another inhaled bronchodilator that starts to work faster than salmeterol does to relieve the attack.
- *For all other adrenergic bronchodilators:* If you are using one of these medicines regularly and you miss a dose, use it as soon as possible. Then use any remaining doses for that day at regularly spaced intervals. Do not double doses.

Storage—To store this medicine:

- Keep out of the reach of children.
- Store away from heat.

- Store the solution form of this medicine away from direct light. Store the inhalation aerosol form of this medicine away from direct sunlight.
- Keep the medicine from freezing.
- Store canister with the nozzle end down.
- Do not store the powder for inhalation forms of these medicines in the bathroom, near the kitchen sink, or in other damp places. Moisture may cause the medicine to break down.
- Do not puncture, break, or burn the inhalation aerosol container, even if it is empty.
- Do not keep outdated medicine or medicine no longer needed. Be sure that any discarded medicine is out of the reach of children.

Precautions While Using This Medicine

It is important that your doctor check your progress at regular intervals to make sure that your medicine is working properly.

If you still have trouble breathing after using one of these medicines, or if your condition becomes worse, check with your doctor at once.

You may also be taking an anti-inflammatory medicine for asthma along with this medicine. *Do not stop taking the anti-inflammatory medicine even if your asthma seems better, unless you are told to do so by your doctor.*

For patients using *salmeterol* or *formoterol*, check with your doctor:

- If you need to use 4 or more inhalations (puffs) a day of a fast-acting inhaled bronchodilator for 2 or more days in a row to relieve asthma attacks.
- If you need to use more than 1 canister (a total of 200 inhalations per canister) of a fast-acting inhaled bronchodilator in a 2-month period to relieve asthma attacks.

For patients using *any of these medicines except salmeterol and formoterol, check with your doctor:*

- If you need more inhalations (puffs) than usual of a fast-acting beta-adrenergic bronchodilator to relieve an acute attack
- If not using an anti-inflammatory medicine and using a fast-acting beta-adrenergic bronchodilator to relieve symptoms more than two times per week
- If you are using an anti-inflammatory medicine and you also are using more than 1 canister per month of a fast-acting beta-adrenergic bronchodilator to relieve symptoms

Side Effects of This Medicine

Along with its needed effects, a medicine may cause some unwanted effects. Although not all of these side effects may occur, if they do occur they may need medical attention.

Check with your doctor immediately if any of the following side effects occur:
Rare
> Dizziness, severe; feeling of choking, irritation, or swelling in throat; flushing or redness of skin; hives; increased shortness of breath; skin rash; swelling of face, lips, or eyelids; tightness in chest or wheezing, troubled breathing

Other side effects may occur that usually do not need medical attention. These side effects may go away during treatment as your body adjusts to the medicine. However, check with

your doctor if any of the following side effects continue or are bothersome:

More common

Fast heartbeat; headache; nervousness; trembling

Less common

Coughing or other bronchial irritation; dizziness or light-headedness; dryness or irritation of mouth or throat

Rare

Chest discomfort or pain; drowsiness or weakness; irregular heartbeat; muscle cramps or twitching; nausea and/or vomiting; restlessness; trouble in sleeping

Not all of the side effects listed above have been reported for each of these medicines, but they have been reported for at least one of them. All of the adrenergic bronchodilators are similar, so any of the above side effects may occur with any of these medicines.

While you are using an adrenergic bronchodilator, you may notice an unusual or unpleasant taste. This may be expected and will go away when you stop using the medicine.

Isoproterenol may cause the saliva to turn pinkish to red. This is to be expected while you are taking this medicine.

Other side effects not listed above may also occur in some patients. If you notice any other effects, check with your doctor.

Revised: 12/27/2000

BRONCHODILATORS, ADRENERGIC   Oral/Injection

Commonly used brand name(s):

In the U.S.—

Adrenalin[3]	EpiPen Jr. Auto-Injector[3]
Alupent[5]	Isuprel[4]
Ana-Guard[3]	Proventil[1]
Brethine[6]	Proventil Repetabs[1]
Bricanyl[6]	Ventolin[1]
EpiPen Auto-Injector[3]	Volmax[1]

In Canada—

Adrenalin[3]	EpiPen Jr. Auto-Injector[3]
Alupent[5]	Isuprel[4]
Bricanyl[6]	Ventolin[1]
EpiPen Auto-Injector[3]	

Other commonly used names are:

Adrenaline
Salbutamol
Orciprenaline

Note: For quick reference the following adrenergic bronchodilators are numbered to match the corresponding brand names.

This information applies to the following medicines:

1. Albuterol (al-BYOO-ter-ole)‡
2. Ephedrine (e-FED-rin)†‡
3. Epinephrine (ep-i-NEF-rin)‡§
4. Isoproterenol (eye-soe-proe-TER-e-nole)‡§
5. Metaproterenol (met-a-proe-TER-e-nol)‡
6. Terbutaline (ter-BYOO-ta-leen)‡

---

†Not commercially available in Canada.
‡Generic name product may be available in the U.S.
§Generic name product may be available in Canada.

Description

Adrenergic bronchodilators are medicines that stimulate the nerves in many parts of the body, causing different effects.

Because these medicines open up the bronchial tubes (air passages) of the lungs, they are used to treat the symptoms of asthma, bronchitis, emphysema, and other lung diseases. They relieve cough, wheezing, shortness of breath, and troubled breathing by increasing the flow of air through the bronchial tubes.

Epinephrine injection (including the auto-injector but not the sterile suspension) is used in the emergency treatment of allergic reactions to insect stings, medicines, foods, or other substances. It relieves skin rash, hives, and itching; wheezing; and swelling of the lips, eyelids, tongue, and inside of the nose.

These medicines may be also used for other conditions as determined by your doctor.

Ephedrine capsules are available without a prescription. However, check with your doctor before taking ephedrine.

All of the other adrenergic bronchodilators are available only with your doctor's prescription.

These medicines are available in the following dosage forms:

Oral

Albuterol
• Oral solution (Canada)
• Syrup (U.S.)
• Tablets (U.S.)
• Extended-release tablets (U.S.)

Ephedrine
• Capsules (U.S.)

Metaproterenol
• Syrup (U.S. and Canada)
• Tablets (U.S. and Canada)

Terbutaline
• Tablets (U.S. and Canada)

Parenteral

Albuterol
• Injection (Canada)

Ephedrine
• Injection (U.S. and Canada)

Epinephrine
• Injection (U.S. and Canada)

Isoproterenol
• Injection (U.S. and Canada)

Terbutaline
• Injection (U.S.)

Before Using This Medicine

In deciding to use a medicine, the risks of taking the medicine must be weighed against the good it will do. This is a decision you and your doctor will make. For adrenergic bronchodilators taken by mouth or given by injection, the following should be considered:

Allergies—Tell your doctor if you have ever had any unusual or allergic reaction to albuterol, ephedrine, epinephrine, isoproterenol, metaproterenol, or terbutaline. Also, tell your doctor if you are allergic to any other substances, such as foods, preservatives, or dyes.

Pregnancy—Some of these medicines can increase blood sugar, blood pressure, and heart rate in the mother, and may increase the heart rate and decrease blood sugar in the infant. Before taking any of these medicines, make sure your doctor knows if you are pregnant or may become pregnant.

Some of these medicines also relax the muscles of the uterus and may delay labor.

- *For albuterol:* Albuterol has not been studied in pregnant women. Studies in animals have shown that albuterol causes birth defects when given in doses many times the usual human dose.
- *For ephedrine:* Ephedrine has not been studied in pregnant women or in animals.
- *For epinephrine:* Epinephrine has been shown to cause birth defects in humans. However, this medicine may be needed during allergic reactions that threaten the mother's life.
- *For isoproterenol:* Studies on birth defects with isoproterenol have not been done in humans. However, there is some evidence that it causes birth defects in animals.
- *For metaproterenol:* Metaproterenol has not been studied in pregnant women. However, studies in animals have shown that metaproterenol causes birth defects and death of the animal fetus when given in doses many times the usual human dose.
- *For terbutaline:* Terbutaline has not been shown to cause birth defects in humans using recommended doses or in animal studies when given in doses many times the usual human dose.

Breast-feeding—
- *For albuterol, isoproterenol, and metaproterenol:* It is not known whether albuterol, isoproterenol, or metaproterenol passes into breast milk. Although most medicines pass into breast milk in small amounts, many of them may be used safely while breast-feeding. Mothers who are taking this medicine and who wish to breast-feed should discuss this with their doctor.
- *For ephedrine:* Ephedrine passes into breast milk and may cause unwanted side effects in babies of mothers using ephedrine.
- *For epinephrine:* Epinephrine passes into breast milk and may cause unwanted side effects in babies of mothers using epinephrine.
- *For terbutaline:* Terbutaline passes into breast milk but has not been shown to cause harmful effects in the infant. Mothers who are taking this medicine and who wish to breast-feed should discuss this with their doctor.

Children— There is no specific information comparing use of isoproterenol, metaproterenol, or terbutaline in children with use in other age groups.

Excitement and nervousness may be more common in children 2 to 6 years of age who take albuterol than in adults and older children.

Infants and children may be especially sensitive to the effects of epinephrine.

Older adults— Older adults may be more sensitive to the side effects of these medicines, such as trembling, high blood pressure, or fast or irregular heartbeats.

Other medicines— Although certain medicines should not be used together at all, in other cases two different medicines may be used together even if an interaction might occur. In these cases, your doctor may want to change the dose, or other precautions may be necessary. When you are taking adrenergic bronchodilators, it is especially important

that your health care professional know if you are taking any of the following:

For all adrenergic bronchodilators
- Amphetamines or
- Appetite suppressants (diet pills) or
- Medicine for colds, sinus problems, or hay fever or other allergies (including nose drops or sprays) or
- Other medicines for asthma or other breathing problems—The chance for side effects may be increased

- Beta-adrenergic blocking agents taken orally or by injection (acebutolol [e.g., Sectral], atenolol [e.g., Tenormin], betaxolol [e.g., Kerlone], bisoprolol [e.g., Zebeta], carteolol [e.g., Cartrol], labetalol [e.g., Normodyne], metoprolol [e.g., Lopressor, Toprol XL], nadolol [e.g., Corgard], oxprenolol [e.g., Trasicor], penbutolol [e.g., Levatol], pindolol [e.g., Visken], propranolol [e.g., Inderal], sotalol [e.g., Sotacor], timolol [e.g., Blocadren])—These medicines may prevent the adrenergic bronchodilators from working properly

- Beta-adrenergic blocking agents used in the eye (betaxolol [e.g., Betoptic], levobunolol [e.g., Betagan], metipranolol [e.g., OptiPranolol], timolol [e.g., Timoptic]—Enough of these medicines may be absorbed from the eye into the blood stream to prevent the adrenergic bronchodilators from working properly

- Cocaine—Unwanted effects of both medicines on the heart may be increased

- Digitalis medicines (e.g., Lanoxin) or
- Quinidine (e.g., Quinaglute Dura-Tabs, Quinidex)—The risk of heart rhythm problems may be increased

- Monoamine oxidase (MAO) inhibitors (furazolidone [e.g., Furoxone], isocarboxazid [e.g., Marplan], phenelzine [e.g., Nardil], procarbazine [e.g., Matulane], selegiline [e.g., Eldepryl], tranylcypromine [e.g., Parnate])—Taking adrenergic bronchodilators while you are taking or within 2 weeks of taking monoamine oxidase (MAO) inhibitors may dramatically increase the effects of MAO inhibitors

- Thyroid hormones—The effect of this medicine may be increased

- Tricyclic antidepressants (amitriptyline [e.g., Elavil], amoxapine [e.g., Asendin], clomipramine [e.g., Anafranil], desipramine [e.g., Norpramin], doxepin [e.g., Sinequan], imipramine [e.g., Tofranil], nortriptyline [e.g., Aventyl, Pamelor], protriptyline [e.g., Vivactil], trimipramine [e.g., Surmontil])—The effects of these medicines on the heart and blood vessels may be increased

Other medical problems— The presence of other medical problems may affect the use of these medicines. Make sure you tell your doctor if you have any other medical problems, especially:
- Convulsions (seizures)—These medicines may make this condition worse

- Diabetes mellitus (sugar diabetes)—These medicines may increase blood sugar, which could change the amount of insulin or other diabetes medicine you need

- Enlarged prostate—Ephedrine may make the condition worse

- Gastrointestinal narrowing—Use of the extended-release dosage form of albuterol may result in a blockage in the intestines.

- Glaucoma—Ephedrine or epinephrine may make the condition worse

- High blood pressure or
- Overactive thyroid—Use of ephedrine or epinephrine may cause severe high blood pressure and other side effects may also be increased

- Parkinson's disease—Epinephrine may make stiffness and trembling worse

- Psychiatric problems—Epinephrine may make problems worse

- Reduced blood flow to the brain—Epinephrine further decreases blood flow, which could make the problem worse

- Reduced blood flow to the heart or
- Heart rhythm problems—These medicines may make these conditions worse

Proper Use of This Medicine

Use this medicine only as directed. Do not use more of it and do not use it more often than your doctor ordered, do not use more than recommended on the label unless otherwise directed by your doctor. To do so may increase the chance of side effects.

If you are using this medicine for asthma, you should use another medicine that works faster than this one for an asthma attack that has already started. *If you do not have another medicine to use for an attack or if you have any questions about this, check with your doctor.*

For patients taking *albuterol extended-release tablets:*
- Swallow the tablet whole.
- Do not crush, break, or chew before swallowing.

For patients using *epinephrine injection:*
- This medicine is for injection only. If you will be giving yourself the injections, make sure you understand exactly how to give them. If you have any questions about this, check with your health care professional.
- When injected into the muscle (intramuscular) this medicine should be injected into the thigh. It should not be injected into the buttocks.
- Do not use the epinephrine solution or suspension if it turns pinkish to brownish in color or if the solution becomes cloudy.
- Keep this medicine ready for use at all times. Also, keep the telephone numbers for your doctor and the nearest hospital emergency room readily available.
- Check the expiration date on the injection regularly. Replace the medicine before that date.

For patients using *epinephrine injection* for an *allergic reaction emergency:*
- If a severe allergic reaction occurs, *use the epinephrine injection immediately.*
- *After using the epinephrine injection, notify your doctor immediately or go to the nearest hospital emergency room. Be sure to tell your doctor that you have used the epinephrine injection.*
- If you have been stung by an insect, remove the insect's stinger with your fingernails, if possible. Be careful not to squeeze, pinch, or push it deeper into the skin. Ice packs or sodium bicarbonate (baking soda) soaks, if available, may then be applied to the area stung.

- If you are using the *epinephrine auto-injector* (automatic injection device):
  —The *epinephrine auto-injector* comes with patient directions. Read them carefully before you actually need to use this medicine. Then, when an emergency arises, you will know how to inject the epinephrine.
  —It is important that you do not remove the safety cap on the auto-injector until you are ready to use it. This prevents accidental activation of the device during storage and handling.
  —To use the epinephrine auto-injector:
    • Remove the gray safety cap.
    • Place the black tip on the thigh, at a right angle (90-degree angle) to the leg.
    • Press hard into the thigh until the auto-injector functions. Hold in place for several seconds. Then remove the auto-injector and discard.
    • Massage the injection area for 10 seconds.

Dosing—The dose of these medicines will be different for different patients. *Follow your doctor's orders or the directions on the label.* The following information includes only the average doses of these medicines. *If your dose is different, do not change it* unless your doctor tells you to do so.

The number of capsules or tablets or teaspoonfuls of solution or syrup that you take, or the amount of injection that you use, depends on the strength of the medicine. Also, *the number of doses you take each day, the time allowed between doses, and the length of time you take the medicine depend on the medical problem for which you are taking it.*

For albuterol
- For symptoms of asthma, chronic bronchitis, emphysema, or other lung disease:
  —For *oral* dosage form (solution):
    • Adults and children 12 years of age and older—2 to 4 milligrams (mg) (1 to 2 teaspoonfuls) three or four times a day.
    • Children 6 to 12 years of age—2 mg (1 teaspoonful) three or four times a day.
    • Children 2 to 6 years of age—Dose is based on body weight and must be determined by your doctor. The usual dose is 0.1 mg per kg (0.045 mg per pound) of body weight up to a maximum dose of 2 mg (1 teaspoonful) three or four times a day.
    • Children up to 2 years of age—Use and dose must be determined by your doctor.
  —For *oral* dosage form (syrup):
    • Adults and children 12 years of age and older—2 to 4 mg (1 to 2 teaspoonfuls) three or four times a day. Then your doctor may increase your dose, if needed.
    • Children 6 to 12 years of age—At first, 2 mg (1 teaspoonful) of albuterol three or four times a day. Then your doctor may increase your dose, if needed.
    • Children 2 to 6 years of age—Dose is based on body weight and must be determined by your doctor. The usual dose is 0.1 mg per kg (0.045 mg per pound) of body weight up to a maximum dose of 2 mg (1 teaspoonful) three or four times a day.

- Children up to 2 years of age—Use and dose must be determined by your doctor.
—For *oral* dosage form (tablets):
  - Adults and children 12 years of age and older—At first, 2 to 4 mg three or four times a day. Then your doctor may increase your dose, if needed.
  - Children 6 to 12 years of age—2 mg three or four times a day.
  - Children up to 6 years of age—Use and dose must be determined by your doctor.
—For *oral* dosage form (extended-release tablets):
  - Adults and children 12 years of age and older—4 to 8 mg every twelve hours.
  - Children 6 to 12 years of age—4 mg every twelve hours.
  - Children up to 6 years of age—Use and dose must be determined by your doctor.
—For *injection* dosage form:
  - Dose is usually based on body weight and must be determined by your doctor. Depending on your condition, this medicine is injected into either a muscle or vein or injected slowly into a vein over a period of time.

For epinephrine
- For *injection* dosage form:
  —For allergic reactions:
  - Adults—At first, 300 to 500 micrograms (mcg) (0.3 to 0.5 mg) injected into a muscle or under the skin. Then the dose may be repeated, if needed, every ten to twenty minutes for up to three doses. In some cases, it may be necessary for 100 to 250 mcg to be injected slowly into a vein by your doctor instead of injecting the dose into a muscle or under the skin.
  - Children—Dose is based on body weight and must be determined by your doctor. The usual dose is 10 mcg per kg (4.5 mcg per pound) of body weight, up to 300 mcg (0.3 mg) a dose, injected into a muscle or under the skin. The dose may be repeated, if needed, every fifteen minutes for up to three doses.
  —For symptoms of bronchial asthma, chronic bronchitis or other lung disease:
  - Adults—Dose is based on body weight and must be determined by your doctor. The usual dose is 10 mcg per kg (4.5 mcg per pound) of body weight, up to 200 to 500 mcg (0.2 to 0.5 mg) a dose, injected under the skin. The dose may be repeated, if needed, every twenty minutes for up to three doses.
  - Children—Dose is based on body weight and must be determined by your doctor. The usual dose is 10 mcg per kg (4.5 mcg per pound) of body weight, up to 500 mcg (0.5 mg) a dose, injected under the skin. The dose may be repeated, if needed, every fifteen minutes for three or four doses or every four hours.

For isoproterenol
- For *injection* dosage form:
  —For symptoms of asthma, chronic bronchitis, emphysema, or other lung disease:
  - Isoproterenol is given by intravenous injection in a doctor's office or hospital.

For metaproterenol
- For *oral* dosage forms (syrup or tablets):
  —For symptoms of asthma, chronic bronchitis, emphysema, or other lung disease:
  - Adults and children 9 years of age and older or weighing 27 kilograms (kg) (59 pounds) or more—20 milligrams (mg) three or four times a day.
  - Children 6 to 9 years of age or weighing up to 27 kg (59 pounds)—10 mg three or four times a day.
  - Children up to 6 years of age—Dose must be determined by your doctor.

For terbutaline
- For symptoms of asthma, chronic bronchitis, emphysema, or other lung disease:
  —For *oral* dosage form (tablets):
  - Adults and adolescents 15 years of age and older—5 milligrams (mg) three times a day. The medicine may be taken about every six hours while you are awake, until three doses have been taken.
  - Children 12 to 15 years of age—2.5 mg three times a day, taken about every six hours.
  - Children 6 to 11 years of age—Dose is based on body weight and must be determined by your doctor.
  - Children up to 6 years of age—Use and dose must be determined by your doctor.
  —For *injection* dosage form:
  - Adults and children 12 years of age or older—250 micrograms (mcg) injected under the skin. The dose may be repeated after fifteen to thirty minutes, if needed. However, not more than 500 mcg should be taken within a four-hour period.
  - Children 6 to 12 years of age—Dose is based on body weight and must be determined by your doctor. The usual dose is 5 to 10 mcg per kg (2.3 to 4.5 mcg per pound) of body weight injected under the skin. The dose may be repeated after fifteen to twenty minutes for up to a total of three doses.
  - Children up to 6 years of age—Use and dose must be determined by your doctor.

Missed dose—If you are using this medicine regularly and you miss a dose, use it as soon as possible. Then use any remaining doses for that day at regularly spaced intervals. Do not double doses.

Storage—To store this medicine:
- Keep out of the reach of children.
- Store away from heat and direct light.
- Do not store the capsule or tablet form of this medicine in the bathroom, near the kitchen sink, or in other damp places. Heat or moisture may cause the medicine to break down.
- Keep the injection or syrup form of this medicine from freezing.
- Do not keep outdated medicine or medicine no longer needed. Be sure that any discarded medicine is out of the reach of children.

Precautions While Using This Medicine

It is important that your doctor check your progress at regular visits to make sure that this medicine is working properly and to check for unwanted effects.

Do not take other medicines unless they have been discussed with your doctor. This especially includes over-the-counter (nonprescription) medicines for appetite control, asthma, colds, cough, hay fever, or sinus problems, since they could increase the unwanted effects of this medicine.

For patients with diabetes:

• This medicine may cause your blood sugar levels to rise, which could change the amount of insulin or diabetes medicine that you need to take.

For patients taking this medicine for asthma:

• *If you still have trouble breathing or if your condition becomes worse (for example, if you have to use an inhaler more frequently to relieve asthma attacks), check with your doctor right away.*

For patients who are using *epinephrine injection:*

• Because epinephrine reduces blood flow to the area where it is injected, it is possible that it could cause damage to the tissues if it is injected in one spot too often. *Check with your doctor right away if you notice severe pain at the place of injection.*

For patients who are using the *epinephrine auto-injector:*

• Do not inject this medicine into your hands or feet. There is already less blood flow to the hands and feet, and epinephrine could make that worse and cause damage to these tissues. *If you accidentally inject epinephrine into your hands or feet, check with your doctor or go to the hospital emergency room right away.*

Side Effects of This Medicine

Along with its needed effects, a medicine may cause some unwanted effects. Although not all of these side effects may occur, if they do occur they may need medical attention.

Check with your doctor immediately if any of the following side effects occur:

Rare

Possible signs of an allergic reaction

Hoarseness; large hive-like swellings on eyelids, face, genitals, hands or feet, lips, throat, tongue; sudden trouble in swallowing or breathing; tightness in throat

Possible signs of a severe reaction that has occurred in children taking albuterol by mouth

Bleeding or crusting sores on lips; chest pain; chills; fever; general feeling of illness; muscle cramps or pain; nausea; painful eyes; painful sores, ulcers, or white spots in mouth or on lips; red or irritated eyes; skin rash or sores, hives, and/or itching; sore throat; vomiting

Check with your doctor as soon as possible if any of the following side effects occur:

More common

Fast heartbeat; irregular heartbeat

Rare

Chest pain; convulsions (seizures); fainting (with isoproterenol); hives; increase in blood pressure (more common with ephedrine or epinephrine); mental problems; muscle cramps or pain; nausea or vomiting; trouble in urinating; unusual tiredness or weakness

Other side effects may occur that usually do not need medical attention. These side effects may go away during treatment as your body adjusts to the medicine. However, check with

your doctor if any of the following side effects continue or are bothersome:

More common

Anxiety (with epinephrine); headache; nervousness; tremor

Less common

Dizziness; feeling of constant movement of self or surroundings; sweating; trouble in sleeping

Although not all of the side effects listed above have been reported for each of these medicines, they have been reported for at least one of them. All of these medicines are similar, so many of the above side effects may occur with any of the medicines.

Other side effects not listed above may also occur in some patients. If you notice any other effects, check with your doctor.

Additional Information

Once a medicine has been approved for marketing for a certain use, experience may show that it is also useful for other medical problems. Although these uses are not included in product labeling, some of the adrenergic bronchodilators are used in certain patients with the following medical conditions:

• Premature labor (terbutaline)
• Bleeding of gums and teeth during dental procedures (epinephrine)
• Priapism (prolonged abnormal erection of penis) (epinephrine)

Other than the above information, there is no additional information relating to proper use, precautions, or side effects for these uses.

Revised: 06/14/99

BRONCHODILATORS, THEOPHYLLINE   Systemic

Commonly used brand name(s):

In the U.S.—

Aerolate Sr[3]
Asmalix[3]
Choledyl[2]
Choledyl SA[2]
Elixophyllin[3]
Lanophyllin[3]
Phyllocontin[1]
Quibron-T Dividose[3]
Quibron-T/SR Dividose[3]
Respbid[3]
Slo-Bid Gyrocaps[3]
Slo-Phyllin[3]
Theo-24[3]

Theobid Duracaps[3]
Theochron[3]
Theo-Dur[3]
Theolair[3]
Theolair-SR[3]
Theo-Time[3]
Theovent Long-Acting[3]
Theo-X[3]
T-Phyl[3]
Truphylline[1]
Truxophyllin[3]
Uni-Dur[3]
Uniphyl[3]

In Canada—

Apo-Oxtriphylline[2]
Apo-Theo LA[3]
Choledyl[2]
Choledyl SA[2]
Phyllocontin[1]
Phyllocontin-350[1]
PMS Oxtriphylline[2]
PMS Theophylline[3]
Pulmophylline[3]

Quibron-T/SR Dividose[3]
Slo-Bid Gyrocaps[3]
Theochron[3]
Theo-Dur[3]
Theolair[3]
Theolair-SR[3]
Theo-SR[3]
Uniphyl[3]

Note: For quick reference, the following theophylline bronchodilators are numbered to match the corresponding brand names.

This information applies to the following medicines:
1. Aminophylline (am-in-OFF-i-lin)‡§
2. Oxtriphylline (ox-TRYE-fi-lin)§
3. Theophylline (thee-OFF-i-lin)‡§

---

‡Generic name product may be available in the U.S.
§Generic name product may be available in Canada.

Description

Aminophylline, oxtriphylline, and theophylline are used to treat and/or prevent the symptoms of bronchial asthma, chronic bronchitis, and emphysema. These medicines relieve cough, wheezing, shortness of breath, and troubled breathing. They work by opening up the bronchial tubes (air passages of the lungs) and increasing the flow of air through them.

Aminophylline and theophylline may also be used for other conditions as determined by your doctor.

The oral liquid, tablet, and capsule dosage forms of these medicines may be used for treatment of the acute attack or for chronic long-term treatment. The enteric-coated and extended-release dosage forms are usually used only for chronic treatment. Sometimes, aminophylline suppositories may be used but they are generally not recommended because of possible poor absorption.

These medicines are available only with your doctor's prescription, in the following dosage forms:

Oral
Aminophylline
  • Oral solution (U.S.)
  • Tablets (U.S. and Canada)
  • Extended-release tablets (U.S. and Canada)
Oxtriphylline
  • Oral solution (Canada)
  • Syrup (Canada)
  • Tablets (U.S. and Canada)
  • Delayed-release tablets (U.S.)
  • Extended-release tablets (U.S. and Canada)
Theophylline
  • Capsules (U.S.)
  • Extended-release capsules (U.S. and Canada)
  • Elixir (U.S. and Canada)
  • Oral solution (U.S. and Canada)
  • Syrup (U.S.)
  • Tablets (U.S. and Canada)
  • Extended-release tablets (U.S. and Canada)

Parenteral
Aminophylline
  • Injection (U.S. and Canada)
Theophylline
  • Injection (U.S. and Canada)

Rectal
Aminophylline
  • Suppositories (U.S.)

Before Using This Medicine

In deciding to use a medicine, the risks of taking the medicine must be weighed against the good it will do. This is a decision you and your doctor will make. For aminophylline, oxtriphylline, or theophylline, the following should be considered:

Allergies—Tell your doctor if you have ever had any unusual or allergic reaction to aminophylline, ethylenediamine (contained in aminophylline), oxtriphylline, or theophylline.

Diet—Make certain your health care professional knows if you are on any special diet, such as a high-protein, low-carbohydrate or a low-protein, high-carbohydrate diet.

Pregnancy—Aminophylline, oxtriphylline, and theophylline are frequently used to treat asthma in pregnant women. Although there are no studies on birth defects in humans, problems have not been reported. Some studies in animals have shown that aminophylline, oxtriphylline, and theophylline can cause birth defects when given in doses many times the human dose.

Because your ability to clear theophylline from your body may decrease later in pregnancy, your doctor may want to take blood samples during your pregnancy to measure the amount of medicine in the blood. This will help your doctor decide whether the dose of this medicine should be changed.

Theophylline crosses the placenta. Use of aminophylline, oxtriphylline, or theophylline during pregnancy may cause unwanted effects such as fast heartbeat, irritability, jitteriness, or vomiting in the newborn infant if the amount of medicine in your blood is too high.

Breast-feeding—Theophylline passes into the breast milk and may cause irritability in nursing babies of mothers taking aminophylline, oxtriphylline, or theophylline.

Children—Very young children and newborn infants require a lower dose than older children. If the amount of theophylline in the blood is too high, side effects are more likely to occur. Your doctor may want to take blood samples to determine whether a dose change is needed.

Older adults—Patients older than 60 years of age are likely to require a lower dose than younger adults. If the amount of theophylline is too high, side effects are more likely to occur. Your doctor may want to take blood samples to determine whether a dose change is needed.

Other medicines—Although certain medicines should not be used together at all, in other cases two different medicines may be used together even if an interaction might occur. In these cases, your doctor may want to change the dose, or other precautions may be necessary. When you are taking aminophylline, oxtriphylline, or theophylline, it is especially important that your health care professional know if you are taking any of the following:
  • Beta-adrenergic blocking agents including those used in the eyes (acebutolol [e.g., Sectral], atenolol [e.g., Tenormin], betaxolol [e.g., Betoptic, Kerlone], bisoprolol [e.g., Zebeta], carteolol [e.g., Cartrol], labetalol [e.g., Normodyne], levobunolol [e.g., Betagan], metipranolol [e.g., OptiPranolol], metoprolol [e.g., Lopressor], nadolol [e.g., Corgard], oxprenolol [e.g., Trasicor], penbutolol [e.g., Levatol], pindolol [e.g., Visken], propranolol [e.g., Inderal], sotalol [e.g., Sotacor], timolol [e.g., Blocadren, Timoptic])—These medicines may prevent aminophylline, oxtriphylline, or theophylline from working properly
  • Cimetidine (e.g., Tagamet) or
  • Ciprofloxacin (e.g., Cipro) or
  • Clarithromycin (e.g., Biaxin) or
  • Enoxacin (e.g., Penetrex) or
  • Erythromycin (e.g., E-Mycin) or
  • Fluvoxamine (e.g., Luvox) or
  • Mexiletine (e.g., Mexitil) or

- Pentoxifylline (e.g., Trental) or
- Propranolol (e.g., Inderal) or
- Tacrine (e.g., Cognex) or
- Thiabendazole or
- Ticlopidine (e.g., Ticlid) or
- Troleandomycin (e.g., TAO)—These medicines may increase the effects of aminophylline, oxtriphylline, or theophylline

- Moricizine (e.g., Ethmozine) or
- Phenytoin (e.g., Dilantin) or
- Rifampin (e.g., Rifadin)—These medicines may decrease the effects of aminophylline, oxtriphylline, or theophylline

- Smoking tobacco or marijuana—Starting or stopping smoking may change the effectiveness of these medicines

Other medical problems—The presence of other medical problems may affect the use of aminophylline, oxtriphylline, or theophylline. Make sure you tell your doctor if you have any other medical problems, especially:

- Convulsions (seizures)—Aminophylline, oxtriphylline, or theophylline may make this condition worse

- Heart failure or
- Liver disease or
- Underactive thyroid—The effects of aminophylline, oxtriphylline, or theophylline may be increased

Proper Use of This Medicine

For patients *taking this medicine by mouth:*
- If you are taking the *capsule, tablet, liquid, or extended-release (not including the once-a-day capsule or tablet) form* of this medicine, *it works best when taken with a glass of water on an empty stomach* (either 30 minutes to 1 hour before meals or 2 hours after meals). In some cases your doctor may want you to take this medicine with meals or right after meals to lessen stomach upset. If you have any questions about how you should be taking this medicine, check with your doctor.
- If you are taking the *once-a-day capsule or tablet form* of this medicine, *some products are to be taken each morning after fasting overnight and at least 1 hour before eating. However, other products are to be taken in the morning or evening with or without food. Be sure you understand exactly how to take the medicine prescribed for you.* Try to take the medicine about the same time each day.
- There are several different forms of aminophylline, oxtriphylline, and theophylline capsules and tablets. If you are taking:
  —*Enteric-coated or delayed-release tablets,* swallow the tablets whole. Do not crush, break, or chew before swallowing.
  —*Extended-release capsules,* swallow the capsule whole. Do not crush, break, or chew before swallowing. Do not open the capsule and sprinkle the beads onto food unless told to do so by your health care professional.
  —*Extended-release tablets,* swallow the tablets whole. Do not break (unless tablet is scored for breaking), crush, or chew before swallowing.

Use this medicine only as directed by your doctor. Do not use more of it, do not use it more often, and do not use it for a longer time than your doctor ordered. To do so may increase the chance of serious side effects.

In order for this medicine to help your medical problem, it must be taken every day in regularly spaced doses as ordered by your doctor. This is necessary to keep a constant amount of this medicine in the blood. To help keep the amount constant, do not miss any doses.

Dosing—When you are taking aminophylline, oxtriphylline, or theophylline, it is very important that you get the exact amount of medicine that you need. The dose of these medicines will be different for different patients. Your doctor will determine the proper dose of these medicines for you. *Follow your doctor's orders or the directions on the label.*

After you begin taking aminophylline, oxtriphylline, or theophylline, it is very important that your doctor check the level of medicine in your blood at regular intervals to find out if your dose needs to be changed. *Do not change your dose of aminophylline, oxtriphylline, or theophylline unless your doctor tells you to do so.*

The number of capsules or tablets or teaspoonfuls of solution or syrup that you take depends on the strength of the medicine. Also, *the number of doses you take each day and the time between doses depend on whether you are taking a short-acting or long-acting form of aminophylline, oxtriphylline, or theophylline.*

Missed dose—If you miss a dose of this medicine, take it as soon as possible. However, if it is almost time for your next dose, skip the missed dose and go back to your regular dosing schedule. Do not double doses.

Storage—To store this medicine:
- Keep out of the reach of children.
- Store away from heat and direct light.
- Do not store the capsule or tablet form of this medicine in the bathroom, near the kitchen sink, or in other damp places. Heat or moisture may cause the medicine to break down.
- Keep the liquid form of this medicine from freezing.
- Do not keep outdated medicine or medicine no longer needed. Be sure that any discarded medicine is out of the reach of children.

Precautions While Using This Medicine

Your doctor should check your progress at regular visits, especially for the first few weeks after you begin using this medicine. A blood test may be taken to help your doctor decide whether the dose of this medicine should be changed.

Do not change brands or dosage forms of this medicine without first checking with your doctor. Different products may not work the same way. If you refill your medicine and it looks different, check with your pharmacist.

A change in your usual behavior or physical well-being may affect the way this medicine works in your body. *Check with your doctor if you:*
- have a fever of 102 °F or higher for at least 24 hours or higher than 100 °F for longer than 24 hours.
- start or stop smoking.
- start or stop taking another medicine.
- change your diet for a long time.

This medicine may add to the central nervous system (CNS) stimulant effects of caffeine-containing foods or beverages such as chocolate, cocoa, tea, coffee, and cola drinks. Avoid eating or drinking large amounts of these foods or beverages while using this medicine. If you have questions about this, check with your doctor.

Before you have myocardial perfusion studies (a medical test that shows how well blood is flowing to your heart), tell the medical doctor in charge that you are taking this medicine. The results of the test may be affected by this medicine.

Side Effects of This Medicine

Along with its needed effects, a medicine may cause some unwanted effects. Although not all of these side effects may occur, if they do occur they may need medical attention.

Check with your doctor as soon as possible if any of the following side effects occur:

Less common
Heartburn and/or vomiting

Rare
Hives, skin rash, or sloughing of skin (with aminophylline only)

Symptoms of toxicity
Abdominal pain, continuing or severe; confusion or change in behavior; convulsions (seizures); dark or bloody vomit; diarrhea; dizziness or lightheadedness; fast and/or irregular heartbeat; nervousness or restlessness, continuing; trembling, continuing

Other side effects may occur that usually do not need medical attention. These side effects may go away during treatment as your body adjusts to the medicine. However, check with your doctor if any of the following side effects continue or are bothersome:

Less common
Headache; fast heartbeat; increased urination; nausea; nervousness; trembling; trouble in sleeping

Other side effects not listed above may also occur in some patients. If you notice any other effects, check with your doctor.

Additional Information

Once a medicine has been approved for marketing for a certain use, experience may show that it is also useful for other medical problems. Although this use is not included in product labeling, aminophylline and theophylline are used in certain patients with the following medical condition:

• Apnea (breathing problem) in newborns

Other than the above information, there is no additional information relating to proper use, precautions, or side effects for this use.

Revised: 8/11/95

BUPROPION   Systemic

Commonly used brand name(s):

In the U.S.—
Wellbutrin
Wellbutrin SR
Zyban

In Canada—
Wellbutrin SR
Zyban

Another commonly used name is amfebutamone.

Description

Bupropion (byoo-PROE-pee-on) is used to relieve mental depression and is used as part of a support program to help you stop smoking.

Bupropion is sold under different brand names for different uses. If you are already taking medicine for mental depression or to help you stop smoking, discuss this with your health care professional before taking bupropion. *It is very important that you receive only one prescription for bupropion at a time*.

This medicine is available only with your doctor's prescription, in the following dosage forms:

Oral
• Extended-release tablets (U.S. and Canada)
• Tablets (U.S.)

Before Using This Medicine

In deciding to use a medicine, the risks of taking the medicine must be weighed against the good it will do. This is a decision you and your doctor will make. For bupropion, the following should be considered:

Allergies—Tell your doctor if you have ever had any unusual or allergic reaction to bupropion. Also tell your health care professional if you are allergic to any other substances, such as foods, preservatives, or dyes.

Pregnancy—Studies have not been done in pregnant women. However, bupropion has not been reported to cause birth defects or other problems in animal studies.

Breast-feeding—Bupropion passes into breast milk. Because it may cause unwanted effects in nursing babies, use of bupropion is not recommended during breast-feeding.

Children—This medicine has been tested in a very small number of patients 6 to 16 years of age and has not been shown to cause different side effects or problems in children than it does in adults. More testing is needed to decide whether bupropion is safe and effective for use in children.

Older adults—This medicine has been tested in a limited number of patients 60 years of age and older and has not been shown to cause different side effects or problems in older people than it does in younger adults.

Other medicines—Although certain medicines should not be used together at all, in other cases two different medicines may be used together even if an interaction might occur. In these cases, your doctor may want to change the dose, or other precautions may be necessary. When you are taking bupropion, it is especially important that your health care professional know if you are taking any of the following:

• Alcohol or
• Antipsychotics (medicine for mental illness) or
• Corticosteriods (cortisone-like medicine) or
• Fluoxetine (e.g., Prozac) or
• Lithium (e.g., Lithane) or
• Maprotiline (e.g., Ludiomil) or
• Theophylline (e.g., Somophyllin-T) or
• Trazodone (e.g., Desyrel) or
• Tricyclic antidepressants (amitriptyline [e.g., Elavil], amoxapine [e.g., Asendin], clomipramine [e.g., Anafranil], desipramine [e.g., Pertofrane], doxepin [e.g., Sinequan], imipramine [e.g., Tofranil], nortriptyline [e.g., Aventyl], protriptyline [e.g., Vivactil], trimipramine [e.g., Surmontil]) or

- Ritonavir (e.g., Norvir)—Using these medicines with bupropion may increase the risk of seizures
- Monoamine oxidase (MAO) inhibitors (furazolidone [e.g., Furoxone], isocarboxazid [e.g., Marplan], phenelzine [e.g., Nardil], procarbazine [e.g., Matulane], selegiline [e.g., Eldepryl], tranylcypromine [e.g., Parnate])—*Do not take bupropion while you are taking or within 14 days of taking an MAO inhibitor* or you may increase the chance of serious side effects; at least 14 days should be allowed between stopping treatment with an MAO inhibitor and starting treatment with bupropion

Other medical problems—The presence of other medical problems may affect the use of bupropion. Make sure you tell your doctor if you have any other medical problems, especially:

- Anorexia nervosa, or history of or
- Brain tumor or
- Bulimia, or history of or
- Drug abuse or
- Head injury, history of or
- Mental retardation or
- Seizure disorders—The risk of seizures may be increased when bupropion is taken by patients with these conditions
- Bipolar disorder (manic-depressive illness) or
- Other nervous, mental, or emotional conditions or
- High blood pressure—Bupropion may make the condition worse
- Heart disease—Higher blood levels of bupropion may result, increasing the chance of side effects, or blood pressure may be increased
- Kidney disease or
- Liver disease—Higher blood levels of bupropion may result, increasing the chance of side effects

---

Proper Use of This Medicine

Use bupropion only as directed by your doctor. Do not use more of it, do not use it more often, and do not use it for a longer time than your doctor ordered. To do so may increase the chance of side effects.

For patients taking the prompt-release tablet form of this medicine
- Take doses at least 4 hours apart to decrease the chance of seizures.

For patients taking the extended-release tablet form of this medicine
- Take doses at least 8 hours apart to decrease the chance of seizures.
- Swallow tablets whole. Do not crush, break, or chew them.

To lessen stomach upset, this medicine may be taken with food, unless your doctor has told you to take it on an empty stomach.

For patients taking this medicine to help stop smoking
- Start taking bupropion 1 week before you plan to stop smoking. A date in the second week that you are taking bupropion should be chosen as the target date on which to stop smoking.
- While you are taking bupropion it is important to participate in a support program to help you stop smoking, as recommended by your doctor.

For patients taking this medicine for mental depression
- Usually this medicine must be taken for several weeks before you feel better. Your doctor should check your progress at regular visits.
- You will probably need to keep taking bupropion for at least 6 months to help prevent the return of the depression.

Dosing—The dose of bupropion will be different for different patients. *Follow your doctor's orders or the directions on the label.* The following information includes only the average doses of bupropion. *If your dose is different, do not change it* unless your doctor tells you to do so.

The number of tablets that you take depends on the strength of the medicine. Also, *the number of doses you take each day, the time allowed between doses, and the length of time you take the medicine depend on the medical problem for which you are taking bupropion.*

- For *oral extended-release* dosage form (tablets):
  —For mental depression:
  - Adults—At first, 150 milligrams (mg) once a day in the morning. Your doctor may increase your dose as needed. However, the dose usually is not more than 200 mg two times a day.
  - Children—Use and dose must be determined by your doctor.
  —To help you stop smoking:
  - Adults—At first, 150 mg once a day. Your doctor may increase your dose as needed. However, the dose usually is not more than 150 mg two times a day.
  - Children—Use and dose must be determined by your doctor.
- For *oral prompt-release* dosage form (tablets):
  —For mental depression:
  - Adults—At first, 100 mg two times a day. Your doctor may increase your dose as needed. However, the dose usually is not more than 150 mg three times a day.
  - Children—Use and dose must be determined by your doctor.

Missed dose—If you are taking the extended-release or the prompt-release form of this medicine and you miss a dose, skip the missed dose and go back to your regular dosing schedule. Do not double doses.

Storage—To store this medicine:
- Keep out of the reach of children.
- Store away from heat and direct light.
- Do not store in the bathroom, near the kitchen sink, or in other damp places. Heat or moisture may cause the medicine to break down.
- Do not keep outdated medicine or medicine no longer needed. Be sure that any discarded medicine is out of the reach of children.

Precautions While Using This Medicine

Your doctor should check your progress at regular visits, especially during the first few months of treatment with this medicine. The amount of bupropion you take may have to be changed often to meet the needs of your condition and to help avoid unwanted effects.

Do not take bupropion within 14 days of taking an MAO inhibitor.

Bupropion is sold under different brand names for different uses. If you are already taking medicine for mental depression or to help you stop smoking, discuss this with your health care professional before taking bupropion. *It is very important that you receive only one prescription for bupropion at a time.*

Drinking of alcoholic beverages should be limited or avoided, if possible, while taking bupropion. This will help prevent seizures.

This medicine may cause some people to feel a false sense of well-being, or to become drowsy, dizzy, or less alert than they are normally. *Make sure you know how you react to this medicine before you drive, use machines, or do anything else that could be dangerous if you are dizzy or are not alert and clearheaded.*

Side Effects of This Medicine

Along with its needed effects, a medicine may cause some unwanted effects. Although not all of these side effects may occur, if they do occur they may need medical attention.

Check with your doctor as soon as possible if any of the following side effects occur:
More common
Agitation; anxiety

Less common
Buzzing or ringing in ears; headache (severe); skin rash, hives, or itching

Rare
Confusion; extreme distrust; fainting; false beliefs that cannot be changed by facts; hallucinations (seeing, hearing, or feeling things that are not there); seizures (convulsions), especially with higher doses; trouble in concentrating

Symptoms of overdose—may be more severe than side effects seen at regular doses, or two or more may occur together
Fast heartbeat; hallucinations (seeing, hearing, or feeling things that are not there); loss of consciousness; nausea; seizures (convulsions); vomiting

Other side effects may occur that usually do not need medical attention. These side effects may go away during treatment as your body adjusts to the medicine. However, check with your doctor if any of the following side effects continue or are bothersome:
More common
Abdominal pain; constipation; decrease in appetite; dizziness; dryness of mouth; increased sweating; nausea or vomiting; trembling or shaking; trouble in sleeping; weight loss (unusual)

Less common
Blurred vision; change in sense of taste; drowsiness; feeling of fast or irregular heartbeat; frequent need to urinate; muscle pain; sore throat; unusual feeling of well-being

Other side effects not listed above may also occur in some patients. If you notice any other effects, check with your doctor.

Revised: 02/22/01

BUSERELIN   Systemic

Commonly used brand name(s):

In Canada—
Suprefact

Description

Buserelin (BYOO-se-rel-in) is used to treat cancer of the prostate gland.

It is similar to a hormone normally released from the hypothalamus gland. When given regularly, buserelin decreases testosterone levels. Reducing the amount of testosterone in the body is one way of treating cancer of the prostate.

Buserelin is available only with your doctor's prescription, in the following dosage forms:
Nasal
• Nasal solution (Canada)
Parenteral
• Injection (Canada)

Before Using This Medicine

In deciding to use a medicine, the risks of taking the medicine must be weighed against the good it will do. This is a decision you and your doctor will make. For buserelin, the following should be considered:

Allergies—Tell your doctor if you have ever had any unusual or allergic reaction to buserelin.

Fertility—Buserelin causes sterility which may be permanent. If you intend to have children, discuss this with your doctor before receiving this medicine.

Older adults—Many medicines have not been studied specifically in older people. Therefore, it may not be known whether they work exactly the same way they do in younger adults. Although there is no specific information comparing use of buserelin in the elderly to use in other age groups, it has been used mostly in elderly patients and is not expected to cause different side effects or problems in older people than it does in younger adults.

Proper Use of This Medicine

Buserelin comes with patient directions. Read these instructions carefully.

For patients using the *injection* form of this medicine:
• Use the syringes provided in the kit. Other syringes may not provide the correct dose. These disposable syringes and needles are already sterilized and designed to be used one time only and then discarded. If you have any questions about the use of disposable syringes, check with your health care professional.
• After use, dispose of the syringes and needles in a safe manner. If a special container is not provided, ask your health care professional about the best way to dispose of syringes and needles.

For patients using the *nasal solution* form of this medicine:
• Use the nebulizer (spray pump) provided. Directions about how to use it are included. If you have any questions about the use of the nebulizer, check with your health care professional.

Use this medicine only as directed by your doctor. Do not use more or less of it, and do not use it more often than your doctor ordered. The exact amount of medicine you need has been carefully worked out. Using too much may increase the chance of side effects, while using too little may not improve your condition.

Buserelin sometimes causes unwanted effects such as hot flashes or decreased sexual ability. It may also cause a temporary increase in pain, trouble in urinating, or weakness in your legs when you begin to use it. However, it is very important that you continue to use the medicine, even after you begin to feel better. *Do not stop using this medicine without first checking with your doctor.*

Dosing—The dose of buserelin will be different for different patients. *Follow your doctor's orders or the directions on the label.* The following information includes only the average doses of buserelin. *If your dose is different, do not change it* unless your doctor tells you to do so.

The number of doses you use each day, the time allowed between doses, and the length of time you use the medicine depend on the medical problem for which you are using buserelin.

- For prostate cancer:
  —For *nasal* dosage forms:
    - Adults: 200 micrograms (mcg) (2 sprays) into each nostril every eight hours.
  —For *injection* dosage forms:
    - Adults: In the beginning, 500 mcg (0.5 milligrams [mg]) injected under the skin every eight hours. After a time, your doctor may lower your dose to 200 mcg (0.2 mg) once a day.

Missed dose—If you miss a dose of this medicine, use it as soon as possible. However, if it is almost time for the next dose, skip the missed dose and go back to your regular dosing schedule. Do not double doses.

Storage—To store this medicine:
- Keep out of the reach of children.
- Store away from heat and direct light.
- Keep the medicine from freezing.
- Do not keep outdated medicine or medicine no longer needed. Dispose of used syringes properly in the container provided. Be sure that any discarded medicine is out of the reach of children.

Precautions While Using This Medicine

It is very important that your doctor check your progress at regular visits to make sure that this medicine is working properly and to check for unwanted effects.

Side Effects of This Medicine

Along with its needed effects, a medicine may cause some unwanted effects. Although not all of these side effects may occur, if they do occur they may need medical attention.

The following side effects are symptoms of a flareup of your condition that may occur during the first few days of treatment. After a few days, these symptoms should lessen. However, they may require medical attention. Check with your doctor if any of the following side effects occur or get worse:

Bone pain; numbness or tingling of hands or feet; trouble in urinating; weakness in legs

Other side effects may occur that usually do not need medical attention. These side effects may go away during treatment as your body adjusts to the medicine. However, check with your doctor if any of the following side effects continue or are bothersome:

More common
Decrease in sexual desire; impotence; sudden sweating and feelings of warmth ("hot flashes")

Less common
Burning, itching, redness, or swelling at place of injection; diarrhea; dry or sore nose (with nasal solution); headache (with nasal solution); increased sweating (with nasal solution); loss of appetite; nausea or vomiting; swelling and increased tenderness of breasts; swelling of feet or lower legs

Other side effects not listed above may also occur in some patients. If you notice any other effects, check with your doctor.

Revised: 07/11/94

BUSPIRONE   Systemic

Commonly used brand name(s):

In the U.S.—
BuSpar
BuSpar DIVIDOSE

In Canada—
BuSpar
Bustab

Description

Buspirone (byoo-SPYE-rone) is used to treat certain anxiety disorders or to relieve the symptoms of anxiety. However, buspirone usually is not used for anxiety or tension caused by the stress of everyday life.

It is not known exactly how buspirone works to relieve the symptoms of anxiety. Buspirone is thought to work by decreasing the amount and actions of a chemical known as serotonin in certain parts of the brain.

Buspirone is available only with your doctor's prescription, in the following dosage form:

Oral
- Tablets (U.S. and Canada)

Before Using This Medicine

In deciding to use a medicine, the risks of taking the medicine must be weighed against the good it will do. This is a decision you and your doctor will make. For buspirone, the following should be considered:

Allergies—Tell your doctor if you have ever had any unusual or allergic reaction to buspirone. Also tell your health care professional if you are allergic to any other substances, such as foods, preservatives, or dyes.

Pregnancy—Buspirone has not been studied in pregnant women. However, buspirone has not been shown to cause birth defects or other problems in animal studies.

Breast-feeding—It is not known whether buspirone passes into the breast milk of humans.

Children—Studies on this medicine have been done only in adult patients, and there is no specific information comparing use of buspirone in children up to 18 years of age with use in other age groups.

Older adults—This medicine has been tested in a limited number of older adults and has not been shown to cause different side effects or problems in older people than it does in younger adults.

Other medicines—Although certain medicines should not be used together at all, in other cases two different medicines may be used together even if an interaction might occur. In these cases, your doctor may want to change the dose, or other precautions may be necessary. When you are taking buspirone, it is especially important that your health care professional know if you are taking any of the following:

- Erythromycin (e.g., ERYC, E.E.S.) or
- Itraconazole (e.g., Sporanox)—Higher blood levels of buspirone may occur, increasing the chance of side effects. Your doctor may change the dose of buspirone that you take
- Monoamine oxidase (MAO) inhibitors (furazolidone [e.g., Furoxone], phenelzine [e.g., Nardil], procarbazine [e.g., Matulane], selegiline at doses more than 10 mg a day [e.g., Eldepryl], tranylcypromine [e.g., Parnate])—Taking buspirone while you are taking monoamine oxidase (MAO) inhibitors may cause high blood pressure

Other medical problems—The presence of other medical problems may affect the use of buspirone. Make sure you tell your doctor if you have any other medical problems, especially:

- Kidney disease or
- Liver disease—Buspirone may be removed from your body more slowly, which may increase the chance of side effects. Your doctor may need to adjust your dose

Proper Use of This Medicine

Take buspirone only as directed by your doctor. Do not take more of it, do not take it more often, and do not take it for a longer time than your doctor ordered. To do so may increase the chance of unwanted effects.

After you begin taking buspirone, 1 to 2 weeks may pass before you begin to feel the effects of this medicine.

Dosing—The dose of buspirone will be different for different patients. *Follow your doctor's orders or the directions on the label*. The following information includes only the average doses of buspirone. *If your dose is different, do not change it* unless your doctor tells you to do so.

The number of tablets that you take depends on the strength of the medicine.

- For *oral* dosage forms (tablets):
  —Adults: To start, 5 milligrams (mg) two or three times a day, or 7.5 mg two times a day. Your doctor may increase your dose by 5 mg a day every few days if needed. However, the dose usually is not more than 60 mg a day.
  —Children up to 18 years of age: Use and dose must be determined by the doctor.
  —Older adults: To start, 5 milligrams (mg) two or three times a day, or 7.5 mg two times a day. Your doctor may increase your dose by 5 mg a day every few days if needed.

Missed dose—If you miss a dose of this medicine, take it as soon as possible. However, if it is almost time for your next dose, skip the missed dose and go back to your regular dosing schedule. Do not double doses.

Storage—To store this medicine:
- Keep out of the reach of children.
- Store away from heat and direct light.
- Do not store in the bathroom, near the kitchen sink, or in other damp places. Heat or moisture may cause the medicine to break down.
- Do not keep outdated medicine or medicine no longer needed. Be sure that any discarded medicine is out of the reach of children.

Precautions While Using This Medicine

If you will be using buspirone regularly for a long time, your doctor should check your progress at regular visits to make sure the medicine does not cause unwanted effects.

Buspirone may cause some people to become dizzy, lightheaded, drowsy, or less alert than they are normally. *Make sure you know how you react to this medicine before you drive, use machines, or do anything else that could be dangerous if you are dizzy or are not alert.*

If you think you or someone else may have taken an overdose of buspirone, get emergency help at once. Some symptoms of an overdose are dizziness or lightheadedness; severe drowsiness or loss of consciousness; stomach upset, including nausea or vomiting; or very small pupils of the eyes.

Side Effects of This Medicine

Along with its needed effects, a medicine may cause some unwanted effects. Although not all of these side effects may occur, if they do occur they may need medical attention.

Check with your doctor as soon as possible if any of the following side effects occur:
  Rare
      Chest pain; confusion; fast or pounding heartbeat; fever; incoordination; mental depression; muscle weakness; numbness, tingling, pain, or weakness in hands or feet; skin rash or hives; stiffness of arms or legs; sore throat; uncontrolled movements of the body

  Symptoms of overdose—may be more severe than side effects seen at regular doses or several may occur together
      Dizziness or lightheadedness; drowsiness (severe) or loss of consciousness; stomach upset, including nausea or vomiting; very small pupils of the eyes

Other side effects may occur that usually do not need medical attention. These side effects may go away during treatment as your body adjusts to the medicine. However, check with your doctor if any of the following side effects continue or are bothersome:
  More common
      Dizziness or lightheadedness, especially when getting up from a sitting or lying position; headache; nausea; restlessness, nervousness, or unusual excitement
  Less common or rare
      Blurred vision; clamminess or sweating; decreased concentration; diarrhea; drowsiness (more common

with doses of more than 20 mg per day); dryness of mouth; muscle pain, spasms, cramps, or stiffness; ringing in the ears; trouble in sleeping, nightmares, or vivid dreams; unusual tiredness or weakness

Other side effects not listed above may also occur in some patients. If you notice any other effects, check with your doctor.

Revised: 03/17/98

BUSULFAN Systemic

Commonly used brand name(s):

In the U.S.—
  Myleran
  Busulfex

In Canada—
  Myleran

Description

Busulfan (byoo-SUL-fan) belongs to the group of medicines known as alkylating agents. It is used to treat some kinds of cancer of the blood. It may also be used as a conditioning regimen prior to progenitor cell transplantation for treatment of chronic myelogenous leukemia.

Busulfan seems to act by interfering with the function of the bone marrow. Since the growth of normal body cells may also be affected by busulfan, other effects will also occur. Some of these may be serious and must be reported to your doctor. Other effects may not be serious but may cause concern. Some effects may not occur for months or years after the medicine is used.

Before you begin treatment with busulfan, you and your doctor should talk about the good this medicine will do as well as the risks of using it.

Busulfan is available only with your doctor's prescription, in the following dosage form:

Oral
- Tablets (U.S. and Canada)

Parenteral
- Injection (U.S.)

Before Using This Medicine

In deciding to use a medicine, the risks of taking the medicine must be weighed against the good it will do. This is a decision you and your doctor will make. For busulfan, the following should be considered:

Allergies—Tell your doctor if you have ever had any unusual or allergic reaction to busulfan.

Pregnancy—Although only one case has been reported, there is a chance that this medicine may cause birth defects if either the male or the female is taking it at the time of conception or if it is taken during pregnancy. In addition, many cancer medicines may cause sterility which could be permanent. Sterility may occur with busulfan and the possibility should be kept in mind.

Be sure that you have discussed this with your doctor before taking this medicine. It is best to use some kind of birth control while you are taking busulfan. Tell your doctor right away if you think you have become pregnant while taking busulfan.

Breast-feeding—It is not known whether busulfan passes into breast milk. However, because this medicine may cause serious side effects, breast-feeding is generally not recommended while you are taking it.

Children—Although there is no specific information comparing use of busulfan in children with use in other age groups, this medicine is not expected to cause different side effects or problems in children than it does in adults.

Older adults—Many medicines have not been studied specifically in older people. Therefore, it may not be known whether they work exactly the same way they do in younger adults. Although there is no specific information comparing use of busulfan in the elderly with use in other age groups, this medicine is not expected to cause different side effects or problems in older people than it does in younger adults.

Other medicines—Although certain medicines should not be used together at all, in other cases two different medicines may be used together even if an interaction might occur. In these cases, your doctor may want to change the dose, or other precautions may be necessary. When taking busulfan it is especially important that your health care professional know if you are taking any of the following:

- Acetaminophen (e.g., Tylenol) or
- Acyclovir (e.g., Zovirax) or
- Amphotericin B by injection (e.g., Fungizone) or
- Anticonvulsants (seizure medicine) or
- Antidiabetics, oral (diabetes medicine you take by mouth) or
- Anti-infectives by mouth or by injection (medicine for infection) or
- Antineoplastics (cancer medicine) or
- Antipsychotics (medicine for mental illness) or
- Antithyroid agents (medicine for overactive thyroid) or
- Azathioprine (e.g., Imuran) or
- Captopril (e.g., Capoten) or
- Carbamazepine (e.g., Tegretol) or
- Chloramphenicol (e.g., Chloromycetin) or
- Colchicine or
- Cyclophosphamide (e.g., Cytoxan)
- Enalapril (e.g., Vasotec) or
- Flecainide (e.g., Tambocor) or
- Flucytosine (e.g., Ancobon) or
- Ganciclovir (e.g., Cytovene) or
- Gold salts (medicine for arthritis) or
- Imipenem and Cilastatin (e.g., Primaxin) or
- Inflammation or pain medicine, except narcotics or
- Interferon (e.g., Intron A, Roferon-A) or
- Itraconazole (e.g., Sporanox) or
- Lisinopril (e.g., Prinivil, Zestril) or
- Maprotiline (e.g., Ludiomil) or
- Mercaptopurine (e.g., Purinethol) or
- Methotrexate (e.g., Rheumatrex) or
- Penicillamine (e.g., Cuprimine) or
- Pimozide (e.g., Orap) or
- Plicamycin (e.g., Mithracin) or
- Procainamide (e.g., Pronestyl) or
- Promethazine (e.g., Phenergan) or
- Ramipril (e.g., Altace) or
- Sulfasalazine (e.g., Azulfidine) or
- Tocainide (e.g., Tonocard) or
- Tricyclic antidepressants (medicine for depression) or
- Trimeprazine (e.g., Temaril) or

- Zidovudine (e.g., AZT, Retrovir) or
- If you have ever been treated with radiation or cancer medicines—Busulfan may increase the effects of these medicines or radiation therapy on the blood
- Probenecid (e.g., Benemid) or
- Sulfinpyrazone (e.g., Anturane)—Busulfan may raise the amount of uric acid in the blood. Since these medicines are used to lower uric acid levels, they may not be as effective in patients taking busulfan

Other medical problems—The presence of other medical problems may affect the use of busulfan. Make sure you tell your doctor if you have any other medical problems, especially:

- Chickenpox (including recent exposure) or
- Herpes zoster (shingles)—Risk of severe disease affecting other parts of the body
- Gout (history of) or
- Kidney stones (or history of)—Busulfan may increase levels of uric acid in the body, which can cause gout or kidney stones
- Head injury or
- Convulsions (seizures, history of)—Busulfan injection and very high doses of oral busulfan can cause convulsions (seizures)
- Infection—Busulfan may decrease your body's ability to fight infection
- Thalassemia—Busulfan may cause increased pressure within the heart in children

Proper Use of This Medicine

Take this medicine only as directed by your doctor. Do not take more or less of it, and do not take it more often than your doctor ordered. The exact amount of medicine you need has been carefully worked out. Taking too much may increase the chance of side effects, while taking too little may not improve your condition.

Take each dose at the same time each day to make sure it has the best effect.

While you are taking this medicine, your doctor may want you to drink extra fluids so that you will pass more urine. This will help prevent kidney problems and keep your kidneys working well.

This medicine sometimes causes nausea and vomiting. However, it is very important that you continue to use the medicine, even if you begin to feel ill. *Do not stop taking this medicine without first checking with your doctor.* Ask your health care professional for ways to lessen these effects.

If you vomit shortly after taking a dose of busulfan, check with your doctor. You will be told whether to take the dose again or to wait until the next scheduled dose.

Dosing—The dose of busulfan will be different for different patients. The dose that is used may depend on a number of things, including what the medicine is being used for, the patient's weight, and whether or not other medicines are also being taken. *If you are taking busulfan at home, follow your doctor's orders or the directions on the label.* If you have any questions about the proper dose of busulfan, ask your doctor.

Missed dose—If you miss a dose of this medicine, skip the missed dose and go back to your regular dosing schedule. Do not double doses.

Storage—To store this medicine:

- Keep out of the reach of children.
- Store away from heat and direct light.
- Do not store in the bathroom, near the kitchen sink, or in other damp places. Heat or moisture may cause the medicine to break down.
- Do not keep outdated medicine or medicine no longer needed. Be sure that any discarded medicine is out of the reach of children.

Precautions While Using This Medicine

It is very important that your doctor check your progress at regular visits to make sure that this medicine is working properly and to check for unwanted effects.

While you are being treated with busulfan, and after you stop treatment with it, *do not have any immunizations (vaccinations) without your doctor's approval.* Busulfan may lower your body's resistance and there is a chance you might get the infection the immunization is meant to prevent. In addition, other persons living in your household should not take oral polio vaccine since there is a chance they could pass the polio virus on to you. Also, avoid persons who have taken oral polio vaccine within the last several months. Do not get close to them, and do not stay in the same room with them for very long. If you cannot take these precautions, you should consider wearing a protective face mask that covers the nose and mouth.

Busulfan can temporarily lower the number of white blood cells in your blood, increasing the chance of getting an infection. It can also lower the number of platelets, which are necessary for proper blood clotting. If this occurs, there are certain precautions you can take, especially when your blood count is low, to reduce the risk of infection or bleeding:

- If you can, avoid people with infections. *Check with your doctor immediately* if you think you are getting an infection or if you get a fever or chills, cough or hoarseness, lower back or side pain, or painful or difficult urination.
- *Check with your doctor immediately* if you notice any unusual bleeding or bruising; black, tarry stools; blood in urine or stools; or pinpoint red spots on your skin.
- Be careful when using a regular toothbrush, dental floss, or toothpick. Your medical doctor, dentist, or nurse may recommend other ways to clean your teeth and gums. Check with your medical doctor before having any dental work done.
- Do not touch your eyes or the inside of your nose unless you have just washed your hands and have not touched anything else in the meantime.
- Be careful not to cut yourself when you are using sharp objects such as a safety razor or fingernail or toenail cutters.
- Avoid contact sports or other situations where bruising or injury could occur.

Before you have any medical tests, tell the medical doctor in charge that you are taking this medicine. The results of some body tissue studies may be affected by this medicine.

Side Effects of This Medicine

Along with its needed effects, a medicine may have some unwanted effects. Although not all of these side effects may occur, if they do occur they may need medical attention.

Also, because of the way these medicines act on the body, there is a chance that they might cause other unwanted effects that may not occur until months or years after the medicine is used. These delayed effects may include certain types of cancer, such as leukemia. Discuss these possible effects with your doctor.

Check with your doctor or nurse immediately if any of the following side effects occur:

More common

Black, tarry stools; blood in urine or stools; cough or hoarseness; fever or chills; inflammation of the mouth; lower back or side pain; painful or difficult urination; pinpoint red spots on skin; unusual bleeding or bruising

Less common

Chest pain; dizziness; fast or irregular breathing; joint pain; light-headedness; puffiness or swelling around face; rapid heartbeat; shortness of breath; sudden, severe decrease in blood pressure; sweating; swelling of fingers, hands, arms, lower legs, or feet; sweating; tingling in lower legs, hands, or feet

Rare

Blurred vision; difficulty swallowing; heartburn; severe upper abdominal and back pain; vomiting blood

Other side effects may occur that usually do not need medical attention. These side effects may go away during treatment as your body adjusts to the medicine. Also, your health care professional may be able to tell you about ways to prevent or reduce some of these side effects. Check with your health care professional if any of the following side effects continue or are bothersome or if you have any questions about them:

More common

Abdominal pain; anxiety; diarrhea; general fatigue or muscle pain; headache; missed or irregular menstrual periods; loss of appetite; nausea and vomiting; rash; trouble in sleeping; weight loss (sudden)

Less common

Bloody nose; confusion; constipation; darkening of skin; depression; dry mouth; inflammation at place of injection; itching; sore throat or cough; stuffy nose, runny nose, or sneezing

After you stop taking busulfan, it may still produce some side effects that need attention. During this period of time, check with your doctor if you notice any of the following:

Black, tarry stools; blood in urine or stools; cough or hoarseness, accompanied by fever or chills; fever or chills; lower back or side pain, accompanied by fever or chills; painful or difficult urination, accompanied by fever or chills; pinpoint red spots on skin; shortness of breath; unusual bleeding or bruising

Other side effects not listed above may also occur in some patients. If you notice any other effects, check with your doctor.

Revised: 10/5/99
Interim revision: 05/02/94; 08/14/98

BUTALBITAL AND ACETAMINOPHEN   Systemic†

Commonly used brand name(s):

In the U.S.—

Amaphen[2]	Fioricet[2]
Anolor-300[2]	Isocet[2]
Anoquan[2]	Medigesic[2]
Arcet[2]	Pacaps[2]
Bancap[1]	Pharmagesic[2]
Bucet[1]	Phrenilin[1]
Butace[2]	Phrenilin Forte[1]
Conten[1]	Repan[2]
Dolmar[2]	Sedapap[1]
Endolor[2]	Tencet[2]
Esgic[2]	Tencon[1]
Esgic-Plus[2]	Triad[2]
Ezol[2]	Triaprin[1]
Femcet[2]	Two-Dyne[2]

Note: For quick reference, the following butalbital and acetaminophens are numbered to match the corresponding brand names.

This information applies to the following medicines:

1. Butalbital and Acetaminophen (byoo-TAL-bi-tal and a-seat-a-MIN-oh-fen)†‡
2. Butalbital, Acetaminophen, and Caffeine (byoo-TAL-bi-tal, a-seat-a-MIN-oh-fen, and KAF-een)†‡

†Not commercially available in Canada.
‡Generic name product may be available in the U.S.

Description

Butalbital and acetaminophen (byoo-TAL-bi-tal and a-seat-a-MIN-oh-fen) combination is a pain reliever and relaxant. It is used to treat tension headaches. Butalbital belongs to the group of medicines called barbiturates (bar-BI-tyoo-rates). Barbiturates act in the central nervous system (CNS) to produce their effects.

When you take butalbital for a long time, your body may get used to it so that larger amounts are needed to produce the same effects. This is called tolerance to the medicine. Also, butalbital may become habit-forming (causing mental or physical dependence) when it is used for a long time or in large doses. Physical dependence may lead to withdrawal side effects when you stop taking the medicine. In patients who get headaches, the first symptom of withdrawal may be new (rebound) headaches.

Some butalbital and acetaminophen combinations also contain caffeine (KAF-een). Caffeine may help to relieve headaches. However, caffeine can also cause physical dependence when it is used for a long time. This may lead to withdrawal (rebound) headaches when you stop taking it.

Butalbital and acetaminophen combination may also be used for other kinds of headaches or other kinds of pain as determined by your doctor.

Butalbital and acetaminophen combinations are available only with your doctor's prescription in the following dosage forms:

Oral

Butalbital and Acetaminophen
- Capsules (U.S.)
- Tablets (U.S.)

Butalbital, Acetaminophen, and Caffeine
- Capsules (U.S.)
- Tablets (U.S.)

Before Using This Medicine

In deciding to use a medicine, the risks of taking the medicine must be weighed against the good it will do. This is a decision you and your doctor will make. For butalbital and acetaminophen combinations, the following should be considered:

Allergies—Tell your doctor if you have ever had any unusual or allergic reaction to butalbital or other barbiturates, or to acetaminophen, aspirin, or caffeine. Also tell your health care professional if you are allergic to any other substances, such as foods, preservatives, or dyes.

Pregnancy—
- *For butalbital:* Barbiturates such as butalbital have been shown to increase the chance of birth defects in humans. Also, one study in humans has suggested that barbiturates taken during pregnancy may increase the chance of brain tumors in the baby. Butalbital may cause breathing problems in the newborn baby if taken just before or during delivery.
- *For acetaminophen:* Although studies on birth defects with acetaminophen have not been done in pregnant women, it has not been reported to cause birth defects or other problems.
- *For caffeine:* Studies in humans have not shown that caffeine (contained in some of these combination medicines) causes birth defects. However, use of large amounts of caffeine during pregnancy may cause problems with the heart rhythm and the growth of the fetus. Also, studies in animals have shown that caffeine causes birth defects when given in very large doses (amounts equal to those present in 12 to 24 cups of coffee a day).

Breast-feeding—
- *For butalbital:* Barbiturates such as butalbital pass into the breast milk and may cause drowsiness, unusually slow heartbeat, shortness of breath, or troubled breathing in nursing babies.
- *For acetaminophen:* Although acetaminophen has not been shown to cause problems in nursing babies, it passes into the breast milk in small amounts.
- *For caffeine:* Caffeine (present in some butalbital and acetaminophen combinations) passes into the breast milk in small amounts. Taking caffeine in the amounts present in these medicines has not been shown to cause problems in nursing babies. However, studies have shown that nursing babies may appear jittery and have trouble in sleeping when their mothers drink large amounts of caffeine-containing beverages. Therefore, breast-feeding mothers who use caffeine-containing medicines should probably limit the amount of caffeine they take in from other medicines or from beverages.

Children—
- *For butalbital:* Although barbiturates such as butalbital often cause drowsiness, some children become excited after taking them.
- *For acetaminophen:* Acetaminophen has been tested in children and, in effective doses, has not been shown to cause different side effects or problems than it does in adults.

- *For caffeine:* There is no specific information comparing use of caffeine in children up to 12 years of age with use in other age groups. However, caffeine is not expected to cause different side effects or problems in children than it does in adults.

Older adults—
- *For butalbital:* Certain side effects, such as confusion, excitement, or mental depression, may be especially likely to occur in elderly patients, who are usually more sensitive than younger adults to the effects of the butalbital in this combination medicine.
- *For acetaminophen:* Acetaminophen has been tested and has not been shown to cause different side effects or problems in older people than it does in younger adults.
- *For caffeine:* Many medicines have not been studied specifically in older people. Therefore, it may not be known whether they work exactly the same way they do in younger adults or if they cause different side effects or problems in older people. There is no specific information comparing use of caffeine in the elderly with use in other age groups.

Other medicines—Although certain medicines should not be used together at all, in other cases two different medicines may be used together even if an interaction might occur. In these cases, your doctor may want to change the dose, or other precautions may be necessary. When you are taking a butalbital and acetaminophen combination, it is especially important that your health care professional know if you are taking any of the following:
- Anticoagulants (blood thinners), or
- Carbamazepine (e.g., Tegretol) or
- Contraceptives, oral (birth control pills) containing estrogen, or
- Corticosteroids (cortisone-like medicines) or
- Corticotropin (e.g., ACTH)—Butalbital may make these medicines less effective

- Antidepressants, tricyclic (amitriptyline [e.g., Elavil], amoxapine [e.g., Asendin], clomipramine [e.g., Anafranil], desipramine [e.g., Pertofrane], doxepin [e.g., Sinequan], imipramine [e.g., Tofranil], nortriptyline [e.g., Aventyl], protriptyline [e.g., Vivactil], trimipramine [e.g., Surmontil]) or
- Central nervous system (CNS) depressants (medicines that often cause drowsiness)—These medicines may add to the effects of butalbital and increase the chance of drowsiness or other side effects

- Divalproex (e.g., Depakote) or
- Valproic acid (e.g., Depakene)—The chance of side effects may be increased

Other medical problems—The presence of other medical problems may affect the use of butalbital and acetaminophen combinations. Make sure you tell your doctor if you have any other medical problems, especially:
- Alcohol abuse (or history of) or
- Drug abuse or dependence (or history of)—Dependence on butalbital may develop; also, acetaminophen may cause liver damage in people who abuse alcohol

- Asthma (or history of), emphysema, or other chronic lung disease or
- Hepatitis or other liver disease or
- Hyperactivity (in children) or

- Kidney disease—The chance of serious side effects may be increased

- Diabetes mellitus (sugar diabetes) or
- Mental depression or
- Overactive thyroid or
- Porphyria (or history of)—Butalbital can make these conditions worse

- Heart disease (severe)—The caffeine in some butalbital and acetaminophen combinations can make some kinds of heart disease worse

Proper Use of This Medicine

Take this medicine only as directed by your doctor. Do not take more of it, do not take it more often, and do not take it for a longer time than your doctor ordered. If butalbital and acetaminophen combination is taken regularly (for example, every day), it may become habit-forming (causing mental or physical dependence). The caffeine in some butalbital and acetaminophen combinations can also increase the chance of dependence. Dependence is especially likely to occur in patients who take these medicines to relieve frequent headaches. Taking too much of this medicine may also lead to liver damage or other medical problems.

This medicine will relieve a headache best if you *take it as soon as the headache begins*. If you get warning signs of a migraine, take this medicine as soon as you are sure that the migraine is coming. This may even stop the headache pain from occurring. *Lying down in a quiet, dark room for a while after taking the medicine also helps to relieve headaches*.

People who get a lot of headaches may need to take a different medicine to help prevent headaches. *It is important that you follow your doctor's directions about taking the other medicine, even if your headaches continue to occur*. Headache-preventing medicines may take several weeks to start working. Even after they do start working, your headaches may not go away completely. However, your headaches should occur less often, and they should be less severe and easier to relieve than before. This will reduce the amount of headache relievers that you need. If you do not notice any improvement after several weeks of headache-preventing treatment, check with your doctor.

Dosing—The dose of butalbital and acetaminophen combination medicines will be different for different patients. *Follow your doctor's orders or the directions on the label*. The following information includes only the average doses of these medicines. *If your dose is different, do not change it* unless your doctor tells you to do so.

The number of capsules or tablets that you take depends on the strength of the medicine.

- For *oral* dosage forms (capsules or tablets):
  —For tension headaches:
  - Adults—One or 2 capsules or tablets every four hours as needed. If your medicine contains 325 or 500 milligrams (mg) of acetaminophen in each capsule or tablet, you should not take more than six capsules or tablets a day. If your medicine contains 650 mg of acetaminophen in each capsule or tablet, you should not take more than four capsules or tablets a day.
  - Children—Dose must be determined by your doctor.

Missed dose—If your doctor has ordered you to take this medicine according to a regular schedule and you miss a dose, take it as soon as you remember. However, if it is almost time for your next dose, skip the missed dose and go back to your regular dosing schedule. *Do not double doses*.

Storage—To store this medicine:
- Keep out of the reach of children. Overdose is especially dangerous in young children.
- Store away from heat and direct light.
- Do not store this medicine in the bathroom, near the kitchen sink, or in other damp places. Heat or moisture may cause the medicine to break down.
- Do not keep outdated medicine or medicine no longer needed. Be sure that any discarded medicine is out of the reach of children.

Precautions While Using This Medicine

Check with your doctor:
- If the medicine stops working as well as it did when you first started using it. This may mean that you are in danger of becoming dependent on the medicine. *Do not try to get better pain relief by increasing the dose*.
- *If you are having headaches more often than you did before you started taking this medicine*. This is especially important if a new headache occurs within 1 day after you took your last dose of this medicine, headaches begin to occur every day, or a headache continues for several days in a row. This may mean that you are dependent on the medicine. *Continuing to take this medicine will cause even more headaches later on*. Your doctor can give you advice on how to relieve the headaches.

Check the labels of all nonprescription (over-the-counter [OTC]) or prescription medicines you now take. If any contain a barbiturate or acetaminophen, check with your health care professional. Taking them together with this medicine may cause an overdose.

The butalbital in this medicine will add to the effects of alcohol and other CNS depressants (medicines that slow down the nervous system, possibly causing drowsiness). Some examples of CNS depressants are antihistamines or medicine for hay fever, other allergies, or colds; sedatives, tranquilizers, or sleeping medicine; other prescription pain medicine; narcotics; other barbiturates; medicine for seizures; muscle relaxants; or anesthetics, including some dental anesthetics. Also, drinking large amounts of alcoholic beverages regularly while taking this medicine may increase the chance of liver damage, especially if you take more of this medicine than your doctor ordered or if you take it regularly for a long time. *Therefore, do not drink alcoholic beverages, and check with your doctor before taking any of the medicines listed above, while you are using this medicine*.

This medicine may cause some people to become drowsy, dizzy, or lightheaded. *Make sure you know how you react to this medicine before you drive, use machines, or do anything else that could be dangerous if you are dizzy or are not alert and clearheaded*.

Before you have any medical tests, tell the person in charge that you are taking this medicine. Caffeine (present in some butalbital and acetaminophen combinations) interferes with the results of certain tests that use dipyridamole (e.g., Persantine) to help show how well blood is flowing to your heart. Caffeine should not be taken for 8 to 12 hours before the test.

The results of other tests may also be affected by butalbital and acetaminophen combinations.

Before having any kind of surgery (including dental surgery) or emergency treatment, tell the medical doctor or dentist in charge that you are taking this medicine. Serious side effects can occur if your medical doctor or dentist gives you certain medicines without knowing that you have taken butalbital.

If you have been taking large amounts of this medicine, or if you have been taking it regularly for several weeks or more, *do not suddenly stop taking it without first checking with your doctor.* Your doctor may want you to reduce gradually the amount you are taking before stopping completely in order to lessen the chance of withdrawal side effects.

If you think you or anyone else may have taken an overdose of this medicine, get emergency help at once. Taking an overdose of this medicine or taking alcohol or CNS depressants with this medicine may lead to unconsciousness or possibly death. Signs of butalbital overdose include severe drowsiness, confusion, severe weakness, shortness of breath or unusually slow or troubled breathing, slurred speech, staggering, and unusually slow heartbeat. Signs of severe acetaminophen poisoning may not occur until 2 to 4 days after the overdose is taken, but treatment to prevent liver damage or death must be started within 24 hours or less after the overdose is taken.

Side Effects of This Medicine

Along with its needed effects, a medicine may cause some unwanted effects. Although not all of these side effects may occur, if they do occur they may need medical attention.

Check with your doctor immediately if any of the following side effects occur, especially if several of them occur together:

Rare

Bleeding or crusting sores on lips; chest pain; fever with or without chills; hive-like swellings (large) on eyelids, face, lips, and/or tongue; muscle cramps or pain; red, thickened, or scaly skin; shortness of breath, troubled breathing, tightness in chest, or wheezing; skin rash, itching, or hives; sores, ulcers, or white spots in mouth (painful); sore throat

Symptoms of overdose

Anxiety, confusion, excitement, irritability, nervousness, restlessness, or trouble in sleeping (severe, especially with products containing caffeine); convulsions (seizures) (for products containing caffeine); diarrhea, especially if occurring together with increased sweating, loss of appetite, and stomach cramps or pain; dizziness, lightheadedness, drowsiness, or weakness, (severe); frequent urination (for products containing caffeine); hallucinations (seeing, hearing, or feeling things that are not there); increased sensitivity to touch or pain (for products containing caffeine); muscle trembling or twitching (for products containing caffeine); nausea or vomiting, sometimes with blood; ringing or other sounds in ears (for products containing caffeine); seeing flashes of "zig-zag" lights (for products containing caffeine); shortness of breath or unusually slow or troubled breathing; slow, fast, or irregular heartbeat; slurred speech; staggering; swelling, pain, or tenderness in the upper abdomen or stomach area; unusual movements of the eyes

Also, check with your doctor as soon as possible if any of the following side effects occur:

Less common

Confusion (mild); mental depression; unusual excitement (mild)

Rare

Bloody or black, tarry stools; bloody urine; pinpoint red spots on skin; swollen or painful glands; unusual bleeding or bruising; unusual tiredness or weakness (mild)

Other side effects may occur that usually do not need medical attention. These side effects may go away during treatment as your body adjusts to the medicine. However, check with your doctor if any of the following side effects continue or are bothersome:

More common

Bloated or "gassy" feeling; dizziness or lightheadedness (mild); drowsiness (mild); nausea, vomiting, or stomach pain (occurring without other symptoms of overdose)

Other side effects not listed above may also occur in some patients. If you notice any other effects, check with your doctor.

Revised: 07/14/92
Interim revision: 07/15/94

BUTALBITAL AND ASPIRIN
Systemic

Commonly used brand name(s):

In the U.S.—

Axotal[1]	Isobutyl[2]
Butalgen[2]	Isolin[2]
Fiorgen[2]	Isollyl[2]
Fiorinal[2]	Laniroif[2]
Fiormor[2]	Lanorinal[2]
Fortabs[2]	Marnal[2]
Isobutal[2]	Vibutal[2]

In Canada—

Fiorinal[2]
Tecnal[2]

Other commonly used names for the butalbital, aspirin, and caffeine combination medicine are butalbital-AC[2] and butalbital compound[2].

Note: For quick reference, the following medicines are numbered to match the corresponding brand names.

This information applies to the following medicines:

1. Butalbital and Aspirin (byoo-TAL-bi-tal and AS-pir-in)†
2. Butalbital, Aspirin#, and Caffeine (byoo-TAL-bi-tal, AS-pir-in, and kaf-EEN)‡

†Not commercially available in Canada.
‡Generic name product may be available in the U.S.
#In Canada, *Aspirin* is a brand name. Acetylsalicylic acid is the generic name in Canada. ASA, a synonym for acetylsalicylic acid, is the term that commonly appears on Canadian product labels.

Description

Butalbital and aspirin combination is a pain reliever and relaxant. It is used to treat tension headaches. Butalbital belongs to the group of medicines called barbiturates. Barbiturates act in the central nervous system (CNS) to produce their effects.

When you use butalbital for a long time, your body may get used to it so that larger amounts are needed to produce the same effects. This is called tolerance to the medicine. Also, butalbital may become habit-forming (causing mental or physical dependence) when it is used for a long time or in large doses. Physical dependence may lead to withdrawal side effects when you stop taking the medicine. In patients who get headaches, the first symptom of withdrawal may be new (rebound) headaches.

Some of these medicines also contain caffeine. Caffeine may help to relieve headaches. However, caffeine can also cause physical dependence when it is used for a long time. This may lead to withdrawal (rebound) headaches when you stop taking it.

Butalbital and aspirin combination is sometimes also used for other kinds of headaches or other kinds of pain, as determined by your doctor.

Butalbital and aspirin combination is available only with your doctor's prescription, in the following dosage forms:

> *Oral*
> Butalbital and Aspirin
> - Tablets (U.S.)
> Butalbital, Aspirin, and Caffeine
> - Capsules (U.S. and Canada)
> - Tablets (U.S. and Canada)

Before Using This Medicine

In deciding to use a medicine, the risks of taking the medicine must be weighed against the good it will do. This is a decision you and your doctor will make. For butalbital and aspirin combinations, the following should be considered:

Allergies—Tell your doctor if you have ever had any unusual or allergic reaction to butalbital or other barbiturates; aspirin or other salicylates, including methyl salicylate (oil of wintergreen); caffeine; or any of the following medicines:

Diclofenac (e.g., Voltaren)
Diflunisal (e.g., Dolobid)
Etodolac (e.g., Lodine)
Fenoprofen (e.g., Nalfon)
Floctafenine (e.g., Idarac)
Flurbiprofen, oral (e.g., Ansaid)
Ibuprofen (e.g., Motrin)
Indomethacin (e.g., Indocin)
Ketoprofen (e.g., Orudis)
Ketorolac (e.g., Toradol)
Meclofenamate (e.g., Meclomen)
Mefenamic acid (e.g., Ponstel)
Nabumetone (e.g., Relafen)
Naproxen (e.g., Naprosyn)
Oxaprozin (e.g., Daypro)
Oxyphenbutazone (e.g., Tandearil)
Phenylbutazone (e.g., Butazolidin)
Piroxicam (e.g., Feldene)
Sulindac (e.g., Clinoril)
Suprofen (e.g., Suprol)
Tenoxicam (e.g., Mobiflex)
Tiaprofenic acid (e.g., Surgam)
Tolmetin (e.g., Tolectin)
Zomepirac (e.g., Zomax)

Also tell your health care professional if you are allergic to any other substances, such as foods, preservatives, or dyes.

Pregnancy—
- *For butalbital:* Barbiturates such as butalbital have been shown to increase the chance of birth defects in humans. Also, one study in humans has suggested that barbiturates taken during pregnancy may increase the chance of brain tumors in the baby. Butalbital may cause breathing problems in the newborn baby if taken just before or during delivery.
- *For aspirin:* Although studies in humans have not shown that aspirin causes birth defects, it has caused birth defects in animal studies. *Do not take aspirin during the last 3 months of pregnancy unless it has been ordered by your doctor.* Some reports have suggested that use of aspirin late in pregnancy may cause a decrease in the newborn's weight and possible death of the fetus or newborn baby. However, the mothers in these reports had been taking much larger amounts of aspirin than are usually recommended. Studies of mothers taking aspirin in the doses that are usually recommended did not show these unwanted effects. There is a chance that regular use of aspirin late in pregnancy may cause unwanted effects on the heart or blood flow in the fetus or in the newborn baby. Also, use of aspirin during the last 2 weeks of pregnancy may cause bleeding problems in the fetus before or during delivery or in the newborn baby. In addition, too much use of aspirin during the last 3 months of pregnancy may increase the length of pregnancy, prolong labor, cause other problems during delivery, or cause severe bleeding in the mother before, during, or after delivery.
- *For caffeine:* Studies in humans have not shown that caffeine causes birth defects. However, use of large amounts of caffeine during pregnancy may cause problems with the heart rhythm and the growth of the fetus. Also, studies in animals have shown that caffeine causes birth defects when given in very large doses (amounts equal to the amount in 12 to 24 cups of coffee a day).

Breast-feeding—Although this combination medicine has not been reported to cause problems, the chance always exists, especially if the medicine is taken for a long time or in large amounts.
- *For butalbital:* Barbiturates such as butalbital pass into the breast milk and may cause drowsiness, unusually slow heartbeat, shortness of breath, or troubled breathing in nursing babies.
- *For aspirin:* Aspirin passes into the breast milk. However, taking aspirin in the amounts present in these combination medicines has not been reported to cause problems in nursing babies.
- *For caffeine:* The caffeine in some of these combination medicines passes into the breast milk in small amounts. Taking caffeine in the amounts present in these medicines has not been reported to cause problems in nursing babies. However, studies have shown that nursing babies may appear jittery and have trouble in sleeping when their mothers drink large amounts of caffeine-containing beverages. Therefore, breast-feeding mothers who use caffeine-containing medicines should probably limit the amount of caffeine they take in from other medicines or from beverages.

Children—
- *For butalbital:* Although barbiturates such as butalbital often cause drowsiness, some children become excited after taking them.

- *For aspirin: Do not give a medicine containing aspirin to a child with fever or other symptoms of a virus infection, especially flu or chickenpox, without first discussing its use with your child's doctor.* This is very important because aspirin may cause a serious illness called Reye's syndrome in children with fever caused by a virus infection, especially flu or chickenpox. Children who do not have a virus infection may also be more sensitive to the effects of aspirin, especially if they have a fever or have lost large amounts of body fluid because of vomiting, diarrhea, or sweating. This may increase the chance of side effects during treatment.
- *For caffeine:* There is no specific information comparing use of caffeine in children up to 12 years of age with use in other age groups. However, caffeine is not expected to cause different side effects or problems in children than it does in adults.

Teenagers—*Teenagers with fever or other symptoms of a virus infection, especially flu or chickenpox, should check with a doctor before taking this medicine.* The aspirin in this combination medicine may cause a serious illness called Reye's syndrome in teenagers with fever caused by a virus infection, especially flu or chickenpox.

Older adults—

- *For butalbital:* Confusion, depression, or excitement may be especially likely to occur in elderly patients, who are usually more sensitive than younger adults to the effects of butalbital.
- *For aspirin:* Elderly patients are more sensitive than younger adults to the effects of aspirin. This may increase the chance of side effects during treatment.
- *For caffeine:* Many medicines have not been studied specifically in older people. Therefore, it may not be known whether they work exactly the same way they do in younger adults or if they cause different side effects or problems in older people. There is no specific information comparing use of caffeine in the elderly with use in other age groups.

Other medicines—Although certain medicines should not be used together at all, in other cases two different medicines may be used together even if an interaction might occur. In these cases, your doctor may want to change the dose, or other precautions may be necessary. When you are taking a butalbital and aspirin combination, it is especially important that your health care professional know if you are taking any of the following:

- Antacids, large amounts taken regularly, especially calcium- and/or magnesium-containing antacids or sodium bicarbonate (baking soda), or
- Urinary alkalizers (medicine that makes the urine less acid, such as acetazolamide [e.g., Diamox], dichlorphenamide [e.g., Daranide], methazolamide [e.g., Neptazane], potassium or sodium citrate and/or citric acid)—These medicines may cause aspirin to be removed from the body faster than usual, which may shorten the time that aspirin is effective; acetazolamide, dichlorphenamide, and methazolamide may also increase the chance of side effects when taken together with aspirin
- Anticoagulants (blood thinners) or
- Heparin—Use of these medicines together with aspirin may increase the chance of bleeding; also, butalbital may cause anticoagulants to be less effective
- Antidepressants, tricyclic (amitriptyline [e.g., Elavil], amoxapine [e.g., Asendin], clomipramine [e.g., Anaf-

ranil], desipramine [e.g., Pertofrane], doxepin [e.g., Sinequan], imipramine [e.g., Tofranil], nortriptyline [e.g., Aventyl], protriptyline [e.g., Vivactil], trimipramine [e.g., Surmontil]) or
- Central nervous system (CNS) depressants (medicines that often cause drowsiness)—These medicines may add to the effects of butalbital and increase the chance of drowsiness or other side effects
- Carbamazepine (e.g., Tegretol) or
- Contraceptives, oral (birth control pills), containing estrogen or
- Corticosteroids (cortisone-like medicines) or
- Corticotropin (e.g., ACTH)—Butalbital may make these medicines less effective
- Divalproex (e.g., Depakote) or
- Methotrexate (e.g., Folex, Mexate) or
- Valproic acid (e.g., Depakene) or
- Vancomycin (e.g., Vancocin)—The chance of serious side effects may be increased
- Probenecid (e.g., Benemid) or
- Sulfinpyrazone (e.g., Anturane)—Aspirin can keep these medicines from working properly for treating gout

Other medical problems—The presence of other medical problems may affect the use of butalbital and aspirin combinations. Make sure you tell your doctor if you have any other medical problems, especially:

- Alcohol abuse (or history of) or
- Drug abuse or dependence (or history of)—Dependence on butalbital may develop
- Asthma, especially if occurring together with other allergies and nasal polyps (or history of), or
- Emphysema or other chronic lung disease or
- Hyperactivity (in children) or
- Kidney disease or
- Liver disease—The chance of serious side effects may be increased
- Diabetes mellitus (sugar diabetes) or
- Mental depression or
- Overactive thyroid or
- Porphyria (or history of)—Butalbital may make these conditions worse
- Gout—Aspirin can make this condition worse and can also lessen the effects of some medicines used to treat gout
- Heart disease (severe)—The caffeine in some of these combination medicines can make some kinds of heart disease worse
- Hemophilia or other bleeding problems or
- Vitamin K deficiency—Aspirin increases the chance of serious bleeding
- Stomach ulcer, especially with a history of bleeding, or other stomach problems—Aspirin can make your condition worse

Proper Use of This Medicine

Take this medicine with food or a full glass (8 ounces) of water to lessen stomach irritation.

Do not take this medicine if it has a strong vinegar-like odor. This odor means the aspirin in it is breaking down. If you have any questions about this, check with your health care professional.

Take this medicine only as directed by your doctor. Do not take more of it, do not take it more often, and do not take it for a longer time than your doctor ordered. If butalbital and aspirin combination is taken regularly (for example, every day), it may become habit-forming (causing mental or physical dependence). The caffeine in some butalbital and aspirin combinations can also increase the chance of dependence. Dependence is especially likely to occur in patients who take this medicine to relieve frequent headaches. Taking too much of this combination medicine can also lead to stomach problems or to other medical problems.

This medicine will relieve a headache best if you *take it as soon as the headache begins*. If you get warning signs of a migraine, take this medicine as soon as you are sure that the migraine is coming. This may even stop the headache pain from occurring. *Lying down in a quiet, dark room for a while after taking the medicine also helps to relieve headaches*.

People who get a lot of headaches may need to take a different medicine to help prevent headaches. *It is important that you follow your doctor's directions about taking the other medicine, even if your headaches continue to occur*. Headache-preventing medicines may take several weeks to start working. Even after they do start working, your headaches may not go away completely. However, your headaches should occur less often, and they should be less severe and easier to relieve than before. This will reduce the amount of headache relievers that you need. If you do not notice any improvement after several weeks of headache-preventing treatment, check with your doctor.

Dosing—The dose of butalbital and aspirin combination medicines will be different for different patients. *Follow your doctor's orders or the directions on the label*. The following information includes only the average doses of the medicine. *If your dose is different, do not change it* unless your doctor tells you to do so.

For Butalbital and Aspirin combination
- For *oral* dosage form (tablets):
  —For tension headaches:
    - Adults—One tablet every four hours as needed. You should not take more than six tablets a day.
    - Children—Dose must be determined by your doctor.

For Butalbital, Aspirin, and Caffeine combination
- For *oral* dosage forms (capsules or tablets):
  —For tension headaches:
    - Adults—One or 2 capsules or tablets every four hours as needed. You should not take more than six capsules or tablets a day.
    - Children—Dose must be determined by your doctor.

Missed dose—If your doctor has ordered you to take this medicine according to a regular schedule and you miss a dose, take it as soon as you remember. However, if it is almost time for your next dose, skip the missed dose and go back to your regular dosing schedule. Do not double doses.

Storage—To store this medicine:
- Keep out of the reach of children. Overdose is especially dangerous in young children.
- Store away from heat and direct light.
- Do not store this medicine in the bathroom, near the kitchen sink, or in other damp places. Heat or moisture may cause the medicine to break down.

- Do not keep outdated medicine or medicine no longer needed. Be sure that any discarded medicine is out of the reach of children.

Precautions While Using This Medicine

Check with your doctor:
- If the medicine stops working as well as it did when you first started using it. This may mean that you are in danger of becoming dependent on the medicine. *Do not try to get better pain relief by increasing the dose*.
- *If you are having headaches more often than you did before you started using this medicine*. This is especially important if a new headache occurs within 1 day after you took your last dose of headache medicine, headaches begin to occur every day, or a headache continues for several days in a row. This may mean that you are dependent on the headache medicine. *Continuing to take this medicine will cause even more headaches later on*. Your doctor can give you advice on how to relieve the headaches.

Check the labels of all nonprescription (over-the-counter [OTC]) and prescription medicines you now take. If any contain a barbiturate, aspirin, or other salicylates, including diflunisal, check with your health care professional. Taking them together with this medicine may cause an overdose.

The butalbital in this medicine will add to the effects of alcohol and other CNS depressants (medicines that slow down the nervous system, possibly causing drowsiness). Some examples of CNS depressants are antihistamines or medicine for hay fever, other allergies, or colds; sedatives, tranquilizers, or sleeping medicine; other prescription pain medicine or narcotics; other barbiturates; medicine for seizures; muscle relaxants; or anesthetics, including some dental anesthetics. Also, stomach problems may be more likely to occur if you drink alcoholic beverages while you are taking aspirin. Therefore, *do not drink alcoholic beverages, and check with your doctor before taking any of the medicines listed above, while you are using this medicine*.

This medicine may cause some people to become drowsy, dizzy, or lightheaded. *Make sure you know how you react to this medicine before you drive, use machines, or do anything else that could be dangerous if you are dizzy or are not alert and clearheaded*.

Before having any kind of surgery (including dental surgery) or emergency treatment, tell the medical doctor or dentist in charge that you are taking this medicine. Serious side effects may occur if your medical doctor or dentist gives you certain other medicines without knowing that you have taken butalbital.

Do not take this medicine for 5 days before any planned surgery, including dental surgery, unless otherwise directed by your medical doctor or dentist. Taking aspirin during this time may cause bleeding problems.

Before you have any medical tests, tell the person in charge that you are taking this medicine. Caffeine (present in some butalbital and aspirin combinations) interferes with the results of certain tests that use dipyridamole (e.g., Persantine) to help show how well blood is flowing to your heart. Caffeine should not be taken for 8 to 12 hours before the test. The results of some other tests may also be affected by butalbital and aspirin combinations.

If you have been taking large amounts of this medicine, or if you have been taking it regularly for several weeks or more, *do not suddenly stop using it without first checking with your doctor*. Your doctor may want you to reduce gradually the amount you are taking before stopping completely, to lessen the chance of withdrawal side effects.

If you think you or anyone else may have taken an overdose of this medicine, get emergency help at once. Taking an overdose of this medicine or taking alcohol or CNS depressants with this medicine may lead to unconsciousness or death. Symptoms of overdose of this medicine include convulsions (seizures); hearing loss; confusion; ringing or buzzing in the ears; severe excitement, nervousness, or restlessness; severe dizziness; severe drowsiness; shortness of breath or troubled breathing; and severe weakness.

Side Effects of This Medicine

Along with its needed effects, a medicine may cause some unwanted effects. Although not all of these side effects may occur, if they do occur they may need medical attention.

The following side effects may mean that a serious allergic reaction is occurring. Check with your doctor or get emergency help immediately if they occur, especially if several of them occur at the same time.

> *Less common or rare*
>> Bluish discoloration or flushing or redness of skin (occurring together with other effects listed in this section); coughing, shortness of breath, troubled breathing, tightness in chest, or wheezing; difficulty in swallowing; dizziness or feeling faint (severe); hive-like swellings (large) on eyelids, face, lips, or tongue; skin rash, itching, or hives; stuffy nose (occurring together with other effects listed in this section)

Also check with your doctor immediately if any of the following side effects occur, especially if several of them occur together:

> *Rare*
>> Bleeding or crusting sores on lips; chest pain; fever with or without chills; red, thickened, or scaly skin; sores, ulcers, or white spots in mouth (painful); sore throat (unexplained); tenderness, burning, or peeling of skin

> *Symptoms of overdose*
>> Anxiety, confusion, excitement, irritability, nervousness, restlessness, or trouble in sleeping (severe, especially with products containing caffeine); convulsions (seizures, with products containing caffeine); diarrhea (severe or continuing); dizziness, lightheadedness, drowsiness, or weakness (severe); frequent urination (for products containing caffeine); hallucinations (seeing, hearing, or feeling things that are not there); increased sensitivity to touch or pain (for products containing caffeine); increased thirst; muscle trembling or twitching (for products containing caffeine); nausea or vomiting (severe or continuing), sometimes with blood; ringing or buzzing in ears (continuing) or hearing loss; seeing flashes of "zig-zag" lights (for products containing caffeine); slow, fast, or irregular heartbeat; slow, fast, irregular, or troubled breathing; slurred speech; staggering; stomach pain (severe); uncontrollable flapping movements of the hands, especially in elderly patients; unusual movements of the eyes; vision problems

Also, check with your doctor as soon as possible if any of the following side effects occur:

> *Less common or rare*
>> Bloody or black, tarry stools; bloody urine; confusion or mental depression; muscle cramps or pain; pinpoint red spots on skin; swollen or painful glands; unusual bleeding or bruising; unusual excitement (mild)

Other side effects may occur that usually do not need medical attention. These side effects may go away during treatment as your body adjusts to the medicine. However, check with your doctor if any of the following side effects continue or are bothersome:

> *More common*
>> Bloated or "gassy" feeling; dizziness or lightheadedness (mild); drowsiness (mild); heartburn or indigestion; nausea, vomiting, or stomach pain (occurring without other symptoms of overdose)

Other side effects not listed above may also occur in some patients. If you notice any other effects, check with your doctor.

Revised: 07/14/92
Interim revision: 07/12/94

BUTALBITAL, ACETAMINOPHEN, CAFFEINE, AND CODEINE
Systemic†

Commonly used brand name(s):

In the U.S.—
> Fioricet with Codeine

†Not commercially available in Canada.

Description

Butalbital, acetaminophen, caffeine, and codeine (byoo-TAL-bi-tal, a-seat-a-MIN-oh-fen, KAF-een, and KOE-deen) combination is a pain reliever and relaxant. It is used to treat tension headaches. Butalbital belongs to the group of medicines called barbiturates (bar-BI-tyoo-rates). Barbiturates act in the central nervous system (CNS) to produce their effects.

Codeine is a narcotic analgesic (nar-KOT-ik an-al-JEE-zik) that acts in the CNS to relieve pain. Many of its side effects are also caused by actions in the CNS.

When you take butalbital or codeine for a long time, your body may get used to it so that larger amounts are needed to produce the same effects. This is called tolerance to the medicine. Also, butalbital and codeine may become habit-forming (causing mental or physical dependence) when it is used for a long time or in large doses. Physical dependence may lead to withdrawal side effects when you stop taking the medicine. In patients who get headaches, the first symptom of withdrawal may be new (rebound) headaches.

Caffeine may help to relieve headaches. However, caffeine can also cause physical dependence when it is used for a long time. This may lead to withdrawal (rebound) headaches when you stop taking it.

Butalbital, acetaminophen, caffeine and codeine combination may also be used for other kinds of headaches or other kinds of pain as determined by your doctor.

Butalbital, acetaminophen, caffeine, and codeine combination is available only with your doctor's prescription in the following dosage forms:

Oral
Butalbital, Acetaminophen, Caffeine, and Codeine
• Capsules (U.S.)

Before Using This Medicine

In deciding to use a medicine, the risks of taking the medicine must be weighed against the good it will do. This is a decision you and your doctor will make. For butalbital, acetaminophen, caffeine, and codeine combination, the following should be considered:

Allergies—Tell your doctor if you have ever had any unusual or allergic reaction to butalbital or other barbiturates, or to acetaminophen, aspirin, caffeine, or codeine. Also tell your health care professional if you are allergic to any other substances, such as foods, preservatives, or dyes.

Pregnancy—
• *For butalbital:* Barbiturates such as butalbital have been shown to increase the chance of birth defects in humans. Also, one study in humans has suggested that barbiturates taken during pregnancy may increase the chance of brain tumors in the baby. Butalbital may cause breathing problems in the newborn baby if taken just before or during delivery.
• *For acetaminophen:* Although studies on birth defects with acetaminophen have not been done in pregnant women, it has not been reported to cause birth defects or other problems.
• *For caffeine:* Studies in humans have not shown that caffeine causes birth defects. However, use of large amounts of caffeine during pregnancy may cause problems with the heart rhythm and the growth of the fetus. Also, studies in animals have shown that caffeine causes birth defects when given in very large doses (amounts equal to those present in 12 to 24 cups of coffee a day).
• *For codeine:* Although studies on birth defects with codeine have not been done in pregnant women, it has not been reported to cause birth defects. However, it may cause breathing problems in the newborn baby if taken just before or during delivery. Codeine did not cause birth defects in animal studies, but it caused slower development of bones and other harmful effects in the fetus.

Breast-feeding—
• *For butalbital:* Barbiturates such as butalbital pass into the breast milk and may cause drowsiness, unusually slow heartbeat, shortness of breath, or troubled breathing in nursing babies.
• *For acetaminophen:* Although acetaminophen has not been shown to cause problems in nursing babies, it passes into the breast milk in small amounts.
• *For caffeine:* Caffeine passes into the breast milk in small amounts. Taking caffeine in the amounts present in these medicines has not been shown to cause problems in nursing babies. However, studies have shown that nursing babies may appear jittery and have trouble in sleeping when their mothers drink large amounts of caffeine-containing beverages. Therefore, breast-feeding mothers who use caffeine-containing medicines should probably limit the amount of caffeine they take in from other medicines or from beverages.
• *For codeine:* Codeine passes into the breast milk in small amounts. However, it has not been reported to cause problems in nursing babies.

Children—
• *For butalbital:* Although barbiturates such as butalbital often cause drowsiness, some children become excited after taking them.
• *For acetaminophen:* Acetaminophen has been tested in children and, in effective doses, has not been shown to cause different side effects or problems than it does in adults.
• *For caffeine:* There is no specific information comparing use of caffeine in children up to 12 years of age with use in other age groups. However, caffeine is not expected to cause different side effects or problems in children than it does in adults.

Older adults—
• *For butalbital:* Certain side effects, such as confusion, excitement, or mental depression, may be especially likely to occur in elderly patients, who are usually more sensitive than younger adults to the effects of the butalbital in this combination medicine.
• *For acetaminophen:* Acetaminophen has been tested and has not been shown to cause different side effects or problems in older people than it does in younger adults.
• *For caffeine:* Many medicines have not been studied specifically in older people. Therefore, it may not be known whether they work exactly the same way they do in younger adults or if they cause different side effects or problems in older people. There is no specific information comparing use of caffeine in the elderly with use in other age groups.
• *For codeine:* Breathing problems may be especially likely to occur in elderly patients, who are usually more sensitive than younger adults to the effects of codeine.

Other medicines—Although certain medicines should not be used together at all, in other cases two different medicines may be used together even if an interaction might occur. In these cases, your doctor may want to change the dose, or other precautions may be necessary. When you are taking butalbital, acetaminophen, caffeine, and codeine combination, it is especially important that your health care professional know if you are taking any of the following:
• Anticoagulants (blood thinners), or
• Carbamazepine (e.g., Tegretol) or
• Contraceptives, oral (birth control pills) containing estrogen, or
• Corticosteroids (cortisone-like medicines) or
• Corticotropin (e.g., ACTH)—Butalbital may make these medicines less effective

• Antidepressants, tricyclic (amitriptyline [e.g., Elavil], amoxapine [e.g., Asendin], clomipramine [e.g., Anafranil], desipramine [e.g., Pertofrane], doxepin [e.g., Sinequan], imipramine [e.g., Tofranil], nortriptyline [e.g., Aventyl], protriptyline [e.g., Vivactil], trimipramine [e.g., Surmontil]) or

- Central nervous system (CNS) depressants (medicines that often cause drowsiness)—These medicines may add to the effects of butalbital or codeine and increase the chance of drowsiness or other side effects
- Divalproex (e.g., Depakote) or
- Valproic acid (e.g., Depakene)—The chance of side effects may be increased
- Naltrexone (e.g., Trexan)—Naltrexone blocks the pain-relieving effect of codeine

Other medical problems—The presence of other medical problems may affect the use of butalbital, acetaminophen, caffeine, and codeine combination. Make sure you tell your doctor if you have any other medical problems, especially:

- Alcohol abuse (or history of) or
- Drug abuse or dependence (or history of)—Dependence on butalbital and codeine may develop; also, acetaminophen may cause liver damage in people who abuse alcohol
- Asthma (or history of), emphysema, or other chronic lung disease or
- Brain disease or head injury or
- Colitis or
- Convulsions (seizures) (history of) or
- Emphysema or other chronic lung disease or
- Enlarged prostate or problems with urination or
- Gallbladder disease or gallstones or
- Hepatitis or other liver disease or
- Hyperactivity (in children) or
- Kidney disease—The chance of serious side effects may be increased
- Diabetes mellitus (sugar diabetes) or
- Mental depression or
- Overactive thyroid or
- Porphyria (or history of)—Butalbital can make these conditions worse
- Heart disease (severe)—The caffeine can make some kinds of heart disease worse

Proper Use of This Medicine

Take this medicine only as directed by your doctor. Do not take more of it, do not take it more often, and do not take it for a longer time than your doctor ordered. If butalbital, acetaminophen, caffeine, and codeine combination is taken regularly (for example, every day), it may become habit-forming (causing mental or physical dependence). The caffeine can also increase the chance of dependence. Dependence is especially likely to occur in patients who take these medicines to relieve frequent headaches. Taking too much of this medicine may also lead to liver damage or other medical problems.

This medicine will relieve a headache best if you *take it as soon as the headache begins.* If you get warning signs of a migraine, take this medicine as soon as you are sure that the migraine is coming. This may even stop the headache pain from occurring. *Lying down in a quiet, dark room for a while after taking the medicine also helps to relieve headaches.*

People who get a lot of headaches may need to take a different medicine to help prevent headaches. *It is important that you follow your doctor's directions about taking the other medicine, even if your headaches continue to occur.* Headache-preventing medicines may take several weeks to start working. Even after they do start working, your headaches may not go away completely. However, your headaches should occur less often, and they should be less severe and easier to relieve than before. This will reduce the amount of headache relievers that you need. If you do not notice any improvement after several weeks of headache-preventing treatment, check with your doctor.

Dosing—The dose of butalbital, acetaminophen, caffeine, and codeine combination will be different for different patients. *Follow your doctor's orders or the directions on the label.* The following information includes only the average doses of these medicines. *If your dose is different, do not change it* unless your doctor tells you to do so.

The number of capsules or tablets that you take depends on the strength of the medicine.

- For *oral* dosage forms (capsules):
  —For tension headaches:
    - Adults—One or 2 capsules every four hours as needed. You should not take more than six capsules a day.
    - Children—Dose must be determined by your doctor.

Missed dose—If your doctor has ordered you to take this medicine according to a regular schedule and you miss a dose, take it as soon as you remember. However, if it is almost time for your next dose, skip the missed dose and go back to your regular dosing schedule. *Do not double doses.*

Storage—To store this medicine:

- Keep out of the reach of children. Overdose is especially dangerous in young children.
- Store away from heat and direct light.
- Do not store this medicine in the bathroom, near the kitchen sink, or in other damp places. Heat or moisture may cause the medicine to break down.
- Do not keep outdated medicine or medicine no longer needed. Be sure that any discarded medicine is out of the reach of children.

Precautions While Using This Medicine

Check with your doctor:

- If the medicine stops working as well as it did when you first started using it. This may mean that you are in danger of becoming dependent on the medicine. *Do not try to get better pain relief by increasing the dose.*
- *If you are having headaches more often than you did before you started taking this medicine.* This is especially important if a new headache occurs within 1 day after you took your last dose of this medicine, headaches begin to occur every day, or a headache continues for several days in a row. This may mean that you are dependent on the medicine. *Continuing to take this medicine will cause even more headaches later on.* Your doctor can give you advice on how to relieve the headaches.

Check the labels of all nonprescription (over-the-counter [OTC]) or prescription medicines you now take. If any contain a barbiturate, acetaminophen, caffeine, or codeine, check with your health care professional. Taking them together with this medicine may cause an overdose.

The butalbital and codeine in this medicine will add to the effects of alcohol and other CNS depressants (medicines that slow down the nervous system, possibly causing drowsiness). Some examples of CNS depressants are antihistamines or medicine for hay fever, other allergies, or colds; sedatives, tranquilizers, or sleeping medicine; other prescription pain medicine; narcotics; other barbiturates; medicine for seizures; muscle relaxants; or anesthetics, including some dental anesthetics. Also, drinking large amounts of alcoholic beverages regularly while taking this medicine may increase the chance of liver damage or stomach problems, especially if you take more of this medicine than your doctor ordered or if you take it regularly for a long time. *Therefore, do not drink alcoholic beverages, and check with your doctor before taking any of the medicines listed above, while you are using this medicine.*

This medicine may cause some people to become drowsy, dizzy, or lightheaded. *Make sure you know how you react to this medicine before you drive, use machines, or do anything else that could be dangerous if you are dizzy or are not alert and clearheaded.*

Before you have any medical tests, tell the person in charge that you are taking this medicine. Caffeine interferes with the results of certain tests that use dipyridamole (e.g., Persantine) to help show how well blood is flowing to your heart. Caffeine should not be taken for 8 to 12 hours before the test. The results of other tests may also be affected by butalbital, acetaminophen, caffeine and codeine combination.

Before having any kind of surgery (including dental surgery) or emergency treatment, tell the medical doctor or dentist in charge that you are taking this medicine. Serious side effects can occur if your medical doctor or dentist gives you certain medicines without knowing that you have taken butalbital or codeine.

If you have been taking large amounts of this medicine, or if you have been taking it regularly for several weeks or more, *do not suddenly stop taking it without first checking with your doctor.* Your doctor may want you to reduce gradually the amount you are taking before stopping completely in order to lessen the chance of withdrawal side effects.

If you think you or anyone else may have taken an overdose of this medicine, get emergency help at once. Taking an overdose of this medicine or taking alcohol or CNS depressants with this medicine may lead to unconsciousness or possibly death. Signs of butalbital or codeine overdose include severe drowsiness, confusion, severe weakness, shortness of breath or unusually slow or troubled breathing, slurred speech, staggering, and unusually slow heartbeat. Signs of severe acetaminophen poisoning may not occur until 2 to 4 days after the overdose is taken, but treatment to prevent liver damage or death must be started within 24 hours or less after the overdose is taken.

Side Effects of This Medicine

Along with its needed effects, a medicine may cause some unwanted effects. Although not all of these side effects may occur, if they do occur they may need medical attention.

Check with your doctor immediately if any of the following side effects occur, especially if several of them occur together:

Rare
  Bleeding or crusting sores on lips; chest pain; fever with or without chills; convulsions, hallucinations, trembling, and/or uncontrolled muscle movements; hive-like swellings (large) on eyelids, face, lips, and/or tongue; mental depression; muscle cramps or pain; red, thickened, or scaly skin; shortness of breath, troubled breathing, tightness in chest, or wheezing;

skin rash, itching, or hives; sores, ulcers, or white spots in mouth (painful); sore throat

Symptoms of overdose
  Anxiety, confusion, excitement, irritability, nervousness, restlessness, or trouble in sleeping (severe); cold and clammy skin; convulsions (seizures); diarrhea, especially if occurring together with increased sweating, loss of appetite, and stomach cramps or pain; dizziness, lightheadedness, drowsiness, or weakness, (severe); frequent urination; hallucinations (seeing, hearing, or feeling things that are not there); increased sensitivity to touch or pain; muscle trembling or twitching; nausea or vomiting, sometimes with blood; ringing or other sounds in ears; seeing flashes of "zig-zag" lights; shortness of breath or unusually slow or troubled breathing; slow, fast, or irregular heartbeat; slurred speech; staggering; swelling, pain, or tenderness in the upper abdomen or stomach area; unusual movements of the eyes

Also, check with your doctor as soon as possible if any of the following side effects occur:

Less common
  Confusion (mild); mental depression; unusual excitement (mild)

Rare
  Bloody or black, tarry stools; bloody urine; pinpoint red spots on skin; swollen or painful glands; unusual bleeding or bruising; unusual tiredness or weakness (mild)

Other side effects may occur that usually do not need medical attention. These side effects may go away during treatment as your body adjusts to the medicine. However, check with your doctor if any of the following side effects continue or are bothersome:

More common
  Bloated or "gassy" feeling; dizziness or lightheadedness (mild); drowsiness (mild); nausea, vomiting, or stomach pain (occurring without other symptoms of overdose)

Other side effects not listed above may also occur in some patients. If you notice any other effects, check with your doctor.

Developed: 05/13/98

BUTENAFINE   Topical

Commonly used brand name(s):

In the U.S.—
Mentax

Description

Butenafine (byoo-TEN-a-feen) is used to treat fungus infections. It works by killing the fungus or preventing its growth. Butenafine is applied to the skin to treat:

- athlete's foot (ringworm of the foot; tinea pedis);
- jock itch (ringworm of the groin; tinea cruris);
- ringworm of the body (tinea corporis).

This medicine is available only with your doctor's prescription, in the following dosage form:

Topical
- Cream (U.S.)

Before Using This Medicine

In deciding to use a medicine, the risks of using the medicine must be weighed against the good it will do. This is a decision you and your doctor will make. For topical butenafine, the following should be considered:

Allergies—Tell your doctor if you have ever had any unusual or allergic reaction to butenafine. Also tell your health care professional if you are allergic to any other substances, such as preservatives or dyes.

Pregnancy—Topical butenafine has not been studied in pregnant women. However, it has not been found to cause birth defects or other problems in studies in animals.

Breast-feeding—It is not known whether topical butenafine passes into breast milk. Although most medicines pass into breast milk in small amounts, many of them may be used safely while breast-feeding. Mothers who are taking this medicine and who wish to breast-feed should discuss this with their doctor.

Children—There is no specific information comparing use of butenafine in children with use in other age groups.

Older adults—Many medicines have not been studied specifically in older people. Therefore, it may not be known whether they work exactly the same way they do in younger adults. Although there is no specific information comparing use of butenafine in the elderly with use in other age groups, clinical studies included older patients. No differences in effects of butenafine were seen in the elderly compared with younger adults.

Proper Use of This Medicine

Apply enough butenafine to cover the affected skin and surrounding areas, and rub in gently.

After applying butenafine, wash your hands to remove any medicine that may be on them.

Keep this medicine away from the eyes and mucous membranes such as the inside of the nose, mouth, or vagina.

Do not bandage or apply an occlusive dressing (airtight covering such as kitchen plastic wrap) over this medicine unless otherwise directed by your doctor. If you have any questions about this, check with your doctor.

To help clear up your skin infection completely, *keep using butenafine for the full time of treatment.* It may sometimes take quite a while for a fungus infection to be cured. If you stop using this medicine too soon, your symptoms will return.

Dosing—The dose of butenafine will be different for different patients. *Follow your doctor's orders or the directions on the label.* The following information includes only the average doses of butenafine. *If your dose is different, do not change it* unless your doctor tells you to do so.
- For *topical* dosage form (cream):
  —For fungus infections:
  - Adults and teenagers—Apply to the affected area(s) of the skin once or twice a day, as ordered by your doctor.
  - Children younger than 12 years of age—Use and dose must be determined by your doctor.

Missed dose—If you miss a dose of this medicine, apply it as soon as possible. However, if it is almost time for your next dose, skip the missed dose and go back to your regular dosing schedule.

Storage—To store this medicine:
- Keep out of the reach of children.
- Store away from heat and direct light.
- Do not store in the bathroom, near the kitchen sink, or in other damp places. Heat or moisture may cause the medicine to break down.
- Do not keep outdated medicine or medicine no longer needed. Be sure that any discarded medicine is out of the reach of children.

Precautions While Using This Medicine

If your skin infection does not improve within 4 weeks, or if it becomes worse, check with your doctor.

To help clear up your skin infection completely and to help make sure it does not return, the following good health habits are important:
- *For patients using butenafine for athlete's foot,* these measures will help keep the feet cool and dry:
  —Carefully dry the feet, especially between the toes, after bathing.
  —Avoid wearing socks made from wool or synthetic materials (for example, rayon or nylon). Instead, wear clean, cotton socks and change them daily or more often if your feet sweat very much.
  —Wear well-ventilated shoes (for example, shoes with holes on top or on the side) or sandals.
  —Use a bland, absorbent powder (for example, talcum powder) or an antifungal powder freely between the toes, on the feet, and in socks and shoes once or twice a day. Be sure to use the powder after butenafine has been applied and has disappeared into the skin. Do not use the powder as the only treatment for your fungus infection.
- *For patients using butenafine for jock itch,* these measures will help reduce chafing and irritation and will also keep the groin area cool and dry:
  —Carefully dry the groin area after bathing.
  —Avoid wearing underwear that is tight-fitting or made from synthetic materials (for example, rayon or nylon). Instead, wear loose-fitting, cotton underwear.
  —Use a bland, absorbent powder (for example, talcum powder) or an antifungal powder freely once or twice a day. Be sure to use the powder after butenafine has been applied and has disappeared into the skin. Do not use the powder as the only treatment for your fungus infection.
- *For patients using butenafine for ringworm of the body,* these measures will help keep the affected area cool and dry:
  —Carefully dry yourself after bathing.
  —Avoid too much heat and humidity if possible. Try to keep moisture from building up on affected areas of the body.
  —Wear loose-fitting clothing.
  —Use a bland, absorbent powder (for example, talcum powder) or an antifungal powder freely once or twice a day. Be sure to use the powder after butenafine has been applied and has disappeared into the skin. Do not use the powder as the only treatment for your fungus infection.

© 2002 MICROMEDEX Thomson Healthcare

Side Effects of This Medicine

Along with its needed effects, a medicine may cause some unwanted effects. Although not all of these side effects may occur, if they do occur they may need medical attention.

Check with your doctor as soon as possible if any of the following side effects occur:

Rare

Blistering, burning, itching, oozing, stinging, swelling, or other signs of skin irritation not present before use of this medicine; rash; redness

Other side effects not listed above may also occur in some patients. If you notice any other effects, check with your doctor.

Developed: 08/07/98

BUTORPHANOL   Nasal-Systemic

Commonly used brand name(s):

In the U.S.—
Stadol NS

In Canada—
Stadol NS

Description

Butorphanol (byoo-TOR-fa-nole) is a narcotic analgesic (pain medicine) that is sprayed into the nose. It is used to relieve moderate or severe pain. It is also used to relieve pain that occurs after an operation.

Narcotic analgesics act in the central nervous system (CNS) to relieve pain. Some of their side effects are also caused by actions in the CNS.

If a narcotic is used for a long time, it may become habit-forming (causing mental or physical dependence). Physical dependence may lead to withdrawal side effects when you stop taking the medicine.

This medicine is available only with your doctor's or dentist's prescription, in the following dosage form:

Nasal
• Nasal solution (U.S. and Canada)

Before Using This Medicine

In deciding to use a medicine, the risks of taking the medicine must be weighed against the good it will do. This is a decision you and your doctor will make. For butorphanol, the following should be considered:

Allergies—Tell your doctor if you have ever had any unusual or allergic reaction to butorphanol or any other narcotic analgesic. Also tell your health care professional if you are allergic to any other substances, such as foods, preservatives, or dyes.

Pregnancy—Nasal butorphanol has not been studied in pregnant women. However, studies in animals have shown that butorphanol causes a decreased pregnancy rate and an increase in stillbirths. Before taking this medicine make sure your doctor knows if you are pregnant or if you may become pregnant.

Too much use of butorphanol during pregnancy may cause the baby to become dependent on the medicine. This may lead to withdrawal side effects after birth.

Breast-feeding—Although butorphanol may pass into the breast milk, it is not expected to cause problems in nursing babies.

Children—Studies on this medicine have been done only in adult patients, and there is no specific information comparing use of butorphanol in children with use in other age groups.

Older adults—Elderly people are especially sensitive to the effects of butorphanol. This may increase the chance of side effects, especially dizziness, during treatment. Studies in older adults show that butorphanol stays in the body for a longer time than it does in younger adults. Your doctor will consider this when deciding on your dose.

Other medicines—Although certain medicines should not be used together at all, in other cases two different medicines may be used together even if an interaction might occur. In these cases, your doctor may want to change the dose, or other precautions may be necessary. When you are taking butorphanol it is especially important that your health care professional know if you are taking any of the following:
• Central nervous system (CNS) depressants (medicines that make you drowsy or less alert) or
• Tricyclic antidepressants (medicines for depression) (amitriptyline [e.g., Elavil], amoxapine [e.g., Asendin], clomipramine [e.g., Anafranil], desipramine [e.g., Pertofrane], doxepin [e.g., Sinequan], imipramine [e.g., Tofranil], nortriptyline [e.g., Aventyl], protriptyline [e.g., Vivactil], trimipramine [e.g., Surmontil])—The chance of side effects may be increased
• Narcotic pain medicine, other—Withdrawal symptoms may occur if a narcotic you are dependent on is replaced by butorphanol.

Other medical problems—The presence of other medical problems may affect the use of butorphanol. Make sure you tell your doctor if you have any other medical problems, especially:
• CNS disease affecting breathing or
• Emphysema, asthma, or other chronic lung disease or
• Head injury—Some of the side effects of butorphanol can be dangerous if you have any of these conditions
• Drug dependence, especially narcotic abuse, or history of, or
• Emotional problems—The chance of side effects may be increased; also, withdrawal symptoms may occur if a narcotic you are dependent on is replaced by butorphanol
• Heart disease or
• Kidney disease or
• Liver disease—The chance of side effects may be increased

Proper Use of This Medicine

You will be given an instruction sheet with your prescription for butorphanol that explains how to use the pump spray unit. If you have any questions about using the unit, ask your health care professional.

To use:
• *Use this medicine only as directed by your medical doctor or dentist.* Do not use more of it, do not use it

more often, and do not use it for a longer time than your medical doctor or dentist told you. This is especially important for elderly patients, who may be more sensitive to the effects of butorphanol. If too much is used, the medicine may become habit-forming (causing mental or physical dependence) or lead to medical problems because of an overdose.

- Remove the protective cover and clip. Before you use each new bottle of butorphanol, the spray pump needs to be started. To do this, point the sprayer away from you and other people or pets. Pump the spray unit firmly about 7 or 8 times. A fine, wide spray should come out by the seventh or eighth time you pump the unit. If the unit is not used for 48 hours or longer, the spray pump should be started again by pumping it 1 or 2 times only.
- Before each use, blow your nose gently.
- For a 1-mg dose, insert the spray tip into one nostril. Close off the other nostril by pressing the side of your nose with your index finger. Tilt your head slightly forward and spray one time. Sniff gently with your mouth closed.
- Remove the spray tip from your nostril. Tilt your head back and sniff gently.
- For a 2-mg dose, repeat these steps using the other nostril.
- Replace the protective cover and clip after each use.

Dosing—The dose of butorphanol will be different for different patients. *Follow your doctor's or dentist's orders or the directions on the label.* The following information includes only the average doses of butorphanol. *If your dose is different, do not change it* unless your doctor or dentist tells you to do so.

- For *nasal* dosage form:
  —For pain:
  - Adults—1 mg (one spray in one nostril). If pain is not relieved within sixty to ninety minutes, another spray (1 mg) in one nostril may be used. This dosing procedure may be repeated in three to four hours as needed. However, if pain is severe, a 2-mg dose (one spray in each nostril) may be used every three to four hours, but it is important to remain lying down if drowsiness or dizziness occurs.
  - Children and teenagers—Use and dose must be determined by your doctor.

Missed dose—If your medical doctor or dentist has told you to use this medicine on a regular schedule and you miss a dose, use it as soon as you remember. However, if it is almost time for your next dose, skip the missed dose and go back to your regular dosing schedule. *Do not double doses.*

Storage—To store this medicine:

- Keep out of the reach of children. Overdose is very dangerous in young children.
- Store away from heat and direct light.
- Keep the medicine from freezing.
- Do not keep outdated medicine or medicine no longer needed. Be sure that any discarded medicine is out of the reach of children.

Precautions While Using This Medicine

Butorphanol will add to the effects of alcohol and other CNS depressants (medicines that make you drowsy or less alert). Some examples of CNS depressants are antihistamines or medicine for hay fever, other allergies, or colds; sedatives, tranquilizers, or sleeping medicine; other prescription pain medicines, including other narcotics; barbiturates; medicine for seizures; muscle relaxants; or anesthetics, including some dental anesthetics. *Do not drink alcoholic beverages, and check with your medical doctor or dentist before taking any of the medicines listed above, while you are using this medicine.*

This medicine may cause some people to become drowsy, dizzy, or lightheaded, or to feel a false sense of well-being. *Make sure you know how you react to this medicine before you drive, use machines, or do anything else that could be dangerous if you are dizzy or are not alert and clearheaded.*

Dizziness, lightheadedness, or fainting may occur, especially in the first hour after use or when you get up suddenly from a lying or sitting position. Getting up slowly may help lessen this problem.

Before having any kind of surgery (including dental surgery) or emergency treatment, tell the medical doctor or dentist in charge that you are using this medicine.

Butorphanol may cause dryness of the mouth. For temporary relief, use sugarless candy or gum, melt bits of ice in your mouth, or use a saliva substitute. However, if dry mouth continues for more than 2 weeks, check with your dentist. Continuing dryness of the mouth may increase the chance of dental disease, including tooth decay, gum disease, and fungus infections.

If you have been using this medicine regularly for several weeks or more, *do not suddenly stop using it without first checking with your doctor.* Your doctor may want you to reduce gradually the amount you are using before stopping completely, in order to lessen the chance of withdrawal side effects.

If you think you or someone else may have used an overdose, get emergency help at once. Using an overdose of this medicine or taking alcohol or CNS depressants with this medicine may lead to unconsciousness or death. Signs of overdose include convulsions (seizures), confusion, severe nervousness or restlessness, severe dizziness, severe drowsiness, slow or troubled breathing, and severe weakness.

Side Effects of This Medicine

Along with its needed effects, a medicine may cause some unwanted effects. Although not all of these side effects may occur, if they do occur they may need medical attention.

Get emergency help immediately if any of the following symptoms of overdose occur:

Cold, clammy skin; confusion; convulsions (seizures); dizziness (severe); drowsiness (severe); nervousness, restlessness, or weakness (severe); small pupils; slow heartbeat; slow or troubled breathing

Also, check with your doctor as soon as possible if any of the following side effects occur:

More common

Difficulty in breathing; fever; nosebleeds; ringing or buzzing in ears; runny nose; sinus congestion; sneezing; sore throat

Less common or rare

Blurred vision; congestion in chest; cough; difficulty in urinating; difficult or painful breathing; ear pain; fainting; hallucinations; itching; sinus congestion with pain; skin rash or hives

Other side effects may occur that usually do not need medical attention. These side effects may go away during treatment as your body adjusts to the medicine. However, check with your doctor if any of the following side effects continue or are bothersome:

More common

Confusion; constipation; dizziness; drowsiness; dry mouth; flushing; headache; irritation inside nose; loss of appetite; nasal congestion; nausea or vomiting; sweating or clammy feeling; trouble in sleeping; unpleasant taste; weakness (severe)

Less common or rare

Anxious feeling; behavior changes; burning, crawling, or prickling feeling on skin; false sense of well-being; feeling hot; floating feeling; nervousness, sometimes with restlessness; pounding heartbeat; stomach pain; strange dreams; trembling

After you stop using this medicine, your body may need time to adjust. The length of time this takes depends on the amount of medicine you were using and how long you used it. During this period of time, check with your doctor if you notice any of the following side effects:

Anxious feeling; diarrhea; nervousness and restlessness

Other side effects not listed above may also occur in some patients. If you notice any other effects, check with your doctor.

Developed: 12/02/96

CABERGOLINE　Systemic

Commonly used brand name(s):

In the U.S.—
Dostinex

Description

Cabergoline (ca-BER-goe-leen) is used to treat different types of medical problems that occur when too much of the hormone prolactin is produced. It can be used to treat certain menstrual problems, fertility problems in men and women, and pituitary prolactinomas (tumors of the pituitary gland).

It works by stopping the brain from making and releasing the prolactin hormone from the pituitary. Cabergoline use is usually stopped when prolactin levels are normal for 6 months. It may be given again if symptoms of too much prolactin occur again.

This medicine is available only with your doctor's prescription, in the following dosage form:

Oral
• Tablets (U.S. and Canada)

Before Using This Medicine

In deciding to use a medicine, the risks of taking the medicine must be weighed against the good it will do. This is a decision you and your doctor will make. For cabergoline, the following should be considered:

Allergies—Tell your doctor if you have ever had any unusual or allergic reaction to cabergoline or other ergot alkaloid medicines. Also tell your health care professional if you are allergic to any other substances, such as foods, preservatives, or dyes.

Pregnancy—Cabergoline has not been shown to cause birth defects or other problems in humans. However, studies in animals have shown that cabergoline causes a decrease in successful pregnancies and other problems. This is because prolactin works differently in animal pregnancies than it does in human pregnancies. Before taking this medicine, make sure your doctor knows if you are pregnant or if you may become pregnant.

Breast-feeding—It is not known whether cabergoline passes into the breast milk. Cabergoline should not be used by breast-feeding women or women planning to breast-feed within a short period of time. Reducing the amount of available prolactin is likely to stop the release of breast milk in breast-feeding women.

Children—Studies of this medicine have been done only in adult patients, and there is no specific information comparing use of cabergoline in children with use in other age groups.

Older adults—Many medicines have not been studied specifically in older people. Therefore, it may not be known whether they work exactly the same way they do in younger adults or if they cause different side effects or problems in older people. There is no specific information comparing use of cabergoline in the elderly with use in other age groups.

Other medicines—Although certain medicines should not be used together at all, in other cases two different medicines may be used together even if an interaction might occur. In these cases, your doctor may want to change the dose, or other precautions may be necessary. When you are taking cabergoline, it is especially important that your health care professional know if you are taking any of the following:

• Antipsychotic medicines (medicines for mental illness) or
• Metoclopramide (e.g., Reglan)—Cabergoline may stop these medicines from working properly and require a change in dose for these medicines

Other medical problems—The presence of other medical problems may affect the use of cabergoline. Make sure you tell your doctor if you have any other medical problems, especially:

• High blood pressure, untreated or
• High blood pressure of pregnancy (or history of)—Cabergoline usually decreases blood pressure but at times it may increase blood pressure and worsen these conditions
• Liver disease, mild to severe—Cabergoline may worsen this condition; a lower dose of cabergoline may be required

Proper Use of This Medicine

Do not take more or less of it than your doctor ordered.

Dosing—The dose of cabergoline will be different for different patients. *Follow your doctor's orders or the directions on the label.* The following information includes only the average doses of cabergoline. *If your dose is different, do not change it* unless your doctor tells you to do so.

- For *oral* dosage form (tablets):
  —For disorders of high prolactin levels or pituitary tumors:
  - Adults—0.25 mg two times a week. Dose may be increased every four weeks as needed, according to body prolactin levels, up to 1 mg two times a week.
  - Children—Use and dose must be determined by the doctor.

Missed dose—If you miss a dose of this medicine, take it as soon as possible within 1 or 2 days. However, if it is almost time for your next dose, check with your doctor to see if you can double your dose.

Storage—To store this medicine:
- Keep out of the reach of children.
- Store away from heat and direct light.
- Do not store in the bathroom, near the kitchen sink, or in other damp places. Heat or moisture may cause the medicine to break down.
- Do not keep outdated medicine or medicine no longer needed. Be sure that any discarded medicine is out of the reach of children.

Precautions While Using This Medicine

It is important that your doctor check your progress at regular visits while you are taking this medicine.

This medicine may cause some people to become drowsy, dizzy, or less alert than they are normally. *Make sure you know how you react to this medicine before you drive, use machines, or do other jobs that require you to be alert.*

Dizziness, lightheadedness, or fainting may occur, especially when you get up from a lying or sitting position. Getting up slowly may help.

Tell your doctor right away if you think you have become pregnant. You and your doctor should discuss whether you should continue to take this medicine during pregnancy.

Check with your doctor right away if you have symptoms of fainting, hallucinations, lightheadedness, stuffy nose, or racing heart.

Side Effects of This Medicine

Along with its needed effects, a medicine may cause some unwanted effects. Although not all of these side effects may occur, if they do occur they may need medical attention.

Check with your doctor as soon as possible if any of the following side effects occur:
  More common
    Abdominal pain; sensation that you are moving in space or that objects are moving around you (vertigo)
  Rare
    Changes in vision; difficulty in concentrating; dizziness or fainting when getting up suddenly from a lying or sitting position; loss of appetite; swelling of hands, ankles, feet, or lower legs; unusually fast heartbeat; weight gain or loss
  Symptoms of overdose
    Fainting; hallucinations; lightheadedness; racing heart; stuffy nose

Other side effects may occur that usually do not need medical attention. These side effects may go away during treatment as your body adjusts to the medicine. However, check with your doctor if any of the following side effects continue or are bothersome:
  More common
    Constipation; dizziness; headache; nausea or stomach discomfort; weakness
  Less common
    Burning, itching, or stinging of the skin; diarrhea; dry mouth or toothache; gas; general feeling of discomfort or illness; hot flashes; mental depression; muscle or joint pain; runny nose; sleepiness; sore throat; trouble in sleeping; vomiting

Other side effects not listed above may also occur in some patients. If you notice any other effects, check with your doctor.

Developed: 06/30/1998
Revised: 03/05/2001

CAFFEINE   Systemic

Commonly used brand name(s):

In the U.S.—

Caffedrine Caplets[1]	NoDoz Maximum Strength
Cafcit[2]	Caplets[1]
Dexitac Stay Alert Stimulant[1]	Pep-Back[1]
Enerjets[1]	Quick Pep[1]
Keep Alert[1]	Ultra Pep-Back[1]
Maximum Strength SnapBack	Vivarin[1]
Stimulant Powders[1]	

In Canada—
Wake-Up[1]

Note: For quick reference, the following caffeine products are numbered to match the corresponding brand names.

This information applies to the following medicines:
1. Caffeine (KAF-feen) ‡
2. Citrated Caffeine (SIH-tray-ted KAF-feen) †
3. Caffeine and Sodium Benzoate (KAF-feen and SOE-dee-um BEN-zo-ate) †‡

†Not commercially available in Canada.
‡Generic name product may be available in the U.S.

Description

Caffeine (KAF-feen) belongs to the group of medicines called central nervous system (CNS) stimulants. It is used to help restore mental alertness when unusual tiredness or weakness or drowsiness occurs. Caffeine's use as an alertness aid should be only occasional. It is not intended to replace sleep and should not be used regularly for this purpose.

Caffeine is also used in combination with ergotamine (for treatment of migraine and cluster headaches) or with certain pain relievers, such as aspirin or aspirin and acetaminophen. When used in this way, caffeine may increase the effectiveness of the other medicines. Caffeine is sometimes used in combination with an antihistamine to overcome the drowsiness caused by the antihistamine.

Citrated caffeine is used to treat breathing problems in premature babies.

Caffeine may also be used for other conditions as determined by your doctor.

Caffeine is present in coffee, tea, soft drinks, cocoa, chocolate, and kola nuts.

Caffeine powder and tablets are available without a prescription; however, your health care professional may have special instructions on its proper use. Citrated caffeine and caffeine and sodium benzoate are to be administered only by or under the supervision of your doctor. Caffeine is available in the following dosage forms:

Oral
  Caffeine
  • Powder (U.S.)
  • Tablets (U.S. and Canada)
  Citrated caffeine
  • Oral solution (U.S.)

Parenteral
  Citrated caffeine
  • Injection (U.S.)

  Caffeine and sodium benzoate
  • Injection (U.S.)

Before Using This Medicine

If you are taking this medicine without a prescription, carefully read and follow any precautions on the label. For caffeine, the following should be considered:

Allergies—Tell your doctor if you have ever had any unusual or allergic reactions to aminophylline, caffeine, dyphylline, oxtriphylline, theobromine (also found in cocoa or chocolate), or theophylline. Also tell your health care professional if you are allergic to any other substances, such as foods, preservatives, or dyes.

Pregnancy—Studies in humans have shown that caffeine may cause miscarriage or may slow the growth of a developing fetus when given in doses greater than 300 mg (an amount equal to three cups of coffee) a day. In addition, use of large amounts of caffeine by the mother during pregnancy may cause problems with the heart rhythm of the fetus. Therefore, it is recommended that pregnant women consume less than 300 mg of caffeine a day. Studies in animals have shown that caffeine causes birth defects when given in very large doses (amounts equal to 12 to 24 cups of coffee a day) and problems with bone growth when given in smaller doses.

Breast-feeding—Caffeine passes into breast milk in small amounts and may build up in the nursing baby. Studies have shown that babies may appear jittery and have trouble in sleeping when their mothers drink large amounts of caffeine-containing beverages.

Children—With the exception of infants, there is no specific information comparing use of caffeine in children with use in other age groups. However, this medicine is not expected to cause different side effects or problems in children than it does in adults.

Older adults—Many medicines have not been studied specifically in older people. Therefore, it may not be known whether they work exactly the same way they do in younger adults or if they cause different side effects or problems in older people. There is no specific information comparing use of caffeine in the elderly with use in other age groups.

Other medicines—Although certain medicines should not be used together at all, in other cases two different medicines may be used together even if an interaction might occur. In these cases, your doctor may want to change the dose, or other precautions may be necessary. When you are taking caffeine, it is especially important that your health care professional know if you are taking any of the following:

• Amantadine (e.g., Symmetrel) or
• Amphetamines (e.g., Desoxyn, Dexedrine) or
• Appetite suppressants (diet pills) or
• Bupropion (e.g., Wellbutrin) or
• Chlophedianol (e.g., Ulone) or
• Cocaine or
• Fluoxetine (e.g., Prozac) or
• Medicine for asthma or other breathing problems or
• Medicine for colds, sinus problems, hay fever or other allergies (including nose drops or sprays) or
• Methylphenidate (e.g., Ritalin) or
• Nabilone (e.g., Cesamet) or
• Other medicines or beverages containing caffeine or
• Paroxetine (e.g., Paxil) or
• Pemoline (e.g., Cylert) or
• Sertraline (e.g., Zoloft)—Using these medicines with caffeine may increase the CNS-stimulant effects, such as nervousness, irritability, or trouble in sleeping, or possibly cause convulsions (seizures) or changes in the rhythm of your heart

• Monoamine oxidase (MAO) inhibitors (furazolidone [e.g., Furoxone], isocarboxazid [e.g., Marplan], phenelzine [e.g., Nardil], procarbazine [e.g., Matulane], selegiline [e.g., Eldepryl], tranylcypromine [e.g., Parnate])— Taking large amounts of caffeine while you are taking or within 2 weeks of taking MAO inhibitors may cause extremely high blood pressure or dangerous changes in the rhythm of your heart; taking small amounts of caffeine may cause mild high blood pressure and fast heartbeat

Other medical problems—The presence of other medical problems may affect the use of caffeine. Make sure you tell your doctor if you have any other medical problems, especially:

• Agoraphobia (fear of being in open places) or
• Anxiety or
• Convulsions (seizures) (in newborn babies) or
• Heart disease, severe or
• High blood pressure or
• Panic attacks or
• Trouble in sleeping—Caffeine may make the condition worse

• Liver disease—Higher blood levels of caffeine may result, increasing the chance of side effects

Proper Use of This Medicine

Take caffeine in powder or tablet form only as directed. Do not take more of it, do not take it more often, and do not take it for a longer time than directed. Taking too much of this medicine may increase the chance of side effects. It may also become habit-forming.

For patients taking the *powder* form of this medicine: Each packet contains one dose of medicine. The contents of the packet may be stirred into water or other liquid and drunk. Or, the powder may be placed on the tongue and washed down with water or other liquid drink.

For patients taking the *oral solution* form of this medicine: Throw away any unused portion of the medicine left in the single-use vial (bottle). Follow the manufacturer's instruction for use.

If you think this medicine is not working properly after you have taken it for a long time, *do not increase the dose*. To do so may increase the chance of side effects.

Dosing—The dose of caffeine will be different for different patients. *Follow the directions on the label.*

- For unusual tiredness or weakness, or drowsiness:
  —For *oral* dosage form (powder):
  - Adults and children 12 years of age and older— The usual dose is 200 milligrams (mg) of caffeine (1 packet) repeated no sooner than every three or four hours. You should not take more than 1600 mg in twenty-four hours.
  - Children up to 12 years of age—Use is not recommended.
  —For *oral* dosage form (tablets):
  - Adults and children 12 years of age and older— The usual dose is 100 to 200 mg of caffeine repeated no sooner than every three or four hours. You should not take more than 1000 mg in twenty-four hours.
  - Children up to 12 years of age—Use is not recommended.
- For breathing problems in premature babies:
  —For *oral* dosage form (oral solution):
  - Newborn babies—At first, the dose is 20 mg (1 milliliter [mL]) per kilogram (kg) (9.1 mg per pound) of body weight given one time. Then, the dose is 5 mg (0.25 mL) per kg (2.3 mg per pound) of body weight given once a day.

Storage—To store this medicine:
- Keep out of the reach of children.
- Store away from heat and direct light.
- Do not store in the bathroom, near the kitchen sink, or in other damp places. Heat or moisture may cause the medicine to break down.
- Do not keep outdated medicine or medicine no longer needed. Be sure that any discarded medicine is out of the reach of children.

Precautions While Using This Medicine

Caffeine powder and tablets are for occasional use only. They are not intended to replace sleep and should not be used regularly for this purpose. If unusual tiredness or weakness or drowsiness continues or returns often, check with your doctor.

Before you have any medical tests, tell the doctor in charge that you are taking this medicine. The results of some tests on the heart may be affected by this medicine.

The recommended dose of this medicine contains about the same amount of caffeine as a cup of coffee. Do not drink large amounts of caffeine-containing coffee, tea, or soft drinks while you are taking this medicine. Also, do not take large amounts of other medicines that contain caffeine. To do so may cause unwanted effects.

The amount of caffeine in some common foods and beverages is as follows:
- Coffee, brewed—40 to 180 milligrams (mg) per cup.
- Coffee, instant—30 to 120 mg per cup.
- Coffee, decaffeinated—3 to 5 mg per cup.

- Tea, brewed American—20 to 90 mg per cup.
- Tea, brewed imported—25 to 110 mg per cup.
- Tea, instant—28 mg per cup.
- Tea, canned iced—22 to 36 mg per 12 ounces.
- Cola and other soft drinks, caffeine-containing—36 to 90 mg per 12 ounces.
- Cola and other soft drinks, decaffeinated—0 mg per 12 ounces.
- Cocoa—4 mg per cup.
- Chocolate, milk—3 to 6 mg per ounce.
- Chocolate, bittersweet—25 mg per ounce.

Caffeine may cause nervousness or irritability, trouble in sleeping, dizziness, or a fast or pounding heartbeat. If these effects occur, discontinue the use of caffeine-containing beverages and medicines, and do not eat large amounts of chocolate-containing products.

To prevent trouble in sleeping, do not take caffeine-containing beverages or medicines too close to bedtime.

Side Effects of This Medicine

Along with its needed effects, a medicine may cause some unwanted effects. Although not all of these side effects may occur, they may be more likely to occur if caffeine is taken in large doses or more often than recommended. If they do occur, they may need medical attention.

Check with your doctor as soon as possible if any of the following side effects occur:

More common

Diarrhea; dizziness; fast heartbeat; hyperglycemia, including blurred vision, drowsiness, dry mouth, flushed dry skin, fruit-like breath odor, increased urination, ketones in urine, loss of appetite, nausea, stomachache, tiredness, troubled breathing, unusual thirst, or vomiting (in newborn babies); hypoglycemia, including anxious feeling, blurred vision, cold sweats, confusion, cool pale skin, drowsiness, excessive hunger, fast heartbeat, nausea, nervousness, restless sleep, shakiness, or unusual tiredness or weakness (in newborn babies); irritability, nervousness, or severe jitters (in newborn babies); nausea (severe); tremors; trouble in sleeping; vomiting

Rare

Abdominal or stomach bloating; dehydration; diarrhea (bloody); unusual tiredness or weakness

Symptoms of overdose

Abdominal or stomach pain; agitation, anxiety, excitement, or restlessness; confusion or delirium; convulsions (seizures)—in acute overdose; dehydration; faster breathing rate; fast or irregular heartbeat; fever; frequent urination; headache; increased sensitivity to touch or pain; irritability; muscle trembling or twitching; nausea and vomiting, sometimes with blood; overextending the body with head and heels bent backward and body bowed forward; painful, swollen abdomen or vomiting (in newborn babies); ringing or other sounds in ears; seeing flashes of "zig-zag" lights; trouble in sleeping; whole-body tremors (in newborn babies)

Other side effects may occur that usually do not need medical attention. These side effects may go away during treatment as your body adjusts to the medicine. However, check with

your doctor if any of the following side effects continue or are bothersome:

More common
Nausea (mild); nervousness or jitters (mild)

After you stop using this medicine, your body may need time to adjust. The length of time this takes depends on the amount of medicine you were using and how long you used it. During this time, check with your doctor if you notice any of the following side effects:

More common
Anxiety; dizziness; headache; irritability; muscle tension; nausea; nervousness; stuffy nose; unusual tiredness

Other side effects not listed above may also occur in some patients. If you notice any other effects, check with your doctor.

Additional Information

Once a medicine has been approved for marketing for a certain use, experience may show that it is also useful for other medical problems. Although these uses are not included in product labeling, caffeine is used in certain patients with the following medical conditions:

- Postoperative infant apnea (breathing problems after surgery in young babies)
- Psychiatric disorders requiring electroconvulsive or shock therapy (ECT)

Other than the above information, there is no additional information relating to proper use, precautions, or side effects for these uses.

Revised: 05/25/2000

CALAMINE Topical

Commonly used brand name(s):

In the U.S.—
Calamox

In Canada—
Diaper Rash Ointment
Onguent de Calamine
Generic name product may be available in U.S. and Canada.

Description

Calamine (KAL-a-meen) is used to relieve the itching, pain, and discomfort of minor skin irritations, such as those caused by poison ivy, poison oak, and poison sumac. This medicine also dries oozing and weeping caused by poison ivy, poison oak, and poison sumac.

Calamine is available without prescription in the following dosage forms:

Topical
- Lotion (U.S. and Canada)
- Ointment (U.S. and Canada)

Before Using This Medicine

If you are using this medicine without a prescription, carefully read and follow any precautions on the label. For calamine, the following should be considered:

Allergies—Tell your doctor if you have ever had any unusual or allergic reaction to calamine. Also tell your health care professional if you are allergic to any other substances, such as foods, preservatives, or dyes.

Pregnancy—Calamine has not been shown to cause birth defects or other problems in humans.

Breast-feeding—Calamine has not been reported to cause problems in nursing babies.

Children—Although there is no specific information comparing use of calamine in children with use in other age groups, this medicine is not expected to cause different side effects or problems in children than it does in adults.

Older adults—Many medicines have not been studied specifically in older people. Therefore, it may not be known whether they work exactly the same way they do in younger adults. Although there is no specific information comparing use of calamine in the elderly with use in other age groups, this medicine is not expected to cause different side effects or problems in older people than it does in younger adults.

Other medicines—Although certain medicines should not be used together at all, in other cases two different medicines may be used together even if an interaction might occur. In these cases, your doctor may want to change the dose, or other precautions may be necessary. Tell your health care professional if you are using any other topical prescription or nonprescription (over-the-counter [OTC]) medicine that is to be applied to the same area of the skin.

Proper Use of This Medicine

Calamine is for external use only. Do not swallow it and do not use it on the eyes or mucous membranes such as the inside of the mouth, nose, genital (sex organs), or anal areas.

To use *calamine lotion:*
- Shake the lotion well before using.
- Moisten a pledget of cotton with the lotion.
- Use the moistened pledget to apply the lotion to the affected skin area(s).
- Allow the medicine to dry on the skin.

To use *calamine ointment:*
- Apply enough medicine to cover affected skin area(s) and rub in gently.

Dosing—*Follow your doctor's orders or the directions on the label*. The following information includes only the average dose of calamine. *If your dose is different, do not change it* unless your doctor tells you to do so.

- For minor skin irritations:
  —For *topical* dosage forms (lotion, ointment):
    - Adults and children—Apply to the affected area(s) of skin as often as needed.

Storage—To store this medicine:
- Keep out of the reach of children.
- Store away from heat and direct light.
- Keep the medicine from freezing. Do not refrigerate.

- Do not keep outdated medicine or medicine no longer needed. Be sure that any discarded medicine is out of the reach of children.

Precautions While Using This Medicine

If your condition gets worse or if it does not improve within 7 days, or if rash or irritation develops, stop using calamine and check with your doctor.

Developed: 05/26/95

CALCIPOTRIENE Topical

Commonly used brand name(s):

In the U.S.—
Dovonex

In Canada—
Dovonex

Another commonly used name is MC 903.

Description

Calcipotriene (kal-si-poe-TRY-een) is used to treat psoriasis. It works by controlling the overproduction of skin cells in areas affected by psoriasis.

Calcipotriene is available only with your doctor's prescription in the following dosage forms:

Topical
- Cream (U.S. and Canada)
- Ointment (U.S. and Canada)
- Solution (U.S. and Canada)

Before Using This Medicine

In deciding to use a medicine, the risks of using the medicine must be weighed against the good it will do. This is a decision you and your doctor will make. For calcipotriene, the following should be considered:

Allergies—Tell your doctor if you have ever had any unusual or allergic reaction to calcipotriene or to other ingredients of the preparation, which you may find listed on the label. Also tell your health care professional if you are allergic to any other substances, such as foods, preservatives, or dyes.

Pregnancy—Calcipotriene has not been studied in pregnant women. However, studies in animals have shown that calcipotriene taken in high doses by mouth causes problems in the mother and the fetus, including birth defects. Before using this medicine, make sure your doctor knows if you are pregnant or if you may become pregnant.

Breast-feeding—It is not known whether calcipotriene passes into breast milk. Although most medicines pass into breast milk in small amounts, many of them may be used safely while breast-feeding. Mothers who are using this medicine and who wish to breast-feed should discuss this with their doctor.

Children—This medicine has been tested in a limited number of children 2 to 14 years of age with psoriasis on less than 30% of the body. When used for 8 weeks or less, the medicine has not been shown to cause different side effects or problems than it does in adults. However, more studies are needed.

Older adults—Skin-related side effects caused by calcipotriene may be more severe when they occur in patients over 65 years of age.

Other medicines—Although certain medicines should not be used together at all, in other cases two different medicines may be used together even if an interaction might occur. In these cases, your doctor may want to change the dose, or other precautions may be necessary. Tell your health care professional if you are taking or using any other prescription or nonprescription (over-the-counter [OTC]) medicine.

Other medical problems—The presence of other medical problems may affect the use of calcipotriene. Make sure you tell your doctor if you have any other medical problems, especially:

- Highly irritated areas of psoriasis on the scalp—Calcipotriene topical solution may increase the skin irritation because of the alcohol in the product
- Hypercalcemia (high blood levels of calcium) or
- Hypercalciuria (high urine levels of calcium) or
- Hypervitaminosis D (high blood levels of vitamin D)—Calcipotriene may increase the chance of kidney stone formation
- Kidney stones (or history of)—Calcipotriene may make this condition worse

Proper Use of This Medicine

Calcipotriene is for external use only. Do not use this medicine orally and do not apply it in your vagina. Use this medicine only as directed. Do not use more of it, do not use it more often, and do not use it for a longer time than your doctor ordered. To do so may increase the chance of side effects.

To help clear up your skin problem completely, it is very important that you keep using calcipotriene for the full time of treatment. Do not miss any doses.

Unless otherwise directed by your doctor, *do not use more than 100 grams of calcipotriene ointment or cream in 1 week* (that is, one 100-gram tube or three 30-gram tubes or six 15-gram tubes in 1 week). Do not use more than 60 milliliters of the topical solution for the scalp in 1 week.

Do not use this medicine on your face, near the eyes, inside your nose or mouth, or on unaffected areas of the skin. If you accidentally get some on these areas, wash it off with water right away.

Use this medicine sparingly in the folds of your skin because it is more likely to cause irritation there.

Wash your hands after using this medicine to avoid accidentally getting the medicine on your face or on unaffected areas of the skin.

Do not use this medicine for treating skin problems other than the one for which it was prescribed by your doctor.

For *cream* and *ointment* dosage forms:
- Apply enough medicine to cover the areas of your skin affected by psoriasis and rub in gently and well. *The treated areas should not be covered (for instance, with a bandage or plastic wrap) after the medicine is applied.*

- If you are being treated with calcipotriene ointment in combination with ultraviolet light (found in sunlight and some special lamps), *do not apply the morning dose of calcipotriene before being treated with the ultraviolet light. It can be applied afterwards.*

For *solution* dosage form:

- Before applying the medicine to your scalp, comb your dry hair to remove any flakes, then part your hair so that you can see the scalp lesions. Apply the solution to the lesions and rub it in gently but completely. *Do not apply the medicine if the lesions are very irritated* because the alcohol in the product may make the irritation worse. Try not to get any medicine on your forehead.

Dosing—*Follow your doctor's orders or the directions on the label.* The following information includes only the average dose of calcipotriene. *If your dose is different, do not change it* unless your doctor tells you to do so.

The length of time you use the medicine depends on the severity of your psoriasis.

- For *topical* dosage form (cream):
  —For psoriasis:
  - Adults—Apply to the affected area(s) of the skin two times a day, in the morning and evening. Treatment may be continued for six to eight weeks or as determined by your doctor.
  - Children—Use and dose must be determined by your doctor.
- For *topical* dosage form (ointment):
  —For psoriasis:
  - Adults—Apply to the affected area(s) of the skin one or two times a day, in the morning and evening. Treatment may be continued for six to eight weeks or as determined by your doctor.
  - Children—Use and dose must be determined by your doctor.
- For *topical* dosage form (solution):
  —For psoriasis:
  - Adults—Apply to the affected area(s) of the scalp two times a day, in the morning and evening. Treatment may be continued for six to eight weeks or as determined by your doctor.
  - Children—Use and dose must be determined by your doctor.

Missed dose—If you miss a dose of this medicine, apply it as soon as possible. However, if it is almost time for your next dose, skip the missed dose and go back to your regular dosing schedule. Do not double doses.

Storage—To store this medicine:

- Keep out of the reach of children.
- Store away from heat and direct light.
- Keep the medicine from freezing. Do not refrigerate.
- Do not keep outdated medicine or medicine no longer needed. Be sure that any discarded medicine is out of the reach of children.
- Keep the topical solution away from open flame.

Precautions While Using This Medicine

Calcipotriene may cause irritation of the affected area(s) of your skin for a short time after you have applied it. Sometimes it may also cause irritation of the surrounding normal skin. If this happens, try not to scratch the area.

If the irritation continues, if you develop rash on your face, or if the medicine causes any other problems for you, *stop using the medicine and check with your doctor.*

You may have to see your doctor regularly while using this medicine so that your doctor can check for any side effects, especially an increase in the level of calcium in your blood or urine, because this may lead to kidney stone formation.

Your doctor may tell you when you should expect to notice an improvement in your condition (usually within 2 to 8 weeks). If your condition has not improved by then or if it becomes worse, check with your doctor.

Side Effects of This Medicine

Along with its needed effects, a medicine may cause some unwanted effects. Although not all of these side effects may occur, if they do occur they may need medical attention.

Check with your doctor as soon as possible if any of the following side effects occur:
More common
  Redness and swelling of skin with itching; skin rash; worsening of psoriasis, including spreading to the face and scalp
Rare—for ointment dosage form only
  Abdominal or stomach pain, constipation, depression, loss of appetite, loss of weight, muscle weakness, nausea, thirst, tiring easily, and vomiting; burning, itching, and pain in hairy areas; pus in the hair follicles; thinning, weakness, or wasting away of skin

Other side effects may occur that usually do not need medical attention. These side effects may go away during treatment as your body adjusts to the medicine. However, check with your doctor if any of the following side effects continue or are bothersome:
More common
  Burning, dryness, irritation, peeling, or redness of skin
Less common or rare—for cream and ointment dosage forms only
  Darkening of treated areas of skin

Other side effects not listed above may also occur in some patients. If you notice any other effects, check with your doctor.

Revised: 08/20/97

CALCITONIN   Nasal-Systemic

Commonly used brand name(s):

In the U.S.—
  Miacalcin

Description

Calcitonin (kal-si-TOE-nin) is used to treat women with postmenopausal osteoporosis (bone loss). It is used together with calcium and vitamin D.

This medicine is available only with your doctor's prescription, in the following dosage form:

Nasal
  - Nasal solution (U.S.)

Before Using This Medicine

In deciding to use a medicine, the risks of using the medicine must be weighed against the good it will do. This is a decision you and your doctor will make. For calcitonin, the following should be considered:

Allergies—Tell your doctor if you have ever had any unusual or allergic reaction to calcitonin or to proteins. Also tell your health care professional if you are allergic to any other substances, such as foods, preservatives, or dyes.

Pregnancy—Calcitonin has not been studied in pregnant women. However, in animal studies, calcitonin has been shown to lower the birth weight of the baby when the mother was given a dose of calcitonin many times the human dose. Calcitonin nasal solution should not be used by women during pregnancy.

Breast-feeding—It is not known whether calcitonin passes into breast milk. However, studies in animals have shown that calcitonin may decrease the flow of milk.

Children—There is no specific information comparing the use of calcitonin in children with use in older age groups.

Older adults—Calcitonin nasal solution has been tested in elderly patients and has not been found to cause different side effects or problems in older people than it does in younger adults.

Other medicines—Although certain medicines should not be used together at all, in other cases two different medicines may be used together even if an interaction might occur. In these cases, your doctor may want to change the dose, or other precautions may be necessary. When you are taking calcitonin, it is especially important that your health care professional know if you are taking any other prescription or nonprescription (over-the-counter [OTC]) medicine.

Proper Use of This Medicine

This medicine usually comes with patient directions. *Read them carefully before using this medicine.* If you have any questions about using the pump spray, ask your doctor, nurse, or pharmacist.

Use this medicine only as directed by your doctor. Do not use more of it and do not use it more often or for a longer time than directed.

To assemble the pump:
- If your medicine and its pump were not already assembled by the pharmacist, carefully follow the instructions provided:
- Remove the bottle of solution from the refrigerator and let it sit until it warms to room temperature (less than 77 °F).
- Lift the blue plastic tab and pull the metal safety seal off the bottle.
- Hold the bottle upright and carefully pull the rubber stopper out of the bottle.
- Hold the spray pump unit and remove the plastic cap from the bottom of the unit.
- Hold the bottle upright and place the spray pump unit into the bottle.
- Turn the spray pump unit clockwise and tighten it until it is securely fastened.

To prepare this medicine:
- *Before you use a new bottle of calcitonin spray, the spray pump will need to be primed (started).* If your pharmacist assembled the unit for you, check to see if it has already been primed by pumping the unit once. If a full spray comes out, the unit has already been primed; if not, you must prime the pump.
- To prime, hold the bottle upright and away from you, then pump it several times until you see a faint spray.
- *Do not prime the pump again before each daily use.*

To use the nose spray:
- Before using the spray, blow your nose gently.
- Keeping your head in an upright position, carefully place the nozzle into one nostril.
- Press the pump toward the bottle one time. *Do not spray more than once.*
- *Do not inhale while spraying.*
- To keep the nosepiece clean, wipe it with a clean tissue and replace the dust cap after use.

Dosing—The dose of calcitonin will be different for different patients. *Follow your doctor's orders or the directions on the label.* The following information includes only the average doses of calcitonin. *If your dose is different, do not change it* unless your doctor tells you to do so.

- For *nasal* dosage form (nose spray):
  —For treatment of women with osteoporosis after menopause:
  - Adults—One spray into one nostril once a day. It is best to spray into the nostril on one side one day and the other side the next day.

Missed dose—If you miss a dose of this medicine, use it as soon as possible. However, if it is almost time for your next dose, skip the missed dose and go back to your regular dosing schedule. Do not double doses.

Storage—To store this medicine:
- Keep out of the reach of children.
- Store in the refrigerator until it is opened for the first time. However, keep the medicine from freezing.
- After the bottle is opened, it may be kept at room temperature (no more than 77 °F) until the medicine is gone (2 weeks). Opened or unopened bottles left at room temperature for more than 30 days must be discarded.
- Do not keep outdated medicine or medicine no longer needed. Be sure that any discarded medicine is out of the reach of children.

Side Effects of This Medicine

Along with its needed effects, a medicine may cause some unwanted effects. Although not all of these side effects may occur, if they do occur they may need medical attention.

Check with your doctor as soon as possible if any of the following side effects occur:

More common
   Crusting, patches, or sores inside the nose; dryness, itching, redness, swelling, tenderness, or other signs of nasal irritation not present before use of this medicine; headaches (severe or continuing); nosebleeds; runny nose

Less common
   Bloody or cloudy urine; breathing difficulty or wheezing (severe); difficult, burning, or painful urination; dizziness; frequent urge to urinate; loss of sense of smell; swollen glands; upper respiratory infection, with chest pain, chills, cough, ear congestion or pain, fever, head congestion, hoarseness or other

voice changes, nasal congestion, runny nose, sneezing, or sore throat

Rare
Hair loss; hives, itching, or skin rash; increased thirst; taste disturbances

Other side effects may occur that usually do not need medical attention. These side effects may go away during treatment as your body adjusts to the medicine. However, check with your doctor if any of the following side effects continue or are bothersome:

More common
Back pain; joint pain

Less common or rare
Abdominal pain; burning, dry, or itching eyes; constipation; diarrhea; flu-like symptoms (fever with or without chills, headache, body ache); flushing; mental depression; muscle pain; nausea; unusual tearing of eyes; unusual tiredness or weakness; upset stomach

Other side effects not listed above may also occur in some patients. If you notice any other effects, check with your doctor.

Developed: 03/23/98

CALCITONIN   Systemic

Commonly used brand name(s):

In the U.S.—
Calcimar[2]
Cibacalcin[1]
Miacalcin[2]

In Canada—
Calcimar[2]

Note: For quick reference, the following calcitonin are numbered to match the corresponding brand names.

This information applies to the following medicines:
1. Calcitonin-Human (kal-si-TOE-nin HYOO-man) †
2. Calcitonin-Salmon (kal-si-TOE-nin SAM-en)

†Not commercially available in Canada.

Description

Calcitonin (kal-si-TOE-nin) is used to treat Paget's disease of bone. It also may be used to prevent continuing bone loss in women with postmenopausal osteoporosis and to treat hypercalcemia (too much calcium in the blood). This medicine may be used to treat other conditions as determined by your doctor.

Calcitonin is available only with your doctor's prescription, in the following dosage forms:

Parenteral
Calcitonin-Human
• Injection (U.S.)
Calcitonin-Salmon
• Injection (U.S. and Canada)

Before Using This Medicine

In deciding to use a medicine, the risks of taking the medicine must be weighed against the good it will do. This is a decision you and your doctor will make. For calcitonin, the following should be considered:

Allergies—Tell your doctor if you have ever had any unusual or allergic reaction to calcitonin or other proteins. Also tell your health care professional if you are allergic to any other substances, such as foods, preservatives, or dyes.

Diet—Make certain your health care professional knows if your diet includes large amounts of calcium-containing foods and/or vitamin D-containing foods, such as milk or other dairy products. Calcium and vitamin D may cause the calcitonin to be less effective in treating a high blood calcium. Also let your health care professional know if you are on any special diet, such as low-sodium or low-sugar diet.

Pregnancy—Calcitonin has not been studied in pregnant women. However, in animal studies, calcitonin has been shown to lower the birth weight of the baby when the mother was given a dose of calcitonin many times the human dose.

Breast-feeding—Calcitonin has not been reported to cause problems in nursing babies. However, studies in animals have shown that calcitonin may decrease the flow of breast milk.

Children—Studies on this medicine have been done only in adult patients, and there is no specific information comparing the use of calcitonin in children with use in other age groups. Therefore, be sure to discuss with your doctor the use of this medicine in children.

Older adults—Many medicines have not been studied specifically in older people. Therefore, it may not be known whether they work exactly the same way they do in younger adults. Although there is no specific information comparing the use of calcitonin in the elderly with use in other age groups, this medicine is not expected to cause different side effects or problems in older people than it does in younger adults. Calcitonin is often used in elderly patients.

Other medicine—Although certain medicines should not be used together at all, in other cases two different medicines may be used together even if an interaction might occur. In these cases, your doctor may want to change the dose, or other precautions may be necessary. Tell your health care professional if you are using any other prescription or non-prescription (over-the-counter [OTC]) medicine.

Proper Use of This Medicine

This medicine is for injection only. If you will be giving yourself the injections, make sure you understand exactly how to give them, including how to fill the syringe before injection. If you have any questions about this, check with your doctor.

Use the calcitonin only when the contents of the syringe are clear and colorless. Do not use it if it looks grainy or discolored.

Dosing—The dose of calcitonin will be different for different patients. *Follow your doctor's orders or the directions on the label.* The following information includes only the average doses of calcitonin. *If your dose is different, do not change it* unless your doctor tells you to do so.

The number of doses you receive, the time allowed between doses, and the length of time you receive the medicine depends on the medical problem for which you are receiving calcitonin.

For calcitonin-human
- For *injection* dosage form:
  —For Paget's disease of bone:
    - Adults—To start, 500 micrograms (mcg) injected under the skin once a day. Your doctor may reduce your dose or increase the time between doses. Or, your doctor may give you a smaller dose to start and increase your dose over two weeks.
    - Children—Dose must be determined by your doctor.

For calcitonin-salmon
- For *injection* dosage form:
  —For Paget's disease of bone:
    - Adults—To start, 100 Units injected into a muscle or under the skin once a day, once every other day, or three times a week. Your doctor may reduce your dose or increase the time between doses.
    - Children—Dose must be determined by your doctor.
  —For hypercalcemia (too much calcium in the blood):
    - Adults—To start, 4 Units per kilogram (kg) (1.8 Units per pound) of body weight injected into a muscle or under the skin every twelve hours. Your doctor may increase your dose or increase the time between doses.
    - Children—Dose must be determined by your doctor.
  —For postmenopausal osteoporosis:
    - Adults—100 Units injected into a muscle or under the skin once a day, once every other day, or three times a week. Or, your doctor may give you a smaller dose to start and increase your dose over two weeks.
    - Children—Dose must be determined by your doctor.

Missed dose—If you miss a dose of this medicine and your dosing schedule is:
- Two doses a day—If you remember within 2 hours of the missed dose, give it right away. Then go back to your regular dosing schedule. But if you do not remember the missed dose until later, skip it and go back to your regular dosing schedule. Do not double doses.
- One dose a day—Give the missed dose as soon as possible. Then go back to your regular dosing schedule. If you do not remember the missed dose until the next day, skip it and go back to your regular dosing schedule. Do not double doses.
- One dose every other day—Give the missed dose as soon as possible if you remember it on the day it should be given. Then go back to your regular dosing schedule. If you do not remember the missed dose until the next day, give it at that time. Then skip a day and start your dosing schedule again.
- One dose three times a week—Give the missed dose the next day. Then set each injection back a day for the rest of the week. Go back to your regular Monday-Wednesday-Friday schedule the following week. Do not double doses.

If you have any questions about this, check with your doctor.

Storage—To store this medicine:
- Keep out of the reach of children.
- Store away from heat and direct light.

- Store *calcitonin-human* at a temperature below 77 °F. Do not refrigerate. Use prepared solution within 6 hours.
- Store *calcitonin-salmon* in the refrigerator. However, keep it from freezing.
- Do not keep outdated medicine or medicine no longer needed. Be sure that any discarded medicine is out of the reach of children.

Precautions While Using This Medicine

Your doctor should check your progress at regular visits to make sure that this medicine does not cause unwanted effects.

If you are using this medicine for hypercalcemia (too much calcium in the blood), your doctor may want you to follow a low-calcium diet. If you have any questions about this, check with your doctor.

Side Effects of This Medicine

Along with its needed effects, a medicine may cause some unwanted effects. Although not all of these side effects may occur, if they do occur they may need medical attention.

Check with your doctor as soon as possible if either of the following side effects occurs:
Rare
   Skin rash or hives

Other side effects may occur that usually do not need medical attention. These side effects may go away during treatment as your body adjusts to the medicine. However, check with your doctor if any of the following side effects continue or are bothersome:
More common
   Diarrhea; flushing or redness of face, ears, hands, or feet; loss of appetite; nausea or vomiting; pain, redness, soreness, or swelling at place of injection; stomach pain
Less common
   Increased frequency of urination
Rare
   Chills; dizziness; headache; pressure in chest; stuffy nose; tenderness or tingling of hands or feet; trouble in breathing; weakness

Other side effects not listed above may also occur in some patients. If you notice any other effects, check with your doctor.

Additional Information

Once a medicine has been approved for marketing for a certain use, experience may show that it is also useful for other medical problems. Although this use is not included in product labeling, calcitonin is used in certain patients with the following medical condition:
- Osteoporosis caused by hormone problems, certain drugs, and other causes

Other than the above information, there is no additional information relating to proper use, precautions, or side effects for this use.

Revised: 05/13/92
Interim revision: 06/27/94

CALCIUM ACETATE   Systemic

Commonly used brand name(s):

In the U.S.—
    PhosLo

Description

Calcium acetate (KAL-see-um ASS-a-tate) is used to treat hyperphosphatemia (too much phosphate in the blood) in patients with kidney disease.

Calcium acetate works by binding with the phosphate in the food you eat, so that it is eliminated from the body without being absorbed.

This medicine is available only with your doctor's prescription, in the following dosage form:

    Oral
      • Tablets (U.S.)

Before Using This Medicine

In deciding to use a medicine, the risks of taking the medicine must be weighed against the good it will do. This is a decision you and your doctor will make. For calcium acetate, the following should be considered:

Allergies—Tell your doctor if you have ever had any unusual or allergic reaction to calcium acetate. Also tell your health care professional if you are allergic to any other substances, such as foods, preservatives, or dyes.

Pregnancy—Studies on the effects of calcium acetate when taken during pregnancy have not been done in either humans or animals.

Breast-feeding—It is not known whether calcium acetate passes into breast milk. Although most medicines pass into breast milk in small amounts, many of them may be used safely while breast-feeding. Mothers who are using this medicine and who wish to breast-feed should discuss this with their doctor.

Children—Studies on this medicine have been done only in adult patients and there is no specific information comparing use of calcium acetate in children with use in other age groups.

Older adults—Many medicines have not been studied specifically in older people. Therefore, it may not be known whether they work exactly the same way they do in younger adults or if they cause different side effects or problems in older people. There is no specific information comparing use of calcium acetate in elderly patients with use in other adults.

Other medicines—Although certain medicines should not be used together at all, in other cases two different medicines may be used together even if an interaction might occur. In these cases, your doctor may want to change the dose, or other precautions may be necessary. When you are taking calcium acetate, it is especially important that your health care professional know if you are taking any of the following:

    • Calcium-containing medicines, other, including antacids—Taking excess calcium may cause too much calcium in the blood or urine, which may increase the chance of side effects
    • Digitalis glycosides (heart medicine)—Use with calcium acetate may cause hypercalcemia (too much calcium in the blood), which could increase the chance of developing an irregular heartbeat

Other medical problems—The presence of other medical problems may affect the use of calcium acetate. Make sure you tell your doctor if you have any other medical problems, especially:

    • Hypercalcemia (too much calcium in the blood)—Calcium acetate may make this condition worse

Proper Use of This Medicine

Take this medicine with meals.

Dosing—The dose of calcium acetate will be different for different patients. *Follow your doctor's orders or the directions on the label.* The following information includes only the average dose of calcium acetate. *If your dose is different, do not change it* unless your doctor tells you to do so.

    • For *oral* dosage form (tablets):
      —For too much phosphate in the blood:
        • Adults—2 tablets three times a day with meals. Your doctor may increase the dose if necessary.
        • Children—Use and dose must be determined by your doctor.

Missed dose—If you miss a dose of this medicine, take it as soon as possible. However, if it is almost time for your next dose, skip the missed dose and go back to your regular dosing schedule. Do not double doses.

Storage—To store this medicine:
    • Keep out of the reach of children.
    • Store away from heat and direct light.
    • Do not store in the bathroom, near the kitchen sink, or in other damp places. Heat or moisture may cause the medicine to break down.
    • Do not keep outdated medicine or medicine no longer needed. Be sure that any discarded medicine is out of the reach of children.

Precautions While Using This Medicine

It is important that your doctor check your progress at regular visits, especially during the first few months of treatment with this medicine, since your dose may have to be adjusted. This is to make sure that this medicine is working properly and does not cause unwanted effects.

Do not take other calcium-containing products including dietary supplements and antacids. Your doctor may adjust the amount of calcium-containing foods you eat. Taking too much calcium while you are taking this medicine can cause hypercalcemia (too much calcium in the blood).

Side Effects of This Medicine

Along with its needed effects, a medicine may cause some unwanted effects. Although not all of these side effects may occur, if they do occur they may need medical attention.

Check with your doctor immediately if any of the following side effects occur:
    Rare—Signs of severe hypercalcemia
      Confusion; full or partial loss of consciousness; incoherent speech

Also, check with your doctor as soon as possible if any of the following side effects occur:
    Rare—Signs of mild hypercalcemia
      Constipation; loss of appetite; nausea or vomiting

Other side effects may occur that usually do not need medical attention. These side effects may go away during treatment

as your body adjusts to the medicine. However, check with your doctor if the following side effect continues or is bothersome:

Less common
Itching

Other side effects not listed above may also occur in some patients. If you notice any other effects, check with your doctor.

Developed: 03/23/98

CALCIUM CHANNEL BLOCKING AGENTS Systemic

Commonly used brand name(s):

In the U.S.—

Adalat[7]	DynaCirc[5]
Adalat CC[7]	Isoptin[9]
Calan[9]	Isoptin SR[9]
Calan SR[9]	Nimotop[8]
Cardene[6]	Plendil[3]
Cardizem[2]	Procardia[7]
Cardizem CD[2]	Procardia XL[7]
Cardizem SR[2]	Vascor[1]
Dilacor-XR[2]	Verelan[9]

In Canada—

Adalat[7]	Novo-Diltazem[2]
Adalat PA[7]	Novo-Nifedin[7]
Adalat XL[7]	Novo-Veramil[9]
Apo-Diltiaz[2]	Nu-Diltiaz[2]
Apo-Nifed[7]	Nu-Nifed[7]
Apo-Verap[9]	Nu-Verap[9]
Cardizem[2]	Plendil[3]
Cardizem SR[2]	Renedil[3]
Isoptin[9]	Sibelium[4]
Isoptin SR[9]	Syn-Diltiazem[2]
Nimotop[8]	Verelan[9]

Note: For quick reference, the following calcium channel blocking agents are numbered to match the corresponding brand names.

This information applies to the following medicines:
1. Bepridil (BE-pri-dil) †
2. Diltiazem (dil-TYE-a-zem) ‡§
3. Felodipine (fe-LOE-di-peen)
4. Flunarizine (floo-NAR-i-zeen) *
5. Isradipine (is-RA-di-peen) †
6. Nicardipine (nye-KAR-de-peen) †‡
7. Nifedipine (nye-FED-i-peen) ‡
8. Nimodipine (nye-MOE-di-peen) ‡
9. Verapamil (ver-AP-a-mil) ‡§

*Not commercially available in the U.S.
†Not commercially available in Canada.
‡Generic name product may be available in the U.S.
§Generic name product may be available in Canada.

Description

Bepridil, diltiazem, felodipine, flunarizine, isradipine, nicardipine, nifedipine, nimodipine, and verapamil belong to the group of medicines called calcium channel blocking agents.

Calcium channel blocking agents affect the movement of calcium into the cells of the heart and blood vessels. As a result, they relax blood vessels and increase the supply of blood and oxygen to the heart while reducing its workload.

Some of the calcium channel blocking agents are used to relieve and control angina pectoris (chest pain).

Some are also used to treat high blood pressure (hypertension). High blood pressure adds to the workload of the heart and arteries. If it continues for a long time, the heart and arteries may not function properly. This can damage the blood vessels of the brain, heart, and kidneys, resulting in a stroke, heart failure, or kidney failure. High blood pressure may also increase the risk of heart attacks. These problems may be less likely to occur if blood pressure is controlled.

Flunarizine is used to prevent migraine headaches.

Nimodipine is used to prevent and treat problems caused by a burst blood vessel around the brain (also known as a ruptured aneurysm or subarachnoid hemorrhage).

Other calcium channel blocking agents may also be used for these and other conditions as determined by your doctor.

These medicines are available only with your doctor's prescription, in the following dosage forms:

Oral
Bepridil
  • Tablets (U.S.)
Diltiazem
  • Extended-release capsules (U.S. and Canada)
  • Tablets (U.S. and Canada)
Felodipine
  • Extended-release tablets (U.S. and Canada)
Flunarizine
  • Capsules (Canada)
Isradipine
  • Capsules (U.S.)
Nicardipine
  • Capsules (U.S.)
Nifedipine
  • Capsules (U.S. and Canada)
  • Extended-release tablets (U.S. and Canada)
Nimodipine
  • Capsules (U.S. and Canada)
Verapamil
  • Extended-release capsules (U.S. and Canada)
  • Tablets (U.S. and Canada)
  • Extended-release tablets (U.S. and Canada)

Parenteral
Diltiazem
  • Injection (U.S. and Canada)
Verapamil
  • Injection (U.S. and Canada)

Before Using This Medicine

In deciding to use a medicine, the risks of taking the medicine must be weighed against the good it will do. This is a decision you and your doctor will make. For the calcium channel blocking agents, the following should be considered:

Allergies—Tell your doctor if you have ever had any unusual or allergic reaction to bepridil, diltiazem, felodipine, flunarizine, isradipine, nicardipine, nifedipine, nimodipine, or verapamil. Also tell your health care professional if you are allergic to any other substances, such as foods, preservatives, or dyes.

Pregnancy—Calcium channel blocking agents have not been studied in pregnant women. However, studies in animals have shown that large doses of calcium channel blocking agents cause birth defects, prolonged pregnancy, poor bone development in the offspring, and stillbirth.

Breast-feeding— Although bepridil, diltiazem, nifedipine, verapamil, and possibly other calcium channel blocking agents, pass into breast milk, they have not been reported to cause problems in nursing babies.

Children— Although there is no specific information comparing use of this medicine in children with use in other age groups, it is not expected to cause different side effects or problems in children than it does in adults.

Older adults— Elderly people may be especially sensitive to the effects of calcium channel blocking agents. This may increase the chance of side effects during treatment.

Other medicines— Although certain medicines should not be used together at all, in other cases two different medicines may be used together even if an interaction might occur. In these cases, your doctor may want to change the dose, or other precautions may be necessary. When taking calcium channel blocking agents it is especially important that your health care professional know if you are taking any of the following:

- Acetazolamide (e.g., Diamox) or
- Amphotericin B by injection (e.g., Fungizone) or
- Corticosteroids (cortisone-like medicine) or
- Dichlorphenamide (e.g., Daranide) or
- Diuretics (water pills) or
- Methazolamide (e.g., Naptazane)—These medicines can cause hypokalemia (low levels of potassium in the body), which can increase the unwanted effects of bepridil
- Beta-adrenergic blocking agents (acebutolol [e.g., Sectral], atenolol [e.g., Tenormin], betaxolol [e.g., Kerlone], carteolol [e.g., Cartrol], labetalol [e.g., Normodyne], metoprolol [e.g., Lopressor], nadolol [e.g., Corgard], oxprenolol [e.g., Trasicor], penbutolol [e.g., Levatol], pindolol [e.g., Visken], propranolol [e.g., Inderal], sotalol [e.g., Sotacor], timolol [e.g., Blocadren])—Effects of both may be increased. In addition, unwanted effects may occur if a calcium channel blocking agent or a beta-blocking agent is stopped suddenly after both have been used together
- Carbamazepine (e.g., Tegretol) or
- Cyclosporine (e.g., Sandimmune) or
- Procainamide (e.g., Pronestyl) or
- Quinidine (e.g., Quinidex)—Effects of these medicines may be increased if they are used with some calcium channel blocking agents
- Digitalis glycosides (heart medicine)—Effects of these medicines may be increased if they are used with some calcium channel blocking agents
- Disopyramide (e.g., Norpace)—Effects of some calcium channel blocking agents on the heart may be increased
- Grapefruit juice—Effects of felodipine may be increased

Also, tell your health care professional if you are using any of the following medicines in the eye:

- Betaxolol (e.g., Betoptic) or
- Levobunolol (e.g., Betagan) or
- Metipranolol (e.g., OptiPranolol) or
- Timolol (e.g., Timoptic)—Effects on the heart and blood pressure may be increased

Other medical problems— The presence of other medical problems may affect the use of the calcium channel blocking agents. Make sure you tell your doctor if you have any other medical problems, especially:

- Heart rhythm problems (history of)—Bepridil can cause serious heart rhythm problems

- Kidney disease or
- Liver disease—Effects of the calcium channel blocking agent may be increased
- Mental depression (history of)—Flunarizine may cause mental depression
- Parkinson's disease or similar problems—Flunarizine can cause parkinsonian-like effects
- Other heart or blood vessel disorders—Calcium channel blocking agents may make some heart conditions worse

Proper Use of This Medicine

Take this medicine exactly as directed even if you feel well and do not notice any signs of chest pain. Do not take more of this medicine and do not take it more often than your doctor ordered. Do not miss any doses.

For patients taking *bepridil:*

- If this medicine causes upset stomach, it can be taken with meals or at bedtime.

For patients taking *diltiazem extended-release capsules:*

- Swallow the capsule whole, without crushing or chewing it.
- *Do not change to another brand without checking with your physician.* Different brands have different doses. If you refill your medicine and it looks different, check with your pharmacist.

For patients taking *felodipine:*

- Do not take this medicine with grapefruit juice.

For patients taking *verapamil extended-release capsules:*

- Swallow the capsule whole, without crushing or chewing it.

For patients taking *felodipine* or *nifedipine extended-release tablets:*

- Swallow the tablet whole, without breaking, crushing, or chewing it.
- If you are taking *Adalat XL* or *Procardia XL*, you may sometimes notice what looks like a tablet in your stool. That is just the empty shell that is left after the medicine has been absorbed into your body.
- If you are taking *Adalat CC*, take the medicine on an empty stomach

For patients taking *verapamil extended-release tablets:*

- Swallow the tablet whole, without crushing or chewing it. However, if your doctor tells you to, you may break the tablet in half.
- Take the medicine with food or milk.

For patients taking this medicine *for high blood pressure:*

- In addition to the use of the medicine your doctor has prescribed, appropriate treatment for your high blood pressure may include weight control and care in the types of food you eat, especially foods high in sodium (salt). Your doctor will tell you which factors are most important for you. You should check with your doctor before changing your diet.
- Many patients who have high blood pressure will not notice any signs of the problem. In fact, many may feel normal. It is very important that you *take your medicine exactly as directed* and that you keep your appointments with your doctor even if you feel well.
- Remember that this medicine will not cure your high blood pressure but it does help control it. Therefore, you must continue to take it as directed if you expect to lower your blood pressure and keep it down. *You may have*

to take high blood pressure medicine for the rest of your life. If high blood pressure is not treated, it can cause serious problems such as heart failure, blood vessel disease, stroke, or kidney disease.

Dosing—The dose of these medicines will be different for different patients. *Follow your doctor's orders or the directions on the label.* The following information includes only the average doses of these medicines. *If your dose is different, do not change it* unless your doctor tells you to do so.

The number of capsules or tablets that you take depends on the strength of the medicine. Also, *the number of doses you take each day, the time allowed between doses, and the length of time you take the medicine depend on the medical problem for which you are taking calcium channel blocking agents.*

For bepridil
- For *oral* dosage form (tablets):
  —For angina (chest pain):
  - Adults—200 to 300 milligrams (mg) once a day.
  - Children—Use and dose must be determined by your doctor.

For diltiazem
- For *long-acting oral* dosage form (extended-release capsules):
  —For high blood pressure:
  - Adults and teenagers:
    —For *Cardizem CD* or *Dilacor-XR:* 180 to 240 milligrams (mg) once a day.
    —For *Cardizem SR:* 60 to 120 mg two times a day.
  - Children—Dose must be determined by your doctor.
- For *regular (short-acting) oral* dosage form (tablets):
  —For angina (chest pain):
  - Adults and teenagers—30 mg three or four times a day. Your doctor may gradually increase your dose as needed.
  - Children—Dose must be determined by your doctor.
- For *injection* dosage form:
  —For arrhythmias (irregular heartbeat):
  - Adults and teenagers—Dose is based on body weight and must be determined by your doctor.
  - Children—Use and dose must be determined by your doctor.

For felodipine
- For *long-acting oral* dosage form (extended-release tablets):
  —For high blood pressure:
  - Adults—5 to 10 milligrams (mg) once a day.
  - Children—Use and dose must be determined by your doctor.
  —For angina (chest pain):
  - Adults—10 mg once a day.
  - Children—Use and dose must be determined by your doctor.

For flunarizine
- For *oral* dosage form (capsules):
  —To prevent headaches:
  - Adults—10 milligrams (mg) once a day in the evening.
  - Children—Dose must be determined by your doctor.

For isradipine
- For *oral* dosage form (capsules):
  —For high blood pressure:
  - Adults—2.5 milligrams (mg) two times a day. Your doctor may increase your dose as needed.
  - Children—Use and dose must be determined by your doctor.

For nicardipine
- For *oral* dosage form (capsules):
  —For high blood pressure or angina (chest pain):
  - Adults and teenagers—20 milligrams (mg) three times a day.
  - Children—Dose must be determined by your doctor.

For nifedipine
- For *regular (short-acting) oral* dosage form (capsules):
  —For high blood pressure or angina (chest pain):
  - Adults and teenagers—10 milligrams (mg) three times a day. Your doctor may increase your dose as needed.
  - Children—Dose must be determined by your doctor.
- For *long-acting oral* dosage form (extended-release tablets):
  —For high blood pressure or angina (chest pain):
  - Adults and teenagers:
    —For *Adalat CC, Adalat XL* or *Procardia XL:* 30 or 60 mg once a day. Your doctor may increase your dose as needed.
    —For *Adalat PA:* 10 or 20 mg two times a day. Your doctor may increase your dose as needed.
  - Children—Dose must be determined by your doctor.

For nimodipine
- For *oral* dosage form (capsules):
  —To treat a burst blood vessel around the brain:
  - Adults—60 milligrams (mg) every four hours.
  - Children—Dose must be determined by your doctor.

For verapamil
- For *regular (short-acting) oral* dosage form (tablets):
  —For angina (chest pain), arrhythmias (irregular heartbeat), or high blood pressure:
  - Adults and teenagers—40 to 120 milligrams (mg) three times a day. Your doctor may increase your dose as needed.
  - Children—Dose is based on body weight and must be determined by your doctor. The usual dose is 4 to 8 mg per kilogram (kg) (1.82 to 3.64 mg per pound) of body weight a day. This is divided into smaller doses.
- For *long-acting oral* dosage form (extended-release capsules):
  —For high blood pressure:
  - Adults and teenagers—240 to 480 mg once a day.
  - Children—Dose must be determined by your doctor.
- For *long-acting oral* dosage form (extended-release tablets):
  —For high blood pressure:
  - Adults and teenagers—120 mg once a day to 240 mg every twelve hours.

- Children—Dose must be determined by your doctor.
- For *injection* dosage form:
  —For arrhythmias (irregular heartbeat):
    - Adults—5 to 10 mg slowly injected into a vein. The dose may be repeated after thirty minutes.
    - Children—Dose is based on body weight and must be determined by your doctor.
      —Infants up to 1 year of age: 100 to 200 micrograms (mcg) per kg (45.5 to 90.9 mcg per pound) of body weight injected slowly into a vein. The dose may be repeated after thirty minutes.
      —Children 1 to 15 years of age: 100 to 300 mcg per kg (45.5 to 136.4 mcg per pound) of body weight injected slowly into a vein. The dose may be repeated after thirty minutes.

Missed dose—If you miss a dose of this medicine, take it as soon as possible. However, if it is almost time for your next dose, skip the missed dose and go back to your regular dosing schedule. Do not double doses.

Storage—To store this medicine:
- Keep out of the reach of children.
- Store away from heat and direct light.
- Do not store in the bathroom, near the kitchen sink, or in other damp places. Heat or moisture may cause the medicine to break down.
- Do not keep outdated medicine or medicine no longer needed. Be sure that any discarded medicine is out of the reach of children.

Precautions While Using This Medicine

It is important that your doctor check your progress at regular visits. This will allow your doctor to make sure the medicine is working properly and to change the dosage if needed.

If you have been using this medicine regularly for several weeks, do not suddenly stop using it. Stopping suddenly may bring on your previous problem. Check with your doctor for the best way to reduce gradually the amount you are taking before stopping completely.

Chest pain resulting from exercise or physical exertion is usually reduced or prevented by this medicine. This may tempt you to be overly active. *Make sure you discuss with your doctor a safe amount of exercise for your medical problem.*

After taking a dose of this medicine you may get a headache that lasts for a short time. This effect is more common if you are taking felodipine, isradipine, or nifedipine. This should become less noticeable after you have taken this medicine for a while. If this effect continues or if the headaches are severe, check with your doctor.

In some patients, tenderness, swelling, or bleeding of the gums may appear soon after treatment with this medicine is started. Brushing and flossing your teeth carefully and regularly and massaging your gums may help prevent this. *See your dentist regularly to have your teeth cleaned. Check with your medical doctor or dentist if you have any questions about how to take care of your teeth and gums, or if you notice any tenderness, swelling, or bleeding of your gums.*

For patients taking *bepridil, diltiazem*, or *verapamil:*
- *Ask your doctor how to count your pulse rate. Then, while you are taking this medicine, check your pulse regularly.* If it is much slower than your usual rate, or less than 50 beats per minute, check with your doctor. A pulse rate that is too slow may cause circulation problems.

For patients taking *flunarizine:*
- This medicine may cause some people to become drowsy or less alert than they are normally. This is more likely to happen when you begin to take it or when you increase the amount of medicine you are taking. *Make sure you know how you react to this medicine before you drive, use machines, or do anything else that could be dangerous if you are not alert.*

For patients taking this medicine *for high blood pressure:*
- *Do not take other medicines unless they have been discussed with your doctor.* This especially includes over-the-counter (nonprescription) medicines for appetite control, asthma, colds, cough, hay fever, or sinus problems, since they may tend to increase your blood pressure.

Side Effects of This Medicine

Along with its needed effects, a medicine may cause some unwanted effects. Although not all of these side effects may occur, if they do occur they may need medical attention.

Not all of the side effects listed below have been reported for each of these medicines, but they have been reported for at least one of them. Since many of the effects of calcium channel blocking agents are similar, some of these side effects may occur with any of these medicines. However, they may be more common with some of these medicines than with others.

Check with your doctor as soon as possible if any of the following side effects occur:

Less common
Breathing difficulty, coughing, or wheezing; irregular or fast, pounding heartbeat; skin rash; slow heartbeat (less than 50 beats per minute—bepridil, diltiazem, and verapamil only); swelling of ankles, feet, or lower legs (more common with felodipine and nifedipine)

For flunarizine only—less common
Loss of balance control; mask-like face; mental depression; shuffling walk; stiffness of arms or legs; trembling and shaking of hands and fingers; trouble in speaking or swallowing

Rare
Bleeding, tender, or swollen gums; chest pain (may appear about 30 minutes after medicine is taken); fainting; painful, swollen joints (for nifedipine only); trouble in seeing (for nifedipine only)

For flunarizine and verapamil only—rare
Unusual secretion of milk

Other side effects may occur that usually do not need medical attention. These side effects may go away during treatment as your body adjusts to the medicine. However, check with your doctor if any of the following side effects continue or are bothersome:

More common
Drowsiness (for flunarizine only); increased appetite and/or weight gain (for flunarizine only)

Less common
Constipation; diarrhea; dizziness or lightheadedness (more common with bepridil and nifedipine); dryness of mouth (for flunarizine only); flushing and feeling

of warmth (more common with nicardipine and nifedipine); headache (more common with felodipine, isradipine, and nifedipine); nausea (more common with bepridil and nifedipine); unusual tiredness or weakness

Other side effects not listed above may also occur in some patients. If you notice any other effects, check with your doctor.

Additional Information

Once a medicine has been approved for marketing for a certain use, experience may show that it is also useful for other medical problems. Although these uses are not included in product labeling, calcium channel blocking agents are used in certain patients with the following medical conditions:

- Hypertrophic cardiomyopathy (a heart condition) (verapamil)
- Raynaud's phenomenon (circulation problems) (nicardipine and nifedipine)

Other than the above information, there is no additional information relating to proper use, precautions, or side effects for these uses.

Revised: 07/14/2000

CALCIUM SUPPLEMENTS   Systemic

Commonly used brand name(s):

In the U.S.—

Alka-Mints[2]	Liquid-Cal[2]
Amitone[2]	Liquid Cal-600[2]
Calcarb 600[2]	Maalox Antacid Caplets[2]
Calci-Chew[2]	Mallamint[2]
Calciday 667[2]	Neo-Calglucon[5]
Calcilac[2]	Nephro-Calci[2]
Calci-Mix[2]	Os-Cal 500[2]
Calcionate[5]	Os-Cal 500 Chewable[2]
Calcium 600[2]	Oysco[2]
Calglycine[2]	Oysco 500 Chewable[2]
Calphosan[9]	Oyst-Cal 500[2]
Cal-Plus[2]	Oystercal 500[2]
Caltrate 600[2]	Posture[13]
Caltrate Jr[2]	Rolaids Calcium Rich[2]
Chooz[2]	Titralac[2]
Citracal[4]	Tums[2]
Citracal Liquitabs[4]	Tums 500[2]
Dicarbosil[2]	Tums E-X[2]
Gencalc 600[2]	

In Canada—

Apo-Cal[2]	Caltrate 600[2]
Calciject[3]	Gramcal[11]
Calcite 500[2]	Nu-Cal[2]
Calcium-Sandoz[5]	Os-Cal[2]
Calcium-Sandoz Forte[11]	Os-Cal Chewable[2]
Calcium Stanley[7]	Tums Extra Strength[2]
Calsan[2]	Tums Regular Strength[2]

Note: For quick reference, the following calcium supplements are numbered to match the corresponding brand names.

This information applies to the following:

1. Calcium Acetate (KAL-see-um ASa-tate) †
2. Calcium Carbonate (KAL-see-um KAR-boh-nate) ‡§
3. Calcium Chloride (KAL-see-um KLOR-ide) ‡§
4. Calcium Citrate (KAL-see-um SIH-trayt) †‡
5. Calcium Glubionate (KAL-see-um gloo-BY-oh-nate) §
6. Calcium Gluceptate (KAL-see-um gloo-SEP-tate) †‡

7. Calcium Gluceptate and Calcium Gluconate (KAL-see-um gloo-SEP-tate and KAL-see-um GLOO-coh-nate) *
8. Calcium Gluconate (KAL-see-um GLOO-coh-nate) ‡§
9. Calcium Glycerophosphate and Calcium Lactate (KAL-see-um gliss-er-o-FOS-fate and KAL-see-um LAK-tate) †
10. Calcium Lactate (KAL-see-um LAK-tate) ‡§
11. Calcium Lactate-Gluconate and Calcium Carbonate (KAL-see-um LAK-tate GLOO-coh-nate and KAL-see-um KAR-boh-nate) *
12. Dibasic Calcium Phosphate (dy-BAY-sic KAL-see-um FOS-fate) †‡
13. Tribasic Calcium Phosphate (try-BAY-sic KAL-see-um FOS-fate) †

Note: This information does *not* apply to calciumcarbonate used as an antacid.

*Not commercially available in the U.S.
†Not commercially available in Canada.
‡Generic name product may be available in the U.S.
§Generic name product may be available in Canada.

Description

Calcium supplements are taken by individuals who are unable to get enough calcium in their regular diet or who have a need for more calcium. They are used to prevent or treat several conditions that may cause hypocalcemia (not enough calcium in the blood). The body needs calcium to make strong bones. Calcium is also needed for the heart, muscles, and nervous system to work properly.

The bones serve as a storage site for the body's calcium. They are continuously giving up calcium to the bloodstream and then replacing it as the body's need for calcium changes from day to day. When there is not enough calcium in the blood to be used by the heart and other organs, your body will take the needed calcium from the bones. When you eat foods rich in calcium, the calcium will be restored to the bones and the balance between your blood and bones will be maintained.

Pregnant women, nursing mothers, children, and adolescents may need more calcium than they normally get from eating calcium-rich foods. Adult women may take calcium supplements to help prevent a bone disease called osteoporosis. Osteoporosis, which causes thin, porous, easily broken bones, may occur in women after menopause, but may sometimes occur in elderly men also. Osteoporosis in women past menopause is thought to be caused by a reduced amount of ovarian estrogen (a female hormone). However, a diet low in calcium for many years, especially in the younger adult years, may add to the risk of developing it. Other bone diseases in children and adults are also treated with calcium supplements.

Calcium supplements may also be used for other conditions as determined by your health care professional.

Injectable calcium is administered only by or under the supervision of your health care professional. Other forms of calcium are available without a prescription.

Calcium supplements are available in the following dosage forms:

Oral
Calcium Carbonate
- Capsules (U.S. and Canada)
- Oral suspension (U.S.)
- Tablets (U.S. and Canada)
- Chewable tablets (U.S. and Canada)
Calcium Citrate
- Tablets (U.S.)

- Tablets for solution (U.S.)

Calcium Glubionate
- Syrup (U.S. and Canada)

Calcium Gluceptate and Calcium Gluconate
- Oral solution (Canada)

Calcium Gluconate
- Tablets (U.S. and Canada)
- Chewable tablets (U.S.)

Calcium Lactate
- Tablets (U.S. and Canada)

Calcium Lactate-Gluconate and Calcium Carbonate
- Tablets for solution (Canada)

Dibasic Calcium Phosphate
- Tablets (U.S.)

Tribasic Calcium Phosphate
- Tablets (U.S.)

Parenteral

Calcium Acetate
- Injection (U.S.)

Calcium Chloride
- Injection (U.S. and Canada)

Calcium Glubionate
- Injection (Canada)

Calcium Gluceptate
- Injection (U.S.)

Calcium Gluconate
- Injection (U.S. and Canada)

Calcium Glycerophosphate and Calcium Lactate
- Injection (U.S.)

A calcium "salt" contains calcium along with another substance, such as carbonate or gluconate. Some calcium salts have more calcium (elemental calcium) than others. For example, the amount of calcium in calcium carbonate is greater than that in calcium gluconate. To give you an idea of how different calcium supplements vary in calcium content, the following chart explains how many tablets of each type of supplement will provide 1000 milligrams of elemental calcium. When you look for a calcium supplement, be sure the number of milligrams on the label refers to the amount of elemental calcium, and not to the strength of each tablet.

Calcium supplement	Strength of each tablet (in milligrams)	Amount of elemental calcium per tablet (in milligrams)	Number of tablets to provide 1000 milligrams of calcium
Calcium carbonate	625	250	4
	650	260	4
	750	300	4
	835	334	3
	1250	500	2
	1500	600	2
Calcium citrate	950	200	5
Calcium gluconate	500	45	22
	650	58	17
	1000	90	11
Calcium lactate	325	42	24
	650	84	12
Calcium phosphate, dibasic	500	115	9
Calcium phosphate, tribasic	800	304	4
	1600	608	2

Importance of Diet

For good health, it is important that you eat a balanced and varied diet. Follow carefully any diet program your health care professional may recommend. For your specific dietary vitamin and/or mineral needs, ask your health care professional for a list of appropriate foods. If you think that you are not getting enough vitamins and/or minerals in your diet, you may choose to take a dietary supplement.

The daily amount of calcium needed is defined in several different ways.

For U.S.—
- Recommended Dietary Allowances (RDAs) are the amount of vitamins and minerals needed to provide for adequate nutrition in most healthy persons. RDAs for a given nutrient may vary depending on a person's age, sex, and physical condition (e.g., pregnancy).
- Daily Values (DVs) are used on food and dietary supplement labels to indicate the percent of the recommended daily amount of each nutrient that a serving provides. DV replaces the previous designation of United States Recommended Daily Allowances (US-RDAs).

For Canada—
- Recommended Nutrient Intakes (RNIs) are used to determine the amounts of vitamins, minerals, and protein needed to provide adequate nutrition and lessen the risk of chronic disease.

Normal daily recommended intakes in milligrams (mg) for calcium are generally defined as follows:

Persons	U.S. (mg)	Canada (mg)
Infants and children		
Birth to 3 years of age	400–800	250–550
4 to 6 years of age	800	600
7 to 10 years of age	800	700–1100
Adolescent and adult males	800–1200	800–1100
Adolescent and adult females	800–1200	700–1100
Pregnant females	1200	1200–1500
Breast-feeding females	1200	1200–1500

Getting the proper amount of calcium in the diet every day and participating in weight-bearing exercise (walking, dancing, bicycling, aerobics, jogging), especially during the early years of life (up to about 35 years of age) is most important in helping to build and maintain bones as dense as possible to prevent the development of osteoporosis in later life.

The following table includes some calcium-rich foods. The calcium content of these foods can supply the daily RDA or RNI for calcium if the foods are eaten regularly in sufficient amounts.

Food (amount)	Milligrams of calcium
Nonfat dry milk, reconstituted (1 cup)	375
Lowfat, skim, or whole milk (1 cup)	290 to 300
Yogurt (1 cup)	275 to 400
Sardines with bones (3 ounces)	370
Ricotta cheese, part skim (½ cup)	340
Salmon, canned, with bones (3 ounces)	285
Cheese, Swiss (1 ounce)	272
Cheese, cheddar (1 ounce)	204
Cheese, American (1 ounce)	174
Cottage cheese, lowfat (1 cup)	154
Tofu (4 ounces)	154
Shrimp (1 cup)	147
Ice milk (¾ cup)	132

Vitamin D helps prevent calcium loss from your bones. It is sometimes called "the sunshine vitamin" because it is made in your skin when you are exposed to sunlight. If you get outside in the sunlight every day for 15 to 30 minutes, you should get all the vitamin D you need. However, in northern locations in winter, the sunlight may be too weak to make vitamin D in the skin. Vitamin D may also be obtained from your diet or from multivitamin preparations. Most milk is fortified with vitamin D.

Do not use bonemeal or dolomite as a source of calcium. The Food and Drug Administration has issued warnings that bonemeal and dolomite could be dangerous because these products may contain lead.

Before Using This Dietary Supplement

If you are taking this dietary supplement without a prescription, carefully read and follow any precautions on the label. For calcium supplements, the following should be considered:

Pregnancy—It is especially important that you are receiving enough calcium when you become pregnant and that you continue to receive the right amount of calcium throughout your pregnancy. The healthy growth and development of the fetus depend on a steady supply of nutrients from the mother. However, taking large amounts of a dietary supplement during pregnancy may be harmful to the mother and/or fetus and should be avoided.

Breast-feeding—It is especially important that you receive the right amount of calcium so that your baby will also get the calcium needed to grow properly. However, taking large amounts of a dietary supplement while breast-feeding may be harmful to the mother and/or baby and should be avoided.

Children—Problems in children have not been reported with intake of normal daily recommended amounts. Injectable forms of calcium should not be given to children because of the risk of irritating the injection site.

Older adults—Problems in older adults have not been reported with intake of normal daily recommended amounts. It is important that older people continue to receive enough calcium in their daily diets. However, some older people may need to take extra calcium or larger doses because they do not absorb calcium as well as younger people. Check with your health care professional if you have any questions about the amount of calcium you should be taking in each day.

Medicines or other dietary supplements—Although certain medicines or dietary supplements should not be used together at all, in other cases they may be used together even if an interaction might occur. In these cases, your health care professional may want to change the dose, or other precautions may be necessary. When you are taking calcium supplements, it is especially important that your health care professional know if you are taking any of the following:

- Calcium-containing medicines, other—Taking excess calcium may cause too much calcium in the blood or urine and lead to medical problems
- Cellulose sodium phosphate (e.g., Calcibind)—Use with calcium supplements may decrease the effects of cellulose sodium phosphate
- Digitalis glycosides (heart medicine)—Use with calcium supplements by injection may increase the chance of irregular heartbeat

- Etidronate (e.g., Didronel)—Use with calcium supplements may decrease the effects of etidronate; etidronate should not be taken within 2 hours of calcium supplements
- Gallium nitrate (e.g., Ganite)—Use with calcium supplements may cause gallium nitrate to not work properly
- Magnesium sulfate (for injection)—Use with calcium supplements may cause either medicine to be less effective
- Phenytoin (e.g., Dilantin)—Use with calcium supplements may decrease the effects of both medicines; calcium supplements should not be taken within 1 to 3 hours of phenytoin
- Tetracyclines (medicine for infection) taken by mouth—Use with calcium supplements may decrease the effects of tetracycline; calcium supplements should not be taken within 1 to 3 hours of tetracyclines

Other medical problems—The presence of other medical problems may affect the use of calcium supplements. Make sure you tell your health care professional if you have any other medical problems, especially:

- Diarrhea or
- Stomach or intestinal problems—Extra calcium or specific calcium preparations may be necessary in these conditions
- Heart disease—Calcium by injection may increase the chance of irregular heartbeat
- Hypercalcemia (too much calcium in the blood) or
- Hypercalciuria (too much calcium in the urine)—Calcium supplements may make these conditions worse
- Hyperparathyroidism or
- Sarcoidosis—Calcium supplements may increase the chance of hypercalcemia (too much calcium in the blood)
- Hypoparathyroidism—Use of calcium phosphate may cause high blood levels of phosphorus which could increase the chance of side effects
- Kidney disease or stones—Too much calcium may increase the chance of kidney stones

Proper Use of This Dietary Supplement

Dosing—The amount of calcium needed to meet normal daily recommended intakes will be different for different individuals. The following information includes only the average amounts of calcium.

- For *oral* dosage form (capsules, chewable tablets, lozenges, oral solution, oral suspension, syrup, tablets, extended-release tablets, tablets for solution):
  - To prevent deficiency, the amount taken by mouth is based on normal daily recommended intakes (Note that the normal daily recommended intakes are expressed as an actual amount of calcium. The salt form [e.g., calcium carbonate, calcium gluconate, etc.] has a different strength):
  For the U.S.
    - Adults and teenagers—800 to 1200 milligrams (mg) per day.
    - Pregnant and breast-feeding females—1200 mg per day.
    - Children 4 to 10 years of age—800 mg per day.
    - Children birth to 3 years of age—400 to 800 mg per day.

For Canada
- Adult and teenage males—800 to 1100 mg per day.
- Adult and teenage females—700 to 1100 mg per day.
- Pregnant and breast-feeding females—1200 to 1500 mg per day.
- Children 7 to 10 years of age—700 to 1100 mg per day.
- Children 4 to 6 years of age—600 mg per day.
- Children birth to 3 years of age—250 to 550 mg per day.

—To treat deficiency:
- Adults, teenagers, and children—Treatment dose is determined by prescriber for each individual based on severity of deficiency.

Drink a full glass (8 ounces) of water or juice when taking a calcium supplement. However, if you are taking calcium carbonate as a phosphate binder in kidney dialysis, it is not necessary to drink a glass of water.

This dietary supplement is best taken 1 to 1½ hours after meals, unless otherwise directed by your health care professional. However, patients with a condition known as achlorhydria may not absorb calcium supplements on an empty stomach and should take them with meals.

For individuals taking *the chewable tablet form* of this dietary supplement:
- Chew the tablets completely before swallowing.

For individuals taking *the syrup form* of this dietary supplement:
- Take the syrup before meals. This will allow the dietary supplement to work faster.
- Mix in water or fruit juice for infants or children.

Take this dietary supplement only as directed. Do not take more of it and do not take it more often than recommended on the label. To do so may increase the chance of side effects.

Missed dose—If you are taking this dietary supplement on a regular schedule and you miss a dose, take it as soon as possible, then go back to your regular dosing schedule.

Storage—To store this dietary supplement:
- Keep out of the reach of children.
- Store away from heat and direct light.
- Do not store in the bathroom, near the kitchen sink, or in other damp places. Heat or moisture may cause the dietary supplement to break down.
- Keep the liquid form of this dietary supplement from freezing.
- Do not keep outdated dietary supplements or those no longer needed. Be sure that any discarded dietary supplement is out of the reach of children.

Precautions While Using This Dietary Supplement

If this dietary supplement has been ordered for you by your health care professional and you will be taking it in large doses or for a long time, your health care professional should check your progress at regular visits. This is to make sure the calcium is working properly and does not cause unwanted effects.

Do not take calcium supplements within 1 to 2 hours of taking other medicine by mouth. To do so may keep the other medicine from working properly.

Unless you are otherwise directed by your health care professional, to make sure that calcium is used properly by your body:
- *Do not take other medicines or dietary supplements containing large amounts of calcium, phosphates, magnesium, or vitamin D unless your health care professional has told you to do so or approved.*
- *Do not take calcium supplements within 1 to 2 hours of eating large amounts of fiber-containing foods, such as bran and whole-grain cereals or breads, especially if you are being treated for hypocalcemia (not enough calcium in your blood).*
- *Do not drink large amounts of alcohol or caffeine-containing beverages (usually more than 8 cups of coffee a day), or use tobacco.*

Some calcium carbonate tablets have been shown to break up too slowly in the stomach to be properly absorbed into the body. If the calcium carbonate tablets you purchase are not specifically labeled as being "USP," check with your pharmacist. He or she may be able to help you determine which tablets are best.

Side Effects of This Dietary Supplement

Along with its needed effects, a dietary supplement may cause some unwanted effects. Although the following side effects occur very rarely when the calcium supplement is taken as recommended, they may be more likely to occur if:
- It is taken in large doses.
- It is taken for a long time.
- It is taken by patients with kidney disease.

Check with your health care professional as soon as possible if any of the following side effects occur:

More common (for injection form only)
> Dizziness; flushing and/or sensation of warmth or heat; irregular heartbeat; nausea or vomiting; skin redness, rash, pain, or burning at injection site; sweating; tingling sensation

Rare
> Difficult or painful urination; drowsiness; nausea or vomiting (continuing); weakness

Early signs of overdose
> Constipation (severe); dryness of mouth; headache (continuing); increased thirst; irritability; loss of appetite; mental depression; metallic taste; unusual tiredness or weakness

Late signs of overdose
> Confusion; drowsiness (severe); high blood pressure; increased sensitivity of eyes or skin to light; irregular, fast, or slow heartbeat; unusually large amount of urine or increased frequency of urination

Other side effects not listed above may also occur in some patients. If you notice any other effects, check with your health care professional.

Additional Information

Once a medicine or dietary supplement has been approved for marketing for a certain use, experience may show that it is also useful for other medical problems. Although this use is not included in product labeling, calcium supplements are used in certain patients with the following medical condition:

- Hyperphosphatemia (too much phosphate in the blood)

Other than the above information, there is no additional information relating to proper use, precautions, or side effects for this use.

Revised: 06/10/92
Interim revision: 08/22/94; 07/18/95

CANDESARTAN AND HYDROCHLOROTHIAZIDE
Systemic—INTRODUCTORY VERSION

Commonly used brand name(s):

In the U.S.—
Atacand HCT

Description

Candesartan belongs to the class of medicines called angiotensin II receptor antagonists. Hydrochlorothiazide belongs to a class of medicines called thiazide diuretics. When these two medicines are combined, they are used to treat high blood pressure (hypertension).

This medicine is available only with your doctor's prescription, in the following dosage forms:

Oral
- Tablets (U.S.)

Before Using This Medicine

In deciding to use a medicine, the risks of taking the medicine must be weighed against the good it will do. This is a decision you and your doctor will make. For the combinations of candesartan and hydrochlorothiazide, the following should be considered:

Allergies—Tell your doctor if you have ever had any unusual or allergic reaction to candesartan, hydrochlorothiazide, or any sulfonamide-type medicines. Also tell your health care provider if you are allergic to any other substances, such as foods, preservatives, or dyes.

Pregnancy—Use of candesartan and hydrochlorothiazide combination during pregnancy, especially during the second and third trimesters (after the first 3 months) can cause adverse effects in the newborn. *Therefore, it is important that you check with your doctor immediately if you think that you may have become pregnant.* Be sure that you have discussed this with your doctor before taking this medicine.

Breast-feeding—It is not known whether candesartan passes into human breast milk. However, it is distributed into animal milk. Thiazides, including hydrochlorothiazide, are distributed into human breast milk.

Children—Studies on this medicine have been done only in adult patients, and there is no specific information comparing use of candesartan and hydrochlorothiazide combination in children with use in other age groups.

Older adults—This medicine has been tested in patients 65 years of age or older and has not been shown to cause

different side effects or problems in older people than it does in younger adults.

Other medicines—Although certain medicines should not be used together at all, in other cases two different medicines may be used together even if an interaction might occur. In these cases, your doctor may want to change the dose, or other precautions may be necessary. When you are taking candesartan and hydrochlorothiazide combination, it is especially important that your health care professional know if you are taking any of the following:

- Lithium (e.g., Eskalith)—Concurrent use may reduce the amount of lithium that is removed from the body, which may lead to lithium toxicity.
- Sympathomimetic agents such as norepinephrine—Hydrochlorothiazide may causse a decreased response to these substances.

Other medical problems—The presence of other medical problems may affect the use of candesartan and hydrochlorothiazide combination. Make sure you tell your doctor if you have any other medical problems, especially:

- Allergy or
- Asthma, bronchial—May have an increased risk of allergic reaction to hydrochlorothiazide
- Congestive heart failure, severe—Lowering of blood pressure by candesartan and hydrochlorothiazide combination may make this condition worse
- Diabetes mellitus—Insulin dosage may need to be adjusted.
- Fluid or electrolyte (e.g., potassium, chloride, sodium) imbalance (due to excessive perspiration, vomiting, diarrhea, etc.)—The side effects of candesartan and hydrochlorothiazide may be increased
- Kidney disease or
- Liver disease—These conditions may be aggravated by candesartan and hydrochlorothiazide
- Sympathectomy—Blood pressure-lowering effects may be increased
- Systemic lupus erythematosus—Candesartan and hydrochlorothiazide combination may trigger or worsen this condition.

Proper Use of This Medicine

Dosing—For patients taking this medicine *for high blood pressure:*

- This medicine works best if there is a constant amount in the blood. To help keep this amount constant, do not miss any doses and take the medicine at the same time each day.
- In addition to the use of the medicine your doctor has prescribed, treatment for your high blood pressure may include weight control and care in the types of foods you eat, especially foods high in sodium. Your doctor will tell you which of these are most important for you. You should check with your doctor before changing your diet.
- Many patients who have high blood pressure will not notice any signs of the problem. In fact, many may feel normal. It is very important that you *take your medicine exactly as directed* and that you keep your appointments with your doctor even if you feel well.
- Remember that this medicine will not cure your high blood pressure but it does help control it. Therefore, you must continue to take it as directed if you expect to lower your blood pressure and keep it down. *You may have to take high blood pressure medicine for the rest of*

your life. If high blood pressure is not treated, it can cause serious problems such as heart failure, blood vessel disease, stroke, or kidney disease.
- This medicine may be taken with or without food.

The dose of candesartan hydrochlorothiazide will be different for different patients. *Follow your doctor's orders or the directions on the label.* The following information includes only the average doses of candesartan and hydrochlorothiazide combination. *If your dose is different, do not change it* unless your doctor tells you to do so.

The number of tablets that you take depends on the strength of the medicine. Also, *the number of doses you take each day, the time allowed between doses, and the length of time you take the medicine depend on the medical problem for which you are taking candesartan and hydrochlorothiazide.*

- For *oral* dosage form (tablets):
  —For high blood pressure:
  - Adults—1 tablet once a day. Your doctor may increase your dose if needed.
  - Children—Use and dose must be determined by your doctor.

Missed dose— If you miss a dose of this medicine, take it as soon as possible. However, if it is almost time for your next dose, skip the missed dose and go back to your regular dosing schedule. Do not double doses.

Storage—To store this medicine:
- Keep out of the reach of children.
- Store away from heat and direct light.
- Do not store in the bathroom, near the kitchen sink, or in other damp places. Heat or moisture may cause the medicine to break down.

Precautions While Using This Medicine

It is important that your doctor check your progress at regular visits to make sure that this medicine is working properly and to check for unwanted effects.

Check with your doctor immediately if you think that you may be pregnant. Candesartan and hydrochlorothiazide may cause birth defects or other problems in the baby if taken during pregnancy.

Do not take other medicines unless they have been discussed with your doctor. This especially includes potassium supplements or salt substitutes that contain potassium, since they may change your blood potassium levels, or over-the-counter (nonprescription) medicines for appetite control, asthma, colds, cough, hay fever, or sinus problems, since they may tend to increase your blood pressure.

Dizziness or light-headedness may occur. Make sure you know how you react to this medicine before you drive, use machines, or do anything else that could be dangerous if you experience these effects.

Check with your doctor right away if you become sick while taking this medicine, especially with severe or continuing nausea and vomiting or diarrhea. These conditions may cause you to lose too much water and lead to low blood pressure.

Dizziness, light-headedness, or fainting also may occur if you exercise or if the weather is hot. Heavy sweating can cause loss of too much water and result in low blood pressure. Use extra care during exercise or hot weather.

Avoid alcoholic beverages until you have discussed their use with your doctor. Alcohol may make the low blood pressure effect worse and/or increase the possibility of dizziness or fainting.

For *diabetic patients:*
- Hydrochlorothiazide may raise blood sugar levels. Check with your doctor if any changes in your blood sugar levels occur.

Side Effects of This Medicine

Along with its needed effects, a medicine may cause some unwanted effects. Although not all of these side effects may occur, if they do occur they may need medical attention.

Check with your doctor as soon as possible if any of the following side effects occur:
Less frequent
  Cough; dizziness; dryness of mouth; fever; increased thirst; irregular heartbeat; light-headedness; muscle cramps; nausea; sore throat; unusual tiredness; vomiting; weak pulse; weakness
Rare
  Arm pain; chest pain; chest tightness; fast or irregular heartbeat; large, hive-like swelling on face, eyelids, lips, tongue, throat, hands, legs, feet, sex organs; shortness of breath

Side effects may occur that usually do not need medical attention. These side effects may go away during treatment as your body adjusts to the medicine. However, check with your doctor if any of the following side effects continue or are bothersome.
Less common
  Back pain; chills; diarrhea; headache; joint pain; loss of appetite; muscle aches and pains; nausea; runny nose; sneezing; sweating; trouble sleeping; unusual tiredness; vomiting

Other side effects not listed above may also occur in some patients. If you notice any other effects, check with your doctor.

Developed: 01/08/2001

CANDESARTAN   Systemic

Commonly used brand name(s):

In the U.S.—
  Atacand

Description

Candesartan (kan-de-SAR-tan) belongs to the class of medicines called angiotensin II inhibitors. It is used to treat high blood pressure (hypertension).

High blood pressure adds to the workload of the heart and arteries. If it continues for a long time, the heart and arteries may not function properly. This can damage the blood vessels of the brain, heart, and kidneys, resulting in a stroke, heart failure, or kidney failure. High blood pressure may also increase the risk of heart attacks. These problems may be less likely to occur if blood pressure is controlled.

Candesartan works by blocking the action of a substance in the body that causes blood vessels to tighten. As a result, candesartan relaxes blood vessels. This lowers blood pressure.

This medicine is available only with your doctor's prescription, in the following dosage form(s):

Oral
- Tablets (U.S.)

Before Using This Medicine

In deciding to use a medicine, the risks of taking the medicine must be weighed against the good it will do. This is a decision you and your doctor will make. For candesartan, the following should be considered:

Allergies—Tell your doctor if you have ever had any unusual or allergic reaction to candesartan. Also tell your health care professional if you are allergic to any other substances, such as foods, preservatives, or dyes.

Pregnancy—Use of candesartan during pregnancy, especially during the second and third trimesters (after the first 3 months) can cause low blood pressure, severe kidney failure, or possibly death in the newborn. *Therefore, it is important that you check with your doctor immediately if you think that you may have become pregnant*. Be sure that you have discussed this with your doctor before taking this medicine.

Breast-feeding—It is not known whether candesartan passes into breast milk. However, candesartan passes into the milk of lactating rats. Because this medicine may cause serious side effects, breast-feeding is generally not recommended while you are taking it.

Children—Studies on this medicine have been done only in adult patients, and there is no specific information comparing use of candesartan in children with use in other age groups.

Older adults—This medicine has been tested in patients 65 years of age or older and has not been shown to cause different side effects or problems in older people than it does in younger adults. However, blood levels of candesartan are increased in the elderly.

Racial differences—Black patients may have a smaller response to the blood pressure-lowering effects of candesartan.

Other medicines—Although certain medicines should not be used together at all, in other cases two different medicines may be used together even if an interaction might occur. In these cases, your doctor may want to change the dose, or other precautions may be necessary. It is important that your health care professional know if you are taking any other medicines.

Other medical problems—The presence of other medical problems may affect the use of candesartan. Make sure you tell your doctor if you have any other medical problems, especially:
- Congestive heart failure (severe)—Lowering of blood pressure by candesartan may make this condition worse
- Dehydration (fluid and electrolyte loss due to excessive perspiration, vomiting, diarrhea, prolonged diuretic therapy, dialysis, or dietary salt restriction)—Blood pressure-lowering effects of candesartan may be increased.
- Kidney disease—Effects of candesartan may make this condition worse.
- Liver disease, severe—Effects of candesartan are unknown.

Proper Use of This Medicine

Take this medicine only as directed by your doctor. Do not take more of it and do not take it more often than your doctor ordered. This medicine also works best when there is a constant amount in the blood. *To help keep the amount constant, do not miss any doses. Also, it is best to take the doses at the same time each day.*

Dosing—The dose of candesartan will be different for different patients. *Follow your doctor's orders or the directions on the label*. The following information includes only the average doses of candesartan. *If your dose is different, do not change it* unless your doctor tells you to do so.

The number of tablets that you take depends on the strength of the medicine.
- For *oral* dosage form (tablets):
  —For high blood pressure:
  - Adults—16 milligrams (mg) once a day. Your doctor may increase your dose as needed.
  - Children—Use and dose must be determined by your doctor.

Missed dose—If you miss a dose of this medicine, take it as soon as possible. However, if it is almost time for your next dose, skip the missed dose and go back to your regular dosing schedule. Do not double doses.

Storage—To store this medicine:
- Keep out of the reach of children.
- Store away from heat and direct light.
- Do not store in the bathroom, near the kitchen sink, or in other damp places. Heat or moisture may cause the medicine to break down.
- Do not keep outdated medicine or medicine no longer needed. Be sure that any discarded medicine is out of the reach of children.

Precautions While Using This Medicine

It is important that your doctor check your progress at regular visits to make sure that this medicine is working properly and to check for unwanted effects.

Check with your doctor immediately if you think that you may be pregnant. Candesartan may cause birth defects or other problems in the baby if taken during pregnancy.

Do not take other medicines unless they have been discussed with your doctor. This especially includes over-the-counter (nonprescription) medicines for appetite control, asthma, colds, cough, hay fever, or sinus problems, since they may tend to increase your blood pressure.

Dizziness or lightheadedness may occur, especially if you have been taking a diuretic (water pill). Make sure you know how you react to this medicine before you drive, use machines, or do anything else that could be dangerous if you experience these effects.

Check with your doctor right away if you become sick while taking this medicine, especially with severe or continuing nausea and vomiting or diarrhea. These conditions may cause you to lose too much water and lead to low blood pressure.

Dizziness, lightheadedness, or fainting also may occur if you exercise or if the weather is hot. Heavy sweating can cause loss of too much water and result in low blood pressure. Use extra care during exercise or hot weather.

Side Effects of This Medicine

Along with its needed effects, a medicine may cause some unwanted effects. Although not all of these side effects may occur, if they do occur they may need medical attention.

Check with your doctor as soon as possible if any of the following side effects occur:

Rare

Chills or fever, cough or hoarseness, lower back or side pain, painful of difficult urination; dizziness, lightheadedness, or fainting; joint pain, lower back or side pain, swelling of feet or lower legs; nosebleeds or bleeding gums

Other side effects may occur that usually do not need medical attention. These side effects may go away during treatment as your body adjusts to the medicine. However, check with your doctor if any of the following side effects continue or are bothersome:

Less common

Back pain; coughing, ear congestion or pain, fever, head congestion, nasal congestion, runny and/or stuffy nose, sneezing, and/or sore throat; headache

Other side effects not listed above may also occur in some patients. If you notice any other effects, check with your doctor.

Developed: 11/23/98

CAPECITABINE   Systemic

Commonly used brand name(s):

In the U.S.—
Xeloda

In Canada—
Xeloda

Description

Capecitabine (ka-pe-SITE-a-been) belongs to the group of medicines called antimetabolites. It is used to treat breast cancer and colorectal cancer.

Capecitabine interferes with the growth of cancer cells, which are eventually destroyed. Since the growth of normal cells may also be affected by the medicine, other effects will also occur. Some of these may be serious and must be reported to your doctor. Other effects may not be serious but may cause concern.

This medicine is available only with your doctor's prescription, in the following dosage form:

Oral
- Tablets (U.S. and Canada)

Before Using This Medicine

In deciding to use a medicine, the risks of taking the medicine must be weighed against the good it will do. This is a decision you and your doctor will make. For capecitabine, the following should be considered:

Allergies—Tell your doctor if you have ever had any unusual or allergic reaction to capecitabine or to fluorouracil. Also tell your health care professional if you are allergic to any other substances, such as foods, preservatives, or dyes.

Pregnancy—It is best to avoid pregnancy during treatment with this medicine. Studies in animals have found that capecitabine causes birth defects and death of the fetus. Be sure that you have discussed this with your doctor before starting treatment with this medicine. Also, tell your doctor right away if you think you have become pregnant while taking this medicine.

Breast-feeding—It is not known whether capecitabine passes into human breast milk. However, because this medicine may cause serious side effects, breast-feeding generally is not recommended while you are taking it.

Children—There is no specific information comparing use of capecitabine in children with use in other age groups.

Older adults—Patients 80 years of age or older may be more sensitive to the effects of capecitabine. Severe diarrhea, nausea, or vomiting may be more likely to occur in these patients.

Other medicines—Although certain medicines should not be used together at all, in other cases two different medicines may be used together even if an interaction might occur. In these cases, your doctor may want to change the dose, or other precautions may be necessary. When you are taking capecitabine, it is especially important that your health care professional knows if you are taking any of the following:

- Amphotericin B by injection (e.g., Fungizone) or
- Antithyroid agents (medicine for overactive thyroid) or
- Azathioprine (e.g., Imuran) or
- Chloramphenicol (e.g., Chloromycetin) or
- Colchicine or
- Flucytosine (e.g., Ancobon) or
- Ganciclovir (e.g., Cytovene) or
- Interferon (e.g., Intron A, Roferon-A) or
- Plicamycin (e.g., Mithracin) or
- Zidovudine (e.g., AZT, Retrovir)
- If you have ever been treated with radiation or cancer medicines—Capecitabine may increase the effects of these medicines or radiation therapy on the blood

- Anticoagulants, coumarin-type (blood thinners)—These medicines can cause increased risk of bleeding

Other medical problems—The presence of other medical problems may affect the use of capecitabine. Make sure you tell your doctor if you have any other medical problems, especially:

- Chickenpox (including recent exposure) or
- Herpes zoster (shingles)—Risk of severe disease affecting other parts of the body

- Heart disease—The risk of a side effect that affects the heart may be increased

- Kidney disease—The risk of side effects that affect the kidneys may be increased

- Liver disease—The amount of capecitabine in the body may be increased in patients with liver disease. Also, the risk of a side effect that affects the liver may be increased
- Infection—Capecitabine decreases your body's ability to fight infection

Proper Use of This Medicine

Each dose of this medicine should be taken within 30 minutes after the end of a meal.

Swallow the tablets with water.

Dosing—The dose of capecitabine will be different for different patients. The dose that is used depends on a number of things, including the patient's body size. *Follow your doctor's orders or the directions on the label*. The following information includes only the average doses of capecitabine. *If your dose is different, do not change it* unless your doctor tells you to do so. If you have any questions about the proper dose of capecitabine, ask your doctor.

- For *oral* dosage form (tablets):
  —For breast cancer:
  - Adults—The starting dose is usually 2500 milligrams (mg) per square meter of body surface area a day, divided into two doses and taken about twelve hours apart within 30 minutes after the end of a meal. However, the dose may have to be decreased if certain side effects occur.
  - Children—Use and dose must be determined by your doctor.

  —For colorectal cancer:
  - Adults—The starting dose is usually 2500 milligrams (mg) per square meter of body surface area a day, divided into two doses and taken about twelve hours apart within 30 minutes after the end of a meal. However, the dose may have to be decreased if certain side effects occur.
  - Children—Use and dose must be determined by your doctor.

Missed dose—If you miss a dose of this medicine, do not take the missed dose at all and do not double the next one. Instead, go back to your regular dosing schedule and check with your doctor.

Storage—To store this medicine:
- Keep out of the reach of children.
- Store away from heat and direct light.
- Do not store in the bathroom, near the kitchen sink, or in other damp places. Heat or moisture may cause the medicine to break down.
- Do not keep outdated medicine or medicine no longer needed. Be sure that any discarded medicine is out of the reach of children.

Precautions While Using This Medicine

It is very important that your doctor check your progress at regular visits to make sure that this medicine is working properly and to check for unwanted effects.

Check with your doctor immediately if you develop a fever of 100.5 °F or higher, or if you notice any other signs of a possible infection. These signs include cough or hoarseness, lower back or side pain, painful or difficult urination, sneezing, sore throat, stuffy nose, and white spots inside the mouth or throat.

Stop taking this medicine and check with your doctor immediately if any of the following occur:
- Diarrhea, moderately severe (four to six stools a day more than usual, or during the night).
- Pain, blistering, peeling, redness, or swelling of the palms of your hands and/or the bottoms of your feet that is severe enough to interfere with your normal activities.
- Nausea that is severe enough to cause you to eat less than usual.
- Vomiting that occurs two times, or more, in a 24-hour period.
- Pain and redness, swelling, or sores or ulcers in your mouth or on your lips that are severe enough to interfere with eating.

If vomiting occurs less often than mentioned above, or if nausea does not cause you to eat less than usual, it is not necessary for you to stop taking the medicine or to check with your doctor (unless these effects are particularly bothersome). Also, you do not need to stop taking the medicine if diarrhea occurs less often than mentioned above or if the other side effects listed are not severe enough to interfere with eating or other daily activities. However, check with your doctor as soon as possible if they occur.

While you are being treated with capecitabine, and after you stop treatment with it, *do not have any immunizations (vaccinations) without your doctor's approval*. Capecitabine may lower your body's resistance and there is a chance you might get the infection the immunization is meant to prevent. In addition, other persons living in your household should not take oral polio vaccine since there is a chance they could pass the polio virus on to you. Also, avoid persons who have taken oral polio vaccine within the last several months. Do not get close to them, and do not stay in the same room with them for very long. If you cannot take these precautions, you should consider wearing a protective face mask that covers the nose and mouth.

Capecitabine can temporarily lower the number of white blood cells in your blood, increasing the chance of getting an infection. It can also lower the number of platelets, which are necessary for proper blood clotting. If this occurs, there are certain precautions you can take, especially when your blood count is low, to reduce the risk of infection or bleeding:
- If you can, avoid people with infections. *Check with your doctor immediately* if you think you are getting an infection or if you get a fever or chills, cough or hoarseness, lower back or side pain, or painful or difficult urination.
- *Check with your doctor immediately* if you notice any unusual bleeding or bruising; black, tarry stools; blood in urine or stools; or pinpoint red spots on your skin.
- Be careful when using a regular toothbrush, dental floss, or toothpick. Your medical doctor, dentist, or nurse may recommend other ways to clean your teeth and gums. Check with your medical doctor before having any dental work done.
- Do not touch your eyes or the inside of your nose unless you have just washed your hands and have not touched anything else in the meantime.
- Be careful not to cut yourself when you are using sharp objects such as a safety razor or fingernail or toenail cutters.

- Avoid contact sports or other situations where bruising or injury could occur.

Side Effects of This Medicine

Along with its needed effects, a medicine may cause some unwanted effects. Although not all of these side effects may occur, if they do occur they may need medical attention.

Stop taking this medicine and check with your doctor immediately if any of the following side effects occur:
More common
Diarrhea (moderately severe [four to six stools a day more than usual, or at night]); pain, blistering, peeling, redness, or swelling of palms of hands and/or bottoms of feet (severe enough to interfere with normal activities); pain and redness, swelling, or sores or ulcers in your mouth or on your lips (severe enough to interfere with eating)
Less common
Nausea (severe, accompanied by loss of appetite); vomiting (severe [occurring two times or more in 24 hours])

Also *check with your doctor immediately* if any of the following side effects occur:
Less common or rare
Abdominal or stomach cramping or pain (severe); blood in urine or stools; bloody or black, tarry stools; chest pain; constipation (severe); cough or hoarseness (accompanied by fever or chills); difficulty in swallowing or pain in back of throat or chest when swallowing; fast or irregular heartbeat; fever or chills; hot, red skin on feet or legs; lower back or side pain (accompanied by fever or chills); painful or difficult urination (accompanied by fever or chills); painful, swollen feet or legs; pain, tenderness, and/or swelling in upper abdominal (stomach) area; pinpoint red spots on skin; shortness of breath, troubled breathing, tightness in chest, and/or wheezing; sneezing, sore throat, and/or stuffy nose; tiredness or weakness (severe); unusual bleeding or bruising; vomiting blood or material that looks like coffee grounds; white spots in mouth or throat; yellow eyes or skin

Also, check with your doctor as soon as possible if any of the following side effects occur:
More common
Abdominal or stomach pain (mild or moderate); blistering, peeling, redness, and/or swelling of palms of hands or bottoms of feet (not severe enough to interfere with daily activities); diarrhea (mild [fewer than four stools a day more than usual]); numbness, pain, tingling, or other unusual sensations in palms of hands or bottoms of feet; pain and redness, swelling, or sores or ulcers in your mouth or on your lips (not severe enough to interfere with eating); unusual tiredness or weakness (mild or moderate)
Less common or rare
Clumsiness or unsteadiness; dark urine; decrease or increase in blood pressure; light-colored stools; problems with coordination; skin rash or itching; swelling of face, fingers, feet, or lower legs; swollen glands; unexplained nosebleeds

Other side effects may occur that usually do not need medical attention. These side effects may go away during treatment as your body adjusts to the medicine. However, check with your doctor if any of the following side effects continue or are bothersome:
More common
Constipation (mild or moderate); loss of appetite (not due to nausea); nausea (not accompanied by loss of appetite); vomiting (mild [once a day or less])
Less common or rare
Changes in fingernails or toenails; dizziness; headache; heartburn; increased sensitivity of skin to sunlight; muscle pain; pain and redness of skin at place of earlier radiation (x-ray) treatment; red, sore eyes; trouble in sleeping

Other side effects not listed above may also occur in some patients. If you notice any other effects, check with your doctor.

Developed: 08/14/1998
Revised: 12/15/2000

CAPREOMYCIN   Systemic

Commonly used brand name(s):
In the U.S.—
Capastat
In Canada—
Capastat

Description

Capreomycin (kap-ree-oh-MYE-sin) is used to treat tuberculosis (TB). It is given with other medicines for TB.

To help clear up your tuberculosis (TB) completely, you must keep taking this medicine for the full time of treatment, even if you begin to feel better. This is very important. It is also important that you do not miss any doses.

Capreomycin is available only with your doctor's prescription, in the following dosage form:
Parenteral
- Injection (U.S. and Canada)

Before Receiving This Medicine

In deciding to use a medicine, the risks of taking the medicine must be weighed against the good it will do. This is a decision you and your doctor will make. For capreomycin, the following should be considered:

Allergies—Tell your doctor if you have ever had any unusual or allergic reaction to capreomycin. Also tell your health care professional if you are allergic to any other substances, such as foods, preservatives, or dyes.

Pregnancy—Capreomycin has not been studied in pregnant women. However, studies in rats given 3½ times the human dose have shown that capreomycin may cause birth defects.

Breast-feeding—It is not known whether capreomycin passes into breast milk. Although most medicines pass into breast milk in small amounts, many of them may be used safely while breast-feeding. Mothers who are taking this medicine and who wish to breast-feed should discuss this with their doctor.

Children—Studies on this medicine have been done only in adult patients, and there is no specific information comparing use of capreomycin in children with use in other age groups.

Older adults—Many medicines have not been studied specifically in older people. Therefore, it may not be known whether they work exactly the same way they do in younger adults or if they cause different side effects or problems in older people. There is no specific information comparing use of capreomycin in the elderly with use in other age groups.

Other medicines—Although certain medicines should not be used together at all, in other cases two different medicines may be used together even if an interaction might occur. In these cases, your doctor may want to change the dose, or other precautions may be necessary. When you are receiving capreomycin, it is especially important that your health care professional know if you are taking any of the following:

- Aminoglycosides by injection (amikacin [e.g., Amikin], gentamicin [e.g., Garamycin], kanamycin [e.g., Kantrex], neomycin [e.g., Mycifradin], netilmicin [e.g., Netromycin], streptomycin, tobramycin [e.g., Nebcin]) or
- Anti-infectives by mouth or by injection (medicine for infection) or
- Carmustine (e.g., BiCNU) or
- Chloroquine (e.g., Aralen) or
- Cisplatin (e.g., Platinol) or
- Combination pain medicine containing acetaminophen and aspirin (e.g., Excedrin) or other salicylates (with large amounts taken regularly) or
- Cyclosporine (e.g., Sandimmune) or
- Deferoxamine (e.g., Desferal) (with long-term use) or
- Gold salts (medicine for arthritis) or
- Hydroxychloroquine (e.g., Plaquenil) or
- Inflammation or pain medicines, except narcotics, or
- Lithium (e.g., Lithane) or
- Methotrexate (e.g., Mexate) or
- Penicillamine (e.g., Cuprimine) or
- Plicamycin (e.g., Mithracin) or
- Quinine (e.g., Quinamm) or
- Streptozocin (e.g., Zanosar) or
- Tiopronin (e.g., Thiola)—Use of any of these medicines with capreomycin may increase the chance of hearing, balance, or kidney side effects

Other medical problems—The presence of other medical problems may affect the use of capreomycin. Make sure you tell your doctor if you have any other medical problems, especially:

- Eighth-cranial-nerve disease (loss of hearing and/or balance)—Capreomycin may cause hearing and balance side effects

- Kidney disease—Capreomycin may cause serious side effects affecting the kidneys

- Myasthenia gravis or
- Parkinson's disease—Capreomycin may cause muscular weakness

Proper Use of This Medicine

To help clear up your infection completely, *it is very important that you keep taking this medicine for the full time of treatment*, even if you begin to feel better after a few weeks. You may have to use it every day for as long as 1 to 2 years or more. If you stop using this medicine too soon, your symptoms may return.

Dosing—The dose of capreomycin will be different for different patients. The following information includes only the average doses of capreomycin. Your dose may be different if you have kidney disease.

- For *injection* dosage form:
  —For treatment of tuberculosis (TB):
    - Adults and adolescents—1 gram of capreomycin injected into the muscle once a day for 60 to 120 days. After this time, 1 gram of capreomycin is injected into the muscle 2 or 3 times a week. This medicine must be given with other medicines to treat tuberculosis (TB).
    - Children—Dose has not been determined.

Side Effects of This Medicine

Along with its needed effects, a medicine may cause some unwanted effects. Although not all of these side effects may occur, if they do occur they may need medical attention.

Check with your doctor as soon as possible if any of the following side effects occur:

More common
   Greatly increased or decreased frequency of urination or amount of urine; increased thirst; loss of appetite; nausea; vomiting

Less common
   Any loss of hearing; clumsiness or unsteadiness; difficulty in breathing; dizziness; drowsiness; fever; irregular heartbeat; itching; muscle cramps or pain; pain, redness, hardness, unusual bleeding, or a sore at the place of injection; ringing or buzzing or a feeling of fullness in the ears; skin rash; swelling; unusual tiredness or weakness

Other side effects not listed above may also occur in some patients. If you notice any other effects, check with your doctor.

Revised: 06/27/94
Interim revision: 10/20/98

CAPSAICIN   Topical

Commonly used brand name(s):
In the U.S.—
   Zostrix
   Zostrix-HP
In Canada—
   Zostrix
   Zostrix-HP

Description

Capsaicin (cap-SAY-sin) is used to help relieve a certain type of pain known as neuralgia (new-RAL-ja). Capsaicin is also used to temporarily help relieve the pain from osteoarthritis (OS-te-o-ar-THRI-tis) or rheumatoid arthritis (ROO-ma-toid ar-THRI-tis). This medicine will not cure any of these conditions.

Neuralgia is a pain from the nerves near the surface of your skin. This pain may occur after an infection with herpes zoster (shingles). It may also occur if you have diabetic neuropathy (di-a-BET-ick new-ROP-a-thee). Diabetic neuropathy is a condition that occurs in some persons with diabetes. The condition causes tingling and pain in the feet and toes. Capsaicin will help relieve the pain of diabetic neuropathy, but it will not cure diabetic neuropathy or diabetes.

Capsaicin may also be used for neuralgias or itching of the skin caused by other conditions as determined by your doctor.

Capsaicin is available without a prescription; however, your doctor may have special instructions on the proper use of this medicine.

Topical
- Cream (U.S. and Canada)

Before Using This Medicine

If you are using this medicine without a prescription, carefully read and follow any precautions on the label. For capsaicin, the following should be considered:

Allergies—Tell your health care professional if you have ever had any unusual or allergic reaction to capsaicin or to the fruit of *Capsicum* plants (for example, hot peppers). Also tell your health care professional if you are allergic to any other substances, such as foods, preservatives, or dyes.

Pregnancy—Capsaicin has not been reported to cause birth defects or other problems in humans.

Breast-feeding—It is not known whether capsaicin passes into breast milk. Although most medicines pass into breast milk in small amounts, many of them may be used safely while breast-feeding. Mothers who are using this medicine and who wish to breast-feed should discuss this with their doctor.

Children—Use is not recommended for infants and children up to 2 years of age, except as directed by your doctor. In children 2 years of age and older, this medicine is not expected to cause different side effects or problems than it does in adults.

Older adults—Many medicines have not been studied specifically in older people. Therefore, it may not be known whether they work exactly the same way they do in younger adults. Although there is no specific information comparing use of capsaicin in the elderly with use in other age groups, this medicine is not expected to cause different side effects or problems in older people than it does in younger adults.

Other medical problems—The presence of other medical problems may affect the use of capsaicin. Make sure you tell your health care professional if you have any other medical problems, especially:
- Broken or irritated skin on area to be treated with capsaicin

Proper Use of This Medicine

If you are using capsaicin for the treatment of neuralgia caused by herpes zoster, do not apply the medicine until the zoster sores have healed.

It is not necessary to wash the areas to be treated before you apply capsaicin, but doing so will not cause harm.

Apply a small amount of cream and use your fingers to rub it well into the affected area so that little or no cream is left on the surface of the skin afterwards.

Wash your hands with soap and water after applying capsaicin to avoid getting the medicine in your eyes or on other sensitive areas of the body. However, if you are using capsaicin for arthritis in your hands, do not wash your hands for at least 30 minutes after applying the cream.

If a bandage is being used on the treated area, it should not be applied tightly.

When you first begin to use capsaicin, a warm, stinging, or burning sensation (feeling) may occur. This sensation is related to the action of capsaicin on the skin and is to be expected. Although this sensation usually disappears after the first several days of treatment, it may last 2 to 4 weeks or longer. Heat, humidity, clothing, bathing in warm water, or sweating may increase the sensation. However, the sensation usually occurs less often and is less severe the longer you use the medicine. Reducing the number of doses of capsaicin that you use each day will not lessen the sensation and may lengthen the period of time that you get the sensation. Also, reducing the number of doses you use may reduce the amount of pain relief that you get.

Capsaicin must be used regularly every day as directed if it is to work properly. Even then, it may not relieve your pain right away. The length of time it takes to work depends on the type of pain you have. In persons with arthritis, pain relief usually begins within 1 to 2 weeks. In most persons with neuralgia, relief usually begins within 2 to 4 weeks, although with head and neck neuralgias, relief may take as long as 4 to 6 weeks.

Once capsaicin has begun to relieve pain, you must continue to use it regularly 3 or 4 times a day to keep the pain from returning. If you stop using capsaicin and your pain returns, you can begin using it again.

Dosing—The dose of capsaicin may be different for different patients. *Follow your doctor's orders or the directions on the label*. The following information includes only the average dose of capsaicin. *If your dose is different, do not change it* unless your doctor tells you to do so.
- For *topical* dosage form (cream):
  —For neuralgias or itching of the skin:
  - Adults and children 2 years of age or older—Apply regularly 3 or 4 times a day and rub well.
  - Children up to 2 years of age—Use and dose must be determined by your doctor.

Missed dose—If you miss a dose of this medicine, use it as soon as possible. However, if it is almost time for your next dose, skip the missed dose and go back to your regular dosing schedule. Do not double doses.

Storage—To store this medicine:
- Keep out of the reach of children.
- Store away from heat and direct light.
- Keep the medicine from freezing. Do not refrigerate.
- Do not keep outdated medicine or medicine no longer needed. Be sure that any discarded medicine is out of the reach of children.

Precautions While Using This Medicine

If capsaicin gets into your eyes or on other sensitive areas of the body, it will cause a burning sensation. If capsaicin gets into your eyes, flush your eyes with water. If capsaicin gets on other sensitive areas of your body, wash the areas with warm (not hot) soapy water.

If your condition gets worse, or does not improve after 1 month, stop using this medicine and check with your doctor.

Side Effects of This Medicine

Along with its needed effects, a medicine may cause some unwanted effects. Although not all of these side effects may occur, if they do occur they may need medical attention. Some side effects may occur that usually do not need medical attention. These side effects may go away during treatment as your body adjusts to the medicine. However, check with your doctor if any of the following side effects continue or are bothersome:

More common
> Warm, stinging, or burning feeling at the place of treatment

Other side effects not listed above may also occur in some patients. If you notice any other effects, check with your doctor.

Revised: 07/14/92
Interim revision: 05/13/98

CARBACHOL   Ophthalmic

Commonly used brand name(s):

In the U.S.—
Carbastat
Carboptic
Isopto Carbachol
Miostat

In Canada—
Carbastat
Isopto Carbachol
Miostat

Another commonly used name is carbamylcholine.

Description

Carbachol (KAR-ba-kole) is used in the eye to treat glaucoma. Sometimes it is also used in eye surgery.

This medicine is available only with your doctor's prescription, in the following dosage forms:

Ophthalmic
- Intraocular solution (U.S. and Canada)
- Ophthalmic solution (eye drops) (U.S. and Canada)

Before Using This Medicine

In deciding to use a medicine, the risks of taking the medicine must be weighed against the good it will do. This is a decision you and your doctor will make. For carbachol, the following should be considered:

Allergies—Tell your doctor if you have ever had any unusual or allergic reaction to carbachol. Also tell your health care professional if you are allergic to any other substances, such as preservatives.

Pregnancy—Studies on effects in pregnancy have not been done in either humans or animals. However, carbachol may be absorbed into the body.

Breast-feeding—Carbachol may be absorbed into the mother's body. However, it is not known whether carbachol passes into breast milk. Although most medicines pass into breast milk in small amounts, many of them may be used safely while breast-feeding. Mothers who are using this medicine and who wish to breast-feed should discuss this with their doctor.

Children—Although there is no specific information comparing use of carbachol in children with use in other age groups, this medicine is not expected to cause different side effects or problems in children than it does in adults.

Older adults—Many medicines have not been studied specifically in older people. Therefore, it may not be known whether they work exactly the same way they do in younger adults. Although there is no specific information comparing use of carbachol in the elderly with use in other age groups, this medicine is not expected to cause different side effects or problems in older people than it does in younger adults.

Other medicines—Although certain medicines should not be used together at all, in other cases two different medicines may be used together even if an interaction might occur. In these cases, your doctor may want to change the dose, or other precautions may be necessary. Tell your health care professional if you are using any other prescription or nonprescription (over-the-counter [OTC]) medicine.

Other medical problems—The presence of other medical problems may affect the use of carbachol. Make sure you tell your doctor if you have any other medical problems, especially:
- Asthma or
- Eye problems (other) or
- Heart disease or
- Overactive thyroid or
- Parkinson's disease or
- Stomach ulcer or other stomach problems or
- Urinary tract blockage—Carbachol may make the condition worse

Proper Use of This Medicine

Use this medicine only as directed. Do not use more of it and do not use it more often than your doctor ordered. To do so may increase the chance of too much medicine being absorbed into the body and the chance of side effects.

To use:
- First, wash your hands. Tilt the head back and, pressing your finger gently on the skin just beneath the lower eyelid, pull the lower eyelid away from the eye to make a space. Drop the medicine into this space. Let go of the eyelid and gently close the eyes. Do not blink. Keep the eyes closed and apply pressure to the inner corner of the eye with your finger for 1 or 2 minutes to allow the medicine to be absorbed by the eye.
- Immediately after using the eye drops, wash your hands to remove any medicine that may be on them.
- To keep the medicine as germ-free as possible, do not touch the applicator tip to any surface (including the eye). Also, keep the container tightly closed.

Dosing—The dose of carbachol will be different for different patients. *Follow your doctor's orders or the directions on the label.* The following information includes only the average doses of carbachol. *If your dose is different, do not change it* unless your doctor tells you to do so.
- For glaucoma:
  —For *ophthalmic solution (eye drops)* dosage form:
    - Adults and children—Use one drop in the eye one to three times a day.

- For use during surgery:
  - —For *intraocular solution* dosage form:
    - Adults and children—Up to 0.5 milliliter (mL), used in the eye during surgery.

Missed dose—If you miss a dose of this medicine, apply it as soon as possible. However, if it is almost time for your next dose, skip the missed dose and go back to your regular dosing schedule. Do not double doses.

Storage—To store this medicine:
- Keep out of the reach of children.
- Store away from heat and direct light.
- Keep the medicine from freezing.
- Do not keep outdated medicine or medicine no longer needed. Be sure that any discarded medicine is out of the reach of children.

Precautions While Using This Medicine

Your doctor should check your eye pressure at regular visits.

After you apply this medicine to your eyes, your pupils may become unusually small. This may cause you to see less well at night or in dim light. *Be especially careful if you drive, use machines, or do anything else at night or in dim light that could be dangerous if you are not able to see well.*

Also, for a short time after you apply this medicine, your vision may be blurred or there may be a change in your near or distance vision. *Make sure your vision is clear before you drive, use machines, or do anything else that could be dangerous if you are not able to see well.*

Side Effects of This Medicine

Along with its needed effects, a medicine may cause some unwanted effects. Although not all of these side effects may occur, if they do occur they may need medical attention.

Check with your doctor as soon as possible if any of the following side effects occur:
Rare
  Veil or curtain appearing across part of vision
Symptoms of too much medicine being absorbed into the body
  Diarrhea, stomach cramps or pain, or vomiting; fainting; flushing or redness of face; frequent urge to urinate; increased sweating; irregular heartbeat; shortness of breath, wheezing, or tightness in chest; unusual tiredness or weakness; watering of mouth

Other side effects may occur that usually do not need medical attention. These side effects may go away during treatment as your body adjusts to the medicine. However, check with your doctor if any of the following side effects continue or are bothersome:
More common
  Blurred vision or change in near or distance vision; eye pain; stinging or burning of the eye
Less common
  Headache; irritation or redness of eyes; twitching of eyelids

Other side effects not listed above may also occur in some patients. If you notice any other effects, check with your doctor.

Revised: 06/21/94
Interim revision: 05/01/95; 09/11/98

CARBAMAZEPINE   Systemic

Commonly used brand name(s):

In the U.S.—

Atretol	Tegretol
Carbatrol	Tegretol-XR
Epitol	

Generic name product may be available.

In Canada—

Apo-Carbamazepine	Taro-Carbamazepine CR
Novo-Carbamaz	Tegretol
Nu-Carbamazepine	Tegretol Chewtabs
Taro-Carbamazepine	Tegretol CR

Description

Carbamazepine (kar-ba-MAZ-e-peen) is used to control some types of seizures in the treatment of epilepsy. It is also used to relieve pain due to trigeminal neuralgia (tic douloureux). It should not be used for other more common aches or pains.

Carbamazepine may also be used for other conditions as determined by your doctor.

This medicine is available only with your doctor's prescription, in the following dosage forms:
Oral
- Oral Suspension (U.S. and Canada)
- Tablets (U.S. and Canada)
- Chewable tablets (U.S. and Canada)
- Extended-release capsules (U.S.)
- Extended-release tablets (U.S. and Canada)

Before Using This Medicine

In deciding to use a medicine, the risks of taking the medicine must be weighed against the good it will do. This is a decision you and your doctor will make. For carbamazepine, the following should be considered:

Allergies—Tell your doctor if you have ever had any unusual or allergic reaction to carbamazepine or to any of the tricyclic antidepressants, such as amitriptyline, amoxapine, clomipramine, desipramine, doxepin, imipramine, nortriptyline, protriptyline, or trimipramine. Also tell your health care professional if you are allergic to any other substances, such as foods, preservatives, or dyes.

Pregnancy—Carbamazepine has not been studied in pregnant women. However, there have been reports of babies having low birth weight, small head size, skull and facial defects, underdeveloped fingernails, and delays in growth when their mothers had taken carbamazepine in high doses during pregnancy. In addition, birth defects have been reported in some babies when the mothers took other medicines for epilepsy during pregnancy. Also, studies in animals have shown that carbamazepine causes birth defects when given in large doses. Therefore, the use of carbamazepine during pregnancy should be discussed with your doctor.

Breast-feeding—Carbamazepine passes into the breast milk, and in some cases the baby may receive enough of it to cause unwanted effects. In animal studies, carbamazepine has affected the growth and appearance of the nursing babies.

Children—Behavior changes are more likely to occur in children.

Older adults—Confusion; restlessness and nervousness; irregular, pounding, or unusually slow heartbeat; and chest pain may be especially likely to occur in elderly patients, who are usually more sensitive than younger adults to the effects of carbamazepine.

Other medicines—Although certain medicines should not be used together at all, in other cases two different medicines may be used together even if an interaction might occur. In these cases, your doctor may want to change the dose, or other precautions may be necessary. When you are taking carbamazepine, it is especially important that your health care professional know if you are taking any of the following:

- Anticoagulants (blood thinners)—The effects of anticoagulants may be decreased; monitoring of blood clotting time may be necessary during and after carbamazepine treatment

- Cimetidine (e.g., Tagamet)—Blood levels of carbamazepine may be increased, leading to an increase in serious side effects

- Clarithromycin (e.g., Biaxin)—Blood levels of carbamazepine may be increased, increasing the risk of unwanted effects

- Corticosteroids (cortisone-like medicine)—The effects of corticosteroids may be decreased

- Diltiazem (e.g., Cardizem) or
- Erythromycin (e.g., E-Mycin, Erythrocin, Ilosone) or
- Propoxyphene (e.g., Darvon) or
- Verapamil (e.g., Calan)—Blood levels of carbamazepine may be increased; these medicines should not be used with carbamazepine

- Estrogens (female hormones) or
- Oral contraceptives (birth control pills) containing estrogen or
- Quinidine—The effects of these medicines may be decreased; use of a nonhormonal method of birth control or an oral contraceptive containing only a progestin may be necessary

- Fluvoxamine (e.g., Luvox)—Blood levels of carbamazepine may be increased, increasing the risk of unwanted effects

- Isoniazid (e.g., INH)—The risk of serious side effects may be increased

- Itraconazole (e.g., Sporanox) or
- Ketoconazole (e.g., Nizoral)—The effects of these medicines may be decreased

- Monoamine oxidase (MAO) inhibitors (furazolidone [e.g., Furoxone], isocarboxazid [e.g., Marplan], phenelzine [e.g., Nardil], procarbazine [e.g., Matulane], selegiline [e.g., Eldepryl], tranylcypromine [e.g., Parnate])—Taking carbamazepine while you are taking or within 2 weeks of taking monoamine oxidase (MAO) inhibitors may cause sudden high body temperature, extremely high blood pressure, and severe convulsions; at least 14 days should be allowed between stopping treatment with one medicine and starting treatment with the other

- Other anticonvulsants (seizure medicine)—The effects of these medicines may be decreased; in addition, if these medicines and carbamazepine are used together during pregnancy, the risk of birth defects may be increased

- Risperidone [e.g., Risperdal]—The effects of risperidone may be decreased

- Tricyclic antidepressants (amitriptyline [e.g., Elavil], amoxapine [e.g., Asendin], clomipramine [e.g., Anafranil], desipramine [e.g., Pertofrane], doxepin [e.g., Sinequan], imipramine [e.g., Tofranil], nortriptyline [e.g., Aventyl], protriptyline [e.g., Vivactil], trimipramine [e.g., Surmontil])—Central nervous system depressant effects of carbamazepine may be increased while the anticonvulsant effects of carbamazepine may be decreased; seizures may occur more frequently

Other medical problems—The presence of other medical problems may affect the use of carbamazepine. Make sure you tell your doctor if you have any other medical problems, especially:

- Alcohol abuse (or history of)—Drinking alcohol may decrease the effectiveness of carbamazepine

- Anemia or other blood problems or
- Behavioral problems or
- Glaucoma or
- Heart or blood vessel disease or
- Problems with urination—Carbamazepine may make the condition worse

- Diabetes mellitus (sugar diabetes)—Carbamazepine may cause increased urine glucose levels

- Kidney disease or
- Liver disease—Higher blood levels of carbamazepine may result, increasing the chance of side effects

---

Proper Use of This Medicine

Carbamazepine suspension and tablets should be taken with meals to lessen the chance of stomach upset (nausea and vomiting). Carbamazepine extended-release capsules do not need to be taken with meals unless they upset your stomach. The contents of these extended-release capsules may be sprinkled over a teaspoonful of applesauce or other similar food; the capsule or its contents should not be crushed or chewed.

It is very important that you take this medicine exactly as directed by your doctor to obtain the best results and lessen the chance of serious side effects. Do not take more of it, do not take it more often, and do not take it for a longer time than your doctor ordered.

If you are taking this medicine for pain relief:

- Carbamazepine is *not* an ordinary pain reliever. It should be used only when a doctor prescribes it for certain kinds of pain. *Do not take carbamazepine for any other aches or pains.*

If you are taking this medicine for epilepsy:

- *Do not suddenly stop taking this medicine without first checking with your doctor.* To keep your seizures under control, it is usually best to gradually reduce the amount of carbamazepine you are taking before stopping completely.

Dosing—The dose of carbamazepine will be different for different patients. *Follow your doctor's orders or the directions on the label.* The following information includes only the average doses of carbamazepine. *If your dose is different, do not change it* unless your doctor tells you to do so.

The number of tablets or teaspoonfuls of suspension that you take depends on the strength of the medicine. Also, *the number of doses you take each day, the time allowed between doses, and the length of time you take the medicine depend on the medical problem for which you are taking carbamazepine.*

- For *oral* dosage form (suspension):
  —For epilepsy:
    - Adults and teenagers—At first, 100 milligrams (mg) taken up to four times a day. Your doctor may increase your dose if needed. However, the dose is usually not more than 1200 mg a day.
    - Children 6 to 12 years of age—At first, 50 mg taken four times a day. Your doctor may increase your dose if needed. However, the dose is usually not more than 1000 mg a day.
    - Children up to 6 years of age—Dose is based on body weight and will be determined by your doctor.
  —For trigeminal neuralgia:
    - Adults and teenagers—At first, 50 mg four times a day. Your doctor may increase your dose if needed. However, the dose is usually not more than 1200 mg a day.
    - Children—Use and dose must be determined by your doctor.
- For *oral* dosage form (tablets and chewable tablets):
  —For epilepsy:
    - Adults and teenagers—At first, 200 mg taken two times a day. Your doctor may increase your dose if needed. However, the dose is usually not more than 1200 mg a day.
    - Children 6 to 12 years of age—At first, 100 mg taken two times a day. Your doctor may increase your dose if needed. However, the dose is usually not more than 1000 mg a day.
    - Children up to 6 years of age—Dose is based on body weight and will be determined by your doctor.
  —For trigeminal neuralgia:
    - Adults and teenagers—At first, 100 mg taken two times a day. Your doctor may increase your dose if needed. However, the dose is usually not more than 1200 mg a day.
    - Children—Use and dose must be determined by your doctor.
- For *oral extended-release capsule* dosage form:
  —For epilepsy:
    - Adults and teenagers—At first, 200 mg taken one or two times a day. Your doctor may increase your dose if needed. However, the dose is usually not more than 1200 mg a day.
    - Children up to 12 years of age—Dose is based on body weight and will be determined by your doctor. However, the dose is usually not more than 1000 mg a day.
  —For trigeminal neuralgia:
    - Adults and teenagers—At first, 200 mg a day. Your doctor may increase your dose if needed. However, the dose is usually not more than 1200 mg a day.
    - Children—Use and dose must be determined by your doctor.
- For *oral extended-release tablet* dosage form:
  —For epilepsy:
    - Adults and teenagers—At first, 100 to 200 mg taken one or two times a day with meals. Your doctor may increase your dose if needed. However, the dose is usually not more than 1200 mg a day.

- Children 6 to 12 years of age—At first, 100 to 200 mg taken in smaller doses during the day. Your doctor may increase your dose if needed. However, the dose is usually not more than 1000 mg a day.
- Children up to 6 years of age—Use and dose must be determined by your doctor.
  —For trigeminal neuralgia:
    - Adults and teenagers—At first, 100 mg taken two times a day. Your doctor may increase your dose if needed. However, the dose is usually not more than 1200 mg a day.
    - Children—Use and dose must be determined by your doctor.

Missed dose—If you miss a dose of this medicine, take it as soon as possible. However, if it is almost time for your next dose, skip the missed dose and go back to your regular dosing schedule. Do not double doses. However, if you miss more than one dose a day, check with your doctor.

Storage—To store this medicine:
- Keep out of the reach of children.
- Store away from heat and direct light.
- *Do not store the tablet forms of carbamazepine in the bathroom, near the kitchen sink, or in other damp places. Heat or moisture may cause the medicine to break down and become less effective.*
- Keep the liquid form of this medicine from freezing.
- Do not keep outdated medicine or medicine no longer needed. Be sure that any discarded medicine is out of the reach of children.

Precautions While Using This Medicine

It is very important that your doctor check your progress at regular visits. Your doctor may want to have certain tests done to see if you are receiving the right amount of medicine or if certain side effects may be occurring without your knowing it. Also, the amount of medicine you are taking may have to be changed often.

This medicine will add to the effects of alcohol and other CNS depressants (medicines that cause drowsiness). Some examples of CNS depressants are antihistamines or medicine for hay fever, other allergies, or colds; sedatives, tranquilizers, or sleeping medicine; prescription pain medicine or narcotics; barbiturates; medicine for seizures; muscle relaxants; or anesthetics, including some dental anesthetics. *Check with your doctor before taking any of the above while you are using this medicine.*

This medicine may cause some people to become drowsy, dizzy, lightheaded, or less alert than they are normally, especially when they are starting treatment or increasing the dose. It may also cause blurred or double vision, weakness, or loss of muscle control in some people. *Make sure you know how you react to this medicine before you drive, use machines, or do anything else that could be dangerous if you are not alert and well-coordinated or able to see well.*

Some people who take carbamazepine may become more sensitive to sunlight than they are normally. Exposure to sunlight, even for brief periods of time, may cause a skin rash, itching, redness or other discoloration of the skin, or a severe sunburn. When you begin taking this medicine:
- Stay out of direct sunlight, especially between the hours of 10:00 a.m. and 3:00 p.m., if possible.

- Wear protective clothing, including a hat. Also, wear sunglasses.
- Apply a sun block product that has a skin protection factor (SPF) of at least 15. Some patients may require a product with a higher SPF number, especially if they have a fair complexion. If you have any questions about this, check with your health care professional.
- Apply a sun block lipstick that has an SPF of at least 15 to protect your lips.
- Do not use a sunlamp or tanning bed or booth.

If you have a severe reaction from the sun, check with your doctor.

Oral contraceptives (birth control pills) containing estrogen may not work properly if you take them while you are taking carbamazepine. Unplanned pregnancies may occur. You should use a different or additional means of birth control while you are taking carbamazepine. If you have any questions about this, check with your health care professional.

For diabetic patients:

- Carbamazepine may affect urine sugar levels. While you are using this medicine, be especially careful when testing for sugar in your urine. If you notice a change in the results of your urine sugar tests or have any questions about this, check with your doctor.

For patients taking the *oral suspension form of Tegretol:*

- Do not take any other liquid medicines at the same time that you take your dose of Tegretol without first checking with your doctor.

Before having any medical tests, tell the medical doctor in charge that you are taking this medicine. The results of some pregnancy tests and the metyrapone test may be affected by this medicine.

Before having any kind of surgery, dental treatment, or emergency treatment, tell the medical doctor or dentist in charge that you are taking this medicine. Taking carbamazepine together with medicines that are used during surgery or dental or emergency treatments may increase the CNS depressant effects and cause other unwanted effects.

Your doctor may want you to carry a medical identification card or bracelet stating that you are taking this medicine.

Side Effects of This Medicine

Along with its needed effects, a medicine may cause some unwanted effects. Although not all of these side effects may occur, if they do occur they may need medical attention.

Check with your doctor immediately if any of the following side effects occur:

Rare

Black, tarry stools; blood in urine or stools; bone or joint pain; cough or hoarseness; darkening of urine; lower back or side pain; nosebleeds or other unusual bleeding or bruising; painful or difficult urination; pain, tenderness, swelling, or bluish color in leg or foot; pale stools; pinpoint red spots on skin; shortness of breath or cough; sores, ulcers, or white spots on lips or in the mouth; sore throat, chills, and fever; swollen or painful glands; unusual tiredness or weakness; wheezing, tightness in chest, or troubled breathing; yellow eyes or skin

Symptoms of overdose

Body spasm in which head and heels are bent backward and body is bowed forward; clumsiness or un-steadiness; convulsions (seizures)—especially in small children; dizziness (severe) or fainting; drowsiness (severe); fast or irregular heartbeat; high or low blood pressure (hypertension or hypotension); irregular, slow, or shallow breathing; large pupils; nausea or vomiting (severe); overactive reflexes followed by underactive reflexes; poor control in body movements (for example, when reaching or stepping); sudden decrease in amount of urine; trembling, twitching, or abnormal body movements

In addition, check with your doctor as soon as possible if any of the following side effects occur:

More common

Blurred vision or double vision; continuous back-and-forth eye movements

Less common

Behavioral changes (especially in children); confusion, agitation, or hostility (especially in the elderly); diarrhea (severe); headache (continuing); increase in seizures; nausea and vomiting (severe); skin rash, hives, or itching; unusual drowsiness

Rare

Chest pain; difficulty in speaking or slurred speech; fainting; frequent urination; irregular, pounding, or unusually slow heartbeat; mental depression with restlessness and nervousness or other mood or mental changes; muscle or stomach cramps; numbness, tingling, pain, or weakness in hands and feet; rapid weight gain; rigidity; ringing, buzzing, or other unexplained sounds in the ears; sudden decrease in amount of urine; swelling of face, hands, feet, or lower legs; trembling; uncontrolled body movements; visual hallucinations (seeing things that are not there)

Other side effects may occur that usually do not need medical attention. These side effects may go away during treatment as your body adjusts to the medicine. However, check with your doctor if any of the following side effects continue or are bothersome:

More common

Clumsiness or unsteadiness; dizziness (mild); drowsiness (mild); lightheadedness; nausea or vomiting (mild)

Less common or rare

Aching joints or muscles; constipation; diarrhea; dryness of mouth; headache; increased sensitivity of skin to sunlight (skin rash, itching, redness or other discoloration of skin, or severe sunburn); increased sweating; irritation or soreness of tongue or mouth; loss of appetite; loss of hair; sexual problems in males; stomach pain or discomfort

Other side effects not listed above may also occur in some patients. If you notice any other effects, check with your doctor.

Additional Information

Once a medicine has been approved for marketing for a certain use, experience may show that it is also useful for other medical problems. Although these uses are not included in product labeling, carbamazepine is used in certain patients with the following medical conditions:

- Neurogenic pain (a type of continuing pain)
- Bipolar disorder (manic-depressive illness)
- Central partial diabetes insipidus (water diabetes)

- Alcohol withdrawal
- Psychotic disorders (severe mental illness)

Other than the above information, there is no additional information relating to proper use, precautions, or side effects for these uses.

Revised: 08/11/98
Interim revision: 01/29/99

CARBETOCIN Systemic*—INTRODUCTORY VERSION

Commonly used brand name(s):

In Canada—
Duratocin

*Not commercially available in the U.S.

Description

Carbetocin (car-bi-TOE-sin) is a hormone used to control bleeding after delivery.

Carbetocin is available only with your doctor's prescription, in the following dosage form:

Parenteral
- Injection (Canada)

Before Using This Medicine

In deciding to use a medicine, the risks of taking this medicine must be weighed against the good it will do. This is a decision you and your doctor will make. For carbetocin, the following should be considered:

Allergies—Tell your doctor if you have ever had any unusual or allergic reaction to oxytocin or carbetocin. Also tell your health care professional if you are allergic to any other substances, such as foods, preservatives, or dyes.

Pregnancy—Carbetocin must not be given before delivery of the baby because it may cause serious problems in the baby and the mother.

Breast-feeding—Although very small amounts of this medicine pass into breast milk, it has not been reported to cause problems in nursing babies.

Other medicines—Although certain medicines should not be used together at all, in other cases two different medicines may be used together even if an interaction might occur. In these cases, your doctor may want to change the dose, or other precautions may be necessary. Tell your health care professional if you are taking any other prescription or nonprescription (over-the-counter [OTC]) medicine.

Other medical problems—The presence of other medical problems may affect the use of carbetocin. Make sure you tell your doctor if you have any other medical problems, especially:

- Heart or blood vessel disease—This medicine should be used with caution

Proper Use of This Medicine

Dosing—The following information includes the average dose of carbetocin.

- For helping to control bleeding after delivery:
  —Adults—100 micrograms (1 mL) injected over 1 minute into a vein beginning after delivery of the baby.

Side Effects of This Medicine

Along with its needed effects, a medicine may cause some unwanted effects. Although not all of these side effects may occur, if they do occur they may need medical attention.

More common
    Abdominal pain; dizziness; faintness; feeling of warmth; headache; light-headedness; itching skin; trembling; unusual tiredness or weakness

Less common
    Chest pain; chills; fast heartbeat; nervousness; pain; pale skin; shortness of breath

Other side effects may occur that usually do not need medical attention. These side effects may go away during treatment as your body adjusts to the medicine. However, check with your doctor if any of the following side effects continue or are bothersome.

More common
    Nausea; vomiting

Less common
    Back pain; metallic taste; sweating

Other side effects not listed above may also occur in some patients. If you notice any other effects, check with your doctor.

Developed: 08/07/2000

CARBOHYDRATES AND ELECTROLYTES Systemic

Commonly used brand name(s):

In the U.S.—

Infalyte[3]	Pedialyte[1]
Kao Lectrolyte[1]	Pedialyte Freezer Pops[1]
Naturalyte[1]	Rehydralyte[1]
Oralyte[1]	Resol‡[1]

In Canada—

Lytren[1]	Pedialyte[1]
Gastrolyte[2]	Rapolyte[2]

Other commonly used names are oral rehydration salts, ORS-bicarbonate, and ORS-citrate. §

Note: For quick reference, the following are numbered to match the corresponding brand names.

This information applies to the following medicines:
1. Dextrose and Electrolytes (DEX-trose and ee-LEK-tro-lites) ‡
2. Oral Rehydration Salts (OR-al ree-hi-DRA-shen solts) *§
3. Rice Syrup Solids and Electrolytes (RIS SIR-ep SOL-ids and ee-LEK-tro-lites) †

*Not commercially available in the U.S.
†Not commercially available in Canada.
‡Generic name product may be available in the U.S.
§Distributed by the World Health Organization (WHO).

- Intestinal blockage—Carbohydrate and electrolytes solution may be harmful if given to patients with this condition

Description

Carbohydrate and electrolytes combination is used to treat or prevent dehydration (the loss of too much water from the body) that may occur with severe diarrhea, especially in babies and young children. Although this medicine does not immediately stop the diarrhea, it replaces the water and some important salts (electrolytes), such as sodium and potassium, that are lost from the body during diarrhea, and helps prevent more serious problems. Some carbohydrate and electrolytes solutions may also be used after surgery when food intake has been stopped.

This medicine is available without a prescription; however, your doctor may have special instructions on the proper use and dose for you or your child.

Carbohydrate and electrolytes combination is available in the following dosage forms:

Oral
- Solution (U.S. and Canada)
- Powder for oral solution (Canada)

Before Using This Medicine

If you are taking this medicine without a prescription, carefully read and follow any precautions on the label. For carbohydrate and electrolytes solutions, the following should be considered:

Allergies—Tell your health care professional if you have ever had any unusual or allergic reaction to medicines containing potassium, sodium, citrates, rice, or sugar. Also tell your health care professional if you are allergic to any other substances, such as foods, preservatives, or dyes.

Pregnancy—Carbohydrate and electrolytes solutions have not been shown to cause birth defects or other problems in humans.

Breast-feeding—This medicine has not been reported to cause problems in nursing babies. Breast-feeding should continue, if possible, during treatment with carbohydrate and electrolytes solution.

Children—This medicine has been tested in children and, in effective doses, appears to be safe and effective in children. This medicine has not been tested in premature infants.

Older adults—This medicine has been tested and has been shown to be well tolerated by older people.

Other medicines—Although certain medicines should not be used together at all, in other cases two different medicines may be used together even if an interaction might occur. In these cases, your doctor may want to change the dose, or other precautions may be necessary. Tell your health care professional if you are taking any other prescription or nonprescription (over-the-counter [OTC]) medicine.

Other medical problems—The presence of other medical problems may affect the use of carbohydrate and electrolytes solutions. Make sure you tell your doctor if you have any other medical problems, especially:
- Difficult urination—This condition may prevent the carbohydrate and electrolytes solution from working properly
- Inability to drink or
- Vomiting (severe and continuing)—Treatment by injection may need to be given to patients with these conditions

Proper Use of This Medicine

For patients using the *commercial powder form* of this medicine:
- Add 7 ounces of boiled, cooled tap water to the entire contents of one powder packet. Shake or stir the container for 2 or 3 minutes until all the powder is dissolved.
- Do not add more water to the solution after it is mixed.
- Do not boil the solution.
- Make and use a fresh solution each day.

For patients using the *freezer pop form* of this medicine:
- Pops should be removed from the box before being placed in the freezer. The pops should be frozen before separating.
- The freezer pop can be eaten without freezing, but tastes best when frozen. To eat the frozen pop, cut the top of the wrapper open and push the pop from the bottom of the plastic sleeve.
- To drink as a liquid, cut the top of the wrapper open and pour the unfrozen pop into a cup or glass.

For patients using the *powder form* of this medicine *distributed by the World Health Organization (WHO)*:
- Add the entire contents of one powder packet to enough drinking water to make one quart (32 ounces) or liter of solution. Shake the container for 2 or 3 minutes until all the powder is dissolved.
- Do not add more water to the solution after it is mixed.
- Do not boil the solution.
- Make and use a fresh solution each day.

Babies and small children should be given the solution slowly, in small amounts, with a spoon, as often as possible, during the first 24 hours of diarrhea.

Take as directed. Do not take it for a longer time than your doctor has recommended. To do so may increase the chance of side effects.

Dosing—The dose of these combination medicines will be different for different patients. *Follow your doctor's orders or the directions on the label.* The following information includes only the average doses of these medicines. *If your dose is different, do not change it* unless your doctor tells you to do so.

For dextrose and electrolytes and for rice syrup solids and electrolytes
- For rehydration (to replace the water and some important salts [electrolytes]):
  —For *oral* dosage form (solution):
  - Adults and children over 10 years of age—Dose is based on body weight and must be determined by your doctor. At first, the usual dose is 50 to 100 milliliters (mL) per kilogram (kg) (23 to 45 mL per pound) of body weight taken over four to six hours. Your doctor may change the dose depending on your thirst and your response to the treatment.
  - Children up to 2 years of age—The dose is based on body weight and must be determined by your doctor. At first, the usual dose is 75 mL per kg (34 mL per pound) of body weight during the first eight hours and 75 mL per kg (34 mL per pound) of body weight during the next sixteen hours. Your doctor may change the dose depending on your

thirst and your response to the treatment. However, the dose is usually not more than 100 mL in any 20-minute period.

- Children 2 to 10 years of age—Dose is based on body weight and must be determined by your doctor. At first, the usual dose is 50 mL per kg (23 mL per pound) of body weight taken over the first four to six hours. Then, the dose is 100 mL per kg (45 mL per pound) of body weight taken over the next eighteen to twenty-four hours. Your doctor may change the dose depending on your thirst and your response to the treatment. However, the dose is usually not more than 100 mL in any 20-minute period.

—For *oral* dosage form (solution for freezer pop):
- Children up to 1 year of age—Use must be determined by your doctor.
- Children older than 1 year of age—Freezer pop may be given as often as desired.

For oral rehydration salts
- For rehydration (to replace the water and some important salts [electrolytes]):
  —For *oral* dosage form (solution):
  - Adults and teenagers—Dose is based on body weight and must be determined by your doctor. At first, the usual dose is 50 to 100 milliliters (mL) of solution per kilogram (kg) (23 to 45 mL per pound) of body weight taken over four to six hours. Your doctor may change the dose depending on your thirst and your response to the treatment.
  - Children—Dose is based on body weight and must be determined by your doctor. At first, the usual dose is 50 to 100 mL per kg (23 to 45 mL per pound) of body weight taken over the first four hours. Your doctor may change the dose depending on your thirst and your response to the treatment.

Storage—To store this medicine:
- Keep out of the reach of children.
- Store away from heat and direct light.
- Do not store the powder packets in the bathroom, near the kitchen sink, or in other damp places. Heat or moisture may cause the medicine to break down.
- Store the liquid in the refrigerator. However, keep the medicine from freezing.
- Make a fresh solution each day. Discard unused solution at the end of each day. Be sure that any discarded medicine is out of the reach of children.

Precautions While Using This Medicine

Eat soft foods, if possible, such as rice cereal, bananas, cooked peas or beans, and potatoes to keep up nutrition until the diarrhea stops and regular food and milk can be taken again. Breast-fed infants should be given breast milk between doses of the solution.

If your diarrhea does not improve in 1 or 2 days, or if it becomes worse, check with your doctor.

Also, *check with your doctor immediately* if your baby or child appears to have severe thirst, doughy skin, sunken eyes, dizziness or lightheadedness, tiredness or weakness, irritability, difficult urination, loss of weight, or convulsions (seizures). These signs may mean that too much water has been lost from the body.

For patients (except nursing babies) using the *powder form* of this medicine:
- Drink plain water whenever thirsty between doses of solution.

For patients taking the *premixed liquid form* of this medicine:
- Do not drink fruit juices or eat foods containing added salt until the diarrhea has stopped.

Side Effects of This Medicine

Along with its needed effects, a medicine may cause some unwanted effects. Although not all of these side effects may occur, if they do occur they may need medical attention.

Check with your doctor as soon as possible if any of the following side effects occur:
Symptoms of too much sodium (salt) in the body
Convulsions (seizures); dizziness; fast heartbeat; high blood pressure; irritability; muscle twitching; restlessness; swelling of feet or lower legs; weakness

Symptoms of too much fluid in the body
Puffy eyelids

Other side effects may occur that usually do not need medical attention. These side effects may go away during treatment as your body adjusts to the medicine. However, check with your doctor if the following side effect continues or is bothersome:
More common
Vomiting (mild)

Other side effects not listed above may also occur in some patients. If you notice any other effects, check with your doctor.

Revised: 12/02/92
Interim revision: 07/20/95; 08/11/97; 05/21/98

CARBOL-FUCHSIN   Topical†

Commonly used brand name(s):

In the U.S.—
Castellani Paint Modified
   (Color)
   Generic name product may be available.
Another commonly used name is Castellani Paint.

†Not commercially available in Canada.

Description

Carbol-fuchsin (kar-bol-FOOK-sin) is used to treat postoperative phenol nail procedures. It may also be used as a first aid antiseptic drying agent in skin conditions where there is too much moisture. This medicine may also be used for other infections as determined by your doctor.

This medicine is available without a prescription; however, your doctor may have special instructions on the use of topical carbol-fuchsin solution for your medical condition.

Topical carbol-fuchsin is available in the following dosage form:

Topical
- Solution (U.S.)

Before Using This Medicine

If you are using this medicine without a prescription, carefully read and follow any precautions on the label. For carbol-fuchsin, the following should be considered:

Allergies—Tell your doctor if you have ever had any unusual or allergic reaction to carbol-fuchsin. Also tell your health care professional if you are allergic to any other substances, such as preservatives or dyes.

Pregnancy—Studies in humans have not shown that carbol-fuchsin causes birth defects or other problems in humans.

Breast-feeding—Carbol-fuchsin has not been reported to cause problems in nursing babies.

Children—If you are treating an infant or child with eczema, do not use carbol-fuchsin more than once a day. Although there is no specific information comparing use of carbol-fuchsin in children treated for other conditions with use in other age groups, this medicine is not expected to cause different side effects or problems in children than it does in adults.

Older adults—Many medicines have not been studied specifically in older people. Therefore, it may not be known whether they work exactly the same way they do in younger adults or if they cause different side effects or problems in older people. There is no specific information comparing use of carbol-fuchsin in the elderly with use in other age groups.

Other medicines—Although certain medicines should not be used together at all, in other cases two different medicines may be used together even if an interaction might occur. In these cases, your doctor may want to change the dose, or other precautions may be necessary. Tell your health care professional if you are using any other topical prescription or nonprescription (over-the-counter [OTC]) medicine that is to be applied to the same area of the skin.

Proper Use of This Medicine

Carbol-fuchsin is a poison if swallowed. Use only on the affected areas as directed. Do not swallow this medicine. Do not use near the eyes or over large areas of the body. Do not use on deep wounds, puncture wounds, animal bites, or serious burns.

Before applying this medicine, wash the affected areas with soap and water, and dry thoroughly.

Using an applicator or swab, apply this medicine only to the affected areas. Do not bandage the area.

Dosing—The dose of carbol-fuchsin will be different for different patients. *Follow your doctor's orders or the directions on the label.* The following information includes only the average doses of carbol-fuchsin. *If your dose is different, do not change it* unless your doctor tells you to do so.

- For *topical* dosage form (solution):
  - For postoperative phenol nail procedures or as a first aid antiseptic drying agent:
    - Adults and children—Apply to the affected area(s) of the skin one to three times a day. Do not use

this medicine for more than one week unless your doctor tells you to do so.

Missed dose—If you miss a dose of this medicine, apply it as soon as possible. However, if it is almost time for your next dose, skip the missed dose and go back to your regular dosing schedule.

Storage—To store this medicine:
- Keep out of the reach of children.
- Store away from heat and direct light.
- Keep the medicine from freezing.
- Do not keep outdated medicine or medicine no longer needed. Be sure that any discarded medicine is out of the reach of children.

Precautions While Using This Medicine

If your skin problem does not improve within 1 week, or if it becomes worse, check with your doctor.

This medicine will stain skin and clothing. Avoid getting it on your clothes. The stain will slowly wear off your skin.

Side Effects of This Medicine

Along with its needed effects, a medicine may cause some unwanted effects. Although not all of these side effects may occur, if they do occur they may need medical attention.

Check with your doctor as soon as possible if the following side effect occurs:

Skin irritation not present before use of this medicine

Other side effects may occur that usually do not need medical attention. These side effects may go away during treatment as your body adjusts to the medicine. However, check with your doctor if the following side effect continues or is bothersome:

Mild, temporary stinging

Other side effects not listed above may also occur in some patients. If you notice any other effects, check with your doctor.

Revised: 06/14/99

CARBONIC ANHYDRASE INHIBITORS   Systemic

Commonly used brand name(s):

In the U.S.—

Ak-Zol[1]	Diamox Sequels[1]
Daranide[2]	MZM[3]
Dazamide[1]	Neptazane[3]
Diamox[1]	Storzolamide[1]

In Canada—

Acetazolam[1]	Diamox Sequels[1]
Apo-Acetazolamide[1]	Neptazane[3]
Diamox[1]	

Another commonly used name for dichlorphenamide is diclofenamide[2].

Note: For quick reference, the following carbonic anhydrase inhibitors are numbered to match the corresponding brand names.

This information applies to the following medicines:
1. Acetazolamide (a-set-a-ZOLE-a-mide) ‡

2. Dichlorphenamide (dye-klor-FEN-a-mide) †
3. Methazolamide (meth-a-ZOLE-a-mide) ‡

---

†Not commercially available in Canada.
‡Generic name product may be available in the U.S.

Description

Carbonic anhydrase inhibitors are used to treat glaucoma. Acetazolamide is also used as an anticonvulsant to control certain seizures in the treatment of epilepsy. It is also sometimes used to prevent or lessen some effects in mountain climbers who climb to high altitudes, and to treat other conditions as determined by your doctor.

These medicines are available only with your doctor's prescription, in the following dosage forms:

Oral
Acetazolamide
- Extended-release capsules (U.S. and Canada)
- Tablets (U.S. and Canada)
Dichlorphenamide
- Tablets (U.S.)
Methazolamide
- Tablets (U.S. and Canada)

Parenteral
Acetazolamide
- Injection (U.S. and Canada)

Before Using This Medicine

In deciding to use a medicine, the risks of taking the medicine must be weighed against the good it will do. This is a decision you and your doctor will make. For carbonic anhydrase inhibitors, the following should be considered:

Allergies—Tell your doctor if you have ever had any unusual or allergic reaction to carbonic anhydrase inhibitors, sulfonamides (sulfa drugs), or thiazide diuretics (a type of water pill). Also tell your health care professional if you are allergic to any other substances, such as foods, preservatives, or dyes.

Pregnancy—Carbonic anhydrase inhibitors have not been studied in pregnant women. However, studies in animals have shown that carbonic anhydrase inhibitors cause birth defects. Before taking this medicine, make sure your doctor knows if you are pregnant or if you may become pregnant.

Breast-feeding—Carbonic anhydrase inhibitors may pass into the breast milk. These medicines are not recommended during breast-feeding, because they may cause unwanted effects in nursing babies. It may be necessary for you to use another medicine or to stop breast-feeding during treatment. Be sure you have discussed this with your doctor.

Children—Although there is no specific information comparing use of carbonic anhydrase inhibitors in children with use in other age groups, these medicines are not expected to cause different side effects or problems in children than they do in adults.

Older adults—Many medicines have not been studied specifically in older people. Therefore, it may not be known whether they work exactly the same way they do in younger adults. Although there is no specific information comparing use of carbonic anhydrase inhibitors in the elderly with use in other age groups, these medicines are not expected to cause different side effects or problems in older people than they do in younger adults.

Other medicines—Although certain medicines should not be used together at all, in other cases two different medicines may be used together even if an interaction might occur. In these cases, your doctor may want to change the dose, or other precautions may be necessary. When you are using carbonic anhydrase inhibitors, it is especially important that your health care professional know if you are using any of the following:
- Amphetamines or
- Mecamylamine (e.g., Inversine) or
- Quinidine (e.g., Quinidex)—Use of carbonic anhydrase inhibitors may increase the chance of side effects
- Methenamine (e.g., Mandelamine)—Use of carbonic anhydrase inhibitors may decrease the effectiveness of methenamine

Other medical problems—The presence of other medical problems may affect the use of carbonic anhydrase inhibitors. Make sure you tell your doctor if you have any other medical problems, especially:
- Diabetes mellitus (sugar diabetes)—Use of carbonic anhydrase inhibitors may increase the patient's blood and urine sugar concentrations
- Emphysema or other chronic lung disease—Use of carbonic anhydrase inhibitors may increase the risk of acidosis (shortness of breath, troubled breathing)
- Gout or
- Low blood levels of potassium or sodium—Use of carbonic anhydrase inhibitors may make the condition worse
- Kidney disease or stones—Higher blood levels of carbonic anhydrase inhibitors may result, which may increase the chance of side effects; also, these medicines may make the condition worse
- Liver disease—Use of carbonic anhydrase inhibitors may increase the risk of electrolyte imbalance and may make the condition worse
- Underactive adrenal gland (Addison's disease)—Use of carbonic anhydrase inhibitors may increase the risk of electrolyte imbalance

---

Proper Use of This Medicine

Take this medicine only as directed. Do not take more of it and do not take it more often than your doctor ordered. To do so may increase the chance of side effects without increasing the effectiveness of this medicine.

This medicine may be taken with meals to lessen the chance of stomach upset. However, if stomach upset (nausea or vomiting) continues, check with your doctor.

This medicine may cause an increase in the amount of urine or in your frequency of urination. If you continue to take the medicine every day, these effects should lessen or stop. To keep the increase in urine from affecting your nighttime sleep:
- If you are to take a single dose a day, take it in the morning after breakfast.
- If you are to take more than one dose a day, take the last dose no later than 6 p.m., unless otherwise directed by your doctor.

However, it is best to plan your dose or doses according to a schedule that will least affect your personal activities and sleep. Ask your health care professional to help you plan the best time to take this medicine.

Dosing—The doses of carbonic anhydrase inhibitors will be different for different patients. *Follow your doctor's orders or the directions on the label*. The following information includes only the average doses of these medicines. *If your dose is different, do not change it* unless your doctor tells you to do so.

The number of capsules or tablets that you take depends on the strength of the medicine. Also, *the number of doses you take each day, the time allowed between doses, and the length of time you take the medicine depend on the medical problem for which you are taking the carbonic anhydrase inhibitor.*

For acetazolamide
- For *oral* dosage form (extended-release capsules):
  —For glaucoma:
    - Adults—500 milligrams (mg) two times a day, in the morning and evening.
    - Children—Use and dose must be determined by your doctor.
  —For altitude sickness:
    - Adults—500 mg one or two times a day.
    - Children—Use and dose must be determined by your doctor.
- For *oral* dosage form (tablets):
  —For glaucoma:
    - Adults—250 mg one to four times a day.
    - Children—Dose is based on body weight and must be determined by your doctor. The usual dose is 10 to 15 mg per kilogram (kg) (4.5 to 6.8 mg per pound) of body weight a day in divided doses.
  —For epilepsy:
    - Adults and children—Dose is based on body weight and must be determined by your doctor. The usual dose is 10 mg per kg (4.5 mg per pound) of body weight a day in divided doses.
  —For altitude sickness:
    - Adults—250 mg two to four times a day.
    - Children—Use and dose must be determined by your doctor.
- For *injection* dosage form:
  —For glaucoma:
    - Adults—500 mg, injected into a muscle or vein, for one dose.
    - Children—Dose is based on body weight and must be determined by your doctor. The usual dose is 5 to 10 mg per kg (2.3 to 4.5 mg per pound) of body weight every six hours, injected into a muscle or vein.

For dichlorphenamide
- For *oral* dosage form (tablets):
  —For glaucoma:
    - Adults—25 to 50 milligrams (mg) one to three times a day.
    - Children—Use and dose must be determined by your doctor.

For methazolamide
- For *oral* dosage form (tablets):
  —For glaucoma:
    - Adults—50 to 100 milligrams (mg) two or three times a day.

- Children—Use and dose must be determined by your doctor.

Missed dose—If you miss a dose of this medicine, take it as soon as possible. However, if it is almost time for your next dose, skip the missed dose and go back to your regular dosing schedule. Do not double doses.

Storage—To store this medicine:
- Keep out of the reach of children.
- Store away from heat and direct light.
- Do not store the capsule or tablet form of this medicine in the bathroom, near the kitchen sink, or in other damp places. Heat or moisture may cause the medicine to break down.
- Do not keep outdated medicine or medicine no longer needed. Be sure that any discarded medicine is out of the reach of children.

Precautions While Using This Medicine

This medicine may cause some people to feel drowsy, dizzy, lightheaded, or more tired than they are normally. *Make sure you know how you react to this medicine before you drive, use machines, or do anything else that could be dangerous if you are not alert.*

It is important that your doctor check your progress at regular visits. Your doctor may want to do certain tests to see if the medicine is working properly or to see if certain side effects may be occurring without your knowing it.

This medicine may cause a loss of potassium from your body. To help prevent this, your doctor may want you to eat or drink foods that have a high potassium content (for example, orange or other citrus fruit juices) or take a potassium supplement. It is very important to follow these directions. Also, it is important not to change your diet on your own. This is more important if you are already on a special diet (as for diabetes) or if you are taking a potassium supplement. Extra potassium may not be necessary and, in some cases, too much potassium could be harmful.

For *diabetic patients:*
- This medicine may raise blood and urine sugar levels. While you are using this medicine, be especially careful in testing for sugar in your blood or urine. If you have any questions about this, check with your doctor.

Your doctor may want you to increase the amount of fluids you drink while you are taking this medicine. This is to prevent kidney stones. However, do not increase the amount of fluids you drink without first checking with your doctor.

For patients taking *acetazolamide as an anticonvulsant:*
- *If you have been taking acetazolamide regularly for several weeks or more, do not suddenly stop taking it.* Your doctor may want you to reduce gradually the amount you are taking before stopping completely.

Side Effects of This Medicine

Along with its needed effects, a medicine may cause some unwanted effects. Although not all of these side effects may occur, if they do occur they may need medical attention.

Check with your doctor immediately if either of the following side effects occurs:
  Rare
    Shortness of breath or trouble in breathing

Also, check with your doctor as soon as possible if any of the following side effects occur:

More common
> Unusual tiredness or weakness

Less common
> Blood in urine; difficult urination; mental depression; pain in lower back; pain or burning while urinating; sudden decrease in amount of urine

Rare
> Bloody or black, tarry stools; clumsiness or unsteadiness; confusion; convulsions (seizures); darkening of urine; fever; hives, itching of skin, skin rash, or sores; muscle weakness (severe); pale stools; ringing or buzzing in the ears; sore throat; trembling; unusual bruising or bleeding; yellow eyes or skin

Symptoms of too much potassium loss
> Dryness of mouth; increased thirst; irregular heartbeats; mood or mental changes; muscle cramps or pain; nausea or vomiting; unusual tiredness or weakness; weak pulse

Also, check with your doctor if you have any changes in your vision (especially problems with seeing faraway objects) when you first begin taking this medicine.

Other side effects may occur that usually do not need medical attention. These side effects may go away during treatment as your body adjusts to the medicine. However, check with your doctor if any of the following side effects continue or are bothersome:

More common
> Diarrhea; general feeling of discomfort or illness; increase in frequency of urination or amount of urine (rare with methazolamide); loss of appetite; metallic taste in mouth; nausea or vomiting; numbness, tingling, or burning in hands, fingers, feet, toes, mouth, lips, tongue, or anus; weight loss

Less common or rare
> Constipation; dizziness or lightheadedness; drowsiness; feeling of choking or lump in the throat; headache; increased sensitivity of eyes to sunlight; loss of taste and smell; nervousness or irritability

Other side effects not listed above may also occur in some patients. If you notice any other effects, check with your doctor.

Revised: 06/21/94
Interim revision: 01/24/95

CARBOPLATIN   Systemic

Commonly used brand name(s):

In the U.S.—
> Paraplatin

In Canada—
> Paraplatin
> Paraplatin-AQ

Description

Carboplatin (KAR-boe-pla-tin) belongs to the group of medicines known as alkylating agents. It is used to treat cancer of the ovaries. It may also be used to treat other kinds of cancer, as determined by your doctor.

Carboplatin interferes with the growth of cancer cells, which eventually are destroyed. Since the growth of normal body cells may also be affected by carboplatin, other effects also will occur. Some of these may be serious and must be reported to your doctor. Other effects may not be serious but may cause concern. Some effects may not occur until months or years after the medicine is used.

Before you begin treatment with carboplatin, you and your doctor should talk about the good this medicine will do as well as the risks of using it.

Carboplatin is to be administered only by or under the immediate supervision of your doctor. It is available in the following dosage form:

Parenteral
> • Injection (U.S. and Canada)

Before Using This Medicine

In deciding to use a medicine, the risks of taking the medicine must be weighed against the good it will do. This is a decision you and your doctor will make. For carboplatin, the following should be considered:

Allergies—Tell your doctor if you have ever had any unusual or allergic reaction to carboplatin, cisplatin, or any other platinum-containing substance.

Pregnancy—There is a chance that this medicine may cause birth defects if either the male or female is taking it at the time of conception or if it is taken during pregnancy. Carboplatin causes toxic or harmful effects and birth defects in rats. In addition, many cancer medicines may cause sterility that could be permanent. Although sterility has not been reported with this medicine, the possibility should be kept in mind.

Be sure that you have discussed these possible effects with your doctor before receiving this medicine. Before receiving carboplatin, make sure your doctor knows if you are pregnant or if you may become pregnant. It is best to use some kind of birth control while you are receiving carboplatin. Tell your doctor right away if you think you have become pregnant while receiving carboplatin.

Breast-feeding—Because carboplatin may cause serious side effects, breast-feeding generally is not recommended while you are receiving this medicine.

Children—Studies on this medicine have been done only in adult patients and there is no specific information comparing use of carboplatin in children with use in other age groups.

Older adults—Some side effects of carboplatin (especially blood problems or numbness or tingling in fingers or toes) may be more likely to occur in the elderly.

Other medicines—Although certain medicines should not be used together at all, in other cases two different medicines may be used together even if an interaction might occur. In these cases, your doctor may want to change the dose, or other precautions may be necessary. When receiving carboplatin it is especially important that your health care professional know if you are taking any of the following:

> • Amphotericin B by injection (e.g., Fungizone) or
> • Antithyroid agents (medicine for overactive thyroid) or
> • Azathioprine (e.g., Imuran) or
> • Chloramphenicol (e.g., Chloromycetin) or

- Colchicine or
- Flucytosine (e.g., Ancobon) or
- Ganciclovir (e.g., Cytovene) or
- Interferon (e.g., Intron A, Roferon-A) or
- Plicamycin (e.g., Mithracin) or
- Zidovudine (e.g., AZT; Retrovir)
- If you have ever been treated with radiation or cancer medicines—Carboplatin may increase the effects of these medicines or radiation therapy on the blood

Other medical problems— The presence of other medical problems may affect the use of carboplatin. Make sure you tell your doctor if you have any other medical problems, especially:

- Chickenpox (including recent exposure) or
- Herpes zoster (shingles)—Risk of severe disease affecting other parts of the body
- Hearing problems—May be worsened by carboplatin
- Infection—Carboplatin decreases your body's ability to fight infection
- Kidney disease—Effects may be increased because of slower removal from the body

Proper Use of This Medicine

This medicine is sometimes given together with certain other medicines. If you are using a combination of medicines, it is important that you receive each one at the proper time. If you are taking some of these medicines by mouth, ask your health care professional to help you plan a way to take them at the right times.

This medicine usually causes nausea and vomiting that sometimes may be severe. However, it is very important that you continue to receive the medicine, even if you begin to feel ill. Ask your health care professional for ways to lessen these effects, especially if they are severe.

Dosing— The dose of carboplatin will be different for different patients. The dose that is used may depend on a number of things, including what the medicine is being used for, the patient's size, and whether or not other medicines are also being taken. *If you are receiving carboplatin at home, follow your doctor's orders or the directions on the label.* If you have any questions about the proper dose of carboplatin, ask your doctor.

Precautions While Using This Medicine

It is very important that your doctor check your progress at regular visits to make sure that this medicine is working properly and to check for unwanted effects.

While you are being treated with carboplatin, and after you stop treatment with it, *do not have any immunizations (vaccinations) without your doctor's approval.* Carboplatin may lower your body's resistance and there is a chance you might get the infection the immunization is meant to prevent. In addition, other persons living in your household should not take oral polio vaccine since there is a chance they could pass the polio virus on to you. Also, avoid persons who have taken oral polio vaccine within the last several months. Do not get close to them, and do not stay in the same room with them for very long. If you cannot take these precautions, you should consider wearing a protective face mask that covers the nose and mouth.

Carboplatin can temporarily lower the number of white blood cells in your blood, increasing the chance of getting an infec-

tion. It can also lower the number of platelets, which are necessary for proper blood clotting. If this occurs, there are certain precautions you can take, especially when your blood count is low, to reduce the risk of infection or bleeding:

- If you can, avoid people with infections. *Check with your doctor immediately* if you think you are getting an infection or if you get a fever or chills, cough or hoarseness, lower back or side pain, or painful or difficult urination.
- *Check with your doctor immediately* if you notice any unusual bleeding or bruising; black, tarry stools; blood in urine or stools; or pinpoint red spots on your skin.
- Be careful when using a regular toothbrush, dental floss, or toothpick. Your medical doctor, dentist, or nurse may recommend other ways to clean your teeth and gums. Check with your health care professional before having any dental work done.
- Do not touch your eyes or the inside of your nose unless you have just washed your hands and have not touched anything else in the meantime.
- Be careful not to cut yourself when you are using sharp objects such as a safety razor or fingernail or toenail cutters.
- Avoid contact sports or other situations where bruising or injury could occur.

Side Effects of This Medicine

Along with its needed effects, a medicine may cause some unwanted effects. Although not all of these side effects may occur, if they do occur they may need medical attention.

Also, because of the way these medicines act on the body, there is a chance that they might cause other unwanted effects that may not occur until months or years after the medicine is used. These delayed effects may include certain types of cancer, such as leukemia. Discuss these possible effects with your doctor.

Check with your doctor as soon as possible if any of the following side effects occur:
More common
  Pain at place of injection

Less common
  Black, tarry stools; blood in urine or stools; cough or hoarseness, accompanied by fever or chills; fever or chills; lower back or side pain, accompanied by fever or chills; numbness or tingling in fingers or toes; painful or difficult urination, accompanied by fever or chills; pinpoint red spots on skin; skin rash or itching; unusual bleeding or bruising; unusual tiredness or weakness

Rare
  Blurred vision; ringing in ears; sores in mouth and on lips; wheezing

Other side effects may occur that usually do not need medical attention. These side effects may go away during treatment as your body adjusts to the medicine. Also, your health care professional may be able to tell you about ways to prevent or reduce some of these side effects. Check with your health care professional if any of the following side effects continue or are bothersome or if you have any questions about them:
More common
  Nausea and vomiting; unusual tiredness or weakness

Less common
  Constipation or diarrhea; loss of appetite

This medicine may cause a temporary loss of hair in some people. After treatment with carboplatin has ended, normal hair growth should return.

Other side effects not listed above may also occur in some patients. If you notice any other effects, check with your doctor.

Additional Information

Once a medicine has been approved for marketing for a certain use, experience may show that it is also useful for other medical problems. Although these uses are not included in product labeling, carboplatin is used in certain patients with the following medical conditions:

- Cancer of the bladder
- Cancer of the breast
- Cancer of the esophagus
- Cancers of the head and neck
- Cancer of the testicles (including seminoma)
- Cancer of the lung
- Cancer of the endometrium (the lining of the uterus)
- Cancer of unknown primary site
- Malignant melanoma (a certain type of skin cancer)
- Retinoblastoma (a certain type of eye cancer)
- Tumors in the brain

Other than the above information, there is no additional information relating to proper use, precautions, or side effects for these uses.

Revised: 01/09/2001

CARBOPROST Systemic

Commonly used brand name(s):

In the U.S.—
Hemabate

In Canada—
Prostin/15M

Description

Carboprost (KAR-boe-prost) is given by injection to cause abortion. It is an oxytocic, which means it acts by causing the uterus to contract the way it does during labor and also helps the cervix to dilate.

Carboprost may also be used for other purposes as determined by your doctor.

Carboprost is to be administered only by or under the immediate care of your doctor. It is available in the following dosage form:

Parenteral
- Injection (U.S. and Canada)

Before Receiving This Medicine

In deciding to use a medicine, the risks of taking the medicine must be weighed against the good it will do. This is a decision you and your doctor will make. For carboprost, the following should be considered:

Allergies—Tell your doctor if you have ever had any unusual or allergic reaction to carboprost or other oxytocics (medicines that stimulate the uterus to contract). Also tell your

health care professional if you are allergic to any other substances, such as foods, preservatives, or dyes.

Other medicines—Although certain medicines should not be used together at all, in other cases two different medicines may be used together even if an interaction might occur. In these cases, your doctor may want to change the dose, or other precautions may be necessary. Tell your doctor if you are taking any prescription or nonprescription (over-the-counter [OTC]) medicine.

Other medical problems—The presence of other medical problems may affect the use of carboprost. Make sure you tell your doctor if you have any other medical problems, especially:

- Adrenal gland disease (history of)—Carboprost stimulates the body to produce steroids
- Anemia—In some patients, abortion with carboprost may result in loss of blood that may require a transfusion
- Asthma (or history of) or
- Lung disease—Carboprost may cause narrowing of the blood vessels in the lungs or narrowing of the lung passages
- Diabetes mellitus (sugar diabetes) (history of)
- Epilepsy (or history of)—Rarely, seizures have occurred with use of carboprost
- Fibroid tumors of the uterus or
- Uterus surgery (history of)—There is an increased risk of rupture of the uterus
- Glaucoma—Rarely, the pressure within the eye has increased during use of carboprost
- Heart or blood vessel disease (or history of) or
- High blood pressure (or history of) or
- Low blood pressure (or history of)—Carboprost may cause changes in heart function or blood pressure changes
- Jaundice (history of)
- Kidney disease (or history of)
- Liver disease (or history of)—The body may not get carboprost out of the bloodstream at the usual rate, which may make the medicine work longer or cause toxic effects

Proper Use of This Medicine

Dosing—The dose of carboprost will be different for different patients. Your doctor will give you the dose of this medicine and follow your care in a hospital or another health care setting. The following information includes only the average doses of carboprost.

- For *injection* dosage form:
  —For causing an abortion in the second trimester of pregnancy (13th to 24th week):
    - Adults—At first, 100 to 250 micrograms (mcg) injected deep into a muscle. Then, 250 to 500 mcg every one and one-half to three and one-half hours for up to two days.
  —For bleeding of the uterus after pregnancy:
    - Adults—250 mcg injected deep into a muscle. Your doctor may repeat this dose every fifteen to ninety minutes as needed.

Side Effects of This Medicine

Along with its needed effects, a medicine may cause some unwanted effects. Although not all of these side effects may occur, if they do occur they may need medical attention.

Tell the health care professional immediately if any of the following side effects occur:

Less common or rare

Fast or slow heartbeat; headache (severe and continuing); hives or skin rash; increased pain of the uterus; pale, cool, blotchy skin on arms or legs; pressing or painful feeling in chest; shortness of breath; swelling of face, inside the nose, and eyelids; tightness in chest; trouble in breathing; weak or absent pulse in arms or legs; wheezing

Check with the health care professional as soon as possible if any of the following side effects occur:

Constipation; pain or inflammation at place of injection; tender or mildly bloated abdomen or stomach

Other side effects may occur that usually do not need medical attention. These side effects usually go away after the medicine is stopped. However, let the health care professional know if any of the following side effects continue or are bothersome:

More common

Diarrhea; nausea; vomiting

Less common or rare

Chills or shivering; dizziness; fever (temporary); flushing or redness of face; headache; stomach cramps or pain

This procedure may result in some effects, which occur after the procedure is completed, that need medical attention. Check with your doctor if you notice any of the following:

Chills or shivering (continuing); fever (continuing); foul-smelling vaginal discharge; increase in uterus bleeding; pain in lower abdomen

Other side effects not listed above may also occur in some patients. If you notice any other effects, check with your health care professional.

Revised: 10/26/92
Interim revision: 06/08/94

CARMUSTINE   Implantation-Local

Commonly used brand name(s):

In the U.S.—
Gliadel Wafer

Another commonly used name is BCNU.

Description

Carmustine (kar-MUS-teen) belongs to the group of medicines known as alkylating agents. It is used to treat certain types of brain cancer.

Carmustine interferes with the growth of cancer cells, which are eventually destroyed. Since the growth of normal body cells may also be affected by carmustine, other effects may also occur.

This medicine is available only with your doctor's prescription, in the following dosage form(s):

Implantation
• Implants (U.S.)

Before Using This Medicine

In deciding to use a medicine, the risks of using the medicine must be weighed against the good it will do. This is a decision you and your doctor will make. For carmustine, the following should be considered:

Allergies—Tell your doctor if you have ever had any unusual or allergic reaction to carmustine. Also tell your health care professional if you are allergic to any other substances, such as foods, preservatives, or dyes.

Pregnancy—The implanted dosage form of carmustine has not been studied in pregnant women or animals. However, studies in animals have shown that carmustine in other dosage forms causes birth defects and other problems. Be sure that you have discussed this before receiving this medicine. Tell your doctor right away if you think you have become pregnant while receiving carmustine.

Breast-feeding—It is not known if carmustine or the components of the wafer pass into the breast milk. However, carmustine is not recommended during breast-feeding, because it may cause unwanted effects in nursing babies.

Children—Studies on this medicine have been done only in adult patients, and there is no specific information comparing use of carmustine in children with use in other age groups.

Older adults—Many medicines have not been studied specifically in older people. Therefore, it may not be known whether they work exactly the same way they do in younger adults or if they cause different side effects or problems in older people. There is no specific information comparing use of carmustine in the elderly with its use in younger adults.

Other medicines—Although certain medicines should not be used together at all, in other cases two different medicines may be used together even if an interaction might occur. In these cases, your doctor may want to change the dose, or other precautions may be necessary. Tell your health care professional if you are taking any other prescription or nonprescription (over-the-counter [OTC]) medicine.

Other medical problems—The presence of other medical problems may affect the use of carmustine. Make sure you tell your doctor if you have any other medical problems.

Precautions While Using This Medicine

It is important that your doctor check your progress at regular visits to make sure this medicine is working properly and to check for unwanted effects.

Side Effects of This Medicine

Along with its needed effects, a medicine may cause some unwanted effects. Although not all of these side effects may occur, if they do occur they may need medical attention.

Check with your doctor as soon as possible if any of the following side effects occur:

More common

Blood in urine; burning, painful, or difficult urination; convulsions (seizures); fever; inability to move legs or arms; lower back or side pain

Less common
> Confusion; extremely severe sleepiness; headache; nausea and vomiting; pain; problems in speaking; rash; stiff neck

Other side effects may occur that usually do not need medical attention. These side effects may go away during treatment as your body adjusts to the medicine. However, check with your doctor if any of the following side effects continue or are bothersome:

More common
> Drowsiness

Other side effects not listed above may also occur in some patients. If you notice any other effects, check with your doctor.

Developed: 08/12/98

CARMUSTINE   Systemic

Commonly used brand name(s):

In the U.S.—
> BiCNU

In Canada—
> BiCNU

Another commonly used name is BCNU.

Description

Carmustine (kar-MUS-teen) belongs to the group of medicines known as alkylating agents. It is used to treat cancer of the lymph system, cancerous brain tumors, and a certain type of cancer in the bone marrow. It may also be used to treat other kinds of cancer, as determined by your doctor.

Carmustine interferes with the growth of cancer cells, which are eventually destroyed. Since the growth of normal body cells may also be affected by carmustine, other effects will also occur. Some of these may be serious and must be reported to your doctor. Other effects, like hair loss, may not be serious but may cause concern. Some effects may not occur for months or years after the medicine is used.

Before you begin treatment with carmustine, you and your doctor should talk about the good this medicine will do as well as the risks of using it.

Carmustine is to be administered only by or under the immediate supervision of your doctor. It is available in the following dosage form:

Parenteral
- Injection (U.S. and Canada)

Before Using This Medicine

In deciding to use a medicine, the risks of taking the medicine must be weighed against the good it will do. This is a decision you and your doctor will make. For carmustine, the following should be considered:

Allergies — Tell your doctor if you have ever had any unusual or allergic reaction to carmustine.

Pregnancy — There is a chance that this medicine may cause birth defects if either the male or female is taking it at the time of conception or if it is taken during pregnancy. Carmustine causes toxic or harmful effects in the fetus of rats and rabbits and causes birth defects in rats at doses about the same as the human dose. In addition, many cancer medicines may cause sterility which could be permanent. Although this has only been reported in animals with this medicine, the possibility should be kept in mind.

Be sure that you have discussed this with your doctor before receiving this medicine. It is best to use some kind of birth control while you are receiving carmustine. Tell your doctor right away if you think you have become pregnant while receiving carmustine.

Breast-feeding — Because carmustine may cause serious side effects, breast-feeding is generally not recommended while you are receiving it.

Children — Although there is no specific information comparing use of carmustine in children with use in other age groups, this medicine is not expected to cause different side effects or problems in children than it does in adults.

Older adults — Many medicines have not been studied specifically in older people. Therefore, it may not be known whether they work exactly the same way they do in younger adults or if they cause different side effects or problems in older people. There is no specific information comparing use of carmustine in the elderly with use in other age groups.

Other medicines — Although certain medicines should not be used together at all, in other cases two different medicines may be used together even if an interaction might occur. In these cases, your doctor may want to change the dose, or other precautions may be necessary. When you are receiving carmustine, it is especially important that your health care professional know if you are taking any of the following:

- Amphotericin B by injection (e.g., Fungizone) or
- Antithyroid agents (medicine for overactive thyroid) or
- Azathioprine (e.g., Imuran) or
- Chloramphenicol (e.g., Chloromycetin) or
- Colchicine or
- Flucytosine (e.g., Ancobon) or
- Ganciclovir (e.g., Cytovene) or
- Interferon (e.g., Intron A, Roferon-A) or
- Plicamycin (e.g., Mithramycin) or
- Zidovudine (e.g., AZT, Retrovir) or
- If you have ever been treated with radiation or cancer medicines—Carmustine may increase the effects of these medicines or radiation therapy on the blood

Other medical problems — The presence of other medical problems may affect the use of carmustine. Make sure you tell your doctor if you have any other medical problems, especially:

- Chickenpox (including recent exposure) or
- Herpes zoster (shingles)—Risk of severe disease affecting other parts of the body
- Infection—Carmustine decreases your body's ability to fight infection
- Kidney disease—Effects of carmustine may be increased because of slower removal from the body
- Liver disease—Carmustine may cause side effects to the liver
- Lung disease—Risk of lung problems caused by carmustine may be increased

Smoking—Increased risk of lung problems.

Proper Use of This Medicine

Carmustine is sometimes given together with certain other medicines. If you are using a combination of medicines, it is important that you receive each one at the proper time. If you are taking some of these medicines by mouth, ask your health care professional to help you plan a way to take them at the right times.

This medicine often causes nausea and vomiting, which usually last no longer than 4 to 6 hours. It is very important that you continue to receive the medicine, even if you begin to feel ill. Ask your health care professional for ways to lessen these effects.

Dosing—The dose of carmustine will be different for different patients. The dose that is used may depend on a number of things, including what the medicine is being used for, the patient's size, and whether or not other medicines are also being taken. *If you are receiving carmustine at home, follow your doctor's orders or the directions on the label.* If you have any questions about the proper dose of carmustine, ask your doctor.

Precautions While Using This Medicine

It is very important that your doctor check your progress at regular visits to make sure that this medicine is working properly and to check for unwanted effects.

While you are being treated with carmustine, and after you stop treatment with it, *do not have any immunizations (vaccinations) without your doctor's approval.* Carmustine may lower your body's resistance and there is a chance you might get the infection the immunization is meant to prevent. In addition, other persons living in your household should not take oral polio vaccine since there is a chance they could pass the polio virus on to you. Also, avoid persons who have taken oral polio vaccine within the last several months. Do not get close to them, and do not stay in the same room with them for very long. If you cannot take these precautions, you should consider wearing a protective face mask that covers the nose and mouth.

Carmustine can temporarily lower the number of white blood cells in your blood, increasing the chance of getting an infection. It can also lower the number of platelets, which are necessary for proper blood clotting. If this occurs, there are certain precautions you can take, especially when your blood count is low, to reduce the risk of infection or bleeding:

- If you can, avoid people with infections. *Check with your doctor immediately* if you think you are getting an infection or if you get a fever or chills, cough or hoarseness, lower back or side pain, or painful or difficult urination.
- *Check with your doctor immediately* if you notice any unusual bleeding or bruising; black, tarry stools; blood in urine or stools; or pinpoint red spots on your skin.
- Be careful when using a regular toothbrush, dental floss, or toothpick. Your medical doctor, dentist, or nurse may recommend other ways to clean your teeth and gums. Check with your medical doctor before having any dental work done.
- Do not touch your eyes or the inside of your nose unless you have just washed your hands and have not touched anything else in the meantime.

- Be careful not to cut yourself when you are using sharp objects such as a safety razor or fingernail or toenail cutters.
- Avoid contact sports or other situations where bruising or injury could occur.

If carmustine accidentally seeps out of the vein into which it is injected, it may damage some tissues and cause scarring. *Tell the doctor or nurse right away if you notice redness, pain, or swelling at the place of injection.*

Side Effects of This Medicine

Along with its needed effects, a medicine may cause some unwanted effects. Some side effects will have signs or symptoms that you can see or feel. Your doctor may watch for others by doing certain tests. Some of the unwanted effects that may be caused by carmustine are listed below. Although not all of these effects may occur, if they do occur, they may need medical attention.

Also, because of the way these medicines act on the body, there is a chance that they might cause other unwanted effects that may not occur until months or years after the medicine is used. These delayed effects may include certain types of cancer, such as leukemia. Discuss these possible effects with your doctor.

Check with your doctor or nurse immediately if any of the following side effects occur:
> *More common*
>> Cough; pain or redness at place of injection; shortness of breath
>
> *Less common*
>> Black, tarry stools; blood in urine or stools; cough or hoarseness, accompanied by fever or chills; fever or chills; lower back or side pain, accompanied by fever or chills; painful or difficult urination, accompanied by fever or chills; pinpoint red spots on skin; unusual bleeding or bruising
>
> *Rare*
>> Decrease in urination; swelling of feet or lower legs

Check with your health care professional as soon as possible if any of the following side effects occur:
> *Less common*
>> Flushing of face; sores in mouth and on lips; unusual tiredness or weakness

This medicine may also cause the following side effects that your doctor will watch for:
> *More common*
>> Low red blood cell count; low white blood cell count; lung problems
>
> *Rare*
>> Liver problems

Other side effects may occur that usually do not need medical attention. These side effects may go away during treatment as your body adjusts to the medicine. Also, your health care professional may be able to tell you about ways to prevent or reduce some of these side effects. Check with your health care professional if any of the following side effects continue or are bothersome or if you have any questions about them:
> *More common*
>> Nausea and vomiting (usually lasting no longer than 4 to 6 hours)

Less common
> Diarrhea; discoloration of skin along vein of injection; dizziness; loss of appetite; skin rash and itching; trouble in swallowing; trouble in walking

This medicine may cause a temporary loss of hair in some people. After treatment with carmustine has ended, normal hair growth should return.

Side effects that affect your lungs (for example, cough and shortness of breath) may be more likely to occur if you smoke.

After you stop receiving carmustine, it may still produce some side effects that need attention. During this period of time check with your health care professional if you notice any of the following:

> Black, tarry stools; blood in urine or stools; cough or hoarseness, accompanied by fever or chills; fever or chills; lower back or side pain, accompanied by fever or chills; painful or difficult urination, accompanied by fever or chills; pinpoint red spots on skin; shortness of breath; unusual bleeding or bruising

Other side effects not listed above may also occur in some patients. If you notice any other effects, check with your health care professional.

Additional Information

Once a medicine has been approved for marketing for a certain use, experience may show that it is also useful for other medical problems. Although these uses are not included in product labeling, carmustine is used in certain patients with the following conditions:

- Cancer of the colon and rectum
- Cancer of the stomach
- Malignant melanoma (a type of skin cancer)
- Mycosis fungoides (tumors on the skin)
- Waldenström's macroglobulinemia (a certain type of cancer of the blood)

Other than the above information, there is no additional information relating to proper use, precautions, or side effects for these uses.

Revised: 07/15/94; 08/14/98

CARVEDILOL   Systemic

Commonly used brand name(s):

In the U.S.—
Coreg

Description

Carvedilol (KAR-ve-dil-ole) belongs to a group of medicines called beta-adrenergic blocking agents, beta-blocking agents, or, more commonly, beta-blockers. Beta-blockers work by affecting the response to some nerve impulses in certain parts of the body. As a result, they decrease the heart's need for blood and oxygen by reducing its workload. They also help the heart to beat more regularly.

Carvedilol is used to treat high blood pressure (hypertension). High blood pressure adds to the workload of the heart and arteries. If it continues for a long time, the heart and arteries may not function properly. This can damage the blood vessels of the brain, heart, and kidneys, resulting in a stroke, heart failure, or kidney failure. High blood pressure may also increase the risk of heart attacks. These problems may be less likely to occur if blood pressure is controlled.

Carvedilol also is used to prevent further worsening of congestive heart failure. Carvedilol may also be used for other conditions as determined by your doctor.

This medicine is available only with your doctor's prescription, in the following dosage form(s):

Oral
- Tablets (U.S.)

Before Using This Medicine

In deciding to use a medicine, the risks of taking the medicine must be weighed against the good it will do. This is a decision you and your doctor will make. For carvedilol, the following should be considered:

Allergies—Tell your doctor if you have ever had any unusual or allergic reaction to carvedilol. Also tell your health care professional if you are allergic to any other substances, such as foods, preservatives, or dyes.

Pregnancy—Carvedilol has not been studied in pregnant women. However, studies in animals have shown that large doses of carvedilol can cause decreased body weight and skeletal problems in rat fetuses. Before taking this medicine, make sure your doctor knows if you are pregnant or may become pregnant.

Breast-feeding—It is not known if carvedilol passes into breast milk; however, it passes into the milk of lactating rats. Because nursing infants may have a serious reaction to carvedilol, breast-feeding is not recommended in women who are taking this medicine.

Children—Studies on this medicine have been done only in adult patients, and there is no specific information comparing use of carvedilol in children with use in other age groups.

Older adults—Although this medicine has not been shown to cause different side effects or problems in older people than it does in younger adults, blood levels of carvedilol may be increased in the elderly. Elderly patients also may experience dizziness more frequently than will younger adults.

Other medicines—Although certain medicines should not be used together at all, in other cases two different medicines may be used together even if an interaction might occur. In these cases, your doctor may want to change the dose, or other precautions may be necessary. When you are taking carvedilol, it is especially important that your health care professional know if you are taking any of the following:

- Antidiabetic agents, sulfonylurea (acetohexamide [e.g., Dymelor], chlorpropamide [e.g., Diabinese], gliclazide [e.g., Diamicron], glipizide [e.g., Glucotrol], glyburide [e.g., DiaBeta, Glynase, or Micronase], tolazamide [e.g., Tolinase], or tolbutamide [e.g., Orinase]) or
- Insulin—Carvedilol may further decrease blood sugar levels
- Calcium channel blocking agents, especially diltiazem (e.g., Cardizem) or verapamil (e.g., Calan)—Carvedilol may make side effects of these medicines worse

Other medical problems—The presence of other medical problems may affect the use of carvedilol. Make sure you

tell your doctor if you have any other medical problems, especially:

- Allergic reaction, severe (that involved facial swelling and/or difficulty breathing), history of or
- Asthma or
- Related bronchospastic conditions, other—Carvedilol may cause a greater reaction to substances that aggravate these conditions and less of a response to treatment of the reaction
- Angina (severe chest pain)—Carvedilol may provoke chest pain
- Bronchial conditions, nonallergic or
- Bronchitis, chronic or
- Emphysema—Carvedilol may aggravate these conditions
- Bradycardia (unusually slow heartbeat) or other heart rate problems or
- Heart or blood vessel disease—Carvedilol may make problems resulting from these conditions worse
- Diabetes mellitus (sugar diabetes) or
- Low blood sugar (hypoglycemia)—Carvedilol may aggravate low blood sugar (hypoglycemia) levels caused by insulin and may delay recovery of blood sugar levels; in patients with diabetes and heart failure, carvedilol may further increase blood sugar levels; in addition, if your diabetes medicine causes your blood sugar to be too low, beta-blockers may cover up some of the symptoms (fast heartbeat)
- Kidney disease or
- Liver disease—Effects of carvedilol may be increased because of slower removal from the body
- Overactive thyroid—Carvedilol may cover up symptoms of this condition, such as a fast heartbeat; suddenly stopping carvedilol may provoke symptoms of this condition

Proper Use of This Medicine

Take this medicine exactly as directed. This medicine works best if you take it at the same time each day; however, do not take more of this medicine and do not take it more often than your doctor ordered. Do not miss any doses.

Take this medicine with food.

Do not interrupt or stop taking this medicine without first checking with your doctor. Your doctor may want you to reduce gradually the amount you are taking before stopping completely. Some conditions may become worse when the medicine is stopped suddenly, which can be dangerous.

Dosing—The dose of carvedilol will be different for different patients. *Follow your doctor's orders or the directions on the label.* The following information includes only the average doses of carvedilol. *If your dose is different, do not change it* unless your doctor tells you to do so.

The number of tablets that you take depends on the strength of the medicine. Also, *the number of doses you take each day, the time allowed between doses, and the length of time you take the medicine depend on the medical problem for which you are taking carvedilol.*

- For *oral* dosage form (tablets):
  —Congestive heart failure:
  - Adults—3.125 mg two times a day, taken with food. Your doctor may increase your dose if needed.

  - Children—Use and dose must be determined by your doctor.
  —Hypertension:
  - Adults—6.25 mg two times a day, taken with food. Your doctor may increase your dose if needed.
  - Children—Use and dose must be determined by your doctor.

Missed dose—If you miss a dose of this medicine, take it as soon as possible. However, if it is almost time for your next dose, skip the missed dose and go back to your regular dosing schedule. Do not double doses.

Storage—To store this medicine:
- Keep out of the reach of children.
- Store away from heat and direct light.
- Do not store in the bathroom, near the kitchen sink, or in other damp places. Heat or moisture may cause the medicine to break down.
- Do not keep outdated medicine or medicine no longer needed. Be sure that any discarded medicine is out of the reach of children.

Precautions While Using This Medicine

It is important that your doctor check your progress at regular visits. This is to make sure the medicine is working for you and to allow the dosage to be changed if needed.

Do not take other medicines unless they have been discussed with your doctor.

This medicine may cause dizziness, lightheadedness, or fainting. Make sure you know how you react to this medicine before you drive, use machines, or do anything else that could be dangerous if you experience these effects.

Dizziness, lightheadedness, or fainting can also occur when standing quickly. Sitting or lying down may help alleviate these effects.

Check with your doctor if you become dizzy or if you faint. Your dosage may need to be adjusted.

Before having any kind of surgery (including dental surgery) or emergency treatment, tell the medical doctor or dentist in charge that you are taking this medicine.

For *diabetic patients:*
- *This medicine may cause changes in your blood sugar levels.* Also, *this medicine may cover up signs of hypoglycemia (low blood sugar),* such as a rapid pulse rate. Check with your physician if you experience these problems.

For *congestive heart failure patients:*
- Check with your physician if you experience weight gain or increased shortness of breath. These may be signs of a worsening of your condition.

For *patients who wear contact lenses:*
- Carvedilol may cause your eyes to form tears less than they do normally. Check with your physician if you experience dry eyes.

Side Effects of This Medicine

Along with its needed effects, a medicine may cause some unwanted effects. Although not all of these side effects may occur, if they do occur they may need medical attention.

Check with your doctor as soon as possible if any of the following side effects occur:

More common

Allergy; chest pain; dizziness, lightheadedness or fainting; pain; shortness of breath; slow heartbeat; generalized swelling or swelling of feet, ankles or lower legs; weight gain

Less common

Blood in urine; fever; itching, dark urine, decreased appetite, yellow eyes or skin, flu-like symptoms, and/ or tenderness on upper right side of body; mental depression; unusual bleeding or bruising

Other side effects may occur that usually do not need medical attention. These side effects may go away during treatment as your body adjusts to the medicine. However, check with your doctor if any of the following side effects continue or are bothersome:

More common

Back pain; diarrhea; prickling or tingling sensation; unusual tiredness or weakness

Less common

Abdominal pain; blurred vision; decreased tearing; headache; increased sweating; joint or muscle pain; nausea; sore throat; stuffy or runny nose; trouble sleeping; vomiting

Other side effects not listed above may also occur in some patients. If you notice any other effects, check with your doctor.

Developed: 08/13/98

CASPOFUNGIN   Systemic— INTRODUCTORY VERSION

Commonly used brand name(s):

In the U.S.—
Cancidas

Description

Caspofungin (kas-poe-FUN-jin) is an antifungal. It is used to help the body overcome serious fungus infections.

This medicine is available only with your doctor's prescription, in the following dosage form:

Parenteral
Injection (U.S.)

Before Using This Medicine

In deciding to use a medicine, the risks of taking the medicine must be weighed against the good it will do. This is a decision you and your doctor will make. For caspofungin, the following should be considered:

Allergies—Tell your doctor if you have ever had any unusual or allergic reaction to caspofungin. Also tell your health care professional if you are allergic to any other substances, such as foods, preservatives, or dyes.

Pregnancy— Caspofungin has not been studied in pregnant women. However, studies in animals have shown that caspofungin causes birth defects or other problems. Before taking this medicine, make sure your doctor knows if you are pregnant or if you may become pregnant.

Breast-feeding—It is not known whether caspofungin passes into breast milk. Although most medicines pass into breast milk in small amounts, many of them may be used safely while breast-feeding. Mothers who are taking this medicine and who wish to breast-feed should discuss this with their doctor.

Children—Studies on this medicine have been done only in adult patients, and there is no specific information comparing the use of caspofungin in children with use in other age groups.

Older adults—Many medicines have not been studied specifically in older people. Therefore, it may not be known whether they work exactly the same way they do in younger adults. Although there is no specific information comparing use of caspofungin in the elderly with use in other age groups, this medicine is not expected to cause different side effects or problems in older people than it does in younger adults.

Other medicines—Although certain medicines should not be used together at all, in other cases two different medicines may be used together even if an interaction might occur. In these cases, your doctor may want to change the dose or other precautions may be necessary. When you are taking caspofungin, it is especially important that your health care professional knows if you are taking any of the following:

- Cyclosporine (e.g., Sandimmune, Neoral)— Use of caspofungin with this medicine may increase the chance of liver problems
- Tacrolimus (e.g., Prograf)—Use of caspofungin may decrease the effects of tacrolimus by decreasing the amount of this medicine in the body; it may be necessary for your doctor to change your dose of tacrolimus

Other medical problems—The presence of other medical problems may affect the use of caspofungin. Make sure you tell your doctor if you have any other medical problems, especially:

- Liver disease, moderate to severe—Higher blood levels of caspofungin may result, increasing the chance of side effects

Proper Use of This Medicine

Dosing—The dose of caspofungin will be different for different patients. The following information includes only the average doses of caspofungin.

- For *injection* dosage form:
  —Adults: At first, the dose is 70 milligrams (mg) injected into a vein. After that, the dose is 50 mg a day injected into a vein.
  —Children: Use and dose must be determined by your doctor.

Side Effects of This Medicine

Along with its needed effects, a medicine may cause some unwanted effects. Although not all of these side effects may occur, if they do occur they may need medical attention.

Check with your doctor as soon as possible if any of the following side effects occur:

Less common

Pain or redness at site of injection

Other side effects may occur that usually do not need medical attention. These side effects may go away during treatment as your body adjusts to the medicine. However, check with your doctor if any of the following side effects continue or are bothersome.

Less common
    Fever; flushing or redness of skin; nausea; vomiting

Other side effects not listed above may also occur in some patients. If you notice any other effects, check with your doctor.

Revised: 03/19/2001

CELECOXIB   Systemic

Commonly used brand name(s):

In the U.S.—
    Celebrex

Description

Celecoxib (sell–a–COKS–ib) is used to relieve some symptoms caused by arthritis, such as inflammation, swelling, stiffness, and joint pain. However, this medicine does not cure arthritis and will help you only as long as you continue to take it.

This medicine is available only with your doctor's prescription, in the following dosage form(s):

Oral
    • Capsules (U.S.)

Before Using This Medicine

In deciding to use a medicine, the risks of taking the medicine must be weighed against the good it will do. This is a decision you and your doctor will make. For celecoxib, the following should be considered:

Allergies—Tell your doctor if you have ever had any unusual or allergic reaction to celecoxib, other nonsteroidal anti-inflammatory drugs, aspirin or other salicylates, or sulfonamide-type medicines. Also tell your health care professional if you are allergic to any other substances, such as foods, preservatives, or dyes.

Pregnancy—Celecoxib has not been studied in pregnant women. However, there is a chance that this medicine may cause unwanted effects on the heart or blood flow of the fetus or newborn baby if it is taken regularly during the last few months of pregnancy. Studies in animals have shown that celecoxib has caused birth defects of the ribs and sternebrae. Before taking this medicine, make sure your doctor knows if you are pregnant or if you may become pregnant.

Breast-feeding—It is not known whether celecoxib passes into breast milk. However, celecoxib may cause unwanted effects in nursing babies. It may be necessary for you to take another medicine or to stop breast-feeding during treatment. Be sure you have discussed the risks and benefits of the medicine with your doctor.

Children—Studies on this medicine have been done only in adult patients, and there is no specific information comparing the use of celecoxib in children with use in older age groups.

Older adults—This medicine has been tested in a limited number of elderly patients 65 years of age and older and has not been shown to cause different side effects or problems in older people than it does in younger adults. However, elderly patients may be more sensitive to the side effects of celecoxib.

Other medicines—Although certain medicines should not be used together at all, in other cases two different medicines may be used together even if an interaction might occur. In these cases, your doctor may want to change the dose, or other precautions may be necessary. When you are taking celecoxib, it is especially important that your health care professional know if you are taking any of the following:
    • Aspirin or
    • Fluconazole (e.g., Diflucan)—The chance of serious side effects may be increased
    • Lithium (e.g., Lithane)—Higher blood levels of celecoxib and an increased chance of side effects may occur

Other medical problems—The presence of other medical problems may affect the use of celecoxib. Make sure you tell your doctor if you have any other medical problems, especially:
    • Alcohol abuse or
    • Bleeding problems or
    • Stomach ulcer or other stomach or intestinal problems or
    • Tobacco use (or recent history of)—The chance of side effects may be increased
    • Anemia or
    • Asthma or
    • Dehydration or
    • Fluid retention (swelling of feet or lower legs) or
    • Heart disease or
    • High blood pressure or
    • Kidney disease or
    • Liver disease—Celecoxib may make these conditions worse

Proper Use of This Medicine

For safe and effective use of this medicine, do not take more of it, do not take it more often, and do not take it for a longer time than ordered by your health care professional. Taking too much of this medicine may increase the chance of unwanted effects.

Dosing—The dose of celecoxib will be different for different patients. *Follow your doctor's orders or the directions on the label.* The following information includes only the average doses of celecoxib. *If your dose is different, do not change it* unless your doctor tells you to do so.

The number of capsules that you take depends on the strength of the medicine. Also, *the number of doses you take each day, the time allowed between doses, and the length of time you take the medicine depend on the medical problem for which you are taking celecoxib.*
    • For *oral* dosage form (capsules):
        —For rheumatoid arthritis:
            • Adults— 100 to 200 mg twice a day.
            • Children—Use and dose must be determined by your doctor.

—For osteoarthritis:
- Adults— 200 mg a day as a single dose or 100 mg twice day.
- Children—Use and dose must be determined by your doctor.

Missed dose—If your health care professional has ordered you to take this medicine according to a regular schedule, and you miss a dose, take it as soon as you remember. However, if it is almost time for your next dose, skip the next dose and go back to your regular dosing schedule. Do not double doses.

Storage—To store this medicine:
- Keep out of the reach of children.
- Do not store in the bathroom, near the kitchen sink, or in other damp places. Heat or moisture may cause the medicine to break down.
- Do not keep outdated medicine or medicine no longer needed. Be sure that any discarded medicine is out of the reach of children.

Precautions While Using This Medicine

If you will be taking this medicine for a long time, your doctor should check your progress at regular visits.

Stomach problems may be more likely to occur if you drink alcoholic beverages while being treated with this medicine. Therefore, *do not regularly drink alcoholic beverages while taking this medicine,* unless otherwise directed by your doctor.

Taking two or more of the nonsteroidal anti-inflammatory drugs together on a regular basis may increase the chance of unwanted effects. Also, taking acetaminophen, aspirin or other salicylates, or ketorolac (e.g., Toradol) regularly while you are taking a nonsteroidal anti-inflammatory drug may increase the chance of unwanted effects. The risk will depend on how much of each medicine you take every day, and on how long you take the medicines together. If your health care professional directs you to take these medicines together on a regular basis, follow his or her directions carefully. However, *do not take acetaminophen or aspirin or other salicylates together with this medicine for more than a few days, and do not take any ketorolac (e.g., Toradol) while you are taking this medicine,* unless your doctor has directed you to do so and is following your progress.

Serious side effects can occur during treatment with this medicine. Sometimes serious side effects can occur without any warning. However, possible warning signs often occur, including swelling of the face, fingers, feet, and/or lower legs; severe stomach pain, black, tarry stools, and/or vomiting of blood or material that looks like coffee grounds; unusual weight gain; and/or skin rash. *Stop taking this medicine and check with your doctor immediately if you notice any of these warning signs.*

Check with your doctor immediately if fever, drowsiness, itching of the skin, tiredness, nausea, or stomach pain occurs; these effects may be the first signs of liver toxicity.

Celecoxib may cause a serious type of allergic reaction called anaphylaxis. Although this is rare, it may occur often in patients who are allergic to aspirin, other nonsteroidal anti-inflammatory drugs, or sulfonamide-type drugs. *Anaphylaxis requires immediate medical attention.* The most serious signs of this reaction are very fast or irregular breathing, gasping for breath, wheezing, or fainting. Other signs may include changes in color of the skin of the face; very fast but irregular heartbeat or pulse; hive-like swellings on the skin; and puffiness or swellings of the eyelids or around the eyes. If these effects occur, get emergency help at once. Ask someone to drive you to the nearest hospital emergency room. If this is not possible, do not try to drive yourself. Call an ambulance, lie down, cover yourself to keep warm, and prop your feet higher than your head. Stay in that position until help arrives.

Side Effects of This Medicine

Along with its needed effects, a medicine may cause some unwanted effects. Although not all of these side effects may occur, if they do occur they may need medical attention.

Check with your doctor as soon as possible if any of the following side effects occur:
More common
   Cough; fever; skin rash; sneezing; sore throat; swelling of face, fingers, feet, and/or lower legs

Less common or rare
   Bloody or black tarry stools; burning feeling in chest or stomach; chills; congestion in chest; cough; diarrhea; fatigue; fever; loss of appetite; muscle aches and pains; nausea; shortness of breath; stomach pain (severe); tenderness in stomach area; unusual weight gain; vomiting of blood or material that looks like coffee grounds; weakness

Symptoms of overdose
   Bloody or black, tarry stools; continuing thirst; dizziness; drowsiness; headache, severe or continuing; nausea and/or vomiting; shortness of breath; stomach pain; sudden decrease in the amount of urine; swelling of face, fingers, and/or lower legs; tightness in chest and/or wheezing; troubled breathing; unusual tiredness or weakness; vomiting of blood or material that looks like coffee grounds; weight gain

Other side effects may occur that usually do not need medical attention. These side effects may go away during treatment as your body adjusts to the medicine. However, check with your doctor if any of the following side effects continue or are bothersome:
More common
   Back pain; dizziness; gas; headache; heartburn; inability to sleep; nausea; pain or burning in throat; stomach pain; stuffy or runny nose

Less common
   Anxiety; blurred vision; buzzing or ringing noise in ears; change in sense of taste; constipation; decreased appetite; depression; difficulty swallowing; dry mouth; fast heartbeat; increased sweating; joint or muscle pain or stiffness; loss of energy or weakness; nervousness; numbness or tingling in fingers and/or toes; pain or burning in throat; pounding heartbeat; sleepiness; sudden sweating and feelings of warmth; unusual tiredness; vomiting

Other side effects not listed above may also occur in some patients. If you notice any other effects, check with your doctor.

Developed: 04/16/1999
Revised: 03/03/2000

CEPHALOSPORINS Systemic

Commonly used brand name(s):

In the U.S.—

Ancef[4]	Keftab[20]
Ceclor[1]	Kefurox[19]
Ceclor CD[1]	Kefzol[4]
Cedax[16]	Mandol[3]
Cefadyl[22]	Maxipime[6]
Cefizox[17]	Mefoxin[12]
Cefobid[9]	Monocid[8]
Cefotan[11]	Omnicef[5]
Ceftin[19]	Rocephin[18]
Cefzil[14]	Suprax[7]
Ceptaz[15]	Tazicef[15]
Claforan[10]	Tazidime[15]
Duricef[2]	Vantin[13]
Fortaz[15]	Velosef[23]
Keflex[20]	Zinacef[19]

In Canada—

Ancef[4]	Keflin[21]
Apo-Cefaclor[1]	Kefurox[19]
Apo-Cephalex[20]	Kefzol[4]
Ceclor[1]	Mandol[3]
Cefizox[17]	Maxipime[6]
Cefotan[11]	Mefoxin[12]
Ceftin[19]	Novo-Lexin[20]
Cefzil[14]	Nu-Cephalex[20]
Ceporacin[21]	PMS-Cephalexin[20]
Ceptaz[15]	Rocephin[18]
Claforan[10]	Suprax[7]
Duricef[2]	Tazidime[15]
Fortaz[15]	Zinacef[19]
Keflex[20]	

Note: For quick reference, the following cephalosporins are numbered to match the corresponding brand names.

This information applies to the following medicines:

1. Cefaclor (SEF-a-klor) ‡
2. Cefadroxil (sef-a-DROX-ill) ‡
3. Cefamandole (sef-a-MAN-dole)
4. Cefazolin (sef-A-zoe-lin) ‡§
5. Cefdinir (sef–DI–neer) ‡
6. Cefepime (SEF-e-pim)
7. Cefixime (sef-IX-eem)
8. Cefonicid (se-FON-i-sid) †
9. Cefoperazone (sef-oh-PER-a-zone) †
10. Cefotaxime (sef-oh-TAKS-eem)
11. Cefotetan (SEF-oh-tee-tan)
12. Cefoxitin (se-FOX-i-tin)
13. Cefpodoxime (sef-pode-OX-eem) †
14. Cefprozil (sef-PROE-zil)
15. Ceftazidime (SEF-tay-zi-deem)
16. Ceftibuten (sef-TYE-byoo-ten) †
17. Ceftizoxime (sef-ti-ZOX-eem)
18. Ceftriaxone (sef-trye-AX-one)
19. Cefuroxime (se-fyoor-OX-eem) ‡
20. Cephalexin (sef-a-LEX-in) ‡
21. Cephalothin (sef-A-loe-thin) *
22. Cephapirin (sef-a-PYE-rin) †
23. Cephradine (SEF-ra-deen) †‡

---

*Not commercially available in the U.S.
†Not commercially available in Canada.
‡Generic name product may be available in the U.S.
§Generic name product may be available in Canada.

Description

Cephalosporins (sef-a-loe-SPOR-ins) are used in the treatment of infections caused by bacteria. They work by killing bacteria or preventing their growth.

Cephalosporins are used to treat infections in many different parts of the body. They are sometimes given with other antibiotics. Some cephalosporins given by injection are also used to prevent infections before, during, and after surgery. However, cephalosporins will not work for colds, flu, or other virus infections.

Cephalosporins are available only with your doctor's prescription, in the following dosage forms:

Oral

Cefaclor
- Capsules (U.S. and Canada)
- Oral suspension (U.S. and Canada)
- Extended-release tablets (U.S.)

Cefadroxil
- Capsules (U.S. and Canada)
- Oral suspension (U.S.)
- Tablets (U.S.)

Cefdinir
- Capsules (U.S.)
- Oral Suspension (U.S.)

Cefixime
- Oral suspension (U.S. and Canada)
- Tablets (U.S. and Canada)

Cefpodoxime
- Oral suspension (U.S.)
- Tablets (U.S.)

Cefprozil
- Oral suspension (U.S. and Canada)
- Tablets (U.S. and Canada)

Ceftibuten
- Capsules (U.S.)
- Oral suspension (U.S.)

Cefuroxime
- Oral suspension (U.S. and Canada)
- Tablets (U.S. and Canada)

Cephalexin
- Capsules (U.S. and Canada)
- Oral suspension (U.S. and Canada)
- Tablets (U.S. and Canada)

Cephradine
- Capsules (U.S.)
- Oral suspension (U.S.)

Parenteral

Cefamandole
- Injection (U.S. and Canada)

Cefazolin
- Injection (U.S. and Canada)

Cefepime
- Injection (U.S. and Canada)

Cefonicid
- Injection (U.S.)

Cefoperazone
- Injection (U.S.)

Cefotaxime
- Injection (U.S. and Canada)

Cefotetan
- Injection (U.S. and Canada)

Cefoxitin
- Injection (U.S. and Canada)

Ceftazidime
- Injection (U.S. and Canada)

Ceftizoxime
- Injection (U.S. and Canada)

Ceftriaxone
- Injection (U.S. and Canada)

Cefuroxime
  • Injection (U.S. and Canada)
Cephalothin
  • Injection (Canada)
Cephapirin
  • Injection (U.S.)

Before Using This Medicine

In deciding to use a medicine, the risks of taking the medicine must be weighed against the good it will do. This is a decision you and your doctor will make. For the cephalosporins, the following should be considered:

Allergies—Tell your doctor if you have ever had any unusual or allergic reaction to any of the cephalosporins, penicillins, penicillin-like medicines, or penicillamine. Also tell your health care professional if you are allergic to any other substances, such as foods, preservatives, or dyes.

Pregnancy—Studies have not been done in humans. However, most cephalosporins have not been reported to cause birth defects or other problems in animal studies. Studies in rabbits have shown that cefoxitin may increase the risk of miscarriages and cause other problems.

Breast-feeding—Most cephalosporins pass into breast milk, usually in small amounts. However, cephalosporins have not been reported to cause problems in nursing babies.

Children—Many cephalosporins have been tested in children and, in effective doses, have not been shown to cause different side effects or problems than they do in adults. However, there are some cephalosporins that have not been tested in children up to 1 year of age.

Older adults—Cephalosporins have been used in the elderly, and they are not expected to cause different side effects or problems in older people than they do in younger adults.

Other medicines—Although certain medicines should not be used together at all, in other cases two different medicines may be used together even if an interaction might occur. In these cases, your doctor may want to change the dose, or other precautions may be necessary. When you are taking a cephalosporin, it is especially important that your health care professional know if you are taking any of the following:

  • Alcohol or alcohol-containing medicine (cefamandole, cefoperazone, and cefotetan only)—Using alcohol and these cephalosporins together may cause abdominal or stomach cramps, nausea, vomiting, headache, dizziness or light-headedness, shortness of breath, sweating, or facial flushing; this reaction usually begins within 15 to 30 minutes after alcohol is consumed and usually goes away over several hours

  • Anticoagulants (blood thinners) or
  • Carbenicillin by injection (e.g., Geopen) or
  • Dipyridamole (e.g., Persantine) or
  • Divalproex (e.g., Depakote) or
  • Heparin (e.g., Hepalean, Liquaemin) or
  • Pentoxifylline (e.g., Trental) or
  • Plicamycin (e.g., Mithracin) or
  • Sulfinpyrazone (e.g., Anturane) or
  • Ticarcillin (e.g., Ticar) or
  • Thrombolytic agents or

  • Valproic acid (e.g., Depakene)—Any of these medicines may increase the chance of bleeding, especially when used with cefamandole, cefoperazone, or cefotetan

  • Iron—Iron supplements, including multivitamins that contain iron, may decrease the effect of cefdinir. However, iron-fortified infant formula does not decrease the effect of cefdinir

  • Probenecid (e.g., Benemid) (except cefoperazone, ceftazidime, or ceftriaxone)—Probenecid increases the blood level of many cephalosporins. Although probenecid may be given with a cephalosporin by your doctor purposely to increase the blood level to treat some infections, in other cases this effect may be unwanted and may increase the chance of side effects

Other medical problems—The presence of other medical problems may affect the use of cephalosporins. Make sure you tell your doctor if you have any other medical problems, especially:

  • Bleeding problems, history of (cefamandole, cefoperazone, and cefotetan only)—These medicines may increase the chance of bleeding

  • Kidney disease—Some cephalosporins need to be given at a lower dose to people with kidney disease. Also, cephalothin, especially, may increase the chance of kidney damage

  • Liver disease (cefoperazone only)—Cefoperazone needs to be given at a lower dose to people with liver and kidney disease

  • Phenylketonuria—Cefprozil oral suspension contains phenylalanine

  • Stomach or intestinal disease, history of (especially colitis, including colitis caused by antibiotics, or enteritis)—Cephalosporins may cause colitis in some patients

---

Proper Use of This Medicine

Cephalosporins may be taken on a full or empty stomach. If this medicine upsets your stomach, it may help to take it with food.

Cefaclor extended-release tablets, cefpodoxime, and cefuroxime axetil should be taken with food to increase absorption of the medicine. Ceftibuten oral suspension should be taken on an empty stomach, at least 2 hours before or 1 hour after a meal.

For patients taking the *oral liquid* form of this medicine:

  • This medicine is to be taken by mouth. Use a specially marked measuring spoon or other device to measure each dose accurately. The average household teaspoon may not hold the right amount of liquid.

  • Do not use after the expiration date on the label since the medicine may not work properly after that date. Check with your pharmacist if you have any questions about this.

To help clear up your infection completely, *keep taking this medicine for the full time of treatment,* even if you begin to feel better after a few days. *If you have a "strep" infection, you should keep taking this medicine for at least 10 days. This is especially important in "strep" infections since serious heart or kidney problems could develop later* if your infection is not cleared up completely. Also, if you stop taking this medicine too soon, your symptoms may return.

This medicine works best when there is a constant amount in the blood or urine. *To help keep the amount constant, do not miss any doses. Also, it is best to take the doses at evenly spaced times, day and night.* For example, if you are to take four doses a day, the doses should be spaced about 6 hours apart. If this interferes with your sleep or other daily activities, or if you need help in planning the best times to take your medicine, check with your health care professional.

Dosing—The dose of these medicines will be different for different patients. *Follow your doctor's orders or the directions on the label.* The following information includes only the average doses of these medicines. Your dose may be different if you have kidney disease. *If your dose is different, do not change it* unless your doctor tells you to do so.

The number of capsules or tablets or teaspoonfuls of suspension that you take depends on the strength of the medicine. Also, *the number of doses you take each day, the time allowed between doses, and the length of time you take the medicine depend on the medical problem for which you are taking a cephalosporin.*

For cefaclor
- For bacterial infections:
  —For *capsule* or *oral suspension* dosage form:
  - Adults and teenagers—250 to 500 milligrams (mg) every eight hours.
  - Infants and children 1 month of age and older—6.7 to 13.4 mg per kilogram (kg) (3.04 to 6.09 mg per pound) of body weight every eight hours, or 10 to 20 mg per kg (4.54 to 9.09 mg per pound) of body weight every twelve hours.
  —For *extended-release tablet* dosage form:
  - Adults and teenagers 16 years of age and older—375 to 500 mg every twelve hours for seven to ten days.
  - Children up to 16 years of age—Use and dose must be determined by your doctor.

For cefadroxil
- For bacterial infections:
  —For *oral* dosage forms (capsules, oral suspension, or tablets):
  - Adults and teenagers—500 milligrams (mg) or 1 gram every twelve hours, or 1 or 2 grams once a day.
  - Children—15 mg per kilogram (kg) (6.81 mg per pound) of body weight every twelve hours, or 30 mg per kg (13.63 mg per pound) of body weight once a day.

For cefamandole
- For bacterial infections:
  —For *injection* dosage form:
  - Adults and teenagers—500 milligrams (mg) to 2 grams every four to eight hours, injected into a muscle or vein.
  - Infants and children 1 month of age and older—8.3 to 50 mg per kilogram (kg) (3.77 to 22.72 mg per pound) of body weight every four to eight hours, injected into a muscle or vein.

For cefazolin
- For bacterial infections:
  —For *injection* dosage form:
  - Adults and teenagers—250 milligrams (mg) to 1.5 grams every six to twelve hours, injected into a muscle or vein.
  - Infants and children 1 month of age and older—6.25 to 25 mg per kilogram (kg) (2.84 to 11.36 mg per pound) of body weight every six hours, or 8.3 to 33.3 mg per kg (3.77 to 15.13 mg per pound) of body weight every eight hours, injected into a muscle or vein.
  - Newborns—20 mg per kg (9.09 mg per pound) of body weight every eight to twelve hours, injected into a vein.

For cefdinir
- For bacterial infections:
  —For *capsule or oral suspension* dosage form:
  - Adults and teenagers—300 milligrams (mg) every twelve hours or 600 mg once a day for 5 to 10 days.
  - Infants and children 6 months of age and older—7 milligrams (mg) per kilogram (3.18 mg per pound) of body weight every twelve hours or 14 mg per kilogram (6.36 mg per pound) once a day for 5 to 10 days.

For cefepime
- For bacterial infections:
  —For *injection* dosage form:
  - Adults and teenagers—500 milligrams to 2 grams every eight to twelve hours, injected into a muscle or vein, for seven to ten days.
  - Infants and children 2 months to 16 years of age—50 milligrams per kilogram body weight injected into muscle or vein, every eight to twelve hours, for seven to ten days.

For cefixime
- For bacterial infections:
  —For *oral* dosage forms (oral suspension or tablets):
  - Adults and teenagers—200 milligrams (mg) every twelve hours, or 400 mg once a day. Gonorrhea is treated with a single, oral dose of 400 mg.
  - Children 6 months to 12 years of age—4 mg per kilogram (kg) (1.81 mg per pound) of body weight every twelve hours, or 8 mg per kg (3.63 mg per pound) of body weight once a day.
  - Infants up to 6 months of age—Use and dose must be determined by your doctor.

For cefonicid
- For bacterial infections:
  —For *injection* dosage form:
  - Adults and teenagers—500 milligrams (mg) to 2 grams every twenty-four hours, injected into a muscle or vein.
  - Children—Use and dose must be determined by your doctor.

For cefoperazone
- For bacterial infections:
  —For *injection* dosage form:
  - Adults and teenagers—1 to 6 grams every twelve hours, or 2 to 4 grams every eight hours, injected into a muscle or vein.
  - Children—Use and dose must be determined by your doctor.

For cefotaxime
- For bacterial infections:
  —For *injection* dosage form:
  - Adults and teenagers—1 to 2 grams every four to twelve hours, injected into a muscle or vein. Gon-

orrhea is usually treated with a single dose of 500 milligrams (mg) or 1 gram, injected into a muscle.
- Children over 50 kg of body weight (110 pounds)—1 to 2 grams every four to twelve hours, injected into a muscle or vein.
- Infants and children 1 month of age and older and up to 50 kg of body weight (110 pounds)—8.3 to 30 mg per kg (3.77 to 13.63 mg per pound) of body weight every four hours, or 12.5 to 45 mg per kg (5.68 to 20.45 mg per pound) of body weight every six hours, injected into a muscle or vein.
- Newborns 1 to 4 weeks of age—50 mg per kg (22.72 mg per pound) of body weight every eight hours, injected into a vein.
- Newborns up to 1 week of age—50 mg per kilogram (kg) (22.72 mg per pound) of body weight every twelve hours, injected into a vein.

For cefotetan
- For bacterial infections:
  —For *injection* dosage form:
  - Adults and teenagers—500 milligrams to 3 grams every twelve hours, or 1 or 2 grams every twenty-four hours, injected into a muscle or vein.
  - Children—Use and dose must be determined by your doctor.

For cefoxitin
- For bacterial infections:
  —For *injection* dosage form:
  - Adults and teenagers—1 to 3 grams every four to eight hours, injected into a vein.
  - Infants and children 3 months of age and older—13.3 to 26.7 milligrams (mg) per kilogram (kg) (6.04 to 12.13 mg per pound) of body weight every four hours, or 20 to 40 mg per kg (9.09 to 18.18 mg per pound) of body weight every six hours, injected into a vein.
  - Infants 1 to 3 months of age—20 to 40 mg per kg (9.09 to 18.18 mg per pound) of body weight every six to eight hours, injected into a vein.
  - Newborns 1 to 4 weeks of age—20 to 40 mg per kg (9.09 to 18.18 mg per pound) of body weight every eight hours, injected into a vein.
  - Premature infants weighing 1500 grams and over to newborns up to 1 week of age—20 to 40 mg per kg (9.09 to 18.18 mg per pound) of body weight every twelve hours, injected into a vein.

For cefpodoxime
- For bacterial infections:
  —For *oral* dosage forms (oral suspension or tablets):
  - Adults and teenagers—100 to 400 milligrams (mg) every twelve hours for five to fourteen days. Gonorrhea is treated with a single, oral dose of 200 mg.
  - Infants and children 5 months to 12 years of age—5 mg per kilogram (kg) (2.27 mg per pound) of body weight every twelve hours for five to ten days, or 10 mg per kg (4.54 mg per pound) of body weight every twenty-four hours for ten days.
  - Infants up to 5 months of age—Use and dose must be determined by your doctor.

For cefprozil
- For bacterial infections:
  —For *oral* dosage forms (oral suspension or tablets):
  - Adults and teenagers—250 or 500 milligrams (mg) every twelve to twenty-four hours for ten days.
  - Children 2 to 12 years of age—7.5 to 20 mg per kilogram (kg) (3.4 to 9.09 mg per pound) of body weight every twelve to twenty-four hours for ten days.
  - Infants and children 6 months to 12 years of age—7.5 to 15 mg per kg (3.4 to 6.81 mg per pound) of body weight every twelve hours for ten days.
  - Infants up to 6 months of age—Use and dose must be determined by your doctor.

For ceftazidime
- For bacterial infections:
  —For *injection* dosage form:
  - Adults and teenagers—250 milligrams (mg) to 2 grams every eight to twelve hours, injected into a muscle or vein. Patients with cystic fibrosis may receive 30 to 50 mg per kilogram (kg) (13.63 to 22.72 mg per pound) of body weight every eight hours, injected into a vein.
  - Infants and children 1 month to 12 years of age—30 to 50 mg per kg (13.63 to 22.72 mg per pound) of body weight every eight hours, injected into a vein.
  - Newborns up to 4 weeks of age—30 mg per kg (13.63 mg per pound) of body weight every twelve hours, injected into a vein.

For ceftibuten
- For bacterial infections:
  —For *oral* dosage forms (capsules or oral suspension):
  - Adults and teenagers—400 milligrams (mg) once a day for ten days.
  - Infants and children 6 months to 12 years of age—9 mg per kilogram (4.09 mg per pound) of body weight once a day for ten days.
  - Infants up to 6 months of age—Use and dose must be determined by your doctor.

For ceftizoxime
- For bacterial infections:
  —For *injection* dosage form:
  - Adults and teenagers—500 milligrams (mg) to 4 grams every eight to twelve hours, injected into a muscle or vein. Gonorrhea is treated with a single dose of 1 gram, injected into a muscle.
  - Infants and children 6 months of age and older—50 mg per kilogram (22.72 mg per pound) of body weight every six to eight hours, injected into a muscle or vein.
  - Infants up to 6 months of age—Use and dose must be determined by your doctor.

For ceftriaxone
- For bacterial infections:
  —For *injection* dosage form:
  - Adults and teenagers—1 to 2 grams every twenty-four hours, or 500 milligrams (mg) to 1 gram every twelve hours, injected into a muscle or vein. Gonorrhea is treated with a single 250-mg dose, injected into a muscle.

- Infants and children—25 to 37.5 mg per kilogram (kg) (11.36 to 17.04 mg per pound) of body weight every twelve hours, or 50 to 75 mg per kg (22.72 to 34.09 mg per pound) of body weight once a day, injected into a muscle or vein. Meningitis is treated with an initial dose of 100 mg per kg, then 100 mg per kg once a day or 50 mg per kg two times a day.

For cefuroxime
- For bacterial infections:
  —For *oral suspension* dosage form:
  - Adults and teenagers—The oral suspension is usually used only for children. Refer to the dosing for cefuroxime tablets.
  - Infants and children 3 months to 12 years of age— 10 to 15 milligrams (mg) per kilogram (kg) (4.54 to 6.81 mg per pound) of body weight every twelve hours for ten days.
  —For *tablet* dosage form:
  - Adults and teenagers—125 to 500 mg every twelve hours. Gonorrhea is treated with a single, oral 1-gram dose.
  - Children up to 12 years of age who can swallow tablets whole—125 or 250 mg every twelve hours for ten days.
  —For *injection* dosage form:
  - Adults and teenagers—750 mg to 3 grams every six to eight hours, injected into a muscle or vein. Gonorrhea is treated with a single dose of 1.5 grams, injected into a muscle; the total 1.5-gram dose is divided into two doses and injected into muscles at two separate places on the body, and given along with a single, oral 1-gram dose of probenecid.
  - Infants and children 1 month of age and older— 12.5 to 80 mg per kg (5.68 to 36.36 mg per pound) of body weight every six to eight hours, injected into a muscle or vein.
  - Newborns—10 to 50 mg per kg (4.54 to 22.72 mg per pound) of body weight every eight to twelve hours, injected into a vein.

For cephalexin
- For bacterial infections:
  —For *oral* dosage forms (capsules, oral suspension, or tablets):
  - Adults and teenagers—250 milligrams (mg) to 1 gram every six to twelve hours.
  - Children 40 kg (88 pounds) of body weight and over—250 mg to 1 gram every six to twelve hours.
  - Children 1 year of age and older and up to 40 kg (88 pounds) of body weight—6.25 to 25 mg per kilogram (kg) (2.84 to 11.36 mg per pound) of body weight every six hours, or 12.5 to 50 mg per kg (5.68 to 22.72 mg per pound) of body weight every twelve hours.
  - Infants and children 1 month to 1 year of age— 6.25 to 12.5 mg per kg (2.84 to 5.68 mg per pound) of body weight every six hours.

For cephalothin
- For bacterial infections:
  —For *injection* dosage form:
  - Adults and teenagers—500 milligrams (mg) to 2 grams every four to six hours, injected into a muscle or vein.

- Children—13.3 to 26.6 mg per kilogram (kg) (6.04 to 12.09 mg per pound) of body weight every four hours, or 20 to 40 mg per kg (9.09 to 18.18 mg per pound) of body weight every six hours, injected into a muscle or vein.

For cephapirin
- For bacterial infections:
  —For *injection* dosage form:
  - Adults and teenagers—500 milligrams (mg) to 1 gram every four to six hours, injected into a muscle or vein.
  - Infants and children 3 months of age and older— 10 to 20 mg per kilogram (kg) (4.54 to 9.09 mg per pound) of body weight every six hours, injected into a muscle or vein.

For cephradine
- For bacterial infections:
  —For *oral* dosage forms (capsules or oral suspension):
  - Adults and teenagers—250 milligrams (mg) to 1 gram every six to twelve hours.
  - Infants and children 9 months of age and older— 6.25 mg to 1 gram per kilogram (kg) (2.84 to 454 mg per pound) of body weight every six hours, or 12.5 to 50 mg per kg (5.68 to 22.72 mg per pound) of body weight every twelve hours.

Missed dose—If you miss a dose of this medicine, take it as soon as possible. This will help to keep a constant amount of medicine in the blood or urine. However, if it is almost time for your next dose, skip the missed dose and go back to your regular dosing schedule. Do not double doses.

Storage—To store this medicine:
- Keep out of the reach of children.
- Store away from heat and direct light.
- Do not store the capsule or tablet form of this medicine in the bathroom, near the kitchen sink, or in other damp places. Heat or moisture may cause the medicine to break down.
- Store the oral liquid form of most cephalosporins in the refrigerator because heat will cause this medicine to break down. However, keep the medicine from freezing. Follow the directions on the label. Cefixime oral suspension (*Suprax*), cefuroxime axetil oral suspension (*Ceftin*), and cefdinir oral suspension (*Omnicef*) do not need to be refrigerated.
- Do not keep outdated medicine or medicine no longer needed. Be sure that any discarded medicine is out of the reach of children.

Precautions While Using This Medicine

If your symptoms do not improve within a few days, or if they become worse, check with your doctor.

For patients with diabetes:
- *This medicine may cause false test results with some urine sugar tests.* Check with your doctor before changing your diet or the dosage of your diabetes medicine.

For patients with phenylketonuria (PKU):
- Cefprozil oral suspension (*Cefzil*) contains phenylalanine. Check with your doctor before taking this medicine.

In some patients, cephalosporins may cause diarrhea:

- Severe diarrhea may be a sign of a serious side effect. *Do not take any diarrhea medicine without first checking with your doctor.* Diarrhea medicines may make your diarrhea worse or make it last longer.
- For mild diarrhea, diarrhea medicine containing kaolin or attapulgite (e.g., *Kaopectate* tablets, *Diasorb*) may be taken. However, other kinds of diarrhea medicine should not be taken. They may make your diarrhea worse or make it last longer.
- If you have any questions about this or if mild diarrhea continues or gets worse, check with your health care professional.

For patients receiving *cefamandole, cefoperazone, or cefotetan by injection:*

- Drinking alcoholic beverages or taking other alcohol-containing preparations (for example, elixirs, cough syrups, tonics, or injections of alcohol) while receiving these medicines may cause problems. The problems may occur if you consume alcohol even several days after you stop taking the cephalosporin. Drinking alcoholic beverages may result in increased side effects such as abdominal or stomach cramps, nausea, vomiting, headache, fainting, fast or irregular heartbeat, difficult breathing, sweating, or redness of the face or skin. These effects usually start within 15 to 30 minutes after you drink alcohol and may not go away for up to several hours. Therefore, *you should not drink alcoholic beverages or take other alcohol-containing preparations while you are receiving these medicines and for several days after stopping them.*

Side Effects of This Medicine

Along with its needed effects, a medicine may cause some unwanted effects. Although not all of these side effects may occur, if they do occur they may need medical attention.

Check with your doctor immediately if any of the following side effects occur:

Less common or rare

Abdominal or stomach cramps and pain (severe); abdominal tenderness; diarrhea (watery and severe, which may also be bloody); fever; unusual bleeding or bruising (more common for cefamandole, cefoperazone, and cefotetan)

Note: Some of these side effects also may occur up to several weeks after you stop taking this medicine.

Rare

Blistering, peeling, or loosening of skin; convulsions (seizures); decrease in urine output; hearing loss (more common with cefuroxime treatment for meningitis); joint pain; loss of appetite, nausea, or vomiting (more common with ceftriaxone); pain, redness, and swelling at place of injection; skin rash, itching, redness, or swelling; trouble in breathing; unusual tiredness or weakness; yellowing of the eyes or skin

Other side effects may occur that usually do not need medical attention. These side effects may go away during treatment as your body adjusts to the medicine. However, check with your doctor if any of the following side effects continue or are bothersome:

More common (less common with some cephalosporins)

Diarrhea (mild); headache; sore mouth or tongue; stomach cramps (mild); vaginal itching or discharge

Other side effects not listed above may also occur in some patients. If you notice any other effects, check with your doctor.

Additional Information

Once a medicine has been approved for marketing for a certain use, experience may show that it is also useful for other medical problems. Although these uses are not included in product labeling, cephalosporins are used in certain patients with the following medical conditions:

- Amoxicillin-resistant sinusitis (treatment)—Cefaclor
- Bacterial endocarditis (Prophylaxis)—Cefadroxil, cefazolin, and cephalexin
- Melioidosis (treatment)—Ceftazidime

Other than the above information, there is no additional information relating to proper use, precautions, or side effects for these uses.

Revised: 08/15/2000

CETRORELIX   Systemic— INTRODUCTORY VERSION

Commonly used brand name(s):

In the U.S.—
Cetrotide

Description

Cetrorelix (set-RO-rel-lix) is a man-made hormone that blocks the effects of Gonadotropin Releasing Hormone (GnRH). GnRH controls another hormone that is called luteinizing hormone (LH), which is the hormone that starts ovulation during the menstrual cycle. When undergoing hormone treatment sometimes premature ovulation can occur, leading to eggs that are not ready for fertilization to be released. Cetrorelix does not allow the premature release of these eggs to occur.

This medicine is available only with your doctor's prescription, in the following dosage form:

Parenteral
- For injection (U.S.)

Before Using This Medicine

In deciding to use a medicine, the risks of taking the medicine must be weighed against the good it will do. This is a decision you and your doctor will make. For cetrorelix, the following should be considered:

Allergies—Tell your health care professional if you have ever had any unusual or allergic reaction to cetrorelix, extrinsic peptide hormones (medicines similar to cetrorelix), mannitol, or any GnRH or GnRH-related medicines. Also tell

your health care professional if you are allergic to any other substances, such as foods, preservatives, or dyes.

Pregnancy—Cetrorelix is not recommended during pregnancy. Before taking this medicine, make sure your doctor knows if you are pregnant, or may become pregnant.

Breast-feeding—It is not known whether cetrorelix passes into the breast milk. However, it is not recommended during breast-feeding because it may cause unwanted effect in nursing babies.

Older adults—Cetrorelix is not intended for use in patients over the age of 65 years.

Proper Use of This Medicine

Take this medicine only as directed by your doctor. If you are to begin on Day 5, count the first day of your menstrual period as Day 1. Beginning on Day 5, take the correct dose every day for as many days as your doctor ordered. To help you to remember to take your dose of medicine, take it at the same time every day.

- Read the paper with information for the patient carefully.
- Understand and use the proper method of safely preparing the medicine.
- Wash your hands with soap and water and use a clean work area to prepare your injection.
- Make sure you clearly understand and carefully follow your doctor's instructions on how to give yourself an injection, including using the proper needle and syringe. Remember to change the site of injection to different areas to prevent skin problems from developing.
- Throw away needles, syringes, bottles, and unused medicine after the injection in a safe manner.

Tell your doctor when you use the last dose of cetrorelix. Cetrorelix often requires that another hormone called human chorionic gonadotropin (hCG) be given as a single dose the day after the last dose of cetrorelix is given. Your doctor will give you this medicine or arrange for you to get this medicine at the right time.

Dosing—The dose of cetrorelix may be different for different patients. *If you are receiving cetrorelix at home, follow your doctor's orders or the directions on the label.* The following information includes only the average doses of cetrorelix. *If your dose is different, do not change it* unless your doctor tells you to do so.

- For *injection* dosage form:
  —For treatment of female infertility:
  - Adults—3 milligrams (mg) injected under the skin one time on Day 7 of your menstrual cycle, or 0.25 mg injected under the skin starting on Day 5 or 6 of your menstrual cycle and continuing until HCG administration occurs.

Missed dose—If you miss a dose of this medicine, discuss with your doctor when you should receive your next dose. Do not double doses. If you have any questions about this, check with your doctor.

Storage—To store this medicine:
- Keep out of the reach of children.
- Keep the packaged tray in the outer carton to protect it from light.
- Do not store in the bathroom, near the kitchen sink, or in other damp places. Heat or moisture may cause the medicine to break down.

- Store the 0.25 mg vials in the refrigerator, keep from freezing.
- Store the 3 mg vials at room temperature.

Precautions While Using This Medicine

It is very important that your doctor check you using ultrasound examination at regular visits to make sure that you are ready for injection with another drug (HCG) to induce ovulation.

Call your doctor immediately if you have taken more of the medication than your doctor ordered.

Side Effects of This Medicine

Along with its needed effects, a medicine may cause some unwanted effects. Although not all of these side effects may occur, if they do occur they may need medical attention.

Check with your doctor immediately if any of the following side effects occur:
  Less common
    Abdominal or stomach pain; continuing or severe nausea, vomiting or diarrhea; decreased amount of urine; feeling of indigestion; moderate to severe bloating; pelvic pain, severe; rapid weight gain; shortness of breath; swelling of lower legs

Other side effects may occur that usually do not need medical attention. These side effects may go away during treatment as your body adjusts to the medicine. However, check with your doctor if any of the following side effects continue or are bothersome.
  More common
    Headache; injection site bruising, itching, swelling, or redness; nausea

Other side effects not listed above may also occur in some patients. If you notice any other effects, check with your doctor.

Developed: 11/03/2000
Revised: 12/21/2000

CEVIMELINE Systemic

Commonly used brand name(s):

In the U.S.—
  Evoxac

Description

Cevimeline (se-VIM-e-leen) is used to treat the symptoms of dry mouth often experienced by patients with Sjogren's syndrome. It works by causing certain mouth glands to produce more saliva.

This medicine is available only with your doctor's prescription, in the following dosage form:

Oral
- Capsules (U.S.)

Before Using This Medicine

In deciding to use a medicine, the risks of taking [using] the medicine must be weighed against the good it will do. This is a decision you and your doctor will make. For cevimeline, the following should be considered:

Allergies—Tell your doctor if you have ever had any unusual or allergic reaction to cevimeline. Also tell your doctor and pharmacist if you are allergic to any other substances, such as foods, preservatives, or dyes.

Pregnancy—Cevimeline has not been studied in women who are pregnant. However, in animal studies, cevimeline caused a reduction in the number of pregnancies. Before taking this medicine, make sure your doctor knows if you are pregnant or if you may become pregnant.

Breast-feeding—It is not known whether cevimeline passes into human breast milk. Although most medicines pass into breast milk in small amounts, many of them may be used safely while breast feeding. Mothers who are taking this medicine and who wish to breast-feed should discuss this with their doctor.

Children—Studies on this medicine have been done only in adult patients, and there is no specific information comparing use of cevimeline in children with use in other age groups.

Older adults—Many medicines have not been studied specifically in older people. Therefore, it may not be known whether they work exactly the same way they do in younger adults. Although there is no specific information comparing use of cevimeline in the elderly with use in other age groups, this medicine is not expected to cause different side effects or problems in older people than it does in younger adults.

Other medicines—Although certain medicines should not be used together at all, in other cases two different medicines may be used together even if an interaction might occur. In these cases, your doctor may want to change the dose, or other precautions may be necessary. When you are taking cevimeline, it is especially important that your doctor and pharmacist know if you are taking any of the following:

- Beta-adrenergic blocking agents (acebutolol, [e.g. Sectral], atenolol [e.g. Tenormin], betaxolol [e.g. Kerlone], carteolol [e.g. Cartrol], labetolol [e.g. Normodyne], metoprolol [e.g. Lopressor], nadolol [e.g. Corgard], oxprenolol [e.g. Trasicor], penbutolol [e.g. Levatol], pindolol [e.g. Visken], propranolol [e.g.Inderal], sotalol [e.g. Sotacor], timolol [e.g. Blocadren])—Disturbances in heart rhythms may occur if these medicines are taken with cevimeline.
- Anticholinergics (medicine for abdominal or stomach spasms or cramps)—Cevimeline may interfere with the effects of these medicines.
- Cholinergics (bethanechol [e.g.Duvoid], donepezil [e.g. Tacrine], physostigmine [e.g. Antilirium], pilocarpine [e.g. Pilocar], pyridostigmine [e.g. Mestinon]—These medicines can add to the effects of cevimeline.

Tell your health care professional if you are taking any other prescription or nonprescription (over-the-counter [OTC]) medicine.

Other medical problems—The presence of other medical problems may affect the use of cevimeline. Make sure you tell your doctor if you have any other medical problems, especially:

- Asthma, uncontrolled, or
- Cholelithiasis (gallstones), or
- Heart disease, or
- Nephrolithiasis (kidney stones), or
- Eye conditions in which contraction of the pupils is undesirable (e.g., acute iritis and narrow-angle glaucoma), or
- Pulmonary disease other than asthma

Proper Use of This Medicine

Dosing—The dose of cevimeline will be different for different patients. *Follow your doctor's orders or the directions on the label.* The following information includes only the average doses of cevimeline. *If your dose is different, do not change it* unless your doctor tells you to do so.

The number of capsules that you take depends on the strength of the medicine. Also, *the number of doses you take each day, the time allowed between doses, and the length of time you take the medicine depend on the medical problem for which you are taking cevimeline.*

- For *oral* dosage form (capsules):
  —For the treatment of dry mouth in patients with Sjogren's syndrome:
    - Adults—30 milligrams three times a day
    - Children—Use and dose must be determined by your doctor.

Missed dose— If you miss a dose of this medicine, take it as soon as possible. However, if it is almost time for your next dose, skip the missed dose and go back to your regular dosing schedule. Do not double doses.

Storage—To store this medicine:

- Keep out of the reach of children.
- Do not store in the bathroom, near the kitchen sink, or in other damp places. heat or moisture may cause the medicine to break down.
- Do not keep outdated medicine or medicine no longer needed. Ask your health care professional how you should dispose of any medicine you do not use. Be sure that any discarded medicine is out of the reach of children.

Precautions While Using This Medicine

If you will be taking this medicine for a long time, *it is very important that your doctor check you at regular visits* for signs of your receiving too much medicine.

If your symptoms do not improve within a few days or if they become worse, check with your doctor.

Do not take other medicines unless they have been discussed with your doctor. This especially includes nonprescription medicines, such as aspirin, and medicines for appetite control, asthma, colds, cough, hay fever, or sinus problems.

This medicine may cause some people to become drowsy, dizzy, or less alert than they are normally. This medicine may also cause a change in vision that could cause you to see less well at night. *Make sure you know how you react to this medicine before you drive, use machines, or do anything else that could be dangerous if you are unable to see well, or if you are dizzy or are not alert.*

Side Effects of This Medicine

Along with its needed effects, a medicine may cause some unwanted effects. Although not all of these side effects may occur, if they do occur they may need medical attention.

Check with your doctor immediately if any of the following side effects occur:

Less common

Difficulty breathing; fast heartbeat; itching

Rare

Chest pain; fainting or light-headedness when getting up from a lying or a sitting position; swelling of gums or tongue

Symptoms of Overdose

Get emergency help immediately if any of the following symptoms of overdose occur:

Blurring or loss of vision; chest pain; cold, clammy skin; diarrhea, continuous and severe; disturbed color vision; dizziness, faintness, or light-headedness when getting up from a lying or sitting position; difficult or labored breathing; fast, pounding, slow, or irregular heartbeat; fast, weak pulse; headache; mental confusion; nausea; pounding in ears; shaking or trembling of hands or feet; shortness of breath; stomach cramps or pain; sweating; tearing of the eyes

Check with your doctor as soon as possible if any of the following side effects occur:

Less common

Bloody or cloudy urine; blurred vision; chest pain; cough; cracks in skin; difficult, burning, or painful urination; dizziness; dry or itching eyes; earache; feeling of constant movement of self or surroundings; itching of vagina, genital, or other skin area; lower back pain; redness or pain in eye; ringing or buzzing in the ears; scaling of skin; shortness of breath; skin rash; soreness or redness of skin; sores, ulcers, or white spots on tongue, lips, or inside of mouth; stiffness of muscles; swelling of hands, ankles, feet, or lower legs; swelling on side of face and jaw, with or without pain; tense muscles

Other side effects may occur that usually do not need medical attention. These side effects may go away during treatment as your body adjusts to the medicine. However, check with your doctor if any of the following side effects continue or are bothersome.

More common

Excessive sweating; nausea; runny or stuffy nose

Less common

Abdominal pain; belching; bloating or swelling of face, hands, feet, or lower legs; bloody nose; bone or joint pain; burning, dry, or itching feeling in eye; change in vision; chills; constipation; cough, mucus-producing; decreased touch sensation; depression; diarrhea; dry mouth; eye pain; feelings of warmth in face, neck, arms, and occasionally, chest; fever; heartburn; hiccups; injury; itching; leg cramps; loss of appetite; migraine headache; mood or mental changes; muscle aches, pain, or stiffness; pain and swelling of eye, eyelid, or inner lining of eye; pain on side of face and jaw; pain, swelling, or redness of joints; postoperative pain; rapid weight gain; shortness of breath; skin disorder; tightness in chest; tooth disorders or pain; trembling or shaking of hands or feet; trouble in sleeping; unusual bleeding or bruising; unusual tiredness or weakness; vomiting; watering of mouth; weight loss

Rare

Abnormal crying; deep, dark, purple bruise; swelling or puffiness of face; temperature sensation changes

Other side effects not listed above may also occur in some patients. If you notice any other effects, check with your doctor.

Developed: 05/25/2000

CHARCOAL, ACTIVATED Oral

Commonly used brand name(s):

In the U.S.—

Actidose-Aqua[1]
Actidose with Sorbitol[2]
CharcoAid[2]
CharcoAid G[1]
CharcoAid 2000[1]
Insta-Char in an Aqueous Base[1]
Insta-Char in an Aqueous Base with Cherry Flavor[1]

Insta-Char Pediatric in an Aqueous Base with Cherry Flavor[1]
Insta-Char Pediatric with Cherry Flavor in a Sorbitol Base[2]
Insta-Char with Cherry Flavor in a Sorbitol Base[2]
Liqui-Char[1]
Liqui-Char with Sorbitol[2]

In Canada—

Aqueous Charcodote[1]
Aqueous Pediatric Charcodote[1]
Charcodote[2]

Charcodote TFS-25[2]
Charcodote TFS-50[2]
Pediatric Charcodote[2]

Note: For quick reference, the following medicines are numbered to match the corresponding brand names.

This information applies to the following medicines:
1. Activated Charcoal (AK-ti-vay-ted CHAR-kole) ‡§
2. Activated Charcoal and Sorbitol (AK-ti-vay-ted CHAR-kole and SOR-bi-tole)

‡Generic name product may be available in the U.S.
§Generic name product may be available in Canada.

Description

Activated charcoal is used in the emergency treatment of certain kinds of poisoning. It helps prevent the poison from being absorbed from the stomach into the body. Sometimes, several doses of activated charcoal are needed to treat severe poisoning. Ordinarily, this medicine is not effective and should not be used in poisoning if corrosive agents such as alkalis (lye) and strong acids, iron, boric acid, lithium, petroleum products (e.g., cleaning fluid, coal oil, fuel oil, gasoline, kerosene, paint thinner), or alcohols have been swallowed, since it will not prevent these poisons from being absorbed into the body.

Some activated charcoal products contain sorbitol. Sorbitol is a sweetener. It also works as a laxative, for the elimination of the poison from the body. *Products that contain sorbitol should be given only under the direct supervision of a doctor because severe diarrhea and vomiting may result.*

Activated charcoal has not been shown to be effective in relieving diarrhea and intestinal gas.

Activated charcoal may be available without a doctor's prescription; however, before using this medicine, call a poison control center, your doctor, or an emergency room for advice. Activated charcoal is available in the following dosage forms:

Oral
  Activated Charcoal
  • Powder (U.S. and Canada)
  • Oral suspension (U.S. and Canada)
  Activated Charcoal and Sorbitol
  • Oral suspension (U.S. and Canada)

Before Using This Medicine

In deciding to use a medicine, the risks of taking the medicine must be weighed against the good it will do. This is a decision you and your doctor will make. For activated charcoal, the following should be considered:

Allergies—Tell your doctor if you have ever had any unusual or allergic reaction to activated charcoal or to fructose (fruit sugar). Also tell your health care professional if you are allergic to any other substances, such as foods, preservatives, or dyes.

Pregnancy—Activated charcoal has not been reported to cause birth defects or other problems in humans.

Breast-feeding—Activated charcoal has not been reported to cause problems in nursing babies.

Children—Activated charcoal should be used only under the direct supervision of your doctor, poison control center, or other health care professional.

Older adults—Many medicines have not been studied specifically in older people. Therefore, it may not be known whether they work exactly the same way they do in younger adults. Although there is no specific information comparing the use of activated charcoal in the elderly, this medicine is not expected to cause different side effects or problems in older people than it does in younger adults.

However, elderly persons with slow digestion are more likely to develop constipation if given more than one dose of activated charcoal.

Other medicines—Although certain medicines should not be used together at all, in other cases two different medicines may be used together even if an interaction might occur. In these cases, your doctor may want to change the dose, or other precautions may be necessary. Tell your health care professional if you are taking any other prescription or nonprescription (over-the-counter [OTC]) medicine.

Other medical problems—The presence of other medical problems may affect the use of activated charcoal. Make sure you tell your doctor if you have any other medical problems, especially:

• Bleeding, intestinal or
• Blockage, intestinal or
• Hole in the intestine—Activated charcoal may make these conditions worse
• Decreased alertness—To prevent activated charcoal from getting into the patient's lungs, it may be necessary to place a tube in the patient's throat before activated charcoal is given
• Dehydration—Use of laxatives, such as sorbitol, is not recommended
• Slow digestion—Activated charcoal may not work properly

• Surgery, recent—Activated charcoal may cause abdominal or stomach problems

Proper Use of This Medicine

Before taking this medicine, call a poison control center, your doctor, or an emergency room for advice. It is a good idea to have these telephone numbers readily available.

To prevent activated charcoal powder from scattering, be careful when opening and adding water to the powder container.

It is very important that you shake the liquid form of this medicine well before taking it, because some might have settled in the bottom. Be sure to drink all the liquid. Then rinse the container with a small amount of water, shake the container, and drink this mixture to get the full dose of activated charcoal.

If you have been told to take both this medicine and ipecac syrup to treat the poisoning, *do not take this medicine until after you have taken the ipecac syrup to cause vomiting and the vomiting has stopped. This usually takes about 30 minutes.*

Do not take this medicine mixed with chocolate syrup, ice cream or sherbet, since they may prevent the medicine from working properly.

If you are taking any other medicine, do not take it within 2 hours of the activated charcoal. Taking other medicines together with activated charcoal may prevent the other medicine from being absorbed by your body. If you have any questions about this, check with your health care professional.

Dosing—The dose of these medicines will be different for different patients. *Follow your doctor's, poison control center's, or other health care professional's orders or the directions on the label.* The following information includes only the average doses of these medicines. *If your dose is different, do not change it* unless your doctor tells you to do so.

For activated charcoal
  • For *oral* dosage form (powder):
    —For treatment of poisoning:
      • Treatment with one dose:
        —Adults and teenagers: Dose is usually 25 to 100 grams mixed with water.
        —Children 1 through 12 years of age: Dose is usually 25 to 50 grams mixed with water, or the dose may be based on body weight. It may be 0.5 to 1 gram per kilogram (kg) (0.23 to 0.45 gram per pound) of body weight mixed with water.
        —Children up to 1 year of age: Dose is usually 10 to 25 grams mixed with water, or the dose may be based on body weight. It may be 0.5 to 1 gram per kg (0.23 to 0.45 gram per pound) of body weight mixed with water.
      • Treatment with more than one dose:
        —Adults and teenagers: At first, the dose is 50 to 100 grams. Then the dose may be 12.5 grams given every hour, 25 grams given every two hours, or 50 grams given every four hours. Each dose should be mixed with water.
        —Children up to 13 years of age: At first, the dose is 10 to 25 grams. Then the dose is based on body weight. It is usually 1 to 2

grams per kg (0.45 to 0.91 gram per pound) of body weight given every two to four hours. Each dose should be mixed with water.
- For *oral* dosage form (oral suspension):
  —For treatment of poisoning:
    - Treatment with one dose:
      —Adults and teenagers: Dose is usually 25 to 100 grams.
      —Children 1 through 12 years of age: Dose is usually 25 to 50 grams, or the dose may be based on body weight. It may be 0.5 to 1 gram per kg (0.23 to 0.45 gram per pound) of body weight.
      —Children up to 1 year of age: Dose is usually 10 to 25 grams, or the dose may be based on body weight. It may be 0.5 to 1 gram per kg (0.23 to 0.45 gram per pound) of body weight.
    - Treatment with more than one dose:
      —Adults and teenagers: At first, the dose is 50 to 100 grams. Then the dose may be 12.5 grams given every hour, 25 grams given every two hours, or 50 grams given every four hours.
      —Children up to 13 years of age: At first, the dose is 10 to 25 grams. Then the dose is based on body weight. It is usually 1 to 2 grams per kg (0.45 to 0.91 gram per pound) of body weight given every two to four hours.

For activated charcoal and sorbitol
- For *oral* dosage form (oral suspension):
  —For treatment of poisoning:
    - Adults and teenagers—Dose is usually 50 to 100 grams of activated charcoal given one time.
    - Children 1 through 12 years of age—Dose is usually 25 to 50 grams of activated charcoal given one time.
    - Children up to 1 year of age—Use is not recommended.

Storage—To store this medicine:
- Keep out of the reach of children.
- Store away from heat and direct light.
- Do not store this medicine in the bathroom, near the kitchen sink, or in other damp places. Heat or moisture may cause the medicine to break down.
- Keep the liquid form of this medicine from freezing.
- Do not keep outdated medicine or medicine no longer needed. Be sure that any discarded medicine is out of the reach of children.

Side Effects of This Medicine

Along with its needed effects, a medicine may cause some unwanted effects. Although not all of these side effects may occur, if they do occur they may need medical attention.

Check with your doctor as soon as possible if the following side effect occurs:
Less common or rare
  Pain or swelling in stomach

Other side effects may occur that usually do not need medical attention. These side effects may go away during treatment as your body adjusts to the medicine. However, check with your doctor if any of the following side effects continue:
More common
  Diarrhea

Less common or rare
  Constipation; vomiting

Activated charcoal will cause your stools to turn black. This is to be expected while you are taking this medicine.

There have not been any other side effects reported with this medicine. However, if you notice any other effects, check with your doctor.

Revised: 06/11/99

CHENODIOL Systemic†

A commonly used name is chenodeoxycholic acid.

†Not commercially available in Canada.

Description

Chenodiol (kee-noe-DYE-ole) is used in the treatment of gallstone disease. It is taken by mouth to dissolve the gallstones.

Chenodiol is used in patients who do not need to have their gallbladder removed or in those in whom surgery is best avoided because of other medical problems. However, chenodiol works only in those patients who have a working gallbladder and whose gallstones are made of cholesterol. Chenodiol works best when these stones are small and of the "floating" type.

Chenodiol is available only with your doctor's prescription, in the following dosage form:
Oral
- Tablets

Before Using This Medicine

In deciding to use a medicine, the risks of taking the medicine must be weighed against the good it will do. This is a decision you and your doctor will make. For chenodiol, the following should be considered:

Allergies—Tell your doctor if you have ever had any unusual or allergic reaction to chenodiol or to other bile acid products.

Diet—If you have gallstones, your doctor may prescribe chenodiol and a personal high-fiber diet for you. Some foods that are high in fiber are whole grain breads and cereals, bran, fruit, and green, leafy vegetables. It has been found that such a diet may help dissolve the stones faster and may keep new stones from forming.

It may also be important for you to go on a reducing diet. However, check with your doctor before going on any diet.

Pregnancy—Chenodiol is not recommended for use during pregnancy. It has been shown to cause liver and kidney problems in animals when given in doses many times the human dose. Be sure you have discussed this with your doctor.

Breast-feeding—It is not known whether chenodiol passes into breast milk. Although most medicines pass into breast milk in small amounts, many of them may be used safely while breast-feeding. Mothers who are taking this medicine and who wish to breast-feed should discuss this with their doctor.

Children—Studies on this medicine have been done only in adult patients, and there is no specific information comparing use of chenodiol in children with use in other age groups.

Older adults—Many medicines have not been studied specifically in older people. Therefore, it may not be known whether they work exactly the same way they do in younger adults. Although there is no specific information comparing use of chenodiol in the elderly with use in other age groups, this medicine is not expected to cause different side effects or problems in older people than it does in younger adults.

Other medicines—Although certain medicines should not be used together at all, in other cases two different medicines may be used together even if an interaction might occur. In these cases, your doctor may want to change the dose, or other precautions may be necessary. Tell your health care professional if you are taking any other prescription or nonprescription (over-the-counter [OTC]) medicine.

Other medical problems—The presence of other medical problems may affect the use of chenodiol. Make sure you tell your doctor if you have any other medical problems, especially:

- Biliary tract problems or
- Blood vessel disease or
- Pancreatitis (inflammation of pancreas)—These conditions may make it necessary to have surgery since treatment with chenodiol would take too long
- Liver disease—Liver disease may become worse with use of chenodiol

Proper Use of This Medicine

Take chenodiol with food or milk for best results, unless otherwise directed by your doctor.

Take chenodiol for the full time of treatment, even if you begin to feel better. If you stop taking this medicine too soon, the gallstones may not dissolve as fast or may not dissolve at all.

Dosing—The dose of chenodiol will be different for different patients. *Follow your doctor's orders or the directions on the label.* The following information includes only the average doses of chenodiol. *If your dose is different, do not change it unless your doctor tells you to do so:*

- For *oral* dosage forms (tablets):
  —For gallstone disease:
    - Adults and children 12 years of age and older— 250 milligrams (mg) a day for the first two weeks of treatment. Your doctor may then increase the dose by 250 mg a day until the proper treatment dose is reached. The treatment dose is based on body weight. It is usually 13 to 16 mg per kilogram (6 to 7 mg per pound) of body weight a day, divided into two doses, taken in the morning and at night. Each dose should be taken with food or milk.
    - Children up to 12 years of age—Use and dose must be determined by your doctor.

Missed dose—If you miss a dose of this medicine, take it as soon as possible. However, if it is almost time for your next dose, skip the missed dose and go back to your regular dosing schedule. Do not double doses.

Storage—To store this medicine:
- Keep out of the reach of children.
- Store away from heat and direct light.

- Do not store in the bathroom, near the kitchen sink, or in other damp places. Heat or moisture may cause the medicine to break down.
- Do not keep outdated medicine or medicine no longer needed. Be sure that any discarded medicine is out of the reach of children.

Precautions While Using This Medicine

Do not take aluminum-containing antacids (e.g., ALternaGel, Maalox) while taking chenodiol. To do so may keep the chenodiol from working properly.

It is important that your doctor check your progress at regular visits. Laboratory tests will have to be done every few months while you are taking this medicine to make sure that the gallstones are dissolving and your liver is working properly.

Check with your doctor immediately if severe abdominal or stomach pain, especially toward the upper right side, and severe nausea and vomiting occur. These symptoms may mean that you have other medical problems or that your gallstone condition needs your doctor's attention.

Side Effects of This Medicine

Along with its needed effects, a medicine may cause some unwanted effects. Although not all of these side effects may occur, if they do occur they may need medical attention.

Check with your doctor as soon as possible if the following side effect occurs:
> *Less common or rare*
> Diarrhea (severe)

Other side effects may occur that usually do not need medical attention. These side effects may go away during treatment as your body adjusts to the medicine. However, check with your doctor if any of the following side effects continue or are bothersome:
> *More common*
> Diarrhea (mild)

> *Less common or rare*
> Constipation; frequent urge for bowel movement; gas or indigestion (usually disappears within 2 to 4 weeks after the beginning of treatment); loss of appetite; nausea or vomiting; stomach cramps or pain

Other side effects not listed above may also occur in some patients. If you notice any other effects, check with your doctor.

Revised: 04/27/94

CHLORAL HYDRATE   Systemic

Commonly used brand name(s):

In the U.S.—
Aquachloral Supprettes
Generic name product may be available.

In Canada—
Novo-Chlorhydrate
PMS-Chloral Hydrate

Description

Chloral hydrate (KLOR-al HYE-drate) belongs to the group of medicines called sedatives and hypnotics. It is sometimes used before surgery or certain procedures to relieve anxiety or tension or to produce sleep. If your child is to take this medicine before a dental or medical procedure, it should be given to the child only at the health care facility where the procedure is to be done. This will allow the health care professional to monitor your child.

Chloral hydrate has been used in the treatment of insomnia (trouble in sleeping) and to help calm or relax patients who are nervous or tense. However, this medicine has generally been replaced by other medicines for the treatment of insomnia and nervousness or tension.

Chloral hydrate has also been used with analgesics (pain medicine) for control of pain following surgery. However, this medicine has generally been replaced by other medicines for control of pain following surgery.

Chloral hydrate comes in different strengths. Serious problems, including deaths, have occurred when children were given the wrong strength. *Make sure your doctor has told your pharmacist both how many milligrams (mg) and how many capsules, teaspoonfuls, or suppositories should be used.* This information is needed to be sure the right amount is given.

This medicine is available only with your doctor's prescription, in the following dosage forms:

Oral
- Capsules (U.S. and Canada)
- Syrup (U.S. and Canada)

Rectal
- Suppositories (U.S.)

Before Using This Medicine

In deciding to use a medicine, the risks of taking the medicine must be weighed against the good it will do. This is a decision you and your doctor will make. For chloral hydrate, the following should be considered:

Allergies—Tell your doctor if you have ever had any unusual or allergic reaction to chloral hydrate. Also tell your health care professional if you are allergic to any other substances, such as foods, preservatives, or dyes.

Pregnancy—Studies on birth defects have not been done in either humans or animals. Too much use of chloral hydrate during pregnancy may cause the baby to become dependent on the medicine. This may lead to withdrawal side effects after birth.

Breast-feeding—Chloral hydrate passes into the breast milk and may cause drowsiness in babies of mothers using this medicine.

Children—This medicine comes in different strengths. Serious problems, including deaths, have occurred when children were given the wrong strength. *Make sure your doctor has told your pharmacist both how many milligrams (mg) and how many capsules, teaspoonfuls, or suppositories your child should receive.* This information is needed to be sure the right amount is given. With proper use, this medicine is not expected to cause different side effects or problems in children than it does in adults.

Older adults—Many medicines have not been studied specifically in older people. Therefore, it may not be known whether they work exactly the same way they do in younger adults. Although there is no specific information comparing use of chloral hydrate in the elderly with use in other age groups, this medicine is not expected to cause different side effects or problems in older people than it does in younger adults.

Other medicines—Although certain medicines should not be used together at all, in other cases two different medicines may be used together even if an interaction might occur. In these cases, your doctor may want to change the dose, or other precautions may be necessary. When you are taking chloral hydrate, it is especially important that your health care professional know if you are taking any of the following:

- Anticoagulants (blood thinners)—Chloral hydrate may change the amount of anticoagulant you need to take
- Central nervous system (CNS) depressants (medicine that causes drowsiness) or
- Tricyclic antidepressants (medicine for depression)— Using these medicines and chloral hydrate together may increase the CNS and other depressant effects

Other medical problems—The presence of other medical problems may affect the use of chloral hydrate. Make sure you tell your doctor if you have any other medical problems, especially:

- Alcohol abuse or dependence (or history of) or
- Drug abuse or dependence (or history of)—Dependence on chloral hydrate may develop

- Colitis or
- Proctitis or inflammation of the rectum—Chloral hydrate used rectally may make the condition worse

- Esophagitis or inflammation of the esophagus, or
- Gastritis or inflammation of the stomach, or
- Stomach ulcers—Chloral hydrate taken by mouth may make the condition worse

- Heart disease—Chloral hydrate may make the condition worse

- Kidney disease or
- Liver disease—Higher blood levels of chloral hydrate may occur, increasing the chance of side effects

- Porphyria—Acute attacks may be set off by chloral hydrate

- Sleep problems in children (especially in those with enlarged tonsils)—Risk of breathing problems may be increased

Proper Use of This Medicine

Use this medicine only as directed by your doctor. Do not use more of it, do not use it more often, and do not use it for a longer time than your doctor ordered. If too much is used, it may become habit-forming.

For patients taking *chloral hydrate capsules:*
- Swallow the capsule whole. Do not chew since the medicine may cause an unpleasant taste.
- Take this medicine with a full glass (8 ounces) of water, fruit juice, or ginger ale to lessen stomach upset.

For patients taking *chloral hydrate syrup:*
- Take each dose of medicine mixed with clear liquid, such as water, apple juice, or ginger ale. This will help to improve flavor and lessen stomach upset.

For patients using *chloral hydrate rectal suppositories:*
- If the suppository is too soft to insert, chill it in the refrigerator for 30 minutes or run cold water over it before removing the foil wrapper.
- To insert suppository—First remove the foil wrapper and moisten the suppository with cold water. Lie down on your side and use your finger to push the suppository well up into the rectum.

Dosing—The dose of chloral hydrate will be different for different patients. *Follow your doctor's orders or the directions on the label.* The following information includes only the average doses of chloral hydrate. *If your dose is different, do not change it* unless your doctor tells you to do so.

This medicine comes in different strengths. *Make sure your doctor has told your pharmacist both how many milligrams (mg) and how many capsules, teaspoonfuls, or suppositories should be used.* This information is needed to be sure the right amount is given.

The number of capsules or teaspoonfuls of syrup that you take, or suppositories that you use, depends on the strength of the medicine. Also, *the number of doses you use each day, the time allowed between doses, and the length of time you use the medicine depend on the medical problem for which you are using chloral hydrate.*
- For *oral* dosage form (capsules or syrup):
  —For trouble in sleeping or sedation before surgery:
  - Adults—500 to 1000 milligrams (mg) taken thirty minutes before bedtime or surgery.
  —For daytime sedation:
  - Adults—250 mg taken three times a day after meals.
  —For sedation before a dental or medical procedure:
  - Children—Dose is based on body weight and must be determined by your doctor. The dose is usually 50 mg per kilogram (kg) (23 mg per pound) of body weight.
  —For sedation before an electroencephalograph (EEG) test:
  - Children—Dose is based on body weight and must be determined by your doctor. The usual dose is 25 mg per kg (11 mg per pound) of body weight.
- For *rectal* dosage form (suppositories):
  —For trouble in sleeping:
  - Adults—500 to 1000 mg at bedtime.
  —For daytime sedation:
  - Adults—325 mg three times a day.
  —For sedation before a dental or medical procedure:
  - Children—Dose is based on body weight and must be determined by your doctor. The dose is usually 50 mg per kg (23 mg per pound) of body weight.
  —For sedation before an electroencephalograph (EEG) test:
  - Children—Dose is based on body weight and must be determined by your doctor. The dose is usually 25 mg per kg (11 mg per pound) of body weight.

Missed dose—If you miss a dose of this medicine, skip the missed dose and go back to your regular dosing schedule. Do not double doses.

Storage—To store this medicine:
- Keep out of the reach of children. Overdose of chloral hydrate is especially dangerous in children.
- Store away from heat and direct light.
- Do not store the capsule form of this medicine in the bathroom, near the kitchen sink, or in other damp places. Heat or moisture may cause the medicine to break down.
- Keep the syrup form of this medicine from freezing.
- Do not keep outdated medicine or medicine no longer needed. Be sure that any discarded medicine is out of the reach of children.

Precautions While Using This Medicine

If you will be using this medicine regularly for a long time:
- Your doctor should check your progress at regular visits to make sure that this medicine does not cause unwanted effects.
- Do not stop using it without first checking with your doctor. Your doctor may want you to reduce gradually the amount you are using before stopping completely.

This medicine will add to the effects of alcohol and other CNS depressants (medicines that slow down the nervous system, possibly causing drowsiness). Some examples of CNS depressants are antihistamines or medicine for hay fever, other allergies, or colds; sedatives, tranquilizers, or sleeping medicine; prescription pain medicine or narcotics; barbiturates; medicine for seizures; muscle relaxants; or anesthetics, including some dental anesthetics. *Check with your doctor before taking any of the above while you are using this medicine.*

If you think you or someone else may have taken an overdose of this medicine, get emergency help at once. Taking an overdose of chloral hydrate or taking alcohol or other CNS depressants with chloral hydrate may lead to unconsciousness and possibly death. Some signs of an overdose are continuing confusion, difficulty in swallowing, convulsions (seizures), severe drowsiness, severe weakness, shortness of breath or troubled breathing, staggering, and slow or irregular heartbeat.

This medicine may cause some people to become dizzy, lightheaded, drowsy, or less alert than they are normally. Even if taken at bedtime, it may cause some people to feel drowsy or less alert on arising. *Make sure you know how you react to this medicine before you drive, use machines, or do anything else that could be dangerous if you are dizzy or are not alert.*

Side Effects of This Medicine

Along with its needed effects, a medicine may cause some unwanted effects. Although not all of these side effects may occur, if they do occur they may need medical attention.

Check with your doctor as soon as possible if any of the following side effects occur:
Less common
  Skin rash or hives
Rare
  Confusion; hallucinations (seeing, hearing, or feeling things that are not there); unusual excitement
Symptoms of overdose
  Confusion (continuing); convulsions (seizures); diffi-

culty in swallowing; drowsiness (severe); low body temperature; nausea, vomiting, or stomach pain (severe); shortness of breath or troubled breathing; slow or irregular heartbeat; slurred speech; staggering; weakness (severe)

Other side effects may occur that do not need medical attention. These side effects may go away during treatment as your body adjusts to the medicine. However, check with your doctor if any of the following side effects continue or are bothersome:

More common
> Nausea; stomach pain; vomiting

Less common
> Clumsiness or unsteadiness; diarrhea; dizziness or lightheadedness; drowsiness; "hangover" effect

After you stop using this medicine, your body may need time to adjust. The length of time this takes depends on the amount of medicine you were using and how long you used it. During this period of time, check with your doctor if you notice any of the following side effects:

> Confusion; hallucinations (seeing, hearing, or feeling things that are not there); nausea or vomiting; nervousness; restlessness; stomach pain; trembling; unusual excitement

Other side effects not listed above may also occur in some patients. If you notice any other effects, check with your doctor.

Revised: 08/02/94
Interim revision: 03/31/95

CHLORAMBUCIL   Systemic

Commonly used brand name(s):

In the U.S.—
Leukeran

In Canada—
Leukeran

Description

Chlorambucil (klor-AM-byoo-sill) belongs to the group of medicines called alkylating agents. It is used to treat cancer of the blood and lymph system. It may also be used to treat other kinds of cancer, as determined by your doctor.

Chlorambucil interferes with the growth of cancer cells, which are eventually destroyed. Since the growth of normal body cells may also be affected by chlorambucil, other effects will also occur. Some of these may be serious and must be reported to your doctor. Other effects may not be serious but may cause concern. Some effects may not occur for months or years after the medicine is used.

Before you begin treatment with chlorambucil, you and your doctor should talk about the good this medicine will do as well as the risks of using it.

Chlorambucil may also be used for other conditions as determined by your doctor.

Chlorambucil is available only with your doctor's prescription, in the following dosage form:

Oral
- Tablets (U.S. and Canada)

Before Using This Medicine

In deciding to use a medicine, the risks of taking the medicine must be weighed against the good it will do. This is a decision you and your doctor will make. For chlorambucil, the following should be considered:

Allergies—Tell your doctor if you have ever had any unusual or allergic reaction to chlorambucil or other cancer medicines.

Pregnancy—This medicine may cause birth defects if either the male or female is taking it at the time of conception or if it is taken during pregnancy. In addition, many cancer medicines may cause sterility which could be permanent. Sterility has been reported with this medicine and the possibility should be kept in mind.

Be sure that you have discussed this with your doctor before taking this medicine. It is best to use some kind of birth control while you are taking chlorambucil. Tell your doctor right away if you think you have become pregnant while taking chlorambucil.

Breast-feeding—Because chlorambucil may cause serious side effects, breast-feeding is generally not recommended while you are taking it.

Children—In general, this medicine has not been shown to cause different side effects or problems in children than it does in adults. However, some children with nephrotic syndrome (a kidney disease) may be more likely to have convulsions (seizures).

Older adults—Many medicines have not been studied specifically in older people. Therefore, it may not be known whether they work exactly the same way they do in younger adults or if they cause different side effects or problems in older people. There is no specific information comparing use of chlorambucil in the elderly with use in other age groups.

Other medicines—Although certain medicines should not be used together at all, in other cases two different medicines may be used together even if an interaction might occur. In these cases, your doctor may want to change the dose, or other precautions may be necessary. When you are taking chlorambucil it is especially important that your health care professional know if you are taking any of the following:
- Amphotericin B by injection (e.g., Fungizone) or
- Antithyroid agents (medicine for overactive thyroid) or
- Chloramphenicol (e.g., Chloromycetin) or
- Colchicine or
- Flucytosine (e.g., Ancobon) or
- Ganciclovir (e.g., Cytovene) or
- Interferon (e.g., Intron A, Roferon-A) or
- Plicamycin (e.g., Mithracin) or
- Zidovudine (e.g., AZT, Retrovir) or
- If you have ever been treated with radiation or cancer medicines—Chlorambucil may increase the effects of these medicines or radiation therapy on the blood

- Azathioprine (e.g., Imuran) or
- Corticosteroids (cortisone-like medicine) or
- Cyclophosphamide (e.g., Cytoxan) or
- Cyclosporine (e.g., Sandimmune) or

- Cytarabine (e.g., Cytosar-U) or
- Mercaptopurine (e.g., Purinethol) or
- Muromonab-CD3 (monoclonal antibody) (e.g., Orthoclone OKT3) or
- Tacrolimus (e.g., Prograf)—There may be an increased risk of infection and development of cancer because chlorambucil decreases the body's ability to fight them

- Probenecid (e.g., Benemid) or
- Sulfinpyrazone (e.g., Anturane)—Chlorambucil may increase the amount of uric acid in the blood. Since these medicines are used to lower uric acid levels, they may not work as well in patients taking chlorambucil

Other medical problems—The presence of other medical problems may affect the use of chlorambucil. Make sure you tell your doctor if you have any other medical problems, especially:

- Chickenpox (including recent exposure) or
- Herpes zoster (shingles)—Risk of severe disease affecting other parts of the body

- Convulsions (seizures) (history of) or
- Head injury—Increased risk of seizures

- Gout or
- Kidney stones (history of)—Chlorambucil may increase levels of uric acid in the body, which can cause gout or kidney stones

- Infection—Chlorambucil decreases your body's ability to fight infection

Proper Use of This Medicine

Take this medicine only as directed by your doctor. Do not take more or less of it, and do not take it more often than your doctor ordered. The exact amount of medicine you need has been carefully worked out. Taking too much may increase the chance of side effects, while taking too little may not improve your condition.

Chlorambucil is sometimes given together with certain other medicines. If you are using a combination of medicines, make sure that you take each one at the proper time and do not mix them. Ask your health care professional to help you plan a way to remember to take your medicines at the right times.

While you are using chlorambucil, your doctor may want you to drink extra fluids so that you will pass more urine. This will help prevent kidney problems and keep your kidneys working well.

This medicine sometimes causes nausea and vomiting. However, it is very important that you continue to use the medicine, even if you begin to feel ill. *Do not stop using this medicine without first checking with your doctor.* Ask your health care professional for ways to lessen these effects.

If you vomit shortly after taking a dose of chlorambucil, check with your doctor. You will be told whether to take the dose again or to wait until the next scheduled dose.

Dosing—The dose of chlorambucil will be different for different patients. The dose that is used may depend on a number of things, including what the medicine is being used for, the patient's weight, and whether or not other medicines are also being taken. *If you are taking chlorambucil at home, follow your doctor's orders or the directions on the label.* If you have any questions about the proper dose of chlorambucil, ask your doctor.

Missed dose—If you miss a dose of this medicine and your dosing schedule is:

- One dose a day—Take the missed dose as soon as possible. Then go back to your regular dosing schedule. However, if you do not remember the missed dose until the next day, do not take it at all. Instead, take your regularly scheduled dose. Do not double doses.
- More than one dose a day—Take the missed dose as soon as possible. Then go back to your regular dosing schedule. However, if it is almost time for your next dose, skip the missed dose and go back to your regular dosing schedule. Do not double doses.

Storage—To store this medicine:

- Keep out of the reach of children.
- Store away from heat and direct light.
- Do not store in the bathroom, near the kitchen sink, or in other damp places. Heat or moisture may cause the medicine to break down.
- Do not keep outdated medicine or medicine no longer needed. Be sure that any discarded medicine is out of the reach of children.

Precautions While Using This Medicine

It is very important that your doctor check your progress at regular visits to make sure this medicine is working properly and to check for unwanted effects.

While you are being treated with chlorambucil, and after you stop treatment with it, *do not have any immunizations (vaccinations) without your doctor's approval.* Chlorambucil may lower your body's resistance and there is a chance you might get the infection the immunization is meant to prevent. In addition, other persons living in your household should not take oral polio vaccine since there is a chance they could pass the polio virus on to you. Also, avoid persons who have taken oral polio vaccine within the last several months. Do not get close to them, and do not stay in the same room with them for very long. If you cannot take these precautions, you should consider wearing a protective face mask that covers the nose and mouth.

Chlorambucil can temporarily lower the number of white blood cells in your blood, increasing the chance of getting an infection. It can also lower the number of platelets, which are necessary for proper blood clotting. If this occurs, there are certain precautions you can take, especially when your blood count is low, to reduce the risk of infection or bleeding:

- If you can, avoid people with infections. *Check with your doctor immediately* if you think you are getting an infection or if you get a fever or chills, cough or hoarseness, lower back or side pain, or painful or difficult urination.
- *Check with your doctor immediately* if you notice any unusual bleeding or bruising; black, tarry stools; blood in urine or stools; or pinpoint red spots on your skin.
- Be careful when using a regular toothbrush, dental floss, or toothpick. Your medical doctor, dentist, or nurse may recommend other ways to clean your teeth and gums. Check with your medical doctor before having any dental work done.
- Do not touch your eyes or the inside of your nose unless you have just washed your hands and have not touched anything else in the meantime.
- Be careful not to cut yourself when you are using sharp objects such as a safety razor or fingernail or toenail cutters.

- Avoid contact sports or other situations where bruising or injury could occur.

Side Effects of This Medicine

Along with its needed effects, a medicine may have some unwanted effects. Although not all of these side effects may occur, if they do occur they may need medical attention.

Also, because of the way these medicines act on the body, there is a chance that they might cause other unwanted effects that may not occur until months or years after the medicine is used. These delayed effects may include certain types of cancer, such as leukemia. Discuss these possible effects with your doctor.

Check with your doctor or nurse immediately if any of the following side effects occur:

Less common
Black, tarry stools; blood in urine or stools; cough or hoarseness, accompanied by fever or chills; fever or chills; lower back or side pain, accompanied by fever or chills; painful or difficult urination, accompanied by fever or chills; pinpoint red spots on skin; sores in mouth and on lips; unusual bleeding or bruising

Rare
Cough; blisters on skin; shortness of breath; skin rash (severe)

Check with your doctor as soon as possible if any of the following side effects occur:

Less common
Joint pain; lower back or side pain; skin rash; swelling of feet or lower legs

Rare
Agitation; confusion; convulsions (seizures); hallucinations (seeing, hearing, or feeling things that are not there); muscle twitching; tremors; trouble in walking; weakness (severe) or paralysis; yellow eyes or skin

Symptoms of overdose (in the order of frequency)
Black, tarry stools; blood in urine or stools; cough or hoarseness, accompanied by fever or chills; fever or chills; lower back or side pain, accompanied by fever or chills; painful or difficult urination, accompanied by fever or chills; pinpoint red spots on skin; unusual bleeding or bruising; agitation; convulsions (seizures); trouble in walking

Other side effects may occur that usually do not need medical attention. These side effects may go away during treatment as your body adjusts to the medicine. Also, your health care professional may be able to tell you about ways to prevent or reduce some of these side effects. Check with your health care professional if any of the following side effects continue or are bothersome or if you have any questions about them:

Less common
Changes in menstrual period; itching of skin; nausea and vomiting

After you stop using chlorambucil, it may still produce some side effects that need attention. During this period of time, check with your doctor if you notice any of the following side effects:
Black, tarry stools; blood in urine or stools; cough or hoarseness (may be accompanied by fever or chills); fever or chills; lower back or side pain, accompanied by fever or chills; painful or difficult urination, accom-

panied by fever or chills; pinpoint red spots on skin; shortness of breath; unusual bleeding or bruising

Other side effects not listed above may also occur in some patients. If you notice any other effects, check with your doctor.

Additional Information

Once a medicine has been approved for marketing for a certain use, experience may show that it is also useful for other medical problems. Although these uses are not included in product labeling, chlorambucil is used in certain patients with the following medical conditions:

- Cancer of the ovaries
- Cancer of the lymph system that affects the skin
- Hairy cell leukemia (a cancer of the blood and bone marrow)
- Nephrotic syndrome (a kidney disease)
- Tumors in the uterus (womb)
- Waldenström's macroglobulinemia (a certain type of cancer of the blood)
- Histiocytosis X (a certain type of cancer found primarily in children)

Other than the above information, there is no additional information relating to proper use, precautions, or side effects for these uses.

Revised: 08/07/2000

CHLORAMPHENICOL   Ophthalmic

Commonly used brand name(s):

In the U.S.—

Ak-Chlor Ophthalmic Ointment	Econochlor Ophthalmic Ointment
Ak-Chlor Ophthalmic Solution	Econochlor Ophthalmic Solution
Chloracol Ophthalmic Solution	I-Chlor Ophthalmic Solution
Chlorofair Ophthalmic Ointment	Ocu-Chlor Ophthalmic Ointment
Chlorofair Ophthalmic Solution	Ocu-Chlor Ophthalmic Solution
Chloromycetin Ophthalmic Ointment	Ophthochlor Ophthalmic Solution
Chloromycetin for Ophthalmic Solution	Spectro-Chlor Ophthalmic Ointment
Chloroptic Ophthalmic Solution	Spectro-Chlor Ophthalmic Solution
Chloroptic S.O.P.	

In Canada—

Ak-Chlor Ophthalmic Solution	Ophtho-Chloram Ophthalmic Solution
Chloromycetin Ophthalmic Ointment	Pentamycetin Ophthalmic Ointment
Chloromycetin for Ophthalmic Solution	Pentamycetin Ophthalmic Solution
Chloroptic Ophthalmic Solution	Sopamycetin Ophthalmic Ointment
Chloroptic S.O.P.	Sopamycetin Ophthalmic Solution
Fenicol Ophthalmic Ointment	

Description

Chloramphenicol (klor-am-FEN-i-kole) belongs to the family of medicines called antibiotics. Chloramphenicol ophthalmic preparations are used to treat infections of the eye. This medicine may be given alone or with other medicines that are taken by mouth for eye infections.

Chloramphenicol is available only with your doctor's prescription, in the following dosage forms:

Ophthalmic
- Ophthalmic ointment (eye ointment) (U.S. and Canada)
- Ophthalmic solution (eye drops) (U.S. and Canada)

Before Using This Medicine

In deciding to use a medicine, the risks of taking the medicine must be weighed against the good it will do. This is a decision you and your doctor will make. For chloramphenicol, the following should be considered:

Allergies—Tell your doctor if you have ever had any unusual or allergic reaction to chloramphenicol. Also tell your health care professional if you are allergic to any other substances, such as preservatives.

Pregnancy—Chloramphenicol ophthalmic preparations have not been shown to cause birth defects or other problems in humans.

Breast-feeding—Chloramphenicol ophthalmic preparations have not been reported to cause problems in nursing babies.

Children—Studies on this medicine have been done only in adult patients, and there is no specific information comparing use of this medicine in children with use in other age groups.

Older adults—Many medicines have not been studied specifically in older people. Therefore, it may not be known whether they work exactly the same way they do in younger adults or if they cause different side effects or problems in older people. There is no specific information comparing use of this medicine in the elderly with use in other age groups.

Other medicines—Although certain medicines should not be used together at all, in other cases two different medicines may be used together even if an interaction might occur. In these cases, your doctor may want to change the dose, or other precautions may be necessary. Tell your health care professional if you are using any other prescription or nonprescription (over-the-counter [OTC]) medicine.

Proper Use of This Medicine

For patients using the *eye drop form* of chloramphenicol:
- Although the bottle may not be full, it contains exactly the amount of medicine your doctor ordered.
- To use:
  —First, wash your hands. Tilt the head back and, pressing your finger gently on the skin just beneath the lower eyelid, pull the lower eyelid away from the eye to make a space. Drop the medicine into this space. Let go of the eyelid and gently close the eyes. Do not blink. Keep the eyes closed and apply pressure to the inner corner of the eye with your finger for 1 or 2 minutes to allow the medicine to come into contact with the infection.
  —If you think you did not get the drop of medicine into your eye properly, use another drop.
  —To keep the medicine as germ-free as possible, do not touch the applicator tip or dropper to any surface

(including the eye). Also, keep the container tightly closed.

To use the *eye ointment form* of chloramphenicol:
- First, wash your hands. Tilt the head back and, pressing your finger gently on the skin just beneath the lower eyelid, pull the lower eyelid away from the eye to make a space. Squeeze a thin strip of ointment into this space. A 1-cm (approximately 1/3-inch) strip of ointment is usually enough, unless you have been told by your doctor to use a different amount. Let go of the eyelid and gently close the eyes. Keep the eyes closed for 1 or 2 minutes to allow the medicine to come into contact with the infection.
- To keep the medicine as germ-free as possible, do not touch the applicator tip to any surface (including the eye). After using chloramphenicol eye ointment, wipe the tip of the ointment tube with a clean tissue and keep the tube tightly closed.

To help clear up your infection completely, *keep using this medicine for the full time of treatment*, even if your symptoms begin to clear up after a few days. If you stop using this medicine too soon, your symptoms may return. *Do not miss any doses.*

Dosing—The dose of chloramphenicol will be different for different patients. *Follow your doctor's orders or the directions on the label*. The following information includes only the average doses of chloramphenicol. *If your dose is different, do not change it* unless your doctor tells you to do so.
- For eye infection:
  —For *ophthalmic ointment* dosage form:
    - Adults and children—Use every three hours.
  —For *ophthalmic solution (eye drops)* dosage form:
    - Adults and children—One drop every one to four hours.

Missed dose—If you miss a dose of this medicine, apply it as soon as possible. However, if it is almost time for your next dose, skip the missed dose and go back to your regular dosing schedule.

Storage—To store this medicine:
- Keep out of the reach of children.
- Store away from heat and direct light.
- Keep the medicine from freezing.
- Do not keep outdated medicine or medicine no longer needed. Be sure that any discarded medicine is out of the reach of children.

Precautions While Using This Medicine

If your symptoms do not improve within a few days, or if they become worse, check with your doctor.

Side Effects of This Medicine

Along with its needed effects, a medicine may cause some unwanted effects. Although not all of these side effects may occur, if they do occur they may need medical attention.

Check with your doctor immediately if any of the following side effects occur:
Rare—may also occur weeks or months after you stop using this medicine
   Pale skin; sore throat and fever; unusual bleeding or bruising; unusual tiredness or weakness

Check with your doctor as soon as possible if any of the following side effects occur:

Less common

Itching, redness, skin rash, swelling, or other sign of irritation not present before use of this medicine

Other side effects may occur that usually do not need medical attention. These side effects may go away during treatment as your body adjusts to the medicine. However, check with your doctor if either of the following side effects continues or is bothersome:

Less common

Burning or stinging

After application, eye ointments may be expected to cause your vision to blur for a few minutes.

Other side effects not listed above may also occur in some patients. If you notice any other effects, check with your doctor.

Revised: 01/15/92
Interim revision: 09/30/93; 12/13/93

CHLORAMPHENICOL   Otic

Commonly used brand name(s):

In the U.S.—
Chloromycetin

In Canada—
Chloromycetin

Description

Chloramphenicol (klor-am-FEN-i-kole) belongs to the family of medicines called antibiotics. Chloramphenicol otic drops are used to treat infections of the ear canal. This medicine may be used alone or with other medicines that are taken by mouth for ear canal infections.

Chloramphenicol is available only with your doctor's prescription, in the following dosage form:

Otic
• Solution (U.S. and Canada)

Before Using This Medicine

In deciding to use a medicine, the risks of using the medicine must be weighed against the good it will do. This is a decision you and your doctor will make. For chloramphenicol otic, the following should be considered:

Allergies—Tell your doctor if you have ever had any unusual or allergic reaction to chloramphenicol. Also tell your health care professional if you are allergic to any other substances, such as preservatives.

Pregnancy—Chloramphenicol otic solution has not been studied in pregnant women. However, using this medication during pregnancy or labor may increase health risks for the child (See *Children*).

Breast-feeding—Chloramphenicol passes into breast milk. Mothers receiving chloramphenicol should not breast-feed their infants.

Children—Gray syndrome may be especially likely to occur in children, who are usually more sensitive than adults to the effects of chloramphenicol. Report any of these effects to your health care professional: blue tone to the skin, changes in blood pressure or heart rate, eating problems, irregular breathing, passage of loose green stools, or stomach bloating with or without vomiting. Your health care professional should monitor blood levels of chloramphenicol if possible.

Older adults—Many medicines have not been studied specifically in older people. Therefore, it may not be known whether they work exactly the same way they do in younger adults or if they cause different side effects or problems in older people. There is no specific information comparing use of this medicine in the elderly with use in other age groups.

Other medicines—Although certain medicines should not be used together at all, in other cases two different medicines may be used together even if an interaction might occur. In these cases, your doctor may want to change the dose, or other precautions may be necessary. Tell your health care professional if you are using any other prescription or nonprescription (over-the-counter [OTC]) medicine. Chloramphenicol may increase the blood levels of these medications: alfentanil, chlorpropamide, phenobarbital, phenytoin, tolbutamide, and warfarin. Phenobarbital and rifampin may reduce the blood levels of chloramphenicol. Concurrent use of chloramphenicol with vitamin B_{12}, folic acid, iron preparations and myelosuppressive agents may inhibit the formation of bone marrow.

Other medical problems—The presence of other medical problems may affect the use of chloramphenicol ear drops. Make sure you tell your doctor if you have any other medical problems, especially:

• Opening in your ear drum—This medicine may cause unwanted effects if it goes past the ear drum into the middle ear
• Sensitivity reaction to chloramphenicol

Proper Use of This Medicine

To use:
• Lie down or tilt the head so that the infected ear faces up. Gently pull the earlobe up and back for adults (down and back for children) to straighten the ear canal. Drop the medicine into the ear canal. Keep the ear facing up for about 1 or 2 minutes to allow the medicine to come into contact with the infection. A sterile cotton plug may be gently inserted into the ear opening to prevent the medicine from leaking out.
• To keep the medicine as germ-free as possible, do not touch the dropper to any surface (including the ear). Also, keep the container tightly closed.

To help clear up your infection completely, *keep using this medicine for the full time of treatment,* even if your symptoms begin to clear up after a few days. If you stop using this medicine too soon, your symptoms may return. *Do not miss any doses.*

Dosing—The dose of otic chloramphenicol will be different for different patients. *Follow your doctor's orders or the directions on the label.* The following information includes only the average doses of otic chloramphenicol. *If your dose is different, do not change it* unless your doctor tells you to do so.

- For *otic solution (ear drops)* dosage form:
  —For infections of the ear canal:
    - Adults and children—Use 2 or 3 drops in the affected ear two to three times a day.

Missed dose—If you miss a dose of this medicine, apply it as soon as possible. However, if it is almost time for your next dose, skip the missed dose and go back to your regular dosing schedule.

Storage—To store this medicine:
- Keep out of the reach of children.
- Store away from heat and direct light.
- Keep the medicine from freezing.
- Do not keep outdated medicine or medicine no longer needed. Be sure that any discarded medicine is out of the reach of children.

Precautions While Using This Medicine

If your symptoms do not improve within a few days, or if they become worse, check with your doctor.

Side Effects of This Medicine

Along with its needed effects, a medicine may cause some unwanted effects. Although not all of these side effects may occur, if they do occur they may need medical attention.

Check with your doctor immediately if any of the following side effects occur:
  Rare—may also occur weeks or months after you stop using this medicine
    Bluish tone to the skin; changes in blood pressure or heart rate; eating problems; irregular breathing; pale skin; passage of loose green stools; sore throat and fever; stomach bloating with or without vomiting; unusual bleeding or bruising; unusual tiredness or weakness

Check with your doctor as soon as possible if any of the following side effects occur:
  Less common
    Blindness or changes in vision; burning, itching, redness, skin rash, swelling, or other sign of irritation not present before use of this medicine; diarrhea; fever; hallucinations; headache; mental confusion; mild depression; nausea; stomach pain; swollen mouth and tongue; unpleasant taste; vomiting

Other side effects not listed above may also occur in some patients. If you notice any other effects, check with your doctor.

Revised: 6/04/99

CHLORAMPHENICOL   Systemic

Commonly used brand name(s):
In the U.S.—
  Chloromycetin
  Generic name product may be available.

In Canada—
  Chloromycetin
  Novochlorocap

Description

Chloramphenicol (klor-am-FEN-i-kole) is used in the treatment of infections caused by bacteria. It works by killing bacteria or preventing their growth.

Chloramphenicol is used to treat serious infections in different parts of the body. It is sometimes given with other antibiotics. However, chloramphenicol should not be used for colds, flu, other virus infections, sore throats or other minor infections, or to prevent infections.

Chloramphenicol should only be used for serious infections in which other medicines do not work. This medicine may cause some serious side effects, including blood problems and eye problems. Symptoms of the blood problems include pale skin, sore throat and fever, unusual bleeding or bruising, and unusual tiredness or weakness. *You and your doctor should talk about the good this medicine will do as well as the risks of taking it.*

Chloramphenicol is available only with your doctor's prescription, in the following dosage forms:
  Oral
    - Capsules (Canada)
  Parenteral
    - Injection (U.S. and Canada)

Before Using This Medicine

In deciding to use a medicine, the risks of taking the medicine must be weighed against the good it will do. This is a decision you and your doctor will make. For chloramphenicol, the following should be considered:

Allergies—Tell your doctor if you have ever had any unusual or allergic reaction to chloramphenicol. Also tell your health care professional if you are allergic to any other substances, such as foods, preservatives, or dyes.

Pregnancy—Chloramphenicol has not been shown to cause birth defects in humans. However, use is not recommended within a week or two of your delivery date. Chloramphenicol may cause gray skin color, low body temperature, bloated stomach, uneven breathing, drowsiness, pale skin, sore throat and fever, unusual bleeding or bruising, unusual tiredness or weakness, or other problems in the infant.

Breast-feeding—Chloramphenicol passes into the breast milk and has been shown to cause unwanted effects, such as pale skin, sore throat and fever, unusual bleeding or bruising, unusual tiredness or weakness, or other problems in nursing babies. It may be necessary for you to take another medicine or to stop breast-feeding during treatment. Be sure you have discussed the risks and benefits of the medicine with your doctor.

Children—Newborn infants are especially sensitive to the side effects of chloramphenicol because they cannot remove the medicine from their body as well as older children and adults.

Older adults—Many medicines have not been studied specifically in older people. Therefore, it may not be known whether they work exactly the same way they do in younger adults or if they cause different side effects or problems in older people. There is no specific information comparing use of chloramphenicol in the elderly with use in other age groups.

Other medicines—Although certain medicines should not be used together at all, in other cases two different medicines may be used together even if an interaction might occur. In these cases, your doctor may want to change the dose, or other precautions may be necessary. When you are taking chloramphenicol, it is especially important that your health care professional know if you are taking any of the following:

- Alfentanil or
- Antidiabetics, oral (diabetes medicine you take by mouth) or
- Phenobarbital or
- Warfarin (e.g., Coumadin)—Use of chloramphenicol with these medicines may increase the chance of side effects of these medicines

- Amphotericin B by injection (e.g., Fungizone) or
- Antineoplastics (cancer medicine) or
- Antithyroid agents (medicine for overactive thyroid) or
- Azathioprine (e.g., Imuran) or
- Colchicine or
- Cyclophosphamide (e.g., Cytoxan) or
- Ethotoin (e.g., Peganone) or
- Flucytosine (e.g., Ancobon) or
- Ganciclovir (e.g., Cytovene) or
- Interferon (e.g., Intron A, Roferon-A) or
- Mephenytoin (e.g., Mesantoin) or
- Mercaptopurine (e.g., Purinethol) or
- Methotrexate (e.g., Mexate) or
- Phenytoin (e.g., Dilantin) or
- Plicamycin (e.g., Mithracin) or
- Zidovudine (e.g., AZT, Retrovir) or
- X-ray treatment—Use of chloramphenicol with any of these medicines or with x-ray treatment may increase the risk of blood problems

- Clindamycin (e.g., Cleocin) or
- Erythromycins (medicine for infection) or
- Lincomycin (e.g., Lincocin)—Use of chloramphenicol with any of these medicines may decrease the effectiveness of these medicines

- Phenytoin (e.g., Dilantin)—Use of chloramphenicol with phenytoin may increase the chance of blood problems or increase the side effects of phenytoin

Other medical problems—The presence of other medical problems may affect the use of chloramphenicol. Make sure you tell your doctor if you have any other medical problems, especially:

- Anemia, bleeding, or other blood problems—Chloramphenicol may cause blood problems

- Liver disease—Patients with liver disease may have an increased risk of side effects

Proper Use of This Medicine

Chloramphenicol is best taken with a full glass (8 ounces) of water on an empty stomach (either 1 hour before or 2 hours after meals), unless otherwise directed by your doctor.

For patients taking the oral liquid form of this medicine:

- Use a specially marked measuring spoon or other device to measure each dose accurately. The average household teaspoon may not hold the right amount of liquid.

To help clear up your infection completely, *keep taking this medicine for the full time of treatment*, even if you begin to feel better after a few days. *Do not miss any doses.*

Dosing—The dose of chloramphenicol will be different for different patients. *Follow your doctor's orders or the directions on the label.* The following information includes only the average doses of chloramphenicol. *If your dose is different, do not change it* unless your doctor tells you to do so.

The number of capsules or teaspoonfuls of suspension that you take depends on the strength of the medicine. Also, *the number of doses you take each day, the time allowed between doses, and the length of time you take the medicine depend on the medical problem for which you are taking chloramphenicol.*

- For infections caused by bacteria:
  —For *oral* dosage forms (capsules and suspension):
    - Adults and teenagers—Dose is based on body weight. The usual dose is 12.5 milligrams (mg) per kilogram (kg) (5.7 mg per pound) of body weight every six hours.
    - Children—
      —Infants up to 2 weeks of age: Dose is based on body weight. The usual dose is 6.25 mg per kg (2.8 mg per pound) of body weight every six hours.
      —Infants 2 weeks of age and older: Dose is based on body weight. The usual dose is 12.5 mg per kg (5.7 mg per pound) of body weight every six hours; or 25 mg per kg (11.4 mg per pound) of body weight every twelve hours.

  —For *injection* dosage form:
    - Adults and teenagers—Dose is based on body weight. The usual dose is 12.5 mg per kg (5.7 mg per pound) of body weight every six hours.
    - Children—
      —Infants up to 2 weeks of age: Dose is based on body weight. The usual dose is 6.25 mg per kg (2.8 mg per pound) of body weight every six hours.
      —Infants 2 weeks of age and older: Dose is based on body weight. The usual dose is 12.5 mg per kg (5.7 mg per pound) of body weight every six hours; or 25 mg per kg (11.4 mg per pound) of body weight every twelve hours.

Missed dose—If you miss a dose of this medicine, take it as soon as possible. However, if it is almost time for your next dose, skip the missed dose and go back to your regular dosing schedule. Do not double doses.

Storage—To store this medicine:

- Keep out of the reach of children.
- Store away from heat and direct light.
- Do not store the capsule form of this medicine in the bathroom, near the kitchen sink, or in other damp places. Heat or moisture may cause the medicine to break down.
- Keep the oral liquid form of this medicine from freezing.
- Do not keep outdated medicine or medicine no longer needed. Be sure that any discarded medicine is out of the reach of children.

Precautions While Using This Medicine

If your symptoms do not improve within a few days, or if they become worse, check with your doctor.

It is very important that your doctor check you at regular visits for any blood problems that may be caused by this medicine.

Chloramphenicol may cause blood problems. These problems may result in a greater chance of infection, slow healing, and bleeding of the gums. Therefore, you should be careful when using regular toothbrushes, dental floss, and toothpicks. Dental work, whenever possible, should be done before you begin taking this medicine or delayed until your blood counts have returned to normal. Check with your medical doctor or dentist if you have any questions about proper oral hygiene (mouth care) during treatment.

For diabetic patients:
- *This medicine may cause false test results with urine sugar tests.* Check with your doctor before changing your diet or the dosage of your diabetes medicine.

Side Effects of This Medicine

Along with its needed effects, a medicine may cause some serious unwanted effects. Although not all of these side effects may occur, if they do occur they may need medical attention.

Stop taking this medicine and get emergency help immediately if any of the following side effects occur:
  Rare—in babies only
    Bloated stomach; drowsiness; gray skin color; low body temperature; uneven breathing; unresponsiveness

Also, *check with your doctor immediately* if any of the following side effects occur:
  Less common
    Pale skin; sore throat and fever; unusual bleeding or bruising; unusual tiredness or weakness (the above side effects may also occur up to weeks or months after you stop taking this medicine)

  Rare
    Confusion, delirium, or headache; eye pain, blurred vision, or loss of vision; numbness, tingling, burning pain, or weakness in the hands or feet; skin rash, fever, or difficulty in breathing

Other side effects may occur that usually do not need medical attention. These side effects may go away during treatment as your body adjusts to the medicine. However, check with your doctor if any of the following side effects continue or are bothersome:
  Less common
    Diarrhea; nausea or vomiting

Other side effects not listed above may also occur in some patients. If you notice any other effects, check with your doctor.

Revised: 05/13/92
Interim revision: 03/17/94; 06/20/95

CHLORDIAZEPOXIDE AND AMITRIPTYLINE   Systemic†

Commonly used brand name(s):

In the U.S.—
  Limbitrol
  Limbitrol DS
  Generic name product may be available.

†Not commercially available in Canada.

Description

Chlordiazepoxide and amitriptyline (klor-dy-az-e-POX-ide and a-mee-TRIP-ti-leen) combination is used to treat mental depression that occurs with anxiety or nervous tension.

This medicine is available only with your doctor's prescription, in the following dosage form:
  Oral
    • Tablets (U.S.)

Before Using This Medicine

In deciding to use a medicine, the risks of taking the medicine must be weighed against the good it will do. This is a decision you and your doctor will make. For chlordiazepoxide and amitriptyline combination, the following should be considered:

Allergies—Tell your doctor if you have ever had any unusual or allergic reaction to chlordiazepoxide (e.g., Librium) or other benzodiazepines (such as alprazolam [e.g., Xanax], bromazepam [e.g., Lectopam], clonazepam [e.g., Klonopin], clorazepate [e.g., Tranxene], diazepam [e.g., Valium], estazolam [e.g., ProSom], flurazepam [e.g., Dalmane], halazepam [e.g., Paxipam], ketazolam [e.g., Loftran], lorazepam [e.g., Ativan], midazolam [e.g., Versed], nitrazepam [e.g., Mogadon], oxazepam [e.g., Serax], prazepam [e.g., Centrax], quazepam [e.g., Doral], temazepam [e.g., Restoril], triazolam [e.g., Halcion]) or to amitriptyline (e.g., Elavil) or other tricyclic antidepressants (such as amoxapine [e.g., Asendin], clomipramine [e.g., Anafranil], desipramine [e.g., Pertofrane], doxepin [e.g., Sinequan], imipramine [e.g., Tofranil], nortriptyline [e.g., Aventyl], protriptyline [e.g., Vivactil], trimipramine [e.g., Surmontil]).

Also tell your health care professional if you are allergic to any other substances, such as foods, preservatives, or dyes.

Pregnancy—
- *Chlordiazepoxide:* Chlordiazepoxide has been reported to increase the chance of birth defects when used during the first 3 months of pregnancy. In addition, overuse of chlordiazepoxide during pregnancy may cause the baby to become dependent on the medicine. This may lead to withdrawal side effects in the baby after birth. Use of chlordiazepoxide during pregnancy, especially during the last weeks, may cause drowsiness, slow heartbeat, shortness of breath, or troubled breathing in the newborn baby. Chlordiazepoxide given just before or during labor may cause weakness in the newborn baby.
- *Amitriptyline:* Studies with amitriptyline have not been done in pregnant women. However, studies in animals have shown amitriptyline to cause birth defects when used in doses many times the human dose. Also, there have been reports of newborns suffering from muscle spasms and heart, breathing, and urinary problems

when their mothers had taken tricyclic antidepressants (such as amitriptyline) immediately before delivery.

Breast-feeding—Chlordiazepoxide may pass into the breast milk and cause drowsiness, slow heartbeat, shortness of breath, or troubled breathing in babies of mothers taking this medicine. Although amitriptyline has also been found in breast milk, it has not been reported to cause problems in nursing babies.

Children—Children may be especially sensitive to the effects of chlordiazepoxide and amitriptyline combination. This may increase the chance of side effects during treatment.

Older adults—Elderly people are especially sensitive to the effects of chlordiazepoxide and amitriptyline combination. This may increase the chance of side effects during treatment.

Other medicines—Although certain medicines should not be used together at all, in other cases 2 different medicines may be used together even if an interaction might occur. In these cases, your doctor may want to change the dose, or other precautions may be necessary. When you are taking chlordiazepoxide and amitriptyline combination, it is especially important that your health care professional know if you are taking any of the following:

- Alcohol or
- Central nervous system (CNS) depressants (medicines that cause drowsiness)—Using these medicines with chlordiazepoxide and amitriptyline combination may increase the CNS depressant effects

- Amphetamines or
- Appetite suppressants (diet pills) or
- Medicine for asthma or other breathing problems or
- Medicine for colds, sinus problems, or hay fever or other allergies (including nose drops or sprays)—Using these medicines with chlordiazepoxide and amitriptyline combination may increase the risk of serious effects on your heart

- Antacids—Taking these medicines with chlordiazepoxide and amitriptyline combination may delay the combination medicine's effects

- Antihypertensives (high blood pressure medicine)—Taking these medicines with chlordiazepoxide and amitriptyline combination may increase the chance of low blood pressure (hypotension)

- Antithyroid agents (medicine for overactive thyroid) or
- Cimetidine (e.g., Tagamet)—Taking these medicines with chlordiazepoxide and amitriptyline combination may increase the chance of serious side effects

- Monoamine oxidase (MAO) inhibitors (furazolidone [e.g., Furoxone], isocarboxazid [e.g., Marplan], phenelzine [e.g., Nardil], procarbazine [e.g., Matulane], selegiline [e.g., Eldepryl], tranylcypromine [e.g., Parnate])—Taking chlordiazepoxide and amitriptyline combination while you are taking or within 2 weeks of taking monoamine oxidase (MAO) inhibitors may cause sudden very high body temperature, extremely high blood pressure, and severe convulsions; however, sometimes certain of these medicines may be used with this combination medicine under close supervision by your doctor

Other medical problems—The presence of other medical problems may affect the use of chlordiazepoxide and am-

itriptyline combination. Make sure you tell your doctor if you have any other medical problems, especially:

- Alcohol abuse (or history of) or
- Drug abuse or dependence (or history of)—Dependence on this medicine may develop

- Bipolar disorder (manic-depressive illness) or
- Blood problems or
- Difficulty in urinating or
- Emphysema, asthma, bronchitis, or other chronic lung disease or
- Enlarged prostate or
- Glaucoma or increased eye pressure or
- Heart disease or
- Mental illness (severe) or
- Myasthenia gravis or
- Porphyria—Chlordiazepoxide and amitriptyline combination may make the condition worse

- Epilepsy or history of seizures—The risk of seizures may be increased

- Hyperactivity—Chlordiazepoxide and amitriptyline combination may cause unexpected effects

- Kidney disease or
- Liver disease—Higher blood levels of chlordiazepoxide and amitriptyline may occur, increasing the chance of side effects

- Overactive thyroid or
- Stomach or intestinal problems—Use of this combination medicine may result in more serious problems

Proper Use of This Medicine

To reduce stomach upset, take this medicine immediately after meals or with food unless your doctor has told you to take it on an empty stomach.

Sometimes this medicine must be taken for several weeks before you begin to feel better. Your doctor should check your progress at regular visits.

Take this medicine only as directed by your doctor. Do not take more of it, do not take it more often, and do not take it for a longer period of time than your doctor ordered. If too much is taken, it may increase unwanted effects or become habit-forming (causing mental or physical dependence).

If you think this medicine is not working properly after you have taken it for a few weeks, *do not increase the dose.* Instead, check with your doctor.

Dosing—The dose of chlordiazepoxide and amitriptyline combination will be different for different patients. *Follow your doctor's orders or the directions on the label.* The following information includes only the average doses of chlordiazepoxide and amitriptyline combination. *If your dose is different, do not change it* unless your doctor tells you to do so.

The number of tablets that you take depends on the strength of the medicine. Also, *the number of doses you take each day, the time allowed between doses, and the length of time you take the medicine depend on the medical problem for which you are taking chlordiazepoxide and amitriptyline combination.*

- For *oral* dosage forms (tablets):
  —Adults and adolescents: To start, 5 milligrams of chlordiazepoxide and 12.5 milligrams of amitriptyline or 10 milligrams of chlordiazepoxide and 25 milligrams of amitriptyline, taken three or four times

a day. The doctor may adjust your dose if needed. However, the dose is usually not greater than 10 milligrams of chlordiazepoxide and 25 milligrams of amitriptyline taken six times a day.

—Children up to 12 years of age: Dose must be determined by the doctor.

Missed dose—If you miss a dose of this medicine, skip the missed dose and go back to your regular dosing schedule. Do not double doses.

Storage—To store this medicine:

- Keep out of the reach of children. Overdose of this medicine is very dangerous in young children.
- Store away from heat and direct light.
- Do not store in the bathroom, near the kitchen sink, or in other damp places. Heat or moisture may cause the medicine to break down.
- Do not keep outdated medicine or medicine no longer needed. Be sure that any discarded medicine is out of the reach of children.

Precautions While Using This Medicine

It is very important that your doctor check your progress at regular visits to allow dose adjustments and help reduce side effects.

Do not stop taking this medicine without first checking with your doctor. Your doctor may want you to reduce gradually the amount you are using before stopping completely. This may help prevent a possible worsening of your condition and reduce the possibility of withdrawal symptoms such as headache, nausea, and/or an overall feeling of discomfort.

This medicine will add to the effects of alcohol and other CNS depressants (medicines that slow down the nervous system, possibly causing drowsiness). Some examples of CNS depressants are antihistamines or medicine for hay fever, other allergies, or colds; sedatives, tranquilizers, or sleeping medicine; prescription pain medicine or narcotics; barbiturates; medicine for seizures; muscle relaxants; or anesthetics, including some dental anesthetics. This effect may last for a few days after you stop taking this medicine. *Check with your doctor before taking any of the above while you are using this medicine.*

For diabetic patients:

- This medicine may affect blood sugar levels. If you notice a change in the results of your blood or urine sugar tests or if you have any questions, check with your doctor.

Before you have any medical tests, tell the medical doctor in charge that you are taking this medicine. The results of the metyrapone test may be affected by this medicine.

Before having any surgery, any dental treatment, or emergency treatment, tell the medical doctor or dentist in charge that you are using this medicine. Taking chlordiazepoxide and amitriptyline combination together with medicines that are used during surgery or dental or emergency treatments may increase the CNS depressant effects.

This medicine may cause some people to become dizzy, lightheaded, drowsy, or less alert than they are normally. Even if taken at bedtime, it may cause some people to feel drowsy or less alert on arising. *Make sure you know how you react to this medicine before you drive, use machines, or do anything else that could be dangerous if you are dizzy or are not alert.*

Dizziness, lightheadedness, or fainting may occur when you get up from a lying or sitting position. Getting up slowly may help. If this problem continues or gets worse, check with your doctor.

Chlordiazepoxide and amitriptyline combination may cause dryness of the mouth. For temporary relief, use sugarless candy or gum, melt bits of ice in your mouth, or use a saliva substitute. However, if your mouth continues to feel dry for more than 2 weeks, check with your medical doctor or dentist. Continuing dryness of the mouth may increase the chance of dental disease, including tooth decay, gum disease, and fungus infections.

Chlordiazepoxide and amitriptyline combination may cause your skin to be more sensitive to sunlight than it is normally. Exposure to sunlight, even for brief periods of time, may cause a skin rash, itching, redness or other discoloration of the skin, or a severe sunburn. When you begin taking this medicine:

- Stay out of direct sunlight, especially between the hours of 10:00 a.m. and 3:00 p.m., if possible.
- Wear protective clothing, including a hat. Also, wear sunglasses.
- Apply a sun block product that has a skin protection factor (SPF) of at least 15. Some patients may require a product with a higher SPF number, especially if they have a fair complexion. If you have any questions about this, check with your health care professional.
- Apply a sun block lipstick that has an SPF of at least 15 to protect your lips.
- Do not use a sunlamp or tanning bed or booth.

If you have a severe reaction from the sun, check with your doctor.

Side Effects of This Medicine

Along with its needed effects, a medicine may cause some unwanted effects. Although not all of these side effects may occur, if they do occur they may need medical attention.

Check with your doctor as soon as possible if any of the following side effects occur:

Less common

Blurred vision or other changes in vision; confusion or hallucinations (seeing, hearing, or feeling things that are not there); constipation; difficulty in urinating; eye pain; fainting; irregular heartbeat; mental depression; shakiness; trouble in sleeping; unusual excitement, nervousness, or irritability

Rare

Convulsions (seizures); increased sensitivity to sunlight; skin rash and itching; sore throat and fever; yellow eyes or skin

Symptoms of overdose

Agitation; confusion; convulsions (seizures); dizziness or lightheadedness (severe); drowsiness (severe); enlarged pupils; fast or irregular heartbeat; fever; hallucinations; muscle stiffness or rigidity; vomiting (severe)

Other side effects may occur that usually do not need medical attention. These side effects may go away during treatment as your body adjusts to the medicine. However, check with your doctor if any of the following side effects continue or are bothersome:

More common

Bloating; clumsiness or unsteadiness; dizziness or

lightheadedness; drowsiness; dryness of mouth or unpleasant taste; headache; weight gain

Less common
> Diarrhea; nausea or vomiting; unusual tiredness or weakness

After you stop using this medicine, your body may need time to adjust. If you took this medicine in high doses or for a long time, this may take up to 2 weeks. *During this time check with your doctor if you notice any of the following side effects:*
> Convulsions (seizures); headache; increased sweating; irritability or restlessness; muscle cramps; nausea or vomiting; stomach cramps; trembling; trouble in sleeping, with vivid dreams

Other side effects not listed above may also occur in some patients. If you notice any other effects, check with your doctor.

Revised: 03/19/93

CHLORDIAZEPOXIDE AND CLIDINIUM Systemic

Commonly used brand name(s):

In the U.S.—
Clindex	Lidox
Clinoxide	Lidoxide
Clipoxide	Zebrax
Librax	

Generic name product may be available.

In Canada—
Apo-Chlorax
Corium
Librax

Description

Chlordiazepoxide and clidinium (klor-dye-az-e-POX-ide and kli-DI-nee-um) is a combination of medicines used to relax the digestive system and to reduce stomach acid. It is used to treat stomach and intestinal problems such as ulcers and colitis.

Chlordiazepoxide belongs to the group of medicines known as benzodiazepines. It is a central nervous system (CNS) depressant (a medicine that slows down the nervous system).

Clidinium belongs to the group of medicines known as anticholinergics. It helps lessen the amount of acid formed in the stomach. Clidinium also helps relieve abdominal or stomach spasms or cramps.

This combination is available only with your doctor's prescription, in the following dosage form:
Oral
> • Capsules (U.S. and Canada)

Before Using This Medicine

In deciding to use a medicine, the risks of taking the medicine must be weighed against the good it will do. This is a decision you and your doctor will make. For chlordiazepoxide and clidinium, the following should be considered:

Allergies—Tell your doctor if you have ever had any unusual or allergic reaction to benzodiazepines such as alprazolam [e.g., Xanax], bromazepam [e.g., Lectopam], chlordiazepoxide [e.g., Librium], clonazepam [e.g., Klonopin], clorazepate [e.g., Tranxene], diazepam [e.g., Valium], flurazepam [e.g., Dalmane], halazepam [e.g., Paxipam], ketazolam [e.g., Loftran], lorazepam [e.g., Ativan], midazolam [e.g., Versed], nitrazepam [e.g., Mogadon], oxazepam [e.g., Serax], prazepam [e.g., Centrax], temazepam [e.g., Restoril], or triazolam [e.g., Halcion], or to clidinium or any of the belladonna alkaloids (atropine, belladonna, hyoscyamine, and scopolamine). Also tell your health care professional if you are allergic to any other substances, such as foods, preservatives, or dyes.

Pregnancy—Clidinium (contained in this combination) has not been studied in pregnant women. However, clidinium has not been shown to cause birth defects or other problems in animal studies. Chlordiazepoxide (contained also in this combination) may cause birth defects if taken during the first 3 months of pregnancy. In addition, too much use of this medicine during pregnancy may cause the baby to become dependent on the medicine. This may lead to withdrawal side effects after birth. Make sure your doctor knows if you are pregnant or if you may become pregnant before taking chlordiazepoxide and clidinium.

Breast-feeding—Chlordiazepoxide may pass into the breast milk and cause unwanted effects, such as excessive drowsiness, in nursing babies. Also, because clidinium tends to decrease the secretions of the body, it is possible that the flow of breast milk may be reduced in some patients.

Children—There is no specific information comparing use of chlordiazepoxide and clidinium in children with use in other age groups. However, children are especially sensitive to the effects of chlordiazepoxide and clidinium. Therefore, this may increase the chance of side effects during treatment.

Older adults—Confusion or memory loss; constipation; difficult urination; drowsiness; dryness of mouth, nose, throat, or skin; and unusual excitement or agitation may be more likely to occur in the elderly, who are usually more sensitive than younger adults to the effects of chlordiazepoxide and clidinium.

Other medicines—Although certain medicines should not be used together at all, in other cases 2 different medicines may be used together even if an interaction might occur. In these cases, your doctor may want to change the dose, or other precautions may be necessary. When you are taking chlordiazepoxide and clidinium it is especially important that your health care professional know if you are taking any of the following:
• Antacids or
• Diarrhea medicine containing kaolin or attapulgite—These medicines may reduce the blood levels of chlordiazepoxide and clidinium, which may decrease their effects; they should be taken at least 2 to 3 hours before or after the chlordiazepoxide and clidinium combination
• Central nervous system (CNS) depressants (medicines that cause drowsiness) or
• Other anticholinergics (medicines for abdominal or stomach spasms or cramps)—Use with chlordiazepoxide and clidinium may increase the side effects of either medicine

- Ketoconazole (e.g., Nizoral)—Chlordiazepoxide and clidinium may reduce the blood level of ketoconazole, which may decrease its effects; therefore, chlordiazepoxide and clidinium should be taken at least 2 hours after ketoconazole

- Potassium chloride (e.g., Kay Ciel)—Use of chlordiazepoxide and clidinium may worsen or cause sores of the stomach or intestine

Other medical problems—The presence of other medical problems may affect the use of chlordiazepoxide and clidinium. Make sure you tell your doctor if you have any other medical problems, especially:

- Difficult urination or
- Dryness of mouth (severe and continuing) or
- Emphysema, asthma, bronchitis, or other chronic lung disease or
- Enlarged prostate or
- Glaucoma or
- Hiatal hernia or
- High blood pressure (hypertension) or
- Intestinal blockage or
- Mental depression or
- Mental illness (severe) or
- Myasthenia gravis or
- Ulcerative colitis (severe)—Use of chlordiazepoxide and clidinium may make these conditions worse

- Drug abuse or dependence—Taking chlordiazepoxide (contained in this combination) may become habit-forming, causing mental or physical dependence

- Kidney disease or
- Liver disease—Higher blood levels of chlordiazepoxide and clidinium may result, possibly increasing the chance of side effects

- Overactive thyroid—Use of chlordiazepoxide and clidinium may further increase the heart rate

Proper Use of This Medicine

Take this medicine about ½ to 1 hour before meals unless otherwise directed by your doctor.

Take this medicine only as directed by your doctor. Do not take more of it, do not take it more often, and do not take it for a longer time than your doctor ordered. If too much is taken, it may become habit-forming.

Dosing—The dose of chlordiazepoxide and clidinium combination will be different for different people. *Follow your doctor's orders or the directions on the label.* The following information includes only the average doses of this combination medicine. *If your dose is different, do not change it* unless your doctor tells you to do so.

- For *oral* dosage form (capsules)
  —To relax the digestive system and to reduce stomach acid:
  - Adults—1 or 2 capsules one to four times a day, thirty to sixty minutes before meals or food. Your doctor may change the dose if needed. However, most people usually will not take more than 8 capsules a day.
  - Children—Dose must be determined by your doctor.
  - Older adults—To start, 1 capsule two times a day. Your doctor may change the dose if needed.

Missed dose—If you miss a dose of this medicine, take it as soon as possible. However, if it is almost time for your next dose, skip the missed dose and go back to your regular dosing schedule. Do not double doses.

Storage—To store this medicine:

- Keep out of the reach of children.
- Store away from heat and direct light.
- Do not store the capsule form of this medicine in the bathroom, near the kitchen sink, or in other damp places. Heat or moisture may cause the medicine to break down.
- Do not keep outdated medicine or medicine no longer needed. Be sure that any discarded medicine is out of the reach of children.

Precautions While Using This Medicine

If you will be taking this medicine regularly for a long time your doctor should check your progress at regular visits.

Do not take this medicine within an hour of taking medicine for diarrhea. Taking them too close together will make this medicine less effective.

This medicine may cause some people to have blurred vision or to become dizzy, lightheaded, drowsy, or less alert than they are normally. *Make sure you know how you react to this medicine before you drive, use machines, or do anything else that could be dangerous if you are dizzy or are not alert or able to see well.*

This medicine will add to the effects of alcohol and other CNS depressants (medicines that slow down the nervous system, possibly causing drowsiness). Some examples of CNS depressants are sedatives, tranquilizers, or sleeping medicine; prescription pain medicine or narcotics; barbiturates; medicine for seizures; muscle relaxants; or anesthetics, including some dental anesthetics. *Check with your doctor before taking any of the above while you are using this medicine and also for a few days after you stop taking it.*

This medicine will often make you sweat less, causing your body temperature to increase. *Use extra care not to become overheated during exercise or hot weather while you are taking this medicine* as this could possibly result in heat stroke. Also, hot baths or saunas may make you feel dizzy or faint while you are taking this medicine.

Your mouth, nose, and throat may feel very dry while you are taking this medicine. For temporary relief of mouth dryness, use sugarless candy or gum, melt bits of ice in your mouth, or use a saliva substitute. However, if your mouth continues to feel dry for more than 2 weeks, check with your dentist. Continuing dryness of the mouth may increase the chance of dental disease, including tooth decay, gum disease, and fungus infections.

Check with your doctor if you develop intestinal problems such as constipation. This is especially important if you are taking other medicine while you are taking chlordiazepoxide and clidinium. If these problems are not corrected, serious complications may result.

If you will be taking this medicine in large doses or for a long time, do not stop taking it without first checking with your doctor. Your doctor may want you to reduce gradually the amount you are taking before stopping completely.

Side Effects of This Medicine

Along with its needed effects, a medicine may cause some unwanted effects. Although not all of these side effects may occur, if they do occur they may need medical attention.

Check with your doctor as soon as possible if any of the following side effects occur:

Less common or rare

Constipation; eye pain; mental depression; skin rash or hives; slow heartbeat, shortness of breath, or troubled breathing; sore throat and fever; trouble in sleeping; unusual excitement, nervousness, or irritability; yellow eyes or skin

Symptoms of overdose

Confusion; difficult urination; drowsiness (severe); dryness of mouth, nose, or throat (severe); fast heartbeat; unusual warmth, dryness, and flushing of skin

Other side effects may occur that usually do not need medical attention. These side effects may go away during treatment as your body adjusts to the medicine. However, check with your doctor if any of the following side effects continue or are bothersome:

More common

Bloated feeling; decreased sweating; dizziness; drowsiness; dryness of mouth; headache

Less common

Blurred vision; decreased sexual ability; loss of memory; nausea; unusual tiredness or weakness

After you stop using this medicine, your body may need time to adjust. The length of time this takes depends on the amount of medicine you were using and how long you used it. During this time check with your doctor if you notice any of the following side effects:

Convulsions (seizures); muscle cramps; nausea or vomiting; stomach cramps; trembling

Other side effects not listed above may also occur in some patients. If you notice any other effects, check with your doctor.

Revised: 01/29/92
Interim revision: 08/10/94

CHLORHEXIDINE   Dental

Commonly used brand name(s):

In the U.S.—
Peridex
PerioGard
Generic name product may be available.

In Canada—
Oro-Clense
Peridex

Description

Chlorhexidine (klor-HEX-i-deen) is used to treat gingivitis. It helps to reduce the inflammation (redness) and swelling of your gums and to reduce gum bleeding.

Gingivitis is caused by the bacteria that grow in the coating (plaque) that forms on your teeth between tooth brushings. Chlorhexidine destroys the bacteria, thereby preventing the gingivitis from occurring. However, chlorhexidine does *not* prevent plaque and tartar from forming; proper tooth brushing and flossing are still necessary and important.

Chlorhexidine is available only with your dentist's or medical doctor's prescription, in the following dosage form:

Dental
• Oral rinse (U.S.)

Before Using This Medicine

In deciding to use a medicine, the risks of using the medicine must be weighed against the good it will do. This is a decision you and your dentist or medical doctor will make. For chlorhexidine, the following should be considered:

Allergies—Tell your dentist or medical doctor if you have ever had any unusual or allergic reaction to this medicine or to skin disinfectants containing chlorhexidine. Also tell your dentist or medical health care professional if you are allergic to any other substances, such as foods, preservatives, or dyes.

Pregnancy—Chlorhexidine has not been studied in pregnant women. However, chlorhexidine has not been shown to cause birth defects or other problems in animal studies.

Breast-feeding—It is not known whether chlorhexidine passes into the breast milk. Although most medicines pass into breast milk in small amounts, many of them may be used safely while breast-feeding. Mothers who are taking this medicine and who wish to breast-feed should discuss this with their dentist or medical doctor.

Children—Studies on this medicine have been done only in adult patients, and there is no specific information comparing use of this medicine in children with use in other age groups.

Older adults—Many medicines have not been studied specifically in older people. Therefore, it may not be known whether they work exactly the same way they do in younger adults or if they cause different side effects or problems in older people. There is no specific information comparing use of this medicine in the elderly with use in other age groups.

Other medicines—Although certain medicines should not be used together at all, in other cases two different medicines may be used together even if an interaction might occur. In these cases, your dentist or medical doctor may want to change the dose, or other precautions may be necessary. Tell your dentist or health care professional if you are using any other prescription or nonprescription (over-the-counter [OTC]) medicine that is to be used in the mouth.

Other medical problems—The presence of other medical problems may affect the use of chlorhexidine. Make sure you tell your dentist or medical doctor if you have any other medical problems, especially:

• Front-tooth fillings (especially those having rough surfaces)—Chlorhexidine may cause staining that, in some cases, may be impossible to remove and may require replacement of the filling

• Gum problems (other)—Use of chlorhexidine may make other gum problems, such as periodontitis, worse

Proper Use of This Medicine

Chlorhexidine oral rinse should be used after you have brushed and flossed your teeth. Rinse the toothpaste completely from your mouth with water before using the oral rinse. Do not eat or drink for several hours after using the oral rinse.

The cap on the original container of chlorhexidine can be used to measure the 15 mL (½ fluid ounce) dose of this medicine. Fill the cap to the "fill line." If you do not receive the dental rinse in its original container, make sure you have a measuring device to measure out the correct dose. Your pharmacist can help you with this.

Swish chlorhexidine around in the mouth for 30 seconds. Then spit out. *Use the medicine full strength.* Do not mix with water before using. *Do not swallow the medicine.*

Dosing—The dose of chlorhexidine oral rinse will be different for different patients. *Follow your dentist's or medical doctor's orders or the directions on the label.* The following information includes only the average doses of chlorhexidine oral rinse. *If your dose is different, do not change it* unless your dentist or medical doctor tells you to do so.

- For *oral rinse* dosage form:
  —For gingivitis:
    - Adults—Use 15 milliliters (mL) as a mouth wash for 30 seconds two times a day.
    - Children up to 18 years of age—Use and dose must be determined by your dentist or medical doctor.

Missed dose—If you miss a dose of this medicine, use it as soon as possible. However, if it is almost time for your next dose, skip the missed dose and go back to your regular dosing schedule. Do not double doses.

Storage—To store this medicine:
- Keep out of the reach of children.
- Store away from heat and direct light.
- Keep the medicine from freezing.
- Do not keep outdated medicine or medicine that is no longer needed. Be sure any discarded medicine is out of the reach of children.

Precautions While Using This Medicine

Chlorhexidine may have a bitter aftertaste. Do not rinse your mouth with water immediately after using chlorhexidine, since doing so will increase the bitterness. Rinsing may also decrease the effect of the medicine.

Chlorhexidine may change the way foods taste to you. Sometimes this effect may last up to 4 hours after you use the oral rinse. In most cases, this effect will become less noticeable as you continue to use the medicine. When you stop using chlorhexidine, your taste should return to normal.

Chlorhexidine may cause staining and an increase in tartar (calculus) on your teeth. Brushing with a tartar-control toothpaste and flossing your teeth daily may help reduce this tartar build-up and staining. In addition, you should visit your dentist at least every 6 months to have your teeth cleaned and your gums examined.

If you think that a child weighing 22 pounds (10 kilograms) or less has swallowed more than 4 ounces of the dental rinse, *get emergency help at once.* In addition, if a child of any age drinks the dental rinse and has symptoms of alcohol intoxication, such as slurred speech, sleepiness, or a staggering or stumbling walk, *get emergency help at once.*

Side Effects of This Medicine

Along with its needed effects, a medicine may cause some unwanted effects. Although not all of these side effects may occur, if they do occur they may need medical attention.

Check with your doctor immediately if any of the following side effects occur:
  Rare
    Signs of allergic reaction (nasal congestion; shortness of breath or troubled breathing; skin rash, hives, or itching; or swelling of face)

Other side effects may occur that usually do not need medical attention. These side effects may go away during treatment as your body adjusts to the medicine. However, check with your dentist or medical doctor if any of the following side effects continue or are bothersome:
  More common
    Change in taste; increase in tartar (calculus) on teeth; staining of teeth, mouth, tooth fillings, and dentures or other mouth appliances
  Less common or rare
    Mouth irritation; swollen glands on side of face or neck; tongue tip irritation

Other side effects not listed above may also occur in some patients. If you notice any other effects, check with your dentist or medical doctor.

Revised: 05/16/94
Interim revision: 08/22/94; 08/14/98

CHLORHEXIDINE   Implantation-Dental

Commonly used brand name(s):

In the U.S.—
  PerioChip

Description

Chlorhexidine (klor-HEX-i-deen) is used to help treat periodontal disease (a disease of your gums), which is caused by bacteria growing beneath the gum line. Chlorhexidine works by killing the bacteria. Up to eight chlorhexidine implants are placed between your teeth and gums in places where the gum has a deep pocket. Your dentist will place the chlorhexidine implants after your teeth have been thoroughly cleaned.

This medicine is available only with your dentist's prescription, in the following dosage form:

  Implantation-Dental
  - Periodontal implants (U.S.)

Before Using This Medicine

In deciding to use a medicine, the risks of using the medicine must be weighed against the good it will do. This is a decision you and your doctor will make. For chlorhexidine periodontal implants, the following should be considered:

Allergies—Tell your dentist if you have ever had any unusual or allergic reaction to chlorhexidine. Also tell your health care professional if you are allergic to any other substances, such as foods, preservatives, or dyes.

Pregnancy—Studies on the effects of chlorhexidine periodontal implants have not been done in either humans or animals. Discuss with your doctor whether or not to use the implants while you are pregnant.

Breast-feeding—It is not known whether chlorhexidine passes into human breast milk. Although most medicines pass into breast milk in small amounts, many of them may be used safely while breast-feeding. Mothers who are using this medicine and who wish to breast-feed should discuss this with their doctor.

Children—Studies on this medicine have been done only in adult patients and there is no specific information comparing use of chlorhexidine implants in children with use in other age groups.

Older adults—Many medicines have not been studied specifically in older people. Therefore, it may not be known whether they work exactly the same way they do in younger adults or if they cause different side effects or problems in older people. There is no specific information comparing use of chlorhexidine implants in the elderly with use in other age groups.

Other medicines—Although certain medicines should not be used together at all, in other cases two different medicines may be used together even if an interaction might occur. In these cases, your doctor may want to change the dose, or other precautions may be necessary. Tell your health care professional if you are using any other prescription or nonprescription (over-the-counter [OTC]) medicine.

Proper Use of This Medicine

Dosing—The number of chlorhexidine implants inserted will be different for different patients. In addition, the following information includes only the average treatment using chlorhexidine implants. If your treatment is different, do not change it unless your dentist tells you to do so.

- For *dental implant* dosage form:
  —For periodontitis:
    - Adults—One implant inserted into each gum pocket that is too deep. Up to 8 implants may be inserted during each treatment. Treatment may be repeated every three months.
    - Children—Use and dose must be determined by your dentist.

It is not necessary to remove the implants; they will dissolve on their own. However, your dentist will want to check the depth of the pockets in your gums every 3 months to see if they need to be treated again.

Precautions While Using This Medicine

For 10 days after the implants have been inserted, do not floss around the teeth and gums that have been treated. Using floss could push the implants out.

Check with your dentist right away if an implant becomes loose or falls out. Chlorhexidine implants are small, orange-brown rectangular chips that are rounded at one end.

Side Effects of This Medicine

Along with its needed effects, a medicine may cause some unwanted effects. Although not all of these side effects may occur, if they do occur they may need medical attention.

Check with your dentist as soon as possible if any of the following side effects occur:
Less common
    Bleeding, tender, or enlarged gums; cough, congestion or tightness in chest, or wheezing

Other side effects may occur that usually do not need medical attention. These side effects may go away during treatment as your body adjusts to the medicine. However, check with your dentist if any of the following side effects continue or are bothersome:
More common
    Tooth, gum, or mouth pain, tenderness, aching, throbbing, soreness, discomfort, or sensitivity (mild to moderate)
Less common
    Indigestion or upset stomach; sore throat; ulcers or sores in mouth

Other side effects not listed above may also occur in some patients. If you notice any other effects, check with your dentist.

Developed: 11/5/98

CHLOROQUINE   Systemic

Commonly used brand name(s):
In the U.S.—
    Aralen
    Aralen HCl
    Generic name product may be available.
In Canada—
    Aralen

Description

Chloroquine (KLOR-oh-kwin) is a medicine used to prevent and treat malaria, a red blood cell infection transmitted by the bite of a mosquito, and to treat some conditions such as liver disease caused by protozoa (tiny one-celled animals).

Malaria transmission occurs in large areas of Central and South America, Hispaniola, sub-Saharan Africa, the Indian subcontinent, Southeast Asia, the Middle East, and Oceania. Country-specific information on malaria can be obtained from the Centers for Disease Control and Prevention (CDC), or from the CDC's web site at *http://www.cdc.gov/travel/yellowbk*.

This medicine may be given alone or with one or more other medicines. It may also be used for other conditions as determined by your doctor.

Chloroquine is available only with your doctor's prescription, in the following dosage forms:
Oral
- Tablets (U.S. and Canada)
Parenteral
- Injection (U.S.)

Before Using This Medicine

In deciding to use a medicine, the risks of taking the medicine must be weighed against the good it will do. This is a decision you and your doctor will make. For chloroquine, the following should be considered:

Allergies—Tell your doctor if you have ever had any unusual or allergic reaction to chloroquine or hydroxychloroquine. Also tell your health care professional if you are allergic to any other substances, such as foods, preservatives, or dyes.

Pregnancy—Unless you are taking chloroquine to treat malaria or liver disease caused by protozoa, use of this medicine is not recommended during pregnancy. In animal

---

studies, chloroquine has been shown to cause damage to the central nervous system (brain and spinal cord) of the fetus, including damage to hearing, sense of balance, bleeding inside the eyes, and other eye problems. However, when given in low doses (once a week) to prevent malaria, this medicine has not been shown to cause birth defects or other problems in humans.

Breast-feeding—Chloroquine passes into breast milk. Chloroquine has not been reported to cause problems in nursing babies. However, babies and children are especially sensitive to the effects of chloroquine. The amount in breast milk is not enough to prevent the infant from getting malaria.

Children—Children are especially sensitive to the effects of chloroquine. This may increase the chance of side effects during treatment. Overdose is especially dangerous in children. Taking as little as 1 tablet (300-mg strength) has resulted in the death of a small child. Children should avoid traveling to areas where there is a chance of getting malaria, unless they can take antimalarial medicines that are more effective than chloroquine.

Older adults—Many medicines have not been studied specifically in older people. Therefore, it may not be known whether they work exactly the same way they do in younger adults or if they cause different side effects or problems in older people. There is no specific information comparing use of chloroquine in the elderly with use in other age groups.

Other medicines—Although certain medicines should not be used together at all, in other cases two different medicines may be used together even if an interaction might occur. In these cases, your doctor may want to change the dose, or other precautions may be necessary. When you are taking chloroquine, it is especially important that your health care professional know if you are taking the following:

- Mefloquine (e.g., Lariam)—Use of chloroquine with mefloquine may increase the chance of convulsions (seizures)

Other medical problems—The presence of other medical problems may affect the use of chloroquine. Make sure you tell your doctor if you have any other medical problems, especially:

- Blood disease (severe)—Chloroquine may cause blood disorders
- Eye or vision problems—Chloroquine, especially in high doses, may cause serious side effects affecting the eyes
- Glucose-6-phosphate dehydrogenase (G6PD) deficiency—Chloroquine may cause serious side effects affecting the blood in patients with this deficiency
- Liver disease—May decrease the removal of chloroquine from the blood, increasing the chance of side effects
- Nerve or brain disease (severe), including convulsions (seizures)—Chloroquine may cause muscle weakness and, at high doses, seizures
- Porphyria—Chloroquine may cause episodes of porphyria to occur more frequently
- Psoriasis—Chloroquine may bring on severe attacks of psoriasis
- Stomach or intestinal disease (severe)—Chloroquine may cause stomach or intestinal irritation

Proper Use of This Medicine

Take this medicine with meals or milk to lessen stomach upset, unless otherwise directed by your doctor.

Keep this medicine out of the reach of children. Children are especially sensitive to the effects of chloroquine and overdose is especially dangerous in children. Taking as little as 1 tablet (300-mg strength) has resulted in the death of a small child.

It is very important that you *take this medicine only as directed*. Do not take more of it, do not take it more often, and do not take it for a longer time than your doctor ordered. To do so may increase the chance of serious side effects.

If you are taking this medicine to help keep you from getting malaria, *keep taking it for the full time of treatment*. If you already have malaria, you should still keep taking this medicine for the full time of treatment even if you begin to feel better after a few days. This will help to clear up your infection completely. If you stop taking this medicine too soon, your symptoms may return.

Chloroquine works best when you take it on a regular schedule. For example, if you are to take it once a week to prevent malaria, it is best to take it on the same day each week. Or if you are to take two doses a day, one dose may be taken with breakfast and the other with the evening meal. *Make sure that you do not miss any doses*. If you have any questions about this, check with your health care professional.

For patients taking chloroquine *to prevent malaria:*

- Your doctor may want you to start taking this medicine 1 to 2 weeks before you travel to an area where there is a chance of getting malaria. This will help you to see how you react to the medicine. Also, it will allow time for your doctor to change to another medicine if you have a reaction to this medicine.
- Also, you should keep taking this medicine while you are in the area and for 4 weeks after you leave the area. No medicine will protect you completely from malaria. However, to protect you as completely as possible, *it is important to keep taking this medicine for the full time your doctor ordered*. Also, if fever develops during your travels or within 2 months after you leave the area, *check with your doctor immediately*.

Dosing—The dose of chloroquine will be different for different patients. *Follow your doctor's orders or the directions on the label*. The following information includes only the average doses of chloroquine. *If your dose is different, do not change it* unless your doctor tells you to do so.

The number of tablets that you take depends on the strength of the medicine. Also, *the number of doses you take each day, the time allowed between doses, and the length of time you take the medicine depend on the medical problem for which you are taking chloroquine.*

- For *oral* dosage form (tablets):
  —For prevention of malaria:
  - Adults—500 milligrams (mg) once every seven days.
  - Children—Dose is based on body weight and must be determined by your doctor. The usual dose is 8.3 mg per kilogram (kg) (3.7 mg per pound) of body weight once every seven days.

—For treatment of malaria:
- Adults—Start with 1 gram. Then, 500 mg six to eight hours after the first dose, and 500 mg once a day on the second and third days of treatment.
- Children—Dose is based on body weight and must be determined by your doctor. The usual dose is 41.7 mg per kg (18.9 mg per pound) of body weight divided up over three days. This dose is given as follows: Start with 16.7 mg per kg (7.5 mg per pound) of body weight, then 8.3 mg per kg (3.7 mg per pound) of body weight six hours, twenty-four hours, and forty-eight hours after the first dose.

—For treatment of liver disease caused by protozoa:
- Adults—At first, start with 250 mg four times a day for two days. Then 250 mg two times a day for at least two to three weeks.
- Children—Dose is based on body weight and must be determined by your doctor. The usual dose is 10 mg per kg (4.5 mg per pound) of body weight a day for three weeks.

- For *injection* dosage form:
  —For treatment of malaria:
  - Adults—200 to 250 mg injected into a muscle. This dose may be repeated in six hours if needed.
  - Children—Dose is based on body weight and must be determined by your doctor. The usual dose is 4.4 mg per kg (2 mg per pound) of body weight injected into a muscle or under the skin. This dose may be repeated in six hours if needed. Chloroquine may also be injected slowly into a vein. If the medicine is given in this way, the dose must be determined by your doctor.
  —For treatment of liver disease caused by protozoa:
  - Adults—200 to 250 mg a day injected into a muscle for ten to twelve days.
  - Children—Dose is based on body weight and must be determined by your doctor. The usual dose is 7.5 mg per kg (3.4 mg per pound) of body weight a day for ten to twelve days.

Missed dose—If you miss a dose of this medicine and your dosing schedule is:
- One dose every seven days—Take the missed dose as soon as possible. Then go back to your regular dosing schedule.
- One dose a day—Take the missed dose as soon as possible. But if you do not remember until the next day, skip the missed dose and go back to your regular dosing schedule. Do not double doses.
- More than one dose a day—Take it right away if you remember within an hour or so of the missed dose. But if you do not remember until later, skip the missed dose and go back to your regular dosing schedule. Do not double doses.

If you have any questions about this, check with your doctor.

Storage—To store this medicine:
- Keep out of the reach of children. Overdose of chloroquine is very dangerous in children.
- Store away from heat and direct light.
- Do not store in the bathroom, near the kitchen sink, or in other damp places. Heat or moisture may cause the medicine to break down.

- Do not keep outdated medicine or medicine no longer needed. Be sure that any discarded medicine is out of the reach of children.

Precautions While Using This Medicine

If you will be taking this medicine for a long time, *it is very important that your doctor check you at regular visits* for any blood problems or muscle weakness that may be caused by this medicine. In addition, *check with your doctor immediately if blurred vision, difficulty in reading, or any other change in vision occurs during or after treatment.* Your doctor may want you to have your eyes checked by an ophthalmologist (eye doctor).

If your symptoms do not improve within a few days or if they become worse, check with your doctor.

Make sure you know how you react to this medicine before you drive, use machines, or do anything else that could be dangerous if you are not able to see well.

Chloroquine may cause blurred vision, difficulty in reading, or other change in vision. It may also cause some people to become lightheaded.

If these reactions are especially bothersome, check with your doctor.

Malaria is spread by mosquitoes. If you are living in, or will be traveling to, an area where there is a chance of getting malaria, the following mosquito-control measures will help to prevent infection:
- Avoid going out between dusk and dawn because it is at these times when mosquitoes most commonly bite.
- If possible, sleep in a screened or air-conditioned room or under mosquito netting, preferably netting coated or soaked with pyrethrum, to avoid being bitten by malaria-carrying mosquitoes.
- Remain in air-conditioned or well-screened rooms to reduce contact with mosquitoes
- Wear long-sleeved shirts or blouses and long trousers to protect your arms and legs, especially from dusk through dawn when mosquitoes are out.
- Apply mosquito repellent, preferably one containing DEET, to uncovered areas of the skin from dusk through dawn when mosquitoes are out.
- Use mosquito coils or sprays to kill mosquitoes in living and sleeping quarters during evening and night-time hours.

Side Effects of This Medicine

Along with its needed effects, a medicine may cause some unwanted effects. Although not all of these side effects may occur, if they do occur they may need medical attention. When this medicine is used for short periods of time, side effects usually are rare. However, when it is used for a long time and/or in high doses, side effects are more likely to occur and may be serious.

Check with your doctor immediately if any of the following side effects occur:
Less common
   Blurred vision; change in vision; eye pain; loss of vision
   Note: The above side effects may also occur or get worse after you stop taking this medicine.
Rare
   Black, tarry stools; blood in urine or stools; convulsions (seizures); cough or hoarseness; feeling faint or

lightheaded; fever or chills; increased muscle weakness; lower back or side pain; mood or other mental changes; painful or difficult urination; pinpoint red spots on skin; ringing or buzzing in ears or any loss of hearing; sore throat; unusual bleeding or bruising; unusual tiredness or weakness

Symptoms of overdose
Drowsiness; headache; increased excitability

Other side effects may occur that usually do not need medical attention. These side effects may go away during treatment as your body adjusts to the medicine. However, check with your doctor if any of the following side effects continue or are bothersome:

More common
Diarrhea; difficulty in seeing to read; headache; itching (more common in black patients); loss of appetite; nausea or vomiting; stomach cramps or pain

Less common
Bleaching of hair or increased hair loss; blue-black discoloration of skin, fingernails, or inside of mouth; skin rash

Other side effects not listed above may also occur in some patients. If you notice any other effects, check with your doctor.

Additional Information

Once a medicine has been approved for marketing for a certain use, experience may show that it is also useful for other medical problems. Although these uses are not included in product labeling, chloroquine is used in certain patients with the following medical conditions:

- Arthritis in children
- High levels of calcium in the blood associated with sarcoidosis
- Rheumatoid arthritis
- Systemic lupus erythematosus (lupus; SLE)
- Various skin disorders

For patients taking chloroquine *for arthritis or lupus:*

- This medicine must be taken regularly as ordered by your doctor in order for it to help you. It may take up to several weeks before you begin to feel better. It may take up to 6 months before you feel the full benefit of this medicine.
- If your symptoms of arthritis do not improve within a few weeks or months, or if they become worse, check with your doctor.

Other than the above information, there is no additional information relating to proper use, precautions, or side effects for these uses.

Revised: 06/02/99

CHLOROXINE   Topical†

Commonly used brand name(s):

In the U.S.—
Capitrol

†Not commercially available in Canada.

Description

Chloroxine (klor-OX-een) is used in the treatment of dandruff and seborrheic dermatitis of the scalp.

This medicine is available only with your doctor's prescription, in the following dosage form:

Topical
- Shampoo (U.S.)

Before Using This Medicine

In deciding to use a medicine, the risks of using the medicine must be weighed against the good it will do. This is a decision you and your doctor will make. For chloroxine, the following should be considered:

Allergies—Tell your doctor if you have ever had any unusual or allergic reaction to chloroxine, clioquinol (iodochlorhydroxyquin), iodoquinol (diiodohydroxyquin), or edetate disodium. Also tell your health care professional if you are allergic to any other substances, such as preservatives or dyes.

Pregnancy—Studies on effects in pregnancy have not been done in either humans or animals.

Breast-feeding—It is not known whether chloroxine passes into the breast milk. However, this medicine has not been reported to cause problems in nursing babies.

Children—Studies on this medicine have been done only in adult patients, and there is no specific information comparing use of this medicine in children with use in other age groups.

Older adults—Many medicines have not been studied specifically in older people. Therefore, it may not be known whether they work exactly the same way they do in younger adults or if they cause different side effects or problems in older people. There is no specific information comparing use of this medicine in the elderly with use in other age groups.

Other medicines—Although certain medicines should not be used together at all, in other cases two different medicines may be used together even if an interaction might occur. In these cases, your doctor may want to change the dose, or other precautions may be necessary. Tell your health care professional if you are using any other topical prescription or nonprescription (over-the-counter [OTC]) medicine that is to be applied to the same area of the skin.

Proper Use of This Medicine

Do not use this medicine if blistered, raw, or oozing areas are present on your scalp, unless otherwise directed by your doctor.

Keep this medicine away from the eyes. If you should accidentally get some in your eyes, flush them thoroughly with cool water. Check with your doctor if eye irritation continues or is bothersome.

To use:
- Shake well before using
- Wet the hair and scalp with lukewarm water. Apply enough chloroxine to the scalp to work up a lather, and rub in well. Allow the lather to remain on the scalp for about 3 minutes, then rinse. Apply the medicine again and rinse thoroughly. Use the medicine two times a week or as directed by your doctor.

Dosing—The dose of chloroxine will be different for different patients. *Follow your doctor's orders or the direc-*

tions on the label. The following information includes only the average doses of chloroxine. *If your dose is different, do not change it* unless your doctor tells you to do so.

- For *topical* dosage form (shampoo):
  —For dandruff or seborrheic dermatitis of the scalp:
    - Adults—Use two times a week.
    - Children—Use and dose must be determined by your doctor.

Missed dose—If you miss a dose of this medicine, apply it as soon as possible.

Storage—To store this medicine:
- Keep out of the reach of children.
- Store away from heat and direct light.
- Keep the medicine from freezing.
- Do not keep outdated medicine or medicine no longer needed. Be sure that any discarded medicine is out of the reach of children.

Precautions While Using This Medicine

This medicine may slightly discolor light-colored hair (for example, bleached, blond, or gray).

Side Effects of This Medicine

Along with its needed effects, a medicine may cause some unwanted effects. Although not all of these side effects may occur, if they do occur they may need medical attention.

Check with your doctor as soon as possible if any of the following side effects occur:
  Irritation or burning of scalp not present before use of this medicine; skin rash

Other side effects may occur that usually do not need medical attention. However, check with your doctor if either of the following side effects continues or is bothersome:
  Dryness or increased itching of scalp

Other side effects not listed above may also occur in some patients. If you notice any other effects, check with your doctor.

Revised: 02/02/00

CHLORZOXAZONE AND ACETAMINOPHEN   Systemic

Commonly used brand name(s):

In Canada—
  Parafon Forte

Another commonly used name for this combination medicine is chlorzoxazone with APAP.

Description

Chlorzoxazone and acetaminophen (klor-ZOX-a-zone and a-seat-a-MIN-oh-fen) combination medicine is used to help relax certain muscles in your body and relieve the pain and discomfort caused by strains, sprains, or other injuries to your muscles. However, this medicine does not take the place of rest, exercise or physical therapy, or other treatment that your doctor may recommend for your medical problem.

Chlorzoxazone acts in the central nervous system (CNS) to produce its muscle relaxant effects. Its actions in the CNS may also produce some of its side effects.

In Canada, this medicine is available without a prescription.

This medicine is available in the following dosage forms:

Oral
  - Tablets (Canada)

Before Using This Medicine

If you are taking this medicine without a prescription, carefully read and follow any precautions on the label. For chlorzoxazone and acetaminophen combination, the following should be considered:

Allergies—Tell your doctor if you have ever had any unusual or allergic reaction to acetaminophen, chlorzoxazone, or aspirin. Also tell your health care professional if you are allergic to any other substances, such as foods, preservatives, or dyes.

Pregnancy—Although studies on birth defects with chlorzoxazone or acetaminophen have not been done in pregnant women, these medicines have not been reported to cause birth defects or other problems.

Breast-feeding—Chlorzoxazone and acetaminophen have not been shown to cause problems in nursing babies. However, acetaminophen passes into the breast milk in small amounts.

Children—Studies on this combination medicine have been done only in adult patients, and there is no specific information about its use in children. However, chlorzoxazone and acetaminophen have been tested separately in children. In effective doses, these medicines have not been shown to cause different side effects or problems in children than they do in adults.

Older adults—Many medicines have not been studied specifically in older people. Therefore, it may not be known whether they work exactly the same way they do in younger adults or if they cause different side effects or problems in older people. There is no specific information comparing use of chlorzoxazone and acetaminophen combination, or of chlorzoxazone alone, in the elderly with use in other age groups. However, acetaminophen has been tested and has not been shown to cause different side effects or problems in older people than it does in younger adults.

Other medicines—Although certain medicines should not be used together at all, in other cases two different medicines may be used together even if an interaction might occur. In these cases, your doctor may want to change the dose, or other precautions may be necessary. When you are taking chlorzoxazone and acetaminophen combination, it is especially important that your health care professional know if you are taking any of the following:
- Antidepressants, tricyclic (amitriptyline [e.g., Elavil], amoxapine [e.g., Asendin], clomipramine [e.g., Anafranil], desipramine [e.g., Pertofrane], doxepin [e.g., Sinequan], imipramine [e.g., Tofranil], nortriptyline [e.g., Aventyl], protriptyline [e.g., Vivactil], trimipramine [e.g., Surmontil]) or
- Central nervous system (CNS) depressants (medicines that often cause drowsiness)—These medicines may add to the effects of chlorzoxazone and increase the chance of drowsiness or other side effects

Other medical problems—The presence of other medical problems may affect the use of chlorzoxazone and acetaminophen combination. Make sure you tell your doctor if you have any other medical problems, especially:

- Alcohol abuse or
- Allergies (asthma, eczema, hay fever, hives) or
- Hepatitis or other liver disease or
- Kidney disease—The chance of side effects may be increased

Proper Use of This Medicine

Take this medicine only as directed. Do not take more of it, do not take it more often, and do not take it for a longer time than directed on the package label or by your doctor. To do so may increase the chance of side effects. This medicine may cause liver damage if too much is taken.

Dosing—The dose of chlorzoxazone and acetaminophen combination will be different for different patients. *Follow your doctor's orders or the directions on the label.* The following information includes only the average doses of this medicine. *If your dose is different, do not change it* unless your doctor tells you to do so.

- For *oral* dosage form (tablets):
  —For relieving painful, stiff muscles:
    - Adults—Two tablets four times a day.
    - Children—Use and dose must be determined by your doctor.

Missed dose—If you miss a dose of this medicine, take it as soon as you remember. However, if it is almost time for your next dose, skip the missed dose and go back to your regular dosing schedule. Do not double doses.

Storage—To store this medicine:

- Keep out of the reach of children.
- Store away from heat and direct light.
- Do not store this medicine in the bathroom, near the kitchen sink, or in other damp places. Heat or moisture may cause the medicine to break down.
- Do not keep outdated medicine or medicine no longer needed. Be sure that any discarded medicine is out of the reach of children.

Precautions While Using This Medicine

If you will be taking this medicine for a long time (for example, for several months at a time), your doctor should check your progress at regular visits.

Check the labels of all nonprescription (over-the-counter [OTC]) and prescription medicines you now take. If any of them contain chlorzoxazone or acetaminophen, check with your doctor or pharmacist. Using any of them together with this medicine may cause an overdose.

This medicine will add to the effects of alcohol and other CNS depressants (medicines that slow down the nervous system, possibly causing drowsiness). Some examples of CNS depressants are antihistamines or medicine for hay fever, other allergies, or colds; sedatives, tranquilizers, or sleeping medicine; prescription pain medicine or narcotics; barbiturates; medicine for seizures; or anesthetics, including some dental anesthetics. Also, the risk of liver damage from acetaminophen may be greater if you use large amounts of alcoholic beverages with acetaminophen. Therefore, *do not drink alcoholic beverages, and check with your doctor before taking any of the medicines listed above, while you are taking this medicine.*

Taking the acetaminophen in this combination medicine together with certain other medicines may increase the chance of unwanted effects. The risk will depend on how much of each medicine you take every day, and on how long you take the medicines together. If your medical doctor or dentist directs you to take these medicines together on a regular basis, follow his or her directions carefully. However, *do not take any of the following medicines together with chlorzoxazone and acetaminophen combination for more than a few days, unless your doctor has directed you to do so and is following your progress.*

> Aspirin or other salicylates
> Diclofenac (e.g., Voltaren)
> Diflunisal (e.g., Dolobid)
> Etodolac (e.g., Lodine)
> Fenoprofen (e.g., Nalfon)
> Floctafenine (e.g., Idarac)
> Flurbiprofen, oral (e.g., Ansaid)
> Ibuprofen (e.g., Motrin)
> Indomethacin (e.g., Indocin)
> Ketoprofen (e.g., Orudis)
> Ketorolac (e.g., Toradol)
> Meclofenamate (e.g., Meclomen)
> Mefenamic acid (e.g., Ponstel)
> Nabumetone (e.g., Relafen)
> Naproxen (e.g., Naprosyn)
> Oxaprozin (e.g., Daypro)
> Phenylbutazone (e.g., Butazolidin)
> Piroxicam (e.g., Feldene)
> Sulindac (e.g., Clinoril)
> Tenoxicam (e.g., Mobiflex)
> Tiaprofenic acid (e.g., Surgam)
> Tolmetin (e.g., Tolectin)

This medicine may cause some people to become drowsy, dizzy, or less alert than they are normally. *Make sure you know how you react to this medicine before you drive, use machines, or do anything else that could be dangerous if you are dizzy or are not alert.*

Acetaminophen may interfere with the results of some medical tests. Before you have any medical tests, tell the doctor in charge if you have taken acetaminophen within the past 3 or 4 days. If possible, it is best to check with the doctor first, to find out whether this medicine may be taken during the 3 or 4 days before the test.

For *diabetic patients:*

- Acetaminophen may cause false results with some blood glucose (sugar) tests. If you notice any change in your test results, or if you have any questions about this possible problem, check with your health care professional. This is especially important if your diabetes is not well-controlled.

If you think that you or anyone else may have taken an overdose of this medicine, get emergency help at once. Signs of overdose of this medicine include fast or irregular breathing and severe muscle weakness. Signs of severe acetaminophen poisoning may not appear for 2 to 4 days after the overdose is taken, but treatment to prevent liver damage or death must be started within 24 hours or less after the overdose is taken.

Side Effects of This Medicine

Along with its needed effects, a medicine may cause some unwanted effects. Although not all of these side effects may occur, if they do occur they may need medical attention.

Check with your doctor immediately if any of the following side effects occur:
> *Rare*
>> Hive-like swellings (large) on face, eyelids, mouth, lips, or tongue; sudden decrease in amount of urine
>
> *Symptoms of overdose*
>> Diarrhea; fast or irregular breathing; increased sweating; loss of appetite; muscle weakness (severe); nausea or vomiting; pain, tenderness, or swelling in upper abdomen or stomach area; stomach cramps or pain

Also, check with your doctor as soon as possible if any of the following side effects occur:
> *Rare*
>> Bloody or black, tarry stools; bloody or cloudy urine; pain in lower back and/or side (severe and/or sharp); pinpoint red spots on skin; skin rash, hives, itching, or redness; sore throat and fever; unusual bleeding or bruising; unusual tiredness or weakness; yellow eyes or skin

Other side effects may occur that usually do not need medical attention. These side effects may go away during treatment as your body adjusts to the medicine. However, check with your doctor if any of the following side effects continue or are bothersome:
> *More common*
>> Dizziness or lightheadedness; drowsiness
>
> *Less common*
>> Constipation; headache; heartburn; unusual excitement, nervousness, restlessness, or irritability

This medicine sometimes causes the urine to turn orange or reddish purple. This is not harmful and will go away when you stop taking the medicine. If you have any questions about this, check with your doctor.

Other side effects not listed above may also occur in some patients. If you notice any other effects, check with your doctor.

Revised: 08/29/94

CHOLECYSTOGRAPHIC AGENTS, ORAL Diagnostic

Commonly used brand name(s):

In the U.S.—

Bilivist[3]	Oragrafin Calcium[3]
Bilopaque[4]	Oragrafin Sodium[3]
Cholebrine[1]	Telepaque[2]

In Canada—
Telepaque[2]

Other—

Biloptin[3]	Felombrine[2]
Cistobil[2]	Jopanonsyre[2]
Colebrin[1]	Lumopaque[4]
Colebrina[1]	Neocontrast[2]
Colegraf[2]	

Another commonly used name for tyropanoate is sodium tyropanoate.

Note: For quick reference, the following oral cholecystographic agents are numbered to match the corresponding brand names.

This information applies to the following medicines:
1. Iocetamic Acid (eye-oh-se-TAM-ik AS-id) †
2. Iopanoic Acid (eye-oh-pa-NOE-ik AS-id)
3. Ipodate (EYE-poe-date) †
4. Tyropanoate (tye-roe-pa-NOE-ate) †

†Not commercially available in Canada.

Description

Oral cholecystographic (ko-le-sis-to-GRAF-ik) agents are radiopaque agents. Radiopaque agents are drugs used to help diagnose certain medical problems. These agents contain iodine, which blocks x-rays. Depending on how the radiopaque agent is given, it localizes or builds up in certain areas of the body. When radiopaque agents are inside the body they will appear white on the x-ray film. This creates the needed distinction, or contrast, between one organ and other tissues. This will help the doctor see any special conditions that may exist in that organ or part of the body.

The oral cholecystographic agents are taken by mouth before x-ray tests to help check for problems of the gallbladder and the biliary tract. Ipodate may also be used for other conditions as determined by your doctor.

These radiopaque agents are to be given only by or under the direct supervision of a doctor. They are available in the following dosage forms:

> *Oral*
> Iocetamic acid
>> • Tablets (U.S.)
>
> Iopanoic acid
>> • Tablets (U.S. and Canada)
>
> Ipodate
>> • Capsules (U.S.)
>> • Oral suspension (U.S.)
>
> Tyropanoate
>> • Capsules (U.S.)

Before Having This Test

In deciding to use a diagnostic test, any risks of the test must be weighed against the good it will do. This is a decision you and your doctor will make. Also, test results may be affected by other things. For cholecystographic agents, the following should be considered:

Allergies—Tell your doctor if you have ever had any unusual or allergic reaction to iodine, to products containing iodine (for example, iodine-containing foods, such as seafoods, cabbage, kale, rape [turnip-like vegetable], turnips, or iodized salt), or to other radiopaque agents. Also tell your doctor if you are allergic to any other substances, such as preservatives.

Pregnancy—Studies on effects in pregnancy have not been done in humans with any of these agents. Studies in animals have been done only with iocetamic acid, which has not been shown to cause birth defects or other problems. However, on rare occasions, other radiopaque agents containing iodine have caused hypothyroidism (underactive thyroid) in the baby when given in late pregnancy. Also, x-rays of the abdomen are usually not recommended during pregnancy. This is to avoid exposing the fetus to radiation. Be sure you have discussed this with your doctor.

Breast-feeding—Iocetamic acid, iopanoic acid, and tyropanoate pass into the breast milk, and the other agents may pass into the breast milk also. However, these radiopaque agents have not been reported to cause problems in nursing babies.

Children—Although there is no specific information comparing use of cholecystographic agents in children with use in other age groups, tests using iopanoic acid and ipodate in children have not shown that these agents cause different side effects or problems in children than they do in adults.

Older adults—Many medicines have not been studied specifically in older people. Therefore, it may not be known whether they work exactly the same way they do in younger adults. Although there is no specific information comparing use of cholecystographic agents in the elderly with use in other age groups, these agents are not expected to cause different side effects or problems in older people than they do in younger adults.

Other medicines—Although certain medicines should not be used together at all, in other cases two different medicines may be used together even if an interaction might occur. In these cases, your doctor may want to change the dose, or other precautions may be necessary. Tell your doctor if you are taking any other prescription or nonprescription (over-the-counter [OTC]) medicine.

Other medical problems—The presence of other medical problems may affect the use of cholecystographic agents. Make sure you tell your doctor if you have any other medical problems, especially:

- Asthma, hay fever, or other allergies (history of) or
- Previous reaction to penicillins or to a skin test for allergies—Patients with these conditions have a greater chance of having a reaction, such as an allergic reaction

- Heart disease—Other problems, such as low blood pressure or slow heartbeat, may occur

- Kidney disease or
- Liver disease (severe)—Serious kidney problems may result

- Overactive thyroid—A sudden increase in symptoms, such as fast heartbeat or palpitations, fatigue, nervousness, excessive sweating, and muscle weakness may occur

---

Preparation for This Test

Dosing—Take this radiopaque agent with water after dinner the evening or evenings before the examination, following the directions of your doctor. Keep drinking an adequate amount of water, unless otherwise directed by your doctor.

Do not eat or drink anything but water after taking the medicine. Also, avoid smoking or chewing gum.

Your doctor may order a special diet or use of a laxative or enema in preparation for your test, depending on the type of test. If you have not received such instructions or if you do not understand them, check with your doctor in advance.

Precautions After Having This Test

Make sure your doctor knows if you are planning to have any future thyroid tests. The results of the thyroid test may be affected, even weeks or months later, by the iodine in this agent.

Side Effects of This Medicine

Along with its needed effects, a medicine may cause some unwanted effects. Although not all of these side effects may occur, if they do occur they may need medical attention.

Check with your health care professional immediately if any of the following side effects occur:
  Rare
    Itching; skin rash or hives; swelling of skin; unusual bleeding or bruising (with iopanoic acid only)

  Symptoms of overdose
    Diarrhea (severe); nausea and vomiting (severe); problems with urination

Other side effects may occur that usually do not need medical attention. These side effects should go away as the effects of the radiopaque agent wear off. However, check with your doctor if any of the following side effects continue or are bothersome:
  More common
    Diarrhea (mild); nausea and vomiting (mild to moderate)

  Less common
    Abdominal or stomach spasms or cramps; diarrhea (severe); difficult or painful urination; dizziness; frequent urge to urinate; headache; heartburn; nausea and vomiting (severe or continuing)

Other side effects not listed above may also occur in some patients. If you notice any other effects, check with your doctor.

Additional Information

Once a medicine has been approved for marketing for a certain use, experience may show that it is also useful for other medical problems. Although not specifically included in product labeling, ipodate is used in certain patients with the following medical condition:
- Graves' disease

In addition to the above information, for patients with Graves' disease taking ipodate:
- Ipodate is used in patients with Graves' disease, who have an overactive thyroid, to reduce the amount of thyroid hormone produced by the thyroid gland.
- *Use this medicine only as directed by your doctor.* Do not take more of it, do not take it more often, and do not take it for a longer period of time than your doctor ordered. To do so may increase the chance of side effects.
- In order for it to work properly, *ipodate must be taken every day, as ordered by your doctor.*
- The information given above in the section *Preparation For This Test* will not apply to you.

Other than the above information, there is no additional information relating to proper use, precautions, or side effects for these uses.

Revised: 06/29/95

CHOLESTYRAMINE Oral

Commonly used brand name(s):

In the U.S.—
Questran
Questran Light

In Canada—
Questran
Questran Light

Description

Cholestyramine (koe-less-TEAR-a-meen) is used to lower high cholesterol levels in the blood. This may help prevent medical problems caused by cholesterol clogging the blood vessels. Cholestyramine is also used to remove substances called bile acids from your body. With some liver problems, there is too much bile acid in your body and this can cause severe itching.

Cholestyramine works by attaching to certain substances in the intestine. Since cholestyramine is not absorbed into the body, these substances also pass out of the body without being absorbed.

Cholestyramine may also be used for other conditions as determined by your doctor.

Cholestyramine is available only with your doctor's prescription, in the following dosage form:

Oral
• Powder (U.S. and Canada)

Before Using This Medicine

In deciding to use a medicine, the risks of taking the medicine must be weighed against the good it will do. This is a decision you and your doctor will make. For cholestyramine, the following should be considered:

Allergies—Tell your doctor if you have ever had any unusual or allergic reaction to cholestyramine. Also tell your health care professional if you are allergic to any other substances, such as foods, preservatives, or dyes.

Pregnancy—Cholestyramine is not absorbed into the body and is not likely to cause problems. However, it may reduce absorption of vitamins into the body. Ask your doctor whether you need to take extra vitamins.

Breast-feeding—Cholestyramine is not absorbed into the body and is not likely to cause problems. However, the reduced absorption of vitamins by the mother may affect the nursing infant.

Children—This medicine has been tested in a limited number of children. In effective doses, the medicine has not been shown to cause different side effects or problems than it does in adults.

Older adults—Side effects may be more likely to occur in patients over 60 years of age, who are usually more sensitive to the effects of cholestyramine.

Other medicines—Although certain medicines should not be used together at all, in other cases two different medicines may be used together even if an interaction might occur. In these cases, your doctor may want to change the dose, or other precautions may be necessary. When you are taking cholestyramine it is especially important that your health care professional know if you are taking any of the following:

• Anticoagulants (blood thinners)—The effects of the anticoagulant may be changed and this may increase the chance of bleeding.

• Digitalis glycosides (heart medicine) or
• Diuretics (water pills) or
• Penicillin G, taken by mouth or
• Phenylbutazone or
• Propranolol (e.g., Inderal) or
• Tetracyclines, taken by mouth (medicine for infection) or
• Thyroid hormones or
• Vancomycin, taken by mouth—Cholestyramine may prevent these medicines from working properly

Other medical problems—The presence of other medical problems may affect the use of cholestyramine. Make sure you tell your doctor if you have any other medical problems, especially:

• Bleeding problems or
• Constipation or
• Gallstones or
• Heart or blood vessel disease or
• Hemorrhoids or
• Stomach ulcer or other stomach problems or
• Underactive thyroid—Cholestyramine may make these conditions worse

• Kidney disease—There is an increased risk of developing electrolyte problems (problems in the blood)

• Phenylketonuria—Phenylalanine in aspartame is included in the sugar-free brand of cholestyramine and should be avoided. Aspartame can cause problems in people with phenylketonuria. Therefore, it is best if you avoid using the sugar-free product.

Proper Use of This Medicine

Take this medicine exactly as directed by your doctor. Try not to miss any doses and do not take more medicine than your doctor ordered.

This medicine should never be taken in its dry form, since it could cause you to choke. Instead, always mix as follows:

• Place the medicine in 2 ounces of any beverage and mix thoroughly. Then add an additional 2 to 4 ounces of beverage and again mix thoroughly (it will not dissolve) before drinking. After drinking all the liquid containing the medicine, rinse the glass with a little more liquid and drink that also, to make sure you get all the medicine.

• You may also mix this medicine with milk in hot or regular breakfast cereals, or in thin soups such as tomato or chicken noodle soup. Or you may add it to some pulpy fruits such as crushed pineapple, pears, peaches, or fruit cocktail.

For patients taking this medicine *for high cholesterol:*

• Importance of diet—Before prescribing medicine for your condition, your doctor will probably try to control your condition by prescribing a personal diet for you. Such a diet may be low in fats, sugars, and/or cholesterol. Many people are able to control their condition by carefully following their doctor's orders for proper diet and exercise. Medicine is prescribed only when additional help is needed. *Follow carefully the special diet your doctor gave you*, since the medicine is effective only when a schedule of diet and exercise is properly followed.

- Also, this medicine is less effective if you are greatly overweight. It may be very important for you to go on a reducing diet. However, check with your doctor before going on any diet.
- Remember that this medicine will not cure your cholesterol problem but it will help control it. Therefore, you must continue to take it as directed if you expect to lower your cholesterol level.

Dosing—The dose of cholestyramine will be different for different patients. *Follow your doctor's orders or the directions on the label*. The following information includes only the average doses of cholestyramine. *If your dose is different, do not change it* unless your doctor tells you to do so.

- For *oral* dosage form (powder for oral suspension):
  —For high cholesterol or pruritus (itching) related to biliary obstruction:
    - Adults—At first, 4 grams one or two times a day before meals. Then, your doctor may increase your dose to 8 to 24 grams a day. This is divided into two to six doses.
    - Children—At first, 4 grams a day. This is divided into two doses and taken before meals. Then, your doctor may increase your dose to 8 to 24 grams a day. This is divided into two or more doses.

Missed dose—If you miss a dose of this medicine, take it as soon as possible. Then go back to your regular dosing schedule. However, if it is almost time for your next dose, skip the missed dose and go back to your regular dosing schedule. Do not double doses.

Storage—To store this medicine:

- Keep out of the reach of children.
- Store away from heat and direct light.
- Do not store in the bathroom, near the kitchen sink, or in other damp places. Heat or moisture may cause the medicine to break down.
- Do not keep outdated medicine or medicine no longer needed. Be sure that any discarded medicine is out of the reach of children.

Precautions While Using This Medicine

It is very important that your doctor check your progress at regular visits. This will allow your doctor to see if the medicine is working properly and to decide if you should continue to take it.

Do not take any other medicine unless prescribed by your doctor since cholestyramine may change the effect of other medicines.

Do not stop taking this medicine without first checking with your doctor. When you stop taking this medicine, your blood cholesterol levels may increase again. Your doctor may want you to follow a special diet to help prevent this from happening.

Side Effects of This Medicine

In some animal studies, cholestyramine was found to cause tumors. It is not known whether cholestyramine causes tumors in humans.

Along with its needed effects, a medicine may cause some unwanted effects. Although not all of these side effects may occur, if they do occur they may need medical attention.

Check with your doctor immediately if any of the following side effects occur:
Rare
Black, tarry stools; stomach pain (severe) with nausea and vomiting

Check with your doctor as soon as possible if any of the following side effects occur:
More common
Constipation
Rare
Loss of weight (sudden)

Other side effects may occur that usually do not need medical attention. These side effects may go away during treatment as your body adjusts to the medicine. However, check with your doctor if any of the following side effects continue or are bothersome:
More common
Heartburn or indigestion; nausea or vomiting; stomach pain
Less common
Belching; bloating; diarrhea; dizziness; headache

Other side effects not listed above may also occur in some patients. If you notice any other effects, check with your doctor.

Additional Information

Once a medicine has been approved for marketing for a certain use, experience may show that it is also useful for other medical problems. Although these uses are not included in product labeling, cholestyramine is used in certain patients with the following medical conditions:

- Digitalis glycoside overdose
- Excess oxalate in the urine

Other than the above information, there is no additional information relating to proper use, precautions, or side effects for these uses.

Revised: 08/02/94

CHONDROCYTES, AUTOLOGOUS CULTURED   Implantation-Local

Commonly used brand name(s):

In the U.S.—
Carticel

Description

Autologous cultured chondrocytes (aw-TOL-a-gus KUL-tured KON-droe-sites) are used, as part of an overall program that includes knee surgery and special exercises, to help repair damaged knee cartilage. Cartilage is a type of tissue that joins together and helps support parts of the body. Autologous cultured chondrocytes are the patient's own cartilage cells. The cells are removed from the patient and sent to a laboratory, where they are processed to increase their number. The cells are then implanted (placed) in the damaged part of the knee. After implantation, the chondrocytes help form new, healthy cartilage.

Before Receiving The Implant

In deciding to use a product or procedure, the risks must be weighed against the good it will do. This is a decision you and your doctor will make. For autologous cultured chondrocyte implantation, the following should be considered:

Allergies—Tell your doctor if you have ever had any unusual or allergic reaction to gentamicin (e.g., Garamycin), an antibiotic used to treat certain infections. Also tell your doctor if you are allergic to beef or other products obtained from cows.

Pregnancy—Tell your doctor if you are pregnant or if you think you might be pregnant. It is not likely that the implanted chondrocytes would affect the fetus. However, you should discuss with your doctor whether you should be having this procedure, and having to use crutches for several weeks afterward, while you are pregnant.

Breast-feeding—It is not likely that the transplanted chondrocytes would affect a nursing baby. However, whether you should be having the procedure at this time, when you are busy caring for an infant, should be discussed with your doctor.

Children—Implantation of autologous cultured chondrocytes has been done only in adults, and there is no information about the effects of this procedure in children.

Older adults—Implantation of autologous cultured chondrocytes has not been studied specifically in older people. There is no information comparing use of this procedure in the elderly with use in other age groups.

Other medical problems—The presence of other medical problems may affect whether you should receive implantation of autologous cultured chondrocytes. Make sure you tell your doctor if you have any other medical problems, especially:

- Cancer near the injured knee—It is not known whether removing and implanting the chondrocyte cells can affect the growth or spread of a nearby cancer

Proper Use of The Implant

Dosing—The amount of autologous cultured chondrocytes needed to repair damaged knee cartilage will be different for different patients. It will depend on the size of the damaged area. Most patients will receive between 0.64 million and 3.3 million cells for each square centimeter of damaged area. (A square centimeter covers an area slightly longer than 3/8 of an inch on each side.)

Precautions After Receiving The Implant

Use crutches to help you walk for the first 6 or 7 weeks after receiving the implant. Walk as normally as possible with the crutches. However, place no more than 25% of your weight on the leg that received the implant. Let the crutches and your other leg hold the rest of your weight. After the first 3 weeks, or when directed by your doctor, you may gradually increase the amount of weight placed on the knee.

Check with your doctor right away if sharp pain occurs in the knee that received the implant, or if "locking" of the knee occurs.

After the implant surgery, your doctor will direct you to start a rehabilitation program that includes exercise. This program is a very important part of your treatment. You will be instructed to start out slowly and to increase gradually the number of times that you do each exercise. To get the most help from this program, *it is very important that you follow the instructions as closely as possible. Do not do different exercises, and do not increase the number of times you do each exercise faster than directed.* If pain or swelling occurs when you increase the amount of exercise you are doing, go back to the last level of exercise until the pain and swelling are gone, then try again. Use ice packs to help reduce the swelling.

Side Effects of The Implant

Along with its needed effects, the implant or the surgical procedure during which the cells are implanted may cause some unwanted effects. Although not all of these side effects may occur, if they do occur they may need medical attention.

Check with your doctor as soon as possible if any of the following side effects occur soon after the implantation procedure:

Less common
Bruising (severe); signs of an infection, such as heat, redness, swelling, and/or oozing at the place of surgery

Rare
Fever and pain (occurring together)

Other side effects may not occur until weeks, months, or even years after the implantation. Check with your doctor if any of the following delayed side effects occur:

More common
"Crackling" sound or pain when moving the knee; stiffness or "catching" of the knee

Less common or rare
Inability to bend the knee; swelling of the knee

Other side effects not listed above may also occur in some patients. If you notice any other effects, check with your doctor.

Developed: 08/14/98
Interim revision: 09/24/98

CHORIOGONADOTROPIN ALFA
Systemic —INTRODUCTORY VERSION

Commonly used brand name(s):

In the U.S.—
Ovidrel

Description

Choriogonadotropin alfa (KOR-ee-o-goe-nad-oh-troe-pin AL-fa) is a substance used to help women become pregnant. It is usually given to women after they have been treated with follicle stimulating hormones, another substance that helps pregnancy occur.

This medicine is available only with your doctor's prescription, in the following dosage form:

Parenteral
- Injection (U.S.)

Before Using This Medicine

In deciding to use a medicine, the risks of using the medicine must be weighed against the good it will do. This is a decision you and your doctor will make. For choriogonadotropin alfa, the following should be considered:

Allergies—Tell your doctor if you have ever had any unusual or allergic reaction to choriogonadotropin alfa. Also tell your health care professional if you are allergic to any other substances, such as foods, preservatives, or dyes.

Pregnancy—Choriogonadotropin alfa is not recommended during pregnancy. Since women using choriogonadotropin alfa may be more likely to have more than one child at a time, the problems of multiple births may be increased for women using this medicine. Also, this medicine has been shown to overstimulate the ovaries (ovarian hyperstimulation syndrome) for a longer time in some women who conceive than in women developing this syndrome who do not become pregnant. Before you use this medicine, make sure your doctor knows if you are pregnant.

Breast-feeding—It is not known whether choriogonadotropin alfa passes into breast milk. Mothers who are taking this medicine and who wish to breast-feed should discuss this with your doctor

Children—Studies on this medicine have been done only in adult patients and there is no information comparing use of choriogonadotropin alfa in children with use in other age groups.

Older adults—Many medicines have not been studied specifically in older people. Therefore it may not be known whether they work exactly the same way they do in younger adults or if they cause different side effects or problems in older people. There is no specific information comparing use of choriogonadotropin alfa in the elderly with use in other age groups.

Other medicines—Although certain medicines should not be used together at all, in other cases two different medicines may be used together even if an interaction might occur. In these cases, your doctor may want to change the dose, or other precautions may be necessary. Tell your health care professional if you are taking any other prescription or nonprescription (over-the-counter [OTC]) medicine.

Other medical problems—The presence of other medical problems may affect the use of choriogonadotropin alfa. Make sure you tell your doctor if you have any other medical problems, especially:

- Abnormal bleeding of uterus (unknown cause)
- Adrenal gland or thyroid disease (not controlled)
- Tumor, brain or sex-dependent
- Ovarian cyst or enlarged ovaries (unknown cause)
- Primary ovarian failure

Proper Use of This Medicine

Dosing—The dose of choriogonadotropin alfa will be different for different patients. *Follow your doctor's orders or the directions on the label.* The following information includes only the average doses of choriogonadotropin alfa. *If your dose is different, do not change it* unless your doctor tells you to do so.

- For *injection* dosage form:
  —For treatment of female infertility:
  - Adults—250 mcg one day after the last dose of the follicle stimulating hormones treatment.
  —For use with assisted reproductive technology (ART):
  - Adults—250 mcg one day after the last dose of the follicle stimulating hormones treatment.

Storage—To store this medicine:

- Keep out of the reach of children
- Store away from heat and direct light
- Store at room temperature or in refrigerator
- Do not store in the bathroom, near the kitchen sink, or in other damp places
- Do not keep outdated medicine or medicine no longer needed. Ask your health care professional how you should dispose of any medicine you do not use. Be sure that any discarded medicine is out of the reach of children.

Precautions While Using This Medicine

It is very important that your doctor check you at regular visits to make sure that the medicine is working and to check for unwanted effects. Your doctor will likely want to monitor the development of the ovarian follicle(s) by measuring the amount of hormones in your bloodstream and by checking the size of the follicle(s) with ultrasound examinations.

Side Effects of This Medicine

Along with its needed effects, a medicine may cause some unwanted effects. Although not all of these side effects may occur, if they do occur they may need medical attention.

Check with your doctor immediately if any of the following side effects occur:
> *Less common*
>> Abdominal pain; aching; bloating stomach; heaviness; pelvic discomfort; rapid weight gain; nausea or vomiting; severe pelvic pain

Other side effects may occur that usually do not need medical attention. These side effects may go away during treatment as your body adjusts to the medicine. However, check with your doctor if any of the following side effects continue or are bothersome.
> *More common*
>> Bruising or pain at site of injection

Other side effects not listed above may also occur in some patients. If you notice any other effects, check with your doctor.

Developed: 12/22/2000

CHORIONIC GONADOTROPIN
Systemic

Commonly used brand name(s):

In the U.S.—
A.P.L.
Pregnyl
Profasi

Generic name product may be available.

In Canada—
    A.P.L.
    Profasi HP
    Generic name product may be available.

Another commonly used name is human chorionic gonadotropin (hCG).

Description

Chorionic gonadotropin (kor-ee-ON-ik goe-NAD-oh-troe-pin) is a drug whose actions are almost the same as those of luteinizing (loo-te-in-eye-ZING) hormone (LH), which is produced by the pituitary gland. It is a hormone also normally produced by the placenta in pregnancy. Chorionic gonadotropin has different uses for females and males.

In females, chorionic gonadotropin is used to help conception occur. It is usually given in combination with other drugs such as menotropins and urofollitropin. Many women being treated with these drugs usually have already tried clomiphene alone (e.g., Serophene) and have not been able to conceive yet. Chorionic gonadotropin is also used in in vitro fertilization (IVF) programs.

In males, LH and chorionic gonadotropin stimulate the testes to produce male hormones such as testosterone. Testosterone causes the enlargement of the penis and testes and the growth of pubic and underarm hair. It also increases the production of sperm.

Although chorionic gonadotropin has been prescribed to help some patients lose weight, it should *never* be used this way. When used improperly, chorionic gonadotropin can cause serious problems.

Chorionic gonadotropin is to be administered only by or under the immediate supervision of your doctor. It is available in the following dosage form:

Parenteral
    • Injection (U.S. and Canada)

Before Using This Medicine

In deciding to use a medicine, the risks of taking the medicine must be weighed against the good it will do. This is a decision you and your doctor will make. For chorionic gonadotropin, the following should be considered:

Allergies—Tell your doctor if you have ever had any unusual or allergic reaction to chorionic gonadotropin. Also tell your health care professional if you are allergic to any other substances, such as foods, preservatives, or dyes.

Pregnancy—If you become pregnant as a result of using this medicine with menotropins (e.g., Pergonal) or urofollitropin (e.g., Metrodin), there is an increased chance of a multiple pregnancy (for example, twins, triplets).

Children—Chorionic gonadotropin, when used for treating cryptorchidism (a birth defect where the testes remain inside the body), has caused the sexual organs of some male children to develop too rapidly.

Other medicines—Although certain medicines should not be used together at all, in other cases two different medicines may be used together even if an interaction might occur. In these cases, your doctor may want to change the dose, or other precautions may be necessary. Tell your health care professional if you are taking any prescription or nonprescription (over-the-counter [OTC]) medicine.

Other medical problems—The presence of other medical problems may affect the use of chorionic gonadotropin.

Make sure you tell your doctor if you have any other medical problems, especially:
    • Cancer of the prostate—Increases in the amount of testosterone in the bloodstream may make this condition worse
    • Cyst on ovary or
    • Fibroid tumors of the uterus—Chorionic gonadotropin can cause further growth of cysts on the ovary or fibroid tumors of the uterus
    • Unusual vaginal bleeding—Irregular vaginal bleeding is a sign that the endometrium is growing too much, of endometrial cancer, or of other hormone imbalances; the increases in estrogen production caused by ovulation can aggravate these problems of the endometrium. If other hormone imbalances are present, they should be treated before beginning ovulation induction

Proper Use of This Medicine

Dosing—The dose of chorionic gonadotropin will be different for different patients. *Follow your doctor's orders or the directions on the label.* The following information includes only the average doses for chorionic gonadotropin. *If your dose is different, do not change it* unless your doctor tells you to do so.

The number of doses you receive each day, the time allowed between doses, and the length of time you receive the medicine depend on the medical problem for which you are receiving chorionic gonadotropin.
    • For *injection* dosage form:
        —For treating men with problems related to low levels of male hormones:
            • Adults—1000 to 4000 Units injected into the muscle two to three times a week. You may need to receive this medicine for several weeks, months, or longer. If you are being treated for a low sperm count and have been on this medicine for six months, your doctor may give you another hormone medicine (menotropin or urofollitropin injection). You may need to receive both of these medicines together for up to twelve more months.
        —To help pregnancy occur in women:
            • Adults—5000 to 10,000 Units injected into the muscle on a day chosen by your doctor. The dose and day will depend on your hormone levels and the other medicines that you have been using.
        —For the treatment of cryptorchidism (condition where testes do not develop properly):
            • Children—1000 to 5000 Units injected into the muscle two to three times a week for up to ten doses.

Precautions While Using This Medicine

It is very important that your doctor check your progress at regular visits to make sure that the medicine is working and to check for unwanted effects.

For women *taking this medicine to become pregnant:*
    • Record your basal body temperature every day if told to do so by your doctor, so that you will know if you have begun to ovulate. It is important that intercourse take place around the time of ovulation to give you the best chance of becoming pregnant. Your doctor will likely want to monitor the development of the ovarian follicle(s) by measuring the amount of estrogen in your blood-

stream and by checking the size of the follicle(s) with ultrasound examinations.

Side Effects of This Medicine

Along with its needed effects, a medicine may cause some other effects. Although not all of these side effects may occur, if they do occur they may need medical attention.

Check with your doctor as soon as possible if any of the following side effects occur:

For females only
   More common
      Bloating (mild); stomach or pelvic pain

   Less common or rare
      Abdominal or stomach pain (severe); bloating (moderate to severe); decreased amount of urine; feeling of indigestion; nausea, vomiting, or diarrhea (continuing or severe); pelvic pain (severe); shortness of breath; swelling of feet or lower legs; weight gain (rapid)

For boys only
   Less common
      Acne; enlargement of penis and testes; growth of pubic hair; increase in height (rapid)

Other side effects may occur that usually do not need medical attention. These side effects may go away during treatment as your body adjusts to the medicine. However, check with your doctor if any of the following side effects continue or are bothersome:

Less common
   Enlargement of breasts; headache; irritability; mental depression; pain at place of injection; tiredness

After you stop receiving this medicine, it may continue to cause some side effects which require medical attention. During this period of time check with your doctor if you notice any of the following side effects:

For females only
   Less common or rare
      Abdominal or stomach pain (severe); bloating (moderate to severe); decreased amount of urine; feeling of indigestion; nausea, vomiting, or diarrhea (continuing or severe); pelvic pain (severe); shortness of breath; weight gain (rapid)

Other side effects not listed above may also occur in some patients. If you notice any other effects, check with your doctor.

Revised: 05/16/2001

CHROMIUM SUPPLEMENTS
Systemic

Commonly used brand name(s):

In the U.S.—
   Chroma-Pak[1]

Note: For quick reference, the following chromium supplements are numbered to match the corresponding brand name.

This information applies to the following:
   1. Chromic Chloride (KROME-ik KLOR-ide) †‡

2. Chromium (KROH-mee-um) ‡§

†Not commercially available in Canada.
‡Generic name product may be available in the U.S.
§Generic name product may be available in Canada.

Description

Chromium supplements are used to prevent or treat chromium deficiency.

The body needs chromium for normal growth and health. For patients who are unable to get enough chromium in their regular diet or who have a need for more chromium, chromium supplements may be necessary. They are generally taken by mouth but some patients may have to receive them by injection. Chromium helps your body use sugar properly. It is also needed for the breakdown of proteins and fats.

Lack of chromium may lead to nerve problems and may decrease the body's ability to use sugar properly.

There is not enough evidence to show that taking chromium supplements improves the way your body uses sugar (glucose tolerance).

Injectable chromium is given by or under the supervision of a health care professional. Other forms are available without a prescription.

Chromium supplements are available in the following dosage forms:

Oral
   Chromium
      • Capsules (U.S.)
      • Tablets (U.S. and Canada)

Parenteral
   Chromic Chloride
      • Injection (U.S.)

Importance of Diet

For good health, it is important that you eat a balanced and varied diet. Follow carefully any diet program your health care professional may recommend. For your specific dietary vitamin and/or mineral needs, ask your health care professional for a list of appropriate foods. If you think that you are not getting enough vitamins and/or minerals in your diet, you may choose to take a dietary supplement.

Chromium is found in various foods, including brewer's yeast, calf liver, American cheese, and wheat germ.

The daily amount of chromium needed is defined in several different ways.

For U.S.—
   • Recommended Dietary Allowances (RDAs) are the amount of vitamins and minerals needed to provide for adequate nutrition in most healthy persons. RDAs for a given nutrient may vary depending on a person's age, sex, and physical condition (e.g., pregnancy).
   • Daily Values (DVs) are used on food and dietary supplement labels to indicate the percent of the recommended daily amount of each nutrient that a serving provides. DV replaces the previous designation of United States Recommended Daily Allowances (US-RDAs).

For Canada—
   • Recommended Nutrient Intakes (RNIs) are used to determine the amounts of vitamins, minerals, and protein needed to provide adequate nutrition and lessen the risk of chronic disease.

Because a lack of chromium is rare, there is no RDA or RNI for it. Normal daily recommended intakes for chromium are generally defined as follows:

- Infants and children—
  Birth to 3 years of age: 10 to 80 micrograms (mcg) a day.
  4 to 6 years of age: 30 to 120 mcg a day.
  7 to 10 years of age: 50 to 200 mcg a day.
- Adolescents and adults—50 to 200 mcg a day.

Before Using This Dietary Supplement

If you are taking this dietary supplement without a prescription, carefully read and follow any precautions on the label. For chromium, the following should be considered:

Allergies—Tell your health care professional if you have ever had any unusual or allergic reaction to chromium. Also tell your health care professional if you are allergic to any other substances, such as foods, preservatives, or dyes.

Pregnancy—It is especially important that you are receiving enough vitamins and minerals when you become pregnant and that you continue to receive the right amount of vitamins and minerals throughout your pregnancy. The healthy growth and development of the fetus depend on a steady supply of nutrients from the mother. However, taking large amounts of a dietary supplement during pregnancy may be harmful to the mother and/or fetus and should be avoided.

Breast-feeding—It is important that you receive the right amounts of vitamins and minerals so that your baby will also get the vitamins and minerals needed to grow properly. However, taking large amounts of a dietary supplement while breast-feeding may be harmful to the mother and/or baby and should be avoided.

Children—Problems in children have not been reported with intake of normal daily recommended amounts.

Older adults—Problems in older adults have not been reported with intake of normal daily recommended amounts.

Medicines or other dietary supplements—Although certain medicines or dietary supplements should not be used together at all, in other cases they may be used together even if an interaction might occur. In these cases, your health care professional may want to change the dose, or other precautions may be necessary. Tell your health care professional if you are using any other dietary supplement or any prescription or over-the-counter (OTC) medication.

Other medical problems—The presence of other medical problems may affect the use of chromium. Make sure you tell your health care professional if you have any other medical problems, especially:

- Diabetes mellitus (sugar diabetes)—Taking chromium supplements when you have a chromium deficiency may cause a change in the amount of insulin you need

Proper Use of This Dietary Supplement

Dosing—The amount of chromium needed to meet normal daily recommended intakes will be different for different individuals. The following information includes only the average amounts of chromium.

- For *oral* dosage forms (capsules and tablets):
  —To prevent deficiency, the amount taken by mouth is based on normal daily recommended intakes:
    - Adults and teenagers—50 to 200 micrograms (mcg) per day.

- Children 7 to 10 years age—50 to 200 mcg per day.
- Children 4 to 6 years of age—30 to 120 mcg per day.
- Children birth to 3 years of age—10 to 80 mcg per day.
  —To treat deficiency:
    - Adults, teenagers, and children—Treatment dose is determined by prescriber for each individual based on severity of deficiency.

Missed dose—If you miss taking chromium supplements for one or more days there is no cause for concern, since it takes some time for your body to become seriously low in chromium. However, if your health care professional has recommended that you take chromium, try to remember to take it as directed every day.

Storage—To store this dietary supplement:

- Keep out of the reach of children.
- Store away from heat and direct light.
- Do not store in the bathroom, near the kitchen sink, or in other damp places. Heat or moisture may cause the dietary supplement to break down.
- Keep the dietary supplement from freezing. Do not refrigerate.
- Do not keep outdated dietary supplements or those no longer needed. Be sure that any discarded dietary supplement is out of the reach of children.

Side Effects of This Dietary Supplement

No side effects or overdoses have been reported for chromium. However, check with your health care professional if you notice any unusual effects while you are taking it.

Revised: 03/24/92
Interim revision: 08/01/94; 05/26/95

CICLOPIROX   Topical

Commonly used brand name(s):

In the U.S.—
Loprox
Penlac Nail Lacquer

In Canada—
Loprox

Description

Ciclopirox (sye-kloe-PEER-ox) is used to treat infections caused by fungus. It works by killing the fungus or preventing its growth.

Ciclopirox cream, gel, or lotion are applied to the skin to treat:

- ringworm of the body (tinea corporis);
- ringworm of the foot (tinea pedis; athlete's foot);
- ringworm of the groin (tinea cruris; jock itch);
- "sun fungus" (tinea versicolor; pityriasis versicolor); and
- certain other fungus infections, such as Candida (Monilia) infections.

Ciclopirox gel may also be applied to the scalp to treat seborrheic dermatitis.

Ciclopirox topical solution (nail lacquer) is applied to the nails to treat ringworm of the nails (tinea unguium).

Ciclopirox is available only with your doctor's prescription, in the following dosage forms:

Topical
- Cream (U.S. and Canada)
- Gel (U.S.)
- Lotion (U.S. and Canada)
- Topical Solution (U.S.)

Before Using This Medicine

In deciding to use a medicine, the risks of taking the medicine must be weighed against the good it will do. This is a decision you and your doctor will make. For ciclopirox, the following should be considered:

Allergies—Tell your doctor if you have ever had any unusual or allergic reaction to ciclopirox. Also tell your health care professional if you are allergic to any other substances, such as preservatives or dyes.

Pregnancy—Ciclopirox has not been studied in pregnant women. However, this medication has not been shown to cause birth defects or other problems in animal studies.

Breast-feeding—It is not known whether ciclopirox passes into breast milk. Although most medicines pass into breast milk in small amounts, many of them may be used safely while breast-feeding. Mothers who are using this medicine and who wish to breast-feed should discuss this with their doctor.

Children—Studies on this medicine have been done only in adult patients, and there is no specific information comparing use of ciclopirox in children under the age of 10 with use in other age groups.

Older adults—Many medicines have not been studied specifically in older people. Therefore, it may not be known whether they work exactly the same way they do in younger adults. Although there is no specific information comparing use of ciclopirox in the elderly with use in other age groups, this medicine is not expected to cause different side effects or problems in older people than it does in younger adults.

Other medicines—Although certain medicines should not be used together at all, in other cases two different medicines may be used together even if an interaction might occur. In these cases, your doctor may want to change the dose, or other precautions may be necessary. Tell your health care professional if you are using any other topical prescription or nonprescription (over-the-counter [OTC]) medicine that is to be applied to the same area of the skin.

Proper Use of This Medicine

For patients using the *cream, gel, or lotion form* of this medicine:
- *Keep this medicine away from the eyes.*
- Apply enough ciclopirox to cover the affected and surrounding skin or scalp areas and rub in gently.

For patients using the *topical solution form* of this medicine:
- *Keep this medicine away from the eyes and mucous membranes*
- This medicine comes with a patient instruction sheet. Read this sheet carefully and follow the directions. If you have any questions on how to use this medicine, be sure to ask your health care professional.
- In addition to daily application of this medicine, you will need to trim your nails as directed, and visit your healthcare professional at regular intervals to have the unattached infected nails removed.

- Do not use nail polish or other nail cosmetic products on the treated nails.
- Do not use near heat or open flame.

When ciclopirox is used to treat certain types of fungus infections of the skin, an occlusive dressing (airtight covering, such as kitchen plastic wrap) should *not* be applied over the medicine. To do so may irritate the skin. *Do not apply an airtight covering over this medicine unless you have been directed to do so by your doctor.*

To help clear up your infection completely, *it is very important that you keep using ciclopirox for the full time of treatment,* even if your symptoms begin to clear up after a few days. Since fungus infections may be very slow to clear up, you may have to continue using this medicine every day for several weeks or more. If you stop using this medicine too soon, your symptoms may return. *Do not miss any doses.*

Dosing—The dose of topical ciclopirox will be different for different patients. *Follow your doctor's orders or the directions on the label.* The following information includes only the average doses of topical ciclopirox. *If your dose is different, do not change it* unless your doctor tells you to do so.

- For *topical* cream and lotion dosage forms:
  —Fungus infections (treatment):
    - Adults and children 10 years of age and over— Apply two times a day, morning and evening.
    - Children up to 10 years of age—Use and dose must be determined by your doctor.
- For *topical* gel dosage form:
  —Fungus infections (treatment) or seborrheic dermatitis (treatment):
    - Adults and children 16 years of age and over— Apply two times a day, morning and evening.
    - Children up to 16 years of age—Use and dose must be determined by your doctor.
- For *topical solution* dosage form:
  —Fungus infections (treatment):
    - Adults —Apply once daily, preferably at bedtime or eight hours before washing.
    - Children up to 18 years of age—Use and dose must be determined by your doctor.

Missed dose—If you miss a dose of this medicine, apply it as soon as possible. However, if it is almost time for your next dose, skip the missed dose and go back to your regular dosing schedule.

Storage—To store this medicine:
- Keep out of the reach of children.
- Store away from heat and direct light.
- Store the topical solution in the carton to protect from light.
- Store the topical solution away from heat and flame.
- Keep the medicine from freezing.
- Do not keep outdated medicine or medicine no longer needed. Be sure that any discarded medicine is out of the reach of children.

Precautions While Using This Medicine

If your skin problem does not improve within 2 to 4 weeks, or if it becomes worse, check with your doctor.

Nail problems treated with the topical solution form of this medicine may take up to 6 months to start improving.

To help clear up your infection completely and to help make sure it does not return, good health habits are also required. The following measures will help reduce chafing and irritation and will also help keep the area cool and dry.

- *For patients using ciclopirox for ringworm of the groin (tinea cruris):*
  - —Avoid wearing underwear that is tight-fitting or made from synthetic materials (for example, rayon or nylon). Instead, wear loose-fitting, cotton underwear.
  - —Use a bland, absorbent powder (for example, talcum powder) or an antifungal powder (for example, tolnaftate) on the skin. It is best to use the powder between applications of ciclopirox.
- *For patients using ciclopirox for ringworm of the foot (tinea pedis):*
  - —Carefully dry the feet, especially between the toes, after bathing.
  - —Avoid wearing socks made from wool or synthetic materials (for example, rayon or nylon). Instead, wear clean, cotton socks and change them daily or more often if the feet sweat freely.
  - —Wear sandals or well-ventilated shoes (for example, shoes with holes on top or on the side).
  - —Use a bland, absorbent powder (for example, talcum powder) or an antifungal powder (for example, tolnaftate) between the toes, on the feet, and in socks and shoes freely once or twice a day. It is best to use the powder between applications of ciclopirox.

If you have any questions about these measures, check with your health care professional.

Side Effects of This Medicine

Along with its needed effects, a medicine may cause some unwanted effects. Although not all of these side effects may occur, if they do occur they may need medical attention.

Check with your doctor as soon as possible if any of the following side effects occur:

Rare
  Burning, itching, redness, swelling, or other signs of irritation not present before use of this medicine

Other side effects not listed above may also occur in some patients. If you notice any other effects, check with your doctor.

Revised: 03/09/00

CIDOFOVIR Systemic

Commonly used brand name(s):

In the U.S.—
  Vistide

Description

Cidofovir (si-DOF-o-veer) is an antiviral. It is used to treat infections caused by viruses.

Cidofovir is used to treat the symptoms of cytomegalovirus (CMV) infection of the eyes (CMV retinitis) in patients with acquired immune deficiency syndrome (AIDS). Cidofovir will not cure this eye infection, but it may help to keep the symptoms from becoming worse.

This medicine is available only with your doctor's prescription, in the following dosage form:

Parenteral
  - Injection (U.S.)

Before Using This Medicine

In deciding to use a medicine, the risks of using the medicine must be weighed against the good it will do. This is a decision you and your doctor will make. For cidofovir, the following should be considered:

Allergies—Tell your doctor if you have ever had any unusual or allergic reaction to cidofovir or probenecid. Also tell your health care professional if you are allergic to any other substances, such as foods, preservatives, or dyes.

Pregnancy—Cidofovir has not been studied in pregnant women. However, in animal studies, cidofovir has been shown to cause harmful effects on both the mother and infant. Discuss with your doctor whether or not you should continue to receive this medicine if you become pregnant.

Breast-feeding—It is not known whether cidofovir passes into breast milk. However, breast-feeding is usually not recommended in AIDS patients because of the risk of passing the AIDS virus on to the infant.

Children—Cidofovir can cause serious side effects, including possible cancer and trouble in having children later. Therefore, it is especially important that you discuss with the child's doctor the good that this medicine may do as well as the risks of using it.

Older adults—Many medicines have not been studied specifically in older people. Therefore, it may not be known whether they work exactly the same way they do in younger adults or if they cause different side effects or problems in older people. There is no specific information comparing use of cidofovir in the elderly with use in other age groups.

Other medicines—Although certain medicines should not be used together at all, in other cases two different medicines may be used together even if an interaction might occur. In these cases, your doctor may want to change the dose, or other precautions may be necessary. When you are receiving cidofovir, it is especially important that your health care professional know if you are taking any of the following:

- Carmustine (e.g., BiCNU) or
- Cisplatin (e.g., Platinol) or
- Combination pain medicine containing acetaminophen and aspirin (e.g., Excedrin) or other salicylates (with large amounts taken regularly) or
- Cyclosporine (e.g., Sandimmune) or
- Deferoxamine (e.g., Desferal) (with long-term use) or
- Gold salts (medicine for arthritis) or
- Inflammation or pain medicine, except narcotics, or
- Lithium (e.g., Lithane) or
- Other anti-infectives (e.g., amphotericin B) or
- Penicillamine (e.g., Cupramine) or
- Streptozocin (e.g., Zanosar) or
- Tiopronin (e.g., Thiola)—Use of these medicines may increase the chance of side effects affecting the kidneys

- Probenecid (e.g., Benemid)—Probenecid is usually given along with cidofovir; however, probenecid may cause other medications you may be taking to be removed from your body more slowly, and there is a possibility that effects of some of these medicines may be increased

Other medical problems—The presence of other medical problems may affect the use of cidofovir. Make sure you tell your doctor if you have any other medical problems, especially:

- Kidney disease—Cidofovir can cause harmful effects on the kidney

Proper Use of This Medicine

To get the best results, *cidofovir must be given for the full time of treatment*. Also, this medicine works best when there is a constant amount in the blood. To help keep the amount constant, cidofovir must be given on a regular schedule.

Dosing—The dose of cidofovir will be different for different patients. *If you are receiving this medicine at home, follow your doctor's orders or the directions on the label*. The following information includes only the average doses of cidofovir. *If your dose is different, do not change it* unless your doctor tells you to do so.

- For *injection* dosage form:
  —For treatment of cytomegalovirus (CMV) retinitis:
  - Adults—Dose is based on body weight and must be determined by your doctor. At first, 5 milligrams (mg) per kilogram (kg) (2.3 mg per pound) of body weight is injected over 1 hour into a vein once a week for two weeks in a row. Then the dose is reduced to 5 mg per kg (2.3 mg per pound) of body weight injected over 1 hour into a vein once every two weeks. Probenecid is taken along with each dose of cidofovir; follow your doctor's instructions for how much and when to take probenecid.
  - Children—Use and dose must be determined by your doctor.

Precautions While Using This Medicine

It is very important that your doctor check you at regular visits for any blood problems that may be caused by this medicine.

It is very important that your ophthalmologist (eye doctor) check your eyes at regular visits since it is still possible that you may have some loss of eyesight during cidofovir treatment.

Side Effects of This Medicine

Along with its needed effects, a medicine may cause some unwanted effects. Although not all of these side effects may occur, if they do occur they may need medical attention.

Medicines like cidofovir can sometimes cause serious side effects such as blood problems and kidney problems; these are described below. Cidofovir has also been found to cause cancer in animals, and there is a chance it could cause cancer in humans as well. Discuss these possible side effects with your doctor.

Check with your doctor immediately if any of the following side effects occur:
More common
    Fever, chills, or sore throat

Also, check with your doctor as soon as possible if any of the following side effects occur:
More common
    Decreased urination; increased thirst and urination
Rare
    Decreased vision or any change in vision

Other side effects may occur that usually do not need medical attention. These side effects may go away during treatment as your body adjusts to the medicine. However, check with your doctor if any of the following side effects continue or are bothersome:
More common
    Diarrhea; headache; loss of appetite; nausea; vomiting
Less common
    Generalized weakness; loss of strength

Other side effects not listed above may also occur in some patients. If you notice any other effects, check with your doctor.

Developed: 07/28/98

CILOSTAZOL   Systemic

Commonly used brand name(s):

In the U.S.—
    Pletal

Description

Cilostazol (sil-OH-sta-zol) improves the flow of blood through blood vessels. It is used to reduce leg pain caused by poor circulation (intermittent claudication). Cilostazol makes it possible to walk farther before having to rest because of leg pain.

Cilostazol works by keeping blood from clotting and by dilating or relaxing the blood vessels.

Cilostazol is available only with your doctor's prescription, in the following dosage form:

Oral
- Tablets (U.S.)

Before Using This Medicine

In deciding to use a medicine, the risks of taking the medicine must be weighed against the good it will do. This is a decision you and your doctor will make. For cilostazol, the following should be considered:

Allergies—Tell your doctor if you have ever had any unusual or allergic reaction to cilostazol. Also tell your healthcare professional if you are allergic to any other substances, such as foods, preservatives, or dyes.

Pregnancy—Tell your doctor if you are pregnant or if you intend to become pregnant. Studies in rats and rabbits have shown that cilostazol may cause some birth defects. Be sure that you have discussed this with your doctor before taking this medicine. Tell your doctor right away if you think you have become pregnant while receiving cilostazol.

Breast-feeding—It is not known whether cilostazol passes into human breast milk. However, cilostazol has been shown to pass into the breast milk of rats. Cilostazol is not recommended during breast-feeding because it may cause unwanted effects in nursing babies.

Children—Studies on this medicine have been done only in adult patients, and there is no specific information comparing the use of cilostazol in children with use in other age groups.

Older adults—This medicine has been tested in a limited number of patients and has not been shown to cause different side effects or problems in older people than it does in younger adults.

Other medicines—Although certain medicines should not be used together at all, in other cases, two different medicines may be used together even if an interaction might occur. In these cases, your doctor may want to change the dose, or other precautions may be necessary. When you are taking cilostazol, it is especially important that your health care professional know if you are taking any of the following:

- Diltiazem (e.g., Cardizem, Cardizem CD, Cardizem SR) or
- Erythromycin (medicine for infection) or
- Fluconazole (e.g., Diflucan) or
- Itraconazole (e.g., Sporanox) or
- Ketoconazole (e.g., Nizoral) or
- Miconazole (e.g., Lotrimin, Monistat) or
- Nefazodone (e.g., Serzone) or
- Omeprazole (e.g., Prilosec) or
- Selective serotonin reuptake inhibitors (fluoxetine [e.g., Prozac], fluvoxamine [e.g., Luvox]), paroxetine [e.g., Paxil], sertraline [e.g., Zoloft])—Use with these medicines may cause high levels of cilostazol, which may increase the chance of side effects

Other medical problems—The presence of other medical problems may affect the use of cilostazol. Make sure you tell your doctor if you have any other medical problems, especially:

- Congestive heart failure or
- Kidney disease—May increase the chance of side effects

Proper Use of This Medicine

To help you remember to take your medicine, try to get into the habit of taking it at the same time each day.

Dosing—The dose of cilostazol will be different for different patients. *Follow your doctor's orders or the directions on the label.* The following information includes on the average doses of cilostazol. *If your dose is different, do not change it* unless your doctor tells you to do so.

- For *oral* dosage form (tablets):
  —For *treatment of peripheral vascular disease (circulation problems):*
    - Adults—100 milligrams (mg) two times a day, taken at least one half-hour before or two hours after breakfast and dinner. In patients who take certain other medicines at the same time as cilostazol, the dose may be 50 mg two times a day.
    - Children—Use and dose must be determined by a doctor.

Missed dose—If you miss a dose of this medicine, take it as soon as possible. However, if it is almost time for your next dose, skip the missed dose and go back to your regular dosing schedule. Do not double doses.

Storage—To store this medicine:

- Keep out of the reach of children.
- Store away from heat and direct light.
- Do not store in the bathroom, near the kitchen sink, or in other damp places. Heat or moisture may cause the medicine to break down.
- Do not keep outdated medicine or medicine no longer needed. Be sure that any discarded medicine is out of the reach of children.

Precautions While Using This Medicine

It may take several weeks for this medicine to work. If you feel that cilostazol is not working, do not stop taking it on your own. Instead, check with your doctor.

Smoking tobacco products, such as cigarettes, may worsen your condition since nicotine may further narrow blood vessels and may also affect how this medicine works. Therefore, it is best to avoid smoking.

You should not take cilostazol with grapefruit juice. You may, however, take it with other citrus juices.

Side Effects of This Medicine

Along with its needed effects, a medicine may cause some unwanted effects. Although not all of these side effects may occur, if they do occur they may need medical attention.

Check with your doctor immediately if any of the following side effects occur:
More common
    Fast or irregular heartbeat; fever

Less common
    Abnormal bleeding; bloody or black tarry stools; bruises and/or red spots on the skin; fainting; nausea, heartburn, and/or indigestion (severe or continuing); nosebleeds; stiff neck; stomach pain, cramping, or burning (severe); swelling of the tongue; vomiting of blood or material that looks like coffee grounds

Symptoms of Overdose
    Diarrhea; dizziness or lightheadedness when getting up from a lying or sitting position; fast or irregular heartbeat; headache (severe)

Other side effects may occur that usually do not need medical attention. These side effects may go away during treatment as your body adjusts to the medicine. However, check with your doctor if any of the following side effects continue or are bothersome:

More common
    Back pain; dizziness; gas; headache; increased cough; pain or stiffness in muscles; pounding heartbeat; runny or stuffy nose; sore throat; swelling of arms or legs
Less common
    Bone pain; burning feeling in throat or chest; difficulty in swallowing; hives; pain or stiffness in joints; ringing or buzzing in ears; swelling of face, fingers, and/or lower legs

Other side effects not listed above may also occur in some patients. If you notice any other effects, check with your doctor.

Developed: 11/02/1999
Revised: 04/20/2001

CINOXACIN   Systemic†

Commonly used brand name(s):

In the U.S.—
Cinobac
Generic name product may be available.

†Not commercially available in Canada.

Description

Cinoxacin (sin-OX-a-sin) is used to prevent and treat infections of the urinary tract. It will not work for other infections or for colds, flu, or other virus infections.

Cinoxacin is available only with your doctor's prescription, in the following dosage form:

Oral
• Capsules (U.S.)

Before Using This Medicine

In deciding to use a medicine, the risks of taking the medicine must be weighed against the good it will do. This is a decision you and your doctor will make. For cinoxacin, the following should be considered:

Allergies—Tell your doctor if you have ever had any unusual or allergic reaction to cinoxacin or to any related medicines such as ciprofloxacin (e.g., Cipro), enoxacin (e.g., Penetrex), lomefloxacin (e.g., Maxaquin), nalidixic acid (e.g., NegGram), norfloxacin (e.g., Noroxin), or ofloxacin (e.g., Floxin). Also tell your health care professional if you are allergic to any other substances, such as foods, preservatives, or dyes.

Pregnancy—Studies have not been done in humans. However, use is not recommended during pregnancy since cinoxacin has been shown to cause bone development problems in young animals.

Breast-feeding—It is not known whether cinoxacin passes into the breast milk. However, other related medicines do pass into the breast milk. Since cinoxacin has been shown to cause bone development problems in young animals, use is not recommended in nursing mothers.

Children—Since this medicine has been shown to cause bone development problems in young animals, its use is not recommended in children up to 18 years of age.

Older adults—Many medicines have not been studied specifically in older people. Therefore, it may not be known whether they work exactly the same way they do in younger adults. Although there is no specific information comparing use of cinoxacin in the elderly with use in other age groups, this medicine is not expected to cause different side effects or problems in older people than it does in younger adults.

Other medical problems—The presence of other medical problems may affect the use of cinoxacin. Make sure you tell your doctor if you have any other medical problems, especially:
• Kidney disease—Patients with kidney disease may have an increased risk of side effects

Proper Use of This Medicine

Cinoxacin may be taken with food, unless you are otherwise directed by your doctor.

Do not give this medicine to infants or children under 18 years of age, unless otherwise directed by your doctor. It has been shown to cause bone development problems in young animals.

To help clear up your infection completely, *keep taking this medicine for the full time of treatment*, even if you begin to feel better after a few days. If you stop taking this medicine too soon, your symptoms may return.

This medicine works best when there is a constant amount in the urine. *To help keep the amount constant, do not miss any doses. Also, it is best to take the doses at evenly spaced times, day and night*. For example, if you are to take 4 doses a day, the doses should be spaced about 6 hours apart. If this interferes with your sleep or other daily activities, or if you need help in planning the best times to take your medicine, check with your health care professional.

Dosing—The dose of cinoxacin will be different for different patients. *Follow your doctor's orders or the directions on the label.* The following information includes only the average doses of cinoxacin. Your dose may be different if you have kidney disease. *If your dose is different, do not change it* unless your doctor tells you to do so.

The number of capsules that you take depends on the strength of the medicine. Also, *the number of doses you take each day, the time allowed between doses, and the length of time you take the medicine depend on whether you are using cinoxacin to prevent or to treat urinary tract infections.*

• For *capsule* dosage form:
—For the *prevention* of urinary tract infections:
• Adults—250 milligrams (mg) at bedtime for up to five months.
• Children up to 18 years of age—Use is generally not recommended because it may cause bone development problems.
—For the *treatment* of urinary tract infections:
• Adults—250 mg every six hours; or 500 mg every twelve hours for seven to fourteen days.
• Children up to 18 years of age—Use is generally not recommended because it may cause bone development problems.

Missed dose—If you miss a dose of this medicine, take it as soon as possible. This will help to keep a constant amount of medicine in the urine. However, if it is almost time for your next dose, skip the missed dose and go back to your regular dosing schedule. Do not double doses.

Storage—To store this medicine:
• Keep out of the reach of children.
• Store away from heat and direct light.
• Do not store in the bathroom, near the kitchen sink, or in other damp places. Heat or moisture may cause the medicine to break down.
• Do not keep outdated medicine or medicine no longer needed. Be sure that any discarded medicine is out of the reach of children.

Precautions While Using This Medicine

If your symptoms do not improve within a few days, or if they become worse, check with your doctor.

This medicine may also cause some people to become dizzy. *Make sure you know how you react to this medicine before you drive, use machines, or do anything else that could be dangerous if you are dizzy.* If this reaction is especially bothersome, check with your doctor.

Some people who take cinoxacin may become more sensitive to sunlight than they are normally. Exposure to sunlight, even for brief periods of time, may cause severe sunburn; skin rash, redness, itching, or discoloration; or vision changes. When you begin taking this medicine:

- Stay out of direct sunlight, especially between the hours of 10:00 a.m. and 3:00 p.m., if possible.
- Wear protective clothing, including a hat and sunglasses.
- Apply a sun block product that has a skin protection factor (SPF) of at least 15. Some patients may require a product with a higher SPF number, especially if they have a fair complexion. If you have any questions about this, check with your health care professional.
- Do not use a sunlamp or tanning bed or booth.

If you have a severe reaction from the sun, check with your doctor.

Side Effects of This Medicine

Along with its needed effects, a medicine may cause some unwanted effects. Although not all of these side effects may occur, if they do occur they may need medical attention.

Check with your doctor as soon as possible if any of the following side effects occur:

Less common
  Skin rash, itching, redness, or swelling

Rare
  Dizziness; headache; increased sensitivity of skin to sunlight

Other side effects may occur that usually do not need medical attention. These side effects may go away during treatment as your body adjusts to the medicine. However, check with your doctor if any of the following side effects continue or are bothersome:

Less common
  Diarrhea; loss of appetite; nausea; stomach cramps; vomiting

Other side effects not listed above may also occur in some patients. If you notice any other effects, check with your doctor.

Revised: 07/19/95

CIPROFLOXACIN   Ophthalmic

Commonly used brand name(s):

In the U.S.—
  Ciloxan

In Canada—
  Ciloxan

Description

Ophthalmic ciprofloxacin (sip-roe-FLOX-a-sin) is used in the eye to treat bacterial infections of the eye (ophthalmic ointment and solution) and corneal ulcers of the eye (ophthalmic solution). Ophthalmic ciprofloxacin works by killing bacteria.

Ciprofloxacin ophthalmic preparation is available only with your doctor's prescription, in the following dosage form:

Ophthalmic
  - Ophthalmic ointment (U.S. and Canada)
  - Ophthalmic solution (eye drops) (U.S. and Canada)

Before Using This Medicine

In deciding to use a medicine, the risks of using the medicine must be weighed against the good it will do. This is a decision you and your doctor will make. For ophthalmic ciprofloxacin, the following should be considered:

Allergies—Tell your doctor if you have ever had any unusual or allergic reaction to ophthalmic or systemic ciprofloxacin (e.g., Cipro) or any related medicines, such as cinoxacin (e.g., Cinobac), norfloxacin (e.g., Chibroxin or Noroxin), ofloxacin (e.g., Floxin), or nalidixic acid (e.g., NegGram). Also tell your health care professional if you are allergic to any other substances, such as foods, preservatives, or dyes.

Pregnancy—Ciprofloxacin has not been studied in pregnant women. However, studies in animals have not shown that ciprofloxacin causes birth defects.

Breast-feeding—It is not known whether ophthalmic ciprofloxin passes into breast milk. However, ciprofloxacin given by mouth does pass into breast milk. Although most medicines pass into breast milk in small amounts, many of them may be used safely while breast-feeding. Mothers who are using this medicine and who wish to breast-feed should discuss this with their doctor.

Children—Use is not recommended in infants and children up to 2 years of age (ophthalmic ointment) and 1 year of age (ophthalmic solution). In children older than 1 or 2 years of age, this medicine is not expected to cause different side effects or problems than it does in adults.

Older adults—Many medicines have not been studied specifically in older people. Therefore, it may not be known whether they work exactly the same way they do in younger adults or if they cause different side effects or problems in older people. There is no specific information comparing use of ophthalmic ciprofloxacin in the elderly with use in other age groups.

Other medicines—Although certain medicines should not be used together at all, in other cases two different medicines may be used together even if an interaction might occur. In these cases, your doctor may want to change the dose, or other precautions may be necessary. Tell your health care professional if you using any other prescription or nonprescription (over-the-counter [OTC]) medicine that is to be used in the eye.

Proper Use of This Medicine

To use the ophthalmic ointment:
- First, wash your hands. Tilt the head back and, pressing your finger gently on the skin just beneath the lower eyelid, pull the lower eyelid away from the eye to make a space. Squeeze a thin strip of ointment into this space. A ½-inch strip of ointment is usually enough, unless you have been told by your doctor to use a different amount. Let go of the eyelid and gently close the eyes. Keep the eyes closed for 1 or 2 minutes to allow the medicine to come into contact with the infection.
- To keep the medicine as germ-free as possible, do not touch the applicator tip to any surface (including the

eye). After using the eye ointment, wipe the tip of the ointment tube with a clean tissue and keep the tube tightly closed.

To use the ophthalmic solution (eye drops):

- First, wash your hands. Then tilt the head back and pull the lower eyelid away from the eye to form a pouch. Drop the medicine into the pouch and gently close the eyes. Do not blink. Keep the eyes closed for 1 or 2 minutes to allow the medicine to come into contact with the infection.
- If you think you did not get the drop of medicine into your eyes properly, use another drop.
- To keep the medicine as germ-free as possible, do not touch the applicator tip to any surface (including the eye). Also, keep the container tightly closed.

To help clear up your eye infection completely, *keep using ophthalmic ciprofloxacin for the full time of treatment,* even if your symptoms have disappeared. *Do not miss any doses.*

Dosing—The dose of ophthalmic ciprofloxacin will be different for different patients. *Follow your doctor's orders or the directions on the label.* The following information includes only the average doses of ophthalmic ciprofloxacin. *If your dose is different, do not change it* unless your doctor tells you to do so.

The number of doses you use each day, the time allowed between doses, and the length of time you use the medicine depend on the medical problem for which you are using ophthalmic ciprofloxacin.

- For *ophthalmic ointment* dosage form:
  —For bacterial conjunctivitis:
  - Adults and children 2 years of age and older— Use a ½-inch strip of eye ointment in each eye three times a day for the first two days, then use a ½-inch strip of eye ointment in each eye two times a day for the next five days.
  - Infants and children up to 2 years of age—Use and dose must be determined by your doctor.
- For *ophthalmic solution* dosage form:
  —For bacterial conjunctivitis:
  - Adults and children 1 year of age and older—Use 1 drop in each eye every two hours, while you are awake, for two days. Then use 1 drop in each eye every four hours, while you are awake, for the next five days. If you think you did not get the drop of medicine into your eyes properly, use another drop.
  - Infants and children up to 1 year of age—Use and dose must be determined by your doctor.
  —For corneal ulcers:
  - Adults and children 1 year of age and older—On day one, use 2 drops in the affected eye every fifteen minutes for six hours, then 2 drops every thirty minutes for the rest of the day, while you are awake. On day two, use 2 drops every hour, while you are awake. On days three through fourteen, use 2 drops every four hours, while you are awake.
  - Infants and children up to 1 year of age—Use and dose must be determined by your doctor.

Missed dose—If you miss a dose of this medicine, use it as soon as possible. However, if it is almost time for your next dose, skip the missed dose and go back to your regular dosing schedule.

Storage—To store this medicine:

- Keep out of the reach of children.
- Store away from heat and direct light.
- Keep the medicine from freezing. Do not refrigerate.
- Do not keep outdated medicine or medicine no longer needed. Be sure that any discarded medicine is out of the reach of children.

Precautions While Using This Medicine

If your eye infection does not improve within a few days, or if it becomes worse, check with your doctor.

This medicine may cause your eyes to become more sensitive to light than they are normally. Wearing sunglasses and avoiding too much exposure to bright light may help lessen the discomfort.

Side Effects of This Medicine

Along with its needed effects, a medicine may cause some unwanted effects. Although not all of these side effects may occur, if they do occur they may need medical attention.

Check with your doctor as soon as possible if any of the following side effects occur:
> *Rare*
>> Allergic reaction, such as skin rash, hives, or itching; blurred vision or other change in vision; eye pain; irritation (severe) or redness of eye; nausea

Other side effects may occur that usually do not need medical attention. These side effects may go away during treatment as your body adjusts to the medicine. However, check with your doctor if any of the following side effects continue or are bothersome:
> *More common*
>> Burning or other discomfort of eye; crusting or crystals in corner of eye
>
> *Less common*
>> Bad taste following use in the eye; feeling of something in eye; itching of eye; redness of the lining of the eyelids
>
> *Rare*
>> Dryness of eye; increased sensitivity of eyes to light; swelling of eyelid; tearing of eye

Other side effects not listed above may also occur in some patients. If you notice any other effects, check with your doctor.

Revised: 06/14/99

CISAPRIDE   Systemic†*

Commonly used brand name(s):

In the U.S.—
Propulsid

In Canada—
Prepulsid

*Not commercially available in the U.S.
†Not commercially available in Canada.

Description

Cisapride (SIS-a-pride) is a medicine that increases the movements or contractions of the stomach and intestines. It is used to treat symptoms such as heartburn caused by a backward flow of stomach acid into the esophagus.

Cisapride will only be available in the U.S. to certain patients who meet eligibility criteria from the manufacturer. Your doctor must enroll in a special program in order to prescribe this medicine for you. Cisapride is not available in Canada.

Before Using This Medicine

In deciding to use a medicine, the risks of taking the medicine must be weighed against the good it will do. This is a decision you and your doctor will make. For cisapride, the following should be considered:

Allergies—Tell your doctor if you have ever had any unusual or allergic reaction to cisapride. Also tell your health care professional if you are allergic to any other substances, such as foods, preservatives, or dyes.

Pregnancy—Cisapride has not been studied in pregnant women. However, studies in animals have shown that cisapride causes harm to the fetus. Before taking this medicine, make sure your doctor knows if you are pregnant or if you may become pregnant.

Breast-feeding—Cisapride passes into breast milk and may cause unwanted effects in nursing babies, particularly if the infant or mother are taking certain other medicines. Be sure you have discussed the risks and benefits of this medicine with your doctor.

Children—Cisapride can cause serious side effects in any patient. Therefore, it is especially important that you discuss with the child's doctor the good that this medicine may do, as well as the risks of using it.

Older adults—Elderly people are especially sensitive to the effects of cisapride. Cisapride stays in the body longer so the dose may be different than in younger people.

Other medicines—Although certain medicines should not be used together at all, in other cases two different medicines may be used together even if an interaction might occur. In these cases, your doctor may want to change the dose, or other precautions may be necessary. When you are taking cisapride, it is especially important that your health care professional know if you are taking any of the following:

- Amantadine (e.g., Symmetrel) or
- Anticholinergics (medicine for abdominal or stomach spasms or cramps) or
- Antidepressants (medicine for depression) or
- Antidyskinetics (medicine for Parkinson's disease or other conditions affecting control of muscles) or
- Antihistamines, except cetirizine (e.g., Reactine), and loratadine (e.g., Claritin) or
- Antipsychotics (medicine for mental illness) or
- Buclizine (e.g., Bucladin) or
- Carbamazepine (e.g., Tegretol) or
- Cyclizine (e.g., Marezine) or
- Cyclobenzaprine (e.g., Flexeril) or
- Disopyramide (e.g., Norpace) or
- Ipratropium (e.g., Atrovent) or
- Meclizine (e.g., Antivert) or
- Orphenadrine (e.g., Norflex) or

- Oxybutynin (e.g., Ditropan) or
- Promethazine (e.g., Phenergan) or
- Trimeprazine (e.g., Temaril)—Cisapride may decrease the absorption of these medicines and cause them to be less effective

- Bepridil (e.g., Bepadin, Vascor) or
- Bumetanide (e.g., Bumex) or
- Clarithromycin (e.g., Biaxin) or
- Erythromycin (e.g., E-Mycin) or
- Ethacrynic acid (e.g., Edecrin) or
- Fluconazole (e.g., Diflucan) or
- Furosemide (e.g., Lasix) or
- Indinavir (e.g., Crixivan) or
- Itraconazole (e.g., Sporanox) or
- Ketoconazole (e.g., Nizoral) or
- Miconazole (e.g., Monistat i.v.) or
- Nefazodone (e.g., Serzone) or
- Nelfinivir (e.g., Viracept) or
- Procainamide (e.g., Pronestyl) or
- Quinidine (e.g., Quinidex) or
- Ritonavir (e.g., Norvir) or
- Saquinavir (e.g., Invirase) or
- Sotalol (e.g., Betapace, Sotacor) or
- Sparfloxacin (e.g., Zagam) or
- Terodiline (e.g., Micturin) or
- Troleandomycin (e.g., Tao)—These medicines may increase the chance of serious side effects and should not be taken with cisapride

- Diuretics (water pills)—These medicines may increase the chance of serious side effects from cisapride

Other medical problems—The presence of other medical problems may affect the use of cisapride. Make sure you tell your doctor if you have any other medical problems, especially:

- Abdominal or stomach bleeding or
- Intestinal blockage—Cisapride may make these conditions worse

- Heart disease or
- Kidney disease, severe, or
- Low potassium blood levels or
- Lung disease, severe—Cisapride may cause an increased risk of serious heart rhythm problems

Proper Use of This Medicine

Take this medicine 15 minutes before meals and at bedtime with a beverage, unless otherwise directed by your doctor.

Grapefruit and grapefruit juice may increase the effects of cisapride by increasing the amount of this medicine in the body. *You should not eat grapefruit or drink grapefruit juice while you are taking this medicine.*

Dosing—The dose of cisapride will be different for different patients. *Follow your doctor's orders or the directions on the label.* The following information includes only the average doses of cisapride. *If your dose is different, do not change it* unless your doctor tells you to do so.

- For *oral* dosage forms (tablets and suspension):
  —For heartburn caused by gastroesophageal reflux:
  - Adults and children 12 years of age and older—5 to 20 milligrams (mg) of cisapride two to four times a day. Cisapride should be taken fifteen minutes before meals and at bedtime.

- Children up to 12 years of age—Dose is based on body weight and must be determined by your doctor. The dose is usually 0.15 to 0.3 mg of cisapride per kilogram (0.07 to 0.14 mg per pound) of body weight three to four times a day, fifteen minutes before meals.

Missed dose—If you miss a dose of this medicine, take it as soon as possible. However, if it is almost time for your next dose, skip the missed dose and go back to your regular dosing schedule. Do not double doses.

Storage—To store this medicine:
- Keep out of the reach of children.
- Store away from heat and direct light.
- Do not store in the bathroom, near the kitchen sink, or in other damp places. Heat or moisture may cause the medicine to break down.
- Do not keep outdated medicine or medicine no longer needed. Be sure that any discarded medicine is out of the reach of children.

Precautions While Using This Medicine

This medicine may cause your body to absorb alcohol more quickly than you normally would. Therefore, you may notice the effects sooner. *Check with your doctor before drinking alcohol while you are using this medicine.*

This medicine may cause some people to become dizzy, drowsy, or less alert than they are normally. *Make sure you know how you react to this medicine before you drive, use machines, or do anything else that could be dangerous if you are dizzy or are not alert.*

Side Effects of This Medicine

Along with its needed effects, a medicine may cause some unwanted effects. Although not all of these side effects may occur, if they do occur they may need medical attention.

Check with your doctor immediately if the following side effects occur:
Rare
  Blurred vision or other changes in vision; convulsions (seizures); dizziness; fainting or feeling faint; fast or racing heartbeat; pounding or irregular heartbeat; swelling of face, hands, lower legs, and/or feet; unusual weight gain

Other side effects may occur that usually do not need medical attention. These side effects may go away during treatment as your body adjusts to the medicine. However, check with your doctor if any of the following side effects continue or are bothersome:
Less common or rare
  Abdominal pain or cramping; constipation; diarrhea; drowsiness; dryness of mouth; gas; headache; heartburn or indigestion; nausea; runny nose; tremor; unusual tiredness or weakness

Other side effects not listed above may also occur in some patients. If you notice any other effects, check with your doctor.

Revised: 12/18/2000

CISPLATIN   Systemic

Commonly used brand name(s):
In the U.S.—
  Platinol
  Platinol-AQ
In Canada—
  Platinol
  Platinol-AQ
  Generic name product may be available.

Description

Cisplatin (sis-PLA-tin) belongs to the group of medicines known as alkylating agents. It is used to treat cancer of the bladder, ovaries, and testicles. It may also be used to treat other kinds of cancer, as determined by your doctor.

Cisplatin interferes with the growth of cancer cells, which are eventually destroyed. Since the growth of normal body cells may also be affected by cisplatin, other effects will also occur. Some of these may be serious and must be reported to your doctor. Other effects may not be serious but may cause concern. Some effects may not occur for months or years after the medicine is used.

Before you begin treatment with cisplatin, you and your doctor should talk about the good this medicine will do as well as the risks of using it.

Cisplatin is to be administered only by or under the immediate supervision of your doctor. It is available in the following dosage form:
  Parenteral
  - Injection (U.S. and Canada)

Before Using This Medicine

In deciding to use a medicine, the risks of taking the medicine must be weighed against the good it will do. This is a decision you and your doctor will make. For cisplatin, the following should be considered:

Allergies—Tell your doctor if you have ever had any unusual or allergic reaction to cisplatin.

Pregnancy—There is a chance that this medicine may cause birth defects if either the male or female is taking it at the time of conception or if it is taken during pregnancy. Cisplatin causes toxic or harmful effects in the fetus in humans and birth defects in mice. In addition, many cancer medicines may cause sterility which could be permanent. Although sterility has not been reported with this medicine, the possibility should be kept in mind.

Be sure that you have discussed this with your doctor before receiving this medicine. It is best to use some kind of birth control while you are receiving cisplatin. Tell your doctor right away if you think you have become pregnant while receiving cisplatin.

Breast-feeding—Because cisplatin may cause serious side effects, breast-feeding is generally not recommended while you are receiving it.

Children—Hearing problems and loss of balance are more likely to occur in children, who are usually more sensitive to the effects of cisplatin.

Older adults—Many medicines have not been studied specifically in older people. Therefore, it may not be known whether they work exactly the same way they do in younger adults or if they cause different side effects or problems in older people. There is no specific information comparing use of cisplatin in the elderly with use in other age groups.

Other medicines—Although certain medicines should not be used together at all, in other cases two different medicines may be used together even if an interaction might occur. In these cases, your doctor may want to change the dose, or other precautions may be necessary. When you are receiving cisplatin, it is especially important that your health care professional know if you are taking any of the following:

- Amphotericin B by injection (e.g., Fungizone) or
- Antithyroid agents (medicine for overactive thyroid) or
- Azathioprine (e.g., Imuran) or
- Chloramphenicol (e.g., Chloromycetin) or
- Colchicine or
- Flucytosine (e.g., Ancobon) or
- Ganciclovir (e.g., Cytovene) or
- Interferon (e.g., Introl A, Roferon-A) or
- Plicamycin (e.g., Mithracin) or
- Zidovudine (e.g., AZT, Retrovir) or
- If you have ever been treated with radiation or cancer medicines—Cisplatin may increase the effects of these medicines or radiation therapy on the blood

- Anti-infectives by mouth or by injection (medicine for infection) or
- Chloroquine (e.g., Aralen) or
- Combination pain medicine containing acetaminophen and aspirin (e.g., Excedrin) or other salicylates (with large amounts taken regularly) or
- Cyclosporine (e.g., Sandimmune) or
- Deferoxamine (e.g., Desferal) (with long-term use) or
- Gold salts (medicine for arthritis) or
- Hydroxychloroquine (e.g., Plaquenil) or
- Inflammation or pain medicine, except narcotics or
- Lithium (e.g., Lithane) or
- Penicillamine (e.g., Cuprimine) or
- Plicamycin (e.g., Mithracin) or
- Quinine (e.g., Quinamm) or
- Tiopronin (e.g., Thiola)—Risk of ear and kidney problems caused by cisplatin is increased

- Probenecid (e.g., Benemid) or
- Sulfinpyrazone (e.g., Anturane)—Cisplatin may raise the amount of uric acid in the blood. Since these medicines are used to lower uric acid levels, they may not work as well in patients receiving cisplatin

Other medical problems—The presence of other medical problems may affect the use of cisplatin. Make sure you tell your doctor if you have any other medical problems, especially:

- Chickenpox (including recent exposure) or
- Herpes zoster (shingles)—Risk of severe disease affecting other parts of the body

- Gout (history of) or
- Kidney stones (history of)—Cisplatin may increase levels of uric acid in the body, which can cause gout or kidney stones

- Hearing problems—May be worsened by cisplatin

- Infection—Cisplatin decreases your body's ability to fight infection

- Kidney disease—Effects of cisplatin may be increased because of slower removal from the body

Proper Use of This Medicine

This medicine is sometimes given together with certain other medicines. If you are using a combination of medicines, it is important that you receive each one at the proper time. If you are taking some of these medicines by mouth, ask your health care professional to help you plan a way to take them at the right times.

While you are receiving this medicine, your doctor may want you to drink extra fluids so that you will pass more urine. This will help prevent kidney problems and keep your kidneys working well.

This medicine usually causes nausea and vomiting that may be severe. However, it is very important that you continue to receive the medicine, even if you begin to feel ill. Ask your health care professional for ways to lessen these effects, especially if they are severe.

Dosing—The dose of cisplatin will be different for different patients. The dose that is used may depend on a number of things, including what the medicine is being used for, the patient's size, and whether or not other medicines are also being taken. *If you are receiving cisplatin at home, follow your doctor's orders or the directions on the label.* If you have any questions about the proper dose of cisplatin, ask your doctor.

Precautions While Using This Medicine

It is very important that your doctor check your progress at regular visits to make sure that this medicine is working properly and to check for unwanted effects.

While you are being treated with cisplatin, and after you stop treatment with it, *do not have any immunizations (vaccinations) without your doctor's approval.* Cisplatin may lower your body's resistance and there is a chance you might get the infection the immunization is meant to prevent. In addition, other persons living in your household should not take oral polio vaccine since there is a chance they could pass the polio virus on to you. Also, avoid persons who have taken oral polio vaccine within the last several months. Do not get close to them, and do not stay in the same room with them for very long. If you cannot take these precautions, you should consider wearing a protective face mask that covers the nose and mouth.

Cisplatin can temporarily lower the number of white blood cells in your blood, increasing the chance of getting an infection. It can also lower the number of platelets, which are necessary for proper blood clotting. If this occurs, there are certain precautions you can take, especially when your blood count is low, to reduce the risk of infection or bleeding:

- If you can, avoid people with infections. *Check with your doctor immediately* if you think you are getting an infection or if you get a fever or chills, cough or hoarseness, lower back or side pain, or painful or difficult urination.
- *Check with your doctor immediately* if you notice any unusual bleeding or bruising; black, tarry stools; blood in urine or stools; or pinpoint red spots on your skin.
- Be careful when using a regular toothbrush, dental floss, or toothpick. Your medical doctor, dentist, or nurse may recommend other ways to clean your teeth and gums. Check with your medical doctor before having any dental work done.

- Do not touch your eyes or the inside of your nose unless you have just washed your hands and have not touched anything else in the meantime.
- Be careful not to cut yourself when you are using sharp objects such as a safety razor or fingernail or toenail cutters.
- Avoid contact sports or other situations where bruising or injury could occur.

If cisplatin accidentally seeps out of the vein into which it is injected, it may damage some tissues and cause scarring. *Tell the doctor or nurse right away if you notice redness, pain, or swelling at the place of injection.*

Side Effects of This Medicine

Along with its needed effects, a medicine may cause unwanted effects. Although not all of these side effects may occur, if they do occur they may need medical attention.

Also, because of the way cancer medicines act on the body, there is a chance that they might cause other unwanted effects that may not occur until months or years after the medicine is used. These delayed effects may include certain types of cancer, such as leukemia. Discuss these possible effects with your doctor.

Check with your doctor or nurse immediately if any of the following side effects occur:

Less common

Black, tarry stools; blood in urine or stools; cough or hoarseness accompanied by fever or chills; dizziness or faintness (during or shortly after a dose); fast heartbeat (during or shortly after a dose); fever or chills; lower back or side pain accompanied by fever or chills; painful or difficult urination accompanied by fever or chills; pain or redness at place of injection; pinpoint red spots on skin; swelling of face (during or shortly after a dose); unusual bleeding or bruising; wheezing (during or shortly after a dose)

Check with your doctor as soon as possible if any of the following side effects occur:

More common

Joint pain; loss of balance; ringing in ears; swelling of feet or lower legs; trouble in hearing; unusual tiredness or weakness

Less common

Convulsions (seizures); loss of reflexes; loss of taste; numbness or tingling in fingers or toes; trouble in walking

Rare

Agitation or confusion; blurred vision; change in ability to see colors (especially blue or yellow); muscle cramps; sores in mouth and on lips

Other side effects may occur that usually do not need medical attention. These side effects may go away during treatment as your body adjusts to the medicine. Also, your health care professional may be able to tell you about ways to prevent or reduce some of these side effects. Check with your health care professional if any of the following side effects continue or are bothersome or if you have any questions about them:

More common

Nausea and vomiting (severe)

Less common

Loss of appetite

After you stop receiving cisplatin, it may still produce some side effects that need attention. During this period of time check with your doctor if you notice any of the following side effects:

Black, tarry stools; blood in urine or stools; convulsions (seizures); cough or hoarseness; decrease in urination; fever or chills; loss of balance; loss of reflexes; loss of taste; lower back or side pain; numbness or tingling in fingers or toes; painful or difficult urination; pinpoint red spots on skin; ringing in ears; swelling of feet or lower legs; trouble in hearing; trouble in walking; unusual bleeding or bruising

Other side effects not listed above may also occur in some patients. If you notice any other effects, check with your doctor.

Additional Information

Once a medicine has been approved for marketing for a certain use, experience may show that it is also useful for other medical problems. Although these uses are not included in product labeling, cisplatin is used in certain patients with the following medical conditions:

- Cancer of the outside layer of the adrenal gland
- Cancer of the breast
- Cancer of the cervix
- Cancer of the endometrium
- Cancer of the esophagus
- Cancer of the stomach
- Cancer of the lung
- Neuroblastoma (a certain type of cancer in nerve tissues that occurs in children)
- Cancer of the prostate
- Cancers of the head and neck
- Cancer of the liver
- Cancer of the thyroid
- Cancer of the anus
- Cancer of the vulva
- Cancer of the bile duct
- Cancer of the skin, including types that spread to other parts of the body
- Cancer of unknown primary site
- Cancer of the lymph system
- Hepatoblastoma (a certain type of liver cancer that occurs in children)
- Thymoma (a cancer of the thymus, which is a small organ that lies under the breastbone)
- Tumors in the ovaries
- Gestational trophoblastic tumors (tumors in the uterus or womb)
- Wilms' tumor (a cancer of the kidneys occurring mainly in children)
- Retinoblastoma (a cancer of the eye occurring mainly in children)
- Cancer of the bones (in children)
- Cancer of the muscles, connective tissues (tendons), vessels that carry blood or lymph, joints, and fat.
- Autoimmune deficiency syndrome (AIDS)–associated Kaposi's sarcoma (a type of cancer of the skin and mucous membranes that is more common in patients with AIDS)

Other than the above information, there is no additional information relating to proper use, precautions, or side effects for these uses.

Revised: 04/13/2001

CITALOPRAM   Systemic

Commonly used brand name(s):

In the U.S.—
Celexa

In Canada—
Celexa

Description

Citalopram (si-TAL-oh-pram) is used to treat mental depression.

Citalopram belongs to a group of medicines known as selective serotonin reuptake inhibitors (SSRIs). These medicines are thought to work by increasing the activity of the chemical serotonin in the brain.

This medicine is available only with your doctor's prescription, in the following dosage form:

Oral
- Tablets (U.S. and Canada)

Before Using This Medicine

In deciding to use a medicine, the risks of taking the medicine must be weighed against the good it will do. This is a decision you and your doctor will make. For citalopram, the following should be considered:

Allergies—Tell your doctor if you have ever had any unusual or allergic reaction to citalopram. Also tell your health care professional if you are allergic to any other substances, such as foods, preservatives, or dyes.

Pregnancy—Studies have not been done in pregnant women. However, studies in animals have shown that citalopram may cause decreased survival rates and slowed growth in offspring when given to the mother in doses many times higher than the usual human dose. Before taking this medicine, make sure your doctor knows if you are pregnant or if you may become pregnant.

Breast-feeding—Citalopram passes into breast milk and may cause unwanted effects, such as drowsiness, decreased feeding, and weight loss in the breast-fed baby. It may be necessary for you to take another medicine or to stop breast-feeding during treatment. Be sure you have discussed the risks and benefits of the medicine with your doctor.

Children—Studies on this medicine have been done only in adult patients, and there is no specific information comparing use of citalopram in children with use in other age groups.

Older adults—This medicine has been tested and has not been shown to cause different side effects or problems in older people than it does in younger adults. However, citalopram is removed from the body more slowly in older people and an older person may need a lower dose than a younger adult.

Other medicines—Although certain medicines should not be used together at all, in other cases two different medicines may be used together even if an interaction might occur. In these cases, your doctor may want to change the dose, or other precautions may be necessary. When you are taking citalopram, it is especially important that your health care professional know if you are taking any of the following:
- Bromocriptine (e.g., Parlodel) or
- Buspirone (e.g., BuSpar) or

- Certain tricyclic antidepressants (amitriptyline [e.g., Elavil], clomipramine [e.g., Anafranil], or imipramine [e.g., Tofranil]) or
- Dextromethorphan (cough medicine) or
- Levodopa (e.g., Sinemet) or
- Lithium (e.g., Eskalith) or
- Meperidine (e.g., Demerol) or
- Moclobemide (e.g., Manerix) or
- Nefazodone (e.g., Serzone) or
- Pentazocine (e.g., Talwin) or
- Selective serotonin reuptake inhibitors, other (fluoxetine [e.g., Prozac], fluvoxamine [e.g., Luvox], paroxetine [e.g., Paxil], sertraline [e.g., Zoloft]) or
- Street drugs (LSD, MDMA [e.g., ecstasy], marijuana) or
- Sumatriptan (e.g., Imitrex) or
- Tramadol (e.g., Ultram) or
- Trazodone (e.g., Desyrel) or
- Tryptophan or
- Venlafaxine (e.g., Effexor)—Using these medicines with citalopram may increase the chance of developing a rare, but very serious, unwanted effect known as the serotonin syndrome. This syndrome may cause confusion, diarrhea, fever, poor coordination, restlessness, shivering, sweating, talking or acting with excitement you cannot control, trembling or shaking, or twitching. If you develop these symptoms, contact your doctor as soon as possible

- Monoamine oxidase (MAO) inhibitors (furazolidone [e.g., Furoxone], isocarboxazid [e.g., Marplan], phenelzine [e.g., Nardil], procarbazine [e.g., Matulane], selegiline [e.g., Eldepryl], tranylcypromine [e.g., Parnate])—*Do not take citalopram while you are taking or within 2 weeks of taking an MAO inhibitor.* If you do, you may develop confusion, agitation, restlessness, stomach or intestinal symptoms, sudden high body temperature, extremely high blood pressure, severe convulsions, or the serotonin syndrome. At least 14 days should pass between stopping treatment with one medicine (citalopram or the MAO inhibitor) and starting treatment with the other

Other medical problems—The presence of other medical problems may affect the use of citalopram. Make sure you tell your doctor if you have any other medical problems, especially:
- Diabetes mellitus (sugar diabetes)—Hypoglycemia has occurred rarely in diabetic patients receiving citalopram
- Kidney disease, severe or
- Liver disease—Higher blood levels of citalopram may occur, increasing the chance of having unwanted effects. You may need to take a lower dose than a person without kidney or liver disease
- Mania (history of)—May be activated
- Seizure disorders (history of)—The risk of having seizures may be increased

Proper Use of This Medicine

Take this medicine only as directed by your doctor to benefit your condition as much as possible. Do not take more of it, do not take it more often, and do not take it for a longer time than your doctor ordered.

Citalopram may be taken with or without food on a full or empty stomach. If your doctor tells you to take it a certain way, follow your doctor's instructions.

You may have to take citalopram for 4 weeks before you begin to feel better. Your doctor should check your progress at regular visits during this time. Also, you may need to keep taking citalopram for 6 months or longer to help prevent the return of the depression.

Dosing—The dose of citalopram will be different for different patients. *Follow your doctor's orders or the directions on the label.* The following information includes only the average doses of citalopram. *If your dose is different, do not change it* unless your doctor tells you to do so.

The number of tablets that you take depends on the strength of the medicine.

- For *oral* dosage form (tablets):
  —For mental depression:
  - Adults—To start, usually 20 milligrams (mg) once a day, taken either in the morning or evening. Your doctor may increase your dose gradually if needed. However, the dose usually is not more than 60 mg a day.
  - Children—Use and dose must be determined by the doctor.
  - Older adults—Usually 20 milligrams (mg) once a day, taken either in the morning or evening. Your doctor may increase your dose gradually if needed. However, the dose usually is not more than 40 mg a day.

Missed dose—Because citalopram may be taken by different patients at different times of the day, you and your doctor should discuss what to do if you miss any doses.

Storage—To store this medicine:
- Keep out of the reach of children.
- Store away from heat and direct light.
- Do not store in the bathroom, near the kitchen sink, or in other damp places. Heat or moisture may cause the medicine to break down.
- Do not keep outdated medicine or medicine no longer needed. Be sure that any discarded medicine is out of the reach of children.

Precautions While Using This Medicine

It is important that your doctor check your progress at regular visits, to allow for changes in your dose and to help reduce any side effects.

Do not take citalopram with or within 14 days of taking an MAO inhibitor (furazolidone, isocarboxazid, phenelzine, procarbazine, selegiline, tranylcypromine). Do not take an MAO inhibitor within 14 days of taking citalopram. If you do, you may develop extremely high blood pressure or convulsions (seizures).

Avoid drinking alcoholic beverages while you are taking citalopram.

This medicine may cause some people to become drowsy, to have trouble thinking, or to have problems with movement. Make sure you know how you react to citalopram before you drive, use machines, or do anything else that could be dangerous if you are not alert or well-coordinated.

Side Effects of This Medicine

Along with its needed effects, a medicine may cause some unwanted effects. Although not all of these side effects may occur, if they do occur they may need medical attention. One rare, but very serious, effect that may occur is the serotonin

syndrome. This syndrome (group of symptoms) is more likely to occur shortly after an increase in citalopram dose.

Check with your doctor as soon as possible if any of the following side effects occur:

More common
Decrease in sexual desire or ability

Less common
Agitation; blurred vision; confusion; fever; increase in frequency of urination or amount of urine produced; lack of emotion; loss of memory; menstrual changes; skin rash or itching; trouble in breathing

Rare
Anxiety; behavior change similar to drunkenness; bleeding gums; breast tenderness or enlargement or unusual secretion of milk (in females); difficulty in concentrating; dizziness or fainting; increased hunger; irregular heartbeat; low blood sodium (confusion, convulsions [seizures], drowsiness, dryness of mouth, increased thirst, lack of energy); mood or mental changes; nervousness; nose bleed; painful urination; purple or red spots on skin; sore throat, fever, and chills; red or irritated eyes; redness, tenderness, itching, burning, or peeling of skin; serotonin syndrome (agitation, confusion, diarrhea, fever, overactive reflexes, poor coordination, restlessness, shivering, sweating, talking or acting with excitement you cannot control, trembling or shaking, twitching); shakiness; slow or irregular heartbeat (less than 50 beats per minute); trouble in holding or releasing urine; unusual or sudden body or facial movements or postures

Symptoms of overdose—more common
Dizziness; drowsiness; fast heartbeat; nausea; sweating; trembling or shaking; vomiting

Symptoms of overdose—rare
Bluish colored skin or lips; confusion; convulsions (seizures); coma; deep or fast breathing with dizziness; fainting; general feeling of discomfort or illness; loss of memory; muscle pain; slow or irregular heartbeat; weakness

Other side effects may occur that usually do not need medical attention. These side effects may go away during treatment as your body adjusts to the medicine. However, check with your doctor if any of the following side effects continue or are bothersome:

More common
Drowsiness; dryness of mouth; nausea; trouble in sleeping

Less common
Abdominal pain; anxiety; change in sense of taste; diarrhea; gas; headache (severe and throbbing); heartburn; increased sweating; increased yawning; loss of appetite; pain in muscles or joints; stuffy or runny nose; tingling, burning, or prickly feelings on skin; tooth grinding; trembling or shaking; unusual increase or decrease in weight; unusual tiredness or weakness; vomiting; watering of mouth

After you stop using this medicine, your body may need time to adjust. The length of time this takes depends on the amount of medicine you were using and how long you used it. During this period of time check with your doctor if you notice any of the following side effects:
Anxiety; dizziness; nervousness; trembling or shaking

Other side effects not listed above may also occur in some patients. If you notice any other effects, check with your doctor.

Developed: 09/02/1998
Revised: 06/02/2000

CITRATES Systemic

Commonly used brand name(s):

In the U.S.—

Bicitra[4]
Citrolith[3]
Oracit[4]
Polycitra-K[2]

Polycitra-K Crystals[2]
Polycitra-LC[5]
Polycitra Syrup[5]
Urocit-K[1]

In Canada—

Oracit[4]

Other commonly used names for sodium citrate and citric acid are Albright's solution and modified Shohl's solution.

Note: For quick reference, the following citrates are numbered to match the corresponding brand names.

This information applies to the following medicines:
1. Potassium Citrate (poe-TASS-ee-um SIH-trayt)
2. Potassium Citrate and Citric Acid (poe-TASS-ee-um SIH-trayt and SIH-trik A-sid)
3. Potassium Citrate and Sodium Citrate (poe-TASS-ee-um SIH-trayt and SOE-dee-um SIH-trayt)
4. Sodium Citrate and Citric Acid (SOE-dee-um SIH-trayt and SIH-trik A-sid)
5. Tricitrates (Try-SIH-trayts)

Description

Citrates (SIH-trayts) are used to make the urine more alkaline (less acid). This helps prevent certain kinds of kidney stones. Citrates are sometimes used with other medicines to help treat kidney stones that may occur with gout. They are also used to make the blood more alkaline in certain conditions.

Citrates are available only with your doctor's prescription, in the following dosage forms:

Oral
Potassium Citrate
- Tablets (U.S.)
Potassium Citrate and Citric Acid
- Oral solution (U.S.)
- Crystals for oral solution (U.S.)
Potassium Citrate and Sodium Citrate
- Tablets (U.S.)
Sodium Citrate and Citric Acid
- Oral solution (U.S. and Canada)
Tricitrates
- Oral solution (U.S.)

Before Using This Medicine

In deciding to use a medicine, the risks of taking the medicine must be weighed against the good it will do. This is a decision you and your doctor will make. For citrates, the following should be considered:

Allergies—Tell your doctor if you have ever had any unusual or allergic reaction to potassium citrate or potassium. Also tell your health care professional if you are allergic to any other substances, such as foods, preservatives, or dyes.

Pregnancy—Studies on effects in pregnancy have not been done in either humans or animals.

Breast-feeding—Although it is not known whether citrates pass into the breast milk, this medicine has not been reported to cause problems in nursing babies.

Children—Although there is no specific information comparing use of citrates in children with use in other age groups, these medicines are not expected to cause different side effects or problems in children than they do in adults.

Older adults—Many medicines have not been studied specifically in older people. Therefore, it may not be known whether they work exactly the same way they do in younger adults or if they cause different side effects or problems in older people. There is no specific information comparing use of citrates in the elderly with use in other age groups.

Other medicines—Although certain medicines should not be used together at all, in other cases two different medicines may be used together even if an interaction might occur. In these cases, your doctor may want to change the dose, or other precautions may be necessary. When you are taking citrates, it is especially important that your health care professional know if you are taking any of the following:

- Amiloride (e.g., Midamor) or
- Benazepril (e.g., Lotensin) or
- Captopril (e.g., Capoten) or
- Digitalis glycosides (heart medicine) or
- Enalapril (e.g., Vasotec) or
- Fosinopril (e.g., Monotril) or
- Heparin (e.g., Panheprin) or
- Lisinopril (e.g., Prinivil; Zestril) or
- Medicines for inflammation or pain (except narcotics) or
- Potassium-containing medicines (other) or
- Quinapril (e.g., Accupron) or
- Ramipril (e.g., Altase) or
- Salt substitutes, low-salt foods or milk or
- Spironolactone (e.g., Aldactone) or
- Triamterene (e.g., Dyrenium)—Use with potassium-containing citrates may further increase potassium blood levels, possibly leading to serious side effects

- Antacids, especially those containing aluminum or sodium bicarbonate—Use with citrates may increase the risk of kidney stones; also, citrates may increase the amount of aluminum in the blood and cause serious side effects, especially in patients with kidney problems

- Methenamine (e.g., Mandelamine)—Use with citrates may make the methenamine less effective

- Quinidine (e.g., Quinidex)—Use with citrates may cause quinidine to build up in the bloodstream, possibly leading to serious side effects

Other medical problems—The presence of other medical problems may affect the use of citrates. Make sure you tell your doctor if you have any other medical problems, especially:

- Addison's disease (underactive adrenal glands) or
- Diabetes mellitus (sugar diabetes) or
- Kidney disease—The potassium in potassium-containing citrates may worsen or cause heart problems in patients with these conditions

- Diarrhea (chronic)—Treatment with citrates may not be effective; a change in dose of citrate may be needed

- Edema (swelling of the feet or lower legs) or
- High blood pressure or

- Toxemia of pregnancy—The sodium in sodium-containing citrates may cause the body to retain (keep) water

- Heart disease—The sodium in sodium-containing citrates may cause the body to retain (keep) water; the potassium in potassium-containing citrates may make heart disease worse

- Intestinal or esophageal blockage—Potassium citrate tablets may cause irritation of the stomach or intestines

- Stomach ulcer or other stomach problems—Potassium citrate-containing products may make these conditions worse

- Urinary tract infection—Citrates may make conditions worse

Proper Use of This Medicine

For patients taking the *tablet form of this medicine:*
- Swallow the tablets whole. Do not crush, chew, or suck the tablet.
- Take with a full glass (8 ounces) of water.
- *If you have trouble swallowing the tablets or they seem to stick in your throat, check with your doctor at once.* If this medicine is not completely swallowed and not properly dissolved, it can cause severe irritation.

For patients taking the *liquid form of this medicine:*
- Dilute with a full glass (6 ounces) of water or juice and drink; follow with additional water, if desired.
- Chill, but do *not* freeze, this medicine before taking it, for a better taste.

For patients taking the *crystals form of this medicine:*
- Add the contents of one packet to at least 6 ounces of cool water or juice.
- Stir well to make sure the crystals are completely dissolved.
- Drink all the mixture to be sure you are taking the correct dose. Follow with additional water or juice, if desired.

Take each dose immediately after a meal or within 30 minutes after a meal or bedtime snack. This helps prevent the medicine from causing stomach pain or a laxative effect.

Drink at least a full glass (8 ounces) of water or other liquid (except milk) every hour during the day (about 3 quarts a day), unless otherwise directed by your doctor. This will increase the flow of urine and help prevent kidney stones.

Take this medicine only as directed by your doctor. Do not take more of it, do not take it more often, and do not take it for a longer time than your doctor ordered. *This is especially important if you are also taking a diuretic (water pill) or digitalis medicine for your heart.*

Dosing—The dose of these single or combination medicines will be different for different patients. *Follow your doctor's orders or the directions on the label.* The following information includes only the average doses of these medicines. *If your dose is different, do not change it* unless your doctor tells you to do so.

The number of tablets that you take or of teaspoonfuls or ounces of solution that you drink depends on the strength of the single or combination medicine. *Also, the number of doses you take each day, the time allowed between doses, and the length of time you take the medicine depend on* the medical problem for which you are taking this single or combination medicine.

For potassium citrate
- For *oral* dosage form (tablets):
  —To make the urine more alkaline (less acidic) and to prevent kidney stones:
  - Adults—At first, 1.08 to 2.16 grams three times a day with meals. Some people may take 1.62 grams four times a day with meals or within thirty minutes after a meal or bedtime snack. Your doctor may change your dose if needed. However, most people usually will not take more than 10.8 grams a day.
  - Children—Dose must be determined by your doctor.

For potassium citrate and citric acid
- For *oral* dosage form (solution):
  —To make the urine or blood more alkaline (less acidic) and to prevent kidney stones:
  - Adults—At first, 2 to 3 teaspoonfuls of solution, mixed with water or juice, four times a day, after meals and at bedtime. Your doctor may change the dose if needed.
  —To make the urine more alkaline (less acidic):
  - Children—At first, 1 to 3 teaspoonfuls of solution, mixed with water or juice, four times a day after meals and at bedtime. Your doctor may change the dose if needed.
- For *oral* dosage form (crystals for solution):
  —To make the urine or blood more alkaline (less acidic) and to prevent kidney stones:
  - Adults—At first, 3.3 grams of potassium citrate, mixed with water or juice, four times a day, after meals and at bedtime. Your doctor may change the dose if needed.
  - Children—Use is not recommended.

For potassium citrate and sodium citrate
- For *oral* dosage form (tablets):
  —To make the urine more alkaline (less acidic) and to prevent kidney stones:
  - Adults—At first, 1 to 4 tablets after meals and at bedtime.
  - Children—Dose must be determined by your doctor.

For sodium citrate and citric acid
- For *oral* dosage form (solution):
  —To make the urine and blood more alkaline (less acidic) and to prevent kidney stones:
  - Adults—At first, 2 to 6 teaspoonfuls of solution four times a day, after meals and at bedtime. The solution should be mixed in one to three ounces of water. Your doctor may change the dose if needed. However, most people will usually not take more than five ounces a day.
  —To make the contents of the stomach less acidic before surgery:
  - Adults—1 to 2 tablespoonfuls as a single dose. You may mix it in one to two tablespoonfuls of water.
  —To make the blood more alkaline (less acidic):
  - Children—At first, 1 to 3 teaspoonfuls of solution four times a day, after meals and at bedtime. The solution should be mixed in one to three ounces of water. Your doctor may change the dose if needed.

For tricitrates
- For *oral* dosage form (solution):
  —To make the urine and blood more alkaline (less acidic) and to prevent kidney stones:
  - Adults—At first, 1 to 2 tablespoonfuls of solution four times a day, after meals and at bedtime. Your doctor may change the dose if needed.
  —To make the contents of the stomach less acidic before surgery:
  - Adults—1 tablespoonful as a single dose. You should mix the solution in one tablespoonful of water.
  —To make the urine or blood more alkaline (less acidic):
  - Children—At first, 5 to 10 mL four times a day after meals and at bedtime. Your doctor may change the dose if needed.

Missed dose—If you miss a dose of this medicine, take it as soon as possible if remembered within 2 hours. However, if it is almost time for your next dose, skip the missed dose and go back to your regular dosing schedule. Do not double doses.

Storage—To store this medicine:
- Keep out of the reach of children.
- Store away from heat and direct light.
- Do not store in the bathroom, near the kitchen sink, or in other damp places. Heat or moisture may cause the medicine to break down.
- Keep the liquid form of this medicine from freezing.
- Do not keep outdated medicine or medicine no longer needed. Be sure that any discarded medicine is out of the reach of children.

Precautions While Using This Medicine

It is important that your doctor check your progress at regular visits. This is to make sure the medicine is working properly and to check for unwanted effects.

Do not eat salty foods or use extra table salt on your food while you are taking citrates. This will help prevent kidney stones and unwanted effects.

Check with your doctor before starting any strenuous physical exercise, especially if you are out of condition and are taking any other medication. Exercise and certain medications may increase the amount of potassium in the blood.

For patients taking *potassium citrate-containing medicines:*
- Do not use salt substitutes and low-salt milk unless told to do so by your doctor. They may contain potassium.
- *Check with your doctor at once if you are taking the tablet form and notice black, tarry stools or other signs of stomach or intestinal bleeding.*
- Do not be alarmed if you notice what appears to be a whole tablet in the stool after taking potassium citrate tablets. Your body has received the proper amount of medicine from the tablet and has expelled the tablet shell. However, it is a good idea to check with your doctor also.
- If you are on a potassium-rich or potassium-restricted diet, check with your health care professional. Potassium citrate-containing medicines contain a large amount of potassium.

For patients taking *sodium citrate-containing medicines:*
- If you are on a sodium-restricted diet, check with your health care professional. Sodium citrate–containing medicines contain a large amount of sodium.

Side Effects of This Medicine

Along with its needed effects, a medicine may cause some unwanted effects. Although not all of these side effects may occur, if they do occur they may need medical attention.

Stop taking this medicine and check with your doctor immediately if any of the following side effects occur:
  Rare
    Abdominal or stomach pain or cramping (severe); black, tarry stools; vomiting (severe), sometimes with blood

Also, check with your doctor as soon as possible if any of the following side effects occur:
  Confusion; convulsions (seizures); dizziness; high blood pressure; irregular or fast heartbeat; irritability; mood or mental changes; muscle pain or twitching; nervousness or restlessness; numbness or tingling in hands, feet, or lips; shortness of breath, difficult breathing, or slow breathing; swelling of feet or lower legs; unexplained anxiety; unpleasant taste; unusual tiredness or weakness; weakness or heaviness of legs

Other side effects may occur that usually do not need medical attention. These side effects may go away during treatment as your body adjusts to the medicine. However, check with your doctor if any of the following side effects continue or are bothersome:
  Less common
    Abdominal or stomach soreness or pain (mild); diarrhea or loose bowel movements; nausea or vomiting

Other side effects not listed above may also occur in some patients. If you notice any other effects, check with your doctor.

Revised: 01/18/93
Interim revision: 08/29/94

CLADRIBINE   Systemic

Commonly used brand name(s):

In the U.S.—
  Leustatin

In Canada—
  Leustatin

Other commonly used names are 2-chlorodeoxyadenosine and 2-CdA.

Description

Cladribine (KLAD-ri-been) belongs to the group of medicines called antimetabolites. It is used to treat hairy cell leukemia, a cancer of the blood and bone marrow. It is also sometimes used to treat other kinds of cancer, as determined by your doctor.

Cladribine interferes with the growth of cancer cells, which are eventually destroyed. Since the growth of normal body cells may also be affected by cladribine, other effects will also occur. Some of these may be serious and must be reported to your doctor. Other effects may not be serious but may cause concern. Some effects may not occur for months or years after the medicine is used.

Before you begin treatment with cladribine, you and your doctor should talk about the good this medicine will do as well as the risks of using it.

Cladribine is to be administered only by or under the immediate supervision of your doctor. It is available in the following dosage form:

Parenteral
- Injection (U.S. and Canada)

Before Using This Medicine

In deciding to use a medicine, the risks of taking the medicine must be weighed against the good it will do. This is a decision you and your doctor will make. For cladribine, the following should be considered:

Allergies—Tell your doctor if you have ever had any unusual or allergic reaction to cladribine.

Pregnancy—There is a chance that this medicine may cause birth defects if either the male or female is taking it at the time of conception or if it is taken during pregnancy. Cladribine has been shown to cause birth defects in mice and rabbits. In addition, many cancer medicines may cause sterility which could be permanent. Although sterility has not been reported with this medicine, fertility problems do occur in male monkeys and the possibility should be kept in mind.

Be sure that you have discussed this with your doctor before receiving this medicine. It is best to use some kind of birth control while you are receiving cladribine. Tell your doctor right away if you think you have become pregnant while receiving cladribine.

Breast-feeding—It is not known whether cladribine passes into breast milk. However, because this medicine may cause serious side effects, breast-feeding is generally not recommended while you are receiving it.

Children—There is no specific information comparing use of cladribine in children with use in other age groups. However, cladribine has been reported to be tested in children with certain types of cancers of the blood.

Older adults—Many medicines have not been studied specifically in older people. Therefore, it may not be known whether they work exactly the same way they do in younger adults. Although there is no specific information comparing use of cladribine in the elderly with use in other age groups, it is not expected to cause different side effects or problems in older people than it does in younger adults.

Other medicines—Although certain medicines should not be used together at all, in other cases two different medicines may be used together even if an interaction might occur. In these cases, your doctor may want to change the dose, or other precautions may be necessary. When you are receiving cladribine it is especially important that your health care professional know if you are taking any of the following:
- Amphotericin B by injection (e.g., Fungizone) or
- Antithyroid agents (medicine for overactive thyroid) or
- Azathioprine (e.g., Imuran) or
- Chloramphenicol (e.g., Chloromycetin) or
- Colchicine or
- Flucytosine (e.g., Ancobon) or
- Ganciclovir (e.g., Cytovene) or
- Interferon (e.g., Intron A, Roferon-A) or
- Plicamycin (e.g., Mithracin) or

- Zidovudine (e.g., AZT, Retrovir) or
- If you have ever been treated with radiation or cancer medicines—Cladribine may increase the effects of these medicines or radiation therapy on the blood

- Probenecid (e.g., Benemid) or
- Sulfinpyrazone (e.g., Anturane)—Cladribine may raise the amount of uric acid in the blood. Since these medicines are used to lower uric acid levels, they may not be as effective in patients receiving cladribine

Other medical problems—The presence of other medical problems may affect the use of cladribine. Make sure you tell your doctor if you have any other medical problems, especially:
- Chickenpox (including recent exposure) or
- Herpes zoster (shingles)—Risk of severe disease affecting other parts of the body

- Gout (history of) or
- Kidney stones (history of)—Cladribine may increase levels of uric acid in the body, which can cause gout or kidney stones

- Infection—Cladribine may decrease your body's ability to fight infection

Proper Use of This Medicine

This medicine may cause mild nausea and may also cause vomiting. However, it is very important that you continue to receive the medicine even if you begin to feel ill. Ask your health care professional for ways to lessen these effects.

Dosing—The dose of cladribine will be different for different patients. The dose that is used may depend on a number of things, including what the medicine is being used for, the patient's weight, and whether or not other medicines are also being taken. *If you are receiving cladribine at home, follow your doctor's orders or the directions on the label.* If you have any questions about the proper dose of cladribine, ask your doctor.

Precautions While Using This Medicine

It is very important that your doctor check your progress at regular visits to make sure that this medicine is working properly and to check for unwanted effects.

While you are being treated with cladribine, and after you stop treatment with it, *do not have any immunizations (vaccinations) without your doctor's approval.* Cladribine may lower your body's resistance and there is a chance you might get the infection the immunization is meant to prevent. In addition, other persons living in your household should not take oral polio vaccine since there is a chance they could pass the polio virus on to you. Also, avoid persons who have taken oral polio vaccine within the last several months. Do not get close to them and do not stay in the same room with them for very long. If you cannot take these precautions, you should consider wearing a protective face mask that covers the nose and mouth.

Cladribine can temporarily lower the number of white blood cells in your blood, increasing the chance of getting an infection. It can also lower the number of platelets, which are necessary for proper blood clotting. If this occurs, there are certain precautions you can take, especially when your blood count is low, to reduce the risk of infection or bleeding:
- If you can, avoid people with infections, colds, or flu. *Check with your doctor immediately* if you think you are getting an infection or if you get a fever or chills,

cough or hoarseness, lower back or side pain, or painful or difficult urination.

- *Check with your doctor immediately* if you notice any unusual bleeding or bruising; black, tarry stools; blood in urine or stools; or pinpoint red spots on your skin.
- Be careful when using a regular toothbrush, dental floss, or toothpick. Your medical doctor, dentist, or nurse may recommend other ways to clean your teeth and gums. Check with your medical doctor before having any dental work done.
- Do not touch your eyes or the inside of your nose unless you have just washed your hands and have not touched anything else in the meantime.
- Be careful not to cut yourself when you are using sharp objects such as a safety razor or fingernail or toenail cutters.
- Avoid contact sports or other situations where bruising or injury could occur.

Side Effects of This Medicine

Along with its needed effects, a medicine may cause some unwanted effects. Some side effects will have signs or symptoms that you can see or feel. Your doctor may watch for others by doing certain tests.

Also, because of the way cancer medicines act on the body, there is a chance that they might cause other unwanted effects that may not occur until months or years after the medicine is used. These delayed effects may include certain types of cancer. Discuss these possible effects with your doctor.

Check with your doctor or nurse immediately if any of the following side effects occur:

More common
> Black, tarry stools; blood in urine; cough or hoarseness, accompanied by fever or chills; fever; lower back or side pain, accompanied by fever or chills; painful or difficult urination, accompanied by fever or chills; pinpoint red spots on skin; unusual bleeding or bruising

Check with your health care professional as soon as possible if any of the following side effects occur:

More common
> Skin rash

Less common
> Pain or redness at place of injection; shortness of breath; stomach pain; swelling of feet or lower legs; unusually fast heartbeat

This medicine may also cause the following side effects that your doctor will watch out for:

More common
> Anemia; low white cell counts in blood

Other side effects may occur that usually do not need medical attention. These side effects may go away during treatment as your body adjusts to the medicine. Also, your health care professional may be able to tell you about ways to prevent or reduce some of these side effects. Check with your health care professional if any of the following side effects continue or are bothersome or if you have any questions about them:

More common
> Headache; loss of appetite; nausea; unusual tiredness; vomiting

Less common
> Constipation; diarrhea; dizziness; general feeling of discomfort or illness; itching; muscle or joint pain; sweating; trouble in sleeping; weakness

Other side effects not listed above may also occur in some patients. If you notice any other effects, check with your doctor.

Additional Information

Once a medicine has been approved for marketing for a certain use, experience may show that it is also useful for other medical problems. Although these uses are not included in product labeling, cladribine is used in certain patients with the following conditions:

- Cancer of the blood and lymph system
- Waldenström's macroglobulinemia (a certain type of cancer of the blood)

Other than the above information, there is no additional information relating to proper use, precautions, or side effects for these uses.

Developed: 07/26/94
Interim revision: 08/15/94; 08/14/98

CLARITHROMYCIN   Systemic

Commonly used brand name(s):

In the U.S.—
> Biaxin

In Canada—
> Biaxin

Description

Clarithromycin (kla-RITH-roe-mye-sin) is used to treat bacterial infections in many different parts of the body. It works by killing bacteria or preventing their growth. It is also used to treat and prevent *Mycobacterium avium* complex (MAC) infection, and to treat duodenal ulcers caused by *Helicobacter pylori*. However, this medicine will not work for colds, flu, or other virus infections. Clarithromycin also may be used for other problems as determined by your doctor.

Clarithromycin is available only with your doctor's prescription, in the following dosage forms:

Oral
- Oral suspension (U.S. and Canada)
- Tablets (U.S. and Canada)

Before Using This Medicine

In deciding to use a medicine, the risks of taking the medicine must be weighed against the good it will do. This is a decision you and your doctor will make. For clarithromycin, the following should be considered:

Allergies—Tell your doctor if you have ever had any unusual or allergic reaction to clarithromycin or to any related medicines, such as erythromycin. Also tell your health care professional if you are allergic to any other substances, such as foods, preservatives, or dyes.

Pregnancy—Clarithromycin has not been studied in pregnant women. However, studies in animals have shown that clarithromycin causes birth defects and other problems. Before taking this medicine, make sure your doctor knows if you are pregnant or if you may become pregnant.

Breast-feeding—Clarithromycin passes into breast milk.

Children—Studies on this medicine have not been done in children up to 6 months of age. In effective doses, the medicine has not been shown to cause different side effects or problems in children over the age of 6 months than it does in adults.

Older adults—This medicine has been tested in a limited number of elderly patients and has not been shown to cause different side effects or problems in older people than it does in younger adults.

Other medicines—Although certain medicines should not be used together at all, in other cases two different medicines may be used together even if an interaction might occur. In these cases, your doctor may want to change the dose, or other precautions may be necessary. When you are taking clarithromycin, it is especially important that your health care professional know if you are taking any of the following:

- Anticoagulants (blood thinners) or
- Astemizole (e.g., Hismanal) or
- Carbamazepine (e.g., Tegretol) or
- Cisapride (e.g., Propulsid) or
- Digoxin (e.g., Lanoxin) or
- Pimozide (e.g., Orap) or
- Terfenadine (e.g., Seldane) or
- Theophylline (e.g., Theodur, Slo-Bid)—Clarithromycin may increase the chance of side effects of these medicines; **astemizole, cisapride, pimozide, and terfenadine should not be taken with clarithromycin**
- Rifabutin (e.g., Mycobutin) or
- Rifampin (e.g., Rifadin)—Rifabutin or rifampin may decrease the amount of clarithromycin in the blood
- Zidovudine (e.g., Retrovir)—Clarithromycin may decrease the amount of zidovudine in the blood

Other medical problems—The presence of other medical problems may affect the use of clarithromycin. Make sure you tell your doctor if you have any other medical problems, especially:

- Kidney disease—Patients with severe kidney disease may have an increased chance of side effects

Proper Use of This Medicine

Clarithromycin may be taken with meals or milk or on an empty stomach.

If you are taking clarithromycin and zidovudine, these medicines should be taken at least 4 hours apart.

To help clear up your infection completely, *keep taking clarithromycin for the full time of treatment,* even if you begin to feel better after a few days. If you stop taking this medicine too soon, your symptoms may return.

If you are using *clarithromycin oral suspension,* use a specially marked measuring spoon or other device to measure each dose accurately. The average household teaspoon may not hold the right amount of liquid.

Dosing—The dose of clarithromycin will be different for different patients. *Follow your doctor's orders or the directions on the label.* The following information includes only the average doses of clarithromycin. Your dose may be different if you have kidney disease. *If your dose is different, do not change it* unless your doctor tells you to do so.

The number of tablets or teaspoonfuls of suspension that you take depends on the strength of the medicine.

- For *oral* dosage forms (suspension and tablets):
  —For bacterial infections:
    - Adults and teenagers—250 to 500 milligrams (mg) every twelve hours for seven to fourteen days.
    - Children 6 months of age and older—7.5 mg per kilogram (kg) (3.4 mg per pound) of body weight every twelve hours for ten days.
    - Infants up to 6 months of age—Use and dose must be determined by your doctor.
  —For prevention or treatment of *Mycobacterium avium* complex (MAC) infection:
    - Adults and teenagers—500 mg two times a day.
    - Children 6 months of age and older—7.5 mg per kg (3.4 mg per pound) of body weight, up to 500 mg, two times a day.
    - Infants up to 6 months of age—Use and dose must be determined by your doctor.
  —For treatment of ulcers associated with *Helicobacter pylori*:
    - Adults and teenagers—500 mg three times a day for fourteen days, in combination with omeprazole or ranitidine bismuth sulfate; or 500 mg every twelve hours in combination with amoxicillin and lansoprazole for fourteen days.
    - Infants and children—Use and dose must be determined by your doctor.

Missed dose—If you miss a dose of this medicine, take it as soon as possible. However, if it is almost time for your next dose, skip the missed dose and go back to your regular dosing schedule. Do not double doses.

Storage—To store this medicine:

- Keep out of the reach of children.
- Store away from heat and direct light.
- Do not store in the bathroom, near the kitchen sink, or in other damp places. Heat or moisture may cause the medicine to break down.
- Do not keep outdated medicine or medicine no longer needed. Be sure that any discarded medicine is out of the reach of children.
- Do not store suspension in the refrigerator.

Precautions While Using This Medicine

Clarithromycin should not be taken with astemizole, cisapride, pimozide, or terfenadine. Doing so may increase the risk of serious side effects affecting the heart.

If your symptoms do not improve within a few days, or if they become worse, check with your doctor.

Side Effects of This Medicine

Along with its needed effects, a medicine may cause some unwanted effects. Although not all of these side effects may occur, if they do occur they may need medical attention. Check with your doctor as soon as possible if any of the following side effects occur:

Rare

Abdominal tenderness; fever; nausea and vomiting; severe abdominal or stomach cramps and pain; shortness of breath; skin rash and itching; unusual bleeding or bruising; watery and severe diarrhea, which may also be bloody; yellow eyes or skin

Other side effects may occur that usually do not need medical attention. These side effects may go away during treatment

as your body adjusts to the medicine. However, check with your doctor if any of the following side effects continue or are bothersome:

Less common
>   Change in sensation of taste; diarrhea (mild); headache

Other side effects not listed above may also occur in some patients. If you notice any other effects, check with your doctor.

Additional Information

Once a medicine has been approved for marketing for a certain use, experience may show that it is also useful for other medical problems. Although this use is not included in product labeling, clarithromycin is used in certain patients with the following medical condition:

- Legionnaires' disease

Other than the above information, there is no additional information relating to proper use, precautions, or side effects for this use.

Revised: 07/24/95
Interim revision: 03/26/98

CLINDAMYCIN   Systemic

Commonly used brand name(s):

In the U.S.—
Cleocin
Cleocin Pediatric
Generic name product may be available.

In Canada—
Dalacin C
Dalacin C Flavored Granules
Dalacin C Phosphate

Description

Clindamycin (klin-da-MYE-sin) is used to treat bacterial infections. It will not work for colds, flu, or other virus infections.

Clindamycin is available only with your doctor's prescription, in the following dosage forms:

Oral
- Capsules (U.S. and Canada)
- Oral solution (U.S. and Canada)

Parenteral
- Injection (U.S. and Canada)

Before Using This Medicine

In deciding to use a medicine, the risks of taking the medicine must be weighed against the good it will do. This is a decision you and your doctor will make. For clindamycin, the following should be considered:

Allergies—Tell your doctor if you have ever had any unusual or allergic reaction to clindamycin, lincomycin, or doxorubicin. Also tell your health care professional if you are allergic to any other substances, such as foods, preservatives, or dyes.

Pregnancy—Clindamycin has not been reported to cause birth defects or other problems in humans.

Breast-feeding—Clindamycin passes into the breast milk. However, clindamycin has not been reported to cause problems in nursing babies.

Children—This medicine has been tested in children and, in effective doses, has not been reported to cause different side effects or problems than it does in adults.

Older adults—Many medicines have not been studied specifically in older people. Therefore, it may not be known whether they work exactly the same way they do in younger adults or if they cause different side effects or problems in older people. There is no specific information comparing use of clindamycin in the elderly with use in other age groups.

Other medicines—Although certain medicines should not be used together at all, in other cases two different medicines may be used together even if an interaction might occur. In these cases, your doctor may want to change the dose, or other precautions may be necessary. When you are taking clindamycin, it is especially important that your health care professional know if you are taking any of the following:

- Chloramphenicol (e.g., Chloromycetin) or
- Diarrhea medicine containing kaolin or attapulgite or
- Erythromycins (medicine for infection)—Taking these medicines along with clindamycin may decrease the effects of clindamycin

Other medical problems—The presence of other medical problems may affect the use of clindamycin. Make sure you tell your doctor if you have any other medical problems, especially:

- Kidney disease (severe) or
- Liver disease (severe)—Severe kidney or liver disease may increase blood levels of this medicine, increasing the chance of side effects

- Stomach or intestinal disease, history of (especially colitis, including colitis caused by antibiotics, or enteritis)— Patients with a history of stomach or intestinal disease may have an increased chance of side effects

Proper Use of This Medicine

For patients taking the *capsule form* of clindamycin:

- *The capsule form of clindamycin should be taken with a full glass (8 ounces) of water or with meals* to prevent irritation of the esophagus (tube between the throat and stomach).

For patients taking the *oral liquid form* of clindamycin:

- Use a specially marked measuring spoon or other device to measure each dose accurately. The average household teaspoon may not hold the right amount of liquid.
- Do not use after the expiration date on the label. The medicine may not work properly after this date. Check with your pharmacist if you have any questions about this.

To help clear up your infection completely, *keep taking this medicine for the full time of treatment,* even if you begin to feel better after a few days. *If you have a "strep" infection, you should keep taking this medicine for at least 10 days. This is especially important in "strep" infections. Serious heart problems could develop later* if your infection is not cleared up completely. Also, if you stop taking this medicine too soon, your symptoms may return.

This medicine works best when there is a constant amount in the blood. *To help keep the amount constant, do not miss any doses. Also, it is best to take each dose at evenly spaced times day and night.* For example, if you are to take 4 doses a day, doses should be spaced about 6 hours apart. If this interferes with your sleep or other daily activities, or if you need help in planning the best times to take your medicine, check with your health care professional.

Dosing—The dose of clindamycin will be different for different patients. *Follow your doctor's orders or the directions on the label.* The following information includes only the average doses of clindamycin. *If your dose is different, do not change it* unless your doctor tells you to do so.

The number of capsules or teaspoonfuls of solution that you take depends on the strength of the medicine. Also, *the number of doses you take each day, the time allowed between doses, and the length of time you take the medicine depend on the medical problem for which you are taking clindamycin.*

- For bacterial infection:
  —For *oral* dosage forms (capsules and solution):
    - Adults and teenagers—150 to 300 milligrams (mg) every six hours.
    - Children—
      —Infants up to 1 month of age: Use and dose must be determined by your doctor.
      —Infants and children 1 month of age and older: Dose is based on body weight. The usual dose is 2 to 5 mg per kilogram (kg) (0.9 to 2.3 mg per pound) of body weight every six hours; or 2.7 to 6.7 mg per kg (1.2 to 3.0 mg per pound) of body weight every eight hours.
  —For *injection* dosage form:
    - Adults and teenagers—300 to 600 mg every six to eight hours injected into a muscle or vein; or 900 mg every eight hours injected into a muscle or vein.
    - Children—
      —Infants up to 1 month of age: Dose is based on body weight. The usual dose is 3.75 to 5 mg per kg (1.7 to 2.3 mg per pound) of body weight every six hours injected into a muscle or vein; or 5 to 6.7 mg per kg (2.3 to 3.0 mg per pound) of body weight every eight hours injected into a muscle or vein.
      —Infants and children 1 month of age and older: Dose is based on body weight. The usual dose is 3.75 to 10 mg per kg (1.7 to 4.5 mg per pound) of body weight every six hours injected into a muscle or vein; or 5 to 13.3 mg per kg (2.3 to 6.0 mg per pound) of body weight every eight hours injected into a muscle or vein.

Missed dose—If you miss a dose of this medicine, take it as soon as possible. This will help to keep a constant amount of medicine in the blood. However, if it is almost time for your next dose, skip the missed dose and go back to your regular dosing schedule. Do not double doses.

Storage—To store this medicine:
- Keep out of the reach of children.
- Store away from heat and direct light.
- Do not store the capsule form of this medicine in the bathroom, near the kitchen sink, or in other damp places. Heat or moisture may cause the medicine to break down.
- Do not refrigerate the oral liquid form of clindamycin. If chilled, the liquid may thicken and be difficult to pour. Follow the directions on the label.
- Do not keep outdated medicine or medicine no longer needed. Be sure that any discarded medicine is out of the reach of children.

Precautions While Using This Medicine

It is important that your doctor check your progress at regular visits.

If your symptoms do not improve within a few days, or if they become worse, check with your doctor.

In some patients, clindamycin may cause diarrhea.
- Severe diarrhea may be a sign of a serious side effect. *Do not take any diarrhea medicine without first checking with your doctor.* Diarrhea medicines, such as loperamide (Imodium A-D) or diphenoxylate and atropine (Lomotil), may make your diarrhea worse or make it last longer.
- For mild diarrhea, diarrhea medicine containing attapulgite (e.g., Kaopectate tablets, Diasorb) may be taken. However, attapulgite may keep clindamycin from being absorbed into the body. Therefore, these diarrhea medicines should be taken at least 2 hours before or 3 to 4 hours after you take clindamycin by mouth.
- If you have any questions about this or if mild diarrhea continues or gets worse, check with your health care professional.

Before having surgery (including dental surgery) with a general anesthetic, tell the medical doctor or dentist in charge that you are taking clindamycin.

Side Effects of This Medicine

Along with its needed effects, a medicine may cause some unwanted effects. Although not all of these side effects may occur, if they do occur they may need medical attention.

Check with your doctor immediately if any of the following side effects occur:
> *More common*
> Abdominal or stomach cramps and pain (severe); abdominal tenderness; diarrhea (watery and severe), which may also be bloody; fever
> (the above side effects may also occur up to several weeks after you stop taking this medicine)

> *Less common*
> Sore throat and fever; skin rash, redness, and itching; unusual bleeding or bruising

Other side effects may occur that usually do not need medical attention. These side effects may go away during treatment as your body adjusts to the medicine. However, check with your doctor if any of the following side effects continue or are bothersome:
> *More common*
> Diarrhea (mild); nausea and vomiting; stomach pain

> *Less common*
> Itching of rectal, or genital (sex organ) areas

Other side effects not listed above may also occur in some patients. If you notice any other effects, check with your doctor.

Revised: 08/12/92
Interim revision: 03/18/94; 04/19/95; 08/14/98

CLINDAMYCIN   Topical

Commonly used brand name(s):

In the U.S.—

Cleocin T Gel   Cleocin T Topical Solution
Cleocin T Lotion   Clinda-Derm

Generic name product may be available.

In Canada—

Dalacin T Topical Solution

Description

Clindamycin (klin-da-MYE-sin) belongs to the family of medicines called antibiotics. Topical clindamycin is used to help control acne. It may be used alone or with one or more other medicines that are used on the skin or taken by mouth for acne. Topical clindamycin may also be used for other problems as determined by your doctor.

Clindamycin is available only with your doctor's prescription, in the following dosage forms:

Topical
- Gel (U.S.)
- Solution (U.S. and Canada)
- Suspension (U.S.)

Before Using This Medicine

In deciding to use a medicine, the risks of using the medicine must be weighed against the good it will do. This is a decision you and your doctor will make. For topical clindamycin, the following should be considered:

Allergies—Tell your doctor if you have ever had any unusual or allergic reaction to this medicine or any of the other clindamycins (by mouth or by injection) or to lincomycin. Also tell your health care professional if you are allergic to any other substances, such as preservatives or dyes.

Pregnancy—Clindamycin has not been studied in pregnant women. However, this medicine has not been shown to cause birth defects or other problems in animal studies.

Breast-feeding—Small amounts of topical clindamycin are absorbed through the skin. It is possible that small amounts of the medicine may pass into the breast milk. However, this medicine has not been reported to cause problems in nursing babies.

Children—Studies on this medicine have been done only in adult patients, and there is no specific information comparing use of this medicine in children up to 12 years of age with use in other age groups.

Older adults—Many medicines have not been studied specifically in older people. Therefore, it may not be known whether they work exactly the same way they do in younger adults. Although there is no specific information comparing use of this medicine in the elderly with use in other age groups, this medicine is not expected to cause different side effects or problems in older people than it does in younger adults.

Other medicines—Although certain medicines should not be used together at all, in other cases two different medicines may be used together even if an interaction might occur. In these cases, your doctor may want to change the dose, or other precautions may be necessary. Tell your health care professional if you are using any other prescription or nonprescription (over-the-counter [OTC]) medicine.

Other medical problems—The presence of other medical problems may affect the use of topical clindamycin. Make sure you tell your doctor if you have any other medical problems, especially:

- History of stomach or intestinal disease (especially colitis, including colitis caused by antibiotics, or enteritis)— These conditions may increase the chance of side effects that affect the stomach and intestines

Proper Use of This Medicine

Before applying this medicine, thoroughly wash the affected areas with warm water and soap, rinse well, and pat dry.

When applying the medicine, use enough to cover the affected area lightly. *You should apply the medicine to the whole area usually affected by acne, not just to the pimples themselves.* This will help keep new pimples from breaking out.

You should avoid washing the acne-affected areas too often. This may dry your skin and make your acne worse. Washing with a mild, bland soap 2 or 3 times a day should be enough, unless you have oily skin. If you have any questions about this, check with your doctor.

Topical clindamycin will not cure your acne. However, to help keep your acne under control, *keep using this medicine for the full time of treatment,* even if your symptoms begin to clear up after a few days. You may have to continue using this medicine every day for months or even longer in some cases. If you stop using this medicine too soon, your symptoms may return. *It is important that you do not miss any doses.*

For patients using the *topical solution form* of clindamycin:

- After washing or shaving, it is best to wait 30 minutes before applying this medicine. The alcohol in it may irritate freshly washed or shaved skin.
- This medicine contains alcohol and is flammable. *Do not use near heat, near open flame, or while smoking.*
- To apply this medicine:
  —This medicine comes in a bottle with an applicator tip, which may be used to apply the medicine directly to the skin. Use the applicator with a dabbing motion instead of a rolling motion (not like a roll-on deodorant, for example). Tilt the bottle and press the tip firmly against your skin. If needed, you can make the medicine flow faster from the applicator tip by slightly increasing the pressure against the skin. If the medicine flows too fast, use less pressure. If the applicator tip becomes dry, turn the bottle upside down and press the tip several times to moisten it.
  —Since this medicine contains alcohol, it will sting or burn. In addition, it has an unpleasant taste if it gets on the mouth or lips. Therefore, *do not get this medicine in the eyes, nose, or mouth, or on other mucous membranes.* Spread the medicine away from these areas when applying. If this medicine does get in the eyes, wash them out immediately, but carefully, with large amounts of cool tap water. If your eyes still burn or are painful, check with your doctor.
- It is important that you do not use this medicine more often than your doctor ordered. It may cause your skin to become too dry or irritated.

For patients using the *topical suspension form* of clindamycin:

- *Shake well* before applying.

Dosing—The dose of topical clindamycin will be different for different patients. *Follow your doctor's orders or the directions on the label.* The following information includes only the average doses of topical clindamycin. *If your dose is different, do not change it* unless your doctor tells you to do so.

The number of doses you use each day, the time allowed between doses, and the length of time you use the medicine depend on the medical problem for which you are using clindamycin.

- For *topical* dosage forms (gel, solution, and suspension):
  —For acne:
    - Adults and children 12 years of age and over— Apply two times a day to areas affected by acne.
    - Infants and children up to 12 years of age—Use and dose must be determined by your doctor.

Missed dose—If you miss a dose of this medicine, apply it as soon as possible. However, if it is almost time for your next dose, skip the missed dose and go back to your regular dosing schedule.

Storage—To store this medicine:
- Keep out of the reach of children.
- Store away from heat and direct light.
- Keep the medicine from freezing.
- Do not keep outdated medicine or medicine no longer needed. Be sure that any discarded medicine is out of the reach of children.

Precautions While Using This Medicine

If your acne does not improve within about 6 weeks, or if it becomes worse, check with your health care professional. However, treatment of acne may take up to 8 to 12 weeks before full improvement is seen.

If your doctor has ordered another medicine to be applied to the skin along with this medicine, it is best to apply them at different times. This may help keep your skin from becoming too irritated. Also, if the medicines are used at or near the same time, they may not work properly.

For patients using the *topical solution form* of clindamycin:
- This medicine may cause the skin to become unusually dry, even with normal use. If this occurs, check with your doctor.

In some patients, clindamycin may cause diarrhea.
- Severe diarrhea may be a sign of a serious side effect. *Do not take any diarrhea medicine without first checking with your doctor.* Diarrhea medicines may make your diarrhea worse or make it last longer.
- For mild diarrhea, only diarrhea medicine containing attapulgite (e.g., Kaopectate, Diasorb) may be taken. Other kinds of diarrhea medicine (e.g., Imodium A.D. or Lomotil) should not be taken. They may make your condition worse or make it last longer.
- If you have any questions about this or if mild diarrhea continues or gets worse, check with your health care professional.

You may continue to use cosmetics (make-up) while you are using this medicine for acne. However, it is best to use only "water-base" cosmetics. Also, it is best not to use cosmetics too heavily or too often. They may make your acne worse. If you have any questions about this, check with your doctor.

Side Effects of This Medicine

Along with its needed effects, a medicine may cause some unwanted effects. Although not all of these side effects may occur, if they do occur they may need medical attention.

Check with your doctor immediately if any of the following side effects occur:
Rare
Abdominal or stomach cramps, pain, and bloating (severe); diarrhea (watery and severe), which may also be bloody; fever; increased thirst; nausea or vomiting; unusual tiredness or weakness; weight loss (unusual)—these side effects may also occur up to several weeks after you stop using this medicine

Also, check with your doctor as soon as possible if any of the following side effects occur:
Less common
Skin rash, itching, redness, swelling, or other sign of irritation not present before use of this medicine

Other side effects may occur that usually do not need medical attention. These side effects may go away during treatment as your body adjusts to the medicine. However, check with your doctor if any of the following side effects continue or are bothersome:
More common
Dryness, scaliness, or peeling of skin (for the topical solution)
Less common
Abdominal pain; diarrhea (mild); irritation or oiliness of skin; stinging or burning feeling of skin

Other side effects not listed above may also occur in some patients. If you notice any other effects, check with your doctor.

Revised: 02/22/94

CLINDAMYCIN   Vaginal

Commonly used brand name(s):

In the U.S.—
Cleocin

In Canada—
Dalacin

Description

Clindamycin (klin-da-MYE-sin) is used to treat certain vaginal infections. It works by killing the bacteria. This medicine will not work for vaginal fungus or yeast infections.

Clindamycin is available only with your doctor's prescription, in the following dosage form:

Vaginal
- Cream (U.S. and Canada)

Before Using This Medicine

In deciding to use a medicine, the risks of taking the medicine must be weighed against the good it will do. This is a decision

you and your doctor will make. For vaginal clindamycin, the following should be considered:

Allergies—Tell your doctor if you have ever had any unusual or allergic reaction to clindamycin or lincomycin (e.g., Lincocin). Also tell your health care professional if you are allergic to any other substances, such as foods, preservatives, or dyes.

Pregnancy—Vaginal clindamycin is used during the second or third trimester of pregnancy. It was found to cause birth defects in one strain of mouse, but has not caused problems in other animals. Vaginal clindamycin has not been reported to cause birth defects or other problems in humans.

Breast-feeding—It is not known whether clindamycin used vaginally passes into the breast milk. Clindamycin taken by mouth does pass into the breast milk and has not been reported to cause problems in nursing babies. Although most medicines pass into the breast milk in small amounts, many of them may be used safely while breast-feeding. Mothers who are using this medicine and who wish to breast-feed should discuss this with their doctor.

Children—Studies on this medicine have been done only in adult patients, and there is no specific information comparing use of vaginal clindamycin in children with use in other age groups.

Older adults—Many medicines have not been studied specifically in older people. Therefore, it may not be known whether they work exactly the same way they do in younger adults or if they cause different side effects or problems in older people. There is no specific information comparing use of vaginal clindamycin in the elderly with use in other age groups.

Other medicines—Although certain medicines should not be used together at all, in other cases two different medicines may be used together even if an interaction might occur. In these cases, your doctor may want to change the dose, or other precautions may be necessary. Tell your health care professional if you are taking or using any other prescription or nonprescription (over-the-counter [OTC]) medicine.

Other medical problems—The presence of other medical problems may affect the use of vaginal clindamycin. Make sure you tell your doctor if you have any other medical problems, especially:

- Stomach or intestinal disease, history of (especially colitis, including colitis caused by antibiotics, or enteritis)— Patients with a history of stomach or intestinal disease may have an increased chance of side effects including diarrhea

Proper Use of This Medicine

Wash your hands before and after using this medicine.

Avoid getting this medicine in your eyes. If this medicine does get into your eyes, rinse them immediately with large amounts of cool tap water. If your eyes still burn or are painful, check with your doctor.

Vaginal clindamycin usually comes with patient directions. Read them carefully before using this medicine.

Use clindamycin vaginal cream exactly as directed by your doctor.

- *To fill the applicator*
  —Remove cap from the tube.
  —Screw one of the applicators onto the tube. Always use a new applicator. Never use one that has been used before.
  —Squeeze the medicine into the applicator slowly until it is full.
  —Remove the applicator from the tube. Replace the cap on the tube.
- *To insert the vaginal cream using the applicator*
  —Relax while lying on your back with your knees bent.
  —Hold the full applicator in one hand. Insert it slowly into the vagina. Stop before it becomes uncomfortable.
  —Slowly press the plunger until it stops.
  —Withdraw the applicator. The medicine will be left behind in the vagina.
- *To care for the applicator*
  —Throw the applicator away after you use it.

To help clear up your infection completely, *it is very important that you keep using this medicine for the full time of treatment*, even if your symptoms begin to clear up after a few days. If you stop using this medicine too soon, your symptoms may return. *Do not miss any doses*. Also, *continue using this medicine even if your menstrual period starts during the time of treatment*.

Dosing—The dose of vaginal clindamycin will be different for different patients. The following information includes only the average dose of vaginal clindamycin. *If your dose is different, do not change it* unless your doctor tells you to do so.

- For *vaginal cream* dosage form:
  —For bacterial vaginosis:
  - Adults and teenagers who are not pregnant—One applicatorful (100 milligrams [mg]) inserted into the vagina once a day, usually at bedtime, for three or seven days.
  - Adults and teenagers who are pregnant—One applicatorful (100 milligrams [mg]) inserted into the vagina once a day, usually at bedtime, for seven days.
  - Children—Use and dose must be determined by your doctor.

Missed dose—If you miss a dose of this medicine, use it as soon as possible. However, if it is almost time for your next dose, skip the missed dose and go back to your regular dosing schedule. Do not double doses.

Storage—To store this medicine:

- Keep out of the reach of children.
- Store away from heat and direct light.
- Keep the medicine from freezing. Do not refrigerate.
- Do not keep outdated medicine or medicine no longer needed. Be sure that any discarded medicine is out of the reach of children.

Precautions While Using This Medicine

If your symptoms do not improve within a few days, or if they become worse, check with your doctor.

It is important that you visit your doctor after you have used all your medicine to make sure that the infection is gone.

This medicine may cause some people to become dizzy. Make sure you know how you react to this medicine before you drive, use machines, or do anything else that could be dangerous if you are dizzy.

Vaginal medicines usually leak out of the vagina during treatment. To keep the medicine from getting on your clothing, wear a minipad or sanitary napkin. Do not use tampons since they may soak up the medicine.

To help clear up your infection completely and make sure it does not return, good health habits are also required.

- Wear cotton panties (or panties or pantyhose with cotton crotches) instead of synthetic (for example, nylon or rayon) panties.
- Wear only freshly washed panties daily.

Do not have sexual intercourse while you are using this medicine. Having sexual intercourse may reduce the strength of the medicine. This may cause the medicine to not work as well.

Do not use latex (rubber) contraceptive products such as condoms, diaphragms, or cervical caps for 72 hours after stopping treatment with vaginal clindamycin cream. The cream contains oils that weaken or harm the latex products, causing them to not work properly to prevent pregnancy. If you have any questions about this, check with your health care professional.

Side Effects of This Medicine

Along with its needed effects, a medicine may cause some unwanted effects. Although not all of these side effects may occur, if they do occur they may need medical attention.

Check with your doctor as soon as possible if any of the following side effects occur:

More common
Itching of the vagina or genital area; pain during sexual intercourse; thick, white vaginal discharge with no odor or with mild odor

Less common
Diarrhea; dizziness; headache; nausea or vomiting; stomach pain or cramps

Rare
Burning, itching, rash, redness, swelling or other signs of skin problems not present before use of this medicine

After you stop using this medicine, your body may need time to adjust. The length of time this takes depends on the amount of medicine you were using and how long you used it. During this period of time, check with your doctor if you notice any of the following side effects:

Itching of the vagina or genital area; pain during sexual intercourse; thick, white vaginal discharge with no odor or with mild odor

Other side effects not listed above may also occur in some patients. If you notice any other effects, check with your doctor.

Revised: 08/11/98

CLIOQUINOL   Topical*

Commonly used brand name(s):

In Canada—
Vioform

Another commonly used name is iodochlorhydroxyquin.

*Not commercially available in the U.S.

Description

Clioquinol (klye-oh-KWIN-ole) belongs to the family of medicines called anti-infectives. Clioquinol topical preparations are used to treat skin infections.

Clioquinol is available without a prescription; however, your doctor may have special instructions on the proper use of this medicine for your medical problem. It is available in the following dosage form:

Topical
- Ointment (Canada)

Before Using This Medicine

If you are using this medicine without a prescription, carefully read and follow any precautions on the label. For clioquinol, the following should be considered:

Allergies—Tell your doctor if you have ever had any unusual or allergic reaction to clioquinol, chloroxine (e.g., Capitrol), hyroxyquinoline or other quinoline derivatives, iodine, or iodine-containing preparations. Also tell your health care professional if you are allergic to any other substances, such as preservatives or dyes.

Pregnancy—Clioquinol topical preparations have not been shown to cause birth defects or other problems in humans.

Breast-feeding—Clioquinol topical preparations have not been reported to cause problems in nursing babies. However, during breast-feeding, keep the infant from contacting the treated skin.

Children—Clioquinol is not recommended in children younger than 2 years of age. Although there is no specific information comparing use of this medicine in children 2 years of age and older with use in other age groups, this medicine is not expected to cause different side effects or problems in children than it does in adults.

Older adults—Many medicines have not been studied specifically in older people. Therefore, it may not be known whether they work exactly the same way they do in younger adults. Although there is no specific information comparing use of this medicine in the elderly with use in other age groups, this medicine is not expected to cause different side effects or problems in older people than it does in younger adults.

Other medicines—Although certain medicines should not be used together at all, in other cases two different medicines may be used together even if an interaction might occur. In these cases, your doctor may want to change the dose, or other precautions may be necessary. Tell your health care professional if you are using any other prescription or nonprescription (over-the-counter [OTC]) medicine.

Other medical problems—The presence of other medical problems may affect the use of clioquinol. Make sure you tell your doctor if you have any other medical problems, especially:

- Kidney disease or
- Liver disease—Caution is advised with clioquinol use in patients with liver or kidney disease

Proper Use of This Medicine

Before applying this medicine, wash the affected area with soap and water, and dry thoroughly.

Do not use this medicine in or around the eyes. If accidental contact occurs, flush eyes with water.

Do not bandage or apply an occlusive dressing (airtight covering, such as kitchen plastic wrap) over this medicine, since it may increase the infection and may cause unwanted drug absorption into the body. If you have any questions about this, check with your doctor.

To use the *ointment form* of this medicine:

- Apply a thin layer of ointment to the affected area and rub in gently. The ointment is recommended for use on dry, crusted lesions.

To help clear up your infection completely, *keep using this medicine for the full time of treatment,* even if your symptoms have disappeared. *Do not miss any doses.*

Dosing—The dose of clioquinol will be different for different patients. *Follow your doctor's orders or the directions on the label.* The following information includes only the average dose of clioquinol. *If your dose is different, do not change it* unless your doctor tells you to do so.

- For *topical* dosage form (ointment):
  —For bacterial or fungus infections:
  - Adults and children 2 years of age and older— Apply to the affected area(s) of the skin two or three times a day.
  - Children younger than 2 years of age—Use is not recommended.

Missed dose—If you miss a dose of this medicine, apply it as soon as possible. However, if it is almost time for your next dose, skip the missed dose and go back to your regular dosing schedule.

Storage—To store this medicine:

- Keep out of the reach of children.
- Store away from heat and direct light.
- Keep the medicine from freezing.
- Do not keep outdated medicine or medicine no longer needed. Be sure that any discarded medicine is out of the reach of children.

Precautions While Using This Medicine

This medicine should not be used for more than 1 week. If your skin problem does not improve in 1 week, or if it becomes worse, check with your doctor.

Clioquinol should not be used to treat large areas of the skin or large open skin lesions. If you have any questions about this, check with your doctor.

This medicine may turn yellow in color when exposed to air. It may stain clothing, skin, hair, and nails yellow. Avoid getting this medicine on your clothing since bleaching may not remove the stain.

Before you have any medical tests, tell the doctor in charge that you are using this medicine. The results of some tests may be affected by this medicine.

Side Effects of This Medicine

Along with its needed effects, a medicine may cause some unwanted effects. Although not all of these side effects may occur, if they do occur they may need medical attention.

Check with your doctor immediately if any of the following side effects occur:
Rare
Burning, itching, rash, redness, swelling, or other sign

of skin irritation not present before use of this medicine or becoming worse during treatment

Other side effects not listed above may also occur in some patients. If you notice any other effects, check with your doctor.

Revised: 5/26/99

CLIOQUINOL AND HYDROCORTISONE   Topical

Commonly used brand name(s):

In the U.S.—
Vioform-Hydrocortisone Cream
Vioform-Hydrocortisone Lotion
Vioform-Hydrocortisone Mild Cream

Vioform-Hydrocortisone Mild Ointment
Vioform-Hydrocortisone Ointment

In Canada—
Vioform-Hydrocortisone Cream
Vioform-Hydrocortisone Mild Cream

Vioform-Hydrocortisone Ointment

Another commonly used name is iodochlorhyroxyquin and hydrocortisone.

Description

Clioquinol and hydrocortisone (klye-oh-KWIN-ole and hye-droe-KOR-ti-sone) is a combined anti-infective and cortisone-like medicine. Clioquinol and hydrocortisone topical preparations are used to treat infections of the skin and to help provide relief from the redness, itching, and discomfort of many skin problems.

Clioquinol and hydrocortisone combination is available only with your doctor's prescription, in the following dosage forms:

Topical
- Cream (U.S. and Canada)
- Lotion (U.S.)
- Ointment (U.S. and Canada)

Before Using This Medicine

In deciding to use a medicine, the risks of taking the medicine must be weighed against the good it will do. This is a decision you and your doctor will make. For clioquinol and hydrocortisone combination, the following should be considered:

Allergies—Tell your doctor if you have ever had any unusual or allergic reaction to clioquinol, hydrocortisone, chloroxine (e.g., Capitrol), iodine, or iodine-containing preparations. Also tell your health care professional if you are allergic to any other substances, such as preservatives or dyes.

Pregnancy—Clioquinol and hydrocortisone topical preparations may be absorbed through the mother's skin. This medicine has not been shown to cause birth defects or other problems in humans. However, studies in animals have shown that it causes birth defects. Use of large amounts on the skin or use for a long time is not recommended during pregnancy.

Breast-feeding—Clioquinol and hydrocortisone topical preparations have not been reported to cause problems in nursing babies.

Children—Clioquinol and hydrocortisone combination is not recommended in children up to 2 years of age. Although there is no specific information comparing use of clioquinol and hydrocortisone combination in children over 2 years of age with use in other age groups, this medicine is not expected to cause different side effects or problems in these children than it does in adults.

Older adults—Many medicines have not been studied specifically in older people. Therefore, it may not be known whether they work exactly the same way they do in younger adults. Although there is no specific information comparing use of clioquinol and hydrocortisone combination in the elderly with use in other age groups, this medicine is not expected to cause different side effects or problems in older people than it does in younger adults.

Other medicines—Although certain medicines should not be used together at all, in other cases two different medicines may be used together even if an interaction might occur. In these cases, your doctor may want to change the dose, or other precautions may be necessary. Tell your health care professional if you are using any other prescription or nonprescription (over-the-counter [OTC]) medicine.

Other medical problems—The presence of other medical problems may affect the use of clioquinol and hydrocortisone topical preparations. Make sure you tell your doctor if you have any other medical problems, especially:

- Skin infection (other)—Use of clioquinol and hydrocortisone topical preparations may make the condition worse

Proper Use of This Medicine

Before applying this medicine, wash the affected area with soap and water, and dry thoroughly.

Do not use this medicine in or around the eyes or on infants and children up to 2 years of age.

To use the *cream form* of this medicine:

- Apply a thin layer of cream to the affected area and rub in gently until cream disappears.

To use the *lotion form* of this medicine:

- Gently squeeze bottle and apply a few drops of lotion to the affected area. Rub in gently until lotion disappears.

To use the *ointment form* of this medicine:

- Apply a thin layer of ointment to the affected area and rub in gently.

Do not bandage or otherwise wrap the area of the skin being treated unless directed to do so by your doctor.

Check with your doctor before using this medicine on any other skin problems. It should not be used on certain kinds of bacterial, virus, or fungus skin infections.

To help clear up your infection completely, *keep using this medicine for the full time of treatment*, even if your symptoms have disappeared. *Do not miss any doses.* However, *do not use this medicine more often or for a longer time than your doctor ordered.* To do so may increase the chance of absorption through the skin and the chance of side effects. In addition, too much use, especially on thin skin areas (for example, face, armpits, groin), may result in thinning of the skin and stretch marks.

Dosing—The dose of clioquinol and hydrocortisone combination will be different for different patients. *Follow your doctor's orders or the directions on the label.* The following information includes only the average dose of clioquinol and hydrocortisone combination. *If your dose is different, do not change it* unless your doctor tells you to do so.

- For *topical* dosage forms (cream, lotion, or ointment):
  —For bacterial and fungus infections:
  - Adults, teenagers, and children 2 years of age and over—Apply to the affected area(s) of the skin three or four times a day.
  - Children up to 2 years of age—Use is not recommended.

Missed dose—If you miss a dose of this medicine, apply it as soon as possible. However, if it is almost time for your next dose, skip the missed dose and go back to your regular dosing schedule.

Storage—To store this medicine:

- Keep out of the reach of children.
- Store away from heat and direct light.
- Keep the medicine from freezing.
- Do not keep outdated medicine or medicine no longer needed. Be sure that any discarded medicine is out of the reach of children.

Precautions While Using This Medicine

If your skin problem does not improve within 1 to 2 weeks, or if it becomes worse, check with your doctor.

This medicine may be absorbed through the skin, and too much use can affect growth. *Children who must use this medicine should be followed closely by their doctor.*

This medicine may stain clothing, skin, hair, and nails yellow. Avoid getting this medicine on your clothing. Bleaching may not remove the stain.

Side Effects of This Medicine

Along with its needed effects, a medicine may cause some unwanted effects. Although not all of these side effects may occur, if they do occur they may need medical attention.

Check with your doctor immediately if any of the following side effects occur:
  Rare
    Blistering, burning, itching, peeling, skin rash, redness, swelling, or other sign of irritation not present before use of this medicine
  With prolonged use
    Thinning of skin with easy bruising

Other side effects not listed above may also occur in some patients. If you notice any other effects, check with your doctor.

Revised: 02/10/92
Interim revision: 07/14/94

CLODRONATE Systemic*— INTRODUCTORY VERSION

Commonly used brand name(s):

In Canada—
  Bonefos

Another commonly used name is disodium clodronate.

*Not commercially available in the U.S.

Description

Clodronate (KLA–dro–nayt) is a medicine used to treat a high level of calcium in the blood caused by changes in the body that happen with cancer. Clodronate also treats the weakening in the bones when cancer has spread to the bones from another part of the body.

This medicine is available only with your doctor's prescription, in the following dosage forms:

Oral
- Capsules (Canada)

Parenteral
- Injection (Canada)

Before Using This Medicine

In deciding to use a medicine, the risks of taking the medicine must be weighed against the good it will do. This is a decision you and your doctor will make. For clodronate, the following should be considered:

Allergies—Tell your doctor if you have ever had any unusual or allergic reaction to clodronate. Also tell your health care professional if you are allergic to any other substances, such as foods, preservatives, or dyes.

Pregnancy—Clodronate has not been studied in pregnant women. However, studies in animals have shown that clodronate causes birth defects. Before taking this medicine, make sure your doctor knows if you are pregnant or if you may become pregnant.

Breast-feeding—It is not known whether clodronate passes into human breast milk. Although most medicines pass into breast milk in small amounts, many of them may be used safely while breast-feeding. Mothers who are taking this medicine and who wish to breast-feed should discuss this with their doctor.

Children—Studies on this medicine have been done only in adult patients, and there is no specific information comparing use of clodronate in children with use in other age groups.

Older adults—Many medicines have not been studied specifically in older people. Therefore, it may not be known whether they work exactly the same way they do in younger adults or if they cause different side effects or problems in older people. There is no specific information comparing use of clodronate in the elderly with use in other age groups.

Other medicines—Although certain medicines should not be used together at all, in other cases two different medicines may be used together even if an interaction might occur. In these cases, your doctor may want to change the dose, or other precautions may be necessary. When you are taking clodronate, it is especially important that your health care professional know if you are taking any of the following:
- Antacids (e.g., Maalox, Mylanta) or
- Calcium supplements (e.g., Tums) or
- Iron supplements (e.g., Geritol)—Taking these medicines and also taking clodronate may cause the clodronate to not work as well
- Calcitonin (e.g., Calcimar, Miacalcin) or
- Corticosteroids (e.g., Prednisone) or
- Loop diuretics (e.g., Lasix, Demadex) or
- Mithramycin (e.g., Mithracin) or
- Phosphate (e.g., found in Centrum, Ensure)—Taking these medicines and also taking clodronate may cause the calcium in your blood to be too low

Other medical problems—The presence of other medical problems may affect the use of clodronate. Make sure you tell your doctor if you have any other medical problems, especially:
- Stomach cramping or pain, nausea, stomach burning—Taking clodronate, especially by mouth, may make your stomach problems worse
- Kidney problems—Taking clodronate may cause your kidney problems to get worse. Your doctor may give you a smaller amount of clodronate to take

Proper Use of This Medicine

Dosing—The dose of clodronate will be different for different patients. *Follow your doctor's orders or the directions on the label.* The following information includes only the average doses of clodronate. *If your dose is different, do not change it* unless your doctor tells you to do so.

The number of capsules that you take depends on the strength of the medicine. Also, *the number of doses you take each day, the time allowed between doses, and the length of time you take the medicine depend on the medical problem for which you are taking clodronate.*
- For *oral* dosage form:
  —For treating hypercalcemia (too much calcium in the blood):
    - Adults—1600 milligrams (mg) to 2400 mg given in one or two divided amounts per day. Your doctor may give you capsules after you have had clodronate through your vein. You should not take more than 3200 mg in a day. You should take clodronate at least two hours before or after food.
    - Children—Use and dosage must be determined by your doctor.

For injection dosage form:
  —For treating hypercalcemia (too much calcium in the blood):
    - Adults—300 mg in a solution to be injected over at least two hours into a vein once a day for two to five days. The treatment will not be longer than seven days. The amount of medicine may be less if you have kidney problems.
    - Children—Use and dosage must be determined by your doctor.

Storage—To store this medicine:
- Keep out of the reach of children. Overdose of clodronate is very dangerous in young children.
- Do not store in the bathroom, near the kitchen sink, or in other damp places. Heat or moisture may cause the medicine to break down.
- Do not keep outdated medicine or medicine no longer needed. Ask your health care professional how you should dispose of any medicine you do not use. Be sure that any discarded medicine is out of the reach of children.

Precautions While Using This Medicine

It is very important that you take adequate fluid before and while taking clodronate.

If you will be taking this medicine for a long time, *it is very important that your doctor see you at regular visits* to check the calcium in your blood and to see how well the clodronate is working.

Side Effects of This Medicine

Along with its needed effects, a medicine may cause some unwanted effects. Although not all of these side effects may occur, if they do occur they may need medical attention.

Check with your doctor immediately if any of the following side effects occur:

Rare

Breathing problems; convulsions (seizures); mood or mental changes; muscle cramps in hands, arms, feet, legs, or face; muscle shaking; problems with urination; sores in throat; stomach cramps or pain; swelling of face, ankles or hands; unusual heartbeats; unusual tiredness or weakness

Symptoms of overdose

Get emergency help immediately if any of the following symptoms of overdose occur

Convulsions (seizures); mood or mental changes; muscle cramps; problems with urination; stomach pain or cramps; trouble breathing; unusual heartbeat

Other side effects may occur that usually do not need medical attention. These side effects may go away during treatment as your body adjusts to the medicine. Also, your health care professional may be able to tell you about ways to prevent or reduce some of these side effects. Check with your health care professional if any of the following side effects continue or are bothersome or if you have any questions about them:

More common

Diarrhea; increased bowel movements; nausea and vomiting

Less common

Cloudy urine; mouth irritation

Other side effects not listed above may also occur in some patients. If you notice any other effects, check with your doctor.

Developed: 03/08/2001

CLOFAZIMINE   Systemic†

Commonly used brand name(s):

In the U.S.—
Lamprene

†Not commercially available in Canada.

Description

Clofazimine (kloe-FA-zi-meen) is taken to treat leprosy (Hansen's disease). It is sometimes given with other medicines for leprosy. When this medicine is used to treat "flare-ups" of leprosy, it may be given with a cortisone-like medicine. Clofazimine may also be used for other problems as determined by your doctor.

This medicine is available only with your doctor's prescription, in the following dosage form:

Oral
• Capsules (U.S.)

Before Using This Medicine

In deciding to use a medicine, the risks of taking the medicine must be weighed against the good it will do. This is a decision you and your doctor will make. For clofazimine, the following should be considered:

Allergies—Tell your doctor if you have ever had any unusual or allergic reaction to clofazimine. Also tell your health care professional if you are allergic to any other substances, such as foods, preservatives, or dyes.

Pregnancy—Clofazimine has not been studied in pregnant women. Although the skin of babies born to mothers who took clofazimine during pregnancy was deeply discolored, this medicine has not been shown to cause birth defects or other problems in humans. A gradual fading of the discoloration may occur over a period of about a year. Some animal studies have not shown that clofazimine causes birth defects. However, studies in mice have shown that clofazimine may cause slow bone formation of the skull and a decrease in successful pregnancies. Before you take clofazimine, make sure your doctor knows if you are pregnant or if you may become pregnant.

Breast-feeding—Clofazimine passes into the breast milk. Use is not recommended in nursing mothers.

Children—Studies on this medicine have been done only in adult patients, and there is no specific information comparing use of clofazimine in children with use in other age groups.

Older adults—Many medicines have not been studied specifically in older people. Therefore, it may not be known whether they work exactly the same way they do in younger adults or if they cause different side effects or problems in older people. There is no specific information comparing use of clofazimine in the elderly with use in other age groups.

Other medicines—Although certain medicines should not be used together at all, in other cases two different medicines may be used together even if an interaction might occur. In these cases, your doctor may want to change the dose, or other precautions may be necessary. Tell your health care professional if you are taking any other prescription or nonprescription (over-the-counter [OTC]) medicine.

Other medical problems—The presence of other medical problems may affect the use of clofazimine. Make sure you tell your doctor if you have any other medical problems, especially:

• Liver disease—Clofazimine may on rare occasion cause hepatitis and liver disease

• Stomach or intestinal problems, history of—Clofazimine often causes some stomach upset, but on rare occasion may cause severe, sharp abdominal pain and burning, which may be a sign of a serious side effect

Proper Use of This Medicine

Clofazimine should be taken with meals or milk.

To help clear up your leprosy completely, *it is very important that you keep taking clofazimine for the full time of treatment*, even if you begin to feel better after a few months. You may have to take it every day for as long as 2 years to life. If you stop taking this medicine too soon, your symptoms may return.

This medicine works best when there is a constant amount in the blood. *To help keep the amount constant, do not* miss any doses. *Also, it is best to take each dose at the same time every day.* If you need help in planning the best time to take your medicine, check with your health care professional.

Dosing—The dose of clofazimine will be different for different patients. *Follow your doctor's orders or the directions on the label.* The following information includes only the average doses of clofazimine. *If your dose is different, do not change it* unless your doctor tells you to do so.

The number of capsules that you take depends on the strength of the medicine. Also, *the number of doses you take each day, the time allowed between doses, and the length of time you take the medicine depend on the medical problem for which you are taking clofazimine.*

- For the *treatment of leprosy (Hansen's disease):*
  - —Adults and teenagers: 50 to 100 milligrams once a day. This medicine must be taken with other medicines for the treatment of Hansen's disease.
  - —Children: Dose must be determined by the doctor.

Missed dose—If you miss a dose of this medicine, take it as soon as possible. However, if it is almost time for your next dose, skip the missed dose and go back to your regular dosing schedule. Do not double doses.

Storage—To store this medicine:
- Keep out of the reach of children.
- Store away from heat and direct light.
- Do not store in the bathroom, near the kitchen sink, or in other damp places. Heat or moisture may cause the medicine to break down.
- Do not keep outdated medicine or medicine no longer needed. Be sure that any discarded medicine is out of the reach of children.

Precautions While Using This Medicine

If your symptoms do not improve within 1 to 3 months, or if they become worse, check with your doctor. It may take up to 6 months before the full benefit of this medicine is seen.

Clofazimine may cause pink or red to brownish-black discoloration of the skin within a few weeks after you start taking it. Because of the skin discoloration, some patients may become depressed. The discoloration will go away when you stop taking this medicine. However, it may take several months or years for the skin to clear up completely. *If skin discoloration causes you to feel very depressed or to have thoughts of suicide, check with your doctor immediately.*

This medicine may cause some people to become dizzy, drowsy, or less alert than they are normally. *Make sure you know how you react to this medicine before you drive, use machines, or do anything else that could be dangerous if you are dizzy or are not alert or able to see well.* If these reactions are especially bothersome, check with your doctor.

Clofazimine may cause your skin to become more sensitive to sunlight than it is normally. Exposure to sunlight, even for brief periods of time, may cause a skin rash, itching, redness or other discoloration of the skin, or a severe sunburn. When you begin taking this medicine:
- Stay out of direct sunlight, especially between the hours of 10:00 a.m. and 3:00 p.m., if possible.
- Wear protective clothing, including a hat. Also, wear sunglasses.
- Apply a sun block product that has a skin protection factor (SPF) of at least 15. Some patients may require a product with a higher SPF number, especially if they have a fair complexion. If you have any questions about this, check with your health care professional.
- Apply a sun block lipstick that has an SPF of at least 15 to protect your lips.
- Do not use a sunlamp or tanning bed or booth.

If you have a severe reaction, check with your doctor.

Clofazimine may also cause dry, rough, or scaly skin. A skin cream, lotion, or oil may help to treat this problem.

Side Effects of This Medicine

Along with its needed effects, a medicine may cause some unwanted effects. Although not all of these side effects may occur, if they do occur they may need medical attention.

Check with your doctor immediately if any of the following side effects occur:
  Rare
    Bloody or black, tarry stools; colicky or burning abdominal or stomach pain; mental depression; yellow eyes or skin—may be an orange color if already have a pink to brownish-black skin or eye discoloration

Other side effects may occur that usually do not need medical attention. These side effects may go away during treatment as your body adjusts to the medicine. However, check with your doctor if any of the following side effects continue or are bothersome:
  More common
    Diarrhea; dry, rough, or scaly skin; loss of appetite; nausea or vomiting; pink or red to brownish-black discoloration of skin and eyes; skin rash and itching

  Less common or rare
    Changes in taste; dryness, burning, itching, or irritation of the eyes; increased sensitivity of skin to sunlight

Clofazimine commonly causes discoloration of the feces, lining of the eyelids, sputum, sweat, tears, and urine. Usually this side effect does not require medical attention, but the discoloration may not go away. However, *clofazimine may also cause bloody or black, tarry stools. This side effect may be a symptom of serious bleeding problems that do require medical attention.*

Other side effects not listed above may also occur in some patients. If you notice any other effects, check with your doctor.

Revised: 02/23/93

CLOFIBRATE   Systemic

Commonly used brand name(s):

In the U.S.—
  Abitrate
  Atromid-S
  Generic name product may be available.

In Canada—
Atromid-S
Claripex
Novofibrate

Description

Clofibrate (kloe-FYE-brate) is used to lower cholesterol and triglyceride (fat-like substances) levels in the blood. This may help prevent medical problems caused by such substances clogging the blood vessels.

Clofibrate may also be used for other conditions as determined by your doctor.

Clofibrate is available only with your doctor's prescription, in the following dosage form:

Oral
- Capsules (U.S. and Canada)

Before Using This Medicine

In addition to its helpful effects in treating your medical problem, this medicine may have some harmful effects.

You may have read or heard about a study called the World Health Organization (WHO) Study. This study compared the effects in patients who used clofibrate with effects in those who used a placebo (sugar pill). The results of this study suggested that clofibrate might increase the patient's risk of cancer, liver disease, and pancreatitis (inflammation of the pancreas), although it might also decrease the risk of heart attack. It may also increase the risk of gallstones and problems from gallbladder surgery. Other studies have not found all of these effects. Be sure you have discussed this with your doctor before taking this medicine.

In deciding to use a medicine, the risks of taking the medicine must be weighed against the good it will do. This is a decision you and your doctor will make. For clofibrate, the following should be considered:

Allergies—Tell your doctor if you have ever had any unusual or allergic reaction to clofibrate. Also tell your health care professional if you are allergic to any other substances, such as foods, preservatives, or dyes.

Diet—Before prescribing medicine for your condition, your doctor will probably try to control your condition by prescribing a personal diet for you. Such a diet may be low in fats, sugars, and/or cholesterol. Many people are able to control their condition by carefully following their doctors' orders for proper diet and exercise. *Medicine is prescribed only when additional help is needed* and is effective only when a schedule of diet and exercise is properly followed.

Also, this medicine is less effective if you are greatly overweight. It may be very important for you to go on a reducing diet. However, check with your doctor before going on any diet.

Make certain your health care professional knows if you are on a low-sodium, low-sugar, or any other special diet. Most medicines contain more than their active ingredient.

Pregnancy—Use of clofibrate is not recommended during pregnancy. Although studies have not been done in pregnant women, studies in rabbits have shown that the fetus may not be able to break down and get rid of this medicine as well as the mother. Because of this, it is possible that clofibrate may be harmful to the fetus if you take it while you are pregnant or for up to several months before you become pregnant. Be sure that you have discussed this with your doctor before taking this medicine, especially if you plan to become pregnant in the near future.

Breast-feeding—Clofibrate passes into breast milk. This medicine is not recommended during breast-feeding because it may cause unwanted effects in nursing babies.

Children—Studies on this medicine have been done only in adult patients, and there is no specific information comparing use of clofibrate in children with use in other age groups. However, use is not recommended in children under 2 years of age since cholesterol is needed for normal development.

Older adults—Many medicines have not been studied specifically in older people. Therefore, it may not be known whether they work exactly the same way they do in younger adults. Although there is no specific information comparing use of clofibrate in the elderly with use in other age groups, this medicine is not expected to cause different side effects or problems in older people than it does in younger adults.

Other medicines—Although certain medicines should not be used together at all, in other cases two different medicines may be used together even if an interaction might occur. In these cases, your doctor may want to change the dose, or other precautions may be necessary. When you are taking clofibrate, it is especially important that your health care professional knows if you are taking the following:
- Anticoagulants (blood thinners)—Use with clofibrate may increase the effects of the anticoagulant

Other medical problems—The presence of other medical problems may affect the use of clofibrate. Make sure you tell your doctor if you have any other medical problems, especially:
- Gallstones or
- Stomach or intestinal ulcer—May make these conditions worse
- Heart disease or
- Kidney disease or
- Liver disease—Higher blood levels may result and increase the risk of side effects
- Underactive thyroid—Clofibrate may cause or make muscle disease worse

Proper Use of This Medicine

Use this medicine only as directed by your doctor. Do not use more or less of it, and do not use it more often or for a longer time than your doctor ordered.

Follow carefully the special diet your doctor gave you. This is the most important part of controlling your condition and is necessary if the medicine is to work properly.

Stomach upset may occur but usually lessens after a few doses. Take this medicine with food or immediately after meals to lessen possible stomach upset.

Dosing—The dose of clofibrate will be different for different patients. *Follow your doctor's orders or the directions on the label.* The following information includes only the average doses of clofibrate. *If your dose is different, do not change it* unless your doctor tells you to do so.

The number of capsules that you take depends on the strength of the medicine.
- For *oral* dosage form (capsules):
  —For high cholesterol:
    - Adults—1.5 to 2 grams a day. This is divided into two to four doses.

- Children—Dose must be determined by your doctor.

Missed dose—If you miss a dose of this medicine, take it as soon as possible. However, if it is almost time for your next dose, skip the missed dose and go back to your regular dosing schedule. Do not double doses.

Storage—To store this medicine:
- Keep out of the reach of children.
- Store away from heat and direct light.
- Do not store in the bathroom, near the kitchen sink, or in other damp places. Heat or moisture may cause the medicine to break down.
- Do not keep outdated medicine or medicine no longer needed. Be sure that any discarded medicine is out of the reach of children.

Precautions While Using This Medicine

It is very important that your doctor check your progress at regular visits. This will allow your doctor to see if the medicine is working properly to lower your cholesterol and triglyceride levels and to decide if you should continue to take it.

Do not stop taking this medicine without first checking with your doctor. When you stop taking this medicine, your blood fat levels may increase again. Your doctor may want you to follow a special diet to help prevent that.

Side Effects of This Medicine

Along with its needed effects, a medicine may cause some unwanted effects. Although not all of these side effects may occur, if they do occur they may need medical attention.

Check with your doctor immediately if you think you have taken an overdose or if any of the following side effects occur:
  Rare
    Chest pain; irregular heartbeat; shortness of breath; stomach pain (severe) with nausea and vomiting

Check with your doctor as soon as possible if any of the following side effects occur:
  Rare
    Blood in urine; cough or hoarseness; decrease in urination; fever or chills; lower back or side pain; painful or difficult urination; swelling of feet or lower legs

Other side effects may occur that usually do not need medical attention. These side effects may go away during treatment as your body adjusts to the medicine. However, check with your doctor if any of the following side effects continue or are bothersome:
  More common
    Diarrhea; nausea
  Less common or rare
    Decreased sexual ability; headache; increased appetite or weight gain (slight); muscle aches or cramps; sores in mouth and on lips; stomach pain, gas, or heartburn; unusual tiredness or weakness; vomiting

Other side effects not listed above may also occur in some patients. If you notice any other effects, check with your doctor.

Additional Information

Once a medicine has been approved for marketing for a certain use, experience may show that it is also useful for other medical problems. Although this use is not included in product labeling, clofibrate is used in certain patients with the following medical condition:
- Certain types of diabetes insipidus (water diabetes)

Other than the above information, there is no additional information relating to proper use, precautions, or side effects for this use.

Revised: 11/24/92
Interim revision: 04/14/94

CLOMIPHENE   Systemic

Commonly used brand name(s):
In the U.S.—
  Clomid
  Milophene
  Serophene
  Generic name product may be available.
In Canada—
  Clomid
  Serophene
Other commonly used names are clomifene and clomifene citrate.

Description

Clomiphene (KLOE-mi-feen) is used as a fertility medicine in some women who are unable to become pregnant.

Clomiphene probably works by changing the hormone balance of the body. In women, this causes ovulation to occur and prepares the body for pregnancy.

Clomiphene may also be used for other conditions in both females and males as determined by your doctor.

The following information applies only to female patients taking clomiphene. Check with your doctor if you are a male and have any questions about the use of clomiphene.

Clomiphene is available only with your doctor's prescription, in the following dosage form:
  Oral
  - Tablets (U.S. and Canada)

Before Using This Medicine

In deciding to use a medicine, the risks of taking the medicine must be weighed against the good it will do. This is a decision you and your doctor will make. For clomiphene, the following should be considered:

Allergies—Tell your doctor if you have ever had any unusual or allergic reaction to clomiphene. Also tell your health care professional if you are allergic to any other substances, such as foods, preservatives, or dyes.

Pregnancy—There is a chance that clomiphene may cause birth defects if it is taken after you become pregnant. *Stop taking this medicine and tell your doctor immediately if you think you have become pregnant* while still taking clomiphene.

If you become pregnant as a result of using this medicine, there is a chance of a multiple birth (for example, twins, triplets) occurring.

Breast-feeding—It is not known if clomiphene passes into breast milk. However, this medicine stops milk from being produced.

Other medicines—Although certain medicines should not be used together at all, in other cases two different medicines may be used together even if an interaction might occur. In these cases, your doctor may want to change the dose, or other precautions may be necessary. When you are taking clomiphene, it is especially important that your health care professional know if you are taking any other prescription or nonprescription (over-the-counter [OTC]) medicine.

Other medical problems—The presence of other medical problems may affect the use of clomiphene. Make sure you tell your doctor if you have any other medical problems, especially:

- Unusually large ovary or
- Cyst on ovary—Clomiphene may cause the cyst to increase in size
- Endometriosis—Inducing ovulation (including using clomiphene) may worsen endometriosis because the body estrogen level is increased; estrogen can cause growth of endometriosis implants
- Fibroid tumors of the uterus—Clomiphene may cause fibroid tumors to increase in size
- Inflamed veins due to blood clots—Clomiphene may make condition worse
- Liver disease (or history of)—Clomiphene may make any liver disease worse
- Mental depression—Existing depression may become worse because of hormone changes caused by clomiphene
- Unusual vaginal bleeding—Some irregular vaginal bleeding is a sign that the lining of the uterus is growing too much or is a sign of cancer of the uterus lining; these problems must be ruled out before clomiphene is used because clomiphene can make these conditions worse

Proper Use of This Medicine

Take this medicine only as directed by your doctor. If you are to begin on Day 5, count the first day of your menstrual period as Day 1. Beginning on Day 5, take the correct dose every day for as many days as your doctor ordered. To help you to remember to take your dose of medicine, take it at the same time every day.

Dosing—The dose of clomiphene will be different for different patients. *Follow your doctor's orders or the directions on the label.* The following information includes only the average doses of clomiphene. *If your dose is different, do not change it* unless your doctor tells you to do so.

- For *oral* dosage form (tablets):
  —For treating infertility:
  - Adults—50 milligrams (mg) a day for five days of a menstrual cycle. The treatment is usually started on the fifth day of your menstrual period. If you do not have menstrual cycles, you can begin taking your medicine at any time. If you do not become pregnant after the first course, your doctor may increase your dose a little at a time up to 250 mg a day. Your treatment may be repeated until you do become pregnant or for up to four treatment cycles.

Missed dose—If you miss a dose of this medicine, take it as soon as possible. If you do not remember until it is time for the next dose, take both doses together; then go back to your regular dosing schedule. If you miss more than one dose, check with your doctor.

Storage—To store this medicine:

- Keep out of the reach of children.
- Store away from heat and direct light.
- Do not store in the bathroom, near the kitchen sink, or in other damp places. Heat or moisture may cause the medicine to break down.
- Do not keep outdated medicine or medicine no longer needed. Be sure that any discarded medicine is out of the reach of children.

Precautions While Using This Medicine

It is very important that your doctor check your progress at regular visits to make sure this medicine is working and to check for unwanted effects.

At certain times in your menstrual cycle, your doctor may want you to use an ovulation prediction test kit. *Follow your doctor's instructions carefully.* Ovulation is controlled by luteinizing hormone (LH). LH is present in the blood and urine in very small amounts during most of the menstrual cycle but rises suddenly for a short time in the middle of the menstrual cycle. This sharp rise, the LH surge, usually causes ovulation within about 30 hours. A woman is most likely to become pregnant if she has intercourse within the 24 hours after detecting the LH surge. Ovulation prediction test kits are used to test for this large amount of LH in the urine. This method is better for predicting ovulation than measuring daily basal body temperature. It is important that intercourse take place at the correct time to give you the best chance of becoming pregnant.

There is a chance that clomiphene may cause birth defects if it is taken after you become pregnant. *Stop taking this medicine and tell your doctor immediately if you think you have become pregnant* while still taking clomiphene.

This medicine may cause blurred vision, difficulty in reading, or other changes in vision. It may also cause some people to become dizzy or lightheaded. *Make sure you know how you react to this medicine before you drive, use machines, or do anything else that could be dangerous if you are not clear-headed or able to see well.* If these reactions are especially bothersome, check with your doctor.

Side Effects of This Medicine

Along with its needed effects, a medicine may cause some unwanted effects. Although not all of these side effects may occur, if they do occur they may need medical attention.

When this medicine is used for a short time at low doses, serious side effects usually are rare. *However, check with your doctor immediately* if any of the following side effects occur:

More common
  Bloating; stomach or pelvic pain

Check with your doctor as soon as possible if any of the following side effects occur:

Less common or rare
  Blurred vision; decreased or double vision or other vision problems; seeing flashes of light; sensitivity of eyes to light; yellow eyes or skin

Other side effects may occur that usually do not need medical attention. These side effects may go away during treatment as your body adjusts to the medicine. However, check with your doctor if any of the following side effects continue or are bothersome:

More common
Hot flashes

Less common or rare
Breast discomfort; dizziness or lightheadedness; headache; heavy menstrual periods or bleeding between periods; mental depression; nausea or vomiting; nervousness; restlessness; tiredness; trouble in sleeping

Other side effects not listed above may also occur in some patients. If you notice any other effects, check with your doctor.

Additional Information

Once a medicine has been approved for marketing for a certain use, experience may show that it is also useful for other medical problems. Although these uses are not included in product labeling, clomiphene is used in certain patients with the following medical conditions:

- Certain problems of the male sexual organs caused by pituitary or hypothalamus gland problems (diagnosis)
- Male infertility caused by low production of sperm
- Problems with the corpus luteum (mature egg)

For males taking this medicine for treatment of infertility caused by low sperm production:

- To help decide on the best treatment for your medical problem, tell your doctor:
  —if you have ever had any unusual or allergic reaction to clomiphene.
  —if you have any of the following medical problems:
    - Liver disease
    - Mental depression
    - Thrombophlebitis
- If you miss a dose of this medicine, take it as soon as possible. If you do not remember until it is time for the next dose, take both doses together; then go back to your regular dosing schedule. If you miss more than one dose, check with your doctor.
- *It is important that your doctor check your progress at regular visits to find out if clomiphene is working and to check for unwanted effects.*
- This medicine may cause vision problems, dizziness, or lightheadedness. *Make sure you know how you react to this medicine before you drive, use machines, or do anything else that could be dangerous if you are not clear-headed or able to see well.*
- Along with its needed effects, a medicine may cause some unwanted effects. Although not all of these side effects may occur, if they do occur they may need medical attention. When this medicine is used for short periods of time at low doses, serious side effects usually are rare. However, check with your doctor if any of the following side effects occur:

Less common or rare
Blurred vision; decreased or double vision or other vision problems; seeing flashes of light; sensitivity of eyes to light; yellow eyes or skin

- Other side effects may occur that usually do not need medical attention. These side effects may go away during treatment as your body adjusts to the medicine. However, check with your doctor if any of the following side effects continue or are bothersome:

Less common or rare
Breast enlargement; dizziness or lightheadedness; headache; mental depression; nausea or vomiting; nervousness; restlessness; tiredness; trouble in sleeping

Other than the above information, there is no additional information relating to proper use, precautions, or side effects for these uses.

Revised: 08/08/95

CLONIDINE   Parenteral-Local

Commonly used brand name(s):

In the U.S.—
Duraclon

Description

Clonidine (KLOE-ni-deen) injection is used with injected pain medicine to treat pain in cancer patients.

Clonidine is to be started under the immediate supervision of your doctor. After your doctor has seen how you respond to clonidine, you may be able to receive this medicine at home.

This medicine is available only with your doctor's prescription, in the following dosage form(s):

Parenteral
- Injection (U.S.)

Before Using This Medicine

In deciding to use a medicine, the risks of using the medicine must be weighed against the good it will do. This is a decision you and your doctor will make. For clonidine, the following should be considered:

Allergies—Tell your doctor if you have ever had any unusual or allergic reaction to clonidine. Also tell your health care professional if you are allergic to any other substances, such as foods, preservatives, or dyes.

Pregnancy—Studies on birth defects with clonidine have not been done in pregnant women. However, it crosses the placenta. Clonidine has not been shown to cause birth defects in animal studies but may cause other problems. Before taking this medicine, make sure your doctor knows if you are pregnant or if you may become pregnant.

Breast-feeding—Clonidine passes into the breast milk. Because this medicine may cause serious side effects, breast-feeding is generally not recommended while you are using it.

Children—Although there is no specific information comparing use of clonidine in children with use in other age groups, this medicine is not expected to cause different side effects or problems in children than it does in adults. This medicine is usually used in children only when the pain is severe and other pain medicines did not help.

Older adults—Many medicines have not been studied specifically in older people. Therefore, it may not be known whether they work exactly the same way they do in younger adults or if they cause different side effects or problems in older people. There is no specific information comparing use of clonidine in the elderly with use in other age groups.

Other medicines—Although certain medicines should not be used together at all, in other cases two different medicines may be used together even if an interaction might occur. In these cases, your doctor may want to change the dose, or other precautions may be necessary. When you are taking clonidine, it is especially important that your health care professional know if you are taking any of the following:

- Beta-adrenergic blocking agents (acebutolol [e.g., Sectral], atenolol [e.g., Tenormin], betaxolol [e.g., Kerlone], bisoprolol [e.g., Zebeta], carteolol [e.g., Cartrol], labetalol [e.g., Normodyne], metoprolol [e.g., Lopressor, Toprol–XL], nadolol [e.g., Corgard], oxprenolol [e.g., Trasicor], penbutolol [e.g., Levatol], pindolol [e.g., Visken], propranolol [e.g., Inderal, Inderal LA], sotalol [e.g., Betapace], timolol [e.g., Blocadren])—These medicines may increase the risk of harmful effects when clonidine treatment is stopped suddenly

Other medical problems—The presence of other medical problems may affect the use of clonidine. Make sure you tell your doctor if you have any other medical problems, especially:

- Anticoagulant therapy or
- Bleeding problems—Bleeding into the area around the spinal cord is possible
- Heart or blood vessel disease—Clonidine may make these conditions worse
- Infection at the place of injection or catheter (tube)—The risk of developing meningitis or an abscess is increased
- Kidney disease—Effects of clonidine may be increased because of slower removal of clonidine from the body
- Pain associated with surgery or
- Pain during or following childbirth—The ability to tolerate some of the potential side effects of clonidine may be decreased

Proper Use of This Medicine

Clonidine is given continuously as an epidural infusion (run around the spinal cord) using an infusion pump. The pump and its tube should be checked regularly to make sure the clonidine flow has not stopped accidentally. The injection or catheter site should also be checked regularly for signs of infection.

If you are using this medicine at home, make sure you understand exactly how to use it.

Dosing—The dose of clonidine will be different for different patients. *Follow your doctor's orders or the directions on the label.* The following information includes only the average doses of clonidine. *If your dose is different, do not change it* unless your doctor tells you to do so.

- For *injection* dosage form:
  —For pain:
    - Adults—30 mcg per hour given as a continuous infusion.
    - Children—Dosage is based on body weight and must be determined by your doctor.

Missed dose—Tell your doctor immediately if you think the clonidine has stopped for any reason.

Storage—To store this medicine:
- Keep out of the reach of children.
- Store away from heat and direct light.
- Keep the medicine from freezing. Do not refrigerate.
- Discard any unused portion of medicine.
- Do not keep outdated medicine or medicine no longer needed. Be sure that any discarded medicine is out of the reach of children.

Precautions While Using This Medicine

This medicine should not be stopped without the doctor's supervision. Serious side effects may occur if clonidine is stopped suddenly.

This medicine may add to the effects of alcohol and other CNS depressants (medicine that may make you drowsy or less alert). Check with your doctor before taking any such depressants while you are using this medicine.

Dizziness, lightheadedness, or fainting may occur, especially when you get up from a lying or sitting position. Getting up slowly may help.

This medicine may cause some people to become drowsy or less alert than they are normally. *Make sure you know how you react to this medicine before you drive, use machines, or do other jobs that require you to be alert.*

Side Effects of This Medicine

Along with its needed effects, a medicine may cause some unwanted effects. Although not all of these side effects may occur, if they do occur they may need medical attention.

Check with your doctor as soon as possible if any of the following side effects occur:

More common
    Dizziness, lightheadedness, or fainting; slow heartbeat
Less common
    Chest pain; extremely shallow or slow breathing; fast heartbeat; fever; hallucinations (seeing, feeling, or hearing things that are not there); mental depression; sleepiness (excessive); vomiting

Other side effects may occur that usually do not need medical attention. These side effects may go away during treatment as your body adjusts to the medicine. However, check with your doctor if any of the following side effects continue or are bothersome:

More common
    Anxiety; confusion; dry mouth; nausea; sleepiness
Less common
    Constipation; ringing, buzzing, or other unexplained noises in the ears; sweating, unusual; weakness

If clonidine use is suddenly stopped, check with your doctor immediately. If you notice any of the following symptoms, report them to your doctor:
    Agitation; headache; nervousness; pounding heartbeat; shaking or trembling

Other side effects not listed above may also occur in some patients. If you notice any other effects, check with your doctor.

Developed: 08/14/98

CLONIDINE   Systemic

Commonly used brand name(s):

In the U.S.—

Catapres	Catapres-TTS-2
Catapres-TTS-1	Catapres-TTS-3

Generic name product may be available.

In Canada—
  Catapres
  Dixarit

Description

Clonidine (KLON-i-deen) belongs to the general class of medicines called antihypertensives. It is used to treat high blood pressure (hypertension).

High blood pressure adds to the work load of the heart and arteries. If it continues for a long time, the heart and arteries may not function properly. This can damage the blood vessels of the brain, heart, and kidneys, resulting in a stroke, heart failure, or kidney failure. Hypertension may also increase the risk of heart attacks. These problems may be less likely to occur if blood pressure is controlled.

Clonidine works by controlling nerve impulses along certain nerve pathways. As a result, it relaxes blood vessels so that blood passes through them more easily. This helps to lower blood pressure.

Clonidine may also be used for other conditions as determined by your doctor.

Clonidine is available only with your doctor's prescription, in the following dosage forms:

Oral
  • Tablets (U.S. and Canada)
Transdermal
  • Skin patch (U.S.)

Before Using This Medicine

In deciding to use a medicine, the risks of taking the medicine must be weighed against the good it will do. This is a decision you and your doctor will make. For clonidine, the following should be considered:

Allergies—Tell your doctor if you have ever had any unusual or allergic reaction to clonidine. Also tell your health care professional if you are allergic to any other substance, such as foods, preservatives, or dyes.

Pregnancy—Clonidine has not been studied in pregnant women. However, studies in animals have shown that clonidine causes harmful effects in the fetus, but not birth defects.

Breast-feeding—Although clonidine passes into breast milk, it has not been reported to cause problems in nursing babies.

Children—Children may be more sensitive than adults to clonidine. Clonidine overdose has been reported when children accidentally took this medicine.

Older adults—Dizziness or faintness may be more likely to occur in the elderly, who are more sensitive than younger adults to the effects of clonidine.

Other medicines—Although certain medicines should not be used together at all, in other cases two different medicines may be used together even if an interaction might occur. In these cases, your doctor may want to change the dose, or other precautions may be necessary. When you are taking clonidine, it is especially important that your health care professional know if you are taking any of the following:
  • Beta-blockers (acebutolol [e.g., Sectral], atenolol [e.g., Tenormin], betaxolol [e.g., Kerlone], carteolol [e.g., Cartrol], labetalol [e.g., Normodyne], metoprolol [e.g., Lopressor], nadolol [e.g., Corgard], oxprenolol [e.g., Trasicor], penbutolol [e.g., Levatol], pindolol [e.g., Visken],

propranolol [e.g., Inderal], sotalol [e.g., Sotacor], timolol [e.g., Blocadren])—These medicines may increase the risk of harmful effects when clonidine treatment is stopped suddenly
  • Tricyclic antidepressants (amitriptyline [e.g., Elavil], amoxapine [e.g., Asendin], clomipramine [e.g., Anafranil], desipramine [e.g., Pertofrane], doxepin [e.g., Sinequan], imipramine [e.g., Tofranil], nortriptyline [e.g., Aventyl], protriptyline [e.g., Vivactil], trimipramine [e.g., Surmontil])—These medicines may decrease clonidine's effects on blood pressure

Other medical problems—The presence of other medical problems may affect the use of clonidine. Make sure you tell your doctor if you have any other medical problems, especially:
  • Heart or blood vessel disease—Clonidine may make these conditions worse
  • Irritated or scraped skin (with transdermal system [skin patch] only)—The effects of clonidine may be increased if the skin patch is placed on an area of scraped or irritated skin because more medicine is absorbed into the body
  • Kidney disease—Effects of clonidine may be increased because of slower removal of clonidine from the body
  • Mental depression (history of) or
  • Raynaud's syndrome—Clonidine may make these conditions worse
  • Polyarteritis nodosa or
  • Scleroderma or
  • Systemic lupus erythematosus (SLE) (with transdermal system [skin patch] only)—Effects of clonidine may be decreased because absorption of this medicine into the body is blocked

Proper Use of This Medicine

For patients taking this medicine *for high blood pressure:*
  • In addition to the use of the medicine your doctor has prescribed, treatment for your high blood pressure may include weight control and care in the types of foods you eat, especially foods high in sodium. Your doctor will tell you which of these are most important for you. You should check with your doctor before changing your diet.
  • Many patients who have high blood pressure will not notice any signs of the problem. In fact, many may feel normal. It is very important that you *take your medicine exactly as directed* and that you keep your appointments with your doctor even if you feel well.
  • Remember that this medicine will not cure your high blood pressure but it does help control it. Therefore, you must continue to use it as directed if you expect to lower your blood pressure and keep it down. *You may have to take high blood pressure medicine for the rest of your life*. If high blood pressure is not treated, it can cause serious problems such as heart failure, blood vessel disease, stroke, or kidney disease.

For patients using the *transdermal system (skin patch):*
  • *Use this medicine exactly as directed by your doctor*. It will work only if applied correctly. *This medicine usually comes with patient instructions. Read them carefully before using.*
  • Do not try to trim or cut the adhesive patch to adjust the

dosage. Check with your doctor if you think the medicine is not working as it should.

- Apply the patch to a clean, dry area of skin on your upper arm or chest. Choose an area with little or no hair and free of scars, cuts, or irritation.
- The system should stay in place even during showering, bathing, or swimming. If the patch becomes loose, cover it with the extra adhesive overlay provided. Apply a new patch if the first one becomes too loose or falls off.
- Each dose is best applied to a different area of skin to prevent skin problems or other irritation.
- After removing a used patch, fold the patch in half with the sticky sides together. Make sure to dispose of it out of the reach of children.

To help you remember to use your medicine, try to get into the habit of using it at regular times. If you are taking the tablets, take them at the same time each day. If you are using the transdermal system (skin patch), try to change it at the same time and day of the week.

Dosing—The dose of clonidine will be different for different patients. *Follow your doctor's orders or the directions on the label.* The following information includes only the average doses of clonidine used for the treatment of high blood pressure. *If your dose is different, do not change it* unless your doctor tells you to do so:

- For *oral* dosage form (tablets):
  —For high blood pressure:
  - Adults—100 mcg (0.1 mg) two times a day. Your doctor may increase your dose up to 200 mcg (0.2 mg) to 600 mcg (0.6 mg) a day taken in divided doses.
  - Children—Use and dose must be determined by your doctor.
- For *transdermal* dosage form (skin patch):
  —For high blood pressure:
  - Adults—One transdermal dosage system (skin patch) applied once a week.
  - Children—Use and dose must be determined by your doctor.

Missed dose—If you miss a dose of this medicine, take it or use it as soon as possible. Then go back to your regular dosing schedule. *If you miss two or more doses of the tablets in a row or if you miss changing the transdermal patch for 3 or more days, check with your doctor right away.* If your body goes without this medicine for too long, your blood pressure may go up to a dangerously high level and some unpleasant effects may occur.

Storage—To store this medicine:

- Keep out of the reach of children.
- Store away from heat and direct light.
- Do not store in the bathroom, near the kitchen sink, or in other damp places. Heat or moisture may cause the medicine to break down.
- Do not keep outdated medicine or medicine no longer needed. Be sure that any discarded medicine is out of the reach of children.

Precautions While Using This Medicine

It is important that your doctor check your progress at regular visits to make sure that this medicine is working properly.

Check with your doctor before you stop using this medicine. Your doctor may want you to reduce gradually the amount you are using before stopping completely.

Make sure that you have enough clonidine on hand to last through weekends, holidays, or vacations. You should not miss any doses. You may want to ask your doctor for another written prescription for clonidine to carry in your wallet or purse. You can then have it filled if you run out of medicine when you are away from home.

For patients taking this medicine *for high blood pressure:*

- *Do not take other medicines unless they have been discussed with your doctor.* This especially includes over-the-counter (nonprescription) medicines for appetite control, asthma, colds, cough, hay fever, or sinus problems, since they may tend to increase your blood pressure.

Clonidine will add to the effects of alcohol and other central nervous system (CNS) depressants (medicines that slow down the nervous system, possibly causing drowsiness). Some examples of CNS depressants are antihistamines or medicine for hay fever, other allergies, or colds; sedatives, tranquilizers, or sleeping medicine; prescription pain medicine or narcotics; barbiturates; medicine for seizures; muscle relaxants; or anesthetics, including some dental anesthetics. *Check with your doctor before taking any of the above while you are using this medicine.*

Clonidine may cause some people to become drowsy or less alert than they are normally. This is more likely to happen when you begin to take it or when you increase the amount of medicine you are taking. *Make sure you know how you react to this medicine before you drive, use machines, or do anything else that could be dangerous if you are not alert.*

Before having any kind of surgery (including dental surgery) or emergency treatment, *tell the medical doctor or dentist in charge that you are using this medicine.*

Dizziness, lightheadedness, or fainting may occur after you take this medicine, especially when you get up from a lying or sitting position. Getting up slowly may help, but if the problem continues or gets worse, check with your doctor.

The dizziness, lightheadedness, or fainting is also more likely to occur if you drink alcohol, stand for long periods of time, exercise, or if the weather is hot. While you are taking clonidine, be careful to limit the amount of alcohol you drink. Also, use extra care during exercise or hot weather or if you must stand for a long time.

Clonidine may cause dryness of the mouth. For temporary relief, use sugarless candy or gum, melt bits of ice in your mouth, or use a saliva substitute. However, if your mouth continues to feel dry for more than 2 weeks, check with your medical doctor or dentist. Continuing dryness of the mouth may increase the chance of dental disease, including tooth decay, gum disease, and fungus infections.

Side Effects of This Medicine

Along with its needed effects, a medicine may cause some unwanted effects. Although not all of these side effects may occur, if they do occur they may need medical attention.

Check with your doctor immediately if any of the following side effects occur:

Signs and symptoms of overdose
>Difficulty in breathing; dizziness (extreme) or faintness; feeling cold; pinpoint pupils of eyes; slow heartbeat; unusual tiredness or weakness (extreme)

Check with your doctor as soon as possible if any of the following side effects occur:

More common—with transdermal system (skin patch) only
>Itching or redness of skin

Less common
>Mental depression; swelling of feet and lower legs

Rare
>Paleness or cold feeling in fingertips and toes; vivid dreams or nightmares

Other side effects may occur that usually do not need medical attention. These side effects may go away during treatment as your body adjusts to the medicine. However, check with your doctor if any of the following side effects continue or are bothersome:

More common
>Constipation; dizziness; drowsiness; dryness of mouth; unusual tiredness or weakness

Less common
>Darkening of skin—with transdermal system (skin patch) only; decreased sexual ability; dizziness, lightheadedness, or fainting, especially when getting up from a lying or sitting position; dry, itching, or burning eyes; loss of appetite; nausea or vomiting; nervousness

After you have been using this medicine for a while, it may cause unpleasant or even harmful effects if you stop taking it too suddenly. After you stop taking this medicine, *check with your doctor immediately* if any of the following occur:
>Anxiety or tenseness; chest pain; fast or pounding heartbeat; headache; increased salivation; nausea; nervousness; restlessness; shaking or trembling of hands and fingers; stomach cramps; sweating; trouble in sleeping; vomiting

Other side effects not listed above may also occur in some patients. If you notice any other effects, check with your doctor.

Additional Information

Once a medicine has been approved for marketing for a certain use, experience may show that it is also useful for other medical problems. Although these uses are not included in product labeling, clonidine is used in certain patients with the following medical conditions:

- Migraine headache
- Symptoms associated with menopause or menstrual discomfort
- Symptoms of withdrawal associated with alcohol, nicotine, or narcotics
- Gilles de la Tourette's syndrome

Other than the above information, there is no additional information relating to proper use, precautions, or side effects for these uses.

Revised: 05/21/99

CLONIDINE AND CHLORTHALIDONE   Systemic†

Commonly used brand name(s):

In the U.S.—
>Combipres
>Generic name product may be available.

†Not commercially available in Canada.

Description

Clonidine and chlorthalidone (KLOE-ni-deen and klor-THAL-i-done) combinations are used in the treatment of high blood pressure (hypertension).

High blood pressure adds to the work load of the heart and arteries. If it continues for a long time, the heart and arteries may not function properly. This can damage the blood vessels of the brain, heart, and kidneys resulting in a stroke, heart failure, or kidney failure. Hypertension may also increase the risk of heart attacks. These problems may be less likely to occur if blood pressure is controlled.

Clonidine works by controlling nerve impulses along certain body nerve pathways. As a result, it relaxes blood vessels so that blood passes through them more easily. The chlorthalidone in this combination is a diuretic (water pill) that helps reduce the amount of water in the body by increasing the flow of urine.

Clonidine and chlorthalidone combination is available only with your doctor's prescription, in the following dosage form:
Oral
- Tablets (U.S.)

Before Using This Medicine

In deciding to use a medicine, the risks of taking the medicine must be weighed against the good it will do. This is a decision you and your doctor will make. For clonidine and chlorthalidone, the following should be considered:

Allergies—Tell your doctor if you have ever had any unusual or allergic reaction to clonidine (oral or skin patch form), chlorthalidone, sulfonamides (sulfa drugs), or other thiazide diuretics (water pills). Also tell your health care professional if you are allergic to any other substance, such as foods, preservatives, or dyes.

Pregnancy—Clonidine has not been studied in pregnant women. However, studies in animals have shown that clonidine does not cause birth defects but does cause other harmful effects in the fetus. When chlorthalidone is used during pregnancy, it may cause side effects including jaundice, blood problems, and low potassium in the newborn infant. Be sure you have discussed this with your doctor before taking this medicine.

Breast-feeding—Both clonidine and chlorthalidone pass into breast milk. Chlorthalidone may decrease the flow of breast milk. Therefore, you should avoid use of clonidine and chlorthalidone combination during the first month of breast-feeding.

Children—Studies on this medicine have been done only in adult patients, and there is no specific information comparing use of clonidine and chlorthalidone combination in children with use in other age groups. However, children may be more sensitive than adults to clonidine. Clonidine overdose has been reported when children accidentally took this medicine.

Older adults—Dizziness or lightheadedness and signs of too much potassium loss may be more likely to occur in the elderly, who are more sensitive to the effects of clonidine and chlorthalidone.

Other medicines—Although certain medicines should not be used together at all, in other cases two different medicines may be used together even if an interaction might occur. In these cases, your doctor may want to change the dose, or other precautions may be necessary. When you are taking clonidine and chlorthalidone, it is especially important that your health care professional know if you are taking any of the following:

- Beta-adrenergic blocking agents (acebutolol [e.g., Sectral], atenolol [e.g., Tenormin], betaxolol [e.g., Kerlone], bisoprolol [e.g., Zebeta], carteolol [e.g., Cartrol], labetalol [e.g., Normodyne], metoprolol [e.g., Lopressor], nadolol [e.g., Corgard], oxprenolol [e.g., Trasicor], penbutolol [e.g., Levatol], pindolol [e.g., Visken], propranolol [e.g., Inderal], sotalol [e.g., Betapace, Sotacor], timolol [e.g., Blocadren])—These medicines may increase the risk of harmful effects when clonidine and chlorthalidone combination treatment is stopped suddenly

- Cholestyramine or
- Colestipol—Use with clonidine and chlorthalidone combination may prevent the chlorthalidone portion of the medicine from working properly; take clonidine and chlorthalidone combination at least 1 hour before or 4 hours after cholestyramine or colestipol

- Digitalis glycosides (heart medicine)—This medicine may cause low potassium in the blood, which may increase the chance of side effects of digitalis glycosides

- Lithium (e.g., Lithane)—Use with clonidine and chlorthalidone combination may cause high blood levels of lithium, which may increase the chance of side effects

- Tricyclic antidepressants (amitriptyline [e.g., Elavil], amoxapine [e.g., Asendin], clomipramine [e.g., Anafranil], desipramine [e.g., Pertofrane], doxepin [e.g., Sinequan], imipramine [e.g., Tofranil], nortriptyline [e.g., Aventyl], protriptyline [e.g., Vivactil], trimipramine [e.g., Surmontil])—These medicines may decrease the effects of clonidine and chlorthalidone combination on blood pressure

Other medical problems—The presence of other medical problems may affect the use of clonidine and chlorthalidone. Make sure you tell your doctor if you have any other medical problems, especially:

- Diabetes mellitus (sugar diabetes)—This medicine may change the amount of diabetes medicine needed

- Gout—This medicine may increase the amount of uric acid in the blood, which can lead to gout

- Heart or blood vessel disease or
- Lupus erythematosus (history of) or
- Mental depression (history of) or
- Pancreatitis (inflammation of the pancreas) or
- Raynaud's syndrome—This medicine may make these conditions worse

- Kidney disease—Effects of this medicine may be increased because of slower removal from the body. If kidney disease is severe, the chlorthalidone portion of this medicine may not work

- Liver disease—If this medicine causes loss of too much water from the body, liver disease can become much worse

Proper Use of This Medicine

This medicine may cause you to have an unusual feeling of tiredness when you begin to take it. You may also notice an increase in the amount of urine or in your frequency of urination. After taking the medicine for a while, these effects should lessen. It is best to plan your doses according to a schedule that will least affect your personal activities and sleep. Ask your health care professional to help you plan the best time to take this medicine.

In addition to the use of the medicine your doctor has prescribed, appropriate treatment for your high blood pressure may include weight control and care in the types of foods you eat, especially foods high in sodium. Your doctor will tell you which factors are most important for you. You should check with your doctor before changing your diet.

Many patients who have high blood pressure will not notice any signs of the problem. In fact, many may feel normal. It is very important that you *take your medicine exactly as directed* and that you keep your appointments with your doctor even if you feel well.

Remember that this medicine will not cure your high blood pressure but it does help control it. Therefore, you must continue to take it as directed if you expect to lower your blood pressure and keep it down. *You may have to take high blood pressure medicine for the rest of your life*. If high blood pressure is not treated, it can cause serious problems such as heart failure, blood vessel disease, stroke, or kidney disease.

To help you remember to take your medicine, try to get into the habit of taking it at the same time each day.

Dosing—The dose of clonidine and chlorthalidone combination will be different for different patients. *Follow your doctor's orders or the directions on the label*. The following information includes only the average doses of clonidine and chlorthalidone combination. *If your dose is different, do not change it* unless your doctor tells you to do so.

The number of tablets that you take depends on the strength of the medicine.

- For *oral* dosage form (tablets):
  —For high blood pressure:
  - Adults—1 tablet one or two times a day.
  - Children—Use and dose must be determined by your doctor.

Missed dose—If you miss a dose of this medicine, take it as soon as possible. Then go back to your regular dosing schedule. *If you miss two or more doses in a row, check with your doctor right away*. If your body goes without this medicine for too long, your blood pressure may go up to a dangerously high level and some unpleasant effects may occur.

Storage—To store this medicine:
- Keep out of the reach of children.
- Store away from heat and direct light.
- Do not store in the bathroom, near the kitchen sink, or in other damp places. Heat or moisture may cause the medicine to break down.

- Do not keep outdated medicine or medicine no longer needed. Be sure that any discarded medicine is out of the reach of children.

Precautions While Using This Medicine

It is important that your doctor check your progress at regular visits to make sure that this medicine is working properly.

Check with your doctor before you stop taking this medicine. Your doctor may want you to reduce gradually the amount you are taking before stopping the medicine completely.

Make sure that you have enough medicine on hand to last through weekends, holidays, or vacations. You should not miss taking any doses. You may want to ask your doctor for another written prescription to carry in your wallet or purse. You can then have it filled if you run out of medicine when you are away from home.

Before having any kind of surgery (including dental surgery) or emergency treatment, *make sure the medical doctor or dentist in charge knows that you are taking this medicine.*

Do not take other medicines unless they have been discussed with your doctor. This especially includes over-the-counter (nonprescription) medicines for appetite control, asthma, colds, cough, hay fever, or sinus problems, since they may tend to increase your blood pressure.

This medicine will add to the effects of alcohol and other central nervous system (CNS) depressants (medicines that slow down the nervous system, possibly causing drowsiness). Some examples of CNS depressants are antihistamines or medicine for hay fever, other allergies, or colds; sedatives, tranquilizers, or sleeping medicine; prescription pain medicine or narcotics; barbiturates; medicine for seizures; muscle relaxants; or anesthetics, including some dental anesthetics. *Check with your doctor before taking any of the above while you are using this medicine.*

This medicine may cause some people to become drowsy or less alert than they are normally. This is more likely to happen when you begin to take it or when you increase the amount of medicine you are taking. *Make sure you know how you react to this medicine before you drive, use machines, or do anything else that could be dangerous if you are not alert.*

Dizziness, lightheadedness, or fainting may occur, especially when you get up from a lying or sitting position. Getting up slowly may help, but if the problem continues or gets worse, check with your doctor.

The dizziness, lightheadedness, or fainting is also more likely to occur if you drink alcohol, stand for long periods of time, exercise, or if the weather is hot. Drinking alcoholic beverages may also make the drowsiness worse. While you are taking this medicine, be careful to limit the amount of alcohol you drink. Also, use extra care during exercise or hot weather or if you must stand for long periods of time.

This medicine may cause a loss of potassium from your body.
- To help prevent this, your doctor may want you to:
  —eat or drink foods that have a high potassium content (for example, orange or other citrus fruit juices), or
  —take a potassium supplement, or
  —take another medicine to help prevent the loss of the potassium in the first place.

- It is very important to follow these directions. Also, it is important not to change your diet on your own. This is more important if you are already on a special diet (as for diabetes), or if you are taking a potassium supplement or a medicine to reduce potassium loss. Extra potassium may not be necessary and, in some cases, too much potassium could be harmful.

Check with your doctor if you become sick and have severe or continuing vomiting or diarrhea. These problems may cause you to lose additional water and potassium.

For *patients with diabetes:*
- The chlorthalidone contained in this medicine may raise blood sugar levels. While you are using this medicine, be sure to test your blood sugar (glucose) level, or test for sugar in your urine.

This medicine may cause your skin to be more sensitive to sunlight than it is normally. Exposure to sunlight, even for brief periods of time, may cause a skin rash, itching, redness or other discoloration of the skin, or a severe sunburn. When you begin taking this medicine:
- Stay out of direct sunlight, especially between the hours of 10:00 a.m. and 3:00 p.m., if possible.
- Wear protective clothing, including a hat. Also, wear sunglasses.
- Apply a sun block product that has a skin protection factor (SPF) of at least 15. Some patients may require a product with a higher SPF number, especially if they have a fair complexion. If you have any questions about this, check with your health care professional.
- Apply a sun block for lips that has an SPF of at least 15 to protect your lips.
- Do not use a sunlamp or tanning bed or booth.

If you have a severe reaction from the sun, check with your doctor.

This medicine may cause dryness of the mouth. For temporary relief, use sugarless candy or gum, melt bits of ice in your mouth, or use a saliva substitute. However, if your mouth continues to feel dry for more than 2 weeks, check with your medical doctor or dentist. Continuing dryness of the mouth may increase the chance of dental disease, including tooth decay, gum disease, and fungus infections.

Side Effects of This Medicine

Along with its needed effects, a medicine may cause some unwanted effects. Although not all of these side effects may occur, if they do occur they may need medical attention.

Check with your doctor immediately if any of the following side effects occur:
Signs and symptoms of overdose
Difficulty in breathing; dizziness (extreme) or faintness; feeling cold; pinpoint pupils of eyes; slow heartbeat; unusual tiredness or weakness (extreme)

Check with your doctor as soon as possible if any of the following side effects occur:
Signs and symptoms of too much potassium loss
Dryness of mouth; increased thirst; irregular heartbeat; mood or mental changes; muscle cramps or pain; nausea or vomiting; weak pulse
Signs and symptoms of too much sodium loss
Confusion; convulsions (seizures); decreased mental activity; irritability; muscle cramps; unusual tiredness or weakness

Less common

Mental depression; swelling of feet and lower legs

Rare

Black, tarry stools; blood in urine or stools; cough or hoarseness; fever or chills; joint pain; lower back or side pain; paleness or cold feeling in fingertips and toes; pinpoint red spots on skin; skin rash or hives; stomach pain (severe) with nausea and vomiting; unusual bleeding or bruising; vivid dreams or nightmares; yellow eyes or skin

Other side effects may occur that usually do not need medical attention. These side effects may go away during treatment as your body adjusts to the medicine. However, check with your doctor if any of the following side effects continue or are bothersome:

More common

Constipation; dizziness; drowsiness; dryness of mouth; unusual tiredness or weakness

Less common

Decreased sexual ability; diarrhea; dizziness or lightheadedness when getting up from a lying or sitting position; dry, itching, or burning eyes; increased sensitivity of skin to sunlight; loss of appetite; nausea or vomiting; nervousness; upset stomach

After you have been using this medicine for a while, it may cause unpleasant or even harmful effects if you stop taking it too suddenly. After you stop taking this medicine, check with your doctor if any of the following occur:

Anxiety or tenseness; chest pain; fast or pounding heartbeat; headache; increased salivation; nausea; nervousness; restlessness; shaking or trembling of hands and fingers; stomach cramps; sweating; trouble in sleeping; vomiting

Other side effects not listed above may also occur in some patients. If you notice any other effects, check with your doctor.

Revised: 05/21/99

CLOPIDOGREL   Systemic

Commonly used brand name(s):

In the U.S.—
Plavix

Description

Clopidogrel (kloh-PID-oh-grel) is used to lessen the chance of heart attack or stroke. It is given to people who have already had a heart attack or stroke or to people with other blood circulation problems that could lead to a stroke or heart attack.

A heart attack or stroke may occur when a blood vessel in the heart or brain is blocked by a blood clot. Clopidogrel reduces the chance that a harmful blood clot will form by preventing certain cells in the blood from clumping together. This effect of clopidogrel may also increase the chance of serious bleeding in some people.

This medicine is available only with your doctor's prescription, in the following dosage form(s):

Oral
- Tablets (U.S.)

Before Using This Medicine

In deciding to use a medicine, the risks of taking the medicine must be weighed against the good it will do. This is a decision you and your doctor will make. For clopidogrel, the following should be considered:

Allergies—Tell your doctor if you have ever had any unusual or allergic reaction to clopidogrel. Also tell your health care professional if you are allergic to any other substances, such as foods, preservatives, or dyes.

Pregnancy—Studies with clopidogrel have not been done in pregnant women. This medicine did not cause birth defects in animal studies. However, discuss with your doctor whether or not you should take this medicine if you are pregnant.

Breast-feeding—It is not known whether clopidogrel passes into breast milk. Although most medicines pass into breast milk in small amounts, many of them may be used safely while breast-feeding. Mothers who are taking this medicine and who wish to breast-feed should discuss this with their doctor.

Children—There is no specific information comparing use of clopidogrel in children with use in other age groups.

Older adults—Although blood levels of clopidogrel may be higher in elderly patients than in younger adults, it is not expected to cause different side effects or problems in older people than it does in other adults.

Other medicines—Although certain medicines should not be used together at all, in other cases two different medicines may be used together even if an interaction might occur. In these cases, your doctor may want to change the dose, or other precautions may be necessary. When you are taking clopidogrel, it is especially important that your health care professional know if you are taking any of the following:

- Inflammation or pain medicine, except narcotics—The chance of serious bleeding may be increased

Other medical problems—The presence of other medical problems may affect the use of clopidogrel. Make sure you tell your doctor if you have any other medical problems, especially:

- Bleeding problems or
- Liver disease (severe) or
- Stomach ulcers—The chance of serious bleeding may be increased

Proper Use of This Medicine

Take this medicine only as directed by your doctor. Clopidogrel will not work properly if you take less of it than directed. Taking more clopidogrel than directed may increase the chance of serious side effects without increasing the helpful effects.

Dosing—The dose of clopidogrel may be different for different patients. *Follow your doctor's orders or the directions on the label.* The following information includes only the average dose of clopidogrel. *If your dose is different, do not change it* unless your doctor tells you to do so.

- For *oral* dosage form (tablets):
  —For prevention of heart attacks or strokes:
  - Adults—1 tablet (75 milligrams [mg]) once a day.
  - Children—It is not likely that clopidogrel would be used to help prevent heart attacks or strokes in children. If a child needs this medicine, however, the dose would have to be determined by the doctor.

Missed dose—If you miss a dose of this medicine, take it as soon as possible. However, if it is almost time for the next dose, skip the missed dose and go back to your regular dosing schedule. Do not double doses.

Storage—To store this medicine:
- Keep out of the reach of children.
- Store away from heat and direct light.
- Do not store in the bathroom, near the kitchen sink, or in other damp places. Heat or moisture may cause the medicine to break down.
- Do not keep outdated medicine or medicine no longer needed. Be sure that any discarded medicine is out of the reach of children.

Precautions While Using This Medicine

Tell all medical doctors, dentists, nurses, and pharmacists you go to that you are taking this medicine. Clopidogrel may increase the risk of serious bleeding during an operation or some kinds of dental work. Therefore, treatment may have to be stopped about 7 days before the operation or dental work is done.

Check with your doctor immediately if you notice bruising or bleeding, especially bleeding that is hard to stop. Bleeding inside the body sometimes appears as bloody or black, tarry stools, or faintness.

Side Effects of This Medicine

Along with its needed effects, a medicine may cause some unwanted effects. Although not all of these side effects may occur, if they do occur they may need medical attention.

Check with your doctor immediately if any of the following side effects occur:

More common
  Red or purple spots on skin, varying in size from pinpoint to large bruises

Less common
  Nosebleed; vomiting of blood or material that looks like coffee grounds

Rare
  Black, tarry stools; blistering, flaking, or peeling of skin; blood in urine or stools; fever, chills, or sore throat; headache (sudden, severe); stomach pain (severe); ulcers, sores, or white spots in mouth; unusual bleeding or bruising; weakness (sudden)

Also, check with your doctor as soon as possible if any of the following side effects occur:

More common
  Chest pain; cough; generalized pain; runny nose; sneezing

Less common
  Fainting; frequent urination; irregular heartbeat; joint pain; painful or difficult urination; shortness of breath; swelling of feet or lower legs

Other side effects may occur that usually do not need medical attention. These side effects may go away during treatment as your body adjusts to the medicine. However, check with your doctor if any of the following side effects continue or are bothersome:

More common
  Abdominal or stomach pain (mild); aching muscles; back pain; dizziness; general feeling of discomfort or illness; headache; heartburn

Less common
  Anxiety; constipation; diarrhea; itching; leg cramps; mental depression; numbness or tingling; nausea; skin rash; trouble in sleeping; unusual tiredness; vomiting; weakness

Other side effects not listed above may also occur in some patients. If you notice any other effects, check with your doctor.

Developed: 05/22/98

CLOTRIMAZOLE   Oral†

Commonly used brand name(s):

In the U.S.—
  Mycelex Troches

†Not commercially available in Canada.

Description

Clotrimazole (kloe-TRIM-a-zole) lozenges are dissolved slowly in the mouth to prevent and treat thrush. Thrush, also called candidiasis or white mouth, is a fungus infection of the mouth and throat. This medicine may also be used for other problems as determined by your doctor.

Clotrimazole is available only with your doctor's prescription, in the following dosage form:

Oral
- Lozenges (U.S.)

Before Using This Medicine

In deciding to use a medicine, the risks of taking the medicine must be weighed against the good it will do. This is a decision you and your doctor will make. For clotrimazole, the following should be considered:

Allergies—Tell your doctor if you have ever had any unusual or allergic reaction to clotrimazole. Also tell your health care professional if you are allergic to any other substances, such as foods, preservatives, or dyes.

Pregnancy—Studies have not been done in humans. Studies in mice, rats, and rabbits given very high doses have not shown that clotrimazole causes birth defects. However, studies in rats and mice given high doses have shown that clotrimazole lozenges may cause other harmful effects in the fetus.

Breast-feeding—It is not known whether clotrimazole passes into breast milk. However, only small amounts of clotrimazole are absorbed into the mother's body. Clotrimazole has not been reported to cause problems in nursing babies.

Children—Although this medicine has not been shown to cause different side effects or problems in children than it does in adults, it should not be given to children under 3 years of age since they may be too young to use the lozenges safely.

Older adults—Many medicines have not been studied specifically in older people. Therefore, it may not be known whether they work exactly the same way they do in younger adults. Although there is no specific information comparing use of clotrimazole lozenges in the elderly with use in other age groups, this medicine is not expected to cause different side effects or problems in older people than it does in younger adults.

Other medicines—Although certain medicines should not be used together at all, in other cases two different medicines may be used together even if an interaction might occur. In these cases, your doctor may want to change the dose, or other precautions may be necessary. Tell your health care professional if you are taking any other prescription or nonprescription (over-the-counter [OTC]) medicine.

Other medical problems—The presence of other medical problems may affect the use of clotrimazole. Make sure you tell your doctor if you have the following medical condition:

- Liver disease—Your doctor may want to monitor your liver function while you are taking this medicine.

Proper Use of This Medicine

Clotrimazole lozenges should be held in the mouth and allowed to dissolve slowly and completely. This may take 15 to 30 minutes. Swallow saliva during this time. *Do not chew the lozenges or swallow them whole.*

Do not give clotrimazole lozenges to infants or children under 3 years of age. They may be too young to use the lozenges safely.

To help clear up your infection completely, *it is very important that you keep using clotrimazole for the full time of treatment,* even if your symptoms begin to clear up after a few days. Since fungus infections may be very slow to clear up, you may have to continue using this medicine every day for two weeks or more. If you stop using this medicine too soon, your symptoms may return. *Do not miss any doses.*

Dosing—The dose of clotrimazole lozenges will be different for different patients. *Follow your doctor's orders or the directions on the label.* The following information includes only the average doses of clotrimazole lozenges. *If your dose is different, do not change it* unless your doctor tells you to do so.

- For the *treatment of thrush:*
  —Adults and children 3 years of age and older: Dissolve one 10-milligram lozenge slowly and completely in your mouth; this dose should be taken five times a day for at least fourteen days.
  —Children up to 3 years of age: This medicine is not recommended in children under 3 years of age since they may be too young to use the lozenges safely.
- For the *prevention of thrush:*
  —Adults and children 3 years of age and older: Dissolve one 10-milligram lozenge slowly and completely in your mouth; this dose should be taken three times a day.

—Children up to 3 years of age: This medicine is not recommended in children under 3 years of age since they may be too young to use the lozenges safely.

Missed dose—If you miss a dose of this medicine, take it as soon as possible. However, if it is almost time for your next dose, skip the missed dose and go back to your regular dosing schedule.

Storage—To store this medicine:
- Keep out of the reach of children.
- Store away from heat and direct light.
- Do not store in the bathroom, near the kitchen sink, or in other damp places. Heat or moisture may cause the medicine to break down.
- Do not keep outdated medicine or medicine no longer needed. Be sure that any discarded medicine is out of the reach of children.

Precautions While Using This Medicine

If your symptoms do not improve within 1 week, or if they become worse, check with your doctor.

Side Effects of This Medicine

Along with its needed effects, a medicine may cause some unwanted effects. The following side effects may go away during treatment as your body adjusts to the medicine. However, check with your doctor if any of these effects continue or are bothersome:

More common
  Abdominal or stomach cramping or pain; diarrhea; itching; nausea or vomiting; unpleasant mouth sensations

Note: Some of the side effects, such as abdominal or stomach cramping or pain or diarrhea, usually occur only when the medicine is swallowed

Other side effects not listed above may also occur in some patients. If you notice any other effects, check with your doctor.

Revised: 10/31/99

CLOTRIMAZOLE   Topical

Commonly used brand name(s):

In the U.S.—

Lotrimin AF Cream	Lotrimin Lotion
Lotrimin AF Lotion	Lotrimin Solution
Lotrimin AF Solution	Mycelex Cream
Lotrimin Cream	Mycelex Solution

Generic name product may be available.

In Canada—

Canesten Cream	Myclo Cream
Canesten Solution	Myclo Solution
Canesten Solution with	Myclo Spray Solution
Atomizer	Neo-Zol Cream
Clotrimaderm Cream	

Description

Clotrimazole (kloe-TRIM-a-zole) topical preparations are used to treat fungus infections.

Some of these preparations are available only with your doctor's prescription. Others are available without a prescription; however, your doctor may have special instructions on the proper dose for your medical condition.

Clotrimazole is available in the following dosage forms:

Topical
- Cream (U.S. and Canada)
- Lotion (U.S.)
- Solution (U.S. and Canada)

Before Using This Medicine

If you are using this medicine without a prescription, carefully read and follow any precautions on the label. For topical clotrimazole, the following should be considered:

Allergies—Tell your doctor if you have ever had any unusual or allergic reaction to clotrimazole. Also tell your health care professional if you are allergic to any other substances, such as preservatives or dyes.

Pregnancy—Clotrimazole has not been studied in pregnant women during the first trimester (3 months). However, clotrimazole used vaginally during the second and third trimesters has not been shown to cause birth defects or other problems in humans.

Breast-feeding—It is not known whether topical clotrimazole passes into the breast milk. Although most medicines pass into breast milk in small amounts, many of them may be used safely while breast-feeding. Mothers who are using this medicine and who wish to breast-feed should discuss this with their doctor.

Children—This medicine has been tested in children and, in effective doses, has not been shown to cause different side effects or problems than it does in adults.

Older adults—Many medicines have not been studied specifically in older people. Therefore, it may not be known whether they work exactly the same way they do in younger adults. Although there is no specific information comparing use of topical clotrimazole in the elderly with use in other age groups, this medicine is not expected to cause different side effects or problems in older people than it does in younger adults.

Other medicines—Although certain medicines should not be used together at all, in other cases two different medicines may be used together even if an interaction might occur. In these cases, your doctor may want to change the dose, or other precautions may be necessary. Tell your health care professional if you are using any other topical prescription or nonprescription (over-the-counter [OTC]) medicine that is to be applied to the same area of the skin.

Proper Use of This Medicine

Apply enough clotrimazole to cover the affected and surrounding skin areas, and rub in gently.

Keep this medicine away from the eyes.

When clotrimazole is used to treat certain types of fungus infections of the skin, an occlusive dressing (airtight covering, such as kitchen plastic wrap) should *not* be applied over the medicine. To do so may cause irritation of the skin. *Do not apply an occlusive dressing over this medicine unless you have been directed to do so by your doctor.*

To help clear up your infection completely, *it is very important that you keep using this medicine for the full time of treatment*, even if your symptoms begin to clear up after a few days. Since fungus infections may be very slow to clear up, you may have to continue using this medicine every day for several weeks or more. If you stop using this medicine too soon, your symptoms may return. *Do not miss any doses.*

Dosing—The dose of topical clotrimazole will be different for different patients. *Follow your doctor's orders or the directions on the label.* The following information includes only the average doses of topical clotrimazole. *If your dose is different, do not change it* unless your doctor tells you to do so:

The number of doses you use each day, the time allowed between doses, and the length of time you use the medicine depend on the medical problem for which you are using clotrimazole.

- For *topical* dosage forms (cream, lotion, and solution):
  —Fungal infections (treatment):
    - Adults and children—Use two times a day, morning and evening.

Missed dose—If you miss a dose of this medicine, apply it as soon as possible. However, if it is almost time for your next dose, skip the missed dose and go back to your regular dosing schedule.

Storage—To store this medicine:
- Keep out of the reach of children.
- Store away from heat and direct light.
- Keep the medicine from freezing.
- Do not keep outdated medicine or medicine no longer needed. Be sure that any discarded medicine is out of the reach of children.

Precautions While Using This Medicine

If your skin problem does not improve within 4 weeks, or if it becomes worse, check with your doctor.

Side Effects of This Medicine

Along with its needed effects, a medicine may cause some unwanted effects. Although not all of these side effects may occur, if they do occur they may need medical attention.

Check with your doctor as soon as possible if any of the following side effects occur:

Skin rash, hives, blistering, burning, itching, peeling, redness, stinging, swelling, or other sign of skin irritation not present before use of this medicine

Other side effects not listed above may also occur in some patients. If you notice any other effects, check with your doctor.

Revised: 03/29/94

CLOTRIMAZOLE AND BETAMETHASONE   Topical

Commonly used brand name(s):

In the U.S.—
Lotrisone

In Canada—
Lotriderm

Description

Clotrimazole and betamethasone (kloe-TRIM-a-zole and bay-ta-METH-a-sone) combination is used to treat fungus infections. Clotrimazole works by killing the fungus or preventing its growth. Betamethasone, a corticosteroid (cortisone-like medicine or steroid), is used to help relieve redness, swelling, itching, and other discomfort of fungus infections.

Clotrimazole and betamethasone cream is applied to the skin to treat:

- athlete's foot (ringworm of the foot; tinea pedis);
- jock itch (ringworm of the groin; tinea cruris); and
- ringworm of the body (tinea corporis).

This medicine may also be used for other fungus infections of the skin as determined by your doctor.

This medicine is available only with your doctor's prescription, in the following dosage form:

Topical
- Cream (U.S. and Canada)

Before Using This Medicine

In deciding to use a medicine, the risks of using the medicine must be weighed against the good it will do. This is a decision you and your doctor will make. For clotrimazole and betamethasone combination, the following should be considered:

Allergies—Tell your doctor if you have ever had any unusual or allergic reaction to this medicine or to clotrimazole (e.g., Gyne-Lotrimin, Lotrimin), betamethasone (e.g., Valisone), butoconazole (e.g., Femstat), econazole (e.g., Ecostatin, Spectazole), ketoconazole (e.g., Nizoral), miconazole (e.g., Monistat, Monistat-Derm), terconazole (e.g., Terazol 7), or to any of the other corticosteroids. Also tell your health care professional if you are allergic to any other substances, such as preservatives or dyes.

Pregnancy—Clotrimazole and betamethasone combination has not been studied in pregnant women. However, for the individual medicines:

- *Clotrimazole*—Clotrimazole (e.g., Gyne-Lotrimin), used in the vagina, has not been shown to cause birth defects or other problems in studies in rats or humans. However, clotrimazole (e.g., Mycelex), given by mouth, has been shown to cause a decrease in successful pregnancies, but no birth defects, in rats and mice.
- *Betamethasone*—Studies in animals have shown that corticosteroids, given by mouth or by injection, may cause birth defects, even at low doses. Also, some of the stronger corticosteroids have been shown to cause birth defects when applied to the skin of animals.

Therefore, this medicine should not be used on large areas of the skin, in large amounts, or for a long time in pregnant patients. Before using this medicine, make sure your doctor knows if you are pregnant or if you may become pregnant.

Breast-feeding—It is not known whether topical clotrimazole and betamethasone combination passes into the breast milk. However, clotrimazole and betamethasone may be absorbed into the mother's body and risk-benefit should be considered.

- *Betamethasone*—Corticosteroids, given by mouth or by injection, do pass into the breast milk. They may cause unwanted effects, such as slower growth rate of nursing babies.

Children—Clotrimazole and betamethasone combination may rarely cause serious side effects. Some of these side effects may be more likely to occur in children, who may absorb greater amounts of this medicine than adults do. Long-term use in children may affect growth and development as well. Therefore, it is especially important that you discuss with the child's doctor the good that this medicine may do, as well as the risks of using it.

Older adults—Many medicines have not been studied specifically in older people. Therefore, it may not be known whether they work exactly the same way they do in younger adults or if they cause different side effects or problems in older people. There is no specific information comparing use of clotrimazole and betamethasone combination in the elderly with use in other age groups.

Other medicines—Although certain medicines should not be used together at all, in other cases two different medicines may be used together even if an interaction might occur. In these cases, your doctor may want to change the dose, or other precautions may be necessary. Tell your health care professional if you are using any other prescription or nonprescription (over-the-counter [OTC]) medicine.

Other medical problems—The presence of other medical problems may affect the use of clotrimazole and betamethasone combination. Make sure you tell your doctor if you have any other medical problems, especially:

- Bacteria infections of the skin or
- Diaper dermatitis (diaper rash) on your child or
- Skin diseases causing impaired circulation, such as stasis dermatitis—Betamethasone may make the condition worse
- Herpes or
- Vaccinia (cowpox) or
- Varicella (chickenpox) or
- Other virus infections of the skin—Betamethasone may speed up the spread of virus infections
- Tuberculosis (TB) of the skin—Betamethasone may make a TB infection worse

Proper Use of This Medicine

Before applying this medicine, wash the affected area with soap and water, and dry thoroughly.

Do not use this medicine in the eyes.

To use:

- *Check with your doctor before using this medicine on any other skin problems.* It should not be used on bacterial or virus infections or on diaper rash. Also, it should only be used on certain kinds of fungus infections of the skin.
- Apply a thin layer of this medicine to the affected area(s) and surrounding skin. Rub in gently and thoroughly.

The use of any kind of occlusive dressing (airtight covering, such as kitchen plastic wrap) over this medicine may increase absorption of the medicine and the chance of irritation and other side effects. Therefore, *do not bandage, wrap, or apply any occlusive dressing over this medicine* unless directed by your doctor. Also, wear loose-fitting clothing when using this medicine on the groin area. When using this medicine on the diaper area of children, *avoid tight-fitting diapers and plastic pants.*

To help clear up your skin infection completely, *keep using this medicine for the full time of treatment,* even if your symptoms have disappeared. *Do not miss any doses*. However, *do not use this medicine more often or for a longer time than your doctor ordered*. To do so may increase absorption through your skin and the chance of side effects. In addition, too much use, especially on thin skin areas (for example, face, armpits, genitals [sex organs], between the toes, groin), may result in thinning of the skin and in stretch marks.

Dosing—*Follow your doctor's orders or the directions on the label*. The following information includes only the average dose of clotrimazole and betamethasone combination. *If your dose is different, do not change it* unless your doctor tells you to do so.

- For *topical cream* dosage form:
  —For jock itch (ringworm of the groin; tinea cruris) or ringworm of the body (tinea corporis):
    • Adults and children 12 years of age and over— Apply to the affected skin and surrounding area(s) two times a day, morning and evening, for 2 weeks.
    • Children up to 12 years of age—Use and dose must be determined by your doctor.
  —For athlete's foot (ringworm of the foot; tinea pedis):
    • Adults and children 12 years of age and over— Apply to the affected skin and surrounding area(s) two times a day, morning and evening, for 4 weeks.
    • Children up to 12 years of age—Use and dose must be determined by your doctor.

Missed dose—If you miss a dose of this medicine, apply it as soon as possible. However, if it is almost time for your next dose, skip the missed dose and go back to your regular dosing schedule.

Storage—To store this medicine:
- Keep out of the reach of children.
- Store away from heat and direct light.
- Keep the medicine from freezing.
- Do not keep outdated medicine or medicine no longer needed. Be sure that any discarded medicine is out of the reach of children.

Precautions While Using This Medicine

If your skin infection does not improve within 1 week for jock itch or ringworm of the body and 2 weeks for athlete's foot, or if it becomes worse, check with your doctor. Redness and itching should get better within 3 to 5 days of therapy.

To help clear up your skin infection completely and to help make sure it does not return, the following good health habits are important:

- For patients using this medicine for *athlete's foot:*
  —Carefully dry the feet, especially between the toes, after bathing.
  —Avoid wearing socks made from wool or synthetic materials (for example, rayon or nylon). Instead, wear clean, cotton socks and change them daily or more often if your feet sweat freely.
  —Wear well-ventilated shoes (for example, shoes with holes) or sandals.
  —Use a bland, absorbent powder (for example, talcum powder) or an antifungal powder freely between the toes, on the feet, and in socks and shoes once or twice a day. Be sure to use the powder after clotrimazole and betamethasone cream has been applied and has disappeared into the skin. Do not use

the powder as the only treatment for your fungus infection.

These measures will help keep the feet cool and dry.

- For patients using this medicine for *jock itch:*
  —Carefully dry the groin area after bathing.
  —Avoid wearing underwear that is tight-fitting or made from synthetic materials (for example, rayon or nylon). Instead, wear loose-fitting, cotton underwear.
  —Use a bland, absorbent powder (for example, talcum powder) or an antifungal powder freely once or twice a day. Be sure to use the powder after clotrimazole and betamethasone cream has been applied and has disappeared into the skin. Do not use the powder as the only treatment for your fungus infection.

These measures will help reduce chafing and irritation and will also help keep the groin area cool and dry.

- For patients using this medicine for *ringworm of the body:*
  —Carefully dry yourself after bathing.
  —Avoid too much heat and humidity if possible. Try to keep moisture from building up on affected areas of the body.
  —Wear well-ventilated clothing.
  —Use a bland, absorbent powder (for example, talcum powder) or an antifungal powder freely once or twice a day. Be sure to use the powder after clotrimazole and betamethasone cream has been applied and has disappeared into the skin. Do not use the powder as the only treatment for your fungus infection.

These measures will help keep the affected areas cool and dry.

If you have any questions about this, check with your health care professional.

For diabetic patients:

- *Rarely, the corticosteroid in this medicine may cause higher blood and urine sugar levels. This is more likely to occur if you have severe diabetes and are using large amounts of this medicine*. Check with your doctor before changing your diet or the dosage of your diabetes medicine.

Side Effects of This Medicine

Along with its needed effects, a medicine may cause some unwanted effects. Although not all of these side effects may occur, if they do occur they may need medical attention.

Check with your doctor immediately if any of the following side effects occur:

Rare

Numbness of the hands and feet; rash; secondary infection; swelling

Less common

Blistering, burning, itching, peeling, dryness, redness, or other signs of skin irritation not present before use of this medicine; hives; stinging

Additional side effects may occur if you use this medicine for a long time. Check with your doctor as soon as possible if any of the following side effects occur:

Acne or oily skin; increased hair growth, especially on the face and body; increased loss of hair, especially on the scalp; pus in the hair follicles; reddish purple lines on arms, face, legs, trunk, or groin; redness and scaling around the mouth; softening of the skin; thinning of skin with easy bruising; white spots

Other side effects not listed above may also occur in some patients. If you notice any other effects, check with your doctor.

Revised: 06/14/99

CLOZAPINE   Systemic

Commonly used brand name(s):

In the U.S.—
   Clozaril
   Generic name product may be available.

In Canada—
   Clozaril

Other—
   Leponex

Description

Clozapine (KLOE-za-peen) is used to treat schizophrenia in patients who have not been helped by or are unable to take other medicines.

Clozapine is available only from pharmacies that agree to participate with your doctor in a plan to monitor your blood tests. You will need to have blood tests done every week for at least 6 months. After that, your doctor will decide if it is safe for you to have blood tests every other week. You will receive enough clozapine to last until your next blood test, but only if the results of your blood tests show that it is safe for you to take this medicine. If any of your blood tests are not normal, you may need to have blood tests more often than every week until they return to normal.

Clozapine is available in the following dosage form:

Oral
   • Tablets (U.S. and Canada)

Before Using This Medicine

In deciding to use a medicine, the risks of taking the medicine must be weighed against the good it will do. This is a decision you and your doctor will make. For clozapine, the following should be considered:

Allergies—Tell your doctor if you have ever had any unusual or allergic reaction to clozapine. Also tell your health care professional if you are allergic to any other substances, such as foods, preservatives, or dyes.

Pregnancy—Clozapine has not been studied in pregnant women. However, clozapine has not been shown to cause birth defects or other problems in animal studies.

Breast-feeding—Clozapine may pass into breast milk and cause drowsiness, trouble in nursing, restlessness or irritability, convulsions (seizures), or heart or blood vessel problems in nursing babies.

Children—Studies on this medicine have been done only in adult patients, and there is no specific information com-paring use of clozapine in children with use in other age groups.

Older adults—Many medicines have not been tested in older people. Therefore, it may not be known whether they work exactly the same way they do in younger adults. Clozapine may be more likely to cause side effects in the elderly, including dizziness and fainting, low blood pressure, and confusion or excitement.

Other medicines—Although certain medicines should not be used together at all, in other cases two different medicines may be used together even if an interaction might occur. In these cases, your doctor may want to change the dose, or other precautions may be necessary. When you are taking clozapine, it is especially important that your health care professional know if you are taking any of the following:

   • Alcohol or
   • Central nervous system (CNS) depressants (medicines that cause drowsiness) or
   • Tricyclic antidepressants (amitriptyline [e.g., Elavil], amoxapine [e.g., Asendin], clomipramine [e.g., Anafranil], desipramine [e.g., Pertofrane], doxepin [e.g., Sinequan], imipramine [e.g., Tofranil], nortriptyline [e.g., Aventyl], protriptyline [e.g., Vivactil], trimipramine [e.g., Surmontil])—Using these medicines or alcohol with clozapine may cause increased drowsiness, low blood pressure, or trouble in breathing

   • Amantadine (e.g., Symmetrel) or
   • Antihypertensives (high blood pressure medicine) or
   • Antipsychotics (medicine for mental illness) or
   • Bromocriptine (e.g., Parlodel) or
   • Certain eye drops used to treat glaucoma (carteolol [e.g., Ocupress], levobunolol [e.g., Betagan], metipranolol [e.g., OptiPranolol], timolol [e.g., Timoptic]) or
   • Diuretics (water pills) or
   • Levodopa (e.g., Dopar) or
   • Medicine for heart disease or
   • Nabilone (e.g., Cesamet) (with high doses) or
   • Narcotic pain medicine or
   • Pentamidine (e.g., Pentam) or
   • Pimozide (e.g., Orap) or
   • Promethazine (e.g., Phenergan) or
   • Trimeprazine (e.g., Temaril)—Using these medicines with clozapine may cause low blood pressure, which can cause dizziness or fainting

   • Amphotericin B by injection (e.g., Fungizone) or
   • Antineoplastics (cancer medicine) or
   • Antithyroid agents (medicine for overactive thyroid) or
   • Azathioprine (e.g., Imuran) or
   • Chlorambucil (e.g., Leukeran) or
   • Chloramphenicol (e.g., Chloromycetin) or
   • Colchicine or
   • Cyclophosphamide (e.g., Cytoxan) or
   • Flucytosine (e.g., Ancobon) or
   • Ganciclovir (e.g., Cytovene) or
   • Interferon (e.g., Intron A, Roferon-A) or
   • Mercaptopurine (e.g., Purinethol) or
   • Methotrexate (e.g., Mexate) or
   • Plicamycin (e.g., Mithracin) or
   • Zidovudine (e.g., AZT, Retrovir)—Taking clozapine with any of these medicines may increase the chance that very serious blood problems will occur

   • Lithium—Using clozapine with lithium may increase the chance that convulsions (seizures), confusion or problems with movement will occur

- Selective serotonin reuptake inhibitors (fluoxetine [e.g., Prozac], fluvoxamine [e.g., Luvox], paroxetine [e.g., Paxil], sertraline [e.g., Zoloft])—These medicines can increase the blood levels of clozapine, which increases the chance that unwanted effects will occur

Other medical problems—The presence of other medical problems may affect the use of clozapine. Make sure you tell your doctor if you have any other medical problems, especially:

- Blood diseases or
- Enlarged prostate or difficult urination or
- Gastrointestinal problems or
- Glaucoma, narrow angle or
- Heart or blood vessel problems—Clozapine may make these conditions worse

- Epilepsy or other seizure disorder—Clozapine may increase the chance that seizures will occur

- Kidney or liver disease—Higher blood levels of clozapine may occur, increasing the chance that unwanted effects will occur

---

Proper Use of This Medicine

Take this medicine exactly as directed. Do not take more of this medicine and do not take it more often than your doctor ordered. Do not miss any doses.

This medicine has been prescribed for your current medical problem only. It must not be given to other people or used for other problems unless you are directed to do so by your doctor.

Dosing—The dose of clozapine will be different for different patients. *Follow your doctor's orders or the directions on the label.* The following information includes only the average doses of clozapine. *If your dose is different, do not change it* unless your doctor tells you to do so.

The number of tablets that you take depends on the strength of the medicine. Also, *the number of doses you take each day, the time allowed between doses, and the length of time you take the medicine depend on your special needs.*

- For *oral* dosage form (tablets):
  —For schizophrenia:
    - Adults—At first, 12.5 milligrams (mg) (one half of a 25-mg tablet) once or twice a day. Your doctor may increase your dose as needed. However, the dose usually is not more than 900 mg a day.
    - Children younger than 16 years of age—Use and dose must be determined by your doctor.

Missed dose—If you miss a dose of this medicine, take it as soon as possible. However, if it is almost time for your next dose, skip the missed dose and go back to your regular dosing schedule. Do not double doses.

If you miss 2 or more days of clozapine doses, talk to your doctor before you start taking it again. You may need to restart this medicine at a lower dose than you were taking before.

Storage—To store this medicine:

- Keep out of the reach of children.
- Store away from heat and direct light.
- Do not store in the bathroom, near the kitchen sink, or in other damp places. Heat or moisture may cause the medicine to break down.

- Do not keep outdated medicine or medicine no longer needed. Be sure that any discarded medicine is out of the reach of children.

Precautions While Using This Medicine

It is important that you have your blood tests done when they are scheduled, and that your doctor check your progress at regular visits. Clozapine can cause some very serious blood problems that you may not be able to feel or see. The pharmacy will give you this medicine only if your blood tests show that it is safe for you to take clozapine. Also, your doctor will make sure the medicine is working properly and change the dosage if needed.

If you do not take clozapine for 2 or more days, talk to your doctor about what to do. You may need to take a lower dose when you first start taking this medicine again.

If you have been using this medicine regularly, do not stop taking it without first checking with your doctor. Your doctor may want you to reduce gradually the amount you are taking before stopping completely. This is to help prevent the illness from suddenly returning.

This medicine will add to the effects of alcohol and other CNS depressants (medicines that slow down the nervous system, possibly causing drowsiness). Some examples of CNS depressants are antihistamines or medicine for hay fever, other allergies, or colds; sedatives, tranquilizers, or sleeping medicine; prescription pain medicine or narcotics; barbiturates; medicine for seizures; muscle relaxants; or anesthetics, including some dental anesthetics. *Check with your doctor before taking any of the above while you are using this medicine.*

Contact your doctor as soon as possible if you develop unusual tiredness or weakness, fever, sore throat, or other symptoms of infection. These can be symptoms of a very serious blood problem.

Clozapine may cause drowsiness, blurred vision or convulsions (seizures). *Do not drive, climb, swim, operate machines or do anything else that could be dangerous* while you are taking this medicine.

Dizziness, lightheadedness, or fainting may occur, especially when you get up from a lying or sitting position. Getting up slowly may help. If this problem continues or gets worse, check with your doctor.

In some patients, clozapine may cause increased watering of the mouth. Other patients, however, may get dryness of the mouth. For temporary relief of mouth dryness, use sugarless gum or candy, melt bits of ice in your mouth, or use a saliva substitute. However, if your mouth continues to feel dry for more than 2 weeks, check with your medical doctor or dentist. Continuing dryness of the mouth may increase the chance of dental disease, including tooth decay, gum disease, and fungus infections.

Side Effects of This Medicine

Along with its needed effects, a medicine may cause some unwanted effects. Some side effects may not have signs or symptoms that you can see or feel. Clozapine can cause some very serious blood problems. Your doctor will watch for these by doing blood tests every week or two for as long as you are taking clozapine and for 4 weeks after you stop taking it. Although not all of these side effects may occur, if they do occur they may need medical attention.

Check with your doctor immediately if any of the following side effects occur:

More common
Fast or irregular heartbeat; fever; low blood pressure

Less common
High blood pressure (severe or continuing headache)

Rare
Chest pain; chills; convulsions (seizures); cough; difficult or fast breathing or sudden shortness of breath; fainting; increased sweating; loss of bladder control; muscle stiffness (severe); sore throat; sores, ulcers, or white spots on lips or in mouth; swelling or pain in leg; unusual bleeding or bruising; unusual tiredness or weakness; unusually pale skin

Check with your doctor as soon as possible if any of the following side effects occur:

More common
Dizziness, especially when getting up from a lying or sitting position

Less common
Blurred vision; confusion; restlessness or need to keep moving; unusual anxiety, nervousness, or irritability

Rare
Absence of or decrease in movement; decreased sexual ability; high blood sugar (increased appetite, increased thirst, increased urination, weakness); lip smacking or puckering; liver problems (dark urine, decreased appetite, nausea, vomiting, yellow eyes or skin); mental depression; puffing of cheeks; rapid or worm-like movements of tongue; trembling or shaking; trouble in sleeping; trouble in urinating; uncontrolled chewing movements; uncontrolled movements of arms and legs

Symptoms of overdose
Convulsions (seizures); dizziness or fainting; drowsiness (severe) or coma; fast, slow, or irregular heartbeat; hallucinations (seeing, hearing, or feeling things that are not there); increased watering of mouth (severe); slow, irregular, or troubled breathing; unusual excitement, nervousness, or restlessness

Other side effects may occur that usually do not need medical attention. These side effects may go away during treatment as your body adjusts to the medicine. However, check with your doctor if any of the following side effects continue or are bothersome:

More common
Constipation; dizziness or lightheadedness (mild); drowsiness; headache (mild); increased watering of mouth; nausea or vomiting; unusual weight gain

Less common
Abdominal discomfort or heartburn; dryness of mouth

Other side effects not listed above may also occur in some patients. If you notice any other effects, check with your doctor.

Revised: 08/07/98

COAL TAR   Topical

Commonly used brand name(s):

In the U.S.—

Alphosyl	Medotar
Aquatar	Pentrax Anti-Dandruff Tar Shampoo
Balnetar Therapeutic Tar Bath	Psorigel
Cutar Water Dispersible Emollient Tar	PsoriNail Topical Solution
Denorex Extra Strength Medicated Shampoo	Taraphilic
	Tarbonis
Denorex Extra Strength Medicated Shampoo with Conditioners	Tarpaste 'Doak'
	T/Derm Tar Emollient
Denorex Medicated Shampoo	Tegrin Lotion for Psoriasis
Denorex Medicated Shampoo and Conditioner	Tegrin Medicated Cream Shampoo
Denorex Mountain Fresh Herbal Scent Medicated Shampoo	Tegrin Medicated Shampoo Concentrated Gel
	Tegrin Medicated Shampoo Extra Conditioning Formula
DHS Tar Gel Shampoo	Tegrin Medicated Shampoo Herbal Formula
DHS Tar Shampoo	Tegrin Medicated Shampoo Original Formula
Doak Oil Forte Therapeutic Bath Treatment	Tegrin Medicated Soap for Psoriasis
Doak Oil Therapeutic Bath Treatment For All-Over Body Care	Tegrin Skin Cream for Psoriasis
Doak Tar Lotion	Tersa-Tar Soapless Tar Shampoo
Doak Tar Shampoo	
Doctar Hair & Scalp Shampoo and Conditioner	T/Gel Therapeutic Conditioner
Doctar Shampoo	T/Gel Therapeutic Shampoo
Estar	Theraplex T Shampoo
Fototar	Zetar Emulsion
Ionil T Plus	Zetar Medicated Antiseborrheic Shampoo
Lavatar	

In Canada—

Alphosyl	Tar Doak
Balnetar	Tarpaste
Denorex	Tersa-Tar Mild Therapeutic Shampoo with Protein and Conditioner
Doak Oil	
Doak Oil Forte	
Estar	Tersa-Tar Therapeutic Shampoo
Lavatar	
Liquor Carbonis Detergens	T-Gel
Pentrax Extra-Strength Therapeutic Tar Shampoo	Zetar Emulsion
	Zetar Shampoo
Psorigel	

Description

Coal tar is used to treat eczema, psoriasis, seborrheic dermatitis, and other skin disorders.

Some of these preparations are available only with your doctor's prescription. Others are available without a prescription; however, your doctor may have special instructions on the proper use of coal tar for your medical condition.

Coal tar is available in the following dosage forms:

Topical
- Cleansing bar (U.S.)
- Cream (U.S. and Canada)
- Gel (U.S. and Canada)
- Lotion (U.S. and Canada)
- Ointment (U.S. and Canada)
- Shampoo (U.S. and Canada)
- Topical solution (U.S. and Canada)
- Topical suspension (U.S. and Canada)

Before Using This Medicine

If you are using this medicine without a prescription, carefully read and follow any precautions on the label. For coal tar, the following should be considered:

Allergies—Tell your doctor if you have ever had any unusual or allergic reaction to coal tar or to any other tar. Also tell your health care professional if you are allergic to any other substances, such as preservatives or dyes.

Pregnancy—Studies on effects in pregnancy have not been done in either humans or animals.

Breast-feeding—It is not known whether coal tar passes into the breast milk. However, this medicine has not been reported to cause problems in nursing babies.

Children—Coal tar products should not be used on infants, unless otherwise directed by your doctor. Studies on this medicine have been done only in adult patients, and there is no specific information comparing use of this medicine in children with use in other age groups.

Older adults—Many medicines have not been studied specifically in older people. Therefore, it may not be known whether they work exactly the same way they do in younger adults or if they cause different side effects or problems in older people. There is no specific information comparing use of this medicine in the elderly with use in other age groups.

Other medicines—Although certain medicines should not be used together at all, in other cases two different medicines may be used together even if an interaction might occur. In these cases, your doctor may want to change the dose, or other precautions may be necessary. Tell your health care professional if you are using any other topical prescription or nonprescription (over-the-counter [OTC]) medicine that is to be applied to the same area of the skin.

Proper Use of This Medicine

Use this medicine only as directed. Do not use more of it and do not use it more often than recommended on the label, unless otherwise directed by your doctor. To do so may increase the chance of side effects.

After applying coal tar, *protect the treated area from direct sunlight and do not use a sunlamp for 72 hours,* unless otherwise directed by your doctor, since a severe reaction may occur. Also, make sure you have removed all the coal tar medicine from your skin before you go back into direct sunlight or use a sunlamp.

Do not apply this medicine to infected, blistered, raw, or oozing areas of the skin.

Keep this medicine away from the eyes. If you should accidentally get some in your eyes, flush them thoroughly with water at once.

To use the *cream or ointment form* of this medicine:
- Apply enough medicine to cover the affected area, and rub in gently.

To use the *gel form* of this medicine:
- Apply enough gel to cover the affected area, and rub in gently. Allow the gel to remain on the affected area for 5 minutes, then remove excess gel by patting with a clean tissue.

To use the *shampoo form* of this medicine:
- Wet the scalp and hair with lukewarm water. Apply a generous amount of shampoo and rub into the scalp, then rinse. Apply the shampoo again, working up a rich lather, and allow to remain on the scalp for 5 minutes. Then rinse thoroughly.

To use the *nonshampoo liquid form* of this medicine:
- Some of these preparations are to be applied directly to dry or wet skin, some are to be added to lukewarm bath water, and some may be applied directly to dry or wet skin or added to lukewarm bath water. Make sure you know exactly how you should use this medicine. If you have any questions about this, check with your health care professional.
- If this medicine is to be applied directly to the skin, apply enough to cover the affected area, and rub in gently.
- Some of these preparations contain alcohol and are flammable. Do not use near heat, near open flame, or while smoking.

Dosing—The dose of coal tar will be different for different patients. *Follow your doctor's orders or the directions on the label.* The following information includes only the average doses of coal tar. *If your dose is different, do not change it* unless your doctor tells you to do so.
- For eczema, psoriasis, seborrheic dermatitis, and other skin disorders:
  —For *cleansing bar* dosage form:
    - Adults—Use one or two times a day, or as directed by your doctor.
    - Children—Use and dose must be determined by your doctor.
  —For *cream* dosage form:
    - Adults—Apply to the affected area(s) of the skin up to four times a day.
    - Children—Use and dose must be determined by your doctor.
  —For *gel* dosage form:
    - Adults—Apply to the affected area(s) of the skin one or two times a day.
    - Children—Use and dose must be determined by your doctor.
  —For *lotion* dosage form:
    - Adults—Apply directly to the affected area(s) of the skin or use as a bath, hand or foot soak, or as a hair rinse, depending on the product.
    - Children—Use and dose must be determined by your doctor.
  —For *ointment* dosage form:
    - Adults—Apply to the affected area(s) of the skin two or three times a day.
    - Children—Use and dose must be determined by your doctor.
  —For *shampoo* dosage form:
    - Adults—Use once a day to once a week or as directed by your doctor.
    - Children—Use and dose must be determined by your doctor.
  —For *topical solution* dosage form:
    - Adults—Apply to wet the skin or scalp, or use as a bath, depending on the product.
    - Children—Use and dose must be determined by your doctor.
  —For *topical suspension* dosage form:
    - Adults—Use as a bath.

- Children—Use and dose must be determined by your doctor.

Missed dose—If you miss a dose of this medicine, apply it as soon as possible. However, if it is almost time for your next dose, skip the missed dose and go back to your regular dosing schedule. Do not double doses.

Storage—To store this medicine:
- Keep out of the reach of children.
- Store away from heat and direct light.
- Keep the medicine from freezing.
- Do not keep outdated medicine or medicine no longer needed. Be sure that any discarded medicine is out of the reach of children.

Precautions While Using This Medicine

If this medicine is used on the scalp, it may temporarily discolor blond, bleached, or tinted hair.

Coal tar may stain the skin or clothing. Avoid getting it on your clothing. The stain on the skin will wear off after you stop using the medicine.

Side Effects of This Medicine

In animal studies, coal tar has been shown to increase the chance of skin cancer.

Along with its needed effects, a medicine may cause some unwanted effects. Although not all of these side effects may occur, if they do occur they may need medical attention.

Check with your doctor as soon as possible if either of the following side effects occurs:

Rare
Skin irritation not present before use of this medicine; skin rash

Other side effects may occur that usually do not need medical attention. These side effects may go away during treatment as your body adjusts to the medicine. However, check with your health care professional if the following side effect continues or is bothersome:

More common
Stinging (mild)—especially for gel and solution dosage forms

Other side effects not listed above may also occur in some patients. If you notice any other effects, check with your health care professional.

Revised: 03/04/92
Interim revision: 06/03/94

COCAINE   Mucosal-Local

Description

Cocaine (KOE-kane) is a local anesthetic. It is applied to certain areas of the body (for example, the nose, mouth, or throat) to cause loss of feeling. This allows some kinds of examinations or surgery to be done without causing pain.

Cocaine can cause psychological dependence (a strong desire to continue using the medicine because of the "high" feeling it produces). This may lead to cocaine abuse (more frequent use and/or use of larger amounts of cocaine) and to an increased chance of serious side effects. Cocaine abuse has caused death from heart or breathing failure.

Use of cocaine as a local anesthetic for an examination or surgery is not likely to cause psychological dependence or other serious side effects. However, if cocaine is absorbed into the body too quickly, serious side effects can occur. Also, some people are especially sensitive to the effects of cocaine. Unwanted effects may occur in these people even with small amounts of the medicine. Before receiving cocaine as a local anesthetic, you should discuss its use with your doctor.

Cocaine is applied only by or under the immediate supervision of your doctor. It is available in the following dosage forms:

Mucosal-Local
- Crystals (U.S. and Canada)
- Solution (U.S.)

Before Receiving This Medicine

In deciding to use a medicine, the risks of taking the medicine must be weighed against the good it will do. This is a decision you and your doctor will make. For cocaine, the following should be considered:

Allergies—Tell your doctor if you have ever had any unusual or allergic reaction to cocaine. Also tell your health care professional if you are allergic to any other substances, such as foods, preservatives, or dyes.

Pregnancy—Studies on birth defects or other problems have not been done in pregnant women receiving cocaine as a local anesthetic. However, studies in women who abused cocaine during pregnancy have shown that cocaine may cause birth defects, decreased birth weight and size, and problems affecting the baby's nervous system. These studies have also shown that too much use of cocaine may cause the baby to be born too soon, sometimes too soon to survive. Cocaine has also been shown to cause birth defects and other unwanted effects in animal studies.

Breast-feeding—Cocaine passes into the breast milk and may cause unwanted effects such as convulsions (seizures), high blood pressure, fast heartbeat, breathing problems, trembling, and unusual irritability in nursing babies. Therefore, after receiving this medicine you should stop breast-feeding your baby for about 2 days.

Children—Cocaine can cause serious side effects in any patient. Therefore, it is especially important that you discuss with the child's doctor the good that this medicine may do as well as the risks of using it.

Older adults—Side effects, including dizziness or lightheadedness or fast or irregular heartbeat, may be especially likely to occur in elderly patients, who are usually more sensitive than younger adults to the effects of cocaine.

Other medicines—Although certain medicines should not be used together at all, in other cases two different medicines may be used together even if an interaction might occur. In these cases, your doctor may want to change the dose, or other precautions may be necessary. When you are receiving cocaine, it is especially important that your health care professional know if you are taking any of the following:
- Amantadine (e.g., Symmetrel) or
- Amphetamines or

- Antimyasthenics (ambenonium [e.g., Mytelase], neostigmine [e.g., Prostigmin], pyridostigmine [e.g., Mestinon]) or
- Appetite suppressants (diet pills), except fenfluramine (e.g., Pondimin), or
- Beta-blockers (acebutolol [e.g., Sectral], atenolol [e.g., Tenormin], betaxolol [e.g., Kerlone], carteolol [e.g., Cartrol], labetalol [e.g., Normodyne], metoprolol [e.g., Lopressor], nadolol [e.g., Corgard], oxprenolol [e.g., Trasicor], penbutolol [e.g., Levatol], pindolol [e.g., Visken], propranolol [e.g., Inderal], sotalol [e.g., Sotacor], timolol [e.g., Blocadren]) or
- Betaxolol (ophthalmic) (e.g., Betoptic) or
- Caffeine (e.g., NoDoz) or
- Chlophedianol (e.g., Ulone) or
- Cyclophosphamide (e.g., Cytoxan) or
- Demecarium (e.g., Humorsol) or
- Echothiophate (e.g., Phospholine Iodide) or
- Guanadrel (e.g., Hylorel) or
- Guanethidine (e.g., Ismelin) or
- Isoflurophate (e.g., Floropryl) or
- Levobunolol (e.g., Betagan) or
- Levodopa (e.g., Dopar) or
- Malathion (e.g., Prioderm) or
- Medicine for asthma or other breathing problems or
- Medicine for colds, sinus problems, or hay fever or other allergies (including nose drops or sprays) or
- Methyldopa (e.g., Aldomet) or
- Methylphenidate (e.g., Ritalin) or
- Metipranolol (e.g., OptiPranolol) or
- Nabilone (e.g., Cesamet) or
- Pemoline (e.g., Cylert) or
- Thiotepa or
- Timolol (ophthalmic) (e.g., Timoptic)—The chance of serious side effects may be increased

- Monoamine oxidase (MAO) inhibitors (furazolidone [e.g., Furoxone], isocarboxazid [e.g., Marplan], phenelzine [e.g., Nardil], procarbazine [e.g., Matulane], selegiline [e.g., Eldepryl], tranylcypromine [e.g., Parnate])—Receiving cocaine while you are taking or within 2 weeks after you have taken an MAO inhibitor may increase the chance of serious side effects.

Also tell your doctor if you have recently used an insecticide (insect killer) or if you have been in an area that was recently treated with an insecticide. Some insecticides can slow the breakdown of cocaine in your body. This increases the chance of serious side effects.

Other medical problems—The presence of other medical problems may affect the use of cocaine. Make sure you tell your doctor if you have any other medical problems, especially:

- Cancer or
- Chest pain, or history of, or
- Convulsions (seizures), history of, or
- Fast or irregular heartbeat or
- Heart or blood vessel disease or
- High blood pressure or
- Liver disease or
- Myocardial infarction ("heart attack"), history of, or
- Overactive thyroid—The chance of serious side effects may be increased

- Tourette's syndrome—Cocaine can make your condition worse

Proper Use of This Medicine

Dosing—The dose of cocaine will be different for different patients. It will depend on the reason a local anesthetic is needed and on the size of the area to which it is being applied. Your doctor or nurse will apply the medicine.

- For *mucosal-local* dosage forms (crystals or solution):
  —For causing loss of feeling before examinations or surgery:
  - Adults and teenagers—Your doctor or nurse will apply the smallest amount of cocaine that will produce the needed effect. The largest amount that is usually used is 400 milligrams (mg).
  - Children up to 12 years of age—Use and dose must be determined by your doctor.

Precautions After Receiving This Medicine

Cocaine and some of its metabolites (substances to which cocaine is broken down in the body) will appear in your blood and urine for several days after you have received the medicine. Tests for possible drug use will then be "positive" for cocaine. If you must have such a test within 5 days or so after receiving cocaine, be sure to tell the person in charge that you have recently received cocaine for medical reasons. It may be helpful to have written information from your doctor stating why the medicine was used, the date on which you received it, and the amount you received.

Side Effects of This Medicine

Along with its needed effects, a medicine may cause some unwanted effects. Although not all of these side effects may occur, if they do occur they may need medical attention.

After cocaine has been applied, your doctor or nurse will closely follow its effects. However, *tell your doctor or nurse immediately* if any of the following side effects occur:
   Signs and symptoms of too much medicine being absorbed into the body
      Abdominal or stomach pain; chills; confusion; dizziness or lightheadedness; excitement, nervousness, restlessness, or any mood or mental changes; fast or irregular heartbeat; general feeling of discomfort or illness; hallucinations (seeing, hearing, or feeling things that are not there); headache (sudden); increased sweating; nausea

Other side effects may occur that usually do not need medical attention. However, check with your doctor if the following side effects continue or are bothersome:
   More common
      Loss of sense of taste or smell (after application to the nose or mouth)

Other side effects not listed above may also occur in some patients. If you notice any other effects, *tell your doctor or nurse immediately.*

Revised: 08/08/92
Interim revision: 07/14/94

COLCHICINE   Systemic

Description

Colchicine (KOL-chi-seen) is used to prevent or treat attacks of gout (also called gouty arthritis). People with gout have too much uric acid in their blood and joints. An attack of gout occurs when uric acid causes inflammation (pain, redness, swelling, and heat) in a joint. Colchicine does not cure gout or take the place of other medicines that lower the amount of uric acid in the body. It prevents or relieves gout attacks by reducing inflammation. Colchicine is not an ordinary pain reliever and will not relieve most kinds of pain.

Colchicine may also be used for other conditions as determined by your doctor.

Colchicine may be used in 2 ways. Most people take small amounts of it regularly for a long time (months or even years) to prevent severe attacks or other problems caused by inflammation. Other people take large amounts of colchicine during a short period of time (several hours) only when the medicine is needed to relieve an attack that is occurring. The chance of serious side effects is much lower with the first (preventive) kind of treatment.

Because some of colchicine's side effects can be very serious, you should discuss with your doctor the good that this medicine can do as well as the risks of using it. Make sure you understand exactly how you are to use it, and follow the instructions carefully, to lessen the chance of unwanted effects.

This medicine is available only with your doctor's prescription, in the following dosage forms:

Oral
- Tablets (U.S. and Canada)

Parenteral
- Injection (U.S.)

Before Using This Medicine

In deciding to use a medicine, the risks of taking the medicine must be weighed against the good it will do. This is a decision you and your doctor will make. For colchicine, the following should be considered:

Allergies—Tell your doctor if you have ever had any unusual or allergic reaction to colchicine. Also tell your health care professional if you are allergic to any other substances, such as foods, preservatives, or dyes.

Pregnancy—Studies in humans taking large amounts of colchicine to relieve attacks have not been done. Fertility problems have occurred in some men taking small amounts of colchicine regularly (preventive treatment), but these problems went away after treatment was stopped. Many other men taking preventive amounts of colchicine have fathered children without stopping treatment. Also, many women receiving preventive treatment with colchicine have become pregnant and given birth to normal, healthy babies. Some women receive preventive amounts of colchicine regularly for a medical condition that can cause fertility problems or miscarriages. Treatment with colchicine does not increase, and may actually decrease, the occurrence of these problems in women with this condition.

Colchicine has caused birth defects and other problems in animal studies.

Breast-feeding—Colchicine passes into breast milk. When breast-feeding mothers receive preventive treatment with one 0.6-milligram (mg) tablet twice a day, the amount that appears in the breast milk is not likely to cause problems in nursing babies. There is no information about whether colchicine can cause problems in nursing babies when the mother takes larger amounts of it. Mothers who are taking this medicine and who wish to breast-feed should discuss this with their doctor.

Children—Studies on the effects of colchicine in patients with gout have been done only in adults. Gout is very rare in children. However, colchicine is used in children 3 years of age and older who need preventive treatment for other medical conditions. It has not been reported to cause different side effects or problems in these children than it does in adults.

Older adults—Elderly people are especially sensitive to the effects of colchicine. Also, colchicine may stay in the body longer in older patients than it does in younger adults. This may increase the chance of side effects during treatment.

Other medicines—Although certain medicines should not be used together at all, in other cases two different medicines may be used together even if an interaction might occur. In these cases, your doctor may want to change the dose, or other precautions may be necessary. When you are taking colchicine, it is especially important that your health care professional know if you are taking any of the following:

- Amphotericin B by injection (e.g., Fungizone) or
- Antineoplastics (cancer medicine) or
- Antithyroid agents (medicine for overactive thyroid) or
- Azathioprine (e.g., Imuran) or
- Chloramphenicol (e.g., Chloromycetin) or
- Cyclophosphamide (e.g., Cytoxan) or
- Flucytosine (e.g., Ancobon) or
- Ganciclovir (e.g., Cytovene) or
- Interferon (e.g., Intron A, Roferon-A) or
- Mercaptopurine (e.g., Purinethol) or
- Methotrexate (e.g., Mexate) or
- Phenylbutazone (e.g., Butazolidin) or
- Plicamycin (e.g., Mithracin) or
- Zidovudine (e.g., Retrovir)—The chance of serious side effects caused by a decrease in the numbers of certain blood cells may be increased

Other medical problems—The presence of other medical problems may affect the use of colchicine. Make sure you tell your doctor if you have any other medical problems, especially:

- Alcohol abuse or
- Intestinal disease or
- Stomach ulcer or other stomach problems—The chance of stomach upset may be increased. Also, colchicine can make some kinds of stomach or intestinal problems worse

- Heart disease or
- Kidney disease or
- Liver disease—The chance of serious side effects may be increased because these conditions can cause colchicine to build up in the body

- Low white blood cell count or
- Low platelet count—The chance of serious side effects may be increased because colchicine can make these conditions worse

Proper Use of This Medicine

Colchicine can build up in the body and cause serious side effects if too much of it is taken or if it is taken too often. Therefore, *do not take more of this medicine, and do not take it more often, than directed by your doctor*. This is especially important for elderly patients, who are more likely than younger adults to have colchicine build up in the body and who are also more sensitive to its effects.

For patients *taking small amounts of colchicine regularly (preventive treatment):*

- Take this medicine regularly as directed by your doctor, even if you feel well. If you are taking colchicine to prevent gout attacks, and you are also taking another medicine to reduce the amount of uric acid in your body, you probably will be able to stop taking colchicine after a while. However, if you stop taking it too soon, your attacks may return or get worse. If you are taking colchicine for certain other medical conditions, you may need to keep taking it for the rest of your life.
- If you are taking colchicine to prevent gout attacks, ask your doctor to recommend other medicine to be taken if an attack occurs. Most people receiving preventive amounts of colchicine should not take extra colchicine to relieve an attack. However, some people cannot take the other medicines that are used for gout attacks and will have to take extra colchicine. If you are one of these people, ask your doctor to tell you the largest amount of colchicine you should take for an attack and how long you should wait before starting to take the smaller preventive amounts again. Be sure to follow these directions carefully.

For patients *taking large amounts of colchicine only when needed to relieve an attack:*

- Start taking this medicine at the first sign of the attack for best results.
- *Stop taking this medicine as soon as the pain is relieved or at the first sign of nausea, vomiting, stomach pain, or diarrhea*. Also, stop taking colchicine when you have taken the largest amount that your doctor ordered for each attack, even if the pain is not relieved or none of these side effects occurs.
- The first few times you take colchicine, keep a record of each dose as you take it. Then, whenever stomach upset (nausea, vomiting, stomach pain, or diarrhea) occurs, count the number of doses you have taken. The next time you need colchicine, stop taking it before that number of doses is reached. For example, if diarrhea occurs after your fifth dose of medicine, take no more than four doses the next time. If taking fewer doses does not prevent stomach upset from occurring after a few treatments, check with your doctor.
- After taking colchicine tablets to treat an attack, *do not take any more colchicine for at least 3 days. Also, after receiving the medicine by injection for an attack, do not take any more colchicine (tablets or injection) for at least 7 days*. Elderly patients may have to wait even longer between treatments and should check with their doctor for directions.
- If you are taking colchicine for an attack of gout, and you are also taking other medicine to reduce the amount of uric acid in your body, *do not stop taking the other medicine*. Continue taking the other medicine as directed by your doctor.

Dosing—The dose of colchicine will be different for different patients. *Follow your doctor's orders or the directions on the label*. The following information includes only the average doses of colchicine. *If your dose is different, do not change it* unless your doctor tells you to do so.

The number of doses you take each day, the time allowed between doses, and the length of time you take the medicine depend on how often your attacks occur and on whether you are taking the medicine to prevent or to relieve attacks. The amount of medicine you take will also depend on how you react to the medicine.

- For *oral* dosage form (tablets):
  - —Adults:
    - For *preventing gout attacks*—Most people start with one 0.5-milligram (mg) or 0.6-mg tablet a day. If gout attacks continue to occur, the doctor may direct you to increase the dose to one tablet two or even three times a day for a while. Some people with mild gout may need only one tablet every other day, or even less.
    - For *treating a gout attack that has already started*—Your doctor will probably recommend one of the following treatment plans:
      - —One or two 0.5-mg or 0.6-mg tablets for the first dose, then one 0.5-mg or 0.6-mg tablet every one or two hours, or
      - —Two 0.5-mg or 0.6-mg tablets or one 1-mg tablet every two hours. For both plans, *stop taking this medicine after you have taken the largest amount ordered by your doctor*. If your doctor has not told you the largest amount that you should take for one attack, *do not take more than 6 mg of this medicine* (a total of twelve 0.5-mg tablets, ten 0.6-mg tablets, or six 1-mg tablets, spread over a period of several hours).
  - —Children: Use and dose must be determined by the doctor.
- For *parenteral* dosage form (injection):
  - —Adults:
    - For *preventing gout attacks*—0.5 or 1 mg one or two times a day, injected into a vein.
    - For *treating an attack of gout that has already started*—1 or 2 mg for the first dose, then 0.5 mg or 1 mg every six to twelve hours, injected into a vein. *After a total of 4 mg has been given, no more colchicine (tablets or injections) should be given for at least seven days*.
  - —Children: Use and dose must be determined by the doctor.

Missed dose—If you are taking colchicine regularly (for example, every day) and you miss a dose, take it as soon as possible. However, if it is almost time for your next dose, skip the missed dose and go back to your regular dosing schedule. Do not double doses.

Storage—To store this medicine:
- Keep out of the reach of children.
- Store away from heat and direct light.
- Do not store this medicine in the bathroom, near the kitchen sink, or in other damp places. Heat or moisture may cause the medicine to break down.
- Do not keep outdated medicine or medicine no longer needed. Be sure that any discarded medicine is out of the reach of children.

Precautions While Using This Medicine

If you must take colchicine for a long time (preventive treatment), your doctor may want to check your progress at regular visits. He or she may also want to check for certain side effects. Finding these side effects early can help to keep them from becoming serious.

Stomach problems may be more likely to occur if you drink large amounts of alcoholic beverages while taking colchicine. Also, drinking too much alcohol may increase the amount of uric acid in your blood. This may lessen the effects of colchicine when it is used to prevent gout attacks. Therefore, people who take colchicine should be careful to limit the amount of alcohol they drink.

For patients taking *small amounts of colchicine regularly (preventive treatment)*:

- Attacks of gout or other problems caused by inflammation may continue to occur during treatment. However, the attacks or other problems should occur less often, and they should not be as severe as they were before you started taking colchicine. Even if you think the colchicine is not working, *do not stop taking it and do not increase the dose.* Check with your doctor instead.

Side Effects of This Medicine

Along with its needed effects, a medicine may cause some unwanted effects. Although not all of these side effects may occur, if they do occur they may need medical attention.

Stop taking this medicine immediately if any of the following side effects occur:

More common
    Diarrhea; nausea or vomiting; stomach pain

If any of these side effects continue for 3 hours or longer after you have stopped taking colchicine, check with your doctor.

Also, *check with your doctor immediately* if any of the following side effects occur:

Rare
    Black, tarry stools; blood in urine or stools; difficulty in breathing when exercising; fever with or without chills; headache; large, hive-like swellings on the face, eyelids, mouth, lips, and/or tongue; pinpoint red spots on skin; sores, ulcers, or white spots on lips or in mouth; sore throat; unusual bleeding or bruising; unusual tiredness or weakness

Signs and symptoms of overdose
    Burning feeling in the stomach, throat, or skin; diarrhea (severe or bloody); nausea, stomach pain, or vomiting (severe)

Note: These side effects are usually the first signs of an overdose of colchicine tablets. They are not likely to occur when too much colchicine has been given by injection. Other signs and symptoms that may occur after an overdose of either the tablets or the injection include bleeding; fast, shallow breathing; convulsions (seizures); fever; and very severe muscle weakness. An overdose of colchicine can cause damage to the blood, heart, intestines, kidneys, liver, lungs, and muscles.

The following side effects may occur after an injection of colchicine. Check with your doctor as soon as possible if any of the following occur at or near the place of injection:

Rare
    Burning, "crawling," or tingling feeling in the skin; pain; peeling of skin; redness; swelling; tenderness

Also, check with your doctor as soon as possible if any of the following side effects occur:

Rare
    Muscle weakness; numbness in fingers or toes (usually mild); skin rash or hives

Other side effects may occur that usually do not need medical attention. However, check with your doctor if either of the following side effects continues or is bothersome:

Less common
    Loss of appetite

With long-term use
    Loss of hair

Other side effects not listed above may also occur in some patients. If you notice any other effects, check with your doctor.

Additional Information

Once a medicine has been approved for marketing for a certain use, experience may show that it is also useful for other medical problems. Although these uses are not included in product labeling, colchicine is used in certain patients with the following medical conditions:

- Amyloidosis
- Behçet's syndrome
- Calcium pyrophosphate deposition disease (pseudogout)
- Cirrhosis of the liver
- Familial Mediterranean fever
- Pericarditis
- Sarcoid arthritis

If you are taking colchicine for any of these conditions, the following information may apply:

- For all of these conditions, colchicine is usually given regularly in small amounts to reduce inflammation (preventive treatment). This usually decreases the occurrence of severe attacks or other problems caused by inflammation.
- Colchicine is not a cure for these conditions. It will help prevent problems caused by inflammation only as long as you continue to take it.
- Some patients with calcium pyrophosphate deposition disease (pseudogout) or familial Mediterranean fever may take larger amounts of colchicine only when an attack occurs, to relieve the attack.

For patients taking colchicine for *familial Mediterranean fever*:

- Preventive treatment with colchicine may be helping you even if it does not reduce the number of severe attacks. Colchicine helps prevent other serious problems, such as kidney disease, that can occur in people with this condition. Therefore, even if you think that the colchicine isn't working, *do not stop taking it.* Check with your doctor instead.

Other than the above information, there is no additional information relating to proper use, precautions, or side effects for these uses.

Revised: 01/31/94

COLESEVELAM   Oral-Local— INTRODUCTORY VERSION

Commonly used brand name(s):

In the U.S.—
   Welchol

Description

Colesevelam (koh-le-SEV-e-lam) is used to lower high cholesterol levels in the blood. This may help prevent medical problems caused by cholesterol clogging the blood vessels.

Colesevelam works by attaching to certain substances in the intestine. Since colesevelam is not absorbed into the body, these substances also pass out of the body without being absorbed.

This medicine is available only with your doctor's prescription, in the following dosage forms:

Oral
- Tablets

Before Using This Medicine

In deciding to use a medicine, the risks of taking the medicine must be weighed against the good it will do. This is a decision you and your doctor will make. For colesevelam, the following should be considered:

Allergies—Tell your doctor if you have ever had any unusual or allergic reaction to colesevelam. Also, tell your doctor and pharmacist if you are allergic to any other substances, such as foods, preservatives, or dyes.

Diet—Before prescribing medicine for your condition, your doctor will probably try to control your condition by prescribing a personal diet for you. Such a diet may be low in fats, sugars, and/or cholesterol. Many people are able to control their condition by carefully following their doctor's orders for proper diet and exercise. *Medicine is prescribed only when additional help is needed* and is effective only when a schedule of diet and exercise is properly followed.

Also, this medicine is less effective if you are greatly overweight. It may be very important for you to go on a reducing diet. However, check with your doctor before going on any diet.

Make certain your health care professional knows if you are on any special diet, such as a low-sodium or low-sugar diet. Most medicines contain more than their active ingredient.

Pregnancy—Colesevelam has not been studied in pregnant women. However, colesevelam has not been shown to cause birth defects or other problems in animal studies.

Breast-feeding—It is not known whether colesevelam passes into breast milk. Although most medicines pass into breast milk in small amounts, many of them may be used safely while breast-feeding. Mothers who are taking this medicine and who wish to breast-feed should discuss this with their doctor.

Children—Studies on this medicine have been done only in adult patients, and there is no specific information comparing use of colesevelam in children with use in other age groups.

Older adults—This medicine has not been shown to cause different side effects or problems in older people than it does in younger adults.

Other medicines—Although certain medicines should not be used together at all, in other cases two different medicines may be used together even if an interaction might occur. In these cases, your doctor may want to change the dose, or other precautions may be necessary. Tell your health care professional if you are taking any other prescription or nonprescription (over-the-counter [OTC]) medicine.

Other medical problems—The presence of other medical problems may affect the use of colesevelam. Make sure you tell your doctor if you have any other medical problems, especially:

- Bowel obstruction or
- Difficulty swallowing or
- Major gastrointestinal surgery (recent) or
- Severe gastrointestinal motility disorders—Colesevelam may make these conditions worse
- Hypersensitivity

Proper Use of This Medicine

Dosing—The dose of colesevelam will be different for different patients. *Follow your doctor's orders or the directions on the label.* The following information includes only the average doses of colesevelam. *If your dose is different, do not change it* unless your doctor tells you to do so.

Also, *the number of doses you take each day, the time allowed between doses, and the length of time you take the medicine depend on the medical problem for which you are taking colesevelam.*

- For high cholesterol:
  - Adults—6 tablets a day. This may be taken as one dose or divided into two doses. The dose should be taken with a meal and liquid.
  - Children—Use and dose must be determined by your doctor.

Missed dose—If you miss a dose of this medicine, skip the missed dose and go back to your regular dosing schedule. Do not double doses.

Storage—To store this medicine:
- Keep out of the reach of children.
- Do not store in the bathroom, near the kitchen sink, or in other damp places. Heat or moisture may cause the medicine to break down.
- Do not keep outdated medicine or medicine no longer needed. Ask your health care professional how you should dispose of any medicine you do not use. Be sure that any discarded medicine is out of the reach of children.

Precautions While Using This Medicine

Your doctor will want to check your progress at regular visits. This will allow your doctor to see if the medicine is working properly to lower your cholesterol levels and to decide if you should continue to take it.

Do not stop taking this medicine without first checking with your doctor. When you stop taking this medicine, your blood cholesterol levels may increase again. Your doctor may want you to follow a special diet to help prevent this from happening.

Side Effects of This Medicine

Along with its needed effects, a medicine may cause some unwanted effects. Although not all of these side effects may occur, if they do occur they may need medical attention.

Check with your doctor as soon as possible if any of the following side effects occur:

Less common

Congestion; cough; dryness or soreness of throat; hoarseness; muscle aches or pain; trouble in swallowing

Other side effects may occur that usually do not need medical attention. These side effects may go away during treatment as your body adjusts to the medicine. Also, your health care professional may be able to tell you about ways to prevent or reduce some of these side effects. Check with your health care professional if any of the following side effects continue or are bothersome or if you have any questions about them:

More common

Acid or sour stomach; belching; constipation; indigestion; stomach discomfort, upset, or pain

Other side effects not listed above may also occur in some patients. If you notice any other effects, check with your doctor.

Developed: 08/14/2000

COLESTIPOL   Oral

Commonly used brand name(s):

In the U.S.—
Colestid

In Canada—
Colestid

Description

Colestipol (koe-LES-ti-pole) is used to lower high cholesterol levels in the blood. This may help prevent medical problems caused by cholesterol clogging the blood vessels.

Colestipol works by attaching to certain substances in the intestine. Since colestipol is not absorbed into the body, these substances also pass out of the body without being absorbed.

Colestipol may also be used for other conditions as determined by your doctor.

Colestipol is available only with your doctor's prescription, in the following dosage form:

Oral
• Powder (U.S. and Canada)

Before Using This Medicine

In deciding to use a medicine, the risks of taking the medicine must be weighed against the good it will do. This is a decision you and your doctor will make. For colestipol, the following should be considered:

Allergies—Tell your doctor if you have ever had any unusual or allergic reaction to colestipol. Also tell your health care professional if you are allergic to any substances, such as foods, preservatives, or dyes.

Diet—Before prescribing medicine for your condition, your doctor will probably try to control your condition by prescribing a personal diet for you. Such a diet may be low in fats, sugars, and/or cholesterol. Many people are able to control their condition by carefully following their doctor's orders for proper diet and exercise. Medicine is prescribed only when additional help is needed and is effective only when a schedule of diet and exercise is properly followed.

Also, this medicine is less effective if you are greatly overweight. It may be very important for you to go on a reducing diet. However, check with your doctor before going on any diet.

Make certain your health care professional knows if you are on a low-sodium, low-sugar, or any other special diet.

Pregnancy—Colestipol is not absorbed into the body and is not likely to cause problems. However, it may reduce absorption of vitamins into the body. Ask your doctor whether you need to take extra vitamins.

Breast-feeding—Colestipol is not absorbed into the body and is not likely to cause problems.

Children—There is no specific information comparing use of colestipol in children with use in other age groups. However, use is not recommended in children under 2 years of age since cholesterol is needed for normal development.

Older adults—Side effects may be more likely to occur in patients over 60 years of age, who are usually more sensitive to the effects of colestipol.

Other medicines—Although certain medicines should not be used together at all, in other cases two different medicines may be used together even if an interaction might occur. In these cases, your doctor may want to change the dose, or other precautions may be necessary. When you are taking colestipol it is especially important that your health care professional knows if you are taking any of the following:

• Anticoagulants (blood thinners)—The effects of the anticoagulant may be altered

• Digitalis glycosides (heart medicine) or
• Diuretics (water pills) or
• Penicillin G, taken by mouth, or
• Propranolol, taken by mouth, or
• Tetracyclines (medicine for infection), taken by mouth, or
• Thyroid hormones or
• Vancomycin, taken by mouth—Colestipol may cause these medicines to be less effective; these medicines should be taken 4 to 5 hours apart from colestipol

Other medical problems—The presence of other medical problems may affect the use of colestipol. Make sure you tell your doctor if you have any other medical problems, especially:

• Bleeding problems or

- Constipation or
- Gallstones or
- Heart or blood vessel disease or
- Hemorrhoids or
- Stomach ulcer or other stomach problems or
- Underactive thyroid—Colestipol may make these conditions worse

- Kidney disease—There is an increased risk of developing electrolyte problems

- Liver disease—Cholesterol levels may be raised

Proper Use of This Medicine

Take this medicine exactly as directed by your doctor. Try not to miss any doses and do not take more medicine than your doctor ordered.

Follow carefully the special diet your doctor gave you. This is the most important part of controlling your condition and is necessary if the medicine is to work properly.

This medicine should never be taken in its dry form, since it could cause you to choke. Instead, always mix as follows:

- Add this medicine to 3 ounces or more of water, milk, flavored drink, or your favorite juice or carbonated drink. If you use a carbonated drink, slowly mix in the powder in a large glass to prevent too much foaming. Stir until it is completely mixed (it will *not* dissolve) before drinking. After drinking all the liquid containing the medicine, rinse the glass with a little more liquid and drink that also, to make sure you get all the medicine.
- You may also mix this medicine with milk in hot or regular breakfast cereals, or in thin soups such as tomato or chicken noodle soup. Or you may add it to some pulpy fruits such as crushed pineapple, pears, peaches, or fruit cocktail.

Dosing—The dose of colestipol will be different for different patients. *Follow your doctor's orders or the directions on the label.* The following information includes only the average doses of colestipol. *If your dose is different, do not change it* unless your doctor tells you to do so.

- For *oral* dosage form (powder for oral suspension):
  —For high cholesterol:
    - Adults—15 to 30 grams a day. This is divided into two to four doses and taken before meals.
    - Children—Use and dose must be determined by your doctor.

Missed dose—If you miss a dose of this medicine, take it as soon as possible. Then go back to your regular dosing schedule. However, if it is almost time for your next dose, skip the missed dose and go back to your regular dosing schedule. Do not double doses.

Storage—To store this medicine:

- Keep out of the reach of children.
- Store away from heat and direct light.
- Do not store in the bathroom, near the kitchen sink or in other damp places. Heat or moisture may cause the medicine to break down.
- Do not keep outdated medicine or medicine no longer needed. Be sure that any discarded medicine is out of the reach of children.

Precautions While Using This Medicine

It is very important that your doctor check your progress at regular visits. This will allow your doctor to see if the medicine is working properly to lower your cholesterol levels and to decide if you should continue to take it.

Do not stop taking this medicine without first checking with your doctor. When you stop taking this medicine, your blood cholesterol levels may increase again. Your doctor may want you to follow a special diet to help prevent this from happening.

Do not take any other medicine unless prescribed by your doctor since colestipol may interfere with other medicines.

Side Effects of This Medicine

Along with its needed effects, a medicine may cause some unwanted effects. Although not all of these side effects may occur, if they do occur they may need medical attention.

Check with your doctor immediately if either of the following side effects occurs:
  Rare
    Black, tarry stools; stomach pain (severe) with nausea and vomiting

Check with your doctor as soon as possible if either of the following side effects occurs:
  More common
    Constipation

  Rare
    Loss of weight (sudden)

Other side effects may occur that usually do not need medical attention. These side effects may go away during treatment as your body adjusts to the medicine. However, check with your doctor if any of the following side effects continue or are bothersome:
  Less common
    Belching; bloating; diarrhea; dizziness; headache; nausea or vomiting; stomach pain

Other side effects not listed above may also occur in some patients. If you notice any other effects, check with your doctor.

Additional Information

Once a medicine has been approved for marketing for a certain use, experience may show that it is also useful for other medical problems. Although these uses are not included in product labeling, colestipol is used in certain patients with the following medical conditions:

- Diarrhea caused by bile acids
- Digitalis glycoside overdose
- Excess oxalate in the urine
- Itching (pruritus) associated with partial biliary obstruction

Other than the above information, there is no additional information relating to proper use, precautions, or side effects for these uses.

Revised: 10/21/92
Interim revision: 04/14/94

COLISTIN, NEOMYCIN, AND HYDROCORTISONE   Otic

Commonly used brand name(s):

In the U.S.—
Coly-Mycin S Otic

In Canada—
Coly-Mycin Otic

Description

Colistin, neomycin, and hydrocortisone (koe-LIS-tin, nee-oh-MYE-sin, and hye-droe-KOR-ti-sone) combination contains two antibiotics and a cortisone-like medicine. It is used in the ear to treat infections of the ear canal and to help provide relief from redness, irritation, and discomfort of certain ear problems.

Colistin, neomycin, and hydrocortisone combination is available only with your doctor's prescription, in the following dosage form:

Otic
• Suspension (U.S. and Canada)

Before Using This Medicine

In deciding to use a medicine, the risks of taking the medicine must be weighed against the good it will do. This is a decision you and your doctor will make. For colistin, neomycin, and hydrocortisone combination, the following should be considered:

Allergies—Tell your doctor if you have ever had any unusual or allergic reaction to this medicine or to any related antibiotics such as amikacin (e.g., Amikin), colistin by mouth or by injection (e.g., Coly-Mycin), gentamicin (e.g., Garamycin), kanamycin (e.g., Kantrex), neomycin by mouth or by injection (e.g., Mycifradin), netilmicin (e.g., Netromycin), paromomycin (e.g., Humatin), polymyxin B (e.g., Aerosporin), streptomycin, or tobramycin (e.g., Nebcin). Also tell your health care professional if you are allergic to any other substances, such as thimerosal or other preservatives.

Pregnancy—Colistin, neomycin, and hydrocortisone otic drops have not been shown to cause birth defects or other problems in humans.

Breast-feeding—Colistin, neomycin, and hydrocortisone otic drops have not been reported to cause problems in nursing babies.

Children—Although there is no specific information comparing use of colistin, neomycin, and hydrocortisone combination in children with use in other age groups, this medicine is not expected to cause different side effects or problems in children than it does in adults.

Older adults—Many medicines have not been studied specifically in older people. Therefore, it may not be known whether they work exactly the same way they do in younger adults. Although there is no specific information comparing use of colistin, neomycin, and hydrocortisone combination in the elderly with use in other age groups, this medicine is not expected to cause different side effects or problems in older people than it does in younger adults.

Other medicines—Although certain medicines should not be used together at all, in other cases two different medicines may be used together even if an interaction might occur. In these cases, your doctor may want to change the dose, or other precautions may be necessary. Tell your health care professional if you are using any other prescription or nonprescription (over-the-counter [OTC]) medicine that is to be used in the ear.

Other medical problems—The presence of other medical problems may affect the use of colistin, neomycin, and hydrocortisone combination. Make sure you tell your doctor if you have any other medical problems, especially:

• Other ear infection or problem, including punctured eardrum—Use of colistin, neomycin, and hydrocortisone combination may make the condition worse or may increase the chance of side effects

• Herpes simplex—Use of hydrocortisone may make the condition worse

Proper Use of This Medicine

Before applying this medicine, thoroughly clean the ear canal and dry it with a sterile cotton applicator.

You may warm the ear drops to body temperature (37 °C or 98.6 °F), but no higher, by holding the bottle in your hand for a few minutes before applying. If this medicine gets too warm, it may break down and not work properly.

To apply this medicine:

• Lie down or tilt the head so that the infected ear faces up. Gently pull the earlobe up and back for adults (down and back for children) to straighten the ear canal. Drop the medicine into the ear canal. Keep the ear facing up for about 5 minutes to allow the medicine to coat the ear canal. (For young children and other patients who cannot stay still for 5 minutes, try to keep the ear facing up for at least 1 or 2 minutes.) Your doctor may have inserted a gauze or cotton wick into your ear and may want you to keep the wick moistened with this medicine. Your doctor also may have other directions for you, such as how long you should keep the wick in your ear or when you should return to your doctor to have the wick replaced. If you have any questions about this, check with your doctor.

To keep the medicine as germ-free as possible, do not touch the dropper to any surface (including the ear). Also, keep the container tightly closed.

Do not use this medicine for more than 10 days unless otherwise directed by your doctor.

To help clear up your infection completely, *keep using this medicine for the full time of treatment,* even if your symptoms begin to clear up after a few days. If you stop using this medicine too soon, your symptoms may return. *Do not miss any doses.*

Dosing—The dose of otic colistin, neomycin, and hydrocortisone combination will be different for different patients. *Follow your doctor's orders or the directions on the label.* The following information includes only the average doses of otic colistin, neomycin, and hydrocortisone combination. *If your dose is different, do not change it* unless your doctor tells you to do so.

• For *otic suspension (ear drops)* dosage form:
  —For infections of the ear canal:
    • Adults—Use four drops in the ear every six to eight hours.

- Children—Use up to three drops in the ear every six to eight hours.

Missed dose—If you miss a dose of this medicine, apply it as soon as possible. However, if it is almost time for your next dose, skip the missed dose and go back to your regular dosing schedule.

Storage—To store this medicine:
- Keep out of the reach of children.
- Store away from heat and direct light.
- Keep the medicine from freezing
- Do not keep outdated medicine or medicine no longer needed. Be sure that any discarded medicine is out of the reach of children.

Precautions While Using This Medicine

If your symptoms do not improve within 1 week, or if they become worse, check with your doctor immediately.

Side Effects of This Medicine

Along with its needed effects, a medicine may cause some unwanted effects. Although not all of these side effects may occur, if they do occur they may need medical attention.

Check with your doctor immediately if any of the following side effects occur:
 More common
  Itching, skin rash, redness, swelling, or other sign of irritation not present before use of this medicine

Other side effects not listed above may also occur in some patients. If you notice any other effects, check with your doctor.

Revised: 05/25/95

COLONY STIMULATING FACTORS
Systemic

Commonly used brand name(s):

In the U.S.—
  Neupogen[1]
  Leukine[2]

In Canada—
  Neupogen[1]

Other commonly used names are:
  Granulocyte colony stimulating factor (G-CSF)[1]
  Granulocyte-macrophage colony stimulating factor (GM-CSF)[2]

Note: For quick reference, the following colony stimulating factors are numbered to match the corresponding brand names.

This information applies to the following medicines:
  1. Filgrastim (fil-GRA-stim)
  2. Sargramostim (sar-GRAM-oh-stim) †

†Not commercially available in Canada.

Description

Filgrastim and sargramostim are synthetic (man-made) versions of substances naturally produced in your body. These substances, called colony stimulating factors, help the bone marrow to make new white blood cells.

When certain cancer medicines fight your cancer cells, they also affect those white blood cells that fight infection. To help prevent infections when these cancer medicines are used, colony stimulating factors may be given. Colony stimulating factors also may be used to help the bone marrow recover after bone marrow transplantation and stem cell transplantation.

Colony stimulating factors are available only with your doctor's prescription, in the following dosage form:
 Parenteral
  Filgrastim
   • Injection (U.S. and Canada)
  Sargramostim
   • Injection (U.S.)

Before Using This Medicine

In deciding to use a medicine, the risks of taking the medicine must be weighed against the good it will do. This is a decision you and your doctor will make. For colony stimulating factors, the following should be considered:

Allergies—Tell your doctor if you have ever had any unusual or allergic reaction to the colony stimulating factor. Also tell your health care professional if you are allergic to any other substances, such as foods, preservatives, or dyes.

Pregnancy—Colony stimulating factors have not been studied in pregnant women.
- *Filgrastim*—In studies in rabbits, filgrastim did not cause birth defects but did cause internal defects, a decrease in average weight, and death of the fetus at high doses.
- *Sargramostim*—Studies on birth defects have not been done in animals.

Breast-feeding—It is not known whether colony stimulating factors pass into human breast milk. However, these medicines have not been reported to cause problems in nursing babies.

Children—Although there is no specific information comparing use of colony stimulating factors in children with use in other age groups, this medicine is not expected to cause different side effects or problems in children than it does in adults. In Canada, data from clinical trials in children indicate that the safety of filgrastim is similar in both adults and children receiving certain cancer medicines.

Older adults—Many medicines have not been studied specifically in older people. Therefore, it may not be known whether they work exactly the same way they do in younger adults. Although there is no specific information comparing use of colony stimulating factors in the elderly with use in other age groups, this medicine has been used in many elderly patients and is not expected to cause different side effects or problems in older people than it does in younger adults.

Other medicines—Although certain medicines should not be used together at all, in other cases two different medicines may be used together even if an interaction might occur. In these cases, your doctor may want to change the dose, or other precautions may be necessary. Tell your health care professional if you are taking any other prescription or nonprescription (over-the-counter [OTC]) medicine.

Other medical problems—The presence of other medical problems may affect the use of colony stimulating factors.

Make sure you tell your doctor if you have any other medical problems, especially:

- Conditions caused by inflammation or immune system problems—There is a chance these may be worsened by colony stimulating factor
- Heart disease—Risk of some unwanted effects (heart rhythm problems, retaining water) may be increased
- Kidney disease or
- Liver disease—May sometimes be worsened by colony stimulating factor
- Lung disease—Colony stimulating factor may cause shortness of breath

Proper Use of This Medicine

If you are injecting this medicine yourself, *use it exactly as directed by your doctor*. Do not use more or less of it, and do not use it more often than your doctor ordered. The exact amount of medicine you need has been carefully worked out. Using too much will increase the risk of side effects, while using too little may not improve your condition.

If you are injecting this medicine yourself, each package of colony stimulating factor will contain a patient instruction sheet. Read this sheet carefully and make sure you understand:

- How to prepare the injection.
- Proper use of disposable syringes.
- How to give the injection.
- How long the injection is stable.

If you have any questions about any of this, check with your health care professional.

Dosing—The dose of colony stimulating factors will be different for different patients. The dose that is used may depend on a number of things, including what the medicine is being used for, the patient's body weight or size, and whether or not other medicines are also being taken. *If you are receiving colony stimulating factors at home, follow your doctor's orders or the directions on the label.* If you have any questions about the proper dose of colony stimulating factors, ask your doctor.

Missed dose—If you miss a dose of this medicine, check with your doctor.

Storage—To store this medicine:

- Keep out of the reach of children.
- Store in the refrigerator.
- Keep the medicine from freezing.
- Do not keep outdated medicine or medicine no longer needed. Ask your health care professional how you should dispose of any medicine you do not use. Be sure that any discarded medicine is out of the reach of children.

Precautions While Using This Medicine

It is very important that your doctor check your progress at regular visits to make sure that this medicine is working properly and to check for unwanted effects.

Colony stimulating factors are used to prevent or reduce the risk of infection while you are being treated with cancer medicines. Because your body's ability to fight infection is reduced, *it is very important that you call your doctor at the first sign of any infection* (for example, if you get a fever or chills) so you can start antibiotic treatment right away.

Colony stimulating factors commonly cause mild bone pain, usually in the lower back or pelvis, about the time the white blood cells start to come back in your bone marrow. The pain is usually mild and lasts only a few days. Your doctor will probably prescribe a mild analgesic (painkiller) for you to take during that time. If you find that the analgesic is not strong enough, talk with your doctor about using something that will make you more comfortable.

Side Effects of This Medicine

Along with its needed effects, a medicine may cause some unwanted effects. Although not all of these side effects may occur, if they do occur they may need medical attention.

The side effects listed below include only those that might be caused by colony stimulating factors. To find out about other side effects that may be caused by the cancer medicines you are also receiving, look under the information about those specific medicines.

Check with your doctor as soon as possible if any of the following side effects occur:
For filgrastim
  Less common
    Redness or pain at the site of subcutaneous (under the skin) injection
  Rare
    Fever; rapid or irregular heartbeat; sores on skin; wheezing
For sargramostim
  Less common
    Fever; redness or pain at the site of subcutaneous (under the skin) injection; shortness of breath; swelling of feet or lower legs; weight gain (sudden)
  Rare
    Chest pain; rapid or irregular heartbeat; sores on skin; wheezing

Other side effects may occur that usually do not need medical attention. These side effects may go away during treatment as your body adjusts to the medicine. However, check with your doctor if any of the following side effects continue or are bothersome:
For both filgrastim and sargramostim
  More common
    Headache; pain in arms or legs; pain in joints or muscles; pain in lower back or pelvis; skin rash or itching
For sargramostin only (in addition to the above)
  Less common or rare
    Dizziness or faintness after first dose of medicine; flushing of face after first dose of medicine; weakness

Other side effects not listed above may also occur in some patients. If you notice any other effects, check with your doctor.

Additional Information

Once a medicine has been approved for marketing for a certain use, experience may show that it also is useful for other medical problems. Although not specifically included in the product labeling, colony stimulating factors are used in certain patients with the following medical conditions:

- Failure or delay of myeloid engraftment after hematopoietic stem cell transplantation
- Myelodysplastic syndromes
- Neutropenia, AIDS-associated
- Neutropenia, drug-induced

Other than the above information, there is no additional information relating to proper use, precautions, or side effects for these uses.

Revised: 04/18/2001

CONJUGATED ESTROGENS AND MEDROXYPROGESTERONE FOR OVARIAN HORMONE THERAPY (OHT)   Systemic†

Commonly used brand name(s):

In the U.S.—
　Premphase[1]
　Prempro[2]

Note: For quick reference, the following estrogens are numbered to match the corresponding brand names.

This information applies to the following medicines
　1. Conjugated Estrogens, and Conjugated Estrogens and Medroxyprogesterone (CON-ju-gate-ed ES-troe-jenz, and CON-ju-gate-ed ES-troe-jenz and me-DROX-ee-proe-JES-te-rone) †
　2. Conjugated Estrogens and Medroxyprogesterone (CON-ju-gate-ed ES-troe-jenz and me-DROX-ee-proe-JES-te-rone) †

†Not commercially available in Canada.

Description

Conjugated estrogens and medroxyprogesterone (CON-ju-gate-ed ES-troe-jenz and me-DROX-ee-proe-JES-te-rone) are estrogen and progestin hormones. Along with other effects, estrogens help females develop sexually at puberty and regulate the menstrual cycle. Progestin lowers the effect of estrogen on the uterus and keeps estrogen-related problems from developing.

Around the time of menopause, the ovaries produce less estrogen. Estrogens are given to:

- Relieve the signs of menopause (vasomotor symptoms of menopause), such as hot flashes and unusual sweating, chills, faintness, or dizziness.
- Treat inflammation of the vagina (atrophic vaginitis) and of the genital area (atrophy of the vulva) by keeping these areas from becoming too dry, itchy, or painful.
- Prevent the loss of bone that begins at the time of menopause. Keeping bones strong decreases the chance of developing weak bones that easily break (osteoporosis). Estrogen use is most effective when it is taken for more than 7 years while you are getting regular exercise and extra calcium. Protection from bone loss can then last for many years after you stop taking the medicine.

There is *no* medical evidence to support the belief that the use of estrogens will keep the patient feeling young, keep the skin soft, or delay the appearance of wrinkles. Nor has it been proven that the use of estrogens during menopause will relieve emotional and nervous symptoms, unless these symptoms are related to the menopausal symptoms, such as hot flashes.

Progestins are not needed if the uterus has been removed (by a surgical method called hysterectomy). In that case, it may be better to receive estrogens alone without the progestin.

Conjugated estrogens and medroxyprogesterone are available only with your doctor's prescription, in the following dosage forms:

　Oral
　　Conjugated Estrogens; Conjugated Estrogens and Medroxyprogesterone
　　- Tablets (U.S.)
　　Conjugated Estrogens and Medroxyprogesterone
　　- Tablets (U.S.)

Before Using This Medicine

In deciding to use a medicine, the risks of taking the medicine must be weighed against the good it will do. This is a decision you and your doctor will make. For conjugated estrogens and medroxyprogesterone, the following should be considered:

Allergies—Tell your doctor if you have ever had any unusual or allergic reaction to estrogens or progestins. Also tell your health care professional if you are allergic to any other substances, such as foods, preservatives, or dyes.

Pregnancy—Conjugated estrogens and medroxyprogesterone are not recommended for use during pregnancy. Becoming pregnant or maintaining a pregnancy is not likely to occur around the time of menopause. Tell your doctor right away if you suspect you are pregnant.

Breast-feeding—Conjugated estrogens and medroxyprogesterone pass into the breast milk. This medicine is not recommended for use during breast-feeding.

Other medicines—Although certain medicines should not be used together at all, in other cases two different medicines may be used together even if an interaction might occur. In these cases, your doctor may want to change the dose, or other precautions may be necessary. When you are taking conjugated estrogens and medroxyprogesterone, it is especially important that your health care professional know if you are taking any of the following:

- Acetaminophen (e.g., Tylenol) (with long-term, high-dose use) or
- Amiodarone (e.g., Cordarone) or
- Anabolic steroids (nandrolone [e.g., Anabolin], oxandrolone [e.g., Anavar], oxymetholone [e.g., Anadrol], stanozolol [e.g., Winstrol]) or
- Androgens (male hormones) or
- Anti-infectives by mouth or by injection (medicine for infection) or
- Antithyroid agents (medicine for overactive thyroid) or
- Carmustine (e.g., BiCNU) or
- Chloroquine (e.g., Aralen) or
- Dantrolene (e.g., Dantrium) or
- Daunorubicin (e.g., Cerubidine) or
- Disulfiram (e.g., Antabuse) or
- Divalproex (e.g., Depakote) or
- Etretinate (e.g., Tegison) or
- Gold salts (medicine for arthritis) or
- Hydroxychloroquine (e.g., Plaquenil) or

- Isoniazid or
- Mercaptopurine (e.g., Purinethol) or
- Methotrexate (e.g., Mexate) or
- Methyldopa (e.g., Aldomet) or
- Naltrexone (e.g., Trexan) (with long-term, high-dose use) or
- Phenothiazines (acetophenazine [e.g., Tindal], chlorpromazine [e.g., Thorazine], fluphenazine [e.g., Prolixin], mesoridazine [e.g., Serentil], perphenazine [e.g., Trilafon], prochlorperazine [e.g., Compazine], promazine [e.g., Sparine], promethazine [e.g., Phenergan], thioridazine [e.g., Mellaril], trifluoperazine [e.g., Stelazine], triflupromazine [e.g., Vesprin], trimeprazine [e.g., Temaril]) or
- Plicamycin (e.g., Mithracin)—Use of these medicines with conjugated estrogens and medroxyprogesterone may increase the chance of problems occurring that affect the liver

- Aminoglutethimide (e.g., Cytadren) or
- Barbiturates, especially phenobarbital or
- Carbamazepine (e.g., Tegretol) or
- Phenytoin (e.g., Dilantin) or
- Rifampin (e.g., Rifadin)—These medicines may decrease the effect of conjugated estrogens or medroxyprogesterone

- Cyclosporine (e.g., Sandimmune)—Conjugated estrogens can prevent cyclosporine's removal from the body; this can lead to cyclosporine causing kidney or liver problems

- Protease inhibitors, such as ritonavir (e.g., Norvir)—May decrease the effect of conjugated estrogens

Other medical problems—The presence of other medical problems may affect the use of conjugated estrogens and medroxyprogesterone. Make sure you tell your doctor if you have any other medical problems, especially:

- Asthma or
- Heart problems or
- Epilepsy or
- High blood pressure or
- Kidney problems, severe or
- Migraine headaches—Rarely, water retention caused by conjugated estrogens or medroxyprogesterone may worsen these conditions; on the other hand, blood pressure and some heart or blood vessel problems can improve for most patients

- Blood clotting problems (or history of during previous estrogen therapy)—Estrogens usually are not used until blood clotting problems stop; using estrogens is usually not a problem for most patients without a history of blood clotting problems due to estrogen use

- Bone cancer or
- Breast cancer or
- Cancer of the uterus (active or suspected) or
- Fibroid tumors of the uterus—Estrogens may interfere with the treatment of breast or bone cancer, worsen cancer of the uterus, or increase the size of fibroid tumors

- Changes in genital or vaginal bleeding of unknown causes—Estrogens may make these conditions worse; some irregular vaginal bleeding may be a sign that the lining of the uterus may be growing too much or is a sign of cancer of the uterus lining

- Diabetes mellitus (sugar diabetes)—Conjugated estrogens or medroxyprogesterone may slightly change the amount of blood sugar for some patients, but for most patients with sugar diabetes, there is no change in blood sugar

- Endometriosis or
- Gallbladder disease or gallstones (or history of) or
- High cholesterol or triglycerides (or family history of) or
- Liver disease, including jaundice (or history of) or
- Pancreatitis (inflammation of pancreas)—Conjugated estrogens or medroxyprogesterone may worsen these conditions; however, using estrogens can lower blood cholesterol in many patients with high cholesterol

Proper Use of This Medicine

Conjugated estrogens and medroxyprogesterone usually come with patient directions. Read them carefully before taking this medicine.

Take this medicine only as directed by your doctor. Do not take more of it and do not take it for a longer period of time than your doctor ordered. The length of time you take the medicine will depend on the medical problem for which you are taking conjugated estrogens and medroxyprogesterone. Discuss with your doctor how long you will need to take these medicines.

If you are taking the estrogen or progestin hormones in a certain order (i.e., conjugated estrogens tablets followed by conjugated estrogens and medroxyprogesterone tablets), *be sure you know in which order you need to take the medicines*. If you have questions about this, ask your health care professional.

Nausea may occur during the first few weeks after you start taking estrogens. This effect usually disappears with continued use. If the nausea is bothersome, it can usually be prevented or reduced by taking each dose with food or immediately after food.

Dosing—The dose of these medicines will be different for different patients. *Follow your doctor's orders or the directions on the label.* The following information includes only the average doses of these medicines. *If your dose is different, do not change it* unless your doctor tells you to do so.

For conjugated estrogens, and conjugated estrogens and medroxyprogesterone
- For *oral* dosage form (tablets):
  —To prevent loss of bone (osteoporosis) or for treating itching or dryness of the genital area (atrophy of the vulva), inflammation of the vagina (atrophic vaginitis), or symptoms of menopause:
  - Adults—One tablet (containing 0.625 mg conjugated estrogens) once a day on Days 1 through 14; then, one tablet (containing 0.625 mg conjugated estrogens and 5 mg medroxyprogesterone) once a day on Days 15 through 28. Repeat cycle.

For conjugated estrogens and medroxyprogesterone
- For *oral* dosage form (tablets):
  —To prevent loss of bone (osteoporosis) or for treating itching or dryness of the genital area (atrophy of the vulva), inflammation of the vagina (atrophic vaginitis), or symptoms of menopause:
  - Adults—One tablet (containing 0.625 mg conjugated estrogens and 2.5 mg medroxyproges-

terone) once a day for twenty-eight days. Repeat cycle. If vaginal bleeding or spotting continues and it is undesired, your doctor may increase your dose to the next highest strength tablet (0.625 mg conjugated estrogens and 5 mg medroxyprogesterone). It should be taken once a day for twenty-eight days. Repeat cycle.

Missed dose—If you miss a dose of this medicine, take it as soon as possible. However, if it is almost time for your next dose, skip the missed dose and go back to your regular dosing schedule. Do not double doses.

Storage—To store this medicine:
- Keep out of the reach of children.
- Store away from heat and direct light.
- Do not store in the bathroom, near the kitchen sink, or in other damp places. Heat or moisture may cause the medicine to break down.
- Do not keep outdated medicine or medicine no longer needed. Be sure that any discarded medicine is out of the reach of children.

Precautions While Using This Medicine

It is very important that your doctor check your progress at regular visits to make sure this medicine does not cause unwanted effects. Plan on going to see your doctor every year, but some doctors require visits more often.

Although the risk for developing breast problems or breast cancer is low, it is still important that you regularly check your breasts for any unusual lumps or discharge, and report any problems to your doctor. You should also have a mammogram (x-ray pictures of the breasts) and breast examination done by your doctor whenever your doctor recommends it.

If your menstrual periods have stopped, they may start again once you begin taking this medicine. This effect will continue for as long as the medicine is taken. However, if taking the continuous treatment (0.625 mg conjugated estrogens and 2.5 mg medroxyprogesterone once a day), monthly bleeding usually stops within 10 months.

Also, vaginal bleeding between your regular menstrual periods may occur during the first 3 months of use. *Do not stop taking your medicine. Check with your doctor* if bleeding continues for an unusually long time, if your period has not started within 45 days of your last period, or if you think you are pregnant.

Tell the doctor in charge that you are taking this medicine before having any laboratory test, because some test results may be affected.

Side Effects of This Medicine

Healthy women rarely have severe side effects from taking conjugated estrogens or medroxyprogesterone to replace estrogen.

Check with your doctor as soon as possible if any of the following side effects occur:
More common
Menstrual periods beginning again, including changing menstrual bleeding pattern for up to 6 months (spotting, breakthrough bleeding, prolonged or heavier vaginal bleeding, or vaginal bleeding completely stopping by 10 months); vaginal itching or irritation, or thick, white vaginal discharge

Less common
Breast lumps; discharge from breast; skin rash
Rare
Pain or tenderness in stomach, side, or abdomen; yellow eyes or skin

Other side effects may occur that usually do not need medical attention. These side effects may go away during treatment as your body adjusts to the medicine. However, check with your doctor if any of the following side effects continue or are bothersome:
More common
Abdominal cramps; breast pain or tenderness; diarrhea; dizziness; enlarged breasts; increase in amount of clear vaginal discharge; itching; joint pain; mental depression; nausea; painful menstrual periods; passing of gas; stomach discomfort following meals; unusual tiredness

Less common
Bloating or swelling of face, ankles, or feet; headaches, including migraine headaches; increase in sexual desire; tense muscles; unusual weight gain or loss

Rare
Mood changes; nervousness; trouble in sleeping; vomiting

Other side effects not listed above may also occur in some patients. If you notice any other effects, check with your doctor.

Revised: 06/30/98

COPPER SUPPLEMENTS Systemic

Commonly used brand name(s):

In the U.S.—
Cupri-Pak[2]

Note: For quick reference, the following copper supplements are numbered to match the corresponding brand names.

This information applies to the following:
1. Copper Gluconate (KOP-er GLOO-coh-nate) †‡
2. Cupric Sulfate (KYOO-prik SUL-fate) †‡

†Not commercially available in Canada.
‡Generic name product may be available in the U.S.

Description

Copper supplements are used to prevent or treat copper deficiency.

The body needs copper for normal growth and health. For patients who are unable to get enough copper in their regular diet or who have a need for more copper, copper supplements may be necessary. They are generally taken by mouth but some patients may have to receive them by injection. Copper is needed to help your body use iron. It is also important for nerve function, bone growth, and to help your body use sugar.

Lack of copper may lead to anemia and osteoporosis (weak bones).

Some conditions may increase your need for copper. These include:

- Burns
- Diarrhea
- Intestine disease
- Kidney disease
- Pancreas disease
- Stomach removal
- Stress, continuing

In addition, premature infants may need additional copper.

Increased need for copper should be determined by your health care professional.

Claims that copper supplements are effective in the treatment of arthritis or skin conditions have not been proven. Use of copper supplements to cause vomiting has caused death and should be avoided.

Injectable copper is given by or under the supervision of a health care professional. Another form of copper is available without a prescription.

Copper supplements are available in the following dosage forms:

Oral
Copper Gluconate
- Tablets (U.S.)

Parenteral
Cupric Sulfate
- Injection (U.S.)

Importance of Diet

For good health, it is important that you eat a balanced and varied diet. Follow carefully any diet program your health care professional may recommend. For your specific dietary vitamin and/or mineral needs, ask your health care professional for a list of appropriate foods. If you think that you are not getting enough vitamins and/or minerals in your diet, you may choose to take a dietary supplement.

Copper is found in various foods, including organ meats (especially liver), seafoods, beans, nuts, and whole-grains. Additional copper can come from drinking water from copper pipes, using copper cookware, and eating farm products sprayed with copper-containing chemicals. Copper may be decreased in foods that have high acid content and are stored in tin cans for a long time.

The daily amount of copper needed is defined in several different ways.

For U.S.—
- Recommended Dietary Allowances (RDAs) are the amount of vitamins and minerals needed to provide for adequate nutrition in most healthy persons. RDAs for a given nutrient may vary depending on a person's age, sex, and physical condition (e.g., pregnancy).
- Daily Values (DVs) are used on food and dietary supplement labels to indicate the percent of the recommended daily amount of each nutrient that a serving provides. DV replaces the previous designation of United States Recommended Daily Allowances (US-RDAs).

For Canada—
- Recommended Nutrient Intakes (RNIs) are used to determine the amounts of vitamins, minerals, and protein needed to provide adequate nutrition and lessen the risk of chronic disease.

There is no RDA or RNI for copper. However, normal daily recommended intakes are generally defined as follows:

- Infants and children—
  Birth to 3 years of age: 0.4 to 1 milligram (mg) per day.
  4 to 6 years of age: 1 to 1.5 mg per day.
  7 to 10 years of age: 1 to 2 mg per day.
- Adolescent and adult males—1.5 to 2.5 mg per day.
- Adolescent and adult females—1.5 to 3 mg per day.

Before Using This Dietary Supplement

If you are taking this dietary supplement without a prescription, carefully read and follow any precautions on the label. For copper supplements, the following should be considered:

Allergies—Tell your health care professional if you are allergic to any substances, such as foods, preservatives, or dyes.

Pregnancy—It is especially important that you are receiving enough vitamins and minerals when you become pregnant and that you continue to receive the right amount of vitamins and minerals throughout your pregnancy. The healthy growth and development of the fetus depend on a steady supply of nutrients from the mother. However, taking large amounts of a dietary supplement in pregnancy may be harmful to the mother and/or fetus and should be avoided.

Breast-feeding—It is important that you receive the right amounts of vitamins and minerals so that your baby will also get the vitamins and minerals needed to grow properly. However, taking large amounts of a dietary supplement while breast-feeding may be harmful to the mother and/or baby and should be avoided.

Children—Problems in children have not been reported with intake of normal daily recommended amounts.

Older adults—Problems in older adults have not been reported with intake of normal daily recommended amounts.

Medicines or other dietary supplements—Although certain medicines or dietary supplements should not be used together at all, in other cases they may be used together even if an interaction might occur. In these cases, your health care professional may want to change the dose, or other precautions may be necessary. When you are taking copper supplements, it is especially important that your health care professional know if you are taking any of the following:

- Penicillamine or
- Trientine or
- Zinc supplements (taken by mouth)—Use with copper supplements may decrease the amount of copper that gets into the body; copper supplements should be taken at least 2 hours after penicillamine, trientine, or zinc supplements

Other medical problems—The presence of other medical problems may affect the use of copper supplements. Make sure you tell your health care professional if you have any other medical problems, especially:

- Biliary disease or
- Liver disease—Taking copper supplements may cause high blood levels of copper, and dosage for copper may have to be changed
- Wilson's disease (too much copper in the body)—Copper supplements may make this condition worse

Proper Use of This Dietary Supplement

Dosing—The amount of copper needed to meet normal daily recommended intakes will be different for different individuals. The following information includes only the average amounts of copper.

- For *oral* dosage form (tablets):
  - —To prevent deficiency, the amount taken by mouth is based on normal daily recommended intakes:
    - Adult and teenage males—1.5 to 2.5 milligrams (mg) per day.
    - Adult and teenage females—1.5 to 3 mg per day.
    - Children 7 to 10 years of age—1 to 2 mg per day.
    - Children 4 to 6 years of age—1 to 1.5 mg per day.
    - Children birth to 3 years of age—0.4 to 1 mg per day.
  - —To treat deficiency:
    - Adults, teenagers, and children—Treatment dose is determined by prescriber for each individual based on the severity of deficiency.

Missed dose—If you miss taking copper supplements for one or more days there is no cause for concern, since it takes some time for your body to become seriously low in copper. However, if your health care professional has recommended that you take copper try to remember to take it as directed every day.

Storage—To store this dietary supplement:

- Keep out of the reach of children.
- Store away from heat and direct light.
- Do not store in the bathroom, near the kitchen sink, or in other damp places. Heat or moisture may cause the dietary supplement to break down.
- Keep the dietary supplement from freezing. Do not refrigerate.
- Do not keep outdated dietary supplements or those no longer needed. Be sure that any discarded dietary supplement is out of the reach of children.

Precautions While Using This Dietary Supplement

Do not take copper supplements and zinc supplements at the same time. It is best to take your copper supplement 2 hours after zinc supplements, to get the full benefit of each.

Side Effects of This Dietary Supplement

Along with its needed effects, a dietary supplement may cause some unwanted effects. Although copper supplements have not been reported to cause any side effects, *check with your health care professional immediately* if any of the following side effects occur as a result of an overdose:

Symptoms of overdose

Black or bloody vomit; blood in urine; coma; diarrhea; dizziness or fainting; headache (severe or continuing); heartburn; loss of appetite; lower back pain; metallic taste; nausea (severe or continuing); pain or burning while urinating; vomiting; yellow eyes or skin

Other side effects not listed above may also occur in some individuals. If you notice any other effects, check with your health care professional.

Revised: 09/01/91
Interim revision: 06/25/92; 08/17/94; 05/26/95

CORTICOSTEROIDS   Dental

Commonly used brand name(s):

In the U.S.—
Kenalog in Orabase[2]   Oracort[2]
Orabase-HCA[1]   Oralone[2]

In Canada—
Kenalog in Orabase[2]

Another commonly used name for hydrocortisone is cortisol.

Note: For quick reference, the following corticosteroids are numbered to match the corresponding brand names.

This information applies to the following medicines:
1. Hydrocortisone (hye-droe-KOR-ti-sone) †
2. Triamcinolone (trye-am-SIN-oh-lone)

†Not commercially available in Canada.

Description

Dental corticosteroids (kor-ti-ko-STER-oyds) are used to relieve the discomfort and redness of some mouth and gum problems. These medicines are like cortisone. They belong to the general family of medicines called steroids.

Dental corticosteroids are available only with your medical doctor's or dentist's prescription in the following dosage forms:

Dental
Hydrocortisone
  • Paste (U.S.)
Triamcinolone
  • Paste (U.S. and Canada)

Before Using This Medicine

In deciding to use a medicine, the risks of taking the medicine must be weighed against the good it will do. This is a decision you and your doctor or dentist will make. For dental corticosteroids, the following should be considered:

Allergies—Tell your doctor or dentist if you have ever had any unusual or allergic reaction to corticosteroids. Also tell your health care professional if you are allergic to any other substances, such as foods, preservatives, or dyes.

Pregnancy—When used properly, these medicines have not been shown to cause problems in humans. Studies on birth defects with dental corticosteroids have not been done in humans. However, studies in animals have shown that topical corticosteroids, such as the hydrocortisone or triamcinolone in this medicine, when applied to the skin in large amounts or used for a long time, could cause birth defects. Studies with dental paste have not been done in animals.

Breast-feeding—When used properly, dental corticosteroids have not been reported to cause problems in nursing babies.

Children—Children and teenagers who must use this medicine should be checked often by their doctor. Dental corticosteroids may be absorbed through the lining of the mouth and, if used too often or for too long a time, may interfere with growth in children. Before using this medicine in children, you should discuss its use with your child's medical doctor or dentist.

Older adults—Although there is no specific information comparing use of dental corticosteroids in the elderly with use in other age groups, these medicines are not expected to cause different side effects or problems in older people than they do in younger adults.

Other medicines—Although certain medicines should not be used together at all, in many cases two different medicines may be used together even if an interaction might occur. In these cases, your doctor or dentist may want to change the dose, or other precautions may be necessary. Tell your health care professional if you are taking or using any other prescription or nonprescription (over-the-counter [OTC]) medicine.

Other medical problems—The presence of other medical problems may affect the use of dental corticosteroids. Make sure you tell your doctor or dentist if you have any other medical problems, especially:

- Diabetes mellitus (sugar diabetes)—Too much use of corticosteroids may cause a loss of control of diabetes by increasing blood and urine glucose. However, this is not likely to happen when dental corticosteroids are used for a short period of time
- Herpes sores or
- Infection or sores of the mouth or throat or
- Tuberculosis—Corticosteroids may make existing infections worse or cause new infections

Proper Use of This Medicine

To use hydrocortisone or triamcinolone dental paste:

- Using a cotton swab, press (do not rub) a small amount of paste onto the area to be treated until the paste sticks and a smooth, slippery film forms. Do not try to spread the medicine because it will become crumbly and gritty.
- Apply the paste at bedtime so the medicine can work overnight. The other applications of the paste should be made following meals.

Do not use corticosteroids more often or for a longer time than your medical doctor or dentist ordered. To do so may increase the chance of absorption through the lining of the mouth and the chance of side effects.

Do not use this medicine for other mouth problems without first checking with your medical doctor or dentist. This medicine should *not* be used on many kinds of bacterial, viral, or fungal infections.

Dosing—The doses of these medicines will be different for different patients. *Follow your doctor's orders or the directions on the label.* The following information includes only the average doses of these medicines. *If your dose is different, do not change it* unless your doctor or dentist tells you to do so.

For hydrocortisone
- For mouth and/or gum problems:
  —Adults: Apply to the affected area two or three times a day, after meals and at bedtime.
  —Children: Dose must be determined by your doctor or dentist.

For triamcinolone
- For mouth and/or gum problems:
  —Adults: Apply to the affected area two or three times a day, after meals and at bedtime.
  —Children: Dose must be determined by your doctor or dentist.

Missed dose—If your medical doctor or dentist has ordered you to use this medicine according to a regular schedule and you miss a dose, use it as soon as you remember. However, if it is almost time for your next dose, skip the missed dose and go back to your regular dosing schedule.

Storage—To store this medicine:
- Keep out of the reach of children.
- Store away from heat and direct light.
- Keep the medicine from freezing.
- Do not keep outdated medicine or medicine no longer needed. Be sure that any discarded medicine is out of the reach of children.

Precautions While Using This Medicine

Check with your medical doctor or dentist:
- if your symptoms do not improve within 1 week.
- if your condition gets worse.

Side Effects of This Medicine

Along with its needed effects, a medicine may cause some unwanted effects. Although not all of these side effects may occur, if they do occur they may need medical attention.

Check with your medical doctor or dentist as soon as possible if the following side effects occur:

> Signs of infection or irritation such as burning, itching, blistering, or peeling not present before use of this medicine

Other side effects not listed above may also occur in some patients. If you notice any other effects, check with your medical doctor or dentist.

Revised: 11/18/92
Interim revision: 06/15/99

CORTICOSTEROIDS   Inhalation

Commonly used brand name(s):

In the U.S.—

AeroBid[4]	Pulmicort Respules[2]
AeroBid-M[4]	Pulmicort Turbuhaler[2]
Azmacort[5]	Vanceril[1]
Beclovent[1]	Vanceril 84 mcg Double
Decadron Respihaler[3]	Strength[1]

In Canada—

Azmacort[5]	Bronalide[4]
Beclodisk[1]	Pulmicort Nebuamp[2]
Becloforte[1]	Pulmicort Turbuhaler[2]
Beclovent[1]	Vanceril[1]
Beclovent Rotacaps[1]	

Other commonly used names are: Beclomethasone dipropionate;[1] Beclomethasone;[1] Beclomethasone dipropionate[1].

Note: For quick reference, the following corticosteroids are numbered to match the corresponding brand names.

This information applies to the following medicines:
1. Beclomethasone (be-kloe-METH-a-sone)
2. Budesonide (byoo-DESS-oh-nide)
3. Dexamethasone (dex-a-METH-a-sone) †
4. Flunisolide (floo-NISS-oh-lide)
5. Triamcinolone (trye-am-SIN-oh-lone)

†Not commercially available in Canada.

Description

Inhalation corticosteroids (kor-ti-koe-STER-oids) are cortisone-like medicines. They are used to help prevent the symptoms of asthma. When used regularly every day, inhalation corticosteroids decrease the number and severity of asthma attacks. However, they will not relieve an asthma attack that has already started.

Inhaled corticosteroids work by preventing certain cells in the lungs and breathing passages from releasing substances that cause asthma symptoms.

This medicine may be used with other asthma medicines, such as bronchodilators (medicines that open up narrowed breathing passages) or other corticosteroids taken by mouth.

Inhalation corticosteroids are available only with your doctor's prescription, in the following dosage forms:

Inhalation
Beclomethasone
- Aerosol (U.S. and Canada)
- Capsules for inhalation (Canada)
- Powder for inhalation (Canada)

Budesonide
- Powder for inhalation (U.S. and Canada)
- Suspension for inhalation (U.S. and Canada)

Dexamethasone
- Aerosol (U.S.)

Flunisolide
- Aerosol (U.S. and Canada)

Triamcinolone
- Aerosol (U.S. and Canada)

Before Using This Medicine

In deciding to use a medicine, the risks of taking the medicine must be weighed against the good it will do. This is a decision you and your doctor will make. For inhalation corticosteroids, the following should be considered:

Allergies—Tell your doctor if you have ever had any unusual or allergic reaction to corticosteroids. Also tell your health care professional if you are allergic to any other substances, such as foods, preservatives, or dyes.

Pregnancy—Although studies in animals have shown that inhaled corticosteroids cause birth defects and other problems, in humans these medicines, when used in regular daily doses during pregnancy to keep the mother's asthma under control, have not been reported to cause breathing problems or birth defects in the newborn. Also, corticosteroids may prevent the effects of poorly controlled asthma, which are known to be harmful to the baby. Before taking an inhaled corticosteroid, make sure your doctor knows if you are pregnant or if you may become pregnant.

Breast-feeding—It is not known whether inhaled corticosteroids pass into breast milk. Although most medicines pass into breast milk in small amounts, many of them may be used safely while breast-feeding. Mothers who are using this medicine and who wish to breast-feed should discuss this with their doctor.

Children—Inhalation corticosteroids have been tested in children and, except for the possibility of slowed growth, in low effective doses, have not been shown to cause different side effects or problems than they do in adults.

Studies have shown that slowed growth or reduced adrenal gland function may occur in some children using inhaled corticosteroids in recommended doses. However, poorly controlled asthma may cause slowed growth, especially when corticosteroids taken by mouth are needed often. Your doctor will want you to use the lowest possible dose of an inhaled corticosteroid that controls asthma. This will lessen the chance of an effect on growth or adrenal gland function. *It is also important that children taking inhaled corticosteroids visit their doctors regularly so that their growth rates may be monitored.*

Regular use of inhaled corticosteroids may allow some children to stop using or decrease the amount of corticosteroids taken by mouth. This also will reduce the risk of slowed growth or reduced adrenal function.

Children who are using inhaled corticosteroids in large doses should avoid exposure to chickenpox or measles. When a child is exposed or the disease develops, the doctor should be contacted and his or her directions should be followed carefully.

Before this medicine is given to a child, you and your child's doctor should talk about the good this medicine will do as well as the risks of using it. Follow the doctor's directions very carefully to lessen the chance that unwanted effects will occur.

Older adults—Many medicines have not been studied specifically in older people. Therefore, it may not be known whether they work exactly the same way they do in younger adults. Although there is no specific information comparing use of inhaled corticosteroids in the elderly with use in other age groups, this medicine is not expected to cause different side effects or problems in older people than it does in younger adults.

Other medicines—Although certain medicines should not be used together at all, in other cases two different medicines may be used together even if an interaction might occur. In these cases, your doctor may want to change the dose, or other precautions may be necessary. Tell your health care professional if you are taking any other prescription or nonprescription (over-the-counter [OTC]) medicine.

Other medical problems—The presence of other medical problems may affect the use of inhaled corticosteroids. Make sure you tell your doctor if you have any other medical problems, especially:

- Cirrhosis (liver disease)—The effect of inhaled corticosteroids may be stronger in patients with this disease
- Glaucoma—Use of this medicine may cause the pressure in the eye to be increased
- Hypothyroidism (decreased production of thyroid hormone)—The effect of inhaled corticosteroids may be stronger in patients with this condition
- Infections, untreated—Using this medicine while an infection is present and is not being treated may cause the infection to get worse.
- Osteoporosis (bone disease)—Inhaled corticosteroids in high doses may make this condition worse in women who are past menopause and who are not receiving an estrogen replacement
- Tuberculosis (history of)—Use of this medicine may cause a tuberculosis infection to occur again

Proper Use of This Medicine

Inhaled corticosteroids will not relieve an asthma attack that has already started. However, your doctor may want you to continue taking this medicine at the usual time, even if you use another medicine to relieve the asthma attack.

Use this medicine only as directed. Do not use more of it and do not use it more often than your doctor ordered. To do so may increase the chance of side effects. Do not stop taking this medicine abruptly. This medicine should be discontinued only under the supervision of your doctor.

In order for this medicine to help prevent asthma attacks, it must be used every day in regularly spaced doses, as ordered by your doctor. Up to 4 to 6 weeks may pass before you begin to notice improvement in your condition. It may take several months before you feel the full effects of this medicine. This may not take as long if you have already been taking certain other medicines for your asthma.

Gargling and rinsing your mouth with water after each dose may help prevent hoarseness, throat irritation, and infection in the mouth. However, do not swallow the water after rinsing. Your doctor may also want you to use a spacer device to lessen these problems.

Inhaled corticosteroids are used with a special inhaler and usually come with patient directions. *Read the directions carefully before using this medicine.* If you do not understand the directions or you are not sure how to use the inhaler, ask your health care professional to show you what to do. Also, *ask your health care professional to check regularly how you use the inhaler to make sure you are using it properly.*

For patients using *beclomethasone, flunisolide, or triamcinolone inhalation aerosol:*

* When you use the inhaler for the first time, or if you have not used it in a while, it may not deliver the right amount of medicine with the first puff. Therefore, before using the inhaler, test or prime it.
* *To test or prime most inhalers:*
  —Insert the metal canister firmly into the clean mouthpiece according to the manufacturer's instructions. Check to make sure the canister is placed properly into the mouthpiece.
  —Take the cover off the mouthpiece and shake the inhaler three or four times.
  —Hold the inhaler well away from you at arm's length and press the top of the canister, spraying the medicine into the air *two* times. The inhaler will now be ready to provide the right amount of medicine when you use it.
* *To use most inhalers:*
  —Using your thumb and one or two fingers, hold the inhaler upright with the mouthpiece end down and pointing toward you.
  —Take the cover off the mouthpiece. Check the mouthpiece and remove any foreign objects. Then gently shake the inhaler three or four times.
  —Hold the mouthpiece away from your mouth and breathe out slowly to the end of a normal breath.
  —Use the inhalation method recommended by your doctor:
    • Open-mouth method—Place the mouthpiece about 1 or 2 inches (2 finger widths) in front of your widely opened mouth. Make sure the inhaler is aimed into your mouth so that the spray does not hit the roof of your mouth or your tongue.
    • Closed-mouth method—Place the mouthpiece in your mouth between your teeth and over your tongue with your lips closed tightly around it. Do not block the mouthpiece with your teeth or tongue.
  —Start to breathe in slowly through your mouth and, at the same time, press the top of the canister one time to get 1 puff of medicine. Continue to breathe

in slowly for 3 to 5 seconds. Count the seconds while inhaling. It is important to press the top of the canister and breathe in slowly at the same time so the medicine gets into your lungs. This step may be difficult at first. If you are using the closed-mouth method and you see a fine mist coming from your mouth or nose, the inhaler is not being used correctly.
  —Hold your breath as long as you can up to 10 seconds. This gives the medicine time to settle in your airways and lungs.
  —Take the mouthpiece away from your mouth and breathe out slowly.
  —If your doctor has told you to inhale more than 1 puff of medicine at each dose, gently shake the inhaler again, and take the next puff, following exactly the same steps you used for the first puff. Press the canister one time for each puff of medicine.
  —When you are finished, wipe off the mouthpiece and replace the cap.
* Your doctor, nurse, or pharmacist may want you to use a spacer device with the inhaler. A spacer helps get the medicine into the lungs and reduces the amount of medicine that stays in your mouth and throat.
  —*To use a spacer device with the inhaler:*
    • Attach the spacer to the inhaler according to the manufacturer's directions. There are different types of spacers available, but the method of breathing remains the same with most spacers.
    • Gently shake the inhaler and spacer three or four times.
    • Hold the mouthpiece of the spacer away from your mouth and breathe out slowly to the end of a normal breath.
    • Place the mouthpiece into your mouth between your teeth and over your tongue with your lips closed around it.
    • Press down on the canister top once to release 1 puff of medicine into the spacer. Within one or two seconds, start to breathe in slowly through your mouth for 3 to 5 seconds. Count the seconds while inhaling. Do not breathe in through your nose.
    • Hold your breath as long as you can up to 10 seconds.
    • Breathe out slowly. Do not remove the mouthpiece from your mouth. Breathe in and out slowly two or three times to make sure the spacer device is emptied.
    • If your doctor has told you to take more than 1 puff of medicine at each dose, gently shake the inhaler and spacer again and take the next puff, following exactly the same steps you used for the first puff. Do not spray more than 1 puff at a time into the spacer.
    • When you are finished, remove the spacer device from the inhaler and replace the cover of the mouthpiece.
* Clean the inhaler mouthpiece, and spacer at least once a week.
  —*To clean the inhaler:*
    • Remove the canister from the inhaler and set the canister aside.
    • Wash the mouthpiece, cap, and spacer with warm, soapy water. Then, rinse well with warm, running water.

- Shake off the excess water and let the inhaler parts air-dry completely before putting the inhaler back together.
- Check with your pharmacist to see if you should save the inhaler piece that comes with this medicine after the medicine is used up. Refill units may be available at a lower cost. However, remember that the inhaler is meant to be used only for the medicine that comes with it. Do not use the inhaler for any other inhalation aerosol medicine, even if the cartridge fits.

For patients using *beclomethasone capsules for inhalation:*
- *Do not swallow the capsules. The medicine will not work if you swallow it.*
- *To load the inhaler:*
  —Make sure your hands are clean and dry.
  —Do not insert the capsule into the inhaler until just before you are ready to use this medicine.
  —Take the inhaler from its container. Hold the inhaler by the mouthpiece and twist the barrel in either direction until it stops.
  —Take a capsule from its container. Hold the inhaler upright with the mouthpiece pointing downward. Press the capsule, with the clear end first, firmly into the raised small hole.
  —Make sure the top of the capsule is even with the top of the hole. This will push the old used capsule shell, if there is one, into the inhaler.
  —Hold the inhaler on its side with the white dot facing up. Twist the barrel quickly until it stops. This will break the capsule into two halves so the powder can be inhaled.
- *To use the inhaler:*
  —Hold the inhaler away from your mouth and breathe out slowly to the end of a normal breath.
  —Keep the inhaler on its side and place the mouthpiece in your mouth. Close your lips around it, and tilt your head slightly back. Do not block the mouthpiece with your teeth or tongue.
  —Breathe in slowly through your mouth until you have taken a full deep breath.
  —Take the inhaler from your mouth and hold your breath as long as you can up to 10 seconds. This gives the medicine time to settle in your airways and lungs.
  —Hold the inhaler well away from your mouth and breathe out to the end of a normal breath.
  —If your doctor has told you to use a second capsule, follow the same steps you used for the first capsule.
  —When you have finished using the inhaler, pull the two halves of the inhaler apart and throw away the empty capsule shells. There is no need to remove the shell left in the small hole, except before cleaning.
  —Put the two halves of the inhaler back together again and place it into its container to keep it clean.
- *To clean the inhaler:*
  —Every two weeks, take the inhaler apart and wash the two halves of the inhaler in clean, warm water. Make sure the empty capsule shell is removed from the small raised hole.
  —Shake out the excess water.
  —Allow all parts of the inhaler to dry before you put it back together.
- The inhaler should be replaced every 6 months.

For patients using *beclomethasone powder for inhalation:*
- *To load the inhaler:*
  —Make sure your hands are clean and dry.
  —Do not insert the cartridge until just before you are ready to use this medicine.
  —Take off the dark brown mouthpiece cover and make sure the mouthpiece is clean.
  —Hold the white cartridge by the exposed corners and gently pull it out until you see the ribbed sides of the cartridge.
  —Squeeze the ribbed sides and take out the cartridge unit from the body of the inhaler.
  —Place the disk containing the medicine onto the white wheel with the numbers facing up. Allow the underside of the disk to fit into the holes of the wheel.
  —Slide the cartridge unit with wheel and disk back into the body of the inhaler. Gently push the cartridge in and pull it out again. The disk will turn.
  —Continue to turn the disk in this way until the number 8 appears in the side indicator window. Each disk has eight blisters containing the medicine. The window will display how many doses you have left after you use it each time, by counting down from 8. For example, when you see the number 1, you have one dose left.
  —To replace the empty disk with a full disk, follow the same steps you used to load the inhaler. Do not throw away the wheel when you discard the empty disk.
- *To use the inhaler:*
  —Hold the inhaler flat in your hand. Lift the rear edge of the lid until it is fully upright.
  —The plastic needle on the front of the lid will break the blister containing one inhalation of medicine. When the lid is raised as far as it will go, both the upper and the lower surfaces of the blister will be pierced. Do not lift the lid if the cartridge is not in the inhaler. Doing this will break the needle and you will need a new inhaler.
  —After the blister is broken open, close the lid. Keeping the inhaler flat and well away from your mouth, breathe out to the end of a normal breath.
  —Raise the inhaler to your mouth, and place the mouthpiece in your mouth.
  —Close your lips around the mouthpiece and tilt your head slightly back. Do not block the mouthpiece with your teeth or tongue. Do not cover the air holes on the side of the mouthpiece.
  —Breathe in through your mouth as fast as you can until you have taken a full deep breath.
  —Hold your breath and remove the mouthpiece from your mouth. Continue holding your breath as long as you can up to 10 seconds before breathing out. This gives the medicine time to settle in your airways and lungs.
  —Hold the inhaler well away from your mouth and breathe out to the end of a normal breath.
  —Prepare the cartridge for your next inhalation. Pull the cartridge out once and push it in once. The disk will turn to the next numbered dose as seen in the indicator window. Do not pierce the blister until just before the inhalation.
- *To clean the inhaler:* Brush away the loose powder each day with the brush provided.
- The inhaler should be replaced every 6 months.

For patients using *budesonide powder for inhalation:*
- *To prime the inhaler:*
  - —Unscrew the cover of the inhaler and lift it off.
  - —Hold the inhaler *upright* with the brown piece pointing downward. Turn the brown piece of the inhaler in one direction as far as it will go. Then twist it back until it clicks. Repeat this step one more time and the inhaler will be primed.
  - —Prime each new inhaler before using it the first time. After it has been primed, it is not necessary to prime it again, even if you put it aside for a long period of time.
- *To load the inhaler:*
  - —Unscrew the cover of the inhaler and lift it off.
  - —Hold the inhaler *upright* with the brown piece pointing downward. Turn the brown piece of the inhaler in one direction as far as it will go. Then twist it back until it clicks.
- *To use the inhaler:*
  - —Hold the inhaler away from your mouth and breathe out slowly to the end of a normal breath.
  - —Place the mouthpiece in your mouth and close your lips around it. Tilt your head slightly back. Do not block the mouthpiece with your teeth or tongue.
  - —Breathe in quickly and evenly through your mouth until you have taken a full deep breath.
  - —Hold your breath and remove the inhaler from your mouth. Continue holding your breath as long as you can up to 10 seconds before breathing out. This gives the medicine time to settle in your airways and lungs.
  - —Hold the inhaler well away from your mouth and breathe out to the end of a normal breath.
  - —Replace the cover on the mouthpiece to keep it clean.
- This inhaler delivers the medicine as a very fine powder. You may not taste, smell, or feel this medicine.
- This inhaler should not be used with a spacer.
- When the indicator window begins to show a red mark, there are about 20 doses left. When the red mark covers the window, the inhaler is empty.

For patients using *budesonide suspension for inhalation:*
- This medicine is to be used in a power-operated nebulizer equipped with a face mask or mouthpiece. Your doctor will advise you on which nebulizer to use. Make sure you understand how to use the nebulizer. If you have any questions about this, check with your doctor.
- Any opened ampul should be protected from light. The medicine in an open ampul must be used promptly after the ampul is opened. Ampuls should be used within 2 weeks after the envelope containing them is opened.
- *To prepare the medicine for use in the nebulizer:*
  - —Remove one ampul from the sheet of five units and shake it gently.
  - —Hold the ampul upright. Open it by twisting off the wing.
  - —Squeeze the contents of the ampul into the cup of the nebulizer. If you use only half of the contents of an ampul, add enough of the sodium chloride solution provided to dilute the solution.
  - —Gently shake the nebulizer. Then attach the face mask to the nebulizer and connect the nebulizer to the air pump.
- *To use the medicine in the nebulizer:*
  - —This medicine should be inhaled over a period of 10 to 15 minutes.

  - —Breathe slowly and evenly, in and out, until no more mist is left in the nebulizer cup.
  - —Rinse your mouth when you are finished with the treatment. Wash your face if you used a face mask.
- *To clean the nebulizer:*
  - —After each treatment, wash the cup of the nebulizer and the mask or mouthpiece in warm water with a mild detergent.
  - —Allow the nebulizer parts to dry before putting them back together again.

Dosing—The dose of these medicines will be different for different patients. *Follow your doctor's orders or the directions on the label.* The following information includes only the average doses of these medicines. *If your dose is different, do not change it* unless your doctor tells you to do so.

For beclomethasone
- For inhalation *aerosol:*
  - —For bronchial asthma:
    - Adults and children 12 years of age and older— For the 42- or 50-mcg-per-metered-spray products: 2 puffs (84 to 100 micrograms [mcg]) three or four times a day, or 4 puffs (168 to 200 mcg) two times a day. In severe asthma, your doctor may want you to take a higher dose. For the 84-mcg-per-metered-spray product: 2 puffs (168 mcg) two times a day. In severe asthma, your doctor may want you to take a higher dose.
    - Children 6 to 12 years of age— For the 42- or 50-mcg-per-metered-spray products: 1 or 2 puffs (42 to 100 mcg) three or four times a day, or 4 puffs (168 to 200 mcg) two times a day. For the 84-mcg-per-metered-spray product: 2 puffs (168 mcg) two times a day.
    - Children up to 6 years of age—Use and dose must be determined by the doctor.
- For *capsules* for inhalation or *powder* for inhalation:
  - —For bronchial asthma:
    - Adults and teenagers 14 years of age and older— At first, 200 mcg three or four times a day. Then your doctor may reduce the dose, based on your condition.
    - Children 6 to 14 years of age—At first, 100 mcg two to four times a day. Then your doctor may reduce the dose, based on your condition.
    - Children up to 6 years of age—Use and dose must be determined by the doctor.

For budesonide
- For *powder* for inhalation:
  - —For bronchial asthma:
    - Adults—200 to 800 micrograms (mcg) two times a day. A lower dose of 200 mcg or 400 mcg once daily, either in the morning or in the evening, may sometimes be used for mild to moderate asthma when the symptoms are well controlled. The higher doses generally are used for patients previously treated with other corticosteroids. Then your doctor may increase or decrease the dose, depending on your condition.
    - Children 6 years of age and older—At first, 200 mcg two times a day. Then your doctor may increase the dose to 400 mcg two times a day, depending on your condition. A lower dose of 200 mcg or 400 mcg once daily, either in the morning or in the evening, may sometimes be used for mild

to moderate asthma when the symptoms are well controlled.

- Children up to 6 years of age—Use and dose must be determined by the doctor.

- For *suspension* for inhalation:
  —For bronchial asthma:
  - Adults and children 8 years of age and older—1000 to 2000 micrograms (mcg) mixed with enough sterile sodium chloride solution for inhalation, if necessary, to make 2 to 4 milliliters (mL). This solution is used in a nebulizer for a period of ten to fifteen minutes. The medicine should be used two times a day.
  - Children 12 months to 8 years of age—250 to 500 mcg mixed with enough sterile sodium chloride solution for inhalation, if necessary, to make 2 to 4 mL. This solution is used in a nebulizer for a period of ten to fifteen minutes. The medicine should be used two times a day.
  - Children up to 12 months of age—Use and dose must be determined by the doctor.

For flunisolide
- For inhalation *aerosol:*
  —For bronchial asthma:
  - Adults and children 6 years of age and older—500 micrograms (mcg) (2 puffs) two times a day, morning and evening.
  - Children up to 6 years of age—Use and dose must be determined by the doctor.

For triamcinolone
- For inhalation *aerosol:*
  —For bronchial asthma:
  - Adults and children 12 years of age and older—At first, 200 micrograms (mcg) (2 puffs) three to four times a day. Then your doctor may reduce the dose, based on your condition. In severe asthma, your doctor may want you to take a higher dose.
  - Children 6 to 12 years of age—At first, 100 to 200 mcg (1 or 2 puffs) three or four times a day. Then your doctor may adjust your dose, based on your condition.
  - Children up to 6 years of age—Use and dose must be determined by the doctor.

Missed dose—If you miss a dose of this medicine, use it as soon as possible. Then use any remaining doses for that day at regularly spaced times.

Storage—To store this medicine:
- Keep out of the reach of children.
- Store away from heat and direct light.
- Do not store the capsule form of this medicine in the bathroom, near the kitchen sink, or in other damp places. Heat or moisture may cause the medicine to break down.
- Keep the aerosol or suspension form of this medicine from getting too cold or freezing. This medicine may be less effective if the container is cold when you use it.
- The 84-mcg-per-metered-spray product of beclomethasone should not be stored for longer than 6 months after it has been removed from its moisture-protective pouch. After 6 months, any remaining medicine should be discarded.
- Do not puncture, break, or burn the aerosol container, even after it is empty.

- Do not keep outdated medicine or medicine no longer needed. Be sure that any discarded medicine is out of the reach of children.

Precautions While Using This Medicine

Check with your doctor if:
- *You go through a period of unusual stress to your body, such as surgery, injury, or infection.*
- *You have an asthma attack that does not improve after you take a bronchodilator medicine.*
- *You are exposed to viral infections, such as chickenpox or measles.*
- *Signs of infection occur, especially in your mouth, throat, or lung.*
- *Your symptoms do not improve or if your condition gets worse.*

Your doctor may want you to carry a medical identification card stating that you are using this medicine and that you may need additional medicine during times of emergency, a severe asthma attack or other illness, or unusual stress.

Before you have any kind of surgery (including dental surgery) or emergency treatment, tell the medical doctor or dentist in charge that you are using this medicine.

For patients who are also regularly taking a corticosteroid by mouth in tablet or liquid form:
- *Do not stop taking the corticosteroid taken by mouth without your doctor's advice, even if your asthma seems better.* Your doctor may want you to reduce gradually the amount you are taking before stopping completely to lessen the chance of unwanted effects.
- When your doctor tells you to reduce the dose, or to stop taking the corticosteroid taken by mouth, follow the directions carefully. Your body may need time to adjust to the change. The length of time this takes may depend on the amount of medicine you were taking and how long you took it. *It is especially important that your doctor check your progress at regular visits during this time.* Ask your doctor if there are special directions you should follow if you have a severe asthma attack, if you need any other medical or surgical treatment, or if certain side effects occur. Be certain that you understand these directions, and follow them carefully.

Side Effects of This Medicine

Along with its needed effects, a medicine may cause some unwanted effects. Although not all of these side effects may occur, if they do occur they may need medical attention.

Check with your doctor immediately if any of the following side effects occur just after you use this medicine:
  Rare
    Shortness of breath, troubled breathing, tightness in chest, or wheezing; signs of hypersensitivity reactions, such as swelling of face, lips, or eyelids

Also, check with your doctor as soon as possible if any of the following side effects occur:
  Less common
    Bruising; burning or pain while urinating, blood in urine, or frequent urge to urinate; chest pain; creamy white, curd-like patches in the mouth or throat and/or pain when eating or swallowing; dizziness or sense of constant movement or surroundings; general feeling of discomfort or illness; irregular or fast heartbeat; itching, rash, or hives; sinus problems; stomach or abdominal pain; swelling of fingers, an-

kles, feet, or lower legs; unusual tiredness or weakness; weight gain

Rare

Bleeding from rectum or bloody stools; blurred vision or other changes in vision; diarrhea or nausea; fainting or feeling faint; fever; frequent urination or unusual thirst; growth inhibition in children; high blood pressure; increased fat deposits in face, neck, and trunk; increased skin pigmentation; loss of appetite; menstrual changes; mood or mental changes; numbness; pain or burning in chest; vomiting

Additional side effects may occur if you take this medicine for a long time. Check with your doctor if any of the following side effects occur:

Pain in back, ribs, arms, or legs (osteoporosis)

Other side effects may occur that usually do not need medical attention. These side effects may go away during treatment as your body adjusts to the medicine. However, check with your doctor if any of the following side effects continue or are bothersome:

More common

Cold-like symptoms; cough; dry mouth or throat; headache; sore throat, hoarseness or voice changes

Less common or rare

Constipation; nosebleeds; trouble in sleeping

Other side effects not listed above may also occur in some patients. If you notice any other effects, check with your doctor.

Revised: 12/04/2000

CORTICOSTEROIDS   Nasal

Commonly used brand name(s):

In the U.S.—

Beconase[1]	Nasarel[4]
Beconase AQ[1]	Nasonex[6]
Dexacort Turbinaire[3]	Rhinocort[2]
Flonase[5]	Vancenase[1]
Nasacort[7]	Vancenase AQ 84 mcg[1]
Nasacort AQ[7]	Vancenase pockethaler[1]
Nasalide[4]	

In Canada—

Beconase[1]	Rhinalar[4]
Flonase[5]	Rhinocort Aqua[2]
Nasacort[7]	Rhinocort Turbuhaler[2]
Nasacort AQ[7]	Vancenase[1]
Nasonex[6]	

Another commonly used name for beclomethasone is beclometasone[1].

Note: For quick reference, the following corticosteroids are numbered to match the corresponding brand names.

This information applies to the following medicines:
1. Beclomethasone (be-kloe-METH-a-sone) §
2. Budesonide (byoo-DES-oh-nide) §
3. Dexamethasone (dex-a-METH-a-sone) †
4. Flunisolide (floo-NISS-oh-lide)
5. Fluticasone (floo-TIC-a-sone)
6. Mometasone (mo-MET-a-sone)
7. Triamcinolone (trye-am-SIN-oh-lone)

†Not commercially available in Canada.
§Generic name product may be available in Canada.

Description

Nasal corticosteroids (kor-ti-ko-STER-oids) are cortisone-like medicines. They belong to the family of medicines called steroids. These medicines are sprayed or inhaled into the nose to help relieve the stuffy nose, irritation, and discomfort of hay fever, other allergies, and other nasal problems. These medicines are also used to prevent nasal polyps from growing back after they have been removed by surgery.

These medicines are available only with your doctor's prescription, in the following dosage forms:

Nasal

Beclomethasone
- Aerosol (U.S. and Canada)
- Suspension (U.S.)

Budesonide
- Aerosol (U.S.)
- Powder (Canada)
- Suspension (Canada)

Dexamethasone
- Aerosol (U.S.)

Flunisolide
- Solution (U.S. and Canada)

Fluticasone
- Suspension (U.S. and Canada)

Mometasone
- Suspension (U.S. and Canada)

Triamcinolone
- Aerosol (U.S. and Canada)
- Suspension (U.S. and Canada)

Before Using This Medicine

In deciding to use a medicine, the risks of taking the medicine must be weighed against the good it will do. This is a decision you and your doctor will make. For corticosteroids, the following should be considered:

Allergies—Tell your doctor if you have ever had any unusual or allergic reaction to corticosteroids. Also tell your health care professional if you are allergic to any other substances, such as foods, preservatives, or dyes.

Pregnancy—In one human study, use of beclomethasone oral inhalation by pregnant women did not cause birth defects or other problems. Other studies on birth defects with beclomethasone, budesonide, dexamethasone, flunisolide, fluticasone, mometasone or triamcinolone have not been done in humans.

In animal studies, corticosteroids taken by mouth or injection during pregnancy were shown to cause birth defects. Also, too much use of corticosteroids during pregnancy, especially during the first trimester, may cause other unwanted effects in the infant, such as slower growth and reduced adrenal gland function.

If corticosteroids are medically necessary during pregnancy to control nasal problems, nasal corticosteroids are generally considered safer than corticosteroids taken by mouth or injection. Also, use of nasal corticosteroids may allow some patients to stop using or decrease the amount of corticosteroids taken by mouth or injection.

Breast-feeding—Use of dexamethasone is not recommended in nursing mothers, since dexamethasone passes into breast milk and may affect the infant's growth.

It is not known whether beclomethasone, budesonide, flunisolide, fluticasone or triamcinolone passes into breast milk. Although most medicines pass into breast milk in small amounts, many of them may be used safely while breast-feeding. Levels of mometasone are not measurable in breast milk, thus exposure is expected to be low. Mothers who are taking these medicines and wish to breast-feed should discuss them with their doctor.

Children—Corticosteroids taken by mouth or injection have been shown to slow or stop growth in children and cause reduced adrenal gland function. If corticosteroids are medically necessary to control nasal problems in a child, nasal corticosteroids are generally considered to be safer than corticosteroids taken by mouth or injection. Prolonged or high-dose use of nasal corticosteroids may potentially affect growth; although, most nasal corticosteroids have not been shown to affect growth. Also, use of most nasal corticosteroids may allow some children to stop using or decrease the amount of corticosteroids taken by mouth or injection.

Before this medicine is given to a child, you and your child's doctor should talk about the good this medicine will do as well as the risks of using it. Follow the doctor's directions very carefully to lessen the chance of unwanted effects.

Older adults—Although there is no specific information comparing use of nasal corticosteroids in the elderly with use in other age groups, they are not expected to cause different side effects or problems in older people than they do in younger adults.

Other medicines—Although certain medicines should not be used together at all, in other cases two different medicines may be used together even if an interaction might occur. In these cases, your doctor may want to change the dose, or other precautions may be necessary. Tell your health care professional if you are taking any prescription or non-prescription (over-the-counter [OTC]) medicines, such as:

- Ephedrine or
- Phenobarbital or
- Rifampin (e.g., Rifadin)—Ephedrine, phenobarbital, and rifampin may decrease the blood levels of nasal corticosteroids, such as dexamethasone, warranting an increase in corticosteroid dose

Other medical problems—The presence of other medical problems may affect the use of corticosteroids. Make sure you tell your doctor if you have any other medical problems, especially:

- Amebiasis—Nasal corticosteroids may make this condition worse
- Asthma—Nasal corticosteroids may make this condition worse
- Diabetes mellitus (sugar diabetes)—Use of dexamethasone may decrease carbohydrate tolerance, worsening blood glucose control and warranting an increase in insulin dosage
- Glaucoma—Long-term use of nasal corticosteroids may worsen glaucoma by increasing the pressure within the eye
- Herpes simplex (virus) infection of the eye or
- Infections (virus, bacteria, or fungus)—Nasal corticosteroids may cover up the signs of these conditions

- Injury to the nose (recent) or
- Nose surgery (recent) or
- Sores in the nose—Nasal corticosteroids may prevent proper healing of these conditions
- Liver disease
- Tuberculosis (active or history of)
- Underactive thyroid
- Weak heart or
- Recent heart attack—Use of dexamethasone may worsen these conditions

Proper Use of This Medicine

This medicine usually comes with patient directions. *Read them carefully before using the medicine.* Beclomethasone, budesonide, dexamethasone, and triamcinolone are used with a special inhaler. If you do not understand the directions, or if you are not sure how to use the inhaler, check with your health care professional.

Before using this medicine, clear the nasal passages by blowing your nose. Then, with the nosepiece inserted into the nostril, aim the spray towards the inner corner of the eye.

In order for this medicine to help you, it must be used regularly as ordered by your doctor. This medicine usually begins to work in about 1 week (for dexamethasone), but up to 3 weeks may pass before you feel its full effects.

Use this medicine only as directed. Do not use more of it and do not use it more often than your doctor ordered. To do so may increase the chance of absorption through the lining of the nose and the chance of unwanted effects.

Check with your doctor before using this medicine for nasal problems other than the one for which it was prescribed, since it should not be used on many bacterial, virus, or fungus nasal infections.

Save the inhaler that comes with beclomethasone or dexamethasone, since refill units may be available at lower cost.

Dosing—The dose of nasal corticosteroids will be different for different patients. *Follow your doctor's orders or the directions on the label.* The following information includes only the average doses of nasal corticosteroids. *If your dose is different, do not change it* unless your doctor tells you to do so.

For beclomethasone
- For allergies or other nasal conditions:
  —For *nasal aerosol* dosage form:
    - Adults and children 6 years of age and older— One spray in each nostril two to four times a day.
    - Children up to 6 years of age—Use and dose must be determined by your doctor.
  —For *nasal suspension* dosage form:
    - Adults and children 6 years of age and older— One or two sprays in each nostril two times a day.
    - Children up to 6 years of age—Use and dose must be determined by your doctor.

For budesonide
- For allergies or other nasal conditions:
  —For *nasal powder* dosage form:
    - Adults and children 6 years of age and older— Two inhalations in each nostril once a day in the morning.
    - Children up to 6 years of age—Use and dose must be determined by your doctor.

—For *nasal suspension* dosage form:
- Adults and children 6 years of age and older—One or two sprays in each nostril one or two times a day.
- Children up to 6 years of age—Use and dose must be determined by your doctor.

For dexamethasone
- For allergies or other nasal conditions:
  —For *nasal aerosol* dosage form:
  - Adults and children 12 years of age and older—Two sprays in each nostril two or three times a day for up to two weeks.
  - Children 6 to 12 years of age—One to two sprays in each nostril two times a day for up to two weeks.
  - Children up to 6 years of age—Use and dose must be determined by your doctor.

For flunisolide
- For allergies or other nasal conditions:
  —For *nasal solution* dosage form:
  - Adults and children 6 years of age and older—One or two sprays in each nostril one to three times a day.
  - Children up to 6 years of age—Use and dose must be determined by your doctor.

For fluticasone
- For allergies or other nasal conditions:
  —For *nasal suspension* dosage form:
  - Adults and children 4 years of age and older—One or two sprays in each nostril one or two times a day.
  - Children up to 4 years of age—Use and dose must be determined by your doctor.

For mometasone
- For allergies or other nasal conditions:
  —For *nasal suspension* dosage form:
  - Adults and children 12 years of age and older—One or two sprays in each nostril one time a day.
  - Children up to 12 years of age—Use and dose must be determined by your doctor.

For triamcinolone
- For allergies or other nasal conditions:
  —For *nasal aerosol* dosage form:
  - Adults and children 6 years of age and older (In Canada, children 12 years of age and older)—One or two sprays in each nostril once a day.
  - Children up to 6 years of age (In Canada, children up to 12 years of age)—Use and dose must be determined by your doctor.
  —For *nasal suspension* dosage form:
  - Adults and children 6 years of age and older—One or two sprays in each nostril one time a day.
  - Children up to 6 years of age—Use and dose must be determined by your doctor.

Missed dose—If you miss a dose of this medicine and remember within an hour or so, use it right away. However, if you do not remember until later, skip the missed dose and go back to your regular dosing schedule. Do not double doses.

Storage—To store this medicine:
- Keep out of the reach of children.
- Store away from heat and direct light.
- Do not store budesonide powder in the bathroom, near the kitchen sink, or in other damp places, especially if the cap has not been tightly screwed back on. Moisture may cause the medicine to break down.
- Keep the medicine from getting too cold or freezing. This medicine may be less effective if it is too cold when you use it.
- Do not puncture, break, or burn the beclomethasone, dexamethasone, or triamcinolone aerosol container, even after it is empty.
- Do not keep outdated medicine or medicine no longer needed. Also, discard any unused beclomethasone or flunisolide solution 3 months after you open the package. Be sure that any discarded medicine is out of the reach of children.

Precautions While Using This Medicine

If you will be using this medicine for more than a few weeks, your doctor should check your progress at regular visits.

Check with your doctor:
- if signs of a nose, sinus, or throat infection occur.
- if your symptoms do not improve within 7 days (for dexamethasone) or within 3 weeks (for beclomethasone, budesonide, flunisolide, fluticasone, mometasone, or triamcinolone).
- if your condition gets worse.

When you are being treated with dexamethasone, and after you stop treatment with it, do not have any immunizations (vaccinations) without your doctor's approval. Dexamethasone may lower your body's resistance and there is a chance you may get the infection the immunization is meant to prevent. In addition, other persons living in your household should not take or have recently taken oral polio vaccine since there is a chance they could pass the polio virus on to you. Also, avoid other persons who have taken oral polio vaccine. Don't get close to them, and do not stay in the same room with them for very long. If you cannot take these precautions, you should consider wearing a protective face mask that covers the nose and mouth.

Side Effects of This Medicine

Along with its needed effects, a medicine may cause some unwanted effects. Although not all of these side effects may occur, if they do occur they may need medical attention.

Check with your doctor as soon as possible if any of the following side effects occur:

Less common or rare
  Bad smell; blindness; bloody mucus or unexplained nosebleeds; blurred or gradual loss of vision; burning or stinging after use of spray or irritation inside nose (continuing); crusting, white patches, or sores inside nose; discharge or redness in eye, eyelid, or inner lining of the eyelid; eye pain; headache; hives; light-headedness or dizziness; loss of sense of taste or smell; muscle pain; nausea or vomiting; ringing in the ears; shortness of breath; skin rash; sore throat, cough, or hoarseness; stomach pains; stuffy, dry, or runny nose or watery eyes (continuing); swelling of eyelids, face, or lips; tightness in chest; troubled breathing; unusual tiredness or weakness; wheezing; white patches in throat

Symptoms of overdose
  Acne; blurred vision; bone fractures; excess hair growth in females; fullness or rounding of the face,

neck, and trunk; high blood pressure; impotence in males; increased urination or thirst; lack of menstrual periods; menstrual changes; muscle wasting and weakness

Other side effects may occur that usually do not need medical attention. These side effects may go away during treatment as your body adjusts to the medicine. However, check with your doctor if any of the following side effects continue or are bothersome:

More common
Burning, dryness, or other irritation inside the nose (mild, lasting only a short time); increase in sneezing; irritation of throat

Less common
Sneezing; itching of throat

Not all of the side effects listed above have been reported for each of these medicines, but they have been reported for at least one of them. All of the nasal corticosteroids are very similar, so any of the above side effects may occur with any of these medicines.

Other side effects not listed above may also occur in some patients. If you notice any other effects, check with your doctor.

Revised: 06/27/2000

CORTICOSTEROIDS   Ophthalmic

Commonly used brand name(s):

In the U.S.—

AK-Dex[2]	Inflamase Forte[6]
AK-Pred[6]	Inflamase Mild[6]
AK-Tate[6]	I-Pred[6]
Baldex[2]	Lite Pred[6]
Decadron[2]	Maxidex[2]
Dexair[2]	Ocu-Dex[2]
Econopred[6]	Ocu-Pred[6]
Econopred Plus[6]	Ocu-Pred-A[6]
Eflone[3]	Ocu-Pred Forte[6]
Flarex[3]	Predair[6]
Fluor-Op[3]	Predair A[6]
FML Forte[3]	Predair Forte[6]
FML Liquifilm[3]	Pred Forte[6]
FML S.O.P.[3]	Pred Mild[6]
HMS Liquifilm[5]	Storz-Dexa[2]
	Ultra Pred[6]

In Canada—

AK-Tate[6]	Inflamase Mild[6]
Betnesol[1]	Maxidex[2]
Cortamed[4]	Ophtho-Tate[6]
Decadron[2]	PMS-Dexamethasone Sodium Phosphate[2]
Diodex[2]	
Flarex[3]	Pred Forte[6]
FML Forte[3]	Pred Mild[6]
FML Liquifilm[3]	R.O.-Dexasone[2]
HMS Liquifilm[5]	Spersadex[2]
Inflamase Forte[6]	

Another commonly used name for hydrocortisone is cortisol[4].

Note: For quick reference, the following corticosteroids are numbered to match the corresponding brand names.

This information applies to the following medicines:
1. Betamethasone (bay-ta-METH-a-sone) *
2. Dexamethasone (dex-a-METH-a-sone) ‡
3. Fluorometholone (flure-oh-METH-oh-lone)
4. Hydrocortisone (hye-droe-KOR-ti-sone) *
5. Medrysone (ME-dri-sone)
6. Prednisolone (pred-NISS-oh-lone) ‡§

*Not commercially available in the U.S.
‡Generic name product may be available in the U.S.
§Generic name product may be available in Canada.

Description

Ophthalmic corticosteroids (kor-ti-ko-STER-oids) (cortisone-like medicines) are used to prevent permanent damage to the eye, which may occur with certain eye problems. They also provide relief from redness, irritation, and other discomfort.

Corticosteroids for use in the eye are available only with your doctor's prescription, in the following dosage forms:

Ophthalmic
Betamethasone
• Solution (eye drops) (Canada)
Dexamethasone
• Ointment (U.S. and Canada)
• Solution (eye drops) (U.S. and Canada)
• Suspension (eye drops) (U.S. and Canada)
Fluorometholone
• Ointment (U.S.)
• Suspension (eye drops) (U.S. and Canada)
Hydrocortisone
• Ointment (Canada)
Medrysone
• Suspension (eye drops) (U.S. and Canada)
Prednisolone
• Solution (eye drops) (U.S. and Canada)
• Suspension (eye drops) (U.S. and Canada)

Before Using This Medicine

In deciding to use a medicine, the risks of taking the medicine must be weighed against the good it will do. This is a decision you and your doctor will make. For ophthalmic corticosteroids, the following should be considered:

Allergies—Tell your doctor if you have ever had any unusual or allergic reaction to corticosteroids. Also tell your health care professional if you are allergic to any other substances, such as foods, preservatives, or dyes.

Pregnancy—Although studies on birth defects with ophthalmic corticosteroids have not been done in humans, these medicines have not been reported to cause birth defects or other problems. However, in animal studies, dexamethasone, fluorometholone, hydrocortisone, and prednisolone caused birth defects when applied to the eyes of pregnant animals. Also, fluorometholone and medrysone caused other unwanted effects in the animal fetus.

Breast-feeding—Ophthalmic corticosteroids have not been reported to cause problems in nursing babies.

Children—Children less than 2 years of age may be especially sensitive to the effects of ophthalmic corticosteroids. This may increase the chance of side effects. If this medicine has been ordered for a young child, you should discuss its use with your child's doctor. Be sure you follow all of the doctor's instructions very carefully.

Older adults—Although there is no specific information about the use of ophthalmic corticosteroids in the elderly, they are not expected to cause different side effects or problems in older people than they do in younger adults.

Other medicines — Although certain medicines should not be used together at all, in other cases two different medicines may be used together even if an interaction might occur. In these cases, your doctor may want to change the dose, or other precautions may be necessary. Tell your health care professional if you are using any other prescription or nonprescription (over-the-counter [OTC]) ophthalmic medicine.

Other medical problems — The presence of other medical problems may affect the use of ophthalmic corticosteroids. Make sure you tell your doctor if you have any other medical problems, especially:

- Cataracts—Corticosteroids may cause cataracts or make them worse
- Diabetes mellitus (sugar diabetes)—Patients with diabetes may be more likely to develop cataracts or glaucoma with the use of corticosteroids
- Glaucoma (or family history of)—Corticosteroids may cause glaucoma or make it worse
- Herpes infection of the eye or
- Tuberculosis of the eye (active or history of) or
- Any other eye infection—Ophthalmic corticosteroids may make existing infections worse or cause new infections

Proper Use of This Medicine

For patients who wear *contact lenses:*

- Use of ophthalmic corticosteroids while you are wearing contact lenses (either hard lenses or soft lenses) may increase the chance of infection. Therefore, do not apply this medicine while you are wearing contact lenses. Also, check with an ophthalmologist (eye doctor) for advice on how long to wait after applying this medicine before inserting your contact lenses. It is possible that you may be directed not to wear contact lenses at all during the entire time of treatment and for a day or two after treatment has been stopped.

For patients using an *ophthalmic solution or suspension (eye drop) form* of this medicine:

- If you are using a suspension form of this medicine, always shake the container very well just before applying the eye drops.
- To use:
  —First, wash your hands. Tilt the head back and, pressing your finger gently on the skin just beneath the lower eyelid, pull the lower eyelid away from the eye to make a space. Drop the medicine into this space. Let go of the eyelid and gently close the eyes. Do not blink. Keep the eyes closed and apply pressure to the inner corner of the eye with your finger for 1 or 2 minutes to allow the medicine to be absorbed by the eye.
  —If you think you did not get the drop of medicine into your eye properly, use another drop.
  —Immediately after using the eye drops, wash your hands to remove any medicine that may be on them.
  —To keep the medicine as germ-free as possible, do not touch the dropper or the applicator tip to any surface (including the eye). Always keep the container tightly closed.

For patients using an *ointment form* of this medicine:

- To use:
  —First, wash your hands. Tilt the head back and, pressing your finger gently on the skin just beneath the lower eyelid, pull the lower eyelid away from the eye to make a space. Squeeze a thin strip of ointment into this space. A 1-cm (approximately ⅓ inch) strip of ointment is usually enough, unless you have been told by your doctor to use a different amount. Let go of the eyelid and gently close the eyes. Keep the eyes closed for 1 or 2 minutes to allow the medicine to come into contact with the irritation.
  —To keep the medicine as germ-free as possible, do not touch the applicator tip to any surface (including the eye). After using the eye ointment, wipe the tip of the ointment tube with a clean tissue. Do not wash the tip with water. Always keep the tube tightly closed.

Do not use corticosteroids more often or for a longer time than your doctor ordered. To do so may increase the chance of side effects, especially in children 2 years of age or younger.

Do not use any leftover medicine for future eye problems without first checking with your doctor. This medicine should not be used if certain kinds of infections are present. To do so may make the infection worse and possibly lead to eye damage.

Dosing — The dose of ophthalmic corticosteroids will be different for different patients. *Follow your doctor's orders or the directions on the label.* The following information includes only the average doses of ophthalmic corticosteroids. *If your dose is different, do not change it* unless your doctor tells you to do so.

For betamethasone
- For eye disorders:
  —For *ophthalmic solution (eye drops)* dosage form:
  - Adults and children—Use one or two drops in the eye every one or two hours, then space the doses further apart as the eye gets better.

For dexamethasone
- For eye disorders:
  —For *ophthalmic ointment* dosage form:
  - Adults and children—Use the ointment in the eye three or four times a day, then space the doses further apart as the eye gets better.
  —For *ophthalmic solution (eye drops)* dosage form:
  - Adults and children—Use one or two drops in the eye up to six times a day.
  —For *ophthalmic suspension (eye drops)* dosage form:
  - Adults and children—Use one or two drops in the eye four to six times a day.

For fluorometholone
- For eye disorders:
  —For *ophthalmic ointment* dosage form:
  - Adults and children—Use the ointment in the eye one to three times a day.
  —For *ophthalmic suspension (eye drops)* dosage form:
  - Adults and children—Use one or two drops in the eye two to four times a day.

For hydrocortisone
- For eye disorders:
  —For *ophthalmic ointment* dosage form:
  - Adults and children—Use the ointment in the eye three or four times a day, then space the doses further apart as the eye gets better.

For medrysone
- For eye disorders:
  —For *ophthalmic suspension (eye drops)* dosage form:
  - Adults and children—Use one drop in the eye up to every four hours.

For prednisolone
- For eye disorders:
  —For *ophthalmic solution (eye drops)* dosage form:
  - Adults and children—Use one or two drops in the eye up to six times a day.
  —For *ophthalmic suspension (eye drops)* dosage form:
  - Adults and children—Use one or two drops in the eye two to four times a day.

Missed dose—If you miss a dose of this medicine, apply it as soon as possible. However, if it is almost time for your next dose, skip the missed dose and go back to your regular dosing schedule.

Storage—To store this medicine:
- Keep out of the reach of children.
- Store away from heat and direct light.
- Keep the medicine from freezing.
- Do not keep outdated medicine or medicine no longer needed. Be sure that any discarded medicine is out of the reach of children.

Precautions While Using This Medicine

If you will be using this medicine for more than a few weeks, an ophthalmologist (eye doctor) should examine your eyes at regular visits to make sure it does not cause unwanted effects.

If your eye condition does not improve after 5 to 7 days, or if it becomes worse, check with your doctor.

Side Effects of This Medicine

Along with its needed effects, a medicine may cause some unwanted effects. Although not all of these side effects may occur, if they do occur they may need medical attention.

Check with your doctor as soon as possible if any of the following side effects occur:
  Less common or rare
    Decreased vision; eye infection; eye pain; gradual blurring or loss of vision; nausea; vomiting

Other side effects may occur that usually do not need medical attention. These side effects may go away during treatment as your body adjusts to the medicine. However, check with your doctor if any of the following side effects continue or are bothersome:
  More frequent
    Blurred vision (mild and temporary, occurs after use of ointments)

  Less common or rare
    Burning, stinging, redness, or watering of the eyes

Other side effects not listed may also occur in some patients. If you notice any other effects, check with your doctor.

Revised: 01/05/94
Interim revision: 05/16/94; 01/27/95

CORTICOSTEROIDS   Otic

Commonly used brand name(s):
In the U.S.—
  Decadron[2]
In Canada—
  Betnesol[1]
  Decadron[2]

Note: For quick reference, the following corticosteroids are numbered to match the corresponding brand names.

This information applies to the following medicines:
  1. Betamethasone (bay-ta-METH-a-sone) *
  2. Dexamethasone (dex-a-METH-a-sone) ‡

*Not commercially available in the U.S.
‡Generic name product may be available in the U.S.

Description

Otic corticosteroids (kor-ti-koe-STE-roids) (cortisone-like medicines) are used in the ear to relieve the redness, itching, and swelling caused by certain ear problems.

Otic corticosteroids are available only with your doctor's prescription, in the following dosage forms:
  Otic
  Betamethasone
  - Solution (Canada)
  Dexamethasone
  - Solution (U.S. and Canada)

Before Using This Medicine

In deciding to use a medicine, the risks of taking the medicine must be weighed against the good it will do. This is a decision you and your doctor will make. For otic corticosteroids, the following should be considered:

Allergies—Tell your doctor if you have ever had any unusual or allergic reaction to corticosteroids. Also tell your health care professional if you are allergic to any other substances, such as certain preservatives or dyes.

Pregnancy—Studies with otic corticosteroids have not been done in pregnant women. However, in animal studies, corticosteroids have been shown to cause birth defects. Before taking this medicine, make sure your doctor knows if you are pregnant or if you may become pregnant.

Breast-feeding—Corticosteroids pass into breast milk. Be sure you have discussed the risks to the child and benefits of the medicine with your doctor.

Children—There is no specific information about the use of otic corticosteroids in children. Children born to mothers taking otic corticosteroid therapy during their pregnancy should be observed for decrease in growth and for hypoadrenalism (anorexia, low blood pressure, and weakness).

Older adults—Although there is no specific information about the use of otic corticosteroids in the elderly, they are not expected to cause different side effects or problems in older people than they do in younger adults.

Other medicines—Although certain medicines should not be used together at all, in other cases two differnet medicines may be used together even if an interaction may occur. In these cases, your doctor may want to change the dose, or other precautions may be necessary. When you are taking otic corticosteroids, it is especially important that your doctor and pharmacist know if you are taking the following:

- Phenytoin (e.g., Dilantin)

Other medical problems—The presence of other medical problems may affect the use of otic corticosteroids. Make sure you tell your doctor if you have any other medical problems, especially:

- Diabetes mellitus (sugar diabetes) or
- Epilepsy—Using otic corticosteroids may worsen this condition
- Heart disease—Irregular heartbeat and change in blood pressure are more likely to occur
- Glaucoma or
- High blood pressure—Otic corticosteroids may increase the pressure in the blood vessels of the eye and throughout the body
- Osteoporosis—Otic corticosteroids increase the risk of bone fractures
- Fungal infections or
- Tuberculosis or
- Viral infections or
- Otitis media, chronic or
- Any other ear infection or condition (or history of)—Otic corticosteroids may worsen existing infections or cause new infections
- Punctured ear drum—Using otic corticosteroids with a punctured ear drum may damage the ear

Proper Use of This Medicine

To use *ear drops:*

- Lie down or tilt the head so that the affected ear faces up. Gently pull the earlobe up and back for adults (down and back for children) to straighten the ear canal. Drop the medicine into the ear canal. Keep the ear facing up for several (about 5) minutes to allow the medicine to run to the bottom of the ear canal. A sterile cotton plug may be gently inserted into the ear opening to prevent the medicine from leaking out. At first, your doctor may want you to put more medicine on the cotton plug during the day to keep it moist.

To keep the medicine as germ-free as possible, do not touch the dropper or applicator tip to any surface (including the ear). Also, keep the container tightly closed.

Do not use corticosteroids more often or for a longer time than your doctor ordered. To do so may increase the chance of side effects.

Do not use any leftover medicine for future ear problems without first checking with your doctor. This medicine should not be used if certain kinds of infections are present. To do so may make the infection worse.

Dosing—The dose of otic corticosteroids will be different for different patients. *Follow your doctor's orders or the directions on the label.* The following information includes only the average doses of otic corticosteroids. *If your dose is different, do not change it* unless your doctor tells you to do so.

For betamethasone
- —For redness, itching, and swelling:
  - Adults and children—Use two or three drops in the ear every two or three hours. After symptoms are relieved, your doctor may lower the dose.

For dexamethasone
- —For redness, itching, and swelling:
  - Adults and children—Use three or four drops in the ear two or three times a day. After symptoms are relieved, your doctor may lower the dose.

Missed dose—If you miss a dose of this medicine, use it as soon as you remember. However, if it is almost time for your next dose, skip the missed dose and go back to your regular dosing schedule. Do not double doses.

Storage—To store this medicine:

- Keep out of the reach of children.
- Store away from heat and direct light.
- Keep the medicine from freezing.
- Do not keep outdated medicine or medicine no longer needed. Be sure that any discarded medicine is out of the reach of children.

Precautions While Using This Medicine

If your condition does not improve within 5 to 7 days, or if it becomes worse, check with your doctor.

While you are being treated with otic corticosteroids, and after you stop treatment, *do not have any immunizatons (vaccinations) without your doctor's approval.* Otic corticosteroids may lower your body's resistance and there is a chance you might get the infection the immunization is trying to prevent. In addition, other persons living in your household should not take or have recently taken oral polio vaccine since there is a chance they could pass the polio virus on to you. Also, avoid other persons who have taken oral polio vaccine. Do not get close to them, and do not stay in the same room with them for very long. If you cannot take these precautions, you should consider wearing a protective face mask that covers the nose and mouth.

Side Effects of This Medicine

Along with its needed effects, a medicine may cause some unwanted effects. The following side effects usually do not need medical attention and may go away during treatment as your body adjusts to the medicine. However, check with your doctor if any of the following side effects continue or are bothersome:

Less common
   Anorexia; black or tarry stools; bone fractures; breathing difficulties; burning or stinging of the ear; chest pain; continual stomach pain or burning; decreased or blurred vision; excess hair growth in females; fainting; flushing; frequent urination; headache; high blood pressure; impaired wound healing; impotence in males; increased sweating; increased thirst; irregular heartbeat; low blood pressure; menstrual changes; muscle cramps; muscle wasting; nausea or vomiting; persistent fungal infections of the ear; rapid weight gain; seizures; stomach bloating; suppressed growth in children; suppressed reaction to skin tests; swelling of feet or lower legs; thin fragile skin; tingling in arms and lower legs or feet; vertigo; weight loss

There have not been any other common or important side effects reported with this medicine. However, if you notice any unusual effects, check with your doctor.

Revised: 08/21/2000

CORTICOSTEROIDS Rectal

Commonly used brand name(s):

In the U.S.—

Anucort-HC[4]	Cortenema[3]
Anu-Med HC[4]	Cortifoam[4]
Anuprep HC[4]	Hemril-HC Uniserts[4]
Anusol-HC[4]	Hemorrhoidal HC[4]
Anutone-HC[4]	Proctocort[4]
Anuzone-HC[4]	Proctosol-HC[4]
Cort-Dome[4]	Rectosol-HC[4]

In Canada—

Betnesol[1]	Entocort[2]
Cortenema[3]	Hycort[3]
Cortifoam[4]	Rectocort[4]
Cortiment-10[4]	Rectovalone[5]
Cortiment-40[4]	

Note: For quick reference, the following rectal corticosteroids are numbered to match the corresponding brand names.

This information applies to the following medicines:
1. Betamethasone (bay-ta-METH-a-sone) *
2. Budesonide (byoo-DES-oh-nide) *
3. Hydrocortisone (hye-droe-KOR-ti-sone) ‡
4. Hydrocortisone acetate (hye-droe-KOR-ti-sone AS-a-tate) ‡
5. Tixocortol (tix-OH-kor-tole) *‡

Another commonly used name for hydrocortisone is cortisol.

*Not commercially available in the U.S.
‡Generic name product may be available in the U.S.

Description

Rectal corticosteroids (kor-ti-ko-STER-oyds) are used to treat mild or moderate ulcerative colitis. They also may be used along with systemic (oral or injection) corticosteroids or other medicines to treat severe disease or mild to moderate disease that has spread too far to be treated effectively by medicine inserted into the rectum alone. Rectal corticosteroids also are used to help relieve swelling, itching, and discomfort of some other rectal problems, including hemorrhoids and inflammation of the rectum caused by radiation therapy.

Rectal corticosteroids are available only with your doctor's prescription in the following dosage forms:

Rectal
- Betamethasone
  - Enema (Canada)
- Budesonide
  - Enema (Canada)
- Hydrocortisone
  - Enema (U.S. and Canada)
- Hydrocortisone acetate
  - Foam (U.S. and Canada)
  - Suppositories (U.S. and Canada)
- Tixocortol
  - Enema (Canada)

Before Using This Medicine

In deciding to use a medicine, the risks of using it must be weighed against the good it will do. This is a decision you and your doctor will make. For rectal corticosteroids, the following should be considered:

Allergies—Tell your doctor if you have ever had any unusual or allergic reaction to any of the corticosteroids. Also tell your health care professional if you are allergic to any other substances, such as food, preservatives, or dyes.

Pregnancy—Betamethasone may change the number and ability of movement of sperm in men. Budesonide crosses the placenta. It is not known whether other rectal corticosteroids cross the placenta. Studies in animals have shown that budesonide, hydrocortisone, and hydrocortisone acetate cause birth defects. Rectal corticosteroids should not be used in large amounts or for a long time by women who are pregnant or who are planning to become pregnant.

Breast-feeding—It is not known whether rectal corticosteroids pass into breast milk. However, systemic (oral and injection) corticosteroids pass into breast milk and may cause problems with growth in nursing babies. It may be necessary for you to take a different medicine or to stop breast-feeding during treatment. Be sure you have discussed with your doctor the risks and benefits of using the medicine.

Children—Children and teenagers who must use this medicine should be checked often by their doctor. Rectal corticosteroids may be absorbed through the lining of the rectum and, rarely, may affect growth, especially if used in large amounts or for a long time. Before using this medicine in children, you should discuss its use with the child's doctor.

Older adults—Many medicines have not been studied specifically in older people. Therefore, it may not be known whether they work exactly the same way they do in younger adults. Although there is no specific information comparing use of rectal corticosteroids in the elderly with use in other age groups, these medicines are not expected to cause different side effects or problems in older people than they do in younger adults.

Other medicines—Although certain medicines should not be used together at all, in other cases two different medicines may be used together even if an interaction may occur. In these cases, your doctor may want to change the dose, or other precautions may be necessary. When you are using rectal corticosteroids, it is especially important that your health care professional know if you are taking any of the following:

- Immunizations (vaccinations)—While you are being treated with this medicine, and even after you stop using it, do not have any immunizations without your doctor's approval
- Skin test injections—Corticosteroids may cause false results in skin tests

Other medical problems—The presence of other medical problems may affect the use of rectal corticosteroids. Make sure you tell your doctor if you have any other medical problems, especially:

- Acute psychosis—This condition may be made worse
- Chickenpox (including recent exposure) or
- Measles (including recent exposure)—Risk of severe disease affecting other parts of the body
- Diabetes mellitus (sugar diabetes)—Corticosteroids may cause a loss of control of diabetes by increasing blood glucose (sugar)
- Glaucoma—Corticosteroids may cause the pressure within the eye to increase
- Heart disease or
- Hypertension (high blood pressure) or
- Kidney disease or
- Myasthenia gravis or
- Overactive thyroid or
- Swelling of blood vessels—Corticosteroids should be used with caution

- Herpes simplex of the eye—Corticosteroids may cause additional problems in the eye

- Ileocolostomy, postsurgical or
- Infection or
- Tuberculosis (active TB, nonactive TB, or past history of)—Corticosteroids may cause slower healing, worsen existing infections, or cause new infections

- Liver disease or
- Underactive thyroid—With these conditions, the body may not eliminate the corticosteroid at the usual rate; therefore, the medicine's effect may be increased

- Osteoporosis—Corticosteroids may worsen osteoporosis because they cause the body to lose more calcium

- Other stomach or intestine problems or
- Severe ulcerative colitis—Corticosteroids may cover up symptoms of a worsening stomach or intestinal condition; a patient would not know if his or her condition was getting worse and would not get medical help when needed

- Stomach ulcer—Corticosteroids may worsen this condition by causing an increase in the amount of acid in the stomach

Proper Use of This Medicine

It is important that your doctor check your progress at regular visits.

For patients using the *enema* form of this medicine:
- This medicine usually comes with patient directions. Read and follow them carefully before using this medicine.

For patients using the *foam* form of this medicine:
- This medicine is used with a special applicator. Do not insert any part of the aerosol container into the rectum.

For patients using the *suppository* form of this medicine:
- If the suppository is too soft to insert, chill it in the refrigerator for 30 minutes or run cold water over it before removing the wrapper.
- To insert the suppository: First remove the wrapper and moisten the suppository with cold water. Lie down on your side and use your finger to push the suppository well up into the rectum.

Do not use rectal corticosteroids in larger amounts, more often, or for a longer time than your doctor ordered. To do so may increase the chance of absorption through the lining of the rectum and the chance of side effects.

Dosing—The dose of rectal corticosteroids may be different for different patients. *Follow your doctor's orders or the directions on the label.* The following information includes only the average doses of corticosteroids. *If your dose is different, do not change it* unless your doctor tells you to do so.

For betamethasone
- For *enema* dosage form:
  —For ulcerative colitis:
    - Adults—The usual dose is 5 milligrams (mg) (1 unit), used as directed, every night for two to four weeks.
    - Children—Dose must be determined by your doctor.

For budesonide
- For *enema* dosage form:
  —For ulcerative colitis:
    - Adults—The usual dose is 2 milligrams (mg) (1 unit), used as directed, every night for four to eight weeks.
    - Children—Use and dose must be determined by your doctor.

For hydrocortisone
- For *enema* dosage form:
  —For ulcerative colitis:
    - Adults—The usual dose is 100 milligrams (mg) (1 unit), used as directed, every night for two or three weeks or until condition improves as determined by your doctor.
    - Children—Dose must be determined by your doctor.

For hydrocortisone acetate
- For *foam* dosage form:
  —For ulcerative colitis:
    - Adults—At first, 1 applicatorful, used as directed, one or two times a day for two or three weeks. Then, the dose may be decreased to 1 applicatorful every other day.
    - Children—Dose must be determined by your doctor.

- For *suppository* dosage form:
  —For ulcerative colitis:
    - Adults—The usual dose is 25 or 30 milligrams (mg) two times a day, in the morning and at night, for two weeks. In more severe cases, the dose may be 25 or 30 mg three times a day or 50 or 60 mg two times a day.
    - Children—Dose must be determined by your doctor.
  —For inflammation of the rectum caused by radiation therapy:
    - Adults—The usual dose is 25 or 30 mg two times a day, in the morning and at night, for six to eight weeks.
    - Children—Dose must be determined by your doctor.
  —For other rectal problems:
    - Adults—The usual dose is 20 to 30 mg a day for three days, or 40 to 80 mg a day as needed.
    - Children—Dose must be determined by your doctor.

For tixocortol
- For *enema* dosage form:
  —For ulcerative colitis:
    - Adults—The usual dose is 250 milligrams (mg) (1 unit), used as directed, at bedtime for twenty-one days in a row.
    - Children—Use and dose must be determined by your doctor.

Missed dose—If you miss a dose of this medicine, use it as soon as you remember. However, if it is almost time for your next dose, skip the missed dose and go back to your regular dosing schedule. Do not double doses.

Storage—To store this medicine:
- Keep out of the reach of children.
- Store away from heat and direct light.

- Do not store suppositories in the bathroom medicine cabinet because the heat or moisture may cause the medicine to break down.
- Keep the medicine from freezing.
- Do not puncture, break, or burn the rectal foam aerosol container, even when it is empty.
- Do not keep outdated medicine or medicine no longer needed. Be sure that any discarded medicine is out of the reach of children.

Precautions While Using This Medicine

Do not stop using this medicine without first checking with your doctor. Your doctor may want you to reduce gradually the amount you are using before you completely stop using it.

Check with your doctor if your condition does not improve within 2 or 3 weeks or if it becomes worse.

Check with your doctor if you notice rectal bleeding, pain, burning, itching, blistering, or any other sign of irritation that you did not have before you started using this medicine.

Use of suppositories may cause staining of clothing or fabric.

Tell the doctor in charge that you are using this medicine:
- *Before having skin tests.*
- *Before having any kind of surgery (including dental surgery) or emergency treatment.*
- *If you get a serious infection or injury.*

Avoid close contact with anyone who has chickenpox or measles. This is especially important for children. *Tell your doctor right away if you think you have been exposed to chickenpox or measles.*

While you are being treated with this medicine, and after you stop taking it, *do not have any immunizations without your doctor's approval.*

For patients with diabetes:
- This medicine may affect blood glucose (sugar) levels. If you notice a change in the results of your blood or urine sugar tests or if you have any questions, check with your doctor.

Side Effects of This Medicine

Along with its needed effects, a medicine may cause some unwanted effects. Although not all of these side effects may occur, if they do occur they may need medical attention.

Check with your doctor as soon as possible if any of the following side effects occur:
Less common or rare
   Burning and itching of skin; chills; depression; diarrhea; false sense of well-being; fever; infection; mood swings; painful, red or itchy, pus-containing blisters in hair follicles; personality changes; rectal bleeding, burning, dryness, itching, or pain not present before therapy; sensation of pins and needles; stabbing pain; straining while passing stool (with tixocortol only)

Additional side effects may occur if you use this medicine for a long time. Check with your doctor as soon as possible if any of the following side effects occur:
   Abdominal or stomach pain; acne; backache; coughing; coughing up blood; decreased resistance to infection; dryness of mouth; eye pain; filling or rounding out of the face; gradual blurring or loss of vision; headache; hunchback; increased thirst; irregular heartbeat; loss of appetite; menstrual irregularities; mood or mental changes; muscle cramps or pain; muscle weakness; nausea or vomiting; nonelevated blue or purplish patch on the skin; osteoporosis or bone fractures; pain in joints; pain or discomfort in the area of a vein; rapid weight gain; reddish purple lines on arms, face, legs, trunk, or groin; redness of eye; sensitivity of eye to light; shortness of breath; skin rash; slow wound healing; stunting of growth (in children); swelling of feet or lower legs; trouble in sleeping; unusual decrease in sexual desire or ability in men; tearing of eyes; unusual increase in hair growth (especially on the face); unusual tiredness or weakness; unusual weight loss; weak pulse

Other side effects may occur that usually do not need medical attention. These side effects may go away during treatment as your body adjusts to the medicine. However, check with your doctor if any of the following side effects continue or are bothersome:
Less common or rare
   Dizziness; dry, scaly skin; increase in appetite; increased sweating; lightened skin color; passing of gas (with budesonide only); sensation of spinning; thin, fragile skin; thinning hair on scalp; unusual weight gain

Other side effects not listed above may also occur in some patients. If you notice any other effects, check with your doctor.

Developed: 07/24/1998

CORTICOSTEROIDS AND ACETIC ACID   Otic

Commonly used brand name(s):

In the U.S.—
   VoSol HC

In Canada—
   VoSol HC

Another commonly used name for hydrocortisone is cortisol.

This information applies to the following corticosteroid and acetic acid combination medicines:
   Hydrocortisone and Acetic Acid (hye-droe-KOR-ti-sone and a-SEE-tik AS-id)

Description

Corticosteroid (kor-ti-koe-STE-roid) and acetic acid combinations are used to treat certain problems of the ear canal. They also help relieve the redness, itching, and swelling that may accompany these conditions.

These medicines may also be used for other conditions as determined by your doctor.

Corticosteroid and acetic acid combinations are available only with your doctor's prescription, in the following dosage form:
Otic
   Hydrocortisone and Acetic Acid
   • Solution (U.S. and Canada)

Before Using This Medicine

In deciding to use a medicine, the risks of using the medicine must be weighed against the good it will do. This is a decision you and your doctor will make. For corticosteroids with acetic acid, the following should be considered:

Allergies—Tell your doctor if you have ever had any unusual or allergic reaction to corticosteroids or acetic acid. Also tell your health care professional if you are allergic to any other substances, such as certain preservatives or dyes.

Pregnancy—Corticosteroids have not been studied in pregnant women. However, studies in animals have shown that corticosteroids cause birth defects. Before taking this medicine, make sure your doctor knows if you are pregnant or if you may become pregnant.

Breast-feeding—Otic corticosteroid and acetic acid combinations pass into breast milk. Possible benefits of otic corticosteroid and acetic acid must be weighed against the potential hazards for the infant.

Children—There is no specific information comparing the use of otic corticosteroids in children under 3 years of age with use in other age groups.

Older adults—Although there is no specific information comparing the use of otic corticosteroids in the elderly with use in other age groups, they are not expected to cause different side effects or problems in older people than they do in younger adults.

Other medicines—Although certain medicines should not be used together at all, in other cases two different medicines may be used together even if an interaction might occur. In these cases, your doctor may want to change the dose, or other precautions may be necessary. When you are taking a corticosteroid and acetic acid combination, it is especially important that your doctor know if you are taking any other prescription or nonprescription (over-the-counter [OTC]) medicine.

Other medical problems—The presence of other medical problems may affect the use of otic corticosteroids. Make sure you tell your doctor if you have any other medical problems, especially:

- Any other ear infection or condition—Otic corticosteroids may worsen existing infections or cause new infections
- Punctured ear drum—Using otic corticosteroids when you have a punctured ear drum may damage the ear

Proper Use of This Medicine

To use:

- Lie down or tilt the head so that the affected ear faces up. Gently pull the ear lobe up and back for adults (down and back for children) to straighten the ear canal. Drop the medicine into the ear canal. Keep the ear facing up for several (about 5) minutes to allow the medicine to run to the bottom of the ear canal. A sterile cotton plug may be gently inserted into the ear opening to prevent the medicine from leaking out. At first, your doctor may want you to put more medicine on the cotton plug during the day to keep it moist.

To keep the medicine as germ-free as possible, avoid touching the dropper or applicator tip to any surface as much as possible (including the ear). Also, always keep the container tightly closed.

For patients using *hydrocortisone and acetic acid ear drops:*
- *Do not wash the dropper or applicator tip*, because water may get into the medicine and make it weaker. If necessary, you may wipe the dropper or applicator tip with a clean tissue.

Do not use corticosteroids more often or for a longer time than your doctor ordered. To do so may increase the chance of side effects.

Do not use any leftover medicine for future ear problems without first checking with your doctor. This medicine should not be used if certain kinds of infections are present. To do so may make the infection worse.

Dosing—The dose of otic corticosteroid and acetic acid combination will be different for different patients. *Follow your doctor's orders or the directions on the label.* The following information includes only the average doses of otic corticosteroid and acetic acid combination. *If your dose is different, do not change it* unless your doctor tells you to do so.

For hydrocortisone and acetic acid
- For *ear drops* dosage form:
  —For ear infections:
  - Adults and children over 3 years of age—Use 3 to 5 drops in the affected ear every four to six hours for the first twenty-four hours, then 5 drops three to four times daily.
  - Children under 3 years of age—Use and dose must be determined by your doctor.

Missed dose—If you miss a dose of this medicine, apply it as soon as possible. However, if it is almost time for your next dose, skip the missed dose and go back to your regular dosing schedule. Do not stop treatment abruptly.

Storage—To store this medicine:
- Keep out of the reach of children.
- Store at room temperature.
- Store away from heat and direct light.
- Keep the medicine from freezing.
- Do not keep outdated medicine or medicine no longer needed. Be sure that any discarded medicine is out of the reach of children.

Precautions While Using This Medicine

If your condition does not improve within 5 to 7 days, or if it becomes worse, check with your doctor.

Side Effects of This Medicine

Along with its needed effects, a medicine may cause some unwanted effects. The following side effects usually do not need medical attention and may go away during treatment as your body adjusts to the medicine or your condition improves. However, check with your doctor if any of the following side effects continue or are bothersome:

Less common
Anorexia, weakness, weight loss (in children); stinging, itching, irritation, or burning of the ear

There have not been any other side effects reported with this medicine. However, if you notice any other effects, check with your doctor.

Revised: 6/04/99

CORTICOSTEROIDS — Glucocorticoid Effects   Systemic

Commonly used brand name(s):

In the U.S.—

Acetocot[9]	Kenacort Diacetate[9]
A-hydroCort[5]	Kenaject-40[9]
Amcort[9]	Kenalog-10[9]
A-MethaPred[6]	Kenalog-40[9]
Aristocort[9]	Ken-Jec 40[9]
Aristocort Forte[9]	Key-Pred[7]
Aristopak[9]	Key-Pred SP[7]
Aristospan[9]	Liquid Pred[8]
Articulose-50[7]	Med-Jec-40[6]
Articulose-L.A.[9]	Medralone 80[6]
Celestone[1]	Medrol[6]
Celestone Phosphate[1]	Meprolone[6]
Celestone Soluspan[1]	Methacort 40[6]
Cinalone 40[9]	Methacort 80[6]
Cinonide 40[9]	Methylcotolone[6]
Clinacort[9]	Meticorten[8]
Clinalog[9]	Mymethasone[4]
Cordrol[8]	Nor-Pred T.B.A.[7]
Cortastat[4]	Orasone 1[8]
Cortastat 10[4]	Orasone 5[8]
Cortastat LA[4]	Orasone 10[8]
Cortef[5]	Orasone 20[8]
Cortone Acetate[3]	Orasone 50[8]
Cotolone[7]	Pediapred[7]
Dalalone[4]	Predacort 50[7]
Dalalone D.P.[4]	Predacorten[6]
Dalalone L.A.[4]	Predacorten 80[6]
Decadrol[4]	Predalone 50[7]
Decadron[4]	Predalone T.B.A.[7]
Decadron Elixir[4]	Predate-50[7]
Decadron-LA[4]	Predate S[7]
Decadron Phosphate[4]	Predate TBA[7]
Decaject[4]	Predcor-25[7]
Decaject-LA[4]	Predcor-50[7]
Delta-Cortef[7]	Predcor-TBA[7]
Deltasone[8]	Predicort-RP[7]
depMedalone 40[6]	Pred-Ject-50[7]
depMedalone 80[6]	Prednicot[8]
Depoject-40[6]	Prednisone Intensol[8]
Depoject-80[6]	Pred-Pak 45[8]
Depo-Medrol[6]	Pred-Pak 79[8]
Depopred[6]	Prelone[7]
Depo-Predate[6]	Primethasone[4]
Dexacorten[4]	Robalog[9]
Dexacorten-LA[4]	Selestoject[1]
Dexamethasone Intensol[4]	Solu-Cortef[5]
Dexasone[4]	Solu-Medrol[6]
Dexasone L.A.[4]	Solurex[4]
Dexone[4]	Solurex LA[4]
Dexone 0.75[4]	Sterapred[8]
Dexone 1.5[4]	Sterapred DS[8]
Dexone 4[4]	Tac-3[9]
Dexone LA[4]	Tramacort-D[9]
Duralone-40[6]	Triam-A[9]
Duralone-80[6]	Triam-Forte[9]
Hexadrol[4]	Triamolone 40[9]
Hexadrol Phosphate[4]	Triamonide 40[9]
Hydrocortone[5]	Tri-Kort[9]
Hydrocortone Acetate[5]	Trilog[9]
Hydrocortone Phosphate[5]	Trilone[9]
Kenacort[9]	Tristoject[9]

In Canada—

A-Hydrocort[5]	Aristocort Intralesional[9]
Apo-Prednisone[8]	Aristospan[9]
Aristocort[9]	Betnesol[1]
Aristocort Forte[9]	Celestone Soluspan[1]

Cortef[5]	Kenacort[9]
Cortisone Acetate-ICN[3]	Kenalog-10[9]
Cortone[3]	Kenalog-40[9]
Decadron[4]	Medrol[6]
Decadron Phosphate[4]	Oradexon[4]
Deltasone[8]	Pediapred[7]
Depo-Medrol[6]	Scheinpharm Triamcine-A[9]
Deronil[4]	Solu-Cortef[5]
Dexasone[4]	Solu-Medrol[6]
Entocort[2]	Winpred[8]
Hexadrol Phosphate[4]	

Another commonly used name for hydrocortisone is cortisol.

Note: For quick reference, the following corticosteroids are numbered to match the corresponding brand names.

This information applies to the following medicines:
1. Betamethasone (bay-ta-METH-a-sone) ‡
2. Budesonide (byoo-DES-oh-nide) *
3. Cortisone (KOR-ti-sone) ‡§
4. Dexamethasone (dex-a-METH-a-sone) ‡§
5. Hydrocortisone (hye-droe-KOR-ti-sone) ‡
6. Methylprednisolone (meth-il-pred-NIS-oh-lone) ‡
7. Prednisolone (pred-NISS-oh-lone) ‡
8. Prednisone (PRED-ni-sone) ‡§
9. Triamcinolone (trye-am-SIN-oh-lone) ‡§

The following information does *not* apply to desoxycorticosterone or fludrocortisone.

*Not commercially available in the U.S.
‡Generic name product may be available in the U.S.
§Generic name product may be available in Canada.

Description

Corticosteroids (kor-ti-koe-STER-oyds) (cortisone-like medicines) are used to provide relief for inflamed areas of the body. They lessen swelling, redness, itching, and allergic reactions. They are often used as part of the treatment for a number of different diseases, such as severe allergies or skin problems, asthma, or arthritis. Corticosteroids may also be used for other conditions as determined by your doctor.

Your body naturally produces certain cortisone-like hormones that are necessary to maintain good health. If your body does not produce enough, your doctor may have prescribed this medicine to help make up the difference.

Corticosteroids are very strong medicines. In addition to their helpful effects in treating your medical problem, they have side effects that can be very serious. If your adrenal glands are not producing enough cortisone-like hormones, taking this medicine is not likely to cause problems unless you take too much of it. If you are taking this medicine to treat another medical problem, be sure that you discuss the risks and benefits of this medicine with your doctor.

These medicines are available only with your doctor's prescription, in the following dosage forms:

Oral
Betamethasone
- Syrup (U.S.)
- Tablets (U.S.)
- Effervescent tablets (Canada)
- Extended-release tablets
Budesonide
- Extended-release capsules (Canada)
Cortisone
- Tablets (U.S. and Canada)
Dexamethasone
- Elixir (U.S.)
- Oral solution (U.S.)

- Tablets (U.S. and Canada)

Hydrocortisone
- Oral suspension (U.S.)
- Tablets (U.S. and Canada)

Methylprednisolone
- Tablets (U.S. and Canada)

Prednisolone
- Oral solution (U.S. and Canada)
- Syrup (U.S.)
- Tablets (U.S.)

Prednisone
- Oral solution (U.S.)
- Syrup (U.S.)
- Tablets (U.S. and Canada)

Triamcinolone
- Syrup (U.S. and Canada)
- Tablets (U.S. and Canada)

Parenteral

Betamethasone
- Injection (U.S. and Canada)

Cortisone
- Injection (U.S. and Canada)

Dexamethasone
- Injection (U.S. and Canada)

Hydrocortisone
- Injection (U.S. and Canada)

Methylprednisolone
- Injection (U.S. and Canada)

Prednisolone
- Injection (U.S.)

Triamcinolone
- Injection (U.S. and Canada)

Before Using This Medicine

In deciding to use a medicine, the risks of taking the medicine must be weighed against the good it will do. This is a decision you and your doctor will make. For corticosteroids, the following should be considered:

Allergies—Tell your doctor if you have ever had any unusual or allergic reaction to corticosteroids. Also tell your health care professional if you are allergic to any other substances, such as foods, preservatives, or dyes.

Diet—If you will be using this medicine for a long time, your doctor may want you to:
- Follow a low-salt diet and/or a potassium-rich diet.
- Watch your calories to prevent weight gain.
- Add extra protein to your diet.

Make certain your health care professional knows if you are already on any special diet, such as a low-sodium or low-sugar diet.

Pregnancy—Studies on birth defects with corticosteroids have not been done in humans. However, studies in animals have shown that corticosteroids cause birth defects.

Breast-feeding—Corticosteroids pass into breast milk and may cause problems with growth or other unwanted effects in nursing babies. Depending on the amount of medicine you are taking every day, it may be necessary for you to take another medicine or to stop breast-feeding during treatment.

Children—Corticosteroids may cause infections such as chickenpox or measles to be more serious in children who catch them. These medicines can also slow or stop growth in children and in growing teenagers, especially when they are

used for a long time. Before this medicine is given to children or teenagers, you should discuss its use with your child's doctor and then carefully follow the doctor's instructions.

Older adults—Older patients may be more likely to develop high blood pressure or osteoporosis (bone disease) from corticosteroids. Women are especially at risk of developing bone disease.

Other medicines—Although certain medicines should not be used together at all, in other cases two different medicines may be used together even if an interaction might occur. In these cases, your doctor may want to change the dose, or other precautions may be necessary. When you are taking corticosteroids, it is especially important that your health care professional know if you are taking any of the following:

- Aminoglutethimide (e.g., Cytadren) or
- Antacids (in large amounts) or
- Barbiturates, except butalbital, or
- Carbamazepine (e.g., Tegretol) or
- Griseofulvin (e.g., Fulvicin) or
- Mitotane (e.g., Lysodren) or
- Phenylbutazone (e.g., Butazolidin) or
- Phenytoin (e.g., Dilantin) or
- Primidone (e.g., Mysoline) or
- Rifampin (e.g., Rifadin)—Use of these medicines may make certain corticosteroids less effective

- Amphotericin B by injection (e.g., Fungizone)—Using corticosteroids with this medicine may decrease the amount of potassium in the blood. Serious side effects could occur if the level of potassium gets too low

- Antidiabetic agents, oral (diabetes medicine taken by mouth) or
- Insulin—Corticosteroids may increase blood glucose (sugar) levels

- Cyclosporine (e.g., Sandimmune)—Use of this medicine with high doses of methylprednisolone may cause convulsions (seizures)

- Digitalis glycosides (heart medicine)—Corticosteroids decrease the amount of potassium in the blood. Digitalis can increase the risk of having an irregular heartbeat or other problems if the amount of potassium in the blood gets too low

- Diuretics (water pills) or
- Medicine containing potassium—Using corticosteroids with diuretics may cause the diuretic to be less effective. Also, corticosteroids may increase the risk of low blood potassium, which is also a problem with certain diuretics. Potassium supplements or a different type of diuretic is used in treating high blood pressure in those people who have problems keeping their blood potassium at a normal level. Corticosteroids may make these medicines less able to do this

- Immunizations (vaccinations)—While you are being treated with this medicine, and even after you stop taking it, do not have any immunizations without your doctor's approval. Also, other people living in your home should not receive the oral polio vaccine, since there is a chance they could pass the polio virus on to you. In addition, you should avoid close contact with other people at school or work who have recently taken the oral polio vaccine

- Ritodrine (e.g., Yutopar)—Serious side effects could occur

- Skin test injections—Corticosteroids may cause false results in skin tests
- Sodium-containing medicine—Corticosteroids cause the body to retain (keep) more sodium (salt) and water. Too much sodium may cause high blood sodium, high blood pressure, and excess body water
- Somatrem (e.g., Protropin) or
- Somatropin (e.g., Humatrope)—Corticosteroids can interfere with the effects of these medicines

Other medical problems—The presence of other medical problems may affect the use of corticosteroids. Make sure you tell your doctor if you have any other medical problems, especially:

- Acquired immunodeficiency syndrome (AIDS) or
- Fungus infection or
- Herpes simplex infection of the eye or
- Human immunodeficiency virus (HIV) infection or
- Infection at the place of treatment or
- Other infection or
- Recent surgery or serious injury or
- *Strongyloides* (worm) infestation or
- Tuberculosis (active TB, nonactive TB, or past history of)—Corticosteroids can cause slower healing, worsen existing infections, or cause new infections

- Chickenpox (including recent exposure) or
- Measles (including recent exposure)—Risk of severe disease affecting other parts of the body

- Diabetes mellitus (sugar diabetes)—Corticosteroids may cause a loss of control of diabetes by increasing blood glucose (sugar)

- Diverticulitis or
- Stomach ulcer or other stomach or intestine problems or
- Ulcerative colitis, severe—Corticosteroids may cover up symptoms of a worsening stomach or intestinal condition. A patient would not know if his or her condition was getting worse and would not get medical help when needed

- Glaucoma—Corticosteroids may cause the pressure within the eye to increase

- Heart disease or
- High blood pressure or
- Kidney disease (especially if you are receiving dialysis) or
- Kidney stones—Corticosteroids cause the body to retain (keep) more salt and water. These conditions may be made worse by this extra body water

- High cholesterol levels—Corticosteroids may increase blood cholesterol levels

- Liver disease or
- Overactive thyroid or
- Underactive thyroid—With these conditions, the body may not eliminate the corticosteroid at the usual rate, which may change the medicine's effect

- Myasthenia gravis—When you first start taking corticosteroids, muscle weakness may occur. Your doctor may want to take special precautions because this could cause problems with breathing

- Osteoporosis (bone disease)—Corticosteroids may worsen bone disease because they cause the body to lose more calcium

- Psychosis—This condition may be made worse
- Systemic lupus erythematosus (SLE)—This condition may cause certain side effects of corticosteroids to occur more easily

Proper Use of This Medicine

For patients taking this medicine by mouth:
- *Take this medicine with food* to help prevent stomach upset. If stomach upset, burning, or pain continues, check with your doctor.
- Stomach problems may be more likely to occur if you drink alcoholic beverages while being treated with this medicine. You should not drink alcoholic beverages while taking this medicine, unless you have first checked with your doctor.

For patients taking *budesonide extended-release capsules:*
- Swallow the capsule whole, without breaking, crushing, or chewing it.

Use this medicine only as directed by your doctor. Do not use more or less of it, do not use it more often, and do not use it for a longer time than your doctor ordered. To do so may increase the chance of side effects.

Dosing—The dose of these medicines will be different for different patients. *Follow your doctor's orders or the directions on the label.* The following information gives the range of doses of these medicines for all uses, which can vary widely. The dose that you are receiving may be very different. *If your dose is different, do not change it* unless your doctor tells you to do so.

The number of capsules, tablets, teaspoonfuls of liquid or amount of injection that you use depends on the strength of the medicine. Also, *the number of doses you take each day, the time allowed between doses, and the length of time you take the medicine depend on the medical problem for which you are taking the corticosteroid. In addition, your doctor may need to change the dose from time to time.*

For betamethasone
- For *oral* dosage forms:
  —Syrup, tablets, effervescent tablets:
  - Adults and teenagers—Dose may range from 0.25 to 7.2 milligrams (mg) a day, as a single dose or divided into several doses.
  - Children—Dose is based on body weight or size and must be determined by your doctor.
  —Extended-release tablets:
  - Adults and teenagers—2 to 6 mg a day.
  - Children—Dose is based on body weight or size and must be determined by your doctor.
- For *injection* dosage form:
  —Adults and teenagers: Dose may range from 1.2 to 12 mg injected into a joint, lesion, muscle, or vein as often as necessary, as determined by your doctor.
  —Children: Dose is based on body weight or size and must be determined by your doctor.

For budesonide
- For *oral* dosage form (extended-release capsules):
  —Adults: At first, the dose is 9 milligrams (mg) a day for up to eight weeks. Then your doctor may decrease the dose to 6 mg a day. Each dose should be taken in the morning before breakfast.

—Children: Use and dose must be determined by your doctor.

For cortisone
- For *oral* dosage form (tablets):
  —Adults and teenagers: 25 to 300 milligrams (mg) a day, as a single dose or divided into several doses.
  —Children: Dose is based on body weight or size and must be determined by your doctor.
- For *injection* dosage form:
  —Adults and teenagers: 20 to 300 mg a day, injected into a muscle.
  —Children: Dose is based on body weight or size and must be determined by your doctor.

For dexamethasone
- For *oral* dosage forms (elixir, oral solution, tablets):
  —Adults and teenagers: 0.5 to 10 milligrams (mg) taken as often as necessary, as determined by your doctor.
  —Children: Dose is based on body weight or size and must be determined by your doctor.
- For *injection* dosage form:
  —Adults and teenagers: 0.2 to 40 mg injected into a joint, lesion, muscle, or vein as often as necessary, as determined by your doctor.
  —Children: Dose is based on body weight or size and must be determined by your doctor.

For hydrocortisone
- For *oral* dosage forms (oral suspension, tablets):
  —Adults and teenagers: 20 to 240 milligrams (mg) a day, as a single dose or divided into several doses.
  —Children: Dose is based on body weight or size and must be determined by your doctor.
- For *injection* dosage form:
  —Adults and teenagers: 15 to 240 mg injected into a joint, lesion, muscle, or vein, or under the skin as often as necessary, as determined by your doctor.
  —Children: Dose is based on body weight or size and must be determined by your doctor.

For methylprednisolone
- For *oral* dosage form (tablets):
  —Adults and teenagers: 4 to 160 milligrams (mg) every one or two days, as a single dose or divided into several doses.
  —Children: Dose is based on body weight or size and must be determined by your doctor.
- For *injection* dosage form:
  —Adults and teenagers: 4 to 80 mg injected into a joint, lesion, muscle, or vein as often as necessary, as determined by your doctor.
  —Children: Dose is based on body weight or size and must be determined by your doctor.

For prednisolone
- For *oral* dosage forms (oral solution, syrup, tablets):
  —Adults and teenagers: 5 to 60 milligrams (mg) taken as often as necessary, as determined by your doctor.
  —Children: Dose is based on body weight or size and must be determined by your doctor.
- For *injection* dosage form:
  —Adults and teenagers: 2 to 100 mg injected into a joint, lesion, muscle, or vein as often as necessary, as determined by your doctor.

—Children: Dose is based on body weight or size and must be determined by your doctor.

For prednisone
- For *oral* dosage forms (oral solution, syrup, tablets):
  —Adults and teenagers: 5 to 200 milligrams (mg) every one or two days, as a single dose or divided into several doses.
  —Children: Dose is based on body weight or size and must be determined by your doctor.

For triamcinolone
- For *oral* dosage forms (syrup, tablets):
  —Adults and teenagers: 2 to 48 milligrams (mg) a day, as a single dose or divided into several doses.
  —Children: Dose is based on body weight or size and must be determined by your doctor.
- For *injection* dosage form:
  —Adults and teenagers: 0.5 to 80 mg injected into a joint, lesion, or muscle, or under the skin as often as necessary, as determined by your doctor.
  —Children: Dose is based on body weight or size and must be determined by your doctor.

Missed dose—If you miss a dose of this medicine and your dosing schedule is:
- One dose every other day—Take the missed dose as soon as possible if you remember it the same morning, then go back to your regular dosing schedule. If you do not remember the missed dose until later, wait and take it the following morning. Then skip a day and start your regular dosing schedule again.
- One dose a day—Take the missed dose as soon as possible, then go back to your regular dosing schedule. If you do not remember until the next day, skip the missed dose and do not double the next one.
- Several doses a day—Take the missed dose as soon as possible, then go back to your regular dosing schedule. If you do not remember until your next dose is due, double the next dose.

If you have any questions about this, check with your health care professional.

Storage—To store this medicine:
- Keep out of the reach of children.
- Store away from heat and direct light.
- Do not store capsules or tablets in the bathroom, near the kitchen sink, or in other damp places. Heat or moisture may cause the medicine to break down.
- Keep the liquid dosage forms of this medicine from freezing.
- Do not keep outdated medicine or medicine no longer needed. Be sure that any discarded medicine is out of the reach of children.

Precautions While Using This Medicine

Your doctor should check your progress at regular visits. Also, your progress may have to be checked after you have stopped using this medicine, since some of the effects may continue.

Do not stop using this medicine without first checking with your doctor. Your doctor may want you to reduce gradually the amount you are using before stopping the medicine completely.

Check with your doctor if your condition reappears or worsens after the dose has been reduced or treatment with this medicine is stopped.

If you will be using corticosteroids for a long time:

- *Your doctor may want you to follow a low-salt diet and/or a potassium-rich diet.*
- Your doctor may want you to watch your calories to prevent weight gain.
- Your doctor may want you to add extra protein to your diet.
- Your doctor may want you to have your eyes examined by an ophthalmologist (eye doctor) before, and also sometime later during treatment.
- Your doctor may want you to carry a medical identification card stating that you are using this medicine.

Tell the doctor in charge that you are using this medicine:

- *Before having skin tests.*
- *Before having any kind of surgery (including dental surgery) or emergency treatment.*
- *If you get a serious infection or injury.*

Avoid close contact with anyone who has chickenpox or measles. This is especially important for children. *Tell your doctor right away if you think you have been exposed to chickenpox or measles.*

While you are being treated with this medicine, and after you stop taking it, *do not have any immunizations without your doctor's approval.* Also, other people living in your home should not receive the oral polio vaccine, since there is a chance they could pass the polio virus on to you. In addition, you should avoid close contact with other people at school or work who have recently taken the oral polio vaccine.

For *patients with diabetes:*

- This medicine may affect blood glucose (sugar) levels. If you notice a change in the results of your blood or urine sugar tests or if you have any questions, check with your doctor.

For patients having this medicine *injected into their joints:*

- If this medicine is injected into one of your joints, you should be careful not to put too much stress or strain on that joint for a while, even if it begins to feel better. Make sure your doctor has told you how much you are allowed to move this joint while it is healing.
- If redness or swelling occurs at the place of injection, and continues or gets worse, check with your doctor.

Side Effects of This Medicine

Corticosteroids may lower your resistance to infections. Also, any infection you get may be harder to treat. Always check with your doctor as soon as possible if you notice any signs of a possible infection, such as sore throat, fever, sneezing, or coughing.

Along with its needed effects, a medicine may cause some unwanted effects. Although not all of these side effects may occur, if they do occur they may need medical attention. When this medicine is used for short periods of time, side effects usually are rare. However, check with your doctor as soon as possible if any of the following side effects occur:

Less common

Decreased or blurred vision; frequent urination; increased thirst

Rare

Blindness (sudden, when injected in the head or neck area); burning, numbness, pain, or tingling at or near place of injection; confusion; excitement; false sense of well-being; hallucinations (seeing, hearing, or feeling things that are not there); mental depression; mistaken feelings of self-importance or being mistreated; mood swings (sudden and wide); redness, swelling, or other sign of allergy or infection at place of injection; restlessness; skin rash or hives

Additional side effects may occur if you take this medicine for a long time. Check with your doctor if any of the following side effects occur:

Abdominal or stomach pain or burning (continuing); acne; bloody or black, tarry stools; changes in vision; eye pain; filling or rounding out of the face; headache; irregular heartbeat; menstrual problems; muscle cramps or pain; muscle weakness; nausea; pain in arms, back, hips, legs, ribs, or shoulders; pitting, scarring, or depression of skin at place of injection; reddish purple lines on arms, face, groin, legs, or trunk; redness of eyes; sensitivity of eyes to light; stunting of growth (in children); swelling of feet or lower legs; tearing of eyes; thin, shiny skin; trouble in sleeping; unusual bruising; unusual increase in hair growth; unusual tiredness or weakness; vomiting; weight gain (rapid); wounds that will not heal

Other side effects may occur that usually do not need medical attention. These side effects may go away during treatment as your body adjusts to the medicine. However, check with your doctor if any of the following side effects continue or are bothersome:

More common

Increased appetite; indigestion; loss of appetite (for triamcinolone only); nervousness or restlessness

Less common or rare

Darkening or lightening of skin color; dizziness or lightheadedness; flushing of face or cheeks; hiccups; increased joint pain (after injection into a joint); increased sweating; nosebleeds (after injection into the nose); sensation of spinning

After you stop using this medicine, your body may need time to adjust. The length of time this takes depends on the amount of medicine you were using and how long you used it. If you have taken large doses of this medicine for a long time, your body may need one year to adjust. During this time, *check with your doctor immediately if any of the following side effects occur:*

Abdominal, stomach, or back pain; dizziness; fainting; fever; loss of appetite (continuing); muscle or joint pain; nausea; reappearance of disease symptoms; shortness of breath; unexplained headaches (frequent or continuing); unusual tiredness or weakness; vomiting; weight loss (rapid)

Other side effects not listed above may also occur in some patients. If you notice any other effects, check with your doctor.

Revised: 06/27/2000

CORTICOSTEROIDS —Low Potency   Topical

Commonly used brand name(s):

In the U.S.—

Aclovate[1]	Dermarest DriCort[7]
Acticort 100[7]	DermiCort[7]
Aeroseb-Dex[4]	Dermtex HC[7]
Aeroseb-HC[7]	DesOwen[3]
Ala-Cort[7]	Epifoam[9]
Ala-Scalp HP[7]	Gynecort[9]
Alphaderm[7]	Gynecort 10[9]
CaldeCORT Anti-Itch[8]	Hi-Cor 1.0[7]
CaldeCORT Light[9]	Hi-Cor 2.5[7]
Carmol-HC[9]	Hydro-Tex[7]
Cetacort[7]	Hytone[7]
Cloderm[2]	LactiCare-HC[7]
Cortaid[8]	Lanacort[9]
Cort-Dome[7]	Lanacort 10[9]
Cortef Feminine Itch[9]	Maximum Strength Cortaid[7]
Corticaine[9]	Nutracort[7]
Cortifair[7]	Penecort[7]
Cortril[7]	Rhulicort[9]
Decaderm[4]	S-T Cort[7]
Decadron[4]	Synacort[7]
Decaspray[4]	Texacort[7]
Delacort[7]	Tridesilon[3]
Dermacort[7]	

In Canada—

Barriere-HC[7]	Emo-Cort Scalp Solution[7]
Cortacet[9]	Hyderm[9]
Cortate[7]	Locacorten[5]
Cortef[8]	Prevex HC[7]
Corticreme[9]	Sarna HC 1.0%[7]
Cortoderm[9]	Sential[7]
Drenison-¼[6]	Tridesilon[3]
Emo-Cort[7]	Unicort[7]

Other commonly used names are:

Cortisol
Fludroxycortide
Flumetasone

Note: For quick reference, the following low potency corticosteroids are numbered to match the corresponding brand names.

This information applies to the following medicines:
1. Alclometasone (al-kloe-MET-a-sone) †
2. Clocortolone (kloe-KOR-toe-lone) †
3. Desonide (DESS-oh-nide) ‡
4. Dexamethasone (dex-a-METH-a-sone) †
5. Flumethasone (floo-METH-a-sone) *
6. Flurandrenolide (flure-an-DREN-oh-lide) (Drenison-¼only)
7. Hydrocortisone (hye-droe-KOR-ti-sone) ‡
8. Hydrocortisone or hydrocortisone acetate (hye-droe-KOR-ti-son or hye-droe-KOR-ti-sonee AS-a-tate) ‡
9. Hydrocortisone acetate (hye-droe-KOR-ti-sone AS-a-tate) ‡

*Not commercially available in the U.S.
†Not commercially available in Canada.
‡Generic name product may be available in the U.S.

Description

Topical corticosteroids (kor-ti-ko-STER-oyds) are used to help relieve redness, swelling, itching, and discomfort of many skin problems. These medicines are like cortisone. They belong to the general family of medicines called steroids.

Most corticosteroids are available only with your doctor's prescription. Some strengths of hydrocortisone are available without a prescription. However, your doctor may have special instructions on the proper use for your medical condition.

Topical corticosteroids are available in the following dosage forms:

Topical
Alclometasone
- Cream (U.S.)
- Ointment (U.S.)
Clocortolone
- Cream (U.S.)
Desonide
- Cream (U.S. and Canada)
- Lotion (U.S.)
- Ointment (U.S. and Canada)
Dexamethasone
- Cream (U.S.)
- Gel (U.S.)
- Topical aerosol (U.S.)
Flumethasone
- Cream (Canada)
- Ointment (Canada)
Flurandrenolide
- Cream 0.0125% (Canada)
- Ointment 0.0125% (Canada)
Hydrocortisone
- Cream (U.S. and Canada)
- Lotion (U.S. and Canada)
- Ointment (U.S. and Canada)
- Topical solution (U.S. and Canada)
Hydrocortisone acetate
- Cream (U.S. and Canada)
- Topical aerosol foam (U.S.)
- Lotion (U.S.)
- Ointment (U.S. and Canada)

Before Using This Medicine

In deciding to use a medicine, the risks of taking the medicine must be weighed against the good it will do. This is a decision you and your doctor will make. For topical corticosteroids, the following should be considered:

Allergies—Tell your doctor if you have ever had any unusual or allergic reaction to corticosteroids. Also tell your health care professional if you are allergic to any other substances, such as foods, preservatives, or dyes.

Pregnancy—When used properly, these medicines have not been shown to cause problems in humans. Studies on birth defects have not been done in humans. However, studies in animals have shown that topical corticosteroids, when applied to the skin in large amounts or used for a long time, could cause birth defects.

Breast-feeding—Topical corticosteroids have not been reported to cause problems in nursing babies when used properly. However, corticosteroids should not be applied to the breasts just before nursing.

Children—Children and teenagers who must use this medicine for a long time should be checked often by their doctor. Other, more potent corticosteroids are absorbed through the skin and can affect growth or cause other unwanted effects. Topical corticosteroids also can be absorbed

© 2002 MICROMEDEX Thomson Healthcare

if they are applied to large areas of skin. These effects are less likely to occur with the use of the lower potency corticosteroids. However, before using this medicine in children, you should discuss its use with your child's doctor.

Older adults—This medicine is not expected to cause different side effects or problems in older people than it does in younger adults.

Other medicines—Although certain medicines should not be used together at all, in other cases two different medicines may be used together even if an interaction might occur. In these cases, your doctor may want to change the dose, or other precautions may be necessary. Tell your health care professional if you are using any other topical prescription or nonprescription (over-the-counter [OTC]) medicine that is to be applied to the same area of the skin.

Other medical problems—The presence of other medical problems may affect the use of topical corticosteroids. Make sure you tell your doctor if you have any other medical problems, especially:

- Diabetes mellitus (sugar diabetes)—Too much use of corticosteroids may cause a loss of control of diabetes by increasing blood and urine glucose. However, this is not likely to happen when topical corticosteroids are used for a short time
- Infection or sores at the place of treatment or
- Tuberculosis—Corticosteroids may make existing infections worse or cause new infections
- Skin conditions that cause thinning of skin with easy bruising—Corticosteroids may make thinning of the skin worse

Proper Use of This Medicine

Be very careful not to get this medicine in your eyes. Wash your hands after using your finger to apply the medicine. If you accidentally get this medicine in your eyes, flush them with water.

Do not bandage or otherwise wrap the skin being treated unless directed to do so by your doctor.

If your doctor has ordered an occlusive dressing (airtight covering, such as kitchen plastic wrap or a special patch) to be applied over this medicine, make sure you know how to apply it. Since occlusive dressings increase the amount of medicine absorbed through your skin and the possibility of side effects, use them only as directed. If you have any questions about this, check with your doctor.

For patients using the *topical aerosol form* of this medicine:

- This medicine usually comes with patient directions. Read them carefully before using this medicine.
- It is important to avoid breathing in the vapors from the spray or getting them in your eyes. If you accidentally get this medicine in your eyes, flush them with water.
- Do not use near heat, near an open flame, or while smoking.

Do not use this medicine more often or for a longer time than your doctor ordered or than recommended on the package label. To do so may increase the chance of absorption through the skin and the chance of side effects.

If this medicine has been prescribed for you, it is meant to treat a specific skin problem. *Do not use it for other skin problems, and do not use nonprescription hydrocortisone for skin problems that are not listed on the package label,*

without first checking with your doctor. Topical corticosteroids should not be used on many kinds of bacterial, viral, or fungal skin infections.

Dosing—The dose of topical corticosteroid will be different for different patients and products. *Follow your doctor's orders or the directions on the label.*

Missed dose—If your doctor has ordered you to use this medicine on a regular schedule and you miss a dose, apply it as soon as possible. But if it is almost time for your next dose, skip the missed dose and apply it at the next regularly scheduled time.

Storage—To store this medicine:
- Keep out of the reach of children.
- Store away from heat and direct light.
- Keep the medicine from freezing.
- Do not puncture, break, or burn aerosol containers, even after they are empty.
- Do not keep outdated medicine or medicine no longer needed. Be sure that any discarded medicine is out of the reach of children.

Precautions While Using This Medicine

Check with your doctor if your symptoms do not improve within 1 week or if your condition gets worse.

Avoid using tight-fitting diapers or plastic pants on a child if this medicine is being used on the child's diaper area. Plastic pants and tight-fitting diapers may increase the chance of absorption of the medicine through the skin and the chance of side effects.

Side Effects of This Medicine

Along with its needed effects, a medicine may cause some unwanted effects. Although not all of these side effects may occur, if they do occur they may need medical attention.

Check with your doctor as soon as possible if any of the following side effects occur:
> *Less common or rare*
>> Blood-containing blisters on skin; burning and itching of skin; increased skin sensitivity; lack of healing of skin condition; numbness in fingers; painful, red or itchy, pus-containing blisters in hair follicles; raised, dark red, wart-like spots on skin, especially when used on the face; skin infection; thinning of skin with easy bruising

Some side effects may occur that usually do not need medical attention. These side effects may go away during treatment as your body adjusts to the medicine. However, check with your doctor if any of the following side effects continue or are bothersome:
> *Less common or rare*—usually mild and transient
>> Burning, dryness, irritation, itching, or redness of skin; increased redness or scaling of skin sores; skin rash

When the gel, lotion, solution, or aerosol form of this medicine is applied, a mild, temporary stinging may be expected.

Other side effects not listed above may also occur in some patients. If you notice any other effects, check with your doctor.

Revised: 11/18/92
Interim revision: 06/15/99

CORTICOSTEROIDS —Medium to Very High Potency   Topical

Commonly used brand name(s):

In the U.S.—

Alphatrex[3]	Kenalog-H[20]
Aristocort[20]	Kenonel[20]
Aristocort A[20]	Lidex[10]
Betatrex[3]	Lidex-E[10]
Beta-Val[3]	Locoid[15]
Cordran[11]	Luxiq[3]
Cordran SP[11]	Maxiflor[7]
Cormax[4]	Maxivate[3]
Cutivate[12]	Olux[4]
Cyclocort[1]	Pandel[16]
Delta-Tritex[20]	Psorcon[7]
Dermabet[3]	Synalar[9]
Diprolene[3]	Synalar-HP[9]
Diprolene AF[3]	Synemol[9]
Diprosone[3]	Teladar[3]
Elocon[18]	Temovate[4]
Florone[7]	Temovate E[4]
Florone E[7]	Temovate Scalp Application[4]
Fluocet[9]	Topicort[6]
Fluocin[10]	Topicort LP[6]
Fluonid[9]	Triderm[20]
Flurosyn[9]	Ultravate[14]
Flutex[20]	Uticort[3]
Halog[13]	Valisone[3]
Halog-E[13]	Valisone Reduced Strength[3]
Kenac[20]	Valnac[3]
Kenalog[20]	Westcort[17]

In Canada—

Aristocort C[20]	Fluonide[9]
Aristocort D[20]	Halog[13]
Aristocort R[20]	Kenalog[20]
Beben[3]	Lidemol[10]
Betacort Scalp Lotion[3]	Lidex[10]
Betaderm[3]	Lyderm[10]
Betaderm Scalp Lotion[3]	Metaderm Mild[3]
Betnovate[3]	Metaderm Regular[3]
Betnovate-½[3]	Nerisone[8]
Celestoderm-V[3]	Nerisone Oily[8]
Celestoderm-V/2[3]	Novobetamet[3]
Cyclocort[1]	Prevex B[3]
Dermovate[4]	Propaderm[2]
Dermovate Scalp Lotion[4]	Synalar[9]
Diprolene[3]	Synamol[9]
Diprosone[3]	Topicort[6]
Drenison[11]	Topicort Mild[6]
Ectosone Mild[3]	Topilene[3]
Ectosone Regular[3]	Topisone[3]
Ectosone Scalp Lotion[3]	Topsyn[10]
Elocom[18]	Triaderm[20]
Eumovate[5]	Trianide Mild[20]
Florone[7]	Trianide Regular[20]
Fluoderm[9]	Valisone Scalp Lotion[3]
Fluolar[9]	Westcort[17]

Other commonly used names are:

Beclometasone
Fludroxycortide
Ulobetasol

Note: For quick reference, the following medium to very high potency corticosteroids are numbered to match the corresponding brand names.

This information applies to the following medicines:

1. Amcinonide (am-SIN-oh-nide)
2. Beclomethasone (be-kloe-METH-a-sone) *
3. Betamethasone (bay-ta-METH-a-sone) ‡
4. Clobetasol (kloe-BAY-ta-sol)
5. Clobetasone (kloe-BAY-ta-sone) *
6. Desoximetasone (des-ox-i-MET-a-sone) ‡
7. Diflorasone (dye-FLOR-a-sone)
8. Diflucortolone (dye-floo-KOR-toe-lone) *
9. Fluocinolone (floo-oh-SIN-oh-lone) ‡
10. Fluocinonide (floo-oh-SIN-oh-nide) ‡
11. Flurandrenolide (flure-an-DREN-oh-lide) (except Drenison-¼)‡
12. Fluticasone (floo-TIK-a-sone) †
13. Halcinonide (hal-SIN-oh-nide)
14. Halobetasol (hal-oh-BAY-ta-sol) †
15. Hydrocortisone butyrate (hye-droe-KOR-ti-sone bue-TEAR-ate) †
16. Hydrocortisone probutate (hye-droe-KOR-ti-sone proe-BYOE-tate) †
17. Hydrocortisone valerate (hye-droe-KOR-ti-sone val-AIR-ate)
18. Mometasone (moe-MET-a-sone)
19. Prednicarbate (PRED-ni-kar-bate) †
20. Triamcinolone (trye-am-SIN-oh-lone)

---

*Not commercially available in the U.S.
†Not commercially available in Canada.
‡Generic name product may be available in the U.S.

Description

Topical corticosteroids (kor-ti-ko-STER-oyds) are used to help relieve redness, swelling, itching, and discomfort of many skin problems. These medicines are like cortisone. They belong to the general family of medicines called steroids.

These corticosteroids are available only with your doctor's prescription. Topical corticosteroids are available in the following dosage forms:

Topical
   Amcinonide
   • Cream (U.S. and Canada)
   • Lotion (U.S. and Canada)
   • Ointment (U.S. and Canada)
   Beclomethasone
   • Cream (Canada)
   • Lotion (Canada)
   Betamethasone
   • Cream (U.S. and Canada)
   • Foam (U.S.)
   • Gel (U.S. and Canada)
   • Lotion (U.S. and Canada)
   • Ointment (U.S. and Canada)
   • Topical aerosol (U.S.)
   Clobetasol
   • Cream (U.S. and Canada)
   • Foam (U.S.)
   • Ointment (U.S. and Canada)
   • Topical solution (U.S. and Canada)
   Clobetasone
   • Cream (Canada)
   • Ointment (Canada)
   Desoximetasone
   • Cream (U.S. and Canada)
   • Gel (U.S. and Canada)
   • Ointment (U.S.)
   Diflorasone
   • Cream (U.S. and Canada)
   • Ointment (U.S. and Canada)
   Diflucortolone
   • Cream (Canada)
   • Ointment (Canada)

Fluocinolone
- Cream (U.S. and Canada)
- Ointment (U.S. and Canada)
- Topical solution (U.S. and Canada)

Fluocinonide
- Cream (U.S. and Canada)
- Gel (U.S. and Canada)
- Ointment (U.S. and Canada)
- Topical solution (U.S. and Canada)

Flurandrenolide
- Cream (U.S. and Canada)
- Lotion (U.S.)
- Ointment (U.S. and Canada)
- Tape (U.S. and Canada)

Fluticasone
- Cream (U.S.)
- Ointment (U.S.)

Halcinonide
- Cream (U.S. and Canada)
- Ointment (U.S. and Canada)
- Topical solution (U.S. and Canada)

Halobetasol
- Cream (U.S.)
- Ointment (U.S.)

Hydrocortisone butyrate
- Cream (U.S.)
- Ointment (U.S.)

Hydrocortisone probutate
- Cream (Canada)

Hydrocortisone valerate
- Cream (U.S. and Canada)
- Ointment (U.S. and Canada)

Mometasone
- Cream (U.S. and Canada)
- Lotion (U.S. and Canada)
- Ointment (U.S. and Canada)

Prednicarbate
- Cream (U.S.)

Triamcinolone
- Cream (U.S. and Canada)
- Lotion (U.S.)
- Ointment (U.S. and Canada)
- Topical aerosol (U.S.)

Before Using This Medicine

In deciding to use a medicine, the risks of taking the medicine must be weighed against the good it will do. This is a decision you and your doctor will make. For corticosteroids, the following should be considered:

Allergies—Tell your doctor if you have ever had any unusual or allergic reaction to corticosteroids. Also tell your health care professional if you are allergic to any other substances, such as foods, preservatives, or dyes.

Pregnancy—When used properly, these medicines have not been shown to cause problems in humans. Studies on birth defects have not been done in humans. However, studies in animals have shown that topical corticosteroids, when applied to the skin in large amounts or used for a long time, could cause birth defects.

Breast-feeding—Topical corticosteroids have not been reported to cause problems in nursing babies when used properly. However, corticosteroids should not be applied to the breasts before nursing.

Children—Children and teenagers who must use this medicine should be checked often by their doctor since this medicine may be absorbed through the skin and can affect growth or cause other unwanted effects.

Older adults—Certain side effects may be more likely to occur in elderly patients since the skin of older adults may be naturally thin. These unwanted effects may include tearing of the skin or blood-containing blisters on the skin.

Other medicines—Although certain medicines should not be used together at all, in other cases two different medicines may be used together even if an interaction might occur. In these cases, your doctor may want to change the dose, or other precautions may be necessary. Tell your health care professional if you are using any other topical prescription or nonprescription (over-the-counter [OTC]) medicine that is to be applied to the same area of the skin.

Other medical problems—The presence of other medical problems may affect the use of topical corticosteroids. Make sure you tell your doctor if you have any other medical problems, especially:
- Cataracts or
- Glaucoma—Corticosteroids may make these medical problems worse, especially when stronger corticosteroids are used in the eye area
- Diabetes mellitus (sugar diabetes)—Too much use of corticosteroids may cause a loss of control of diabetes by increasing blood and urine glucose. However, this is not likely to happen when topical corticosteroids are used for a short time
- Infection or sores at the place of treatment (unless your doctor also prescribed medicine for the infection) or
- Tuberculosis—Corticosteroids may make existing infections worse or cause new infections
- Skin conditions that cause thinning of skin with easy bruising—Corticosteroids may make thinning of the skin worse

Proper Use of This Medicine

Be very careful not to get this medicine in your eyes. Wash your hands after using your finger to apply the medicine. If you accidentally get this medicine in your eyes, flush them with water.

Do not bandage or otherwise wrap the skin being treated unless directed to do so by your doctor.

If your doctor has ordered an occlusive dressing (airtight covering, such as kitchen plastic wrap or a special patch) to be applied over this medicine, make sure you know how to apply it. Since occlusive dressings increase the amount of medicine absorbed through your skin and the possibility of side effects, use them only as directed. If you have any questions about this, check with your doctor.

For patients using the *foam form* of this medicine:
- This medicine usually comes with patient directions. Read them carefully before using this medicine.
- Do not use near heat, near an open flame, or while smoking.

For patients using the *topical aerosol form* of this medicine:
- This medicine usually comes with patient directions. Read them carefully before using this medicine.
- It is important to avoid breathing in the vapors from the spray or getting them in your eyes. If you accidentally get this medicine in your eyes, flush them with water.
- Do not use near heat, near an open flame, or while smoking.

© 2002 MICROMEDEX Thomson Healthcare

For patients using *flurandrenolide tape:*
- This medicine usually comes with patient directions. Read them carefully before using this medicine.

Do not use this medicine more often or for a longer time than your doctor ordered. To do so may increase the chance of absorption through the skin and the chance of side effects. In addition, too much use, especially on areas with thinner skin (for example, face, armpits, groin), may result in thinning of the skin and stretch marks or other unwanted effects.

Do not use this medicine for other skin problems without first checking with your doctor. Topical corticosteroids should not be used on many kinds of bacterial, viral, or fungal skin infections.

Dosing — The dose of topical corticosteroid will be different for different patients and products. *Follow your doctor's orders or the directions on the label.*

Missed dose — If your doctor has ordered you to use this medicine on a regular schedule and you miss a dose, apply it as soon as possible. However, if it is almost time for your next dose, skip the missed dose and apply it at the next regularly scheduled time.

Storage — To store this medicine:
- Keep out of the reach of children.
- Store away from heat and direct light.
- Keep the medicine from freezing.
- Do not puncture, break, or burn aerosol containers, even after they are empty.
- Do not keep outdated medicine or medicine no longer needed. Be sure that any discarded medicine is out of the reach of children.

Precautions While Using This Medicine

Check with your doctor if your symptoms do not improve within 1 week or if your condition gets worse.

Avoid using tight-fitting diapers or plastic pants on a child if this medicine is being used on the child's diaper area. Plastic pants or tight-fitting diapers may increase the chance of absorption of the medicine through the skin and the chance of side effects.

Side Effects of This Medicine

Along with its needed effects, a medicine may cause some unwanted effects. Although not all of these side effects may occur, if they do occur they may need medical attention.

Check with your doctor as soon as possible if any of the following side effects occur:
Less frequent or rare
  Blood-containing blisters on skin; burning and itching of skin; increased skin sensitivity (for some brands of betamethasone lotion); lack of healing of skin condition; loss of top skin layer (for tape dosage forms); numbness in fingers; painful, red or itchy, pus-containing blisters in hair follicles; raised, dark red, wart-like spots on skin, especially when used on the face; skin infection; thinning of skin with easy bruising

Additional side effects may occur if you use this medicine improperly or for a long time. Check with your doctor if any of the following side effects occur:
Rare
  Acne or oily skin; backache; blurring or loss of vision (occurs gradually if certain products have been used near the eye); burning and itching of skin with pinhead-sized red blisters; eye pain (if certain products have been used near the eye); filling or rounding out of the face; increased blood pressure; irregular heartbeat; irregular menstrual periods; irritability; irritation of skin around mouth; loss of appetite; mental depression; muscle cramps, pain, or weakness; nausea; rapid weight gain or loss; reddish purple lines (stretch marks) on arms, face, legs, trunk, or groin; skin color changes; softening of skin; stomach bloating, burning, cramping, or pain; swelling of feet or lower legs; tearing of the skin; unusual bruising; unusual decrease in sexual desire or ability (in men); unusual increase in hair growth, especially on the face; unusual loss of hair, especially on the scalp; unusual tiredness or weakness; vomiting; weakness of the arms, legs, or trunk (severe); worsening of infections

Some side effects may occur that usually do not need medical attention. These side effects may go away during treatment as your body adjusts to the medicine. However, check with your doctor if any of the following side effects continue or are bothersome:
Less frequent or rare — usually mild and transient
  Burning, dryness, irritation, itching, or redness of skin; increased redness or scaling of skin sores; skin rash

When the foam, gel, lotion, solution, or aerosol form of this medicine is applied, a mild, temporary stinging may be expected.

Other side effects not listed above may also occur in some patients. If you notice any other effects, check with your doctor.

Revised: 03/01/2001

COUGH/COLD COMBINATIONS
Systemic

Commonly used brand name(s):

In the U.S.—

Actagen-C Cough[50]	Alka-Seltzer Plus Night-Time Cold Liqui-Gels[62]	Aprodine with Codeine[50]
Actifed with Codeine Cough[50]	Allerfrin with Codeine[50]	Atuss DM[26] Atuss EX[114] Atuss HD[27]
Alka-Seltzer Plus Cold and Cough[58]	All-Nite Cold Formula[62]	Banex-LA[146] Banex Liquid[145]
Alka-Seltzer Plus Cold and Cough Medicine Liqui-Gels[60]	Ambenyl Cough[1] Ambenyl-D Decongestant Cough Formula[136]	Benylin Expectorant[111] Benylin Multi-Symptom[136]
Alka-Seltzer Plus Flu & Body Aches[57]	Ambophen[1] Amgenal Cough[1] Ami-Tex[145]	Bromanate DC Cough[21] Bromanyl[1]
Alka-Seltzer Plus Flu & Body Aches Medicine Liqui-Gels[127]	Ami-Tex LA[146] Anaplex HD[27] Anatuss[134]	Bromarest DX Cough[23] Bromatane DX Cough[23]
Alka-Seltzer Plus Night-Time Cold[61]	Anatuss DM[136] Anatuss LA[147] Anti-Tuss DM Expectorant[111]	Bromfed-DM[23] Bromotuss with Codeine[1]

Bromphen DC with
Codeine
Cough[21]
Bromphen DX
Cough[23]
Broncholate[142]
Bronkotuss
Expectorant[95]
Brontex[108]
Brotane DX
Cough[23]
Calcidrine[107]
Carbinoxamine
Compound[24]
Carbinoxamine
Compound-
Drops[24]
Carbodec DM[24]
Carbodec DM
Drops[24]
Cardec DM[24]
Cardec DM Drops[24]
Cardec DM
Pediatric[24]
Cerose-DM[26]
Cheracol[108]
Cheracol D
Cough[111]
Cheracol Plus[32]
Children's Formula
Cough[111]
Children's Tylenol
Cold Plus Cough
Multi
Symptom[60]
Chlorgest-HD[27]
Citra Forte[17]
Co-Apap[60]
Co-Complex DM
Caplets[127]
Codamine[122]
Codamine
Pediatric[122]
Codan[105]
Codegest
Expectorant[132]
Codehist DH[33]
Codiclear DH[114]
Codimal DH[49]
Codimal DM[48]
Codimal PH[47]
Comtrex Cough
Formula[141]
Comtrex Daytime
Caplets[127]
Comtrex Daytime
Maximum
Strength
Cold, Cough,
and Flu
Relief[127]
Comtrex Daytime
Maximum
Strength Cold
and Flu
Relief[127]
Comtrex Maximum
Strength Multi-
Symptom Liqui-
Gels[57]
Comtrex Multi-
Symptom Cold
Reliever[57]

Comtrex Multi-
Symptom
Maximum
Strength Non-
Drowsy
Caplets[127]
Comtrex
Nighttime[60]
Comtrex
Nighttime
Maximum
Strength Cold,
Cough and Flu
Relief[60]
Comtrex Nighttime
Maximum
Strength Cold
and Flu
Relief[60]
Concentrin[136]
Conex[146]
Conex with
Codeine
Liquid[132]
Congess JR[147]
Congess SR[147]
Congestac
Caplets[147]
Contac Cold/Flu
Day Caplets[127]
Contac Severe
Cold & Flu
Caplets[57]
Contac Severe
Cold & Flu
Non-Drowsy
Caplets[127]
Contuss[145]
Cophene-S[30]
Cophene-X[130]
Cophene XP[137]
Cophene-XP[74]
Co-Tuss V[114]
C-Tussin
Expectorant[132]
Decohistine DH[33]
Deconamine
CX[137]
Deconsal II[147]
Deconsal
Pediatric[144]
Deproist
Expectorant
with Codeine[135]
Despec[145]
Despec SF[145]
Despec-SR
Caplets[146]
De-Tuss[125]
Detussin
Expectorant[137]
Detussin Liquid[125]
Dexafed Cough[129]
Diabetic Tussin
DM[111]
Dihistine DH[33]
Dihistine
Expectorant[135]
Dilaudid Cough[117]
Dimacol
Caplets[136]
Dimetane-DC
Cough[21]

Dimetane-DX
Cough[23]
Dimetapp DM[22]
Dimetapp DM Cold
& Cough[22]
Dimetapp
Maximum
Strength Cold &
Cough Liqui-
Gels[22]
Donatussin[72]
Donatussin DC[131]
Donatussin
Drops[96]
Dondril[26]
Dorcol Children's
Cough[136]
Drixoral Cough &
Congestion
Liquid Caps[124]
Drixoral Cough &
Sore Throat
Liquid Caps[103]
Dura-Gest[145]
Duratex[145]
Duratuss[147]
Duratuss HD[137]
Dura-Vent[146]
ED-TLC[27]
ED Tuss HC[27]
Effective Strength
Cough Formula[3]
Effective Strength
Cough Formula
with Deconges-
tant[124]
Endagen-HD[27]
Endal[144]
Endal
Expectorant[132]
Endal-HD[27]
Endal-HD Plus[27]
Enomine[145]
Entex[145]
Entex LA[146]
Entex Liquid[145]
Entex PSE[147]
Entuss-D[139]
Entuss-D Jr[137]
Entuss
Expectorant[115]
Eudal-SR[147]
Exgest LA[146]
Expressin 400
Caplets[147]
Extra Action
Cough[111]
Father John's
Medicine
Plus[73]
Fendol[148]
Fenesin DM[111]
Gelpirin-CCF[102]
Genatuss DM[111]
Genite[62]
Glycofed[147]
Glycotuss-dM[111]
Glydeine Cough[108]
GP-500[147]
Guaifed[147]
Guaifed-PD[147]
Guaifenex
PPA 75[146]

Guaifenex PSE
60[147]
Guaifenex PSE
120[147]
GuaiMAX-D[147]
Guaipax[146]
Guaitab[147]
Guaivent[147]
Guaivent PD[147]
Guai-Vent/PSE[147]
GuiaCough CF[133]
GuiaCough PE[147]
Guiamid D.M.
Liquid[111]
Guiatuss A.C.[108]
Guiatuss CF[133]
Guiatuss DAC[135]
Guiatuss-DM[111]
Guiatussin with
Codeine Liquid[108]
Guiatussin DAC[135]
Guiatussin w/
Dextrometh-
orphan[111]
Guiatuss PE[147]
Halotussin-DM[111]
Histinex DM[22]
Histinex HC[27]
Histinex PV[35]
Histussin HC[27]
Humibid DM[111]
Humibid DM
Pediatric[111]
Humibid
Guaifenesin
Plus[147]
Hycodan[105]
Hycomine[122]
Hycomine
Compound[56]
Hycomine
Pediatric[122]
Hycotuss
Expectorant[114]
Hydromet[105]
Hydromine[122]
Hydromine
Pediatric[122]
Hydropane[105]
Hydrophen[122]
Improved Sino-
Tuss[55]
Iobid DM[111]
Iodal HD[27]
Iohist DM[22]
Iophen-C Liquid[109]
Iophen DM[112]
Iosal II[147]
Iotussin HC[27]
Ipsatol Cough
Formula for
Children and
Adults[133]
Kiddy Koff[133]
KIE[143]
Kolephrin/DM
Cough and Cold
Medication[60]
Kolephrin
GG/DM[111]
Kophane Cough
and Cold
Formula[32]

Kwelcof Liquid[114]
Lanatuss
Expectorant[98]
Liqui-Histine DM[22]
Mapap Cold
Formula[60]
Marcof
Expectorant[116]
Med-Hist Exp[137]
Med-Hist HC[27]
Midahist DH[33]
Muco-Fen DM[111]
Myminic
Expectorant[146]
Myminicol[32]
Myphetane DC
Cough[21]
Myphetane DX
Cough[23]
Mytussin AC[108]
Mytussin DAC[135]
Mytussin DM[111]
Naldecon-CX Adult
Liquid[132]
Naldecon-DX Adult
Liquid[133]
Naldecon-DX
Children's
Syrup[133]
Naldecon-DX
Pediatric
Drops[133]
Naldecon-EX
Children's
Syrup[146]
Naldecon-EX
Pediatric
Drops[146]
Naldecon Senior
DX[111]
Nalex[147]
Nalex DH[119]
Nalex Jr[147]
Nasabid[147]
Nasatab LA[147]
Nasatuss[27]
Norel[145]
Novagest
Expectorant w/
Codeine[135]
Novahistine DH
Liquid[33]
Novahistine DMX
Liquid[136]
Novahistine
Expectorant[135]
Nucochem
Expectorant[135]
Nucochem
Pediatric
Expectorant[135]
Nucofed[123]
Nucofed
Expectorant[135]
Nucofed Pediatric
Expectorant[135]
Nucotuss
Expectorant[135]
Nucotuss Pediatric
Expectorant[135]
Nytcold Medicine[62]
Nytime Cold
Medicine Liquid[62]

Omnicol[52]
Ordrine AT[120]
Ornex Severe Cold
No Drowsiness
Caplets[127]
PanMist-JR[147]
Para-Hist HD[27]
Partuss LA[146]
PediaCare Cough-
Cold[34]
PediaCare Night
Rest Cough-
Cold Liquid[34]
Pediacof Cough[71]
PediaPressin
Pediatric
Drops[136]
Pedituss Cough[71]
Pentazine VC w/
Codeine[6]
Phanatuss[111]
Phanatussin[85]
Phenameth DM[7]
Phenameth VC
with Codeine[45]
Phenergan with
Codeine[6]
Phenergan with
Dextrometh-
orphan[7]
Phenergan VC
with Codeine[45]
Phenhist DH w/
Codeine[33]
Phenhist
Expectorant[135]
Phenylfenesin
L.A[146]
Pherazine w/
Codeine[6]
Pherazine DM[7]
Pherazine VC with
Codeine[45]
Pneumotussin
HC[114]
Polaramine
Expectorant[100]
Poly-Histine-CS[21]
Poly-Histine-DM[22]
Primatuss Cough
Mixture 4[3]
Primatuss Cough
Mixture 4D[136]
Profen II[46]
Profen-LA[146]
Promethazine DM[7]
Promethazine VC
w/Codeine[45]
Prometh w/
Dextrometh-
orphan[7]
Promethist w/
Codeine[45]
Prometh VC with
Codeine[45]
Prominic
Expectorant[146]
Prominicol Cough[79]
Promist HD
Liquid[35]
Protuss-D[138]
Pseudo-Car DM[24]
P-V-Tussin[36]

Quelidrine Cough[67]
Rentamine Pediatric[25]
Rescaps-D S.R.[120]
Rescon-DM[34]
Rescon-GG[144]
Respa-1st[147]
Respa-DM[111]
Respaire-60 SR[147]
Respaire-120 SR[147]
Rhinosyn-DM[34]
Rhinosyn-DMX Expectorant[111]
Rhinosyn-X[136]
Robafen AC Cough[108]
Robafen CF[133]
Robafen DAC[135]
Robafen DM[111]
Robitussin A-C[108]
Robitussin-CF[133]
Robitussin Cold and Cough Liqui-Gels[136]
Robitusssin Cold, Cough & Flu Liqui-Gels[141]
Robitussin-DAC[135]
Robitussin-DM[111]
Robitussin Maximum Strength Cough and Cold[124]
Robitussin Night Relief[64]
Robitussin Night-Time Cold Formula[62]
Robitussin-PE[147]
Robitussin Pediatric Cough & Cold[124]
Robitussin Severe Congestion Liqui-Gels[147]
Rolatuss Expectorant[70]
Rolatuss w/ Hydrocodone[41]
Rondamine-DM Drops[24]
Rondec-DM[24]
Rondec-DM Drops[24]
Ru-Tuss DE[147]
Ru-Tuss Expectorant[136]
Ru-Tuss with Hydrocodone Liquid[41]
Rymed[147]
Rymed Liquid[147]
Rymed-TR Caplets[146]
Ryna-C Liquid[33]
Ryna-CX Liquid[135]
Rynatuss[25]
Rynatuss Pediatric[25]
Safe Tussin 30[111]
Saleto-CF[126]
Scot-Tussin DM[3]

Scot-Tussin Senior Clear[111]
Silaminic Expectorant[146]
Sildec-DM[24]
Sildec-DM Oral Drops[24]
Sildicon-E Pediatric Drops[146]
Silexin Cough[111]
Siltapp w/ Dextromethorphan Cough & Cold[22]
Sil-Tex[145]
Siltussin-CF[133]
Siltussin DM[111]
Sinufed Timecelles[147]
Sinupan[144]
Sinutab Non-Drying No Drowsiness Liquid Caps[147]
SINUvent[146]
Snaplets-DM[121]
Snaplets-EX[146]
Snaplets-Multi[32]
SRC Expectorant[137]
Stamoist E[147]
Stamoist LA[146]
Statuss Expectorant[132]
Statuss Green[41]
S-T Forte[82]
S-T Forte 2[4]
Sudafed Children's Non-Drowsy Cold & Cough[136]
Sudafed Cold & Cough Liquid Caps[141]
Sudafed Children's Cold & Cough[136]
Sudafed Non-Drowsy Non-Drying Sinus Liquid Caps[147]
Sudafed Severe Cold Formula[127]
Sudafed Severe Cold Formula Caplets[127]
Sudal 60/500[147]
Sudal 120/600[147]
Suppressin DM[111]
Suppressin DM Caplets[111]
Suppressin DM Plus[129]
Syracol CF[111]
TheraFlu Flu, Cold & Cough Medicine[60]
TheraFlu Maximum Strength Non-Drowsy Formula Flu, Cold & Cough Medicine[127]

TheraFlu Maximum Strength Non-Drowsy Formula Flu, Cold & Cough Medicine Caplets[127]
TheraFlu Nighttime Maximum Strength Flu, Cold & Cough[60]
Threamine DM[32]
T-Koff[28]
Tolu-Sed Cough[108]
Tolu-Sed DM[111]
Touro DM[111]
Touro LA Caplets[147]
Triacin C Cough[50]
Triafed w/Codeine[50]
Triaminic AM Non-Drowsy Cough and Decongestant[124]
Triaminic-DM Cough Relief[121]
Triaminic Expectorant[146]
Triaminic Expectorant with Codeine[132]
Triaminic Expectorant DH[81]
Triaminic Night Time[34]
Triaminicol Multi-Symptom Cold and Cough Medicine[32]
Triaminic Sore Throat Formula[127]
Triaminic Triaminicol[32]
Tricodene[8]
Tricodene Forte[32]
Tricodene NN[32]
Tricodene Pediatric[121]
Tricodene Sugar Free[3]
Trifed-C Cough[50]
Triminol Cough[32]
Triphenyl Expectorant[146]
Tri-Tannate Plus Pediatric[25]
Tusquelin[68]
Tuss-Ade[120]
Tussafed[24]
Tussafed Drops[24]
Tussafin Expectorant[137]
Tuss-Allergine Modified T.D.[120]
Tussar-2[135]
Tussar DM[34]
Tussar SF[135]
Tuss-DA[124]
Tuss-DM[111]
Tussex Cough[129]
Tussigon[105]

Tussionex Pennkinetic[4]
Tussi-Organidin DM NR Liquid[111]
Tussi-Organidin DM-S NR Liquid[111]
Tussi-Organidin NR Liquid[108]
Tussi-Organidin-S NR Liquid[108]
Tussirex[91]
Tuss-LA[147]
Tusso-DM[112]
Tussogest[120]
Tylenol Cold and Flu No Drowsiness Powder[127]
Tylenol Cold Medication[60]
Tylenol Cold Medication Caplets[60]
Tylenol Cold Medication, Non-Drowsy Caplets[127]
Tylenol Cold Medication, Non-Drowsy Gelcaps[127]
Tylenol Cold Multi-Symptom[60]
Tylenol Maximum Strength Flu Gelcaps[127]

In Canada—
Actifed DM[51]
Ambenyl Cough[10]
Benylin Codeine D-E[135]
Benylin DM-D[124]
Benylin DM-D for Children[124]
Benylin DM-D-E[136]
Benylin DM-D-E Extra Strength[136]
Benylin DM-E[111]
Benylin DM-E Extra Strength[111]
Benylin 4 Flu[141]
Biohisdex DM[38]
Biohisdine DM[38]
Buckley's DM[124]
Caldomine-DH Forte[44]
Caldomine-DH Pediatric[44]
Calmydone[39]
Calmylin #2[124]
Calmylin #3[136]
Calmylin #4[13]
Calmylin Codeine D-E[135]
Calmylin Cough & Flu[141]
Calmylin DM-D-E Extra Strength[136]
Calmylin DM-E[111]
Calmylin Original with Codeine[12]

Tylenol Multi-Symptom Cough[103]
Tylenol Multi-Symptom Cough with Decongestant[127]
Tyrodone[125]
ULR-LA[146]
Unituss HC[27]
Uni-tussin DM[111]
Unproco[111]
Vanex Expectorant[137]
Vanex Grape[30]
Vanex-HD[27]
V-Dec-M[147]
Versacaps[147]
Vicks Children's NyQuil Cold/ Cough Relief[34]
Vicks 44 Cough and Cold Relief Non-Drowsy LiquiCaps[124]
Vicks 44D Cough and Head Congestion[124]
Vicks DayQuil Multi-Symptom Cold/Flu LiquiCaps[141]
Vicks DayQuil Multi-Symptom Cold/Flu Relief[141]

Calmylin Pediatric[124]
Cheracol[106]
CoActifed[50]
CoActifed Expectorant[86]
Coristex-DH[119]
Coristine-DH[119]
CoSudafed[123]
CoSudafed Expectorant[135]
Cotridin[50]
Cotridin Expectorant[86]
Dimetane Expectorant[93]
Dimetane Expectorant-C[65]
Dimetane Expectorant-DC[66]
Dimetapp-C[19]
Dimetapp-DM[20]
Entex LA[146]
Histenol[127]
Hycodan[105]
Hycomine[84]
Hycomine-S Pediatric[84]
Mercodol with Decapryn[39]
Mersyndol with Codeine[9]
Neo Citran Day Caps Extra Strength Caplets[127]

Vicks DayQuil Sinus Pressure and Congestion Relief Caplets[146]
Vicks 44E Cough & Chest Congestion[111]
Vicks 44M Cough, Cold and Flu Relief[60]
Vicks 44M Cough, Cold au Relief LiquiCaps[60]
Vicks NyQuil Hot Therapy[62]
Vicks NyQuil Multi-Symptom Cold/ Flu LiquiCaps[62]
Vicks NyQuil Multi-Symptom Cold/ Flu Relief[62]
Vicks Pediatric 44D Cough & Head Decongestion[124]
Vicks Pediatric 44E[111]
Vicks Pediatric 44M Multi-Symptom Cough & Cold[34]
Vicodin Tuss[114]
Zephrex[147]
Zephrex-LA[147]

NeoCitran DM Coughs and Colds[40]
Novahistex C[118]
Novahistex DH[119]
Novahistex DH Expectorant[131]
Novahistex DM w/ Decongestant[124]
Novahistex DM Expectorant w/ Decongestant[136]
Novahistex Expectorant w/ Decongestant[147]
Novahistine DH[119]
Novahistine DM w/ Decongestant[124]
Novahistine DM Expectorant w/ Decongestant[136]
Omni-Tuss[77]
Ornade-DM 10[32]
Ornade-DM 15[32]
Ornade-DM 30[32]
Ornade Expectorant[97]
Penntuss[2]
Pharmasave Children's Cough Syrup[124]
Pharmasave DM+ Decongestant/ Expectorant[136]
Pharmasave DM+ Expectorant[111]

Phenergan Expectorant[103]
Phenergan Expectorant w/ Codeine[18]
Phenergan VC Expectorant[101]
Phenergan VC Expectorant w/ Codeine[83]
Promatussin DM[46]
Promatusssin DM Children's Syrup[46]
Robitussin A-C[15]
Robitussin-CF[133]
Robitussin with Codeine[15]
Robitussin Cough & Cold[136]
Robitussin Cough & Cold Liqui-Fills[136]
Robitussin-DM[111]
Robitussin-PE[147]
Robitussin Pediatric Cough & Cold[124]
Sinutab with Codeine[59]
Sudafed Cold & Flu Gelcaps[141]
Sudafed Cough & Cold Extra Strength Caplets[127]
Sudafed DM[124]
Tantacol DM[43]
Tanta Cough Syrup[111]
Triaminic DM Day Time for Children[133]
Triaminic-DM Expectorant[78]

Triaminic DM NightTime for Children[34]
Triaminic Expectorant[99]
Triaminic Expectorant DH[81]
Triaminicol DM[34]
Tussaminic C Forte[42]
Tussaminic C Pediatric[42]
Tussaminic DH Forte[44]
Tussaminic DH Pediatric[44]
Tussilyn DM[34]
Tussionex[5]
Tuss-Ornade Spansules[31]
Tylenol Children's Cold DM Medication[60]
Tylenol Cold and Flu[60]
Tylenol Cold Medication Extra Strength Day-time Caplets[127]
Tylenol Cold Medication Extra Strength Night-time Caplets[60]
Tylenol Cold Medication Regular Strength Day-time Caplets[127]
Tylenol Cold Medication Regular Strength Night-time Caplets[60]

Tylenol Cough Extra Strength Caplets[104]
Tylenol Cough Medication with Decongestant, Regular Strength[127]
Tylenol Cough Medication Regular Strength[104]
Tylenol Extra Strength Cold and Flu Medication Powder[60]
Tylenol Junior Strength Cold DM Medication[60]
Vicks Children's NyQuil[34]
Vicks Cough Syrup[128]
Vicks DayQuil Liquicaps[141]
Vicks Formula 44-D[124]
Vicks Formula 44-d Pediatric[124]
Vicks Formula 44E[111]
Vicks Formula 44e Pediatric[111]
Vicks Formula 44M[60]
Vicks NyQuil[62]
Vicks NyQuil LiquiCaps[62]

Note: For quick reference the following cough/cold combinations are numbered to match the preceding corresponding brand names.

Antihistamine and antitussive combinations—
1. Bromodiphenhydramine and Codeine (broe-moe-dye-fen-HYE-dra-meen and KOE-deen) †‡
2. Chlorpheniramine and Codeine (klor-fen-EER-a-meen and KOE-deen) *
3. Chlorpheniramine and Dextromethorphan (klor-fen-EER-a-meen and dex-troe-meth-OR-fan) †
4. Chlorpheniramine and Hydrocodone (klor-fen-EER-a-meen and hye-droe-KOE-done) †
5. Phenyltoloxamine and Hydrocodone (fen-ill-tole-OX-a-meen and hye-droe-KOE-done) *
6. Promethazine and Codeine (proe-METH-a-zeen and KOE-deen) †‡
7. Promethazine and Dextromethorphan (proe-METH-a-zeen and dex-troe-meth-OR-fan) †
8. Pyrilamine and Codeine (peer-ILL-a-meen and KOE-deen) †

Antihistamine, antitussive, and analgesic combinations—
9. Doxylamine, Codeine, and Acetaminophen (dox-ILL-a-meen, KOE-deen, and a-seat-a-MIN-oh-fen) *

Antihistamine, antitussive, and expectorant combinations—
10. Bromodiphenhydramine, Diphenhydramine, Codeine, Ammonium Chloride, and Potassium Guaiacolsulfonate (broe-moe-dye-fen-HYE-dra-meen, dye-fen-HYE-dra-meen, KOE-

deen, a-MOE-nee-um KLOR-ide, and poe-TAS-ee-um gwye-a-kol-SUL-fon-ate) *
11. No product available
12. Diphenhydramine, Codeine, and Ammonium Chloride (dye-fen-HYE-dra-meen, KOE-deen, and a-MOE-nee-um KLOR-ide) *
13. Diphenhydramine, Dextromethorphan, and Ammonium Chloride (dye-fen-HYE-dra-meen, dex-troe-meth-OR-fan, and a-MOE-nee-um KLOR-ide) *
14. No product available
15. Pheniramine, Codeine, and Guaifenesin (fen-EER-a-meen, KOE-deen, and gwye-FEN-e-sin) *
16. Pheniramine, Pyrilamine, Hydrocodone, Potassium Citrate, and Ascorbic Acid (fen-EER-a-meen, peer-ILL-a-meen, hye-droe-KOE-done, poe-TAS-ee-um SI-trate, and a-SKOR-bik AS-id) †
17. Pheniramine, Pyrilamine, Hydrocodone, Potassium Citrate, and Ascorbic Acid or Chlorpheniramine, Pheniramine, Pyrilamine, Phenylephrine, Hydrocodone, Salicylamide, Caffeine, and Ascorbic Acid (fen-EER-a-meen, peer-ILL-a-meen, hye-droe-KOE-done, poe-TAS-ee-um SI-trate, and a-SKOR-bik AS-id or klor-fen-EER-a-meen, fen-EER-a-meen, peer-ILL-a-meen, fen-ill-EF-rin, hye-droe-KOE-done, sal-i-SILL-a-mide, kaf-EEN, and a-SKOR-bik AS-id) †
18. Promethazine, Codeine, and Potassium Guaiacolsulfonate (proe-METH-a-zeen, KOE-deen, and poe-TAS-ee-um gwye-a-kol-SUL-fon-ate) *

Antihistamine, decongestant, and antitussive combinations—
19. Brompheniramine, Phenylephrine, Phenylpropanolamine, and Codeine (brome-fen-EER-a-meen, fen-ill-EF-rin, fen-ill-proe-pa-NOLE-a-meen, and KOE-deen) *
20. Brompheniramine, Phenylephrine, Phenylpropanolamine, and Dextromethorphan (brome-fen-EER-a-meen, fen-ill-EF-rin, fen-ill-proe-pa-NOLE-a-meen, and dex-troe-meth-OR-fan) *
21. Brompheniramine, Phenylpropanolamine, and Codeine (brome-fen-EER-a-meen, fen-ill-proe-pa-NOLE-a-meen, and KOE-deen) †
22. Brompheniramine, Phenylpropanolamine, and Dextromethorphan (brome-fen-EER-a-meen, fen-ill-proe-pa-NOLE-a-meen, and dex-troe-meth-OR-fan) †
23. Brompheniramine, Pseudoephedrine, and Dextromethorphan (brome-fen-EER-a-meen, soo-doe-e-FED-rin, and dex-troe-meth-OR-fan) †
24. Carbinoxamine, Pseudoephedrine, and Dextromethorphan (kar-bi-NOX-a-meen, soo-doe-e-FED-rin, and dex-troe-meth-OR-fan) †
25. Chlorpheniramine, Ephedrine, Phenylephrine, and Carbetapentane (klor-fen-EER-a-meen, e-FED-rin, fen-ill-EF-rin, and kar-bay-ta-PEN-tane) †
26. Chlorpheniramine, Phenylephrine, and Dextromethorphan (klor-fen-EER-a-meen, fen-ill-EF-rin, and dex-troe-meth-OR-fan) †
27. Chlorpheniramine, Phenylephrine, and Hydrocodone (klor-fen-EER-a-meen, fen-ill-EF-rin, and hye-droe-KOE-done) †
28. Chlorpheniramine, Phenylephrine, Phenylpropanolamine, and Codeine (klor-fen-EER-a-meen, fen-ill-EF-rin, fen-ill-proe-pa-NOLE-a-meen, and KOE-deen) †
29. No product available
30. Chlorpheniramine, Phenylephrine, Phenylpropanolamine, and Dihydrocodeine (klor-fen-EER-a-meen, fen-ill-EF-rin, fen-ill-proe-pa-NOLE-a-meen, and dye-hye-droe-KOE-deen) †
31. Chlorpheniramine, Phenylpropanolamine, and Caramiphen (klor-fen-EER-a-meen, fen-ill-proe-pa-NOLE-a-meen, and kar-AM-i-fen) *
32. Chlorpheniramine, Phenylpropanolamine, and Dextromethorphan (klor-fen-EER-a-meen, fen-ill-proe-pa-NOLE-a-meen, and dex-troe-meth-OR-fan)
33. Chlorpheniramine, Pseudoephedrine, and Codeine (klor-fen-EER-a-meen, soo-doe-e-FED-rin, and KOE-deen) †

34. Chlorpheniramine, Pseudoephedrine, and Dextromethorphan (klor-fen-EER-a-meen, soo-doe-e-FED-rin, and dex-troe-meth-OR-fan)

35. Chlorpheniramine, Pseudoephedrine, and Hydrocodone (klor-fen-EER-a-meen, soo-doe-e-FED-rin, and hye-droe-KOE-done) †

36. Chlorpheniramine, Pseudoephedrine, and Hydrocodone or Pseudoephedrine and Hydrocodone (klor-fen-EER-a-meen, soo-doe-e-FED-rin, and hye-droe-KOE-done or soo-doe-e-FED-rin and hye-droe-KOE-done) †

37. No product available

38. Diphenylpyraline, Phenylephrine, and Dextromethorphan (dye-fen-il-PEER-a-leen, fen-ill-EF-rin, and dex-troe-meth-OR-fan) *

39. Doxylamine, Etafedrine, and Hydrocodone (dox-ILL-a-meen, et-a-FED-rin, and hye-droe-KOE-done) *

40. Pheniramine, Phenylephrine, and Dextromethorphan (fen-EER-a-meen, fen-ill-EF-rin, and dex-troe-meth-OR-fan) *

41. Pheniramine, Pyrilamine, Phenylephrine, Phenylpropanolamine, and Hydrocodone (fen-EER-a-meen, peer-ILL-a-meen, fen-ill-EF-rin, fen-ill-proe-pa-NOLE-a-meen, and hye-droe-KOE-done) †

42. Pheniramine, Pyrilamine, Phenylpropanolamine, and Codeine (fen-EER-a-meen, peer-ILL-a-meen, fen-ill-proe-pa-NOLE-a-meen, and KOE-deen) *

43. Pheniramine, Pyrilamine, Phenylpropanolamine, and Dextromethorphan (fen-EER-a-meen, peer-ILL-a-meen, fen-ill-proe-pa-NOLE-a-meen, and dex-troe-meth-OR-fan) *

44. Pheniramine, Pyrilamine, Phenylpropanolamine, and Hydrocodone (fen-EER-a-meen, peer-ILL-a-meen, fen-ill-proe-pa-NOLE-a-meen, and hye-droe-KOE-done) *

45. Promethazine, Phenylephrine, and Codeine (proe-METH-a-zeen, fen-ill-EF-rin, and KOE-deen) †

46. Promethazine, Pseudoephedrine, and Dextromethorphan (proe-METH-a-zeen, soo-doe-e-FED-rin, and dex-troe-meth-OR-fan) *

47. Pyrilamine, Phenylephrine, and Codeine (peer-ILL-a-meen, fen-ill-EF-rin, and KOE-deen) †

48. Pyrilamine, Phenylephrine, and Dextromethorphan (peer-ILL-a-meen, fen-ill-EF-rin, and dex-troe-meth-OR-fan) †

49. Pyrilamine, Phenylephrine, and Hydrocodone (peer-ILL-a-meen, fen-ill-EF-rin, and hye-droe-KOE-done) †

50. Triprolidine, Pseudoephedrine, and Codeine (trye-PROE-li-deen, soo-doe-e-FED-rin, and KOE-deen)

51. Triprolidine, Pseudoephedrine, and Dextromethorphan (trye-PROE-li-deen, soo-doe-e-FED-rin, and dex-troe-meth-OR-fan) *

Antihistamine, decongestant, antitussive, and analgesic combinations—

52. Chlorpheniramine, Phenindamine, Phenylephrine, Dextromethorphan, Acetaminophen, Salicylamide, Caffeine, and Ascorbic Acid (klor-fen-EER-a-meen, fen-IN-da-meen, fen-ill-EF-rin, dex-troe-meth-OR-fan, a-seat-a-MIN-oh-fen, sal-i-SILL-a-mide, kaf-EEN, and a-SKOR-bik AS-id)

53. Chlorpheniramine, Pheniramine, Pyrilamine, Phenylephrine, Hydrocodone, Salicylamide, Caffeine, and Ascorbic Acid (klor-fen-EER-a-meen, fen-EER-a-meen, peer-ILL-a-meen, fen-ill-EF-rin, hye-droe-KOE-done, sal-i-SILL-a-mide, kaf-EEN, and a-SKOR-bik AS-id) †

54. No product available

55. Chlorpheniramine, Phenylephrine, Dextromethorphan, Acetaminophen, and Salicylamide (klor-fen-EER-a-meen, fen-ill-EF-rin, dex-troe-meth-OR-fan, a-seat-a-MIN-oh-fen, and sal-i-SILL-a-mide) †

56. Chlorpheniramine, Phenylephrine, Hydrocodone, Acetaminophen, and Caffeine (klor-fen-EER-a-meen, fen-ill-EF-rin, hye-droe-KOE-done, a-seat-a-MIN-oh-fen, and kaf-EEN) †

57. Chlorpheniramine, Phenylpropanolamine, Dextromethorphan, and Acetaminophen (klor-fen-EER-a-meen, fen-ill-proe-pa-NOLE-a-meen, dex-troe-meth-OR-fan, and a-seat-a-MIN-oh-fen) †

58. Chlorpheniramine, Phenylpropanolamine, Dextromethorphan, and Aspirin (klor-fen-EER-a-meen, fen-ill-proe-pa-NOLE-a-meen, dex-troe-meth-OR-fan, and AS-pir-in) †

59. Chlorpheniramine, Pseudoephedrine, Codeine, and Acetaminophen (klor-fen-EER-a-meen, soo-doe-e-FED-rin, KOE-deen, and a-seat-a-MIN-oh-fen) *

60. Chlorpheniramine, Pseudoephedrine, Dextromethorphan, and Acetaminophen (klor-fen-EER-a-meen, soo-doe-e-FED-rin, dex-troe-meth-OR-fan, and a-seat-a-MIN-oh-fen)

61. Doxylamine, Phenylpropanolamine, Dextromethorphan, and Aspirin (dox-ILL-a-meen, fen-ill-proe-pa-NOLE-a-meen, dex-troe-meth-OR-fan, and AS-pir-in) †

62. Doxylamine, Pseudoephedrine, Dextromethorphan, and Acetaminophen (dox-ILL-a-meen, soo-doe-e-FED-rin, dex-troe-meth-OR-fan, and a-seat-a-MIN-oh-fen)

63. No product available

64. Pyrilamine, Pseudoephedrine, Dextromethorphan, and Acetaminophen (peer-ILL-a-meen, soo-doe-e-FED-rin, dex-troe-meth-OR-fan, and a-seat-a-MIN-oh-fen) †

Antihistamine, decongestant, antitussive, and expectorant combinations—

65. Brompheniramine, Phenylephrine, Phenylpropanolamine, Codeine, and Guaifenesin (brome-fen-EER-a-meen, fen-ill-EF-rin, fen-ill-proe-pa-NOLE-a-meen, KOE-deen, and gwye-FEN-e-sin) *

66. Brompheniramine, Phenylephrine, Phenylpropanolamine, Hydrocodone, and Guaifenesin (brome-fen-EER-a-meen, fen-ill-EF-rin, fen-ill-proe-pa-NOLE-a-meen, hye-droe-KOE-done, and gwye-FEN-e-sin) *

67. Chlorpheniramine, Ephedrine, Phenylephrine, Dextromethorphan, Ammonium Chloride, and Ipecac (klor-fen-EER-a-meen, e-FED-rin, fen-ill-EF-rin, dex-troe-meth-OR-fan, a-MOE-nee-um KLOR-ide, and IP-e-kak) †

68. Chlorpheniramine, Phenylephrine, Phenylpropanolamine, Dextromethorphan, Potassium Guaiacolsulfonate, and Ipecac (klor-fen-EER-a-meen, fen-ill-EF-rin, fen-ill-proe-pa-NOLE-a-meen, dex-troe-meth-OR-fan, poe-TAS-see-um gwye-a-kol-SUL-fon-ate, and IP-e-kak) †

69. No product available

70. Chlorpheniramine, Phenylephrine, Codeine and Ammonium Chloride (klor-fen-EER-a-meen, fen-ill-EF-rin, KOE-deen, and a-MOE-nee-um KLOR-ide) †

71. Chlorpheniramine, Phenylephrine, Codeine, and Potassium Iodide (klor-fen-EER-a-meen, fen-ill-EF-rin, KOE-deen, and por-TAS-ee-um EYE-oh-dyed) †

72. Chlorpheniramine, Phenylephrine, Dextromethorphan, and Guaifenesin (klor-fen-EER-a-meen, fen-ill-EF-rin, dex-troe-meth-OR-fan, and gwye-FEN-e-sin) †

73. Chlorpheniramine, Phenylephrine, Dextromethorphan, Guaifenesin, and Ammonium Chloride (klor-fen-EER-a-meen, fen-ill-EF-rin, dex-troe-meth-OR-fan, gwye-FEN-e-sin, and a-MOE-nee-um KLOR-ide) †

74. Chlorpheniramine, Phenylephrine, Phenylpropanolamine, Carbetapentane, and Potassium Guaiacolsulfonate (klor-fen-EER-a-meen, fen-ill-EF-rin, fen-ill-proe-pa-NOLE-a-meen, kar-bay-ta-PEN-tane, and poe-TAS-see-um gwye-a-kol-SUL-fon-ate) †

75. No product available

76. No product available

77. Chlorpheniramine, Phenyltoloxamine, Ephedrine, Codeine, and Guaiacol Carbonate (klor-fen-EER-a-meen, fen-ill-tole-OX-a-meen, e-FED-rin, KOE-deen, and GYWE-a-kole KAR-bone-ate) *

78. Chlorpheniramine, Pseudoephedrine, Dextromethorphan, and Guaifenesin (klor-fen-EER-a-meen, soo-doe-e-FED-rin, dex-troe-meth-OR-fan, and gwye-FEN-e-sin) *

79. Pheniramine, Pyrilamine, Phenylpropanolamine, Dextromethorphan, and Ammonium Chloride (fen-EER-a-meen, peer-ILL-a-meen, fen-ill-proe-pa-NOLE-a-meen, dex-troe-meth-OR-fan, and a-MOE-nee-um KLOR-ide) †

80. No product available

81. Pheniramine, Pyrilamine, Phenylpropanolamine, Hydrocodone, and Guaifenesin (fen-EER-a-meen, peer-ILL-a-meen, fen-ill-proe-pa-NOLE-a-meen, hye-droe-KOE-done, and gwye-FEN-e-sin)

82. Pheniramine, Phenylephrine, Phenylpropanolamine, Hydrocodone, and Guaifenesin (fen-EER-a-meen, fen-ill-EF-rin,

fen-ill-proe-pa-NOLE-a-meen, hye-droe-KOE-done, and gwye-FEN-e-sin) †

83. Promethazine, Phenylephrine, Codeine, and Potassium Guaiacolsulfonate (pro-METH-a-zeen, fen-ill-EF-rin, KOE-deen, and poe-TAS-see-um gwye-a-kol-SUL-fon-ate) *

84. Pyrilamine, Phenylephrine, Hydrocodone, and Ammonium Chloride (peer-ILL-a-meen, fen-ill-EF-rin, hye-droe-KOE-done, and a-MOE-nee-um KLOR-ide) *

85. Pyrilamine, Phenylpropanolamine, Dextromethorphan, Guaifenesin, Potassium Citrate, and Citric Acid (peer-ILL-a-meen, fen-ill-proe-pa-NOLE-a-meen, dex-troe-meth-OR-fan, gwye-FEN-e-sin, poe-TAS-ee-um SI-trate, and SI-trik AS-id) †

86. Triprolidine, Pseudoephedrine, Codeine, and Guaifenesin (trye-PROE-li-deen, soo-doe-e-FED-rin, KOE-deen, and gwye-FEN-e-sin) *

Antihistamine, decongestant, antitussive, expectorant, and analgesic combinations—

87. No product available
88. No product available
89. No product available
90. No product available
91. Pheniramine, Phenylephrine, Codeine, Sodium Citrate, Sodium Salicylate, and Caffeine (fen-EER-a-meen, fen-ill-EF-rin, KOE-deen, SOE-dee-um SI-trate, SOE-dee-um sa-LI-sill-ate, and kaf-EEN) †
92. No product available

Antihistamine, decongestant, and expectorant combinations—

93. Brompheniramine, Phenylephrine, Phenylpropanolamine, and Guaifenesin (brome-fen-EER-a-meen, fen-ill-EF-rin, fen-ill-proe-pa-NOLE-a-meen, and gwye-FEN-e-sin) *
94. No product available
95. Chlorpheniramine, Ephedrine, and Guaifenesin (klor-fen-EER-a-meen, e-FED-rin, and gwye-FEN-e-sin) †
96. Chlorpheniramine, Phenylephrine, and Guaifenesin (klor-fen-EER-a-meen, fen-ill-EF-rin, and gwye-FEN-e-sin) †
97. Chlorpheniramine, Phenylpropanolamine, and Guaifenesin (klor-fen-EER-a-meen, fen-ill-proe-pa-NOLE-a-meen, and gwye-FEN-e-sin) *
98. Chlorpheniramine, Phenylpropanolamine, Guaifenesin, Sodium Citrate, and Citric Acid (klor-fen-EER-a-meen, fen-ill-proe-pa-NOLE-a-meen, gwye-FEN-e-sin, SOE-dee-um SI-trate, and SI-trik AS-id) †
99. Chlorpheniramine, Pseudoephedrine, and Guaifenesin (klor-fen-EER-a-meen, soo-doe-e-FED-rin, and gwye-FEN-e-sin) *
100. Dexchlorpheniramine, Pseudoephedrine, and Guaifenesin (dex-klor-fen-EER-a-meen, soo-doe-e-FED-rin, and gwye-FEN-e-sin) †
101. Promethazine, Phenylephrine, and Potassium Guaiacolsulfonate (pro-METH-a-zeen, fen-ill-EF-rin, and poe-TAS-see-um gwye-a-kol-SUL-fon-ate) *

Antihistamine, decongestant, expectorant, and analgesic combinations—

102. Chlorpheniramine, Phenylpropanolamine, Guaifenesin, and Acetaminophen (klor-fen-EER-a-meen, fen-ill-proe-pa-NOLE-a-meen, gwye-FEN-e-sin, and a-seat-a-MIN-oh-fen) †

Antihistamine and expectorant combination—

103. Promethazine and Potassium Guaiacolsulfonate (pro-METH-a-zeen and poe-TAS-see-um gwye-a-kol-SUL-fon-ate) *

Antitussive and analgesic combination—

104. Dextromethorphan and Acetaminophen (dex-troe-meth-OR-fan and a-seat-a-MIN-oh-fen)

Antitussive and anticholinergic combination—

105. Hydrocodone and Homatropine (hye-droe-KOE-done and hoe-MA-troe-peen) ‡

Antitussive and expectorant combinations—

106. Codeine, Ammonium Chloride, and Guaifenesin (KOE-deen, a-MOE-nee-um KLOR-ide, and gwye-FEN-e-sin) *
107. Codeine and Calcium Iodide (KOE-deen and KAL-see-um EYE-oh-dyed) †
108. Codeine and Guaifenesin (KOE-deen and gwye-FEN-e-sin) †‡

109. Codeine and Iodinated Glycerol (KOE-deen and EYE-oh-di-nay-ted GLI-ser-ole) †
110. No product available
111. Dextromethorphan and Guaifenesin (dex-troe-meth-OR-fan and gwye-FEN-e-sin)
112. Dextromethorphan and Iodinated Glycerol (dex-troe-meth-OR-fan and EYE-oh-di-nay-ted GLI-ser-ole) †
113. No product available
114. Hydrocodone and Guaifenesin (hye-droe-KOE-done and gwye-FEN-e-sin) †‡
115. Hydrocodone and Guaifenesin or Hydrocodone and Potassium Guaiacolsulfonate (hye-droe-KOE-done and gwye-FEN-e-sin or hye-droe-KOE-done and poe-TAS-see-um gwye-a-kol-SUL-fon-ate) †‡
116. Hydrocodone and Potassium Guaiacolsulfonate (hye-droe-KOE-done and poe-TAS-see-um gwye-a-kol-SUL-fon-ate) †
117. Hydromorphone and Guaifenesin (hye-droe-MOR-fone and gwye-FEN-e-sin) †

Decongestant and antitussive combinations—

118. Phenylephrine and Codeine (fen-ill-EF-rin and KOE-deen) *
119. Phenylephrine and Hydrocodone (fen-ill-EF-rin and hye-droe-KOE-done)
120. Phenylpropanolamine and Caramiphen (fen-ill-proe-pa-NOLE-a-meen and kar-AM-i-fen) †
121. Phenylpropanolamine and Dextromethorphan (fen-ill-proe-pa-NOLE-a-meen and dex-troe-meth-OR-fan) †
122. Phenylpropanolamine and Hydrocodone (fen-ill-proe-pa-NOLE-a-meen and hye-droe-KOE-done) †‡
123. Pseudoephedrine and Codeine (soo-doe-e-FED-rin and KOE-deen)
124. Pseudoephedrine and Dextromethorphan (soo-doe-e-FED-rin and dex-troe-meth-OR-fan)
125. Pseudoephedrine and Hydrocodone (soo-doe-e-FED-rin and hye-droe-KOE-done) †

Decongestant, antitussive, and analgesic combinations—

126. Phenylpropanolamine, Dextromethorphan, and Acetaminophen (fen-ill-proe-pa-NOLE-a-meen, dex-troe-meth-OR-fan, and a-seat-a-MIN-oh-fen) †
127. Pseudoephedrine, Dextromethorphan, and Acetaminophen (soo-doe-e-FED-rin, dex-troe-meth-OR-fan, and a-seat-a-MIN-oh-fen)

Decongestant, antitussive, and expectorant combinations—

128. Ephedrine, Carbetapentane, and Guaifenesin (e-FED-rin, kar-bay-ta-PEN-tane, and gwye-FEN-e-sin) *
129. Phenylephrine, Dextromethorphan, and Guaifenesin (fen-ill-EF-rin, dex-troe-meth-OR-fan, and gwye-FEN-e-sin) †
130. Phenylephrine, Phenylpropanolamine, Carbetapentane, and Potassium Guaiacolsulfonate (fen-ill-EF-rin, fen-ill-proe-pa-NOLE-a-meen, kar-bay-ta-PEN-tane, and poe-TAS-see-um gwye-a-kol-SUL-fon-ate) †
131. Phenylephrine, Hydrocodone, and Guaifenesin (fen-ill-EF-rin, hye-droe-KOE-done, and gwye-FEN-e-sin)
132. Phenylpropanolamine, Codeine, and Guaifenesin (fen-ill-proe-pa-NOLE-a-meen, KOE-deen, and gwye-FEN-e-sin) †
133. Phenylpropanolamine, Dextromethorphan, and Guaifenesin (fen-ill-proe-pa-NOLE-a-meen, dex-troe-meth-OR-fan, and gwye-FEN-e-sin) †
134. Phenylpropanolamine, Dextromethorphan, and Guaifenesin or Phenylpropanolamine, Dextromethorphan, Guaifenesin, and Acetaminophen (fen-ill-proe-pa-NOLE-a-meen, dex-troe-meth-OR-fan, and gwye-FEN-e-sin or fen-ill-proe-pa-NOLE-a-meen, dex-troe-meth-OR-fan, gwye-FEN-e-sin, and a-seat-a-MIN-oh-fen) †
135. Pseudoephedrine, Codeine, and Guaifenesin (soo-doe-e-FED-rin, KOE-deen, and gwye-FEN-e-sin) ‡
136. Pseudoephedrine, Dextromethorphan, and Guaifenesin (soo-doe-e-FED-rin, dex-troe-meth-OR-fan, and gwye-FEN-e-sin)
137. Pseudoephedrine, Hydrocodone, and Guaifenesin (soo-doe-e-FED-rin, hye-droe-KOE-done, and gwye-FEN-e-sin) †
138. Pseudoephedrine, Hydrocodone, and Potassium Guaiacolsulfonate (soo-doe-e-FED-rin, hye-droe-KOE-done, and poe-TAS-ee-um gwye-a-kol-SUL-fon-ate) †

139. Pseudoephedrine, Hydrocodone, and Guaifenesin or Pseudoephedrine, Hydrocodone, and Potassium Guaiacolsulfonate (soo-doe-e-FED-rin, hye-droe-KOE-done, and gwye-FEN-e-sin or soo-doe-e-FED-rin, hye-droe-KOE-done, and poe-TAS-ee-um gwye-a-kol-SUL-fon-ate) †

Decongestant, antitussive, expectorant, and analgesic combinations—

140. Phenylpropanolamine, Dextromethorphan, Guaifenesin, and Acetaminophen (fen-ill-proe-pa-NOLE-a-meen, dex-troe-meth-OR-fan, gwye-FEN-e-sin, and a-seat-a-MIN-oh-fen) †
141. Pseudoephedrine, Dextromethorphan, Guaifenesin, and Acetaminophen (soo-doe-e-FED-rin, dex-troe-meth-OR-fan, gwye-FEN-e-sin, and a-seat-a-MIN-oh-fen)

Decongestant and expectorant combinations—

142. Ephedrine and Guaifenesin (e-FED-rin and gwye-FEN-e-sin) †
143. Ephedrine and Potassium Iodide (e-FED-rin and poe-TAS-ee-um EYE-oh-dyed) †
144. Phenylephrine and Guaifenesin (fen-ill-EF-rin and gwye-FEN-e-sin) †
145. Phenylephrine, Phenylpropanolamine, and Guaifenesin (fen-ill-EF-rin, fen-ill-proe-pa-NOLE-a-meen, and gwye-FEN-e-sin) †
146. Phenylpropanolamine and Guaifenesin (fen-ill-proe-pa-NOLE-a-meen and gwye-FEN-e-sin) ‡
147. Pseudoephedrine and Guaifenesin (soo-doe-e-FED-rin and gwye-FEN-e-sin) ‡

Decongestant, expectorant, and analgesic combination—

148. Phenylephrine, Guaifenesin, Acetaminophen, Salicylamide and Caffeine (fen-ill-EF-rin, gwye-FEN-e-sin, a-seat-a-MIN-oh-fen, sal-i-SILL-a-mide and kaf-EEN) †

---

*Not commercially available in the U.S.
†Not commercially available in Canada.
‡Generic name product may be available in the U.S.

Description

Cough/cold combinations are used mainly to relieve the cough due to colds, influenza, or hay fever. They are not to be used for the chronic cough that occurs with smoking, asthma, or emphysema or when there is an unusually large amount of mucus or phlegm (pronounced flem) with the cough.

Cough/cold combination products contain more than one ingredient. For example, some products may contain an antihistamine, a decongestant, and an analgesic, in addition to a medicine for coughing. If you are treating yourself, it is important to select a product that is best for your symptoms. Also, in general, it is best to buy a product that includes only those medicines you really need. If you have questions about which product to buy, check with your pharmacist.

Since different products contain ingredients that will have different precautions and side effects, it is important that you know the ingredients of the medicine you are taking. The different kinds of ingredients that may be found in cough/cold combinations include:

Antihistamines—Antihistamines are used to relieve or prevent the symptoms of hay fever and other types of allergy. They also help relieve some symptoms of the common cold, such as sneezing and runny nose. They work by preventing the effects of a substance called histamine, which is produced by the body. Some examples of antihistamines contained in these combinations are: bromodiphenhydramine (broe-moe-dye-fen-HYE-dra-meen), brompheniramine (brome-fen-EER-a-meen), carbinoxamine (kar-bi-NOX-a-meen), chlorpheniramine (klor-fen-EER-a-meen), dexchlorpheniramine (dex-

klor-fen-EER-a-meen), diphenhydramine (dye-fen-HYE-dra-meen), doxylamine (dox-ILL-a-meen), phenindamine (fen-IN-da-meen), pheniramine (fen-EER-a-meen), phenyltoloxamine (fen-ill-tole-OX-a-meen), pyrilamine (peer-ILL-a-meen), promethazine (proe-METH-a-zeen), and triprolidine (trye-PROE-li-deen).

Decongestants—Decongestants, such as ephedrine (e-FED-rin), phenylephrine (fen-ill-EF-rin), phenylpropanolamine (fen-ill-proe-pa-NOLE-a-meen), and pseudoephedrine (soo-doe-e-FED-rin), produce a narrowing of blood vessels. This leads to clearing of nasal congestion. However, this effect may also increase blood pressure in patients who have high blood pressure.

Antitussives—To help relieve coughing these combinations contain either a narcotic [codeine (KOE-deen), dihydrocodeine (dye-hye-droe-KOE-deen), hydrocodone (hye-droe-KOE-done) or hydromorphone (hye-droe-MOR-fone)] or a nonnarcotic [carbetapentane (kar-bay-ta-PEN-tane), caramiphen (kar-AM-i-fen), or dextromethorphan (dex-troe-meth-OR-fan)] antitussive. These antitussives act directly on the cough center in the brain. Narcotics may become habit-forming, causing mental or physical dependence, if used for a long time. Physical dependence may lead to withdrawal side effects when you stop taking the medicine.

Expectorants—Guaifenesin (gwye-FEN-e-sin) works by loosening the mucus or phlegm in the lungs. Other ingredients added as expectorants (for example, ammonium chloride, calcium iodide, iodinated glycerol, ipecac, potassium guaiacolsulfonate, potassium iodide, and sodium citrate) have not been proven to be effective. In general, the best thing you can do to loosen mucus or phlegm is to drink plenty of water.

Analgesics—Analgesics, such as acetaminophen (a-seat-a-MIN-oh-fen), aspirin, and other salicylates [such as salicylamide (sal-i-SILL-a-mide) and sodium salicylate (SOE-dee-um sa-LI-sill-ate)] are used in these combination medicines to help relieve the aches and pain that may occur with the common cold.

The use of too much acetaminophen and salicylates at the same time may cause kidney damage or cancer of the kidney or urinary bladder. This may occur if large amounts of both medicines are taken together for a long time. However, taking the recommended amounts of combination medicines that contain both acetaminophen and a salicylate for short periods of time has not been shown to cause these unwanted effects.

Anticholinergics—Anticholinergics such as homatropine (hoe-MA-troe-peen) may help produce a drying effect in the nose and chest.

Some of these combinations are available only with your doctor's prescription. Others are available without a prescription; however, your health care professional may have special instructions on the proper dose of the medicine for your medical condition.

Cough/cold combinations are available in the following dosage forms:

Antihistamine and antitussive combinations—
Oral
Bromodiphenhydramine and Codeine
• Syrup (U.S.)
Chlorpheniramine and Codeine
• Oral suspension (Canada)

Chlorpheniramine and Dextromethorphan
  • Oral solution (U.S.)
Chlorpheniramine and Hydrocodone
  • Oral solution (U.S.)
  • Oral suspension (U.S.)
Phenyltoloxamine and Hydrocodone
  • Oral suspension (Canada)
  • Tablets (Canada)
Promethazine and Codeine
  • Oral solution (U.S.)
  • Syrup (U.S.)
Promethazine and Dextromethorphan
  • Oral solution (U.S.)
  • Syrup (U.S.)
Pyrilamine and Codeine
  • Oral solution (U.S.)

Antihistamine, antitussive, and analgesic combinations—
Oral
Doxylamine, Codeine, and Acetaminophen
  • Tablets (Canada)

Antihistamine, antitussive, and expectorant combinations—
Oral
Bromodiphenhydramine, Diphenhydramine, Codeine, Ammonium Chloride, and Potassium Guaiacolsulfonate
  • Syrup (Canada)
Diphenhydramine, Codeine, and Ammonium Chloride
  • Syrup (Canada)
Diphenhydramine, Dextromethorphan, and Ammonium Chloride
  • Syrup (Canada)
Pheniramine, Codeine, and Guaifenesin
  • Syrup (Canada)
Pheniramine, Pyrilamine, Hydrocodone, Potassium Citrate, and Ascorbic Acid
  • Syrup (U.S.)
Promethazine, Codeine, and Potassium Guaiacolsulfonate
  • Syrup (Canada)

Antihistamine, decongestant, and antitussive combinations—
Oral
Brompheniramine, Phenylephrine, Phenylpropanolamine, and Codeine
  • Syrup (Canada)
Brompheniramine, Phenylephrine, Phenylpropanolamine, and Dextromethorphan
  • Elixir (Canada)
  • Tablets (Canada)
Brompheniramine, Phenylpropanolamine, and Codeine
  • Syrup (U.S.)
Brompheniramine, Phenylpropanolamine, and Dextromethorphan
  • Capsules (U.S.)
  • Elixir (U.S.)
  • Oral solution (U.S.)
  • Syrup (U.S.)
Brompheniramine, Pseudoephedrine, and Dextromethorphan
  • Syrup (U.S.)

Carbinoxamine, Pseudoephedrine, and Dextromethorphan
  • Oral solution (U.S.)
  • Syrup (U.S.)
Chlorpheniramine, Ephedrine, Phenylephrine, and Carbetapentane
  • Oral suspension (U.S.)
  • Tablets (U.S.)
Chlorpheniramine, Phenylephrine, and Dextromethorphan
  • Oral solution (U.S.)
  • Syrup (U.S.)
  • Tablets (U.S.)
Chlorpheniramine, Phenylephrine, and Hydrocodone
  • Oral solution (U.S.)
  • Syrup (U.S.)
Chlorpheniramine, Phenylephrine, Phenylpropanolamine, and Codeine
  • Oral solution (U.S.)
Chlorpheniramine, Phenylephrine, Phenylpropanolamine, and Dihydrocodeine
  • Oral solution (U.S.)
  • Syrup (U.S.)
Chlorpheniramine, Phenylpropanolamine, and Caramiphen
  • Extended-release capsules (Canada)
Chlorpheniramine, Phenylpropanolamine, and Dextromethorphan
  • Granules (U.S.)
  • Oral solution (U.S. and Canada)
  • Syrup (U.S.)
  • Tablets (U.S.)
Chlorpheniramine, Pseudoephedrine, and Codeine
  • Elixir (U.S.)
  • Oral solution (U.S.)
Chlorpheniramine, Pseudoephedrine, and Dextromethorphan
  • Chewable tablets (U.S.)
  • Oral solution (U.S. and Canada)
  • Syrup (U.S. and Canada)
Chlorpheniramine, Pseudoephedrine, and Hydrocodone
  • Oral solution (U.S.)
  • Syrup (U.S.)
Diphenylpyraline, Phenylephrine, and Dextromethorphan
  • Oral solution (Canada)
Doxylamine, Etadefrine, and Hydrocodone
  • Syrup (Canada)
Pheniramine, Phenylephrine, and Dextromethorphan
  • Oral solution (Canada)
Pheniramine, Pyrilamine, Phenylephrine, Phenylpropanolamine, and Hydrocodone
  • Oral solution (U.S.)
Pheniramine, Pyrilamine, Phenylpropanolamine, and Codeine
  • Syrup (Canada)
Pheniramine, Pyrilamine, Phenylpropanolamine, and Dextromethorphan
  • Syrup (Canada)
Pheniramine, Pyrilamine, Phenylpropanolamine, and Hydrocodone
  • Oral solution (Canada)
  • Syrup (Canada)

Promethazine, Phenylephrine, and Codeine
- Oral solution (U.S.)
- Syrup (U.S.)

Promethazine, Pseudoephedrine, and Dextromethorphan
- Syrup (Canada)

Pyrilamine, Phenylephrine, and Codeine
- Syrup (U.S.)

Pyrilamine, Phenylephrine, and Dextromethorphan
- Syrup (U.S.)

Pyrilamine, Phenylephrine, and Hydrocodone
- Syrup (U.S.)

Triprolidine, Pseudoephedrine, and Codeine
- Oral solution (Canada)
- Syrup (U.S.)
- Tablets (Canada)

Triprolidine, Pseudoephedrine, and Dextromethorphan
- Oral solution (Canada)
- Tablets (Canada)

Antihistamine, decongestant, antitussive, and analgesic combinations—
Oral

Chlorpheniramine, Phenindamine, Phenylephrine, Dextromethorphan, Acetaminophen, Salicylamide, Caffeine, and Ascorbic Acid
- Tablets (U.S.)

Chlorpheniramine, Pheniramine, Pyrilamine, Phenylephrine, Hydrocodone, Salicylamide, Caffeine, and Ascorbic Acid
- Capsules (U.S.)

Chlorpheniramine, Phenylephrine, Dextromethorphan, Acetaminophen, and Salicylamide
- Tablets (U.S.)

Chlorpheniramine, Phenylephrine, Hydrocodone, Acetaminophen, and Caffeine
- Tablets (U.S.)

Chlorpheniramine, Phenylpropanolamine, Dextromethorphan, and Acetaminophen
- Capsules (U.S.)
- Effervescent tablets (U.S.)
- Oral solution (U.S.)
- Tablets (U.S.)

Chlorpheniramine, Phenylpropanolamine, Dextromethorphan, and Aspirin
- Effervescent tablets (U.S.)

Chlorpheniramine, Pseudoephedrine, Codeine, and Acetaminophen
- Tablets (Canada)

Chlorpheniramine, Pseudoephedrine, Dextromethorphan, and Acetaminophen
- Capsules (U.S.)
- Chewable tablets (U.S. and Canada)
- Oral solution (U.S. and Canada)
- Syrup (Canada)
- Tablets (U.S. and Canada)

Doxylamine, Phenylpropanolamine, Dextromethorphan, and Aspirin
- Effervescent tablets (U.S.)

Doxylamine, Pseudoephedrine, Dextromethorphan, and Acetaminophen
- Capsules (U.S.)
- Oral solution (U.S.)

Pyrilamine, Pseudoephedrine, Dextromethorphan, and Acetaminophen
- Oral solution (U.S.)

Antihistamine, decongestant, antitussive, and expectorant combinations—
Oral

Brompheniramine, Phenylephrine, Phenylpropanolamine, Codeine, and Guaifenesin
- Oral solution (Canada)

Brompheniramine, Phenylephrine, Phenylpropanolamine, Hydrocodone, and Guaifenesin
- Oral solution (Canada)

Chlorpheniramine, Ephedrine, Phenylephrine, Dextromethorphan, Ammonium Chloride, and Ipecac
- Syrup (U.S.)

Chlorpheniramine, Phenylephrine, Codeine, and Ammonium Chloride
- Oral solution (U.S.)

Chlorpheniramine, Phenylephrine, Codeine, and Potassium Iodide
- Syrup (U.S.)

Chlorpheniramine, Phenylephrine, Dextromethorphan, and Guaifenesin
- Syrup (U.S.)

Chlorpheniramine, Phenylephrine, Dextromethorphan, Guaifenesin, and Ammonium Chloride
- Oral solution (U.S.)

Chlorpheniramine, Phenylephrine, Phenylpropanolamine, Carbetapentane, and Potassium Guaiacolsulfonate
- Syrup (U.S.)

Chlorpheniramine, Phenylephrine, Phenylpropanolamine, Dextromethorphan, Potassium Guaicolsulfonate, and Ipecac
- Syrup (U.S.)

Chlorpheniramine, Phenyltoloxamine, Ephedrine, Codeine, and Guaiacol Carbonate
- Oral suspension (Canada)

Chlorpheniramine, Pseudoephedrine, Dextromethorphan and Guaifenesin
- Oral solution (Canada)

Pheniramine, Pyrilamine, Phenylpropanolamine, Dextromethorphan, and Ammonium Chloride
- Syrup (U.S.)

Pheniramine, Pyrilamine, Phenylpropanolamine, Hydrocodone, and Guaifenesin
- Oral solution (U.S.)
- Elixir (Canada)

Pheniramine, Phenylephrine, Phenylpropanolamine, Hydrocodone, and Guaifenesin
- Oral solution (U.S.)
- Syrup (U.S.)

Promethazine, Phenylephrine, Codeine, and Potassium Guaiacolsulfonate
- Syrup (Canada)

Pyrilamine, Phenylephrine, Hydrocodone, and Ammonium Chloride
- Syrup (Canada)

Pyrilamine, Phenylpropanolamine, Dextromethorphan, Guaifenesin, Potassium Citrate, and Citric Acid
- Syrup (U.S.)

Triprolidine, Pseudoephedrine, Codeine, and Guaifenesin
- Oral solution (Canada)

Antihistamine, decongestant, antitussive, expectorant, and analgesic combinations—
Oral
Pheniramine, Phenylephrine, Codeine, Sodium Citrate, Sodium Salicylate, and Caffeine
• Oral solution (U.S.)

Antihistamine, decongestant, and expectorant combinations—
Oral
Brompheniramine, Phenylephrine, Phenylpropanolamine, and Guaifenesin
• Oral solution (Canada)
Chlorpheniramine, Ephedrine, and Guaifenesin
• Oral solution (U.S.)
Chlorpheniramine, Phenylephrine, and Guaifenesin
• Oral solution (U.S.)
Chlorpheniramine, Phenylpropanolamine, and Guaifenesin
• Oral solution (Canada)
Chlorpheniramine, Phenylpropanolamine, Guaifenesin, Sodium Citrate, and Citric Acid
• Oral solution (U.S.)
Chlorpheniramine, Pseudoephedrine, and Guaifenesin
• Extended-release tablets (Canada)
• Oral solution (Canada)
Dexchlorpheniramine, Pseudoephedrine, and Guaifenesin
• Oral solution (U.S.)
Promethazine, Phenylephrine, and Potassium Guaiacolsulfonate
• Syrup (Canada)

Antihistamine, decongestant, expectorant, and analgesic combinations—
Oral
Chlorpheniramine, Phenylpropanolamine, Guaifenesin, and Acetaminophen
• Tablets (U.S.)

Antitussive and analgesic combination—
Oral
Dextromethorphan and Acetaminophen
• Capsules (U.S.)
• Oral solution (U.S.)
• Oral suspension (Canada)
• Tablets (U.S.)

Antitussive and anticholinergic combination—
Oral
Hydrocodone and Homatropine (Canadian product does not contain homatropine)
• Syrup (U.S. and Canada)
• Tablets (U.S. and Canada)

Antitussive and expectorant combinations—
Oral
Codeine, Ammonium Chloride, and Guaifenesin
• Syrup (Canada)
Codeine and Calcium Iodide
• Syrup (U.S.)
Codeine and Guaifenesin
• Oral solution (U.S.)
• Syrup (U.S.)
• Tablets (U.S.)
Codeine and Iodinated Glycerol
• Oral solution (U.S.)

Dextromethorphan and Guaifenesin
• Capsules (U.S.)
• Extended-release capsules (U.S.)
• Oral solution (U.S.)
• Syrup (U.S. and Canada)
• Tablets (U.S.)
• Extended-release tablets (U.S.)
Dextromethorphan and Iodinated Glycerol
• Oral solution (U.S.)
Hydrocodone and Guaifenesin
• Oral solution (U.S.)
• Syrup (U.S.)
• Tablets (U.S.)
Hydrocodone and Potassium Guaiacolsulfonate
• Oral solution (U.S.)
• Syrup (U.S.)
Hydromorphone and Guaifenesin
• Syrup (U.S.)

Decongestant and antitussive combinations—
Oral
Phenylephrine and Codeine
• Oral solution (Canada)
Phenylephrine and Hydrocodone
• Oral solution (Canada)
• Syrup (Canada)
Phenylpropanolamine and Caramiphen
• Extended-release capsules (U.S.)
Phenylpropanolamine and Dextromethorphan
• Granules (U.S.)
• Oral solution (U.S.)
• Syrup (U.S.)
Phenylpropanolamine and Hydrocodone
• Oral solution (U.S.)
• Syrup (U.S.)
Pseudoephedrine and Codeine
• Capsules (U.S.)
• Syrup (U.S. and Canada)
• Tablets (Canada)
Pseudoephedrine and Dextromethorphan
• Capsules (U.S.)
• Oral solution (U.S. and Canada)
• Syrup (Canada)
Pseudoephedrine and Hydrocodone
• Oral solution (U.S.)
• Syrup (U.S.)
• Tablets (U.S.)

Decongestant, antitussive, and analgesic combinations—
Oral
Phenylpropanolamine, Dextromethorphan, and Acetaminophen
• Tablets (U.S.)
Pseudoephedrine, Dextromethorphan, and Acetaminophen
• Capsules (U.S.)
• Oral solution (U.S.)
• Oral suspension (Canada)
• Tablets (U.S. and Canada)

Decongestant, antitussive, and expectorant combinations—
Oral
Ephedrine, Carbetapentane, and Guaifenesin
• Syrup (Canada)

Phenylephrine, Dextromethorphan, and Guaifenesin
- Syrup (U.S.)

Phenylephrine, Phenylpropanolamine, Carbetapentane and Potassium Guaiacolsulfonate
- Capsules (U.S.)

Phenylephrine, Hydrocodone, and Guaifenesin
- Oral solution (Canada)
- Syrup (U.S.)

Phenylpropanolamine, Codeine, and Guaifenesin
- Oral solution (U.S.)
- Syrup (U.S.)

Phenylpropanolamine, Dextromethorphan, and Guaifenesin
- Oral solution (U.S.)
- Syrup (U.S. and Canada)

Pseudoephedrine, Codeine, and Guaifenesin
- Oral solution (U.S. and Canada)
- Syrup (U.S. and Canada)

Pseudoephedrine, Dextromethorphan, and Guaifenesin
- Capsules (U.S. and Canada)
- Oral solution (U.S. and Canada)
- Syrup (U.S. and Canada)
- Tablets (U.S.)

Pseudoephedrine, Hydrocodone, and Guaifenesin
- Elixir (U.S.)
- Oral solution (U.S.)
- Syrup (U.S.)
- Tablets (U.S.)

Pseudoephedrine, Hydrocodone, and Potassium Guaiacolsulfonate
- Oral solution (U.S.)

Decongestant, antitussive, expectorant, and analgesic combinations—
Oral

Phenylpropanolamine, Dextromethorphan, Hydrocodone, Guaifenesin, and Acetaminophen
- Tablets (U.S.)

Pseudoephedrine, Dextromethorphan, Guaifenesin, and Acetaminophen
- Capsules (U.S.)
- Oral solution (U.S. and Canada)
- Syrup (Canada)
- Tablets (U.S.)

Decongestant and expectorant combinations—
Oral

Ephedrine and Guaifenesin
- Syrup (U.S.)

Ephedrine and Potassium Iodide
- Syrup (U.S.)

Phenylephrine and Guaifenesin
- Oral solution (U.S.)
- Extended-release capsules (U.S.)
- Extended-release tablets (U.S.)

Phenylephrine, Phenylpropanolamine, and Guaifenesin
- Capsules (U.S.)
- Oral solution (U.S.)

Phenylpropanolamine and Guaifenesin
- Granules (U.S.)
- Oral solution (U.S.)
- Syrup (U.S.)
- Tablets (U.S.)
- Extended-release tablets (U.S. and Canada)

Pseudoephedrine and Guaifenesin
- Capsules (U.S.)
- Extended-release capsules (U.S.)
- Oral solution (U.S. and Canada)
- Syrup (U.S. and Canada)
- Tablets (U.S.)
- Extended-release tablets (U.S.)

Decongestant, expectorant, and analgesic combination—
Oral

Phenylephrine, Guaifenesin, Acetaminophen, Salicylamide and Caffeine
- Tablets (U.S.)

Before Using This Medicine

If you are taking this medicine without a prescription, carefully read and follow any precautions on the label. For cough/cold combinations, the following should be considered:

Allergies—Tell your doctor if you have ever had any unusual or allergic reaction to any of the ingredients contained in this medicine. Also tell your health care professional if you are allergic to any other substances, such as foods, preservatives, or dyes. In addition, if this medicine contains *aspirin or other salicylates*, before taking it, check with your doctor if you have ever had any unusual or allergic reaction to any of the following medicines:

Aspirin or other salicylates
Diclofenac (e.g., Voltaren)
Diflunisal (e.g., Dolobid)
Fenoprofen (e.g., Nalfon)
Floctafenine
Flurbiprofen, by mouth (e.g., Ansaid)
Ibuprofen (e.g., Motrin)
Indomethacin (e.g., Indocin)
Ketoprofen (e.g., Orudis)
Ketorolac (e.g., Toradol)
Meclofenamate (e.g., Meclomen)
Mefenamic acid (e.g., Ponstel)
Methyl salicylate (oil of wintergreen)
Naproxen (e.g., Naprosyn)
Oxyphenbutazone (e.g., Tandearil)
Phenylbutazone (e.g., Butazolidin)
Piroxicam (e.g., Feldene)
Sulindac (e.g., Clinoril)
Suprofen (e.g., Suprol)
Tiaprofenic acid (e.g., Surgam)
Tolmetin (e.g., Tolectin)
Zomepirac (e.g., Zomax)

Diet—Make certain your health care professional knows if you are on any special diet, such as a low-sodium or low-sugar diet.

Pregnancy—The occasional use of a cough/cold combination is not likely to cause problems in the fetus or in the newborn baby. However, when these medicines are used at higher doses and/or for a long time, the chance that problems might occur may increase. For the individual ingredients of these combinations, the following information should be considered before you decide to use a particular cough/cold combination:

- *Acetaminophen*—Studies on birth defects have not been done in humans. However, acetaminophen has not been shown to cause birth defects or other problems in humans.

- *Alcohol*—Some of these combination medicines contain a large amount of alcohol. Too much use of alcohol during pregnancy may cause birth defects.
- *Antihistamines*—Antihistamines have not been shown to cause problems in humans.
- *Caffeine*—Studies in humans have not shown that caffeine causes birth defects. However, studies in animals have shown that caffeine causes birth defects when given in very large doses (amounts equal to the amount of caffeine contained in 12 to 24 cups of coffee a day).
- *Codeine*—Although studies on birth defects with codeine have not been done in humans, it has not been reported to cause birth defects in humans. Codeine has not been shown to cause birth defects in animal studies, but it caused other unwanted effects. Also, regular use of narcotics during pregnancy may cause the baby to become dependent on the medicine. This may lead to withdrawal side effects after birth. In addition, narcotics may cause breathing problems in the newborn baby if taken by the mother just before delivery.
- *Hydrocodone*—Although studies on birth defects with hydrocodone have not been done in humans, it has not been reported to cause birth defects in humans. However, hydrocodone has been shown to cause birth defects in animals when given in very large doses. Also, regular use of narcotics during pregnancy may cause the baby to become dependent on the medicine. This may lead to withdrawal side effects after birth. In addition, narcotics may cause breathing problems in the newborn baby if taken by the mother just before delivery.
- *Iodides (e.g., calcium iodide and iodinated glycerol)*—Not recommended during pregnancy. Iodides have caused enlargement of the thyroid gland in the fetus and resulted in breathing problems in newborn babies whose mothers took iodides in large doses for a long period of time.
- *Phenylephrine*—Studies on birth defects with phenylephrine have not been done in either humans or animals.
- *Phenylpropanolamine*—Studies on birth defects with phenylpropanolamine have not been done in either humans or animals. However, it seems that women who take phenylpropanolamine in the weeks following delivery are more likely to suffer mental or mood changes.
- *Pseudoephedrine*—Studies on birth defects with pseudoephedrine have not been done in humans. In animal studies pseudoephedrine did not cause birth defects but did cause a decrease in average weight, length, and rate of bone formation in the animal fetus when given in high doses.
- *Salicylates (e.g., aspirin)*—Studies on birth defects in humans have been done with aspirin, but not with salicylamide or sodium salicylate. Salicylates have not been shown to cause birth defects in humans. However, salicylates have been shown to cause birth defects in animals. Some reports have suggested that too much use of aspirin late in pregnancy may cause a decrease in the newborn's weight and possible death of the fetus or newborn infant. However, the mothers in these reports had been taking much larger amounts of aspirin than are usually recommended. Studies of mothers taking aspirin in the doses that are usually recommended did not show these unwanted effects. However, there is a chance that regular use of salicylates late in pregnancy may cause

unwanted effects on the heart or blood flow in the fetus or newborn baby. Use of salicylates, especially aspirin, during the last 2 weeks of pregnancy may cause bleeding problems in the fetus before or during delivery, or in the newborn baby. Also, too much use of salicylates during the last 3 months of pregnancy may increase the length of pregnancy, prolong labor, cause other problems during delivery, or cause severe bleeding in the mother before, during, or after delivery. *Do not take aspirin during the last 3 months of pregnancy unless it has been ordered by your doctor.*

Breast-feeding—If you are breast-feeding, the chance that problems might occur depends on the ingredients of the combination. For the individual ingredients of these combinations, the following apply:

- *Acetaminophen*—Acetaminophen passes into the breast milk. However, it has not been reported to cause problems in nursing babies.
- *Alcohol*—Alcohol passes into the breast milk. However, the amount of alcohol in recommended doses of this medicine does not usually cause problems in nursing babies.
- *Antihistamines*—Small amounts of antihistamines pass into the breast milk. Antihistamine-containing medicine is not recommended for use while breast-feeding since most antihistamines are especially likely to cause side effects, such as unusual excitement or irritability, in the baby. Also, since antihistamines tend to decrease the secretions of the body, the flow of breast milk may be reduced in some patients.
- *Caffeine*—Small amounts of caffeine pass into the breast milk and may build up in the nursing baby. However, the amount of caffeine in recommended doses of this medicine does not usually cause problems in nursing babies.
- *Decongestants (e.g., ephedrine, phenylephrine, phenylpropanolamine, pseudoephedrine)*—Phenylephrine and phenylpropanolamine have not been reported to cause problems in nursing babies. Ephedrine and pseudoephedrine pass into the breast milk and may cause unwanted effects in nursing babies (especially newborn and premature babies).
- *Iodides (e.g., calcium iodide and iodinated glycerol)*—These medicines pass into the breast milk and may cause unwanted effects, such as underactive thyroid, in the baby.
- *Narcotic antitussives (e.g., codeine, dihydrocodeine, hydrocodone, and hydromorphone)*—Small amounts of codeine have been shown to pass into the breast milk. However, the amount of codeine or other narcotic antitussives in recommended doses of this medicine has not been reported to cause problems in nursing babies.
- *Salicylates (e.g., aspirin)*—Salicylates pass into the breast milk. Although salicylates have not been reported to cause problems in nursing babies, it is possible that problems may occur if large amounts are taken regularly.

Children—Very young children are usually more sensitive to the effects of this medicine. *Before giving any of these combination medicines to a child, check the package label very carefully. Some of these medicines are too strong for use in children.* If you are not certain whether a specific product can be given to a child, or if you have any questions about the amount to give, check with your health care professional, especially if it contains:

- *Antihistamines*—Nightmares, unusual excitement, nervousness, restlessness, or irritability may be more likely to occur in children taking antihistamines.
- *Decongestants (e.g., ephedrine, phenylephrine, phenylpropanolamine, pseudoephedrine)*—Increases in blood pressure may be more likely to occur in children taking decongestants. Also, mental changes may be more likely to occur in young children taking phenylpropanolamine-containing combinations.
- *Narcotic antitussives (e.g., codeine, hydrocodeine, hydrocodone, and hydromorphone)*—Breathing problems may be especially likely to occur in children younger than 2 years of age taking narcotic antitussives. Also, unusual excitement or restlessness may be more likely to occur in children receiving these medicines.
- *Salicylates (e.g., aspirin)—Do not give medicines containing aspirin or other salicylates to a child with a fever or other symptoms of a virus infection, especially flu or chickenpox, without first discussing its use with your child's doctor.* This is very important because salicylates may cause a serious illness called Reye's syndrome in children with fever caused by a virus infection, especially flu or chickenpox. Also, children may be more sensitive to the aspirin or other salicylates contained in some of these medicines, especially if they have a fever or have lost large amounts of body fluid because of vomiting, diarrhea, or sweating.

Teenagers—*Do not give medicines containing aspirin or other salicylates to a teenager with a fever or other symptoms of a virus infection, especially flu or chickenpox, without first discussing its use with your child's doctor.* This is very important because salicylates may cause a serious illness called Reye's syndrome in teenagers with fever caused by a virus infection, especially flu or chickenpox.

Older adults—The elderly are usually more sensitive to the effects of this medicine, especially if it contains:

- *Antihistamines*—Confusion, difficult or painful urination, dizziness, drowsiness, feeling faint, or dryness of mouth, nose, or throat may be more likely to occur in elderly patients. Also, nightmares or unusual excitement, nervousness, restlessness, or irritability may be more likely to occur in the elderly taking antihistamines.
- *Decongestants (e.g., ephedrine, phenylephrine, phenylpropanolamine, pseudoephedrine)*—Confusion, hallucinations, drowsiness, or convulsions (seizures) may be more likely to occur in the elderly, who are usually more sensitive to the effects of this medicine. Also, increases in blood pressure may be more likely to occur in elderly persons taking decongestants.

Other medicines—Although certain medicines should not be used together at all, in other cases two different medicines may be used together even if an interaction might occur. In these cases, your doctor may want to change the dose, or other precautions may be necessary. Tell your health care professional if you are taking *any* other prescription or nonprescription (over-the-counter [OTC]) medicine, for example, aspirin or other medicine for allergies. Some medicines may change the way this medicine affects your body. Also, the effect of other medicines may be increased or reduced by some of the ingredients in this medicine. Check with

your health care professional about which medicines you should not take with this medicine.

Other medical problems—The presence of other medical problems may affect the use of the cough/cold combination medicine. Make sure you tell your doctor if you have any other medical problems, especially:

- Alcohol abuse (or history of)—Acetaminophen-containing medicines increase the chance of liver damage; also, some of the liquid medicines contain a large amount of alcohol

- Anemia or
- Gout or
- Hemophilia or other bleeding problems or
- Stomach ulcer or other stomach problems—These conditions may become worse if you are taking a combination medicine containing aspirin or another salicylate

- Brain disease or injury or
- Colitis or
- Convulsions (seizures) (history of) or
- Diarrhea or
- Gallbladder disease or gallstones—These conditions may become worse if you are taking a combination medicine containing codeine, dihydrocodeine, hydrocodone, or hydromorphone

- Cystic fibrosis (in children)—Side effects of iodinated glycerol may be more likely in children with cystic fibrosis

- Diabetes mellitus (sugar diabetes)—Decongestants may put diabetic patients at greater risk of having heart or blood vessel disease

- Emphysema, asthma, or chronic lung disease (especially in children)—Salicylate-containing medicine may cause an allergic reaction in which breathing becomes difficult

- Enlarged prostate or
- Urinary tract blockage or difficult urination—Some of the effects of anticholinergics (e.g., homatropine) or antihistamines may make urinary problems worse

- Glaucoma—A slight increase in inner eye pressure may occur with the use of anticholinergics (e.g., homatropine) or antihistamines, which may make the condition worse

- Heart or blood vessel disease or
- High blood pressure—Decongestant-containing medicine may increase the blood pressure and speed up the heart rate; also, caffeine-containing medicine, if taken in large amounts, may speed up the heart rate

- Kidney disease—This condition may increase the chance of side effects of this medicine because the medicine may build up in the body

- Liver disease—Liver disease increases the chance of side effects because the medicine may build up in the body; also, if liver disease is severe, there is a greater chance that aspirin-containing medicine may cause bleeding

- Thyroid disease—If an overactive thyroid has caused a fast heart rate, the decongestant in this medicine may cause the heart rate to speed up further; also, if the medicine contains narcotic antitussives (e.g., codeine), iodides (e.g., iodinated glycerol), or salicylates, the thyroid problem may become worse

Proper Use of This Medicine

To help loosen mucus or phlegm in the lungs, *drink a glass of water after each dose of this medicine*, unless otherwise directed by your doctor.

Take this medicine only as directed. Do not take more of it and do not take it more often than recommended on the label, unless otherwise directed by your doctor. To do so may increase the chance of side effects.

For patients *taking the extended-release capsule or tablet form of this medicine:*

- Swallow the capsule or tablet whole.
- Do not crush, break, or chew before swallowing.
- If the capsule is too large to swallow, you may mix the contents of the capsule with applesauce, jelly, honey, or syrup and swallow without chewing.

For patients *taking a combination medicine containing an antihistamine and/or aspirin or other salicylate:*

- Take with food or a glass of water or milk to lessen stomach irritation, if necessary.

If a combination medicine containing aspirin has a strong vinegar-like odor, do not use it. This odor means the medicine is breaking down. If you have any questions about this, check with your pharmacist.

Missed dose—If you must take this medicine regularly and you miss a dose, take it as soon as possible. However, if it is almost time for your next dose, skip the missed dose and go back to your regular dosing schedule. Do not double doses.

Storage—To store this medicine:

- Keep this medicine out of the reach of children. Overdose is very dangerous in young children.
- Store away from heat and direct light.
- Do not store the capsule or tablet form of this medicine in the bathroom, near the kitchen sink, or in other damp places. Heat or moisture may cause the medicine to break down.
- Keep the liquid form of this medicine from freezing. Do not refrigerate the syrup.
- Do not keep outdated medicine or medicine no longer needed. Be sure that any discarded medicine is out of the reach of children.

Precautions While Using This Medicine

If your cough has not improved after 7 days or if you have a high fever, skin rash, continuing headache, or sore throat with the cough, check with your doctor. These signs may mean that you have other medical problems.

For patients *taking antihistamine-containing medicine:*

- Before you have any skin tests for allergies, tell the doctor in charge that you are taking this medicine. The results of the test may be affected by the antihistamine in this medicine.
- This medicine will add to the effects of alcohol and other CNS depressants (medicines that slow down the nervous system, possibly causing drowsiness). Some examples of CNS depressants are antihistamines or medicine for hay fever, other allergies, or colds; sedatives, tranquilizers, or sleeping medicine; prescription pain medicine or narcotics; barbiturates; medicine for seizures; muscle relaxants; or anesthetics, including some dental anesthetics. *Check with your doctor before taking any of the above while you are taking this medicine.*
- This medicine may cause some people to become drowsy, dizzy, or less alert than they are normally. *Make sure you know how you react to this medicine before you drive, use machines, or do anything else that could be dangerous if you are dizzy or are not alert.*
- When taking antihistamines on a regular basis, make sure your doctor knows if you are taking large amounts of aspirin at the same time (as in arthritis or rheumatism). Effects of too much aspirin, such as ringing in the ears, may be covered up by the antihistamine.
- Antihistamines may cause dryness of the mouth. For temporary relief, use sugarless candy or gum, melt bits of ice in your mouth, or use a saliva substitute. However, if your mouth continues to feel dry for more than 2 weeks, check with your medical doctor or dentist. Continuing dryness of the mouth may increase the chance of dental disease, including tooth decay, gum disease, and fungus infections.

For patients *taking decongestant-containing medicine:*

- This medicine may add to the central nervous system (CNS) stimulant and other effects of phenylpropanolamine (PPA)-containing diet aids. *Do not use medicines for diet or appetite control while taking this medicine unless you have checked with your doctor.*
- This medicine may cause some people to be nervous or restless or to have trouble in sleeping. If you have trouble in sleeping, *take the last dose of this medicine for each day a few hours before bedtime.* If you have any questions about this, check with your doctor.
- Before having any kind of surgery (including dental surgery) or emergency treatment, tell the medical doctor or dentist in charge that you are taking this medicine.

For patients *taking narcotic antitussive (codeine, dihydrocodeine, hydrocodone, or hydromorphone)-containing medicine:*

- This medicine will add to the effects of alcohol and other CNS depressants (medicines that slow down the nervous system, possibly causing drowsiness). Some examples of CNS depressants are antihistamines or medicine for hay fever, other allergies, or colds; sedatives, tranquilizers, or sleeping medicine; prescription pain medicine or narcotics; barbiturates; medicine for seizures; muscle relaxants; or anesthetics, including some dental anesthetics. *Check with your doctor before taking any of the above while you are taking this medicine.*
- This medicine may cause some people to become drowsy, dizzy, less alert than they are normally, or to feel a false sense of well-being. *Make sure you know how you react to this medicine before you drive, use machines, or do anything else that could be dangerous if you are dizzy or are not alert and clearheaded.*
- Nausea or vomiting may occur after taking a narcotic antitussive. This effect may go away if you lie down for a while. However, if nausea or vomiting continues, check with your doctor.
- Dizziness, lightheadedness, or fainting may be especially likely to occur when you get up suddenly from a lying or sitting position. Getting up slowly may help lessen this problem.

- Before having any kind of surgery (including dental surgery) or emergency treatment, tell the medical doctor or dentist in charge that you are taking this medicine.

For patients *taking iodide (calcium iodide, iodinated glycerol, or potassium iodide)-containing medicine:*

- Make sure your doctor knows if you are planning to have any future thyroid tests. The results of the thyroid test may be affected by the iodine in this medicine.

For patients *taking analgesic-containing medicine:*

- *Check the label of all nonprescription (over-the-counter [OTC]), and prescription medicines you now take.* If any contain acetaminophen or aspirin or other salicylates, including diflunisal or bismuth subsalicylate, be especially careful. Taking them while taking a cough/cold combination medicine that already contains them may lead to overdose. If you have any questions about this, check with your health care professional.
- Do not take aspirin-containing medicine for 5 days before any surgery, including dental surgery, unless otherwise directed by your medical doctor or dentist. Taking aspirin during this time may cause bleeding problems.

For *diabetic patients taking aspirin- or sodium salicylate-containing medicine:*

- False urine sugar test results may occur:
  —If you take 8 or more 325-mg (5-grain) doses of aspirin every day for several days in a row.
  —If you take 8 or more 325-mg (5-grain), or 4 or more 500-mg (10-grain) doses of sodium salicylate.
- Smaller doses or occasional use of aspirin or sodium salicylate usually will not affect urine sugar tests. If you have any questions about this, check with your health care professional, especially if your diabetes is not well controlled.

For patients *taking homatropine-containing medicine:*

- This medicine may make you sweat less, causing your body temperature to increase. *Use extra care not to become overheated during exercise or hot weather while you are taking this medicine,* since overheating may result in heat stroke. Also, hot baths or saunas may make you feel dizzy or faint while you are taking this medicine.

Side Effects of This Medicine

Along with its needed effects, a medicine may cause some unwanted effects. Although serious side effects occur rarely when this medicine is taken as recommended, they may be more likely to occur if:

- too much medicine is taken.
- it is taken in large doses.
- it is taken for a long period of time.

Get emergency help immediately if any of the following symptoms of overdose occur:
  For narcotic antitussive (codeine, dihydrocodeine, hydrocodone, or hydromorphone)-containing
    Cold, clammy skin; confusion (severe); convulsions (seizures); drowsiness or dizziness (severe); nervousness or restlessness (severe); pinpoint pupils of eyes; slow heartbeat; slow or troubled breathing; weakness (severe)

  For acetaminophen-containing
    Diarrhea; increased sweating; loss of appetite; nausea

or vomiting; stomach cramps or pain; swelling or tenderness in the upper abdomen or stomach area
  For salicylate-containing
    Any loss of hearing; bloody urine; confusion; convulsions (seizures); diarrhea (severe or continuing); dizziness or lightheadedness; drowsiness (severe); excitement or nervousness (severe); fast or deep breathing; fever; hallucinations (seeing, hearing, or feeling things that are not there); increased sweating; nausea or vomiting (severe or continuing); shortness of breath or troubled breathing (for salicylamide only); stomach pain (severe or continuing); uncontrollable flapping movements of the hands, especially in elderly patients; unusual thirst; vision problems
  For decongestant-containing
    Fast, pounding, or irregular heartbeat; headache (continuing and severe); nausea or vomiting (severe); nervousness or restlessness (severe); shortness of breath or troubled breathing (severe or continuing)

Also, check with your doctor as soon as possible if any of the following side effects occur:
  For all combinations
    Skin rash, hives, and/or itching
  For antihistamine- or anticholinergic-containing
    Clumsiness or unsteadiness; convulsions (seizures); drowsiness (severe); dryness of mouth, nose, or throat (severe); flushing or redness of face; hallucinations (seeing, hearing, or feeling things that are not there); restlessness (severe); shortness of breath or troubled breathing; slow or fast heartbeat
  For iodine-containing
    Headache (continuing); increased watering of mouth; loss of appetite; metallic taste; skin rash, hives, or redness; sore throat; swelling of face, lips, or eyelids
  For acetaminophen-containing
    Unexplained sore throat and fever; unusual tiredness or weakness; yellow eyes or skin

Other side effects may occur that usually do not need medical attention. These side effects may go away during treatment as your body adjusts to the medicine. However, check with your doctor if any of the following side effects continue or are bothersome:
    Constipation; decreased sweating; difficult or painful urination; dizziness or lightheadedness; drowsiness; dryness of mouth, nose, or throat; false sense of well-being; increased sensitivity of skin to sun; nausea or vomiting; nightmares; stomach pain; thickening of mucus; trouble in sleeping; unusual excitement, nervousness, restlessness, or irritability; unusual tiredness or weakness

Not all of the side effects listed above have been reported for each of these medicines, but they have been reported for at least one of them. There are some similarities among these combination medicines, so many of the above side effects may occur with any of these medicines.

Other side effects not listed above may also occur in some patients. If you notice any other effects, check with your doctor.

Revised: 09/03/92
Interim revision: 08/11/95; 08/28/96; 09/28/98

CROMOLYN Inhalation

Commonly used brand name(s):

In the U.S.—
Intal
Generic name product may be available.

In Canada—

Intal	Novo-cromolyn
Intal Inhaler	PMS-Sodium Cromoglycate
Intal Syncroner	

Other commonly used names are cromoglicic acid, cromoglycic acid, sodium cromoglicate, and sodium cromoglycate.

Description

Cromolyn (KROE-moe-lin) is used to prevent the symptoms of asthma. When it is used regularly, cromolyn lessens the number and severity of asthma attacks by reducing inflammation in the lungs. Cromolyn is also used just before exposure to conditions or substances (for example, exercise, allergens, such as pollen, aspirin, chemicals, cold air, or air pollutants) that cause bronchospasm (wheezing or difficulty in breathing). Cromolyn will not help an asthma or bronchospasm attack that has already started.

Cromolyn may be used alone or with other asthma medicines, such as bronchodilators (medicines that open up narrowed breathing passages) or corticosteroids (cortisone-like medicines).

Cromolyn inhalation works by acting on certain inflammatory cells in the lungs to prevent them from releasing substances that cause asthma symptoms or bronchospasm.

This medicine is available only with your doctor's prescription, in the following dosage forms:

Inhalation
- Capsules for inhalation (Canada)
- Inhalation aerosol (U.S. and Canada)
- Inhalation solution (U.S. and Canada)

It is very important that you read and understand the following information. If any of it causes you special concern, check with your doctor. Also, *if you have any questions* or if you want more information about this medicine or your medical problem, *ask your doctor, nurse, or pharmacist.*

Before Using This Medicine

In deciding to use a medicine, the risks of using the medicine must be weighed against the good it will do. This is a decision you and your doctor will make. For cromolyn inhalation, the following should be considered:

Allergies—Tell your doctor if you have ever had any unusual or allergic reaction to cromolyn or to any other inhalation aerosol medicine. Also, tell your health care professional if you are allergic to any other substances, such as preservatives.

Pregnancy—Cromolyn has not been studied in pregnant women. However, when taken during pregnancy to control the mother's asthma, cromolyn has not been shown to cause birth defects or other problems in the baby. Studies in animals have shown that cromolyn causes a reduction in the number of successful pregnancies and a decrease in the weight of the animal fetus only when given by injection in very large amounts. Before taking this medication, make sure your doctor knows if you are pregnant or if you may become pregnant.

Breast-feeding—It is not known whether cromolyn passes into the breast milk. However, this medicine has not been reported to cause problems in nursing babies. Although most medicines pass into breast milk in small amounts, many of them may be used safely while breast-feeding. Mothers who are using this medicine and who wish to breast-feed should discuss this with their doctor.

Children—Although there is no specific information comparing the use of cromolyn in children with use in other age groups, this medicine is not expected to cause different side effects or problems in children than it does in adults. The inhalation solution form of this medicine should not be used in children younger than 2 years of age, and the inhalation aerosol should not be used in children younger than 5 years of age.

Older adults—Many medicines have not been studied specifically in older people. Therefore, it may not be known whether they work exactly the same way they do in younger adults. Although there is no specific information comparing the use of cromolyn inhalation in the elderly with use in other age groups, this medicine is not expected to cause different side effects or problems in older people than it does in younger adults.

Other medical problems—The presence of other medical problems may affect the use of cromolyn. Make sure you tell your doctor if you have any other medical problems, especially:

- Heart disease or
- Irregular heartbeat—The propellants used to deliver the medicine in the aerosol inhaler may worsen these conditions

Proper Use of This Medicine

Cromolyn oral inhalation is used to help prevent symptoms of asthma or bronchospasm (wheezing or difficulty in breathing). Cromolyn will not relieve an asthma or a bronchospasm attack that has already started. It is important to use cromolyn at regular times as directed by your doctor.

Use cromolyn inhalation only as directed. Do not use more of it and do not use it more often than your doctor ordered. To do so may increase the chance of side effects.

Cromolyn inhalation usually comes with patient directions. Read them carefully before using this medicine. If you do not understand the directions that come with the inhaler or if you are not sure how to use the inhaler, ask your health care professional to show you how to use it. Also, ask your health care professional to check regularly how you use the inhaler to make sure you are using it properly.

For patients using *cromolyn inhalation aerosol:*

- The cromolyn aerosol canister provides about 112 or 200 inhalations, depending on the size of the canister your doctor ordered. You should try to keep a record of the number of inhalations you use so you will know when the canister is almost empty. This canister, unlike some other aerosol canisters, cannot be floated in water to test its fullness.
- When you use the inhaler for the first time, or if you have not used it in a while, the inhaler may not deliver the right

amount of medicine with the first puff. Therefore, before using the inhaler, test or prime it.

- *To test or prime the inhaler:*
  —Insert the medicine container (canister) firmly into the clean mouthpiece according to the manufacturer's directions. Check to make sure the canister is placed properly into the mouthpiece.
  —Take the cap off the mouthpiece and shake the inhaler three or four times.
  —Hold the inhaler well away from you at arm's length and press the top of the canister, spraying the medicine one time into the air. The inhaler will now be ready to provide the right amount of medicine when you use it.
- *To use the inhaler:*
  —Using your thumb and one or two fingers, hold the inhaler upright, with the mouthpiece end down and pointing toward you.
  —Take the cap off the mouthpiece. Check the mouthpiece to make sure it is clear. Do not use the inhaler with any other mouthpieces.
  —Gently shake the inhaler three or four times.
  —Hold the mouthpiece away from your mouth and breathe out slowly and completely to the end of a normal breath.
  —Use the inhalation method recommended by your doctor.
    - Open-mouth method: Place the mouthpiece about 1 to 2 inches (2 fingerwidths) in front of your widely opened mouth. Make sure the inhaler is aimed into your mouth so the spray does not hit the roof of your mouth or your tongue. Avoid spraying in eyes.
    - Closed-mouth method: Place the mouthpiece in your mouth between your teeth and over your tongue with your lips closed tightly around it. Make sure your tongue or teeth are not blocking the opening.
  —Tilt your head back a little. Start to breathe in slowly through your mouth. At the same time, press the top of the canister once to get one puff of medicine. Continue to breathe in slowly for 3 to 4 seconds until you have taken a full deep breath. It is important to press down on the canister and breathe in slowly at the same time so the medicine gets into your lungs. This step may be difficult at first. If you are using the closed-mouth method and you see a fine mist coming from your mouth or nose, the inhaler is not being used correctly.
  —Hold your breath as long as you can up to 10 seconds (count slowly to ten). This gives the medicine time to settle into your airways and lungs.
  —Take the mouthpiece away from your mouth and breathe out slowly.
  —If your doctor has told you to inhale more than 1 puff of medicine at each dose, wait about 1 minute between puffs. Then, gently shake the inhaler again, and take the second puff following exactly the same steps you used for the first puff. Breathe in only one puff at a time.
  —When you are finished using the inhaler, wipe off the mouthpiece and replace the cap.
  —Keep track of the number of sprays you have used from the inhaler, and discard the inhaler after the labeled maximum number of sprays has been used.

Your doctor may want you to use a spacer device with the inhaler. A spacer makes the inhaler easier to use. It allows more of the medicine to reach your lungs, rather than staying in your mouth and throat.

- *To use a spacer device with the inhaler:*
  —Attach the spacer to the inhaler according to the manufacturer's directions. There are different types of spacers available, but the method of breathing remains the same with most spacers.
  —Gently shake the inhaler and spacer well.
  —Hold the mouthpiece of the spacer away from your mouth and breathe out slowly and completely.
  —Place the mouthpiece of the spacer into your mouth between your teeth and over your tongue with your lips closed around it.
  —Press down on the canister top once to release one puff of medicine into the spacer. Then, within 1 or 2 seconds, begin to breathe in slowly and deeply through your mouth for 5 to 10 seconds. Count the seconds while inhaling.
  —Hold your breath as long as you can up to 10 seconds (count slowly to 10).
  —Breathe out slowly.
  —Wait a minute between puffs. Then, gently shake the inhaler and spacer again and take the second puff, following exactly the same steps you used for the first puff. Do not spray more than one puff at a time into the spacer.
  —When you are finished using the inhaler, remove the spacer device from the inhaler and replace the cap.

Clean the inhaler, mouthpiece, and spacer at least once a week.
- *To clean the inhaler:*
  —Remove the canister from the inhaler and set the canister aside. Do not get the canister wet.
  —Wash the mouthpiece, cap, and the spacer in warm soapy water. Rinse well with warm, running water.
  —Shake off the excess water and let the inhaler parts air dry completely before putting the inhaler back together.

For patients using *cromolyn capsules for inhalation:*
- *Do not swallow the capsules. The medicine will not work if you swallow it.*
- This medicine is used with a special inhaler, either the *Spinhaler* or the *Halermatic.* If you do not understand the directions that come with the inhaler or if you are not sure how to use the inhaler, ask your health care professional to show you how to use it. Also, ask your health care professional to check regularly how you use the inhaler to make sure you are using it properly.
- If you are using *cromolyn capsules for inhalation* with the *Spinhaler:*
  —*To load the Spinhaler:*
    - Make sure your hands are clean and dry.
    - Insert the capsule into the inhaler just before using this medicine.
    - Hold the inhaler upright with the mouthpiece pointing down. Unscrew the body of the inhaler from the mouthpiece.
    - Keep the mouthpiece pointing down and the propeller on the spindle. Remove the foil from the capsule and insert the colored end of the cromolyn capsule firmly into the cup of the propeller. Avoid

too much handling of the capsule, because moisture from your hands may make the capsule soft.
- Make sure the propeller moves freely.
- Screw the body of the inhaler back into the mouthpiece and make certain that it is fastened well.
- While keeping the inhaler upright with the mouthpiece pointing down, slide the grey outer sleeve down firmly until it stops. This will puncture the capsule. Then slide the sleeve up as far as it will go. This step may be repeated a second time to make sure the capsule is punctured.

—*To use the Spinhaler:*
- Check to make sure the mouthpiece is properly attached to the body of the inhaler.
- Hold the inhaler away from your mouth and breathe out slowly to the end of a normal breath.
- Place the mouthpiece in your mouth, close your lips around it, and tilt your head back. Do not block the mouthpiece with your teeth or tongue.
- Take a deep and rapid breath. You should hear and feel the vibrations of the rotating propeller as you breathe in.
- Take the inhaler from your mouth and hold your breath for a few seconds or as long as possible.
- Hold the inhaler away from your mouth and breathe out slowly and completely to the end of a normal breath. Do not breathe out through the inhaler because this may prevent the inhaler from working properly.
- Keep taking inhalations of this medicine until all the powder from the capsule is inhaled. A light dusting of powder remaining in the capsule is normal and is not a sign that the inhaler is not working properly.
- Throw away the empty capsule. Then return the inhaler to the container and replace the lid on the container.

—*To clean the Spinhaler:*
- At least once a week, brush off any powder left sticking to the propeller.
- Take the inhaler apart and wash the parts of the inhaler with clean, warm water.
- Wash the inside of the propeller shaft by moving the propeller on and off the steel spindle under water.
- Shake out the excess water.
- Allow all parts of the inhaler to dry completely before putting it back together.
- The Spinhaler should be replaced after 6 months.

- If you are using *cromolyn capsules for inhalation* with the *Halermatic:*

  —*To load the Halermatic:*
  - Make sure your hands are clean and dry.
  - Insert the capsule cartridge into the inhaler just before using this medicine.
  - Remove the mouthpiece cover. Then pull off the mouthpiece.
  - Push a cromolyn capsule cartridge firmly down to the bottom of the slot.
  - Slide the mouthpiece back on the body of the inhaler. Push down slowly as far as the mouthpiece will go. This punctures the capsule cartridge and lifts it into the rotation chamber. Do not repeat this step because the capsule cartridge needs to be punctured only once.

—*To use the Halermatic:*
- Hold the inhaler away from your mouth and breathe out slowly to the end of a normal breath.
- Place the mouthpiece in your mouth, close your lips around it, and tilt your head back. Do not block the flow of medicine into the lungs with your teeth or tongue.
- Breathe in quickly and steadily through the mouthpiece.
- Hold your breath for a few seconds to keep the medicine in the lungs as long as possible. Then take the inhaler away from your mouth.
- Hold the inhaler well away from your mouth and breathe out to the end of a normal breath. Do not breathe out through the inhaler because this may prevent the inhaler from working properly.
- Keep taking inhalations of this medicine until all the powder from the capsule is inhaled. A light dusting of powder remaining in the capsule is normal and is not a sign that the inhaler is not working properly.
- Throw away the empty capsule cartridge.

—*To clean the Halermatic:*
- Brush away powder deposits each day with a brush.
- When powder deposits build up, wipe them away with a slightly damp cloth.
- The mouthpiece may be washed separately if necessary. However, do not wet the blue-based body of the inhaler. Be sure the mouthpiece grid is dry before putting the inhaler back together.
- The Halermatic should be replaced every 6 months.

For patients using *cromolyn inhalation solution:*
- Cromolyn inhalation solution comes in a small glass container called an ampul. The ampul must be broken gently to empty the contents. If you do not understand the manufacturer's directions, ask your health care professional to show you what to do.
- Do not use the solution in the ampul if it is cloudy or contains particles.
- *To break and empty the ampul:*
  —The glass ampul is weak at each end so the ends can be broken easily by hand.
  —Hold the ampul away from the nebulizer and your face when you break it. Hold the ampul at an angle and carefully break off the lower end. No solution will come out.
  —Turn the ampul over so the open end faces up. Place a forefinger carefully over the open end.
  —Keep your finger firmly in place and break off the lower end of the ampul.
  —To empty the ampul, hold it over the bowl of the nebulizer unit and remove your finger to let the solution flow out.
  —Throw away any solution left in the nebulizer after you have taken your treatment.
- Use this medicine only in a power-operated nebulizer that has an adequate flow rate and is equipped with a face mask or mouthpiece. Your doctor will advise you on which nebulizer to use. Make sure you understand exactly how to use it. Hand-squeezed bulb nebulizers cannot be used with this medicine. If you have any questions about this, check with your doctor.

For patients using *cromolyn oral inhalation* regularly (for example, every day):

- *In order for cromolyn to work properly, it must be inhaled every day in regularly spaced doses as ordered by your doctor.* Up to 4 weeks may pass before you feel the full effects of the medicine.

Dosing—The dose of cromolyn will be different for different patients. *Follow your doctor's orders or the directions on the label.* The following information includes only the average doses of cromolyn inhalation. *If your dose is different, do not change it* unless your doctor tells you to do so.

The number of doses you take each day, the time allowed between doses, and the length of time you take the medicine depend on the medical problem for which you are taking cromolyn inhalation.

- For *inhalation aerosol* dosage form:
  —For prevention of asthma symptoms:
  - Adults and children 5 years of age or older—2 inhalations (puffs) taken four times a day with doses spaced four to six hours apart.
  - Children up to 5 years of age—Cromolyn inhalation aerosol should not be used in children younger than 5 years of age.
  —For prevention of bronchospasm caused by exercise or a condition or substance:
  - Adults and children 5 years of age or older—2 inhalations (puffs) taken at least ten to fifteen (but not more than sixty) minutes before exercise or exposure to any condition or substance that may cause an attack.
  - Children up to 5 years of age—Cromolyn inhalation aerosol should not be used in children younger than 5 years of age.

- For *capsule for inhalation* dosage form:
  —For prevention of asthma symptoms:
  - Adults and children 2 years of age or older—20 mg (contents of 1 capsule) used in an inhaler, taken four times a day with doses spaced four to six hours apart.
  - Children up to 2 years of age—The capsule for inhalation should not be used in children younger than 2 years of age.
  —For prevention of bronchospasm caused by exercise or a condition or substance:
  - Adults and children 2 years of age or older—20 mg (contents of 1 capsule) used in an inhaler, taken at least ten to fifteen (but not more than sixty) minutes before exercise or exposure to any condition or substance that may cause an attack.
  - Children up to 2 years of age—The capsule for inhalation should not be used in children younger than 2 years of age.

- For *inhalation solution* dosage form:
  —For prevention of asthma symptoms:
  - Adults and children 2 years of age or older—20 mg (contents of 1 ampul) used in a nebulizer. This medicine should be used four times a day with doses spaced four to six hours apart. Use a new ampul of solution for each dose.
  - Children up to 2 years of age—Cromolyn inhalation solution should not be used in children younger than 2 years of age.

  —For prevention of bronchospasm caused by exercise or a condition or substance:
  - Adults and children 2 years of age or older—20 mg (contents of 1 ampul) used in a nebulizer. This medicine should be used at least ten to fifteen (but not more than sixty) minutes before exercise or exposure to any condition or substance that may cause an attack. Use a new ampul of solution for each dose.
  - Children up to 2 years of age—Cromolyn inhalation solution should not be used in children younger than 2 years of age.

Missed dose—If you are using cromolyn regularly and you miss a dose, use it as soon as possible. Then use any remaining doses for that day at regularly spaced times.

Storage—To store this medicine:

- Keep out of the reach of children.
- Store the aerosol or solution form of this medicine at room temperature away from heat or cold. Keep this medicine from freezing.
- Store the capsule or solution form of this medicine away from direct light. Store the aerosol form of this medicine away from direct sunlight.
- Do not store the capsule form of this medicine in the bathroom, near the kitchen sink, or in other damp places. Heat or moisture may cause the medicine to break down.
- Do not puncture, break, or burn the aerosol container, even if it is empty.
- Do not keep outdated medicine or medicine no longer needed. Be sure that any discarded medicine is out of the reach of children.

Precautions While Using This Medicine

If your symptoms do not improve within 4 weeks or if your condition becomes worse after you begin using cromolyn, check with your doctor.

If you are also taking a corticosteroid or a bronchodilator for your asthma along with this medicine, do not stop taking the corticosteroid or bronchodilator even if your asthma seems better, unless you are told to do so by your doctor.

Dryness of the mouth or throat or irritation of the throat may occur after you use this medicine. Gargling and rinsing your mouth or taking a drink of water after each dose may help prevent these effects.

Side Effects of This Medicine

Along with its needed effects, a medicine may cause some unwanted effects. Although not all of these side effects may occur, if they do occur they may need medical attention.

Check with your doctor as soon as possible if any of the following side effects occur:
Rare
   Difficulty in swallowing; hives; increased wheezing or difficulty in breathing; itching of skin; low blood pressure; shortness of breath; swelling of face, lips, or eyelids; tightness in chest

Other side effects may occur that usually do not need medical attention. These side effects may go away during treatment as your body adjusts to the medicine. However, check with

your doctor if any of the following side effects continue or are bothersome:

More common
Coughing; nausea; throat irritation or dryness

If you are using the cromolyn inhalation aerosol, you may notice an unpleasant taste. This may be expected and will go away when you stop using the medicine.

Other side effects not listed above may also occur in some patients. If you notice any other effects, check with your doctor.

Revised: 5/18/99

CROMOLYN   Nasal

Commonly used brand name(s):

In the U.S.—
Children's Nasalcrom
Nasalcrom

In Canada—
Apo-Cromolyn
Cromolyn Nasal Solution
Gen-Cromoglycate

Another commonly used name is sodium cromoglycate.

Description

Cromolyn (KROE-moe-lin) nasal solution is used to help prevent or treat the symptoms (sneezing, wheezing, runny nose, itching) of seasonal (short-term) or chronic (long-term) allergic rhinitis. Cromolyn powder for nasal inhalation is used to help prevent seasonal (short-term) allergic rhinitis.

This medicine works by acting on certain cells in the body, called mast cells, to prevent them from releasing substances that cause the allergic reaction.

When cromolyn is used to treat chronic (long-term) allergic rhinitis, an antihistamine and/or a nasal decongestant may be used with this medicine, especially during the first few weeks of treatment.

Nasal cromolyn is available without a prescription in the U.S., however, in Canada, it requires a prescription from your doctor. It is available in the following dosage forms:

Nasal
• Nasal solution (U.S. and Canada)

Before Using This Medicine

In deciding to use a medicine, the risks of using the medicine must be weighed against the good it will do. This is a decision you and your doctor will make. For nasal cromolyn, the following should be considered:

Allergies—Tell your doctor if you have ever had any unusual or allergic reaction to cromolyn. Also tell your health care professional if you are allergic to any other substances, such as foods, preservatives, or dyes.

Pregnancy—Nasal cromolyn has not been shown to cause birth defects in humans. However, studies in animals have shown that cromolyn, when given by injection in very large amounts, causes a decrease in successful pregnancies and a decrease in the weight of the animal fetus. Before using this medicine, make sure your doctor knows if you are pregnant or if you may become pregnant.

Breast-feeding—It is not known whether cromolyn passes into the breast milk. Although most medicines pass into breast milk in small amounts, many of them may be used safely while breast-feeding. Mothers who are using this medicine and who wish to breast-feed should discuss this with their doctor.

Children—Studies on this medicine have been done only in adult patients, and there is no specific information comparing use of nasal cromolyn in children up to 6 years of age (in Canada, up to 5 years of age) with use in other age groups. In older children, this medicine is not expected to cause different side effects or problems than it does in adults.

Older adults—Many medicines have not been studied specifically in older people. Therefore, it may not be known whether they work exactly the same way they do in younger adults. Although there is no specific information comparing use of nasal cromolyn in the elderly with use in other age groups, this medicine is not expected to cause different side effects or problems in older people than it does in younger adults.

Other medicines—Although certain medicines should not be used together at all, in other cases two different medicines may be used together even if an interaction might occur. In these cases, your doctor may want to change the dose, or other precautions may be necessary. When you are taking nasal cromolyn, it is especially important that your doctor and pharmacist know if you are taking any other prescription or nonprescription (over-the-counter [OTC]) medicine.

Other medical problems—The presence of other medical problems may affect the use of nasal cromolyn. Make sure you tell your doctor if you have any other medical problems, especially:
• Kidney disease or
• Liver disease—Diseases of these body systems may alter the concentration of nasal cromolyn in the body
• Polyps or growths inside the nose—Cromolyn may not work if nasal passages are blocked

Proper Use of This Medicine

This medicine usually comes with patient directions. Read them carefully before using the medicine.

Before using this medicine, clear the nasal passages by blowing your nose.

To use:
• Cromolyn solution is used with a special spray device.
• To keep clean, wipe the nosepiece with a clean tissue and replace the dust cap after use.
• To avoid spreading an infection, do not use the container for more than one person.

Use this medicine only as directed. Do not use more of it and do not use it more often than your doctor ordered. To do so may increase the chance of side effects.

In order for this medicine to work properly, it must be used every day in regularly spaced doses as ordered by your doctor:
• For patients using cromolyn for *seasonal (short-term) allergic rhinitis*, up to 1 week may pass before you begin to feel better.

© 2002 MICROMEDEX Thomson Healthcare

• For patients using cromolyn for *chronic (long-term) allergic rhinitis*, up to 2 to 4 weeks may pass before you feel the full effects of this medicine, although you may begin to feel better after 1 week.

Dosing—The dose of nasal cromolyn will be different for different patients. *Follow your doctor's orders or the directions on the label.* The following information includes only the average doses of nasal cromolyn. *If your dose is different, do not change it* unless your doctor tells you to do so.

- For *nasal solution* dosage form:
  —For allergic rhinitis:
  • Adults and children 6 years of age (in Canada, 5 years of age) and older—One spray into each nostril three to six times a day until condition is better; then, one spray in each nostril every eight to twelve hours.
  • Children up to 6 years of age (in Canada, up to 5 years of age)—Use and dose must be determined by your doctor.

Missed dose—If you miss a dose of this medicine, use it as soon as possible. Then use any remaining doses for that day at regularly spaced intervals. Do not double doses.

Storage—To store this medicine:
- Keep out of the reach of children.
- Store away from heat and direct light.
- Keep the solution from freezing.
- Do not keep outdated medicine or medicine no longer needed. Be sure that any discarded medicine is out of the reach of children.

Precautions While Using This Medicine

If your symptoms do not improve or if your condition becomes worse, check with your doctor.

Side Effects of This Medicine

Along with its needed effects, a medicine may cause some unwanted effects. Although not all of these side effects may occur, if they do occur they may need medical attention.

Check with your doctor as soon as possible if any of the following side effects occur:

Rare
Allergic reaction (coughing; difficulty in swallowing; hives or itching; swelling of face, lips, or eyelids; wheezing or difficulty in breathing); nosebleeds; skin rash

Other side effects may occur that usually do not need medical attention. These side effects may go away during treatment as your body adjusts to the medicine. However, check with your doctor if any of the following side effects continue or are bothersome:

More common
Burning, stinging, or irritation inside of nose; flushing; increase in sneezing

Less common
Cough; headache; postnasal drip; unpleasant taste

Other side effects not listed above may also occur in some patients. If you notice any other effects, check with your doctor.

Revised: 6/04/99

CROMOLYN   Ophthalmic

Commonly used brand name(s):

In the U.S.—
Crolom

In Canada—
Opticrom
Vistacrom

Other commonly used names are cromoglicic acid, cromoglycic acid, and sodium cromoglycate.

Description

Cromolyn (KROE-moe-lin) ophthalmic solution is used in the eye to treat certain disorders of the eye caused by allergies. It works by acting on certain cells, called mast cells, to prevent them from releasing substances that cause the allergic reaction.

Cromolyn is available only with your doctor's prescription, in the following dosage form:

Ophthalmic
• Ophthalmic solution (eye drops) (U.S. and Canada)

Before Using This Medicine

In deciding to use a medicine, the risks of using the medicine must be weighed against the good it will do. This is a decision you and your doctor will make. For ophthalmic cromolyn, the following should be considered:

Allergies—Tell your doctor if you have ever had any unusual or allergic reaction to cromolyn. Also tell your health care professional if you are allergic to any other substances, such as foods, preservatives, or dyes.

Pregnancy—Cromolyn has not been studied in pregnant women. Studies in animals have shown that cromolyn causes a decrease in successful pregnancies and a decrease in the weight of the animal fetus when given by injection in very large amounts. However, it is unlikely that ophthalmic cromolyn will cause problems in humans when used in the eye as directed.

Breast-feeding—It is not known whether cromolyn passes into the breast milk. Although most medicines pass into breast milk in small amounts, many of them may be used safely while breast-feeding. Mothers who are taking this medicine and who wish to breast-feed should discuss this with their doctor.

Children—Studies on this medicine have been done only in adult patients, and there is no specific information comparing use of cromolyn in children up to 4 years of age with use in other age groups. For older children, this medicine is not expected to cause different side effects or problems than it does in adults.

Older adults—Many medicines have not been studied specifically in older people. Therefore, it may not be known whether they work exactly the same way they do in younger adults. Although there is no specific information comparing use of ophthalmic cromolyn in the elderly with use in other age groups, this medicine is not expected to cause different side effects or problems in older people than it does in younger adults.

Proper Use of This Medicine

To use the *eye drops:*

- First, wash your hands. Tilt the head back and, pressing your finger gently on the skin just beneath the lower eyelid, pull the lower eyelid away from the eye to make a space. Drop the medicine into this space. Let go of the eyelid and gently close the eyes. Do not blink. Keep the eyes closed for 1 or 2 minutes to allow the medicine to be absorbed by the eye.
- If you think you did not get the drop of medicine into your eye properly, use another drop.
- To keep the medicine as germ-free as possible, do not touch the applicator tip to any surface (including the eye). Also, keep the container tightly closed.

Use cromolyn eye drops only as directed. Do not use more of this medicine and do not use it more often than your doctor ordered. To do so may increase the chance of side effects.

In order for this medicine to work properly, it must be used every day in regularly spaced doses as ordered by your doctor. A few days may pass before you begin to feel better. However, in some conditions, it may take several weeks before you begin to feel better.

Dosing—The dose of ophthalmic cromolyn will be different for different patients. *Follow your doctor's orders or the directions on the label.* The following information includes only the average doses of ophthalmic cromolyn. *If your dose is different, do not change it* unless your doctor tells you to do so.

- For *ophthalmic solution (eye drops)* dosage form:
  —For eye allergies:
  - Adults and children 4 years of age and older— Use one or two drops four to six times a day in regularly spaced doses.
  - Children up to 4 years of age—Use and dose must be determined by your doctor.

Missed dose—If you miss a dose of this medicine, use it as soon as possible. Then go back to your regular dosing schedule.

Storage—To store this medicine:

- Keep out of the reach of children.
- Store away from heat and direct light.
- Keep the medicine from freezing.
- Do not keep outdated medicine or medicine no longer needed. Be sure that any discarded medicine is out of the reach of children.

Precautions While Using This Medicine

If your symptoms do not improve or if your condition becomes worse, check with your doctor.

Side Effects of This Medicine

Along with its needed effects, a medicine may cause some unwanted effects. Although not all of these side effects may occur, if they do occur they may need medical attention.

Check with your doctor as soon as possible if any of the following side effects occur:

Rare

Rash or redness around the eyes; swelling of the membrane covering the white part of the eye, redness of the white part of the eye, styes, or other eye irritation not present before therapy

Other side effects may occur that usually do not need medical attention. These side effects may go away during treatment as your body adjusts to the medicine. However, check with your doctor if any of the following side effects continue or are bothersome:

More common

Burning or stinging of eye (mild and temporary)

Less common or rare

Dryness or puffiness around the eye; watering or itching of eye (increased)

Other side effects not listed above may also occur in some patients. If you notice any other effects, check with your doctor.

Revised: 04/19/94
Interim revision: 07/10/95

CROMOLYN   Oral

Commonly used brand name(s):

In the U.S.—
Gastrocrom

In Canada—
Nalcrom

Another commonly used name is sodium cromoglycate.

Description

Cromolyn (KROE-moe-lin) is used to treat the symptoms of mastocytosis. Mastocytosis is a rare condition caused by too many mast cells in the body. These mast cells release substances that cause the symptoms of the disease, such as abdominal pain, nausea, vomiting, diarrhea, headache, flushing or itching of skin, or hives.

Cromolyn works by acting on the mast cells in the body to prevent them from releasing substances that cause the symptoms of mastocytosis.

Cromolyn is available only with your doctor's prescription, in the following dosage form:

Oral

- Capsules (U.S. and Canada)
- Ampuls (U.S.)

Before Using This Medicine

In deciding to use a medicine, the risks of taking the medicine must be weighed against the good it will do. This is a decision you and your doctor will make. For oral cromolyn, the following should be considered:

Allergies—Tell your doctor if you have ever had any unusual or allergic reaction to cromolyn. Also tell your health care professional if you are allergic to any other substances, such as foods, preservatives, or dyes.

Diet—Make certain your health care professional knows if you are on any special diet, such as a low-sodium diet. This medicine contains sodium.

Pregnancy—Cromolyn has not been studied in pregnant women. However, studies in animals have shown that cromolyn, when given by injection in very large amounts, causes a decrease in successful pregnancies and a decrease in the weight of the animal fetus. Before using this medicine, make sure your doctor knows if you are pregnant or if you may become pregnant.

Breast-feeding—It is not known whether cromolyn passes into the breast milk. Although most medicines pass into breast milk in small amounts, many of them may be used safely while breast-feeding. Mothers who are taking this medicine and who wish to breast-feed should discuss this with their doctor.

Children—Although there is no specific information comparing use of oral cromolyn in children with use in other age groups, this medicine is not expected to cause different side effects or problems in children than it does in adults. This medicine is usually used in children two years of age and older. However, it may be used in children younger than two years of age if their disease is severe.

Older adults—Many medicines have not been studied specifically in older people. Therefore, it may not be known whether they work exactly the same way they do in younger adults. Although there is no specific information comparing use of oral cromolyn in the elderly with use in other age groups, this medicine is not expected to cause different side effects or problems in older people than it does in younger adults.

Other medicines—Although certain medicines should not be used together at all, in other cases two different medicines may be used together even if an interaction might occur. In these cases, your doctor may want to change the dose, or other precautions may be necessary. Tell your health care professional if you are taking any other prescription or nonprescription (over-the-counter [OTC]) medicine.

Other medical problems—The presence of other medical problems may affect the use of oral cromolyn. Make sure you tell your doctor if you have any other medical problems, especially:
- Kidney disease or
- Liver disease—The effects of cromolyn may be increased, which may increase the chance of side effects

---

Proper Use of This Medicine

Unless otherwise directed by your doctor, it is best to take oral cromolyn as follows:

Capsules
- Open the cromolyn capsule(s) and pour all of the powder into one-half glass (4 ounces) of hot water. Stir the solution until the powder is completely dissolved and the solution is clear. Then add an equal amount (one-half glass) of cold water to the solution while stirring.
- Be sure to drink all of the liquid to get the full dose of medicine.
- Do not mix this medicine with fruit juice, milk, or food because they may keep the medicine from working properly.
- It is important to take this medicine at regular intervals for best results.

Ampuls
- Break open the ampul(s) and squeeze contents into a glass of water and stir well.
- Be sure to drink all of the liquid to get the full dose of medicine.
- It is important to take this medicine at regular intervals for best results.

- Do not use the ampul if it appears cloudy or discolored.

Take cromolyn only as directed. Do not take more of it and do not take it more often than your doctor ordered. To do so may increase the chance of side effects.

Dosing—The dose of cromolyn will be different for different patients. *Follow your doctor's orders or the directions on the label.* The following information includes only the average doses of cromolyn. *If your dose is different, do not change it* unless your doctor tells you to do so.
- For *oral* dosage form (capsules and ampuls):
  —For symptoms of mastocytosis:
  - Adults and children 12 years of age and older— 200 milligrams (mg) dissolved or mixed in water and taken four times a day, thirty minutes before meals and at bedtime.
  - Children 2 to 12 years of age—100 mg dissolved or mixed in water and taken four times a day, thirty minutes before meals and at bedtime. Your doctor may increase the dose if your symptoms are not under control within two to three weeks after you begin taking this medicine.
  - Infants and children up to 2 years of age—Dose is based on body weight and must be determined by your doctor. The dose is usually 20 mg per kilogram (kg) (9.1 mg per pound) of body weight a day. This dose is divided into four doses. Your doctor may increase the dose if your symptoms are not under control within two to three weeks after you begin taking this medicine.
  - Premature infants—Use is not recommended.

Missed dose—If you miss a dose of this medicine, take it as soon as possible. Then take any remaining doses for that day at regularly spaced times.

Storage—To store this medicine:
- Keep out of the reach of children.
- Store away from heat and light, in a tightly closed container.
- Do not store the capsule form of this medicine in the bathroom, near the kitchen sink, or in other damp places. Heat or moisture may cause the medicine to break down.
- Do not keep outdated medicine or medicine no longer needed. Be sure that any discarded medicine is out of the reach of children.
- Store ampuls in their foil pouch until you are ready to use them.

Precautions While Using This Medicine

If your symptoms do not improve or if your condition becomes worse, check with your doctor.

Side Effects of This Medicine

Along with its needed effects, a medicine may cause some unwanted effects. Although not all of these side effects may occur, if they do occur they may need medical attention.

Check with your doctor immediately if any of the following side effects occur:
Rare
  Coughing; difficulty in swallowing; hives or itching of skin; swelling of face, lips, or eyelids; wheezing or difficulty in breathing

Also, check with your doctor as soon as possible if the following side effect occurs:

Less common
Skin rash

Other side effects may occur that usually do not need medical attention. These side effects may go away during treatment as your body adjusts to the medicine. However, check with your doctor if any of the following side effects continue or are bothersome:

More common
Diarrhea; headache

Less common
Abdominal pain; irritability; muscle pain; nausea; trouble in sleeping

Note: If the above side effects occur in patients with mastocytosis, they are usually only temporary and could be symptoms of the disease.

Other side effects not listed above may also occur in some patients. If you notice any other effects, check with your doctor.

Revised: 08/14/98

CYCLANDELATE   Systemic*

A commonly used brand name is—
Cyclospasmol

* Not commercially available in the U.S.

Description

Cyclandelate (sye-KLAN-de-late) belongs to the group of medicines commonly called vasodilators. These medicines increase the size of blood vessels. Cyclandelate is used to treat problems resulting from poor blood circulation.

Cyclandelate is available in the following dosage form:

Oral
• Tablets (Canada)

Before Using This Medicine

In deciding to use a medicine, the risks of taking the medicine must be weighed against the good it will do. This is a decision you and your doctor will make. For cyclandelate, the following should be considered:

Allergies—Tell your doctor if you have ever had any unusual or allergic reaction to cyclandelate. Also tell your health care professional if you are allergic to any other substances, such as foods, preservatives, or dyes.

Pregnancy—Studies on effects in pregnancy have not been done in either humans or animals.

Breast-feeding—It is not known whether cyclandelate passes into breast milk. However, cyclandelate has not been reported to cause problems in nursing babies.

Children—Studies on this medicine have been done only in adult patients, and there is no specific information comparing use of cyclandelate in children with use in other age groups.

Older adults—Many medicines have not been studied specifically in older people. Therefore, it may not be known whether they work exactly the same way they do in younger

adults. Although there is no specific information comparing use of cyclandelate in the elderly with use in other age groups, this medicine is not expected to cause different side effects or problems in older people than in younger adults.

Other medicines—Although certain medicines should not be used together at all, in other cases two different medicines may be used together even if an interaction might occur. In these cases, your doctor may want to change the dose, or other precautions may be necessary. Tell your health care professional if you are taking any other prescription or nonprescription (over-the-counter [OTC]) medicine, or if you smoke.

Other medical problems—The presence of other medical problems may affect the use of cyclandelate. Make sure you tell your doctor if you have any other medical problems, especially:

• Angina (chest pain) or
• Bleeding problems or
• Glaucoma or
• Hardening of the arteries or
• Heart attack (recent) or
• Stroke (recent)—The chance of unwanted effects may be increased

Proper Use of This Medicine

If this medicine upsets your stomach, it may be taken with meals, milk, or antacids.

Dosing—The dose of cyclandelate will be different for different patients. *Follow your doctor's orders or the directions on the label.* The following information includes only the average doses of cyclandelate. *If your dose is different, do not change it* unless your doctor tells you to do so.

The number of tablets that you take depends on the strength of the medicine.

• For *oral* dosage form (tablets):
  —For treating poor circulation:
  • Adults—At first, 1.2 to 1.6 grams a day. This is taken in divided doses before meals and at bedtime. Then, your doctor will gradually lower your dose to 400 to 800 milligrams (mg) a day. This is divided into two to four doses.
  • Children—Use and dose must be determined by your doctor.

Missed dose—If you miss a dose of this medicine, take it as soon as you remember. Then go back to your regular dosing schedule. However, if it is almost time for your next dose, skip the missed dose and go back to your regular dosing schedule. Do not double doses.

Storage—To store this medicine:
• Keep out of the reach of children.
• Store away from heat and direct light.
• Do not store in the bathroom, near the kitchen sink, or in other damp places. Heat or moisture may cause the medicine to break down.
• Do not keep outdated medicine or medicine no longer needed. Be sure that any discarded medicine is out of the reach of children.

Precautions While Using This Medicine

It may take some time for this medicine to work. If you feel that the medicine is not working, do not stop taking it on your own. Instead, check with your doctor.

The helpful effects of this medicine may be decreased if you smoke.

Dizziness may occur, especially when you get up from a lying or sitting position or climb stairs. Getting up slowly may help. If this problem continues or gets worse, check with your doctor.

Side Effects of This Medicine

Along with its needed effects, a medicine may cause some unwanted effects. The following side effects may go away during treatment as your body adjusts to the medicine. However, check with your doctor if any of these effects continue or are bothersome:

Less common
 Belching, heartburn, nausea, or stomach pain; dizziness; fast heartbeat; flushing of face; headache; sweating; tingling sensation in face, fingers, or toes; weakness

Other side effects not listed above may also occur in some patients. If you notice any other effects, check with your doctor.

Revised: 10/15/92
Interim revision: 04/14/94; 08/18/97

CYCLOBENZAPRINE   Systemic

Commonly used brand name(s):

In the U.S.—
 Flexeril
 Generic name product may be available.

In Canada—
 Flexeril

Description

Cyclobenzaprine (sye-kloe-BEN-za-preen) is used to help relax certain muscles in your body. It helps relieve the pain, stiffness, and discomfort caused by strains, sprains, or injuries to your muscles. However, this medicine does not take the place of rest, exercise or physical therapy, or other treatment that your doctor may recommend for your medical problem. Cyclobenzaprine acts on the central nervous system (CNS) to produce its muscle relaxant effects. Its actions on the CNS may also cause some of this medicine's side effects.

Cyclobenzaprine may also be used for other conditions as determined by your doctor.

Cyclobenzaprine is available only with your doctor's prescription, in the following dosage form:

Oral
 • Tablets (U.S. and Canada)

Before Using This Medicine

In deciding to use a medicine, the risks of taking the medicine must be weighed against the good it will do. This is a decision you and your doctor will make. For cyclobenzaprine, the following should be considered:

Allergies—Tell your doctor if you have ever had any unusual or allergic reaction to cyclobenzaprine. Also tell your health care professional if you are allergic to any other substances, such as foods, preservatives, or dyes.

Pregnancy—Studies on birth defects with cyclobenzaprine have not been done in humans. However, cyclobenzaprine has not been shown to cause birth defects or other problems in animal studies.

Breast-feeding—It is not known whether cyclobenzaprine passes into breast milk. Although most medicines pass into the breast milk in small amounts, many of them may be used safely while breast-feeding. Mothers who are taking this medicine and who wish to breast-feed should discuss this with their doctor.

Children—Studies on this medicine have been done only in adult patients, and there is no specific information comparing use of cyclobenzaprine in children with use in other age groups.

Teenagers—Studies on this medicine have been done only in adult patients, and there is no specific information comparing use of cyclobenzaprine in teenagers up to 15 years of age with use in other age groups.

Older adults—Many medicines have not been studied specifically in older people. Therefore, it may not be known whether they work exactly the same way they do in younger adults or if they cause different side effects or problems in older people. There is no specific information comparing use of cyclobenzaprine in the elderly with use in other age groups.

Other medicines—Although certain medicines should not be used together at all, in other cases two different medicines may be used together even if an interaction might occur. In these cases, your doctor may want to change the dose, or other precautions may be necessary. When you are taking cyclobenzaprine, it is especially important that your health care professional know if you are taking any of the following:

• Alcohol or
• Central nervous system (CNS) depressants (medicines that cause drowsiness) or
• Tricyclic antidepressants (amitriptyline [e.g., Elavil], amoxapine [e.g., Asendin], clomipramine [e.g., Anafranil], desipramine [e.g., Pertofrane], doxepin [e.g., Sinequan], imipramine [e.g., Tofranil], nortriptyline [e.g., Aventyl], protriptyline [e.g., Vivactil], trimipramine [e.g., Surmontil])—The chance of side effects may be increased

• Monoamine oxidase (MAO) inhibitors (furazolidone [e.g., Furoxone], phenelzine [e.g., Nardil], procarbazine [e.g., Matulane], selegiline (e.g., Eldepryl), tranylcypromine [e.g., Parnate])—Taking cyclobenzaprine while you are taking or within 2 weeks of taking MAO inhibitors may increase the chance of side effects

Other medical problems—The presence of other medical problems may affect the use of cyclobenzaprine. Make sure you tell your doctor if you have any other medical problems, especially:

• Glaucoma or
• Problems with urination—Cyclobenzaprine can make your condition worse

- Heart or blood vessel disease or
- Overactive thyroid—The chance of side effects may be increased

Proper Use of This Medicine

Take this medicine only as directed by your doctor. Do not take more of it and do not take it more often than your doctor ordered. To do so may increase the chance of serious side effects.

Dosing—The dose of cyclobenzaprine will be different for different people. *Follow your doctor's orders or the directions on the label.* The following information includes only the average doses of cyclobenzaprine. *If your dose is different, do not change it* unless your doctor tells you to do so.

- For the *oral* dosage form (tablets):
  —For relaxing stiff muscles:
  - Adults and teenagers 15 years of age and older— The usual dose is 10 milligrams (mg) three times a day. The largest amount should be no more than 60 mg (six 10-mg tablets) a day.
  - Children and teenagers up to 15 years of age— Dose must be determined by your doctor.

Missed dose—If you miss a dose of this medicine and remember within an hour or so of the missed dose, take it right away. Then go back to your regular dosing schedule. But if you do not remember until later, skip the missed dose and go back to your regular dosing schedule. Do not double doses.

Storage—To store this medicine:
- Keep out of the reach of children.
- Store away from heat and direct light.
- Do not store this medicine in the bathroom, near the kitchen sink, or in other damp places. Heat or moisture may cause the medicine to break down.
- Do not keep outdated medicine or medicine no longer needed. Be sure that any discarded medicine is out of the reach of children.

Precautions While Using This Medicine

This medicine will add to the effects of alcohol and other CNS depressants (medicines that slow down the nervous system, possibly causing drowsiness). Some examples of CNS depressants are antihistamines or medicine for hay fever, other allergies, or colds; sedatives, tranquilizers, or sleeping medicine; prescription pain medicine or narcotics; barbiturates; medicine for seizures; other muscle relaxants; or anesthetics, including some dental anesthetics. *Check with your doctor before taking any of the above while you are using this medicine.*

This medicine may cause some people to have blurred vision or to become drowsy, dizzy, or less alert than they are normally. *Make sure you know how you react to this medicine before you drive, use machines, or do anything else that could be dangerous if you are dizzy or are not alert and able to see well.*

Cyclobenzaprine may cause dryness of the mouth. For temporary relief, use sugarless candy or gum, melt bits of ice in your mouth, or use a saliva substitute. However, if your mouth continues to feel dry for more than 2 weeks, check with your medical doctor or dentist. Continuing dryness of the mouth may increase the chance of dental disease, including tooth decay, gum disease, and fungus infections.

Side Effects of This Medicine

Along with its needed effects, a medicine may cause some unwanted effects. Although not all of these side effects may occur, if they do occur they may need medical attention.

The following side effects may mean that you are having a serious allergic reaction to the medicine. *Get emergency help right away if any of them occur:*
  Rare
    Changes in the skin color of the face; fast or irregular breathing; large swellings that look like hives on the face, eyelids, mouth, lips, and/or tongue; puffiness or swelling of the eyelids or the area around the eyes; shortness of breath, troubled breathing, tightness in chest, and/or wheezing; skin rash, hives, or itching

Also, check with your doctor immediately if any of the following side effects occur:
  Rare
    Fainting
  Symptoms of overdose
    Convulsions (seizures); drowsiness (severe); dry, hot, flushed skin; fast or irregular heartbeat; hallucinations (seeing, hearing, or feeling things that are not there); increase or decrease in body temperature; troubled breathing; unexplained muscle stiffness; unusual nervousness or restlessness (severe); vomiting (occurring together with other symptoms of overdose)

Also, check with your doctor as soon as possible if any of the following side effects occur:
  Rare
    Clumsiness or unsteadiness; confusion; mental depression or other mood or mental changes; problems in urinating; ringing or buzzing in the ears; skin rash, hives, or itching occurring without other symptoms of an allergic reaction listed above; unusual thoughts or dreams; yellow eyes or skin

Other side effects may occur that usually do not need medical attention. These side effects may go away during treatment as your body adjusts to the medicine. However, check with your doctor if any of the following side effects continue or are bothersome:
  More common
    Blurred vision; dizziness or lightheadedness; drowsiness; dryness of mouth
  Less common or rare
    Bloated feeling or gas, indigestion, nausea or vomiting, or stomach cramps or pain; constipation; diarrhea; excitement or nervousness; frequent urination; general feeling of discomfort or illness; headache; muscle twitching; numbness, tingling, pain, or weakness in hands or feet; pounding heartbeat; problems in speaking; trembling; trouble in sleeping; unpleasant taste or other taste changes; unusual muscle weakness; unusual tiredness

Other side effects not listed above may also occur in some patients. If you notice any other effects, check with your doctor.

Additional Information

Once a medicine has been approved for marketing for a certain use, experience may show that it is also useful for other medical problems. Although this use is not included in product labeling, cyclobenzaprine is used in certain patients with fibromyalgia syndrome (also called fibrositis or fibrositis syndrome).

There is no additional information relating to proper use, precautions, or side effects for this use of cyclobenzaprine.

Revised: 06/03/99

CYCLOPENTOLATE   Ophthalmic

Commonly used brand name(s):

In the U.S.—

Ak-Pentolate	Ocu-Pentolate
Cyclogyl	Pentolair
Cylate	

Generic name product may be available.

In Canada—

Ak-Pentolate	Cyclogyl
Diopentolate	Minims Cyclopentolate

Description

Cyclopentolate (sye-kloe-PEN-toe-late) is used to dilate (enlarge) the pupil. It is used before eye examinations (such as cycloplegic refraction or ophthalmoscopy).

This medicine is available only with your doctor's prescription, in the following dosage form:

Ophthalmic
- Ophthalmic solution (eye drops) (U.S. and Canada)

Before Using This Medicine

In deciding to use a medicine, the risks of using the medicine must be weighed against the good it will do. This is a decision you and your doctor will make. For cyclopentolate, the following should be considered:

Allergies—Tell your doctor if you have ever had any unusual or allergic reaction to cyclopentolate. Also tell your health care professional if you are allergic to any other substances, such as preservatives.

Pregnancy—Cyclopentolate may be absorbed into the body. However, studies on effects in pregnancy have not been done in either humans or animals.

Breast-feeding—Cyclopentolate may be absorbed into the mother's body. It is not known whether cyclopentolate passes into the breast milk. However, cyclopentolate has not been reported to cause problems in nursing babies.

Children—Infants and young children and children with blond hair or blue eyes may be especially sensitive to the effects of cyclopentolate. This may increase the chance of side effects during treatment.

Older adults—Elderly people are especially sensitive to the effects of cyclopentolate. This may increase the chance of side effects during treatment.

Other medicines—Although certain medicines should not be used together at all, in other cases two different medicines may be used together even if an interaction might occur. In these cases, your doctor may want to change the dose, or other precautions may be necessary. Tell your health care professional if you are using any other prescription or nonprescription (over-the-counter [OTC]) medicine.

Other medical problems—The presence of other medical problems may affect the use of cyclopentolate. Make sure you tell your doctor if you have any other medical problems, especially:

- Brain damage (in children) or
- Down's syndrome (mongolism) (in children and adults) or
- Glaucoma or
- Spastic paralysis (in children)—Cyclopentolate may make the condition worse

Proper Use of This Medicine

To use:
- First, wash your hands. Tilt the head back and with the index finger of one hand, press gently on the skin just beneath the lower eyelid and pull the lower eyelid away from the eye to make a space. Drop the medicine into this space. Let go of the eyelid and gently close the eyes. Do not blink. Keep the eyes closed and apply pressure to the inner corner of the eye with your finger for 2 or 3 minutes, to allow the medicine to be absorbed. *This is especially important in infants.*
- Immediately after using the eye drops, wash your hands to remove any medicine that may be on them. If you are using the eye drops for an infant or child, be sure to wash the infant's or child's hands also, and do not let any of the medicine get in the infant's or child's mouth.
- To keep the medicine as germ-free as possible, do not touch the applicator tip to any surface (including the eye). Also, keep the container tightly closed.

Use this medicine only as directed. Do not use more of it and do not use it more often than your doctor ordered. To do so may increase the chance of too much medicine being absorbed into the body and the chance of side effects.

Dosing—The dose of cyclopentolate will be different for different patients. *Follow your doctor's orders or the directions on the label.* The following information includes only the average doses of cyclopentolate. *If your dose is different, do not change it unless your doctor tells you to do so.*

- For *ophthalmic solution (eye drops)* dosage form:
  —For eye examinations:
    - Adults—One drop 40 to 50 minutes before the exam. Dose may be repeated in five to ten minutes.
    - Children—One drop 40 to 50 minutes before the exam. After five to ten minutes, another drop may be used.
    - Babies—One drop of 0.5% solution.

Missed dose—If you miss a dose of this medicine, apply it as soon as possible. However, if it is almost time for your next dose, skip the missed dose and go back to your regular dosing schedule. Do not double doses.

Storage—To store this medicine:
- Keep out of the reach of children. Overdose of this medicine is very dangerous for infants and children.

- Store away from heat and direct light.
- Keep the medicine from freezing.
- Do not keep outdated medicine or medicine no longer needed. Be sure that any discarded medicine is out of the reach of children.

Precautions While Using This Medicine

After you apply this medicine to your eyes:

- Your pupils will become unusually large and you will have blurring of vision, especially for close objects. *Make sure your vision is clear before you drive, use machines, or do anything else that could be dangerous if you are not able to see well.*
- Your eyes will become more sensitive to light than they are normally. When you go out during the daylight hours, even on cloudy days, *wear sunglasses that block ultraviolet (UV) light to protect your eyes from sunlight and other bright lights.* Ordinary sunglasses may not protect your eyes. If you have any questions about the kind of sunglasses to wear, check with your doctor.

If these side effects continue for longer than 36 hours after you have stopped using this medicine, check with your doctor.

Side Effects of This Medicine

Along with its needed effects, a medicine may cause some unwanted effects. Although not all of these side effects may occur, if they do occur they may need medical attention.

Check with your doctor as soon as possible if any of the following side effects occur:

Symptoms of too much medicine being absorbed into the body

Clumsiness or unsteadiness; confusion; constipation, full feeling, passing gas, or stomach cramps or pain; fast or irregular heartbeat; convulsions (seizures); fever; flushing or redness of face; hallucinations (seeing, hearing, or feeling things that are not there); passing urine less often; skin rash; slurred speech; swollen stomach (in infants); thirst or dryness of mouth; unusual behavior, such as disorientation to time or place, failure to recognize people, hyperactivity, or restlessness, especially in children; unusual drowsiness, tiredness, or weakness

Other side effects may occur that usually do not need medical attention. These side effects may go away during treatment as your body adjusts to the medicine. However, check with your doctor if any of the following side effects continue or are bothersome:

Blurred vision; burning of eye; eye irritation not present before therapy; increased sensitivity of eyes to light

Other side effects not listed above may also occur in some patients. If you notice any other effects, check with your doctor.

Additional Information

Once a medicine has been approved for marketing for a certain use, experience may show that it is also useful for other medical problems. Although this use is not included in product labeling, cyclopentolate is used in certain patients with the following medical conditions:

- Posterior synechiae
- Uveitis

Other than the above information, there is no additional information relating to proper use, precautions, or side effects for these uses.

Revised: 08/13/98

CYCLOPHOSPHAMIDE   Systemic

Commonly used brand name(s):

In the U.S.—
Cytoxan
Neosar
Generic name product may be available.

In Canada—
Cytoxan
Procytox

Description

Cyclophosphamide (sye-kloe-FOSS-fa-mide) belongs to the group of medicines called alkylating agents. It is used to treat cancer of the ovaries, breast, blood and lymph system, nerves (found primarily in children), retinoblastoma (a cancer of the eye found primarily in children), multiple myeloma (cancer in the bone marrow), and mycosis fungoides (tumors on the skin).

Cyclophosphamide is also used for treatment of some kinds of kidney disease.

Cyclophosphamide may also be used for other conditions as determined by your doctor.

Cyclophosphamide interferes with the growth of cancer cells, which are eventually destroyed. Since the growth of normal body cells may also be affected by cyclophosphamide, other effects will also occur. Some of these may be serious and must be reported to your doctor. Other effects, like hair loss, may not be serious but may cause concern. Some effects may not occur for months or years after the medicine is used.

Before you begin treatment with cyclophosphamide, you and your doctor should talk about the good this medicine will do as well as the risks of using it.

Cyclophosphamide is available only with your doctor's prescription, in the following dosage forms:

Oral
- Oral solution (U.S. and Canada)
- Tablets (U.S. and Canada)

Parenteral
- Injection (U.S. and Canada)

Before Using This Medicine

In deciding to use a medicine, the risks of taking the medicine must be weighed against the good it will do. This is a decision you and your doctor will make. For cyclophosphamide, the following should be considered:

Allergies—Tell your doctor if you have ever had any unusual or allergic reaction to cyclophosphamide.

Pregnancy—This medicine may cause several different birth defects if either the male or female is taking it at the time of conception or if it is taken during pregnancy. In addition, many cancer medicines may cause sterility. Although sterility occurs commonly with cyclophosphamide, it is usually only temporary.

Be sure that you have discussed this with your doctor before taking this medicine. It is best to use some kind of birth control while you are taking cyclophosphamide. Tell your doctor right away if you think you have become pregnant while taking cyclophosphamide.

Breast-feeding—Cyclophosphamide passes into the breast milk. Because this medicine may cause serious side effects, breast-feeding is generally not recommended while you are taking it.

Children—This medicine has been tested in children and has not been shown to cause different side effects or problems than it does in adults.

Older adults—Many medicines have not been studied specifically in older people. Therefore, it may not be known whether they work exactly the same way they do in younger adults. Although there is no specific information comparing use of cyclophosphamide in the elderly with use in other age groups, it is not expected to cause different side effects or problems in older people than it does in younger adults.

Other medicines—Although certain medicines should not be used together at all, in other cases two different medicines may be used together even if an interaction might occur. In these cases, your doctor may want to change the dose, or other precautions may be necessary. When you are taking or receiving cyclophosphamide, it is especially important that your health care professional know if you are taking any of the following:

- Amphotericin B by injection (e.g., Fungizone) or
- Antithyroid agents (medicine for overactive thyroid) or
- Chloramphenicol (e.g., Chloromycetin) or
- Colchicine or
- Flucytosine (e.g., Ancobon) or
- Ganciclovir (e.g., Cytovene) or
- Interferon (e.g., Intron A, Roferon-A) or
- Methotrexate or
- Plicamycin (e.g., Mithracin) or
- Zidovudine (e.g., AZT, Retrovir) or
- If you have ever been treated with radiation or cancer medicines—Cyclophosphamide may increase the effects of these medicines or radiation therapy on the blood
- Cocaine—Cyclophosphamide may increase the effects and toxicity of this medicine
- Cytarabine—Cyclophosphamide may increase the effects of this medicine on the heart and blood
- Azathioprine (e.g., Imuran) or
- Chlorambucil (e.g., Leukeran) or
- Corticosteroids (cortisone-like medicine) or
- Cyclosporine (e.g., Sandimmune) or
- Mercaptopurine (e.g., Purinethol) or
- Muromonab-CD3 (monoclonal antibody) (e.g., Orthoclone OKT3)—There may be an increased risk of infection and development of cancer because cyclophosphamide reduces the body's ability to fight them
- Probenecid (e.g., Benemid) or
- Sulfinpyrazone (e.g., Anturane)—Cyclophosphamide may increase the amount of uric acid in the blood. Since these medicines are used to lower uric acid levels, they may not work as well in patients taking cyclophosphamide

Other medical problems—The presence of other medical problems may affect the use of cyclophosphamide. Make sure you tell your doctor if you have any other medical problems, especially:

- Chickenpox (including recent exposure) or
- Herpes zoster (shingles)—Risk of severe disease affecting other parts of the body
- Gout (history of) or
- Kidney stones (history of)—Cyclophosphamide may increase levels of uric acid in the body, which can cause gout or kidney stones
- Infection—Cyclophosphamide can decrease your body's ability to fight infection
- Kidney disease—Effects of cyclophosphamide may be increased because of slower removal from the body
- Liver disease—The effect of cyclophosphamide may be decreased
- Prior removal of adrenal gland(s)—Toxic effects of cyclophosphamide may be increased, dosage adjustment may be necessary
- Tumor cell accumulation—Increased risk of tumor cells entering the bone marrow, due to bone marrow depression from high doses of cyclophosphamide

Proper Use of This Medicine

Take this medicine only as directed by your doctor. Do not take more or less of it, and do not take it more often than your doctor ordered. The exact amount of medicine you need has been carefully worked out. Taking too much may increase the chance of side effects, while taking too little may not improve your condition.

Cyclophosphamide is sometimes given together with certain other medicines. If you are using a combination of medicines, make sure that you take each one at the proper time and do not mix them. Ask your health care professional to help you plan a way to remember to take your medicines at the right times.

While you are using cyclophosphamide, it is important that you drink extra fluids so that you will pass more urine. Also, empty your bladder frequently, including at least once during the night. This will help prevent kidney and bladder problems and keep your kidneys working well. Cyclophosphamide passes from the body in the urine. If too much of it appears in the urine or if the urine stays in the bladder too long, it can cause dangerous irritation. *Follow your doctor's instructions carefully about how much fluid to drink every day.* Some patients may have to drink up to 7 to 12 cups (3 quarts) of fluid a day.

Usually it is best to take cyclophosphamide first thing in the morning, to reduce the risk of bladder problems. However, your doctor may want you to take it with food in smaller doses over the day, to lessen stomach upset or help the medicine work better. Follow your doctor's instructions carefully about when to take cyclophosphamide.

Cyclophosphamide often causes nausea, vomiting, and loss of appetite. However, it is very important that you continue to use the medicine even if you begin to feel ill. *Do not stop taking this medicine without first checking with your doctor.* Ask your health care professional for ways to lessen these effects.

If you vomit shortly after taking a dose of cyclophosphamide, check with your doctor. You will be told whether to take the dose again or to wait until the next scheduled dose.

Dosing—The dose of cyclophosphamide will be different for different patients. The dose that is used may depend on a number of things, including what the medicine is being used for, the patient's weight, whether the medicine is being given by mouth or by injection, and whether or not other medicines are also being taken. *If you are taking or receiving cyclophosphamide at home, follow your doctor's orders or the directions on the label.* If you have any questions about the proper dose of cyclophosphamide, ask your doctor.

Missed dose—If you miss a dose of this medicine, do not take the missed dose at all and do not double the next one. Instead, go back to your regular dosing schedule and check with your doctor.

Storage—To store this medicine:
- Keep out of the reach of children.
- Store away from heat and direct light.
- Do not store in the bathroom, near the kitchen sink, or in other damp places. Heat or moisture may cause the medicine to break down.
- Store the oral solution form of this medicine in the refrigerator. Keep it from freezing.
- Do not keep outdated medicine or medicine no longer needed. Be sure that any discarded medicine is out of the reach of children.

Precautions While Using This Medicine

It is very important that your doctor check your progress at regular visits to make sure that this medicine is working properly and to check for unwanted effects.

While you are being treated with cyclophosphamide, and after you stop treatment with it, *do not have any immunizations (vaccinations) without your doctor's approval.* Cyclophosphamide may lower your body's resistance and there is a chance you might get the infection the immunization is meant to prevent. In addition, other persons living in your house should not take oral polio vaccine since there is a chance they could pass the polio virus on to you. Also, avoid persons who have recently taken oral polio vaccine within the last several months. Do not get close to them, and do not stay in the same room with them for very long. If you cannot take these precautions, you should consider wearing a protective face mask that covers the nose and mouth.

Before having any kind of surgery, including dental surgery, or emergency treatment, make sure the medical doctor or dentist in charge knows that you are taking this medicine, especially if you have taken it within the last 10 days.

Cyclophosphamide can temporarily lower the number of white blood cells in your blood, increasing the chance of getting an infection. It can also lower the number of platelets, which are necessary for proper blood clotting. If this occurs, there are certain precautions you can take, especially when your blood count is low, to reduce the risk of infection or bleeding:
- If you can, avoid people with infections. *Check with your doctor immediately* if you think you are getting an infection or if you get a fever or chills, cough or hoarseness, lower back or side pain, or painful or difficult urination.
- *Check with your doctor immediately* if you notice any unusual bleeding or bruising; black, tarry stools; blood in urine or stools; or pinpoint red spots on your skin.
- Be careful when using a regular toothbrush, dental floss, or toothpick. Your medical doctor, dentist, or nurse may recommend other ways to clean your teeth and gums.

Check with your medical doctor before having any dental work done.
- Do not touch your eyes or the inside of your nose unless you have just washed your hands and have not touched anything else in the meantime.
- Be careful not to cut yourself when you are using sharp objects such as a safety razor or fingernail or toenail cutters.
- Avoid contact sports or other situations where bruising or injury could occur.

Before you have any medical tests, tell the medical doctor in charge that you are taking this medicine. The results of some tests may be affected by this medicine.

Side Effects of This Medicine

Along with its needed effects, a medicine may cause some unwanted effects. Although not all of these side effects may occur, if they do occur they may need medical attention.

Also, because of the way these medicines act on the body, there is a chance that they might cause other unwanted effects that may not occur until months or years after the medicine is used. These may include certain types of cancer, such as leukemia or bladder cancer. Discuss these possible effects with your doctor.

Check with your doctor or nurse immediately if any of the following side effects occur:
  More common
      Cough or hoarseness; fever or chills; lower back or side pain; missing menstrual periods; painful or difficult urination
  With high doses and/or long-term treatment
      Blood in urine; dizziness, confusion, or agitation; fast heartbeat; joint pain; shortness of breath; swelling of feet or lower legs; unusual tiredness or weakness
  Less common
      Black, tarry stools or blood in stools; pinpoint red spots on skin; unusual bleeding or bruising
  Rare
      Frequent urination; redness, swelling, or pain at site of injection; sores in mouth and on lips; sudden shortness of breath; unusual thirst; yellow eyes or skin

Other side effects may occur that usually do not need medical attention. These side effects may go away during treatment as your body adjusts to the medicine. Also, your health care professional may be able to tell you about ways to prevent or reduce some of these side effects. Check with your health care professional if any of the following side effects continue or are bothersome or if you have any questions about them:
  More common
      Darkening of skin and fingernails; loss of appetite; nausea or vomiting
  Less common
      Diarrhea or stomach pain; flushing or redness of face; headache; increased sweating; skin rash, hives, or itching; swollen lips

Cyclophosphamide may cause a temporary loss of hair in some people. After treatment has ended, normal hair growth should return, although the new hair may be a slightly different color or texture.

After you stop using cyclophosphamide, it may still produce some side effects that need attention. During this period of time, *check with your doctor immediately* if you notice the following side effect:

Blood in urine

Other side effects not listed above may also occur in some patients. If you notice any other effects, check with your doctor.

Additional Information

Once a medicine has been approved for marketing for a certain use, experience may show that it is also useful for other medical problems. Although these uses are not included in product labeling, cyclophosphamide is used in certain patients with the following medical conditions:

- Cancer of the bladder
- Cancer in the bones
- Cancer of the cervix
- Cancer of the endometrium
- Cancers of the lungs
- Cancer of the prostate
- Cancer of the testicles
- Cancer of the adrenal cortex (the outside layer of the adrenal gland)
- Ewing's sarcoma (a certain type of bone cancer)
- Germ cell tumors in the ovaries (a cancer in the egg-making cells in the ovary)
- Gestational trophoblastic tumors (a certain type of tumor in the uterus/womb)
- Soft tissue sarcomas (a cancer of the muscles, tendons, vessels that carry blood or lymph, joints, and fat)
- Thymoma (a cancer in the thymus, a small organ beneath the breastbone)
- Tumors in the brain
- Waldenström's macroglobulinemia (a certain type of cancer of the blood)
- Wilms' tumor (a cancer of the kidney found primarily in children)
- Histiocytosis X (a certain type of cancer found primarily in children)
- Organ transplant rejection (prevention)
- Rheumatoid arthritis
- Wegener's granulomatosis
- Systemic lupus erythematosus
- Systemic dermatomyositis or
- Multiple sclerosis (a disease of the nervous system)

Other than the above information, there is no additional information relating to proper use, precautions, or side effects for these uses.

Revised: 07/19/2000

CYCLOSERINE   Systemic†

Commonly used brand name(s):

In the U.S.—
Seromycin

†Not commercially available in Canada.

Description

Cycloserine (sye-kloe-SER-een) belongs to the family of medicines called antibiotics. It is used to treat tuberculosis (TB). When cycloserine is used for TB, it is given with other medicines for TB. Cycloserine may also be used for other conditions as determined by your doctor.

To help clear up your tuberculosis (TB) completely, you must keep taking this medicine for the full time of treatment, even if you begin to feel better. This is very important. It is also important that you do not miss any doses.

Cycloserine is available only with your doctor's prescription, in the following dosage form:

Oral
- Capsules (U.S.)

Before Using This Medicine

In deciding to use a medicine, the risks of taking the medicine must be weighed against the good it will do. This is a decision you and your doctor will make. For cycloserine, the following should be considered:

Allergies—Tell your doctor if you have ever had any unusual or allergic reaction to cycloserine. Also, tell your health care professional if you are allergic to any other substances, such as foods, preservatives, or dyes.

Pregnancy—Cycloserine has not been shown to cause birth defects or other problems in humans.

Breast-feeding—Cycloserine passes into the breast milk. However, cycloserine has not been reported to cause problems in nursing babies.

Children—Although there is no specific information comparing use of cycloserine in children with use in other age groups, this medicine is not expected to cause different side effects or problems in children than it does in adults.

Older adults—Many medicines have not been studied specifically in older people. Therefore, it may not be known whether they work exactly the same way they do in younger adults. Although there is no specific information comparing use of cycloserine in the elderly with use in other age groups, this medicine is not expected to cause different side effects or problems in older people than it does in younger adults.

Other medicines—Although certain medicines should not be used together at all, in other cases two different medicines may be used together even if an interaction might occur. In these cases, your doctor may want to change the dose, or other precautions may be necessary. When you are taking cycloserine, it is especially important that your health care professional know if you are taking the following:

- Ethionamide (e.g., Trecator-SC)—Ethionamide may increase the risk of nervous system side effects, especially seizures

Other medical problems—The presence of other medical problems may affect the use of cycloserine. Make sure you tell your doctor if you have any other medical problems, especially:

- Alcohol abuse (or history of) or
- Convulsive disorders such as seizures or epilepsy—Cycloserine may increase the risk of seizures in patients who drink alcohol or have a history of seizures
- Kidney disease—Cycloserine is removed from the body through the kidneys, and patients with kidney disease may need an adjustment in dose or the medicine may need to be discontinued
- Mental disorders such as mental depression, psychosis, or severe anxiety—Cycloserine may cause anxiety, mental depression, or psychosis

Proper Use of This Medicine

Cycloserine may be taken after meals if it upsets your stomach.

To help clear up your infection completely, *it is very important that you keep taking this medicine for the full time of treatment*, even if you begin to feel better after a few weeks. If you are taking this medicine for TB, you may have to take it every day for as long as 1 to 2 years or more. If you stop taking this medicine too soon, your symptoms may return.

This medicine works best when there is a constant amount in the blood or urine. *To help keep the amount constant, do not miss any doses. Also, it is best to take the doses at evenly spaced times day and night*. For example, if you are to take 2 doses a day, the doses should be spaced about 12 hours apart. If this interferes with your sleep or other daily activities, or if you need help in planning the best times to take your medicine, check with your health care professional.

Dosing—The dose of cycloserine will be different for different patients. *Follow your doctor's orders or the directions on the label*. The following information includes only the average doses of cycloserine. *If your dose is different, do not change it* unless your doctor tells you to do so.

- For the *oral* dosage form (capsules):
  —For treatment of tuberculosis:
  - Adults and teenagers—250 milligrams (mg) two times a day to start. Your doctor may slowly increase your dose up to 250 mg three or four times a day. This medicine must be taken along with other medicines to treat tuberculosis.
  - Children—Use and dose must be determined by your doctor. Doses of 10 to 20 mg per kilogram (4.5 to 9.1 mg per pound) of body weight per day have been used. This medicine must be taken along with other medicines to treat tuberculosis.

Missed dose—If you do miss a dose of this medicine, take it as soon as possible. This will help to keep a constant amount of medicine in the blood or urine. However, if it is almost time for your next dose, skip the missed dose and go back to your regular dosing schedule. Do not double doses.

Storage—To store this medicine:
- Keep out of the reach of children.
- Store away from heat and direct light.
- Do not store in the bathroom, near the kitchen sink, or in other damp places. Heat or moisture may cause the medicine to break down.
- Do not keep outdated medicine or medicine no longer needed. Be sure that any discarded medicine is out of the reach of children.

Precautions While Using This Medicine

It is very important that your doctor check your progress at regular visits.

If your symptoms do not improve within 2 to 3 weeks, or if they become worse, check with your doctor.

If cycloserine causes you to feel very depressed or to have thoughts of suicide, check with your doctor immediately. Your doctor will probably want to change your medicine.

This medicine may cause some people to become dizzy, drowsy, or less alert than they are normally. *Make sure you know how you react to this medicine before you drive, use machines, or do anything else that could be dan-*

gerous if you are dizzy or are not alert. If these reactions are especially bothersome, check with your doctor.

Some of cycloserine's side effects (for example, convulsions [seizures]) may be more likely to occur if you drink alcoholic beverages regularly while you are taking this medicine. Therefore, *you should not drink alcoholic beverages while you are taking this medicine*.

Side Effects of This Medicine

Along with its needed effects, a medicine may cause some unwanted effects. Although not all of these side effects may occur, if they do occur they may need medical attention.

Check with your doctor immediately if any of the following side effects occur:
> *More common*
>> Anxiety; confusion; dizziness; drowsiness; increased irritability; increased restlessness; mental depression; muscle twitching or trembling; nervousness; nightmares; other mood or mental changes; speech problems; thoughts of suicide
>
> *Less common*
>> Convulsions (seizures); numbness, tingling, burning pain, or weakness in the hands or feet; skin rash

Other side effects may occur that usually do not need medical attention. These side effects may go away during treatment as your body adjusts to the medicine. However, check with your doctor if the following side effect continues or is bothersome:
> *More common*
>> Headache

Other side effects not listed above may also occur in some patients. If you notice any other effects, check with your doctor.

Additional Information

Once a medicine has been approved for marketing for a certain use, experience may show that it is also useful for other medical problems. Although this use is not included in product labeling, ethambutol is used in certain patients with the following medical condition:

- Atypical mycobacterial infections, such as *Mycobacterium avium* complex (MAC)

Other than the above information, there is no additional information relating to proper use, precautions, or side effects for this use.

Revised: 05/02/94

CYCLOSPORINE   Systemic

Commonly used brand name(s):

In the U.S.—
Neoral
Sandimmune
SangCya

In Canada—
Neoral
Sandimmune

Some other commonly used names are ciclosporin and cyclosporin A.

Description

Cyclosporine (SYE-kloe-spor-een) belongs to the group of medicines known as immunosuppressive agents. It is used to reduce the body's natural immunity in patients who receive organ (for example, kidney, liver, and heart) transplants.

When a patient receives an organ transplant, the body's white blood cells will try to get rid of (reject) the transplanted organ. Cyclosporine works by preventing the white blood cells from doing this.

Cyclosporine also is used to treat severe cases of psoriasis and rheumatoid arthritis.

Cyclosporine may also be used for other conditions, as determined by your doctor.

Cyclosporine is a very strong medicine. It may cause side effects that could be very serious, such as high blood pressure and kidney and liver problems. It may also reduce the body's ability to fight infections. You and your doctor should talk about the good this medicine will do as well as the risks of using it.

Cyclosporine is available only with your doctor's prescription, in the following dosage forms:

Oral
- Capsules (U.S. and Canada)
- Oral solution (U.S. and Canada)

Parenteral
- Injection (U.S. and Canada)

Before Using This Medicine

In deciding to use a medicine, the risks of taking the medicine must be weighed against the good it will do. This is a decision you and your doctor will make. For cyclosporine, the following should be considered:

Allergies—Tell your doctor if you have ever had any unusual or allergic reaction to cyclosporine.

Pregnancy—Studies have not been done in humans. However, some women who received cyclosporine during pregnancy delivered their babies prematurely, and some babies were smaller than average when they were born. Additionally, some babies had birth defects. It is not certain that these birth defects occurred because of the use of cyclosporine by the mothers.

Studies in rats and rabbits have shown that cyclosporine at toxic doses (2 to 5 times the human dose) causes birth defects or death of the fetus.

Breast-feeding—Cyclosporine passes into breast milk. There is a chance that it could cause the same side effects in the baby that it does in people taking it. It may be necessary for you to stop breast-feeding during treatment. Be sure you have discussed the risks and benefits of the medicine with your doctor.

Children—This medicine has been tested in children and, in effective doses, has not been shown to cause different side effects or problems than it does in adults.

Older adults—Older people are more likely to experience some side effects (e.g., high blood pressure and kidney problems) than are younger adults.

Other medicines—Although certain medicines should not be used together at all, in other cases two different medicines may be used together even if an interaction might occur. In these cases, your doctor may want to change the dose, or other precautions may be necessary. When you are taking cyclosporine, it is especially important that your health care professional knows if you are taking any of the following:

- Amiloride (e.g., Midamor) or
- Spironolactone (e.g., Aldactone) or
- Triamterene (e.g., Dyrenium)—Since both cyclosporine and these medicines increase the amount of potassium in the body, potassium levels could become too high

- Allopurinol (e.g., Zyloprim) or
- Androgens (male hormones) or
- Bromocriptine (e.g., Parlodel) or
- Cimetidine (e.g., Tagamet) or
- Clarithromycin (e.g., Biaxin) or
- Danazol (e.g., Danocrine) or
- Diltiazem (e.g., Cardizem) or
- Erythromycins (medicine for infection) or
- Estrogens (female hormones) or
- Fluconazole (e.g., Diflucan) or
- Human immunodeficiency virus (HIV) protease inhibitors (e.g., Crixivan, Fortovase, Invirase, Norvir, Viracept) or
- Itraconazole (e.g., Sporanox) or
- Ketoconazole (e.g., Nizoral) or
- Nefazodone (e.g., Serzone) or
- Nicardipine (e.g., Cardene) or
- Verapamil (e.g., Calan, Covera-HS, Isoptin, Verelan)—May increase effects of cyclosporine by increasing the amount of cyclosporine in the body

- Azathioprine (e.g., Imuran) or
- Chlorambucil (e.g., Leukeran) or
- Corticosteroids (cortisone-like medicine) or
- Cyclophosphamide (e.g., Cytoxan) or
- Mercaptopurine (e.g., Purinethol) or
- Muromonab-CD3 (monoclonal antibody) (e.g., Orthoclone OKT3)—There may be an increased risk of infection and cancer because both cyclosporine and these medicines decrease the body's ability to fight them

- Coal tar (e.g., Balnetar, Zetar) or
- Methoxsalen (e.g., Oxsoralen) or
- Radiation therapy or
- Trioxsalen (e.g., Trisoralen)—There may be increased risk of some skin cancers

- Lovastatin (e.g., Mevacor) or
- Simvastatin (e.g., Zocor)—May increase the risk of muscle problems and kidney problems

Other medical problems—The presence of other medical problems may affect the use of cyclosporine. Make sure you tell your doctor if you have any other medical problems, especially:

- Cancer or
- Precancerous skin changes—Cyclosporine can make these conditions worse

- Chickenpox (including recent exposure) or
- Herpes zoster (shingles)—Risk of severe disease affecting other parts of the body

- High blood pressure—Cyclosporine can cause high blood pressure

- Hyperkalemia (too much potassium in the blood)—Cyclosporine can make this condition worse

- Infection—Cyclosporine decreases the body's ability to fight infection

- Intestine problems—Effects may be decreased because cyclosporine cannot be absorbed into the body

- Kidney disease—Cyclosporine can have harmful effects on the kidney when it is taken for long periods of time

- Liver disease—Effects of cyclosporine may be increased because of slower removal of the medicine from the body

---

Proper Use of This Medicine

Take this medicine only as directed by your doctor. Do not take more or less of it and do not take it more often than your doctor ordered. The exact amount of medicine you need has been carefully worked out. Taking too much may increase the chance of side effects, while taking too little may not improve your condition.

To help you remember to take your medicine, try to get into the habit of taking it at the same time each day. This will also help cyclosporine work better by keeping a constant amount in the blood.

Absorption of this medicine may be changed if you change your diet. This medicine should be taken consistently with respect to meals. You should not change the type or amount of food you eat unless you discuss it with your health care professional. If this medicine upsets your stomach, your doctor may recommend that you take it with meals. However, check with your doctor before you decide to do this on your own.

Grapefruit and grapefruit juice may increase the effects of cyclosporine by increasing the amount of this medicine in the body. *You should not eat grapefruit or drink grapefruit juice while you are taking this medicine.*

This medicine is to be taken by mouth even if it comes in a dropper bottle. The amount you should take is to be measured only with the specially marked dropper provided with your prescription. The dropper should be wiped with a clean towel after it is used, and stored in its container.

To make *Sandimmune®* taste better, mix it in a glass container with milk, chocolate milk, or orange juice (preferably at room temperature). To make *Neoral®* taste better, mix it in a glass container with apple juice or orange juice (preferably at room temperature). Do not use a wax-lined or plastic disposable container. Stir it well, then drink it immediately. After drinking all the liquid containing the medicine, rinse the glass with a little more liquid and drink that also, to make sure you get all the medicine. Dry the dropper used to measure the cyclosporine, but do not rinse it with water.

Do not stop taking this medicine without first checking with your doctor. You may have to take medicine for the rest of your life to prevent your body from rejecting the transplant.

Dosing—The dose of cyclosporine will be different for different patients. *Follow your doctor's orders or the directions on the label.* The following information includes only the average doses of cyclosporine. *If your dose is different, do not change it* unless your doctor tells you to do so.

The number of capsules or teaspoonfuls of oral solution that you take depends on the strength of the medicine. Also, *the number of doses you take each day, the time allowed between doses, and the length of time you take the medicine depend on the medical problem for which you are taking cyclosporine.*

- For *oral* dosage forms (capsules, oral solution):
  —For transplant rejection:
    - Adults, teenagers, or children: Dose is based on body weight. The usual dose in the beginning is 12 to 15 milligrams (mg) per kilogram (kg) (5.5 to 6.8 mg per pound) of body weight a day. After a period of time, the dose may be decreased to 5 to 10 mg per kg (2.3 to 4.5 mg per pound) of body weight a day.
  —For rheumatoid arthritis:
    - Adults or teenagers: Dose is based on body weight. The usual dose is 2.5 to 4 mg per kg (1.1 to 1.8 mg per pound) of body weight a day.
    - Children—Use and dose must be determined by your doctor.
  —For psoriasis:
    - Adults or teenagers: Dose is based on body weight. The usual dose is 2.5 to 4 mg per kg (1.1 to 1.8 mg per pound) of body weight a day.
    - Children—Use and dose must be determined by your doctor.
- For *injection* dosage form:
  —For transplant rejection:
    - Adults, teenagers, or children: Dose is based on body weight. The usual dose is 2 to 6 mg per kg (0.9 to 2.7 mg per pound) of body weight a day.

Missed dose—If you miss a dose of cyclosporine and remember it within 12 hours, take the missed dose as soon as you remember. However, if it is almost time for the next dose, skip the missed dose, go back to your regular dosing schedule, and check with your doctor. Do not double doses.

Storage—To store this medicine:

- Keep out of the reach of children.
- Store away from heat and direct light.
- Do not store in the bathroom, near the kitchen sink, or in other damp places. Heat or moisture may cause the medicine to break down.
- Do not store the oral solution in the refrigerator.
- Do not keep outdated medicine or medicine no longer needed. Be sure that any discarded medicine is out of the reach of children.

Precautions While Using This Medicine

It is very important that your doctor check your progress at regular visits. Your doctor will want to do laboratory tests to make sure that cyclosporine is working properly and to check for unwanted effects.

While you are being treated with cyclosporine, and after you stop treatment with it, *it is important to see your doctor about the immunizations (vaccinations) you should receive. Do not have any immunizations without your doctor's approval.* Cyclosporine lowers your body's resistance and there is a chance you might get the infection the immunization is meant to prevent. However, it may be especially important to receive certain immunizations to prevent a disease. In addition, other persons living in your house should not take oral polio vaccine since there is a chance they could pass the polio virus on to you. Also, avoid persons who have recently taken oral polio vaccine. Do not get close to them, and do not stay in the same room with them for very long. If you cannot take these precautions, you should consider wearing a protective face mask that covers the nose and mouth.

In some patients (usually younger patients), tenderness, swelling, or bleeding of the gums may appear soon after treatment with cyclosporine is started. Brushing and flossing your teeth, carefully and regularly, and massaging your gums may help prevent this. *See your dentist regularly to have your teeth cleaned. Check with your medical doctor or dentist if you have any questions about how to take care of your teeth and gums, or if you notice any tenderness, swelling, or bleeding of your gums.*

Side Effects of This Medicine

Along with its needed effects, a medicine may cause some unwanted effects. Some side effects will have signs or symptoms that you can see or feel. Your doctor will watch for others by doing certain tests.

Also, because of the way that cyclosporine acts on the body, there is a chance that it may cause effects that may not occur until years after the medicine is used. These delayed effects may include certain types of cancer, such as lymphomas or skin cancers. You and your doctor should discuss the good this medicine will do as well as the risks of using it.

Check with your doctor or nurse immediately if any of the following side effects occur:

Rare
   Blood in urine; flushing of face and neck (for injection only); wheezing or shortness of breath (for injection only)

Check with your doctor as soon as possible if any of the following side effects occur:

More common
   Bleeding, tender, or enlarged gums

Less common
   Convulsions (seizures); fever or chills; frequent urge to urinate; vomiting

Rare
   Confusion; general feeling of discomfort and illness; irregular heartbeat; numbness or tingling in hands, feet, or lips; shortness of breath or difficult breathing; stomach pain (severe) with nausea and vomiting; unexplained nervousness; unusual tiredness or weakness; weakness or heaviness of legs; weight loss

This medicine may also cause the following side effects that your doctor will watch for:

More common
   High blood pressure; kidney problems

Less common
   Liver problems; changes in blood chemistry

Other side effects may occur that usually do not need medical attention. These side effects may go away during treatment as your body adjusts to the medicine. However, check with your doctor if any of the following side effects continue or are bothersome:

More common
   Increase in hair growth; trembling and shaking of hands

Less common
   Acne or oily skin; headache; leg cramps; nausea

Other side effects not listed above may also occur in some patients. If you notice any other effects, check with your doctor.

Additional Information

Once a medicine has been approved for marketing for a certain use, experience may show that it is also useful for other medical problems. Although not specifically included in the product labeling, cyclosporine is used in certain patients with the following medical conditions:

* Bone marrow transplantation
* Nephrotic syndrome

For patients receiving bone marrow transplantation, cyclosporine may work by preventing the cells from the transplanted bone marrow from attacking the cells of the patient's own body.

The doses of cyclosporine for patients receiving bone marrow transplantation and for patients with nephrotic syndrome are based on the patients' body weight. The usual starting dose for patients receiving bone marrow transplantation is 12.5 milligrams (mg) per kilogram (kg) (5.7 mg per pound) of body weight a day. The dose of cyclosporine for patients with nephrotic syndrome is 3.5 to 5 mg per kg (1.6 to 2.3 mg per pound) of body weight a day.

The side effects that patients experience when they receive cyclosporine for bone marrow transplantation or nephrotic syndrome are similar to those side effects experienced by patients receiving cyclosporine for organ transplantation.

Other than the above information, there is no additional information relating to proper use, precautions, or side effects for these uses.

Revised: 07/23/98
Interim revision: 10/20/98, 02/26/99

CYPROTERONE   Systemic*

Commonly used brand name(s):

In Canada—
   Androcur®

* Not commercially available in the U.S.

Description

Cyproterone (SYE-proe-te-rone) is used to treat cancer of the prostate gland. The prostate gland is present only in males; therefore, females do not get prostate cancer.

This medicine blocks the effect of the male hormone testosterone in the body. This decreases the amount of testosterone produced in the body and is one way of treating this type of cancer.

This medicine is available only with your doctor's prescription, in the following dosage forms:

Oral
   • Tablets (Canada)
Parenteral
   • Injection (Canada)

Before Using This Medicine

In deciding to use a medicine, the risks of using the medicine must be weighed against the good it will do. This is a decision you and your doctor will make. For cyproterone, the following should be considered:

Allergies—Tell your doctor if you have ever had any unusual or allergic reaction to cyproterone. Also tell your doctor and pharmacist if you are allergic to any other substances, such as foods, preservatives, or dyes.

Pregnancy—Studies on effects in pregnancy have not been done in either humans or animals.

Breast-feeding— It is not known whether cyproterone passes into the breast milk. However, this medicine has not been reported to cause problems in nursing babies.

Children—Studies on this medicine have been done only in adult patients, and there is no specific information comparing use of cyproterone in children with use in other age groups.

Older adults—Many medicines have not been studied specifically in older people. Therefore, it may not be known whether they work exactly the same way they do in younger adults or if they cause different side effects or problems in older people. There is no specific information comparing use of cyproterone in the elderly with use in other age groups.

Other medicines—Although certain medicines should not be used together at all, in other cases two different medicines may be used together even if an interaction might occur. In these cases, your doctor may want to change the dose, or other precautions may be necessary. When you are taking cyproterone, it is especially important that your health care professional know if you are receiving any of the following:

- Ethinyl estradiol (eg, Estinyl)—Concurrent use with cyproterone may cause blood clotting problems

Other medical problems—The presence of other medical problems may affect the use of cyproterone. Make sure you tell your doctor if you have any other medical problems, especially:

- Blood clots (or history of) or
- Circulation disease (or history of) or
- Stroke (or history of)—If these conditions already are already present, cyproterone may have a greater chance of causing blood clot problems
- Cardiac disease—May make the condition worse
- Depressive tendencies—May cause depression to occur
- Diabetes mellitus (sugar diabetes)—May cause a loss of control of diabetes by increasing blood and urine sugar
- Liver disease—Effects of cyproterone may be increased because of its slower removal from the body

Proper Use of This Medicine

At first, cyproterone often causes loss of strength and energy or tiredness. However, these effects are lessened after about the third month of treatment and it is very important that you continue to receive this medication.

This medication should not be discontinued even if improvement of the disease occurs.

Dosing—The dose of cyproterone will be different for different patients. The dose that is used may depend on a number of things, including what the medicine is being used for, the patient's body size, and whether or not other medicines are also being taken. *If you are taking or receiving cyproterone at home, follow your doctor's orders or the directions on the label.* If you have any questions about the proper dose of cyproterone, ask your doctor.

- For *oral* dosage form:
  —For treating prostate cancer:
  - Adults—100 to 200 milligrams (mg) (2 to 4 tablets) a day divided into 2 to 3 doses and taken after meals.
- For *injection* dosage form:
  —For treating prostate cancer:
  - Adult—300 mg (3 mL) injected into a muscle once a week.

Missed dose—If you miss a dose of this medicine, take it as soon as possible. However, if it is almost time for your next dose, skip the missed dose and go back to your regular dosing schedule. Do not double doses.

Storage—To store this medicine:

- Keep out of the reach of children.
- Do not store in the bathroom, near the kitchen sink, or in other damp places. Heat or moisture may cause the medicine to break down.
- Keep the medicine from freezing.
- Do not keep outdated medicine or medicine no longer needed. Ask your health care professional how you should dispose of any medicine you do not use. Be sure that any discarded medicine is out of the reach of children.

Precautions While Using This Medicine

It is very important that your doctor check your progress at regular visits. This will allow your doctor to see if the medicine is working properly and to decide if you should continue to take it.

This medicine may cause some people to become drowsy, dizzy, or less alert than they are normally. *Make sure you know how you react to this medicine before you drive, use machines, or do anything else that could be dangerous if you are dizzy or are not alert.*

Cyproterone may cause your skin to be more sensitive to sunlight than it is normally. Exposure to sunlight, even for brief periods of time, may cause a skin rash, itching, redness or other discoloration of the skin, or a severe sunburn. When you begin taking this medicine:

- Stay out of direct sunlight, especially between the hours of 10:00 a.m. and 3:00 p.m., if possible.
- Wear protective clothing, including a hat. Also, wear sunglasses.
- Apply a sun block product that has a skin protection factor (SPF) of at least 15. Some patients may require a product with a higher SPF number, especially if they have a fair complexion. If you have any questions about this, check with your health care professional.
- Apply a sun block lipstick that has an SPF of at least 15 to protect your lips.
- Do not use a sunlamp or tanning bed or booth.

If you have a severe reaction from the sun, check with your doctor.

While you are taking cyproterone, be careful to limit the amount of alcohol you drink.

Side Effects of This Medicine

Along with its needed effects, a medicine may cause some unwanted effects. Although not all of these side effects may occur, if they do occur they may need medical attention.

Check with your doctor as soon as possible if any of the following side effects occur:

Less common or rare

Abdominal pain or tenderness; agitation; back pain; black, tarry stools; blisters on skin; bloody urine; blurred vision; chest pain; chills; clay colored stools; confusion; cough; dark urine; decreased appetite; decreased urine output; difficulty swallowing; dilated neck veins; dizziness; drowsiness; dry mouth; fainting or light-headedness when getting up from a lying or sitting position; fast heartbeat; fatigue; fever; flushed, dry skin; fruit-like breath odor; general feeling of discomfort or illness; hallucinations; headache, sudden and severe; hives; inability to speak; increased blood pressure; increased hunger; increased thirst; increased urination; irregular breathing; irregular heartbeat; itching; loss of consciousness; lower back/side pain; mood or mental changes; nausea and vomiting; painful or difficult urination; pains in chest, groin, or legs, especially calves of legs; puffiness or swelling of the eyelids or around the eyes, face, lips or tongue; red, thickened, or scaly skin; seizures; shortness of breath; skin rash; slurred speech; sores, ulcers, or white spots on lips or in mouth; sore throat; stiff neck; stomachache; sudden loss of coordination; sweating; swelling of feet or lower legs; swollen and/or painful glands; temporary blindness; tightness in chest; unexplained weight loss; unusual bleeding or bruising; vision changes; weakness in arm and/or leg on one side of the body, sudden and severe; wheezing; yellow eyes or skin

Other side effects may occur that usually do not need medical attention. These side effects may go away during treatment as your body adjusts to the medicine. However, check with your doctor if any of the following side effects continue or are bothersome.

More Common

Decreased interest in sexual intercourse; inability to have or keep an erection; increase in sexual ability, desire, drive, or performance; increased interest in sexual intercourse; loss in sexual ability, desire, drive, or performance; swelling of the breasts or breast soreness in both females and males; unexpected or excess milk flow from breasts

Less common or rare

Bleeding, blistering, burning, coldness, or discoloration of skin; change in walking and balance; clumsiness or unsteadiness; hair loss; inability to move legs or arms; increased sensitivity of skin to sunlight; increase in bowel movements; loose stools; loss of strength or energy; muscle pain or weakness; paralysis of one side of the body; redness or other discoloration of skin; severe sunburn; soft stools; tiredness or weakness; unusual increase in hair growth; weight gain

Other side effects not listed above may also occur in some patients. If you notice any other effects, check with your doctor.

Developed: 05/02/00

CYSTEAMINE   Systemic†

Commonly used brand name(s):

In the U.S.—
Cystagon

†Not commercially available in Canada.

Description

Cysteamine (sis-TEE-a-meen) is used to prevent damage that may be caused by the buildup of cystine crystals in organs such as the kidneys. This medicine works by removing the extra cystine from the cells of the body.

Oral
- Capsules (U.S.)

Before Using This Medicine

In deciding to use a medicine, the risks of taking the medicine must be weighed against the good it will do. This is a decision you and your doctor will make. For cysteamine, the following should be considered:

Allergies—Tell your health care professional if you have ever had any unusual or allergic reaction to cysteamine or penicillamine. Also tell your health care professional if you are allergic to any other substances, such as foods, preservatives, or dyes.

Pregnancy—Cysteamine has not been studied in pregnant women. However, studies in animals have shown that cysteamine causes a decrease in fertility and a decrease in survival of their offspring. Before taking this medicine, make sure your health care professional knows if you are pregnant or if you may become pregnant.

Breast-feeding—It is not known whether cysteamine passes into breast milk. Since cysteamine has been reported to cause problems in nursing animals, it may be necessary for you to stop taking this medicine or to stop breast-feeding during treatment.

Children—This medicine has been tested in children and, in effective doses, has not been shown to cause different side effects or problems than it does in adults.

Older adults—Many medicines have not been studied specifically in older people. Therefore, it may not be known whether they work exactly the same way they do in younger adults or if they cause different side effects or problems in older people. There is no specific information comparing use of cysteamine in the elderly with use in other age groups.

Other medical problems—The presence of other medical problems may affect the use of cysteamine. Make sure you tell your doctor if you have any other medical problems, especially:

- Blood problems (or a history of) or
- Convulsions (seizures) or
- Liver disease—Cysteamine may make these conditions worse

Proper Use of This Medicine

If you vomit your dose of cysteamine within 20 minutes of taking it, take the dose again. However, if you vomit the dose a second time, do not repeat the dose but wait and take your next dose as scheduled. Also, if vomiting occurs more than 20 minutes after you take your dose, do not repeat the dose.

It is important that you follow any special instructions from your doctor, such as taking dietary supplements. These supplements will replace minerals lost through the kidneys.

For children under 6 years of age, the capsule may be opened and the contents of the capsule sprinkled on food or mixed in formula.

Dosing—The dose of cysteamine will be different for different patients. *Follow your health care professional's or-*

ders or the directions on the label. The following information includes only the average doses of cysteamine. *If your dose is different, do not change it* unless your health care professional tells you to do so.

- For *oral* dosage form (capsules):
  —To prevent buildup of cystine crystals in the kidney:
    • Adults and teenagers—The starting dose must be determined by your doctor. Your doctor may gradually increase your dose.
    • Children—The starting dose is based on body size and must be determined by your doctor. Your doctor may gradually increase your dose.

Missed dose—If you miss a dose of this medicine, take it as soon as possible. However, if it is almost time for your next dose, skip the missed dose and go back to your regular dosing schedule. Do not double doses.

Storage—To store this medicine:
- Keep out of the reach of children.
- Store away from heat and direct light.
- Do not store in the bathroom, near the kitchen sink, or in other damp places. Heat or moisture may cause the medicine to break down.
- Keep the medicine from freezing. Do not refrigerate.
- Do not keep outdated medicine or medicine no longer needed. Be sure that any discarded medicine is out of the reach of children.

Precautions While Using This Medicine

Your doctor should check your progress at regular visits to make sure that this medicine is working properly and does not cause unwanted effects.

This medicine may cause some people to become dizzy or drowsy. Make sure you know how you react to this medicine before you drive, use machines, or do anything else that could be dangerous if you are dizzy or are not alert.

Side Effects of This Medicine

Along with its needed effects, a medicine may cause some unwanted effects. Although not all of these side effects may occur, if they do occur they may need medical attention.

Check with your doctor as soon as possible if any of the following side effects occur:
More common
Abdominal pain; diarrhea; drowsiness; fever; loss of appetite; nausea or vomiting; skin rash
Less common
Confusion; dizziness; headache; mental depression; sore throat; trembling
Rare
Convulsions (seizures); increased thirst; unusual tiredness or weakness

Other side effects may occur that usually do not need medical attention. These side effects may go away during treatment as your body adjusts to the medicine. However, check with your doctor if any of the following side effects continue or are bothersome:
Less common
Breath odor; constipation

Other side effects not listed above may also occur in some patients. If you notice any other effects, check with your doctor.

Developed: 01/31/96

CYTARABINE   Systemic

Commonly used brand name(s):
In the U.S.—
Cytosar-U
Generic name product may be available.
In Canada—
Cytosar
Other commonly used names are ara-C and cytosine arabinoside.

Description

Cytarabine (sye-TARE-a-been) belongs to the group of medicines called antimetabolites. It is used to treat some kinds of cancers of the blood. It may also be used to treat other kinds of cancer, as determined by your doctor.

Cytarabine interferes with the growth of cancer cells, which are eventually destroyed. Since the growth of normal body cells may also be affected by cytarabine, other effects will also occur. Some of these may be serious and must be reported to your doctor. Other effects, like hair loss, may not be serious but may cause concern. Some effects may not occur for months or years after the medicine is used.

Before you begin treatment with cytarabine, you and your doctor should talk about the good this medicine will do as well as the risks of using it.

Cytarabine is to be administered only by or under the immediate supervision of your doctor. It is available in the following dosage form:
Parenteral
- Injection (U.S. and Canada)

Before Using This Medicine

In deciding to use a medicine, the risks of taking the medicine must be weighed against the good it will do. This is a decision you and your doctor will make. For cytarabine, the following should be considered:

Allergies—Tell your doctor if you have ever had any unusual or allergic reaction to cytarabine.

Pregnancy—This medicine may cause birth defects (such as defects of the arms, legs, or ears, which occurred in two babies) if either the male or female is taking it at the time of conception or if it is taken during pregnancy. In addition, many cancer medicines may cause sterility. Although sterility has been reported with this medicine, it is usually only temporary.

Be sure that you have discussed this with your doctor before taking this medicine. It is best to use some kind of birth control while you are receiving cytarabine. Tell your doctor right away if you think you have become pregnant while receiving cytarabine.

Breast-feeding—Because cytarabine may cause serious side effects, breast-feeding is generally not recommended while you are receiving it.

Children—Although there is no specific information comparing use of cytarabine in children with use in other age groups, this medicine is not expected to cause different side effects or problems in children than it does in adults.

Older adults—Many medicines have not been studied specifically in older people. Therefore, it may not be known whether they work exactly the same way they do in younger adults. Although there is no specific information comparing use of cytarabine in the elderly with use in other age groups, this medicine is not expected to cause different side effects or problems in older people than it does in younger adults.

Other medicines—Although certain medicines should not be used together at all, in other cases two different medicines may be used together even if an interaction might occur. In these cases, your doctor may want to change the dose, or other precautions may be necessary. When you are receiving cytarabine, it is especially important that your health care professional know if you are taking any of the following:

- Amphotericin B by injection (e.g., Fungizone) or
- Antithyroid agents (medicine for overactive thyroid) or
- Azathioprine (e.g., Imuran) or
- Chloramphenicol (e.g., Chloromycetin) or
- Colchicine or
- Flucytosine (e.g., Ancobon) or
- Ganciclovir (e.g., Cytovene) or
- Interferon (e.g., Intron A, Roferon-A) or
- Plicamycin (e.g., Mithracin) or
- Zidovudine (e.g., AZT, Retrovir) or
- If you have ever been treated with radiation or cancer medicines—Cytarabine may increase the effects of these medicines or radiation therapy on the blood

- Azathioprine (e.g., Imuran) or
- Chlorambucil (e.g., Leukeran) or
- Corticosteroids (cortisone-like medicine) or
- Cyclosporine (e.g., Sandimmune) or
- Mercaptopurine (e.g., Purinethol) or
- Muromonab-CD3 (monoclonal antibody) (e.g., Orthoclone OKT3) or
- Tacrolimus (e.g., Prograf)—There may be an increased risk of infection because cytarabine decreases your body's ability to fight it

- Probenecid (e.g., Benemid) or
- Sulfinpyrazone (e.g., Anturane)—Cytarabine may raise the concentration of uric acid in the blood. Since these medicines are used to lower uric acid levels, they may not work as well in patients receiving cytarabine

Other medical problems—The presence of other medical problems may affect the use of cytarabine. Make sure you tell your doctor if you have any other medical problems, especially:

- Chickenpox (including recent exposure) or
- Herpes zoster (shingles)—Risk of severe disease affecting other parts of the body

- Gout (history of) or
- Kidney stones (history of)—Cytarabine may increase levels of uric acid in the body, which can cause gout or kidney stones

- Infection—Cytarabine can decrease your body's ability to fight infection

- Kidney disease or
- Liver disease—Effects of cytarabine may be increased because of slower removal from the body

Proper Use of This Medicine

This medicine is sometimes given together with certain other medicines. If you are using a combination of medicines, it is important that you receive each one at the proper time. If you are taking some of these medicines by mouth, ask your health care professional to help you plan a way to take them at the right times.

While you are receiving this medicine, your doctor may want you to drink extra fluids so that you will pass more urine. This will help prevent kidney problems and keep your kidneys working well.

This medicine often causes nausea and vomiting. However, it is very important that you continue to receive the medicine even if you begin to feel ill. Ask your health care professional for ways to lessen these effects.

Dosing—The dose of cytarabine will be different for different patients. The dose that is used may depend on a number of things, including what the medicine is being used for, the patient's weight, and whether or not other medicines are also being taken. *If you are receiving cytarabine at home, follow your doctor's orders or the directions on the label.* If you have any questions about the proper dose of cytarabine, ask your doctor.

Precautions While Using This Medicine

It is very important that your doctor check your progress at regular visits to make sure that this medicine is working properly and to check for unwanted effects.

While you are being treated with cytarabine, and after you stop treatment with it, *do not have any immunizations (vaccinations) without your doctor's approval.* Cytarabine may lower your body's resistance and there is a chance you might get the infection the immunization is meant to prevent. In addition, other persons living in your household should not take oral polio vaccine since there is a chance they could pass the polio virus on to you. Also, avoid persons who have taken oral polio vaccine. Do not get close to them and do not stay in the same room with them for very long. If you cannot take these precautions, you should consider wearing a protective face mask that covers the nose and mouth.

Cytarabine can temporarily lower the number of white blood cells in your blood, increasing the chance of getting an infection. It can also lower the number of platelets, which are necessary for proper blood clotting. If this occurs, there are certain precautions you can take, especially when your blood count is low, to reduce the risk of infection or bleeding:

- If you can, avoid people with infections. *Check with your doctor immediately* if you think you are getting an infection or if you get a fever or chills, cough or hoarseness, lower back or side pain, or painful or difficult urination.
- *Check with your doctor immediately* if you notice any unusual bleeding or bruising; black, tarry stools; blood in urine or stools; or pinpoint red spots on your skin.
- Be careful when using a regular toothbrush, dental floss, or toothpick. Your medical doctor, dentist, or nurse may recommend other ways to clean your teeth and gums. Check with your medical doctor before having any dental work done.
- Do not touch your eyes or the inside of your nose unless you have just washed your hands and have not touched anything else in the meantime.
- Be careful not to cut yourself when you are using sharp objects such as a safety razor or fingernail or toenail cutters.
- Avoid contact sports or other situations where bruising or injury could occur.

Side Effects of This Medicine

Along with its needed effects, a medicine may cause some unwanted effects. Although not all of these side effects may occur, if they do occur they may need medical attention.

Also, because of the way these medicines act on the body, there is a chance that they might cause other unwanted effects that may not occur until months or years after the medicine is used. These delayed effects may include certain types of cancer, such as leukemia. Discuss these possible effects with your doctor.

Check with your doctor or nurse immediately if any of the following side effects occur:

Less common

Black, tarry stools; blood in urine; cough or hoarseness; fever or chills; lower back or side pain; painful or difficult urination; pinpoint red spots on skin; unusual bleeding or bruising

Check with your health care professional as soon as possible if any of the following side effects occur:

More common

Sores in mouth and on lips

Less common

Joint pain; numbness or tingling in fingers, toes, or face; swelling of feet or lower legs; unusual tiredness

Rare

Bone or muscle pain; chest pain; decrease in urination; difficulty in swallowing; fainting spells; general feeling of discomfort or illness or weakness; heartburn; irregular heartbeat; pain at place of injection; reddened eyes; shortness of breath; skin rash; weakness; yellow eyes or skin

Other side effects may occur that usually do not need medical attention. These side effects may go away during treatment as your body adjusts to the medicine. Also, your health care professional may be able to tell you about ways to prevent or reduce some of these side effects. Check with your health care professional if any of the following side effects continue or are bothersome or if you have any questions about them:

More common

Loss of appetite; nausea and vomiting

Less common or rare

Diarrhea; dizziness; headache; itching of skin; skin freckling

This medicine may cause a temporary loss of hair in some people. After treatment with cytarabine has ended, normal hair growth should return.

After you stop receiving cytarabine, it may still produce some side effects that need attention. During this period of time check with your doctor if you notice any of the following:

Black, tarry stools; blood in urine or stools; cough or hoarseness; fever or chills; lower back or side pain; painful or difficult urination; pinpoint red spots on skin; unusual bleeding or bruising

Other side effects not listed above may also occur in some patients. If you notice any other effects, check with your doctor.

Additional Information

Once a medicine has been approved for marketing for a certain use, experience may show that it is also useful for other medical problems. Although these uses are not included in product labeling, cytarabine is used in certain patients with the following medical conditions:

• Cancer of the lymph system
• Cancer of the brain and spinal cord

Other than the above information, there is no additional information relating to proper use, precautions, or side effects for these uses.

Revised: 06/18/98

CYTARABINE, LIPOSOMAL
Intrathecal†

Commonly used brand name(s):

In the U.S.—

DepoCyt

Generic name product may be available.

†Not commercially available in Canada.

Description

Liposomal cytarabine (LIP-oh-som-al sye-TARE-a-been) belongs to the group of medicines known as antineoplastics. It is used to treat cancer of the lymph system that has spread to the brain.

Liposomal cytarabine interferes with the growth of cancer cells, which are eventually destroyed. Since the growth of normal cells may also be affected by the medicine, other effects may also occur. Some of these may be serious and must be reported to your doctor. Some effects may occur after treatment with liposomal cytarabine has been stopped.

Before you begin treatment with liposomal cytarabine, you and your doctor should talk about the good this medicine will do as well as the risks of using it.

Liposomal cytarabine is to be administered only by or under the immediate supervision of your doctor. It is available in the following dosage form:

Parenteral

• Injection (U.S.)

Before Using This Medicine

In deciding to use a medicine, the risks of taking the medicine must be weighed against the good it will do. This is a decision you and your doctor will make. For liposomal cytarabine, the following should be considered:

Allergies—Tell your doctor if you have ever had any unusual or allergic reaction to cytarabine or liposomal cytarabine. Also tell your doctor and pharmacist if you are allergic to any other substances, such as foods, preservatives, or dyes.

Pregnancy—Liposomal cytarabine has not been studied in humans, but has been found to cause birth defects or other problems in rats and mice.

Be sure that you have discussed this with your doctor before starting treatment with this medicine. It is best to use birth control while you are receiving liposomal cytarabine. Also, tell your doctor right away if you think you have become pregnant during treatment.

Breast-feeding—It is not known whether liposomal cytarabine passes into the breast milk. However, liposomal cytarabine is not recommended during breast-feeding because it may cause unwanted effects in nursing babies.

Children—Studies on this medicine have been done only in adult patients, and there is no specific information comparing use of liposomal cytarabine in children with use in other age groups.

Older adults—Many medicines have not been studied specifically in older people. Therefore, it may not be known whether they work exactly the same way they do in younger adults or if they cause different side effects or problems in older people. There is no specific information comparing use of liposomal cytarabine in the elderly with use in other age groups.

Other medicines—Although certain medicines should not be used together at all, in other cases two different medicines may be used together even if an interaction might occur. In these cases, your doctor may want to change the dose, or other precautions may be necessary. Tell your doctor and pharmacist if your are taking any other prescription or nonprescription (over-the-counter [OTC]) medicine.

Other medical problems—The presence of other medical problems may affect the use of liposomal cytarabine. Make sure you tell your doctor if you have any other medical problems, especially:

- Active meningitis—Use is not recommended
- Blockage to cerebrospinal fluid flow— Increased risk of neurotoxicity

Proper Use of This Medicine

This medicine often causes nausea and vomiting. *However, it is very important that you continue to receive the medicine, even if you begin to feel ill.* Ask your health care professional for ways to lessen these effects.

Dosing—The dose of liposomal cytarabine will be different for different patients. The dose that is used may depend on a number of things, including the patient's weight and whether or not other medicines are also being taken. If you have any questions about the proper dose of cytarabine, ask your doctor.

Precautions While Using This Medicine

It is very important that your doctor check your progress at regular visits to make sure that this medicine is working properly and to check for unwanted effects.

Side Effects of This Medicine

Along with its needed effects, a medicine may cause some unwanted effects. Although not all of these side effects may occur, if they do occur they may need medical attention.

Check with your doctor as soon as possible if any of the following side effects occur:

More common
>Back pain; fever; headache; nausea; neck pain or rigidity; sleepiness; vomiting; weakness

Less common
>Black, tarry stools; blood in urine or stools; chills; cough or hoarseness; lower back or side pain; painful or difficult urination; pinpoint red spots on skin; sore throat; swelling of fingers, hands, arms, lower legs, or feet; unusual bleeding or bruising

Rare
>Fast or irregular breathing; puffiness or swelling around the face; shortness of breath; sudden, severe decrease in blood pressure; unusual tiredness

Other side effects may occur that usually do not need medical attention. These side effects may go away during treatment as your body adjusts to the medicine. However, check with your doctor if any of the following side effects continue or are bothersome:

Less common
>Constipation; urinary incontinence

Other side effects not listed above may also occur in some patients. If you notice any other effects, check with your doctor.

Developed: 08/19/99

DACARBAZINE   Systemic

Commonly used brand name(s):

In the U.S.—
>DTIC-Dome
>Generic name product may be available.

In Canada—
>DTIC

Description

Dacarbazine (da-KAR-ba-zeen) belongs to the group of medicines called alkylating agents. It is used to treat cancer of the lymph system and malignant melanoma (a type of skin cancer). It may also be used to treat other kinds of cancer, as determined by your doctor.

Dacarbazine interferes with the growth of cancer cells, which are eventually destroyed. Since the growth of normal body cells may also be affected by dacarbazine, other effects will also occur. Some of these may be serious and must be reported to your doctor. Other effects, like hair loss, may not be serious but may cause concern. Some effects may not occur for months or years after the medicine is used.

Before you begin treatment with dacarbazine, you and your doctor should talk about the good this medicine will do as well as the risks of using it.

Dacarbazine is to be administered only by or under the immediate supervision of your doctor. It is available in the following dosage form:

Parenteral
- Injection (U.S. and Canada)

Before Using This Medicine

In deciding to use a medicine, the risks of taking the medicine must be weighed against the good it will do. This is a decision you and your doctor will make. For dacarbazine, the following should be considered:

Allergies—Tell your doctor if you have ever had any unusual or allergic reaction to dacarbazine.

Pregnancy—There is a chance that this medicine may cause birth defects if either the male or female is taking it at the time of conception or if it is taken during pregnancy. In addition, many cancer medicines may cause sterility, which could be permanent. Although sterility has not been reported with this medicine, the possibility should be kept in mind. Dacarbazine has caused birth defects and a decrease in successful pregnancies in animal studies involving rats and rabbits given doses several times the usual human adult dose.

Be sure that you have discussed this with your doctor before taking this medicine. It is best to use some kind of birth control while you are receiving dacarbazine. Tell your doctor right away if you think you have become pregnant while receiving dacarbazine.

Breast-feeding—It is not known whether dacarbazine passes into breast milk. However, because this medicine may cause serious side effects, breast-feeding is generally not recommended while you are receiving it.

Children—Studies on this medicine have been done only in adult patients and there is no specific information comparing use of dacarbazine in children with use in other age groups.

Older adults—Many medicines have not been studied specifically in older people. Therefore, it may not be known whether they work exactly the same way they do in younger adults or if they cause different side effects or problems in older people. There is no specific information about the use of dacarbazine in the elderly.

Other medicines—Although certain medicines should not be used together at all, in other cases two different medicines may be used together even if an interaction might occur. In these cases, your doctor may want to change the dose, or other precautions may be necessary. When receiving dacarbazine it is especially important that your health care professional know if you are taking any of the following:

- Amphotericin B by injection (e.g., Fungizone) or
- Antithyroid agents (medicine for overactive thyroid) or
- Azathioprine (e.g., Imuran) or
- Chloramphenicol (e.g., Chloromycetin) or
- Colchicine or
- Flucytosine (e.g., Ancobon) or
- Ganciclovir (e.g., Cytovene) or
- Interferon (e.g., Intron A, Roferon-A) or
- Plicamycin (e.g., Mithracin) or
- Zidovudine (e.g., AZT, Retrovir) or
- If you have ever been treated with radiation or cancer medicines—Dacarbazine may increase the effects of these medicines or radiation therapy on the blood

Other medical problems—The presence of other medical problems may affect the use of dacarbazine. Make sure you tell your doctor if you have any other medical problems, especially:

- Chickenpox (including recent exposure) or
- Herpes zoster (shingles)—Risk of severe disease affecting other parts of the body
- Infection—Dacarbazine can decrease your body's ability to fight infection
- Kidney disease or
- Liver disease—Effects of dacarbazine may be increased because of slower removal from the body

Proper Use of This Medicine

Dacarbazine is sometimes given together with certain other medicines. If you are using a combination of medicines, it is important that you receive each one at the proper time. If you are taking some of these medicines by mouth, ask your health care professional to help you plan a way to remember to take them at the right times.

This medicine often causes nausea, vomiting, and loss of appetite. The injection may also cause a feeling of burning or pain. However, it is very important that you continue to receive the medicine, even if you have discomfort or begin to feel ill. After 1 or 2 days, your stomach upset should lessen. Ask your health care professional for ways to lessen these effects.

Dosing—The dose of dacarbazine will be different for different patients. The dose that is used may depend on a number of things, including what the medicine is being used for, the patient's weight, and whether or not other medicines are also being taken. *If you are receiving dacarbazine at home, follow your doctor's orders or the directions on the label.* If you have any questions about the proper dose of dacarbazine, ask your doctor.

Precautions While Using This Medicine

It is very important that your doctor check your progress at regular visits to make sure that this medicine is working properly and to check for unwanted effects.

While you are being treated with dacarbazine, and after you stop treatment with it, *do not have any immunizations (vaccinations) without your doctor's approval.* Dacarbazine may lower your body's resistance and there is a chance you might get the infection the immunization is meant to prevent. In addition, other persons living in your household should not take oral polio vaccine since there is a chance they could pass the polio virus on to you. Also, avoid persons who have taken oral polio vaccine within the last several months. Do not get close to them, and do not stay in the same room with them for very long. If you cannot take these precautions, you should consider wearing a protective face mask that covers the nose and mouth.

Dacarbazine can temporarily lower the number of white blood cells in your blood, increasing the chance of getting an infection. It can also lower the number of platelets, which are necessary for proper blood clotting. If this occurs, there are certain precautions you can take, especially when your blood count is low, to reduce the risk of infection or bleeding:

- If you can, avoid people with infections. *Check with your doctor immediately* if you think you are getting an infection or if you get a fever or chills, cough or hoarseness, lower back or side pain, or painful or difficult urination.
- *Check with your doctor immediately* if you notice any unusual bleeding or bruising; black, tarry stools; blood in urine or stools; or pinpoint red spots on your skin.
- Be careful when using a regular toothbrush, dental floss, or toothpick. Your medical doctor, dentist, or nurse may recommend other ways to clean your teeth and gums. Check with your medical doctor before having any dental work done.
- Do not touch your eyes or the inside of your nose unless you have just washed your hands and have not touched anything else in the meantime.
- Be careful not to cut yourself when you are using sharp objects such as a safety razor or fingernail or toenail cutters.
- Avoid contact sports or other situations where bruising or injury could occur.

If dacarbazine accidentally seeps out of the vein into which it is injected, it may damage some tissues and cause scarring. *Tell the doctor or nurse right away if you notice redness, pain, or swelling at the place of injection.*

Side Effects of This Medicine

Along with its needed effects, a medicine may cause some unwanted effects. Although not all of these side effects may occur, if they do occur they may need medical attention.

Also, because of the way these medicines act on the body, there is a chance that they might cause other unwanted effects that may not occur until months or years after the medicine is used. These delayed effects may include certain types of cancer, such as leukemia. Discuss these possible effects with your doctor.

Check with your doctor or nurse immediately if any of the following side effects occur:
More common
Redness, pain, or swelling at place of injection
Less common
Black, tarry stools; blood in urine or stools; cough or hoarseness, accompanied by fever or chills; fever or chills; lower back or side pain, accompanied by fever or chills; painful or difficult urination, accompanied by fever or chills; pinpoint red spots on skin; unusual bleeding or bruising
Rare
Shortness of breath; stomach pain; swelling of face; yellow eyes or skin

Check with your health care professional as soon as possible if the following side effect occurs:
Rare
Sores in mouth and on lips

Other side effects may occur that usually do not need medical attention. These side effects may go away during treatment as your body adjusts to the medicine. Also, your health care professional may be able to tell you about ways to prevent or reduce some of these side effects. Check with your health care professional if any of the following side effects continue or are bothersome or if you have any questions about them:
More common
Loss of appetite; nausea or vomiting (should lessen after 1 or 2 days)
Less common
Feelings of uneasiness; flushing of face; muscle pain; numbness of face

This medicine may cause a temporary loss of hair in some people. After treatment with dacarbazine has ended, normal hair growth should return.

After you stop receiving dacarbazine, it may still produce some side effects that need attention. During this period of time check with your doctor if you notice any of the following:
Black, tarry stools; blood in urine or stools; cough or hoarseness, accompanied by fever or chills; fever or chills; lower back or side pain, accompanied by fever or chills; painful or difficult urination, accompanied by fever or chills; pinpoint red spots on skin; unusual bleeding or bruising

Other side effects not listed above may also occur in some patients. If you notice any other effects, check with your doctor.

Additional Information

Once a medicine has been approved for marketing for a certain use, experience may show that it is also useful for other medical problems. Although these uses are not included in product labeling, dacarbazine is used in certain patients with the following medical conditions:
• Cancer of the islet cells (a part of the pancreas)
• Soft tissue sarcomas (a cancer of the muscles, tendons, vessels that carry blood or lymph, joints, and fat)

Other than the above information, there is no additional information relating to proper use, precautions, or side effects for these uses.

Revised: 07/11/94
Interim revision: 08/14/98

DACLIZUMAB Systemic

Commonly used brand name(s):
In the U.S.—
Zenapax
Another commonly used name is dacliximab.

Description

Daclizumab (da-KLIZ-yoo-mab) belongs to a group of medicines known as immunosuppressive agents. It is used to lower the body's natural immunity in patients who receive kidney transplants.

When a patient receives a kidney transplant, the body's white blood cells will try to get rid of (reject) the transplanted kidney. Daclizumab works by preventing the white blood cells from getting rid of the transplanted kidney. The effect of daclizumab on the white blood cells may also reduce the body's ability to fight infections.

Daclizumab is to be administered only by or under the immediate supervision of your doctor. It is available in the following dosage form:
Parenteral
• Injection (U.S.)

Before Using This Medicine

In deciding to use a medicine, the risks of receiving the medicine must be weighed against the good it will do. This is a decision you and your doctor will make. For daclizumab, the following should be considered:

Allergies—Tell your doctor if you have ever had any unusual or allergic reaction to daclizumab. Also tell your health care professional if you are allergic to any other substances.

Pregnancy—Daclizumab crosses the placenta. However, daclizumab has not been studied in pregnant women.

Breast-feeding—It is not known if daclizumab passes into breast milk. Breast-feeding is not recommended for patients receiving daclizumab.

Children—Studies on the use of daclizumab in children have not been completed. However, daclizumab may cause high blood pressure and dehydration more often in children than it does in adults.

Older adults—Many medicines have not been studied specifically in older people. Therefore, it may not be known whether they work exactly the same way they do in younger adults or if they cause different side effects or problems in older people. There is no specific information comparing use of daclizumab in the elderly with use in other age groups.

Other medical problems—The presence of other medical problems may affect the use of daclizumab. Make sure you tell your doctor if you have any other medical problems, especially:

- Cancer—Daclizumab may make this condition worse
- Diabetes mellitus (sugar diabetes)—Daclizumab can increase the amount of sugar in the blood
- Infection—Daclizumab may decrease the body's ability to fight infection

Proper Use of This Medicine

Dosing—The dose of daclizumab will be different for different patients. Your doctor will decide what dose should be used for you based on your body weight. The following information includes only the average doses of daclizumab.

- For injection dosage form:
  —To prevent kidney transplant rejection:
  - Adults or children—1 milligram (mg) per kilogram (kg) (0.45 mg per pound) of body weight.

Precautions While Receiving This Medicine

If you are continuing your course of therapy with daclizumab after you are discharged from the hospital, it is very important that your doctor check your progress at regular visits. Your doctor will want to do laboratory tests to make sure daclizumab is working properly.
Dental—It is important to maintain good dental hygiene and see a dentist regularly for teeth cleaning.

If you are a woman of childbearing age, you should use effective contraception while receiving this medicine.

Side Effects of This Medicine

Along with its needed effects, a medicine may cause some unwanted effects. Although not all of these side effects may occur, if they do occur they may need medical attention.

Check with your doctor immediately if any of the following side effects occur:
Less common
Chest pain; coughing; dizziness; fever; nausea; rapid heart rate; red, tender, oozing skin at incision; shortness of breath; swelling of the feet or lower legs; trembling or shaking of the hands or feet; vomiting; weakness
Rare
Frequent urination

Other side effects may occur that usually do not need medical attention. These side effects may go away during treatment as your body adjusts to the medicine. However, check with your doctor if any of the following side effects continue or are bothersome:
Less common
Constipation; diarrhea; headache; heartburn; joint pain; muscle pain; slow wound healing; trouble in sleeping

Other side effects not listed above may also occur in some patients. If you notice any other effects, check with your doctor.

Developed: 04/03/98

DACTINOMYCIN   Systemic

Commonly used brand name(s):

In the U.S.—
Cosmegen

In Canada—
Cosmegen
Another commonly used name is actinomycin-D.

Description

Dactinomycin (dak-ti-noe-MYE-sin) belongs to the group of medicines known as antineoplastics. It is used to treat some kinds of cancer of the bones and soft tissue, including muscles and tendons; Wilms' tumor (a cancer of the kidney found primarily in children); tumors in the uterus or womb; and cancer of the testicles.

Dactinomycin interferes with the growth of cancer cells, which are eventually destroyed. Since the growth of normal body cells may also be affected by dactinomycin, other effects will also occur. Some of these may be serious and must be reported to your doctor. Other effects, like hair loss, may not be serious but may cause concern. Some effects may not occur for months or years after the medicine is used.

Before you begin treatment with dactinomycin, you and your doctor should talk about the good this medicine will do as well as the risks of using it.

Dactinomycin is to be administered only by or under the immediate supervision of your doctor. It is available in the following dosage form:
Parenteral
- Injection (U.S. and Canada)

Before Using This Medicine

In deciding to use a medicine, the risks of taking the medicine must be weighed against the good it will do. This is a decision you and your doctor will make. For dactinomycin, the following should be considered:

Allergies—Tell your doctor if you have ever had any unusual or allergic reaction to dactinomycin.

Pregnancy—There is a chance that this medicine may cause birth defects if either the male or female is receiving it at the time of conception or if it is taken during pregnancy. Studies have shown that dactinomycin causes birth defects in animals. In addition, many cancer medicines may cause sterility which could be permanent. Although sterility has not been reported with this medicine, the possibility should be kept in mind.

Be sure that you have discussed this with your doctor before receiving this medicine. It is best to use some kind of birth control while you are receiving dactinomycin. Tell your doctor right away if you think you have become pregnant while receiving dactinomycin.

Breast-feeding—It is not known whether dactinomycin passes into breast milk. However, because this medicine may cause serious side effects, breast-feeding is generally not recommended while you are receiving it.

Children—Because of increased toxicity, use of dactinomycin in infants less than 6 to 12 months of age is not recommended.

Older adults—Many medicines have not been studied specifically in older people. Therefore, it may not be known whether they work exactly the same way they do in younger adults or if they cause different side effects or problems in older people. There is no specific information about the use of dactinomycin in the elderly.

Other medicines—Although certain medicines should not be used together at all, in other cases two different medicines may be used together even if an interaction might occur. In these cases, your doctor may want to change the dose, or other precautions may be necessary. When receiving dactinomycin it is especially important that your health care professional know if you are taking any of the following:

- Amphotericin B by injection (e.g., Fungizone) or
- Antithyroid agents (medicine for overactive thyroid) or
- Azathioprine (e.g., Imuran) or
- Chloramphenicol (e.g., Chloromycetin) or
- Flucytosine (e.g., Ancobon) or
- Ganciclovir (e.g., Cytovene) or
- Interferon (e.g., Intron A, Roferon-A) or
- Plicamycin (e.g., Mithramycin) or
- Zidovudine (e.g., AZT, Retrovir) or
- If you have ever been treated with radiation or cancer medicine—Dactinomycin may increase the effects of these medicines or radiation therapy on the blood

- Probenecid (e.g., Benemid) or
- Sulfinpyrazone (e.g., Anturane)—Dactinomycin may increase concentrations of uric acid in the blood. Since these medicines are used to lower uric acid levels, they may not be as effective in patients receiving dactinomycin

Other medical problems—The presence of other medical problems may affect the use of dactinomycin. Make sure you tell your doctor if you have any other medical problems, especially:

- Chickenpox (including recent exposure) or
- Herpes zoster (shingles)—Risk of severe disease affecting other parts of the body

- Gout (or history of) or
- Kidney stones—Dactinomycin may increase levels of uric acid in the body, which can cause gout or kidney stones

- Infection—Dactinomycin can decrease your body's ability to fight infection

- Liver disease—Effects of dactinomycin may be increased

Proper Use of This Medicine

Dactinomycin is sometimes given together with certain other medicines. If you are receiving a combination of medicines, it is important that you receive each one at the proper time. If you are taking some of these medicines by mouth, ask your health care professional to help you plan a way to remember to take them at the right times.

This medicine often causes nausea and vomiting. However, it is very important that you continue to receive the medicine, even if you begin to feel ill. Ask your health care professional for ways to lessen these effects.

Dosing—The dose of dactinomycin will be different for different patients. The dose that is used may depend on a number of things, including what the medicine is being used for, the patient's weight, and whether or not other medicines are also being taken. *If you are receiving dactinomycin at home, follow your doctor's orders or the directions on the label.* If you have any questions about the proper dose of dactinomycin, ask your doctor.

Precautions While Using This Medicine

It is very important that your doctor check your progress at regular visits to make sure that this medicine is working properly and to check for unwanted effects.

While you are being treated with dactinomycin, and after you stop treatment with it, *do not have any immunizations (vaccinations) without your doctor's approval.* Dactinomycin may lower your body's resistance, and there is a chance you might get the infection the immunization is meant to prevent. In addition, other persons living in your household should not take oral polio vaccine since there is a chance they could pass the polio virus on to you. Also, avoid persons who have taken oral polio vaccine within the last several months. Do not get close to them, and do not stay in the same room with them for very long. If you cannot take these precautions, you should consider wearing a protective face mask that covers the nose and mouth.

Dactinomycin can temporarily lower the number of white blood cells in your blood increasing the chance of getting an infection. It can also lower the number of platelets, which are necessary for proper blood clotting. If this occurs, there are certain precautions you can take, especially when your blood count is low, to reduce the risk of infection or bleeding:

- If you can, avoid people with infections. *Check with your doctor immediately* if you think you are getting an infection or if you get a fever or chills, cough or hoarseness, lower back or side pain, or painful or difficult urination.
- *Check with your doctor immediately* if you notice any unusual bleeding or bruising; black, tarry stools; blood in urine or stools; or pinpoint red spots on your skin.
- Be careful when using a regular toothbrush, dental floss, or toothpick. Your medical doctor, dentist, or nurse may recommend other ways to clean your teeth and gums. Check with your medical doctor before having any dental work done.
- Do not touch your eyes or the inside of your nose unless you have just washed your hands and have not touched anything else in the meantime.
- Be careful not to cut yourself when you are using sharp objects such as a safety razor or fingernail or toenail cutters.
- Avoid contact sports or other situations where bruising or injury could occur.

If dactinomycin accidentally seeps out of the vein into which it is injected, it may severely damage some tissues and cause scarring. *Tell the health care professional right away if you notice redness, pain, or swelling at the place of injection.*

Side Effects of This Medicine

Along with its needed effects, a medicine may cause some unwanted effects. Although not all of these side effects may occur, if they do occur they may need medical attention.

Also, because of the way these medicines act on the body, there is a chance that they might cause other unwanted effects that may not occur until months or years after the medicine is used. These delayed effects may include certain types of cancer, such as leukemia. Discuss these possible effects with your doctor.

Check with your doctor or nurse immediately if any of the following side effects occur:

Less common
> Black, tarry stools; blood in urine or stools; cough or hoarseness accompanied by fever or chills; fever or chills; lower back or side pain accompanied by fever or chills; painful or difficult urination accompanied by fever or chills; pinpoint red spots on skin; unusual bleeding or bruising

Rare
> Pain at place of injection; wheezing

Check with your health care professional as soon as possible if any of the following side effects occur:

More common
> Diarrhea (continuing); difficulty in swallowing; heartburn; sores in mouth and on lips; stomach pain (continuing); unusual tiredness or weakness

Rare
> Joint pain; swelling of feet or lower legs; yellow eyes or skin

Other side effects may occur that usually do not need medical attention. These side effects may go away during treatment as your body adjusts to the medicine. Also, your health care professional may be able to tell you about ways to prevent or reduce some of these side effects. Check with your health care professional if any of the following side effects continue or are bothersome or if you have any questions about them:

More common
> Darkening of skin; nausea and vomiting; redness of skin; skin rash or acne

This medicine often causes a temporary loss of hair, sometimes including the eyebrows. After treatment with dactinomycin has ended, normal hair growth should return.

After you stop receiving dactinomycin, it may still produce some side effects that need attention. During this period of time check with your doctor if you notice any of the following:
> Black, tarry stools; blood in urine or stools; cough or hoarseness accompanied by fever or chills; diarrhea; fever or chills; lower back or side pain accompanied by fever or chills; painful or difficult urination accompanied by fever or chills; pinpoint red spots on skin; sores in mouth and on lips; stomach pain; unusual bleeding or bruising; yellow eyes or skin

Other side effects not listed above may also occur in some patients. If you notice any other effects, check with your doctor.

Additional Information

Once a medicine has been approved for marketing for a certain use, experience may show that it is also useful for other medical problems. Although these uses are not included in product labeling, dactinomycin is used in certain patients with the following medical conditions:

- Kaposi's sarcoma (a type of cancer of the skin and mucuous membranes)
- Osteosarcoma (a type of bone cancer found primarily in children)

Other than the above information, there is no additional information relating to proper use, precautions, or side effects for these uses.

Revised: 07/11/94
Interim revision: 06/03/99

DALTEPARIN   Systemic

Commonly used brand name(s):

In the U.S.—
Fragmin

In Canada—
Fragmin

Description

Dalteparin (dal-TE-pa-rin) is used to prevent deep venous thrombosis, a condition in which harmful blood clots form in the blood vessels of the legs. These blood clots can travel to the lungs and can become lodged in the blood vessels of the lungs, causing a condition called pulmonary embolism. Dalteparin is used for several days after abdominal surgery, while you are unable to walk. It is during this time that blood clots are most likely to form. Dalteparin also may be used for other conditions as determined by your doctor.

Dalteparin is available only with your doctor's prescription, in the following dosage form:

Parenteral
- Injection (U.S. and Canada)

Before Using This Medicine

In deciding to use a medicine, the risks of taking the medicine must be weighed against the good it will do. This is a decision you and your doctor will make. For dalteparin, the following should be considered:

Allergies—Tell your doctor if you have ever had any unusual or allergic reaction to dalteparin or heparin. Also tell your health care professional if you are allergic to any other substances, such as foods, especially pork or pork products, preservatives, or dyes.

Pregnancy—Dalteparin has not been studied in pregnant women. However, it has not been shown to cause birth defects or other problems in animals.

Breast-feeding—It is not known whether this medicine passes into breast milk. Although most medicines pass into breast milk in small amounts, many of them may be used safely while breast-feeding. Mothers who are using this medicine and who wish to breast-feed should discuss this with their doctor.

Children—Studies on this medicine have been done only in adult patients, and there is no specific information com-

paring use of dalteparin in children with use in other age groups.

Older adults— This medicine has been tested and has not been shown to cause different side effects or problems in older people than it does in younger adults.

Other medicines— Although certain medicines should not be used together at all, in other cases two different medicines may be used together even if an interaction might occur. In these cases, your doctor may want to change the dose, or other precautions may be necessary. When you are using dalteparin, it is especially important that your health care professional know if you are taking any of the following:

- Aspirin or
- Inflammation or pain medicine, except narcotics, or
- Ticlopidine—Using any of these medicines together with dalteparin may increase the risk of bleeding

Other medical problems— The presence of other medical problems may affect the use of dalteparin. Make sure you tell your doctor if you have any other medical problems, especially:

- Bleeding problems or
- Eye problems caused by diabetes or high blood pressure or
- Heart infection or
- High blood pressure (hypertension) or
- Kidney disease or
- Liver disease or
- Stomach or intestinal ulcer (active) or
- Stroke—The risk of bleeding may be increased

Also, tell your doctor if you have received dalteparin or heparin before and had a reaction to either of them called thrombocytopenia (a low platelet count in the blood), or if new blood clots formed while you were receiving the medicine.

In addition, *tell your doctor if you have recently had medical surgery*. This may increase the risk of serious bleeding when you are taking dalteparin.

Proper Use of This Medicine

If you are using dalteparin at home, your health care professional will teach you how to inject yourself with the medicine. *Be sure to follow the directions carefully. Check with your health care professional if you have any problems using the medicine.*

Put used syringes in a puncture-resistant, disposable container, or dispose of them as directed by your health care professional.

Dosing—The dose of dalteparin will be different for different patients. *Follow your doctor's orders or the directions on the label.* The following information includes only the average doses of dalteparin. *If your dose is different, do not change it* unless your doctor tells you to do so.

- For *injection* dosage form:
  —For prevention of deep venous thrombosis (leg clots) and pulmonary embolism (lung clots):
    - Adults—The dose will be determined by your doctor, based on your condition.
    - Children—Use and dose must be determined by your doctor.
  —For prevention of blood clots after unstable angina (chest pain) or non–Q-wave myocardial infarction (a type of heart attack)

- Adults—120 International Units (IU) per kilogram of body weight injected under the skin (but no more than 10,000 IU) given every 12 hours for 5 to 8 days. Unless your doctor recommends otherwise, aspirin should be given 75 to 165 milligrams daily.
- Children—Use and dose must be determined by your doctor.

Missed dose— If you miss a dose of this medicine, use it as soon as possible. However, if it is almost time for your next dose, skip the missed dose and go back to your regular dosing schedule. Do not double doses.

Storage— To store this medicine:

- Keep out of the reach of children.
- Store away from heat and direct light.
- Keep the medicine from freezing. Do not refrigerate.
- Do not keep outdated medicine or medicine no longer needed. Be sure that any discarded medicine is out of the reach of children.

Precautions While Using This Medicine

Tell all your medical doctors and dentists that you are using this medicine.

Check with your doctor immediately if you notice any of the following side effects:

- Bruising or bleeding, especially bleeding that is hard to stop. (Bleeding inside the body sometimes appears as bloody or black, tarry stools or causes faintness.)
- Back pain; burning, pricking, tickling, or tingling sensation; leg weakness; numbness; paralysis; or problems with bowel or bladder function.

Side Effects of This Medicine

Along with its needed effects, a medicine may cause some unwanted effects. Although not all of these side effects may occur, if they do occur they may need medical attention.

Stop using this medicine and check with your doctor immediately if any of the following side effects occur:
More common
    Deep, dark purple bruise, pain, or swelling at place of injection

Less common
    Bleeding of gums; coughing up blood; difficulty in breathing or swallowing; dizziness; headache; increased menstrual flow or vaginal bleeding; nosebleeds; paralysis; prolonged bleeding from cuts; red or dark brown urine; red or black, tarry stools; shortness of breath; unexplained pain, swelling, or discomfort, especially in the chest, abdomen, joints, or muscles; unusual bruising; vomiting of blood or coffee ground-like material; weakness

Rare
    Back pain; bleeding from mucous membranes; bluish or black discoloration, flushing, or redness of skin; burning, pricking, tickling, or tingling sensation; coughing; feeling faint; fever; leg weakness; numbness; problems with bowel or bladder function; skin rash (which may consist of pinpoint, purple-red spots), hives, or itching; sloughing of skin at place of injection; swelling of eyelids, face, or lips; tightness in chest or wheezing

Other side effects not listed above may also occur in some patients. If you notice any other effects, check with your doctor.

Developed: 1/6/1996
Revised: 12/18/2000
Interim revision: 07/28/1998

DANAPAROID Systemic

Commonly used brand name(s):

In the U.S.—
Orgaran

Description

Danaparoid (da-NAP-a-roid) is used to prevent deep venous thrombosis, a condition in which harmful blood clots form in the blood vessels of the legs. These blood clots can travel to the lungs and can become lodged in the blood vessels of the lungs, causing a condition called pulmonary embolism. Danaparoid is used for several days after hip replacement surgery, while you are unable to walk. It is during this time that blood clots are most likely to form. Danaparoid also may be used for other conditions as determined by your doctor.

Danaparoid is available only with your doctor's prescription, in the following dosage form:

Parenteral
• Injection (U.S.)

Before Using This Medicine

In deciding to use a medicine, the risks of using the medicine must be weighed against the good it will do. This is a decision you and your doctor will make. For danaparoid, the following should be considered:

Allergies—Tell your doctor if you have ever had any unusual or allergic reaction to danaparoid or heparin. Also tell your health care professional if you are allergic to any other substances, such as foods, especially pork or pork products, preservatives, or dyes.

Pregnancy—Danaparoid has not been studied in pregnant women. However, it has not been found to cause birth defects in animals.

Breast-feeding—It is not known whether this medicine passes into breast milk. Although most medicines pass into breast milk in small amounts, many of them may be used safely while breast-feeding. Mothers who are using this medicine and who wish to breast-feed should discuss this with their doctor.

Children—Studies on this medicine have been done only in adult patients, and there is no specific information comparing use of danaparoid in children with use in other age groups.

Older adults—Many medicines have not been studied specifically in older people. Therefore, it may not be known whether they work exactly the same way they do in younger adults or if they cause different side effects or problems in older people. There is no specific information comparing use of danaparoid in the elderly with use in other age groups.

Other medicines—Although certain medicines should not be used together at all, in other cases two different medicines may be used together even if an interaction might occur. In these cases, your doctor may want to change the dose, or other precautions may be necessary. Tell your health care professional if you are using any other prescription or nonprescription (over-the-counter [OTC]) medicine.

Other medical problems—The presence of other medical problems may affect the use of danaparoid. Make sure you tell your doctor if you have any other medical problems, especially:

• Bleeding problems or
• Heart infection or
• High blood pressure (hypertension) or
• Kidney disease or
• Stomach or intestinal ulcer (active) or
• Stroke—The risk of bleeding may be increased

Also, tell your doctor if you have received danaparoid before and had a reaction to it called thrombocytopenia (a low platelet count in the blood), or if new blood clots formed while you were receiving the medicine.

In addition, *tell your doctor if you have recently had medical surgery*. This may increase the risk of serious bleeding when you are taking danaparoid.

Proper Use of This Medicine

If you are using danaparoid at home, your health care professional will teach you how to inject yourself with the medicine. *Be sure to follow the directions carefully. Check with your health care professional if you have any problems using the medicine.*

Put used syringes in a puncture-resistant, disposable container, or dispose of them as directed by your health care professional.

Dosing—The dose of danaparoid may be different for different patients. *Follow your doctor's orders or the directions on the label.* The following information includes only the average doses of danaparoid. *If your dose is different, do not change it* unless your doctor tells you to do so.

• For *injection* dosage form:
   —For prevention of deep venous thrombosis (leg clots) and pulmonary embolism (lung clots):
   • Adults—750 anti-factor Xa units, injected under the skin, two times a day for up to fourteen days after surgery.
   • Children—Use and dose must be determined by your doctor.

Missed dose—If you miss a dose of this medicine, use it as soon as possible. However, if it is almost time for your next dose, skip the missed dose and go back to your regular dosing schedule. Do not double doses.

Storage—To store this medicine:
• Keep out of the reach of children.
• Store away from heat and direct light.
• Keep the medicine from freezing. Do not refrigerate.
• Do not keep outdated medicine or medicine no longer needed. Be sure that any discarded medicine is out of the reach of children.

Precautions While Using This Medicine

Tell all your medical doctors and dentists that you are using this medicine.

Check with your doctor immediately if you notice any of the following side effects:

- Bruising or bleeding, especially bleeding that is hard to stop. Bleeding inside the body sometimes appears as bloody or black, tarry stools, or faintness.
- Back pain; burning, pricking, tickling, or tingling sensation; leg weakness; numbness; paralysis; or problems with bowel or bladder function.

Side Effects of This Medicine

Along with its needed effects, a medicine may cause some unwanted effects. Although not all of these side effects may occur, if they do occur they may need medical attention.

Stop using this medicine and check with your doctor immediately if any of the following side effects occur:

Less common
Bleeding gums; coughing up blood; difficulty in breathing or swallowing; dizziness; headache; increased menstrual flow or vaginal bleeding; nosebleeds; paralysis; prolonged bleeding from cuts; red or dark brown urine; red or black, tarry stools; shortness of breath; unexplained pain, swelling, or discomfort, especially in the chest, abdomen, joints, or muscles; unusual bruising; vomiting of blood or coffee ground-like material; weakness

Rare
Back pain; burning, pricking, tickling, or tingling sensation; leg weakness; numbness; problems with bowel or bladder function

Also, check with your doctor as soon as possible if any of the following side effects occur:

Less common
Fever

Rare
Skin rash

Other side effects may occur that usually do not need medical attention. These side effects may go away during treatment as your body adjusts to the medicine. However, check with your doctor if any of the following side effects continue or are bothersome:

More common
Pain at injection site

Less common
Constipation; nausea

Other side effects not listed above may also occur in some patients. If you notice any other effects, check with your doctor.

Developed: 07/10/98

DANAZOL   Systemic

Commonly used brand name(s):

In the U.S.—
Danocrine
Generic name product may be available.

In Canada—
Cyclomen

Description

Danazol (DA-na-zole) may be used for a number of different medical problems. These include treatment of:

- pain and/or infertility due to endometriosis;
- a tendency for females to develop cysts in the breasts (fibrocystic breast disease); or
- hereditary angioedema, which causes swelling of the face, arms, legs, throat, windpipe, bowels, or sexual organs.

Danazol may also be used for other conditions as determined by your doctor.

This medicine is available only with your doctor's prescription, in the following dosage form:

Oral
- Capsules (U.S. and Canada)

Before Using This Medicine

In deciding to use a medicine, the risks of taking the medicine must be weighed against the good it will do. This is a decision you and your doctor will make. For danazol, the following should be considered:

Allergies—Tell your doctor if you have ever had any unusual or allergic reaction to danazol, androgens (male hormones), or anabolic steroids. Also tell your health care professional if you are allergic to any other substances, such as foods, preservatives, or dyes.

Pregnancy—Danazol is not recommended for use during pregnancy, since it may cause a female baby to develop certain male characteristics.

Breast-feeding—Breast-feeding is not recommended while you are taking this medicine because it may cause unwanted effects in the baby.

Children—Danazol may cause male-like changes in female children and cause premature sexual development in male children. It may also slow or stop growth in any child.

Older adults—Many medicines have not been studied specifically in older people. Therefore, it may not be known whether they work exactly the same way they do in younger adults. Although there is no specific information comparing use of danazol in the elderly with use in other age groups, danazol has effects similar to androgens (male hormones). Androgens used in older males may increase the risk of developing prostate enlargement or cancer.

Other medicines—Although certain medicines should not be used together at all, in other cases two different medicines may be used together even if an interaction might occur. In these cases, your doctor may want to change the dose, or other precautions may be necessary. When you are taking danazol, it is especially important that your health care professional know if you are taking any of the following:

- Anticoagulants (blood thinners)—Danazol may increase the effects of these medicines and possibly increase the risk of severe bleeding
- Tacrolimus (e.g., Prograf)—Danazol may increase the effects of tacrolimus by increasing the amount of that medicine in the body

Other medical problems—The presence of other medical problems may affect the use of danazol. Make sure you tell your doctor if you have any other medical problems, especially:

- Blood clotting disorders or

- Severe liver disease or
- Tumor caused by too much male hormones or
- Tumor on the genitals or
- Unusual bleeding from the vagina—Danazol should not be used when these conditions exist
- Porphyria—This condition may be made worse
- Diabetes mellitus (sugar diabetes)—Danazol may increase blood glucose (sugar) levels
- Epilepsy or
- Heart disease or
- Kidney disease or
- Migraine headaches—These conditions can be made worse by the fluid retention (keeping too much body water) that can be caused by danazol

Proper Use of This Medicine

In order for danazol to help you, *it must be taken regularly for the full time of treatment* as ordered by your doctor.

Dosing—The dose of danazol will be different for different patients. *Follow your doctor's orders or the directions on the label.* The following information includes only the average doses of danazol. *If your dose is different, do not change it* unless your doctor tells you to do so.

The number of capsules that you take depends on the strength of the medicine. Also, *the number of doses you take each day, the time allowed between doses, and the length of time you take the medicine depend on the medical problems for which you are taking danazol.*

- For *capsules* dosage form:
  —Adults and teenagers:
  - For treatment of endometriosis: 100 to 400 milligrams (mg) two times a day for at least three to six months, and possibly for nine months.
  - For treatment of fibrocystic breast disease: 50 to 200 mg two times a day for six months or until signs of the disease go away, whichever comes first.
  - For prevention of attacks of hereditary angioedema: 200 mg two or three times a day. The dose may be lowered, depending upon your condition.
  —Children: Dose must be determined by your doctor.

Missed dose—If you miss a dose of this medicine, take it as soon as possible. However, if it is almost time for your next dose, skip the missed dose and go back to your regular dosing schedule. Do not double doses.

Storage—To store this medicine:
- Keep out of the reach of children.
- Store away from heat and direct light.
- Do not store in the bathroom, near the kitchen sink, or in other damp places. Heat or moisture may cause the medicine to break down.
- Do not keep outdated medicine or medicine no longer needed. Be sure that any discarded medicine is out of the reach of children.

Precautions While Using This Medicine

Your doctor should check your progress at regular visits to make sure that this medicine does not cause unwanted effects.

Contact your doctor if you are a female and have a larger clitoris (sexual organ), deepening of your voice, or un-natural hair growth after taking danazol. Your doctor may advise you to stop taking the medicine so these effects do not get worse.

For patients with diabetes:
- This medicine may affect blood glucose (sugar) levels. If you notice a change in the results of your blood or urine glucose test or if you have any questions about this, check with your doctor.

Danazol may cause your skin to be more sensitive to sunlight than it is normally. Exposure to sunlight, even for brief periods of time, may cause a skin rash, itching, redness, or other discoloration of the skin, or a severe sunburn. When you begin taking this medicine:
- Stay out of direct sunlight, especially between the hours of 10:00 a.m. and 3:00 p.m., if possible.
- Wear protective clothing, including a hat. Also, wear sunglasses.
- Apply a sun block product that has a skin protection factor (SPF) of a least 15. Some patients may require a product with a higher SPF number, especially if they have a fair complexion. If you have questions about this, check with your health care professional.
- Apply a sun block lipstick that has an SPF of at least 15 to protect your lips.
- Do not use a sunlamp or tanning bed or booth.

If you have a severe reaction from the sun, check with your doctor.

If you are taking danazol for *endometriosis* or *fibrocystic breast disease:*
- During the time you are taking danazol, your menstrual period may not be regular or you may not have a menstrual period at all. This is to be expected when you are taking this medicine. If regular menstruation does not begin within 60 to 90 days after you stop taking this medicine, check with your doctor.
- During the time you are taking danazol, you should use birth control methods that do not contain hormones. If you have any questions about this, check with your health care professional.
- *If you suspect that you may have become pregnant, stop taking this medicine and check with your doctor.* Continued use of danazol during pregnancy may cause male-like changes in female babies.

Side Effects of This Medicine

Along with its needed effects, a medicine may cause some unwanted effects. Although not all of these side effects may occur, if they do occur they may need medical attention.

Check with your doctor as soon as possible if any of the following side effects occur:
For both females and males
  Less common
    Acne; dark-colored urine; increased oiliness of hair or skin; muscle cramps or spasms; swelling of feet or lower legs; unusual tiredness or weakness; weight gain (rapid)

  Rare
    Bleeding gums; bloating, pain or tenderness of abdomen or stomach; blood in urine; burning, numbness, pain, or tingling in all fingers except

the smallest finger; changes in vision; chest pain; chills; complete or partial numbness or weakness on one side of body; cough; coughing up blood; diarrhea; difficulty in speaking; difficulty in swallowing; discharge from nipple; eye pain; fast heartbeat; fever; headache; hives or other skin rash; joint pain; light-colored stools; loss of appetite (continuing); loss of muscle coordination; more frequent nosebleeds; muscle aches; nausea; purple- or red-colored, or other spots on body or inside the mouth or nose; restlessness; shortness of breath; sore throat; sweating; tingling, numbness, or weakness in legs, which may move upward to arms, trunk, or face; unusual bruising or bleeding; unusual tiredness, weakness, or general feeling of illness; vomiting; yellow eyes or skin

For females only
More common
Decrease in breast size; irregular menstrual periods; weight gain

Rare
Enlarged clitoris; hoarseness or deepening of voice; unnatural hair growth

For males only
Rare
Changes in semen; decrease in size of testicles

Other side effects may occur that usually do not need medical attention. These side effects may go away during treatment as your body adjusts to the medicine. However, check with your doctor if any of the following side effects continue or are bothersome:

For both females and males
Less common
Flushing or redness of skin; mood or mental changes; nervousness

Rare
Increased sensitivity of skin to sunlight

For females only
Less common
Burning, dryness, or itching of vagina; vaginal bleeding

Other side effects not listed above may also occur in some patients. If you notice any other effects, check with your doctor.

Additional Information

Once a medicine has been approved for marketing for a certain use, experience may show that it is also useful for other medical problems. Although these uses may not be included in product labeling, danazol is used in certain patients with the following medical conditions:

- Gynecomastia (excess breast development in males)
- Menorrhagia (excessively long menstrual periods)
- Precocious puberty in females (premature sexual development)

Other than the above information, there is no additional information relating to proper use, precautions, or side effects for these uses.

Revised: 06/09/99

DANTROLENE   Systemic

Commonly used brand name(s):

In the U.S.—
Dantrium
Dantrium Intravenous

In Canada—
Dantrium
Dantrium Intravenous

Description

Dantrolene (DAN-troe-leen) is used to help relax certain muscles in your body. It relieves the spasms, cramping, and tightness of muscles caused by certain medical problems such as multiple sclerosis (MS), cerebral palsy, stroke, or injury to the spine. Dantrolene does not cure these problems, but it may allow other treatment, such as physical therapy, to be more helpful in improving your condition. Dantrolene acts directly on the muscles to produce its relaxant effects.

Dantrolene is also used to prevent or treat a medical problem called malignant hyperthermia that may occur in some people during or following surgery or anesthesia. Malignant hyperthermia consists of a group of symptoms including very high fever, fast and irregular heartbeat, and breathing problems. It is believed that the tendency to develop malignant hyperthermia is inherited.

Dantrolene has been shown to cause cancer and noncancerous tumors in some animals (but not in others) when given in large doses for a long time. It is not known whether long-term use of dantrolene causes cancer or tumors in humans. Before taking this medicine, be sure that you have discussed this with your doctor.

This medicine is available only with your doctor's prescription, in the following dosage forms:

Oral
- Capsules (U.S. and Canada)

Parenteral
- Injection (U.S. and Canada)

Before Using This Medicine

In deciding to use a medicine, the risks of taking the medicine must be weighed against the good it will do. This is a decision you and your doctor will make. For dantrolene, the following should be considered:

Allergies—Tell your doctor if you have ever had any unusual or allergic reaction to dantrolene. Also tell your health care professional if you are allergic to any other substances, such as foods, preservatives, or dyes.

Pregnancy—Dantrolene has not been shown to cause birth defects or other problems in humans.

Breast-feeding—Use of dantrolene is not recommended during breast-feeding.

Children—This medicine has been tested in children 5 years of age and older and has not been shown to cause different side effects or problems than it does in adults.

Older adults—Many medicines have not been studied specifically in older people. Therefore, it may not be known whether they work exactly the same way they do in younger adults or if they cause different side effects or problems in

older people. There is no specific information comparing use of dantrolene in the elderly with use in other age groups.

Other medicines—Although certain medicines should not be used together at all, in other cases two different medicines may be used together even if an interaction might occur. In these cases, your doctor may want to change the dose, or other precautions may be necessary. When you are taking dantrolene, it is especially important that your health care professional know if you are taking any of the following:

- Acetaminophen (e.g., Tylenol) (with long-term, high-dose use) or
- Amiodarone (e.g., Cordarone) or
- Anabolic steroids (dromostanolone [e.g., Drolban], ethylestrenol [e.g., Maxibolin], nandrolone [e.g., Anabolin], oxandrolone [e.g., Anavar], oxymetholone [e.g., Anadrol], stanozolol [e.g., Winstrol]) or
- Androgens (male hormones) or
- Anti-infectives by mouth or by injection (medicine for infection) or
- Antithyroid agents (medicine for overactive thyroid) or
- Carbamazepine (e.g., Tegretol) or
- Carmustine (e.g., BiCNU) or
- Central nervous system (CNS) depressants (medicine that causes drowsiness) or
- Chloroquine (e.g., Aralen) or
- Daunorubicin (e.g., Cerubidine) or
- Disulfiram (e.g., Antabuse) or
- Divalproex (e.g., Depakote) or
- Estrogens (female hormones) or
- Etretinate (e.g., Tegison) or
- Gold salts (medicine for arthritis) or
- Hydroxychloroquine (e.g., Plaquenil) or
- Mercaptopurine (e.g., Purinethol) or
- Methotrexate (e.g., Mexate) or
- Methyldopa (e.g., Aldomet) or
- Naltrexone (e.g., Trexan) (with long-term, high-dose use) or
- Oral contraceptives (birth control pills) containing estrogen or
- Phenothiazines (acetophenazine [e.g., Tindal], chlorpromazine [e.g., Thorazine], fluphenazine [e.g., Prolixin], mesoridazine [e.g., Serentil], perphenazine [e.g., Trilafon], prochlorperazine [e.g., Compazine], promazine [e.g., Sparine], promethazine [e.g., Phenergan], thioridazine [e.g., Mellaril], trifluoperazine [e.g., Stelazine], triflupromazine [e.g., Vesprin], trimeprazine [e.g., Temaril]) or
- Phenytoin (e.g., Dilantin) or
- Plicamycin (e.g., Mithracin) or
- Tricyclic antidepressants (medicine for depression) (amitriptyline [e.g., Elavil], amoxapine [e.g., Asendin], clomipramine [e.g., Anafranil], desipramine [e.g., Pertofrane], doxepin [e.g., Sinequan], imipramine [e.g., Tofranil], nortriptyline [e.g., Aventyl], protriptyline [e.g., Vivactil], trimipramine [e.g., Surmontil]) or
- Valproic acid (e.g., Depakene)—The chance of side effects may be increased

Other medical problems—The presence of other medical problems may affect the use of dantrolene. Make sure you tell your doctor if you have any other medical problems, especially:

- Emphysema, asthma, bronchitis, or other chronic lung disease or
- Heart disease or

- Liver disease, such as hepatitis or cirrhosis (or history of)—The chance of serious side effects may be increased

---

Proper Use of This Medicine

If you are unable to swallow the capsules, you may empty the number of capsules needed for one dose into a small amount of fruit juice or other liquid. Stir gently to mix the powder with the liquid before drinking. Drink the medicine right away. Rinse the glass with a little more liquid and drink that also to make sure that you have taken all of the medicine.

Dantrolene may be taken with or without food or on a full or empty stomach. However, if your doctor tells you to take the medicine a certain way, take it exactly as directed.

Take this medicine only as directed by your doctor. Do not take more of it and do not take it more often than your doctor ordered. Dantrolene may cause liver damage or other unwanted effects if too much is taken.

Dosing—The dose of dantrolene will be different for different patients. *Follow your doctor's orders or the directions on the label.* The following information includes only the average doses of dantrolene. *If your dose is different, do not change it* unless your doctor tells you to do so:

The number of capsules that you take depends on the strength of the medicine. Also, the number of doses you take each day, the time allowed between doses, and the length of time you take the medicine depend on the medical problem for which you are taking dantrolene.

- For *oral* dosage form (capsules):
  —For prevention or treatment of a malignant hyperthermic crisis:
  - Adults—Dose is based on body weight and must be determined by your doctor. The usual dose is 4 to 8 milligrams (mg) per kilogram (kg) (1.8 to 3.6 mg per pound) of body weight per day in divided doses. The doctor will instruct you exactly when and how often to take your medicine.
  —To relieve spasms:
  - Adults—To start, 25 mg once a day. The doctor may increase your dose as needed and tolerated. However, the dose is usually not more than 100 mg four times a day.
  - Children—Dose is based on body weight and must be determined by your doctor. To start, the dose is usually 0.5 mg per kg (0.23 mg per pound) of body weight once a day. The doctor may increase the dose as needed and tolerated. However, the dose is usually not more than 3 mg per kg or 100 mg four times a day.

- For *injection* dosage form:
  —For prevention or treatment of a malignant hyperthermia crisis:
  - Adults, teenagers, and children—Dose is based on body weight and must be determined by your doctor.

Missed dose—If you miss a dose of this medicine and remember within an hour or so of the missed dose, take it right away. Then go back to your regular dosing schedule. But if you do not remember until later, skip the missed dose and go back to your regular dosing schedule. Do not double doses.

Storage—To store this medicine:
- Keep out of the reach of children.
- Store away from heat and direct light.
- Do not store this medicine in the bathroom, near the kitchen sink, or in other damp places. Heat or moisture may cause the medicine to break down.
- Do not keep outdated medicine or medicine no longer needed. Be sure that any discarded medicine is out of the reach of children.

Precautions While Using This Medicine

If you will be taking dantrolene for a long time (for example, for several months at a time), your doctor should check your progress at regular visits. It may be necessary to have certain blood tests to check for unwanted effects while you are taking dantrolene.

This medicine will add to the effects of alcohol and other CNS depressants (medicines that slow down the nervous system, possibly causing drowsiness). Some examples of CNS depressants are antihistamines or medicine for hay fever, other allergies, or colds; sedatives, tranquilizers, or sleeping medicine; prescription pain medicine or narcotics; barbiturates; medicine for seizures; other muscle relaxants; or anesthetics, including some dental anesthetics. Therefore, *do not drink alcoholic beverages, and check with your doctor before taking any of the medicines listed above, while you are using this medicine.*

This medicine may cause drowsiness, dizziness or lightheadedness, vision problems, or muscle weakness in some people. *Make sure you know how you react to this medicine before you drive, use machines, or do anything else that could be dangerous if you are dizzy or are not alert, well-coordinated, and able to see well.*

Side Effects of This Medicine

Along with its needed effects, a medicine may cause some unwanted effects. Although not all of these side effects may occur, if they do occur they may need medical attention. Serious side effects are very rare when dantrolene is taken for a short time (for example, when it is used for a few days before, during, or after surgery or anesthesia to prevent or treat malignant hyperthermia). However, serious side effects may occur, especially when the medicine is taken for a long time.

Check with your doctor immediately if any of the following side effects occur:
Less common
Convulsions (seizures); pain, tenderness, changes in skin color, or swelling of foot or leg; shortness of breath or slow or troubled breathing

Also, check with your doctor as soon as possible if any of the following side effects occur:
Less common
Bloody or dark urine; chest pain; confusion; constipation (severe); diarrhea (severe); difficult urination; mental depression; skin rash, hives, or itching; yellow eyes or skin

Other side effects may occur that usually do not need medical attention. These side effects may go away during treatment as your body adjusts to the medicine. However, check with your doctor if any of the following side effects continue or are bothersome:

More common
Diarrhea (mild); dizziness or lightheadedness; drowsiness; general feeling of discomfort or illness; muscle weakness; nausea or vomiting; unusual tiredness
Less common
Abdominal or stomach cramps or discomfort; blurred or double vision or any change in vision; chills and fever; constipation (mild); difficulty in swallowing; frequent urge to urinate or uncontrolled urination; headache; loss of appetite; slurring of speech or other speech problems; sudden decrease in amount of urine; trouble in sleeping; unusual nervousness

Other side effects not listed above may also occur in some patients. If you notice any other effects, check with your doctor.

Revised: 05/10/93

DAPIPRAZOLE Ophthalmic

Commonly used brand name(s):

In the U.S.—
Rev-Eyes

In Canada—
Rev-Eyes

Description

Dapiprazole (da-PI-pray-zole) is used in the eye to reduce the size of the pupil after certain kinds of eye examinations.

Some eye examinations are best done when your pupil (the black center of the colored part of your eye) is very large, so the doctor can see into your eye better. This medicine helps to reduce the size of your pupil back to its normal size after the eye examination.

Dapiprazole is available in the following dosage form:
Ophthalmic
- Ophthalmic solution (eye drops) (U.S. and Canada)

Before Using This Medicine

In deciding to use a medicine, the risks of using the medicine must be weighed against the good it will do. This is a decision you and your doctor will make. For dapiprazole, the following should be considered:

Allergies—Tell your doctor if you have ever had any unusual or allergic reaction to dapiprazole. Also tell your health care professional if you are allergic to any other substances, such as foods, preservatives, or dyes.

Pregnancy—Dapiprazole has not been studied in pregnant women. However, dapiprazole has not been shown to cause birth defects or other problems in animal studies.

Breast-feeding—It is not known whether dapiprazole passes into the breast milk. However, this medicine has not been reported to cause problems in nursing babies.

Children—Studies on this medicine have been done only in adult patients, and there is no specific information comparing use of dapiprazole in children with use in other age groups.

Older adults—Many medicines have not been studied specifically in older people. Therefore, it may not be known whether they work exactly the same way they do in younger adults. Although there is no specific information comparing use of dapiprazole in the elderly with use in other age groups, this medicine is not expected to cause different side effects or problems in older people than it does in younger adults.

Other medicines—Although certain medicines should not be used together at all, in other cases two different medicines may be used together even if an interaction might occur. In these cases, your doctor may want to change the dose, or other precautions may be necessary. Tell your health care professional if you are using any other ophthalmic (eye) prescription or nonprescription (over-the-counter [OTC]) medicine.

Other medical problems—The presence of other medical problems may affect the use of dapiprazole. Make sure you tell your doctor if you have any other medical problems, especially:

- Eye problems, other—Use of dapiprazole may make the condition worse

Proper Use of This Medicine

Dosing—The dose of dapiprazole will be different for different patients. *Follow your doctor's orders or the directions on the label.* The following information includes only the average doses of dapiprazole. *If your dose is different, do not change it* unless your doctor tells you to do so.

- For *ophthalmic solution (eye drops)* dosage form:
  —For reduction of size of pupil of eye:
    - Adults—Two drops, then two drops in five minutes, following eye examination.
    - Children—Use and dose must be determined by your doctor.

Precautions While Using This Medicine

Even after using this medicine, you may have blurred vision or other vision problems. If any of these occur, *do not drive, use machines, or do anything else that could be dangerous if you are not able to see well.*

This medicine may cause your eyes to become more sensitive to light than they are normally. Wearing sunglasses and avoiding too much exposure to bright light may help lessen the discomfort.

Side Effects of This Medicine

Along with its needed effects, a medicine may cause some unwanted effects. Although not all of these side effects may occur, if they do occur they may need medical attention.

Check with your doctor as soon as possible if any of the following side effects occur:
  Less common
    Irritation (severe) or swelling of the clear part of the eye

Other side effects may occur that usually do not need medical attention. These side effects may go away during treatment as your body adjusts to the medicine. However, check with your doctor if any of the following side effects continue or are bothersome:
  More common
    Burning of eye when medicine is applied; redness of the white part of the eye

Less common
  Blurring of vision; browache; drooping of upper eyelid; dryness of eye; headache; increased sensitivity of eye to light; itching of eye; redness of eyelid; swelling of eyelid; swelling of the membrane covering the white part of the eye; tearing of eye

Other side effects not listed above may also occur in some patients. If you notice any other effects, check with your doctor.

Revised: 04/13/92
Interim revision: 08/16/93

DAPSONE   Systemic

Commonly used brand name(s):

In Canada—
  Avlosulfon
  Generic name product may be available.

Another commonly used name is DDS.

Description

Dapsone (DAP-sone), a sulfone, belongs to the family of medicines called anti-infectives.

Dapsone is used to treat leprosy (Hansen's disease) and to help control dermatitis herpetiformis, a skin problem. When it is used to treat leprosy, dapsone may be given with one or more other medicines. Dapsone may also be used for other conditions as determined by your doctor.

Dapsone is available only with your doctor's prescription, in the following dosage form:

Oral
  - Tablets (U.S. and Canada)

Before Using This Medicine

In deciding to use a medicine, the risks of taking the medicine must be weighed against the good it will do. This is a decision you and your doctor will make. For dapsone, the following should be considered:

Allergies—Tell your doctor if you have ever had any unusual or allergic reaction to dapsone or sulfonamides. Also tell your health care professional if you are allergic to any other substances, such as foods, preservatives, or dyes.

Pregnancy—Studies have not been done in humans or animals. However, reports on the use of dapsone in humans have not shown that this medicine causes birth defects or other problems.

Breast-feeding—Dapsone passes into the breast milk. Dapsone may cause blood problems in nursing babies with glucose-6-phosphate dehydrogenase (G6PD) deficiency. Breast-feeding may need to be stopped because of the risks to the baby.

Children—Although there is no specific information comparing use of dapsone in children with use in other age groups, this medicine is not expected to cause different side effects or problems in children than it does in adults.

Older adults—Many medicines have not been studied specifically in older people. Therefore, it may not be known whether they work exactly the same way they do in younger adults or if they cause different side effects or problems in older people. There is no specific information comparing use of dapsone in the elderly with use in other age groups.

Other medicines—Although certain medicines should not be used together at all, in other cases two different medicines may be used together even if an interaction might occur. In these cases, your doctor may want to change the dose, or other precautions may be necessary. When you are taking dapsone, it is especially important that your health care professional knows if you are taking any of the following:

- Acetohydroxamic acid (e.g., Lithostat) or
- Antidiabetics, oral (diabetes medicine you take by mouth) or
- Furazolidone (e.g., Furoxone) or
- Methyldopa (e.g., Aldomet) or
- Nitrofurantoin (e.g., Furadantin) or
- Primaquine or
- Procainamide (e.g., Pronestyl) or
- Quinidine (e.g., Quinidex) or
- Quinine (e.g., Quinamm) or
- Sulfonamides (sulfa medicine) or
- Vitamin K (e.g., AquaMEPHYTON, Synkayvite)—Use of dapsone with these medicines may increase the chance of side effects affecting the blood
- Dideoxyinosine (e.g., ddI, Videx)—Use of dideoxyinosine with dapsone may decrease the effectiveness of dapsone

Other medical problems—The presence of other medical problems may affect the use of dapsone. Make sure you tell your doctor if you have any other medical problems, especially:

- Anemia (severe) or
- Glucose-6-phosphate dehydrogenase (G6PD) deficiency or
- Methemoglobin reductase deficiency—There is an increased risk of severe blood disorders and a decrease in red blood cell survival
- Liver disease—Dapsone may on rare occasion cause liver damage

Proper Use of This Medicine

For patients taking dapsone for leprosy:

- To help clear up your leprosy completely or to keep it from coming back, *it is very important that you keep taking this medicine for the full time of treatment,* even if you begin to feel better after a few weeks or months. You may have to take it every day for as long as 3 years or more, or for life. If you stop taking this medicine too soon, your symptoms may return.
- This medicine works best when there is a constant amount in the blood. *To help keep the amount constant, do not miss any doses. Also, it is best to take each dose at the same time every day.* If you need help in planning the best time to take your medicine, check with your health care professional.

For patients taking dapsone for dermatitis herpetiformis:

- Your doctor may want you to follow a gluten-free diet. If you have any questions about this, check with your doctor.

Dosing—The dose of dapsone will be different for different patients. *Follow your doctor's orders or the directions on the label.* The following information includes only the average

doses of dapsone. *If your dose is different, do not change it* unless your doctor tells you to do so.

The number of tablets that you take depends on the strength of the medicine. Also, *the number of doses you take each day, the time allowed between doses, and the length of time you take the medicine depend on the medical problem for which you are taking dapsone.*

- For *oral* dosage form (tablets):
  —For Hansen's disease (leprosy):
  - Adults and teenagers—50 to 100 milligrams (mg) once a day; or 1.4 mg per kilogram (kg) (0.6 mg per pound) of body weight once a day. Dapsone should be taken with other medicines to treat Hansen's disease.
  - Children—Dose is based on body weight. The usual dose is 1.4 mg per kg (0.6 mg per pound) of body weight once a day. Dapsone should be taken with other medicines to treat Hansen's disease.
  —For dermatitis herpetiformis:
  - Adults and teenagers—50 mg once a day to start. Your doctor will increase your dose, up to 300 mg once a day, until your symptoms are controlled. Then your dose will be decreased to the lowest dose that will still control your symptoms.
  - Children—Dose is based on body weight. The usual dose is 2 mg per kg (0.9 mg per pound) of body weight once a day to start. Your doctor will increase your dose until your symptoms are controlled. Then your dose will be decreased to the lowest dose that will still control your symptoms.

Missed dose—You may skip a missed dose if it does not make your symptoms come back or get worse. If your symptoms do come back or get worse, take the missed dose as soon as possible. Then go back to your regular dosing schedule.

Storage—To store this medicine:

- Keep out of the reach of children.
- Store away from heat and direct light.
- Do not store in the bathroom, near the kitchen sink, or in other damp places. Heat or moisture may cause the medicine to break down.
- Do not keep outdated medicine or medicine no longer needed. Be sure that any discarded medicine is out of the reach of children.

Precautions While Using This Medicine

It is very important that your doctor check your progress at regular visits.

If your symptoms do not improve within 2 to 3 months (for leprosy), or within a few days (for dermatitis herpetiformis), or if they become worse, check with your doctor.

Side Effects of This Medicine

Along with its needed effects, a medicine may cause some unwanted effects. Although not all of these side effects may occur, if they do occur they may need medical attention.

Check with your doctor immediately if any of the following side effects occur:

More common

Back, leg, or stomach pains; bluish fingernails, lips, or skin; difficult breathing; fever; loss of appetite; pale skin; skin rash; unusual tiredness or weakness

Rare

> Itching, dryness, redness, scaling, or peeling of the skin, or loss of hair; mood or other mental changes; numbness, tingling, pain, burning, or weakness in hands or feet; sore throat; unusual bleeding or bruising; yellow eyes or skin

Other side effects may occur that usually do not need medical attention. These side effects may go away during treatment as your body adjusts to the medicine. However, check with your doctor if any of the following side effects continue or are bothersome:

Rare

> Headache; loss of appetite; nausea or vomiting; nervousness; trouble in sleeping

Other side effects not listed above may also occur in some patients. If you notice any other effects, check with your doctor.

Additional Information

Once a medicine has been approved for marketing for a certain use, experience may show that it is also useful for other medical problems. Although these uses are not specifically included in product labeling, dapsone is used in certain patients with the following medical conditions:

- Actinomycotic mycetoma
- Granuloma annulare
- Malaria (prevention of)
- Pemphigoid
- *Pneumocystis carinii* pneumonia
- Pyoderma gangrenosum
- Relapsing polychondritis
- Subcorneal pustular dermatosis
- Systemic lupus erythematosus

For patients taking this medicine for *Pneumocystis carinii* pneumonia (PCP):

- To help clear up PCP completely or to keep it from coming back, *it is very important that you keep taking this medicine for the full time of treatment.*
- If you miss a dose of this medicine, take it as soon as possible. This will help keep a constant amount of medicine in the blood. However, if it is almost time for your next dose, skip the missed dose and go back to your regular dosing schedule. Do not double doses.
- If your symptoms do not improve within 1 week, or if they become worse, check with your doctor.

Other than the above information, there is no additional information relating to proper use, precautions, or side effects for these uses.

Revised: 06/26/92
Interim revision: 03/17/94

DAUNORUBICIN   Systemic

Commonly used brand name(s):

In the U.S.—
   Cerubidine

In Canada—
   Cerubidine

Description

Daunorubicin (daw-noe-ROO-bi-sin) belongs to the general group of medicines known as antineoplastics. It is used to treat some kinds of cancer.

Daunorubicin seems to interfere with the growth of cancer cells, which are eventually destroyed. Since the growth of normal body cells may also be affected by daunorubicin, other effects will also occur. Some of these may be serious and must be reported to your doctor. Other effects, like hair loss, may not be serious but may cause concern. Some effects may not occur for months or years after the medicine is used.

Before you begin treatment with daunorubicin, you and your doctor should talk about the good this medicine will do as well as the risks of using it.

Daunorubicin is to be administered only by or under the immediate supervision of your doctor. It is available in the following dosage form:

Parenteral
- Injection (U.S. and Canada)

Before Using This Medicine

In deciding to use a medicine, the risks of taking the medicine must be weighed against the good it will do. This is a decision you and your doctor will make. For daunorubicin, the following should be considered:

Allergies—Tell your doctor if you have ever had any unusual or allergic reaction to daunorubicin.

Pregnancy—This medicine may cause birth defects if either the male or female is receiving it at the time of conception or if it is taken during pregnancy. In addition, many cancer medicines may cause sterility which could be permanent. Although sterility has been reported only in male dogs with this medicine, the possibility of an effect in human males should be kept in mind.

Be sure that you have discussed this with your doctor before receiving this medicine. It is best to use some kind of birth control while you are receiving daunorubicin. Tell your doctor right away if you think you have become pregnant while receiving daunorubicin.

Breast-feeding—Because daunorubicin may cause serious side effects, breast-feeding is generally not recommended while you are receiving it.

Children—Although daunorubicin is used in children, there is no specific information comparing use in children with use in other age groups.

Older adults—Heart problems are more likely to occur in the elderly, who are usually more sensitive to the effects of daunorubicin. The elderly may also be more likely to have blood problems.

Other medicines—Although certain medicines should not be used together at all, in other cases two different medicines may be used together even if an interaction might occur. In these cases, your doctor may want to change the dose, or other precautions may be necessary. When receiving daunorubicin it is especially important that your health care professional know if you are taking any of the following:

- Amphotericin B by injection (e.g., Fungizone) or
- Antithyroid agents (medicine for overactive thyroid) or
- Azathioprine (e.g., Imuran) or

- Chloramphenicol (e.g., Chloromycetin) or
- Colchicine or
- Flucytosine (e.g., Ancobon) or
- Ganciclovir (e.g., Cytovene) or
- Interferon (e.g., Intron A, Roferon-A) or
- Plicamycin (e.g., Mithracin) or
- Zidovudine (e.g., AZT, Retrovir) or
- If you have ever been treated with radiation or cancer medicines—Daunorubicin may increase the effects of these medicines or radiation therapy on the blood

- Probenecid (e.g., Benemid) or
- Sulfinpyrazone (e.g., Anturane)—Daunorubicin may raise the concentration of uric acid in the blood. Since these medicines are used to lower uric acid levels, they may not be as effective in patients receiving daunorubicin

Other medical problems— The presence of other medical problems may affect the use of daunorubicin. Make sure you tell your doctor if you have any other medical problems, especially:

- Chickenpox (including recent exposure) or
- Herpes zoster (shingles)—Risk of severe disease affecting other parts of the body

- Gout (history of) or
- Kidney stones—Daunorubicin may increase uric acid in the body, which can cause gout or kidney stones

- Heart disease—Risk of heart problems caused by daunorubicin may be increased

- Infection—Daunorubicin can decrease your body's ability to fight infection

- Kidney disease or
- Liver disease—Effects of daunorubicin may be increased because of slower removal from the body

Proper Use of This Medicine

Daunorubicin is sometimes given together with certain other medicines. If you are using a combination of medicines, it is important that you receive each one at the proper time. If you are taking some of these medicines by mouth, ask your health care professional to help you plan a way to take them at the right times.

While you are receiving daunorubicin, your doctor may want you to drink extra fluids so that you will pass more urine. This will help prevent kidney problems and keep your kidneys working well.

This medicine often causes nausea and vomiting. However, it is very important that you continue to receive it, even if you begin to feel ill. Ask your health care professional for ways to lessen these effects.

Dosing— The dose of daunorubicin will be different for different patients. The dose that is used may depend on a number of things, including what the medicine is being used for, the patient's size, and whether or not other medicines are also being taken. *If you are receiving daunorubicin at home, follow your doctor's orders or the directions on the label.* If you have any questions about the proper dose of daunorubicin, ask your doctor.

Precautions While Using This Medicine

It is very important that your doctor check your progress at regular visits to make sure that this medicine is working properly and to check for unwanted effects.

While you are being treated with daunorubicin, and after you stop treatment with it, *do not have any immunizations (vaccinations) without your doctor's approval.* Daunorubicin may lower your body's resistance and there is a chance you might get the infection the immunization is meant to prevent. In addition, other persons living in your household should not take oral polio vaccine since there is a chance they could pass the polio virus on to you. Also, avoid persons who have taken oral polio vaccine. Do not get close to them, and do not stay in the same room with them for very long. If you cannot take these precautions, you should consider wearing a protective face mask that covers the nose and mouth.

Daunorubicin can temporarily lower the number of white blood cells in your blood, increasing the chance of getting an infection. It can also lower the number of platelets, which are necessary for proper blood clotting. If this occurs, there are certain precautions you can take, especially when your blood count is low, to reduce the risk of infection or bleeding:

- If you can, avoid people with infections. *Check with your doctor immediately* if you think you are getting an infection or if you get a fever or chills, cough or hoarseness, lower back or side pain, or painful or difficult urination.
- *Check with your doctor immediately* if you notice any unusual bleeding or bruising; black, tarry stools; blood in urine or stools; or pinpoint red spots on your skin.
- Be careful when using a regular toothbrush, dental floss, or toothpick. Your medical doctor, dentist, or nurse may recommend other ways to clean your teeth and gums. Check with your medical doctor before having any dental work done.
- Do not touch your eyes or the inside of your nose unless you have just washed your hands and have not touched anything else in the meantime.
- Be careful not to cut yourself when you are using sharp objects such as a safety razor or fingernail or toenail cutters.
- Avoid contact sports or other situations where bruising or injury could occur.

If daunorubicin accidentally seeps out of the vein into which it is injected, it may damage some tissues and cause scarring. *Tell the doctor or nurse right away if you notice redness, pain, or swelling at the place of injection.*

Side Effects of This Medicine

Along with its needed effects, a medicine may cause some unwanted effects. Although not all of these side effects may occur, if they do occur they may need medical attention.

Also, because of the way these medicines act on the body, there is a chance that they might cause other unwanted effects that may not occur until months or years after the medicine is used. These delayed effects may include certain types of cancer, such as leukemia. Discuss these possible effects with your doctor.

Check with your doctor or nurse immediately if any of the following side effects occur:

Less common
Cough or hoarseness; fever or chills; irregular heartbeat; lower back or side pain; pain at place of injection; painful or difficult urination; shortness of breath; swelling of feet and lower legs

Rare
Black, tarry stools; blood in urine or stools; pinpoint red spots on skin; unusual bleeding or bruising

Check with your health care professional as soon as possible if any of the following side effects occur:

More common

Sores in mouth and on lips

Less common

Joint pain

Rare

Skin rash or itching

Other side effects may occur that usually do not need medical attention. These side effects may go away during treatment as your body adjusts to the medicine. Also, your health care professional may be able to tell you about ways to prevent or reduce some of these side effects. Check with your health care professional if any of the following side effects continue or are bothersome or if you have any questions about them:

More common

Nausea and vomiting

Less common or rare

Darkening or redness of skin; diarrhea

Daunorubicin causes the urine to turn reddish in color, which may stain clothes. This is not blood. It is perfectly normal and lasts for only 1 or 2 days after each dose is given.

This medicine often causes a temporary and total loss of hair. After treatment with daunorubicin has ended, normal hair growth should return.

After you stop receiving daunorubicin, it may still produce some side effects that need attention. During this period of time *check with your doctor immediately* if you notice any of the following side effects:

Irregular heartbeat; shortness of breath; swelling of feet and lower legs

Other side effects not listed above may also occur in some patients. If you notice any other effects, check with your health care professional.

Revised: 07/11/94

DAUNORUBICIN, LIPOSOMAL
Systemic†

Commonly used brand name(s):

In the U.S.—
DaunoXome

†Not commercially available in Canada.

Description

Liposomal daunorubicin (LIP-oh-som-al daw-noe-ROO-bi-sin) belongs to the general group of medicines known as antineoplastics. It is used to treat advanced acquired immunodeficiency syndrome (AIDS)-associated Kaposi's sarcoma (KS), a kind of skin cancer.

Liposomal daunorubicin seems to interfere with the growth of cancer cells, which eventually are destroyed. Since the growth of normal body cells also may be affected by liposomal daunorubicin, other effects will occur. Some of these may be serious and must be reported to your doctor. Other effects, like hair loss, may not be serious but may cause concern.

Some effects may not occur until months or years after the medicine is used.

Before you begin treatment with liposomal daunorubicin, you and your doctor should talk about the good this medicine will do as well as the risks of using it.

Liposomal daunorubicin is to be administered only by or under the immediate supervision of your doctor. It is available in the following dosage form:

Parenteral
- Injection (U.S.)

Before Receiving This Medicine

In deciding to use a medicine, the risks of taking the medicine must be weighed against the good it will do. This is a decision you and your doctor will make. For liposomal daunorubicin, the following should be considered:

Allergies—Tell your doctor if you have ever had any unusual or allergic reaction to liposomal daunorubicin. Also, tell your health care professional if you are allergic to any other substances, such as preservatives.

Pregnancy—Liposomal daunorubicin has not been studied in pregnant women. However, studies in rats have shown that liposomal daunorubicin at low doses causes birth defects or death of the fetus.

Before receiving this medicine, make sure your doctor knows if you are pregnant or may become pregnant. It is best to use some kind of birth control while you are receiving liposomal daunorubicin. Tell your doctor right away if you think you have become pregnant while receiving liposomal daunorubicin.

Breast-feeding—Because liposomal daunorubicin may cause serious side effects in the infant, breast-feeding is generally not recommended while you are receiving it.

Children—There is no specific information comparing the use of liposomal daunorubicin in children with use in any other age group. Safety and efficacy of liposomal daunorubicin in children have not been established.

Older adults—There is no specific information comparing the use of liposomal daunorubicin in the elderly with use in any other age group. Safety and efficacy of liposomal daunorubicin in the elderly have not been established.

Other medicines—Although certain medicines should not be used together at all, in other cases two different medicines may be used together even if an interaction might occur. In these cases, your doctor may want to change the dose, or other precautions may be necessary. When you are taking liposomal daunorubicin, it is especially important that your health care professional know if you are taking any of the following:

- Amphotericin B by injection (e.g., Fungizone) or
- Antithyroid agents (medicine for overactive thyroid) or
- Azathioprine (e.g., Imuran) or
- Chloramphenicol (e.g., Chloromycetin) or
- Colchicine or
- Cyclophosphamide (e.g., Cytoxan) or
- Flucytosine (e.g., Ancobon) or
- Ganciclovir (e.g., Cytovene) or
- Interferon (e.g., Intron A, Roferon-A) or
- Mercaptopurine (e.g., Purinethol) or
- Methotrexate (e.g., Mexate) or
- Plicamycin (e.g., Mithracin) or
- Zidovudine (e.g., AZT, Retrovir) or
- If you have ever been treated with radiation or cancer medicines—Liposomal daunorubicin may increase the

effects of these medicines or radiation therapy on the blood
- Probenecid (e.g., Benemid) or
- Sulfinpyrazone (e.g., Anturane)—Liposomal daunorubicin may raise the concentration of uric acid in the blood. Since these medicines are used to lower uric acid levels, they may not be as effective in patients receiving liposomal daunorubicin

Other medical problems— The presence of other medical problems may affect the use of liposomal daunorubicin. Make sure you tell your doctor if you have any other medical problems, especially:
- Chickenpox (including recent exposure) or
- Herpes zoster (shingles)—Risk of severe disease affecting other parts of the body
- Gout (history of) or
- Kidney stones—Liposomal daunorubicin may increase uric acid in the body, which can cause gout or kidney stones
- Heart disease—Risk of heart problems caused by liposomal daunorubicin may be increased
- Infection—Liposomal daunorubicin can decrease your body's ability to fight infection
- Kidney disease or
- Liver disease—Effects of liposomal daunorubicin may be increased because of slower removal from the body

Proper Use of This Medicine

Liposomal daunorubicin is sometimes given together with certain other medicines. If you are using a combination of medicines, it is important that you receive each one at the proper time. If you are taking some of these medicines by mouth, ask your health care professional to help you plan a way to take them at the right times.

While you are receiving liposomal daunorubicin, your doctor may want you to drink extra fluids so that you will pass more urine. This will help prevent kidney problems and keep your kidneys working well.

This medicine often causes nausea and vomiting. However, it is very important that you continue to receive it even if you begin to feel ill. Ask your health care professional for ways to lessen these effects.

Dosing— The dose of liposomal daunorubicin will be different for different patients. The dose that is used may depend on a number of things, including what the medicine is being used for, the patient's size, and whether or not other medicines are also being taken. *If you are receiving liposomal daunorubicin at home, follow your doctor's orders or the directions on the label.* If you have any questions about the proper dose of liposomal daunorubicin, ask your doctor.

Precautions While Using This Medicine

It is very important that your doctor check your progress at regular visits to make sure that this medicine is working properly and to check for unwanted effects.

While you are being treated with liposomal daunorubicin, and after you stop treatment with it, *do not have any immunizations (vaccinations) without your doctor's approval.* Liposomal daunorubicin may lower your body's resistance and there is a chance you might get the infection the immunization is meant to prevent. In addition, other persons living in your household should not take oral poliovirus vaccine since there is a chance they could pass the poliovirus on to you. Also, avoid persons who have taken oral poliovirus vaccine. Do not get close to them, and do not stay in the same room with them for very long. If you cannot take these precautions, you should consider wearing a protective face mask that covers the nose and the mouth.

Liposomal daunorubicin can temporarily lower the number of white blood cells in your blood, increasing the chance of getting infection. It can also lower the number of platelets, which are necessary for proper blood clotting. If this occurs, there are certain precautions you can take, especially when your blood count is low, to reduce the risk of infection or bleeding:
- If you can, avoid people with infection. *Check with your doctor immediately* if you think you are getting an infection or if you get a fever or chills, cough or hoarseness, lower back or side pain, or painful or difficult urination.
- *Check with your doctor immediately* if you notice any unusual bleeding or bruising; black, tarry stools; blood in urine or stools; or pinpoint red spots on your skin.
- Be careful when using a regular toothbrush, dental floss, or toothpick. Your medical doctor, dentist, or nurse may recommend other ways to clean your teeth and gums. Check with your medical doctor before having any dental work done.
- Do not touch your eyes or the inside of your nose unless you have just washed your hands and have not touched anything else in the meantime.
- Be careful not to cut yourself when you are using sharp objects such as safety razor or fingernail or toenail cutters.
- Avoid contact sports or other situations where bruising or injury can occur.

Side Effects of This Medicine

Along with its needed effects, a medicine may cause some unwanted effects. Although not all of these side effects may occur, if they do occur they may need medical attention.

Check with your doctor as soon as possible if any of the following side effects occur:
More common
  Cough or hoarseness; fever or chills; lower back or side pain; painful or difficult urination; shortness of breath; sore throat; troubled breathing; weakness or numbness in arms or legs

Less common
  Black, tarry stools; blood in urine or stools; bloody vomit; chest pain; coughing up blood; fainting; fast heartbeat; irregular heartbeat; pinpoint red spots on skin; producing large amounts of pale, dilute urine; sores in mouth and on lips; swelling of abdomen, face, fingers, hands, feet, or lower legs; unusual bleeding or bruising; unusual nighttime urination; unusual tiredness or weakness; weight gain

Other side effects may occur that usually do not need medical attention. These side effects may go away during treatment as your body adjusts to the medicine. However, check with your doctor if any of the following side effects continue or are bothersome:
More common
  Abdominal pain; back pain; chest tightness; diarrhea;

feeling unusually cold; flushing; headache; nausea and vomiting; shivering; skin rash or itching

Less common

Bleeding after defecation; bleeding gums; constipation; difficulty swallowing; dizziness; dry mouth; dry, irritated, itching, or red eyes; extreme feeling of sleepiness; eye pain; frequent urge to defecate; pain in joints or muscles; pain at site of injection; painful, red, hot, or irritated hair follicles; red, hot, or irritated skin at site of injection; ringing sound in ears; sleeplessness; swelling or lump under skin at site of injection; tooth pain; uncomfortable swelling around anus; uncontrollable movement of body

Symptoms of overdose

Black, tarry stools; blood in urine or stools; cough or hoarseness; fever or chills; lower back or side pain; painful or difficult urination; pinpoint red spots on skin; sore throat; sores in mouth and on lips; unusual bleeding or bruising

Liposomal daunorubicin causes the urine to turn reddish in color, which may stain clothes. This is not blood. It is to be expected and only lasts for 1 or 2 days after each dose is given.

This medicine often causes a temporary and total loss of hair. After treatment with liposomal daunorubicin has ended, normal hair growth should return.

Other side effects not listed above may also occur in some patients. If you notice any other effects, check with your doctor.

Developed: 06/23/98

DECONGESTANTS AND ANALGESICS Systemic

Commonly used brand name(s):

In the U.S.—

Actifed Sinus Daytime[8]
Actifed Sinus Daytime Caplets[8]
Advil Cold and Sinus[10]
Advil Cold and Sinus Caplets[10]
Alka-Seltzer Plus Sinus Medicine[7]
Allerest No-Drowsiness Caplets[8]
Aspirin-Free Bayer Select Sinus Pain Relief Caplets[8]
BC Cold Powder Non-Drowsy Formula[7]
Coldrine[8]
Contac Allergy/Sinus Day Caplets[8]
Contac Non-Drowsy Formula Sinus Caplets[8]
Dimetapp Sinus Caplets[10]
Dristan Cold Caplets[8]
Dristan Sinus Caplets[8]
Dynafed Maximum Strength[8]
Motrin IB Sinus[10]
Motrin IB Sinus Caplets[10]
Ornex Maximum Strength Caplets[8]
Ornex No Drowsiness Caplets[8]

PhenAPAP Without Drowsiness[8]
Rhinocaps[4]
Saleto D Caplets[6]
Sinarest No-Drowsiness Caplets[8]
Sine-Aid IB Caplets[10]
Sine-Aid Maximum Strength[8]
Sine-Aid Maximum Strength Caplets[8]
Sine-Aid Maximum Strength Gelcaps[8]
Sine-Off Maximum Strength No Drowsiness Formula Caplets[8]
Sinus Excedrin Extra Strength[8]
Sinus Excedrin Extra Strength Caplets[8]
Sinus-Relief[8]
Sinutab Sinus Maximum Strength Without Drowsiness[8]
Sinutab Sinus Maximum Strength Without Drowsiness Caplets[8]
Sinutrol 500 Caplets[8]

Sudafed Sinus Maximum Strength Without Drowsiness[8]
Sudafed Sinus Maximum Strength Without Drowsiness Caplets[8]
TheraFlu Sinus Maximum Strength Caplets[8]
Tylenol Sinus Maximum Strength[8]

Tylenol Sinus Maximum Strength Caplets[8]
Tylenol Sinus Maximum Strength Gelcaps[8]
Tylenol Sinus Maximum Strength Geltabs[8]
Ursinus Inlay[9]
Vicks DayQuil Sinus Pressure & Pain Relief Caplets[10]

In Canada—

Coricidin Non-Drowsy Sinus Formula[7]
Dilotab[3]
Dimetapp-A Sinus[2]
Dristan N.D. Caplets[8]
Dristan N.D. Extra Strength Caplets[8]
Emertabs[5]
Neo Citran Extra Strength Sinus[1]

Sinutab No Drowsiness Caplets[8]
Sinutab No Drowsiness Extra Strength Caplets[8]
Sudafed Head Cold and Sinus Extra Strength Caplets[8]
Tylenol Sinus Medication Regular Strength Caplets[8]
Tylenol Sinus Medication Extra Strength Caplets[8]

Note: In November 2000, the Food and Drug Administration (FDA) issued a public health warning regarding phenylpropanolamine (PPA) due to the risk of hemorrhagic stroke. The FDA, supported by results of a research program, requested that manufacturers voluntarily discontinue marketing products that contain PPA and that consumers work with their healthcare providers to select alternative products.

Note: For quick reference, the following decongestants and analogs are numbered to match the corresponding brand names.

This information applies to the following medicines:

1. Phenylephrine and Acetaminophen (fen-ill-EF-rin and a-seat-a-MIN-oh-fen) *
2. Phenylephrine, Phenylpropanolamine, and Acetaminophen (fen-ill-EF-rin, fen-ill-proe-pa-NOLE-a-meen, and a-seat-a-MIN-oh-fen) *
3. Phenylpropanolamine and Acetaminophen (fen-ill-proe-pa-NOLE-a-meen and a-seat-a-MIN-oh-fen)
4. Phenylpropanolamine, Acetaminophen, and Aspirin (fen-ill-proe-pa-NOLE-a-meen, a-seat-a-MIN-oh-fen, and AS-pir-in) †
5. Phenylpropanolamine, Acetaminophen, and Caffeine (fen-ill-proe-pa-NOLE-a-meen, a-seat-a-MIN-oh-fen, and kaf-EEN) *
6. Phenylpropanolamine, Acetaminophen, Salicylamide, and Caffeine (fen-ill-proe-pa-NOLE-a-meen, a-seat-a-MIN-oh-fen, sal-i-SILL-a-mide, and kaf-EEN) †
7. Phenylpropanolamine and Aspirin (fen-ill-proe-pa-NOLE-a-meen and AS-pir-in)
8. Pseudoephedrine and Acetaminophen (soo-doe-e-FED-rin and a-seat-a-MIN-oh-fen)
9. Pseudoephedrine and Aspirin (soo-doe-e-FED-rin and AS-pir-in) †
10. Pseudoephedrine and Ibuprofen (soo-doe-e-FED-rin and eye-byoo-PRO-fen)

*Not commercially available in the U.S.
†Not commercially available in Canada.

Description

Decongestant and analgesic combinations are taken by mouth to relieve sinus and nasal congestion (stuffy nose) and headache of colds, allergy, and hay fever.

Decongestants, such as phenylephrine, phenylpropanolamine (also known as PPA), and pseudoephedrine produce a narrowing of blood vessels. This leads to clearing of nasal congestion, but it may also cause an increase in blood pressure in patients who have high blood pressure.

Analgesics, such as acetaminophen, ibuprofen, and salicylates (e.g., aspirin, salicylamide), are used in these combination medicines to help relieve headache and sinus pain.

Acetaminophen and salicylates may cause kidney damage or cancer of the kidney or urinary bladder if large amounts of both medicines are taken together for a long time. However, taking the recommended amounts of combination medicines that contain both acetaminophen and a salicylate for short periods of time has not been shown to cause these unwanted effects.

These medicines are available without a prescription. However, your doctor may have special instructions on the proper dose of these medicines for your medical condition. They are available in the following dosage forms:

Oral

Phenylephrine and Acetaminophen
- For oral solution (Canada)

Phenylephrine, Phenylpropanolamine, and Acetaminophen
- Tablets (Canada)

Phenylpropanolamine and Acetaminophen
- Oral solution (U.S.)
- Tablets (Canada)

Phenylpropanolamine, Acetaminophen, and Aspirin
- Capsules (U.S.)

Phenylpropanolamine, Acetaminophen, and Caffeine
- Tablets (Canada)

Phenylpropanolamine, Acetaminophen, Salicylamide, and Caffeine
- Tablets (U.S.)

Phenylpropanolamine and Aspirin
- For oral solution (U.S.)
- Effervescent tablets (U.S.)
- Tablets (Canada)

Pseudoephedrine and Acetaminophen
- Capsules (U.S.)
- Tablets (U.S. and Canada)

Pseudoephedrine and Aspirin
- Tablets (U.S.)

Pseudoephedrine and Ibuprofen
- Tablets (U.S. and Canada)

Before Using This Medicine

If you are taking this medicine without a prescription, carefully read and follow any precautions on the label. For decongestant and analgesic combinations, the following should be considered:

Allergies—Tell your doctor if you have ever had any unusual or allergic reaction to any of the ingredients contained in this medicine.

If this medicine contains *aspirin, salicylamide,* or *ibuprofen,* before taking it check with your doctor if you have ever had any unusual or allergic reaction to any of the following medicines:

Aspirin or other salicylates
Diclofenac (e.g., Voltaren)
Diflunisal (e.g., Dolobid)
Etodolac (e.g., Lodine)
Fenoprofen (e.g., Nalfon)
Floctafenine (e.g., Idarac)
Flurbiprofen, by mouth (e.g., Ansaid)
Ibuprofen (e.g., Motrin)
Indomethacin (e.g., Indocin)
Ketoprofen (e.g., Orudis)
Ketorolac (e.g., Toradol)

Meclofenamate (e.g., Meclomen)
Mefenamic acid (e.g., Ponstel)
Methyl salicylate (oil of wintergreen)
Nabumetone (e.g., Relafen)
Naproxen (e.g., Naprosyn)
Oxaprozin (e.g., Daypro)
Oxyphenbutazone (e.g., Tandearil)
Phenylbutazone (e.g., Butazolidin)
Piroxicam (e.g., Feldene)
Sulindac (e.g., Clinoril)
Suprofen (e.g., Suprol)
Tenoxicam (e.g., Mobiflex)
Tiaprofenic acid (e.g., Surgam)
Tolmetin (e.g., Tolectin)
Zomepirac (e.g., Zomax)

Also tell your health care professional if you are allergic to any other substances, such as foods, preservatives, or dyes.

Pregnancy—The occasional use of decongestant and analgesic combinations at the doses recommended on the label is not likely to cause problems in the fetus or in the newborn baby. However, for the individual ingredients of these combinations, the following information applies:

- *Alcohol*—Some of these combination medicines contain large amounts of alcohol. Too much use of alcohol during pregnancy may cause birth defects.
- *Caffeine*—Studies in humans have not shown that caffeine causes birth defects. However, studies in animals have shown that caffeine causes birth defects when given in very large doses (amounts equal to the amount of caffeine contained in 12 to 24 cups of coffee a day).
- *Ibuprofen*—Studies on birth defects have not been done in humans. However, there is a chance that ibuprofen may cause unwanted effects on the heart or blood flow of the fetus or newborn baby if it is taken regularly during the last few months of pregnancy.
- *Phenylephrine*—Studies on birth defects have not been done in either humans or animals with phenylephrine.
- *Phenylpropanolamine*—Studies on birth defects have not been done in either humans or animals with phenylpropanolamine. However, it seems that women who take phenylpropanolamine in the weeks following delivery are more likely to suffer mental or mood changes.
- *Pseudoephedrine*—Studies on birth defects with pseudoephedrine have not been done in humans. In animal studies pseudoephedrine did not cause birth defects. However, when given to animals in high doses, pseudoephedrine did cause a decrease in average weight, length, and rate of bone formation in the animal fetus.
- *Salicylates (e.g., aspirin)*—Studies on birth defects in humans have been done with aspirin, but not with salicylamide. Although salicylates have been shown to cause birth defects in animals, they have not been shown to cause birth defects in humans. Regular use of salicylates late in pregnancy may cause unwanted effects on the heart or blood flow in the fetus or newborn baby. Use of salicylates during the last 2 weeks of pregnancy may cause bleeding problems in the fetus before or during delivery, or in the newborn baby. Also, too much use of salicylates during the last 3 months of pregnancy may increase the length of pregnancy, prolong labor and cause other problems during delivery, or cause severe bleeding in the mother before, during, or after delivery. *Do not take aspirin during the last 3*

months of pregnancy unless it has been ordered by your doctor.

Breast-feeding—If you are breast-feeding the chance that problems might occur depends on the ingredients of the combination. For the individual ingredients of these combinations, the following apply:

- *Acetaminophen*—Acetaminophen passes into the breast milk. However, it has not been reported to cause problems in nursing babies.
- *Alcohol*—Alcohol passes into the breast milk. However, the amount of alcohol in recommended doses of this medicine does not usually cause problems in nursing babies.
- *Caffeine*—Small amounts of caffeine pass into the breast milk and may build up in the nursing baby. However, the amount of caffeine in recommended doses of this medicine does not usually cause problems in nursing babies.
- *Decongestants (e.g., phenylephrine, phenylpropanolamine, pseudoephedrine)*—Decongestants may pass into the breast milk and may cause unwanted effects in nursing babies of mothers taking this medicine.
- *Salicylates (e.g., aspirin, salicylamide)*—Salicylates pass into the breast milk. Although salicylates have not been reported to cause problems in nursing babies, it is possible that problems may occur if large amounts are taken regularly.

Children—Very young children are usually more sensitive to the effects of this medicine. *Before giving any of these combination medicines to a child, check the package label very carefully. Some of these medicines are too strong for use in children.* If you are not certain whether a specific product can be given to a child, or if you have any questions about the amount to give, check with your health care professional, especially if it contains:

- *Decongestants (e.g., phenylephrine, phenylpropanolamine, pseudoephedrine)*—Increases in blood pressure may be more likely to occur in children taking decongestants. Also, mental changes may be more likely to occur in young children taking phenylpropanolamine-containing combinations.
- *Salicylates (e.g., aspirin)*—Do not give aspirin or other salicylates to a child with a fever or other symptoms of a virus infection, especially flu or chickenpox, without first discussing its use with your child's doctor. This is very important because salicylates may cause a serious illness called Reye's syndrome in these children. Also, children may be more sensitive to the aspirin or other salicylates contained in some of these medicines, especially if they have a fever or have lost large amounts of body fluid because of vomiting, diarrhea, or sweating.

Teenagers—*Do not give aspirin or other salicylates to a teenager with a fever or other symptoms of a virus infection, especially flu or chickenpox, without first discussing its use with your child's doctor.* This is very important because salicylates may cause a serious illness called Reye's syndrome in these individuals.

Older adults—The elderly are usually more sensitive to the effects of this medicine.

Other medicines—Although certain medicines should not be used together at all, in other cases two different medicines may be used together even if an interaction might occur. In these cases, your doctor may want to change the dose, or other precautions may be necessary. Tell your health care professional if you are taking *any* other prescription or nonprescription (over-the-counter [OTC]) medicine, for example, aspirin or other medicine for allergies. Some medicines may change the way this medicine affects your body. Also, the effect of other medicines may be increased or reduced by some of the ingredients in this medicine. Check with your health care professional about which medicines you should not take together with this medicine.

Other medical problems—The presence of other medical problems may affect the use of decongestant and analgesic combinations. Make sure you tell your doctor if you have any other medical problems, especially:

- Alcohol abuse—Acetaminophen-containing medicine increases the chance of liver damage
- Anemia—Taking aspirin-, salicylamide-, or ibuprofen-containing medicine may make the anemia worse
- Asthma, allergies, and nasal polyps, history of—Taking salicylate- or ibuprofen-containing medicine may cause an allergic reaction in which breathing becomes difficult
- Diabetes mellitus (sugar diabetes)—The decongestant in this medicine may put the patient with diabetes at a greater risk of having heart or blood vessel disease
- Gout—Aspirin-containing medicine may make the gout worse and reduce the benefit of the medicines used for gout
- Hepatitis or other liver disease—Liver disease increases the chance of side effects because the medicine is not broken down and may build up in the body; also, if liver disease is severe there is a greater chance that aspirin-containing medicine may cause bleeding, and that ibuprofen-containing medicine may cause serious kidney damage
- Heart or blood vessel disease or
- High blood pressure—The decongestant in this medicine may cause the blood pressure to increase and may also speed up the heart rate; also, caffeine-containing medicine if taken in large amounts may increase the heart rate; ibuprofen-containing medicine may cause the blood pressure to increase
- Hemophilia or other bleeding problems—Aspirin- or ibuprofen-containing medicine increases the chance of bleeding
- Kidney disease—The kidneys may be affected, especially if too much of this medicine is taken for a long time
- Mental illness (history of)—The decongestant in this medicine may increase the chance of mental side effects
- Overactive thyroid—If an overactive thyroid has caused a fast heart rate, the decongestant in this medicine may cause the heart rate to speed up further
- Stomach ulcer or other stomach problems—Salicylate- or ibuprofen-containing medicine may make the ulcer worse or cause bleeding of the stomach
- Systemic lupus erythematosus (SLE)—Ibuprofen-containing medicine may put the patient with SLE at a greater risk of having unwanted effects on the central nervous system and/or kidneys

- Ulcers, sores, or white spots in the mouth—This may be a sign of a serious side effect of ibuprofen-containing medicine; if you already have ulcers or sores in the mouth you and your doctor may not be able to tell when this side effect occurs

Proper Use of This Medicine

Take this medicine only as directed. Do not take more of it and do not take it more often than recommended on the label, unless otherwise directed by your doctor. To do so may increase the chance of side effects.

For *aspirin- or salicylamide-containing medicines:*
- If this medicine irritates your stomach, you may take it with food or a glass of water or milk to lessen the irritation.
- *If a combination medicine containing aspirin has a strong vinegar-like odor, do not use it.* This odor means the medicine is breaking down. If you have any questions about this, check with your pharmacist.

For *ibuprofen-containing medicines:*
- To lessen stomach upset, these medicines may be taken with food or an antacid.
- Take with a full glass (8 ounces) of water. Also, do not lie down for about 15 to 30 minutes after taking the medicine. Doing so may cause irritation that may lead to trouble in swallowing.

Dosing—The dose of these combination medicines will be different for different products. *Follow the directions on the box if you are buying this medicine without a prescription. Or, follow your doctor's orders if this medicine was prescribed.* The following information includes only the average doses for these combinations.

The number of capsules or tablets or teaspoonfuls of liquid that you take depends on the strengths of the medicines.

There is a large variety of decongestant and analgesic combination products on the market. Some products are for use in adults only, while others may be used in children. If you have any questions about this, check with your health care professional.
- For *oral* dosage forms (capsules, liquid, or tablets):
  —For sinus pain and congestion:
    - Adults and children 12 years of age and older: 1 to 2 capsules or tablets every four to six hours.
    - Children up to 6 years of age: Use and dose must be determined by your doctor.
    - Children 6 to 12 years of age: 1 tablet, 4 to 6 chewable tablets, or 1 to 2 teaspoonfuls of liquid every four hours.

Missed dose—If you must take this medicine regularly and you miss a dose, take it as soon as possible. However, if it is almost time for your next dose, skip the missed dose and go back to your regular dosing schedule. Do not double doses.

Storage—To store this medicine:
- Keep this medicine out of the reach of children. Overdose is very dangerous in young children.
- Store away from heat and direct light.
- Do not store the capsule or tablet form of this medicine in the bathroom, near the kitchen sink, or in other damp places. Heat or moisture may cause the medicine to break down.
- Keep the liquid form of this medicine from freezing.

- Do not keep outdated medicine or medicine no longer needed. Be sure that any discarded medicine is out of the reach of children.

Precautions While Using This Medicine

Check with your doctor if your symptoms do not improve or become worse, or if you have a high fever.

This medicine may add to the central nervous system (CNS) stimulant and other effects of phenylpropanolamine (PPA)-containing diet aids. *Do not use medicines for diet or appetite control while taking this medicine unless you have checked with your doctor.*

This medicine may cause some people to become nervous or restless or to have trouble in sleeping. If you have trouble in sleeping, *take the last dose of this medicine for each day a few hours before bedtime.* If you have any questions about this, check with your doctor.

Before having any kind of surgery (including dental surgery) or emergency treatment, tell the medical doctor or dentist in charge that you are taking this medicine.

Check the label of all over-the-counter (OTC), nonprescription, and prescription medicines you now take. If any of them contain acetaminophen, aspirin, other salicylates such as bismuth subsalicylate (e.g., Pepto Bismol) or magnesium salicylate (e.g., Nuprin Backache Caplets), or salicylic acid (present in some shampoos and skin products), *check with your health care professional. Using any of them together with this medicine may cause an overdose.*

Do not drink alcoholic beverages while taking this medicine. Stomach problems may be more likely to occur if you drink alcoholic beverages while you are taking aspirin or ibuprofen. Also, liver damage may be more likely to occur if you drink large amounts of alcoholic beverages while you are taking acetaminophen.

If you think that you or anyone else may have taken an overdose of this medicine, get emergency help at once. Taking an overdose of a salicylate may cause unconsciousness or death. The first sign of an aspirin overdose may be ringing or buzzing in the ears. Other signs include convulsions (seizures), hearing loss, confusion, severe drowsiness or tiredness, severe excitement or nervousness, and unusually fast or deep breathing. Signs of severe acetaminophen overdose may not appear until 2 to 4 days after the overdose is taken, but treatment to prevent liver damage or death must be started within 24 hours or less after the overdose is taken.

For patients *taking aspirin-containing medicine:*
- Do not take aspirin-containing medicine for 5 days before any surgery, including dental surgery, unless otherwise directed by your medical doctor or dentist. Taking aspirin during this time may cause bleeding problems.

For diabetic patients *taking salicylate-containing medicine:*
- False urine sugar test results may occur if you take 8 or more 325-mg (5-grain) doses of aspirin every day for several days in a row. Smaller doses or occasional use of aspirin usually will not affect urine sugar tests. If you have any questions about this, check with your health care professional, especially if your diabetes is not well controlled.

For patients *taking ibuprofen-containing medicine:*
- This medicine may cause some people to become confused, drowsy, dizzy, lightheaded, or less alert than they

are normally. It may also cause blurred vision or other vision problems in some people. *Make sure you know how you react to this medicine before you drive, use machines, or do anything else that could be dangerous if you are dizzy or are not alert and able to see well.*

Side Effects of This Medicine

Along with its needed effects, a medicine may cause some unwanted effects. Although serious side effects occur rarely when this medicine is taken as recommended, they may be more likely to occur if:
- too much medicine is taken
- it is taken in large doses
- it is taken for a long period of time

Get emergency help immediately if any of the following symptoms of overdose occur:
For all combinations
Convulsions (seizures); dizziness or lightheadedness (severe); fast, slow, or irregular heartbeat; hallucinations (seeing, hearing, or feeling things that are not there); headache (continuing and severe); increased sweating; mood or mental changes; nausea or vomiting (severe or continuing); nervousness or restlessness (severe); shortness of breath or troubled breathing; stomach cramps or pain (severe or continuing); swelling or tenderness in the upper abdomen or stomach area; trouble in sleeping

For acetaminophen-containing only
Diarrhea; loss of appetite

For aspirin- or salicylamide-containing only
Any loss of hearing; changes in behavior (in children); confusion; diarrhea (severe or continuing); drowsiness or tiredness (severe, especially in children); fast or deep breathing (especially in children); ringing or buzzing in ears (continuing); uncontrollable flapping movements of the hands, (especially in elderly patients); unexplained fever; unusual thirst; vision problems

Also, check with your doctor as soon as possible if any of the following side effects occur:
More common
Nausea, vomiting, or stomach pain (mild—for combinations containing aspirin or ibuprofen)

Less common or rare
Bloody or black, tarry stools; bloody or cloudy urine; blurred vision or any changes in vision or eyes; changes in facial skin color; changes in hearing; changes or problems with urination; difficult or painful urination; fever; headache, severe, with fever and stiff neck; increased blood pressure; muscle cramps or pain; skin rash, hives, or itching; sores, ulcers, or white spots on lips or in mouth; swelling of face, fingers, feet, or lower legs; swollen and/or painful glands; unexplained sore throat and fever; unusual bleeding or bruising; unusual tiredness or weakness; vomiting of blood or material that looks like coffee grounds; weight gain (unusual); yellow eyes or skin

Other side effects may occur that usually do not need medical attention. These side effects may go away during treatment as your body adjusts to the medicine. However, check with your doctor if any of the following side effects continue or are bothersome:

More common
Heartburn or indigestion (for medicines containing salicylate or ibuprofen); nervousness or restlessness
Less common
Drowsiness (for medicines containing salicylamide)

Not all of the side effects listed above have been reported for each of these medicines, but they have been reported for at least one of them. There are some similarities among these combination medicines, so many of the above side effects may occur with any of these medicines.

Other side effects not listed above may also occur in some patients. If you notice any other effects, check with your doctor.

Revised: 12/18/2000

DEFEROXAMINE   Systemic

Commonly used brand name(s):

In the U.S.—
Desferal

In Canada—
Desferal
Another commonly used name is desferrioxamine.

Description

Deferoxamine (dee-fer-OX-a-meen) is used to remove excess iron from the body. This may be necessary in certain patients with anemia who must receive many blood transfusions. It is also used to treat acute iron poisoning, especially in small children.

Deferoxamine combines with iron in the bloodstream. The combination of iron and deferoxamine is then removed from the body by the kidneys. By removing the excess iron, the medicine lessens damage to various organs and tissues of the body. This medicine may be used for other conditions as determined by your doctor.

Deferoxamine is to be administered only by or under the immediate supervision of your doctor. It is available in the following dosage form:

Parenteral
- Injection (U.S. and Canada)

Before Receiving This Medicine

In deciding to use a medicine, the risks of taking the medicine must be weighed against the good it will do. This is a decision you and your doctor will make. For deferoxamine, the following should be considered:

Allergies—Tell your doctor if you have ever had any unusual or allergic reaction to deferoxamine. Also tell your health care professional if you are allergic to any other substances, such as foods, preservatives, or dyes.

Pregnancy—Deferoxamine has not been shown to cause birth defects or other problems in humans. However, in animal studies this medicine caused birth defects when given in doses just above the recommended human dose. In general, deferoxamine is not recommended for women who may become pregnant or for use during early pregnancy, unless the woman's life is in danger from too much iron.

Breast-feeding—It is not known whether deferoxamine passes into breast milk. Although most medicines pass into breast milk in small amounts, many of them may be used safely while breast-feeding. Mothers who are taking this medicine and who wish to breast-feed should discuss this with their doctor.

Children—Deferoxamine is not used for long-term treatment of children up to 3 years of age. Also, younger patients are more likely to develop hearing and vision problems with the use of deferoxamine in high doses for a long time.

Older adults—The combination of deferoxamine and vitamin C should be used with caution in older patients, since this combination may be more likely to cause heart problems in these patients than in younger adults.

Other medicines—Although certain medicines should not be used together at all, in other cases two different medicines may be used together even if an interaction might occur. In these cases, your doctor may want to change the dose, or other precautions may be necessary. When you are receiving deferoxamine, it is especially important that your health care professional know if you are taking the following:

- Ascorbic acid (vitamin C)—Use with deferoxamine may be harmful to body tissues, especially in the elderly

Other medical problems—The presence of other medical problems may affect the use of deferoxamine. Make sure you tell your doctor if you have any other medical problems, especially:

- Kidney disease—Patients with kidney disease may be more likely to have side effects

Proper Use of This Medicine

Deferoxamine may sometimes be given at home to patients who do not need to be in the hospital. If you are receiving this medicine at home, *make sure you clearly understand and carefully follow your doctor's instructions.*

Dosing—The dose of deferoxamine will be different for different patients. *Follow your doctor's orders or the directions on the label.* The following information includes only the average doses of deferoxamine. *If your dose is different, do not change it* unless your doctor tells you to do so.

- For *injection* dosage form:
  —For acute iron toxicity:
  - Adults and children over 3 years of age—Dose is based on body weight and must be determined by your doctor. The usual dose is 90 milligrams (mg) per kilogram (kg) (41 mg per pound) of body weight, followed by 45 mg per kg (20 mg per pound) of body weight, injected into a muscle every four to twelve hours. If it is injected into a vein, the usual dose is 15 mg per kg (7 mg per pound) of body weight per hour every eight hours.
  - Children up to 3 years of age—The usual dose is 15 mg per kg (7 mg per pound) of body weight per hour, injected into a vein.
  —For chronic iron toxicity:
  - Adults and children over 3 years of age—The usual dose is 500 mg to 1 gram a day, injected into a muscle. Or, the medicine may be injected under the skin by an infusion pump. The usual dose is 1 to 2 grams (20 to 40 mg per kg [9 to

18 mg per pound] of body weight) a day, injected under the skin, over a period of eight to twenty-four hours. If you are receiving blood transfusions, the usual dose is 500 mg to 1 gram a day, injected into a muscle. An extra 2 grams of the medicine is injected into a vein with each unit of blood at a rate of 15 mg per kg of body weight per hour.
  - Children up to 3 years of age—Use and dose must be determined by your doctor. The usual dose is 10 mg per kg (5 mg per pound) of body weight a day, injected under the skin.

Storage—To store this medicine:
- Keep out of the reach of children.
- Store away from heat and direct light.
- Store the mixed medicine at room temperature for no longer than recommended by your doctor or the manufacturer. Do not refrigerate.
- Do not keep outdated medicine or medicine that is no longer needed. Be sure any discarded medicine is out of the reach of children.

Precautions While Receiving This Medicine

It is important that your doctor check your progress at regular visits to make sure that this medicine is working properly and to prevent unwanted effects. Certain blood and urine tests must be done regularly to check for the need for dosage changes.

Deferoxamine may cause some people, especially younger patients, to have hearing and vision problems within a few weeks after they start taking it. *If you notice any problems with your vision, such as blurred vision, difficulty in seeing at night, or difficulty in seeing colors, or difficulty with your hearing, check with your doctor as soon as possible.* The dose of deferoxamine may need to be adjusted.

Do not take vitamin C unless your doctor has told you to do so.

Side Effects of This Medicine

Along with its needed effects, a medicine may cause some unwanted effects. Although not all of these side effects may occur, if they do occur they may need medical attention.

Check with your doctor as soon as possible if any of the following side effects occur:
More common
Bluish fingernails, lips, or skin; blurred vision or other problems with vision; convulsions (seizures); difficulty in breathing (wheezing), or fast breathing; fast heartbeat; hearing problems; pain or swelling at place of injection; redness or flushing of skin; skin rash, hives, or itching
Less common
Diarrhea; difficult urination; fever; leg cramps; stomach and muscle cramps; stomach discomfort; unusual bleeding or bruising

Hearing and vision problems are more likely to occur in younger patients taking high doses and on long-term treatment.

Deferoxamine may cause the urine to turn orange-rose in color. This is to be expected while you are using this medicine.

Other side effects not listed above may also occur in some patients. If you notice any other effects, check with your doctor.

Additional Information

Once a medicine has been approved for marketing for a certain use, experience may show that it is also useful for other medical problems. Although this use is not included in product labeling, deferoxamine is used in certain patients with the following medical condition:

- Aluminum toxicity (too much aluminum in the body)

Other than the above information, there is no additional information relating to proper use, precautions, or side effects for this use.

Revised: 06/22/2000

DELAVIRDINE   Systemic

Commonly used brand name(s):

In the U.S.—
Rescriptor

Description

Delavirdine (de-la-VIR-deen) is used, in combination with other medicines, in the treatment of the infection caused by the human immunodeficiency virus (HIV). HIV is the virus that causes acquired immune deficiency syndrome (AIDS).

Delavirdine will not cure or prevent HIV infection or AIDS; however, it helps keep HIV from reproducing and appears to slow down the destruction of the immune system. This may help delay the development of problems usually related to AIDS or HIV disease. Delavirdine will not keep you from spreading HIV to other people. People who receive this medicine may continue to have other problems usually related to AIDS or HIV disease.

This medicine is available only with your doctor's prescription, in the following dosage form:

Oral
- Tablets (U.S.)

Before Using This Medicine

In deciding to use a medicine, the risks of taking the medicine must be weighed against the good it will do. This is a decision you and your doctor will make. For delavirdine, the following should be considered:

Allergies—Tell your doctor if you have ever had any unusual or allergic reaction to delavirdine. Also tell your health care professional if you are allergic to any other substances, such as foods, preservatives, or dyes.

Pregnancy—Delavirdine has not been studied in pregnant women. However, studies in animals have shown that delavirdine causes birth defects when given in doses higher than those given to humans. Before taking this medicine, make sure your doctor knows if you are pregnant or if you may become pregnant.

Breast-feeding—It is not known whether delavirdine passes into the breast milk. However, if your baby does not

already have the AIDS virus, there is a chance you could pass it to your baby by breast-feeding. Talk to your doctor first if you are thinking about breast-feeding your baby.

Older adults—Delavirdine has not been studied specifically in older people. Therefore, it is not known whether it causes different side effects or problems in the elderly than it does in younger adults.

Other medicines—Although certain medicines should not be used together at all, in other cases two different medicines may be used together even if an interaction might occur. In these cases, your doctor may want to change the dose, or other precautions may be necessary. When you are taking delavirdine, it is especially important that your health care professional know if you are taking any of the following:

- Amphetamines or
- Astemizole (e.g., Hismanal) or
- Benzodiazepines (alprazolam [e.g., Xanax], chlordiazepoxide [e.g., Librium], clonazepam [e.g., Klonopin], clorazepate [e.g., Tranxene], diazepam [e.g., Valium], estazolam [e.g., ProSom], flurazepam [e.g., Dalmane], halazepam [e.g., Paxipam], lorazepam [e.g., Ativan], oxazepam [e.g., Serax], prazepam [e.g., Centrax], quazepam [e.g., Doral], temazepam [e.g., Restoril], triazolam [e.g., Halcion]) or
- Calcium channel blocking agents (bepridil [e.g., Vasocor], diltiazem [e.g., Cardizem], felodipine [e.g., Plendil], flunarizine [e.g., Sibelium], isradipine [e.g., DynaCirc], nicardipine [e.g., Cardene], nifedipine [e.g., Adalat, Procardia], nimodipine [e.g., Nimotop], verapamil [e.g., Calan, Isoptin]) or
- Cisapride (e.g., Propulsid) or
- Ergot alkaloids (dihydroergotamine [e.g., D.H.E. 45], ergoloid mesylates [e.g., Hydergine], ergonovine [e.g., Ergotrate], ergotamine [e.g., Gynergen], methylergonovine [e.g., Methergine], methysergide [e.g., Sansert]) or
- Terfenadine (e.g., Seldane)—Delavirdine may interfere with the removal of these medicines from the body, which could lead to serious side effects

- Carbamazepine (e.g., Tegretol) or
- Phenobarbital or
- Phenytoin (e.g., Dilantin)—Use of these medicines with delavirdine may decrease the effects of delavirdine

- Cimetidine (e.g., Tagamet) or
- Famotidine (e.g., Pepcid) or
- Nizatidine (e.g., Axid) or
- Ranitidine (e.g., Zantac)—Use of these medicines may interfere with absorption of delavirdine into the body and could decrease its effects

- Clarithromycin (e.g., Biaxin)—Use of this medicine with delavirdine may increase the amount of both medicines in the body

- Indinavir (e.g., Crixivan)—Use of this medicine with delavirdine may increase the amount of indinavir in the body

- Rifabutin (e.g., Mycobutin)—Use of this medicine with delavirdine may increase the amount of rifabutin and decrease the amount of delavirdine in the body

- Rifampin (e.g., Rifadin)—Use of this medicine with delavirdine may decrease the amount of delavirdine in the body

Other medical problems—The presence of other medical problems may affect the use of delavirdine. Make sure

you tell your doctor if you have any other medical problems, especially:

- Liver disease—Effects of delavirdine may be increased because of slower removal from the body

Proper Use of This Medicine

This medicine can be taken with our without food.

It is best to swallow the tablets whole. However, if swallowing is difficult, the tablets can be put in a glass of water (at least 3 ounces), allowed to sit for a few minutes, and then stirred to mix. Drink the mixture right away. Then rinse the glass with water and drink that rinse to make sure the full dose is taken.

Do not take any antacid medications within 1 hour of the time you take delavirdine. They may prevent delavirdine from being absorbed into the body.

Take this medicine exactly as directed by your doctor. Do not take it more often, and do not take it for a longer time than your doctor ordered. Also, do not stop taking this medicine without checking with your doctor first.

Keep taking delavirdine for the full time of treatment, even if you begin to feel better.

Dosing—The dose of delavirdine will be different for different patients. *Follow your doctor's orders or the directions on the label.* The following information includes only the average doses of delavirdine. *If your dose is different, do not change it* unless your doctor tells you to do so.

- For *oral* dosage form (tablets):
  —For treatment of HIV infection:
  - Adults—400 mg three times a day.
  - Children younger than 16 years of age—Use and dose must be determined by your doctor.

Missed dose—If you miss a dose of this medicine, take it as soon as you remember. However, if it is almost time for your next dose, skip the missed dose and go back to your regular dosing schedule. Do not double doses.

Storage—To store this medicine:

- Keep out of the reach of children.
- Store away from heat and direct light.
- Do not store in the bathroom, near the kitchen sink, or in other damp places. Heat or moisture may cause the medicine to break down.
- Do not keep outdated medicine or medicine no longer needed. Be sure that any discarded medicine is out of the reach of children.

Precautions While Using This Medicine

It is very important that your doctor check your progress at regular visits.

Side Effects of This Medicine

Along with its needed effects, a medicine may cause some unwanted effects. Although not all of these side effects may occur, if they do occur they may need medical attention.

Check with your doctor as soon as possible if any of the following side effects occur:

More common
Skin rash (severe) with itching

Less common
Blisters; eye inflammation; fever; joint aches; muscle aches; sores in mouth; swelling

Rare
Difficulty in breathing

Other side effects may occur that usually do not need medical attention. These side effects may go away during treatment as your body adjusts to the medicine. However, check with your doctor if any of the following side effects continue or are bothersome:

More common
Diarrhea; headache; nausea; unusual tiredness or weakness

Less common
Vomiting

Other side effects not listed above may also occur in some patients. If you notice any other effects, check with your doctor.

Developed: 07/28/98

DENILEUKIN DIFTITOX   Systemic†

Commonly used brand name(s):

In the U.S.—
Ontak
Generic name product may be available.

†Not commercially available in Canada.

Description

Denileukin diftitox (DEN-i-loo-kin DIF-ti-toks) is used to treat cutaneous T-cell lymphoma, a rare type of cancer that affects certain white blood cells and causes lesions to develop on the skin.

Denileukin diftitox interferes with the growth of cancer cells, which are eventually destroyed. Since the growth of normal cells may also be affected by the medicine, other effects may also occur. Some of these may be serious and must be reported to your doctor. Some effects may occur after treatment with denileukin diftitox.

Denileukin diftitox is to be administered only by or under the supervision of your doctor or other health care professional. It is available in the following dosage form(s):

Parenteral
- Injection (U.S.)

Before Using This Medicine

In deciding to use a medicine, the risks of taking the medicine must be weighed against the good it will do. This is a decision you and your doctor will make. For denileukin diftitox, the following should be considered:

Allergies—Tell your doctor if you have ever had any unusual or allergic reaction to denileukin diftitox, diptheria toxin, or interleukin-2. Also tell your health care professional if your are allergic to any other substances, such as foods, preservatives, or dyes.

Pregnancy—Denileukin diftitox has not been studied in pregnant women. Before taking this medicine, make sure your doctor knows if you are pregnant or if you may become pregnant.

Breast-feeding—It is not known whether denileukin diftitox passes into human breast milk. However, breast-feeding is not recommended while you are receiving this medicine.

Children—Studies on this medicine have been done only in adult patients, and there is no specific information comparing use of denileukin diftitox in children with use in other age groups.

Older adults—Adverse effects such as anorexia, hypotension, anemia, confusion, rash, nausea, and/or vomiting may be especially likely to occur in elderly patients who may be more sensitive than younger adults to the effects of denileukin diftitox.

Other medical problems—The presence of other medical problems may affect the use of denileukin diftitox. Make sure to tell your doctor if you have any other medical problems, especially heart disease.

Proper Use of This Medicine

Dosing—The dose of denileukin diftitox will be different for different patients. The dose that is used may depend on a number of things, including your size. Denileukin diftitox usually is given by a doctor or nurse in the hospital or outpatient clinic. If you have any questions about the proper dose of denileukin diftitox, ask your doctor.

Precautions While Using This Medicine

It is very important that your doctor check your progress at regular visits to make sure that this medicine is working properly and to check for unwanted effects.

Side Effects of This Medicine

Along with its needed effects, a medicine may cause some unwanted effects. Although not all of these side effects may occur, if they do occur they may need medical attention.

Check with your doctor immediately if any of the following side effects occur:

More common
> Back pain; chest pain; dizziness or faintness; difficulty swallowing; fast or irregular heartbeat; fever or chills; infection; rash; shortness of breath; swelling of face, feet, or lower legs; warmth and flushing of skin

Less common
> Abdominal pain, severe; black, tarry stools; cloudy urine; blood in urine or stools; cloudy urine; cough or hoarseness accompanied by fever or chills; headache, severe; loss of coordination; lower back pain or side pain accompanied by fever or chills; painful or difficult urination accompanied by fever or chills; pain in groin or leg; pinpoint red spots on skin; slurring of speech; sudden vision changes; swelling or pain at injection site; unusual bleeding or bruising; weakness of arm and leg

Rare
> Decreased urination, accompanied by nausea and loss of appetite

Check with your doctor as soon as possible if any of the following side effects occur:

More common
> Difficulty swallowing; loss of strength or energy; nausea; pain in joints and muscles; unusual tiredness or weakness; vomiting

Rare
> Dry, puffy skin; increased heart rate; loss of appetite; weight gain

Other side effects may occur that usually do not need medical attention. These side effects may go away during treatment as your body adjusts to the medicine. However, check with your doctor if any of the following side effects continue or are bothersome:

More common
> Cough; diarrhea; skin rash; sore throat

Less common or rare
> Confusion; constipation; indigestion; numbness or tingling of fingers, toes, or face; runny nose; trouble in sleeping

Some side effects of denileukin diftitox may not develop until long after you have received the medicine, sometimes up to two weeks later.

Other side effects not listed above may also occur in some patients. If you notice any other effects, check with your doctor.

Developed: 9/23/99

DESMOPRESSIN   Systemic

Commonly used brand name(s):

In the U.S.—
DDAVP Injection   DDAVP Tablets
DDAVP Nasal Spray   Stimate Nasal Spray
DDAVP Rhinal Tube
Generic name product may be available.

In Canada—
DDAVP Injection   DDAVP Tablets
DDAVP Spray   Octostim
DDAVP Rhinyle Nasal
   Solution

Description

Desmopressin (des-moe-PRES-in) is a hormone taken through the nose, by mouth, or given by injection to prevent or control the frequent urination, increased thirst, and loss of water associated with diabetes insipidus (water diabetes). It is used also to control bed-wetting and frequent urination and increased thirst associated with certain types of brain injuries or brain surgery. Desmopressin works by acting on the kidneys to reduce the flow of urine.

Desmopressin is also given by injection to treat some patients with certain bleeding problems such as hemophilia or von Willebrand's disease.

Desmopressin is available only with your doctor's prescription, in the following dosage forms:

Nasal
> • Nasal solution (U.S. and Canada)

Oral
> • Tablets (U.S. and Canada)

Parenteral
> • Injection (U.S. and Canada)

Before Using This Medicine

In deciding to use a medicine, the risks of taking the medicine must be weighed against the good it will do. This is a decision you and your doctor will make. For desmopressin, the following should be considered:

Allergies—Tell your doctor if you have ever had any unusual or allergic reaction to desmopressin. Also tell your health care professional if you are allergic to any other substances, such as foods, preservatives, or dyes.

Pregnancy—Studies have not been done in pregnant women. Desmopressin has been used before and during pregnancy to treat diabetes insipidus and has not been shown to cause birth defects.

Breast-feeding—Desmopressin passes into breast milk in very small amounts. However, it has not been reported to cause problems in nursing babies.

Children—Infants may be more sensitive to the effects of desmopressin.

Older adults—Some side effects (confusion, continuing headache, drowsiness, problem with urination, weight gain) may be especially likely to occur in elderly patients, who are usually more sensitive than younger adults to the effects of desmopressin.

Other medicines—Although certain medicines should not be used together at all, in other cases two different medicines may be used together even if an interaction might occur. In these cases, your doctor may want to change the dose, or other precautions may be necessary. Tell your health care professional if you are taking any other prescription or nonprescription (over-the-counter [OTC]) medicine.

Other medical problems—The presence of other medical problems may affect the use of desmopressin. Make sure you tell your doctor if you have any other medical problems, especially:

- Cystic fibrosis or
- Dehydration—Loss of sodium from the blood and serious side effects may be more likely to occur in patients with these conditions

- Headache, severe, or migraine or
- Heart or blood vessel disease or
- High blood pressure—Large doses of desmopressin can cause an increase or decrease in blood pressure

- Stuffy nose caused by cold or allergy—May prevent nasal desmopressin from being absorbed through the lining of the nose into the blood stream

Proper Use of This Medicine

Use this medicine only as directed. Do not use more of it and do not use it more often than your doctor ordered. To do so may increase the chance of side effects.

For patients using the *nasal solution form* of this medicine:
- This medicine usually comes with patient directions. Read them carefully before using this medicine.
- *Do not use the nasal spray more times than the number indicated on the label*. If you do, you may not receive the correct amount of medicine.

Dosing—When you are using desmopressin, it is very important that you get the exact amount of medicine that you need. The dose of desmopressin will be different for different

patients. Your doctor will determine the proper dose of desmopressin for you.

The number of doses you use each day, the time allowed between doses, and the length of time you use the medicine depend on the medical problem for which you are using desmopressin.

- For *nasal* dosage form (nasal solution):
  - —For preventing or controlling diabetes insipidus (water diabetes):
    - Adults and teenagers—At first, 10 micrograms (mcg) inhaled in a nostril at bedtime. Your doctor may increase the dose gradually each night if needed. Then, your doctor may want you to use 10 to 40 mcg. The dose may be used as a single dose or it may be divided into two or three doses a day.
    - Children 3 months to 12 years of age—Dose is based on body weight and must be determined by your doctor. It is usually 0.25 mcg per kilogram (kg) (0.11 mcg per pound) of body weight. The dose is inhaled in a nostril one or two times a day.
    - Children up to 3 months of age—Dose must be determined by your doctor.
  - —For controlling bed-wetting:
    - Adults, teenagers, and children 6 years of age or older—At first, 10 mcg inhaled into each nostril at bedtime. Then, your doctor may change the dose to 10 to 40 mcg a day.
    - Children up to 6 years of age—Dose must be determined by your doctor.

- For *oral* dosage form (tablets):
  - —For preventing or controlling diabetes insipidus (water diabetes):
    - Adults, teenagers, and children—At first, 0.05 milligram (mg) two times a day. Then, your doctor may change the dose to 0.1 to 0.8 mg. The dose may be divided into several doses a day.
  - —For controlling bed-wetting:
    - Adults, teenagers, and children 6 years of age or older—At first, 0.2 mg once a day at bedtime. Then, your doctor may increase the dose to as much as 0.6 mg a day.
    - Children up to 6 years of age—Dose must be determined by your doctor.

- For *parenteral* dosage form (injection):
  - —For preventing or controlling frequent urination:
    - Adults and teenagers—2 to 4 mcg or 0.025 mcg per kg (0.011 mcg per pound) of body weight injected into a muscle, vein, or under the skin. This dose is usually divided into two doses a day, one given in the morning, and the other given in the evening.
    - Children—0.4 mcg or 0.025 mcg per kg (0.011 mcg per pound) of body weight injected into a muscle, vein, or under the skin once a day.
  - —For treating some bleeding problems such as hemophilia or von Willebrand's disease:
    - Adults, teenagers, and children 11 months of age or older weighing more than 10 kg (22 pounds)—The dose is based on body weight and must be determined by your doctor. It is usually 0.3 mcg per kg (0.14 mcg per pound) of body weight mixed in 50 milliliters (mL) of 0.9% sodium chloride. This solution is injected into a vein slowly over fifteen

to thirty minutes. Your doctor may repeat this treatment if needed.

- Children 11 months of age or older weighing 10 kg (22 pounds) or less—The dose is based on body weight and must be determined by your doctor. It is usually 0.3 mcg per kg (0.14 mcg per pound) of body weight mixed in 10 mL of 0.9% sodium chloride. This solution is injected into a vein slowly over fifteen to thirty minutes. Your doctor may repeat this treatment if needed.
- Children up to 11 months of age—Use is not recommended.

Missed dose—If you miss a dose of this medicine and your dosing schedule is:

- One dose a day—Use the missed dose as soon as possible. Then go back to your regular dosing schedule. However, if you do not remember the missed dose until the next day, skip the missed dose and go back to your regular dosing schedule. Do not double doses.
- More than one dose a day—Use the missed dose as soon as possible. Then go back to your regular dosing schedule. However, if it is almost time for your next dose, skip the missed dose and go back to your regular dosing schedule. Do not double doses.

Storage—To store this medicine:

- Keep out of the reach of children.
- Store away from heat and direct light.
- Do not store tablets in the bathroom, near the kitchen sink, or in other damp places. Heat or moisture may cause the medicine to break down.
- Store as directed on the label or by your health care professional. Keep the medicine from freezing.
- Do not keep outdated medicine or medicine no longer needed. Be sure that any discarded medicine is out of the reach of children.

Side Effects of This Medicine

Along with its needed effects, a medicine may cause some unwanted effects. Although not all of these effects may occur, if they do occur they may need medical attention.

Check with your doctor immediately if any of the following side effects occur:
 Rare
  Chills; confusion; convulsions (seizures); decreased urination; drowsiness; fever; headache (continuing); shortness of breath, tightness in chest, trouble in breathing, or wheezing; skin rash, hives, or itching; weight gain (rapid)

Check with your doctor as soon as possible if the following side effect occurs:
 Rare
  Fast heartbeat

Other side effects may occur that usually do not need medical attention. These side effects may go away during treatment as your body adjusts to the medicine. However, check with your doctor if any of the following side effects continue or are bothersome:
 Less common or rare
  Abdominal or stomach cramps; flushing or redness of skin; nausea; pain in the vulva (genital area outside of the vagina)

With intranasal (through the nose) use
  Cough; nosebleed; runny or stuffy nose; sneezing; sore throat
With intravenous use
  Pain, redness, or swelling at place of injection

Other side effects not listed above may also occur in some patients. If you notice any other effects, check with your doctor.

Additional Information

Once a medicine has been approved for marketing for a certain use, experience may show that it is also useful for other medical problems. Although this use is not included in product labeling, desmopressin is used in certain patients to determine the cause of Cushing's syndrome.

Other than the above information, there is no additional information relating to proper use, precautions, or side effects for this use.

Revised: 06/04/99

DEXRAZOXANE Systemic

Commonly used brand name(s):

In the U.S.—
 Zinecard

Description

Dexrazoxane (dex-ray-ZOKS-ane) is used to help prevent or lessen a toxic effect to your heart that is caused by certain medicines that are used to treat cancer.

This medicine is available only with your doctor's prescription, in the following dosage form(s):

 Parenteral
  - Injection (U.S.)

Before Using This Medicine

In deciding to use a medicine, the risks of using the medicine must be weighed against the good it will do. This is a decision you and your doctor will make. For dexrazoxane, the following should be considered:

Allergies—Tell your doctor if you have ever had any unusual or allergic reaction to dexrazoxane.

Pregnancy—Dexrazoxane has not been studied in pregnant women. However, studies in animals have shown that dexrazoxane causes birth defects. Before taking this medicine, make sure your doctor knows if you are pregnant or if you may become pregnant.

Breast-feeding—It is not known whether dexrazoxane passes into the breast milk. However, dexrazoxane is not recommended during breast-feeding, because it may cause unwanted effects in nursing infants.

Children—Studies on this medicine have been done only in adult patients, and there is no specific information comparing use of dexrazoxane in children with use in other age groups.

Older adults—Many medicine have not been studies specifically on older people. Therefore, it may not be known whether they work exactly the same way they do in younger adults or if they cause different side effects or problems in older people. There is no specific information comparing the use of dexrazoxane in the elderly with use in other age groups.

Other medicines—Although certain medicines should not be used together at all, in other cases two different medicines may be used together even if an interaction might occur. In these cases, your doctor may want to change the dose, or other precautions may be necessary. When you are taking dexrazoxane, it is especially important that your health care professional know if you are taking any of the following:

- Amphotericin B by injection (e.g., Fungizone) or
- Antithyroid agents (medicine for overactive thyroid) or
- Azathioprine (e.g., Imuran) or
- Chloramphenicol (e.g., Chloromycetin) or
- Colchicine or
- Flucytosine (e.g., Ancobon) or
- Ganciclovir (e.g., Cytovene) or
- Interferon (e.g., Intron A, Roferon-A) or
- Plicamycin (e.g., Mithracin) or
- Zidovudine (e.g., AZT, Retrovir)—Dexrazoxane may increase the effects of these medicines on the blood

Proper Use of This Medicine

Dosing—The dose of dexrazoxane will be different for different patients. The dose that is used may depend on a number of things, including your size and the dose of the cancer medicine being used with dexrazoxane. If you have any questions about the proper dose of dexrazoxane, ask your doctor.

Side Effects of This Medicine

Along with its needed effects, a medicine may cause some unwanted effects. Although not all of these side effects may occur, if they do occur they may need medical attention.

Check with your doctor immediately if the following side effect occurs:

> *Less common*
>> Pain at place of injection

Other side effects not listed above may also occur in some patients. If you notice any other effects, check with your doctor.

Developed: 08/14/98

DEXTROMETHORPHAN   Systemic

Commonly used brand name(s):
In the U.S.—

Benylin Adult Formula Cough Syrup
Benylin Pediatric Cough Suppressant
Cough-X
Creo-Terpin
Delsym Cough Formula
Diabe-TUSS DM Syrup
Hold DM
Pertussin CS Children's Strength
Pertussin DM Extra Strength
Robitussin Maximum Strength Cough Suppressant
Robitussin Pediatric Cough Suppressant

Sucrets 4 Hour Cough Suppressant
Trocal
Vicks 44 Cough Relief

In Canada—
Balminil DM
Balminil DM Children
Benylin DM
Benylin DM 12 Hour
Benylin DM for Children
Benylin DM for Children 12 Hour
Broncho-Grippol-DM
Calmylin #1
Delsym
Koffex DM
Novahistex DM
Novahistine DM
Robitussin Pediatric
Triaminic DM Long Lasting for Children

Description

Dextromethorphan (dex-troe-meth-OR-fan) is used to relieve coughs due to colds or influenza (flu). It should not be used for chronic cough that occurs with smoking, asthma, or emphysema or when there is an unusually large amount of mucus or phlegm (flem) with the cough.

Dextromethorphan relieves cough by acting directly on the cough center in the brain.

This medicine is available without a prescription; however, your doctor may have special instructions on the proper use of this medicine for your medical condition. It is available in the following dosage forms:

> *Oral*
>> Lozenges (U.S.)
>> Extended-release oral suspension (U.S. and Canada)
>> Syrup (U.S. and Canada)

Before Using This Medicine

If you are taking this medicine without a prescription, carefully read and follow any precautions on the label. For dextromethorphan, the following should be considered:

Allergies—Tell your doctor if you have ever had any unusual or allergic reaction to dextromethorphan or its other ingredients such as, alcohol, artificial sweetener, benzocaine, glucose, granulated sugar, menthol, natural honey flavoring, sucralose, sucrose, or sugar. Also tell your health care professional if you are allergic to any other substances, such as foods, preservatives, or dyes.

Diet—Make certain your health care professional knows if you are on a low-sodium, low-sugar, or any other special diet. Most medicines contain more than their active ingredient, and many liquid medicines contain alcohol.

Pregnancy—Dextromethorphan has not been studied in pregnant women. Before taking this medicine, make sure your doctor knows if you are pregnant or if you may become pregnant.

Breast-feeding—It is not known whether dextromethorphan passes into breast milk. However, dextromethorphan has not been reported to cause problems in nursing babies.

Children—Although there is no specific information comparing use of dextromethorphan in children with use in other age groups, this medicine is not expected to cause different side effects or problems in children than it does in adults.

Older adults—Many medicines have not been studied specifically in older people. Therefore, it may not be known whether they work exactly the same way they do in younger adults or if they cause different side effects or problems in older people. There is no specific information comparing use of dextromethorphan in the elderly with use in other age groups.

Other medicines—Although certain medicines should not be used together at all, in other cases 2 different medicines may be used together even if an interaction might occur. In these cases, your doctor may want to change the dose, or other precautions may be necessary. When you are taking dextromethorphan it is especially important that your health care professional know if you are taking any of the following:

- Amiodarone (e.g., Cordarone) or
- Fluoxetine (e.g., Prozac) or
- Quinidine—Taking dextromethorphan with any of these medicines may result in increased side effects of dextromethorphan
- Central nervous system (CNS) depressants (medicines that cause drowsiness)—The CNS depressant effects of either these medicines or dextromethorphan may be increased
- Monoamine oxidase (MAO) inhibitors (furazolidone [e.g., Furoxone], phenelzine [e.g., Nardil], procarbazine [e.g., Matulane], selegiline [e.g., Eldepryl], tranylcypromine [e.g., Parnate])—Taking dextromethorphan if you are taking MAO inhibitors or have taken them within the past 2 to 3 weeks may cause coma, dizziness, excited or unusual behavior, fever, high blood pressure, nausea, sluggishness, spasms, and tremors
- Smoking tobacco—Since dextromethorphan decreases coughing, it makes it difficult to get rid of the mucus that may collect in the lungs and airways resulting from smoking

Other medical problems—The presence of other medical problems may affect the use of dextromethorphan. Make sure you tell your doctor if you have any other medical problems, especially:

- Asthma—Since dextromethorphan decreases coughing, it makes it difficult to get rid of the mucus that collects in the lungs and airways during asthma
- Diabetes (sugar diabetes)—Some products contain sugar and may affect control of blood glucose monitoring
- Liver disease—Dextromethorphan may build up in the body and cause unwanted effects
- Chronic bronchitis or
- Emphysema or
- Mucus or phlegm with cough—Since dextromethorphan decreases coughing, it makes it difficult to get rid of the mucus that may collect in the lungs and airways with some diseases
- Slowed breathing—Dextromethorphan may slow the rate of breathing even further

Proper Use of This Medicine

Use this medicine only as directed by your doctor or the directions on the label. Do not use more of it, do not use it more often, and do not use it for a longer time than your doctor or the label says. Although this effect has happened only rarely, dextromethorphan has become habit-forming (causing mental or physical dependence) in some persons who used too much for a long time.

Dosing—The dose of dextromethorphan will be different for different patients. *Follow your doctor's orders or the directions on the label.* The following information includes only the average doses of dextromethorphan. *If your dose is different, do not change it* unless your doctor tells you to do so.

The number of capsules or tablets or teaspoonfuls of suspension or syrup that you take depends on the strength of the medicine.

- For *lozenge* dosage form:
  —For cough:
    - Adults and children 12 years of age and older—5 to 15 mg every two to four hours, as needed.
    - Children younger than 2 years of age—Use and dose must be determined by your doctor.
    - Children 2 to 6 years of age—5 mg every four hours, as needed.
    - Children 6 to 12 years of age—5 to 15 mg every two to six hours, as needed.
- For *syrup* dosage form:
  —For cough:
    - Adults and children 12 years of age and older— 30 mg every six to eight hours, as needed.
    - Children younger than 2 years of age—Use and dose must be determined by your doctor.
    - Children 2 to 6 years of age—3.5 mg every four hours or 7.5 mg every six to eight hours, as needed.
    - Children 6 to 12 years of age—7 mg every four hours or 15 mg every six to eight hours, as needed.
- For *extneded-release oral suspension* dosage form:
  —For cough:
    - Adults and children 12 years of age and older— 60 mg every twelve hours, as needed.
    - Children younger than 2 years of age—Use and dose must be determined by your doctor.
    - Children 2 to 6 years of age—15 mg every twelve hours, as needed.
    - Children 6 to 12 years of age—30 mg every twelve hours, as needed.

Missed dose—If you must take this medicine regularly and you miss a dose, take it as soon as possible. However, if it is almost time for your next dose, skip the missed dose and go back to your regular dosing schedule. Do not double doses.

Storage—To store this medicine:

- Store away from heat and direct light.
- Keep out of the reach of children.
- Do not store the tablet form of this medicine in the bathroom, near the kitchen sink, or in other damp places. Heat or moisture may cause the medicine to break down.
- Keep the liquid form of this medicine from freezing.
- Do not keep outdated medicine or medicine no longer needed. Be sure that any discarded medicine is out of the reach of children.

Precautions While Using This Medicine

If your cough has not improved after 7 days, if sore throat has not improved after 2 days, if you have a high fever, skin rash, or continuing headache with the cough, or if asthma or high blood pressure is present, check with your doctor. These signs may mean that you have other medical problems.

Dissolve lozenges in the mouth with caution, to lessen the risk of choking.

Side Effects of This Medicine

Along with its needed effects, a medicine may cause some unwanted effects. Although not all of these side effects may occur, if they do occur they may need medical attention.

Check with your doctor as soon as possible if any of the following side effects occur:
Symptoms of overdose
 Blurred vision; confusion; difficulty in urination; drowsiness or dizziness; nausea or vomiting (severe); shakiness and unsteady walk; slowed breathing; unusual excitement, nervousness, restlessness, or irritability (severe)

Other side effects may occur that usually do not need medical attention. These side effects may go away during treatment as your body adjusts to the medicine. However, check with your health care professional if any of the following side effects continue or are bothersome:
Less common or rare
 Confusion; constipation; dizziness (mild); drowsiness (mild); headache; nausea or vomiting; stomach pain

Other side effects not listed above may also occur in some patients. If you notice any other effects, check with your doctor.

Revised: 6/11/99

DEXTROTHYROXINE Systemic†*

* Not commercially available in the U.S.
† Not commercially available in Canada.

Description

Dextrothyroxine (dex-troe-thye-ROX-een) is used to lower high cholesterol levels in the blood. However, it has generally been replaced by safer medicines for the treatment of high cholesterol.

Dextrothyroxine is available only with your doctor's prescription, in the following dosage form:
Oral
 • Tablets (other countries)

Before Using This Medicine

In deciding to use a medicine, the risks of taking the medicine must be weighed against the good it will do. This is a decision you and your doctor will make. For dextrothyroxine, the following should be considered:

Allergies—Tell your doctor if you have ever had any unusual or allergic reaction to dextrothyroxine. Also tell your health care professional if you are allergic to any other substances, such as foods, preservatives, or dyes.

Diet—Before prescribing medicine for your condition, your doctor will probably try to control your condition by prescribing a personal diet for you. Such a diet may be low in fats, sugars, and/or cholesterol. Many people are able to control their condition by carefully following their doctor's orders for proper diet and exercise. *Medicine is prescribed only when additional help is needed* and is effective only when a schedule of diet and exercise is properly followed.

Also, this medicine is less effective if you are greatly overweight. It may be very important for you to go on a weight-reducing diet. However, check with your doctor before going on any diet.

Make certain your health care professional knows if you are on any special diet, such as a low-sodium or low-sugar diet.

Pregnancy—Dextrothyroxine has not been studied in pregnant women. However, studies in animals have not shown that dextrothyroxine causes birth defects or other problems. Before taking this medicine, make sure your doctor knows if you are pregnant or if you may become pregnant.

Breast-feeding—It is not known whether dextrothyroxine passes into breast milk. Although most medicines pass into breast milk in small amounts, many of them may be used safely while breast-feeding. Mothers who are taking this medicine and who wish to breast-feed should discuss this with their doctor.

Children—There is no specific information comparing use of dextrothyroxine in children to use in other age groups. However, use is not recommended in children under 2 years of age since cholesterol is needed for normal development.

Older adults—Side effects are more likely to occur in the elderly, who are usually more sensitive to the effects of dextrothyroxine.

Other medicines—Although certain medicines should not be used together at all, in other cases two different medicines may be used together even if an interaction might occur. In these cases, your doctor may want to change the dose, or other precautions may be necessary. When you are taking dextrothyroxine, it is especially important that your health care professional know if you are taking any of the following:
 • Anticoagulants (blood thinners)—The effects of the anticoagulant may be altered; a change in dosage of the anticoagulant may be necessary
 • Cholestyramine (e.g., Questran) or
 • Colestipol (e.g., Colestid)—The effects of dextrothyroxine may decrease; these two medicines should be taken at least 4 to 5 hours before or after dextrothyroxine

Other medical problems—The presence of other medical problems may affect the use of dextrothyroxine. Make sure you tell your doctor if you have any other medical problems, especially:
 • Diabetes mellitus (sugar diabetes)—Blood sugar levels may be increased
 • Heart or blood vessel disease or
 • High blood pressure or
 • Overactive thyroid—Dextrothyroxine may make these conditions worse
 • Kidney disease—Higher blood levels of dextrothyroxine may result and increase the chance of side effects
 • Liver disease—May lead to an increase in cholesterol blood levels
 • Underactive thyroid—There may be an increased sensitivity to the effects of dextrothyroxine

Proper Use of This Medicine

Take this medicine exactly as directed by your doctor. Try not to miss any doses and do not take more medicine than your doctor ordered.

Remember that this medicine will not cure your cholesterol problem but it does help control it. Therefore, you must continue to take it as directed if you expect to lower your cholesterol level.

Follow carefully the special diet your doctor gave you. This is the most important part of controlling your condition, and is necessary if the medicine is to work properly.

Dosing—The dose of dextrothyroxine will be different for different patients. *Follow your doctor's orders or the directions on the label.* The following information includes only the average doses of dextrothyroxine. *If your dose is different, do not change it* unless your doctor tells you to do so.

The number of tablets that you take depends on the strength of the medicine.

- For *tablets* dosage form:
  —For treatment of high cholesterol:
  - Adults—1 to 8 milligrams (mg) a day.
  - Children up to two years of age—Use is not recommended.
  - Children two years of age and older—50 to 100 micrograms (0.05 to 0.1 mg) per kilogram of body weight a day.

Missed dose—If you miss a dose of this medicine, take it as soon as possible. However, if it is almost time for your next dose, skip the missed dose and go back to your regular dosing schedule. Do not double doses.

Storage—To store this medicine:

- Keep out of the reach of children.
- Store away from heat and direct light.
- Do not store in the bathroom, near the kitchen sink, or in other damp places. Heat or moisture may cause the medicine to break down.
- Do not keep outdated medicine or medicine no longer needed. Be sure that any discarded medicine is out of the reach of children.

Precautions While Using This Medicine

It is very important that your doctor check your progress at regular visits. This will allow your doctor to see if the medicine is working properly to lower your cholesterol levels and if you should continue to take it.

Do not stop taking this medicine without first checking with your doctor. When you stop taking this medicine, your blood cholesterol levels may increase again. Your doctor may want you to follow a special diet to help prevent this from happening.

Before having any kind of surgery (including dental surgery) or emergency treatment, *tell the medical doctor or dentist in charge that you are taking this medicine.*

Side Effects of This Medicine

Along with its needed effects, a medicine may cause some unwanted effects. Although not all of these side effects may occur, if they do occur they may need medical attention.

Check with your doctor immediately if any of the following side effects occur:
 Rare
  Chest pain; fast or irregular heartbeat; stomach pain (severe) with nausea and vomiting

Check with your doctor as soon as possible if the following side effects occur, since they may indicate too much medicine is being taken:
 Rare
  Changes in appetite; changes in menstrual periods; diarrhea; fast or irregular heartbeat; fever; hand tremors; headache; increase in urination; irritability, nervousness, or trouble in sleeping; leg cramps; shortness of breath; skin rash or itching; sweating, flushing, or increased sensitivity to heat; unusual weight loss; vomiting

Other side effects not listed above may also occur in some patients. If you notice any other effects, check with your doctor.

Revised: 04/22/93
Interim revision: 07/18/98

DEZOCINE   Systemic†

Commonly used brand name(s):

In the U.S.—
 Dalgan

†Not commercially available in Canada.

Description

Dezocine (DEZ-oh-seen) belongs to the group of medicines known as narcotic analgesics (nar-KOT-ik an-al-JEE-zicks). Narcotic analgesics act in the central nervous system (CNS) to relieve pain. Some of their side effects are also caused by actions in the CNS.

Dezocine is available only with your doctor's prescription. It is available in the following dosage form:

Parenteral
 - Injection (U.S.)

Before Using This Medicine

In deciding to use a medicine, the risks of using the medicine must be weighed against the good it will do. This is a decision you and your doctor will make. For dezocine, the following should be considered:

Allergies—Tell your doctor if you have ever had any unusual or allergic reaction to dezocine. Also tell your health care professional if you are allergic to any other substances, such as foods, preservatives, or dyes.

Pregnancy—Studies on birth defects with dezocine have not been done in pregnant women. Dezocine did not cause birth defects in animal studies. However, the birth weights of the newborn animals were lower than normal, probably because the pregnant animals ate less than usual.

Too much use of a narcotic during pregnancy may cause the baby to become dependent on the medicine. This may lead to withdrawal side effects after birth. Also, narcotics may cause breathing problems in the newborn infant if taken just before delivery.

Breast-feeding—It is not known whether dezocine passes into the breast milk. However, it has not been reported to cause problems in nursing babies.

Children—Studies on this medicine have been done only in adult patients, and there is no specific information comparing use of dezocine in patients up to 18 years of age with use in other age groups.

Older adults—Elderly people are especially sensitive to the effects of narcotic analgesics such as dezocine. This may increase the chance of side effects, especially breathing problems, during treatment.

Other medicines—Although certain medicines should not be used together at all, in other cases two different medicines may be used together even if an interaction might occur. In these cases, your doctor may want to change the dose, or other precautions may be necessary. When you are using dezocine, it is especially important that your health care professional know if you are taking any of the following:

- Central nervous system (CNS) depressants, including other narcotics, or
- Tricyclic antidepressants (amitriptyline [e.g., Elavil], amoxapine [e.g., Asendin], clomipramine [e.g., Anafranil], desipramine [e.g., Pertofrane], doxepin [e.g., Sinequan], imipramine [e.g., Tofranil], nortriptyline [e.g., Aventyl], protriptyline [e.g., Vivactil], trimipramine [e.g., Surmontil])—The chance of side effects may be increased

- Naltrexone (e.g., Trexan)—Dezocine may not be effective in people taking naltrexone

Other medical problems—The presence of other medical problems may affect the use of dezocine. Make sure you tell your doctor if you have any other medical problems, especially:

- Alcohol abuse, or history of, or
- Drug dependence, especially narcotic abuse, or history of, or
- Emotional problems—The chance of side effects may be increased; also, withdrawal symptoms may occur if a narcotic you are dependent on is replaced by dezocine

- Brain disease or head injury or
- Colitis or other intestinal disease or
- Diarrhea or
- Emphysema, asthma, or other chronic lung disease or
- Enlarged prostate or problems with urination—Some of the side effects of narcotic analgesics can be dangerous if these conditions are present

- Heart or blood vessel disease, severe, or
- Gallbladder disease or gallstones or
- Kidney disease or
- Liver disease or
- Underactive thyroid—The chance of side effects may be increased

Proper Use of This Medicine

Some narcotic analgesics given by injection may be used at home by patients who do not need to be in the hospital. If you are using dezocine at home, *make sure you clearly understand and carefully follow your doctor's directions.*

Take this medicine only as directed by your doctor. Do not use more of it, do not use it more often, and do not use it for a longer time than your doctor ordered. This is especially important for elderly patients, who are more sensitive than younger adults to the effects of narcotic analgesics. If too much is taken, the medicine may become habit-forming (causing mental or physical dependence) or lead to medical problems because of an overdose.

Dosing—The dose of dezocine will be different for different patients. *Follow your doctor's orders or the directions on the label.* The following information includes only the average doses of dezocine. *If your dose is different, do not change it* unless your doctor tells you to do so.

The number of milliliters (mL) of injection that you use for each dose depends on the strength of the medicine.

- For *parenteral* dosage form (injection):
  —For pain:
  - Adults—The usual dose is 10 milligrams (mg), injected into a muscle every three to six hours as needed. Some people may need only 5 mg and others may need 15 or 20 mg. The medicine may also be injected into a vein in a dose of 2.5 to 10 mg every two to four hours as needed. The total amount used in twenty-four hours should not be more than 120 mg. Elderly people, people who are very ill, and people with breathing problems may have to use lower doses than other adults.
  - Children and teenagers up to 18 years of age—Use and dose must be determined by your doctor.

Missed dose—If your doctor has ordered you to use dezocine according to a regular schedule and you miss a dose, use it as soon as you remember. However, if it is almost time for your next dose, skip the missed dose and go back to your regular dosing schedule. *Do not double doses.*

Storage—To store this medicine:
- Keep out of the reach of children. Overdose is very dangerous in young children.
- Store away from heat and direct light.
- Keep the medicine from freezing.
- Do not keep outdated medicine or medicine no longer needed. Be sure that any discarded medicine is out of the reach of children.

Precautions While Using This Medicine

Dezocine will add to the effects of alcohol and other CNS depressants (medicines that slow down the nervous system, possibly causing drowsiness). Some examples of CNS depressants are antihistamines or medicine for hay fever, other allergies, or colds; sedatives, tranquilizers, or sleeping medicine; other prescription pain medicines including other narcotics; barbiturates; medicine for seizures; muscle relaxants; or anesthetics, including some dental anesthetics. *Do not drink alcoholic beverages, and check with your doctor before taking any of the medicines listed above, while you are using this medicine.*

This medicine may cause some people to become drowsy, dizzy, or lightheaded. *Make sure you know how you react to this medicine before you drive, use machines, or do anything else that could be dangerous if you are dizzy or are not alert.*

Dizziness, lightheadedness, or fainting may occur, especially when you get up suddenly from a lying or sitting position. Getting up slowly may help lessen this problem. Also, lying down for a while may help relieve these effects.

Nausea or vomiting may occur, especially after the first couple of doses. This effect may go away if you lie down for a while. However, if nausea or vomiting continues, check with your doctor.

Before having any kind of surgery (including dental surgery) or emergency treatment, tell the health care professional in charge that you are taking this medicine. Serious side effects may occur if your health care professional gives you certain medicines without knowing that you are using dezocine.

If you think you or someone else may have taken an overdose, get emergency help at once. Taking an overdose of this medicine or taking alcohol or CNS depressants with it may lead to unconsciousness or death. Signs of overdose of narcotic analgesics include convulsions (seizures), confusion, severe nervousness or restlessness, severe dizziness, severe drowsiness, slow or troubled breathing, and severe weakness.

Side Effects of This Medicine

Along with its needed effects, a medicine may cause some unwanted effects. Although not all of these side effects may occur, if they do occur they may need medical attention.

Get emergency help immediately if any of the following symptoms of overdose occur:
> Cold, clammy skin; confusion, nervousness, or restlessness (severe); convulsions (seizures); dizziness (severe); drowsiness (severe); low blood pressure; pinpoint pupils of eyes; slow heartbeat; slow or troubled breathing; weakness (severe)

Also, check with your doctor as soon as possible if any of the following side effects occur:
> *Rare*
> > Chest pain; coughing occurring together with breathing problems; difficult, decreased, or frequent urination; difficult, slow, or shallow breathing; increase or decrease in blood pressure; irregular heartbeat; mental depression or other mood or mental changes; skin rash or itching; swelling of face, fingers, lower legs, or feet; weight gain

Other side effects may occur that usually do not need medical attention. These side effects may go away during treatment as your body adjusts to the medicine. However, check with your doctor if any of the following side effects continue or are bothersome:
> *More common*
> > Drowsiness; nausea or vomiting
> *Less common or rare*
> > Abdominal or stomach pain; anxiety or crying; blurred or double vision; confusion; constipation; diarrhea; dizziness or lightheadedness; flushing or redness of skin; slurred speech

After you stop using this medicine, your body may need time to adjust. The length of time this takes depends on the amount of medicine you were using and how long you used it. During this period of time check with your doctor if you notice any of the following side effects:
> Body aches; diarrhea; fast heartbeat; fever, runny nose, or sneezing; gooseflesh; increased sweating; in-

creased yawning; loss of appetite; nausea or vomiting; nervousness, restlessness, or irritability; shivering or trembling; stomach cramps; trouble in sleeping; unusually large pupils of eyes; weakness

Other side effects not listed above may also occur in some patients. If you notice any other effects, check with your doctor.

Revised: 08/29/94

DIAZOXIDE   Oral

Commonly used brand name(s):

In the U.S.—
Proglycem

In Canada—
Proglycem

Description

Diazoxide (dye-az-OX-ide) when taken by mouth is used in the treatment of hypoglycemia (low blood sugar). It works by preventing release of insulin from the pancreas.

Diazoxide is available only with your doctor's prescription, in the following dosage forms:

> *Oral*
> > Capsules (U.S. and Canada)
> > Suspension (U.S. and Canada)

Before Using This Medicine

In deciding to use a medicine, the risks of taking the medicine must be weighed against the good it will do. This is a decision you and your doctor will make. For diazoxide, the following should be considered:

Allergies—Tell your doctor if you have ever had any unusual or allergic reaction to diazoxide, sulfonamides (sulfa medicine), or thiazide diuretics (certain types of water pills). Also tell your health care professional if you are allergic to any other substances, such as foods, preservatives, or dyes.

Pregnancy—Studies have not been done in pregnant women. However, too much use of diazoxide during pregnancy may cause unwanted effects (high blood sugar, loss of hair or increased hair growth, blood problems) in the baby. Studies in animals have shown that diazoxide causes some birth defects (in the skeleton, heart, and pancreas) and other problems (delayed birth, decrease in successful pregnancies).

Breast-feeding—It is not known whether diazoxide passes into breast milk. However, this medicine has not been reported to cause problems in nursing babies.

Children—Infants are more likely to retain (keep) body water because of diazoxide. In some infants, this may lead to certain types of heart problems. Also, a few children who received diazoxide for prolonged periods (longer than 4 years) developed changes in their facial structure.

Older adults—Many medicines have not been tested in older people. Therefore, it may not be known whether they work exactly the same way they do in younger adults or if they cause different side effects or problems in older people.

There is no specific information comparing use of oral diazoxide in the elderly with use in other age groups.

Other medicines—Although certain medicines should not be used together at all, in other cases two different medicines may be used together even if an interaction might occur. In these cases, your doctor may want to change the dose, or other precautions may be necessary. When you are taking diazoxide, it is especially important that your health care professional know if you are taking any of the following:

- Amantadine (e.g., Symmetrel) or
- Antidepressants (medicine for depression) or
- Antihypertensives (high blood pressure medicine) or
- Antipsychotics (medicines for mental illness) or
- Bromocriptine (e.g., Parlodel) or
- Cyclandelate (e.g., Cyclospasmol) or
- Deferoxamine (e.g., Desferal) or
- Diuretics (water pills) or
- Hydralazine (e.g., Apresoline) or
- Isoxsuprine (e.g., Vasodilan) or
- Levobunolol (e.g., Betagan) (use in the eye) or
- Levodopa (e.g., Dopar) or
- Medicine for heart disease or
- Metipranolol (e.g., OptiPranolol) or
- Nabilone (e.g., Cesamet) (with high doses) or
- Narcotic pain medicine or
- Nicotinyl alcohol (e.g., Roniacol) or
- Nimodipine (e.g., Nimotop) or
- Nylidrin (e.g., Arlidin) or
- Papaverine (e.g., Pavabid) or
- Pentamidine (e.g., Pentam) or
- Pimozide (e.g., Orap) or
- Promethazine (e.g., Phenergan) or
- Timolol (e.g., Timoptic) (use in the eye) or
- Trimeprazine (e.g., Temaril)—Use of any of these medicines with diazoxide may cause low blood pressure

- Ethotoin (e.g., Peganone) or
- Mephenytoin (e.g., Mesantoin) or
- Phenytoin (e.g., Dilantin)—Any of these medicines and diazoxide may be less effective if they are taken at the same time

Other medical problems—The presence of other medical problems may affect the use of diazoxide. Make sure you tell your doctor if you have any other medical problems, especially:

- Angina (chest pain)
- Gout—Diazoxide may make this condition worse
- Heart attack (recent)
- Heart or blood vessel disease
- Kidney disease—The effects of diazoxide may last longer because the kidney may not be able to get the medicine out of the bloodstream as it normally would
- Liver disease
- Stroke (recent)

Proper Use of This Medicine

Take this medicine only as directed by your doctor. Do not take more or less of it than your doctor ordered, and take it at the same time each day.

Follow carefully the special diet your doctor gave you. This is an important part of controlling your condition, and is necessary if the medicine is to work properly.

Test for sugar in your urine or blood with a diabetic urine or blood test kit as directed by your doctor. This is a convenient way to make sure your condition is being controlled, and it provides an early warning when it is not. Your doctor may also want you to test your urine for acetone.

Dosing—The dose of diazoxide will be different for different patients. *Follow your doctor's orders or the directions on the label.* The following information includes only the average doses of diazoxide. *If your dose is different, do not change it* unless your doctor tells you to do so.

The number of capsules that you take depends on the strength of the medicine.

- For *oral* dosage forms (capsules or suspension):
  —For treating hypoglycemia (low blood sugar):
    - Adults, teenagers, and children—Dose is based on body weight and must be determined by your doctor. At first, the usual dose is 1 milligram (mg) per kilogram (kg) (0.45 mg per pound) of body weight every eight hours. Then, your doctor may increase your dose to 3 to 8 mg per kg (1.4 to 3.6 mg per pound) of body weight a day. This dose may be divided into two or three doses.
    - Newborn babies and infants—Dose is based on body weight and must be determined by your doctor. At first, the usual dose is 3.3 mg per kg (1.5 mg per pound) of body weight every eight hours. Then, your doctor may increase the dose to 8 to 15 mg per kg (3.6 to 6.8 mg per pound) of body weight a day. This dose may be divided into two or three doses.

Missed dose—If you miss a dose of this medicine, take it as soon as possible. However, if it is almost time for your next dose, skip the missed dose and go back to your regular dosing schedule. Do not double doses.

Storage—To store this medicine:

- Keep out of the reach of children.
- Store away from heat and direct light.
- Do not store in the bathroom, near the kitchen sink, or in other damp places. Heat or moisture may cause the medicine to break down.
- Keep the oral liquid form of this medicine from freezing.
- Do not keep outdated medicine or medicine no longer needed. Be sure that any discarded medicine is out of the reach of children.

Precautions While Using This Medicine

It is very important that your doctor check your progress at regular visits, especially during the first few weeks of treatment, to make sure that this medicine is working properly.

Before you have any kind of surgery, dental treatment, or emergency treatment, *tell the medical doctor or dentist in charge that you are using this medicine.*

Do not take any other medicine, unless prescribed or approved by your doctor, since some may interfere with this medicine's effects. This especially includes over-the-counter (OTC) or nonprescription medicine such as that for colds, cough, asthma, hay fever, or appetite control.

Check with your doctor right away if symptoms of high blood sugar (hyperglycemia) occur. These symptoms usually include:

Drowsiness

Flushed, dry skin
Fruit-like breath odor
Increased urination
Loss of appetite (continuing)
Unusual thirst

These symptoms may occur if the dose of the medicine is too high, or if you have a fever or infection or are experiencing unusual stress.

Check with your doctor as soon as possible also if these symptoms of low blood sugar (hypoglycemia) occur:

Anxiety
Chills
Cold sweats
Cool pale skin
Drowsiness
Excessive hunger
Fast pulse
Headache
Nausea
Nervousness
Shakiness
Unusual tiredness or weakness

Symptoms of both low blood sugar and high blood sugar must be corrected before they progress to a more serious condition. In either situation, you should check with your doctor immediately.

Side Effects of This Medicine

Along with its needed effects, a medicine may cause some unwanted effects. Although not all of these side effects may occur, if they do occur they may need medical attention.

Stop taking this medicine and get emergency help immediately if any of the following side effects occur:
   Rare
      Chest pain caused by exercise or activity; confusion; numbness of the hands; shortness of breath (unexplained)

Check with your doctor as soon as possible if any of the following side effects occur:
   More common
      Decreased urination; swelling of feet or lower legs; weight gain (rapid)

   Less common
      Fast heartbeat
   Rare
      Fever; skin rash; stiffness of arms or legs; trembling and shaking of hands and fingers; unusual bleeding or bruising

Other side effects may occur that usually do not need medical attention. These side effects may go away during treatment as your body adjusts to the medicine. However, check with your doctor if any of the following side effects continue or are bothersome:
   Less common
      Changes in ability to taste; constipation; increased hair growth on forehead, back, arms, and legs; loss of appetite; nausea and vomiting; stomach pain

This medicine may cause a temporary increase in hair growth in some people when it is used for a long time. After treatment with diazoxide has ended, normal hair growth should return.

Other side effects not listed above may also occur in some patients. If you notice any other effects, check with your doctor.

Revised: 12/15/92
Interim revision: 05/24/94

DICLOFENAC   Topical— INTRODUCTORY VERSION

Commonly used brand name(s):

In the U.S.—
   Solaraze

Description

Diclofenac (di-KLO-fen-ack) belongs to the family of medicines called antineoplastics. Antineoplastics are used to treat cancer by killing cancer cells.

When applied to the skin, diclofenac is used to treat actinic keratosis, a skin problem that may be cancer or may become cancerous if not treated. The exact way that topical diclofenac helps this condition is unknown.

This medicine is available only with your doctor's prescription, in the following dosage forms:
   Topical
   • Gel (U.S)

Before Using This Medicine

In deciding to use a medicine, the risks of using the medicine must be weighed against the good it will do. This is a decision you and your doctor will make. For topical diclofenac, the following should be considered:

Allergies—Tell your doctor if you have ever had any unusual or allergic reaction to diclofenac. Also tell your doctor and pharmacist if you are allergic to any other substances, such as foods, preservatives, or dyes.

Pregnancy—Tell your doctor if you are pregnant or if you intend to become pregnant. Diclofenac should not be used late in pregnancy because there is a chance that it could cause birth defects. Be sure that you have discussed this with your doctor before using this medicine.

Breast-feeding—It is not known whether diclofenac passes into breast milk. However, diclofenac is not recommended for use during breast-feeding because it may cause unwanted effects in nursing babies.

Children— Studies on this medicine have been done only in adult patients, and there is no specific information comparing use of diclofenac on the skin in children with use in other age groups.

Older adults— Many medicines have not been studied specifically in older people. Therefore, it may not be known whether they work exactly the same way they do in younger adults. Although there is no specific information comparing use of diclofenac on the skin in the elderly with use in other age groups, this medicine is not expected to cause different side effects or problems in older people than it does in younger adults.

Other medicines—Although certain medicines should not be used together at all, in other cases two different medicines may be used together even if an interaction might occur. In these cases, your doctor may want to change the dose, or other precautions may be necessary. When you are using diclofenac on the skin, it is especially important that your doctor and pharmacist know if you are taking any of the following:

- Medicines for inflammation and pain (non-narcotic), including aspirin—The risk of serious side effects may be increased

Other medical problems—The presence of other medical problems may affect the use of diclofenac. Make sure you tell your doctor if you have any other medical problems, especially:

- Stomach or intestinal ulcers or bleeding—Diclofenac may make these conditions worse

- Kidney disease or
- Liver disease—Effects of this medicine may be increased because of slower removal of the medicine from the body

Proper Use of This Medicine

Keep using this medicine for the full time of treatment. However, *do not use this medicine more often or for a longer time than your doctor ordered.* Apply enough medicine each time to cover the entire affected area.

Diclofenac may cause redness, soreness, scaling, and peeling of the affected skin. Do not stop using this medicine without first checking with your doctor. If the reaction is very uncomfortable, check with your doctor.

Apply this medicine very carefully, and avoid getting any in your eyes. Do not apply this medicine to areas with broken skin or open wounds, infection, or severely peeling skin.

Dosing—The dose of diclofenac will be different for different patients. *Follow your doctor's orders or the directions on the label.* The following information includes only the average doses of diclofenac. *If your dose is different, do not change it* unless your doctor tells you to do so.

The amount of gel that you use depends on the strength of the medicine. Also, *the number of doses you take each day, the time allowed between doses, and the length of time you take the medicine depend on the medical problem for which you are taking diclofenac*

- For *topical* dosage form (gel):
  —For actinic keratosis:
    - Adults—Apply to affected skin 2 times a day

Missed dose—If you miss a dose of this medicine, use it as soon as possible. However, if it is almost time for your next dose, skip the missed dose and go back to your regular dosing schedule. Do not double the amount of medicine you use.

Storage—To store this medicine:

- Keep out of the reach of children
- Keep the medicine from freezing
- Protect from heat
- Do not keep outdated medicine or medicine no longer needed. Ask your health care professional how you should dispose of any medicine you do not use. Be sure that any discarded medicine is out of the reach of children.

Precautions While Using This Medicine

It is very important that your doctor check your progress at regular visits to make sure that this medicine is working properly and to check for unwanted effects.

If your symptoms become worse, check with your doctor.

While using this medicine, your skin may become more sensitive to sunlight than usual, and too much sunlight may increase the effects of the medicine. During this period of time:

- Stay out of direct sunlight, especially between the hours of 10:00 a.m. and 3:00 p.m., if possible.
- Wear protective clothing, including a hat and sunglasses.
- Do not use a sunlamp or tanning bed or booth.
- Make sure you have discussed the use of a sun block product with your doctor.

If you have a severe reaction from the sun, check with your doctor.

Side Effects of This Medicine

Along with it's needed effects, a medicine may cause some unwanted effects. Although not all of these side effects may occur, if they do occur they may need medical attention.

Check with you doctor as soon as possible if any of the following side effects occur:

More common

Application site reactions, including skin rash, pain, tingling or burning sensation; itching skin; flu-like syndrome (bodyache; headache; fever, with or without chills)

Less common or rare

Application site reactions, including swelling; increased skin sensitivity; or skin rash, itching, redness, or pain caused by reaction from exposure to sun; blood in the urine; cough; decrease in body movement; dry, itching, or burning eyes; eye pain; fever; headaches, including migraines; high blood pressure; increased sensitivity of eyes to light; infection; nasal congestion; pain or tenderness around eyes and cheekbones; redness or swelling of eyes; shortness of breath; skin rash other than at the application site; sore throat; tightness in chest; troubled breathing; ulcers or sores on skin, other than at the application site; wheezing

Side effects may occur that usually do not need medical attention. These side effects may go away during treatment as your body adjusts to the medicine. However, check with your doctor if any of the following side effects continue or are bothersome.

More common

burning skin; dry skin; red skin; scaly skin; thickened skin; tingling skin

Less common

Acne; back pain; belching; bleeding skin; chest pain; diarrhea; heartburn; indigestion; joint pain; lack or loss of strength; loss or thinning of hair; muscle pain; neck pain; runny nose; stomach upset or pain

Other side effects not listed above may also occur in some patients. If you notice any other effects, check with your doctor.

Developed: 12/06/2000

DICLOFENAC AND MISOPROSTOL
Systemic

Commonly used brand name(s):

In the U.S.—
Arthrotec 50
Arthrotec 75

In Canada—
Arthrotec 50
Arthrotec 75

Description

Diclofenac and misoprostol (dye-KLOE-fen-ak and mye-soe-PROST-ole) combination is used for patients with arthritis who may develop stomach ulcers from taking nonsteroidal anti-inflammatory drugs (NSAIDs) alone.

Diclofenac is a NSAID used in this combination medicine to help relieve some symptoms of arthritis, such as inflammation, swelling, stiffness, and joint pain.

Misoprostol is used in this combination medicine to prevent stomach ulcers.

This medicine is available only with your doctor's prescription, in the following dosage form(s):

Oral
• Tablets (U.S. and Canada)

Before Using This Medicine

In deciding to use a medicine, the risks of taking the medicine must be weighed against the good it will do. This is a decision you and your doctor will make. For diclofenac and misoprostol combination, the following should be considered:

Allergies—Tell your doctor if you have ever had any unusual or allergic reaction to diclofenac or other nonsteroidal anti-inflammatory drugs (NSAIDs), to misoprostol, or to any of the following medicines:

• Aspirin or other salicylates
• Prostaglandin analogs

Also tell your health care professional if you are allergic to any other substances, such as foods, preservatives, or dyes.

Pregnancy—*Diclofenac and misoprostol combination must not be used during pregnancy.*

Before starting to take diclofenac and misoprostol combination, you must have had a negative pregnancy test within the previous 2 weeks. Also, you must start taking this combination only on the second or third day of your next normal menstrual period. In addition, it will be necessary that you use an effective form of birth control while taking this medicine. Be sure that you have discussed this with your doctor before taking diclofenac and misoprostol combination.

Studies on birth defects with the diclofenac and misoprostol combination have not been done. However, there is a chance that diclofenac may cause unwanted effects on the heart or blood flow of the fetus or newborn baby if taken regularly during the last few months of pregnancy. Also, studies in animals have shown that diclofenac, if taken late in pregnancy, may increase the length of pregnancy, prolong labor, or cause other problems during delivery. Diclofenac caused unwanted effects on the formation of bones in animals.

Misoprostol has been shown to cause contractions and bleeding of the uterus. It may also cause miscarriage.

Breast-feeding—It is not known whether diclofenac and misoprostol combination passes into breast milk. Diclofenac passes into breast milk. Diclofenac and misoprostol combination is not recommended for use during breast-feeding.

Children—Studies on this medicine have been done only in adult patients, and there is no specific information comparing use of diclofenac and misoprostol combination in children with use in other age groups.

Older adults—Certain side effects, such as confusion, swelling of the face, feet, or lower legs, or sudden decrease in the amount of urine, may be especially likely to occur in elderly patients, who are usually more sensitive than younger adults to the effects of nonsteroidal anti-inflammatory drugs. Also, elderly people are more likely than younger adults to get sick if this medicine causes stomach problems.

Other medicines—Although certain medicines should not be used together at all, in other cases two different medicines may be used together even if an interaction might occur. In these cases, your doctor may want to change the dose, or other precautions may be necessary. When you are taking diclofenac and misoprostol combination, it is especially important that your health care professional know if you are taking any of the following:

• Anticoagulants (blood thinners) or
• Corticosteroids (e.g., prednisone or other cortisone-like medicines)—The chance of bleeding may be increased

• Aspirin—The chance of serious side effects may be increased if aspirin is used together with diclofenac and misoprostol combination on a regular basis

• Cyclosporine (e.g., Sandimmune) or
• Digitalis glycosides (heart medicine) or
• Lithium (e.g., Lithane) or
• Methotrexate (e.g., Mexate)—Higher blood levels of these medicines and an increased chance of side effects may occur

• Amiloride (e.g., Midamor) or
• Spironolactone (e.g., Aldactone) or
• Triamterene (e.g., Dyrenium)—May cause high blood levels of potassium, which may increase the chance of side effects

Other medical problems—The presence of other medical problems may affect the use of diclofenac and misoprostol combination. Make sure you tell your doctor if you have any other medical problems, especially:

• Alcohol abuse or
• Bleeding problems or
• Hepatitis or other liver disease or
• Kidney disease (or history of) or
• Tobacco use (or recent history of) or
• Stomach ulcer, or other stomach or intestinal problems or
• Systemic lupus erythematosus—The chance of side effects may be increased

• Anemia or
• Asthma or
• Dehydration or
• Fluid retention (swelling of feet or lower legs) or
• Heart disease or
• High blood pressure or
• Low platelet count or
• Low white blood cell count or
• Porphyria (liver) or

• Volume depletion—Diclofenac and misoprostol combination may make these conditions worse

Proper Use of This Medicine

For safe and effective use of this medicine, do not take more of it, do not take it more often, and do not take it for a longer time than ordered by your health care professional. Taking too much of this medicine may increase the chance of unwanted effects.

Do not take diclofenac and misoprostol combination with magnesium-containing antacids. Antacids may be taken with diclofenac and misoprostol combination, if needed, to help relieve stomach pain, unless you are otherwise directed by your doctor. However, do not take magnesium-containing antacids, since they may cause diarrhea or worsen the diarrhea that is sometimes caused by the diclofenac and misoprostol combination.

Do not chew, crush, or dissolve tablets.

Do not give this medication to another person.

Diclofenac and misoprostol combination should be taken with meals.

Dosing—The dose of diclofenac and misoprostol combination will be different for different patients. *Follow your doctor's orders or the directions on the label.* The following information includes only the average doses of diclofenac and misoprostol combination. *If your dose is different, do not change it* unless your doctor tells you to do so.

The number of tablets that you take depends on the strength of the medicine. Also, *the number of doses you take each day, the time allowed between doses, and the length of time you take the medicine depend on the medical problem for which you are taking diclofenac and misoprostol combination.*

- For *oral* dosage form (tablets):
  —For osteoarthritis:
    - Adults—1 tablet of Arthrotec 50 three times a day.
    - Children—Use and dose must be determined by your doctor.
  —For rheumatoid arthritis:
    - Adults—1 tablet of Arthrotec 50 three or four times a day.
    - Children—Use and dose must be determined by your doctor.
  —For osteoarthritis or rheumatoid arthritis (for patients who are unable to tolerate other doses):
    - Adults—1 tablet of Arthrotec 50 two times a day or 1 tablet of Arthrotec 75 two times a day.
    - Children—Use and dose must be determined by your doctor.

Missed dose—If you miss a dose of this medicine, take it as soon as possible. However, if it is almost time for your next dose, skip the missed dose and go back to your regular dosing schedule. Do not double doses.

Storage—To store this medicine:
- Keep out of the reach of children.
- Store away from heat and direct light.
- Do not store in the bathroom, near the kitchen sink, or in other damp places. Heat or moisture may cause the medicine to break down.

• Do not keep outdated medicine or medicine no longer needed. Be sure that any discarded medicine is out of the reach of children.

Precautions While Using This Medicine

Misoprostol may cause miscarriage if taken during pregnancy. Therefore, if you suspect that you may have become pregnant, stop taking this medicine immediately and check with your doctor.

This medicine may cause diarrhea in some people. The diarrhea will usually disappear within a few days as your body adjusts to the medicine. However, check with your doctor if the diarrhea is severe and/or does not stop after a week.

If you will be taking this medicine for a long time, your doctor should check your progress at regular visits. Your doctor may want to do certain tests to find out if unwanted effects are occurring. The tests are very important because serious side effects, including ulcers, bleeding, blood, or liver problems, can occur without any warning.

Stomach problems may be more likely to occur if you drink alcoholic beverages while being treated with this medicine. Therefore, *do not regularly drink alcoholic beverages while taking this medicine,* unless otherwise directed by your doctor.

Taking nonsteroidal anti-inflammatory drugs together with this medicine on a regular basis may increase the chance of unwanted effects. Also, taking acetaminophen, aspirin or other salicylates, or ketorolac (e.g., Toradol) regularly while you are taking a diclofenac and misoprostol combination may increase the chance of unwanted effects. The risk will depend on how much of each medicine you take every day, and on how long you take the medicine together. If your health care professional directs you to take these medicines together on a regular basis, follow his or her directions carefully. However, *do not take acetaminophen or aspirin or other salicylates together with this medicine for more than a few days, and do not take any ketorolac (e.g., Toradol) while you are taking this medicine, unless your doctor has directed you to do so and is following your progress.*

Side Effects of This Medicine

Along with its needed effects, a medicine may cause some unwanted effects. Although not all of these side effects may occur, if they do occur they may need medical attention.

Check with your doctor as soon as possible if any of the following side effects occur:
Less common
  Black, tarry stools; bleeding or crusting sores on lips; blood in urine or stools; bruises and/or red spots on the skin; chest pain; chills; confusion; continuing thirst; convulsions (seizures); cough or hoarseness; disorientation; drowsiness; fainting; fever with or without chills; fluid retention; general feeling of illness; heartburn and/or indigestion; increased blood pressure; increased heart rate; increased weight gain; itching of the skin; irregular heartbeat; large, flat, blue or purplish patches on the skin; light-headedness or dizziness; lower back or side pain; mental depression; muscle cramps; nausea; painful or difficult urination; pounding heartbeat; psychotic reaction; rectal bleeding; seeing, hearing, or feeling things that are not there; severe headache; severe

hepatic reactions; severe stomach pain, cramping or burning; shortness of breath, troubled breathing, tightness in chest, and/or wheezing; skin rash; sores, ulcers, or white spots on lips or in mouth; sore throat; stiff neck and/or back; sudden decrease in the amount of urine; swelling and/or tenderness in upper stomach; swelling of face, fingers, feet, and/or lower legs; unusual bleeding or bruising; unusual tiredness or weakness; vomiting of material that looks like coffee grounds; yellow eyes or skin

Rare
   Changes in facial skin color; fast or irregular breathing; puffiness or swelling of the eyelids or around the eyes

Symptoms of overdose
   Confusion; diarrhea; drowsiness; fever; nausea and/or vomiting; pounding heartbeat; convulsions (seizures); shortness of breath; slow heartbeat; stomach pain; trembling or shaking

Other side effects may occur that usually do not need medical attention. These side effects may go away during treatment as your body adjusts to the medicine. However, check with your doctor if any of the following side effects continue or are bothersome:

More common
   Diarrhea; gas; heartburn

Less common
   Abnormal vision; acne; change in sense of taste; decreased appetite; dry mouth; irritability or nervousness; loss of hair; muscle pain; decrease in sexual ability; tingling, burning, or prickling sensations; trembling or shaking; trouble swallowing; vaginal bleeding

Other side effects not listed above may also occur in some patients. If you notice any other effects, check with your doctor.

Developed: 05/27/98
Revised: 4/20/00

DIDANOSINE   Systemic

Commonly used brand name(s):

In the U.S.—
   Videx

In Canada—
   Videx

Another commonly used name is ddI.

Description

Didanosine (di-DAN-oe-seen) (also known as ddI) is used in the treatment of the infection caused by the human immunodeficiency virus (HIV). HIV is the virus responsible for acquired immune deficiency syndrome (AIDS).

Didanosine (ddI) will not cure or prevent HIV infection or AIDS; however, it helps keep HIV from reproducing and appears to slow down the destruction of the immune system. This may help delay the development of problems usually related to AIDS or HIV disease. Didanosine will not keep you from spreading HIV to other people. People who receive this medicine may continue to have the problems usually related to AIDS or HIV disease.

Didanosine may cause some serious side effects, including pancreatitis (inflammation of the pancreas). Symptoms of pancreatitis include stomach pain, and nausea and vomiting. Didanosine may also cause peripheral neuropathy. Symptoms of peripheral neuropathy include tingling, burning, numbness, and pain in the hands or feet. *Check with your doctor if any new health problems or symptoms occur while you are taking didanosine.*

Didanosine is available only with your doctor's prescription, in the following dosage forms:

Oral
   • Capsules, delayed-release (U.S.)
   • Oral solution, buffered powder (U.S.)
   • Oral suspension, pediatric powder (U.S. and Canada)
   • Tablets, buffered—chewable and for oral suspension (U.S. and Canada)

Before Using This Medicine

In deciding to use a medicine, the risks of taking the medicine must be weighed against the good it will do. This is a decision you and your doctor will make. For didanosine, the following should be considered:

Allergies—Tell your doctor if you have ever had any unusual or allergic reaction to didanosine. Also tell your health care professional if you are allergic to any other substances, such as foods, preservatives, or dyes.

Diet—Make certain your health care professional knows if you are on any special diet, such as a low-sodium (low-salt) diet. Didanosine chewable tablets and the oral solution packets contain a large amount of sodium. Also, didanosine tablets contain phenylalanine, which must be restricted in patients with phenylketonuria.

Pregnancy—Didanosine crosses the placenta. Studies in pregnant women have not been done. However, didanosine has not been shown to cause birth defects or other problems in animal studies. Also, it is not known whether didanosine reduces the chances that a baby born to an HIV-infected mother will also be infected. Before taking this medicine, make sure your doctor knows if you are pregnant or if you may become pregnant. This is especially important when taking didanosine together with stavudine.

Breast-feeding—It is not known whether didanosine passes into human breast milk. However, if your baby does not already have the AIDS virus, there is a chance that you could pass it to your baby by breast-feeding. Talk to your doctor first if you are thinking about breast-feeding your baby.

Children—Didanosine can cause serious side effects in any patient. Therefore, it is especially important that you discuss with your child's doctor the good that this medicine may do as well as the risks of using it. Your child must be carefully followed, and frequently seen, by the doctor while taking didanosine.

Older adults—Many medicines have not been studied specifically in older people. Therefore, it may not be known whether they work exactly the same way they do in younger adults or if they cause different side effects or problems in older people. There is no specific information comparing use of didanosine in the elderly with use in other age groups.

Other medicines—Although certain medicines should not be used together at all, in other cases 2 different medicines may be used together even if an interaction might occur. In these cases, your doctor may want to change the dose, or other precautions may be necessary. When you are taking didanosine, it is especially important that your health care professional know if you are taking any of the following:

- Alcohol or
- Asparaginase (e.g., Elspar) or
- Azathioprine (e.g., Imuran) or
- Estrogens (female hormones) or
- Furosemide (e.g., Lasix) or
- Methyldopa (e.g., Aldomet) or
- Pentamidine (e.g., Pentam, Pentacarinat) or
- Sulfonamides (e.g., Bactrim, Septra) or
- Sulindac (e.g., Clinoril) or
- Thiazide diuretics (e.g., Diuril, Hydrodiuril) or
- Valproic acid (e.g., Depakote)—Use of these medicines with didanosine may increase the chance of pancreatitis (inflammation of the pancreas)

- Allopurinol (e.g., Lopurin, Purinol)—This medicine should not be used with didanosine; use of this medicine will increase the amount of didanosine in your body to abnormally high levels

- Chloramphenicol (e.g., Chloromycetin) or
- Cisplatin (e.g., Platinol) or
- Ethambutol (e.g., Myambutol) or
- Ethionamide (e.g., Trecator-SC) or
- Hydralazine (e.g., Apresoline) or
- Isoniazid (e.g., Nydrazid) or
- Lithium (e.g., Eskalith, Lithobid) or
- Metronidazole (e.g., Flagyl) or
- Nitrous oxide or
- Phenytoin (e.g., Dilantin) or
- Stavudine (e.g., D4T) or
- Vincristine (e.g., Oncovin) or
- Zalcitabine (e.g., HIVID)—Use of these medicines with didanosine may increase the chance of peripheral neuropathy (tingling, burning, numbness, or pain in your hands or feet)

- Ciprofloxacin (e.g., Cipro) or
- Enoxacin (e.g., Penetrex) or
- Itraconazole (e.g., Sporanox) or
- Ketoconazole (e.g., Nizoral) or
- Lomefloxacin (e.g., Maxaquin) or
- Norfloxacin (e.g., Noroxin) or
- Ofloxacin (e.g., Floxin)—Use of these medicines with didanosine may keep these medicines from working properly; these medicines should be taken at least 2 hours before or 2 hours after taking didanosine

- Dapsone (e.g., Avlosulfon)—Use of dapsone with didanosine may increase the chance of peripheral neuropathy (tingling, burning, numbness, or pain in your hands or feet); it may also keep dapsone from working properly; dapsone should be taken at least 2 hours before or 2 hours after taking didanosine

- Ganciclovir (e.g., Cytovene)—Use of these medicines with didanosine may keep these medicines from working

properly; these medicines should be taken at least 2 hours after taking didanosine

- Nitrofurantoin (e.g., Macrodantin)—Use of nitrofurantoin with didanosine may increase the chance of pancreatitis (inflammation of the pancreas) and peripheral neuropathy (tingling, burning, numbness, or pain in your hands or feet)

- Delavirdine (e.g., Rescriptor) or
- Indinavir (e.g., Crixivan)—Use of these medicines with didanosine may keep these medicines from working properly; these medicines should be taken at least 1 hour before taking didanosine

- Tetracyclines (e.g., Achromycin, Minocin)—Use of tetracyclines with didanosine may increase the chance of pancreatitis (inflammation of the pancreas); it may also keep the tetracycline from working properly; tetracyclines should be taken at least 2 hours before or 2 hours after taking didanosine

Other medical problems—The presence of other medical problems may affect the use of didanosine. Make sure you tell your doctor if you have any other medical problems, especially:

- Alcoholism, active, or
- Increased blood triglycerides (substance formed in the body from fats in foods) or
- Pancreatitis (or a history of)—Patients with these medical problems may be at increased risk of pancreatitis (inflammation of the pancreas)

- Edema or
- Heart disease or
- High blood pressure or
- Kidney disease or
- Liver disease or
- Toxemia of pregnancy—The salt contained in the didanosine tablets and the oral solution packets may make these conditions worse

- Gouty arthritis—Didanosine may cause an attack or worsen gout

- Peripheral neuropathy—Didanosine may make this condition worse

- Phenylketonuria (PKU)—Didanosine tablets contain phenylalanine, which must be restricted in patients with PKU

Proper Use of This Medicine

Take this medicine exactly as directed by your doctor. Do not take more of it, do not take it more often, and do not take it for a longer time than your doctor ordered. Also, do not stop taking this medicine without checking with your doctor first. However, stop taking didanosine and call your doctor right away if you get severe nausea, vomiting, and stomach pain.

Otherwise, keep taking didanosine for the full time of treatment, even if you begin to feel better.

For patients taking *didanosine delayed-release capsules:*
- Capsules should be swallowed intact.

For patients taking *didanosine for oral solution, buffered powder:*
- Open the foil packet and pour its contents into approximately 1/2 glass (4 ounces) of water. *Do not mix with fruit juice* or other acid-containing drinks.

- Stir for approximately 2 to 3 minutes until the powder is dissolved.
- Drink at once.

For patients taking *didanosine for oral suspension, pediatric powder:*

- Use a specially marked measuring spoon or other device to measure each dose accurately. The average household teaspoon may not hold the right amount of liquid.

For patients taking *didanosine tablets, buffered—chewable and for oral suspension:*

- Tablets should be thoroughly chewed or crushed or mixed in at least 1 ounce of water before swallowing. The tablets are hard and some people may find them difficult to chew. If the tablets are mixed in water, stir well until a uniform suspension is formed and take at once. For additional flavoring, mix the prepared suspension with 1 ounce of clear apple juice.
- *Two tablets must be taken together by patients over 1 year of age.* These tablets contain a special buffer to keep didanosine from being destroyed in the stomach. In order to get the correct amount of buffer, 2 tablets always need to be taken together. Infants from 6 to 12 months of age will get enough buffer from just 1 tablet. For 1-tablet dose, a ½ ounce of clear apple juice may be added as a flavor enhancer.

Didanosine should be taken on an empty stomach since food may decrease the absorption in the stomach and keep it from working properly. Didanosine should be taken at least 2 hours before or 2 hours after you eat.

This medicine works best when there is a constant amount in the blood. *To help keep the amount constant, do not miss any doses.* If you need help in planning the best times to take your medicine, check with your health care professional.

Dosing—The dose of didanosine will be different for different patients. *Follow your doctor's orders or the directions on the label.* The following information includes only the average doses of didanosine. *If your dose is different, do not change it* unless your doctor tells you to do so.

The number of capsules, tablets or teaspoonfuls of solution or suspension that you take depends on the strength of the medicine.

- For the treatment of advanced HIV infection or AIDS:
  - —For *oral* dosage form (capsules, delayed-release):
    - Adults and teenagers—Dose is based on body weight.
      - —For patients weighing less than 60 kilograms (kg) (132 pounds): 250 milligrams (mg) once daily.
      - —For patients weighing 60 kg (132 pounds) or more: 400 mg once daily.
    - Children—The oral capsules are usually not used for small children.
  - —For *oral* dosage form (solution, buffered powder):
    - Adults and teenagers—Dose is based on body weight.
      - —For patients weighing less than 60 kilograms (kg) (132 pounds): 167 mg every twelve hours.
      - —For patients weighing 60 kg (132 pounds) or more: 250 mg every twelve hours.
    - Children—The oral solution is usually not used for small children.
  - —For *oral* dosage form (suspension, pediatric powder):
    - Adults and teenagers—The pediatric oral suspension is usually not used in adults and teenagers.
    - Children—Dose is based on body size and must be determined by your doctor.
  - —For *oral* dosage form (tablets):
    - Adults and teenagers—Dose is based on body weight.
      - —For patients weighing less than 60 kg (132 pounds): 125 mg every twelve hours, or 250 mg once daily.
      - —For patients weighing 60 kg (132 pounds) or more: 200 mg every twelve hours, or 400 mg once daily.
    - Children—Dose is based on body size and must be determined by your doctor.

Missed dose—If you do miss a dose of this medicine, take it as soon as possible. However, if it is almost time for your next dose, skip the missed dose and go back to your regular dosing schedule. Do not double doses.

Only take medicine that your doctor has prescribed specifically for you. Do not share your medicine with others.

Storage—To store this medicine:

- Keep out of the reach of children.
- Store away from heat and direct light.
- Do not store in the bathroom, near the kitchen sink, or in other damp places. Heat or moisture may cause the medicine to break down.
- Do not keep outdated medicine or medicine no longer needed. Be sure that any discarded medicine is out of the reach of children.

Precautions While Using This Medicine

It is very important that your doctor check your progress at regular visits.

Do not take any other medicines without checking with your doctor first. To do so may increase the chance of side effects from didanosine.

HIV may be acquired from or spread to other people through infected body fluids, including blood, vaginal fluid, or semen. *If you are infected, it is best to avoid any sexual activity involving an exchange of body fluids with other people. If you do have sex, always wear (or have your partner wear) a condom ("rubber").* Only use condoms made of latex, and *use them every time you have vaginal, anal, or oral sex.* The use of a spermicide (such as nonoxynol-9) may also help prevent transmission of HIV if it is not irritating to the vagina, rectum, or mouth. Spermicides have been shown to kill HIV in lab tests. Do not use oil-based jelly, cold cream, baby oil, or shortening as a lubricant—these products can cause the condom to break. Lubricants without oil, such as *K-Y jelly*, are recommended. Women may wish to carry their own condoms. Birth control pills and diaphragms will help protect against pregnancy, but they will not prevent someone from giving or getting the AIDS virus. *If you inject drugs,* get help to stop. *Do not share needles or equipment with anyone.* In some cities, more than half of the drug users are infected and sharing even 1 needle or syringe can spread the virus. If you have any questions about this, check with your health care professional.

Side Effects of This Medicine

Along with its needed effects, a medicine may cause some unwanted effects. Although not all of these side effects may occur, if they do occur they may need medical attention.

Check with your doctor immediately if any of the following side effects occur:
Less common
Nausea and vomiting; stomach pain; tingling, burning, numbness, and pain in the hands or feet

Rare
Convulsions (seizures); fever and chills; shortness of breath; skin rash and itching; sore throat; swelling of feet or lower legs; unusual bleeding and bruising; unusual tiredness and weakness; yellow skin and eyes

Other side effects may occur that usually do not need medical attention. These side effects may go away during treatment as your body adjusts to the medicine. However, check with your doctor if any of the following side effects continue or are bothersome:
More common
Anxiety; diarrhea; difficulty in sleeping; dryness of mouth; headache; irritability; restlessness

Other side effects not listed above may also occur in some patients. If you notice any other effects, check with your doctor.

Developed: 06/22/1994
Revised: 02/23/2001

DIFENOXIN AND ATROPINE
Systemic†

Commonly used brand name(s):

In the U.S.—
Motofen

†Not commercially available in Canada.

Description

Difenoxin and atropine (dye-fen-OX-in and A-troe-peen) combination medicine is used along with other measures to treat severe diarrhea in adults. Difenoxin helps stop diarrhea by slowing down the movements of the intestines.

Since difenoxin is chemically related to some narcotics, it may be habit-forming if taken in doses that are larger than prescribed. To help prevent possible abuse, atropine (an anticholinergic) has been added. If higher-than-normal doses of the combination are taken, the atropine will cause unpleasant effects, making it unlikely that such doses will be taken again.

Difenoxin and atropine combination medicine should not be used in children. Children with diarrhea should be given solutions of carbohydrates (sugars) and electrolytes (important salts) to replace the water and important salts that are lost from the body during diarrhea.

This medicine is available only with your doctor's prescription, in the following dosage form:
Oral
• Tablets (U.S.)

Before Using This Medicine

In deciding to use a medicine, the risks of taking the medicine must be weighed against the good it will do. This is a decision you and your doctor will make. For difenoxin and atropine, the following should be considered:

Allergies—Tell your doctor if you have ever had any unusual or allergic reaction to difenoxin or atropine. Also tell your health care professional if you are allergic to any other substances, such as foods, preservatives, or dyes.

Pregnancy—Difenoxin and atropine combination has not been studied in pregnant women. However, studies in rats have shown that difenoxin and atropine combination, when given in doses many times the human dose, increases the delivery time and the chance of death of the newborn.

Breast-feeding—Both difenoxin and atropine pass into the breast milk. Although it is not known how much of these drugs pass into the breast milk, difenoxin and atropine combination could cause serious effects in the nursing baby. Be sure you have discussed the risks and benefits of this medicine with your doctor.

Children—This medicine should not be used in children. Children, especially very young children, are very sensitive to the effects of difenoxin and atropine. This may increase the chance of side effects during treatment. Also, the fluid loss caused by diarrhea may result in a severe condition. For this reason, it is very important that a sufficient amount of liquids be given to replace the fluid lost by the body. If you have any questions about this, check with your health care professional.

Older adults—Shortness of breath or difficulty in breathing may be more likely to occur in elderly patients, who are usually more sensitive than younger adults to the effects of difenoxin. Also, the fluid loss caused by diarrhea may result in a severe condition. For this reason, elderly persons should not take this medicine without first checking with their doctor. It is also very important that a sufficient amount of liquids be taken to replace the fluid lost by the body. If you have any questions about this, check with your health care professional.

Other medicines—Although certain medicines should not be used together at all, in other cases two different medicines may be used together even if an interaction might occur. In these cases, your doctor may want to change the dose, or other precautions may be necessary. When you are taking difenoxin and atropine, it is especially important that your health care professional know if you are taking any of the following:

• Antibiotics, such as cephalosporins (e.g., Ceftin, Keflex), clindamycin (e.g., Cleocin), erythromycins (e.g., E.E.S., PCE), tetracyclines (e.g., Achromycin, Doryx)—These antibiotics may cause diarrhea. Difenoxin and atropine may make the diarrhea caused by antibiotics worse or make it last longer
• Central nervous system (CNS) depressants (medicines that cause drowsiness)—Effects, such as drowsiness,

of CNS depressants or of difenoxin and atropine may become greater

- Monoamine oxidase (MAO) inhibitors (furazolidone [e.g., Furoxone], isocarboxazid [e.g., Marplan], phenelzine [e.g., Nardil], procarbazine [e.g., Matulane], tranylcypromine [e.g., Parnate])—Taking difenoxin and atropine while you are taking or within 2 weeks of taking MAO inhibitors may cause severe side effects; these medicines should not be used together

- Naltrexone (e.g., Trexan)—Withdrawal side effects may occur in patients who have become addicted to the difenoxin in this combination medicine; also, naltrexone will make this medicine less effective against diarrhea

- Other anticholinergics (medicine to help reduce stomach acid and abdominal or stomach spasms or cramps)—Use of other anticholinergics with this combination medicine may increase the effects of the atropine in this combination; however, this is not likely to happen with the usual doses of difenoxin and atropine

Other medical problems—The presence of other medical problems may affect the use of difenoxin and atropine. Make sure you tell your doctor if you have any other medical problems, especially:

- Alcohol abuse (or history of) or
- Drug abuse (history of)—There is a greater chance that this medicine may become habit-forming

- Colitis (severe)—A more serious problem of the colon may develop if you use this medicine

- Down's syndrome—Side effects may be more likely and severe in these patients

- Dysentery—This condition may get worse; a different kind of treatment may be needed

- Emphysema, asthma, bronchitis, or other chronic lung disease—There is a greater chance that this medicine may cause breathing problems in patients who have any of these conditions

- Enlarged prostate or
- Urinary tract blockage or difficult urination—Problems with urination may develop with the use of this medicine

- Gallbladder disease or gallstones—Use of this medicine may cause spasms of the biliary tract and make the condition worse

- Glaucoma—Severe pain in the eye may occur with the use of this medicine; however, the chance of this happening is low

- Heart disease—This medicine may have some effects on the heart, which may make the condition worse

- Hiatal hernia—The atropine in this medicine may make this condition worse; however, the chance of this happening is low

- High blood pressure (hypertension)—The atropine in this medicine may cause an increase in blood pressure; however, the chance of this happening is low

- Intestinal blockage—This medicine may make the condition worse

- Kidney disease—The atropine in this medicine may build up in the body and cause side effects

- Liver disease—The chance of central nervous system (CNS) side effects, including coma, may be greater in patients who have this condition

- Myasthenia gravis—This medicine may make the condition worse

- Overactive or underactive thyroid—Unwanted effects on breathing and heart rate may occur

- Overflow incontinence—This medicine may make the condition worse

Proper Use of This Medicine

If this medicine upsets your stomach, your doctor may want you to take it with food.

Take this medicine only as directed by your doctor. Do not take more of it, do not take it more often, and do not take it for a longer time than your doctor ordered. If too much is taken, it may become habit-forming.

Importance of diet and fluids while treating diarrhea:
- *In addition to using medicine for diarrhea, it is very important that you replace the fluid lost by the body and follow a proper diet.* For the first 24 hours you should eat gelatin and drink plenty of caffeine-free clear liquids, such as ginger ale, decaffeinated cola, decaffeinated tea, and broth. During the next 24 hours you may eat bland foods, such as cooked cereals, bread, crackers, and applesauce. Fruits, vegetables, fried or spicy foods, bran, candy, caffeine, and alcoholic beverages may make the condition worse.
- If too much fluid has been lost by the body due to the diarrhea a serious condition may develop. Check with your doctor as soon as possible if any of the following symptoms of too much fluid loss occur:
  Decreased urination
  Dizziness and lightheadedness
  Dryness of mouth
  Increased thirst
  Wrinkled skin

Dosing—The dose of difenoxin and atropine combination medicine will be different for different patients. *Follow your doctor's orders or the directions on the label.* The following information includes only the average doses of difenoxin and atropine combination. *If your dose is different, do not change it* unless your doctor tells you to do so.
- For *oral dosage form (tablets):*
  —For severe diarrhea:
  - Adults and teenagers—The first dose is usually 2 milligrams (mg). After that, the dose is 1 mg taken after each loose stool or every three or four hours as needed. *Do not take more than 8 mg in any twenty-four-hour period.*
  - Children—Use is not recommended.

Missed dose—If you are taking this medicine on a regular schedule and you miss a dose, take it as soon as possible. However, if it is almost time for your next dose, skip the missed dose and go back to your regular dosing schedule. Do not double doses.

Storage—To store this medicine:
- Keep out of the reach of children. Overdose is especially dangerous in children, and even part of an adult's pill can cause serious problems in children.
- Store away from heat and direct light.

- Do not store in the bathroom, near the kitchen sink, or in other damp places. Heat or moisture may cause the medicine to break down.
- Do not keep outdated medicine or medicine no longer needed. Be sure that any discarded medicine is out of the reach of children.

Precautions While Using This Medicine

Your doctor should check your progress at regular visits if you will be taking this medicine regularly for a long time.

Check with your doctor if your diarrhea does not stop after 2 days or if you develop a fever.

This medicine will add to the effects of alcohol and other CNS depressants (medicines that slow down the nervous system, possibly causing drowsiness). Some examples of CNS depressants are antihistamines or medicine for hay fever, other allergies, or colds; sedatives, tranquilizers, or sleeping medicine; prescription pain medicine or narcotics; barbiturates; medicine for seizures; muscle relaxants; or anesthetics, including some dental anesthetics. *Check with your doctor before taking any of the above while you are taking this medicine.*

If you think you or someone else in your home may have taken an overdose of this medicine, get emergency help at once. Taking an overdose of this medicine may lead to unconsciousness and possibly death. Symptoms of overdose include severe drowsiness; fast heartbeat; shortness of breath or troubled breathing; and unusual warmth, dryness, and flushing of skin.

Before having any kind of surgery (including dental surgery) or emergency treatment, tell the medical doctor or dentist in charge that you are using this medicine.

This medicine may cause some people to become dizzy, drowsy, or less alert than they are normally. Even if taken at bedtime, it may cause some people to feel drowsy or less alert on arising. *Make sure you know how you react to this medicine before you drive, use machines, or do anything else that could be dangerous if you are dizzy or are not alert.*

Side Effects of This Medicine

Along with its needed effects, a medicine may cause some unwanted effects. Although not all of these side effects may occur, if they do occur they may need medical attention.

When this medicine is used for short periods of time at low doses, side effects usually are rare. However, check with your doctor immediately if any of the following side effects are severe and occur suddenly, since they may be signs of a more severe and dangerous problem with your bowels:

Bloating; constipation; loss of appetite; stomach pain (severe) with nausea and vomiting

Check with your doctor also if any of the following effects occur, since they may be signs of an overdose of this medicine:

Blurred vision (continuing) or changes in near vision; drowsiness (severe); dryness of mouth, nose, and throat (severe); fast heartbeat; shortness of breath or troubled breathing (severe); unusual excitement, nervousness, restlessness, or irritability; unusual warmth, dryness, and flushing of skin

Other side effects may occur that usually do not need medical attention. These side effects may go away during treatment as your body adjusts to the medicine. However, check with your doctor if any of the following side effects continue, worsen, or are bothersome:

Less common or rare

Blurred vision; confusion; difficult urination; dizziness or lightheadedness; drowsiness; dryness of skin and mouth; fever; headache; trouble in sleeping; unusual tiredness or weakness

After you stop using this medicine, your body may need time to adjust. The length of time this takes depends on the amount of medicine you were using and how long you used it. During this period of time check with your doctor if you notice any of the following side effects:

Increased sweating; muscle cramps; nausea or vomiting; shivering or trembling; stomach cramps

Other side effects not listed above may also occur in some patients. If you notice any other effects, check with your doctor.

Revised: 07/15/94

DIGITALIS MEDICINES   Systemic

Commonly used brand name(s):

In the U.S.—

Lanoxicaps[2]	Lanoxin Injection[2]
Lanoxin[2]	Lanoxin Injection Pediatric[2]
Lanoxin Elixir Pediatric[2]	

In Canada—

Digitaline[1]	Lanoxin Injection[2]
Lanoxin[2]	Lanoxin Pediatric Injection[2]
Lanoxin Pediatric Elixir[2]	Novo-Digoxin[2]

Note: For quick reference, the following digitalis medicines are numbered to match the corresponding brand names.

This information applies to the following medicines:

1. Digitoxin (di-ji-TOX-in) *
2. Digoxin (di-JOX-in) ‡§

*Not commercially available in the U.S.
‡Generic name product may be available in the U.S.
§Generic name product may be available in Canada.

Description

Digitalis medicines are used to improve the strength and efficiency of the heart, or to control the rate and rhythm of the heartbeat. This leads to better blood circulation and reduced swelling of hands and ankles in patients with heart problems.

Although digitalis has been prescribed to help some patients lose weight, it should *never* be used in this way. When used improperly, digitalis can cause serious problems.

Digitalis medicines are available only with your doctor's prescription, in the following dosage forms:

Oral

Digitoxin

- Tablets (Canada)

Digoxin

- Capsules (U.S.)
- Elixir (U.S. and Canada)
- Tablets (U.S. and Canada)

Parenteral
Digoxin
• Injection (U.S. and Canada)

Before Using This Medicine

In deciding to use a medicine, the risks of taking the medicine must be weighed against the good it will do. This is a decision you and your doctor will make. For digitalis medicines, the following should be considered:

Allergies—Tell your doctor if you have ever had any unusual or allergic reaction to digitalis medicines. Also tell your health care professional if you are allergic to any other substances, such as foods, preservatives, or dyes.

Pregnancy—Digitalis medicines pass from the mother to the fetus. However, studies on effects in pregnancy have not been done in either humans or animals. Make sure your doctor knows if you are pregnant or if you may become pregnant before taking digitalis medicines.

Breast-feeding—Digoxin passes into breast milk. Although most medicines pass into breast milk in small amounts, many of them may be used safely while breast-feeding. Mothers who are taking this medicine and who wish to breast-feed should discuss this with their doctor.

Children—This medicine has been tested in children and, in effective doses, has not been shown to cause different side effects or problems than it does in adults. However, the dose is very different for babies and children, and it is important to follow your doctor's instructions exactly.

Older adults—Signs and symptoms of overdose may be especially likely to occur in elderly patients, who are usually more sensitive than younger adults to the effects of digitalis medicines.

Other medicines—Although certain medicines should not be used together at all, in other cases two different medicines may be used together even if an interaction might occur. In these cases, your doctor may want to change the dose, or other precautions may be necessary. When you are taking or receiving digitalis medicines it is especially important that your health care professional know if you are taking any other medicines because they may affect the levels of digitalis in the body and cause side effects. The following medicines are especially important:

• Amphetamines or
• Appetite suppressants (diet pills) or
• Medicine for asthma or other breathing problems or
• Medicine for colds, sinus problems, or hay fever or other allergies (including nose drops or sprays)—May increase the risk of heart rhythm problems

• Antiarrhythmic or other heart medicine, such as amiodarone (e.g., Cordarone) taken within the last 3 months or
• Calcium channel blocking agents (bepridil [e.g., Bepadin, Vascor], diltiazem [e.g., Cardizem, Cardizem CD, Cardizem SR], felodipine [e.g., Plendil], flunarizine [e.g., Sibelium], isradipine [e.g., DynaCirc], nicardipine [e.g., Cardene], nifedipine [e.g., Adalat, Procardia, Procardia XL], nimodipine [e.g., Nimotop], nisoldipine [e.g., Sular], verapamil [e.g., Calan, Calan SR, Isoptin, Isoptin SR, Verelan]) or
• Propafenone (e.g., Rythmol) or

• Quinidine (e.g., Quinidex)—May cause levels of digitalis medicines in the body to be higher than usual, which could lead to overdose
• Beta-adrenergic blocking agents (acebutolol [e.g., Sectral], atenolol [e.g., Tenormin], betaxolol [e.g., Kerlone], bisoprolol [e.g., Zebeta], carteolol [e.g., Cartrol], carvedilol [e.g., Coreg], labetalol [e.g., Normodyne], metoprolol [e.g., Lopressor], nadolol [e.g., Corgard], oxprenolol [e.g., Trasicor], penbutolol [e.g., Levatol], pindolol [e.g., Visken], propranolol [e.g., Inderal], sotalol [e.g., Sotacor], timolol [e.g., Blocadren])—Effects on slowing the heartbeat may be increased
• Diuretics (water pills)—These medicines can cause hypokalemia (low levels of potassium in the body), which can increase the unwanted effects of digitalis medicines

Other medical problems—The presence of other medical problems may affect the use of digitalis medicines. Make sure you tell your doctor if you have any other medical problems, especially:

• Electrolyte disorders or
• Heart disease or
• Lung disease (severe)—The heart may be more sensitive to the effects of digitalis medicines
• Heart rhythm problems—Digitalis medicines may make certain heart rhythm problems worse
• Kidney disease or
• Liver disease—Effects may be increased because of slower removal of digitalis medicines from the body
• Thyroid disease—Patients with low or high thyroid gland activity may be more or less sensitive to the effects of digitalis medicines

Proper Use of This Medicine

To keep your heart working properly, *take this medicine exactly as directed even though you may feel well.* Do not take more of it than your doctor ordered and do not miss any doses. Take the medicine at the same time each day. This medicine works best when there is a constant amount in the blood.

For patients taking the *liquid form of digoxin:*
• This medicine is to be taken by mouth even if it comes in a dropper bottle. The amount you should take is to be measured only with the specially marked dropper.

Dosing—When you are taking digitalis medicines, it is very important that you get the exact amount of medicine that you need. The dose of digitalis medicine will be different for different patients. Your doctor will determine the proper dose of digitalis medicine for you. *Follow your doctor's orders or the directions on the label.*

After you begin taking digitalis medicines, your doctor may sometimes check your blood level of digitalis medicine to find out if your dose needs to be changed. *Do not change your dose of digitalis medicine* unless your doctor tells you to do so.

The number of capsules, tablets, drops, or dropperfuls of solution that you take depends on the strength of the medicine.

Missed dose—If you miss a dose of this medicine, and you remember it within 12 hours, take it as soon as you remember. However, if you do not remember until later, do not take the missed dose at all and do not double the next one. Instead, go back to your regular dosing schedule. If you have any questions about this or if you miss doses for 2 or more days in a row, check with your doctor.

Storage—To store this medicine:

- Keep out of the reach of children.
- Store away from heat and direct light.
- Do not store in the bathroom, near the kitchen sink, or in other damp places. Heat or moisture may cause the medicine to break down.
- Do not keep outdated medicine or medicine no longer needed. Be sure that any discarded medicine is out of the reach of children.

Precautions While Using This Medicine

It is important that your doctor check your progress at regular visits to make sure the medicine is working properly. This will allow your doctor to make any changes in directions for taking it, if necessary.

Do not stop taking this medicine without first checking with your doctor. Stopping suddenly may cause a serious change in heart function.

Keep this medicine out of the reach of children. Digitalis medicines are a major cause of poisoning in children.

Watch for signs and symptoms of overdose while you are taking digitalis medicine. Follow your doctor's directions carefully. The amount of this medicine needed to help most people is very close to the amount that could cause serious problems from overdose. Some early warning signs of overdose are loss of appetite, nausea, vomiting, diarrhea, or problems in seeing. Other signs of overdose are changes in the rate or rhythm of the heartbeat (becoming irregular or slow), palpitations (feeling of pounding in the chest), and/or fainting. In infants and small children, the earliest signs of overdose are changes in the rate and rhythm of the heartbeat. Children may not show the other symptoms as soon as adults.

Your doctor may want you to carry a medical identification card or bracelet stating that you are taking this medicine.

Do not take any other medicine without consulting your doctor. Many over-the-counter (OTC) or nonprescription medicines contain ingredients that interfere with digitalis medicines or that may make your condition worse. These medicines include antacids; laxatives; asthma remedies; cold, cough, or sinus preparations; medicine for diarrhea; and weight reducing or diet medicines.

For patients taking the *tablet or capsule* form of this medicine:

- This medicine may look like other tablets or capsules you now take. It is very important that you do not get the medicines mixed up since this may have serious results. Ask your pharmacist for ways to avoid mix-ups with medicines that look alike.

Side Effects of This Medicine

Along with its needed effects, a medicine may cause some unwanted effects. Although not all of these side effects may occur, if they do occur they may need medical attention.

Check with your doctor as soon as possible if any of the following side effects or symptoms occur:

In adults
   Anxiety, blurred or yellow vision, confusion, dizziness, mental depression, feeling of not caring, headache, loss of appetite, seeing or hearing things that are not there, and/or weakness; diarrhea, loss of ap-

petite, lower stomach pain, nausea, and/or vomiting; irregular or slow heartbeat, palpitations (feeling of pounding in the chest), and/or fainting

Rare
   Skin rash; nosebleeds or bleeding gums

With long-term use
   Breast enlargement in males

In infants and children
   The above signs and symptoms also can occur in infants and children, but heartbeat rate or rhythm side effects are more common initially than stomach upset, loss of appetite, changes in vision, or other side effects.

Other side effects not listed above may also occur in some patients. If you notice any other effects, check with your doctor.

Revised: 03/02/99

DIHYDROERGOTAMINE   Nasal-Systemic

Commonly used brand name(s):

In the U.S.—
   Migranal

Description

Dihydroergotamine (dye-hye-droe-er-GOT-a-meen) belongs to the group of medicines called ergot alkaloids. It is a nasal solution used to help relieve migraine headaches. Nasal dihydroergotamine is not an ordinary pain reliever. It will not relieve any kind of pain other than throbbing headaches.

Nasal dihydroergotamine may cause blood vessels in the body to constrict (become narrower). This action can lead to serious effects that are caused by a decrease in the flow of blood (blood circulation) to many parts of the body. Be sure that you discuss with your doctor the risks of using this medicine as well as the good it can do.

This medicine is available only with your doctor's prescription, in the following dosage form(s):

Nasal
   - Nasal solution (US)

Before Using This Medicine

In deciding to use a medicine, the risks of using the medicine must be weighed against the good it will do. This is a decision you and your doctor will make. For nasal dihydroergotamine, the following should be considered:

Allergies—Tell your doctor if you have ever had any unusual or allergic reaction to dihydroergotamine or any other ergot alkaloid. Also tell your health care professional if you are allergic to any other substances, such as foods, preservatives, or dyes.

Pregnancy—Use of nasal dihydroergotamine by pregnant women may cause serious harm to the fetus. Therefore, *nasal dihydroergotamine should not be used during pregnancy.*

Breast-feeding—Use of nasal dihydroergotamine is not recommended for nursing mothers. Nasal dihydroergotamine may pass into the breast milk and may cause unwanted effects, such as vomiting, diarrhea, weak pulse, changes in blood pressure, or convulsions (seizures) in nursing babies. Nasal dihydroergotamine may also decrease the flow of breast milk.

Children—There is no specific information comparing use of nasal dihydroergotamine in children with use in other age groups.

Older adults—There is no specific information comparing use of nasal dihydroergotamine in older adults with use in other age groups.

Other medicines—Although certain medicines should not be used together at all, in other cases two different medicines may be used together even if an interaction might occur. In these cases, your doctor may want to change the dose, or other precautions may be necessary. When you are taking nasal dihydroergotamine, it is especially important that your health care professional know if you are using any of the following:

- Cocaine or
- Epinephrine by injection [e.g., Epi-Pen] or
- Other ergot medicines (ergoloid mesylates [e.g., Hydergine], ergonovine [e.g., Ergotrate], methylergonovine [e.g., Methergine], methysergide [e.g., Sansert] or
- Sumatriptan [e.g., Imitrex]—The chance of serious side effects caused by nasal dihydroergotamine may be increased.

Other medical problems—The presence of other medical problems may affect the use of nasal dihydroergotamine. Make sure you tell your doctor if you have any other medical problems, especially:

- Heart or blood vessel disease or
- Hypertension (high blood pressure) or
- Kidney disease or
- Liver disease or
- Infection—The chance of serious side effects caused by nasal dihydroergotmine may be increased. Heart or blood vessel disease and high blood pressure sometimes do not cause any symptoms, so some people do not know that they have these problems. Before deciding whether you should use nasal dihydroergotamine, your doctor may need to do some tests to make sure that you do not have any of these conditions.

Proper Use of This Medicine

It is important to use this medicine properly. Make sure that you read the patient directions carefully before using this medicine.

Do not use nasal dihydroergotamine for a headache that is different from your usual migraine. Instead, check with your doctor.

To relieve your migraine as soon as possible, use nasal dihydroergotamine as soon as the headache begins. Even if you get warning signals of a coming migraine (an aura), *you should wait until the headache pain starts before using nasal dihydroergotamine.*

Lying down in a quiet, dark room for a while after you use this medicine may help relieve your migraine.

If you feel much better after a dose of nasal dihydroergotamine, but your headache comes back or gets worse after a while, you may use more nasal dihydroergotamine. However,

use this medicine only as directed by your doctor. Do not use more of it, and do not use it more often, than directed.

Your doctor may direct you to take another medicine to help prevent headaches. *It is important that you follow your doctor's directions, even if your headaches continue to occur.* Headache-preventing medicines may take several weeks to start working. Even after they do start working, your headaches should occur less often, and they should be less severe, and easier to relieve. This can reduce the amount of nasal dihydroergotamine or other pain medicines that you need. If you do not notice any improvement after several weeks of headache-preventing treatment, check with your doctor.

Dosing—The dose of nasal dihydroergotamine will be different for different patients. *Follow your doctor's orders or the directions on the label.* The following information includes only the average doses of nasal dihydroergotamine. *If your dose is different, do not change it* unless your doctor tells you to do so.

- For *nasal* dosage form (nasal solution):
  - —For migraine headaches:
    - Adults—One spray (0.5 mg) in each nostril. After 15 minutes, another spray (0.5 mg) in each nostril should be used.
    - Children—Use and dose must be determined by your doctor.

Storage—To store this medicine:

- Keep out of the reach of children.
- Store away from heat and direct light.
- Do not store in the bathroom, near the kitchen sink, or in other damp places. Heat or moisture may cause the medicine to break down.
- Do not keep outdated medicine or medicine no longer needed. Be sure that any discarded medicine is out of the reach of children.

Precautions While Using This Medicine

Drinking alcoholic beverages can make headaches worse or cause new headaches to occur. People who suffer from severe headaches should probably avoid alcoholic beverages, especially during a headache.

Some people feel drowsy or dizzy during or after a migraine attack, or after taking nasal dihydroergotamine to relieve a migraine headache. As long as you are feeling drowsy or dizzy, *do not drive, use machines or do anything else that could be dangerous if you are dizzy or are not alert.*

Side Effects of This Medicine

Along with its needed effects, a medicine may cause some unwanted effects. Although not all of these side effects may occur, if they do occur they may need medical attention.

Check with your doctor as soon as possible if any of the following side effects occur:

Less common or rare

Chest pain; cough, fever, sneezing, or sore throat; feeling of heaviness in chest; irregular heartbeat; itching of the skin; numbness and tingling of face, fingers, or toes; pain in arms, legs, or lower back; pain in back, chest or left arm; pale bluish-colored or cold hands or feet; shortness of breath or troubled breathing; weak or absent pulses in legs

Symptoms of overdose

   Confusion; convulsions (seizures); delirium; dizziness; headaches; nausea and/or vomiting; numbness, tingling, and/or pain in the legs or arms; shortness of breath; stomach pain

Other side effects may occur that usually do not need medical attention. These side effects may go away during treatment as your body adjusts to the medicine. However, check with your doctor if any of the following side effects continue or are bothersome:

More common

   Burning or tingling sensation, dryness, soreness, or pain in the nose; change in sense of taste; diarrhea; dizziness; dry mouth; fatigue; headache; increased sweating; nausea and or vomiting; muscle stiffness; runny and or stuffy nose; sudden sweatings and feelings of warmth; sensation of burning, warmth, or heat; sore throat; sleepiness; unexplained nose bleeds; unusual tiredness or weakness

Less common

   Anxiety; blurred vision; cold clammy skin; confusion; congestion in chest; cough; decreased appetite; depression; difficulty swallowing; dizziness or light-headedness when getting up from a lying or sitting position; ear pain; eye pain; fever; heartburn; increased watering of eyes; increased watering of the mouth; increased yawning; muscle weakness; nervousness; pinpoint red spots on skin; pounding heartbeat; red or irritated eyes; ringing or buzzing in ears; skin rash; stomach pain; sudden fainting; swelling of face, fingers, feet, or lower legs; trembling or shaking of hands or feet; trouble in sleeping; unusual feeling of well being

Other side effects not listed above may also occur in some patients. If you notice any other effects, check with your doctor.

Developed: 07/08/98

DIMETHYL SULFOXIDE Mucosal

Commonly used brand name(s):

In the U.S.—
   Rimso-50
   Generic name product may be available.
In Canada—
   Rimso-50
Another commonly used name is DMSO.

Description

Dimethyl sulfoxide (dye-METH-il sul-FOX-ide) is a purified preparation used in the bladder to relieve the symptoms of the bladder condition called interstitial cystitis. A catheter (tube) or syringe is used to put the solution into the bladder where it is allowed to remain for about 15 minutes. Then, the solution is expelled by urinating.

Interstitial cystitis is the only human use for dimethyl sulfoxide that is approved by the U.S. Food and Drug Administration (FDA).

Claims that dimethyl sulfoxide is effective for treating various types of arthritis, ulcers in scleroderma, muscle sprains and

strains, bruises, infections of the skin, burns, wounds, and mental conditions have not been proven.

Although other preparations of dimethyl sulfoxide are available for industrial and veterinary (animal) use, they must not be used by humans, because of their unknown purity. Impurities in these preparations may cause serious unwanted effects in humans. Even if dimethyl sulfoxide is applied to the skin, it is absorbed into the body through the skin and mucous membranes.

This medicine is available only with your doctor's prescription, in the following dosage form:

Topical
   • Bladder irrigation (U.S. and Canada)

Before Using This Medicine

In deciding to use a medicine, the risks of taking the medicine must be weighed against the good it will do. This is a decision you and your doctor will make. For dimethyl sulfoxide, the following should be considered:

Allergies—Tell your doctor if you have ever had any unusual or allergic reaction to dimethyl sulfoxide. Also tell your health care professional if you are allergic to any other substances, such as preservatives.

Pregnancy—Dimethyl sulfoxide has not been studied in pregnant women. However, some studies in animals have shown that dimethyl sulfoxide causes birth defects when used on the skin and when given in high doses by injection. Before using this medicine, make sure your doctor knows if you are pregnant or if you may become pregnant.

Breast-feeding—Dimethyl sulfoxide is absorbed into the body. It is not known whether dimethyl sulfoxide passes into the breast milk. However, this medicine has not been reported to cause problems in nursing babies.

Children—Studies on this medicine have been done only in adult patients, and there is no specific information comparing use of this medicine in children with use in other age groups.

Older adults—Many medicines have not been studied specifically in older people. Therefore, it may not be known whether they work exactly the same way they do in younger adults or if they cause different side effects or problems in older people. There is no specific information comparing use of this medicine in the elderly with use in other age groups.

Other medicines—Although certain medicines should not be used together at all, in other cases two different medicines may be used together even if an interaction might occur. In these cases, your doctor may want to change the dose, or other precautions may be necessary. Tell your health care professional if you are using any other prescription or nonprescription (over-the-counter [OTC]) medicine.

Proper Use of This Medicine

Dosing—The dose of dimethyl sulfoxide will be different for different patients. The following information includes only the average doses of dimethyl sulfoxide. *Your dose may be different.*

   • For *bladder irrigation* dosage form:
      —For interstitial cystitis of bladder:
         • Adults—50 mL (milliliters) of a 50% solution is instilled into the bladder and left there for fifteen minutes. The treatment is repeated every two weeks until relief is obtained; then the treatment is repeated less often.

- Children—Use and dose must be determined by your doctor.

Side Effects of This Medicine

Along with its needed effects, a medicine may cause some unwanted effects. Although not all of these side effects may occur, if they do occur they may need medical attention.

Check with your doctor immediately if any of the following side effects occur:

Nasal congestion; shortness of breath or troubled breathing; skin rash, hives, or itching; swelling of face

Some patients may have some discomfort during the time this medicine is being put into the bladder. However, the discomfort usually becomes less each time the medicine is used.

Dimethyl sulfoxide may cause you to have a garlic-like taste within a few minutes after the medicine is put into the bladder. This effect may last for several hours. It may also cause your breath and skin to have a garlic-like odor, which may last up to 72 hours.

Other side effects not listed above may also occur in some patients. If you notice any other effects, check with your doctor.

Revised: 03/04/92
Interim revision: 03/28/94

DINOPROSTONE   Cervical/Vaginal

Commonly used brand name(s):

In the U.S.—
 Cervidil
 Prepidil
 Prostin E$_2$
In Canada—
 Prepidil
 Prostin E$_2$
Other commonly used names are prostaglandin E$_2$ or PGE$_2$.

Description

Dinoprostone (dye-noe-PROST-one) works by causing the cervix to thin and dilate (open) and the uterus to contract (cramp) the way it does during labor.

Dinoprostone may also be used for other purposes as determined by your doctor.

Dinoprostone is to be administered only by or under the immediate care of your doctor. It is available in the following dosage forms:

Cervical
 • Gel (U.S. and Canada)
Vaginal
 • Gel (Canada)
 • Suppositories (U.S.)
 • System (U.S.)

Before Receiving This Medicine

In deciding to use a medicine, the risks of taking the medicine must be weighed against the good it will do. This is a decision you and your doctor will make. For dinoprostone, the following should be considered:

Allergies—Tell your doctor if you have ever had any unusual or allergic reaction to dinoprostone, misoprostol, oxytocin or other medicines that stimulate the uterus to contract.

Other medicines—Although certain medicines should not be used together at all, in other cases two different medicines may be used together even if an interaction might occur. In these cases, your doctor may want to change the dose, or other precautions may be necessary. When you are receiving dinoprostone, it is especially important that your doctor knows if you are using any other vaginal prescription or nonprescription (over-the-counter [OTC]) medicine.

Other medical problems—The presence of other medical problems may affect the use of dinoprostone. Make sure you tell your doctor if you have any other medical problems, especially:

- Anemia (or history of)—Dinoprostone, when used in doses that stimulate the uterus to contract, may result in loss of blood in some patients that may require a blood transfusion
- Asthma (or history of, including childhood asthma) or
- Lung disease—Dinoprostone may cause narrowing of the blood vessels in the lungs or narrowing of the lung passages, especially when it is used in doses that stimulate the uterus to contract
- Epilepsy (or history of)—Rarely, seizures have occurred with dinoprostone when it is used in doses that stimulate the uterus to contract
- Glaucoma—Rarely, the pressure within the eye has increased and constriction of the pupils has occurred during the use of medicines like dinoprostone; this may also be a problem with dinoprostone when it is used in doses that stimulate the uterus to contract
- Heart or blood vessel disease (or history of) or
- High blood pressure (or history of) or
- Low blood pressure (history of)—Dinoprostone may cause changes in heart function or blood pressure changes; two patients with a history of heart disease had heart attacks when dinoprostone was used in doses that stimulated the uterus to contract
- Kidney disease (or history of) or
- Liver disease (or history of)—The body may not remove dinoprostone from the blood stream at the usual rate, which may make the dinoprostone work longer or cause an increased chance of side effects, especially when dinoprostone is used in doses that stimulate the uterus to contract
- Problems during delivery, history of or
- Surgery of uterus (history of) or
- Unusual vaginal bleeding—There is an increased risk of problems occurring with dinoprostone when it is used in doses that stimulate the uterus to contract

Proper Use of This Medicine

After dinoprostone is given, you will need to lie down for 10 minutes to 2 hours so that the medicine can be absorbed. The length of time you must remain lying down will depend on what form of the medicine you are using.

Dosing—The dose of dinoprostone will be different for different patients. The following information includes only the average doses for dinoprostone. Your doctor will give you the dose of this medicine and follow your care in a hospital or other health care setting.

- For *cervical* dosage form (gel):
  —To thin and widen the opening of the cervix just before labor:
    - Adults and teenagers—Your doctor will insert 0.5 milligram (mg) (one application) of dinoprostone into the canal of your cervix. You should remain lying on your back for at least ten to thirty minutes after it has been applied.
- For *vaginal* dosage form (gel):
  —To cause the uterus to contract for labor:
    - Adults and teenagers—Your doctor will insert 1 milligram (mg) (one applicatorful) of dinoprostone into your vagina. You should remain lying on your back for at least thirty minutes after it has been applied. You may need another dose of 1 to 2 mg six hours after the first dose.
- For *vaginal* dosage form (suppositories):
  —To cause the uterus to contract to abort a pregnancy:
    - Adults and teenagers—Your doctor will insert 20 milligrams (mg) (one suppository) into your vagina every three to five hours as needed. You should remain lying on your back for at least ten minutes after it has been inserted.
- For *vaginal* dosage form (system):
  —To thin and widen the opening of the cervix just before labor:
    - Adults and teenagers—Your doctor will insert 10 milligrams (mg) (one system) into your vagina. You should remain lying on your back for at least two hours after it has been inserted.

Side Effects of This Medicine

Along with its needed effects, a medicine may cause some unwanted effects. Although not all of these side effects may occur, if they do occur they may need medical attention.

Tell the health care professional immediately if any of the following side effects occur:

Less common or rare
> Fast or slow heartbeat; hives; increased pain of the uterus; pale, cool, blotchy skin on arms or legs; pressing or painful feeling in chest; shortness of breath; swelling of face, inside the nose, and eyelids; tightness in chest; trouble in breathing; weak or absent pulse in arms or legs; wheezing

Other side effects may occur that usually do not need medical attention. These side effects usually go away after the medicine is stopped. However, let the health care professional know if any of the following side effects continue or are bothersome:

More common
> Abdominal or stomach cramps; diarrhea; fever; nausea; vomiting

Less common or rare
> Chills or shivering; constipation; flushing; headache; swelling of the genital area (vulva); tender or mildly bloated abdomen or stomach

This procedure may still result in some effects, which occur after the procedure is completed, that need medical attention. Check with your doctor if any of the following side effects occur:

> Chills or shivering (continuing); fever (continuing); foul-smelling vaginal discharge; pain in lower abdomen; unusual increase in bleeding of the uterus

Other side effects not listed above may also occur in some patients. If you notice any other effects, check with your health care professional.

Additional Information

Once a medicine has been approved for marketing for a certain use, experience may show that it is also useful for other medical problems. Although these uses are not included in product labeling, dinoprostone is used in certain patients with the following medical condition:

- Unusual increase in bleeding of the uterus after delivery (postpartum hemorrhage)

Other than the above information, there is no additional information relating to proper use, precautions, or side effects for this use.

Revised: 08/20/97

DIPHENIDOL   Systemic†

A commonly used name is difenidol.

†Not commercially available in Canada.

Description

Diphenidol (dye-FEN-i-dole) is used to relieve or prevent nausea, vomiting, and dizziness caused by certain medical problems.

Before Using This Medicine

In deciding to use a medicine, the risks of taking the medicine must be weighed against the good it will do. This is a decision you and your doctor will make. For diphenidol, the following should be considered:

Allergies—Tell your doctor if you have ever had any unusual or allergic reaction to diphenidol. Also tell your health care professional if you are allergic to any other substances, such as foods, preservatives, or dyes.

Pregnancy—Diphenidol has not been shown to cause birth defects or other problems in human or animal studies.

Breast-feeding—Diphenidol has not been reported to cause problems in nursing babies.

Children—There is no specific information comparing use of diphenidol for dizziness in children with use in other age groups. Also, there is no specific information about the use of diphenidol for nausea and vomiting in children who weigh less than 22.8 kilograms (50 pounds).

Older adults—Many medicines have not been studied specifically in older people. Therefore, it may not be known whether they work exactly the same way they do in younger adults or if they cause different side effects or problems in older people. There is no specific information comparing use of diphenidol in the elderly with use in other age groups.

Other medicines—Although certain medicines should not be used together at all, in other cases two different medicines may be used together even if an interaction might occur. In these cases, your doctor may want to change the dose, or other precautions may be necessary. When you are

taking diphenidol, it is especially important that your health care professional know if you are taking any of the following:

- Central nervous system (CNS) depressants (medicines that cause drowsiness) or
- Tricyclic antidepressants (medicine for depression)— Using these medicines with diphenidol may increase the CNS depressant effects

Other medical problems—The presence of other medical problems may affect the use of diphenidol. Make sure you tell your doctor if you have any other medical problems, especially:

- Enlarged prostate or
- Glaucoma or
- Intestinal blockage or
- Low blood pressure or
- Stomach ulcer—Diphenidol may make the condition worse

- Kidney disease or
- Urinary tract blockage—Higher blood levels of diphenidol may occur, increasing the chance of side effects

Proper Use of This Medicine

If you are taking diphenidol to prevent nausea and vomiting, it may be taken with food or a glass of water or milk to lessen stomach irritation, unless otherwise directed by your doctor. However, if you are already suffering from nausea and vomiting, it is best to keep the stomach empty, and this medicine should be taken only with a small amount of water.

Take this medicine only as directed. Do not take more of it and do not take it more often than directed by your doctor. To do so may increase the chance of side effects.

Dosing—The dose of diphenidol will be different for different patients. *Follow your doctor's orders or the directions on the label.* The following information includes only the average doses of diphenidol. *If your dose is different, do not change it* unless your doctor tells you to do so.

The number of tablets that you take depends on the strength of the medicine. Also, *the number of doses you take each day, the time allowed between doses, and the length of time you take the medicine depend on the medical problem for which you are taking diphenidol.*

- For *oral* dosage form (tablets):
  —Adults: 25 to 50 milligrams (mg) every four hours as needed.
  —Children: The dose is based on body weight and must be determined by the doctor.

Missed dose—If your doctor has ordered you to take this medicine on a regular schedule and you miss a dose, take it as soon as possible. However, if it is almost time for your next dose, skip the missed dose and go back to your regular dosing schedule. Do not double doses.

Storage—To store this medicine:

- Keep out of the reach of children.
- Store away from heat and direct light.
- Do not store the tablet form of this medicine in the bathroom, near the kitchen sink, or in other damp places. Heat or moisture may cause the medicine to break down.
- Do not keep outdated medicine or medicine no longer needed. Be sure that any discarded medicine is out of the reach of children.

Precautions While Using This Medicine

This medicine will add to the effects of alcohol and other CNS depressants (medicines that make you drowsy or less alert). Some examples of CNS depressants are antihistamines or medicine for hay fever, other allergies, or colds; sedatives, tranquilizers, or sleeping medicine; prescription pain medicine or narcotics; barbiturates; medicine for seizures; muscle relaxants; or anesthetics, including some dental anesthetics. *Check with your doctor before taking any of the above while you are using this medicine.*

This medicine may cause some people to have blurred vision or to become dizzy, drowsy, or less alert than they are normally. *Make sure you know how you react to this medicine before you drive, use machines, or do anything else that could be dangerous if you are dizzy or are not alert or able to see well.*

Side Effects of This Medicine

Along with its needed effects, a medicine may cause some unwanted effects. Although not all of these side effects may occur, if they do occur they may need medical attention.

Check with your doctor as soon as possible if any of the following side effects occur:
  Rare
    Confusion; hallucinations (seeing, hearing, or feeling things that are not there)
  Symptoms of overdose
    Drowsiness (severe); shortness of breath or troubled breathing; unusual tiredness or weakness (severe)

Other side effects may occur that usually do not need medical attention. These side effects may go away during treatment as your body adjusts to the medicine. However, check with your doctor if any of the following side effects continue or are bothersome:
  More common
    Drowsiness
  Less common or rare
    Blurred vision; dizziness; dryness of mouth; headache; heartburn; nervousness, restlessness, or trouble in sleeping; skin rash; stomach upset or pain; unusual tiredness or weakness

Other side effects not listed above may also occur in some patients. If you notice any other effects, check with your doctor.

Revised: 01/29/99

DIPHENOXYLATE AND ATROPINE
Systemic

Commonly used brand name(s):

In the U.S.—
Lofene	Lomotil
Logen	Lonox
Lomocot	Vi-Atro

Generic name product may be available.

In Canada—
Lomotil

Description

Diphenoxylate and atropine (dye-fen-OX-i-late and A-troe-peen) is a combination medicine used along with other measures to treat severe diarrhea in adults. Diphenoxylate helps stop diarrhea by slowing down the movements of the intestines.

Since diphenoxylate is chemically related to some narcotics, it may be habit-forming if taken in doses that are larger than prescribed. To help prevent possible abuse, atropine (an anticholinergic) has been added. If higher than normal doses of the combination are taken, the atropine will cause unpleasant effects, making it unlikely that such doses will be taken again.

Diphenoxylate and atropine combination medicine should not be used in children. Children with diarrhea should be given solutions of carbohydrates (sugars) and important salts (electrolytes) to replace the water, sugars, and important salts that are lost from the body during diarrhea. For more information on these solutions, see the Carbohydrates and Electrolytes (Systemic) monograph.

This medicine is available only with your doctor's prescription in the following dosage forms:

Oral
- Oral solution (U.S.)
- Tablets (U.S. and Canada)

Before Using This Medicine

In deciding to use a medicine, the risks of taking the medicine must be weighed against the good it will do. This is a decision you and your doctor will make. For diphenoxylate and atropine, the following should be considered:

Allergies—Tell your doctor if you have ever had any unusual or allergic reaction to diphenoxylate or atropine. Also tell your health care professional if you are allergic to any other substances, such as foods, preservatives, or dyes.

Pregnancy—Studies have not been done in humans. In animal studies this medicine given in larger doses than the usual human dose has not been shown to cause birth defects. However, some studies in rats have shown that this medicine reduces the weight gain of the pregnant rat and lessens the chance of conceiving or becoming pregnant when given in doses many times the usual human dose.

Breast-feeding—Although both diphenoxylate and atropine pass into the breast milk, this medicine has not been shown to cause problems in nursing babies.

Children—This medicine should not be used in children. Children, especially very young children, are very sensitive to the effects of diphenoxylate and atropine. This may increase the chance of side effects during treatment. Also, the fluid loss caused by diarrhea may result in a severe condition. For this reason, it is very important that a sufficient amount of liquids be given to replace the fluid lost by the body. If you have any questions about this, check with your health care professional.

Older adults—Shortness of breath or difficulty in breathing may be especially likely to occur in elderly patients, who are usually more sensitive than younger adults to the effects of diphenoxylate. Also, the fluid loss caused by diarrhea may result in a severe condition. For this reason, elderly persons should not take this medicine without first checking with their doctor. It is also very important that a sufficient amount of liquids be taken to replace the fluid lost by the

body. If you have any questions about this, check with your health care professional.

Other medicines—Although certain medicines should not be used together at all, in other cases two different medicines may be used together even if an interaction might occur. In these cases, your doctor may want to change the dose, or other precautions may be necessary. When you are taking diphenoxylate and atropine, it is especially important that your health care professional know if you are taking any of the following:

- Antibiotics, such as cephalosporins (e.g., Ceftin, Keflex), clindamycin (e.g., Cleocin), erythromycins (e.g., E.E.S., PCE), tetracyclines (e.g., Achromycin, Doryx)—These antibiotics may cause diarrhea. Diphenoxylate and atropine may make the diarrhea caused by antibiotics worse or make it last longer
- Central nervous system (CNS) depressants (medicines that cause drowsiness)—Effects, such as drowsiness, of CNS depressants or of diphenoxylate and atropine may become greater
- Monoamine oxidase (MAO) inhibitors (furazolidone [e.g., Furoxone], isocarboxazid [e.g., Marplan], phenelzine [e.g., Nardil], procarbazine [e.g., Matulane], selegiline [e.g., Eldepryl], tranylcypromine [e.g., Parnate])—Taking diphenoxylate and atropine while you are taking or within 2 weeks of taking MAO inhibitors may cause severe side effects; these medicines should not be used together
- Opioid (narcotic) antagonists (naltrexone [e.g., ReVia])—Withdrawal side effects may occur in patients who have become addicted to the diphenoxylate in this combination medicine; also, naltrexone will make this medicine less effective against diarrhea
- Other anticholinergics (medicine to help reduce stomach acid and abdominal or stomach spasms or cramps)—Use of other anticholinergics with this combination medicine may increase the effects of the atropine in this combination; however, this is not likely to happen with the usual doses of diphenoxylate and atropine

Other medical problems—The presence of other medical problems may affect the use of diphenoxylate and atropine. Make sure you tell your doctor if you have any other medical problems, especially:

- Alcohol abuse (or history of) or
- Drug abuse (history of)—There is a greater chance that this medicine will become habit-forming
- Colitis (severe)—A more serious problem of the colon may develop if you use this medicine
- Down's syndrome—Side effects may be more likely and severe in these patients
- Dysentery—This condition may get worse; a different kind of treatment may be needed
- Emphysema, asthma, bronchitis, or other chronic lung disease—There is a greater chance that this medicine may cause serious breathing problems in patients who have any of these conditions
- Enlarged prostate or
- Urinary tract blockage or difficult urination—Severe problems with urination may develop with the use of this medicine
- Gallbladder disease or gallstones—Use of this medicine may cause spasms of the biliary tract and make the condition worse

- Glaucoma—Severe pain in the eye may occur with the use of this medicine; however, the chance of this happening is small
- Heart disease—This medicine may have some effects on the heart, which may make the condition worse
- Hiatal hernia—The atropine in this medicine may make this condition worse; however, the chance of this happening is small
- High blood pressure (hypertension)—The atropine in this medicine may cause an increase in blood pressure; however, the chance of this happening is small
- Intestinal blockage—This medicine may make the condition worse
- Kidney disease—The atropine in this medicine may build up in the body and cause side effects
- Liver disease—The chance of central nervous system (CNS) side effects, including coma, may be greater in patients who have this condition
- Myasthenia gravis—This medicine may make the condition worse
- Overactive or underactive thyroid—Unwanted effects on breathing and heart rate may occur
- Overflow incontinence—This medicine may make the condition worse

Proper Use of This Medicine

If this medicine upsets your stomach, your doctor may want you to take it with food.

Take this medicine only as directed by your doctor. Do not take more of it, do not take it more often, and do not take it for a longer time than your doctor ordered. If too much is taken, it may become habit-forming.

For patients taking the liquid form of this medicine:
- This medicine is to be taken by mouth even if it comes in a dropper bottle. The amount to be taken is to be measured with the specially marked dropper.

Importance of diet and fluids while treating diarrhea:
- *In addition to using medicine for diarrhea, it is very important that you replace the fluid lost by the body and follow a proper diet.* For the first 24 hours you should eat gelatin and drink plenty of caffeine-free clear liquids, such as ginger ale, decaffeinated cola, decaffeinated tea, and broth. During the next 24 hours you may eat bland foods, such as cooked cereals, bread, crackers, and applesauce. Fruits, vegetables, fried or spicy foods, bran, candy, caffeine, and alcoholic beverages may make the condition worse.
- If too much fluid has been lost by the body due to the diarrhea a serious condition may develop. Check with your doctor as soon as possible if any of the following signs or symptoms of too much fluid loss occur:
  Decreased urination
  Dizziness and light-headedness
  Dryness of mouth
  Increased thirst
  Wrinkled skin

Dosing—The dose of diphenoxylate and atropine combination medicine will be different for different patients. *Follow your doctor's orders or the directions on the label.* The following information includes only the average doses of diphenoxylate and atropine combination. *If your dose is different, do not change it* unless your doctor tells you to do so.

- For severe diarrhea:
  —For *oral* dosage form (oral solution):
    - Adults and teenagers—At first, the dose is 5 milligrams (mg) (2 teaspoonfuls) three or four times a day. Then, the dose is usually 5 mg (2 teaspoonfuls) once a day, as needed.
    - Children up to 12 years of age—Use is not recommended.
  —For *oral* dosage form (tablets):
    - Adults and teenagers—At first, the dose is 5 mg (2 tablets) three or four times a day. Then, the dose is usually 5 mg (2 tablets) once a day, as needed.
    - Children up to 12 years of age—Use is not recommended.

Missed dose—If you are taking this medicine on a regular schedule and you miss a dose, take it as soon as possible. However, if it is almost time for your next dose, skip the missed dose and go back to your regular dosing schedule. Do not double doses.

Storage—To store this medicine:
- Keep out of the reach of children since overdose is especially dangerous in children.
- Store away from heat and direct light.
- Do not store the tablet form of this medicine in the bathroom, near the kitchen sink, or in other damp places. Heat or moisture may cause the medicine to break down.
- Keep the liquid form of this medicine from freezing.
- Do not keep outdated medicine or medicine no longer needed. Be sure that any discarded medicine is out of the reach of children.

Precautions While Using This Medicine

Your doctor should check your progress at regular visits if you will be taking this medicine regularly for a long time.

Check with your doctor if your diarrhea does not stop after two days or if you develop a fever.

This medicine will add to the effects of alcohol and other CNS depressants (medicines that slow down the nervous system, possibly causing drowsiness). Some examples of CNS depressants are antihistamines or medicine for hay fever, other allergies, or colds; sedatives, tranquilizers, or sleeping medicine; prescription pain medicine or narcotics; barbiturates; medicine for seizures; muscle relaxants; or anesthetics, including some dental anesthetics. *Check with your doctor before taking any of the above while you are taking this medicine.*

If you think you or anyone else may have taken an overdose, get emergency help at once. Taking an overdose of this medicine may lead to unconsciousness and possibly death. Signs or symptoms of overdose include severe drowsiness; shortness of breath or troubled breathing; fast heartbeat; and unusual warmth, dryness, and flushing of the skin.

Before having any kind of surgery (including dental surgery) or emergency treatment, tell the medical doctor or dentist in charge that you are taking this medicine.

This medicine may cause some people to become dizzy, drowsy, or less alert than they are normally. Even if taken at bedtime, it may cause some people to feel drowsy or less alert on arising. *Make sure you know how you react to this medicine before you drive, use machines, or do anything else that could be dangerous if you are dizzy or are not alert.*

Side Effects of This Medicine

Along with its needed effects, a medicine may cause some unwanted effects. Although not all of these side effects may occur, if they do occur they may need medical attention.

When this medicine is used for short periods of time at low doses, side effects usually are rare. However, check with your doctor immediately if any of the following side effects are severe and occur suddenly, since they may be signs of a more severe and dangerous problem with your bowels:

Bloating; constipation; loss of appetite; stomach pain (severe) with nausea and vomiting

Check with your doctor immediately also if the following effects occur, since they may be signs of an overdose of this medicine:

Blurred vision (continuing) or changes in near vision; drowsiness (severe); dryness of mouth, nose, and throat (severe); fast heartbeat; shortness of breath or troubled breathing (severe); unusual excitement, nervousness, restlessness, or irritability; unusual warmth, dryness, and flushing of the skin

Other side effects may occur that usually do not need medical attention. These side effects may go away during treatment as your body adjusts to the medicine. However, check with your doctor if any of the following side effects continue, worsen, or are bothersome:

Less common or rare

Blurred vision; confusion; difficult urination; dizziness or light-headedness; drowsiness; dryness of skin and mouth; fever; headache; increased body temperature; mental depression; numbness of hands or feet; skin rash or itching; swelling of the gums

After you stop using this medicine, your body may need time to adjust. The length of time this takes depends on the amount of medicine you were using and how long you used it. During this time check with your doctor if you notice any of the following side effects:

Rare

Increased sweating; muscle cramps; nausea or vomiting; shivering or trembling; stomach cramps

Other side effects not listed above may also occur in some patients. If you notice any other effects, check with your doctor.

Revised: 12/09/99

DIPHTHERIA AND TETANUS TOXOIDS   Systemic

A commonly used name for diphtheria and tetanus toxoids for pediatric use is DT[1].

A commonly used name for tetanus and diphtheria toxoids for adult use is Td[2].

This information applies to the following medicines:
1. Diphtheria and Tetanus Toxoids for Pediatric Use (dif-THEE-ree-a and TET-n-us)
2. Tetanus and Diphtheria Toxoids for Adult Use (TET-n-us and dif-THEE-ree-a)

Description

Diphtheria and Tetanus Toxoids (also known as DT and Td) is a combination immunizing agent given by injection to prevent diphtheria and tetanus.

Diphtheria is a serious illness that can cause breathing difficulties, heart problems, nerve damage, pneumonia, and possibly death. The risk of serious complications and death is greatest in very young children and in the elderly.

Tetanus (also known as lockjaw) is a serious illness that causes convulsions (seizures) and severe muscle spasms that can be strong enough to cause bone fractures of the spine. Tetanus causes death in 30 to 40 percent of cases.

Immunization with diphtheria and tetanus toxoids for pediatric use (DT) is recommended for infants and children from 6 weeks of age (8 weeks in Canada) up until their 7th birthday.

Children 7 years of age and older and adults should be immunized with tetanus and diphtheria toxoids for adult use (Td). In addition, these children and adults should receive booster doses of Td every 10 years for the rest of their lives.

Diphtheria and tetanus are serious diseases that can cause life-threatening illnesses. Although some serious side effects can occur after a dose of DT or Td, these are rare. The chance of your child catching one of these diseases and being permanently injured or dying as a result is much greater than the chance of your child getting a serious side effect from the DT or Td vaccine.

DT and Td are available in the following dosage form:

Parenteral
• Injection (U.S. and Canada)

Before Receiving This Vaccine

In deciding to use a vaccine, the risks of using the vaccine must be weighed against the good it will do. This is a decision you and your doctor will make. For DT and Td, the following should be considered:

Allergies—Tell your doctor if you have ever had any unusual or allergic reaction to diphtheria toxoid, tetanus toxoid, DT, or Td. Also tell your health care professional if you are allergic to any other substances, such as preservatives.

Pregnancy—This vaccine has not been shown to cause birth defects or other problems in humans. Immunization of a pregnant woman can prevent her newborn baby from getting tetanus at birth.

Breast-feeding—This vaccine has not been shown to cause problems in nursing babies.

Children—For infants up to 6 weeks of age, use of DT or Td is not recommended.

For infants and children 6 weeks up to 7 years of age, Td is not recommended. DT is used instead.

For children 7 years of age and older, DT is not recommended. Td is used instead.

Older adults—DT is not recommended. Td is used instead. Td is not expected to cause different side effects or problems in older people than it does in younger adults. However, Td may be slightly less effective in older people than in younger adults.

Other medical problems—The presence of other medical problems may affect the use of DT or Td. Make sure you

tell your doctor if you have any other medical problems, especially:

- Fever or
- Infection or illness (severe)—Use of DT or Td may make the condition worse or may increase the chance of side effects

Proper Use of This Vaccine

Dosing—The doses of DT and Td will be different for different patients. The following information includes only the average doses of DT and Td.

For DT

- For *injection* dosage form:
  —For prevention of diphtheria and tetanus:
  - Children up to 6 weeks of age—Use is not recommended.
  - Children 6 weeks to 1 year of age—One dose is given every four to eight weeks for a total of three doses. A fourth dose is given six to twelve months after the third dose. A booster (fifth) dose is given when the child is four to six years of age. The booster (fifth) dose is given only if the fourth dose was given before the child's fourth birthday. The doses are injected into a muscle.
  - Children 1 to 7 years of age—One dose is given at the first visit to the doctor, followed by a second dose four to eight weeks later. A third dose is given six to twelve months after the second dose. A booster (fourth) dose is given when the child is four to six years of age. The booster (fourth dose) is given only if the third dose was given before the child's fourth birthday. The doses are injected into a muscle.
  - Adults and children 7 years of age and over—Use is not recommended. Td should be used instead.

For Td

- For *injection* dosage form:
  —For prevention of diphtheria and tetanus:
  - Children up to 7 years of age—Use is not recommended. DT should be used instead.
  - Adults and children 7 years of age and over—One dose is given at the first visit to the doctor, followed by a second dose four to eight weeks later. A third dose is given six to twelve months after the second dose. You should receive a booster dose every ten years. In addition, if you get a wound that is unclean or hard to clean, you may need an emergency booster injection if it has been more than five years since your last booster dose. The doses are injected into a muscle.

Side Effects of This Medicine

Along with its needed effects, a medicine may cause some unwanted effects. Although not all of these side effects may occur, if they do occur they may need medical attention. *It is very important that you tell your doctor about any side effect that occurs after a dose of DT or Td,* even if the side effect has gone away without treatment. Some types of side effects may mean that you should not receive any more doses of DT or Td.

Get emergency help immediately if any of the following side effects occur:

Rare—Symptoms of allergic reaction

Difficulty in breathing or swallowing; hives; itching, especially of feet or hands; reddening of skin, especially around ears; swelling of eyes, face, or inside of nose; unusual tiredness or weakness (sudden and severe)

Check with your doctor as soon as possible if any of the following side effects occur:

Rare

Confusion; convulsions (seizures); excessive sleepiness; fever over 39.4 °C (103 °F); headache or vomiting (severe or continuing); hives; itching; joint aches or pain; skin rash; swelling, blistering, pain, or other severe reaction at the place of injection (generally starts within 2 to 8 hours after the injection); unusual irritability

Other side effects may occur that usually do not need medical attention. However, check with your doctor if any of the following side effects continue or are bothersome:

More common—For DT and Td

Redness or hard lump at the place of injection (this may last for a few days; however, less often, the hard lump may last for a few weeks)

More common—For DT only

Fever under 39.4 °C (103 °F); swelling, pain, or tenderness at the place of injection (this may last for a few days)

Less common—For DT and Td

Dent or indentation at the place of injection

Less common—For DT only

Crying (continuing); drowsiness; fretfulness; loss of appetite; vomiting

Less common—For Td only

Chills; fast heartbeat; fever under 39.4 °C (103 °F); general feeling of discomfort or illness; headache; muscle aches; swelling of glands in armpit; unusual tiredness or weakness

Other side effects not listed above may also occur in some patients. If you notice any other effects, check with your doctor.

Developed: 04/26/95

DIPHTHERIA AND TETANUS TOXOIDS AND PERTUSSIS VACCINE ADSORBED   Systemic

Commonly used brand name(s):

In the U.S.—

Acel-Imune	Infanrix
Certiva	Tripedia

Generic name product may be available.

In Canada—

Infanrix

Other commonly used names are acellular DTP, DTaP, DTP, DTwP, and whole-cell DTP.

Description

Diphtheria and tetanus toxoids and pertussis (dif-THEER-ee-a and TET-n-us and per-TUS-iss) vaccine (also known as DTP) is a combination immunizing agent given by injection to prevent diphtheria, tetanus, and pertussis.

Diphtheria is a serious illness that can cause breathing difficulties, heart problems, nerve damage, pneumonia, and possibly death. The risk of serious complications and death is greater in very young children and in the elderly.

Tetanus (also known as lockjaw) is a serious illness that causes convulsions (seizures) and severe muscle spasms that can be strong enough to cause bone fractures of the spine. Tetanus causes death in 30 to 40 percent of cases.

Pertussis (also known as whooping cough) is a serious disease that causes severe spells of coughing that can interfere with breathing. Pertussis also can cause pneumonia, long-lasting bronchitis, seizures, brain damage, and death.

Immunization against diphtheria, tetanus, and pertussis is recommended for all infants and children from 2 months of age up to their 7th birthday. Children 7 years of age and older and adults should receive immunizing agents that contain only diphtheria and tetanus toxoids and not pertussis vaccine. Adults should receive the diphtheria and tetanus injections every 10 years for the rest of their lives.

Diphtheria, tetanus, and pertussis are serious diseases that can cause life-threatening illnesses. Although some serious side effects can occur after a dose of DTP (usually from the pertussis vaccine in DTP), this rarely happens. The chance of your child catching one of these diseases and being permanently injured or dying as a result is much greater than the chance of your child getting a serious side effect from the DTP vaccine.

DTP is available in the following dosage form:

Parenteral
- Injection (U.S. and Canada)

Before Receiving This Vaccine

In deciding to use a medicine, the risks of taking the medicine must be weighed against the good it will do. This is a decision you and your doctor will make. For DTP, the following should be considered:

Allergies—Tell your doctor if your child has ever had any unusual or allergic reaction to diphtheria toxoid, tetanus toxoid, pertussis vaccine, or DTP. Also tell your health care professional if your child is allergic to any other substances, such as preservatives.

Pregnancy—Studies on effects in pregnancy have not been done in either humans or animals.

Breast-feeding—DTP has not been reported to cause problems in nursing babies.

Children—Use is not recommended for infants up to 2 months of age.

Teenagers—Use is not recommended for persons older than 7 years of age.

Older adults—Use is not recommended for persons older than 7 years of age.

Other medical problems—The presence of other medical problems may affect the use of DTP. Make sure you tell your doctor if your child has any other medical problems, especially:
- Allergic reaction to a previous dose of DTP or
- Brain disease or
- Fever—Use of DTP may make the condition worse or may increase the chance of side effects

Proper Use of This Vaccine

Dosing—The dose of DTP will be different for different patients. The following information includes only the average doses of DTP.

- For *injection* dosage form:
  —For prevention of diphtheria, tetanus, and pertussis:
    - Adults and children 7 years of age and older—Use is not recommended.
    - Children 2 months to 7 years of age—One dose every four to eight weeks for a total of three doses, then a fourth dose six to twelve months after the third dose. A booster dose should be given at 4, 5, or 6 years of age. (The booster dose is given only if the fourth dose was given before the child's 4th birthday.)

Precautions After Receiving This Vaccine

At the time of the DTP injection, your doctor may give your child a dose of acetaminophen (or another medicine that helps prevent fever). This is to help prevent some of the side effects of DTP. Your doctor may also want your child to take this medicine every 4 hours for 24 hours after your child receives the DTP injection. Check with your doctor if you have any questions.

Side Effects of This Vaccine

Along with its needed effects, a vaccine may cause some unwanted effects. Although not all of these side effects may occur, if they do occur they may need medical attention. *It is very important that you tell your doctor about any side effect that occurs after a dose of DTP*, even though the side effect may have gone away without treatment. Some types of side effects may mean that your child should not receive any more doses of DTP.

Get emergency help immediately if any of the following side effects occur:
Less frequent
    Collapse; crying for 3 or more hours
Rare
    Confusion; convulsions (seizures); difficulty in breathing or swallowing; fever of 105 °F (40.5 °C) or more; headache (severe or continuing); hives; irritability (unusual); itching, especially of feet or hands; periods of unconsciousness or lack of awareness; reddening of skin, especially around ears; sleepiness (unusual and continuing); swelling of eyes, face, or inside of nose; unusual tiredness, weakness (sudden and severe); vomiting (severe or continuing)

Other side effects may occur that usually do not need medical attention. These side effects may go away as your child's body adjusts to the vaccine. However, check with your doctor if any of the following side effects continue or are bothersome:
More common
    Fever between 100.4 and 102.2 °F (38 and 39 °C) (may occur with fretfulness, drowsiness, vomiting, and loss of appetite); lump at place of injection (may be present for a few weeks after injection); redness, swelling, tenderness, or pain at place of injection
Less common
    Fever between 102.2 and 104 °F (39 and 40 °C) (may

occur with fretfulness, drowsiness, vomiting, and loss of appetite)

Rare

Fever between 104 and 105 °F (40 and 40.5 °C) (may occur with fretfulness, drowsiness, vomiting, and loss of appetite); skin rash; swollen glands on side of neck (following DTP injection into arm)

Other side effects not listed above may also occur in some patients. If you notice any other effects, check with your doctor.

Revised: 02/02/99

DIPHTHERIA AND TETANUS TOXOIDS AND PERTUSSIS VACCINE ADSORBED AND HAEMOPHILUS B CONJUGATE VACCINE   Systemic

Commonly used brand name(s):

In the U.S.—
Tetramune

In Canada—
DPT-Hib
Tetramune

Other commonly used names are DTP-HbOC, DTP-Hib, and DTP-PRP-D.

Description

Diphtheria and tetanus toxoids and pertussis (dif-THEER-ee-a and TET-n-us and per-TUSS-iss) vaccine (also known as DTP vaccine) combined with Haemophilus b conjugate (hem-OFF-fil-us BEE KON-ja-gat) vaccine (also known as Hib vaccine) is a combination immunizing agent used to prevent illness caused by diphtheria, tetanus, pertussis, and *Haemophilus influenzae* type b (Hib) bacteria. The vaccine works by causing the body to produce its own protection (antibodies) against these diseases. This combination vaccine is also known as DTP-Hib vaccine.

Diphtheria is a serious illness that can cause breathing difficulties, heart problems, nerve damage, pneumonia, and possibly death. The risk of serious complications and death is greater in very young children and in the elderly.

Tetanus (also known as lockjaw) is a serious illness that causes convulsions (seizures) and severe muscle spasms that can be strong enough to cause bone fractures of the spine. Tetanus causes death in 30 to 40 percent of cases.

Pertussis (also known as whooping cough) is a serious disease that causes severe spells of coughing that can interfere with breathing. Pertussis can also cause pneumonia, long-lasting bronchitis, seizures, brain damage, and death.

Infection by *Haemophilus influenzae* type b (Hib) bacteria can cause life-threatening illnesses, such as meningitis, which affects the brain; epiglottitis, which can cause death by suffocation; pericarditis, which affects the heart; pneumonia, which affects the lungs; and septic arthritis, which affects the bones and joints. Hib meningitis causes death in 5 to 10% of children who are infected. Also, approximately 30% of children who survive Hib meningitis are left with some type of serious permanent damage, such as mental retardation, deafness, epilepsy, or partial blindness.

DTP-Hib vaccine is available in the following dosage form:

Parenteral
• Injection (U.S. and Canada)

Before Receiving This Vaccine

In deciding to use a vaccine, the risks of receiving the vaccine must be weighed against the good it will do. This is a decision you and your doctor will make. For DTP-Hib vaccine, the following should be considered:

Allergies—Tell your doctor if your child has ever had any unusual or allergic reaction to diphtheria toxoid, tetanus toxoid, pertussis vaccine, DTP vaccine, Haemophilus b conjugate vaccine, Hib vaccine, or Haemophilus b polysaccharide vaccine. Also tell your health care professional if your child is allergic to any other substances, such as thimerosal or other preservatives.

Children—This vaccine is not recommended for children younger than 2 months of age or older than 7 years of age.

Other medical problems—The presence of other medical problems may affect the use of DTP-Hib vaccine. Make sure you tell your doctor if your child has any other medical problems, especially:

• Brain disease or
• Central nervous system (CNS) disease or family history of or
• Convulsions (seizures) or family history of—Use of the vaccine may make the condition worse or may increase the chance of side effects

• Fever or
• Serious illness—The symptoms of the condition may be confused with some of the possible side effects of the vaccine

Proper Use of This Vaccine

Dosing—The number of doses of DTP-Hib vaccine will be different for different patients. The following information includes only the average doses of DTP-Hib vaccine.

• For *injection* dosage form:
—For prevention of diphtheria, tetanus, pertussis, and *Haemophilus influenzae* type b illnesses:
• Children up to 2 months of age—Use is not recommended.
• Children 2 to 6 months of age at the first dose—Three doses, at least two months apart. Then a fourth dose at 12 to 18 months of age after at least 6 months have passed since the third dose. The doses are injected into a muscle.
• Children 7 to 11 months of age at the first dose—Two doses, at least two months apart, followed by additional doses of either this vaccine, DTP vaccine, or Hib vaccine, depending on the immunization schedule. The doses are injected into a muscle.
• Children 12 to 14 months of age at the first dose—One dose, followed by additional doses of either this vaccine, DTP vaccine, or Hib vaccine, depending on the immunization schedule. The doses are injected into a muscle.

- Children 15 to 59 months of age at the first dose—One dose, followed by additional doses of DTP vaccine to complete the immunization schedule for DTP. The doses are injected into a muscle.
- Adults and children 7 years of age and older—Use is not recommended.

After Receiving This Vaccine

At the time of the DTP-Hib vaccine injection, your doctor may give your child a dose of acetaminophen (or another medicine that helps prevent fever). This is to help prevent some of the side effects of this vaccine. Your doctor may also want your child to take this medicine every 4 hours for 24 hours after your child receives this vaccine. Check with your doctor if you have any questions.

This vaccine may interfere with laboratory tests that check for Hib disease. Make sure your doctor knows that your child has received DTP-Hib vaccine if your child is treated for a severe infection during the 2 weeks after your child receives this vaccine.

Side Effects of This Vaccine

Along with its needed effects, a vaccine may cause some unwanted effects. Although not all of these side effects may occur, if they do occur they may need medical attention. *It is very important that you tell your doctor about any side effect that occurs after a dose of DTP-Hib vaccine*, even if the side effect goes away without treatment. Some types of side effects may mean that your child should not receive any more doses of DTP-Hib vaccine.

Get emergency help immediately if any of the following side effects occur:
> *Rare*
>> Collapse; confusion; convulsions (seizures); crying for three or more hours; fever of 40.5 °C (105 °F) or more; headache (severe or continuing); irritability (unusual and continuing); periods of unconsciousness or lack of awareness; sleepiness (unusual and continuing); vomiting (severe or continuing)

Check with your doctor immediately if any of the following side effects occur:
> *Rare*
>> Symptoms of allergic reactions—Difficulty in breathing or swallowing; hives; itching (especially of feet or hands); reddening of skin (especially around ears); swelling of eyes, face, or inside of nose; unusual tiredness or weakness (sudden and severe)

Other side effects may occur that usually do not need medical attention. These side effects may go away as your child's body adjusts to the vaccine. However, check with your doctor if any of the following side effects continue or are bothersome:
> *More common*
>> Drowsiness; fever of up to 102.2 °F (39 °C) (usually lasts less than 48 hours and may occur with fretfulness, drowsiness, vomiting, and loss of appetite); fretfulness; irritability; lump at place of injection (may be present for a few weeks after injection); redness, warm feeling, swelling, tenderness, or pain at place of injection

> *Less common*
>> Diarrhea; fever between 102.2 and 104 °F (39 and 40 °C) (usually lasts less than 48 hours and may occur with fretfulness, drowsiness, vomiting, and

loss of appetite); hard lump at place of injection (may be present for a few days after injection); loss of appetite; vomiting

> *Rare*
>> Fever between 104 and 104.8 °F (40 and 40.4 °C) (usually lasts less than 48 hours and may occur with fretfulness, drowsiness, vomiting, and loss of appetite); lack of interest; reduced physical activity; skin rash

Other side effects not listed above may also occur in some patients. If you notice any other effects, check with your doctor.

Developed: 11/27/96

DIPIVEFRIN   Ophthalmic

Commonly used brand name(s):

In the U.S.—
> AKPro
> Propine C Cap B.I.D.
> Generic name product may be available.

In Canada—
> DPE
> Ophtho-Dipivefrin
> Propine

Another commonly used name is dipivefrine.

Description

Dipivefrin (dye-PI-ve-frin) is used to treat certain types of glaucoma.

This medicine is available only with your doctor's prescription, in the following dosage form:
> *Ophthalmic*
>> • Ophthalmic solution (eye drops) (U.S. and Canada)

Before Using This Medicine

In deciding to use a medicine, the risks of taking the medicine must be weighed against the good it will do. This is a decision you and your doctor will make. For dipivefrin, the following should be considered:

Allergies—Tell your doctor if you have ever had any unusual or allergic reaction to dipivefrin or epinephrine. Also tell your health care professional if you are allergic to any other substances, such as preservatives.

Pregnancy—Dipivefrin has not been studied in pregnant women. However, this medication has not been shown to cause birth defects or other problems in animal studies.

Breast-feeding—Dipivefrin may be absorbed into the body, but it is not known whether dipivefrin passes into the breast milk.

Children—Studies on this medicine have been done only in adult patients, and there is no specific information comparing use of this medicine in children with use in other age groups.

Older adults—Many medicines have not been studied specifically in older people. Therefore, it may not be known whether they work exactly the same way they do in younger adults. Although there is no specific information comparing use of this medicine in the elderly with use in other age groups, this medicine is not expected to cause different side effects or problems in older people than it does in younger adults.

Other medicines—Although certain medicines should not be used together at all, in other cases two different medicines may be used together even if an interaction might occur. In these cases, your doctor may want to change the dose, or other precautions may be necessary. Tell your health care professional if you are using any other prescription or nonprescription (over-the-counter [OTC]) medicine.

Other medical problems—The presence of other medical problems may affect the use of dipivefrin. Make sure you tell your doctor if you have any other medical problems, especially:

- Eye disease or problems (other)—Dipivefrin may make the condition worse

Proper Use of This Medicine

Use this medicine only as directed. Do not use more of it and do not use it more often than your doctor ordered. To do so may increase the chance of too much medicine being absorbed into the body and the chance of side effects.

To use:

- First, wash your hands. Tilt the head back and, pressing your finger gently on the skin just beneath the lower eyelid, pull the lower eyelid away from the eye to make a space. Drop the medicine into this space. Let go of the eyelid and gently close the eyes. Do not blink. Keep the eyes closed and apply pressure to the inner corner of the eye with your finger for 1 or 2 minutes to allow the medicine to be absorbed by the eye.
- Immediately after using the eye drops, wash your hands to remove any medicine that may be on them.
- To keep the medicine as germ-free as possible, do not touch the applicator tip to any surface (including the eye). Also, keep the container tightly closed.
- If you are using the medicine with the compliance cap (C Cap):
  —Before using the eye drops for the first time, make sure the number 1 or the correct day of the week appears in the window on the cap.
  —Remove the cap and use the eye drops as directed.
  —Replace the cap. Holding the cap between your thumb and forefinger, rotate the bottle until the cap clicks to the next station. This will tell you your next dose.
  —After every dose, rotate the bottle until the cap clicks to the position that tells you your next dose.

Dosing—The dose of dipivefrin will be different for different patients. *Follow your doctor's orders or the directions on the label.* The following information includes only the average doses of dipivefrin. *If your dose is different, do not change it* unless your doctor tells you to do so.

- For *ophthalmic solution* (eye drops) dosage form:
  —For glaucoma:
  - Adults—One drop every twelve hours.
  - Children—Use and dose must by determined by your doctor.

Missed dose—If you miss a dose of this medicine, apply the missed dose as soon as possible. However, if it is almost time for your next dose, skip the missed dose and go back to your regular dosing schedule. Do not double doses.

Storage—To store this medicine:

- Keep out of the reach of children.
- Store away from heat and direct light.
- Keep the medicine from freezing.
- Do not keep outdated medicine or medicine no longer needed. Be sure that any discarded medicine is out of the reach of children.

Precautions While Using This Medicine

Your doctor should check your eye pressure at regular visits.

Side Effects of This Medicine

Along with its needed effects, a medicine may cause some unwanted effects. Although not all of these side effects may occur, if they do occur they may need medical attention.

Check with your doctor as soon as possible if any of the following side effects occur:

Rare
> Fast or irregular heartbeat; increase in blood pressure; itching, pain, redness, or swelling of eye or eyelid (severe), or other irritation of the eye; skin rash or hives; watering of eyes (severe and continuing)

Other side effects may occur that usually do not need medical attention. These side effects may go away during treatment as your body adjusts to the medicine. However, check with your doctor if any of the following side effects continue or are bothersome:

Less common
> Blurred vision; burning or stinging of the eye; headache; increased sensitivity of eyes to light; large pupils

Other side effects not listed above may also occur in some patients. If you notice any other effects, check with your doctor.

Revised: 01/13/99

DIPYRIDAMOLE AND ASPIRIN
Systemic

Commonly used brand name(s):

In the U.S.—
Aggrenox

In Canada—
Aggrenox

Other commonly used names are.

Aspirin: acetylsalicylic acid ASA salicylic acid acetate.

Description

Dipyridamole (dye-peer-ID-a-mole) and aspirin (AS-pir-in) is used to lessen the chance of stroke that may occur when a blood vessel in the brain is blocked by blood clots. It is given only when there is a larger-than-usual chance that these problems may occur. For example, it is given to people who have had a stroke, because dangerous blood clots are especially likely to occur in these patients. Dipyridamole and aspirin work by helping to prevent dangerous blood clots from forming.

This medicine is available only with your doctor's prescription, in the following dosage forms:

Oral
- Capsule (extended-release dipyridamole and immediate-release aspirin) (U.S.and Canada)

Before Using This Medicine

In deciding to use a medicine, the risks of taking the medicine must be weighed against the good it will do. This is a decision you and your doctor will make. For dipyridamole and aspirin the following should be considered:

Allergies—Tell your doctor if you have ever had any unusual or allergic reaction to dipyridamole, aspirin, or inflammation or pain medicine (excluding narcotics). Also tell your doctor and pharmacist if you are allergic to any other substances, such as foods, preservatives, or dyes.

Pregnancy—
- *Dipyridamole*—Dipyridamole has not been studied in pregnant women. However, dipyridamole has not been shown to cause birth defects or other problems in animal studies.
- *Aspirin*—Aspirin has been shown to cause bleeding problems in mother and fetus in humans, especially during the last 3 months of pregnancy. Be sure you have discussed this with your doctor.

Breast-feeding—Dipyridamole and aspirin are passed into breast milk in small amount. Mothers who are taking this medicine and who wish to breast-feed should discuss this with their doctor.

Children—
- *Dipyridamole*—There is no specific information comparing use of dipyridamole in children with use in other age groups.
- *Aspirin—Do not give aspirin to a child or a teenager with a fever or other symptoms of a virus infection, especially flu or chickenpox, without first discussing its use with your child's doctor.* This is very important because salicylates may cause a serious illness called Reye's syndrome in children and teenagers caused by a virus infection, especially flu or chickenpox.

Older adults—
- *Dipyridamole*—Dipyridamole has not been studied specifically in older people taking the medicine regularly to prevent blood clots from forming. Although there is no specific information comparing this use of dipyridamole in the elderly with use in other age groups, it is not expected to cause different side effects or problems in older people than it does in younger adults.
- *Aspirin*—Elderly people are especially sensitive to the effects of aspirin. However, this is not expected to limit the usefulness of this drug.

Other medicines—Although certain medicines should not be used together at all, in other cases two different medicines may be used together even if an interaction might occur. In these cases, your doctor may want to change the dose, or other precautions may be necessary. When you are taking dipyridamole and aspirin, it is especially important that your health care professional know if you are taking any of the following:
- Probenecid (e.g. Benemid) or
- Sulfinpyrazone (e.g. Anturane)—may decrease the effects of these drugs

- Methotrexate (e.g. Rheumatrex)—may increase the toxicity of methotrexate, especially in older people with kidney disease
- Anticoagulants (blood thinners) such as heparin (e.g., Liquaemin) or
- Warfarin (e.g. Coumadin) or
- Inflammation or pain medicines, except narcotics—may increase the chance of bleeding

Other medical problems—The presence of other medical problems may affect the use of dipyridamole and aspirin. Make sure you tell your doctor if you have any other medical problems, especially:
- Alcohol use, chronic or
- Vitamin K deficiency or other bleeding problems—The chance of bleeding may be increased
- Asthma, allergies, and nasal polyps (history of) or
- Heart disease or
- Liver disease or
- Low blood pressure—The side effects may be increased
- Glucose-6-phosphate dehydrogenase enzyme deficiency—This condition may worsen, increasing risk of anemia
- Gout—The medicine used to treat this condition may not work properly
- Kidney disease—This condition may be made worse
- Stomach inflammation or ulcer—These conditions may worsen, increasing the risk of bleeding

Proper Use of This Medicine

The capsules must be swallowed whole. Do not chew them, crush them or break them up before taking.

Dosing—The dose of dipyridamole and aspirin will be different for different patients. *Follow your doctor's orders or the directions on the label.* The following information includes only the average doses of dipyridamole and aspirin. *If your dose is different, do not change it* unless your doctor tells you to do so.

- For preventing stroke:
  —For *oral* dosage form (capsules):
  - Adults—The usual dose is one capsule twice a day, one in the morning and one in the evening.
  - Children—Use is not recommended.

Missed dose—If you miss a dose of this medicine, take it as soon as possible. However, if it is almost time for your next dose, skip the missed dose and go back to your regular dosing schedule. Do not double doses.

Storage—To store this medicine:
- Keep out of the reach of children.
- Do not store in the bathroom, near the kitchen sink, or in other damp places. heat or moisture may cause the medicine to break down.
- Do not keep outdated medicine or medicine no longer needed. Ask your health care professional how you should dispose of any medicine you do not use. Be sure that any discarded medicine is out of the reach of children.

Precautions While Using This Medicine

Dipyridamole and aspirin combination provide better protection against the formation of blood clots than either of the medicines used alone. However, the risk of bleeding may also be increased. To reduce the risk of bleeding:

- *Do not take aspirin, or any combination medicine containing aspirin in addition to this medicine unless the same doctor who directed you to take dipyridamole and aspirin also directs you to take aspirin.*
- If you need a medicine to relieve pain or a fever, your doctor may not want you to take extra aspirin. It is a good idea to discuss this with your doctor, so that you will know ahead of time what medicine to take.
- Your doctor should check your progress at regular visits.

Tell all medical doctors and dentists you go to that you are taking dipyridamole and aspirin.

Dizziness, lightheadedness, or fainting may occur, especially when you get up from a lying or sitting position. Getting up slowly may help. If this problem continues or gets worse, check with your doctor.

Do not stop taking this medicine for any reason without first checking with the doctor who directed you to take it.

Side Effects of This Medicine

Along with its needed effects, a medicine may cause some unwanted effects. Although not all of these side effects may occur, if they do occur they may need medical attention.

Check with your doctor immediately if any of the following side effects occur:
 Confusion, difficulty in speaking, slow speech, inability to speak, inability to move arms, legs, or facial muscles, or double vision; difficulty breathing, tightness in chest, or wheezing
Symptoms of overdose
 Get emergency help immediately if any of the following symptoms of overdose occur
  Blurred vision; Continuing ringing or buzzing or other unexplained noise in ears, or hearing loss; dizziness, faintness, or lightheadedness when getting up from a lying or sitting position sudden, sweating, or unusual tiredness or weakness; fast or irregular heartbeat; restlessness; warm feeling, flushes

Check with your doctor as soon as possible if any of the following side effects occur shortly after you start taking this medicine:
More common
 Stomach or abdomen pain; vomiting
Less common
 Bloody or black, tarry stools, blood or coffee ground materials in the vomit, or bleeding from the rectum; convulsions (seizures); memory loss; pale skin, troubled breathing, exertional, unusual bleeding or bruising; purple or red spots on skin
Rare
 Abdominal fullness, gaseous abdominal pain, recurrent fever, chills, clay-colored stools, loss of appetite, nausea, yellow eyes or skin; blood in the urine; collection of blood under skin, deep, dark purple bruise; cough; noisy breathing; shortness of breath; itching, pain, redness, or swelling of eye or eyelid watering of eyes, or severe skin rash or hives

Other side effects may occur that usually do not need medical attention. These side effects may go away during treatment as your body adjusts to the medicine. However, check with

your doctor if any of the following side effects continue or are bothersome.
More common
 Diarrhea; headache; pain, swelling, or redness in joints, muscle pain or stiffness, or difficulty in moving; stomach discomfort upset or pain, heartburn, belching, acid or sour stomach, or indigestion
Less common or rare
 Back pain; bloody mucous, or unexplained nosebleeds; burning feeling in chest or stomach tenderness in stomach area stomach upset indigestion; loss of strength or energy; rectal pain or swelling; sleepiness or unusual drowsiness; taste loss

Other side effects not listed above may also occur in some patients. If you notice any other effects, check with your doctor.

Developed: 05/02/00
Revised: 02/21/2001

DIPYRIDAMOLE—Diagnostic
Systemic

Commonly used brand name(s):
In the U.S.—
 Persantine
 Generic name product may be available.

In Canada—

Apo-Dipyridamole FC	Novo-Dipiradol
Apo-Dipyridamole SC	Persantine

Description

Dipyridamole (dye-peer-ID-a-mole) is used as part of a medical test that shows how well blood is flowing to your heart. The test can show your doctor whether any of the blood vessels that bring blood to the heart are blocked or in danger of becoming blocked. Your doctor can then decide on the best treatment for you. Exercise (for example, walking on a treadmill) is usually used to give your doctor this information. Dipyridamole is used instead of exercise for people who are not able to exercise at all, or cannot exercise hard enough.

The dose of dipyridamole that is used to test how well blood is flowing to your heart will be different for different patients and depends on your body weight.

For information on other uses of dipyridamole, see Dipyridamole—Therapeutic (Systemic).

Dipyridamole is available only with your doctor's prescription, in the following dosage forms:
Oral
- Tablets (U.S. and Canada)
Parenteral
- Injection (U.S. and Canada)

Before Having This Test

In deciding to use a diagnostic test, any risks of the test must be weighed against the good it will do. This is a decision you and your doctor will make. Also, test results may be affected by other things. For dipyridamole, the following should be considered:

Allergies—Tell your doctor if you have ever had any unusual or allergic reaction to dipyridamole. Also tell your health care professional if you are allergic to any other substances, such as foods, preservatives, or dyes.

Pregnancy—Although studies have not been done in pregnant women, dipyridamole has not been reported to cause birth defects or other problems in humans. However, studies in animals have shown that dipyridamole decreased the number of successful pregnancies in female rats given many times the maximum human dose.

Breast-feeding—Although dipyridamole passes into breast milk, it has not been reported to cause problems in nursing babies.

Children—This medicine has been tested only in adults and in children older than 12 years of age. There is no specific information comparing use of dipyridamole in children younger than 12 years of age with use in other age groups.

Older adults—Dipyridamole for diagnostic use has been tested in older people. It has not been shown to cause different side effects or problems in older people than it does in younger adults.

Other medicines—Although certain medicines should not be used together at all, in other cases two different medicines may be used together even if an interaction might occur. In these cases, your doctor may want to change the dose, or other precautions may be necessary. Before you receive dipyridamole, it is especially important that your doctor knows if you are taking any of the following:

- Aminophylline (e.g., Phyllocontin) or
- Caffeine (e.g., NoDoz) or
- Dyphylline (e.g., Lufyllin) or
- Oxtriphylline (e.g., Choledyl) or
- Theophylline (e.g., Theo-Dur)—These medicines will interfere with the results of this test. Caffeine should not be taken for 8 to 12 hours before the test. It is present in many medicines (for example, stay-awake products, pain relievers, and medicines for relieving migraine headaches) and foods or beverages (for example, coffee, tea, colas or other soft drinks, cocoa, and chocolate). If you are not sure whether any medicine you are taking contains caffeine, check with your pharmacist

The other medicines listed here are used to treat asthma or other lung or breathing problems. They should not be taken for about 36 hours before the test. However, *do not stop taking the medicine on your own.* Instead, at least 3 or 4 days before the test, tell the doctor in charge of giving the test that you are taking the medicine. He or she can call the doctor who ordered the medicine for you, and together they will decide whether you should stop taking the medicine for a while.

- Aspirin or
- Carbenicillin by injection (e.g., Geopen) or
- Cefamandole (e.g., Mandol) or
- Cefoperazone (e.g., Cefobid) or
- Cefotetan (e.g., Cefotan) or
- Divalproex (e.g., Depakote) or
- Heparin or
- Inflammation or pain medicine, except narcotics, or
- Pentoxifylline (e.g., Trental) or
- Plicamycin (e.g., Mithracin) or
- Sulfinpyrazone (e.g., Anturane) or
- Ticarcillin (e.g., Ticar) or
- Ticlopidine (e.g., Ticlid) or
- Valproic acid (e.g., Depakene)—The chance of bleeding may be increased

Other medical problems—The presence of other medical problems may affect the use of dipyridamole. Make sure you tell your doctor if you have any other medical problems, especially:

- Asthma or history of or
- Chest pain—The chance of side effects may be increased
- Low blood pressure—Large amounts of dipyridamole can make your condition worse

Side Effects of This Medicine

Along with its needed effects, a medicine may cause some unwanted effects. Although not all of these side effects may occur, if they do occur they may need medical attention.

While you are receiving dipyridamole, and for a while after you have received it, your doctor will closely follow its effects. If necessary, your doctor can give you a medicine that will stop any unwanted effects. *Tell your doctor right away if you notice any of the following side effects:*

More common
 Chest pain

Less common or rare
 Decreased sensitivity to touch; dizziness, sweating, or sudden, severe headache; headache (severe and throbbing); fast breathing; fast heartbeat; muscle stiffness; sharp pain in either or both sides of the chest; shortness of breath, troubled breathing, tightness in chest, or wheezing; skin rash or itching

Other side effects may occur that usually do not need medical attention. These side effects may go away in a little while. However, check with your doctor if they continue or are bothersome:

More common
 Abdominal or stomach cramps; diarrhea; dizziness or lightheadedness; headache

Less common
 Flushing; nausea or vomiting; weakness

Other side effects not listed above may also occur in some patients. If you notice any other effects, check with your doctor.

Revised: 5/20/99
Interim revision: 5/20/99

DIPYRIDAMOLE—Therapeutic
Systemic

Commonly used brand name(s):
In the U.S.—
 Persantine
 Generic name product may be available.

In Canada—

Apo-Dipyridamole FC	Novo-Dipiradol
Apo-Dipyridamole SC	Persantine

Description

Dipyridamole (dye-peer-ID-a-mole) is used to lessen the chance of stroke or other serious medical problems that may occur when a blood vessel is blocked by blood clots. It is given only when there is a larger-than-usual chance that these problems may occur. For example, it is given to people who have had diseased heart valves replaced by mechanical valves, because dangerous blood clots are especially likely to occur in these patients. Dipyridamole works by helping to prevent dangerous blood clots from forming.

Dipyridamole may also be used for other heart and blood conditions as determined by your doctor.

Dipyridamole is also sometimes used as part of a medical test that shows how well blood is flowing to your heart. For information on this use of dipyridamole, see Dipyridamole—Diagnostic (Systemic).

Dipyridamole is available only with your doctor's prescription, in the following dosage forms:

Oral
- Tablets (U.S. and Canada)

Parenteral
- Injection (U.S. and Canada)

Before Using This Medicine

In deciding to use a medicine, the risks of taking the medicine must be weighed against the good it will do. This is a decision you and your doctor will make. For dipyridamole, the following should be considered:

Allergies—Tell your doctor if you have ever had any unusual or allergic reaction to dipyridamole. Also tell your health care professional if you are allergic to any other substances, such as foods, preservatives, or dyes.

Pregnancy—Although studies have not been done in pregnant women, dipyridamole has not been reported to cause birth defects or other problems in humans. However, studies in animals have shown that dipyridamole decreased the number of successful pregnancies in female rats given many times the maximum human dose.

Breast-feeding—Although dipyridamole passes into breast milk, it has not been reported to cause problems in nursing babies.

Children—This medicine has been tested only in adults and in children older than 12 years of age. There is no specific information comparing use of dipyridamole in children younger than 12 years of age with use in other age groups.

Older adults—Dipyridamole has not been studied specifically in older people taking the medicine regularly to prevent blood clots from forming. Although there is no specific information comparing this use of dipyridamole in the elderly with use in other age groups, it is not expected to cause different side effects or problems in older people than it does in younger adults.

Other medicines—Although certain medicines should not be used together at all, in other cases two different medicines may be used together even if an interaction might occur. In these cases, your doctor may want to change the dose, or other precautions may be necessary. When you are taking dipyridamole, it is especially important that your health care professional know if you are taking any of the following:

- Aspirin or
- Carbenicillin by injection (e.g., Geopen) or
- Cefamandole (e.g., Mandol) or
- Cefoperazone (e.g., Cefobid) or
- Cefotetan (e.g., Cefotan) or
- Divalproex (e.g., Depakote) or
- Heparin or
- Inflammation or pain medicine, except narcotics, or
- Pentoxifylline (e.g., Trental) or
- Plicamycin (e.g., Mithracin) or

- Sulfinpyrazone (e.g., Anturane) or
- Ticarcillin (e.g., Ticar) or
- Ticlopidine (e.g., Ticlid) or
- Valproic acid (e.g., Depakene)—The chance of bleeding may be increased

Other medical problems—The presence of other medical problems may affect the use of dipyridamole. Make sure you tell your doctor if you have any other medical problems, especially:

- Chest pain—The chance of side effects may be increased

- Low blood pressure—Large amounts of dipyridamole can make your condition worse

Proper Use of This Medicine

This medicine works best when there is a constant amount in the blood. To help keep the amount constant, *dipyridamole must be taken in regularly spaced doses*, as ordered by your doctor.

This medicine works best when taken with a full glass (8 ounces) of water at least 1 hour before or 2 hours after meals. However, to lessen stomach upset, your doctor may want you to take the medicine with food or milk.

Dosing—The dose of dipyridamole will be different for different patients. *Follow your doctor's orders or the directions on the label.* The following information includes only the average doses of dipyridamole. *If your dose is different, do not change it* unless your doctor tells you to do so.

- For preventing blood clots:
   —For *oral* dosage form (tablets):
      - Adults—The usual dose is 75 to 100 milligrams (mg) four times a day taken together with an anticoagulant (blood-thinning) medicine.
      - Children—Use and dose must be determined by your doctor.

Missed dose—If you miss a dose of this medicine, take it as soon as possble. However, if it is within 4 hours of your next scheduled dose, skip the missed dose and go back to your regular dosing schedule. Do not double doses.

Storage—To store this medicine:
- Keep out of the reach of children.
- Store away from heat and direct light.
- Do not store in the bathroom, near the kitchen sink, or in other damp places. Heat or moisture may cause the medicine to break down.
- Do not keep outdated medicine or medicine no longer needed. Be sure that any discarded medicine is out of the reach of children.

Precautions While Using This Medicine

Dipyridamole is sometimes used together with an anticoagulant (blood thinner) or aspirin. The combination of medicines may provide better protection against the formation of blood clots than any of the medicines used alone. However, the risk of bleeding may also be increased when dipyridamole is taken with aspirin. To reduce the risk of bleeding:

- *Do not take aspirin, or any combination medicine containing aspirin, unless the same doctor who directed you to take dipyridamole also directs you to take aspirin.* This is especially important if you are taking an anticoagulant together with dipyridamole.
- If you have been directed to take aspirin together with dipyridamole, *take only the amount of aspirin ordered*

by your doctor. If you need a medicine to relieve pain or a fever, your doctor may not want you to take extra aspirin. It is a good idea to discuss this with your doctor, so that you will know ahead of time what medicine to take.

• Your doctor should check your progress at regular visits.

Tell all medical doctors and dentists you go to that you are taking dipyridamole, and whether or not you are taking an anticoagulant (blood thinner) or aspirin together with it.

Dizziness, lightheadedness, or fainting may occur, especially when you get up from a lying or sitting position. Getting up slowly may help. If this problem continues or gets worse, check with your doctor.

Side Effects of This Medicine

Along with its needed effects, a medicine may cause some unwanted effects. Although not all of these side effects may occur, if they do occur they may need medical attention.

Check with your doctor as soon as possible if any of the following side effects occur shortly after you start taking this medicine:

Rare
  Chest pain; gallstones; tightness or swelling of neck; yellow eyes or skin

Other side effects may occur that usually do not need medical attention. These side effects may go away during treatment as your body adjusts to the medicine. However, check with your doctor if they continue or are bothersome:

More common
  Abdominal or stomach cramps; diarrhea; dizziness or lightheadedness

Less common
  Flushing; headache; nausea or vomiting; weakness

Rare
  General discomfort and/or unusual tiredness or weakness; hair loss; joint pain or swelling; muscle pain; runny nose; sneezing

Other side effects not listed above may also occur in some patients. If you notice any other effects, check with your doctor.

Revised: 5/20/99

DIRITHROMYCIN   Systemic†

Commonly used brand name(s):

In the U.S.—
  Dynabac

†Not commercially available in Canada.

Description

Dirithromycin (dye-RITH-roe-mye-sin) is used to treat bacterial infections in many different parts of the body. It works by killing bacteria or preventing their growth. However, this medicine will not work for colds, flu, or other virus infections.

Dirithromycin is available only with your doctor's prescription, in the following dosage form:

  Oral
  • Tablets (U.S.)

Before Using This Medicine

In deciding to use a medicine, the risks of taking the medicine must be weighed against the good it will do. This is a decision you and your doctor will make. For dirithromycin, the following should be considered:

Allergies—Tell your doctor if you have ever had any unusual or allergic reaction to dirithromycin or to any related medicines, such as erythromycin. Also tell your health care professional if you are allergic to any other substances, such as foods, preservatives, or dyes.

Pregnancy—Dirithromycin has not been studied in pregnant women. However, studies in animals have shown that dirithromycin causes birth defects and other problems at high doses. Before taking this medicine, make sure your doctor knows if you are pregnant or if you may become pregnant.

Breast-feeding—It is not known whether dirithromycin passes into breast milk. Although most medicines pass into breast milk in small amounts, many of them may be used safely while breast-feeding. Mothers who are taking this medicine and who wish to breast-feed should discuss this with their doctor.

Children—Studies on this medicine have been only in adult patients, and there is no specific information comparing use of dirithromycin in children with use in other age groups.

Older adults—This medicine has been tested in a limited number of elderly patients and has not been shown to cause different side effects or problems in older people than it does in younger adults.

Other medicines—Although certain medicines should not be used together at all, in other cases two different medicines may be used together even if an interaction might occur. In these cases, your doctor may want to change the dose, or other precautions may be necessary. Tell your health care professional if you are taking any other prescription or nonprescription (over-the-counter [OTC]) medicine.

Other medical problems—The presence of other medical problems may affect the use of dirithromycin. Make sure you tell your doctor if you have any other medical problems, especially:

• Liver disease—Patients with moderate to severe liver disease may have an increased chance of side effects

Proper Use of This Medicine

Dirithromycin should be taken with food or within 1 hour after eating.

To help clear up your infection completely, *keep taking dirithromycin for the full time of treatment*, even if you begin to feel better after a few days. If you stop taking this medicine too soon, your symptoms may return.

Do not cut, crush, or chew dirithromycin tablets.

Dosing—The dose of dirithromycin will be different for different patients. *Follow your doctor's orders or the directions on the label.* The following information includes only the average doses of dirithromycin. *If your dose is different, do not change it* unless your doctor tells you to do so.

- For *oral* dosage form (tablets):
  - —For bacterial infections:
    - Adults and teenagers—500 milligrams (mg) once a day for seven to fourteen days.
    - Children up to 12 years of age—Use and dose must be determined by your doctor.

Missed dose—If you miss a dose of this medicine, take it as soon as possible. However, if it is almost time for your next dose, skip the missed dose and go back to your regular dosing schedule. Do not double doses.

Storage—To store this medicine:
- Keep out of the reach of children.
- Store away from heat and direct light.
- Do not store in the bathroom, near the kitchen sink, or in other damp places. Heat or moisture may cause the medicine to break down.
- Do not keep outdated medicine or medicine no longer needed. Be sure that any discarded medicine is out of the reach of children.

Precautions While Using This Medicine

If your symptoms do not improve within a few days, or if they become worse, check with your doctor.

Side Effects of This Medicine

Along with its needed effects, a medicine may cause some unwanted effects. Although not all of these side effects may occur, if they do occur they may need medical attention.

Check with your doctor as soon as possible if any of the following side effects occur:

Rare
> Abdominal tenderness; fever; severe abdominal or stomach cramps and pain; watery and severe diarrhea, which may also be bloody

Other side effects may occur that usually do not need medical attention. These side effects may go away during treatment as your body adjusts to the medicine. However, check with your doctor if any of the following side effects continue or are bothersome:

Less common
> Diarrhea; dizziness; headache; nausea; vomiting; weakness

Other side effects not listed above may also occur in some patients. If you notice any other effects, check with your doctor.

Developed: 06/24/96

DISOPYRAMIDE Systemic

Commonly used brand name(s):

In the U.S.—
Norpace
Norpace CR

Generic name product may be available.

In Canada—
Norpace CR
Rythmodan
Rythmodan-LA

Description

Disopyramide (dye-soe-PEER-a-mide) is used to treat abnormal heart rhythms.

It is available only with your doctor's prescription, in the following dosage forms:

Oral
- Capsules (U.S. and Canada)
- Extended-release capsules (U.S.)
- Extended-release tablets (Canada)

Before Using This Medicine

In deciding to use a medicine, the risks of taking the medicine must be weighed against the good it will do. This is a decision you and your doctor will make. For disopyramide, the following should be considered:

Allergies—Tell your doctor if you have ever had any unusual or allergic reaction to disopyramide. Also tell your health care professional if you are allergic to any other substance, such as foods, preservatives, or dyes.

Pregnancy—Disopyramide has not been studied in pregnant women. However, use of disopyramide in a small number of pregnant women seems to show that this medicine may cause contractions of the uterus. Studies in animals have shown that disopyramide increases the risk of miscarriages. Before taking this medicine, make sure your doctor knows if you are pregnant or if you may become pregnant.

Breast-feeding—Disopyramide passes into breast milk.

Children—This medicine has been tested in children and has not been shown to cause different side effects or problems than it does in adults.

Older adults—Some side effects, such as difficult urination and dry mouth, may be especially likely to occur in elderly patients, who are usually more sensitive than younger adults to the effects of disopyramide.

Other medicines—Although certain medicines should not be used together at all, in other cases two different medicines may be used together even if an interaction might occur. In these cases, your doctor may want to change the dose, or other precautions may be necessary. When you are taking disopyramide, it is especially important that your health care professional know if you are taking any of the following:

- Antidepressants, tricyclic, such as amitriptyline (e.g., Elavil), clomipramine (e.g., Anafranil), desipramine (e.g., Norpramin), doxepin (e.g., Sinequan), imipramine (e.g., Tofranil), and nortriptyline (e.g., Pamelor) or
- Astemizole (e.g., Hismanal) or
- Chloroquine (e.g., Aralen) or
- Clarithromycin (e.g., Biaxin) or
- Cisapride (e.g., Propulsid) or
- Diphenhydramine (e.g., Benadryl) or
- Erythromycin (e.g., Erythrocin, Erytab) or
- Fludrocortisone (e.g., Florinef) or
- Halofantrine (e.g., Halfan) or
- Haloperidol (e.g., Haldol) or
- Indapamide (e.g., Lozol) or
- Maprotiline (e.g., Ludiomil) or
- Other heart medicine, including amiodarone (e.g., Cordarone); bepridil (e.g., Bepadin, Vascor); beta-adrenergic blocking agents, such as propranolol (e.g., Inderal) or sotalol (e.g., Betapace, Sotacor); diltiazem (e.g., Cardizem); encainide (e.g., Encaid); flecainide

(e.g., Tambocor); ibutilide (e.g., Corvert); lidocaine (e.g., Xylocaine); procainamide (e.g., Procanbid); propafenone (e.g., Rythmol); quinidine (e.g., Quinidex); tocainide (e.g., Tonocard); and verapamil (e.g., Calan, Isoptin) or

- Pentamidine (e.g., NebuPent, Pentam) or
- Phenothiazines (chlorpromazine [e.g., Thorazine], prochlorperazine [e.g., Compazine], thioridazine [e.g., Mellaril]) or
- Pimozide (e.g., Orap) or
- Risperidone (e.g., Risperdal) or
- Sparfloxacin (e.g., Zagam) or
- Tamoxifen (e.g., Nolvadex) or
- Thiothixene (e.g., Navane) or
- Trimethoprim and sulfamethoxazole combination (e.g., Bactrim, Septra)—Effects on the heart may be increased

Other medical problems—The presence of other medical problems may affect the use of disopyramide. Make sure you tell your doctor if you have any other medical problems, especially:

- Diabetes mellitus (sugar diabetes)—Disopyramide may cause low blood sugar
- Difficult urination or
- Enlarged prostate—Disopyramide may cause difficult urination
- Electrolyte disorders—Disopyramide may worsen heart rhythm problems
- Glaucoma (history of) or
- Myasthenia gravis—Disopyramide may aggravate these conditions
- Kidney disease or
- Liver disease—Effects may be increased because of slower removal of disopyramide from the body
- Low blood pressure or
- Other heart disorders—Effects of disopyramide on the heart may make these conditions worse
- Malnutrition, long term—Disopyramide may cause low blood sugar

Proper Use of This Medicine

Take disopyramide exactly as directed by your doctor even though you may feel well. Do not take more medicine than ordered.

For patients taking the *extended-release capsules:*
- Swallow the capsule whole without breaking, crushing, or chewing.

For patients taking the *extended-release tablets:*
- Do not crush or chew the tablet.

This medicine works best when there is a constant amount in the blood. *To help keep the amount constant, do not miss any doses. Also, it is best to take the doses at evenly spaced times day and night.* For example, if you are to take four doses a day, the doses should be spaced about 6 hours apart. If this interferes with your sleep or other daily activities, or if you need help in planning the best times to take your medicine, check with your health care professional.

Dosing—The dose of disopyramide will be different for different patients. *Follow your doctor's orders or the directions on the label.* The following information includes only the average doses of disopyramide. *If your dose is different, do not change it* unless your doctor tells you to do so.

The number of tablets or capsules that you take depends on the strength of the medicine.
- For *treatment* of arrhythmias:
  —For *short-acting oral* dosage form (capsules):
    - Adults—100 to 150 mg taken every six to eight hours.
    - Children—Dose is based on body weight and age and must be determined by your doctor. The dose is usually 6 to 30 mg per kilogram (kg) (2.73 to 13.64 mg per pound) of body weight per day. This dose is evenly divided and taken every six hours.
  —For *long-acting oral* dosage forms (extended-release capsules or tablets):
    - Adults—200 or 400 mg every twelve hours.
    - Children—Use is not recommended.

Missed dose—*If you miss a dose of this medicine, take it as soon as possible unless the next scheduled dose is in less than 4 hours.* If you do not remember until later, skip the missed dose and go back to your regular dosing schedule. Do not double doses.

Storage—To store this medicine:
- Keep out of the reach of children.
- Store away from heat and direct light.
- Do not store in the bathroom, near the kitchen sink, or in other damp places. Heat or moisture may cause the medicine to break down.
- Do not keep outdated medicine or medicine no longer needed. Be sure that any discarded medicine is out of the reach of children.

Precautions While Using This Medicine

Your doctor should check your progress at regular visits to make sure the medicine is working properly.

Do not stop taking this medicine without first checking with your doctor. Stopping suddenly may cause a serious change in heart function.

Dizziness, lightheadedness, or fainting may occur, especially when you get up from a lying or sitting position. This is due to lowered blood pressure. Getting up slowly may help. This effect does not occur often at doses of disopyramide usually used; however, *make sure you know how you react to this medicine before you drive, use machines, or do anything else that could be dangerous if you are not alert.* If the problem continues or gets worse, check with your doctor.

Disopyramide may rarely cause hypoglycemia (low blood sugar) in some people. (See Side Effects of This Medicine.) *If these signs appear, eat or drink a food containing sugar and call your doctor right away.*

This medicine may cause blurred vision or other vision problems. If any of these occur, *do not drive, use machines, or do anything else that could be dangerous if you are not able to see well.*

Disopyramide may cause dryness of the eyes, mouth, and nose. For temporary relief of mouth dryness, use sugarless candy or gum, melt bits of ice in your mouth, or use a saliva substitute. However, if dry mouth continues for more than 2 weeks, check with your medical doctor or dentist. Continuing dryness of the mouth may increase the chance of dental disease, including tooth decay, gum disease, and oral yeast infections.

This medicine often will make you sweat less, allowing your body temperature to increase. *Use extra care not to become overheated during exercise or hot weather while you are taking this medicine,* since becoming overheated could possibly result in heatstroke.

Side Effects of This Medicine

Along with its needed effects, a medicine may cause some unwanted effects. Although not all of these side effects may occur, if they do occur they may need medical attention.

Check with your doctor as soon as possible if any of the following side effects occur:

More common
Dizziness, feeling of faintness; fainting; heartbeat sensations; shortness of breath; unusual tiredness

Less common
Chest pain; fast or slow heartbeat, rapid weight gain, swelling of feet or lower legs; lightheadedness; rash and/or itching

Rare
Enlargement of breasts in men; fever; mental depression; nosebleeds or bleeding gums; sore throat and fever; yellow eyes or skin

Signs and symptoms of hypoglycemia (low blood sugar)
Anxious feeling; chills; cold sweats; confusion; cool, pale skin; drowsiness; fast heartbeat; headache; hunger (excessive); nausea; nervousness; shakiness; unsteady walk; unusual tiredness or weakness

Other side effects may occur that usually do not need medical attention. These side effects may go away during treatment as your body adjusts to the medicine. However, check with your health care professional if any of the following side effects continue or are bothersome:

More common
Blurred vision; constipation; dry eyes, mouth, nose, or throat; problems with urination

Less common
Bloating or stomach pain; diarrhea; headache; impotence; loss of appetite; muscle weakness; nausea; nervousness; trouble in sleeping

Other side effects not listed above may also occur in some patients. If you notice any other effects, check with your doctor.

Revised: 3/16/99

DISULFIRAM   Systemic

Commonly used brand name(s):

In the U.S.—
Antabuse
Generic name product may be available.

In Canada—
Antabuse

Description

Disulfiram (dye-SUL-fi-ram) is used to help overcome your drinking problem. It is not a cure for alcoholism, but rather will discourage you from drinking.

Disulfiram is available only with your doctor's prescription, in the following dosage form:
Oral
• Tablets (U.S. and Canada)

Before Using This Medicine

In deciding to use a medicine, the risks of taking the medicine must be weighed against the good it will do. This is a decision you and your doctor will make. For disulfiram, the following should be considered:

Allergies—Tell your doctor if you have had any unusual or allergic reactions to disulfiram, rubber, pesticides, or fungicides.

Diet—In addition to beverages, alcohol is found in many other products. Reading the list of ingredients on foods and other products before using them will help you to avoid alcohol. Do not use alcohol-containing foods such as sauces and vinegars.

Pregnancy—Disulfiram has not been studied in pregnant women. However, there have been a few reports of birth defects in infants whose mothers took disulfiram during pregnancy. Before taking this medicine, make sure your doctor knows if you are pregnant or if you may become pregnant.

Breast-feeding—Disulfiram has not been reported to cause problems in nursing babies.

Children—Studies on this medicine have been done only in adult patients, and there is no specific information comparing use of disulfiram in children with use in other age groups.

Older adults—Many medicines have not been studied specifically in older people. Therefore, it may not be known whether they work exactly the same way they do in younger adults or if they cause different side effects or problems in older people. There is no specific information comparing use of disulfiram in the elderly with use in other age groups.

Other medicines—Although certain medicines should not be used together at all, in other cases 2 different medicines may be used together even if an interaction might occur. In these cases, your doctor may want to change the dose, or other precautions may be necessary. When you are taking disulfiram, it is especially important that your health care professional know if you are taking any of the following:

• Anticoagulants (blood thinners)—Taking disulfiram may increase the effects of anticoagulants, changing the amount you need to take

• Ethotoin (e.g., Peganone) or
• Mephenytoin (e.g., Mesantoin) or
• Phenytoin (e.g., Dilantin)—Taking these medicines with disulfiram may change the amount of anticonvulsant medicine you need to take

• Isoniazid (e.g., INH, Nydrazid)—Disulfiram may increase central nervous system (CNS) effects, such as dizziness, clumsiness, irritability, or trouble in sleeping

• Metronidazole (e.g., Flagyl) or
• Paraldehyde (e.g., Paral)—These medicines should not be taken with or within several days of disulfiram because serious side effects may occur

Ethylene dibromide or organic solvents (such as chemicals which may contain alcohol, acetaldehyde, paraldehyde, or other related chemicals used in factories and in hobbies [e.g., paint thinner])—Make sure you tell your doctor if you will come in contact with or breathe the fumes of ethylene dibromide or organic solvents while you are taking disulfiram.

Other medical problems—The presence of other medical problems may affect the use of disulfiram. Make sure you tell your doctor if you have any other medical problems, especially:

- Asthma or other lung disease, severe, or
- Diabetes mellitus (sugar diabetes) or
- Epilepsy or other seizure disorder or
- Heart or blood vessel disease or
- Kidney disease or
- Liver disease or cirrhosis of the liver or
- Underactive thyroid—A disulfiram-alcohol reaction may make the condition worse

- Depression or
- Severe mental illness—Disulfiram may make the condition worse

- Skin allergy—Disulfiram may cause an allergic reaction

Proper Use of This Medicine

Before you take the first dose of this medicine, *make sure you have not taken any alcoholic beverage or alcohol-containing product or medicine* (for example, tonics, elixirs, and cough syrups) *during the past 12 hours*. If you are not sure about the alcohol content of medicines you may have taken, check with your health care professional.

Take this medicine every day as directed by your doctor. The medicine is usually taken each morning. However, if it makes you drowsy, ask your doctor if you may take it at bedtime instead.

Dosing—The dose of disulfiram will be different for different patients. *Follow your doctor's orders or the directions on the label*. The following information includes only the average doses of disulfiram. *If your dose is different, do not change it* unless your doctor tells you to do so.

- For *oral* dosage form (tablets):
  - To help overcome drinking problems:
    - Adults and teenagers—At first, the dose is 500 milligrams (mg) or less, once a day for one or two weeks. Then, your doctor may lower your dose to 125 to 500 mg (usually to 250 mg) once a day.
    - Children—Use and dose must be determined by your doctor.

Storage—To store this medicine:

- Keep out of the reach of children.
- Store away from heat and direct light.
- Do not store in the bathroom, near the kitchen sink, or in other damp places. Heat or moisture may cause the medicine to break down.
- Do not keep outdated medicine or medicine no longer needed. Be sure that any discarded medicine is out of the reach of children.

Precautions While Using This Medicine

Do not drink any alcohol, even small amounts, while you are taking this medicine and for 14 days after you stop taking it, because the alcohol may make you very sick. In addition to beverages, alcohol is found in many other products. Reading the list of ingredients on foods and other products before using them will help you to avoid alcohol. You can also avoid alcohol if you:

- Do not use alcohol-containing foods, products, or medicines, such as elixirs, tonics, sauces, vinegars, cough syrups, mouth washes, or gargles.

- *Do not come in contact with or breathe in the fumes of chemicals that may contain alcohol, acetaldehyde, paraldehyde, or other related chemicals*, such as paint thinner, paint, varnish, or shellac.
- *Use caution when using alcohol-containing products that are applied to the skin*, such as some transdermal (stick-on patch) medicines or rubbing alcohol, back rubs, after-shave lotions, colognes, perfumes, toilet waters, or after-bath preparations. Using such products while you are taking disulfiram may cause headache, nausea, or local redness or itching because the alcohol in these products may be absorbed into your body. Before using alcohol-containing products on your skin, first test the product by applying some to a small area of your skin. Allow the product to remain on your skin for 1 or 2 hours. If no redness, itching, or other unwanted effects occur, you should be able to use the product.
- *Do not use any alcohol-containing products on raw skin or open wounds*.

Check with your doctor if you have any questions.

Some of the symptoms you may experience if you use any alcohol while taking this medicine are:

    Blurred vision
    Chest pain
    Confusion
    Dizziness or fainting
    Fast or pounding heartbeat
    Flushing or redness of face
    Increased sweating
    Nausea and vomiting
    Throbbing headache
    Troubled breathing
    Weakness

These symptoms will last as long as there is any alcohol left in your system, from 30 minutes to several hours. On rare occasions, if you have a severe reaction or have taken a large enough amount of alcohol, a heart attack, unconsciousness, convulsions (seizures), and death may occur.

Your doctor may want you to carry an identification card stating that you are using this medicine. This card should list the symptoms most likely to occur if alcohol is taken, and the doctor, clinic, or hospital to be contacted in case of an emergency. These cards may be available from the manufacturer. Ask your health care professional if you have any questions about this.

If you will be taking this medicine for a long period of time (for example, for several months at a time), your doctor should check your progress at regular visits.

Before buying or using any liquid prescription or nonprescription medicine, check with your pharmacist to see if it contains any alcohol.

This medicine may cause some people to become drowsy or less alert than they are normally. If this occurs, *do not drive, use machines, or do anything else that could be dangerous if you are not alert.*

Disulfiram will add to the effects of other CNS depressants (medicines that slow down the nervous system, possibly causing drowsiness). Some examples of CNS depressants are antihistamines or medicine for hay fever, other allergies, or colds; sedatives, tranquilizers, or sleeping medicine; prescription pain medicine or narcotics; barbiturates; medicine for seizures; muscle relaxants; or anesthetics, including some dental anesthetics. *Check with your doctor before taking any of the above while you are using this medicine.*

Side Effects of This Medicine

Along with its needed effects, a medicine may cause some unwanted effects. Although not all of these side effects may occur, if they do occur they may need medical attention.

Check with your doctor as soon as possible if any of the following side effects occur:

Less common
> Eye pain or tenderness or any change in vision; mood or mental changes; numbness, tingling, pain, or weakness in hands or feet

Rare
> Darkening of urine; light gray-colored stools; severe stomach pain; yellow eyes or skin

Other side effects may occur that usually do not need medical attention. These side effects may go away during treatment as your body adjusts to the medicine. However, check with your doctor if any of the following side effects continue or are bothersome:

More common
> Drowsiness

Less common or rare
> Decreased sexual ability in males; headache; metallic or garlic-like taste in mouth; skin rash; unusual tiredness

Other side effects not listed above may also occur in some patients. If you notice any other effects, check with your doctor.

Revised: 01/27/92
Interim revision: 07/20/94

DIURETICS, LOOP   Systemic

Commonly used brand name(s):

In the U.S.—

Bumex[1]	Lasix[3]
Edecrin[2]	Myrosemide[3]

In Canada—

Apo-Furosemide[3]	Lasix Special[3]
Edecrin[2]	Novosemide[3]
Furoside[3]	Uritol[3]
Lasix[3]	

Note: For quick reference, the following loop diuretics are numbered to match the corresponding brand names.

This information applies to the following medicines:
1. Bumetanide (byoo-MET-a-nide) †‡
2. Ethacrynic Acid (eth-a-KRIN-ik AS-id)
3. Furosemide (fur-OH-se-mide) ‡§

†Not commercially available in Canada.
‡Generic name product may be available in the U.S.
§Generic name product may be available in Canada.

Description

Loop diuretics are given to help reduce the amount of water in the body. They work by acting on the kidneys to increase the flow of urine.

Furosemide is also used to treat high blood pressure (hypertension) in those patients who are not helped by other medicines or in those patients who have kidney problems.

High blood pressure adds to the work load of the heart and arteries. If it continues for a long time, the heart and arteries may not function properly. This can damage the blood vessels of the brain, heart, and kidneys, resulting in a stroke, heart failure, or kidney failure. High blood pressure may also increase the risk of heart attacks. These problems may be less likely to occur if blood pressure is controlled.

Loop diuretics may also be used for other conditions as determined by your doctor.

This medicine is available only with your doctor's prescription, in the following dosage forms:

Oral
> Bumetanide
> • Tablets (U.S.)
> Ethacrynic Acid
> • Oral solution (U.S. and Canada)
> • Tablets (U.S. and Canada)
> Furosemide
> • Oral solution (U.S. and Canada)
> • Tablets (U.S. and Canada)

Parenteral
> Bumetanide
> • Injection (U.S.)
> Ethacrynic Acid
> • Injection (U.S. and Canada)
> Furosemide
> • Injection (U.S. and Canada)

Before Using This Medicine

In deciding to use a medicine, the risks of taking the medicine must be weighed against the good it will do. This is a decision you and your doctor will make. For loop diuretics, the following should be considered:

Allergies—Tell your doctor if you have ever had any unusual or allergic reaction to bumetanide, ethacrynic acid, furosemide, sulfonamides (sulfa drugs), or thiazide diuretics (water pills). Also tell your health care professional if you are allergic to any other substances, such as foods, preservatives, or dyes.

Pregnancy—Studies have not been done in pregnant women. However, studies in animals have shown this medicine to cause harmful effects.

In general, diuretics are not useful for normal swelling of feet and hands that occurs during pregnancy. Diuretics should not be taken during pregnancy unless recommended by your doctor.

Breast-feeding—These medicines have not been reported to cause problems in nursing babies. Furosemide passes into breast milk; it is not known whether bumetanide or ethacrynic acid passes into breast milk.

Children—Although there is no specific information comparing the use of loop diuretics in children with use in any other age group, these medicines are not expected to cause different side effects in children than they do in adults.

Older adults—Dizziness, lightheadedness, or signs of too much potassium loss may be more likely to occur in the elderly, who are more sensitive to the effects of this medicine. Elderly patients may also be more likely to develop blood clots.

Other medicines—Although certain medicines should not be used together at all, in other cases two different medicines may be used together even if an interaction might occur. In these cases, your doctor may want to change the dose, or other precautions may be necessary. When you are taking loop diuretics, it is especially important that your health care professional know if you are taking *any* other medicines.

Other medical problems—The presence of other medical problems may affect the use of loop diuretics. Make sure you tell your doctor if you have any other medical problems, especially:

- Diabetes mellitus (sugar diabetes)—Loop diuretics may increase the amount of sugar in the blood

- Gout or
- Hearing problems or
- Pancreatitis (inflammation of the pancreas)—Loop diuretics may make these conditions worse

- Heart attack, recent—Use of loop diuretics after a recent heart attack may increase the chance of side effects

- Kidney disease (severe) or
- Liver disease—Higher blood levels of the loop diuretic may occur, which may increase the chance of side effects

- Lupus erythematosus (history of)—Ethacrynic acid and furosemide may make this condition worse

---

Proper Use of This Medicine

This medicine may cause you to have an unusual feeling of tiredness when you begin to take it. You may also notice an increase in the amount of urine or in your frequency of urination. After you have taken the medicine for a while, these effects should lessen. In general, to keep the increase in urine from affecting your sleep:

- If you are to take a single dose a day, take it in the morning after breakfast.
- If you are to take more than one dose a day, take the last dose no later than 6 p.m., unless otherwise directed by your doctor.

However, it is best to plan your dose or doses according to a schedule that will least affect your personal activities and sleep. Ask your health care professional to help you plan the best time to take this medicine.

To help you remember to take your medicine, try to get into the habit of taking it at the same time each day.

For patients taking the *oral liquid form* of furosemide:

- This medicine is to be taken by mouth even if it comes in a dropper bottle. If this medicine does not come in a dropper bottle, use a specially marked measuring spoon or other device to measure each dose accurately, since the average household teaspoon may not hold the right amount of liquid.

For patients taking this medicine for *high blood pressure:*

- In addition to the use of the medicine your doctor has prescribed, appropriate treatment for your high blood pressure may include weight control and care in the types of foods you eat, especially foods high in sodium. Your doctor will tell you which factors are most important for you. You should check with your doctor before changing your diet.
- Many patients who have high blood pressure will not notice any signs of the problem. In fact, many may feel normal. It is very important that you *take your medicine*

exactly as directed and that you keep your appointments with your doctor even if you feel well.

- Remember that this medicine will not cure your high blood pressure but it does help control it. Therefore, you must continue to take it as directed if you expect to lower your blood pressure and keep it down. *You may have to take high blood pressure medicine for the rest of your life.* If high blood pressure is not treated, it can cause serious problems such as heart failure, blood vessel disease, stroke, or kidney disease.

If this medicine upsets your stomach, it may be taken with meals or milk. If stomach upset (nausea, vomiting, or stomach pain) continues or gets worse, or if you suddenly get severe diarrhea, check with your doctor.

Dosing—The dose of loop diuretics will be different for different patients. *Follow your doctor's orders or the directions on the label.* The following information includes only the average doses of loop diuretics. *If your dose is different, do not change it* unless your doctor tells you to do so.

The number of tablets or teaspoonfuls of solution that you take depends on the strength of the medicine. Also, *the number of doses you take each day, the time allowed between doses, and the length of time you take the medicine depend on the medical problem for which you are taking loop diuretics.*

For bumetanide
- For *oral* dosage form (tablets):
  —To lower the amount of water in the body:
  - Adults—0.5 to 2 milligrams (mg) once a day. Your doctor may increase your dose if needed.
  - Children—Dose must be determined by your doctor.
- For *injection* dosage form:
  —To lower the amount of water in the body:
  - Adults—0.5 to 1 mg injected into a muscle or a vein every two to three hours as needed.
  - Children—Dose must be determined by your doctor.

For ethacrynic acid
- For *oral* dosage form (oral solution or tablets):
  —To lower the amount of water in the body:
  - Adults—50 to 200 milligrams (mg) a day. This may be taken as a single dose or divided into smaller doses.
  - Children—At first, 25 mg a day. Your doctor may increase your dose as needed.
- For *injection* dosage form:
  —To lower the amount of water in the body:
  - Adults—50 mg injected into a vein every two to six hours as needed.
  - Children—Dose is based on body weight and must be determined by your doctor. The usual dose is 1 mg per kilogram (kg) (0.45 mg per pound) of body weight injected into a vein.

For furosemide
- For *oral* dosage form (oral solution or tablets):
  —To lower the amount of water in the body:
  - Adults—At first, 20 to 80 milligrams (mg) once a day. Then, your doctor may increase your dose as needed. Your doctor may tell you to take a dose once a day, two or three times a day, or every other day.
  - Children—Dose is based on body weight and must be determined by your doctor. The usual dose is 2 mg per kilogram (kg) (0.91 mg per

pound) of body weight for one dose. Then, your doctor may increase your dose every six to eight hours as needed.

—For high blood pressure:
  • Adults—40 mg two times a day. Your doctor may increase your dose.

• For *injection* dosage form:
  —To lower the amount of water in the body:
    • Adults—At first, 20 to 40 mg injected into a muscle or a vein for one dose. Then, your doctor may increase your dose every two hours as needed. Once the medicine is working, the dose is injected into a muscle or a vein one or two times a day.
    • Children—Dose is based on body weight and must be determined by your doctor. The usual dose is 1 mg per kg (0.45 mg per pound) of body weight injected into a muscle or a vein for one dose. Your doctor may increase your dose every two hours as needed.
  —For very high blood pressure:
    • Adults—40 to 200 mg injected into a vein.

Missed dose—If you miss a dose of this medicine, take it as soon as possible. However, if it is almost time for your next dose, skip the missed dose and go back to your regular dosing schedule. Do not double doses.

Storage—To store this medicine:
  • Keep out of the reach of children.
  • Store away from heat and direct light.
  • Do not store in the bathroom, near the kitchen sink, or in other damp places. Heat or moisture may cause the medicine to break down.
  • Keep the oral liquid form of this medicine from freezing.
  • Do not keep outdated medicine or medicine no longer needed. Be sure that any discarded medicine is out of the reach of children.

Precautions While Using This Medicine

It is important that your doctor check your progress at regular visits to make sure that this medicine is working properly.

This medicine may cause a loss of potassium from your body:
  • To help prevent this, your doctor may want you to:
    —eat or drink foods that have a high potassium content (for example, orange or other citrus fruit juices), or
    —take a potassium supplement, or
    —take another medicine to help prevent the loss of the potassium in the first place.
  • It is very important to follow these directions. Also, it is important not to change your diet on your own. This is more important if you are already on a special diet (as for diabetes), or if you are taking a potassium supplement or a medicine to reduce potassium loss. Extra potassium may not be necessary and, in some cases, too much potassium could be harmful.

To prevent the loss of too much water and potassium, tell your doctor if you become sick, especially with severe or continuing nausea and vomiting or diarrhea.

Before having any kind of surgery (including dental surgery) or emergency treatment, make sure the medical doctor or dentist in charge knows that you are taking this medicine.

Dizziness, lightheadedness, or fainting may occur, especially when you get up from a lying or sitting position. This is more likely to occur in the morning. *Getting up slowly may help.* When you get up from lying down, sit on the edge of the bed with your feet dangling for 1 or 2 minutes. Then stand up slowly. If the problem continues or gets worse, check with your doctor.

The dizziness, lightheadedness, or fainting is also more likely to occur if you drink alcohol, stand for long periods of time, exercise, or if the weather is hot. *While you are taking this medicine, be careful to limit the amount of alcohol you drink. Also, use extra care during exercise or hot weather or if you must stand for long periods of time.*

For *diabetic patients:*
  • This medicine may affect blood sugar levels. While you are using this medicine, be especially careful in testing for sugar in your blood or urine.

For patients taking this medicine for *high blood pressure:*
  • *Do not take other medicines unless they have been discussed with your doctor.* This especially includes over-the-counter (nonprescription) medicines for appetite control, asthma, colds, cough, hay fever, or sinus problems, since they may tend to increase your blood pressure.

For patients taking *furosemide:*
  • Furosemide may cause your skin to be more sensitive to sunlight than it is normally. Exposure to sunlight, even for brief periods of time, may cause a skin rash, itching, redness or other discoloration of the skin, or a severe sunburn. When you begin taking this medicine:
    —Stay out of direct sunlight, especially between the hours of 10:00 a.m. and 3:00 p.m., if possible.
    —Wear protective clothing, including a hat. Also, wear sunglasses.
    —Apply a sun block product that has a skin protection factor (SPF) of at least 15. Some patients may require a product with a higher SPF number, especially if they have a fair complexion. If you have any questions about this, check with your health care professional.
    —Apply a sun block lipstick that has an SPF of at least 15 to protect your lips.
    —Do not use a sunlamp or tanning bed or booth.

If you have a severe reaction from the sun, check with your doctor.

Side Effects of This Medicine

Along with its needed effects, a medicine may cause some unwanted effects. Although not all of these side effects may occur, if they do occur they may need medical attention.

Check with your doctor as soon as possible if any of the following side effects occur:
  Rare
    Black, tarry stools; blood in urine or stools; cough or hoarseness; fever or chills; joint pain; lower back or side pain; painful or difficult urination; pinpoint red spots on skin; ringing or buzzing in ears or any loss of hearing—more common with ethacrynic acid; skin rash or hives; stomach pain (severe) with nausea and vomiting; unusual bleeding or bruising; yellow eyes or skin; yellow vision—for furosemide only

  Signs and symptoms of too much potassium loss
    Dryness of mouth; increased thirst; irregular heartbeat; mood or mental changes; muscle cramps or pain; nausea or vomiting; unusual tiredness or weakness; weak pulse

Other side effects may occur that usually do not need medical attention. These side effects may go away during treatment as your body adjusts to the medicine. However, check with your doctor if any of the following side effects continue or are bothersome:

More common

Dizziness or lightheadedness when getting up from a lying or sitting position

Less common or rare

Blurred vision; chest pain—with bumetanide only; confusion—with ethacrynic acid only; diarrhea—more common with ethacrynic acid; headache; increased sensitivity of skin to sunlight—with furosemide only; loss of appetite—more common with ethacrynic acid; nervousness—with ethacrynic acid only; premature ejaculation or difficulty in keeping an erection—with bumetanide only; redness or pain at place of injection; stomach cramps or pain

Other side effects not listed above may also occur in some patients. If you notice any other effects, check with your doctor.

Additional Information

Once a medicine has been approved for marketing for a certain use, experience may show that it is also useful for other medical problems. Although these uses are not included in product labeling, loop diuretics are used in certain patients with the following medical conditions:

- Hypercalcemia (too much calcium in the blood)
- Diagnostic aid for kidney disease

Other than the above information, there is no additional information relating to proper use, precautions, or side effects for these uses.

Revised: 08/02/94
Interim revision: 04/24/95

DIURETICS, POTASSIUM-SPARING
Systemic

Commonly used brand name(s):

In the U.S.—
Aldactone[2]
Dyrenium[3]
Midamor[1]

In Canada—

Aldactone[2]   Midamor[1]
Dyrenium[3]   Novospiroton[2]

Note: For quick reference, the following potassium-sparing diuretics are numbered to match the corresponding brand names.

This information applies to the following medicines:
1. Amiloride (a-MILL-oh-ride) ‡
2. Spironolactone (speer-on-oh-LAK-tone) ‡
3. Triamterene (trye-AM-ter-een)

‡Generic name product may be available in the U.S.

Description

Potassium-sparing diuretics are commonly used to help reduce the amount of water in the body. Unlike some other diuretics, these medicines do not cause your body to lose potassium.

Amiloride and spironolactone are also used to treat high blood pressure (hypertension). High blood pressure adds to the workload of the heart and arteries. If the condition continues for a long time, the heart and arteries may not function properly. This can damage the blood vessels of the brain, heart, and kidneys, resulting in a stroke, heart failure, or kidney failure. High blood pressure may also increase the risk of heart attacks. These problems may be less likely to occur if blood pressure is controlled.

Spironolactone is also used to help increase the amount of potassium in the body when it is getting too low.

Potassium-sparing diuretics help to reduce the amount of water in the body by acting on the kidneys to increase the flow of urine. This also helps to lower blood pressure.

These medicines can also be used for other conditions as determined by your doctor.

Potassium-sparing diuretics are available only with your doctor's prescription, in the following dosage forms:

Oral

Amiloride
- Tablets (U.S. and Canada)
Spironolactone
- Tablets (U.S. and Canada)
Triamterene
- Capsules (U.S.)
- Tablets (Canada)

Before Using This Medicine

In deciding to use a medicine, the risks of taking the medicine must be weighed against the good it will do. This is a decision you and your doctor will make. For potassium-sparing diuretics, the following should be considered:

Allergies—Tell your doctor if you have ever had any unusual or allergic reaction to amiloride, spironolactone, or triamterene. Also tell your health care professional if you are allergic to any other substances, such as foods, preservatives, or dyes.

Pregnancy—Studies have not been done in pregnant women. However, this medicine has not been shown to cause birth defects or other problems in animals.

In general, diuretics are not useful for normal swelling of feet and hands that occurs during pregnancy. Diuretics should not be taken during pregnancy unless recommended by your doctor.

Breast-feeding—Although amiloride, spironolactone, and triamterene may pass into breast milk, these medicines have not been reported to cause problems in nursing babies.

Children—This medicine has been tested in children and, in effective doses, has not been shown to cause different side effects or problems in children than it does in adults.

Older adults—Signs and symptoms of too much potassium are more likely to occur in the elderly, who are more sensitive than younger adults to the effects of this medicine.

Other medicines—Although certain medicines should not be used together at all, in other cases two different medicines may be used together even if an interaction might occur. In these cases, your doctor may want to change the dose, or other precautions may be necessary. When you are taking potassium-sparing diuretics, it is especially important that your health care professional know if you are taking any of the following:

- Angiotensin-converting enzyme (ACE) inhibitors (benazepril [e.g., Lotensin], captopril [e.g., Capoten], enalapril [e.g., Vasotec], fosinopril [e.g., Monopril], lisinopril [e.g., Prinivil, Zestril], quinapril [e.g., Accupril], ramipril [e.g., Altace]) or
- Cyclosporine (e.g., Sandimmune) or
- Potassium-containing medicines or supplements—Use with potassium-sparing diuretics may cause high blood levels of potassium, which may increase the chance of side effects
- Digoxin—Use with spironolactone may cause high blood levels of digoxin, which may increase the chance of side effects
- Lithium (e.g., Lithane)—Use with potassium-sparing diuretics may cause high blood levels of lithium, which may increase the chance of side effects

Other medical problems—The presence of other medical problems may affect the use of potassium-sparing diuretics. Make sure you tell your doctor if you have any other medical problems, especially:

- Diabetes mellitus (sugar diabetes) or
- Kidney disease or
- Liver disease—Higher blood levels of potassium may occur, which may increase the chance of side effects
- Gout or
- Kidney stones (history of)—Triamterene may make these conditions worse
- Menstrual problems or breast enlargement—Spironolactone may make these conditions worse

Proper Use of This Medicine

This medicine may cause you to have an unusual feeling of tiredness when you begin to take it. You may also notice an increase in the amount of urine or in your frequency of urination. After you have taken the medicine for a while, these effects should lessen. In general, to keep the increase in urine from affecting your sleep:

- If you are to take a single dose a day, take it in the morning after breakfast.
- If you are to take more than one dose a day, take the last dose no later than 6 p.m., unless otherwise directed by your doctor.

However, it is best to plan your dose or doses according to a schedule that will least affect your personal activities and sleep. Ask your health care professional to help you plan the best time to take this medicine.

To help you remember to take your medicine, try to get into the habit of taking it at the same time each day.

If this medicine upsets your stomach, it may be taken with meals or milk. If stomach upset (nausea, vomiting, stomach pain or cramps) continues, check with your doctor.

For patients taking this medicine for *high blood pressure:*

- In addition to the use of the medicine your doctor has prescribed, treatment for your high blood pressure may include weight control and care in the types of foods you eat, especially foods high in sodium. Your doctor will tell you which of these are most important for you. You should check with your doctor before changing your diet.
- Many patients who have high blood pressure will not notice any signs of the problem. In fact, many may feel normal. It is very important that you *take your medicine exactly as directed* and that you keep your appointments with your doctor even if you feel well.
- Remember that this medicine will not cure your high blood pressure but it does help control it. Therefore, you must continue to take it as directed if you expect to lower your blood pressure and keep it down. *You may have to take high blood pressure medicine for the rest of your life.* If high blood pressure is not treated, it can cause serious problems such as heart failure, blood vessel disease, stroke, or kidney disease.

Dosing—The dose of potassium-sparing diuretics will be different for different patients. *Follow your doctor's orders or the directions on the label.* The following information includes only the average doses of potassium-sparing diuretics. *If your dose is different, do not change it* unless your doctor tells you to do so.

The number of capsules or tablets that you take depends on the strength of the medicine. Also, *the number of doses you take each day, the time allowed between doses, and the length of time you take the medicine depend on the medical problem for which you are taking potassium-sparing diuretics.*

For amiloride
- For *oral* dosage form (tablets):
  —For high blood pressure or to lower the amount of water in the body:
  - Adults—5 to 10 milligrams (mg) once a day.
  - Children—Dose must be determined by your doctor.

For spironolactone
- For *oral* dosage form (tablets):
  —To lower the amount of water in the body:
  - Adults—At first, 25 to 200 milligrams (mg) a day. This is divided into two to four doses. Your doctor may increase your dose as needed.
  - Children—Dose is based on body weight and must be determined by your doctor. The usual dose is 1 to 3 mg per kilogram (kg) (0.45 to 1.36 mg per pound) of body weight a day. The dose may be taken as a single dose or divided into two to four doses. Your doctor may increase your dose as needed.
  —For high blood pressure:
  - Adults—At first, 50 to 100 milligrams (mg) a day. This may be taken as a single dose or divided into two to four doses. Your doctor may gradually increase your dose up to 200 mg a day.
  - Children—Dose is based on body weight and must be determined by your doctor. The usual dose is 1 to 3 mg per kg (0.45 to 1.36 mg per pound) of body weight a day. The dose may be taken as a single dose or divided into two to four doses. Your doctor may increase your dose as needed.
  —To treat high aldosterone levels in the body:
  - Adults—100 to 400 mg a day. This is divided into two to four doses and taken until you have surgery. If you are not having surgery, your doses may be smaller.
  —For detecting high aldosterone levels in the body:
  - Adults—400 mg a day, taken in two to four divided doses. Your doctor may want you to take this dose

for as little as four days or as long as three to four weeks. Follow your doctor's instructions.
—To treat low potassium levels in the blood:
• Adults—25 to 100 mg a day. This may be taken as a single dose or divided into two to four doses.

For triamterene
• For *oral* dosage form (capsules or tablets):
—To lower the amount of water in the body:
• Adults—100 mg twice a day. Your doctor may gradually increase your dose.
• Children—Dose is based on body weight and must be determined by your doctor. To start, the usual dose is 2 to 4 mg per kilogram (kg) (0.9 to 1.82 mg per pound) of body weight a day or every other day. This is divided into smaller doses. Your doctor may increase your dose as needed.

Missed dose—If you miss a dose of this medicine, take it as soon as possible. However, if it is almost time for your next dose, skip the missed dose and go back to your regular dosing schedule. Do not double doses.

Storage—To store this medicine:
• Keep out of the reach of children.
• Store away from heat and direct light.
• Do not store in the bathroom, near the kitchen sink, or in other damp places. Heat or moisture may cause the medicine to break down.
• Do not keep outdated medicine or medicine no longer needed. Be sure that any discarded medicine is out of the reach of children.

Precautions While Using This Medicine

It is important that your doctor check your progress at regular visits to make sure that this medicine is working properly.

This medicine does not cause a loss of potassium from your body as some other diuretics (water pills) do. Therefore, it is not necessary for you to get extra potassium in your diet, and too much potassium could even be harmful. Since salt substitutes and low-sodium milk may contain potassium, do not use them unless told to do so by your doctor.

Check with your doctor if you become sick and have severe or continuing nausea, vomiting, or diarrhea. These problems may cause you to lose additional water, which could be harmful, or to lose potassium, which could lessen the medicine's helpful effects.

Before having any kind of surgery (including dental surgery) or emergency treatment, tell the medical doctor or dentist in charge that you are taking this medicine.

Before you have any medical tests, tell the doctor in charge that you are taking this medicine. The results of some tests may be affected by this medicine.

For patients taking this medicine for *high blood pressure:*
• *Do not take other medicines unless they have been discussed with your doctor.* This especially includes over-the-counter (nonprescription) medicines for appetite control, asthma, colds, cough, hay fever, or sinus problems, since these medicines may tend to increase your blood pressure.

For patients taking *triamterene:*
• This medicine may cause your skin to be more sensitive to sunlight than it is normally. Exposure to sunlight, even for brief periods of time, may cause a skin rash, itching,

redness or other discoloration of the skin, or a severe sunburn. When you begin taking this medicine:
—Stay out of direct sunlight, especially between the hours of 10:00 a.m. and 3:00 p.m., if possible.
—Wear protective clothing, including a hat. Also, wear sunglasses.
—Apply a sun block product that has a skin protection factor (SPF) of at least 15. Some patients may require a product with a higher SPF number, especially if they have a fair complexion. If you have any questions about this, check with your health care professional.
—Apply a sun block lipstick that has an SPF of at least 15 to protect your lips.
—Do not use a sunlamp or tanning bed or booth.
—If you have a severe reaction from the sun, check with your doctor.

Side Effects of This Medicine

In rats, spironolactone has been found to increase the risk of tumors. It is not known if spironolactone increases the chance of tumors in humans.

Check with your doctor as soon as possible if any of the following side effects occur:
Rare
For amiloride, spironolactone, and triamterene
Skin rash or itching; shortness of breath
For spironolactone and triamterene only (in addition to effects listed above)
Cough or hoarseness; fever or chills; lower back or side pain; painful or difficult urination
For triamterene only (in addition to effects listed above)
Black, tarry stools; blood in urine or stools; bright red tongue; burning, inflamed feeling in tongue; cracked corners of mouth; lower back pain (severe); pinpoint red spots on skin; unusual bleeding or bruising; weakness
Signs and symptoms of too much potassium
Confusion; irregular heartbeat; nervousness; numbness or tingling in hands, feet, or lips; shortness of breath or difficult breathing; unusual tiredness or weakness; weakness or heaviness of legs

Other side effects may occur that usually do not need medical attention. These side effects may go away during treatment as your body adjusts to the medicine. However, check with your doctor if any of the following side effects continue or are bothersome:
More common (less common with amiloride and triamterene)
Nausea and vomiting; stomach cramps and diarrhea
Less common
For amiloride, spironolactone, and triamterene
Dizziness; headache
For amiloride and spironolactone only (in addition to effects listed above)
Decreased sexual ability
For amiloride only (in addition to effects listed above)
Constipation; muscle cramps
For spironolactone only (in addition to effects listed above for spironolactone)
Breast tenderness in females; clumsiness; deep-

ening of voice in females; enlargement of breasts in males; inability to have or keep an erection; increased hair growth in females; irregular menstrual periods; sweating

For triamterene only (in addition to effects listed above for triamterene)
   Increased sensitivity of skin to sunlight

Signs and symptoms of too little sodium
   Drowsiness; dryness of mouth; increased thirst; lack of energy

For *male patients:*
- Spironolactone sometimes causes enlarged breasts in males, especially when they take large doses of it for a long time. Breasts usually decrease in size gradually over several months after this medicine is stopped. If you have any questions about this, check with your doctor.

Other side effects not listed above may also occur in some patients. If you notice any other effects, check with your doctor.

Additional Information

Once a medicine has been approved for marketing for a certain use, experience may show that it is also useful for other medical problems. Although these uses are not included in product labeling, spironolactone is used in certain patients with the following medical conditions:
- Polycystic ovary syndrome
- Hirsutism, female (increased hair growth)
- Congestive heart failure, severe

Other than the above information, there is no additional information relating to proper use, precautions, or side effects for these uses.

Revised: 04/26/00

DIURETICS, POTASSIUM-SPARING, AND HYDROCHLOROTHIAZIDE
Systemic

Commonly used brand name(s):

In the U.S.—
Aldactazide[2]   Moduretic[1]
Dyazide[3]   Spirozide[2]
Maxzide[3]

In Canada—
Aldactazide[2]   Moduret[1]
Apo-Triazide[3]   Novo-Spirozine[2]
Dyazide[3]   Novo-Triamzide[3]

Note: For quick reference, the following medicines are numbered to match the corresponding brand names.

This information applies to the following medicines:
1. Amiloride and Hydrochlorothiazide (a-MILL-oh-ride and hye-droe-klor-oh-THYE-a-zide) ‡
2. Spironolactone and Hydrochlorothiazide (speer-on-oh-LAK-tone and hye-droe-klor-oh-THYE-a-zide) ‡
3. Triamterene and Hydrochlorothiazide (trye-AM-ter-een and hye-droe-klor-oh-THYE-a-zide) ‡

‡Generic name product may be available in the U.S.

Description

This medicine is a combination of two diuretics (water pills). It is commonly used to help reduce the amount of water in the body.

This combination is also used to treat high blood pressure (hypertension). High blood pressure adds to the work load of the heart and arteries. If it continues for a long time, the heart and arteries may not function properly. This can damage the blood vessels of the brain, heart, and kidneys, resulting in a stroke, heart failure, or kidney failure. High blood pressure may also increase the risk of heart attacks. These problems may be less likely to occur if blood pressure is controlled.

Diuretics help to reduce the amount of water in the body by acting on the kidneys to increase the flow of urine. This also helps to lower blood pressure.

This combination is also used to treat problems caused by too little potassium in the body.

This medicine is available only with your doctor's prescription, in the following dosage forms:

Oral
   Amiloride and Hydrochlorothiazide
   - Tablets (U.S. and Canada)
   Spironolactone and Hydrochlorothiazide
   - Tablets (U.S. and Canada)
   Triamterene and Hydrochlorothiazide
   - Capsules (U.S.)
   - Tablets (U.S. and Canada)

Before Using This Medicine

In deciding to use a medicine, the risks of taking the medicine must be weighed against the good it will do. This is a decision you and your doctor will make. For potassium-sparing diuretics and hydrochlorothiazide, the following should be considered:

Allergies—Tell your doctor if you have ever had any unusual or allergic reaction to amiloride, spironolactone, triamterene, sulfonamides (sulfa drugs), bumetanide, furosemide, acetazolamide, dichlorphenamide, methazolamide, or to hydrochlorothiazide or any of the other thiazide diuretics. Also tell your health care professional if you are allergic to any other substances, such as foods, preservatives, or dyes.

Pregnancy—In general, diuretics are not useful for normal swelling of feet and hands that occurs during pregnancy. They should not be taken during pregnancy unless recommended by your doctor.

Breast-feeding—Hydrochlorothiazide and spironolactone pass into breast milk. It is not known whether amiloride or triamterene passes into breast milk. Hydrochlorothiazide may also decrease the flow of breast milk. Therefore, you should avoid use of potassium-sparing diuretic and hydrochlorothiazide combinations during the first month of breast-feeding.

Children—Studies on this combination medicine have been done only in adult patients, and there is no specific information comparing use of potassium-sparing diuretic and hydrochlorothiazide combinations in children with use in other age groups.

Older adults—Dizziness or lightheadedness and signs and symptoms of too much potassium in the body or too little potassium in the body may be more likely to occur in the elderly, who are more sensitive than younger adults to the effects of this medicine.

Other medicines—Although certain medicines should not be used together at all, in other cases two different medicines may be used together even if an interaction might occur. In these cases, your doctor may want to change the dose, or other precautions may be necessary. When you are taking potassium-sparing diuretics and hydrochlorothiazide, it is especially important that your health care professional know if you are taking any of the following:

- Angiotensin-converting enzyme (ACE) inhibitors (benazepril [e.g., Lotensin], captopril [e.g., Capoten], enalapril [e.g., Vasotec], fosinopril [e.g., Monopril], lisinopril [e.g., Prinivil, Zestril], quinapril [e.g., Accupril], ramipril [e.g., Altace]) or
- Cyclosporine (e.g., Sandimmune) or
- Potassium-containing medicines or supplements—Use with potassium-sparing diuretic and hydrochlorothiazide combinations may cause high blood levels of potassium, which may increase the chance of side effects

- Cholestyramine or
- Colestipol—Use with potassium-sparing diuretic and hydrochlorothiazide combinations may prevent the diuretic from working properly; take the diuretic at least 1 hour before or 4 hours after cholestyramine or colestipol

- Digitalis glycosides (heart medicine)—Use with diuretics may cause high blood levels of digoxin, which may increase the chance of side effects

- Lithium (e.g., Lithane)—Use with diuretics may cause high blood levels of lithium, which may increase the chance of side effects

Other medical problems—The presence of other medical problems may affect the use of potassium-sparing diuretics and hydrochlorothiazide. Make sure you tell your doctor if you have any other medical problems, especially:

- Diabetes mellitus (sugar diabetes) or
- Kidney disease or
- Liver disease—Higher blood levels of potassium may occur, which may increase the chance of side effects

- Gout (history of) or
- Kidney stones (history of)—Triamterene and hydrochlorothiazide combination may make these conditions worse

- Heart or blood vessel disease—These medicines may cause high cholesterol levels or high triglyceride levels

- Lupus erythematosus (history of) or
- Pancreatitis (inflammation of pancreas)—Potassium-sparing diuretic and hydrochlorothiazide combinations may make these conditions worse

- Menstrual problems in women or breast enlargement in men—Spironolactone and hydrochlorothiazide combination may make these conditions worse

Proper Use of This Medicine

This medicine may cause you to have an unusual feeling of tiredness when you begin to take it. You may also notice an increase in the amount of urine or in your frequency of urination. After you have taken the medicine for a while, these effects should lessen. In general, to keep the increase in urine from affecting your sleep:

- If you are to take a single dose a day, take it in the morning after breakfast.
- If you are to take more than one dose a day, take the last dose no later than 6 p.m., unless otherwise directed by your doctor.

However, it is best to plan your dose or doses according to a schedule that will least affect your personal activities and sleep. Ask your health care professional to help you plan the best time to take this medicine.

To help you remember to take your medicine, try to get into the habit of taking it at the same time each day.

If this medicine upsets your stomach, it may be taken with meals or milk. If stomach upset (nausea, vomiting, stomach pain, or cramps) continues, check with your doctor.

For patients taking this medicine for *high blood pressure:*

- In addition to the use of the medicine your doctor has prescribed, treatment for your high blood pressure may include weight control and care in the types of foods you eat, especially foods high in sodium. Your doctor will tell you which of these are most important for you. You should check with your doctor before changing your diet.
- Many patients who have high blood pressure will not notice any signs of the problem. In fact, many may feel normal. It is very important that you *take your medicine exactly as directed* and that you keep your appointments with your doctor even if you feel well.
- Remember that this medicine will not cure your high blood pressure but it does help control it. Therefore, you must continue to take it as directed if you expect to lower your blood pressure and keep it down. *You may have to take high blood pressure medicine for the rest of your life.* If high blood pressure is not treated, it can cause serious problems such as heart failure, blood vessel disease, stroke, or kidney disease.

Dosing—The dose of potassium-sparing diuretic and hydrochlorothiazide combinations will be different for different patients. *Follow your doctor's orders or the directions on the label.* The following information includes only the average doses of potassium-sparing diuretic and hydrochlorothiazide combinations. *If your dose is different, do not change it unless your doctor tells you to do so.*

The number of capsules or tablets that you take depends on the strength of the medicine. Also, *the number of doses you take each day depends on the strength of the medicine and the medical problem for which you are taking potassium-sparing diuretic and hydrochlorothiazide combinations.*

For amiloride and hydrochlorothiazide combination
- For *oral* dosage form (tablets):
  —For high blood pressure or lowering the amount of water in the body:
    - Adults—1 or 2 tablets a day.
    - Children—Dose must be determined by your doctor.

For spironolactone and hydrochlorothiazide combination
- For *oral* dosage form (tablets):
  —For high blood pressure or lowering the amount of water in the body:
    - Adults—1 to 4 tablets a day.
    - Children—Dose is based on body weight and must be determined by your doctor.

For triamterene and hydrochlorothiazide combination
- For *oral* dosage form (capsules):
  —For high blood pressure or lowering the amount of water in the body:
    - Adults—1 or 2 capsules once a day.
    - Children—Dose must be determined by your doctor.
- For *oral* dosage form (tablets):
  —For high blood pressure or lowering the amount of water in the body:
    - Adults—1 to 4 tablets a day, depending on the strength of your tablet.
    - Children—Dose must be determined by your doctor.

Missed dose—If you miss a dose of this medicine, take it as soon as possible. However, if it is almost time for your next dose, skip the missed dose and go back to your regular dosing schedule. Do not double doses.

Storage—To store this medicine:
- Keep out of the reach of children.
- Store away from heat and direct light.
- Do not store in the bathroom, near the kitchen sink, or in other damp places. Heat or moisture may cause the medicine to break down.
- Do not keep outdated medicine or medicine no longer needed. Be sure that any discarded medicine is out of the reach of children.

Precautions While Using This Medicine

It is important that your doctor check your progress at regular visits to make sure that this medicine is working properly.

This medicine may cause a loss or increase of potassium in your body. Your doctor may have special instructions about whether or not you need to eat or drink foods or beverages that have a high potassium content (for example, orange or other citrus fruit juices), taking a potassium supplement, or using salt substitutes. Since too much potassium can be harmful, it is important not to change your diet on your own. Tell your doctor if you are already on a special diet (as for diabetes). Since salt substitutes and low-sodium milk may contain potassium, do not use them unless told to do so by your doctor. Check with your health care professional if you need a list of foods that are high in potassium or if you have any questions.

Check with your doctor if you become sick and have severe or continuing vomiting or diarrhea. These problems may cause you to lose additional water and potassium and lead to low blood pressure.

For *diabetic patients:*
- Hydrochlorothiazide (contained in this combination medicine) may raise blood sugar levels. While you are taking this medicine, be especially careful in testing for sugar in your blood or urine.

Potassium-sparing diuretics and hydrochlorothiazide may cause your skin to be more sensitive to sunlight than it is normally. Exposure to sunlight, even for brief periods of time, may cause a skin rash, itching, redness or other discoloration of the skin, or a severe sunburn. When you begin taking this medicine:
- Stay out of direct sunlight, especially between the hours of 10:00 a.m. and 3:00 p.m., if possible.
- Wear protective clothing, including a hat. Also, wear sunglasses.
- Apply a sun block product that has a skin protection factor (SPF) of at least 15. Some patients may require a product with a higher SPF number, especially if they have a fair complexion. If you have any questions about this, check with your health care professional.
- Apply a sun block lipstick that has an SPF of at least 15 to protect your lips.
- Do not use a sunlamp or tanning bed or booth.

If you have a severe reaction from the sun, check with your doctor.

Before having any kind of surgery (including dental surgery) or emergency treatment, tell the medical doctor or dentist in charge that you are taking this medicine.

For patients taking *triamterene and hydrochlorothiazide combination:*
- Do not change brands of triamterene and hydrochlorothiazide without first checking with your doctor. Different products may not work the same way. If you refill your medicine and it looks different, check with your pharmacist.

For patients taking this medicine for *high blood pressure:*
- *Do not take other medicines unless they have been discussed with your doctor.* This especially includes over-the-counter (nonprescription) medicines for appetite control, asthma, colds, cough, hay fever, or sinus problems, since they may tend to increase your blood pressure.

Tell the doctor in charge that you are taking this medicine before you have any medical tests. The results of some tests may be affected by this medicine.

Side Effects of This Medicine

In rats, spironolactone has been found to increase the risk of development of tumors. However, the doses given were many times the dose of spironolactone given to humans. It is not known whether spironolactone causes tumors in humans.

Along with its needed effects, a medicine may cause some unwanted effects. Although not all of these side effects may occur, if they do occur they may need medical attention.

Check with your doctor as soon as possible if any of the following side effects occur:
Rare
　Black, tarry stools; blood in urine or stools; cough or hoarseness; fever or chills; joint pain; lower back or side pain; painful or difficult urination; pinpoint red spots on skin; skin rash or hives; stomach pain (severe) with nausea and vomiting; unusual bleeding or bruising; yellow eyes or skin

Signs and symptoms of changes in potassium
　Confusion; dryness of mouth; increased thirst; irregular heartbeat; mood or mental changes; muscle cramps or pain; numbness or tingling in hands, feet, or lips; shortness of breath or difficulty breathing; unusual tiredness or weakness; weak pulse; weakness or heaviness of legs

Reported for triamterene only (rare)
　Bright red tongue; burning, inflamed feeling in tongue; cracked corners of mouth

Other side effects may occur that usually do not need medical attention. These side effects may go away during treatment as your body adjusts to the medicine. However, check with your doctor if any of the following side effects continue or are bothersome:

More common (less common with triamterene)
Loss of appetite; nausea and vomiting; stomach cramps and diarrhea; upset stomach

Less common
Decreased sexual ability; dizziness or lightheadedness when getting up from a lying or sitting position; headache; increased sensitivity of skin to sunlight

Reported for amiloride only (less common)
Constipation

Reported for spironolactone only (less common)
Breast tenderness in females; deepening of voice in females; enlargement of breasts in males; increased hair growth in females; irregular menstrual periods; sweating

Spironolactone sometimes causes enlarged breasts in males, especially when they take large doses of it for a long time. Breasts usually decrease in size gradually over several months after this medicine is stopped. If you have any questions about this, check with your doctor.

Other side effects not listed above may also occur in some patients. If you notice any other effects, check with your doctor.

Revised: 08/03/94

DIURETICS, THIAZIDE   Systemic

Commonly used brand name(s):

In the U.S.—

Aquatensen[6]	Metahydrin[10]
Diucardin[5]	Microzide[4]
Diulo[7]	Mykrox[7]
Diuril[2]	Naqua[10]
Enduron[6]	Naturetin[1]
Esidrix[4]	Oretic[4]
Hydro-chlor[4]	Renese[8]
Hydro-D[4]	Saluron[5]
HydroDIURIL[4]	Thalitone[3]
Hydromox[9]	Trichlorex[10]
Hygroton[3]	Zaroxolyn[7]

In Canada—

Apo-Chlorthalidone[3]	Neo-Codema[4]
Apo-Hydro[4]	Novo-Hydrazide[4]
Diuchlor H[4]	Novo-Thalidone[3]
Duretic[6]	Uridon[3]
HydroDIURIL[4]	Urozide[4]
Hygroton[3]	Zaroxolyn[7]
Naturetin[1]	

Note: For quick reference, the following thiazide diuretics are numbered to match the corresponding brand names.

This information applies to the following medicines:
1. Bendroflumethiazide (ben-droe-floo-meth-EYE-a-zide)
2. Chlorothiazide (klor-oh-THYE-a-zide) †‡
3. Chlorthalidone (klor-THAL-i-doan) ‡§
4. Hydrochlorothiazide (hye-droe-klor-oh-THYE-a-zide) ‡§
5. Hydroflumethiazide (hye-droe-floo-meth-EYE-a-zide) †‡
6. Methyclothiazide (meth-ee-kloe-THYE-a-zide) ‡

7. Metolazone (me-TOLE-a-zone)
8. Polythiazide (pol-i-THYE-a-zide) †
9. Quinethazone (kwin-ETH-a-zone) †
10. Trichlormethiazide (trye-klor-meth-EYE-a-zide) †‡

†Not commercially available in Canada.
‡Generic name product may be available in the U.S.
§Generic name product may be available in Canada.

Description

Thiazide or thiazide-like diuretics are commonly used to treat high blood pressure (hypertension). High blood pressure adds to the workload of the heart and arteries. If it continues for a long time, the heart and arteries may not function properly. This can damage the blood vessels of the brain, heart, and kidneys, resulting in a stroke, heart failure, or kidney failure. High blood pressure may also increase the risk of heart attacks. These problems may be less likely to occur if blood pressure is controlled.

Thiazide diuretics are also used to help reduce the amount of water in the body by increasing the flow of urine. They may also be used for other conditions as determined by your doctor.

Thiazide diuretics are available only with your doctor's prescription, in the following dosage forms:

Oral
Bendroflumethiazide
• Tablets (U.S. and Canada)
Chlorothiazide
• Oral suspension (U.S.)
• Tablets (U.S.)
Chlorthalidone
• Tablets (U.S. and Canada)
Hydrochlorothiazide
• Capsules (U.S.)
• Oral solution (U.S.)
• Tablets (U.S. and Canada)
Hydroflumethiazide
• Tablets (U.S.)
Methyclothiazide
• Tablets (U.S. and Canada)
Metolazone
• Tablets (U.S. and Canada)
Polythiazide
• Tablets (U.S.)
Quinethazone
• Tablets (U.S.)
Trichlormethiazide
• Tablets (U.S.)

Parenteral
Chlorothiazide
• Injection (U.S.)

Before Using This Medicine

In deciding to use a medicine, the risks of taking the medicine must be weighed against the good it will do. This is a decision you and your doctor will make. For thiazide diuretics, the following should be considered:

Allergies—Tell your doctor if you have ever had any unusual or allergic reaction to sulfonamides (sulfa drugs), bumetanide, furosemide, acetazolamide, dichlorphenamide, methazolamide, or to any of the thiazide diuretics. Also tell

your health care professional if you are allergic to any other substances, such as foods, preservatives, or dyes.

Pregnancy—When this medicine is used during pregnancy, it may cause side effects including jaundice, blood problems, and low potassium in the newborn infant. In addition, although this medicine has not been shown to cause birth defects or other problems in animals, studies have not been done in humans.

In general, diuretics are not useful for normal swelling of feet and hands that occurs during pregnancy. They should not be taken during pregnancy unless recommended by your doctor.

Breast-feeding—Thiazide diuretics pass into breast milk. These medicines also may decrease the flow of breast milk. Therefore, you should avoid use of thiazide diuretics during the first month of breast-feeding.

Children—Although there is no specific information comparing the use of thiazide diuretics in children with use in other age groups, these medicines are not expected to cause different side effects or problems in children than they do in adults. However, extra caution may be necessary in infants with jaundice, because these medicines can make the condition worse.

Older adults—Dizziness or lightheadedness and signs of too much potassium loss may be more likely to occur in the elderly, who are more sensitive than younger adults to the effects of thiazide diuretics.

Other medicines—Although certain medicines should not be used together at all, in other cases two different medicines may be used together even if an interaction might occur. In these cases, your doctor may want to change the dose, or other precautions may be necessary. When you are taking thiazide diuretics, it is especially important that your health care professional know if you are taking any of the following:

- Cholestyramine or
- Colestipol—Use with thiazide diuretics may prevent the diuretic from working properly; take the diuretic at least 1 hour before or 4 hours after cholestyramine or colestipol
- Digitalis glycosides (heart medicine)—Use with thiazide diuretics may cause high blood levels of digoxin, which may increase the chance of side effects
- Lithium (e.g., Lithane)—Use with thiazide diuretics may cause high blood levels of lithium, which may increase the chance of side effects

Other medical problems—The presence of other medical problems may affect the use of thiazide diuretics. Make sure you tell your doctor if you have any other medical problems, especially:

- Diabetes mellitus (sugar diabetes)—Thiazide diuretics may increase the amount of sugar in the blood
- Gout (history of) or
- Lupus erythematosus (history of) or
- Pancreatitis (inflammation of the pancreas)—Thiazide diuretics may make these conditions worse
- Heart or blood vessel disease—Thiazide diuretics may cause high cholesterol levels or high triglyceride levels
- Liver disease or
- Kidney disease (severe)—Higher blood levels of the thiazide diuretic may occur, which may prevent the thiazide diuretic from working properly

Proper Use of This Medicine

This medicine may cause you to have an unusual feeling of tiredness when you begin to take it. You may also notice an increase in the amount of urine or in your frequency of urination. After you have taken the medicine for a while, these effects should lessen. In general, to keep the increase in urine from affecting your sleep:

- If you are to take a single dose a day, take it in the morning after breakfast.
- If you are to take more than one dose a day, take the last dose no later than 6 p.m., unless otherwise directed by your doctor.

However, it is best to plan your dose or doses according to a schedule that will least affect your personal activities and sleep. Ask your health care professional to help you plan the best time to take this medicine.

Take each dose at the same time each day. This medicine works best if there is a constant amount in the blood.

For patients taking this medicine for *high blood pressure:*

- In addition to the use of the medicine your doctor has prescribed, appropriate treatment for your high blood pressure may include weight control and care in the types of foods you eat, especially foods high in sodium. Your doctor will tell you which factors are most important for you. You should check with your doctor before changing your diet.
- Many patients who have high blood pressure will not notice any signs of the problem. In fact, many may feel normal. It is very important that you *take your medicine exactly as directed* and that you keep your appointments with your doctor even if you feel well.
- Remember that this medicine will not cure your high blood pressure but it does help control it. Therefore, you must continue to take it as directed if you expect to lower your blood pressure and keep it down. *You may have to take high blood pressure medicine for the rest of your life.* If high blood pressure is not treated, it can cause serious problems such as heart failure, blood vessel disease, stroke, or kidney disease.

For patients taking the *oral liquid form of hydrochlorothiazide*, which comes in a dropper bottle:

- This medicine is to be taken by mouth. The amount you should take is to be measured only with the specially marked dropper.

Dosing—The dose of these medicines will be different for different patients. *Follow your doctor's orders or the directions on the label.* The following information includes only the average doses of these medicines. *If your dose is different, do not change it* unless your doctor tells you to do so.

The number of tablets or teaspoonfuls of solution or suspension that you take depends on the strength of the medicine. Also, *the number of doses you take each day, the time allowed between doses, and the length of time you take the medicine depend on the medical problem for which you are taking thiazide diuretics.*

For bendroflumethiazide
- For *oral* dosage form (tablets):
  —To lower the amount of water in the body:
    - Adults—At first, 2.5 to 10 milligrams (mg) one or two times a day. Then, your doctor may lower your

dose to 2.5 to 5 mg once a day. Or your doctor may want you to take this dose once every other day or once a day for only three to five days out of the week.

- Children—Dose is based on body weight and must be determined by your doctor. The usual dose is 50 to 100 micrograms (mcg) per kilogram (kg) (22.7 to 45.4 mcg per pound) of body weight once a day.

—For high blood pressure:

- Adults—2.5 to 20 mg a day. This may be taken as a single dose or divided into two doses.
- Children—Dose is based on body weight and must be determined by your doctor. The usual dose is 50 to 400 mcg per kg (22.7 to 181.8 mcg per pound) of body weight a day. This may be taken as a single dose or divided into two doses.

For chlorothiazide

- For *oral* dosage forms (oral suspension or tablets):
  —To lower the amount of water in the body:
  - Adults—500 to 1000 milligrams (mg) every twelve to twenty-four hours.
  - Children—Dose is based on body weight and must be determined by your doctor.
  —For high blood pressure:
  - Adults—500 to 1000 mg a day. This may be taken as a single dose or divided into smaller doses.
  - Children—Dose is based on body weight and must be determined by your doctor.

- For *injection* dosage form:
  —To lower the amount of water in the body:
  - Adults—500 to 1000 mg once or twice daily injected into a vein.
  - Children—Use and dose must be determined by your doctor.
  —For high blood pressure:
  - Adults—500 to 1000 mg once or twice daily, injected into a vein.
  - Children—Use and dose must be determined by your doctor.

For chlorthalidone

- For *oral* dosage form (tablets):
  —To lower the amount of water in the body:
  - Adults—30 to 120 milligrams (mg) once a day or on alternate days.
  - Children—Dose is based on body weight and must be determined by your doctor.
  —For high blood pressure:
  - Adults—15 to 50 mg once a day.
  - Children—Dose is based on body weight and must be determined by your doctor.

For hydrochlorothiazide

- For *oral* dosage forms (oral solution or tablets):
  —To lower the amount of water in the body:
  - Adults—25 to 100 milligrams (mg) one or two times a day. Or your doctor may want you to take this dose once every other day or once a day for three to five days out of the week.
  - Children—Dose is based on body weight and must be determined by your doctor.
  —For high blood pressure:
  - Adults—12.5 to 100 mg a day. This may be taken as a single dose or divided into two doses.

- Children—Dose is based on body weight and must be determined by your doctor.

For hydroflumethiazide

- For *oral* dosage form (tablets):
  —To lower the amount of water in the body:
  - Adults—25 to 100 milligrams (mg) one or two times a day. Or your doctor may want you to take this dose once every other day or once a day for three to five days out of the week.
  - Children—Dose is based on body weight and must be determined by your doctor.
  —For high blood pressure:
  - Adults—50 to 100 mg a day. This may be taken as a single dose or divided into two doses.
  - Children—Dose is based on body weight and must be determined by your doctor.

For methyclothiazide

- For *oral* dosage form (tablets):
  —To lower the amount of water in the body:
  - Adults—2.5 to 10 milligrams (mg) once a day. Or your doctor may want you to take this dose once every other day or once a day for three to five days out of the week.
  - Children—Dose is based on body weight and must be determined by your doctor.
  —For high blood pressure:
  - Adults—2.5 to 5 mg once a day.
  - Children—Dose is based on body weight and must be determined by your doctor.

For metolazone

- For *oral* dosage form (*extended* metolazone tablets):
  —To lower the amount of water in the body:
  - Adults—5 to 20 milligrams (mg) once a day.
  - Children—Dose must be determined by your doctor.
  —For high blood pressure:
  - Adults—2.5 to 5 mg once a day.
  - Children—Dose must be determined by your doctor.

- For *oral* dosage form (*prompt* metolazone tablets):
  —For high blood pressure:
  - Adults—At first, 500 micrograms (mcg) once a day. Then, 500 to 1000 mcg once a day.
  - Children—Dose must be determined by your doctor.

For polythiazide

- For *oral* dosage form (tablets):
  —To lower the amount of water in the body:
  - Adults—1 to 4 milligrams (mg) once a day. Or your doctor may want you to take this dose once every other day or once a day for three to five days out of the week.
  - Children—Dose is based on body weight and must be determined by your doctor.
  —For high blood pressure:
  - Adults—2 to 4 mg once a day.
  - Children—Dose is based on body weight and must be determined by your doctor.

For quinethazone

- For *oral* dosage form (tablets):
  —To lower the amount of water in the body or for high blood pressure:

- Adults—50 to 200 milligrams (mg) a day. This may be taken as a single dose or divided into two doses.
- Children—Dose must be determined by your doctor.

For trichlormethiazide
- For *oral* dosage form (tablets):
  —To lower the amount of water in the body:
    - Adults—1 to 4 milligrams (mg) once a day. Or your doctor may want you to take this dose once every other day or once a day for three to five days out of the week.
    - Children—Dose is based on body weight and must be determined by your doctor.
  —For high blood pressure:
    - Adults—1 to 4 mg once a day.
    - Children—Dose is based on body weight and must be determined by your doctor.

Missed dose—If you miss a dose of this medicine, take it as soon as possible. However, if it is almost time for your next dose, skip the missed dose and go back to your regular dosing schedule. Do not double doses.

Storage—To store this medicine:
- Keep out of the reach of children.
- Store away from heat and direct light.
- Do not store in the bathroom, near the kitchen sink, or in other damp places. Heat or moisture may cause the medicine to break down.
- Keep the oral liquid form of this medicine from freezing.
- Do not keep outdated medicine or medicine no longer needed. Be sure that any discarded medicine is out of the reach of children.

Precautions While Using This Medicine

It is important that your doctor check your progress at regular visits to make sure that this medicine is working properly.

This medicine may cause a loss of potassium from your body:
- To help prevent this, your doctor may want you to:
  —eat or drink foods that have a high potassium content (for example, orange or other citrus fruit juices), or
  —take a potassium supplement, or
  —take another medicine to help prevent the loss of the potassium in the first place.
- It is very important to follow these directions. Also, it is important not to change your diet on your own. This is more important if you are already on a special diet (as for diabetes), or if you are taking a potassium supplement or a medicine to reduce potassium loss. Extra potassium may not be necessary and, in some cases, too much potassium could be harmful.

Check with your doctor if you become sick and have severe or continuing vomiting or diarrhea. These problems may cause you to lose additional water and potassium.

For *diabetic patients:*
- Thiazide diuretics may raise blood sugar levels. While you are using this medicine, be especially careful in testing for sugar in your blood or urine.

Thiazide diuretics may cause your skin to be more sensitive to sunlight than it is normally. Exposure to sunlight, even for brief periods of time, may cause a skin rash, itching, redness or other discoloration of the skin, or a severe sunburn. When you begin taking this medicine:
- Stay out of direct sunlight, especially between the hours of 10:00 a.m. and 3:00 p.m., if possible.
- Wear protective clothing, including a hat. Also, wear sunglasses.
- Apply a sun block product that has a skin protection factor (SPF) of at least 15. Some patients may require a product with a higher SPF number, especially if they have a fair complexion. If you have any questions about this, check with your health care professional.
- Apply a sun block lipstick that has an SPF of at least 15 to protect your lips.
- Do not use a sunlamp or tanning bed or booth.

If you have a severe reaction from the sun, check with your doctor.

For patients taking this medicine for *high blood pressure:*
- *Do not take other medicines unless they have been discussed with your doctor.* This especially includes over-the-counter (nonprescription) medicines for appetite control, asthma, colds, cough, hay fever, or sinus problems, since they may tend to increase your blood pressure.

Side Effects of This Medicine

Along with its needed effects, a medicine may cause some unwanted effects. Although not all of these side effects may occur, if they do occur they may need medical attention.

Check with your doctor as soon as possible if any of the following side effects occur:
Rare
 Black, tarry stools; blood in urine or stools; cough or hoarseness; fever or chills; joint pain; lower back or side pain; painful or difficult urination; pinpoint red spots on skin; skin rash or hives; stomach pain (severe) with nausea and vomiting; unusual bleeding or bruising; yellow eyes or skin

Signs and symptoms of too much potassium loss
 Dryness of mouth; increased thirst; irregular heartbeat; mood or mental changes; muscle cramps or pain; nausea or vomiting; unusual tiredness or weakness; weak pulse

Signs and symptoms of too much sodium loss
 Confusion; convulsions; decreased mental activity; irritability; muscle cramps; unusual tiredness or weakness

Other side effects may occur that usually do not need medical attention. These side effects may go away during treatment as your body adjusts to the medicine. However, check with your doctor if any of the following side effects continue or are bothersome:
Less common
 Decreased sexual ability; diarrhea; dizziness or lightheadedness when getting up from a lying or sitting position; increased sensitivity of skin to sunlight; loss of appetite; upset stomach

Other side effects not listed above may also occur in some patients. If you notice any other effects, check with your doctor.

Additional Information

Once a medicine has been approved for marketing for a certain use, experience may show that it is also useful for other medical problems. Although these uses are not specifically included in product labeling, thiazide diuretics are used in certain patients with the following medical conditions:

- Diabetes insipidus (water diabetes)
- Kidney stones (calcium-containing)

For patients taking this medicine for *diabetes insipidus (water diabetes):*

- Some thiazide diuretics are used in the treatment of diabetes insipidus (water diabetes). In patients with water diabetes, this medicine causes a decrease in the flow of urine and helps the body hold water. Thus, the information given above about increased urine flow will not apply to you.

Other than the above information, there is no additional information relating to proper use, precautions, or side effects for these uses.

Revised: 06/07/92
Interim revision: 06/30/94; 06/12/98

DOCETAXEL   Systemic

Commonly used brand name(s):

In the U.S.—
Taxotere

In Canada—
Taxotere

Description

Docetaxel (doe-se-TAX-el) belongs to the group of medicines called antineoplastics. It is used to treat breast cancer and non-small cell lung cancer.

Docetaxel interferes with the growth of cancer cells, which are eventually destroyed. Since the growth of normal body cells may also be affected by docetaxel, other effects will also occur. Some of these may be serious and must be reported to your doctor. Other effects may not be serious but may cause concern. Some effects may not occur for months or years after the medicine is used.

Docetaxel may also be used to treat other conditions as determined by your doctor.

Before you begin treatment with docetaxel, you and your doctor should talk about the good this medicine will do as well as the risks of using it.

Docetaxel is to be administered only by or under the immediate supervision of your doctor. It is available in the following dosage form:

Parenteral
- Injection (U.S. and Canada)

Before Using This Medicine

In deciding to use a medicine, the risks of taking the medicine must be weighed against the good it will do. This is a decision you and your doctor will make. For docetaxel, the following should be considered:

Allergies—Tell your doctor if you have ever had any unusual or allergic reaction to docetaxel.

Pregnancy—Tell your doctor if you are pregnant or if you intend to become pregnant. Studies in rats and rabbits have shown that docetaxel causes miscarriages and deaths of the fetus, as well as problems in the mother.

Be sure that you have discussed this with your doctor before taking this medicine. It is best to use some kind of birth control while you are receiving docetaxel. Tell your doctor right away if you think you have become pregnant while receiving docetaxel.

Breast-feeding—It is not known whether docetaxel passes into breast milk. However, because this medicine may cause serious side effects, breast-feeding is generally not recommended while you are receiving it.

Children—Docetaxel has been studied in a limited number of children. The study showed that children are especially sensitive to the effects of docetaxel and cannot be given usual doses of the medicine.

Older adults—This medicine has been tested in elderly patients and has not been shown to cause different side effects or problems in older people than it does in younger adults.

Other medicines—Although certain medicines should not be used together at all, in other cases two different medicines may be used together even if an interaction might occur. In these cases, your doctor may want to change the dose, or other precautions may be necessary. When you are receiving docetaxel, it is especially important that your health care professional know if you are taking any of the following:

- Amphotericin B by injection (e.g., Fungizone) or
- Antithyroid agents (medicine for overactive thyroid) or
- Azathioprine (e.g., Imuran) or
- Chloramphenicol (e.g., Chloromycetin) or
- Colchicine or
- Flucytosine (e.g., Ancobon) or
- Ganciclovir (e.g., Cytovene) or
- Interferon (e.g., Intron A, Roferon-A) or
- Plicamycin (e.g., Mithracin) or
- Zidovudine (e.g., AZT, Retrovir) or
- If you have ever been treated with x-rays or cancer medicines—Docetaxel may increase the effects of these medicines or radiation therapy on the blood

- Erythromycins (medicine for infection) or
- Ketoconazole (e.g., Nizoral) or
- Midazolam (e.g., Versed) or
- Orphenadrine (e.g., Norflex) or
- Testosterone (male hormone) or
- Troleandomycin—Higher blood levels of docetaxel may occur, increasing the chance of serious side effects

Other medical problems—The presence of other medical problems may affect the use of docetaxel. Make sure you tell your doctor if you have any other medical problems, especially:

- Alcohol abuse or history of—The risk of some side effects affecting the muscles and nerves may be increased

- Chickenpox (including recent exposure) or
- Herpes zoster (shingles)—Risk of severe disease affecting other parts of the body

- Fluid in lungs—docetaxel may make your condition worse
- Infection—Docetaxel may decrease your body's ability to fight infection
- Liver disease—The chance of serious side effects is greatly increased

Proper Use of This Medicine

This medicine often causes nausea and vomiting, which is usually mild. However, it is very important that you continue to receive the medicine even if you begin to feel ill. Ask your health care professional for ways to lessen these effects.

Your doctor may direct you to take a corticosteroid medicine such as dexamethasone (e.g., Decadron), starting the day before you receive an injection of docetaxel and continuing for a few days after a docetaxel treatment. This other medicine decreases the chance of an allergic reaction to docetaxel and certain other side effects. *It is very important that you take each dose of the corticosteroid medicine as directed.*

Dosing—The dose of docetaxel will be different for different patients. The dose that is used may depend on a number of things, including what the medicine is being used for, the patient's size, and whether or not other medicines are also being taken. *If you are receiving docetaxel at home, follow your doctor's orders or the directions on the label.* If you have any questions about the proper dose of docetaxel, ask your doctor.

Precautions While Using This Medicine

It is very important that your doctor check your progress at regular visits to make sure that this medicine is working properly and to check for unwanted effects.

While you are being treated with docetaxel, and after you stop treatment with it, *do not have any immunizations (vaccinations) without your doctor's approval.* Docetaxel may lower your body's resistance and there is a chance you might get the infection the immunization is meant to prevent. In addition, other persons living in your household should not take oral polio vaccine since there is a chance they could pass the polio virus on to you. Also, avoid persons who have taken oral polio vaccine within the past several months. Do not get close to them and do not stay in the same room with them for very long. If you cannot take these precautions, you should consider wearing a protective face mask that covers the nose and mouth.

Docetaxel can temporarily lower the number of white blood cells in your blood, increasing the chance of getting an infection. It can also lower the number of platelets, which are necessary for proper blood clotting. If this occurs, there are certain precautions you can take, especially when your blood count is low, to reduce the risk of infection or bleeding:

- If you can, avoid people with infections. *Check with your doctor immediately* if you think you are getting an infection or if you get a fever or chills, cough or hoarseness, lower back or side pain, or painful or difficult urination.
- *Check with your doctor immediately* if you notice any unusual bleeding or bruising; black, tarry stools; blood in urine or stools; or pinpoint red spots on your skin.
- Be careful when using a regular toothbrush, dental floss, or toothpick. Your medical doctor, dentist, or nurse may recommend other ways to clean your teeth and gums.

Check with your medical doctor before having any dental work done.
- Do not touch your eyes or the inside of your nose unless you have just washed your hands and have not touched anything else in the meantime.
- Be careful not to cut yourself when you are using sharp objects such as a safety razor or fingernail or toenail cutters.
- Avoid contact sports or other situations where bruising or injury could occur.

Side Effects of This Medicine

Along with its needed effects, a medicine may cause some unwanted effects. Some side effects will have signs or symptoms that you can see or feel. Your doctor may watch for others by doing certain tests.

Also, because of the way these medicines act on the body, there is a chance that they might cause other unwanted effects that may not occur until months or years after the medicine is used. These delayed effects may include certain types of cancer. Discuss these possible effects with your doctor.

Check with your doctor immediately if any of the following side effects occur:
Less common
  Black, tarry stools; blood in urine or stools; cough or hoarseness (accompanied by fever or chills); difficult or painful urination (accompanied by fever or chills); fever or chills; lower back or side pain (accompanied by fever or chills); noisy, rattling breathing; pinpoint red spots on skin; troubled breathing while at rest; unusual bleeding or bruising
Rare
  Chest pain; fast or irregular heartbeat; shortness of breath

Docetaxel sometimes causes allergic reactions, especially during the first few treatments. *Tell your doctor or nurse right away if you notice back pain or itching during an injection.* Your doctor or nurse will be watching out for other signs of an allergic reaction while you are receiving this medicine, and will be ready to treat any serious effects right away.

Check with your doctor as soon as possible if any of the following side effects occur:
More common
  Swelling of abdomen, face, fingers, hands, feet, or lower legs; unusual tiredness or weakness; weight gain
Less common
  Red, scaly, swollen, or peeling areas of skin (severe)
Rare
  Decrease in blood pressure, sometimes with dizziness or fainting; increase in blood pressure, sometimes with dizziness or headaches

This medicine may also cause the following side effects that your doctor will watch out for:
More common
  Anemia; low white blood cell count
Less common
  High or low blood pressure; low platelet count in blood

Other side effects may occur that usually do not need medical attention. These side effects may go away during treatment as your body adjusts to the medicine. Also, your health care professional may be able to tell you about ways to prevent or reduce some of these side effects. Check with your health care professional if any of the following side effects continue or are bothersome or if you have any questions about them:

More common

> Burning, numbness, tingling, or pain in arms, hands, legs, or feet; diarrhea; nausea; skin rash or redness (mild); sores or ulcers on the lips or tongue or inside the mouth; weakness in arms, hands, legs, or feet

Less common

> Change in color of fingernails or toenails; dry, red, hot, or irritated skin at place of injection; headache; loosening or loss of fingernails or toenails, sometimes painful; pain in joints or muscles; pain, swelling, or lump under the skin at place of injection; vomiting

This medicine usually causes a temporary loss of hair. After treatment with docetaxel has ended, normal hair growth should return.

Other side effects not listed above may also occur in some patients. If you notice any other effects, check with your doctor.

Additional Information

Once a medicine has been approved for marketing for a certain use, experience may show that it is also useful for other medical problems. Although these uses are not included in the product labeling, docetaxel is used in certain patients with the following medical conditions:

- Bladder cancer
- Head and neck cancer
- Lung cancer, small cell
- Ovarian cancer
- Prostate cancer

Other than the above information, there is no additional information relating to proper use, precautions, or side effects for these uses.

Developed: 09/17/1997
Revised: 08/16/2000

DOCOSANOL   Topical—
INTRODUCTORY VERSION

Commonly used brand name(s):

In the U.S.—
Abreva

Description

Docosanol (doe-KOE-san-ole) belongs to the family of medicines called antivirals. Antivirals are used to treat infections caused by viruses. Usually they work for only one kind or group of virus infections.

Topical docosanol is used to treat the symptoms of herpes simplex virus infections around the mouth. Although topical docosanol will not cure herpes simplex, it may help relieve the pain and discomfort and may help the sores (if any) heal faster.

Docosanol is available over the counter in the following dosage form:

Topical
- Cream (U.S.)

Before Using This Medicine

In deciding to use a medicine, the risks of using the medicine must be weighed against the good it will do. This is a decision you and your doctor will make. For docosanol, the following should be considered:

Allergies—Tell your doctor if you have ever had any unusual or allergic reaction to docosanol. Also tell your health care professional if you are allergic to any other substances, such as preservatives or dyes.

Pregnancy—Topical docosanol has not been studied in pregnant women. However, this medicine has not been shown to cause birth defects or other problems in animal studies using rats or rabbits.

Breast-feeding—It is not known whether docosanol passes into breast milk. Although most medicines pass into breast milk in small amounts, many of them may be used safely while breast-feeding. Mothers who are taking this medicine and who wish to breast-feed should discuss this with their doctor.

Children—Although there is no specific information comparing use of docosanol in children with use in other age groups, this medicine is not expected to cause different side effects or problems in children than it does in adults.

Older adults—Many medicines have not been studied specifically in older people. Therefore, it may not be known whether they work exactly the same way they do in younger adults or if they cause different side effects or problems in older people. There is no specific information comparing use of docosanol in the elderly with use in other age groups.

Other medicines—Although certain medicines should not be used together at all, in other cases two different medicines may be used together even if an interaction might occur. In these cases, your doctor may want to change the dose, or other precautions may be necessary. Tell your health care professional if you are using any other topical prescription or nonprescription OTC medicine that is to be applied to the same area of the skin.

Proper Use of This Medicine

Do not use this medicine in or around the eyes or on the genitalia.

Docosanol is best used as soon as possible after the signs and symptoms of herpes infection (for example, pain, burning, or blisters) begin to appear.

Apply the medication to the sores (blisters); rub in gently and completely.

To help clear up your herpes infection, *continue using docosanol for the full time of treatment. Do not miss any doses.* However, *do not use this medicine more often or for a longer time than your health care professional or the OTC label indicates.*

Dosing—The dose of topical docosanol can be different for different patients. *Follow your doctor's orders. You may also follow the directions on the label if you are 12 years of age or older.* The following information includes only the average dose of topical docosanol. *If your dose is different, do not change it* unless your doctor tells you to do so.

- For *topical* dosage form (cream):
  —Adults and adolescents:
    - Apply to the affected area(s), five times a day until sore is healed.
    - Rub in gently and completely
  —Children under 12 years of age
    - Use and dosage must be determined by your doctor.

Storage—To store this medicine:

- Keep out of the reach of children.
- Do not keep outdated medicine or medicine no longer needed. Ask your health care professional how you should dispose of any medicine you do not use. Be sure that any discarded medicine is out of the reach of children.

Side Effects of This Medicine

Along with its needed effects, a medicine may cause some unwanted effects. Although not all of these side effects may occur, if they do occur they may need medical attention.

Side effects may occur that usually do not need medical attention. These side effects may go away during treatment as your body adjusts to the medicine. However, check with your doctor if any of the following side effects continue or are bothersome.

More common
  Headache

Less common
  Surface problems including: acne; burning; dryness; itching; rash; redness; soreness; swelling

Other side effects not listed above may also occur in some patients. If you notice any other effects, check with your doctor.

Revised: 12/22/2000

DOFETILIDE Systemic

Commonly used brand name(s):

In the U.S.—
  Tikosyn

Description

Dofetilide (DOH−fet−a−lyed) belongs to the group of medicines known as antiarrhythmics. It is used to correct irregular heartbeats to a normal rhythm

Dofetilide produces its helpful effects by slowing nerve impulses in the heart.

This medicine is available only with your doctor's prescription, in the following dosage forms:

Oral
  - Capsules (U.S)

Before Using This Medicine

In deciding to use a medicine, the risks of taking the medicine must be weighed against the good it will do. This is a decision you and your doctor will make. The following should be considered:

Allergies—Tell your doctor if you have ever had any unusual or allergic reaction to dofetilide.

Pregnancy—Dofetilide has not been studied in pregnant women. However, studies in animals have shown that dofetilide causes birth defects. Before taking this medicine, make sure your doctor knows if you are pregnant or if you may become pregnant.

Breast-feeding—It is not known whether dofetilide passes into breast milk. However, the manufacturer does not recommend breast-feeding while taking dofetilide.

Children—Studies on this medicine have been done only in adult patients, and there is no specific information comparing use of dofetilide in children less than 18 years of age with use in other age groups.

Older adults—This medicine has been tested in patients 65 to 89 years old and has not been shown to cause different side effects or problems in older people than it does in younger adults.

Other medicines—Although certain medicines should not be used together at all, in other cases two different medicines may be used together even if an interaction might occur. In these cases, your doctor may want to change the dose, or other precautions may be necessary. When you are taking dofetilide, it is especially important that your doctor and pharmacist know if you are taking any of the following:

- Antiarrhythmic or other heart medicine, such as amiodarone (e.g., Cordarone) taken within the last 3 months or
- Antibiotics like macrolides or trimethoprim, alone or in combination with sulfamethoxazole (e.g., Biaxin, E-Mycin, ERYC, Ery-Tab, Trimpex, Bactrim, Septra) or
- Bepridil (e.g., Vascor) or
- Cimetidine (e.g., Tagamet) or
- Cisapride (e.g., Propulsid) or
- Ketoconazole (e.g., Nizoral) or
- Megestrol (e.g., Megace) or
- Phenothiazines like prochlorperazine or trifluoperazine (e.g., Compazine, Stelazine) or
- Tricyclic antidepressants like amitriptyline or desipramine (e.g., Elavil or Norpramin) or
- Verapamil (e.g., Calan, Covera-HS, isoptin SR, Verelan)—may cause irregular heartbeats

Other medical problems—The presence of other medical problems may affect the use of dofetilide. Make sure you tell your doctor if you have any other medical problems, especially:

- Electrolyte disorders, such as low potassium or magnesium levels or
- Heart rhythm problems—may cause irregular heartbeats
- Liver disease (severe)—Safety in this condition is unknown
- Kidney disease—Higher blood levels may occur, which may increase the chance of side effects. Your doctor may need to change your dose.

Proper Use of This Medicine

Patient information about dofetilide is available. Read this information carefully.

Use this medicine exactly as directed by your doctor. Do not use more or less of it, and do not use it more often than your doctor ordered. This medicine works best when there is a constant amount in the body. *To help keep the amount constant, it is best to take the doses at the same time every day.*

Dosing—The dose of dofetilide will be different for different patients. *Follow your doctor's orders or the directions on the label.* The following information includes only the average doses of dofetilide. *If your dose is different, do not change it* unless your doctor tells you to do so.

The number of capsules that you take depends on the strength of the medicine.
- For *oral* dosage form (capsules):
  —For abnormal heart rhythm:
  - Adults—125 to 500 micrograms (mcg) two times a day.
  - Children—Use and dose must be determined by your doctor.

Missed dose—If you do miss a dose of this medicine, skip the missed dose and go back to your regular dosing schedule. Do not double doses.

Storage—
- Keep out of the reach of children. Overdose of dofetilide is very dangerous in young children.
- Do not store in the bathroom, near the kitchen sink, or in other damp places. Heat or moisture may cause the medicine to break down.

Precautions While Using This Medicine

It is very important that your doctor check your progress at regular visits to make sure that this medicine is working properly and to check for unwanted effects. This will allow for changes to be made in the amount of medicine you are taking, if necessary.

Other medicines: Do not take other medicines unless they have been discussed with your doctor. This especially includes nonprescription medicines, such as Tagamet and Tagamet HB.

Side Effects of This Medicine

Along with its needed effects, a medicine may cause some unwanted effects. Although not all of these side effects may occur, if they do occur they may need medical attention.

Check with your doctor as soon as possible if any of the following side effects occur:
More common
  dizziness; fainting; fast or irregular heartbeat
Less common
  Chest pain; confusion ; facial or flaccid paralysis; numbness or tingling of the hands, feet or face; paralysis; pounding, slow heartbeat; slurred speech; swelling of the ankles, arms, face, feet, fingers, legs, lips, tongue, and/or throat; troubled breathing; unexplained shortness of breath; unusual tiredness or weakness; weight gain; yellow eyes or skin

Other side effects may occur that usually do not need medical attention. These side effects may go away during treatment as your body adjusts to the medicine. However, check with your doctor if any of the following side effects continue or are bothersome:
Less common
  Abdominal or stomach pain; accidental injury; back pain; chills; cough; diarrhea; fever; flu-like symptoms; general feeling of discomfort or illness; headache; joint pain; loss of appetite; migraine; muscle aches and pains; nausea; rash; runny nose; shivering; sneezing; sore throat; sweating; trouble sleeping; vomiting

Other side effects not listed above may also occur in some patients. If you notice any other effects, check with your doctor.

Developed: 03/16/00

DOLASETRON   Systemic

Commonly used brand name(s):
In the U.S.—
  Anzemet

Description

Dolasetron (dol-A-se-tron) is used to prevent and treat the nausea and vomiting that may occur after treatment with anticancer medicines (chemotherapy) or after surgery.

This medicine is available only with your doctor's prescription, in the following dosage forms:
Oral
  • Tablets (U.S.)
Parenteral
  • Injection (U.S.)

Before Using This Medicine

In deciding to use a medicine, the risks of taking the medicine must be weighed against the good it will do. This is a decision you and your doctor will make. For dolasetron, the following should be considered:

Allergies—Tell your doctor if you have ever had any unusual or allergic reaction to dolasetron. Also tell your health care professional if you are allergic to any other substances, such as foods, preservatives, or dyes.

Pregnancy—Dolasetron has not been studied in pregnant women. However, this medicine has not been shown to cause birth defects or other problems in animal studies.

Breast-feeding—It is not known whether dolasetron passes into the breast milk. Although most medicines pass into breast milk in small amounts, many of them may be used safely while breast-feeding. Mothers who are taking this medicine and who wish to breast-feed should discuss this with their doctor.

Children—This medicine has been tested in a limited number of children between 2 and 17 years of age with cancer. In effective doses, this medicine has not been shown to cause different side effects or problems than it does in adults.

Older adults—This medicine has not been shown to cause different side effects or problems in older people than it does in younger adults.

Other medicines—Although certain medicines should not be used together at all, in other cases two different medicines may be used together even if an interaction might occur. In these cases, your doctor may want to change the dose, or other precautions may be necessary. When you are taking dolasetron, it is especially important that your health care professional know if you are taking any other prescription or nonprescription (over-the-counter [OTC]) medicines.

Other medical problems—The presence of other medical problems may affect the use of dolasetron. Make sure you tell your doctor if you have any other medical problems.

Proper Use of This Medicine

Dosing—The dose of dolasetron will be different for different patients. *Follow your doctor's orders or the directions on the label.* The following information includes only the average doses of dolasetron. *If your dose is different, do not change it* unless your doctor tells you to do so.

The number of tablets that you take depends on the strength of the medicine. Also, *the number of doses you take each day, the time allowed between doses, and the length of time you take the medicine depend on the medical problem for which you are taking dolasetron.*

- For *oral* dosage form (tablets):
  —For prevention of nausea and vomiting after anticancer medicine:
  - Adults—100 milligrams (mg) given within one hour before the anticancer medicine is given.
  - Children 2 to 16 years of age—1.8 mg per kilogram (kg) (0.82 mg per pound) of body weight given within one hour before the anticancer medicine is given. The dose generally is not greater than 100 mg.
  - Children up to 2 years of age—Use and dose must be determined by your doctor.
  —For prevention of nausea and vomiting after surgery:
  - Adults—100 mg given within two hours before surgery.
  - Children 2 to 16 years of age—1.2 mg per kg (0.55 mg per pound) of body weight given within two hours before surgery. The dose generally is not greater than 100 mg.
  - Children up to 2 years of age—Use and dose must be determined by your doctor.
- For *injection* dosage form:
  —For prevention of nausea and vomiting after anticancer medicine:
  - Adults—100 milligrams (mg) given into a vein approximately 30 minutes before the anticancer medicine is given.
  - Children 2 to 16 years of age—1.8 mg per kilogram (kg) (0.82 mg per pound) of body weight given into a vein approximately 30 minutes before the anticancer medicine is given. The dose generally is not greater than 100 mg.
  - Children up to 2 years of age—Use and dose must be determined by your doctor.
  —For prevention of nausea and vomiting after surgery:
  - Adults—12.5 mg given into a vein approximately 15 minutes before anesthesia (medicine to put you to sleep during surgery) is ended.
  - Children 2 to 16 years of age—0.35 mg per kg (0.16 mg per pound) of body weight given into a vein approximately 15 minutes before anesthesia (medicine to put you to sleep during surgery) is ended. The dose generally is not greater than 12.5 mg.
  - Children up to 2 years of age—Use and dose must be determined by your doctor.
  —For treatment of nausea and vomiting after surgery:
  - Adults—12.5 mg given into a vein as soon as nausea and vomiting start.
  - Children 2 to 16 years of age—0.35 mg per kg (0.16 mg per pound) of body weight given into a vein as soon as nausea and vomiting start. The dose generally is not greater than 12.5 mg.
  - Children up to 2 years of age—Use and dose must be determined by your doctor.

Storage—To store this medicine:
- Keep out of the reach of children.
- Store away from heat and direct light.
- Do not store in the bathroom, near the kitchen sink, or in other damp places. Heat or moisture may cause the medicine to break down.
- Keep the medicine from freezing. Do not refrigerate.
- Do not keep outdated medicine or medicine no longer needed. Be sure that any discarded medicine is out of the reach of children.

Side Effects of This Medicine

Along with its needed effects, a medicine may cause some unwanted effects. Although not all of these side effects may occur, if they do occur they may need medical attention.

Check with your doctor as soon as possible if any of the following side effects occur:
Less common
   High or low blood pressure

Rare
   Blood in the urine; chest pain; decrease in amount of urine; fast heartbeat; pain; painful urination or trouble in urinating; severe stomach pain with nausea or vomiting; skin rash, hives, and/or itching; slow or irregular heartbeat; swelling of face; swelling of feet or lower legs; troubled breathing

Other side effects may occur that usually do not need medical attention. These side effects may go away during treatment as your body adjusts to the medicine. However, check with your doctor if any of the following side effects continue or are bothersome:
More common
   Diarrhea; headache
Less common
   Abdominal or stomach pain; dizziness or lightheadedness; fever or chills; unusual tiredness

Other side effects not listed above may also occur in some patients. If you notice any other effects, check with your doctor.

Developed: 03/25/98

DOMPERIDONE Systemic— INTRODUCTORY VERSION

Commonly used brand name(s):

In Canada—
Motilium®

Description

Domperidone (dom-PER-i-done) is a medicine that increases the movements or contractions of the stomach and bowel. Domperidone is also used to treat nausea and vomiting caused by other drugs used to treat Parkinson's Disease.

Domperidone is to be given only by or under the immediate supervision of your doctor. It is available in the following dosage forms:

Oral
- Tablets (Canada)

Before Receiving This Medicine

In deciding to use a medicine, the risks of taking the medicine must be weighed against the good it will do. This is a decision you and your doctor will make. For domperidone the following should be considered:

Allergies—Tell your doctor if you have ever had any unusual or allergic reaction to domperidone.

Pregnancy—domperidone has not been studied in pregnant women. However, domperidone has not been shown to cause birth defects or other problems in animal studies.

Breast-feeding—Domperidone passes into the breast milk, but it is not known if domperidone will cause unwanted effects in the newborn. It may be necessary for you to take another medicine or to stop breast-feeding during treatment. Be sure you have discussed the risks and benefits of the medicine with your doctor.

Children—Studies on this medicine have been done only in adult patients, and there is no specific information comparing use of domperidone in children with use in other age groups.

Older adults—Many medicines have not been studied specifically in older people. Therefore, it may not be known whether they work exactly the same way they do in younger adults or if they cause different side effects or problems in older people. There is no specific information comparing the use of domperidone in the elderly with use in other age groups.

Other medicines—Although certain medicines should not be used together at all, in other cases two different medicines may be used together even if an interaction might occur. In these cases, your doctor may want to change the dose, or other precautions may be necessary. Tell your doctor or pharmacist if you are taking any other prescription or nonprescription (over-the-counter [OTC]) medicine, especially:

- Monoamine oxidase (MAO) inhibitors (furazolidone [e.g., Furoxone], phenelzine [e.g., Nardil], procarbazine [e.g., Matulane], selegilene [e.g., Eldepryl], tranylcypromine [e.g., Parnate])

Other medical problems—The presence of other medical problems may affect the use of domperidone. Make sure you tell your doctor if you have any other medical problems, especially:

- Bleeding from the stomach or other problems involving the bowels
- Pituitary (brain) tumor
- Liver disease
- Medicine sensitivity to domperidone

Proper Use of This Medicine

Dosing—The dose of domperidone will be different for different patients. *Follow your doctor's orders or the directions on the label*. The following information includes only the average doses of domperidone. *If your dose is different, do not change it* unless your doctor tells you to do so.

The number of tablets of that you take depends on the strength of the medicine. Also, *the number of doses you take each day, the time allowed between doses, and the length of time you take the medicine depend on the medical problem for which you are taking domperidone.*

- For *oral* dosage form (tablets):
  —Treatment of gastrointestinal motility disorders:
    - Adults—10 milligrams (mg) three to four times daily. Some patients may require higher doses up to 20 mg three or four times daily.
  —Nausea and vomiting:
    - Adults—20 milligrams (mg) three to four times daily.

Missed dose—If you miss a dose of this medicine, take it as soon as possible. However, if it is almost time for your next dose, skip the missed dose and go back to your regular dosing schedule. Do not double doses.

Storage—To store this medicine:
- Keep out of the reach of children.
- Store away from heat and direct light.
- Do not store in the bathroom, near the kitchen sink, or in other damp places. Heat or moisture may cause the medicine to break down.
- Do not keep outdated medicine or medicine no longer needed. Be sure that any discarded medicine is out of the reach of children.

Precautions While Receiving This Medicine

It is very important that your doctor check your progress at regular visits. This will allow your doctor to see if the medicine is working properly and to decide if you should continue to take it.

If your symptoms do not improve within a few days or if they become worse, check with your doctor.

Side Effects of This Medicine

Along with its needed effects, a medicine may cause some unwanted effects. Although not all of these side effects may occur, if they do occur they may need medical attention.
Symptoms of overdose

Get emergency help immediately if any of the following symptoms of overdose occur
    Difficulty in speaking; disorientation; dizziness; fainting; irregular heartbeat; light-headedness; loss of balance or muscle control

Check with your doctor immediately if any of the following side effects occur:

Less common

    Loss of balance or muscle control; swelling of the mouth

Rare

    Fast, irregular, pounding, or racing heartbeat or pulse; swelling of face, hands, lower legs, or feet

Other side effects may occur that usually do not need medical attention. These side effects may go away during treatment as your body adjusts to the medicine. However, check with your doctor if any of the following side effects continue or are bothersome.

Less common

    Breast milk flowing from the nipple; dry mouth; swelling of the breast in the male; headache; hives; hot flashes; itching of skin; itching, redness, pain, or swelling of eye; menstrual irregularities; pain in the breast

Rare

    Change in need to urinate; change in appetite; constipation; diarrhea; burning, difficult, or painful urination; difficulty in speaking; dizziness; drowsiness; heartburn; irritability; lack or loss of strength; leg cramps; mental dullness; nervousness; palpitations; sluggishness; stomach cramps; thirst; tiredness; weakness

Developed: 10/09/2000

DONEPEZIL   Systemic

Commonly used brand name(s):

In the U.S.—
    Aricept

Another commonly used name is E2020.

Description

Donepezil (doe-NEP-ah-zil) is used to treat the symptoms of mild to moderate Alzheimer's disease. Donepezil will not cure Alzheimer's disease, and it will not stop the disease from getting worse. However, it can improve thinking ability in some patients.

This medicine is available only with your doctor's prescription, in the following dosage form:

Oral
• Tablets (U.S. and Canada)

Before Using This Medicine

In deciding to use a medicine, the risks of taking the medicine must be weighed against the good it will do. This is a decision you and your doctor will make. For donepezil, the following should be considered:

Allergies—Tell your doctor if you have ever had any unusual or allergic reaction to donepezil, or to biperiden (e.g., Akineton), bupivacaine (e.g., Marcaine), methylphenidate (e.g., Ritalin), paroxetine (e.g., Paxil), rifabutin (e.g., Mycobutin), or trihexyphenidyl (e.g., Artane). Also tell your health care professional if you are allergic to any other substances, such as foods, preservatives, or dyes.

Pregnancy—Studies have not been done in pregnant women. However, studies in pregnant animals have shown that donepezil may cause unwanted effects on the offspring when the mother is given doses many times higher than the human dose. Before taking this medicine, make sure your doctor knows if you are pregnant or if you may become pregnant.

Breast-feeding—It is not known whether donepezil passes into breast milk. Because of the possibility of serious unwanted effects in the nursing infant, it is important that you discuss the use of this medicine with your doctor if you wish to breast-feed.

Children—Studies on this medicine have been done only in adult patients, and there is no specific information comparing use of donepezil in children with use in other age groups.

Older adults—In studies done to date that have included older adults, some side effects of donepezil have been shown to occur more frequently in older people than in younger adults.

Other medicines—Although certain medicines should not be used together at all, in other cases two different medicines may be used together even if an interaction might occur. In these cases, your doctor may want to change the dose, or other precautions may be necessary. When you are taking donepezil, it is especially important that your health care professional know if you are taking any other prescription or nonprescription (over-the-counter [OTC]) medicines.

Other medical problems—The presence of other medical problems may affect the use of donepezil. Make sure you tell your doctor if you have any other medical problems, especially:

• Asthma or
• Lung disease or
• Peptic ulcers, or history of or
• Seizures, or history of or
• Urinary tract blockage—Donepezil may make these conditions worse

• Heart problems—Donepezil may have unwanted effects on heart rate

• Liver problems—Higher blood levels of donepezil may result and increase the chance of side effects

Proper Use of This Medicine

Take this medicine exactly as directed by your doctor in order to improve your condition as much as possible. Do not take more of it or less of it, and do not take it more or less often than your doctor ordered.

Donepezil should be taken at bedtime unless otherwise directed by your doctor. It may be taken with or without food, on a full or empty stomach.

Dosing—The dose of donepezil will be different for different patients. *Follow your doctor's orders or the directions on the label.* The following information includes only the average doses of donepezil. *If your dose is different, do not change it* unless your doctor tells you to do so.

The number of tablets that you take depends on the strength of the medicine.

- For *oral* dosage form (tablets):
  —For Alzheimer's disease:
    - Adults—5 milligrams (mg) taken at bedtime. Your doctor may increase your dose as needed. However, the dose usually is not more than 10 mg a day.
    - Children—Use and dose must be determined by your doctor.

Missed dose—If you miss a dose of this medicine, skip the missed dose and go back to your regular dosing schedule. Do not double doses.

Storage—To store this medicine:

- Keep out of the reach of children.
- Store away from heat and direct light.
- Do not store in the bathroom, near the kitchen sink, or in other damp places. Heat or moisture may cause the medicine to break down.
- Keep the medicine from freezing. Do not refrigerate.
- Do not keep outdated medicine or medicine no longer needed. Be sure that any discarded medicine is out of the reach of children.

Precautions While Using This Medicine

It is important that your doctor check your progress at regular visits. This is necessary to allow dose adjustments and to reduce any unwanted effects.

Before you have any kind of surgery, dental treatment, or emergency treatment, tell the medical doctor or dentist in charge that you are using this medicine. Taking donepezil together with certain medicines that are used during surgery or dental or emergency treatments may increase the effects of those medicines and cause unwanted effects.

This medicine may cause some people to become dizzy or drowsy, to have blurred vision, or to have problems with clumsiness or unsteadiness. *Make sure you know how you react to this medicine before you drive, use machines, or do anything else that could be dangerous if you are not alert, well-coordinated, and able to see clearly.*

If you think that you or someone else may have taken an overdose of this medicine, get emergency help at once. Taking an overdose of this medicine may cause convulsions (seizures) or serious effects on your heart and your breathing. Signs of overdose include increased watering of mouth, increased sweating, low blood pressure, muscle weakness, severe nausea, severe vomiting, slow heartbeat, and troubled breathing.

Side Effects of This Medicine

Along with its needed effects, a medicine may cause some unwanted effects. Although not all of these side effects may occur, if they do occur they may need medical attention.

Check with your doctor as soon as possible if any of the following side effects occur:
More common
  Diarrhea; loss of appetite; muscle cramps; nausea; trouble in sleeping; unusual tiredness or weakness; vomiting
Less common
  Abnormal dreams; constipation; dizziness; drowsiness; fainting; frequent urination; headache; joint pain,

stiffness, or swelling; mental depression; pain; unusual bleeding or bruising; weight loss
Rare
  Black, tarry stools; bloating; bloody or cloudy urine; blurred vision; burning, prickling, or tingling sensations; cataract; chills; clumsiness or unsteadiness; confusion; cough; decreased urination; difficult or painful urination; dryness of mouth; eye irritation; fever; flushing of skin; frequent urge to urinate; high or low blood pressure; hives; hot flashes; increased heart rate and breathing; increase in sexual desire or performance; increased sweating; increased urge to urinate during the night; irregular heartbeat; itching; loss of bladder control; loss of bowel control; mood or mental changes, including abnormal crying, aggression, agitation, delusions, irritability, nervousness, or restlessness; nasal congestion; pain in chest, upper stomach, or throat; problems with speech; runny nose; severe thirst; shortness of breath; sneezing; sore throat; sunken eyes; tightness in chest; tremor; troubled breathing; wheezing; wrinkled skin
Symptoms of overdose
  Convulsions (seizures); increased sweating; increased watering of mouth; increasing muscle weakness; low blood pressure; severe nausea; severe vomiting; slow heartbeat; troubled breathing

Other side effects not listed above may also occur in some patients. If you notice any other effects, check with your doctor.

Developed: 6/11/99

DORNASE ALFA   Inhalation

Commonly used brand name(s):
In the U.S.—
  Pulmozyme
In Canada—
  Pulmozyme
Other commonly used names are: rhDNase and DNase I.

Description

Dornase alfa (DOR-nayse AL-fa) is used in the management of cystic fibrosis. It is used every day with other cystic fibrosis medicines, especially antibiotics, bronchodilators (medicines that open up narrowed breathing passages), and corticosteroids (cortisone-like medicines).

Cystic fibrosis is a condition in which thick mucus is formed in the lungs and breathing passages. The mucus blocks the airways and increases the chance of lung infections. The infections then cause the mucus to become even thicker, making it more difficult to breathe.

Dornase alfa will not cure cystic fibrosis. However, when it is used every day, it helps make breathing easier and reduces the number of serious lung infections that require treatment with antibiotics.

Dornase alfa is available only with your doctor's prescription, in the following dosage form:

Inhalation
• Inhalation solution (U.S. and Canada)

Before Using This Medicine

In deciding to use a medicine, the risks of taking the medicine must be weighed against the good it will do. This is a decision you and your doctor will make. For dornase alfa, the following should be considered:

Allergies—Tell your doctor if you have ever had any unusual or allergic reaction to dornase alfa. Also tell your health care professional if you are allergic to any other substances, such as foods, preservatives, or dyes.

Pregnancy—Dornase alfa has not been studied in pregnant women. However, this medicine has not been shown to cause birth defects or other problems in animals.

Breast-feeding—It is not known whether dornase alfa passes into human breast milk. Although most medicines pass into breast milk in small amounts, many of them may be used safely while breast-feeding. Mothers who are using this medicine and who wish to breast-feed should discuss this with their doctor.

Children—Dornase alfa has been studied in children 3 months of age and older and has not been shown to cause different side effects or problems in children than it does in adults, although coughing, runny or stuffy nose, and skin rashes were more common in children 3 months to 5 years of age than in other age groups.

Older adults—Many medicines have not been studied specifically in older people. Therefore, it may not be known whether they work exactly the same way they do in younger adults. Although there is no specific information comparing use of dornase alfa in the elderly with use in other age groups, this medicine is not expected to cause different side effects or problems in older people than it does in younger adults.

Other medicines—Although certain medicines should not be used together at all, in other cases two different medicines may be used together even if an interaction might occur. In these cases, your doctor may want to change the dose, or other precautions may be necessary. Tell your health care professional if you are taking any other prescription or nonprescription (over-the-counter [OTC]) medicine.

Proper Use of This Medicine

Dornase alfa usually comes with patient instructions. Read them carefully before using this medicine.

Dornase alfa is packaged in small plastic containers called ampuls. Each ampul contains one full dose of dornase alfa. *Do not use an ampul that has already been opened. Also, do not use an ampul of this medicine after the expiration date printed on the package.*

Do not use dornase alfa solution if it is cloudy or discolored.

Dornase alfa must be used in a nebulizer with a compressor. Only the following nebulizers and compressors should be used with this medicine:

• Hudson T Up-draft II disposable jet nebulizer used with the Pulmo-Aide compressor
• Marquest Acorn II disposable jet nebulizer used with the Pulmo-Aide compressor
• Reusable PARI LC Jet+ nebulizer used with the PARI PRONEB compressor
• Reusable PARI BABY nebulizer used with the PARI PRONEB compressor

Your health care professional will help you decide which nebulizer and compressor to use.

It is very important that you *use dornase alfa only as directed.* Use the mouthpiece provided with the nebulizer. Do not use a face mask with the nebulizer because less medicine will get into your lungs. Infants and chlidren unable to inhale and exhale through the mouth for the entire nebulizer treatment may use the PARI BABY nebulizer with the supplied face mask. *Make sure you understand exactly how to use this medicine in the nebulizer.*

In order to receive the full effects of this medicine, *you must use it every day as ordered by your doctor.* If possible, dornase alfa should be used at about the same time each day. You may notice some improvement in your condition within the first week of treatment. However, some patients may not feel the full effects of this medicine for weeks or months.

If you are taking any other medicines for cystic fibrosis, keep taking them as you did before you started using dornase alfa, unless otherwise directed by your doctor. However, *do not put any other inhaled medicine in the nebulizer at the same time that you use dornase alfa.* Other inhaled medicines may be used in a clean nebulizer before or after your treatment with dornase alfa.

To prepare the nebulizer for use:
• Wash your hands well with soap and water before putting the nebulizer together and preparing the medicine. This will help prevent infection.
• Put the nebulizer together only on a clean surface. If dirt or germs get on the nebulizer or in the medicine, they may cause infection.
• After you put the nebulizer together, test the compressor (following the manufacturer's directions) to make sure it works properly. If you have any questions about this, ask your health care professional.

To prepare the medicine for use in the nebulizer:
• Remove one ampul of dornase alfa from the refrigerator. Hold the tab at the base of the ampul firmly. Twist off the top of the ampul, but do not squeeze the body of the ampul while doing so.
• Take the cap off the nebulizer cup. Turn the opened ampul upside down over the cup. Squeeze the ampul gently until all the contents are emptied into the cup. *It is very important that you use the full dose of this medicine.*
• Replace the cap on the nebulizer cup. Connect the nebulizer and compressor, following the manufacturer's directions.
• Turn on the compressor. Make sure there is mist coming from the nebulizer.

To use the medicine in the nebulizer:
• Place the mouthpiece between your teeth and on top of your tongue. Close your lips around the mouthpiece. Be sure that you do not block the airflow with your tongue or teeth.
• Breathe normally, in and out, through your mouth. *Do not breathe through your nose.* If you have trouble breathing only through your mouth, use a nose clip.

- During treatment, moisture may collect in the long connecting tube of the nebulizer. This should be expected. However, if you notice a leak or feel moisture coming from the nebulizer during the treatment, turn off the compressor. Then check to make sure the nebulizer cap is sealed correctly before you continue the treatment.
- When the nebulizer begins "spitting," gently tap the nebulizer cup. Continue breathing until the cup is empty or no more mist comes from the nebulizer.
- If you have to stop the treatment for some reason or if you start coughing during the treatment, turn off the compressor. To begin the treatment again, turn on the compressor and continue as before.
- The complete treatment usually takes 10 to 15 minutes. *Be sure to inhale the full dose of dornase alfa.*

After using dornase alfa:
- Turn off the compressor. Then take apart the nebulizer system.
- Follow the manufacturer's directions for care and cleaning of your nebulizer and compressor.

Dosing—The dose of dornase alfa will be different for different patients. *Follow your doctor's orders or the directions on the label.* The following information includes only the average doses of dornase alfa. *If your dose is different, do not change it* unless your doctor tells you to do so.
- For *inhalation* dosage form (inhalation solution):
  —For cystic fibrosis:
    - Adults and children 5 years of age and older—The usual dose is 2.5 milligrams (mg) (one ampul), used in a nebulizer once a day for about 10 to 15 minutes. However, your doctor may want you to use this medicine two times a day at regularly spaced times.
    - Children 3 months to 5 years of age—The usual dose is 2.5 milligrams (mg) (one ampul), used in a nebulizer once a day for about 10 to 15 minutes.
    - Children up to 3 months of age—Use and dose must be determined by your doctor.

Missed dose—If you miss a dose of this medicine, use it as soon as possible. However, if it is almost time for your next dose, skip the missed dose and go back to your regular dosing schedule.

Storage—To store this medicine:
- Keep out of the reach of children
- Store away from heat and light.
- Store the medicine in the refrigerator in the foil pouches. However, keep the medicine from freezing. Do not leave this medicine out of the refrigerator for longer than 24 hours. If an ampul of medicine is left out for longer than this, it should be thrown away and a new ampul should be used.
- Do not keep outdated medicine or medicine no longer needed. Be sure that any discarded medicine is out of the reach of children.

Precautions While Using This Medicine

If your condition becomes worse while you are using this medicine, check with your doctor.

Side Effects of This Medicine

Along with its needed effects, a medicine may cause some unwanted effects. The following side effects may go away during treatment as your body adjusts to the medicine. However, check with your doctor if any of the following side effects continue or are bothersome:

More common
  Chest pain or discomfort; hoarseness; sore throat

Less common
  Difficulty breathing; fever; redness, itching, pain, swelling, or other irritation of eyes; runny or stuffy nose; skin rash; upset stomach

Other side effects not listed above may also occur in some patients. If you notice any other effects, check with your doctor.

Revised: 07/24/97
Interim revision: 07/29/98

DORZOLAMIDE   Ophthalmic†

Commonly used brand name(s):

In the U.S.—
  Trusopt

†Not commercially available in Canada.

Description

Dorzolamide (dor-ZOLE-a-mide) is a carbonic anhydrase inhibitor that is used in the eye. It is used to treat increased pressure in the eye caused by open-angle glaucoma. It is also used to treat a condition called hypertension of the eye.

Dorzolamide is available only with your doctor's prescription, in the following dosage form:

Ophthalmic
- Ophthalmic solution (eye drops) (U.S.)

Before Using This Medicine

In deciding to use a medicine, the risks of using the medicine must be weighed against the good it will do. This is a decision you and your doctor will make. For ophthalmic dorzolamide, the following should be considered:

Allergies—Tell your doctor if you have ever had any unusual or allergic reaction to ophthalmic dorzolamide or to any of the sulfonamides (sulfa medicines); furosemide (e.g., Lasix) or thiazide diuretics (water pills); oral antidiabetics (diabetes medicine you take by mouth); or the carbonic anhydrase inhibitor-type glaucoma medicine you take by mouth (for example, acetazolamide [e.g., Diamox], dichlorphenamide [e.g., Daranide], or methazolamide [e.g., Neptazane]). Also tell your health care professional if you are allergic to any other substances, such as benzalkonium chloride or other preservatives.

Pregnancy—Ophthalmic dorzolamide has not been studied in pregnant women. However, one animal study has shown that this medicine, when given in very high doses, causes toxicity in the mother and birth defects in the fetus. Before using this medicine, make sure your doctor knows if you are pregnant or if you may become pregnant.

Breast-feeding—It is not known whether ophthalmic dorzolamide passes into breast milk. However, other carbonic anhydrase inhibitors may pass into breast milk. These medicines are not recommended during breast-feeding, because they may cause unwanted effects in nursing babies. It may be necessary for you to use another medicine or to stop breast-feeding during treatment. Be sure you have discussed this with your doctor.

Children—Studies on this medicine have been done only in adult patients and there is no specific information comparing use of ophthalmic dorzolamide in children with use in other age groups.

Older adults—This medicine has been tested in a limited number of patients 65 years of age or older and has not been shown to cause different side effects or problems in older people than it does in younger adults.

Other medicines—Although certain medicines should not be used together at all, in other cases two different medicines may be used together even if an interaction might occur. In these cases, your doctor may want to change the dose, or other precautions may be necessary. When you are using ophthalmic dorzolamide, it is especially important that your health care professional know if you are using any of the following:

- Silver preparations for the eye, such as silver nitrate—Ophthalmic dorzolamide should not be used with ophthalmic silver preparations, since a chemical reaction may occur

Other medical problems—The presence of other medical problems may affect the use of ophthalmic dorzolamide. Make sure you tell your doctor if you have any other medical problems, especially:

- Kidney disease, severe, or
- Liver disease—Use of ophthalmic dorzolamide may lead to increased side effects from the medication
- Kidney stones—Use of ophthalmic dorzolamide may make this condition worse

Proper Use of This Medicine

To use: First, wash your hands. Tilt the head back and, pressing your finger gently on the skin just beneath the lower eyelid, pull the lower eyelid away from the eye to make a space. Drop the medicine into this space. Let go of the eyelid and gently close the eyes. Do not blink. Keep the eyes closed and apply pressure to the inner corner of the eye with your finger for 1 or 2 minutes to allow the medicine to be absorbed by the eye.

Use this medicine only as directed. Do not use more of it and do not use it more often than your doctor ordered. To do so may increase the chance of too much medicine being absorbed into the body and the chance of side effects.

If your doctor ordered two different eye drops to be used together, wait at least 10 minutes between the times you apply the medicines. This will help to keep the second medicine from "washing out" the first one.

Dosing—The dose of ophthalmic dorzolamide will be different for different patients. *Follow your doctor's orders or the directions on the label.* The following information includes only the average doses of ophthalmic dorzolamide. *If your dose is different, do not change it* unless your doctor tells you to do so.

- For *ophthalmic* dosage form (eye drops):
  —For glaucoma or hypertension of the eye:
  - Adults and teenagers—Use one drop in the eye three times a day.

- Children—Use and dose must be determined by your doctor.

Missed dose—If you miss a dose of this medicine, use it as soon as possible. However, if it is almost time for your next dose, skip the missed dose and go back to your regular dosing schedule. Do not double doses.

Storage—To store this medicine:
- Keep out of the reach of children.
- Store away from heat and direct light.
- Keep the medicine from freezing. Do not refrigerate.
- Do not keep outdated medicine or medicine no longer needed. Be sure that any discarded medicine is out of the reach of children.

Precautions While Using This Medicine

It is important that your doctor check your progress at regular visits. Your doctor may want to do certain tests to see if the medicine is working properly or to see if certain side effects may be occurring without your knowing it.

If itching, redness, swelling, or other signs of eye or eyelid irritation occur, check with your doctor. These signs may mean that you are allergic to ophthalmic dorzolamide.

This medicine may cause some people to have blurred vision for a short time. *Make sure you know how you react to this medicine before you drive, use machines, or do anything else that could be dangerous if you cannot see properly.* Also, since blurred vision may be a sign of a side effect that needs medical attention, check with your doctor if it continues.

Ophthalmic dorzolamide may cause your eyes to become more sensitive to light than they are normally. Wearing sunglasses and avoiding too much exposure to bright light may help lessen the discomfort. If the discomfort continues, check with your doctor.

Side Effects of This Medicine

Along with its needed effects, a medicine may cause some unwanted effects. Although not all of these side effects may occur, if they do occur they may need medical attention.

Check with your doctor as soon as possible if any of the following side effects occur:
More common
  Itching, redness, swelling, or other sign of eye or eyelid irritation
Rare
  Blurred vision; eye pain; skin rash; symptoms of kidney stone (blood in urine, nausea or vomiting, or pain in side, back, or abdomen); tearing

Other side effects may occur that usually do not need medical attention. These side effects may go away during treatment as your body adjusts to the medicine. However, check with your doctor if any of the following side effects continue or are bothersome:
More common
  Bitter taste; burning, stinging, or discomfort when medicine is applied; feeling of something in eye; sensitivity of eyes to light
Less common
  Dryness of eyes; headache; nausea; unusual tiredness or weakness

Other side effects not listed above may also occur in some patients. If you notice any other effects, check with your doctor.

Developed: 01/31/96

DORZOLAMIDE AND TIMOLOL
Ophthalmic

Commonly used brand name(s):

In the U.S.—
    Cosopt

Description

Dorzolamide (dor-ZOLE-a-mide) and timolol (TYE-moe-lole) combination medicine contains a carbonic anhydrase inhibitor (dorzolamide) and a beta-adrenergic blocking agent (timolol). It is used in the eye to treat increased pressure in the eye caused by open-angle glaucoma and a condition called hypertension of the eye.

This medicine is available only with your doctor's prescription, in the following dosage form:

Ophthalmic
   • Ophthalmic solution (eye drops) (U.S.)

Before Using This Medicine

In deciding to use a medicine, the risks of using the medicine must be weighed against the good it will do. This is a decision you and your doctor will make. For ophthalmic dorzolamide and timolol, the following should be considered:

Allergies—Tell your doctor if you have ever had any unusual or allergic reaction to carbonic anhydrase inhibitors (either ophthalmic or systemic), such as acetazolamide, brinzolamide, dichlorphenamide, dorzolamide, or methazolamide.

In addition, tell your doctor if you have ever had any unusual or allergic reaction to any of the beta-adrenergic blocking agents (either ophthalmic or systemic), such as acebutolol, atenolol, betaxolol, bisoprolol, carteolol, labetalol, levobunolol, metipranolol, metoprolol, nadolol, oxprenolol, penbutolol, pindolol, propranolol, sotalol, or timolol.

Also, tell your doctor if you have ever had any unusual or allergic reaction to sulfonamides (sulfa drugs) or thiazide diuretics (a type of water pill).

Furthermore, tell your health care professional if you are allergic to any other substances, such as benzalkonium chloride or other preservatives.

Pregnancy—This medicine has not been studied in pregnant women. However, studies in animals given very high doses of this medicine by mouth have shown that this medicine causes birth defects or other problems. Before using this medicine, make sure your doctor knows if you are pregnant or if you may become pregnant.

Breast-feeding—Although it is not known whether dorzolamide passes into the breast milk, timolol has been found to pass into the breast milk and it is possible that it could cause unwanted effects in nursing babies. Mothers who are using this medicine and who wish to breast-feed should discuss this with their doctor.

Children—Studies on this medicine have been done only in adult patients, and there is no specific information comparing use of this medicine in children with use in other age groups.

Older adults—Many medicines have not been studied specifically in older people. Therefore, it may not be known whether they work exactly the same way they do in younger adults or if they cause different side effects or problems in older people. There is no specific information comparing use of this medicine in the elderly with use in other age groups.

Other medicines—Although certain medicines should not be used together at all, in other cases two different medicines may be used together even if an interaction might occur. In these cases, your doctor may want to change the dose, or other precautions may be necessary. When you are using this medicine, it is especially important that your health care professional know if you are taking any of the following:

• Beta-adrenergic blocking agents you take by mouth (acebutolol [e.g., Sectral], atenolol [e.g., Tenormin], betaxolol [e.g., Kerlone], bisoprolol [e.g., Zebeta], carteolol [e.g., Cartrol], labetalol [e.g., Normodyne], metoprolol [e.g., Lopressor], nadolol [e.g., Corgard], oxprenolol [e.g., Trasicor], penbutolol [e.g., Levatol], pindolol [e.g., Visken], propranolol [e.g., Inderal], sotalol [e.g., Sotacor], timolol [e.g., Blocadren])—The effects of both the timolol in the ophthalmic dorzolamide and timolol combination and the systemic beta-adrenergic blocking agents may be increased

• Calcium channel blocking agents (bepridil [e.g, Vascar], diltiazem [e.g., Cardizem], felodipine [e.g., Plendil], flunarizine [e.g., Sibelium], isradipine [e.g., DynaCirc], nicardipine [e.g., Cardene], nifedipine [e.g., Procardia], nimodipine [e.g., Nimotop], verapamil [e.g., Calan] or

• Digitalis glycosides (heart medicine) when used together with calcium channel blocking agents—Unwanted effects on the heart may be increased

• Carbonic anhydrase inhibitor–type glaucoma medicine you take by mouth (for example, acetazolamide [e.g., Diamox], dichlorphenamide [e.g., Daranide], or methazolamide [e.g., Neptazane])—Effects of these medicines on the body may be increased

• Quinidine (e.g., Cardioquin) or
• Reserpine (e.g., Serpasil) and other catecholamine-depleting medicines—Effects of the ophthalmic dorzolamide and timolol combination may be increased, possibly leading to slow heartbeat, low blood pressure, and fainting

Other medical problems—The presence of other medical problems may affect the use of this medicine. Make sure you tell your doctor if you have any other medical problems, especially:

• Allergy, history of—Severity and duration of allergic reactions to other substances may be increased

• Asthma or
• Bronchitis or
• Emphysema or
• Lung problems, other—This medicine can increase trouble in breathing

• Bradycardia (unusually slow heartbeat) or
• Heart problems, other—There is a risk of further decreased heart function

• Diabetes mellitus (sugar diabetes) or
• Hypoglycemia—If your blood sugar becomes too low, this medicine may cover up some of the symptoms

- Kidney disease, severe—Effects of this medicine may be increased because of its slower removal from the body
- Myasthenia gravis—This medicine may make this condition worse
- Overactive thyroid—This medicine may cover up fast heartbeat, which is a sign of overactive thyroid

Proper Use of This Medicine

To use:
The bottle is only partially full to provide proper drop control.

First, wash your hands. Tilt the head back and, pressing your finger gently on the skin just beneath the lower eyelid, pull the lower eyelid away from the eye to make a space. Drop the medicine into this space. Let go of the eyelid and gently close the eyes. Do not blink. Keep the eyes closed and apply pressure to the inner corner of the eye with your finger for 1 or 2 minutes to allow the medicine to be absorbed by the eye.

Immediately after using the eye drops, wash your hands to remove any medicine that may be on them.

To keep the medicine as germ-free as possible, do not touch the applicator tip to any surface (including the eye). Also, keep the container tightly closed. Serious damage to the eye and possible loss of vision may result from using contaminated eye drops.

Use this medicine only as directed by your doctor. Do not use more of it and do not use it more often than your doctor ordered. To do so may increase the chance of too much medicine being absorbed into the body and the chance of side effects.

If your doctor ordered two different eye drops to be used together, wait at least 10 minutes between the times you apply the medicines. This will help to keep the second medicine from "washing out" the first one.

Dosing—The dose of this medicine will be different for different patients. *Follow your doctor's orders or the directions on the label.* The following information includes only the average doses of this medicine. *If your dose is different, do not change it* unless your doctor tells you to do so.

- For *ophthalmic* dosage form (eye drops):
  —For glaucoma or hypertension of the eye:
    - Adults—Use 1 drop of the medicine in the affected eye(s) two times a day.
    - Children—Use and dose must be determined by your doctor.

Missed dose—If you miss a dose of this medicine, use it as soon as you remember. However, if it is almost time for the next dose, skip the missed dose and go back to your regular dosing schedule. Do not double doses.

Storage—To store this medicine:
- Keep out of the reach of children.
- Store away from heat and direct light.
- Keep the medicine from freezing.
- Do not keep outdated medicine or medicine no longer needed. Be sure that any discarded medicine is out of the reach of children.

Precautions While Using This Medicine

It is important that your doctor check your progress at regular visits to make sure that this medicine is working properly and is not causing unwanted effects.

If itching, redness, swelling, or other signs of eye or eyelid irritation occur, stop using this medicine and check with your doctor. These signs may mean that you are allergic to this medicine.

Before you have any kind of surgery, dental treatment, or emergency treatment, tell the medical doctor or dentist in charge that you are using this medicine. This medicine contains an ophthalmic beta-adrenergic blocking agent. Using an ophthalmic beta-adrenergic blocking agent during this time may cause an increased risk of side effects.

It is very important that you check with your doctor if you get an injury or infection in your eye or if you are scheduled to have eye surgery. Your doctor will tell you whether to keep using the same container of eye drops or whether you should start using a fresh bottle of eye drops.

For diabetic patients:
- *This medicine may cover up some signs of hypoglycemia (low blood sugar).* If you notice a change in the results of your blood or urine sugar tests or if you have any questions, check with your doctor.

This medicine contains benzalkonium chloride, which may be absorbed by contact lenses. Take soft contact lenses out before using this medicine. Lenses may be put back in 15 minutes after using the medicine.

Side Effects of This Medicine

Along with its needed effects, a medicine may cause some unwanted effects. Although not all of these side effects may occur, if they do occur they may need medical attention.

Check with your doctor as soon as possible if any of the following side effects occur:
More common
Blurred vision; feeling of something in eye; itching of the eye; redness of eye and lining of eyelid; sensitivity of eyes to light

Less common
Back, abdominal, or stomach pain; change in vision; coughing, shortness of breath, troubled breathing, tightness in chest, or wheezing; discharge from eye; dizziness; eye or eyelid pain, swelling, discomfort, or irritation; increased blood pressure; increased frequency of urination or painful urination; itching of eyelid; seeing flashes or sparks of light; seeing floating spots before the eyes; swelling of lining of eyelid; tiny bumps on lining of eyelid

Rare
Blood in urine; chest pain; diarrhea; lightheadedness or fainting; headache or weakness, severe and sudden; mental depression; nausea or vomiting; pain, numbness, tingling, or burning feeling in hands or feet; skin rash; slow heartbeat; unusual tiredness or weakness

Other side effects may occur that usually do not need medical attention. These side effects may go away during treatment as your body adjusts to the medicine. However, check with your doctor if any of the following side effects continue or are bothersome:
More common
Bitter, sour, or unusual taste; burning or stinging of the eye (when medicine is applied)

Less common
Cold- or flu-like symptoms; crusting or scales on eyelid; dryness of eyes; headache; indigestion or upset

stomach; sore throat; stuffy or runny nose; tearing of eye

Other side effects not listed above may also occur in some patients. If you notice any other effects, check with your doctor.

Developed: 09/25/98
Interim revision: 12/28/98

DOXAZOSIN Systemic

Commonly used brand name(s):

In the U.S.—
Cardura

In Canada—
Cardura–1
Cardura–2
Cardura–4

Description

Doxazosin (dox-AY-zoe-sin) belongs to the general class of medicines called antihypertensives. It is used to treat high blood pressure (hypertension).

High blood pressure adds to the workload of the heart and arteries. If it continues for a long time, the heart and arteries may not function properly. This can damage the blood vessels of the brain, heart, and kidneys, resulting in a stroke, heart failure, or kidney failure. High blood pressure may also increase the risk of heart attacks. These problems may be less likely to occur if blood pressure is controlled.

Doxazosin works by relaxing blood vessels so that blood passes through them more easily. This helps to lower blood pressure.

Doxazosin is also used to treat benign (noncancerous) enlargement of the prostate (benign prostatic hyperplasia [BPH]). Benign enlargement of the prostate is a problem that can occur in men as they get older. The prostate gland is located below the bladder. As the prostate gland enlarges, certain muscles in the gland may become tight and get in the way of the tube that drains urine from the bladder. This can cause problems in urinating, such as a need to urinate often, a weak stream when urinating, or a feeling of not being able to empty the bladder completely.

Doxazosin helps relax the muscles in the prostate and the opening of the bladder. This may help increase the flow of urine and/or decrease the symptoms. However, doxazosin will not shrink the prostate. The prostate may continue to get larger. This may cause the symptoms to become worse over time. Therefore, even though doxazosin may lessen the problems caused by enlarged prostate now, surgery still may be needed in the future.

Doxazosin is available only with your doctor's prescription, in the following dosage form:
Oral
- Tablets (U.S. and Canada)

Before Using This Medicine

In deciding to use a medicine, the risks of taking the medicine must be weighed against the good it will do. This is a decision you and your doctor will make. For doxazosin, the following should be considered:

Allergies—Tell your doctor if you have ever had any unusual or allergic reaction to doxazosin, prazosin, or terazosin. Also tell your health care professional if you are allergic to any other substances, such as foods, preservatives, or dyes.

Pregnancy—Doxazosin has not been studied in pregnant women. However, studies in rabbits have shown that doxazosin given at very high doses may cause death of the fetus. Before taking this medicine, make sure your doctor knows if you are pregnant or if you may become pregnant.

Breast-feeding—It is not known whether doxazosin passes into breast milk. However, doxazosin passes into the milk of lactating rats. Although most medicines pass into breast milk in small amounts, many of them may be used safely while breast-feeding. Mothers who are taking this medicine and who wish to breast-feed should discuss this with their doctor.

Children—Studies on this medicine have been done only in adult patients, and there is no specific information comparing use of doxazosin in children with use in other age groups.

Older adults—Dizziness, lightheadedness, or fainting may be especially likely to occur in elderly patients with high blood pressure, because these patients are usually more sensitive than younger adults to the effects of doxazosin.

Other medicines—Although certain medicines should not be used together at all, in other cases two different medicines may be used together even if an interaction might occur. In these cases, your doctor may want to change the dose, or other precautions may be necessary. Tell your health care professional if you are using any other prescription or nonprescription (over-the-counter [OTC]) medicine.

Other medical problems—The presence of other medical problems may affect the use of doxazosin. Make sure you tell your doctor if you have any other medical problems, especially:
- Kidney disease—Possible increased sensitivity to the effects of doxazosin
- Liver disease—The effects of doxazosin may be increased, which may increase the chance of side effects

Proper Use of This Medicine

To help you remember to take your medicine, try to get into the habit of taking it at the same time each day.

For patients *taking this medicine for high blood pressure:*
- In addition to the use of the medicine your doctor has prescribed, treatment for your high blood pressure may include weight control and care in the types of foods you eat, especially foods high in sodium. Your doctor will tell you which of these are most important for you. You should check with your doctor before changing your diet.
- Many patients who have high blood pressure will not notice any signs of the problem. In fact, many may feel normal. It is very important that you *take your medicine exactly as directed* and that you keep your appointments with your doctor even if you feel well.
- Remember that doxazosin will not cure your high blood pressure but it does help control it. Therefore, you must continue to take it as directed if you expect to lower your blood pressure and keep it down. *You may have to take*

high blood pressure medicine for the rest of your life. If high blood pressure is not treated, it can cause serious problems such as heart failure, blood vessel disease, stroke, or kidney disease.

For patients *taking this medicine for benign enlargement of the prostate:*

- Remember that doxazosin will not shrink the size of your prostate but it does help to relieve the symptoms of this condition. You may still need to have surgery later.
- It may take up to 2 weeks before your symptoms improve.

Dosing—The dose of doxazosin will be different for different patients. *Follow your doctor's orders or the directions on the label.* The following information includes only the average doses of doxazosin. *If your dose is different, do not change it* unless your doctor tells you to do so.

The number of tablets that you take depends on the strength of the medicine.

- For *oral* dosage form (tablets):
  —For benign enlargement of the prostate:
  - Adults—At first, 1 milligram (mg) once a day, in the morning or in the evening. Your doctor may increase your dose slowly up to 8 mg once a day.
  —For high blood pressure:
  - Adults—1 mg once a day to start. Your doctor may increase your dose slowly to as much as 16 mg once a day.
  - Children—Use and dose must be determined by your doctor.

Missed dose—If you miss a dose of this medicine, take it as soon as possible. However, if it is almost time for your next dose, skip the missed dose and go back to your regular dosing schedule. Do not double doses.

If you miss several doses, call your doctor to see at what dose you should start again.

Storage—To store this medicine:

- Keep out of the reach of children.
- Store away from heat and direct light.
- Do not store in the bathroom, near the kitchen sink, or in other damp places. Heat or moisture may cause the medicine to break down.
- Do not keep outdated medicine or medicine no longer needed. Be sure that any discarded medicine is out of the reach of children.

Precautions While Using This Medicine

It is important that your doctor check your progress at regular visits to make sure that this medicine is working properly. This is especially important for elderly patients, who may be more sensitive to the effects of this medicine.

For patients *taking this medicine for high blood pressure:*

- *Do not take other medicines unless they have been discussed with your doctor.* This especially includes over-the-counter (nonprescription) medicines for appetite control, asthma, colds, cough, hay fever, or sinus problems, since they may tend to increase your blood pressure.

Dizziness, lightheadedness, or sudden fainting may occur after you take this medicine, especially when you get up from a lying or sitting position. These effects are more likely to occur when you take the first dose of this medicine. Taking the first dose at bedtime may prevent problems. However, *be especially careful if you need to get up during the night.* These effects may also occur with any doses you take after the first dose. Getting up slowly may help lessen this problem. *If you feel dizzy, lie down so that you do not faint.* Then sit for a few moments before standing to prevent the dizziness from returning.

The dizziness, lightheadedness, or sudden fainting is more likely to occur if you drink alcohol, stand for a long time, exercise, or if the weather is hot. *While you are taking this medicine, be careful to limit the amount of alcohol you drink. Also, use extra care during exercise or hot weather or if you must stand for a long time.*

Doxazosin may cause some people to become drowsy or less alert than they are normally. *Make sure you know how you react to this medicine before you drive, use machines, or do anything else that could be dangerous if you are dizzy, drowsy, or are not alert.* After you have taken several doses of this medicine, these effects should lessen.

The possibility of priapism, a painful or prolonged erection of the penis, is a rare side effect that can occur when taking doxazosin and must have immediate medical attention.

Side Effects of This Medicine

Along with its needed effects, a medicine may cause some unwanted effects. Although not all of these side effects may occur, if they do occur they may need medical attention.

Check with your doctor as soon as possible if any of the following side effects occur:
More common
  Dizziness or lightheadedness

Less common
  Dizziness or lightheadedness when getting up from a lying or sitting position; fainting (sudden); fast and pounding heartbeat; irregular heartbeat; shortness of breath; swelling of feet or lower legs
Rare
  Painful or prolonged erection of the penis (called priapism), although extremely rare, must have immediate medical attention. If painful or prolonged erection occurs, call your doctor or go to an emergency room as soon as possible

Other side effects may occur that usually do not need medical attention. These side effects may go away during treatment as your body adjusts to the medicine. However, check with your doctor if any of the following side effects continue or are bothersome:
More common
  Headache; unusual tiredness

Less common
  Nausea; nervousness, restlessness, unusual irritability; runny nose; sleepiness or drowsiness

Other side effects not listed above may also occur in some patients. If you notice any other effects, check with your doctor.

Revised: 05/21/99

DOXEPIN   Topical

Commonly used brand name(s):

In the U.S.—
   Zonalon

In Canada—
   Zonalon

Description

Topical doxepin (DOX-e-pin) is used to relieve itching in patients with certain types of eczema. It appears to work by preventing the effects of histamine, which is a substance produced by the body that causes itching.

Doxepin is available only with your doctor's prescription in the following dosage form:

Topical
- Cream (U.S. and Canada)

Before Using This Medicine

In deciding to use a medicine, the risks of using the medicine must be weighed against the good it will do. This is a decision you and your doctor will make. For topical doxepin, the following should be considered:

Allergies—Tell your doctor if you have ever had any unusual or allergic reaction to doxepin. Also tell your health care professional if you are allergic to any other substances, such as foods, preservatives, or dyes.

Pregnancy—Doxepin has not been studied in pregnant women. However, doxepin has not been shown to cause birth defects or other problems in animal studies.

Breast-feeding—Doxepin passes into the breast milk. Oral doxepin has been shown to cause unwanted effects in the breast-fed baby. Therefore, it may be necessary for you to use another medicine or to stop breast-feeding during treatment with topical doxepin. Be sure you have discussed the risk and benefits of the medicine with your doctor.

Children—Studies on this medicine have been done only in adult patients, and there is no specific information comparing use of doxepin in children with use in other age groups.

Older adults—Many medicines have not been studied specifically in older people. Therefore, it may not be known whether they work exactly the same way they do in younger adults. Although there is no specific information comparing use of doxepin in the elderly with use in other age groups, this medicine is not expected to cause different side effects or problems in older people than it does in younger adults.

Other medicines—Although certain medicines should not be used together at all, in other cases two different medicines may be used together even if an interaction might occur. In these cases, your doctor may want to change the dose, or other precautions may be necessary. When you are using topical doxepin, it is especially important that your health care professional know if you are taking any of the following:

- Alcohol or
- Central nervous system (CNS) depressants (medicines that cause drowsiness) or
- Tricyclic antidepressants (medicines for depression)— Drinking alcohol or using these medicines with topical

doxepin may cause increased CNS depressant effects such as drowsiness

- Cimetidine (e.g., Tagamet)
- Debrisoquine (e.g., Declinax)
- Dextromethorphan (e.g., Benylin DM)
- Medicines that correct heart rhythm problems, (encainide [e.g., Enkaid], flecainide [e.g., Tambocor], propafenone [e.g., Rythmol], quinidine [e.g., Cardioquin])— Using these medicines with topical doxepin may increase the chance of side effects
- Monoamine oxidase (MAO) inhibitors (furazolidone [e.g., Furoxone], isocarboxazid [e.g., Marplan], phenelzine [e.g., Nardil], procarbazine [e.g., Matulane], selegiline [e.g., Eldepryl], tranylcypromine [e.g., Parnate])— Using topical doxepin while you are taking or within 2 weeks of taking MAO inhibitors may cause sudden high body temperature, excitability, severe convulsions, and even death; however, sometimes some of these medicines may be used together under close supervision by your doctor

Other medical problems—The presence of other medical problems may affect the use of topical doxepin. Make sure you tell your doctor if you have any other medical problems, especially:

- Glaucoma or
- Urinary tract blockage or difficult urination—Using topical doxepin may make these conditions worse

Proper Use of This Medicine

Topical doxepin is *for external use only*. Do not use this medicine orally, do not use it on the eyes, or inside of the vagina.

Use this medicine exactly as directed. Do not use more of it, do not use it more often, and do not use it for more than 8 days. Also, do not apply it to an area of skin larger than recommended by your doctor. To do so may increase the chance of side effects.

Apply a thin layer of doxepin cream to only the affected area(s) of the skin and rub in gently.

To help clear up your skin problem it is very important that you keep using topical doxepin for the full time of treatment. Do not miss any doses.

Do not cover with a bandage or otherwise wrap the area of skin being treated. This may increase the amount of medicine that gets into the bloodstream, thereby increasing the chance of side effects.

Dosing—The dose of topical doxepin will be different for different patients. *Follow your doctor's orders or the directions on the label.* The following information includes only the average dose of topical doxepin. *If your dose is different, do not change it* unless your doctor tells you to do so.

The number of doses you apply each day, the time allowed between doses, and the length of time you use the medicine depend on the severity of the medical problem for which you are using topical doxepin.

- For *topical* dosage form (cream):
  - —For itching due to eczema:
    - Adults—Apply a thin layer to the affected area(s) of the skin four times a day. Space the doses or

applications at least three or four hours apart. Treatment may be continued for up to eight days.
- Children—Use and dose must be determined by your doctor.

Missed dose—If you miss a dose of this medicine, apply it as soon as possible. However, if it is almost time for your next dose, skip the missed dose and go back to your regular dosing schedule. Do not double doses.

Storage—To store this medicine:
- Keep out of the reach of children.
- Store away from heat and direct light.
- Keep the medicine from freezing. Do not refrigerate.
- Do not keep outdated medicine or medicine no longer needed. Be sure that any discarded medicine is out of the reach of children.

Precautions While Using This Medicine

If your skin problem does not improve after 8 days or if it becomes worse, check with your doctor.

This medicine will add to the effects of alcohol (alcoholic beverages or other alcohol-containing preparations [e.g., elixirs, cough syrups, tonics]) and other CNS depressants (medicines that slow down the nervous system, possibly causing drowsiness). Some examples of CNS depressants are antihistamines or medicine for hay fever, other allergies, or colds; sedatives, tranquilizers, or sleeping medicine; prescription pain medicine or narcotics; barbiturates; medicine for seizures; muscle relaxants; or anesthetics, including some dental anesthetics. *Check with your doctor before taking any of the above while you are using this medicine.*

Topical doxepin may cause some people to become drowsy. Make sure you know how to react to this medicine before you drive, use machines, or do other jobs that require you to be alert. If too much drowsiness occurs, it may be necessary to use less medicine, use it less often, or stop using it completely. However, check with your doctor first before lessening your dose or stopping use of this medicine.

This medicine may cause dryness of the mouth. For temporary relief, use sugarless gum or candy, or melt bits of ice in your mouth, or use a saliva substitute. However, if your mouth continues to feel dry for more than 2 weeks, check with your medical doctor or dentist. Continuing dryness of the mouth may increase the chance of dental disease, including tooth decay, gum disease, and fungus infections.

Side Effects of This Medicine

Along with its needed effects, a medicine may cause some unwanted effects. Although not all of these side effects may occur, if they do occur they may need medical attention.

Check with your doctor as soon as possible if any of the following side effects occur:
More common
Burning, crawling, or tingling sensation of the skin; swelling at the site of application; worsening of eczema and itching
Rare
Fever
Symptoms of overdose
Abdominal pain and swelling; blurring of vision; convulsions (seizures); decreased awareness or responsiveness; difficulty in breathing; difficulty in passing urine; dizziness, fainting, or lightheadedness; drowsiness; enlarged pupils; excessive dryness of mouth; extremely high fever or body temperature; extremely low body temperature; fast heartbeat; increased or excessive unconscious or jerking movements; incurable constipation; irregular heartbeat; unconsciousness; vomiting; weak pulse

Other side effects may occur that usually do not need medical attention. These side effects may go away during treatment as your body adjusts to the medicine. However, check with your doctor if any of the following side effects continue or are bothersome:
More common
Burning and/or stinging at the site of application; changes in taste; dizziness; drowsiness; dryness and tightness of skin; dryness of mouth and/or lips; emotional changes; headache; thirst; unusual tiredness or weakness
Less common
Anxiety; irritation, tingling, scaling, and cracking of skin; nausea

Other side effects not listed above may also occur in some patients. If you notice any other effects, check with your doctor.

Developed: 05/26/95

DOXORUBICIN   Systemic

Commonly used brand name(s):

In the U.S.—
Adriamycin PFS
Adriamycin RDF
Rubex
Generic name product may be available.

In Canada—
Adriamycin PFS
Adriamycin RDF

Description

Doxorubicin (dox-oh-ROO-bi-sin) belongs to the general group of medicines known as antineoplastics. It is used to treat some kinds of cancers of the blood; lymph system; bladder; breast; stomach; lung; ovaries; thyroid; nerves; kidneys; bones; and soft tissues, including muscles and tendons. It may also be used to treat other kinds of cancer, as determined by your doctor.

Doxorubicin seems to interfere with the growth of cancer cells, which are then eventually destroyed by the body. Since the growth of normal body cells may also be affected by doxorubicin, other effects will also occur. Some of these may be serious and must be reported to your doctor. Other effects, like hair loss, may not be serious but may cause concern. Some effects may not occur until months or years after the medicine is used.

Before you begin treatment with doxorubicin, you and your doctor should talk about the good this medicine will do as well as the risks of using it.

Doxorubicin is to be administered only by or under the supervision of your doctor. It is available in the following dosage form:

Parenteral
- Injection (U.S. and Canada)

Before Using This Medicine

In deciding to use a medicine, the risks of taking the medicine must be weighed against the good it will do. This is a decision you and your doctor will make. For doxorubicin, the following should be considered:

Allergies—Tell your doctor if you have ever had any unusual or allergic reaction to doxorubicin or lincomycin.

Pregnancy—There is a chance that this medicine may cause birth defects if either the male or female is receiving it at the time of conception or if it is taken by the mother during pregnancy. Studies in rats and rabbits have shown that doxorubicin causes birth defects in the fetus and other problems (including miscarriage). In addition, many cancer medicines may cause sterility, which could be permanent. Although sterility has been reported in animals and humans with this medicine, this is less likely to occur in humans than in animals.

Be sure that you have discussed these possible effects with your doctor before receiving this medicine. Before receiving doxorubicin make sure your doctor knows if you are pregnant or if you may become pregnant. It is best to use some kind of birth control while you are receiving doxorubicin. Tell your doctor right away if you think you have become pregnant while receiving doxorubicin.

Breast-feeding—Because doxorubicin may cause serious side effects, breast-feeding is generally not recommended while you are receiving this medicine.

Children—Heart problems are more likely to occur in children younger than 2 years of age, who are usually more sensitive to the effects of doxorubicin.

Older adults—Heart problems are more likely to occur in the elderly, who are usually more sensitive to the effects of doxorubicin. The elderly may also be more likely to have blood problems.

Other medicines—Although certain medicines should not be used together at all, in other cases two different medicines may be used together even if an interaction might occur. In these cases, your doctor may want to change the dose, or other precautions may be necessary. When receiving doxorubicin it is especially important that your health care professional know if you are taking any of the following:
- Amphotericin B by injection (e.g., Fungizone) or
- Antithyroid agents (medicine for overactive thyroid) or
- Azathioprine (e.g., Imuran) or
- Chloramphenicol (e.g., Chloromycetin) or
- Colchicine or
- Flucytosine (e.g., Ancobon) or
- Ganciclovir (e.g., Cytovene) or
- Interferon (e.g., Intron A, Roferon-A) or
- Plicamycin (e.g., Mithracin) or
- Zidovudine (e.g., AZT, Retrovir) or
- If you have ever been treated with radiation or cancer medicines—Doxorubicin may increase the effects of these medicines or radiation therapy on the blood
- If you have ever been treated with radiation to your chest—Risk of heart problems caused by doxorubicin may be increased

- Probenecid (e.g., Benemid) or
- Sulfinpyrazone (e.g., Anturane)—Doxorubicin may raise the concentration of uric acid in the blood. Since these medicines are used to lower uric acid levels, they may not work as well in patients receiving doxorubicin

Other medical problems—The presence of other medical problems may affect the use of doxorubicin. Make sure you tell your doctor if you have any other medical problems, especially:
- Chickenpox (including recent exposure) or
- Herpes zoster (shingles)—Risk of severe disease affecting other parts of the body
- Gout or
- Kidney stones—Doxorubicin may increase levels of uric acid in the body, which can cause gout or kidney stones
- Heart disease—Risk of heart problems caused by doxorubicin may be increased
- Liver disease—Effects of doxorubicin may be increased because of its slower removal from the body

Proper Use of This Medicine

Doxorubicin is sometimes given together with certain other medicines. If you are receiving a combination of medicines, it is important that you receive each one at the proper time. If you are taking some of these medicines by mouth, ask your health care professional to help you plan a way to take them at the right times.

While you are using this medicine, your doctor may want you to drink extra fluids so that you will pass more urine. This will help prevent kidney problems and keep your kidneys working well.

Doxorubicin often causes nausea and vomiting. However, it is very important that you continue to receive the medication, even if you begin to feel ill. Ask your health care professional for ways to lessen these effects.

Dosing—The dose of doxorubicin will be different for different patients. The dose that is used may depend on a number of things, including what the medicine is being used for, the patient's body size, and whether or not other medicines are also being taken. *If you are receiving doxorubicin at home, follow your doctor's orders or the directions on the label.* If you have any questions about the proper dose of doxorubicin, ask your doctor.

Precautions While Using This Medicine

It is very important that your doctor check your progress at regular visits to make sure that this medicine is working properly and to check for unwanted effects.

While you are being treated with doxorubicin, and after you stop treatment with it, *do not have any immunizations (vaccinations) without your doctor's approval.* Doxorubicin may lower your body's resistance, and there is a chance you might get the infection the immunization is meant to prevent. In addition, other persons living in your household should not take oral polio vaccine, since there is a chance they could pass the polio virus on to you. Also, avoid persons who have taken oral polio vaccine within the last several months. Do not get close to them, and do not stay in the same room with them for very long. If you cannot take these precautions, you should consider wearing a protective face mask that covers the nose and mouth.

Doxorubicin can temporarily lower the number of white blood cells in your blood, increasing the chance of getting an infection. It can also lower the number of platelets, which are necessary for proper blood clotting. If this occurs, there are certain precautions you can take, especially when your blood count is low, to reduce the risk of infection or bleeding:

- If you can, avoid people with infections. *Check with your doctor immediately* if you think you are getting an infection or if you get a fever or chills, cough or hoarseness, lower back or side pain, or painful or difficult urination.
- *Check with your doctor immediately* if you notice any unusual bleeding or bruising; black, tarry stools; blood in urine or stools; or pinpoint red spots on your skin.
- Be careful when using a regular toothbrush, dental floss, or toothpick. Your medical doctor, dentist, or nurse may recommend other ways to clean your teeth and gums. Check with your medical doctor before having any dental work done.
- Do not touch your eyes or the inside of your nose unless you have just washed your hands and have not touched anything else in the meantime.
- Be careful not to cut yourself when you are using sharp objects such as a safety razor or fingernail or toenail cutters.
- Avoid contact sports or other situations where bruising or injury could occur.

If doxorubicin accidentally seeps out of the vein into which it is injected, it may damage some tissues and cause scarring. *Tell the doctor or nurse right away if you notice redness, pain, or swelling at the place of injection.*

Side Effects of This Medicine

Along with its needed effects, a medicine may cause some unwanted effects. Although not all of these side effects may occur, if they do occur they may need medical attention.

Also, because of the way these medicines act on the body, there is a chance that they might cause other unwanted effects that may not occur until months or years after the medicine is used. These delayed effects may include certain types of cancer, such as leukemia. Discuss these possible effects with your doctor.

Check with your doctor or nurse immediately if any of the following side effects occur:
Less common
  Fast or irregular heartbeat; pain at place of injection; shortness of breath; swelling of feet and lower legs
Rare
  Black, tarry stools; blood in urine; pinpoint red spots on skin; unusual bleeding or bruising; wheezing

Check with your health care professional as soon as possible if any of the following side effects occur:
More common
  Sores in mouth and on lips
Less common
  Cough or hoarseness accompanied by fever or chills; darkening or redness of skin (if you recently had radiation treatment); fever or chills; joint pain; lower back or side pain accompanied by fever or chills; painful or difficult urination accompanied by fever or chills; red streaks along injected vein; stomach pain
Rare
  Skin rash or itching

Other side effects may occur that usually do not need medical attention. These side effects may go away during treatment as your body adjusts to the medicine. Also, your health care professional may be able to tell you about ways to prevent or reduce some of these side effects. Check with your health care professional if any of the following side effects continue or are bothersome or if you have any questions about them:
More common
  Nausea and vomiting
Less common
  Darkening of soles, palms, or nails; diarrhea

Doxorubicin causes the urine to turn reddish in color, which may stain clothes. This is not blood. It is to be expected and only lasts for 1 or 2 days after each dose is given.

This medicine often causes a temporary and total loss of hair. After treatment with doxorubicin has ended, normal hair growth should return.

After you stop receiving doxorubicin, it may still produce some side effects that need attention. During this period of time, *check with your doctor or nurse immediately* if you notice any of the following side effects:
  Fast or irregular heartbeat; shortness of breath; swelling of feet and lower legs

Other side effects not listed above may also occur in some patients. If you notice any other effects, check with your health care professional.

Additional Information

Once a medicine has been approved for marketing for a certain use, experience may show that it is also useful for other medical problems. Although these uses are not included in product labeling, doxorubicin is used in certain patients with the following medical conditions:

- Autoimmune deficiency syndrome (AIDS)-associated Kaposi's sarcoma (a type of cancer of the skin and mucous membranes that is more common in patients with AIDS)
- Cancer of the adrenal cortex (the outside layer of the adrenal gland)
- Cancer of the cervix
- Cancer of the endometrium
- Cancer of the esophagus
- Cancers of the head and neck
- Cancer of the liver
- Cancer of the pancreas
- Cancer of the prostate
- Cancer of the thymus (a small organ found under the breast bone)
- Carcinoid tumors
- Chronic lymphocytic leukemia (a type of cancer of the blood and lymph system)
- Ewing's sarcoma (a type of cancer found in the bone)
- Gestational trophoblastic tumors (tumors in the uterus or womb)
- Hepatoblastoma (a certain type of liver cancer that occurs in children)
- Multiple myeloma (a certain type of cancer of the blood)
- Non-small cell lung cancer (a certain type of lung cancer usually associated with prior smoking, passive smoking, or radon exposure)
- Retinoblastoma (a type of eye cancer found primarily in children)
- Tumors in the ovaries

Other than the above information, there is no additional information relating to proper use, precautions, or side effects for these uses.

Revised: 06/17/98
Interim revision: 06/15/99

DOXORUBICIN, LIPOSOMAL
Systemic

Commonly used brand name(s):

In the U.S.—
Doxil

In Canada—
Caelyx

Description

Liposomal doxorubicin (LIP-oh-som-al dox-oh-ROO-bi-sin) belongs to the general group of medicines known as antineoplastics. It is used to treat some kinds of cancer.

Liposomal doxorubicin seems to interfere with the growth of cancer cells, which are eventually destroyed. Since the growth of normal body cells may also be affected by liposomal doxorubicin, other effects will also occur. Some of these may be serious and must be reported to your doctor. Other effects, like hair loss, may not be serious but may cause concern. Some effects may not occur for months or years after the medicine is used.

Before you begin treatment with liposomal doxorubicin, you and your doctor should talk about the good this medicine will do as well as the risks of using it.

Liposomal doxorubicin is to be administered only by or under the immediate supervision of your doctor. It is available in the following dosage form:

Parenteral
• Injection (U.S. and Canada)

Before Receiving This Medicine

In deciding to use a medicine, the risks of taking the medicine must be weighed against the good it will do. This is a decision you and your doctor will make. For liposomal doxorubicin, the following should be considered:

Allergies—Tell your doctor if you have ever had any unusual or allergic reaction to liposomal doxorubicin. Also tell your health care professional if you are allergic to any other substances, such as preservatives.

Pregnancy—This medicine may cause birth defects if either the male or the female parent is receiving it at the time of conception or if it is taken by the mother during pregnancy. In addition, many cancer medicines may cause sterility, which may be permanent. Although sterility has been reported only in male dogs treated with the active ingredient of this medicine, the possibility of an effect in human males should be kept in mind.

Be sure that you have discussed this with your doctor before receiving this medicine. It is best to use some kind of birth control while you are receiving liposomal doxorubicin. Tell your doctor right away if you think you have become pregnant while receiving liposomal doxorubicin.

Breast-feeding—Because liposomal doxorubicin may cause serious side effects in a nursing baby, breast-feeding is generally not recommended while you are receiving it.

Children—There is no specific information comparing the use of liposomal doxorubicin in children with use in any other age group. Safety and efficacy of liposomal doxorubicin in children have not been established. However, problems are more likely to occur in children younger than 2 years of age, who are usually more sensitive to the effects of the active ingredient, doxorubicin.

Older adults— This medicine has been tested in a limited number of patients 60 years of age or older and has not been shown to cause different side effects in older people than it does in younger adults. However, problems are more likely to occur in the elderly, who are usually more sensitive to the effects of the active ingredient, doxorubicin. The elderly are also more likely to have blood problems.

Other medicines—Although certain medicines should not be used together at all, in other cases two different medicines may be used together even if an interaction might occur. In these cases, your doctor may want to change the dose, or other precautions may be necessary. When you are taking liposomal doxorubicin, it is especially important that your health care professional know if you are taking any of the following:

• Amphotericin B by injection (e.g., Fungizone) or
• Antithyroid agents (medicine for overactive thyroid) or
• Azathioprine (e.g., Imuran) or
• Chloramphenicol (e.g., Chloromycetin) or
• Colchicine or
• Flucytosine (e.g., Ancobon) or
• Ganciclovir (e.g., Cytovene) or
• Interferon (e.g., Intron A, Roferon-A) or
• Plicamycin (e.g., Mithracin) or
• Zidovudine (e.g., AZT, Retrovir) or
• If you have ever been treated with radiation or cancer medicines—Liposomal doxorubicin may increase the effects of these medicines or radiation therapy on the blood

• Daunorubicin (e.g., Cerubidine) or
• Doxorubicin (e.g., Adriamycin) or
• Idarubicin (e.g., Idamycin) or
• Mitoxantrone (e.g., Novantrone)—Concurrent use of maximum cumulative doses of other anthracyclines with liposomal doxorubicin may increase risk of heart damage or blood problems. Concurrent use may increase risk of liver problems.

Other medical problems—The presence of other medical problems may affect the use of liposomal doxorubicin. Make sure you tell your doctor if you have any other medical problems, especially:

• Chickenpox (including recent exposure) or
• Herpes zoster (shingles)—Risk of severe disease affecting other parts of the body

• Heart disease—Risk of heart problems caused by liposomal doxorubicin may be increased

• Infection—Liposomal doxorubicin can decrease your body's ability to fight infection

• Liver disease—Effects of liposomal doxorubicin may be increased because of slower removal from the body

Proper Use of This Medicine

Liposomal doxorubicin is sometimes given together with certain other medicines. If you are using a combination of medicines, it is important that you receive each one at the proper time. If you are taking some of these medicines by mouth, ask your health care professional to help you plan a way to take them at the right times.

While you are receiving liposomal doxorubicin, your doctor may want you to drink extra fluids so that you will pass more urine. This will help prevent kidney problems and keep your kidneys working well.

This medicine often causes nausea and vomiting. However, it is very important that you continue to receive it, even if you begin to feel ill. Ask your health care professional for ways to lessen these effects.

Dosing—The dose of liposomal doxorubicin will be different for different patients. The dose that is used may depend on a number of things, including what the medicine is being used for, the patient's size, and whether or not other medicines are also being taken. *If you are receiving liposomal doxorubicin at home, follow your doctor's orders or the directions on the label.* If you have any questions about the proper dose of liposomal doxorubicin, ask your doctor.

Precautions While Using This Medicine

It is very important that your doctor check your progress at regular visits to make sure that this medicine is working properly and to check for unwanted effects.

While you are being treated with liposomal doxorubicin, and after you stop treatment with it, *do not have any immunizations (vaccinations) without your doctor's approval.* Liposomal doxorubicin may lower your body's resistance and there is a chance you might get the infection the immunization is meant to prevent. In addition, other persons living in your household should not take oral poliovirus vaccine since there is a chance they could pass the poliovirus on to you. Also, avoid persons who have taken oral poliovirus vaccine. Do not get close to them, and do not stay in the same room with them for very long. If you cannot take these precautions, you should consider wearing a protective face mask that covers the nose and the mouth.

Liposomal doxorubicin can temporarily lower the number of white blood cells in your blood, increasing the chance of getting an infection. It can also lower the number of platelets, which are necessary for proper blood clotting. If this occurs, there are certain precautions you can take, especially when your blood count is low, to reduce the risk of infection or bleeding:

- If you can, avoid people with infections. *Check with your doctor immediately* if you think you are getting an infection or if you get a fever or chills, cough or hoarseness, lower back or side pain, or painful or difficult urination.
- *Check with your doctor immediately* if you notice any unusual bleeding or bruising; black, tarry stools; blood in urine or stools; or pinpoint red spots on your skin.
- Do not touch your eyes or the inside of your nose unless you have just washed your hands and have not touched anything else in the meantime.

- Be careful not to cut yourself when you are using sharp objects such as a safety razor or fingernail or toenail cutters.
- Avoid contact sports or other situations where bruising or injury can occur.

If liposomal doxorubicin accidentally seeps out of the vein into which it is injected, it may damage some tissues and cause scarring. *Tell the doctor or nurse right away if you notice redness, pain, or swelling at the place of injection.*

Be careful when using a regular toothbrush, dental floss, or toothpick. Your medical doctor, dentist, or nurse may recommend other ways to clean your teeth and gums. Check with your medical doctor before having any dental work done.

Side Effects of This Medicine

Along with its needed effects, a medicine may cause some unwanted effects. Although not all of these side effects may occur, if they do occur they may need medical attention.

Check with your doctor as soon as possible if any of the following side effects occur:
More common—in any treatment group
    Black, tarry stools; blood in urine or stools; chills; cough or hoarseness; facial swelling; fever; headache; loss of strength and energy; low blood pressure; lower back or side pain; painful or difficult urination; pinpoint red spots on skin; shortness of breath; sore throat; sores in mouth and on lips; unusual bleeding or bruising; unusual tiredness or weakness

Less common—in any treatment group
    Skin rash or itching

Rare—in any treatment group
    Yellowing of the eyes and skin

Less common—for patients being treated for Kaposi's sarcoma
    Cough; darkening or redness of skin; fast or irregular heartbeat; fever; pain at place of injection; reddening of skin; scaling of skin on hands and feet; shortness of breath; swelling of the feet and lower legs; swelling of skin; troubled breathing; ulceration of skin; wheezing

Rare—for patients being treated for Kaposi's sarcoma
    Blurred or loss of vision; eye pain; flushed, dry skin; frequent urination; fruit-like breath odor; unusual thirst

More common—for patients being treated for ovarian cancer
    Reddening of skin; scaling of skin on hands and feet; swelling of skin; ulceration of skin

Less common—for patients being treated for ovarian cancer
    Chest pain; decreased urination; rapid weight gain; bloating or swelling of face, hands, lower legs, and/or feet; fever or chills; cough or hoarseness; lower back or side pain; painful or difficult urination

Rare—for patients being treated for ovarian cancer
    Cough; difficulty swallowing; fast or irregular heartbeat; hives; pain at place of injection; puffiness or swelling of the eyelids or around the eyes, face, lips or tongue; shortness of breath; swelling of the feet and lower legs; tightness in chest; wheezing

Symptoms of overdose

Black, tarry stools; blood in urine or stools; cough or hoarseness accompanied by fever or chills; fever or chills; lower back or side pain accompanied by fever or chills; painful or difficult urination accompanied by fever or chills; pinpoint red spots on skin; sores in mouth and on lips; unusual bleeding or bruising

Other side effects may occur that usually do not need medical attention. These side effects may go away during treatment as your body adjusts to the medicine. However, check with your doctor if any of the following side effects continue or are bothersome:

More common—in any treatment group

Diarrhea; nausea; vomiting

Less common—in any treatment group

Back pain; difficulty swallowing; dizziness

More common—for patients being treated for Kaposi's sarcoma

Creamy white, curd-like patches in mouth or throat; pain when eating or swallowing

Less common—for patients being treated for Kaposi's sarcoma

Constipation; headache

More common—for patients being treated for ovarian cancer

Abdominal or stomach pain; loss of appetite; changes in the lining of the mouth or nose; constipation; headache; pain; rash; sore throat; tingling, burning, or prickly sensations

Less common—for patients being treated for ovarian cancer

Anxiety; bad, unusual, or unpleasant (after)taste; burning, dry, or itching eyes; difficulty swallowing; change in taste; excessive tearing; itching skin; muscle aches; redness, pain, swelling of eye, eyelid, or inner lining of eyelid; trouble sleeping

Rare—for patients being treated for ovarian cancer

Shakiness and unsteady walk; clumsiness, unsteadiness, trembling, or other problems with muscle control or coordination; change in sense of smell; chills; cough; fever; general feeling of discomfort or illness; increased white vaginal discharge; joint pain; nausea; shivering; sore throat; sweating; thinking abnormal; vomiting

Liposomal doxorubicin causes the urine to turn reddish in color, which may stain clothes. This is not blood. It is to be expected and only lasts for 1 or 2 days after each dose is given.

Other side effects may occur that usually do not need medical attention. These side effects may go away during treatment as your body adjusts to the medicine. Also, your health care professional may be able to tell you about ways to prevent or reduce some of these side effects. Check with your health care professional if any of the following side effects continue or are bothersome or if you have any questions about them:

More common—for patients being treated for ovarian cancer

Dry skin

Less common—for patients being treated for ovarian cancer

Change in skin color

This medicine often causes a temporary and total loss of hair. After treatment with liposomal doxorubicin has ended, normal hair growth should return.

After you stop using this medicine, your body may need time to adjust. The length of time this takes depends on the amount of medicine you were using and how long you used it. During this period of time, *check with your doctor or nurse immediately* if you notice any of the following side effects:

Fast or irregular heartbeat; shortness of breath; swelling of feet and lower legs

Other side effects not listed above may also occur in some patients. If you notice any other effects, check with your doctor.

Additional Information

Once a medicine has been approved for marketing for a certain use, experience may show that it is also useful for other medical problems. Although these uses are not included in product labeling, liposomal doxorubicin is used in certain patients with the following medical conditions:

• Cancer of the breast

Other than the above information, there is no additional information relating to proper use, precautions, or side effects for these uses.

Developed: 06/30/1998
Revised: 02/16/2001

DOXYCYCLINE   Dental

Commonly used brand name(s):

In the U.S.—
Atridox

Description

Doxycycline (dox-i-SYE-kleen) periodontal system contains the antibiotic doxycycline and is used to help treat periodontal disease (a disease of your gums), which is caused by bacteria growing beneath the gum line. Doxycycline works by preventing the growth of the bacteria. Doxycycline periodontal system is placed in deep gum pockets next to your teeth in order to reduce the depth of the pockets.

This medicine will be applied by your dentist, and is available in the following dosage form(s):

Dental
• Periodontal system (U.S.)

Before Using This Medicine

In deciding to use a medicine, the risks of using the medicine must be weighed against the good it will do. This is a decision you and your dentist or doctor will make. For doxycycline periodontal system, the following should be considered:

Allergies—Tell your dentist if you have ever had any unusual or allergic reaction to doxycycline or to other tetracyclines. Also tell your health care professional if you are allergic to any other substances, such as foods, preservatives, or dyes.

Pregnancy—Use of doxycycline periodontal system is not recommended during the last half of pregnancy. Tetracyclines, such as doxycycline, may cause the unborn infant's teeth to become discolored and may slow down the growth of the infant's teeth and bones if they are used during that time.

Breast-feeding—Use of doxycycline periodontal system is not recommended, since tetracyclines, such as doxycycline, pass into breast milk. They may cause unwanted effects in the breast-fed baby. It may be necessary for you to stop breast-feeding during treatment with doxycycline periodontal system. Be sure you have discussed the risks and benefits of the medicine with your dentist and doctor.

Children—In infants and children up to 8 years of age: Tetracyclines, such as doxycycline, may cause permanent discoloration of teeth and slow down the growth of bones. Use is not recommended.

In children 8 years of age and older: The safety and effectiveness of doxycycline periodontal system have not been established.

Older adults—Many medicines have not been studied specifically in older people. Therefore, it may not be known whether they work exactly the same way they do in younger adults or if they cause different side effects or problems in older people. There is no specific information comparing use of doxycycline periodontal system in the elderly with use in other age groups.

Other medicines—Although certain medicines should not be used together at all, in other cases two different medicines may be used together even if an interaction might occur. In these cases, your dentist or doctor may want to change the dose, or other precautions may be necessary. While you are receiving doxycycline periodontal system, it is especially important that your health care professional know if you are taking any of the following:

- Oral contraceptives (birth control pills) containing estrogen—Use of birth control pills with tetracyclines, such as doxycycline, may decrease the effect of the birth control pills and increase the chance of unwanted pregnancy

Other medical problems—The presence of other medical problems may affect the use of doxycycline periodontal system. Make sure you tell your dentist if you have any other medical problems, especially:

- Candidiasis (yeast infection) of the mouth—May make the condition worse

Proper Use of This Medicine

The treatment period for the doxycycline periodontal system is the 7 days after your dentist inserts it. If the system comes loose or falls out before the 7 days are up, check with your dentist.

Doxycycline periodontal system does not have to be removed by the dentist; it will dissolve. The dental dressing or adhesive that holds the system in place may fall out naturally. However, if the dental dressing or adhesive is still present after 7 days, it should be removed by the dentist.

Tetracyclines, such as doxycycline, should not be used in children up to 8 years of age. Tetracyclines may cause per-

manently discolored teeth and other problems in this age group.

Dosing—The dose of doxycycline periodontal system will be different for different patients. The following information includes only the average doses of doxycycline periodontal system.

- For *dental* dosage form:
  - —For antibacterial (dental):
    - Adults—Doxycycline periodontal system is placed by your dentist into one or more deep gum pockets next to your teeth. A dental dressing or adhesive will be placed on top to help keep the system in place. The treatment may be repeated four months later.
    - Infants and children up to 8 years of age—Use is not recommended. Tetracyclines, such as doxycycline, can permanently discolor teeth.
    - Children 8 years of age and older—Use and dose must be determined by your dentist.

Precautions While Using This Medicine

Oral contraceptives (birth control pills) containing estrogen may not work properly if you take them while you are using doxycycline periodontal system. Unplanned pregnancies may occur. You should use a different or additional means of birth control during the cycle in which doxycycline periodontal system is in place. If you have any questions about this, check with your health care professional.

For 7 days after receiving doxycycline periodontal system, do not floss or brush around the teeth that have been treated. Brushing or flossing may loosen the system or cause it to fall out.

Tetracyclines, such as doxycycline, may cause your skin to be more sensitive to sunlight than it is normally. Exposure to sunlight, even for brief periods of time, may cause a skin rash, itching, redness or other discoloration of the skin, or a severe sunburn. For a period of 7 days after receiving doxycycline periodontal system:

- Stay out of direct sunlight, especially between the hours of 10:00 a.m. and 3:00 p.m., if possible.
- Wear protective clothing, including a hat. Also, wear sunglasses.
- Apply a sun block product that has a skin protection factor (SPF) of at least 15. Some patients may require a product with a higher SPF number, especially if they have a fair complexion. If you have any questions about this, check with your health care professional.
- Apply a sun block lipstick that has an SPF of at least 15 to protect your lips.
- Do not use a sunlamp or tanning bed or booth.

You may still be sensitive to sunlight or sunlamps for 2 weeks to several months or more after the 7-day treatment period of doxycycline periodontal system. *If you have a severe reaction, check with your doctor.*

Dental—Use of doxycycline periodontal system is not recommended during the last half of pregnancy or in infants and children up to 8 years of age. Tetracyclines, such as doxycycline, may cause permanent discoloration of teeth and slow down the growth of bones. In addition, systemic tetracyclines, such as doxycycline, may favor the growth of oral candidiasis (yeast infection of the mouth).

Side Effects of This Medicine

Along with its needed effects, a medicine may cause some unwanted effects. Although not all of these side effects may occur, if they do occur they may need medical attention.

Check with your dentist or doctor as soon as possible if any of the following side effects occur:

Less common
> High blood pressure; looseness of tooth; tooth or gum pain (severe or continuing)

Other side effects may occur that usually do not need medical attention. These side effects may go away during treatment as your body adjusts to the medicine. However, check with your dentist or doctor if any of the following side effects continue or are bothersome:

More common
> Common cold–like symptoms; gum discomfort, pain, or soreness; headache; pressure sensitivity of tooth; toothache

Less common
> Abdominal bloating and/or stomach or pelvic pain; cough; diarrhea; gum redness; indigestion, upset stomach, or stomachache; influenza-like symptoms; mouth pain or soreness; muscle aches; sensitivity of tooth to heat or cold; shortness of breath; sleeplessness; sore throat; stuffy head, postnasal drip, or nasal congestion

Other side effects not listed above may also occur in some patients. If you notice any other effects, check with your dentist or doctor.

Developed: 12/22/98

DOXYCYCLINE—For Dental Use
Systemic

Commonly used brand name(s):

In the U.S.—
> Periostat

Description

Doxycycline (dox-i-SYE-kleen) belongs to the group of medicines known as tetracyclines. Although tetracyclines are antibiotics that are usually used to treat some types of infections, this form of doxycycline is used to help treat periodontitis (a disease of the gums).

The exact way doxycycline works on the gums is not known, but may involve blocking the effect of an enzyme called collagenase.

This medicine is available only with your doctor's prescription, in the following dosage form:

Oral
> • Capsules (U.S.)

Before Using This Medicine

In deciding to use a medicine, the risks of taking the medicine must be weighed against the good it will do. This is a decision you and your doctor will make. For doxycycline, the following should be considered:

Allergies—Tell your doctor if you have ever had any unusual or allergic reaction to doxycycline or to other tetracyclines. Also tell your health care professional if you are allergic to any other substances, such as foods, preservatives, or dyes.

Pregnancy—Use of doxycycline is not recommended during the last half of pregnancy. Tetracyclines, such as doxycycline, may cause the unborn infant's teeth to become discolored and may slow down the growth of the infant's teeth and bones if they are taken during that time.

Breast-feeding—Use of doxycycline is not recommended since tetracyclines, such as doxycycline, pass into breast milk. Tetracyclines may cause the nursing baby's teeth to become discolored and may slow down the growth of the baby's teeth. It may be necessary for you to stop breast-feeding during treatment with doxycyline. Be sure you have discussed the risks and benefits of the medicine with your dentist and doctor.

Children—Tetracyclines may cause permanent discoloration of teeth and slow down the growth of bones. Doxycycline should not be given to children up to 8 years of age unless directed by the child's doctor.

Older adults—Many medicines have not been studied specifically in older people. Therefore, it may not be known whether they work exactly the same way they do in younger adults or if they cause different side effects or problems in older people. There is no specific information comparing use of doxycycline in the elderly with use in other age groups.

Other medicines—Although certain medicines should not be used together at all, in other cases two different medicines may be used together even if an interaction might occur. In these cases, your doctor may want to change the dose, or other precautions may be necessary. When you are taking doxycycline, it is especially important that your health care professional know if you are taking any of the following:

> • Anticoagulants (blood thinners)—Tetracyclines may decrease clotting of blood, which could increase the effects of the blood thinner

> • Antacids or
> • Bismuth subsalicylate (e.g., Pepto-Bismol) or
> • Iron-containing medicine—Use of these medicines with doxycycline may decrease the amount of doxycycline absorbed into the body and decrease its effects

> • Oral contraceptives (birth control pills)—Use of birth control pills with tetracyclines may decrease the effect of the birth control pills and increase the chance of unwanted pregnancy

> • Penicillins—Tetracyclines may decrease the effects of penicillins against infection

Proper Use of This Medicine

It is best if this medicine is taken 1 hour before the morning and evening meals.

Take this medicine with a full glass (8 ounces) of water while you are standing up, to prevent irritation of the esophagus (tube between the throat and stomach) or stomach.

Dosing—The dose of doxycycline will be different for different patients. *Follow your doctor's orders or the directions on the label.* The following information includes only the average doses of doxycycline. *If your dose is different, do not change it* unless your doctor tells you to do so.

- For *oral* dosage form (capsules):
  —For periodontitis (gum disease):
  - Adults—20 mg twice a day.
  - Children—Use in children up to 8 years of age is not recommended. Tetracyclines, such as doxycycline, can permanently discolor teeth.
  - Children 8 years of age and older—Use and dose must be determined by your dentist or doctor.

Missed dose—If you miss a dose of this medicine, take it as soon as possible. However, if it is almost time for the next dose, skip the missed dose and go back to your regular dosing schedule. Do not double doses.

Storage—To store this medicine:
- Keep out of the reach of children.
- Store away from heat and direct light.
- Do not store in the bathroom, near the kitchen sink, or in other damp places. Heat or moisture may cause the medicine to break down.
- Do not keep outdated medicine or medicine no longer needed. Be sure that any discarded medicine is out of the reach of children.

Precautions While Using This Medicine

Do not take antacids or bismuth subsalicylate within 1 to 2 hours of taking doxycycline. In addition, *do not take iron-containing medicines* (including vitamin preparations containing iron) within 2 to 3 hours of taking doxycycline. To do so may keep doxycycline from working properly.

Oral contraceptives (birth control pills) may not work properly if you take them while you are taking tetracyclines. Unplanned pregnancies may occur. *You should use a different or additional means of birth control while you are taking doxycycline.* If you have any questions about this, check with your doctor.

Before having surgery (including dental surgery) with a general anesthetic, tell the medical doctor or dentist in charge that you are taking doxycycline.

Some people who take tetracyclines may become more sensitive to sunlight than they are normally. Exposure to sunlight, even for brief periods of time, may cause severe sunburn; skin rash, redness, itching, or discoloration; or vision changes. When you begin taking this medicine:

- Stay out of direct sunlight, especially between the hours of 10:00 a.m. and 3:00 p.m., if possible.
- Wear protective clothing, including a hat and sunglasses.
- Apply a sun block product that has a skin protection factor (SPF) of at least 15. Some patients may require a product with a higher SPF number, especially if they have a fair complexion. If you have any questions about this, check with your health care professional.
- Do not use a sunlamp or tanning bed or booth.

If you have a severe reaction from the sun, check with your doctor.

Side Effects of This Medicine

Along with its needed effects, a medicine may cause some unwanted effects. Although not all of these side effects may occur, if they do occur they may need medical attention.

Check with your dentist or doctor as soon as possible if any of the following side effects occur:
  Rare
    Increased sensitivity of skin to sunlight; itching of the rectal or genital areas; sore mouth or tongue

Other side effects may occur that usually do not need medical attention. These side effects may go away during treatment as your body adjusts to the medicine. However, check with your doctor if any of the following side effects continue or are bothersome:
  Less common
    Diarrhea; heartburn; joint pain; nausea

Other side effects not listed above may also occur in some patients. If you notice any other effects, check with your doctor.

Developed: 01/14/99

DRONABINOL   Systemic

Commonly used brand name(s):

In the U.S.—
  Marinol

In Canada—
  Marinol

Another commonly used name is delta-9-tetrahydrocannabinol (THC).

Description

Dronabinol (droe-NAB-i-nol) is used to prevent the nausea and vomiting that may occur after treatment with cancer medicines. It is used only when other kinds of medicine for nausea and vomiting do not work. Dronabinol is also used to increase appetite in patients with acquired immunodeficiency syndrome (AIDS).

Dronabinol is available only with your doctor's prescription. Prescriptions cannot be refilled, and you must obtain a new prescription from your doctor each time you need this medicine. It is available in the following dosage form:

  Oral
  - Capsules (U.S. and Canada)

Before Using This Medicine

In deciding to use a medicine, the risks of taking the medicine must be weighed against the good it will do. This is a decision you and your doctor will make. For dronabinol, the following should be considered:

Allergies—Tell your doctor if you have ever had any unusual or allergic reaction to dronabinol, marijuana products, or sesame oil. Also tell your health care professional if you are allergic to any other substances, such as foods, preservatives, or dyes.

Pregnancy—Studies have not been done in pregnant women. However, studies in animals have shown that dronabinol, given in doses many times the usual human dose, increases the risk of death of the fetus and decreases the number of live babies born.

Breast-feeding—Dronabinol passes into human breast milk. There is a possibility that serious unwanted effects may occur in the nursing infant.

Children—Although there is no specific information comparing use of dronabinol in children with use in other age groups, the effects that this medicine may have on the mind may be of special concern in children. Children should be watched closely while they are taking this medicine.

Older adults—This medicine has been tested in a limited number of patients up to 82 years of age and has not been shown to cause different side effects or problems in older people than it does in younger adults. However, the effects this medicine may have on the mind may be of special concern in the elderly. Therefore, older people should be watched closely while they are taking this medicine.

Other medicines—Although certain medicines should not be used together at all, in other cases two different medicines may be used together even if an interaction might occur. In these cases, your doctor may want to change the dose, or other precautions may be necessary. When you are taking dronabinol, it is especially important that your health care professional know if you are taking any of the following:

- Central nervous system (CNS) depressants (medicine that causes drowsiness) or
- Tricyclic antidepressants (medicine for depression)—Taking these medicines with dronabinol may increase the CNS depressant effects

Other medical problems—The presence of other medical problems may affect the use of dronabinol. Make sure you tell your doctor if you have any other medical problems, especially:

- Alcohol abuse (or history of) or
- Drug abuse or dependence (or history of)—Dependence on dronabinol may develop
- Bipolar disorder (manic or depressive states) or
- Heart disease or
- High blood pressure (hypertension) or
- Severe mental illness—Dronabinol may make the condition worse

Proper Use of This Medicine

Take this medicine only as directed by your physician. Do not take more of it, do not take it more often, and do not take it for a longer time than your doctor ordered. If too much is taken, it may lead to medical problems because of an overdose.

Dosing—The dose of dronabinol will be different for different patients. *Follow your doctor's orders or the directions on the label.* The following information includes only the average doses of dronabinol. *If your dose is different, do not change it* unless your doctor tells you to do so.

The number of capsules that you take depends on the strength of the medicine. Also, *the number of doses you take each day, the time allowed between doses, and the length of time you take the medicine depend on the medical problem for which you are taking dronabinol.*

- For *oral* dosage form (capsules):
  —For nausea and vomiting caused by cancer medicines:
    - Adults and teenagers—Dose is based on body surface area. Your doctor will tell you how much medicine to take and when to take it.

- Children—Dose is based on body surface area and must be determined by your doctor.
  —For increasing appetite in patients with AIDS:
    - Adults and teenagers—To start, 2.5 milligrams (mg) two times a day, taken before lunch and supper. Your doctor may change your dose depending on your condition. However, the dose is usually not more than 20 mg a day.
    - Children—Use and dose must be determined by your doctor.

Missed dose—If you miss a dose of this medicine, take it as soon as you remember. However, if it is almost time for your next dose, skip the missed dose and go back to your regular dosing schedule. *Do not double doses.*

Storage—To store this medicine:

- Keep out of the reach of children. Overdose is very dangerous in young children.
- Store away from heat and direct light.
- Do not store this medicine in the bathroom, near the kitchen sink, or in other damp places. Heat or moisture may cause the medicine to break down.
- Keep this medicine in the refrigerator but keep it from freezing.
- Do not keep outdated medicine or medicine no longer needed. Be sure that any discarded medicine is out of the reach of children.

Precautions While Using This Medicine

Dronabinol will add to the effects of alcohol and other CNS depressants (medicines that make you drowsy or less alert). Some examples of CNS depressants are antihistamines or medicine for hay fever, other allergies, or colds; sedatives, tranquilizers, or sleeping medicine; prescription pain medicines including other narcotics; barbiturates; medicine for seizures; muscle relaxants; or anesthetics, including some dental anesthetics. *Check with your doctor before taking any of the above while you are taking this medicine.*

This medicine may cause some people to become drowsy, dizzy, or lightheaded, or to feel a false sense of well-being. *Make sure you know how you react to this medicine before you drive, use machines, or do anything else that could be dangerous if you are dizzy or are not alert and clearheaded.*

Dizziness, lightheadedness, or fainting may occur, especially when you get up suddenly from a lying or sitting position. Getting up slowly may help lessen this problem.

If you think you or someone else may have taken an overdose of dronabinol, get emergency help at once. Taking an overdose of this medicine or taking alcohol or CNS depressants with this medicine may lead to severe mental effects. Signs of overdose include changes in mood, confusion, hallucinations, mental depression, nervousness or anxiety, and fast or pounding heartbeat.

Side Effects of This Medicine

Along with its needed effects, a medicine may cause some unwanted effects. Although not all of these side effects may occur, if they do occur they may need medical attention.

Check with your doctor as soon as possible if any of the following side effects occur:

Less common (may also be signs of overdose)
Amnesia (memory loss); changes in mood; confusion;

delusions; feelings of unreality; hallucinations (seeing, hearing, or feeling things that are not there); mental depression; nervousness or anxiety; fast or pounding heartbeat

Symptoms of overdose

Being forgetful; change in your sense of smell, taste, sight, sound, or touch; change in how fast you think time is passing; constipation; decrease in motor co-ordination; drowsiness (severe); dryness of mouth (severe); false sense of well-being; fast or pounding heartbeat; feeling dizzy or lightheaded, especially when getting up from a lying or sitting position; feeling sluggish; mood changes; panic reaction; problems in urinating; redness of eyes; seizures; slurred speech; unusual drowsiness or dullness

Other side effects may occur that usually do not need medical attention. These side effects may go away during treatment as your body adjusts to the medicine. However, check with your doctor if any of the following side effects continue or are bothersome:

More common

Clumsiness or unsteadiness; dizziness; drowsiness; false sense of well-being; nausea; trouble thinking; vomiting

Less common or rare

Blurred vision or any changes in vision; dryness of mouth; feeling faint or lightheaded, especially when getting up from a lying or sitting position; flushing of face; restlessness; unusual tiredness or weakness

Other side effects not listed above may also occur in some patients. If you notice any other effects, check with your doctor.

Revised: 02/21/2001

DROPERIDOL   Systemic

Commonly used brand name(s):

In the U.S.—
Inapsine
In Canada—
Inapsine

Description

Droperidol (droe-PER-i-dole) is used to produce sleepiness or drowsiness before surgery or certain procedures. It is also used to prevent nausea and vomiting after surgery.

This medicine is available only with your doctor's prescription, in the following dosage form(s):

Parenteral
- Injection (U.S. and Canada)

Before Receiving This Medicine

In deciding to use a medicine, the risks of using the medicine must be weighed against the good it will do. This is a decision you and your doctor will make. For droperidol, the following should be considered:

Allergies—Tell your doctor if you have ever had any un-usual or allergic reaction to droperidol, haloperidol, or similar medicines. Also tell your health care professional if you are allergic to any other substances, such as foods, preserva-tives, or dyes.

Pregnancy—Droperidol has been used in some pregnant patients. There was no increase in premature births or birth defects when droperidol was used. Droperidol has been used in patients undergoing cesarean section. Newborn babies whose mothers received droperidol did not have an increase in breathing problems.

Breast-feeding—Droperidol passes into breast milk. Breast-feeding is not recommended while you are receiving droperidol.

Children—Droperidol has not been studied in children up to 2 years of age. There is no specific information comparing the use of droperidol in children with use in other age groups. However, based on experience with similar drugs, children may be more likely than older patients to experience side effects after receiving droperidol, such as muscle spasms in the tongue, face, neck, and back, and inability to move the eyes.

Older adults—Older patients may be more likely than younger adult patients to experience dizziness and excessive sleepiness from droperidol.

Other medicines—Although certain medicines should not be used together at all, in other cases two different med-icines may be used together even if an interaction might occur. In these cases, your doctor may want to change the dose, or other precautions may be necessary. Tell your health care professional if you are taking any other drugs, including nonprescription (over-the-counter [OTC]) medicine.

Other medical problems—The presence of other med-ical problems may affect the use of droperidol. Make sure you tell your doctor if you have any other medical problems, es-pecially:
- Alcoholism or
- Hypokalemia (too little potassium in the blood) or
- Hypomagnesemia (too little magnesium in the blood) or
- Irregular heartbeat—Droperidol may increase the risk of irregular heartbeats
- Epilepsy—The risk of seizures may be increased
- Heart disease or
- Mental depression or
- Parkinsonism—Droperidol may worsen these condi-tions
- Hypovolemia—The risk of dizziness may be increased
- Liver disease—The risk of side effects may be in-creased
- Pheochromocytoma—High blood pressure and rapid heart rate may occur

Proper Use of This Medicine

Dosing—The dose of droperidol will be different for dif-ferent patients. Your health care professional will decide on the right amount for you, depending on:
- Your age;
- Your general physical condition;
- The reason you are receiving droperidol; and
- Other medicines you are taking or will receive before or after droperidol is given.

Precautions After Receiving This Medicine

For patients going home within a few hours after surgery:
- Droperidol and other medicines that may be given during surgery may cause some people to feel drowsy, tired, or weak for up to a few days afterwards. Therefore, for at least 24 hours (or longer if necessary) after receiving this medicine, do not drive, use machines, or do anything else that could be dangerous if you are dizzy or are not alert.
- Unless otherwise directed by your medical doctor, do not drink alcoholic beverages or take other central nervous system (CNS) depressants (medicines that slow down the nervous system, possibly causing drowsiness) for about 24 hours after you have received this medicine. To do so may add to the effects of droperidol. Some examples of CNS depressants are antihistamines or medicine for hay fever, other allergies, or colds; sedatives, tranquilizers, or sleeping medicine; prescription pain medicine or narcotics; barbiturates; medicine for seizures; and muscle relaxants.

Side Effects of This Medicine

Along with its needed effects, a medicine may cause some unwanted effects. Although not all of these side effects may occur, if they do occur they may need medical attention.

Check with your doctor as soon as possible if any of the following side effects occur:

Less common
Anxiety; high blood pressure; restlessness

Rare
Fever; fixed upward position of the eyeballs; spasm of the muscles of the tongue, face, neck, and back

Side effects are possible for one or two days after you receive droperidol. During this period of time, check with your doctor if you notice any of the side effects listed above.

Symptoms of overdose
Dizziness; fixed upward position of the eyeballs; restlessness; slowed breathing; spasm of the muscles of the tongue, face, neck, and back

Other side effects may occur that usually do not need medical attention. However, check with your doctor if any of the following side effects continue or are bothersome:

More common
Drowsiness; lightheadedness; rapid heart rate

Other side effects not listed above may also occur in some patients. If you notice any other effects, check with your doctor.

Additional Information

Once a medicine has been approved for marketing for a certain use, experience may show that it is also useful for other medical problems. Although these uses are not included in product labeling, droperidol is used in certain patients with the following medical condition:
- Severe agitation and combativeness

For patients receiving this medicine for severe agitation and combativeness, the dose administered will depend on the degree of agitation and the size of the patient.

Developed: 05/21/98

DYPHYLLINE   Systemic†

Commonly used brand name(s):

In the U.S.—

Dilor	Lufyllin
Dilor-400	Lufyllin-400

Generic name product may be available.

†Not commercially available in Canada.

Description

Dyphylline (DYE-fi-lin) is used to treat and/or prevent the symptoms of bronchial asthma, chronic bronchitis, and emphysema. It works by opening up the bronchial tubes (air passages of the lungs) and increasing the flow of air through them.

This medicine is available only with your doctor's prescription, in the following dosage forms:

Oral
- Elixir (U.S.)
- Tablets (U.S.)

Parenteral
- Injection (U.S.)

Before Using This Medicine

In deciding to use a medicine, the risks of taking the medicine must be weighed against the good it will do. This is a decision you and your doctor will make. For dyphylline, the following should be considered:

Allergies—Tell your doctor if you have ever had any unusual or allergic reaction to aminophylline, caffeine, dyphylline, oxtriphylline, theobromine, or theophylline. Also tell your health care professional if you are allergic to any other substances, such as foods, preservatives, or dyes.

Pregnancy—Dyphylline has not been studied in pregnant women. Before taking this medicine, make sure your doctor knows if you are pregnant or if you may become pregnant.

Breast-feeding—Dyphylline passes into breast milk. However, this medicine has not been reported to cause problems in nursing babies.

Children—Use of other bronchodilator medicines is preferred.

Older adults—As in younger patients, use of other bronchodilator medicines is preferred. Also, older patients with kidney disease may require a lower dose of dyphylline than do older adults without kidney disease.

Other medicines—Although certain medicines should not be used together at all, in other cases two different medicines may be used together even if an interaction might occur. In these cases, your doctor may want to change the dose, or other precautions may be necessary. When you are taking dyphylline, it is especially important that your health care provider know if you are taking any of the following:
- Beta-blockers including ophthalmics (acebutolol [e.g., Sectral], atenolol [e.g., Tenormin], betaxolol [e.g., Betoptic, Kerlone], bisoprolol [e.g., Zebeta], carteolol [e.g., Cartrol], labetalol [e.g., Normodyne], levobunolol [e.g., Betagan], metipranolol [e.g., OptiPranolol], metoprolol [e.g., Lopressor], nadolol [e.g., Corgard], oxprenolol [e.g., Trasicor], penbutolol [e.g., Levatol], pindolol [e.g., Visken], propranolol [e.g., Inderal], sotalol [e.g., So-

tacor], timolol [e.g., Blocadren, Timoptic])—These medicines may prevent dyphylline from working properly

- Probenecid (e.g., Benemid)—This medicine may increase the effects of dyphylline

- Xanthine-derivatives (aminophylline [e.g., Somophyllin], caffeine [e.g., NoDoz], Oxtriphylline [e.g., Choledyl], theophylline [e.g., Somophyllin-T])—The chance of side effects may be increased

Other medical problems—The presence of other medical problems may affect the use of dyphylline. Make sure you tell your doctor if you have any other medical problems, especially:

- Heart or blood vessel disease or
- Stomach ulcer (or history of) or other stomach problems—Dyphylline may make these conditions worse

- Heart failure or
- Kidney disease—The effects of dyphylline may be increased

Proper Use of This Medicine

For patients *taking this medicine by mouth:*

This medicine works best when there is a constant amount in the blood. To help keep the amount constant, dyphylline must be taken at regularly spaced times, as ordered by your doctor. Do not miss any doses.

This medicine also works best when taken with a glass of water on an empty stomach (either 30 minutes to 1 hour before meals or 2 hours after meals). However, in some cases your doctor may want you to take this medicine with meals or right after meals to lessen stomach upset.

Dosing—The dose of dyphylline will be different for different patients. *Follow your doctor's orders or the directions on the label.* The following information includes only the average doses of dyphylline. *If your dose is different, do not change it* unless your doctor tells you to do so.

The number of tablets or teaspoonfuls of elixir that you take depends on the strength of the medicine. Also, *the number of doses you take each day, the time allowed between doses, and the length of time you take the medicine depend on the medical problem for which you are taking dyphylline.*

- For *oral* dosage forms (elixir or tablets):
  —For asthma, bronchitis, or emphysema:
  - Adults—Dose is based on body weight. The usual dose is 15 milligrams (mg) per kilogram (6.8 mg per pound) of body weight up to four times a day (about six hours apart).
  - Children—Dose must be determined by your doctor.

Missed dose—If you miss a dose of this medicine, take it as soon as possible. However, if it is almost time for your next dose, skip the missed dose and go back to your regular dosing schedule. Do not double doses.

Storage—To store this medicine:

- Keep out of the reach of children.
- Store away from heat and direct light.
- Do not store tablets in the bathroom, near the kitchen sink, or in other damp places. Heat or moisture may cause the medicine to break down.
- Keep the liquid form of this medicine from freezing. Do not refrigerate.

- Do not keep outdated medicine or medicine no longer needed. Be sure that any discarded medicine is out of the reach of children.

Precautions While Using This Medicine

Your doctor should check your progress at regular visits, especially during the first few weeks of your treatment with this medicine.

This medicine may add to the central nervous system (CNS) stimulant effects of caffeine-containing foods or beverages such as chocolate, cocoa, tea, coffee, and cola drinks. *Avoid eating or drinking large amounts of these foods or beverages while using this medicine.* If you have questions about this, check with your doctor.

Before you have any kind of surgery that requires general anesthesia, tell the medical doctor in charge that you are using this medicine.

Side Effects of This Medicine

Along with its needed effects, a medicine may cause some unwanted effects. Although not all of these side effects may occur, if they do occur they may need medical attention.

Check with your doctor as soon as possible if any of the following side effects occur:

Less common
 Heartburn; vomiting

Symptoms of overdose
 Abdominal pain (continuing or severe); confusion or change in behavior; convulsions (seizures); dark or bloody vomit; diarrhea; fast and irregular heartbeat; fast heartbeat (continuing); nervousness or restlessness (continuing); trembling (continuing)

Other side effects may occur that usually do not need medical attention. These side effects may go away during treatment as your body adjusts to the medicine. However, check with your doctor if any of the following side effects continue or are bothersome:

Less common
 Fast heartbeat; headache; increased urination; nausea; nervousness; trembling; trouble in sleeping

Other side effects not listed above may also occur in some patients. If you notice any other effects, check with your doctor.

Developed: 07/10/95

ECONAZOLE Topical

Commonly used brand name(s):

In the U.S.—
 Spectazole

In Canada—
 Ecostatin

Description

Econazole (e-KONE-a-zole) belongs to the family of medicines called antifungals, which are used to treat infections caused by a fungus. They work by killing the fungus or preventing its growth.

Econazole cream is applied to the skin to treat fungus infections. These include:

- ringworm of the body (tinea corporis);
- ringworm of the foot (tinea pedis; athlete's foot);
- ringworm of the groin (tinea cruris; jock itch);
- tinea versicolor (sometimes called "sun fungus"); and
- certain other fungus infections, such as Candida (Monilia) infections.

Econazole is available only with your doctor's prescription, in the following dosage form:

Topical
- Cream (U.S. and Canada)

Before Using This Medicine

In deciding to use a medicine, the risks of using the medicine must be weighed against the good it will do. This is a decision you and your doctor will make. For topical econazole, the following should be considered:

Allergies—Tell your doctor if you have ever had any unusual or allergic reaction to econazole. Also tell your health care professional if you are allergic to any other substances, such as preservatives or dyes.

Pregnancy—Topical econazole has not been studied in pregnant women. Oral econazole has not been shown to cause birth defects in animal studies; however, it has been shown to cause other problems. Before using this medicine, make sure your doctor knows if you are pregnant or if you may become pregnant.

Breast-feeding—It is not known whether topical econazole passes into the breast milk. However, econazole, when given by mouth, does pass into the milk of rats and has caused problems in the young. Although most medicines pass into breast milk in small amounts, many of them may be used safely while breast-feeding. Mothers who are taking this medicine and who wish to breast-feed should discuss this with their doctor.

Children—Although there is no specific information comparing use of this medicine in children with use in other age groups, this medicine is not expected to cause different side effects or problems in children than it does in adults.

Older adults—Many medicines have not been studied specifically in older people. Therefore, it may not be known whether they work exactly the same way they do in younger adults. Although there is no specific information comparing use of econazole in the elderly with use in other age groups, this medicine is not expected to cause different side effects or problems in older people than it does in younger adults.

Other medicines—Although certain medicines should not be used together at all, in other cases two different medicines may be used together even if an interaction might occur. In these cases, your doctor may want to change the dose, or other precautions may be necessary. Tell your health care professional if you are using any other prescription or nonprescription (over the counter [OTC]) medicine.

Proper Use of This Medicine

Apply enough econazole to cover the affected and surrounding skin areas, and massage in gently.

Keep this medicine away from the eyes.

When econazole is used to treat certain types of fungus infections of the skin, an occlusive dressing (airtight covering,

such as kitchen plastic wrap) should *not* be applied over the medicine. To do so may cause irritation of the skin. *Do not apply an airtight covering over this medicine unless you have been directed to do so by your doctor.*

To help clear up your infection completely, *it is very important that you keep using econazole for the full time of treatment,* even if your symptoms begin to clear up after a few days. Since fungus infections may be very slow to clear up, you may have to continue using this medicine every day for several weeks or more. If you stop using this medicine too soon, your symptoms may return. *Do not miss any doses.*

Dosing—The dose of topical econazole will be different for different patients. *Follow your doctor's orders or the directions on the label.* The following information includes only the average dose of topical econazole. *If your dose is different, do not change it* unless your doctor tells you to do so.

- For *topical* dosage form (cream):
  —For fungus infections:
    - Adults and children—Apply to the affected skin and surrounding areas, one or two times a day, for two to four weeks. If you have to use the cream two times a day, apply it in the morning and evening.

Missed dose—If you miss a dose of this medicine, apply it as soon as possible. However, if it is almost time for your next dose, skip the missed dose and go back to your regular dosing schedule.

Storage—To store this medicine:
- Keep out of the reach of children.
- Store away from heat and direct light.
- Keep the medicine from freezing.
- Do not keep outdated medicine or medicine no longer needed. Be sure that any discarded medicine is out of the reach of children.

Precautions While Using This Medicine

If your skin problem does not improve within 2 weeks or more, or if it becomes worse, check with your doctor.

To help clear up your infection completely and to help make sure it does not return, good health habits are also required.

- For patients using econazole for ringworm of the groin (tinea cruris; jock itch):
  —Avoid wearing underwear that is tight-fitting or made from synthetic materials (for example, rayon or nylon). Instead, wear loose-fitting, cotton underwear.
  —Use a bland, absorbent powder (for example, talcum powder) or an antifungal powder (for example, tolnaftate) on the skin. It is best not to use econazole cream or any other antifungal cream at the same time that you use the powder.

These measures will help reduce chafing and irritation and will also help keep the groin area cool and dry.

- For patients using econazole for ringworm of the foot (tinea pedis; athlete's foot):
  —Carefully dry the feet, especially between the toes, after bathing.
  —Avoid wearing socks made from wool or synthetic materials (for example, rayon or nylon). Instead,

wear clean, cotton socks and change them daily or more often if the feet sweat freely.

—Wear well-ventilated shoes (for example, shoes with holes) or sandals.

—Use a bland, absorbent powder (for example, talcum powder) or an antifungal powder (for example, tolnaftate) between the toes, on the feet, and in socks and shoes freely once or twice a day. It is best not to use econazole cream or any other antifungal cream at the same time that you use the powder.

These measures will help keep the feet cool and dry.

If you have any questions about this, check with your health care professional.

Side Effects of This Medicine

Along with its needed effects, a medicine may cause some unwanted effects. Although not all of these side effects may occur, if they do occur they may need medical attention.

Check with your doctor as soon as possible if any of the following side effects occur:

Less common
Burning, itching, stinging, redness, or other sign of irritation not present before use of this medicine

Rare
Skin rash with itching

Other side effects not listed above may also occur in some patients. If you notice any other effects, check with your doctor.

Revised: 06/14/99

EFAVIRENZ   Systemic

Commonly used brand name(s):

In the U.S.—
Sustiva

Description

Efavirenz (ef-FAH-ver-enz) is used with other medicines in the treatment of the infection caused by the human immunodeficiency virus (HIV). HIV is the virus that causes acquired immune deficiency syndrome (AIDS).

Efavirenz will not cure or prevent HIV infection or AIDS; however, it helps keep HIV from reproducing and appears to slow down the destruction of the immune system. This may help delay the development of problems that usually result from AIDS or HIV disease. Efavirenz will not keep you from spreading HIV to other people. People who receive this medicine may continue to have some of the problems usually related to AIDS or HIV disease.

This medicine is available only with your doctor's prescription, in the following dosage form(s):

Oral
• Capsules (U.S.)

Before Using This Medicine

In deciding to use a medicine, the risks of taking the medicine must be weighed against the good it will do. This is a decision you and your doctor will make. For efavirenz, the following should be considered:

Allergies—Tell your doctor if you have ever had any unusual or allergic reaction to efavirenz. Also tell your health care professional if you are allergic to any other substances, such as foods, preservatives, or dyes.

Pregnancy—Efavirenz has not been studied in pregnant women. However, studies in animals have found that it causes birth defects and other problems. A pregnancy test is recommended before starting treatment with efavirenz. In addition, it is recommended that women with the potential to become pregnant use two methods of contraception. One method of contraception should be a reliable barrier contraceptive, such as condoms, and the other method should be an oral or other hormone contraceptive. Before taking efavirenz, make sure your doctor knows if you are pregnant or if you may become pregnant.

Breast-feeding—It is not known whether efavirenz passes into the breast milk. However, breast-feeding is not recommended in patients with HIV infection because of the risk of passing the virus on to the nursing infant.

Children—Children have a higher risk of developing a rash, which is sometimes severe, while taking this medicine. Your doctor may suggest that an additional medicine, an antihistamine, be taken to prevent a rash from occurring. The appearance of a rash should be reported to your doctor as soon as possible.

Older adults—Many medicines have not been studied specifically in older people. Therefore, it may not be known whether they work exactly the same way they do in younger adults or if they cause different side effects or problems in older people. There is no specific information comparing use of efavirenz in the elderly with use in other age groups.

Other medicines—Although certain medicines should not be used together at all, in other cases two different medicines may be used together even if an interaction might occur. In these cases, your doctor may want to change the dose, or other precautions may be necessary. *It is important that you inform your health care professional of any prescription or nonprescription (OTC) medicine you are taking, especially if you are taking any of the following:*

• Amprenavir (e.g., Agenerase)—Efavirenz may decrease the amount of this medicine in the body

• Astemizole (e.g., Hismanal) or
• Cisapride (e.g., Propulsid)—Efavirenz may increase the amount of these medicines in the body, which may cause cardiac arrythmias (irregular heartbeat)

• Ergot derivatives (e.g., Gerimal, Hydergine, Hydergine LC, Ergotrate, Methergine, Bellergal-S)—Efavirenz may increase the amount of these medicines in the body, which could lead to breathing problems

• Indinavir (e.g., Crixivan)—Efavirenz may decrease the amount of this medicine in the body

• Midazolam (e.g., Versed) or
• Triazolam (e.g., Halcion)—Efavirenz may increase the amount of these medicines in the body, which may lead to severe drowsiness

• Rifabutin (e.g., Mycobutin)—Efavirenz may decrease the amount of this medicine in the body

• Ritonavir (e.g., Norvir)—Taking efavirenz with this medicine may increase the chance of side effects

• Saquinavir (e.g., Invirase)—Efavirenz may decrease the amount of this medicine in the body

- Warfarin (e.g., Coumadin)—Efavirenz may either increase or decrease the amount of warfarin in the body

Other medical problems—The presence of other medical problems may affect the use of efavirenz. Make sure you tell your doctor if you have any other medical problems, especially:

- Hepatitis B or C (history of) or
- Liver disease—Efavirenz may cause unwanted effects in the liver

Proper Use of This Medicine

Take this medicine exactly as directed by your doctor. Do not take it more often, and do not take it for a longer time than your doctor ordered. Also, do not stop taking this medicine without checking with your doctor first.

Keep taking efavirenz for the full time of treatment even if you begin to feel better. It is also important that you continue taking all other medicines for HIV infection your doctor has instructed you to take.

Efavirenz may be taken with or without meals. However, meals high in fat should be avoided because the amount of efavirenz absorbed into the body may be increased, which might increase the chance of side effects.

The central nervous system (CNS) side effects that may occur with this medicine usually lessen after you have taken the medicine for a while. Also, taking efavirenz at bedtime, especially during the first 2 to 4 weeks, may lessen these side effects.

Dosing—The dose of efavirenz will be different for different patients. *Follow your doctor's orders or the directions on the label.* The following information includes only the average doses of efavirenz. *If your dose is different, do not change it* unless your doctor tells you to do so.

The number of capsules that you take depends on the strength of the medicine.

- For *oral* dosage form (capsules):
  —For treatment of HIV infection:
    - Adults—600 milligrams (mg) once a day, taken with other medicines.
    - Children 3 years of age and older (by weight)—
      10 to 15 kilograms (22 to 33 pounds) of body weight: 200 mg once a day, taken with other medicines.
      15 to 20 kilograms (33 to 44 pounds) of body weight: 250 mg once a day, taken with other medicines.
      20 to 25 kilograms (44 to 55 pounds) of body weight: 300 mg once a day, taken with other medicines.
      25 to 32.5 kilograms (55 to 71.5 pounds) of body weight: 350 mg once a day, taken with other medicines.
      32.5 to 40 kilograms (71.5 to 88 pounds) of body weight: 400 mg once a day, taken with other medicines.
      40 kilograms (88 pounds) of body weight or over: 600 mg once a day, taken with other medicines.
    - Children up to 3 years of age—Use and dose must be determined by your doctor.

Missed dose—If you miss a dose of this medicine, take it as soon as you remember. However, if it is almost time for your next dose, skip the missed dose and go back to your regular dosing schedule. Do not double doses.

Storage—To store this medicine:

- Keep out of the reach of children.
- Store away from heat and direct light.
- Do not store in the bathroom, near the kitchen sink, or in other damp places. Heat or moisture may cause the medicine to break down.
- Do not keep outdated medicine or medicine no longer needed. Be sure that any discarded medicine is out of the reach of children.

Precautions While Using This Medicine

Efavirenz may cause dizziness, difficulty in concentrating, or drowsiness. *Make sure you know how you react to this medicine before you drive, use machines, or do anything else that could be dangerous if you are dizzy or are not alert.*

Check with your physician before taking efavirenz with alcohol or other medicines that affect the central nervous system (CNS). The use of alcohol or other medicines that affect the CNS with efavirenz may worsen the side effects of this medicine, such as dizziness, poor concentration, drowsiness, unusual dreams, and trouble in sleeping. Some examples of medicines that affect the CNS are antihistamines or medicine for hay fever, other allergies, or colds; sedatives, tranquilizers, or sleeping medicine; medicine for depression; medicine for anxiety; prescription pain medicine or narcotics; barbiturates; medicine for attention deficit and hyperactivity disorder; medicine for seizures; muscle relaxants; or anesthetics, including some dental anesthetics.

Efavirenz does not decrease the risk of transmitting the HIV infection to others through sexual contact or by contamination through blood.

Women of childbearing potential should use two forms of birth control while taking this medicine, a barrier method of contraception and an oral or other hormonal method of contraception.

Side Effects of This Medicine

Along with its needed effects, a medicine may cause some unwanted effects. Although not all of these side effects may occur, if they do occur they may need medical attention.

Check with your doctor as soon as possible if any of the following side effects occur:
More common
    Depression; skin rash or itching
Less common
    Blood in urine; difficult or painful urination; pain in lower back and/or side
Rare
    Abdominal pain; changes in vision; blistering; clumsiness or unsteadiness; confusion; convulsions (seizures); cough; dark urine; delusions; double vision; fainting; fast or pounding heartbeat; fever or chills; headache (severe and throbbing); hives; inappropriate behavior; loss of appetite; mood or mental changes (severe); muscle cramps or pain; nausea or vomiting; nerve pain; open sores; pain, tenderness, bluish color, or swelling of leg or foot; rapid weight gain; seeing, hearing, or feeling things that are not there; sense of constant movement of self or surroundings; sores, ulcers, or white spots in mouth or on lips; speech disorder; swelling and/or tenderness in upper abdominal or stomach area; swelling of hands, arms, feet, or legs; thoughts of

suicide or attempts at suicide; tightness in chest; tingling, burning, or prickling sensations; tingling, burning, numbness, or pain in the hands, arms, feet, or legs; tremor; troubled breathing; unusual tiredness; weight loss; wheezing; yellow eyes or skin

Other side effects may occur that usually do not need medical attention. These side effects may go away during treatment as your body adjusts to the medicine. However, check with your doctor if any of the following side effects continue or are bothersome:

More common

Diarrhea; dizziness; drowsiness; fatigue; headache; increased sweating; poor concentration; trouble in sleeping

Less common or rare

Abnormally decreased sensitivity, particularly to touch; agitation or anxiety; belching; change in sense of taste or smell; dry mouth; excessive gas; false sense of well-being; flaking and falling off of skin; flushing; general feeling of discomfort; heartburn; indigestion; joint pain; lack of feeling or emotion; loss of hair; loss of memory; loss of sense of reality; mood changes; nervousness; pain; painful, red, hot or irritated hair follicles; ringing in the ears; stomach discomfort; unusual dreams; weakness

Other side effects not listed above may also occur in some patients. If you notice any other effects, check with your doctor.

Developed: 12/14/98

EFLORNITHINE Topical— INTRODUCTORY VERSION

Commonly used brand name(s):

In the U.S.—
Vaniqa

Description

Eflornithine (ee–FLOOR–nith–een) is used to slow down bodily substances called enzymes that help hair grow. The effect is slower facial hair growth.

This medicine is available only with your doctor's prescription, in the following dosage form:

Topical
• Cream (U.S.)

Before Using This Medicine

In deciding to use a medicine, the risks of using the medicine must be weighed against the good it will do. This is a decision you and your doctor will make. For eflornithine, the following should be considered:

Allergies—Tell your doctor if you have ever had any unusual or allergic reaction to eflornithine. Also tell your health care professional if you are allergic to any other substances or topical medications.

Pregnancy—Studies with eflornithine have not been done in pregnant women. In animal studies, when taken by mouth, eflornithine has been shown to cause birth defects or other problems. If you are pregnant or plan to become pregnant, discuss with your doctor whether you should use this medicine during pregnancy.

Breast-feeding—It is not known whether eflornithine passes into breast milk. Mothers who are taking this medicine and wish to breast-feed should discuss this with their doctor.

Children—There is no specific information comparing use of eflornithine in children under the age of 12 years with use in other age groups. However, this medicine is not expected to cause different side effects or problems in older children than it does in adults.

Older adults—This medicine has been tested and has not been shown to cause different side effects or problems in older people than it does in younger adults.

Other medicines—Although certain medicines should not be used together at all, in other cases two different medicines may be used together even if an interaction might occur. In these cases, your doctor may want to change the dose, or other precautions may be necessary. Tell your health care professional if you are using any other topical prescription or nonprescription (over-the-counter [OTC]) medicine that is to be applied to the same area of the skin.

Proper Use of This Medicine

This medicine comes with a patient instruction sheet. Read this sheet carefully and follow the directions. If you have any questions on how to use this medicine, be sure to ask your health care professional.

This medicine is usually used on the face and nearby involved areas under the chin only. Do not get the medicine in your eyes, nose, or mouth. Rinse thoroughly with water and contact your doctor if the medicine gets in the eyes

You need to continue your normal hair removal procedures while using this medicine, and the medicine should be applied at least five minutes after the unwanted hair has been removed. You should wait until the medicine dries before applying cosmetics or sunscreen.

Do not wash the treated areas for at least 4 hours after applying the medicine.

Dosing—The dose of eflornithine will be different for different patients. *Follow your doctor's orders or the directions on the label.* The following information includes only the average dose of eflornithine. *If your dose is different, do not change it* unless your doctor tells you to do so.

• For *topical* dosage form (cream):
—For reduced rate of facial hair growth in women.
• Adults and children 12 years of age or older— Coat the problem areas on the face and nearby areas under the chin with the medicine two times a day with the second treatment coming at least eight hours after the first.
• Children under 12 years of age—Use and dose must be determined by your doctor.

Missed dose—If you forget or miss a dose of this medicine, apply it as soon as possible. However, if it is almost time for your next dose, skip the missed dose and go back to your regular dosing schedule. Do not double doses.

Storage—To store this medicine:
• Keep out of the reach of children.
• Store away from heat and direct light.
• Store at 15°C–30°C (59°F–86°F).
• Keep the medicine from freezing.

- Do not keep outdated medicine or medicine no longer needed. Be sure that any discarded medicine is out of the reach of children.

Precautions While Using This Medicine

If skin irritation occurs, reduce the frequency of treatments. If irritation continues, stop using the medicine and contact your doctor.

If no improvement is seen after six months of treatment, stop using the medicine and contact your doctor.

If condition gets worse while you use the medicine, stop the medicine and contact your doctor.

Side Effects of This Medicine

Side effects may occur that usually do not need medical attention. These side effects may go away during treatment as your body adjusts to the medicine. However, check with your doctor if any of the following side effects continue or are bothersome.

More common
   Acne; stinging skin

Less common
   Burning or bleeding skin; chapped, red lips; chronic acne; hair bumps; numbness; rash; reddening of skin; swelling of lips; tingling skin

Other side effects not listed above may also occur in some patients. If you notice any other effects, check with your doctor.

Revised: 10/30/00

EMEDASTINE   Ophthalmic

Commonly used brand name(s):

In the U.S.—
   Emadine

Description

Emedastine (em-e-DAS-teen) ophthalmic solution is used to treat symptoms of the eye caused by allergic conjunctivitis. It works by preventing the effects of a substance called histamine, which is produced in certain cells in your eyes and which causes the allergic reaction.

This medicine is available only with your doctor's prescription, in the following dosage form:

Ophthalmic
   - Ophthalmic solution (eye drops) (U.S.)

Before Using This Medicine

In deciding to use a medicine, the risks of using the medicine must be weighed against the good it will do. This is a decision you and your doctor will make. For emedastine, the following should be considered:

Allergies—Tell your doctor if you have ever had any unusual or allergic reaction to emedastine. Also tell your health care professional if you are allergic to any other substances, such as preservatives.

Pregnancy—Emedastine has not been studied in pregnant women. However, studies in animals have shown that emedastine, when given in very high doses to some types of animals, causes birth defects. Before using this medicine, make sure your doctor knows if you are pregnant or if you may become pregnant.

Breast-feeding—It is not known whether enough ophthalmic emedastine is absorbed by the body to pass into breast milk. However, be sure you have discussed the risks and benefits of the medicine with your doctor.

Children—Studies on this medicine have been done only in adult patients, and there is no specific information comparing use of ophthalmic emedastine in children younger than 3 years of age with use in other age groups.

Older adults—Many medicines have not been studied specifically in older people. Therefore, it may not be known whether they work exactly the same way they do in younger adults or if they cause different side effects or problems in older people. There is no specific information comparing use of ophthalmic emedastine in the elderly with use in other age groups.

Proper Use of This Medicine

Do not wear contact lenses if your eyes are red. If your eyes are not red, contact lenses should be removed before you use this medicine. Also, you should wait at least 10 minutes after using this medicine before putting the contact lenses back in.

To use:

- First, wash your hands. Tilt the head back and, pressing your finger gently on the skin just beneath the lower eyelid, pull the lower eyelid away from the eye to make a space. Drop the medicine into this space. Let go of the eyelid and gently close the eyes. Do not blink. Keep the eyes closed for 1 to 2 minutes to allow the medicine to be absorbed by the eye. If you think you did not get the drop of medicine into your eye properly, use another drop. *To keep the medicine as germ-free as possible, do not touch the applicator tip to any surface (including the eye)*. Also, keep the container tightly closed.

Dosing—The dose of emedastine will be different for different patients. *Follow your doctor's orders or the directions on the label*. The following information includes only the average doses of emedastine. *If your dose is different, do not change it* unless your doctor tells you to do so.

- For *ophthalmic* dosage form (eye drops):
   —For eye allergy:
      - Adults and children 3 years of age and older— Use one drop in the affected eye one to four times a day.
      - Children younger than 3 years of age—Use and dose must be determined by your doctor.

Missed dose—If you miss a dose of this medicine, use it as soon as possible. However, if it is almost time for your next dose, skip the missed dose and go back to your regular dosing schedule.

Storage—To store this medicine:
- Keep out of the reach of children.
- Store away from heat and direct light.
- Keep the medicine from freezing. Do not refrigerate.
- Do not keep outdated medicine or medicine no longer needed. Be sure that any discarded medicine is out of the reach of children.

Precautions While Using This Medicine

If your symptoms do not improve or if your condition becomes worse, check with your doctor.

Side Effects of This Medicine

Along with its needed effects, a medicine may cause some unwanted effects. Although not all of these side effects may occur, if they do occur they may need medical attention.

Check with your doctor as soon as possible if any of the following side effects occur:

Less common
> Abnormal dreams; blurred vision or other change in vision; eye redness, irritation, or pain; tearing, discomfort, or other eye irritation not present before therapy or becoming worse during therapy; weakness

Other side effects may occur that usually do not need medical attention. These side effects may go away during treatment as your body adjusts to the medicine. However, check with your doctor if any of the following side effects continue or are bothersome:

More common
> Headache

Less common
> Bad taste; burning or stinging of the eye; dry eye; feeling of something in the eye; itching; skin rash; stuffy or runny nose

Other side effects not listed above may also occur in some patients. If you notice any other effects, check with your doctor.

Developed: 08/13/98

ENALAPRIL AND DILTIAZEM
Systemic—INTRODUCTORY VERSION

Description

Enalapril (e-NAL-a-pril) and diltiazem (dil-TYE-a-zem) combination belongs to the class of medicines called high blood pressure medicines (antihypertensives). It is used to treat high blood pressure (hypertension).

High blood pressure adds to the workload of the heart and arteries. If it continues for a long time, the heart and arteries may not function properly. This can damage the blood vessels of the brain, heart, and kidneys, resulting in a stroke, heart failure, or kidney failure. High blood pressure may also increase the risk of heart attacks. These problems may be less likely to occur if blood pressure is controlled.

The exact way in which this medicine works is not known. Enalapril is a type of medicine known as an angiotensin-converting enzyme (ACE) inhibitor. It blocks an enzyme in the body that is necessary in producing a substance that causes blood vessels to tighten. Diltiazem is a type of medicine known as a calcium channel blocker. Calcium channel blocking agents affect the movement of calcium into the cells of the heart and blood vessels. The actions of both medicines relax blood vessels, lower blood pressure, and increase the supply of blood and oxygen to the heart.

This medicine was withdrawn from the U.S. market in December 1999.

Before Using This Medicine

In deciding to use a medicine, the risks of taking the medicine must be weighed against the good it will do. This is a decision you and your doctor will make. For enalapril and diltiazem combination, the following should be considered:

Allergies—Tell your doctor if you have ever had any unusual or allergic reaction to enalapril or diltiazem, as well as to any other ACE inhibitor (benazepril, captopril, fosinopril, lisinopril, moexipril, quinapril, ramipril, or trandolapril). Also tell your health care professional if you are allergic to any other substances, such as foods, preservatives, or dyes.

Pregnancy—Studies with this combination medicine have not been done in pregnant women. However, use of ACE inhibitors during pregnancy, especially in the second and third trimesters (after the first 3 months) can cause low blood pressure, kidney failure, an underdeveloped skull, or even death in newborns. Diltiazem has caused problems in animals, including birth defects, pregnancy that continues too long, poor bone development, and stillbirth. *Therefore, it is important that you check with your doctor immediately if you think that you may be pregnant.* Be sure that you have discussed this with your doctor before taking this combination medicine.

Breast-feeding—Diltiazem and enalapril pass into breast milk. Breast-feeding is not recommended in women who are taking this medicine.

Children—Studies on this medicine have been done only in adult patients, and there is no specific information comparing use of enalapril and diltiazem in children with use in other age groups.

Older adults—Although this medicine has not been shown to cause different side effects or problems in older people than it does in younger adults, blood levels of the diltiazem component may be increased in the elderly and elderly people may be more sensitive to the effects of this combination medicine.

Racial differences—Black patients may be less sensitive to the blood pressure-lowering effects of this medicine. In addition, the risk of a serious allergic reaction involving swelling of the face, mouth, hands, or feet may be increased in black patients.

Other medicines—Although certain medicines should not be used together at all, in other cases two different medicines may be used together even if an interaction might occur. In these cases, your doctor may want to change the dose, or other precautions may be necessary. When you are taking this medicine, it is especially important that your health care professional know if you are taking any of the following:

- Beta-blockers (acebutolol [e.g., Sectral], atenolol [e.g., Tenormin], betaxolol [e.g., Kerlone], bisoprolol [e.g., Zebeta], carteolol [e.g., Cartrol], carvedilol [e.g., Coreg], labetalol [e.g., Normodyne], metoprolol [e.g., Lopressor], nadolol [e.g., Corgard], oxprenolol [e.g., Trasicor], penbutolol [e.g., Levatol], pindolol [e.g., Visken], propranolol [e.g., Inderal], sotalol [e.g., Sotacor], timolol [e.g., Blocadren])—Effects of these medicines and diltiazem on the heart may be increased

- Digitalis glycosides (heart medicine [e.g., Lanoxin])—Effects of these medicines may be increased

- Diuretics (water pills)—Blood pressure lowering effect may be increased

- Potassium-containing medicines or supplements or
- Salt substitutes that contain potassium—Use of these substances with ACE inhibitors may result in an unusually high potassium level in the blood, which can lead to irregular heart rhythm and other problems

Also, tell your health care professional if you are using any of the following medicines in the eye:

- Betaxolol (e.g., Betoptic) or
- Carteolol (e.g., Ocupress) or
- Levobunolol (e.g., Betagan) or
- Metipranolol (e.g., OptiPranolol) or
- Timolol (e.g., Timoptic)—Effects on heart and blood pressure may be increased

Other medical problems—The presence of other medical problems may affect the use of this medicine. Make sure you tell your doctor if you have any other medical problems, especially:

- Bee-sting allergy treatments or
- Dialysis—Increased risk of serious allergic reaction occurring
- Dehydration—Lowering effects on blood pressure may be increased
- Diabetes mellitus (sugar diabetes)—Increased risk of potassium levels in the body becoming too high
- Heart attack or stroke or
- Heart or blood vessel disease or
- Hypotension (low blood pressure)—Further lowering of blood pressure may make problems resulting from these conditions worse
- Heart rate or rhythm problems—Diltiazem may make these problems worse
- Kidney disease—Effects may be increased because of slower removal of the medicine from the body
- Liver disease—Diltiazem has been reported to cause liver problems in animals
- Scleroderma or
- Systemic lupus erythematosus (SLE)—Increased risk of blood problems caused by ACE inhibitors
- Previous reaction to an ACE inhibitor involving hoarseness; swelling of face, mouth, hands, or feet; or sudden trouble in breathing—Reaction is more likely to occur with this medicine

Proper Use of This Medicine

Take this medicine exactly as directed by your doctor, at the same time each day. Do not take more of it and do not take it more often than directed.

Swallow the tablets whole, without breaking, crushing, or chewing them.

Dosing—The dose of this medicine will be different for different patients. *Follow your doctor's orders or the directions on the label.* The following information includes only the average doses of this medicine. *If your dose is different, do not change it* unless your doctor tells you to do so.

- For *oral* dosage form (extended-release tablets):
  —For high blood pressure:
  - Adults—1 or 2 tablets a day.
  - Children—Use and dose must be determined by your doctor.

Missed dose—If you miss a dose of this medicine, take it as soon as possible. However, if it is almost time for your next dose, skip the missed dose and go back to your regular dosing schedule. Do not double doses.

Storage—To store this medicine:

- Keep out of the reach of children.
- Store away from heat and direct light.
- Do not store in the bathroom, near the kitchen sink, or in other damp places. Heat or moisture may cause the medicine to break down.
- Do not keep outdated medicine or medicine no longer needed. Be sure that any discarded medicine is out of the reach of children.

Precautions While Using This Medicine

It is very important that your doctor check your progress at regular visits. This will allow your doctor to make sure the medicine is working properly, to check for unwanted effects, and to change the dosage if needed.

If you think that you may have become pregnant, check with your doctor immediately. Use of this medicine, especially during the second and third trimesters (after the first 3 months) of pregnancy, may cause serious injury or even death to the unborn child.

Do not take any other medicines, potassium supplements, or salt substitutes that contain potassium unless approved or prescribed by your doctor.

Dizziness, lightheadedness, or fainting may occur after the first dose, especially if you have been taking a diuretic (water pill). Make sure you know how you react to the medicine before you drive, use machines, or do other things that could be dangerous if you experience these effects.

Call your doctor if you faint or feel lightheaded while you are taking this medicine.

Check with your doctor if you notice any signs of fever, sore throat, or chills. These could be symptoms of an infection resulting from low white blood cell counts.

Check with your doctor if you notice difficult breathing or swelling of the face, arms, or legs. These could be symptoms of a serious allergic reaction.

Check with your doctor if you become sick while taking this medicine, especially with severe or continuing vomiting or diarrhea. These conditions may cause you to lose too much water, possibly resulting in low blood pressure.

Dizziness, lightheadedness, or fainting may also occur if you exercise or if the weather is hot. Heavy sweating can cause loss of too much water and result in low blood pressure. Use extra care during exercise or hot weather.

Before having any kind of surgery (including dental surgery) or emergency treatment, tell the medical doctor or dentist in charge that you are taking this medicine.

Side Effects of This Medicine

Along with its needed effects, a medicine may cause some unwanted effects. Although not all of these side effects may occur, if they do occur they may need medical attention.

Check with your doctor immediately if any of the following side effects occur:
  Rare
    Swelling of face, mouth, hands, or feet; trouble in swallowing or breathing (sudden) accompanied by hoarseness

Check with your doctor as soon as possible if any of the following side effects occur:

Less common
> Dizziness, lightheadedness, or fainting; slow heartbeat; swelling of ankles, feet, or lower legs

Rare
> Bleeding gums, nosebleeds, or pale skin; chest pain; fever, chills, or sore throat; unusual bleeding or bruising; yellow eyes or skin

Signs and symptoms of too much potassium in the body
> Confusion; irregular heartbeat; nervousness; numbness or tingling in hands, feet, or lips; shortness of breath; weakness or heaviness of legs

Other side effects may occur that usually do not need medical attention. These side effects may go away during treatment as your body adjusts to the medicine. However, check with your doctor if any of the following side effects continue or are bothersome:

Less common
> Abdominal pain; cough (dry, persistent); nausea; skin rash or other irritation; unusual tiredness

Other side effects not listed above may also occur in some patients. If you notice any other effects, check with your doctor.

Developed: 08/10/1998
Revised: 10/13/2000

ENALAPRIL AND FELODIPINE
Systemic

Commonly used brand name(s):

In the U.S.—
> Lexxel

Description

Enalapril (e-NAL-a-pril) and felodipine (fe-LOE-di-peen) combination belongs to the class of medicines called high blood pressure medicines (antihypertensives). This medicine is used to treat high blood pressure (hypertension).

High blood pressure adds to the workload of the heart and arteries. If it continues for a long time, the heart and arteries may not function properly. This can damage the blood vessels of the brain, heart, and kidneys, resulting in a stroke, heart failure, or kidney failure. High blood pressure may also increase the risk of heart attacks. These problems may be less likely to occur if blood pressure is controlled.

The exact way in which this medicine works is not known. Enalapril is a type of medicine known as an angiotensin-converting enzyme (ACE) inhibitor. It blocks an enzyme in the body that is necessary in producing a substance that causes blood vessels to tighten. Felodipine is a type of medicine known as a calcium channel blocker. Calcium channel blocking agents affect the movement of calcium into the cells of the heart and blood vessels. The actions of both medicines relax blood vessels, lower blood pressure, and increase the supply of blood and oxygen to the heart.

This medicine is available only with your doctor's prescription, in the following dosage form:

Oral
> • Tablets (U.S.)

Before Using This Medicine

In deciding to use a medicine, the risks of taking the medicine must be weighed against the good it will do. This is a decision you and your doctor will make. For enalapril and felodipine combination, the following should be considered:

Allergies—Tell your doctor if you have ever had any unusual or allergic reaction to enalapril or felodipine, as well as to any other ACE inhibitor (benazepril, captopril, fosinopril, lisinopril, moexipril, quinapril, ramipril, or trandolapril). Also tell your health care professional if you are allergic to any other substances, such as foods, preservatives, or dyes.

Pregnancy—Studies with this combination medicine have not been done in pregnant women. However, use of any of the ACE inhibitors during pregnancy, especially in the second and third trimesters (after the first 3 months), can cause low blood pressure, kidney failure, an underdeveloped skull, or even death in newborns. Felodipine can cause birth defects and problems with labor and delivery. *Therefore, it is important that you check with your doctor immediately if you think that you may be pregnant.* Be sure that you have discussed this with your doctor before taking this combination medicine.

Breast-feeding—Enalapril passes into breast milk. It is not known if felodipine passes into breast milk; however, felodipine passes into the milk of lactating rats. Use of this combination medicine is not recommended in women who are breast-feeding.

Children—Studies on this medicine have been done only in adult patients, and there is no specific information comparing use of enalapril and felodipine in children with use in other age groups.

Older adults—Although this medicine has not been shown to cause different side effects or problems in older people than it does in younger adults, blood levels of the felodipine component may be increased in the elderly.

Racial differences—Black patients may be less sensitive to the blood pressure-lowering effects of this medicine. In addition, the risk of a serious allergic reaction involving swelling of the face, mouth, hands, or feet may be increased.

Other medicines—Although certain medicines should not be used together at all, in other cases two different medicines may be used together even if an interaction might occur. In these cases, your doctor may want to change the dose, or other precautions may be necessary. When you are taking this medicine, it is especially important that your health care professional know if you are taking any of the following:

> • Carbamazepine (e.g., Tegretol) or
> • Phenytoin (e.g., Dilantin) or
> • Phenobarbital—Effects of felodipine may be greatly decreased
> • Diuretics (water pills)—Effects on blood pressure may be increased
> • Potassium-containing supplements or
> • Salt substitutes that contain potassium—Use of these substances with ACE inhibitors may result in an unusually high potassium level in the blood, which can lead to irregular heart rhythm and other problems

Other medical problems— The presence of other medical problems may affect the use of this medicine. Make sure you tell your doctor if you have any other medical problems, especially:

- Bee-sting allergy treatments or
- Dialysis—Increased risk of serious allergic reaction occurring
- Dehydration—Lowering effects on blood pressure may be increased
- Diabetes mellitus (sugar diabetes)—Increased risk of potassium levels in the body becoming too high
- Heart attack or stroke or
- Heart or blood vessel disease or
- Hypotension (low blood pressure)—Further lowering of blood pressure may make problems resulting from these conditions worse
- Kidney disease or
- Liver disease—Effects may be increased because of slower removal from the body
- Previous reaction to any ACE inhibitor involving hoarseness; swelling of the face, mouth, hands, or feet; or sudden trouble in swallowing or breathing—Reaction is more likely to occur again
- Scleroderma or
- Systemic lupus erythematosus (SLE) (or history of)—Increased risk of blood problems caused by ACE inhibitors

Proper Use of This Medicine

Take this medicine exactly as directed by your doctor, at the same time each day. Do not take more of it and do not take it more often than directed.

Swallow the tablets whole, without breaking, crushing, or chewing them.

If felodipine is taken with grapefruit juice, its effects may be increased. Check with your doctor before taking this medicine with grapefruit juice.

Dosing— The dose of this medicine will be different for different patients. *Follow your doctor's orders or the directions on the label.* The following information includes only the average doses of this medicine. *If your dose is different, do not change it* unless your doctor tells you to do so.

- For *oral* dosage form (tablets):
  - —For high blood pressure:
    - Adults—1 tablet once a day to start. Your doctor may increase your dose up to 4 tablets once a day if needed, to equal 20 mg enalapril and 10 mg felodipine extended-release.
    - Children—Use and dose must be determined by your doctor.

Missed dose— If you miss a dose of this medicine, take it as soon as possible. However, if it is almost time for your next dose, skip the missed dose and go back to your regular dosing schedule. Do not double doses.

Storage— To store this medicine:
- Keep out of the reach of children.
- Store away from heat and direct light.
- Do not store in the bathroom, near the kitchen sink, or in other damp places. Heat or moisture may cause the medicine to break down.
- Do not keep outdated medicine or medicine no longer needed. Be sure that any discarded medicine is out of the reach of children.

Precautions While Using This Medicine

It is very important that your doctor check your progress at regular visits. This will allow your doctor to make sure the medicine is working properly, to check for unwanted effects, and to change the dosage if needed.

If you think that you may have become pregnant, check with your doctor immediately. Use of this medicine, especially during the second and third trimesters (after the first 3 months) of pregnancy, may cause serious injury or even death to the unborn child.

Do not take any other medicines, potassium supplements, or salt substitutes that contain potassium unless approved or prescribed by your doctor.

Dizziness, lightheadedness, or fainting may occur after the first dose, especially if you have been taking a diuretic (water pill). Make sure you know how you react to the medicine before you drive, use machines, or do other things that could be dangerous if you experience these effects.

Call your doctor if you faint or feel lightheaded while you are taking this medicine.

Check with your doctor if you notice any signs of fever, sore throat, or chills. These could be symptoms of an infection developing as a result of low white blood cell counts.

Check with your doctor if you notice difficult breathing or swelling of the face, arms, or legs. These could be symptoms of a serious allergic reaction.

Check with your doctor if you become sick while taking this medicine, especially with severe or continuing vomiting or diarrhea. These conditions may cause you to lose too much water, possibly resulting in low blood pressure.

Dizziness, lightheadedness, or fainting may also occur if you exercise or if the weather is hot. Heavy sweating can cause loss of too much water and result in low blood pressure. Use extra care during exercise or hot weather.

Before having any kind of surgery (including dental surgery) or emergency treatment, tell the medical doctor or dentist in charge that you are taking this medicine.

Side Effects of This Medicine

Along with its needed effects, a medicine may cause some unwanted effects. Although not all of these side effects may occur, if they do occur they may need medical attention.

Check with your doctor immediately if any of the following side effects occur:
  Rare
    Swelling of face, mouth, hands, or feet; trouble in swallowing or breathing (sudden), accompanied by hoarseness

Check with your doctor as soon as possible if any of the following side effects occur:
  Less common
    Dizziness, lightheadedness, or fainting; swelling of ankles, feet, or lower legs
  Rare
    Chills, fever, and sore throat; unusual bleeding or bruising; yellow eyes or skin

Signs and symptoms of too much potassium in the body
Confusion; irregular heartbeat; nervousness; numbness or tingling in hands, feet, or lips; shortness of breath; weakness or heaviness of legs

Other side effects may occur that usually do not need medical attention. These side effects may go away during treatment as your body adjusts to the medicine. However, check with your doctor if any of the following side effects continue or are bothersome:

More common
Headache

Less common
Cough (dry, persistent); flushing; swelling of the gums; unusual tiredness

Other side effects not listed above may also occur in some patients. If you notice any other effects, check with your doctor.

Developed: 08/11/98
Interim revision: 06/14/99

ENCAINIDE   Systemic†

A commonly used brand name is—
Enkaid

†Not commercially available in Canada.

Description

Encainide (en-KAY-nide) belongs to the group of medicines known as antiarrhythmics. It is used to correct irregular heartbeats to a normal rhythm.

Encainide produces its helpful effects by slowing nerve impulses in the heart and making the heart tissue less sensitive.

There is a chance that encainide may cause new heart rhythm problems when it is used. Since it has been shown to cause severe problems in some patients, it is only used to treat serious heart rhythm problems. Discuss this possible effect with your doctor.

This medicine is available only from your doctor in the following dosage form:

Oral
• Capsules

Before Using This Medicine

In deciding to use a medicine, the risks of taking the medicine must be weighed against the good it will do. This is a decision you and your doctor will make. For encainide, the following should be considered:

Allergies—Tell your doctor if you have ever had any unusual or allergic reaction to encainide. Also tell your health care professional if you are allergic to any other substances, such as foods, preservatives, or dyes.

Pregnancy—Encainide has not been studied in pregnant women. However, this medicine has not been shown to cause birth defects or other problems in animal studies, but has been shown to reduce fertility in rats. Before taking encainide, make sure your doctor knows if you are pregnant or if you may become pregnant.

Breast-feeding—Encainide passes into the milk of some animals and may also pass into the milk of humans. However, this medicine has not been reported to cause problems in nursing babies.

Children—Studies on this medicine have been done only in adult patients. Therefore, be sure to discuss with your doctor the use of this medicine in children.

Older adults—Many medicines have not been tested in older people. Therefore, it may not be known whether they work exactly the same way they do in younger adults or if they cause different side effects or problems in older people. There is no specific information about the use of encainide in the elderly.

Other medical problems—The presence of other medical problems may affect the use of encainide. Make sure you tell your doctor if you have any other medical problems, especially:

• Diabetes mellitus—Encainide may raise blood sugar levels

• Kidney disease—Effects of encainide may be increased because of slower removal from the body

• Liver disease—Effects of encainide may be changed

• Recent heart attack—Risk of irregular heartbeats may be increased

• If you have a pacemaker—Encainide may interfere with the pacemaker and require more careful follow-up by the doctor

Proper Use of This Medicine

Take encainide exactly as directed by your doctor, even though you may feel well. Do not take more or less of it than your doctor ordered.

This medicine works best when there is a constant amount in the blood. *To help keep the amount constant, do not miss any doses. Also, it is best to take each dose at evenly spaced times day and night.* For example, if you are to take 3 doses a day, doses should be spaced about 8 hours apart. If you need help in planning the best times to take your medicine, check with your health care professional.

Dosing—The dose of encainide will be different for different patients. *Follow your doctor's orders or the directions on the label.* The following information includes only the average doses of encainide. *If your dose is different, do not change it* unless your doctor tells you to do so.

• For *oral* dosage form (capsules):
—For irregular heartbeat:
• Adults—25 to 50 milligrams (mg) every eight hours.
• Children—Use and dose must be determined by your doctor.

Missed dose—If you miss a dose of encainide and remember within 4 hours, take it as soon as possible. However, if you do not remember until later, skip the missed dose and go back to your regular dosing schedule. Do not double doses.

Storage—To store this medicine:
• Keep out of the reach of children.
• Store away from heat and direct light.

- Do not store in the bathroom, near the kitchen sink, or in other damp places. Heat or moisture may cause the medicine to break down.
- Do not keep outdated medicine or medicine no longer needed. Be sure that any discarded medicine is out of the reach of children.

Precautions While Using This Medicine

It is important that your doctor check your progress at regular visits to make sure the medicine is working properly. This will allow changes to be made in the amount of medicine you are taking, if necessary.

Your doctor may want you to carry a medical identification card or bracelet stating that you are using this medicine.

Before having any kind of surgery (including dental surgery) or emergency treatment, tell the medical doctor or dentist in charge that you are taking this medicine.

Encainide may cause some people to become dizzy or lightheaded. Make sure you know how you react to this medicine before you drive, use machines, or do anything else that could be dangerous if you are dizzy.

Side Effects of This Medicine

Along with its needed effects, a medicine may cause some unwanted effects. Although not all of these side effects may occur, if they do occur they may need medical attention.

Check with your doctor as soon as possible if any of the following side effects occur:

More common
Chest pain; fast or irregular heartbeat

Rare
Shortness of breath; swelling of feet or lower legs; trembling or shaking

Other side effects may occur that usually do not need medical attention. These side effects may go away during treatment as your body adjusts to the medicine. However, check with your doctor if any of the following side effects continue or are bothersome:

Less common
Blurred or double vision; dizziness; headache; nausea; pain in arms or legs; skin rash; unusual tiredness or weakness

Other side effects not listed above may also occur in some patients. If you notice any other effects, check with your doctor.

Revised: 06/08/93
Interim revision: 01/26/95

ENOXAPARIN   Systemic

Commonly used brand name(s):

In the U.S.—
Lovenox

In Canada—
Lovenox

Description

Enoxaparin (e-nox-a-PA-rin) is used to prevent deep venous thrombosis, a condition in which harmful blood clots form in the blood vessels of the legs. This medicine is used for several days after hip or knee replacement surgery, and in some cases following abdominal surgery, while you are unable to walk. It is during this time that blood clots are most likely to form. In addition, enoxaparin is used to prevent blood clots from forming in the arteries of the heart during certain types of angina and heart attacks. Enoxaparin also may be used for other conditions as determined by your doctor.

Enoxaparin is available only with your doctor's prescription, in the following dosage form:

Parenteral
- Injection (U.S. and Canada)

Before Using This Medicine

In deciding to use a medicine, the risks of taking the medicine must be weighed against the good it will do. This is a decision you and your doctor will make. For enoxaparin, the following should be considered:

Allergies—Tell your doctor if you have ever had any unusual or allergic reaction to enoxaparin or to heparin. Also tell your health care professional if you are allergic to any other substances, such as foods, especially pork or pork products, preservatives, or dyes.

Pregnancy—Enoxaparin has not been studied in pregnant women. However, it has not been shown to cause birth defects or other problems in animal studies.

Breast-feeding—It is not known whether this medicine passes into breast milk. Although most medicines pass into breast milk in small amounts, many of them may be used safely while breast-feeding. Mothers who are using this medicine and who wish to breast-feed should discuss this with their doctor.

Children—Studies on this medicine have been done only in adult patients, and there is no specific information comparing use of enoxaparin in children with use in other age groups.

Older adults—This medicine has been tested and has not been shown to cause different side effects or problems in older people than it does in younger adults.

Other medicines—Although certain medicines should not be used together at all, in other cases two different medicines may be used together even if an interaction might occur. In these cases, your doctor may want to change the dose, or other precautions may be necessary. When you are using enoxaparin, it is especially important that your health care professional know if you are taking any of the following:

- Aspirin or
- Divalproex (e.g., Depakote) or
- Inflammation or pain medicine, except narcotics, or
- Plicamycin (e.g., Mithracin) or
- Sulfinpyrazone (e.g., Anturane) or
- Thrombolytic agents or
- Ticlopidine (e.g., Ticlid) or
- Valproic acid (e.g., Depakene)—Using any of these medicines together with enoxaparin may increase the risk of bleeding

Other medical problems—The presence of other medical problems may affect the use of enoxaparin. Make sure you tell your doctor if you have any other medical problems, especially:

- Blood disease or bleeding problems or
- Blood vessel problems or
- Heart infection or
- High blood pressure (hypertension) or
- Kidney disease or
- Liver disease or
- Stomach ulcer (active) or
- Threatened miscarriage—The risk of bleeding may be increased

Also, tell your doctor if you have received enoxaparin or heparin before and had a reaction to either of them called thrombocytopenia, or if new blood clots formed while you were receiving the medicine.

In addition, *tell your doctor if you have recently given birth, fallen or suffered a blow to the body or head, or had medical or dental surgery.* These events may increase the risk of serious bleeding when you are taking enoxaparin.

Proper Use of This Medicine

If you are using enoxaparin at home, your health care professional will teach you how to inject yourself with the medicine. *Be sure to follow the directions carefully. Check with your health care professional if you have any problems using the medicine.*

Put used syringes in a puncture-resistant, disposable container, or dispose of them as directed by your health care professional.

Dosing—The dose of enoxaparin will be different for different patients. *Follow your doctor's orders or the directions on the label.* The following information includes only the average doses of enoxaparin. *If your dose is different, do not change it* unless your doctor tells you to do so.

- For *injection* dosage form:
  —For prevention of deep venous thrombosis (hip or knee replacement surgery):
    - Adults—30 milligrams (mg) injected under the skin every twelve hours for seven to ten days. Alternatively, for hip replacement surgery, the dose may be 40 mg injected under the skin once a day for three weeks.
    - Children—Use and dose must be determined by your doctor.
  —For prevention of deep venous thrombosis (abdominal surgery):
    - Adults—40 mg injected under the skin once a day for seven to ten days.
    - Children—Use and dose must be determined by your doctor.
  —For prevention of coronary arterial thrombosis:
    - Adults—1 mg per kilogram (kg) (0.45 mg per pound) of body weight injected under the skin every twelve hours for two to eight days.
    - Children—Use and dose must be determined by your doctor.

Missed dose—If you miss a dose of this medicine, use it as soon as possible. However, if it is almost time for your next dose, skip the missed dose and go back to your regular dosing schedule. Do not double doses.

Storage—To store this medicine:

- Keep out of the reach of children.
- Store away from heat and direct light.
- Keep the medicine from freezing. Do not refrigerate.
- Do not keep outdated medicine or medicine no longer needed. Be sure that any discarded medicine is out of the reach of children.

Precautions While Using This Medicine

Tell all your medical doctors and dentists that you are using this medicine.

Check with your doctor immediately if you notice any of the following side effects:

- Bruising or bleeding, especially bleeding that is hard to stop. Bleeding inside the body sometimes appears as bloody or black, tarry stools, or faintness.
- Back pain; burning, pricking, tickling, or tingling sensation; leg weakness; numbness; paralysis; or problems with bowel or bladder function.

Side Effects of This Medicine

Along with its needed effects, a medicine may cause some unwanted effects. Although not all of these side effects may occur, if they do occur they may need medical attention.

Stop using this medicine and check with your doctor immediately if any of the following side effects occur:

Less common
  Blood in urine; bloody or black, tarry stools; bruising; chest discomfort; collection of blood under the skin; confusion; continuing bleeding or oozing from the nose and/or mouth, or surgical wound; convulsions; coughing up blood; fever; headache; irritability; lightheadedness; moderate to severe pain or numbness in the arms, legs, hands, feet; nosebleed; shortness of breath; swelling of hands and/or feet; unusual bleeding; unusual tiredness or weakness; vomiting of blood or material that looks like coffee grounds

Rare
  Back pain; burning, pricking, tickling, or tingling sensation; chest pain; dizziness or lightheadedness when getting up from a lying or sitting position; fast or irregular heartbeat; leg weakness; paralysis; problems with bowel or bladder function; skin rash or hives; sudden fainting; swelling of the face, genitals, mouth, or tongue

Other side effects may occur that usually do not need medical attention. These side effects may go away during treatment as your body adjusts to the medicine. However, check with your doctor if any of the following side effects continue or are bothersome:

Less common
  Increased menstrual bleeding; irritation, pain, or redness at place of injection; nausea; vomiting

Other side effects not listed above may also occur in some patients. If you notice any other effects, check with your doctor.

Developed: 11/22/93
Interim revision: 07/28/98

ENTACAPONE   Systemic

Commonly used brand name(s):

In the U.S.—
    Comtan

Description

Entacapone (in-TACK-a-pohn) is used in combination with levodopa/carbidopa to treat Parkinson's disease, sometimes referred to as shaking palsy. Some patients experience signs and symptoms of end-of-dose "wearing-off" effect despite taking levodopa/carbidopa. Entacapone enhances the effect of levodopa/carbidopa. By improving muscle control, this medicine allows more normal movements of the body.

This medicine is available only with your doctor's prescription, in the following dosage forms:

- Tablets (U.S.)

Before Using This Medicine

In deciding to use a medicine, the risks of taking entacapone must be weighed against the good it will do. This is a decision you and your doctor will make. For entacapone, the following should be considered:

Allergies—Tell your doctor if you have ever had any unusual or allergic reaction to entacapone. Also tell your doctor and pharmacist if you are allergic to any other substances, such as foods, preservatives, or dyes.

Pregnancy—Entacapone has not been studied in pregnant women. However, studies in animals have shown that entacapone causes problems with the development of offspring. Before taking this medicine, make sure your doctor knows if you are pregnant or if you may become pregnant.

Breast-feeding—It is not known whether entacapone passes into breast milk.

Children—Studies on this medicine have been done only in adult patients. There is no identified potential use of entacapone in children.

Older adults—Many medicines have not been tested in older people. Therefore, it may not be known whether they work exactly the same way they do in younger adults or if they cause different side effects or problems in older people. In studies done to date that included elderly people, entacapone did not cause different side effects or problems in older people than it did in younger adults.

Other medicines—Although certain medicines should not be used together at all, in other cases two different medicines may be used together even if an interaction might occur. In these cases, your doctor may want to change the dose, or other precautions may be necessary. When you are taking entacapone, it is especially important that your doctor and pharmacist know if you are taking any of the following:

- Apomorphine (e.g., Zydis) or
- Bitolterol (e.g., Tornalate) or
- Epinephrine (e.g., Adrenalin) or
- Isoetherine (e.g., Bronkosol) or
- Isoproterenol (e.g., Isuprel) or
- Methyldopa (e.g., Aldomet)—Taking these medications with entacapone may cause a fast or irregular heartbeat and excessive changes in blood pressure.
- Monoamine oxidase (MAO) inhibitors (furazolidone [e.g., Furoxone]. isocarboxazid [e.g., Marplan], phenelzine [e.g., Nardil], procarbazine [e.g., Matulane], tranylcypromine [e.g., Parnate])—Taking these medicines with entacapone may cause serious unwanted effects.

Note: Entacapone may be taken with the selective monoamine oxidase (MAO) inhibitor selegiline (e.g., Eldepryl).

Other medical problems—The presence of other medical problems may affect the use of entacapone. Make sure you tell your doctor if you have any other medical problems, especially:

- Liver problems—Side effects of entacapone may be increased because of a slower removal from the body.

Proper Use of This Medicine

Take this medicine only as directed by your doctor, to help your condition as much as possible. Do not take more or less of it, and do not take it more or less often than your doctor ordered.

Dosing—The dose of entacapone will be different for different patients. *Follow your doctor's orders or the directions on the label.* The following information includes only the average doses of entacapone. *If your dose is different, do not change it* unless your doctor tells you to do so.

Entacapone is always used in combination with levodopa/carbidopa (Sinemet); never alone.

The number of times a day you take the tablets depends on how often you take levodopa/carbidopa (Sinemet).

- For *oral* dosage form (tablets):
    —For Parkinson's disease:
      - Adults—200 mg with each levodopa/carbidopa (Sinemet) dose. Entacapone may be taken up to 8 times a day, and the total daily dose is usually not more than 1600 mg.
      - Children—Use and dose must be determined by your doctor.

Missed dose—Always take with your levodopa/carbidopa (Sinemet). If you miss a dose of this medicine, take it as soon as possible. However, if your next scheduled dose is within 2 hours, skip the missed dose and go back to your regular dosing schedule. Do not double doses.

Storage—To store this medicine:

- Keep out of the reach of children.
- Do not store in the bathroom, near the kitchen sink, or in other damp places. Heat or moisture may cause the medicine to break down.
- Do not keep outdated medicine or medicine no longer needed. Ask your health care professional how you should dispose of any medicine you do not use. Be sure that any discarded medicine is out of the reach of children.

Precautions While Using This Medicine

It is important that your doctor check your progress at regular visits to make sure that this medicine is working properly and to check for unwanted effects.

Do not stop taking entacapone without first checking with your doctor. Your doctor may want you to gradually reduce the amount you are taking before stopping completely.

Nausea may occur, especially when you first start taking this medicine. Also, an increase in body movements and twitching, twisting, or uncontrolled movements of the tongue, lips, face, arms or legs may occur. Your doctor may need to adjust your dose of levodopa/carbidopa if these movements occur.

This medicine may cause some people to become dizzy or drowsy. *Make sure you know how you react to this medicine before you drive, use machines, or do anything else that could be dangerous if you are not alert.*

Dizziness, lightheadedness, or fainting may occur, especially when you get up from a lying or sitting position. Getting up slowly may help. If you should have this problem, check with your doctor.

Hallucinations (seeing, hearing, or feeling things that are not there) may occur in some patients.

Entacapone may cause your urine to turn brownish orange. This effect is harmless and will go away after you stop taking the medicine.

Side Effects of This Medicine

Along with its needed effects, a medicine may cause some unwanted effects. Although not all of these side effects may occur, if they do occur they may need medical attention.

Check with your doctor as soon as possible if any of the following side effects occur:

More common
Absence of or decrease in body movements; hyperactivity; increase in body movements; seeing, hearing, or feeling things that are not there; twitching; twisting; uncontrolled repetitive movements of tongue, lips, face, arms, or legs

Less common
Fever or chills; cough or hoarseness; lower back or side pain; painful or difficult urination

Rare
Confusion; muscle cramps; pain; shortness of breath; stiffness; weakness; unusual tiredness

Other side effects may occur that usually do not need medical attention. These side effects may go away during treatment as your body adjusts to the medicine. However, check with your doctor if any of the following side effects continue or are bothersome.

More common
Abdominal pain; constipation; diarrhea; dizziness; fatigue; nausea

Less common
Acid or sour stomach; anxiety; belching; bruising; burning feeling in chest or stomach; heartburn; difficult or labored breathing; dry mouth; indigestion; insomnia; irritability; loss of strength or energy; muscle pain or weakness; nervousness; passing gas; sleepiness or unusual drowsiness; small, red spots on skin; stomach discomfort, upset or pain; sweating increased; restlessness; tenderness in stomach area; tightness in chest; tremor; shortness of breath; unusual or unpleasant (after)taste; unusual weak feeling; wheezing

This medicine may cause your urine to turn brownish orange. This effect is harmless and will go away after you stop taking the medicine.

Other side effects not listed above may also occur in some patients. If you notice any other effects, check with your doctor.

Developed: 03/10/2000

EPINEPHRINE   Ophthalmic

Commonly used brand name(s):

In the U.S.—
Epifrin[1]   Eppy/N[2]
Epinal[2]   Glaucon[1]

In Canada—
Epifrin[1]

Note: For quick reference, the following medicines are numbered to match the corresponding brand names.

This information applies to the following medicines:
1. Epinephrine (ep-i-NEF-rin) ‡
2. Epinephryl Borate (ep-i-NEF-rill BOR-ate) †

†Not commercially available in Canada.
‡Generic name product may be available in the U.S.

Description

Ophthalmic epinephrine is used to treat certain types of glaucoma. It may also be used in eye surgery.

This medicine is available only with your doctor's prescription, in the following dosage forms:

Ophthalmic
Epinephrine
• Ophthalmic solution (eye drops) (U.S. and Canada)
Epinephryl Borate
• Ophthalmic solution (eye drops) (U.S.)

Before Using This Medicine

In deciding to use a medicine, the risks of taking the medicine must be weighed against the good it will do. This is a decision you and your doctor will make. For epinephrine, the following should be considered:

Allergies—Tell your doctor if you have ever had any unusual or allergic reaction to epinephrine. Also tell your health care professional if you are allergic to any other substances, such as sulfites or other preservatives.

Pregnancy—Ophthalmic epinephrine may be absorbed into the body. However, studies on effects in pregnancy have not been done in either humans or animals.

Breast-feeding—Ophthalmic epinephrine may be absorbed into the body. However, it is not known whether epinephrine passes into the breast milk.

Children—Studies on this medicine have been done only in adult patients, and there is no specific information comparing use of this medicine in children with use in other age groups.

Older adults—Many medicines have not been studied specifically in older people. Therefore, it may not be known whether they work exactly the same way they do in younger adults. Although there is no specific information comparing use of this medicine in the elderly with use in other age groups, this medicine is not expected to cause different side effects or problems in older people than it does in younger adults.

Other medicines—Although certain medicines should not be used together at all, in other cases two different medicines may be used together even if an interaction might occur. In these cases, your doctor may want to change the dose, or other precautions may be necessary. Tell your health care professional if you are using any other prescription or nonprescription (over-the-counter [OTC]) medicine.

Other medical problems—The presence of other medical problems may affect the use of epinephrine. Make sure you tell your doctor if you have any other medical problems, especially:

- Bronchial asthma or
- Diabetes mellitus (sugar diabetes) or
- Eye disease (other) or
- Heart or blood vessel disease or
- High blood pressure or
- Overactive thyroid—Epinephrine may make the condition worse
- Dental surgery on gums—Dental surgery may include the use of epinephrine in topical or injection form. Use of ophthalmic epinephrine during this time may increase blood levels of the medicine and increase the chance of side effects

Proper Use of This Medicine

Use this medicine only as directed. Do not use more of it and do not use it more often than your doctor ordered. To do so may increase the chance of too much medicine being absorbed into the body and the chance of side effects.

To use:

- First, wash your hands. Tilt the head back and, pressing your finger gently on the skin just beneath the lower eyelid, pull the lower eyelid away from the eye to make a space. Drop the medicine into this space. Let go of the eyelid and gently close the eyes. Do not blink. Keep the eyes closed and apply pressure to the inner corner of the eye with your finger for 1 or 2 minutes to allow the medicine to be absorbed by the eye.
- Immediately after using the eye drops, wash your hands to remove any medicine that may be on them.
- To keep the medicine as germ-free as possible, do not touch the applicator tip to any surface (including the eye). Also, keep the container tightly closed.

For patients using *epinephrine ophthalmic solution:*

- Do not use if the solution turns pinkish or brownish in color, or if it becomes cloudy.

For patients using *epinephryl borate ophthalmic solution:*

- The color of this solution may vary from colorless to amber yellow. Do not use if the solution turns dark brown or becomes cloudy.

Dosing—The dose of ophthalmic epinephrine will be different for different patients. *Follow your doctor's orders or the directions on the label.* The following information includes only the average doses of ophthalmic epinephrine. *If your dose is different, do not change it* unless your doctor tells you to do so.

For epinephrine and epinephryl borate

- For *ophthalmic solution (eye drops)* dosage forms:
  —For glaucoma:
    - Adults and teenagers—One drop one or two times a day.
    - Children—Use and dose must be determined by your doctor.

Missed dose—If you miss a dose of this medicine, apply the missed dose as soon as possible. However, if it is almost time for your next dose, skip the missed dose and go back to your regular dosing schedule. Do not double doses.

Storage—To store this medicine:

- Keep out of the reach of children.
- Store away from heat and direct light.
- Keep the medicine from freezing.
- Do not keep outdated medicine or medicine no longer needed. Be sure that any discarded medicine is out of the reach of children.

Precautions While Using This Medicine

Your doctor should check your eye pressure at regular visits.

This medicine may cause blurred vision or other vision problems for a short time after it is applied. If any of these occur, *do not drive, use machines, or do anything else that could be dangerous if you are not able to see well.*

Side Effects of This Medicine

Along with its needed effects, a medicine may cause some unwanted effects. Although not all of these side effects may occur, if they do occur they may need medical attention.

Check with your doctor as soon as possible if any of the following side effects occur:
> *Less common*
>> Blurred or decreased vision
>
> *Symptoms of too much medicine being absorbed into the body*
>> Fast, irregular, or pounding heartbeat; feeling faint; increased sweating; paleness; trembling

Other side effects may occur that usually do not need medical attention. These side effects may go away during treatment as your body adjusts to the medicine. However, check with your doctor if any of the following side effects continue or are bothersome:
> *More common*
>> Headache or browache; stinging, burning, redness, or other eye irritation; watering of eyes
>
> *Less common*
>> Eye pain or ache

Other side effects not listed above may also occur in some patients. If you notice any other effects, check with your doctor.

Revised: 11/28/94

EPIRUBICIN   Systemic

Commonly used brand name(s):

In the U.S.—
Ellence

In Canada—
Pharmorubicin PFS

Description

Epirubicin (ep-ee-ROO-bi-sin) belongs to the general group of medicines known as antineoplastics. It is used to treat some kinds of cancers of the breast; lung; lymph system; stomach; and ovaries. It may also be used to treat other kinds of cancer, as determined by your doctor.

Epirubicin seems to interfere with the growth of cancer cells, which are then eventually destroyed by the body. Since the growth of normal body cells may also be affected by epirubicin, other effects will also occur. Some of these may be serious and must be reported to your doctor. Other effects, like hair loss, may not be serious but may cause concern. Some effects may not occur until months or years after the medicine is used.

Before you begin treatment with epirubicin, you and your doctor should talk about the good this medicine will do as well as the risks of using it.

Epirubicin is to be administered only by or under the supervision of your doctor. It is available in the following dosage form:

Parenteral
- Injection (U.S. and Canada)

Before Using This Medicine

In deciding to use a medicine, the risks of taking the medicine must be weighed against the good it will do. This is a decision you and your doctor will make. For epirubicin, the following should be considered:

Allergies—Tell your doctor if you have ever had any unusual or allergic reaction to daunorubicin, doxorubicin, epirubicin, idarubicin, or mitoxantrone.

Pregnancy—There is a chance that this medicine may cause birth defects if either the male or female is receiving it at the time of conception or if it is taken by the mother during pregnancy. Studies in rats and rabbits have shown that epirubicin causes birth defects in the fetus and other problems (including miscarriage). In addition, many cancer medicines may cause sterility, which could be permanent. Although sterility has been reported in animals and humans with this medicine, this is less likely to occur in humans than in animals.

Be sure that you have discussed these possible effects with your doctor before receiving this medicine. Before receiving epirubicin make sure your doctor knows if you are pregnant or if you may become pregnant. It is best to use some kind of birth control while you are receiving epirubicin. Tell your doctor right away if you think you have become pregnant while receiving epirubicin.

Breast-feeding—It is not known whether epirubicin passes into breast milk. However, epirubicin is not recommended during breast-feeding, because it may cause unwanted effects in nursing babies.

Children—Studies on this medicine have been done only in adult patients, and there is no specific information comparing use of epirubicin in children with use in other age groups. Heart problems are more likely to occur in children younger than 2 years of age.

Older adults—Heart problems are more likely to occur in the elderly, who may have existing heart disease. The elderly may also be more likely to have blood problems. Also, elderly patients may not be able to metabolize the medication as quickly as younger patients, which may put them at risk for added toxicity.

Other medicines—Although certain medicines should not be used together at all, in other cases two different medicines may be used together even if an interaction might occur. In these cases, your doctor may want to change the dose, or other precautions may be necessary. When receiving epirubicin it is especially important that your health

care professional know if you are taking any of the following:

- Acetaminophen (e.g., Tylenol) (with long-term, high-dose use) or
- Amiodarone (e.g., Cordarone) or
- Anabolic steroids, nandrolone [e.g., Anabolin], oxandrolone [e.g., Anawar], oxymetholone [e.g., Anadrol], stanozolol [e.g., Winstrol]) or
- Androgens (male hormones) or
- Carmustine (e.g., BiCNU) or
- Chloroquine (e.g., Aralen) or
- Dantrolene (e.g., Dantrium) or
- Disulfiram (e.g., Antabuse) or
- Divalproex (e.g., Depakote) or
- Estrogens (female hormones) or
- Etretinate (e.g., Tegison) or
- Hydroxychloroquine (e.g., Plaquenil) or
- Methyldopa (e.g., Aldomet) or
- Naltrexone (e.g., Trexan) (with long-term, high-dose use) or
- Oral contraceptives (birth control pills) containing estrogen or
- Phenothiazines (acetophenazine [e.g., Tindal], chlorpromazine [e.g., Thorazine], fluphenazine [e.g., Prolixin], mesoridazine [e.g., Serentil], perphenazine [e.g., Trilafon], prochlorperazine [e.g., Compazine], promazine [e.g., Sparine], promethazine [e.g., Phenergan], thioridazine [e.g., Mellaril], trifluoperazine [e.g., Stelazine], triflupromazine [e.g., Vesprin], trimeprazine [e.g., Temaril]) or
- Phenytoin (e.g., Dilantin) or
- Valproic acid (e.g., Depakene)—Concurrent use of these agents with epirubicin may increase risk of liver problems

- Acyclovir (e.g., Zovirax) or
- Anticonvulsants (seizure medicine) or
- Antidiabetics, oral (diabetes medicine taken by mouth) or
- Antipsychotics (medicine for mental illness) or
- Captopril (e.g., Capoten) or
- Enalapril (e.g., Vasotec) or
- Flecainide (e.g., Tambocor) or
- Imipenem or
- Inflammation or pain medicine, except narcotics or
- Lisinopril (e.g., Prinivil, Zestril) or
- Maprotiline (e.g., Ludiomil) or
- Penicillamine (e.g., Cuprimine) or
- Pimozide (e.g., Orap) or
- Procainamide (e.g., Pronestyl) or
- Promethazine (e.g., Phenergan) or
- Ramipril (e.g., Altace) or
- Sulfasalazine (e.g., Azulfidine) or
- Tiopronin (e.g., Thiola) or
- Tocainide (e.g., Tonocard) or
- Tricyclic antidepressants (medicine for depression) or
- Trimeprazine (e.g., Temaril)—Concurrent use of these agents with epirubicin may cause blood disorders

- Amphotericin B, injection (e.g., Fungizone) or
- Antineoplastics, other (cancer medicine) or
- Azathioprine (e.g., Imuran) or
- Chloramphenicol (e.g., Chloromycetin) or
- Colchicine or
- Cyclophosphamide (e.g. Cytoxan) or
- Flucytosine (e.g. Ancoban) or
- Ganciclovir (e.g., Cytovene) or
- Interferon (e.g., Intron A, Roferon-A) or

- Zidovudine (e.g., AZT, Retrovir)—Concurrent use of these agents with epirubicin increases the risk of infection
- Anti-infectives, by mouth or injection (medicine for infection) or
- Carbamazepine (e.g., Tegretol) or
- Gold salts (medicine for arthritis)—Concurrent use with epirubicin may cause blood disorders and increase risk of liver problems
- Antithyroid agents (medicine for overactive thyroid) or
- Mercaptopurine (e.g., Purinethol) or
- Methotrexate (e.g., Rheumatrex) or
- Plicamycin (e.g., Mithracin)—Concurrent use with epirubicin increases the risk of infection and may increase the risk of liver problems
- Bepridil (e.g., Vascor) or
- Diltiazem (e.g., Cardizem) or
- Flunarizine (e.g., Sibelium) or
- Isradipine (e.g., DynaCirc) or
- Nicardipine (e.g., Cardene) or
- Nifedipine (e.g., Procardia) or
- Nimodipine (e.g., Nimotop) or
- Verapamil (e.g., Calan) or
- other heart medicines—Concurrent use of these agents with epirubicin may contribute to heart damage and failure
- Cimetidine (e.g., Tagamet)—Cimetidine increases the amount of time epirubicin stays in the body.
- Daunorubicin (e.g., Cerubidine) or
- Doxorubicin (e.g., Adriamycin) or
- Idarubicin (e.g., Idamycin) or
- Mitoxantrone (e.g., Novantrone)—Concurrent use of maximum cumulative doses of other anthracyclines with epirubicin may increase risk of heart damage, secondary leukemia, and stomach and blood problems. Concurrent use may increase risk of liver problems.
- If you have ever been treated with radiation or cancer medicines—Epirubicin may increase the effects of these medicines or radiation therapy on the blood
- If you have ever been treated with radiation to your chest—Risk of heart problems caused by epirubicin may be increased

Other medical problems—The presence of other medical problems may affect the use of epirubicin. Make sure you tell your doctor if you have any other medical problems, especially:

- Bone marrow depression or
- Viral, fungal, or bacterial infection—There may be an increased risk of infections or worsening infections because of the body's reduced ability to fight them
- Heart disease—Risk of heart problems caused by epirubicin may be increased
- Kidney disease or
- Liver disease—Effects of epirubicin may be increased because of its slower removal from the body
- Tumor cell infiltration of bone marrow—Increased susceptibility for cancer to spread to bone marrow

Proper Use of This Medicine

Epirubicin is sometimes given together with certain other medicines. *If you are receiving a combination of medicines, it is important that you receive each one at the proper time.* If you are taking some of these medicines by mouth, ask your health care professional to help you plan a way to take them at the right times.

While you are using this medicine, your doctor may want you to drink extra fluids so that you will pass more urine. This will help prevent kidney problems and keep your kidneys working well.

Epirubicin often causes nausea and vomiting. However, it is very important that you continue to receive the medication, even if you begin to feel ill. Ask your health care professional for ways to lessen these effects.

Dosing—The dose of epirubicin will be different for different patients. The dose that is used may depend on a number of things, including what the medicine is being used for, the patient's body size, and whether or not other medicines are also being taken. *If you are taking or receiving epirubicin at home, follow your doctor's orders or the directions on the label.* If you have any questions about the proper dose of epirubicin, ask your doctor.

Precautions While Using This Medicine

It is very important that your doctor check your progress at regular visits to make sure that this medicine is working properly and to check for unwanted effects.

While you are being treated with epirubicin, and after you stop treatment with it, *do not have any immunizations (vaccinations) without your doctor's approval.* Epirubicin may lower your body's resistance, and there is a chance you might get the infection the immunization is meant to prevent. In addition, other persons living in your household should not take oral polio vaccine, since there is a chance they could pass the polio virus on to you. Also, avoid persons who have taken oral polio vaccine within the last several months. Do not get close to them, and do not stay in the same room with them for very long. If you cannot take these precautions, you should consider wearing a protective face mask that covers the nose and mouth.

Epirubicin can temporarily lower the number of white blood cells in your blood, increasing the chance of getting an infection. It can also lower the number of platelets, which are necessary for proper blood clotting. If this occurs, there are certain precautions you can take, especially when your blood count is low, to reduce the risk of infection or bleeding:

- If you can, avoid people with infections. *Check with your doctor immediately* if you think you are getting an infection or if you get a fever or chills, cough or hoarseness, lower back or side pain, or painful or difficult urination.
- *Check with your doctor immediately* if you notice any unusual bleeding or bruising; black, tarry stools; blood in urine or stools; or pinpoint red spots on your skin.
- Be careful when using a regular toothbrush, dental floss, or toothpick. Your medical doctor, dentist, or nurse may recommend other ways to clean your teeth and gums. Check with your medical doctor before having any dental work done.
- Do not touch your eyes or the inside of your nose unless you have just washed your hands and have not touched anything else in the meantime.
- Be careful not to cut yourself when you are using sharp objects such as a safety razor or fingernail or toenail cutters.
- Avoid contact sports or other situations where bruising or injury could occur.

If epirubicin accidentally leaks out of the vein into which it is injected, it may damage some tissues and cause scarring. *Tell the doctor or nurse right away if you notice redness, pain, or swelling at the place of injection.*

Side Effects of This Medicine

Along with its needed effects, a medicine may cause some unwanted effects. Although not all of these side effects may occur, if they do occur they may need medical attention.

Also, because of the way these medicines act on the body, there is a chance that they might cause other unwanted effects that may not occur until months or years after the medicine is used. These delayed effects may include certain types of cancer, such as leukemia. Discuss these possible effects with your doctor.

Check with your doctor or nurse immediately if any of the following side effects occur:

More common
Bleeding, redness, or ulcers in mouth or throat; cough or hoarseness; fever or chills; lower back or side pain; painful or difficult urination; pain or burning in mouth or throat; sores in mouth or on lips

Less common
Black, tarry stools; blood in urine or stools; pinpoint red spots on skin; redness or discharge of the eye, eyelid, or lining of the eyelid; red streaks along injected vein; unusual bleeding or bruising

Rare
Darkening or redness of skin at place of irradiation; fast or irregular heartbeat; joint pain; pain, redness, or warmth at place of injection; skin rash or itching; swelling of abdomen, lower legs, and feet; swelling or tenderness of lymph nodes, abdomen, side or lower back; wheezing, difficulty breathing or shortness of breath

Symptoms of overdose
Abdominal swelling or tenderness; black, tarry stools or blood in stools; difficulty in urination; fast or irregular heartbeat; high fever; shortness of breath; stomach pain; swelling of the lining of the mouth, nose or throat; vomiting

Other side effects may occur that usually do not need medical attention. These side effects may go away during treatment as your body adjusts to the medicine. Also, your health care professional may be able to tell you about ways to prevent or reduce some of these side effects. Check with your health care professional if any of the following side effects continue or are bothersome or if you have any questions about them:

More common
Lack of menstrual periods; nausea and vomiting

Less common
Diarrhea; hot flashes

Rare
Darkening of soles, palms, or nails; loss of appetite or weight loss

Epirubicin causes the urine to turn reddish in color, which may stain clothes. This is not blood. It is to be expected and only lasts for 1 or 2 days after each dose is given.

This medicine often causes a temporary and total loss of hair. After treatment with epirubicin has ended, normal hair growth should return.

After you stop receiving epirubicin, it may still produce some side effects that need attention. During this period of time, *check with your doctor or nurse immediately* if you notice any of the following side effects:

Fast or irregular heartbeat; shortness of breath; swelling of abdomen, feet, and lower legs

Other side effects not listed above may also occur in some patients. If you notice any other effects, check with your health care professional.

Additional Information

Once a medicine has been approved for marketing for a certain use, experience may show that it is also useful for other medical problems. Although these uses are not included in the product labeling, epirubicin is used in certain patients with the following medical condition:

• Cancer of the muscles, connective tissues (tendons), vessels that carry blood or lymph, joints, and fat

Developed: 11/04/99
Revised: 03/30/2001

EPOETIN   Systemic

Commonly used brand name(s):

In the U.S.—
Epogen
Procrit

In Canada—
Eprex

Other commonly used names are human erythropoietin, recombinant; EPO; and r-HuEPO.

Description

Epoetin (eh-POH-ee-tin) is a man-made version of human erythropoietin (EPO). EPO is produced naturally in the body, mostly by the kidneys. It stimulates the bone marrow to produce red blood cells. If the body does not produce enough EPO, severe anemia can occur. This often occurs in people whose kidneys are not working properly. Epoetin is used to treat severe anemia in these people.

Epoetin may also be used to prevent or treat anemia caused by other conditions, such as AIDS, cancer, or surgery, as determined by your doctor.

Epoetin is given by injection. It is available only with your doctor's prescription and is available in the following dosage form:

Parenteral
• Injection (U.S. and Canada)

Before Using This Medicine

In deciding to use a medicine, the risks of taking the medicine must be weighed against the good it will do. This is a decision you and your doctor will make. For epoetin, the following should be considered:

Allergies—Tell your doctor if you have ever had any unusual or allergic reaction to epoetin or to human albumin. Also tell your health care professional if you are allergic to any other substances, such as foods, preservatives, or dyes.

Pregnancy—Epoetin has not been reported to cause birth defects or other problems in humans. However, it did cause problems, including unwanted effects on the bones and spine, in some animal studies.

Breast-feeding—It is not known whether epoetin passes into the breast milk. However, it has not been reported to cause problems in nursing babies.

Children—This medicine has been tested in children and, in effective doses, has not been shown to cause different side effects or problems than it does in adults.

Older adults—Epoetin has been given to elderly people. However, there is no specific information about whether epoetin works the same way it does in younger adults or whether it causes different side effects or problems in older people.

Other medicines—Although certain medicines should not be used together at all, in other cases two different medicines may be used together even if an interaction might occur. In these cases, your doctor may want to change the dose, or other precautions may be necessary. When you are taking epoetin, it is important that your health care professional know if you are taking any other prescription or nonprescription (over-the-counter [OTC]) medicine.

Other medical problems—The presence of other medical problems may affect the use of epoetin. Make sure you tell your doctor if you have any other medical problems, especially:

- Aluminum poisoning
- Blood clots (history of) or other problems with the blood or
- Folic acid, iron, or vitamin B_{12} deficiencies
- Heart or blood vessel disease or
- High blood pressure—The chance of side effects may be increased
- Infection, inflammation, or cancer
- Bone problems or
- Porphyrin (red blood cell pigment) metabolism disorder—Symptoms include change in color of urine, increased sun sensitivity, abdominal pain, and nerve swelling
- Sickle cell anemia—Epoetin may not work properly
- Seizures (history of)—The chance of seizures may be increased

Proper Use of This Medicine

Epoetin is usually given by a health care professional after a dialysis treatment. However, medicines given by injection are sometimes used at home. If you will be using epoetin at home, your health care professional will teach you how the injections are to be given. You will also have a chance to practice giving them. *Be certain that you understand exactly how the medicine is to be injected.*

Dosing—The dose of epoetin will be different for different patients. *Follow your doctor's orders or the directions on the label.* The following information includes only the average doses of epoetin. *If your dose is different, do not change it* unless your doctor tells you to do so.

- For *injection* dosage form:
  —For *severe anemia:*
  - Adults and teenagers—Dose is based on body weight and must be determined by your doctor. The usual dose is 50 to 100 Units per kilogram (kg) (23 to 45 Units per pound) of body weight three times a week, injected into a vein or under the skin. Your doctor may then gradually decrease the dose every four weeks or more until the lowest effective dose is reached.
  - Children 1 month to 12 years of age—Dose is based on body weight and must be determined by your doctor. The usual dose is 50 Units per kg (23 Units per pound) of body weight three times a week, injected into a vein or under the skin. Your doctor may then gradually decrease the dose every four weeks or more until the lowest effective dose is reached.
  - Children up to 1 month of age—Use and dose must be determined by your doctor.

Missed dose—If you miss a dose of this medicine, use it as soon as possible. However, if it is almost time for your next dose, skip the missed dose and go back to your regular dosing schedule. Do not double doses.

Storage—To store this medicine:

- Keep out of the reach of children.
- Store in the refrigerator. However, keep the medicine from freezing.
- Do not keep outdated medicine or medicine no longer needed. Be sure that any discarded medicine is out of the reach of children.

Precautions While Using This Medicine

Epoetin sometimes causes convulsions (seizures), especially during the first 90 days of treatment. During this time, it is best to avoid driving, operating heavy machinery, or other activities that could cause a serious injury if a seizure occurs while you are performing them.

People with severe anemia usually feel very tired and sick. When epoetin begins to work, usually in about 6 weeks, most people start to feel better. Some people are able to be more active. However, epoetin only corrects anemia. It has no effect on kidney disease or any other medical problem that needs regular medical attention. Therefore, even if you are feeling much better, *it is very important that you do not miss any appointments with your doctor or any dialysis treatments.*

Many people with kidney problems need to be on a special diet. Also, people with high blood pressure (which may be caused by kidney disease or by epoetin treatment) may need to be on a special diet and/or to take medicine to keep their blood pressure under control. After their anemia has been corrected, some people feel so much better that they want to eat more than before. To keep your kidney disease or your high blood pressure from getting worse, *it is very important that you follow your special diet and take your medicines regularly*, even if you are feeling better.

In addition to epoetin, your body needs iron to make red blood cells. Your doctor may direct you to take iron supplements. He or she may also direct you to take certain vitamins that help the iron work better. *Be sure to follow your doctor's orders carefully*, because epoetin will not work properly if there is not enough iron in your body.

Side Effects of This Medicine

Along with its needed effects, a medicine may cause some unwanted effects. Although not all of these side effects may occur, if they do occur they may need medical attention.

Check with your doctor immediately if any of the following side effects occur:

   More common–in any treatment group
      Chest pain; shortness of breath

   Less common–in any treatment group
      Convulsions (seizures)

Also, check with your doctor as soon as possible if any of the following side effects occur:

   More common—for patients being treated for anemia due to chronic kidney failure
      Headache; increased blood pressure; swelling of face, fingers, ankles, feet, or lower legs; vision problems; weight gain

   Rare—for patients being treated for anemia due to chronic kidney failure
      Skin rash or hives

   More common—for patients being treated for anemia due to chronic kidney failure who require dialysis (in addition to those listed above)
      Cough; fast heartbeat; fever; sneezing; sore throat

   More common—for zidovudine-treated HIV-infected patients
      Fever; headache; skin rash or hives

   More common—for cancer patients on chemotherapy
      Cough, sneezing or sore throat; fever; swelling of face, fingers, ankles, feet or lower legs; weight gain

   More common—for surgical patients
      Blood in urine, lower back pain, or pain or burning while urinating; fever; headache; increased blood pressure; skin rash or hives; swelling of face, fingers, ankles, feet or lower legs; swelling or pain in legs; weight gain

Other side effects may occur that usually do not need medical attention. These side effects may go away during treatment as your body adjusts to the medicine. Epoetin sometimes causes an influenza-like reaction, with symptoms such as muscle aches, bone pain, chills, shivering, and sweating, occurring about 1 or 2 hours after an injection. These symptoms usually go away within 12 hours. However, check with your doctor if this influenza-like reaction or any of the following side effects continue or are bothersome:

   More common—in all treatment groups
      Diarrhea; dizziness; nausea or vomiting

   More common—for patients being treated for anemia due to chronic kidney failure (in addition to those listed above)
      Bone or joint pain, muscle aches, chills, shivering, sweating; general feeling of tiredness or weakness; itching or stinging at site of injection; loss of strength or energy; muscle pain or weakness

   More common—for patients being treated for anemia due to chronic kidney failure who require dialysis (in addition to those listed above)
      Abdominal pain and swelling; constipation; cough; fever; sore throat; weight loss

   More common—for zidovudine-treated HIV-infected patients
      Congestion in the lungs; cough; general feeling of tiredness or weakness; itching or stinging at site of injection; loss of strength or energy; muscle pain or weakness

   More common—for cancer patients on chemotherapy
      General feeling of tiredness or weakness; loss of

strength or energy; muscle pain or weakness; tingling, burning or prickly sensation

   More common—for surgical patients
      Anxiety; constipation; heartburn or belching, acid or sour stomach; inability to sleep; itching or stinging at site of injection; skin pain; stomach discomfort, upset or pain

Other side effects not listed above may also occur in some patients. If you notice any other effects, check with your doctor.

Additional Information

For patients receiving epoetin who do not have anemia caused by kidney disease:

• The information about the importance of keeping dialysis appointments and following a special diet for people with kidney problems does not apply to you. However, your doctor may have other special directions for you to follow. Be sure to follow these directions carefully, even if you feel much better after receiving epoetin for a while.

Revised: 03/02/00

EPOPROSTENOL   Systemic

Commonly used brand name(s):

In the U.S.—
   Flolan

In Canada—
   Flolan

Other commonly used names are Prostacyclin, PGI$_2$, and PGX.

Description

Epoprostenol (e-poe-PROST-en-ole) belongs to a group of agents called prostaglandins. Prostaglandins occur naturally in the body and are involved in many biological functions. Epoprostenol is used to treat the symptoms of primary pulmonary hypertension, or the high blood pressure that occurs in the main artery that carries blood from the right side of the heart (the ventricle) to the lungs. When the smaller blood vessels in the lungs become more resistant to blood flow, the right ventricle must work harder to pump enough blood through the lungs. Epoprostenol works by relaxing blood vessels and increasing the supply of blood to the lungs, reducing the workload of the heart.

This medicine is available only with your doctor's prescription, in the following dosage form(s):

   Parenteral
      • Injection (U.S. and Canada)

Before Using This Medicine

In deciding to use a medicine, the risks of using the medicine must be weighed against the good it will do. This is a decision you and your doctor will make. For epoprostenol, the following should be considered:

Allergies—Tell your health care professional if you are allergic to any other substances, such as foods, preservatives, or dyes.

Pregnancy—Epoprostenol has not been studied in pregnant women and, although epoprostenol has not been shown to cause birth defects or other problems in animals, it is not recommended for use in pregnant women unless absolutely necessary. Before taking this medicine, make sure your doctor knows if you are pregnant or if you may become pregnant.

Breast-feeding—It is not known whether epoprostenol passes into breast milk. Although most medicines pass into breast milk in small amounts, many of them may be used safely while breast-feeding. Mothers who are taking this medicine and who wish to breast-feed should discuss this with their doctor.

Children—Although there is no specific information comparing use of this medicine in children with use in other age groups, this medicine is not expected to cause different side effects or problems in children than it does in adults.

Older adults—Many medicines have not been studied specifically in older people. Therefore, it may not be known whether they work exactly the same way they do in younger adults or if they cause different side effects or problems in older people. There is no specific information comparing use of epoprostenol in the elderly with use in other age groups.

Other medicines—Although certain medicines should not be used together at all, in other cases two different medicines may be used together even if an interaction might occur. In these cases, your doctor may want to change the dose, or other precautions may be necessary. It is important that your health care professional know if you are taking any prescription or nonprescription (over-the-counter [OTC]) medicines.

Other medical problems—The presence of other medical problems may affect the use of epoprostenol. Make sure you tell your doctor if you have any other medical problems, especially:

- Heart disease or
- Lung disease—Epoprostenol may make these conditions worse

Proper Use of This Medicine

Your doctor or nurse will teach you how to prepare the medicine and use the pump for administering the medicine. Epoprostenol must be administered continuously by a portable pump that is operated by a small computer. The medicine will be delivered directly to the heart through a catheter that will be inserted into a vein in the chest.

Epoprostenol should be reconstituted only with the sterile diluent that is supplied with this medicine. The reconstituted medicine should not be mixed with other solutions or medicines. Use the following procedure for reconstituting your daily supply:

- Clear an area to work in and clean the area with alcohol. Gather your supplies. Wash your hands thoroughly with soap and water and then open all packages. Remove the vial cap from the vial containing the sterile diluent, clean the tops of the vials with alcohol swabs, and let the vial tops dry before proceeding.

To withdraw the sterile diluent
- If not already attached, attach a needle to the syringe. Gently pull the plunger out slightly and push it back to break the syringe seal. Draw air into the syringe that is about equal to the amount of sterile diluent you've been instructed to withdraw from the vial. Insert the needle at an angle, completely through the rubber seal of the vial. Turn the vial and syringe upside down (the syringe-vial unit is now vertical) and carefully press the plunger, injecting some or all of the air into the vial. Then aim the tip of the needle into the fluid and carefully pull the plunger slowly back to withdraw the diluent and/or allow the pressure to fill the syringe with the diluent. Continue pushing the remaining air into the vial, allowing the liquid to enter the syringe until the prescribed amount of diluent has been drawn into the syringe. Without withdrawing the needle, tap the syringe gently so that any air bubbles trapped in the syringe rise toward the top of the syringe. If air bubbles appear, depress the plunger gently to force the air bubbles out (into the vial) and then withdraw enough additional diluent to restore the needed volume in the syringe. (Holding the syringe-vial as a unit in a vertical position and keeping the needle tip in the fluid while withdrawing the diluent may help minimize the amount of air drawn into the syringe.) Once the required volume has been drawn into the syringe, let the syringe-vial pressure equalize and slowly withdraw the needle from the vial.

To reconstitute the epoprostenol
- Insert the same needle through the rubber seal of the vial of epoprostenol and inject the sterile diluent gently onto the side of the vial. The flow of the sterile diluent should be directed toward the side of the vial and injected slowly in order to prevent the medicine from foaming. Once the pressure has equalized, withdraw the needle from the vial. Gently swirl the vial to mix the epoprostenol. Turn the vial upside down to catch any undissolved powder near the top of the vial. Never shake the vials. Repeat this process if you need to mix more than one vial of epoprostenol.

To draw out the reconstituted epoprostenol
- Wipe the top of the reconstituted epoprostenol vial with an alcohol swab and let it dry. Change the needle on the syringe and then gently pull back the syringe plunger and fill the syringe with the amount of air that is equal to the amount of reconstituted epoprostenol you have been instructed to withdraw. Insert the needle through the seal of the vial and inject the air into the vial. Be sure to keep the needle tip below the fluid line and then pull the plunger back gently to withdraw the reconstituted epoprostenol into the syringe. Remove any air that may be trapped in the syringe as described above. Withdraw the needle and replace the needle cap on the syringe.

To inject the reconstituted epoprostenol into the cassette
- Remove the end cap from the cassette tubing. Carefully remove the needle from the syringe (be sure to discard the needle in an appropriate manner) and attach the syringe to the cassette tubing. Hold the cassette in one hand and push the plunger to inject the reconstituted solution into the cassette (alternatively, you may find it useful to use a tabletop or other solid structure to steady the plunger while pushing down on the syringe to inject the solution). When the syringe is empty, clamp the cassette tubing near the syringe. Disconnect the syringe and replace the cassette tubing end cap.

To inject the remaining diluent into the partially filled cassette
- Using a 60 mL syringe, attach a new needle to the syringe and follow the above procedures for breaking

the syringe seal and wiping the tops of the sterile diluent vials. Fill the syringe with the amount of air that is equal to the amount of sterile diluent you will remove from the first vial. Insert the needle through the rubber seal and slowly inject some of the air into the vial, allowing the fluid to flow into the syringe. Continue to push air gently into the vial until all of the fluid in the vial has flowed into the syringe. Remove any air that may be in the syringe as described above. Allow the pressure to equalize before you pull the needle out or you may lose fluid from the syringe. (If this occurs, the whole process needs to be repeated.) Withdraw the needle and replace the needle cap on the syringe. You may find it easier to hold the larger syringe in an upside down, vertical position while withdrawing the fluid in the vial.

To inject the sterile diluent into the cassette
- Uncap the clamped cassette tube and carefully remove the needle from the syringe (discarding the needle in an appropriate manner). Attach the syringe to the cassette tubing. Unclamp the cassette tubing and carefully inject the solution into the cassette. When the syringe is empty, clamp the cassette tube near the syringe and disconnect the syringe. Replace the cap on the cassette tube. If more diluent is needed to fill the cassette, repeat steps 6 and 7 with an additional vial of diluent; however, after completing the transfer of all of the required diluent, clamp the tubing, but leave the syringe attached to the cassette tubing while you mix the solution. Gently turn the cassette upside down at least 10 times to thoroughly mix the reconstituted epoprostenol with the additional diluent.

To remove air from the cassette
- To remove the air from inside the cassette, slowly turn the cassette until all of the small bubbles of air join to form one air pocket. Tilt the cassette gently so that the air pocket is in the corner where the tubing connects to the cassette. Unclamp the tube and pull back the plunger of the syringe until you see fluid fill the tubing. Clamp the tube near the connector and remove the syringe and replace the cap on the tubing. Label the cassette with the current time and date. Store the cassette in the refrigerator (preferably, on the top shelf to avoid spilling any food or drink on it) until it is time to use it. Make up a new cassette each day and use the cassette you refrigerated the day before so that you will always have a back-up cassette.

To use the pump
- The instructions for the use of the pump may vary depending on the particular make and model of the pump. Your doctor or nurse will give detailed instructions on how to use and care for the particular pump and accessories that you will use for administering your medicine. These instructions should include how to change the pump battery, cassette, and tubing. Remember to change the gel packs every 12 hours or every 8 hours if the surrounding temperature approaches 86 °F.
- Maintain sterile technique at all times. If you suspect that you have contaminated anything, throw away the accessories and begin again.

Dosing—The dose of epoprostenol will be different for different patients and will be determined by your doctor. The amount of medicine you take may have to be increased gradually by your doctor. It must never be stopped suddenly. *Follow your doctor's orders or the directions on the label.* The following information includes only the average doses of epoprostenol. *If your dose is different, do not change it* unless your doctor tells you to do so.

The amount of medicine that you take depends on the concentration of the reconstituted medicine and the rate at which the infusion pump delivers the medicine.
- For *injection* dosage form:
  —For primary pulmonary hypertension and pulmonary hypertension secondary to scleroderma spectrum of disease:
  - Adults—Initially, 2 nanograms per kilogram (kg) (0.9 nanogram per pound) of body weight per minute. Your doctor may increase your dose as necessary.
  - Children—Use and dose must be determined by your doctor.

Missed dose—*Epoprostenol has to be administered by a continuous intravenous infusion and it must never be stopped suddenly.*

Storage—To store this medicine:
- Keep out of the reach of children.
- Do not keep outdated medicine, or medicine no longer needed. Be sure that any discarded medicine is out of the reach of children.

Unopened vials
- Store unopened vials away from heat and direct light.
- Keep the medicine and the diluent from freezing.
- Do not store unopened vials in the bathroom, near the kitchen sink, or in other damp places. Heat or moisture may cause the medicine to break down.

Reconstituted injection
- Store the reconstituted injection in the refrigerator, away from direct light. However, keep the medicine from freezing. Any medicine that has been frozen should be thrown away. Reconstituted solutions should be kept either in the refrigerator or in a cold pouch, or a combination of the two, for no more than 48 hours. Do not expose reconstituted solution to temperatures higher than 25 °C (77 °F).
- If the reconstituted solution has particles in it or is discolored, it should be discarded.

Precautions While Using This Medicine

It is important that your doctor check your progress at regular visits. This will allow your doctor to make sure the medicine is working properly and to change the dosage if needed.

Be sure to report any signs of infection at the catheter site to your doctor. Also, if you develop a sudden fever, contact your doctor as soon as possible.

Avoid the use of saunas, hot baths, or sunbathing, or other situations that may cause blood vessels to dilate, resulting in low blood pressure and increasing the possibility of dizziness, light-headedness, or fainting.

Do not suddenly stop using this medicine. Stopping suddenly may bring on symptoms of your condition and can be dangerous. Check with your doctor before stopping completely.

Your doctor may want you to carry a medical identification card stating that you are using this medicine.

Side Effects of This Medicine

Along with its needed effects, a medicine may cause some unwanted effects. Although not all of these side effects may occur, if they do occur they may need medical attention.

Check with your doctor immediately if any of the following side effects occur:

Signs and symptoms that can occur with initial dosage adjustments and/or dosage excess

Diarrhea; fast heartbeat; headache; light-headedness or fainting; nausea; redness of face or neck (flushing); vomiting

Check with your doctor as soon as possible if any of the following side effects occur:

More common

Anxiety and/or nervousness; diarrhea; dizziness; flu or infection-like symptoms, such as chills, confusion, delirium, light-headedness or fainting, fast heartbeat, fever, and/or rapid, shallow breathing; headache; jaw pain (when chewing); local infection at the catheter site; pain at injection site; pain in muscles or bones; redness of face (flushing); unusual bleeding such as nosebleeds or bleeding gums or bruising

Less common

Altered or abnormal touch sensation or sensitivity

If you stop using this medicine abruptly or your dosage is reduced suddenly, symptoms of your condition may recur. If your medicine is suddenly stopped or reduced, *check with your doctor immediately*, especially if any of the following side effects occur:

Difficult or labored breathing; dizziness; fainting; weakness

Other side effects not listed above may also occur in some patients. If you notice any other effects, check with your doctor.

Developed: 01/04/1999
Revised: 09/04/2000

EPROSARTAN   Systemic

Commonly used brand name(s):

In the U.S.—
Teveten

Description

Eprosartan (ep-roe-SAR-tan) belongs to the class of medicines called angiotensin II inhibitors. It is used to treat high blood pressure (hypertension).

High blood pressure adds to the workload of the heart and arteries. If it continues for a long time, the heart and arteries may not function properly. This can damage the blood vessels of the brain, heart, and kidneys, resulting in a stroke, heart failure, or kidney failure. High blood pressure may also increase the risk of heart attacks. These problems may be less likely to occur if blood pressure is controlled.

Eprosartan works by blocking the action of a substance in the body that causes blood vessels to tighten. As a result, eprosartan relaxes blood vessels. This lowers blood pressure.

This medicine is available only with your doctor's prescription, in the following dosage form:

Oral
- Tablets (U.S.)

Before Using This Medicine

In deciding to use a medicine, the risks of taking the medicine must be weighed against the good it will do. This is a decision you and your doctor will make. For eprosartan, the following should be considered:

Allergies—Tell your doctor if you have ever had any unusual or allergic reaction to eprosartan or to any other substances, such as foods, preservatives, or dyes.

Pregnancy—Use of eprosartan during pregnancy, especially during the second and third trimesters (after the first 3 months) can cause low blood pressure, severe kidney failure, or possibly death in the newborn. *Therefore, it is important that you check with your doctor immediately if you think that you may have become pregnant.* Be sure that you have discussed this with your doctor before taking this medicine.

Breast-feeding—It is not known whether eprosartan passes into breast milk. However, eprosartan passes into the milk of lactating animals. Because this medicine may cause serious side effects in nursing infants, breast-feeding is generally not recommended while you are taking it.

Children—Studies on this medicine have been done only in adult patients, and there is no specific information comparing use of eprosartan in children with use in other age groups.

Older adults—This medicine has been tested in patients 65 years of age or older and has not been shown to cause different side effects or problems in older people than it does in younger adults.

Other medicines—Although certain medicines should not be used together at all, in other cases two different medicines may be used together even if an interaction might occur. In these cases, your doctor may want to change the dose, or other precautions may be necessary. Tell your health care professional if you are using any other prescription or nonprescription (over-the-counter [OTC]) medicine.

Other medical problems—The presence of other medical problems may affect the use of eprosartan. Make sure you tell your doctor if you have any other medical problems, especially:

- Congestive heart failure (severe)—Lowering of blood pressure by eprosartan may make this condition worse

- Dehydration or salt depletion—Blood pressure-lowering effects of eprosartan may be increased

- Kidney disease—Effects of eprosartan may make this condition worse

Proper Use of This Medicine

Take this medicine only as directed by your doctor. Do not take more of it and do not take it more often than your doctor ordered. This medicine also works best when there is a constant amount in the blood. *To help keep the amount constant, do not miss any doses. Also, it is best to take the doses at the same time each day.*

Dosing—The dose of eprosartan will be different for different patients. *Follow your doctor's orders or the directions on the label.* The following information includes only the average doses of eprosartan. *If your dose is different, do not change it* unless your doctor tells you to do so.

The number of tablets that you take depends on the strength of the medicine.

- For *oral* dosage form (tablets):
  —For high blood pressure:
  - Adults—400 to 800 milligrams (mg) a day. The dose may be taken once a day or divided into two doses.
  - Children—Use and dose must be determined by your doctor.

Missed dose—If you miss a dose of this medicine, take it as soon as possible. However, if it is almost time for your next dose, skip the missed dose and go back to your regular dosing schedule. Do not double doses.

Storage—To store this medicine:

- Keep out of the reach of children.
- Store away from heat and direct light.
- Do not keep outdated medicine or medicine no longer needed. Ask your health care professional how you should dispose of any medicine you do not use. Be sure that any discarded medicine is out of the reach of children.

Precautions While Using This Medicine

It is important that your doctor check your progress at regular visits to make sure that this medicine is working properly and to check for unwanted effects.

Check with your doctor immediately if you think that you may be pregnant. Eprosartan may cause birth defects or other problems in the baby if taken during pregnancy.

Do not take other medicines unless they have been discussed with your doctor. This especially includes over-the-counter (nonprescription) medicines for appetite control, asthma, colds, cough, hay fever, or sinus problems, since they may increase your blood pressure.

Dizziness or light-headedness may occur, especially if you have been taking a diuretic (water pill). Make sure you know how you react to this medicine before you drive, use machines, or do anything else that could be dangerous if you experience these effects.

Check with your doctor right away if you become sick while taking this medicine, especially with severe or continuing nausea and vomiting or diarrhea. These conditions may cause you to lose too much water and lead to low blood pressure.

Dizziness, light-headedness, or fainting also may occur if you exercise or if the weather is hot. Heavy sweating can cause loss of too much water and result in low blood pressure. Use extra care during exercise or hot weather.

Side Effects of This Medicine

Along with its needed effects, a medicine may cause some unwanted effects. Although not all of these side effects may occur, if they do occur they may need medical attention.

Check with your doctor as soon as possible if any of the following side effects occur:

Less common
Burning or painful urination or changes in urinary frequency; cough, fever, or sore throat

Rare
Dizziness, light-headedness, or fainting; swollen face, lips, limbs, or tongue

Other side effects may occur that usually do not need medical attention. These side effects may go away during treatment as your body adjusts to the medicine. However, check with your doctor if any of the following side effects continue or are bothersome:

Less common or rare
Abdominal pain; joint pain; unusual tiredness

Other side effects not listed above may also occur in some patients. If you notice any other effects, check with your doctor.

Developed: 12/16/99

ERGOLOID MESYLATES   Systemic

Commonly used brand name(s):

In the U.S.—
Gerimal
Hydergine
Hydergine LC
Generic name product may be available.

In Canada—
Hydergine

Another commonly used name is dihydrogenated ergot alkaloids.

Description

Ergoloid mesylates (ER-goe-loid MESS-i-lates) belongs to the group of medicines known as ergot alkaloids. It is used to treat some mood, behavior, or other problems that may be due to changes in the brain from Alzheimer's disease or multiple small strokes.

This medicine is different from other ergot alkaloids such as ergotamine and methysergide. It is not useful for treating migraine headache. The exact way ergoloid mesylates acts on the body is not known.

This medicine is available only with your doctor's prescription, in the following dosage forms:

Oral
- Capsules (U.S.)
- Oral solution (U.S.)
- Tablets (U.S. and Canada)

Sublingual (under-the-tongue)
- Tablets (U.S.)

Before Using This Medicine

In deciding to use a medicine, the risks of taking the medicine must be weighed against the good it will do. This is a decision

you and your doctor will make. For ergoloid mesylates, the following should be considered:

Allergies—Tell your doctor if you have ever had any unusual or allergic reaction to ergot alkaloids. Also tell your health care professional if you are allergic to any other substances, such as foods, preservatives, or dyes.

Other medicines—Although certain medicines should not be used together at all, in other cases 2 different medicines may be used together even if an interaction might occur. In these cases, your doctor may want to change the dose, or other precautions may be necessary. Tell your health care professional if you are taking any other prescription or non-prescription (over-the-counter [OTC]) medicine.

Other medical problems—The presence of other medical problems may affect the use of ergoloid mesylates. Make sure you tell your doctor if you have any other medical problems, especially:

- Liver disease—Higher blood levels of ergoloid mesylates may occur, increasing the chance of side effects
- Low blood pressure or
- Other mental problems or
- Slow heartbeat—Ergoloid mesylates may make the condition worse

Proper Use of This Medicine

Take this medicine only as directed by your doctor. Do not take more or less of it, and do not take it more often or for a longer period of time than your doctor ordered. To do so may increase the chance of unwanted effects.

For patients taking the *sublingual (under-the-tongue) tablets:*

- Dissolve the tablet under your tongue. The sublingual tablet should not be chewed or swallowed, since it works much faster when absorbed through the lining of the mouth. Do not eat, drink, or smoke while a tablet is dissolving.

Dosing—The dose of ergoloid mesylates will be different for different patients. *Follow your doctor's orders or the directions on the label.* The following information includes only the average doses of ergoloid mesylates. *If your dose is different, do not change it* unless your doctor tells you to do so.

The number of tablets or milliliters of oral solution that you take depends on the strength of the medicine. Also, *the number of doses you take each day, the time allowed between doses, and the length of time you take the medicine depend on the medical problem for which you are taking ergoloid mesylates.*

- For *oral* dosage forms (capsules, tablets, sublingual tablets, or oral solution):
  - Adults: 1 to 2 milligrams (mg) three times a day.

Missed dose—If you miss a dose of this medicine, skip the missed dose and go back to your regular dosing schedule. Do not double doses. If you have any questions about this, or if you miss two or more doses in a row, check with your doctor.

Storage—To store this medicine:
- Keep out of the reach of children.
- Store away from heat and direct light.
- Do not store in the bathroom, near the kitchen sink, or in other damp places. Heat or moisture may cause the medicine to break down.

- Keep the oral solution from freezing.
- Do not keep outdated medicine or medicine no longer needed. Be sure that any discarded medicine is out of the reach of children.

Precautions While Using This Medicine

It is important that your doctor check your progress at regular visits to make sure this medicine is working and to check for unwanted effects.

It may take several weeks for this medicine to work. *However, do not stop taking this medicine without first checking with your doctor.*

Side Effects of This Medicine

Along with its needed effects, a medicine may cause some unwanted effects. Although not all of these side effects may occur, if they do occur they may need medical attention.

Check with your doctor as soon as possible if any of the following side effects occur:
> *Less common or rare*
>> Dizziness or lightheadedness when getting up from a lying or sitting position; drowsiness; skin rash; slow pulse
> *Signs and symptoms of overdose*
>> Blurred vision; dizziness; fainting; flushing; headache; loss of appetite; nausea or vomiting; stomach cramps; stuffy nose

Other side effects may occur that usually do not need medical attention. These side effects may go away during treatment as your body adjusts to the medicine. However, check with your doctor if any of the following side effects continue or are bothersome:
> *Less common or rare*
>> Soreness under tongue (with sublingual use)

Other side effects not listed above may also occur in some patients. If you notice any other effects, check with your doctor.

Revised: 04/16/93

ERGONOVINE/ METHYLERGONOVINE Systemic

Commonly used brand name(s):

In the U.S.—
Ergotrate[1]
Methergine[2]

In Canada—
Ergotrate Maleate[1]

Other commonly used names are:

Ergometrine[1], Methylergometrine[2].

Note: For quick reference, the following medicines are numbered to match the corresponding brand names.

This information applies to the following medicines
1. Ergonovine (er-goe-NOE-veen) §
2. Methylergonovine (meth-ill-er-goe-NOE-veen) †

†Not commercially available in Canada.
§Generic name product may be available in Canada.

Description

Ergonovine and methylergonovine belong to the group of medicines known as ergot alkaloids. These medicines are usually given to stop excessive bleeding that sometimes occurs after abortion or a baby is delivered. They work by causing the muscle of the uterus to contract.

Ergonovine and methylergonovine may also be used for other conditions as determined by your doctor.

These medicines are available only on prescription and are to be administered only by or under the supervision of your doctor. They are available in the following dosage forms:

Oral
> Ergonovine
> • Tablets (U.S. and Canada)
> Methylergonovine
> • Tablets (U.S.)

Parenteral
> Ergonovine
> • Injection (U.S. and Canada)
> Methylergonovine
> • Injection (U.S.)

Before Using This Medicine

In deciding to use a medicine, the risks of taking the medicine must be weighed against the good it will do. This is a decision you and your doctor will make. For ergonovine and methylergonovine, the following should be considered:

Allergies—Tell your doctor if you have ever had any unusual or allergic reaction to ergonovine, methylergonovine, or other ergot medicines. Also tell your health care professional if you are allergic to any other substances, such as foods, preservatives, or dyes.

Breast-feeding—This medicine passes into the breast milk and may cause unwanted effects, such as vomiting; decreased circulation in the hands, lower legs, and feet; diarrhea; weak pulse; unstable blood pressure; or convulsions (seizures) in infants of mothers taking large doses.

Children—Although there is no specific information comparing use of ergonovine or methylergonovine in children with use in other age groups, these medicines are not expected to cause different problems in children than they do in adults.

Older adults—Many medicines have not been studied specifically in older people. Therefore, it may not be known whether they work exactly the same way they do in younger adults or if they cause different side effects or problems in older people. There is no specific information comparing use of ergonovine or methylergonovine in the elderly with use in other age groups.

Other medicines—Although certain medicines should not be used together at all, in other cases two different medicines may be used together even if an interaction might occur. In these cases, your doctor may want to change the dose, or other precautions may be necessary. When you are taking ergonovine or methylergonovine it is especially important that your health care professional know if you are taking any of the following:

• Bromocriptine (e.g., Parlodel) or
• Other ergot alkaloids (dihydroergotamine [e.g., D.H.E. 45], ergoloid mesylates [e.g., Hydergine], ergotamine [e.g., Gynergen], methysergide [e.g., Sansert])—Use of these medicines with ergonovine or methylergonovine may increase the chance of side effects of these medicines.

• Nitrates or
• Other medicines for angina—Use of these medicines with ergonovine or methylergonovine may keep these medicines from working properly

Other medical problems—The presence of other medical problems may affect the use of ergonovine or methylergonovine. Make sure you tell your doctor if you have any other medical problems, especially:

• Angina (chest pain) or other heart problems or
• Blood vessel disease or
• High blood pressure (or history of) or
• Stroke (history of)—These medicines may cause changes in how the heart works or blood pressure changes

• Infection—Infections may cause an increased sensitivity to the effect of these medicines

• Kidney disease

• Liver disease—The body may not remove these medicines from the bloodstream at the usual rate, which may make the medicine work longer or increase the chance for side effects

• Raynaud's phenomenon—Use of these medicines may cause worsening of the blood vessel narrowing that occurs with this disease

Proper Use of This Medicine

Take this medicine only as directed by your doctor. Do not take more of it, do not take it more often, and do not take it for a longer time than your doctor ordered. If too much is taken or if it is taken for a longer time than your doctor ordered, it may cause serious effects.

Dosing—The dose of ergonovine or methylergonovine will be different for different patients. *Follow your doctor's orders or the directions on the label.* The following information includes only the average doses of ergonovine and methylergonovine. *If your dose is different, do not change it* unless your doctor tells you to do so.

For ergonovine
• For *oral* dosage forms (tablets):
—For treatment of excessive uterine bleeding:
 • Adults—0.2 to 0.4 milligram, swallowed or placed under the tongue every six to twelve hours. Usually this medicine is taken for forty-eight hours or less.

• For *injection* dosage form:
—For treatment of excessive uterine bleeding:
 • Adults—0.2 milligram, injected into a muscle or vein. This dose can be repeated up to five times if needed, with a two- to four-hour wait between doses.

For methylergonovine
• For *oral* dosage forms (tablets):
—For treatment of excessive uterine bleeding:
 • Adults—0.2 to 0.4 milligram, taken every six to twelve hours. Usually this medicine is taken for forty-eight hours or less.

• For *injection* dosage form:
—For treatment of excessive uterine bleeding:
 • Adults—0.2 milligram, injected into a muscle or vein. This dose can be repeated up to five times

if needed, with a two- to four-hour wait between doses.

Missed dose—If you miss a dose of this medicine, do not take the missed dose at all and do not double the next one. Instead, go back to your regular dosing schedule. If you have any questions about this, check with your doctor.

Storage—To store this medicine:

- Keep out of the reach of children.
- Store away from heat and direct light.
- Do not store in the bathroom, near the kitchen sink, or in other damp places. Heat or moisture may cause the medicine to break down.
- Do not keep outdated medicine or medicine no longer needed. Be sure that any discarded medicine is out of the reach of children.

Precautions While Using This Medicine

If you have an infection or illness of any kind, check with your doctor before taking this medicine, since you may be more sensitive to its effects.

Side Effects of This Medicine

Along with its needed effects, a medicine may cause some unwanted effects. Although not all of these side effects may occur, if they do occur they may need medical attention.

Check with the health care professional immediately if any of the following side effects occur:

Less common
Chest pain

Rare
Blurred vision; convulsions (seizures); crushing chest pain; headache (sudden and severe); irregular heartbeat; unexplained shortness of breath

Check with your doctor as soon as possible if any of the following side effects occur:

Less common
Slow heartbeat

Rare
Itching of skin; pain in arms, legs, or lower back; pale or cold hands or feet; weakness in legs

Symptoms of overdose
Bluish color of skin or inside of nose or mouth; chest pain; cool, pale, or numb arms or legs; confusion; cramping of the uterus (severe); decreased breathing rate; drowsiness; heartbeat changes; muscle pain; small pupils; tingling, itching, and cool skin; trouble in breathing; unconsciousness; unusual thirst; weak or absent pulse in arms or legs; weak pulse

With long-term use
Dry, shriveled-looking skin on hands, lower legs, or feet; false feeling of insects crawling on the skin; pain and redness in an arm or leg; paralysis of one side of the body

Other side effects may occur that usually do not need medical attention. These side effects may go away during treatment as your body adjusts to the medicine. However, check with your doctor if any of the following side effects continue or are bothersome:

More common
Cramping of the uterus; nausea; vomiting

Less common
Abdominal or stomach pain; diarrhea; dizziness; headache (mild and temporary); ringing in the ears; stuffy nose; sweating; unpleasant taste

Other side effects not listed above may also occur in some patients. If you notice any other effects, check with your doctor.

Revised: 06/07/93

ERGOTAMINE, BELLADONNA ALKALOIDS, AND PHENOBARBITAL Systemic

Commonly used brand name(s):

In the U.S.—
Bellergal-S

In Canada—
Bellergal
Bellergal Spacetabs

Description

Ergotamine, belladonna alkaloids, and phenobarbital (er-GOT-a-meen, bell-a-DON-a AL-ka-loids, and feen-oh-BAR-bi-tal) combination is used to treat some symptoms of menopause (such as hot flashes, sweating, restlessness, and trouble in sleeping). However, it is not effective against other problems that may occur after menopause, such as osteoporosis. This medicine is also used to prevent migraine or cluster headaches in people who get these headaches often. It is not used to treat a headache that has already started. This combination medicine may also be used for other problems as determined by your doctor.

The phenobarbital in this combination medicine belongs to the group of medicines known as barbiturates.

This medicine is available only with your doctor's prescription, in the following dosage forms:

Oral
- Tablets (Canada)
- Extended-release tablets (U.S. and Canada)

Before Using This Medicine

In deciding to use a medicine, the risks of taking the medicine must be weighed against the good it will do. This is a decision you and your doctor will make. For ergotamine, belladonna alkaloids, and phenobarbital combination, the following should be considered:

Allergies—Tell your doctor if you have ever had any unusual or allergic reaction to ergotamine or other ergot medicines, atropine, belladonna, or barbiturates. Also tell your health care professional if you are allergic to any other substances, such as foods, preservatives, or dyes.

Pregnancy—
- *For ergotamine*—Ergotamine is not recommended for use during pregnancy since it has been shown to increase the chance of early labor, which could result in a miscarriage.
- *For belladonna alkaloids*—Belladonna alkaloids have not been shown to cause problems in humans.

- *For phenobarbital*—Barbiturates such as phenobarbital have been shown to increase the chance of birth defects. Also, when taken during pregnancy, barbiturates may cause bleeding problems in the newborn baby. Be sure that you have discussed these problems with your doctor before taking this medicine.

Breast-feeding—

- *For ergotamine*—Ergotamine passes into the breast milk and may cause unwanted effects, such as vomiting, diarrhea, weak pulse, unstable blood pressure, or convulsions (seizures), in nursing babies whose mothers take large amounts of the medicine. Large amounts of ergotamine may also decrease the flow of breast milk.
- *For belladonna alkaloids*—Although belladonna alkaloids pass into the breast milk, the amount of belladonna alkaloids in this combination medicine has not been shown to cause problems in nursing babies. However, because the belladonna alkaloids tend to decrease the secretions of the body, it is possible that the flow of breast milk may be reduced in some patients.
- *For phenobarbital*—Phenobarbital passes into the breast milk. Taking this combination medicine two or three times a day is not likely to cause problems in nursing babies. However, larger amounts of the medicine may cause drowsiness, unusually slow heartbeat, shortness of breath, or troubled breathing in nursing babies.

Be sure that you discuss these possible problems with your doctor before taking this medicine.

Children—Children may be especially sensitive to the effects of the belladonna alkaloids and the phenobarbital in this combination medicine. This may increase the chance of side effects during treatment. Although there is no specific information about the use of ergotamine in children, it is not expected to cause different side effects or problems in children than it does in adults.

Older adults—Elderly people are especially sensitive to the effects of ergotamine, belladonna alkaloids, and barbiturates such as phenobarbital. This may increase the chance of side effects during treatment.

Other medicines—Although certain medicines should not be used together at all, in other cases two different medicines may be used together even if an interaction might occur. In these cases, your doctor may want to change the dose, or other precautions may be necessary. When you are taking this combination medicine, it is especially important that your health care professional know if you are taking any of the following:

- Antacids or
- Diarrhea medicine containing kaolin or attapulgite—These medicines may decrease the effects of the belladonna alkaloids and the phenobarbital in this combination medicine; to prevent this, take the 2 medicines at least 1 hour apart
- Anticoagulants (blood thinners)—The phenobarbital in this combination medicine may decrease the effects of anticoagulants; a change in the dose of anticoagulant may be needed
- Anticholinergics (medicine for abdominal or stomach spasms or cramps) or
- Carbamazepine (e.g., Tegretol) or
- Central nervous system (CNS) depressants (medicine that causes drowsiness) or
- Cocaine or

- Contraceptives, oral, (birth control pills) containing estrogens or progestins or
- Digitalis glycosides (heart medicine) or
- Monoamine oxidase (MAO) inhibitors (furazolidone [e.g., Furoxone], isocarboxazid [e.g., Marplan], phenelzine [e.g., Nardil], procarbazine [e.g., Matulane], selegiline [e.g., Eldepryl], tranylcypromine [e.g., Parnate] (taken currently or within the past 2 weeks) or
- Other ergot medicines (dihydroergotamine [e.g., D.H.E. 45], ergoloid mesylates [e.g., Hydergine], ergonovine [e.g., Ergotrate], methylergonovine [e.g., Methergine], methysergide [e.g., Sansert]) or
- Other medicines for migraine that contain ergotamine in combination with other ingredients, such as ergotamine and caffeine (e.g., Cafergot), or
- Potassium chloride (e.g., Kay Ciel) or
- Tricyclic antidepressants (amitriptyline [e.g., Elavil], amoxapine [e.g., Asendin], clomipramine [e.g., Anafranil], desipramine [e.g., Pertofrane], doxepin [e.g., Sinequan], imipramine [e.g., Tofranil], nortriptyline [e.g., Aventyl], protriptyline [e.g., Vivactil], trimipramine [e.g., Surmontil])—The chance of serious side effects may be increased
- Ketoconazole (e.g., Nizoral)—The belladonna alkaloids in this combination medicine may reduce the effects of ketoconazole; to prevent this, take the ergotamine, belladonna alkaloids, and phenobarbital combination at least 2 hours after taking ketoconazole

Other medical problems—The presence of other medical problems may affect the use of this combination medicine. Make sure you tell your doctor if you have any other medical problems, especially:

- Asthma (or history of), emphysema, or other chronic lung disease or
- Brain damage (in children) or
- Difficult urination or
- Down's syndrome (mongolism) or
- Dry mouth (severe and continuing) or
- Enlarged prostate or
- Heart or blood vessel disease or
- High blood pressure (severe) or
- Hyperactivity (in children) or
- Infection or
- Intestinal blockage or other intestinal problems or
- Itching (severe) or
- Kidney disease or
- Liver disease or
- Overactive thyroid or
- Porphyria or
- Spastic paralysis (in children) or
- Urinary tract blockage—The chance of side effects may be increased
- Glaucoma—The belladonna alkaloids in this combination medicine may make your condition worse

Also tell your doctor if you have recently had an angioplasty (a procedure done to improve the flow of blood in a blocked blood vessel) or surgery on a blood vessel, because the chance of side effects caused by the ergotamine in this combination medicine may be increased.

Proper Use of This Medicine

Take this medicine only as directed by your doctor. If the amount you are to take does not seem to work, do not take more than your doctor ordered. Instead, check with your doctor. Taking too much of this medicine or taking it too often may cause serious effects such as nausea and vomiting; cold, painful hands or feet; or even gangrene. Also, if too much is used, it may become habit-forming.

To take the *extended-release tablet* form of this medicine:

- Swallow the tablet whole.
- Do not crush, break, or chew the tablet before swallowing it.

Dosing—The dose of this combination medicine will be different for different patients. *Follow your doctor's orders or the directions on the label.* The following information includes only the average doses of this medicine. *If your dose is different, do not change it* unless your doctor tells you to do so.

- For *oral tablet* dosage form:
  —For relieving symptoms of menopause and for preventing headaches:
    - Adults—One tablet in the morning, one tablet at noon, and two tablets at bedtime.
    - Children—Use and dose must be determined by your doctor.
- For *oral extended-release tablet* dosage form:
  —For relieving symptoms of menopause and for preventing headaches:
    - Adults—One tablet in the morning and one tablet in the evening.
    - Children—Use and dose must be determined by your doctor.

Missed dose—If you miss a dose of this medicine, skip the missed dose and go back to your regular dosing schedule. Do not double doses.

Storage—To store this medicine:

- Keep out of the reach of children since overdose is especially dangerous in children.
- Store away from heat and direct light.
- Do not store in the bathroom, near the kitchen sink, or in other damp places. Heat and moisture may cause the medicine to break down.
- Do not keep outdated medicine or medicine no longer needed. Be sure that any discarded medicine is out of the reach of children.

Precautions While Using This Medicine

If you have been taking this medicine regularly, *do not stop taking it without first checking with your doctor.* Your doctor may want you to reduce gradually the amount you are using before stopping completely.

Do not take antacids or medicine for diarrhea within 1 hour of taking this medicine. Taking them too close together will make the belladonna alkaloids less effective.

This medicine will add to the effects of alcohol and other CNS depressants (medicines that slow down the nervous system, possibly causing drowsiness). Some examples of CNS depressants are antihistamines or medicine for hay fever, other allergies, or colds; sedatives, tranquilizers, or sleeping medicine; prescription pain medicine or narcotics; other barbiturates; medicine for seizures; muscle relaxants; or anesthetics, including some dental anesthetics. *Check with your doctor before taking any of the above while you are taking this medicine.* Also, alcohol may make headaches worse, so it is best to avoid alcoholic beverages if you are taking this medicine to prevent headaches.

This medicine may cause some people to have blurred vision or to become drowsy, dizzy, lightheaded, or less alert than they are normally. *Make sure you know how you react to this medicine before you drive, use machines, or do anything else that could be dangerous if you are dizzy or are not alert and able to see well.*

Since smoking may increase some of the harmful effects of this medicine, it is best to avoid smoking while you are using it. If you have any questions about this, check with your doctor.

This medicine may make you more sensitive to cold temperatures, especially if you have blood circulation problems. It tends to decrease blood circulation in the skin, fingers, and toes. Dress warmly during cold weather and be careful during prolonged exposure to cold, such as in winter sports. This is especially important for elderly people, who are more likely than younger adults to already have problems with their circulation.

Belladonna alkaloids (contained in this combination medicine) will often make you sweat less, causing your body temperature to increase. *Use extra care not to become overheated during exercise or hot weather while you are taking this medicine,* as overheating may result in a heat stroke. Also, hot baths or saunas may make you feel dizzy or faint while you are taking this medicine. This is especially important in children taking this medicine.

This medicine may cause your eyes to become more sensitive to light than they are normally. Wearing sunglasses may help lessen the discomfort from bright light.

If you have a serious infection or illness of any kind, check with your doctor before taking this medicine, since you may be more sensitive to its effects.

This medicine may cause dryness of the mouth, nose and throat. For temporary relief of mouth dryness, use sugarless candy or gum, melt bits of ice in your mouth, or use a saliva substitute. However, if dry mouth continues for more than 2 weeks, check with your medical doctor or dentist. Continuing dryness of the mouth may increase the chance of dental disease, including tooth decay, gum disease, and fungus infections.

Side Effects of This Medicine

Along with its needed effects, a medicine may cause some unwanted effects. Although not all of these side effects may occur, if they do occur they may need medical attention.

Check with your doctor immediately if the following side effects occur, because they may mean that you are developing a problem with blood circulation:

Less common or rare
> Anxiety or confusion (severe); change in vision; chest pain; increase in blood pressure; pain in arms, legs, or lower back, especially if pain occurs in your calves or heels while you are walking; pale, bluish-colored, or cold hands or feet (not caused by cold temperatures and occurring together with other side effects listed in this section); red or violet-colored blisters on the skin of the hands or feet

Also check with your doctor immediately if any of the following side effects occur since they may be symptoms of an overdose:
> Convulsions (seizures); diarrhea, nausea, vomiting, or stomach pain or bloating (severe) occurring together with other signs of overdose or of problems with blood circulation; dizziness, drowsiness, or weakness (severe), occurring together with other signs of overdose

or of problems with blood circulation; fast or slow heartbeat; shortness of breath; unusual excitement

Also check with your doctor as soon as possible if any of the following side effects occur:

More common

Swelling of face, fingers, feet, and/or lower legs

Less common or rare

Skin rash, hives, or itching; sore throat and fever; unusual bleeding or bruising; weakness in legs; yellow eyes or skin

Other side effects may occur that usually do not need medical attention. These side effects may go away during treatment as your body adjusts to the medicine. However, check with your doctor if any of the following side effects continue or are bothersome:

More common

Constipation; decreased sweating; dizziness or lightheadedness; drowsiness; dryness of mouth, nose, throat, or skin

Less common or rare

Blurred vision, diarrhea, nausea, or vomiting (occurring without other signs of overdose or blood circulation problems); difficult urination (especially in older men); difficulty in swallowing; increased sensitivity of eyes to sunlight; loss of memory; reduced sweating; unusual excitement (especially in older adults); unusual tiredness or weakness

After you stop taking this medicine, your body may need time to adjust. The length of time this takes depends on the amount of medicine you were taking and how long you took it. During this time check with your doctor if your headaches or other symptoms begin again or worsen.

Other side effects not listed above may also occur in some patients. If you notice any other effects, check with your doctor.

Revised: 08/30/94

ERYTHROMYCIN   Ophthalmic

Commonly used brand name(s):

In the U.S.—
Ilotycin
Generic name product may be available.

In Canada—
Ilotycin

Description

Erythromycin (eh-rith-roe-MYE-sin) belongs to the family of medicines called antibiotics. Erythromycin ophthalmic preparations are used to treat infections of the eye. They also may be used to prevent certain eye infections of newborn babies, such as neonatal conjunctivitis and ophthalmia neonatorum. They may be used with other medicines for some eye infections.

Erythromycin is available only with your doctor's prescription, in the following dosage form:

Ophthalmic
• Ophthalmic ointment (U.S. and Canada)

Before Using This Medicine

In deciding to use a medicine, the risks of taking the medicine must be weighed against the good it will do. This is a decision you and your doctor will make. For ophthalmic erythromycin, the following should be considered:

Allergies—Tell your doctor if you have ever had any unusual or allergic reaction to this or any of the other erythromycins. Also tell your health care professional if you are allergic to any other substances, such as preservatives.

Pregnancy—Ophthalmic erythromycin has not been shown to cause birth defects or other problems in humans.

Breast-feeding—Ophthalmic erythromycin has not been reported to cause problems in nursing babies.

Children—Studies on this medicine have been done only in adult patients, and there is no specific information comparing use of this medicine in children with use in other age groups.

Older adults—Many medicines have not been studied specifically in older people. Therefore, it may not be known whether they work exactly the same way they do in younger adults or if they cause different side effects or problems in older people. There is no specific information comparing use of this medicine in the elderly with use in other age groups.

Proper Use of This Medicine

To use:

• First, wash your hands. Tilt the head back and, pressing your finger gently on the skin just beneath the lower eyelid, pull the lower eyelid away from the eye to make a space. Squeeze a thin strip of ointment into this space. A 1-cm (approximately 1/3-inch) strip of ointment is usually enough, unless you have been told by your doctor to use a different amount. Let go of the eyelid and gently close the eyes. Keep the eyes closed for 1 or 2 minutes to allow the medicine to come into contact with the infection.

• To keep the medicine as germ-free as possible, do not touch the applicator tip to any surface (including the eye). After using erythromycin eye ointment, wipe the tip of the ointment tube with a clean tissue and keep the tube tightly closed.

To help clear up your infection completely, *keep using this medicine for the full time of treatment*, even if your symptoms begin to clear up after a few days. If you stop using this medicine too soon, your symptoms may return. *Do not miss any doses.*

Dosing—The dose of ophthalmic erythromycin will be different for different patients. *Follow your doctor's orders or the directions on the label.* The following information includes only the average doses of ophthalmic erythromycin. *If your dose is different, do not change it* unless your doctor tells you to do so.

• For *ophthalmic ointment* dosage form:

—For treatment of eye infections:

• Adults and children—Use in the eyes up to six times a day as directed by your doctor.

—For prevention of neonatal conjunctivitis and ophthalmia neonatorum:

• Newborn babies—Use in the eyes once at birth.

Missed dose—If you do miss a dose of this medicine, apply it as soon as possible. However, if it is almost time for your next dose, skip the missed dose and go back to your regular dosing schedule.

Storage—To store this medicine:

- Keep out of the reach of children.
- Store away from heat and direct light.
- Keep the medicine from freezing.
- Do not keep outdated medicine or medicine no longer needed. Be sure that any discarded medicine is out of the reach of children.

Precautions While Using This Medicine

If your symptoms do not improve within a few days, or if they become worse, check with your doctor.

After application, eye ointments usually cause your vision to blur for a few minutes.

Side Effects of This Medicine

Along with its needed effects, a medicine may cause some unwanted effects.

Check with your doctor as soon as possible if the following side effect occurs:

Rare
    Eye irritation not present before therapy

Other side effects not listed above may also occur in some patients. If you notice any other effects, check with your doctor.

Revised: 11/28/94

ERYTHROMYCIN   Topical

Commonly used brand name(s):

In the U.S.—

Akne-Mycin	Ery-Sol
A/T/S	Erythra-Derm
Emgel	ETS
Erycette	Staticin
EryDerm	Theramycin Z
Erygel	T-Stat
Erymax	

Generic name product may be available.

In Canada—
Sans-Acne
Staticin

Description

Erythromycin (eh-rith-roe-MYE-sin) belongs to the family of medicines called antibiotics. Erythromycin topical preparations are used on the skin to help control acne. They may be used alone or with one or more other medicines that are applied to the skin or taken by mouth for acne. They may also be used for other problems, such as skin infections, as determined by your doctor.

Erythromycin is available only with your doctor's prescription, in the following dosage forms:

Topical
- Gel (U.S.)
- Ointment (U.S.)
- Pledgets (U.S.)
- Solution (U.S. and Canada)

Before Using This Medicine

In deciding to use a medicine, the risks of taking the medicine must be weighed against the good it will do. This is a decision you and your doctor will make. For topical erythromycin, the following should be considered:

Allergies—Tell your doctor if you have ever had any unusual or allergic reaction to this or any of the other erythromycins. Also tell your health care professional if you are allergic to any other substances, such as preservatives or dyes.

Pregnancy—Topical erythromycin has not been studied in pregnant women. However, this medication has not been shown to cause birth defects or other problems in animal studies.

Breast-feeding—It is not known whether topical erythromycin passes into the breast milk. Erythromycin, given by mouth or by injection, does pass into the breast milk. However, erythromycin topical preparations have not been reported to cause problems in nursing babies.

Children—Erythromycin topical solution has been tested in children 12 years of age and older and, in effective doses, has not been shown to cause different side effects or problems than it does in adults.

Older adults—Many medicines have not been studied specifically in older people. Therefore, it may not be known whether they work exactly the same way they do in younger adults. Although there is no specific information comparing use of topical erythromycin in the elderly with use in other age groups, this medicine is not expected to cause different side effects or problems in older people than it does in younger adults.

Other medicines—Although certain medicines should not be used together at all, in other cases two different medicines may be used together even if an interaction might occur. In these cases, your doctor may want to change the dose, or other precautions may be necessary. Tell your health care professional if you are using any other topical prescription or nonprescription (over-the-counter [OTC]) medicine that is to be applied to the same area of the skin.

Proper Use of This Medicine

Before applying this medicine, thoroughly wash the affected area with warm water and soap, rinse well, and pat dry. After washing or shaving, it is best to wait 30 minutes before applying the pledget (swab), topical gel, or topical liquid form. The alcohol in them may irritate freshly washed or shaved skin.

This medicine will not cure your acne. However, to help keep your acne under control, *keep using this medicine for the full time of treatment*, even if your symptoms begin to clear up after a few days. You may have to continue using this medicine every day for months or even longer in some cases. If you stop using this medicine too soon, your symptoms may return. *It is important that you do not miss any doses.*

Dosing—The dose of topical erythromycin will be different for different patients. *Follow your doctor's orders or the directions on the label*. The following information includes only the average doses of topical erythromycin. *If your dose is different, do not change it unless* your doctor tells you to do so.

- For acne:
  —For *gel* dosage form:
    • Adults—Apply to the affected area(s) of the skin two times a day, morning and evening.
    • Children—Dose must be determined by your doctor.
  —For *ointment* dosage form:
    • Adults, teenagers, and children—Apply to the affected area(s) of the skin two times a day, morning and evening.
  —For *pledgets* dosage form:
    • Adults, teenagers, and children—Apply to the affected area(s) of the skin two times a day.
  —For *topical solution* dosage form:
    • Adults, teenagers, and children 12 years of age and over—Apply to the affected area(s) of the skin two times a day, morning and evening.
    • Children up to 12 years of age—Dose must be determined by your doctor.

Missed dose—If you miss a dose of this medicine, apply it as soon as possible. However, if it is almost time for your next dose, skip the missed dose and go back to your regular dosing schedule.

For patients using the pledget (swab), topical gel, or topical liquid form of erythromycin:

- These forms contain alcohol and are flammable. *Do not use near heat, near open flame, or while smoking.*
- It is important that you do not use this medicine more often than your doctor ordered. It may cause your skin to become too dry or irritated.
- Also, you should avoid washing the acne-affected areas too often. This may dry your skin and make your acne worse. Washing with a mild, bland soap 2 or 3 times a day should be enough, unless you have oily skin. If you have any questions about this, check with your doctor.
- To use:
  —The topical liquid form of this medicine may come in a bottle with an applicator tip, which may be used to apply the medicine directly to the skin. Use the applicator with a dabbing motion instead of a rolling motion (not like a roll-on deodorant, for example). If the medicine does not come in an applicator bottle, you may moisten a pad with the medicine and then rub the pad over the whole affected area. Or you may also apply this medicine with your fingertips. Be sure to wash the medicine off your hands afterward.
  —Apply a thin film of medicine, using enough to cover the affected area lightly. *You should apply the medicine to the whole area usually affected by acne, not just to the pimples themselves.* This will help keep new pimples from breaking out.
  —The pledget (swab) form should be rubbed over the whole affected area. You may use extra pledgets (swabs), if needed, to cover larger areas.
  —Since these medicines contain alcohol, they may sting or burn. Therefore, *do not get these medicines in the eyes, nose, mouth, or on other mucous membranes.* Spread the medicine away from these areas when applying. If these medicines do get in the eyes, wash them out immediately, but carefully, with large amounts of cool tap water. If

your eyes still burn or are painful, check with your doctor.

Storage—To store this medicine:
- Keep out of the reach of children.
- Store away from heat and direct light.
- Keep the medicine from freezing.
- Do not keep outdated medicine or medicine no longer needed. Be sure that any discarded medicine is out of the reach of children.

Precautions While Using This Medicine

If your acne does not improve within 3 to 4 weeks, or if it becomes worse, check with your health care professional. However, treatment of acne may take up to 8 to 12 weeks before you see full improvement.

For patients using the pledget (swab), topical gel, or topical liquid form of erythromycin:

- If your doctor has ordered another medicine to be applied to the skin along with this medicine, it is best to wait at least 1 hour before you apply the second medicine. This may help keep your skin from becoming too irritated. Also, if the medicines are used too close together, they may not work properly.
- After application of this medicine to the skin, mild stinging or burning may be expected and may last up to a few minutes or more.
- This medicine may also cause the skin to become unusually dry, even with normal use. If this occurs, check with your doctor.
- You may continue to use cosmetics (make-up) while you are using this medicine for acne. However, it is best to use only "water-base" cosmetics. Also, it is best not to use cosmetics too heavily or too often. They may make your acne worse. If you have any questions about this, check with your doctor.

Side Effects of This Medicine

Along with its needed effects, a medicine may cause some unwanted effects. The following side effects may go away during treatment as your body adjusts to the medicine.

However, check with your doctor if any of the following side effects continue or are bothersome:
For erythromycin ointment
  Less common
    Peeling; redness

For erythromycin pledget (swab), topical gel, or topical liquid form
  More common
    Dry or scaly skin; irritation; itching; stinging or burning feeling

  Less common
    Peeling; redness

Other side effects not listed above may also occur in some patients. If you notice any other effects, check with your doctor.

Revised: 09/18/2000
Interim revision: 09/18/2000

ERYTHROMYCIN AND BENZOYL PEROXIDE   Topical†

Commonly used brand name(s):

In the U.S.—
   Benzamycin

---

†Not commercially available in Canada.

Description

Erythromycin and benzoyl peroxide (eh-rith-roe-MYE-sin and BEN-zoe-ill per-OX-ide) combination is used to help control acne.

This medicine is applied to the skin. It may be used alone or with other medicines that are applied to the skin or taken by mouth for acne.

Erythromycin and benzoyl peroxide combination is available only with your doctor's prescription, in the following dosage form:

   Topical
   • Topical gel (U.S.)

Before Using This Medicine

In deciding to use a medicine, the risks of using the medicine must be weighed against the good it will do. This is a decision you and your doctor will make. For erythromycin and benzoyl peroxide combination, the following should be considered:

Allergies—Tell your doctor if you have ever had any unusual or allergic reaction to this medicine, to any of the other erythromycins, or to benzoyl peroxide (e.g., PanOxyl). Also tell your health care professional if you are allergic to any other substances, such as preservatives or dyes.

Pregnancy—Studies on effects in pregnancy have not been done in either humans or animals. However, the benzoyl peroxide in this medicine may be absorbed into the body. Before using this medicine, make sure your doctor knows if you are pregnant or if you may become pregnant.

Breast-feeding—It is not known whether topical erythromycin or topical benzoyl peroxide passes into the breast milk. Erythromycin (e.g., E-Mycin), given by mouth or by injection, does pass into the breast milk. In addition, the benzoyl peroxide in this medicine may be absorbed into the mother's body. However, erythromycin and benzoyl peroxide combination has not been reported to cause problems in nursing babies.

Children—Studies on this medicine have been done only in adult patients, and there is no specific information comparing use of this medicine in children up to 12 years of age with use in other age groups.

Older adults—Many medicines have not been studied specifically in older people. Therefore, it may not be known whether they work exactly the same way they do in younger adults or if they cause different side effects or problems in older people. There is no specific information comparing use of this medicine in the elderly with use in other age groups.

Other medicines—Although certain medicines should not be used together at all, in other cases two different medicines may be used together even if an interaction might occur. In these cases, your doctor may want to change the dose, or other precautions may be necessary. Tell your health care professional if you are using any other topical prescription or nonprescription (over-the-counter [OTC]) medicine that is to be applied to the same area of the skin.

Proper Use of This Medicine

Do not use this medicine on raw or irritated skin.

Before applying this medicine, thoroughly wash the affected area(s) with warm water and soap, rinse well, and gently pat dry. After washing or shaving, it is best to wait 30 minutes before applying the medicine. The alcohol in it may irritate freshly washed or shaved skin.

Avoid washing the acne-affected area(s) too often. This may dry your skin and make your acne worse. Washing with a mild, bland soap 2 or 3 times a day should be enough, unless you have oily skin. If you have any questions about this, check with your doctor.

To use:
   • *Use this medicine only as directed.* Do not use more of it and do not use it more often than your doctor ordered. To do so may cause your skin to become too dry or irritated.
   • After washing the affected area(s), you may apply this medicine with your fingertips. However, be sure to wash the medicine off your hands afterward.
   • Apply and rub in a thin film of medicine, using enough to cover the affected area(s) lightly. *You should apply the medicine to the whole area usually affected by acne, not just to the pimples themselves.*
   • Since this medicine contains alcohol, it may sting or burn. Therefore, *do not get this medicine in or around your eyes, nose, or mouth, or on other mucous membranes.* Spread the medicine away from these areas when applying. If this medicine does get in your eyes, wash them out immediately, but carefully, with large amounts of cool tap water. If your eyes still burn or are painful, check with your doctor.

Do not use this medicine after the expiration date on the label. The medicine may not work properly. Get a fresh supply from your pharmacist. Check with your pharmacist if you have any questions about this.

To help keep your acne under control, *keep using this medicine for the full time of treatment.* You may have to continue using this medicine every day for months or even longer in some cases.

Dosing—The dose of erythromycin and benzoyl peroxide combination will be different for different patients. *Follow your doctor's orders or the directions on the label.* The following information includes only the average dose of erythromycin and benzoyl peroxide combination. *If your dose is different, do not change it unless your doctor tells you to do so.*

   • For *gel* dosage form:
      —For acne:
         • Adults and children 12 years of age and over—Apply to the affected area(s) of the skin two times a day, morning and evening, or as directed by your doctor.
         • Children up to 12 years of age—Dose must be determined by your doctor.

Missed dose—If you miss a dose of this medicine, apply it as soon as possible. However, if it is almost time for your next dose, skip the missed dose and go back to your regular dosing schedule.

© 2002 MICROMEDEX Thomson Healthcare

Storage—To store this medicine:
- Keep out of the reach of children.
- Store in the refrigerator. Heat will cause this medicine to break down. However, keep the medicine from freezing. Follow the directions on the label.
- Do not keep outdated medicine or medicine no longer needed. Be sure that any discarded medicine is out of the reach of children.

Precautions While Using This Medicine

If your acne does not improve within 3 to 4 weeks, or if it becomes worse, check with your health care professional. However, treatment of acne may take up to 8 to 12 weeks before you see full improvement.

If your doctor has ordered another medicine to be applied to the skin along with this medicine, it is best to apply the second medicine at least 1 hour after you apply the first medicine. This may help keep your skin from becoming too irritated. Also, if the medicines are used too close together, they may not work properly.

Mild stinging or burning of the skin may be expected after this medicine is applied. These effects may last up to a few minutes or more. If irritation continues, check with your doctor. You may have to use the medicine less often. Follow your doctor's directions.

This medicine may also cause the skin to become unusually dry, even with normal use. If this occurs, check with your doctor.

This medicine may bleach hair or colored fabrics.

You may continue to use cosmetics (make-up) while you are using this medicine for acne. However, it is best to use only "oil-free" cosmetics. Also, it is best not to use cosmetics too heavily or too often. They may make your acne worse. If you have any questions about this, check with your doctor.

Side Effects of This Medicine

Along with its needed effects, a medicine may cause some unwanted effects. Although not all of these side effects may occur, if they do occur they may need medical attention.

Check with your doctor as soon as possible if any of the following side effects occur:

Less common or rare
  Burning, blistering, crusting, itching, severe redness, or swelling of the skin; painful irritation of the skin; skin rash

Symptoms of topical overdose
  Burning, itching, scaling, redness, or swelling of the skin (severe)

Other side effects may occur that usually do not need medical attention. These side effects may go away during treatment as your body adjusts to the medicine. However, check with your doctor if any of the following side effects continue or are bothersome:

Less common
  Dryness or peeling of the skin; feeling of warmth, mild stinging, or redness of the skin

Other side effects not listed above may also occur in some patients. If you notice any other effects, check with your doctor.

Revised: 06/26/92
Interim revision: 07/06/94

ERYTHROMYCIN AND SULFISOXAZOLE   Systemic

Commonly used brand name(s):

In the U.S.—
  Eryzole
  Pediazole
  Generic name product may be available.

In Canada—
  Pediazole

Description

Erythromycin and sulfisoxazole (er-ith-roe-MYE-sin and sulfi-SOX-a-zole) is a combination antibiotic used to treat ear infections in children. It also may be used for other problems as determined by your doctor. It will not work for colds, flu, or other virus infections.

Erythromycin and sulfisoxazole combination is available only with your doctor's prescription, in the following dosage form:

Oral
  • Suspension (U.S. and Canada)

Before Using This Medicine

In deciding to use a medicine, the risks of taking the medicine must be weighed against the good it will do. This is a decision you and your doctor will make. For erythromycin and sulfisoxazole, the following should be considered:

Allergies—Tell your doctor if you have ever had any unusual or allergic reaction to the erythromycins or sulfa medicines, furosemide (e.g., Lasix) or thiazide diuretics (water pills), oral antidiabetics (diabetes medicine you take by mouth), or glaucoma medicine you take by mouth (for example, acetazolamide [e.g., Diamox], dichlorphenamide [e.g., Daranide], methazolamide [e.g., Neptazane]). Also tell your health care professional if you are allergic to any other substances, such as foods, preservatives, or dyes.

Pregnancy—Studies have not been done in humans with either erythromycins or sulfa medicines. In addition, erythromycins have not been shown to cause birth defects or other problems in humans. However, studies in mice, rats, and rabbits have shown that some sulfa medicines cause birth defects, including cleft palate and bone problems.

Breast-feeding—Erythromycins and sulfa medicines pass into the breast milk. This medicine is not recommended for use during breast-feeding. It may cause liver problems, anemia, and other unwanted effects in nursing babies, especially those with glucose-6-phosphate dehydrogenase (G6PD) deficiency.

Children—This medicine has been tested in children over the age of 2 months and has not been shown to cause different side effects or problems than it does in adults. This medicine should not be given to infants under 2 months of age unless directed by the child's doctor, because it may cause unwanted effects.

Older adults—This medicine is intended for use in children and is not generally used in adult patients.

Other medicines—Although certain medicines should not be used together at all, in other cases two different medicines may be used together even if an interaction might occur. In these cases, your doctor may want to change the dose, or other precautions may be necessary. When you are taking erythromycin and sulfisoxazole, it is especially important that your health care professional know if you are taking any of the following:

- Acetaminophen (e.g., Tylenol) (with long-term, high-dose use) or
- Amiodarone (e.g., Cordarone) or
- Anabolic steroids (nandrolone [e.g., Anabolin], oxandrolone [e.g., Anavar], oxymetholone [e.g., Anadrol], stanozolol [e.g., Winstrol]) or
- Androgens (male hormones) or
- Antithyroid agents (medicine for overactive thyroid) or
- Carbamazepine (e.g., Tegretol) or
- Carmustine (e.g., BiCNU) or
- Chloroquine (e.g., Aralen) or
- Dantrolene (e.g., Dantrium) or
- Daunorubicin (e.g., Cerubidine) or
- Disulfiram (e.g., Antabuse) or
- Divalproex (e.g., Depakote) or
- Estrogens (female hormones) or
- Etretinate (e.g., Tegison) or
- Gold salts (medicine for arthritis) or
- Hydroxychloroquine (e.g., Plaquenil) or
- Mercaptopurine (e.g., Purinethol) or
- Methotrexate (e.g., Mexate, Rheumatrex) or
- Methyldopa (e.g., Aldomet) or
- Naltrexone (e.g., Trexan) (with long-term, high-dose use) or
- Other anti-infectives by mouth or by injection (medicine for infection) or
- Phenothiazines (acetophenazine [e.g., Tindal], chlorpromazine [e.g., Thorazine], fluphenazine [e.g., Prolixin], mesoridazine [e.g., Serentil], perphenazine [e.g., Trilafon], prochlorperazine [e.g., Compazine], promazine [e.g., Sparine], promethazine [e.g., Phenergan], thioridazine [e.g. Mellaril], trifluoperazine [e.g., Stelazine], triflupromazine [e.g., Vesprin], trimeprazine [e.g., Temaril]) or
- Phenytoin (e.g., Dilantin) or
- Plicamycin (e.g., Mithracin) or
- Valproic acid (e.g., Depakene)—Use of erythromycin and sulfisoxazole with any of these medicines may increase the chance of side effects affecting the liver

- Acetohydroxamic acid (e.g., Lithostat) or
- Dapsone or
- Furazolidone (e.g., Furoxone) or
- Nitrofurantoin (e.g., Furadantin) or
- Primaquine or
- Procainamide (e.g., Pronestyl) or
- Quinidine (e.g., Quinidex) or
- Quinine (e.g., Quinamm) or
- Sulfoxone (e.g., Diasone)—Use of erythromycin and sulfisoxazole with these medicines may increase the chance of side effects

- Alfentanil (e.g., Alfenta)—Long-term use of erythromycin and sulfisoxazole may increase the action of alfentanil and increase the chance of side effects

- Aminophylline (e.g., Truphylline) or
- Caffeine (e.g., NoDoz) or
- Oxtriphylline (e.g., Choledyl) or
- Theophylline (e.g., Slo-Phyllin, Theo-Dur)—Use of erythromycin and sulfisoxazole with these medicines may increase the side effects of these medicines

- Astemizole (e.g., Hismanal) or
- Terfenadine (e.g., Seldane)—Use of astemizole or terfenadine with erythromycin and sulfisoxazole may cause heart problems, such as an irregular heartbeat; these medicines should not be used together

- Anticoagulants (blood thinners) or
- Antidiabetics, oral (diabetes medicine you take by mouth) or
- Ethotoin (e.g., Peganone) or
- Mephenytoin (e.g., Mesantoin)—Use of erythromycin and sulfisoxazole with these medicines may increase the effects of these medicines, thereby increasing the chance of side effects

- Chloramphenicol (e.g., Chloromycetin) or
- Clindamycin (e.g., Cleocin) or
- Lincomycin (e.g., Lincocin)—Use of erythromycin and sulfisoxazole with these medicines may decrease the effectiveness of these medicines

- Cyclosporine (e.g., Sandimmune, Neoral)—Use of any of these medicines with erythromycin and sulfisoxazole may increase the side effects of these medicines

- Methenamine (e.g., Mandelamine)—Use of erythromycin and sulfisoxazole with this medicine may, on rare occasion, increase the chance of side effects affecting the kidneys

- Oral contraceptives (birth control pills) containing estrogen—Use of erythromycin and sulfisoxazole with oral contraceptives may decrease the effectiveness of oral contraceptives, increasing the chance of breakthrough bleeding and pregnancy. Also, the use of erythromycin and sulfisoxazole with oral contraceptives containing estrogen may increase the chance of side effects affecting the liver.

- Vitamin K (e.g., AquaMEPHYTON, Synkayvite)—Patients taking erythromycin and sulfisoxazole may have an increased need for vitamin K

Other medical problems—The presence of other medical problems may affect the use of erythromycin and sulfisoxazole. Make sure you tell your doctor if you have any other medical problems, especially:

- Anemia or other blood problems or
- Glucose-6-phosphate dehydrogenase (G6PD) deficiency—Erythromycin and sulfisoxazole may increase the chance of blood problems

- Heart disease—High doses of erythromycin and sulfisoxazole may increase the chance of side effects in patients with a history of an irregular heartbeat

- Kidney disease or
- Liver disease—Patients with liver or kidney disease may have an increased chance of side effects

- Loss of hearing—High doses of erythromycin and sulfisoxazole may increase the chance for hearing loss in some patients

- Porphyria—Erythromycin and sulfisoxazole may increase the chance of a porphyria attack

---

Proper Use of This Medicine

Erythromycin and sulfisoxazole combination is best taken with extra amounts of water and may be taken with food. *Additional amounts of water should be taken several times every day*, unless otherwise directed by your doctor. Drinking extra water will help to prevent some unwanted effects (e.g., kidney stones) of sulfa medicines.

Do not give this medicine to infants under 2 months of age, unless otherwise directed by your doctor. Sulfa medicines may cause liver problems in these infants.

Use a specially marked measuring spoon or other device to measure each dose accurately. The average household teaspoon may not hold the right amount of liquid.

Do not use after the expiration date on the label. The medicine may not work properly after that date. Check with your pharmacist if you have any questions about this.

To help clear up your infection completely, *keep taking this medicine for the full time of treatment*, even if you begin to feel better after a few days. If you stop taking this medicine too soon, your symptoms may return.

This medicine works best when there is a constant amount in the blood. *To help keep the amount constant, do not miss any doses. Also, it is best to take the doses at evenly spaced times, day and night.* For example, if you are to take 4 doses a day, the doses should be spaced about 6 hours apart. If this interferes with your sleep or other daily activities, or if you need help in planning the best times to take your medicine, check with your health care professional.

Dosing—The dose of erythromycin and sulfisoxazole combination will be different for different patients. *Follow your doctor's orders or the directions on the label.* The following information includes only the average doses of erythromycin and sulfisoxazole combination. *If your dose is different, do not change it* unless your doctor tells you to do so.

- For *oral* dosage form (suspension):
  - For infections caused by bacteria:
    - Adults and teenagers—This medicine is used only in children.
    - Children up to 2 months of age—Use is not recommended.
    - Children 2 months of age and older—Dose is based on body weight:
    For the four-times-a-day dosing schedule
      - Children weighing less than 8 kilograms (kg) (under 18 pounds): Dose must be determined by your doctor.
      - Children weighing 8 to 16 kg (18 to 35 pounds): 1/2 teaspoonful (2.5 milliliters [mL]) every six hours for ten days.
      - Children weighing 16 to 24 kg (35 to 53 pounds): 1 teaspoonful (5 mL) every six hours for ten days.
      - Children weighing 24 to 32 kg (53 to 70 pounds): 1 1/2 teaspoonfuls (7.5 mL) every six hours for ten days.
      - Children weighing more than 32 kg (over 70 pounds): 2 teaspoonfuls (10 mL) every six hours for ten days.
    For the three-times-a-day dosing schedule
      - Children weighing less than 6 kg (under 13 pounds): Dose must be determined by your doctor.
      - Children weighing 6 to 12 kg (13 to 26 pounds): 1/2 teaspoonful (2.5 mL) every eight hours for ten days.
      - Children weighing 12 to 18 kg (26 to 40 pounds): 1 teaspoonful (5 mL) every eight hours for ten days.
      - Children weighing 18 to 24 kg (40 to 53 pounds): 1 1/2 teaspoonfuls (7.5 mL) every eight hours for ten days.
      - Children weighing 24 to 30 kg (53 to 66 pounds): 2 teaspoonfuls (10 mL) every eight hours for ten days.
      - Children weighing more than 30 kg (over 66 pounds): 2 1/2 teaspoonfuls (12.5 mL) every eight hours for ten days.

Missed dose—If you miss a dose of this medicine, take it as soon as possible. This will help to keep a constant amount of medicine in the blood. However, if it is almost time for your next dose, skip the missed dose and go back to your regular dosing schedule. Do not double the dose.

Storage—To store this medicine:
- Keep out of the reach of children.
- Store away from heat and direct light.
- Store in the refrigerator because heat will cause this medicine to break down. However, keep the medicine from freezing. Follow the directions on the label.
- Do not keep outdated medicine or medicine no longer needed. Be sure that any discarded medicine is out of the reach of children.

Precautions While Using This Medicine

It is very important that your doctor check you at regular visits for any blood problems that may be caused by this medicine, especially if you will be taking this medicine for a long time.

If your symptoms do not improve within a few days, or if they become worse, check with your doctor.

Erythromycin and sulfisoxazole may cause your skin to be more sensitive to sunlight than it is normally. Exposure to sunlight, even for brief periods of time, may cause a skin rash, itching, redness or other discoloration of the skin, or a severe sunburn. When you begin taking this medicine:
- Stay out of direct sunlight, especially between the hours of 10:00 a.m. and 3:00 p.m., if possible.
- Wear protective clothing, including a hat. Also, wear sunglasses.
- Apply a sun block product that has a skin protection factor (SPF) of at least 15. Some patients may require a product with a higher SPF number, especially if they have a fair complexion. If you have any questions about this, check with your health care professional.
- Apply a sun block lipstick that has an SPF of at least 15 to protect your lips.
- Do not use a sunlamp or tanning bed or booth.

If you have a severe reaction from the sun, check with your doctor.

Erythromycin and sulfisoxazole combination may cause blood problems. These problems may result in a greater chance of infection, slow healing, and bleeding of the gums. Therefore, you should be careful when using regular toothbrushes, dental floss, and toothpicks. Dental work should be delayed until your blood counts have returned to normal. Check with your medical doctor or dentist if you have any questions about proper oral hygiene (mouth care) during treatment.

Side Effects of This Medicine

Along with its needed effects, a medicine may cause some unwanted effects. Although not all of these side effects may occur, if they do occur they may need medical attention.

Check with your doctor immediately if any of the following side effects occur:

More common
Itching; skin rash

Less common
Aching of joints and muscles; difficulty in swallowing; nausea or vomiting; pale skin; redness, blistering, peeling, or loosening of skin; skin rash; sore throat and fever; stomach pain, severe; unusual bleeding or bruising; unusual tiredness or weakness; yellow eyes or skin

Rare
Blood in urine; dark or amber urine; irregular or slow heartbeat; temporary loss of hearing (with kidney disease and high doses); lower back pain; pain or burning while urinating; pale stools; recurrent fainting; severe stomach pain; swelling of front part of neck

In addition to the side effects listed above, check with your doctor as soon as possible if the following side effect occurs:

More common
Increased sensitivity to sunlight

Other side effects may occur that usually do not need medical attention. These side effects may go away during treatment as your body adjusts to the medicine. However, check with your doctor if any of the following side effects continue or are bothersome:

More common
Abdominal or stomach cramping and discomfort; diarrhea; headache; loss of appetite; nausea or vomiting

Less common
Sore mouth or tongue

Other side effects not listed above may also occur in some patients. If you notice any other effects, check with your doctor.

Additional Information

Once a medicine has been approved for marketing for a certain use, experience may show that it is also useful for other medical problems. Although this use is not specifically included in product labeling, erythromycin and sulfisoxazole combination is used in certain patients with the following medical condition:

- Sinusitis (sinus infection)

Other than the above information, there is no additional information relating to proper use, precautions, or side effects for this use.

Revised: 06/14/99

ERYTHROMYCINS Systemic

Commonly used brand name(s):

In the U.S.—

E-Base[1]	Erythrocin[6]
E-Mycin[1]	Erythrocot[6]
ERYC[1]	Ilotycin [1]
Ery-Tab	Ilotycin[4]
E.E.S.[3]	Ilosone[2]
EryPed[3]	My-E[6]
Erythro[3]	PCE[1]
Erythrocin[5]	Wintrocin[6]

In Canada—

Apo-Erythro[1]	Erythrocin[5]
Apo-Erythro E-C[1]	Erythrocin[6]
Apo-Erythro-ES[3]	Erythromid[1]
Apo-Erythro-S[6]	Ilosone[2]
E-Mycin[1]	Ilotycin[4]
E.E.S.[3]	Novo-rythro[2]
Erybid[1]	Novo-rythro[6]
EryPed[3]	Novo-rythro Encap[1]
ERYC-250[1]	PCE[1]
ERYC-333[1]	

Note: For quick reference, the following erythromycins are numbered to match the corresponding brand names.

This information applies to the following medicines:
1. Erythromycin Base (er-ith-roe-MYE-sin) ‡§
2. Erythromycin Estolate (er-ith-roe-MYE-sin ESS-toe-layt) ‡
3. Erythromycin Ethylsuccinate (er-ith-roe-MYE-sin eth-ill-SUK-sin-ayt) ‡
4. Erythromycin Gluceptate (er-ith-roe-MYE-sin gloo-SEP-tayt)
5. Erythromycin Lactobionate (er-ith-roe-MYE-sin lak-toe-BYE-oh-nayt) ‡
6. Erythromycin Stearate (er-ith-roe-MYE-sin STEER-ate) ‡

‡Generic name product may be available in the U.S.
§Generic name product may be available in Canada.

Description

Erythromycins (eh-rith-roe-MYE-sins) are used to treat many kinds of infections. Erythromycins are also used to prevent "strep" infections in patients with a history of rheumatic heart disease who may be allergic to penicillin.

These medicines may also be used to treat Legionnaires' disease and for other problems as determined by your doctor. They will not work for colds, flu, or other virus infections.

Erythromycins are available only with your doctor's prescription, in the following dosage forms:

Oral
Erythromycin Base
- Delayed-release capsules (U.S. and Canada)
- Delayed-release tablets (U.S. and Canada)
- Tablets (U.S. and Canada)
Erythromycin Estolate
- Capsules (U.S. and Canada)
- Oral suspension (U.S. and Canada)
- Tablets (U.S. and Canada)
Erythromycin Ethylsuccinate
- Chewable tablets (U.S. and Canada)
- Oral suspension (U.S. and Canada)
- Tablets (U.S. and Canada)
Erythromycin Stearate
- Oral suspension (Canada)
- Tablets (U.S. and Canada)

Parenteral
Erythromycin Gluceptate
- Injection (U.S. and Canada)

Erythromycin Lactobionate
- Injection (U.S. and Canada)

Before Using This Medicine

In deciding to use a medicine, the risks of taking the medicine must be weighed against the good it will do. This is a decision you and your doctor will make. For erythromycins, the following should be considered:

Allergies—Tell your doctor if you have ever had any unusual or allergic reaction to erythromycins, or any related medicines, such as azithromycin or clarithromycin. Also tell your health care professional if you are allergic to any other substances, such as foods, preservatives, or dyes.

Pregnancy—Erythromycin estolate has caused side effects involving the liver in some pregnant women. However, none of the erythromycins has been shown to cause birth defects or other problems in human babies.

Breast-feeding—Erythromycins pass into the breast milk. However, erythromycins have not been shown to cause problems in nursing babies.

Children—This medicine has been tested in children and, in effective doses, has not been shown to cause different side effects or problems in children than it does in adults.

Older adults—This medicine has been tested and has not been shown to cause different side effects or problems in older people than it does in younger adults. However, older adults may be at increased risk of hearing loss, especially if they are taking high doses of erythromycin and/or have kidney or liver disease.

Other medicines—Although certain medicines should not be used together at all, in other cases two different medicines may be used together even if an interaction might occur. In these cases, your doctor may want to change the dose, or other precautions may be necessary. When you are taking or receiving erythromycins, it is especially important that your health care professional know if you are taking any of the following:

- Acetaminophen (e.g., Tylenol) (with long-term, high-dose use) or
- Amiodarone (e.g., Cordarone) or
- Anabolic steroids (nandrolone [e.g., Anabolin], oxandrolone [e.g., Anavar], oxymetholone [e.g., Anadrol], stanozolol [e.g., Winstrol]) or
- Androgens (male hormones) or
- Antithyroid agents (medicine for overactive thyroid) or
- Carmustine (e.g., BiCNU) or
- Chloroquine (e.g., Aralen) or
- Dantrolene (e.g., Dantrium) or
- Daunorubicin (e.g., Cerubidine) or
- Disulfiram (e.g., Antabuse) or
- Divalproex (e.g., Depakote) or
- Estrogens (female hormones) or
- Etretinate (e.g., Tegison) or
- Gold salts (medicine for arthritis) or
- Hydroxychloroquine (e.g., Plaquenil) or
- Mercaptopurine (e.g., Purinethol) or
- Methotrexate (e.g., Mexate) or
- Methyldopa (e.g., Aldomet) or
- Naltrexone (e.g., Trexan) (with long-term, high-dose use) or
- Oral contraceptives (birth control pills) containing estrogen or
- Other anti-infectives by mouth or by injection (medicine for infection) or
- Phenothiazines (acetophenazine [e.g., Tindal], chlorpromazine [e.g., Thorazine], fluphenazine [e.g., Prolixin], mesoridazine [e.g., Serentil], perphenazine [e.g., Trilafon], prochlorperazine [e.g., Compazine], promazine [e.g., Sparine], promethazine [e.g., Phenergan], thioridazine [e.g., Mellaril], trifluoperazine [e.g., Stelazine], triflupromazine [e.g., Vesprin], trimeprazine [e.g., Temaril]) or
- Phenytoin (e.g., Dilantin) or
- Plicamycin (e.g., Mithracin) or
- Valproic acid (e.g., Depakene)—Use of these medicines with erythromycins, especially erythromycin estolate, may increase the chance of liver problems

- Aminophylline (e.g., Somophyllin) or
- Caffeine (e.g., NoDoz) or
- Oxtriphylline (e.g., Choledyl) or
- Theophylline (e.g., Somophyllin-T, Theo-Dur)—Use of these medicines with erythromycins may increase the chance of side effects from aminophylline, caffeine, oxtriphylline, or theophylline

- Astemizole (e.g., Hismanal) or
- Terfenadine (e.g., Seldane)—Use of astemizole or terfenadine with erythromycins may cause heart problems, such as an irregular heartbeat; these medicines should not be used together

- Carbamazepine (e.g., Tegretol)—Use of carbamazepine with erythromycin may increase the side effects of carbamazepine or increase the chance of liver problems

- Chloramphenicol (e.g., Chloromycetin) or
- Clindamycin (e.g., Cleocin) or
- Lincomycin (e.g., Lincocin)—Use of these medicines with erythromycins may decrease the effectiveness of these other antibiotics

- Cyclosporine (e.g., Sandimmune) or
- Warfarin (e.g., Coumadin)—Use of any of these medicines with erythromycins may increase the side effects of these medicines

Other medical problems—The presence of other medical problems may affect the use of erythromycins. Make sure you tell your doctor if you have any other medical problems, especially:

- Heart disease—High doses of erythromycin may increase the chance of side effects in patients with a history of an irregular heartbeat

- Liver disease—Erythromycins, especially erythromycin estolate, may increase the chance of side effects involving the liver

- Loss of hearing—High doses of erythromycins may, on rare occasion, cause hearing loss, especially if you have kidney or liver disease

Proper Use of This Medicine

Generally, erythromycins are best taken with a full glass (8 ounces) of water on an empty stomach (at least 1 hour before or 2 hours after meals). If stomach upset occurs, these medicines may be taken with food. If you have questions about the erythromycin medicine you are taking, check with your health care professional.

For patients taking the *oral liquid form* of this medicine:

- This medicine is to be taken by mouth even if it comes in a dropper bottle. If this medicine does not come in a dropper bottle, use a specially marked measuring spoon or other device to measure each dose accurately. The average household teaspoon may not hold the right amount of liquid.
- Do not use after the expiration date on the label. The medicine may not work properly after that date. Check with your pharmacist if you have any questions about this.

For patients taking the *chewable tablet form* of this medicine:

- Tablets must be chewed or crushed before they are swallowed.

For patients taking the *delayed-release capsule form (with enteric-coated pellets)* or the *delayed-release tablet form* of this medicine:

- Swallow capsules or tablets whole. Do not break or crush. If you are not sure about which type of capsule or tablet you are taking, check with your pharmacist.

To help clear up your infection completely, *keep taking this medicine for the full time of treatment,* even if you begin to feel better after a few days. *If you have a "strep" infection, you should keep taking this medicine for at least 10 days. This is especially important in "strep" infections. Serious heart problems could develop later* if your infection is not cleared up completely. Also, if you stop taking this medicine too soon, your symptoms may return.

This medicine works best when there is a constant amount in the blood. *To help keep the amount constant, do not miss any doses. Also, it is best to take the doses at evenly spaced times day and night.* For example, if you are to take 4 doses a day, the doses should be spaced about 6 hours apart. If this interferes with your sleep or other daily activities, or if you need help in planning the best times to take your medicine, check with your health care professional.

Dosing—The dose of erythromycin will be different for different patients. *Follow your doctor's orders or the directions on the label.* The following information includes only the average doses of erythromycin. *If your dose is different, do not change it* unless your doctor tells you to do so.

The number of capsules or tablets or teaspoonfuls of suspension that you take depends on the strength of the medicine. Also, *the number of doses you take each day, the time allowed between doses, and the length of time you take the medicine depend on the medical problem for which you are taking erythromycin.*

For erythromycin base
- For *oral* dosage forms (capsules, tablets):
  - For treatment of infections:
    - Adults and teenagers—250 to 500 milligrams (mg) two to four times a day.
    - Children—Dose is based on body weight. The usual dose is 7.5 to 12.5 mg per kilogram (kg) (3.4 to 5.6 mg per pound) of body weight four times a day, or 15 to 25 mg per kg (6.8 to 11.4 mg per pound) of body weight two times a day.

  - For prevention of heart infections:
    - Adults and teenagers—Take 1 gram one hour before your dental appointment or surgery, then 500 mg six hours after taking the first dose.
    - Children—Dose is based on body weight. The usual dose is 20 mg per kg (9.1 mg per pound) of body weight one hour before the dental appointment or surgery, then 10 mg per kg (4.5 mg per pound) of body weight six hours after taking the first dose.

For erythromycin estolate
- For *oral* dosage forms (capsules, oral suspension, tablets):
  - For treatment of infections:
    - Adults and teenagers—250 to 500 milligrams (mg) two to four times a day.
    - Children—Dose is based on body weight. The usual dose is 7.5 to 12.5 mg per kilogram (kg) (3.4 to 5.6 mg per pound) of body weight four times a day, or 15 to 25 mg per kg (6.8 to 11.4 mg per pound) of body weight two times a day.
  - For prevention of heart infections:
    - Adults and teenagers—Take 1 gram one hour before your dental appointment or surgery, then 500 mg six hours after taking the first dose.
    - Children—Dose is based on body weight. The usual dose is 20 mg per kg (9.1 mg per pound) of body weight one hour before the dental appointment or surgery, then 10 mg per kg (4.5 mg per pound) of body weight six hours after taking the first dose.

For erythromycin ethylsuccinate
- For *oral* dosage forms (oral suspension, tablets):
  - For treatment of infections:
    - Adults and teenagers—400 to 800 milligrams (mg) two to four times a day.
    - Children—Dose is based on body weight. The usual dose is 7.5 to 12.5 mg per kilogram (kg) (3.4 to 5.6 mg per pound) of body weight four times a day, or 15 to 25 mg per kg (6.8 to 11.4 mg per pound) of body weight two times a day.
  - For prevention of heart infections:
    - Adults and teenagers—Take 1.6 grams one hour before your dental appointment or surgery, then 800 mg six hours after taking the first dose.
    - Children—Dose is based on body weight. The usual dose is 20 mg per kg (9.1 mg per pound) of body weight one hour before the dental appointment or surgery, then 10 mg per kg (4.5 mg per pound) of body weight six hours after taking the first dose.

For erythromycin gluceptate
- For *injection* dosage forms:
  - For treatment of infections:
    - Adults and teenagers—250 to 500 milligrams (mg) injected into a vein every six hours; or 3.75 to 5 mg per kilogram (kg) (1.7 to 2.3 mg per pound) of body weight injected into a vein every six hours.
    - Children—Dose is based on body weight. The usual dose is 3.75 to 5 mg per kg (1.7 to 2.3 mg per pound) of body weight injected into a vein every six hours.

For erythromycin lactobionate
- For *injection* dosage forms:
  - —For treatment of infections:
    - Adults and teenagers—250 to 500 milligrams (mg) injected into a vein every six hours; or 3.75 to 5 mg per kilogram (kg) (1.7 to 2.3 mg per pound) of body weight injected into a vein every six hours.
    - Children—Dose is based on body weight. The usual dose is 3.75 to 5 mg per kg (1.7 to 2.3 mg per pound) of body weight injected into a vein every six hours.

For erythromycin stearate
- For *oral* dosage forms (oral suspension, tablets):
  - —For treatment of infections:
    - Adults and teenagers—250 to 500 milligrams (mg) two to four times a day.
    - Children—Dose is based on body weight. The usual dose is 7.5 to 12.5 mg per kilogram (kg) (3.4 to 5.6 mg per pound) of body weight four times a day; or 15 to 25 mg per kg (6.8 to 11.4 mg per pound) of body weight two times a day.
  - —For prevention of heart infections:
    - Adults and teenagers—Take 1 gram one hour before your dental appointment or surgery, then 500 mg six hours after taking the first dose.
    - Children—Dose is based on body weight. The usual dose is 20 mg per kg (9.1 mg per pound) of body weight one hour before the dental appointment or surgery, then 10 mg per kg (4.5 mg per pound) of body weight six hours after taking the first dose.

Missed dose—If you miss a dose of this medicine, take it as soon as possible. This will help to keep a constant amount of medicine in the blood. However, if it is almost time for your next dose, skip the missed dose and go back to your regular dosing schedule. Do not double doses.

Storage—To store this medicine:
- Keep out of the reach of children.
- Store away from heat and direct light.
- Do not store the capsule or tablet form of erythromycins in the bathroom, near the kitchen sink, or in other damp places. Heat or moisture may cause the medicine to break down.
- Store the oral liquid form of some erythromycins in the refrigerator because heat will cause this medicine to break down. However, keep the medicine from freezing. Follow the directions on the label.
- Do not keep outdated medicine or medicine no longer needed. Be sure that any discarded medicine is out of the reach of children.

Precautions While Using This Medicine

If your symptoms do not improve within a few days, or if they become worse, check with your doctor.

Side Effects of This Medicine

Along with its needed effects, a medicine may cause some unwanted effects. Although not all of these side effects may occur, if they do occur they may need medical attention.

Check with your doctor immediately if any of the following side effects occur:

Less common

Fever; nausea; skin rash, redness, or itching; stomach pain (severe); unusual tiredness or weakness; vomiting; yellow eyes or skin—with erythromycin estolate (rare with other erythromycins)

Less common—with erythromycin injection only

Pain, swelling, or redness at place of injection

Rare

Fainting (repeated); irregular or slow heartbeat; loss of hearing (temporary)

Other side effects may occur that usually do not need medical attention. These side effects may go away during treatment as your body adjusts to the medicine. However, check with your doctor if any of the following side effects continue or are bothersome:

More common

Abdominal or stomach cramping and discomfort; diarrhea; nausea or vomiting

Less common

Sore mouth or tongue; vaginal itching and discharge

Other side effects not listed above may also occur in some patients. If you notice any other effects, check with your doctor.

Additional Information

Once a medicine has been approved for marketing for a certain use, experience may show that it is also useful for other medical problems. Although these uses are not included in product labeling, erythromycins are used in certain patients with the following medical conditions:

- Acne
- Actinomycosis
- Anthrax
- Chancroid
- Gastroparesis
- Lyme disease
- Lymphogranuloma venereum
- Relapsing fever

Other than the above information, there is no additional information relating to proper use, precautions, or side effects for these uses.

Revised: 07/22/94

ESOMEPRAZOLE Systemic— INTRODUCTORY VERSION

Commonly used brand name(s):

In the U.S.—
Nexium

Description

Esomeprazole (e-so-MEP-ra-zole) is used to treat conditions in which there is too much acid in the stomach. It is used to treat duodenal ulcers and gastroesophageal reflux disease

(GERD). This is a condition in which the acid in the stomach washes back up into the esophagus. Sometimes esomeprazole is used along with antibiotics to treat ulcers associated with infection caused by the *H. pylori* bacteria (germ).

Esomeprazole works by decreasing the amount of acid produced by the stomach.

This medicine is available only with your doctor's prescription, in the following dosage forms:

Oral
- Delayed-release capsules (U.S.)

Before Using This Medicine

In deciding to use a medicine, the risks of taking the medicine must be weighed against the good it will do. This is a decision you and your doctor will make. For esomeprazole, the following should be considered:

Allergies—Tell your doctor if you have ever had any unusual or allergic reaction to esomeprazole. Also tell your health care professionfal if you are allergic to any other substances, such as foods, preservatives, or dyes.

Pregnancy—Esomeprazole has not been studied in pregnant women. However, esomeprazole has not been shown to cause birth defects or other problems in animal studies.

Breast-feeding—It is not known whether esomeprazole passes in human breast milk. Since this medicine has been shown to cause unwanted effects in animals, it may be necessary for you to take another medicine or to stop breast-feeding during treatment. Be sure you have discussed the risks and benefits of the medicine with your doctor.

Children—Studies on this medicine have been done only in adult patients, and there is no specific information comparing the use of esomeprazole in children with use in other age groups.

Older adults—This medicine has been tested and has not been shown to cause different side effects or problems in older people than it does in younger adults.

Other medicines—Although certain medicines should not be used together at all, in other cases two different medicines may be used together even if an interaction might occur. In these cases, your doctor may want to change the dose, or other precautions may be necessary. Tell your health care professional if you are taking any other prescription or nonprescription (over-the-counter [OTC]) medicine.

Other medical problems—The presence of other medical problems may affect the use of esomeprazole. Make sure you tell your doctor if you have any other medical problems, especially:
- Liver disease or a history of liver disease—This condition may cause esomeprazole to build up in the body

Proper Use of This Medicine

Take esomeprazole at least one hour before a meal.

Swallow the capsule whole. Do not crush, break, or chew the capsule. If you cannot swallow the capsule whole, you may open it and sprinkle the granules contained in the capsule on one tablespoonful of applesauce or yogurt and swallow it immediately; or you may mix the granules in some tap water or fruit juice and drink it immediately. Juices you may use include apple or orange juice. *Do not chew or crush the granules.*

Take this medicine for the full time of treatment, even if you begin to feel better. Also, keep your appointments with your doctor for check-ups so that your doctor will be better able to tell you when to stop taking this medicine.

Dosing—The dose of esomeprazole will be different for different patients. *Follow your doctor's orders or the directions on the label.* The following information includes only the average doses of esomeprazole. *If your dose is different, do not change it* unless your doctor tells you to do so.

The number of doses you take each day and the length of time you take the medicine depend on the medical problem for which you are taking esomeprazole
- To treat gastroesophageal reflux disease (GERD):
  - Adults—20 or 40 milligrams (mg) taken once a day for 4 to 8 weeks.
  - Children up to 18 years of age—Use and dose must be determined by your doctor.
- To prevent gastroesophageal reflux disease (GERD):
  - Adults—20 mg taken once a day.
  - Children up to 18 years of age—Use and dose must be determined by your doctor.
- To treat ulcers related to infection with *H. pylori*
  - Adults—40 mg once daily, plus amoxicillin 1000 mg (1 gram) plus clarithromycin 500 mg, taken together before meals twice a day for ten days
  - Children up to 18 years of age—Use and dose must be determined by your doctor.

Missed dose—If you miss a dose of this medicine, take it as soon as possible. However, if it is almost time for your next dose, skip the missed dose and go back to your regular dosing schedule. Do not double doses.

Storage—To store this medicine:
- Keep out of the reach of children.
- Do not store in the bathroom, near the kitchen sink, or in other damp places. Heat or moisture may cause the medicine to break down.
- Store away from heat and direct light.
- Do not keep outdated medicine or medicine no longer needed. Ask your health care professional how you should dispose of any medicine you do not use. Be sure that any discarded medicine is out of the reach of children.

Precautions While Using This Medicine

It is very important that your doctor check you at regular visits. If your condition does not improve, or if it becomes worse, discuss this with your doctor.

Side Effects of This Medicine

Along with its needed effects, a medicine may cause some unwanted effects.

The following side effects may go away during treatment as your body adjusts to the medicine. Also, your health care professional may be able to tell you about ways to prevent or reduce some of these side effects. Check with your health care professional if any of the following side effects continue or are bothersome or if you have any questions about them:
More common
Abdominal pain; diarrhea; headache

Less common
Constipation; dryness of mouth; gas; nausea

Other side effects not listed above may also occur in some patients. If you notice any other effects, check with your doctor.

Developed: 05/17/2001

ESTRAMUSTINE Systemic

Commonly used brand name(s):

In the U.S.—
Emcyt

In Canada—
Emcyt

Other—
Estracyt

Description

Estramustine (ess-tra-MUSS-teen) belongs to the general group of medicines called antineoplastics. It is used to treat some cases of prostate cancer.

Estramustine is a combination of two medicines, an estrogen and mechlorethamine. The way that estramustine works against cancer is not completely understood. However, it seems to interfere with the growth of cancer cells, which are eventually destroyed.

Estramustine is available only with your doctor's prescription, in the following dosage form:

Oral
• Capsules (U.S. and Canada)

Before Using This Medicine

In deciding to use a medicine, the risks of taking the medicine must be weighed against the good it will do. This is a decision you and your doctor will make. For estramustine, the following should be considered:

Allergies—Tell your doctor if you have ever had any unusual or allergic reaction to estramustine, estrogens, or mechlorethamine.

Pregnancy—There is a chance that this medicine may cause birth defects if the male is taking it at the time of conception. It may also cause permanent sterility after it has been taken for a while. Be sure that you have discussed this with your doctor before taking this medicine. Before taking estramustine, make sure your doctor knows if you intend to have children.

Older adults—Many medicines have not been studied specifically in older people. Therefore, it may not be known whether they work exactly the same way they do in younger adults or if they cause different side effects or problems in older people. There is no specific information comparing use of estramustine in the elderly with use in other age groups.

Other medicines—Although certain medicines should not be used together at all, in other cases two different medicines may be used together even if an interaction might occur. In these cases, your doctor may want to change the dose, or other precautions may be necessary. When you are taking estramustine, it is especially important that your health care professional know if you are taking any of the following:

• Acetaminophen (e.g., Tylenol) (with long-term, high-dose use) or
• Amiodarone (e.g., Cordarone) or
• Anabolic steroids (nandrolone [e.g., Anabolin], oxandrolone [e.g., Anavar], oxymetholone [e.g., Anadrol], stanozolol [e.g., Winstrol]) or
• Androgens (male hormones) or
• Anti-infectives by mouth or by injection (medicine for infection) or
• Antithyroid agents (medicine for overactive thyroid) or
• Carbamazepine (e.g., Tegretol) or
• Carmustine (e.g., BiCNU) or
• Chloroquine (e.g., Aralen) or
• Dantrolene (e.g., Dantrium) or
• Disulfiram (e.g., Antabuse) or
• Divalproex (e.g., Depakote) or
• Estrogens (female hormones) or
• Etretinate (e.g., Tegison) or
• Gold salts (medicine for arthritis) or
• Hydroxychloroquine (e.g., Plaquenil) or
• Mercaptopurine (e.g., Purinethol) or
• Methotrexate (e.g., Mexate) or
• Methyldopa (e.g., Aldomet) or
• Naltrexone (e.g., Trexan) (with long-term, high-dose use) or
• Oral contraceptives (birth control pills) containing estrogen or
• Phenothiazines (acetophenazine [e.g., Tindal], chlorpromazine [e.g., Thorazine], fluphenazine [e.g., Prolixin], mesoridazine [e.g., Serentil], perphenazine [e.g., Trilafon], prochlorperazine [e.g., Compazine], promazine [e.g., Sparine], promethazine [e.g., Phenergan], thioridazine [e.g., Mellaril], trifluoperazine [e.g., Stelazine], triflupromazine [e.g., Vesprin], trimeprazine [e.g., Temaril]) or
• Phenytoin (e.g., Dilantin) or
• Plicamycin (e.g., Mithracin) or
• Valproic acid (e.g., Depakene)—May increase the risk of liver problems

• Tobacco, smoking—Smoking causes narrowing of blood vessels and may increase the risk of serious circulation problems, which can lead to stroke or heart attack

Other medical problems—The presence of other medical problems may affect the use of estramustine. Make sure you tell your doctor if you have any other medical problems, especially:

• Asthma or
• Epilepsy or
• Mental depression (or history of) or
• Migraine headaches or
• Kidney disease—Fluid retention sometimes caused by estramustine may worsen these conditions

• Blood clots (or history of) or
• Stroke (or history of) or
• Recent heart attack or stroke—May be worsened because of blood vessel problems caused by estramustine

• Chickenpox (including recent exposure) or
• Herpes zoster (shingles)—Risk of severe disease affecting other parts of the body

- Diabetes mellitus (sugar diabetes)—Estramustine may change the amount of antidiabetic medicine needed
- Gallbladder disease (or history of)—May be worsened by estramustine
- Heart or blood vessel disease—Estramustine can cause circulation problems
- Jaundice or hepatitis (or history of) or other liver disease—Effects, including liver problems, may be increased
- Stomach ulcer—May be aggravated by estramustine

Proper Use of This Medicine

Use this medicine only as directed by your doctor. Do not use more or less of it, and do not use it more often than your doctor ordered. The exact amount of medicine you need has been carefully worked out. Taking too much may increase the chance of side effects, while taking too little may not improve your condition.

Do not take estramustine within 1 hour before or 2 hours after meals or after the time you take milk, milk formulas, or other dairy products, since they may keep the medicine from working properly.

This medicine commonly causes nausea and sometimes causes vomiting. However, it may have to be taken for several weeks to months to be effective. Even if you begin to feel ill, *do not stop using this medicine without first checking with your doctor.* Ask your health care professional for ways to lessen these effects.

If you vomit shortly after taking a dose of estramustine, check with your doctor. You will be told whether to take the dose again or to wait until the next scheduled dose.

Dosing—The dose of estramustine will be different for different patients. The dose that is used may depend on a number of things, including what the medicine is being used for, the patient's size, and whether or not other medicines are also being taken. *If you are taking estramustine at home, follow your doctor's orders or the directions on the label.* If you have any questions about the proper dose of estramustine, ask your doctor.

Missed dose—If you miss a dose of this medicine, skip the missed dose and go back to your regular dosing schedule. Do not double doses.

Storage—To store this medicine:
- Keep out of the reach of children.
- Store in the refrigerator, away from direct light.
- Do not store in the bathroom, near the kitchen sink, or in other damp places. Heat or moisture may cause the medicine to break down.
- Do not keep outdated medicine or medicine no longer needed. Be sure that any discarded medicine is out of the reach of children.

Precautions While Using This Medicine

It is very important that your doctor check your progress at regular visits to make sure that the medicine is working properly and does not cause unwanted effects.

While you are being treated with estramustine, and after you stop treatment with it, *do not have any immunizations (vaccinations) without your doctor's approval.* Estramustine may lower your body's resistance and there is a chance you might get the infection the immunization is meant to prevent.

In addition, other persons living in your household should not take oral polio vaccine since there is a chance they could pass the polio virus on to you. Also, avoid persons who have recently taken oral polio vaccine. Do not get close to them and do not stay in the same room with them for very long. If you cannot take these precautions, you should consider wearing a protective face mask that covers the nose and mouth.

Side Effects of This Medicine

Along with its needed effects, a medicine may cause some unwanted effects. Although not all of these side effects may occur, if they do occur they may need medical attention.

Check with your doctor immediately if any of the following side effects occur. If your doctor is not available, go to the nearest hospital emergency room.
> *Rare*
>> Black, tarry stools; blood in urine or stools; cough or hoarseness; fever or chills; headaches (severe or sudden); loss of coordination (sudden); lower back or side pain; painful or difficult urination; pains in chest, groin, or leg (especially calf of leg); pinpoint red spots on skin; shortness of breath (sudden, for no apparent reason); slurred speech (sudden); unusual bleeding or bruising; vision changes (sudden); weakness or numbness in arm or leg

Check with your doctor as soon as possible if any of the following side effects occur:
> *More common*
>> Swelling of feet or lower legs
> *Rare*
>> Skin rash or fever; unusual tiredness or weakness

Other side effects may occur that usually do not need medical attention. These side effects may go away during treatment as your body adjusts to the medicine. However, check with your doctor if any of the following side effects continue or are bothersome or if you have any questions about them:
> *More common*
>> Breast tenderness or enlargement; decreased interest in sex; diarrhea; nausea
> *Less common*
>> Trouble in sleeping; vomiting

Other side effects not listed above may also occur in some patients. If you notice any other effects, check with your doctor.

Revised: 07/11/94

ESTROGENS   Systemic

Commonly used brand name(s):

In the U.S.—

Alora[4]	Depogen[4]
Aquest[5]	Dioval 40[4]
Climara[4]	Dioval XX[4]
Delestrogen[4]	Dura-Estrin[4]
depGynogen[4]	Duragen-20[4]
Depo-Estradiol[4]	E-Cypionate[4]

Estinyl[7]
Estrace[4]
Estraderm[4]
Estragyn 5[5]
Estragyn LA 5[4]
Estra-L 40[4]
Estratab[3]
Estro-Cyp[4]
Estrofem[4]
Estro-L.A.[4]
Estrone '5'[5]
FemPatch[4]
Gynogen L.A. 20[4]
Gynogen L.A. 40[4]
Kestrone-5[5]

Menaval-20[4]
Menest[3]
Ogen.625[6]
Ogen 1.25[6]
Ogen 2.5[6]
Ortho-Est.625[6]
Ortho-Est 1.25[6]
Premarin[1]
Premarin Intravenous[1]
Stilphostrol[2]
Valergen-10[4]
Valergen-20[4]
Valergen-40[4]
Vivelle[4]
Wehgen[5]

In Canada—
C.E.S.[1]
Delestrogen[4]
Estinyl[7]
Estrace[4]
Estraderm[4]
Femogex[4]

Honvol[2]
Ogen[6]
Premarin[1]
Premarin Intravenous[1]
Stilbestrol[2]
Vivelle[4]

Other commonly used names are:

DES
Fosfestrol
Oestradiol
Oestrone
Piperazine estrone sulfate
Stilboestrol

Note: For quick reference, the following estrogens are numbered to match the corresponding brand names.

This information applies to the following medicines
1. Conjugated Estrogens (CON-ju-gate-ed ES-troe-jenz) §
2. Diethylstilbestrol (dye-eth-il-stil-BES-trole)
3. Esterified Estrogens (es-TAIR-i-fyed Es-troe-jenz)
4. Estradiol (es-tra-DYE-ole) ‡
5. Estrone (ES-trone) †‡
6. Estropipate (es-troe-PIH-pate) ‡
7. Ethinyl Estradiol (ETH-in-il es-tra-DYE-ole)

---

†Not commercially available in Canada.
‡Generic name product may be available in the U.S.
§Generic name product may be available in Canada.

Description

Estrogens (ES-troe-jenz) are female hormones. They are produced by the body and are necessary for the normal sexual development of the female and for the regulation of the menstrual cycle during the childbearing years.

The ovaries begin to produce less estrogen after menopause (the change of life). This medicine is prescribed to make up for the lower amount of estrogen. Estrogens help relieve signs of menopause, such as hot flashes and unusual sweating, chills, faintness, or dizziness.

Estrogens are prescribed for several reasons:

- to provide additional hormone when the body does not produce enough of its own, such as during menopause or when female puberty (development of female sexual organs) does not occur on time. Other conditions include a genital skin condition (vulvar atrophy), inflammation of the vagina (atrophic vaginitis), or ovary problems (female hypogonadism or failure or removal of both ovaries).
- to help prevent weakening of bones (osteoporosis) in women past menopause.

- in the treatment of selected cases of breast cancer in men and women.
- in the treatment of cancer of the prostate in men.

Estrogens may also be used for other conditions as determined by your doctor.

There is *no* medical evidence to support the belief that the use of estrogens will keep the patient feeling young, keep the skin soft, or delay the appearance of wrinkles. Nor has it been proven that the use of estrogens during menopause will relieve emotional and nervous symptoms, unless these symptoms are caused by other menopausal symptoms, such as hot flashes or hot flushes.

Estrogens are available only with your doctor's prescription, in the following dosage forms:

Oral
Conjugated Estrogens
- Tablets (U.S. and Canada)
Diethylstilbestrol
- Tablets (U.S. and Canada)
Esterified Estrogens
- Tablets (U.S. and Canada)
Estradiol
- Tablets (U.S. and Canada)
Estropipate
- Tablets (U.S. and Canada)
Ethinyl Estradiol
- Tablets (U.S. and Canada)

Parenteral
Conjugated Estrogens
- Injection (U.S. and Canada)
Diethylstilbestrol
- Injection (U.S. and Canada)
Estradiol
- Injection (U.S. and Canada)
Estrone
- Injection (U.S.)

Topical
Estradiol
- Transdermal system (skin patch) (U.S. and Canada)

Before Using This Medicine

In deciding to use a medicine, the risks of taking the medicine must be weighed against the good it will do. This is a decision you and your doctor will make. For estrogens, the following should be considered:

Allergies—Tell your doctor if you have ever had any unusual or allergic reaction to estrogens. Also tell your health care professional if you are allergic to any other substances, such as foods, preservatives, or dyes.

Pregnancy—Estrogens are not recommended for use during pregnancy or right after giving birth. Becoming pregnant or maintaining a pregnancy is not likely to occur around the time of menopause.

Certain estrogens have been shown to cause serious birth defects in humans and animals. Some daughters of women who took diethylstilbestrol (DES) during pregnancy have developed reproductive (genital) tract problems and, rarely, cancer of the vagina or cervix (opening to the uterus) when they reached childbearing age. Some sons of women who took DES during pregnancy have developed urinary-genital tract problems.

Breast-feeding—Use of this medicine is not recommended in nursing mothers. Estrogens pass into the breast milk and their possible effect on the baby is not known.

Older adults—This medicine has been tested and has not been shown to cause different side effects or problems in older women than it does in younger women.

Other medicines—Although certain medicines should not be used together at all, in other cases two different medicines may be used together even if an interaction might occur. In these cases, your doctor may want to change the dose, or other precautions may be necessary. When you are taking estrogens, it is especially important that your health care professional know if you are taking any of the following:

- Acetaminophen (e.g., Tylenol) (with long-term, high-dose use) or
- Amiodarone (e.g., Cordarone) or
- Anabolic steroids (nandrolone [e.g., Anabolin], oxandrolone [e.g., Anavar], oxymetholone [e.g., Anadrol], stanozolol [e.g., Winstrol]) or
- Androgens (male hormones) or
- Anti-infectives by mouth or by injection (medicine for infection) or
- Antithyroid agents (medicine for overactive thyroid) or
- Carbamazepine (e.g., Tegretol) or
- Carmustine (e.g., BiCNU) or
- Chloroquine (e.g., Aralen) or
- Dantrolene (e.g., Dantrium) or
- Daunorubicin (e.g., Cerubidine) or
- Disulfiram (e.g., Antabuse) or
- Divalproex (e.g., Depakote) or
- Etretinate (e.g., Tegison) or
- Gold salts (medicine for arthritis) or
- Hydroxychloroquine (e.g., Plaquenil) or
- Isoniazid or
- Mercaptopurine (e.g., Purinethol) or
- Methotrexate (e.g., Mexate) or
- Methyldopa (e.g., Aldomet) or
- Naltrexone (e.g., Trexan) (with long-term, high-dose use) or
- Oral contraceptives (birth control pills) containing estrogen or
- Phenothiazines (acetophenazine [e.g., Tindal], chlorpromazine [e.g., Thorazine], fluphenazine [e.g., Prolixin], mesoridazine [e.g., Serentil], perphenazine [e.g., Trilafon], prochlorperazine [e.g., Compazine], promazine [e.g., Sparine], promethazine [e.g., Phenergan], thioridazine [e.g., Mellaril], trifluoperazine [e.g., Stelazine], triflupromazine [e.g., Vesprin], trimeprazine [e.g., Temaril]) or
- Phenytoin (e.g., Dilantin) or
- Plicamycin (e.g., Mithracin) or
- Valproic acid (e.g., Depakene)—Use of these medicines with estrogens may increase the chance of problems occurring that affect the liver
- Cyclosporine (e.g., Sandimmune)—Estrogens can prevent cyclosporine's removal from the body; this can lead to cyclosporine causing kidney or liver problems
- Protease inhibitors, such as ritonavir (e.g., Norvir)—May decrease the effect of estrogens

Other medical problems—The presence of other medical problems may affect the use of estrogens. Make sure you tell your doctor if you have any other medical problems, especially:

For all patients
- Blood clotting problems (or history of during previous estrogen therapy)—Estrogens usually are not used until blood clotting problems stop; using estrogens is not a problem for most patients without a history of blood clotting problems due to estrogen use
- Breast cancer or
- Bone cancer or
- Cancer of the uterus or
- Fibroid tumors of the uterus—Estrogens may interfere with the treatment of breast or bone cancer or worsen cancer of the uterus when these conditions are present
- Changes in genital or vaginal bleeding of unknown causes—Use of estrogens may delay diagnosis or worsen condition. The reason for the bleeding should be determined before estrogens are used
- Endometriosis or
- High cholesterol or triglycerides (or history of) or
- Gallbladder disease or gallstones (or history of) or
- Liver disease (or history of) or
- Pancreatitis (inflammation of pancreas)—Estrogens may worsen these conditions. Although estrogens can improve blood cholesterol, they can worsen blood triglycerides for some people

For males treated for breast or prostate cancer
- Blood clots or
- Heart or circulation disease or
- Stroke—Males with these medical problems may be more likely to have clotting problems while taking estrogens; the high doses of estrogens used to treat male breast or prostate cancer have been shown to increase the chances of heart attack, phlebitis (inflamed veins) caused by a blood clot, or blood clots in the lungs

---

Proper Use of This Medicine

Estrogens usually come with patient information or directions. Read them carefully before taking this medicine.

Take this medicine only as directed by your doctor. Do not take more of it and do not take or use it for a longer time than your doctor ordered. For patients taking any of the estrogens by mouth, try to take the medicine at the same time each day to reduce the possibility of side effects and to allow it to work better.

For patients taking any of the estrogens by mouth or by injection:
- Nausea may occur during the first few weeks after you start taking estrogens. This effect usually disappears with continued use. If the nausea is bothersome, it can usually be prevented or reduced by taking each dose with food or immediately after food.

For patients using the transdermal (skin patch) form of estradiol:
- Wash and dry your hands thoroughly before and after handling the patch.
- Apply the patch to a clean, dry, nonoily skin area of your lower abdomen, hips below the waist, or buttocks that has little or no hair and is free of cuts or irritation. The manufacturer of the 0.025-mg patch recommends that its patch be applied to the buttocks only. Furthermore, each new patch should be applied to a new site of application. For instance, if the old patch is taken off the left buttock, then apply the new patch to the right buttock.

- *Do not apply to the breasts.* Also, do not apply to the waistline or anywhere else where tight clothes may rub the patch loose.
- Press the patch firmly in place with the palm of your hand for about 10 seconds. Make sure there is good contact, especially around the edges.
- If a patch becomes loose or falls off, you may reapply it or discard it and apply a new patch.
- Each dose is best applied to a different area of skin on your lower abdomen, hips below the waist, or buttocks so that at least 1 week goes by before the same area is used again. This will help prevent skin irritation.

Dosing—The dose of these medicines will be different for different patients. *Follow your doctor's orders or the directions on the label.* The following information includes only the average doses of these medicines. *If your dose is different, do not change it* unless your doctor tells you to do so.

The number of tablets that you take or the amount of injection you use depends on the strength of the medicine. Also, *the number of doses you take or use each day or patches you apply each week, the time allowed between doses, and the length of time you take or use the medicine depend on the medical problem for which you are taking, using, or applying estrogen.*

For conjugated estrogens
- For *oral* dosage form (tablets):
  —For treating breast cancer in women after menopause and in men:
  - Adults—10 milligrams (mg) three times a day for at least three months.
  —For treating a genital skin condition (vulvar atrophy), inflammation of the vagina (atrophic vaginitis), or symptoms of menopause:
  - Adults—0.3 to 1.25 mg a day. Your doctor may want you to take the medicine each day or only on certain days of the month.
  —To prevent loss of bone (osteoporosis):
  - Adults—0.625 mg a day. Your doctor may want you to take the medicine each day or only on certain days of the month.
  —For treating ovary problems (female hypogonadism or for starting puberty):
  - Adults and teenagers—2.5 to 7.5 mg a day. This dose is divided up and taken in smaller doses. Your doctor may want you to take the medicine only on certain days of the month.
  —For treating ovary problems (failure or removal of both ovaries):
  - Adults—1.25 mg a day. Your doctor may want you to take the medicine each day or only on certain days of the month.
  —For treating prostate cancer:
  - Adults—1.25 to 2.5 mg three times a day.
- For *injection* dosage form:
  —For controlling abnormal bleeding of the uterus:
  - Adults—25 mg injected into a muscle or vein. This may be repeated in six to twelve hours if needed.

For diethylstilbestrol
- For *oral* dosage form (tablets):
  —For treating prostate cancer:
  - Adults—At first, 1 to 3 milligrams (mg) a day. Later, your doctor may decrease your dose to 1 mg a day.

For diethylstilbestrol diphosphate
- For *oral* dosage form (tablets):
  —For treating prostate cancer:
  - Adults—50 to 200 milligrams (mg) three times a day.
- For *injection* dosage form:
  —For treating prostate cancer:
  - Adults—At first, 500 mg is mixed in solution with sodium chloride or dextrose injection and injected slowly into a vein. Your doctor may increase your dose to 1 gram a day for five or more straight days as needed. Then, your doctor may lower your dose to between 250 and 500 mg one or two times a week.

For esterified estrogens
- For *oral* dosage form (tablets):
  —For treating breast cancer in women after menopause and in men:
  - Adults—10 milligrams (mg) three times a day for at least three months.
  —For treating a genital skin condition (vulvar atrophy) or inflammation of the vagina (atrophic vaginitis), or to prevent loss of bone (osteoporosis):
  - Adults—0.3 to 1.25 mg a day. Your doctor may want you to take the medicine each day or only on certain days of the month.
  —For treating ovary problems (failure or removal of both ovaries):
  - Adults—1.25 mg a day. Your doctor may want you to take the medicine each day or only on certain days of the month.
  —For treating ovary problems (female hypogonadism):
  - Adults—2.5 to 7.5 mg a day. This dose may be divided up and taken in smaller doses. Your doctor may want you to take the medicine each day or only on certain days of the month.
  —For treating symptoms of menopause:
  - Adults—0.625 to 1.25 mg a day. Your doctor may want you to take the medicine each day or only on certain days of the month.
  —For treating prostate cancer:
  - Adults—1.25 to 2.5 mg three times a day.

For estradiol
- For *oral* dosage form (tablets):
  —For treating breast cancer in women after menopause and in men:
  - Adults—10 milligrams (mg) three times a day for at least three months.
  —For treating a genital skin condition (vulvar atrophy), inflammation of the vagina (atrophic vaginitis), ovary problems (female hypogonadism or failure or removal of both ovaries), or symptoms of menopause:
  - Adults—0.5 to 2 mg a day. Your doctor may want you to take the medicine each day or only on certain days of the month.
  —For treating prostate cancer:
  - Adults—1 to 2 mg three times a day.
  —To prevent loss of bone (osteoporosis):
  - Adults—0.5 mg a day. Your doctor may want you to take the medicine each day or only on certain days of the month.
- For *transdermal* dosage form (skin patches):
  —For treating a genital skin condition (vulvar atrophy), inflammation of the vagina (atrophic vaginitis), symptoms of menopause, ovary problems (female

hypogonadism or failure or removal of both ovaries), or to prevent loss of bone (osteoporosis):

For the Climara or FemPatch patches

- Adults—0.025 to 0.1 milligram (mg) (one patch) applied to the skin and worn for one week. Then, remove that patch and apply a new one. A new patch should be applied once a week for three weeks. During the fourth week, you may or may not wear a patch. Your health care professional will tell you what you should do for this fourth week. After the fourth week, you will repeat the cycle.

For the Alora, Estraderm, or Vivelle patches

- Adults—0.025 to 0.1 mg (one patch) applied to the skin and worn for one half of a week. Then, remove that patch and apply and wear a new patch for the rest of the week. A new patch should be applied two times a week for three weeks. During the fourth week, you may or may not apply new patches. Your health care professional will tell you what you should do for this fourth week. After the fourth week, you will repeat the cycle.

For estradiol cypionate

- For *injection* dosage form:
  - —For treating ovary problems (female hypogonadism):
    - Adults—1.5 to 2 milligrams (mg) injected into a muscle once a month.
  - —For treating symptoms of menopause:
    - Adults—1 to 5 mg injected into a muscle every three to four weeks.

For estradiol valerate

- For *injection* dosage form:
  - —For treating a genital skin condition (vulvar atrophy), inflammation of the vagina (atrophic vaginitis), symptoms of menopause, or ovary problems (female hypogonadism or failure or removal of both ovaries):
    - Adults—10 to 20 milligrams (mg) injected into a muscle every four weeks as needed.
  - —For treating prostate cancer:
    - Adults—30 mg injected into a muscle every one or two weeks.

For estrone

- For *injection* dosage form:
  - —For controlling abnormal bleeding of the uterus:
    - Adults—2 to 5 milligrams (mg) a day, injected into a muscle for several days.
  - —For treating a genital skin condition (vulvar atrophy), inflammation of the vagina (atrophic vaginitis), or symptoms of menopause:
    - Adults—0.1 to 0.5 mg injected into a muscle two or three times a week. Your doctor may want you to receive the medicine each week or only during certain weeks of the month.
  - —For treating ovary problems (female hypogonadism or failure or removal of both ovaries):
    - Adults—0.1 to 1 mg a week. This is injected into a muscle as a single dose or divided into more than one dose. Your doctor may want you to receive the medicine each week or only during certain weeks of the month.
  - —For treating prostate cancer:
    - Adults—2 to 4 mg injected into a muscle two or three times a week.

For estropipate

- For oral dosage form (tablets):
  - —For treating a genital skin condition (vulvar atrophy), inflammation of the vagina (atrophic vaginitis), or symptoms of menopause:
    - Adults—0.75 to 6 milligrams (mg) a day. Your doctor may want you to take the medicine each day or only on certain days of the month.
  - —For treating ovary problems (female hypogonadism or failure or removal of both ovaries):
    - Adults—1.5 to 9 mg a day. Your doctor may want you to take the medicine each day or only on certain days of the month.
  - —To prevent loss of bone (osteoporosis):
    - Adults—0.75 mg a day. Your doctor may want you to take the medicine each day for twenty-five days of a thirty-one–day cycle.

For ethinyl estradiol

- For *oral* dosage form (tablets):
  - —For treating breast cancer in women after menopause and in men:
    - Adults—1 milligram (mg) three times a day.
  - —For treating ovary problems (female hypogonadism or failure or removal of both ovaries):
    - Adults—0.05 mg one to three times a day for three to six months. Your doctor may want you to take the medicine each day or only on certain days of the month.
  - —For treating prostate cancer:
    - Adults—0.15 to 3 mg a day.
  - —For treating symptoms of menopause:
    - Adults—0.02 to 0.05 mg a day. Your doctor may want you to take the medicine each day or only on certain days of the month.

For ethinyl estradiol and norethindrone

- For *oral* dosage form (tablets):
  - —For treating symptoms of menopause:
    - Adults—1 tablet (5 mcg ethinyl estradiol and 1 mg of norethindrone) each day
  - —To prevent loss of bone (osteoporosis):
    - Adults—1 tablet (5 mcg ethinyl estradiol and 1 mg of norethindrone) each day

Missed dose—

- For patients taking any of the estrogens by mouth: If you miss a dose of this medicine, take it as soon as possible. However, if it is almost time for your next dose, skip the missed dose and go back to your regular dosing schedule. Do not double doses.
- For patients using the transdermal (skin patch) form of estradiol: If you forget to apply a new patch when you are supposed to, apply it as soon as possible. However, if it is almost time for the next patch, skip the missed one and go back to your regular schedule. Always remove the old patch before applying a new one. Do not apply more than one patch at a time.

Storage—To store this medicine:

- Keep out of the reach of children.
- Store away from heat and direct light.
- Do not store in the bathroom medicine cabinet because the heat or moisture may cause the medicine to break down.
- Keep the injection form of this medicine from freezing.

- Do not keep outdated medicine or medicine no longer needed. Be sure that any discarded medicine is out of the reach of children.

Precautions While Using This Medicine

It is very important that your doctor check your progress at regular visits to make sure this medicine does not cause unwanted effects. These visits will usually be every year, but some doctors require them more often.

In some patients using estrogens, tenderness, swelling, or bleeding of the gums may occur. Brushing and flossing your teeth carefully and regularly and massaging your gums may help prevent this. See your dentist regularly to have your teeth cleaned. Check with your medical doctor or dentist if you have any questions about how to take care of your teeth and gums, or if you notice any tenderness, swelling, or bleeding of your gums.

It is not yet known whether the use of estrogens increases the risk of breast cancer in women. Therefore, it is very important that you regularly check your breasts for any unusual lumps or discharge. Report any problems to your doctor. You should also have a mammogram (x-ray pictures of the breasts) done if your doctor recommends it. Because breast cancer has occurred in men taking estrogens, regular breast self-exams and exams by your doctor for any unusual lumps or discharge should be done.

If your menstrual periods have stopped, they may start again. This effect will continue for as long as the medicine is taken. However, if taking the continuous treatment (0.625 mg conjugated estrogens and 2.5 mg medroxyprogesterone once a day), monthly bleeding usually stops within 10 months.

Also, vaginal bleeding between your regular menstrual periods may occur during the first 3 months of use. Do not stop taking your medicine. *Check with your doctor if bleeding continues for an unusually long time, if your period has not started within 45 days of your last period, or if you think you are pregnant.*

Tell the doctor in charge that you are taking this medicine before having any laboratory test because some results may be affected.

Side Effects of This Medicine

Women rarely have severe side effects from taking estrogens to replace estrogen. Discuss these possible effects with your doctor:

- The prolonged use of estrogens has been reported to increase the risk of endometrial cancer (cancer of the lining of the uterus) in women after menopause. This risk seems to increase as the dose and the length of use increase. When estrogens are used in low doses for less than 1 year, there is less risk. The risk is also reduced if a progestin (another female hormone) is added to, or replaces part of, your estrogen dose. If the uterus has been removed by surgery (total hysterectomy), there is no risk of endometrial cancer.
- It is not yet known whether the use of estrogens increases the risk of breast cancer in women. Although some large studies show an increased risk, most studies and information gathered to date do not support this idea. Breast cancer has been reported in men taking estrogens.

The following side effects may be caused by blood clots, which could lead to stroke, heart attack, or death. These side effects occur rarely, and, when they do occur, they occur in men treated for cancer using high doses of estrogens. *Get emergency help immediately* if any of the following side effects occur:

Rare—for males being treated for breast or prostate cancer only

Headache (sudden or severe); loss of coordination (sudden); loss of vision or change of vision (sudden); pains in chest, groin, or leg, especially in calf of leg; shortness of breath (sudden and unexplained); slurring of speech (sudden); weakness or numbness in arm or leg

Also, check with your doctor as soon as possible if any of the following side effects occur:

More common

Breast pain (in females and males); increased breast size (in females and males); swelling of feet and lower legs; weight gain (rapid)

Less common or rare

Changes in vaginal bleeding (spotting, breakthrough bleeding, prolonged or heavier bleeding, or complete stoppage of bleeding); lumps in, or discharge from, breast (in females and males); pains in stomach, side, or abdomen; yellow eyes or skin

Other side effects may occur that usually do not need medical attention. These side effects may go away during treatment as your body adjusts to the medicine. However, check with your doctor if any of the following side effects continue or are bothersome:

More common

Bloating of stomach; cramps of lower stomach; loss of appetite; nausea; skin irritation or redness where skin patch was worn

Less common

Diarrhea (mild); dizziness (mild); headaches (mild); migraine headaches; problems in wearing contact lenses; unusual decrease in sexual desire (in males); unusual increase in sexual desire (in females); vomiting (usually with high doses)

Also, many women who are taking estrogens with a progestin (another female hormone) will start having monthly vaginal bleeding, similar to menstrual periods, again. This effect will continue for as long as the medicine is taken. However, monthly bleeding will not occur in women who have had the uterus removed by surgery (total hysterectomy).

Other side effects not listed above may also occur in some patients. If you notice any other effects, check with your doctor.

Additional Information

Once a medicine has been approved for marketing for a certain use, experience may show that it is also useful for other medical problems. Although these uses are not included in product labeling, estrogen is used in certain patients with the following medical conditions:

- Osteoporosis caused by lack of estrogen before menopause
- Atherosclerotic disease (hardening of the arteries)
- Turner's syndrome (a genetic disorder)

Other than the above information, there is no additional information relating to proper use, precautions, or side effects for these uses.

Revised: 01/16/2001

ESTROGENS   Vaginal

Commonly used brand name(s):

In the U.S.—

Estrace[3]   Ortho Dienestrol[2]
Estring[3]   Premarin[1]
Ogen[5]

In Canada—

Estring[3]   Ortho Dienestrol[2]
Oestrilin[4]   Premarin[1]

Other commonly used names are dienoestrol[2], oestradiol[3], and piperazine estrone sulfate[5].

Note: For quick reference, the following estrogens are numbered to match the corresponding brand names.

This information applies to the following medicines

1. Conjugated Estrogens (CON-ju-gate-ed ES-troe-jenz)
2. Dienestrol (dye-en-ES-trole)
3. Estradiol (es-tra-DYE-ole)
4. Estrone (ES-trone) *
5. Estropipate (es-troe-PIH-pate) †

---

*Not commercially available in the U.S.
†Not commercially available in Canada.

Description

Estrogens (ES-troe-jenz) are hormones produced by the body. Among other things, estrogens help develop and maintain female organs.

When your body is in short supply of this hormone, replacing it can ease uncomfortable changes that occur in the vagina, vulva (female genitals), and urethra (part of the urinary system). Conditions that are treated with vaginal estrogens include a genital skin condition (vulvar atrophy), inflammation of the vagina (atrophic vaginitis), and inflammation of the urethra (atrophic urethritis).

Estrogens work partly by increasing a normal clear discharge from the vagina and making the vulva and urethra healthy. Using or applying an estrogen relieves or lessens:

- Dryness and soreness in the vagina
- Itching, redness, or soreness of the vulva
- Feeling an urge to urinate more often then is needed or experiencing pain while urinating
- Pain during sexual intercourse

When used vaginally or on the skin, most estrogens are absorbed into the bloodstream and cause some, but not all, of the same effects as when they are taken by mouth. Estrogens used vaginally at very low doses for treating local problems of the genitals and urinary system will not protect against osteoporosis or stop the hot flushes caused by menopause.

Estrogens for vaginal use are available only with your doctor's prescription, in the following dosage forms:

Vaginal
Conjugated Estrogens
- Cream (U.S. and Canada)

Dienestrol
- Cream (U.S. and Canada)
Estradiol
- Cream (U.S.)
- Insert (or ring) (U.S. and Canada)
Estrone
- Cream (Canada)
- Suppositories (Canada)
Estropipate
- Cream (U.S.)

Before Using This Medicine

In deciding to use a medicine, the risks of using the medicine must be weighed against the good it will do. This is a decision you and your doctor will make. For vaginal estrogens, the following should be considered:

Allergies—Tell your doctor if you have ever had any unusual or allergic reaction to estrogens or to parabens. Also tell your health care professional if you are allergic to any other substances, such as foods, preservatives, or dyes.

Pregnancy—Estrogens are not recommended for use during pregnancy, since an estrogen called diethylstilbestrol (DES) that is no longer taken for hormone replacement has caused serious birth defects in humans and animals.

Breast-feeding—Use of this medicine is not recommended in nursing mothers. Estrogens pass into the breast milk.

Older adults—This medicine has been tested and has not been shown to cause different side effects or problems in older people than it does in younger adults.

Other medicines—Although certain medicines should not be used together at all, in other cases two different medicines may be used together even if an interaction might occur. In these cases, your doctor may want to change the dose, or other precautions may be necessary. Tell your health care professional if you are taking or using any other prescription or nonprescription (over-the-counter [OTC]) medicine.

Other medical problems—The presence of other medical problems may affect the use of estrogens. Make sure you tell your doctor if you have any other medical problems, especially:

- Blood clotting problems—Although worsening of a blood clotting condition is unlikely, some doctors do not prescribe vaginal estrogens for patients with blood clotting problems or a history of these problems

- Certain cancers, including cancers of the breast, bone, or uterus (active or suspected)—Estrogens may interfere with the treatment of breast or bone cancer or worsen cancer of the uterus when these conditions are present

- Endometriosis or
- Fibroid tumors of the uterus—Estrogens may worsen endometriosis or increase the size of fibroid tumors

- Irritation or infection of the vagina—Usually estrogens decrease infections or irritation of the vagina, but sometimes these conditions may become worse

- Liver disease, severe—Estrogens may worsen the condition in some cases; however, many doctors recommend vaginal use of estrogen because it has less effect on the liver than when estrogens are taken by mouth

---

- Physical problems within the vagina, such as narrow vagina, vaginal stenosis, or vaginal prolapse—Estradiol vaginal insert may be more likely to slip out of place or cause problems, such as irritation of the vagina

- Unusual genital or vaginal bleeding of unknown causes—Use of estrogens may delay diagnosis or worsen the condition. The reason for the bleeding should be determined before estrogens are used

Proper Use of This Medicine

Vaginal estrogen products usually come with patient directions. *Read them carefully before using this medicine.*

Wash your hands before and after using the medicine. Also, keep the medicine out of your eyes. If this medicine does get into your eyes, wash them out immediately, but carefully, with large amounts of tap water. If your eyes still burn or are painful, check with your doctor.

Use this medicine only as directed. Do not use more of it and do not use it for a longer time than your doctor ordered. It can take up to 4 months to see the full effect of the estrogens. Your doctor may reconsider continuing your estrogen treatment or may lower your dose several times within the first one or two months, and every 3 to 6 months after that. Sometimes a switch to oral estrogens may be required for added benefits or for higher doses. When using the estradiol vaginal insert, you will need to replace it every 3 months or remove it after 3 months.

For vaginal creams or suppositories—Vaginal creams and some vaginal suppositories are inserted with a plastic applicator. Directions for using the applicator are supplied with your medicine. If you do not see your dose marked on the applicator, ask your health care professional for more information.

- *To fill the applicator for cream dosage forms:*
  - Break the metal seal at the opening of the tube by using the point on the top of the cap.
  - Screw the applicator onto the tube.
  - Squeeze the medicine into the applicator slowly until it is measured properly.
  - Remove the applicator from the tube. Replace the cap on the tube.
- *To fill the applicator for suppository dosage form*
  - Place the suppository into the applicator.
- *To place the dose using the applicator for cream and suppository dosage forms:*
  - Relax while lying on your back with your knees bent or stand with one foot on a chair.
  - Hold the full applicator in one hand. Slide the applicator slowly into the vagina. Stop before it becomes uncomfortable.
  - Slowly press the plunger until it stops.
  - Withdraw the applicator. The medicine will be left behind in the vagina.
- *To care for the applicator for cream and suppository dosage forms:*
  - Clean the applicator after use by pulling the plunger out of the applicator and washing both parts completely in warm, soapy water. *Do not use hot or boiling water.*
  - Rinse well.
  - After drying the applicator, replace the plunger.

For vaginal insert dosage form
- *To place the vaginal insert*
  - Relax while lying on your back with your knees bent or stand with one foot on a chair.
  - Pinch or press the sides of the vaginal insert together, between your forefinger and middle finger.
  - With one hand, part the folds of skin around your vagina.
  - Slide the vaginal insert slowly into the upper third of your vagina. Stop before it becomes uncomfortable. The exact location is not too important but it should be comfortable.
  - If it seems uncomfortable, then carefully push the vaginal insert higher into the vagina.
- *To remove the vaginal insert*
  - Stand with one foot on a chair.
  - Slide one finger into the vagina and hook it around the closest part of the vaginal insert.
  - Slowly pull the vaginal insert out.
  - Dispose of the vaginal insert by wrapping it up and throwing it into the trash. *Do not flush it down the toilet.*

Dosing—The dose of vaginal estrogens will be different for different women. *Follow your doctor's orders or the directions on the label.* The following information includes only the average doses of these medicines. *If your dose is different, do not change it* unless your doctor tells you to do so.

For conjugated estrogens
- For *vaginal* dosage form (cream):
  - For treating a genital skin condition (vulvar atrophy) and inflammation of the vagina (atrophic vaginitis):
    - Adults: 0.3 to 1.25 milligrams (mg) of conjugated estrogens (one half to two grams of cream) inserted into the vagina once a day or as directed by your doctor to achieve the lowest dose possible. Usually your doctor will want you to use this medicine for only three weeks of each month (three weeks on and one week off).

For dienestrol
- For *vaginal* dosage form (cream):
  - For treating a genital skin condition (vulvar atrophy) and inflammation of the vagina (atrophic vaginitis):
    - Adults: At first, one applicatorful of 0.01% cream inserted into the vagina one or two times a day for one to two weeks, decreasing the dose by one half over two and four weeks. After four weeks, your doctor will probably ask you to use the medicine less often, such as one applicatorful one to three times a *week* and for only three weeks of each month (three weeks on and one week off).

For estradiol
- For *vaginal* dosage form (cream):
  - For treating a genital skin condition (vulvar atrophy) and inflammation of the vagina (atrophic vaginitis):
    - Adults: 200 to 400 micrograms (mcg) of estradiol (two to four grams of cream) inserted into the vagina once a day for one to two weeks, decreasing the dose by one half over two and four weeks. After four weeks, your doctor will probably ask you to use the medicine less often, such as 100 mcg (one gram of cream) one to three times a *week*

and for only three weeks of each month (three weeks on and one week off).

- For *vaginal* dosage form (insert):
  - —For treating a genital skin condition (vulvar atrophy), inflammation of the vagina (atrophic vaginitis) in postmenopausal women, and inflammation of the urethra (urethritis) in postmenopausal women:
    - Adults: 2 milligrams (mg) of estradiol (7.5 mcg released every twenty-four hours with continuous use) and replaced every three months.

For estrone

- For *vaginal* dosage form (cream):
  - —For treating a genital skin condition (vulvar atrophy) and inflammation of the vagina (atrophic vaginitis) in postmenopausal women:
    - Adults: 2 to 4 milligrams (mg) of estrone (two to four grams of cream) inserted into the vagina once a day or as directed by your doctor.
- For *vaginal* dosage form (suppository):
  - —For treating a genital skin condition (vulvar atrophy) and inflammation of the vagina (atrophic vaginitis) in postmenopausal women:
    - Adults: 250 to 500 micrograms (mcg) inserted into the vagina once a day or as directed by your doctor.

For estropipate

- For *vaginal* dosage form (cream):
  - —For treating a genital skin condition (vulvar atrophy) and inflammation of the vagina (atrophic vaginitis):
    - Adults: 3 to 6 milligrams (mg) of estropipate (two to four grams of cream) inserted into the vagina once a day. Your doctor will probably ask you to use the medicine for only three weeks of each month (three weeks on and one week off).

Missed dose— When using the suppository or cream several times a week: If you miss a dose of this medicine and remember it within 1 or 2 days of the missed dose, use the missed dose as soon as possible. However, if it is almost time for your next dose, skip the missed dose and go back to your regular dosing schedule. Do not double doses.

When using the cream or suppositories more than several times a week: If you miss a dose of this medicine, use it as soon as possible if remembered within 12 hours of the missed dose. However, if it is almost time for your next dose, skip the missed dose and go back to your regular dosing schedule. Do not double doses.

Storage— To store this medicine:

- Keep out of the reach of children.
- Store away from heat and direct light.
- Keep the medicine from freezing.
- Do not keep outdated medicine or medicine no longer needed. Be sure that any discarded medicine is out of the reach of children.

Precautions While Using This Medicine

It is very important that your doctor check your progress at regular visits to make sure this medicine does not cause unwanted effects. Plan on going to see your doctor every year, but some doctors require visits more often.

It is not yet known whether the use of vaginal estrogens increases the risk of breast cancer in women. Therefore, it is very important that you regularly check your breasts for any unusual lumps or discharge. Report any problems to your doctor. You should also have a mammogram (x-ray pictures of the breasts) done if your doctor recommends it.

If you think that you may be pregnant, stop using the medicine immediately and check with your doctor.

Tell the doctor in charge that you are using this medicine before having any laboratory test, because some test results may be affected.

For vaginal creams

- Avoid using latex condoms, diaphragms, or cervical caps for up to 72 hours after using estrogen vaginal creams. Certain estrogen products may contain oils in the creams that can weaken latex (rubber) products and cause condoms to break or leak, or cervical caps or diaphragms to wear out sooner. Check with your health care professional to make sure the vaginal estrogen product you are using can be used with latex devices.
- This medicine is often used at bedtime to increase effectiveness through better absorption.
- Vaginal creams or suppositories will melt and leak out of the vagina. A minipad or sanitary napkin will protect your clothing. *Do not use tampons* (like those used for menstrual periods) since they may soak up the medicine and make the medicine less effective.
- Avoid exposing your male sexual partner to your vaginal estrogen cream or suppository by not having sexual intercourse right after using these medicines. Your male partner might absorb the medicine through his penis if it comes in contact with the medicine.

For estradiol vaginal insert

- It is not necessary to remove the vaginal insert for sexual intercourse unless desired.
- If you do take it out or if it accidentally slips or comes out of the vagina, you can replace the vaginal insert in the vagina after washing it with lukewarm water. *Never use hot or boiling water.*
- If it slips down, gently push it upwards back into place.
- Replace the vaginal insert every 3 months.

Side Effects of This Medicine

The risk of any serious adverse effect is unlikely for most women using low doses of estrogens vaginally. Even women with special risks have used vaginal estrogens without problems.

Check with your doctor as soon as possible if any of the following side effects occur:

Less common

Breast pain; enlarged breasts; itching of the vagina or genitals; headache; nausea; stinging or redness of the genital area; thick, white vaginal discharge without odor or with a mild odor

Rare

Feeling of vaginal pressure (with use of estradiol vaginal insert); vaginal burning or pain (with use of estradiol vaginal insert); unusual or unexpected uterine bleeding or spotting

Other side effects may occur that usually do not need medical attention. These side effects may go away during treatment as your body adjusts to the medicine. However, check with

your doctor if any of the following side effects continue or are bothersome:

Less common
Abdominal or back pain; clear vaginal discharge (usually means the medicine is working)

Also, many women who are using estrogens with a progestin (another female hormone) will start having monthly vaginal bleeding, similar to menstrual periods, again. This effect will continue for as long as the medicine is taken. However, monthly bleeding will not occur in women who have had the uterus removed by surgery (total hysterectomy).

Other side effects not listed above may also occur in some patients. If you notice any other effects, check with your doctor.

Revised: 08/20/97

ESTROGENS AND PROGESTINS (OVARIAN HORMONE THERAPY)
Systemic

Commonly used brand name(s):

In the U.S.—
femhrt[2]
Ortho-Prefest[1]
Activella[3]

Other commonly used names are:
Ethinylestradiol [Ethinyl estradiol]
Ethinyloestradiol [Ethinyl estradiol]
Norethindrone [Norethisterone]

Note: For quick reference, the following estrogens and progestins are numbered to match the corresponding brand names.

This information applies to the following medicines:
1. 17 beta-estradiol and norgestimate (seh-ven-TEEN BAY-tuh es-tra-DYE-ole and nor-JES-ti-mate)
2. Ethinyl estradiol and norethindrone (ETH-in-il es-tra-DYE-ole and nor-eth-IN-drone)
3. Estradiol and norethindrone (es-tra-DYE-ole and nor-eth-IN-drone)

Description

Estrogens (ES-troe-jenz) and progestins (pro-GEST-ins) are female hormones. They are produced by the body and are necessary for the normal sexual development of the female and for the regulation of the menstrual cycle during the childbearing years.

The ovaries begin to produce less estrogen after menopause (the change of life). This medicine is prescribed to make up for the lower amount of estrogen. Estrogens help relieve signs of menopause, such as hot flashes and unusual sweating, chills, faintness, or dizziness. Progestins help to regulate the effects of estrogens.

Estrogens are prescribed for several reasons:
- to provide additional hormone when the body does not produce enough of its own, such as during menopause. They can also help to relieve a genital skin condition called vaginal or vulvar atrophy.
- to help prevent weakening of bones (osteoporosis) in women past menopause.

Estrogens may also be used for other conditions as determined by your doctor.

There is *no* medical evidence to support the belief that the use of estrogens will keep the patient feeling young, keep the skin soft, or delay the appearance of wrinkles. Nor has it been proven that the use of estrogens during menopause will relieve emotional and nervous symptoms, unless these symptoms are caused by other menopausal symptoms, such as hot flashes or hot flushes.

Estrogens and progestins are available only with your doctor's prescription, in the following dosage forms:

Oral
17 beta-estradiol and norgestimate
- Tablets (U.S.)
Ethinyl estradiol and norethindrone
- Tablets (U.S.)
Estradiol and norethindrone
- Tablets (U.S.)

Before Using This Medicine

In deciding to use a medicine, the risks of taking the medicine must be weighed against the good it will do. This is a decision you and your doctor will make. For estrogens and progestins, the following should be considered:

Allergies—Tell your doctor if you have ever had any unusual or allergic reaction to estrogens or progestins. Also tell your health care professional if you are allergic to any other substances, such as foods, preservatives, or dyes

Pregnancy—Estrogens and progestins are not recommended for use during pregnancy or right after giving birth. Becoming pregnant or maintaining a pregnancy is not likely to occur around the time of menopause.

Breast-feeding—Estrogens and progestins pass into the breast milk and can change the content or lower the amount of breast milk. Use of this medicine is not recommended in nursing mothers.

Older adults—Many medicines have not been studied specifically in older people. Therefore, it may not be known whether they work exactly the same way they do in younger adults or if they cause different side effects or problems in older people. There is no specific information comparing use of estrogens and progestins in the elderly with use in other age groups.

Other medicines—Although certain medicines should not be used together at all, in other cases two different medicines may be used together even if an interaction might occur. In these cases, your doctor may want to change the dose, or other precautions may be necessary. When you are taking estrogens and progestins, it is especially important that your health care professional know if you are taking any of the following:
- Cyclosporine (e.g., Sandimmune)—Estrogens can prevent cyclosporine's removal from the body; this can lead to kidney or liver problems caused by too much cyclosporine

Other medical problems—The presence of other medical problems may affect the use of estrogens and progestins. Make sure you tell your doctor if you have any other medical problems, especially:
- Blood clotting problems (or history of during previous estrogen therapy)—Estrogens usually are not used until

blood clotting problems stop; using estrogens is not a problem for most patients without a history of blood clotting problems due to estrogen use

- Breast cancer or
- Bone cancer or
- Cancer of the uterus or
- Fibroid tumors of the uterus—Estrogens may interfere with the treatment of breast or bone cancer or worsen cancer of the uterus when these conditions are present

- Changes in genital or vaginal bleeding of unknown causes—Use of estrogens may delay diagnosis or worsen condition. The reason for the bleeding should be determined before estrogens are used

- Endometriosis or
- High cholesterol or triglycerides (or history of) or
- Pancreatitis (inflammation of pancreas)—Estrogens may worsen these conditions; while estrogens can improve blood cholesterol, they may worsen blood triglycerides for some people

Proper Use of This Medicine

Estrogens and progestins usually come with patient information or directions. Read them carefully before taking this medicine.

Take this medicine only as directed by your doctor. Do not take more of it and do not take or use it for a longer time than your doctor ordered. Try to take the medicine at the same time each day to reduce the possibility of side effects and to allow it to work better.

For patients taking estrogens and progestins by mouth:

- Nausea may occur during the first few weeks after you start taking estrogens. This effect usually disappears with continued use. If the nausea is bothersome, it can usually be prevented or reduced by taking each dose with food or immediately after food.

Dosing—The dose of these medicines will be different for different patients. *Follow your doctor's orders or the directions on the label.* The following information includes only the average doses of these medicines. *If your dose is different, do not change it* unless your doctor tells you to do so.

For 17 beta-estradiol and norgestimate
- For *oral* dosage forms (tablets)
  —For treating a genital skin condition (vaginal or vulvar atrophy), or vasomotor symptoms of menopause:
  - Adults—Oral, 1 mg estradiol for three days followed by 1 mg of estradiol combined with 0.09 mg of norgestimate for three days. The regimen is repeated continuously without interruption.
  —To prevent loss of bone (osteoporosis):
  - Adults—Oral, 1 mg estradiol for three days followed by 1mg of estradiol combined with 0.09 mg of norgestimate for three days. The regimen is repeated continuously without interruption.

For ethinyl estradiol and norethindrone
- For *oral* dosage forms (tablets)
  —For treating vasomotor symptoms of menopause:
  - Adults—Oral, 5 mcg (0.05 mg) ethinyl estradiol and 1 mg norethindrone once daily.
  —To prevent loss of bone (osteoporosis):
  - Adults—Oral, 5 mcg (0.05 mg) ethinyl estradiol and 1 mg norethindrone once daily.

For estradiol and norethindrone
- For *oral* dosage forms (tablets)
  —For treating vasomotor symptoms of menopause or treatment of vaginal or vulvar atrophy:
  - Adults—Oral, 1 mg estradiol and 0.5 mg norethindrone once daily.
  —To prevent loss of bone (osteoporosis):
  - Adults—Oral, 1 mg estradiol and 0.5 mg norethindrone once daily.

Missed dose—If you miss a dose of this medicine, take it as soon as possible. However, if it is almost time for your next dose, skip the missed dose and take only your next regularly scheduled dose. Do not double doses.

Storage—To store this medicine:
- Keep out of the reach of children.
- Store away from heat and direct light.
- Do not store in the bathroom medicine cabinet because the heat or moisture may cause the medicine to break down.
- Do not keep outdated medicine or medicine no longer needed. Be sure that any discarded medicine is out of the reach of children.

Precautions While Using This Medicine

It is very important that your doctor check your progress at regular visits to make sure this medicine does not cause unwanted effects. These visits will usually be every year, but some doctors require them more often.

It is not yet known whether the use of estrogens increases the risk of breast cancer in women. Therefore, it is very important that you regularly check your breasts for any unusual lumps or discharge. Report any problems to your doctor. You should also have a mammogram (x-ray pictures of the breasts) done if your doctor recommends it. Because breast cancer has occurred in men taking estrogens, regular breast self-exams and exams by your doctor for any unusual lumps or discharge should be done.

Tell the doctor in charge that you are taking this medicine before having any laboratory test because some results may be affected.

Side Effects of This Medicine

Women rarely have severe side effects from taking estrogens to replace estrogen. Discuss these possible effects with your doctor:

- The prolonged use of estrogens has been reported to increase the risk of endometrial cancer (cancer of the lining of the uterus) in women after menopause. This risk seems to increase as the dose and the length of use increase. When estrogens are used in low doses for less than 1 year, there is less risk. The risk is also reduced if a progestin (another female hormone) is added to, or replaces part of, your estrogen dose. If the uterus has been removed by surgery (total hysterectomy), there is no risk of endometrial cancer, and no need to take an estrogen and progestin combination.
- It is not yet known whether the use of estrogens increases the risk of breast cancer in women. Although some large studies show an increased risk, most studies and information gathered to date do not support this idea.

Check with your doctor as soon as possible if any of the following side effects occur:

More common

Breast pain or tenderness; dizziness or light-headedness; headache; swelling of feet and lower legs; rapid weight gain; vaginal bleeding

Rare

Breast lumps; change in vaginal discharge; discharge from nipple; nausea and vomiting; pains in stomach, side, or abdomen; pain or feeling of pressure in pelvis; yellow eyes or skin; severe or sudden headache; sudden loss of coordination; pains in chest, groin, or leg, especially calf; sudden and unexplained shortness of breath; sudden slurred speech; sudden vision changes; weakness or numbness in arm or leg

Other side effects may occur that usually do not need medical attention. These side effects may go away during treatment as your body adjusts to the medicine. However, check with your doctor if any of the following side effects continue or are bothersome:

More common

Back pain; dizziness; general feeling of tiredness; bloating or gas; flu-like symptoms; mental depression; muscle aches; nausea—taking tablet with food may decrease; vaginitis

Other side effects not listed above may also occur in some patients. If you notice any other effects, check with your doctor.

Developed: 04/10/2000
Revised: 08/08/2000

ESTROGENS AND PROGESTINS ORAL CONTRACEPTIVES   Systemic

Commonly used brand name(s):

In the U.S.—

Alesse[3]	Necon 1/35[5]
Brevicon[5]	Necon 1/50[6]
Demulen 1/35[2]	Necon 10/11[5]
Demulen 1/50[2]	N.E.E. 1/35[5]
Desogen[1]	N.E.E. 1/50[5]
Estrostep[4]	Nelova 0.5/35E[5]
Estrostep Fe[4]	Nelova 1/35E[5]
Genora 0.5/35[5]	Nelova 1/50M[6]
Genora 1/35[5]	Nelova 10/11[5]
Genora 1/50[6]	Nordette[3]
Intercon 0.5/35[5]	Norethin 1/35E[5]
Intercon 1/35[5]	Norethin 1/50M[6]
Intercon 1/50[6]	Norinyl 1+35[5]
Jenest[5]	Norinyl 1+50[5]
Levlen[3]	Ortho-Cept[1]
Levlite[3]	Ortho-Cyclen[7]
Levora 0.15/30[3]	Ortho-Novum 1/35[5]
Loestrin 1/20[4]	Ortho-Novum 1/50[6]
Loestrin Fe 1/20[4]	Ortho-Novum 7/7/7[5]
Loestrin 1.5/30[4]	Ortho-Novum 10/11[5]
Loestrin Fe 1.5/30[4]	Ortho Tri-Cyclen[7]
Lo/Ovral[8]	Ovcon-35[5]
Mircette[1]	Ovcon-50[5]
ModiCon[5]	Ovral[8]
Necon 0.5/35[5]	Tri-Levlen[3]

Tri-Norinyl[5]	Zovia 1/35E[2]
Triphasil[3]	Zovia 1/50E[2]
Trivora[3]	

In Canada—

Brevicon 0.5/35[5]	Ortho 1/35[5]
Brevicon 1/35[5]	Ortho 7/7/7[5]
Cyclen[7]	Ortho 10/11[5]
Demulen 30[2]	Ortho-Cept[1]
Demulen 50[2]	Ortho-Novum 1/50[6]
Loestrin 1.5/30[4]	Ovral[8]
Marvelon[1]	Select 1/35[5]
Minestrin 1/20[4]	Synphasic[5]
Min-Ovral[3]	Tri-Cyclen[7]
Norinyl 1/50[6]	Triphasil[3]
Ortho 0.5/35[5]	Triquilar[3]

Other commonly used names are:

Ethinylestradiol [Ethinyl estradiol]
Ethinyloestradiol [Ethinyl estradiol]
Ethynodiol [Ethynodiol diacetate]
Etynodiol [Ethynodiol diacetate]
Etynodiol acetate [Ethynodiol diacetate]
Norethindrone [Norethisterone]

Note: For quick reference, the following estrogens and progestins are numbered to match the corresponding brand names.

This information applies to the following medicines

1. Desogestrel and Ethinyl Estradiol (des-oh-JES-trel and ETH-in-il es-tra-DYE-ole)
2. Ethynodiol Diacetate and Ethinyl Estradiol (e-thye-noe-DYE-ole dye-AS-e-tate and ETH-in-il es-tra-DYE-ole)
3. Levonorgestrel and Ethinyl Estradiol (LEE-voh-nor-jes-trel and ETH-in-il es-tra-DYE-ole)
4. Norethindrone Acetate and Ethinyl Estradiol (nor-eth-IN-drone AS-e-tate and ETH-in-il es-tra-DYE-ole)
5. Norethindrone and Ethinyl Estradiol (nor-eth-IN-drone and ETH-in-il es-tra-DYE-ole)
6. Norethindrone and Mestranol (nor-eth-IN-drone and MES-tra-nole)
7. Norgestimate and Ethinyl Estradiol (nor-JES-ti-mate and ETH-in-il es-tra-DYE-ole)
8. Norgestrel and Ethinyl Estradiol (nor-JES-trel and ETH-in-il es-tra-DYE-ole)

For information about norethindrone (e.g., Micronor) or norgestrel (e.g., Ovrette) when used as single-ingredient oral contraceptives, see Progestins—For Contraceptive Use (Systemic).

Description

Oral contraceptives are known also as the Pill, OCs, BCs, BC tablets, or birth control pills. This medicine usually contains two types of hormones, estrogens (ES-troh-jenz) and progestins (proh-JES-tins) and, when taken properly, prevents pregnancy. It works by stopping a woman's egg from fully developing each month. The egg can no longer accept a sperm and fertilization is prevented. Although oral contraceptives have other effects that help prevent a pregnancy from occurring, this is the main action.

Sometimes a woman's egg can still develop even though the medication is taken once each day, especially when more than 24 hours pass between two doses. In almost all cases when the medicine was taken properly and an egg develops, fertilization can still be stopped by oral contraceptives. This is because oral contraceptives also thicken cervical mucus at the opening of the uterus. This makes it hard for the partner's sperm to reach the egg. In addition, oral contraceptives change the uterus lining just enough so that an egg will not stop in the uterus to develop. All of these effects make it difficult to become pregnant when properly taking an oral contraceptive.

No contraceptive method is 100 percent effective. *Studies show that fewer than one of each one hundred women correctly using oral contraceptives becomes pregnant during the first year of use.* Birth control methods such as having surgery to become sterile or not having sex are more effective. Using condoms, diaphragms, progestin-only oral contraceptives, or spermicides is not as effective as using oral contraceptives containing estrogens and progestins. Discuss with your health care professional your options for birth control.

The triphasic cycle product of norgestimate and ethinyl estradiol (the brand name *Ortho Tri-Cyclen*) can improve acne in females who also need contraception.

Sometimes these preparations can be used for other conditions as determined by your doctor.

Oral contraceptives are available only with your doctor's prescription, in the following dosage forms:

Oral
Desogestrel and Ethinyl Estradiol
  • Tablets (U.S. and Canada)
Ethynodiol Diacetate and Ethinyl Estradiol
  • Tablets (U.S. and Canada)
Levonorgestrel and Ethinyl Estradiol
  • Tablets (U.S. and Canada)
Norethindrone Acetate and Ethinyl Estradiol
  • Tablets (U.S. and Canada)
Norethindrone and Ethinyl Estradiol
  • Tablets (U.S. and Canada)
Norethindrone and Mestranol
  • Tablets (U.S. and Canada)
Norgestimate and Ethinyl Estradiol
  • Tablets (U.S. and Canada)
Norgestrel and Ethinyl Estradiol
  • Tablets (U.S. and Canada)

Before Using This Medicine

In deciding to use a medicine, the risks of taking the medicine must be weighed against the good it will do. If you are using oral contraceptives for contraception you should understand how their benefits and risks compare to those of other birth control methods. This is a decision you, your sexual partner, and your doctor will make. For oral contraceptives, the following should be considered:

Allergies—Tell your doctor if you have ever had any unusual or allergic reaction to estrogens or progestins. Also tell your health care professional if you are allergic to any other substances, such as foods, preservatives, or dyes.

Diet—Make certain your health care professional knows if you are on any special diet, such as a low-sodium or low-sugar diet.

Pregnancy—Oral contraceptives are not recommended for use during pregnancy and should be discontinued if you become pregnant or think you are pregnant. In rare cases when oral contraceptives have been taken early in a pregnancy, problems in the fetus have not occurred. Women who are not breast-feeding may begin to take oral contraceptives two weeks after having a baby.

Breast-feeding—Oral contraceptives pass into the breast milk and can change the content or lower the amount of breast milk. Also, they may shorten a woman's ability to breast-feed by about 1 month, especially when the mother is only partially breast-feeding. Because the amount of hormones is so small in low-dose contraceptives, your doctor may allow you to begin using an oral contraceptive after you have been breast-feeding for a while. However, it may be necessary for you to use another method of birth control or to stop breast-feeding while taking oral contraceptives.

Teenagers—This medicine is frequently used for birth control in teenage females and has not been shown to cause different side effects or problems than it does in adults. Some teenagers may need extra information on the importance of taking this medication exactly as prescribed.

Other medicines—Although certain medicines should not be used together at all, in other cases two different medicines may be used together even if an interaction might occur. In these cases, your doctor may want to change the dose, or other precautions may be necessary. When you are taking oral contraceptives, it is especially important that your health care professional know if you are taking any of the following:

  • Amiodarone (e.g., Cordarone) or
  • Anabolic steroids (nandrolone [e.g., Anabolin], oxandrolone [e.g., Anavar], oxymetholone [e.g., Anadrol], stanozolol [e.g., Winstrol]) or
  • Androgens (male hormones) or
  • Anti-infectives by mouth or by injection (medicine for infection) or
  • Barbiturates or
  • Carbamazepine (e.g., Tegretol) or
  • Carmustine (e.g., BiCNU) or
  • Dantrolene (e.g., Dantrium) or
  • Daunorubicin (e.g., Cerubidine) or
  • Disulfiram (e.g., Antabuse) or
  • Divalproex (e.g., Depakote) or
  • Estrogens (female hormones) or
  • Etretinate (e.g., Tegison) or
  • Gold salts (medicine for arthritis) or
  • Griseofulvin (e.g., Fulvicin) or
  • Hydroxychloroquine (e.g., Plaquenil) or
  • Mercaptopurine (e.g., Purinethol) or
  • Methotrexate (e.g., Mexate) or
  • Methyldopa (e.g., Aldomet) or
  • Naltrexone (e.g., Trexan) (with long-term, high-dose use) or
  • Phenothiazines (acetophenazine [e.g., Tindal], chlorpromazine [e.g., Thorazine], fluphenazine [e.g., Prolixin], mesoridazine [e.g., Serentil], perphenazine [e.g., Trilafon], prochlorperazine [e.g., Compazine], promazine [e.g., Sparine], promethazine [e.g., Phenergan], thioridazine [e.g., Mellaril], trifluoperazine [e.g., Stelazine], triflupromazine [e.g., Vesprin], trimeprazine [e.g., Temaril]) or
  • Phenylbutazone (e.g., Butazolidin) or
  • Phenytoin (e.g., Dilantin) or
  • Plicamycin (e.g., Mithracin) or
  • Primidone (e.g., Mysoline) or
  • Rifabutin (e.g., Mycobutin) or
  • Rifampin (e.g., Rifadin) or
  • Troleandomycin (e.g., TAO)—These medicines may increase the chance of liver problems if taken with oral contraceptives; also, these medicines may decrease the effect of oral contraceptives and increase your chance of pregnancy. Use of an additional form of birth control is recommended unless directed otherwise by your health care professional

- Corticosteroids (cortisone-like medicine) or
- Theophylline—Oral contraceptives may increase the effects of these medicines and increase the chance of problems occurring
- Cyclosporine—Oral contraceptives increase the effect of cyclosporine and increase the chance of problems occurring
- Ritonavir (e.g., Norvir) or
- Troglitazone (e.g., Rezulin)—These medicines may decrease the effect of oral contraceptives and increase your chance of pregnancy. Use of an additional form of birth control is recommended unless directed otherwise by your health care professional
- Smoking, tobacco—Smoking may decrease the effect of oral contraceptives and increase the chance of causing serious blood clot, vein, or heart problems

Other medical problems—The presence of other medical problems may affect the use of oral contraceptives. Make sure you tell your doctor if you have any other medical problems, especially:

- Abnormal changes in menstrual or uterine bleeding or
- Endometriosis or
- Fibroid tumors of the uterus—Oral contraceptives usually improve these female conditions but sometimes they can make them worse or make the diagnosis of these problems more difficult
- Blood clots (or history of) or
- Heart or circulation disease or
- Stroke (or history of)—If these conditions are already present, oral contraceptives may have a greater chance of causing blood clots or circulation problems, especially in women who smoke tobacco. Otherwise, oral contraceptives may help prevent circulation and heart disease if you are healthy and do not smoke
- Breast disease (not involving cancer)—Oral contraceptives usually protect against certain breast diseases, such as breast cysts or breast lumps; however, your doctor may want to follow your condition more closely
- Cancer, including breast cancer (or history of or family history of)—Oral contraceptives may worsen some cancers, especially when breast, cervical, or uterine cancers already exist. Use of oral contraceptives is not recommended if you have any of these conditions. If you have a family history of breast disease, oral contraceptives may still be a good choice but you may need to be tested more often
- Chorea gravidarum or
- Gallbladder disease or gallstones (or history of) or
- High blood cholesterol or
- Liver disease (or history of, including jaundice during pregnancy) or
- Mental depression (or history of)—Oral contraceptives may make these conditions worse or, rarely, cause them to occur again. Oral contraceptives may still be a good choice but you may need to be tested more often
- Diabetes mellitus (sugar diabetes)—Use of oral contraceptives may cause an increase, usually only a small increase, in your blood sugar and usually does not affect the amount of diabetes medicine that you take. You or your doctor will want to test for any changes in your blood sugar for 12 to 24 months after starting to take oral

contraceptives in case the dose of your diabetes medicine needs to be changed
- Epilepsy (seizures) (or history of) or
- Heart or circulation problems or
- High blood pressure (hypertension) or
- Migraine headaches—Oral contraceptives may cause fluid build-up and may cause these conditions to become worse; however, some people have fewer migraine headaches when they use oral contraceptives

Proper Use of This Medicine

To make using oral contraceptives as safe and reliable as possible, you should understand how and when to take them and what effects may be expected.

A paper with information for the patient will be given to you with your filled prescription, and will provide many details concerning the use of oral contraceptives. Read this paper carefully and ask your health care professional if you need additional information or explanation.

Take this medicine with food to help prevent nausea that might occur during the first few weeks. Nausea usually disappears with continued use or if the medicine is taken at bedtime.

When you begin to use oral contraceptives, your body will require at least 7 days to adjust before a pregnancy will be prevented. You will need to use an additional birth control method for at least 7 days. Some doctors recommend using an additional method of birth control for the first cycle (or 3 weeks) to ensure full protection. Follow the advice of your doctor or other health care professional.

Try to take the doses no more than 24 hours apart to reduce the possibility of side effects and to prevent pregnancy. Since one of the most important factors in the proper use of oral contraceptives is taking every dose exactly on schedule, you should never let your tablet supply run out. When possible, try to keep an extra month's supply of tablets on hand and replace it monthly.

It is very important that you keep the tablets in their original container and take the tablets in the same order that they appear in the container. The containers help you keep track of which tablets to take next. Different colored tablets in the same package contain different amounts of hormones or are placebos (tablets that do not contain hormones). *The effectiveness of the medicine is reduced if the tablets are taken out of order.*

- *Monophasic (one-phase) cycle* dosing schedule: Most available dosing schedules are monophasic. If you are taking tablets of one strength (color) for 21 days, you are using a monophasic schedule. For the 28-day monophasic cycle you will also take an additional 7 inactive tablets, which are another color. If you are taking the brand name *Mircette*, the last seven tablets of the 28-day cycle contains two inactive tablets (for Days 22 and 23) and five tablets (for Days 24 through 28) that contain a low dose of estrogen. Taking the last 7 tablets is not required for full protection against pregnancy but they do help to replace estrogen.
- *Biphasic (two-phase) cycle* dosing schedule: If you are using a biphasic twenty-one–day schedule, you are taking tablets of one strength (color) for either seven or ten days, depending on the medication prescribed (the first phase). You then take tablets of a second strength

(color) for the next eleven or fourteen days, depending on the medication prescribed (the second phase). At this point, you will have taken a total of twenty-one tablets. For the twenty-eight-day biphasic cycle you will also take an additional seven inactive tablets, which are a third color.

- *Triphasic (three-phase) cycle* dosing schedule: If you are using a triphasic twenty-one-day schedule, you are taking tablets of one strength (color) for five, six or seven days, depending on the medicine prescribed (the first phase). You then take tablets of a second strength (color) for the next five, seven, or nine days, depending on the medicine prescribed (the second phase). After that, you take tablets of a third strength (color) for the next five, seven, nine, or ten days, depending on the medicine prescribed (the third phase). At this point, you will have taken a total of twenty-one tablets. For the twenty-eight-day triphasic cycle you will also take an additional seven inactive tablets, which are a fourth color.

If you are taking one of the brand name products *Estrostep Fe* or *Loestrin Fe* each of the last seven tablets that you will take on Days 21 through 28 of your cycle contains iron. These tablets are also a different color from the other tablets in your package. They help to replace some of the iron you lose when you have a menstrual period.

Dosing—Your health care professional may begin your dose on the first day of your menstrual period (called Day-1 start) or on Sunday (called Sunday start). *When you begin on a certain day it is important that you follow that schedule, even when you miss a dose. Do not change your schedule on your own.* If the schedule that you have been put on is not convenient, check with your health care professional about changing schedules.

- For *oral* dosage forms (monophasic, biphasic, or triphasic tablets):
  —For contraception:
    - Adults and teenagers:
      —For the twenty-one-day cycle: Take 1 tablet a day for twenty-one days. Skip seven days. Then repeat the cycle.
      —For the twenty-eight-day cycle: Take 1 tablet a day for twenty-eight days. Then repeat the cycle.

- For *oral* dosage forms (norgestimate and ethinyl estradiol triphasic tablets):
  —To treat acne:
    - Adults and teenagers 15 years of age and over:
      —For the twenty-one-day cycle: Take 1 tablet a day for twenty-one days. Skip seven days. Then repeat the cycle.
      —For the twenty-eight-day cycle: Take 1 tablet a day for twenty-eight days. Then repeat the cycle.
    - Teenagers up to 15 years of age—Use and dose must be determined by your doctor.

Missed dose—*Follow your doctor's orders or the directions on the label* if you miss a dose of this medicine. The following information includes only some of the ways to handle missed doses. Your health care professional may want you to stop taking the medicine and use other birth control methods for the rest of the month until you have your menstrual period. Then your health care professional can tell you how to begin taking your medicine again.

For monophasic, biphasic, or triphasic cycles:
- If you miss the first tablet of a new cycle—Take the missed tablet as soon as you remember and take the next tablet at the usual time. You may take 2 tablets in one day. Then continue your regular dosing schedule. Also, use another birth control method until you have taken seven days of your tablets after the last missed dose.
- If you miss 1 tablet during the cycle—Take the missed tablet as soon as you remember. Take the next tablet at the usual time. You may take 2 tablets in one day. Then continue your regular dosing schedule.
- If you miss 2 tablets in a row in the first or second week—Take 2 tablets on the day that you remember and 2 tablets the next day. Then continue taking 1 tablet a day. Also use another birth control method until you begin a new cycle.
- If you miss 2 tablets in a row in the third week; or
- If you miss 3 or more tablets in a row at any time during the cycle—
  Using a Day-1 start: Throw out your current cycle and begin taking a new cycle. Also, use another birth control method until you have taken seven days of your tablets after the last missed dose. You may not have a menstrual period this month. But if you miss two menstrual periods in a row, call your health care professional.
  Using a Sunday start: Keep taking one tablet a day from your current pack until Sunday. Then, on Sunday, throw out your old pack and begin a new pack. Also use another birth control method until you have taken seven days of your tablets after the last missed dose. You may not have a menstrual period this month. But if you miss two menstrual periods in a row, call your health care professional.

If you miss any of the last seven (inactive) tablets of a twenty-eight–day cycle, there is no danger of pregnancy. However, the first tablet (active) of the next month's cycle must be taken on the regularly scheduled day, in spite of any missed doses, if pregnancy is to be avoided. The active and inactive tablets are colored differently for your convenience.

Storage—To store this medicine:
- Keep out of the reach of children.
- Store away from heat and direct light.
- Do not store in the bathroom, near the kitchen sink, or in other damp places. Heat and moisture may cause the medicine to break down.
- Do not keep outdated medicine or medicine no longer needed. Be sure that any discarded medicine is out of the reach of children.

Precautions While Using This Medicine

It is very important that your doctor check your progress at regular visits to make sure this medicine does not cause unwanted effects. These visits will usually be every 6 to 12 months, but some doctors require them more often.

Tell the medical doctor or dentist in charge that you are taking this medicine before any kind of surgery (including dental surgery) or emergency treatment. Your doctor will decide whether you should continue taking this medicine.

The following medicines may reduce the effectiveness of oral contraceptives. *You should use an additional method of birth control during each cycle in which any of the following medicines are used:*

> Ampicillin
> Barbiturates
> Carbamazepine (e.g., Tegretol)
> Griseofulvin (e.g., Fulvicin)
> Penicillin V
> Phenytoin (e.g., Dilantin)
> Primidone (e.g., Mysoline)
> Rifampin (e.g., Rifadin)
> Ritonavir (e.g., Norvir)
> Tetracyclines (medicine for infection)
> Troglitazone (e.g., Rezulin)

Check with your doctor if you have any questions about this.

Vaginal bleeding of various amounts may occur between your regular menstrual periods during the first 3 months of use. This is sometimes called spotting when slight, or breakthrough bleeding when heavier. If this should occur:

- Continue on your regular dosing schedule.
- The bleeding usually stops within 1 week.
- Check with your doctor if the bleeding continues for more than 1 week.
- After you have been taking oral contraceptives on schedule and for more than 3 months and bleeding continues, check with your doctor.

Missed menstrual periods may occur:

- If you have not taken the medicine exactly as scheduled. Pregnancy must be considered as a possibility.
- If the medicine is not the right strength or type for your needs.
- If you stop taking oral contraceptives, especially if you have taken oral contraceptives for 2 or more years.

Check with your doctor if you miss any menstrual periods so that the cause may be determined.

In some patients using estrogen-containing oral contraceptives, tenderness, swelling, or bleeding of the gums may occur. Brushing and flossing your teeth carefully and regularly and massaging your gums may help prevent this. See your dentist regularly to have your teeth cleaned. Check with your medical doctor or dentist if you have any questions about how to take care of your teeth and gums, or if you notice any tenderness, swelling, or bleeding of your gums. Also, it has been shown that estrogen-containing oral contraceptives may cause a healing problem called dry socket after a tooth has been removed. If you are going to have a tooth removed, tell your dentist or oral surgeon that you are taking oral contraceptives.

Some people who take oral contraceptives may become more sensitive to sunlight than they are normally. When you begin taking this medicine, avoid too much sun and do not use a sunlamp until you see how you react to the sun, especially if you tend to burn easily. If you have a severe reaction, check with your doctor. Some people may develop brown, blotchy spots on exposed areas. These spots usually disappear gradually when the medicine is stopped.

If you suspect that you may have become pregnant, stop taking this medicine immediately and check with your doctor.

If you are scheduled for any laboratory tests, tell your doctor that you are taking birth control pills.

Check with your doctor before refilling an old prescription, especially after a pregnancy. You will need another physical examination and your doctor may change your prescription.

Side Effects of This Medicine

Healthy women who do not smoke cigarettes have almost no chance of having a severe side effect from taking oral contraceptives. For most women, more problems occur because of pregnancy than will occur from taking oral contraceptives. But for some women who have special health problems, oral contraceptives can cause some unwanted effects. Some of these unwanted effects include benign (not cancerous) liver tumors, liver cancer, or blood clots or related problems, such as a stroke. Although these effects are very rare, they can be serious enough to cause death. You may want to discuss these effects with your doctor.

Smoking cigarettes during the use of oral contraceptives has been found to greatly increase the chances of these serious side effects occurring. *To reduce the risk of serious side effects, do not smoke cigarettes while you are taking oral contraceptives.*

The following side effects may be caused by blood clots. *Get emergency help immediately* if any of the following side effects occur:

Rare
> Abdominal or stomach pain (sudden, severe, or continuing); coughing up blood; headache (severe or sudden); loss of coordination (sudden); loss of vision or change in vision (sudden); pains in chest, groin, or leg (especially in calf of leg); shortness of breath (sudden or unexplained); slurring of speech (sudden); weakness, numbness, or pain in arm or leg (unexplained)

Check with your doctor as soon as possible if any of the following side effects occur:

More common—usually less common after the first 3 months of oral contraceptive use
> Changes in the uterine bleeding pattern at menses or between menses, such as decreased bleeding at menses, breakthrough bleeding or spotting between periods, prolonged bleeding at menses, complete stopping of menstrual bleeding that occurs over several months in a row, or stopping of menstrual bleeding that only occurs sometimes

Less common
> Headaches or migraines (although headaches may lessen in many users, in others, they may increase in number or become worse); increased blood pressure; vaginal infection with vaginal itching or irritation, or thick, white, or curd-like discharge

For women with diabetes mellitus
> Mild increase of blood sugar—Faintness, nausea, pale skin, or sweating

Rare
> Mental depression; swelling, pain, or tenderness in upper abdominal area

For women who smoke tobacco
> Pains in stomach, side, or abdomen; yellow eyes or skin

For women with a history of breast disease
> Lumps in breast

Other side effects may occur that usually do not need medical attention. These side effects may go away during treatment as your body adjusts to the medicine. However, check with your doctor if any of the following side effects continue or are bothersome:

More common

Abdominal cramping or bloating; acne (usually less common after first 3 months and may improve if acne already exists); breast pain, tenderness, or swelling; dizziness; nausea; swelling of ankles and feet; unusual tiredness or weakness; vomiting

Less common

Brown, blotchy spots on exposed skin; gain or loss of body or facial hair; increased or decreased interest in sexual intercourse; increased sensitivity of skin to sunlight; weight gain or loss

Other side effects not listed above may also occur in some patients. If you notice any other effects, check with your doctor.

Additional Information

Once a medicine has been approved for marketing for a certain use, experience may show that it is also useful for other medical problems. Although these uses are not included in product labeling, oral contraceptives are used in certain patients with the following medical conditions:

- Amenorrhea (stopping of menses for several consecutive months)
- Dysfunctional uterine bleeding (abnormal uterine bleeding)
- Dysmenorrhea (painful menstrual bleeding)
- Hypermenorrhea (excessive menstrual bleeding)
- Emergency contraception within 72 hours of unprotected intercourse
- Endometriosis (painful bleeding from uterine-like tissue that can grow in different parts of the female body)
- Hirsutism in females (male-like hair growth)
- Hyperandrogenism, ovarian (excessive production of male hormones)
- Polycystic ovary syndrome (many problems that include amenorrhea, hirsutism, infertility, and many tiny cysts or sacs usually in both ovaries)

For patients taking this medicine for *emergency contraception:*

- Must be taken with food within 72 hours of unprotected sexual intercourse. One single course (2 doses 12 hours apart) is a one-time emergency protection. Using more than one course in a month will reduce the effectiveness.
- Because the hormones are strong, watch for danger signs. Call your doctor if you experience any severe pains in your leg, stomach, or chest; any vision or breathing changes; yellowing of skin; headaches; numbness; or trouble in speaking.
- You may experience nausea so take it with food and call your doctor if you vomit the medicine.
- Your menstrual period may start earlier than usual. If it doesn't start, call your doctor.

For patients taking this medicine for *hirsutism:*

- You may need to use oral contraceptives for 6 to 12 months before you see less new hair growth.

For patients taking this medicine for *endometriosis:*

- Sometimes instead of following the directions on the oral contraceptive's package, your doctor may ask you to follow different directions, such as taking the active tablets in the package each day without stopping for 6 to 9 months. This means that after 21 days you will start a new package of pills. If you are not sure about how to take this medicine, discuss any questions with your health care professional.
- Also, your symptoms of endometriosis may worsen at first but with continued use of the oral contraceptives your symptoms should lessen and your condition improve.

Other than the above information, there is no additional information relating to proper use, precautions, or side effects for these uses.

Revised: 07/29/98

ETANERCEPT   Systemic

Commonly used brand name(s):

In the U.S.—
Enbrel

Description

Etanercept (ee-tan-NER-cept) is injected under the skin to reduce signs and symptoms of rheumatoid arthritis, such as joint swelling, pain, tiredness, and duration of morning stiffness.

This medicine is available only with your doctor's prescription, in the following dosage form(s):

Parenteral
- Injection (U.S.)

Before Using This Medicine

In deciding to use a medicine, the risks of using the medicine must be weighed against the good it will do. This is a decision you and your doctor will make. For etanercept, the following should be considered:

Allergies—Tell your doctor if you have ever had any unusual or allergic reaction to etanercept or any of its components. Also tell your health care professional if you are allergic to any other substances, such as foods, preservatives, or dyes.

The needle cover on the pre-filled diluent syringe is made from latex (rubber product). If you are allergic to latex (rubber products), talk to your doctor before using.

Pregnancy—Etanercept has not been studied in pregnant women. Etanercept has not been shown to cause birth defects or other problems in animal studies.

Breast-feeding—It is not known whether etanercept passes into breast milk. However, etanercept may possibly cause serious side effects in nursing infants. Mothers who are using this medicine and who wish to breast-feed should discuss this with their doctor.

Children—Etanercept has been tested in children 4 to 17 years of age. Studies indicate that etanercept may reduce signs and symptoms in patients with juvenile rheumatoid arthritis. Stomach pain and vomiting were seen more often in children than in adults.

Older adults—Etanercept has been tested in elderly patients and has not been found to cause different side effects or problems in older people than it does in younger adults.

Other medicines—Tell your health care professional if you are using *any* other prescription, nonprescription (over-the-counter [OTC]) medicine, or vaccinations.

Other medical problems—The presence of other medical problems may affect the use of etanercept. Make sure you tell your doctor if you have any other medical problems, especially:

- Diseases of the central nervous system, such as multiple sclerosis—Etanercept may make these diseases worse in susceptible patients
- Cancer (or history of) or
- Diabetes mellitus (sugar diabetes) or
- Disease of the immune system (or history of) or
- Infections—Etanercept may decrease the body's ability to fight infection
- Blood disorders—Etanercept may make these diseases worse or cause them to appear in susceptible patients

Proper Use of This Medicine

If you are injecting this medicine yourself, each package of etanercept will contain a patient instruction sheet. Read this sheet carefully and make sure you understand:

- How to prepare the injection
- How to give the injection
- Proper use and disposal of syringes
- How long the injection is stable
- How to store the medication

Dosing—The dose of etanercept may be different for different patients. Your doctor will decide on the right dose for you.

- For *injection* dosage form:
  —For the reduction of signs and symptoms of rheumatoid arthritis:
    - Adults—25 mg injected under the skin twice a week.
    - Children 4 to 17 years of age—0.4 milligrams (mg) per kg (0.88 mg per pound) of body weight, injected under the skin twice a week.
    - Children under 4 years of age—Use and dose must be determined by your doctor.

Missed dose—If you miss a dose of this medicine, use it as soon as possible. However, if it is almost time for your next dose, skip the missed dose and go back to your regular dosing schedule. Do not double doses.

Storage—To store this medicine:

- Keep out of the reach of children.
- Store in the refrigerator. However, keep the medicine from freezing.
- Do not keep outdated medicine or medicine no longer needed. Be sure that any discarded medicine is out of the reach of children.

Precautions While Using This Medicine

It is important that your doctor check your progress at regular visits to make sure that this medicine is working properly and to check for unwanted effects.

Your body's ability to fight infection may be reduced while you are being treated with etanercept, *it is very important that you call your doctor at the first signs of any infection* (for example, if you get a fever or chills).

While you are being treated with etanercept, *do not have any immunizations (vaccinations) without your doctor's approval.*

Side Effects of This Medicine

Along with its needed effects, a medicine may cause some unwanted effects. Although not all of these side effects may occur, if they do occur they may need medical attention.

Check with your doctor as soon as possible if any of the following side effects occur:

More common
Chills; cough; fever; skin rash on face, scalp, or stomach; sneezing

Less common
Congestion in chest; dizziness; fainting; fast heartbeat; frequent or painful urination; headache; itching, pain, redness, or swelling on the skin; joint or muscle pain; joint or muscle stiffness, tightness, or rigidity; light-headedness; nausea and/or vomiting; stomach discomfort and/or pain; wheezing

Rare
Black, tarry stools; headache; nosebleeds; pale skin; shortness of breath; sores, ulcers, or white spots on lips or in mouth; swollen or painful glands; tightness in chest; unusual tiredness or weakness; unusual bleeding or bruising; wheezing

Other side effects may occur that usually do not need medical attention. These side effects may go away during treatment as your body adjusts to the medicine. However, check with your doctor if any of the following side effects continue or are bothersome:

More common
Abdominal pain—more common in children; nausea and vomiting—more common in children; pain or burning in throat; redness and/or itching, pain, or swelling at the site of injection (under the skin); runny or stuffy nose

Less common
Depression; diarrhea; heartburn; loss of energy or weakness

Other side effects not listed above also may occur in some patients. If you notice any other effects, check with your doctor.

Developed: 06/03/1999
Revised: 11/01/2000

ETHAMBUTOL   Systemic

Commonly used brand name(s):

In the U.S.—
Myambutol

In Canada—
Etibi
Myambutol

Description

Ethambutol (e-THAM-byoo-tole) is used to treat tuberculosis (TB). It is used with other medicines for TB. This medicine may also be used for other problems as determined by your doctor.

To help clear up your tuberculosis (TB) infection completely, you must keep taking this medicine for the full time of treatment, even if you begin to feel better. This is very important. It is also important that you do not miss any doses.

Ethambutol is available only with your doctor's prescription, in the following dosage form:

> *Oral*
> • Tablets (U.S. and Canada)

Before Using This Medicine

In deciding to use a medicine, the risks of taking the medicine must be weighed against the good it will do. This is a decision you and your doctor will make. For ethambutol, the following should be considered:

Allergies—Tell your doctor if you have ever had any unusual or allergic reaction to ethambutol. Also tell your health care professional if you are allergic to any other substances, such as foods, preservatives, or dyes.

Pregnancy—Pregnant women with tuberculosis (TB) should be treated with TB medicines, including ethambutol. Ethambutol has not been shown to cause birth defects or other problems in humans. However, studies in animals have shown that ethambutol causes cleft palate, skull and spine defects, absence of one eye, and hare lip.

Breast-feeding—Ethambutol passes into breast milk. However, ethambutol has not been shown to cause problems in nursing babies.

Children—This medicine has been tested in children 13 years of age or older and has not been shown to cause different side effects or problems than it does in adults. Ethambutol may be used for children with TB when other medicines cannot be used. However, ethambutol is usually not used in children up to 6 years of age because it may be hard to tell if they are having side effects affecting their eyes.

Older adults—Many medicines have not been studied specifically in older people. Therefore, it may not be known whether they work exactly the same way they do in younger adults. Although there is no specific information comparing use of ethambutol in the elderly with its use in other age groups, this medicine is not expected to cause different side effects or problems in older people than it does in younger adults.

Other medicines—Although certain medicines should not be used together at all, in other cases two different medicines may be used together even if an interaction might occur. In these cases, your doctor may want to change the dose, or other precautions may be necessary. Tell your health care professional if you are taking any other prescription or nonprescription (over-the-counter [OTC]) medicine.

Other medical problems—The presence of other medical problems may affect the use of ethambutol. Make sure you tell your doctor if you have any other medical problems, especially:

> • Gouty arthritis—Ethambutol may cause or worsen attacks of gout

> • Kidney disease—Patients with kidney disease may be more likely to have side effects

> • Optic neuritis (eye nerve damage)—Ethambutol may cause or worsen eye disease

Proper Use of This Medicine

Ethambutol may be taken with food if this medicine upsets your stomach.

To help clear up your tuberculosis (TB) completely, *it is very important that you keep taking this medicine for the full time of treatment*, even if you begin to feel better after a few weeks. You may have to take it every day for as long as 1 to 2 years or more. *It is important that you do not miss any doses.*

Dosing—The dose of ethambutol will be different for different patients. *Follow your doctor's orders or the directions on the label.* The following information includes only the average doses of ethambutol. *If your dose is different, do not change it* unless your doctor tells you to do so.

The number of tablets that you take depends on the strength of the medicine.

> • For *oral* dosage form (tablets):
>> —For the treatment of tuberculosis (TB):
>>> • Adults and children 13 years of age and older—15 to 25 milligrams (mg) per kilogram (kg) (6.8 to 11.4 mg per pound) of body weight once a day. Instead, your doctor may tell you to take 50 mg per kg (22.8 mg per pound) of body weight, up to a total of 2.5 grams, two times a week. Another dose that your doctor may tell you to take is 25 to 30 mg per kg (11.4 to 13.6 mg per pound) of body weight, up to a total of 2.5 grams, three times a week. Ethambutol must be taken with other medicines to treat tuberculosis.
>>> • Infants and children up to 13 years of age—Use and dose must be determined by your doctor.

Missed dose—If you miss a dose of this medicine, take it as soon as possible. However, if it is almost time for your next dose, skip the missed dose and go back to your regular dosing schedule. Do not double doses.

Storage—To store this medicine:
> • Keep out of the reach of children.
> • Store away from heat and direct light.
> • Do not store in the bathroom, near the kitchen sink, or in other damp places. Heat or moisture may cause the medicine to break down.
> • Do not keep outdated medicine or medicine no longer needed. Be sure that any discarded medicine is out of the reach of children.

Precautions While Using This Medicine

If your symptoms do not improve within 2 to 3 weeks, or if they become worse, check with your doctor.

It is very important that your doctor check your progress at regular visits.

Check with your doctor immediately if blurred vision, eye pain, red-green color blindness, or loss of vision occurs during treatment. Your doctor may want you to have your eyes checked by an ophthalmologist (eye doctor). *Also, make sure you know how you react to this medicine be-*

fore you drive, use machines, or do anything else that could be dangerous if you are not alert or able to see well.

Side Effects of This Medicine

Along with its needed effects, a medicine may cause some unwanted effects. Although not all of these side effects may occur, if they do occur they may need medical attention.

Check with your doctor immediately if any of the following side effects occur:

Less common
Chills; pain and swelling of joints, especially big toe, ankle, or knee; tense, hot skin over affected joints

Rare
Blurred vision, eye pain, red-green color blindness, or any loss of vision (more common with high doses); fever; joint pain; numbness, tingling, burning pain, or weakness in hands or feet; skin rash

Other side effects may occur that usually do not need medical attention. These side effects may go away during treatment as your body adjusts to the medicine. However, check with your doctor if any of the following side effects continue or are bothersome:

Less common
Abdominal pain; confusion; headache; loss of appetite; nausea and vomiting

Other side effects not listed above may also occur in some patients. If you notice any other effects, check with your doctor.

Additional Information

Once a medicine has been approved for marketing for a certain use, experience may show that it is also useful for other medical problems. Although this use is not included in product labeling, ethambutol is used in certain patients with the following medical condition:

- Atypical mycobacterial infections, such as *Mycobacterium avium* complex (MAC)

Other than the above information, there is no additional information relating to proper use, precautions, or side effects for this use.

Revised: 08/15/97

ETHAMBUTOL AND ISONIAZID
Systemic†

†Not commercially available in Canada.

Description

Ethambutol (e-THAM-byoo-tole) and isoniazid (eye-soe-NYE-a-zid) is a combination anti-infective medicine. This combination medicine is used to treat tuberculosis (TB). It may be given in combination with other medicines to treat TB.

This medicine may cause some serious side effects, including damage to the liver. Liver damage is more likely to occur in patients older than 50 years of age. You and your doctor should talk about the good this medicine will do, as well as the risks of taking it.

To help clear up your TB infection completely, you must keep taking this medicine for the full time of treatment, even if you begin to feel better. This is very important. It is also important that you do not miss any doses.

Ethambutol and isoniazid combination is available only with your doctor's prescription, in the following dosage form:

Oral
- Tablets (Africa, Asia, and Latin America)

Before Using This Medicine

In deciding to use a medicine, the risks of taking the medicine must be weighed against the good it will do. This is a decision you and your doctor will make. For ethambutol and isoniazid combination, the following should be considered:

Allergies—Tell your doctor if you have ever had any unusual or allergic reaction to ethambutol, ethionamide (e.g., Trecator-SC), isoniazid, niacin (e.g., Nicobid, nicotinic acid), or pyrazinamide. Also tell your health care professional if you are allergic to any other substances, such as foods, preservatives, or dyes.

Pregnancy—Pregnant women with tuberculosis (TB) should be treated with TB medicines, including ethambutol and isoniazid. Ethambutol and isoniazid have not been shown to cause birth defects or other problems in humans. However, studies in animals have shown that ethambutol causes cleft palate, skull and spine defects, absence of one eye, and harelip.

Breast-feeding—Both ethambutol and isoniazid pass into the breast milk. However, ethambutol and isoniazid have not been reported to cause problems in nursing babies.

Children—Ethambutol or combination medications containing ethambutol may be used for children with TB when other medicines cannot be used. However, ethambutol or combination medications containing ethambutol usually are not used in children younger than 6 years of age because it may be hard to tell if they are having side effects affecting their eyes.

Older adults—Hepatitis may be especially likely to occur in patients older than 50 years of age, who are usually more sensitive than younger adults to the effects of isoniazid.

Other medicines—Although certain medicines should not be used together at all, in other cases two different medicines may be used together even if an interaction might occur. In these cases, your doctor may want to change the dose, or other precautions may be necessary. When you are taking ethambutol and isoniazid combination, it is especially important that your health care professional know if you are taking any of the following:

- Alcohol or
- Carbamazepine (e.g., Tegretol) or
- Disulfiram (e.g., Antabuse) or
- Ketoconazole (e.g., Nizoral) or
- Phenytoin (e.g., Dilantin) or
- Rifampin (e.g., Rifadin)—These medicines may increase the chance of side effects if taken with ethambutol and isoniazid combination

Other medical problems—The presence of other medical problems may affect the use of this medicine. Make sure

you tell your doctor if you have any other medical problems, especially:

- Alcohol abuse (or history of) or
- Liver disease—There may be an increased chance of hepatitis with daily drinking of alcohol or in patients with liver disease
- Gouty arthritis—Ethambutol and isoniazid combination may cause or worsen attacks of gout
- Kidney disease (severe)—There may be an increased chance of side effects in patients with severe kidney disease
- Optic neuritis (eye nerve damage)—Ethambutol and isoniazid combination may cause or worsen eye disease
- Seizure disorders such as epilepsy—There may be an increased chance of convulsions (seizures) in some patients

Proper Use of This Medicine

If ethambutol and isoniazid combination upsets your stomach, take it with food. Antacids may also help. However, do not take aluminum-containing antacids within 1 hour of taking this medicine. They may keep this medicine from working properly.

To help clear up your tuberculosis (TB) completely, *it is very important that you keep taking this medicine for the full time of treatment*, even if you begin to feel better after a few weeks. You may have to take it every day for as long as 6 months to 2 years. *It is important that you do not miss any doses.*

Your doctor may also want you to take pyridoxine (vitamin B$_6$) every day to help prevent or lessen some of the side effects of isoniazid. This usually is not needed in children, who receive enough pyridoxine in their diet. If it is needed, *it is very important to take pyridoxine every day along with this medicine. Do not miss any doses.*

Dosing—The dose of ethambutol and isoniazid combination will be different for different patients. *Follow your doctor's orders or the directions on the label.* The following information includes only the average doses of ethambutol and isoniazid combination. *If your dose is different, do not change it* unless your doctor tells you to do so.

- For *oral* dosage form (tablets):
  —For treatment of tuberculosis:
    - Adults and teenagers—800 mg ethambutol and 300 mg isoniazid once a day.
    - Children up to 13 years of age—Dose must be determined by your doctor.

Missed dose—If you miss a dose of this medicine, take it as soon as possible. However, if it is almost time for your next dose, skip the missed dose and go back to your regular dosing schedule. Do not double doses.

Storage—To store this medicine:

- Keep out of the reach of children.
- Store away from heat and direct light.
- Do not store the tablet form of this medicine in the bathroom, near the kitchen sink, or in other damp places. Heat or moisture may cause the medicine to break down.
- Do not keep outdated medicine or medicine no longer needed. Be sure that any discarded medicine is out of the reach of children.

Precautions While Using This Medicine

It is very important that your doctor check your progress at regular visits. Also, check with your doctor immediately if blurred vision, red-green color blindness, or loss of vision, with or without eye pain, occurs during treatment. Your doctor may want you to have your eyes checked by an ophthalmologist (eye doctor).

Also, make sure you know how you react to this medicine before you drive, use machines, or do anything else that could be dangerous if you are not alert or able to see well.

If your symptoms do not improve within 2 to 3 weeks, or if they become worse, check with your doctor.

Certain foods such as cheese (Swiss or Cheshire) or fish (tuna, skipjack, or Sardinella) may rarely cause reactions in some patients taking this medicine. Check with your doctor if redness or itching of the skin, hot feeling, fast or pounding heartbeat, sweating, chills or clammy feeling, headache, or light-headedness occurs while you are taking this medicine.

Liver problems may be more likely to occur if you drink alcoholic beverages regularly while you are taking this medicine. Also, the regular use of alcohol may keep this medicine from working properly. Therefore, *you should strictly limit the amount of alcoholic beverages you drink while you are taking this medicine.*

If this medicine causes you to feel very tired or very weak, or causes clumsiness, unsteadiness, a loss of appetite, nausea, numbness, tingling, burning, or pain in the hands and feet, or vomiting, check with your doctor immediately. These may be early warning signs of more serious liver or nerve problems that could develop later.

For diabetic patients:
- *This medicine may cause false test results with some urine sugar tests.* Check with your doctor before changing your diet or the dosage of your diabetes medicine.

Side Effects of This Medicine

Along with its needed effects, a medicine may cause some unwanted effects. Although not all of these side effects may occur, if they do occur they may need medical attention.

Check with your doctor immediately if any of the following side effects occur:
More common
    Clumsiness or unsteadiness; dark urine; loss of appetite; nausea; numbness, tingling, burning, or pain in hands and feet; unusual tiredness or weakness; vomiting; yellow eyes or skin

Less common
    Chills; pain and swelling of joints, especially big toe, ankle, or knee; tense, hot skin over affected joints

Rare
    Blurred vision or loss of vision, with or without eye pain; convulsions (seizures); fever; joint pain; mental depression; mood or other mental changes; skin rash; sore throat; unusual bleeding or bruising

Other side effects may occur that usually do not need medical attention. These side effects may go away during treatment as your body adjusts to the medicine. However, check with

your doctor if any of the following side effects continue or are bothersome:

More common

Confusion; diarrhea; disorientation; headache; stomach pain

Developed: 02/02/99

ETCHLORVYNOL   Systemic†

Commonly used brand name(s):

In the U.S.—
Placidyl
Generic name product may be available.

†Not commercially available in Canada.

Description

Ethchlorvynol (eth-klor-VI-nole) is used to treat insomnia (trouble in sleeping). However, it has generally been replaced by other medicines for the treatment of insomnia. If ethchlorvynol is used regularly (for example, every day) to help produce sleep, it is usually not effective for more than 1 week.

This medicine is available only with your doctor's prescription, in the following dosage form:

Oral
• Capsules (U.S.)

Before Using This Medicine

In deciding to use a medicine, the risks of taking the medicine must be weighed against the good it will do. This is a decision you and your doctor will make. For ethchlorvynol, the following should be considered:

Allergies—Tell your doctor if you have ever had any unusual or allergic reaction to ethchlorvynol or tartrazine (FD&C Yellow No. 5). Also tell your health care professional if you are allergic to any other substances, such as foods, preservatives, or dyes.

Pregnancy—Ethchlorvynol has not been studied in pregnant women. However, use of ethchlorvynol during the first 6 months of pregnancy is not recommended because studies in animals have shown that high doses of ethchlorvynol increase the chance of stillbirths and decrease the chance of the newborn surviving. Taking ethchlorvynol during the last 3 months of pregnancy may cause slow heartbeat, shortness of breath, troubled breathing, or withdrawal side effects in the newborn baby.

Breast-feeding—It is not known whether ethchlorvynol passes into the breast milk. However, this medicine may cause unwanted effects in nursing babies. Be sure you have discussed the risks and benefits of the medicine with your doctor.

Children—Studies on this medicine have been done only in adult patients and there is no specific information comparing use of ethchlorvynol in children with use in other age groups.

Older adults—Elderly people may be especially sensitive to the effects of ethchlorvynol. This may increase the chance of side effects during treatment.

Other medicines—Although certain medicines should not be used together at all, in other cases 2 different medicines may be used together even if an interaction might occur. In these cases, your doctor may want to change the dose, or other precautions may be necessary. When you are taking ethchlorvynol, it is especially important that your health care professional know if you are taking any of the following:

• Anticoagulants (blood thinners)—Ethchlorvynol may change the amount of anticoagulant you need to take
• Central nervous system (CNS) depressants (medicine that causes drowsiness) or
• Tricyclic antidepressants (medicine for depression)—Using these medicines together with ethchlorvynol may increase the CNS and other depressant effects

Other medical problems—The presence of other medical problems may affect the use of ethchlorvynol. Make sure you tell your doctor if you have any other medical problems, especially:

• Alcohol abuse (or history of) or
• Drug abuse or dependence (or history of)—Dependence on ethchlorvynol may develop
• Kidney disease or
• Liver disease—Higher blood levels of ethchlorvynol may result and increase the chance of side effects
• Mental depression or
• Porphyria—Ethchlorvynol may make the condition worse

Proper Use of This Medicine

Ethchlorvynol is best taken with food or a glass of milk to lessen the possibility of dizziness, clumsiness, or unsteadiness, which may occur shortly after you take this medicine.

Take this medicine only as directed by your doctor. Do not take more of it, do not take it more often, and do not take it for a longer time than your doctor ordered. If too much is taken, it may become habit-forming.

Dosing—The dose of ethchlorvynol will be different for different patients. *Follow your doctor's orders or the directions on the label.* The following information includes only the average doses of ethchlorvynol. *If your dose is different, do not change it* unless your doctor tells you to do so.

• For *oral* dosage forms (capsules):
—Adults: 500 to 1000 milligrams at bedtime.
—Children: Dose must be determined by the doctor.

Storage—To store this medicine:

• Keep out of the reach of children. Overdose of ethchlorvynol is especially dangerous in children.
• Store away from heat and direct light.
• Do not store in the bathroom, near the kitchen sink, or in other damp places. Heat or moisture may cause the medicine to break down.
• Do not keep outdated medicine or medicine no longer needed. Be sure that any discarded medicine is out of the reach of children.

Precautions While Using This Medicine

If you will be taking this medicine regularly for a long time:

• Your doctor should check your progress at regular visits.
• Do not stop taking it without first checking with your doctor. Your doctor may want you to reduce gradually the amount you are taking before stopping completely.

This medicine will add to the effects of alcohol and other CNS depressants (medicines that cause drowsiness). Some examples of CNS depressants are antihistamines or medicine for hay fever, other allergies, or colds; sedatives, tranquilizers, or sleeping medicine; prescription pain medicine or narcotics; barbiturates; medicine for seizures; muscle relaxants; or anesthetics, including some dental anesthetics. *Check with your doctor before taking any of the above while you are taking this medicine.*

If you think you or someone else may have taken an overdose of this medicine, get emergency help at once. Taking an overdose of etchchlorvynol or taking alcohol or other CNS depressants with ethchlorvynol may lead to unconsciousness and possibly death. Some signs of an overdose are continuing confusion, severe weakness, shortness of breath or slow or troubled breathing, slurred speech, staggering, and slow heartbeat.

This medicine may cause some people to become dizzy, lightheaded, drowsy, or less alert than they are normally. Even if taken at bedtime, it may cause some people to feel drowsy or less alert on arising. *Make sure you know how you react to this medicine before you drive, use machines, or do anything else that could be dangerous if you are dizzy or are not alert.*

Side Effects of This Medicine

Along with its needed effects, a medicine may cause some unwanted effects. Although not all of these side effects may occur, if they do occur they may need medical attention.

Check with your doctor as soon as possible if any of the following side effects occur:

Less common
> Skin rash or hives; dizziness or faintness; unusual excitement, nervousness, or restlessness

Rare
> Darkening of urine, itching, pale stools, yellow eyes or skin; unusual bleeding or bruising

Symptoms of overdose
> Confusion (continuing); decrease in or other change in vision; double vision; fever, chills, or sore throat; low body temperature; numbness, tingling, pain, or weakness in hands or feet; overactive reflexes; pale skin; shakiness and unsteady walk, clumsiness, unsteadiness, trembling, or other problems with muscle control or coordination; shortness of breath or slow or troubled breathing; slow heartbeat; slurred speech; trembling; unusual bleeding or bruising; unusual movements of the eyes; unusual tiredness or weakness (severe)

Other side effects may occur that usually do not need medical attention. These side effects may go away during treatment as your body adjusts to the medicine. However, check with your doctor if any of the following side effects continue or are bothersome:

More common
> Blurred vision; dizziness or light-headedness; low blood pressure; indigestion; nausea or vomiting; numbness of face; stomach pain; unpleasant aftertaste; unusual tiredness or weakness

Less common
> Clumsiness or unsteadiness; confusion; drowsiness (daytime)

After you stop using this medicine, your body may need time to adjust. If you took this medicine in high doses or for a long time, this may take up to 2 weeks. During this period of time check with your doctor if you notice any of the following side effects:

> Confusion as to time, place, or person; convulsions (seizures); dizziness; hallucinations (seeing, hearing, or feeling things that are not there); loss of appetite; memory loss; muscle twitching; nausea or vomiting; restlessness, nervousness, or irritability; slurred speech; sweating; trembling; trouble in sleeping; weakness; weight loss, unexplained

Other side effects not listed above may also occur in some patients. If you notice any other effects, check with your doctor.

Revised: 03/14/00

ETHINAMATE   Systemic*†

*Not commercially available in the U.S.
†Not commercially available in Canada.

Description

Ethinamate (e-THIN-a-mate) is used to treat insomnia (trouble in sleeping). However, it has generally been replaced by other medicines for the treatment of insomnia. If ethinamate is used regularly (for example, every day) to help produce sleep, it is usually not effective for more than 7 days.

Note: This medicine is not available in the U.S. or Canada.

Before Using This Medicine

In deciding to use a medicine, the risks of taking the medicine must be weighed against the good it will do. This is a decision you and your doctor will make. For ethinamate, the following should be considered:

Allergies—Tell your doctor if you have ever had any unusual or allergic reaction to ethinamate. Also tell your health care professional if you are allergic to any other substances, such as foods, preservatives, or dyes.

Pregnancy—Studies on birth defects have not been done in either humans or animals.

Breast-feeding—It is not known whether ethinamate passes into the breast milk. However, this medicine has not been reported to cause problems in nursing babies.

Children—Studies on this medicine have been done only in adult patients, and there is no specific information about its use in children.

Older adults—Elderly people may be especially sensitive to the effects of ethinamate. This may increase the chance of side effects during treatment.

Other medicines—Although certain medicines should not be used together at all, in other cases 2 different medicines may be used together even if an interaction might occur. In these cases, your doctor may want to change the dose, or other precautions may be necessary. When taking ethinamate it is especially important that your health care professional know if you are taking any of the following:

- Central nervous system (CNS) depressants, other— Using these medicines together may increase the CNS and other depressant effects

Other medical problems— The presence of other medical problems may affect the use of ethinamate. Make sure you tell your doctor if you have any other medical problems, especially:

- Alcohol abuse (or history of) or
- Drug abuse or dependence (or history of)—Dependence on ethinamate may develop
- Mental depression—Ethinamate may make the condition worse

Proper Use of This Medicine

Take this medicine only as directed by your doctor. Do not take more of it, do not take it more often, and do not take it for a longer time than your doctor ordered. If too much is taken, it may become habit-forming.

Storage— To store this medicine:

- Keep out of the reach of children. Overdose of ethinamate is especially dangerous in children.
- Store away from heat and direct light.
- Do not store in the bathroom, near the kitchen sink, or in other damp places. Heat or moisture may cause the medicine to break down.
- Do not keep outdated medicine or medicine no longer needed. Be sure that any discarded medicine is out of the reach of children.

Precautions While Using This Medicine

If you will be taking this medicine regularly for a long time:

- Your doctor should check your progress at regular visits.
- Do not stop taking it without first checking with your doctor. Your doctor may want you to reduce gradually the amount you are taking before stopping completely.

This medicine will add to the effects of alcohol and other CNS depressants (medicines that slow down the nervous system, possibly causing drowsiness). Some examples of CNS depressants are antihistamines or medicine for hay fever, other allergies, or colds; sedatives, tranquilizers, or sleeping medicine; prescription pain medicine or narcotics; barbiturates; medicine for seizures; muscle relaxants; or anesthetics, including some dental anesthetics. *Check with your doctor before taking any of the above while you are taking this medicine.*

If you think you or someone else may have taken an overdose of this medicine, get emergency help at once. Taking an overdose of ethinamate or taking alcohol or other CNS depressants with ethinamate may lead to unconsciousness and possibly death. Some signs of an overdose are confusion, severe weakness, shortness of breath or slow or troubled breathing, slurred speech, staggering, and slow heartbeat.

This medicine may cause some people to become drowsy or less alert than they are normally. Even if taken at bedtime, it may cause some people to feel drowsy or less alert on arising. *Make sure you know how you react to this medicine before you drive, use machines, or do anything else that could be dangerous if you are not alert.*

Side Effects of This Medicine

Along with its needed effects, a medicine may cause some unwanted effects. Although not all of these side effects may occur, if they do occur they may need medical attention.

Check with your doctor as soon as possible if any of the following side effects occur:

Less common
  Skin rash; unusual excitement (especially in children)

Rare
  Unusual bleeding or bruising

Symptoms of overdose
  Confusion; shortness of breath or slow or troubled breathing; slow heartbeat; slurred speech; staggering; weakness (severe)

Other side effects may occur that usually do not need medical attention. These side effects may go away during treatment as your body adjusts to the medicine. However, check with your doctor if any of the following side effects continue or are bothersome:

Less common
  Indigestion; nausea; stomach pain; vomiting

Rare
  Drowsiness (daytime)

After you stop using this medicine, your body may need time to adjust. The length of time this takes depends on the amount of medicine you were using and how long you used it. During this period of time check with your doctor if you notice any of the following side effects:

  Confusion; convulsions (seizures); hallucinations (seeing, hearing, or feeling things that are not there); restlessness, nervousness, or irritability; trembling; trouble in sleeping

Other side effects not listed above may also occur in some patients. If you notice any other effects, check with your doctor.

Revised: 10/16/2000
Interim revision: 10/16/2000

ETHIONAMIDE   Systemic†

Commonly used brand name(s):

In the U.S.—
  Trecator-SC

†Not commercially available in Canada.

Description

Ethionamide (e-thye-ON-am-ide) is used with other medicines to treat tuberculosis (TB). Ethionamide may also be used for other problems as determined by your doctor.

To help clear up your tuberculosis (TB) completely, you must keep taking this medicine for the full time of treatment, even if you begin to feel better. This is very important. It is also important that you do not miss any doses.

Ethionamide is available only with your doctor's prescription, in the following dosage form:

Oral
- Tablets (U.S.)

Before Using This Medicine

In deciding to use a medicine, the risks of taking the medicine must be weighed against the good it will do. This is a decision you and your doctor will make. For ethionamide, the following should be considered:

Allergies—Tell your doctor if you have ever had any unusual or allergic reaction to ethionamide, isoniazid (e.g., INH; Nydrazid), pyrazinamide, or niacin (e.g., Nicobid; nicotinic acid). Also tell your health care professional if you are allergic to any other substances, such as foods, preservatives, or dyes.

Pregnancy—Ethionamide causes birth defects in rats and rabbits given doses greater than the usual human dose. However, women with tuberculosis (TB) should be treated with medicines to treat TB. If you have any concerns, talk to your doctor.

Breast-feeding—It is not known whether ethionamide passes into breast milk. Although most medicines pass into breast milk in small amounts, many of them may be used safely while breast-feeding. Mothers who are taking this medicine and who wish to breast-feed should discuss this with their doctor.

Children—Although there is no specific information comparing use of ethionamide in children with use in other age groups, this medicine is not expected to cause different side effects or problems in children than it does in adults.

Older adults—Many medicines have not been studied specifically in older people. Therefore, it may not be known whether they work exactly the same way they do in younger adults or if they cause different side effects or problems in older people. There is no specific information comparing use of ethionamide in the elderly with use in other age groups.

Other medicines—Although certain medicines should not be used together at all, in other cases two different medicines may be used together even if an interaction might occur. In these cases, your doctor may want to change the dose, or other precautions may be necessary. When you are taking ethionamide, it is especially important that your health care professional know if you are taking any of the following:
- Cycloserine—Use of ethionamide with cycloserine may increase the chance for nervous system side effects, such as convulsions (seizures)

Other medical problems—The presence of other medical problems may affect the use of ethionamide. Make sure you tell your doctor if you have any other medical problems, especially:
- Diabetes mellitus (sugar diabetes)—Diabetes may be harder to control in patients taking ethionamide
- Liver disease (severe)—Patients with severe liver disease may have an increased chance of side effects

Proper Use of This Medicine

Ethionamide may be taken with or after meals if it upsets your stomach.

To help clear up your tuberculosis (TB) completely, *it is very important that you keep taking this medicine for the full time of treatment*, even if you begin to feel better after a few weeks. You may have to take it every day for 1 to 2 years or more. *It is important that you do not miss any doses.*

Your doctor may also want you to take pyridoxine (e.g., Hexa-Betalin; vitamin B$_6$) every day to help prevent or lessen some of the side effects of ethionamide. If so, *it is very important to take pyridoxine every day along with this medicine. Do not miss any doses.*

Dosing—The dose of ethionamide will be different for different patients. *Follow your doctor's orders or the directions on the label.* The following information includes only the average doses of ethionamide. *If your dose is different, do not change it* unless your doctor tells you to do so.
- For *oral* dosage form (tablets):
  —For the treatment of tuberculosis (TB):
  - Adults and teenagers—250 milligrams (mg) every eight to twelve hours. Ethionamide must be taken with other medicines to treat tuberculosis.
  - Children—Dose is based on body weight. The usual dose is 4 to 5 mg per kilogram of body weight every eight hours. Ethionamide must be taken with other medicines to treat tuberculosis.

Missed dose—If you do miss a dose of either of these medicines, take it as soon as possible. However, if it is almost time for your next dose, skip the missed dose and go back to your regular dosing schedule. Do not double doses.

Storage—To store this medicine:
- Keep out of the reach of children.
- Store away from heat and direct light.
- Do not store in the bathroom, near the kitchen sink, or in other damp places. Heat or moisture may cause the medicine to break down.
- Do not keep outdated medicine or medicine no longer needed. Be sure that any discarded medicine is out of the reach of children.

Precautions While Using This Medicine

If your symptoms do not improve within 2 to 3 weeks, or if they become worse, check with your doctor.

It is very important that your doctor check your progress at regular visits. Also, *check with your doctor immediately if blurred vision or any loss of vision, with or without eye pain, occurs during treatment.* Your doctor may want you to have your eyes checked by an ophthalmologist (eye doctor).

Since this medicine may cause blurred vision or loss of vision, *make sure you know how you react to this medicine before you drive, use machines, or do anything else that could be dangerous if you are not able to see well.*

If this medicine causes clumsiness; unsteadiness; or numbness, tingling, burning, or pain in the hands and feet, check with your doctor immediately. These may be early warning symptoms of more serious nerve problems that could develop later.

Side Effects of This Medicine

Along with its needed effects, a medicine may cause some unwanted effects. Although not all of these side effects may occur, if they do occur they may need medical attention.

Check with your doctor immediately if any of the following side effects occur:

Less common
> Clumsiness or unsteadiness; confusion; mental depression; mood or other mental changes; numbness, tingling, burning, or pain in hands and feet; yellow eyes or skin

Rare
> Blurred vision or loss of vision, with or without eye pain; changes in menstrual periods; coldness; decreased sexual ability (in males); difficulty in concentrating; dry, puffy skin; faster heartbeat; increased hunger; nervousness; shakiness; skin rash; swelling of front part of neck; weight gain

Other side effects may occur that usually do not need medical attention. These side effects may go away during treatment as your body adjusts to the medicine. However, check with your doctor if any of the following side effects continue or are bothersome:

More common
> Dizziness (especially when getting up from a lying or sitting position); loss of appetite; metallic taste; nausea or vomiting; sore mouth

Less common or rare
> Enlargement of the breasts (in males)

Other side effects not listed above may also occur in some patients. If you notice any other effects, check with your doctor.

Additional Information

Once a medicine has been approved for marketing for a certain use, experience may show that it is also useful for other medical problems. Although these uses are not included in product labeling, ethionamide is used in certain patients with the following medical conditions:

- Atypical mycobacterial infections, such as *Mycobacterium avium* complex (MAC)
- Leprosy (Hansen's disease)

Other than the above information, there is no additional information relating to proper use, precautions, or side effects for these uses.

Revised: 06/22/94

ETIDRONATE   Systemic

Commonly used brand name(s):
In the U.S.—
Didronel
In Canada—
Didronel
Another commonly used name is EHDP.

Description

Etidronate (eh-tih-DROE-nate) is used to treat Paget's disease of bone. It may also be used to treat or prevent a certain type of bone problem that may occur after hip replacement surgery or spinal injury.

Etidronate is also used to treat hypercalcemia (too much calcium in the blood) that may occur with some types of cancer.

This medicine is available only with your doctor's prescription, in the following dosage forms:

Oral
- Tablets (U.S. and Canada)
Parenteral
- Injection (U.S.)

Before Using This Medicine

In deciding to use a medicine, the risks of taking the medicine must be weighed against the good it will do. This is a decision you and your doctor will make. For etidronate, the following should be considered:

Allergies—Tell your doctor if you have ever had any unusual or allergic reaction to etidronate. Also tell your health care professional if you are allergic to any other substances, such as foods, preservatives, or dyes.

Diet—Make certain your health care professional knows if your diet includes large amounts of calcium, such as milk or other dairy products, or if you are on any special diet, such as a low-sodium or low-sugar diet. Calcium in the diet may prevent the absorption of oral etidronate.

Pregnancy—Studies have not been done in humans. However, studies in rats injected with large doses of etidronate have shown that etidronate causes deformed bones in the fetus.

Breast-feeding—It is not known if etidronate passes into breast milk. However, this medicine has not been reported to cause problems in nursing babies.

Children—Some changes in bone growth may occur in children, but will usually go away when the medicine is stopped.

Older adults—When etidronate is given by injection along with a large amount of fluids, older people tend to retain (keep) the excess fluid.

Other medicines—Although certain medicines should not be used together at all, in other cases two different medicines may be used together even if an interaction might occur. In these cases, your doctor may want to change the dose, or other precautions may be necessary. When you are taking etidronate, it is especially important that your health care professional know if you are taking any of the following:

- Antacids containing calcium, magnesium, or aluminum or
- Mineral supplements or other medicines containing calcium, iron, magnesium, or aluminum—These medicines may decrease the effects of etidronate, and should be taken at least 2 hours before or after taking etidronate

Other medical problems—The presence of other medical problems may affect the use of etidronate. Make sure you tell your doctor if you have any other medical problems, especially:

- Bone fracture, especially of arm or leg—Etidronate may increase the risk of bone fractures
- Intestinal or bowel disease—Etidronate may increase the risk of diarrhea
- Kidney disease—High blood levels of etidronate may result causing serious side effects

Proper Use of This Medicine

Take etidronate with water on an empty stomach at least 2 hours before or after food (midmorning is best) or at bedtime. Food may decrease the amount of etidronate absorbed by your body.

Take etidronate only as directed. Do not take more of it, do not take it more often, and do not take it for a longer time than your doctor ordered. To do so may increase the chance of side effects.

In some patients, etidronate takes up to 3 months to work. If you feel that the medicine is not working, do not stop taking it on your own. Instead, check with your doctor.

It is important that you eat a well-balanced diet with an adequate amount of calcium and vitamin D (found in milk or other dairy products). Too much or too little of either may increase the chance of side effects while you are taking etidronate. Your doctor can help you choose the meal plan that is best for you. *However, do not take any food, especially milk, milk formulas, or other dairy products, or antacids, or mineral supplements, or other medicines that are high in calcium or iron (high amounts of these minerals may also be in some vitamin preparations), magnesium, or aluminum* within 2 hours of taking etidronate. To do so may keep this medicine from working properly.

Dosing—The dose of etidronate will be different for different patients. *Follow your doctor's order or the directions on the label.* The following information includes only the average doses of etidronate. *If your dose is different, do not change it* unless your doctor tells you to do so.

- For *oral* dosage form (tablets):
  - —For treating Paget's disease of bone:
    - Adults—Dose is based on body weight and must be determined by your doctor. The dose to start is 5 milligrams (mg) per kilogram (kg) (2.3 mg per pound) of body weight a day, usually as a single dose, for not more than six months. Some people may need 6 to 10 mg per kg (2.7 to 4.6 mg per pound) of body weight a day for not more than six months. Others may need 11 to 20 mg per kg (5 to 9.1 mg per pound) of body weight a day for not more than three months. Your doctor may change your dose depending on your response to treatment.
    - Children—Dose must be determined by your doctor.
  - —For treating or preventing a certain type of bone problem that may occur after hip replacement:
    - Adults—Dose is based on body weight and must be determined by your doctor. The usual dose is 20 mg per kg (9.1 mg per pound) of body weight a day for one month before surgery, and for three months after surgery.
    - Children—Dose must be determined by your doctor.
  - —For treating or preventing a certain type of bone problem that may occur after spinal injury:
    - Adults—Dose is based on body weight and must be determined by your doctor. The usual dose is 20 mg per kg (9.1 mg per pound) of body weight a day for two weeks, beginning as soon as possible after your injury. Your doctor may then decrease your dose to 10 mg per kg (4.5 mg per pound) of body weight for an additional ten weeks.
    - Children—Dose must be determined by your doctor.
  - —For treating hypercalcemia (too much calcium in the blood):
    - Adults—Dose is based on body weight and must be determined by your doctor. The usual dose is 20 mg per kg (9.1 mg per pound) of body weight a day for thirty days. Treatment usually does not continue beyond ninety days.
    - Children—Dose must be determined by your doctor.
- For *injection* dosage form:
  - —For treating hypercalcemia (too much calcium in the blood):
    - Adults—Dose is based on body weight and must be determined by your doctor. The usual dose is 7.5 mg per kg (3.4 mg per pound) of body weight, injected slowly into your vein over 2 hours. This dose is repeated for two more days. Your doctor may repeat the treatment after at least seven days.
    - Children—Dose must be determined by your doctor.

Missed dose—If you miss a dose of this medicine, take it as soon as possible. However, if it is almost time for your next dose, skip the missed dose and go back to your regular dosing schedule. Do not double doses.

Storage—To store this medicine:
- Keep out of the reach of children.
- Store away from heat and direct light.
- Do not store in the bathroom, near the kitchen sink, or in other damp places. Heat or moisture may cause the medicine to break down.
- Do not keep outdated medicine or medicine no longer needed. Be sure that any discarded medicine is out of the reach of children.

Precautions While Using This Medicine

It is important that your doctor check your progress at regular visits even if you are between treatments and are not taking this medicine. If your condition has improved and your doctor has told you to stop taking etidronate, your progress must still be checked. The results of laboratory tests or the occurrence of certain symptoms will tell your doctor if more medicine must be taken. Your doctor may want you to begin another course of treatment after you have been off the medicine for at least 3 months.

If this medicine causes you to have nausea or diarrhea and it continues, check with your doctor. The dose may need to be changed.

If bone pain occurs or worsens during treatment, check with your doctor.

Side Effects of This Medicine

Along with its needed effects, a medicine may cause some unwanted effects. Although not all of these side effects may occur, if they do occur they may need medical attention.

Check with your doctor as soon as possible if any of the following side effects occur:

More common

    Bone pain or tenderness (increased, continuing, or returning—in patients with Paget's disease)

Less common
    Bone fractures, especially of the thigh bone
Rare
    Hives; skin rash or itching; swelling of the arms, legs, face, lips, tongue, and/or throat

Other side effects may occur that usually do not need medical attention. These side effects may go away during treatment as your body adjusts to the medicine. However, check with your doctor if any of the following side effects continue or are bothersome:
    More common—at higher doses
        Diarrhea; nausea
    Less common—with injection
        Loss of taste or metallic or altered taste

Other side effects not listed above may also occur in some patients. If you notice any other effects, check with your doctor.

Revised: 08/19/92
Interim revision: 08/10/94

ETOPOSIDE   Systemic

Commonly used brand name(s):

In the U.S.—
    VePesid
    Etopophos
    Toposar
    Generic name product may be available.

In Canada—
    VePesid
Another commonly used name is VP-16.

Description

Etoposide (e-toe-POE-side) belongs to the group of medicines known as antineoplastic agents. It is used to treat cancer of the testicles and certain types of lung cancer. It is also sometimes used to treat some other kinds of cancer in both males and females.

The exact way that etoposide acts against cancer is not known. However, it seems to interfere with the growth of the cancer cells, which are eventually destroyed. Since the growth of normal body cells may also be affected by etoposide, other effects will also occur. Some of these may be serious and must be reported to your doctor. Other effects, like hair loss, may not be serious but may cause concern. Some effects may not occur until months or years after the medicine is used.

Before you begin treatment with etoposide, you and your doctor should talk about the good this medicine will do as well as the risks of using it.

This medicine is available only with your doctor's prescription, in the following dosage forms:
    Oral
        • Capsules (U.S. and Canada)
    Parenteral
        • Injection (U.S. and Canada)

Before Using This Medicine

In deciding to use a medicine, the risks of taking the medicine must be weighed against the good it will do. This is a decision you and your doctor will make. For etoposide, the following should be considered:

Allergies—Tell your doctor if you have ever had any unusual or allergic reaction to etoposide.

Pregnancy—There is a good chance that this medicine will cause birth defects if it is being used at the time of conception or during pregnancy. In addition, many cancer medicines may cause sterility, which could be permanent. Although sterility has not been reported with etoposide, the possibility should be kept in mind.

Be sure that you have discussed this with your doctor before receiving this medicine. Before taking etoposide make sure your doctor knows if you are pregnant or if you may become pregnant. It is best to use some kind of birth control while you are taking etoposide. Tell your doctor right away if you think you have become pregnant while taking etoposide.

Breast-feeding—Because etoposide may cause serious side effects, breast-feeding is generally not recommended while you are receiving it.

Children—Although this medicine has been used in children, there is no specific information comparing use of etoposide in children with use in other age groups. However, children who receive high doses may be more likely to have a serious allergic reaction to this medicine.

Older adults—Many medicines have not been studied specifically in older people. Therefore, it may not be known whether they work exactly the same way they do in younger adults or if they cause different side effects or problems in older people. There is no specific information comparing use of etoposide in the elderly with use in other age groups.

Other medicines—Although certain medicines should not be used together at all, in other cases two different medicines may be used together even if an interaction might occur. In these cases, your doctor may want to change the dose, or other precautions may be necessary. When you are taking or receiving etoposide, it is especially important that your health care professional know if you are taking any of the following:

• Amphotericin B by injection (e.g., Fungizone) or
• Antithyroid agents (medicine for overactive thyroid) or
• Azathioprine (e.g., Imuran) or
• Chloramphenicol (e.g., Chloromycetin) or
• Colchicine or
• Flucytosine (e.g., Ancobon) or
• Ganciclovir (e.g., Cytovene) or
• Interferon (e.g., Intron A, Roferon-A) or
• Plicamycin (e.g., Mithracin) or
• Zidovudine (e.g., AZT, Retrovir) or
• If you have ever been treated with radiation or cancer medicines—Etoposide may increase the effects of these medicines or radiation therapy on the blood

Other medical problems—The presence of other medical problems may affect the use of etoposide. Make sure you tell your doctor if you have any other medical problems, especially:

• Chickenpox (including recent exposure) or
• Herpes zoster (shingles)—Risk of severe disease affecting other parts of the body

- Infection—Etoposide can decrease your body's ability to fight infection
- Kidney disease or
- Liver disease—Effects of etoposide may be increased because of slower removal from the body

Proper Use of This Medicine

Take etoposide only as directed by your doctor. Do not use more or less of it, and do not use it more often than your doctor ordered. The exact amount of medicine you need has been carefully worked out. Taking too much may increase the chance of side effects, while taking too little may not improve your condition.

Etoposide is sometimes given together with certain other medicines. If you are using a combination of medicines, make sure that you take each one at the proper time and do not mix them. If you are taking some of these medicines by mouth, ask your health care professional to help you plan a way to remember to take your medicines at the right times.

Etoposide often causes nausea, vomiting, and loss of appetite, which may be severe. However, it is very important that you continue to receive the medicine, even if you begin to feel ill. Ask your health care professional for ways to lessen these effects.

If you vomit shortly after taking a dose of etoposide, check with your doctor. You will be told whether to take the dose again or to wait until the next dose.

Dosing—The dose of etoposide will be different for different patients. The dose that is used may depend on a number of things, including what the medicine is being used for, the patient's size, whether the medicine is being given by mouth or by injection, and whether or not other medicines are also being taken. *If you are taking or receiving etoposide at home, follow your doctor's orders or the directions on the label*. If you have any questions about the proper dose of etoposide, ask your doctor.

Missed dose—If you miss a dose of this medicine, do not take the missed dose at all and do not double the next one. Instead, go back to your regular dosing schedule and check with your doctor.

Storage—To store this medicine:
- Keep out of the reach of children.
- Store in the refrigerator.
- Do not store in the bathroom, near the kitchen sink, or in other damp places. Heat or moisture may cause the medicine to break down.
- Do not keep outdated medicine or medicine no longer needed. Be sure that any discarded medicine is out of the reach of children.

Precautions While Using This Medicine

It is very important that your doctor check your progress at regular visits to make sure that etoposide is working properly and to check for unwanted effects.

While you are being treated with etoposide, and after you stop treatment with it, *do not have any immunizations (vaccinations) without your doctor's approval*. Etoposide may lower your body's resistance and there is a chance you might get the infection the immunization is meant to prevent. In addition, other persons living in your household should not take oral polio vaccine since there is a chance they could pass the polio virus on to you. Also, avoid persons who have taken oral polio vaccine within the last several months. Do not get close to them and do not stay in the same room with them for very long. If you cannot take these precautions, you should consider wearing a protective face mask that covers the nose and mouth.

Etoposide can temporarily lower the number of white blood cells in your blood, increasing the chance of your getting an infection. It can also lower the number of platelets, which are necessary for proper blood clotting. If this occurs, there are certain precautions you can take, especially when your blood count is low, to reduce the risk of infection or bleeding:

- If you can, avoid people with infections. *Check with your doctor immediately* if you think you are getting an infection or if you get a fever or chills, cough or hoarseness, lower back or side pain, or have painful or difficult urination.
- *Check with your doctor immediately* if you notice any unusual bleeding or bruising; black, tarry stools; blood in urine or stools; or pinpoint red spots on your skin.
- Be careful when using a regular toothbrush, dental floss, or toothpick. Your medical doctor, dentist, or nurse may recommend other ways to clean your teeth and gums. Check with your medical doctor before having any dental work done.
- Do not touch your eyes or the inside of your nose unless you have just washed your hands and have not touched anything else in the meantime.
- Be careful not to cut yourself when you are using sharp objects such as a safety razor or fingernail or toenail cutters.
- Avoid contact sports or other situations where bruising or injury could occur.

Side Effects of This Medicine

Along with its needed effects, a medicine may cause some unwanted effects. Although not all of these side effects may occur, if they do occur they may need medical attention.

Also, because of the way these medicines act on the body, there is a chance that they might cause other unwanted effects that may not occur until months or years after the medicine is used. These delayed effects may include certain types of cancer, such as leukemia. Discuss these possible effects with your doctor.

Check with your doctor or nurse immediately if any of the following side effects occur:
Rare
    Fast heartbeat; loss of consciousness; shortness of breath; sweating; swelling of face or tongue; tightness in throat; wheezing

Check with your health care professional as soon as possible if any of the following side effects occur:
More common
    Unusual tiredness or weakness

Less common
    Black, tarry stools; blood in urine or stools; cough or hoarseness, accompanied by fever or chills; fever or chills; lower back or side pain, accompanied by fever or chills; painful or difficult urination, accompanied by fever or chills; pinpoint red spots on skin; sores in mouth or on lips; unusual bleeding or bruising

Rare
    Back pain; difficulty in walking; numbness or tingling in

fingers and toes; pain at place of injection; skin rash or itching; weakness

Other side effects may occur that usually do not need medical attention. These side effects may go away during treatment as your body adjusts to the medicine. Also, your health care professional may be able to tell you about ways to prevent or reduce some of these side effects. Check with your health care professional if any of the following side effects continue or are bothersome or if you have any questions about them:

More common
    Loss of appetite; nausea and vomiting

Less common
    Diarrhea

This medicine often causes a temporary loss of hair. After treatment with etoposide has ended, normal hair growth should return.

Other side effects not listed above may also occur in some patients. If you notice any other effects, check with your doctor or nurse.

Additional Information

Once a medicine has been approved for marketing for a certain use, experience may show that it is also useful for other medical problems. Although these uses are not included in product labeling, etoposide is used in certain patients with the following medical conditions:

- Autoimmune deficiency syndrome (AIDS)-associated Kaposi's sarcoma (a type of cancer of the skin and mucous membranes that is more common in patients with AIDS)
- Cancer of the adrenal cortex (the outside layer of the adrenal gland)
- Cancers of the blood and lymph system
- Cancer in the bone
- Cancer of the endometrium
- Cancer of the lung (a certain type of lung cancer usually associated with prior smoking, passive smoking, or radon exposure)
- Cancer of the lymph system (a part of the body's immune system) that affects the skin
- Cancer of the stomach
- Cancers of the soft tissues of the body, including the muscles, connective tissues (tendons), vessels that carry blood or lymph, or fat
- Cancer of unknown primary site
- Ewing's sarcoma (a type of cancer found in the bone)
- Gestational trophoblastic tumors (tumors in the uterus or womb)
- Hepatoblastoma (a certain type of liver cancer that occurs in children)
- Multiple myeloma (a certain type of cancer of the blood)
- Neuroblastoma (a cancer of the nerves that usually occurs in children)
- Retinoblastoma (a cancer of the eye that usually occurs in children)
- Thymoma (a cancer of the thymus, which is a small organ that lies under the breastbone)
- Tumors in the brain
- Wilms' tumor (a cancer of the kidney that usually occurs in children)
- Cancer of the ovaries (a type of cancer found in the egg-making cells)

Other than the above information, there is no additional information relating to proper use, precautions, or side effects for these uses.

Revised: 02/20/2001

ETRETINATE   Systemic†

†Not commercially available in Canada.

Description

Etretinate (e-TRET-i-nate) is used to treat severe psoriasis. It is usually used only after other medicines have been tried and have failed to help the psoriasis.

Etretinate must not be used to treat women who are able to bear children unless other forms of treatment have been tried first and have failed. Etretinate must not be taken during pregnancy, because it causes birth defects in humans. In addition, if you take etretinate, you must plan on never having children in the future. If you are able to bear children, it is very important that you read, understand, and follow the pregnancy warnings for etretinate.

It is also recommended that etretinate not be used to treat children unless all other forms of treatment have been tried first and have failed. Etretinate may interfere with bone growth. In addition, children may be more sensitive to the side effects of the medicine.

This medicine was withdrawn from the U.S. market in March 1998 and the Canadian market in January 1996.

Before Using This Medicine

In deciding to use a medicine, the risks of taking the medicine must be weighed against the good it will do. This is a decision you and your doctor will make. For etretinate, the following should be considered:

Allergies—Tell your doctor if you have ever had any unusual or allergic reaction to etretinate, isotretinoin, tretinoin, or vitamin A-like preparations. Also tell your health care professional if you are allergic to any other substances, such as foods, preservatives, or dyes.

Pregnancy—*Etretinate must not be taken during pregnancy, because it causes birth defects in humans. In addition, since it is not known how long pregnancy should be avoided after treatment stops, you must plan on never having children if you are treated with etretinate.* If you are able to bear children, you must have a pregnancy test within 2 weeks before beginning treatment with etretinate to make sure you are not pregnant. Therapy with etretinate will then be started on the second or third day of your next normal menstrual period. *Also, etretinate must not be taken unless an effective form of contraception (birth control) is used for at least 1 month before beginning treatment. Contraception must be continued during treatment and for as long as you are able to become pregnant after etretinate is stopped. Be sure you have discussed this information with your doctor.*

Breast-feeding—It is not known whether etretinate passes into the breast milk. However, etretinate is not recommended during breast-feeding or if you plan to breast-feed in the future, because it may cause unwanted effects in nursing babies.

Children—It is recommended that etretinate not be used to treat children, unless all other forms of treatment have been tried first and have failed. Etretinate may interfere with bone growth. In addition, children may be more sensitive to the side effects of the medicine.

Older adults—Many medicines have not been studied specifically in older people. Therefore, it may not be known whether they work exactly the same way they do in younger adults or if they cause different side effects or problems in older people. There is no specific information comparing use of etretinate in the elderly with use in other age groups.

Other medicines—Although certain medicines should not be used together at all, in other cases two different medicines may be used together even if an interaction might occur. In these cases, your doctor may want to change the dose, or other precautions may be necessary. When you are using etretinate, it is especially important that your health care professional know if you are using any of the following:

- Abrasive or medicated soaps or cleansers or
- Cosmetics or soaps that dry the skin or
- Medicated cosmetics or "cover-ups" or
- Topical acne preparation or preparation containing a peeling agent, such as benzoyl peroxide, resorcinol, salicylic acid, sulfur, or tretinoin (vitamin A acid), or
- Topical alcohol-containing preparation, such as aftershave lotion, astringent, cologne, perfume, or shaving cream or lotion, or
- Topical medicine for the skin, other—Use of etretinate with these products will increase the chance of dryness and other irritation of the skin

- Isotretinoin (e.g., Accutane) or
- Methotrexate (e.g., Mexate) or
- Tretinoin (vitamin A acid) (e.g., Retin-A) or
- Vitamin A or any preparation containing vitamin A (e.g., Alphalin)—Use of etretinate with these products will cause an increase in side effects

- Tetracyclines (medicine for infection)—Use of etretinate may increase the chance of the side effect called pseudotumor cerebri, which is a swelling of the brain

Other medical problems—The presence of other medical problems may affect the use of etretinate. Make sure you tell your doctor if you have any other medical problems, especially:

- Alcoholism or excess use of alcohol (or history of) or
- Diabetes mellitus (sugar diabetes) (or a family history of) or
- Heart or blood vessel disease (or history of increased risk of or family history of) or
- High triglyceride (a fat-like substance) levels in the blood (history of or a family history of) or
- Severe weight problems—Use of etretinate may increase blood levels of triglyceride (a fat-like substance), which may increase the chance of heart or blood vessel problems in patients who have a family history of high triglycerides, are greatly overweight, are diabetic, or use a lot of alcohol. For persons with diabetes mellitus, use of etretinate may also change blood sugar levels

- Liver disease (or history of or family history of)—Use of etretinate may make the condition worse

Proper Use of This Medicine

Take each dose of etretinate with milk or a fatty food. This is important because taking fats with etretinate will help your body absorb the medicine better. *However, you should follow a low-fat diet during the rest of the day* because eating a high-fat diet while you are taking this medicine may cause high triglyceride (fat-like substance) levels in the blood. This may increase the chance of heart and blood vessel disease.

It is very important that you take etretinate only as directed. Do not take more of it, do not take it more often, and do not take it for a longer period of time than your doctor ordered. To do so may increase the chance of side effects.

Dosing—The dose of etretinate will be different for different patients. *Follow your doctor's orders or the directions on the label.* The following information includes only the average doses of etretinate. *If your dose is different, do not change it* unless your doctor tells you to do so.

The number of capsules that you take depends on the strength of the medicine. Also, *the number of doses you take each day, the time allowed between doses, and the length of time you take the medicine depend on the medical problem for which you are taking etretinate.*

- For *oral* dosage form (capsules):
  —For psoriasis:
  - Adults and teenagers—Dose is based on body weight and must be determined by your doctor. The usual dose is 0.75 to 1 milligram (mg) per kilogram (kg) (0.34 to 0.45 mg per pound) of body weight a day, divided into several doses.
  - Children—Use is usually not recommended.

Missed dose—If you miss a dose of this medicine, take it as soon as possible with milk or a fatty food. However, if it is almost time for your next dose, skip the missed dose and go back to your regular dosing schedule. Do not double doses.

Storage—To store this medicine:
- Keep out of the reach of children.
- Store away from heat and direct light.
- Do not store in the bathroom, near the kitchen sink, or in other damp places. Heat or moisture may cause the medicine to break down.
- Do not keep outdated medicine or medicine no longer needed. Be sure that any discarded medicine is out of the reach of children.

Precautions While Using This Medicine

Your doctor should check your progress at regular visits to make sure this medicine does not cause unwanted effects.

Etretinate causes birth defects in humans if taken during pregnancy. In addition, it is not known how long pregnancy should be avoided after treatment stops, to prevent birth defects. Therefore, you must plan on never having children if you are treated with etretinate. For as long as you are able to become pregnant, you must use a reliable form of birth control. In addition, you must not change your birth control method unless you have checked with your doctor first. If you suspect that you may have become pregnant while taking etretinate, stop taking the medicine immediately and check with your doctor. Also, if you become pregnant at any time after you have stopped taking this medicine, check with your doctor as soon as possible. In either case, you should talk to your doctor about the risks of continuing the pregnancy.

It is not known how long etretinate stays in the blood. *Therefore, to prevent the possibility of a pregnant patient receiving your blood, you must plan on never donating blood to a blood bank if you are being treated with etretinate or if you have ever been treated with etretinate.*

Do not take vitamin A or any vitamin supplement containing vitamin A while you are taking this medicine. To do so may increase the chance of side effects.

Drinking too much alcohol while you are taking this medicine may cause high triglyceride (fat-like substance) levels in the blood. This may increase the chance of heart and blood vessel disease. Therefore, *while taking this medicine, do not drink alcoholic beverages or, at least, reduce the amount you usually drink.* If you have any questions about this, check with your doctor.

For *diabetic patients:*

- This medicine may affect blood sugar levels. If you notice a change in the results of your blood or urine sugar tests or if you have any questions, check with your doctor.

In some patients, etretinate may cause a decrease in night vision. This decrease may occur suddenly. If it does occur, *do not drive, use machines, or do anything else that could be dangerous if you are not able to see well.* Also, check with your doctor.

Etretinate may cause dryness of the eyes. Therefore, if you wear contact lenses, your eyes may be more sensitive to them while you are taking etretinate and for several weeks or longer after you stop taking it. To help relieve dryness of the eyes, check with your doctor about using an eye lubricating solution, such as artificial tears. If your eyes become inflamed, check with your doctor.

Some people who take this medicine may become more sensitive to sunlight than they are normally. When you begin taking this medicine:

- Stay out of direct sunlight, especially between the hours of 10:00 a.m. and 3:00 p.m., if possible.
- Wear protective clothing, including a hat and sunglasses.
- Apply a sun block product that has a skin protection factor (SPF) of at least 15. Some patients may require a product with a higher SPF number, especially if they have a fair complexion. If you have any questions about this, check with your health care professional.
- Do not use a sunlamp or tanning bed or booth.

If you have a severe reaction, check with your doctor.

This medicine may cause dryness of the mouth and nose. For temporary relief of mouth dryness, use sugarless candy or gum, melt bits of ice in your mouth, or use a saliva substitute. However, if dry mouth continues for more than 2 weeks, check with your medical doctor or dentist. Continuing dryness of the mouth may increase the chance of dental disease, including tooth decay, gum disease, and fungus infections.

During the first month of treatment with etretinate, your psoriasis may seem to get worse before it gets better. There may be more redness or itching, but this usually goes away during treatment. It may take 2 or 3 months before the full effects of etretinate are seen. If irritation or other symptoms of your condition become severe, check with your doctor.

Side Effects of This Medicine

Along with its needed effects, a medicine may cause some unwanted effects. Although not all of these side effects may occur, if they do occur they may need medical attention.

Stop taking this medicine and check with your doctor immediately if any of the following side effects occur:
Less common
Blurred or double vision or other changes in vision; dark-colored urine; flu-like symptoms; yellow eyes or skin
Rare
Headache (severe or continuing); nausea and vomiting

Check with your doctor as soon as possible if any of the following side effects occur:
More common
Bone or joint pain, tenderness, or stiffness; burning, redness, itching, feeling of dryness, pain, tenderness, excessive tearing (continuing), or other sign of inflammation or irritation of eyes; cramps or pain in upper abdomen or stomach area; muscle cramps; unusual bruising
Less common
Change in hearing, earache or pain in ear, or drainage from ear
Rare
Bleeding or inflammation of gums; confusion; mental depression; mood or mental changes

Other side effects may occur that usually do not need medical attention. These side effects may go away during treatment as your body adjusts to the medicine. However, check with your doctor if any of the following side effects continue or are bothersome:
More common
Changes in appetite; chapped lips; dryness of nose or nosebleeds; dryness, redness, scaling, itching, rash, or other sign of inflammation or irritation of the skin; headache (mild); increased sensitivity to contact lenses (may occur during and after treatment); increased sensitivity of skin to sunlight; peeling of skin on fingertips, palms of hands, or soles of feet; thinning of hair; unusual thirst; unusual tiredness
Less common
Dizziness; dryness of mouth; fever; nausea (mild); redness or soreness around fingernails; loosening of the fingernails; soreness of tongue; soreness, cracking, swelling, or unusual redness of lips

Other side effects not listed above may also occur in some patients. If you notice any other effects, check with your doctor.

Revised: 10/13/2000
Interim revision: 10/13/2000

EXEMESTANE   Systemic

Commonly used brand name(s):

In the U.S.—
Aromasin

In Canada—
Aromasin

Description

Exemestane (ex-uh-MESS-tane) is a medicine that is used to treat breast cancer in women whose disease has progressed while they were taking tamoxifen (ta-MOX-i-fen).

Many breast cancer tumors grow in response to estrogen. Exemestane interferes with the production of estrogen in the body. As a result, the amount of estrogen that the tumor is exposed to is reduced, limiting the growth of the tumor. This medicine is meant to be used only by women who have already stopped menstruating.

Before you begin treatment with exemestane, you and your doctor should talk about the good this medicine will do as well as the risks of using it.

Exemestane is available only with your doctor's prescription, in the following dosage form:

Oral
• Tablets (U.S.and Canada)

Before Using This Medicine

In deciding to use a medicine, the risks of taking the medicine must be weighed against the good it will do. This is a decision you and your doctor will make. For exemestane, the following should be considered:

Allergies—Tell your doctor if you have ever had any unusual or allergic reaction to exemestane. Also tell your health care professional if you are allergic to any other substances, such as foods, preservatives, or dyes.

Pregnancy—Exemestane is meant to be used only by women who have experienced menopause and can no longer become pregnant, however, it is important to tell your doctor if you think you might be pregnant. If this medicine is taken by a pregnant woman for any reason it may cause harm to, and possibly even death of, the fetus.

Breast-feeding—It is not known whether exemestane passes into human milk. Studies in animals have shown that exemestane passes into rat milk. Because this medicine may cause serious side effects, breast-feeding is generally not recommended while you are taking it.

Older adults—Many medicines have not been studied specifically in older people. Therefore, it may not be known whether they work exactly the same way they do in younger adults. Although there is no specific information comparing use of exemestane in the elderly with use in other age groups, this medicine is not expected to cause different side effects or problems in older people than it does in younger adults.

Other medicines—Although certain medicines should not be used together at all, in other cases two different medicines may be used together even if an interaction might occur. In these cases, your doctor may want to change the dose, or other precautions may be necessary. Tell your health care professional if you are taking any other prescription or nonprescription (over-the-counter [OTC]) medicine including the following:

• Estrogens—Exemestane may not work as well

Other medical problems—The presence of other medical problems may affect the use of exemestane. Make sure you tell your doctor if you have any other medical problems, especially:

• Kidney disease or
• Liver disease—It is not known whether moderate or severe kidney or liver disease may increase the chance of side effects during treatment

Proper Use of This Medicine

Use this medicine only as directed by your doctor. Do not use more or less of it, and do not use it more often than your doctor ordered. The exact amount of medicine you need has been carefully worked out. Taking too much may increase the chance of side effects, while taking too little may not improve your condition.

Dosing—The dose of exemestane will be different for different patients. *Follow your doctor's orders or the directions on the label.* The following information includes only the average doses of exemestane. *If your dose is different, do not change it* unless your doctor tells you to do so.
• For *oral* dosage form (tablets)
—For breast cancer in postmenopausal women:
• Adults—25 milligrams (mg) once a day after a meal.

Missed dose—If you miss a dose of this medicine, do not take the missed dose at all and do not double the next one. Instead, go back to your regular dosing schedule and check with your doctor.

Storage—To store this medicine:
• Keep out of the reach of children.
• Store away from heat and direct light.
• Do not store in the bathroom, near the kitchen sink, or in other damp places. Heat or moisture may cause the medicine to break down.
• Do not keep outdated medicine or medicine no longer needed. Be sure that any discarded medicine is out of the reach of children.

Precautions While Using This Medicine

It is very important that your doctor check your progress at regular visits to make sure that this medicine is working properly and to check for unwanted effects.

Side Effects of This Medicine

Along with its needed effects, a medicine may cause some unwanted effects. Although not all of these side effects may occur, if they do occur they may need medical attention.

Check with your doctor as soon as possible if any of the following side effects occur:
More common
Cough or hoarseness; difficult or labored breathing; fever or chills; increased blood pressure; lower back or side pain; mental depression; shortness of breath; swelling of hands, ankles, feet, or lower legs; tightness in chest
Less common
Chest pain; difficult, burning, or painful urination; fre-

quent urge to urinate; headache; sore throat; unexplained broken bones; wheezing

Other side effects may occur that usually do not need medical attention. These side effects may go away during treatment as your body adjusts to the medicine. However, check with your doctor if any of the following side effects continue or are bothersome:

More common
> Abdominal or stomach pain; anxiety; constipation; diarrhea; dizziness; general feeling of discomfort or illness; general feeling of tiredness or weakness; hot flashes; increased sweating; loss of appetite; nausea and vomiting; pain; trouble in sleeping

Less common
> Back pain; bone pain; burning, tingling or prickly sensations; confusion; decreased sense of touch; increased appetite; itching; joint pain; loss of hair; rash; runny nose; stomach upset; weakness, generalized

Other side effects not listed above may also occur in some patients. If you notice any other effects, check with your doctor.

Developed: 03/14/00
Revised: 12/08/00

FACTOR IX   Systemic

Commonly used brand name(s):

In the U.S.—

AlphaNine SD	Mononine
Bebulin VH	Profilnine SD
BeneFix	Proplex T
Konyne 80	

In Canada—

AlphaNine SD	BeneFix
Bebulin VH	Immunine VH

Other commonly used names are Christmas factor, plasma thromboplastin component (PTC), and prothrombin complex concentrate (PCC).

Description

Factor IX is a protein produced naturally in the body. It helps the blood form clots to stop bleeding. Injections of factor IX are used to treat hemophilia B, which is sometimes called Christmas disease. This is a condition in which the body does not make enough factor IX. If you do not have enough factor IX and you become injured, your blood will not form clots as it should, and you may bleed into and damage your muscles and joints.

Injections of one form of factor IX, called factor IX complex, also are used to treat certain people with hemophilia A. In hemophilia A, sometimes called classical hemophilia, the body does not make enough factor VIII, and, just as in hemophilia B, the blood cannot form clots as it should. Injections of factor IX complex may be used in patients in whom the medicine used to treat hemophilia A is no longer effective. Injections of factor IX complex also may be used for other conditions as determined by your doctor.

The factor IX product that your doctor will give you is obtained naturally from human blood or artificially by a man-made process. Factor IX obtained from human blood has been treated and is not likely to contain harmful viruses such as hepatitis B virus, hepatitis C (non-A, non-B) virus, or human immunodeficiency virus (HIV), the virus that causes acquired immunodeficiency syndrome (AIDS). The man-made factor IX product does not contain these viruses.

Factor IX is available only with your doctor's prescription, in the following dosage form:

Parenteral
• Injection (U.S. and Canada)

Before Using This Medicine

In deciding to use a medicine, the risks of using the medicine must be weighed against the good it will do. This is a decision you and your doctor will make. For factor IX, the following should be considered:

Allergies—Tell your doctor if you have ever had any unusual or allergic reaction to injections of factor IX, hamster protein, or mouse protein. Also tell your health care professional if you are allergic to any other substances, such as foods, preservatives, or dyes.

Pregnancy—Studies on effects in pregnancy have not been done in either humans or animals.

Breast-feeding—It is not known whether the ingredients in factor IX products pass into breast milk. Although most medicines pass into breast milk in small amounts, many of them may be used safely while breast-feeding. Mothers who are using this medicine and who wish to breast-feed should discuss this with their doctor.

Children—Blood clots may be especially likely to occur in premature and newborn babies, who are usually more sensitive than adults to the effects of injections of factor IX.

Older adults—This medicine has been tested and has not been shown to cause different side effects or problems in older people than it does in younger adults.

Other medicines—Although certain medicines should not be used together at all, in other cases two different medicines may be used together even if an interaction might occur. In these cases, your doctor may want to change the dose, or other precautions may be necessary. Tell your health care professional if you are using any other prescription or nonprescription (over-the-counter [OTC]) medicine.

Other medical problems—The presence of other medical problems may affect the use of factor IX products. Make sure you tell your doctor if you have any other medical problems, especially:
• Blood clots or a history of medical problems caused by blood clots or
• Liver disease—Risk of bleeding or developing blood clots may be increased

Proper Use of This Medicine

Some medicines given by injection may sometimes be given at home to patients who do not need to be in the hospital. If you are using this medicine at home, your health care professional will teach you how to prepare and inject the medicine. You will have a chance to practice preparing and injecting it. *Be sure that you understand exactly how the medicine is to be prepared and injected.*

To prepare this medicine:
- Take the dry medicine and the liquid (diluent) out of the refrigerator and *bring them to room temperature*, as directed by your doctor.
- When injecting the liquid (diluent) into the dry medicine, *aim the stream of liquid (diluent) against the wall of the container of dry medicine* to prevent foaming.
- *Swirl the container gently to dissolve the medicine. Do not shake the container.*

Use this medicine right away. It should not be kept longer than 3 hours after it has been prepared.

A plastic disposable syringe and filter needle must be used with this medicine. The medicine may stick to the inside of a glass syringe, and you may not receive a full dose.

Do not reuse syringes and needles. Put used syringes and needles in a puncture-resistant disposable container, or dispose of them as directed by your health care professional.

Dosing—The dose of factor IX will be different for different patients. The dose you receive will be based on:
- The condition for which you are using this medicine.
- Your body weight.
- The amount of factor IX your body is able to make.
- How much, how often, and where in your body you are bleeding.
- Whether or not your body has built up a defense (antibody) against this medicine.

Your dose of this medicine may even be different at different times. It is important that you *follow your doctor's orders.*

Missed dose—If you miss a dose of this medicine, check with your doctor as soon as possible for instructions.

Storage—To store this medicine:
- Keep out of the reach of children.
- Some factor IX products must be stored in the refrigerator, and some may be kept at room temperature for short periods of time. Store this medicine as directed by your doctor or the manufacturer.
- Do not keep outdated medicine or medicine no longer needed. Be sure that any discarded medicine is out of the reach of children.

Precautions While Using This Medicine

If you were recently diagnosed with hemophilia B, you should receive hepatitis A and hepatitis B vaccines to reduce even further your risk of getting hepatitis A or hepatitis B from factor IX products.

After a while, your body may build up a defense (antibody) against this medicine. *Tell your doctor if this medicine seems to be less effective than usual.*

It is recommended that you carry identification stating that you have hemophilia A or hemophilia B. If you have any questions about what kind of identification to carry, check with your health care professional.

Side Effects of This Medicine

Along with its needed effects, a medicine may cause some unwanted effects. Although not all of these side effects may occur, if they do occur they may need medical attention.

Check with your doctor immediately if any of the following side effects occur, because they may mean that you are having a serious allergic reaction to the medicine:
Less common or rare
Changes in facial skin color; fast or irregular breathing; puffiness or swelling of the eyelids or around the eyes; shortness of breath, troubled breathing, tightness in chest, and/or wheezing; skin rash, hives, and/or itching

Also, check with your doctor immediately if any of the following side effects occur, because they may mean that you are developing a problem with blood clotting:
More common
Bluish coloring (especially of the hands and feet); convulsions; dizziness or lightheadedness when getting up from a lying or sitting position; increased heart rate; large blue or purplish patches in the skin (at places of injection); nausea or vomiting; pains in chest, groin, or legs (especially calves); persistent bleeding from puncture sites, gums, or inner linings of the nose and/or mouth, or blood in the stool or urine; severe pain or pressure in the chest and/or the neck, back, or left arm; severe, sudden headache; shortness of breath or fast breathing; sudden loss of coordination; sudden and unexplained slurred speech, vision changes, and/or weakness or numbness in arm or leg

Also, check with your doctor immediately if any of the following side effects occur, because they may mean that your medicine is being given too fast:
Less common
Burning or stinging at place of injection; changes in blood pressure or pulse rate; chills; drowsiness; fever; headache; nausea or vomiting; redness of face; shortness of breath

Other side effects not listed above may also occur in some patients. If you notice any other effects, check with your doctor.

Revised: 08/15/97

FACTOR VIIA   Systemic†

Commonly used brand name(s):

In the U.S.—
NovoSeven

Other commonly used names are coagulation factor VIIa (recombinant), eptacog alfa, factor 7, proconvertin, recombinant activated factor VIIa, recombinant coagulation factor VIIa, recombinant factor VIIa, and rFVIIa.

†Not commercially available in Canada.

Description

Factor VIIa is a man-made protein produced to replicate the naturally occurring activated factor VII (factor VIIa) in the body. Factor VIIa is used to stop bleeding of injuries for patients with hemophilia by helping the blood to clot. This man-made protein, factor VIIa, is used in people who have Hemophilia A or Hemophilia B, who have also formed antibodies against other clotting proteins that help bleeding to stop. Patients using factor VIIa are usually male.

Factor VIIa is to be administered only by or under the supervision of your doctor or other health care professional. It is available in the following dosage form(s):

Parenteral
- Injection (U.S.)

Before Using This Medicine

In deciding to use a medicine, the risks of using the medicine must be weighed against the good it will do. This is a decision you and your doctor will make. For factor VIIa, the following should be considered:

Allergies—Tell your doctor if you have ever had any unusual or allergic reaction to factor VIIa or to any products that contain mouse, hamster, or cow proteins. Also tell your doctor and pharmacist if you are allergic to any other substances, such as foods, preservatives, or dyes.

Pregnancy—Studies on effects in pregnancy have not been done in humans.

Breast-feeding—It is not known whether factor VIIa passes into breast milk. However, because this medicine may cause serious side effects, breast-feeding is generally not recommended while you are receiving it.

Children—This medicine has been tested in children and no side effects or problems were found that were different from those seen in adults.

Older adults—No information is available about the use of factor VIIa in older adults.

Other medicines—Although certain medicines should not be used together at all, in other cases two different medicines may be used together even if an interaction might occur. In these cases, your doctor may want to change the dose, or other precautions may be necessary. When you are taking factor VIIa, it is especially important that your doctor and pharmacist know if you are taking any of the following:
- Activated prothrombin complex concentrates (ie, FEIBA, Autoplex T) or
- Prothrombin complex concentrates (ie, AlphaNine, BeneFix)—May increase the risk of side effects

Other medical problems—The presence of medical problems may affect the use of factor VIIa. Make sure to tell your doctor if you have any medical problems, especially:
- Blood clots or a history of medical problems caused by blood clots or
- Heart disease or
- Infection or
- Injury (crush)—These conditions may increase the risk of bleeding

Proper Use of This Medicine

This medicine is to be used in a medical setting under the direct supervision of a doctor.

Dosing—The dose of factor VIIa will be different for different patients. The dose you receive will be based on:
- Your body weight.
- How much, how often, and where in your body you are bleeding.

Precautions While Using This Medicine

If you notice early signs of a hypersensitivity reaction such as hives, skin rash, tightness of the chest or wheezing, lightheadedness or dizziness, notify your physician immediately.

Side Effects of This Medicine

Along with its needed effects, a medicine may cause some unwanted effects. Although not all of these side effects may occur, if they do occur they may need medical attention.

Check with your doctor as soon as possible if any of the following side effects occur:

More common
   Bleeding problems; fever; high blood pressure; joint or muscle pain and/or stiffness

Less common or rare
   Bloating or swelling of face, hands, lower legs, and/or feet; bluish color hands or feet; blurred vision; changes in facial color; chest pain; chills; cold sweats; confusion; continuing thirst; cough; dizziness; excessive sweating; faintness; fast heartbeat; hives and/or itching; large flat blue or purplish patches on the skin; lightheadedness when getting up from a lying or sitting position; persistent bleeding or oozing from puncture sites or mucous membranes [bowel, mouth, nose, or urinary bladder]; puffiness or swelling of eyelids or around the eyes; shakiness; slurred speech; shortness of breath; skin rash; slow or irregular heartbeat [less than 50 beats per minute]; sneezing; sore throat; sudden decrease in the amount urine; swelling of face, fingers, feet, and/or lower legs; troubled breathing, tightness in chest, and/or wheezing; unusual tiredness or weakness; weight gain (unusual).

Other side effects may occur that usually do not need medical attention. These side effects may go away during treatment as your body adjusts to the medicine. However, check with your doctor if any of the following side effects continue or are bothersome:

Less common or rare
   Burning or stinging at the injection site; changes in blood pressure or pulse rate; drowsiness; flushing [redness of face]; headache; pinpoint red or purple spots on skin; nausea or vomiting

Other side effects not listed above may also occur in some patients. If you notice any other effects, check with your doctor.

Additional Information

Once a medicine has been approved for marketing for a certain use, experience may show that it is also useful for other medical problems. Although this use is not included in product labeling, factor VIIa is used in certain patients with the following medical conditions:
- Factor VII deficiency

Other than the above information, there is no additional information relating to proper use, precautions, or side effects for this use.

Developed: 05/09/2000

FAMCICLOVIR   Systemic

Commonly used brand name(s):

In the U.S.—
   Famvir

In Canada—
   Famvir

Description

Famciclovir (fam-SYE-kloe-veer) is used to treat the symptoms of herpes zoster (also known as shingles), a herpes virus infection of the skin. It is used to treat and suppress recurrent episodes of genital herpes infection. This medicine is also used to treat recurrent herpes virus infections of the mucous membranes (lips and mouth) and genitals in HIV-infected patients. Although famciclovir will not cure genital herpes or herpes zoster, it does help relieve the pain and discomfort and helps the sores heal faster.

Famciclovir is available only with your doctor's prescription, in the following dosage form:

Oral
   • Tablets (U.S. and Canada)

Before Using This Medicine

In deciding to use a medicine, the risks of taking the medicine must be weighed against the good it will do. This is a decision you and your doctor will make. For famciclovir, the following should be considered:

Allergies—Tell your doctor if you have ever had any unusual or allergic reaction to famciclovir. Also tell your health care professional if you are allergic to any other substances, such as foods, sulfites or other preservatives, or dyes.

Pregnancy—Famciclovir has not been studied in pregnant women. However, famciclovir has not been shown to cause birth defects or other problems in animal studies.

Breast-feeding—It is not known whether famciclovir passes into the breast milk of humans; however, it does pass into the milk of rats. Famciclovir is not recommended during breast-feeding because it may cause unwanted effects in nursing babies.

Children—Studies on this medicine have been done only in adult patients, and there is no specific information comparing use of famciclovir in children with use in other age groups.

Older adults—Famciclovir has been used in the elderly and has not been shown to cause different side effects or problems in older people than it does in younger adults.

Other medicines—Although certain medicines should not be used together at all, in other cases two different medicines may be used together even if an interaction might occur. In these cases, your doctor may want to change your dose or other precautions may be necessary. Tell your health care professional if you are taking any other prescription or nonprescription (over-the-counter [OTC]) medicine.

Other medical problems—The presence of other medical problems may affect the use of famciclovir. Make sure you tell your doctor if you have any other medical problems, especially:

• Kidney disease—Kidney disease may increase blood levels of this medicine, increasing the chance of side effects

Proper Use of This Medicine

Famciclovir is best used within 48 hours after the symptoms of shingles (for example, pain, burning, blisters) begin to appear, or within 6 hours after the symptoms of recurrent genital herpes (for example, pain, blisters) begin to appear.

Famciclovir may be taken with meals.

To help clear up your herpes infection, *keep taking famciclovir for the full time of treatment*, even if your symptoms begin to clear up after a few days. *Do not miss any doses.* However, *do not use this medicine more often or for a longer time than your doctor ordered.*

Dosing—The dose of famciclovir will be different for different patients. *Follow your doctor's orders or the directions on the label.* The following information includes only the average doses of famciclovir. Your dose may be different if you have kidney disease. *If your dose is different, do not change it* unless your doctor tells you to do so.

• For *oral* dosage form (tablets):
   —For treatment of shingles:
      • Adults—500 milligrams (mg) every eight hours for seven days.
      • Children—Use and dose must be determined by your doctor.
   —For suppression of recurrent genital herpes:
      • Adults—250 mg two times a day for up to one year.
      • Children—Use and dose must be determined by your doctor.
   —For treatment of recurrent genital herpes:
      • Adults—125 mg two times a day for five days.
      • Children—Use and dose must be determined by your doctor.
   —For treatment of recurrent herpes virus infections of the mucous membranes (lips and mouth) and genitals in HIV-infected patients:
      • Adults—500 mg two times a day for seven days.
      • Children—Use and dose must be determined by your doctor.

Missed dose—If you miss a dose of this medicine, take it as soon as possible. However, if it is almost time for your next dose, skip the missed dose and go back to your regular dosing schedule. Do not double doses.

Storage—To store this medicine:
• Keep out of the reach of children.
• Store away from heat and direct light.
• Do not store the tablets in the bathroom, near the kitchen sink, or in other damp places. Heat or moisture may cause the medicine to break down.
• Do not keep outdated medicine or medicine no longer needed. Be sure that any discarded medicine is out of the reach of children.

Precautions While Using This Medicine

If your symptoms do not improve within a few days, or if they become worse, check with your doctor.

The areas affected by herpes should be kept as clean and dry as possible. Also, wear loose-fitting clothing to avoid irritating the sores (blisters).

Side Effects of This Medicine

Along with its needed effects, a medicine may cause some unwanted effects. Although not all of these side effects may occur, if they do occur they may need medical attention.

Side effects may occur that usually do not need medical attention. These side effects may go away during treatment as your body adjusts to the medicine. However, check with your doctor if any of the following side effects continue or are bothersome:

More common
    Headache
Less common
    Diarrhea; dizziness; nausea; unusual tiredness or weakness; vomiting

Other side effects not listed above may also occur in some patients. If you notice any other effects, check with your doctor.

Developed: 11/28/94
Interim revision: 04/04/00

FELBAMATE   Systemic†

Commonly used brand name(s):

In the U.S.—
    Felbatol
Another commonly used name is FBM.

    †Not commercially available in Canada.

Description

Felbamate (FEL-ba-mate) is used to control some types of seizures in the treatment of epilepsy. Felbamate acts on the central nervous system (CNS) to make it more difficult for seizures to start or to continue. This medicine cannot cure epilepsy and will only work to control seizures for as long as you continue to use it.

Felbamate is available only with your doctor's prescription, in the following dosage forms:

Oral
    • Suspension (U.S.)
    • Tablets (U.S.)

Before Using This Medicine

In deciding to use a medicine, the risks of taking the medicine must be weighed against the good it will do. This is a decision you and your doctor will make. For felbamate, the following should be considered:

Allergies—Tell your doctor if you have ever had any unusual or allergic reaction to felbamate or to medicines like felbamate such as carbromal, carisoprodol (Soma, Rela), mebutamate, meprobamate (Equanil, Miltown), or tybamate (Tybatran). Also tell your health care professional if you are allergic to any other substances, such as foods, preservatives, or dyes.

Pregnancy—Felbamate has not been studied in pregnant women. However, studies in pregnant animals have shown that felbamate may cause lowered birth weight and lowered survival of offspring when given to the mother in doses more than one and one-half times the usual human dose. Before taking this medicine, make sure your doctor knows if you are pregnant or if you may become pregnant.

Breast-feeding—Felbamate passes into breast milk. However, it is not known whether this medicine causes problems in nursing babies.

Children—This medicine has some very serious unwanted effects. Children may not be able to tell their parent or guardian or their doctor if they have symptoms of these effects, such as chills or stomach pain. Felbamate should be used in children only if other medicines have not controlled their seizures.

Older adults—Many medicines have not been studied specifically in older people. Therefore, it may not be known whether they work exactly the same way they do in younger adults or if they cause different side effects or problems in older people. There is no specific information comparing use of felbamate in the elderly with use in other age groups. However, older people are more likely to have other illnesses and to use other medicines that may affect the way felbamate works. Your doctor may start with a lower felbamate dose or may increase the dose more slowly.

Other medicines—Although certain medicines should not be used together at all, in other cases two different medicines may be used together even if an interaction might occur. In these cases, your doctor may want to change the dose, or other precautions may be necessary. When you are taking felbamate, it is especially important that your health care professional know if you are taking any of the following:

• Carbamazepine (e.g., Tegretol) or
• Phenytoin (e.g., Dilantin) or
• Valproic acid (e.g., Depakene)—Higher or lower blood levels of these medicines or felbamate may occur, which may increase the chance of unwanted effects; your doctor may need to change the dose of either these medicines or felbamate

Other medical problems—The presence of other medical problems may affect the use of felbamate. Make sure you tell your doctor if you have any other medical problems, especially:

• Anemia or other blood problems (or history of) or
• Liver problems (or history of)—Felbamate may make the condition worse

Proper Use of This Medicine

Take this medicine only as directed by your doctor, to benefit your condition as much as possible. Do not take more of it, do not take it more often, and do not take it for a longer time than your doctor ordered.

For patients taking the *oral liquid form* of this medicine:
• Shake the bottle well before measuring the dose.
• Use a specially marked measuring spoon, a plastic syringe, or a small marked measuring cup to measure each dose accurately. The average household teaspoon may not hold the right amount of liquid.

To lessen stomach upset, felbamate may be taken with food, unless your doctor has told you to take it on an empty stomach.

Dosing—The dose of felbamate will be different for different patients. *Follow your doctor's orders or the directions on the label.* The following information includes only the average doses of felbamate. *If your dose is different, do not change it* unless your doctor tells you to do so.

The number of tablets or teaspoonfuls of suspension that you take depends on the strength of the medicine.

- For *oral* dosage forms (suspension or tablets):
  —For epilepsy:
  - Adults and teenagers 14 years of age and older— At first, usually 1200 milligrams (mg) a day, divided into three or four smaller doses. Your doctor may increase the dose gradually over several weeks if needed. However, the dose is usually not more than 3600 mg a day.
  - Children 2 to 14 years of age—At first, usually 15 mg per kilogram (kg) [6.8 mg per pound] of body weight per day, divided into smaller doses that are given three or four times during the day. Your doctor may increase the dose gradually over a few weeks if needed. However, the dose is usually not more than 45 mg per kg [20.5 mg per pound] or 3600 mg per day, whichever is less.

Missed dose—If you miss a dose of this medicine, take it as soon as possible. However, if it is almost time for your next dose, skip the missed dose and go back to your regular dosing schedule. Do not double doses.

Storage—To store this medicine:
- Keep out of the reach of children.
- Store away from heat and direct sunlight.
- Do not store in the bathroom, near the kitchen sink, or in other damp places. Heat or moisture may cause the medicine to break down.
- Do not keep outdated medicine or medicine no longer needed. Be sure that any discarded medicine is out of the reach of children.

Precautions While Using This Medicine

It is important that your doctor check your progress at regular visits. This is necessary to allow dose adjustments and to test for serious unwanted effects.

Do not stop taking felbamate without first checking with your doctor. Your doctor may want you to gradually reduce the amount you are taking before stopping completely. Stopping the medicine suddenly may cause your seizures to return or to occur more often.

Felbamate may cause blurred vision, double vision, or other changes in vision. It may also cause some people to become dizzy or drowsy. *Make sure you know how you react to this medicine before you drive, use machines, or do anything else that could be dangerous if you are not alert or able to see well.* If these reactions are especially bothersome, check with your doctor.

Side Effects of This Medicine

Felbamate may cause some serious side effects, including blood problems and liver problems. *You and your doctor should discuss the good this medicine will do as well as the risks of receiving it.*

Along with its needed effects, a medicine may cause some unwanted effects. Some side effects will have signs or symptoms that you can see or feel. Your doctor may watch for others by doing certain tests. Although not all of these side effects may occur, if they do occur they may need medical attention.

Check with your doctor immediately if any of the following side effects occur:
  More common
    Fever; purple or red spots on skin
  Rare
    Black or tarry stools; blood in urine or stools; chills; continuing headache; continuing stomach pain; continuing vomiting; dark-colored urine; general feeling of tiredness or weakness; light-colored stools; nosebleeds or other unusual bruising or bleeding; shortness of breath, trouble in breathing, wheezing, or tightness in chest; sore throat; sores, ulcers, or white spots on lips or in mouth; swelling of face; swollen or painful glands; yellow eyes or skin

Check with your doctor as soon as possible if any of the following side effects occur:
  More common
    Walking in unusual manner
  Less common
    Agitation, aggression, or other mood or mental changes; clumsiness or unsteadiness; skin rash; trembling or shaking
  Rare
    Chest pain; hives or itching; muscle cramps; nasal congestion; pain; sensitivity of skin to sunlight; swollen lymph nodes

Other side effects may occur that usually do not need medical attention. These side effects may go away during treatment as your body adjusts to the medicine. However, check with your doctor if any of the following side effects continue or are bothersome:
  More common
    Change in your sense of taste; constipation; difficulty in sleeping; dizziness; headache; indigestion; loss of appetite; nausea; stomach pain; vomiting
  Less common
    Blurred or double vision; coughing; diarrhea; drowsiness; ear congestion or pain; runny nose; sneezing; weight loss

This medicine may also cause the following side effects that your doctor will watch for:
  Rare
    Blood problems

Other side effects not listed above may also occur in some patients. If you notice any other effects, check with your doctor.

Developed: 08/30/94
Interim revision: 10/06/94; 03/28/95

FENOFIBRATE   Systemic

Commonly used brand name(s):

In the U.S.—
  Tricor

In Canada—
  Apo-Feno
  Lipidil
  Gen-Fenofibrate

Description

Fenofibrate (fen-o-FI-brate) is used to lower triglyceride (fat-like substances) levels in the blood. This may help prevent the development of pancreatitis (inflammation of the pancreas) caused by high levels of triglycerides in the blood.

This medicine is available only with your doctor's prescription, in the following dosage form(s):

Oral
- Capsules (U.S.)

Before Using This Medicine

In addition to its helpful effects in treating your medical problem, this type of medicine may have some harmful effects.

Results of large studies using other agents that are similar to fenofibrate seem to suggest that fenofibrate may increase the patient's risk of cancer, pancreatitis (inflammation of the pancreas), gallstones, and problems from gallbladder surgery.

Studies with fenofibrate in rats found an increased risk of liver and pancreatic tumors when doses up to 6 times the human dose were given for a long time.

Be sure you have discussed this with your doctor before taking this medicine.

In deciding to use a medicine, the risks of taking the medicine must be weighed against the good it will do. This is a decision you and your doctor will make. For fenofibrate, the following should be considered:

Allergies—Tell your doctor if you have ever had any unusual or allergic reaction to fenofibrate. Also tell your health care professional if you are allergic to any other substances, such as foods, preservatives, or dyes.

Diet—Before prescribing medicine for your condition, your doctor will probably try to control your condition by prescribing a personal diet for you. Such a diet may be low in fats, sugars, and/or cholesterol. Many people are able to control their condition by carefully following their doctor's orders for proper diet and exercise. *Medicine is prescribed only when additional help is needed* and is effective only when a schedule of diet and exercise is properly followed.

Pregnancy—Fenofibrate has not been studied in pregnant women. However, studies in animals have shown that high doses of fenofibrate may increase the number of fetal deaths, decrease birth weight, or cause some skeletal defects. Before taking this medicine, make sure your doctor knows if you are pregnant or if you may become pregnant.

Breast-feeding—It is not known whether fenofibrate passes into breast milk. Studies in animals have shown that high doses of fenofibrate may increase the risk of some kinds of tumors. Therefore, this medicine is not recommended for use during breast-feeding.

Children—Studies on this medicine have been done only in adult patients, and there is no specific information comparing use of fenofibrate in children with use in other age groups.

Older adults—Although the effects of fenofibrate have not been fully tested in older people, this medicine has been tested in a limited number of patients 77 through 87 years of age and has not been shown to cause problems when given to older people.

Other medicines—Although certain medicines should not be used together at all, in other cases two different medicines may be used together even if an interaction might occur. In these cases, your doctor may want to change the dose, or other precautions may be necessary. When you are taking fenofibrate, it is especially important that your health care professional know if you are taking any of the following:

- Anticoagulants (blood thinners)—Use with fenofibrate may increase the effect of the anticoagulant and increase the risk of bleeding
- Cyclosporine—Use with fenofibrate may cause kidney problems or make them worse
- HMG-CoA reductase inhibitors (atorvastatin [e.g., Lipitor], cerivastatin [e.g., Baycol], fluvastatin [e.g., Lescol], lovastatin [e.g., Mevacor], pravastatin [e.g., Pravacol], simvastatin [e.g., Zocor])—Use with fenofibrate may cause muscle or kidney problems or make them worse

Other medical problems—The presence of other medical problems may affect the use of fenofibrate. Make sure you tell your doctor if you have any other medical problems, especially:

- Gallbladder disease or
- Gallstones or
- Liver disease—Fenofibrate may make these conditions worse
- Kidney disease—Higher blood levels of fenofibrate may result, which may increase the chance of side effects or make kidney problems worse

Proper Use of This Medicine

Use this medicine only as directed by your doctor. Take the medication at the same time each day to maintain the medication's effect. Do not use more or less of it, and do not use it more often than your doctor ordered.

Follow carefully the special diet your doctor gave you. This is the most important part of controlling your condition and is necessary if the medicine is to work properly.

This medicine is usually taken once a day. This medicine works best if it is taken with a meal.

Dosing—The dose of fenofibrate will be different for different patients. *Follow your doctor's orders or the directions on the label.* The following information includes only the average doses of fenofibrate. *If your dose is different, do not change it* unless your doctor tells you to do so:

- For *oral* dosage form (capsules):
  —For hyperlipidemia (to lower triglycerides):
  - Adults—At first, 67 milligrams (mg) once a day with a meal. Your doctor may increase your dose as needed.
  - Children—Use and dose must be determined by your doctor.

Missed dose—If you miss a dose of this medicine, take it as soon as possible. However, if it is almost time for your next dose, skip the missed dose and go back to your regular dosing schedule. Do not double doses.

Storage—To store this medicine:
- Keep out of the reach of children.
- Store away from heat and direct light.
- Do not store in the bathroom, near the kitchen sink, or in other damp places. Heat or moisture may cause the medicine to break down.

• Do not keep outdated medicine or medicine no longer needed. Be sure that any discarded medicine is out of the reach of children.

Precautions While Using This Medicine

It is very important that your doctor check your progress at regular visits. This will allow your doctor to see if the medicine is working properly to lower your triglyceride levels and to decide if you should continue to take it.

Check with your doctor right away if you experience unexplained muscle pain, tenderness, or weakness, especially if accompanied by unusual tiredness or fever.

Check with your doctor right away if you think that you may be pregnant. Fenofibrate may cause birth defects or other problems in the baby if taken during pregnancy.

Check with your doctor right away if you have signs of an infection, such as a fever, sore throat, or chills.

Side Effects of This Medicine

Along with its needed effects, a medicine may cause some unwanted effects. Although not all of these side effects may occur, if they do occur they may need medical attention.

Check with your doctor immediately if any of the following side effects occur:
Rare
Chills, fever, or sore throat

Check with your doctor as soon as possible if any of the following side effects occur:
Less common
Chills, fever, muscle aches and pains, or nausea and/or vomiting; hives; infections; itching (generalized); skin rash
Rare
Bloating or pain of the stomach; chronic indigestion; cough and shortness of breath or troubled breathing; dark urine; general ill feeling; loss of appetite; muscle cramps, pain, stiffness, swelling, or weakness; nausea; unusual bleeding or bruising; unusual tiredness; vomiting; yellow eyes or skin

Other side effects may occur that usually do not need medical attention. These side effects may go away during treatment as your body adjusts to the medicine. However, check with your doctor if any of the following side effects continue or are bothersome:
Less common
Belching; constipation; decreased sexual drive; dizziness; eye irritation; gas; increased sensitivity of the skin to sunlight; stuffy nose

Other side effects not listed above may also occur in some patients. If you notice any other effects, check with your doctor.

Developed: 05/11/98

FENTANYL   Systemic

Commonly used brand name(s):
In the U.S.—
Actiq

Description

Fentanyl (FEN-ta-nil) belongs to the group of medicines called narcotic analgesics (nar-KOT-ik an-al-GEE-ziks). Narcotic analgesics are used to relieve pain. The transmucosal form of fentanyl is used to treat breakthrough cancer pain. Breakthrough episodes of cancer pain are the flares of pain which "breakthrough" the medication used to control the persistent pain. Transmucosal fentanyl is only used in patients who are already taking narcotic analgesics.

Fentanyl acts in the central nervous system (CNS) to relieve pain. Some of its side effects are also caused by actions in the CNS. When a narcotic is used for a long time, it may become habit-forming (causing mental or physical dependence). However, people who have continuing pain should not let the fear of dependence keep them from using narcotics to relieve their pain. Mental dependence (addiction) is not likely to occur when narcotics are used for this purpose. Physical dependence may lead to withdrawal side effects if treatment is stopped suddenly. However, severe withdrawal side effects can usually be prevented by reducing the dose gradually over a period of time before treatment is stopped completely. Your health care professional will take this into consideration when deciding on the amount of transmucosal fentanyl you should receive.

This medicine is available only with your doctor's prescription, in the following dosage form(s):
Oral
• Transmucosal (U.S.)

Before Using This Medicine

In deciding to use a medicine, the risks of using the medicine must be weighed against the good it will do. This is a decision you and your doctor will make. For transmucosal fentanyl, the following should be considered:

Allergies—Tell your doctor if you have ever had any unusual or allergic reaction to fentanyl, including the stick-on patch. Also tell your health care professional if you are allergic to any other substances, such as foods, preservatives, or dyes.

Pregnancy—Although studies on birth defects with fentanyl have not been done in pregnant women, it has not been reported to cause birth defects.

Breast-feeding—Fentanyl passes into breast milk. Nursing babies whose mothers are using this medicine regularly may receive enough of it to cause unwanted effects such as drowsiness or breathing problems. A mother who wishes to breast-feed and who needs treatment for continuing pain should discuss the risks and benefits of different pain treatments with her health care professional.

Children—Studies with transmucosal fentanyl have been done only in adult patients, and there is no specific information comparing use of transmucosal fentanyl in children with use in other age groups. *It contains a medicine in an amount which can be fatal to a child.* Patients and their caregivers should keep transmucosal fentanyl out of the reach of children and discard open units properly.

Older adults—Elderly people may be especially sensitive to the effects of narcotic analgesics. This may increase the chance of side effects during treatment. Your health care professional will take this into consideration when deciding on the amount of transmucosal fentanyl you should receive.

Other medicines—Although certain medicines should not be used together at all, in other cases two different medicines may be used together even if an interaction might occur. In these cases, your doctor may want to change the dose, or other precautions may be necessary. When you are using transmucosal fentanyl, it is especially important that your health care professional know if you are taking any other dosage form of fentanyl (e.g., injection, patch) or nonprescription (over-the-counter [OTC] medicine) or any of the following:

- Alcohol or
- Central nervous system (CNS) depressants (medicines that cause drowsiness), including other narcotics or
- Erythromycin (e.g., E-Mycin) or
- Itraconazole (e.g., Diflucan) or
- Ketoconazole (e.g., Nizoral) or
- Ritanovir (e.g., Norvir)—These medicines may add to the effects of transmucosal fentanyl. This may increase the chance of serious side effects.
- Monoamine oxidase (MAO) inhibitors (furazolidone [e.g., Furoxone], phenelzine [e.g., Nardil], procarbazine [e.g., Matulane], selegilene [e.g., Eldepryl], tranylcypromine [e.g., Parnate]—Taking transmucosal fentanyl while you are taking or within 2 weeks of taking MAO inhibitors may cause an increased chance of serious side effects

Other medical problems—The presence of other medical problems may affect the use of transmucosal fentanyl. Make sure you tell your doctor if you have any other medical problems, especially:

- Alcohol abuse or history of or
- Drug dependence, especially narcotic abuse or dependence, history of or
- Kidney disease or
- Liver disease—The chance of side effects may be increased
- Emphysema or other chronic lung disease or
- Head injuries—Some of the side effects of transmucosal fentanyl can cause serious problems in people who have these medical problems
- Slow heartbeat—Transmucosal fentanyl can make this condition worse

Proper Use of This Medicine

Transmucosal fentanyl contains a medicine in an amount which can be fatal to a child. Patients and their caregivers should keep transmucosal fentanyl out of the reach of children and discard open units properly.

Transmucosal fentanyl comes with patient instructions. Read them carefully before using the product.

How to use transmucosal fentanyl:
- Keep medication in sealed pouch until ready to use.
- The foil package should be opened with scissors immediately prior to product use.
- Place the medicine in mouth between the cheek and lower gum, occasionally moving the medicine from one side to the other using the handle.
- The medicine should be sucked, not chewed.
- Suck the medicine over a 15-minute period.

Dosing—The dose of transmucosal fentanyl will be different for different patients. *Follow your doctor's orders or the directions on the label.* The following information includes only the average doses of transmucosal fentanyl. *If*

your dose is different, do not change it unless your doctor tells you to do so.

The number of units that you use will depend on the strength of the medicine. Also, *the number of doses you use each day, the time allowed between doses, and the length of time you take the medicine depend on the medical problem for which you are using transmucosal fentanyl.*

- For *oral transmucosal* dosage form:
  —For cancer pain:
  - Adults—The initial dose to treat episodes of breakthrough cancer pain in patients who are already receiving and who are tolerant to opioid therapy for their underlying persistent cancer pain is 200 micrograms. Redosing may start 15 minutes after the previous dose has been completed (30 minutes after the start of the previous dose). Patients should not use more than 2 units per episode of breakthrough pain. Patients should record their use over several episodes of breakthrough cancer pain and review their experience with their physicians to determine if a dosage adjustment is warranted.
  - Children—Use and dose must be determined by the doctor.

Missed dose—If your medical doctor has ordered you to use this medicine according to a regular schedule and you miss a dose, use it as soon as you remember. However, if it is almost time for your next dose, skip the missed dose and go back to your regular dosing schedule. *Do not double doses.*

Storage—To store this medicine:
- Keep out of the reach of children.
- Store away from heat and direct light.
- Do not store in the bathroom, near the kitchen sink, or in other damp places. Heat or moisture may cause the medicine to break down.
- Do not keep outdated medicine or medicine no longer needed. Be sure that any discarded medicine is out of the reach of children.
- Do not use if the foil pouch has been opened.
- A temporary storage bottle is provided as part of the Actiq ° Welcome Kit. This container is to be used by patients or their caregivers in the event that a partially consumed unit cannot be disposed of promptly. If additional assistance is required, refer to 1-800-615-0187.

Precautions While Using This Medicine

Transmucosal fentanyl contains a medicine in an amount which can be fatal to a child. Patients and their caregivers should keep transmucosal fentanyl out of the reach of children and discard open units properly.

Check with your health care professional at regular times while using fentanyl. Be sure to report any side effects.

Transmucosal fentanyl comes with patient instructions. Read them carefully before using the product.

This medicine will add to the effects of alcohol and other CNS depressants (medicines that can make you drowsy or less alert). Some examples of CNS depressants are antihistamines or medicine for hay fever, other allergies, or colds; sedatives, tranquilizers, or sleeping medicine; other prescription pain medicine or narcotics; barbiturates; medicine for seizures; muscle relaxants; or anesthetics, including some dental anesthetics. *Check with your health care profes-*

sional before taking any of the other medicines listed above while you are using this medicine.

Transmucosal fentanyl may cause some people to become drowsy, dizzy, or lightheaded, or to feel a false sense of well-being. *Make sure you know how you react to this medicine before you drive, use machines, or do anything else that could be dangerous if you are dizzy or not alert and clear-headed.* These effects usually go away after a few days of treatment, when your body gets used to the medicine. However, *check with your health care professional if drowsiness that is severe enough to interfere with your activities continues for more than a few days.*

Dizziness, lightheadedness, or even fainting may occur when you get up suddenly from a lying or sitting position. Getting up slowly may help lessen this problem. Also, lying down for a while may relieve dizziness or lightheadedness.

Using narcotics for a long time can cause severe constipation. To prevent this, your health care professional may direct you to take laxatives, drink a lot of fluids, or increase the amount of fiber in your diet. Be sure to follow the directions carefully, because continuing constipation can lead to more serious problems.

Before having any kind of surgery (including dental surgery) or emergency treatment, tell the medical doctor or dentist in charge that you are using this medicine. Serious side effects can occur if your medical doctor or dentist gives you certain other medicines without knowing that you are using transmucosal fentanyl.

If you have been using this medicine regularly for several weeks or more, *do not suddenly stop using it without first checking with your health care professional.* You may be directed to reduce gradually the amount you are using before stopping treatment completely to lessen the chance of withdrawal side effects.

Using too much transmucosal fentanyl, or taking too much of another narcotic while using transmucosal fentanyl, may cause an overdose. If this occurs, get emergency help right away. An overdose can cause severe breathing problems (breathing may even stop), unconsciousness, and death. Serious signs of an overdose include very slow breathing (fewer than 8 breaths a minute) and drowsiness that is so severe that you are not able to answer when spoken to or, if asleep, cannot be awakened. Other signs of an overdose may include cold, clammy skin; low blood pressure; pinpoint pupils of eyes; and slow heartbeat. *It may be best to have a family member or a friend check on you several times a day when you start using a narcotic regularly, and whenever your dose is increased,* so that he or she can get help for you if you cannot do so yourself.

Side Effects of This Medicine

Along with its needed effects, a medicine may cause some unwanted effects. Although not all of these side effects may occur, if they do occur they may need medical attention.

Check with your doctor as soon as possible if any of the following side effects occur:
More common
Dizziness, feeling faint, lightheadedness, unusual tiredness or weakness; shortness of breath
Less common
Anxiety; confusion; decrease in urine volume; decreased frequency of urination; drowsiness; false sense of well-being; nervousness; seeing, hearing, or feeling things that are not there
Symptoms of overdose
Cold, clammy skin; convulsions (seizures); feeling faint; pinpoint pupils of the eyes; severe dizziness, drowsiness, nervousness, restlessness, or weakness; slow or troubled breathing

Other side effects may occur that usually do not need medical attention. These side effects may go away during treatment as your body adjusts to the medicine. However, check with your doctor if any of the following side effects continue or are bothersome:
More common
Constipation; dry mouth; nausea and/or vomiting

After you stop using this medicine, your body may need time to adjust. The length of time this takes depends on the amount of medicine you were using and how long you used it. During this period of time check with your doctor if you notice any of the following side effects:
Diarrhea; nausea and/or vomiting; restlessness or irritability; speech disorder; stomach cramps; trouble in sleeping; weakness

Other side effects not listed above may also occur in some patients. If you notice any other effects, check with your doctor.

Developed: 06/14/99
Revised: 10/20/99

FENTANYL   Transdermal-Systemic

Commonly used brand name(s):

In the U.S.—
Duragesic

In Canada—
Duragesic

Description

Fentanyl (FEN-ta-nil) belongs to the group of medicines called narcotic analgesics (nar-KOT-ik an-al-GEE-ziks). Narcotic analgesics are used to relieve pain. The transdermal system (skin patch) form of fentanyl is used to treat chronic pain (pain that continues for a long time).

Fentanyl acts in the central nervous system (CNS) to relieve pain. Some of its side effects are also caused by actions in the CNS.

When a narcotic is used for a long time, it may become habit-forming (causing mental or physical dependence). However, *people who have continuing pain should not let the fear of dependence keep them from using narcotics to relieve their pain.* Mental dependence (addiction) is not likely to occur when narcotics are used for this purpose. Physical dependence may lead to withdrawal side effects if treatment is stopped suddenly. However, severe withdrawal side effects can usually be prevented by reducing the dose gradually over a period of time before treatment is stopped completely.

This medicine is available only with your doctor's prescription. Prescriptions for transdermal fentanyl cannot be refilled. You will need to obtain a new prescription from your doctor each

---

time you need the medicine. This medicine is available in the following dosage form:

Transdermal
- Transdermal system (stick-on skin patch) (U.S. and Canada)

Before Using This Medicine

In deciding to use a medicine, the risks of using the medicine must be weighed against the good it will do. This is a decision you and your health care professional will make. For fentanyl, the following should be considered:

Allergies—Tell your health care professional if you have ever had any unusual or allergic reaction to fentanyl, alfentanil (e.g., Alfenta), or sufentanil (e.g., Sufenta). Also tell your health care professional if you are allergic to any other substances, including the adhesives that keep stick-on bandages in place.

Pregnancy—Although studies on birth defects with fentanyl have not been done in pregnant women, it has not been reported to cause birth defects. However, using any narcotic regularly during pregnancy may cause physical dependence in the fetus. This may lead to withdrawal side effects after birth. Also, use of this medicine near the end of pregnancy may cause drowsiness and breathing problems in newborn babies.

Breast-feeding—Fentanyl passes into the breast milk. Nursing babies whose mothers are using this medicine regularly may receive enough of it to cause unwanted effects such as drowsiness, breathing problems, and physical dependence. Similar effects may also occur with some other narcotics if they are taken regularly in large amounts. A mother who wishes to breast-feed and who needs treatment for continuing pain should discuss the risks and benefits of different pain treatments with her health care professional.

Children—Studies with the fentanyl skin patch have been done only in adult patients, and there is no specific information comparing the use of this medicine in children with use in other age groups.

Teenagers—Studies with the fentanyl skin patch have been done only in patients 18 years of age and older. There is no specific information comparing the use of this medicine in teenagers with use in other age groups.

Older adults—Elderly people are especially sensitive to the effects of narcotic analgesics. This may increase the chance of side effects, especially breathing problems, during treatment. Your health care professional will take this into consideration when deciding on the amount of transdermal fentanyl you should receive.

Other medicines—Although certain medicines should not be used together at all, in other cases two different medicines may be used together even if an interaction might occur. In these cases, your health care professional may want to change the dose, or other precautions may be necessary. When you are using fentanyl, it is especially important that your health care professional know if you are taking any of the following:

- Buprenorphine (e.g., Buprenex) or
- Dezocine (e.g., Dalgan) or
- Nalbuphine (e.g., Nubain) or
- Pentazocine (e.g., Talwin)—Like all narcotic analgesics, these medicines may add to the effects of fentanyl, which may increase the chance of side effects or overdose. However, buprenorphine, dezocine, nalbuphine,

and pentazocine sometimes decrease the effects of fentanyl, so that fentanyl might be less effective in relieving pain. Also, these medicines can cause withdrawal side effects if they are given to someone who is physically dependent on fentanyl

- Central nervous system (CNS) depressants (medicines that cause drowsiness), including other narcotics, or
- Tricyclic antidepressants—These medicines may add to the effects of fentanyl. This may increase the chance of serious side effects

- Naltrexone (e.g., Trexan)—Fentanyl will not be effective in people taking naltrexone

Other medical problems—The presence of other medical problems may affect the use of fentanyl. Make sure you tell your health care professional if you have any other medical problems, especially:

- Alcohol abuse, or history of, or
- Drug dependence, especially narcotic abuse or dependence, or history of, or
- Emotional problems or
- Kidney disease or
- Liver disease or
- Underactive thyroid—The chance of side effects may be increased

- Brain tumor or
- Diarrhea caused by antibiotic treatment or poisoning or
- Emphysema, asthma, or other chronic lung disease or
- Enlarged prostate or problems with urination or
- Gallbladder disease or gallstones or
- Intestinal problems such as colitis or Crohn's disease—Some of the side effects of fentanyl can cause serious problems in people who have these medical problems

- Slow heartbeat—Fentanyl can make this condition worse

Proper Use of This Medicine

Transdermal fentanyl comes with patient instructions. Read them carefully before using the product. If you do not receive any printed instructions with the medicine, check with your pharmacist.

To use:
- *Use this medicine exactly as directed by your doctor.* It will work only if it has been applied correctly.
- Fentanyl skin patches are packaged in sealed pouches. *Do not remove the patch from the sealed pouch until you are ready to apply it.*
- When handling the skin patch, *be careful not to touch the adhesive (sticky) surface with your hand.* The adhesive part of the system contains some fentanyl, which can be absorbed into your body too fast through the skin of your hand. If any of the medicine does get on your hand, *rinse the area right away with a lot of clear water. Do not use soap or other cleansers.*
- *Be careful not to tear the patch or make any holes in it.* Damage to a patch may allow fentanyl to pass into your skin too quickly. This can cause an overdose.
- Apply the patch to a dry, flat skin area on your upper arm, chest, or back. *Choose a place where the skin is not very oily and is free of scars, cuts, burns, or any other skin irritations. Also, do not apply this medicine to areas that have received radiation (x-ray) treatment.*

- The patch will stay in place better if it is applied to an area with little or no hair. If you need to apply the patch to a hairy area, you may first clip the hair with scissors, *but do not shave it off*.
- If you need to clean the area before applying the medicine, *use only plain water. Do not use soaps, other cleansers, lotions, or anything that contains oils or alcohol*. Be sure that the skin is completely dry before applying the medicine.
- Remove the liner covering the sticky side of the skin patch. Then press the patch firmly in place, using the palm of your hand, for about 30 seconds. Make sure that the entire adhesive surface is attached to your skin, especially around the edges.
- If you need to apply more than 1 patch at a time, *place the patches far enough apart so that the edges do not touch or overlap each other*.
- Wash your hands with a lot of clear water after applying the medicine. Do not use soap or other cleansers.
- Remove the patch after 72 hours (3 days). *Choose a different place on your skin to apply the next patch. If possible, use a place on the other side of your body. Wait at least 3 days before using the first area again.*

After a patch is applied, the fentanyl it contains passes into the skin a little at a time. A certain amount of the medicine must build up in the skin before it is absorbed into the body. Therefore, up to a day may pass before the first dose begins to work. Your health care professional may need to change the dose during the first several applications (each kept in place for 3 days) before finding the amount that works best for you. Even if you feel that the medicine is not working, *do not increase the amount of transdermal fentanyl that you apply*. Instead, check with your health care professional.

You will probably need to take a faster-acting narcotic to relieve pain during the first few days of transdermal fentanyl treatment. You may continue to need another narcotic while your dose of fentanyl is being adjusted, and also to relieve any "break through" pain that occurs later on. *Be sure that you do not take more of the other narcotic, and do not take it more often, than directed. Taking other narcotics together with fentanyl can increase the chance of an overdose.*

Dosing—The dose of transdermal fentanyl will be different for different patients. *Follow your doctor's orders or the directions on the label*. The following information includes only the average doses of this medicine. *If your dose is different, do not change it* unless your doctor tells you to do so.
- For *transdermal* dosage form (stick-on patch):
  —For relief of severe, continuing pain:
    - Adults—If you have not already been using other narcotics regularly, your first dose will probably be one patch that releases 25 micrograms (mcg) of fentanyl every hour. If you have already been using other narcotics regularly, your first dose will depend on the amount of other narcotic you have been taking every day. If necessary, your health care professional will change the dose after 3 days, when the first patch is replaced. The size of the new dose will depend on how well the medicine is working and on whether you had any side effects during the first 3-day application. Other changes in dose may be needed later on. Some people may need to use more than one patch at a time.
    - Children—Use and dose must be determined by the doctor.

Missed dose—If you miss a dose of this medicine, apply it as soon as possible. Remove the new patch 3 days after applying it.

Storage—To store this medicine:
- Keep out of the reach of children.
- Store away from heat and direct light.
- Do not keep outdated medicine or medicine no longer needed. To dispose of this medicine, first fold the patch in half, with the sticky side inside. If the patch has not been used, take it out of the pouch and remove the liner that covers the sticky side of the patch before folding it in half. Then flush it down the toilet right away.

Precautions While Using This Medicine

Check with your health care professional at regular times while using fentanyl. Be sure to report any side effects.

After you have been using this medicine for a while, "break through" pain may occur more often than usual, and it may not be relieved by your regular dose of medicine. If this occurs, *do not increase the amount of transdermal fentanyl or other narcotic that you are taking without first checking with your health care professional*.

This medicine will add to the effects of alcohol and other CNS depressants (medicines that can make you drowsy or less alert). Some examples of CNS depressants are antihistamines or medicine for hay fever, other allergies, or colds; sedatives, tranquilizers, or sleeping medicine; other prescription pain medicine or narcotics; barbiturates; medicine for seizures; muscle relaxants; or anesthetics, including some dental anesthetics. You will probably be directed to take other pain relievers if you still have pain while using transdermal fentanyl. However, *check with your health care professional before taking any of the other medicines listed above while you are using this medicine*.

Fentanyl may cause some people to become drowsy, dizzy, or lightheaded, or to feel a false sense of well-being. *Make sure you know how you react to this medicine before you drive, use machines, or do anything else that could be dangerous if you are dizzy or not alert and clearheaded*. These effects usually go away after a few days of treatment, when your body gets used to the medicine. However, *check with your health care professional if drowsiness that is severe enough to interfere with your activities continues for more than a few days*.

Dizziness, lightheadedness, or even fainting may occur when you get up suddenly from a lying or sitting position. *Getting up slowly may help lessen this problem*. Also, lying down for a while may relieve dizziness or lightheadedness.

Nausea or vomiting may occur, especially during the first several days of treatment. Lying down for a while may relieve these effects. However, if they are especially bothersome or if they continue for more than a few days, check with your health care professional. You may be able to take another medicine to help prevent these problems.

Using narcotics for a long time can cause severe constipation. To prevent this, your health care professional may direct you to take laxatives, drink a lot of fluids, or increase the amount of fiber in your diet. *Be sure to follow the directions carefully*, because continuing constipation can lead to more serious problems.

Heat can cause the fentanyl in the patch to be absorbed into your body faster. This may increase the chance of serious side effects or an overdose. While you are using this medicine, *do not use a heating pad, a sunlamp, or a heated water bed, and do not take sunbaths or long baths or showers in hot water.* Also, *check with your health care professional if you get a fever.*

Before having any kind of surgery (including dental surgery) or emergency treatment, tell the medical doctor or dentist in charge that you are using this medicine. Serious side effects can occur if your medical doctor or dentist gives you certain other medicines without knowing that you are using fentanyl.

You may bathe, shower, or swim while wearing a fentanyl skin patch. However, be careful to wash and dry the area around the patch gently. Rubbing may cause the patch to get loose or come off. If this does occur, throw away the patch and apply a new one in a different place. Make sure the area is completely dry before applying the new patch.

If you have been using this medicine regularly for several weeks or more, *do not suddenly stop using it without first checking with your health care professional.* You may be directed to reduce gradually the amount you are using before stopping treatment completely, or to take another narcotic for a while, to lessen the chance of withdrawal side effects.

Using too much transdermal fentanyl, or taking too much of another narcotic while using transdermal fentanyl, may cause an overdose. If this occurs, get emergency help right away. An overdose can cause severe breathing problems (breathing may even stop), unconsciousness, and death. Serious signs of an overdose include very slow breathing (fewer than 8 breaths a minute) and drowsiness that is so severe that you are not able to answer when spoken to or, if asleep, cannot be awakened. Other signs of an overdose may include cold, clammy skin; low blood pressure; pinpoint pupils of eyes; and slow heartbeat. *It may be best to have a family member or a friend check on you several times a day when you start using a narcotic regularly, and whenever your dose is increased,* so that he or she can get help for you if you cannot do so yourself.

Side Effects of This Medicine

Along with its needed effects, a medicine may cause some unwanted effects. Although not all of these side effects may occur, if they do occur they may need medical attention.

Get emergency help immediately if the following signs of overdose occur:
Cold, clammy skin; convulsions (seizures); drowsiness that is so severe that you are not able to answer when spoken to or, if asleep, cannot be awakened; low blood pressure; pinpoint pupils of eyes; slow heartbeat; very slow (fewer than 8 breaths a minute) or troubled breathing

Also, check with your doctor as soon as possible if any of the following side effects occur:
More common
Decrease in amount of urine or in the frequency of urination; hallucinations (seeing, hearing, or feeling things that are not there)
Less common
Chest pain; difficulty in speaking; fainting; irregular heartbeat; mood or mental changes; problems with

walking; redness, swelling, itching, or bumps on the skin at place of application; spitting blood
Rare
Any change in vision; bladder pain; difficulty in speaking; fever with or without chills; fluid-filled blisters on skin; frequent urge to urinate; noisy breathing, shortness of breath, tightness in chest, or wheezing; red, thickened, or scaly skin; swelling of abdomen or stomach area; swollen and/or painful glands; unusual bruising

Other side effects may occur that usually do not need medical attention. These side effects may go away during treatment as your body adjusts to the medicine. However, check with your doctor if any of the following side effects continue or are bothersome:
More common
Abdominal or stomach pain that was not present before treatment; confusion; constipation; diarrhea; dizziness, drowsiness, or lightheadedness; false sense of well-being; feeling anxious; headache; indigestion; loss of appetite; nausea or vomiting; nervousness; sweating; weakness
Less common
Bloated feeling or gas; feeling anxious and restless at the same time; feeling of crawling, tingling, or burning of the skin; memory loss; unusual dreams

After you stop using this medicine, your body may need time to adjust. The length of time this takes depends on the amount of medicine you were using and how long you used it. During this period of time check with your doctor if you notice any of the following side effects:
Body aches; diarrhea; fast heartbeat; fever, runny nose, or sneezing; gooseflesh; increased sweating; increased yawning; loss of appetite; nausea or vomiting; nervousness, restlessness, or irritability; shivering or trembling; stomach cramps; trouble in sleeping; unusually large pupils of eyes; weakness

Other side effects not listed above may also occur in some patients. If you notice any other effects, check with your doctor.

Developed: 07/27/94

FEXOFENADINE Systemic

Commonly used brand name(s):

In the U.S.—
Allegra

Description

Fexofenadine (fex-oh-FEN-a-deen) is an antihistamine. It is used to relieve the symptoms of hay fever and hives of the skin.

Antihistamines work by preventing the effects of a substance called histamine, which is produced by the body. Histamine can cause itching, sneezing, runny nose, and watery eyes. Also, in some persons histamine can close up the bronchial tubes (air passages of the lungs) and make breathing difficult.

Histamine can also cause some persons to have hives, with severe itching of the skin.

This medicine is available only with your doctor's prescription, in the following dosage form:

Oral
- Capsules (U.S.)
- Tablets (U.S. and Canada)

Before Using This Medicine

In deciding to use a medicine, the risks of taking the medicine must be weighed against the good it will do. This is a decision you and your doctor will make. For fexofenadine, the following should be considered:

Allergies—Tell your doctor if you have ever had any unusual or allergic reaction to fexofenadine. Also tell your health care professional if you are allergic to any other substances, such as foods, preservatives, or dyes.

Pregnancy—In animal studies, this medicine did not cause birth defects but did cause a decrease in weight of the infant. Discuss with your doctor whether or not you should continue to use this medicine if you become pregnant.

Breast-feeding—It is not known whether fexofenadine passes into breast milk. Although most medicines pass into breast milk in small amounts, many of them may be used safely while breast-feeding. Mothers who are taking this medicine and who wish to breast-feed should discuss this with their doctor.

Children—This medicine has been tested in children 6 years of age and older and, in effective doses, has not been shown to cause different side effects or problems than it does in adults. There is no specific information comparing use of fexofenadine in children up to 6 years of age.

Older adults—Fexofenadine has been tested in patients 65 years of age and older and has not been shown to cause different side effects or problems in older people than it does in younger adults.

Other medicines—Although certain medicines should not be used together at all, in other cases two different medicines may be used together even if an interaction might occur. In these cases, your doctor may want to change the dose, or other precautions may be necessary. Tell your health care professional if you are taking or using any other prescription or nonprescription (over-the-counter [OTC]) medicine, especially antacids that contain aluminum and magnesium hydroxide (e.g., Maalox, Mylanta).

Other medical problems—The presence of other medical problems may affect the use of fexofenadine. Make sure you tell your doctor if you have any other medical problems, especially:
- Kidney disease—Effects of fexofenadine may be increased because of slower removal from the body

Proper Use of This Medicine

Dosing—The dose of fexofenadine may be different for different patients. *Follow your doctor's orders or the directions on the label.* The following information includes only the average doses of fexofenadine. *If your dose is different, do not change it* unless your doctor tells you to do so.
- For *oral* dosage form (capsules, tablets):
  —For symptoms of hay fever:
    - Adults and children 12 years of age and older— 60 milligrams (mg) two times a day, or 180 mg once a day.

- Children 6 to 11 years of age—30 mg two times a day
- Children younger than 6 years of age—Use and dose must be determined by your doctor.
—For symptoms of chronic hives
  - Adults and children 12 years of age and older— 60 mg two times a day.
  - Children 6 to 11 years of age—30 mg two times a day.
  - Children younger than 6 years of age—Use and dose must be determined by your doctor.

Missed dose—If you miss a dose of this medicine, take it as soon as you remember. However, if it is almost time for your next dose, skip the missed dose and go back to your regular dosing schedule. Do not double doses.

Storage—To store this medicine:
- Keep out of the reach of children.
- Store away from heat and direct light in a tightly closed container.
- Do not store in the bathroom, near the kitchen sink, or in other damp places. Heat or moisture may cause the medicine to break down.
- Do not keep outdated medicine or medicine no longer needed. Be sure that any discarded medicine is out of the reach of children.

Side Effects of This Medicine

Along with its needed effects, a medicine may cause some unwanted effects. Although not all of these side effects may occur, if they do occur they may need medical attention.

The following side effects usually do not need medical attention. These side effects may go away during treatment as your body adjusts to the medicine. However, check with your doctor if any of the following side effects continue or are bothersome.

Less common
  Back pain; coughing; dizziness; drowsiness; earache; fever; headache; nausea; pain or tenderness around eyes or cheekbones; painful menstrual bleeding; ringing or buzzing in ears; runny or stuffy nose; stomach upset; unusual feeling of tiredness; viral infection (such as cold and flu)

Other side effects not listed above may also occur in some patients. If you notice any other effects, check with your doctor.

Developed: 08/12/1998
Revised: 06/27/2000

FEXOFENADINE AND PSEUDOEPHEDRINE   Systemic

Commonly used brand name(s):

In the U.S.—
Allegra-D

Description

Fexofenadine (fex-oh-FEN-a-deen) is an antihistamine and pseudoephedrine (soo-doe-e-FED-rin) is a decongestant. The combination of these two medicines is used to treat the nasal congestion (stuffy nose), sneezing, and runny nose caused by hay fever.

This medicine is available only with your doctor's prescription, in the following dosage form:

Oral
- Extended-release tablets (U.S.)

Before Using This Medicine

In deciding to use a medicine, the risks of taking the medicine must be weighed against the good it will do. This is a decision you and your doctor will make. For fexofenadine and pseudoephedrine combination, the following should be considered:

Allergies—Tell your doctor if you have ever had any unusual or allergic reaction to fexofenadine or pseudoephedrine, or to amphetamine, dextroamphetamine (e.g., Dexedrine), ephedrine (e.g., Ephed II), epinephrine (e.g., Adrenalin), isoproterenol (e.g., Isuprel), metaproterenol (e.g., Alupent), methamphetamine (e.g., Desoxyn), norepinephrine (e.g., Levophed), phenylephrine (e.g., Neo-Synephrine), Phenylpropanolamine (e.g., Dexatrim), or terbutaline (e.g., Brethine). Also tell your health care professional if you are allergic to any other substances, such as foods, preservatives, or dyes.

Pregnancy—In animal studies, this medicine did not cause birth defects but did cause a decrease in weight of newborn and bone formation in the ribs. Discuss with your doctor whether or not you should continue to use this medicine if you become pregnant.

Breast-feeding—It is not known whether fexofenadine passes into breast milk, but pseudoephedrine does pass into breast milk. Discuss with your doctor the risks of breast-feeding while taking this medicine.

Children—Use is not recommended in infants and children up to 12 years of age. In children 12 years of age and older, this medicine is not expected to cause different side effects or problems than it does in adults.

Older adults—Some side effects may be more likely to occur in elderly patients, who are usually more sensitive to the effects of this medicine.

Other medicines—Although certain medicines should not be used together at all, in other cases two different medicines may be used together even if an interaction might occur. In these cases, your doctor may want to change the dose, or other precautions may be necessary. When you are taking this medicine, it is especially important that your health care professional know if you are taking any of the following:

- Monoamine oxidase (MAO) inhibitors (furazolidone [e.g., Furoxone], isocarboxazid [e.g., Marplan], phenelzine [e.g., Nardil], procarbazine [e.g., Matulane], selegiline [e.g., Eldepryl], tranylcypromine [e.g., Parnate])—If you are now taking, or have taken within the past 2 weeks, any of the MAO inhibitors, the side effects of pseudoephedrine may become more severe; these medicines should not be used together

Other medical problems—The presence of other medical problems may affect the use of this medicine. Make sure you tell your doctor if you have any other medical problems, especially:

- Diabetes mellitus (sugar diabetes)—Use of this medicine may cause an increase in blood glucose levels

- Enlarged prostate or

- Urinary tract blockage or difficult urination—Use of this medicine may cause urination to be more difficult

- Glaucoma or
- Increased pressure in the eye—Use of this medicine may make the condition worse

- Heart or blood vessel disease or
- High blood pressure—Use of this medicine may make the condition worse

- Kidney disease—Effects may be increased because of slower removal of the medicine from the body

- Overactive thyroid—Serious effects on the heart may occur

Proper Use of This Medicine

Swallow the extended-release tablet whole. Do not crush, break, or chew it before swallowing.

This medicine is best taken on an empty stomach (either one hour before or two hours after a meal).

Dosing—The dose of this medicine may be different for different patients. *Follow your doctor's orders or the directions on the label*. The following information includes only the average doses of this medicine. *If your dose is different, do not change it* unless your doctor tells you to do so.

- For *oral* dosage form (extended-release tablets):
  —For symptoms of hay fever:
    - Adults—1 tablet two times a day.
    - Children—Use and dose must be determined by your doctor.

Missed dose—If you miss a dose of this medicine, take it as soon as you remember. However, if it is almost time for the next dose, skip the missed dose and go back to your regular dosing schedule. Do not double doses.

Storage—To store this medicine:
- Keep out of the reach of children.
- Store away from heat and direct light in a tightly closed container.
- Do not store in the bathroom, near the kitchen sink, or in other damp places. Heat or moisture may cause the medicine to break down.
- Do not keep outdated medicine or medicine no longer needed. Be sure that any discarded medicine is out of the reach of children.

Side Effects of This Medicine

Along with its needed effects, a medicine may cause some unwanted effects. Although not all of these side effects may occur, if they do occur they may need medical attention.

Check with your doctor as soon as possible if any of the following side effects occur:
More common
　Trouble in sleeping
Less common
　Cough; dizziness; irregular heartbeat; nervousness; sore throat

Other side effects may occur that usually do not need medical attention. These side effects may go away during treatment as your body adjusts to the medicine. However, check with your doctor if any of the following side effects continue or are bothersome:
More common
　Headache; nausea

Less common
> Abdominal or stomach pain; agitation; anxiety; back pain; dry mouth; heartburn

Other side effects not listed above may also occur in some patients. If you notice any other effects, check with your doctor.

Developed: 08/12/98

FINASTERIDE   Systemic

Commonly used brand name(s):

In the U.S.—
> Propecia
> Proscar

In Canada—
> Proscar

Description

Note: Women of childbearing potential should not use or handle crushed finasteride tablets. Finasteride can cause birth defects in male fetuses.

Finasteride (fin-AS-tur-ide) belongs to the group of medicines called enzyme inhibitors. It is used to treat urinary problems caused by enlargement of the prostate (benign prostatic hyperplasia or BPH). In men with very enlarged prostates and mild to moderate symptoms (difficulty urinating, decreased flow of urination, hesitation at the beginning of urination, getting up at night to urinate), finasteride may decrease the severity of symptoms.

Finasteride blocks an enzyme called 5-alpha-reductase, which is necessary to change testosterone to another hormone that causes the prostate to grow. As a result, the size of the prostate is decreased. The effect of finasteride on the prostate lasts only as long as the medicine is taken. If it is stopped, the prostate begins to grow again.

Finasteride also is used by some balding men to stimulate hair growth. If hair growth is going to occur with the use of finasteride, it usually occurs after the medicine has been used for about 3 months and lasts only as long as the medicine continues to be used. The new hair will be lost within 1 year after finasteride treatment is stopped.

Finasteride is available only with your doctor's prescription, in the following dosage form:

Oral
- Tablets (U.S. and Canada)

Before Using This Medicine

In deciding to use a medicine, the risks of taking the medicine must be weighed against the good it will do. This is a decision you and your doctor will make. For finasteride, the following should be considered:

Allergies—Tell your doctor if you have ever had any unusual or allergic reaction to finasteride. Also tell your health care professional if you are allergic to any other substances, such as foods, preservatives, or dyes.

Pregnancy—Women who are or may become pregnant should not take finasteride or should not be exposed to crushed finasteride tablets, because it can cause changes in the genitals (sex organs) of male fetuses.

Older adults—This medicine has been tested and has not been shown to cause different side effects or problems in older people than it does in younger adults.

Other medicines—Although certain medicines should not be used together at all, in other cases two different medicines may be used together even if an interaction might occur. In these cases, your doctor may want to change the dose, or other precautions may be necessary. Tell your health care professional if you are taking any other prescription or nonprescription (over-the-counter [OTC]) medicine.

Proper Use of This Medicine

Finasteride tablets may be crushed to make them easier to swallow. However, women who are or may become pregnant should not handle crushed finasteride tablets.

For patients taking this medicine for *benign prostatic hyperplasia* (BPH):
- To help you remember to take your medicine, try to get into the habit of taking it at the same time each day.
- Remember that this medicine does not cure BPH but it does help reduce the size of the prostate. Therefore, you must continue to take it if you expect to keep the size of your prostate down. *You may have to take this medicine for at least 6 months to see the full effect.* You may have to take this medicine for the rest of your life. Do not stop taking this medicine without first discussing it with your doctor.
- This medicine helps to reduce urinary problems in men with BPH. In general, it is best to avoid drinking fluids, especially coffee or alcohol, in the evening. Then your sleep will not be disturbed by your need to urinate during the night.

For individuals taking this medicine for *hair growth:*
- You may have to take this medicine for at least 3 months to see an effect. The effect will last only as long as the medicine continues to be used. The new hair will be lost within 1 year after finasteride is stopped.

Dosing—The dose of finasteride will be different for different patients. *Follow your doctor's orders or the directions on the label.* The following information includes only the average dose of finasteride. *If your dose is different, do not change it* unless your doctor tells you to do so:
- For *oral* dosage form (tablets):
  —For treatment of benign prostatic hyperplasia (BPH):
  - Adults—5 milligrams (mg) once a day.
  —For hair growth:
  - Adults—1 mg once a day.

Missed dose—If you miss a dose of this medicine, take it as soon as possible. However, if it is almost time for your next dose, skip the missed dose and go back to your regular dosing schedule. Do not double doses.

Storage—To store this medicine:
- Keep out of the reach of children.
- Store away from heat and direct light.
- Do not store in the bathroom, near the kitchen sink, or in other damp places. Heat or moisture may cause the medicine to break down.
- Do not keep outdated medicine or medicine no longer needed. Be sure that any discarded medicine is out of the reach of children.

© 2002 MICROMEDEX Thomson Healthcare

Precautions While Using This Medicine

Women who are or who may become pregnant should not handle crushed finasteride tablets. There is a risk that the medicine could get into the pregnant woman's body and cause birth defects in a male fetus.

Side Effects of This Medicine

Along with its needed effects, a medicine may cause some unwanted effects. Although not all of these side effects may occur, if they do occur they may need medical attention.

Check with your doctor as soon as possible if any of the following side effects occur:

Less common

Breast enlargement and tenderness; skin rash; swelling of lips

Note: Breast enlargement and tenderness, skin rash and swelling of lips are more likely to occur with the 5-mg dose.

Other side effects may occur that usually do not need medical attention. The following side effects may go away during treatment as your body adjusts to the medicine. However, check with your doctor if any of the following side effects continue or are bothersome:

Less common or rare

Abdominal pain; back pain; decreased libido (decreased interest in sex); decreased volume of ejaculate (decreased amount of semen); diarrhea; dizziness; headache; impotence (inability to have or keep an erection)

Note: A decrease in the amount of semen during ejaculation should not affect your sexual performance and is not a sign of any change in fertility.

Other side effects not listed above may also occur in some patients. If you notice any other effects, check with your doctor.

Revised: 04/27/98

FLAVOXATE   Systemic

Commonly used brand name(s):

In the U.S.—
Urispas

In Canada—
Urispas

Description

Flavoxate (fla-VOX-ate) belongs to the group of medicines called antispasmodics. It is taken by mouth to help decrease muscle spasms of the bladder and relieve difficult urination.

Flavoxate is available only with your doctor's prescription, in the following dosage form:

Oral
• Tablets (U.S. and Canada)

Before Using This Medicine

In deciding to use a medicine, the risks of taking the medicine must be weighed against the good it will do. This is a decision you and your doctor will make. For flavoxate, the following should be considered:

Allergies—Tell your doctor if you have ever had any unusual or allergic reaction to flavoxate. Also tell your health care professional if you are allergic to any other substances, such as foods, preservatives, or dyes.

Pregnancy—Flavoxate has not been studied in pregnant women. However, flavoxate has not been shown to cause birth defects or other problems in animal studies.

Breast-feeding—It is not known whether flavoxate passes into breast milk. Although most medicines pass into breast milk in small amounts, many of them may be used safely while breast-feeding. Mothers who are taking this medicine and who wish to breast-feed should discuss this with their doctor.

Children—Studies on this medicine have been done only in adult patients and in children over 12 years of age. Flavoxate is not recommended for children younger than 12 years of age because safety and efficacy have not been established.

Older adults—Confusion may be especially likely to occur in elderly patients, who are usually more sensitive than younger adults to the effects of flavoxate.

Other medicines—Although certain medicines should not be used together at all in other cases two different medicines may be used together even if an interaction might occur. In these cases, your doctor may want to change the dose, or other precautions may be necessary. Tell your health care professional if you are taking any other prescription or nonprescription (over-the-counter [OTC]) medicine.

Other medical problems—The presence of other medical problems may affect the use of flavoxate. Make sure you tell your doctor if you have any other medical problems, especially:

• Bleeding (severe) or
• Glaucoma or
• Intestinal blockage or other intestinal or stomach problems or
• Urinary tract blockage—Use of flavoxate may make these conditions worse
• Enlarged prostate—Use of flavoxate may cause difficult urination

Proper Use of This Medicine

This medicine is usually taken with water on an empty stomach. However, your doctor may want you to take it with food or milk to lessen stomach upset.

Take this medicine only as directed. Do not take more of it, do not take it more often, and do not take it for a longer time than your doctor ordered. To do so may increase the chance of side effects.

Dosing—The dose of flavoxate will be different for different patients. *Follow your doctor's orders or the directions on the label.* The following information includes only the average dose of flavoxate. *If your dose is different, do not change it* unless your doctor tells you to do so. The number of tablets that you take depends on the strength of the medicine.

• Adults and children 12 years of age and older: 100 to 200 milligrams three or four times a day.
• Children up to 12 years of age: Use and dose must be determined by the doctor.

Missed dose—If you miss a dose of this medicine, take it as soon as possible. However, if it is almost time for your

next dose, skip the missed dose and go back to your regular dosing schedule. Do not double doses.

Storage— To store this medicine:

- Keep out of the reach of children.
- Store away from heat and direct light.
- Do not store in the bathroom, near the kitchen sink, or in other damp places. Heat or moisture may cause the medicine to break down.
- Do not keep outdated medicine or medicine no longer needed. Be sure that any discarded medicine is out of the reach of children.

Precautions While Using This Medicine

This medicine may cause your eyes to become more sensitive to light than they are normally. Wearing sunglasses may help lessen the discomfort from bright light.

This medicine may cause some people to become drowsy or have blurred vision. *Make sure you know how you react to this medicine before you drive, use machines, or do anything else that could be dangerous if you are not alert or able to see well.*

Flavoxate may make you sweat less, causing your body temperature to increase. *Use extra care not to become overheated during exercise or hot weather while you are taking this medicine,* since overheating may result in heat stroke. Also, hot baths or saunas may make you feel dizzy or faint while you are taking this medicine.

Your mouth and throat may feel very dry while you are taking this medicine. For temporary relief of mouth dryness, use sugarless candy or gum, melt bits of ice in your mouth, or use a saliva substitute. However, if your mouth continues to feel dry for more than 2 weeks, check with your medical doctor or dentist. Continuing dryness of the mouth may increase the chance of dental disease, including tooth decay, gum disease, and fungus infections.

Side Effects of This Medicine

Along with its needed effects, a medicine may cause some unwanted effects. Although not all of these side effects may occur, if they do occur they may need medical attention.

Check with your doctor as soon as possible if any of the following side effects occur:

Rare
Confusion; eye pain; skin rash or hives; sore throat and fever

Symptoms of overdose
Clumsiness or unsteadiness; dizziness (severe); drowsiness (severe); fever; flushing or redness of face; hallucinations (seeing, hearing, or feeling things that are not there); shortness of breath or troubled breathing; unusual excitement, nervousness, restlessness, or irritability

Other side effects may occur that usually do not need medical attention. These side effects may go away during treatment as your body adjusts to the medicine. However, check with your doctor if any of the following side effects continue or are bothersome:

More common
Drowsiness; dryness of mouth and throat

Less common or rare
Blurred vision; constipation; difficult urination; difficulty concentrating; dizziness; fast heartbeat; headache;

increased sensitivity of eyes to light; increased sweating; nausea or vomiting; nervousness; stomach pain

Other side effects not listed above may also occur in some patients. If you notice any other effects, check with your doctor.

Revised: 02/23/00

FLECAINIDE   Systemic

Commonly used brand name(s):

In the U.S.—
Tambocor
Generic name product may be available.

In Canada—
Tambocor

Description

Flecainide (FLEK-a-nide) belongs to the group of medicines known as antiarrhythmics. It is used to correct irregular heartbeats to a normal rhythm.

Flecainide produces its helpful effects by slowing nerve impulses in the heart and making the heart tissue less sensitive.

There is a chance that flecainide may cause new or make worse existing heart rhythm problems when it is used. Since it has been shown to cause severe problems in some patients, it is only used to treat serious heart rhythm problems. Discuss this possible effect with your doctor.

This medicine is available only with your doctor's prescription, in the following dosage form:

Oral
- Tablets (U.S. and Canada)

Before Using This Medicine

In deciding to use a medicine, the risks of taking the medicine must be weighed against the good it will do. This is a decision you and your doctor will make. For flecainide, the following should be considered:

Allergies— Tell your doctor if you have ever had any unusual or allergic reaction to flecainide, lidocaine, tocainide, or anesthetics. Also tell your health care professional if you are allergic to any other substances, such as foods, preservatives, or dyes.

Pregnancy— Flecainide has not been studied in pregnant women. However, studies in one kind of rabbit given about 4 times the usual human dose have shown that flecainide causes birth defects. Before taking flecainide, make sure your doctor knows if you are pregnant or if you may become pregnant.

Breast-feeding— Flecainide passes into breast milk. However, this medicine has not been shown to cause problems in nursing babies.

Children— Studies on this medicine have been done only in adult patients, and there is no specific information comparing use of flecainide in children with use in other age groups.

Older adults—Elderly people are especially sensitive to the effects of flecainide. Flecainide may be more likely to cause irregular heartbeat in the elderly.

Other medicines—Although certain medicines should not be used together at all, in other cases two different medicines may be used together even if an interaction might occur. In these cases, your doctor may want to change the dose, or other precautions may be necessary. When you are taking flecainide it is especially important that your health care professional knows if you are taking any of the following:

- Other medicine for heart rhythm problems—Both wanted and unwanted effects on the heart may increase

Other medical problems—The presence of other medical problems may affect the use of flecainide. Make sure you tell your doctor if you have any other medical problems, especially:

- Congestive heart failure—Flecainide may make this condition worse

- Kidney disease or
- Liver disease—Effects of flecainide may be increased because of slower removal from the body

- Recent heart attack—Risk of irregular heartbeats may be increased

- If you have a pacemaker—Flecainide may interfere with the pacemaker and require more careful follow-up by the doctor

Proper Use of This Medicine

Take flecainide exactly as directed by your doctor, even though you may feel well. Do not take more medicine than ordered.

This medicine works best when there is a constant amount in the blood. *To help keep this amount constant, do not miss any doses. Also, it is best to take the doses 12 hours apart, in the morning and at night*, unless otherwise directed by your doctor. If you need help in planning the best times to take your medicine, check with your health care professional.

Dosing—The dose of flecainide will be different for different patients. *Follow your doctor's orders or the directions on the label.* The following information includes only the average doses of flecainide. *If your dose is different, do not change it* unless your doctor tells you to do so.

The number of tablets that you take depends on the strength of the medicine.

- For *oral* dosage form (tablets):
  —For correcting irregular heartbeat:
    - Adults—50 to 150 milligrams (mg) every twelve hours.
    - Children—Use and dose must be determined by your doctor.

Missed dose—If you miss a dose of flecainide and remember within 6 hours, take it as soon as possible. However, if you do not remember until later, skip the missed dose and go back to your regular dosing schedule. Do not double doses.

Storage—To store this medicine:

- Keep out of the reach of children.
- Store away from heat and direct light.
- Do not store in the bathroom, near the kitchen sink, or in other damp places. Heat or moisture may cause the medicine to break down.
- Do not keep outdated medicine or medicine no longer needed. Be sure that any discarded medicine is out of the reach of children.

Precautions While Using This Medicine

It is important that your doctor check your progress at regular visits to make sure the medicine is working properly. This will allow for changes to be made in the amount of medicine you are taking, if necessary.

Your doctor may want you to carry a medical identification card or bracelet stating that you are using this medicine.

Before having any kind of surgery (including dental surgery) or emergency treatment, tell the medical doctor or dentist in charge that you are taking this medicine.

Flecainide may cause some people to become dizzy, lightheaded, or less alert than they are normally. *Make sure you know how you react to this medicine before you drive, use machines, or do anything else that could be dangerous if you are dizzy or are not alert.*

If you have been using this medicine regularly for several weeks, do not suddenly stop using it. Check with your doctor for the best way to reduce gradually the amount you are taking before stopping completely.

Side Effects of This Medicine

Along with its needed effects, a medicine may cause some unwanted effects. Although not all of these side effects may occur, if they do occur they may need medical attention.

Check with your doctor as soon as possible if any of the following side effects occur:
Less common
  Chest pain; irregular heartbeat; shortness of breath; swelling of feet or lower legs; trembling or shaking

Rare
  Yellow eyes or skin

Other side effects may occur that usually do not need medical attention. These side effects may go away during treatment as your body adjusts to the medicine. However, check with your doctor if any of the following side effects continue or are bothersome:
More common
  Blurred vision or seeing spots; dizziness or lightheadedness

Less common
  Anxiety or mental depression; constipation; headache; nausea or vomiting; skin rash; stomach pain or loss of appetite; unusual tiredness or weakness

Other side effects not listed above may also occur in some patients. If you notice any other effects, check with your doctor.

Revised: 09/24/92
Interim revision: 04/29/94; 08/18/97

FLOXURIDINE   Systemic†

Commonly used brand name(s):

In the U.S.—
  FUDR
  Generic name product may be available.

†Not commercially available in Canada.

Description

Floxuridine (flox-YOOR-i-deen) belongs to the group of medicines known as antimetabolites. It is used to treat some kinds of cancer.

Floxuridine interferes with the growth of cancer cells, which are eventually destroyed. Since the growth of normal body cells may also be affected by floxuridine, other effects will also occur. Some of these may be serious and must be reported to your doctor. Other effects, like hair loss, may not be serious but may cause concern. Some effects may not occur for months or years after the medicine is used.

Before you begin treatment with floxuridine, you and your doctor should talk about the good this medicine will do as well as the risks of using it.

Floxuridine is to be administered only by or under the immediate supervision of your doctor. It is available in the following dosage form:

  Parenteral
  • Injection (U.S.)

Before Using This Medicine

In deciding to use a medicine, the risks of taking the medicine must be weighed against the good it will do. This is a decision you and your doctor will make. For floxuridine, the following should be considered:

Allergies—Tell your doctor if you have ever had any unusual or allergic reaction to floxuridine.

Pregnancy—There is a chance that this medicine may cause birth defects if either the male or female is receiving it at the time of conception or if it is taken during pregnancy. Floxuridine has been shown to cause birth defects in mice and rats. In addition, many cancer medicines may cause sterility which could be permanent. Although sterility has not been reported with this medicine, the possibility should be kept in mind.

Be sure that you have discussed this with your doctor before receiving this medicine. It is best to use some kind of birth control while you are receiving floxuridine. Tell your doctor right away if you think you have become pregnant while receiving floxuridine.

Breast-feeding—Tell your doctor if you are breast-feeding or if you intend to breast-feed during treatment with this medicine. Because floxuridine may cause serious side effects, breast-feeding is generally not recommended while you are receiving it.

Children—There is no specific information comparing use of floxuridine in children with use in other age groups.

Older adults—Many medicines have not been studied specifically in older people. Therefore, it may not be known whether they work exactly the same way they do in younger adults or if they cause different side effects or problems in older people. Although there is no specific information comparing use of floxuridine in the elderly with use in other age groups, this medicine is not expected to cause different side effects or problems in older people than it does in younger adults.

Other medicines—Although certain medicines should not be used together at all, in other cases two different medicines may be used together even if an interaction might occur. In these cases, your doctor may want to change the dose, or other precautions may be necessary. When you are receiving floxuridine, it is especially important that your health care professional know if you are taking any of the following:

  • Amphotericin B by injection (e.g., Fungizone) or
  • Antithyroid agents (medicine for overactive thyroid) or
  • Azathioprine (e.g., Imuran) or
  • Chloramphenicol (e.g., Chloromycetin) or
  • Colchicine or
  • Flucytosine (e.g., Ancobon) or
  • Ganciclovir (e.g., Cytovene) or
  • Interferon (Intron A, Roferon-A) or
  • Plicamycin (e.g., Mithracin) or
  • Zidovudine (e.g., AZT, Retrovir) or
  • If you have ever been treated with radiation or cancer medicines—Floxuridine may increase the effects of these medicines or radiation on the blood

Other medical problems—The presence of other medical problems may affect the use of floxuridine. Make sure you tell your doctor if you have any other medical problems, especially:

  • Chickenpox (including recent exposure) or
  • Herpes zoster (shingles)—Risk of severe disease affecting other parts of the body
  • Hepatitis (history of)—Increased risk of hepatitis
  • Kidney disease or
  • Liver disease (other)—Effects of floxuridine may be increased because of slower removal from the body
  • Infection—Floxuridine can decrease your body's ability to fight infection

Proper Use of This Medicine

Floxuridine sometimes causes nausea and vomiting. *Tell your doctor if this occurs, especially if you have stomach pain.*

Dosing—The dose of floxuridine will be different for different patients. The dose that is used may depend on a number of things, including what the medicine is being used for, the patient's weight, and whether or not other medicines are also being taken. *If you are receiving floxuridine at home, follow your doctor's orders or the directions on the label.* If you have any questions about the proper dose of floxuridine, ask your doctor.

Precautions While Using This Medicine

It is very important that your doctor check your progress at regular visits to make sure that this medicine is working properly and to check for unwanted effects.

While you are being treated with floxuridine, and after you stop treatment with it, *do not have any immunizations (vaccinations) without your doctor's approval.* Floxuridine may lower your body's resistance and there is a chance you might get the infection the immunization is meant to prevent. In addition, other persons living in your household should not take oral polio vaccine since there is a chance they could pass the polio virus on to you. Also, avoid persons who have recently taken oral polio vaccine. Do not get close to them and do not stay in the same room with them for very long. If you cannot take these precautions, you should consider wearing a protective face mask that covers the nose and mouth.

Side Effects of This Medicine

Along with its needed effects, a medicine may cause some unwanted effects. Although not all of these side effects may occur, if they do occur they may need medical attention.

Also, because of the way these medicines act on the body, there is a chance that they might cause other unwanted effects that may not occur until months or years after the medicine is used. These delayed effects may include certain types of cancer, such as leukemia. Discuss these possible effects with your doctor.

Check with your doctor or nurse immediately if any of the following side effects occur:

More common
 Diarrhea; sores in mouth and on lips; stomach pain or cramps

Less common
 Black, tarry stools; heartburn; nausea and vomiting; scaling or redness of hands or feet; swelling or soreness of the tongue

Rare
 Blood in urine or stools; cough or hoarseness; fever or chills; lower back or side pain; painful or difficult urination; pinpoint red spots on skin; trouble in walking; unusual bleeding or bruising; yellow eyes or skin

Other side effects may occur that usually do not need medical attention. These side effects may go away during treatment as your body adjusts to the medicine. Also, your health care professional may be able to tell you about ways to prevent or reduce some of these side effects. Check with your health care professional if any of the following side effects continue or are bothersome or if you have any questions about them:

Less common or rare
 Loss of appetite; skin rash or itching

This medicine sometimes causes temporary thinning of hair. After treatment with floxuridine has ended, normal hair growth should return.

Other side effects not listed above may also occur in some patients. If you notice any other effects, check with your health care professional.

Revised: 07/26/94

FLUCYTOSINE   Systemic

Commonly used brand name(s):

In the U.S.—
 Ancobon

In Canada—
 Ancotil

Other commonly used names are 5-fluorocytosine and 5-FC.

Description

Flucytosine (floo-SYE-toe-seen) belongs to the group of medicines called antifungals. It is used to treat certain fungus infections.

Flucytosine is available only with your doctor's prescription, in the following dosage form:

Oral
 • Capsules (U.S. and Canada)

Before Using This Medicine

In deciding to use a medicine, the risks of taking the medicine must be weighed against the good it will do. This is a decision you and your doctor will make. For flucytosine, the following should be considered:

Allergies—Tell your doctor if you have ever had any unusual or allergic reaction to flucytosine. Also tell your health care professional if you are allergic to any other substances, such as foods, preservatives, or dyes.

Pregnancy—Flucytosine has not been reported to cause birth defects or other problems in humans. However, studies in rats have shown that flucytosine causes birth defects.

Breast-feeding—It is not known if flucytosine passes into breast milk. Discuss with your doctor whether or not you should discontinue breast-feeding while using this medicine.

Children—Although there is no specific information comparing use of flucytosine in children with use in other age groups, this medicine is not expected to cause different side effects or problems in children than it does in adults.

Older adults—Many medicines have not been studied specifically in older people. Therefore, it may not be known whether they work exactly the same way they do in younger adults. Although there is no specific information comparing use of flucytosine in the elderly with use in other age groups, this medicine is not expected to cause different side effects or problems in older people than it does in younger adults.

Other medicines—Although certain medicines should not be used together at all, in other cases two different medicines may be used together even if an interaction might occur. In these cases, your doctor may want to change the dose, or other precautions may be necessary. When you are taking flucytosine, it is especially important that your health care professional knows if you are taking any of the following:
 • Amphotericin B by injection (e.g., Fungizone) or
 • Antineoplastics (cancer medicine) or
 • Antithyroid agents (medicine for overactive thyroid) or
 • Azathioprine (e.g., Imuran) or
 • Chloramphenicol (e.g., Chloromycetin) or
 • Colchicine or
 • Cyclophosphamide (e.g., Cytoxan) or
 • Ganciclovir (e.g., Cytovene) or
 • Interferon (e.g., Intron A, Roferon-A) or
 • Mercaptopurine (e.g., Purinethol) or
 • Methotrexate (e.g., Mexate) or
 • Plicamycin (e.g., Mithracin) or
 • Zidovudine (e.g., AZT, Retrovir) or
 • X-ray treatment—Use of flucytosine with any of these medicines may increase the chance for side effects of the blood

Other medical problems—The presence of other medical problems may affect the use of flucytosine. Make sure

you tell your doctor if you have any other medical problems, especially:

- Blood disease—Flucytosine may cause blood problems
- Kidney disease—Patients with kidney disease may have an increased chance of side effects
- Liver disease—Flucytosine may cause liver side effects

Proper Use of This Medicine

In some patients this medicine may cause nausea or vomiting. If you are taking more than 1 capsule for each dose, you may space them out over a period of 15 minutes to help lessen the nausea or vomiting. If this does not help or if you have any questions, check with your doctor.

To help clear up your infection completely, *keep taking this medicine for the full time of treatment,* even if you begin to feel better after a few days. *Do not miss any doses.*

Dosing—The dose of flucytosine will be different for different patients. *Follow your doctor's orders or the directions on the label.* The following information includes only the average doses of flucytosine. *If your dose is different, do not change it* unless your doctor tells you to do so.

- For *oral* dosage form (capsules):
  —For fungus infections:
    - Adults and children—Dose is based on body weight. The usual dose is 12.5 to 37.5 milligrams (mg) per kilogram (kg) (5.7 to 17 mg per pound) of body weight every six hours.

Missed dose—If you miss a dose of this medicine, take it as soon as possible. However, if it is almost time for your next dose, skip the missed dose and go back to your regular dosing schedule. Do not double doses.

Storage—To store this medicine:

- Keep out of the reach of children.
- Store away from heat and direct light.
- Do not store in the bathroom, near the kitchen sink, or in other damp places. Heat or moisture may cause the medicine to break down.
- Do not keep outdated medicine or medicine no longer needed. Be sure that any discarded medicine is out of the reach of children.

Precautions While Using This Medicine

Your doctor should check your progress at regular visits to make sure that this medicine does not cause unwanted effects.

Flucytosine may cause blood problems. These problems may result in a greater chance of infection, slow healing, and bleeding of the gums. Therefore, you should be careful when using regular toothbrushes, dental floss, and toothpicks. Dental work, whenever possible, should be done before you begin taking this medicine or delayed until your blood counts have returned to normal. Check with your medical doctor or dentist if you have any questions about proper oral hygiene (mouth care) during treatment.

Flucytosine may cause your skin to be more sensitive to sunlight than it is normally. Exposure to sunlight, even for brief periods of time, may cause skin rash, itching, redness, or other discoloration of the skin, or a severe sunburn. When you begin taking this medicine:

- Stay out of direct sunlight, especially between the hours of 10:00 a.m. and 3:00 p.m., if possible.

- Wear protective clothing, including a hat. Also, wear sunglasses.
- Apply a sun block product that has a skin protection factor (SPF) of at least 15. Some patients may require a product with a higher SPF number, especially if they have a fair complexion. If you have any questions about this, check with your health care professional.
- Apply a sun block lipstick that has an SPF of at least 15 to protect your lips.
- Do not use a sunlamp or tanning bed or booth.

If you have a severe reaction from the sun, check with your doctor.

This medicine may also cause some people to become dizzy, lightheaded, drowsy, or less alert than they are normally. *Make sure you know how you react to this medicine before you drive, use machines, or do anything else that could be dangerous if you are dizzy or are not alert.* If these reactions are especially bothersome, check with your doctor.

Side Effects of This Medicine

Along with its needed effects, a medicine may cause some unwanted effects. Although not all of these side effects may occur, if they do occur they may need medical attention.

Check with your doctor immediately if any of the following side effects occur:
  More common
    Skin rash, redness, or itching; sore throat and fever; unusual bleeding or bruising; unusual tiredness or weakness; yellow eyes or skin

  Less common
    Confusion; hallucinations (seeing, hearing, or feeling things that are not there); increased sensitivity of skin to sunlight

Other side effects may occur that usually do not need medical attention. These side effects may go away during treatment as your body adjusts to the medicine. However, check with your doctor if any of the following side effects continue or are bothersome:
  More common
    Abdominal pain; diarrhea; loss of appetite; nausea or vomiting

  Less common
    Dizziness or lightheadedness; drowsiness; headache

Other side effects not listed above may also occur in some patients. If you notice any other effects, check with your doctor.

Revised: 3/8/00

FLUDARABINE   Systemic

Commonly used brand name(s):

In the U.S.—
Fludara

In Canada—
Fludara

Description

Fludarabine (floo-DARE-a-been) belongs to the group of medicines called antimetabolites. It is used to treat chronic lymphocytic leukemia (CLL), a type of cancer.

Fludarabine interferes with the growth of cancer cells, which are eventually destroyed. Since the growth of normal body cells may also be affected by fludarabine, other effects will also occur. Some of these may be serious and must be reported to your doctor. Other effects may not be serious but may cause concern. Some effects may not occur for months or years after the medicine is used.

Before you begin treatment with fludarabine, you and your doctor should talk about the good this medicine will do as well as the risks of using it.

Fludarabine is to be administered only by or under the immediate supervision of your doctor. It is available in the following dosage form:

Parenteral
- Injection (U.S. and Canada)

Before Using This Medicine

In deciding to use a medicine, the risks of taking the medicine must be weighed against the good it will do. This is a decision you and your doctor will make. For fludarabine, the following should be considered:

Allergies—Tell your doctor if you have ever had any unusual or allergic reaction to fludarabine.

Pregnancy—There is a chance that this medicine may cause birth defects if either the male or female is taking it at the time of conception or if it is taken during pregnancy. Fludarabine has been shown to cause birth defects in rats and rabbits. In addition, many cancer medicines may cause sterility which could be permanent. Although sterility has not been reported with this medicine, it does occur in animals and the possibility should be kept in mind.

Be sure that you have discussed this with your doctor before taking this medicine. It is best to use some kind of birth control while you are receiving fludarabine. Tell your doctor right away if you think you have become pregnant while receiving fludarabine.

Breast-feeding—It is not known whether fludarabine passes into breast milk. However, because this medicine may cause serious side effects, breast-feeding is generally not recommended while you are receiving it.

Children—There is no specific information comparing use of fludarabine in children with use in other age groups.

Older adults—Many medicines have not been studied specifically in older people. Therefore, it may not be known whether they work exactly the same way they do in younger adults. Although there is no specific information comparing use of fludarabine in the elderly with use in other age groups, it is not expected to cause different side effects or problems in older people than it does in younger adults.

Other medicines—Although certain medicines should not be used together at all, in other cases two different medicines may be used together even if an interaction might occur. In these cases, your doctor may want to change the dose, or other precautions may be necessary. When receiving fludarabine it is especially important that your health care professional know if you are taking any of the following:
- Amphotericin B by injection (e.g., Fungizone) or
- Antithyroid agents (medicine for overactive thyroid) or
- Azathioprine (e.g., Imuran) or
- Chloramphenicol (e.g., Chloromycetin) or
- Colchicine or
- Flucytosine (e.g., Ancobon) or
- Ganciclovir (e.g., Cytovene) or
- Interferon (e.g., Intron A, Roferon-A) or
- Plicamycin (e.g., Mithracin) or
- Zidovudine (e.g., AZT, Retrovir) or
- If you have ever been treated with radiation or cancer medicines—Fludarabine may increase the effects of these medicines or radiation therapy on the blood
- Probenecid (e.g., Benemid) or
- Sulfinpyrazone (e.g., Anturane)—Fludarabine may raise the amount of uric acid in the blood. Since these medicines are used to lower uric acid levels, they may not be as effective in patients receiving fludarabine

Other medical problems—The presence of other medical problems may affect the use of fludarabine. Make sure you tell your doctor if you have any other medical problems, especially:
- Chickenpox (including recent exposure) or
- Herpes zoster (shingles)—Risk of severe disease affecting other parts of the body
- Gout (history of) or
- Kidney stones (history of)—Fludarabine may increase levels of uric acid in the body, which can cause gout or kidney stones
- Infection—Fludarabine may decrease your body's ability to fight infection
- Kidney disease—Effects of fludarabine may be increased because of slower removal from the body

Proper Use of This Medicine

This medicine may cause nausea and vomiting. However, it is very important that you continue to receive the medicine even if you begin to feel ill. Ask your health care professional for ways to lessen these effects.

Dosing—The dose of fludarabine will be different for different patients. The dose that is used may depend on a number of things, including what the medicine is being used for, the patient's size, and whether or not other medicines are also being taken. *If you are receiving fludarabine at home, follow your doctor's orders or the directions on the label.* If you have any questions about the proper dose of fludarabine, ask your doctor.

Precautions While Using This Medicine

It is very important that your doctor check your progress at regular visits to make sure that this medicine is working properly and to check for unwanted effects.

While you are being treated with fludarabine, and after you stop treatment with it, *do not have any immunizations (vaccinations) without your doctor's approval.* Fludarabine may lower your body's resistance and there is a chance you might get the infection the immunization is meant to prevent. In addition, other persons living in your household should not take oral polio vaccine since there is a chance they could pass the polio virus on to you. Also, avoid persons who have recently taken oral polio vaccine. Do not get close to them and do not stay in the same room with them for very long. If you cannot take these precautions, you should consider wearing a protective face mask that covers the nose and mouth.

Fludarabine can temporarily lower the number of white blood cells in your blood, increasing the chance of getting an infection. It can also lower the number of platelets, which are necessary for proper blood clotting. If this occurs, there are certain precautions you can take, especially when your blood count is low, to reduce the risk of infection or bleeding:

- If you can, avoid people with infections. *Check with your doctor immediately* if you think you are getting an infection or if you get a fever or chills, cough or hoarseness, lower back or side pain, or painful or difficult urination.
- *Check with your doctor immediately* if you notice any unusual bleeding or bruising; black, tarry stools; blood in urine or stools; or pinpoint red spots on your skin.
- Be careful when using a regular toothbrush, dental floss, or toothpick. Your medical doctor, dentist, or nurse may recommend other ways to clean your teeth and gums. Check with your medical doctor before having any dental work done.
- Do not touch your eyes or the inside of your nose unless you have just washed your hands and have not touched anything else in the meantime.
- Be careful not to cut yourself when you are using sharp objects such as a safety razor or fingernail or toenail cutters.
- Avoid contact sports or other situations where bruising or injury could occur.

Side Effects of This Medicine

Along with its needed effects, a medicine may cause some unwanted effects. Although not all of these side effects may occur, if they do occur they may need medical attention.

Also, because of the way cancer medicines act on the body, there is a chance that they might cause other unwanted effects that may not occur until months or years after the medicine is used. These delayed effects may include certain types of cancer. Discuss these possible effects with your doctor.

Check with your doctor or nurse immediately if any of the following side effects occur:

More common
  Cough or hoarseness; fever or chills; lower back or side pain; painful or difficult urination; shortness of breath

Less common
  Black, tarry stools; blood in urine; pinpoint red spots on skin; unusual bleeding or bruising

Check with your health care professional as soon as possible if any of the following side effects occur:

More common
  Pain

Less common
  Agitation or confusion; blurred vision; loss of hearing; numbness or tingling in fingers, toes, or face; sores in mouth and on lips; swelling of feet or lower legs; unusual tiredness or weakness

Other side effects may occur that usually do not need medical attention. These side effects may go away during treatment as your body adjusts to the medicine. Also, your health care professional may be able to tell you about ways to prevent or reduce some of these side effects. Check with your health

care professional if any of the following side effects continue or are bothersome or if you have any questions about them:

More common
  Diarrhea; nausea or vomiting; skin rash

Less common
  Aching muscles; general feeling of discomfort or illness; headache; loss of appetite

This medicine may rarely cause a temporary loss of hair in some people. After treatment with fludarabine has ended, normal hair growth should return.

After you stop treatment with fludarabine, it may still produce some side effects that need attention. During this period of time, check with your doctor if you notice the following:

Rare
  Cough or hoarseness; fever or chills; loss of vision; lower back or side pain; painful or difficult urination

Other side effects not listed above may also occur in some patients. If you notice any other effects, check with your doctor.

Revised: 08/02/94

FLUDROCORTISONE   Systemic

Commonly used brand name(s):

In the U.S.—
  Florinef

In Canada—
  Florinef

Description

Fludrocortisone (floo-droe-KOR-tis-sone) is a corticosteroid (kor-ti-koe-STE-roid) (cortisone-like medicine). It belongs to the family of medicines called steroids. Your body naturally produces similar corticosteroids, which are necessary to maintain the balance of certain minerals and water for good health. If your body does not produce enough corticosteroids, your doctor may have prescribed this medicine to help make up the difference.

Fludrocortisone may also be used to treat other medical conditions as determined by your doctor.

Fludrocortisone is available only with your doctor's prescription, in the following dosage form:

Oral
  • Tablets (U.S. and Canada)

Before Using This Medicine

In deciding to use a medicine, the risks of taking the medicine must be weighed against the good it will do. This is a decision you and your doctor will make. For fludrocortisone, the following should be considered:

Allergies—Tell your doctor if you have ever had any unusual or allergic reaction to fludrocortisone. Also tell your health care professional if you are allergic to any other substances, such as foods, preservatives, or dyes.

Diet—Your doctor may want you to control the amount of sodium in your diet. When fludrocortisone is used to treat certain types of kidney diseases, too much sodium may cause high blood sodium, high blood pressure, and excess body water.

Pregnancy—Studies on birth defects in humans or animals have not been done with fludrocortisone. However, it is possible that too much use of this medicine during pregnancy may cause the baby to have an underactive adrenal gland after birth.

Breast-feeding—Fludrocortisone passes into the breast milk and may cause problems with growth or other unwanted effects in the nursing baby.

Children—Fludrocortisone may slow or stop growth in children or growing adolescents when used for a long time. The natural production of corticosteroids by the body may also be decreased by the use of this medicine. Before this medicine is given to a child or adolescent, you and your child's doctor should talk about the good this medicine will do as well as the risks of using it. Follow the doctor's directions very carefully to lessen the chance that these unwanted effects will occur.

Older adults—Many medicines have not been studied specifically in older people. Therefore, it may not be known whether they work exactly the same way they do in younger adults or if they cause different side effects or problems in older people. There is no specific information comparing the use of fludrocortisone in the elderly with its use in other age groups.

Other medicines—Although certain medicines should not be used together at all, in other cases two different medicines may be used together even if an interaction might occur. In these cases, your doctor may want to change the dose, or other precautions may be necessary. When you are taking fludrocortisone, it is especially important that your health care professional know if you are taking any of the following:

- Acetazolamide (e.g., Diamox) or
- Amphotericin B by injection (e.g., Fungizone) or
- Azlocillin (e.g., Azlin) or
- Capreomycin (e.g., Capastat) or
- Carbenicillin by injection (e.g., Geopen) or
- Corticotropin (ACTH) or
- Dichlorphenamide (e.g., Daranide) or
- Diuretics (water pills) or
- Insulin or
- Laxatives (with overdose or chronic misuse) or
- Methazolamide (e.g., Neptazane) or
- Mezlocillin (e.g., Mezlin) or
- Piperacillin (e.g., Pipracil) or
- Salicylates or
- Sodium bicarbonate (e.g., baking soda) or
- Ticarcillin (e.g., Ticar) or
- Ticarcillin and clavulanate (e.g., Timentin) or
- Vitamin B$_{12}$ (e.g., AlphaRedisol, Rubramin-PC) (when used in megaloblastic anemia) or
- Vitamin D—Fludrocortisone and these medicines decrease the amount of potassium in the blood, which may increase the chance of severe low blood potassium

- Alcohol—Alcohol and fludrocortisone decrease the amount of potassium in the blood, which may increase the chance of severe low blood potassium; alcohol may also make fludrocortisone less effective by causing the body to get rid of it faster

- Barbiturates or
- Carbamazepine (e.g., Tegretol) or

- Griseofulvin (e.g., Fulvicin) or
- Phenylbutazone (e.g., Butazolidin) or
- Phenytoin (e.g., Dilantin) or
- Primidone (e.g., Mysoline) or
- Rifampin (e.g., Rifadin)—Using these medicines may make fludrocortisone less effective because they cause the body to get rid of it faster

- Digitalis glycosides (heart medicine)—Fludrocortisone decreases the amount of potassium in the blood, which may increase the chance of irregular heartbeat

- Other corticosteroids (cortisone-like medicine)—Using any corticosteroid medicine with fludrocortisone will cause the body to get rid of both medicines faster. This may make either or both medicines less effective. Also, fludrocortisone and other corticosteroids decrease the amount of potassium in the blood, which may increase the chance of severe low blood potassium

- Sodium-containing medicine—When using fludrocortisone to treat certain types of kidney diseases, too much sodium may cause high blood sodium, high blood pressure, and excess body water

Other medical problems—The presence of other medical problems may affect the use of fludrocortisone. Make sure you tell your doctor if you have any other medical problems, especially:

- Bone disease—Fludrocortisone may make bone disease worse because it causes more calcium to pass into the urine

- Edema (swelling of feet or lower legs) or
- Heart disease or
- High blood pressure or
- Kidney disease—Fludrocortisone causes the body to retain (keep) more salt and water. These conditions may be made worse by this extra body water

- Liver disease or
- Thyroid disease—The body may not get fludrocortisone out of the bloodstream at the usual rate, which may increase the effect of fludrocortisone or cause more side effects

Proper Use of This Medicine

Take this medicine only as directed by your doctor. Do not take more or less of it, do not take it more often, and do not take it for a longer time than your doctor ordered. To do so may increase the chance of side effects.

Dosing—The dose of fludrocortisone will be different for different patients. *Follow your doctor's orders or the directions on the label.* The following information includes only the average doses of fludrocortisone. *If your dose is different, do not change it* unless your doctor tells you to do so.

- For *oral* dosage forms (tablets):
  —Adults
  - For adrenal gland deficiency: 50 to 200 micrograms a day.
  - For adrenogenital syndrome: 100 to 200 micrograms a day.
  —Children: For adrenal gland deficiency: 50 to 100 micrograms a day.

Missed dose—If you miss a dose of this medicine, take it as soon as you remember. However, if it is almost time for

your next dose, skip the missed dose and go back to your regular dosing schedule. Do not double doses.

Storage—To store this medicine:

- Keep out of the reach of children.
- Store away from heat and direct light.
- Do not store in the bathroom, near the kitchen sink, or in other damp places. Heat or moisture may cause the medicine to break down.
- Do not keep outdated medicine or medicine no longer needed. Be sure that any discarded medicine is out of the reach of children.

Precautions While Using This Medicine

Your doctor should check your progress at regular visits to make sure this medicine does not cause unwanted effects.

If you will be using this medicine for a long time, your doctor may want you to carry a medical identification card stating that you are using this medicine.

While you are taking fludrocortisone, be careful to limit the amount of alcohol you drink.

Side Effects of This Medicine

Along with its needed effects, a medicine may cause some unwanted effects. Although not all of these side effects may occur, if they do occur they may need medical attention.

Check with your doctor immediately if any of the following side effects occur:

Less common or rare
Cough; difficulty swallowing; hives; irregular breathing or shortness of breath; irregular heartbeat; redness and itching of skin; redness of eyes; swelling of nasal passages, face, or eyelids; swollen neck veins; unusual tiredness or weakness

Check with your doctor as soon as possible if any of the following side effects occur:

Less common or rare
Dizziness; headache (severe or continuing); loss of appetite; muscle cramps or pain; nausea; swelling of feet or lower legs; weakness in arms, legs, or trunk (severe); weight gain (rapid); vomiting

Other side effects not listed above may also occur in some patients. If you notice any other effects, check with your doctor.

Additional Information

Once a medicine has been approved for marketing for a certain use, experience may show that it is also useful for other medical problems. Although these uses are not included in product labeling, fludrocortisone is used in certain patients with the following medical conditions:

- Idiopathic orthostatic hypotension (a certain type of low blood pressure)
- Too much acid in the blood, caused by kidney disease

Other than the above information, there is no additional information relating to proper use, precautions, or side effects for these uses.

Revised: 06/15/93

FLUOROQUINOLONES   Systemic

Commonly used brand name(s):

In the U.S.—

Avelox[6]	Maxaquin[5]
Cipro[1]	Noroxin[7]
Cipro I.V.[1]	Penetrex[2]
Floxin[8]	Tequin[3]
Floxin I.V.[8]	Zagam[9]
Levaquin[4]	

In Canada—

Cipro[1]	Levaquin[4]
Cipro I.V.[1]	Noroxin[7]
Floxin[8]	

Note: For quick reference, the following fluoroquinolones are numbered to match the corresponding brand names.

This information applies to the following medicines:
1. Ciprofloxacin (sip-roe-FLOX-a-sin)
2. Enoxacin (en-OX-a-sin) †
3. Gatifloxacin (gat-i-FLOX-a-sin) †
4. Levofloxacin (lee-voe-FLOX-a-sin)
5. Lomefloxacin (loe-me-FLOX-a-sin) †
6. Moxifloxacin (mox-i-FLOX-a-sin) †
7. Norfloxacin (nor-FLOX-a-sin)
8. Ofloxacin (oe-FLOX-a-sin)
9. Sparfloxacin (spar-FLOX-a-sin) †

†Not commercially available in Canada.

Description

Fluoroquinolones (flu-roe-KWIN-a-lones) are used to treat bacterial infections in many different parts of the body. They work by killing bacteria or preventing their growth. However, these medicines will not work for colds, flu, or other virus infections. Fluoroquinolones may also be used for other problems as determined by your doctor.

Fluoroquinolones are available only with your doctor's prescription, in the following dosage forms:

Oral
Ciprofloxacin
- Oral suspension (U.S.)
- Tablets (U.S. and Canada)
Enoxacin
- Tablets (U.S.)
Gatifloxacin
- Tablets (U.S.)
Levofloxacin
- Tablets (U.S. and Canada)
Lomefloxacin
- Tablets (U.S.)
Moxifloxacin
- Tablets (U.S.)
Norfloxacin
- Tablets (U.S. and Canada)
Ofloxacin
- Tablets (U.S. and Canada)
Sparfloxacin
- Tablets (U.S.)

Parenteral
Ciprofloxacin
- Injection (U.S. and Canada)
Gatifloxacin
- Injection (U.S.)
Levofloxacin
- Injection (U.S. and Canada)

Ofloxacin
- Injection (U.S.)

Before Using This Medicine

In deciding to use a medicine, the risks of taking the medicine must be weighed against the good it will do. This is a decision you and your doctor will make. For the fluoroquinolones, the following should be considered:

Allergies—Tell your doctor if you have ever had any unusual or allergic reaction to any of the fluoroquinolones or to any related medicines such as cinoxacin (e.g., Cinobac) or nalidixic acid (e.g., NegGram). Also tell your health care professional if you are allergic to any other substances, such as foods, preservatives, or dyes.

Pregnancy—Studies have not been done in humans. However, use is not recommended during pregnancy since fluoroquinolones have been reported to cause bone development problems in young animals.

Breast-feeding—Some of the fluoroquinolones are known to pass into human breast milk. Since fluoroquinolones have been reported to cause bone development problems in young animals, breast-feeding is not recommended during treatment with these medicines.

Children—Use is not recommended for infants or children since fluoroquinolones have been shown to cause bone development problems in young animals. However, your doctor may choose to use one of these medicines if other medicines cannot be used.

Teenagers—Use is not recommended for teenagers younger than 18 years of age since fluoroquinolones have been shown to cause bone development problems in young animals. However, your doctor may choose to use one of these medicines if other medicines cannot be used.

Older adults—These medicines have been tested and, in effective doses, have not been shown to cause different side effects or problems in older people than they do in younger adults.

Other medicines—Although certain medicines should not be used together at all, in other cases two different medicines may be used together even if an interaction might occur. In these cases, your doctor may want to change the dose, or other precautions may be necessary. When you are taking a fluoroquinolone, it is especially important that your health care professional know if you are taking any of the following:

- Aminophylline or
- Oxtriphylline (e.g., Choledyl) or
- Theophylline (e.g., Elixophyllin, Theo-Dur)—Ciprofloxacin, enoxacin,, and norfloxacin may increase the chance of side effects of aminophylline, oxtriphylline, or theophylline

- Amiodarone (e.g., Cordarone) or
- Astemizole (e.g., Hismanal) or
- Bepridil (e.g., Vascor) or
- Cisapride (e.g., Propulsid) or
- Disopyramide (e.g., Norpace) or
- Erythromycin (e.g., E-Mycin) or
- Pentamidine (e.g., NebuPent) or
- Phenothiazines (acetophenazine [e.g., Tindal], chlorpromazine [e.g., Ormazine, Thorazine Spansule, ThorProm], fluphenazine [e.g., Permitil, Prolixin], mesoridazine [e.g., Serentil], methotrimeprazine [e.g., Nozinan], pericyazine [e.g., Neuleptil], perphenazine [e.g., Trilafon], prochlorperazine [e.g., Compazine], promazine [e.g., Primazine, Sparine], thioridazine [e.g., Mellaril], trifluoperazine [e.g., Stelazine], triflupromazine [e.g., Vesprin]) or
- Procainamide (e.g., Pronestyl) or
- Quinidine (e.g., Quinidex) or
- Sotalol (e.g., Sotacor) or
- Terfenadine (e.g., Seldane) or
- Tricyclic antidepressants (amitriptyline [e.g., Elavil, Endep], amoxapine [e.g., Asendin], clomipramine [e.g., Anafranil], desipramine [e.g., Norpramin], doxepin [e.g., Sinequan], imipramine [e.g., Norfranil, Tipramine, Tofranil], nortriptyline [e.g., Aventyl, Pamelor], protriptyline [e.g., Vivactil], trimipramine [e.g., Surmontil])—Use of these medicines with gatifloxacin, moxifloxacin or sparfloxacin may cause heart problems, such as an irregular heartbeat

- Antacids, aluminum-, calcium-, and/or magnesium-containing, or
- Didanosine (e.g., Videx, ddl) or
- Iron supplements or
- Sucralfate (e.g., Carafate)—Antacids, didanosine, iron, or sucralfate may keep any of the fluoroquinolones from working properly

- Caffeine—Ciprofloxacin, enoxacin, and norfloxacin may increase the chance of side effects of caffeine; caffeine should *not* be taken during treatment with enoxacin

- Phenytoin (e.g., Dilantin)—Ciprofloxacin may keep phenytoin from working properly

- Warfarin (e.g., Coumadin)—Ciprofloxacin and norfloxacin may increase the effect of warfarin, increasing the chance of bleeding

Other medical problems—The presence of other medical problems may affect the use of fluoroquinolones. Make sure you tell your doctor if you have any other medical problems, especially:

- Brain or spinal cord disease, including hardening of the arteries in the brain or epilepsy or other seizures—Fluoroquinolones may cause nervous system side effects

- Diabetes mellitus (sugar diabetes)—Levofloxacin may cause changes in blood sugar, which could lead to problems in controlling blood sugar

- Heart disease— Gatifloxacin, moxifloxacin or sparfloxacin may make this problem worse

- Kidney disease or
- Liver disease—Patients with kidney disease or liver disease may have an increased chance of side effects with any of the fluoroquinolones

- Sensitivity of the skin to sunlight (previous)—Patients taking sparfloxacin or any of the other fluoroquinolones may have an increased risk of severe reactions to sunlight

- Tendinitis (previous)—Fluoroquinolones may increase the risk of tendon injury

Proper Use of This Medicine

Do not take fluoroquinolones if you are pregnant. Do not give fluoroquinolones to infants, children, or teenagers unless otherwise directed by your doctor. These medicines have been shown to cause bone development problems in young animals.

Fluoroquinolones are best taken with a full glass (8 ounces) of water. Several additional glasses of water should be taken every day, unless you are otherwise directed by your doctor. Drinking extra water will help to prevent some unwanted effects of ciprofloxacin and norfloxacin.

Enoxacin or norfloxacin should be taken on an empty stomach.

Ciprofloxacin, gatifloxacin, levofloxacin, lomefloxacin, moxifloxacin, ofloxacin, or sparfloxacin may be taken with meals or on an empty stomach.

To help clear up your infection completely, *keep taking your medicine for the full time of treatment,* even if you begin to feel better after a few days. If you stop taking this medicine too soon, your symptoms may return.

This medicine works best when there is a constant amount in the blood or urine. *To help keep the amount constant, do not miss any doses. Also, it is best to take the doses at evenly spaced times, day and night.* For example, if you are to take two doses a day, the doses should be spaced about 12 hours apart. If this interferes with your sleep or other daily activities, or if you need help in planning the best times to take your medicine, check with your health care professional.

Dosing—The dose of fluoroquinolones will be different for different patients. *Follow your doctor's orders or the directions on the label.* The following information includes only the average doses of fluoroquinolones. Your dose may be different if you have kidney disease. *If your dose is different, do not change it* unless your doctor tells you to do so.

The number of tablets or amount of oral suspension that you take depends on the strength of the medicine. Also, *the number of doses you take each day, the time allowed between doses, and the length of time you take the medicine depend on the medical problem for which you are using a fluoroquinolone.*

For ciprofloxacin
- For *oral* dosage form (oral suspension or tablets):
  —Adults: 100 to 750 milligrams (mg) every twelve hours for three to twenty-eight days, depending on the medical problem being treated. Bone and joint infections are usually treated for at least four to six weeks. Gonorrhea is usually treated with a single oral dose of 250 mg. Inhalational anthrax is usually treated for sixty days with 500 mg every twelve hours.
  —Children up to 18 years of age: This medicine is not recommended for use in infants, children, or teenagers, except in the case of inhalational anthrax. Inhalational anthrax is usually treated for sixty days with 15 mg per kilogram (kg) (6.8 mg per pound) of body weight every twelve hours.
- For *injection* dosage form:
  —Adults: 200 to 400 mg every eight to twelve hours.
  —Children up to 18 years of age: This medicine is not recommended for use in infants, children, or teenagers, except in the case of inhalational anthrax. Inhalational anthrax is usually treated for sixty days with 10 mg per kg (4.5 mg per pound) of body weight every twelve hours.

For enoxacin
- For *oral* dosage form (tablets):
  —Adults: 200 to 400 mg every twelve hours for seven to fourteen days, depending on the medical problem being treated. Gonorrhea is usually treated with a single oral dose of 400 mg.

—Children up to 18 years of age: This medicine is not recommended for use in infants, children, or teenagers.

For gatifloxacin
- For *oral* dosage form (tablets):
  —Adult: 200 to 400 mg every twenty-four hours for seven to fourteen days, depending on the medical problems being treated. Gonorrhea and certain bladder infection are usually treated with a single oral dose of 400 mg.
  —Children up to 18 years of age: This medicine is not recommended for use in infants, children, or teenagers.
- For *injection* dosage form:
  —Adults: 200 to 400 mg every twenty four hours for seven to fourteen days, depending on the medical problems being treated. Gonorrhea and certain bladder infection are usually treated with a single oral dose of 400 mg.
  —Children up to 18 years of age: This medicine is not recommended for use in infants, children, or teenagers.

For levofloxacin
- For *oral* dosage form (tablets):
  —Adults: 250 to 500 mg once a day for seven to fourteen days, depending on the medical problem being treated.
  —Children up to 18 years of age: This medicine is not recommended for use in infants, children, or teenagers.
- For *injection* dosage form:
  —Adults: 250 to 500 mg, injected slowly into a vein, once a day for seven to fourteen days, depending on the medical problem being treated.
  —Children up to 18 years of age: This medicine is not recommended for use in infants, children, or teenagers.

For lomefloxacin
- For *oral* dosage form (tablets):
  —Adults: 400 mg once a day for three to fourteen days, depending on the medical problem being treated.
  —Children up to 18 years of age: This medicine is not recommended for use in infants, children, or teenagers.

For moxifloxacin
- For *oral* dosage form (tablets):
  —Adult: 400 mg once a day for five to ten days, depending on the medical problem being treated.
  —Children up to 18 years of age: This medicine is not recommended for use in infants, children, or teenagers.

For norfloxacin
- For *oral* dosage form (tablets):
  —Adults: 400 mg every twelve hours for three to twenty-eight days, depending on the medical problem being treated. Gonorrhea is usually treated with a single oral dose of 800 mg.
  —Children up to 18 years of age: This medicine is not recommended for use in infants, children, or teenagers.

For ofloxacin
- For *oral* dosage form (tablets):
  —Adults: 200 to 400 mg every twelve hours for three to fourteen days, depending on the medical problem

being treated. Prostatitis is usually treated for six weeks. Gonorrhea is usually treated with a single oral dose of 400 mg.

—Children up to 18 years of age: This medicine is not recommended for use in infants, children, or teenagers.

- For *injection* dosage form:
  —Adults: 200 to 400 mg, injected slowly into a vein, every twelve hours for three to fourteen days, depending on the medical problem being treated. Prostatitis is usually treated for six weeks. Gonorrhea is usually treated with a single dose of 400 mg.
  —Children up to 18 years of age: This medicine is not recommended for use in infants, children, or teenagers.

For sparfloxacin
- For *oral* dosage form (tablets):
  —Adults: 400 mg on the first day, then 200 mg once a day for an additional nine days.
  —Children up to 18 years of age: This medicine is not recommended for use in infants, children, or teenagers.

Missed dose—If you miss a dose of this medicine, take it as soon as possible. This will help to keep a constant amount of medicine in the blood or urine. However, if it is almost time for your next dose, skip the missed dose and go back to your regular dosing schedule. Do not double doses.

Storage—To store this medicine:
- Keep out of the reach of children.
- Store away from heat and direct light.
- Ciprofloxacin oral suspension may be refrigerated. However, keep this medicine from freezing.
- Do not store in the bathroom, near the kitchen sink, or in other damp places. Heat or moisture may cause the medicine to break down.
- Do not keep outdated medicine or medicine no longer needed. Be sure that any discarded medicine is out of the reach of children.

Precautions While Using This Medicine

If your symptoms do not improve within a few days, or if they become worse, check with your doctor.

If you are taking aluminum- or magnesium-containing antacids, or sucralfate, do not take them at the same time that you take this medicine. It is best to take these medicines at least 6 hours before or 2 hours after taking ciprofloxacin; at least 8 hours before or 2 hours after taking enoxacin; at least 4 hours after taking gatifloxacin; at least 4 hours before or 4 hours after taking sparfloxacin; at least 2 hours before or 2 hours after taking levofloxacin, norfloxacin, or ofloxacin; at least 4 hours before or 2 hours after taking lomefloxacin, and at least 4 hours before and 8 hours after taking moxifloxacin. These medicines may keep fluoroquinolones from working properly.

If you are taking enoxacin, you should not take any caffeine-containing products (e.g., coffee, tea, chocolate, certain carbonated beverages). Taking any of these caffeine-containing products while you are taking enoxacin may increase the effects of caffeine.

Some people who take fluoroquinolones, especially sparfloxacin, may become more sensitive to sunlight than they are normally. Exposure to sunlight, even for brief periods of time, may cause severe sunburn, or skin rash, redness, itching, or discoloration. When you begin taking this medicine:

- Stay out of direct sunlight, especially between the hours of 10:00 a.m. and 3:00 p.m., if possible.
- Wear protective clothing, including a hat and sunglasses.
- Apply a sun block product that has a skin protection factor (SPF) of at least 15. Some patients may require a product with a higher SPF number, especially if they have a fair complexion. If you have any questions about this, check with your health care professional.
- Do not use a sunlamp or tanning bed or booth.

Stay out of direct sunlight and artificial light (e.g., sunlamp, tanning bed or booth) for the next 5 days or until the reaction has stopped.

If you get a skin rash or other signs of an allergic reaction, stop taking the fluoroquinolone and check with your doctor.

Fluoroquinolones may also cause some people to become dizzy, lightheaded, drowsy, or less alert than they are normally. *Make sure you know how you react to this medicine before you drive, use machines, or do anything else that can be dangerous if you are dizzy or are not alert.* If these reactions are especially bothersome, check with your doctor.

Fluoroquinolones may rarely cause inflammation or even tearing of a tendon (the cord that attaches muscles to bones). *If you get sudden pain in a tendon after exercise (for example, in your ankle, back of the knee or leg, shoulder, elbow, or wrist), stop taking the fluoroquinolone and check with your doctor.* Rest and do not exercise until the doctor has made sure that you have not injured or torn the tendon.

For patients with diabetes taking insulin or diabetes medicine by mouth: Levofloxacin may cause hypoglycemia (low blood sugar) in some patients. *Symptoms of low blood sugar must be treated before they lead to unconsciousness (passing out).* Different people may feel different symptoms of low blood sugar. *If you experience symptoms of low blood sugar, stop taking levofloxacin and check with your doctor right away:*

- Symptoms of low blood sugar can include: Anxious feeling, behavior change similar to being drunk, blurred vision, cold sweats, confusion, cool pale skin, difficulty in concentrating, drowsiness, excessive hunger, headache, nausea, nervousness, rapid heartbeat, shakiness, unusual tiredness or weakness.

Side Effects of This Medicine

Along with its needed effects, a medicine may cause some unwanted effects. Although not all of these side effects may occur, if they do occur they may need medical attention.

Check with your doctor immediately if any of the following side effects occur:

More common—For sparfloxacin
    Fainting; irregular or slow heart rate

Less common—More common for lomefloxacin and sparfloxacin
    Blistering of skin; sensation of skin burning; skin itching, rash, redness, or swelling

Rare
    Abdominal or stomach cramps and pain (severe); abdominal tenderness; agitation; blisters on mucous membranes, with fever; bloody or cloudy urine; con-

fusion; dark or amber urine; diarrhea (watery and severe, which may also be bloody); dizziness, faintness, feeling of warmth or heat, flushing or redness of skin especially on face and neck, headache, lightheadedness, sweating, weakness; fever; hallucinations (seeing, hearing, or feeling things that are not there); irregular or fast heart rate; joint pain; loss of appetite; pain at site of injection—for ciprofloxacin or ofloxacin injection; pain in calves, radiating to heels; pale stools; peeling of the skin; shakiness or tremors; shortness of breath; stomach pain; swelling of face or neck; swelling of calves, feet, or lower legs; unusual tiredness or weakness; yellow eyes or skin

Other side effects may occur that usually do not need medical attention. These side effects may go away during treatment as your body adjusts to the medicine. However, check with your doctor if any of the following side effects continue or are bothersome:

More common
   Abdominal or stomach pain or discomfort (mild); diarrhea (mild); dizziness; drowsiness; headache; lightheadedness; nausea or vomiting; nervousness; trouble in sleeping; vaginal pain and discharge

Less frequent or rare
   Abnormal dream; back pain; change in sense of taste; difficulty in urination; increased sensitivity of skin to sunlight; muscle pain; sore mouth or tongue, or white patches in mouth and/or on tongue; vaginal yeast infection; vision problems

Other side effects not listed above may also occur in some patients. If you notice any other effects, check with your doctor.

Additional Information

Once a medicine has been approved for marketing for a certain use, experience may show that it is also useful for other medical problems. Although these uses are not included in product labeling, fluoroquinolones are used in certain patients with the following medical conditions:

- Chancroid
- Pulmonary exacerbations (airway infections) in cystic fibrosis

Other than the above information, there is no additional information relating to proper use, precautions, or side effects for these uses.

Revised: 12/18/2000

FLUOROURACIL   Systemic

Commonly used brand name(s):

In the U.S.—
   Adrucil
   Generic name product may be available.

In Canada—
   Adrucil
   Generic name product may be available.
   Another commonly used name is 5-FU.

Description

Fluorouracil (flure-oh-YOOR-a-sill) belongs to the group of medicines known as antimetabolites. It is used to treat cancer of the colon, rectum, breast, stomach, and pancreas. It may also be used to treat other kinds of cancer, as determined by your doctor.

Fluorouracil interferes with the growth of cancer cells, which are eventually destroyed. Since the growth of normal body cells may also be affected by fluorouracil, other effects will also occur. Some of these may be serious and must be reported to your doctor. Other effects, like hair loss, may not be serious but may cause concern. Some effects may not occur for months or years after the medicine is used.

Before you begin treatment with fluorouracil, you and your doctor should talk about the good this medicine will do as well as the risks of using it.

Fluorouracil is to be administered only by or under the immediate supervision of your doctor. It is available in the following dosage form:

Parenteral
   • Injection (U.S. and Canada)

Before Using This Medicine

In deciding to use a medicine, the risks of taking the medicine must be weighed against the good it will do. This is a decision you and your doctor will make. For fluorouracil, the following should be considered:

Allergies—Tell your doctor if you have ever had any unusual or allergic reaction to fluorouracil.

Pregnancy—Tell your doctor if you are pregnant or if you intend to have children. There is a chance that this medicine may cause birth defects if either the male or female is receiving it at the time of conception or if it is taken during pregnancy. Fluorouracil has been reported to cause birth defects in mice given doses slightly higher than the human dose. Also, there has been one case of a baby born with several birth defects after the mother received fluorouracil. In addition, many cancer medicines may cause sterility. Although sterility has been reported with this medicine, it is usually only temporary; the possibility should be kept in mind.

Be sure that you have discussed this with your doctor before receiving this medicine. It is best to use some kind of birth control while you are receiving fluorouracil. Tell your doctor right away if you think you have become pregnant while receiving fluorouracil.

Breast-feeding—Tell your doctor if you are breast-feeding or if you intend to breast-feed during treatment with this medicine. It is not known whether fluorouracil passes into breast milk. However, because fluorouracil may cause serious side effects, breast-feeding is generally not recommended while you are receiving it.

Children—Although there is no specific information comparing use of fluorouracil in children with use in other age groups, it is not expected to cause different side effects or problems in children than it does in adults.

Older adults—Many medicines have not been studied specifically in older people. Therefore, it may not be known whether they work exactly the same way they do in younger adults. Although there is no specific information comparing use of fluorouracil in the elderly with use in other age groups, it is not expected to cause different side effects or problems in older people than it does in younger adults.

Other medicines—Although certain medicines should not be used together at all, in other cases two different medicines may be used together even if an interaction might occur. In these cases, your doctor may want to change the dose, or other precautions may be necessary. When you are receiving fluorouracil, it is especially important that your health care professional know if you are taking any of the following:

- Amphotericin B by injection (e.g., Fungizone) or
- Antithyroid agents (medicine for overactive thyroid) or
- Azathioprine (e.g., Imuran) or
- Chloramphenicol (e.g., Chloromycetin) or
- Colchicine or
- Flucytosine (e.g., Ancobon) or
- Ganciclovir (e.g., Cytovene) or
- Interferon (e.g., Intron A, Roferon-A) or
- Plicamycin (e.g., Mithracin) or
- Zidovudine (e.g., AZT, Retrovir) or
- Warfarin (e.g. Coumadin)
- If you have ever been treated with radiation or cancer medicines—Fluorouracil may increase the effects of these medicines or radiation on the blood

Other medical problems—The presence of other medical problems may affect the use of fluorouracil. Make sure you tell your doctor if you have any other medical problems, especially:

- Chickenpox (including recent exposure) or
- Herpes zoster (shingles)—Risk of severe disease affecting other parts of the body
- Infection—Fluorouracil can decrease your body's ability to fight infection
- Kidney disease or
- Liver disease—Effects of fluorouracil may be increased because of slower removal from the body

Proper Use of This Medicine

This medicine is sometimes given together with certain other medicines. If you are using a combination of medicines, it is important that you receive each one at the proper time. If you are taking some of these medicines by mouth, ask your health care professional to help you plan a way to remember to take them at the right times.

Fluorouracil often causes nausea and vomiting. However, it is very important that you continue to receive the medicine, even if your stomach is upset. Ask your health care professional for ways to lessen these effects.

Dosing—The dosing of fluorouracil will be different for different patients. The dose that is used may depend on a number of things, including what the medicine is being used for, the patient's weight, and whether or not other medicines are also being taken. *If you are receiving fluorouracil at home, follow your doctor's orders or the directions on the label.* If you have any questions about the proper dose of fluorouracil, ask your doctor.

Precautions While Using This Medicine

It is very important that your doctor check your progress at regular visits to make sure that this medicine is working properly and to check for unwanted effects.

While you are being treated with fluorouracil, and after you stop treatment with it, *do not have any immunizations (vaccinations) without your doctor's approval.* Fluorouracil may lower your body's resistance and there is a chance you might get the infection the immunization is meant to prevent. In addition, other persons living in your household should not take oral polio vaccine since there is a chance they could pass the polio virus on to you. Also, avoid persons who have taken oral polio vaccine within the last several months. Do not get close to them and do not stay in the same room with them for very long. If you cannot take these precautions, you should consider wearing a protective face mask that covers the nose and mouth.

Fluorouracil can temporarily lower the number of white blood cells in your blood, increasing the chance of getting an infection. It can also lower the number of platelets, which are necessary for proper blood clotting. If this occurs, there are certain precautions you can take, especially when your blood count is low, to reduce the risk of infection or bleeding:

- If you can, avoid people with infections. *Check with your doctor immediately* if you think you are getting an infection or if you get a fever or chills, cough or hoarseness, lower back or side pain, or painful or difficult urination.
- *Check with your doctor immediately* if you notice any unusual bleeding or bruising; black, tarry stools; blood in urine or stools; or pinpoint red spots on your skin.
- Be careful when using a regular toothbrush, dental floss, or toothpick. Your medical doctor, dentist, or nurse may recommend other ways to clean your teeth and gums. Check with your medical doctor before having any dental work done.
- Do not touch your eyes or the inside of your nose unless you have just washed your hands and have not touched anything else in the meantime.
- Be careful not to cut yourself when you are using sharp objects such as a safety razor or fingernail or toenail cutters.
- Avoid contact sports or other situations where bruising or injury could occur.

Side Effects of This Medicine

Along with its needed effects, a medicine may cause some unwanted effects. Although not all of these side effects may occur, if they do occur they may need medical attention.

Also, because of the way these medicines act on the body, there is a chance that they might cause other unwanted effects that may not occur until months or years after the medicine is used. These delayed effects may include certain types of cancer, such as leukemia. Discuss these possible effects with your doctor.

Check with your doctor or nurse immediately if any of the following side effects occur:

More common
   Diarrhea; heartburn; sores in mouth and on lips

Less common
   Black, tarry stools; cough or hoarseness, accompanied by fever or chills; fever or chills; lower back or side pain, accompanied by fever or chills; nausea and vomiting (severe); painful or difficult urination, accompanied by fever or chills; stomach cramps

Rare
   Blood in urine or stools; pinpoint red spots on skin; unusual bleeding or bruising

Check with your health care professional as soon as possible if any of the following side effects occur:

Rare
> Chest pain; cough; shortness of breath; tingling of hands and feet, followed by pain, redness, and swelling; trouble with balance

Other side effects may occur that usually do not need medical attention. These side effects may go away during treatment as your body adjusts to the medicine. Also, your health care professional may be able to tell you about ways to prevent or reduce some of these side effects. Check with your health care professional if any of the following side effects continue or are bothersome or if you have any questions about them:

More common
> Loss of appetite; nausea and vomiting; skin rash and itching; weakness

Less common
> Dry or cracked skin

This medicine often causes a temporary loss of hair. After treatment with fluorouracil has ended, normal hair growth should return.

After you stop receiving fluorouracil, it may still produce some side effects that need attention. During this period of time, *check with your doctor or nurse immediately* if you notice any of the following:

> Black, tarry stools; blood in urine or stools; cough or hoarseness, accompanied by fever or chills; fever or chills; lower back or side pain, accompanied by fever or chills; painful or difficult urination, accompanied by fever or chills; pinpoint red spots on skin; unusual bleeding or bruising

Other side effects not listed above may also occur in some patients. If you notice any other effects, check with your health care professional.

Additional Information

Once a medicine has been approved for marketing for a certain use, experience may show that it is also useful for other medical problems. Although these uses are not included in product labeling, fluorouracil is used in certain patients with the following medical conditions:

- Cancer of the outside layer of the adrenal gland
- Cancer of the anus
- Cancer of the bladder
- Cancer of the cervix
- Cancer of the endometrium
- Cancer of the ovaries
- Cancer of the esophagus
- Cancer of the head and neck
- Cancer of the penis
- Cancer of the liver
- Cancer of the prostate
- Cancer of the skin
- Cancer of the vulva
- Carcinoid tumors
- Hepatoblastoma (a certain type of liver cancer that occurs in children)
- Glaucoma, during and after certain surgery (trabeculectomy)

Other than the above information, there is no additional information relating to proper use, precautions, or side effects for these uses.

Revised: 05/04/2001

FLUOROURACIL   Topical

Commonly used brand name(s):

In the U.S.—
> Efudex
> Fluoroplex

In Canada—
> Efudex
> Fluoroplex

Another commonly used name is 5-FU.

Description

Fluorouracil (flure-oh-YOOR-a-sill) belongs to the group of medicines known as antimetabolites. When applied to the skin, it is used to treat certain skin problems, including cancer or conditions that could become cancerous if not treated.

Fluorouracil interferes with the growth of abnormal cells, which are eventually destroyed.

Fluorouracil is available only with your doctor's prescription, in the following dosage forms:

Topical
- Cream (U.S. and Canada)
- Topical solution (U.S. and Canada)

Before Using This Medicine

In deciding to use a medicine, the risks of using the medicine must be weighed against the good it will do. This is a decision you and your doctor will make. For topical fluorouracil, the following should be considered:

Allergies—Tell your doctor if you have ever had any unusual or allergic reaction to fluorouracil.

Pregnancy—Tell your doctor if you are pregnant or if you intend to become pregnant. Although fluorouracil applied to the skin has not been shown to cause problems in humans, some of it is absorbed through the skin and there is a chance that it could cause birth defects. Be sure that you have discussed this with your doctor before using this medicine.

Breast-feeding—Although fluorouracil applied to the skin has not been shown to cause problems in nursing babies, some of it is absorbed through the skin.

Children—There is no specific information comparing use of fluorouracil on the skin in children with use in other age groups.

Older adults—Many medicines have not been studied specifically in older people. Therefore, it may not be known whether they work exactly the same way they do in younger adults or if they cause different side effects or problems in older people. Although there is no specific information comparing use of fluorouracil on the skin in the elderly with use in other age groups, this medicine is not expected to cause different side effects or problems in older people than it does in younger adults.

Other medical problems—The presence of other medical problems may affect the use of fluorouracil on the skin. Make sure you tell your doctor if you have any other medical problems, especially:

- Other skin problems—May be aggravated

Proper Use of This Medicine

Keep using this medicine for the full time of treatment. However, *do not use this medicine more often or for a longer time than your doctor ordered.* Apply enough medicine each time to cover the entire affected area with a thin layer.

After washing the area with soap and water and drying carefully, use a cotton-tipped applicator or your fingertips to apply the medicine in a thin layer to your skin.

If you apply this medicine with your fingertips, make sure you *wash your hands immediately afterwards,* to prevent any of the medicine from accidentally getting in your eyes or mouth.

Fluorouracil may cause redness, soreness, scaling, and peeling of affected skin after 1 or 2 weeks of use. This effect may last for several weeks after you stop using the medicine and is to be expected. Sometimes a pink, smooth area is left when the skin treated with this medicine heals. This area will usually fade after 1 to 2 months. Do not stop using this medicine without first checking with your doctor. If the reaction is very uncomfortable, check with your doctor.

Dosing—The dose of fluorouracil will be different for different patients. *Follow your doctor's orders or the directions on the label.* The following information includes only the average doses of fluorouracil. *If your dose is different, do not change it* unless your doctor tells you to do so.

- For *cream* dosage form:
  —For precancerous skin condition caused by the sun:
    - Adults—Use the 1% cream on the affected areas of skin one or two times a day. The 5% cream is sometimes used on the hands.
    - Children—Use and dose must be determined by your doctor.
  —For skin cancer:
    - Adults—Use the 5% cream on the affected areas of skin two times a day. Treatment may continue for several weeks.
    - Children—Use and dose must be determined by your doctor.
- For *topical solution* dosage form:
  —For precancerous skin condition caused by the sun:
    - Adults—Use the 1% solution on the affected areas of skin one or two times a day. The 2% or 5% solution is sometimes used on the hands.
    - Children—Use and dose must be determined by your doctor.
  —For skin cancer:
    - Adults—Use the 5% solution on the affected areas of skin two times a day. Treatment may continue for several weeks.
    - Children—Use and dose must be determined by your doctor.

Missed dose—If you miss a dose of this medicine, apply it as soon as you remember. However, if more than a few hours have passed, skip the missed dose and go back to your regular dosing schedule. If you miss more than one dose, check with your doctor.

Storage—To store this medicine:
- Keep out of the reach of children.
- Store away from heat and direct light.
- Do not store in the bathroom, near the kitchen sink, or in other damp places. Heat or moisture may cause the medicine to break down.
- Protect the solution from freezing.
- Do not keep outdated medicine or medicine no longer needed. Be sure that any discarded medicine is out of the reach of children.

Precautions While Using This Medicine

It is very important that your doctor check your progress at regular visits to make sure that this medicine is working properly and to check for unwanted effects.

Apply this medicine very carefully when using it on your face. Avoid getting any in your eyes, nose, or mouth.

While using this medicine, and for 1 or 2 months after you stop using it, your skin may become more sensitive to sunlight than usual and too much sunlight may increase the effect of the drug. *During this period of time:*

- Stay out of direct sunlight, especially between the hours of 10:00 a.m. and 3:00 p.m., if possible.
- Wear protective clothing, including a hat and sunglasses.
- Apply a sun block product that has a skin protection factor (SPF) of at least 15. Some patients may require a product with a higher SPF number, especially if they have a fair complexion. If you have any questions about this, check with your health care professional.
- Do not use a sunlamp or tanning bed or booth.

If you have a severe reaction from the sun, check with your doctor.

Side Effects of This Medicine

Along with its needed effects, a medicine may cause some unwanted effects. Although not all of these side effects may occur, if they do occur they may need medical attention.

Check with your doctor immediately if the following side effects occur:
    Redness and swelling of normal skin

Other side effects may occur that usually do not need medical attention. These side effects may go away during treatment as your body adjusts to the medicine. However, check with your doctor if any of the following side effects continue, worsen, or are bothersome:
    More common
        Burning feeling where medicine is applied; increased sensitivity of skin to sunlight; itching; oozing; skin rash; soreness or tenderness of skin
    Less common or rare
        Darkening of skin; scaling; watery eyes

Other side effects not listed above may also occur in some patients. If you notice any other effects, check with your doctor.

Revised: 06/09/93
Interim revision: 05/02/94

FLUOXETINE   Systemic

Commonly used brand name(s):

In the U.S.—
    Prozac
    Prozac Weekly
    Sarafem

In Canada—
    Prozac

Description

Fluoxetine (floo-OX-e-teen) is used to treat mental depression. It is also used to treat obsessive-compulsive disorder, bulimia nervosa, and premenstrual dysphoric disorder.

Fluoxetine also may be used for other conditions as determined by your doctor.

Fluoxetine belongs to a group of medicines known as selective serotonin reuptake inhibitors (SSRIs). These medicines are thought to work by increasing the activity of a chemical called serotonin in the brain.

This medicine is available only with your doctor's prescription, in the following dosage forms:

Oral
- Capsules (U.S. and Canada)
- Oral Solution (U.S. and Canada)
- Tablets (U.S.)

Before Using This Medicine

In deciding to use a medicine, the risks of taking the medicine must be weighed against the good it will do. This is a decision you and your doctor will make. For fluoxetine, the following should be considered:

Allergies—Tell your doctor if you have ever had any unusual or allergic reaction to fluoxetine. Also tell your health care professional if you are allergic to any other substances, such as foods, preservatives, or dyes.

Pregnancy—One study of babies whose mothers had taken fluoxetine while they were pregnant found some problems in the babies, such as premature birth, jitteriness, and trouble in breathing or nursing. However, four other studies did not find any problems in babies or young children whose mothers had taken fluoxetine while they were pregnant. Tell your doctor if you are pregnant or if you may become pregnant while you are taking this medicine.

Breast-feeding—Fluoxetine passes into breast milk. A study of 11 breast-fed babies whose mothers were taking fluoxetine found no effect on the babies. However, another baby whose mother was taking this medicine had vomiting, watery stools, crying, and sleep problems. Be sure you have discussed the risks and benefits of this medicine with your doctor.

Children—This medicine has been tested in a limited number of children 7 to 18 years of age. These studies indicate that fluoxetine may help to treat depression and obsessive-compulsive disorder in children. However, unusual excitement, restlessness, irritability, and trouble in sleeping may be especially likely to occur in children, who seem to be more sensitive than adults to the effects of fluoxetine. More study is needed to be sure fluoxetine is safe and effective in children.

Older adults—Many medicines have not been tested in older people. Therefore, it may not be known whether they work exactly the same way they do in younger adults or if they cause different side effects or problems in older people. In studies done to date that included elderly people, fluoxetine did not cause different side effects or problems in older people than it did in younger adults.

Other medicines—Although certain medicines should not be used together at all, in other cases two different medicines may be used together even if an interaction might occur. In these cases, your doctor may want to change the dose, or other precautions may be necessary. When you are taking fluoxetine, it is especially important that your health care professional know if you are taking any of the following:

- Alprazolam (e.g., Xanax)—Higher blood levels of alprazolam may occur and its effects may be increased
- Anticoagulants (blood thinners) or
- Digitalis glycosides (heart medicine)—Higher or lower blood levels of these medicines or fluoxetine may occur, increasing the chance of unwanted effects. Your doctor may need to see you more often, especially when you first start or when you stop taking fluoxetine. Your doctor also may need to change the dose of either medicine
- Astemizole (e.g., Hismanal)—Higher blood levels of astemizole may occur, which increases the chance of having a very serious change in the rhythm of your heartbeat
- Buspirone (e.g., BuSpar) or
- Bromocriptine (e.g., Parlodel) or
- Dextromethorphan (cough medicine) or
- Levodopa (e.g., Sinemet) or
- Lithium (e.g., Eskalith) or
- Meperidine (e.g., Demerol) or
- Nefazodone (e.g., Serzone) or
- Pentazocine (e.g., Talwin) or
- Selective serotonin reuptake inhibitors, other (citalopram [Celexa], fluvoxamine [e.g., Luvox], paroxetine [e.g., Paxil], sertraline [e.g., Zoloft]) or
- Street drugs (LSD, MDMA [e.g., ecstasy], marijuana) or
- Sumatriptan (e.g., Imitrex) or
- Tramadol (e.g., Ultram) or
- Trazodone (e.g., Desyrel) or
- Tryptophan or
- Venlafaxine (e.g., Effexor)—Using these medicines with fluoxetine or within 5 weeks of stopping fluoxetine may increase the chance of developing a rare, but very serious, unwanted effect known as the serotonin syndrome. This syndrome may cause confusion, diarrhea, fever, poor coordination, restlessness, shivering, sweating, talking or acting with excitement you cannot control, trembling or shaking, or twitching. If you develop these symptoms contact your doctor as soon as possible. Taking tramadol with fluoxetine increases the chance of having convulsions (seizures). Also, taking tryptophan with fluoxetine may result in increased agitation or restlessness and intestinal or stomach problems
- Moclobemide (e.g., Manerex)—The risk of developing serious unwanted effects, including the serotonin syndrome, is increased. Use of moclobemide with fluoxetine is not recommended. Also, it is recommended that 7 days be allowed between stopping treatment with moclobemide and starting treatment with fluoxetine, and it is recommended that 5 weeks be allowed between stopping treatment with fluoxetine and starting treatment with moclobemide
- Monoamine oxidase (MAO) inhibitors (furazolidone [e.g., Furoxone], phenelzine [e.g., Nardil], procarbazine [e.g., Matulane], selegiline [e.g., Eldepryl], tranylcypromine [e.g., Parnate])—*Do not take fluoxetine while you are taking or within 2 weeks of taking an MAO inhibitor*. If you do, you may develop confusion, agitation, restlessness, stomach or intestinal problems, sudden high body temperature, extremely high blood pressure, and severe convulsions. At least 14 days

should be allowed between stopping treatment with an MAO inhibitor and starting treatment with fluoxetine. If you have been taking fluoxetine, at least 5 weeks should be allowed between stopping treatment with fluoxetine and starting treatment with an MAO inhibitor

- Phenytoin (e.g., Dilantin) or
- Tricyclic antidepressants (amitriptyline [e.g., Elavil], amoxapine [e.g., Asendin], clomipramine [e.g., Anafranil], desipramine [e.g., Pertofrane], doxepin [e.g., Sinequan], imipramine [e.g., Tofranil], nortriptyline [e.g., Aventyl], protriptyline [e.g., Vivactil], trimipramine [e.g., Surmontil])—Higher blood levels of these medicines may occur, which increases the chance of having serious side effects. Your doctor may want to see you more often and may need to change the doses of your medicines. Also, taking amitriptyline, clomipramine, or imipramine with fluoxetine may increase the chance of developing the serotonin syndrome

Other medical problems—The presence of other medical problems may affect the use of fluoxetine. Make sure you tell your doctor if you have any other medical problems, especially:

- Brain disease or mental retardation or
- Seizures, history of—The chance of having seizures may be increased
- Diabetes—The amount of insulin or oral antidiabetic medicine that you need to take may change
- Kidney disease or
- Liver disease—Higher blood levels of fluoxetine may occur, increasing the chance of side effects
- Parkinson's disease—May become worse
- Weight loss—Fluoxetine may cause weight loss. This weight loss is usually small, but if a large weight loss occurs, it may be harmful in some patients

Proper Use of This Medicine

Take this medicine only as directed by your doctor, to benefit your condition as much as possible. Do not take more of it, do not take it more often, and do not take it for a longer time than your doctor ordered.

If this medicine upsets your stomach, it may be taken with food.

If you are taking fluoxetine for depression, it may take 4 weeks or longer before you begin to feel better. Also, you may need to keep taking this medicine for 6 months or longer to stop the depression from returning. If you are taking fluoxetine for obsessive-compulsive disorder, it may take 5 weeks or longer before you begin to get better. Your doctor should check your progress at regular visits during this time.

If you are taking fluoxetine for bulimia nervosa, you may begin to get better after 1 week. However, it may take 4 weeks or longer before you get better.

Dosing—The dose of fluoxetine will be different for different patients and for different medical problems. *Follow your doctor's orders or the directions on the label.* The following information includes only the average doses of fluoxetine. *If your dose is different, do not change it unless your doctor tells you to do so:*

The number of capsules or teaspoonfuls of solution that you take depends on the strength of the medicine. Also, *the number of doses you take each day, the time allowed between doses, and the length of time you take the medicine depend on the medical problem for which you are taking fluoxetine.*

- For *oral* dosage forms (capsules or solution):
  —For depression or obsessive-compulsive disorder:
    - Adults—At first, usually 20 milligrams (mg) a day, taken as a single dose in the morning. Your doctor may increase the dose if needed. However, the dose usually is not more than 80 mg a day. Once your depression is under control, your doctor may wish to change you to a weekly dose. In this case, you will usually take a 90-mg capsule as a single dose one day per week.
    - Children—Use and dose must be determined by your doctor.
  —For bulimia nervosa:
    - Adults—Usually 60 milligrams (mg) a day, taken as a single dose in the morning. Your doctor may start with a lower dose and increase it gradually. The dose usually is not more than 80 mg a day.
    - Children—Use and dose must be determined by your doctor.
  —For premenstrual dysphoric disorder:
    - Adults—At first, usually 20 milligrams (mg) a day, taken as a single dose in the morning. Your doctor may increase the dose if needed. However, the dose usually is not more than 80 mg a day.
    - Children—Use and dose must be determined by your doctor.

Missed dose—If you miss a dose of this medicine, it is not necessary to make up the missed dose. Skip the missed dose and continue with your next scheduled dose. Do not double doses.

Storage—To store this medicine:

- Keep out of the reach of children.
- Store away from heat and direct light.
- Keep the oral solution form of this medicine from freezing.
- Do not store in the bathroom, near the kitchen sink, or in other damp places. Heat or moisture may cause the medicine to break down.
- Do not keep outdated medicine or medicine no longer needed. Be sure that any discarded medicine is out of the reach of children.

Precautions While Using This Medicine

It is important that your doctor check your progress at regular visits, to allow dosage adjustments and help reduce any side effects.

Do not take fluoxetine within 2 weeks of taking a monoamine oxidase (MAO) inhibitor (furazolidone, phenelzine, procarbazine, selegiline, or tranylcypromine) and do not take an MAO inhibitor for at least 5 weeks after taking fluoxetine. If you do, you may develop extremely high blood pressure or convulsions.

Avoid drinking alcohol while you are taking fluoxetine.

If you develop a skin rash or hives, stop taking fluoxetine and check with your doctor as soon as possible.

For diabetic patients:

- This medicine may affect blood sugar levels. If you notice a change in the results of your blood or urine sugar tests or if you have any questions, check with your doctor.

This medicine may cause some people to become drowsy or less able to think clearly, or to have poor muscle control. *Make sure you know how you react to fluoxetine before you drive, use machines, or do anything else that could be dangerous if you are not alert and well able to control your movements.*

Side Effects of This Medicine

Along with its needed effects, a medicine may cause some unwanted effects. Although not all of these side effects may occur, if they do occur they may need medical attention.

Check with your doctor as soon as possible if any of the following side effects occur:

More common
Decreased sexual drive or ability; inability to sit still; restlessness; skin rash, hives, or itching

Less common
Chills or fever; joint or muscle pain

Rare
Breast enlargement or pain; convulsions (seizures); fast or irregular heartbeat; purple or red spots on skin; symptoms of hypoglycemia (low blood sugar), including anxiety or nervousness, chills, cold sweats, confusion, cool pale skin, difficulty in concentration, drowsiness, excessive hunger, fast heartbeat, headache, shakiness or unsteady walk, or unusual tiredness or weakness; symptoms of hyponatremia (low blood sodium), including confusion, convulsions (seizures), drowsiness, dryness of mouth, increased thirst, lack of energy; symptoms of serotonin syndrome, including diarrhea, fever, increased sweating, mood or behavior changes, overactive reflexes, racing heartbeat, restlessness, shivering or shaking; talking, feeling, and acting with excitement and activity you cannot control; trouble in breathing; unusual or incomplete body or facial movements; unusual secretion of milk, in females

Symptoms of overdose—May be more severe than side effects that may occur from regular doses, or several symptoms may occur together
Agitation and restlessness; convulsions (seizures); drowsiness; fast heartbeat; nausea and vomiting; talking, feeling, and acting with excitement and activity you cannot control; trembling or shaking

Other side effects may occur that usually do not need medical attention. These side effects may go away during treatment as your body adjusts to the medicine. However, check with your doctor if any of the following side effects continue or are bothersome:

More common
Anxiety or nervousness; decreased appetite; diarrhea; drowsiness; headache; increased sweating; nausea; tiredness or weakness; trembling or shaking; trouble in sleeping

Less common or rare
Abnormal dreams; change in sense of taste; changes in vision; chest pain; constipation; dizziness or lightheadedness; dryness of mouth; feeling of warmth or heat; flushing or redness of skin, especially on face and neck; frequent urination; hair loss; increased appetite; increased sensitivity of skin to sunlight; menstrual pain; stomach cramps, gas, or pain; vomiting; weight loss; yawning

After you stop taking fluoxetine, your body may need time to adjust. The length of time this takes depends on the amount of medicine you were using and how long you used it. During this period of time, check with your doctor if you notice any of the following side effects:
Anxiety; dizziness; feeling that body or surroundings are turning; general feeling of discomfort or illness; headache; nausea; sweating; unusual tiredness or weakness

Other side effects not listed above may also occur in some patients. If you notice any other effects, check with your doctor.

Revised: 04/19/01

FLUTICASONE   Inhalation-Local

Commonly used brand name(s):

In the U.S.—
Flovent
Flovent Rotadisk

In Canada—
Flovent
Flovent Diskus

Description

Fluticasone (floo-TIK-a-sone) belongs to the family of medicines known as corticosteroids (cortisone-like medicines). It is used to help prevent the symptoms of asthma. When used regularly every day, inhaled fluticasone decreases the number and severity of asthma attacks. However, it will not relieve an asthma attack that has already started.

Inhaled fluticasone works by preventing certain cells in the lungs and breathing passages from releasing substances that cause asthma symptoms.

This medicine may be used with other asthma medicines, such as bronchodilators (medicines that open up narrowed breathing passages) or other corticosteroids taken by mouth.

This medicine is available only with your doctor's prescription, in the following dosage form(s):

Inhalation
- Aerosol (U.S. and Canada)
- Powder for inhalation (U.S. and Canada)

Before Using This Medicine

In deciding to use a medicine, the risks of using the medicine must be weighed against the good it will do. This is a decision you and your doctor will make. For inhaled fluticasone, the following should be considered:

Allergies—Tell your doctor if you have ever had any unusual or allergic reaction to fluticasone. Also tell your health care professional if you are allergic to any other substances, such as foods, especially milk, preservatives, or dyes.

Pregnancy—Inhaled fluticasone has not been studied in pregnant women. However, in animal studies, fluticasone given by injection was shown to cause birth defects. Also, too much use of corticosteroids during pregnancy may cause other unwanted effects in the infant, such as slower growth and reduced adrenal gland function.

Breast-feeding—It is not known whether inhaled fluticasone passes into breast milk. However, in animals given fluticasone by injection, the medicine did pass into breast milk. Although most medicines pass into breast milk in small amounts, many of them may be used safely while breast-feeding. Mothers who are taking this medicine and who wish to breast-feed should discuss this with their doctor.

Children—Corticosteroids taken by mouth or injection have been shown to slow or stop growth in children and cause reduced adrenal gland function. If enough fluticasone is absorbed following inhalation, it is possible it also could cause these effects. Your doctor will want you to use the lowest possible dose of fluticasone that controls asthma. This will lessen the chance of an effect on growth or adrenal gland function. *It is also important that children taking fluticasone visit their doctors regularly so that their growth rates may be monitored.* Children who are taking this medicine may be more susceptible to infections, such as chickenpox or measles. Care should be taken to avoid exposure to chickenpox or measles. If the child is exposed or the disease develops, the doctor should be contacted and his or her directions should be followed carefully. Before this medicine is given to a child, you and your child's doctor should talk about the good this medicine will do as well as the risks of using it.

Older adults—Inhaled fluticasone has been studied in elderly patients and has not been found to cause different side effects or other problems than it does in younger adults.

Other medicines—Although certain medicines should not be used together at all, in other cases two different medicines may be used together even if an interaction might occur. In these cases, your doctor may want to change the dose, or other precautions may be necessary. Tell your health care professional if you are taking any prescription or nonprescription (over-the-counter [OTC]) medicines.

Other medical problems—The presence of other medical problems may affect the use of inhaled fluticasone. Make sure you tell your doctor if you have any other medical problems, especially:

- Herpes simplex (virus) infection of the eye or
- Infections (virus, bacteria, or fungus)—Inhaled fluticasone may make these infections worse
- Tuberculosis (active or history of)—Inhaled fluticasone may cause this infection to start up again

Proper Use of This Medicine

Inhaled fluticasone is used to prevent asthma attacks. It is not used to relieve an attack that has already started. For relief of an asthma attack that has already started, you should use another medicine. If you do not have another medicine to use for an attack or if you have any questions about this, check with your health care professional.

Use this medicine only as directed. Do not use more of it and do not use it more often than your doctor ordered. To do so may increase the chance of side effects. The full benefit of this medicine may take 1 to 2 weeks or longer to achieve.

In order for this medicine to help prevent asthma attacks, it must be used every day in regularly spaced doses, as ordered by your doctor.

Gargling and rinsing your mouth with water after each dose may help prevent hoarseness, throat irritation, and infection in the mouth. However, do not swallow the water after rinsing.

Inhaled fluticasone is used with a special inhaler and usually comes with patient directions. *Read the directions carefully before using this medicine.* If you do not understand the directions or you are not sure how to use the inhaler, ask your health care professional to show you what to do. Also, *ask your health care professional to check regularly how you use the inhaler to make sure you are using it properly.*

For patients using the *inhalation aerosol:*

- When you use the inhaler for the first time, or if you have not used it for 4 weeks or longer, it may not deliver the right amount of medicine with the first puff. Therefore, before using the inhaler, prime it by spraying the medicine into the air four times. (Spray the inhaler once into the air if it has not been used in 1 to 3 weeks.) The inhaler will now be ready to give the right amount of medicine when you use it.
- To use the inhaler:
  —Shake the inhaler well for 15 seconds immediately before each use.
  —Take the cap off the mouthpiece (the strap will stay attached to the actuator). Check the mouthpiece and remove any foreign objects. Make sure the canister is fully and firmly inserted into the actuator.
  —Hold the mouthpiece away from your mouth and breathe out slowly and completely.
  —Use the inhalation method recommended by your doctor.
    - Open-mouth method—Place the mouthpiece about 1 or 2 inches (two fingerwidths) in front of your widely opened mouth. Make sure the inhaler is aimed into your mouth so that the spray does not hit the roof of your mouth or your tongue.
    - Closed-mouth method—Place the mouthpiece in your mouth between your teeth and over your tongue, with your lips closed tightly around it. Do not block the mouthpiece with your teeth or tongue.
  —Tilt your head back a little. Start to breathe in slowly and deeply through your mouth and, at the same time, press the top of the canister one time to get one puff of the medicine. Continue to breathe in slowly for 5 to 10 seconds. Count the seconds while inhaling. It is important to press the top of the canister and breathe in slowly at the same time so the medicine is pulled into your lungs. This step may be difficult at first. If you are using the closed-mouth method and you see a fine mist coming from your mouth or nose, the inhaler is not being used correctly.
  —Hold your breath as long as you can up to 10 seconds. This gives the medicine time to settle in your airways and lungs. Take the mouthpiece away from your mouth and breathe out slowly.
  —If your doctor has told you to inhale more than one puff of medicine at each dose, wait about 30 seconds and then gently shake the inhaler again, and take the second puff following exactly the same steps you used for the first puff.
  —When you are finished, wipe off the mouthpiece and replace the cover to keep the mouthpiece clean and free of foreign objects.
- Clean the inhaler and mouthpiece at least once a day to prevent buildup of medicine and blockage of the mouthpiece.

—To clean the inhaler:
- Remove the metal canister from the inhaler and set it aside.
- Rinse the mouthpiece and cover and plastic case in warm, running water.
- Shake off the excess water and let the inhaler parts air dry completely before replacing the metal canister and cover.

For patients using the *powder for inhalation:*
- *To load the inhaler:*
  - Make sure your hands are clean and dry.
  - Do not insert the disk until just before you are ready to use the medicine.
  - Take off the mouthpiece cover and make sure that the mouthpiece is clean.
  - Hold the corners of the white tray and pull out gently until you can see all of the plastic ridges on the sides of the tray.
  - Put your finger and thumb on the ridges, squeeze inward, and gently pull the tray out of the body of the inhaler.
  - Place a disk on the wheel with the numbers facing up, and then slide the tray back into the inhaler.
  - Hold the corners of the tray and slide the tray out and in. This will rotate the disk.
  - Continue to turn the disk in this way until the number 4 appears in the small window. Each disk has four blisters containing the medicine. The window will display how many inhalations you have left after you use it each time. For example, when you see the number 1, you have one inhalation left.
  - To replace the empty disk with a full disk, follow the same steps you used to load the inhaler. Do not throw away the wheel when you discard the empty disk.
- *To use the inhaler:*
  - Hold the inhaler flat in your hand. Lift the rear edge of the lid until it is fully upright.
  - The plastic needle on the front of the lid will break the blister containing one inhalation of medicine. When the lid is raised as far as it will go, both the upper and the lower surfaces of the blister will be pierced. Do not lift the lid if the cartridge is not in the inhaler. Doing this will break the needle and you will need a new inhaler.
  - After the blister is broken open, close the lid. Keeping the inhaler flat and well away from your mouth, breathe out to the end of a normal breath.
  - Raise the inhaler to your mouth, and place the mouthpiece in your mouth.
  - Close your lips around the mouthpiece and tilt your head slightly back. Do not bite down on the mouthpiece. Do not block the mouthpiece with your teeth or tongue. Do not cover the air holes on the side of the mouthpiece.
  - Breathe in through your mouth as steadily and as deeply as you can until you have taken a full deep breath.
  - Hold your breath and remove the mouthpiece from your mouth. Continue holding your breath as long as you can up to 10 seconds before breathing out. This gives the medicine time to settle in your airways and lungs.
  - Hold the inhaler well away from your mouth and breathe out to the end of a normal breath.

—Prepare the cartridge for your next inhalation. Pull the cartridge out once and push it in once. The disk will turn to the next numbered dose as seen in the indicator window. Do not pierce the blister until just before the inhalation.
—If your doctor has told you to inhale more than one puff of medicine at each dose, take the second puff following exactly the same steps you used for the first puff.
—When you are finished, wipe off the mouthpiece and replace the cover to keep the mouthpiece clean and free of foreign objects.
- *To clean the inhaler:*
  - Remove the tray from the body of the inhaler.
  - Hold the wheel between your forefinger and thumb and pull upward to separate it from the tray.
  - Use the brush that is stored in the rear of the body of the inhaler to brush away any powder left behind on the parts of the inhaler.
  - Replace the wheel and push it down firmly until it snaps back into place.
  - Replace the tray and mouthpiece cover.
  or
  - Separate the parts of the inhaler using the steps outlined above.
  - Rinse the parts of the inhaler with warm water and let them air dry before reassembling them as described above.

  The inhaler should be cleaned once a week.

Dosing—The dose of inhaled fluticasone will be different for different patients. *Follow your doctor's orders or the directions on the label.* The following information includes only the average doses of inhaled fluticasone. *If your dose is different, do not change it* unless your doctor tells you to do so.

The number of puffs that you take or disks that you use depends on the strength of the medicine.
- For bronchial asthma
  - For inhalation *aerosol:*
    - Adults and children 12 years of age and older— 88 to 880 micrograms (mcg) two times a day, morning and evening. Canadian labeling recommends—For adults and children 16 and older: 100 to 1000 mcg two times a day.
    - Children younger than 12 years of age—Use and dose must be determined by your doctor. Canadian labeling recommends—For children 4 to 16 years of age: 50 to 100 mcg two times a day; For children up to 4 years of age: Use and dose must be determined by your doctor.
  - For *powder* for inhalation:
    - Adults and children older than 11 years of age— 100 to 1000 mcg two times a day.
    - Children 4 to 11 years of age—50 to 100 mcg two times a day.
    - Children younger than 4 years of age—Use and dose must be determined by your doctor.

    Canadian labeling recommends—For children 4 to 16 years of age: 50 to 100 mcg two times a day.

Missed dose—If you miss a dose of this medicine, use it as soon as you remember. Then use any remaining doses for that day at regularly spaced times. Do not double doses.

Storage—To store this medicine:
- Keep out of the reach of children.
- Store away from heat and direct light.

- Do not store the powder (disk) form of this medicine in the bathroom, near the kitchen sink, or in other damp places. Heat or moisture may cause the medicine to break down.
- Keep the aerosol form of this medicine from freezing. This medicine may be less effective if the container is cold when you use it.
- Do not puncture, break, or burn the aerosol container, even after it is empty.
- The blisters should be used within 2 months after opening the moisture-protective foil wrap or before the expiration date, whichever comes first.
- Do not keep outdated medicine or medicine no longer needed. Be sure that any discarded medicine is out of the reach of children.

Precautions While Using This Medicine

Check with your doctor if:
- *You go through a period of unusual stress to your body, such as surgery, injury, or infection.*
- *You have an asthma attack that does not improve after you take a bronchodilator medicine.*
- *Your asthma symptoms do not improve or your condition worsens.*
- *You are exposed to the chickenpox or measles.*

Your doctor may want you to carry a medical identification card stating that you are using this medicine and that you may need additional medicine during times of emergency, a severe asthma attack or other illness, or unusual stress.

Before you have any kind of surgery (including dental surgery) or emergency treatment, tell the medical doctor or dentist in charge that you are using this medicine.

Side Effects of This Medicine

Along with its needed effects, a medicine may cause some unwanted effects. Although not all of these side effects may occur, if they do occur they may need medical attention.

Check with your doctor immediately if any of the following side effects occur:

More common
   White patches in mouth and throat

Less common
   Diarrhea; ear ache; fever; lower abdominal pain; nausea; pain on passing urine; redness or discharge of the eye, eyelid, or lining of the eye; shortness of breath; sore throat; trouble in swallowing; vaginal discharge (creamy white) and itching; vomiting

Rare
   Blindness, blurred vision, eye pain; large hives; bone fractures; diabetes mellitus [increased hunger, thirst, or urination]; excess facial hair in women; fullness or roundness of face, neck, and trunk; growth reduction in children or adolescents; heart problems; high blood pressure; hives and skin rash; impotence in males; lack of menstrual periods; muscle wasting; numbness and weakness of hands and feet; weakness; swelling of face, lips, or eyelids; tightness in chest, troubled breathing, or wheezing

Other side effects may occur that usually do not need medical attention. These side effects may go away during treatment as your body adjusts to the medicine. However, check with your doctor if any of the following side effects continue or are bothersome:

More common
   Cough; general aches and pains or general feeling of illness; greenish-yellow mucus in nose; headache; hoarseness or other voice changes; loss of appetite; runny, sore, or stuffy nose; unusual tiredness; weakness

Less common
   Bloody mucus or unexplained nosebleeds; dizziness; eye irritation; feeling 'faint'; giddiness; irregular or painful menstrual periods; irritation due to inhalant; joint pain; migraines; mouth irritation; muscle soreness, sprain, or strain; sneezing; stomach pain or burning

Rare
   Aggression; agitation; bruising; depression; itching; restlessness; weight gain

Other side effects not listed above may also occur in some patients. If you notice any other effects, check with your doctor.

Developed: 08/12/1998
Revised: 06/22/2000

FLUTICASONE AND SALMETEROL
Inhalation-Local—INTRODUCTORY VERSION

Commonly used brand name(s):

In the U.S.—
   Advair Diskus

In Canada—
   Advair Diskus

Description

Fluticasone (floo-TIK-a-sone) and salmeterol (sal-ME-te-role) is a combination of two medicines that are used to help control the symptoms of asthma and improve lung function. However, this medicine will not relieve an asthma attack that has already started.

Inhaled fluticasone belongs to the family of medicines known as corticosteroids (cortisone-like medicines). It works by preventing certain cells in the lungs and breathing passages from releasing substances that cause asthma symptoms. It will not relieve an asthma attack that has already started.

Inhaled salmeterol is a long-acting bronchodilator and it belongs to the family of medicines known as bronchodilators. Bronchodilators are medicines that are breathed in through the mouth to open up the bronchial tubes (air passages) of the lungs. Salmeterol is different than other bronchodilators because it does not act quickly enough to relieve an asthma attack that has already started.

This medicine must be used with a short-acting beta$_2$ agonist (e.g. albuterol) for the treatment of an asthma attack or asthma symptoms that need immediate attention.

This medicine is available only with your doctor's prescription, in the following dosage form:

Inhalation
- Inhalation powder (U.S. and Canada)

Before Using This Medicine

In deciding to use a medicine, the risks of using the medicine must be weighed against the good it will do. This is a decision you and your doctor will make. For fluticasone and salmeterol, the following should be considered:

Allergies—Tell your doctor if you have ever had any unusual or allergic reaction to fluticasone or salmeterol.

Pregnancy—The combination of fluticasone and salmeterol has not been studied in pregnant women. However, studies in animals have shown that the fluticasone and salmeterol causes problems. Before taking this medicine, make sure your doctor knows if you are pregnant or plan to become pregnant.

Breast-feeding—It is not known whether the combination of fluticasone and salmeterol passes into breast milk. Although most medicines pass into breast milk in small amounts, many of them may be used safely while breast-feeding. Mothers who are taking this medicine and who wish to breast-feed should discuss this with their doctor.

Children—Corticosteroids taken by mouth or injection have been shown to slow or stop growth in children and cause reduced adrenal gland function. If enough fluticasone is absorbed following inhalation, it is possible it also could cause these effects. Your doctor will want you to use the lowest possible dose of fluticasone that controls asthma. This will lessen the chance of an effect on growth or adrenal gland function. *It is also important that children taking fluticasone visit their doctors regularly so that their growth rates may be monitored.* Children who are taking this medicine may be more susceptible to infections, such as chickenpox or measles. Care should be taken to avoid exposure to chickenpox or measles. If the child is exposed or the disease develops, the doctor should be contacted and his or her directions should be followed carefully. Before this medicine is given to a child, you and your child's doctor should talk about the good this medicine will do as well as the risks of using it.

Older adults—Many medicines have not been studied specifically in older people. Therefore, it may not be known whether they work exactly the same way they do in younger adults. Although there is no specific information comparing the use of fluticasone and salmeterol in the elderly with other age groups, this medicine has been used in in elderly patients and is not expected to cause different side effects or problems in older people than it does in younger adults. Elderly people who have cardiovascular disease may have increased chances of side effects from this medicine.

Other medicines—Although certain medicines should not be used together at all, in other cases two different medicines may be used together even if an interaction might occur. In these cases, your doctor may want to change the dose, or other precautions may be necessary. When you are taking fluticasone and salmeterol, it is especially important that your doctor and pharmacist know if you are taking any of the following:

- Tricyclic antidepressants (amitriptyline [e.g., Elavil], amoxapine [e.g., Asendin], clomipramine [e.g., Anafranil], desipramine [e.g., Norpramin], doxepin [e.g., Sinequan], imipramine [e.g., Tofranil], nortriptyline [e.g., Pamelor], protriptyline [e.g., Vivactil], trimipramine [e.g., Surmontil]) or
- Monoamine oxidase (MAO) inhibitors (isocarboxazid [e.g., Marplan], phenelzine [e.g., Nardil], procarbazine [e.g., Matulane], selegiline [e.g., Eldepryl], tranylcypromine [e.g., Parnate])—Taking fluticasone and salmeterol while you are taking or within 2 weeks of taking MAO inhibitors may increase side effects

- Beta-adrenergic receptor blocking agents (acebutolol [e.g., Sectral], atenolol [e.g., Tenormin], betaxolol [e.g., Kerlone], bisoprolol [e.g., Zebeta], carteolol [e.g., Cartrol], carvedilol [e.g., Coreg], celiprolol [e.g., Cardem], esmolol [e.g., Brevibloc], labetalol [e.g., Normodyne], metoprolol [e.g., Lopressor], nadolol [e.g., Corgard], oxprenolol [e.g., Trasicor], penbutolol [e.g., Levatol], pindolol [e.g., Visken], propranolol [e.g., Inderal], sotalol [e.g., Betapace], timolol [e.g., Blocadren])—Use of these medicines can block the beneficial effect of salmeterol

Other medical problems—The presence of other medical problems may affect the use of fluticasone and salmeterol combination. Make sure you tell your doctor if you have any other medical problems, especially:

- Chickenpox (including recent exposure) or
- Measles or
- Herpes simplex (virus) infection of the eye or
- Infections (virus, bacteria, or fungus) or
- Tuberculosis (active or history of)—Inhaled fluticasone can reduce the body's ability to fight off these infections

- Heart or blood vessel disease or
- High blood pressure or
- Overactive thyroid or
- Seizures—This medicine may worsen these conditions

Proper Use of This Medicine

Inhaled fluticasone and salmeterol is used to prevent asthma attacks. It is not used to relieve an asthma attack that has already started. For relief of an asthma attack that has already started, you should use another medicine. If you do not have another medicine to use for an attack or if you have any questions about this, check with your health care professional.

Use this medicine only as directed. Do not use more of it and do not use it more often than your doctor ordered. To do so may increase the chance of side effects.

In order for this medicine to help prevent asthma attacks, it must be used every day in regularly spaced doses, as ordered by your doctor.

Rinsing your mouth with water after each dose may help prevent hoarseness, throat irritation, and infection in the mouth. However, do not swallow the water after rinsing.

Inhaled fluticasone and salmeterol is used with a special inhaler that comes with patient directions. *Read the directions carefully before using this medicine.* If you do not understand the directions or you are not sure how to use the inhaler, ask your health care professional to show you what to do. Also, *ask your health care professional to check regularly how you use the inhaler to make sure you are using it properly.*

To use the inhaler:

- To open the inhaler, push the thumbgrip away from you as far as it will go. You will hear a click and feel a snap. When open, the mouthpiece will appear.
- Slide the mouthpiece lever away from you as far as it will go until it clicks. The inhaler is now ready to use. If you close the inhaler or push the lever again, you will lose medicine.
- Turn your head away from the inhaler, and breathe out to the end of a normal breath. Do not breathe into the inhaler.
- Holding the inhaler level, put the mouthpiece between your lips and teeth, and close your lips around the mouthpiece. Do not bite down on the mouthpiece. Do not block the mouthpiece with your teeth and tongue.
- Breathe in through your mouth as deeply as you can until you have taken a full deep breath. Do not breathe through your nose.
- Hold your breath and remove the mouthpiece from your mouth. Continue holding your breath as long as you can up to 10 seconds before breathing out slowly. This gives the medicine time to settle in your airways and lungs.
- Turn your head away from the inhaler, and breathe out slowly to the end of a normal breath. Do not breathe into the inhaler.
- If your doctor has told you to inhale more than one puff of medicine at each dose, take the second puff following exactly the same steps you used for the first puff.
- When you are finished, close the inhaler. Place your thumb on the thumbgrip, and slide it back toward you as far as it will go. You will hear it click shut.
- Keep the inhaler dry. Do not wash the mouthpiece, or any other part of the inhaler. You may use a dry cloth to wipe it clean.
- The inhaler has a window that shows the number of doses remaining. This tells you when you are getting low on medicine. The doses counting down from 5 to 0 will show up in red to remind you to refill your prescription.

Dosing—The dose of inhaled fluticasone and salmeterol will be different for different patients. *Follow your doctor's orders or the direction on the label*. The following information includes only the average doses of inhaled fluticasone and salmeterol. *If your dose is different, do not change it unless your doctor tells you to do so.*

- For inhalation
  —For bronchial asthma
    - Adults and children 12 years of age and older: One inhalation twice a day.
    - Children up to 12 years of age: Use and dose must be determined by your doctor.

Missed dose—If you miss a dose of this medicine skip the missed dose and go back to your regular dosing schedule. Do not double doses.

Storage—To store this medicine:

- Keep out of the reach of children.
- Store at room temperature.
- Do not store in the bathroom, near the kitchen sink, or in other damp places. Heat or moisture may cause the medicine to break down.
- Store away from direct heat or sunlight.
- Do not keep outdated medicine or medicine no longer needed. Be sure that any discarded medicine is out of the reach of children.

The inhaler contents should be used within 1 month after opening the moisture-protective foil wrap or before the expiration date, whichever comes first.

Precautions While Using This Medicine

Check with your doctor if your asthma symptoms do not improve or your condition worsens. Check with your doctor if you notice:

- Your short-acting inhaler does not seem to work as well as it used to
- You need to use your short-acting inhaler more often
- You have a significant decrease in your peak flow when measured as directed by your doctor

Side Effects of This Medicine

Along with its needed effects, a medicine may cause some unwanted effects. Although not all of these side effects may occur, if they do occur they may need medical attention.

Check with your doctor as soon as possible if any of the following side effects occur:

Black, tarry stools; burning, tingling, numbness or pain in the hands, arms, feet, or legs; chills; cough; fever; difficulty breathing; noisy breathing; painful or difficult urination; sensation of pins and needles; sore throat; sores, ulcers or white spots on lips or in mouth; stabbing pain in extremities; swollen glands; unusual bleeding or bruising; wheezing

Symptoms of overdose

Get emergency help immediately if any of the following symptoms of overdose occur:

Darkening of skin; diarrhea; dizziness; fainting; loss of appetite; mental depression; nausea; skin rash; unusual tiredness or weakness; vomiting; chest pain or tightness; shortness of breath; dry mouth; fatigue; blurred vision; flushed, dry skin; fruit-like breath odor; headache; increased hunger; increased thirst; high blood pressure; convulsions (seizures); decreased urine output; mood changes; muscle pain or cramps; numbness or tingling in hands, feet, or lips; confusion; faintness, or light-headedness when getting up from a lying or sitting position; sudden sweating; trouble in sleeping; general feeling of discomfort or illness; nervousness; fast, pounding, or irregular heartbeat or pulse; palpitations; tremors

Other side effects may occur that usually do not need medical attention. These side effects may go away during treatment as your body adjusts to the medicine. Also, your health care professional may be able to tell you about ways to prevent or reduce some of these side effects. Check with your health care professional if any of the following side effects continue or are bothersome or if you have any questions about them:

More common

Body aches or pain; choking; congestion; dryness of throat; high-pitched noise when breathing; hoarseness; runny nose; sneezing; trouble in swallowing; voice changes

Less common

Abdominal or stomach pain; cough producing mucus; flu-like symptoms; irritation or inflammation of eye; muscle pain; pain or tenderness around eyes and cheekbones; sleep disorders; stuffy nose; tremors; white patches in the mouth or throat or on the tongue

Other side effects not listed above may also occur in some patients. If you notice any other effects, check with your doctor.

Revised: 02/06/2001

FLUVOXAMINE   Systemic

Commonly used brand name(s):

In the U.S.—
Luvox

In Canada—
Luvox

Description

Fluvoxamine (floo-VOX-a-meen) is used to treat obsessive-compulsive disorder.

This medicine may also be used for other conditions as determined by your doctor.

Fluvoxamine belongs to a group of medicines known as selective serotonin reuptake inhibitors (SSRIs). These medicines are thought to work by increasing the activity of a chemical called serotonin in the brain.

This medicine is available only with your doctor's prescription, in the following dosage form:

Oral
  • Tablets (U.S. and Canada)

Before Using This Medicine

In deciding to use a medicine, the risks of taking the medicine must be weighed against the good it will do. This is a decision you and your doctor will make. For fluvoxamine, the following should be considered:

Allergies—Tell your doctor if you have ever had any unusual or allergic reaction to fluvoxamine. Also tell your health care professional if you are allergic to any other substances, such as foods, preservatives, or dyes.

Pregnancy—Fluvoxamine has not been studied in pregnant women. However, studies in animals have shown that fluvoxamine may cause lower survival rates in offspring when given to the mother in doses less than the maximum recommended human dose. Before taking this medicine, make sure your doctor knows if you are pregnant or if you may become pregnant.

Breast-feeding—Fluvoxamine passes into breast milk. However, the effects of this medicine in nursing babies are not known.

Children—This medicine has been tested in children and, in effective doses, has not been shown to cause different side effects or problems than it does in adults. Because fluvoxamine may cause weight loss or a decrease in appetite, children who will be taking fluvoxamine for a long time should have their weight and growth measured by the doctor regularly.

Older adults—Fluvoxamine has been tested in a limited number of older adults and has not been shown to cause different side effects or problems in older people than it does in younger adults. However, fluvoxamine may be removed from the body more slowly in older adults and an older adult may receive a lower dose than a younger adult.

Other medicines—Although certain medicines should not be used together at all, in other cases two different medicines may be used together even if an interaction might occur. In these cases, your doctor may want to change the dose, or other precautions may be necessary. When you are taking fluvoxamine, it is especially important that your doctor and pharmacist know if you are taking any of the following:

  • Alprazolam (e.g., Xanax) or
  • Bromazepam (e.g., Lectopam) or
  • Clozapine (e.g., Clozaril) or
  • Metoprolol (e.g., Lopressor) or
  • Midazolam (e.g., Versed) or
  • Propranolol (e.g., Inderal) or
  • Theophylline (e.g., Theo-Dur) or
  • Triazolam (e.g., Halcion) or
  • Tricyclic antidepressants (amitriptyline [e.g., Elavil], amoxapine [e.g., Asendin], clomipramine [e.g., Anafranil], desipramine [e.g., Pertofrane], doxepin [e.g., Sinequan], imipramine [e.g., Tofranil], nortriptyline [e.g., Aventyl], protriptyline [e.g., Vivactil], trimipramine [e.g., Surmontil]) or
  • Warfarin (e.g., Coumadin)—Higher blood levels of these medicines may occur, causing unwanted effects. Your doctor may want to see you more often if you are taking one of these medicines with fluvoxamine. Your doctor may also change the dose of these medicines or may change you to a different medicine.

  • Astemizole (e.g., Hismanal) or
  • Cisapride (e.g., Propulsid) or
  • Terfenadine (e.g., Seldane)—*Do not take any of these medicines while you are taking fluvoxamine* or a very serious heart problem may occur.

  • Buspirone (e.g., BuSpar) or
  • Bromocriptine (e.g., Parlodel) or
  • Dexfenfluramine (e.g., Redux) or
  • Dextromethorphan (e.g., Robitussin DM) or
  • Dihydroergotamine (e.g., D.H.E. 45) or
  • Fenfluramine (e.g., Pondimin) or
  • Levodopa (e.g., Sinemet) or
  • Lithium (e.g., Eskalith) or
  • Meperidine (e.g., Demerol) or
  • Moclobemide (e.g., Manerex) or
  • Nefazodone (e.g., Serzone) or
  • Pentazocine (e.g., Talwin) or
  • Selective serotonin reuptake inhibitors, other (fluoxetine [e.g., Prozac], paroxetine [e.g., Paxil], sertraline [e.g., Zoloft]) or
  • Street drugs (LSD, MDMA [e.g., ecstasy], marijuana) or
  • Sumatriptan (e.g., Imitrex) or
  • Tramadol (e.g., Ultram) or
  • Trazodone (e.g., Desyrel) or
  • Tryptophan or
  • Venlafaxine (e.g., Effexor)—Using these medicines with fluvoxamine may increase the chance of developing a rare, but very serious, unwanted effect known as the serotonin syndrome. Symptoms of this syndrome include agitation, confusion, diarrhea, fever, overactive reflexes, poor coordination, restlessness, shivering, sweating, talking or acting with excitement you cannot control, trembling or shaking, or twitching. If you develop these symptoms (usually three or more occur together) check with your doctor as soon as possible

- Diazepam (e.g., Valium)—Higher blood levels of diazepam may occur, causing unwanted effects. Taking diazepam while you are taking fluvoxamine is not recommended

- Monoamine oxidase (MAO) inhibitors (furazolidone [e.g., Furoxone], phenelzine [e.g., Nardil], procarbazine [e.g., Matulane], selegiline [e.g., Eldepryl], tranylcypromine [e.g., Parnate])—*Do not take fluvoxamine while you are taking or within 2 weeks of taking an MAO inhibitor*, or you may develop agitation, coma, severe muscle stiffness, sudden high body temperature, or extremely high blood pressure. At least 14 days should be allowed between stopping treatment with one medicine and starting treatment with the other

Other medical problems—The presence of other medical problems may affect the use of fluvoxamine. Make sure you tell your doctor if you have any other medical problems, especially:

- Brain disease or mental retardation or
- Seizures, history of—The risk of seizures may be increased

- Liver disease—Higher blood levels of fluvoxamine may occur, increasing the chance of side effects

- Mania or hypomania, history of—The condition may be activated

Proper Use of This Medicine

Take this medicine only as directed by your doctor to benefit your condition as much as possible. Do not take more of it, do not take it more often, and do not take it for a longer time than your doctor ordered.

Fluvoxamine may be taken with or without food or on a full or empty stomach. However, if your doctor tells you to take the medicine a certain way, take it exactly as directed.

If you are taking fluvoxamine for obsessive-compulsive disorder, you may have to take it for up to 10 or 12 weeks before you begin to feel better. Your doctor should check your progress at regular visits during this time.

Dosing—The dose of fluvoxamine will be different for different patients. *Follow your doctor's orders or the directions on the label.* The following information includes only the average doses of fluvoxamine. *If your dose is different, do not change it* unless your doctor tells you to do so.

The number of tablets that you take depends on the strength of the medicine.

- For *oral* dosage form (tablets):
  —For treatment of obsessive-compulsive disorder:
  - Adults—At first, 50 milligrams (mg) once a day at bedtime. Your doctor may increase your dose if needed. However, the dose usually is not more than 300 mg a day. If your daily dose is higher than 100 mg, your doctor may want you to take it in two divided doses.
  - Children younger than 8 years of age—Use and dose must be determined by your doctor.
  - Children 8 to 17 years of age—At first, 25 mg once a day at bedtime. Your doctor may increase your dose if needed. However, the dose usually is not more than 200 mg a day. If your daily dose is higher than 50 mg, your doctor may want you to take it in two divided doses.

Missed dose—If you miss a dose of fluvoxamine and your dosing schedule is:

- One time a day—Take the missed dose as soon as possible if remembered the same day and go back to your regular dosing schedule. Do not double doses.
- Two times a day—Skip the missed dose and go back to your regular dosing schedule. Do not double doses.

Storage—To store this medicine:

- Keep out of the reach of children.
- Store away from heat and direct light.
- Do not store in the bathroom, near the kitchen sink, or in other damp places. Heat or moisture may cause the medicine to break down.
- Do not keep outdated medicine or medicine no longer needed. Be sure that any discarded medicine is out of the reach of children.

Precautions While Using This Medicine

It is important that your doctor check your progress at regular visits, to allow for changes in your dose and to help reduce any side effects.

Do not take astemizole, cisapride, or terfenadine while you are taking fluvoxamine. If you do, you may develop a very serious heart problem.

Do not take fluvoxamine if you have taken a monoamine oxidase (MAO) inhibitor in the past 14 days. Do not start taking an MAO inhibitor within 14 days of stopping fluvoxamine. If you do, you may develop agitation, coma, extreme muscle stiffness, sudden high body temperature, or other severe unwanted effects.

Avoid drinking alcohol while taking fluvoxamine.

Check with your doctor as soon as possible if you develop a skin rash, hives, or itching while you are taking fluvoxamine.

Fluvoxamine may cause some people to become drowsy or less able to think clearly, or to have blurred vision or poor muscle control. *Make sure you know how you react to this medicine before you drive, use machines, or do anything else that could be dangerous if you are not alert, able to see clearly, or able to control your movements well.*

Do not stop taking this medicine without first checking with your doctor. Your doctor may want you to reduce gradually the amount you are taking before stopping completely. This is to decrease the chance of having discontinuation symptoms.

Side Effects of This Medicine

Along with its needed effects, a medicine may cause some unwanted effects. Although not all of these side effects may occur, if they do occur they may need medical attention.

Check with your doctor as soon as possible if any of the following side effects occur:
More common
    Change in sexual performance or desire
Less common
    Behavior, mood, or mental changes; trouble in breathing; trouble in urinating; twitching
Rare
    Absence of or decrease in body movements; blurred vision; clumsiness or unsteadiness; convulsions (seizures); inability to move eyes; increase in body movements; menstrual changes; nose bleeds; red

or irritated eyes; redness, tenderness, itching, burning or peeling of skin; skin rash; sore throat, fever, and chills; unusual bruising; unusual, incomplete, or sudden body or facial movements; unusual secretion of milk, in females; weakness

Rare—Symptoms of serotonin syndrome (usually three or more occur together)

Agitation; confusion; diarrhea; fever; overactive reflexes; poor coordination; restlessness; shivering; sweating; talking or acting with excitement you cannot control; trembling or shaking; twitching

Symptoms of overdose—may be more severe than usual side effects, or two or more may occur together

Coma; convulsions (seizures); diarrhea; dizziness; drowsiness; dryness of mouth; fast or slow heartbeat; large pupils; low blood pressure; nausea; trembling or shaking; trouble in urinating; twitching; vomiting

Other side effects may occur that usually do not need medical attention. These side effects may go away during treatment as your body adjusts to the medicine. However, check with your doctor if any of the following side effects continue or are bothersome:

More common

Constipation; dizziness; drowsiness; headache; nausea; trouble in sleeping; unusual tiredness; vomiting

Less common

Abdominal pain; change in sense of taste; decreased appetite; diarrhea; dryness of mouth; feeling of constant movement of self or surroundings; feeling of fast or irregular heartbeat; frequent urination; heartburn; increased sweating; trembling or shaking; unusual weight gain or loss

After you stop using this medicine, your body may need time to adjust. The length of time this takes depends on the amount of medicine you were using and how long you used it. During this period of time check with your doctor if you notice any of the following side effects:

Confusion; decreased energy; dizziness; headache; irritability; nausea; problems with memory; weakness

Other side effects not listed above may also occur in some patients. If you notice any other effects, check with your doctor.

Additional Information

Once a medicine has been approved for marketing for a certain use, experience may show that it is also useful for other medical problems. Although this use is not included in product labeling, fluvoxamine is used in certain patients with the following medical condition:

- Mental depression

If you are taking fluvoxamine for mental depression, you may have to take it for 3 weeks or longer before you begin to feel better. Your doctor should check your progress at regular visits during this time.

Other than the above information, there is no additional information relating to proper use, precautions, or side effects for this use.

Developed: 04/16/98
Interim revision: 08/07/98

FOLIC ACID (VITAMIN B₉)
Systemic

Commonly used brand name(s):

In the U.S.—
Folvite
Generic name product may be available.

In Canada—
Apo-Folic
Folvite
Novo-Folacid

Another commonly used name is Vitamin B₉.

Description

Vitamins (VYE-ta-mins) are compounds that you *must* have for growth and health. They are needed in small amounts only and are usually available in the foods that you eat. Folic acid (FOE-lik AS-id) (vitamin B₉) is necessary for strong blood.

Lack of folic acid may lead to anemia (weak blood). Your health care professional may treat this by prescribing folic acid for you.

Some conditions may increase your need for folic acid. These include:

- Alcoholism
- Anemia, hemolytic
- Diarrhea (continuing)
- Fever (prolonged)
- Hemodialysis
- Illness (prolonged)
- Intestinal diseases
- Liver disease
- Stress (continuing)
- Surgical removal of stomach

In addition, infants smaller than normal, breast-fed infants, or those receiving unfortified formulas (such as evaporated milk or goat's milk) may need additional folic acid.

Increased need for folic acid should be determined by your health care professional.

Some studies have found that folic acid taken by women before they become pregnant and during early pregnancy may reduce the chances of certain birth defects (neural tube defects).

Claims that folic acid and other B vitamins are effective for preventing mental problems have not been proven. Many of these treatments involve large and expensive amounts of vitamins.

Injectable folic acid is given by or under the direction of your health care professional. Another form of folic acid is available without a prescription.

Folic acid is available in the following dosage forms:

Oral
- Tablets (U.S. and Canada)

Parenteral
- Injection (U.S. and Canada)

Importance of Diet

For good health, it is important that you eat a balanced and varied diet. Follow carefully any diet program your health care professional may recommend. For your specific dietary vitamin and/or mineral needs, ask your health care professional for a list of appropriate foods. If you think that you are not getting enough vitamins and/or minerals in your diet, you may choose to take a dietary supplement.

Folic acid is found in various foods, including vegetables, especially green vegetables; potatoes; cereal and cereal products; fruits; and organ meats (for example, liver or kidney). It is best to eat fresh fruits and vegetables whenever possible since they contain the most vitamins. Food processing may destroy some of the vitamins. For example, heat may reduce the amount of folic acid in foods.

Vitamins alone will not take the place of a good diet and will not provide energy. Your body also needs other substances found in food such as protein, minerals, carbohydrates, and fat. Vitamins themselves often cannot work without the presence of other foods.

The daily amount of folic acid needed is defined in several different ways.

For U.S.—
- Recommended Dietary Allowances (RDAs) are the amount of vitamins and minerals needed to provide for adequate nutrition in most healthy persons. RDAs for a given nutrient may vary depending on a person's age, sex, and physical condition (e.g., pregnancy).
- Daily Values (DVs) are used on food and dietary supplement labels to indicate the percent of the recommended daily amount of each nutrient that a serving provides. DV replaces the previous designation of United States Recommended Daily Allowances (USRDAs).

For Canada—
- Recommended Nutrient Intakes (RNIs) are used to determine the amounts of vitamins, minerals, and protein needed to provide adequate nutrition and lessen the risk of chronic disease.

Normal daily recommended intakes in micrograms (mcg) for folic acid are generally defined as follows:

Persons	U.S. (mcg)	Canada (mcg)
Infants and children		
Birth to 3 years of age	25–100	50–80
4 to 6 years of age	75–400	90
7 to 10 years of age	100–400	125–180
Adolescent and adult males	150–400	150–220
Adolescent and adult females	150–400	145–190
Pregnant females	400–800	445–475
Breast-feeding females	260–800	245–275

Before Using This Dietary Supplement

In deciding to use folic acid, the risks of taking it must be weighed against the good it will do. This is a decision you and your health care professional will make. For folic acid, the following should be considered:

Allergies—Tell your health care professional if you have ever had any unusual or allergic reaction to folic acid. Also tell your health care professional if you are allergic to any other substances, such as foods, preservatives, or dyes.

Pregnancy—It is especially important that you are receiving enough vitamins when you become pregnant and that you continue to receive the right amount of vitamins, especially folic acid, throughout your pregnancy. The healthy growth and development of the fetus depend on a steady supply of nutrients from the mother. However, taking large amounts of a dietary supplement in pregnancy may be harmful to the mother and/or fetus and should be avoided.

Your health care professional may recommend that you take folic acid alone or as part of a multivitamin supplement before you become pregnant and during early pregnancy. Folic acid may reduce the chances of your baby being born with a certain type of birth defect (neural tube defects).

Breast-feeding—It is especially important that you receive the right amounts of vitamins so that your baby will also get the vitamins needed to grow properly. However, taking large amounts of a dietary supplement while breast-feeding may be harmful to the mother and/or baby and should be avoided.

Children—Problems in children have not been reported with intake of normal daily recommended amounts.

Older adults—Problems in older adults have not been reported with intake of normal daily recommended amounts.

Medicines or other dietary supplements—Although certain medicines or dietary supplements should not be used together at all, in other cases they may be used together even if an interaction might occur. In these cases, your health care professional may want to change the dose, or other precautions may be necessary. Tell your health care professional if you are taking any other dietary supplement or any prescription or nonprescription (over-the-counter [OTC]) medicine.

Other medical problems—The presence of other medical problems may affect the use of folic acid. Make sure you tell your health care professional if you have any other medical problems, especially:
- Pernicious anemia (a type of blood problem)—Taking folic acid while you have pernicious anemia may cause serious side effects. You should be sure that you do not have pernicious anemia before beginning folic acid supplementation

Proper Use of This Dietary Supplement

Dosing—The amount of folic acid needed to meet normal daily recommended intakes will be different for different individuals. The following information includes only the average amounts of folic acid.
- For *oral* dosage form (tablets):
  —To prevent deficiency, the amount taken by mouth is based on normal daily recommended intakes:
  For the U.S.
  - Adult and teenage males—150 to 400 micrograms (mcg) per day.
  - Adult and teenage females—150 to 400 mcg per day.
  - Pregnant females—400 to 800 mcg per day.
  - Breast-feeding females—260 to 800 mcg per day.
  - Children 7 to 10 years of age—100 to 400 mcg per day.
  - Children 4 to 6 years of age—75 to 400 mcg per day.
  - Children birth to 3 years of age—25 to 100 mcg per day.
  For Canada
  - Adult and teenage males—150 to 220 mcg per day.
  - Adult and teenage females—145 to 190 mcg per day.
  - Pregnant females—445 to 475 mcg per day.

- Breast-feeding females—245 to 275 mcg per day.
- Children 7 to 10 years of age—125 to 180 mcg per day.
- Children 4 to 6 years of age—90 mcg per day.
- Children birth to 3 years of age—50 to 80 mcg per day.
  —To treat deficiency:
  - Adults, teenagers, and children—Treatment dose is determined by prescriber for each individual based on the severity of deficiency.

Missed dose—If you miss taking a vitamin for one or more days there is no cause for concern, since it takes some time for your body to become seriously low in vitamins. However, if your health care professional has recommended that you take this vitamin, try to remember to take it as directed every day.

Storage—To store this dietary supplement:

- Keep out of the reach of children.
- Store away from heat and direct light.
- Do not store in the bathroom, near the kitchen sink, or in other damp places. Heat or moisture may cause the dietary supplement to break down.
- Do not keep outdated dietary supplements or those no longer needed. Be sure that any discarded dietary supplement is out of the reach of children.

Side Effects of This Dietary Supplement

Along with its needed effects, a dietary supplement may cause some unwanted effects. Although folic acid does not usually cause any side effects, check with your health care professional as soon as possible if any of the following side effects occur:

Rare

Fever; general weakness or discomfort; reddened skin; shortness of breath; skin rash or itching; tightness in chest; troubled breathing; wheezing

Other side effects not listed above may also occur in some individuals. If you notice any other effects, check with your health care professional.

Revised: 05/20/92
Interim revision: 08/17/94; 05/01/95;12/30/99

FOLLITROPIN ALFA   Systemic—
INTRODUCTORY VERSION

Commonly used brand name(s):

In the U.S.—
  Gonal-F

Description

Follitropin alfa (fol-li-TROE-pin AL-fa) is a hormone identical to follicle-stimulating hormone (FSH) produced by the pituitary gland. FSH helps to develop eggs in the ovaries.

Follitropin alfa is used as a fertility medicine to develop eggs in women who have not been able to become pregnant because of problems in ovulation. Also, many women wanting to become pregnant will use this medicine while enrolled in a fertility program (assisted reproductive technology [ART]) that uses procedures such as in vitro fertilization (IVF) or embryo transfer (ET). Follitropin alfa may be used with other medicines for these purposes.

Follitropin alfa is also used as a fertility medicine to help men with low sperm counts produce more sperms. Treatment with human chorionic gonadotropin should come before treatment with follitropin alfa. This pretreatment elevates the amount of testosterone to the correct level. Treatment with human chorionic gonadotropin should continue as long as follitropin alfa is being used.

Some patients may be treated with another hormone called gonadotropin-releasing hormone agonist (GnRHa) before starting treatment with follitropin alfa. GnRHa reduces the amount of FSH released from the pituitary gland. This is done so that the doctor can replace their FSH with follitropin alfa in the proper amounts each day to achieve fertility.

This medicine is available only with your doctor's prescription, in the following dosage form(s):

Parenteral
  - For injection (U.S.)

Before Using This Medicine

In deciding to use a medicine, the risks of using the medicine must be weighed against the good it will do. This is a decision you and your doctor will make. For follitropin alfa, the following should be considered:

Allergies—Tell your doctor if you have ever had any unusual or allergic reaction to follitropin alfa or similar drugs. Also tell your health care professional if you are allergic to any other substances, such as foods, preservatives, or dyes.

Pregnancy—Follitropin alfa is not needed or recommended for use during pregnancy. Since women using follitropin alfa may be more likely to have more than one child at a time, the problems of multiple births may be increased for women using this medicine. Also, this medicine has been shown to overstimulate the ovaries (ovarian hyperstimulation syndrome) for a longer time in some women who conceive than in women developing this syndrome who do not become pregnant. Signs of this syndrome include severe abdominal pain, nausea, rapid weight gain, and vomiting. Before you use this medicine, make sure your doctor knows if you are pregnant.

Breast-feeding—It is not known whether follitropin alfa passes into the breast milk. However, this medicine has not been reported to cause problems in nursing babies.

Other medicines—Although certain medicines should not be used together at all, in other cases two different medicines may be used together even if an interaction might occur. In these cases, your doctor may want to change the dose, or other precautions may be necessary. Tell your doctor and pharmacist if you are taking any other prescription or nonprescription (over-the-counter [OTC]) medicine.

Other medical problems—The presence of other medical problems may affect the use of follitropin alfa. Make sure you tell your doctor if you have any other medical problems, especially:

- Abnormal bleeding of genitals or uterus (unknown cause)—Use of follitropin alfa may make the diagnosis of this problem more difficult
- Adrenal gland or thyroid disease (not controlled) or
- Asthma or
- Tumor, brain or
- Tumor, sex hormone-dependent—Use of follitropin alfa may make these conditions worse

Ovarian cyst or enlarged ovaries—Use of follitropin alfa may increase the size of a cyst on an ovary or increase the size of enlarged ovaries

Primary testicular failure—Follitropin alfa will not work in patients who no longer are able to produce sperms

Primary ovarian failure—Follitropin alfa will not work in patients whose ovaries no longer develop eggs

Proper Use of This Medicine

To make using follitropin alfa as safe and reliable as possible, you should understand how and when to use this medicine and what effects may be expected. A paper with information for the patient will be given to you with your filled prescription and will provide many details concerning the use of follitropin alfa. *Read this paper carefully* and ask your health care professional for any additional information or explanation.

Sometimes follitropin alfa can be given by injection at home. If you are using this medicine at home:

- Understand and use the proper method of safely preparing the medicine if you are going to prepare your own medicine.
- Wash yours hands with soap and water and use a clean work area to prepare your injection.
- Make sure you clearly understand and carefully follow your doctor's instructions on how to give yourself an injection, including using the proper needle and syringe.
- Do not inject more or less of the medicine than your doctor ordered.
- Remember to move the site of injection to different areas to prevent skin problems from developing.
- Throw away needles, syringes, bottles, and unused medicine after the injection in a safe manner.

Tell your doctor when you use the last dose of follitropin alfa. Follitropin alfa often requires that another hormone called human chorionic gonadotropin (hCG) be given as a single dose the day after the last dose of follitropin alfa is given. Your doctor will give you this medicine or arrange for you to get this medicine at the right time.

Dosing—The dose of follitropin alfa will be different for different patients. *Follow your doctor's orders or the directions on the label*. The following information includes only the average doses of follitropin alfa. *If your dose is different, do not change it* unless your doctor tells you to do so.

- For *injection* dosage form:
  —For treatment of female infertility:
    - Adults—75 international units (IU) injected under the skin once a day for approximately fourteen days. The dose may be increased at weekly intervals by 37.5 IU, up to a total dose of 300 IU once a day. Using follitropin alfa for longer than fourteen days may be needed, but only if directed by your doctor. Report when you receive your last dose of follitropin alfa because you may be given an injection of hCG twenty-four hours later. If abdominal pain occurs with the use of follitropin alfa, report it to your doctor immediately, discontinue treatment, do not receive the dose of hCG, and avoid sexual intercourse.
  —For use with assisted reproductive technology (ART) procedures:
    - Adults—150 international units (IU) injected under the skin once a day for five days beginning on Day 2 or Day 3 of your menstrual cycle. After five days, your dose may be increased by 75 to 150 IU every

three to five days, up to a total dose of 450 IU once a day, for up to five more days. Some patients may start treatment at a dose of 225 IU once a day. Using follitropin alfa for longer than ten days may be needed, but only if directed by your doctor. Report when you receive your last dose of follitropin alfa because you may be given an injection of hCG twenty-four hours later.
  — For treatment of male infertility
    - Adults—150 international units (IU) injected under the skin three times a week in conjunction with 1000 USP Units of human chorionic gonadotropin (hCG) three times a week. Your dose may be increased up to 300 IU three times a week, and the treatment may last up to eighteen months.

Missed dose—If you miss a dose of this medicine, discuss with your doctor when you should receive your next dose. Do not double doses. If you have any questions about this, check with your doctor.

Storage—To store this medicine:
- Keep out of the reach of children.
- Store away from heat and direct light.
- Do not store in the bathroom, near the kitchen sink, or in other damp places.
- Do not keep outdated medicine or medicine no longer needed. Be sure that any discarded medicine is out of the reach of children.

Precautions While Using This Medicine

It is very important that *your doctor check your progress often at regular visits* to make sure that the medicine is working properly and to check for unwanted effects. Your doctor will probably want to follow the developing eggs inside the ovaries by doing an ultrasound examination and measuring hormones in your blood stream. *After you no longer receive follitropin alfa, your progress still must be checked for at least 2 weeks.*

If your doctor has asked you to record your basal body temperatures (BBTs) daily, make sure that you do this every day. Using a BBT record or some other method, your doctor will help you decide when you are most fertile and when ovulation occurs. It is important that sexual intercourse take place around the time when you are most fertile to give you the best chance of becoming pregnant. *Follow your doctor's directions carefully.*

If abdominal pain occurs with use of follitropin alfa, discontinue treatment and report the problem to your doctor immediately. Do not receive the injection of human chorionic gonadotropin (hCG) and avoid sexual intercourse.

This medicine may cause some people to become dizzy. If this side effect occurs, *do not drive, use machines, or do anything else that could be dangerous if you are not alert* while you are using follitropin alfa and for 24 hours after you stop using it.

Side Effects of This Medicine

Along with its needed effects, a medicine may cause some unwanted effects. Although not all of these side effects may occur, if they do occur they may need medical attention.

Stop taking this medicine and get emergency help immediately if any of the following side effects occur:
  Abdominal pain (severe), nausea, vomiting, and weight gain (rapid)

Check with your doctor as soon as possible if any of the following side effects occur:

More common

For patients treated for female infertility or patients pretreated with a gonadotropin-releasing hormone agonist (GnRHa) undergoing assisted reproduction technologies (ART)

Abdominal bloating; diarrhea; flu or cold-like symptoms, such as body aches or pain, coughing, fever, headache, loss of voice, runny nose, and unusual tiredness or weakness; nausea; passing of gas; vaginal bleeding between menstrual periods

For patients treated for female infertility

Acne; breast pain or tenderness; mood swings

Less common

For patients treated for female infertility or patients pretreated with GnRHa undergoing ART

Dizziness; painful menstrual periods; redness, pain, or swelling at injection site; sleepiness; vaginal bleeding unrelated to menstrual periods (heavy); white vaginal discharge

For patients treated for female infertility

Fainting; light-headedness; migraine headache; nervousness; stomach discomfort

For patients treated pretreated with a GnRHa undergoing ART

Fast, racing heartbeat; itching of skin; loss of appetite; thirst (unusual)

After you stop using this medicine, your body may need time to adjust. The length of time this takes depends on the amount of medicine you were using and how long you used it. During this period of time *check with your doctor immediately* if you notice any of the following side effects:

Abdominal pain (severe), nausea, vomiting, and weight gain (rapid)

Other side effects not listed above may also occur in some patients. If you notice any other effects, check with your doctor.

Developed: 1/26/1998
Revised: 12/28/2000

FOLLITROPIN BETA   Systemic

Commonly used brand name(s):

In the U.S.—
Follistim

In Canada—
Puregon

Description

Follitropin beta (fol-li-TROE-pin BAY-ta) is a hormone identical to follicle-stimulating hormone (FSH) produced by the pituitary gland. FSH helps to develop eggs in the ovaries.

Follitropin beta is used as a fertility medicine to develop eggs in women who have not been able to become pregnant because of problems in ovulation. Also, many women wanting to become pregnant will use this medicine while enrolled in a fertility program that uses procedures such as in vitro fertilization (IVF) or embryo transfer (ET). Follitropin beta may be used with other medicines for these purposes.

Some patients may be treated with another hormone called gonadotropin-releasing hormone agonist (GnRHa) before starting treatment with follitropin beta. GnRHa reduces the amount of FSH released from the pituitary gland. This is done so that the doctor can replace their FSH by using follitropin beta in the proper amounts each day to achieve fertility.

Follitropin beta is available only with your doctor's prescription, in the following dosage form(s):

Parenteral
• For injection (U.S.)

Before Using This Medicine

In deciding to use a medicine, the risks of using the medicine must be weighed against the good it will do. This is a decision you and your doctor will make. For follitropin beta, the following should be considered:

Allergies—Tell your doctor if you have ever had any unusual reaction to follitropin beta or similar medicines. Also tell your health care professional if you are allergic to any other substances, such as foods, preservatives, or dyes.

Pregnancy—Follitropin beta is not needed or recommended for use during pregnancy. Since women using follitropin beta may be more likely to have more than one child at a time, the problems of multiple births may be increased for women using this medicine. Also, this medicine has been shown to overstimulate the ovaries (ovarian hyperstimulation syndrome [OHSS]) for a longer time in some women who become pregnant than in women developing this syndrome who do not become pregnant. Signs of this syndrome include severe abdominal pain, nausea, rapid weight gain, and vomiting. Before using this medicine, make sure your doctor knows if you are pregnant.

Breast-feeding—It is not known whether follitropin beta passes into the breast milk. However, this medicine has not been reported to cause problems in nursing babies.

Other medicines—Although certain medicines should not be used together at all, in other cases two different medicines may be used together even if an interaction might occur. In these cases, your doctor may want to change the dose, or other precautions may be necessary. Tell your doctor and pharmacist if you are taking any other prescription or nonprescription (over-the-counter [OTC]) medicine.

Other medical problems—The presence of other medical problems may affect the use of follitropin beta. Make sure you tell your doctor if you have any other medical problems, especially:

• Abnormal bleeding of genitals or uterus (unknown cause)—Use of follitropin beta may make the diagnosis of this problem more difficult

• Adrenal gland or thyroid disease (not controlled) or
• Asthma or
• Tumors, brain or
• Tumors, sex hormone-dependent—Use of follitropin beta may make these conditions worse

• Ovarian cyst or enlarged ovaries—Use of follitropin beta may increase the size of a cyst on an ovary or increase the size of enlarged ovaries

• Primary ovarian failure—Follitropin will not work in patients whose ovaries no longer develop eggs

Proper Use of This Medicine

To make using follitropin beta as safe and reliable as possible, you should understand how and when to use this medicine and what effects may be expected. A paper with information for the patient will be given to you with your filled prescription, and will provide many details concerning the use of follitropin beta. *Read this paper carefully* and ask your health care professional for any additional information or explanation.

Sometimes follitropin beta can be given by injection at home. If you are using this medicine at home:

- Understand and use the proper method of safely preparing the medicine if you are going to prepare your own medicine.
- Wash your hands with soap and water and use a good, clean work area to prepare your injection.
- Make sure you clearly understand and carefully follow your doctor's instructions on how to give yourself an injection, including using the proper needle and syringe.
- Do not inject more or less of the medicine than your doctor ordered.
- Remember to move the site of injection to different areas to prevent skin problems from developing.
- Throw away needles, syringes, bottles, and unused medicine after the injection in a safe manner.

Tell your doctor when you use your last dose of follitropin beta. Follitropin beta often requires that another hormone called human chorionic gonadotropin (hCG) be given as a single dose the day after the last dose of follitropin beta is given. Your doctor will give you this medicine or arrange for you to get this medicine at the right time.

Dosing—The dose of follitropin beta will be different for different patients. *Follow your doctor's orders or the directions on the label.* The following information includes only the average doses of follitropin beta. *If your dose is different, do not change it* unless your doctor tells you to do so.

- For *injection* dosage form:
  —For treatment of female infertility:
  - Adults—75 international units (IU) injected under the skin or into a muscle once a day for up to fourteen days. The dose may be increased at weekly intervals by 37.5 IU, up to a total dose of 300 IU a day. Tell your doctor when you receive your last dose of follitropin beta. If abdominal pain occurs with the use of follitropin beta, report it to your doctor immediately, discontinue treatment, do not receive the dose of hCG, and avoid sexual intercourse.
  —For use with assisted reproductive technology (ART) procedures:
  - Adults—150 international units (IU) injected under the skin or into a muscle once a day for four days beginning on Day 2 or Day 3 of your menstrual cycle. Then your dose may be increased by 75 to 150 IU up to a total daily dose of 600 IU. Some patients may start at 375 IU. Tell your doctor when you receive your last dose of follitropin beta.

Missed dose—If you miss a dose of this medicine, discuss with your doctor when you should receive your next dose. Do not double doses. If you have any questions about this, check with your doctor.

Storage—To store this medicine:
- Keep out of the reach of children.
- Store away from heat and direct light.
- Do not store in the bathroom, near the kitchen sink, or in other damp places. Heat or moisture may cause the medicine to break down.
- Do not keep outdated medicine or medicine no longer needed. Be sure that any discarded medicine is out of the reach of children.

Precautions While Using This Medicine

It is very important that *your doctor check your progress often at regular visits, such as every other day,* to make sure that the medicine is working properly and to check for unwanted effects. Your doctor will probably want to follow the developing eggs inside the ovaries by doing an ultrasound examination and measuring hormones in your blood stream. *After you no longer receive follitropin beta, your progress still must be checked every other day for at least 2 weeks.*

If your doctor has asked you to record your basal body temperature (BBT) daily, make sure that you do this every day. Using a BBT record or some other method, your doctor will help you decide when you are most fertile and when ovulation occurs. It is important that sexual intercourse take place around the time when you are most fertile to give you the best chance of becoming pregnant. *Follow your doctor's directions carefully.*

If abdominal pain occurs with use of follitropin beta, discontinue treatment and report the problem to your doctor immediately. Do not receive the injection of hCG and avoid sexual intercourse.

This medicine may cause some people to become dizzy. If this side effect occurs, *do not drive, use machines, or do anything else that could be dangerous if you are not alert* while you are using follitropin beta and for 24 hours after you stop using it.

Side Effects of This Medicine

Along with its needed effects, a medicine may cause some unwanted effects. Although not all of these side effects may occur, if they do occur they may need medical attention.

There is a rare chance that serious lung and blood problems can occur with use of follitropin beta. Discuss these possible effects with your doctor.

Stop taking this medicine and get emergency help immediately if any of the following side effects occur:
Abdominal pain (severe), nausea, vomiting, and weight gain (rapid)

Check with your doctor as soon as possible if any of the following side effects occur:
Less common
For patients treated for female infertility or patients pretreated with a gonadotropin-releasing hormone agonist (GnRHa) undergoing assisted reproduction technologies (ART)
Abdominal pain
For patients pretreated with a GnRHa undergoing ART
Redness, pain, or swelling at injection site

The following side effects have not been reported for follitropin beta, but may occur because they have been reported for similar medicines. Some of these side effects may go away during treatment as your body adjusts to the medicine. However, check with your doctor if any of the following side effects continue or are bothersome:

> Body aches or pain; breast tenderness; chills; difficulty in breathing; dizziness; dry skin; fast, racing heart; fever; hair loss; headache; hives; nausea; quick, shallow breathing; skin rash; unusual tiredness

After you stop using this medicine, your body may need time to adjust. The length of time this takes depends on the amount of medicine you were using and how long you used it. During this period of time *check with your doctor immediately* if you notice any of the following side effects:

> Abdominal pain (severe), nausea, vomiting, and weight gain (rapid)

Other side effects not listed above may also occur in some patients. If you notice any other effects, check with your doctor.

Developed: 2/24/98

FOMIVIRSEN   Parenteral-Local

Commonly used brand name(s):

In the U.S.—
> Vitravene

Description

Fomivirsen (foe-MI-vir-sen) is an antiviral medicine that is injected into the eye (intravitreal). It is used to treat a serious condition called cytomegalovirus (CMV) retinitis in persons who have acquired immune deficiency syndrome (AIDS). Fomivirsen will not cure this eye infection, but it may help to keep the symptoms from becoming worse.

This medicine is available only with your doctor's prescription, in the following dosage form:

> *Parenteral-Local*
> • Intravitreal injection (injection in the eye) (U.S.)

Before Using This Medicine

In deciding to use a medicine, the risks of using the medicine must be weighed against the good it will do. This is a decision you and your doctor will make. For fomivirsen, the following should be considered:

Allergies—Tell your doctor if you have ever had any unusual or allergic reaction to fomivirsen. Also tell your health care professional if you are allergic to any other substances, such as certain preservatives.

Pregnancy—Studies on effects in pregnancy have not been done in either humans or animals. Before being treated with this medicine, make sure your doctor knows if you are pregnant or if you may become pregnant.

Breast-feeding—It is not known whether fomivirsen injected into the eye passes into breast milk. Discuss with your doctor whether or not you should breast-feed while you are being treated with this medicine.

Children—Studies with this medicine have been done only in adult patients and there is no specific information comparing use of fomivirsen in children with use in other age groups.

Older adults—Many medicines have not been studied specifically in older people. Therefore, it may not be known whether they work exactly the same way they do in younger adults or if they cause different side effects or problems in older people. There is no specific information comparing use of fomivirsen in the elderly with use in other age groups.

Other medicines—Although certain medicines should not be used together at all, in other cases two different medicines may be used together even if an interaction might occur. In these cases, your doctor may want to change the dose, or other precautions may be necessary. When you are taking fomivirsen, it is especially important that your health care professional know if you are receiving any of the following:

> • Cidofovir injection (e.g., Vistide)—Possibility of increased eye inflammation

Proper Use of This Medicine

This medicine will not cure CMV retinitis, although it may help keep it from getting worse. In addition, it will not help other symptoms of CMV (for example, in the lungs or colon).

Dosing—The dose of fomivirsen may be different for different patients. The following information includes only the average doses of fomivirsen.

> • For *parenteral-local* dosage form (ophthalmic injection):
> —For CMV retinitis:
> • Adults—The usual starting dose is 330 micrograms injected into the eye once every other week for two doses. Then the same dose is used once every four weeks for as long as it is needed.
> • Children—Use and dose must be determined by your doctor.

Precautions While Using This Medicine

It is very important that your doctor check your progress at regular visits to make sure the medicine is working properly and to watch for unwanted effects.

Side Effects of This Medicine

Along with its needed effects, a medicine may cause some unwanted effects. Although not all of these side effects may occur, if they do occur they may need medical attention.

Check with your doctor as soon as possible if any of the following side effects occur:

More common
> Abnormal vision; blurred vision; change in how colors look; decreased vision or other changes in vision; eye pain; redness of eye; seeing flashes or sparks of light; seeing floating spots before eyes; sensitivity of eye to light; veil or curtain appearing across part of vision; watering of eye

Less common
> Decreased ability to see to the side when looking straight ahead; itching, redness, or soreness at place of injection; pain on moving the eye; soreness of eye; swelling of the eye

Other side effects may occur that usually do not need medical attention. These side effects may go away during treatment as your body adjusts to the medicine. However, check with your doctor if any of the following side effects continue or are bothersome:

More common
> Abdominal or stomach pain; diarrhea; headache; nausea; skin rash; vomiting; weakness

Less common
> Back pain; cough; dizziness; loss of appetite; sweating; tightness in chest; weight loss

Other side effects not listed above may also occur in some patients. If you notice any other effects, check with your doctor.

Developed: 5/17/99

FORMOTEROL Inhalation-Local— INTRODUCTORY VERSION

Commonly used brand name(s):

In the U.S.—
Foradil

In Canada—
Oxeze

Description

Formoterol (for–MOE–tur–all) belongs to the family of medicines known as β_2-agonists. It is used to help prevent the symptoms of asthma. When used regularly every day, inhaled formoterol decreases the number and severity of asthma attacks. However, it will not relieve an asthma attack that has already started.

Inhaled formoterol works by preventing certain cells in the lungs and breathing passages from releasing substances that cause asthma symptoms.

This medicine should be taken with other asthma medicines known as corticosteroids

This medicine is available only with your doctor's prescription, in the following dosage form:

Inhalation
- Powder for inhalation (U.S. and Canada)

Before Using This Medicine

In deciding to use a medicine, the risks of taking the medicine must be weighed against the good it will do. This is a decision you and your doctor will make. For formoterol, the following should be considered:

Allergies—Tell your doctor if you have ever had any unusual or allergic reaction to formoterol or inhaled lactose. Also tell your doctor and pharmacist if you are allergic to any other substances, such as foods, preservatives, or dyes.

Pregnancy—Formoterol has not been studied in pregnant women. However, animal studies in which pregnant rabbits were given 7000 to 11000 times the recommended human dose of formoterol have found an increase in the number of birth defects and other negative effects on the fetus

Breast-feeding—It is not known if inhaled formoterol is distributed in human breast milk. However, it is distributed in rat milk. Mothers who are taking this medicine and who wish to breast-feed should discuss this with their doctor.

Children—Studies on this medicine been done only in patients 6 years of age and older, and there is no specific information comparing use of formoterol in children less than 6 years of age with use in other age groups.

Older adults—Many medicines have not been studied specifically in older people. Therefor, it may not be known whether they work exactly the same way they do in younger adults or if they cause different side effects or problems in older people. There is no specific information comparing use of formoterol in the elderly with use in other age groups.

Other medicines—Although certain medicines should not be used together at all, in other cases two different medicines may be used together even if an interaction might occur. In these cases, your doctor may want to change the dose, or other precautions may be necessary. When you are taking formoterol, it is especially important that your doctor and pharmacist know if you are taking any of the following:

- Antidepressants, tricyclic (amitriptyline [e.g. Elavil], amoxapine [e.g. Asendin], clomipramine [e.g. Anafranil], desipramine [e.g. Norpramin], doxepin [e.g. Adapin, Sinequan, or Zonalon], imipramine [e.g., Tofranil], nortriptyline [e.g. Aventyl or Pamelor], protriptyline [e.g. Vivactil]) or
- Disopyramide (e.g. Norpace) or
- Monoamine oxidase inhibitors (furazolidine [e.g., Furoxone], isocarboxazid [e.g. Marplan], phenelzine [e.g. Nardil], procarbazine [e.g., Matulane], selegiline [e.g., Eldepryl], tranylcypromine [e.g. Parnate]) or
- Phenothiazines (methdilazine [e.g. Tacaryl], promethazine [e.g. Phenergan], trimeprazine [e.g. Temaril]) or
- Procainamide (e.g. Procan SR, Procanbid, or Pronestyl) or
- Quinidine (e.g. Quinaglute) or
- Terfenadine (e.g. Seldane)
- Beta-receptor blocking agents (acebutolol [e.g. Sectral], atenolol [e.g. Tenormin], betoxolol [e.g. Frisium], bisoprolol [e.g. Zebeta], carteolol [e.g. Cartrol or Ocupress], carvedilol [e.g. Coreg], esmolol [e.g. Brevibloc], labetalol [e.g. Normodyne or Trandate], metoprolol [e.g. Lopresor or Toprol XL], nadolol [e.g. Corgard], oxprenolol [e.g. Trasicor], penbutolol [e.g. Levatol], pindolol [e.g. Visken], propranolol [e.g. Inderal], sotalol [e.g. Betapace], or timolol [e.g. Blocadren or Timoptic]

Other medical problems—The presence of other medical problems may affect the use of formoterol. Make sure you tell your doctor if you have any other medical problems, especially:

- Acutely deteriorating asthma
- Blocked heart or
- High blood pressure or
- Irregular heartbeat or
- Structural problems with the heart or
- Weak heart, unable to circulate blood effectively—Risk of increased side effects
- Diabetes—Risk of increased side effects
- Overactive thyroid—Risk of increased side effects

Proper Use of This Medicine

Dosing—*Inhaled formoterol is used to prevent asthma attacks. It is not used to relieve an attack that has already started.* For relief of an asthma attack that has already started, you should use another medicine. If you do not have another medicine to use for an attack or if you have any questions about this, check with your health care professional.

In order for this medicine to help prevent asthma attacks, it must be used every day in regularly spaced doses, as ordered by your doctor.

Inhaled formoterol is used with a special inhaler and usually comes with patient directions. *Read the directions carefully before using this medicine.* If you do not understand the directions or you are not sure how to use the inhaler, ask your health care professional to show you what to do. Also, *ask your health care professional to check regularly how you use the inhaler to make sure you are using it properly.*

The dose of formoterol will be different for different patients. *Follow your doctor's orders or the directions on the label.* The following information includes only the average doses of formoterol. *If your dose is different, do not change it* unless your doctor tells you to do so.

The number of inhaled doses that you take depends on the strength of the medicine.

- For *powder* for inhalation:
  —Adults and children 6 years of age and older—6 or 12 mcg by oral inhalation every 12 hours
  —Children younger than 6 years of age—use and dose must be determined by your doctor

Missed dose— If you miss a dose of this medicine, take it as soon as possible. However, if it is almost time for your next dose, skip the missed dose and go back to your regular dosing schedule. Do not double doses.

Storage—To store this medicine:

- Keep out of the reach of children.
- Do not store in the bathroom, near the kitchen sink, or in other damp places. Heat or moisture may cause the medicine to break down.
- Keep the medicine from freezing. Do not refrigerate.
- Do not keep outdated medicine or medicine no longer needed. Ask your health care professional how you should dispose of any medicine you do not use. Be sure that any discarded medicine is out of the reach of children.

Precautions While Using This Medicine

If you will be taking this medicine for a long time, *it is very important that your doctor check you at regular visits* for any blood or heart problems that may be caused by this medicine.

If your symptoms do not improve within a few days or if they become worse, check with your doctor.

You may also be taking an anti-inflammatory medicine along with this medicine. *Do not stop taking the anti-inflammatory medicine even if your asthma seems better, unless you are told to do so by your doctor*

Side Effects of This Medicine

Along with its needed effects, a medicine may cause some unwanted effects. Although not all of these side effects may occur, if they do occur they may need medical attention.

Check with your doctor immediately if any of the following side effects occur:

Rare
  Convulsions; cough; decreased urine; difficulty breathing; dry mouth; fainting; fast pounding, or irregular heartbeat or pulse palpitations; increased thirst; irregular heartbeat; loss of appetite; noisy breathing; shortness of breath; tightness in chest; wheezing

Symptoms of overdose

  Get emergency help immediately if any of the following symptoms of overdose occur
    Blurred vision; dizziness or light-headedness; increased hunger or thirst; increased urination; shortness of breath; troubled breathing

Other side effects may occur that usually do not need medical attention. These side effects may go away during treatment as your body adjusts to the medicine. However, check with your doctor if any of the following side effects continue or are bothersome.

More common
  Headache

Less common
  Cramps

Rare
  Agitation; hives or welts; itching; redness of skin; restlessness; skin rash; trouble sleeping

Developed: 03/05/2001

FOSCARNET   Systemic†

Commonly used brand name(s):

In the U.S.—
  Foscavir

Other commonly used names are phosphonoformic acid and PFA.

†Not commercially available in Canada.

Description

Foscarnet (foss-KAR-net) is used to treat the symptoms of cytomegalovirus (CMV) infection of the eyes in patients with acquired immune deficiency syndrome (AIDS). Foscarnet will not cure this eye infection, but it may help to control worsening of the symptoms. It is also used to treat herpes simplex virus (HSV) infections of the skin and mucous membranes in people who are immunocompromised and whose infections did not improve with other therapy. Foscarnet may also be used for other serious viral infections as determined by your doctor. However, it does not work in treating certain viruses, such as the common cold or the flu.

Foscarnet is administered only by or under the supervision of your doctor. It is available in the following dosage form:

Parenteral
  • Injection (U.S.)

Before Using This Medicine

In deciding to use a medicine, the risks of taking the medicine must be weighed against the good it will do. This is a decision you and your doctor will make. For foscarnet, the following should be considered:

Allergies—Tell your doctor if you have ever had any unusual or allergic reaction to foscarnet. Also tell your health

care professional if you are allergic to any other substances, such as foods, preservatives, or dyes.

Pregnancy—Foscarnet has not been studied in pregnant women. However, studies in animals have shown that foscarnet causes birth defects. Before taking this medicine, make sure your doctor knows if you are pregnant or if you may become pregnant.

Breast-feeding—It is not known whether foscarnet passes into the breast milk. Although most medicines pass into breast milk in small amounts, many of them may be used safely while breast-feeding. Mothers who are taking this medicine and who wish to breast-feed should discuss this with their doctor.

Children—There is no specific information comparing use of foscarnet in children with use in other age groups. Foscarnet can cause serious side effects in any patient. Therefore, it is especially important that you discuss with the child's doctor the good that this medicine may do as well as the risks of using it.

Older adults—Many medicines have not been studied specifically in older people. Therefore, it may not be known whether they work exactly the same way they do in younger adults or if they cause different side effects or problems in older people. There is no specific information comparing use of foscarnet in the elderly with use in other age groups.

Other medicines—Although certain medicines should not be used together at all, in other cases 2 different medicines may be used together even if an interaction might occur. In these cases, your doctor may want to change the dose, or other precautions may be necessary. When you are taking foscarnet, it is especially important that your health care professional know if you are taking any of the following:

- Carmustine (e.g., BiCNU) or
- Cisplatin (e.g., Platinol) or
- Combination pain medicine containing acetaminophen and aspirin (e.g., Excedrin) or other salicylates (with large amounts taken regularly) or
- Cyclosporine (e.g., Sandimmune) or
- Deferoxamine (e.g., Desferal) (with long-term use) or
- Gold salts (medicine for arthritis) or
- Inflammation or pain medicine, except narcotics, or
- Lithium (e.g., Lithane) or
- Methotrexate (e.g., Mexate) or
- Other anti-infectives (e.g., amphotericin B) or
- Penicillamine (e.g., Cupramine) or
- Plicamycin (e.g., Mithracin) or
- Streptozocin (e.g., Zanosar) or
- Tiopronin (e.g., Thiola)—Use of these medicines may increase the chance of side effects affecting the kidneys
- Pentamidine (e.g., Pentam)—Use of pentamidine injection with foscarnet may lower the level of important minerals (calcium and magnesium) in the blood; it may also increase the chance of side effects affecting the kidneys

Other medical problems—The presence of other medical problems may affect the use of foscarnet. Make sure you tell your doctor if you have any other medical problems, especially:

- Anemia—Foscarnet may cause or worsen anemia
- Dehydration or
- Kidney disease—Patients who are dehydrated or have kidney disease may have an increased chance of side effects

Proper Use of This Medicine

To ensure the best response, foscarnet must be given for the full time of treatment. Also, this medicine works best when there is a constant amount in the blood. To help keep the amount constant, foscarnet must be given on a regular schedule.

Several glasses of water should be taken every day, unless otherwise directed by your doctor. Drinking extra water will help to prevent some unwanted effects foscarnet has on the kidneys.

This medicine may cause sores on the genitals (sex organs). Washing your genitals after urination may decrease the chance of your developing this problem.

Dosing—The dose of foscarnet will be different for different patients. *Follow your doctor's orders or the directions on the label.* The following information includes only the average doses of foscarnet. *If your dose is different, do not change it* unless your doctor tells you to do so.

- For *injection* dosage form:
  —For cytomegalovirus (CMV) retinitis induction (first stage of dosing):
  - Adults and children—The usual dose is 60 milligrams (mg) per kilogram (kg) (27.3 mg per pound) of body weight every eight hours for fourteen to twenty-one days. Each dose is injected slowly into a vein by an infusion pump over at least one hour.
  —For CMV retinitis maintenance (second stage of dosing):
  - Adults and children—The usual dose is 90 to 120 mg per kg (41 to 54.5 mg per pound) of body weight once a day. This dose is injected slowly into a vein by an infusion pump over at least two hours.
  —For herpes simplex infections:
  - Adults and children—The usual dose is 40 mg per kg (18.2 mg per pound) of body weight given either every eight or every twelve hours. This dose is injected slowly into a vein by an infusion pump over at least one hour. Treatment is usually continued for two to three weeks or until the infection in healed.

Precautions After Receiving This Medicine

It is very important that your doctor check your progress at regular visits. This will allow your doctor to check for possible unwanted effects.

It is also *very important that your ophthalmologist (eye doctor) check your eyes* at regular visits since you may have some loss of eyesight due to retinitis even while you are receiving foscarnet.

Side Effects of This Medicine

Along with their needed effects, medicines like foscarnet can sometimes cause serious side effects such as kidney problems; these are described below. Foscarnet may also decrease the amount of calcium in your blood, causing you to have a tingling sensation around your mouth, and pain or numbness in your hands and feet. If this occurs, especially while you are receiving the medicine, notify your health care professional immediately.

Along with its needed effects, a medicine may cause some unwanted effects. Although not all of these side effects may occur, if they do occur they may need medical attention.

Check with your doctor immediately if any of the following side effects occur:

More common

Increased or decreased frequency of urination or amount of urine; increased thirst

Less common

Convulsions (seizures); fever, chills, and sore throat; muscle twitching; pain at place of injection; pain or numbness in hands or feet; tingling sensation around mouth; tremor; unusual tiredness and weakness

Rare

Sores or ulcers on the mouth or throat, penis, or vulva

Other side effects may occur that usually do not need medical attention. These side effects may go away during treatment as your body adjusts to the medicine. However, check with your doctor if any of the following side effects continue or are bothersome:

More common

Abdominal or stomach pain; anxious feeling; confusion; dizziness; headache; loss of appetite; nausea and vomiting; unusual tiredness or weakness

Other side effects not listed above may also occur in some patients. If you notice any other effects, check with your doctor.

Additional Information

Once a medicine has been approved for marketing for a certain use, experience may show that it is also useful for other medical problems. Although these uses are not included in product labeling, foscarnet is used in certain patients with the following medical conditions:

- Cytomegalovirus infections in places other than the eyes, such as the lungs, esophagus, or intestines
- Varicella-zoster infection (shingles) that does not respond to treatment with acyclovir in patients with HIV infection

Other than the above information, there is no additional information relating to proper use, precautions, or side effects for these uses.

Revised: 07/22/94
Interim revision: 09/25/98

FOSFOMYCIN   Systemic

Commonly used brand name(s):

In the U.S.—
Monurol

Description

Fosfomycin (fos-foe-MYE-sin) is an antibiotic. It is used to treat urinary tract infection and cystitis (bladder infection) in women.

This medicine is available only with your doctor's prescription, in the following dosage form:

Oral
- Powder for solution (U.S.)

Before Using This Medicine

In deciding to use a medicine, the risks of taking the medicine must be weighed against the good it will do. This is a decision you and your doctor will make. For fosfomycin, the following should be considered:

Allergies—Tell your doctor if you have ever had any unusual or allergic reaction to fosfomycin. Also tell your health care professional if you are allergic to any other substances, such as foods, preservatives, or dyes.

Pregnancy—Fosfomycin has not been studied in pregnant women. However, it does pass through the placenta from the mother to the baby. In animals, fosfomycin has been shown to cause some harmful effects in the mother and the infant.

Breast-feeding—It is not known whether fosfomycin passes into breast milk. Although most medicines pass into breast milk in small amounts, many of them may be used safely while breast-feeding. Mothers who receive this medicine and who wish to breast-feed should discuss this with their doctor.

Other medicines—Although certain medicines should not be used together at all, in other cases two different medicines may be used together even if an interaction might occur. In these cases, your doctor may want to change the dose, or other precautions may be necessary. Tell your doctor and pharmacist if you are taking any other prescription or nonprescription (over-the-counter [OTC]) medicine.

Other medical problems—The presence of other medical problems may affect the use of fosfomycin. Make sure you tell your doctor if you have any other medical problems, especially:

- Kidney disease—Effects of fosfomycin may be increased because of slower removal from the body

Proper Use of This Medicine

Fosfomycin powder must be dissolved in water before it is taken. Take the medicine as soon as it has dissolved.

This medicine can be taken with or without food.

Dosing—The dose of fosfomycin may be different for different patients. *Follow your doctor's orders or the directions on the label.* The following information includes only the average doses of fosfomycin. *If your dose is different, do not change it* unless your doctor tells you to do so.

- For *oral* dosage form (powder for solution):
  —For treatment of bladder infection:
    - Adults—3 grams (one packet) dissolved in water taken one time.
    - Children—Use and dose must be determined by your doctor.

Storage—To store this medicine:

- Keep out of the reach of children.
- Store away from heat and direct light.
- Do not store in the bathroom, near the kitchen sink, or in other damp places. Heat or moisture may cause the medicine to break down.
- Do not keep outdated medicine or medicine no longer needed. Be sure that any discarded medicine is out of the reach of children.

Precautions While Using This Medicine

Check with your doctor if your symptoms do not improve within 2 or 3 days or if they become worse.

Side Effects of This Medicine

Along with its needed effects, a medicine may cause some unwanted effects. Although not all of these side effects may occur, if they do occur they may need medical attention.

Check with your doctor as soon as possible if any of the following side effects occur:

More common
Vaginal discharge and pain

Other side effects may occur that usually do not need medical attention. These side effects may go away during treatment as your body adjusts to the medicine. However, check with your doctor if any of the following side effects continue or are bothersome:

More common
Diarrhea; headache; nausea
Less common
Abdominal or stomach pain; back pain; dizzinesss; heartburn; indigestion; pain; painful menstruation; runny or stuffy nose; skin rash; sore throat; weakness

Other side effects not listed above may also occur in some patients. If you notice any other effects, check with your doctor.

Developed: 07/28/98

FRAMYCETIN   Ophthalmic*— INTRODUCTORY VERSION

Commonly used brand name(s):

In Canada—
Soframycin Ophthalmic

*Not commercially available in the U.S.

Description

Framycetin (Fram-E-see-tin) belongs to the family of medicines called antibiotics. Framycetin ophthalmic preparations are used to treat infections of the eye.

Framycetin is available only with your doctor's prescription, in the following dosage forms:

Ophthalmic
• Ophthalmic ointment (Canada)
• Ophthalmic solution (eye drops) (Canada)

Before Using This Medicine

In deciding to use a medicine, the risks of using the medicine must be weighed against the good it will do. This is a decision you and your doctor will make. For framycetin, the following should be considered:

Allergies—Tell your doctor if you have ever had any unusual or allergic reaction to framycetin or related antibiotics, such as neomycin (e.g., Mycifradin), paromomycin (e.g., Humatin), or kanamycin (e.g., Kantrex). Also tell your health care professional if you are allergic to any other substances, such as preservatives.

Pregnancy—Studies on effects in pregnancy have not been done in either humans or animals.

Breast-feeding—Framycetin has not been reported to cause problems in nursing babies.

Children—Studies on this medicine have been done only in adult patients, and there is no specific information comparing use of framycetin in children with use in other age groups.

Older adults—Many medicines have not been studied specifically in older people. Therefore, it may not be known whether they work exactly the same way they do in younger adults or if they cause different side effects or problems in older people. There is no specific information comparing use of framycetin in the elderly with use in other age groups.

Proper Use of This Medicine

For patients using the *eye drops form* of this medicine:
• The bottle is only partially full to provide proper drop control.
• First, wash your hands. Tilt the head back and, pressing your finger gently on the skin just beneath the lower eyelid, pull the lower eyelid away from the eye to make a space. Drop the medicine into this space. Let go of the eyelid and gently close the eyes. Do not blink. Keep the eyes closed and apply pressure to the inner corner of the eye with your finger for 1 or 2 minutes to allow the medicine to be absorbed by the eye.
• Remove any excess solution around the eye with a clean tissue, being careful not to touch the eye.

For patients using the *eye ointment form* of this medicine:
• First, wash your hands. Tilt the head back and with the index finger of one hand, press gently on the skin just beneath the lower eyelid and pull the lower eyelid away from the eye to make a space. Squeeze a thin strip of ointment into this space. A 1-cm (approximately ⅓-inch) strip of ointment is usually enough unless otherwise directed by your doctor. Let go of the eyelid and gently close the eyes and keep them closed for 1 or 2 minutes, to allow the medicine to come into contact with the infection.
• To keep the medicine as germ-free as possible, do not touch the applicator tip to any surface (including the eye). After using framycetin eye ointment, wipe the tip of the ointment tube with a clean tissue and keep the tube tightly closed.

To help clear up your infection completely, *keep using this medicine for the full time of treatment*, even if your symptoms have disappeared. *Do not miss any doses.*

Dosing—The dose of ophthalmic framycetin will be different for different patients. *Follow your doctor's orders or the directions on the label.* The following information includes only the average doses of ophthalmic framycetin. *If your dose is different, do not change it* unless your doctor tells you to do so.
• For *ophthalmic ointment* dosage form:
   —For eye infections:
   • Adults—Apply to affected eye 2 or 3 times per day, or at bedtime if the drops have been used during the day.
   • Children—Use and dose must be determined by your doctor.

- For *ophthalmic solution (eye drops)* dosage form:
  —For eye infections:
    - Adults—Apply 1 or 2 drops to affected eye every one or two hours for the first two or three days. Your doctor may then instruct you to decrease your dose to 1 or 2 drops to affected eye 3 or 4 times per day.
    - Children—Use and dose must be determined by your doctor.

Missed dose—If you do miss a dose of this medicine, apply it as soon as possible. However, if it is almost time for your next dose, skip the missed dose and go back to your regular dosing schedule.

Storage—To store this medicine:
- Keep out of the reach of children.
- Do not keep outdated medicine or medicine no longer needed. Ask your health care professional how you should dispose of any medicine you do not use. Be sure that any discarded medicine is out of the reach of children.

Precautions While Using This Medicine

If your symptoms do not improve within a few days, or if they become worse, check with your doctor.

Side Effects of This Medicine

A medicine may cause some unwanted effects. If you notice any side effects, check with your doctor.

Developed: 08/17/2000

FRUCTOSE, DEXTROSE, AND PHOSPHORIC ACID   Oral

Commonly used brand name(s):

In the U.S.—
Emetrol

In Canada—
Emetrol

Description

Fructose, dextrose, and phosphoric acid (FRUK-tose, DEX-trose, and fos-FOR-ik AS-id) combination is used to treat nausea and vomiting. However, this combination has not been proven to be effective.

This medicine is available without a prescription; however, your doctor may have special instructions on the proper use and dose for your medical problem. Fructose, dextrose, and phosphoric acid combination is available in the following dosage form:

Oral
- Oral solution (U.S. and Canada)

Before Using This Medicine

If you are taking this medicine without a prescription, carefully read and follow any precautions on the label. For fructose, dextrose, and phosphoric acid combination, the following should be considered:

Allergies—Tell your doctor if you have ever had any unusual or allergic reaction to fructose, dextrose, or phosphoric acid.

Pregnancy—Studies on effects in pregnancy have not been done in either humans or animals.

Breast-feeding—This medicine has not been reported to cause problems in nursing babies.

Children—The fluid loss caused by vomiting may result in a severe condition, especially in children under 3 years of age. Do not give medicine for vomiting to children without first checking with their doctor.

Older adults—The fluid loss caused by vomiting may result in a severe condition. Elderly persons should not take any medicine for vomiting without first checking with their doctor.

Other medical problems—The presence of other medical problems may affect the use of fructose, dextrose, and phosphoric acid. Make sure you tell your doctor if you have any other medical problems, especially:
- Appendicitis, symptoms of, or
- Inflamed bowel, symptoms of—Make sure nausea and vomiting are not due to appendicitis or inflamed bowel before using this product. These conditions may become more severe if they are not treated by your doctor
- Diabetes mellitus—The sugars contained in this medicine may cause problems in diabetics
- Fructose intolerance, hereditary—The fructose in this medicine may cause severe side effects in patients with this condition

Proper Use of This Medicine

For safe use of this medicine:
- Follow your doctor's instructions if this medicine was prescribed.
- Follow the manufacturer's package directions if you are treating yourself.

Do not dilute this medicine with other liquids. Also, do not drink any other liquids immediately before or after taking this medicine. To do so may keep this medicine from working properly.

Dosing—The dose of this combination product will be different for different patients. *Follow your doctor's orders or the directions on the label.* The following information includes only the average doses. *If your dose is different, do not change it* unless your doctor tells you to do so.
- For *oral* dosage form (oral solution):
  —For morning sickness:
    - Pregnant women: One or two tablespoonfuls upon arising and every three hours as needed.
  —For nausea:
    - Adults: One or two tablespoonfuls. Dose may be repeated every fifteen minutes until nausea stops. You should not take this product for more than one hour (5 doses) without checking with your doctor.
    - Children over 3 years of age: One or two teaspoonfuls. Dose may be repeated every fifteen minutes until nausea stops. This product should not be taken for more than one hour (5 doses) without checking with your doctor.

- Children under 3 years of age: Use is not recommended.

Storage—To store this medicine:
- Keep out of the reach of children.
- Store away from heat and direct light.
- Keep the medicine from freezing.
- Do not keep outdated medicine or medicine no longer needed. Be sure that any discarded medicine is out of the reach of children.

Precautions While Using This Medicine

Check with your doctor if your nausea and vomiting continue or become worse after you have taken this medicine.

Do not take this medicine if you have any signs of appendicitis or inflamed bowel (such as stomach or lower abdominal pain, cramping, bloating, soreness, or continuing or severe nausea or vomiting). Instead, check with your doctor as soon as possible.

Side Effects of This Medicine

Along with its needed effects, a medicine may cause some unwanted effects. Although not all of these side effects may occur, if they do occur they may need medical attention.

Stop using this medicine and check with your doctor as soon as possible if any of the following side effects occur:
Signs of fructose intolerance
Fainting; swelling of face, arms, and legs; unusual bleeding; vomiting; weight loss; yellow eyes or skin

Other side effects may occur that usually do not need medical attention. These side effects may go away during treatment as your body adjusts to the medicine. However, check with your doctor if any of the following side effects continue or are bothersome:
Less common—more common with large doses
Diarrhea; stomach or abdominal pain

Other side effects not listed above may also occur in some patients. If you notice any other effects, check with your doctor.

Revised: 05/12/93

FUSIDIC ACID   Systemic*

Commonly used brand name(s):
In Canada—
Fusidin Leo

*Not commercially available in the U.S.

Description

Fusidic acid (Fu-SID-ick ass-id) is a substance that is used to treat bacterial infections. It will not work for colds, flu, or other virus infections.

Fusidic acid is available only with your doctor's prescription, in the following dosage forms:
Oral
- Oral solution (Canada)
- Tablets (Canada)

Parenteral
- Injection (Canada)

Before Using This Medicine

In deciding to use a medicine, the risks of taking fusidic acid must be weighed against the good it will do. This is a decision you and your doctor will make. For fusidic acid, the following should be considered:

Allergies—Tell your doctor if you have ever had any unusual or allergic reaction to fusidic acid. Also tell your doctor and pharmacist if you are allergic to any other substances, such as foods, preservatives, or dyes.

Pregnancy—Studies on effects in pregnancy have not been done in either humans or animals.

Breast-feeding—It is not known whether fusidic acid passes into breast milk. Although most medicines pass into breast milk in small amounts, many of them may be used safely while breast-feeding. Mothers who are taking this medicine and who wish to breast-feed should discuss this with their doctor.

Other medicines—Although certain medicines should not be used together at all, in other cases two different medicines may be used together even if an interaction might occur. In these cases, your doctor may want to change the dose, or other precautions may be necessary. When you are taking fusidic acid, it is especially important that your doctor and pharmacist know if you are taking any of the following:
- Lincomycin (eg, Lincocin) or
- Rifampin (eg, Rifadin)—may interfere with your liver
- Amino acid solution (Aminosyn) or
- Whole blood products—may be at risk for damage to the red blood cells

Although certain medicines should not be used together at all, in other cases two different medicines may be used together even if an interaction might occur. In these cases, your doctor may want to change the dose, or other precautions may be necessary. Tell your doctor and pharmacist if you are using any other prescription or nonprescription (over-the-counter [OTC]) medicine.

Other medical problems—The presence of other medical problems may affect the use of fusidic acid. Make sure you tell your doctor if you have any other medical problems, especially:
- Liver disease—May be worsened by fusidic acid

Proper Use of This Medicine

Dosing—The dose of fusidic acid may be different for different patients. *Follow your doctor's orders or the directions on the label.* The following information includes only the average doses of fusidic acid. *If your dose is different, do not change it* unless your doctor tells you to do so.

The number of tablets or teaspoonfuls of suspension that you take depends on the strength of the medicine. Also, *the number of doses you take each day, the time allowed between doses, and the length of time you take the medicine depend on the medical problem for which you are taking fusidic acid*
- For *oral* dosage form (tablets):
  —Osteomyelitis (bone and joint infections) or skin and soft tissue infections:
    - Adults—500 mg (2 tablets) three times daily

- For *oral* dosage form (suspension):
  —Osteomyelitis (bone and joint infections) or skin and soft tissue infections:
  - Adults—15 milliliters three times daily
  - Children—Up to 1 year of age: 1 milliliter (mL) per kilogram DAILY divided into 3 equal doses; 1 to 5 years of age is 5 mL three times daily; 6 to 12 years of age is 10 mL three times daily.
- For *injection* dosage form:
  —Osteomyelitis (bone and joint infections) or skin and soft tissue infections:
  - Adults—500 milligrams three times daily
  - Children—Up to 1 year of age to 12 years: 20 milligrams/kilogram DAILY divided into 3 equal doses, infused over at least 2 hours.

Missed dose—If you miss a dose of this medicine, take it as soon as possible. However, if it is within 2 hours for your next dose, skip the missed dose and go back to your regular dosing schedule. Do not double doses.

Storage—To store this medicine:

- Keep out of the reach of children.
- Keep the oral liquid form of this medicine out of direct sunlight.
- Keep the oral liquid form of this medicine from freezing.
- Keep the injection for of this medicine at room temperature.
- Do not keep outdated medicine or medicine no longer needed. Ask your health care professional how you should dispose of any medicine you do not use. Be sure that any discarded medicine is out of the reach of children.

Precautions While Using This Medicine

If your symptoms do not improve within a few days or if they become worse, check with your doctor.

Do not take other medicines unless they have been discussed with your doctor. This especially includes nonprescription medicines, such as aspirin, and medicines for appetite control, asthma, colds, cough, hay fever, or sinus problems.

Side Effects of This Medicine

Along with its needed effects, a medicine may cause some unwanted effects. Although not all of these side effects may occur, if they do occur they may need medical attention.

Check with your doctor immediately if any of the following side effects occur:

Rare
  Unusual tiredness or weakness; yellow eyes or skin

Other side effects may occur that usually do not need medical attention. These side effects may go away during treatment as your body adjusts to the medicine. However, check with your doctor if any of the following side effects continue or are bothersome.

Less common
  Loss of appetite; nausea; abdominal or stomach pain; increase in bowel movements; loose stools

Other side effects not listed above may also occur in some patients. If you notice any other effects, check with your doctor.

Developed: 04/17/00

GABAPENTIN   Systemic

Commonly used brand name(s):

In the U.S.—
  Neurontin

In Canada—
  Neurontin

Another commonly used name is GBP.

Description

Gabapentin (GA-ba-pen-tin) is used to help control some types of seizures in the treatment of epilepsy. This medicine cannot cure epilepsy and will only work to control seizures for as long as you continue to take it.

Gabapentin is available only with your doctor's prescription, in the following dosage form:

Oral
  - Capsules (U.S. and Canada)
  - Oral Solution (U.S.)
  - Tablets (U.S.)

Before Using This Medicine

In deciding to use a medicine, the risks of taking the medicine must be weighed against the good it will do. This is a decision you and your doctor will make. For gabapentin, the following should be considered:

Allergies—Tell your doctor if you have ever had any unusual or allergic reaction to gabapentin. Also tell your health care professional if you are allergic to any other substances, such as foods, preservatives, or dyes.

Pregnancy—Gabapentin has not been studied in pregnant women. However, studies in pregnant animals have shown that gabapentin may cause bone or kidney problems in offspring when given to the mother in doses larger than the largest human dose. Before taking this medicine, make sure your doctor knows if you are pregnant or if you may become pregnant.

Breast-feeding—It is not known whether gabapentin passes into breast milk. Although most medicines pass into breast milk in small amounts, many of them may be used safely while breast-feeding. Mothers who are taking this medicine and who wish to breast-feed should discuss this with their doctor.

Children—This medicine has been tested in children 3 years to 12 years of age and, in effective doses, has not been shown to cause different side effects or problems than it does in adults.

Teenagers—This medicine has been tested in a small number of patients 12 to 18 years of age. In effective doses, gabapentin has not been shown to cause different side effects or problems than it does in adults.

Older adults—Gabapentin is removed from the body more slowly in elderly people than in younger people. Higher blood levels may occur, which may increase the chance of unwanted effects. Your doctor may give you a different gabapentin dose than a younger person would receive.

Other medicines—Although certain medicines should not be used together at all, in other cases two different medicines may be used together even if an interaction might occur. In these cases, your doctor may want to change the dose, or other precautions may be necessary. When you are

taking gabapentin, it is especially important that your health care professional know if you are taking any of the following:

- Antacids (e.g., Maalox)—Lower blood levels of gabapentin may occur, so gabapentin may not work properly; gabapentin should be taken at least 2 hours after any antacid is taken.

Other medical problems—The presence of other medical problems may affect the use of gabapentin. Make sure you tell your doctor if you have any other medical problems, especially:

- Kidney disease—Higher blood levels of gabapentin may occur, which may increase the chance of unwanted effects; your doctor may need to change your dose

Proper Use of This Medicine

Take this medicine only as directed by your doctor, to help your condition as much as possible. Do not take more or less of it, and do not take it more or less often than your doctor ordered.

Gabapentin may be taken with or without food or on a full or empty stomach. However, if your doctor tells you to take the medicine a certain way, take it exactly as directed.

When taking gabapentin 3 times a day, do not allow more than 12 hours to pass between any 2 doses.

If you have trouble swallowing capsules, you may open the gabapentin capsule and mix the medicine with applesauce or juice. Mix only one dose at a time just before taking it. *Do not mix any doses to save for later*, because the medicine may change over time and may not work properly.

Dosing—The dose of gabapentin will be different for different patients. *Follow your doctor's orders or the directions on the label*. The following information includes only the average doses of gabapentin. *If your dose is different, do not change it* unless your doctor tells you to do so.

The number of capsules that you take depends on the strength of the medicine.

- For *oral* dosage form (capsules):
  —For epilepsy:
  - Adults and teenagers 12 years of age and older— At first, 300 milligrams (mg) three times a day. Your doctor may increase the dose gradually if needed. However, the dose is usually not more than 3600 mg a day.
  - Children 3 to 12 years of age—Dose is based on body weight. To start, 10 to 15 mg per kilogram (4.5 to 6.8 mg per pound) of body weight a day, divided into three doses. Your doctor may increase your dose as needed. The usual dose for children 5 years of age and older is 25 to 35 mg per kilogram (11.3 to 15.9 mg per pound) of body weight a day, divided into three doses. The usual dose for children 3 to 5 years of age is 40 mg per kilogram (18.1 mg per pound) of body weight a day, divided into three doses.
  - Children less than 3 years of age—Use and dose must be determined by your doctor.
  - Older adults—Dose must be determined by your doctor, but it is usually not more than 400 mg three times a day.
- For *oral* dosage form (oral solution):
  —For epilepsy:
  - Adults and teenagers 12 years of age and older— At first, 300 milligrams (mg) three times a day.

Your doctor may increase the dose gradually if needed. However, the dose is usually not more than 3600 mg a day.
  - Children 3 to 12 years of age—Dose is based on body weight. To start, 10 to 15 mg per kilogram (4.5 to 6.8 mg per pound) of body weight a day, divided into three doses. Your doctor may increase your dose as needed. The usual dose for children 5 years of age and older is 25 to 35 mg per kilogram (11.3 to 15.9 mg per pound) of body weight a day, divided into three doses. The usual dose for children 3 to 5 years of age is 40 mg per kilogram (18.1 mg per pound) of body weight a day, divided into three doses.
  - Children less than 3 years of age—Use and dose must be determined by your doctor.
  - Older adults—Dose must be determined by your doctor, but it is usually not more than 400 mg three times a day.
- For *oral* dosage form (tablets):
  —For epilepsy:
  - Adults and teenagers 12 years of age and older— At first, 300 milligrams (mg) three times a day. Your doctor may increase the dose gradually if needed. However, the dose is usually not more than 3600 mg a day.
  - Children 3 to 12 years of age—Dose is based on body weight. To start, 10 to 15 mg per kilogram (4.5 to 6.8 mg per pound) of body weight a day, divided into three doses. Your doctor may increase your dose as needed. The usual dose for children 5 years of age and older is 25 to 35 mg per kilogram (11.3 to 15.9 mg per pound) of body weight a day, divided into three doses. The usual dose for children 3 to 5 years of age is 40 mg per kilogram (18.1 mg per pound) of body weight a day, divided into three doses.
  - Children less than 3 years of age—Use and dose must be determined by your doctor.
  - Older adults—Dose must be determined by your doctor, but it is usually not more than 400 mg three times a day.

Note: This medicine may be given as a combination of any of the forms it comes in.

Missed dose—If you miss a dose of this medicine, take it as soon as possible. However, if it is less than 2 hours until your next dose, take the missed dose right away, and take the next dose 1 to 2 hours later. Then go back to your regular dosing schedule. Do not double doses.

Storage—To store this medicine:

- Keep out of the reach of children.
- Store away from heat and direct light.
- Do not store the capsule or tablet forms of this medicine in the bathroom, near the kitchen sink, or in other damp places. Heat or moisture may cause the medicine to break down.
- Store the liquid form of this medicine in the refrigerator. However, keep the medicine from freezing.
- Do not keep outdated medicine or medicine no longer needed. Be sure that any discarded medicine is out of the reach of children.

Precautions While Using This Medicine

It is important that your doctor check your progress at regular visits, especially for the first few months you take gabapentin. This is necessary to allow dose adjustments and to reduce any unwanted effects.

This medicine will add to the effects of alcohol and other CNS depressants (medicines that make you drowsy or less alert). Some examples of CNS depressants are antihistamines or medicine for hay fever, other allergies, or colds; sedatives, tranquilizers, or sleeping medicine; prescription pain medicine or narcotics; barbiturates; other medicines for seizures; muscle relaxants; or anesthetics, including some dental anesthetics. *Check with your medical doctor or dentist before taking any of the above while you are taking gabapentin.*

Gabapentin may cause blurred vision, double vision, clumsiness, unsteadiness, dizziness, drowsiness, or trouble in thinking. *Make sure you know how you react to this medicine before you drive, use machines, or do anything else that could be dangerous if you are not alert, well-coordinated, or able to think or see well.* If these reactions are especially bothersome, check with your doctor.

Before you have any medical tests, tell the doctor in charge that you are taking gabapentin. The results of dipstick tests for protein in the urine may be affected by this medicine.

Do not stop taking gabapentin without first checking with your doctor. Stopping the medicine suddenly may cause your seizures to return or to occur more often. Your doctor may want you to gradually reduce the amount you are taking before stopping completely.

Side Effects of This Medicine

Along with its needed effects, a medicine may cause some unwanted effects. Although not all of these side effects may occur, if they do occur they may need medical attention.

Check with your doctor as soon as possible if any of the following side effects occur:

More common
> Clumsiness or unsteadiness; continuous, uncontrolled, back-and-forth and/or rolling eye movements

More common in patients 3 to 12 years of age
> Aggressive behaviors or other behavior problems; anxiety; concentration problems and change in school performance; crying; false sense of well-being; hyperactivity or increase in body movements; mental depression; reacting too quickly, too emotionally, or overreacting; rapidly changing moods; restlessness; suspiciousness or distrust

Less common
> Depression, irritability, or other mood or mental changes; loss of memory

Rare
> Cough or hoarseness; fever or chills; lower back or side pain; painful or difficult urination

Symptoms of overdose
> Diarrhea; double vision; drowsiness; sluggishness; slurred speech

Other side effects may occur that usually do not need medical attention. These side effects may go away during treatment as your body adjusts to the medicine. However, check with your doctor if any of the following side effects continue or are bothersome:

More common
> Blurred or double vision; dizziness; drowsiness; muscle ache or pain; swelling of hands, feet, or lower legs; trembling or shaking; unusual tiredness or weakness

Less common
> Back pain; constipation; decrease in sexual desire or ability; diarrhea; dryness of mouth or throat; frequent urination; headache; indigestion; low blood pressure; nausea; noise in ears; runny nose; slurred speech; trouble in sleeping; trouble in thinking; twitching; vomiting; weakness or loss of strength; weight gain

Other side effects not listed above also may occur in some patients. If you notice any other effects, check with your doctor.

Revised: 01/29/2001

GALANTAMINE   Systemic— INTRODUCTORY VERSION

Commonly used brand name(s):

In the U.S.—
> Reminyl

Description

Galantamine (ga-LAN-ta-meen) is used to treat the symptoms of mild to moderate Alzheimer's disease. Galantamine will not cure Alzheimer's disease, and it will not stop the disease from getting worse. However, galantamine can improve thinking ability in some patients with Alzheimer's disease

In Alzheimer's disease, many chemical changes take place in the brain. One of the earliest and biggest changes is that there is less of a chemical called acetylcholine (ACh). ACh helps the brain to work properly. Galantamine slows the breakdown of ACh, so it can build up and have a greater effect. However, as Alzheimer's disease gets worse, there will be less and less ACh, so galantamine may not work as well.

This medicine is available only with your doctor's prescription, in the following dosage forms:

Oral
> • Tablets (U.S.)

Before Using This Medicine

In deciding to use a medicine, the risks of taking the medicine must be weighed against the good it will do. This is a decision you and your doctor will make. For galantamine the following should be considered:

Allergies—Tell your doctor if you have ever had any unusual or allergic reaction to galantamine. Also tell your doctor and pharmacist if you are allergic to any other substances, such as foods, preservatives, or dyes.

Pregnancy—Galantamine has not been studied in pregnant women. Galantamine has been shown to cause birth defects or other problems in animal studies.

Breast-feeding—It is not known whether galantamine passes into breast milk. Mothers who are taking this medicine and who wish to breast-feed should discuss this with their doctor. Use in breast-feeding mothers is not indcated.

Children—Studies on this medicine have been done only in adult patients, and there is no specific information comparing use of galantamine in children with use in other age groups. Use in children is not recommended.

Older adults—Galantamine levels are higher in older adults than in healthy young subjects.

Other medicines—Although certain medicines should not be used together at all, in other cases two different medicines may be used together even if an interaction might occur. In these cases, your doctor may want to change the dose, or other precautions may be necessary. Tell your health care professional if you are taking any other prescription or nonprescription (over-the-counter [OTC]) medicine.

Other medical problems—The presence of other medical problems may affect the use of galantamine. Make sure you tell your doctor if you have any other medical problems, especially:

- Asthma (or history of) or
- Heart problems, including slow heartbeat or heart block (slow and irregular heartbeat), or
- Stomach ulcer (or history of) or
- Urinary tract blockage or difficult urination—Galantamine may make these conditions worse
- Epilepsy or history of seizures—Galantamine may cause seizures

Proper Use of This Medicine

Dosing—*Take this medicine only as directed by your doctor.* Do not take more or less of it, and do not take it more or less often than your doctor ordered. Taking too much may increase the chance of side effects, while taking too little may not improve your condition.

The dose of galantamine will be different for different patients. *Follow your doctor's orders or the directions on the label.* The following information includes only the average doses of galantamine. *If your dose is different, do not change it* unless your doctor tells you to do so.

The number of tablets that you take depends on the strength of the medicine. Also, *the number of doses you take each day, the time allowed between doses, and the length of time you take the medicine depend on the medical problem for which you are taking galantamine.*

- For *oral* dosage form (tablets):
  - For treatment of Alzheimer's disease:
    - Adults—To start, take 4 mg (milligrams) two times a day. Your doctor may increase your dose gradually if you are doing well on this medicine.

Missed dose—If you miss a dose of this medicine, take it as soon as possible. However, if you do not remember within a few hours, skip the missed dose and go back to your regular dosing schedule. Do not double doses. Do not take your morning and evening doses close together.

Storage—To store this medicine:

- Keep out of the reach of children.
- Do not store in the bathroom, near the kitchen sink, or in other damp places. Heat or moisture may cause the medicine to break down.
- Do not keep outdated medicine or medicine no longer needed. Ask your health care professional how you should dispose of any medicine you do not use. Be sure that any discarded medicine is out of the reach of children.

Precautions While Using This Medicine

It is very important that your doctor check you at regular visits.

Tell your doctor if your symptoms get worse, or if you notice any new symptoms.

Do not take other medicines unless they have been discussed with your doctor. This especially includes nonprescription medicines, such as aspirin, and medicines for appetite control, asthma, colds, cough, hay fever, or sinus problems.

Galantamine causes a large number of patients to have problems with their stomachs and intestines. Tell your doctor about any nausea, vomiting, diarrhea, stomach pain or loss of appetite.

If you think you or someone else may have taken an overdose of galantamine, get emergency help at once. Taking an overdose of galantaminee may lead to convulsions (seizures) or shock. Some signs of shock are large pupils, irregular breathing, and fast weak pulse. Other signs of an overdose are severe nausea and vomiting, increasing muscle weakness, greatly increased sweating, and greatly increased watering of the mouth.

Side Effects of This Medicine

Along with its needed effects, a medicine may cause some unwanted effects. Although not all of these side effects may occur, if they do occur they may need medical attention.

Check with your doctor as soon as possible if any of the following side effects occur:
  Symptoms of overdose
    Cramping; defecation or urination, uncontrolled; dizziness; drooling; fainting; increased sweating; low blood pressure; muscle weakness; seizures; slow heart beat; severe nausea or vomiting; slow or troubled breathing; tearing of the eyes; watering of the mouth

Other side effects may occur that usually do not need medical attention. These side effects may go away during treatment as your body adjusts to the medicine. However, check with your doctor if any of the following side effects continue or are bothersome:
  More common
    Loss of appetite; weight loss; diarrhea; nausea; vomiting
  Less common
    Abdominal pain; pale skin; troubled breathing with activity; slow or irregular heartbeat (less than 50 beats per minute); light-headedness; dizziness or fainting; unusual tiredness or weakness; indigestion; headache; blood in urine; lower back pain; pain or burning while urinating; trouble sleeping; unable to sleep; sleepiness; sleeplessness; stuffy nose; unusual bleeding or bruising; unusual drowsiness; high or low blood pressure; tremor

Other side effects not listed above may also occur in some patients. If you notice any other effects, check with your doctor.

Developed: 05/17/2001

GANCICLOVIR   Implantation-Ophthalmic

Commonly used brand name(s):

In the U.S.—
   Vitrasert

Description

Ganciclovir (gan-SYE-kloe-veer) is an antiviral medicine that is used in an implant that is inserted into the eye during surgery. The ganciclovir implant is used to treat a serious condition called cytomegalovirus (CMV) retinitis in persons who have acquired immune deficiency syndrome (AIDS). Ganciclovir will not cure this eye infection, but it may help to keep the symptoms from becoming worse.

After your eye has used up all the medicine in the implant (generally within 5 to 8 months), the implant is removed by surgery and, at the same time, another implant can be inserted.

The surgery, the implant containing this medicine, or the medicine itself may cause some serious side effects, including detachment of the retina, formation of a cataract, and eye infections. *Before you receive this implant, you and your doctor should talk about the good this medicine and surgery will do as well as the risks involved.*

This medicine is available only with your doctor's prescription, in the following dosage form:

   Ophthalmic
   • Intravitreal implant (eye implant) (U.S.)

Before Receiving This Medicine

In deciding to use a medicine, the risks of using the medicine must be weighed against the good it will do. This is a decision you and your doctor will make. For ganciclovir, the following should be considered:

Allergies—Tell your doctor if you have ever had any unusual or allergic reaction to ganciclovir or acyclovir. Also tell your health care professional if you are allergic to any other substances, such as certain preservatives.

Pregnancy—The ganciclovir eye implant has not been studied in pregnant women. However, in animals, ganciclovir given by injection has caused cancer and birth defects. Discuss these possible effects with your doctor.

Breast-feeding—It is not known whether ganciclovir from an eye implant passes into breast milk. However, because ganciclovir given by injection to animals has caused serious unwanted effects, it is recommended that breast-feeding be stopped during treatment with this medicine.

Children—There is no specific information comparing use of ganciclovir eye implants in children younger than 9 years of age with use in other age groups.

Older adults—Many medicines have not been studied specifically in older people. Therefore, it may not be known whether they work exactly the same way they do in younger adults or if they cause different side effects or problems in older people. There is no specific information comparing use of ganciclovir eye implants in the elderly with use in other age groups.

Other medicines—Although certain medicines should not be used together at all, in other cases two different med-icines may be used together even if an interaction might occur. In these cases, your doctor may want to change the dose, or other precautions may be necessary. Tell your health care professional if you are taking or using any other prescription or nonprescription (over-the-counter [OTC]) medicine.

Other medical problems—The presence of other medical problems may affect the use of ganciclovir. Make sure you tell your doctor if you have any other medical problems, especially:

   • Blood problems or
   • Eye infection—Surgery on the eye is not recommended

Precautions After Receiving This Medicine

It is very important that your doctor check your progress at regular visits. This is to make sure the medicine is working properly and to check for any problems from the surgery, implant, or medicine. This will also help the doctor determine when all of the medicine in the implant has been used up, so it can be removed.

You may notice blurred or decreased vision in the eye where the implant has been placed. This is to be expected and will last for 2 to 4 weeks after the surgery to insert the implant into the eye. *Tell your doctor if the blurred or decreased vision gets worse, lasts for more than 4 weeks, or gets better for a while and then gets worse again. Also, tell your doctor right away if any other changes in your vision occur.* These may be signs of complications from the surgery.

Side Effects of This Medicine

Along with its needed effects, a medicine may cause some unwanted effects. Although not all of these side effects may occur, if they do occur they may need medical attention.

Also, ganciclovir has been found to cause cancerous tumors in animals. Discuss these possible effects with your doctor.

Check with your doctor as soon as possible if any of the following side effects occur:
   More common—Usually occur within the first 2 months after the surgery
      Decrease in vision (severe); seeing flashes or sparks of light; seeing floating spots before the eyes, or a veil or curtain appearing across part of vision

   Less common—Usually occur within the first 2 months after the surgery
      Blurred vision or other change in vision; decreased vision or other change in vision; eye pain or tearing; red or bloodshot eye; sensitivity of eye to light

   Rare—Usually occur within the first 2 months after the surgery
      Eye irritation; swelling of the membrane covering the white part of the eye

Other side effects may occur that usually do not need medical attention. These side effects may go away during treatment as your body adjusts to the medicine. However, check with your doctor if the following side effect continues or is bothersome:
   More common
      Decrease in vision lasting approximately 2 to 4 weeks

Other side effects not listed above may also occur in some patients. If you notice any other effects, check with your doctor.

Developed: 08/14/98

GANCICLOVIR   Systemic

Commonly used brand name(s):

In the U.S.—
Cytovene
Cytovene-IV

In Canada—
Cytovene

Another commonly used name is DHPG.

Description

Ganciclovir (gan-SYE-kloe-vir) is an antiviral. It is used to treat infections caused by viruses.

Ganciclovir is used to treat the symptoms of cytomegalovirus (CMV) infection of the eyes in people whose immune system is not working fully. This includes patients with acquired immune deficiency syndrome (AIDS). Ganciclovir will not cure this eye infection, but it may help to keep the symptoms from becoming worse. It is also used to help prevent CMV infection in patients who receive organ or bone marrow transplants, as well as in patients with advanced human immunodeficiency virus (HIV) infection. Ganciclovir may be used for other serious CMV infections as determined by your doctor. However, it does not work in treating certain viruses, such as the common cold or the flu.

This medicine may cause some serious side effects, including anemia and other blood problems. Before you begin treatment with ganciclovir, you and your doctor should talk about the good this medicine will do as well as the risks of using it.

Ganciclovir is to be administered only by or under the supervision of your doctor. It is available in the following dosage forms:

Oral
  • Capsules (U.S. and Canada)
Parenteral
  • Injection (U.S. and Canada)

Before Receiving This Medicine

In deciding to use a medicine, the risks of taking the medicine must be weighed against the good it will do. This is a decision you and your doctor will make. For ganciclovir, the following should be considered:

Allergies—Tell your doctor if you have ever had any unusual or allergic reaction to acyclovir or ganciclovir. Also tell your health care professional if you are allergic to any other substances, such as foods, preservatives, or dyes.

Pregnancy—Use of ganciclovir during pregnancy should be avoided whenever possible since ganciclovir has caused cancer and birth defects in animal studies. The use of birth control is recommended during ganciclovir therapy. Men should use a condom while receiving ganciclovir, and for at least 90 days following treatment. Also, animal studies have shown that ganciclovir causes a decrease in fertility.

Breast-feeding—Breast-feeding should be stopped during treatment with this medicine because ganciclovir may cause serious unwanted effects in nursing babies.

Children—Ganciclovir can cause serious side effects in any patient. Therefore, it is especially important that you discuss with the child's doctor the good that this medicine may do as well as the risks of using it.

Older adults—Many medicines have not been studied specifically in older people. Therefore, it may not be known whether they work exactly the same way they do in younger adults or if they cause different side effects or problems in older people. There is no specific information comparing use of ganciclovir in the elderly with use in other age groups.

Other medicines—Although certain medicines should not be used together at all, in other cases two different medicines may be used together even if an interaction might occur. In these cases, your doctor may want to change the dose, or other precautions may be necessary. When you are taking ganciclovir, it is especially important that your health care professional know if you are taking any of the following:

  • Amphotericin B by injection (e.g., Fungizone) or
  • Antineoplastics (cancer medicine) or
  • Antithyroid agents (medicine for overactive thyroid) or
  • Azathioprine (e.g., Imuran) or
  • Chloramphenicol (e.g., Chloromycetin) or
  • Colchicine or
  • Cyclophosphamide (e.g., Cytoxan) or
  • Flucytosine (e.g., Ancobon) or
  • Interferon (e.g., Intron A, Roferon-A) or
  • Mercaptopurine (e.g., Purinethol) or
  • Zidovudine (e.g., AZT, Retrovir)—Caution should be used if these medicines and ganciclovir are used together; receiving ganciclovir while you are using these medicines may make anemia and other blood problems worse

  • Carmustine (e.g., BiCNU) or
  • Cisplatin (e.g., Platinol) or
  • Combination pain medicine containing acetaminophen and aspirin (e.g., Excedrin) or other salicylates (with large amounts taken regularly) or
  • Cyclosporine (e.g., Sandimmune) or
  • Deferoxamine (e.g., Desferal) (with long-term use) or
  • Gold salts (medicine for arthritis) or
  • Inflammation or pain medicine, except narcotics, or
  • Lithium (e.g., Lithane) or
  • Other anti-infectives (e.g., amphotericin B) or
  • Penicillamine (e.g., Cupramine) or
  • Streptozocin (e.g., Zanosar) or
  • Tiopronin (e.g., Thiola)—Use of these medicines may increase the chance of side effects affecting the kidneys

  • Methotrexate (e.g., Mexate) or
  • Plicamycin (e.g., Mithracin)—These medicines may increase the chance of side effects affecting the blood and the kidneys

Other medical problems—The presence of other medical problems may affect the use of ganciclovir. Make sure you tell your doctor if you have any other medical problems, especially:

  • Kidney disease—Ganciclovir may build up in the blood in patients with kidney disease, increasing the chance of side effects

  • Low platelet count or

• Low white blood cell count—Ganciclovir may make these blood diseases worse

Proper Use of This Medicine

It is *important that you take ganciclovir capsules with food*. This is to make sure the medicine is fully absorbed into the body and will work properly.

To get the best results, *ganciclovir must be given for the full time of treatment*. Also, this medicine works best when there is a constant amount in the blood. To help keep the amount constant, ganciclovir must be given on a regular schedule.

Dosing—The dose of ganciclovir will be different for different patients. *Follow your doctor's orders or the directions on the label*. The following information includes only the average doses of ganciclovir. *If your dose is different, do not change it* unless your doctor tells you to do so.

• For *oral* dosage form (capsules):
  —For treatment of CMV retinitis after you have received ganciclovir injection for at least fourteen to twenty-one days:
    • Adults and teenagers—1000 milligrams (mg) three times a day with food; or 500 mg six times a day, every three hours with food, during waking hours.
    • Children—Use and dose must be determined by your doctor.
  —For prevention of CMV disease in transplant patients and patients with advanced HIV infection:
    • Adults and teenagers—1000 mg three times a day with food.
    • Children—Use and dose must be determined by your doctor.

• For *injection* dosage form:
  —For treatment of CMV retinitis:
    • Adults and teenagers—Dose is based on body weight and must be determined by your doctor. At first, 5 mg per kilogram (2.3 mg per pound) of body weight is injected into a vein every twelve hours for fourteen to twenty-one days. Then, 5 mg per kilogram (2.3 mg per pound) of body weight is injected into a vein once a day for seven days of the week; or 6 mg per kilogram (2.7 mg per pound) of body weight is injected into a vein once a day for five days of the week.
    • Children—Use and dose must be determined by your doctor.
  —For prevention of CMV in transplant patients:
    • Adults and teenagers—Dose is based on body weight and must be determined by your doctor. At first, 5 mg per kilogram (2.3 mg per pound) of body weight is injected into a vein every twelve hours for seven to fourteen days. Then the dose is reduced to 5 mg per kilogram (2.3 mg per pound) of body weight once a day for seven days of the week; or 6 mg per kilogram (2.7 mg per pound) of body weight is injected into a vein once a day for five days of the week.
    • Children—Use and dose must be determined by your doctor.

Precautions After Receiving This Medicine

Ganciclovir can lower the number of white blood cells in your blood, increasing the chance of getting an infection. It can also lower the number of platelets, which are necessary for proper blood clotting. If this occurs, there are certain precautions you can take to reduce the risk of infection or bleeding:

• *Check with your doctor immediately* if you think you are getting an infection or if you get a fever or chills.
• *Check with your doctor immediately* if you notice any unusual bleeding or bruising; black, tarry stools; blood in urine or stools; or pinpoint red spots on your skin.
• Be careful when using a regular toothbrush, dental floss, or toothpick. Your medical doctor, dentist, or nurse may recommend other ways to clean your teeth and gums. Check with your medical doctor before having any dental work done.
• Be careful not to cut yourself when you are using sharp objects such as a safety razor or fingernail or toenail cutters.

The *use of birth control is recommended for both men and women*. Women should use effective birth control methods while receiving this medicine. Men should use a condom during treatment with this medicine and for at least 90 days after treatment has been completed.

It is very important that your doctor check you at regular visits for any blood problems that may be caused by this medicine.

If you have CMV retinitis: It is also very important that your ophthalmologist (eye doctor) check your eyes at regular visits since it is still possible that you may have some loss of eyesight during ganciclovir treatment.

Side Effects of This Medicine

Along with its needed effects, a medicine may cause some unwanted effects. Although not all of these side effects may occur, if they do occur they may need medical attention.

Medicines like ganciclovir can sometimes cause serious side effects such as blood problems; these are described below. Discuss these possible effects with your doctor.

Check with your doctor immediately if any of the following side effects occur:
  More common
    For oral capsules and injection into the vein only
      Sore throat and fever; unusual bleeding or bruising

  Less common
    For oral capsules and injection into the vein only
      Mood or other mental changes; nervousness; pain at place of injection; skin rash; tremor; unusual tiredness and weakness

  For injection into the eye only
    Decreased vision or any change in vision

Other side effects may occur that usually do not need medical attention. These side effects may go away during treatment as your body adjusts to the medicine. However, check with your doctor if any of the following side effects continue or are bothersome:
  Less common
    Abdominal or stomach pain; loss of appetite; nausea and vomiting

Other side effects not listed above may also occur in some patients. If you notice any other effects, check with your doctor.

Revised: 04/04/2001

GANIRELIX Systemic

Commonly used brand name(s):

In the U.S.—
Antagon

Description

Ganirelix (ga-ni-REL-iks) is used as a fertility medicine to prevent premature luteinizing hormone (LH) surges in women undergoing the fertility procedure of controlled ovarian hyperstimulation. LH is involved in ovulation, which is the development of eggs in the ovaries. Ganirelix may help reduce the need for follicle-stimulating hormone (FSH), which is also involved in ovulation.

Ganirelix is available only with your doctor's prescription in the following dosage form:

Parenteral
- For injection (U.S)

Before Using This Medicine

In deciding to use a medicine, the risks of taking the medicine must be weighed against the good it will do. This is a decision you and your doctor will make. For ganirelix, the following should be considered:

Allergies—Tell your doctor if you have ever had any unusual or allergic reaction to ganirelix or other related medicines. Also tell your health care professional if you have any allergies to any other substances, such as foods, preservatives, or dyes.

Pregnancy—Ganirelix is not recommended during pregnancy. It has been shown to cause problems in animals. Be sure you have discussed this with your doctor.

Breast-feeding—It is not known whether ganirelix passes into breast milk. It is recommended that you avoid ganirelix if you are breast-feeding.

Other medicines—Although certain medicines should not be used together at all, in other cases two different medicines may be used together even if an interaction might occur. In these cases, your doctor may want to change the dose, or other precautions may be necessary. Tell your health care professional if you are taking any other prescription or nonprescription (over-the-counter [OTC]) medicine.

Other medical problems—The presence of other medical problems may affect the use of ganirelix. Make sure you tell your doctor if you have any other medical problems.

Proper Use of This Medicine

To make using ganirelix as safe and reliable as possible, you should understand how and when to use this medicine and what effects may be expected. A paper with information for the patient will be given to you with your filled prescription and will provide many details concerning the use of ganirelix.

Read this paper carefully and ask your health care professional for any additional information or explanation.

Sometimes ganirelix can be given by injection at home. If you are using this medicine at home:

- Understand and use the proper method of safely preparing the medicine if you are going to prepare your own medicine.
- Wash your hands with soap and water and use a clean work area to prepare your injection.
- Make sure you clearly understand and carefully follow your doctor's instructions on how to give yourself an injection, including using the proper needle and syringe.
- Do not inject more or less of the medicine than your doctor ordered.
- Remember to move the site of injection to different areas to prevent skin problems from developing.
- Throw away needles, syringes, bottles, and unused medicine after the injection in a safe manner.
- Tell your doctor when you use your last dose of ganirelix. Your doctor will give you another medicine called human chorionic gonadotrophin (hCG) or arrange for you to get this medicine at the right time.

Dosing—The dose of ganirelix will be different for different patients. *If you are receiving ganirelix at home, follow your doctor's orders or the directions on the label.* If you have any questions about the proper dose of ganirelix, ask your doctor.

The following information includes only the average doses of ganirelix. *If your dose is different, do not change it* unless your doctor tells you to do so.

- For *injection* dosage form:
  —For treatment of female infertility:
    - Adults—After receiving FSH treatment on Day 2 or 3 of your menstrual cycle, 250 micrograms (mcg) of ganirelix is injected under the skin once a day during the early to midfollicular phase (about Day 7 or Day 8 of your menstrual cycle).

Missed dose—If you miss a dose of this medicine, do not inject the missed dose at all and do not double the next one. Check with your doctor for further instructions.

Storage—To store this medicine:
- Keep out of the reach of children.
- Store away from heat and direct light.
- Do not store in the bathroom, near the kitchen sink, or in other damp places.
- Do not keep outdated medicine or medicine no longer needed. Be sure that any discarded medicine is out of the reach of children.

Precautions While Using This Medicine

It is very important that *your doctor check your progress often at regular visits* to make sure that the medicine is working properly and to check for unwanted effects. Your doctor will probably want to follow the developing eggs inside the ovaries by doing an ultrasound examination and measuring hormones in your blood stream.

If your doctor has asked you to record your basal body temperatures (BBTs) daily, make sure that you do this every day. Using a BBT record or some other method, your doctor will help you decide when you are most fertile and when ovulation occurs. It is important that sexual intercourse take place around the time when you are most fertile to give you the best chance of becoming pregnant. *Follow your doctor's directions carefully.*

If severe abdominal pain occurs with use of ganirelix, discontinue treatment and report the problem to your doctor immediately. Do not receive the injection of human chorionic gonadotropin (hCG) and avoid sexual intercourse.

Side Effects of This Medicine

Along with its needed effects, a medicine may cause some unwanted effects. Although not all of these side effects may occur, if they do occur they may need medical attention.

Stop taking this medicine and get emergency help immediately if any of the following side effects occur:
 Less common
  Abdominal pain (severe); nausea and vomiting; weight gain (rapid)

Check with your doctor as soon as possible if any of the following side effects occur:
 Less common
  Nausea; vaginal bleeding

Other side effects may occur that usually do not need medical attention. These side effects may go away during treatment as your body adjusts to the medicine. However, check with your doctor if any of the following side effects continue to occur or are bothersome:
 Less common
  Headache; redness, pain or swelling at injection site

Other side effects not listed above may also occur in some patients. If you notice any other effects, check with your doctor.

Developed: 11/8/99

GEMCITABINE   Systemic

Commonly used brand name(s):
In the U.S.—
 Gemzar
In Canada—
 Gemzar

Description

Gemcitabine (jem-SITE-a-been) belongs to the group of medicines called antimetabolites. It is used to treat cancer of the pancreas and lung. It may also be used to treat other kinds of cancer, as determined by your doctor.

Gemcitabine interferes with the growth of cancer cells, which are eventually destroyed. Since the growth of normal cells may also be affected by the medicine, other effects will also occur. Some of these may be serious and must be reported to your doctor. Other effects, like hair loss, may not be serious but may cause concern. Some effects may occur after treatment with gemcitabine has been stopped.

This medicine is available only with your doctor's prescription, in the following dosage form:
 Parenteral
  • Injection (U.S. and Canada)

Before Using This Medicine

In deciding to use a medicine, the risks of taking the medicine must be weighed against the good it will do. This is a decision you and your doctor will make. For gemcitabine, the following should be considered:

Allergies—Tell your doctor if you have ever had any unusual or allergic reaction to gemcitabine.

Pregnancy—Tell your doctor if you are pregnant. Studies in mice and rabbits have shown that gemcitabine causes birth defects and death of the fetus, as well as problems in the mother.

Be sure that you have discussed this with your doctor before starting treatment with this medicine. It is best to use birth control while you are receiving gemcitabine. Also, tell your doctor right away if you think you have become pregnant during treatment.

Breast-feeding—It is not known whether gemcitabine passes into breast milk. However, because this medicine may cause serious side effects, breast-feeding is generally not recommended while you are receiving it.

Children—There is no specific information comparing use of gemcitabine in children with use in other age groups.

Older adults—Gemcitabine has been tested in elderly patients and has not been shown to cause different side effects or problems in older people than it does in younger adults. However, seriously low blood counts tend to occur more often in elderly patients.

Other medicines—Although certain medicines should not be used together at all, in other cases two different medicines may be used together even if an interaction might occur. In these cases, your doctor may want to change the dose, or other precautions may be necessary. When you are taking gemcitabine, it is especially important that your health care professional know if you are taking any of the following:
 • Amphotericin B by injection (e.g., Fungizone) or
 • Antithyroid agents (medicine for overactive thyroid) or
 • Azathioprine (e.g., Imuran) or
 • Chloramphenicol (e.g., Chloromycetin) or
 • Colchicine or
 • Flucytosine (e.g., Ancobon) or
 • Ganciclovir (e.g., Cytovene) or
 • Interferon (e.g., Intron A, Roferon-A) or
 • Plicamycin (e.g., Mithracin) or
 • Zidovudine (e.g., AZT, Retrovir) or
 • If you have ever been treated with radiation or other cancer medicines—The risk of developing seriously low blood counts may be increased. Also, gemcitabine can cause problems, sometimes serious, in areas treated by radiation

 • Azathioprine (e.g., Imuran) or
 • Chlorambucil (e.g., Leukeran) or
 • Corticosteroids (cortisone-like medicine) or
 • Cyclosporine (e.g., Sandimmune) or
 • Mercaptopurine (e.g., Purinethol) or
 • Muromonab-CD3 (monoclonal antibody) (e.g., Orthoclone OKT3) or
 • Tacrolimus (e.g., Prograf)—There may be an increased risk of infection because gemcitabine decreases your body's ability to fight it

Other medical problems—The presence of other medical problems may affect the use of gemcitabine. Make sure

you tell your doctor if you have any other medical problems, especially:

- Chickenpox (including recent exposure) or
- Herpes zoster (shingles)—Risk of severe disease spreading to other parts of the body
- Infection—Gemcitabine can decrease your body's ability to fight infection
- Kidney disease or
- Liver disease, severe—These conditions sometimes increase the effects of medicines by causing them to be removed from the body more slowly

Proper Use of This Medicine

Gemcitabine often causes nausea and vomiting. It can also cause flu-like symptoms such as chills, fever, general feeling of illness, headache, muscle pain, and weakness. It is very important that you continue to receive the medicine even if it makes you feel ill. Ask your health care professional for ways to lessen these effects.

Dosing—The dose of gemcitabine will be different for different patients. The dose that is used may depend on a number of things, including the type of cancer being treated, the patient's size, and whether or not other treatments are also being given. *If you are receiving gemcitabine at home, follow your doctor's orders or the directions on the label.* If you have any questions about the proper dose of gemcitabine, ask your doctor.

Precautions While Using This Medicine

It is very important that your doctor check your progress at regular visits to make sure that this medicine is working properly. Blood tests will be needed to check for unwanted effects.

While you are being treated with gemcitabine, and after you stop treatment with it, *do not have any immunizations (vaccinations) without your doctor's approval.* Gemcitabine may lower your body's resistance, and there is a chance you might get the infection that the immunization is meant to prevent. In addition, other persons living in your household should not take oral polio vaccine, since there is a chance they could pass the polio virus on to you. Also, avoid persons who have taken oral polio vaccine within the past several months. Do not get close to them and do not stay in the same room with them for very long. If you cannot take these precautions, you should consider wearing a protective face mask that covers the nose and mouth.

Check with your doctor immediately if shortness of breath occurs or worsens while you are being treated with gemcitabine.

Gemcitabine can temporarily lower the number of white blood cells in your blood, increasing the chance of getting an infection. It can also lower the number of platelets, which are needed for proper blood clotting. If this occurs, there are certain precautions you can take, especially when your blood count is low, to reduce the risk of infection or bleeding:

- If you can, avoid people with infections. *Check with your doctor immediately* if you think you are getting an infection or if you get a fever or chills, cough or hoarseness, lower back or side pain, or painful or difficult urination.
- *Check with your doctor immediately* if you notice any unusual bleeding or bruising; black, tarry stools; blood in urine or stools; or pinpoint red spots on your skin.

- Be careful when using a regular toothbrush, dental floss, or toothpick. Your medical doctor, dentist, or nurse may recommend other ways to clean your teeth and gums. Also, check with your medical doctor before having any dental work done.
- Do not touch your eyes or the inside of your nose unless you have just washed your hands and have not touched anything else in the meantime.
- Be careful not to cut yourself when you are using sharp objects such as a safety razor or fingernail or toenail cutters.
- Avoid contact sports or other situations where bruising or injury could occur.

Side Effects of This Medicine

Along with its needed effects, a medicine may cause some unwanted effects. Although not all of these side effects may occur, if they do occur they may need medical attention.

Check with your doctor immediately if any of the following side effects occur:
More common
  Shortness of breath

Less common
  Cough or hoarseness (accompanied by fever or chills); fever or chills; headache (sudden and severe); lower back or side pain (accompanied by fever or chills); painful or difficult urination (accompanied by fever or chills); pain in chest, arm, or back; pressure or squeezing in chest; slurred speech or inability to speak; troubled breathing, tightness in chest, and/or wheezing; weakness in arm and/or leg on one side of the body (sudden and severe)

Rare
  Coughing; noisy or rattling breathing

The following side effects may mean that you are having a serious allergic reaction to this medicine, especially if they occur together with breathing problems. *Check with your doctor immediately* if any of them occur:
Rare
  Change in skin color of the face; skin rash, hives, and/or itching; swelling or puffiness of the face, especially the eyelids or area around the eyes

Also, check with your doctor as soon as possible if any of the following side effects occur:

More common
  Black, tarry stools; blood in urine or stools; cloudy urine; fever; pinpoint red spots on skin; skin rash, with or without itching; swelling of fingers, feet, or lower legs; unusual bleeding or bruising; unusual tiredness or weakness

Less common
  Fast or irregular heartbeat; high blood pressure

Rare
  Increased or decreased urination; yellow eyes or skin

Some of the above side effects may occur, or continue to occur, after treatment with gemcitabine has ended. Check with your doctor if you notice any of them after you stop receiving the medicine.

Other side effects may occur that usually do not need medical attention. These side effects may go away during treatment as your body adjusts to the medicine. However, check with

your doctor if any of the following side effects continue or are bothersome:

More common
Constipation; diarrhea; general feeling of illness; loss of appetite; muscle pain; nausea and vomiting; runny nose; sweating; trouble in sleeping

Less common
Drowsiness (severe); irritation, pain, or redness at place of injection; numbness or tingling of hands or feet; sores, ulcers, or white spots on lips and in mouth

Gemcitabine may also cause a temporary loss of hair in some people. After treatment with gemcitabine has ended, normal hair growth should return.

Other side effects not listed above may also occur in some patients. If you notice any other effects, check with your doctor.

Additional Information

Once a medicine has been approved for marketing for a certain use, experience may show that it is also useful for other medical problems. Although this use is not included in product labeling, gemcitabine is used in certain patients with the following medical conditions:

- Bladder cancer
- Breast cancer
- Cancer of the lymph system
- Epithelial ovarian cancer

Other than the above information, there is no additional information relating to proper use, precautions, or side effects for this use.

Developed: 08/21/1997
Revised: 04/04/2001

GEMFIBROZIL   Systemic

Commonly used brand name(s):

In the U.S.—
Lopid
Generic name product may be available.

In Canada—
Lopid   Novo-Gemfibrozil
Apo-Gemfibrozil   Nu-Gemfibrozil
Gen-Fibro

Description

Gemfibrozil (gem-FI-broe-zil) is used to lower cholesterol and triglyceride (fat-like substances) levels in the blood. This may help prevent medical problems caused by such substances clogging the blood vessels.

Gemfibrozil is available only with your doctor's prescription, in the following dosage forms:

Oral
- Capsules (Canada)
- Tablets (U.S. and Canada)

Before Using This Medicine

In addition to its helpful effects in treating your medical problem, this type of medicine may have some harmful effects.

Results of a large study using gemfibrozil seem to show that it may cause a higher rate of some cancers in humans. In addition, the action of gemfibrozil is similar to that of another medicine called clofibrate. Studies with clofibrate have suggested that it may increase the patient's risk of cancer, liver disease, pancreatitis (inflammation of the pancreas), gallstones and problems from gallbladder surgery, although it may also decrease the risk of heart attacks. Other studies have not found all of these effects.

Studies with gemfibrozil in rats found an increased risk of liver tumors when doses up to 10 times the human dose were given for a long time.

Be sure you have discussed this with your doctor before taking this medicine.

In deciding to use a medicine, the risks of taking the medicine must be weighed against the good it will do. This is a decision you and your doctor will make. For gemfibrozil, the following should be considered:

Allergies—Tell your doctor if you have ever had any unusual or allergic reaction to gemfibrozil. Also tell your health care professional if you are allergic to any other substances, such as foods, preservatives, or dyes.

Diet—Before prescribing medicine for your condition, your doctor will probably try to control your condition by prescribing a personal diet for you. Such a diet may be low in fats, sugars, and/or cholesterol. Many people are able to control their condition by carefully following their doctor's orders for proper diet and exercise. *Medicine is prescribed only when additional help is needed* and is effective only when a schedule of diet and exercise is properly followed.

Also, this medicine is less effective if you are greatly overweight. It may be very important for you to go on a reducing diet. However, check with your doctor before going on any diet.

Make certain your health care professional knows if you are on a low-sodium, low-sugar, or any other special diet. Most medicines contain more than their active ingredient.

Pregnancy—Gemfibrozil has not been studied in pregnant women. However, studies in animals have shown that high doses of gemfibrozil may increase the number of fetal deaths, decrease birth weight, or cause some skeletal defects. Before taking this medicine, make sure your doctor knows if you are pregnant or if you may become pregnant.

Breast-feeding—It is not known whether gemfibrozil passes into breast milk. However, studies in animals have shown that high doses of gemfibrozil may increase the risk of some kinds of tumors. Therefore, you should consider this when deciding whether to breast-feed your baby while taking this medicine.

Children—There is no specific information about the use of gemfibrozil in children. However, use is not recommended in children under 2 years of age since cholesterol is needed for normal development.

Older adults—Many medicines have not been studied specifically in older people. Therefore, it may not be known whether they work exactly the same way they do in younger adults or if they cause different side effects or problems in

older people. There is no specific information comparing use of gemfibrozil in the elderly with use in other age groups.

Other medicines—Although certain medicines should not be used together at all, in other cases two different medicines may be used together even if an interaction might occur. In these cases, your doctor may want to change the dose, or other precautions may be necessary. When you are taking gemfibrozil it is especially important that your health care professional know if you are taking any of the following:

- Anticoagulants (blood thinners)—Use with gemfibrozil may increase the effect of the anticoagulant

- Lovastatin—Use with gemfibrozil may cause muscle or kidney problems or make them worse

Other medical problems—The presence of other medical problems may affect the use of gemfibrozil. Make sure you tell your doctor if you have any other medical problems, especially:

- Gallbladder disease or
- Gallstones—Gemfibrozil may make these conditions worse

- Kidney disease or
- Liver disease—Higher blood levels of gemfibrozil may result, which may increase the chance of side effects; a decrease in the dose of gemfibrozil may be needed

Proper Use of This Medicine

Use this medicine only as directed by your doctor. Do not use more or less of it, and do not use it more often or for a longer time than your doctor ordered.

This medicine is usually taken twice a day. If you are taking 2 doses a day, it is best to take the medicine 30 minutes before your breakfast and evening meal.

Follow carefully the special diet your doctor gave you. This is the most important part of controlling your condition and is necessary if the medicine is to work properly.

Dosing—The dose of gemfibrozil will be different for different patients. *Follow your doctor's orders or the directions on the label.* The following information includes only the average doses of gemfibrozil. *If your dose is different, do not change it* unless your doctor tells you to do so:

- For *oral* dosage forms (tablets):
  - Adults: 600 milligrams two times a day to be taken thirty minutes before the morning and evening meals.

Missed dose—If you miss a dose of this medicine, take it as soon as possible. However, if it is almost time for your next dose, skip the missed dose and go back to your regular dosing schedule. Do not double doses.

Storage—To store this medicine:

- Keep out of the reach of children.
- Store away from heat and direct light.
- Do not store in the bathroom, near the kitchen sink, or in other damp places. Heat or moisture may cause the medicine to break down.
- Do not keep outdated medicine or medicine no longer needed. Be sure that any discarded medicine is out of the reach of children.

Precautions While Using This Medicine

It is very important that your doctor check your progress at regular visits. This will allow your doctor to see if the

medicine is working properly to lower your cholesterol and triglyceride levels and to decide if you should continue to take it.

Do not stop taking this medication without first checking with your doctor. When you stop taking this medicine, your blood cholesterol levels may increase again. Your doctor may want you to follow a special diet to help prevent this from happening.

Side Effects of This Medicine

Along with its needed effects, a medicine may cause some unwanted effects. Although not all of these side effects may occur, if they do occur they may need medical attention.

Check with your doctor immediately if any of the following side effects occur:

Rare
    Cough or hoarseness; fever or chills; lower back or side pain; painful or difficult urination; stomach pain (severe) with nausea and vomiting

Check with your doctor as soon as possible if either of the following side effects occurs:

Rare
    Muscle pain; unusual tiredness or weakness

Other side effects may occur that usually do not need medical attention. These side effects may go away during treatment as your body adjusts to the medicine. However, check with your doctor if any of the following side effects continue or are bothersome:

More common
    Stomach pain, gas, or heartburn
Less common
    Diarrhea; nausea or vomiting; skin rash

Other side effects not listed above may also occur in some patients. If you notice any other effects, check with your doctor.

Revised: 05/24/93
Interim revision: 06/28/95; 08/12/98

GEMTUZUMAB OZOGAMICIN
Systemic†—INTRODUCTORY VERSION

Commonly used brand name(s):

In the U.S.—
    Mylotarg

†Not commercially available in Canada.

Description

Gemtuzumab (gem-TOO-ze-mab) is a monoclonal antibody. It is used to treat a certain type of leukemia which has recurred in patients who are 60 years of age or older. Gemtuzumab is an alternative to chemotherapy for these patients.

This medicine is to be administered only by or under the immediate supervision of your doctor. It is available in the following dosage form:

Parenteral
- Injection (U.S.)

Before Using This Medicine

In deciding to use a medicine, the risks of taking the medicine must be weighed against the good it will do. This is a decision you and your doctor will make. For gemtuzumab, the following should be considered:

Allergies—Tell your doctor if you have ever had any unusual or allergic reaction to gemtuzumab, anti-CD33 antibody, or calicheamicin derivatives. Also tell your doctor and pharmacist if you are allergic to any other substances, such as foods, preservatives, or dyes.

Pregnancy—Gemtuzumab may cause harm to the fetus when administered during pregnancy. There are no adequate, well-controlled studies in pregnant women. You should avoid becoming pregnant while receiving gemtuzumab. However, this medicine may be needed in serious diseases or other situations that threaten the mother's life. Be sure you have discussed this with your doctor.

Breast-feeding—It is not known if gemtuzumab passes into the breast milk. However, due to potential serious side effects in nursing babies from gemtuzumab, a decision should be made whether to stop nursing or to stop the drug.

Children—Studies on this medicine have been done only in adult patients, and there is no specific information comparing use of gemtuzumab in children with use in other age groups.

Older adults—Many medicines have not been studied specifically in older people. Therefore, it may not be known whether they work exactly the same way they do in younger adults or if they cause different side effects or problems in older people. There is no specific information comparing use of gemtuzumab in the elderly with use in other age groups. However, laboratory values associated with liver problems were observed more often in patients 60 years old or older.

Other medicines—Although certain medicines should not be used together at all, in other cases two different medicines may be used together even if an interaction might occur. In these cases, your doctor may want to change the dose, or other precautions may be necessary. When you are taking gemtuzumab, it is especially important that your doctor or pharmacist know if you are taking any of the following:

- Alpha interferons (e.g., Intron A, Roferon-A) or
- Amphotericin B by injection (e.g., Fungizone) or
- Antineoplastics, other (cancer medicine) or
- Antithyroid agents (medicine for overactive thyroid) or
- Azathioprine (e.g., Imuran) or
- Chloramphenicol (e.g., Chloromycetin) or
- Colchicine or
- Cyclophosphamide (e.g., Cytoxan) or
- Flucytosine (e.g., Ancoban) or
- Ganciclovir (e.g., Cytovene) or
- Mercaptopurine (e.g., Purinethol) or
- Methotrexate (e.g., Rheumatrex) or
- Plicamycin (e.g., Mithracin) or
- Zidovudine (e.g., AZT, Retrovir)—Concurrent use of these agents with gemtuzumab increases the risk of infection

Other medical problems—The presence of other medical problems may affect the use of gemtuzumab. Make sure you tell your doctor if you have any other medical problems, especially:

- Chickenpox (including recent exposure) or
- Herpes zoster (shingles)—Risk of severe disease affecting other parts of the body
- Infection—Risk increased by gemtuzumab
- Liver disease—May be worsened by gemtuzumab

Proper Use of This Medicine

Dosing—The dose of gemtuzumab will be different for different patients. The dose that is used may depend on a number of things, including your size. Gemtuzumab is usually given by a doctor or nurse in the hospital or outpatient clinic. If you have any questions about the proper dose of gemtuzumab, ask your doctor.

Precautions While Using This Medicine

It is very important that your doctor check you at regular visits to make sure this medication is working properly and to check for any unwanted effects.

While you are being treated with gemtuzumab, and after you stop treatment with it, *do not have any immunizations (vaccinations) without your doctor's approval.* Gemtuzumab may lower your body's resistance and there is a chance you might get the infection the immunization is meant to prevent. In addition, other persons living in your household should not take oral polio vaccine since there is a chance they could pass the polio virus on to you. Also, avoid persons who have taken oral polio vaccine within the last several months. Do not get close to them, and do not stay in the same room with them for very long. If you cannot take these precautions, you should consider wearing a protective face mask that covers the nose and mouth.

Gemtuzumab can temporarily lower the number of white blood cells in your blood, increasing the chance of getting an infection. It can also lower the number of platelets, which are necessary for proper blood clotting. If this occurs, there are certain precautions you can take, especially when your blood count is low, to reduce the risk of infection or bleeding:

- If you can, avoid people with infections. *Check with your doctor immediately* if you think you are getting an infection or if you get a fever or chills, cough or hoarseness, lower back or side pain, or painful or difficult urination.
- *Check with your doctor immediately* if you notice any unusual bleeding or bruising; black, tarry stools; blood in urine or stools; or pinpoint red spots on your skin.
- Be careful when using a regular toothbrush, dental floss, or toothpick. Your medical doctor, dentist, or nurse may recommend other ways to clean your teeth and gums. Check with your medical doctor before having any dental work done.
- Do not touch your eyes or the inside of your nose unless you have just washed your hands and have not touched anything else in the meantime.
- Be careful not to cut yourself when you are using sharp objects such as a safety razor or fingernail or toenail cutters.
- Avoid contact sports or other situations where bruising or injury could occur.

Side Effects of This Medicine

Along with its needed effects, a medicine may cause some unwanted effects. Although not all of these side effects may occur, if they do occur they may need medical attention.

Black, tarry stools; bloating or swelling of face, arms, hands, lower legs, or feet; blood in stools or urine; bluish color of fingernails, lips, skin, palms, or nail beds; blurred vision; burning or stinging of skin; chest pain; chills; confusion; convulsions (seizures); cough or hoarseness; cracked lips; decrease or increase in urine; diarrhea; difficulty in swallowing; dizziness; dry mouth; excessive sweating; fainting; fast heartbeat; fatigue; fever; flushed, dry skin; fruit-like breath odor; headache, sudden and severe; heavy, nonmenstrual vaginal bleeding; inability to speak; increased thirst or hunger; irregular heartbeat; light-headedness; lower back pain or side pain; loss of appetite; mood changes; muscle pain or cramps; muscle trembling or twitching; nausea or vomiting; numbness or tingling in hands, feet, or lips; pain or burning while urinating; painful cold sores or blisters on lips, nose, eyes, or genitals; pale skin; persistent bleeding or oozing from puncture sites, mouth, or nose; palpitations; pinpoint red spots on skin; pounding in the ears; red or purplish patches or spots on skin; rapid, shallow breathing; rapid weight gain; severe or continuing dull nervousness; shortness of breath; slurred speech; sneezing; sore throat; sores, ulcers, or white spots on lips, tongue, or inside mouth; stomachache; swelling or inflammation of the mouth; swollen glands; temporary blindness; tightness in chest; tingling of hands or feet; troubled breathing, exertional; unexplained nosebleeds; unusual bleeding or bruising; unusual tiredness or weakness; unusual weight gain or loss; weakness in arm and/or leg on one side of the body, sudden and severe; wheezing; yellow eyes or skin

Other side effects may occur that usually do not need medical attention. These side effects may go away during treatment as your body adjusts to the medicine. However, check with your doctor if any of the following side effects continue or are bothersome.

More common

Acid or sour stomach; belching; difficulty in moving; dry, red, hot, or irritated skin; full or bloated feeling or pressure in the stomach; heartburn; indigestion; lack or loss of strength; muscle pain or stiffness; pain, swelling, or redness in joints; runny, stuffy nose; stomach discomfort upset; swelling of abdominal or stomach area; trouble in sleeping

Other side effects not listed above may also occur in some patients. If you notice any other effects, check with your doctor.

Developed: 08/28/2000

GENTAMICIN   Ophthalmic

Commonly used brand name(s):

In the U.S.—

Garamycin	Gentafair
Genoptic Liquifilm	Gentak
Genoptic S.O.P.	Ocu-Mycin
Gentacidin	Spectro-Genta

Generic name product may be available.

In Canada—

Alcomicin
Garamycin

Another commonly used name is gentamycin.

Description

Gentamicin (jen-ta-MYE-sin) belongs to the family of medicines called antibiotics. Gentamicin ophthalmic preparations are used to treat infections of the eye.

Gentamicin is available only with your doctor's prescription, in the following dosage forms:

Ophthalmic
- Ophthalmic ointment (U.S. and Canada)
- Ophthalmic solution (eye drops) (U.S. and Canada)

Before Using This Medicine

In deciding to use a medicine, the risks of using the medicine must be weighed against the good it will do. This is a decision you and your doctor will make. For ophthalmic gentamicin, the following should be considered:

Allergies—Tell your doctor if you have ever had any unusual or allergic reaction to this medicine or to any related antibiotic, such as amikacin (e.g., Amikin), gentamicin by injection (e.g., Garamycin), kanamycin (e.g., Kantrex), neomycin (e.g., Mycifradin), netilmicin (e.g., Netromycin), streptomycin, or tobramycin (e.g., Nebcin). Also tell your health care professional if you are allergic to any other substances, such as preservatives.

Pregnancy—Gentamicin ophthalmic preparations have not been shown to cause birth defects or other problems in humans.

Breast-feeding—Gentamicin ophthalmic preparations have not been reported to cause problems in nursing babies.

Children—There is no specific information comparing use of this medicine in babies up to one month of age with use in other age groups.

Older adults—Many medicines have not been studied specifically in older people. Therefore, it may not be known whether they work exactly the same way they do in younger adults or if they cause different side effects or problems in older people. There is no specific information comparing use of this medicine in the elderly with use in other age groups.

Proper Use of This Medicine

For patients using the *eye drop form* of this medicine:

- The bottle is only partially full to provide proper drop control.
- To use:
  - First, wash your hands. Tilt the head back and with the index finger of one hand, press gently on the skin just beneath the lower eyelid and pull the lower eyelid away from the eye to make a space. Drop the medicine into this space. Let go of the eyelid and gently close the eyes. Do not blink. Keep the eyes closed for 1 or 2 minutes, to allow the medicine to come into contact with the infection.
- If you think you did not get the drop of medicine into your eye properly, use another drop.
- Avoid wearing contact lenses during treatment

- To keep the medicine as germ-free as possible, do not touch the applicator tip to any surface (including the eye). Also, keep the container tightly closed.

For patients using the *eye ointment form* of this medicine:
- First, wash your hands. Tilt the head back and with the index finger of one hand, press gently on the skin just beneath the lower eyelid and pull the lower eyelid away from the eye to make a space. Squeeze a thin strip of ointment into this space. A 1-cm (approximately ⅓-inch) strip of ointment is usually enough unless otherwise directed by your doctor. Let go of the eyelid and gently close the eyes and keep them closed for 1 or 2 minutes, to allow the medicine to come into contact with the infection.
- To keep the medicine as germ-free as possible, do not touch the applicator tip to any surface (including the eye). After using gentamicin eye ointment, wipe the tip of the ointment tube with a clean tissue and keep the tube tightly closed.

To help clear up your infection completely, *keep using this medicine for the full time of treatment*, even if your symptoms have disappeared. *Do not miss any doses.*

Dosing—The dose of ophthalmic gentamicin will be different for different patients. *Follow your doctor's orders or the directions on the label*. The following information includes only the average doses of ophthalmic gentamicin. *If your dose is different, do not change it* unless your doctor tells you to do so.
- For *ophthalmic ointment* dosage form:
  —For eye infections:
  - Adults and children—Use every eight to twelve hours.
- For *ophthalmic solution (eye drops)* dosage form:
  —For mild to moderate eye infections:
  - Adults and children—One to two drops every four hours.
  —For severe eye infections:
  - Adults and children—One to two drops as often as once every hour as directed by your doctor.

Missed dose—If you do miss a dose of this medicine, apply it as soon as possible. However, if it is almost time for your next dose, skip the missed dose and go back to your regular dosing schedule.

Storage—To store this medicine:
- Keep out of the reach of children.
- Store away from heat and direct light.
- Keep the medicine from freezing.
- Do not keep outdated medicine or medicine no longer needed. Be sure that any discarded medicine is out of the reach of children.

Precautions While Using This Medicine

If your symptoms do not improve within a few days, or if they become worse, check with your doctor.

Side Effects of This Medicine

Along with its needed effects, a medicine may cause some unwanted effects. Although not all of these side effects may occur, if they do occur they may need medical attention.

Check with your doctor immediately if any of the following side effects occur:
  Less common
    Itching, redness, swelling, or other sign of irritation not present before use of this medicine; redness of eye, eyelid, or inner lining of eyelid
  Rare
    Black, tarry stools; blood in urine or stools; or unusual bleeding or swelling; blurred vision, eye pain, sensitivity to light, and/or tearing; seeing, hearing, or feeling things that are not there; hallucinations

Other side effects may occur that usually do not need medical attention. These side effects may go away during treatment as your body adjusts to the medicine. However, check with your doctor if any of the following side effects continue or are bothersome:
  Less common
    Burning or stinging

After application, eye ointments usually cause your vision to blur for a few minutes.

Other side effects not listed above may also occur in some patients. If you notice any other effects, check with your doctor.

Revised: 07/19/2000

GENTAMICIN   Otic

Commonly used brand name(s):

In Canada—
  Garamycin Otic Solution

Description

Gentamicin (jen-ta-MYE-sin) belongs to the family of medicines called antibiotics. Gentamicin otic preparations are used to treat infections of the ear canal.

Gentamicin is available only with your doctor's prescription, in the following dosage form:
  Otic
  - Solution (Canada)

Before Using This Medicine

In deciding to use a medicine, the risks of using the medicine must be weighed against the good it will do. This is a decision you and your doctor will make. For gentamicin otic preparations, the following should be considered:

Allergies—Tell your doctor if you have ever had any unusual or allergic reaction to this medicine or to any related antibiotics such as amikacin (e.g., Amikin), gentamicin by injection (e.g., Garamycin), kanamycin (e.g., Kantrex), neomycin (e.g., Mycifradin), netilmicin (e.g., Netromycin), streptomycin, or tobramycin (e.g., Nebcin). Also tell your health care professional if you are allergic to any other substances, such as preservatives.

Pregnancy—Studies with gentamicin have not been done in pregnant women. However, studies in animals have shown that gentamicin causes decreased kidney development, kidney weight, and overall body weight. Before taking this medicine, make sure your doctor knows if you are pregnant or if you may become pregnant.

Breast-feeding—Gentamicin otic preparations have not been reported to cause problems in nursing babies.

Children—There is no specific information comparing use of gentamicin otic solution in children up to 6 years of age with use in other age groups.

Older adults—Many medicines have not been studied specifically in older people. Therefore, it may not be known whether they work exactly the same way they do in younger adults. Although there is no specific information comparing use of this medicine in the elderly with use in other age groups, this medicine is not expected to cause different side effects or problems in older people than it does in younger adults.

Other medical problems—The presence of other medical problems may affect the use of gentamicin otic preparations. Make sure you tell your doctor if you have any other medical problems, especially:

- Any other ear infection or problem (including punctured or absent eardrum)—Use of gentamicin otic preparations in persons with this condition may lead to systemic absorption, and increase the chance of side effects

Proper Use of This Medicine

To use:
- Lie down or tilt the head so that the infected ear faces up. Gently pull the earlobe up and back for adults (down and back for children) to straighten the ear canal. Drop the medicine into the ear canal. Keep the ear facing up for about 1 or 2 minutes to allow the medicine to come into contact with the infection. A sterile cotton plug may be gently inserted into the ear opening to prevent the medicine from leaking out.
- To keep the medicine as germ-free as possible, do not touch the applicator tip to any surface (including the ear). Also, keep the container tightly closed.

To help clear up your infection completely, *keep using this medicine for the full time of treatment*, even if your symptoms have disappeared. *Do not miss any doses.*

Dosing—The dose of gentamicin otic will be different for different patients. *Follow your doctor's orders or the directions on the label*. The following information includes only the average doses of gentamicin otic. *If your dose is different, do not change it* unless your doctor tells you to do so.

- For *ear drops* dosage form:
  —For ear infections:
  - Adults and children 6 years of age and older—Place three or four drops in the infected ear three times a day.
  - Children younger than 6 years of age—Use and dose must be determined by your doctor.

Missed dose—If you miss a dose of this medicine, apply it as soon as possible. However, if it is almost time for your next dose, skip the missed dose and go back to your regular dosing schedule.

Storage—To store this medicine:
- Keep out of the reach of children.
- Store away from heat and direct light.

- Keep the medicine from freezing.
- Do not keep outdated medicine or medicine no longer needed. Be sure that any discarded medicine is out of the reach of children.

Precautions While Using This Medicine

If your symptoms do not improve within a few days, or if they become worse, check with your doctor.

Side Effects of This Medicine

Along with its needed effects, a medicine may cause some unwanted effects. Although not all of these side effects may occur, if they do occur they may need medical attention.

Check with your doctor immediately if any of the following side effects occur:
  Less common
    Itching, redness, swelling, or other sign of irritation not present before use of this medicine

Other side effects may occur that usually do not need medical attention. These side effects may go away during treatment as your body adjusts to the medicine. However, check with your doctor if either of the following side effects continues or is bothersome:
  Less common
    Burning or stinging in the ear

Other side effects not listed above may also occur in some patients. If you notice any other effects, check with your doctor.

Revised: 6/09/99

GENTIAN VIOLET   Topical†

†Not commercially available in Canada.

Description

Gentian violet (JEN-shun VYE-oh-let) belongs to the group of medicines called antifungals. Topical gentian violet is used to treat some types of fungus infections inside the mouth (thrush) and of the skin.

Gentian violet is available without a prescription; however, your doctor may have special instructions on the proper use of gentian violet for your medical condition.

Gentian violet is available in the following dosage form:

Topical
- Solution (U.S.)

Before Using This Medicine

If you are using this medicine without a prescription, carefully read and follow any precautions on the label. For gentian violet, the following should be considered:

Allergies—Tell your doctor if you have ever had any unusual or allergic reaction to gentian violet. Also tell your health care professional if you are allergic to any other substances, such as preservatives or dyes.

Pregnancy—Gentian violet topical solution has not been shown to cause birth defects or other problems in humans.

Breast-feeding—Gentian violet topical solution has not been reported to cause problems in nursing babies.

Children—Although there is no specific information comparing use of this medicine in children with use in other age groups, this medicine is not expected to cause different side effects or problems in children than it does in adults.

Older adults—Many medicines have not been studied specifically in older people. Therefore, it may not be known whether they work exactly the same way they do in younger adults. Although there is no specific information comparing use of this medicine in the elderly with use in other age groups, this medicine is not expected to cause different side effects or problems in older people than it does in younger adults.

Other medical problems—The presence of other medical problems may affect the use of gentian violet. Make sure you tell your doctor if you have any other medical problems, especially:

- Ulcerative skin condition on the face—Use of gentian violet may cause tattooing of the area

Proper Use of This Medicine

Using a cotton swab, apply enough gentian violet to cover only the affected area.

If you are applying this medicine to affected areas in the mouth, avoid swallowing any of the medicine.

If you are using this medicine in a child's mouth, make sure you understand exactly how to apply it so that it is not swallowed. If you have any questions about this, check with your health care professional.

Do not apply an occlusive dressing (airtight covering, such as kitchen plastic wrap) over this medicine. It may cause irritation of the skin.

To help clear up your infection completely, *keep using this medicine for the full time of treatment*, even if your condition has improved. *Do not miss any doses.*

Dosing—The dose of gentian violet will be different for different patients. *Follow your doctor's orders or the directions on the label.* The following information includes only the average dose of gentian violet. *If your dose is different, do not change it* unless your doctor tells you to do so.

- For *topical solution* dosage form:
  —For fungus infections:
    - Adults and children—Apply to the affected area(s) of the skin two or three times a day for three days.

Missed dose—If you miss a dose of this medicine, apply it as soon as possible. However, if it is almost time for your next dose, skip the missed dose and go back to your regular dosing schedule.

Storage—To store this medicine:

- Keep out of the reach of children.
- Store away from heat and direct light.
- Keep the medicine from freezing.
- Do not keep outdated medicine or medicine no longer needed. Be sure that any discarded medicine is out of the reach of children.

Precautions While Using This Medicine

Gentian violet will stain the skin and clothing. Avoid getting the medicine on your clothes.

Side Effects of This Medicine

Along with its needed effects, a medicine may cause some unwanted effects. Although not all of these side effects may occur, if they do occur they may need medical attention.

Check with your doctor as soon as possible if the following side effect occurs:

Skin irritation not present before use of this medicine

Other side effects not listed above may also occur in some patients. If you notice any other effects, check with your doctor.

Revised: 06/23/92
Interim revision: 06/22/94

GLATIRAMER ACETATE   Systemic

Commonly used brand name(s):

In the U.S.—
Copaxone

Another commonly used name is copolymer-1.

Description

Glatiramer acetate (gla-TIR-a-mer ASS-a-tate) is used in the treatment of the relapsing-remitting form of multiple sclerosis (MS). This medicine will not cure MS, but may extend the time between relapses.

This medicine is available only with your doctor's prescription, in the following dosage form(s):

Parenteral
- Injection (U.S.)

Before Using This Medicine

In deciding to use a medicine, the risks of taking the medicine must be weighed against the good it will do. This is a decision you and your doctor will make. For glatiramer acetate, the following should be considered:

Allergies—Tell your doctor if you have ever had any unusual or allergic reaction to glatiramer acetate. Also tell your health care professional if you are allergic to any other substances, such as foods, preservatives, or dyes.

Pregnancy—Glatiramer acetate has not been studied in pregnant women. However, this medicine has not been shown to cause birth defects or other problems in animal studies.

Breast-feeding—It is not known whether glatiramer acetate passes into the breast milk. Although most medicines pass into breast milk in small amounts, many of them may be used safely while breast-feeding. Mothers who are taking this medicine and who wish to breast-feed should discuss this with their doctor.

Children—Studies on this medicine have been done only in adult patients, and there is no specific information comparing use of glatiramer acetate in children with use in other age groups.

Older adults—Many medicines have not been studied specifically in older people. Therefore, it may not be known whether they work exactly the same way they do in younger adults or if they cause different side effects or problems in older people. There is no specific information comparing the use of glatiramer acetate in the elderly with use in other age groups.

Other medicines—Although certain medicines should not be used together at all, in other cases two different medicines may be used together even if an interaction might occur. In these cases, your doctor may want to change the dose, or other precautions may be necessary. Tell your health care professional if you are taking any other prescription or nonprescription (over-the-counter [OTC]) medicine.

Other medical problems—The presence of other medical problems may affect the use of glatiramer acetate. Make sure you tell your doctor if you have any other medical problems.

Proper Use of This Medicine

Use this medicine exactly as directed by your doctor in order to help your condition as much as possible.

Special patient directions come with glatiramer acetate injection. *Read the directions carefully before using the medicine.*

It is important to follow several steps to prepare your glatiramer acetate injection correctly. Before injecting the medication, you need to:

- Gather the items you will need on a clean cloth or towel in a well-lighted area.
- Wash your hands with soap and water. Do not touch your hair or skin afterwards.
- Remove the plastic cover from the glatiramer acetate vial and use an alcohol swab to wipe the rubber top. Do not touch the rubber top after it has been wiped.
- Remove the plastic cover from the diluent vial and use a fresh alcohol swab to wipe the rubber top. Do not touch the rubber top after it has been wiped.
- Let both rubber tops dry for a few seconds.

It is important that you do not touch the tops of the vials or the needles in order to keep everything sterile. Also, use only the diluent (sterile water) provided with the glatiramer acetate to dilute the medicine for injection.

To mix the water and the powder:
- Remove one 3-milliliter (3-mL) syringe from its protective wrapper. Make sure the needle is tightly in place by slightly twisting the plastic cover over the needle. Do not touch the needle itself.
- Hold the syringe in one hand and pull the plastic cover straight off the needle with the other hand. Do not touch the needle.
- Pull the plunger of the syringe back to draw 1.1 mL of air into the syringe. Insert the needle through the rubber top of the diluent (sterile water) vial while it is upright and push the plunger all the way in to inject 1.1 mL of air into the vial.
- Turn the vial upside down using one hand and make sure the tip of the needle is covered by solution. With

your other hand, pull back the plunger to withdraw 1.1 mL of diluent into the syringe.
- Pull the syringe out of the vial, and place the vial on the clean surface.
- With the vial of glatiramer acetate still on the table, insert the needle of the syringe through the rubber top and slowly inject the diluent into the vial. The best way is to do this is to point the needle toward the inside wall of the vial, instead of injecting the diluent directly onto the cake of medicine. Remove the needle and syringe from the glatiramer acetate vial, and put the plastic cover back on the needle.
- Gently swirl the vial until all the medication dissolves. Do not shake the vial. Check the solution to make sure it is clear. Do not use the medicine if you can see anything solid in the solution or if the solution is cloudy. Let the vial sit and warm up for about 5 minutes.

To prepare the injection syringe:
- Remove one 1-mL syringe from its protective wrapper. Make sure the needle is tightly in place by slightly twisting the plastic cover over the needle. Remove the cover from the needle, but do not touch the needle itself.
- Pull the plunger back to the 1 mL mark.
- Insert the needle into the rubber top of the glatiramer acetate vial and push the plunger all the way in to inject the air.
- Then turn the vial upside down and slowly withdraw the solution into the syringe to the 1 mL mark. Make sure the tip of the needle is below the level of the solution.
- While still holding the vial and syringe upside down and the needle still in the vial, check the syringe for air bubbles.
- Tap the side of the syringe to make the air bubbles float to the top of the syringe.
- Inject the air back into the vial. You will probably need to draw a little more solution into the syringe to bring the level back to the 1 mL mark.
- Make sure your dose is correct by checking that the position of the plunger is at the 1 mL mark.
- Then remove the needle from the vial, put the plastic cover back on the needle, and place it on a clean surface.

To give yourself the injection:

Before you self-inject the glatiramer acetate dose, decide where you will inject yourself. There are seven injection sites on your body, and you should not use any site more than once each week. Marking a calendar will help you keep track of the sites you have used each day. Try to be consistent and give yourself the injection at the same time each day. Choose a time when you feel strongest.

- Clean the injection site with a fresh alcohol wipe, and let it dry.
- Pick up the 1-mL syringe you already filled with glatiramer acetate. Hold the syringe as you would a pencil, using the hand you write with. Remove the plastic cover from the needle, but do not touch the needle itself.
- Pinch about a 2-inch fold of skin between your thumb and index finger.
- Insert the needle into the 2-inch fold of skin. It may help to steady you hand by resting the heel of your hand against your body.
- When the needle is all the way in, release the fold of skin.

- Inject the medicine by holding the syringe steady while pushing down on the plunger. The injection should take just a few seconds.
- Pull the needle straight out.
- Press a dry clean cotton ball on the injection site for a few seconds, but do not massage it.
- Put the plastic cover back on the needle.

To dispose of needles and syringes:

Needles, syringes and vials should be used for only one injection. *Place all used syringes, needles, and vials in a hard-walled plastic container,* such as a liquid laundry detergent container. Keep the cover of this container tight and out of the reach of children. When the container is full, check with your physician or nurse about proper disposal, as laws vary from state to state.

Dosing—The dose of glatiramer acetate will be different for different patients. *Follow your doctor's orders or the directions on the label.* The following information includes only the average doses of glatiramer acetate. *If your dose is different, do not change it* unless your doctor tells you to do so.

For *injection* dosage form:
—For multiple sclerosis (MS):
- Adults—20 milligrams (mg) once a day, given subcutaneously (under the skin).
- Children—Use and dose must be determined by your doctor.

Missed dose—If you miss a dose of this medicine, take the missed dose as soon as possible. However, if you do not remember the missed dose until the next day, skip the missed dose and go back to your regular dosing schedule. Do not double doses.

Storage—To store this medicine:
- Keep out of the reach of children.
- Store away from direct light.
- Store the vials of glatiramer acetate in the refrigerator. If refrigeration is not available, the vials may be kept for up to 1 week at room temperature, as long as the temperature does not go above 86 °F.
- Store the vials of diluent at room temperature, as long as the temperature does not go above 86 °F.
- Do not keep outdated medicine or medicine no longer needed. Be sure that any discarded medicine is out of the reach of children.

Precautions While Using This Medicine

Do not stop using this medicine without first checking with your doctor.

Side Effects of This Medicine

Along with its needed effects, a medicine may cause some unwanted effects. Although not all of these side effects may occur, if they do occur they may need medical attention.

The most commonly occurring side effects of glatiramer acetate are redness, pain, inflammation, itching, or a lump at the site of the injection. Some patients have reported a rare reaction that started immediately after the injection and consisted of flushing, chest tightness with racing or pounding heartbeat, anxiety, and difficulty in breathing. The symptoms of this reaction generally lasted approximately fifteen minutes and resolved without any further problems. However, if you inject glatiramer acetate and experience dizziness, hives and itching, sweating, chest pain, difficulty in breathing, or other uncomfortable changes in your general health, call your doctor immediately. If symptoms become severe, or you cannot reach your doctor, call 911 or the appropriate emergency phone number in your area for assistance.

Also, check with your doctor as soon as possible if any of the following side effects occur:

More common
Anxiety; bleeding, hard lump, hives or welts, itching, pain, redness, or swelling at the place of injection; chest pain; excessive muscle tone; flushing; irregular or pounding heartbeat; joint pain; neck pain; swelling or puffiness of face; swollen lymph glands; troubled breathing; vaginal yeast infection

Less common
Agitation; bloating or swelling; chills; confusion; fainting; fever; infections; migraine; muscle aches; pain; purple spots under the skin; skin rash; small lumps under the skin; spasm of throat; strong urge to urinate; swelling of fingers, arms, feet, or legs; tightness in chest or wheezing

Rare
Back pain; blood in urine; continuous, uncontrolled back-and-forth and/or rolling eye movements; decreased sexual ability; diarrhea; ear pain; fast breathing; fast or racing heartbeat; high blood pressure; irritation of mouth and tongue (thrush); loss of appetite; menstrual pain or changes; sensation of motion, usually whirling, either of oneself or of one's surroundings; speech problems; suspicious Papanicolaou test (Pap test) results; vision problems

Other side effects may occur that usually do not need medical attention. These side effects may go away during treatment as your body adjusts to the medicine. However, check with your doctor if any of the following side effects continue or are bothersome:

More common
Increased sweating; nausea; trembling; unusual tiredness or weakness; vomiting

Less common
Runny nose; weight gain

Other side effects not listed above may also occur in some patients. If you notice any other effects, check with your doctor.

Developed: 05/21/98

GLUCAGON   Systemic

Commonly used brand name(s):

In the U.S.—
Glucagon Diagnostic Kit
Glucagon Emergency Kit
Glucagon Emergency Kit for Low Blood Sugar
Generic name product may be available.

In Canada—
Glucagon Emergency Kit

Description

Glucagon (GLOO-ka-gon) belongs to the group of medicines called hormones. It is an emergency medicine used to treat severe hypoglycemia (low blood sugar) in patients with diabetes who have passed out or cannot take some form of sugar by mouth.

Glucagon is also used during x-ray tests of the stomach and bowels to improve test results by relaxing the muscles of the stomach and bowels. This also makes the testing more comfortable for the patient.

Glucagon also may be used for other conditions as determined by your doctor.

Glucagon is available only with your doctor's prescription, in the following dosage form:

Parenteral
  • Injection (U.S. and Canada)

Before Using This Medicine

In deciding to use a medicine, the risks of taking the medicine must be weighed against the good it will do. This is a decision you and your doctor will make. For glucagon, the following should be considered:

Allergies—Tell your doctor if you have ever had any unusual or allergic reaction to glucagon or to beef or pork products, including insulin. Also, tell your health care professional if you are allergic to any other substances, such as foods, preservatives, or dyes.

Pregnancy—Glucagon has not been studied in pregnant women. However, glucagon has not been shown to cause birth defects or other problems in animal studies.

Breast-feeding—It is not known whether glucagon passes into breast milk. However, this medicine has not been reported to cause problems in nursing babies.

Children—This medicine has been tested in children and, in effective doses, has not been shown to cause different side effects or problems than it does in adults.

Older adults—Many medicines have not been studied specifically in older people. Therefore, it may not be known whether they work exactly the same way they do in younger adults. Although there is no specific information comparing use of glucagon in the elderly with use in other age groups, it is not expected to cause different side effects or problems in older people than it does in younger adults.

Other medicines—Although certain medicines should not be used together at all, in other cases two different medicines may be used together even if an interaction might occur. In these cases, your doctor may want to change the doses or other precautions may be necessary. Tell your health care professional if you are using any other prescription or nonprescription (over-the-counter [OTC]) medicine.

Other medical problems—The presence of other medical problems may affect the use of glucagon. Make sure you tell your doctor if you have any other medical problems, especially:
  • Diabetes mellitus—When glucagon is used for test or x-ray procedures in patients with diabetes that is well-controlled, a rise in blood sugar may occur; otherwise, glucagon is an important part of the management of diabetes because it is used to treat hypoglycemia (low blood sugar)
  • Insulinoma (tumors of the pancreas gland that make too much insulin) (or history of)—Blood sugar concentrations may decrease

  • Pheochromocytoma—Glucagon can cause high blood pressure

Proper Use of This Medicine

Glucagon is an emergency medicine and must be used only as directed by your doctor. *Make sure that you and a member of your family or a friend understand exactly when and how to use this medicine before it is needed.*

Glucagon is packaged in a kit with a vial of powder containing the medicine and a syringe filled with liquid to mix with the medicine. *Directions for mixing and injecting the medicine are in the package. Read the directions carefully* and ask your health care professional for additional explanation, if necessary.

Glucagon should not be mixed after the expiration date printed on the kit and on one vial. *Check the date regularly and replace the medicine before it expires.* The printed expiration date does not apply after mixing, when any unused portion must be discarded.

Dosing—The dose of glucagon will be different for different patients. *Follow your doctor's orders or the directions on the label.* The following information includes only the average doses of glucagon. *If your dose is different, do not change it* unless your doctor tells you to do so.
  • As an *emergency treatment for hypoglycemia:*
    —Adults and children weighing 20 kilograms (kg) (44 pounds) or more: 1 milligram (mg). The dose may be repeated after fifteen minutes if necessary.
    —Children weighing up to 20 kg (44 pounds): 0.5 mg or 20 to 30 micrograms (mcg) per kg (9.1 to 13.6 mcg per pound) of body weight. The dose may be repeated after fifteen minutes if necessary.

Storage—To store this medicine:
  • Keep out of the reach of children.
  • Store away from heat and direct light.
  • Store the unmixed medicine at room temperature.
  • Do not store the unmixed medicine in the bathroom, near the kitchen sink, or in other damp places. Heat or moisture may cause the medicine to break down.
  • Do not keep outdated medicine or medicine no longer needed. Be sure that any discarded medicine is out of the reach of children.

Precautions While Using This Medicine

Patients with diabetes should be aware of the symptoms of hypoglycemia (low blood sugar). These symptoms may develop in a very short time and may result from:
  • using too much insulin ("insulin reaction") or as a side effect from oral antidiabetic medicines.
  • delaying or missing a scheduled snack or meal.
  • sickness (especially with vomiting or diarrhea).
  • exercising more than usual.

Unless corrected, hypoglycemia will lead to unconsciousness, convulsions (seizures), and possibly death. Early symptoms of hypoglycemia include: anxious feeling, behavior change similar to being drunk, blurred vision, cold sweats, confusion, cool pale skin, difficulty in concentrating, drowsiness, excessive hunger, fast heartbeat, headache, nausea, nervousness, nightmares, restless sleep, shakiness, slurred speech, and unusual tiredness or weakness.

Symptoms of hypoglycemia can differ from person to person. It is important that you learn your own signs of low blood sugar so that you can treat it quickly. It is a good idea also to check your blood sugar to confirm that it is low.

You should know what to do if symptoms of low blood sugar occur. Eating or drinking something containing sugar when symptoms of low blood sugar first appear will usually prevent them from getting worse, and will probably make the use of glucagon unnecessary. Good sources of sugar include glucose tablets or gel, corn syrup, honey, sugar cubes or table sugar (dissolved in water), fruit juice, or nondiet soft drinks. If a meal is not scheduled soon (1 hour or less), you should also eat a light snack, such as crackers and cheese or half a sandwich or drink a glass of milk to keep your blood sugar from going down again. You should not eat hard candy or mints because the sugar will not get into your blood stream quickly enough. You also should not eat foods high in fat such as chocolate because the fat slows down the sugar entering the blood stream. After 10 to 20 minutes, check your blood sugar again to make sure it is not still too low.

Tell someone to take you to your doctor or to a hospital right away if the symptoms do not improve after eating or drinking a sweet food. Do not try to drive yourself.

If severe symptoms such as convulsions (seizures) or unconsciousness occur, the patient with diabetes should not be given anything to eat or drink. There is a chance that he or she could choke from not swallowing correctly. Glucagon should be administered and the patient's doctor should be called at once.

If it becomes necessary to inject glucagon, a family member or friend should know the following:

- *After the injection, turn the patient on his or her left side.* Glucagon may cause some patients to vomit and this position will reduce the possibility of choking.
- The patient should become conscious in less than 15 minutes after glucagon is injected, but if not, a second dose may be given. *Get the patient to a doctor or to hospital emergency care as soon as possible* because being unconscious too long can be harmful.
- When the patient is conscious and can swallow, give him or her some form of sugar. Glucagon is not effective for much longer than 1½ hours and is used only until the patient is able to swallow. Fruit juice, corn syrup, honey, and sugar cubes or table sugar (dissolved in water) all work quickly. Then, if a snack or meal is not scheduled for an hour or more, the patient should also eat some crackers and cheese or half a sandwich, or drink a glass of milk. This will prevent hypoglycemia from occurring again before the next meal or snack.
- The patient or caregiver should continue to monitor the patient's blood sugar. For about 3 to 4 hours after the patient regains consciousness, the blood sugar should be checked every hour.
- *If nausea and vomiting prevent the patient from swallowing some form of sugar for an hour after glucagon is given, medical help should be obtained.*

Keep your doctor informed of any hypoglycemic episodes or use of glucagon even if the symptoms are successfully controlled and there seem to be no continuing problems. Complete information is necessary for the doctor to provide the best possible treatment of any condition.

Replace your supply of glucagon as soon as possible, in case another hypoglycemic episode occurs.

You should wear a medical identification (I.D.) bracelet or chain at all times. In addition, you should carry an I.D. card that lists your medical condition and medicines.

Side Effects of This Medicine

Along with its needed effects, a medicine may cause some unwanted effects. Although not all of these side effects may occur, if they do occur they may need medical attention.

Get emergency help immediately if any of the following side effects occur:
Less common
    Dizziness; lightheadedness; trouble in breathing
Symptoms of overdose
    Diarrhea; irregular heartbeat; loss of appetite; muscle cramps or pain; nausea (continuing); vomiting (continuing); weakness of arms, legs, and trunk (severe)

Check with your doctor as soon as possible if the following side effect occurs:
Less common
    Skin rash

Other side effects may occur that usually do not need medical attention. These side effects may go away during treatment as your body adjusts to the medicine. However, check with your doctor if any of the following side effects continue or are bothersome:
Less common or rare
    Fast heartbeat; nausea; vomiting

Other side effects not listed above may also occur in some patients. If you notice any other effects, check with your doctor.

Additional Information

Once a medicine has been approved for marketing for a certain use, experience may show that it is also useful for other medical problems. Although these uses are not included in product labeling, glucagon is used in certain patients with the following medical conditions or undergoing certain medical procedures:

- Overdose of beta-adrenergic blocking medicines
- Overdose of calcium channel blocking medicines
- Removing food or an object stuck in the esophagus
- Hysterosalpingography (x-ray examination of the uterus and fallopian tubes)

Other than the above information, there is no additional information relating to proper use, precautions, or side effects for these uses.

Revised: 01/29/99

GLUTETHIMIDE   Systemic†

†Not commercially available in Canada.

Description

Glutethimide (gloo-TETH-i-mide) is used to treat insomnia (trouble in sleeping). However, it has generally been replaced by safer and more effective medicines for the treatment of insomnia. If glutethimide is used regularly (for example, every day) to help produce sleep, it is usually not effective for more than 7 days.

Before Using This Medicine

In deciding to use a medicine, the risks of taking the medicine must be weighed against the good it will do. This is a decision you and your doctor will make. For glutethimide the following should be considered:

Allergies—Tell your doctor if you have ever had any unusual or allergic reaction to glutethimide. Also tell your health care professional if you are allergic to any other substances, such as foods, preservatives, or dyes.

Pregnancy—Studies of effects in pregnancy have not been done in either humans or animals. However, too much use of glutethimide during pregnancy may cause the baby to become dependent on the medicine. This may lead to withdrawal side effects after birth.

Breast-feeding—Glutethimide passes into the breast milk and may cause drowsiness in nursing babies.

Children—Studies on this medicine have been done only in adult patients and there is no specific information comparing use of glutethimide in children with use in other age groups.

Older adults—Elderly people may be especially sensitive to the effects of glutethimide. This may increase the chance of side effects during treatment.

Other medicines—Although certain medicines should not be used together at all, in other cases 2 different medicines may be used together even if an interaction might occur. In these cases, your doctor may want to change the dose, or other precautions may be necessary. When you are taking glutethimide it is especially important that your health care professional know if you are taking any of the following:

- Anticoagulants (blood thinners)—Glutethimide may change the amount of anticoagulant you need to take

- Central nervous system (CNS) depressants, other (medicine that causes drowsiness) or
- Tricyclic antidepressants (medicine for depression)— Using these medicines together with glutethimide may increase the CNS and other depressant effects

Other medical problems—The presence of other medical problems may affect the use of glutethimide. Make sure you tell your doctor if you have any other medical problems, especially:

- Enlarged prostate or
- Intestinal blockage or
- Irregular heartbeat or
- Porphyria or
- Stomach ulcer or
- Urinary tract blockage—Glutethimide may make the condition worse

- Kidney disease—Higher blood levels of glutethimide may result and increase the chance of side effects

Proper Use of This Medicine

Take this medicine only as directed by your doctor. Do not take more of it, do not take it more often, and do not take it for a longer time than your doctor ordered. If too much is taken, it may become habit-forming.

Dosing—The dose of glutethimide will be different for different patients. *Follow your doctor's orders or the directions on the label*. The following information includes only the average doses of glutethimide. *If your dose is different, do not change it* unless your doctor tells you to do so.

- For *oral* dosage forms (capsules or tablets):
  —Adults: 250 to 500 milligrams (1 capsule or tablet) at bedtime.
  —Children: Dose must be determined by the doctor.

Storage—To store this medicine:

- Keep out of the reach of children since overdose is especially dangerous in children.
- Store away from heat and direct light.
- Do not store in the bathroom, near the kitchen sink, or in other damp places. Heat or moisture may cause the medicine to break down.
- Do not keep outdated medicine or medicine no longer needed. Be sure that any discarded medicine is out of the reach of children.

Precautions While Using This Medicine

If you will be taking this medicine regularly for a long time:

- Your doctor should check your progress at regular visits.
- Do not stop taking it without first checking with your doctor. Your doctor may want you to reduce gradually the amount you are taking before stopping completely.

This medicine will add to the effects of alcohol and other CNS depressants (medicines that slow down the nervous system, possibly causing drowsiness). Some examples of CNS depressants are antihistamines or medicine for hay fever, other allergies, or colds; sedatives, tranquilizers, or sleeping medicine; prescription pain medicine or narcotics; barbiturates; medicine for seizures; muscle relaxants; or anesthetics, including some dental anesthetics. *Check with your doctor before taking any of the above while you are using this medicine.*

Before you have any medical tests, tell the doctor in charge that you are taking this medicine. The results of the metyrapone test may be affected by this medicine.

If you think you or someone else may have taken an overdose of this medicine, get emergency help at once. Taking an overdose of glutethimide or taking alcohol or other CNS depressants with glutethimide may lead to unconsciousness and possibly death. Some signs of an overdose are continuing confusion, severe weakness, shortness of breath or slow or troubled breathing, convulsions (seizures), slurred speech, staggering, and slow heartbeat.

This medicine may cause some people to become dizzy, drowsy, or less alert than they are normally. Even if taken at bedtime, it may cause some people to feel drowsy or less alert on arising. *Make sure you know how you react to this medicine before you drive, use machines, or do anything else that could be dangerous if you are dizzy or are not alert.*

Side Effects of This Medicine

Along with its needed effects, a medicine may cause some unwanted effects. Although not all of these side effects may occur, if they do occur they may need medical attention.

Check with your doctor as soon as possible if any of the following side effects occur:

Less common
    Skin rash

Rare
    Sore throat and fever; unusual bleeding or bruising; unusual excitement; unusual tiredness or weakness

Symptoms of overdose
    Bluish coloration of skin; confusion (continuing); convulsions (seizures); fever; low body temperature; memory problems; muscle spasms or twitching; shortness of breath or slow or troubled breathing; slow heartbeat; slowness or loss of reflexes; slurred speech; staggering; trembling; trouble in concentrating; weakness (severe)

Other side effects may occur that usually do not need medical attention. These side effects may go away during treatment as your body adjusts to the medicine. However, check with your doctor if any of the following side effects continue or are bothersome:

More common
    Drowsiness (daytime)

Less common
    Blurred vision; clumsiness or unsteadiness; confusion; dizziness; "hangover" effect; headache; nausea; vomiting

After you stop using this medicine, your body may need time to adjust. The length of time this takes depends on the amount of medicine you were using and how long you used it. During this period of time check with your doctor if you notice any of the following side effects:

Convulsions (seizures); fast heartbeat; hallucinations (seeing, hearing, or feeling things that are not there); increased dreaming; muscle cramps or spasms; nausea or vomiting; nightmares; stomach cramps or pain; trembling; trouble in sleeping

Other side effects not listed above may also occur in some patients. If you notice any other effects, check with your doctor.

Revised: 05/12/93
Interim revision: 10/03/97

GLYBURIDE AND METFORMIN
Systemic—INTRODUCTORY VERSION

Commonly used brand name(s):

In the U.S.—
    Glucovance

Description

Glyburide and Metformin (GLYE-byoor-ide and met-FOR-min) combination is used to treat high blood sugar levels that are caused by a type of diabetes mellitus or sugar diabetes called type 2 diabetes. Normally, after you eat, your pancreas releases insulin to help your body store excess sugar for later use. This process occurs during normal digestion of food. In type 2 diabetes, your body does not work properly to store

the excess sugar and the sugar remains in your bloodstream. Chronic high blood sugar can lead to serious health problems in the future. Proper diet is the first step in managing type 2 diabetes but often medicines are needed to help your body. With two actions, the combination of glyburide and metformin helps your body cope with high blood sugar. Glyburide stimulates the release of insulin from the pancreas, directing your body to store blood sugar. Metformin has three different actions: it slows the absorption of sugar in your small intestine; it also stops your liver from converting stored sugar into blood sugar; and it helps your body use your natural insulin more efficiently.

This medicine is available only with your doctor's prescription, in the following dosage form:

Oral
    • Tablets (U.S.)

Before Using This Medicine

In deciding to use a medicine, the risks of taking the medicine must be weighed against the good it will do. This is a decision you and your doctor will make. For glyburide and metformin, the following should be considered:

Allergies—Tell your doctor if you have ever had any unusual or allergic reaction to glyburide or metformin. Also, tell your health care professional if you are allergic to any other substances, such as foods, preservatives, or dyes.

Pregnancy—Glyburide and metformin combination has not been studied in pregnant women or animals. However, independent studies with glyburide and also with metformin have not shown that either medicine causes birth defects or other problems in animal studies. It is easier during pregnancy to control your blood sugar by using injections of insulin rather than by taking oral diabetes medicines. Close control of your blood sugar can reduce the chance of your baby gaining too much weight, having birth defects, or having high blood sugar before birth. Before taking this medicine, make sure your doctor knows if you are pregnant or if you may become pregnant.

Breast-feeding—It is not known whether glyburide or metformin passes into human breast milk. Although most medicines pass into breast milk in small amounts, many of them may be used safely while breast-feeding. Mothers who are taking this medicine and who wish to breast-feed should discuss this with their doctor.

Children—Studies on this medicine have been done only in adult patients, and there is no specific information comparing use of glyburide and metformin in children with use in other age groups.

Older adults—This medicine has been tested and has not been shown to cause different side effects or problems in older people than it does in younger adults.

Other medicines—Although certain medicines should not be used together at all, in other cases two different medicines may be used together even if an interaction might occur. In these cases, your doctor may want to change the dose, or other precautions may be necessary. When you are taking glyburide and metformin, it is especially important that your health care professional know if you are taking any of the following:

    • Alcohol—Drinking alcohol may increase the risk of developing lactic acidosis and/or very low blood sugar.

- Beta-adrenergic blocking agents (acebutolol [e.g., Sectral], atenolol [e.g., Tenormin], betaxolol [e.g., Kerlone], bisoprolol [e.g., Zebeta], carteolol [e.g., Cartrol], labetalol [e.g., Normodyne], metoprolol [e.g., Lopressor], nadolol [e.g., Corgard], oxprenolol [e.g., Trasicor], penbutolol [e.g., Levatol], pindolol [e.g., Visken], propranolol [e.g., Inderal], sotalol [e.g., Betapace], timolol [e.g., Blocadren])—Beta-adrenergic blocking agents can hide the symptoms of low blood sugar. Because of this, a person with diabetes might not recognize that he or she has low blood sugar and might not take immediate steps to treat it.
- Cimetidine (e.g., Tagamet) or
- Furosemide (e.g., Lasix)—Use with a medicine that contains metformin may cause high blood levels of metformin, which may increase the chance of low blood sugar or other side effects.

Other medical problems—The presence of other medical problems may affect the use of glyburide and metformin. Make sure you tell your doctor if you have any other medical problems, especially:

- Acid in the blood (acidosis or ketoacidosis) or
- Surgery (major)—Use of insulin is best to help control diabetes in patients with these conditions.

- Blood poisoning or
- Dehydration (severe) or
- Heart or blood vessel disorders or
- Kidney disease or
- Liver disease—Lactic acidosis can occur in these conditions and chances of it occurring are even greater with a medicine that contains metformin.

- Kidney, heart, or other problems that require medical tests or examinations that use certain medicines called contrast agents, with x-ray exams—Because this medicine contains metformin, your doctor should advise you to stop taking it before you have any medical exams or diagnostic tests that might cause less urine output than usual; you may be advised to start taking the medicine again 48 hours after the exams or tests if your kidney function is tested and found to be normal.

Proper Use of This Medicine

Follow carefully the special meal plan your doctor gave you. This is the most important part of controlling your condition, and is necessary if the medicine is to work properly. Also, exercise regularly and test for sugar in your blood or urine as directed.

Glyburide and metformin combination should be taken with meals to help reduce the gastrointestinal side effects that may occur during the first few weeks of treatment.

Dosing—The dose of the glyburide and metformin combination will be different for different patients. *Follow your doctor's orders or the directions on the label.* The following information includes only the average doses of glyburide and metformin. *If your dose is different, do not change it* unless your doctor tells you to do so.

- For *oral* dosage form (tablets):
  —For type 2 diabetes:
    - For first-time treatment:
      —Adults: At first, 1.25 milligrams (mg) of glyburide and 250 mg of metformin one or two times a day with meals. Then, your doctor may increase your dose a little at a time every two weeks until your blood sugar is controlled.
      —Children: Use and dose must be determined by your doctor.
    - For patients previously treated with a sulfonylurea antidiabetic agent and/or metformin:
      —Adults: At first, 2.5 mg of glyburide and 500 mg of metformin or 5 mg of glyburide and 500 mg of metformin two times a day, with the morning and evening meals. Then, your doctor may increase your dose a little at a time until your blood sugar is controlled.
      —Children: Use and dose must be determined by your doctor.

Storage—To store this medicine:
- Keep out of the reach of children.
- Do not store in the bathroom, near the kitchen sink, or in other damp places. Heat or moisture may cause the medicine to break down.
- Keep the medicine from freezing. Do not refrigerate.
- Do not keep outdated medicine or medicine no longer needed. Ask your health care professional how you should dispose of any medicine you do not use. Be sure that any discarded medicine is out of the reach of children.

Precautions While Using This Medicine

Your doctor will want to check your progress at regular visits, especially during the first few weeks that you take this medicine.

Under certain conditions, too much metformin can cause lactic acidosis. *Symptoms of lactic acidosis are severe and quick to appear* and usually occur when other health problems not related to the medicine are present and are very severe, such as a heart attack or kidney failure. Symptoms of lactic acidosis include abdominal or stomach discomfort; decreased appetite; diarrhea; fast, shallow breathing; general feeling of discomfort; muscle pain or cramping; and unusual sleepiness, tiredness, or weakness.

If symptoms of lactic acidosis occur, you should get immediate emergency medical help.

It is very important to follow carefully any instructions from your health care team about:

- Alcohol—Drinking alcohol may cause severe low blood sugar. Discuss this with your health care team.
- Other medicines—Do not take other medicines unless they have been discussed with your doctor. This especially includes nonprescription medicines such as aspirin, and medicines for appetite control, asthma, colds, cough, hay fever, or sinus problems.
- Counseling—Other family members need to learn how to prevent side effects or help with side effects if they occur. Also, patients with diabetes may need special counseling about diabetes medicine dosing changes that might occur because of lifestyle changes, such as changes in exercise and diet. Furthermore, counseling on contraception and pregnancy may be needed because of the problems that can occur in patients with diabetes during pregnancy.
- Travel—Keep a recent prescription and your medical history with you. Be prepared for an emergency as you would normally. Make allowances for changing time

zones and keep your meal times as close as possible to your usual meal times.

In case of emergency—There may be a time when you need emergency help for a problem caused by your diabetes. You need to be prepared for these emergencies. It is a good idea to wear a medical identification (ID) bracelet or neck chain at all times. Also, carry an ID card in your wallet or purse that says that you have diabetes and a list of all your medicines.

Symptoms of hypoglycemia (low blood sugar) include anxiety; behavior change similar to being drunk; blurred vision; cold sweats; confusion; cool, pale skin; difficulty in thinking; drowsiness; excessive hunger; fast heartbeat; headache (continuing); nausea; nervousness; nightmares; restless sleep; shakiness; slurred speech; or unusual tiredness or weakness.

Glyburide and metformin combination can cause low blood sugar. However, it also can occur if you delay or miss a meal or snack, drink alcohol, exercise more than usual, cannot eat because of nausea or vomiting, take certain medicines, or take glyburide and metformin with another type of diabetes medicine. *Symptoms of low blood sugar must be treated before they lead to unconsciousness (passing out).* Different people feel different symptoms of low blood sugar. *It is important that you learn which symptoms of low blood sugar you usually have so that you can treat it quickly.*

If symptoms of low blood sugar occur, *eat glucose tablets or gel, corn syrup, honey, or sugar cubes; or drink fruit juice, nondiet soft drink, or sugar dissolved in water.* Also, check your blood for low blood sugar. *Glucagon is used in emergency situations when severe symptoms such as seizures (convulsions) or unconsciousness occur.* Have a glucagon kit available, along with a syringe or needle, and know how to use it. Members of your household also should know how to use it.

Symptoms of hyperglycemia (high blood sugar) include blurred vision; drowsiness; dry mouth; flushed, dry skin; fruitlike breath odor; increased urination (frequency and volume); ketones in urine; loss of appetite; sleepiness; stomachache, nausea, or vomiting; tiredness; troubled breathing (rapid and deep); unconsciousness; or unusual thirst.

High blood sugar may occur if you do not exercise as much as usual, have a fever or infection, do not take enough or skip a dose of your diabetes medicine, or overeat or do not follow your meal plan.

If symptoms of high blood sugar occur, *check your blood sugar level and then call your health care professional for instructions.*

Side Effects of This Medicine

Along with its needed effects, a medicine may cause some unwanted effects. Although not all of these side effects may occur, if they do occur they may need medical attention.

Check with your doctor immediately if any of the following side effects occur:
More common
   Convulsions (seizures); unconsciousness
Rare
   Lactic acidosis, including abdominal discomfort, decreased appetite, diarrhea, fast shallow breathing, general feeling of discomfort, muscle pain or

cramping, unusual sleepiness, or unusual tiredness or weakness

Check with your doctor as soon as possible if any of the following side effects occur:
More common
   Cough; fever; hypoglycemia (low blood sugar), including anxious feeling, behavior change similar to being drunk, blurred vision, cold sweats, confusion, cool pale skin, difficulty in concentrating, drowsiness, excessive hunger, fast heartbeat, headache (continuing), nausea, nervousness, nightmares, restless sleep, shakiness, slurred speech, or unusual tiredness or weakness; sneezing; sore throat

Other side effects may occur that usually do not need medical attention. These side effects may go away during treatment as your body adjusts to the medicine. However, check with your doctor if any of the following side effects continue or are bothersome.
More common
   Dizziness; headache; vomiting

Other side effects not listed above may also occur in some patients. If you notice any other effects, check with your doctor.

Developed: 12/07/2000

GLYCERIN   Systemic

Commonly used brand name(s):

In the U.S.—
   Glyrol
   Osmoglyn
   Generic name product may be available.

Description

Glycerin (GLI-ser-in), when taken by mouth, is used to treat certain conditions in which there is increased eye pressure, such as glaucoma. It may also be used before eye surgery to reduce pressure in the eye.

Glycerin may also be used for other conditions as determined by your doctor.

This medicine is available only with your doctor's prescription, in the following dosage form:
Oral
   • Oral solution (U.S.)

Before Using This Medicine

In deciding to use a medicine, the risks of taking the medicine must be weighed against the good it will do. This is a decision you and your doctor will make. For glycerin, the following should be considered:

Allergies—Tell your doctor if you have ever had any unusual or allergic reaction to glycerin. Also tell your health care professional if you are allergic to any other substances, such as foods, preservatives, or dyes.

Pregnancy—Studies on effects in pregnancy have not been done in either humans or animals.

Breast-feeding—It is not known whether glycerin passes into breast milk. This medicine has not been reported to cause problems in nursing babies.

Children—Although there is no specific information comparing use of glycerin in children with use in other age groups, this medicine is not expected to cause different side effects or problems in children than it does in adults.

Older adults—Glycerin reduces water in the body, and there may be an increased risk that elderly patients taking it could become dehydrated.

Other medicines—Although certain medicines should not be used together at all, in other cases two different medicines may be used together even if an interaction might occur. In these cases, your doctor may want to change the dose, or other precautions may be necessary. Tell your health care professional if you are taking any other prescription or nonprescription (over-the-counter [OTC]) medicine.

Other medical problems—The presence of other medical problems may affect the use of glycerin. Make sure you tell your doctor if you have any other medical problems, especially:

- Diabetes mellitus (sugar diabetes)—Use of glycerin may increase the chance of dehydration (loss of too much body water)
- Confused mental states or
- Heart disease or
- Kidney disease—Glycerin may make these conditions worse

Proper Use of This Medicine

It is very important that you take this medicine only as directed. Do not take more of it and do not take it more often than your doctor ordered.

To improve the taste of this medicine, mix it with a small amount of unsweetened lemon, lime, or orange juice, pour over cracked ice, and sip through a straw.

Dosing—The dose of glycerin will be different for different patients. *Follow your doctor's orders or the directions on the label.* The following information includes only the average doses of glycerin. *If your dose is different, do not change it* unless your doctor tells you to do so.

- For *oral* dosage form (oral solution):
  —To lower pressure in the eye:
  - Adults—Dose is based on body weight and must be determined by your doctor. The usual dose is 1 to 2 grams per kilogram (kg) (0.45 to 0.91 grams per pound) of body weight taken one time. Then, additional doses of 500 milligrams (mg) per kg (227 mg per pound) of body weight every six hours may be taken if needed.
  - Children—Dose is based on body weight and must be determined by your doctor. The usual dose is 1 to 1.5 grams per kg (0.45 to 0.68 grams per pound) of body weight taken one time. The dose may be repeated in four to eight hours if needed.

Missed dose—If you miss a dose of this medicine, take it as soon as possible. However, if it is almost time for your next dose, skip the missed dose and go back to your regular dosing schedule. Do not double doses.

Storage—To store this medicine:
- Keep out of the reach of children.
- Store away from heat and direct light.
- Do not store in the bathroom, near the kitchen sink, or in other damp places. Heat or moisture may cause the medicine to break down.
- Keep the medicine from freezing.
- Do not keep outdated medicine or medicine no longer needed. Be sure that any discarded medicine is out of the reach of children.

Precautions While Using This Medicine

Your doctor should check your progress at regular visits to make sure that this medicine is working properly.

In some patients, headaches may occur when this medicine is taken. To help prevent or relieve the headache, lie down while you are taking this medicine and for a short time after taking it. If headaches become severe or continue, check with your doctor.

Side Effects of This Medicine

Along with its needed effects, a medicine may cause some unwanted effects. Although not all of these side effects may occur, if they do occur they may need medical attention.

Check with your doctor as soon as possible if either of the following side effects occurs:
Less common
  Confusion
Rare
  Irregular heartbeat

Other side effects may occur that usually do not need medical attention. These side effects may go away during treatment as your body adjusts to the medicine. However, check with your doctor if any of the following side effects continue or are bothersome:
More common
  Headache; nausea or vomiting
Less common
  Diarrhea; dizziness; dryness of mouth or increased thirst

Other side effects not listed above may also occur in some patients. If you notice any other effects, check with your doctor.

Additional Information

Once a medicine has been approved for marketing for a certain use, experience may show that it is also useful for other medical problems. Although this use is not included in product labeling, glycerin is used in certain patients with the following medical conditions:

- Cerebral edema (swelling of the brain)

Other than the above information, there is no additional information relating to proper use, precautions, or side effects for these uses.

Revised: 08/03/94

GOLD COMPOUNDS   Systemic

Commonly used brand name(s):

In the U.S.—
Myochrysine[3]
Ridaura[1]
Solganal[2]

In Canada—
Myochrysine[3]
Ridaura[1]

Note: For quick reference, the following gold compounds are numbered to match the corresponding brand names.

This information applies to the following medicines:
1. Auranofin (au-RANE-oh-fin)
2. Aurothioglucose (aur-oh-thye-oh-GLOO-kose)
3. Gold Sodium Thiomalate (gold SO-dee-um thye-oh-MAH-late)‡

‡Generic name product may be available in the U.S.

Description

The gold compounds are used in the treatment of rheumatoid arthritis. They may also be used for other conditions as determined by your doctor.

In addition to the helpful effects of this medicine in treating your medical problem, it has side effects that can be very serious. Before you take this medicine, you should discuss with your doctor the good that this medicine will do as well as the risks of using it.

Auranofin is available only with your doctor's prescription. The other gold compounds are given by your health care professional.

These medicines are available in the following dosage forms:

Oral
Auranofin
• Capsules (U.S. and Canada)

Parenteral
Aurothioglucose
• Injection (U.S.)
Gold sodium thiomalate
• Injection (U.S. and Canada)

Before Using This Medicine

In deciding to use a medicine, the risks of taking the medicine must be weighed against the good it will do. This is a decision you and your doctor will make. For gold compounds, the following should be considered:

Allergies—Tell your doctor if you have ever had any unusual or allergic reaction to gold or other metals, if you have received a gold compound before and developed serious side effects from it, or if any medicine you have taken has caused an allergy or a reaction that affected your blood. Also tell your health care professional if you are allergic to any other substances, such as foods, preservatives, or dyes.

Pregnancy—Studies on birth defects with gold compounds have not been done in humans. However, studies in animals have shown that gold compounds may cause birth defects.

Breast-feeding—Aurothioglucose and gold sodium thiomalate pass into the breast milk and may cause unwanted effects in nursing babies. It is not known whether auranofin passes into the breast milk.

Children—Auranofin has been tested only in adult patients and there is no specific information about its use in children. However, aurothioglucose and gold sodium thiomalate have been tested in children and have not been shown to cause different side effects or problems than they do in adults.

Older adults—These medicines have been tested and have not been shown to cause different side effects or problems in older people than they do in younger adults.

Other medicines—Although certain medicines should not be used together at all, in other cases two different medicines may be used together even if an interaction might occur. In these cases, your doctor may want to change the dose, or other precautions may be necessary. When you are taking a gold compound, it is important that your health care professional know if you are taking *any* other prescription or nonprescription (over-the-counter [OTC]) medicine, especially:

• Penicillamine (e.g., Cuprimine)—The chance of side effects may be increased.

Other medical problems—The presence of other medical problems may affect the use of gold compounds. Make sure you tell your doctor if you have any other medical problems, especially:

• Blood or blood vessel disease or
• Colitis or
• Kidney disease (or history of) or
• Lupus erythematosus or
• Sjögren's syndrome or
• Skin disease—The chance of unwanted effects may be increased

Proper Use of This Medicine

In order for this medicine to work, it must be taken regularly as ordered by your doctor. Continue receiving the injections or taking auranofin even if you think the medicine is not working. You may not notice the effects of this medicine until after three to six months of regular use.

For patients taking *auranofin:*
• *Do not take more of this medicine than ordered by your doctor*. Taking too much auranofin may increase the chance of serious unwanted effects.

If you have any questions about this, check with your doctor.

Dosing—The dose of these medicines will be different for different patients. *Follow your doctor's orders or the directions on the label*. The following information includes only the average doses of these medicines. *If your dose is different, do not change it* unless your doctor tells you to do so.

For auranofin
• For *oral* dosage form (capsules):
   —For arthritis:
      • Adults—6 milligrams (mg) once a day or 3 mg twice a day. After six months, your doctor may increase the dose to 3 mg three times a day.
      • Children—Dose must be determined by your doctor.

For aurothioglucose
• For *injection* dosage form:
   —For arthritis:
      • Adults and teenagers—10 milligrams (mg) for the first dose, then 25 mg once a week for the next two weeks, then 25 or 50 mg once a week. The

medicine is injected into a muscle. After several months, the injections may be given less often (25 or 50 mg every two weeks for a while, then every three or four weeks).

- Children 6 to 12 years of age—2.5 mg for the first dose, then 6.25 mg once a week for the next two weeks, then 12.5 mg once a week. The medicine is injected into a muscle. After several months, the injections may be given less often (6.25 or 12.5 mg every three or four weeks).
- Children younger than 6 years of age—Dose must be determined by your doctor.

For gold sodium thiomalate
- For *injection* dosage form:
  —For arthritis:
  - Adults and teenagers—10 milligrams (mg) for the first dose, then 25 mg a week later, then 25 or 50 mg once a week. The medicine is injected into a muscle. After several months, the injections may be given less often (25 or 50 mg every two weeks for a while, then every three or four weeks).
  - Children—10 mg for the first dose, then 1 mg per kilogram (about 0.45 mg per pound) of body weight, but not more than a total of 50 mg, once a week. The medicine is injected into a muscle. After several months, the same dose may be given less often (every two weeks for a while, then every three or four weeks).

Missed dose—For patients taking *auranofin:* If you miss a dose of this medicine, and your dosing schedule is—

- One dose a day—Take the missed dose as soon as possible. However, if you do not remember until the next day, skip the missed dose and go back to your regular dosing schedule. Do not double doses.
- More than one dose a day—Take the missed dose as soon as possible. However, if it is almost time for your next dose, skip the missed dose and go back to your regular dosing schedule. Do not double doses.

Storage—To store this medicine:
- Keep out of the reach of children.
- Store away from heat and direct light.
- Do not store this medicine in the bathroom, near the kitchen sink, or in other damp places. Heat or moisture may cause the medicine to break down.
- Do not keep outdated medicine or medicine no longer needed. Be sure that any discarded medicine is out of the reach of children.

Precautions While Using This Medicine

Gold compounds may cause some people to become more sensitive to sunlight than they are normally. These people may break out in a rash after being in the sun, or a skin rash that is already present may become worse. To protect yourself, it is best to:

- Stay out of direct sunlight, especially between the hours of 10:00 a.m. and 3:00 p.m., if possible.
- Wear protective clothing.
- Ask your doctor if you may apply a sun block product. Products that have a skin protection factor (SPF) of at least 15 work best, but some patients may require a product with a higher SPF number, especially if they have a fair complexion.
- Do not use a sunlamp or tanning bed or booth.

If you have a severe reaction from the sun, check with your doctor.

For patients taking *auranofin:*
- Your doctor should check your progress at regular visits. Blood and urine tests may be needed to make certain that this medicine is not causing unwanted effects.

For patients receiving *gold injections:*
- Immediately following an injection of this medicine, side effects such as dizziness, feeling faint, flushing or redness of the face, nausea or vomiting, increased sweating, or unusual weakness may occur. These will usually go away after you lie down for a few minutes. If any of these effects continue or become worse, or if you notice any other effects within 10 minutes or so after receiving an injection, tell your health care professional right away.
- Joint pain may occur for 1 or 2 days after you receive an injection of this medicine. This effect usually disappears after the first few injections. However, if this continues or is bothersome, check with your doctor.

Side Effects of This Medicine

Gold compounds have been shown to cause tumors and cancer of the kidney when given to animals in large amounts for a long time. However, these effects have not been reported in humans receiving gold compounds for arthritis. If you have any questions about this, check with your doctor.

Along with its needed effects, a medicine may cause some unwanted effects. Although not all of these side effects may occur, side effects may occur at any time during treatment with this medicine *and up to many months after treatment has ended*, and they may need medical attention.

Check with your doctor as soon as possible if any of the following side effects occur:

More common
  Irritation or soreness of tongue—less common with auranofin; metallic taste—less common with auranofin; skin rash or itching; redness, soreness, swelling, or bleeding of gums—rare with auranofin; ulcers, sores, or white spots on lips or in mouth or throat

Less common
  Bloody or cloudy urine; hives

Rare
  Abdominal or stomach pain, cramping, or burning (severe); bloody or black, tarry stools; confusion; convulsions (seizures); coughing, hoarseness, difficulty in breathing, shortness of breath, tightness in chest, or wheezing; dark urine; decreased urination; decreased vision; difficulty in swallowing; feeling of something in the eye; fever; hair loss; hallucinations (hearing, seeing, or feeling things that are not there); irritation of nose, throat, or upper chest area, possibly with hoarseness or coughing; irritation of vagina; nausea, vomiting, or heartburn (severe and/or continuing); numbness, tingling, pain, or weakness, especially in the face, hands, arms, or feet; pale stools; painful or difficult urination; pain in lower back, side, or lower abdomen (stomach) area; pain, redness, itching, or tearing of eyes; pinpoint red spots on skin; problems with muscle coordination; red, thickened, or scaly skin; sore throat and fever with or without chills; swelling of face, fingers, an-

kles, lower legs, or feet; swellings (large) on face, eyelids, mouth, lips, and/or tongue; swollen and/or painful glands; unusual bleeding or bruising; unusual tiredness or weakness; vomiting of blood or material that looks like coffee grounds; yellow eyes or skin

Other side effects may occur that usually do not need medical attention. These side effects may go away during treatment as your body adjusts to the medicine. However, check with your doctor if the following side effects continue or are bothersome:

More common with auranofin; rare with injections
Abdominal or stomach cramps or pain (mild or moderate); bloated feeling, gas, or indigestion (mild or moderate); decrease or loss of appetite; diarrhea or loose stools; nausea or vomiting (mild or moderate)

Less common
Constipation—with auranofin; joint pain—with injections

Some patients receiving auranofin have noticed changes in the taste of certain foods. If you notice a metallic taste while receiving any gold compound, check with your doctor as soon as possible. If you notice any other taste changes while you are taking auranofin, it is not necessary to check with your doctor unless you find this effect especially bothersome.

Other side effects not listed above may also occur in some patients. If you notice any other effects, check with your doctor.

Revised: 10/31/99

GONADORELIN   Systemic

Commonly used brand name(s):

In the U.S.—
Factrel

In Canada—
Factrel
Lutrepulse
Relisorm

Other commonly used names are luteinizing hormone–releasing hormone (LHRH), luteinizing hormone–releasing factor dihydrochloride (for gonadorelin hydrochloride), luteinizing hormone–releasing factor diacetate tetrahydrate (for gonadorelin acetate), and luteinizing hormone–/follicle-stimulating hormone–releasing hormone (LH/FSH-RH).

Description

Gonadorelin (goe-nad-oh-RELL-in) is a medicine that is the same as gonadotropin-releasing hormone (GnRH) that is naturally released from the hypothalamus gland. GnRH causes the pituitary gland to release other hormones (luteinizing hormone [LH] and follicle-stimulating hormone [FSH]). LH and FSH control development in children and fertility in adults.

Gonadorelin is used to test how well the hypothalamus and the pituitary glands are working. It is also used to cause ovulation (release of an egg from the ovary) in women who do not have regular ovulation and menstrual periods because the hypothalamus gland does not release enough GnRH.

Gonadorelin may also be used for other conditions as determined by your doctor.

Gonadorelin is available in the following dosage form:

Parenteral
• Injection (U.S. and Canada)

Before Using This Medicine

In deciding to use a medicine, the risks of using the medicine must be weighed against the good it will do. This is a decision you and your doctor will make. For gonadorelin, the following should be considered:

Allergies—Tell your doctor if you have ever had any unusual or allergic reaction to gonadorelin. Also tell your health care professional if you are allergic to any other substances, such as foods, preservatives, or dyes.

Pregnancy—Gonadorelin has not been shown to cause birth defects or problems in humans when given in the first three months of pregnancy. If you become pregnant while using this medicine, there is an increased chance of a multiple pregnancy, such as having twins and triplets. Also, gonadorelin has not been shown to cause birth defects or other problems in animal studies.

Breast-feeding—It is not known if gonadorelin passes into the breast milk. Gonadorelin has not been reported to cause problems in nursing babies.

Children—Gonadorelin, used as a test, has been studied only in children 12 years of age and older. The medicine has not caused different side effects or problems in children 12 years of age and older than it does in adults. Children up to 12 years of age may not be sensitive to the effects of gonadorelin. Infants may be very sensitive to the effects of gonadorelin and use in infants is not recommended.

Teenagers—Gonadorelin has been tested in a limited number of teenagers and, in effective doses, has not been shown to cause different side effects or problems in teenagers than it does in adults.

Other medicines—Although certain medicines should not be used together at all, in other cases two different medicines may be used together even if an interaction might occur. In these cases, your doctor may want to change the dose, or other precautions may be necessary. When you are using gonadorelin, it is especially important that your health care professional know if you are taking any of the following:

• Infertility therapy agents, such as clomiphene (e.g., Clomid)—When using gonadorelin to cause ovulation, the use of other infertility therapy agents at the same time may increase the chance of causing problems of the ovaries

Other medical problems—The presence of other medical problems may affect the use of gonadorelin. Make sure you tell your doctor if you have any other medical problems, especially:

• Gonadotropin-releasing hormone adenoma—Although this condition is rare, use of gonadorelin when this condition exists may cause problems in the pituitary gland and could result in sudden blindness
• Any condition that may be made worse by estrogens, progestins, or androgens, such as a hormone-dependent tumor—The increase of estrogens and progestins in women or androgens in men that can result from use of multiple doses of gonadorelin may make a tumor worse if the tumor depends on estrogens, progestins, or androgens for growth

Proper Use of This Medicine

If you are having a test done with gonadorelin, one or more samples of your blood will be taken. Then gonadorelin is given by an intravenous (into a vein) or a subcutaneous (under the skin) injection. At regular times after the medicine is given, more blood samples will be taken. Then the results of the test will be studied.

Some medicines given by injection or by injection pump may sometimes be given at home to patients who do not need to be in the hospital. If you are using this medicine at home, *make sure you clearly understand and carefully follow your doctor's instructions.*

For *Lutrepulse* pump—The *Lutrepulse* pump is a device containing gonadorelin. It automatically injects the medicine into a vein. The pump will be attached to a belt that is placed around your waist. Tubing from the pump will be taped to your chest, shoulder, and arm, as the tubing goes up your chest to your shoulder and then comes down your arm. A needle will be attached to the end of the tubing. It is inserted into a vein on the inner part of the crook of your elbow. A dressing is used to keep the needle protected. *You will need to know how to take care of the equipment and the injection site.*

To care for the pump:

- When showering or bathing, remove the belt with the device from your abdomen and any tape attached to your stomach and chest without removing the tape, tubing, or needle from your arm. The device is not waterproof. You will need to hang it outside on the railing of the shower and carefully shower without pulling the needle and tubing from your arm.
- When getting into bed, you must also remove the device from the abdomen as stated above, without removing the tape, tubing, or needle from your arm. Place the device above your pillow, then pin it to your bedsheets so that it does not fall off the bed. This will give you freedom of movement while sleeping.
- Know the warning signals that your pump can produce to alert you to problems, such as low battery, among other messages. *Do not try to take the pump apart yourself. Call your health care professional for directions if warning signals sound.*

To care for the injection site:

- *Inspect the injection site daily. Report to doctor if the skin at the injection site becomes red or swollen, if you experience fever or chills, if the needle comes out of your arm, if blood is seen in the tubing, or if the tubing becomes disconnected from the pump.*
- Keep the protective dressing in place over the needle, replacing it if it gets wet or dirty.
- Avoid putting pressure on the needle placed in your arm.
- Carefully keep the tubing taped to your skin to keep it securely in place and to prevent it from kinking.
- The needle should be replaced every 48 hours.

Dosing—The dose of gonadorelin will be different for different patients. *Follow your doctor's orders.* The following information includes only the average doses of gonadorelin.

- For *injection* dosage form (for *Lutrepulse* pump):
  —For treating amenorrhea or infertility in women caused by pituitary or hypothalamus problems:
  - Adults—5 microgram (mcg) injected by the pump into a vein or under the skin slowly over 1 minute, every ninety minutes for twenty-one days. As determined by doctor, dose may be changed slowly,

decreased to 1 mcg or increased to 20 mcg if needed.
  - Children up to 18 years of age—Use and dose must be determined by the doctor.

- For *injection* dosage form (single-dose injection):
  —For testing the hypothalamus and pituitary glands:
  - Adults—0.1 milligram (mg) injected once as a single dose under the skin or into a vein.
  - Children 12 years of age and older—2 micrograms (mcg) per kilogram (kg) (0.9 mcg per pound) of body weight, not to exceed a single dose of 100 mcg, injected once under the skin or into vein.
  - Children up to 12 years of age—Use and dose must be determined by doctor.

For *Lutrepulse* pump

It is very important that your doctor check your progress at regular visits. This will allow the doctor to see if the medicine is working properly and to decide if you should continue to use it.

If you are using gonadorelin to help you become pregnant, *closely follow your doctor's advice on the best times to have sexual intercourse.* Your doctor can help you decide when having sexual intercourse will not result in a pregnancy with twins or triplets.

Tell your doctor when you suspect you are pregnant.

Side Effects of This Medicine

Along with its needed effects, a medicine may cause some unwanted effects. Although the following side effects usually occur rarely with the use of repeated injections, they require immediate medical attention. *Get emergency help immediately* if any of the following side effects occur:

With repeated doses
   Difficulty in breathing; flushing (continuing); rapid heartbeat

Check with your doctor as soon as possible if any of the following side effects occur:

With repeated doses
   Hardening of skin at place of injection; hives

With single or repeated doses
   Itching, pain, redness or swelling of skin at place of injection; skin rash (at place of injection or over entire body)

Other side effects may occur that usually do not need medical attention. These side effects may go away during treatment as your body adjusts to the medicine. However, check with your doctor if any of the following side effects continue or are bothersome:

Less common
   With single dose
      Abdominal or stomach discomfort; flushing (lasting only a short time); headaches; lightheadedness; nausea

Other side effects not listed above may also occur in some patients. If you notice any other effects, check with your doctor.

Additional Information

Once a medicine has been approved for marketing for a certain use, experience may show that it is also useful for other

medical problems. Although not specifically included in product labeling, gonadorelin is used in certain patients with the following medical conditions:

- Delayed puberty
- Infertility in males caused by pituitary or hypothalamus problems

Other than the above information, there is no additional information relating to proper use, precautions, or side effects for these uses.

Revised: 06/29/98

GOSERELIN   Systemic

Commonly used brand name(s):

In the U.S.—
Zoladex
Zoladex 3-Month

In Canada—
Zoladex
Zoladex LA

Description

Goserelin (GOE-se-rel-in) is a hormone similar to the one normally released from the hypothalamus gland in the brain. It is used to treat a number of medical problems. These include:

- Cancer of the prostate in men;
- Cancer of the breast in women if it develops before or around the time of menopause;
- Endometriosis, a painful condition caused by extra tissue growing inside or outside of the uterus; and
- Thinning of the lining of the uterus before surgery on the uterus.

When given regularly as an implant, goserelin works every day to decrease the amount of estrogen and testosterone in the blood.

Reducing the amount of estrogen in the body is one way of treating endometriosis and cancer of the breast, and can help thin the uterus lining before surgery. Goserelin prevents the growth of tissue associated with endometriosis in adult women during treatment and for up to 6 months after treatment is discontinued.

Reducing the amount of testosterone in the body is one way of treating cancer of the prostate.

Suppressing estrogen can thin the bones or slow their growth. This is a problem for adult women whose bones are no longer growing like the bones of children. This is why goserelin is used only for up to 6 months in adult women treated for endometriosis.

Goserelin is to be given only by or under the supervision of your doctor. It is injected under the skin and is available in the following dosage form:

Parenteral
- Implants (U.S. and Canada)

Before Using This Medicine

In deciding to use a medicine, the risks of taking the medicine must be weighed against the good it will do. This is a decision you and your doctor will make. For goserelin, the following should be considered:

Allergies—Tell your doctor if you have ever had any unusual or allergic reaction to goserelin, buserelin, gonadorelin, histrelin, leuprolide, or nafarelin.

Fertility—During use of goserelin, and usually for a short time after discontinuing it, the medicine decreases fertility in men by reducing sperm counts and in many women by suppressing egg development. Be sure you have discussed this with your doctor before receiving the medicine.

Pregnancy—Goserelin is not recommended for use during pregnancy. This medicine may cause birth defects if taken by a woman during pregnancy or may cause a miscarriage to occur. *Use of a nonhormonal contraceptive is recommended for women who are taking goserelin. Although the chance of becoming pregnant is decreased while you are taking this medicine, a pregnancy can still occur. Tell your doctor immediately if you think you have become pregnant.*

Breast-feeding—It is not known whether goserelin passes into breast milk. However, use of goserelin is not recommended during breast-feeding because it may cause unwanted effects in nursing babies.

Children—Studies of this medicine have been done only in adult patients, and there is no specific information comparing use of goserelin in children younger than 18 years of age with use in other age groups. Endometriosis is not likely to occur before puberty.

Older adults—Many medicines have not been tested in older people. Therefore, it may not be known whether they work exactly the same way they do in younger adults. Although there is no specific information comparing use of goserelin in the elderly to use in other age groups, it has been used mostly in elderly patients and is not expected to cause different side effects or problems in older people than it does in younger adults.

Other medicines—Although certain medicines should not be used together at all, in other cases two medicines may be used together even if an interaction might occur. In these cases, your doctor may want to change the dose, or other precautions may be necessary. Tell your doctor and pharmacist if you are taking any other prescription or nonprescription (over-the-counter [OTC]) medicine.

Other medical problems—The presence of other medical problems may affect the use of goserelin. Make sure you tell your doctor if you have any other medical problems, especially:

- Changes in vaginal bleeding from an unknown cause— Gonadorelin may delay diagnosis or worsen condition. The reason for the bleeding should be determined before goserelin is used

- Conditions that increase the chances of developing thinning bones or
- Osteoporosis (brittle bones), history of, or family history of—It is important that your doctor know if you already have an increased risk of osteoporosis. Some things that can increase your risk for having osteoporosis include cigarette smoking, alcohol abuse, and a family history of osteoporosis or easily broken bones. Some medicines, such as corticosteroids (cortisone-like medicines) or anticonvulsants (seizure medicine), can also cause thinning of the bones when used for a long time

- Nerve problems caused by bone lesions in the spine (in treatment of cancer of the prostate) or
- Problems in passing urine (in treatment of cancer of the prostate)—Conditions may get worse for a short time after goserelin treatment is started

Proper Use of This Medicine

Goserelin sometimes causes unwanted effects such as hot flashes or decreased sexual ability. However, it is very important that you continue to receive the medicine, even after you begin to feel better. *Do not stop treatment with this medicine without first checking with your doctor.*

Dosing—The dose of goserelin will be different for different patients. Goserelin implants are usually given by a doctor in the office or hospital. The following information includes only the average dose of goserelin:

- For *implants* dosage form:
  —For treating cancer of the breast:
  - Adults—3.6 milligrams (mg) (one implant) injected under the skin of the upper abdomen every twenty-eight days.
  - Children up to 18 years of age—Use and dose must be determined by the doctor.
  —For treating cancer of the prostate:
  - Adults—3.6 milligrams (mg) (one implant) injected under the skin of the upper abdomen every twenty-eight days or 10.8 mg (one implant) injected under the skin of the upper abdomen every twelve weeks.
  - Children up to 18 years of age—Use and dose must be determined by the doctor.
  —For treating endometriosis:
  - Adults—3.6 milligrams (mg) (one implant) injected under the skin of the upper abdomen every twenty-eight days for six months.
  - Children up to 18 years of age—Use must be determined by the doctor.
  —For thinning the uterus before surgery of the uterus:
  - Adults—3.6 milligrams (mg) (one implant) injected under the skin of the upper abdomen every twenty-eight days for two doses.
  - Children up to 18 years of age—Use and dose must be determined by the doctor.

Missed dose—If you miss getting a dose of this medicine, receive it as soon as possible.

Precautions While Using This Medicine

It is very important that your doctor check your progress at regular visits to make sure that this medicine is working properly and to check for unwanted effects.

For women—

- During the time you are receiving goserelin, your menstrual period may not be regular or you may not have a menstrual period at all. This is to be expected when being treated with this medicine. If regular menstrual periods continue during treatment or do not begin within 2 to 3 months after you stop using this medicine, check with your health care professional.
- To prevent pregnancy if you are sexually active and able to become pregnant, you should use birth control methods that do not contain hormones, such as vaginal spermicides with condoms, a diaphragm, or a cervical

cap. If you have any questions about this, check with your health care professional.

- *If you suspect you are pregnant, check with your doctor immediately.* There is a chance goserelin could cause problems to the unborn baby if taken during a pregnancy.

Side Effects of This Medicine

Along with its needed effects, a medicine may cause some unwanted effects. Although not all of these side effects may occur, if they do occur they may need medical attention.

Get emergency help immediately if any of the following side effects occur:
For adults
  Less common
    Fast or irregular heartbeat

  Rare
    Bone, muscle, or joint pain; changes in skin color of face; fainting; fast or irregular breathing; numbness or tingling of hands or feet; puffiness or swelling of the eyelids or around the eyes; shortness of breath; skin rash, hives, and/or itching; sudden, severe decrease in blood pressure and collapse; tightness in chest or wheezing; troubled breathing

For males only
  Rare
    Pains in chest; pain in groin or legs (especially in calves of legs)

Check with your doctor as soon as possible if any of the following side effects occur:
For females only
  Rare
    Anxiety; deepening of voice; increased hair growth; mental depression; mood changes; nervousness

Other side effects may occur that usually do not need medical attention. These side effects may go away during treatment as your body adjusts to the medicine. However, check with your doctor if any of the following side effects continue or are bothersome:
For females and males
  More common
    Sudden sweating and feelings of warmth (also called hot flashes)

  Less common
    Blurred vision; burning, itching, redness, or swelling at place of injection; decreased interest in sexual intercourse; dizziness; headache; nausea or vomiting; swelling and increased tenderness of breasts; swelling of feet or lower legs; trouble in sleeping; weight gain

For females only
  More common
    Light, irregular vaginal bleeding; stopping of menstrual periods

  Less common
    Burning, dryness, or itching of vagina; pelvic pain

For males only
  Less common
    Bone pain; constipation; decreased size of testicles; inability to have or keep an erection

Other side effects not listed above may also occur in some patients. If you notice any other effects, check with your doctor.

Revised: 06/09/2000

GRANISETRON   Systemic

Commonly used brand name(s):

In the U.S.—
   Kytril
In Canada—
   Kytril

Description

Granisetron (gra-NI-se-tron) is used to prevent the nausea and vomiting that may occur after treatment with anticancer medicines (chemotherapy) or with radiation therapy.

Granisetron is to be given only by or under the immediate supervision of your doctor. It is available in the following dosage forms:

Oral
   • Tablets (U.S. and Canada)
Parenteral
   • Injection (U.S. and Canada)

Before Receiving This Medicine

In deciding to use a medicine, the risks of taking the medicine must be weighed against the good it will do. This is a decision you and your doctor will make. For granisetron, the following should be considered:

Allergies—Tell your doctor if you have ever had any unusual or allergic reaction to granisetron, dolasetron, or ondansetron. Also tell your health care professional if you are allergic to any other substances, such as foods, preservatives, or dyes.

Pregnancy—Granisetron has not been studied in pregnant women. However, granisetron has not been shown to cause birth defects or other problems in animal studies.

Breast-feeding—It is not known whether granisetron passes into breast milk. Although most medicines pass into breast milk in small amounts, many of them may be used safely while breast-feeding. Mothers who are taking this medicine and who wish to breast-feed should discuss this with their doctor.

Children—This medicine has been tested in children 2 years of age and older and, in effective doses, has not been shown to cause different side effects or problems than it does in adults.

Older adults—This medicine has been tested in a limited number of patients 65 years of age or older and has not been shown to cause different side effects or problems in older people than it does in younger adults.

Other medicines—Although certain medicines should not be used together at all, in other cases two different medicines may be used together even if an interaction might occur. In these cases, your doctor may want to change the dose, or other precautions may be necessary. Tell your health care professional if you are taking any other prescription or nonprescription (over-the-counter [OTC]) medicine.

Other medical problems—The presence of other medical problems may affect the use of granisetron. Make sure you tell your doctor if you have any other medical problems.

Proper Use of This Medicine

Dosing—The dose of granisetron will be different for different patients. The following information includes only the average doses of granisetron.

• For prevention of nausea and vomiting caused by anticancer medicine:
   —For *oral* dosage form (tablets):
      • Adults and teenagers—Dose is usually 1 milligram (mg) taken up to one hour before the anticancer medicine. The 1-mg dose is taken again twelve hours after the first dose. Alternatively, 2 mg may be taken as one dose, up to one hour before the anticancer medicine.
      • Children—Dose must be determined by your doctor.
   —For *injection* dosage form:
      • Adults and children 2 years of age or older—Dose is based on body weight and must be determined by your doctor. It is usually 10 micrograms (mcg) per kilogram (kg) (4.5 mcg per pound) of body weight. It is injected into a vein over a period of five minutes, beginning within thirty minutes before the anticancer medicine is given.
      • Children up to 2 years of age—Dose must be determined by your doctor.
• For prevention of nausea and vomiting caused by radiation therapy:
   —For *oral* dosage form (tablets):
      • Adults and teenagers—Dose is 2 milligrams (two 1 milligram tablets) taken within 1 hour of radiation.
      • Children—Dose must be determined by your doctor.

Precautions While Receiving This Medicine

Check with your doctor if severe nausea and vomiting occur after receiving the anticancer medicine.

Side Effects of This Medicine

Along with its needed effects, a medicine may cause some unwanted effects. Although not all of these side effects may occur, if they do occur they may need medical attention.

Check with your doctor as soon as possible if any of the following side effects occur:
   Less common
      Fever
   Rare
      Chest pain; fainting; irregular heartbeat; shortness of breath; skin rash, hives, and itching

Other side effects may occur that usually do not need medical attention. These side effects may go away during treatment as your body adjusts to the medicine. However, check with your doctor if any of the following side effects continue or are bothersome:
   More common
      Abdominal pain; constipation; diarrhea; headache; unusual tiredness or weakness

Less common

Agitation; dizziness; drowsiness; heartburn; indigestion; sour stomach; trouble in sleeping; unusual taste in mouth

Additional Information

Once a medicine has been approved for marketing for a certain use, experience may show that it is also useful for other medical problems. Although this use is not included in product labeling, granisetron injection is used in certain patients to prevent the nausea and vomiting that may occur after cancer radiation treatment in patients undergoing bone marrow transplantation.

Other than the above information, there is no additional information relating to proper use, precautions, or side effects for this use.

Developed: 12/16/1994
Revised: 08/15/2000

GRISEOFULVIN   Systemic

Commonly used brand name(s):

In the U.S.—

Fulvicin P/G
Fulvicin-U/F
Grifulvin V
Grisactin
Grisactin Ultra
Gris-PEG

Generic name product may be available.

In Canada—

Fulvicin U/F

Description

Griseofulvin (gri-see-oh-FUL-vin) belongs to the group of medicines called antifungals. It is used to treat fungus infections of the skin, hair, fingernails, and toenails. This medicine may be taken alone or used along with medicines that are applied to the skin for fungus infections.

Griseofulvin is available only with your doctor's prescription, in the following dosage forms:

Oral
- Capsules (U.S.)
- Suspension (U.S.)
- Tablets (U.S. and Canada)

Before Using This Medicine

In deciding to use a medicine, the risks of taking the medicine must be weighed against the good it will do. This is a decision you and your doctor will make. For griseofulvin, the following should be considered:

Allergies—Tell your doctor if you have ever had any unusual or allergic reaction to penicillins, penicillamine (e.g., Cuprimine), or griseofulvin. Also tell your health care professional if you are allergic to any other substances, such as foods, preservatives, or dyes.

Diet—Griseofulvin is absorbed best when it is taken with a high fat meal, such as a cheeseburger, whole milk, or ice cream. Tell your doctor if you are on a low-fat diet.

Pregnancy—Griseofulvin should not be used during pregnancy. The birth of twins that were joined together has been reported, although rarely, in women who took griseofulvin during the first 3 months of pregnancy. In addition, studies in rats and dogs have shown that griseofulvin causes birth defects and other problems.

Breast-feeding—It is not known if griseofulvin is excreted in breast milk. However, griseofulvin has not been reported to cause problems in nursing babies.

Children—This medicine has been tested in a limited number of children 2 years of age or older. In effective doses, the medicine has not been shown to cause different side effects or problems than it does in adults.

Older adults—Many medicines have not been studied specifically in older people. Therefore, it may not be known whether they work exactly the same way they do in younger adults. Although there is no specific information comparing use of griseofulvin in the elderly with use in other age groups, this medicine is not expected to cause different side effects or problems in older people than it does in younger adults.

Other medicines—Although certain medicines should not be used together at all, in other cases two different medicines may be used together even if an interaction might occur. In these cases, your doctor may want to change the dose, or other precautions may be necessary. When you are taking griseofulvin, it is especially important that your health care professional knows if you are taking any of the following:

- Anticoagulants (blood thinners)—Griseofulvin may decrease the effectiveness of anticoagulants in some patients
- Oral contraceptives (birth control pills) containing estrogen—Griseofulvin may decrease the effectiveness of birth control pills, which may result in breakthrough bleeding and unwanted pregnancies

Other medical problems—The presence of other medical problems may affect the use of griseofulvin. Make sure you tell your doctor if you have any other medical problems, especially:

- Liver disease—Griseofulvin may on rare occasion cause side effects affecting the liver
- Lupus erythematosus or lupus-like diseases—Griseofulvin may worsen lupus symptoms in patients who have lupus erythematosus or lupus-like diseases
- Porphyria—Griseofulvin may increase attacks of porphyria in patients with acute intermittent porphyria

Proper Use of This Medicine

Griseofulvin is best taken with or after meals, especially fatty ones (for example, whole milk or ice cream). This lessens possible stomach upset and helps to clear up the infection by helping your body absorb the medicine better. *However, if you are on a low-fat diet, check with your doctor.*

For patients taking the *oral liquid form of griseofulvin:*
- Use a specially marked measuring spoon or other device to measure each dose accurately. The average household teaspoon may not hold the right amount of liquid.

To help clear up your infection completely, *keep taking this medicine for the full time of treatment,* even if you begin to feel better after a few days. *Do not miss any doses.*

Dosing—The dose of griseofulvin will be different for different patients. *Follow your doctor's orders or the directions on the label.* The following information includes only the average doses of griseofulvin. *If your dose is different, do not change it* unless your doctor tells you to do so.

The number of capsules or tablets or teaspoonfuls of suspension that you take depends on the strength of the medicine. Also, *the number of doses you take each day, the time allowed between doses, and the length of time you take the medicine depend on the medical problem for which you are taking griseofulvin.*

- For microsize capsules, tablets, and suspension:
  —Adults and teenagers:
  - Treatment of fungus infections of the feet and nails—500 milligrams (mg) every twelve hours.
  - Treatment of fungus infections of the scalp, skin, and groin—250 mg every twelve hours; or 500 mg once a day.
  —Children:
  - Treatment of fungus infections—Dose is based on body weight. The usual dose is 5 mg per kilogram (kg) (2.3 mg per pound) of body weight every twelve hours; or 10 mg per kg (4.6 mg per pound) of body weight once a day.
- For ultramicrosize tablets:
  —Adults and teenagers:
  - Treatment of fungus infections of the feet and nails—250 to 375 mg every twelve hours.
  - Treatment of fungus infections of the scalp, skin, and groin—125 to 187.5 mg every twelve hours; or 250 to 375 mg once a day.
  —Infants and children up to 2 years of age:
  - Treatment of fungus infections—Use and dose must be determined by your doctor.
  —Children 2 years of age and over:
  - Treatment of fungus infections—Dose is based on body weight. The usual dose is 2.75 to 3.65 mg per kg (1.25 to 1.7 mg per pound) of body weight every twelve hours; or 5.5 to 7.3 mg per kg (2.5 to 3.3 mg per pound) of body weight once a day.

Missed dose—If you miss a dose of this medicine, take it as soon as possible. However, if it is almost time for your next dose, skip the missed dose and go back to your regular dosing schedule. Do not double doses.

Storage—To store this medicine:
- Keep out of the reach of children.
- Store away from heat and direct light.
- Do not store the capsule or tablet form of this medicine in the bathroom, near the kitchen sink, or in other damp places. Heat or moisture may cause the medicine to break down.
- Keep the oral liquid form of this medicine from freezing.
- Do not keep outdated medicine or medicine no longer needed. Be sure that any discarded medicine is out of the reach of children.

Precautions While Using This Medicine

Your doctor should check your progress at regular visits to make sure that griseofulvin does not cause unwanted effects.

Oral contraceptives (birth control pills) containing estrogen may not work properly if you take them while you are taking griseofulvin. Unplanned pregnancies may occur. You should use a different or additional means of birth control while you are taking griseofulvin and for one month after stopping griseofulvin. If you have any questions about this, check with your health care professional.

Griseofulvin may increase the effects of alcohol. If taken with alcohol it may also cause fast heartbeat, flushing, increased sweating, or redness of the face. Therefore, if you have this reaction, do not drink alcoholic beverages while you are taking this medicine, unless you have first checked with your doctor.

This medicine may cause some people to become dizzy or less alert than they are normally. *Make sure you know how you react to this medicine before you drive, use machines, or do other things that could be dangerous if you are dizzy or are not alert.* If these reactions are especially bothersome, check with your doctor.

Griseofulvin may cause your skin to be more sensitive to sunlight than it is normally. Exposure to sunlight, even for brief periods of time, may cause a skin rash, itching, redness or other discoloration of the skin, or a severe sunburn. When you begin taking this medicine:
- Stay out of direct sunlight, especially between the hours of 10:00 a.m. and 3:00 p.m., if possible.
- Wear protective clothing, including a hat. Also, wear sunglasses.
- Apply a sun block product that has a skin protection factor (SPF) of at least 15. Some patients may require a product with a higher SPF number, especially if they have a fair complexion. If you have any questions about this, check with your health care professional.
- Apply a sun block lipstick that has an SPF of at least 15 to protect your lips.
- Do not use a sunlamp or tanning bed or booth.

If you have a severe reaction from the sun, check with your doctor.

Side Effects of This Medicine

Griseofulvin has been shown to cause liver and thyroid tumors in some animals. *You and your doctor should discuss the good this medicine will do, as well as the risks of taking it.*

Along with its needed effects, a medicine may cause some unwanted effects. Although not all of these side effects may occur, if they do occur they may need medical attention.

Check with your doctor as soon as possible if any of the following side effects occur:
Less common
  Confusion; increased sensitivity of skin to sunlight; skin rash, hives, or itching; soreness or irritation of mouth or tongue
Rare
  Numbness, tingling, pain, or weakness in hands or feet; sore throat and fever; yellow eyes or skin

Other side effects may occur that usually do not need medical attention. These side effects may go away during treatment as your body adjusts to the medicine. However, check with your doctor if any of the following side effects continue or are bothersome:
More common
  Headache
Less common
  Diarrhea; dizziness; nausea or vomiting; stomach pain; trouble in sleeping; unusual tiredness

Other side effects not listed above may also occur in some patients. If you notice any other effects, check with your doctor.

Revised: 08/08/2000

GROWTH HORMONE   Systemic

Commonly used brand name(s):

In the U.S.—

Genotropin[2]	Nutropin AQ[2]
Genotropin Miniquick[2]	Protropin[1]
Humatrope[2]	Saizen[2]
Norditropin[2]	Serostim[2]
Nutropin[2]	

In Canada—

Humatrope[2]	Protropin[1]
Nutropin[2]	Saizen[2]
Nutropin AQ[2]	Serostim[2]

Note: For quick reference, the following growth hormones are numbered to match the corresponding brand names.

This information applies to the following medicines:
1. Somatrem (SOE-ma-trem)
2. Somatropin, Recombinant (soe-ma-TROE-pin, re-KOM-binant)

Description

Somatrem and somatropin are man-made versions of human growth hormone. Growth hormone is naturally produced by the pituitary gland and is necessary to stimulate growth in children. Man-made growth hormone may be used in children who have certain conditions that cause failure to grow normally. These conditions include growth hormone deficiency (inability to produce enough growth hormone), kidney disease, and Turner's syndrome. Growth hormone is also used in adults to treat growth failure and to treat weight loss caused by acquired immunodeficiency syndrome (AIDS).

This medicine is available only with your doctor's prescription, in the following dosage forms:

Parenteral
Somatrem
• Injection (U.S. and Canada)
Somatropin, Recombinant
• Injection (U.S. and Canada)

Before Using This Medicine

In deciding to use a medicine, the risks of taking the medicine must be weighed against the good it will do. This is a decision you and your doctor will make. For growth hormone, the following should be considered:

Allergies—Tell your doctor if you have ever had any unusual or allergic reaction to growth hormone. Also tell your health care professional if you are allergic to any other substances, such as foods, preservatives, or dyes.

Pregnancy—Growth hormone has not been studied in pregnant women. However, in animal studies, growth hormone has not been shown to cause birth defects or other problems.

Breast-feeding—It is not known whether growth hormone passes into breast milk.

Children—There is no specific information comparing use of growth hormone in children with acquired immunodeficiency syndrome (AIDS) with use in other age groups.

Older adults—Many medicines have not been studied specifically in older people. Therefore, it may not be known whether they work exactly the same way they do in younger adults. Although there is no specific information comparing use of growth hormone in the elderly with use in other age groups, it is not expected to cause different side effects or problems in older people than it does in younger adults.

Other medicines—Although certain medicines should not be used together at all, in other cases two different medicines may be used together even if an interaction might occur. In these cases, your doctor may want to change the dose, or other precautions may be necessary. When you are taking growth hormone, it is especially important that your health care professional know if you are taking any of the following:

• Corticosteroids (cortisone-like medicines)—These medicines can interfere with the effects of growth hormone

Other medical problems—The presence of other medical problems may affect the use of growth hormone. Make sure you tell your doctor if you have any other medical problems, especially:

• Brain tumor—Growth hormone should not be used in patients who have a brain tumor that is still growing
• Diabetes mellitus (sugar diabetes)—Growth hormone may prevent insulin from working as well as it should; your doctor may have to change your dose of insulin
• Underactive thyroid—This condition can interfere with the effects of growth hormone

Proper Use of This Medicine

Some medicines given by injection may sometimes be given at home to patients who do not need to be in the hospital. If you are using this medicine at home, your health care professional will teach you how to prepare and inject the medicine. You will have a chance to practice preparing and injecting it. *Be certain that you understand exactly how the medicine is to be prepared and injected.*

It is important to follow any instructions from your doctor about the careful selection and rotation of injection sites on your body. This will help to prevent skin problems.

Put used needles and syringes in a puncture-resistant disposable container or dispose of them as directed by your health care professional. *Do not reuse needles and syringes.*

Dosing—The dose of these medicines will be different for different patients. *Follow your doctor's orders or the directions on the label.* The following information includes only the average doses of these medicines. *If your dose is different, do not change it* unless your doctor tells you to do so.

For somatrem
• For *injection* dosage form:
—For treatment of growth failure caused by growth hormone deficiency:
• Children—Dose is based on body weight and must be determined by your doctor. The usual total weekly dose is 0.3 milligram (mg) per kilogram (kg) (0.136 mg per pound) of body weight. This is divided into smaller doses and usually is injected under the skin, but may be injected into a muscle as determined by your doctor.

For somatropin
• For *injection* dosage form:
—For treatment of growth failure caused by growth hormone deficiency:
• Adults—Dose is based on body weight and must be determined by your doctor. At first, it is usually 0.006 milligram (mg) per kilogram (kg) (0.0027 mg

per pound) of body weight injected under the skin once a day. Your doctor may then increase the dose if needed.

- Children—Dose is based on body weight and must be determined by your doctor. The usual total weekly dose is 0.16 to 0.3 mg per kg (0.073 to 0.136 mg per pound) of body weight. This is divided into smaller doses and usually is injected under the skin, but may be injected into a muscle as determined by your doctor.
- Children using Norditropin Cartridges—Dose is based on body weight and must be determined by your doctor. The usual dose is 0.024 to 0.034 mg per kg (0.011 to 0.015 mg per pound of body weight) injected under the skin, 6 to 7 days a week. The dose is given using a Nordipen™ injection device.

—For treatment of growth failure caused by kidney disease:

- Children—Dose is based on body weight and must be determined by your doctor. The usual total weekly dose is 0.35 mg per kg (0.16 mg per pound) of body weight. This is divided into smaller daily doses and is injected under the skin or into a muscle.

—For treatment of growth failure caused by Turner's syndrome:

- Children—Dose is based on body weight and must be determined by your doctor. The usual total weekly dose is 0.375 mg per kg (0.17 mg per pound) of body weight. This is divided into smaller doses and is injected under the skin.

—For treatment of weight loss caused by acquired immunodeficiency disease (AIDS):

- Adults weighing more than 121 pounds (55 kg)—6 mg injected under the skin once a day at bedtime.
- Adults weighing 99 to 121 pounds (45 to 55 kg)—5 mg injected under the skin once a day at bedtime.
- Adults weighing 77 to 98 pounds (35 to 44 kg)—4 mg injected under the skin once a day at bedtime.
- Adults weighing less than 77 pounds (35 kg)—Dose is based on body weight and must be determined by your doctor. It is usually 0.1 mg per kg (0.045 mg per pound) of body weight injected under the skin once a day at bedtime.
- Children—Use and dose must be determined by your doctor.

Storage—To store this medicine:

- Keep out of the reach of children.
- Store away from heat and direct light.
- Store at temperature directed by your health care professional or the manufacturer.
- Do not keep outdated medicine or medicine no longer needed. Be sure that any discarded medicine is out of the reach of children.

Precautions While Using This Medicine

It is important that your doctor check your progress at regular visits.

Side Effects of This Medicine

Leukemia has been reported in a few patients after treatment with growth hormone. However, it is not definitely known whether the leukemia was caused by the growth hormone. Leukemia has also been reported in patients whose bodies do not make enough growth hormone and who have not yet been treated with man-made growth hormone. However, discuss this possible effect with your doctor.

If growth hormone is given to children or adults with normal growth, who do not need growth hormone, serious unwanted effects may occur because levels in the body become too high. These effects include the development of diabetes; abnormal growth of bones and internal organs such as the heart, kidneys, and liver; atherosclerosis (hardening of the arteries); and hypertension (high blood pressure).

Along with its needed effects, a medicine may cause some unwanted effects. Although not all of these side effects may occur, if they do occur they may need medical attention. Check with your doctor as soon as possible if any of the following side effects occur:

More common
Ear infection or other ear problems (in patients with Turner's syndrome)

Rare
Abdominal pain or bloating; changes in vision; depression of skin at place of injection; headache; limp; nausea and vomiting; pain and swelling at place of injection; pain in hip or knee; skin rash or itching

Other side effects may occur that usually do not need medical attention. These side effects may go away during treatment as your body adjusts to the medicine. However, check with your doctor if any of the following side effects continue or are bothersome:

Less common or rare
Carpal tunnel syndrome; enlargement of breasts; increased growth of birthmarks; joint pain; muscle pain; swelling of hands, feet, or lower legs; unusual tiredness or weakness

Other side effects not listed above may also occur in some patients. If you notice any other effects, check with your doctor.

Revised: 12/05/2000

GUAIFENESIN   Systemic

Commonly used brand name(s):

In the U.S.—

Anti-Tuss	Humibid Sprinkle
Breonesin	Hytuss
Diabetic Tussin EX	Hytuss-2X
Fenesin	Naldecon Senior EX
Gee-Gee	Organidin NR
Genatuss	Pneumomist
Glycotuss	Robitussin
Glytuss	Scot-tussin Expectorant
Guiatuss	Sinumist-SR
Halotussin	Touro EX
Humibid L.A.	Uni-tussin

Generic name product may be available.

In Canada—
Balminil Expectorant
Benylin-E
Calmylin Expectorant
Resyl
Robitussin

Another commonly used name is glyceryl guaiacolate.

Description

Guaifenesin (gwye-FEN-e-sin) is used to help coughs caused by colds or similar illnesses clear mucus or phlegm (pronounced flem) from the chest. It works by thinning the mucus or phlegm in the lungs.

Some guaifenesin preparations are available only with your doctor's prescription. Others are available without a prescription; however, your doctor may have special instructions on the proper dose of guaifenesin for your medical condition. Guaifenesin is available in the following dosage forms:

Oral
- Capsules (U.S.)
- Extended-release capsules (U.S.)
- Oral solution (U.S.)
- Syrup (U.S. and Canada)
- Tablets (U.S. and Canada)
- Extended-release tablets (U.S.)

Before Using This Medicine

If you are taking this medicine without a prescription, carefully read and follow any precautions on the label. For guaifenesin, the following should be considered:

Allergies—Tell your doctor if you have ever had any unusual or allergic reaction to guaifenesin. Also tell your health care professional if you are allergic to any other substances, such as foods, preservatives, or dyes.

Pregnancy—Several groups of women taking guaifenesin during pregnancy have been studied. In one group, when guaifenesin was taken during the first 3 months of pregnancy, the babies had more inguinal hernias than expected. However, more birth defects than expected did not occur in the babies of other groups of women taking guaifenesin during pregnancy. Studies have not been done in animals.

Breast-feeding—It is not known whether guaifenesin passes into breast milk. However, guaifenesin has not been reported to cause problems in nursing babies.

Children—Although there is no specific information comparing use of guaifenesin in children with use in other age groups, this medicine is not expected to cause different side effects or problems in children than it does in adults. However, check with your doctor before using this medicine in children who have a chronic cough, such as occurs with asthma, or who have an unusually large amount of mucus or phlegm with the cough. Children with these conditions may need a different kind of medicine. Also, guaifenesin should not be given to children younger than 2 years of age unless you are directed to do so by your doctor.

Older adults—Many medicines have not been studied specifically in older people. Therefore, it may not be known whether they work exactly the same way they do in younger adults. Although there is no specific information comparing use of guaifenesin in the elderly with use in other age groups, this medicine is not expected to cause different side effects or problems in older people than it does in younger adults.

Proper Use of This Medicine

Drinking plenty of water while taking guaifenesin may help loosen mucus or phlegm in the lungs.

For patients taking the *extended-release capsule* form of this medicine:
- Swallow the capsule whole, or open the capsule and sprinkle the contents on soft food such as applesauce, jelly, or pudding and swallow without crushing or chewing.

For patients taking the *extended-release tablet* form of this medicine:
- If the tablet has a groove in it, you may carefully break it into two pieces along the groove. Then swallow the pieces whole, without crushing or chewing them.
- If the tablet does not have a groove in it, it must be swallowed whole. Do not break, crush, or chew it before swallowing.

Dosing—The dose of guaifenesin will be different for different patients. *Follow your doctor's orders or the directions on the label.* The following information includes only the average doses of guaifenesin. *If your dose is different, do not change it* unless your doctor tells you to do so.
- For *regular (short-acting) oral* dosage forms (capsules, oral solution, syrup, or tablets):
  —For cough:
    - Adults—200 to 400 milligrams (mg) every four hours.
    - Children younger than 2 years of age—Use and dose must be determined by your doctor.
    - Children 2 to 6 years of age—50 to 100 mg every four hours.
    - Children 6 to 12 years of age—100 to 200 mg every four hours.
- For *long-acting oral* dosage forms (extended-release capsules or tablets):
  —For cough:
    - Adults—600 to 1200 mg every twelve hours.
    - Children younger than 2 years of age—Use is not recommended.
    - Children 2 to 6 years of age—300 mg every twelve hours.
    - Children 6 to 12 years of age—600 mg every twelve hours.

Missed dose—If you must take this medicine regularly and you miss a dose, take it as soon as possible. However, if it is almost time for your next dose, skip the missed dose and go back to your regular dosing schedule. Do not double doses.

Storage—To store this medicine:
- Keep out of the reach of children.
- Store away from heat and direct light.
- Do not store the capsule or tablet form of this medicine in the bathroom, near the kitchen sink, or in other damp places. Heat or moisture may cause the medicine to break down.
- Do not refrigerate the syrup form of this medicine.
- Do not keep outdated medicine or medicine no longer needed. Be sure that any discarded medicine is out of the reach of children.

Precautions While Using This Medicine

If your cough has not improved after 7 days or if you have a fever, skin rash, continuing headache, or sore throat with the cough, check with your doctor. These signs may mean that you have other medical problems.

Side Effects of This Medicine

Along with its needed effects, a medicine may cause some unwanted effects. Although not all of these side effects may occur, if they do occur they may need medical attention. Some side effects may occur that usually do not need medical attention. These side effects may go away during treatment as your body adjusts to the medicine.

However, check with your doctor if any of the following side effects continue or are bothersome:

Less common or rare
　　Diarrhea; dizziness; headache; hives; nausea or vomiting; skin rash; stomach pain

Other side effects not listed above may also occur in some patients. If you notice any other effects, check with your doctor.

Revised: 06/27/00

GUANABENZ Systemic†

Commonly used brand name(s):

In the U.S.—
　Wytensin

　†Not commercially available in Canada.

Description

Guanabenz (GWAHN-a-benz) belongs to the general class of medicines called antihypertensives. It is used to treat high blood pressure (hypertension).

High blood pressure adds to the work load of the heart and arteries. If it continues for a long time, the heart and arteries may not function properly. This can damage the blood vessels of the brain, heart, and kidneys, resulting in a stroke, heart failure, or kidney failure. High blood pressure may also increase the risk of heart attacks. These problems may be less likely to occur if blood pressure is controlled.

Guanabenz works by controlling nerve impulses along certain nerve pathways. As a result, it relaxes blood vessels so that blood passes through them more easily. This helps to lower blood pressure.

Guanabenz is available only with your doctor's prescription, in the following dosage form:

Oral
　• Tablets (U.S.)

Before Using This Medicine

In deciding to use a medicine, the risks of taking the medicine must be weighed against the good it will do. This is a decision you and your doctor will make. For guanabenz, the following should be considered:

Allergies—Tell your doctor if you have ever had any unusual or allergic reaction to guanabenz. Also tell your health care professional if you are allergic to any other substance, such as foods, preservatives, or dyes.

Pregnancy—Guanabenz has not been studied in pregnant women. However, studies in rats have shown that guanabenz given in doses 9 to 10 times the maximum human dose caused a decrease in fertility. In addition, 3 to 6 times the maximum human dose caused birth defects (in the skeleton) in mice, and 6 to 9 times the maximum human dose caused death of the fetus in rats. Before taking this medicine, make sure your doctor knows if you are pregnant or if you may become pregnant.

Breast-feeding—It is not known whether guanabenz passes into the breast milk. However, this medicine has not been reported to cause problems in nursing babies.

Children—Studies on this medicine have been done only in adult patients, and there is no specific information comparing use of guanabenz in children with use in other age groups.

Older adults—Many medicines have not been studied specifically in older people. Therefore, it may not be known whether they work exactly the same way they do in younger adults or if they cause different side effects or problems in older people. There is no specific information comparing use of guanabenz in the elderly with use in other age groups. However, dizziness, faintness, or drowsiness may be more likely to occur in the elderly, who are usually more sensitive to the effects of guanabenz.

Other medicines—Although certain medicines should not be used together at all, in other cases two different medicines may be used together even if an interaction might occur. In these cases, your doctor may want to change the dose, or other precautions may be necessary. When you are taking guanabenz, it is especially important that your health care professional know if you are taking any of the following:

• Beta-blockers (acebutolol [e.g., Sectral], atenolol [e.g., Tenormin], betaxolol [Kerlone], bisoprolol [e.g., Zebeta], carteolol [e.g., Cartrol], labetalol [e.g., Normodyne], metoprolol [e.g., Lopressor], nadolol [e.g., Corgard], oxprenolol [e.g., Trasicor], penbutolol [e.g., Levatol], pindolol [e.g., Visken], propranolol [e.g., Inderal], sotalol [e.g., Sotacor], timolol [e.g., Blocadren])—Effects on blood pressure may be increased. Also, the risk of unwanted effects when guanabenz treatment is stopped suddenly may be increased

Other medical problems—The presence of other medical problems may affect the use of guanabenz. Make sure you tell your doctor if you have any other medical problems, especially:

• Heart or blood vessel disease—Lowering blood pressure may make some conditions worse

• Kidney disease or
• Liver disease—Effects of guanabenz may be increased because of slower removal of guanabenz from the body

Proper Use of This Medicine

In addition to the use of the medicine your doctor has prescribed, treatment for your high blood pressure may include weight control and care in the types of foods you eat, especially foods high in sodium. Your doctor will tell you which of these are most important for you. You should check with your doctor before changing your diet.

Many patients who have high blood pressure will not notice any signs of the problem. In fact, many may feel normal. It is very important that you *take your medicine exactly as directed* and that you keep your appointments with your doctor even if you feel well.

Remember that this medicine will not cure your high blood pressure but it does help control it. Therefore, you must continue to take it as directed if you expect to lower your blood pressure and keep it down. *You may have to take high blood pressure medicine for the rest of your life.* If high blood pressure is not treated, it can cause serious problems such as heart failure, blood vessel disease, stroke, or kidney disease.

To help you remember to take your medicine, try to get into the habit of taking it at the same time each day.

Dosing—The dose of guanabenz will be different for different patients. *Follow your doctor's orders or the directions on the label.* The following information includes only the average doses of guanabenz. *If your dose is different, do not change it* unless your doctor tells you to do so.

The number of tablets that you take depends on the strength of the medicine.
- For *oral* dosage form (tablets):
  —For high blood pressure:
  - Adults—At first, 4 milligrams (mg) two times a day. Then, your doctor may gradually increase your dose.
  - Children—Use and dose must be determined by your doctor.

Missed dose—
- If you miss a dose of this medicine, take it as soon as possible. However, if it is almost time for your next dose, skip the missed dose and go back to your regular dosing schedule. Do not double doses.
- If you miss two or more doses in a row, check with your doctor. If your body suddenly goes without this medicine, some unpleasant effects may occur. If you have any questions about this, check with your doctor.

Storage—To store this medicine:
- Keep out of the reach of children.
- Store away from heat and direct light.
- Do not store in the bathroom, near the kitchen sink, or in other damp places. Heat or moisture may cause the medicine to break down.
- Do not keep outdated medicine or medicine no longer needed. Be sure that any discarded medicine is out of the reach of children.

Precautions While Using This Medicine

It is important that your doctor check your progress at regular visits to make sure that this medicine is working properly.

Check with your doctor before you stop taking guanabenz. Your doctor may want you to reduce gradually the amount you are taking before stopping completely.

Before having any kind of surgery (including dental surgery) or emergency treatment, tell the medical doctor or dentist in charge that you are using this medicine.

Do not take other medicines unless they have been discussed with your doctor. This especially includes over-the-counter (nonprescription) medicines for appetite control, asthma, colds, cough, hay fever, or sinus problems, since they may tend to increase your blood pressure.

Guanabenz will add to the effects of alcohol and other CNS depressants (medicines that slow down the nervous system, possibly causing drowsiness). Some examples of CNS depressants are antihistamines or medicine for hay fever, other allergies, or colds; sedatives, tranquilizers, or sleeping medicine; prescription pain medicine or narcotics; barbiturates; medicine for seizures; muscle relaxants; or anesthetics, including some dental anesthetics. *Check with your doctor before taking any of the above while you are using this medicine.*

Guanabenz may cause some people to become dizzy, drowsy, or less alert than they are normally. *Make sure you know how you react to this medicine before you drive, use machines, or do anything else that could be dangerous if you are dizzy or are not alert.*

Guanabenz may cause dryness of the mouth, nose, and throat. For temporary relief of mouth dryness, use sugarless candy or gum, melt bits of ice in your mouth, or use a saliva substitute. However, if your mouth continues to feel dry for more than 2 weeks, check with your medical doctor or dentist. Continuing dryness of the mouth may increase the chance of dental disease, including tooth decay, gum disease, and fungus infections.

Side Effects of This Medicine

Along with its needed effects, a medicine may cause some unwanted effects. Although not all of these side effects may occur, if they do occur they may need medical attention.

Check with your doctor as soon as possible if any of the following side effects occur:
Signs and symptoms of overdose
  Dizziness (severe); irritability; nervousness; pinpoint pupils; slow heartbeat; unusual tiredness or weakness

Other side effects may occur that usually do not need medical attention. These side effects may go away during treatment as your body adjusts to the medicine. However, check with your doctor if any of the following side effects continue or are bothersome:
More common
  Dizziness; drowsiness; dryness of mouth; weakness
Less common or rare
  Decreased sexual ability; headache; nausea

After you have been using this medicine for a while, unpleasant effects may occur if you stop taking it too suddenly. After you stop taking this medicine, check with your doctor if any of the following effects occur:
  Anxiety or tenseness; chest pain; fast or irregular heartbeat; headache; increased salivation; increase in sweating; nausea or vomiting; nervousness or restlessness; shaking or trembling of hands or fingers; stomach cramps; trouble in sleeping

Other side effects not listed above may also occur in some patients. If you notice any other effects, check with your doctor.

Revised: 06/28/96

HAEMOPHILUS B CONJUGATE VACCINE Systemic

Commonly used brand name(s):

In the U.S.—
Act-Hib[4]   Pedvaxhib[3]
Hibtiter[1]   Prohibit[2]

In Canada—
Act-Hib[4]   Pedvaxhib[3]
Hibtiter[1]   Prohibit[2]

Other commonly used names are: HbOC, PRP-D, PRP-OMP, and PRP-T.

This information applies to the following medicines:
1. Haemophilus b Conjugate Vaccine (HbOC—Diphtheria CRM$_{197}$ Protein Conjugate)‡§
2. Haemophilus b Conjugate Vaccine (PRP-D—Diphtheria Toxoid Conjugate)‡§
3. Haemophilus b Conjugate Vaccine (PRP-OMP—Meningococcal Protein Conjugate)§
4. Haemophilus b Conjugate Vaccine (PRP-T—Tetanus Protein Conjugate)‡§

‡Generic name product may be available in the U.S.
§Generic name product may be available in Canada.

Description

Haemophilus b conjugate (hem-OFF-fil-us BEE KON-ja-gat) vaccine is an active immunizing agent used to prevent infection by *Haemophilus influenza* type b (Hib) bacteria. The vaccine works by causing your body to produce its own protection (antibodies) against the disease.

Haemophilus b conjugate vaccine is an haemophilus b vaccine that has been prepared by adding a diphtheria-, meningococcal-, or tetanus-related substance. However, this vaccine does *not* take the place of the regular diphtheria or tetanus toxoid injections (for example, DTP, DT, or T) that children should receive, the regular tetanus toxoid or diphtheria and tetanus toxoid injections (for example T or Td) that adults should receive, or the meningococcal vaccine injection that some children and adults should receive.

Infection by *Haemophilus influenza* type b (Hib) bacteria can cause life-threatening illnesses, such as meningitis, which affects the brain; epiglottitis, which can cause death by suffocation; pericarditis, which affects the heart; pneumonia, which affects the lungs; and septic arthritis, which affects the bones and joints. Hib meningitis causes death in 5 to 10% of children who are infected. Also, approximately 30% of children who survive Hib meningitis are left with some type of serious permanent damage, such as mental retardation, deafness, epilepsy, or partial blindness.

Immunization against Hib is recommended for all children 2 months up to 5 years of age (i.e., up to the 5th birthday).

Immunization against Hib may also be recommended for adults and children over 5 years of age with certain medical problems.

This vaccine is to be administered only by or under the supervision of your doctor or other authorized health care professional. It is available in the following dosage form:

Parenteral
• Injection (U.S. and Canada)

Before Receiving This Vaccine

In deciding to use a medicine, the risks of taking the medicine must be weighed against the good it will do. This is a decision you and your doctor will make. For haemophilus b conjugate vaccine, the following should be considered:

Allergies—Tell your doctor if you have ever had any unusual or allergic reaction to haemophilus b conjugate vaccine, haemophilus b polysaccharide vaccine, diphtheria or tetanus toxoid, or meningococcal vaccine. Also tell your health care professional if you are allergic to any other substances, such as preservatives.

Pregnancy—Studies on effects in pregnancy have not been done in either humans or animals.

Breast-feeding—This vaccine has not been reported to cause problems in nursing babies.

Children—This vaccine is not recommended for children less than 2 months of age.

Older adults—Many medicines have not been studied specifically in older people. Therefore, it may not be known whether they work exactly the same way they do in younger adults. Although there is no specific information comparing use of this vaccine in the elderly with use in other age groups, this vaccine is not expected to cause different side effects or problems in older people than it does in younger adults.

Other medicines—Although certain medicines should not be used together at all, in other cases two different medicines may be used together even if an interaction might occur. In these cases, your doctor may want to change the dose, or other precautions may be necessary. Tell your health care professional if you are using any other prescription or nonprescription (over-the-counter [OTC]) medicine.

Other medical problems—The presence of other medical problems may affect the use of haemophilus b conjugate vaccine. Make sure you tell your doctor if you have any other medical problems, especially:

• Fever or
• Serious illness—The symptoms of the condition may be confused with some of the possible side effects of the vaccine

Proper Use of This Vaccine

Dosing—Haemophilus b conjugate vaccine is an haemophilus b vaccine that has been prepared by adding a diphtheria-, meningococcal-, or tetanus-related substance to it. If the vaccine was prepared using a diphtheria-related substance, it is called either HbOC or PRP-D. If the vaccine was prepared using a meningococcal-related substance, it is called PRP-OMP. If the vaccine was prepared using a tetanus-related substance, it is called PRP-T. *All of these subtypes of haemophilus b conjugate vaccine work the same way*, but may be given at different ages or times.

The dose of haemophilus b conjugate vaccine will be different for different patients. The following information includes only the average doses of haemophilus b conjugate vaccine.

• For prevention of *Haemophilus influenzae* type b infection:
  —For *HbOC or PRP-T injection* dosage form:
  • Adults and children 5 years of age and older—Use and dose must be determined by your doctor.
  • Infants 2 to 6 months of age at the first dose—Three doses, two months apart, then a booster dose at fifteen months of age. The doses are injected into a muscle.
  • Children 7 to 11 months of age at the first dose—Two doses, two months apart, then a booster

dose at fifteen months of age. The doses are injected into a muscle.
- Children 12 to 14 months of age at the first dose—One dose, then a booster dose at fifteen months of age. The doses are injected into a muscle.
- Children 15 to 59 months of age at the first dose—One dose injected into a muscle.

—For *PRP-D injection* dosage form:
- Adults and children 5 years of age and older—Use and dose must be determined by your doctor.
- Infants and children up to 15 months of age—Use is not recommended.
- Children 15 to 59 months of age at the first dose—One dose injected into a muscle.

—For *PRP-OMP injection* dosage form:
- Adults and children 5 years of age and older—Use and dose must be determined by your doctor.
- Infants 2 to 6 months of age at the first dose—Two doses, two months apart, then a booster dose at twelve months of age. The doses are injected into a muscle.
- Children 7 to 11 months of age at the first dose—Two doses, two months apart, then a booster dose at fifteen months of age. The doses are injected into a muscle.
- Children 12 to 14 months of age at the first dose—One dose, then a booster dose at fifteen months of age. The doses are injected into a muscle.
- Children 15 to 59 months of age at the first dose—One dose injected into a muscle.

After Receiving This Vaccine

This vaccine may interfere with laboratory tests that check for Hib disease. Make sure your doctor knows that you have received Hib vaccine if you are treated for a severe infection during the 2 weeks after you receive this vaccine.

Side Effects of This Vaccine

Along with its needed effects, a vaccine may cause some unwanted effects. Although not all of these side effects may occur, if they do occur they may need medical attention.

Get emergency help immediately if any of the following side effects occur:
  Symptoms of allergic reactions
    Difficulty in breathing or swallowing; hives; itching (especially of feet or hands); reddening of skin (especially around ears); swelling of eyes, face, or inside of nose; unusual tiredness or weakness (sudden and severe)

Check with your doctor immediately if the following side effect occurs:
  Rare
  Convulsions (seizures)

Other side effects may occur that usually do not need medical attention. However, check with your doctor if any of the following side effects continue or are bothersome:
  More common
    Fever of up to 102 °F (39 °C) (usually lasts less than 48 hours); irritability; loss of appetite; lack of interest; redness at place of injection; reduced physical activity; tenderness at place of injection; tiredness
  Less common
    Diarrhea; fever over 102 °F (39 °C) (usually lasts less

than 48 hours); hard lump, swelling, or warm feeling at place of injection; skin rash; vomiting

Other side effects not listed above may also occur in some patients. If you notice any other effects, check with your doctor.

Revised: 08/04/2000

HAEMOPHILUS B POLYSACCHARIDE VACCINE
Systemic†

Commonly used names are:
  Haemophilus influenzae type b polysaccharide vaccine, HbPV, Hib CPS, Hib polysaccharide vaccine, PRP

†Not commercially available in Canada.

Description

Haemophilus b polysaccharide (hem-OFF-fil-us BEE pol-i-SAK-ka-ryd) vaccine is an active immunizing agent used to prevent infection by *Haemophilus influenzae* type b (Hib) bacteria. The vaccine works by causing your body to produce its own protection (antibodies) against the disease.

The following information applies only to the Haemophilus b polysaccharide vaccine.

Infection by *Haemophilus influenzae* type b (Hib) bacteria can cause life-threatening illnesses, such as meningitis, which affects the brain; epiglottitis, which can cause death by suffocation; pericarditis, which affects the heart; pneumonia, which affects the lungs; and septic arthritis, which affects the bones and joints. Hib meningitis causes death in 5 to 10% of children who are infected. Also, approximately 30% of children who survive Hib meningitis are left with some type of serious permanent damage, such as mental retardation, deafness, epilepsy, or partial blindness.

Immunization against Hib is recommended for all children 24 months up to 5 years of age (i.e., up to the 5th birthday). In addition, immunization is recommended for children 18 to 24 months of age, especially:
- Children attending day-care facilities.
- Children with chronic illnesses associated with increased risk of Hib disease. These illnesses include asplenia, sickle cell disease, antibody deficiency syndromes, immunosuppression, and Hodgkin's disease.
- Children 18 to 24 months of age who have already had Hib disease. These children may get the disease again if they are not immunized. Children who developed Hib disease when 24 months of age or older do not need to be immunized, since most children in this age group will develop antibodies against the disease.
- Children with human immunodeficiency virus (HIV) infection or acquired immunodeficiency syndrome (AIDS).
- Children of certain racial groups, such as American Indian and Alaskan Eskimo. Children in these groups seem to be at increased risk of Hib disease.
- Children living close together with groups of other persons. Close living conditions increase a child's risk of being exposed to persons who have Hib infection or who carry the bacteria.

It is recommended that children immunized when they were 18 to 24 months of age receive a second dose of vaccine, since these children may not produce enough antibodies to fully protect them from Hib disease. Children who were first immunized when they were 24 months of age or older do not need to be reimmunized.

This vaccine is available only from your doctor or other authorized health care professional, in the following dosage form:

Parenteral
- Injection

Before Receiving This Vaccine

In deciding to use a medicine, the risks of taking the medicine must be weighed against the good it will do. This is a decision you and your doctor will make. For haemophilus b polysaccharide vaccine, the following should be considered:

Allergies—Tell your doctor if you have ever had any unusual or allergic reaction to haemophilus b polysaccharide vaccine or haemophilus b conjugate vaccine. Also tell your health care professional if you are allergic to any other substances, such as preservatives.

Children—This vaccine is not recommended for children less than 18 months of age.

Other medicines—Although certain medicines should not be used together at all, in other cases two different medicines may be used together even if an interaction might occur. In these cases, your doctor may want to change the dose, or other precautions may be necessary. Tell your health care professional if you are using any other prescription or nonprescription (over-the-counter [OTC]) medicine.

Other medical problems—The presence of other medical problems may affect the use of haemophilus b polysaccharide vaccine. Make sure you tell your doctor if you have any other medical problems, especially:

- Fever or
- Serious illness—The symptoms of the condition may be confused with the possible side effects of the vaccine

Proper Use of This Vaccine

Dosing—The dose of haemophilus b polysaccharide vaccine will be different for different patients. The following information includes only the average doses of haemophilus b polysaccharide vaccine.

- For *injection* dosage form:
  - For prevention of *Haemophilus influenzae* type b infection:
    - Adults and children 5 years of age and older— Use is not recommended.
    - Children up to 18 months of age—Use is not recommended.
    - Children 18 to 24 months of age—Use and dose must be determined by your doctor.
    - Children 24 months to 5 years of age—One dose injected under the skin or into a muscle.

Side Effects of This Vaccine

Along with its needed effects, a vaccine may cause some unwanted effects. Although not all of these side effects may occur, if they do occur they may need medical attention.

Get emergency help immediately if any of the following side effects occur:
Symptoms of allergic reaction
Difficulty in breathing or swallowing; hives; itching (especially of feet or hands); reddening of skin (especially around ears); swelling of eyes, face, or inside of nose; unusual tiredness or weakness (sudden and severe)

Check with your doctor immediately if the following side effect occurs:
Rare
Convulsions (seizures)

Other side effects may occur that usually do not need medical attention. However, check with your doctor if any of the following side effects continue or are bothersome:
More common
Diarrhea; fever up to 102 °F (39 °C) (usually lasts less than 48 hours); irritability; lack of appetite; lack of interest; redness at place of injection; reduced physical activity; tenderness at place of injection

Less common
Fever over 102 °F (39 °C) (usually lasts less than 48 hours); hard lump at place of injection; itching; joint aches or pains; skin rash; swelling at place of injection; trouble in sleeping; vomiting

Other side effects not listed above may also occur in some patients. If you notice any other effects, check with your doctor.

Revised: 06/21/93
Interim revision: 03/29/94

HALOPERIDOL   Systemic

Commonly used brand name(s):

In the U.S.—
Haldol
Haldol Decanoate
Generic name product may be available.

In Canada—

Apo-Haloperidol	Novo-Peridol
Haldol	Peridol
Haldol LA	PMS Haloperidol

Description

Haloperidol (ha-loe-PER-i-dole) is used to treat nervous, mental, and emotional conditions. It is also used to control the symptoms of Tourette's disorder. Haloperidol may also be used for other conditions as determined by your doctor.

Haloperidol is available only with your doctor's prescription, in the following dosage forms:

Oral
- Solution (U.S. and Canada)
- Tablets (U.S. and Canada)
Parenteral
- Injection (U.S. and Canada)

Before Using This Medicine

In deciding to use a medicine, the risks of taking the medicine must be weighed against the good it will do. This is a decision you and your doctor will make. For haloperidol, the following should be considered:

Allergies—Tell your doctor if you have ever had any unusual or allergic reaction to haloperidol. Also tell your health care professional if you are allergic to any other substances, such as foods, preservatives, or dyes.

Pregnancy—Haloperidol has not been studied in pregnant women. However, studies in animals given 2 to 20 times the usual maximum human dose of haloperidol have shown reduced fertility, delayed delivery, cleft palate, and an increase in the number of stillbirths and newborn deaths.

Breast-feeding—Haloperidol passes into breast milk. Animal studies have shown that haloperidol in breast milk causes drowsiness and unusual muscle movements in the nursing offspring. Breast-feeding is not recommended during treatment with haloperidol.

Children—Side effects, especially muscle spasms of the neck and back, twisting movements of the body, trembling of fingers and hands, and inability to move the eyes are more likely to occur in children, who usually are more sensitive than adults to the effects of haloperidol.

Older adults—Constipation, dizziness or fainting, drowsiness, dryness of mouth, trembling of the hands and fingers, and symptoms of tardive dyskinesia (such as rapid, worm-like movements of the tongue or any other uncontrolled movements of the mouth, tongue, or jaw, and/or arms and legs) are especially likely to occur in elderly patients, who are usually more sensitive than younger adults to the effects of haloperidol.

Other medicines—Although certain medicines should not be used together at all, in other cases 2 different medicines may be used together even if an interaction might occur. In these cases, your doctor may want to change the dose, or other precautions may be necessary. When you are taking haloperidol, it is especially important that your health care professional know if you are taking any of the following:

- Amoxapine (e.g., Asendin) or
- Metoclopramide (e.g., Reglan) or
- Metyrosine (e.g., Demser) or
- Other antipsychotics (medicine for mental illness) or
- Pemoline (e.g., Cylert) or
- Pimozide (e.g., Orap) or
- Promethazine (e.g., Phenergan) or
- Rauwolfia alkaloids (alseroxylon [e.g., Rauwiloid], deserpidine [e.g., Harmonyl], rauwolfia serpentina [e.g., Raudixin], reserpine [e.g., Serpasil]) or
- Trimeprazine (e.g., Temaril)—Taking these medicines with haloperidol may increase the frequency and severity of certain side effects
- Central nervous system (CNS) depressants (medicine that causes drowsiness) or
- Tricyclic antidepressants (medicine for depression)—Taking these medicines with haloperidol may result in increased CNS and other depressant effects, and in an increased chance of low blood pressure (hypotension)
- Epinephrine (e.g., Adrenalin)—Severe low blood pressure or irregular heartbeat may occur
- Levodopa (e.g., Dopar, Larodopa)—Haloperidol may interfere with the effects of this medicine

- Lithium (e.g., Eskalith, Lithane)—Although lithium and haloperidol are sometimes used together, their use must be closely monitored by your doctor, who may change the amount of medicine you need to take

Other medical problems—The presence of other medical problems may affect the use of haloperidol. Make sure you tell your doctor if you have any other medical problems, especially:

- Alcohol abuse—The risk of heat stroke may be increased
- Difficult urination or
- Glaucoma or
- Heart or blood vessel disease or
- Lung disease or
- Parkinson's disease—Haloperidol may make the condition worse
- Epilepsy—The risk of seizures may be increased
- Kidney disease or
- Liver disease—Higher blood levels of haloperidol may occur, increasing the chance of side effects
- Overactive thyroid—Serious unwanted effects may occur

Proper Use of This Medicine

If this medicine upsets your stomach, it may be taken with food or milk to lessen stomach irritation.

For patients taking the *liquid form of this medicine:*
- This medicine is to be taken by mouth even if it comes in a dropper bottle. Each dose is to be measured with the specially marked dropper provided with your prescription. Do not use other droppers since they may not deliver the correct amount of medicine.
- This medicine should be mixed with water or a beverage such as orange juice, apple juice, tomato juice, or cola and taken immediately after mixing. Haloperidol should not be mixed with tea or coffee, since they cause the medicine to separate out of solution.

Take this medicine only as directed by your doctor. Do not take more of it, do not take it more often, and do not take it for a longer time than your doctor ordered. This is particularly important for children or elderly patients, since they may react very strongly to this medicine.

Continue taking this medicine for the full time of treatment. *Sometimes haloperidol must be taken for several days to several weeks before its full effect is reached.*

Dosing—The dose of haloperidol will be different for different patients. *Follow your doctor's orders or the directions on the label.* The following information includes only the average doses of haloperidol. *If your dose is different, do not change it* unless your doctor tells you to do so.

The number of tablets or dropperfuls of solution that you take or injections that you receive depends on the strength of the medicine. Also, *the number of doses you take each day, the time allowed between doses, and the length of time you take the medicine depend on the medical problem for which you are using haloperidol.*

- For *oral* dosage forms (solution and tablets):
  —Adults and adolescents: To start, 500 micrograms to 5 milligrams two or three times a day. Your doctor may increase your dose if needed. However, the dose is usually not more than 100 milligrams a day.

—Children 3 to 12 years of age or weighing 15 to 40 kilograms (33 to 88 pounds): Dose is based on body weight. The usual dose is 25 to 150 micrograms per kilogram (11 to 68 micrograms per pound) a day, taken in smaller doses two or three times a day.

—Children up to 3 years of age: Dose must be determined by the doctor.

—Older adults: To start, 500 micrograms to 2 milligrams two or three times a day. The doctor may increase your dose if needed.

• For *short-acting injection* dosage form:

—Adults and adolescents: To start, 2 to 5 milligrams, usually injected into a muscle. The dose may be repeated every one to eight hours, depending on your condition.

—Children: Dose must be determined by the doctor.

• For *long-acting or depot injection* dosage form:

—Adults and adolescents: To start, the dose is usually 10 to 15 times the daily oral dose you were taking, injected into a muscle once a month. The doctor may adjust how much of this medicine you need and how often you will need it, depending on your condition.

—Children: Dose must be determined by the doctor.

Missed dose—If you miss a dose of this medicine, take it as soon as possible. Then take any remaining doses for that day at regularly spaced intervals. Do not double doses.

Storage—To store this medicine:

• Keep out of the reach of children.
• Store away from heat and direct light.
• Do not store the tablet form of this medicine in the bathroom, near the kitchen sink, or in other damp places. Heat or moisture may cause the medicine to break down.
• Keep the liquid form of this medicine from freezing.
• Do not keep outdated medicine or medicine no longer needed. Be sure that any discarded medicine is out of the reach of children.

Precautions While Using This Medicine

Your doctor should check your progress at regular visits, especially during the first few months of treatment with this medicine. The amount of haloperidol you take may be changed often to meet the needs of your condition. This also helps prevent side effects.

Do not stop taking this medicine without first checking with your doctor. Your doctor may want you to reduce gradually the amount you are taking before stopping completely. This will allow your body time to adjust and help avoid a worsening of your medical condition.

This medicine will add to the effects of alcohol and other CNS depressants (medicines that slow down the nervous system, possibly causing drowsiness). Some examples of CNS depressants are antihistamines or medicine for hay fever, other allergies, or colds; sedatives, tranquilizers, or sleeping medicine; prescription pain medicine or narcotics; barbiturates; medicine for seizures; muscle relaxants; or anesthetics, including some dental anesthetics. *Check with your doctor before taking any of the above while you are taking this medicine.*

This medicine may cause some people to become dizzy, drowsy, or less alert than they are normally, especially as the amount of medicine is increased. Even if you take haloperidol at bedtime, you may feel drowsy or less alert on arising. *Make sure you know how you react to this medicine before you drive, use machines, or do anything else that could be dangerous if you are dizzy or are not alert.*

Although not a problem for many patients, dizziness, light-headedness, or fainting may occur, especially when you get up from a lying or sitting position. Getting up slowly may help. However, if the problem continues or gets worse, check with your doctor.

This medicine will often make you sweat less, causing your body temperature to increase. *Use extra care not to become overheated during exercise or hot weather while you are taking this medicine, since overheating may result in heat stroke.* Also, hot baths or saunas may make you feel dizzy or faint while you are taking this medicine.

Before using any prescription or over-the-counter (OTC) medicine for colds or allergies, check with your doctor. These medicines may increase the chance of heat stroke or other unwanted effects, such as dizziness, dry mouth, blurred vision, and constipation, while you are taking haloperidol.

Before having any kind of surgery, dental treatment, or emergency treatment, tell the medical doctor or dentist in charge that you are using this medicine. Taking haloperidol together with medicines that are used during surgery or dental or emergency treatments may increase the CNS depressant effects.

Haloperidol may cause your skin to be more sensitive to sunlight than it is normally. Exposure to sunlight, even for brief periods of time, may cause a skin rash, itching, redness or other discoloration of the skin, or a severe sunburn. When you begin taking this medicine:

• Stay out of direct sunlight, especially between the hours of 10:00 a.m. and 3:00 p.m., if possible.
• Wear protective clothing, including a hat. Also, wear sunglasses.
• Apply a sun block product that has a skin protection factor (SPF) of at least 15. Some patients may require a product with a higher SPF number, especially if they have a fair complexion. If you have any questions about this, check with your health care professional.
• Apply a sun block lipstick that has an SPF of at least 15 to protect your lips.
• Do not use a sunlamp or tanning bed or booth.

If you have a severe reaction from the sun, check with your doctor.

Haloperidol may cause dryness of the mouth. For temporary relief, use sugarless candy or gum, melt bits of ice in your mouth, or use a saliva substitute. However, if your mouth continues to feel dry for more than 2 weeks, check with your medical doctor or dentist. Continuing dryness of the mouth may increase the chance of dental disease, including tooth decay, gum disease, and fungus infections.

If you are taking the liquid form of this medicine, avoid getting it on your skin because it may cause a skin rash or other irritation.

If you are *receiving this medicine by injection:*

• The effects of the long-acting injection form of this medicine may last for up to 6 weeks. *The precautions and side effects information for this medicine applies during this time.*

Side Effects of This Medicine

Along with its needed effects, haloperidol can sometimes cause serious side effects. Tardive dyskinesia (a movement disorder) may occur and may not go away after you stop using the medicine. Signs of tardive dyskinesia include fine, worm-like movements of the tongue, or other uncontrolled movements of the mouth, tongue, cheeks, jaw, or arms and legs. Other serious but rare side effects may also occur. These include severe muscle stiffness, fever, unusual tiredness or weakness, fast heartbeat, difficult breathing, increased sweating, loss of bladder control, and seizures (neuroleptic malignant syndrome). *You and your doctor should discuss the good this medicine will do as well as the risks of taking it.*

Stop taking haloperidol and get emergency help immediately if any of the following side effects occur:
Rare
  Convulsions (seizures); difficult or fast breathing; fast heartbeat or irregular pulse; fever (high); high or low blood pressure; increased sweating; loss of bladder control; muscle stiffness (severe); unusually pale skin; unusual tiredness or weakness

Check with your doctor as soon as possible if any of the following side effects occur:
More common
  Difficulty in speaking or swallowing; inability to move eyes; loss of balance control; mask-like face; muscle spasms, especially of the neck and back; restlessness or need to keep moving (severe); shuffling walk; stiffness of arms and legs; trembling and shaking of fingers and hands; twisting movements of body; weakness of arms and legs
Less common
  Decreased thirst; difficulty in urination; dizziness, lightheadedness, or fainting; hallucinations (seeing or hearing things that are not there); lip smacking or puckering; puffing of cheeks; rapid or worm-like movements of tongue; skin rash; uncontrolled chewing movements; uncontrolled movements of arms and legs
Rare
  Confusion; hot, dry skin, or lack of sweating; increased blinking or spasms of eyelid; muscle weakness; sore throat and fever; uncontrolled twisting movements of neck, trunk, arms, or legs; unusual bleeding or bruising; unusual facial expressions or body positions; yellow eyes or skin
Symptoms of overdose
  Difficulty in breathing (severe); dizziness (severe); drowsiness (severe); muscle trembling, jerking, stiffness, or uncontrolled movements (severe); unusual tiredness or weakness (severe)

Other side effects may occur that usually do not need medical attention. These side effects may go away during treatment as your body adjusts to the medicine. However, check with your doctor if any of the following side effects continue or are bothersome:
More common
  Blurred vision; changes in menstrual period; constipation; dryness of mouth; swelling or pain in breasts (in females); unusual secretion of milk; weight gain
Less common
  Decreased sexual ability; drowsiness; increased sensitivity of skin to sun (skin rash, itching, redness or other discoloration of skin, or severe sunburn); nausea or vomiting

Some side effects, such as trembling of fingers and hands, or uncontrolled movements of the mouth, tongue, and jaw, may occur after you have stopped taking this medicine. If you notice any of these effects, check with your doctor as soon as possible.

Other side effects not listed above may also occur in some patients. If you notice any other effects, check with your doctor.

Additional Information

Once a medicine has been approved for marketing for a certain use, experience may show that it is also useful for other medical problems. Although these uses are not included in product labeling, haloperidol is used in certain patients with the following medical conditions:

- Huntington's chorea (an hereditary movement disorder)
- Infantile autism
- Nausea and vomiting caused by cancer chemotherapy

Other than the above information, there is no additional information relating to proper use, precautions, or side effects for these uses.

Revised: 03/19/93
Interim revision: 08/04/95

HEADACHE MEDICINES, ERGOT DERIVATIVE-CONTAINING
Systemic

Commonly used brand name(s):

In the U.S.—

Cafergot[3]	Ergomar[2]
Cafertine[3]	Ergostat[2]
Cafetrate[3]	Gotamine[3]
D.H.E. 45[1]	Migergot[3]
Ercaf[3]	Wigraine[3]
Ergo-Caff[3]	

In Canada—

Cafergot[3]	Gravergol[7]
Cafergot-PB[5]	Gynergen[2]
Dihydroergotamine-Sandoz[1]	Medihaler Ergotamine[2]
Ergodryl[8]	Megral[6]
Ergomar[2]	Wigraine[4]

Note: For quick reference, the following ergot derivative-containing headache medicines are numbered to match the corresponding brand names.

This information applies to the following medicines:
1. Dihydroergotamine (dye-hye-droe-er-GOT-a-meen)
2. Ergotamine (er-GOT-a-meen)
3. Ergotamine and Caffeine (er-GOT-a-meen and kaf-EEN) ‡
4. Ergotamine, Caffeine, and Belladonna Alkaloids (er-GOT-a-meen, kaf-EEN, and bell-a-DON-a AL-ka-loids) *
5. Ergotamine, Caffeine, Belladonna Alkaloids, and Pentobarbital (er-GOT-a-meen, kaf-EEN, bell-a-DON-a AL-ka-loids, and pen-toe-BAR-bi-tal) *

6. Ergotamine, Caffeine, and Cyclizine (er-GOT-a-meen, kaf-EEN, and SYE-kli-zeen) *
7. Ergotamine, Caffeine, and Dimenhydrinate (er-GOT-a-meen, kaf-EEN, and dye-men-HYE-dri-nate) *
8. Ergotamine, Caffeine, and Diphenhydramine (er-GOT-a-meen, kaf-EEN, and dye-fen-HYE-dra-mine) *

---

*Not commercially available in the U.S.
‡Generic name product may be available in the U.S.

Description

Dihydroergotamine and ergotamine belong to the group of medicines known as ergot alkaloids. They are used to treat severe, throbbing headaches, such as migraine and cluster headaches. Dihydroergotamine and ergotamine are not ordinary pain relievers. They will not relieve any kind of pain other than throbbing headaches. Because these medicines can cause serious side effects, they are usually used for patients whose headaches are not relieved by acetaminophen, aspirin, or other pain relievers.

Dihydroergotamine and ergotamine may cause blood vessels in the body to constrict (become narrower). This effect can lead to serious side effects that are caused by a decrease in the flow of blood (blood circulation) to many parts of the body.

The caffeine present in many ergotamine-containing combinations helps ergotamine work better and faster by causing more of it to be quickly absorbed into the body. The belladonna alkaloids, cyclizine, dimenhydrinate, and diphenhydramine in some combinations help to relieve nausea and vomiting, which often occur together with the headaches. Cyclizine, dimenhydinate, diphenhydramine, and pentobarbital also help the patient relax and even sleep. This also helps relieve headaches.

Dihydroergotamine is also used for other conditions, as determined by your doctor.

These medicines are available only with your doctor's prescription, in the following dosage forms:

Oral
Ergotamine
  • Inhalation aerosol (Canada)
  • Sublingual tablets (U.S. and Canada)
  • Tablets (Canada)
Ergotamine and Caffeine
  • Tablets (U.S. and Canada)
Ergotamine, Caffeine, and Belladonna Alkaloids
  • Tablets (Canada)
Ergotamine, Caffeine, Belladonna Alkaloids, and Pentobarbital
  • Tablets (Canada)
Ergotamine, Caffeine, and Cyclizine
  • Tablets (Canada)
Ergotamine, Caffeine, and Dimenhydrinate
  • Capsules (Canada)
Ergotamine, Caffeine, and Diphenhydramine
  • Capsules (Canada)

Parenteral
Dihydroergotamine
  • Injection (U.S. and Canada)

Rectal
Ergotamine and Caffeine
  • Suppositories (U.S. and Canada)
Ergotamine, Caffeine, and Belladonna Alkaloids
  • Suppositories (Canada)
Ergotamine, Caffeine, Belladonna Alkaloids, and Pentobarbital
  • Suppositories (Canada)

Before Using This Medicine

In deciding to use a medicine, the risks of taking the medicine must be weighed against the good it will do. This is a decision you and your doctor will make. For these headache medicines, the following should be considered:

Allergies—Tell your doctor if you have ever had any unusual or allergic reaction to atropine, belladonna, pentobarbital or other barbiturates, caffeine, cyclizine, dimenhydrinate, diphenhydramine, or an ergot medicine. Also tell your health care professional if you are allergic to any other substances, such as foods, preservatives, or dyes.

Pregnancy—Use of dihydroergotamine or ergotamine by pregnant women may cause serious harm, including death of the fetus and miscarriage. Therefore, *these medicines should not be used during pregnancy.*

Breast-feeding—
  • *For dihydroergotamine and ergotamine:* These medicines pass into the breast milk and may cause unwanted effects, such as vomiting, diarrhea, weak pulse, changes in blood pressure, or convulsions (seizures) in nursing babies. Large amounts of these medicines may also decrease the flow of breast milk.
  • *For caffeine:* Caffeine passes into the breast milk. Large amounts of it may cause the baby to appear jittery or to have trouble in sleeping.
  • *For belladonna alkaloids, cyclizine, dimenhydrinate, and diphenhydramine:* These medicines have drying effects. Therefore, it is possible that they may reduce the amount of breast milk in some people. Dimenhydrinate passes into the breast milk. Cylizine may also pass into the breast milk.
  • *For pentobarbital:* Pentobarbital passes into the breast milk. Large amounts of it may cause unwanted effects such as drowsiness in nursing babies.

Be sure that you discuss these possible problems with your doctor before taking any of these medicines.

Children—
  • *For dihydroergotamine and ergotamine:* These medicines are used to relieve severe, throbbing headaches in children 6 years of age or older. They have not been shown to cause different side effects or problems in children than they do in adults. However, these medicines can cause serious side effects in any patient. Therefore, it is especially important that you discuss with the child's doctor the good that this medicine may do as well as the risks of using it.
  • *For belladonna alkaloids:* Young children, especially children with spastic paralysis or brain damage, may be especially sensitive to the effects of belladonna alkaloids. This may increase the chance of side effects during treatment.
  • *For cyclizine, dimenhydrinate, diphenhydramine, and pentobarbital:* Although these medicines often cause drowsiness, some children become excited after taking them.

Older adults—
  • *For dihydroergotamine and ergotamine:* The chance of serious side effects caused by decreases in blood flow is increased in elderly people receiving these medicines.

- *For belladonna alkaloids, cyclizine, dimenhydrinate, diphenhydramine, and pentobarbital:* Elderly people are more sensitive than younger adults to the effects of these medicines. This may increase the chance of side effects such as excitement, depression, dizziness, drowsiness, and confusion.

Other medicines—Although certain medicines should not be used together at all, in other cases two different medicines may be used together even if an interaction might occur. In these cases, your doctor may want to change the dose, or other precautions may be necessary. Many medicines can add to or decrease the effects of the belladonna alkaloids, caffeine, cyclizine, dimenhydrinate, diphenhydramine, or pentobarbital present in some of these headache medicines. Therefore, you should tell your health care professional if you are taking *any* other prescription or nonprescription (over-the-counter [OTC]) medicine. This is especially important if any medicine you take causes excitement, trouble in sleeping, dryness of the mouth, dizziness, or drowsiness.

When you are taking dihydroergotamine or ergotamine, it is especially important that your health care professional know if you are taking any of the following:

- Cocaine or
- Epinephrine by injection [e.g., Epi-Pen] or
- Other ergot medicines (ergoloid mesylates [e.g., Hydergine], ergonovine [e.g., Ergotrate], methylergonovine [e.g., Methergine], methysergide [e.g., Sansert])—The chance of serious side effects caused by dihydroergotamine or ergotamine may be increased

Other medical problems—The presence of other medical problems may affect the use of these headache medicines. Make sure you tell your doctor if you have any other medical problems, especially:

- Agoraphobia (fear of open or public places) or
- Panic attacks or
- Stomach ulcer or
- Trouble in sleeping (insomnia)—Caffeine can make your condition worse
- Diarrhea—Rectal dosage forms (suppositories) will not be effective if you have diarrhea
- Difficult urination or
- Enlarged prostate or
- Glaucoma (not well controlled) or
- Heart or blood vessel disease or
- High blood pressure (not well controlled) or
- Infection or
- Intestinal blockage or other intestinal problems or
- Itching (severe) or
- Kidney disease or
- Liver disease or
- Mental depression or
- Overactive thyroid or
- Urinary tract blockage—The chance of side effects may be increased

Also, tell your doctor if you need, or if you have recently had, an angioplasty (a procedure done to improve the flow of blood in a blocked blood vessel) or surgery on a blood vessel. The chance of serious side effects caused by dihydroergotamine or ergotamine may be increased.

Proper Use of This Medicine

Use this medicine only as directed by your doctor. Do not use more of it, and do not use it more often, than directed. If the amount you are to use does not relieve your headache, check with your doctor. Taking too much dihydroergotamine or ergotamine, or taking it too often, may cause serious effects, especially in elderly patients. Also, if a headache medicine (especially ergotamine) is used too often for migraines, it may lose its effectiveness or even cause a type of physical dependence. If this occurs, your headaches may actually get worse.

This medicine works best if you:

- *Use it at the first sign of headache or migraine attack. If you get warning signals of a coming migraine, take it before the headache actually starts.*
- *Lie down in a quiet, dark room until you are feeling better.*

Your doctor may direct you to take another medicine to help prevent headaches. *It is important that you follow your doctor's directions, even if your headaches continue to occur.* Headache-preventing medicines may take several weeks to start working. Even after they do start working, your headaches may not go away completely. However, your headaches should occur less often, and they should be less severe and easier to relieve. This can reduce the amount of dihydroergotamine, ergotamine, or pain relievers that you need. If you do not notice any improvement after several weeks of headache-preventing treatment, check with your doctor.

For patients using *dihydroergotamine:*

- Dihydroergotamine is given only by injection. Your health care professional will teach you how to inject yourself with the medicine. Be sure to follow the directions carefully. Check with your health care professional if you have any problems using the medicine.

For patients using *ergotamine inhalation* [e.g., Medihaler Ergotamine]:

- This medicine comes with patient directions. Read them carefully before using the medicine, and check with your health care professional if you have any questions.
- To use the inhaler—Remove the cap, then shake the container well. After breathing out, place the mouthpiece of the inhaler in your mouth. Aim it at the back of the throat. Breathe in; at the same time, press the vial down into the adapter. After inhaling the medicine, hold your breath as long as you can.

For patients using the *sublingual (under-the-tongue) tablets of ergotamine:*

- To use—Place the tablet under your tongue and let it remain there until it disappears. The sublingual tablet should not be chewed or swallowed, because it works faster when it is absorbed into the body through the lining of the mouth. Do not eat, drink, or smoke while the tablet is under your tongue.

For patients using *rectal suppository forms of a headache medicine:*

- If the suppository is too soft to use, chill it in the refrigerator for 30 minutes or run cold water over it before removing the foil wrapper.
- If you have been directed to use part of a suppository, you should divide the suppository into pieces that all contain the same amount of medicine. To do this, use a sharp knife and carefully cut the suppository lengthwise (from top to bottom) into pieces that are the same size. The suppository will be easier to cut if it has been kept in the refrigerator.

• To insert the suppository—First remove the foil wrapper and moisten the suppository with cold water. Lie down on your side and use your finger to push the suppository well up into the rectum.

Dosing—The dose of these headache medicines will be different for different patients. *Follow your doctor's orders or the directions on the label.* The following information includes only the average doses of these medicines. *If your dose is different, do not change it* unless your doctor tells you to do so.

For dihydroergotamine
• Adults: For relieving a migraine or cluster headache— 1 mg. If your headache is not better, and no side effects are occurring, a second 1-mg dose may be used at least one hour later.
• Children 6 years of age and older: For relieving a migraine headache—It is not likely that a child will be receiving dihydrogergotamine at home. If a child needs the medicine, the dose will have to be determined by the doctor.

For ergotamine
• Some headache medicines contain only ergotamine. Some of them contain other medicines along with the ergotamine. The number of tablets, capsules, or suppositories that you need for each dose depends on the amount of ergotamine in them. The size of each dose, and the number of doses that you take, also depends on the reason you are taking the medicine and on how you react to the medicine.
• For *oral* (capsule or tablet) and *sublingual* (under-the-tongue tablet) dosage forms:
  —Adults:
    • For relieving a migraine or cluster headache—1 or 2 mg of ergotamine. If your headache is not better, and no side effects are occurring, a second dose and even a third dose may be taken; however the doses should be taken at least 30 minutes apart. People who usually need more than one dose of the medicine, and who do not get side effects from it, may be able to take a larger first dose of not more than 3 mg of ergotamine. This may provide better relief of the headache with only one dose. *The medicine should not be taken more often than 2 times a week, at least five days apart.*
    • For preventing cluster headaches—The dose of ergotamine, and the number of doses you need every day, will depend on how many headaches you usually get each day. For some people, 1 or 2 mg of ergotamine once a day may be enough. Other people may need to take 1 or 2 mg of ergotamine 2 or 3 times a day.
    • For all uses— *Do not take more than 6 mg of ergotamine a day in the form of capsules or tablets.*
  —Children 6 years of age and older: For relieving migraine headaches—1 mg of ergotamine. If the headache is not better, and no side effects are occurring, a second dose and even a third dose may be taken; however, the doses should be taken at least 30 minutes apart. *Children should not take more than 3 mg of ergotamine a day in the form of capsules or tablets. Also, this medicine should not be taken more often than 2 times a week, at least five days apart.*

• For *rectal suppository* dosage forms:
  —Adults: For relieving migraine or cluster headaches—Usually 1 mg of ergotamine, but the dose may range from half of this amount to up to 2 mg. If your headache is not better, and no side effects are occurring, a second dose and even a third dose may be used; however the doses should be taken at least 30 minutes apart. People who usually need more than one dose of the medicine, and who do not get side effects from it, may be able to use a larger first dose of not more than 3 mg. This may provide better relief of the headache with only one dose. *Adults should not use more than 4 mg of ergotamine a day in suppository form. Also, this medicine should not be used more often than 2 times a week, at least five days apart.*
  —Children 6 years of age and older: For relieving migraine headaches—One-half or 1 mg of ergotamine. *Children should not receive more than 1 mg a day of ergotamine in suppository form. Also, this medicine should not be used more often than 2 times a week, at least five days apart.*
• For the *oral inhalation* dosage form:
  —Adults: For relieving a migraine or cluster headache—1 spray (1 inhalation). Another inhalation may be used at least 5 minutes later, if needed. Up to a total of 6 inhalations a day may be used, at least 5 minutes apart. *This medicine should not be used more often than 2 times a week, at least five days apart.*
  —Children: To be determined by the doctor.

Storage—To store this medicine:
• Keep out of the reach of children since overdose is especially dangerous in children.
• Store away from heat and direct light.
• Do not store in the bathroom, near the kitchen sink, or in other damp places. Heat or moisture may cause the medicine to break down.
• Suppositories should be stored in a cool place, but not allowed to freeze. Some manufacturers recommend keeping them in a refrigerator; others do not. Follow the directions on the package. However, cutting the suppository into smaller pieces, if you need to do so, will be easier if the suppository is kept in the refrigerator.
• Do not puncture, break, or burn the ergotamine inhalation aerosol container, even after it is empty.
• Do not keep outdated medicine or medicine no longer needed. Be sure that any discarded medicine is out of the reach of children.

Precautions While Using This Medicine

Check with your doctor:
• If your migraine headaches are worse than they were before you started using this medicine, or your headache medicine stops working as well as it did when you first started using it. This may mean that you are in danger of becoming dependent on the headache medicine. *Do not try to get better relief by increasing the dose.*
• If your migraine headaches are occurring more often than they did before you started using this medicine. This is especially important if a new headache occurs within 1 day after you took your last dose of headache medicine, or if you are having headaches every day. This may mean that you are dependent on the headache

medicine. *Continuing to take this medicine will cause even more headaches later on.* Your doctor can give you advice on how to relieve the headaches.

Drinking alcoholic beverages can make headaches worse or cause new headaches to occur. People who suffer from severe headaches should probably avoid alcoholic beverages, especially during a headache.

Smoking may increase some of the harmful effects of dihydroergotamine or ergotamine. It is best to avoid smoking for several hours after taking these medicines.

Dihydroergotamine and ergotamine may make you more sensitive to cold temperatures, especially if you have blood circulation problems. They tend to decrease blood flow in the skin, fingers, and toes. Dress warmly during cold weather and be careful during prolonged exposure to cold temperatures. This is especially important for older patients, who are more likely than younger adults to already have problems with their circulation.

If you have a serious infection or illness of any kind, check with your doctor before using this medicine, since you may be more sensitive to its effects.

For patients using *ergotamine inhalation* [e.g., Medihaler Ergotamine]:

- Cough, hoarseness, or throat irritation may occur. Gargling and rinsing your mouth after each dose may help prevent the hoarseness and irritation. However, check with your doctor if these or any other side effects continue or are bothersome.

For patients taking one of the combination medicines that contains *caffeine:*

- Caffeine may interfere with the results of a test that uses dipyridamole (e.g., Persantine) to help find out how well your blood is flowing through certain blood vessels. You should not have any caffeine for at least 12 hours before the test.

Caffeine may also interfere with some other laboratory tests. Before having any other laboratory tests, tell the person in charge if you have taken a medicine that contains caffeine.

For patients taking one of the combination medicines that contains *belladonna alkaloids, cyclizine, dimenhydrinate, diphenhydramine, or pentobarbital:*

- These medicines may cause some people to have blurred vision or to become drowsy, dizzy, lightheaded, or less alert than they are normally. These effects may be especially severe if you also take CNS depressants (medicines that slow down the nervous system, possibly causing drowsiness) together with one of these combination medicines. Some examples of CNS depressants are antihistamines or medicine for hay fever, other allergies, or colds; sedatives, tranquilizers, or sleeping medicine; prescription pain medicine or narcotics; barbiturates; medicine for seizures; muscle relaxants; and antiemetics (medicines that prevent or relieve nausea or vomiting). If you are not able to lie down for a while, *make sure you know how you react to this medicine or combination of medicines before you drive, use machines, or do anything else that could be dangerous if you are dizzy or are not alert and able to see well.*
- Belladonna alkaloids, cyclizine, dimenhydrinate, and diphenhydramine may cause dryness of the mouth, nose, and throat. For temporary relief of mouth dryness, use

sugarless candy or gum, melt bits of ice in your mouth, or use a saliva substitute.

- Belladonna alkaloids may interfere with certain laboratory tests that check the amount of acid in your stomach. They should not be taken for 24 hours before the test.
- Cyclizine, dimenhydrinate, and diphenhydramine may interfere with skin tests that show whether you are allergic to certain substances. They should not be taken for 3 days before the test.

Side Effects of This Medicine

Along with its needed effects, a medicine may cause some unwanted effects. Although not all of these side effects may occur, if they do occur they may need medical attention.

Check with your doctor immediately if the following side effects occur, because they may mean that you are developing a problem with blood circulation:

Less common or rare

Anxiety or confusion (severe); change in vision; chest pain; increase in blood pressure; pain in arms, legs, or lower back, especially if pain occurs in your calves or heels while you are walking; pale, bluish-colored, or cold hands or feet (not caused by cold temperatures and occurring together with other side effects listed in this section); red or violet-colored blisters on the skin of the hands or feet

Also check with your doctor immediately if any of the following side effects occur, because they may mean that you have taken an overdose of the medicine:

Less common or rare

Convulsions (seizures); diarrhea, nausea, vomiting, or stomach pain or bloating (severe) occurring together with other signs of overdose or of problems with blood circulation; dizziness, drowsiness, or weakness (severe), occurring together with other signs of overdose or of problems with blood circulation; fast or slow heartbeat; diarrhea; headaches, more often and/or more severe than before; problems with moving bowels, occurring together with pain or discomfort in the rectum (with rectal suppositories only); shortness of breath; unusual excitement

The following side effects may go away after a little while. *Do not take any more medicine while they are present.* If any of them occur together with other signs of problems with blood circulation, *check with your doctor right away.* Even if any of the following side effects occur without other signs of problems with blood circulation, *check with your doctor if any of them continue for more than one hour:*

More common

Itching of skin; coldness, numbness, or tingling in fingers, toes, or face; weakness in legs

Also, check with your doctor as soon as possible if you notice any of the following side effects:

More common

Swelling of face, fingers, feet, or lower legs

Other side effects may occur that usually do not need medical attention. These side effects may go away after a little while. However, check with your doctor if any of the following side effects continue or are bothersome:

More common

Diarrhea, nausea, or vomiting (occurring without other signs of overdose or problems with blood circulation); dizziness or drowsiness (occurring without other signs of overdose or problems with blood circulation, especially with combinations containing cyclizine, dimenhydrinate, diphenhydramine, or pentobarbital); nervousness or restlessness; dryness of mouth (especially with combinations containing belladonna alkaloids, cyclizine, dimenhydrinate, or diphenhydramine)

After you stop taking this medicine, your body may need time to adjust. The length of time this takes depends on the amount of medicine you were taking and how long you took it. During this time check with your doctor if your headaches begin again or worsen.

Other side effects not listed above may also occur in some patients. If you notice any other effects, check with your doctor.

Additional Information

Once a medicine has been approved for marketing for a certain use, experience may show that it is also useful for other medical problems. Although this use is not specifically included in product labeling, dihydroergotamine is sometimes used together with another medicine (heparin) to help prevent blood clots that may occur after certain kinds of surgery. It is also used to prevent or treat low blood pressure in some patients.

For patients receiving this medicine for *preventing blood clots:*

- You may need to receive this medicine two or three times a day for several days in a row. This may increase the chance of problems caused by decreased blood flow. Your health care professional will be following your progress, to make sure that this medicine is not causing problems with blood circulation.

For patients using this medicine to *prevent or treat low blood pressure:*

- Take this medicine every day as directed by your doctor.
- The dose of dihydroergotamine will depend on whether the medicine is going to be injected under the skin or into a muscle, and, sometimes, on the weight of the patient. For these reasons, the dose will have to be determined by your doctor.
- Your doctor will need to check your progress at regular visits, to make sure that the medicine is working properly without causing side effects.
- This medicine is less likely to cause problems with blood circulation in patients with low blood pressure than it is in patients with normal or high blood pressure.
- In patients being treated for low blood pressure, an increase in blood pressure is the wanted effect, not a side effect that may need medical attention.

Other than the above information, there is no additional information relating to proper use, precautions, or side effects for these uses.

Revised: 09/08/92

HEPARIN Systemic

Commonly used brand name(s):

In the U.S.—
  Calciparine
  Liquaemin
  Generic name product may be available.

In Canada—
  Calcilean   Hepalean
  Calciparine   Heparin Leo

Description

Heparin (HEP-a-rin) is an anticoagulant. It is used to decrease the clotting ability of the blood and help prevent harmful clots from forming in the blood vessels. This medicine is sometimes called a blood thinner, although it does not actually thin the blood. Heparin will not dissolve blood clots that have already formed, but it may prevent the clots from becoming larger and causing more serious problems.

Heparin is often used as a treatment for certain blood vessel, heart, and lung conditions. Heparin is also used to prevent blood clotting during open-heart surgery, bypass surgery, and dialysis. It is also used in low doses to prevent the formation of blood clots in certain patients, especially those who must have certain types of surgery or who must remain in bed for a long time.

Heparin is available only with your doctor's prescription, in the following dosage form:

Parenteral
  - Injection (U.S. and Canada)

Before Using This Medicine

In deciding to use a medicine, the risks of taking the medicine must be weighed against the good it will do. This is a decision you and your doctor will make. For heparin, the following should be considered:

Allergies—Tell your doctor if you have ever had any unusual or allergic reaction to heparin, to beef, or to pork. Also tell your health care professional if you are allergic to any other substances, such as foods, preservatives, or dyes.

Pregnancy—Heparin has not been shown to cause birth defects or bleeding problems in the baby. However, use during the last 3 months of pregnancy or during the month following the baby's delivery may cause bleeding problems in the mother.

Breast-feeding—Heparin does not pass into the breast milk. However, heparin can rarely cause bone problems in the nursing mother. This effect has been reported to occur when heparin is used for 2 weeks or more. Be sure to discuss this with your doctor.

Children—Heparin has been tested in children and, in effective doses, has not been shown to cause different side effects or problems than it does in adults.

Older adults—Bleeding problems may be more likely to occur in elderly patients, especially women, who are usually more sensitive than younger adults to the effects of heparin.

Other medicines—Although certain medicines should not be used together at all, in other cases two different medicines may be used together even if an interaction might occur. In these cases, your doctor may want to change the

dose, or other precautions may be necessary. When you are taking heparin, it is especially important that your health care professional know if you are taking any of the following:

- Aspirin or
- Carbenicillin by injection (e.g., Geopen) or
- Cefamandole (e.g., Mandol) or
- Cefoperazone (e.g., Cefobid) or
- Cefotetan (e.g., Cefotan) or
- Dipyridamole (e.g., Persantine) or
- Divalproex (e.g., Depakote) or
- Medicine for inflammation or pain, except narcotics, or
- Medicine for overactive thyroid or
- Pentoxifylline (e.g., Trental) or
- Plicamycin (e.g., Mithracin) or
- Probenecid (e.g., Benemid) or
- Sulfinpyrazone (e.g., Anturane) or
- Ticarcillin (e.g., Ticar) or
- Valproic acid (e.g., Depakene)—Using any of these medicines together with heparin may increase the risk of bleeding

Also, tell your doctor if you are now receiving any kind of medicine by intramuscular (IM) injection.

Other medical problems—The presence of other medical problems may affect the use of heparin. Make sure you tell your doctor if you have any other medical problems, especially:

- Allergies or asthma (history of)—The risk of an allergic reaction to heparin may be increased

- Blood disease or bleeding problems or
- Colitis or stomach ulcer (or history of) or
- Diabetes mellitus (sugar diabetes) (severe) or
- High blood pressure (hypertension) or
- Kidney disease or
- Liver disease or
- Tuberculosis (active)—The risk of bleeding may be increased

Also, tell your doctor if you have received heparin before and had a reaction to it called thrombocytopenia, or if new blood clots formed while you were receiving the medicine.

In addition, it is important that you tell your doctor if you have recently had any of the following conditions or medical procedures:

- Childbirth or
- Falls or blows to the body or head or
- Heavy or unusual menstrual bleeding or
- Insertion of intrauterine device (IUD) or
- Medical or dental surgery or
- Spinal anesthesia or
- X-ray (radiation) treatment—The risk of serious bleeding may be increased

Proper Use of This Medicine

If you are using these injections at home, make sure your doctor has explained exactly how this medicine is to be given.

To obtain the best results without causing serious bleeding, *use this medicine exactly as directed by your doctor. Be certain that you are using the right amount of heparin, and that you use it according to schedule.* Be especially careful that you do not use more of it, do not use it more often, and do not use it for a longer time than your doctor ordered.

Your doctor should check your progress at regular visits. A blood test must be taken regularly to see how fast your blood is clotting so that your doctor can decide on the proper amount of heparin you should be receiving each day.

Dosing—The dose of heparin will be different for different patients and must be determined by your doctor. The dose you receive will be based on the type of heparin you receive, the condition for which you are receiving heparin, and your body weight.

Missed dose—If you miss a dose of this medicine, use it as soon as possible. However, if it is almost time for your next dose, do not use the missed dose at all and do not double the next one. *Doubling the dose may cause bleeding.* Instead, go back to your regular dosing schedule. It is best to keep a record of each dose as you use it to avoid mistakes. Be sure to give your doctor a record of any doses you miss. If you have any questions about this, check with your doctor.

Storage—To store this medicine:

- Keep out of the reach of children.
- Store away from heat and direct light.
- Keep the medicine from freezing.
- Do not keep outdated medicine or medicine no longer needed. Be sure that any discarded medicine is out of the reach of children.

Precautions While Using This Medicine

Do not take aspirin while using this medicine. Many nonprescription (over-the-counter [OTC]) medicines and some prescription medicines contain aspirin. Check the labels of all medicines you take. Also, do not take ibuprofen unless it has been ordered by your doctor. In addition, there are many other medicines that may change the way heparin works or increase the chance of bleeding if they are used together with heparin. It is best to check with your health care professional before taking any other medicine while you are using heparin.

Tell all medical doctors and dentists you visit that you are using this medicine.

It is recommended that you carry identification stating that you are using heparin. If you have any questions about what kind of identification to carry, check with your health care professional.

While you are using this medicine, it is very important that you avoid sports and other activities that may cause you to be injured. Report to your doctor any falls, blows to the body or head, or other injuries, since serious bleeding inside the body may occur without your knowing about it.

Take special care in brushing your teeth and in shaving. Use a soft toothbrush and floss gently. Also, it is best to use an electric shaver rather than a blade.

Side Effects of This Medicine

Since many things can affect the way your body reacts to this medicine, you should always watch for signs of unusual bleeding. Unusual bleeding may mean that your body is getting more heparin than it needs.

Along with its needed effects, a medicine may cause some unwanted effects. Although not all of these side effects may occur, if they do occur they may need medical attention.

Check with your doctor immediately if any of the following signs and symptoms of bleeding inside the body occur:

> Abdominal or stomach pain or swelling; back pain or backaches; blood in urine; bloody or black, tarry stools; constipation; coughing up blood; dizziness; headaches (severe or continuing); joint pain, stiffness, or swelling; vomiting of blood or material that looks like coffee grounds

Also, *check with your doctor immediately* if any of the following side effects occur, since they may mean that you are having a serious allergic reaction to the medicine:

> Changes in the skin color of the face; fast or irregular breathing; puffiness or swelling of the eyelids or around the eyes; shortness of breath, troubled breathing, tightness in chest, and/or wheezing; skin rash, hives, and/or itching

Also, check with your doctor as soon as possible if any of the following occur:

> Bleeding from gums when brushing teeth; heavy bleeding or oozing from cuts or wounds; unexplained bruising or purplish areas on skin; unexplained nosebleeds; unusually heavy or unexpected menstrual bleeding

Other side effects that may need medical attention may occur while you are using this medicine. Check with your doctor as soon as possible if any of the following side effects occur:

> *Less common or rare*
> Back or rib pain (with long-term use only); change in skin color, especially near the place of injection or in the fingers, toes, arms, or legs; chest pain; chills and/or fever; collection of blood under skin (blood blister) at place of injection; decrease in height (with long-term use only); frequent or persistent erection; irritation, pain, redness, or ulcers at place of injection; itching and burning feeling, especially on the bottom of the feet; nausea and/or vomiting; numbness or tingling in hands or feet; pain, coldness, or blue color of skin of arms or legs; peeling of skin; runny nose; tearing of eyes; unusual hair loss (with long-term use only)

Other side effects not listed above may also occur in some patients. If you notice any other effects, check with your doctor.

Revised: 08/01/90
Interim revision: 08/23/94

HEPATITIS A VACCINE INACTIVATED   Systemic

Commonly used brand name(s):

In the U.S.—
> Havrix
> Vaqta

In Canada—
> Havrix
> Vaqta

Description

Hepatitis (hep-ah-TY-tiss) A is a serious disease of the liver that can cause death. It is caused by the hepatitis A virus (HAV), and is spread most often through infected food or water. Hepatitis A may also be spread by close person-to-person contact with infected persons (such as between persons living in the same household). Although some infected persons do not appear to be sick, they are still able to spread the virus to others.

Hepatitis A is less common in the U.S. and other areas of the world that have a higher level of sanitation and good water and sewage (waste) systems. However, it is a significant health problem in parts of the world that do not have such systems. If you are traveling to certain countries or remote (out-of-the-way) areas, hepatitis A vaccine will help protect you from hepatitis A disease.

It is recommended that persons 2 years of age and older be vaccinated with hepatitis A vaccine when traveling to the following parts of the world:

- Africa.
- Asia (except Japan).
- parts of the Caribbean.
- Central and South America.
- eastern Europe.
- the Mediterranean basin.
- the Middle East.
- Mexico.

Hepatitis A vaccine is also recommended for all persons 2 years of age and older who live in areas that have frequent outbreaks of hepatitis A disease or who may be at increased risk of infection from hepatitis A virus. These persons include:

- Military personnel.
- Persons living in or moving to areas that have a high rate of HAV infection.
- Persons who may be exposed to the hepatitis A virus repeatedly due to a high rate of hepatitis A disease, such as Alaskan Eskimos and Native Americans.
- Persons engaging in high-risk sexual activity, such as homosexual and bisexual males.
- Persons who use illegal injectable drugs.
- Persons living in a community experiencing an outbreak of hepatitis A.
- Persons working in facilities for the mentally retarded.
- Employees of child day-care centers.
- Persons who work with hepatitis A virus in the laboratory.
- Persons who handle primate animals.
- Persons with hemophilia.
- Food handlers.
- Persons with chronic liver disease.

Hepatitis A vaccine is to be used only by or under the supervision of a doctor. It is available in the following dosage form:

Parenteral
- Injection (U.S. and Canada)

Before Receiving This Vaccine

In deciding to use a medicine, the risks of taking the medicine must be weighed against the good it will do. This is a decision you and your doctor will make. For hepatitis A vaccine, the following should be considered:

Allergies—Tell your doctor if you have ever had any unusual or allergic reaction to hepatitis A vaccine. Also tell your health care professional if you are allergic to any other substances, such as preservatives.

Pregnancy—Studies on effects in pregnancy have not been done in either humans or animals. However, since the vaccine does not contain contagious particles, it is not expected to cause problems during pregnancy.

Breast-feeding—This vaccine has not been reported to cause problems in nursing babies.

Children—Hepatitis A vaccine is not recommended for infants and children younger than 2 years of age. For children 2 years of age and older, this vaccine is not expected to cause different side effects or problems than it does in adults.

Older adults—Many medicines have not been studied specifically in older people. Therefore, it may not be known whether they work exactly the same way they do in younger adults. Although there is no specific information comparing use of hepatitis A vaccine in the elderly with use in other age groups, this vaccine is not expected to cause different side effects or problems in older people than it does in younger adults.

Other medicines—Although certain medicines should not be used together at all, in other cases two different medicines may be used together even if an interaction might occur. In these cases, your doctor may want to change the dose, or other precautions may be necessary. Tell your health care professional if you are taking any other prescription or nonprescription (over-the-counter [OTC]) medicine.

Other medical problems—The presence of other medical problems may affect the use of hepatitis A vaccine. Make sure you tell your doctor if you have any other medical problems.

Proper Use of This Vaccine

Dosing—The dose of hepatitis A vaccine will be different for different patients. *Follow your doctor's orders*. The following information includes only the average doses of hepatitis A vaccine.

- For *injection* dosage form:
  —For prevention of hepatitis A disease:
  - Adults—One adult dose injected into a muscle. A booster (repeat) dose may be needed six to twelve months after the first dose.
  - Children 2 to 18 years of age—One or two pediatric doses injected into a muscle. A booster (repeat) dose may be needed six to twelve months after the first dose.
  - Children up to 2 years of age—Use is not recommended.

Side Effects of This Vaccine

Along with its needed effects, a vaccine may cause some unwanted effects. Although not all of these side effects may occur, if they do occur they may need medical attention. *It is very important that you tell your doctor about any side effects that occur after a dose of hepatitis A vaccine*, even though the side effect may have gone away without treatment. Some types of side effects may mean that you should not receive any more doses of hepatitis A vaccine.

Get emergency help immediately if any of the following side effects occur:
  Rare
    Difficulty in breathing or swallowing; hives; itching, es-

pecially of feet or hands; reddening of skin, especially around ears; swelling of eyes, face, or inside of nose; unusual tiredness or weakness (sudden and severe)

Other side effects may occur that usually do not need medical attention. However, check with your doctor if any of the following side effects continue or are bothersome:
  More common
    Soreness at place of injection
  Less common
    Fever of 37.7 °C (100 °F) or higher; general feeling of discomfort or illness; headache; lack of appetite; nausea; tenderness or warmth at injection site
  Rare
    Aches or pain in joints or muscles; diarrhea or stomach cramps or pain; itching; swelling of glands in armpits or neck; vomiting; welts

Other side effects not listed above may also occur in some patients. If you notice any other effects, check with your doctor.

Developed: 02/06/97
Interim revision: 07/31/98

HEPATITIS B VACCINE RECOMBINANT   Systemic

Commonly used brand name(s):

In the U.S.—
Engerix-B
Recombivax HB

Recombivax HB Dialysis
Formulation

In Canada—
Engerix-B
Recombivax HB

Recombivax HB Dialysis
Formulation

Another commonly used name is HB vaccine.

Description

Hepatitis (hep-ah-TY-tiss) B vaccine recombinant is used to prevent infection by the hepatitis B virus. The vaccine works by causing your body to produce its own protection (antibodies) against the disease.

Hepatitis B vaccine recombinant is made without any human blood or blood products or any other substances of human origin and cannot give you the hepatitis B virus (HBV) or the human immunodeficiency virus (HIV).

HBV infection is a major cause of serious liver diseases, such as virus hepatitis and cirrhosis, and a type of liver cancer called primary hepatocellular carcinoma.

Pregnant women who have hepatitis B infection or are carriers of hepatitis B virus can give the disease to their babies when they are born. These babies often suffer serious long-term illnesses from the disease.

Immunization against hepatitis B disease is recommended for all newborn babies, infants, children, and adolescents up to 19 years old. It is also recommended for adults who live in areas that have a high rate of hepatitis B disease or who may be at increased risk of infection from hepatitis B virus. These adults include:

- Sexually active homosexual and bisexual males, including those with HIV infection.
- Sexually active heterosexual persons with multiple partners.
- Persons who may be exposed to the virus by means of blood, blood products, or human bites, such as health care workers, employees in medical facilities, patients and staff of live-in facilities and day-care programs for the developmentally disabled, morticians and embalmers, police and fire department personnel, and military personnel.
- Persons who have kidney disease or who undergo blood dialysis for kidney disease.
- Persons with blood clotting disorders who receive transfusions of clotting-factor concentrates.
- Household and sexual contacts of HBV carriers.
- Persons in areas with high risk of HBV infection [in the population], such as Alaskan Eskimos, Pacific Islanders, Haitian and Indochinese immigrants, and refugees from areas that have a high rate of hepatitis B disease; persons accepting orphans or adoptees from these areas; and travelers to these areas.
- Persons who use illegal injection drugs.
- Prisoners.

This vaccine is available only from your doctor or other authorized health care professional, in the following dosage form:

Parenteral
- Injection (U.S. and Canada)

Before Receiving This Vaccine

In deciding to use a medicine, the risks of using the medicine must be weighed against the good it will do. This is a decision you and your doctor will make. For hepatitis B recombinant vaccine, the following should be considered:

Allergies—Tell your doctor if you have ever had any unusual or allergic reaction to this vaccine or to the hepatitis B vaccine made from human plasma. Also tell your health care professional if you are allergic to any other substances, such as foods (especially yeast). The vaccine is made by using yeast; persons allergic to yeast may also be allergic to the vaccine.

Pregnancy—Studies on effects in pregnancy have not been done in either humans or animals. However, the vaccine is not expected to cause problems during pregnancy.

Breast-feeding—It is not known whether hepatitis B vaccine passes into the breast milk. However, the vaccine is not expected to cause problems in nursing babies.

Children—Hepatitis B vaccine has been tested in newborns, infants, and children and, in effective doses, has not been shown to cause different side effects or problems than it does in adults. The vaccine strength for use in dialysis patients has been studied only in adult patients, and there is no specific information about its use in children receiving dialysis.

Teenagers—Hepatitis B vaccine is very effective when administered to adolescents and young adults. It is recommended that all adolescents who have not previously received three doses of hepatitis B vaccine should start or complete the vaccine series at 11 to 12 years of age. Hepatitis B vaccine has not been shown to cause different side effects

or problems in adolescents and young adults than it does in other age groups.

Older adults—This vaccine is not expected to cause different side effects or problems in older people than it does in younger adults. However, persons over 50 years of age may not become as immune to the virus as do younger adults.

Other medicines—Although certain medicines should not be used together at all, in other cases two different medicines may be used together even if an interaction might occur. In these cases, your doctor may want to change the dose, or other precautions may be necessary. Tell your health care professional if you are using any other prescription or nonprescription (over-the-counter [OTC]) medicine.

Other medical problems—The presence of other medical problems may affect the use of hepatitis B vaccine. Make sure you tell your doctor if you have any other medical problems, especially:

- Allergic reaction to hepatitis B vaccine, history of—Use of hepatitis B vaccine is not recommended

Proper Use of This Vaccine

Dosing—The dose of hepatitis B vaccine will be different for different patients. *Follow your doctor's orders*. The following information includes only the average doses of hepatitis B vaccine.

- For *injection* dosage form:
  —For prevention of hepatitis B infection:
    - Adults, adolescents, and older children—2.5 to 20 micrograms (mcg) injected into the arm muscle during the first office visit, then one month and six months after the first dose, for a total of three doses.
    - Adults who also receive or will receive blood dialysis—40 mcg injected into the arm muscle during the first office visit, then one month and six months after the first dose, for a total of three doses; or 40 mcg injected into the arm muscle during the first office visit, then one month, two months, and six months after the first dose, for a total of four doses.
    - Infants and young children—2.5 to 20 mcg injected into the thigh muscle during the first office visit, then one month and six months after the first dose, for a total of three doses.
    - Newborn babies—2.5 to 20 mcg injected into the thigh muscle at birth or within seven days of birth, then one month and six months after the first dose, for a total of three doses; or 10 or 20 mcg injected into the thigh muscle at birth or within seven days of birth, then one month, two months, and twelve months after the first dose, for a total of four doses.

Side Effects of This Vaccine

Along with its needed effects, a vaccine may cause some unwanted effects. Although not all of these side effects may occur, if they do occur they may need medical attention.

Get emergency help immediately if any of the following side effects occur:

  Symptoms of allergic reaction—Rare
    Difficulty in breathing or swallowing; hives; itching, especially of feet or hands; reddening of skin, especially around ears; swelling of eyes, face, or inside of nose; unusual tiredness or weakness (sudden and severe)

Check with your doctor as soon as possible if any of the following side effects occur:

Rare

Aches or pain in joints, fever, or skin rash or welts (may occur days or weeks after receiving the vaccine); blurred vision or other vision changes; muscle weakness or numbness or tingling of arms and legs

Other side effects may occur that usually do not need medical attention. However, check with your doctor if any of the following side effects continue or are bothersome:

More common

Soreness at the place of injection

Less common

Dizziness; fever of 37.7 °C (100 °F) or higher; hard lump, redness, swelling, pain, itching, purple spot, tenderness, or warmth at place of injection; headache; unusual tiredness or weakness

Rare

Aches or pain in muscles; back pain or stiffness or pain in neck or shoulder; chills; diarrhea or stomach cramps or pain; general feeling of discomfort or illness; increased sweating; headache (mild), sore throat, runny nose, or fever (mild); itching; lack of appetite or decreased appetite; nausea or vomiting; sudden redness of skin; swelling of glands in armpit or neck; trouble in sleeping; welts

Other side effects not listed above may also occur in some patients. If you notice any other effects, check with your doctor.

Revised: 06/20/97

HISTAMINE H$_2$-RECEPTOR ANTAGONISTS   Systemic

Commonly used brand name(s):

In the U.S.—

Axid[3]	Pepcid RPD[2]
Axid AR[3]	Tagamet[1]
Mylanta AR Acid Reducer[2]	Tagamet HB[1]
Pepcid[2]	Zantac[4]
Pepcid I.V.[2]	Zantac EFFERdose Granules[4]
Pepcid AC Acid Controller[2]	Zantac EFFERdose Tablets[4]

In Canada—

Acid Control[2]	Novo-Ranitidine[4]
Act[2]	Nu-Cimet[1]
Apo-Cimetidine[1]	Nu-Famotidine[2]
Apo-Famotidine[2]	Nu-Ranit[4]
Apo-Nizatidine[3]	Pepcid[2]
Apo-Ranitidine[4]	Pepcid AC[2]
Axid[3]	Pepcid I.V.[2]
Dyspep HB[2]	Peptol[1]
Gen-Cimetidine[1]	PMS-Cimetidine[1]
Gen-Famotidine[2]	Tagamet[1]
Gen-Ranitidine[4]	Ulcidine[2]
Maalox H2 Acid Controller[2]	Ulcidine-HB[2]
Novo-Cimetine[1]	Zantac[4]
Novo-Famotidine[2]	Zantac 75[4]

Note: For quick reference, the following histamine H$_2$-receptor antagonists are numbered to match the corresponding brand names.

This information applies to the following medicines:

1. Cimetidine (sye-MET-i-deen) ‡§
2. Famotidine (fa-MOE-ti-deen) §
3. Nizatidine (ni-ZA-ti-deen)
4. Ranitidine (ra-NIT-ti-deen) ‡

‡Generic name product may be available in the U.S.
§Generic name product may be available in Canada.

Description

Histamine H$_2$-receptor antagonists, also known as H$_2$-blockers, are used to treat duodenal ulcers and prevent their return. They are also used to treat gastric ulcers and for some conditions, such as Zollinger-Ellison disease, in which the stomach produces too much acid. In over-the-counter (OTC) strengths, these medicines are used to relieve and/or prevent heartburn, acid indigestion, and sour stomach. H$_2$-blockers may also be used for other conditions as determined by your doctor.

H$_2$-blockers work by decreasing the amount of acid produced by the stomach.

They are available in the following dosage forms:

Oral

Cimetidine
- Oral solution (U.S. and Canada)
- Tablets (U.S. and Canada)

Famotidine
- Oral suspension (U.S.)
- Tablets (U.S. and Canada)
- Chewable tablets (U.S. and Canada)
- Oral disintegrating tablets (U.S.)

Nizatidine
- Capsules (U.S. and Canada)
- Tablets (U.S.)

Ranitidine
- Capsules (U.S.)
- Effervescent granules (U.S.)
- Syrup (U.S. and Canada)
- Tablets (U.S. and Canada)
- Effervescent tablets (U.S.)

Parenteral

Cimetidine
- Injection (U.S. and Canada)

Famotidine
- Injection (U.S. and Canada)

Ranitidine
- Injection (U.S. and Canada)

Before Using This Medicine

In deciding to use a medicine, the risks of taking the medicine must be weighed against the good it will do. This is a decision you and your doctor will make. For H$_2$-blockers, the following should be considered:

Allergies—Tell your doctor if you have ever had any unusual or allergic reaction to cimetidine, famotidine, nizatidine, or ranitidine.

Pregnancy—H$_2$-blockers have not been studied in pregnant women. In animal studies, famotidine and ranitidine have not been shown to cause birth defects or other problems. However, one study in rats suggested that cimetidine may affect male sexual development. More studies are needed to confirm this. Also, studies in rabbits with very high doses have shown that nizatidine causes miscarriages and low birth weights. Make sure your doctor knows if you are pregnant or if you may become pregnant before taking H$_2$-blockers.

Breast-feeding—Cimetidine, famotidine, nizatidine, and ranitidine pass into the breast milk and may cause unwanted effects, such as decreased amount of stomach acid and increased excitement, in the nursing baby. It may be necessary for you to take another medicine or to stop breast-feeding during treatment. Be sure you have discussed the risks and benefits of the medicine with your doctor.

Children—This medicine has been tested in children and, in effective doses, has not been shown to cause different side effects or problems than it does in adults when used for short periods of time.

Older adults—Confusion and dizziness may be especially likely to occur in elderly patients, who are usually more sensitive than younger adults to the effects of H$_2$-blockers.

Other medicines—Although certain medicines should not be used together at all, in other cases two different medicines may be used together even if an interaction might occur. In these cases, your doctor may want to change the dose, or other precautions may be necessary. When you are taking or receiving H$_2$-blockers it is especially important that your health care professional know if you are taking any of the following:

- Aminophylline (e.g., Somophyllin) or
- Anticoagulants (blood thinners) or
- Caffeine (e.g., NoDoz) or
- Metoprolol (e.g., Lopressor) or
- Oxtriphylline (e.g., Choledyl) or
- Phenytoin (e.g., Dilantin) or
- Propranolol (e.g., Inderal) or
- Theophylline (e.g., Somophyllin-T) or
- Tricyclic antidepressants (amitriptyline [e.g., Elavil], amoxapine [e.g., Asendin], clomipramine [e.g., Anafranil], desipramine [e.g., Pertofrane], doxepin [e.g., Sinequan], imipramine [e.g., Tofranil], nortriptyline [e.g., Aventyl], protriptyline [e.g., Vivactil], trimipramine [e.g., Surmontil])—Use of these medicines with cimetidine has been shown to increase the effects of cimetidine. This is less of a problem with ranitidine and has not been reported for famotidine or nizatidine. However, all of the H$_2$-blockers are similar, so drug interactions may occur with any of them

- Itraconazole (e.g., Sporanox) or
- Ketoconazole (e.g., Nizoral)—H$_2$-blockers may decrease the effects of itraconazole or ketoconazole; H$_2$-blockers should be taken at least 2 hours after these medicines

Other medical problems—The presence of other medical problems may affect the use of H$_2$-blockers. Make sure you tell your doctor if you have any other medical problems, especially:

- Kidney disease or
- Liver disease—The H$_2$-blocker may build up in the bloodstream, which may increase the risk of side effects

- Phenylketonuria (PKU)—Some H$_2$-blockers contain aspartame. Aspartame is converted to phenylalanine in the body and must be used with caution in patients with PKU. The Pepcid AC brand of famotidine chewable tablets contains 1.4 mg of phenylalanine per 10-mg dose. The Pepcid RPD brand of famotidine oral dispersible tablets contains 1.05 mg of phenylalanaine per 20-mg dose. The Zantac brand of ranitidine EFFERdose tablets and EFFERdose granules contain 16.84 mg of phenyl-alanine per 150-mg dose

- Weakened immune system (difficulty fighting infection)—Decrease in stomach acid caused by H$_2$-blockers may increase the possibility of a certain type of infection

Proper Use of This Medicine

For patients taking the *nonprescription strengths* of these medicines for heartburn, acid indigestion, and sour stomach:

- Do not take the maximum daily dosage continuously for more than 2 weeks, unless directed to do so by your doctor.
- If you have trouble in swallowing, or persistent abdominal pain, see your doctor promptly. These may be signs of a serious condition that may need different treatment.

For patients taking the *prescription strengths* of these medicines for more serious problems:

- One dose a day—Take it at bedtime, unless otherwise directed.
- Two doses a day—Take one in the morning and one at bedtime.
- Several doses a day—Take them with meals and at bedtime for best results.

It may take several days before this medicine begins to relieve stomach pain. To help relieve this pain, antacids may be taken with the H$_2$-blocker, unless your doctor has told you not to use them. However, you should wait one-half to one hour between taking the antacid and the H$_2$-blocker.

Take this medicine for the full time of treatment, even if you begin to feel better. Also, it is important that you keep your appointments with your doctor for check-ups so that your doctor will be better able to tell you when to stop taking this medicine.

For patients taking *famotidine chewable tablets:*

- Chew the tablets well before swallowing.

For patients taking *famotidine oral disintegrating tablets:*

- Make sure your hands are dry.
- Leave tablets in unopened package until the time of use, then open the pack and remove the tablet.
- Immediately place the tablet on the tongue.
- The tablet will dissolve in seconds, and you may swallow it with your saliva. You do not need to drink water or other liquid to swallow the tablet.

For patients taking *ranitidine effervescent granules or tablets:*

- Remove the foil wrapping and dissolve the dose in 6 to 8 ounces of water before drinking.

Dosing—The dose of histamine H$_2$-receptor antagonists (also called H$_2$-blockers) will be different for different patients. *Follow your doctor's orders or the directions on the label.* The following information includes only the average doses of these medicines. *If your dose is different, do not change it unless your doctor tells you to do so.*

The number of capsules or tablets or teaspoonfuls of solution, suspension, or syrup that you take depends on the strength of the medicine. Also, *the number of doses you take each day, the time allowed between doses, and the length of time you take the medicine depend on the medical problem for which you are taking the H$_2$-receptor antagonist.*

For cimetidine
- For *oral* dosage forms (solution and tablets):
  - —To treat duodenal or gastric ulcers:
    - Older adults, adults, and teenagers—300 milligrams (mg) four times a day, with meals and at bedtime. Some people may take 400 or 600 mg two times a day, on waking up and at bedtime. Others may take 800 mg at bedtime.
    - Children—20 to 40 mg per kilogram (kg) (9.1 to 18.2 mg per pound) of body weight a day, divided into four doses, taken with meals and at bedtime.
  - —To prevent duodenal ulcers:
    - Older adults, adults, and teenagers—300 mg two times a day, on waking up and at bedtime. Instead some people may take 400 mg at bedtime.
    - Children—Dose must be determined by your doctor.
  - —To treat heartburn, acid indigestion, and sour stomach:
    - Adults and teenagers—100 to 200 mg with water when symptoms start. The dose may be repeated once in twenty-four hours. Do not take more than 400 mg in twenty-four hours.
    - Children—Dose must be determined by your doctor.
  - —To prevent heartburn, acid indigestion, and sour stomach:
    - Adults and teenagers—100 to 200 mg with water up to one hour before eating food or drinking beverages you expect to cause symptoms. Do not take more than 400 mg in twenty-four hours.
    - Children—Dose must be determined by your doctor.
  - —To treat conditions in which the stomach produces too much acid:
    - Adults—300 mg four times a day, with meals and at bedtime. Your doctor may change the dose if needed.
    - Children—Dose must be determined by your doctor.
  - —To treat gastroesophageal reflux disease:
    - Adults—800 to 1600 mg a day, divided into smaller doses. Treatment usually lasts for 12 weeks.
    - Children—Dose must be determined by your doctor.
- For *injectable* dosage form:
  - —To treat duodenal ulcers, gastric ulcers or conditions in which the stomach produces too much acid:
    - Older adults, adults, and teenagers—300 mg injected into muscle, every six to eight hours. Or, 300 mg injected slowly into a vein every six to eight hours. Instead, 900 mg may be injected slowly into a vein around the clock at the rate of 37.5 mg per hour. Some people may need 150 mg at first, before beginning the around-the-clock treatment.
    - Children—5 to 10 mg per kg (2.3 to 4.5 mg per pound) of body weight injected into a vein or muscle, every six to eight hours.
  - —To prevent stress-related bleeding:
    - Older adults, adults, and teenagers—50 mg per hour injected slowly into a vein around the clock for up to 7 days.
    - Children—Dose must be determined by your doctor.

For famotidine
- For *oral* dosage forms (suspension, tablets, chewable tablets, and oral disintegrating tablets):
  - —To treat duodenal ulcers:
    - Older adults, adults, and teenagers—40 milligrams (mg) once a day at bedtime. Some people may take 20 mg two times day.
    - Children—Dose must be determined by your doctor.
  - —To prevent duodenal ulcers:
    - Older adults, adults, and teenagers—20 mg once a day at bedtime.
    - Children—Dose must be determined by your doctor.
  - —To treat gastric ulcers:
    - Older adults, adults, and teenagers—40 mg once a day at bedtime.
    - Children—Dose must be determined by your doctor.
  - —To treat heartburn, acid indigestion, and sour stomach:
    - Adults and teenagers—10 mg with water when symptoms start. The dose may be repeated once in twenty-four hours. Do not take more than 20 mg in twenty-four hours.
    - Children—Dose must be determined by your doctor.
  - —To prevent heartburn, acid indigestion, and sour stomach:
    - Adults and teenagers—10 mg taken one hour before eating a meal you expect to cause symptoms. The dose may be repeated once in twenty-four hours. Do not take more than 20 mg in twenty-four hours.
    - Children—Dose must be determined by your doctor.
  - —To treat conditions in which the stomach produces too much acid:
    - Older adults, adults, and children—20 mg every six hours. Your doctor may change the dose if needed.
    - Children—Dose must be determined by your doctor.
  - —To treat gastroesophageal reflux disease:
    - Older adults, adults, and teenagers—20 mg two times a day, usually for up to 6 weeks.
    - Children weighing more than 10 kg (22 pounds)—1 to 2 mg per kilogram (kg) (0.5 to 0.9 mg per pound) of body weight a day divided into two doses.
    - Children weighing less than 10 kg (22 pounds)—1 to 2 mg per kg (0.5 to 0.9 mg per pound) of body weight a day, divided into three doses.
- For *injectable* dosage form:
  - —To treat duodenal ulcers, gastric ulcers, or conditions in which the stomach produces too much acid:
    - Older adults, adults, and teenagers—20 mg injected into a vein, every twelve hours.
    - Children—Dose must be determined by your doctor.

For nizatidine
- For *oral* dosage forms (capsules and tablets):
  - —To treat duodenal or gastric ulcers:
    - Older adults, adults, and teenagers—300 milligrams (mg) once a day at bedtime. Some people may take 150 mg two times a day.

- Children—Dose must be determined by your doctor.
—To prevent duodenal ulcers:
  - Adults and teenagers—150 mg once a day at bedtime.
  - Children—Dose must be determined by your doctor.
—To prevent heartburn, acid indigestion, and sour stomach:
  - Adults and teenagers—75 mg taken thirty to sixty minutes before eating a meal you expect to cause symptoms. The dose may be repeated once in twenty-four hours.
  - Children—Dose must be determined by your doctor.
—To treat gastroesophageal reflux disease:
  - Adults and teenagers—150 mg two times a day.
  - Children—Dose must be determined by your doctor.

For ranitidine
- For *oral* dosage forms (effervescent granules, syrup, tablets, effervescent tablets):
—To treat duodenal ulcers:
  - Older adults, adults, and teenagers—150 milligrams (mg) two times a day. Some people may take 300 mg once a day at bedtime.
  - Children—2 to 4 mg per kilogram (kg) (1 to 2 mg per pound) of body weight per day, usually given as two divided doses. However, your total dose will not be more than 300 mg a day.
—To prevent duodenal ulcers:
  - Older adults, adults, and teenagers—150 mg at bedtime.
  - Children—Dose must be determined by your doctor.
—To treat gastric ulcers:
  - Older adults, adults, and teenagers—150 mg two times a day.
  - Children—2 to 4 mg per kilogram (1 to 2 mg per pound) of body weight per day, usually given as two divided doses. However, your total dose will not be more than 300 mg a day.
—To treat heartburn, acid indigestion, and sour stomach:
  - Adults and teenagers—75 mg with water when symptoms start. The dose may be repeated once in twenty-four hours. Do not take more than 150 mg in twenty-four hours.
  - Children—Dose must be determined by your doctor.
—To prevent heartburn, acid indigestion, and sour stomach:
  - Adults and teenagers—75 mg with water taken thirty to sixty minutes before eating a meal or drinking beverages you expect to cause symptoms. Do not take more than 150 mg in twenty-four hours.
  - Children—Dose must be determined by your doctor.
—To treat some conditions in which the stomach produces too much acid:
  - Older adults, adults, and teenagers—150 mg two times a day. Your doctor may change the dose if needed.

- Children—Dose must be determined by your doctor.
—To treat gastroesophageal reflux disease:
  - Older adults, adults, and teenagers—150 mg two times a day. Your dose may be increased if needed.
  - Children—5 to 10 mg per kg (2.3 to 4.6 mg per pound) of body weight a day, usually divided and given in two doses during the day. However, most children usually will not take more than 300 mg a day.
- For *injectable* dosage form:
—To treat duodenal ulcers, gastric ulcers, or conditions in which the stomach produces too much acid:
  - Older adults, adults, and teenagers—50 mg injected into a muscle every six to eight hours. Or, 50 mg injected slowly into a vein every six to eight hours. Instead, you may receive 6.25 mg per hour injected slowly into a vein around the clock. However, most people will usually not need more than 400 mg a day.
—To treat duodenal or gastric ulcers:
  - Children—2 to 4 mg per kg (1 to 2 mg per pound) of body weight a day, injected slowly into a vein.

Missed dose—If you miss a dose of this medicine, take it as soon as possible. However, if it is almost time for your next dose, skip the missed dose and go back to your regular dosing schedule. Do not double doses.

Storage—To store this medicine:
- Keep out of the reach of children.
- Store away from heat and direct light.
- Do not store the capsule or tablet form of this medicine in the bathroom, near the kitchen sink, or in other damp places. Heat or moisture may cause the medicine to break down.
- Keep the liquid form of this medicine from freezing.
- Do not keep outdated medicine or medicine no longer needed. Be sure that any discarded medicine is out of the reach of children.

Precautions While Using This Medicine

Some tests may be affected by this medicine. Tell the doctor in charge that you are taking this medicine before:
- You have any skin tests for allergies.
- You have any tests to determine how much acid your stomach produces.

Remember that certain medicines, such as aspirin, and certain foods and drinks (e.g., citrus products, carbonated drinks, etc.) irritate the stomach and may make your problem worse.

Cigarette smoking tends to decrease the effect of H$_2$-blockers by increasing the amount of acid produced by the stomach. This is more likely to affect the stomach's nighttime production of acid. While taking H$_2$-blockers, stop smoking completely, or at least do not smoke after taking the last dose of the day.

Drinking alcoholic beverages while taking an H$_2$-receptor antagonist has been reported to increase the blood levels of alcohol. You should consult your health care professional for guidance.

Check with your doctor if your ulcer pain continues or gets worse.

Side Effects of This Medicine

Along with its needed effects, a medicine may cause some unwanted effects. Although not all of these side effects may occur, if they do occur they may need medical attention.

Check with your doctor as soon as possible if any of the following side effects occur:

Rare

Abdominal pain; back, leg, or stomach pain; bleeding or crusting sores on lips; blistering, burning, redness, scaling, or tenderness of skin; blisters on palms of hands and soles of feet; changes in vision or blurred vision; confusion; coughing or difficulty in swallowing; dark-colored urine; dizziness; fainting; fast, pounding, or irregular heartbeat; fever and/or chills; flu-like symptoms; general feeling of discomfort or illness; hives; inflammation of blood vessels; joint pain; light-colored stools; mood or mental changes, including anxiety, agitation, confusion, hallucinations (seeing, hearing, or feeling things that are not there), mental depression, nervousness, or severe mental illness; muscle cramps or aches; nausea, vomiting, or loss of appetite; pain; peeling or sloughing of skin; red or irritated eyes; shortness of breath; skin rash or itching; slow heartbeat; sore throat; sores, ulcers, or white spots on lips, in mouth, or on genitals; sudden difficult breathing; swelling of face, lips, mouth, tongue, or eyelids; swelling of hands or feet; swollen or painful glands; tightness in chest; troubled breathing; unusual bleeding or bruising; unusual tiredness or weakness; unusually slow or irregular breathing; wheezing; yellow eyes or skin

Other side effects may occur that usually do not need medical attention. These side effects may go away during treatment as your body adjusts to the medicine. However, check with your doctor if any of the following side effects continue or are bothersome:

Less common or rare

Constipation; decreased sexual ability (especially in patients with Zollinger-Ellison disease who have received high doses of cimetidine for at least 1 year); decrease in sexual desire; diarrhea; difficult urination; dizziness; drowsiness; dryness of mouth or skin; headache; increased or decreased urination; increased sweating; loss of hair; ringing or buzzing in ears; runny nose; swelling of breasts or breast soreness in females and males; trouble in sleeping

Not all of the side effects listed above have been reported for each of these medicines, but they have been reported for at least one of them. All of the H_2-blockers are similar, so any of the above side effects may occur with any of these medicines.

Other side effects not listed above may also occur in some patients. If you notice any other effects, check with your doctor.

Additional Information

Once a medicine has been approved for marketing for a certain use, experience may show that it is also useful for other medical problems. Although these uses are not included in product labeling, H_2-blockers are used in certain patients with the following medical conditions:

- Damage to the stomach and/or intestines due to stress or trauma
- Hives
- Pancreatic problems
- Stomach or intestinal ulcers (sores) resulting from damage caused by medication used to treat rheumatoid arthritis

Other than the above information, there is no additional information relating to proper use, precautions, or side effects for these uses.

Revised: 05/29/2000

HISTRELIN   Systemic

Commonly used brand name(s):

In the U.S.—
Supprelin

Description

Histrelin (his-TREL-in) is a hormone similar to one normally released from the hypothalamus gland in the brain. Histrelin is used in the treatment of central precocious puberty (CPP), a condition that causes early puberty in boys (before 9.5 years of age) and in girls (before 8 years of age). Histrelin works by decreasing the amount of estrogen and testosterone in the blood.

When given regularly to boys and girls, this medicine helps to delay early puberty, slowing down the development of breasts in girls and the development of genital areas in boys and girls. This medicine delays puberty in a child only as long as the child continues to receive it.

Suppressing estrogen can cause thinning of the bones or slowing of their growth. Slowing the growth of bones is a positive effect in girls and boys whose bones grow too fast when puberty begins too early. Boys and girls may benefit by adding inches to their adult height when histrelin helps their bones grow at the proper and expected rate for children.

This medicine is available only with your doctor's prescription, in the following dosage form(s):

Parenteral
- Injection (U.S.)

Before Using This Medicine

In deciding to use a medicine, the risks of using the medicine must be weighed against the good it will do. This is a decision you and your doctor will make. For histrelin, the following should be considered:

Allergies—Tell your doctor if you have ever had any unusual or allergic reaction to histrelin or to gonadotropin-releasing hormone-like medicines. Also tell your health care professional if you are allergic to any other substances, such as foods, preservatives, or dyes.

Pregnancy—Histrelin use is not recommended during pregnancy. Histrelin has not been studied in pregnant women. It has been shown to cause problems in animals, such as low birth weights and a decrease in the number of successful pregnancies.

Breast-feeding— It is not known whether histrelin passes into breast milk. However, use of histrelin is not recommended during breast-feeding because it may cause unwanted effects in nursing babies.

Children— When used to treat a child for central precocious puberty, histrelin will stop having an effect soon after the child stops using it, and puberty should occur normally. It is not known if using histrelin around the time of puberty will cause changes in a boy's or a girl's future ability to have babies. Their chances of having children are thought to be normal.

It is especially important that you discuss with the child's doctor the good that this medicine may do as well as the risks of using it.

Proper Use of This Medicine

You will be given a fact sheet with your prescription for histrelin that explains how to prepare and give the injection. *Carefully read the fact sheet.* If you have any questions about using histrelin, ask your health care professional.

There are several important steps that will help you successfully prepare the histrelin injection. To draw the histrelin up into the syringe correctly, you need to follow these steps:

- Remove a bottle of medicine from the refrigerator and allow it to warm to room temperature before injecting it.
- Wash your hands with soap and water.
- Open the syringe packaging.
- Look at the medicine to make sure it is clear and colorless. Do not use it if it seems to be even a little discolored.
- Remove the colored protective cap on the bottle. Do *not* remove the rubber stopper.
- Wipe the top of the bottle with an alcohol swab.
- Pull the plunger on the syringe back until it is at the amount you were asked to inject.
- Remove the needle cover from the syringe.

How to prepare the histrelin dose:

- Gently push the needle through the top of the rubber stopper with the bottle standing upright.
- Push plunger in all the way to inject air into the bottle.
- Turn the bottle with syringe upside down in one hand. Be sure the tip of the needle is covered by the histrelin. With your other hand, draw the plunger back slowly to draw the correct dose of histrelin into the syringe.
- Check the dose. Hold the syringe with the scale at eye level to see that the proper dose is withdrawn and to check for air bubbles. To remove air bubbles, tap gently on the measuring scale of the syringe to move any bubbles to the top of the syringe near the needle. Then, push the histrelin slowly back into the bottle and draw up the dose again.
- If the dose measures too low in the syringe, withdraw more solution from the bottle. If there is too much histrelin in the syringe, put some back into the bottle. Then check the dose again.
- Remove the needle from the bottle and re-cover the needle with its plastic cap.

Choose the proper area of the body, such as the upper arms, thighs, or abdomen, to inject the dose of histrelin. The site should be changed between injections as directed by your doctor.

How to inject the histrelin dose:

- After you have prepared the syringe and chosen the area of the body to inject, you are ready to inject the histrelin into the fatty part of the skin.
  - Clean the area where the injection is to be given with an alcohol swab or with soap and water. Let the area dry.
  - Pinch up a large area of skin and hold it firmly. With your other hand, hold the syringe like a pencil. Push the needle straight into the pinched-up skin at a 45-degree angle for a child. Be sure the needle is all the way in. It is not necessary to draw back on the syringe each time to check for blood (also called routine aspiration).
  - Push the plunger all the way down, using less than 5 seconds to inject the dose. Let go of the skin. Hold an alcohol swab near the needle and pull the needle straight out of the skin in the same direction that you inserted it.
  - Press the alcohol swab against the injection area for several seconds. Do not rub.
  - Throw away the vial with any remaining medicine in it. It does not have a preservative and will not keep until the next day.

For patients using *disposable syringes:*

- *Manufacturers of disposable syringes recommend that they be used only once,* because the sterility of a reused syringe cannot be guaranteed. The syringe should be thrown away safely. It should not be used even once if the needle is bent or has come into contact with any surface other than the cleaned, swabbed area of the skin. *Do not wipe the needle with alcohol.*
- Used syringes and needles should be destroyed. Be careful when you recap, bend, or break a needle, because these actions increase the chances of a needle-stick injury. It is best to put used syringes and needles in a disposable container that is puncture-resistant (such as an empty plastic liquid laundry detergent or bleach bottle) or to use a needle-clipping device. The chance of a syringe being reused by someone else is lower if the plunger is taken out of the barrel and broken in half when you dispose of a syringe.

Use this medicine only as directed by your doctor. Do not use more or less of it, and do not use it more often than your doctor ordered. The exact amount of medicine you need has been carefully worked out. *Using too much may increase the chance of unwanted side effects, while using too little may not control the onset of puberty.*

Many boys and girls who have central precocious puberty will not feel sick or will not understand the importance of using the medicine regularly. *It is very important that the medicine is used exactly as directed and that the proper amount is used at the proper time.* It works best when there is a constant amount in the blood. To help keep the amount of histrelin in the blood constant, histrelin must be given on a regular schedule.

Dosing— The dose of histrelin will be different for different patients. *Follow your doctor's orders or the directions on the label.* The following information includes only the average doses of histrelin. *If your dose is different, do not change it* unless your doctor tells you to do so.

- For *injection* dosage form:
  - Central precocious puberty:
    - Children up to 2 years of age—Use and dose must be determined by the doctor. Children 2

years of age and older—10 micrograms (mcg) per kilogram (kg) (4.5 micrograms per pound) of body weight injected under the skin once a day and given every twenty-four hours.

Missed dose—Check with your doctor if you miss a dose of this medicine.

Storage—To store this medicine:
- Keep out of the reach of children.
- Store away from heat and direct light.
- Store in the refrigerator. However, keep the medicine from freezing.
- Do not keep outdated medicine or medicine no longer needed. Be sure that any discarded medicine is out of the reach of children.

Precautions While Using This Medicine

All scheduled visits to the doctor should be kept. This is especially important for children using the medicine for treatment of central precocious puberty as their condition improves. *The child's progress still must be checked by the doctor after the medicine is no longer being used.*

Tell the doctor if histrelin does not stop puberty from progressing within 6 to 8 weeks after starting treatment with histrelin. You may notice puberty progressing in your child for the first few weeks of therapy. These signs should stop within 4 weeks after your child begins treatment with histrelin.

This medicine may cause blurred vision, difficulty in reading, or other changes in vision. It may also cause some people to feel dizzy or lightheaded and impair their ability to use machines or do dangerous tasks. *If these problems occur, report them to your doctor.*

Side Effects of This Medicine

In the first few weeks of therapy, you may notice puberty progressing in your child, including light vaginal bleeding and breast enlargement in girls. Within 4 weeks after histrelin has had time to begin working properly, you should see signs in boys and girls that puberty is stopping.

Along with its needed effects, a medicine may cause some unwanted effects. Although not all of these side effects may occur, if they do occur they may need medical attention.

Check with your doctor immediately if any of the following side effects occur:
Less common
Bloody mucus in nose or unexplained nosebleeds; convulsion; difficulty in swallowing; feeling of fast or irregular heartbeat; flushing of skin; increased blood pressure; itching or redness of skin; lightheadedness; loss of consciousness; migraine headaches; swelling of skin; trouble in breathing

Check with your doctor as soon as possible if any of the following side effects occur:
More common
Headache; redness, swelling, and itching of skin at place of injection; skin rash; vaginal bleeding (for a short-term, occurring within first 3 weeks of therapy initiation); white vaginal discharge

Less common
Anxiety; blood in urine; breast swelling, pain, or discharge; brownish vaginal discharge with odor; chills; conduct disorder; cough; difficulty in seeing; dizziness; earache; feeling of warmth; frequent urge to urinate; hair loss; increased sensitivity of eyes to light; irritation or itching of vaginal area; loss of appetite; lower back pain; mental depression; nervousness; pain in chest, legs, joints, or neck; pain or burning while urinating; paleness of skin; red or purple spots on skin, varying in size from pinpoint to large bruises; seeing two objects instead of just one; sore throat; sudden sweating; thickened patches of skin; trembling or shaking; unusual tiredness or weakness

Other side effects may occur that usually do not need medical attention. These side effects may go away during treatment as your body adjusts to the medicine. However, check with your doctor if any of the following side effects continue or are bothersome:
More common
Abdominal pain or cramping; diarrhea; nausea; vomiting

Less common
Constipation; increased appetite; increased thirst

Other side effects not listed above also may occur in some patients. If you notice any other effects, check with your doctor.

Developed: 04/27/98

HMG-COA REDUCTASE INHIBITORS   Systemic

Commonly used brand name(s):

In the U.S.—

Baycol[2]	Mevacor[4]
Lescol[3]	Pravachol[5]
Lipitor[1]	Zocor[6]

In Canada—

Baycol[2]	Mevacor[4]
Lescol[3]	Pravachol[5]
Lipitor[1]	Zocor[6]

Other commonly used names are:
Epistatin
Eptastatin
Mevinolin
Synvinolin

Note: For quick reference, the following HMG-CoA reductase inhibitors are numbered to match the corresponding brand names.

This information applies to the following medicines:
1. Atorvastatin (a-TOR-va-sta-tin)
2. Cerivastatin (se-RIV-a-sta-tin)
3. Fluvastatin (FLOO-va-sta-tin)
4. Lovastatin (LOE-va-sta-tin)
5. Pravastatin (PRA-va-stat-in)
6. Simvastatin (SIM-va-stat-in)

Description

Atorvastatin, cerivastatin, fluvastatin, lovastatin, pravastatin, and simvastatin are used to lower levels of cholesterol and other fats in the blood. This may help prevent medical problems caused by cholesterol clogging the blood vessels.

These medicines belong to the group of medicines called 3-hydroxy-3-methylglutaryl coenzyme A (HMG-CoA) reductase inhibitors. They work by blocking an enzyme that is needed by the body to make cholesterol. Thus, less cholesterol is made.

HMG-CoA reductase inhibitors are available only with your doctor's prescription, in the following dosage forms:

Oral
    Atorvastatin
    • Tablets (U.S. and Canada)
    Cerivastatin
    • Tablets (U.S. and Canada)
    Fluvastatin
    • Capsules (U.S. and Canada)
    Lovastatin
    • Tablets (U.S. and Canada)
    Pravastatin
    • Tablets (U.S. and Canada)
    Simvastatin
    • Tablets (U.S. and Canada)

Before Using This Medicine

In deciding to use a medicine, the risks of taking the medicine must be weighed against the good it will do. This is a decision you and your doctor will make. For HMG-CoA reductase inhibitors, the following should be considered:

Allergies—Tell your doctor if you have ever had any unusual or allergic reaction to HMG-CoA reductase inhibitors. Also tell your health care professional if you are allergic to any other substances, such as foods, preservatives, or dyes.

Diet—Before prescribing medicines to lower your cholesterol, your doctor will probably try to control your condition by prescribing a personal diet for you. Such a diet will be lower in total fat, particularly saturated fat, and dietary cholesterol. Many people are able to control their condition by carefully following their doctor's orders for proper diet and exercise. *Medicine is prescribed only when additional help is needed* and is effective only when a schedule of diet and exercise is properly followed.

Also, this medicine is less effective if you are greatly overweight. It may be very important for you to go on a reducing diet. However, check with your doctor before going on any diet.

Pregnancy—HMG-CoA reductase inhibitors should not be used during pregnancy or by women who plan to become pregnant in the near future. These medicines block formation of cholesterol, which is necessary for the fetus to develop properly. HMG-CoA reductase inhibitors may cause birth defects or other problems in the baby if taken during pregnancy. An effective form of birth control should be used during treatment with these medicines. *Check with your doctor immediately if you think you have become pregnant while taking this medicine.* Be sure you have discussed this with your doctor.

Breast-feeding—These medicines are not recommended for use during breast-feeding because they may cause unwanted effects in nursing babies.

Children—Studies on this medicine have been done only in adult patients, and there is no specific information comparing use of HMG-CoA reductase inhibitors in children with use in other age groups. However, atorvastatin, lovastatin, and simvastatin have been used in a limited number of children under 18 years of age. Early information seems to show that these medicines may be effective in children, but their long-term safety has not been studied.

Older adults—This medicine has been tested in a limited number of patients 65 years of age or older and has not been shown to cause different side effects or problems in older people than it does in younger adults.

Other medicines—Although certain medicines should not be used together at all, in other cases two different medicines may be used together even if an interaction might occur. In these cases, your doctor may want to change the dose, or other precautions may be necessary. When you are taking HMG-CoA reductase inhibitors, it is especially important that your health care professional know if you are taking any of the following:

• Cyclosporine (e.g., Sandimmune) or
• Gemfibrozil (e.g., Lopid) or
• Niacin—Use of these medicines with an HMG-CoA reductase inhibitor may increase the risk of developing muscle problems and kidney failure

• Digoxin (e.g., Lanoxin)—Use with atorvastatin, fluvastatin, or simvastatin may increase blood levels of digoxin, increasing the risk of side effects

• Oral contraceptives, (birth control tablets)—Atorvastatin may increase the blood levels of the birth control hormones, increasing the risk of side effects

Other medical problems—The presence of other medical problems may affect the use of HMG-CoA reductase inhibitors. Make sure you tell your doctor if you have any other medical problems, especially:

• Alcohol abuse (or history of) or
• Liver disease—Use of this medicine may make liver problems worse

• Convulsions (seizures), not well-controlled, or
• Organ transplant with therapy to prevent transplant rejection or
• If you have recently had major surgery—Patients with these conditions may be at risk of developing problems that may lead to kidney failure

Proper Use of This Medicine

Use this medicine only as directed by your doctor. Do not use more or less of it, and do not use it more often or for a longer time than your doctor ordered.

Remember that this medicine will not cure your condition but it does help control it. Therefore, you must continue to take it as directed if you expect to keep your cholesterol levels down.

Follow carefully the special diet your doctor gave you. This is the most important part of controlling your condition, and is necessary if the medicine is to work properly.

For patients taking *atorvastatin:*
    Do not take this medicine with large amounts of grapefruit juice

For patients taking *lovastatin:*
    • This medicine works better when it is taken with food. If you are taking this medicine once a day, take it with the evening meal. If you are taking more than one dose a day, take each dose with a meal or snack.

Dosing—The dose of these medicines will be different for different patients. *Follow your doctor's orders or the directions on the label.* The following information includes only the average doses of these medicines. *If your dose is different, do not change it* unless your doctor tells you to do so.

The number of capsules or tablets that you take depends on the strength of the medicine.

For atorvastatin
- For *oral* dosage form (tablets):
  —For high cholesterol:
  - Adults—10 to 80 milligrams (mg) once a day.
  - Children—Use and dose must be determined by your doctor.

For cerivastatin
- For *oral* dosage form (tablets):
  —For high cholesterol:
  - Adults—0.4 milligrams (mg) once a day in the evening.
  - Children—Use and dose must be determined by your doctor.

For fluvastatin
- For *oral* dosage form (capsules):
  —For high cholesterol:
  - Adults—20 to 40 milligrams (mg) once a day in the evening.
  - Children—Use and dose must be determined by your doctor.

For lovastatin
- For *oral* dosage form (tablets):
  —For high cholesterol:
  - Adults— 20 to 80 milligrams (mg) a day taken as a single dose or divided into smaller doses. Take with evening meals.
  - Children—Use and dose must be determined by your doctor.

For pravastatin
- For *oral* dosage form (tablets):
  —For high cholesterol:
  - Adults—10 to 40 mg once a day at bedtime.
  - Children—Use and dose must be determined by your doctor.

For simvastatin
- For *oral* dosage form (tablets):
  —For high cholesterol:
  - Adults—5 to 80 mg a day.
  - Children—Use and dose must be determined by your doctor.

Missed dose—If you miss a dose of this medicine, take it as soon as possible. However, if it is almost time for your next dose, skip the missed dose and go back to your regular dosing schedule. Do not double doses.

Storage—To store this medicine:
- Keep out of the reach of children.
- Store away from heat and direct light.
- Do not store in the bathroom, near the kitchen sink, or in other damp places. Heat or moisture may cause the medicine to break down.
- Keep the medicine from freezing. Do not refrigerate.
- Do not keep outdated medicine or medicine no longer needed. Be sure that any discarded medicine is out of the reach of children.

Precautions While Using This Medicine

It is very important that your doctor check your progress at regular visits. This will allow your doctor to see if the medicine is working properly to lower your cholesterol levels and that it does not cause unwanted effects.

Check with your doctor immediately if you think that you may be pregnant. HMG-CoA reductase inhibitors may cause birth defects or other problems in the baby if taken during pregnancy.

Do not stop taking this medicine without first checking with your doctor. When you stop taking this medicine, your blood cholesterol levels may increase again. Your doctor may want you to follow a special diet to help prevent this from happening.

Before having any kind of surgery (including dental surgery) or emergency treatment, tell the medical doctor or dentist in charge that you are taking this medicine.

Side Effects of This Medicine

Along with its needed effects, a medicine may cause some unwanted effects. Although not all of these side effects may occur, if they do occur they may need medical attention.

Check with your doctor as soon as possible if any of the following side effects occur:
Less common or rare
  Fever; muscle aches or cramps; severe stomach pain; unusual tiredness or weakness

Other side effects may occur that usually do not need medical attention. These side effects may go away during treatment as your body adjusts to the medicine. However, check with your doctor if any of the following side effects continue or are bothersome:
More common
  Constipation; diarrhea; dizziness; gas; headache; heartburn; nausea; skin rash; stomach pain
Rare
  Decreased sexual ability; trouble in sleeping

Other side effects not listed above may also occur in some patients. If you notice any other effects, check with your doctor.

Revised: 03/28/2001

HYALURONATE SODIUM   Systemic

Commonly used brand name(s):

In the U.S.—
  Hyalgan
Another commonly used name is hyaluronic acid.

Description

Hyaluronate (hye-a-loo-ROE-nate) is similar to a substance that occurs naturally in joints and that helps joints work properly by acting like a lubricant and shock absorber. This medicine is injected directly into the knee to relieve pain caused by osteoarthritis.

This medicine is to be administered only by or under the immediate supervision of your doctor. It is available in the following dosage form:

Parenteral
- Injection (U.S.)

Before Receiving This Medicine

In deciding to use a medicine, the risks of using the medicine must be weighed against the good it will do. This is a decision you and your doctor will make. For hyaluronate, the following should be considered:

Allergies—Tell your doctor if you have ever had any unusual or allergic reaction to hyaluronate or to bird protein, feathers, or egg products. Also tell your health care professional if you are allergic to any other substances, such as foods, preservatives, or dyes.

Pregnancy—Studies have not been done in pregnant woman. However, studies in animals did not find that hyaluronate causes birth defects or other problems.

Breast-feeding—It is not known whether hyaluronate passes into breast milk. Although most medicines pass into breast milk in small amounts, many of them may be used safely while breast-feeding. Mothers who are taking this medicine and who wish to breast-feed should discuss this with their doctor.

Children—Studies on this medicine have been done only in adult patients, and there is no specific information comparing use of hyaluronate in children with use in other age groups.

Older adults—Many medicines have not been studied specifically in older people. Therefore, it may not be known whether they work exactly the same way they do in younger adults or if they cause different side effects or problems in older people. There is no specific information comparing use of hyaluronate in the elderly with the use in other age groups.

Other medical problems—The presence of other medical problems may affect the use of hyaluronate. Make sure you tell your doctor if you have any other medical problems, especially:

- Skin infection or other problems at the place where the injection is to be given—This medicine should not be injected there.

Proper Use of This Medicine

Dosing—The dose of hyaluronate may be different for different patients. The following information includes only the average doses of hyaluronate.

- For *parenteral* dosage form (injection):
  —For knee pain caused by osteoarthritis:
  - Adults—By injection into the knee, 20 milligrams (mg) once a week (one week apart) for a total of five injections.
  - Children—Use and dose must be determined by your doctor.

Precautions While Using This Medicine

For the first 48 hours after you receive this medicine, avoid strenuous activities or prolonged (more than 1 hour) activities that put a lot of weight on your legs, such as jogging, heavy lifting, playing tennis, or standing on your feet for a long period of time.

Side Effects of This Medicine

Along with its needed effects, a medicine may cause some unwanted effects. Although not all of these side effects may occur, if they do occur they may need medical attention.

Check with your doctor immediately if any of the following side effects occur:

Less common

> Blue color or flushing or redness of skin; cough; difficulty in swallowing; dizziness or feeling faint (severe); fever; redness or pain at place of injection; skin rash, hives, and/or itching; stuffy nose; swelling of eyelids, face, or lips; tightness in chest, troubled breathing, and/or wheezing

Other side effects may occur that usually do not need medical attention. These side effects may go away during treatment as your body adjusts to the medicine. However, check with your doctor if any of the following side effects continue or are bothersome:

More common

> Diarrhea; headache; itching of the skin; large, nonelevated blue or purplish patches in the skin; loss of appetite; nausea and/or vomiting; stomach pain; swelling of the knee

Other side effects not listed above may also occur in some patients. If you notice any other effects, check with your doctor.

Developed: 05/01/98

HYALURONATE SODIUM DERIVATIVE Systemic

Commonly used brand name(s):

In the U.S.—
> Synvisc

Another commonly used name is hylan G-F 20.

Description

Hyaluronate (hye-a-loo-ROE-nate) sodium derivative is similar to a substance that occurs naturally in joints that helps joints work properly by acting like a lubricant and shock absorber. This medicine is injected into the knee to relieve pain caused by osteoarthritis.

This medicine is to be administered only by or under the immediate supervision of your doctor. It is available only with your doctor's prescription, in the following dosage form(s):

Parenteral
- Injection (U.S.)

Before Using This Medicine

In deciding to use a medicine, the risks of using the medicine must be weighed against the good it will do. This is a decision you and your doctor will make. For hyaluronate sodium derivative, the following should be considered:

Allergies—Tell your doctor if you have ever had any unusual or allergic reaction to hyaluronate sodium derivative, other hylans, hyaluronate sodium, bird protein, feathers, or egg products. Also tell your health care professional if you are allergic to any other substances, such as foods, preservatives, or dyes.

Pregnancy—Studies have not been done in pregnant women.

Breast-feeding— It is not known whether hyaluronate sodium derivative passes into breast milk. Although most medicines pass into breast milk in small amounts, many of them may be used safely while breast-feeding. Mothers who are using this medicine and who wish to breast-feed should discuss this with their doctor.

Children— Studies on this medicine have been done only in adult patients, and there is no specific information comparing the use of hyaluronate sodium derivative in children with use in other age groups.

Older adults—Many medicines have not been studied specifically in older people. Therefore, it may not be known whether they work exactly the same way they do in younger adults or if they cause different side effects or problems in older people. There is no specific information comparing use of hyaluronate sodium derivative in the elderly with use in other age groups.

Other medical problems— The presence of other medical problems may affect the use of hyaluronate sodium derivative. Make sure you tell your doctor if you have any other medical problems, especially:

- Skin or knee joint infections or other problems at the place where the injection is to be given—This medicine should not be injected there

Proper Use of This Medicine

Dosing—The dose of hyaluronate sodium derivative will be different for different patients. The following information includes only the average doses of hyaluronate sodium derivative.

- For *parenteral* dosage form (injection):
  —For knee pain caused by osteoarthritis:
  - Adults—By injection into the knee, 16 milligrams (mg) once a week (one week apart) for a total of three injections.
  - Children—Use and dose must be determined by your doctor.

Precautions While Using This Medicine

For the first 48 hours after you receive this medicine, avoid strenuous activities or prolonged (more than 1 hour) activities that put a lot of weight on your legs, such as jogging, heavy lifting, playing tennis, or standing on your feet for a long period of time.

Side Effects of This Medicine

Along with its needed effects, a medicine may cause some unwanted effects. Although not all of these side effects may occur, if they do occur they may need medical attention.

Check with your doctor as soon as possible if any of the following side effects occur:
Rare
Difficulty breathing; hives; shortness of breath

Other side effects may occur that usually do not need medical attention. These side effects may go away during treatment as your body adjusts to the medicine. However, check with your doctor if any of the following side effects continue or are bothersome:
More common
Knee pain; pain at the injection site; swelling of the knee

Rare
Calf cramps; dizziness; facial flushing with swelling of the lips; headache; infection of the joint; itching of the skin; muscle pain; nausea; pain on one side of the body with anxiety, nausea, and tiredness; rapid heartbeat; skin rash

Other side effects not listed above may also occur in some patients. If you notice any other effects, check with your doctor.

Developed: 07/08/98
Interim revision: 10/15/98

HYDRALAZINE Systemic

Commonly used brand name(s):
In the U.S.—
Generic name product may be available.
In Canada—

Apo-Hydral	Apresoline
Apo-Hydralazine	Novo-Hylazin

Description

Hydralazine (hye-DRAL-a-zeen) belongs to the general class of medicines called antihypertensives. It is used to treat high blood pressure (hypertension). It is also used to control high blood pressure in the mother during pregnancy (preeclampsia or eclampsia) or in emergency situations when blood pressure is extremely high (hypertensive crisis).

High blood pressure adds to the workload of the heart and arteries. If it continues for a long time, the heart and arteries may not function properly. This can damage the blood vessels of the brain, heart, and kidneys, resulting in a stroke, heart failure, or kidney failure. High blood pressure may also increase the risk of heart attacks. These problems may be less likely to occur if blood pressure is controlled.

Hydralazine works by relaxing blood vessels and increasing the supply of blood and oxygen to the heart while reducing its workload.

Hydralazine may also be used for other conditions as determined by your doctor.

Hydralazine is available only with your doctor's prescription, in the following dosage forms:
Oral
- Oral solution (must be prepared by the pharmacist)
- Tablets (U.S. and Canada)
Parenteral
- Injection (U.S. and Canada)

Before Using This Medicine

In deciding to use a medicine, the risks of taking the medicine must be weighed against the good it will do. This is a decision you and your doctor will make. For hydralazine, the following should be considered:

Allergies—Tell your doctor if you have ever had any unusual or allergic reaction to hydralazine. Also tell your health care professional if you are allergic to any other substances, such as foods, preservatives, or dyes.

Pregnancy—Although hydralazine often is used to reduce high blood pressure in pregnant women, extensive studies of hydralazine in pregnant women have not been done. However, blood problems and other problems have been reported in infants of mothers who took hydralazine during pregnancy. In addition, studies in mice have shown that high doses of hydralazine cause birth defects (cleft palate, defects in head and face bones). These birth defects also occurred in rabbits, but did not occur in rats. Before taking this medicine, make sure your doctor knows if you are pregnant or if you may become pregnant.

Breast-feeding—Hydralazine passes into breast milk. Although most medicines pass into breast milk in small amounts, many of them may be used safely while breast-feeding. Mothers who are taking this medicine and who wish to breast-feed should discuss this with their doctor.

Children—Although there is no specific information comparing use of hydralazine in children with use in other age groups, this medicine is not expected to cause different side effects or problems in children than it does in adults. However, the oral solution contains aspartame, which is converted to phenylalanine in the body. Children with phenylketonuria cannot process phenylalanine and high levels of this substance in body fluids may cause brain damage.

Older adults—Many medicines have not been studied specifically in older people. Therefore, it may not be known whether they work exactly the same way they do in younger adults. Although there is no specific information comparing use of hydralazine in the elderly with use in other age groups, this medicine is not expected to cause different side effects or problems in older people than it does in younger adults.

Other medicines—Although certain medicines should not be used together at all, in other cases two different medicines may be used together even if an interaction might occur. In these cases, your doctor may want to change the dose, or other precautions may be necessary. When you are taking hydralazine, it is especially important that your health care professional know if you are taking the following:

- Diazoxide (e.g., Proglycem)—Effect on blood pressure may be increased

Other medical problems—The presence of other medical problems may affect the use of hydralazine. Make sure you tell your doctor if you have any other medical problems, especially:

- Heart or blood vessel disease or
- Stroke—Lowering blood pressure may make problems resulting from these conditions worse
- Kidney disease—Effects may be increased because of slower removal of hydralazine from the body
- Phenylketonuria—The oral solution of hydralazine contains aspartame, which is converted to phenylalanine in the body. Patients with phenylketonuria cannot process phenylalanine and high levels of this substance in body fluids may cause brain damage

---

Proper Use of This Medicine

For patients taking this medicine *for high blood pressure:*

- In addition to the use of the medicine your doctor has prescribed, treatment for your high blood pressure may include weight control and care in the types of foods you eat, especially foods high in sodium. Your doctor will tell you which of these are most important for you. You should check with your doctor before changing your diet.

- Many patients who have high blood pressure will not notice any signs of the problem. In fact, many may feel normal. It is very important that you *take your medicine exactly as directed* and that you keep your appointments with your doctor even if you feel well.
- Remember that hydralazine will not cure your high blood pressure but it does help control it. Therefore, you must continue to take it as directed if you expect to lower your blood pressure and keep it down. *You may have to take high blood pressure medicine for the rest of your life.* If high blood pressure is not treated, it can cause serious problems such as heart failure, blood vessel disease, stroke, or kidney disease.

For patients taking the *oral solution form of hydralazine:*

- The oral solution may be mixed with fruit juice or applesauce. If mixed with fruit juice or applesauce, take immediately after mixing. Be sure to take all of the mixture to get the full dose of the medicine.

This medicine works best if there is a constant amount in the blood. To help keep this amount constant, do not miss any doses and take the medicine at the same times each day.

Dosing—The dose of hydralazine will be different for different patients. *Follow your doctor's orders or the directions on the label.* The following information includes only the average doses of hydralazine. *If your dose is different, do not change it* unless your doctor tells you to do so.

The number of tablets or teaspoonfuls of oral solution that you take depends on the strength of the medicine.

- For *oral* dosage forms (oral solution and tablets):
  —For high blood pressure:
    - Adults—40 to 200 milligrams (mg) per day divided into two or four doses
    - Children—Dose is based on body weight. The usual dose is 0.75 to 7.5 mg per kilogram (kg) (0.34 to 3.4 mg per pound) of body weight a day. This is divided into two or four doses.

- For *injection* dosage form:
  —For high blood pressure:
    - Adults—5 to 40 mg injected into a muscle or a vein. Your doctor may repeat the dose as needed.
    - Children—Dose is based on body weight. The usual dose is 1.7 to 3.5 mg per kg (0.77 to 1.6 mg per pound) of body weight a day. This is divided into four to six doses and injected into a muscle or a vein.
  —For high blood pressure during pregnancy:
    - Adults—5 mg injected into a vein every fifteen to twenty minutes.

Missed dose—If you miss a dose of this medicine, take it as soon as possible. However, if it is almost time for your next dose, skip the missed dose and go back to your regular dosing schedule. Do not double doses.

Storage—To store this medicine:

- Keep out of the reach of children.
- Store away from heat and direct light.
- Store the oral solution form of hydralazine in the refrigerator because heat will cause this medicine to break down. However, keep the medicine from freezing.
- Do not store in the bathroom, near the kitchen sink, or in other damp places. Heat or moisture may cause the medicine to break down.
- Do not keep outdated medicine or medicine no longer needed. Be sure that any discarded medicine is out of the reach of children.

Precautions While Using This Medicine

It is important that your doctor check your progress at regular visits to make sure that this medicine is working properly.

Hydralazine may cause some people to have headaches or to feel dizzy. *Make sure you know how you react to this medicine before you drive, use machines, or do anything else that could be dangerous if you are dizzy or are not alert.*

The oral solution contains 1.4 milligrams (mg) of phenylalanine per teaspoonful (5 mL). Patients with phenylketonuria cannot process phenylalanine and high levels of this substance in body fluids may cause brain damage.

For patients taking this medicine *for high blood pressure:*
- *Do not take other medicines unless they have been discussed with your doctor.* This especially includes over-the-counter (nonprescription) medicines for appetite control, asthma, colds, cough, hay fever, or sinus problems, since they may tend to increase your blood pressure.

Side Effects of This Medicine

Along with its needed effects, a medicine may cause some unwanted effects. Although not all of these side effects may occur, if they do occur they may need medical attention.

In general, side effects with hydralazine are rare at lower doses. However, check with your doctor as soon as possible if any of the following occur:

Less common
> Blisters on skin; chest pain; general feeling of discomfort or illness or weakness; joint pain; muscle pain; numbness, tingling, pain, or weakness in hands or feet; skin rash or itching; sore throat and fever; swelling of feet or lower legs; swelling of lymph glands

Rare
> Fever; general feeling of discomfort or illness; sore throat; weakness

Other side effects may occur that usually do not need medical attention. These side effects may go away during treatment as your body adjusts to the medicine. However, check with your doctor if any of the following side effects continue or are bothersome:

More common
> Diarrhea; fast heartbeat; headache; loss of appetite; nausea or vomiting; pounding heartbeat

Less common
> Constipation; dizziness or lightheadedness; redness or flushing of face; shortness of breath; stuffy nose; watery eyes

Other side effects not listed above may also occur in some patients. If you notice any other effects, check with your doctor.

Additional Information

Once a medicine has been approved for marketing for a certain use, experience may show that it is also useful for other medical problems. Although this use is not specifically included in product labeling, hydralazine is used in certain patients with the following medical condition:
- Congestive heart failure

Other than the above information, there is no additional information relating to proper use, precautions, or side effects for this use.

Revised: 08/08/96
Interim revision: 08/24/98

HYDROCODONE AND IBUPROFEN
Systemic

Commonly used brand name(s):

In the U.S.—
> Vicoprofen

Description

Hydrocodone and ibuprofen (hye-droe-KOE-done and eye-byoo-PROE-fen) combination is used to relieve pain.

The hydrocodone is a narcotic analgesic that acts in the central nervous system to relieve pain. If hydrocodone is used for a long time, it may become habit-forming (causing mental or physical dependence). Physical dependence may lead to withdrawal side effects when you stop taking the medicine. Since hydrocodone and ibuprofen combination is only used for short-term (10 days or less) relief of pain, physical dependence will probably not occur.

Ibuprofen is a nonsteroidal anti-inflammatory drug (NSAID) used in this combination to relieve inflammation, swelling, and pain.

This medicine is available only with your doctor's prescription, in the following dosage form(s):

Oral
- Tablets (U.S.)

Before Using This Medicine

In deciding to use a medicine, the risks of taking the medicine must be weighed against the good it will do. This is a decision you and your doctor will make. For hydrocodone and ibuprofen combination, the following should be considered:

Allergies—Tell your doctor if you have ever had any unusual or allergic reaction to aspirin, hydrocodone or other narcotic analgesics, or ibuprofen or other nonsteroidal anti-inflammatory drugs (NSAIDs). Also tell your health care professional if you are allergic to any other substances, such as foods, preservatives, or dyes.

Pregnancy—Studies on birth defects with hydrocodone and ibuprofen combination have not been done in pregnant women. However, there is a chance that the ibuprofen in this combination may cause unwanted effects on the heart or blood flow of the fetus or newborn baby if they are taken during the last few months of pregnancy. Also, too much use during pregnancy of a narcotic analgesic like the hydrocodone in the combination may cause the baby to become dependent on the medicine. This may lead to withdrawal side effects after birth. Before taking this medicine, make sure your doctor knows if you are pregnant or if you may become pregnant.

Breast-feeding—It is not known whether hydrocodone and ibuprofen combination passes into breast milk. However, hydrocodone and ibuprofen combination is not recommended for use during breast-feeding because it may cause unwanted effects in nursing babies.

Children—Studies on this medicine have been done only in adult patients, and there is no specific information comparing use of hydrocodone and ibuprofen combination in children with its use in other age groups.

Older adults—Elderly people are especially sensitive to the effects of hydrocodone and ibuprofen combination. This may increase the chance of side effects during treatment. Constipation may be especially likely to occur in elderly patients.

Other medicines—Although certain medicines should not be used together at all, in other cases two different medicines may be used together even if an interaction might occur. In these cases, your doctor may want to change the dose, or other precautions may be necessary. When you are taking hydrocodone and ibuprofen combination, it is especially important that your health care professional know if you are taking any of the following:

- Alcohol or
- Central nervous system (CNS) depressants (medicine that causes drowsiness) or
- Monoamine oxidase (MAO) inhibitors (furazolidone [e.g., Furoxone], phenelzine [e.g., Nardil], procarbazine [e.g., Matulane], selegiline [e.g., Eldepryl], tranylcypromine [e.g., Parnate] or
- Tricyclic antidepressants (amitriptyline [e.g., Elavil], amoxapine [e.g., Asendin], clomipramine [e.g., Anafranil], desipramine [e.g., Pertofrane], doxepin [e.g., Sinequan], imipramine [e.g., Tofranil], nortriptyline [e.g., Aventyl], protriptyline [e.g., Vivactil], trimipramine [e.g., Surmontil]—The chance of side effects may be increased
- Anticoagulants (blood thinners)—The chance of bleeding may be increased
- Angiotensin-converting enzyme (ACE) inhibitors (benazepril [e.g., Lotensin], captopril [e.g., Capoten], enalapril [e.g., Vasotec], fosinopril [e.g., Monopril], lisinopril [e.g., Prinivil, Zestril], quinapril [e.g., Accupril], ramipril [e.g., Altace] or
- Diuretics (water pills)—Hydrocodone and ibuprofen combination may decrease the effects of these medicines; the chance of kidney problems also may be increased
- Lithium (e.g., Lithane) or
- Methotrexate (e.g., Mexate)—Higher blood levels of these medicines and an increased chance of side effects may occur

Other medical problems—The presence of other medical problems may affect the use of hydrocodone and ibuprofen combination. Make sure you tell your doctor if you have any other medical problems, especially:

- Asthma or other chronic lung disease or
- Brain disease or head injury or
- Enlarged prostate or problems with urination—Side effects of hydrocodone and ibuprofen combination may be dangerous with these conditions
- Abdominal conditions or
- Anemia or
- Alcohol abuse, or history of, or
- Bleeding problems or
- Dehydration or
- Drug dependence, especially narcotic abuse, or history of or
- Heart disease or
- Kidney disease or
- Liver disease or
- Stomach ulcer or
- Tobacco use or
- Underactive thyroid—The chance of side effects may be increased

Proper Use of This Medicine

For safe and effective use of this medicine, do not take more of it, do not take it more often, and do not take it for a longer time than ordered by your health care professional. Taking too much of this medicine may increase the chance of unwanted effects.

Dosing—The dose of hydrocodone and ibuprofen combination will be different for different patients. *Follow your doctor's orders or the directions on the label.* The following information includes only the average doses of hydrocodone and ibuprofen combination. *If your dose is different, do not change it* unless your doctor tells you to do so.

The number of doses you take each day, the time allowed between doses, and the length of time you take the medicine depend on the medical problem for which you are taking hydrocodone and ibuprofen combination.

- For *oral* dosage form (tablets):
  —For pain:
    - Adults—1 tablet of Vicoprofen every four to six hours as needed.
    - Children—Use and dose must be determined by your doctor.

Missed dose—If you miss a dose of this medicine, take it as soon as possible. However, if it is almost time for your next dose, skip the missed dose and go back to your regular dosing schedule. Do not double doses.

Storage—To store this medicine:
- Keep out of the reach of children.
- Store away from heat and direct light.
- Do not store in the bathroom, near the kitchen sink, or in other damp places. Heat or moisture may cause the medicine to break down.
- Do not keep outdated medicine or medicine no longer needed. Be sure that any discarded medicine is out of the reach of children.

Precautions While Using This Medicine

Hydrocodone and ibuprofen combination will add to the effects of alcohol and other central nervous system (CNS) depressants (medicines that slow down the nervous system, possibly causing drowsiness). Some examples of CNS depressants are antihistamines or medicine for hay fever, other allergies, or colds; sedatives, tranquilizers, sleeping medicine, or other prescription pain medication. *Do not drink alcoholic beverages, and check with your medical doctor or dentist before taking any of the medicines listed above, while you are using this medicine.*

This medicine may cause some people to become drowsy, dizzy, or lightheaded, or to feel a false sense of well-being. *Make sure you know how you react to this medicine before you drive, use machines, or do anything else that could be dangerous if you are dizzy or are not alert and clearheaded.* If these reactions are especially bothersome, check with your doctor.

Dizziness, lightheadedness, or fainting may occur, especially when getting up suddenly from a lying or sitting position. Getting up slowly may lessen this problem.

Before having any kind of surgery (including dental surgery) or emergency treatment, tell the medical doctor or dentist in charge that you are taking this medicine.

Hydrocodone and ibuprofen combination may cause dryness of the mouth. For temporary relief, use sugarless candy or gum, melt bits of ice in your mouth, or use a saliva substitute. However, if dry mouth continues for more than 2 weeks, check with your dentist. Continuing dryness of the mouth may increase the chance of dental disease, including tooth decay, gum disease, and fungus infections.

Side Effects of This Medicine

Along with its needed effects, a medicine may cause some unwanted effects. Although not all of these side effects may occur, if they do occur they may need medical attention.

Check with your doctor as soon as possible if any of the following side effects occur:

Less common or rare
> Bloody stools; burning feeling in chest or stomach; congestion in chest; changes in facial skin color; cough; diarrhea; difficulty in swallowing; fast or irregular breathing; fever; frequent urge to urinate; heartburn; inability to urinate; irregular heartbeat; lightheadedness or dizziness; loss of bladder control; puffiness or swelling of the eyelids or around the eyes; ringing or buzzing in the ears; shortness of breath, troubled breathing, tightness in chest and/or wheezing; skin rash, hives, and/or itching; stomach pain; tenderness in stomach

Symptoms of overdose
> Blurred vision; cold or clammy skin; confusion; difficulty hearing or ringing or buzzing in ears; dizziness; general feeling of illness; headache; mood or mental changes; nausea and/or vomiting; severe drowsiness; severe stomach pain; skin rash; slow heartbeat; slow or troubled breathing; stiff neck and/or back; swelling of the face, fingers, feet, or lower legs

Other side effects may occur that usually do not need medical attention. These side effects may go away during treatment as your body adjusts to the medicine. However, check with your doctor if any of the following side effects continue or are bothersome:

More common
> Anxiety; constipation; dry mouth; gas; increased sweating; nausea and/or vomiting; nervousness; pounding heartbeat; sleepiness; swelling of feet or lower legs; trouble in sleeping; unusual tiredness or weakness

Less common or rare
> Confusion; decreased appetite; decrease in sexual ability; depression; headache; heartburn; increased thirst; irritability; mood or mental changes; mouth ulcers; pain or burning in throat; runny nose; sensation of burning, warmth, heat, numbness, tightness, or tingling; slurred speech; stomach upset; thinking abnormalities; trembling or shaking of hands or feet; unexplained weight loss; unusual feeling of well-being; visual disturbances

Other side effects not listed above may also occur in some patients. If you notice any other effects, check with your doctor.

Developed: 07/13/98

HYDROXYCHLOROQUINE
Systemic

Commonly used brand name(s):

In the U.S.—
> Plaquenil

In Canada—
> Plaquenil

Description

Hydroxychloroquine (hye-drox-ee-KLOR-oh-kwin) belongs to the family of medicines called antiprotozoals. *Protozoa* are tiny, one-celled animals. Some are parasites that can cause many different kinds of infections in the body.

This medicine is used to prevent and to treat malaria and to treat some conditions such as liver disease caused by *protozoa*. It is also used in the treatment of arthritis to help relieve inflammation, swelling, stiffness, and joint pain and to help control the symptoms of lupus erythematosus (lupus; SLE).

This medicine may be given alone or with one or more other medicines. It may also be used for other conditions as determined by your doctor.

Hydroxychloroquine is available only with your doctor's prescription, in the following dosage form:

Oral
> • Tablets (U.S. and Canada)

Before Using This Medicine

In deciding to use a medicine, the risks of taking the medicine must be weighed against the good it will do. This is a decision you and your doctor will make. For hydroxychloroquine, the following should be considered:

Allergies—Tell your doctor if you have ever had any unusual or allergic reaction to hydroxychloroquine or chloroquine. Also tell your health care professional if you are allergic to any other substances, such as foods, preservatives, or dyes.

Pregnancy—Unless you are taking it for malaria or liver disease caused by *protozoa*, use of this medicine is not recommended during pregnancy. In animal studies, hydroxychloroquine has been shown to cause damage to the central nervous system (brain and spinal cord) of the fetus, including damage to hearing and sense of balance, bleeding inside the eyes, and other eye problems. However, when given in low doses (once a week) to prevent malaria, this medicine has not been shown to cause birth defects or other problems in pregnant women.

Breast-feeding—A very small amount of hydroxychloroquine passes into the breast milk. It has not been reported to cause problems in nursing babies to date. However, babies and children are especially sensitive to the effects of hydroxychloroquine.

Children—Children are especially sensitive to the effects of hydroxychloroquine. This may increase the chance of side effects during treatment. Overdose is especially dangerous in children. Taking as few as 3 or 4 tablets (250-milligrams [mg] strength) of chloroquine has resulted in death in small children. Because hydroxychloroquine is so similar to chloroquine, it is probably just as toxic.

Older adults—Many medicines have not been studied specifically in older people. Therefore, it may not be known whether they work exactly the same way they do in younger adults or if they cause different side effects or problems in older people. There is no specific information comparing use of hydroxychloroquine in the elderly with use in other age groups.

Other medicines—Although certain medicines should not be used together at all, in other cases 2 different medicines may be used together even if an interaction might occur. In these cases, your doctor may want to change the dose, or other precautions may be necessary. Tell your health care professional if you are taking any other prescription or non-prescription (over-the-counter [OTC]) medicine.

Other medical problems—The presence of other medical problems may affect the use of hydroxychloroquine. Make sure you tell your doctor if you have any other medical problems, especially:

- Blood disease (severe)—Hydroxychloroquine may cause blood disorders
- Eye or vision problems—Hydroxychloroquine may cause serious eye side effects, especially in high doses
- Glucose-6-phosphate dehydrogenase (G6PD) deficiency—Hydroxychloroquine may cause serious blood side effects in patients with this deficiency
- Kidney disease—There may be an increased chance of side effects in patients with kidney disease
- Liver disease—May decrease the removal of hydroxychloroquine from the blood, increasing the chance of side effects
- Nerve or brain disease (severe), including convulsions (seizures)—Hydroxychloroquine may cause muscle weakness and, in high doses, seizures
- Porphyria—Hydroxychloroquine may worsen the symptoms of porphyria
- Psoriasis—Hydroxychloroquine may bring on severe attacks of psoriasis
- Stomach or intestinal disease (severe)—Hydroxychloroquine may cause stomach irritation

Proper Use of This Medicine

Take this medicine with meals or milk to lessen possible stomach upset, unless otherwise directed by your doctor.

Keep this medicine out of the reach of children. Children are especially sensitive to the effects of hydroxychloroquine and overdose is especially dangerous in children. Taking as few as 3 or 4 tablets (250-mg strength) of chloroquine has resulted in death in small children. Hydroxychloroquine is probably just as dangerous.

It is very important that you *take this medicine only as directed.* Do not take more of it, do not take it more often, and do not take it for a longer time than your doctor ordered. To do so may increase the chance of serious side effects.

If you are taking this medicine to help keep you from getting malaria, *keep taking it for the full time of treatment.* If you already have malaria, you should still keep taking this medicine for the full time of treatment even if you begin to feel better after a few days. This will help to clear up your infection completely. If you stop taking this medicine too soon, your symptoms may return.

Hydroxychloroquine works best when you take it on a regular schedule. For example, if you are to take it once a week to prevent malaria, it is best to take it on the same day each week. Or if you are to take 2 doses a day, 1 dose may be taken with breakfast and the other with the evening meal.

Make sure that you do not miss any doses. If you have any questions about this, check with your health care professional.

Dosing—The dose of hydroxychloroquine will be different for different patients. *Follow your doctor's orders or the directions on the label.* The following information includes only the average doses of hydroxychloroquine. *If your dose is different, do not change it* unless your doctor tells you to do so.

The number of doses you take each day, the time allowed between doses, and the length of time you take the medicine depend on the medical problem for which you are taking hydroxychloroquine.

- For *tablets* dosage form:
  —For prevention of malaria:
  - Adults—400 milligrams (mg) once every seven days.
  - Children—Dose is based on body weight and must be determined by your doctor. The usual dose is 6.4 mg per kilogram (kg) (2.9 mg per pound) of body weight once every seven days.
  —For treatment of malaria:
  - Adults—800 mg as a single dose. This may sometimes be followed by a dose of 400 mg six to eight hours after the first dose, then 400 mg once a day on the second and third days.
  - Children—Dose is based on body weight and must be determined by your doctor. The usual dose is 32 mg per kg (14.5 mg per pound) of body weight taken over a period of three days.
  —For treatment of arthritis:
  - Adults—Dose is based on body weight and must be determined by your doctor. The usual dose is 6.5 mg per kg (2.9 mg per pound) of body weight per day.

Missed dose—If you miss a dose of this medicine, take it as soon as possible. However, if it is almost time for your next dose, skip the missed dose and go back to your regular dosing schedule. Do not double doses.

For patients taking hydroxychloroquine *to prevent malaria:*

- Your doctor may want you to start taking this medicine 1 to 2 weeks before you travel to an area where there is a chance of getting malaria. This will help you to see how you react to the medicine. Also, it will allow time for your doctor to change to another medicine if you have a reaction to this medicine.
- Also, you should keep taking this medicine while you are in the area and for 4 to 6 weeks after you leave the area. No medicine will protect you completely from malaria. However, to protect you as completely as possible, *it is important to keep taking this medicine for the full time your doctor ordered.* Also, if fever develops during your travels or within 2 months after you leave the area, *check with your doctor immediately.*

For patients taking hydroxychloroquine *for arthritis or lupus:*

- This medicine must be taken regularly as ordered by your doctor in order for it to help you. It may take up to several weeks before you begin to feel better. It may take up to 6 months before you feel the full benefit of this medicine.

For patients *unable to swallow hydroxychloroquine tablets:*

- Your pharmacist can crush the tablets and put each dose in a capsule. Contents of the capsules may then be mixed with a teaspoonful of jam, jelly, or jello. Be sure you take all the food in order to get the full dose of medicine.

Storage—To store this medicine:

- Keep out of the reach of children. Overdose of hydroxychloroquine is very dangerous in children.
- Store away from heat and direct light.
- Do not store in the bathroom, near the kitchen sink, or in other damp places. Heat or moisture may cause the medicine to break down.
- Do not keep outdated medicine or medicine no longer needed. Be sure that any discarded medicine is out of the reach of children.

Precautions While Using This Medicine

Check with your doctor immediately if blurred vision, difficulty in reading, or any other change in vision occurs during or after long-term treatment. Your doctor may want you to have your eyes checked by an ophthalmologist (eye doctor).

If your symptoms do not improve within a few days (or a few weeks or months for arthritis), or if they become worse, check with your doctor.

Hydroxychloroquine may cause blurred vision, difficulty in reading, or other change in vision. It may also cause some people to become dizzy or lightheaded. *Make sure you know how you react to this medicine before you drive, use machines, or do anything else that could be dangerous if you are dizzy or are not alert or able to see well.* If these reactions are especially bothersome, check with your doctor.

Malaria is spread by mosquitoes. If you are living in, or will be traveling to, an area where there is a chance of getting malaria, the following mosquito-control measures will help to prevent infection:

- If possible, sleep under mosquito netting to avoid being bitten by malaria-carrying mosquitoes.
- Wear long-sleeved shirts or blouses and long trousers to protect your arms and legs, especially from dusk through dawn when mosquitoes are out.
- Apply mosquito repellent to uncovered areas of the skin from dusk through dawn when mosquitoes are out.

Side Effects of This Medicine

Along with its needed effects, a medicine may cause some unwanted effects. Although not all of these side effects may occur, if they do occur they may need medical attention. When this medicine is used for short periods of time, side effects usually are rare. However, when it is used for a long time and/or in high doses, side effects are more likely to occur and may be serious.

Check with your doctor immediately if any of the following side effects occur:
Less common
   Blurred vision or any other change in vision—this side effect may also occur or get worse after you stop taking this medicine
Rare
   Convulsions (seizures); increased muscle weakness; mood or other mental changes; ringing or buzzing in ears or any loss of hearing; sore throat and fever;

unusual bleeding or bruising; unusual tiredness; weakness
Symptoms of overdose
   Drowsiness; headache; increased excitability

Other side effects may occur that usually do not need medical attention. These side effects may go away during treatment as your body adjusts to the medicine. However, check with your doctor if any of the following side effects continue or are bothersome:
More common
   Diarrhea; difficulty in seeing to read; headache; itching (more common in black patients); loss of appetite; nausea or vomiting; stomach cramps or pain
Less common
   Bleaching of hair or increased hair loss; blue-black discoloration of skin, fingernails, or inside of mouth; dizziness or lightheadedness; nervousness or restlessness; skin rash

Other side effects not listed above may also occur in some patients. If you notice any other effects, check with your doctor.

Additional Information

Once a medicine has been approved for marketing for a certain use, experience may show that it is also useful for other medical problems. Although these uses are not included in product labeling, hydroxychloroquine is used in certain patients with the following medical conditions:

- Arthritis, juvenile
- Hypercalcemia, sarcoid-associated
- Polymorphous light eruption
- Porphyria cutanea tarda
- Urticaria, solar
- Vasculitis, chronic cutaneous

Other than the above information, there is no additional information relating to proper use, precautions, or side effects for these uses.

Revised: 12/30/94
Interim revision: 05/24/99

HYDROXYPROPYL CELLULOSE
Ophthalmic

Commonly used brand name(s):

In the U.S.—
   Lacrisert

In Canada—
   Lacrisert

Description

Hydroxypropyl cellulose (hye-drox-ee-PROE-pil SELL-yoo-lose) belongs to the group of medicines known as artificial tears. It is inserted in the eye to relieve dryness and irritation caused by reduced tear flow that occurs in certain eye diseases.

This medicine is available only with your doctor's prescription, in the following dosage form:

Ophthalmic
- Ocular system (eye system) (U.S. and Canada)

Before Using This Medicine

In deciding to use a medicine, the risks of using the medicine must be weighed against the good it will do. This is a decision you and your doctor will make. For hydroxypropyl cellulose, the following should be considered:

Allergies—Tell your doctor if you have ever had any unusual or allergic reaction to hydroxypropyl cellulose. Also tell your health care professional if you are allergic to any other substances, such as preservatives.

Pregnancy—Hydroxypropyl cellulose has not been shown to cause birth defects or other problems in humans.

Breast-feeding—Hydroxypropyl cellulose has not been reported to cause problems in nursing babies.

Children—Although there is no specific information comparing use of this medicine in children with use in other age groups, this medicine is not expected to cause different side effects or problems in children than it does in adults.

Older adults—Many medicines have not been studied specifically in older people. Therefore, it may not be known whether they work exactly the same way they do in younger adults. Although there is no specific information comparing use of this medicine in the elderly with use in other age groups, this medicine is not expected to cause different side effects or problems in older people than it does in younger adults.

Proper Use of This Medicine

To use:
- This medicine usually comes with patient directions. Read them carefully before using this medicine. It is very important that you understand how to insert this eye system properly. If you have any questions about this, check with your doctor.
- Before opening the package containing this medicine, wash your hands thoroughly with soap and water.
- If the eye system accidentally comes out of your eye, as sometimes occurs when the eye is rubbed, do not put it back in the eye, since it may be contaminated. Instead, insert another eye system if needed.
- You may have to use this medicine for several weeks before your eye symptoms get better.

Dosing—The dose of hydroxypropyl cellulose will be different for different patients. *Follow your doctor's orders or the directions on the label.* The following information includes only the average doses of hydroxypropyl cellulose. *If your dose is different, do not change it* unless your doctor tells you to do so.

The number of doses you use, the time allowed between doses, and the length of time you use the medicine depend on the medical problem for which you are using hydroxypropyl cellulose.

- For *eye system* dosage form:
  —For dry eyes or eye irritation:
  - Adults and children—Place one insert in the eye each day.

Missed dose—If you forget to insert an eye system at the proper time, insert it as soon as possible. Then go back to your regular dosing schedule.

Storage—To store this medicine:
- Keep out of the reach of children.
- Store away from heat and direct light.
- Do not keep outdated medicine or medicine no longer needed. Be sure that any discarded medicine is out of the reach of children.

Precautions While Using This Medicine

This medicine may cause blurred vision for a short time after each dose is applied. *Make sure your vision is clear before you drive, use machines, or do anything else that could be dangerous if you are not able to see well.*

This medicine may also cause your eyes to become more sensitive to light than they are normally. Wearing sunglasses and avoiding too much exposure to bright light may help lessen the discomfort.

If your eye symptoms get worse or if you get new eye symptoms, remove the eye system and check with your doctor as soon as possible.

Side Effects of This Medicine

Along with its needed effects, a medicine may cause some unwanted effects. The following side effects may go away during treatment as your body adjusts to the medicine.

However, check with your doctor if any of these effects continue or are bothersome:

Less common
Blurred vision; eye redness or discomfort or other irritation not present before use of this medicine; increased sensitivity of eyes to light; matting or stickiness of eyelashes; swelling of eyelids; watering of eyes

Other side effects not listed above may also occur in some patients. If you notice any other effects, check with your doctor.

Revised: 06/21/93

HYDROXYPROPYL METHYLCELLULOSE   Ophthalmic

Commonly used brand name(s):

In the U.S.—

Artificial Tears	Moisture Drops
Bion Tears	Nature's Tears
Gonak	Ocucoat
Goniosoft	Ocucoat PF
Goniosol	Tearisol
Isopto Alkaline	Tears Naturale
Isopto Plain	Tears Naturale II
Isopto Tears	Tears Naturale Free
Just Tears	Tears Renewed
Lacril	Ultra Tears

In Canada—

Eyelube	Ocutears
Isopto Tears	Tears Naturale
Methocel	Tears Naturale II
Moisture Drops	Tears Naturale Free

Another commonly used name is hypromellose.

Description

Hydroxypropyl methylcellulose (hye-drox-ee-PROE-pil meth-ill-SELL-yoo-lose) belongs to the group of medicines known as artificial tears. It is used to relieve dryness and irritation caused by reduced tear flow. It helps prevent damage to the eye in certain eye diseases. Hydroxypropyl methylcellulose may also be used to moisten hard contact lenses and artificial eyes. In addition, it may be used in certain eye examinations.

Some of these preparations are available only with your doctor's prescription. Others are available without a prescription; however, your doctor may have special instructions on the proper use of this medicine for your medical problem.

Hydroxypropyl methylcellulose is available in the following dosage form:

Ophthalmic
- Ophthalmic solution (eye drops) (U.S. and Canada)

Before Using This Medicine

If you are using this medicine without a prescription, carefully read and follow any precautions on the label. For hydroxypropyl methylcellulose, the following should be considered:

Allergies—Tell your doctor if you have ever had any unusual or allergic reaction to hydroxypropyl methylcellulose. Also tell your health care professional if you are allergic to any other substances, such as preservatives.

Pregnancy—Hydroxypropyl methylcellulose has not been shown to cause birth defects or other problems in humans.

Breast-feeding—Hydroxypropyl methylcellulose has not been reported to cause problems in nursing babies.

Children—Although there is no specific information comparing use of hydroxypropyl methylcellulose in children with use in other age groups, this medicine is not expected to cause different side effects or problems in children than it does in adults.

Older adults—Many medicine have not been studied specifically in older people. Therefore, it may not be known whether they work exactly the same way they do in younger adults. Although there is no specific information comparing use of hydroxypropyl methylcellulose in the elderly with use in other age groups, this medicine is not expected to cause different side effects or problems in older people than it does in younger adults.

Proper Use of This Medicine

To use:
- First, wash your hands. Then tilt the head back and pull the lower eyelid away from the eye to form a pouch. Drop the medicine into the pouch and gently close the eyes. Do not blink. Keep the eyes closed for 1 or 2 minutes to allow the medicine to be absorbed.
- To keep the medicine as germ-free as possible, do not touch the applicator tip to any surface (including the eye). Also, keep the container tightly closed.

For patients *wearing hard contact lenses:*
- Take care not to float the lens from your eye when applying this medicine. If you have any questions about this, check with your health care professional.

Dosing—The dose of hydroxypropyl methylcellulose will be different for different patients. *Follow your doctor's orders or the directions on the label.* The following information includes only the average doses of hydroxypropyl methylcellulose. *If your dose is different, do not change it* unless your doctor tells you to do so.

The number of doses you use each day, the time allowed between doses, and the length of time you use the medicine depend on the medical problem for which you are using hydroxypropyl methylcellulose.

- For dry eyes:
  —For *ophthalmic solution (eye drops)* dosage form:
    - Adults and children—Use 1 drop three or four times a day.

Storage—To store this medicine:
- Keep out of the reach of children.
- Store away from heat and direct light.
- Keep the medicine from freezing.
- Do not keep outdated medicine or medicine no longer needed. Be sure that any discarded medicine is out of the reach of children.

Precautions While Using This Medicine

If you experience eye pain, changes in vision, continued redness or irritation of the eye, or if your symptoms continue for more than 3 days or become worse, check with your doctor.

Side Effects of This Medicine

Along with its needed effects, a medicine may cause some unwanted effects. Although not all of these side effects may occur, if they do occur they may need medical attention.

Check with your doctor as soon as possible if the following side effect occurs:
Eye irritation not present before use of this medicine

Other side effects may occur that usually do not need medical attention. These side effects may go away during treatment as your body adjusts to the medicine. However, check with your health care professional if any of the following side effects continue or are bothersome:
Less common—more common with 1% solution
Blurred vision; matting or stickiness of eyelashes

Other side effects not listed above may also occur in some patients. If you notice any other effects, check with your health care professional.

Revised: 08/14/95

HYDROXYPROPYL METHYLCELLULOSE   Parenteral-Local

Commonly used brand name(s):

In the U.S.—
Ocucoat

Another commonly used name is hypromellose.

Description

Hydroxypropyl methylcellulose (hye-drox-ee-PROE-pil meth-ill-SELL-yoo-lose) is used as a surgical aid in certain eye surgeries, such as cataract removal and lens implantation procedures. It helps maintain the shape of the eye during surgery as well as protect the tissues of the eye from damage due to surgical instruments.

This medicine is available only with your doctor's prescription, in the following dosage form(s):

Parenteral-Local
- Injection (U.S.)

Before Using This Medicine

In deciding to use a medicine, the risks of using the medicine must be weighed against the good it will do. This is a decision you and your doctor will make. For hydroxypropyl methylcellulose, the following should be considered:

Allergies—Tell your doctor if you have ever had any unusual or allergic reaction to hydroxypropyl methylcellulose. Also tell your health care professional if you are allergic to any other substances, such as foods, preservatives, or dyes.

Pregnancy—Hydroxypropyl methylcellulose has not been reported to cause birth defects or other problems in humans.

Breast-feeding—Hydroxypropyl methylcellulose has not been reported to cause problems in nursing babies.

Children—There is no specific information comparing use of hydroxypropyl methylcellulose in children with use in other age groups.

Older adults—Many medicines have not been studied specifically in older people. Therefore, it may not be known whether they work exactly the same way they do in younger adults or if they cause different side effects or problems in older people. There is no specific information comparing use of hydroxypropyl methylcellulose in the elderly with use in other age groups.

Other medicines—Although certain medicines should not be used together at all, in other cases two different medicines may be used together even if an interaction might occur. In these cases, your doctor may want to change the dose, or other precautions may be necessary. Tell your doctor if you are using any other ophthalmic prescription or nonprescription (over-the-counter [OTC]) medicine.

Other medical problems—The presence of other medical problems may affect the use of hydroxypropyl methylcellulose. Make sure you tell your doctor if you have any other medical problems, especially:

- Glaucoma—An increase in the pressure inside your eye may occur following the surgery

Proper Use of This Medicine

Dosing—Hydroxypropyl methylcellulose will be administered during the surgical procedure.

- For *injection* dosage form:
  —For use as an opthalmic surgical aid:
  - Adults—Hydroxypropyl methylcellulose is injected into the eye to maintain the shape of the eye and to replace fluid lost during the surgery. The solution is removed at the end of the surgery.
  - Children—Use and dose must be determined by your doctor.

Side Effects of This Medicine

Along with its needed effects, a medicine may cause some unwanted effects. Although not all of these side effects may occur, if they do occur they may need medical attention.

Check with your doctor as soon as possible if any of the following side effects occur:
Rare
 Blurred vision or other change in vision; pooling of a whitish fluid visible on the colored part of the eye; sensitivity to light; tearing; throbbing pain in eye

Other side effects not listed above may also occur in some patients. If you notice any other effects, check with your doctor.

Developed: 10/28/98

HYDROXYUREA   Systemic

Commonly used brand name(s):
In the U.S.—
 Hydrea
 Droxia
In Canada—
 Hydrea

Description

Hydroxyurea (hye-DROX-ee-yoo-REE-ah) belongs to the group of medicines called antimetabolites. It is used to treat some kinds of cancer and to prevent painful episodes associated with sickle cell anemia.

Hydroxyurea seems to interfere with the growth of cancer cells, which are eventually destroyed. Since the growth of normal body cells may also be affected by hydroxyurea, other effects will also occur. Some of these may be serious and must be reported to your doctor. Other effects may not be serious but may cause concern. Some effects may not occur for months or years after the medicine is used.

When used in sickle cell anemia, hydroxyurea appears to increase the flexibility of sickled cells.

Before you begin treatment with hydroxyurea, you and your doctor should talk about the good this medicine will do as well as the risks of using it.

Hydroxyurea is available only with your doctor's prescription, in the following dosage form:

Oral
- Capsules (U.S. and Canada)

Before Using This Medicine

In deciding to use a medicine, the risks of taking the medicine must be weighed against the good it will do. This is a decision you and your doctor will make. For hydroxyurea, the following should be considered:

Allergies—Tell your doctor if you have ever had any unusual or allergic reaction to hydroxyurea.

Pregnancy—Tell your doctor if you are pregnant or if you intend to have children. There is a chance that this medicine may cause birth defects if either the male or female is taking it at the time of conception or if it is taken during pregnancy. Studies have shown that hydroxyurea causes birth defects in animals. In addition, many cancer medicines may cause sterility. Although sterility seems to be only temporary with this medicine, the possibility should be kept in mind.

Be sure that you have discussed this with your doctor before taking this medicine. It is best to use some kind of birth control while you are taking hydroxyurea. Tell your doctor right away if you think you have become pregnant while taking hydroxyurea.

Breast-feeding—Hydroxyurea passes into human breast milk. Tell your doctor if you are breast-feeding or if you intend to breast-feed during treatment with this medicine. Because hydroxyurea may cause serious side effects, breast-feeding is not recommended while you are taking it.

Children—Side effects may be likely to occur in children, who may be more sensitive to the effects of hydroxyurea.

Older adults—Side effects may be more likely to occur in the elderly, who may be more sensitive to the effects of hydroxyurea.

Other medicines—Although certain medicines should not be used together at all, in other cases two different medicines may be used together even if an interaction might occur. In these cases, your doctor may want to change the dose, or other precautions may be necessary. When you are taking hydroxyurea, it is especially important that your health care professional know if you are taking any of the following:

- Amphotericin B by injection (e.g., Fungizone) or
- Antithyroid agents (medicine for overactive thyroid) or
- Azathioprine (e.g., Imuran) or
- Chloramphenicol (e.g., Chloromycetin) or
- Colchicine or
- Cyclophosphamide (e.g., Cytoxan) or
- Flucytosine (e.g., Ancobon) or
- Ganciclovir (e.g., Cytovene) or
- Interferon (e.g., Intron A, Roferon-A) or
- Mercaptopurine (e.g., Purinethol) or
- Methotrexate (e.g., Rheumatrex) or
- Plicamycin (e.g., Mithracin) or
- Zidovudine (e.g., AZT, Retrovir) or
- If you have ever been treated with x-rays or other cancer medicines—Hydroxyurea may increase the effects of these medicines or radiation therapy on the blood

- Probenecid (e.g., Benemid) or
- Sulfinpyrazone (e.g., Anturane)—Hydroxyurea may increase the amount of uric acid in the blood. Since these medicines are used to lower uric acid levels, they may not be as effective in patients taking hydroxyurea

- Abacavir (e.g., ABC, Ziagen) or
- Abacavir/Lamivudine/Zidovudine (e.g., Trizivir) or
- Amprenavir (e.g., Agenerase) or
- Delavirdine (e.g., Rescriptor) or
- Didanosine (e.g., ddI, Videx) or
- Efavirenz (e.g., Sustiva) or
- Indinavir (e.g., Crixivan) or
- Lamivudine (e.g., 3TC, Epivir) or
- Lamivudine/Zidovudine (e.g., Combivir) or
- Lopinavir/Ritonavir (e.g., Kaletra) or
- Nelfinavir (e.g., Viracept) or
- Nevirapine (e.g., Viramune) or
- Ritonavir (e.g., Norvir) or

- Saquinavir (e.g., Fortovase) or
- Saquinavir mesylate (e.g., Invirase) or
- Stavudine (e.g. D4T, Zerit) or
- Zalcitabine (e.g., ddC, HIVID) or
- Zidovudine (e.g., AZT, Retrovir, ZDV)—Hydroxyurea may increase the effects of these medicines on the liver, pancreas, and nerves

Other medical problems—The presence of other medical problems may affect the use of hydroxyurea. Make sure you tell your doctor if you have any other medical problems, especially:

- Anemia or
- Leukopenia or
- Neutropenia or
- Thrombocytopenia—May worsen and affect the decision to continue therapy

- Chickenpox (including recent exposure) or
- Herpes zoster (shingles)—Risk of severe disease affecting other parts of the body

- Gout or
- Kidney stones—Hydroxyurea may increase levels of uric acid in the body, which can cause gout or kidney stones

- Infection (especially AIDS or HIV)—Hydroxyurea may decrease your body's ability to fight infection or cause serious liver, pancreas, or peripheral nerve reactions with certain specific HIV treatments

- Kidney disease—Effects may be increased because of slower removal of hydroxyurea from the body

---

Proper Use of This Medicine

Take hydroxyurea only as directed by your doctor. Do not use more or less of it, and do not use it more often than your doctor ordered. The exact amount of medicine you need has been carefully worked out. Taking too much may increase the chance of side effects, while taking too little may not improve your condition.

For patients who *cannot swallow the capsules*:
- The contents of the capsule may be emptied into a glass of water and then taken immediately. Some powder may float on the surface of the water, but that is just filler from the capsule.

This medicine is sometimes given together with certain other medicines. If you are using a combination of medicines, make sure that you take each one at the right time and do not mix them. Ask your health care professional to help you plan a way to take your medicine at the right times.

While you are using this medicine, your doctor may want you to drink extra fluids so that you will pass more urine. This will help prevent kidney problems and keep your kidneys working well.

This medicine commonly causes nausea, vomiting, and diarrhea. *However, it is very important that you continue to use the medicine, even if you begin to feel ill*. Ask your health care professional for ways to lessen these effects.

If you vomit shortly after taking a dose of hydroxyurea, check with your doctor. You will be told whether to take the dose again or to wait until the next scheduled dose.

Dosing—The dose of hydroxyurea will be different for different patients. The dose that is used may depend on a number of things, including what the medicine is being used for, the patient's weight, and whether or not other medicines are also being taken. *If you are taking hydroxyurea at home, follow your doctor's orders or the directions on the label.* If you have any questions about the proper dose of hydroxyurea, ask your doctor.

Missed dose—If you miss a dose of this medicine, do not take the missed dose at all and do not double the next one. Instead, go back to your regular dosing schedule and check with your doctor.

Storage—To store this medicine:
- Keep out of the reach of children.
- Store away from heat and direct light.
- Do not store in the bathroom, near the kitchen sink, or in other damp places. Heat or moisture may cause the medicine to break down.
- Do not keep outdated medicine or medicine no longer needed. Be sure that any discarded medicine is out of the reach of children.

Precautions While Using This Medicine

It is very important that your doctor check your progress at regular visits to make sure that this medicine is working properly and to check for unwanted effects.

While you are being treated with hydroxyurea, and after you stop treatment with it, *do not have any immunizations (vaccinations) without your doctor's approval.* Hydroxyurea may lower your body's resistance and there is a chance you might get the infection the immunization is meant to prevent. In addition, other persons living in your household should not take oral polio vaccine since there is a chance they could pass the polio virus on to you. Also, avoid persons who have recently taken oral polio vaccine. Do not get close to them and do not stay in the same room with them for very long. If you cannot take these precautions, you should consider wearing a protective face mask that covers the nose and mouth.

Hydroxyurea can temporarily lower the number of white blood cells in your blood, increasing the chance of getting an infection. It can also lower the number of platelets, which are necessary for proper blood clotting. If this occurs, there are certain precautions you can take, especially when your blood count is low, to reduce the risk of infection or bleeding:
- If you can, avoid people with infections. *Check with your doctor immediately* if you think you are getting an infection or if you get a fever or chills, cough or hoarseness, lower back or side pain, or painful or difficult urination.
- *Check with your doctor immediately* if you notice any unusual bleeding or bruising; black, tarry stools; blood in urine or stools; or pinpoint red spots on your skin.
- Be careful when using a regular toothbrush, dental floss, or toothpick. Your medical doctor, dentist, or nurse may recommend other ways to clean your teeth and gums. Check with your medical doctor before having any dental work done.
- Do not touch your eyes or the inside of your nose unless you have just washed your hands and have not touched anything else in the meantime.
- Be careful not to cut yourself when you are using sharp objects such as a safety razor or fingernail or toenail cutters.
- Avoid contact sports or other situations where bruising or injury could occur.

Side Effects of This Medicine

Along with their needed effects, medicines like hydroxyurea can sometimes cause unwanted effects such as blood problems and other side effects. These and others are described below. Also, because of the way these medicines act on the body, there is a chance that they might cause other unwanted effects that may not occur until months or years after the medicine is used. These delayed effects may include certain types of cancer, such as leukemia. Ask your health care professional for ways to lessen these effects.

Although not all of these side effects may occur, if they do occur they may need medical attention.

Check with your doctor or nurse immediately if any of the following side effects occur:
> *More common*
>> Cough or hoarseness; fever or chills; lower back or side pain; painful or difficult urination
>
> *Less common*
>> Black, tarry stools; blood in urine or stools; pinpoint red spots on skin; unusual bleeding or bruising

Check with your doctor as soon as possible if any of the following side effects occur:
> *Less common*
>> Blackening of fingernails and toenails; sores in mouth and on lips
>
> *Rare*
>> Confusion; convulsions (seizures); difficulty in urination; dizziness; hallucinations (seeing, hearing, or feeling things that are not there); headache; joint pain; swelling of feet or lower legs
>
> *Symptoms of overdose*
>> Scaling of skin on hands and feet; severe darkening of skin color; soreness; sores in mouth and on lips; swelling of palms and soles of feet; violet flushing of the skin

Other side effects may occur that usually do not need medical attention. These side effects may go away during treatment as your body adjusts to the medicine. Also, your health care professional may be able to tell you about ways to prevent or reduce some of these side effects. Check with your health care professional if any of the following side effects continue or are bothersome or if you have any questions about them:
> *More common*
>> Diarrhea; drowsiness; loss of appetite; nausea or vomiting
>
> *Less common*
>> Constipation; redness of skin at place of irradiation; skin rash and itching

Hydroxyurea may cause temporary loss of hair in some people. After treatment has ended, normal hair growth should return, although the new hair may be a slightly different color or texture.

After you stop taking hydroxyurea, your body may need time to adjust. The length of time this takes depends on the amount of medicine you were using and how long you used it. During this period of time check with your doctor as soon as possible if you notice any of the following side effects:
> Black, tarry stools; blood in urine; cough or hoarseness; fever or chills; lower back or side pain; painful or difficult urination; pinpoint red spots on skin; unusual bleeding or bruising

Other side effects not listed above may also occur in some patients. If you notice any other effects, check with your doctor.

Revised: 05/03/2001

IDARUBICIN   Systemic

Commonly used brand name(s):

In the U.S.—
   Idamycin

In Canada—
   Idamycin

Description

Idarubicin (eye-da-RUE-bi-sin) belongs to the general group of medicines known as antineoplastics. It is used to treat some kinds of cancer, including leukemia.

Idarubicin seems to interfere with the growth of cancer cells, which are eventually destroyed. Since the growth of normal body cells may also be affected by idarubicin, other effects will also occur. Some of these may be serious and must be reported to your doctor. Other effects, like hair loss, may not be serious but may cause concern. Some effects may not occur for months or years after the medicine is used.

Before you begin treatment with idarubicin, you and your doctor should talk about the good this medicine will do as well as the risks of using it.

Idarubicin is to be administered only by or under the supervision of your doctor. It is available in the following dosage form:

Parenteral
   • Injection (U.S. and Canada)

Before Using This Medicine

In deciding to use a medicine, the risks of taking the medicine must be weighed against the good it will do. This is a decision you and your doctor will make. For idarubicin, the following should be considered:

Allergies—Tell your doctor if you have ever had any unusual or allergic reaction to idarubicin.

Pregnancy—There is a chance that this medicine may cause birth defects if either the male or female is receiving it at the time of conception or if it is taken during pregnancy. Studies in rats and rabbits have shown that idarubicin causes birth defects in the fetus and other problems (including miscarriage). In addition, many cancer medicines may cause sterility which could be permanent. Although sterility has been reported only in male dogs with this medicine, the possibility of an effect in human males should be kept in mind.

Be sure that you have discussed these possible effects with your doctor before receiving this medicine. It is best to use some kind of birth control while you are receiving idarubicin. Tell your doctor right away if you think you have become pregnant while receiving idarubicin. Before receiving idarubicin make sure your doctor knows if you are pregnant or if you may become pregnant.

Breast-feeding—Because idarubicin may cause serious side effects, breast-feeding is generally not recommended while you are receiving it.

Children—There is no specific information comparing use of idarubicin in children with use in other age groups.

Older adults—Heart problems are more likely to occur in the elderly, who are usually more sensitive to the effects of idarubicin.

Other medicines—Although certain medicines should not be used together at all, in other cases two different medicines may be used together even if an interaction might occur. In these cases, your doctor may want to change the dose, or other precautions may be necessary. When you are receiving idarubicin, it is especially important that your health care professional know if you have ever been treated with x-rays or cancer medicines or if you are taking any of the following:

- Amphotericin B by injection (e.g., Fungizone) or
- Antithyroid agents (medicine for overactive thyroid) or
- Azathioprine (e.g., Imuran) or
- Chloramphenicol (e.g., Chloromycetin) or
- Colchicine or
- Flucytosine (e.g., Ancobon) or
- Ganciclovir (e.g., Cytovene) or
- Interferon (e.g., Intron A, Roferon-A) or
- Plicamycin (e.g., Mithracin) or
- Zidovudine (e.g., AZT, Retrovir)—Idarubicin may increase the effects of these medicines or radiation therapy on the blood

- Probenecid (e.g., Benemid) or
- Sulfinpyrazone (e.g., Anturane)—Idarubicin may raise the concentration of uric acid in the blood, which these medicines are used to lower

Other medical problems—The presence of other medical problems may affect the use of idarubicin. Make sure you tell your doctor if you have any other medical problems, especially:

- Chickenpox (including recent exposure) or
- Herpes zoster (shingles)—Risk of severe disease affecting other parts of the body

- Gout or
- Kidney stones—Idarubicin may increase levels of a chemical called uric acid in the body, which can cause gout or kidney stones

- Heart disease—Risk of heart problems caused by idarubicin may be increased

- Kidney disease or
- Liver disease—Effects may be increased because of slower removal of idarubicin from the body

Proper Use of This Medicine

Idarubicin is sometimes given together with certain other medicines. If you are receiving a combination of medicines, it is important that you receive each one at the proper time. If you are taking some of these medicines by mouth, ask your health care professional to help you plan a way to take them at the right times.

While you are receiving this medicine, your doctor may want you to drink extra fluids so that you will pass more urine. This will help prevent kidney problems and keep your kidneys working well.

Idarubicin often causes nausea and vomiting. However, it is very important that you continue to receive it, even if you begin to feel ill. Ask your health care professional for ways to lessen these effects.

Dosing—The dose of idarubicin will be different for different patients. The dose that is used may depend on a number of things, including what the medicine is being used for, the patient's size, and whether or not other medicines are also being taken. *If you are receiving idarubicin at home, follow your doctor's orders or the directions on the label.* If you have any questions about the proper dose of idarubicin, ask your doctor.

Precautions While Using This Medicine

It is very important that your doctor check your progress at regular visits to make sure that this medicine is working properly and to check for unwanted effects.

While you are being treated with idarubicin, and after you stop treatment with it, *do not have any immunizations (vaccinations) without your doctor's approval.* Idarubicin may lower your body's resistance, and there is a chance you might get the infection the immunization is meant to prevent. In addition, other persons living in your household should not take oral polio vaccine since there is a chance they could pass the polio virus on to you. Also, avoid persons who have taken oral polio vaccine. Do not get close to them, and do not stay in the same room with them for very long. If you cannot take these precautions, you should consider wearing a protective face mask that covers the nose and mouth.

Idarubicin can temporarily lower the number of white blood cells in your blood, increasing the chance of getting an infection. It can also lower the number of platelets, which are necessary for proper blood clotting. If this occurs, there are certain precautions you can take, especially when your blood count is low, to reduce the risk of infection or bleeding:

- If you can, avoid people with infections. *Check with your doctor immediately* if you think you are getting an infection or if you get a fever or chills, cough or hoarseness, lower back or side pain, or painful or difficult urination.
- *Check with your doctor immediately* if you notice any unusual bleeding or bruising; black, tarry stools; blood in urine or stools; or pinpoint red spots on your skin.
- Be careful when using a regular toothbrush, dental floss, or toothpick. Your medical doctor, dentist, or nurse may recommend other ways to clean your teeth and gums. Check with your medical doctor before having any dental work done.
- Do not touch your eyes or the inside of your nose unless you have just washed your hands and have not touched anything else in the meantime.
- Be careful not to cut yourself when you are using sharp objects such as a safety razor or fingernail or toenail cutters.
- Avoid contact sports or other situations where bruising or injury could occur.

If idarubicin accidentally seeps out of the vein into which it is injected, it may damage some tissues and cause scarring. *Tell the health care professional right away if you notice redness, pain, or swelling at the place of injection.*

Side Effects of This Medicine

Along with its needed effects, a medicine may cause some unwanted effects. Although not all of these side effects may occur, if they do occur they may need medical attention.

Also, because of the way cancer medicines act on the body, there is a chance that they might cause other unwanted effects that may not occur until months or years after the medicine is used. These delayed effects may include certain types of cancer. Discuss these possible effects with your doctor.

Check with your health care professional immediately if any of the following side effects occur:
> *More common*
>> Black, tarry stools; blood in urine or stools; cough or hoarseness; fever or chills; lower back or side pain; painful or difficult urination; pinpoint red spots on skin; unusual bleeding or bruising
> *Less common*
>> Fast or irregular heartbeat; pain at place of injection; shortness of breath; swelling of feet and lower legs
> *Rare*
>> Stomach pain (severe)

Check with your health care professional as soon as possible if any of the following side effects occur:
> *More common*
>> Sores in mouth and on lips
> *Less common*
>> Joint pain
> *Rare*
>> Skin rash or hives

Other side effects may occur that usually do not need medical attention. These side effects may go away during treatment as your body adjusts to the medicine. Also, your health care professional may be able to tell you about ways to prevent or reduce some of these side effects. Check with your health care professional if any of the following side effects continue or are bothersome or if you have any questions about them:
> *More common*
>> Diarrhea or stomach cramps; headache; nausea and vomiting
> *Less common*
>> Darkening or redness of skin (after x-ray treatment); numbness or tingling of fingers, toes, or face

Idarubicin causes the urine to turn reddish in color, which may stain clothes. This is not blood. It is perfectly normal and lasts for only a day or two after each dose is given.

This medicine often causes a temporary and total loss of hair. After treatment with idarubicin has ended, normal hair growth should return.

After you stop receiving idarubicin, it may still produce some side effects that need attention. During this period of time, *check with your health care professional immediately* if you notice any of the following side effects:
> Fast or irregular heartbeat; shortness of breath; swelling of feet and lower legs

Other side effects not listed above may also occur in some patients. If you notice any other effects, check with your health care professional.

Revised: 03/09/2001

IDOXURIDINE   Ophthalmic

Commonly used brand name(s):

In the U.S.—
 Herplex Liquifilm
 Stoxil

In Canada—
 Herplex Liquifilm
 Stoxil

Description

Idoxuridine (eye-dox-YOOR-i-deen) belongs to the family of medicines called antivirals. Idoxuridine is used to treat virus infections of the eye.

Idoxuridine is available only with your doctor's prescription, in the following dosage forms:

Ophthalmic
 • Ophthalmic ointment (U.S. and Canada)
 • Ophthalmic solution (eye drops) (U.S. and Canada)

Before Using This Medicine

In deciding to use a medicine, the risks of using the medicine must be weighed against the good it will do. This is a decision you and your doctor will make. For idoxuridine, the following should be considered:

Allergies—Tell your doctor if you have ever had any unusual or allergic reaction to idoxuridine or to iodine or iodine-containing preparations. Also tell your health care professional if you are allergic to any other substances, such as preservatives.

Pregnancy—Idoxuridine ophthalmic preparations have not been shown to cause birth defects or other problems in humans. However, studies in animals have shown that idoxuridine causes protruding eyes (eyes that stick out too far) and deformed front legs in rabbits. Before using this medicine, make sure your doctor knows if you are pregnant or if you may become pregnant.

Breast-feeding—It is not known whether idoxuridine passes into the breast milk. Although most medicines pass into breast milk in small amounts, many of them may be used safely while breast-feeding. Mothers who are using this medicine and who wish to breast-feed should discuss this with their doctor.

Children—Studies on this medicine have been done only in adult patients, and there is no specific information comparing use of this medicine in children with use in other age groups.

Older adults—Many medicines have not been studied specifically in older people. Therefore, it may not be known whether they work exactly the same way they do in younger adults or if they cause different side effects or problems in older people. There is no specific information comparing use of idoxuridine in the elderly with use in other age groups.

Other medicines—Although certain medicines should not be used together at all, in other cases two different medicines may be used together even if an interaction might occur. In these cases, your doctor may want to change the dose, or other precautions may be necessary. When you are using idoxuridine, it is especially important that your health care professional know if you are using the following:

 • Eye product containing boric acid—Boric acid may interact with the idoxuridine preparation causing a gritty substance to form or may interact with the preservative in the idoxuridine preparation causing a toxic effect in the eye

Proper Use of This Medicine

For patients using the *eye drop form* of idoxuridine:
 • The bottle is only partially full to provide proper drop control.
 • To use:
  —First, wash your hands. Then tilt the head back and pull the lower eyelid away from the eye to form a pouch. Drop the medicine into the pouch and gently close the eyes. Do not blink. Keep the eyes closed for 1 or 2 minutes to allow the medicine to come into contact with the infection.
  —If you think you did not get the drop of medicine into your eye properly, use another drop.
  —To keep the medicine as germ-free as possible, do not touch the applicator tip to any surface (including the eye). Also, keep the container tightly closed.

For patients using the *eye ointment form* of idoxuridine:
 • To use:
  —First, wash your hands. Then pull the lower eyelid away from the eye to form a pouch. Squeeze a thin strip of ointment into the pouch. A 1-cm (approximately ⅓-inch) strip of ointment is usually enough unless otherwise directed by your doctor. Gently close the eyes and keep them closed for 1 or 2 minutes to allow the medicine to come into contact with the infection.
  —To keep the medicine as germ-free as possible, do not touch the applicator tip to any surface (including the eye). After using idoxuridine eye ointment, wipe the tip of the ointment tube with a clean tissue and keep the tube tightly closed.

Do not use this medicine more often or for a longer time than your doctor ordered. To do so may cause problems in the eyes. If you have any questions about this, check with your doctor.

To help clear up your infection completely, *keep using this medicine for the full time of treatment*, even though your symptoms may have disappeared. *Do not miss any doses*.

Dosing—The dose of idoxuridine will be different for different patients. *Follow your doctor's orders or the directions on the label*. The following information includes only the average doses of idoxuridine. *If your dose is different, do not change it* unless your doctor tells you to do so.

The number of doses you use each day, the time allowed between doses, and the length of time you use the medicine depend on the medical problem for which you are using idoxuridine.

 • For virus infections of the eye:
  —For *eye ointment* dosage form:
   • Adults and children—Use every four hours during the day (five times a day).

—For *eye solution (eye drops)* dosage form:
- Adults and children—Use every hour during the day and every two hours during the night. After the eye condition gets better, use every two hours during the day and every four hours during the night.

Missed dose—If you miss a dose of this medicine, apply it as soon as possible. However, if it is almost time for your next dose, skip the missed dose and go back to your regular dosing schedule.

Storage—To store this medicine:
- Keep out of the reach of children.
- Store in the refrigerator or in a cool place because heat will cause this medicine to break down. However, keep the medicine from freezing. Follow the directions on the label.
- Do not keep outdated medicine or medicine no longer needed. Be sure that any discarded medicine is out of the reach of children.

Precautions While Using This Medicine

It is very important that your doctor check your progress at regular visits.

If your symptoms do not improve within a week, or if they become worse, check with your doctor.

This medicine may cause your eyes to become more sensitive to light than they are normally. Wearing sunglasses and avoiding too much exposure to bright light may help lessen the discomfort.

Side Effects of This Medicine

Along with its needed effects, a medicine may cause some unwanted effects. Although not all of these side effects may occur, if they do occur they may need medical attention.

Check with your doctor as soon as possible if any of the following side effects occur:
Less common
Increased sensitivity of eyes to light; itching, redness, swelling, pain, or other sign of irritation not present before use of this medicine

Rare
Blurring, dimming, or haziness of vision

Other side effects may occur that usually do not need medical attention. These side effects may go away during treatment as your body adjusts to the medicine. However, check with your doctor if the following side effect continues or is bothersome:
Less common
Excess flow of tears

After application, eye ointments usually cause your vision to blur for a few minutes.

Other side effects not listed above may also occur in some patients. If you notice any other effects, check with your doctor.

Revised: 06/21/93

IFOSFAMIDE   Systemic

Commonly used brand name(s):

In the U.S.—
IFEX

In Canada—
IFEX

Description

Ifosfamide (eye-FOS-fa-mide) belongs to the group of medicines called alkylating agents. It is used to treat cancer of the testicles as well as some other kinds of cancer. Another medicine, called mesna, is usually given along with ifosfamide to prevent bladder problems that can be caused by ifosfamide.

Ifosfamide interferes with the growth of cancer cells, which are eventually destroyed. Since the growth of normal body cells may also be affected by ifosfamide, other effects will also occur. Some of these may be serious and must be reported to your doctor. Other effects, like hair loss, may not be serious but may cause concern. Some effects may not occur until months or years after the medicine is used.

Before you begin treatment with ifosfamide, you and your doctor should talk about the good this medicine will do as well as the risks of using it.

Ifosfamide is to be administered only by or under the immediate supervision of your doctor. It is available in the following dosage form:
Parenteral
- Injection (U.S. and Canada)

Before Using This Medicine

In deciding to use a medicine, the risks of taking the medicine must be weighed against the good it will do. This is a decision you and your doctor will make. For ifosfamide, the following should be considered:

Allergies—Tell your doctor if you have ever had any unusual or allergic reaction to ifosfamide.

Pregnancy—Tell your doctor if you are pregnant or if you intend to have children. There is a chance that this medicine may cause birth defects if either the male or female is taking it at the time of conception or if it is taken during pregnancy. Ifosfamide causes birth defects in animals. In addition, many cancer medicines may cause sterility that could be permanent. Although sterility has not been reported with this medicine, the possibility should be kept in mind.

Be sure that you have discussed this with your doctor before taking this medicine. It is best to use some kind of birth control while you are receiving ifosfamide. Tell your doctor right away if you think you have become pregnant while receiving ifosfamide.

Breast-feeding—Tell your doctor if you are breast-feeding or if you intend to breast-feed during treatment with this medicine. Because ifosfamide may cause serious side effects in the nursing infant, breast-feeding is generally not recommended while you are receiving it.

Children—Although there is no specific information comparing use of ifosfamide in children with use in other age groups, this medicine is not expected to cause different side effects or problems in children than it does in adults.

Older adults—Many medicines have not been studied specifically in older people. Therefore, it may not be known whether they work exactly the same way they do in younger adults or if they cause different side effects or problems in older people. There is no specific information comparing use of ifosfamide in the elderly with use in other age groups.

Other medicines—Although certain medicines should not be used together at all, in other cases two different medicines may be used together even if an interaction might occur. In these cases, your doctor may want to change the dose, or other precautions may be necessary. When you are taking ifosfamide, it is especially important that your health care professional know if you are taking any of the following:

- Amphotericin B by injection (e.g., Fungizone) or
- Antithyroid agents (medicine for overactive thyroid) or
- Azathioprine (e.g., Imuran) or
- Chloramphenicol (e.g., Chloromycetin) or
- Colchicine or
- Flucytosine (e.g., Ancobon) or
- Ganciclovir (e.g., Cytovene) or
- Interferon (e.g., Intron A, Roferon-A) or
- Plicamycin (e.g., Mithracin) or
- Zidovudine (e.g., AZT, Retrovir) or
- If you have ever been treated with x-rays or cancer medicines—Ifosfamide may increase the effects of these medicines or radiation therapy on the blood

Other medical problems—The presence of other medical problems may affect the use of ifosfamide. Make sure you tell your doctor if you have any other medical problems, especially:

- Chickenpox (including recent exposure) or
- Herpes zoster (shingles)—Risk of severe disease affecting other parts of the body
- Infection—Ifosfamide can decrease your body's ability to fight infection
- Kidney disease—Effects may be increased because of slower removal of ifosfamide from the body
- Liver disease—Effects may be increased or decreased because the liver both makes ifosfamide work and removes it from the body

Proper Use of This Medicine

Ifosfamide is sometimes given together with certain other medicines. If you are using a combination of medicines, make sure that you take each one at the proper time and do not mix them. Ask your health care professional to help you plan a way to remember to take your medicines at the right times.

While you are receiving ifosfamide, it is important that you drink extra fluids so that you will pass more urine. Also, empty your bladder frequently, including at least once during the night. This will help prevent kidney and bladder problems and keep your kidneys working well. Ifosfamide passes from the body in the urine. If too much of it appears in the urine or if the urine stays in the bladder too long, it can cause dangerous irritation. Follow your doctor's instructions carefully about how much fluid to drink every day. Some patients may have to drink up to 7 to 12 cups (3 quarts) of fluid a day.

Ifosfamide often causes nausea and vomiting. However, it is very important that you continue to receive the medicine even if you begin to feel ill. Ask your health care professional for ways to lessen these effects.

Dosing—The dose of ifosfamide will be different for different patients. The dose that is used may depend on a number of things, including what the medicine is being used for, the patient's size, and whether or not other medicines are also being taken. *If you are receiving ifosfamide at home, follow your doctor's orders or the directions on the label.* If you have any questions about the proper dose of ifosfamide, ask your doctor.

Precautions While Using This Medicine

It is very important that your doctor check your progress at regular visits to make sure that this medicine is working properly and to check for unwanted effects.

While you are being treated with ifosfamide, and after you stop treatment with it, *do not have any immunizations (vaccinations) without your doctor's approval.* Ifosfamide may lower your body's resistance and there is a chance you might get the infection the immunization is meant to prevent. In addition, other persons living in your house should not take oral polio vaccine since there is a chance they could pass the polio virus on to you. Also, avoid persons who have taken oral polio vaccine within the past several months. Do not get close to them, and do not stay in the same room with them for very long. If you cannot take these precautions, you should consider wearing a protective face mask that covers the nose and mouth.

Ifosfamide can temporarily lower the number of white blood cells in your blood, increasing the chance of getting an infection. It can also lower the number of platelets, which are necessary for proper blood clotting. If this occurs, there are certain precautions you can take to reduce the risk of infection or bleeding:

- If you can, avoid people with infections. *Check with your doctor immediately* if you think you are getting an infection or if you get a fever or chills, cough or hoarseness, lower back or side pain, or have painful or difficult urination.
- *Check with your doctor immediately* if you notice any unusual bleeding or bruising; black, tarry stools; blood in urine or stools; or pinpoint red spots on your skin.
- Be careful when using a regular toothbrush, dental floss, or toothpick. Your medical doctor, dentist, or nurse may recommend other ways to clean your teeth and gums. Check with your medical doctor before having any dental work done.
- Do not touch your eyes or the inside of your nose unless you have just washed your hands and have not touched anything else in the meantime.
- Be careful not to cut yourself when you are using sharp objects such as a safety razor or fingernail or toenail cutters.
- Avoid contact sports or other situations where bruising or injury could occur.

Side Effects of This Medicine

Along with their needed effects, medicines like ifosfamide can sometimes cause unwanted effects such as blood problems, loss of hair, and problems with the bladder. These and others are described below. Also, because of the way these medicines act on the body, there is a chance that they might cause other unwanted effects that may not occur until months or years after the medicine is used. These may include certain types of cancer, such as leukemia. Discuss these possible effects with your doctor.

Although not all of these side effects may occur, if they do occur they may need medical attention.

Check with your doctor immediately if any of the following side effects occur:

More common
Blood in urine; frequent urination; painful urination

Less common
Cough or hoarseness accompanied by fever or chills; fever or chills; lower back or side pain accompanied by fever or chills

Rare
Black, tarry stools; blood in stools; pinpoint red spots on skin; unusual bleeding or bruising

Check with your doctor as soon as possible if any of the following side effects occur:

More common
Agitation; confusion; hallucinations (seeing, hearing, or feeling things that are not there); unusual tiredness

Less common
Dizziness; redness, swelling, or pain at place of injection

Rare
Convulsions (seizures); cough or shortness of breath; sores in mouth and on lips

Other side effects may occur that usually do not need medical attention. These side effects may go away during treatment as your body adjusts to the medicine. Also, your health care professional may be able to tell you about ways to prevent or reduce some of these side effects. Check with your doctor if any of the following side effects continue or are bothersome or if you have any questions about them:

More common
Nausea and vomiting

Ifosfamide often causes a temporary loss of hair. After treatment has ended, normal hair growth should return.

After you stop receiving ifosfamide, it may still produce some side effects that need attention. During this period of time, *check with your doctor immediately* if you notice the following side effect:
Blood in urine

Other side effects not listed above may also occur in some patients. If you notice any other effects, check with your doctor.

Additional Information

Once a medicine has been approved for marketing for a certain use, experience may show that it is also useful for other medical problems. Although these uses are not included in product labeling, ifosfamide is used in certain patients with the following medical conditions:
- Acute lymphocytic leukemia (a type of cancer of the blood)
- Cancer of the bladder
- Cancer of the bone (including Ewing's sarcoma)
- Cancer of the breast
- Cancer of the cervix
- Cancer of the endometrium
- Cancers of the head and neck
- Cancer of the lung

- Cancer of the ovaries
- Lymphomas
- Neuroblastoma (a certain type of brain cancer)
- Tumors in the ovaries
- Wilms' tumor (a cancer of the kidneys occurring mainly in children)

Other than the above information, there is no additional information relating to proper use, precautions, or side effects for these uses.

Revised: 06/30/98
Interim revision: 06/08/99

IMATINIB   Systemic—INTRODUCTORY VERSION

Commonly used brand name(s):

In the U.S.—
Gleevec

Description

Imatinib (i-MAT-in-ib) is a new type of medication that prevents and stops the growth of cancer cells. It helps your body fight against a type of cancer called chronic myeloid leukemia or CML. CML is caused by a genetic problem in which your body makes too many abnormal white blood cells which can cause you to become sick more often and also to feel weak or tired. Imatinib helps your body to stop making these abnormal white blood cells.

Before you begin treatment with imatinib, you and your doctor should talk about the good this medicine will do as well as the risks of using it.

This medicine is available only with your doctor's prescription, in the following dosage form:

Oral
- Capsules (U.S.)

Before Using This Medicine

In deciding to use a medicine, the risks of taking the medicine must be weighed against the good it will do. This is a decision you and your doctor will make. For imatinib, the following should be considered:

Allergies—Tell your doctor if you have ever had any unusual or allergic reaction to imatinib. Also tell your health care professional if you are allergic to any other substances, such as foods, preservatives, or dyes.

Pregnancy—Imatinib has not been studied in pregnant women. However, studies in animals have shown that imatinib causes birth defects and other problems with pregnancy. Before taking this medicine, make sure your doctor knows if you are pregnant or if you may become pregnant. This medicine may be needed in serious diseases or other situations that threaten the mother's life. Be sure you have discussed this with your doctor.

Breast-feeding—It is not known whether imatinib passes into human breast milk. However, imatinib is not recommended during breast-feeding, because it may cause unwanted effects in nursing babies.

Children—Studies on this medicine have been done only in adult patients, and there is no specific information comparing use of imatinib in children with use in other age groups. Safety and effectiveness have not been established in children under 18 years of age.

Older adults—This medicine has been tested and has not been shown to cause different side effects or problems in older people than it does in younger adults. Fluid retention may be more likely to occur in elderly patients, who may be more sensitive than younger adults to the effects of imatinib.

Other medicines—Although certain medicines should not be used together at all, in other cases two different medicines may be used together even if an interaction might occur. In these cases, your doctor may want to change the dose, or other precautions may be necessary. When you are taking imatinib, it is especially important that your doctor and pharmacist know if you are taking any of the following:

- Amphotericin B by injection (e.g., Fungizone) or
- Antineoplastics (cancer medicines) or
- Antithyroid agents (medicine for overactive thyroid) or
- Azathioprine (e.g., Imuran) or
- Chloramphenicol (e.g., Chloromycetin) or
- Colchicine or
- Cyclophosphamide (e.g., Cytoxan) or
- Flucytosine (e.g., Ancobon) or
- Ganciclovir (e.g., Cytovene) or
- Interferon (e.g., Intron A, Roferon-A) or
- Mercaptopurine (e.g., Purinethol) or
- Methotrexate (e.g., Rheumatrex) or
- Plicamycin (e.g., Mithracin) or
- Zidovudine (e.g., AZT, Retrovir)—Concurrent use of these medicines with imatinib increases the risk of infection.
- If you have ever been treated with x-rays or other cancer medicines—Imatinib may increase the effects of these medicines or radiation therapy on the blood.
- Carbamazepine (e.g., Tegretol) or
- Dexamethasone (e.g., Decadron) or
- Phenobarbital (e.g., Luminal) or
- Phenytoin (e.g., Dilantin) or
- Rifampicin (e.g., Rifampin) or
- St. John's Wort—These medications may decrease the amount of imatinib in your body.
- Clarithromycin (e.g., Biaxin) or
- Erythromycin (e.g., E-Mycin, Erythrocin) or
- Itraconazole (e.g., Sporanox) or
- Ketoconazole (e.g., Nizoral)—These medications may increase the amount of imatinib in your body.
- Cyclosporine (e.g., Sandimmune) or
- Pimozide (e.g., Orap)—Imatinib may increase the amount of these medications in your blood to possibly harmful levels.
- Warfarin (e.g., Coumadin)—Imatinib may interfere with the metabolism of warfarin, which can cause clotting problems.

Other medical problems—The presence of other medical problems may affect the use of imatinib. Make sure you tell your doctor if you have any other medical problems, especially:

- Anemia or
- Platelet problems or
- White blood cell problems—May worsen and affect the decision to continue therapy
- Chickenpox (including recent exposure) or
- Herpes zoster (shingles)—Risk of severe disease affecting other parts of the body
- Liver disease—Effects may be increased because of slower removal of imatinib from the body
- Infection—Imatinib may decrease your body's ability to fight infection

Proper Use of This Medicine

Take imatinib only as directed by your doctor. Do not use more or less of it, and do not use it more often than your doctor ordered. The exact amount of medicine you need has been carefully worked out. Taking too much may increase the chance of side effects, while taking too little may not improve your condition.

This medicine should be taken with a tall glass of water and a meal.

Dosing—The dose of imatinib will be different for different patients. The dose that is used may depend on a number of things, how you are responding to the medicine and whether or not it is affecting your blood cells. *If you are taking imatinib at home, follow your doctor's orders or the directions on the label*. If you have any questions about the proper dose of imatinib, ask your doctor.

Missed dose—If you miss a dose of this medicine, do not take the missed dose at all and do not double the next one. Instead, go back to your regular dosing schedule and check with your doctor.

Storage—To store this medicine:

- Keep out of the reach of children.
- Store away from heat and direct light.
- Do not store in the bathroom, near the kitchen sink, or in other damp places. Heat or moisture may cause the medicine to break down.
- Do not keep outdated medicine or medicine no longer needed. Be sure that any discarded medicine is out of the reach of children.

Precautions While Using This Medicine

It is very important that your doctor check your progress at regular visits to make sure that this medicine is working properly and to check for unwanted effects.

While you are being treated with imatinib, and after you stop treatment with it, *do not have any immunizations (vaccinations) without your doctor's approval*. Imatinib may lower your body's resistance and there is a chance you might get the infection the immunization is meant to prevent. In addition, other persons living in your household should not take oral polio vaccine since there is a chance they could pass the polio virus on to you. Also, avoid persons who have recently taken oral polio vaccine. Do not get close to them and do not stay in the same room with them for very long. If you cannot take these precautions, you should consider wearing a protective face mask that covers the nose and mouth.

Imatinib can temporarily lower the number of white blood cells in your blood, increasing the chance of getting an infection. It can also lower the number of platelets, which are necessary for proper blood clotting. If this occurs, there are certain precautions you can take, especially when your blood count is low, to reduce the risk of infection or bleeding:

- If you can, avoid people with infections. *Check with your doctor immediately* if you think you are getting an infection or if you get a fever or chills, cough or hoarseness, lower back or side pain, or painful or difficult urination.
- *Check with your doctor immediately* if you notice any unusual bleeding or bruising; black, tarry stools; blood in urine or stools; or pinpoint red spots on your skin.
- Be careful when using a regular toothbrush, dental floss, or toothpick. Your medical doctor, dentist, or nurse may recommend other ways to clean your teeth and gums. Check with your medical doctor before having any dental work done.
- Do not touch your eyes or the inside of your nose unless you have just washed your hands and have not touched anything else in the meantime.
- Be careful not to cut yourself when you are using sharp objects such as a safety razor or fingernail or toenail cutters.
- Avoid contact sports or other situations where bruising or injury could occur.

Side Effects of This Medicine

Along with its needed effects, a medicine may cause some unwanted effects. Although not all of these side effects may occur, if they do occur they may need medical attention.

Check with your doctor as soon as possible if any of the following side effects occur:

More common (>25%)
> Black, tarry stools; bleeding problems; bloating or swelling of face, hands, lower legs, and/or feet; chest pain; chills; cough; decreased urination; fever; painful or difficult urination; pale skin; rapid weight gain; shortness of breath; sore throat; sores, ulcers, or white spots on lips or in mouth; swollen glands; trouble breathing, exertional; unusual bleeding or bruising; unusual tiredness or weakness

Less common (10–25%)
> Convulsions (seizures); dry mouth; increased thirst; irregular heartbeat; loss of appetite; mood changes; muscle pain or cramps; nausea and vomiting; numbness or tingling in hands, feet, or lips; small red or purple spots on skin; sneezing; tightness in chest; wheezing

Other side effects may occur that usually do not need medical attention. These side effects may go away during treatment as your body adjusts to the medicine. However, check with your doctor if any of the following side effects continue or are bothersome.

More common (>25%)
> Bone pain; increased bowel movements; loose stools; skin rash

Less common (10–25%)
> Bloody nose; constipation; headache; joint pain; loss of appetite; night sweats; weight loss

Rare (<10%)
> Acid indigestion; sore throat; stuffy nose; itching skin; upset stomach; weight gain

Other side effects not listed above may also occur in some patients. If you notice any other effects, check with your doctor.

Developed: 06/08/2001

IMIGLUCERASE   Systemic

Commonly used brand name(s):

In the U.S.—
> Cerezyme

In Canada—
> Cerezyme

Description

Imiglucerase (im-i-GLOO-ser-ase) is used to treat Gaucher's disease caused by the lack of a certain enzyme, glucocerebrosidase, in the body. This enzyme is necessary for your body to use fats.

Imiglucerase is available only from your doctor in the following dosage form:

Parenteral
- Injection (U.S. and Canada)

Before Using This Medicine

In deciding to use a medicine, the risks of taking the medicine must be weighed against the good it will do. This is a decision you and your doctor will make. For imiglucerase, the following should be considered:

Allergies—Tell your doctor if you have ever had any unusual or allergic reaction to alglucerase or imiglucerase. Also tell your health care professional if you are allergic to any other substances, such as foods, preservatives, or dyes.

Pregnancy—Studies on effects in pregnancy have not been done in either humans or animals.

Breast-feeding—It is not known whether imiglucerase passes into human breast milk. Although most medicines pass into breast milk in small amounts, many of them may be used safely while breast-feeding. Mothers who are taking this medicine and who wish to breast-feed should discuss this with their doctor.

Children—Although there is no specific information comparing use of imiglucerase in children with use in other age groups, this medicine is not expected to cause different side effects or problems in children than it does in adults.

Older adults—Many medicines have not been studied specifically in older people. Therefore, it may not be known whether they work exactly the same way they do in younger adults or if they cause different side effects or problems in older people. There is no specific information comparing use of imiglucerase in the elderly with use in other age groups.

Other medicines—Although certain medicines should not be used together at all, in other cases two different medicines may be used together even if an interaction might occur. In these cases, your doctor may want to change the dose, or other precautions may be necessary. Tell your health care professional if you are taking any other prescription or nonprescription (over-the-counter [OTC]) medicines.

Proper Use of This Medicine

This medicine helps control and reverse problems caused by Gaucher's disease. Therefore, you must continue to receive it if you expect to keep your condition under control. You may have to receive imiglucerase for the rest of your life. If Gaucher's disease is not treated, it can cause serious blood, liver, skeletal, or spleen problems.

Dosing—The dose of imiglucerase will be different for different patients. *Follow your doctor's orders*. The following information includes only the average doses of imiglucerase:

- For Gaucher's disease:
  —For *injection* dosage form:
    - Adults and children—The dose is based on body weight and must be determined by your doctor. The usual dose is 15 to 60 Units per kilogram (kg) (6.8 to 27 Units per pound) of body weight injected into a vein over one to two hours. The dose may be repeated several times a week to once every 2 weeks, depending on your condition. Later your doctor may lower your dose.

Precautions While Using This Medicine

It is important that your doctor check your progress while you are receiving imiglucerase to make sure that the dosage is correct for you.

Side Effects of This Medicine

Along with its needed effects, a medicine may cause some unwanted effects. Although not all of these side effects may occur, if they do occur they may need medical attention.

The following side effects may go away during treatment as your body adjusts to the medicine. However, check with your doctor if any of the following side effects continue or are bothersome:

Less common
  Abdominal discomfort; decrease in blood pressure, decrease in frequency of urination; dizziness; headache; itching; nausea; rash

Other side effects not listed above may also occur in some patients. If you notice any other effects, check with your doctor.

Developed: 06/16/95
Interim revision: 08/13/98

IMIPENEM AND CILASTATIN
Systemic

Commonly used brand name(s):

In the U.S.—
  Primaxin IM
  Primaxin IV

In Canada—
  Primaxin

Description

Imipenem and cilastatin (i-mi-PEN-em and sye-la-STAT-in) combination is used in the treatment of infections caused by bacteria. It works by killing bacteria or preventing their growth. This medicine will not work for colds, flu, or other virus infections.

Imipenem and cilastatin combination is used to treat infections in many different parts of the body. It is sometimes given with other antibiotics.

This medicine is available only with your doctor's prescription, in the following dosage form:

Parenteral
  - Injection (U.S. and Canada)

Before Receiving This Medicine

In deciding to use a medicine, the risks of taking the medicine must be weighed against the good it will do. This is a decision you and your doctor will make. For imipenem and cilastatin, the following should be considered:

Allergies—Tell your doctor if you have ever had any unusual or allergic reaction to imipenem and cilastatin, penicillins or cephalosporins. Also tell your health care professional if you are allergic to any other substances, such as foods, preservatives, or dyes.

Pregnancy—Studies have not been done in humans. However, imipenem and cilastatin combination has not been reported to cause birth defects or other problems in animal studies.

Breast-feeding—It is not known whether imipenem or cilastatin passes into the breast milk. However, this medicine has not been reported to cause problems in nursing babies.

Children—This medicine has been tested in a limited number of children 12 years of age and older and, in effective doses, has not been reported to cause different side effects or problems in children than it does in adults.

Older adults—Many medicines have not been studied specifically in older people. Therefore, it may not be known whether they work exactly the same way they do in younger adults. Although there is no specific information comparing use of imipenem and cilastatin in the elderly with use in other age groups, this medicine is not expected to cause different side effects or problems in older people than it does in younger adults.

Other medicines—Although certain medicines should not be used together at all, in other cases two different medicines may be used together even if an interaction might occur. In these cases, your doctor may want to change the dose, or other precautions may be necessary. Tell your health care professional if you are taking any other prescription or nonprescription (over-the-counter [OTC]) medicine.

Other medical problems—The presence of other medical problems may affect the use of imipenem and cilastatin. Make sure you tell your doctor if you have any other medical problems, especially:

- Central nervous system (CNS) disorders (for example, brain disease or history of seizures)—Patients with nervous system disorders, including seizures, may be more likely to have side effects

- Kidney disease—Patients with kidney disease may be more likely to have side effects

Proper Use of This Medicine

To help clear up your infection completely, *imipenem and cilastatin combination must be given for the full time of treatment*, even if you begin to feel better after a few days. Also, this medicine works best when there is a constant amount in the blood or urine. To help keep the amount constant, it must be given on a regular schedule.

Dosing—The dose of imipenem and cilastatin combination will be different for different patients. *Follow your doctor's* *orders or the directions on the label.* The following information includes only the average doses of imipenem and cilastatin combination. *If your dose is different, do not change it* unless your doctor tells you to do so.

- For *injection* dosage form:
  —For bacterial infections:
  - Adults and children 12 years of age and over—250 milligrams (mg) to 1 gram injected into a vein every six to eight hours; or 500 to 750 mg injected into a muscle every twelve hours, depending on how severe your infection is.
  - Children up to 12 years of age—Use and dose must be determined by your doctor.

Precautions While Using This Medicine

Some patients may develop tremors or seizures while receiving this medicine. If you already have a history of seizures and you are taking anticonvulsants, you should continue to take them unless otherwise directed by your doctor.

In some patients, imipenem and cilastatin combination may cause diarrhea.

- Severe diarrhea may be a sign of a serious side effect. *Do not take any diarrhea medicine without first checking with your doctor.* Diarrhea medicines may make your diarrhea worse or make it last longer.
- For mild diarrhea, diarrhea medicine containing kaolin (e.g., Kaopectate liquid) or attapulgite (e.g., Kaopectate tablets, Diasorb) may be taken. However, other kinds of diarrhea medicine should not be taken. They may make your diarrhea worse or make it last longer.
- If you have any questions about this or if mild diarrhea continues or gets worse, check with your health care professional.

Side Effects of This Medicine

Along with its needed effects, a medicine may cause some unwanted effects. Although not all of these side effects may occur, if they do occur they may need medical attention.

Check with your health care professional immediately if any of the following side effects occur:

More common
Confusion; convulsions (seizures); dizziness; pain at place of injection; skin rash, hives, itching, fever, or wheezing; tremors

Less common
Dizziness; increased sweating; nausea or vomiting; unusual tiredness or weakness

Rare
Fever; severe abdominal or stomach cramps and pain; watery and severe diarrhea, which may also be bloody (these side effects may also occur up to several weeks after you stop receiving this medicine)

Other side effects may occur that usually do not need medical attention. These side effects may go away during treatment as your body adjusts to the medicine. However, check with your doctor if the following side effects continue or are bothersome:

More common
Diarrhea; nausea and vomiting

Other side effects not listed above may also occur in some patients. If you notice any other effects, check with your doctor.

Additional Information

Once a medicine has been approved for marketing for a certain use, experience may show that it is also useful for other medical problems. Although these uses are not included in product labeling, imipenem and cilastatin combination is used in certain patients with the following medical conditions:

- Febrile neutropenia (treatment)
- Melioidosis (treatment)

Other than the above information, there is no additional information relating to proper use, precautions, or side effects for its use.

Revised: 08/08/2000

IMIQUIMOD   Topical

Commonly used brand name(s):

In the U.S.—
Aldara

Description

Imiquimod (i-MI-kwi-mod) is used to treat external warts around the genital and rectal areas called condyloma acuminatum. It is not used on warts inside the vagina, penis, or rectum.

It works by aiding the immune system to help protect the body from viruses that cause warts. The medicine does not fight the viruses that cause warts directly. It does help to relieve and control wart production.

This medicine is available only with your doctor's prescription, in the following dosage form:

Topical
- Cream (U.S. and Canada)

Before Using This Medicine

In deciding to use a medicine, the risks of using the medicine must be weighed against the good it will do. This is a decision you and your doctor will make. For imiquimod, the following should be considered:

Allergies—Tell your doctor if you have ever had any unusual or allergic reaction to imiquimod. Also tell your health care professional if you are allergic to any other substances, such as foods, preservatives, or dyes.

Pregnancy—Imiquimod has not been shown to cause birth defects or other problems in humans. However, studies in animals using doses higher than recommended for humans have shown that imiquimod causes bone problems or low birth weight in pregnancies. Before taking this medicine, make sure your doctor knows if you are pregnant or if you may become pregnant.

Breast-feeding—It is not known whether imiquimod passes into breast milk. However, this medicine has not been reported to cause problems in nursing babies.

Children—Studies of this medicine have been done only in adult patients, and there is no specific information comparing use of imiquimod in children up to 18 years of age with use in other age groups.

Older adults—Many medicines have not been studied specifically in older people. Therefore, it may not be known whether they work exactly the same way they do in younger adults or if they cause different side effects or problems in older people. There is no specific information comparing use of imiquimod in the elderly with use in other age groups.

Other medicines—Although certain medicines should not be used together at all, in other cases two different medicines may be used together even if an interaction might occur. In these cases, your doctor may want to change the dose, or other precautions may be necessary. Tell your doctor and pharmacist if you are using any other topical prescription or nonprescription (over-the counter [OTC]) medicine that is to be applied to the same area of the skin.

Other medical problems—The presence of other medical problems may affect the use of imiquimod. Make sure you tell your doctor if you have any other medical problems, especially:

- Skin problems, genital or
- Surgery, genital (recent)—Imiquimod may cause skin irritation and redness of skin for these conditions

Proper Use of This Medicine

To apply the medicine:

- *Wash your hands before and after using the medicine.* Avoid getting the medicine into your eyes.
- *Use the medicine only as directed by your doctor.* Do not use more of it, do not use it more often, and do not use it longer than directed.
- Allow medicine to stay on skin for 6 to 10 hours, then wash area thoroughly with soap and water.
- Throw out any unused cream from the single-dose packet.
- *Do not apply an occlusive dressing* (airtight covering, such as kitchen plastic wrap) over the medicine, unless told to do so by your doctor. To do so may cause irritation of the skin. Other materials that are not airtight, such as cotton gauze or cotton underclothes, may be used.

Dosing—The dose of imiquimod will be different for different patients. *Follow your doctor's orders or the directions on the label.* The following information includes only the average doses of imiquimod. *If your dose is different, do not change it* unless your doctor tells you to do so.

- For *topical* dosage form (cream):
  —For warts on the skin outside of the genital or rectal areas (condyloma acuminatum):
    - Adults—Apply a thin film to wart once every other day (three times a week) before normal sleeping hours. Rub in well and leave on for six to ten hours. Remove medicine from wart by washing with mild soap and water. Continue treatment until wart is gone or for up to sixteen weeks.
    - Children—Use and dose must be determined by doctor.

Missed dose—If you miss a dose of this medicine, wait until the next evening to apply it. Then go back to your regular dosing schedule.

Storage—To store this medicine:

- Keep out of the reach of children.
- Store away from heat and direct light.
- Keep the medicine from freezing. Do not refrigerate.
- Do not keep outdated medicine or medicine no longer needed. Be sure that any discarded medicine is out of the reach of children.

Precautions While Using This Medicine

If you notice severe skin irritation or flu-like symptoms (diarrhea, fatigue, fever, headache, or muscle pain), check with your doctor. It may be necessary for you to *reduce the number of times a day that you use the medicine or to stop using the medicine* for a short time until your skin is less irritated or your flu-like symptoms disappear.

Avoid having genital, oral, or anal sex while the medicine is on your skin. Make sure you *wash the cream off your skin before you engage in any sexual activity.* Also, the medicine contains oils that can weaken latex (rubber) condoms, diaphragms, or cervical caps causing them not to work properly to prevent pregnancy.

Do not use any other skin product on the same skin area on which you use this medicine, unless directed otherwise by your doctor.

Do not share your medicine with others, even if you think that they have the same condition you have.

Side Effects of This Medicine

Along with its needed effects, a medicine may cause some unwanted effects. Although not all of these side effects may occur, if they do occur they may need medical attention.

Check with your doctor as soon as possible if any of the following side effects occur:

More common
　Blisters on skin; itching in genital or other skin areas; open sores or scabs on skin; redness of skin (severe); scaling

Symptoms of overdose
　Flu-like symptoms, including diarrhea, fatigue, fever, headache, or muscle pain

Other side effects may occur that usually do not need medical attention. These side effects may go away during treatment as your body adjusts to the medicine. However, check with your doctor if any of the following side effects continue or are bothersome:

More common
　Burning or stinging of skin (mild); flaking of skin; pain, soreness, or tenderness of skin (mild); rash; redness of skin (mild); swelling at place of application

Less common
　Lightening of the treated skin

Other side effects not listed above may also occur in some patients. If you notice any other effects, check with your doctor.

Developed: 06/30/98
Revised: 08/30/99

IMMUNE GLOBULIN INTRAVENOUS (HUMAN) Systemic

Commonly used brand name(s):

In the U.S.—

Gamimune N 5%	Gammar-P IV
Gamimune N 10%	Iveegam
Gamimune N 5% S/D	Polygam S/D
Gamimune N 10% S/D	Sandoglobulin
Gammagard S/D	Venoglobulin–I
Gammagard S/D 0.5 g	Venoglobulin-S

In Canada—

Gamimune N 5%	Gamimune N 10% S/D
Gamimune N 10%	Iveegam
Gamimune N 5% S/D	

Other commonly used names are IGIV and IVIG.

Description

Immune globulin intravenous (IGIV) belongs to a group of medicines known as immunizing agents. IGIV is used to prevent or treat some illnesses that can occur when your body does not produce enough of its own immunity to prevent those diseases.

IGIV should be administered only by or under the supervision of your doctor or other health care professional. IGIV is available in the following dosage form:

Parenteral
- Injection (U.S. and Canada)

Before Using This Medicine

In deciding to use a medicine, the risks of taking the medicine must be weighed against the good it will do. This is a decision you and your doctor will make. For immune globulin intravenous (IGIV), the following should be considered:

Allergies—Tell your doctor if you have ever had any unusual or allergic reaction to intramuscular or intravenous immune globulins. Also tell your health care professional if you are allergic to any other substances, such as foods, preservatives, or dyes.

Diet—Make certain your health care professional knows if you are on any special diet, such as a low-sodium or low-sugar diet.

Pregnancy—Studies on effects in pregnancy have not been done in either humans or animals.

Breast-feeding—It is not known whether IGIV passes into the breast milk. Although most medicines pass into breast milk in small amounts, many of them may be used safely while breast-feeding. Mothers who are using this medicine and who wish to breast-feed should discuss this with their doctor.

Children—Although there is no specific information comparing use of IGIV in children with use in other age groups, this medicine is not expected to cause different side effects or problems in children than it does in adults.

Older adults—Many medicines have not been studied specifically in older people. Therefore, it may not be known whether they work exactly the same way they do in younger adults. Although there is no specific information comparing use of IGIV in the elderly with use in other age groups, this medicine is not expected to cause different side effects or problems in older people than it does in younger adults.

Other medicines—Although certain medicines should not be used together at all, in other cases two different medicines may be used together even if an interaction might occur. In these cases, your doctor may want to change the dose, or other precautions may be necessary. When receiving IGIV it is especially important that your health care professional know if you are taking any of the following:

- Live virus vaccines—IGIV may affect the degree of protection provided by live virus vaccines. Also, live virus vaccines may interfere with the therapeutic effects of IGIV

Other medical problems—The presence of other medical problems may affect the use of IGIV. Make sure you tell your doctor if you have any other medical problems, especially:

- Diabetes mellitus or
- Heart problems or
- Immunoglobulin A (IgA) deficiencies or
- Kidney problems or
- Severe allergic reaction to IGIV—IGIV may make the conditions worse

Proper Use of This Medicine

Waiting at least 2 to 3 weeks after receiving live virus vaccines before receiving IGIV, depending on the vaccine received.

Waiting at least 5 to 11 months after receiving IGIV before receiving live virus vaccines, depending on the vaccine to be received.

Dosing—The dose of IGIV will be different for different patients. Doses are based on body weight and the condition for which you are being treated. *If you are receiving IGIV at home, follow your doctor's orders or the directions on the label.* If you have any questions about the proper dose of IGIV, ask your doctor.

Side Effects of This Medicine

Along with its needed effects, a medicine may cause some unwanted effects. Although not all of these side effects may occur, if they do occur they may need medical attention.

Check with your doctor as soon as possible if any of the following side effects occur:

More common
  Fast or pounding heartbeat; troubled breathing

Less common
  Bluish coloring of lips or nailbeds; burning sensation in head; faintness or lightheadedness; unusual tiredness or weakness; wheezing

Rare
  Difficulty in breathing or swallowing; hives; itching, especially of feet or hands; reddening of skin, especially around ears; swelling of eyes, face, or inside of nose; unusual tiredness or weakness (sudden and severe)

Other side effects may occur that usually do not need medical attention. These side effects may go away during treatment as your body adjusts to the medicine. However, check with your doctor if any of the following side effects continue or are bothersome:

More common
  Backache or pain; general feeling of discomfort or ill-

ness; headache; joint pain; muscle pain; nausea; vomiting

Less common
Chest or hip pain; leg cramps; redness, rash, or pain at place of injection

Other side effects not listed above may also occur in some patients. If you notice any other effects, check with your doctor.

Additional Information

Once a medicine has been approved for marketing for a certain use, experience may show that it is also useful for other medical problems. Although these uses are not included in product labeling, IGIV is used in certain patients with the following medical conditions:

- Chronic parvovirus B19 infection (treatment)
- Chronic inflammatory demyelinating polyneuropathies (treatment)
- Dermatomyositis (treatment)
- Guillain-Barré syndrome (treatment)
- Hyperimmunoglobulinemia E syndrome (treatment)
- Infections in low-birth-weight preterm high-risk neonates (prophylaxis and treatment adjunct)
- Lambert-Eaton myasthenic syndrome (treatment)
- Multifocal motor neuropathy (treatment)
- Relapsing-remitting multiple sclerosis (treatment)

Other than the above information, there is no additional information relating to proper use, precautions, or side effects for its use.

Revised: 08/07/2000

INDAPAMIDE   Systemic

Commonly used brand name(s):

In the U.S.—
Lozol
Generic name product may be available.

In Canada—

Lozide	Novo-Indapamide
Apo-Indapamide	Nu-Indapamide
Gen-Indapamide	

Description

Indapamide (in-DAP-a-mide) belongs to the group of medicines known as diuretics. It is commonly used to treat high blood pressure (hypertension).

High blood pressure adds to the workload of the heart and arteries. If it continues for a long time, the heart and arteries may not function properly. This can damage the blood vessels of the brain, heart, and kidneys resulting in a stroke, heart failure, or kidney failure. High blood pressure may also increase the risk of heart attacks. These problems may be less likely to occur if blood pressure is controlled.

Indapamide is also used to help reduce the amount of water in the body by increasing the flow of urine.

Indapamide is available only with your doctor's prescription, in the following dosage form:

Oral
- Tablets (U.S. and Canada)

Before Using This Medicine

In deciding to use a medicine, the risks of taking the medicine must be weighed against the good it will do. This is a decision you and your doctor will make. For indapamide, the following should be considered:

Allergies—Tell your doctor if you have ever had any unusual or allergic reaction to indapamide or other sulfonamide-type medicines. Also tell your health care professional if you are allergic to any other substances, such as foods, preservatives, or dyes.

Pregnancy—Indapamide has not been studied in pregnant women. However, indapamide has not been shown to cause birth defects or other problems in animal studies.

In general, diuretics are not useful for normal swelling of feet and hands that occurs during pregnancy. Diuretics should not be taken during pregnancy unless recommended by your doctor.

Breast-feeding—It is not known whether indapamide passes into breast milk. However, this medicine has not been reported to cause problems in nursing babies.

Children—Studies on this medicine have been done only in adult patients, and there is no specific information comparing use of indapamide in children with use in other age groups.

Older adults—Dizziness or lightheadedness and signs and symptoms of too much potassium loss are more likely to occur in the elderly, who are usually more sensitive than younger adults to the effects of indapamide.

Other medicines—Although certain medicines should not be used together at all, in other cases two different medicines may be used together even if an interaction might occur. In these cases, your doctor may want to change the dose, or other precautions may be necessary. When you are taking indapamide, it is especially important that your health care professional know if you are taking any of the following:

- Digitalis glycosides (heart medicine)—Use with indapamide may increase the chance of side effects of digitalis glycosides
- Lithium (e.g., Lithane)—Use with indapamide may cause high blood levels of lithium, which may increase the chance of side effects

Other medical problems—The presence of other medical problems may affect the use of indapamide. Make sure you tell your doctor if you have any other medical problems, especially:

- Diabetes mellitus (sugar diabetes) or
- Gout (history of)—Indapamide may make these conditions worse
- Kidney disease—May prevent indapamide from working properly
- Liver disease—Higher blood levels of indapamide may occur, which may increase the chance of side effects

Proper Use of This Medicine

Indapamide may cause you to have an unusual feeling of tiredness when you begin to take it. You may also notice an increase in the amount of urine or in your frequency of urination. After taking the medicine for a while, these effects should lessen. In general, to keep the increase in urine from affecting your sleep:

- If you are to take a single dose a day, take it in the morning after breakfast.
- If you are to take more than one dose a day, take the last dose no later than 6 p.m., unless otherwise directed by your doctor.

However, it is best to plan your dose or doses according to a schedule that will least affect your personal activities and sleep. Ask your health care professional to help you plan the best time to take this medicine.

To help you remember to take indapamide, try to get into the habit of taking it at the same time each day.

For patients taking indapamide for *high blood pressure:*

- In addition to the use of the medicine your doctor has prescribed, treatment for your high blood pressure may include weight control and care in the types of foods you eat, especially foods high in sodium. Your doctor will tell you which of these are most important for you. You should check with your doctor before changing your diet.
- Many patients who have high blood pressure will not notice any signs of the problem. In fact, many may feel normal. It is very important that you *take your medicine exactly as directed* and that you keep your appointments with your doctor even if you feel well.
- Remember that this medicine will not cure your high blood pressure but it does help control it. Therefore, you must continue to take it as directed if you expect to lower your blood pressure and keep it down. *You may have to take high blood pressure medicine for the rest of your life.* If high blood pressure is not treated, it can cause serious problems such as heart failure, blood vessel disease, stroke, or kidney disease.

Dosing—The dose of indapamide will be different for different patients. *Follow your doctor's orders or the directions on the label.* The following information includes only the average doses of indapamide. *If your dose is different, do not change it* unless your doctor tells you to do so:

- For *oral* dosage forms (tablets):
  —Adults: 2.5 to 5 milligrams once a day.

Missed dose—If you miss a dose of this medicine, take it as soon as possible. However, if it is almost time for your next dose, skip the missed dose and go back to your regular dosing schedule. Do not double doses.

Storage—To store this medicine:

- Keep out of the reach of children.
- Store away from heat and direct light.
- Do not store in the bathroom, near the kitchen sink, or in other damp places. Heat or moisture may cause the medicine to break down.
- Do not keep outdated medicine or medicine no longer needed. Be sure that any discarded medicine is out of the reach of children.

Precautions While Using This Medicine

It is important that your doctor check your progress at regular visits to make sure that indapamide is working properly.

This medicine may cause a loss of potassium from your body:

- To help prevent this, your doctor may want you to:
  —eat or drink foods that have a high potassium content (for example, orange or other citrus fruit juices), or
  —take a potassium supplement, or
  —take another medication to help prevent the loss of the potassium in the first place.
- It is very important to follow these directions. Also, it is important not to change your diet on your own. This is more important if you are already on a special diet (as for diabetes), or if you are taking a potassium supplement or a medicine to reduce potassium loss. Extra potassium may not be necessary and, in some cases, too much potassium could be harmful.

Check with your doctor if you become sick and have severe or continuing vomiting or diarrhea. These problems may cause you to lose additional water and potassium.

For patients taking this medicine for *high blood pressure:*

- *Do not take other medicines unless they have been discussed with your doctor.* This especially includes over-the-counter (nonprescription) medicines for appetite control, asthma, colds, hay fever, or sinus problems, since they may tend to increase your blood pressure.

Side Effects of This Medicine

Along with its needed effects, a medicine may cause some unwanted effects. Although not all of these side effects may occur, if they do occur they may need medical attention.

Check with your doctor as soon as possible if any of the following side effects occur:
Signs and symptoms of an imbalance of water or potassium in the body
　　Dryness of mouth; increased thirst; irregular heartbeat; mood or mental changes; muscle cramps or pain; nausea or vomiting; unusual tiredness or weakness; weak pulse
Rare
　　Skin rash, itching, or hives

Other side effects may occur that usually do not need medical attention. These side effects may go away during treatment as your body adjusts to the medicine. However, check with your doctor if any of the following side effects continue or are bothersome:
Less common or rare
　　Diarrhea; dizziness or lightheadedness, especially when getting up from a lying or sitting position; headache; loss of appetite; trouble in sleeping; stomach upset

Other side effects not listed above may also occur in some patients. If you notice any other effects, check with your doctor.

Revised: 01/20/93; 08/18/98

INDINAVIR   Systemic

Commonly used brand name(s):

In the U.S.—
　　Crixivan

Description

Indinavir (in-DIN-a-veer) is used, alone or in combination with other medicines, in the treatment of the infection caused by the human immunodeficiency virus (HIV). HIV is the virus that causes acquired immune deficiency syndrome (AIDS).

Indinavir will not cure or prevent HIV infection or AIDS; however, it helps keep HIV from reproducing and appears to slow down the destruction of the immune system. This may help delay the development of problems usually related to AIDS or HIV disease. Indinavir will not keep you from spreading HIV to other people. People who receive this medicine may continue to have other problems usually related to AIDS or HIV disease.

This medicine is available only with your doctor's prescription, in the following dosage form:

Oral
- Capsules (U.S.)

Before Using This Medicine

In deciding to use a medicine, the risks of taking the medicine must be weighed against the good it will do. This is a decision you and your doctor will make. For indinavir, the following should be considered:

Allergies—Tell your doctor if you have ever had any unusual or allergic reaction to indinavir. Also tell your health care professional if you are allergic to any other substances, such as foods, preservatives, or dyes.

Pregnancy—Indinavir has not been studied in pregnant women. However, it has caused increased levels of a substance called bilirubin in the mother, which can cause jaundice. It is not known if it causes this effect in the baby. Before taking this medicine, make sure your doctor knows if you are pregnant or if you may become pregnant.

Breast-feeding—It is not known whether indinavir passes into the breast milk in humans. However, it does pass into the milk in animals. Because it can cause serious unwanted effects, breast-feeding is usually not recommended while you are taking indinavir.

Older adults—Indinavir has not been studied specifically in older people. Therefore, it is not known whether it causes different side effects or problems in the elderly than it does in younger adults.

Other medicines—Although certain medicines should not be used together at all, in other cases two different medicines may be used together even if an interaction might occur. In these cases, your doctor may want to change the dose, or other precautions may be necessary. When you are taking indinavir, it is especially important that your health care professional know if you are taking any of the following:

- Astemizole (e.g., Hismanal) or
- Cisapride (e.g., Propulsid) or
- Midazolam (e.g., Versed) or
- Terfenadine (e.g., Seldane) or
- Triazolam (e.g., Halcion)—There is a possibility that indinavir may interfere with the removal of these medicines from the body, which could lead to serious side effects
- Didanosine (e.g., Videx)—It is recommended that this medicine and indinavir be taken at least 1 hour apart so that both will be absorbed properly from the stomach

- Ketoconazole (e.g., Nizoral)—Use of this medicine with indinavir may increase the amount of indinavir in the body
- Rifabutin (e.g., Mycobutin)—Use of this medicine with indinavir may increase the amount of both rifabutin and indinavir in the body
- Rifampin (e.g., Rifadin)—Use of this medicine with indinavir may decrease the amount of indinavir in the body

Other medical problems—The presence of other medical problems may affect the use of indinavir. Make sure you tell your doctor if you have any other medical problems, especially:

- Liver disease—Effects of indinavir may be increased because of slower removal from the body

Proper Use of This Medicine

This medicine should be taken with water 1 hour before or 2 hours after a meal. Indinavir may also be taken with other liquids (skim milk, juice, coffee, or tea) or with a light meal (dry toast with jelly, juice, coffee with skim milk and sugar, or corn flakes with skim milk and sugar).

While you are taking indinavir, it is important that you drink extra fluids so that you will pass more urine. This will help prevent possible kidney stones. *Follow your doctor's instructions carefully about how much fluid to drink.* Usually you will need to drink at least 48 ounces (1.5 liters) of fluids every day during your treatment.

Take this medicine exactly as directed by your doctor. Do not take it more often, and do not take it for a longer time than your doctor ordered. Also, do not stop taking this medicine without checking with your doctor first.

Keep taking indinavir for the full time of treatment, even if you begin to feel better.

This medicine works best when there is a constant amount in the blood. *To help keep the amount constant, do not miss any doses. Also, it is best to take the doses at evenly spaced times, day and night.* For example, if you are to take three doses a day, the doses should be spaced about 8 hours apart. If you need help in planning the best times to take your medicine, check with your health care professional.

Only take medicine that your doctor has prescribed specially for you. Do not share your medicine with others.

Dosing—The dose of indinavir may be different for different patients. *Follow your doctor's orders or the directions on the label.* The following information includes only the average doses of indinavir. *If your dose is different, do not change it* unless your doctor tells you to do so.

The number of capsules that you take depends on the strength of the medicine.

- For *oral* dosage form (capsules):
  —For treatment of HIV infection:
    - Adults—800 mg every eight hours.
    - Children—Use and dose must be determined by your doctor.

Missed dose—If you miss a dose of this medicine, take it as soon as you remember. However, if it is almost time for your next dose, skip the missed dose and go back to your regular dosing schedule. Do not double doses.

Storage—To store this medicine:
- Keep out of the reach of children.
- Store away from heat and direct light.

- Indinavir capsules are very sensitive to moisture. Keep them in their original container and leave the drying packet in the container.
- Do not store in the bathroom, near the kitchen sink, or in other damp places. Heat or moisture may cause the medicine to break down.
- Do not keep outdated medicine or medicine no longer needed. Be sure that any discarded medicine is out of the reach of children.

Precautions While Using This Medicine

Do not take any other medicines without checking with your doctor first. To do so may increase the chance of side effects from indinavir.

It is very important that your doctor check your progress at regular visits to make sure this medicine is working properly and to check for unwanted effects.

Side Effects of This Medicine

Along with its needed effects, a medicine may cause some unwanted effects. Although not all of these side effects may occur, if they do occur they may need medical attention.

Check with your doctor immediately if any of the following side effects occur:
  More common
    Blood in urine; sharp back pain just below ribs

Also, check with your doctor as soon as possible if any of the following side effects occur:
  Rare
    Confusion; dehydration; dry or itchy skin; fatigue; fruity mouth odor; increased hunger; increased thirst; increased urination; nausea; vomiting; weight loss

Other side effects may occur that usually do not need medical attention. These side effects may go away during treatment as your body adjusts to the medicine. However, check with your doctor if any of the following side effects continue or are bothersome:
  More common
    Abdominal or stomach pain; change in sense of taste; diarrhea; difficulty in sleeping; generalized weakness; headache
  Less common
    Dizziness; sleepiness

Other side effects not listed above may also occur in some patients. If you notice any other effects, check with your doctor.

Developed: 07/28/98

INFLIXIMAB   Systemic†

Commonly used brand name(s):

In the U.S.—
  Remicade
Another commonly used name is cA2.

†Not commercially available in Canada.

Description

Infliximab (in-FLIX-i-mab) is a monoclonal antibody. It is used to treat Crohn's disease in patients who have not been helped by other medicines and also in patients who have a type of Crohn's disease in which fistulas form. It is also used to treat rheumatoid arthritis.

This medicine is available only with your doctor's prescription, in the following dosage form:
- Injection (U.S.)

Before Using This Medicine

In deciding to use a medicine, the risks of using the medicine must be weighed against the good it will do. This is a decision you and your doctor will make. For infliximab, the following should be considered:

Allergies—Tell your doctor if you have ever had any unusual or allergic reaction to infliximab or to rodents (such as rats or mice). Mouse cells are used in the preparation of infliximab. Also tell your health care professional if you are allergic to any other substances, such as foods, preservatives, or dyes.

Pregnancy—Studies have not been done in either humans or animals. It is not known if infliximab causes harmful effects on the fetus. Before receiving this medicine, make sure your doctor knows if you are pregnant or if you may become pregnant.

Breast-feeding—It is not known whether infliximab passes into breast milk. Because of the risk of harmful effects in the nursing baby, it may be necessary for you to stop breast-feeding during treatment. Be sure you have discussed the risks and benefits of the medicine with your doctor.

Children—Studies on this medicine have been done only in adult patients, and there is no specific information comparing use of infliximab in children with use in other age groups.

Older adults—Many medicines have not been studied specifically in older people. Therefore, it may not be known whether they work exactly the same way they do in younger adults or if they cause different side effects or problems in older people. There is no specific information comparing use of infliximab in the elderly with use in other age groups. However, older adults generally get more infections than do younger adults, and it is not known if infliximab may affect the number of infections that older people get.

Proper Use of This Medicine

Dosing—The dose of infliximab will be different for different patients. Infliximab is usually given by a doctor or nurse. The following information includes only the average dose of infliximab.

- For treatment of Crohn's disease:
    Adults—5 milligrams (mg) per kilogram (kg) (2.27 mg per pound) of body weight, injected into a vein.
    Children—Use and dose must be determined by your doctor.
- For treatment of Rheumatoid arthritis:
    Adults—3 milligrams (mg) per kilogram (kg) (1.36 mg per pound) of body weight, injected into a vein
    Children—Use and dose must be determined by your doctor.

Storage—To store this medicine:
- Keep out of the reach of children.
- Store away from heat and direct light.
- Do not store in the bathroom, near the kitchen sink, or in other damp places. Heat or moisture may cause the medicine to break down.
- Store in the refrigerator. However, keep the medicine from freezing.
- Do not keep outdated medicine or medicine no longer needed. Be sure that any discarded medicine is out of the reach of children.

Precautions While Using This Medicine

Infliximab may cause chest pain, fever, chills, itching, hives, flushing of face, or troubled breathing within a few hours after you receive it. *Check with your doctor or nurse immediately* if you have any of these symptoms.

Side Effects of This Medicine

Along with its needed effects, a medicine may cause some unwanted effects. Although not all of these side effects may occur, if they do occur they may need medical attention.

Check with your doctor immediately if any of the following side effects occur:
More common
> Chest pain; chills; fever; flushing of face; hives; itching; troubled breathing

Check with your doctor as soon as possible if any of the following side effects occur:
More common
> Abdominal pain; cough; dizziness; fainting; headache; muscle pain; nasal congestion; nausea; runny nose; shortness of breath; sneezing; sore throat; tightness in chest; unusual tiredness or weakness; vomiting; wheezing

Less common
> Back pain; bloody or cloudy urine; cracks in skin at the corners of mouth; diarrhea; difficult or painful urination; frequent urge to urinate; high blood pressure; low blood pressure; pain; pain or tenderness around eyes and cheekbones; skin rash; soreness or irritation of mouth or tongue; soreness or redness around fingernails or toenails; vaginal burning or itching and discharge; white patches in mouth and/or on tongue

Rare
> Abscess (swollen, red, tender area of infection containing pus); back or side pain; black, tarry stools; blood in urine or stools; bone or joint pain; constipation; falls; feeling of fullness; general feeling of illness; hernia (bulge of tissue through the wall of the abdomen); infection; irregular or pounding heartbeat; pain in rectum; pain spreading from the abdomen to the left shoulder; pinpoint red spots on skin; stomach pain (severe); swollen or painful glands; tendon injury; unusual bleeding or bruising; weight loss (unusual); yellow skin and eyes

Developed: 05/05/1999
Revised: 08/29/2000

INFLUENZA VIRUS VACCINE
Systemic

Commonly used brand name(s):

In the U.S.—
FluShield
Fluvirin
Fluzone
Generic name product may be available.

In Canada—
Fluviral
Fluviral S/F
Fluzone

Another commonly used name is flu vaccine.

Description

Influenza (in-floo-EN-za) virus vaccine is used to prevent infection by the influenza viruses. The vaccine works by causing your body to produce its own protection (antibodies) against the disease. It is also known as a "flu shot."

There are many kinds of influenza viruses, but not all will cause problems in any given year. Therefore, before the influenza vaccine for each year is produced, the World Health Organization (WHO) and the U.S. and Canadian Public Health Services decide which influenza viruses will be most likely to cause influenza infection that year. Then they include the antigens (substances that cause protective antibodies to be formed) to these viruses in the influenza vaccine made available. Usually, the U.S. and Canada use the same influenza vaccine; however, they are not required to do so.

It is necessary to receive an influenza vaccine injection each year, since influenza infections are usually caused by different kinds of influenza viruses each year and because the protection gained by the vaccine lasts less than a year.

Influenza is a virus infection of the throat, bronchial tubes, and lungs. Influenza infection causes fever, chills, cough, headache, and muscle aches and pains in your back, arms, and legs. In addition, adults and children weakened by other diseases or medical conditions and persons 50 years of age and over, even if they are healthy, may get a much more serious illness and may have to be treated in a hospital. Each year thousands of people die as a result of an influenza infection.

The best way to help prevent influenza infection is to get an influenza vaccination each year, usually in early November. Immunization (administration of vaccine) against influenza is approved for infants 6 months of age and over, all children, and all adults.

This vaccine is to be administered only by or under the supervision of your doctor or other health care professional. It is available in the following dosage form:

Parenteral
- Injection (U.S. and Canada)

Before Receiving This Vaccine

In deciding to use a medicine, the risks of taking the medicine must be weighed against the good it will do. This is a decision you and your doctor will make. For influenza vaccine, the following should be considered:

Allergies—Tell your doctor if you have ever had any unusual or allergic reaction to influenza vaccine or to antibiotics, such as gentamicin, streptomycin, or other aminoglycosides. Influenza vaccine available in the U.S. or Canada may contain these antibiotics in very small amounts. Also tell your health care professional if you are allergic to any other substances, such as foods (especially eggs) or preservatives (especially sodium bisulfite or thimerosal). Influenza vaccine is grown in the fluids of chick embryos.

Pregnancy—Influenza vaccine has not been shown to cause birth defects or other problems in humans.

Breast-feeding—Influenza vaccine has not been reported to cause problems in nursing babies.

Children—*Use is not recommended for infants up to 6 months of age*. In addition, only a split-virus influenza vaccine should be given to children 6 months to 12 years of age. Some side effects of the vaccine, such as fever, unusual tiredness or weakness, or aches or pains in muscles, are more likely to occur in infants and children, who are usually more sensitive than adults to the effects of influenza vaccine.

Older adults—This vaccine is not expected to cause different side effects or problems in older persons than it does in younger adults. However, elderly persons may not become as immune to head and upper chest influenza infections as younger adults, although the vaccine may still be effective in preventing lower chest influenza infections and other complications of influenza.

Other medicines—Although certain medicines should not be used together at all, in other cases two different medicines may be used together even if an interaction might occur. In these cases, your doctor may want to change the dose, or other precautions may be necessary. Tell your health care professional if you are using any other prescription or nonprescription (over-the-counter [OTC]) medicine.

Other medical problems—The presence of other medical problems may affect the use of influenza vaccine. Make sure you tell your doctor if you have any other medical problems, especially:

- Bronchitis, pneumonia, or other illness involving lungs or bronchial tubes—Use of influenza vaccine may make the condition worse

- Guillain Barré syndrome, history of—Use of influenza vaccine may cause a recurrence of the symptoms of the condition

- Severe illness with fever—The symptoms of the condition may be confused with the possible side effects of the vaccine

Proper Use of This Vaccine

Dosing—The dose of influenza vaccine will be different for different patients. *Follow your doctor's orders*. The following information includes only the average dose of influenza vaccine.

- For *injection* dosage form:
    - To help prevent influenza infection:
        - Adults and children 9 years of age and older—One injection each year.
        - Children 6 months to 9 years of age—One or two injections, depending on whether the child has received influenza vaccine in the past. The dose is given each year. If two doses are needed, they should be spaced 4 weeks apart.

Side Effects of This Vaccine

In 1976, a number of persons who received the "swine flu" influenza vaccine developed Guillain-Barré syndrome (GBS). Most of these persons were over 25 years of age. Although only 10 out of one million persons receiving the vaccine actually developed GBS, this number was 6 times more than would normally have been expected. Most of the persons who got GBS recovered completely from the paralysis it caused.

It is assumed that the "swine flu" virus included in the 1976 vaccine caused the problem, but this has not been proven. Since that time, the "swine flu" virus has not been used in influenza vaccines, and there has been no recurrence of GBS associated with influenza vaccinations.

Along with its needed effects, a vaccine may cause some unwanted effects. Although not all of these side effects may occur, if they do occur they may need medical attention.

Get emergency help immediately if any of the following side effects occur:
   Symptoms of allergic reaction
       Difficulty in breathing or swallowing; hives; itching, especially of feet or hands; reddening of skin, especially around ears; swelling of eyes, face, or inside of nose; unusual tiredness or weakness (sudden and severe)

Other side effects may occur that usually do not need medical attention. These side effects generally do not last for more than 1 or 2 days. However, check with your doctor if any of the following side effects continue or are bothersome:
   More common
       Tenderness, redness, or hard lump at place of injection
   Less common
       Fever, general feeling of discomfort or illness, or aches or pains in muscles

Other side effects not listed above may also occur in some patients. If you notice any other effects, check with your doctor.

Revised: 06/12/2001

INSULIN   Systemic

Commonly used brand name(s):

In the U.S.—

Humulin 50/50[14]	Novolin N PenFill[13]
Humulin 70/30[14]	Novolin N Prefilled[13]
Humulin 70/30 Pen[14]	Novolin 70/30 PenFill[14]
Humulin L[10]	Novolin 70/30 Prefilled[14]
Humulin N[13]	Novolin R[7]
Humulin N Pen[13]	Novolin R PenFill[7]
Humulin R[7]	Novolin R Prefilled[7]
Humulin R, Regular U-500	NPH Iletin II[11]
(Concentrated)[7]	NPH Purified Insulin[11]
Humulin U[5]	Regular (Concentrated) Iletin
Lente Iletin II[8]	II, U-500[6]
Lente[8]	Regular Iletin II[6]
Novolin 70/30[14]	Regular Insulin[6]
Novolin L[10]	Velosulin BR[1]
Novolin N[13]	

In Canada—

Humulin 10/90[14]	Novolin ge NPH Penfill[13]
Humulin 20/80[14]	Novolin ge 10/90 Penfill[14]
Humulin 30/70[14]	Novolin ge 20/80 Penfill[14]
Humulin 40/60[14]	Novolin ge 30/70 Penfill[14]
Humulin 50/50[14]	Novolin ge 40/60 Penfill[14]
Humulin-L[10]	Novolin ge 50/50 Penfill[14]
Humulin-N[13]	Novolin ge Toronto[7]
Humulin-R[7]	Novolin ge Toronto Penfill[7]
Humulin-U[5]	Novolin ge Ultralente[5]
Lente Iletin[8]	NPH Iletin[11]
Lente Iletin II[8]	NPH Iletin II[11]
Novolin ge 30/70[14]	Regular Iletin II[6]
Novolin ge Lente[10]	Velosulin Human[1]
Novolin ge NPH[13]	

Other commonly used names are:

Lente insulin, L[9]
NPH insulin, NPH[12]
Regular insulin, R1[2]
Semilente insulin, S[15]
Ultralente insulin, U[4]

Note: For quick reference, the following insulins are numbered to match the corresponding brand names.

This information applies to the following medicines:

1. Buffered Insulin Human (R) (IN-su-lin)
2. Buffered Insulin Human (R) or Insulin (R) or Insulin Human (R)
3. Extended Insulin Zinc (U)*†
4. Extended Insulin Zinc (U) or Extended Insulin Human Zinc (U)*†
5. Extended Insulin Human Zinc (U)
6. Insulin (R)
7. Insulin Human (R)
8. Insulin Zinc (L)
9. Insulin Zinc (L) or Insulin Human Zinc (L)
10. Insulin Human Zinc (L)
11. Isophane Insulin (NPH) (EYE-so-fayn)
12. Isophane Insulin (NPH) or Isophane Insulin Human (NPH)
13. Isophane Insulin Human (NPH)
14. Isophane Insulin Human and Insulin Human (NPH and R)
15. Prompt Insulin Zinc (S)*†

---

*Not commercially available in the U.S.
†Not commercially available in Canada.

Description

Insulin (IN-su-lin) is one of many hormones that helps the body turn the food we eat into energy. Also, insulin helps us store energy that we can use later. After we eat, insulin works by causing sugar (glucose) to go from the blood into our body's cells to make fat, sugar, and protein. When we need more energy between meals, insulin will help us use the fat, sugar, and protein that we have stored. This occurs whether we make our own insulin in the pancreas gland or take it by injection.

Diabetes mellitus (sugar diabetes) is a condition in which the body does not make enough insulin to meet its needs or does not properly use the insulin it makes. Without insulin, glucose cannot get into the body's cells. Without glucose, the cells will not work properly.

To work properly, the amount of insulin you use must be balanced against the amount and type of food you eat and the amount of exercise you do. If you change your diet, your exercise, or both without changing your insulin dose, your blood glucose level can drop too low or rise too high. A prescription is not necessary to purchase most insulin. However, your doctor must first determine your insulin needs and provide you with special instructions for control of your diabetes.

Insulin can be obtained from beef or pork pancreas glands. Another type of insulin that you may use is called human insulin. It is just like the insulin made by humans but it is made by methods called semi-synthetic or recombinant DNA. All types of insulin must be injected because, if taken by mouth, insulin is destroyed in the stomach.

Insulin is available in the following dosage forms:

Parenteral

Buffered Insulin Human (a regular insulin)
• Injection (U.S. and Canada)
Extended Insulin Zinc (an ultralente insulin)
• Injection
Extended Insulin Human Zinc (an ultralente insulin)
• Injection (U.S. and Canada)
Insulin (a regular insulin)
• Injection (U.S. and Canada)
Insulin Human (a regular insulin)
• Injection (U.S. and Canada)
Insulin Zinc (a lente insulin)
• Injection (U.S. and Canada)
Insulin Human Zinc (a lente insulin)
• Injection (U.S. and Canada)
Isophane Insulin (an NPH insulin)
• Injection (U.S. and Canada)
Isophane Insulin Human (an NPH insulin)
• Injection (U.S. and Canada)
Isophane Insulin Human and Insulin Human (an NPH and a regular insulin)
• Injection (U.S. and Canada)
Prompt Insulin Zinc (a semilente insulin)
• Injection

Before Using This Medicine

In deciding to use a medicine, the risks of taking the medicine must be weighed against the good it will do. This is a decision you and your doctor will make. For insulin, the following should be considered:

Allergies—Tell your doctor if you have ever had any reactions to insulin, especially in the skin area where you injected the insulin. Also, tell your health care professional if you are allergic to any other substances, such as foods, preservatives, or dyes.

Pregnancy—The amount of insulin you need changes during and after pregnancy. It is especially important for your health and your baby's health that your blood sugar be closely controlled. Close control of your blood sugar can reduce the chance of your baby gaining too much weight, having birth defects, or having high or low blood sugar. Be sure to tell your doctor if you plan to become pregnant or if you think you are pregnant.

Breast-feeding—Insulin does not pass into breast milk and will not affect the nursing infant. However, most women need less insulin while breast-feeding than they needed before. You will need to test your blood sugar often for several months in case your insulin dose needs to be changed.

Children—Children are especially sensitive to the effects of insulin before puberty (the time when sexual changes occur). Therefore, low blood sugar may be especially likely to occur.

Teenagers—Use in teenagers is similar to use in older age groups. The insulin need may be higher during puberty and lower after puberty.

Older adults—Use in older adults is similar to use in other age groups. However, sometimes the first signs of low or high blood sugar are missing or not easily seen in older patients. This may increase the chance of low blood sugar during treatment. Also, some older people may have vision problems or other medical problems that make it harder for them to measure and inject the medicine. Special training and equipment may be needed.

Other medicines—Although certain medicines should not be used together at all, in other cases two different medicines may be used together even if an interaction might occur. In these cases, your doctor may want to change the dose, or other precautions may be necessary. *Do not take any other medicine, unless prescribed or approved by your doctor.* When you are using insulin, it is especially important that your health care professional know if you are taking any of the following:

- Alcohol—Small amounts of alcohol taken with meals do not usually cause a problem; however, larger amounts of alcohol taken for a long time or in one sitting without food can increase the effect of insulin to lower the blood sugar level. This can keep the blood sugar low for a longer period of time than normal
- Beta-adrenergic blocking agents (acebutolol [e.g., Sectral], atenolol [e.g., Tenormin], betaxolol [e.g., Kerlone], bisoprolol [e.g., Zebeta], carteolol [e.g., Cartrol], labetalol [e.g., Normodyne], metoprolol [e.g., Lopressor], nadolol [e.g., Corgard], oxprenolol [e.g., Trasicor], penbutolol [e.g., Levatol], pindolol [e.g., Visken], propranolol [e.g., Inderal], sotalol [e.g., Sotacor], timolol [e.g., Blocadren])—Beta-adrenergic blocking agents may increase the chance of developing either high or low blood sugar levels. Also, they can cover up symptoms of low blood sugar (such as fast heartbeat). Because of this, a person with diabetes might not recognize that he or she has low blood sugar and might not take immediate steps to treat it. Beta-adrenergic blocking agents can also cause a low blood sugar level to last longer than normal
- Corticosteroids (e.g., prednisone or other cortisone-like medicines)—Corticosteroids taken over several weeks, applied to the skin over a long period of time, or injected into a joint may increase the blood sugar level. Higher doses of insulin may be needed during corticosteroid treatment and for a period of time after corticosteroid treatment ends
- Pentamidine (e.g., NebuPent)—Your dose of pentamidine or insulin or both may need to be adjusted if your pancreas can still make some insulin because pentamidine may cause your pancreas to release its insulin too fast. This effect at first lowers the blood sugar but then causes high blood sugar

Other medical problems—The presence of other medical problems may affect the dose of insulin you need. Be sure to tell your doctor if you have any other medical problems, especially:

- Changes in female hormones for some women (e.g., during puberty, pregnancy, or menstruation) or
- High fever or
- Infection, severe or
- Mental stress or
- Overactive adrenal gland, not properly controlled or

- Other conditions that cause high blood sugar—These conditions increase blood sugar and may increase the amount of insulin you need to take, make it necessary to change the time when you inject the insulin dose, and increase the need to take blood sugar tests

- Diarrhea or
- Gastroparesis (slow stomach emptying) or
- Intestinal blockage or
- Vomiting or
- Other conditions that delay food absorption or stomach emptying—These conditions may slow the time it takes to break down and absorb your meal from your stomach or intestines, which may change the amount of insulin you need, make it necessary to change the time when you inject the insulin dose, and increase the need to take blood sugar tests

- Injury or
- Surgery—Effects of insulin may be increased or decreased; the amount and type of insulin you need may change rapidly

- Kidney disease or
- Liver disease—Effects of insulin may be increased or decreased, partly because of slower removal of insulin from the body; this may change the amount of insulin you need

- Overactive thyroid, not properly controlled—Effects of insulin may be increased or decreased, partly because of faster removal of insulin from the body. Until your thyroid condition is controlled, the amount of insulin you need may change, make it necessary to change the time when you inject the insulin dose, and increase the need to take blood sugar tests

- Underactive adrenal gland, not properly controlled or
- Underactive pituitary gland, not properly controlled or
- Other conditions that cause low blood sugar—These conditions lower blood sugar and may lower the amount of insulin you need, make it necessary for you to change the time when you inject the insulin dose, and increase the need to take blood sugar tests

---

Proper Use of This Medicine

Make sure you have the type (beef and pork, pork, or human) and the strength of insulin that your doctor ordered for you. You may find that keeping an insulin label with you is helpful when buying insulin supplies.

The concentration (strength) of insulin is measured in USP Insulin Units and USP Insulin Human Units and is usually expressed in terms such as U-100 insulin. Insulin doses are measured and injected with specially marked insulin syringes. *The appropriate syringe is chosen based on your insulin dose to make measuring the dose easy to read. This helps you measure your dose accurately.* These syringes come in three sizes: 3/10 cubic centimeters (cc) measuring up to 30 USP Units of insulin, ½ cc measuring up to 50 USP Units of insulin, and 1 cc measuring up to 100 USP Units of insulin.

It is important to follow any instructions from your doctor about the careful selection and rotation of injection sites on your body.

There are several important steps that will help you successfully prepare your insulin injection. To draw the insulin up into the syringe correctly, you need to follow these steps:

- Wash your hands with soap and water.

- If your insulin contains zinc or isophane (normally cloudy), be sure that it is completely mixed. Mix the insulin by slowly rolling the bottle between your hands or gently tipping the bottle over a few times.
- Never shake the bottle vigorously (hard).
- Do not use the insulin if it looks lumpy or grainy, seems unusually thick, sticks to the bottle, or seems to be even a little discolored. Do not use the insulin if it contains crystals or if the bottle looks frosted. Regular insulin (short-acting) should be used only if it is clear and colorless.
- Remove the colored protective cap on the bottle. Do *not* remove the rubber stopper.
- Wipe the top of the bottle with an alcohol swab.
- Remove the needle cover from the insulin syringe.

How to prepare your insulin dose if you are using one type of insulin:
- Draw air into the syringe by pulling back on the plunger. The amount of air should be equal to your insulin dose.
- Gently push the needle through the top of the rubber stopper with the bottle standing upright.
- Push plunger in all the way to inject air into the bottle.
- Turn the bottle with syringe upside down in one hand. Be sure the tip of the needle is covered by the insulin. With your other hand, draw the plunger back slowly to draw the correct dose of insulin into the syringe.
- Check your dose. Hold the syringe with the scale at eye level to see that the proper dose is withdrawn and to check for air bubbles. Tap gently on the measuring scale of the syringe to move any bubbles to the top of the syringe near the needle. Then, push the insulin slowly back into the bottle and draw up your dose again.
- If your dose measures too low in the syringe, withdraw more solution from the bottle. If there is too much insulin in the syringe, put some back into the bottle. Then check your dose again.
- Remove the needle from the bottle and re-cover the needle.

How to prepare your insulin dose if you are using two types of insulin:
- When you mix regular insulin with another type of insulin, *always* draw the regular insulin into the syringe first. When you mix two types of insulins other than regular insulin, it does not matter in what order you draw them into the syringe.
- After you decide on a certain order for drawing up your insulin, you should use the same order each time.
- Some mixtures of insulins have to be injected immediately. Others may be stable for longer periods of time, which means that you can wait before you inject the mixture. Check with your health care professional to find out which type you have.
- Draw air into the syringe by pulling back on the plunger. The amount of air in the syringe should be equal to the part of the dose that you will be taking from the first bottle. Inject the air into the first bottle. *Do not draw the insulin yet.* Next, draw into the syringe an amount of air equal to the part of the dose that you will be taking from the *second* bottle. Inject the air into the second bottle.
- Return to the first bottle of the combination. With the plunger at zero, draw the first insulin dose of the combination (usually regular insulin) into the syringe.
- Check your dose. Hold the syringe with the scale at eye level to help you see that the proper dose is withdrawn and to check for air bubbles. Tap gently on the meas-

uring scale of the syringe to move any bubbles to the top of the syringe near the needle.
- At this point, if the first part of the dose measures too low in the syringe, you can withdraw more solution from the bottle. If there is too much insulin in your syringe, put some back into the bottle. Then check your dose again.
- Then, without moving the plunger, insert the needle into the second bottle of insulin and withdraw the dose. Sometimes withdrawing a little bit more insulin from the second bottle than needed will help you correct the second dose more easily when you remove the air bubbles.
- Again, check that the proper dose is withdrawn. The syringe will now contain two types of insulin. It is important *not* to squirt *any* extra solution from the syringe back into the bottle. Doing so might change the insulin in the bottle. Throw away any extra insulin in the syringe.
- *If you are not sure that you have done this correctly,* throw away the dose into the sink and begin the steps again. *Do not place any of the solutions back into either bottle.* You can use the same syringe to begin the procedure again.
- If you prepared your mixture ahead of time, gently turn the filled syringe back and forth to remix the insulins before you inject them. Do not shake the syringe.

How to inject your insulin dose:
- After you have prepared your syringe and chosen the area of your body to inject, you are ready to inject the insulin into the fatty skin.
  —Clean the area where the injection is to be given with an alcohol swab or with soap and water. Let the area dry.
  —Pinch up a large area of skin and hold it firmly. With your other hand, hold the syringe like a pencil. Push the needle straight into the pinched-up skin at a 90-degree angle for an adult or at a 45-degree angle for a child. Be sure the needle is all the way in. It is not necessary to draw back on the syringe each time to check for blood (also called routine aspiration).
  —Push the plunger all the way down, using less than 5 seconds to inject the dose. Let go of the skin. Hold an alcohol swab near the needle and pull the needle straight out of the skin.
  —Press the swab against the injection area for several seconds. Do not rub.
  —If you are either thin or greatly overweight, you may be given special instructions for giving yourself insulin injections.

How to use special injection devices:
- It is important to follow the information that comes with your insulin and with the device you use for injecting your insulin. This will ensure proper use and proper insulin dosing. If you need more information about this, ask your health care professional.

For patients using an *automatic injector* (with a disposable syringe):
- After the dose is drawn, the disposable syringe is placed inside the automatic injector. Pressing a button on the device quickly plunges the needle into the skin, releasing the insulin dose.

For patients using *a continuous subcutaneous infusion insulin pump:*

- Buffered regular human insulin, when available, is the recommended insulin for insulin pumps. Otherwise non-buffered regular insulin can be used.
- The pump consists of a tube, with a needle on the end of it that is taped to the abdomen, and a computerized device that is worn at the waist. Insulin is received continuously from the pump. A button is pressed at mealtime to release an extra insulin dose.
- It is important to follow the pump manufacturer's directions on how to load the syringe and/or pump reservoir. If you do not load the syringe and/or pump properly, you may not get the correct insulin dose.
- Check the infusion tubing and infusion-site dressing as often as your health care professional recommends to make sure the pump is working properly.

For patients using *disposable syringes:*

- Manufacturers of disposable syringes recommend that they be used only once, because the sterility of a reused syringe cannot be guaranteed. However, some patients prefer to reuse a syringe until its needle becomes dull. Most insulins have chemicals added that keep them from growing the bacteria that are usually found on the skin. However, the syringe should be thrown away when the needle becomes dull, has been bent, or has come into contact with any surface other than the cleaned and swabbed area of skin. If you plan to reuse a syringe, the needle must be recapped after each use. Check with your health care professional to find out the best way to reuse syringes.

For patients using an *insulin pen device* (cartridge and disposable needles):

- Change the dose by rotating the head of the pen. Put the pen next to your skin and press the plunger to inject the medicine. Some pen devices can only inject certain doses of insulin with each injection. Injection amounts can be different for different pen devices. To receive the right dose, you might have to count the number of times you press the plunger. Also, these devices use special cartridges of isophane insulin (NPH), regular insulin (R), or a mixture of these two types.

For patients using *nondisposable syringes* (glass syringe and metal needle):

- These types of syringes and needles may be used repeatedly if they are sterilized after each use. You should get an instruction sheet that tells you how to do this. If you need more information about this, ask your health care professional.

For patients using *a spray injector* (device without needles):

- The dose is measured by rotating part of the device. Insulin is drawn up into the spray device from an insulin bottle. Pressing a button forcefully sprays the insulin dose into the skin. This involves a wider area of skin than an injection would.

Laws in some states require that used insulin syringes and needles be destroyed. Be careful when you recap, bend, or break a needle, because these actions increase the chances of a needle-stick injury. It is best to put used syringes and needles in a disposable container that is puncture-resistant (such as an empty plastic liquid laundry detergent or bleach bottle) or to use a needle-clipping device. The chance of a syringe being reused by someone else is smaller if the plunger is taken out of the barrel and broken in half when you dispose of a syringe.

Use this medicine only as directed. Do not use more or less insulin than recommended by your doctor. To do so may increase the chance of serious side effects.

Your doctor will give you instructions about diet, exercise, how to test your blood sugar levels, and how to adjust your dose when you are sick.

- Diet—The daily number of calories in the meal plan should be adjusted by your doctor or a registered dietitian to help you reach and maintain a healthy body weight. In addition, regular meals and snacks are arranged to meet the energy needs of your body at different times of the day. *It is very important that you carefully follow your meal plan.*
- Exercise—Ask your doctor what kind of exercise to do, the best time to do it, and how much you should do each day.
- Blood tests—This is the best way to tell whether your diabetes is being controlled properly. Blood sugar testing helps you and your health care team adjust your insulin dose, meal plan, and exercise schedule.
- Changes in dose—Your doctor may change the first dose of the day. A change in the first dose of the day might change your blood sugar later in the day or change the amount of insulin you should use in other doses later that day. *That is why your doctor should know any time your dose changes, even temporarily, unless you have been told otherwise.*
- On sick days—When you become sick with a cold, fever, or the flu, you need to take your usual insulin dose, even if you feel too ill to eat. This is especially true if you have nausea, vomiting, or diarrhea. Infection usually increases your need for insulin. Call your doctor for specific instructions. Continue taking your insulin and try to stay on your regular meal plan. However, if you have trouble eating solid food, drink fruit juices, nondiet soft drinks, or clear soups, or eat small amounts of bland foods. A dietitian or your doctor can give you a list of foods and the amounts to use for sick days. Test your blood sugar level at least every 4 hours while you are awake and check your urine for ketones. If ketones are present, call your doctor at once. If you have severe or prolonged vomiting, check with your doctor. Even when you start feeling better, let your doctor know how you are doing.

Dosing—The dose of these medicines will be different for different patients. *Follow your doctor's orders or the directions on the label.* The following information applies to the average doses of these medicines. *If your dose is different, do not change it* unless your doctor tells you to do so.

The number of injections that you receive each day depends on the strength or type of the medicine. Also, *the number of doses you receive each day, the time allowed between doses, and the length of time you receive the medicine depend on the amount of sugar in your blood or urine.*

For regular insulin (R)—Crystalline zinc, human buffered, and human regular insulins

- For *injection* dosage form:
  —For treating sugar diabetes (diabetes mellitus):
    - Adults and teenagers—The dose is based on your blood sugar and must be determined by your doctor. The medicine is injected under the skin fifteen or thirty minutes before meals and/or a bed-

time snack. Also, your doctor may want you to use more than one type of insulin.
- Children—Dose is based on your blood sugar and body weight and must be determined by your doctor.

For isophane insulin (NPH)—Isophane and human isophane insulins
- For *injection* dosage form:
  —For treating sugar diabetes (diabetes mellitus):
  - Adults and teenagers—The dose is based on your blood sugar and must be determined by your doctor. The medicine is injected under the skin thirty to sixty minutes before a meal and/or a bedtime snack. Also, your doctor may want you to use more than one type of insulin.
  - Children—Dose is based on your blood sugar and body weight and must be determined by your doctor.

For isophane insulin human/insulin human (NPH/R)—Human isophane/human regular insulin
- For *injection* dosage form:
  —For treating sugar diabetes (diabetes mellitus):
  - Adults and teenagers—The dose is based on your blood sugar and must be determined by your doctor. The medicine is injected under the skin fifteen to thirty minutes before breakfast. You may need a dose before another meal or at bedtime. Also, your doctor may want you to use more than one type of insulin.
  - Children—Dose is based on your blood sugar and body weight and must be determined by your doctor.

For insulin zinc (L)—Lente and human lente insulins
- For *injection* dosage form:
  —For treating sugar diabetes (diabetes mellitus):
  - Adults and teenagers—The dose is based on your blood sugar and must be determined by your doctor. The medicine is injected under the skin thirty minutes before breakfast. You may need a dose before another meal and/or a bedtime snack. Also, your doctor may want you to use more than one type of insulin.
  - Children—Dose is based on your blood sugar and body weight and must be determined by your doctor.

For insulin zinc extended (U)—Ultralente and human ultralente insulins
- For *injection* dosage form:
  —For treating sugar diabetes (diabetes mellitus):
  - Adults and teenagers—The dose is based on your blood sugar and must be determined by your doctor. The medicine is injected under the skin thirty to sixty minutes before a meal and/or a bedtime snack. Your doctor may want you to use more than one type of insulin.
  - Children—Dose is based on your blood sugar and body weight and must be determined by your doctor.

For prompt insulin zinc (S)—Semilente insulin
- For *injection* dosage form:
  —For treating sugar diabetes (diabetes mellitus):
  - Adults and teenagers—The dose is based on your blood sugar and must be determined by your

doctor. The medicine is injected under the skin thirty to sixty minutes before breakfast. You may need a dose thirty minutes before another meal and/or a bedtime snack. Your doctor may want you to use more than one type of insulin.
- Children—Dose is based on your blood sugar and body weight and must be determined by your doctor.

Storage—To store this medicine:
- Unopened bottles of insulin should be refrigerated until needed and may be used until the printed expiration date on the label. Insulin should never be frozen. Remove the insulin from the refrigerator and allow it to reach room temperature before injecting it.
- An insulin bottle in use may be kept at room temperature for up to 1 month. Insulin that has been kept at room temperature for longer than a month should be thrown away.
- Storing prefilled syringes in the refrigerator with the needle pointed up reduces problems that can occur, such as crystals forming in the needle and blocking it up.
- Do not expose insulin to extremely hot temperatures or to sunlight. Extreme heat will cause insulin to become less effective much more quickly.

Precautions While Using This Medicine

It is very important that your doctor check your progress at regular visits, especially during the first few weeks of insulin treatment.

It is very important to follow carefully any instructions from your health care team about:
- Alcohol—Drinking alcohol may cause severe low blood sugar. Discuss this with your health care team.
- Tobacco—If you have been smoking for a long time and suddenly stop, your dosage of insulin may need to be reduced. If you decide to quit, tell your doctor first.
- Other medicines—Do not take other medicines unless they have been discussed with your doctor. This especially includes nonprescription medicines such as aspirin, and medicines for appetite control, asthma, colds, cough, hay fever, or sinus problems.
- Counseling—Other family members need to learn how to prevent side effects or help with side effects if they occur. Also, patients with diabetes, especially teenagers, may need special counseling about insulin dosing changes that might occur because of lifestyle changes, such as changes in exercise and diet. Furthermore, counseling on contraception and pregnancy may be needed because of the problems that can occur in women with diabetes who become pregnant.
- Travel—Keep a recent prescription and your medical history with you. Be prepared for an emergency as you would normally. Make allowances for changing time zones, keep your meal times as close as possible to your usual meal times, and store insulin properly.

In case of emergency —There may be a time when you need emergency help for a problem caused by your diabetes. You need to be prepared for these emergencies. It is a good idea to:
- Wear a medical identification (ID) bracelet or neck chain at all times. Also, carry an ID card in your wallet or purse that says that you have diabetes and lists all of your medicines.

© 2002 MICROMEDEX Thomson Healthcare

- Keep an extra supply of insulin and syringes with needles on hand in case high blood sugar occurs.
- Keep some kind of quick-acting sugar handy to treat low blood sugar.
- Have a glucagon kit available in case severe low blood sugar occurs. Check and replace any expired kits regularly.

Too much insulin can cause low blood sugar (also called hypoglycemia or insulin reaction). *Symptoms of low blood sugar must be treated before they lead to unconsciousness (passing out).* Different people may feel different symptoms of low blood sugar. *It is important that you learn what symptoms of low blood sugar you usually have so that you can treat it quickly.*

- Symptoms of low blood sugar can include: anxious feeling, behavior change similar to being drunk, blurred vision, cold sweats, confusion, cool pale skin, difficulty in concentrating, drowsiness, excessive hunger, fast heartbeat, headache, nausea, nervousness, nightmares, restless sleep, shakiness, slurred speech, and unusual tiredness or weakness.
- The symptoms of low blood sugar may develop quickly and may result from:
  —delaying or missing a scheduled meal or snack.
  —exercising more than usual.
  —drinking a significant amount of alcohol.
  —taking certain medicines.
  —using too much insulin.
  —sickness (especially with vomiting or diarrhea).
- Know what to do if symptoms of low blood sugar occur. Eating some form of quick-acting sugar when symptoms of low blood sugar first appear will usually prevent them from getting worse. Good sources of sugar include:
  —Glucose tablets or gel, fruit juice or nondiet soft drink (4 to 6 ounces [one-half cup]), corn syrup or honey (1 tablespoon), sugar cubes (six one-half inch size), or table sugar (dissolved in water).
    - If a snack is not scheduled for an hour or more you should also eat a light snack, such as cheese and crackers, half a sandwich, or drink an 8-ounce glass of milk.
    - Do not use chocolate because its fat slows down the sugar entering into the blood stream.
  —Glucagon is used in emergency situations such as unconsciousness. Have a glucagon kit available and know how to prepare and use it. Members of your household also should know how and when to use it.

High blood sugar (hyperglycemia) is another problem related to uncontrolled diabetes. *If you have any symptoms of high blood sugar, contact your health care team right away.* If high blood sugar is not treated, severe hyperglycemia can occur, leading to ketoacidosis (diabetic coma) and death.

- The symptoms of mild high blood sugar appear more slowly than those of low blood sugar. Symptoms can include: blurred vision; drowsiness; dry mouth; flushed and dry skin; fruit-like breath odor; increased urination (frequency and volume); loss of appetite; stomachache, nausea, or vomiting; tiredness; troubled breathing (rapid and deep); and unusual thirst.
- Symptoms of severe high blood sugar (called ketoacidosis or diabetic coma) that need immediate hospitalization include: flushed and dry skin, fruit-like breath odor, ketones in urine, passing out, and troubled breathing (rapid and deep).

- High blood sugar symptoms may occur if you:
  —have diarrhea, a fever, or an infection.
  —do not take enough insulin or skip a dose of insulin.
  —do not exercise as much as usual.
  —overeat or do not follow your meal plan.
- Know what to do if high blood sugar occurs. Your doctor may recommend changes in your insulin dose or meal plan to avoid high blood sugar. Symptoms of high blood sugar must be corrected before they progress to more serious conditions. Check with your doctor often to make sure you are controlling your blood sugar. Your doctor might discuss the following with you:
  —Increasing your insulin dose when you plan to eat an unusually large dinner, such as on holidays. This type of increase is called an anticipatory dose.
  —Decreasing your dose for a short time for special needs, such as when you cannot exercise as you normally do. Changing only one type of insulin dose (usually the first dose) and anticipating how the change may affect other doses during the day. Contacting your doctor if you need a permanent change in dose.
  —Delaying a meal if your blood glucose is over 200 mg/dL to allow time for your blood sugar to go down. An extra insulin dose may be needed if your blood sugar does not come down shortly.
  —Not exercising if your blood glucose is over 240 mg/dL and reporting this to your doctor immediately.
  —Being hospitalized if ketoacidosis or diabetic coma occurs.

Side Effects of This Medicine

Along with its needed effects, a medicine may cause some unwanted effects. Although not all of these side effects may occur, if they do occur they may need medical attention.

Check with your doctor immediately if any of the following side effects occur:
> *More common*
> Convulsions (seizures); unconsciousness

Also, check with your doctor as soon as possible if any of the following side effects occur:
> *More common*
> Low blood sugar (mild), including anxious feeling, behavior change similar to being drunk, blurred vision, cold sweats, confusion, cool pale skin, difficulty in concentrating, drowsiness, excessive hunger, fast heartbeat, headache, nausea, nervousness, nightmares, restless sleep, shakiness, slurred speech, unusual tiredness or weakness; weight gain

> *Rare*
> Depressed skin at the place of injection; swelling of face, fingers, feet, or ankles; thickening of the skin at the place of injection

Not all of the side effects listed above have been reported for each of these medicines, but they have been reported for at least one of them. All of the insulins are similar, so any of the above side effects may occur with any of these medicines.

Other side effects not listed above may also occur in some patients. If you notice any other effects, check with your doctor.

Additional Information

Once a medicine has been approved for marketing for a certain use, experience may show that it is also useful for other medical problems. Although this use is not included in product labeling, regular insulin is used in certain patients:

- To test for growth hormone deficiency
- To prevent complications of diabetes, including eye problems (retinopathy), kidney disease (nephropathy), and nerve damage (neuropathy)

Other than the above information, there is no additional information relating to proper use, precautions, or side effects for this use.

Revised: 04/06/2001

INSULIN ASPART Systemic†—
INTRODUCTORY VERSION

Commonly used brand name(s):

In the U.S.—
NovoLog

†Not commercially available in Canada.

Description

Insulin aspart (IN-su-lin AS-part) is a fast-acting type of human insulin. Insulin is used by people with sugar diabetes to help keep blood sugar levels under control. If you have sugar diabetes, your body cannot make enough or does not use insulin properly. So, you must take additional insulin to regulate your blood sugar and keep your body healthy. This is very important as too much sugar in your blood can be harmful to your health. Since insulin aspart acts faster than regular human insulin, you normally should use insulin aspart with a longer-acting insulin.

This medicine is available only with your doctor's prescription, in the following dosage forms:

Parenteral
- Injection (U.S.)

Before Using This Medicine

In deciding to use a medicine, the risks of taking the medicine must be weighed against the good it will do. This is a decision you and your doctor will make. For insulin aspart, the following should be considered:

Allergies—Tell your doctor if you have ever had any unusual or allergic reaction to insulin aspart. Also tell your health care professional if you are allergic to any other substances, such as foods, preservatives, or dyes.

Pregnancy—The amount of insulin or insulin aspart you need changes during pregnancy. It is especially important for your health and your baby's health that your blood sugar be closely controlled before you become pregnant and throughout pregnancy.

Breast-feeding—It is not known whether insulin aspart passes into human breast milk. Although most medicines, including human insulin, pass into breast milk in small amounts, many of them may be used safely while breast-feeding.

Mothers who are taking this medicine and who wish to breast-feed should discuss this with their doctor.

Children—Studies on this medicine have been done only in adult patients, and there is no specific information comparing use of insulin aspart in children with use in other age groups.

Older adults—This medicine has been tested in a limited number of patients 65 years of age or older and has not been shown to cause different side effects or problems in older people than it does in younger adults.

Other medicines—Although certain medicines should not be used together at all, in other cases two different medicines may be used together even if an interaction might occur. In these cases, your doctor may want to change the dose, or other precautions may be necessary. When you are taking insulin aspart, it is especially important that your doctor and pharmacist know if you are taking any of the following:

- Beta-adrenergic blocking agents (acebutolol [e.g., Sectral], atenolol [e.g., Tenormin], betaxolol [e.g., Kerlone], bisoprolol [e.g., Zebeta], carteolol [e.g., Cartrol], labetalol [e.g., Normodyne, Trandate], metoprolol [e.g., Lopressor], nadolol [e.g., Corgard], oxprenolol [e.g., Trasicor], penbutolol [e.g., Levatol], pindolol [e.g., Visken], propranolol [e.g., Inderal], sotalol [e.g., Betapace], timolol [e.g., Blocadren]) or
- Clonidine (e.g., Catapres, Duraclon) or
- Guanethidine (e.g., Ismelin) or
- Reserpine (e.g., Serpasil)—These medicines may hide symptoms of low blood sugar (such as fast heartbeat). Thus, a person with diabetes might not recognize that he or she has low blood sugar and might not take immediate steps to treat it

Other medical problems—The presence of other medical problems may affect the use of insulin aspart. Make sure you tell your doctor if you have any other medical problems, especially:

- Hypoglycemia (low blood sugar)—If you have low blood sugar and take insulin, your blood sugar may reach dangerously low levels

- Kidney disease or
- Liver disease—Effects of insulin aspart may be increased or decreased; your doctor may need to change your insulin dose

Proper Use of This Medicine

It is best to use a different place on the body for each injection (e.g., abdomen, thigh, or upper arm). If you have questions about this, contact a member of your health care team.

When used as a mealtime insulin, insulin aspart should be taken within 5-10 minutes before the meal or immediately before the meal.

Follow carefully the special meal plan your doctor gave you. This is the most important part of controlling your condition, and is necessary if the medicine is to work properly. Also, exercise regularly and test for sugar in your blood or urine as directed.

Dosing—The dose of insulin aspart will be different for different patients. *Follow your doctor's orders or the directions on the label.*

- For *injection* dosage form:
  —For diabetes mellitus (sugar diabetes):
  - Adults—The dose is based on your blood sugar and must be determined by your doctor.
  - Children—Use and dose must be determined by your doctor.

Storage—To store this medicine:

- Keep out of the reach of children.
- Store away from heat and direct light.
- Store in the refrigerator. However, keep the medicine from freezing.
- After a cartridge has been inserted into a pen, store the cartridge and pen at room temperature, not in the refrigerator.
- Do not keep outdated medicine or medicine no longer needed. Be sure that any discarded medicine is out of the reach of children.

Precautions While Using This Medicine

Your doctor will want to check your progress at regular visits, especially during the first few weeks you take this medicine.

It is very important to follow carefully any instructions from your health care team about:

- Alcohol—Drinking alcohol may cause severe low blood sugar. Discuss this with your health care team.
- Other medicines—Do not take other medicines during the time you are taking insulin aspart unless they have been discussed with your doctor. This especially includes nonprescription medicines such as aspirin, and medicines for appetite control, asthma, colds, cough, hay fever, or sinus problems.
- Counseling—Other family members need to learn how to prevent side effects or help with side effects if they occur. Also, patients with diabetes may need special counseling about diabetes medicine dosing changes that might occur because of lifestyle changes, such as changes in exercise and diet. Furthermore, counseling on contraception and pregnancy may be needed because of the problems that can occur in patients with diabetes during pregnancy.
- Travel—Keep a recent prescription and your medical history with you. Be prepared for an emergency as you would normally. Make allowances for changing time zones and keep your meal times as close as possible to your usual meal times.

In case of emergency—There may be a time when you need emergency help for a problem caused by your diabetes. You need to be prepared for these emergencies. It is a good idea to:

- Wear a medical identification (ID) bracelet or neck chain at all times. Also, carry an ID card in your wallet or purse that says that you have diabetes and a list of all of your medicines.

Too much insulin aspart can cause hypoglycemia (low blood sugar). *Symptoms of low blood sugar include* anxiety; behavior change similar to being drunk; blurred vision; cold sweats; confusion; depression; difficulty in thinking; dizziness or light-headedness; drowsiness; excessive hunger; fast heartbeat; headache; irritability or abnormal behavior; nervousness; nightmares; restless sleep; shakiness; slurred speech; and tingling in the hands, feet, lips, or tongue.

Low blood sugar also can occur if you use insulin aspart with another antidiabetic medicine, delay or miss a meal or snack, exercise more than usual, drink alcohol, or cannot eat because of nausea or vomiting or have diarrhea.

If symptoms of low blood sugar occur, *eat glucose tablets or gel to relieve the symptoms.* Also, check your blood for low blood sugar. *Get to a doctor or a hospital right away if the symptoms do not improve. Someone should call for emergency help immediately if severe symptoms such as convulsions (seizures) or unconsciousness occur.* Have a glucagon kit available, along with a syringe and needle, and know how to use it. Members of your household also should know how to use it.

Symptoms of high blood sugar include blurred vision; drowsiness; dry mouth; flushed, dry skin; fruit-like breath odor; increased urination; ketones in urine; loss of appetite; stomachache, nausea, or vomiting; tiredness; troubled breathing (rapid and deep); unconsciousness; and unusual thirst.

Hyperglycemia (high blood sugar) may occur if you do not take enough or skip a dose of your antidiabetic medicine, overeat or do not follow your meal plan, have a fever or infection, or do not exercise as much as usual.

If symptoms of high blood sugar occur, *check your blood sugar level and then call your doctor for instructions.*

Side Effects of This Medicine

Along with its needed effects, a medicine may cause some unwanted effects. Although not all of these side effects may occur, if they do occur they may need medical attention.

Check with your doctor immediately if any of the following side effects occur:

    More common
       Convulsions (seizures); unconsciousness

Check with your doctor as soon as possible if any of the following side effects occur:

    More common
       Low blood sugar; anxious feeling; behavior change similar to being drunk; blurred vision; cold sweats; confusion; depression; difficulty in thinking; dizziness or light-headedness; drowsiness; excessive hunger; fast heartbeat; headache; irritability or abnormal behavior; nervousness; nightmares; restless sleep; shakiness; slurred speech; tingling in the hands, feet, lips, or tongue

    Less common or rare
       Depression of the skin at place of injection; thickening of the skin at place of injection; dryness of mouth; irregular heartbeat; increased thirst; loss of appetite; mood or mental changes; muscle cramps or pain; nausea or vomiting; shortness of breath; unusual tiredness or weakness; fast or weak pulse; sweating; skin rash or itching over the whole body; wheezing; feeling of pressure, itching, redness, soreness, stinging; swelling, or tingling at place of injection

Other side effects not listed above may also occur in some patients. If you notice any other effects, check with your doctor.

Developed: 01/18/2001

INSULIN GLARGINE   Systemic—INTRODUCTORY VERSION

Commonly used brand name(s):

In the U.S.—
   Lantus

Description

Insulin glargine (IN-su-lin GLARE-jeen) is a type of insulin. Insulin is one of many hormones that help the body turn the food we eat into energy. This is done by using the glucose (sugar) in the blood as quick energy. Also, insulin helps us store energy that we can use later. When you have diabetes mellitus (sugar diabetes), your body does not produce enough insulin, or the insulin produced is not used properly. This causes you to have too much sugar in your blood. Like other types of insulin, insulin glargine is used to keep your blood sugar level close to normal. Insulin glargine is a long-acting insulin that works slowly over about 24 hours. You may have to use insulin glargine in combination with another type of insulin or with a type of oral diabetes medicine to keep your blood sugar under control.

This medicine is available only with your doctor's prescription, in the following dosage forms:

   Parenteral
   • Injection (U.S.)

Before Using This Medicine

In deciding to use a medicine, the risks of taking the medicine must be weighed against the good it will do. This is a decision you and your doctor will make. For insulin glargine, the following should be considered:

Allergies—Tell your doctor if you have ever had any unusual or allergic reaction to insulin glargine. Also tell your health care professional if you are allergic to any other substances, such as foods, preservatives, or dyes.

Pregnancy—The amount of insulin or insulin glargine you need changes during pregnancy. It is especially important for your health and your baby's health that your blood sugar be closely controlled.

Breast-feeding—It is not known whether insulin glargine passes into breast milk. However, your insulin glargine dosage, your meal plan, or both may need adjustment.

Children—This medicine has been tested in a limited number of children 6 years of age or older. In effective doses, the medicine has not been shown to cause different side effects or problems than it does in adults.

Older adults—This medicine has been tested in a limited number of patients 65 years of age or older and has not been shown to cause different side effects or problems in older people than it does in younger adults.

Other medicines—Although certain medicines should not be used together at all, in other cases two different medicines may be used together even if an interaction might occur. In these cases, your doctor may want to change the dose, or other precautions may be necessary. When you are taking insulin glargine, it is especially important that your health care professional know if you are taking any of the following:
   • Beta-adrenergic blocking agents (acebutolol [e.g., Sectral], atenolol [e.g., Tenormin], betaxolol [e.g., Kerlone], bisoprolol [e.g., Zebeta], carteolol [e.g., Cartrol], labetalol [e.g., Normodyne, Trandate], metoprolol [e.g., Lopressor], nadolol [e.g., Corgard], oxprenolol [e.g., Trasicor], penbutolol [e.g., Levatol], pindolol [e.g., Visken], propranolol [e.g., Inderal], sotalol [e.g., Betapace], timolol [e.g., Blocadren]) or
   • Clonidine (e.g., Catapres) or
   • Guanethidine (e.g., Ismelin) or
   • Reserpine (e.g., Serpalan)—These medicines may hide symptoms of low blood sugar (such as fast heartbeat). Because of this, a person with diabetes might not recognize that he or she has low blood sugar and might not take immediate steps to treat it

Other medical problems—The presence of other medical problems may affect the use of insulin glargine. Make sure you tell your doctor if you have any other medical problems, especially:
   • Emotional disturbances or
   • Infection or
   • Stress—These conditions increase blood sugar and may increase the amount of insulin or insulin glargine you need
   • Kidney disease or
   • Liver disease—Effects of insulin glargine may be increased; this may change the amount of insulin glargine you need

Proper Use of This Medicine

Dosing— *Each package of insulin glargine contains a patient information sheet. Read this sheet carefully and make sure you understand:*
   • How to prepare the medicine.
   • How to inject the medicine.
   • How to dispose of syringes, needles, and injection devices.

It is best to use a different place on the body for each injection (e.g., abdomen, thigh, or upper arm). If you have questions about this, contact a member of your health care team.

Since insulin glargine lowers the blood glucose over 24 hours, it should be taken once daily at bedtime

Follow carefully the special meal plan your doctor gave you. This is the most important part of controlling your condition, and is necessary if the medicine is to work properly. Also, exercise regularly and test for sugar in your blood or urine as directed.

The dose of insulin glargine will be different for different patients. *Follow your doctor's orders or the directions on the label.*
   • For *injection* dosage form:
      —For diabetes mellitus (sugar diabetes):
         • Adults, teenagers, and children 6 years of age or older—The dose is based on your blood sugar and must be determined by your doctor.
         • Children up to 6 years of age—Use and dose must be determined by your doctor.

Storage—To store this medicine:
   • Keep out of the reach of children.
   • Store away from heat and direct light.
   • Store in the refrigerator. However, keep the medicine from freezing.
   • After a cartridge has been inserted into a pen, store the cartridge and pen at room temperature, not in the refrigerator.

- Do not keep outdated medicine or medicine no longer needed. Be sure that any discarded medicine is out of the reach of children.

Precautions While Using This Medicine

Your doctor will want to check your progress at regular visits, especially during the first few weeks you take this medicine.

It is very important to follow carefully any instructions from your health care team about:

- Alcohol—Drinking alcohol may cause severe low blood sugar. Discuss this with your health care team.
- Other medicines—Do not take other medicines during the time you are taking insulin glargine unless they have been discussed with your doctor. This especially includes nonprescription medicines such as aspirin, and medicines for appetite control, asthma, colds, cough, hay fever, or sinus problems.
- Counseling—Other family members need to learn how to prevent side effects or help with side effects if they occur. Also, patients with diabetes may need special counseling about diabetes medicine dosing changes that might occur because of lifestyle changes, such as changes in exercise and diet. Furthermore, counseling on contraception and pregnancy is needed because of the problems that can occur in patients with diabetes during pregnancy.
- Travel—Keep a recent prescription and your medical history with you. Be prepared for an emergency as you would normally. Make allowances for changing time zones and keep your meal times as close as possible to your usual meal times.

In case of emergency—There may be a time when you need emergency help for a problem caused by your diabetes. You need to be prepared for these emergencies. It is a good idea to:

- Wear a medical identification (ID) bracelet or neck chain at all times. Also, carry an ID card in your wallet or purse that says that you have diabetes and a list of all of your medicines.
- Keep an extra supply of insulin glargine and syringes with needles or injection devices on hand in case high blood sugar occurs.
- Keep some kind of quick-acting sugar handy to treat low blood sugar.
- Have a glucagon kit and a syringe and needle available in case severe low blood sugar occurs. Check and replace any expired kits regularly.

Too much insulin glargine can cause hypoglycemia (low blood sugar). Low blood sugar also can occur if you use insulin glargine with another antidiabetic medicine, delay or miss a meal or snack, exercise more than usual, or drink alcohol. *Symptoms of low blood sugar must be treated before they lead to unconsciousness (passing out).* Different people may feel different symptoms of low blood sugar. *It is important that you learn which symptoms of low blood sugar you usually have so that you can treat it quickly.*

Symptoms of low blood sugar include anxiety; behavior change similar to being drunk; blurred vision; cold sweats; confusion; difficulty in thinking; dizziness or lightheadedness; drowsiness; excessive hunger; fast heartbeat; headache; irritability or abnormal behavior; nervousness; nightmares; restless sleep; shakiness; slurred speech; and tingling in the hands, feet, lips, or tongue.

If symptoms of low blood sugar occur, *eat glucose tablets or gel, corn syrup, honey, or sugar cubes; or drink fruit juice, nondiet soft drink, or sugar dissolved in water to relieve the symptoms.* Also, check your blood for low blood sugar. *Get to a doctor or a hospital right away if the symptoms do not improve. Someone should call for emergency help immediately if severe symptoms such as convulsions (seizures) or unconsciousness occur.* Have a glucagon kit available, along with a syringe and needle, and know how to use it. Members of your household also should know how to use it.

Hyperglycemia (high blood sugar) may occur if you do not take enough or skip a dose of your antidiabetic medicine, overeat or do not follow your meal plan, have emotional stress or infection, or do not exercise as much as usual.

Symptoms of high blood sugar include blurred vision; drowsiness; dry mouth; flushed, dry skin; fruit-like breath odor; increased urination; ketones in urine; loss of appetite; stomachache, nausea, or vomiting; tiredness; troubled breathing (rapid and deep); unconsciousness; and unusual thirst.

If symptoms of high blood sugar occur, *check your blood sugar level and then call your doctor for instructions.*

Side Effects of This Medicine

Along with its needed effects, a medicine may cause some unwanted effects. Although not all of these side effects may occur, if they do occur they may need medical attention.

Check with your doctor immediately if any of the following side effects occur:
More common
Convulsions (seizures); unconsciousness

Check with your doctor as soon as possible if any of the following side effects occur:
More common
Low blood sugar, including anxious feeling; behavior change similar to being drunk; blurred vision; cold sweats; confusion; cool, pale skin; difficulty in thinking; dizziness or lightheadedness; drowsiness; excessive hunger; fast heartbeat; headache; nausea; nervousness; nightmares; restless sleep; shakiness; slurred speech; and tingling in the hands, feet, lips, or tongue

Less common or rare
Allergic reaction, including fast pulse, shortness of breath, skin rash or itching over the entire body, sweating, and wheezing

Other side effects may occur that usually do not need medical attention. These side effects may go away during treatment as your body adjusts to the medicine. However, check with your doctor if any of the following side effects continue or are bothersome.
Less common or rare
Bloating or swelling of face, hands, lower legs, and/or feet; depression of skin at injection site; injection site pain; local allergy, including itching, redness, or swelling at injection site; thickening of skin at injection site

Other side effects not listed above may also occur in some patients. If you notice any other effects, check with your doctor.

Developed: 08/07/2000

INSULIN LISPRO   Systemic

Commonly used brand name(s):

In the U.S.—
   Humalog

Description

Insulin lispro (IN-su-lin LYE-sproe) is a type of insulin. Insulin is one of many hormones that help the body turn the food we eat into energy. This is done by using the glucose (sugar) in the blood as quick energy. Also, insulin helps us store energy that we can use later. When you have diabetes mellitus (sugar diabetes), your body does not produce enough insulin, or the insulin produced is not used properly. This causes you to have too much sugar in your blood. Like other types of insulin, insulin lispro is used to keep your blood sugar level close to normal. Insulin lispro works faster than other types of insulin; therefore, you may have to use insulin lispro in combination with another type of insulin or with a type of oral diabetes medicine called a sulfonylurea to keep your blood sugar under control.

This medicine is available only with your doctor's prescription, in the following dosage form:

   Parenteral
   • Injection (U.S.)

Before Using This Medicine

In deciding to use a medicine, the risks of taking the medicine must be weighed against the good it will do. This is a decision you and your doctor will make. For insulin lispro, the following should be considered:

Allergies—Tell your doctor if you have ever had any unusual or allergic reaction to insulin lispro. Also tell your health care professional if you are allergic to any other substances, such as foods, preservatives, or dyes.

Pregnancy—The amount of insulin or insulin lispro you need changes during pregnancy. It is especially important for your health and your baby's health that your blood sugar be closely controlled.

Breast-feeding—It is not known whether insulin lispro passes into breast milk. However, your insulin lispro dosage, your meal plan, or both may need adjustment.

Children— This medicine has been tested in a limited number of children 3 years of age or older. In effective doses, the medicine has not been shown to cause different side effects or problems than it does in adults.

Older adults— This medicine has been tested in a limited number of patients 65 years of age or older and has not been shown to cause different side effects or problems in older people than it does in younger adults.

Other medicines—Although certain medicines should not be used together at all, in other cases two different medicines may be used together even if an interaction might occur. In these cases, your doctor may want to change the dose, or other precautions may be necessary. When you are taking insulin lispro, it is especially important that your health care professional know if you are taking any of the following:
   • Beta-adrenergic blocking agents (acebutolol [e.g., Sectral], atenolol [e.g., Tenormin], betaxolol [e.g., Kerlone], bisoprolol [e.g., Zebeta], carteolol [e.g., Cartrol], labetalol [e.g., Normodyne, Trandate], metoprolol [e.g., Lo-

pressor], nadolol [e.g., Corgard], oxprenolol [e.g., Trasicor], penbutolol [e.g., Levatol], pindolol [e.g., Visken], propranolol [e.g., Inderal], sotalol [e.g., Betapace], timolol [e.g., Blocadren])—These medicines may hide symptoms of low blood sugar (such as fast heartbeat). Because of this, a person with diabetes might not recognize that he or she has low blood sugar and might not take immediate steps to treat it

Other medical problems—The presence of other medical problems may affect the use of insulin lispro. Make sure you tell your doctor if you have any other medical problems, especially:
   • Diarrhea or
   • Underactive adrenal gland or
   • Underactive pituitary gland or
   • Vomiting—These conditions lower blood sugar and may lower the amount of insulin or insulin lispro you need

   • Fever or
   • Infection—These conditions increase blood sugar and may increase the amount of insulin or insulin lispro you need

   • Kidney disease or
   • Liver disease—Effects of insulin lispro may be increased or decreased; this may change the amount of insulin lispro you need

Proper Use of This Medicine

Each package of insulin lispro contains a patient information sheet. Read this sheet carefully and make sure you understand:
   • How to prepare the medicine.
   • How to inject the medicine.
   • How to dispose of syringes, needles, and injection devices.

It is best to use a different place on the body for each injection (e.g., abdomen, thigh, or upper arm). If you have questions about this, contact a member of your health care team.

When used as a mealtime insulin, insulin lispro should be taken within 15 minutes before the meal or immediately after the meal.

Follow carefully the special meal plan your doctor gave you. This is the most important part of controlling your condition, and is necessary if the medicine is to work properly. Also, exercise regularly and test for sugar in your blood or urine as directed.

Dosing—The dose of insulin lispro will be different for different patients. *Follow your doctor's orders or the directions on the label.*
   • For *injection* dosage form:
      —For diabetes mellitus (sugar diabetes):
         • Adults and teenagers—The dose is based on your blood sugar and must be determined by your doctor.
         • Children—Use and dose must be determined by your doctor.

Storage—To store this medicine:
   • Keep out of the reach of children.
   • Store away from heat and direct light.
   • Store in the refrigerator. However, keep the medicine from freezing.

- After a cartridge has been inserted into a pen, store the cartridge and pen at room temperature, not in the refrigerator.
- Do not keep outdated medicine or medicine no longer needed. Be sure that any discarded medicine is out of the reach of children.

Precautions While Using This Medicine

Your doctor will want to check your progress at regular visits, especially during the first few weeks you take this medicine.

It is very important to follow carefully any instructions from your health care team about:

- Alcohol—Drinking alcohol may cause severe low blood sugar. Discuss this with your health care team.
- Other medicines—Do not take other medicines during the time you are taking insulin lispro unless they have been discussed with your doctor. This especially includes nonprescription medicines such as aspirin, and medicines for appetite control, asthma, colds, cough, hay fever, or sinus problems.
- Counseling—Other family members need to learn how to prevent side effects or help with side effects if they occur. Also, patients with diabetes may need special counseling about diabetes medicine dosing changes that might occur because of lifestyle changes, such as changes in exercise and diet. Furthermore, counseling on contraception and pregnancy may be needed because of the problems that can occur in patients with diabetes during pregnancy.
- Travel—Keep a recent prescription and your medical history with you. Be prepared for an emergency as you would normally. Make allowances for changing time zones and keep your meal times as close as possible to your usual meal times.

In case of emergency—There may be a time when you need emergency help for a problem caused by your diabetes. You need to be prepared for these emergencies. It is a good idea to:

- Wear a medical identification (ID) bracelet or neck chain at all times. Also, carry an ID card in your wallet or purse that says that you have diabetes and a list of all of your medicines.
- Keep an extra supply of insulin lispro and syringes with needles or injection devices on hand in case high blood sugar occurs.
- Keep some kind of quick-acting sugar handy to treat low blood sugar.
- Have a glucagon kit and a syringe and needle available in case severe low blood sugar occurs. Check and replace any expired kits regularly.

Too much insulin lispro can cause hypoglycemia (low blood sugar). Low blood sugar also can occur if you use insulin lispro with another antidiabetic medicine, delay or miss a meal or snack, exercise more than usual, drink alcohol, or cannot eat because of nausea or vomiting or have diarrhea. *Symptoms of low blood sugar must be treated before they lead to unconsciousness (passing out).* Different people may feel different symptoms of low blood sugar. *It is important that you learn which symptoms of low blood sugar you usually have so that you can treat it quickly.*

Symptoms of low blood sugar include anxiety; behavior change similar to being drunk; blurred vision; cold sweats; confusion; depression; difficulty in thinking; dizziness or light-headedness; drowsiness; excessive hunger; fast heartbeat; headache; irritability or abnormal behavior; nervousness; nightmares; restless sleep; shakiness; slurred speech; and tingling in the hands, feet, lips, or tongue.

If symptoms of low blood sugar occur, *eat glucose tablets or gel, corn syrup, honey, or sugar cubes; or drink fruit juice, nondiet soft drink, or sugar dissolved in water to relieve the symptoms.* Also, check your blood for low blood sugar. *Get to a doctor or a hospital right away if the symptoms do not improve. Someone should call for emergency help immediately if severe symptoms such as convulsions (seizures) or unconsciousness occur.* Have a glucagon kit available, along with a syringe and needle, and know how to use it. Members of your household also should know how to use it.

Hyperglycemia (high blood sugar) may occur if you do not take enough or skip a dose of your antidiabetic medicine, overeat or do not follow your meal plan, have a fever or infection, or do not exercise as much as usual.

Symptoms of high blood sugar include blurred vision; drowsiness; dry mouth; flushed, dry skin; fruit-like breath odor; increased urination; ketones in urine; loss of appetite; stomachache, nausea, or vomiting; tiredness; troubled breathing (rapid and deep); unconsciousness; and unusual thirst.

If symptoms of high blood sugar occur, *check your blood sugar level and then call your doctor for instructions.*

Side Effects of This Medicine

Along with its needed effects, a medicine may cause some unwanted effects. Although not all of these side effects may occur, if they do occur they may need medical attention.

Check with your doctor immediately if any of the following side effects occur:

> *More common*
> Convulsions (seizures); unconsciousness

Check with your doctor as soon as possible if any of the following side effects occur:

> *More common*
> Low blood sugar, including anxious feeling; behavior change similar to being drunk; blurred vision; cold sweats; confusion; depression; difficulty in thinking; dizziness or lightheadedness; drowsiness; excessive hunger; fast heartbeat; headache; irritability or abnormal behavior; nervousness; nightmares; restless sleep; shakiness; slurred speech; and tingling in the hands, feet, lips, or tongue

> *Less common or rare*
> Depression of the skin at place of injection; dryness of mouth; fast or weak pulse; increased thirst; irregular heartbeat; itching, redness, or swelling at place of injection; mood or mental changes; muscle cramps or pain; nausea or vomiting; shortness of breath; skin rash or itching over the whole body; sweating; thickening of the skin at place of injection; unusual tiredness or weakness; wheezing

Other side effects not listed above may also occur in some patients. If you notice any other effects, check with your doctor.

Developed: 08/04/98
Revised: 05/02/2001

INTERFERON ALFACON-1
Systemic

Commonly used brand name(s):

In the U.S.—
   Infergen

Description

Interferon (in-ter-FEER-on) is a substance naturally produced in cells in the body to help fight infections. There also are synthetic (man-made) versions of this substance, such as interferon alfacon-1. Interferon alfacon-1 is used to treat hepatitis C, a type of infection of the liver, in adults who also have other types of liver disease.

This medicine is available only with your doctor's prescription, in the following dosage form:

   Parenteral
   • Injection (U.S.)

Before Using This Medicine

In deciding to use a medicine, the risks of using the medicine must be weighed against the good it will do. This is a decision you and your doctor will make. For interferon alfacon-1, the following should be considered:

Allergies—Tell your doctor if you have ever had any unusual or allergic reaction to interferon alfacon-1 or to any other alpha interferon. Also tell your health care professional if you are allergic to any other substances, such as foods, preservatives, or dyes.

Pregnancy—Interferon alfacon-1 has not been studied in pregnant women. However, studies in animals have shown that interferon alfacon-1 causes the fetus to abort and other problems. Before taking this medicine, make sure your doctor knows if you are pregnant or if you plan to become pregnant.

Breast-feeding—It is not known whether interferon alfacon-1 passes into breast milk. However, because this medicine may cause serious side effects in nursing babies, breast-feeding may not be recommended while you are receiving it. Discuss with your doctor whether you should breast-feed while you are receiving interferon alfacon-1.

Children—Studies on this medicine have been done only in adult patients, and there is no specific information comparing use of interferon alfacon-1 in children with use in other age groups. However, use in children less than 18 years of age is not recommended.

Teenagers—Studies on this medicine have been done only in adult patients, and there is no specific information comparing use of interferon alfacon-1 in teenagers with use in other age groups. However, use in adolescent patients less than 18 years of age is not recommended.

Older adults—Many medicines have not been studied specifically in older people. Therefore, it may not be known whether they work exactly the same way they do in younger adults or if they cause different side effects or problems in older people. There is no specific information comparing use of interferon alfacon-1 in the elderly with use in other age groups.

Other medicines—Although certain medicines should not be used together at all, in other cases two different medicines may be used together even if an interaction might occur. In these cases, your doctor may want to change the dose, or other precautions may be necessary. Tell your health care professional if you are taking any other prescription or nonprescription (over-the-counter [OTC]) medicine.

Other medical problems—The presence of other medical problems may affect the use of interferon alfacon-1. Make sure you tell your doctor if you have any other medical problems, especially:

   • Decreased bone marrow production or other blood problems or
   • Heart disease or
   • Liver disease or
   • Mental problems (or history of) or
   • Thyroid disease—Interferon alfacon-1 may make these conditions worse
   • Problems with an overactive immune system—Interferon alfacon-1 may make the immune system even more active

Proper Use of This Medicine

If you are injecting this medicine yourself, *use it exactly as directed by your doctor*. Do not use more or less of it, and do not use it more often than your doctor ordered. The exact amount of medicine you need has been carefully worked out. Using too much will increase the risk of side effects, while using too little may not improve your condition.

To help clear up your infection completely, interferon alfacon-1 must be used for the full time of treatment, even if you begin to feel better after a few days or weeks. *It is also very important that you receive your injection at the same time for each day of treatment.*

Each package of interferon alfacon-1 contains a patient instruction sheet. Read this sheet carefully and make sure you understand:

   • How to prepare the injection.
   • Proper use of disposable syringes.
   • How to give the injection.
   • How long the injection is stable.
If you have any questions about any of this, check with your health care professional.

Dosing—The dose of interferon alfacon-1 will be different for different patients. *If you are receiving interferon alfacon-1 at home, follow your doctor's orders or the directions on the label*. If you have any questions about the proper dose of interferon alfacon-1, ask your doctor.

   • For *injection* dosage form:
      —For hepatitis C:
         • Adults—9 micrograms per dose, injected under the skin, three times per week at intervals of at least forty-eight hours, for twenty-four weeks.
         • Children—Use is not recommended.

Missed dose—If you miss a dose of this medicine, do not give the missed dose at all and do not double the next one. Check with your doctor for further instructions.

Storage—To store this medicine:

- Keep out of the reach of children.
- Store in the refrigerator. However, keep the medicine from freezing.
- Do not keep outdated medicine or medicine no longer needed. Ask your health care professional how you should dispose of any medicine you do not use. Be sure that any discarded medicine is out of the reach of children.

Precautions While Using This Medicine

It is very important that your doctor check your progress at regular visits to make sure that this medicine is working properly and to check for unwanted effects. It is also important that you tell your doctor if you notice any changes in your ability to see clearly.

Do not change to another brand of alpha interferon without checking with your physician. Different kinds of alpha interferon have different doses. If you refill your medicine and it looks different, check with your pharmacist.

This medicine commonly causes a flu-like reaction, with aching muscles, fever and chills, and headache. To prevent problems from your temperature going too high, your doctor may ask you to take acetaminophen before each dose of interferon alfacon-1. You may also need to take acetaminophen after a dose of interferon alfacon-1 to bring your temperature down. *Follow your doctor's instructions carefully about taking your temperature, and how much and when to take the acetaminophen.*

In some patients, this medicine may cause mental depression. *Tell your doctor right away:*

- if you or anyone else notices unusual changes in your mood.
- if you start having early-morning sleeplessness or unusually vivid dreams or nightmares.

Interferon alfacon-1 can lower the number of white blood cells in your blood temporarily, increasing the chance of getting an infection. It can also lower the number of platelets, which are necessary for proper blood clotting. If this occurs, there are certain precautions you can take, especially when your blood count is low, to reduce the risk of infection or bleeding:

- If you can, avoid people with infections. *Check with your doctor immediately* if you think you are getting an infection or if you get a fever or chills, cough or hoarseness, lower back or side pain, or painful or difficult urination.
- *Check with your doctor immediately* if you notice any unusual bleeding or bruising; black, tarry stools; blood in urine or stools; or pinpoint red spots on your skin.
- Be careful when using a regular toothbrush, dental floss, or toothpick. Your medical doctor, dentist, or nurse may recommend other ways to clean your teeth and gums. Check with your medical doctor before having any dental work done.
- Do not touch your eyes or the inside of your nose unless you have just washed your hands and have not touched anything else in the meantime.
- Be careful not to cut yourself when you are using sharp objects, such as a safety razor or fingernail or toenail cutters.
- Avoid contact sports or other situations where bruising or injury could occur.

Interferon alfacon-1 may cause some people to become unusually tired or dizzy, or less alert than they are normally.

Make sure you know how you react to this medicine before you drive, use machines, or do anything else that could be dangerous if you are dizzy or if you are not alert.

Side Effects of This Medicine

Along with its needed effects, a medicine may cause some unwanted effects. Although not all of these side effects may occur, if they do occur they may need medical attention.

Check with your doctor as soon as possible if any of the following side effects occur:
More common
Anxiety; black, tarry stools; blood in urine or stools; confusion; cough or hoarseness; fever or chills; lower back or side pain; mental depression; nervousness; painful or difficult urination; pinpoint red spots on skin; redness at place of injection; trouble in sleeping; trouble in thinking or concentrating; unusual bleeding or bruising
Less common
Chest pain; irregular heartbeat; numbness or tingling of fingers, toes, or face
Rare
Blurred vision or loss of vision; skin rash, hives, or itching

Other side effects may occur that usually do not need medical attention. These side effects may go away during treatment as your body adjusts to the medicine. However, check with your doctor if any of the following side effects continue or are bothersome:
More common
Abdominal pain; aching muscles; decreased appetite; diarrhea; dizziness; general feeling of discomfort or illness; headache; heartburn or indigestion; nausea or vomiting; pain in back or joints; sore throat; unusual tiredness or weakness

Interferon alfacon-1 may cause a temporary loss of some hair. After treatment has ended, normal hair growth should return.

Other side effects not listed above may also occur in some patients. If you notice any other effects, check with your doctor.

Developed: 03/12/98

INTERFERON, BETA-1A   Systemic

Commonly used brand name(s):

In the U.S.—
Avonex

In Canada—
Avonex
Rebif

Description

Interferon beta-1a (in-ter-FEER-on BAY-ta) is used to treat the relapsing forms of multiple sclerosis (MS). This medicine will not cure MS, but it may slow some disabling effects and decrease the number of relapses of the disease.

Interferon beta-1a is also used to treat genital warts.

This medicine is available only with your doctor's prescription, in the following dosage form(s):

Parenteral
- Injection (U.S. and Canada)

Before Using This Medicine

In deciding to use a medicine, the risks of taking the medicine must be weighed against the good it will do. This is a decision you and your doctor will make. For interferon beta-1a, the following should be considered:

Allergies—Tell your doctor if you have ever had any unusual or allergic reaction to interferons or human albumin. Also tell your health care professional if you are allergic to any other substances, such as foods, preservatives, or dyes.

Pregnancy—Interferon beta-1a has not been studied in pregnant women. However, studies in animals have shown that interferon beta-1a may cause miscarriages. Be sure your doctor knows if you are pregnant or if you may become pregnant.

Breast-feeding—It is not known whether interferon beta-1a passes into breast milk. Because of the possibility of serious unwanted effects in the nursing infant, it is important that you discuss the use of this medicine with your doctor if you wish to breast-feed.

Children—Studies on this medicine have been done only in adult patients, and there is no specific information comparing use of interferon beta-1a in children with use in other age groups.

Older adults—Many medicines have not been studied specifically in older people. Therefore, it may not be known whether they work exactly the same way they do in younger adults. Although there is no specific information comparing use of interferon beta-1a in the elderly with use in other age groups, this medicine is not expected to cause different side effects or problems in older people than it does in younger adults.

Other medicines—Although certain medicines should not be used together at all, in other cases two different medicines may be used together even if an interaction might occur. In these cases, your doctor may want to change the dose, or other precautions may be necessary. Tell your health care professional if you are taking any other prescription or nonprescription (over-the-counter [OTC]) medicine.

Other medical problems—The presence of other medical problems may affect the use of interferon beta-1a. Make sure you tell your doctor if you have any other medical problems, especially:
- Heart disease—Some side effects of this medicine may be harmful to patients with serious heart problems
- Mental depression or thoughts of suicide—This medicine may make the condition worse
- Seizure disorder—The risk of seizures may be increased

Proper Use of This Medicine

If you are injecting this medicine yourself, *use it exactly as directed by your doctor.*

Special patient directions come with interferon beta-1a injection. *Read the directions carefully before using the medicine.* Make sure you understand:
- How to prepare the injection.
- Proper use of disposable syringes.

- How to give the injection.
- How long the injection is stable.

If you have any questions about any of this, check with your health care professional.

Dosing—*If you are receiving interferon beta-1a at home, follow your doctors orders or the directions on the label.* If you have any questions about the proper dose of interferon beta-1a, ask your doctor.
- For *injection* dosage form:
  —For multiple sclerosis (MS):
  - Adults
    —For *Avonex*
    - 30 micrograms (mcg) once a week, injected into a muscle.
    —For *Rebif*
    - 22 micrograms (mcg) 3 times a week, injected under the skin
  - Children—Use and dose must be determined by the physician.
  —For genital warts:
  - Adults
    —For *Rebif*
    - 3.67 micrograms (mcg) per lesion 3 times a week for 3 weeks

Missed dose—If you miss a dose of this medicine, take it as soon as remembered. The next injection should be scheduled at least 48 hours later.

Storage—To store this medicine:
- Keep out of the reach of children.
- Store away from direct light.
- Store prefilled syringes or vials of interferon beta-1a in the refrigerator. Do not freeze. If refrigeration is not available, the vials that have not been mixed with diluent may be kept for up to 30 days at room temperature, as long as the temperature does not go above 77 °F.
- Do not keep outdated medicine or medicine no longer needed. Be sure that any discarded medicine is out of the reach of children.

Precautions While Using This Medicine

It is very important that your doctor check your progress at regular visits to make sure that this medicine is working properly and to check for unwanted effects.

This medicine commonly causes a flu-like reaction, with aching muscles, chills, fever, headache, joint pain, and nausea. Your doctor may ask you to take acetaminophen to help control these effects. *Follow your doctor's instructions carefully about how much and when to take acetaminophen.*

Side Effects of This Medicine

Along with its needed effects, a medicine may cause some unwanted effects. Although not all of these side effects may occur, if they do occur they may need medical attention.

Check with your doctor as soon as possible if any of the following side effects occur:

More common
  Chills; diarrhea; fever; flu-like symptoms including headache, joint pain, muscle aches, and nausea; pain; unusual bleeding or bruising; unusual tiredness or weakness

Less common
  Abdominal pain; chest pain; clumsiness or unsteadi-

ness; convulsions (seizures); coughing; decreased hearing; difficulty in swallowing; dizziness; fainting; flushing; hives or itching; mood changes, especially with thoughts of suicide; muscle spasms; pain or discharge from the vagina; pelvic discomfort, aching, or heaviness; redness, swelling, or tenderness at place of injection; runny or stuffy nose; skin lesions; sneezing; sore throat; speech problems; swelling of face, lips, or eyelids; troubled breathing; wheezing

Rare
Earache; general feeling of discomfort or illness; loss of appetite; painful blisters on trunk of body—also known as shingles; painful cold sores or blisters on lips, nose, eyes, or genitals

Other side effects may occur that usually do not need medical attention. These side effects may go away during treatment as your body adjusts to the medicine. However, check with your doctor if any of the following side effects continue or are bothersome:

More common
Heartburn; indigestion; sour stomach

Less common
Hair loss; trouble in sleeping

Other side effects not listed above may also occur in some patients. If you notice any other effects, check with your doctor.

Developed: 06/01/98
Revised: 05/01/00

INTERFERON, BETA-1B   Systemic

Commonly used brand name(s):

In the U.S.—
Betaseron

Description

Interferon beta-1b (in-ter-FEER-on BAY-ta) is used to treat the relapsing-remitting form of multiple sclerosis (MS). This medicine will not cure MS, but may decrease the number of relapses of the disease.

This medicine is available only with your doctor's prescription, in the following dosage form(s):

Parenteral
• Injection (U.S.)

Before Using This Medicine

In deciding to use a medicine, the risks of taking the medicine must be weighed against the good it will do. This is a decision you and your doctor will make. For interferon beta-1b, the following should be considered:

Allergies—Tell your doctor if you have ever had any unusual or allergic reaction to interferons or human albumin. Also tell your health care professional if you are allergic to any other substances, such as foods, preservatives, or dyes.

Pregnancy—Interferon beta-1b has not been studied in pregnant women. However, studies in animals have shown that it may cause miscarriages. Be sure your doctor knows if you are pregnant or if you may become pregnant.

Breast-feeding—It is not known whether interferon beta-1b passes into breast milk. Because of the possibility of serious unwanted effects in the nursing infant, it is important that you discuss the use of this medicine with your doctor if you wish to breast-feed.

Children—Studies on this medicine have been done only in adult patients, and there is no specific information comparing use of interferon beta-1b in children with use in other age groups.

Older adults—Many medicines have not been studied specifically in older people. Therefore, it may not be known whether they work exactly the same way they do in younger adults. Although there is no specific information comparing use of interferon beta-1b in the elderly with use in other age groups, this medicine is not expected to cause different side effects or problems in older people than it does in younger adults.

Other medicines—Although certain medicines should not be used together at all, in other cases two different medicines may be used together even if an interaction might occur. In these cases, your doctor may want to change the dose, or other precautions may be necessary. Tell your health care professional if you are taking any other prescription or nonprescription (over-the-counter [OTC]) medicine.

Other medical problems—The presence of other medical problems may affect the use of interferon beta-1b. Make sure you tell your doctor if you have any other medical problems, especially:
• Mental depression or thoughts of suicide—This medicine may make the condition worse

Proper Use of This Medicine

Use this medicine exactly as directed by your doctor in order to help your condition as much as possible.

Taking interferon beta-1b at bedtime may help lessen the flu-like symptoms.

Special patient directions come with interferon beta-1b. *Read the directions carefully before using this medicine.*

It is important to follow several steps to prepare your interferon beta-1b injection correctly. Before injecting the medication, you need to:
• Collect the items you will need before you begin.
• Wash your hands thoroughly with soap and water. Do not touch your hair or skin afterwards.
• Make sure the needle guards are on the needles tightly.
• Remove the plastic cap from the interferon beta-1b and the diluent vial. Use an alcohol wipe to clean the tops of the vials. Move the alcohol wipe in one direction and use one wipe per vial. Leave the alcohol wipe on top of each vial until you are ready to use it.

In order to keep everything sterile, it is important that you do not touch the tops of the vials or the needles. If you do touch a stopper, clean it with a fresh alcohol wipe. If you touch a needle, or if the needle touches any surface, throw away the entire syringe and start over with a new syringe. Also, use only the diluent (sodium chloride 0.54%) provided with the interferon beta-1b to dilute the medicine for injection.

To mix the contents of one vial:
• Resting your hands on a stable surface, remove the needle cover on the 3-mL syringe by pulling the cover straight off the needle. Do not touch the needle itself.
• Pull back the plunger of the syringe back to the 1.2-mL mark.

- Holding the vial of diluent for interferon beta-1b on a stable surface, slowly insert the needle straight through the stopper into the top of the vial.
- Push in the plunger all the way to gently inject 1.2 mL of air into the vial. Leave the needle in the vial of diluent.
- Turn the vial upside down using one hand and make sure the tip of the needle is covered by solution. With your other hand, slowly pull back the plunger of the syringe to withdraw 1.2 mL of diluent into the syringe.
- Keeping the vial upside down, gently tap the syringe until any air bubbles that formed rise to the top of the barrel of the syringe.
- Carefully push in the plunger to eject only the air through the needle. Remove the needle/syringe from the vial of diluent.
- Holding the interferon beta-1b vial on a stable surface, slowly insert the needle of the syringe (containing 1.2 mL of diluent) all the way through the stopper of the vial.
- Push the plunger down slowly, directing the needle toward the side of the vial to allow the diluent to run down the inside wall. Injecting the diluent directly onto the white cake of medicine will cause excess foaming.
- Remove the needle/syringe from the vial of interferon beta-1b.
- Roll the vial between your hands gently to completely dissolve the white cake of medicine.
- Check the solution to make sure it is clear. If you can see anything solid in the solution or if the solution is discolored, discard it and start again.

To prepare the injection syringe:
- Remove the needle guard from the 1-mL syringe and pull back the plunger to the 1-mL mark.
- Insert the needle of the 1-mL syringe through the stopper of the vial of interferon beta-1b solution.
- Gently push the plunger all the way down to inject air into the vial.
- Turn the vial of interferon beta-1b solution upside down, keeping the needle tip in the liquid.
- Pull back the plunger of the syringe to withdraw 1 mL of liquid into the syringe.
- Hold the syringe with the needle pointing upward. Tap the syringe gently until any air bubbles that formed rise to the top of the barrel of the syringe.
- Carefully push in the plunger to eject only the air through the needle.
- Remove the needle/syringe from the vial. Replace the needle guard on the syringe.
- Throw away the unused portion of the solution remaining in the vial.

The injection should be administered immediately after mixing. If the injection is delayed, refrigerate the solution and inject it within 3 hours.

To give yourself the injection:

Before you self-inject the interferon beta-1b dose, decide where you will inject yourself. There are eight areas for injection, and each area has an upper, a middle, and a lower injection site. To help prevent injection site reactions, select a site in an area different from the area where you last injected yourself. You should not choose the same area for two injections in a row. Keeping a record of your injections will help make sure you rotate areas.

Do not self-inject into any area in which you feel lumps, bumps, firm knots, or pain. Do not use any area in which the skin is discolored, depressed, red, scabbed, tender, or has broken open. Talk to your doctor or other health care professional about these or any other unusual conditions that you find. If you experience a break in the skin or drainage of fluid from the injection site, contact your doctor before continuing injections with interferon beta-1b.

- Clean the injection site with a fresh alcohol wipe, and let it air dry.
- Pick up the 1-mL syringe you already filled with interferon beta-1b. Hold the syringe as you would a pencil or dart. Remove the needle guard from the needle, but do not touch the needle itself.
- Gently pinch the skin together around the site, to lift it up a bit.
- Resting your wrist on the skin near the site, stick the needle straight into the skin at a 90° angle with a quick, firm motion.
- Using a slow steady push, inject the medicine by pushing the plunger all the way in until the syringe is empty.
- Hold a swab on the injection site. Remove the needle by pulling straight out.
- Gently massage the injection site with a dry cotton ball or gauze.

To dispose of needles and syringes:

Needles, syringes, and vials should be used for only one injection. *Place all used syringes, needles, and vials in a syringe disposal unit or in a hard-walled plastic container,* such as a liquid laundry detergent container. Keep the cover closed tightly, and keep the container out of the reach of children. When the container is full, check with your physician or nurse about proper disposal, as laws vary from state to state.

Dosing—The dose of interferon beta-1b will be different for different patients. *Follow your doctor's orders or the directions on the label.* The following information includes only the average doses of interferon beta-1b. *If your dose is different, do not change it* unless your doctor tells you to do so.
- For *injection* dosage form:
  —For multiple sclerosis (MS):
    - Adults—0.25 milligrams (mg) every other day.
    - Children—Use and dose must be determined by your doctor.

Missed dose—If you miss a dose of this medicine, take it as soon as remembered. The next injection should be scheduled about 48 hours later.

Storage—To store this medicine:
- Keep out of the reach of children.
- Store away from heat and direct light.
- Store in the refrigerator. However, keep the medicine from freezing. If refrigeration is not available, vials may be kept for up to 7 days at room temperature, as long as the temperature does not go above 86 °F.
- Do not keep outdated medicine or medicine no longer needed. Be sure that any discarded medicine is out of the reach of children.

Side Effects of This Medicine

Along with its needed effects, a medicine may cause some unwanted effects. Although not all of these side effects may occur, if they do occur they may need medical attention.

Check with your doctor as soon as possible if any of the following side effects occur:
More common
   Abdominal pain; break in the skin at place of injection,

with blue-black discoloration, swelling, or drainage of fluid; flu-like symptoms including chills, fever, generalized feeling of discomfort or illness, increased sweating, and muscle pain; headache or migraine; hives, itching, or swelling at place of injection; hypertension (high blood pressure); irregular or pounding heartbeat; pain at place of injection; redness or feeling of heat at place of injection; stuffy nose

Less common
Breast pain; bloody or cloudy urine; changes in vision; cold hands and feet; difficult, burning, or painful urination; fast or racing heartbeat; frequent urge to urinate; pain; pelvic pain; swollen glands; troubled breathing; unusual weight gain

Rare
Abnormal growth in breast; benign lumps in breast; bleeding problems; bloating or swelling; changes in menstrual periods; confusion; convulsions (seizures); cyst (abnormal growth filled with fluid or semisolid material); decreased sexual ability in males; dry, puffy skin; feeling cold; hyperactivity; increased muscle tone; increased urge to urinate; loss of memory; mental depression with thoughts of suicide; problems in speaking; red, itching, or swollen eyes; swelling of front part of neck; unusual weight loss

Other side effects may occur that usually do not need medical attention. These side effects may go away during treatment as your body adjusts to the medicine. However, check with your doctor if any of the following side effects continue or are bothersome:

More common
Constipation; diarrhea; dizziness; laryngitis (loss of voice); menstrual pain or other changes; unusual tiredness or weakness

Less common
Anxiety; drowsiness; hair loss; nervousness; vomiting

Other side effects not listed above may also occur in some patients. If you notice any other effects, check with your doctor.

Developed: 06/16/98

INTERFERON, GAMMA   Systemic†

Commonly used brand name(s):

In the U.S.—
Actimmune

---

†Not commercially available in Canada.

Description

Gamma interferon (GAM-a in-ter-FEER-on) is a synthetic (man-made) version of a substance naturally produced by cells in the body to help fight infections and tumors. Gamma interferon is used to treat chronic granulomatous disease and osteopetrosis.

Gamma interferon is available only with your doctor's prescription, in the following dosage form:

Parenteral
• Injection (U.S.)

Before Using This Medicine

In deciding to use a medicine, the risks of taking the medicine must be weighed against the good it will do. This is a decision you and your doctor will make. For gamma interferon, the following should be considered:

Allergies—Tell your doctor if you have ever had any unusual or allergic reaction to gamma interferon.

Pregnancy—Gamma interferon has not been studied in pregnant women. However, in monkeys given 100 times the human dose of gamma interferon and in mice, there was an increase in deaths of the fetus. Also, in mice, toxic doses of gamma interferon caused bleeding of the uterus.

Breast-feeding—It is not known whether gamma interferon passes into the breast milk. However, because this medicine may cause serious side effects, breast-feeding may not be recommended while you are receiving it. Discuss with your doctor whether or not you should breast-feed while you are receiving gamma interferon.

Children—Studies on this medicine have been done mostly in children and it is not expected to cause different side effects or problems than it does in adults.

Older adults—Many medicines have not been studied specifically in older people. Therefore, it may not be known whether they work exactly the same way they do in younger adults or if they cause different side effects or problems in older people. There is no specific information comparing use of gamma interferon in the elderly with use in other age groups.

Other medicines—Although certain medicines should not be used together at all, in other cases two different medicines may be used together even if an interaction might occur. In these cases, your doctor may want to change the dose, or other precautions may be necessary. Tell your health care professional if you are taking any other prescription or nonprescription (over-the-counter [OTC]) medicine.

Other medical problems—The presence of other medical problems may affect the use of gamma interferon. Make sure you tell your doctor if you have any other medical problems, especially:

• Convulsions (seizures) or
• Mental problems (or history of)—Risk of problems affecting the central nervous system may be increased

• Heart disease or
• Multiple sclerosis or
• Systemic lupus erythematosus—May be worsened by gamma interferon

---

Proper Use of This Medicine

If you are injecting this medicine yourself, *use it exactly as directed by your doctor*. Do not use more or less of it, and do not use it more often than your doctor ordered. The exact amount of medicine you need has been carefully worked out. Using too much will increase the risk of side effects, while using too little may not improve your condition.

Each package of gamma interferon contains a patient instruction sheet. Read this sheet carefully and make sure you understand:

- How to prepare the injection.
- Proper use of disposable syringes.
- How to give the injection.
- How long the injection is stable.

If you have any questions about any of this, check with your health care professional.

While you are using gamma interferon, your doctor may want you to drink extra fluids. This will help prevent low blood pressure due to loss of too much water.

Gamma interferon often causes flu-like symptoms, which can be severe. This effect is less likely to cause problems if you inject your gamma interferon at bedtime.

Dosing—The dose of gamma interferon will be different for different patients. The dose that is used may depend on a number of things, including the patient's body size. *If you are receiving gamma interferon at home, follow your doctor's orders or the directions on the label.* If you have any questions about the proper dose of gamma interferon, ask your doctor.

Missed dose—If you miss a dose of this medicine, do not give the missed dose at all and do not double the next one. Check with your doctor for further instructions.

Storage—To store this medicine:

- Keep out of the reach of children.
- Store in the refrigerator.
- Keep the medicine from freezing.
- Discard any unopened vials that are left at room temperature for more than 12 hours.
- Do not keep outdated medicine or medicine no longer needed. Ask your health care professional how you should dispose of any medicine you do not use. Be sure that any discarded medicine is out of the reach of children.

Precautions While Using This Medicine

It is very important that your doctor check your progress at regular visits to make sure that this medicine is working properly and to check for unwanted effects.

This medicine commonly causes a flu-like reaction, with aching muscles, fever and chills, and headache. To prevent problems from your temperature going too high, your doctor may ask you to take acetaminophen before each dose of gamma interferon. You may also need to take it after a dose to bring your temperature down. *Follow your doctor's instructions carefully about taking your temperature, and how much and when to take the acetaminophen.*

Side Effects of This Medicine

Along with its needed effects, a medicine may cause some unwanted effects. Although not all of these side effects may occur, if they do occur they may need medical attention.

Check with your doctor as soon as possible if any of the following side effects occur:

Rare
Black, tarry stools; blood in urine or stools; confusion; cough or hoarseness; loss of balance control; lower back or side pain; mask-like face; painful or difficult urination; pinpoint red spots on skin; shuffling walk; stiffness of arms or legs; trembling and shaking of hands and fingers; trouble in speaking or swallowing; trouble in thinking or concentrating; trouble in walking; unusual bleeding or bruising

Other side effects may occur that usually do not need medical attention. These side effects may go away during treatment as your body adjusts to the medicine. However, check with your doctor if any of the following side effects continue or are bothersome:

More common
Aching muscles; diarrhea; fever and chills; general feeling of discomfort or illness; headache; nausea or vomiting; skin rash; unusual tiredness

Less common
Back pain; dizziness; joint pain; loss of appetite; weight loss

Other side effects not listed above may also occur in some patients. If you notice any other effects, check with your doctor.

Revised: 4/18/00

INTERFERONS, ALPHA   Systemic

Commonly used brand name(s):

In the U.S.—
Alferon N[4]
Roferon-A[1]
Intron A[2]

In Canada—
Roferon-A[1]
Intron A[2]
Wellferon[3]

Note: For quick reference, the following alpha interferons are numbered to match the corresponding brand names.

This information applies to the following medicines:

1. Interferon Alfa-2a, Recombinant
2. Interferon Alfa-2b, Recombinant
3. Interferon Alfa-n1 (Ins)*
4. Interferon Alfa-n3†

*Not commercially available in the U.S.
†Not commercially available in Canada.

Description

Interferons (in-ter-FEER-ons) are substances naturally produced by cells in the body to help fight infections and tumors. They may also be synthetic (man-made) versions of these substances. Alpha interferons are used to treat hairy cell leukemia, malignant melanoma, and AIDS-related Kaposi's sarcoma. They are also used to treat laryngeal papillomatosis (growths in the respiratory tract) in children, genital warts, and some kinds of hepatitis.

Alpha interferons may also be used for other conditions as determined by your doctor.

Alpha interferons are available only with your doctor's prescription, in the following dosage form:

Parenteral
Interferon Alfa-2a, Recombinant
• Injection (U.S. and Canada)
Interferon Alfa-2b, Recombinant
• Injection (U.S. and Canada)

Interferon Alfa-n1 (Ins)
  • Injection (Canada)
Interferon Alfa-n3
  • Injection (U.S.)

Before Using This Medicine

In deciding to use a medicine, the risks of taking the medicine must be weighed against the good it will do. This is a decision you and your doctor will make. For interferons, the following should be considered:

Allergies—Tell your doctor if you have ever had any unusual or allergic reaction to alpha interferon or to proteins, such as egg white or immunoglobulin.

Pregnancy—Alpha interferons have not been shown to cause birth defects or other problems in humans. However, in monkeys given 20 to 500 times the human dose of recombinant interferon alfa-2a or given 90 to 180 times the usual dose of recombinant interferon alfa-2b, there was an increase in death of the fetuses.

Breast-feeding—It is not known whether alpha interferons pass into breast milk. However, because this medicine may cause serious side effects, breast-feeding may not be recommended while you are receiving it. Discuss with your doctor whether or not you should breast-feed while you are receiving alpha interferon.

Children—There is no specific information comparing use of alpha interferon for cancer or genital warts in children with use in other age groups.

Teenagers—Alpha interferons may cause changes in the menstrual cycle. Discuss this possible effect with your doctor.

Older adults—Some side effects of alpha interferons (chest pain, irregular heartbeat, unusual tiredness, confusion, mental depression, trouble in thinking or concentrating) may be more likely to occur in the elderly, who are usually more sensitive to the effects of alpha interferons.

Other medicines—Although certain medicines should not be used together at all, in other cases two different medicines may be used together even if an interaction might occur. In these cases, your doctor may want to change the dose, or other precautions may be necessary. Tell your health care professional if you are taking any other prescription or nonprescription (over-the-counter [OTC]) medicine.

Other medical problems—The presence of other medical problems may affect the use of alpha interferons. Make sure you tell your doctor if you have any other medical problems, especially:

  • Bleeding problems—May be worsened by recombinant interferon alfa-2b
  • Chickenpox (including recent exposure) or
  • Herpes zoster (shingles)—Risk of severe disease affecting other parts of the body
  • Convulsions (seizures) or
  • Mental problems (or history of)—Risk of problems affecting the central nervous system may be increased
  • Diabetes mellitus (sugar diabetes) or
  • Heart attack (recent) or
  • Heart disease or
  • Kidney disease or
  • Liver disease or
  • Lung disease—May be worsened by alpha interferons
  • Problems with overactive immune system—Alpha interferons make the immune system even more active

  • Thyroid disease—Recombinant interferon alfa-2b can cause thyroid problems when it is used to treat hepatitis

Proper Use of This Medicine

If you are injecting this medicine yourself, *use it exactly as directed by your doctor*. Do not use more or less of it, and do not use it more often than your doctor ordered. The exact amount of medicine you need has been carefully worked out. Using too much will increase the risk of side effects, while using too little may not improve your condition.

Each package of alpha interferon contains a patient instruction sheet. Read this sheet carefully and make sure you understand:

  • How to prepare the injection.
  • Proper use of disposable syringes.
  • How to give the injection.
  • How long the injection is stable.

If you have any questions about any of this, check with your health care professional.

While you are using alpha interferon, your doctor may want you to drink extra fluids. This will help prevent low blood pressure due to loss of too much water.

Alpha interferons often cause unusual tiredness, which can be severe. This effect is less likely to cause problems if you inject your interferon at bedtime.

Dosing—The dose of alpha interferons will be different for different patients. The dose that is used may depend on a number of things, including what the medicine is being used for, the patient's size, and whether or not other medicines are also being taken. *If you are receiving alpha interferons at home, follow your doctor's orders or the directions on the label*. If you have any questions about the proper dose of alpha interferons, ask your doctor.

Missed dose—If you miss a dose of this medicine, do not inject the missed dose at all and do not double the next one. Check with your doctor for further instructions.

Storage—To store this medicine:
  • Keep out of the reach of children.
  • Store in the refrigerator.
  • Keep the medicine from freezing.
  • Do not keep outdated medicine or medicine no longer needed. Ask your health care professional how you should dispose of any medicine you do not use. Be sure that any discarded medicine is out of the reach of children.

Precautions While Using This Medicine

It is very important that your doctor check your progress at regular visits to make sure that this medicine is working properly and to check for unwanted effects.

Do not change to another brand of alpha interferon without checking with your physician. Different kinds of alpha interferon have different doses. If you refill your medicine and it looks different, check with your pharmacist.

This medicine will add to the effects of alcohol and other CNS depressants (medicines that slow down the nervous system, possibly causing drowsiness). Some examples of CNS depressants are antihistamines or medicine for hay fever, other allergies, or colds; sedatives, tranquilizers, or sleeping medicine; prescription pain medicine or narcotics; barbiturates; medicine for seizures; muscle relaxants; or anesthetics, including some dental anesthetics. *Check with your doctor before drinking alcohol or taking any of the above while you are using this medicine.*

Alpha interferon may cause some people to become unusually tired or dizzy, or less alert than they are normally. *Make sure you know how you react to this medicine before you drive, use machines, or do anything else that could be dangerous if you are dizzy or if you are not alert.*

This medicine commonly causes a flu-like reaction, with aching muscles, fever and chills, and headache. To prevent problems from your temperature going too high, your doctor may ask you to take acetaminophen (e.g., *Anacin-3, Tylenol*) before each dose of interferon. You may also need to take it after a dose to bring your temperature down. *Follow your doctor's instructions carefully about taking your temperature, and how much and when to take the acetaminophen.*

Alpha interferon can lower the number of white blood cells in your blood temporarily, increasing the chance of getting an infection. It can also lower the number of platelets, which are necessary for proper blood clotting. If this occurs, there are certain precautions you can take, especially when your blood count is low, to reduce the risk of infection or bleeding:

• If you can, avoid being close to people with infections. *Check with your doctor immediately* if you think you are getting an infection or if you get a fever or chills, cough or hoarseness, lower back or side pain, or have painful or difficult urination.

• *Check with your doctor immediately* if you notice any unusual bleeding or bruising; black, tarry stools; blood in urine or stools; or pinpoint red spots on your skin.

• Be careful when using a regular toothbrush, dental floss, or toothpick. Your medical doctor, dentist, or nurse may recommend other ways to clean your teeth and gums. Check with your medical doctor before having any dental work done.

• Do not touch your eyes or the inside of your nose unless you have just washed your hands and have not touched anything else in the meantime.

• Be careful not to cut yourself when you are using sharp objects such as a safety razor or fingernail or toenail cutters.

• Avoid contact sports or other situations where bruising or injury could occur.

Side Effects of This Medicine

Along with its needed effects, a medicine may cause some unwanted effects. Although not all of these side effects may occur, if they do occur they may need medical attention.

Because this medicine is used for many different conditions and in many different doses, the actual frequency of side effects may vary. In general, side effects are less common with low doses than with high doses. Also, when alpha interferon is used for genital warts, very little of it gets into the rest of the body, so side effects are generally less common than in other conditions.

Check with your doctor as soon as possible if any of the following side effects occur:

Less common
Confusion; mental depression; nervousness; numbness or tingling of fingers, toes, and face; trouble in sleeping; trouble in thinking or concentrating

Rare
Black, tarry stools; blood in urine or stools; chest pain; cough or hoarseness accompanied by fever or

chills; fever or chills (beginning after 3 weeks of treatment); irregular heartbeat; lower back or side pain accompanied by fever or chills; painful or difficult urination accompanied by fever or chills; pinpoint red spots on skin; unusual bleeding or bruising

Other side effects may occur that usually do not need medical attention. These side effects may go away during treatment as your body adjusts to the medicine. However, check with your doctor if any of the following side effects continue or are bothersome:

More common
Aching muscles; change in taste or metallic taste; fever and chills (should lessen after the first 1 or 2 weeks of treatment); general feeling of discomfort or illness; headache; loss of appetite; nausea and vomiting; skin rash; unusual tiredness

Less common or rare
Back pain; blurred vision; diarrhea; dizziness; dryness of mouth; dry skin or itching; increased sweating; joint pain; leg cramps; sores in mouth and on lips; weight loss

Alpha interferon may cause a temporary loss of some hair. After treatment has ended, normal hair growth should return.

Other side effects not listed above may also occur in some patients. If you notice any other effects, check with your doctor.

Additional Information

Once a medicine has been approved for marketing for a certain use, experience may show that it is also useful for other medical problems. Although these uses are not included in product labeling, alpha interferons are used in certain patients with the following medical conditions:

• Bladder cancer
• Carcinoid tumors
• Chronic myelocytic leukemia
• Kidney cancer
• Laryngeal papillomatosis (growths on larynx)
• Lymphomas, non-Hodgkin's
• Multiple myeloma
• Mycosis fungoides
• Ovarian cancer
• Polycythemia vera (a type of cancer of the blood)
• Skin cancer
• Thrombocytosis

Other than the above information, there is no additional information relating to proper use, precautions, or side effects for these uses.

Revised: 06/24/98
Interim revision: 07/07/98

IODINE   Topical†

†Not commercially available in Canada.

Description

Topical iodine (EYE -oh-din) is used to prevent and treat infections that may occur in minor scrapes and cuts. It works by killing bacteria that can cause infections.

This medicine is available in the following dosage form:

Topical
- Tincture (U.S.)

Before Using This Medicine

If you are using this medicine without a prescription, carefully read and follow any precautions on the label. For topical iodine, the following should be considered:

Allergies—Tell your doctor if you have ever had any unusual or allergic reaction to iodine. Also tell your health care professional if you are allergic to any other substances, such as foods, preservatives, or dyes.

Pregnancy—Use of topical iodine is not recommended during pregnancy because it has been shown to cause thyroid problems in the newborn infant. Before using this medicine, make sure your doctor knows if you are pregnant or you may become pregnant.

Breast-feeding—Topical iodine passes into the breast milk and has been shown to cause unwanted effects, such as thyroid problems in nursing babies. It may be necessary for you to use another medicine or to stop breast-feeding during treatment. Be sure you have discussed the risks and benefits of the medicine with your doctor.

Children—Use of topical iodine is not recommended for newborn infants because it may cause skin and thyroid problems.

Older adults—Many medicines have not been studied specifically in older people. Therefore, it may not be known whether they work exactly the same way they do in younger adults. Although there is no specific information comparing use of topical iodine in the elderly with use in other age groups, this medicine is not expected to cause different side effects or problems in older people than it does in younger adults.

Other medicines—Although certain medicines should not be used together at all, in other cases two different medicines may be used together even if an interaction might occur. In these cases, your doctor may want to change the dose, or other precautions may be necessary. Tell your health care professional if you are using any other topical prescription or nonprescription (over-the-counter [OTC]) medicine that is to be applied to the same area of the skin.

Other medical problems—The presence of other medical problems may affect the use of topical iodine. Make sure you tell your doctor if you have any other medical problems, especially:
- Animal bites or
- Deep wounds or
- Serious burns—The chance of side effects may be increased

Proper Use of This Medicine

Use this medicine only as directed.

This medicine is for external use only. Do not swallow it.

Keep this medicine away from the eyes because it may cause irritation. If you should accidentally get some in your eyes, wash it away with water immediately.

Do not use topical iodine on deep, puncture wounds, animal bites, or serious burns. To do so may increase the chance of side effects.

Do not cover the wound to which you have applied topical iodine with a tight dressing or bandage since this may increase the chance of side effects.

Dosing—*Follow your doctor's orders or the directions on the label before using this medicine.* The following information includes only the average doses of iodine. *If your dose is different, do not change it* unless your doctor tells you to do so.
- For *topical* dosage form (tincture):
  —For minor bacterial skin infections:
    - Adults and children 1 month of age and over—Use when necessary, according to the directions on the label or your doctor's instructions. Do not use for more than ten days.
    - Infants and children under 1 month of age—Use is not recommended.

To help clear up your infection completely, it *is very important that you keep using topical iodine for the full time of treatment. Do not miss any doses.*

Missed dose—If you miss a dose of this medicine, apply it as soon as possible. However, if it is almost time for your next dose, skip the missed dose and go back to your regular dosing schedule.

Storage—To store this medicine:
- Keep out of the reach of children.
- Store away from heat and direct light.
- Keep the medicine from freezing. Do not refrigerate.
- Do not keep outdated medicine or medicine no longer needed. Be sure that any discarded medicine is out of the reach of children.

Precautions While Using This Medicine

Check with your doctor if the skin problem for which you are using topical iodine becomes worse, or if you develop a constant irritation such as itching or burning that was not present before you started using this medicine.

This medicine can stain your skin and clothing. Alcohol may be used to remove iodine stain on the skin. Stains on clothing can be removed by washing and rinsing them in ammonia diluted with water. Stains on starched linens can be removed by washing them in soap and water.

Side Effects of This Medicine

Along with its needed effects, a medicine may cause some unwanted effects. Although not all of these side effects may occur, if they do occur they may need medical attention.

Check with your doctor as soon as possible if any of the following side effects occur:
Rare
  Blistering, crusting, irritation, itching, or reddening of skin

Symptoms of overdose (when swallowed)
  Abdominal or stomach pain; diarrhea; fever; nausea; not being able to pass urine; thirst, severe; vomiting

Other side effects not listed above may also occur in some patients. If you notice any other effects, check with your doctor.

Developed: 02/22/94

IPECAC   Oral

Description

Ipecac (IP-e-kak) is used in the emergency treatment of certain kinds of poisoning. It is used to cause vomiting of the poison.

Only the syrup form of ipecac should be used. A bottle of ipecac labeled as being Ipecac Fluidextract or Ipecac Tincture should not be used. These dosage forms are too strong and may cause serious side effects or death. Only ipecac syrup contains the proper strength of ipecac for treating poisonings.

Ordinarily, this medicine should not be used if strychnine, corrosives such as alkalies (lye) and strong acids, or petroleum distillates such as kerosene, gasoline, coal oil, fuel oil, paint thinner, or cleaning fluid have been swallowed. It may cause seizures, additional injury to the throat, or pneumonia.

Ipecac should not be used to cause vomiting as a means of losing weight. If used regularly for this purpose, serious heart problems or even death may occur.

This medicine in amounts of more than 1 ounce is available only with your doctor's prescription. It is available in ½- and 1-ounce bottles without a prescription. However, before using ipecac syrup, call a poison control center, your doctor, or an emergency room for advice.

Oral
- Syrup (U.S. and Canada)

Before Using This Medicine

Before using this medicine to cause vomiting in poisoning, call a poison control center, your doctor, or an emergency room for advice. It is a good idea to have these telephone numbers readily available. In addition, before you use ipecac, the following should be considered:

Pregnancy—Studies on effects in pregnancy have not been done in either humans or animals.

Children—Infants and very young children are at a greater risk of choking with their own vomit (or getting vomit in their lungs). Therefore, it is especially important to call a poison control center, your doctor, or an emergency room for instructions before giving ipecac to an infant or young child.

Older adults—This medicine has been tested and has not been shown to cause different side effects or problems in older people than it does in younger adults.

Other medical problems—The presence of other medical problems may affect the use of ipecac. Make sure you tell your doctor or the person you talk to at the poison control center or the emergency room if you have any other medical problems, especially:
- Heart disease—There is an increased risk of heart problems, such as unusually fast heartbeat, if the ipecac is not vomited

Proper Use of This Medicine

It is very important that you take this medicine only as directed. Do not take more of it and do not take it more often than recommended on the label, unless otherwise directed. When too much ipecac is used, it can cause damage to the heart and other muscles, and may even cause death.

Do not give this medicine to unconscious or very drowsy persons, since the vomited material may enter the lungs and cause pneumonia.

To help this medicine cause vomiting of the poison, adults should drink 1 full glass (8 ounces) of water and children should drink ½ to 1 full glass (4 to 8 ounces) of water immediately after taking this medicine. Water may be given first in the case of a small or scared child.

Do not take this medicine with milk, milk products, or with carbonated beverages. Milk or milk products may prevent this medicine from working properly, and carbonated beverages may cause swelling of the stomach.

If vomiting does not occur within 20 to 30 minutes after you have taken the first dose of this medicine, take a second dose. If vomiting does not occur after you have taken the second dose, you must immediately see your doctor or go to an emergency room.

If you have been told to take both this medicine and activated charcoal to treat the poisoning, *do not take the activated charcoal until after you have taken this medicine to cause vomiting and vomiting has stopped. This takes usually about 30 minutes.*

Dosing—The dose of ipecac will be different for different patients. *Follow your doctor's orders or the directions on the label.* The following information includes only the average doses of ipecac. *If your dose is different, do not change it unless your doctor tells you to do so.*

- For *oral* dosage form (syrup):
  —For treatment of poisoning:
  - Adults and teenagers—The usual dose is 15 to 30 milliliters (mL) (1 to 2 tablespoonfuls), followed immediately by one full glass (240 mL) of water. The dose may be repeated one time after twenty to thirty minutes if vomiting does not occur.
  - Children 1 to 12 years of age—The usual dose is 15 mL (1 tablespoonful). One-half to one full glass (120 to 240 mL) of water should be taken right before or right after the dose. The dose may be repeated one time after twenty to thirty minutes if vomiting does not occur.
  - Children 6 months to 1 year of age—The usual dose is 5 to 10 mL (1 to 2 teaspoonfuls). One-half to one full glass (120 to 240 mL) of water should be taken right before or right after the dose. The dose may be repeated one time after twenty to thirty minutes if vomiting does not occur.
  - Children up to 6 months of age—Ipecac must be given only under the direction of your doctor.

Storage—To store this medicine:
- Keep out of the reach of children since overdose is very dangerous in children.
- Store away from heat and direct light.
- Keep the syrup from freezing.
- Do not keep outdated medicine or medicine no longer needed. Be sure that any discarded medicine is out of the reach of children.
- Do not keep a bottle of ipecac that has been opened. Ipecac may evaporate over a period of time. It is best to replace it with a new one.

Side Effects of This Medicine

Along with its needed effects, a medicine may cause some unwanted effects. Although side effects usually do not occur with recommended doses of ipecac, if they do occur they may need medical attention.

Check with your doctor as soon as possible if any of the following side effects occur:

Symptoms of overdose (may also occur if ipecac is taken regularly)

Diarrhea; fast or irregular heartbeat; nausea or vomiting (continuing more than 30 minutes); stomach cramps or pain; troubled breathing; unusual tiredness or weakness; weakness, aching, and stiffness of muscles, especially those of the neck, arms, and legs

Other side effects not listed above may also occur in some patients. If you notice any other effects, check with your doctor.

Revised: 08/04/94

IPRATROPIUM   Inhalation

Commonly used brand name(s):

In the U.S.—
Atrovent

In Canada—
Apo-Ipravent
Atrovent
Kendral-Ipratropium

Description

Ipratropium (I-pra-TROE-pee-um) is a bronchodilator (medicine that opens up narrowed breathing passages). It is taken by inhalation to help control the symptoms of lung diseases, such as asthma, chronic bronchitis, and emphysema. Ipratropium helps decrease coughing, wheezing, shortness of breath, and troubled breathing by increasing the flow of air into the lungs.

When ipratropium inhalation is used to treat acute, severe attacks of asthma, bronchitis, or emphysema, it is used only in combination with other bronchodilators.

Ipratropium is available only with your doctor's prescription, in the following dosage forms:

Inhalation
• Inhalation aerosol (U.S. and Canada)
• Inhalation solution (U.S. and Canada)

Before Using This Medicine

In deciding to use a medicine, the risks of using the medicine must be weighed against the good it will do. This is a decision you and your doctor will make. For ipratropium, the following should be considered:

Allergies—Tell your doctor if you have ever had any unusual or allergic reaction to ipratropium, atropine, belladonna, hyoscyamine, or scopolamine, or to other inhalation aerosol medicines. Also tell your health care professional if you are allergic to soya lecithin or related food substances such as soybeans and peanuts.

Pregnancy—Ipratropium has not been studied in pregnant women. However, it has not been shown to cause birth defects or other problems in animal studies.

Breast-feeding—It is not known whether ipratropium passes into the breast milk. Although most medicines pass into breast milk in small amounts, many of them may be used safely while breast-feeding. Mothers who are using this medicine and who wish to breast-feed should discuss this with their doctor.

Children—This medicine has been tested in children and, in effective doses, has not been shown to cause different side effects or problems in children than it does in adults.

Older adults—Ipratropium inhalation has been tested in patients 65 years of age or older. This medicine is not expected to cause different side effects or problems in older people than it does in younger adults.

Other medicines—Although certain medicines should not be used together at all, in other cases two different medicines may be used together even if an interaction might occur. In these cases, your doctor may want to change the dose, or other precautions may be necessary. When you are taking ipratropium, it is especially important that your health care professional know if you are taking any other prescription or nonprescription (over-the-counter [OTC]) medicine.

Other medical problems—The presence of other medical problems may affect the use of ipratropium. Make sure you tell your doctor if you have any other medical problem, especially:

• Difficult urination—Ipratropium may make the condition worse

• Glaucoma—Ipratropium may make the condition worse if it gets into the eyes

Proper Use of This Medicine

Ipratropium is used to help control the symptoms of lung diseases, such as chronic bronchitis, emphysema, and asthma. However, for treatment of bronchospasm or asthma attacks that have already started, ipratropium is used only in combination with other bronchodilators.

It is very important that you use ipratropium only as directed. Do not use more of it and do not use it more often than your doctor ordered. To do so may increase the chance of side effects.

Keep the spray or solution away from the eyes because this medicine may cause irritation or blurred vision. Closing your eyes while you are inhaling ipratropium may keep the medicine from getting into your eyes. Rinsing your eyes with cool water may help if any medicine does get into your eyes.

Ipratropium usually comes with patient directions. Read them carefully before using this medicine.

If you are taking this medicine every day to help control your symptoms, it must be taken at regularly spaced times as ordered by your doctor.

Dosing—The dose of ipratropium will be different for different patients. *Follow your doctor's orders or the directions on the label.* The following information includes only the average doses of ipratropium. *If your dose is different, do not change it* unless your doctor tells you to do so.

- For symptoms of chronic obstructive pulmonary disease, such as chronic bronchitis or emphysema:
  —For *inhalation aerosol* dosage form:
  - Adults and children 12 years of age and older—2 to 4 inhalations (puffs) three or four times a day, at regularly spaced times. Some patients may need up to 6 to 8 puffs three times a day.
  —For *inhalation solution* dosage form:
  - Adults and children 12 years of age and older—250 to 500 mcg used in a nebulizer three or four times a day, every six to eight hours.
- For symptoms of asthma:
  —For *inhalation aerosol* dosage form:
  - Adults and children 12 years of age and older—1 to 4 inhalations (puffs) four times a day, at regularly spaced times, as needed.
  - Children up to 12 years of age—1 or 2 inhalations (puffs) three or four times a day, at regularly spaced times, as needed.
  —For *inhalation solution* dosage form:
  - Adults and children 12 years of age and older—500 mcg used in a nebulizer three or four times a day, every six to eight hours, as needed.
  - Children 5 to 12 years of age—125 to 250 mcg used in a nebulizer three or four times a day, every four to six hours as needed.
  - Children up to 5 years of age—Use and dose must be determined by your doctor.

Missed dose—If you use ipratropium inhalation regularly and you miss a dose of this medicine, use it as soon as possible. Then use any remaining doses for that day at regularly spaced times.

Storage—To store this medicine:
- Keep out of the reach of children.
- Store away from heat.
- Store the solution form of this medicine away from direct light. Store the aerosol form of this medicine away from direct sunlight.
- Keep the medicine from freezing.
- Store any opened bottles of the solution form of this medicine in the refrigerator.
- Do not puncture, break, or burn the aerosol container, even if it is empty.
- Do not keep outdated medicine or medicine no longer needed. Be sure that any discarded medicine is out of the reach of children.

For patients using *ipratropium inhalation aerosol:*
- If you do not understand the directions or you are not sure how to use the inhaler, ask your health care professional to show you how to use it. Also, ask your health care professional to check regularly how you use the inhaler to make sure you are using it properly.
- When you use the inhaler for the first time, or if you have not used it for a while, the inhaler may not give the right amount of medicine with the first puff. Therefore, before using the inhaler, test or prime it.
- *To test or prime the inhaler:*
  —Insert the canister firmly into the clean mouthpiece according to the manufacturer's instructions. Check to make sure it is placed properly into the mouthpiece.
  —Take the cap off the mouthpiece and shake the inhaler three or four times.
  —Hold the inhaler away from you at arm's length and press the top of the canister, spraying the medicine once into the air. The inhaler will now be ready to give the right amount of medicine when you use it.
- *To use the inhaler:*
  —Using your thumb and one or two fingers, hold the inhaler upright, with the mouthpiece end down and pointing toward you.
  —Take the cap off the mouthpiece. Check the mouthpiece to make sure it is clear. Then, gently shake the inhaler three or four times.
  —Breathe out slowly to the end of a normal breath.
  —Use the inhalation method recommended by your doctor:
  - Open-mouth method—Place the mouthpiece about 1 or 2 inches (2 fingerwidths) in front of your widely opened mouth. Make sure the inhaler is aimed into your mouth so the spray does not hit the roof of your mouth or your tongue.
  - Closed-mouth method—Place the mouthpiece in your mouth between your teeth and over your tongue with your lips closed tightly around it. Make sure your tongue or teeth are not blocking the opening.
  —Start to breathe in slowly and deeply through your mouth. At the same time, press the top of the canister once to get one puff of medicine. Continue to breathe in slowly for 5 to 10 seconds. Count the seconds while breathing in. It is important to press the canister and breathe in slowly at the same time so the medicine gets into your lungs. This step may be difficult at first. If you are using the closed-mouth method and you see a fine mist coming from your mouth or nose, the inhaler is not being used correctly.
  —Hold your breath as long as you can up to 10 seconds. This gives the medicine time to settle into your airways and lungs.
  —Take the mouthpiece away from your mouth and breathe out slowly.
  —If your doctor has told you to inhale more than one puff of medicine at each dose, gently shake the inhaler again, and take the second puff following exactly the same steps you used for the first puff. Press the canister one time for each puff of medicine.
  —When you are finished, wipe off the mouthpiece and replace the cap.
- Your doctor may want you to use a spacer device or holding chamber with the inhaler. A spacer helps get the medicine into the lungs and reduces the amount of medicine that stays in your mouth and throat.
  —*To use a spacer device with the inhaler:*
  - Attach the spacer to the inhaler according to the manufacturer's directions. There are different types of spacers available, but the method of breathing remains the same with most spacers.
  - Gently shake the inhaler and spacer three or four times.
  - Hold the mouthpiece of the spacer away from your mouth and breathe out slowly to the end of a normal breath.
  - Place the mouthpiece into your mouth between your teeth and over your tongue with your lips closed around it.

- Press the top of the canister once to release one puff of medicine into the spacer. Within 1 or 2 seconds, start to breathe in slowly and deeply through your mouth for 5 to 10 seconds. Count the seconds while inhaling. Do not breathe in through your nose.
- Hold your breath as long as you can up to 10 seconds.
- Take the mouthpiece away from your mouth and breathe out slowly.
- If your doctor has told you to take more than one puff of medicine at each dose, gently shake the inhaler and spacer again and take the next puff, following exactly the same steps you used for the first puff. Do not put more than one puff of medicine into the spacer at a time.
- When you are finished, remove the spacer device from the inhaler and replace the cap.

- Clean the inhaler, mouthpiece, and spacer at least twice a week.
  —*To clean the inhaler:*
  - Remove the canister from the inhaler and set aside.
  - Wash the mouthpiece, cap, and the spacer with warm, soapy water. Then, rinse well with warm, running water.
  - Shake off the excess water and let the inhaler parts air dry completely before putting the inhaler back together.

- The ipratropium canister provides about 200 inhalations. You should keep a record of the number of inhalations you use so you will know when the canister is almost empty. This canister, unlike other aerosol canisters, cannot be floated in water to test its fullness.

For patients using *ipratropium inhalation solution:*
- Use this medicine only in a power-operated nebulizer with an adequate flow rate and equipped with a face mask or mouthpiece. Your doctor will tell you which nebulizer to use. Make sure you understand exactly how to use it. If you have any questions about this, check with your doctor.
- *To prepare the medicine for use in the nebulizer:*
  —*If you are using the single-dose vial of ipratropium:*
  - Break away one vial by pulling it firmly from the strip.
  - Twist off the top to open the vial. Use the contents of the vial as soon as possible after opening it.
  - Squeeze the contents of the vial into the cup of the nebulizer. If your doctor has told you to use less than a full vial of solution, use a syringe to withdraw the correct amount of solution from the vial and add it to the nebulizer cup. Be sure to throw away the syringe after one use.
  —*If you are using the multiple-dose bottle of ipratropium:*
  - Use a syringe to withdraw the correct amount of solution from the bottle and add it to the nebulizer cup. Do not use the same syringe more than once.
- If you have been told to dilute the ipratropium inhalation solution in the nebulizer cup with the sodium chloride solution provided, use a new syringe to add the sodium chloride solution to the cup as directed by your health care professional.

- If your doctor told you to use another inhalation solution with the ipratropium inhalation solution, add that solution also to the nebulizer cup.
- *To use the nebulizer:*
  —Gently shake the nebulizer cup to mix the solutions well.
  —Connect the nebulizer tube to the air or oxygen pump and begin the treatment. Adjust the mask, if you are using one, to prevent mist from getting into your eyes.
  —Use the method of breathing your doctor told you to use to take the treatment. One way is to breathe slowly and deeply through the mask or mouthpiece. Another way is to breathe in and out normally with the mouthpiece in your mouth, taking a deep breath every 1 or 2 minutes. Continue to breathe in the medicine as instructed until no more mist is formed in the nebulizer cup or until you hear a sputtering (spitting or popping) sound.
  —When you have finished, replace the caps on the solutions. Store the bottles of solution in the refrigerator until the next treatment.
  —Clean the nebulizer according to the manufacturer's directions.

Precautions While Using This Medicine

Check with your doctor at once if your symptoms do not improve within 30 minutes after using a dose of this medicine or if your condition gets worse.

For patients using *ipratropium inhalation solution:*
- *If you are also using cromolyn inhalation solution, do not mix that solution with the ipratropium inhalation solution containing the preservative benzalkonium chloride for use in a nebulizer.* To do so will cause the solution to become cloudy. However, if your condition requires you to use cromolyn inhalation solution with ipratropium inhalation solution, it may be mixed with ipratropium inhalation solution that is preservative-free.

Side Effects of This Medicine

Along with its needed effects, a medicine may cause some unwanted effects. Although not all of these side effects may occur, if they do occur they may require medical attention.

Check with your doctor as soon as possible if any of the following side effects occur:
  Rare
    Constipation (continuing) or lower abdominal pain or bloating; increased wheezing, tightness in chest, or difficulty in breathing; severe eye pain; skin rash or hives; swelling of face, lips, or eyelids

Other side effects may occur that usually do not need medical attention. These side effects may go away during treatment as your body adjusts to the medicine. However, check with your doctor if any of the following side effects continue or are bothersome:
  More common
    Cough; dryness of mouth; unpleasant taste
  Less common or rare
    Blurred vision or other changes in vision; burning eyes; difficult urination; dizziness; headache; nausea; nervousness; pounding heartbeat; sweating; trembling

Other side effects not listed above may also occur in some patients. If you notice any other effects, check with your doctor.

Revised: 06/21/96

IPRATROPIUM   Nasal

Commonly used brand name(s):

In the U.S.—
Atrovent

In Canada—
Atrovent

Description

Ipratropium (i-pra-TROE-pee-um) nasal spray is used to relieve runny nose (rhinorrhea).

The 0.03% nasal solution is used to relieve a runny nose associated with allergic and nonallergic perennial rhinitis. However, it does not relieve the nasal congestion, sneezing, or postnasal drip associated with allergic or nonallergic perennial rhinitis.

The 0.06% nasal solution is used for 4 days to relieve a runny nose associated with the common cold. However, it does not relieve the nasal congestion or sneezing associated with the common cold.

When this medicine is sprayed into your nose, it works by preventing the glands in your nose from producing large amounts of fluid.

Ipratropium is available only with your doctor's prescription, in the following dosage form:

Nasal
- Nasal solution (nasal spray) (U.S. and Canada)

Before Using This Medicine

In deciding to use a medicine, the risks of using the medicine must be weighed against the good it will do. This is a decision you and your doctor will make. For ipratropium nasal spray, the following should be considered:

Allergies—Tell your doctor if you have ever had any unusual or allergic reaction to ipratropium, atropine, belladonna, hyoscyamine, or scopolamine, or to other nasal medicines.

Pregnancy—Ipratropium has not been studied in pregnant women. However, it has not been shown to cause birth defects in animal studies.

Breast-feeding—It is not known whether ipratropium nasal spray passes into the breast milk. Although most medicines pass into breast milk in small amounts, many of them may be used safely while breast-feeding. Mothers who are using this medicine and who wish to breast-feed should discuss this with their doctor.

Children—Although there is no specific information comparing the use of ipratropium nasal spray in children with use in other age groups, this medicine is not expected to cause different side effects or problems in children than it does in adults.

Older adults—Many medicines have not been studied specifically in older people. Therefore, it may not be known whether they work exactly the same way they do in younger adults. Although there is no specific information comparing the use of ipratropium nasal spray in the elderly with use in other age groups, this medicine is not expected to cause different side effects in older people than it does in younger adults.

Other medicines—Although certain medicines should not be used together at all, in other cases two different medicines may be used together even if an interaction might occur. In these cases, your doctor may want to change the dose, or other precautions may be necessary. Tell your health care professional if you are taking any other prescription or nonprescription (over-the-counter [OTC]) medicine.

Other medical problems—The presence of other medical problems may affect the use of ipratropium nasal spray. Make sure you tell your doctor if you have any other medical problem, especially:

- Bladder neck obstruction or
- Enlarged prostate—Ipratropium nasal may make the condition worse

- Glaucoma, angle-closure—If ipratropium nasal is sprayed into the eyes, it may make the condition worse

Proper Use of This Medicine

It is very important that you use ipratropium nasal spray only as directed. Do not use more of it and do not use it more often than your doctor ordered. To do so may increase the chance of side effects.

Keep the nasal spray away from your eyes. If the nasal spray gets in your eyes, immediately flush your eyes with cool tap water for several minutes. If you get the nasal spray in your eyes, you may experience an increased sensitivity to light (which may last a few hours), blurring of vision, or eye pain. If eye pain or blurred vision occurs, check with your doctor as soon as possible.

Ipratropium nasal spray usually comes with patient directions. Read them carefully before using this medicine.

If you do not understand the directions or if you are not sure how to use the ipratropium nasal spray, ask your health care professional to show you how to use it.

When you use the nasal spray for the first time or if you have not used it for a while, the spray device may not deliver the right amount of medicine with the first spray. Therefore, before using the nasal spray, prime the device to make sure it works properly.

To prime the nasal spray device:
- The nasal spray pump must be primed before the nasal spray is used for the first time.
- To prime the pump, hold the bottle with your thumb at the base and your index and middle fingers on the white shoulder area. Make sure the bottle points upright and away from your eyes.
- Press your thumb firmly and quickly against the bottle seven times. The pump is now primed and can be used.
- Your pump should not have to be reprimed unless you have not used the medication for more than 24 hours. Repriming the pump will only require two sprays. However, if you have not used your nasal spray for more than seven days, repriming the pump will require seven sprays.

To use the nasal spray:

- Before using the nasal spray, blow your nose gently to clear your nostrils.
- Remove the clear plastic dust cap and the green safety clip from the nasal spray pump. The safety clip prevents the accidental discharge of the spray when you are not using it.
- Close one nostril by gently placing your finger against the side of your nose, tilt your head slightly forward and, keeping the bottle upright, insert the nasal tip into the other nostril. Point the tip toward the back and outer side of the nose.
- Press firmly and quickly upwards with the thumb at the base while holding the white shoulder portion of the pump between your index and middle fingers. Do *not* breathe in while spraying.
- After spraying the nostril and removing the unit, sniff deeply and breathe out through the nose. Tilt your head backwards for a few seconds to let the spray spread over the back of the nose.
- Repeat these steps for the second spray in the first nostril and for the two sprays in the other nostril.
- Replace the clear plastic dust cap and the green safety clip.
- You should not take extra doses of the nasal spray without checking with your doctor.

To clean the nasal spray device:

- If the nasal tip becomes clogged, remove the clear plastic dust cap and the green safety clip.
- Hold the nasal tip under running warm tap water for about a minute.
- Dry the nasal tip, reprime the nasal spray pump (see above, *To prime the nasal spray device*), and replace the clear plastic dust cap and green safety clip.

Dosing—The dose of ipratropium nasal spray will be different for different patients. *Follow your doctor's orders or the directions on the label.* The following information includes only the average doses of ipratropium nasal spray. *If your dose is different, do not change it* unless your doctor tells you to do so:

- For the 0.03% *nasal* spray:
  —For runny nose associated with allergic and nonallergic perennial rhinitis:
  - Adults and children 6 years of age and older—2 sprays of the 0.03% nasal solution into each nostril two or three times a day.
  - Children up to 6 years of age—Use and dose must be determined by your doctor.
- For the 0.06% *nasal* spray:
  —For runny nose associated with the common cold:
  - Adults and children 5 years of age and older—2 sprays of the 0.06% nasal solution into each nostril three or four times a day. Do not use the medicine for more than 4 days.
  - Children up to 5 years of age—Use and dose must be determined by your doctor.

Missed dose—If you are using ipratropium nasal spray regularly and you miss a dose of this medicine, use it as soon as possible. However, if it is almost time for your next dose, skip the missed dose and go back to your regular dosing schedule. Do not double doses.

Storage—To store this medicine:

- Keep out of the reach of children.
- Store away from heat and direct sunlight.
- Keep the medicine from freezing.
- Do not keep outdated medicine or medicine no longer needed. Be sure that any discarded medicine is out of the reach of children.

Precautions While Using This Medicine

Some improvement in your runny nose is usually seen during the first full day of treatment. However:

- If you are using the 0.03% nasal spray for runny nose associated with allergic and nonallergic perennial rhinitis, and *your symptoms do not improve within one or two weeks or if your condition becomes worse, check with your doctor.*
- If you are using the 0.06% nasal spray for runny nose associated with the common cold, and *your condition becomes worse, check with your doctor.*

Ipratropium nasal spray may cause dryness of the mouth or throat. For temporary relief, use sugarless candy or gum, melt bits of ice in your mouth, or use a saliva substitute. However, if your mouth continues to feel dry for more than 2 weeks, check with your medical doctor or dentist. Continuing dryness of the mouth may increase the chance of dental disease, including tooth decay, gum disease, and fungus infections.

Side Effects of This Medicine

Along with its needed effects, a medicine may cause some unwanted effects. Although not all of these side effects may occur, if they do occur they may require medical attention.

Check with your doctor as soon as possible if any of the following side effects occur:
For the 0.03% nasal spray
  Less common
    Nasal dryness; nosebleeds; sore throat
  Rare
    Blurred vision; dizziness; eye redness, irritation, or pain; pain or cramping in abdomen; painful or difficult urination
For the 0.06% nasal spray used for 4 days
  Less common
    Nasal dryness; nosebleeds
  Rare
    Blurred vision; dizziness; eye redness or pain; fast, slow, or irregular heartbeat; pain or cramping in abdomen; painful or difficult urination; ringing or buzzing in ears; sore throat

Other side effects may occur that usually do not need medical attention. These side effects may go away during treatment as your body adjusts to the medicine. However, check with your doctor if any of the following side effects continue or are bothersome:
For the 0.03% nasal spray
  Less common or rare
    Dry mouth or throat; increased nasal congestion or runny nose; nasal itching, burning, or irritation; nausea
For the 0.06% nasal spray
  Less common or rare
    Dry mouth or throat; increased nasal congestion

Other side effects not listed above may occur in some patients. If you notice any other effects, check with your doctor.

Revised: 06/11/99

IPRATROPIUM AND ALBUTEROL
Inhalation-Local

Commonly used brand name(s):

In the U.S.—
Combivent; DuoNeb

Another commonly used name for albuterol is salbutamol.

Description

Ipratropium (i-pra-TROE-pee-um) and albuterol (al-BYOO-ter-ol) combination is a bronchodilator (medicine that opens up narrowed breathing passages). It is taken by inhalation to help control the symptoms of lung diseases, such as asthma, chronic bronchitis, and emphysema.

Ipratropium in combination with albuterol helps decrease coughing, wheezing, shortness of breath, and troubled breathing by increasing the flow of air into the lungs.

This medicine is available only with your doctor's prescription, in the following dosage form:

Inhalation
- Inhalation aerosol (U.S.)
- Inhalation solution (U.S.)

Before Using This Medicine

In deciding to use a medicine, the risks of using the medicine must be weighed against the good it will do. This is a decision you and your doctor will make. For ipratropium and albuterol combination, the following should be considered:

Allergies—Tell your doctor if you have ever had any unusual or allergic reaction to albuterol, ipratropium, atropine, belladonna, hyoscyamine, or scopolamine, or to other inhalation aerosol medicines. Also tell your health care professional if you are allergic to soya lecithin or related food substances such as soybeans and peanuts.

Pregnancy—Ipratropium and albuterol have not been studied in pregnant women. However, studies in animals have shown that albuterol causes birth defects when given in doses comparable to the maximum human dose. Ipratropium has not been found to cause birth defects or other problems in animal studies.

Breast-feeding—It is not known whether ipratropium or albuterol passes into breast milk. Although most medicines pass into breast milk in small amounts, many of them may be used safely while breast-feeding. Mothers who are using this medicine and who wish to breast-feed should discuss this with their doctor.

Children—Studies comparing the effects of the inhalation aerosol dosage form of ipratropium and albuterol in children with those in other age groups have not been done.

Older adults—Ipratropium and albuterol combination has been tested in elderly patients and has not been found to cause different side effects or problems in older people than it does in younger adults.

Other medicines—Although certain medicines should not be used together at all, in other cases two different medicines may be used together even if an interaction might occur. In these cases, your doctor may want to change the dose, or other precautions may be necessary. When you are taking ipratropium and albuterol combination, it is especially important that your health care professional know if you are taking any other prescription or nonprescription (over-the-counter [OTC]) medicine.

Other medical problems—The presence of other medical problems may affect the use of ipratropium and albuterol combination. Make sure you tell your doctor if you have any other medical problems, especially:
- Difficult urination—This medicine may make the condition worse
- Glaucoma—This medicine may make the condition worse if it gets into the eyes
- Heart rhythm problems or
- High blood pressure (hypertension) or
- Problems with blood circulation to the heart—The albuterol contained in this combination medicine can cause unwanted effects on the heart in some patients

Proper Use of This Medicine

This medicine usually comes with patient directions. Read them carefully before using this medicine. If you do not understand the directions or you are not sure how to use the inhaler or nebulizer, ask your doctor, nurse, or pharmacist to show you how to use it.

When you use the inhaler for the first time, or if you have not used it for more than 24 hours, the inhaler may not give the right amount of medicine with the first puff. Therefore, before using the inhaler, prime it by spraying the medicine into the air three times. The inhaler will now be ready to give the right amount of medicine when you use it.

When you use the inhalation solution, make sure you use a jet nebulizer that is connected to an air compressor with a good air flow. Use a face mask or mouthpiece to inhale the medicine.

Keep the spray away from the eyes because this medicine may cause irritation or blurred vision. This is especially important for people with glaucoma. Closing your eyes while you are inhaling this medicine may help keep it out of your eyes.

It is very important that you use ipratropium and albuterol combination only as directed. Do not use more of it and do not use it more often than directed. To do so may increase the chance of serious side effects.

Dosing—The dose of ipratropium and albuterol combination will be different for different patients. *Follow your doctor's orders or the directions on the label.* The following information includes only the average doses of this medicine. *If your dose is different, do not change it* unless your doctor tells you to do so.

- For *inhalation* aerosol dosage form:
  - For symptoms of chronic obstructive pulmonary disease:
    - Adults—2 puffs four times a day and as needed. No more than a total of 12 puffs should be used in any twenty-four-hour period.
    - Children—Use and dose must be determined by your doctor.
- For *inhalation solution* dosage form (used with a nebulizer):
  - For symptoms of chronic obstructive pulmonary disease:
    - Adults—Use on 3 mL (mililiter) vial in the nebulizer 4 times a day. You may have 2 additional treatments per day if needed.
    - Children—Use and dose must be determined by your doctor.

Missed dose—If you are using ipratropium and albuterol combination regularly and you miss a dose, use it as soon as possible. Then use any remaining doses for that day at regularly spaced intervals.

Storage— To store this medicine:
- Keep out of the reach of children.
- Store away from heat and direct light. Keep unused vials of inhalation solution in the foil pouch or carton.
- Do not store in the bathroom, near the kitchen sink, or in other damp places. Heat or moisture may cause the medicine to break down.
- Do not keep outdated medicine or medicine no longer needed. Be sure that any discarded medicine is out of the reach of children.

Precautions While Using This Medicine

Check with your doctor at once if difficulty in breathing continues after using a dose of this medicine or if your condition gets worse.

Side Effects of This Medicine

Along with its needed effects, a medicine may cause some unwanted effects. Although not all of these side effects may occur, if they do occur they may need medical attention.

Check with your doctor as soon as possible if any of the following side effects occur:
Rare
> Chest discomfort or pain; fast or irregular heartbeat; shortness of breath or wheezing; skin rash or hives; swelling of the face, lips, eyelids, mouth, or throat

Other side effects may occur that usually do not need medical attention. These side effects may go away during treatment as your body adjusts to the medicine. However, check with your doctor if any of the following side effects continue or are bothersome:
Less common or rare
> Change in sense of taste; coughing; dizziness; dryness of mouth; headache; nausea; nervousness; tremor

Other side effects not listed above may also occur in some patients. If you notice any other effects, check with your doctor.

Developed: 07/29/98
Revised: 07/03/2001

IRBESARTAN   Systemic

Commonly used brand name(s):

In the U.S.—
Avapro

Description

Irbesartan (ir-be-SAR-tan) belongs to the class of medicines called angiotensin II inhibitor antihypertensives. It is used to treat high blood pressure (hypertension).

High blood pressure adds to the workload of the heart and arteries. If it continues for a long time, the heart and arteries may not function properly. This can damage the blood vessels of the brain, heart, and kidneys, resulting in a stroke, heart failure, or kidney failure. High blood pressure also may increase the risk of heart attacks. These problems may be less likely to occur if blood pressure is controlled.

Irbesartan works by blocking the action of a substance in the body that causes blood vessels to tighten. As a result, irbesartan relaxes blood vessels. This lowers blood pressure.

This medicine is available only with your doctor's prescription, in the following dosage form(s):
Oral
- Tablets (U.S.)

Before Using This Medicine

In deciding to use a medicine, the risks of taking the medicine must be weighed against the good it will do. This is a decision you and your doctor will make. For irbesartan, the following should be considered:

Allergies— Tell your doctor if you have ever had any unusual or allergic reaction to irbesartan. Also tell your health care professional if you are allergic to any other substances, such as foods, preservatives, or dyes.

Pregnancy— Use of irbesartan during pregnancy, especially during the second and third trimesters (after the first 3 months), can cause low blood pressure, severe kidney failure, or even death in the newborn. *Therefore, it is important that you check with your doctor immediately if you think that you may have become pregnant.* Be sure that you have discussed this with your doctor before taking this medicine.

Breast-feeding— It is not known whether irbesartan passes into breast milk. However, irbesartan passes into the milk of lactating rats. Because this medicine may cause serious side effects, breast-feeding is generally not recommended while you are taking it.

Children— Studies on this medicine have been done only in adult patients, and there is no specific information comparing use of irbesartan in children with use in other age groups.

Older adults— This medicine has been tested in patients 65 years of age or older and has not been shown to cause different side effects or problems in older people than it does in younger adults. However, blood levels of irbesartan may be increased in the elderly and elderly patients may be more sensitive to the effects of irbesartan.

Other medicines— Although certain medicines should not be used together at all, in other cases two different medicines may be used together even if an interaction might occur. In these cases, your doctor may want to change the dose, or other precautions may be necessary. When you are taking irbesartan, it is especially important that your health care professional know if you are taking any of the following:
- Diuretics (water pills)—Effects on blood pressure may be increased

Other medical problems— The presence of other medical problems may affect the use of irbesartan. Make sure you tell your doctor if you have any other medical problems, especially:
- Congestive heart failure, severe—Lowering of blood pressure by irbesartan may make this condition worse
- Dehydration—Blood pressure–lowering effects of irbesartan may be increased.
- Kidney disease—Effects of irbesartan may be increased because of slower removal of medicine from the body.

Proper Use of This Medicine

Take this medicine only as directed by your doctor. Do not take more of it and do not take it more often than your doctor ordered. This medicine works best when there is a constant amount in the blood. *To help keep the amount constant, do not miss any doses. Also, it is best to take the doses at the same time each day.*

Dosing—The dose of irbesartan will be different for different patients. *Follow your doctor's orders or the directions on the label.* The following information includes only the average doses of irbesartan. *If your dose is different, do not change it* unless your doctor tells you to do so.

The number of tablets that you take depends on the strength of the medicine.

- For *oral* dosage form (tablets):
  —For high blood pressure:
  - Adults—75 or 150 milligrams (mg) once a day. Your doctor may increase your dose if needed.
  - Children—Use and dose must be determined by your doctor.

Missed dose—If you miss a dose of this medicine, take it as soon as possible. However, if it is almost time for your next dose, skip the missed dose and go back to your regular dosing schedule. Do not double doses.

Storage—To store this medicine:

- Keep out of the reach of children.
- Store away from heat and direct light.
- Do not store in the bathroom, near the kitchen sink, or in other damp places. Heat or moisture may cause the medicine to break down.
- Do not keep outdated medicine or medicine no longer needed. Be sure that any discarded medicine is out of the reach of children.

Precautions While Using This Medicine

It is important that your doctor check your progress at regular visits to make sure that this medicine is working properly and to check for unwanted effects.

Check with your doctor immediately if you think that you may be pregnant. Irbesartan may cause birth defects or other problems in the baby if taken during pregnancy.

Do not take other medicines unless they have been discussed with your doctor. This especially includes over-the-counter (nonprescription) medicines for appetite control, asthma, colds, cough, hay fever, or sinus problems, since they may tend to increase your blood pressure.

Dizziness or lightheadedness may occur, especially if you have been taking a diuretic (water pill). *Make sure you know how you react to this medicine before you drive, use machines, or do anything else that could be dangerous if you experience these effects.*

Check with your doctor right away if you become sick while taking this medicine, especially with severe or continuing nausea and vomiting or diarrhea. These conditions may cause you to lose too much water and lead to low blood pressure.

Dizziness, lightheadedness, or fainting may also occur if you exercise or if the weather is hot. Heavy sweating can cause loss of too much water and result in low blood pressure. Use extra care during exercise or hot weather.

Side Effects of This Medicine

Along with its needed effects, a medicine may cause some unwanted effects. Although not all of these side effects may occur, if they do occur they may need medical attention.

Check with your doctor as soon as possible if any of the following side effects occur:
  Rare
    Dizziness, lightheadedness, or fainting

Other side effects may occur that usually do not need medical attention. These side effects may go away during treatment as your body adjusts to the medicine. However, check with your doctor if any of the following side effects continue or are bothersome:
  Less common
    Anxiety and/or nervousness; cold-like symptoms; belching, heartburn, and stomach discomfort; cold symptoms; diarrhea; headache; muscle or bone pain; unusual tiredness

Other side effects not listed above may also occur in some patients. If you notice any other effects, check with your doctor.

Developed: 08/10/98

IRINOTECAN   Systemic

Commonly used brand name(s):

In the U.S.—
  Camptosar

In Canada—
  Camptosar

Another commonly used name is CPT-11.

Description

Irinotecan (eye-ri-noe-TEE-kan) belongs to the group of medicines called antineoplastics. It is used to treat cancer of the colon or rectum.

Irinotecan interferes with the growth of cancer cells, which are eventually destroyed. Since the growth of normal cells may also be affected by the medicine, other effects may also occur. Some of these may be serious and must be reported to your doctor. Other effects, like hair loss, may not be serious but may cause concern. Some effects may occur after treatment with irinotecan has been stopped. Be sure that you have discussed with your doctor the possible side effects of this medicine as well as the good it can do.

This medicine is available only with your doctor's prescription, in the following dosage form(s):

  Parenteral
  - Injection (U.S. and Canada)

Before Using This Medicine

In deciding to use a medicine, the risks of using the medicine must be weighed against the good it will do. This is a decision you and your doctor will make. For irinotecan, the following should be considered:

Allergies—Tell your doctor if you have ever had any unusual or allergic reaction to irinotecan. Also tell your health care professional if you are allergic to any other substances.

Pregnancy—Tell your doctor if you are pregnant. Studies in rats and rabbits have shown that irinotecan causes birth defects and deaths of fetuses.

Be sure that you have discussed this with your doctor before starting treatment with this medicine. It is best to use birth control while you are receiving irinotecan. Also, tell your doctor right away if you think you have become pregnant during treatment.

Breast-feeding—It is not known whether irinotecan passes into breast milk. However, because this medicine may cause serious side effects, breast-feeding is generally not recommended while you are receiving it.

Children—Studies on this medicine have been done only in adult patients, and there is no specific information comparing use of irinotecan in children with use in other age groups.

Older adults—This medicine has been tested in patients 65 years of age and older and has not been shown to cause different side effects or problems in older people than it does in younger adults. However, severe diarrhea caused by irinotecan may occur more often in elderly patients.

Other medicines—Although certain medicines should not be used together at all, in other cases two different medicines may be used together even if an interaction might occur. In these cases, your doctor may want to change the dose, or other precautions may be necessary. When you are taking irinotecan, it is especially important that your health care professional know if you are taking any of the following:

- Amphotericin B by injection (e.g., Fungizone) or
- Antithyroid agents (medicine for overactive thyroid) or
- Azathioprine (e.g., Imuran) or
- Chloramphenicol (e.g., Chloromycetin) or
- Colchicine or
- Flucytosine (e.g., Ancobon) or
- Ganciclovir (e.g., Cytovene) or
- Interferon alfa (e.g., Intron A, Roferon-A) or
- Plicamycin (e.g., Mithracin) or
- Zidovudine (e.g., AZT, Retrovir) or
- If you have ever been treated with radiation or other cancer medicines—The risk of dangerously low blood counts may be increased

- Azathioprine (e.g., Imuran) or
- Chlorambucil (e.g., Leukeran) or
- Corticosteroids (cortisone-like medicine) or
- Cyclophosphamide (e.g., Cytoxan) or
- Cyclosporine (e.g., Sandimmune) or
- Mercaptopurine (e.g., Purinethol) or
- Muromonab-CD3 (monoclonal antibody) (e.g., Orthoclone OKT3) or
- Mycophenolate (e.g., CellCept) or
- Tacrolimus (e.g., Prograf)—The risk of infection may be increased because these medicines and irinotecan can all decrease your body's resistance to infection

- Diuretics (water pills)—There may be an increased risk of serious problems caused by loss of body fluid if severe diarrhea or vomiting occurs during irinotecan treatment

- Laxatives—Use of laxatives together with irinotecan may increase the risk of severe diarrhea

Other medical problems—The presence of other medical problems may affect the use of irinotecan. Make sure you tell your doctor if you have any other medical problems, especially:

- Chickenpox (including recent exposure) or
- Herpes zoster (shingles)—Irinotecan may cause these

conditions to get worse and spread to other parts of your body

- Infection—Irinotecan may decrease your body's ability to fight an infection
- Liver disease—The risk of dangerously low white blood cell counts may be increased
- Lung disease—An unusual side effect consisting of fever and of shortness of breath and other problems with the lungs has occurred, very rarely, in some people with lung disease who received irinotecan

Proper Use of This Medicine

Irinotecan often causes nausea and vomiting. *It is very important that you continue to receive the medicine* even if it makes you feel ill. Ask your health care professional about ways to lessen these effects.

Dosing—The dose of irinotecan will be different for different patients. The dose that is used may depend on a number of things, including the patient's size and whether or not other treatments are also being given. *If you are receiving irinotecan at home, follow your doctor's orders or the directions on the label.* If you have any questions about the proper dose of this medicine, ask your doctor.

Precautions While Using This Medicine

It is very important that your doctor check your progress at regular visits to make sure that this medicine is working properly and to check for unwanted effects. Some of the side effects of this medicine do not have any symptoms and must be found with a blood test.

While you are being treated with irinotecan, and after you stop treatment with it, *do not have any immunizations (vaccinations) without your doctor's approval.* Irinotecan may lower your body's resistance, and there is a chance you might get the infection the immunization is meant to prevent. In addition, other persons living in your household should not take oral polio vaccine, since there is a chance they could pass the polio virus on to you. Also, avoid persons who have taken oral polio vaccine within the past several months. Do not get close to them and do not stay in the same room with them for very long. If you cannot take these precautions, you should consider wearing a protective face mask that covers the nose and mouth.

Irinotecan may cause diarrhea, which can last long enough and be severe enough to cause serious medical problems. If diarrhea occurs while you are being treated with irinotecan:

- *Check with your doctor immediately.* Be sure to let your doctor know if the diarrhea started during an irinotecan injection or less than 24 hours afterwards. Also, be sure to tell your doctor if you had any other symptoms, such as stomach cramps or sweating, before the diarrhea started. This means that you are having a certain kind of diarrhea that may need to be treated by your doctor.
- If diarrhea first occurs more than 24 hours after a dose of irinotecan, *start taking loperamide (e.g., Imodium A-D)* as soon as you notice that your bowel movements are occurring more often, or are looser, than usual. Loperamide is available without a prescription. Buy some of it ahead of time, so that you will have it on hand in case it is needed. Unless otherwise directed by your doctor, take 4 milligrams (mg) of loperamide (2 capsules or tablets, or 4 teaspoonfuls of the oral solution dosage

form) for the first dose, then 2 mg (1 capsule or tablet, or 2 teaspoonfuls of the oral solution dosage form) every two hours. To interrupt your sleep less often, you may take 4 mg of loperamide every four hours during the night. Continue taking loperamide, day and night, until you have not had any diarrhea for twelve hours. *It is very important that you follow these (or your doctor's) directions, even though they are different from the directions on the nonprescription (over-the-counter [OTC]) loperamide package label.* The largest amount of loperamide recommended on the package label for use in a twenty-four-hour period (8 mg) is not enough for treating diarrhea caused by irinotecan.

- Diarrhea causes loss of body fluid, which can lead to dehydration, a serious medical problem. To prevent this, *it is very important that you replace the lost fluid.* While you have diarrhea, and for a day or two after the diarrhea has stopped, *drink plenty of clear liquids,* such as ginger ale, caffeine-free cola, decaffeinated tea, and broth. *Ask your doctor about the amount of liquid you should be drinking every day.* Also, ask your doctor whether you should use a sports drink (e.g., Gatorade), which contains other substances, such as sodium and potassium, that may be lost along with body fluid. *Follow your doctor's directions very carefully.*
- Because alcohol and caffeine can increase fluid loss, you should not drink beverages or take any medicines that contain them while you have diarrhea. Also, avoid eating foods that may make diarrhea worse, such as bran, raw fruits or vegetables, or fatty, fried, or spicy foods.
- Vomiting can also increase the amount of fluid lost by the body and increase the risk of dehydration. *If vomiting occurs at the same time as diarrhea, check with your doctor right away.*
- Signs of too much fluid loss (dehydration) include decreased urination, dizziness or light-headedness, dryness of the mouth, fainting, increased thirst, and wrinkled skin. If any of these occur, *check with your doctor immediately.*

Irinotecan can temporarily lower the number of white blood cells in your blood, increasing the chance of getting an infection. It can also lower the number of platelets, which are needed for proper blood clotting. If this occurs, there are certain precautions you can take, especially when your blood count is low, to reduce the risk of infection or bleeding:

- If you can, avoid people with infections. *Check with your doctor immediately* if you think you are getting an infection or if you get a fever or chills, cough or hoarseness, lower back or side pain, or painful or difficult urination.
- *Check with your doctor immediately* if you notice any unusual bleeding or bruising; black, tarry stools; blood in urine or stools; or pinpoint red spots on your skin.
- Be careful when using a regular toothbrush, dental floss, or toothpick. Your medical doctor, dentist, or nurse may recommend other ways to clean your teeth and gums. Also, check with your medical doctor before having any dental work done.
- Do not touch your eyes or the inside of your nose unless you have just washed your hands and have not touched anything else in the meantime.
- Be careful not to cut yourself when you are using sharp objects such as a safety razor or fingernail or toenail cutters.

- Avoid contact sports or other situations where bruising or injury could occur.

Side Effects of This Medicine

Along with its needed effects, a medicine may cause some unwanted effects. Although not all of these side effects may occur, if they do occur they may need medical attention.

Check with your doctor immediately if any of the following side effects occur:
More common
Diarrhea, with or without stomach cramps or sweating; fever; shortness of breath or troubled breathing

Less common
Cough or hoarseness (accompanied by fever or chills); dizziness or light-headedness; fainting; fever or chills; lower back or side pain (accompanied by fever or chills); painful or difficult urination (accompanied by fever or chills); runny or stuffy nose; sore throat; swelling of abdomen or stomach area; swelling of face, fingers, feet, or lower legs

The side effects listed above may occur, or continue to occur, after treatment with irinotecan has ended. Check with your doctor if you notice any of them after you stop receiving the medicine.

Also, check with your doctor as soon as possible if any of the following side effects occur:
More common
Black, tarry stools; blood in urine or stools; pinpoint red spots on skin; unusual bleeding or bruising; Unusual tiredness or weakness (severe)

Less common
Decreased urination; dryness of mouth; increased thirst; sores, ulcers, or white spots on lips or in mouth; wrinkled skin

Rare
fast or irregular breathing; puffiness or swelling of the eyelids or around the eyes; skin rash, hives, and/or itching; tightness in chest and/or wheezing

Other side effects may occur that usually do not need medical attention. These side effects may go away during treatment as your body adjusts to the medicine. However, check with your doctor if any of the following side effects continue or are bothersome:
More common
Abdominal (stomach) cramps or pain; constipation; decrease in or loss of appetite; nausea and vomiting; weakness; weight loss

Less common
Bloated feeling or gas; headache; increased sweating; indigestion; skin rash

Irinotecan may also cause a temporary loss of hair in some people. After treatment with irinotecan has ended, normal hair growth should return.

Irinotecan sometimes causes flushing of the face. This effect is harmless and does not need medical treatment.

Other side effects not listed above may also occur in some patients. If you notice any other effects, check with your doctor.

Developed: 06/27/1998
Revised: 04/04/2001

IRON SUPPLEMENTS   Systemic

Commonly used brand name(s):

In the U.S.—

DexFerrum[4]	Ferretts[1]
Femiron[1]	Ferrlecit[8]
Feosol[3]	Fumasorb[1]
Feostat[1]	Fumerin[1]
Feostat Drops[1]	Hemocyte[1]
Feratab[3]	Hytinic[5]
Fer-gen-sol[3]	InFeD[4]
Fergon[2]	Ircon[1]
Fer-In-Sol Capsules[3]	Mol-Iron[3]
Fer-In-Sol Drops[3]	Nephro-Fer[1]
Fer-In-Sol Syrup[3]	Niferex[5]
Fer-Iron Drops[3]	Niferex-150[5]
Fero-Gradumet[3]	Nu-Iron[5]
Ferospace[3]	Nu-Iron 150[5]
Ferralet[2]	Simron[2]
Ferralet Slow Release[2]	Slow Fe[3]
Ferralyn Lanacaps[3]	Span-FF[1]
Ferra-TD[3]	Venofer[7]

In Canada—

Apo-Ferrous Gluconate[2]	Neo-Fer[1]
Apo-Ferrous Sulfate[3]	Novoferrogluc[2]
DexIron[4]	Novoferrosulfa[3]
Fer-In-Sol Drops[3]	Novofumar[1]
Fer-In-Sol Syrup[3]	Palafer[1]
Fertinic[2]	PMS-Ferrous Sulfate[3]
Jectofer[6]	Slow Fe[3]

Note: For quick reference, the following iron supplements are numbered to match the corresponding brand names.

This information applies to the following:
1. Ferrous Fumarate (FER-us FYOO-ma-rate) ‡
2. Ferrous Gluconate (FER-us GLOO-koe-nate) ‡§
3. Ferrous Sulfate (FER-us SUL-fate) ‡§
4. Iron Dextran (DEX-tran)
5. Iron-Polysaccharide (pol-i-SAK-a-ride) †
6. Iron Sorbitol (SOR-bi-tole) *
7. Iron Sucrose (SU-crose) †
8. Sodium Ferric Gluconate (SO-dee-um FAIR-ic GLU-con-ate)†

---

*Not commercially available in the U.S.
†Not commercially available in Canada.
‡Generic name product may be available in the U.S.
§Generic name product may be available in Canada.

Description

Iron is a mineral that the body needs to produce red blood cells. When the body does not get enough iron, it cannot produce the number of normal red blood cells needed to keep you in good health. This condition is called iron deficiency (iron shortage) or iron deficiency anemia.

Although many people in the U.S. get enough iron from their diet, some must take additional amounts to meet their needs. For example, iron is sometimes lost with slow or small amounts of bleeding in the body that you would not be aware of and which can only be detected by your doctor. Your doctor can determine if you have an iron deficiency, what is causing the deficiency, and if an iron supplement is necessary.

Lack of iron may lead to unusual tiredness, shortness of breath, a decrease in physical performance, and learning problems in children and adults, and may increase your chance of getting an infection.

Some conditions may increase your need for iron. These include:
- Bleeding problems

- Burns
- Hemodialysis
- Intestinal diseases
- Stomach problems
- Stomach removal
- Use of medicines to increase your red blood cell count

In addition, infants, especially those receiving breast milk or low-iron formulas, may need additional iron.

Increased need for iron supplements should be determined by your health care professional.

Injectable iron is administered only by or under the supervision of your health care professional. Other forms of iron are available without a prescription; however, your health care professional may have special instructions on the proper use and dose for your condition.

Iron supplements are available in the following dosage forms:

Oral
Ferrous Fumarate
- Capsules (Canada)
- Extended-release capsules (U.S.)
- Solution (U.S.)
- Suspension (U.S. and Canada)
- Tablets (U.S. and Canada)
- Chewable tablets (U.S.)

Ferrous Gluconate
- Capsules (U.S.)
- Elixir (U.S.)
- Syrup (Canada)
- Tablets (U.S. and Canada)
- Extended-release tablets (U.S.)

Ferrous Sulfate
- Capsules (U.S.)
- Extended-release capsules (U.S.)
- Elixir (U.S.)
- Solution (U.S. and Canada)
- Tablets (U.S. and Canada)
- Enteric-coated tablets (U.S. and Canada)
- Extended-release tablets (U.S. and Canada)

Iron-Polysaccharide
- Capsules (U.S.)
- Elixir (U.S.)
- Tablets (U.S.)

Parenteral
Iron Dextran
- Injection (U.S. and Canada)
Iron Sorbitol
- Injection (Canada)
Iron Sucrose
- Injection (U.S.)
Sodium Ferric Gluconate
- Injection (U.S.)

Importance of Diet

For good health, it is important that you eat a balanced and varied diet. Follow carefully any diet program your health care professional may recommend. For your specific dietary vitamin and/or mineral needs, ask your health care professional for a list of appropriate foods. If you think that you are not getting enough vitamins and/or minerals in your diet, you may choose to take a dietary supplement.

Iron is found in the diet in two forms—heme iron, which is well absorbed, and nonheme iron, which is poorly absorbed. The best dietary source of absorbable (heme) iron is lean red meat. Chicken, turkey, and fish are also sources of iron, but they contain less than red meat. Cereals, beans, and some vegetables contain poorly absorbed (nonheme) iron. Foods rich in vitamin C (e.g., citrus fruits and fresh vegetables), eaten with small amounts of heme iron-containing foods, such as meat, may increase the amount of nonheme iron absorbed from cereals, beans, and other vegetables. Some foods (e.g., milk, eggs, spinach, fiber-containing, coffee, tea) may decrease the amount of nonheme iron absorbed from foods. Additional iron may be added to food from cooking in iron pots.

The daily amount of iron needed is defined in several different ways.

For U.S.—
- Recommended Dietary Allowances (RDAs) are the amount of vitamins and minerals needed to provide for adequate nutrition in most healthy persons. RDAs for a given nutrient may vary depending on a person's age, sex, and physical condition (e.g., pregnancy).
- Daily Values (DVs) are used on food and dietary supplement labels to indicate the percent of the recommended daily amount of each nutrient that a serving provides. DV replaces the previous designation of United States Recommended Daily Allowances (US-RDAs).

For Canada—
- Recommended Nutrient Intakes (RNIs) are used to determine the amounts of vitamins, minerals, and protein needed to provide adequate nutrition and lessen the risk of chronic disease.

Normal daily recommended intakes in milligrams (mg) for iron are generally defined as follows (Note that the RDA and RNI are expressed as an actual amount of iron, which is referred to as "elemental" iron. The product form [e.g., ferrous fumarate, ferrous gluconate, ferrous sulfate] has a different strength):

Persons	U.S. (mg)	Canada (mg)
Infants and children		
Birth to 3 years of age	6–10	0.3–6
4 to 6 years of age	10	8
7 to 10 years of age	10	8–10
Adolescent and adult males	10	8–10
Adolescent and adult females	10–15	8–13
Pregnant females	30	17–22
Breast-feeding females	15	8–13

Before Using This Dietary Supplement

If you are taking this dietary supplement without a prescription, carefully read and follow any precautions on the label. For iron supplements, the following should be considered:

Allergies—Tell your health care professional if you have ever had any unusual or allergic reaction to iron medicine. Also tell your health care professional if you are allergic to any other substances, such as foods, preservatives, or dyes.

Pregnancy—It is especially important that you are receiving enough vitamins and minerals when you become pregnant and that you continue to receive the right amount of vitamins and minerals throughout your pregnancy. Healthy fetal growth and development depend on a steady supply of nutrients from mother to fetus. During the first 3 months of pregnancy, a proper diet usually provides enough iron. However, during the last 6 months, in order to meet the increased needs of the developing baby, an iron supplement may be recommended by your health care professional.

However, taking large amounts of a dietary supplement in pregnancy may be harmful to the mother and/or fetus and should be avoided.

Breast-feeding—It is especially important that you receive the right amounts of vitamins and minerals so that your baby will also get the vitamins and minerals needed to grow properly. Iron normally is present in breast milk in small amounts. When prescribed by a health care professional, iron preparations are not known to cause problems during breast-feeding. However, nursing mothers are advised to check with their health care professional before taking iron supplements or any other medication. Taking large amounts of a dietary supplement while breast-feeding may be harmful to the mother and/or infant and should be avoided.

Children—Problems in children have not been reported with intake of normal daily recommended amounts. Iron supplements, when prescribed by your health care professional, are not expected to cause different side effects in children than they do in adults. However, it is important to follow the directions carefully, since iron overdose in children is especially dangerous.

Studies on sodium ferric gluconate have been done only in adult patients, and there is no specific information comparing the use of sodium ferric gluconate in children with use in other age groups.

Older adults—Problems in older adults have not been reported with intake of normal daily recommended amounts. Elderly people sometimes do not absorb iron as easily as younger adults and may need a larger dose. If you think you need to take an iron supplement, check with your health care professional first. Only your health care professional can decide if you need an iron supplement and how much you should take.

Medicines or other dietary supplements—Although certain medicines or dietary supplements should not be used together at all, in other cases they may be used together even if an interaction might occur. In these cases, your health care professional may want to change the dose, or other precautions may be necessary. When you are taking iron supplements, it is especially important that your health care professional know if you are taking any of the following:

- Acetohydroxamic acid (e.g., Lithostat)—Use with iron supplements may cause either medicine to be less effective

- Antacids—Use with iron supplements may make the iron supplements less effective; iron supplements should be taken 1 or 2 hours before or after antacids

- Dimercaprol—Iron supplements and dimercaprol may combine in the body to form a harmful chemical

- Etidronate or
- Fluoroquinolones (e.g., ciprofloxacin, enoxacin, lomefloxacin, norfloxacin, ofloxacin) or
- Tetracyclines (taken by mouth) (medicine for infection)—Use with iron supplements may make these medicines less effective; iron supplements should be taken 2 hours before or after these medicines

Other medical problems—The presence of other medical problems may affect the use of iron supplements. Make sure you tell your health care professional if you have any other medical problems, especially:

- Alcohol abuse (or history of) or
- Blood transfusions (with high red blood cell iron content) or
- Kidney infection or
- Liver disease or
- Porphyria cutaneous tarda—Higher blood levels of the iron supplement may occur, which may increase the chance of side effects
- Arthritis (rheumatoid) or
- Asthma or allergies or
- Heart disease—The injected form of iron may make these conditions worse
- Colitis or other intestinal problems or
- Iron overload conditions (e.g., hemochromatosis, hemosiderosis) or
- Stomach ulcer—Iron supplements may make these conditions worse
- Other anemias—Iron supplements may increase iron to toxic levels in anemias not associated with iron deficiency

Proper Use of This Dietary Supplement

Dosing—The amount of iron needed to meet normal daily recommended intakes will be different for different individuals. The following information includes only the average amounts of iron.

- For *oral* dosage forms (capsules, tablets, oral solution):
  —To prevent deficiency, the amount taken by mouth is based on normal daily recommended intakes:
  For the U.S.
  - Adult and teenage males—10 milligrams (mg) per day.
  - Adult and teenage females—10 to 15 mg per day.
  - Pregnant females—30 mg per day.
  - Breast-feeding females—15 mg per day.
  - Children 7 to 10 years of age—10 mg per day.
  - Children 4 to 6 years of age—10 mg per day.
  - Children birth to 3 years of age—6 to 10 mg per day.
  For Canada
  - Adult and teenage males—8 to 10 mg per day.
  - Adult and teenage females—8 to 13 mg per day.
  - Pregnant females—17 to 22 mg per day.
  - Breast-feeding females—8 to 13 mg per day.
  - Children 7 to 10 years of age—8 to 10 mg per day.
  - Children 4 to 6 years of age—8 mg per day.
  - Children birth to 3 years of age—0.3 to 6 mg per day.
  —To treat deficiency:
  - Adults, teenagers, and children— The dose will be determined by your doctor, based on your condition.
- For injection dosage forms:
  - Adults, teenagers, and children— The dose will be determined by your doctor, based on your condition.

After you start using this dietary supplement, continue to return to your health care professional to see if you are benefiting from the iron. Some blood tests may be necessary for this.

Iron is best absorbed when taken on an empty stomach, with water or fruit juice (adults: full glass or 8 ounces; children: ½ glass or 4 ounces), about 1 hour before or 2 hours after meals. However, to lessen the possibility of stomach upset, iron may be taken with food or immediately after meals.

For safe and effective use of iron supplements:
- Follow your health care professional's instructions if this dietary supplement was prescribed.
- Follow the manufacturer's package directions if you are treating yourself. If you think you still need iron after taking it for 1 or 2 months, check with your health care professional.

Liquid forms of iron supplement tend to stain the teeth. To prevent, reduce, or remove these stains:
- Mix each dose in water, fruit juice, or tomato juice. You may use a drinking tube or straw to help keep the iron supplement from getting on the teeth.
- When doses of liquid iron supplement are to be given by dropper, the dose may be placed well back on the tongue and followed with water or juice.
- Iron stains on teeth can usually be removed by brushing with baking soda (sodium bicarbonate) or medicinal peroxide (hydrogen peroxide 3%).

Missed dose—If you miss a dose of this dietary supplement, skip the missed dose and go back to your regular dosing schedule. Do not double doses.

Storage—To store this dietary supplement:
- Keep out of the reach of children because iron overdose is especially dangerous in children. As few as 3 or 4 adult iron tablets can cause serious poisoning in small children. Vitamin-iron products for use during pregnancy and flavored vitamins with iron often cause iron overdose in small children.
- Store away from heat and direct light.
- Do not store in the bathroom, near the kitchen sink, or in other damp places. Heat or moisture may cause the dietary supplement to break down.
- Keep the liquid form of this dietary supplement from freezing.
- Do not keep outdated dietary supplements or those no longer needed. Be sure that any discarded dietary supplement is out of the reach of children.

Precautions While Using This Dietary Supplement

When iron is combined with certain foods it may lose much of its value. If you are taking iron, the following foods should be avoided, or only taken in very small amounts, for at least 1 hour before or 2 hours after you take iron:

Cheese and yogurt
Eggs
Milk
Spinach
Tea or coffee
Whole-grain breads and cereals and bran

Do not take iron supplements and antacids or calcium supplements at the same time. It is best to space doses of these 2 products 1 to 2 hours apart, to get the full benefit from each medicine or dietary supplement.

If you are taking iron supplements *without a prescription:*
- Do not take iron supplements by mouth if you are receiving iron injections. To do so may result in iron poisoning.
- Do not regularly take large amounts of iron for longer than 6 months without checking with your health care professional. People differ in their need for iron, and those with certain medical conditions can gradually become poisoned by taking too much iron over a period of time. Also, unabsorbed iron can mask the presence of

blood in the stool, which may delay discovery of a serious condition.

If you have been taking a long-acting or coated iron tablet and your stools have *not* become black, check with your health care professional. The tablets may not be breaking down properly in your stomach, and you may not be receiving enough iron.

It is important to keep iron preparations out of the reach of children. Keep a 1-ounce bottle of *syrup* of ipecac available at home to be taken in case of an iron overdose emergency when a doctor, poison control center, or emergency room orders its use.

If you think you or anyone else has taken an overdose of iron medicine:

- *Immediate medical attention is very important.*
- *Call your doctor, a poison control center, or the nearest hospital emergency room at once.* Always keep these phone numbers readily available.
- *Follow any instructions given to you.* If syrup of ipecac has been ordered and given, do not delay going to the emergency room while waiting for the ipecac syrup to empty the stomach, since it may require 20 to 30 minutes to show results.
- *Go to the emergency room without delay.*
- *Take the container of iron with you.*

Early signs of iron overdose may not appear for up to 60 minutes or more. Do not delay going to the emergency room while waiting for signs to appear.

Side Effects of This Dietary Supplement

Along with its needed effects, a dietary supplement may cause some unwanted effects. Although not all of these effects may occur, if they do occur they may need medical attention.

Check with your health care professional if any of the following side effects occur:

More common—with injection only
    Backache, groin, side, or muscle pain; chest pain; chills; dizziness; fainting; fast heartbeat; fever with increased sweating; flushing; headache; metallic taste; nausea or vomiting; numbness, pain, or tingling of hands or feet; pain or redness at injection site; redness of skin; skin rash or hives; swelling of mouth or throat; troubled breathing

More common—when taken by mouth only
    Abdominal or stomach pain; cramping (continuing) or soreness

Less common or rare—with injection only
    Double vision; general unwell feeling; weakness without feeling dizzy or faint

Less common or rare—when taken by mouth only
    Chest or throat pain, especially when swallowing; stools with signs of blood (red or black color)

Early symptoms of iron overdose
    Diarrhea (may contain blood); fever; nausea; stomach pain or cramping (sharp); vomiting, severe (may contain blood)

    Note: Symptoms of iron overdose may not occur for up to 60 minutes or more after the overdose was taken. By this time you should have had emergency room treatment. Do not delay going to emergency room while waiting for signs to appear.

Late symptoms of iron overdose
    Bluish-colored lips, fingernails, and palms of hands; convulsions (seizures); drowsiness; pale, clammy skin; shallow and rapid breathing; unusual tiredness or weakness; weak and fast heartbeat

Other side effects may occur that usually do not need medical attention. These side effects may go away during treatment as your body adjusts to the dietary supplement. However, check with your health care professional if any of the following side effects continue or are bothersome:

More common
    Constipation; diarrhea; leg cramps; nausea; vomiting

Less common
    Darkened urine; heartburn; stained teeth

Stools commonly become dark green or black when iron preparations are taken by mouth. This is caused by unabsorbed iron and is harmless. However, in rare cases, black stools of a sticky consistency may occur along with other side effects such as red streaks in the stool, cramping, soreness, or sharp pains in the stomach or abdominal area. Check with your health care professional immediately if these side effects appear.

If you have been receiving injections of iron, you may notice a brown discoloration of your skin. This color usually fades within several weeks or months.

Other side effects not listed above may also occur in some individuals. If you notice any other effects, check with your health care professional.

Revised: 12/13/2000

ISOMETHEPTENE, DICHLORALPHENAZONE, AND ACETAMINOPHEN Systemic†

Commonly used brand name(s):

In the U.S.—

Amidrine	Migrapap
Duradrin	Migquin
I.D.A	Migratine
Iso-Acetazone	Migrazone
Isocom	Migrend
Midchlor	Migrex
Midrin	Mitride

Generic name product may be available.

†Not commercially available in Canada.

Description

Isometheptene, dichloralphenazone, and acetaminophen (eye-soe-meth-EP-teen, dye-klor-al-FEN-a-zone, and a-seat-a-MIN-oh-fen) combination is used to treat certain kinds of headaches, such as "tension" headaches and migraine headaches. This combination is not used regularly (for example, every day) to prevent headaches. It should be taken only after headache pain begins, or after a warning sign that a migraine is coming appears. Isometheptene helps to relieve throbbing headaches, but it is not an ordinary pain reliever. Dichloralphenazone helps you to relax, and acetaminophen relieves pain.

This medicine is available only with your doctor's prescription, in the following dosage form:

Oral
- Capsules (U.S.)

Before Using This Medicine

In deciding to use a medicine, the risks of taking the medicine must be weighed against the good it will do. This is a decision you and your doctor will make. For this combination medicine, the following should be considered:

Allergies—Tell your doctor if you have ever had any unusual or allergic reaction to acetaminophen or to this combination medicine. Also tell your health care professional if you are allergic to any other substances, such as foods, preservatives, or dyes.

Pregnancy—Studies with this combination medicine have not been done in either humans or animals.

Breast-feeding—Acetaminophen passes into the breast milk in small amounts. However, this medicine has not been shown to cause problems in nursing babies.

Children—Studies with this medicine have been done only in adult patients, and there is no specific information about its use in children.

Older adults—Many medicines have not been tested in older people. Therefore, it may not be known whether they work exactly the same way they do in younger adults or if they cause different side effects or problems in older people. There is no specific information comparing use of this combination medicine in the elderly with use in other age groups.

Other medicines—Although certain medicines should not be used together at all, in other cases two different medicines may be used together even if an interaction might occur. In these cases, your doctor may want to change the dose, or other precautions may be necessary. When you are taking this combination medicine, it is especially important that your health care professional know if you are taking any of the following:

- Monoamine oxidase (MAO) inhibitors (furazolidone [e.g., Furoxone], isocarboxazid [e.g., Marplan], phenelzine [e.g., Nardil], procarbazine [e.g., Matulane], selegiline [e.g., Eldepryl], tranylcypromine [e.g., Parnate])—Taking this combination medicine while you are taking or within 2 weeks of taking a monoamine oxidase (MAO) inhibitor may increase the chance of side effects

Other medical problems—The presence of other medical problems may affect the use of this medicine. Make sure you tell your doctor if you have any other medical problems, especially:

- Alcohol abuse or
- Heart attack (recent) or
- Heart or blood vessel disease or
- Kidney disease or
- Liver disease or
- Stroke (recent) or
- Virus infection of the liver (viral hepatitis)—The chance of side effects may be increased

- Glaucoma, not well controlled, or
- High blood pressure (hypertension), not well controlled—The isometheptene in this combination medicine may make these conditions worse

Proper Use of This Medicine

Take this medicine only as directed by your doctor. Do not take more of it, do not take it more often than directed, and do not take it every day for several days in a row. If the amount you are to take does not relieve your headache, check with your doctor. If a headache medicine is used too often, it may lose its effectiveness or even cause a type of physical dependence. If this occurs, your headaches may actually get worse. Also, taking too much acetaminophen can cause liver damage.

This medicine works best if you:

- *Take it as soon as the headache begins.* If you get warning signals of a migraine, take this medicine as soon as you are sure that the migraine is coming. This may even stop the headache pain from occurring.
- *Lie down in a quiet, dark room until you are feeling better.*

People who get a lot of headaches may need to take a different medicine to help prevent headaches. *It is important that you follow your doctor's directions, even if your headaches continue to occur.* Headache-preventing medicines may take several weeks to start working. Even after they do start working, your headaches may not go away completely. However, your headaches should occur less often, and they should be less severe and easier to relieve, than before. This will reduce the amount of headache relievers that you need. If you do not notice any improvement after several weeks of headache-preventing treatment, check with your doctor.

Dosing—The dose of this combination medicine will be different for different patients. *Follow your doctor's orders or the directions on the label.* The following information includes only the average doses of this medicine. *If your dose is different, do not change it unless your doctor tells you to do so.*

- *For "tension" headaches:*
  —Adults: 1 or 2 capsules every 4 hours, as needed. Not more than 8 capsules a day.
  —Children: Dose must be determined by the doctor.
- *For migraine headaches:*
  —Adults: 2 capsules for the first dose, then 1 capsule every hour, as needed. Not more than 5 capsules in 12 hours.
  —Children: Dose must be determined by the doctor.

Storage—To store this medicine
- Keep out of the reach of children.
- Store away from heat and direct light.
- Do not store in the bathroom, near the kitchen sink, or in other damp places. Heat and moisture may cause the medicine to break down.
- Do not keep outdated medicine or medicine no longer needed. Be sure that any discarded medicine is out of the reach of children.

Precautions While Using This Medicine

Check with your doctor:
- *If the medicine stops working as well as it did when you first started using it.* This may mean that you are in danger of becoming dependent on the medicine. *Do not try to get better relief by increasing the dose.*
- *If you are having headaches more often than you did before you started using this medicine.* This is espe-

cially important if a new headache occurs within 1 day after you took your last dose of headache medicine, headaches begin to occur every day, or a headache continues for several days in a row. This may mean that you are dependent on the medicine. *Continuing to take this medicine will cause even more headaches later on.* Your doctor can give you advice on how to relieve the headaches.

Check the labels of all nonprescription (over-the-counter [OTC]) and prescription medicines you now take. Taking other medicines that contain acetaminophen together with this medicine may lead to an overdose. If you have any questions about this, check with your health care professional.

This medicine may cause some people to become drowsy, dizzy, or less alert than they are normally. These effects may be especially severe if you also take CNS depressants (medicines that slow down the nervous system, possibly causing drowsiness) together with this medicine. Some examples of CNS depressants are antihistamines or medicine for hay fever, other allergies, or colds; sedatives, tranquilizers, or sleeping medicine; prescription pain medicine or narcotics; barbiturates; medicine for seizures; muscle relaxants; antiemetics (medicines that prevent or relieve nausea or vomiting), and anesthetics. If you are not able to lie down for a while, *make sure you know how you react to this medicine or combination of medicines before you drive, use machines, or do anything else that could be dangerous if you are drowsy or dizzy or are not alert.*

Do not drink alcoholic beverages while taking this medicine. To do so may increase the chance of liver damage caused by acetaminophen, especially if you drink large amounts of alcoholic beverages regularly. Also, because drinking alcoholic beverages may make your headaches worse or cause new headaches to occur, people who often get headaches should probably avoid alcohol.

Side Effects of This Medicine

Along with its needed effects, a medicine may cause some unwanted effects. Although not all of these side effects may occur, if they do occur they may need medical attention.

Check with your doctor as soon as possible if any of the following side effects occur:

Less common
Unusual tiredness or weakness

Rare
Black, tarry stools; blood in urine or stools; pinpoint red spots on skin; skin rash, hives, or itching; sore throat and fever; unusual bleeding or bruising; yellow eyes or skin

Symptoms of dependence on this medicine
Headaches, more severe and/or more frequent than before

Symptoms of acetaminophen overdose
Diarrhea; increased sweating; loss of appetite; nausea or vomiting; pain, tenderness, and/or swelling in the upper abdominal (stomach) area; stomach cramps or pain

Other side effects may occur that usually do not need medical attention. These side effects may go away during treatment as your body adjusts to the medicine. However, check with your doctor if any of the following side effects continue or are bothersome:

More common
Drowsiness

Rare
Dizziness; fast or irregular heartbeat

Other side effects not listed above may also occur in some patients. If you notice any other effects, check with your doctor.

Revised: 12/22/99

ISONIAZID Systemic

Commonly used brand name(s):

In the U.S.—
Laniazid
Nydrazid
Generic name product may be available.

In Canada—
Isotamine
PMS Isoniazid

Another commonly used name is INH.

Description

Isoniazid (eye-soe-NYE-a-zid) is used to treat tuberculosis (TB) or prevent its return (reactivation). It may be given alone, or in combination with other medicines, to treat TB or to prevent its return (reactivation). This medicine may also be used for other problems as determined by your doctor.

This medicine may cause some serious side effects, including damage to the liver. Liver damage is more likely to occur in patients over 50 years of age. You and your doctor should talk about the good this medicine will do, as well as the risks of taking it.

If you are being treated for active tuberculosis (TB): To help clear up your TB infection completely, you must keep taking this medicine for the full time of treatment, even if you begin to feel better. This is very important. It is also important that you do not miss any doses.

Isoniazid is available only with your doctor's prescription, in the following dosage forms:

Oral
• Syrup (U.S. and Canada)
• Tablets (U.S. and Canada)
Parenteral
• Injection (U.S.)

Before Using This Medicine

In deciding to use a medicine, the risks of taking the medicine must be weighed against the good it will do. This is a decision you and your doctor will make. For isoniazid, the following should be considered:

Allergies—Tell your doctor if you have ever had any unusual or allergic reaction to isoniazid, ethionamide (e.g., Trecator-SC), pyrazinamide, or niacin (e.g., Nicobid, nicotinic acid). Also tell your health care professional if you are allergic to any other substances, such as foods, preservatives, or dyes.

Diet—Make certain your health care professional knows if you are on a low-sodium, low-sugar, or any other special diet. Most medicines contain more than just the active ingredient, and many liquid medicines contain alcohol.

Pregnancy—Isoniazid has not been shown to cause birth defects or other problems in humans or animals. Studies in rats and rabbits have shown that isoniazid may increase the risk of fetal death. However, tuberculosis is a very serious disease and many women have been treated with isoniazid during pregnancy with no problems occurring in their babies.

Breast-feeding—Isoniazid passes into the breast milk. However, isoniazid has not been reported to cause problems in nursing babies. Also, there is not enough isoniazid in breast milk to protect or treat babies who have been exposed to tuberculosis.

Children—Isoniazid can cause serious side effects in any patient. Therefore, it is especially important that you discuss with the child's doctor the good that this medicine may do as well as the risks of using it.

Older adults—Hepatitis may be especially likely to occur in patients over 50 years of age, who are usually more sensitive than younger adults to the effects of isoniazid.

Other medicines—Although certain medicines should not be used together at all, in other cases two different medicines may be used together even if an interaction might occur. In these cases, your doctor may want to change the dose, or other precautions may be necessary. When you are taking or receiving isoniazid it is especially important that your health care professional know if you are taking any of the following:

- Acetaminophen (e.g., Tylenol) (with long-term, high-dose use) or
- Alfentanil (e.g., Alfenta) or
- Amiodarone (e.g., Cordarone) or
- Anabolic steroids (nandrolone [e.g., Anabolin], oxandrolone [e.g., Anavar], oxymetholone [e.g., Anadrol], stanozolol [e.g., Winstrol]) or
- Androgens (male hormones) or
- Antithyroid agents (medicine for overactive thyroid) or
- Carmustine (e.g., BiCNU) or
- Chloroquine (e.g., Aralen) or
- Dantrolene (e.g., Dantrium) or
- Daunorubicin (e.g., Cerubidine) or
- Disulfiram (e.g., Antabuse) or
- Divalproex (e.g., Depakote) or
- Estrogens (female hormones) or
- Etretinate (e.g., Tegison) or
- Gold salts (medicine for arthritis) or
- Hydroxychloroquine (e.g., Plaquenil) or
- Mercaptopurine (e.g., Purinethol) or
- Methotrexate (e.g., Mexate) or
- Methyldopa (e.g., Aldomet) or
- Naltrexone (e.g., Trexan) (with long-term, high-dose use) or
- Oral contraceptives (birth control pills) containing estrogen or
- Phenothiazines (acetophenazine [e.g., Tindal], chlorpromazine [e.g., Thorazine], fluphenazine [e.g., Prolixin], mesoridazine [e.g., Serentil], perphenazine [e.g., Trilafon], prochlorperazine [e.g., Compazine], promazine [e.g., Sparine], promethazine [e.g., Phenergan], thioridazine [e.g., Mellaril], trifluoperazine [e.g., Stelazine], triflupromazine [e.g., Vesprin], trimeprazine [e.g., Temaril]) or

- Plicamycin (e.g., Mithracin) or
- Valproic acid (e.g., Depakene)—These medicines may increase the chance of liver damage if taken with isoniazid
- Carbamazepine (e.g., Tegretol) or
- Phenytoin (e.g., Dilantin)—These medicines may increase the chance of liver damage if taken with isoniazid. There may also be an increased chance of side effects of carbamazepine and phenytoin
- Disulfiram (e.g., Antabuse)—This medicine may increase the chance of liver damage and side effects, such as dizziness, lack of coordination, irritability, and trouble in sleeping
- Ketoconazole (e.g., Nizoral) or
- Rifampin (e.g., Rifadin)—Use of these medicines with isoniazid can lower the blood levels of ketoconazole or rifampin, decreasing their effects

Other medical problems—The presence of other medical problems may affect the use of isoniazid. Make sure you tell your doctor if you have any other medical problems, especially:

- Alcohol abuse (or history of) or
- Liver disease—There may be an increased chance of hepatitis with daily drinking of alcohol or in patients with liver disease
- Kidney disease (severe)—There may be an increased chance of side effects in patients with severe kidney disease
- Seizure disorders such as epilepsy—There may be an increased chance of seizures (convulsions) in some patients

Proper Use of This Medicine

If you are taking isoniazid by mouth and it upsets your stomach, take it with food. Antacids may also help. However, do not take aluminum-containing antacids within 1 hour of taking isoniazid. They may keep this medicine from working properly.

For patients taking the *oral liquid form* of isoniazid:
- Use a specially marked measuring spoon or other device to measure each dose accurately. The average household teaspoon may not hold the right amount of liquid.

To help clear up your tuberculosis (TB) completely, *it is very important that you keep taking this medicine for the full time of treatment*, even if you begin to feel better after a few weeks. You may have to take it every day for as long as 6 months to 2 years. *It is important that you do not miss any doses.*

Your doctor may also want you to take pyridoxine (e.g., Hexa-Betalin, vitamin B$_6$) every day to help prevent or lessen some of the side effects of isoniazid. This is not usually needed in children, who receive enough pyridoxine in their diet. If it is needed, *it is very important to take pyridoxine every day along with this medicine. Do not miss any doses.*

Dosing—The dose of isoniazid will be different for different patients. *Follow your doctor's orders or the directions on the label.* The following information includes only the average doses of isoniazid. *If your dose is different, do not change it* unless your doctor tells you to do so.

The number of tablets or teaspoonfuls of syrup that you take depends on the strength of the medicine.

- For *oral* dosage forms (tablets, syrup):
  —For preventing the return (reactivation) of tuberculosis:
  - Adults and teenagers—300 milligrams (mg) once a day.
  - Children—Dose is based on body weight. The usual dose is 10 mg per kilogram (kg) (4.5 mg per pound) of body weight, up to 300 mg, once a day.
  —For treatment of tuberculosis:
  - Adults and teenagers—300 mg once a day; or 15 mg per kg (6.8 mg per pound) of body weight, up to 900 mg, two times a week or three times a week, depending on the schedule your doctor chooses for you.
  - Children—Dose is based on body weight. The usual dose is 10 to 20 mg per kg (4.5 to 9.1 mg per pound) of body weight, up to 300 mg, once a day; or 20 to 40 mg per kg (9.1 to 18.2 mg per pound) of body weight, up to 900 mg, two times a week or three times a week, depending on the schedule your doctor chooses for you.
- For *injection* dosage form:
  —For preventing the return (reactivation) of tuberculosis:
  - Adults and teenagers—300 mg once a day.
  - Children—Dose is based on body weight. The usual dose is 10 mg per kg (4.5 mg per pound) of body weight, up to 300 mg, once a day.
  —For treatment of tuberculosis:
  - Adults and teenagers—300 mg once a day; or 15 mg per kg (6.8 mg per pound) of body weight, up to 900 mg, two times a week or three times a week, depending on the schedule your doctor chooses for you.
  - Children—Dose is based on body weight. The usual dose is 10 to 20 mg per kg (4.5 to 9.1 mg per pound) of body weight, up to 300 mg, once a day; or 20 to 40 mg per kg (9.1 to 18.2 mg per pound) of body weight, up to 900 mg, two times a week or three times a week, depending on the schedule your doctor chooses for you.

Missed dose—If you miss a dose of this medicine, take it as soon as possible. However, if it is almost time for your next dose, skip the missed dose and go back to your regular dosing schedule. Do not double doses.

Storage—To store this medicine:
- Keep out of the reach of children.
- Store away from heat and direct light.
- Do not store the tablet form of this medicine in the bathroom, near the kitchen sink, or in other damp places. Heat or moisture may cause the medicine to break down.
- Keep the oral liquid form of this medicine from freezing.
- Do not keep outdated medicine or medicine no longer needed. Be sure that any discarded medicine is out of the reach of children.

Precautions While Using This Medicine

It is very important that your doctor check your progress at regular visits. Also, check with your doctor immediately if blurred vision or loss of vision, with or without eye pain, occurs during treatment. Your doctor may want you to have your eyes checked by an ophthalmologist (eye doctor).

If your symptoms do not improve within 2 to 3 weeks, or if they become worse, check with your doctor.

Certain foods such as cheese (Swiss or Cheshire) or fish (tuna, skipjack, or Sardinella) may rarely cause reactions in some patients taking isoniazid. Check with your doctor if redness or itching of the skin, hot feeling, fast or pounding heartbeat, sweating, chills or clammy feeling, headache, or lightheadedness occurs while you are taking this medicine.

Liver problems may be more likely to occur if you drink alcoholic beverages regularly while you are taking this medicine. Also, the regular use of alcohol may keep this medicine from working properly. Therefore, *you should strictly limit the amount of alcoholic beverages you drink while you are taking this medicine.*

If this medicine causes you to feel very tired or very weak; or causes clumsiness; unsteadiness; a loss of appetite; nausea; numbness, tingling, burning, or pain in the hands and feet; or vomiting, check with your doctor immediately. These may be early warning signs of more serious liver or nerve problems that could develop later.

For diabetic patients:
- *This medicine may cause false test results with some urine sugar tests.* Check with your doctor before changing your diet or the dosage of your diabetes medicine.

Side Effects of This Medicine

Along with its needed effects, a medicine may cause some unwanted effects. Although not all of these side effects may occur, if they do occur they may need medical attention.

Check with your doctor immediately if any of the following side effects occur:
More common
   Clumsiness or unsteadiness; dark urine; loss of appetite; nausea or vomiting; numbness, tingling, burning, or pain in hands and feet; unusual tiredness or weakness; yellow eyes or skin
Rare
   Blurred vision or loss of vision, with or without eye pain; convulsions (seizures); fever and sore throat; joint pain; mental depression; mood or other mental changes; skin rash; unusual bleeding or bruising

Other side effects may occur that usually do not need medical attention. These side effects may go away during treatment as your body adjusts to the medicine. However, check with your doctor if any of the following side effects continue or are bothersome:
More common
   Diarrhea; stomach pain
For injection form
   Irritation at the place of injection

Dark urine and yellowing of the eyes or skin (signs of liver problems) are more likely to occur in patients over 50 years of age.

Other side effects not listed above may also occur in some patients. If you notice any other effects, check with your doctor.

Revised: 06/30/2000

ISOTRETINOIN   Systemic

Commonly used brand name(s):

In the U.S.—
Accutane

In Canada—
Accutane Roche

Description

Isotretinoin (eye-soe-TRET-i-noyn) is used to treat severe, disfiguring nodular acne. It should be used only after other acne medicines have been tried and have failed to help the acne. Isotretinoin may also be used to treat other skin diseases as determined by your doctor.

Isotretinoin must not be used to treat women who are able to bear children unless other forms of treatment have been tried first and have failed. Isotretinoin must not be taken during pregnancy because it causes birth defects in humans. If you are able to bear children, it is very important that you read, understand, and follow the pregnancy warnings for isotretinoin.

This medicine is available only with your doctor's prescription and should be prescribed only by a doctor who has special knowledge of the diagnosis and treatment of severe, uncontrollable cystic acne.

Isotretinoin is available in the following dosage form:

Oral
- Capsules (U.S. and Canada)

Before Using This Medicine

In deciding to use a medicine, the risks of taking the medicine must be weighed against the good it will do. This is a decision you and your doctor will make. For isotretinoin, the following should be considered:

Allergies—Tell your doctor if you have ever had any unusual or allergic reaction to isotretinoin, acitretin, tretinoin, or vitamin A preparations. Also tell your health care professional if you are allergic to any other substances, such as foods, preservatives (such as parabens), or dyes.

Pregnancy—*Isotretinoin must not be taken during pregnancy because it causes birth defects in humans. In addition, isotretinoin must not be taken if there is a chance that you may become pregnant during treatment or within 1 month following treatment.*

Breast-feeding—It is not known whether isotretinoin passes into breast milk. However, isotretinoin is not recommended during breast-feeding because it may cause unwanted effects in nursing babies.

Children—Children may be especially sensitive to the effects of isotretinoin. This may increase the chance of side effects during treatment.

Older adults—Many medicines have not been studied specifically in older people. Therefore, it may not be known whether they work exactly the same way they do in younger adults or if they cause different side effects or problems in older people. There is no specific information comparing use of isotretinoin in the elderly with use in other age groups.

Other medicines—Although certain medicines should not be used together at all, in other cases two different medicines may be used together even if an interaction might occur. In these cases, your doctor may want to change the dose, or other precautions may be necessary. When you are using isotretinoin, it is especially important that your health care professional know if you are using any of the following:

- Acitretin (e.g., Soriatane) or
- Tretinoin, oral (e.g., Vesanoid)—Use of isotretinoin with these medicines may result in an increase in side effects
- Tetracyclines, oral (medicine for infection)—Use of isotretinoin with these medicines may increase the chance of a side effect called pseudotumor cerebri, which is a swelling and pressure on the brain

Other medical problems—The presence of other medical problems may affect the use of isotretinoin. Make sure you tell your doctor if you have any other medical problems, especially:

- Alcoholism or excess use of alcohol (or history of) or
- Diabetes mellitus (sugar diabetes) (or a family history of) or
- Family history of high triglyceride (a fat-like substance) levels in the blood or
- Severe weight problems—Use of isotretinoin may increase blood levels of triglyceride (a fat-like substance), which may increase the chance of heart or blood vessel problems in patients who have a family history of high triglycerides, are greatly overweight, are diabetic, or use a lot of alcohol. For persons with diabetes mellitus, use of isotretinoin also may change blood sugar levels

Proper Use of This Medicine

Isotretinoin comes with patient information. It is very important that you read and understand this information. Be sure to ask your doctor about anything you do not understand.

Isotretinoin must not be taken by women of reproductive age unless two effective forms of contraception (birth control) have been used for at least 1 month before the beginning of treatment. Contraception must be continued during the period of treatment, which is up to 20 weeks, and for 1 month after isotretinoin is stopped. Be sure you have discussed this information with your doctor. In addition, you will be asked to sign an informed consent form stating that you understand the above information.

If you are a woman who is able to have children, you must have a pregnancy blood test within 1 week before beginning treatment with isotretinoin to make sure you are not pregnant. Treatment with isotretinoin will then be started within the week, on the second or third day of your next normal menstrual period. In addition, you must have a pregnancy blood test each month while you are taking this medicine and one month after treatment is completed.

Take isotretinoin with food.

It is very important that you take isotretinoin only as directed. Do not take more of it, do not take it more often, and do not take it for a longer time than your doctor ordered. To do so may increase the chance of side effects.

Dosing—The dose of isotretinoin will be different for different patients. *Follow your doctor's orders or the directions on the label.* The following information includes only the average doses of isotretinoin. *If your dose is different, do not change it* unless your doctor tells you to do so.

The number of capsules that you take depends on the strength of the medicine. Also, *the number of doses you take each day, the time allowed between doses, and the length of time you take the medicine depend on the medical problem for which you are taking isotretinoin.*

- For *oral* dosage form (capsules):
  —For acne:
  - Adults and teenagers—Dose is based on body weight and must be determined by your doctor. The usual dose is 0.5 to 1 milligram (mg) per kilogram (kg) (0.23 to 0.45 mg per pound) of body weight a day.
  - Children—Use is usually not recommended.

Missed dose—If you miss a dose of this medicine, take it as soon as possible. However, if it is almost time for your next dose, skip the missed dose and go back to your regular dosing schedule. Do not double doses.

Storage—To store this medicine:

- Keep out of the reach of children.
- Store away from heat and direct light.
- Do not store in the bathroom, near the kitchen sink, or in other damp places. Heat or moisture may cause the medicine to break down.
- Do not keep outdated medicine or medicine no longer needed. Be sure that any discarded medicine is out of the reach of children.

Precautions While Using This Medicine

Your doctor should check your progress at regular visits to make sure this medicine does not cause unwanted effects.

Isotretinoin causes birth defects in humans if taken during pregnancy. Therefore, if you suspect that you may have become pregnant, stop taking this medicine immediately and check with your doctor.

During the first 3 weeks you are taking isotretinoin, your skin may become irritated. Also, your acne may seem to get worse before it gets better. *Check with your doctor if your skin condition does not improve within 1 to 2 months after starting this medicine or at any time your skin irritation becomes severe.* Full improvement continues after you stop taking isotretinoin and may take up to 6 months. Your health care professional can help you choose the right skin products to reduce skin dryness and irritation.

Do not donate blood to a blood bank while you are taking isotretinoin or for 30 days after you stop taking it. This is to prevent the possibility of a pregnant patient receiving the blood containing the medicine.

In some patients, isotretinoin may cause a decrease in night vision. This decrease may occur suddenly. If it does occur, *do not drive, use machines, or do anything else that could be dangerous if you are not able to see well.* Also, check with your doctor.

Isotretinoin may cause dryness of the eyes. Therefore, if you wear contact lenses, your eyes may be more sensitive to them during the time you are taking isotretinoin and for up to about 2 weeks after you stop taking it. To help relieve dryness of the eyes, check with your doctor about using an eye-lubricating solution, such as artificial tears. If eye inflammation occurs, check with your doctor.

Isotretinoin may cause dryness of the mouth and nose. For temporary relief of mouth dryness, use sugarless candy or gum, melt bits of ice in your mouth, or use a saliva substitute. However, if dry mouth continues for more than 2 weeks, check with your medical doctor or dentist. Continuing dryness of the mouth may increase the chance of dental disease, including tooth decay, gum disease, and fungus infections.

Avoid overexposing your skin to sunlight, wind, or cold weather. Your skin will be more prone to sunburn, dryness, or irritation, especially during the first 2 or 3 weeks of treatment. However, you should not stop taking this medicine unless the skin irritation becomes too severe. *Do not use a sunlamp.*

To help isotretinoin work properly, regularly use sunscreen or sunblocking lotions with a sun protection factor (SPF) of at least 15. Also, wear protective clothing and hats.

Do not take vitamin A or any vitamin supplement containing vitamin A while taking this medicine, unless otherwise directed by your doctor. To do so may increase the chance of side effects.

For diabetic patients:

- This medicine may affect blood sugar levels. If you notice a change in the results of your blood or urine sugar tests or if you have any questions, check with your doctor.

Side Effects of This Medicine

Along with its needed effects, a medicine may cause some unwanted effects. Although not all of these side effects may occur, if they do occur they may need medical attention.

Check with your doctor as soon as possible if any of the following side effects occur:

More common

Bone or joint pain; burning, redness, itching, or other signs of eye inflammation; difficulty in moving; nosebleeds; scaling, redness, burning, pain, or other signs of inflammation of lips; skin infection or rash

Rare

Abdominal or stomach pain (severe); attempts at suicide or thoughts of suicide (usually stops after medicine is stopped); back pain; bleeding or inflammation of gums; blurred vision or other changes in vision; changes in behavior; decreased vision after sunset or before sunrise (sudden or may continue after medicine is stopped); diarrhea (severe); headache (severe or continuing); mental depression; nausea and vomiting; pain or tenderness of eyes; pain, tenderness, or stiffness in muscles (long-term treatment); rectal bleeding; yellow eyes or skin

Other side effects may occur that usually do not need medical attention. These side effects may go away during treatment as your body adjusts to the medicine. However, check with your doctor if any of the following side effects continue or are bothersome:

More common

Crusting of skin; difficulty in wearing contact lenses (may continue after medicine is stopped); dryness of mouth or nose; dryness of eyes (may continue after treatment is stopped); dryness or itching of skin; headache (mild); increased sensitivity of skin to sunlight; peeling of skin on palms of hands or soles of feet; stomach upset; thinning of hair (may continue after treatment is stopped); unusual tiredness

Other side effects not listed above may also occur in some patients. If you notice any other effects, check with your doctor.

Additional Information

Once a medicine has been approved for marketing for a certain use, experience may show that it is also useful for other medical problems. Although these uses are not included in product labeling, isotretinoin is used in certain patients with the following medical conditions:

- Folliculitis, gram-negative (bacterial infection of skin on face beginning near the nose)
- Hidradenitis suppurativa (sweat gland problem)
- Rosacea (red skin disorder of the face, usually of the nose and cheeks)
- Thickened or patchy skin disorders, such as keratosis follicularis, palmoplantar keratoderma, lamellar ichthyosis, or pityriasis rubra pilaris

Other than the above information, there is no additional information relating to proper use, precautions, or side effects for these uses.

Revised: 08/13/98

KAOLIN AND PECTIN   Oral

Commonly used brand name(s):

In the U.S.—
Kao-Spen
Kapectolin
K-P
Generic name product may be available.

In Canada—
Donnagel-MB

Description

Kaolin and pectin (KAY-oh-lin and PEK-tin) combination medicine is used to treat diarrhea.

Kaolin is a clay-like powder believed to work by attracting and holding onto the bacteria or germ that may be causing the diarrhea.

This medicine is available without a prescription; however, the product's directions and warnings should be carefully followed. In addition, your doctor may have special instructions on the proper dose or use of kaolin and pectin combination medicine for your medical condition. Kaolin and pectin combination is available in the following dosage form:

Oral
- Oral suspension (U.S. and Canada)

Before Using This Medicine

If you are taking this medicine without a prescription, carefully read and follow any precautions on the label. For kaolin and pectin combination, the following should be considered:

Pregnancy—This medicine is not absorbed into the body and is not likely to cause problems.

Breast-feeding—This medicine is not absorbed into the body and is not likely to cause problems.

Children—The fluid loss caused by diarrhea may result in a severe condition. For this reason, antidiarrheals must not be given to young children (under 3 years of age) without first checking with their doctor. In older children with diarrhea, antidiarrheals may be used, but it is also very important that a sufficient amount of liquids be given to replace the fluid lost by the body. If you have any questions about this, check with your health care professional.

Older adults—The fluid loss caused by diarrhea may result in a severe condition. For this reason, elderly persons with diarrhea, in addition to using an antidiarrheal, must receive a sufficient amount of liquids to replace the fluid lost by the body. If you have any questions about this, check with your health care professional.

Other medicines—Although certain medicines should not be used together at all, in other cases two different medicines may be used together even if an interaction might occur. In these cases, your doctor may want to change the dose, or other precautions may be necessary. Tell your health care professional if you are taking any other prescription or nonprescription (over-the-counter [OTC]) medicine.

Other medical problems—The presence of other medical problems may affect the use of kaolin and pectin. Make sure you tell your doctor if you have any other medical problems, especially:

- Dysentery—This condition may get worse; a different kind of treatment may be needed

Proper Use of This Medicine

Do not use kaolin and pectin combination to treat your diarrhea if you have a fever or if there is blood or mucus in your stools. Contact your doctor.

Take this medicine, following the directions in the product package, after each loose bowel movement until the diarrhea is controlled, unless otherwise directed by your doctor.

Importance of diet and fluid intake while treating diarrhea:
- *In addition to using medicine for diarrhea, it is very important that you replace the fluid lost by the body and follow a proper diet.* For the first 24 hours you should eat gelatin and drink plenty of clear liquids, such as ginger ale, decaffeinated cola, decaffeinated tea, and broth. During the next 24 hours you may eat bland foods, such as cooked cereals, bread, crackers, and applesauce. Fruits, vegetables, fried or spicy foods, bran, candy, and caffeine and alcoholic beverages may make the condition worse.
- If too much fluid has been lost by the body due to the diarrhea, a serious condition may develop. Check with your doctor as soon as possible if any of the following signs or symptoms of too much fluid loss occur:
  Decreased urination
  Dizziness and lightheadedness
  Dryness of mouth
  Increased thirst
  Wrinkled skin

Dosing—The dose of kaolin and pectin combination will be different for different patients. *Follow your doctor's orders or the directions on the label.* The following information includes only the average doses of kaolin and pectin.

The number of tablespoonfuls of suspension that you take depends on the strength of the medicine.
- For diarrhea:
  —For *oral* dosage form (suspension):
    - Adults—The usual dose is 4 to 8 tablespoonfuls (60 to 120 milliliters [mL]) taken after each loose bowel movement.
    - Children 12 years of age and over—The usual

dose is 3 to 4 tablespoonfuls (45 to 60 mL) taken after each loose bowel movement.
- Children 6 to 12 years of age—The usual dose is 2 to 4 tablespoonfuls (30 to 60 mL) taken after each loose bowel movement.
- Children 3 to 6 years of age—The usual dose is 1 to 2 tablespoonfuls (15 to 30 mL) taken after each loose bowel movement.
- Children up to 3 years of age—Use and dose must be determined by your doctor.

Storage—To store this medicine:
- Keep out of the reach of children.
- Store away from heat and direct light.
- Keep this medicine from freezing.
- Do not keep outdated medicine or medicine no longer needed. Be sure that any discarded medicine is out of the reach of children.

Precautions While Using This Medicine

Check with your doctor if your diarrhea does not stop after 1 or 2 days or if you develop a fever.

If you are taking any other medicine, do not take it within 2 to 3 hours of taking kaolin and pectin. Taking the medicines together may prevent the other medicine from being absorbed by your body. If you have any questions about this, check with your health care professional.

Side Effects of This Medicine

Along with its needed effects, a medicine may cause some unwanted effects. No serious side effects have been reported for this medicine. However, this medicine may cause constipation in some patients, especially if they take a lot of it. Check with your doctor as soon as possible if constipation continues or is bothersome.

Other side effects not listed above may also occur in some patients. If you notice any other effects, check with your doctor.

Revised: 08/04/94

KETOCONAZOLE   Topical

Commonly used brand name(s):

In the U.S.—
Nizoral Cream
Nizoral A-D Shampoo
Nizoral Shampoo

In Canada—
Nizoral Cream
Nizoral Shampoo

Description

Ketoconazole (kee-toe-KOE-na-zole) is used to treat infections caused by a fungus or yeast. It works by killing the fungus or yeast or preventing its growth.

Ketoconazole cream is used to treat:
- Athlete's foot (tinea pedis; ringworm of the foot);
- Ringworm of the body (tinea corporis);
- Ringworm of the groin (tinea cruris; jock itch);
- Seborrheic dermatitis;
- "Sun fungus" (tinea versicolor; pityriasis versicolor); and
- Yeast infection of the skin (cutaneous candidiasis).

Ketoconazole 1% shampoo is used to treat dandruff.

Ketoconazole 2% shampoo is used to treat "sun fungus" (tinea versicolor; pityriasis versicolor).

This medicine may also be used for other fungus infections of the skin as determined by your doctor.

Ketoconazole is available without a doctor's prescription, in the following dosage form:

Topical
- Shampoo (1%) (U.S.)

Ketoconazole is available only with your doctor's prescription, in the following dosage forms:

Topical
- Cream (U.S. and Canada)
- Shampoo (2%) (U.S. and Canada)

Before Using This Medicine

In deciding to use a medicine, the risks of using the medicine must be weighed against the good it will do. This is a decision you and your doctor will make. For topical ketoconazole, the following should be considered:

Allergies—Tell your doctor if you have ever had any unusual or allergic reaction to ketoconazole, miconazole or other imidazoles, or sulfites. The cream form of ketoconazole contains sulfites. Also tell your health care professional if you are allergic to any other substances, such as preservatives or dyes.

Pregnancy—Ketoconazole has not been studied in pregnant women. However, studies in animals have shown that ketoconazole causes birth defects or other problems. Before using this medicine, make sure your doctor knows if you are pregnant or if you may become pregnant.

Breast-feeding—It is not known whether topical ketoconazole, used on a regular basis, is absorbed into the mother's body enough to pass into the breast milk. However, the cream was not absorbed through the skin after a single dose was applied to the chest, back, and arms of volunteers. Also, the shampoo was not absorbed through the skin after frequent shampooing by volunteers. Therefore, it is unlikely to cause problems in nursing babies.

Children—Studies on this medicine have been done only in adult patients, and there is no specific information comparing use of this medicine in children with use in other age groups.

Older adults—Many medicines have not been studied specifically in older people. Therefore, it may not be known whether they work exactly the same way they do in younger adults or if they cause different side effects or problems in older people. There is no specific information comparing use of topical ketoconazole in the elderly with use in other age groups.

Other medicines—Although certain medicines should not be used together at all, in other cases two different medicines may be used together even if an interaction might occur. In these cases, your doctor may want to change the dose, or other precautions may be necessary. Tell your health care professional if you are using any other prescription or nonprescription (over-the-counter [OTC]) medicine.

Proper Use of This Medicine

Keep this medicine away from the eyes.

For patients using the *cream form* of this medicine:
- Apply enough ketoconazole cream to cover the affected and surrounding skin areas, and rub in gently.
- To help clear up your infection completely, *it is very important that you keep using ketoconazole cream for the full time of treatment,* even if your symptoms begin to clear up after a few days. Since fungus or yeast infections may be very slow to clear up, you may have to continue using this medicine every day for up to several weeks. If you stop using this medicine too soon, your symptoms may return. *Do not miss any doses.*

For patients using the *1% shampoo form* of this medicine:
- Wet your hair and scalp well with water.
- Apply enough shampoo to work up a good lather and gently massage it over your entire scalp.
- Rinse your hair and scalp with warm water.
- Repeat application.
- Rinse your hair and scalp well with warm water, and dry your hair.

For patients using the *2% shampoo form* of this medicine:
- Wet your hair and scalp well with water.
- Apply the shampoo to the skin of the affected area and a wide margin surrounding this area.
- Work up a good lather and leave it in place for 5 minutes.
- Rinse your hair and scalp well with warm water, and dry your hair.

Dosing—The dose of topical ketoconazole will be different for different patients. *Follow your doctor's orders or the directions on the label.* The following information includes only the average doses of topical ketoconazole. *If your dose is different, do not change it* unless your doctor tells you to do so.

The number of doses you use each day, the time allowed between doses, and the length of time you use the medicine depend on the medical problem for which you are using topical ketoconazole.

- For *cream* dosage form:
  —For cutaneous candidiasis, tinea corporis, tinea cruris, tinea pedis, or pityriasis versicolor:
    - Adults—Apply once a day to the affected skin and surrounding area.
    - Children—Use and dose must be determined by your doctor.
  —For seborrheic dermatitis:
    - Adults—Apply two times a day to the affected skin and surrounding area.
    - Children—Use and dose must be determined by your doctor.
- For *1% shampoo* dosage form:
  —For dandruff:
    - Adults—Use every 3 or 4 days for up to 8 weeks. Then use only as needed to keep dandruff under control.
    - Children—Use and dose must be determined by your doctor.
- For *2% shampoo* dosage form:
  —For pityriasis versicolor:
    - Adults—Use once.
    - Children—Use and dose must be determined by your doctor.

Missed dose—If you miss a dose of this medicine, apply it as soon as possible. However, if it is almost time for your next dose, skip the missed dose and go back to your regular dosing schedule.

Storage—To store this medicine:
- Keep out of the reach of children.
- Store away from heat and direct light.
- Keep the medicine from freezing.
- Do not keep outdated medicine or medicine no longer needed. Be sure that any discarded medicine is out of the reach of children.

Precautions While Using This Medicine

If your skin problem does not improve within:
- 2 weeks for cutaneous candidiasis, pityriasis versicolor, tinea corporis, or tinea cruris;
- 4 weeks for seborrheic dermatitis; or
- 4 to 6 weeks for tinea pedis;
or if it becomes worse, check with your doctor.

For patients using the *cream form* of this medicine:
- *To help clear up your infection completely and to help make sure it does not return, good health habits are also required.*
- For patients using ketoconazole cream for *athlete's foot* (tinea pedis; ringworm of the foot), the following instructions will help keep the feet cool and dry.
  —Avoid wearing socks made from wool or synthetic materials (for example, rayon or nylon). Instead, wear clean, cotton socks and change them daily or more often if your feet sweat a lot.
  —Wear sandals or well-ventilated shoes (for examples, shoes with holes).
  —Use a bland, absorbent powder (for example, talcum powder) or an antifungal powder between the toes, on the feet, and in socks and shoes one or two times a day. It is best to use the powder between the times you use ketoconazole cream. If you have any questions about these instructions, check with your health care professional.
- For patients using ketoconazole cream for *ringworm of the groin* (tinea cruris; jock itch), the following instructions will help reduce chafing and irritation and will also help keep the groin area cool and dry.
  —Avoid wearing underwear that is tight-fitting or made from synthetic materials (for example, rayon or nylon). Instead, wear loose-fitting, cotton underwear.
  —Use a bland, absorbent powder (for example, talcum powder) or an antifungal powder on the skin. It is best to use the powder between the times you use ketoconazole cream. If you have any questions about these instructions, check with your health care professional.

Side Effects of This Medicine

Along with its needed effects, a medicine may cause some unwanted effects. Although not all of these side effects may occur, if they do occur they may need medical attention.

Check with your doctor as soon as possible if any of the following side effects occur:
Less common—For cream or shampoo
  Itching, stinging, or irritation not present before use of this medicine

Rare—For cream
  Skin rash

Other side effects may occur that usually do not need medical attention. These side effects may go away during treatment as your body adjusts to the medicine. However, check with your doctor if any of the following side effects continue or are bothersome:

Less common—For shampoo
  Dry skin; dryness or oiliness of the hair and scalp

Other side effects not listed above may also occur in some patients. If you notice any other effects, check with your doctor.

Revised: 06/14/99

KETOROLAC   Ophthalmic

Commonly used brand name(s):

In the U.S.—
  Acular

In Canada—
  Acular

Description

Ophthalmic ketorolac (kee-toe-ROLE-ak) is an anti-inflammatory medicine. It is used in the eye to treat itching caused by seasonal allergic conjunctivitis (an allergy that occurs at only certain times of the year). Ophthalmic ketorolac is also used to treat inflammation of the eye following cataract surgery.

This medicine may also be used to prevent or treat other conditions, as determined by your ophthalmologist (eye doctor).

Ophthalmic
  • Ophthalmic solution (eye drops) (U.S. and Canada)

Before Using This Medicine

In deciding to use a medicine, the risks of using the medicine must be weighed against the good it will do. This is a decision you and your doctor will make. For ophthalmic ketorolac, the following should be considered:

Allergies—Tell your doctor if you have ever had any unusual or allergic reaction to aspirin or other salicylates, ophthalmic ketorolac, systemic ketorolac (e.g., Toradol), diclofenac (e.g., Voltaren), or any of the other ophthalmic or systemic anti-inflammatory medicines. Also tell your health care professional if you are allergic to any other substances, such as preservatives.

Pregnancy—Ophthalmic ketorolac has not been studied in pregnant women. However, studies in some animals have shown that ophthalmic ketorolac causes birth defects. Before using this medicine, make sure your doctor knows if you are pregnant or if you may become pregnant.

Breast-feeding—Ophthalmic ketorolac has not been reported to cause problems in nursing babies.

Children—Studies on this medicine have been done only in adult patients, and there is no specific information comparing use of ophthalmic ketorolac in children with use in other age groups.

Older adults—Many medicines have not been studied specifically in older people. Therefore, it may not be known whether they work exactly the same way they do in younger adults. Although there is no specific information comparing use of ophthalmic ketorolac in the elderly with use in other age groups, this medicine is not expected to cause different side effects or problems in older people than it does in younger adults.

Other medicines—Although certain medicines should not be used together at all, in other cases two different medicines may be used together even if an interaction might occur. In these cases, your doctor may want to change the dose, or other precautions may be necessary. Tell your health care professional if you are using any other ophthalmic prescription or nonprescription (over-the-counter [OTC]) medicine.

Other medical problems—The presence of other medical problems may affect the use of ophthalmic ketorolac. Make sure you tell your doctor if you have any other medical problems, especially:

• Hemophilia or
• Other bleeding problems—The possiblity of bleeding may be increased during eye surgery

Proper Use of This Medicine

To use:
• First, wash your hands. Tilt the head back and, pressing your finger gently on the skin just beneath the lower eyelid, pull the lower eyelid away from the eye to make a space. Drop the medicine into this space. Let go of the eyelid and gently close the eyes. Do not blink. Keep the eyes closed for 1 or 2 minutes to allow the medicine to be absorbed by the eye.
• If you think you did not get the drop of medicine into your eye properly, use another drop.
• To keep the medicine as germ-free as possible, do not touch the applicator tip to any surface (including the eye). Also, keep the container tightly closed.

Dosing—The dose of ophthalmic ketorolac will be different for different patients. *Follow your doctor's orders or the directions on the label.* The following information includes only the average dose of ophthalmic ketorolac. *If your dose is different, do not change it* unless your doctor tells you to do so.

• For *ophthalmic solution (eye drops)* dosage form:
  —For itching of the eye
    • Adults—Use one drop in each eye four times a day for up to one week or as directed by your doctor.
    • Children—Use and dose must be determined by your doctor.
  —For inflammation of the eye following cataract surgery
    • Adults—Use one drop in the affected eye(s) four times a day beginning twenty-four hours after surgery and continuing for two weeks.
    • Children—Use and dose must be determined by your doctor.

Missed dose—If you miss a dose of this medicine, use it as soon as possible. However, if it is almost time for your next dose, skip the missed dose and go back to your regular dosing schedule. Do not double doses.

Storage—To store this medicine:
• Keep out of the reach of children.

© 2002 MICROMEDEX Thomson Healthcare

- Store away from heat and direct light.
- Keep the medicine from freezing. Do not refrigerate.
- Do not keep outdated medicine or medicine no longer needed. Be sure that any discarded medicine is out of the reach of children.

Precautions While Using This Medicine

If your symptoms do not improve within a few days, or if they become worse, check with your doctor.

While applying this medicine, your eyes will probably sting or burn for a short time. This is to be expected.

Side Effects of This Medicine

Along with its needed effects, a medicine may cause some unwanted effects. Although not all of these side effects may occur, if they do occur they may need medical attention.

Check with your doctor as soon as possible if any of the following side effects occur:

Less common or rare

Burning, itching, redness, swelling, tearing, or other sign of eye irritation not present before therapy or becoming worse during therapy; skin rash around eye

Other side effects may occur that usually do not need medical attention. These side effects may go away during treatment as your body adjusts to the medicine. However, check with your doctor if any of the following side effects continue or are bothersome:

More common

Stinging or burning of eye when medicine is applied

Other side effects not listed above may also occur in some patients. If you notice any other effects, check with your doctor.

Developed: 08/11/94
Interim revision: 11/20/98

KETOROLAC   Systemic

Commonly used brand name(s):

In the U.S.—
Toradol

In Canada—
Toradol

Description

Ketorolac (kee-toe-ROLE-ak) is used to relieve moderately severe pain, usually pain that occurs after an operation or other painful procedure. It belongs to the group of medicines called nonsteroidal anti-inflammatory drugs (NSAIDs). Ketorolac is not a narcotic and is not habit-forming. It will not cause physical or mental dependence, as narcotics can. However, ketorolac is sometimes used together with a narcotic to provide better pain relief than either medicine used alone.

Ketorolac has side effects that can be very dangerous. The risk of having a serious side effect increases with the dose of ketorolac and with the length of treatment. Therefore, ketorolac should not be used for more than 5 days. Before using this medicine, you should discuss with your doctor the good that this medicine can do as well as the risks of using it.

Ketorolac is available only with your doctor's prescription, in the following dosage forms:

Oral
- Tablets (U.S. and Canada)

Parenteral
- Injection (U.S. and Canada)

Before Using This Medicine

In deciding to use a medicine, the risks of taking the medicine must be weighed against the good it will do. This is a decision you and your doctor will make. For ketorolac, the following should be considered:

Allergies—Tell your doctor if you have ever had any unusual or allergic reaction to ketorolac or to any of the following medicines:

Aspirin or other salicylates
Diclofenac (e.g., Voltaren)
Diflunisal (e.g., Dolobid)
Etodolac (e.g., Lodine)
Fenoprofen (e.g., Nalfon)
Floctafenine (e.g., Idarac)
Flurbiprofen (e.g., Ansaid)
Ibuprofen (e.g., Motrin)
Indomethacin (e.g., Indocin)
Ketoprofen (e.g., Orudis)
Meclofenamate (e.g., Meclomen)
Mefenamic acid (e.g., Ponstel)
Nabumetone (e.g., Relafen)
Naproxen (e.g., Naprosyn)
Oxaprozin (e.g., Daypro)
Phenylbutazone (e.g., Butazolidin)
Piroxicam (e.g., Feldene)
Sulindac (e.g., Clinoril)
Tenoxicam (e.g., Mobiflex)
Tiaprofenic acid (e.g., Surgam)
Tolmetin (e.g., Tolectin)

Also tell your health care professional if you are allergic to any other substances, such as foods, preservatives, or dyes.

Pregnancy—Studies on birth defects with ketorolac have not been done in pregnant women. However, it crosses the placenta. There is a chance that regular use of ketorolac during the last few months of pregnancy may cause unwanted effects on the heart or blood flow of the fetus or newborn baby. Ketorolac has not been shown to cause birth defects in animal studies. However, animal studies have shown that, if taken late in pregnancy, ketorolac may increase the length of pregnancy, prolong labor, or cause other problems during delivery.

Breast-feeding—Ketorolac passes into the breast milk and may cause unwanted effects in nursing babies. It may be necessary for you to use another pain reliever or to stop breast-feeding during treatment. Be sure that you have discussed the use of this medicine with your doctor.

Children—Studies on this medicine have been done only in adult patients, and there is no specific information comparing use of ketorolac in children up to 16 years of age with use in other age groups.

Older adults—Stomach or intestinal problems, swelling of the face, feet, or lower legs, or sudden decrease in the amount of urine may be especially likely to occur in elderly patients, who are usually more sensitive than younger adults to the effects of ketorolac. Also, elderly people are more likely than younger adults to get very sick if the medicine causes stomach problems. Studies in older adults have shown that ketorolac stays in the body longer than it does in younger people. Your doctor will consider this when deciding on how much ketorolac should be given for each dose and how often it should be given.

Other medicines—Although certain medicines should not be used together at all, in other cases two different medicines may be used together even if an interaction might occur. In these cases, your doctor may want to change the dose, or other precautions may be necessary. When you are using ketorolac, it is especially important that your health care professional know if you are taking any of the following:

- Anticoagulants (blood thinners) or
- Cefamandole (e.g., Mandol) or
- Cefoperazone (e.g., Cefobid) or
- Cefotetan (e.g., Cefotan) or
- Heparin or
- Plicamycin (e.g., Mithracin) or
- Valproic acid (e.g., Depakene)—Use of any of these medicines together with ketorolac may increase the chance of bleeding

- Aspirin or other salicylates or
- Other medicine for inflammation or pain, except narcotics—The chance of serious side effects may be increased

- Lithium (e.g., Lithane) or
- Methotrexate (e.g., Mexate)—Higher blood levels of lithium or methotrexate and an increased chance of side effects may occur

- Probenecid (e.g., Benemid)—Higher blood levels of ketorolac and an increased chance of side effects may occur

Other medical problems—The presence of other medical problems may affect the use of ketorolac. Make sure you tell your doctor if you smoke tobacco or if you have any other medical problems, especially:

- Alcohol abuse or
- Diabetes mellitus (sugar diabetes) or
- Edema (swelling of face, fingers, feet or lower legs caused by too much fluid in the body) or
- Kidney disease or
- Liver disease (severe) or
- Systemic lupus erythematosus (SLE)—The chance of serious side effects may be increased

- Asthma or
- Heart disease or
- High blood pressure—Ketorolac may make your condition worse.

- Bleeding in the brain (history of) or
- Hemophilia or other bleeding problems—Ketorolac may increase the chance of serious bleeding

- Bleeding from the stomach or intestines (history of) or
- Colitis, stomach ulcer, or other stomach or intestinal problems (or history of)—Ketorolac may make stomach or intestinal problems worse. Also, bleeding from the stomach or intestines is more likely to occur during ketorolac treatment in people with these conditions

Proper Use of This Medicine

For patients taking *ketorolac tablets:*
- To lessen stomach upset, ketorolac tablets should be taken with food (a meal or a snack) or with an antacid.
- Take this medicine with a full glass of water. Also, do not lie down for about 15 to 30 minutes after taking it. This

helps to prevent irritation that may lead to trouble in swallowing.

For patients using *ketorolac injection:*
- Medicines given by injection are sometimes used at home. If you will be using ketorolac at home, your health care professional will teach you how the injections are to be given. You will also have a chance to practice giving injections. Be certain that you understand exactly how the medicine is to be injected.

For safe and effective use of this medicine, do not use more of it, do not use it more often, and do not use it for more than 5 days. Using too much of this medicine increases the chance of unwanted effects, especially in elderly patients.

Ketorolac should be used only when it is ordered by your doctor for treating certain kinds of pain. Because of the risk of serious side effects, do not save any leftover ketorolac for use in the future, and do not share it with other people.

Dosing—The dose of ketorolac will be different for different patients. *Follow your doctor's orders or the directions on the label.* The following information includes only the average doses of ketorolac. *If your dose is different, do not change it* unless your doctor tells you to do so.

- For *oral* dosage form (tablets):
  —For pain:
    - Adults (patients 16 years of age and older)—One 10-milligram (mg) tablet four times a day, four to six hours apart. Some people may be directed to take two tablets for the first dose only.
    - Children up to 16 years of age—Use and dose must be determined by your doctor.

- For *injection* dosage form:
  —For pain:
    - Adults (patients 16 years of age and older)—15 or 30 mg, injected into a muscle or a vein four times a day, at least 6 hours apart. This amount of medicine may be contained in 1 mL or in one-half (0.5) mL of the injection, depending on the strength. Some people who do not need more than one injection may receive one dose of 60 mg, injected into a muscle.
    - Children up to 16 years of age—Use and dose must be determined by your doctor.

Missed dose—If you have been directed to use this medicine according to a regular schedule, and you miss a dose, use it as soon as possible. However, if it is almost time for your next dose, skip the missed dose and go back to your regular dosing schedule. Do not double doses.

Storage—To store this medicine:
- Keep out of the reach of children.
- Store away from heat and direct light.
- Do not store ketorolac tablets in the bathroom, near the kitchen sink, or in other damp places. Heat or moisture may cause the medicine to break down.
- Keep the injection form of ketorolac from freezing. Do not store it in the refrigerator.
- Do not keep outdated medicine or medicine no longer needed. Be sure that any discarded medicine is out of the reach of children.

Precautions While Using This Medicine

Taking certain other medicines together with ketorolac may increase the chance of unwanted effects. The risk will depend on how much of each medicine you take every day, and on how long you take the medicines together. Therefore, do not take acetaminophen (e.g., Tylenol) together with ketorolac for more than a few days, unless otherwise directed by your medical doctor or dentist. Also, *do not take any of the following medicines together with ketorolac, unless your medical doctor or dentist has directed you to do so and is following your progress:*

> Aspirin or other salicylates
> Diclofenac (e.g., Voltaren)
> Diflunisal (e.g., Dolobid)
> Etodolac (e.g., Lodine)
> Fenoprofen (e.g., Nalfon)
> Floctafenine (e.g., Idarac)
> Flurbiprofen (e.g., Ansaid)
> Ibuprofen (e.g., Motrin)
> Indomethacin (e.g., Indocin)
> Ketoprofen (e.g., Orudis)
> Meclofenamate (e.g., Meclomen)
> Mefenamic acid (e.g., Ponstel)
> Nabumetone (e.g., Relafen)
> Naproxen (e.g., Naprosyn)
> Oxaprozin (e.g., Daypro)
> Phenylbutazone (e.g., Butazolidin)
> Piroxicam (e.g., Feldene)
> Sulindac (e.g., Clinoril)
> Tenoxicam (e.g., Mobiflex)
> Tiaprofenic acid (e.g., Surgam)
> Tolmetin (e.g., Tolectin)
> Zomepirac (e.g., Zomax)

Ketorolac may cause some people to become dizzy or drowsy. If either of these side effects occurs, *do not drive, use machines, or do anything else that could be dangerous if you are not alert.*

Side Effects of This Medicine

Along with its needed effects, a medicine may cause some unwanted effects. Although not all of these side effects may occur, if they do occur they may need medical attention.

Stop using this medicine and check with your doctor immediately if any of the following side effects occur:
> *Rare*
> > Bleeding from the rectum or bloody or black, tarry stools; bleeding or crusting sores on lips; blue lips and fingernails; chest pain; convulsions; fainting; shortness of breath, fast, irregular, noisy, or troubled breathing, tightness in chest, and/or wheezing; vomiting of blood or material that looks like coffee grounds

Also, check with your doctor as soon as possible if any of the following side effects occur:
> *More common*
> > Swelling of face, fingers, lower legs, ankles, and/or feet; weight gain (unusual)
> *Less common*
> > Bruising (not at place of injection); high blood pressure; skin rash or itching; small, red spots on skin; sores, ulcers, or white spots on lips or in mouth
> *Rare*
> > Abdominal or stomach pain, cramping, or burning (severe); bloody or cloudy urine; blurred vision of other vision change; burning, red, tender, thick, scaly, or peeling skin; cough or hoarseness; dark urine; decrease in amount of urine (sudden); fever with severe headache, drowsiness, confusion, and stiff neck or back; fever with or without chills or sore throat; general feeling of illness; hallucinations (seeing, hearing, or feeling things that are not there); hearing loss; hives; increase in amount of urine or urinating often; light-colored stools; loss of appetite; low blood pressure; mood changes or unusual behavior; muscle cramps or pain; nausea, heartburn, and/or indigestion (severe and continuing); nosebleeds; pain in lower back and/or side; pain, tenderness, and/or swelling in the upper abdominal area; painful or difficult urination; pale skin; puffiness or swelling of the eyelids or around the eyes; ringing or buzzing in ears; runny nose; severe restlessness; swollen and/or painful glands; swollen tongue; thirst (continuing); unusual tiredness or weakness; yellow eyes or skin

Other side effects may occur that usually do not need medical attention. These side effects may go away during treatment as your body adjusts to the medicine. However, check with your doctor if any of the following side effects continue or are bothersome:
> *More common*
> > Abdominal or stomach pain (mild or moderate); bruising at place of injection; diarrhea; dizziness; drowsiness; headache; indigestion; nausea
> *Less common or rare*
> > Bloating or gas; burning or pain at place of injection; constipation; feeling of fullness in abdominal or stomach area; increased sweating; vomiting

Other side effects not listed above may also occur in some patients. If you notice any other effects, check with your doctor.

Additional Information

Once a medicine has been approved for marketing for a certain use, experience may show that it is also useful for other medical problems. Although these uses are not included in product labeling, ketorolac is used in certain patients with the following medical conditions:

- Pain after surgery in children

Other than the above information, there is no additional information relating to proper use, precautions, or side effects for these uses.

Revised: 08/17/2000

KETOTIFEN   Ophthalmic†

Commonly used brand name(s):

In the U.S.—
> Zaditor

†Not commercially available in Canada.

Description

Ketotifen (kee-toe-TYE-fen) ophthalmic (eye) solution is used to temporarily prevent itching of the eye caused by a condition known as allergic conjunctivitis. It works by acting on certain cells, called mast cells, to prevent them from releasing substances that cause the allergic reaction.

This medicine is available only with your doctor's prescription, in the following dosage forms:

Ophthalmic
- Ophthalmic solution (eye drops) (U.S.)

Before Using This Medicine

In deciding to use a medicine, the risks of taking the medicine must be weighed against the good it will do. This is a decision you and your doctor will make. For ketotifen, the following should be considered:

Allergies—Tell your doctor if you have ever had any unusual or allergic reaction to ketotifen. Also tell your health care professional if you are allergic to any other substances, such as preservatives.

Pregnancy—Ketotifen has not been studied in pregnant women. However, studies in animals have shown that ketotifen, when given in very high doses to some types of animals, causes birth defects. Before using this medicine, make sure your doctor knows if you are pregnant or if you may become pregnant.

Breast-feeding—It is not known whether ketotifen passes into human breast milk. However, it does pass into the milk of animals with nursing young. Mothers who are taking this medicine and who wish to breast-feed should discuss this with their doctor.

Children—Studies on this medicine have been done only in adult patients, and there is no specific information comparing use of ketotifen in children younger than 3 years of age with use in other age groups.

Older adults—Many medicines have not been studied specifically in older people. Therefore, it may not be known whether they work exactly the same way they do in younger adults or if they cause different side effects or problems in older people. There is no specific information comparing use of ophthalmic ketotifen in the elderly with use in other age groups.

Other medicines—Although certain medicines should not be used together at all, in other cases two different medicines may be used together even if an interaction might occur. In these cases, your doctor may want to change the dose, or other precautions may be necessary. Tell your health care professional if you are taking or using any other prescription or nonprescription (over-the-counter [OTC]) medicine.

Proper Use of This Medicine

Do not wear contact lenses if your eyes are red. Also, do not use this medicine to treat irritation related to contact lens use. If you wear contact lenses: Take out your contact lenses before using ketotifen eye drops. Wait at least 10 minutes after putting the eye drops in before putting the contact lenses back in.

To use the *eye drops:*
- First, wash your hands. Tilt the head back and, pressing your finger gently on the skin just beneath the lower eyelid, pull the lower eyelid away from the eye to make a space. Drop the medicine into this space. Let go of the eyelid and gently close the eyes. Do not blink. Keep the eyes closed for 1 to 2 minutes to allow the medicine to be absorbed by the eye.
- If you think you did not get the drop of medicine into your eye properly, use another drop.

- *To keep the medicine as germ-free as possible, do not touch the applicator tip to any surface (including the eye).* Also, keep the container tightly closed.

Dosing—The dose of ketotifen will be different for different patients. *Follow your doctor's orders or the directions on the label.* The following information includes only the average doses of ophthalmic ketotifen. *If your dose is different, do not change it* unless your doctor tells you to do so.
- For *ophthalmic* dosage form (eye drops):
  - For prevention of itching of the eye due to allergic conjunctivitis (eye allergy):
    - Adults and children 3 years of age and older—Use one drop in each affected eye every 8 to 12 hours.
    - Children up to 3 years of age—Use and dose must be determined by your doctor.

Missed dose—If you miss a dose of this medicine, use it as soon as possible. However, if it is almost time for your next dose, skip the missed dose and go back to your regular dosing schedule. Do not double doses.

Storage—To store this medicine:
- Keep out of the reach of children.
- Store away from heat and direct light.
- Keep the medicine from freezing.
- Do not keep outdated medicine or medicine no longer needed. Ask your health care professional how you should dispose of any medicine you do not use. Be sure that any discarded medicine is out of the reach of children.

Precautions While Using This Medicine

If your symptoms do not improve or if your condition becomes worse, check with your doctor.

Side Effects of This Medicine

Along with its needed effects, a medicine may cause some unwanted effects. Although not all of these side effects may occur, if they do occur they may need medical attention.

Check with your doctor as soon as possible if any of the following side effects occur:
More common
　Eye redness and swelling
Less common
　Eye discharge; eye discomfort; eye pain; hives; increased itching of eyes; rash.

Other side effects may occur that usually do not need medical attention. These side effects may go away during treatment as your body adjusts to the medicine. However, check with your doctor if any of the following side effects continue or are bothersome:
More common
　Headaches; stuffy or runny nose
Less common
　Burning or stinging of eyes; dry eyes; eyelid disorder; eye sensitivity to light; fever, tiredness, achiness, and sore throat; increase in size of pupils; sore throat; tearing.

Other side effects not listed above may also occur in some patients. If you notice any other effects, check with your doctor.

Developed: 9/30/99

KETOTIFEN   Systemic—
INTRODUCTORY VERSION

Commonly used brand name(s):

In Canada—
Apo-Ketotifen
Novo-Ketotifen
Zaditen

Description

Ketotifen (kee-toe-TYE-fen) is a type of asthma medication which, when taken every day and used along with other antiasthma medications, may reduce the frequency, severity, and duration of asthma symptoms or attacks in children. It may also lead to a reduction in daily requirements of other antiasthma medications. Ketotifen is not effective for the prevention or treatment of acute asthma attacks. Ketotifen works by inhibiting certain substances in the body that are known to cause inflammation and symptoms of asthma.

This medicine is available only with your doctor's prescription, in the following dosage forms:

Oral
- Syrup (Canada)
- Tablets (Canada)

Before Using This Medicine

In deciding to use a medicine, the risks of taking the medicine must be weighed against the good it will do. This is a decision you and your doctor will make. For ketotifen, the following should be considered:

Allergies—Tell your doctor if you have ever had any unusual or allergic reaction to ketotifen. Also tell your health care professional if you are allergic to any other substances, such as foods, preservatives, or dyes.

Diet—Make certain your health care professional knows if you are on any special diet, such as a low-sugar diet. The syrup contains carbohydrates.

Pregnancy—Ketotifen has not been studied in pregnant women. However, studies in animals have shown that ketotifen crosses the placenta and, at high doses, cause problems. Before using this medicine, make sure your doctor knows if you are pregnant or if you may become pregnant.

Breast-feeding—It is not known whether ketotifen passes into human breast milk. However, it does pass into the milk of rats. It may be necessary for you to take another medicine or to stop breast-feeding during treatment. Be sure you have discussed the risks and benefits of the medicine with your doctor.

Children—This medicine has been tested in children and, in effective doses, has not been shown to cause different side effects or problems than it does in adults.

Older adults—Many medicines have not been studied specifically in older people. Therefore, it may not be known whether they work exactly the same way they do in younger adults or if they cause different side effects or problems in older people. There is no specific information comparing use of ketotifen in the elderly with use in other age groups.

Other medicines—Although certain medicines should not be used together at all, in other cases two different medicines may be used together even if an interaction might occur. In these cases, your doctor may want to change the dose, or other precautions may be necessary. When you are taking ketotifen, it is especially important that your health care professional knows if you are taking any of the following:

- Antidiabetic agents, oral—May increase the risk of bruising or bleeding and affect blood sugar concentrations

- Alcohol or
- Antihistamines or
- Hypnotics or
- Sedatives—May increase the chance of side effects (i.e., drowsiness)

Other medical problems—The presence of other medical problems may affect the use of ketotifen. Make sure you tell your doctor if you have any other medical problems, especially:

- Diabetes mellitus (sugar diabetes)—May alter low-sugar diet (syrup contains carbohydrates)

- Epilepsy—May increase risk of convulsions (seizures)

Proper Use of This Medicine

Ketotifen is used to help prevent asthma attacks. It will not relieve an asthma attack that has already started.

Ketotifen must be taken continuously in order to be effective.

Continue taking your current asthma medications until instructed otherwise by your doctor.

Ketotifen may be taken with or without food.

Dosing—The dose of ketotifen will be different for different patients. *Follow your doctor's orders or the directions on the label.* The following information includes only the average doses of ketotifen. *If your dose is different, do not change it* unless your doctor tells you to do so.

- For *oral* dosage form (tablets and syrup):
  —For asthma:
    - Adults and children 3 years of age and older—The usual dose is 1 milligram (mg) (1 tablet or 5 milliliters [mL] of syrup) twice daily, once in the morning and once in the evening.
    - Infants and children from 6 months to 3 years of age—Dose is based on body weight and must be determined by the doctor. It is usually 0.25 mL (50 mcg or 0.05 mg) of syrup per kilogram (kg) (110 micrograms [mcg] or 0.110 mg per pound) of body weight twice daily, once in the morning and once in the evening.

Missed dose—If you miss a dose of this medicine, take it as soon as possible. However, if it is almost time for your next dose, skip the missed dose and go back to your regular dosing schedule. Do not double doses.

Storage—To store this medicine:
- Keep out of the reach of children.
- Do not store tablets in the bathroom, near the kitchen sink, or in other damp places. Heat or moisture may cause the medicine to break down.
- Do not keep outdated medicine or medicine no longer needed. Ask your health care professional how you should dispose of any medicine you do not use. Be sure that any discarded medicine is out of the reach of children.

Precautions While Using This Medicine

It is very important that your doctor check your progress at regular visits. This will allow your doctor to see if the medicine is working properly and to decide if you should continue to take it. If your symptoms worsen, you should check with your doctor.

This medicine may cause some people to become drowsy, dizzy, or less alert than they are normally. *Make sure you know how you react to this medicine before you drive, use machines, or do anything else that could be dangerous if you are dizzy or are not alert.*

This medicine may cause some people to become excited, irritable, or nervous or to have trouble in sleeping. These are symptoms of central nervous system stimulation and are especially likely to occur in children.

For patients with diabetes:
- The syrup form of this medicine may affect blood sugar levels. If you notice a change in the results of your blood or urine sugar tests or if you have any questions, check with your doctor.

Side Effects of This Medicine

Along with its needed effects, a medicine may cause some unwanted effects. Although not all of these side effects may occur, if they do occur they may need medical attention.

Check with your doctor as soon as possible if any of the following side effects occur:

Less common
Chills; cough; diarrhea; fever; general feeling of discomfort or illness; headache; joint pain; loss of appetite; muscle aches and pains; nausea; runny nose; shivering; sore throat; sweating; trouble sleeping; unusual tiredness or weakness; vomiting

Rare
Abdominal or stomach pain; blistering, itching, peeling, or redness of skin; bloody or cloudy urine; clay-colored stools; convulsions; dark urine; difficult, burning, or painful urination; dizziness; frequent urge to urinate; muscle spasm or jerking of all extremities; rash; sudden loss of consciousness; unpleasant breath odor; vomiting of blood; yellow eyes or skin

Symptoms of overdose
Get emergency help immediately if any of the following symptoms of overdose occur
Blurred vision; confusion; convulsions; disorientation; dizziness; drowsiness (severe); faintness or lightheadedness when getting up from a lying or sitting position; fast, pounding, or irregular heartbeat or pulse; hyperexcitability; loss of consciousness; palpitations; sweating; unusual tiredness or weakness

Other side effects may occur that usually do not need medical attention. These side effects may go away during treatment as your body adjusts to the medicine. However, check with your doctor if any of the following side effects continue or are bothersome.

More common
Weight gain

Less common or rare
Bloody nose; drowsiness; dryness of mouth; excitation; increased appetite; irritability; nervousness; swelling of eyelids; unexplained nosebleeds

Other side effects not listed above may also occur in some patients. If you notice any other effects, check with your doctor.

Developed: 08/02/2000

LAMIVUDINE   Systemic

Commonly used brand name(s):

In the U.S.—
Epivir
Epivir-HBV
In Canada—
3TC
Heptovir

Description

Lamivudine (la-MI-vyoo-deen) is used in the treatment of the infection caused by the human immunodeficiency virus (HIV). HIV is the virus that causes acquired immune deficiency syndrome (AIDS). Lamivudine is taken together with zidovudine (AZT) or other medications used to treat HIV. Lamivudine is also used to treat hepatitis B virus (HBV) infections.

Lamivudine will not cure or prevent HIV infection or AIDS; however, it helps keep HIV from reproducing and appears to slow down the destruction of the immune system. This may help delay the development of problems usually related to AIDS or HIV disease. Lamivudine will not keep you from spreading HIV to other people. People who receive this medicine may continue to have other problems usually related to AIDS or HIV disease. Lamivudine is not a cure for the hepatitis B virus; the long-term effects of the drug on the infection and the liver are unknown at this time.

Lamivudine is available only with your doctor's prescription, in the following dosage forms:

Oral
- Oral solution (U.S. and Canada)
- Tablets (U.S. and Canada)

Before Using This Medicine

In deciding to use a medicine, the risks of taking the medicine must be weighed against the good it will do. This is a decision you and your doctor will make. For lamivudine, the following should be considered:

Allergies—Tell your doctor if you have ever had any unusual or allergic reaction to lamivudine. Also tell your health care professional if you are allergic to any other substances, such as foods, preservatives, or dyes.

Pregnancy—Lamivudine crosses the placenta. Studies in animals have shown that lamivudine causes birth defects when given in very high doses. Before taking this medicine, make sure your doctor knows if you are pregnant or if you may become pregnant. Ask your doctor to register you with the Pregnancy Registry, to monitor the effect of treatment on you and your baby.

Breast-feeding—Lamivudine passes into the breast milk. If your baby does not already have the AIDS virus, there is a chance that you could pass it to your baby by breast-feeding. Talk to your doctor first if you are thinking about breast-feeding your baby.

Children—Lamivudine can cause serious side effects. In one study, children with advanced AIDS were more likely than children who were less ill to develop pancreatitis (inflammation of the pancreas) and peripheral neuropathy (a problem involving the nerves). Therefore, it is especially important that you discuss with your child's doctor the good that this medicine may do as well as the risks of using it. Your child must be seen frequently and your child's progress carefully followed by the doctor while the child is taking lamivudine.

Older adults—Lamivudine has not been studied specifically in older people. Therefore, it is not known whether it causes different side effects or problems in the elderly than it does in younger adults.

Other medicines—Although certain medicines should not be used together at all, in other cases two different medicines may be used together even if an interaction might occur. In these cases, your doctor may want to change the dose, or other precautions may be necessary. Tell your health care professional if you are taking any other prescription or nonprescription (over-the-counter [OTC]) medicine.

Other medical problems—The presence of other medical problems may affect the use of lamivudine. Make sure you tell your doctor if you have any other medical problems, especially:

- Inflamed pancreas or
- Nerve damage—These conditions may occur or worsen when taking lamivudine
- Kidney disease—Patients with kidney disease may have an increased chance of side effects
- Untreated or unrecognized human immunodeficiency virus—For patients with hepatitis B virus, your physician will talk to you about HIV before you begin taking lamivudine. You may be tested for HIV. Lamivudine tablets and oral solution for hepatitis B virus contain lower amounts of the drug than the tablets and solution for HIV. If you start on the lower-dose medication and later learn that you have HIV, the higher-dose lamivudine may not then be effective against the infection caused by HIV.

Proper Use of This Medicine

Take this medicine exactly as directed by your doctor. Do not take more of it, do not take it more often, and do not take it for a longer time than your doctor ordered. Also, do not stop taking lamivudine or zidovudine without checking with your doctor first.

Keep taking lamivudine for the full time of treatment, even if you begin to feel better.

This medicine works best when there is a constant amount in the blood. *To help keep the amount constant, do not miss any doses.* If you need help in planning the best times to take your medicine, check with your health care professional.

If you are using *lamivudine oral suspension*, use a specially marked measuring spoon or other device to measure each dose accurately. The average household teaspoon may not hold the right amount of liquid.

Only take medicine that your doctor has prescribed specifically for you. Do not share your medicine with others.

Dosing—The dose of lamivudine will be different for different patients. *Follow your doctor's orders or the directions on the label.* The following information includes only the average doses of lamivudine. Your dose may be different if you have kidney disease. *If your dose is different, do not change it* unless your doctor tells you to do so:

- For *oral* dosage forms (oral solution and tablets):
  - —For treatment of hepatitis B infection:
    - Adults —100 milligrams (mg) once a day.
    - Children younger than 16 years of age—Use and dose must be determined by your doctor.
  - —For treatment of HIV infection or AIDS:
    - Adults weighing 50 kilograms (kg) (110 pounds) or more—150 milligrams (mg) twice a day together with other HIV medications.

- Adults weighing less than 50 kg (110 pounds)— 2 mg per kg of body weight twice a day together with other HIV medications.
- Children 3 months to 16 years of age—4 mg per kg of body weight, up to 150 mg per dose, twice a day together with other HIV medications.
- Children younger than 3 months of age—Use and dose must be determined by your doctor.

Note: Patients that require treatment for both hepatitis B and either AIDS or HIV should follow the dosing schedule for HIV or AIDS

Missed dose—If you miss a dose of this medicine, take it as soon as possible. However, if it is almost time for your next dose, skip the missed dose and go back to your regular dosing schedule. Do not double doses.

Storage—To store this medicine:
- Keep out of the reach of children.
- Store away from heat and direct light.
- Do not store in the bathroom, near the kitchen sink, or in other damp places. Heat or moisture may cause the medicine to break down.
- Do not keep outdated medicine or medicine no longer needed. Be sure that any discarded medicine is out of the reach of children.

Precautions While Using This Medicine

It is very important that your doctor check your progress at regular visits.

Do not take any other medicines without checking with your doctor first. To do so may increase the chance of side effects from lamivudine.

Side Effects of This Medicine

Along with its needed effects, a medicine may cause some unwanted effects. Although not all of these side effects may occur, if they do occur they may need medical attention.

Check with your doctor immediately if any of the following side effects occur:
  More common—especially in children
    Abdominal or stomach pain (severe); feeling of fullness; nausea; tingling, burning, numbness, or pain in the hands, arms, feet, or legs; vomiting

  Rare
    Abdominal discomfort; decreased appetite; diarrhea; fast, shallow breathing; feeling of fullness; fever, chills, or sore throat; general feeling of discomfort; muscle pain or cramping; nausea; shortness of breath; skin rash; sleepiness; unusual tiredness or weakness

Other side effects may occur that usually do not need medical attention. These side effects may go away during treatment as your body adjusts to the medicine. However, check with your doctor if any of the following side effects continue or are bothersome:
  More common
    Canker sores; ear discharge; ear swelling; redness of skin; sores, ulcers, or white spots on lips or tongue or inside the mouth; swollen and painful spots on neck, armpit, or groin; unusually warm skin

  Less common
    Abdominal or stomach pain; cough; dizziness; headache; trouble in sleeping; vomiting

Rare
   Hair loss

Other side effects not listed above may also occur in some patients. If you notice any other effects, check with your doctor.

Additional Information

Once a medicine has been approved for marketing for a certain use, experience may show that it is also useful for other medical problems. Although this use is not included in product labeling, lamivudine is used in certain patients with the following medical condition:

- Human immunodeficiency virus (HIV) infection due to occupational exposure (possible prevention of)

Other than the above information, there is no additional information relating to proper use, precautions, or side effects for this use.

Developed: 08/08/96
Revised: 2/28/01

LAMIVUDINE AND ZIDOVUDINE
Systemic†

Commonly used brand name(s):

In the U.S.—
   Combivir

   †Not commercially available in Canada.

Description

Lamivudine (la-MI-vyoo-deen) and zidovudine (zye-DOE-vyoo-deen) combination is used in the treatment of human immunodeficiency virus (HIV) infection. HIV is the virus that causes acquired immune deficiency syndrome (AIDS).

Lamivudine and zidovudine combination will not cure or prevent HIV infection or the symptoms of AIDS; however, it helps keep HIV from reproducing, and appears to slow down the destruction of the immune system. This may help delay the development of serious health problems usually related to AIDS or HIV infection. Lamivudine and zidovudine combination will not keep you from spreading HIV to other people. People who receive this medicine may continue to have other problems usually related to AIDS or HIV infection.

The zidovudine component of this combination medicine may cause some serious side effects, including bone marrow problems. Symptoms of bone marrow problems include fever, chills, sore throat, pale skin, and unusual tiredness or weakness. These problems may require blood transfusion or temporarily stopping treatment with lamivudine and zidovudine combination. Check with your doctor if any new health problems or symptoms occur while you are taking lamivudine and zidovudine combination.

This medicine is available only with your doctor's prescription, in the following dosage form:

Oral
   - Tablets (U.S.)

Before Using This Medicine

In deciding to use a medicine, the risks of taking the medicine must be weighed against the good it will do. This is a decision you and your doctor will make. For lamivudine and zidovudine combination, the following should be considered:

Allergies—Tell your doctor if you have ever had any unusual or allergic reaction to lamivudine or zidovudine. Also tell your health care professional if you are allergic to any other substances, such as foods, preservatives, or dyes.

Pregnancy—Lamivudine and zidovudine combination has not been studied in pregnant women. However, studies in animals have shown that zidovudine causes birth defects when given in very high doses. Before taking this lamivudine and zidovudine combination, make sure your doctor knows if you are pregnant or if you may become pregnant.

Breast-feeding—Zidovudine passes into breast milk. It is not known whether lamivudine passes into breast milk. However, if your baby does not already have the AIDS virus, there is a chance that you could pass it to your baby by breast-feeding. Talk to your doctor first if you are thinking about breast-feeding your baby.

Children—Either lamivudine or zidovudine used alone may cause serious side effects, and children should receive less of these medicines than adults. However, lamivudine and zidovudine combination contains a fixed amount of each medicine that cannot be decreased. Therefore, lamivudine and zidovudine combination is not recommended for children less than 12 years of age, or children who weigh less than 50 kilograms (110 pounds) because the amounts of lamivudine and zidovudine in this product cannot be adjusted for smaller body sizes.

Teenagers—Lamivudine and zidovudine combination contains a fixed amount of each medicine that cannot be decreased. Therefore, this medicine is not recommended for patients who weigh less than 50 kilograms (110 pounds) because the amounts of lamivudine and zidovudine in this product cannot be adjusted for smaller body sizes.

Older adults—Many medicines have not been studied specifically in older people. Therefore, it may not be known whether they work exactly the same way they do in younger adults or if they cause different side effects or problems in older people. Many older people have problems with their liver, heart and kidneys. Your doctor may change the amount of medicine you take because of other health problems.

Other medicines—Although certain medicines should not be used together at all, in other cases two different medicines may be used together even if an interaction might occur. In these cases, your doctor may want to change the dose, or other precautions may be necessary. When you are taking lamivudine and zidovudine combination, it is especially important that your health care professional know if you are taking any of the following:

- Amphotericin B by injection (e.g., Fungizone) or
- Antineoplastics (cancer medicine) or
- Azathioprine (e.g., Imuran) or
- Chloramphenicol (e.g., Chloromycetin) or
- Clozapine (e.g., Clozaril) or
- Colchicine or
- Didanosine (e.g., Videx) or
- Eflornithine (e.g., Ornidyl) or
- Flucytosine (e.g., Ancobon) or
- Ganciclovir (e.g., Cytovene) or
- Interferon (e.g., Intron A, Roferon-A)

- Uracil mustard—Taking lamivudine and zidovudine combination while you are using or receiving these medicines may make anemia or other blood problems worse
- Lamivudine (e.g., Epivir) or
- Zidovudine (e.g., Retrovir)—Using additional lamivudine or zidovudine with the combination product may increase the chance of side effects of lamivudine or zidovudine

Other medical problems—The presence of other medical problems may affect the use of lamivudine and zidovudine combination. Make sure you tell your doctor if you have any other medical problems, especially:

- Blood problems, including decreased bone marrow production—Lamivudine and zidovudine combination may make these conditions worse
- Kidney disease or
- Liver disease—Patients with kidney or liver disease may experience an increase in side effects

Proper Use of This Medicine

Lamivudine and zidovudine combination may be taken with food or on an empty stomach.

Take this medicine exactly as directed by your doctor. Do not take more of it, do not take it more often, and do not take it for a longer time than your doctor ordered. Also, do not stop taking lamivudine and zidovudine combination without checking with your doctor first.

Keep taking lamivudine and zidovudine combination for the full time of treatment, even if you begin to feel better.

This medicine works best when there is a constant amount in the blood. *To help keep the amount constant, do not miss any doses.* If you need help in planning the best times to take your medicine, check with your health care professional.

Only take medicine that your doctor has prescribed specifically for you. Do not share your medicine with others.

Dosing—Lamivudine and zidovudine combination contains a fixed amount of each medicine.

- For *oral* dosage form (tablets):
    —For human immunodeficiency virus (HIV) infection:
    - Adults and teenagers who weigh more than 50 kilograms (kg) (110 pounds)—150 milligrams (mg) of lamivudine and 300 mg of zidovudine (equivalent to one tablet) two times a day.
    - Adults and teenagers who weigh 50 kg (110 pounds) or less—Use is not recommended.
    - Children—Use is not recommended.

Missed dose—If you miss a dose of this medicine, take it as soon as possible. However, if it is almost time for your next dose, skip the missed dose and go back to your regular dosing schedule. Do not double doses.

Storage—To store this medicine:

- Keep out of the reach of children.
- Store away from heat and direct light.
- Do not store in the bathroom, near the kitchen sink, or in other damp places. Heat or moisture may cause the medicine to break down.
- Do not keep outdated medicine or medicine no longer needed. Be sure that any discarded medicine is out of the reach of children.

Precautions While Using This Medicine

It is very important that your doctor check your progress at regular visits. Lamivudine and zidovudine combination may cause blood problems, and your doctor will want to test your blood regularly.

Do not take any other medicines without checking with your doctor first. To do so may increase the chance of side effects from lamivudine and zidovudine combination.

Side Effects of This Medicine

Along with its needed effects, a medicine may cause some unwanted effects. Although not all of these side effects may occur, if they do occur they may need medical attention.

Check with your doctor as soon as possible if any of the following side effects occur:
More common
    Chills; fever; pale skin; sore throat; unusual tiredness or weakness
Less common
    Abdominal pain (severe); burning, tingling, numbness, or pain in the hands, arms, feet, or legs; muscle tenderness and weakness; nausea; skin rash; vomiting; yellow eyes or skin

Other side effects may occur that usually do not need medical attention. These side effects may go away during treatment as your body adjusts to the medicine. However, check with your doctor if any of the following side effects continue or are bothersome:
More common
    Headache
Less common
    Abdominal pain (mild); coughing; decreased appetite; diarrhea; dizziness; trouble in sleeping

Other side effects not listed above may also occur in some patients. If you notice any other effects, check with your doctor.

Developed: 02/23/98
Revised: 03/14/01

LAMOTRIGINE Systemic

Commonly used brand name(s):

In the U.S.—
    Lamictal

In Canada—
    Lamictal

Another commonly used name is LTG.

Description

Lamotrigine (la-MOE-tri-jeen) is used to help control some types of seizures in the treatment of epilepsy. This medicine cannot cure epilepsy and will only work to control seizures for as long as you continue to take it.

Lamotrigine is available only with your doctor's prescription, in the following dosage form:

Oral
- Chewable/Dispersible Tablets (U.S.)
- Tablets (U.S. and Canada)

Before Using This Medicine

In deciding to use a medicine, the risks of taking the medicine must be weighed against the good it will do. This is a decision you and your doctor will make. For lamotrigine, the following should be considered:

Allergies—Tell your doctor if you have ever had any unusual or allergic reaction to lamotrigine. Also tell your health care professional if you are allergic to any other substances, such as foods, preservatives, or dyes.

Pregnancy—Lamotrigine has not been studied in pregnant women. However, if you might become pregnant while taking lamotrigine, your doctor may want you to take folic acid supplements. Studies in animals have shown that lamotrigine, even when given to the mother in doses smaller than the largest human dose, may cause some offspring to die. Before taking this medicine, make sure your doctor knows if you are pregnant or if you may become pregnant.

Breast-feeding—Lamotrigine passes into breast milk. However, it is not known whether this medicine causes problems in nursing babies. Mothers who are taking lamotrigine and who wish to breast-feed should discuss this with their doctor.

Children—Skin rashes may be more likely to occur in children younger than 16 years of age than in adults. Some of these rashes may be serious and life-threatening. It is especially important that you discuss with the child's doctor the good that this medicine may do as well as the risks of using it.

Older adults—Lamotrigine is removed from the body more slowly in elderly people than in younger people. Higher blood levels of the medicine may occur, which may increase the chance of unwanted effects. Your doctor may give you a different lamotrigine dose than a younger person would receive.

Other medicines—Although certain medicines should not be used together at all, in other cases two different medicines may be used together even if an interaction might occur. In these cases, your doctor may want to change the dose, or other precautions may be necessary. When you are taking lamotrigine, it is especially important that your health care professional know if you are taking any of the following:
- Carbamazepine (e.g., Tegretol) or
- Phenobarbital (e.g., Luminal) or
- Phenytoin (e.g., Dilantin) or
- Primidone (e.g., Mysoline) or
- Valproic acid (e.g., Depakote)—These medicines may increase or decrease the blood levels of lamotrigine, which may increase the chance of unwanted effects; your doctor may need to change the dose of either these medicines or lamotrigine

Other medical problems—The presence of other medical problems may affect the use of lamotrigine. Make sure you tell your doctor if you have any other medical problems, especially:
- Heart disease—It is not clear if patients who have problems with heart rhythms will have increased problems while taking lamotrigine
- Kidney disease or

- Liver disease—Higher blood levels of lamotrigine may occur, which may increase the chance of unwanted effects; your doctor may need to change your dose
- Thalassemia—Lamotrigine may cause your body to stop making or to make fewer red blood cells

Proper Use of This Medicine

Take lamotrigine only as directed by your doctor to help your condition as much as possible and to decrease the chance of unwanted effects. Do not take more or less of this medicine, and do not take it more or less often than your doctor ordered.

Lamotrigine may be taken with or without food or on a full or empty stomach. However, if your doctor tells you to take the medicine a certain way, take it exactly as directed.

If you are taking the *chewable/dispersible tablets:* These tablets may be swallowed whole, chewed and swallowed, or dispersed in a small amount of liquid and swallowed. If the tablets are chewed, they should be followed with a small amount of water or diluted fruit juice to aid in swallowing. If tablets are to be dispersed: Place tablets in enough water or diluted fruit juice to cover the tablets (about a teaspoonful), wait until the tablets are completely dispersed (about 1 minute), then swirl the solution and swallow it immediately.

Dosing—The dose of lamotrigine will be different for different patients, and depends on what other medicines you are taking. *Follow your doctor's orders or the directions on the label.* The following information includes only the average doses of lamotrigine. *If your dose is different, do not change it* unless your doctor tells you to do so.

The number of tablets that you take depends on the strength of the medicine.
- For *oral* dosage forms (tablets):
  —For treatment of epilepsy:
    - Adults *not* taking valproic acid (e.g., Depakote) but taking carbamazepine (e.g., Tegretol), phenobarbital (e.g., Luminal), phenytoin (e.g., Dilantin), and/or primidone (e.g., Mysoline)—At first, 50 milligrams (mg) of lamotrigine once a day for two weeks, then a total of 100 mg divided into two smaller doses each day for two weeks. After this, your doctor may increase the dose gradually if needed. However, the dose is usually not more than 500 mg a day.
    - Adults taking valproic acid (e.g., Depakote) and also taking carbamazepine (e.g., Tegretol), phenobarbital (e.g., Luminal), phenytoin (e.g., Dilantin), and/or primidone (e.g., Mysoline)—At first, 25 mg of lamotrigine once every other day for two weeks, then 25 mg once every day for two weeks. After this, your doctor may increase the dose gradually if needed. However, the dose is usually not more than 400 mg a day.
    - Children 2 to 12 years of age:
      —Children *not* taking valproic acid (e.g., Depakote) but taking carbamazepine (e.g., Tegretol), phenobarbital (e.g., Luminal), phenytoin (e.g., Dilantin), and/or primidone (e.g., Mysoline): At first, 0.6 milligrams (mg) per kilogram (kg) (0.27 mg per pound) of body weight of lamotrigine once a day for two weeks, then 1.2 mg/kg (0.54 mg per pound) of body weight divided into two smaller doses each day for

two weeks. After this, your doctor may increase the dose gradually if needed. However, the dose is usually not more than 400 mg a day.

—Children taking valproic acid (e.g., Depakote) and also taking carbamazepine (e.g., Tegretol), phenobarbital (e.g., Luminal), phenytoin (e.g., Dilantin), and/or primidone (e.g., Mysoline): At first, 0.15 mg per kg (0.07 mg per pound) of body weight of lamotrigine given in one dose or two smaller doses each day for two weeks, then 0.3 mg/kg (0.136 mg per pound) of body weight given in one dose or two smaller doses each day for two weeks. After this, your doctor may increase the dose gradually if needed. However, the dose is usually not more than 200 mg a day.

• Children older than 12 years of age usually receive the adult dose.

Missed dose—If you miss a dose of this medicine, take it as soon as possible. However, if it is almost time for your next dose, skip the missed dose and go back to your regular dosing schedule. Do not double doses.

Storage—To store this medicine:
• Keep out of the reach of children.
• Store away from heat and direct light.
• Do not store in the bathroom, near the kitchen sink, or in other damp places. Heat or moisture may cause the medicine to break down.
• Do not keep outdated medicine or medicine no longer needed. Be sure that any discarded medicine is out of the reach of children.

Precautions While Using This Medicine

It is important that your doctor check your progress at regular visits, especially during the first few months of your treatment with lamotrigine. This will allow your doctor to change your dose, if necessary, and will help reduce any unwanted effects.

This medicine may increase the effects of alcohol and other central nervous system (CNS) depressants (medicines that make you drowsy or less alert). Some examples of CNS depressants are antihistamines or medicine for hay fever, other allergies, or colds; sedatives, tranquilizers, or sleeping medicine; prescription pain medicine or narcotics; barbiturates; medicine for seizures; muscle relaxants; or anesthetics, including some dental anesthetics. *Check with your doctor before taking any of the above while you are using this medicine.*

Lamotrigine may cause blurred vision, double vision, clumsiness, unsteadiness, dizziness, or drowsiness. *Make sure you know how you react to this medicine before you drive, use machines, or do anything else that could be dangerous if you are not alert, well-coordinated, or able to see well.* If these reactions are especially bothersome, check with your doctor.

Skin rash may be a sign of a serious unwanted effect. *Check with your doctor immediately if you develop a rash, fever, flu-like symptoms, or swollen glands, or if your seizures increase.*

Do not stop taking lamotrigine without first checking with your doctor. Stopping this medicine suddenly may cause your seizures to return or to occur more often. Your doctor

may want you to gradually reduce the amount you are taking before stopping completely.

Side Effects of This Medicine

Along with its needed effects, a medicine may cause some unwanted effects. Although not all of these side effects may occur, if they do occur they may need medical attention.

Check with your doctor immediately if any of the following side effects occur:

More common
　Skin rash

Less common
　Increase in seizures

Rare
　Blistering, peeling, or loosening of skin; dark-colored urine; fever, chills, and/or sore throat; flu-like symptoms; itching; muscle cramps, pain, or weakness; red or irritated eyes; small red or purple spots on skin; sores, ulcers, or white spots on lips or in mouth; swelling of face, mouth, hands, or feet; swollen lymph nodes; trouble in breathing; unusual bleeding or bruising; unusual tiredness or weakness; yellow eyes or skin

Symptoms of overdose
　Clumsiness or unsteadiness (severe); coma; continuous, uncontrolled back and forth and/or rolling eye movements (severe); dizziness (severe); drowsiness (severe); dryness of mouth (severe); headache (severe); increased heart rate; slurred speech (severe)

Check with your doctor as soon as possible if any of the following side effects occur:

More common
　Blurred or double vision or other changes in vision; clumsiness or unsteadiness; poor coordination

Less common
　Anxiety, confusion, depression, irritability, or other mood or mental changes; chest pain; continuous, uncontrolled back and forth and/or rolling eye movements; infection

Rare
　Memory loss

Other side effects may occur that usually do not need medical attention. These side effects may go away during treatment as your body adjusts to the medicine. However, check with your doctor if any of the following side effects continue or are bothersome:

More common
　Dizziness (more common in women); drowsiness; headache; nausea; vomiting

Less common
　Constipation; diarrhea; dryness of mouth; indigestion; loss of strength; menstrual pain; pain; runny nose; slurred speech; trembling or shaking; trouble in sleeping; unusual weight loss

Other side effects not listed above may also occur in some patients. If you notice any other effects, check with your doctor.

Developed: 05/23/96
Revised: 05/21/99

LANSOPRAZOLE   Systemic

Commonly used brand name(s):

In the U.S.—
Prevacid

In Canada—
Prevacid

Description

Lansoprazole (lan-SOE-pra-zole) is used to treat certain conditions in which there is too much acid in the stomach. It is used to treat duodenal and gastric ulcers and gastroesophageal reflux disease (GERD), a condition in which the acid in the stomach washes back up into the esophagus. Sometimes lansoprazole is used in combination with antibiotics to treat ulcers associated with infection caused by the *H. pylori* bacteria (germ).

Lansoprazole is also used to treat Zollinger-Ellison disease, a condition in which the stomach produces too much acid.

Lansoprazole works by decreasing the amount of acid produced by the stomach.

This medicine is available only with your doctor's prescription.

Oral
- Delayed-release capsules (U.S. and Canada)

Before Using This Medicine

In deciding to use a medicine, the risks of taking the medicine must be weighed against the good it will do. This is a decision you and your doctor will make. For lansoprazole, the following should be considered:

Allergies—Tell your doctor if you have ever had any unusual or allergic reaction to lansoprazole. Also tell your health care professional if you are allergic to any other substances, such as foods, preservatives, or dyes.

Pregnancy—Studies have not been done in humans. However, studies in animals have not shown that lansoprazole causes harm to the fetus.

Breast-feeding—Lansoprazole may pass into the breast milk. Since this medicine has been shown to cause unwanted effects such as tumors in animals, it may be necessary for you to take another medicine or to stop breast-feeding during treatment. Be sure you have discussed the risks and benefits of the medicine with your doctor.

Children—There is no specific information comparing the use of lansoprazole in children with use in other age groups.

Older adults—In studies done to date that have included older adults, lansoprazole did not cause different side effects or problems than it did in younger adults.

Other medicines—Although certain medicines should not be used together at all, in other cases two different medicines may be used together even if an interaction might occur. In these cases, your doctor may want to change the dose, or other precautions may be necessary. When you are taking lansoprazole, it is especially important that your health care professional know if you are taking any of the following:
- Sucralfate (e.g., Carafate)—Lansoprazole should be taken at least 30 minutes before sucralfate so that lansoprazole will be properly absorbed

Proper Use of This Medicine

Take lansoprazole before a meal, preferably in the morning.

Swallow the capsule whole. Do not crush, break, or chew the capsule. If you cannot swallow the capsule whole, you may open it and sprinkle the granules contained in the capsule on one tablespoonful of applesauce and swallow it immediately; or you may mix the granules in some fruit or vegetable juice and drink it immediately. Juices you may use include apple, cranberry, grape, orange, pineapple, prune, tomato, and V-8 vegetable juice. *Do not chew or crush the granules.*

Take this medicine for the full time of treatment, even if you begin to feel better. Also, keep your appointments with your doctor for check-ups so that your doctor will be better able to tell you when to stop taking this medicine.

Dosing—The dose of lansoprazole will be different for different patients. *Follow your doctor's orders or the directions on the label.* The following information includes only the average doses of lansoprazole. *If your dose is different, do not change it* unless your doctor tells you to do so.

The number of doses you take each day and the length of time you take the medicine depend on the medical problem for which you are taking lansoprazole.
- For *oral* dosage form (delayed-release capsule):
  —To treat gastroesophageal reflux disease (GERD):
  - Adults—15 to 30 mg once a day, preferably taken in the morning before a meal.
  - Children up to 18 years of age—Use and dose must be determined by your doctor.
  —To treat duodenal ulcers:
  - Adults—At first, 15 milligrams (mg) once a day, preferably taken in the morning before a meal. Your doctor may increase your dose if needed.
  - Children up to 18 years of age—Use and dose must be determined by your doctor.
  —To treat duodenal ulcers related to infection with *H. pylori*:
  - Adults—30 mg plus amoxicillin 1000 mg (1 gram) plus clarithromycin 500 mg, taken together before meals twice a day for ten to fourteen days. Alternatively, your doctor may want you to take lansoprazole 30 mg plus amoxicillin 1000 mg (1 gram) before meals three times a day for fourteen days.
  - Children up to 18 years of age—Use and dose must be determined by your doctor.
  —To treat gastric ulcers:
  - Adults—15 to 30 mg once a day, preferably taken in the morning before a meal.
  - Children up to 18 years of age—Use and dose must be determined by your doctor.
  —To treat conditions in which the stomach produces too much acid:
  - Adults—At first, 60 mg once a day, preferably taken in the morning before a meal. Your doctor may increase your dose if needed.
  - Children up to 18 years of age—Use and dose must be determined by your doctor.

Missed dose—If you miss a dose of this medicine, take it as soon as possible. However, if it is almost time for your next dose, skip the missed dose and go back to your regular dosing schedule. Do not double doses.

Storage—To store this medicine:
- Keep out of the reach of children.
- Store away from heat and direct light.
- Do not store in the bathroom, near the kitchen sink, or in other damp places. Heat or moisture may cause the medicine to break down.
- Do not keep outdated medicine or medicine no longer needed. Be sure that any discarded medicine is out of the reach of children.

Precautions While Using This Medicine

It is important that your doctor check your progress at regular intervals. If your condition does not improve, or if it becomes worse, discuss this with your doctor.

Side Effects of This Medicine

Along with its needed effects, a medicine may cause some unwanted effects. Although not all of these side effects may occur, if they do occur they may need medical attention.

Check with your doctor as soon as possible if any of the following side effects occur:

More common
> Diarrhea; skin rash or itching

Less common
> Abdominal or stomach pain; increased or decreased appetite; joint pain; nausea; vomiting

Rare
> Anxiety; cold or flu-like symptoms; constipation; increased cough; mental depression; muscle pain; rectal bleeding; unusual bleeding or bruising

Other side effects may occur that usually do not need medical attention. These side effects may go away during treatment as your body adjusts to the medicine. However, check with your doctor if any of the following side effects continue or are bothersome:

More common
> Dizziness; headache

Other side effects not listed above may also occur in some patients. If you notice any other effects, check with your doctor.

Revised: 06/11/99

LATANOPROST   Ophthalmic

Commonly used brand name(s):

In the U.S.—
> Xalatan

Description

Latanoprost (la-TA-noe-prost) is used to treat certain kinds of glaucoma. It is also used to treat a condition called hypertension of the eye. Latanoprost appears to work by increasing the outflow of fluid from the eye. This lowers the pressure in the eye.

This medicine is available only with your doctor's prescription, in the following dosage form(s):

Ophthalmic
- Ophthalmic solution (eye drops) (U.S.)

Before Using This Medicine

In deciding to use a medicine, the risks of using the medicine must be weighed against the good it will do. This is a decision you and your doctor will make. For latanoprost, the following should be considered:

Allergies—Tell your doctor if you have ever had any unusual or allergic reaction to latanoprost. Also tell your health care professional if you are allergic to any other substances, such as benzalkonium chloride or other preservatives.

Pregnancy—Latanoprost has not been studied in pregnant women. However, latanoprost has been shown to cause death of the fetus when given to pregnant rabbits in doses many times larger than the human dose. Before using this medicine, make sure your doctor knows if you are pregnant or if you may become pregnant.

Breast-feeding—It is not known whether latanoprost passes into the breast milk. Although most medicines pass into breast milk in small amounts, many of them may be used safely while breast-feeding. Mothers who are using this medicine and who wish to breast-feed should discuss this with their doctor.

Children—Studies on this medicine have been done only in adult patients, and there is no specific information comparing use of latanoprost in children with use in other age groups.

Older adults—Many medicines have not been studied specifically in older people. Therefore, it may not be known whether they work exactly the same way they do in younger adults. Although there is no specific information comparing use of latanoprost in the elderly with use in other age groups, this medicine has been used mostly in elderly patients and is not expected to cause different side effects or problems in older people than it does in younger adults.

Other medicines—Although certain medicines should not be used together at all, in other cases two different medicines may be used together even if an interaction might occur. In these cases, your doctor may want to change the dose, or other precautions may be necessary. When you are using latanoprost, it is especially important that your health care professional know if you are taking any of the following:
- Thimerosal-containing ophthalmic medications—A precipitation occurs (a solid settles out of the solution) when latanoprost is applied at the same time as a thimerosal-containing ophthalmic medicine; you should wait at least 5 minutes between using these two types of eye drops

Other medical problems—The presence of other medical problems may affect the use of latanoprost. Make sure you tell your doctor if you have any other medical problems, especially:
- Eye disease, such as iritis or uveitis—Use of latanoprost may make the condition worse
- Eye problems, such as loss of the lens of the eye or
- Intraocular lens (IOL) replacement—May be more prone to an adverse reaction called macular edema
- Kidney disease or
- Liver disease—Higher blood levels of latanoprost may result, which may lead to increased side effects

Proper Use of This Medicine

Use this medicine only as directed. Do not use more of it and do not use it more often than your doctor ordered. To do so may increase the chance of too much medicine being absorbed into the body and the chance of side effects.

If your doctor ordered two different eye drops to be used together, wait at least 5 minutes between the times you apply the medicines. This will help to keep the second medicine from "washing out" the first one.

It is important that your doctor check your eye pressure at regular visits to make certain that your glaucoma is being controlled.

Contact lenses should be removed before you use this medicine. You should wait at least 15 minutes after using the eye drops before reinserting them.

To use the *eye drops:*
- First, wash your hands. Tilt the head back and, pressing your finger gently on the skin just beneath the lower eyelid, pull the lower eyelid away from the eye to make a space. Drop the medicine into this space. Let go of the eyelid and gently close the eyes. Do not blink. Keep the eyes closed and apply pressure to the inner corner of the eye with your finger for 1 or 2 minutes to allow the medicine to be absorbed by the eye.
- Immediately after using the eye drops, wash your hands to remove any medicine that may be on them.
- *To keep the medicine as germ-free as possible, do not touch the applicator tip to any surface (including the eye).* Also, keep the container tightly closed.

Dosing—The dose of latanoprost will be different for different patients. *Follow your doctor's orders or the directions on the label.* The following information includes only the average dose of latanoprost. *If your dose is different, do not change it* unless your doctor tells you to do so.
- For *ophthalmic solution (eye drops)* dosage form:
  —For glaucoma or hypertension of the eye:
  - Adults—Use one drop in the affected eye(s) once a day in the evening.
  - Children—Use and dose must be determined by your doctor.

Missed dose—If you miss a dose of this medicine, use it as soon as possible. However, if you do not remember the missed dose until the next day, skip the missed dose and go back to your regular dosing schedule. Do not double doses.

Storage—To store this medicine:
- Keep out of the reach of children.
- Store away from heat and direct light.
- Before the bottle has been opened for the first time, store in the refrigerator. After the bottle has been opened, store at room temperature (up to 25 °C [77 °F]) for up to 6 weeks, or in the refrigerator. However, keep the medicine from freezing.
- Do not keep outdated medicine or medicine no longer needed. Be sure that any discarded medicine is out of the reach of children.

Precautions While Using This Medicine

While you are using latanoprost, the iris (colored part) of your treated eye(s) may slowly become more brown in color. This is more likely to happen if you have blue-brown, gray-brown, green-brown, or yellow-brown eyes. The change in color of the iris is noticeable usually within several months or years from the start of treatment with latanoprost. *In addition, there may be a darkening of eyelid skin color. Also, your eyelashes may become longer, thicker, and darker. These changes to the iris, eyelid, and lashes may be permanent even if you stop using latanoprost. Also, these changes to the iris, eyelid, and lashes will affect only the eye being treated with latanoprost. Therefore, if only one eye is being treated, only that eye may develop darker iris, eyelid, and eyelashes and other changes to the eyelashes, and you may have differently appearing eyes.* Check with your doctor if you have any questions about this.

Latanoprost may cause your eyes to become more sensitive to light than they are normally. Wearing sunglasses and avoiding too much exposure to bright light may help lessen the discomfort.

Side Effects of This Medicine

Along with its needed effects, a medicine may cause some unwanted effects. Although not all of these side effects may occur, if they do occur they may need medical attention.

Check with your doctor immediately if any of the following side effects occur:
Less common
  Eyelid crusting, redness, swelling, discomfort, or pain
Rare
  Cough; difficulty breathing; noisy breathing; redness of eye or inside of eyelid; shortness of breath; swelling of the eye; tightness in chest; wheezing

Check with your doctor as soon as possible if any of the following side effects occur:
More common
  Blurred vision, eye irritation, or tearing; darkening of eyelid skin color; increase in brown color in colored part of eye; longer, thicker, and darker eyelashes
Less common
  Angina pectoris or other chest pain; cold or flu symptoms; eye pain; pain in muscles, joints, or back; skin rash
Rare
  Discharge from the eye; double vision or other change in vision; fever; sensitivity of eye to light; sore throat

Other side effects may occur that usually do not need medical attention. These side effects may go away during treatment as your body adjusts to the medicine. However, check with your doctor if any of the following side effects continue or are bothersome:
More common
  Burning of eye; feeling of something in eye; itching of eye; stinging of eye
Less common
  Dryness of eye

Other side effects not listed above may also occur in some patients. If you notice any other effects, check with your doctor.

Developed: 08/12/98
Revised: 4/18/00

LAXATIVES   Oral

Commonly used brand name(s):

In the U.S.—

Afko-Lube[46]
Afko-Lube Lax[40]
Agoral
  Marshmallow[26]
Agoral Raspberry[26]
Alaxin[47]
Alophen[35]
Alphamul[33]
Alramucil Orange[7]
Alramucil Regular[7]
Bilagog[19]
Bilax[42]
Bisac-Evac[28]
Black-Draught[29]
Black-Draught
  Lax-Senna[37]
Carter's Little Pills[28]
Cholac[14]
Chronulac[14]
Cillium[6]
Citroma[16]
Citrucel Orange
  Flavor[3]
Citrucel Sugar-
  Free Orange
  Flavor[3]
Colace[46]
Colax[44]
Cologel[3]
Constilac[14]
Constulose[14]
Correctol[28]
Correctol Caplets[28]
Correctol Herbal
  Tea[37]
Correctol Stool
  Softener Soft
  Gels[46]
Dacodyl[28]
DC Softgels[46]
Decholin[34]
Deficol[28]
Dialose[46]
Dialose Plus[44]
Diocto[46]
Diocto-C[40]
Diocto-K[46]
Diocto-K Plus[40]
Dioctolose Plus[40]
Dioeze[46]
Diosuccin[46]
Di-Sosul[46]
Di-Sosul Forte[40]
Docucal-P[44]
Docu-K Plus[40]
DOK[46]
DOK Softgels[46]
D.O.S. Softgels[46]
Dosaflex[37]
Doxidan Liqui-
  Gels[40]
Dr. Caldwell
  Senna Laxative[37]
DSMC Plus[40]
D-S-S[46]
D-S-S plus[40]
Dulcolax[28]

Duosol[46]
Duphalac[14]
Effer-syllium[7]
Emulsoil[33]
Enulose[14]
Epsom salts[19]
Equalactin[4]
Evac-U-Gen[35]
Evac-U-Lax[35]
Evalose[14]
Ex-Lax[35]
Ex-Lax Gentle
  Nature Pills[38]
Ex-Lax Maximum
  Relief Formula[35]
Ex-Lax Pills[35]
Extra Gentle Ex-
  Lax[44]
FemiLax[44]
Fiberall[7]
Fibercon Caplets[4]
Fiber-Lax[4]
FiberNorm[4]
Fleet Laxative[28]
Fleet Mineral Oil[25]
Fleet Phospho-
  Soda[20]
Fleet Soflax
  Gelcaps[46]
Fleet Soflax
  Overnight
  Gelcaps[40]
Fletcher's
  Castoria[37]
Genasoft Plus
  Softgels[40]
Gentle Laxative[28]
Haley's M-O[21]
Hepahydrin[34]
Heptalac[14]
Herbal Laxative[38]
Hydrocil Instant[7]
Kasof[46]
Kellogg's Castor
  Oil[33]
Kondremul Plain[25]
Konsyl[5]
Konsyl-D[7]
Konsyl Easy Mix[7]
Konsyl-Orange[7]
Konsyl-Orange
  Sugar Free[7]
Laxinate 100[46]
Lax-Pills[35]
Liqui-Doss[25]
Mag-Ox 400[18]
Maltsupex[1]
Maox 420[18]
Medilax[35]
Metamucil[7]
Metamucil Apple
  Crisp Fiber
  Wafers[7]
Metamucil
  Cinnamon Spice
  Fiber Wafers[7]

Metamucil Orange
  Flavor[7]
Metamucil
  Smooth, Citrus
  Flavor[7]
Metamucil
  Smooth, Orange
  Flavor[7]
Metamucil Smooth
  Sugar-Free,
  Citrus Flavor[7]
Metamucil Smooth
  Sugar-Free,
  Orange Flavor[7]
Metamucil Smooth
  Sugar-Free,
  Regular Flavor[7]
Metamucil Sugar-
  Free, Lemon-
  Lime Flavor[7]
Metamucil Orange
  Flavor[7]
Metamucil Sugar-
  Free, Orange
  Flavor[7]
Milkinol[25]
MiraLax[15]
Mitrolan[4]
Modane[35]
Modane Bulk[7]
Modane Plus[44]
Modane Soft[46]
Molatoc[46]
Molatoc-CST[40]
Mylanta Natural
  Fiber
  Supplement[7]
Mylanta Sugar
  Free Natural
  Fiber
  Supplement[7]
Naturacil[6]
Nature's Remedy[31]
Neolax[42]
Neoloid[33]
Nytilax[38]
Perdiem[9]
Perdiem Fiber[6]
Peri-Colace[40]
Peri-Dos Softgels[40]
Petrogalar Plain[25]
Phenolphthalein
  Petrogalar[26]
Phillips'
  Chewable[17]
Phillips'
  Concentrated[17]
Phillips' Gelcaps[44]
Phillips' LaxCaps[44]
Phillips' Milk of
  Magnesia[17]
Portalac[14]
Pro-Cal-Sof[46]
Pro-Lax[7]
Prompt[11]
Pro-Sof[46]
Pro-Sof Plus[40]

Prulet[35]
Purge[33]
Regulace[40]
Regulax SS[46]
Reguloid Natural[7]
Reguloid Natural
  Sugar Free[7]
Reguloid Orange[7]
Reguloid Orange
  Sugar Free[7]
Senexon[37]
Senna-Gen[37]

Senokot[37]
Senokot
  Children's
  Syrup[38]
Senokot-S[45]
Senokot XTRA[38]
Senolax[37]
Serutan[7]
Serutan Toasted
  Granules[8]
Silace[46]
Silace-C[40]

Stulex[46]
Sulfolax[46]
Surfak[46]
Syllact[6]
Syllamalt[2]
Trilax[43]
Unilax[44]
Veracolate[32]
V-Lax[7]
X-Prep Liquid[37]
Zymenol[25]

In Canada—

Acilac[14]
Agarol Plain[22]
Agarol
  Strawberry[23]
Agarol Vanilla[23]
Albert Docusate[46]
Apo-Bisacodyl[28]
Bicholate Lilas[32]
Bisacolax[28]
Caroid[32]
Carter's Little
  Pills[35]
Chronulac[14]
Citro-Mag[16]
Colace[46]
Correctol[28]
Correctol Stool
  Softener Soft
  Gels[46]
Doss[41]
Doxidan[44]
Dulcodos[39]
Dulcolax[28]
Ex-Lax[35]
Ex-Lax Light
  Formula[44]
Ex-Lax Pills[35]
Feen-a-Mint Pills[28]
Fibrepur[25]

Fletcher's
  Castoria[38]
Glysennid[38]
Herbal Laxative[37]
Karacil[7]
Kondremul[25]
Lactulax[14]
Lansoÿl[25]
Lansoÿl Sugar
  Free[25]
Laxavite[32]
Laxilose[14]
Laxit[28]
Magnolax[21]
Metamucil[7]
Metamucil
  Orange
  Flavor[7]
Metamucil Sugar
  Free[7]
Metamucil Sugar-
  Free, Orange
  Flavor[7]
Mitrolan[4]
Mucinum[36]
Natural Source
  Fibre Laxative[7]
Nature's Remedy[31]
Nujol[25]

Peri-Colace[40]
Phillips' Magnesia
  Tablets[17]
Phillips' Milk of
  Magnesia[17]
PMS-Bisacodyl[28]
PMS-Docusate
  Calcium[46]
PMS-Docusate
  Sodium[46]
PMS-Lactulose[14]
PMS-Phosphates[20]
PMS-Sennosides[38]
Prodiem Plain[7]
Prodiem Plus[10]
Pro-Lax[15]
Regulex[46]
Regulex-D[41]
Senokot[37]
Senokot-S[45]
SenoKot XTRA[38]
Silace[46]
Soflax[46]
Surfak[46]
Vitalax Super
  Smooth Sugar
  Free Orange
  Flavor[7]
Vitalax Unflavored[7]

Note: For quick reference the following laxatives are numbered to
       match the corresponding brand names.

Bulk-forming laxatives—
1. Malt Soup Extract (malt soup EX-tract) †
2. Malt Soup Extract and Psyllium (malt soup EX-tract and SILL-i-yum)†
3. Methylcellulose (meth-ill-SELL-yoo-lose) †‡
4. Polycarbophil (pol-i-KAR-boe-fil)
5. Polycarbophil and Psyllium (pol-i-KAR-boe-fil and SILL-i-yum)†
6. Psyllium (SILL-i-yum)†
7. Psyllium Hydrophilic Mucilloid (SILL-i-yum hye-droe-FILL-ik MYOO-sill-oid)
8. Psyllium Hydrophilic Mucilloid and Carboxymethylcellulose (SILL-i-yum hye-droe-FILL-ik MYOO-sill-oid and kar-box-ee-meth-ill-SELL-yoo-lose) †

Bulk-forming and stimulant combinations—
9. Psyllium and Senna (SILL-i-yum and SEN-na) †
10. Psyllium Hydrophilic Mucilloid and Senna (SILL-i-yum hye-droe-FILL-ik MYOO-sill-oid and SEN-na) *
11. Psyllium Hydrophilic Mucilloid and Sennosides (SILL-i-yum hye-droe-FILL-ik MYOO-sill-oid and SEN-no-sydes) †

Bulk-forming, stimulant, and stool softener (emollient) combinations—
12. Product not available

Bulk-forming and stool softener (emollient) combinations—
13. Product not available

Hyperosmotic laxatives—Lactulose:
14. Lactulose (LAC-tu-los) ‡§

Hyperosmotic laxatives—Polymer:
15. Polyethylene glycol 3350 (pol-ee-ETH-ill-een GLYE-cal) ‡§

Hyperosmotic laxatives—Saline:
16. Magnesium Citrate (mag-NEE-zhum SI-trate) ‡§
17. Magnesium Hydroxide (mag-NEE-zhum hye-DROX-ide) ‡§
18. Magnesium Oxide (mag-NEE-zhum OX-ide) †
19. Magnesium Sulfate (mag-NEE-zhum SUL-fate) †‡
20. Sodium Phosphate (SOE-dee-um FOS-fate) †‡

Hyperosmotic and lubricant combinations—
21. Milk of Magnesia and Mineral Oil (milk of mag-NEE-zha and MIN-er-al oil) †
22. Mineral Oil and Glycerin (MIN-er-al oil and GLIH-ser-in) *

Hyperosmotic, lubricant, and stimulant combinations—
23. Mineral Oil, Glycerin, and Phenolphthalein (MIN-er-al oil, GLIH-ser-in, and fee-nole-THAY-leen) *

Hyperosmotic and stimulant combinations—
24. Milk of Magnesia and Cascara Sagrada (milk of mag-NEE-zha and kas-KAR-a sa-GRA-da) †‡

Lubricant laxatives—
25. Mineral Oil (MIN-er-al oil) ‡§

Lubricant and stimulant combinations—
26. Mineral Oil and Phenolphthalein (MIN-er-al oil and fee-nole-THAY-leen) †
27. Product not available

Stimulant laxatives—
28. Bisacodyl (bis-a-KOE-dill) ‡
29. Casanthranol (cas-SAN-thrah-nole) †
30. Cascara Sagrada (kas-KAR-a sa-GRA-da) ‡§
31. Cascara Sagrada and Aloe (kas-KAR-a sa-GRA-da and AL-owe)
32. CascaraSagrada and Phenolphthalein (kas-KAR-a sa-GRA-da and fee-nole-THAY-leen)
33. Castor Oil (KAS-tor) ‡§
34. Dehydrocholic Acid (dee-hye-droe-KOE-lik acid) †‡
35. Phenolphthalein (fee-nole-THAY-leen)
36. Phenolphthalein and Senna (fee-nole-THAY-leen and SEN-na) *
37. Senna (SEN-na)
38. Sennosides (SEN-no-sides) §

Stimulant and stool softener (emollient) combinations—
39. Bisacodyl and Docusate (bis-a-KOE-dill and doc-CUE-sayt)*
40. Casanthranol and Docusate (cas-SAN-thrah-nole and doc-CUE-sayt) ‡
41. Danthron and Docusate (DAN-thron and doc-CUE-sayt) *
42. Dehydrocholic Acid and Docusate (dee-hye-droe-KOE-lik acid and doc-CUE-sayt) †
43. Dehydrocholic Acid, Docusate, and Phenolphthalein (dee-hye-droe-KOE-lik acid, doc-CUE-day, and fee-nole-THAY-leen) †
44. dee-hye-droe-KOE-lik acid, doc-CUE-sayt, and fee-nole-THAY-leen Phenolphthalein and Docusate (fee-nole-THAY-leen and doc-CUE-sayt)
45. Sennosides and Docusate (SEN-no-sides and doc-CUE-sayt)

Stool softener (emollient) laxatives—
46. Docusate (doc-CUE-sayt) ‡§
47. Poloxamer188 (pol-OX-a-mer188) †

---

*Not commercially available in the U.S.
†Not commercially available in Canada.
‡Generic name product may be available in the U.S.
§Generic name product may be available in Canada.

Description

Oral laxatives are medicines taken by mouth to encourage bowel movements to relieve constipation.

There are several different types of oral laxatives and they work in different ways. Since directions for use are different for each type, it is important to know which one you are taking. The different types of oral laxatives include:

Bulk-formers—Bulk-forming laxatives are not digested but absorb liquid in the intestines and swell to form a soft, bulky stool. The bowel is then stimulated normally by the presence of the bulky mass. Some bulk-forming laxatives, like psyllium and polycarbophil, may be prescribed by your doctor to treat diarrhea.

Hyperosmotics—Hyperosmotic laxatives encourage bowel movements by drawing water into the bowel from surrounding body tissues. This provides a soft stool mass and increased bowel action.

There are three types of hyperosmotic laxatives taken by mouth—the saline, the lactulose, and the polymer types. The *saline type* is often called "salts." They are used for rapid emptying of the lower intestine and bowel. They are not used for long-term or repeated correction of constipation. With smaller doses than those used for the laxative effect, some saline laxatives are used as antacids. The information that follows applies only to their use as laxatives. Sodium phosphate may also be prescribed for other conditions as determined by your doctor.

The *lactulose type* is a special sugar-like laxative that works the same way as the saline type. However, it produces results much more slowly and is often used for long-term treatment of chronic constipation. Lactulose may sometimes be used in the treatment of certain medical conditions to reduce the amount of ammonia in the blood. It is available only with your doctor's prescription.

The *polymer type* is a polyglycol (polyethylene glycol), a large molecule that causes water to be retained in the stool; this will soften the stool and increase the number of bowel movements. It is used for short periods of time to treat constipation.

Lubricants—Lubricant laxatives, such as mineral oil, taken by mouth encourage bowel movements by coating the bowel and the stool mass with a waterproof film. This keeps moisture in the stool. The stool remains soft and its passage is made easier.

Stimulants—Stimulant laxatives, also known as contact laxatives, encourage bowel movements by acting on the intestinal wall. They increase the muscle contractions that move along the stool mass. Stimulant laxatives are a popular type of laxative for self-treatment. However, they also are more likely to cause side effects. One of the stimulant laxatives, dehydrocholic acid, may also be used for treating certain conditions of the biliary tract.

Stool softeners (emollients)—Stool softeners encourage bowel movements by helping liquids mix into the stool and prevent dry, hard stool masses. This type of laxative has been said not to *cause* a bowel movement but instead *allows* the patient to have a bowel movement without straining.

Combinations—There are many products that you can buy for constipation that contain more than one type of laxative. For example, a product may contain both a stool softener and a stimulant laxative. In general, combination products may be more likely to cause side effects because of the multiple ingredients. In addition, they may not offer any advantage over products containing only one type of laxative. *If you are taking a combination laxative, make certain* *you know the proper use and precautions for each of the different ingredients.*

Most laxatives (except saline laxatives) may be used to provide relief:

- during pregnancy.
- for a few days after giving birth.
- during preparation for examination or surgery.
- for constipation of bedfast patients.
- for constipation caused by other medicines.
- following surgery when straining should be avoided.
- following a period of poor eating habits or a lack of physical exercise in order to develop normal bowel function (bulk-forming laxatives only).
- for some medical conditions that may be made worse by straining, for example:
  Heart disease
  Hemorrhoids
  Hernia (rupture)
  High blood pressure (hypertension)
  History of stroke

Saline laxatives have more limited uses and may be used to provide rapid results:

- during preparation for examination or surgery.
- for elimination of food or drugs from the body in cases of poisoning or overdose.
- for simple constipation that happens on occasion (although another type of laxative may be preferred).
- in supplying a fresh stool sample for diagnosis.

Most laxatives are available without a prescription; however, your doctor may have special instructions for the proper use and dose for your medical condition. They are available in the following dosage forms:

Oral

Bulk-forming laxatives—
Malt Soup Extract
- Powder (U.S.)
- Oral solution (U.S.)
- Tablets (U.S.)
Malt Soup Extract and Psyllium
- Powder (U.S.)
Methylcellulose
- Capsules (U.S.)
- Granules (U.S.)
- Powder (U.S.)
- Oral solution (U.S.)
- Tablets (U.S.)
Polycarbophil
- Tablets (U.S.)
- Chewable tablets (U.S. and Canada)
Psyllium
- Caramels (U.S.)
- Granules (U.S.)
- Powder (U.S.)
Psyllium Hydrophilic Mucilloid
- Granules (U.S. and Canada)
- Powder (U.S. and Canada)
- Effervescent powder (U.S.)
- For oral suspension (Canada)
- Wafers (U.S.)
Psyllium Hydrophilic Mucilloid and Carboxymethyl-cellulose
- Granules (U.S.)

Bulk-forming and stimulant combinations—
Psyllium and Senna
- Granules (U.S.)

Psyllium Hydrophilic Mucilloid and Senna
- Granules (Canada)
Psyllium Hydrophilic Mucilloid and Sennosides
- Powder (U.S.)

Hyperosmotic laxative—Lactulose:
Lactulose
- Solution (U.S. and Canada)

Hyperosmotic laxative—Polyethylene Glycol:
Polyethylene glycol 3350
- Powder (U.S. and Canada)

Hyperosmotic laxatives—Saline:
Magnesium Citrate
- Oral solution (U.S. and Canada)
Magnesium Hydroxide
- Milk of magnesia (U.S. and Canada)
- Tablets (U.S. and Canada)
Magnesium Oxide
- Tablets (U.S.)
Magnesium Sulfate
- Crystals (U.S. and Canada)
- Tablets (U.S.)
Sodium Phosphate
- Effervescent powder (U.S.)
- Oral solution (U.S. and Canada)

Hyperosmotic and lubricant combinations—
Milk of Magnesia and Mineral Oil
- Emulsion (U.S. and Canada)
Mineral Oil and Glycerin
- Emulsion (Canada)

Hyperosmotic, lubricant, and stimulant combination—
Mineral Oil, Glycerin, and Phenolphthalein
- Emulsion (Canada)

Hyperosmotic and stimulant combination—
Milk of Magnesia and Cascara Sagrada
- Oral Suspension (U.S.)

Lubricant laxatives—
Mineral Oil
- Oil (U.S. and Canada)
- Emulsion (U.S. and Canada)
- Gel (Canada)
- Oral suspension (U.S.)

Lubricant and stimulant combinations—
Mineral Oil and Phenolphthalein
- Emulsion (U.S.)
- Oral suspension (U.S.)

Stimulant laxatives—
Bisacodyl
- Tablets (U.S. and Canada)
Casanthranol
- Syrup (U.S.)
Cascara Sagrada
- Fluidextract (U.S. and Canada)
- Tablets (U.S. and Canada)
Cascara Sagrada and Aloe
- Tablets (U.S. and Canada)
Cascara Sagrada and Phenolphthalein
- Tablets (U.S. and Canada)
Castor Oil
- Oil (U.S. and Canada)
- Emulsion (U.S.)
Dehydrocholic Acid
- Tablets (U.S.)

Phenolphthalein
- Tablets (U.S. and Canada)
- Chewable tablets (U.S. and Canada)

Phenolphthalein and Senna
- Tablets (Canada)

Senna
- Granules (U.S.)
- Oral solution (U.S. and Canada)
- For oral solution (U.S.)
- Syrup (U.S.)
- Tablets (U.S. and Canada)

Sennosides
- Granules (U.S. and Canada)
- Oral solution (Canada)
- Syrup (U.S. and Canada)
- Tablets (U.S. and Canada)

Stimulant and stool softener (emollient) combinations—

Bisacodyl and Docusate
- Tablets (Canada)

Casanthranol and Docusate
- Capsules (U.S. and Canada)
- Syrup (U.S.)
- Tablets (U.S.)

Danthron and Docusate
- Capsules (Canada)
- Tablets (Canada)

Dehydrocholic Acid and Docusate
- Capsules (U.S.)
- Tablets (U.S.)

Dehydrocholic Acid, Docusate, and Phenolphthalein
- Capsules (U.S.)

Phenolphthalein and Docusate
- Capsules (U.S. and Canada)
- Tablets (U.S. and Canada)

Sennosides and Docusate
- Tablets (U.S. and Canada)

Stool softener (emollient) laxatives—

Docusate
- Capsules (U.S. and Canada)
- Oral solution (U.S. and Canada)
- Syrup (U.S. and Canada)
- Tablets (U.S.)

Poloxamer 188
- Capsules (U.S.)

Before Using This Medicine

Importance of diet, fluids, and exercise to prevent constipation—Laxatives are to be used to provide short-term relief only, unless otherwise directed by a doctor. A proper diet containing roughage (whole grain breads and cereals, bran, fruit, and green, leafy vegetables), with 6 to 8 full glasses (8 ounces each) of liquids each day, and daily exercise are most important in maintaining healthy bowel function. Also, for individuals who have problems with constipation, foods such as pastries, puddings, sugar, candy, cake, and cheese may make the constipation worse.

If you are taking this medicine without a prescription, carefully read and follow any precautions on the label. For oral laxatives, the following should be considered:

Allergies—Tell your doctor if you have ever had any unusual or allergic reaction to laxatives. Also tell your health care professional if you are allergic to any other substances, such as foods, preservatives, or dyes.

Diet—Make certain your health care professional knows if you are on any special diet, such as a low-sodium or low-sugar diet. Some laxatives have large amounts of sodium or sugars in them.

Pregnancy—Although laxatives are often used during pregnancy, some types are better than others. Stool softeners (emollient) laxatives and bulk-forming laxatives are probably used most often. If you are using a laxative during pregnancy, remember that:

- Some laxatives (in particular, the bulk-formers) contain a large amount of sodium or sugars, which may have possible unwanted effects such as increasing blood pressure or causing water to be held in the body.
- Saline laxatives containing magnesium, potassium, or phosphates may have to be avoided if your kidney function is not normal.
- Mineral oil is usually not used during pregnancy because of possible unwanted effects on the mother or infant. Mineral oil may interfere with the absorption of nutrients and vitamins in the mother. Also, if taken for a long time during pregnancy, mineral oil may cause severe bleeding in the newborn infant.
- Stimulant laxatives may cause unwanted effects in the expectant mother if improperly used. Castor oil in particular should not be used as it may cause contractions of the womb.

Breast-feeding—Laxatives containing cascara, danthron, and phenolphthalein may pass into the breast milk. Although the amount of laxative in the milk is generally thought to be too small to cause problems in the baby, your doctor should be told if you plan to use such laxatives. Some reports claim that diarrhea has been caused in the infant.

Children—*Laxatives should not be given to young children (up to 6 years of age) unless prescribed by their doctor.* Since children usually cannot describe their symptoms very well, they should be checked by a doctor before being given a laxative. The child may have a condition that needs other treatment. If so, laxatives will not help, and may even cause unwanted effects or make the condition worse.

Mineral oil should not be given to young children (up to 6 years of age) because a form of pneumonia may be caused by the inhalation of oil droplets into the lungs.

Also, bisacodyl tablets should not be given to children up to 6 years of age because if chewed they may cause stomach irritation.

Older adults—Mineral oil should not be taken by bedridden elderly persons because a form of pneumonia may be caused by the inhalation of oil droplets into the lungs. Also, stimulant laxatives (e.g., bisacodyl, casanthranol, or phenolphthalein), if taken too often, may worsen weakness, lack of coordination, or dizziness and light-headedness.

Polyethylene glycol 3350 should be discontinued if diarrhea occurs, especially in elderly persons in nursing homes.

Other medicines—Although certain medicines should not be used together at all, in other cases two different medicines may be used together even if an interaction might occur. In these cases, your doctor may want to change the dose, or other precautions may be necessary. When you are taking oral laxatives, it is especially important that your health care professional know if you are taking any of the following:

- Anticoagulants, oral (blood thinners you take by mouth) or

© 2002 MICROMEDEX Thomson Healthcare

- Digitalis glycosides (heart medicine)—The use of magnesium-containing laxatives may reduce the effects of these medicines
- Ciprofloxacin (e.g., Cipro) or
- Etidronate (e.g., Didronel) or
- Sodium polystyrene sulfonate—Use of magnesium-containing laxatives will keep these medicines from working
- Tetracyclines taken by mouth (medicine for infection)— Use of bulk-forming or magnesium-containing laxatives will keep the tetracycline medicine from working

Other medical problems— The presence of other medical problems may affect the use of oral laxatives. Make sure you tell your doctor if you have any other medical problems, especially:

- Appendicitis (or signs of) or
- Rectal bleeding of unknown cause—These conditions need immediate attention by a doctor
- Colostomy or
- Intestinal blockage or
- Ileostomy—The use of laxatives may create other problems if these conditions are present
- Diabetes mellitus (sugar diabetes)—Diabetic patients should be careful since some laxatives contain large amounts of sugars, such as dextrose, galactose, and/or sucrose
- Heart disease or
- High blood pressure—Some laxatives contain large amounts of sodium, which may make these conditions worse
- Kidney disease—Magnesium and potassium (contained in some laxatives) may build up in the body if kidney disease is present; a serious condition may develop
- Swallowing difficulty—Mineral oil should not be used since it may get into the lungs by accident and cause pneumonia; also, bulk-forming laxatives may get lodged in the esophagus of patients who have difficulty in swallowing

Proper Use of This Medicine

For safe and effective use of your laxative:

- Follow your doctor's instructions if this laxative was prescribed.
- Follow the manufacturer's package directions if you are treating yourself.

With all kinds of laxatives, at least 6 to 8 glasses (8 ounces each) of liquids should be taken each day. This will help make the stool softer.

For *patients taking laxatives containing a bulk-forming ingredient:*

- Do not try to swallow in the dry form. Take with liquid.
- To allow bulk-forming laxatives to work properly and to prevent intestinal blockage, it is necessary to drink plenty of fluids during their use. Each dose should be taken in or with a full glass (8 ounces) or more of cold water or fruit juice. This will provide enough liquid for the laxative to work properly. A second glass of water or juice by itself is often recommended with each dose for best effect and to avoid side effects.
- When taking a product that contains only a bulk-forming ingredient, results often may be obtained in 12 hours.

However, this may not occur for some individuals until after 2 or 3 days.

For *patients taking laxatives containing a stool softener (emollient):*

- Liquid forms may be taken in milk or fruit juice to improve flavor.
- When taking a product that contains only a stool softener, results usually occur 1 to 2 days after the first dose. However, this may not occur for some individuals until after 3 to 5 days.

For *patients taking laxatives containing a hyperosmotic ingredient:*

- Each dose should be taken in or with a full glass (8 ounces) or more of cold water or fruit juice. This will provide enough liquid for the laxative to work properly. A second glass of water or juice by itself is often recommended with each dose for best effect and, in the case of saline laxatives, to prevent you from becoming dehydrated.
- The unpleasant taste produced by some hyperosmotic laxatives may be improved by following each dose with citrus fruit juice or citrus-flavored carbonated beverage.
- Lactulose may not produce laxative results for 24 to 48 hours.
- Polyethylene glycol may not produce laxative results for 2 to 4 days.
- Saline laxatives usually produce results within ½ to 3 hours following a dose. When a larger dose is taken on an empty stomach, the results are quicker. When a smaller dose is taken with food, the results are delayed. Therefore, large doses of saline laxatives are usually not taken late in the day on an empty stomach.

For *patients taking laxatives containing mineral oil:*

- Mineral oil should not be taken within 2 hours of meals because of possible interference with food digestion and absorption of nutrients and vitamins.
- Mineral oil is usually taken at bedtime (but not while lying down) for convenience and because it requires about 6 to 8 hours to produce results.

For *patients taking laxatives containing a stimulant ingredient:*

- Stimulant laxatives are usually taken on an empty stomach for rapid effect. Results are slowed if taken with food.
- Many stimulant laxatives (but not castor oil) are often taken at bedtime to produce results the next morning (although some may require 24 hours or more).
- *Castor oil* is not usually taken late in the day because its results occur within 2 to 6 hours.
- The unpleasant taste of *castor oil* may be improved by chilling in the refrigerator for at least an hour and then stirring the dose into a full glass of cold orange juice just before it is taken. Also, flavored preparations of castor oil are available.
- *Bisacodyl tablets* are specially coated to allow them to work properly without causing irritation and/or nausea. To protect this coating, do not chew, crush, or take the tablets within an hour of milk or antacids.
- Because of the way *phenolphthalein* works in the body, a single dose may cause a laxative effect in some people for up to 3 days.

Dosing— There are a large number of laxative products on the market. The dose of laxatives will be different for different products. The number of capsules or tablets or teaspoonfuls of crystals, gel, granules, liquid, or powder that you use; the number of caramels or wafers that you eat; or the number of pieces of gum that you chew depends on the strength of the medicine. *Follow your doctor's orders if this medicine was prescribed, or follow the directions on the box if you are buying this medicine without a prescription.*

Storage—To store this medicine:

- Keep out of the reach of children.
- Store away from heat and direct light.
- Do not store the capsule, tablet, granules, or powder form of this medicine in the bathroom, near the kitchen sink, or in other damp places. Heat or moisture may cause the medicine to break down.
- Keep the liquid form of this medicine from freezing.
- Do not keep outdated medicine or medicine no longer needed. Be sure that any discarded medicine is out of the reach of children.

Precautions While Using This Medicine

Do not take any type of laxative:

- *if you have signs of appendicitis or inflamed bowel* (such as stomach or lower abdominal pain, cramping, bloating, soreness, nausea, or vomiting). Instead, check with your doctor as soon as possible.
- *for more than 1 week* unless your doctor has prescribed or ordered a special schedule for you. This is true even when you have had no results from the laxative.
- *within 2 hours of taking other medicine* because the desired effect of the other medicine may be reduced.
- *if you do not need it,* as for the common cold, "to clean out your system," or as a "tonic to make you feel better."
- *if you miss a bowel movement for a day or two.*
- *if you develop a skin rash* while taking a laxative or if you had a rash the last time you took it. Instead, check with your doctor.

If you notice a sudden change in bowel habits or function that lasts longer than 2 weeks, or that keeps returning off and on, check with your doctor before using a laxative. This will allow the cause of your problem to be determined before it may become more serious.

The "laxative habit"—Laxative products are overused by many people. Such a practice often leads to dependence on the laxative action to produce a bowel movement. In severe cases, overuse of some laxatives has caused damage to the nerves, muscles, and tissues of the intestines and bowel. If you have any questions about the use of laxatives, check with your health care professional.

Many laxatives often contain large amounts of sugars, carbohydrates, and sodium. If you are on a low-sugar, low-caloric, or low-sodium diet, check with your health care professional before using a laxative.

For *patients taking laxatives containing mineral oil:*

- Mineral oil should not be taken often or for long periods of time because:
    - gradual build-up in body tissues may create additional problems.
    - the use of mineral oil may interfere with the body's ability to absorb certain food nutrients and vitamins A, D, E, and K.
- Large doses of mineral oil may cause some leakage from the rectum. The use of absorbent pads or a de-

crease in dose may be necessary to prevent the soiling of clothing.
- Do not take mineral oil within 2 hours of a stool softener (emollient laxative). The stool softener may increase the amount of mineral oil absorbed.

For *patients taking laxatives containing a stimulant ingredient:*

- Stimulant laxatives are most often associated with:
    - overuse and the laxative habit.
    - skin rashes.
    - intestinal cramping after dosing (especially if taken on an empty stomach).
    - potassium loss.

Side Effects of This Medicine

Along with its needed effects, a medicine may cause some unwanted effects. Although not all of these side effects may occur, if they do occur they may need medical attention.

Check with your doctor as soon as possible if any of the following side effects occur:

For bulk-forming-containing
> Difficulty in breathing; intestinal blockage; skin rash or itching; swallowing difficulty (feeling of lump in throat)

For hyperosmotic-containing
> Confusion; dizziness or light-headedness; irregular heartbeat; muscle cramps; unusual tiredness or weakness

For stimulant-containing
> Confusion; irregular heartbeat; muscle cramps; pink to red coloration of alkaline urine and stools (for phenolphthalein only); pink to red, red to violet, or red to brown coloration of alkaline urine (for cascara, danthron, and/or senna only); skin rash; unusual tiredness or weakness; yellow to brown coloration of acid urine (for cascara, phenolphthalein, and/or senna only)

For stool softener (emollient)-containing
> Skin rash

Other side effects may occur that usually do not need medical attention. These side effects are less common and may go away during treatment as your body adjusts to the medicine. However, check with your doctor if any of the following side effects continue or are bothersome:

For hyperosmotic-containing
> Bloating; cramping; diarrhea; nausea; gas; increased thirst

For lubricant-containing
> Skin irritation surrounding rectal area

For stimulant-containing
> Belching; cramping; diarrhea; nausea

For stool softener (emollient)-containing
> Stomach and/or intestinal cramping; throat irritation (liquid forms only)

Other side effects not listed above may also occur in some patients. If you notice any other effects, check with your doctor.

Additional Information

Once a medicine has been approved for marketing for a certain use, experience may show that it is also useful for other

medical problems. Although this use is not included in product labeling, psyllium hydrophilic mucilloid is used in certain patients with high cholesterol (hypercholesterolemia).

For patients taking psyllium hydrophilic mucilloid for *high cholesterol:*

- Importance of diet—Before prescribing medicine for your condition, your doctor will probably try to control your condition by prescribing a personal diet for you. Such a diet may be low in fats, sugars, and/or cholesterol. Many people are able to control their condition by carefully following their doctor's orders for proper diet and exercise. Medicine is prescribed only when additional help is needed. *Follow carefully the special diet your doctor gave you*, since the medicine is effective only when a schedule of diet and exercise is properly followed.
- Do not try to swallow the powder form of this medicine in the dry form. Mix with liquid following the directions in the package.
- Remember that this medicine will not cure your cholesterol problem but it will help control it. Therefore, you must continue to take it as directed by your doctor if you expect to lower your cholesterol level.

Other than the above information, there is no additional information relating to proper use, precautions, or side effects for this use.

Revised: 09/29/2000

LAXATIVES   Rectal

Commonly used brand name(s):

In the U.S.—

Bisco-Lax[1]	Fleet Enema Mineral Oil[4]
Ceo-Two[5]	Fleet Glycerin Laxative[3]
Dacodyl[1]	Fleet Laxative[1]
Deficol[1]	Sani-Supp[3]
Dulcolax[1]	Senokot[6]
Fleet Babylax[3]	Theralax[1]
Fleet Bisacodyl[1]	Therevac Plus[2]
Fleet Enema[7]	Therevac-SB[2]
Fleet Enema for Children[7]	

In Canada—

Apo-Bisacodyl[1]	Fleet Pediatric Enema[7]
Bisacolax[1]	Gent-L-Tip[7]
Dulcolax[1]	Laxit[1]
Enemol[7]	PMS-Bisacodyl[1]
Fleet Enema[7]	Senokot[6]
Fleet Enema Mineral Oil[4]	

Note: For quick reference, the following laxatives are numbered to match the corresponding brand names.

This information applies to the following medicines:
1. Bisacodyl (bis-a-KOE-dill) ‡§
2. Docusate (DOK-yoo-sate) †
3. Glycerin (GLI-ser-in) ‡§
4. Mineral Oil
5. Potassium Bitartrate and Sodium Bicarbonate (pot-TAS-ee-um bye-TAR-trayte and SOE-dee-um bye-KAR-boe-nate) †
6. Senna
7. Sodium Phosphates (SOE-dee-um FOS-fates)

---

†Not commercially available in Canada.
‡Generic name product may be available in the U.S.
§Generic name product may be available in Canada.

Description

Rectal laxatives are used as enemas or suppositories to produce bowel movements in a short time.

There are several different types of rectal laxatives and they work in different ways. Since directions for use are different for each type, it is important to know which one you are taking. The different types of rectal laxatives include:

Carbon dioxide-releasing—Carbon dioxide-releasing laxatives (e.g., potassium bitartrate and sodium bicarbonate) are suppositories that encourage bowel movements by forming carbon dioxide, a gas. This gas pushes against the intestinal wall, causing contractions that move along the stool mass.

Hyperosmotic—Hyperosmotic laxatives (e.g., glycerin; sodium phosphates) draw water into the bowel from surrounding body tissues. This provides a soft stool mass and increased bowel action.

Lubricant—Mineral oil coats the bowel and the stool mass with a waterproof film. This keeps moisture in the stool. The stool remains soft and its passage is made easier.

Stimulants—Stimulant laxatives (e.g., bisacodyl; senna), also known as contact laxatives, act on the intestinal wall. They increase the muscle contractions that move along the stool mass.

Stool softeners (emollients)—Stool softeners (emollient laxatives—e.g., docusate) encourage bowel movements by helping liquids mix into the stool and prevent dry, hard stool masses. This type of laxative has been said not to *cause* a bowel movement but instead *allows* the patient to have a bowel movement without straining.

Rectal laxatives may provide relief in a number of situations such as:

- before giving birth.
- for a few days after giving birth.
- preparation for examination or surgery.
- to aid in developing normal bowel function following a period of poor eating habits or a lack of physical exercise (glycerin suppositories only).
- following surgery when straining should be avoided.
- constipation caused by other medicines.

Some of these laxatives are available only with your doctor's prescription. Others are available without a prescription; however, your doctor may have special instructions for the proper use and dose for your medical condition. They are available in the following dosage forms:

Rectal
Bisacodyl
- Rectal solution (U.S. and Canada)
- Suppositories (U.S. and Canada)
Docusate
- Rectal solution (U.S.)
Glycerin
- Rectal solution (U.S.)
- Suppositories (U.S. and Canada)
Mineral Oil
- Enema (U.S. and Canada)
Potassium Bitartrate and Sodium Bicarbonate
- Suppositories (U.S.)
Senna
- Suppositories (U.S. and Canada)

Sodium Phosphates
- Enema (U.S. and Canada)

Before Using This Medicine

Importance of diet, fluids, and exercise to prevent constipation—Laxatives are to be used to provide short-term relief only, unless otherwise directed by your doctor. A proper diet containing roughage (whole grain breads and cereals, bran, fruit, and green, leafy vegetables), with 6 to 8 full glasses (8 ounces each) of liquids each day, and daily exercise are most important in maintaining healthy bowel function. Also, for individuals who have problems with constipation, foods such as pastries, puddings, sugar, candy, cake, and cheese may make the constipation worse.

If you are using this medicine without a prescription, carefully read and follow any precautions on the label. For rectal laxatives, the following should be considered:

Allergies—Tell your doctor if you have ever had any unusual or allergic reaction to rectal laxatives. Also tell your health care professional if you are allergic to any other substances, such as preservatives or dyes.

Children—*Laxatives should not be given to young children (up to 6 years of age) unless prescribed by their doctor.* Since children cannot usually describe their symptoms very well, they should be checked by a doctor before being given a laxative. The child may have a condition that needs other treatment. If so, laxatives will not help and may even cause unwanted effects or make the condition worse.

Also, weakness, increased sweating, and convulsions (seizures) may be especially likely to occur in children receiving enemas or rectal solutions, since they may be more sensitive than adults to their effects.

Older adults—Weakness, increased sweating, and convulsions (seizures) may be especially likely to occur in elderly patients, since they may be more sensitive than younger adults to the effects of rectal laxatives.

Other medical problems—The presence of other medical problems may affect the use of rectal laxatives. Make sure you tell your doctor if you have any other medical problems, especially:
- Appendicitis (or signs of) or
- Rectal bleeding of unknown cause—These conditions need immediate attention by a doctor
- Intestinal blockage—The use of laxatives may create other problems if this condition is present

Proper Use of This Medicine

For safe and effective use of laxatives:
- Follow your doctor's orders if this laxative was prescribed.
- Follow the manufacturer's package directions if you are treating yourself.

For patients using *the enema or rectal solution form* of this medicine:
- This medicine usually comes with patient directions. Read them carefully before using this medicine.
- Lubricate anus with petroleum jelly before inserting the enema applicator.
- Gently insert the rectal tip of the enema applicator to prevent damage to the rectal wall.

- Results often may be obtained with:
  —bisacodyl enema in 15 minutes to 1 hour.
  —docusate enema in 2 to 15 minutes.
  —glycerin enema in 15 minutes to 1 hour.
  —mineral oil enema in 2 to 15 minutes.
  —senna enema in 30 minutes, but may not occur for some individuals for up to 2 hours.
  —sodium phosphates enema in 2 to 5 minutes.

For patients using *the suppository form* of this medicine:
- If the suppository is too soft to insert, chill the suppository in the refrigerator for 30 minutes or run cold water over it, before removing the foil wrapper.
- To insert suppository: First remove the foil wrapper and moisten the suppository with cold water. Lie down on your side and use your finger to push the suppository well up into the rectum.
- Results often may be obtained with:
  —bisacodyl suppositories in 15 minutes to 1 hour.
  —carbon dioxide-releasing suppositories in 5 to 30 minutes.
  —glycerin suppositories in 15 minutes to 1 hour.
  —senna suppositories in 30 minutes, but may not occur for some individuals for up to 2 hours.

Dosing—There are a large number of laxative products on the market. The dose of laxatives will be different for different products. The amount of enema or the number of suppositories that you use depends on the strength of the medicine. *Follow your doctor's orders if this medicine was prescribed, or follow the directions on the box if you are buying this medicine without a prescription.*

Storage—To store this medicine:
- Keep out of the reach of children.
- Store away from heat and direct light.
- Do not store in the bathroom, near the kitchen sink, or in other damp places. Heat or moisture may cause the medicine to break down.
- Do not keep outdated medicine or medicine no longer needed. Be sure that any discarded medicine is out of the reach of children.

Precautions While Using This Medicine

Do not use any type of laxative:
- *if you have signs of appendicitis or inflamed bowel* (such as stomach or lower abdominal pain, cramping, bloating, soreness, nausea, or vomiting). Instead, check with your doctor as soon as possible.
- *more often than your doctor prescribed. This is true even when you have had no results from the laxative.*
- *if you do not need it,* as for the common cold, "to clean out your system," or as a "tonic to make you feel better."
- *if you miss a bowel movement for a day or two.*

If you notice a sudden change in bowel habits or function that lasts longer than 2 weeks, or keeps returning off and on, check with your doctor before using a laxative. This will allow the cause of your problem to be determined before it becomes more serious.

The "laxative habit"—Laxative products are overused by many people. Such a practice often leads to dependence on the laxative action to produce a bowel movement. In severe cases, overuse of some laxatives has caused damage to the nerves, muscles, and tissues of the intestines and bowel. If you have any questions about the use of laxatives, check with your health care professional.

For patients using *the enema or rectal solution form* of this medicine:

- *Check with your doctor if you notice rectal bleeding, blistering, pain, burning, itching, or other sign of irritation not present before you started using this medicine.*

For patients using *the suppository form* of this medicine:

- Do not lubricate the suppository with mineral oil or petroleum jelly before inserting into the rectum. To do so may affect the way the suppository works. Moisten only with water.

Side Effects of This Medicine

Along with its needed effects, a medicine may cause some unwanted effects. Although not all of these side effects may occur, if they do occur they may need medical attention.

Check with your doctor as soon as possible if any of the following side effects occur:

Less common
    Rectal bleeding, blistering, burning, itching, or pain (with enemas only)

Other side effects may occur that usually do not need medical attention. These side effects may go away during treatment as your body adjusts to the medicine. However, check with your doctor if the following side effect continues or is bothersome:

Less common
    Skin irritation surrounding rectal area

Other side effects not listed above may also occur in some patients. If you notice any other effects, check with your doctor.

Revised: 06/25/93
Interim revision: 08/01/95; 07/31/96

LEFLUNOMIDE   Systemic

Commonly used brand name(s):

In the U.S.—
    Arava

Description

Leflunomide (le-FLUN-o-mide) is used to relieve some symptoms caused by rheumatoid arthritis, such as inflammation, swelling, stiffness, and joint pain. This medicine works by stopping the body from producing too many of the immune cells that are responsible for the swelling and inflammation.

This medicine is available only with your doctor's prescription, in the following dosage form(s):

Oral
    • Tablets (U.S.)

Before Using This Medicine

In deciding to use a medicine, the risks of taking the medicine must be weighed against the good it will do. This is a decision you and your doctor will make. For leflunomide, the following should be considered:

Allergies—Tell your doctor if you have ever had any unusual or allergic reaction to leflunomide. Also tell your health care professional if you are allergic to any other substances, such as foods, preservatives, or dyes.

Pregnancy—*Leflunomide must not be taken during pregnancy because it may cause birth defects in humans.* Women of childbearing age are advised to use reliable contraception before receiving leflunomide.

Breast-feeding—It is not known whether leflunomide passes into the breast milk. However, leflunomide is not recommended during breast-feeding, because it may cause unwanted effects in nursing babies.

Children—Although there is no specific information comparing use of leflunomide in children with use in any other age group, use is not recommended in children up to 18 years of age.

Older adults—Many medicines have not been studied specifically in older people. Therefore, it may not be known whether they work exactly the same way as they do in younger adults or if they cause different side effects or problems in older people. There is no specific information comparing use of leflunomide in the elderly with use in other age groups.

Males—Studies have not been done in animals or humans to determine if leflunomide will cause birth defects in the children of men taking leflunomide at the time of conception. However, it is recommended that men taking this medicine use condoms as a form of birth control during sexual intercourse. Men taking leflunomide who intend to father a child, should stop taking the medicine and tell their doctor immediately.

Other medicines—Although certain medicines should not be used together at all, in other cases two different medicines may be used together even if an interaction might occur. In these cases, your doctor may want to change the dose, or other precautions may be necessary. Tell your health care professional if you are taking *any* other prescription or nonprescription (over-the-counter [OTC] medicine.

Other medical problems—The presence of other medical problems may affect the use of leflunomide. Make sure you tell your doctor if you have any other medical problems, especially:

- Disease of the immune system or
- Infections, severe—Leflunomide may decrease the body's ability to fight infection
- Liver disease, including hepatitis B or C or
- Renal disease—The chance of side effects may be increased

Proper Use of This Medicine

Take this medicine only as directed by your doctor. Do not take more or less of it, and do not take it more often than your doctor ordered.

Dosing—The dose of leflunomide will be different for different patients. *Follow your doctor's orders or the directions on the label.* The following information includes only the average doses of leflunomide. *If your dose is different, do not change it* unless your doctor tells you to do so.

- For *oral* dosage form (tablets):
    —For rheumatoid arthritis:
        • Adults—At first, 100 mg once a day for three days, then 20 mg once a day. Your doctor may decrease the dose as needed.
        • Children—Use and dose must be determined by your doctor.

Missed dose—If you miss a dose of this medicine, take it as soon as possible. However, if you do not remember the missed dose until the next day, skip the missed dose and go back to your regular dosing schedule. Do not double doses.

Storage—To store this medicine:
- Keep out of the reach of children.
- Store away from heat and direct light.
- Do not store in the bathroom, near the kitchen sink, or in other damp places. Heat or moisture may cause the medicine to break down.
- Do not keep outdated medicine or medicine no longer needed. Be sure that any discarded medicine is out of the reach of children.

Precautions While Using This Medicine

It is important that your doctor check your progress at regular visits to make sure that this medicine is working properly and to check for unwanted effects.

Leflunomide may cause birth defects in humans if taken during pregnancy. Therefore, if you suspect that you may have become pregnant, stop taking this medicine immediately and check with your doctor.

Leflunomide may cause birth defects in the children of the men taking it during the time of conception. Therefore, men taking leflunomide should use condoms as a form of birth control during sexual intercourse. A man intending to father a child should stop taking this medicine and check with his doctors.

Do not drink alcohol while using this medicine. Alcohol can increase the chance of liver problems.

While you are being treated with leflunomide, and after you stop treatment with it, *do not have any immunizations (vaccinations) without your doctor's approval.*

Side Effects of This Medicine

Along with its needed effects, a medicine may cause some unwanted effects. Although not all of these side effects may occur, if they do occur they may need medical attention.

Check with your doctor as soon as possible if any of the following side effects occur:
  More common
    Bloody or cloudy urine; congestion in chest; cough; difficult, burning, or painful urination; difficult or painful breathing; dizziness; fever; frequent urge to urinate; headache; loss of appetite; nausea and/or vomiting; sneezing; sore throat; yellow eyes and/or skin
  Less common
    Burning feeling in chest or stomach; burning, prickling, or tingling sensation in fingers and/or toes; chest pain; diarrhea; fast heartbeat; indigestion; joint or muscle pain or stiffness; pounding heartbeat; severe stomach pain; shortness of breath; tenderness in stomach area; unusual tiredness or weakness

Other side effects may occur that usually do not need medical attention. These side effects may go away during treatment as your body adjusts to the medicine. However, check with your doctor if any of the following side effects continue or are bothersome:
  More common
    Back pain; hair loss; heartburn; skin rash; stomach pain; weight loss (unexplained)
  Less common
    Acne; anxiety; constipation; decreased appetite; dry

mouth; gas; irritation or soreness of mouth; itching of the skin; pain or burning in throat; red or irritated eyes; runny nose

Other side effects not listed above may also occur in some patients. If you notice any other effects, check with your doctor.

Developed: 12/1/98

LETROZOLE   Systemic

Commonly used brand name(s):
In the U.S.—
  Femara
In Canada—
  Femara

Description

Letrozole (LET-roe-zole) is used to treat certain types of breast cancer in women. Female hormones that occur naturally in the body can increase the growth of some breast cancers. Letrozole works by decreasing the amounts of these hormones in the body. This medicine is meant to be used only by women who have already stopped menstruating.

This medicine is available only with your doctor's prescription, in the following dosage form:
  Oral
    • Tablets (U.S. and Canada)

Before Using This Medicine

In deciding to use a medicine, the risks of taking the medicine must be weighed against the good it will do. This is a decision you and your doctor will make. For letrozole, the following should be considered:

Allergies—Tell your doctor if you have ever had any unusual or allergic reaction to letrozole. Also tell your health care professional if you are allergic to any other substances, such as foods, preservatives, or dyes.

Pregnancy—This medicine is meant to be used only by women who are no longer able to have children. If this medicine is taken by a pregnant woman for any reason it may cause harm to, and possibly even death of, the fetus.

Older adults—This medicine has been tested and has not been shown to cause different effects in older women than in younger adults.

Other medical problems—The presence of other medical problems may affect the use of letrozole. Make sure you tell your doctor if you have any other medical problems, especially:
- Kidney disease or
- Liver disease—Problems are not likely to occur in people with mild kidney or liver disease. However, it is not known whether severe kidney or liver disease may increase the chance of side effects during treatment

Proper Use of This Medicine

Take this medicine only as directed by your doctor. Do not take more of it, and do not take it more often than your doctor ordered.

Dosing—The dose of letrozole may be different for different patients. *Follow your doctor's orders or the directions on the label.* The following information includes only the average dose of letrozole. *If your dose is different, do not change it* unless your doctor tells you to do so.

- For *oral* dosage form (tablets):
  —For breast cancer:
  - Adults—One 2.5-milligram tablet a day.

Missed dose—If you miss a dose of this medicine, take it as soon as you remember. However, if you do not remember until the next day, skip the missed dose and go back to your regular dosing schedule. Do not double the next day's dose.

Storage—To store this medicine:

- Keep out of the reach of children.
- Store away from heat and direct light.
- Do not store in the bathroom, near the kitchen sink, or in other damp places. Heat or moisture may cause the medicine to break down.
- Do not keep outdated medicine or medicine no longer needed. Be sure that any discarded medicine is out of the reach of children.

Precautions While Using This Medicine

It is very important that your doctor check your progress at regular visits to make sure that the medicine is working properly and does not cause unwanted effects.

Side Effects of This Medicine

Along with its needed effects, a medicine may cause some unwanted effects. Although not all of these side effects may occur, if they do occur they may need medical attention.

The following side effects may be caused by blood clots, which could lead to a heart attack or a stroke. *Stop taking this medicine and get emergency help immediately* if any of the following side effects occur:

More common
  Shortness of breath
Less common
  Chest pain
Rare
  Continuing or severe nervousness; cough; dizziness or lightheadedness; fainting; fast heartbeat; heart attack; increased sweating; nausea; pain in chest, groin, or legs, especially the calves; severe, sudden headache; slurred speech; severe and sudden, unexplained shortness of breath; sudden loss of coordination; sudden, severe weakness or numbness in arm or leg; vision changes

Also, check with your doctor as soon as possible if any of the following side effects occur:

Less common
  Bone fracture; breast pain; chills, fever, or flu-like symptoms; mental depression; swelling of feet or lower legs
Rare
  Vaginal bleeding

Other side effects may occur that usually do not need medical attention. These side effects may go away during treatment as your body adjusts to the medicine. However, check with your doctor if any of the following side effects continue or are bothersome:

More common
  Back pain; bone pain; hot flashes (sudden sweating and feeling of warmth); joint pain; muscle pain
Less common
  Anxiety; confusion; constipation; diarrhea; dry mouth; headache; increased thirst and urination; loss of appetite or weight loss; metallic taste; skin rash or itching; sleepiness; spinning or whirling sensation causing loss of balance; stomach pain or upset; trouble sleeping; unusual tiredness; vomiting; weakness; weight gain

Letrozole sometimes causes a loss of hair.

Other side effects not listed above may also occur in some patients. If you notice any other effects, check with your doctor.

Developed: 08/14/1998
Revised: 02/13/2001

LEUCOVORIN   Systemic

Commonly used brand name(s):

In the U.S.—
  Wellcovorin
  Generic name product may be available.

Other commonly used names are citrovorum factor and folinic acid.

Description

Leucovorin (loo-koe-VOR-in) is used as an antidote to the harmful effects of methotrexate (a cancer medicine) that is given in high doses. It is used also to prevent or treat certain kinds of anemia. Leucovorin acts the same way in the body as folic acid, which may be low in these patients.

Leucovorin is also used along with fluorouracil (a cancer medicine) to treat cancer of the colon (bowel).

Leucovorin is available only with a prescription and is to be given only by or under the supervision of your doctor. It is available in the following dosage forms:

Oral
  - Tablets (U.S. and Canada)
Parenteral
  - Injection (U.S. and Canada)

Before Using This Medicine

In deciding to use a medicine, the risks of taking the medicine must be weighed against the good it will do. This is a decision you and your doctor will make. For leucovorin, the following should be considered:

Allergies—Tell your doctor if you have ever had any unusual or allergic reaction to leucovorin. Also tell your health care professional if you are allergic to any other substance, such as foods, sulfites or other preservatives, or dyes.

Pregnancy—Studies on effects in pregnancy have not been done in either humans or animals.

Breast-feeding—It is not known whether leucovorin passes into the breast milk. However, it has not been reported to cause problems in nursing babies.

Children—In children with seizures, leucovorin may increase the number of seizures that occur.

Older adults—Many medicines have not been studied specifically in older people. Therefore, it may not be known whether they work exactly the same way they do in younger adults or if they cause different side effects or problems in older people. There is no specific information comparing use of leucovorin in the elderly with use in other age groups.

Other medicines—Although certain medicines should not be used together at all, in other cases two different medicines may be used together even if an interaction might occur. In these cases, your doctor may want to change the dose, or other precautions may be necessary. Tell your health care professional if you are taking any other prescription or nonprescription (over-the-counter [OTC]) medicine.

Other medical problems—The presence of other medical problems may affect the use of leucovorin. If you are taking leucovorin as an antidote to methotrexate, make sure you tell your doctor if you have any other medical problems, especially:

- Kidney disease—Levels of methotrexate may be increased because of its slower removal from the body, so the dose of leucovorin may not be enough to block the unwanted effects of methotrexate

- Nausea and vomiting—Not enough leucovorin may be absorbed into the body to block the unwanted effects of methotrexate

Proper Use of This Medicine

It is very important that you *take leucovorin exactly as directed*, especially when it is being taken to counteract the harmful effects of cancer medicine. *Do not miss any doses. Also, it is best to take the doses at evenly spaced times day and night.* For example, if you are to take 4 doses a day, the doses should be spaced about 6 hours apart. If this interferes with your sleep or other daily activities, or if you need help in planning the best times to take your medicine, check with your health care professional.

Do not stop taking leucovorin without checking with your doctor. It is very important that you get exactly the right amount.

Dosing—The dose of leucovorin will be different for different patients. *Follow your doctor's orders or the directions on the label.* The following information includes only the average doses of leucovorin. *If your dose is different, do not change it* unless your doctor tells you to do so.

The number of tablets or doses of injection that you take depends on the strength of the medicine. Also, *the number of doses you take each day, the time allowed between doses, and the length of time you take the medicine depend on the medical problem for which you are taking leucovorin.*

- For use as an antidote to methotrexate:
  - —For *oral* (tablets) or *injection* dosage forms:
    - Adults, teenagers, and children—Dose is based on body size and must be determined by your doctor.
- For use as an antidote to other medicines:
  - —For *oral* (tablets) or *injection* dosage forms:
    - Adults, teenagers, and children—Dose may range from 0.4 milligrams (mg) to 15 mg a day and must be determined by your doctor.

- For certain kinds of anemia:
  - —For *oral* (tablets) or *injection* dosage forms:
    - Adults, teenagers, and children—Up to 1 mg a day.
- For colon cancer:
  - —For *injection* dosage forms:
    - Adults and teenagers—Dose is based on body size and must be determined by your doctor.
    - Children—Dose must be determined by your doctor.

Missed dose—If you miss a dose of leucovorin or if you vomit shortly after taking a dose, *check with your doctor right away.* Your doctor may want you to take extra leucovorin to make up for what you missed. Do not take more medicine on your own, however, since it is very important that you receive just the right dose at the right time.

Storage—To store this medicine:

- Keep out of the reach of children.
- Store away from heat and direct light.
- Do not store in the bathroom, near the kitchen sink, or in other damp places. Heat or moisture may cause the medicine to break down.
- Do not keep outdated medicine or medicine no longer needed. Be sure that any discarded medicine is out of the reach of children.

Side Effects of This Medicine

Along with its needed effects, a medicine may cause some unwanted effects. Leucovorin usually does not cause any side effects.

However, *check with your doctor immediately* if any of the following side effects occur shortly after you receive this medicine:

　Rare
　　Skin rash, hives, or itching; wheezing

Check with your doctor as soon as possible if the following side effect occurs:

　Rare—reported with use in treatment of cancer
　　Convulsions (seizures)

Other side effects not listed above may also occur in some patients. If you notice any other effects, check with your doctor.

Additional Information

Once a medicine has been approved for marketing for a certain use, experience may show that it is also useful for other medical problems. Although these uses are not included in the product labeling, leucovorin is used in certain patients with the following medical conditions:

- Ewing's sarcoma (type of cancer found in the bone)
- Gestational trophoblastic tumors (tumors in the uterus or womb)
- Head and neck cancer
- Non-Hodgkin's lymphoma (cancer of the lymph system)

Other than the above information, there is no additional information relating to proper use, precautions, or side effects for these uses.

Revised: 08/14/2000

LEUPROLIDE   Systemic

Commonly used brand name(s):

In the U.S.—

Lupron	Lupron Depot-3 Month
Lupron Depot	22.5 mg
Lupron Depot-Ped	Lupron Depot-4 Month 30 mg
Lupron Depot-3 Month	Viadur
11.25 mg	

In Canada—

Lupron	Lupron-3 Month SR Depot
Lupron Depot	22.5 mg

Another commonly used name is leuprorelin.

Description

Leuprolide (loo-PROE-lide) may be used for a number of different medical problems. These include treatment of:

- anemia caused by bleeding of uterine leiomyomas (tumors in the uterus);
- cancer of the prostate gland in men;
- central precocious puberty (CPP), a condition that causes early puberty in boys (before 9 years of age) and in girls (before 8 years of age);
- pain due to endometriosis in women.

Leuprolide is similar to a hormone normally released from the hypothalamus gland.

When given regularly to men and boys, leuprolide decreases testosterone levels. Reducing the amount of testosterone in the body is one way of treating cancer of the prostate.

When given regularly to women and girls, leuprolide decreases estrogen levels. Reducing the amount of estrogen in the body is one way of treating endometriosis. By shrinking tumors in the uterus, leuprolide helps stop anemia by decreasing the vaginal bleeding from these tumors. Iron supplements should be used to help treat the anemia.

When given to boys and girls experiencing early puberty, leuprolide slows down the development of the genital areas in both sexes and breast development in girls. This medicine delays puberty in a child only as long as the child continues to receive it.

Suppressing estrogen can cause thinning of the bones or slowing of their growth. This is a problem for adult women whose bones are no longer growing like the bones of children. Slowing the growth of bones is a positive effect in girls and boys whose bones grow too fast when puberty begins too early. Boys and girls may benefit by adding inches to their adult height when leuprolide helps their bones grow at the proper and expected rate for children.

Leuprolide is available only with your doctor's prescription, in the following dosage form:

Parenteral
- Injection (U.S. and Canada)
- Implant (U.S.)

Before Using This Medicine

In deciding to use a medicine, the risks of taking the medicine must be weighed against the good it will do. This is a decision you and your doctor will make. For leuprolide, the following should be considered:

Allergies—Tell your doctor if you have ever had any unusual or allergic reaction to leuprolide, buserelin, gonadorelin, histrelin, nafarelin, or to benzyl alcohol, a preservative present in some of the leuprolide products.

Pregnancy—Tell your doctor if you intend to have children.

- For men: Leuprolide may cause sterility which probably is only temporary. Be sure that you have discussed this with your doctor before receiving this medicine.
- For women: There is a chance that leuprolide may cause birth defects if it is taken after you become pregnant. It could also cause a miscarriage if taken during pregnancy. *Stop using this medicine and tell your doctor immediately if you think you have become pregnant while receiving this medicine.*

Breast-feeding—It is not known whether leuprolide passes into breast milk. However, use of leuprolide is not recommended during breast-feeding because it may cause unwanted effects in nursing babies.

Children—Leuprolide will stop having an effect on a child treated for central precocious puberty soon after the child stops using it, and puberty will advance normally. It is not known if using leuprolide around the time of puberty causes changes in boys' and girls' future abilities to have babies. Their chances of having children later are thought to be normal. It is especially important that you discuss with the child's doctor the good that this medicine may do as well as the risks of using it.

Older adults—Many medicines have not been studied specifically in older people. Therefore, it may not be known whether they work exactly the same way they do in younger adults. Although there is no specific information comparing use of leuprolide in the elderly to use in other age groups, it is not expected to cause different side effects or problems in older people than it does in younger adults.

Other medicines—Although certain medicines should not be used together at all, in other cases two medicines may be used together even if an interaction might occur. In these cases, your doctor may want to change the dose, or other precautions may be necessary. Tell your doctor and pharmacist if you are taking any other prescription or nonprescription (over-the-counter [OTC]) medicine.

Other medical problems—The presence of other medical problems may affect the use of leuprolide. Make sure you tell your doctor if you have any other medical problems, especially:

- Changes in vaginal bleeding from an unknown cause (for use for endometriosis or anemia due to tumors of the uterus)—Leuprolide may delay diagnosis or worsen condition. The reason for the bleeding should be determined before leuprolide is used

- Conditions that increase the chances of developing thinning bones or
- Osteoporosis (brittle bones), history of, or family history of—It is important that your doctor know if you already have an increased risk of osteoporosis. Some things that can increase your risk for having osteoporosis include cigarette smoking, alcohol abuse, and a family history of osteoporosis or easily broken bones. Some medicines, such as corticosteroids (cortisone-like medicines) or anticonvulsants (seizure medicine), can also cause thinning of the bones when used for a long time

- Nerve problems caused by bone lesions in spine (for use for cancer of the prostate) and

- Problems in passing urine (for use for cancer of the prostate)—Conditions may get worse for a short time after leuprolide treatment is started

Proper Use of This Medicine

Leuprolide comes with patient directions. Read these instructions carefully.

Use the syringes provided in the kit. Other syringes may not provide the correct dose. These disposable syringes and needles are already sterilized and are designed to be used one time only and then discarded. If you have any questions about the use of disposable syringes, check with your health care professional.

Use this medicine only as directed by your doctor. Do not use more or less of it, and do not use it more often than your doctor ordered. The exact amount of medicine you need has been carefully worked out. Using too much may increase the chance of side effects, while using too little may not improve your condition.

For adult patients receiving leuprolide for *anemia caused by tumors of the uterus* or for *endometriosis:*

- Leuprolide sometimes causes unwanted effects such as hot flashes or decreased interest in sex. It may also cause a temporary increase in pain when you first begin to use it. However, it is very important that you continue to use the medicine, even after you begin to feel better. *Do not stop using this medicine without first checking with your doctor.*

For adult patients receiving leuprolide for *cancer of the prostate:*

- Leuprolide sometimes causes unwanted effects such as hot flashes or decreased sexual ability. It may also cause a temporary increase in pain or difficulty in urinating, as well as temporary numbness or tingling of hands or feet or weakness when you first begin to use it. However, it is very important that you continue to use the medicine, even after you begin to feel better. *Do not stop using this medicine without first checking with your doctor.*

Dosing—The dose of leuprolide will be different for different patients. *Follow your doctor's orders or the directions on the label.* The following information includes only the average doses of leuprolide. *If your dose is different, do not change it* unless your doctor tells you to do so:

- For *short-acting (daily)* injection dosage forms:
  —For *cancer of the prostate:*
  - Adults—1 milligram (mg) injected under the skin once a day.
  —For *central precocious puberty:*
  - Children—Dose is based on body weight and must be determined by your doctor. It is injected under the skin once a day. The dose should be changed over time as weight changes.

- For *long-acting (1-month)* injection dosage forms:
  —For *anemia caused by tumors of the uterus:*
  - Adults—3.75 milligrams (mg) injected into a muscle once a month for up to three months.
  —For *cancer of the prostate:*
  - Adults—7.5 milligrams (mg) injected into a muscle once a month.

—For *central precocious puberty:*
  - Children—Dose is based on body weight and must be determined by the doctor. It is injected into a muscle once a month. The dose should be changed over time as weight changes.
—For *endometriosis:*
  - Adults—3.75 milligrams (mg) injected into a muscle once a month for up to six months.

- For *long-acting (3-month)* injection dosage forms:
  —For *anemia caused by tumors of the uterus:*
  - Adults—11.25 milligrams (mg) injected into a muscle as a single injection to last for three months.
  —For *cancer of the prostate:*
  - Adults—22.5 milligrams (mg) injected into a muscle once every three months.
  —For *endometriosis:*
  - Adults—11.25 milligrams (mg) injected into a muscle once every three months for up to six months.

- For *long-acting (4-month)* injection dosage form:
  —For *cancer of the prostate:*
  - Adults—30 milligrams (mg) injected into a muscle once every four months.

- For *long-acting (12-month)* implant dosage form:
  —For *cancer of the prostate:*
  - Adults—one implant every 12 months.

Missed dose—If you are using this medicine every day and you miss a dose, give it as soon as possible. However, if you do not remember until the next day, skip the missed dose and go back to your regular dosing schedule. Do not double doses.

If you are using this medicine once a month or every 3 to 12 months and you miss a dose, receive it as soon as possible, and go back to your regular dosing schedule.

Storage—To store this medicine:
- Keep out of the reach of children.
- Store away from heat and direct light.
- Keep the medicine from freezing.
- Do not keep outdated medicine or medicine no longer needed. Dispose of used syringes properly in the container provided. Be sure that any discarded medicine is out of the reach of children.

Precautions While Using This Medicine

It is very important that your doctor check your progress at regular visits to make sure that this medicine is working properly and to check for unwanted effects.

For patients receiving leuprolide for *endometriosis* or for *anemia caused by tumors of the uterus:*

- During the time you are receiving leuprolide, your menstrual period may not be regular or you may not have a menstrual period at all. This is to be expected when being treated with this medicine. If regular menstruation does not begin within 60 to 90 days after you stop receiving this medicine, check with your doctor.
- During the time you are receiving leuprolide, you should use birth control methods that do not contain hormones. If you have any questions about this, check with your health care professional.
- *If you suspect you may have become pregnant, stop using this medicine and check with your doctor.*

There is a chance that continued use of leuprolide during pregnancy could cause birth defects or a miscarriage.

Side Effects of This Medicine

Along with its needed effects, a medicine may cause some unwanted effects. Although not all of these side effects may occur, if they do occur they may need medical attention.

Get emergency help immediately if any of the following side effects occur:

For adults
  Less common
    Fast or irregular heartbeat
  Rare
    Bone, muscle, or joint pain; changes in skin color of face; fainting; fast or irregular breathing; numbness or tingling of hands or feet; puffiness or swelling of the eyelids or around the eyes; shortness of breath; skin rash, hives, and/or itching; sudden, severe decrease in blood pressure and collapse; tightness in chest or wheezing; troubled breathing

For males only (adults)
  Rare
    Pains in chest; pain in groin or legs (especially in calves of legs)

Check with your doctor as soon as possible if any of the following side effects occur:

For females only (adults)
  Rare
    Anxiety; deepening of voice; increased hair growth; mental depression; mood changes; nervousness

For children
  Rare
    Body pain; burning, itching, redness, or swelling at place of injection; skin rash

For females only (children)—expected in first few weeks
  Rare
    Vaginal bleeding (continuing); white vaginal discharge (continuing)

Other side effects may occur that usually do not need medical attention. These side effects may go away during treatment as your body adjusts to the medicine. However, check with your doctor if any of the following side effects continue or are bothersome:

For adults
  More common
    Sudden sweating and feelings of warmth (also called hot flashes)
  Less common
    Blurred vision; bleeding, bruising, burning, itching, pain, redness, or swelling at place of injection; decreased interest in sexual intercourse; dizziness; headache; nausea or vomiting; swelling of feet or lower legs; swelling or increased tenderness of breasts; trouble in sleeping; weight gain

For females only (adults)
  More common
    Light, irregular vaginal bleeding; stopping of menstrual periods
  Less common
    Burning, dryness, or itching of vagina; pelvic pain

For males only (adults)
  Less common
    Bone pain; constipation; decreased size of testicles; inability to have or keep an erection

Other side effects not listed above may also occur in some patients. If you notice any other effects, check with your doctor.

Additional Information

Once a medicine has been approved for marketing for a certain use, experience may show that it is also useful for other medical problems. Although this use is not included in product labeling, leuprolide is used in certain patients with the following medical condition:

• Cancer of the breast

Other than the above information, there is no additional information relating to proper use, precautions, or side effects for this use.

Revised: 09/05/2000

LEVALBUTEROL   Inhalation-Local

Commonly used brand name(s):

In the U.S.—
  Xopenex

Description

Levalbuterol (lee-val-BYOO-ter-ole) belongs to the family of adrenergic bronchodilators. Levalbuterol is used to prevent or treat chest tightness, shortness of breath, troubled breathing and wheezing associated with bronchospasm.

This medicine is breathed in through the mouth by using a nebulizer and compressor. Levalbuterol opens up the bronchial tubes (air passages) of the lungs.

This medicine is available only with your doctor's prescription, in the following dosage form:

Inhalation
  • Solution (U.S.)

Before Using This Medicine

In deciding to use a medicine, the risks of using the medicine must be weighed against the good it will do. This is a decision you and your doctor will make. For levalbuterol, the following should be considered:

Allergies—Tell your doctor if you have ever had any unusual or allergic reaction to levalbuterol, albuterol, or other inhaled asthma medicines. Also tell your health care professional if you are allergic to any other substances, such as foods, preservatives, or dyes.

Pregnancy—Levalbuterol has not been studied in pregnant women. However, studies in animals have shown that albuterol, a very similar medicine, may cause birth defects or other problems. Levalbuterol has the potential to interfere with contractions during labor. Before taking this medicine, make sure your doctor knows if you are pregnant or may become pregnant.

Breast-feeding—It is not known whether levalbuterol passes into breast milk. Although most medicines pass into breast milk in small amounts, many of them may be used safely while breast-feeding. Mothers who are taking this medicine and who wish to breast-feed should discuss this with their doctor.

Children—This medicine has been tested in children 12 years of age and older. In effective doses, this medicine has not been shown to cause different side effects or problems than it does in other age groups.

Older adults—Many medicines have not been studied specifically in older people. Therefore, it may not be known whether they work exactly the same as they do in young adults. Although there is limited information comparing the use of levalbuterol in the elderly with use in other age groups, this medicine is not expected to cause different side effects or problems in older people than it does in younger adults. Your doctor may want to begin with a lesser dose and increase the dosage as tolerated.

Other medicines—Although certain medicines should not be used together at all, in other cases two different medicines may be used together even if an interaction might occur. In these cases, your doctor may want to change the dose, or other precautions may be necessary. Tell your doctor and pharmacist if you are taking any other prescription or nonprescription (over-the-counter [OTC]) medicines, including the following:

- Aerosol bronchodilators, short-acting (albuterol [e.g., Proventil, Ventolin], bitolterol [e.g., Tornalate], ephedrine [OTC], epinephrine [OTC, e.g., Primatene], isoetharine [e.g., Bronkosol], isoproterenol [e.g., Isuprel], pirbuterol [e.g., Maxair], terbutaline [e.g., Brethaire])—Using levalbuterol while you are using short-acting aerosol bronchodilators may cause some heart problems

- Beta-adrenergic blocking agents, systemic (acebutolol [e.g., Sectral], atenolol [e.g., Tenormin], betaxolol [e.g., Kerlone], carteolol [e.g., Cartrol], labetolol [e.g., Normodyne], metoprolol [e.g., Lopressor], nadolol [e.g., Corgard], oxprenolol [e.g., Trasicor], penbutolol [e.g., Levatol], pindolol [e.g., Visken], propranolol [e.g., Inderal], sotalol [e.g., Betapace, Sotacor], timolol [e.g., Blocadren])—Using levalbuterol while you are using beta-adrenergic blocking agents may block the relaxation of smooth muscle in the lungs to ease breathing

- Digoxin—Levalbuterol may decrease the levels of digoxin in the blood. Blood levels of digoxin should be monitored when possible

- Diuretics, non-potassium-sparing (bumetanide [e.g., Bumex], ethacrynic acid [e.g., Edecrin], furosemide [e.g., Lasix], indapamide [e.g., Lozol], thiazide diuretics [water pills])—Use may worsen salt imbalance in the blood

- Methylxanthines (caffeine, theophylline [e.g., Theo-Dur])—Using levalbuterol with methylxanthines may result in irregular heartbeat

- Monoamine oxidase (MAO) inhibitors (furazolidone [e.g., Furoxone], phenelzine [e.g., Nardil], procarbazine [e.g., Matulane], selegiline [e.g., Eldepryl], tranylcypromine [e.g., Parnate]) or

- Tricyclic antidepressants (amitriptyline [e.g., Elavil], amoxapine [e.g., Asendin], clomipramine [e.g., Anafranil], desipramine [e.g., Norpramin, Pertofrane], doxepin [e.g., Sinequan], imipramine [e.g., Tofranil], nortriptyline [e.g., Aventyl, Pamelor], protriptyline [e.g., Vivactil], trimipramine [e.g., Surmontil])—Taking levalbuterol while you are taking, or within 2 weeks of taking, MAO inhibitors or tricyclic antidepressants may cause a change in blood pressure or pulse rate

Other medical problems—The presence of other medical problems may affect the use of levalbuterol. Make sure you tell your doctor if you have any other medical problems, especially:

- Heart disease (irregular heartbeat or decreased blood flow through the heart) or
- High blood pressure—Use of levalbuterol may worsen these conditions

- Diabetes mellitus (sugar diabetes)—Levalbuterol may worsen blood glucose control

- Hyperthyroidism (overactive thyroid)

- Seizures—Concurrent use may worsen this condition

Proper Use of This Medicine

These medicines come with patient directions. Read them carefully before using the medicine. If you do not understand the directions or if you are not sure how to use the medicine, ask your health care professional to show you what to do. Also, ask your health care professional to check regularly how you use the medicine to make sure you are using it properly.

Use this medicine only as directed. Do not use more of it and do not use it more often than recommended on the label, unless otherwise directed by your doctor. Using the medicine more often may increase the chance of serious unwanted effects. Deaths have occurred when too much of an inhalation bronchodilator medicine was used.

For patients using the inhalation solution dosage form:
- *If you are using this medicine in a nebulizer, make sure you understand exactly how to use it. If you have any questions about this, check with your health care professional.*
- *Do not use if solution becomes cloudy.*
- *Do not mix another inhalation medicine with levalbuterol in the nebulizer unless told to do so by your health care professional.*

Dosing—The dose of levalbuterol will be different for different patients. *Follow your doctor's orders or the directions on the label.* The following information includes only the average doses of levalbuterol. *If your dose is different, do not change it* unless your doctor tells you to do so.

- For *inhalation solution* dosage form:
  —For preventing or treating bronchospasm:
  - Adults and children 12 years of age and older—This medicine is used in a nebulizer and is taken by inhalation over a period of five to fifteen minutes. The usual dose is 0.63 milligrams (mg) to 1.25 mg three times a day, every six to eight hours.
  - Children up to 12 years of age—Use and dose must be determined by your doctor.

Missed dose—If you miss a dose of this medicine, use it as soon as possible. However, if it is almost time for your next dose, skip the missed dose and go back to your regular dosing schedule. Do not double doses.

If your dosing schedule is different from all of the above and you miss a dose of this medicine, or if you have any questions about this, check with your doctor.

Storage—To store this medicine:
- Keep out of the reach of children.
- Store away from heat and direct light, in the foil pouch.
- Do not keep outdated medicine or medicine no longer needed. Be sure that any discarded medicine is out of the reach of children.
- Once a foil pouch is opened, use the medicine within 2 weeks.

Precautions While Using This Medicine

It is important that your doctor check your progress at regular intervals to make sure that your medicine is working properly.

If you still have trouble breathing after using one of this medicine, if your condition becomes worse, or if you are using more medicine than the amount prescribed, check with your doctor at once.

Do not add or stop taking inhaled or other asthma medicines without first checking with your doctor.

Side Effects of This Medicine

Along with its needed effects, a medicine may cause some unwanted effects. Although not all of these side effects may occur, if they do occur they may need medical attention.

Check with your doctor as soon as possible if any of the following side effects occur:

More common
Fast heartbeat

Less common or rare
Chest pain or tightness; dizziness; feeling "faint"; high or low blood pressure; hives; light-headedness; shortness of breath; troubled breathing; wheezing

Symptoms of overdose
Chest pain; dizziness; dry mouth; fatigue; general feeling of discomfort or illness; headache; high blood pressure; impaired consciousness; irregular or fast heartbeat; light-headedness; nausea; nervousness; seizures; sleeplessness; sweating; tremor

Other side effects not listed above may also occur in some patients. If you notice any other effects, check with your doctor.

Additional Information

Other than the above information, there is no additional information relating to proper use, precautions, or side effects for use in preventing or treating bronchospasm.

Revised: 6/14/99

LEVAMISOLE   Systemic

Commonly used brand name(s):

In Canada—
Ergamisol

Description

Levamisole (lee-VAM-i-sole) is used with another cancer medicine (fluorouracil) to help make it work better against cancer of the colon.

Levamisole is available only with your doctor's prescription in the following dosage form:

Oral
- Tablets (Canada)

Before Using This Medicine

In deciding to use a medicine, the risks of taking the medicine must be weighed against the good it will do. This is a decision you and your doctor will make. For levamisole, the following should be considered:

Allergies—Tell your doctor if you have ever had any unusual or allergic reaction to levamisole or to any other medicines.

Pregnancy—Levamisole has not been studied in pregnant women. However, studies in rats and rabbits have not shown that levamisole causes birth defects or other problems.

Breast-feeding—It is not known whether levamisole passes into the breast milk in humans, although it passes into cows' milk. However, this medicine has not been reported to cause problems in nursing babies.

Children—Studies on this medicine have been done only in adult patients, and there is no specific information comparing use of levamisole in children with use in other age groups.

Older adults—Many medicines have not been studied specifically in older people. Therefore, it may not be known whether they work exactly the same way they do in younger adults or if they cause different side effects or problems in older people. Although there is no specific information comparing use of levamisole in the elderly with use in other age groups, this medicine has been used in elderly patients and is not expected to cause different side effects or problems in older people than it does in younger adults.

Other medicines—Although certain medicines should not be used together at all, in other cases two different medicines may be used together even if an interaction might occur. In these cases, your doctor may want to change the dose, or other precautions may be necessary. Tell your health care professional if you are taking any other prescription or nonprescription (over-the-counter [OTC]) medicine.

Other medical problems—The presence of other medical problems may affect the use of levamisole. Make sure you tell your doctor if you have any other medical problems, especially:
- Infection—Levamisole may decrease your body's ability to fight infection

Proper Use of This Medicine

Take this medicine only as directed by your doctor. Do not take more or less of it, and do not take it more often than your doctor ordered. The exact amount of medicine you need has been carefully worked out. Taking too much may increase the chance of side effects, while taking too little may not improve your condition.

If you vomit shortly after taking a dose of levamisole, check with your doctor. You will be told whether to take the dose again or to wait until the next scheduled dose.

Dosing—The dose of levamisole will be different for different patients. The dose that is used may depend on a number of things, including what the medicine is being used for and whether or not other medicines are also being taken. *If you are taking levamisole at home, follow your doctor's orders or the directions on the label.* If you have any questions about the proper dose of levamisole, ask your doctor.

Missed dose—If you miss a dose of this medicine, do not take the missed dose at all and do not double the next one. Instead, go back to your regular dosing schedule and check with your doctor.

Storage—To store this medicine:
- Keep out of the reach of children.
- Store away from heat and direct light.
- Do not store in the bathroom, near the kitchen sink, or in other damp places. Heat or moisture may cause the medicine to break down.
- Do not keep outdated medicine or medicine no longer needed. Be sure that any discarded medicine is out of the reach of children.

Precautions While Using This Medicine

It is very important that your doctor check your progress at regular visits to make sure that this medicine is working properly and to check for unwanted effects.

Side Effects of This Medicine

Along with its needed effects, a medicine may cause some unwanted effects. Although not all of these side effects may occur, if they do occur they may need medical attention.

Check with your doctor immediately if any of the following side effects occur:
Less common
Fever or chills; unusual feeling of discomfort or weakness
Rare
Black, tarry stools; blood in urine or stools; cough or hoarseness; lower back or side pain; painful or difficult urination; pinpoint red spots on skin; unusual bleeding or bruising

Check with your doctor as soon as possible if the following side effects occur:
Less common
Sores in mouth and on lips
Rare
Blurred vision; confusion; convulsions (seizures); lip smacking or puffing; numbness, tingling, or pain in face, hands, or feet; paranoia (feelings of persecution); puffing of cheeks; rapid or worm-like movements of tongue; trembling or shaking; trouble in walking; uncontrolled movements of arms and legs

Other side effects may occur that usually do not need medical attention. These side effects may go away during treatment as your body adjusts to the medicine. Also, your health care professional may be able to tell you about ways to prevent or reduce some of these side effects. However, check with your doctor if any of the following side effects continue or are bothersome:

More common
Diarrhea; metallic taste; nausea
Less common
Anxiety or nervousness; dizziness; headache; mental depression; nightmares; pain in joints or muscles; skin rash or itching; trouble in sleeping; unusual tiredness or sleepiness; vomiting

Levamisole may cause a temporary loss of hair in some people. After treatment has ended, normal hair growth should return.

Other side effects not listed above may also occur in some patients. If you notice any other effects, check with your doctor.

Revised: 02/20/2001

LEVETIRACETAM   Systemic

Commonly used brand name(s):

In the U.S.—
Keppra

Description

Levetiracetam (lev-a-tir-ASS-a-tam) is used to help control some types of seizures in the treatment of epilepsy. This medicine cannot cure epilepsy and will only work to control seizures for as long as you continue to take it.

This medicine is available only with your doctor's prescription, in the following dosage forms:

Oral
- Tablets (U.S.)

Before Using This Medicine

In deciding to use a medicine, the risks of taking the medicine must be weighed against the good it will do. This is a decision you and your doctor will make. For levetiracetam the following should be considered:

Allergies—Tell your doctor if you have ever had any unusual or allergic reaction to levetiracetam. Also tell your doctor and pharmacist if you are allergic to any other substances, such as foods, preservatives, or dyes.

Pregnancy—Levetiracetam has not been studied in pregnant women. However, studies in animals have shown that levetiracetam causes birth defects. Before taking this medicine, make sure your doctor knows if you are pregnant or if you may become pregnant.

Breast-feeding— It is not known whether levetiracetam passes into breast milk. Although most medicines pass into breast milk in small amounts, many of them may be used safely while breast-feeding. Mothers who are taking this medicine and who wish to breast-feed should discuss this with their doctor.

Children—Studies on this medicine have been done only in adult patients, and there is no specific information comparing use of levetiracetam in children with use in other age groups.

Older adults—This medicine has been tested in a limited number of patients 65 years of age and older and has not been shown to cause different side effects or problems in older people than it does in younger adults.

Other medicines—Although certain medicines should not be used together at all, in other cases two different medicines may be used together even if an interaction might occur. In these cases, your doctor may want to change the dose, or other precautions may be necessary. Tell your health care professional if you are taking any other prescription or nonprescription (over-the-counter [OTC]) medicine.

Other medical problems—The presence of other medical problems may affect the use of levetiracetam. Make sure you tell your doctor if you have any other medical problems, especially:

- Kidney problems—Higher blood levels of levetiracetam may occur, which may increase the chance of unwanted effects; your doctor may need to change your dose.

Proper Use of This Medicine

Take this medicine only as directed by your doctor, to help your condition as much as possible. Do not take it more or less often than your doctor ordered.

Levetiracetam may be taken with or without food or on a full or empty stomach. However, if your doctor tells you to take the medicine a certain way, take it exactly as directed.

Dosing—The dose of levetiracetam will be different for different patients. *Follow your doctor's orders or the directions on the label.* The following information includes only the average doses of levetiracetam. *If your dose is different, do not change it* unless your doctor tells you to do so.

- For *oral* dosage form (tablets):
  —For epilepsy:
    - Adults—At first, 500 milligrams (mg) two times a day. Your doctor may increase the dose gradually if needed. However, the dose is usually not more than 3000 mg a day.
    - Children—Use and dose must be determined by your doctor.

Missed dose—If you miss a dose of this medicine, take it as soon as possible. However, if it is less than 2 hours until your next dose, take the missed dose right away, and take the next dose 1 to 2 hours later. Then go back to your regular dosing schedule. Do not double doses.

Storage—To store this medicine:

- Keep out of the reach of children.
- Store away from heat and direct light.
- Do not store in the bathroom, near the kitchen sink, or in other damp places. Heat or moisture may cause the medicine to break down.
- Do not keep outdated medicine or medicine no longer needed. Ask your health care professional how you should dispose of any medicine you do not use. Be sure that any discarded medicine is out of the reach of children.

Precautions While Using This Medicine

It is important that your doctor check your progress at regular visits, especially for the first few months you take levetiracetam. This is necessary to allow dose adjustments and to reduce any unwanted effects.

This medicine may cause some people to become drowsy, dizzy, or less alert than they are normally. *Make sure you know how you react to this medicine before you drive, use machines, or do anything else that could be dangerous if you are dizzy or are not alert*

Do not stop taking levetiracetam without first checking with your doctor. Stopping the medicine suddenly may cause your seizures to return or to occur more often. Your doctor may want you to gradually reduce the amount you are taking before stopping completely.

Side Effects of This Medicine

Along with its needed effects, a medicine may cause some unwanted effects. Although not all of these side effects may occur, if they do occur they may need medical attention.

Check with your doctor as soon as possible if any of the following side effects occur:
Less common
  Clumsiness or unsteadiness; cough or hoarseness; crying; depersonalization; depression; double vision; fever or chills; headache; loss of memory or problems with memory; lower back or side pain; mood or mental changes; nervousness; outburst of anger; pain or tenderness around eyes and cheekbones; painful or difficult urination; paranoia; problems with muscle control or coordination; quick to react or overreact; rapidly changing emotional moods; shortness of breath or troubled breathing; stuffy or runny nose; tightness of chest or wheezing

Other side effects may occur that usually do not need medical attention. These side effects may go away during treatment as your body adjusts to the medicine. However, check with your doctor if any of the following side effects continue or are bothersome:
More common
  Cough; dizziness; dryness or soreness of throat; fever; hoarseness; loss of strength or energy; muscle pain or weakness; pain; runny nose; sleepiness or unusual drowsiness; tender, swollen glands in neck; trouble in swallowing; unusual weak feeling; voice changes
Less common
  Burning, crawling, itching, numbness, prickling, "pins and needles," or tingling feelings; cough increased; dizziness or light-headedness; feeling of constant movement of self or surroundings; loss of appetite; sensation of spinning; weight loss;

Other side effects not listed above may also occur in some patients. If you notice any other effects, check with your doctor.

Developed: 04/14/2000

LEVOBETAXOLOL   Ophthalmic†

Commonly used brand name(s):
In the U.S.—
  Betaxon
Another commonly used name is
L-betaxolol

†Not commercially available in Canada.

Description

Levobetaxolol (lee-voh-be-TAKS-oh-lol) is used to treat glaucoma and other conditions of the eye in which the pressure in the eye is too high (ocular hypertension).

This medicine is available only with your doctor's prescription, in the following dosage form:

Ophthalmic
- Ophthalmic suspension (eye drops) (U.S.)

Before Using This Medicine

In deciding to use a medicine, the risks of using the medicine must be weighed against the good it will do. This is a decision you and your doctor will make. For levobetaxolol, the following should be considered:

Allergies—Tell your doctor if you have ever had any unusual or allergic reaction to levobetaxolol or any other beta-adrenergic receptor blocking agent. Also tell your health care professional if you are allergic to any other substances, such as foods, preservatives, or dyes.

Pregnancy—Levobetaxolol has not been studied in pregnant women. However, studies in animals have shown that levobetaxolol causes birth defects and fertility problems. Before taking this medicine, make sure your doctor knows if you are pregnant or if you may become pregnant.

Breast-feeding—It is not known whether levobetaxolol passes into human breast milk. Although most medicines pass into breast milk in small amounts, many of them may be safely used while breast-feeding. Mothers who are taking this medicine and wish to breast-feed should discuss this with their doctor.

Children—Studies on this medicine have been done only in adult patients. There is no specific information comparing use of levobetaxolol in children with use in other age groups.

Older adults—This medicine has been tested and has not been shown to cause different side effects or problems in older people than it does in younger adults.

Other medicines—Although certain medicines should not be used together at all, in other cases two different medicines may be used together even if an interaction might occur. In these cases, your doctor may want to change the dose, or other precautions may be necessary. When you are taking levobetaxolol, it is especially important that your health care professional know if you are taking any of the following:

- Beta-adrenergic receptor blocking agents, systemic (acebutolol [e.g., Sectral], atenolol [e.g.,Tenormin], Betaxolol [e.g., Kerlone], Bisoprolol [e.g., Zebeta], Carteolol [e.g., Cartrol], Labetalol [e.g., Trandate], metoprolol [e.g., Lopressor], nadolol [e.g., Corgard], oxprenolol [e.g., Transicor], penbutolol [e.g., Levatol], pindolol [e.g.,Visken], propranolol [e.g., Inderal], sotalol [e.g., Betapace], or timolol [e.g., Blocadren]) or
- Reserpine (e.g., Serpalan)—Use of these medicines with levobetaxolol may increase the chance of side effects

Other medical problems—The presence of other medical problems may affect the use of levobetaxolol. Make sure you tell your doctor if you have any other medical problems, especially:

- Allergic reactions, severe (history of)—Levobetaxolol may reduce the effectiveness of the medicine (epinephrine) used to treat severe allergic reactions

- Asthma or other lung disease—Severe breathing problems may occur
- Diabetes mellitus (sugar diabetes) or
- Hypoglycemia (low blood sugar)—Levobetaxolol may cover up some of the signs and symptoms of low blood sugar
- Glaucoma, angle-closure—In patients with this type of glaucoma, levobetaxolol must be used with another type of medicine because it does not work well alone
- Heart block (history of) or
- Heart failure (history of)—Levobetaxolol may have a negative effect on heart rate and blood pressure
- Heart disease, severe—Levobetaxolol should not be used in patients with this condition
- Myasthenic conditions—Levobetaxolol may make muscle weakness worse
- Surgery, major—Levobetaxolol may lessen the heart's ability to tolerate the effects of the anesthetic (medicine to cause loss of feeling before and during surgery)
- Thyrotoxicosis (overactive thyroid)—Levobetaxolol may cover up some of the signs and symptoms of an overactive thyroid

Proper Use of This Medicine

If you wear contact lenses, make sure you take them out before using this medicine.

Shake the medicine well before using it.

To use:
- First, wash your hands. With the middle finger, apply pressure to the inside corner of the eye (and continue to apply pressure for 1 or 2 minutes after the medicine has been placed in the eye).Tilt the head back and with the index finger of the same hand, pull the lower eyelid away from the eye to form a pouch. Drop the medicine into the pouch and gently close the eyes. Do not blink. Keep the eyes closed for 1 or 2 minutes to allow the medicine to be absorbed.
- Immediately after using the eye drops, wash your hands to remove any medicine that may be on them.
- To keep the medicine as germ-free as possible, do not touch the dropper to any surface (including the eye). Also, keep the container tightly closed.

Dosing—The dose of ophthalmic levobetaxolol may be different for different patients. *Follow your doctor's orders or the directions on the label.* The following information includes only the average doses of levobetaxolol. *If your dose is different, do not change it* unless your doctor tells you to do so.

- For *ophthalmic* dosage form (suspension):
  —For open-angle glaucoma or ocular hypertension
    - Adults—Use one drop in each affected eye two times a day
    - Children—Use and dose must be determined by your doctor.

Missed dose—If you miss a dose of this medicine, apply it as soon as possible. However, if it is almost time for your next dose, skip the missed dose and go back to your regular dosing schedule. Do not double doses.

Storage—To store this medicine:
- Keep the bottle in an upright position.
- Keep out of the reach of children.

- Do not store in the bathroom, near the kitchen sink, or in other damp places. Heat or moisture may cause the medicine to break down.
- Protect from light.
- Do not keep outdated medicine or medicine no longer needed. Ask your health care professional how you should dispose of any medicine you do not use. Be sure that any discarded medicine is out of the reach of children.

Precautions While Using This Medicine

It is very important that your doctor check your progress at regular visits, to make sure that this medicine is working and to check for unwanted effects.

Before you have any kind of surgery, dental treatment, or emergency treatment, tell the medical doctor or dentist in charge that you are using this medicine. Using levobetaxolol during this time may cause an increased risk of side effects.

This medicine may cause blurred vision. It also may cause some people to become dizzy or lightheaded. *Make sure that you know how you react to this medicine before you drive, use machines, or do anything else that could be dangerous if you are not alert or able to see well.*

For patients with diabetes:
- *Levobetaxolol may cover up some of the signs of hypoglycemia (low blood sugar).* If you notice a change in the results of your blood or urine sugar tests or if you have any questions, check with your doctor.

Side Effects of This Medicine

Along with its needed effects, a medicine may cause some unwanted effects. Although not all of these side effects may occur, if they do occur they may need medical attention.

Check with your doctor immediately if any of the following side effects occur:
Less common
Difficult breathing, labored breathing, tightness in chest, wheezing, or shortness of breath; fast, pounding, or irregular heartbeat; slow or irregular heartbeat

Check with your doctor as soon as possible if any of the following side effects occur:
Less common
Accidental injury; ankle, knee, or great toe pain; ankle, knee, or great toe swelling; bloody or cloudy urine; blurred or decreased vision; breast pain; confusion, faintness, or lightheadedness; cough, mucus-producing; difficult, burning, or painful urination; dizziness; dry, puffy skin; earache, buzzing, or ringing in ears; fatigue with or without increased hunger, increased thirst, or increased urination; feeling of constant movement; fever or chills; headache with pounding in ears; loss of appetite; lower back or side pain; muscle stiffness or tightness; pain or tenderness around eyes or cheekbones; red, scaling, or crusted skin; runny or stuffy nose; weight gain

Other side effects may occur that usually do not need medical attention. These side effects may go away during treatment as your body adjusts to the medicine. However, check with your doctor if any of the following side effects continue or are bothersome.
More common
Eye pain and discomfort (when the medicine is applied)
Less common
Acid or sour stomach, with belching; change in taste; constipation; cough; difficulty in swallowing; dry skin; dryness or soreness of throat; ear pain; feeling very anxious or nervous; headache; heartburn and indigestion; hoarseness; pain, redness, warmth, or swelling of muscles; pain, swelling, redness, or stiffness of joints; thinning or loss of hair

Other side effects not listed above may also occur in some patients. If you notice any other effects, check with your doctor.

Developed: 05/10/00

LEVOCABASTINE   Ophthalmic

Commonly used brand name(s):

In the U.S.—
Livostin

In Canada—
Livostin

Description

Levocabastine (lee-voe-KAB-as-teen) is used to treat certain disorders of the eye caused by allergies. It works by preventing the effects of a substance called histamine, which is produced in certain cells in your eyes and which causes the allergic reaction.

Levocabastine is available only with your doctor's prescription, in the following dosage form:

Ophthalmic
- Ophthalmic suspension (eye drops) (U.S. and Canada)

Before Using This Medicine

In deciding to use a medicine, the risks of using the medicine must be weighed against the good it will do. This is a decision you and your doctor will make. For levocabastine, the following should be considered:

Allergies—Tell your doctor if you have ever had any unusual or allergic reaction to levocabastine. Also tell your health care professional if you are allergic to any other substances, such as preservatives.

Pregnancy—Levocabastine has not been studied in pregnant women. However, studies in animals have shown that levocabastine, when given in very high doses, causes birth defects. Before using this medicine, make sure your doctor knows if you are pregnant or if you may become pregnant.

Breast-feeding—Although levocabastine passes into the breast milk, it has not been reported to cause problems in nursing babies. However, be sure you have discussed the risks and benefits of the medicine with your doctor.

Children—Studies on this medicine have been done only in adult patients and there is no specific information comparing use of levocabastine in children up to 12 years of age with use in other age groups.

Older adults—Many medicines have not been studied specifically in older people. Therefore, it may not be known whether they work exactly the same way they do in younger adults or if they cause different side effects or problems in older people. There is no specific information comparing use of levocabastine in the elderly with use in other age groups.

Other medicines—Although certain medicines should not be used together at all, in other cases two different medicines may be used together even if an interaction might occur. In these cases, your doctor may want to change the dose, or other precautions may be necessary. Tell your health care professional if you are using any other prescription or nonprescription (over the-counter [OTC]) medicine.

Proper Use of This Medicine

To use the *eye drops:*
- First, wash your hands. Tilt the head back and, pressing your finger gently on the skin just beneath the lower eyelid, pull the lower eyelid away from the eye to make a space. Drop the medicine into this space. Let go of the eyelid and gently close the eyes. Do not blink. Keep the eyes closed for 1 or 2 minutes to allow the medicine to be absorbed by the eye.
- If you think you did not get the drop of medicine into your eye properly, use another drop.
- To keep the medicine as germ-free as possible, do not touch the applicator tip to any surface (including the eye). Also, keep the container tightly closed.

In order for this medicine to work properly, it must be used every day in regularly spaced doses as ordered by your doctor. A few days may pass before you begin to feel better.

Dosing—The dose of levocabastine will be different for different patients. *Follow your doctor's orders or the directions on the label.* The following information includes only the average dose of levocabastine. *If your dose is different, do not change it* unless your doctor tells you to do so.
- For *ophthalmic suspension (eye drops) dosage* form:
  —For eye allergy:
    - Adults and children 12 years of age and older— Use one drop in each eye four times a day.
    - Children up to 12 years of age—Use and dose must be determined by your doctor.

Missed dose—If you miss a dose of this medicine, use it as soon as possible. Then go back to your regular dosing schedule.

Storage—To store this medicine:
- Keep out of the reach of children.
- Store away from heat and direct light.
- Keep the medicine from freezing. Do not refrigerate.
- Do not keep outdated medicine or medicine no longer needed. Be sure that any discarded medicine is out of the reach of children.

Precautions While Using This Medicine

If your symptoms do not improve within 3 days or if your condition becomes worse, check with your doctor.

After application of this medicine to the eye, occasional stinging or burning may occur.

Side Effects of This Medicine

Along with its needed effects, a medicine may cause some unwanted effects. Although not all of these side effects may occur, if they do occur they may need medical attention.

Check with your doctor as soon as possible if any of the following side effects occur:
Less common
  Headache

Rare
  Change in vision or trouble in seeing; cough; eye pain; nausea; redness, tearing, discharge, or other eye irritation not present before therapy or becoming worse during therapy; skin rash; sore throat; swelling of eyelids; troubled breathing; unusual tiredness or weakness

Other side effects may occur that usually do not need medical attention. These side effects may go away during treatment as your body adjusts to the medicine. However, check with your doctor if any of the following side effects continue or are bothersome:
More common
  Burning or stinging when medicine is applied

Less common
  Dry eyes; dry mouth; feeling sleepy

Other side effects not listed above may also occur in some patients. If you notice any other effects, check with your doctor.

Developed: 08/11/94
Interim revision: 09/28/98

LEVODOPA   Systemic

Commonly used brand name(s):

In the U.S.—
Atamet[1]
Larodopa[2]

Sinemet[1]
Sinemet CR[1]

In Canada—
Apo-Levocarb[1]
Nu-Levocarb[1]

Sinemet[1]
Sinemet CR[1]

Note: For quick reference, the following medicines are numbered to match the corresponding brand names.

This information applies to the following medicines:
1. Carbidopa and Levodopa (kar-bi-DOE-pa and lee-voe-DOE-pa) ‡§
2. Levodopa (LEE-voe-doe-pa)

Description

Levodopa is used alone or in combination with carbidopa to treat Parkinson's disease, sometimes referred to as shaking palsy. Some patients require the combination of medicine, while others benefit from levodopa alone. By improving muscle control, this medicine allows more normal movements of the body.

Levodopa alone or in combination is available only with your doctor's prescription. It is available in the following dosage forms:

Oral
Carbidopa and Levodopa
- Tablets (U.S. and Canada)
- Extended-release tablets (U.S. and Canada)
Levodopa
- Tablets (U.S.)

Before Using This Medicine

In deciding to use a medicine, the risks of taking the medicine must be weighed against the good it will do. This is a decision you and your doctor will make. For levodopa and for carbidopa and levodopa combination, the following should be considered:

Allergies—Tell your doctor if you have ever had any unusual or allergic reaction to levodopa alone or in combination with carbidopa. Also tell your health care professional if you are allergic to any other substances, such as foods, preservatives, or dyes.

Diet—Since protein may interfere with the body's response to levodopa, high protein diets should be avoided. Intake of normal amounts of protein should be spaced equally throughout the day, or taken as directed by your doctor.

For patients taking levodopa by itself:

Pyridoxine (vitamin B_6) has been found to reduce the effects of levodopa when levodopa is taken by itself. This does not happen with the combination of carbidopa and levodopa. *If you are taking levodopa by itself, do not take vitamin products containing vitamin B_6 during treatment, unless prescribed by your doctor.*

Large amounts of pyridoxine are also contained in some foods such as bananas, egg yolks, lima beans, meats, peanuts, and whole grain cereals. Check with your doctor about how much of these foods you may have in your diet while you are taking levodopa. Also, ask your health care professional for help when selecting vitamin products.

Pregnancy—Studies have not been done in pregnant women. However, studies in animals have shown that levodopa affects the baby's growth both before and after birth if given during pregnancy in doses many times the human dose.

Breast-feeding—Levodopa, alone and in carbidopa and levodopa combination, passes into breast milk and may cause unwanted side effects in the nursing baby. Also, levodopa may reduce the flow of breast milk.

Children—Studies on this medicine have been done only in adult patients, and there is no specific information comparing use of levodopa or carbidopa in children with use in other age groups.

Older adults—Elderly people are especially sensitive to the effects of levodopa. This may increase the chance of side effects during treatment.

Other medicines—Although certain medicines should not be used together at all, in other cases two different medicines may be used together even if an interaction might occur. In these cases, your doctor may want to change the dose, or other precautions may be necessary. When you are taking levodopa or carbidopa and levodopa combination, it is especially important that your health care professional know if you are taking any of the following:

- Cocaine—Cocaine use by individuals taking levodopa, alone or in combination with carbidopa, may cause an irregular heartbeat

- Haloperidol (e.g., Haldol) or
- Phenothiazines (acetophenazine [e.g., Tindal], chlorpromazine [e.g., Thorazine], fluphenazine [e.g., Prolixin], mesoridazine [e.g., Serentil], perphenazine [e.g., Trilafon], prochlorperazine [e.g., Compazine], promazine [e.g., Sparine], promethazine [e.g., Phenergan], thioridazine [e.g., Mellaril], trifluoperazine [e.g., Stelazine], triflupromazine [e.g., Vesprin], trimeprazine [e.g., Temaril]) or
- Thioxanthenes (chlorprothixene [e.g., Taractan], thiothixene [e.g., Navane])—Taking these medicines with levodopa may lessen the effects of levodopa

- Monoamine oxidase (MAO) inhibitors (furazolidone [e.g., Furoxone], isocarboxazid [e.g., Marplan], phenelzine [e.g., Nardil], procarbazine [e.g., Matulane], tranylcypromine [e.g., Parnate])—Taking levodopa while you are taking or within 2 weeks of taking monoamine oxidase (MAO) inhibitors may cause sudden extremely high blood pressure; at least 14 days should be allowed between stopping treatment with one medicine and starting treatment with the other medicine

- Pyridoxine (vitamin B_6 [e.g., Hexa-Betalin]), present in some foods and vitamin formulas (for levodopa used alone)—Pyridoxine reverses the effects of levodopa

- Selegiline—Dosage of levodopa or carbidopa and levodopa combination may need to be decreased

Other medical problems—The presence of other medical problems may affect the use of levodopa. Make sure you tell your doctor if you have any other medical problems, especially:

- Diabetes mellitus (sugar diabetes)—The amount of insulin or antidiabetic medicine that you need to take may change
- Emphysema, asthma, bronchitis, or other chronic lung disease or
- Glaucoma or
- Heart or blood vessel disease or
- Hormone problems or
- Melanoma (a type of skin cancer) (or history of) or
- Mental illness—Levodopa may make the condition worse
- Kidney disease or
- Liver disease—Higher blood levels of levodopa may occur, increasing the chance of side effects
- Seizure disorders, such as epilepsy (history of)—The risk of seizures may be increased
- Stomach ulcer (history of)—The ulcer may occur again

Proper Use of This Medicine

At first, levodopa may be taken with a meal or a snack, so that any effects like stomach upset will be lessened. Later, as your body becomes accustomed to the medicine, it should be taken on an empty stomach so that it works better. Be sure to talk to your doctor about the best time for you to take this medicine.

Take this medicine only as directed. Do not take more or less of it, and do not take it more often than your doctor ordered.

For patients taking *carbidopa and levodopa extended-release tablets:*

- Swallow the tablet whole without crushing or chewing, unless your doctor tells you not to. If your doctor tells you to, you may break the tablet in half.

Some people must take this medicine for several weeks or months before full benefit is received. *Do not stop taking it even if you do not think it is working.* Instead, check with your doctor.

Dosing—The dose of levodopa or carbidopa and levodopa combination will be different for different patients. *Follow your doctor's orders or the directions on the label.* The following information includes only the average doses of levodopa or carbidopa and levodopa combination. *If your dose is different, do not change it* unless your doctor tells you to do so.

The number of tablets that you take depends on the strength of the medicine. Also, *the number of doses you take each day, the time allowed between doses, and the length of time you take the medicine depend on your special needs.*
For levodopa
- For Parkinson's disease:
  —For *oral* dosage form (tablets):
    - Adults and teenagers—At first, 250 milligrams (mg) two to four times a day. Your doctor may increase your dose if needed. However, the dose is usually not more than 8000 mg (8 grams) a day.
    - Children up to 12 years of age—Use and dose must be determined by your doctor.

For levodopa and carbidopa combination
- For Parkinson's disease:
  —For *oral tablet* dosage form:
    - Adults—At first, 1 tablet three or four times a day. Your doctor may need to change your dose, depending on how you respond to this combination medicine.
    - Children and teenagers—Use and dose must be determined by your doctor.
  —For *oral extended-release tablet* dosage form:
    - Adults—At first, 1 tablet two times a day. However, you may need to take more than this. Your doctor will decide the right dose for you, depending on your condition and the other medicines you may be taking for Parkinson's disease.
    - Children and teenagers—Use and dose must be determined by your doctor.

Missed dose—If you miss a dose of this medicine, take it as soon as possible. However, if your next scheduled dose is within 2 hours, skip the missed dose and go back to your regular dosing schedule. Do not double doses.

Storage—To store this medicine:
- Keep out of the reach of children.
- Store away from heat and direct light.
- Do not store in the bathroom, near the kitchen sink, or in other damp places. Heat or moisture may cause the medicine to break down.
- Do not keep outdated medicine or medicine no longer needed. Be sure that any discarded medicine is out of the reach of children.

Precautions While Using This Medicine

Before having any kind of surgery (including dental surgery) or emergency treatment, tell the medical doctor or dentist in charge that you are taking this medicine.

For *patients with diabetes:*
- This medicine may cause test results for urine sugar or ketones to be wrong. Check with your doctor before depending on home tests using the paper-strip or tablet method.

This medicine may cause some people to become dizzy, confused, or have blurred or double vision. *Make sure you know how you react to this medicine before you drive, use machines, or do anything else that could be dangerous if you are not alert or not able to see well.*

Dizziness, lightheadedness, or fainting may occur, especially when you get up from a lying or sitting position. Getting up slowly may help. If the problem continues or gets worse, check with your doctor.

For patients taking levodopa by itself:
- Pyridoxine (vitamin B_6) has been found to reduce the effects of levodopa when levodopa is taken by itself. This does not happen with the combination of carbidopa and levodopa. *If you are taking levodopa by itself, do not take vitamin products containing vitamin B_6 during treatment, unless prescribed by your doctor.*
- Large amounts of pyridoxine are also contained in some foods such as bananas, egg yolks, lima beans, meats, peanuts, and whole grain cereals. Check with your doctor about how much of these foods you may have in your diet while you are taking levodopa. Also, ask your health care professional for help when selecting vitamin products.

As your condition improves and your body movements become easier, *be careful not to overdo physical activities. Injuries resulting from falls may occur.* Physical activities must be increased gradually to allow your body to adjust to changing balance, circulation, and coordination. *This is especially important in the elderly.*

Side Effects of This Medicine

Along with its needed effects, a medicine may cause some unwanted effects. Although not all of these side effects may occur, if they do occur they may need medical attention.

Check with your doctor as soon as possible if any of the following side effects occur:
More common
  Abnormal thinking: holding false beliefs that cannot be changed by fact; agitation; anxiety; clenching or grinding of teeth; clumsiness or unsteadiness; confusion; difficulty swallowing; dizziness; excessive watering of mouth; false sense of well being; feeling faint; general feeling of discomfort or illness; hallucinations (seeing, hearing, or feeling things that are not there); hand tremor, increased; nausea or vomiting; numbness; unusual and uncontrolled movements of the body, including the face, tongue, arms, hands, head, and upper body; unusual tiredness or weakness

Less common
  Blurred vision; difficult urination; difficulty opening

mouth; dilated (large) pupils; dizziness or lightheadedness when getting up from a lying or sitting position; double vision; fast, irregular, or pounding heartbeat; hot flashes; increased blinking or spasm of eyelids; loss of bladder control; mental depression; other mood or mental changes; skin rash; unusual weight gain or loss

Rare

Back or leg pain; bloody or black tarry stools; chills; convulsions (seizures); fever; high blood pressure; inability to move eyes; loss of appetite; pain, tenderness, or swelling of foot or leg; pale skin; prolonged, painful, inappropriate penile erection; sore throat; stomach pain; swelling of face; swelling of feet or lower legs; vomiting of blood or material that looks like coffee grounds

Other side effects may occur that usually do not need medical attention. These side effects may go away during treatment as your body adjusts to the medicine. However, check with your doctor if any of the following side effects continue or are bothersome:

More common

Abdominal pain; dryness of mouth; loss of appetite; nightmares; passing gas

Less common

Constipation; diarrhea; flushing of skin; headache; hiccups; increased sweating; muscle twitching; trouble in sleeping

This medicine may sometimes cause the urine, saliva, and sweat to be darker in color than usual. The urine may at first be reddish, then turn to nearly black after being exposed to air. Some bathroom cleaning products will produce a similar effect when in contact with urine containing this medicine. This is to be expected during treatment with this medicine. Also, this medicine may cause a bitter taste, or a burning sensation of the tongue.

Other side effects not listed above may also occur in some patients. If you notice any other effects, check with your doctor.

Revised: 06/15/99

LEVODOPA AND BENSERAZIDE
Systemic—INTRODUCTORY VERSION

Commonly used brand name(s):

In Canada—
　　Prolopa®

Description

Levodopa and Benserazide (lee-voe-DOE-pa AND ben-sir-A-zide) is used to treat Parkinson's disease, sometimes called shaking palsy or paralysis agitans. This medicine works to increase and extend the effects of levodopa, and may help to slow the progress of Parkinson's disease.

This medicine is available only with your doctor's prescription, in the following dosage forms:

Oral
- Capsules (Canada)

Before Using This Medicine

Diet—Since protein may interfere with the body's response to levodopa, high protein diets should be avoided. Intake of normal amounts of protein should be spaced equally throughout the day, or taken as directed by your doctor.

Pregnancy—Studies have not been done in pregnant women. However, studies in animals have shown that levodopa affects the baby's growth both before and after birth if given during pregnancy.

Breast-feeding—Levodopa and benserazide passes into breast milk and may cause unwanted side effects in the nursing baby. Also, levodopa may reduce the flow of breast milk.

Children—Studies on this medicine have been done only in adult patients, and there is no specific information comparing use of levodopa or benserazide in children with use in other age groups.

Other medicines—Although certain medicines should not be used together at all, in other cases two different medicines may be used together even if an interaction might occur. In these cases, your doctor may want to change the dose, or other precautions may be necessary. When you are taking levodopa and benserazide, it is especially important that your doctor and pharmacist know if you are taking any of the following:

Other medications, especially anesthetics, antihypertensive agents, MAO inhibitors, reserpine, phenothiazines, psychotherapeutic agents, sympathomimetics, and tricyclic antidepressants; high-protein foods.

- Anesthetics

- Antihypertensive agents—May decrease blood pressure even more as seen with levodopa therapy

- Monoamine oxidase (MAO) inhibitors—Taking levodopa while you are taking or within 2 weeks of taking monoamine oxidase (MAO) inhibitors may cause sudden extremely high blood pressure

- Reserpine or
- Phenothiazines or
- Tricyclic antidepressants—Levodopa and benserazide therapy may make the patients depression worse or increase the risk of suicidal tendencies

Tell your health care professional if you are taking any other prescription or nonprescription (over-the-counter [OTC]) medicine."

Other medical problems—The presence of other medical problems may affect the use of levodopa and benserazide. Make sure you tell your doctor if you have any other medical problems, especially:

- Blood disorder or
- History of heart attack or arrhythmias or
- Kidney disease or
- Liver disease or
- Melanoma (a type of skin cancer) (or history of) or
- Mental illness—Levodopa may make the condition worse

- Seizure disorders, such as epilepsy (history of)—The risk of seizures may be increased

- Stomach ulcer (history of)—The ulcer may occur again

Proper Use of This Medicine

At first, levodopa and benserazide may be taken with a meal or a snack, so that any effects like stomach upset will be lessened. Later, as your body becomes accustomed to the medicine, it should be taken on an empty stomach so that it works better. Be sure to talk to your doctor about the best time for you to take this medicine.

The levodopa and benserazide capsules should be swallowed whole and not opened or dissolved in liquid.

Take this medicine only as directed. Do not take more or less of it, and do not take it more often than your doctor ordered.

Some people must take this medicine for several weeks or months before full benefit is received. *Do not stop taking it even if you do not think it is working*. Instead, check with your doctor.

Dosing—The dose of levodopa or carbidopa and levodopa combination will be different for different patients. *Follow your doctor's orders or the directions on the label*. The following information includes only the average doses of levodopa or carbidopa and levodopa combination. *If your dose is different, do not change it* unless your doctor tells you to do so.

The number of tablets that you take depends on the strength of the medicine. Also, *the number of doses you take each day, the time allowed between doses, and the length of time you take the medicine depend on your special needs*.

For levodopa and benserazide
- For Parkinson's disease—start of therapy:
  —For *oral* dosage form (capsules):
    - Adults—At first, 1 capsule of Prolopa® 100–25 (levodopa 100 milligrams (mg) and benserazide 25 mg) twice daily. Your doctor may increase your dose if needed. However, the dose is usually not more than 4 to 8 capsules of Prolopa® 100–25 per day (400 to 800 mg levodopa) divided into 4 to 6 doses. If you are already on levodopa, the doctor will start you on a lower dose of Prolopa®. After time, the previous levodopa therapy will be replaced with the levodopa and benserazide combination.
    - Children up to 18 years of age—Use and dose must be determined by your doctor.

- For Parkinson's disease—maintain therapy:
  —For *oral* dosage form (capsules):
    - Adults—After several weeks, the doctor will determine your optimal dose of levodopa and benserazide. Your doctor may then switch you to Prolopa® 200–50 (levodopa 200 milligrams (mg) and benserazide 50 mg) to make it more convenient to match your optimal dose. Some patients may require frequent dosing in which case your doctor may use Prolopa® 50–12.5 (50 mg levodopa and 12.5 mg benserazide). Frequent dosing may be used to maximize your dose and minimize any side effects. During the first year of therapy, the total daily dose of levodopa should not exceed 1000 to 1200 mg.
    - Children up to 18 years of age—Use and dose must be determined by your doctor.

Missed dose—If you miss a dose of this medicine, take it as soon as possible. However, if your next scheduled dose is within 2 hours, skip the missed dose and go back to your regular dosing schedule. Do not double doses.

Storage—To store this medicine:
- Keep out of the reach of children.
- Store away from heat and direct light.
- Do not store in the bathroom, near the kitchen sink, or in other damp places. Heat or moisture may cause the medicine to break down.
- Do not keep outdated medicine or medicine no longer needed. Be sure that any discarded medicine is out of the reach of children.

Precautions While Using This Medicine

Before having any kind of surgery (including dental surgery) or emergency treatment, tell the medical doctor or dentist in charge that you are taking this medicine.

This medicine may cause some people to become dizzy, confused, or have blurred or double vision. *Make sure you know how you react to this medicine before you drive, use machines, or do anything else that could be dangerous if you are not alert or not able to see well.*

Dizziness, light-headedness, or fainting may occur, especially when you get up from a lying or sitting position. Getting up slowly may help. If the problem continues or gets worse, check with your doctor.

As your condition improves and your body movements become easier, *be careful not to overdo physical activities. Injuries resulting from falls may occur.* Physical activities must be increased gradually to allow your body to adjust to changing balance, circulation, and coordination. *This is especially important in the elderly.*

Side Effects of This Medicine

Along with its needed effects, a medicine may cause some unwanted effects. Although not all of these side effects may occur, if they do occur they may need medical attention.

Check with your doctor immediately if any of the following side effects occur:
  More common
    Absence of or decrease in body movement; increased blinking or twitching of eyelids; involuntary movements of the limbs and facial muscles; disorder marked especially by sadness, inactivity, difficulty with thinking and concentration, or feelings of dejec-

tion and hopelessness; twitching, twisting, uncontrolled repetitive movements of tongue, lips, face, arms, or legs; inability to move eyes increased blinking or spasms; sudden freezing, hypotonia and postural instability; , muscle twitching; fearfulness, suspiciousness, or other mental changes; agitation, delusions, hallucinations

Less common
A condition where you have a constricted pupil, drooping of the upper eyelid, an absence of sweating over the affected side of the face; a twisting of the neck to one side; bleeding gums; blurred vision; burning while urinating; change in the color of urine or blood in urine; chest pain or tightness; chills, swollen neck, and sore throat sometimes with local ulceration; color changes in skin color; confusion, dizziness, faintness, or light-headedness when getting up from lying or sitting position; difficulty in swallowing; dizziness; fainting; fast, slow, or irregular heartbeat; flushing; inability to move eyes; nosebleeds; pain or tenderness swelling of foot or leg; pounding feeling in the ears; seizures; severe stomach pain; stomach pain or ulcer; swollen glands; unusual bleeding or bruising; unusual tiredness or weakness; vomiting of blood or material that looks like coffee grounds

Other side effects may occur that usually do not need medical attention. These side effects may go away during treatment as your body adjusts to the medicine. However, check with your doctor if any of the following side effects continue or are bothersome.

Less common
Absence of or decrease in body movement loss or impairment of voluntary activity; belching; bitter taste; bizarre breathing; bloating or swelling of face, hands, lower legs, and/or feet; blurred vision; burning sensation of the tongue; change in urinary frequency; change in walking and balance; clenching, gnashing, or grinding teeth; constipation; cough; dark sweat; dark urine; decrease in urine production; diarrhea; dilated pupils; double vision; dry mouth; excessive watering of mouth; false or unusual sense of well-being; fatigue and malaise; fever; general feeling of discomfort or illness; hair loss; hallucinations and delusion; headache; hiccups; hoarseness; impairment in ability to think; increased hand tremor; increased in sexual ability or desire; loss of bladder control; low back pain; mood or mental changes; muscle or bone pain; muscle spasm and twitching; nervousness, restlessness, irritability, insomnia; passing gas; rash; shakiness and unsteady walk, clumsiness, trembling problems with muscle control or coordination; stomach problems; tightness of the mouth, lips or tongue; trouble sleeping; unusual tiredness or weakness

Other side effects not listed above may also occur in some patients. If you notice any other effects, check with your doctor.

Developed: 10/11/2000

LEVOFLOXACIN Ophthalmic— INTRODUCTORY VERSION

Commonly used brand name(s):

In the U.S.—
Quixin

Description

Ophthalmic levofloxacin (lee-voh-FLOKS-a-sin) is used in the eye to treat bacterial infections of the eye. Ophthalmic levofloxacin works by killing bacteria.

This medicine is available only with your doctor's prescription, in the following dosage form:

Ophthalmic
• Ophthalmic solution (eye drops) (U.S.)

Before Using This Medicine

In deciding to use a medicine, the risks of using the medicine must be weighed against the good it will do. This is a decision you and your doctor will make. For levofloxacin, the following should be considered:

Allergies—Tell your doctor if you have ever had any unusual or allergic reaction to levofloxacin or any related medicines, such as cinoxacin (e.g., Cinobac), ciprofloxacin (e.g., Cipro or Ciloxan), norfloxacin (e.g., Chibroxin or Noroxin), ofloxacin (e.g., Floxin), or nalidixic acid (e.g., NegGram). Also tell your health care professional if you are allergic to any other substances, such as foods, preservatives, or dyes.

Pregnancy—Levofloxacin has not been studied in pregnant women. Before taking this medicine, make sure your doctor knows if you are pregnant or if you may become pregnant.

Breast-feeding—It is not known whether levofloxacin passes into breast milk. However, similar medicines do pass into breast milk. Be sure you have discussed the risks and benefits with your doctor.

Children—Use is not recommended in infants under 1 year of age. In children older than 1 year, this medicine is not expected to cause different side effects or problems than it does in adults.

Older adults—Many medicines have not been studied specifically in older people. Therefore, it may not be known whether they work exactly the same way they do in younger adults. Although there is no specific information comparing use of levofloxacin in the elderly with use in other age groups, this medicine is not expected to cause different side effects or problems in older people than it does in younger adults.

Other medicines—Although certain medicines should not be used together at all, in other cases two different medicines may be used together even if an interaction might occur. In these cases, your doctor may want to change the dose, or other precautions may be necessary. Tell your health care professional if you using any other prescription or nonprescription (over-the-counter [OTC]) medicine that is to be used in the eye.

Proper Use of This Medicine

Dosing—To use levofloxacin ophthalmic solution (eye drops):

- First, wash your hands. Then tilt the head back and pull the lower eyelid away from the eye to form a pouch. Drop the medicine into the pouch and gently close the eyes. Do not blink. Keep the eyes closed for 1 or 2 minutes to allow the medicine to come into contact with the infection.
- If you think you did not get the drop of medicine into your eyes properly, use another drop.
- To keep the medicine as germ-free as possible, do not touch the applicator tip to any surface (including the eye). Also, keep the container tightly closed.

To help clear up your eye infection completely, *keep using ophthalmic levofloxacin for the full time of treatment,* even if your symptoms have disappeared. *Do not miss any doses. Follow your doctor's orders or the directions on the label.* The following information includes only the average doses of levofloxacin. *If your dose is different, do not change it* unless your doctor tells you to do so.

The number of doses you take each day, the time allowed between doses, and the length of time you take the medicine depend on the medical problem for which you are taking levofloxacin.

- For *ophthalmic solution* dosage form:
  —For bacterial conjunctivitis:
  - Adults and children 1 year of age and older—Days 1 and 2: Put one to two drops in the affected eye(s) every two hours while awake. Do not put drops in more than 8 times a day. Days 3 through 7: Put one to two drops in the affected eye(s) every 4 hours while awake. Do not put drops in more than 4 times a day.
  - Infants and children up to 1 year of age—Use and dose must be determined by your doctor.

Missed dose— If you miss a dose of this medicine, use it as soon as possible. However, if it is almost time for your next dose, skip the missed dose and go back to your regular dosing schedule.

Storage—To store this medicine:

- Keep out of the reach of children.
- Store away from heat and direct light.
- Keep the medicine from freezing. Do not refrigerate.
- Do not keep outdated medicine or medicine no longer needed. Ask your health care professional how you should dispose of any medicine you do not use. Be sure that any discarded medicine is out of the reach of children.

Precautions While Using This Medicine

If your eye infection does not improve within a few days, or if it becomes worse, check with your doctor.

This medicine may cause your eyes to become more sensitive to light than they are normally. Wearing sunglasses and avoiding too much exposure to bright light may help lessen the discomfort.

Side Effects of This Medicine

Along with its needed effects, a medicine may cause some unwanted side effects. Many side effects that occur do not need medical attention. These side effects may go away during treatment as your body adjusts to the medicine. However, check with your doctor if any of the following side effects continue or are bothersome.

Less common

Itching, pain, redness or swelling of eye or eyelid; watering of eyes; decreased vision; fever; feeling of having something in the eye; headache; hoarseness; eye burning, dryness, itching, or pain; increased sensitivity of eyes to light; body aches or pain; congestion; dryness or soreness of throat; runny nose; swelling of the eyelid; tender, swollen glands in neck; trouble in swallowing; voice changes

Other side effects not listed above may also occur in some patients. If you notice any other effects, check with your doctor.

Developed: 10/20/2000

LIDOCAINE   Topical

Commonly used brand name(s):

In the U.S.—
    Lidoderm

Description

Lidocaine (LYE-doe-kane) belongs to the family of medicines called local anesthetics (an-ess-THET-iks). When lidocaine is applied to the skin, it produces numbness by deadening the nerve endings in the skin. Lidocaine topical systems are used to relieve pain and discomfort associated with herpes zoster virus infection of the skin (shingles).

Lidocaine is available only with your doctor's prescription, in the following dosage form(s):

Topical
- Topical system (U.S.)

Before Using This Medicine

In deciding to use a medicine, the risks of taking the medicine must be weighed against the good it will do. This is a decision you and your doctor will make. For lidocaine, the following should be considered:

Allergies—Tell your doctor if you have ever had any unusual or allergic reaction to lidocaine or other local anesthetics given by injection or applied to any part of the body as a liquid, cream, ointment, or spray. Also tell your health care professional if you are allergic to any other substances, such as foods, preservatives, or dyes.

Pregnancy—Lidocaine has not been studied in pregnant women. However, lidocaine has not been shown to cause birth defects or other problems in animal studies.

Breast-feeding—Small amounts of lidocaine pass into breast milk. Many medicines that pass into breast milk in small amounts may be used safely while breast-feeding.

Mothers who are using this medicine and who wish to breast-feed should discuss this with their doctor.

Children—Studies on this medicine have been done only in adult patients, and there is no specific information comparing use of lidocaine topical systems in children with use in other age groups.

Older adults—Many medicines have not been studied specifically in older people. Therefore, it may not be known whether they work exactly the same way they do in younger adults or if they cause different side effects or problems in older people. There is no specific information comparing use of lidocaine topical systems in the elderly with use in other age groups.

Other medicines—Although certain medicines should not be used together at all, in other cases two different medicines may be used together even if an interaction might occur. In these cases, your doctor may want to change the dose, or other precautions may be necessary. When you are using lidocaine topical systems, it is especially important that your health care professional know if you are taking or using any other prescription or nonprescription medicine.

Other medical problems—The presence of other medical problems may affect the use of lidocaine topical systems. Make sure to tell your doctor if you have any other medical problems, especially:

- Broken or inflamed skin, burns, or open wounds at the place of application—More of this medicine can be absorbed into the body quickly, which increases the chance of side effects
- Liver disease (severe)—The risk of side effects may be increased because of slower removal of lidocaine from the body

Proper Use of This Medicine

Unless otherwise directed by your health care professional, do not apply this medicine to open wounds, burns or broken or inflamed skin.

Be careful not to get any of this medicine in your eyes, because it can cause severe eye irritation. If any of the medicine does get into your eye, immediately wash out the eye with water and protect the eye until sensation returns. Check with your doctor.

Use only as directed by your health care professional; avoid applying more than the recommended number of topical systems or using the topical systems for longer than the recommended wearing time.

Clothing may be worn over the area of application.

Dosing—The dose of lidocaine topical systems will be different for different patients. *Follow your doctor's orders or the directions on the label.* The following information includes only the average doses of lidocaine topical systems. If your dose is different, *do not change it* unless your doctor tells you to do so.

For relieving pain caused by herpes zoster virus infection of the skin (shingles) in adult patients—Remove release liner and apply topical system to skin, covering the most painful area(s). Apply no more than 3 systems at one time and do not leave on for longer than twelve hours within a twenty-four hour period. Topical systems may be cut into smaller sizes with scissors prior to removal of the release liner.

Storage—To store this medicine:

- Keep out of the reach of children.
- Keep envelope sealed at all times when not in use.
- Store away from heat.
- Keep the medicine from freezing. Do not refrigerate.
- Do not keep outdated medicine or medicine no longer needed. Be sure that any discarded medicine is out of the reach of children and pets.

Precautions While Using This Medicine

If irritation or a burning sensation occurs during application, remove the system(s) and do not reapply until the irritation subsides.

Wash hands after handling systems.

Avoid contact with eyes.

Store and dispose of topical systems out of the reach of children and pets. Chewing or ingesting new or used topical systems could result in serious adverse effects.

Side Effects of This Medicine

Along with its needed effects, a medicine may cause some unwanted effects. Although not all of these side effects may occur, if they do occur they may need medical attention.

Get emergency help immediately if any of the following side effects occur:
  Symptoms of allergic reaction
    Rare
        Cough; difficulty swallowing or tongue swelling; dizziness or fainting; hives or swelling of eyelids, face or lips; itching or skin rash; stuffy nose; chest tightness, shortness of breath, troubled breathing, or wheezing

  Signs of too much medicine being absorbed into the body
    Rare
        Blurred or double vision; confusion; dizziness, light-headedness or drowsiness; feeling hot, cold, or numb; muscle twitching or trembling; nausea or vomiting; ringing or buzzing in the ears; shortness of breath or trouble breathing; unusual excitement, nervousness, or restlessness; unusual tiredness or weakness

    Note: The above side effects are not likely to occur when usual amounts of this medicine are used properly. However, they may occur if the medicine is used too often, applied to broken or inflamed skin, applied to very large areas, or kept on the skin too long.

Other side effects may occur that usually do not need medical attention. These side effects may go away during treatment as your body adjusts to the medicine. However, check with your doctor if any of the following side effects continue or are bothersome:
  More common
      Rash, hives, swelling, or abnormal sensation at the site of application

Other side effects not listed above may also occur in some patients. If you notice any other effects, check with your doctor.

Developed: 12/02/99

LINDANE   Topical

Commonly used brand name(s):

In the U.S.—

Bio-Well	Kwell
GBH	Kwildane
G-well	Scabene
Kildane	Thionex

Generic name product may be available.

In Canada—

GBH	Kwellada
Hexit	PMS Lindane

Another commonly used name for lindane is gamma benzene hexachloride.

Description

Lindane (LIN-dane), formerly known as gamma benzene hexachloride, is an insecticide and is used to treat scabies and lice infestations.

Lindane cream and lotion are usually used to treat only scabies infestation. Lindane shampoo is used to treat only lice infestations.

Lindane is available only with your doctor's prescription, in the following dosage forms:

Topical
- Cream (U.S. and Canada)
- Lotion (U.S. and Canada)
- Shampoo (U.S. and Canada)

Before Using This Medicine

In deciding to use a medicine, the risks of using the medicine must be weighed against the good it will do. This is a decision you and your doctor will make. For lindane, the following should be considered:

Allergies—Tell your doctor if you have ever had any unusual or allergic reaction to lindane. Also tell your health care professional if you are allergic to any other substances, such as preservatives or dyes.

Pregnancy—Lindane is absorbed through the skin and could possibly cause toxic effects in the central nervous system (CNS) of the unborn baby. *Use lindane only as directed by your doctor. Do not use more of it, do not use it more often, and do not use it for a longer time than your doctor ordered. In addition, you should not be treated with lindane more than twice during your pregnancy.*

Breast-feeding—Lindane is absorbed through the mother's skin and is present in breast milk. Even though lindane has not been reported to cause problems in nursing babies, you should use another method of feeding your baby for 2 days after you use lindane. Be sure you have discussed this with your doctor.

Children—Infants and children are especially sensitive to the effects of lindane. This may increase the chance of side effects during treatment. In addition, use of lindane is not recommended in premature infants.

Older adults—Absorption of lindane may be increased in the elderly. This may increase the chance of problems during treatment with this medicine.

Other medicines—Although certain medicines should not be used together at all, in other cases two different medicines may be used together even if an interaction might occur. In these cases, your doctor may want to change the dose, or other precautions may be necessary. When you are using lindane, it is especially important that your health care professional know if you are using any other prescription or nonprescription (over-the-counter [OTC]) medicine.

Other medical problems—The presence of other medical problems may affect the use of lindane. Make sure you tell your doctor if you have any other medical problems, especially:

- Seizure disorder—Use of lindane may make the condition worse
- Skin rash or raw or broken skin—Condition may increase the absorption of lindane and the chance of side effects

Proper Use of This Medicine

Lindane is poisonous. Keep it away from the mouth because it is harmful and may be fatal if swallowed.

Use lindane only as directed by your doctor. Do not use more of it, do not use it more often, and do not use it for a longer time than your doctor ordered. To do so may increase the chance of absorption through the skin and the chance of lindane poisoning.

Keep lindane away from the eyes. If you should accidentally get some in your eyes, flush them thoroughly with water at once and contact your doctor.

Do not use lindane on open wounds, such as cuts or sores on the skin or scalp. To do so may increase the chance of lindane poisoning.

When applying lindane to another person, you should wear plastic disposable or rubber gloves, especially if you are pregnant or are breast-feeding. This will prevent lindane from being absorbed through your skin. If you have any questions about this, check with your doctor.

Lindane usually comes with patient directions. Read them carefully before using lindane.

Your sexual partner or partners, especially, and all members of your household may need to be treated also, since the infestation may spread to persons in close contact. If these persons have not been checked for an infestation or if you have any questions about this, check with your doctor.

To use the *cream or lotion form of lindane for scabies:*
- If your skin has any cream, lotion, ointment, or oil on it, wash, rinse, and dry your skin well before applying lindane.
- If you take a warm bath or shower before using lindane, dry the skin well before applying it.
- Apply enough lindane to your dry skin to cover the entire skin surface from the neck down, including the soles of your feet, and rub in well.
- Leave lindane on for no more than 8 hours, then remove by washing thoroughly.

To use the *shampoo form of lindane for lice:*
- If your hair has any cream, lotion, ointment, or oil-based product on it, shampoo, rinse, and dry your hair and scalp well before applying lindane.
- If you apply this shampoo in the shower or in the bathtub, make sure the shampoo is not allowed to run down on other parts of your body. Also, do not apply this shampoo in a bathtub where the shampoo may run into the bath water in which you are sitting. To do so may increase

the chance of absorption through the skin. When you rinse out the shampoo, be sure to thoroughly rinse your entire body also to remove any shampoo that may have gotten on it.
- Apply enough shampoo to your dry hair (1 ounce or less for short hair, 1½ ounces for medium length hair, and 2 ounces or less for long hair) to thoroughly wet the hair and skin or scalp of the affected and surrounding hairy areas.
- Thoroughly rub the shampoo into the hair and skin or scalp and allow to remain in place for 4 minutes. Then, use just enough water to work up a good lather.
- Rinse thoroughly and dry with a clean towel.
- When the hair is dry, comb with a fine-toothed comb to remove any remaining nits (eggs) or nit shells.
- *Do not use as a regular shampoo.*

Dosing—*Follow your doctor's orders or the directions on the label*. The following information includes only the average doses of lindane. *If your dose is different, do not change it* unless your doctor tells you to do so.
- For cream and lotion dosage forms:
  —For scabies:
  - Adults and children—Apply to the affected area(s) of the skin one time.
  - Premature infants—Use is not recommended.
- For shampoo dosage form:
  —For lice:
  - Adults and children—Apply to the scalp or the affected area(s) of the skin one time. Treatment may be repeated after seven days if necessary.
  - Premature infants—Use is not recommended.

Storage—To store this medicine:
- Keep out of the reach of children.
- Store away from heat and direct light.
- Keep lindane from freezing.
- Do not keep outdated lindane or lindane no longer needed. Be sure that any discarded lindane is out of the reach of children.

Precautions While Using This Medicine

To help prevent reinfestation or spreading of the infestation to other persons:
- For scabies—All recently worn underwear and pajamas and used sheets, pillowcases, and towels should be washed in very hot water or dry-cleaned.
- For lice—All recently worn clothing and used bed linens and towels should be washed in very hot water or dry-cleaned.

Side Effects of This Medicine

In infants and children, the risk of lindane being absorbed through the skin and causing unwanted side effects is greater than in adults. In premature newborn infants, use of lindane is not recommended, because lindane may be more likely to be absorbed through their skin than through the skin of older infants. You should discuss these possible effects with your doctor.

Along with its needed effects, a medicine may cause some unwanted effects. Although not all of these side effects may occur, if they do occur they may need medical attention.

Check with your doctor as soon as possible if any of the following side effects occur:

Rare
Skin irritation not present before use of lindane; skin rash
Symptoms of lindane poisoning
Convulsions (seizures); dizziness, clumsiness, or unsteadiness; fast heartbeat; muscle cramps; nervousness, restlessness, or irritability; vomiting

After you stop using lindane, itching may occur and continue for 1 to several weeks. If this continues longer or is bothersome, check with your doctor.

Other side effects not listed above may also occur in some patients. If you notice any other effects, check with your doctor.

Revised: 08/15/94

LINEZOLID   Systemic— INTRODUCTORY VERSION

Commonly used brand name(s):
In the U.S.—
Zyvox

Description

Linezolid (li-NE-zoh-lid) belongs to the family of medicines called antibiotics. Antibiotics are medicines used in the treatment of infections caused by bacteria. They work by killing bacteria or preventing their growth. Linezolid will not work for colds, flu, or other virus infections.

Linezolid is used to treat infections of the blood, lungs, and skin. It may also be used for other conditions as determined by your doctor. It is given by injection or orally. It is used mainly for serious infection for which other medicines may not work.

This medicine is available only with your doctor's prescription, in the following dosage forms:
Oral
- Oral Suspension (U.S.)
- Tablets (U.S.)
Parenteral
- Injection (U.S.)

Before Using This Medicine

In deciding to use a medicine, the risks of taking the medicine must be weighed against the good it will do. This is a decision you and your doctor will make. For linezolid, the following should be considered:

Allergies—Tell your doctor if you have ever had any unusual or allergic reaction to linezolid. Also tell your health care professional if you are allergic to any other substances, such as foods, preservatives, or dyes.

Pregnancy—Linezolid has not been studied in pregnant women. Before taking this medicine, make sure your doctor knows if you are pregnant of if you may become pregnant.

Breast-feeding— It is not known whether linezolid passes into breast milk. Although most medicines pass into breast milk in small amounts, many of them may be used safely while breast-feeding. Mothers who are taking this medicine and who wish to breast-feed should discuss this with their doctor.

Children—Studies on this medicine have been done only in adult patients, and there is no specific information comparing use of linezolid in children with use in other age groups.

Older adults—This medicine has been tested and has not been shown to cause different side effects or problems in older people than it does in younger adults.

Other medicines—Although certain medicines should not be used together at all, in other cases two different medicines may be used together even if an interaction might occur. In these cases, your doctor may want to change the dose, or other precautions may be necessary. When you are taking linezolid, it is especially important that your health care professional know if you are taking any of the following:

- Citalopram (e.g., Celexa) or
- Clomipramine (e.g., Anafranil) or
- Fluvoxamine (e.g., Luvox) or
- Moclobemide (e.g., Manerix) or
- Monoamine oxidase (MAO) inhibitors (furazolidone [e.g., Furoxone], phenylzine [e.g., Nardil], procarbazine [e.g., Matulane], selegiline [e.g., Eldepryl], tranylcypromine [e.g., Parnate]) or
- Nefazodone (e.g., Serzone) or
- Paroxetine (e.g., Paxil) or
- Sertraline (e.g., Zoloft) or
- Sibutramine (e.g., Meridia) or
- Tryptophan (e.g., Alti-Tryptophan) or
- Venlafaxine (e.g., Effexor)—Using these medicines with linezolid may increase the chance of developing a rare, but very serious, unwanted effect known as the serotonin syndrome
- Pseudoephedrine (e.g., Rondex®, Sudafed®)—Using pseudoephedrine with linezolid may cause an increase in your blood pressure

Other medical problems—The presence of other medical problems may affect the use of linezolid. Make sure you tell your doctor if you have any other medical problems, especially:

- Phenylketonuria—The oral suspension contains phenylalanine, which may cause side effects; however, the other dosage forms do not contain phenylalanine

Proper Use of This Medicine

- The *liquid form of linezolid* should be gently mixed by turning the bottle upside down 3 to 5 times before each dose. Do not shake this product.
- Do not use after the expiration date on the label. The medicine may not work properly after that date. If you have any questions about this, check with your pharmacist.

To help clear up your infection completely, *keep taking this medicine for the full time of treatment*, even if you begin to feel better after a few days. Also, it works best when there is a constant amount in the blood. To help keep the amount constant, linezolid must be given on a regular schedule.

Dosing—The dose of linezolid will be different for different patients. *Follow your doctor's orders or the directions on the label. Also, the number of doses you take each day, the time allowed between doses, and the length of time you take the medicine depend on the medical problem for which you are taking linezolid.*

- For *oral* dosage forms:
  - Adults—400 or 600 mg every 12 hours.
  - Children—Dose must be determined by your doctor.
- For *parenteral* dosage form (injection):
  - Adults—600 mg every 12 hours.
  - Children—Dose must be determined by your doctor.

Missed dose—If you miss a dose of this medicine, take it as soon as possible. However, if it is almost time for your next dose, skip the missed dose and go back to your regular dosing schedule. Do not double doses.

Storage—To store this medicine:

- Store at room temperature.
- Do not store in the bathroom, near the kitchen sink, or in other damp places. Heat or moisture may cause the medicine to break down.
- Do not keep outdated medicine or medicine no longer needed. Ask your health care professional how you should dispose of any medicine you do not use. Be sure that any discarded medicine is out of the reach of children.

Precautions While Using This Medicine

If your symptoms do not improve within a few days or if they become worse, check with your doctor.

Linezolid can lower the number of white blood cells in your blood temporarily, increasing the chance of getting an infection. It can also lower the number of platelets, which are necessary for proper blood clotting. If this occurs, there are certain precautions your doctor may ask you to take, especially when your blood count is low, to reduce the risk of infection or bleeding:

- If you can, avoid people with infections. *Check with your doctor immediately* if you think you are getting an infection or if you get a fever or chills.
- *Check with your doctor immediately* if you notice any unusual bleeding or bruising.
- Do not touch your eyes or the inside of your nose unless you have just washed your hands and have not touched anything else in the meantime.
- Be careful not to cut yourself when you are using sharp objects such as a safety razor or fingernail or toenail cutters.
- Avoid contact sports or other situations where bruising or injury could occur.

When taken with certain foods or drinks, linezolid can cause an increase in blood pressure. To avoid this, *do not eat large amounts of foods or drink beverages that have a high tyramine content* (most common in foods that are aged, fermented, pickled, or smoked to increase their flavor, such as aged cheeses; air-dried, fermented, or smoked fish, meat, or poultry; sauerkraut; soy sauce; red wine; or tap beer. If a list of these foods and beverages is not given to you, ask your health care professional to provide one.

Side Effects of This Medicine

Along with its needed effects, a medicine may cause some unwanted effects. Although not all of these side effects may occur, if they do occur they may need medical attention.

More common
  Diarrhea
Less common or rare
  Abdominal or stomach cramps or pain (severe); black, tarry stools; blood in urine or stools; chills; cough;

© 2002 MICROMEDEX Thomson Healthcare

diarrhea (severe and watery, may also be bloody); discharge from the vagina; fever; headache; hoarseness; itching of the vagina; lower back or side pain; painful or difficult urination; pinpoint red spots on skin; shortness of breath; sore mouth or tongue; unusual bleeding or bruising; unusual tiredness or weakness; white patches in mouth, tongue, or throat

Other side effects may occur that usually do not need medical attention. These side effects may go away during treatment as your body adjusts to the medicine. However, check with your doctor if any of the following side effects continue or are bothersome.

More common
    Nausea

Less common or rare
    Bad taste in the mouth; change in sense of taste; change in color of tongue; dizziness; loss of taste; vomiting

Other side effects not listed above may also occur in some patients. If you notice any other effects, check with your doctor.

Developed: 08/17/2000
Revised: 05/02/2001

LITHIUM   Systemic

Commonly used brand name(s):

In the U.S.—

Cibalith-S	Lithobid
Eskalith	Lithonate
Eskalith CR	Lithotabs
Lithane	

Generic name product may be available.

In Canada—

Carbolith	Lithane
Duralith	Lithizine

Description

Lithium (LITH-ee-um) is used to treat the manic stage of bipolar disorder (manic-depressive illness). Manic-depressive patients experience severe mood changes, ranging from an excited or manic state (for example, unusual anger or irritability or a false sense of well-being) to depression or sadness. Lithium is used to reduce the frequency and severity of manic states. Lithium may also reduce the frequency and severity of depression in bipolar disorder.

It is not known how lithium works to stabilize a person's mood. However, it does act on the central nervous system. It helps you to have more control over your emotions and helps you cope better with the problems of living.

It is important that you and your family understand all the effects of lithium. These effects depend on your individual condition and response and the amount of lithium you use. You also must know when to contact your doctor if there are problems with the medicine's use. Lithium may also be used for other conditions as determined by your doctor.

This medicine is available only with your doctor's prescription, in the following dosage forms:

Oral
 • Capsules (U.S. and Canada)
 • Slow-release capsules (Canada)
 • Syrup (U.S.)
 • Tablets (U.S. and Canada)
 • Extended-release tablets (U.S. and Canada)

Before Using This Medicine

In deciding to use a medicine, the risks of taking the medicine must be weighed against the good it will do. This is a decision you and your doctor will make. For lithium, the following should be considered:

Allergies—Tell your doctor if you have ever had any unusual or allergic reaction to lithium. Also tell your health care professional if you are allergic to any other substances, such as foods, preservatives, or dyes.

Diet—Make certain your health care professional knows if you are on a low-sodium or low-salt diet. Too little salt in your diet could lead to serious side effects.

Pregnancy—Lithium is not recommended for use during pregnancy, especially during the first 3 months. Studies have shown that lithium may rarely cause thyroid problems and heart or blood vessel defects in the baby. It has also been shown to cause muscle weakness and severe drowsiness in newborn babies of mothers taking lithium near time of delivery.

Breast-feeding—Lithium passes into the breast milk. It has been reported to cause unwanted effects such as muscle weakness, lowered body temperature, and heart problems in nursing babies. Before taking this medicine, be sure you have discussed with your doctor the risks and benefits of breast-feeding.

Children—Lithium may cause weakened bones in children during treatment.

Older adults—Unusual thirst, an increase in amount of urine, diarrhea, drowsiness, loss of appetite, muscle weakness, trembling, slurred speech, nausea or vomiting, goiter, or symptoms of underactive thyroid are especially likely to occur in elderly patients, who are often more sensitive than younger adults to the effects of lithium.

Other medicines—Although certain medicines should not be used together at all, in other cases 2 different medicines may be used together even if an interaction might occur. In these cases, your doctor may want to change the dose, or other precautions may be necessary. When you are taking lithium, it is especially important that your health care professional know if you are taking any of the following:

 • Acetazolamide (e.g., Diamox)
 • Antipsychotics (medicine for mental illness)—Blood levels of both medicines may change, increasing the chance of serious side effects

 • Diuretics (water pills) or
 • Inflammation or pain medicine, except narcotics—Higher blood levels of lithium may occur, increasing the chance of serious side effects

 • Medicine for asthma, bronchitis, emphysema, sinusitis, or cystic fibrosis that contains the following:
    Calcium iodide or
    Iodinated glycerol or

Potassium iodide—Unwanted effects on the thyroid gland may occur

Other medical problems—The presence of other medical problems may affect the use of lithium. Make sure you tell your doctor if you have any other medical problems, especially:

- Brain disease or
- Schizophrenia—You may be especially sensitive to lithium, and mental effects (such as increased confusion) may occur
- Diabetes mellitus (sugar diabetes)—Lithium may increase the blood levels of insulin; the dose of insulin you need to take may change
- Difficult urination or
- Infection (severe, occurring with fever, prolonged sweating, diarrhea, or vomiting) or
- Kidney disease—Higher blood levels of lithium may occur, increasing the chance of serious side effects
- Epilepsy or
- Goiter or other thyroid disease, or
- Heart disease or
- Parkinson's disease or
- Psoriasis—Lithium may make the condition worse
- Leukemia (history of)—Lithium may cause the leukemia to occur again

Proper Use of This Medicine

Take this medicine after a meal or snack. Doing so will reduce stomach upset, tremors, or weakness and may also prevent a laxative effect.

For patients taking the *long-acting or slow-release form* of lithium:

- Swallow the tablet or capsule whole.
- Do not break, crush, or chew before swallowing.

For patients taking the *syrup form* of lithium:

- Dilute the syrup in fruit juice or another flavored beverage before taking.

During treatment with lithium, drink 2 or 3 quarts of water or other fluids each day, and use a normal amount of salt in your food, unless otherwise directed by your doctor.

Take this medicine exactly as directed. Do not take more or less of it, do not take it more or less often, and do not take it for a longer time than your doctor ordered. To do so may increase the chance of unwanted effects.

Sometimes lithium must be taken for 1 to several weeks before you begin to feel better.

In order for lithium to work properly, it must be taken every day in regularly spaced doses as ordered by your doctor. This is necessary to keep a constant amount of lithium in your blood. To help keep the amount constant, do not miss any doses and *do not stop taking the medicine even if you feel better.*

Dosing—The dose of lithium will be different for different patients. *Follow your doctor's orders or the directions on the label.* The following information includes only the average doses of lithium. *If your dose is different, do not change it unless your doctor tells you to do so.*

The number of capsules or tablets or teaspoonfuls of syrup that you take depends on the strength of the medicine. Also, *the number of doses you take each day, the time allowed between doses, and the length of time you take the medicine depend on the medical problem for which you are using lithium.*

- For *short-acting oral* dosage forms (capsules, tablets, syrup):
  - —Adults and adolescents: To start, 300 to 600 milligrams three times a day.
  - —Children up to 12 years of age: The dose is based on body weight. To start, the usual dose is 15 to 20 milligrams per kilogram of body weight (6.8 to 9 milligrams per pound) a day, given in smaller doses two or three times during the day.
- For *long-acting oral* dosage forms (slow-release capsules, extended-release tablets):
  - —Adults and adolescents: 300 to 600 milligrams three times a day, or 450 to 900 milligrams two times a day.
  - —Children up to 12 years of age: Dose must be determined by the doctor.

Missed dose—If you miss a dose of this medicine, take it as soon as possible. However, if it is within 4 hours (about 6 hours for extended-release tablets or slow-release capsules) of your next dose, skip the missed dose and go back to your regular dosing schedule. Do not double doses.

Storage—To store this medicine:

- Keep out of the reach of children.
- Store away from heat and direct light.
- Do not store in the bathroom, near the kitchen sink, or in other damp places. Heat or moisture may cause the medicine to break down.
- Keep the syrup form of this medicine from freezing.
- Do not keep outdated medicine or medicine no longer needed. Be sure that any discarded medicine is out of the reach of children.

Precautions While Using This Medicine

Your doctor should check your progress at regular visits to make sure that the medicine is working properly and that possible side effects are avoided. Laboratory tests may be necessary.

Lithium may not work properly if you drink large amounts of caffeine-containing coffee, tea, or colas.

This medicine may cause some people to become dizzy, drowsy, or less alert than they are normally. *Make sure you know how you react to this medicine before you drive, use machines, or do anything else that could be dangerous if you are dizzy or are not alert.*

Use extra care in hot weather and during activities that cause you to sweat heavily, such as hot baths, saunas, or exercising. The loss of too much water and salt from your body could lead to serious side effects from this medicine.

If you have an infection or illness that causes heavy sweating, vomiting, or diarrhea, check with your doctor. The loss of too much water and salt from your body could lead to serious side effects from lithium.

Do not go on a diet to lose weight and do not make a major change in your diet without first checking with your doctor. Improper dieting could cause the loss of too much water and salt from your body and could lead to serious side effects from this medicine.

For patients taking the *slow-release capsules or the extended-release tablets:*

- Do not use this medicine interchangeably with other lithium products.

It is important that you and your family know the early symptoms of lithium overdose or toxicity and when to call the doctor.

Side Effects of This Medicine

Along with its needed effects, a medicine may cause some unwanted effects. Although not all of these side effects may occur, if they do occur they may need medical attention.

Check with your doctor immediately if any of the following side effects occur:

Early symptoms of overdose or toxicity
Diarrhea; drowsiness; lack of coordination; loss of appetite; muscle weakness; nausea or vomiting; slurred speech; trembling

Late symptoms of overdose or toxicity
Blurred vision; clumsiness or unsteadiness; confusion; convulsions (seizures); dizziness; increase in amount of urine; ringing in the ears; trembling (severe)

Check with your doctor as soon as possible if any of the following side effects occur:

Less common
Confusion, poor memory or lack of awareness; fainting; fast or slow heartbeat; frequent urination; irregular pulse; increased thirst; stiffness of arms or legs; troubled breathing (especially during hard work or exercise); slurred speech; unusual tiredness or weakness; weight gain

Rare
Blue color and pain in fingers and toes; coldness of arms and legs; dizziness; eye pain; headache; noises in the ears; vision problems

Signs of low thyroid function
Dry, rough skin; hair loss; hoarseness; mental depression; sensitivity to cold; swelling of feet or lower legs; swelling of neck; unusual excitement

Other side effects may occur that usually do not need medical attention. These side effects may go away during treatment as your body adjusts to the medicine. However, check with your doctor if any of the following side effects continue or are bothersome:

More common
Increased frequency of urination or loss of bladder control—more common in women than in men, usually beginning 2 to 7 years after start of treatment; increased thirst; nausea (mild); trembling of hands (slight)

Less common
Acne or skin rash; bloated feeling or pressure in the stomach; muscle twitching (slight)

Other side effects not listed above may also occur in some patients. If you notice any other effects, check with your doctor.

Additional Information

Once a medicine has been approved for marketing for a certain use, experience may show that it is also useful for other medical problems. Although these uses are not included in product labeling, lithium is used in certain patients with the following medical conditions:

- Cluster headaches
- Mental depression
- Neutropenia (a blood condition in which there is a decreased number of a certain type of white blood cells)

Other than the above information, there is no additional information relating to proper use, precautions, or side effects for these uses.

Revised: 02/02/00

LODOXAMIDE   Ophthalmic

Commonly used brand name(s):

In the U.S.—
Alomide

In Canada—
Alomide

Another commonly used name is lodoxamide trometamol.

Description

Lodoxamide (loe-DOX-a-mide) ophthalmic solution is used in the eye to treat certain disorders of the eye caused by allergies. It works by acting on certain cells, called mast cells, to prevent them from releasing substances that cause the allergic reaction.

Lodoxamide is available only with your doctor's prescription, in the following dosage form:

Ophthalmic
- Ophthalmic solution (eye drops) (U.S. and Canada)

Before Using This Medicine

In deciding to use a medicine, the risks of using the medicine must be weighed against the good it will do. This is a decision you and your doctor will make. For lodoxamide, the following should be considered:

Allergies—Tell your doctor if you have ever had any unusual or allergic reaction to lodoxamide. Also tell your health care professional if you are allergic to any other substances, such as foods, preservatives, or dyes.

Pregnancy—Lodoxamide has not been studied in pregnant women. However, lodoxamide has not been shown to cause birth defects or other problems in animal studies.

Breast-feeding—It is not known whether lodoxamide passes into the breast milk. Although most medicines pass into breast milk in small amounts, many of them may be used safely while breast-feeding. Mothers who are using this medicine and who wish to breast-feed should discuss this with their doctor.

Children—Studies on this medicine have been done only in adult patients, and there is no specific information com-

paring use of lodoxamide in children up to 2 years of age with use in other age groups. For older children, this medicine is not expected to cause different side effects or problems than it does in adults.

Older adults—Many medicines have not been studied specifically in older people. Therefore, it may not be known whether they work exactly the same way they do in younger adults or if they cause different side effects or problems in older people. There is no specific information comparing use of lodoxamide in the elderly with use in other age groups.

Proper Use of This Medicine

To use the *eye drops:*
- First, wash your hands. Tilt the head back and, pressing your finger gently on the skin just beneath the lower eyelid, pull the lower eyelid away from the eye to make a space. Drop the medicine into this space. Let go of the eyelid and gently close the eyes. Do not blink. Keep the eyes closed for 1 or 2 minutes to allow the medicine to be absorbed by the eye.
- If you think you did not get the drop of medicine into your eye properly, use another drop.
- To keep the medicine as germ-free as possible, do not touch the applicator tip to any surface (including the eye). Also, keep the container tightly closed.

In order for this medicine to work properly, it should be used every day in regularly spaced doses as ordered by your doctor.

Dosing—The dose of ophthalmic lodoxamide will be different for different patients. *Follow your doctor's orders or the directions on the label.* The following information includes only the average doses of ophthalmic lodoxamide. *If your dose is different, do not change it* unless your doctor tells you to do so.
- For *ophthalmic solution (eye drops)* dosage form:
  —For eye allergies:
  - Adults and children 2 years of age and older— Use one drop four times a day at regularly spaced times for up to three months.
  - Children up to 2 years of age—Use and dose must be determined by your doctor.

Missed dose—If you miss a dose of this medicine, use it as soon as possible. Then go back to your regular dosing schedule.

Storage—To store this medicine:
- Keep out of the reach of children.
- Store away from heat and direct light.
- Keep the medicine from freezing.
- Do not keep outdated medicine or medicine no longer needed. Be sure that any discarded medicine is out of the reach of children.

Precautions While Using This Medicine

If your symptoms do not improve or if your condition becomes worse, check with your doctor.

Side Effects of This Medicine

Along with its needed effects, a medicine may cause some unwanted effects. Although not all of these side effects may occur, if they do occur they may need medical attention.

Check with your doctor as soon as possible if any of the following side effects occur:
Less common
  Blurred vision; feeling of something in eye, itching, discomfort, redness, tearing or discharge, or other eye or eyelid irritation (not present before you started using this medicine or becoming worse while you are using this medicine)
Rare
  Dizziness; mucus from eye, eye pain, or swelling of eye or eyelid (not present before you started using this medicine or becoming worse while you are using this medicine); headache; sensitivity of eyes to light; skin rash

Other side effects may occur that usually do not need medical attention. These side effects may go away during treatment as your body adjusts to the medicine. However, check with your doctor if any of the following side effects continue or are bothersome:
More common
  Burning or stinging (when medicine is applied)
Less common or rare
  Aching eyes; crusting in corner of eye or on eyelid; drowsiness or sleepiness; dryness of nose or eyes; feeling of heat in eye; heat sensation on body; nausea or stomach discomfort; scales on eyelid or eyelash; sneezing; sticky feeling of eyes; tired eyes

Other side effects not listed above may also occur in some patients. If you notice any other effects, check with your doctor.

Developed: 03/29/94
Interim revision: 09/30/98

LOMUSTINE   Systemic

Commonly used brand name(s):

In the U.S.—
  CeeNU

In Canada—
  CeeNU

Another commonly used name is CCNU.

Description

Lomustine (loe-MUS-teen) belongs to the group of medicines known as alkylating agents. It is used to treat some kinds of cancer.

Lomustine interferes with the growth of cancer cells, which are eventually destroyed. Since the growth of normal body cells may also be affected by lomustine, other effects will also occur. Some of these may be serious and must be reported to your doctor. Other effects, like hair loss, may not be serious but may cause concern. Some effects may not occur for months or years after the medicine is used.

Before you begin treatment with lomustine, you and your doctor should talk about the good this medicine will do as well as the risks of using it.

Lomustine is available only with your doctor's prescription, in the following dosage form:

Oral
- Capsules (U.S. and Canada)

Before Using This Medicine

In deciding to use a medicine, the risks of taking the medicine must be weighed against the good it will do. This is a decision you and your doctor will make. For lomustine, the following should be considered:

Allergies—Tell your doctor if you have ever had any unusual or allergic reaction to lomustine.

Pregnancy—Tell your doctor if you are pregnant or if you intend to have children. There is a chance that this medicine may cause birth defects if either the male or female is taking it at the time of conception or if it is taken during pregnancy. Lomustine causes birth defects in rats and causes toxic or harmful effects in the fetus of rats and rabbits at doses about the same as the human dose. In addition, many cancer medicines may cause sterility which could be permanent. Sterility has been reported in animals and humans with this medicine.

Be sure that you have discussed this with your doctor before taking this medicine. It is best to use some kind of birth control while you are taking lomustine. Tell your doctor right away if you think you have become pregnant while taking lomustine.

Breast-feeding—Tell your doctor if you are breast-feeding or if you intend to breast-feed during treatment with this medicine. Because lomustine may cause serious side effects, breast-feeding is generally not recommended while you are receiving it.

Children—Although there is no specific information comparing use of lomustine in children with use in other age groups, this medicine is not expected to cause different side effects or problems in children than it does in adults.

Older adults—Many medicines have not been studied specifically in older people. Therefore, it may not be known whether they work exactly the same way they do in younger adults or if they cause different side effects or problems in older people. There is no specific information comparing use of lomustine in the elderly with use in other age groups.

Other medicines—Although certain medicines should not be used together at all, in other cases two different medicines may be used together even if an interaction might occur. In these cases, your doctor may want to change the dose, or other precautions may be necessary. When you are taking lomustine, it is especially important that your health care professional know if you have ever been treated with x-rays or cancer medicines or if you are taking any of the following:

- Amphotericin B by injection (e.g., Fungizone) or
- Antithyroid agents (medicine for overactive thyroid) or
- Azathioprine (e.g., Imuran) or
- Chloramphenicol (e.g., Chloromycetin) or
- Colchicine or
- Flucytosine (e.g., Ancobon) or
- Ganciclovir (e.g., Cytovene) or
- Interferon (e.g., Intron A, Roferon-A) or
- Plicamycin (e.g., Mithracin) or
- Zidovudine (e.g., AZT, Retrovir)—Lomustine may increase the effects of these medicines or radiation therapy on the blood

Other medical problems—The presence of other medical problems may affect the use of lomustine. Make sure you tell your doctor if you have any other medical problems, especially:

- Chickenpox (including recent exposure) or
- Herpes zoster (shingles)—Risk of severe disease affecting other parts of the body
- Infection—Lomustine can decrease your body's ability to fight infection
- Kidney disease—Effects of lomustine may be increased because of slower removal from the body
- Lung disease—Risk of lung problems caused by lomustine may be increased

Proper Use of This Medicine

Take this medicine only as directed by your doctor. Do not take more or less of it than your doctor ordered. The exact amount of medicine you need has been carefully worked out. Taking too much may increase the chance of side effects, while taking too little may not improve your condition.

In order that you receive the proper dose of lomustine, there may be two or more different types of capsules in the container. This is not an error. It is important that you take all of the capsules in the container as one dose so that you receive the right dose of the medicine.

This medicine is sometimes given together with certain other medicines. If you are using a combination of medicines, make sure that you take each one at the right time and do not mix them. Ask your health care professional to help you plan a way to remember to take your medicines at the right times.

Nausea and vomiting occur often after lomustine is taken, but usually last less than 24 hours. Loss of appetite may last for several days. This medicine is best taken on an empty stomach at bedtime so that it will cause less stomach upset. Ask your health care professional for other ways to lessen these effects.

If you vomit shortly after taking a dose of lomustine, check with your doctor. You may be told to take the dose again.

Dosing—The dose of lomustine will be different for different patients. The dose that is used may depend on a number of things, including what the medicine is being used for, the patient's size, and whether or not other medicines are also being taken. *If you are taking lomustine at home, follow your doctor's orders or the directions on the label.* If you have any questions about the proper dose of lomustine, ask your doctor.

Precautions While Using This Medicine

It is important that your doctor check your progress at regular visits to make sure that this medicine is working properly and to check for unwanted effects.

While you are being treated with lomustine, and after you stop treatment with it, *do not have any immunizations (vaccinations) without your doctor's approval.* Lomustine may lower your body's resistance and there is a chance you might get the infection the immunization is meant to prevent. In addition, other persons living in your household should not take oral polio vaccine since there is a chance they could pass the polio virus on to you. Also, avoid persons who have recently taken oral polio vaccine. Do not get close to them, and do not stay in the same room with them for very long. If you cannot take these precautions, you should consider wearing a protective face mask that covers the nose and mouth.

Lomustine can temporarily lower the number of white blood cells in your blood, increasing the chance of getting an infection. It can also lower the number of platelets, which are necessary for proper blood clotting. If this occurs, there are certain precautions you can take, especially when your blood count is low, to reduce the risk of infection or bleeding:

- If you can, avoid people with infections. *Check with your doctor immediately* if you think you are getting an infection or if you get a fever or chills, cough or hoarseness, lower back or side pain, or painful or difficult urination.
- *Check with your doctor immediately* if you notice any unusual bleeding or bruising; black, tarry stools; blood in urine or stools; or pinpoint red spots on your skin.
- Be careful when using a regular toothbrush, dental floss, or toothpick. Your medical doctor, dentist, or nurse may recommend other ways to clean your teeth and gums. Check with your medical doctor before having any dental work done.
- Do not touch your eyes or the inside of your nose unless you have just washed your hands and have not touched anything else in the meantime.
- Be careful not to cut yourself when you are using sharp objects such as a safety razor or fingernail or toenail cutters.
- Avoid contact sports or other situations where bruising or injury could occur.

Side Effects of This Medicine

Along with their needed effects, medicines like lomustine can sometimes cause unwanted effects such as blood problems, loss of hair, and other side effects; these are described below. Also, because of the way these medicines act on the body, there is a chance that they might cause other unwanted effects that may not occur until months or years after the medicine is used. These delayed effects may include certain types of cancer, such as leukemia. Discuss these possible effects with your doctor.

Although not all of these side effects may occur, if they do occur they may need medical attention.

Check with your doctor or nurse immediately if any of the following side effects occur:

Less common
Black, tarry stools; blood in urine or stools; cough or hoarseness; fever or chills; lower back or side pain; painful or difficult urination; pinpoint red spots on skin; unusual bleeding or bruising

Check with your doctor as soon as possible if any of the following side effects occur:

Less common
Awkwardness; confusion; decrease in urination; slurred speech; sores in mouth and on lips; swelling of feet or lower legs; unusual tiredness or weakness

Rare
Cough; shortness of breath

Other side effects may occur that usually do not need medical attention. These side effects may go away during treatment as your body adjusts to the medicine. Also, your health care professional may be able to tell you about ways to prevent or reduce some of these side effects. Check with your health care professional if any of the following side effects continue or are bothersome or if you have any questions about them:

More common
Loss of appetite; nausea and vomiting (usually last less than 24 hours)

Less common
Darkening of skin; diarrhea; skin rash and itching

This medicine may cause a temporary loss of hair in some people. After treatment with lomustine has ended, normal hair growth should return.

After you stop using this medicine, it may still produce some side effects that need attention. During this period of time, check with your doctor if you notice any of the following side effects:

Black, tarry stools; blood in urine or stools; cough or hoarseness; fever or chills; lower back or side pain; painful or difficult urination; pinpoint red spots on skin; unusual bleeding or bruising

Other side effects not listed above may also occur in some patients. If you notice any other effects, check with your doctor.

Revised: 08/09/92
Interim revision: 06/21/94

LOPERAMIDE Oral

Commonly used brand name(s):

In the U.S.—
Imodium
Imodium A-D
Imodium A-D Caplets
Kaopectate II
Maalox Anti-Diarrheal
Pepto Diarrhea Control
Generic name product may be available.

In Canada—
Apo-Loperamide
Diarr-Eze
Imodium
Loperacap
Nu-Loperamide
PMS-Loperamide
Rho-Loperamide

Description

Loperamide (loe-PER-a-mide) is a medicine used along with other measures to treat diarrhea. Loperamide helps stop diarrhea by slowing down the movements of the intestines.

In the U.S., loperamide capsules are available only with your doctor's prescription, while the liquid form and the tablet form are available without a prescription. In Canada, all the dosage forms are available without a prescription.

Loperamide is available in the following dosage forms:

Oral
- Capsules (U.S. and Canada)
- Oral solution (U.S. and Canada)
- Tablets (U.S. and Canada)

Before Using This Medicine

If you are taking this medicine without a prescription, carefully read and follow any precautions on the label. For loperamide, the following should be considered:

Allergies—Tell your doctor if you have ever had any unusual or allergic reaction to loperamide. Also tell your health

care professional if you are allergic to any other substances, such as foods, preservatives, or dyes.

Pregnancy—Studies have not been done in humans. However, studies in animals have not shown that loperamide causes cancer or birth defects or lessens the chances of becoming pregnant even when given in doses many times the human dose.

Breast-feeding—It is not known whether loperamide passes into breast milk. Although most medicines pass into breast milk in small amounts, many of them may be used safely while breast-feeding. Mothers who are taking this medicine and who wish to breast-feed should discuss this with their doctor.

Children—This medicine should not be used in children under 6 years of age unless directed by a doctor. Children, especially very young children, are very sensitive to the effects of loperamide. This may increase the chance of side effects during treatment. Also, the fluid loss caused by diarrhea may result in a serious health problem (dehydration). Loperamide may hide the symptoms of dehydration. For these reasons, do not give medicine for diarrhea to children without first checking with their doctor. If you have any questions about this, check with your health care professional.

Older adults—The fluid loss caused by diarrhea may result in a serious health problem (dehydration). Loperamide may hide the symptoms of dehydration. For this reason, elderly persons with diarrhea, in addition to using medicine for diarrhea, must receive a sufficient amount of liquids to replace the fluid lost by the body. If you have any questions about this, check with your health care professional.

Other medicines—Although certain medicines should not be used together at all, in other cases two different medicines may be used together even if an interaction might occur. In these cases, your doctor may want to change the dose, or other precautions may be necessary. When you are taking loperamide, it is especially important that your health care professional know if you are taking any of the following:

- Antibiotics such as cephalosporins (e.g., Ceftin, Keflex), clindamycin (e.g., Cleocin), erythromycins (e.g., E.E.S., PCE), tetracyclines (e.g., Achromycin, Doryx)—These antibiotics may cause diarrhea; loperamide may make the diarrhea caused by antibiotics worse or make it last longer

- Narcotic pain medicine—There is a greater chance that severe constipation may occur if loperamide is used together with narcotic pain medicine

Other medical problems—The presence of other medical problems may affect the use of loperamide. Make sure you tell your doctor if you have any other medical problems, especially:

- Colitis (severe)—A more serious problem of the colon may develop if you use loperamide

- Dysentery—This condition may get worse; a different kind of treatment may be needed

- Liver disease—The chance of severe central nervous system (CNS) side effects may be greater in patients with liver disease

Proper Use of This Medicine

Do not use loperamide to treat your diarrhea if you have a fever or if there is blood or mucus in your stools. Contact your doctor.

For safe and effective use of this medicine:
- *Follow your doctor's instructions if this medicine was prescribed.*
- Follow the manufacturer's package directions if you are treating yourself.

Use a specially marked measuring spoon or other device to measure each dose accurately. The average household teaspoon may not hold the right amount of liquid.

Importance of diet and fluid intake while treating diarrhea:
- *In addition to using medicine for diarrhea, it is very important that you replace the fluid lost by the body and follow a proper diet.* For the first 24 hours, you should eat gelatin, and drink plenty of caffeine-free clear liquids, such as ginger ale, decaffeinated cola, decaffeinated tea, and broth. During the next 24 hours you may eat bland foods, such as cooked cereals, bread, crackers, and applesauce. Fruits, vegetables, fried or spicy foods, bran, candy, caffeine, and alcoholic beverages may make the condition worse.
- If too much fluid has been lost by the body due to the diarrhea, a serious condition (dehydration) may develop. Check with your doctor as soon as possible if any of the following signs or symptoms of too much fluid loss occur:
  Decreased urination
  Dizziness and lightheadedness
  Dryness of mouth
  Increased thirst
  Wrinkled skin

Dosing—The dose of loperamide will be different for different patients. *Follow your doctor's orders or the directions on the label.* The following information includes only the average doses of loperamide. *If your dose is different, do not change it* unless your doctor tells you to do so.
- For diarrhea:
  —For *oral* dosage form (capsules):
  - Adults and teenagers—The usual dose is 4 milligrams (mg) (2 capsules) after the first loose bowel movement, and 2 mg (1 capsule) after each loose bowel movement after the first dose has been taken. No more than 16 mg (8 capsules) should be taken in any twenty-four-hour period.
  - Children 8 to 12 years of age—The usual dose is 2 mg (1 capsule) three times a day.
  - Children 6 to 8 years of age—The usual dose is 2 mg (1 capsule) two times a day.
  - Children up to 6 years of age—Use is not recommended unless directed by your doctor.
  —For *oral* dosage form (oral solution):
  - Adults and teenagers—The usual dose is 4 teaspoonfuls (4 mg) after the first loose bowel movement, and 2 teaspoonfuls (2 mg) after each loose bowel movement after the first dose has been taken. No more than 8 teaspoonfuls (8 mg) should be taken in any twenty-four-hour period.
  - Children 9 to 11 years of age—The usual dose is 2 teaspoonfuls (2 mg) after the first loose bowel movement, and 1 teaspoonful (1 mg) after each loose bowel movement after the first dose has been taken. No more than 6 teaspoonfuls (6 mg) should be taken in any twenty-four-hour period.
  - Children 6 to 8 years of age—The usual dose is 2 teaspoonfuls (2 mg) after the first loose bowel movement, and 1 teaspoonful (1 mg) after each loose bowel movement after the first dose has

been taken. No more than 4 teaspoonfuls (4 mg) should be taken in any twenty-four-hour period.

- Children up to 6 years of age—Use is not recommended unless directed by your doctor.

—For *oral* dosage form (tablets):

- Adults and teenagers—The usual dose is 4 mg (2 tablets) after the first loose bowel movement, and 2 mg (1 tablet) after each loose bowel movement after the first dose has been taken. No more than 8 mg (4 tablets) should be taken in any twenty-four-hour period.
- Children 9 to 11 years of age—The usual dose is 2 mg (1 tablet) after the first loose bowel movement, and 1 mg (½ tablet) after each loose bowel movement after the first dose has been taken. No more than 6 mg (3 tablets) should be taken in any twenty-four-hour period.
- Children 6 to 8 years of age—The usual dose is 2 mg (1 tablet) after the first loose bowel movement, and 1 mg (½ tablet) after each loose bowel movement after the first dose has been taken. No more than 4 mg (2 tablets) should be taken in any twenty-four-hour period.
- Children up to 6 years of age—Use is not recommended unless directed by your doctor.

Missed dose—If you must take this medicine regularly and you miss a dose, skip the missed dose and go back to your regular dosing schedule. Do not double doses.

Storage—To store this medicine:

- Keep out of the reach of children
- Store away from heat and direct light.
- Do not store the capsule or tablet form of this medicine in the bathroom, near the kitchen sink, or in other damp places. Heat or moisture may cause the medicine to break down.
- Keep the liquid form of this medicine from freezing.
- Do not keep outdated medicine or medicine no longer needed. Be sure that any discarded medicine is out of the reach of children.

Precautions While Using This Medicine

Loperamide should not be used for more than 2 days, unless directed by your doctor. If you will be taking this medicine regularly for a long time, your doctor should check your progress at regular visits.

Check with your doctor if your diarrhea does not stop after two days or if you develop a fever.

Side Effects of This Medicine

Along with its needed effects, a medicine may cause some unwanted effects. *When this medicine is used for short periods of time at low doses, side effects usually are rare.*

However, *check with your doctor immediately* if any of the following side effects are severe and occur suddenly since they may be signs of a more severe and dangerous problem with your bowels:

Rare

Bloating; constipation; loss of appetite; stomach pain (severe) with nausea and vomiting

Also, check with your doctor as soon as possible if the following side effect occurs:

Rare

Skin rash

Other side effects may occur that usually do not need medical attention. These side effects may go away during treatment as your body adjusts to the medicine. However, check with your doctor if any of the following side effects continue or are bothersome:

Rare

Dizziness or drowsiness; dryness of mouth

Other side effects not listed above may also occur in some patients. If you notice any other effects, check with your doctor.

Revised: 01/25/95
Interim revision: 08/14/98

LOPINAVIR AND RITONAVIR
Systemic†—INTRODUCTORY VERSION

Commonly used brand name(s):

In the U.S.—
Kaletra

†Not commercially available in Canada.

Description

The combination of lopinavir and ritonavir (low-PIN-a-veer and ri-TOE-na-veer) is used in the treatment of the infection caused by the human immunodeficiency virus (HIV). HIV is the virus responsible for acquired immune deficiency syndrome (AIDS). It is used to slow the progression of disease in patients infected with HIV who have advanced symptoms, early symptoms, or no symptoms at all.

Lopinavir and ritonavir will not cure or prevent HIV infection or AIDS; however, it helps keep HIV from reproducing and appears to slow down the destruction of the immune system. This may help delay the development of problems usually related to AIDS or HIV disease. Lopinavir and ritonavir will not keep you from spreading HIV to other people. People who receive this medicine may continue to have other problems usually related to AIDS or HIV disease.

This medicine is available only with your doctor's prescription, in the following dosage forms:

Oral
- Capsules (U.S.)
- Oral solution (U.S.)

Before Using This Medicine

In deciding to use a medicine, the risks of taking the medicine must be weighed against the good it will do. This is a decision you and your doctor will make. For lopinavir and ritonavir, the following should be considered:

Allergies—Tell your doctor if you have ever had any unusual or allergic reaction to lopinavir or ritonavir. Also tell your health care professional if you are allergic to any other substances, such as foods, preservatives, or dyes.

Pregnancy—Lopinavir and ritonavir has not been studied in pregnant women. However, it has been found to cause birth defects and other problems in animals at doses many times the human dose. Before taking this medicine, make sure your doctor knows if you are pregnant or if you may become pregnant.

Breast-feeding—It is not known whether lopinavir and ritonavir pass into breast milk. However, because of the possibility that this medicine could cause unwanted effects in nursing babies and the risk of passing HIV on to the infant, breast-feeding is usually not recommended.

Children—This medicine has been tested in children 6 months of age and older and, in effective doses, has not been shown to cause different side effects or problems than it does in adults.

Older adults—Many medicines have not been studied specifically in older people. Therefore, it may not be known whether they work exactly the same way they do in younger adults or if they cause different side effects or problems in older people. There is no specific information comparing use of lopinavir and ritonavir in the elderly with use in other age groups.

Other medicines—Although certain medicines should not be used together at all, in other cases two different medicines may be used together even if an interaction might occur. In these cases, your doctor may want to change the dose, or other precautions may be necessary. When you are taking lopinavir and ritonavir, it is especially important that your health care professional knows if you are taking any of the following:

- Amiodarone (e.g., Cordarone) or
- Bepridil (e.g., Vascor) or
- Quinidine (e.g., Quinidex)—Levels of these medicines in the body may be increased and cause toxic effects to the heart.

- Astemizole (e.g. Hismanal) or
- Cisapride (e.g., Propulsid) or
- Flecainide (e.g., Tambocor) or
- Pimozide (e.g., Orap) or
- Propafenone (e.g., Rythmol) or
- Terfenadine (e.g., Seldane)—These medicines should not be taken with lopinavir and ritonavir due to the chance of serious heart rhythm problems.

- Atorvastatin (e.g., Lipitor) or
- Cerivastatin (e.g., Baycol) or
- Lovastatin (e.g., Mevacor) or
- Simvastatin (e.g., Zocor)—Simvastatin and lovastatin should not be taken with lopinavir and ritonavir due to the risk of serious effects on muscle tissue; atorvastatin and cerivastatin doses should be as low as possible to avoid adverse effects

- Carbamazepine (e.g., Tegretol) or
- Dexamethasone (e.g., Decadron) or
- Phenobarbitol (e.g., Luminal) or
- Phenytoin (e.g., Dilantin)—These medicines may reduce the effectiveness of lopinavir and ritonavir by lowering the amount of lopinavir present in the body.

- Clarithromycin (e.g., Biaxin)—Use of lopinavir and ritonavir may increase the amount of clarithromycin in the body; patients with abnormal kidney function may need to have their dose adjusted

- Cyclosporine (e.g., Sandimmune, Neoral) or
- Felodipine (e.g., Plendil) or
- Nicardipine (e.g., Cardene) or
- Nifedipine (e.g., Procardia) or
- Sirolimus (e.g., Rapamune) or
- Tacrolimus (e.g., Prograf)—Use of lopinavir and ritonavir may increase the amount of these medicines in the body, which may lead to increased side effects

- Dihydroergotamine (e.g. D.H.E., Migranal) or
- Ergonovine (e.g., Ergotrate) or
- Ergotamine (e.g., Ergostat) or
- Methylergonovine (e.g., Methergine) or
- Midazolam (e.g., Versed) or
- Triazolam (e.g., Halcion)—These medicines should not be taken with lopinavir and ritonavir because serious side effects could occur

- Efavirenz (e.g., Sustiva) or
- Nevirapine (e.g., Viramune)—The dose of lopinavir and ritonavir might need to be increased when taken with these medicines.

- Ethinyl estradiol—Lopinavir and ritonavir may cause this medicine to be less effective; therefore, alternative or additional birth control methods should be used when birth control pills containing ethinyl estradiol are taken with lopinavir and ritonavir.

- Ketoconazole (e.g., Nizoral) or
- Itraconazole (e.g., Sporonox)—High doses are not recommended when taken with lopinavir and ritonavir

- Rifabutin (e.g., Mycobutin)—Doses of this medicine should be decreased and patients should be monitored more closely when this medicine is taken with lopinavir and ritonavir.

- Rifampin (e.g., Rifadin) or
- St. John's wort—Lopinavir and ritonavir may not work properly if taken with these medicines

- Sildenafil (e.g., Viagra)—Use of lopinavir and ritonavir may increase the amount of this medicine in the body, which may lead to increased side effects; your doctor may decrease your sildenafil dose

- Warfarin (e.g., Coumadin)—The amount of warfarin in the blood may be affected; bleeding times should be closely watched by your doctor

Other medical problems—The presence of other medical problems may affect the use of lopinavir and ritonavir. Make sure you tell your doctor if you have any other medical problems, especially:

- Diabetes mellitus (sugar diabetes)—Lopinavir and ritonavir may increase blood sugar; it may be necessary to adjust your dose of insulin or oral diabetes medicine

- Hemophilia—Lopinavir and ritonavir may increase the risk of major bleeding.

- Liver problems or
- Hepatitis B or
- Hepatitis C—Effects of lopinavir and ritonavir may be increased because of slower removal of the medicines from the body

- Pancreatitis (history of)—The chance that this condition will return is increased

---

Proper Use of This Medicine

A paper with information about lopinavir and ritonavir will be given to you with your filled prescription. Read this paper carefully and ask your health care professional if you need additional information or explanation.

It is important that lopinavir and ritonavir be taken with food.

Take this medicine exactly as directed by your doctor. Do not take it more often and do not take it for a longer time than your doctor ordered. Also, do not stop taking this medicine without checking with your doctor first.

Dosing—The dose of lopinavir and ritonavir will be different for different patients. *Follow your doctor's orders or the directions on the label.* The following information includes only the average doses of lopinavir and ritonavir. *If your dose is different, do not change it* unless your doctor tells you to do so.

The number of capsules or teaspoonfuls of lopinavir and ritonavir that you take depends on the strength of the medicine.

- For *oral* dosage form (capsules):
  —For treatment of HIV infection:
    - Adults: 400 milligrams (mg) of lopinavir and 100 mg of ritonavir (3 capsules) twice a day with food.
    - Children: This dosage form is usually not used for children. Please refer to the oral solution dosage form.
- For *oral* dosage form (oral solution):
  —For treatment of HIV infection:
    - Adults and adolescents: 400 mg of lopinavir and 100 mg of ritonavir (5 milliliters [mL]) twice a day with food.
    - Children 6 months to 12 years of age: Dose is based on body weight and must be determined by your doctor.
    - Children less than 6 months of age: Use and dose must be determined by your doctor.

Missed dose—If you miss a dose of this medicine, take it as soon as possible. However, if it is almost time for your next dose, skip the missed dose and go back to your regular dosing schedule. Do not double doses.

Storage—To store this medicine:
- Keep out of the reach of children.
- Store in the refrigerator. However, keep the medicine from freezing.
- Avoid high heat.
- Do not keep outdated medicine or medicine no longer needed. Ask your health care professional how you should dispose of any medicine you do not use. Be sure that any discarded medicine is out of the reach of children.

Precautions While Using This Medicine

It is very important that your doctor check your progress at regular visits to make sure this medicine is working properly and to check for unwanted effects.

If you are taking the oral solution form of this medicine, you should limit the amount of alcohol you drink. The oral solution contains 42% alcohol.

Side Effects of This Medicine

Along with its needed effects, a medicine may cause some unwanted effects. Although not all of these side effects may occur, if they do occur they may need medical attention.
    Less common
        Bloating; blurred vision; chills; constipation; darkened urine; dry mouth; fast heart beat; fatigue; fever; flushed, dry skin; fruit-like breath odor; increased hunger; increased thirst; increased urination; indigestion; loss of appetite; loss of consciousness; nausea; pains in stomach, side, or abdomen, possibly moving to the back; sweating; troubled breathing; unexplained weight loss; vomiting; yellow eyes or skin

Other side effects may occur that usually do not need medical attention. These side effects may go away during treatment as your body adjusts to the medicine. However, check with your doctor if any of the following side effects continue or are bothersome.
    More common
        Diarrhea
    Less common
        Abnormal stools; headache; lack or loss of strength; pain; rash; trouble in sleeping

Other side effects may occur that do not require medical attention.
    More common
        Redistribution of body fat

Other side effects not listed above may also occur in some patients. If you notice any other effects, check with your doctor.

Developed: 01/18/2001

LORACARBEF   Systemic†

Commonly used brand name(s):

In the U.S.—
    Lorabid

†Not commercially available in Canada.

Description

Loracarbef (loe-ra-KAR-bef) is used to treat bacterial infections in many different parts of the body. It works by killing bacteria or preventing their growth. This medicine will not work for colds, flu, or other virus infections.

Loracarbef is available only with your doctor's prescription, in the following dosage forms:
    Oral
        - Capsules (U.S.)
        - Oral suspension (U.S.)

Before Using This Medicine

In deciding to use a medicine, the risks of taking the medicine must be weighed against the good it will do. This is a decision you and your doctor will make. For loracarbef, the following should be considered:

Allergies—Tell your doctor if you have ever had any unusual or allergic reaction to loracarbef or to any related medicines such as penicillins or cephalosporins. Also tell your health care professional if you are allergic to any other substances, such as foods, preservatives, or dyes.

Pregnancy—Loracarbef has not been studied in pregnant women. However, loracarbef has not been shown to cause birth defects or other problems in animal studies.

Breast-feeding—It is not known whether loracarbef passes into breast milk.

Children—This medicine has been tested in a limited number of children 6 months of age and older. In effective doses, the medicine has not been shown to cause different side effects or problems than it does in adults.

Older adults—This medicine has been tested in a limited number of elderly patients and has not been shown to cause different side effects or problems in older people than it does in younger adults.

Other medicines—Although certain medicines should not be used together at all, in other cases two different medicines may be used together even if an interaction might occur. In these cases, your doctor may want to change the dose, or other precautions may be necessary. When you are taking loracarbef, it is especially important that your health care professional know if you are taking any of the following:

- Probenicid (e.g., Benemid)—Probenecid increases the blood level of loracarbef, increasing the chance of side effects

Other medical problems—The presence of other medical problems may affect the use of loracarbef. Make sure you tell your doctor if you have any other medical problems, especially:

- Kidney disease—Kidney disease may increase the blood level of loracarbef, increasing the chance of side effects

Proper Use of This Medicine

Loracarbef should be taken at least 1 hour before or at least 2 hours after meals.

To help clear up your infection completely, *keep taking loracarbef for the full time of treatment*, even if you begin to feel better after a few days. *If you have a "strep" infection, you should keep taking this medicine for at least 10 days. This is especially important in "strep" infections. Serious heart problems could develop later* if your infection is not cleared up completely. Also, if you stop taking this medicine too soon, your symptoms may return.

This medicine works best when there is a constant amount in the blood or urine. *To help keep the amount constant, do not miss any doses. Also, it is best to take the doses at evenly spaced times, day and night.* If this interferes with your sleep or other daily activities, or if you need help in planning the best times to take your medicine, check with your health care professional.

Dosing—The dose of loracarbef will be different for different patients. *Follow your doctor's orders or the directions on the label.* The following information includes only the average doses of loracarbef. Your dose may be different if you have kidney disease. *If your dose is different, do not change it* unless your doctor tells you to do so.

The number of capsules or teaspoonfuls of suspension that you take depends on the strength of the medicine. Also, *the number of doses you take each day, the time allowed between doses, and the length of time you take the medicine depend on the medical problem for which you are taking loracarbef.*

- For *oral* dosage forms (capsules or oral suspension):
    —For bronchitis:
    - Adults and children 13 years of age and older—200 to 400 milligrams (mg) every twelve hours for seven days.
    - Children 6 months to 12 years of age—Use and dose to be determined by your doctor.

—For otitis media (ear infection):
- Children 6 months to 12 years of age—Dose is based on body weight and must be determined by your doctor.
—For pneumonia:
- Adults and children 13 years of age and older—400 mg every twelve hours for fourteen days.
- Children 6 months to 12 years of age—Use and dose to be determined by your doctor.
—For sinusitis:
- Adults and children 13 years of age and older—400 mg every twelve hours for ten days.
- Children 6 months to 12 years of age—Use and dose to be determined by your doctor.
—For skin and soft tissue infections:
- Adults and children 13 years of age and older—200 mg every twelve hours for seven days.
- Children 6 months to 12 years of age—Dose is based on body weight and must be determined by your doctor.
—For streptococcal pharyngitis ("strep throat"):
- Adults and children 13 years of age and older—200 mg every twelve hours for ten days.
- Children 6 months to 12 years of age—Dose is based on body weight and must be determined by your doctor.
—For urinary tract infections:
- Adults and children 13 years of age and older—200 to 400 mg every twelve to twenty-four hours for seven to fourteen days.
- Children 6 months to 12 years of age—Use and dose to be determined by your doctor.

Missed dose—If you do miss a dose of this medicine, take it as soon as possible. This will help to keep a constant amount of medicine in the blood or urine. However, if it is almost time for your next dose, skip the missed dose and go back to your regular dosing schedule. Do not double doses.

Storage—To store this medicine:
- Keep out of the reach of children.
- Store away from heat and direct light.
- Do not store the capsule form of this medicine in the bathroom, near the kitchen sink, or in other damp places. Heat or moisture may cause the medicine to break down.
- Do not keep outdated medicine or medicine no longer needed. Be sure that any discarded medicine is out of the reach of children.

Precautions While Using This Medicine

If your symptoms do not improve within a few days, or if they become worse, check with your doctor.

In some patients, loracarbef may cause diarrhea.
- Severe diarrhea may be a sign of a serious side effect. *Do not take any diarrhea medicine without first checking with your doctor.* Diarrhea medicines may make your diarrhea worse or last longer.
- For mild diarrhea, diarrhea medicine containing kaolin or attapulgite (e.g., Kaopectate tablets, Diasorb) may be taken. However, other kinds of diarrhea medicine should not be taken. They may make your diarrhea worse or last longer.
- If you have any questions about this or if mild diarrhea continues or gets worse, check with your health care professional.

Side Effects of This Medicine

Along with its needed effects, a medicine may cause some unwanted effects. Although not all of these side effects may occur, if they do occur they may need medical attention.

Check with your doctor as soon as possible if any of the following side effects occur:

More common
    Itching; skin rash

Other side effects may occur that usually do not need medical attention. These side effects may go away during treatment as your body adjusts to the medicine. However, check with your doctor if any of the following side effects continue or are bothersome:

More common
    Diarrhea; loss of appetite; nausea and vomiting; stomach pain

Rare
    Dizziness; drowsiness; headache; itching or discharge from the vagina; nervousness; trouble in sleeping

Other side effects not listed above may also occur in some patients. If you notice any other effects, check with your doctor.

Revised: 08/18/93
Interim revision: 06/20/95

LOSARTAN   Systemic†

Commonly used brand name(s):

In the U.S.—
    Cozaar

†Not commercially available in Canada.

Description

Losartan (loe-SAR-tan) is used to treat high blood pressure (hypertension). High blood pressure adds to the work load of the heart and arteries. If it continues for a long time, the heart and arteries may not function properly. This can damage the blood vessels of the brain, heart, and kidneys, resulting in a stroke, heart failure, or kidney failure. High blood pressure may also increase the risk of heart attacks. These problems may be less likely to occur if blood pressure is controlled.

Losartan works by blocking the action of a substance in the body that causes blood vessels to tighten. As a result, losartan relaxes blood vessels. This lowers blood pressure.

Losartan is available only with your doctor's prescription, in the following dosage form:

Oral
    • Tablets (U.S.)

Before Using This Medicine

In deciding to use a medicine, the risks of taking the medicine must be weighed against the good it will do. This is a decision you and your doctor will make. For losartan, the following should be considered:

Allergies—Tell your doctor if you have ever had any unusual or allergic reaction to losartan. Also tell your health care professional if you are allergic to any other substances, such as foods, preservatives, or dyes.

Diet—Make certain your health care professional knows if you are on any special diet, such as a low-sodium diet.

Pregnancy—Use of losartan during pregnancy, especially during the second and third trimesters (after the first three months) can cause low blood pressure, severe kidney failure, or even death in the newborn. *Therefore, it is important that you check with your doctor immediately if you think that you may be pregnant.* Be sure that you have discussed this with your doctor before taking this medicine.

Breast-feeding—It is not known whether losartan passes into breast milk. However, losartan passes into the milk of lactating rats.

Children—Studies on this medicine have been done only in adult patients, and there is no specific information comparing use of losartan in children with use in other age groups.

Older adults—This medicine has been tested in a limited number of patients 65 years of age or older and has not been shown to cause different side effects or problems in older people than it does in younger adults.

Other medicines—Although certain medicines should not be used together at all, in other cases two different medicines may be used together even if an interaction might occur. In these cases, your doctor may want to change the dose, or other precautions may be necessary. When you are taking losartan, it is especially important that your health care professional know if you are taking any of the following:

• Diuretics (water pills)—Effects on blood pressure may be increased. In addition, some diuretics make the increase in potassium in the blood caused by losartan even greater

Other medical problems—The presence of other medical problems may affect the use of losartan. Make sure you tell your doctor if you have any other medical problems, especially:

• Kidney disease or
• Liver disease—Effects may be increased because of slower removal of losartan from the body

Proper Use of This Medicine

To help you remember to take your medicine, try to get into the habit of taking it at the same time each day.

In addition to the use of the medicine your doctor has prescribed, treatment for your high blood pressure may include weight control and care in the types of foods you eat, especially foods high in sodium. Your doctor will tell you which of these are most important for you. You should check with your doctor before changing your diet.

Many patients who have high blood pressure will not notice any signs of the problem. In fact, many may feel normal. It is very important that you *take your medicine exactly as directed* and that you keep your appointments with your doctor even if you feel well.

Remember that this medicine will not cure your high blood pressure but it does help control it. Therefore, you must continue to take it as directed if you expect to lower your blood pressure and keep it down. *You may have to take high blood pressure medicine for the rest of your life.* If high blood pressure is not treated, it can cause serious problems such as heart failure, blood vessel disease, stroke, or kidney disease.

This medicine may be taken with or without food.

Dosing—The dose of losartan will be different for different patients. *Follow your doctor's orders or the directions on the label.* The following information includes only the average doses of losartan. *If your dose is different, do not change it* unless your doctor tells you to do so.

The number of tablets that you take depends on the strength of the medicine.

- For *oral* dosage form (tablets):
  —For high blood pressure:
    - Adults—25 to 100 milligrams (mg) a day. The dose may be taken once a day or divided into two doses.
    - Children—Use and dose must be determined by your doctor.

Missed dose—If you miss a dose of this medicine, take it as soon as possible. However, if it is almost time for your next dose, skip the missed dose and go back to your regular dosing schedule. Do not double doses.

Storage—To store this medicine:

- Keep out of the reach of children.
- Store away from heat and direct light.
- Do not store in the bathroom, near the kitchen sink, or in other damp places. Heat or moisture may cause the medicine to break down.
- Keep the medicine from freezing. Do not refrigerate.
- Do not keep outdated medicine or medicine no longer needed. Be sure that any discarded medicine is out of the reach of children.

Precautions While Using This Medicine

Check with your doctor immediately if you think that you may be pregnant. Losartan may cause birth defects or other problems in the baby if taken during pregnancy.

It is important that your doctor check your progress at regular visits to make sure that this medicine is working properly and to check for unwanted effects.

Do not take other medicines unless they have been discussed with your doctor. This especially includes over-the-counter (nonprescription) medicines for appetite control, asthma, colds, cough, hay fever, or sinus problems, since they may tend to increase your blood pressure.

Dizziness or lightheadedness may occur after the first dose of this medicine, especially if you have been taking a diuretic (water pill). Make sure you know how you react to this medicine before you drive, use machines, or do anything else that could be dangerous if you are dizzy.

Check with your doctor right away if you become sick while taking this medicine, especially with severe or continuing nausea and vomiting or diarrhea. These conditions may cause you to lose too much water and lead to low blood pressure.

Dizziness, lightheadedness, or fainting may also occur if you exercise or if the weather is hot. Heavy sweating can cause loss of too much water and result in low blood pressure. Use extra care during exercise or hot weather.

Avoid alcoholic beverages until you have discussed their use with your doctor. Alcohol may make the low blood pressure effect worse and/or increase the possibility of dizziness or fainting.

Side Effects of This Medicine

Along with its needed effects, a medicine may cause some unwanted effects. Although not all of these side effects may occur, if they do occur they may need medical attention.

Check with your doctor immediately if any of the following side effects occur:
  Rare
    Hoarseness; swelling of face, mouth, hands, or feet; trouble in swallowing or breathing (sudden)

Check with your doctor as soon as possible if any of the following side effects occur:
  Less common
    Cough, fever or sore throat; dizziness

Other side effects may occur that usually do not need medical attention. These side effects may go away during treatment as your body adjusts to the medicine. However, check with your doctor if any of the following side effects continue or are bothersome:
  More common
    Headache

  Less common
    Back pain; diarrhea; fatigue; nasal congestion

  Rare
    Cough, dry; leg pain; muscle cramps or pain; sinus problems; trouble in sleeping

Other side effects not listed above may also occur in some patients. If you notice any other effects, check with your doctor.

Developed: 08/15/95
Interim revision: 09/21/95

LOTEPREDNOL   Ophthalmic

Commonly used brand name(s):

In the U.S.—
  Alrex
  Lotemax

Description

Loteprednol (loe-te-PRED-nol) belongs to the group of medicines known as corticosteroids (cortisone-like medicines). It is used to treat inflammation (redness) of the eye, which may occur with certain eye problems or following eye surgery. This medicine is also used to temporarily treat the symptoms of the eye caused by a condition known as seasonal allergic conjunctivitis (seasonal eye allergy).

This medicine is available only with your doctor's prescription, in the following dosage form:

  Ophthalmic
    - Eye drops (U.S.)

Before Using This Medicine

In deciding to use a medicine, the risks of using the medicine must be weighed against the good it will do. This is a decision

you and your doctor will make. For ophthalmic loteprednol, the following should be considered:

Allergies—Tell your doctor if you have ever had any unusual or allergic reaction to loteprednol, other cortisone-like medicines, or benzalkonium chloride. Also tell your health care professional if you are allergic to any other substances, such as foods, preservatives, or dyes.

Pregnancy—Ophthalmic loteprednol has not been studied in pregnant women. However, studies in animals given loteprednol by mouth have shown that loteprednol in high doses causes birth defects or other unwanted effects in the animal fetus. Before using this medicine, make sure your doctor knows if you are pregnant or if you may become pregnant.

Breast-feeding—It is not known whether enough loteprednol is absorbed from the eye to get into breast milk. Discuss with your doctor whether or not to breast-feed while using this medicine.

Children—There is no specific information comparing use of ophthalmic loteprednol in children with use in other age groups.

Older adults—Many medicines have not been studied specifically in older people. Therefore, it may not be known whether they work exactly the same way they do in younger adults or if they cause different side effects or problems in older people. There is no specific information comparing use of ophthalmic loteprednol in the elderly with use in other age groups.

Other medicines—Although certain medicines should not be used together at all, in other cases two different medicines may be used together even if an interaction might occur. In these cases, your doctor may want to change the dose, or other precautions may be necessary. Tell your health care professional if you are taking or using any other prescription or nonprescription (over-the-counter [OTC]) medicine.

Other medical problems—The presence of other medical problems may affect the use of ophthalmic loteprednol. Make sure you tell your doctor if you have any other medical problems, especially:

- Certain eye diseases that cause the cornea to get thin—Use of ophthalmic loteprednol could cause a hole to form (perforation)
- Fungus infection of the eye or
- Herpes infection of the eye or
- Virus infection of the eye or
- Yeast infection of the eye or
- Any other eye infection—Ophthalmic loteprednol may make existing infections worse or cause new infections
- Glaucoma—Prolonged use of corticosteroids may result in glaucoma; caution should be used when corticosteroids are used in patients who have glaucoma

Proper Use of This Medicine

Shake the container very well before applying the eye drops.

If you are using the 0.5% strength of this medicine: *Do not wear soft contact lenses while you are using this medicine.*

If you are using the 0.2% strength of this medicine: *If your eyes are red, you should not wear contact lenses.* If your eyes are not red, soft contact lenses should be removed before you use this medicine. You should wait at least 10 min-

utes after using the eye drops before reinserting the contact lenses.

To use:
- First, wash your hands. Tilt your head back and, pressing your finger gently on the skin just beneath the lower eyelid, pull the lower eyelid away from the eye to make a space. Drop the medicine into this space. Let go of the eyelid and gently close the eyes. Do not blink. Keep the eyes closed and apply pressure to the inner corner of the eye with your finger for 1 or 2 minutes to allow the medicine to be absorbed by the eye.
- If you think you did not get the drop of medicine into your eye properly, use another drop.
- *To keep the medicine as germ-free as possible, do not touch the applicator tip to any surface (including the eye).* Also, keep the container tightly closed.

Dosing—The dose of ophthalmic loteprednol will be different for different patients. The amount that you use depends on the strength of the eye drops, as well as what they are being used for. *Follow your doctor's orders or the directions on the label.* The following information includes only the average doses of ophthalmic loteprednol. *If your dose is different, do not change it* unless your doctor tells you to do so.

- For *ophthalmic suspension* dosage form (eye drops):
  —For seasonal allergic conjunctivitis:
  - Adults—Use one drop of the 0.2% eye suspension in the affected eye four times a day.
  - Children—Use and dose must be determined by your doctor.
  —For inflammation after surgery:
  - Adults—Use one or two drops of the 0.5% eye suspension in the affected eye four times a day beginning twenty-four hours after surgery and continuing throughout the first two weeks after surgery.
  - Children—Use and dose must be determined by your doctor.
  —For other eye problems as determined by your doctor:
  - Adults—Use one or two drops of the 0.5% eye suspension in the affected eye four times a day. During the first week your doctor may want you to use the eye drops more often.
  - Children—Use and dose must be determined by your doctor.

Missed dose—If you miss a dose of this medicine, use it as soon as you remember. However, if it is almost time for the next dose, skip the missed dose and go back to your regular dosing schedule. Do not double doses.

Storage—To store this medicine:
- Keep out of the reach of children.
- Do not freeze.
- Do not keep outdated medicine or medicine no longer needed. Be sure that any discarded medicine is out of the reach of children.

Precautions While Using This Medicine

If you will be using this medicine for more than few weeks, an ophthalmologist (eye doctor) should examine your eyes at regular visits to make sure it does not cause unwanted effects.

If your symptoms do not improve or if your condition becomes worse, check with your doctor.

Side Effects of This Medicine

Along with its needed effects, a medicine may cause some unwanted effects. Although not all of these side effects may occur, if they do occur they may need medical attention.

Check with your doctor as soon as possible if any of the following side effects occur:

More common
Blurred vision or other change in vision; redness or swelling of the eye; swelling of the membrane covering the white part of the eye

Less common
Discharge from the eye; eye discomfort, irritation, or pain; increased sensitivity of eye to light; redness of eyelid or inner lining of eyelid; tiny bumps on the inner lining of eyelid

Other side effects may occur that usually do not need medical attention. These side effects may go away during treatment as your body adjusts to the medicine. However, check with your doctor if any of the following side effects continue or are bothersome:

More common
Burning when medicine is applied; dry eye; feeling of something in the eye; headache; itching; runny nose; sore throat; tearing or watery eye

Other side effects not listed above may also occur in some patients. If you notice any other effects, check with your doctor.

Developed: 08/14/98

LOXAPINE   Systemic

Commonly used brand name(s):

In the U.S.—
Loxitane
Loxitane C
Loxitane IM
Generic name product may be available.

In Canada—
Loxapac

Description

Loxapine (LOX-a-peen) is used to treat nervous, mental, and emotional conditions.

Loxapine is available only with your doctor's prescription, in the following dosage forms:

Oral
• Solution (U.S. and Canada)
• Capsules (U.S.)
• Tablets (Canada)
Parenteral
• Injection (U.S. and Canada)

Before Using This Medicine

In deciding to use a medicine, the risks of taking the medicine must be weighed against the good it will do. This is a decision you and your doctor will make. For loxapine, the following should be considered:

Allergies—Tell your doctor if you have ever had any unusual or allergic reaction to loxapine or amoxapine. Also tell your health care professional if you are allergic to any other substances, such as foods, preservatives, or dyes.

Pregnancy—Loxapine has not been shown to cause birth defects or other problems in humans. However, animal studies have shown unwanted effects in the fetus.

Breast-feeding—It is not known if loxapine passes into breast milk.

Children—Studies on this medicine have been done only in adult patients, and there is no specific information comparing use of loxapine in children with use in other age groups.

Older adults—Elderly patients are usually more sensitive than younger adults to the effects of loxapine. Constipation, dizziness or fainting, drowsiness, dry mouth, trembling of the hands and fingers, and symptoms of tardive dyskinesia (such as rapid, worm-like movements of the tongue or any other uncontrolled movements of the mouth, tongue, or jaw, and/or arms and legs) are especially likely to occur in elderly patients.

Other medicines—Although certain medicines should not be used together at all, in other cases 2 different medicines may be used together even if an interaction might occur. In these cases, your doctor may want to change the dose, or other precautions may be necessary. When you are taking loxapine, it is especially important that your health care professional know if you are taking any of the following:

• Amoxapine (e.g., Asendin) or
• Methyldopa (e.g., Aldomet) or
• Metoclopramide (e.g., Reglan) or
• Metyrosine (e.g., Demser) or
• Other antipsychotics (medicine for mental illness) or
• Pemoline (e.g., Cylert) or
• Pimozide (e.g., Orap) or
• Promethazine (e.g., Phenergan) or
• Rauwolfia alkaloids (alseroxylon [e.g., Rauwiloid], deserpidine [e.g., Harmonyl], rauwolfia serpentina [e.g., Raudixin], reserpine [e.g., Serpasil]) or
• Trimeprazine (e.g., Temaril)—Taking these medicines with loxapine may increase the chance and seriousness of some side effects

• Central nervous system (CNS) depressants (medicine that causes drowsiness) or
• Tricyclic antidepressants (medicine for depression)—Taking these medicines with loxapine may increase the CNS depressant effects

• Guanadrel (e.g., Hylorel) or
• Guanethidine (e.g., Ismelin)—Loxapine may decrease the effects of these medicines

Other medical problems—The presence of other medical problems may affect the use of loxapine. Make sure you tell your doctor if you have any other medical problems, especially:

• Alcohol abuse—CNS depressant effects may be increased

• Difficult urination or
• Enlarged prostate or
• Glaucoma (or predisposition to) or
• Parkinson's disease—Loxapine may make the condition worse

- Heart or blood vessel disease—An increased risk of low blood pressure (hypotension) or changes in the rhythm of your heart may occur
- Liver disease—Higher blood levels of loxapine may occur, increasing the chance of side effects
- Seizure disorders—Loxapine may increase the risk of seizures

Proper Use of This Medicine

This medicine may be taken with food or a full glass (8 ounces) of water or milk to reduce stomach irritation.

For patients taking the *oral solution:*

- Measure the solution only with the dropper provided by the manufacturer. This will give a more accurate dose.

The liquid medicine must be mixed with orange juice or grapefruit juice just before you take it to make it easier to take.

Do not take more of this medicine, do not take it more often, and do not take it for a longer time than your doctor ordered. To do so may increase the chance of unwanted effects.

Dosing—The dose of loxapine will be different for different patients. *Follow your doctor's orders or the directions on the label.* The following information includes only the average doses of loxapine. *If your dose is different, do not change it* unless your doctor tells you to do so.

The number of capsules or tablets or amount of solution that you take depends on the strength of the medicine. Also, *the number of doses you take each day, the time allowed between doses, and the length of time you take the medicine depend on the medical problem for which you are taking loxapine.*

- For *oral* dosage forms (capsules, oral solution, or tablets):
  —Adults: To start, 10 milligrams taken two times a day. Your doctor may increase your dose if needed.
  —Children up to 16 years of age: The dose must be determined by the doctor.
- For *injection* dosage form:
  —Adults: 12.5 to 50 milligrams every four to six hours, injected into a muscle.
  —Children up to 16 years of age: The dose must be determined by the doctor.

Missed dose—If you miss a dose of this medicine, take it as soon as possible. However, if it is within one hour of your next dose, skip the missed dose and go back to your regular dosing schedule. Do not double doses.

Storage—To store this medicine:

- Keep out of the reach of children.
- Store away from heat and direct light.
- Do not store the capsule or tablet form of this medicine in the bathroom, near the kitchen sink, or in other damp places. Heat or moisture may cause the medicine to break down.
- Keep the liquid form of this medicine from freezing.
- Do not keep outdated medicine or medicine no longer needed. Be sure that any discarded medicine is out of the reach of children.

Precautions While Using This Medicine

Your doctor should check your progress at regular visits, especially during the first few months of treatment with this medicine. The amount of loxapine you take may be changed often to meet the needs of your condition and to help avoid side effects.

Do not stop taking this medicine without first checking with your doctor. Your doctor may want you to reduce gradually the amount you are taking before stopping completely. This will allow your body time to adjust and to keep your condition from becoming worse.

This medicine will add to the effects of alcohol and other CNS depressants (medicines that slow down the nervous system, possibly causing drowsiness). Some examples of CNS depressants are antihistamines or medicine for hay fever, other allergies, or colds; sedatives, tranquilizers, or sleeping medicine; prescription pain medicine or narcotics; barbiturates; medicine for seizures; or anesthetics, including some dental anesthetics. *Check with your doctor before taking any of the above while you are taking this medicine.*

Do not take this medicine within two hours of taking antacids or medicine for diarrhea. Taking loxapine and antacids or medicine for diarrhea too close together may make this medicine less effective.

This medicine may cause some people to become drowsy or less alert than they are normally, especially as the amount of medicine is increased. Even if you take this medicine at bedtime, you may feel drowsy or less alert on arising. *Make sure you know how you react to this medicine before you drive, use machines, or do anything else that could be dangerous if you are not alert.*

Although it is not a problem for most patients, dizziness, lightheadedness, or fainting may occur, especially when you get up from a lying or sitting position. Getting up slowly may help. However, if the problem continues or gets worse, check with your doctor.

Loxapine may cause your skin to be more sensitive to sunlight than it is normally. Exposure to sunlight, even for brief periods of time, may cause a skin rash, itching, redness or other discoloration of the skin, or a severe sunburn. When you begin taking this medicine:

- Stay out of direct sunlight, especially between the hours of 10:00 a.m. and 3:00 p.m., if possible.
- Wear protective clothing, including a hat. Also, wear sunglasses.
- Apply a sun block product that has a skin protection factor (SPF) of at least 15. Some patients may require a product with a higher SPF number, especially if they have a fair complexion. If you have any questions about this, check with your health care professional.
- Apply a sun block lipstick that has an SPF of at least 15 to protect your lips.
- Do not use a sunlamp or tanning bed or booth.

If you have a severe reaction from the sun, check with your doctor.

Loxapine may cause dryness of the mouth. For temporary relief, use sugarless candy or gum, melt bits of ice in your mouth, or use a saliva substitute. However, if your mouth continues to feel dry for more than 2 weeks, check with your medical doctor or dentist. Continuing dryness of the mouth may increase the chance of dental disease, including tooth decay, gum disease, and fungus infections.

Before having any kind of surgery, dental treatment, or emergency treatment, tell the medical doctor or dentist in charge that you are taking this medicine. Taking loxapine together with medicines that are used during surgery or dental or emergency treatments may increase the CNS depressant effects.

Side Effects of This Medicine

Along with its needed effects, loxapine can sometimes cause serious side effects. Tardive dyskinesia (a movement disorder) may occur and may not go away after you stop using the medicine. Signs of tardive dyskinesia include fine, worm-like movements of the tongue, or other uncontrolled movements of the mouth, tongue, cheeks, jaw, or arms and legs. Other serious but rare side effects may also occur. These include severe muscle stiffness, fever, unusual tiredness or weakness, fast heartbeat, difficult breathing, increased sweating, loss of bladder control, and seizures (neuroleptic malignant syndrome). *You and your doctor should discuss the good this medicine will do as well as the risks of taking it.*

Stop taking loxapine and get emergency help immediately if any of the following side effects occur:
Rare
Convulsions (seizures); difficult or fast breathing; fast heartbeat or irregular pulse; fever (high); high or low blood pressure; increased sweating; loss of bladder control; muscle stiffness (severe); unusually pale skin; unusual tiredness or weakness

Check with your doctor immediately if any of the following side effects occur:
More common
Lip smacking or puckering; puffing of cheeks; rapid or fine, worm-like movements of tongue; uncontrolled chewing movements; uncontrolled movements of arms or legs

Also, check with your doctor as soon as possible if any of the following side effects occur:
More common (occurring with increase of dosage)
Difficulty in speaking or swallowing; loss of balance control; mask-like face; restlessness or desire to keep moving; shuffling walk; slowed movements; stiffness of arms and legs; trembling and shaking of fingers and hands

Less common
Constipation (severe); difficult urination; inability to move eyes; muscle spasms, especially of the neck and back; skin rash; twisting movements of the body

Rare
Sore throat and fever; increased blinking or spasms of eyelid; uncontrolled twisting movements of neck, trunk, arms, or legs; unusual bleeding or bruising; unusual facial expressions or body positions; yellow eyes or skin

Symptoms of overdose
Dizziness (severe); drowsiness (severe); muscle trembling, jerking, stiffness, or uncontrolled movements (severe); troubled breathing (severe); unusual tiredness or weakness (severe)

Other side effects may occur that usually do not need medical attention. These side effects may go away during treatment as your body adjusts to the medicine. However, check with your doctor if any of the following side effects continue or are bothersome:
More common
Blurred vision; confusion; dizziness, lightheadedness, or fainting; drowsiness; dryness of mouth

Less common
Constipation (mild); decreased sexual ability; enlargement of breasts (males and females); headache; in-creased sensitivity of skin to sun; missing menstrual periods; nausea or vomiting; trouble in sleeping; unusual secretion of milk; weight gain

Certain side effects of this medicine may occur after you have stopped taking it. Check with your doctor as soon as possible if you notice any of the following effects after you have stopped taking loxapine:
Dizziness; nausea and vomiting; rapid or worm-like movements of the tongue; stomach upset or pain; trembling of fingers and hands; uncontrolled chewing movements

Other side effects not listed above may also occur in some patients. If you notice any other effects, check with your doctor.

Additional Information

Once a medicine has been approved for marketing for a certain use, experience may show that it is also useful for other medical problems. Although this use is not included in product labeling, loxapine is used in certain patients with the following medical condition:

• Anxiety associated with mental depression

Other than the above information, there is no additional information relating to proper use, precautions, or side effects for this use.

Revised: 01/29/93

L-TRYPTOPHAN   Systemic— INTRODUCTORY VERSION

Commonly used brand name(s):

In Canada—
Alti-Tryptophan

Other commonly used names are
Tryptophan

Description

L-tryptophan (L-TRIP-toe-fan) is used along with other medications to treat mental depression. Also, L-tryptophan is used along with lithium to treat bipolar disorder.

L-tryptophan is available in the following dosage forms:
Oral
• Capsules (Canada)
• Tablets (Canada)

Before Using This Medicine

If you are taking this medicine without a prescription, carefully read and follow any precautions on the label. For L-tryptophan, the following should be considered:

Allergies—Tell your doctor if you have ever had any unusual or allergic reaction to L-tryptophan. Also tell your doctor and pharmacist if you are allergic to any other substances, such as foods, preservatives, or dyes.

Pregnancy—L-tryptophan has not been shown to cause birth defects or other problems in humans.

Breast-feeding— It is not known whether L-tryptophan

passes into breast milk. However, L-tryptophan has not been reported to cause problems in nursing babies.

Children—Studies on this medicine have been done only in adult patients, and there is no specific information comparing use of L-tryptophan in children with use in other age groups.

Older adults—Many medicines have not been studied specifically in older people. Therefore, it may not be known whether they work exactly the same way they do in younger adults or if they cause different side effects or problems in older people. There is no specific information comparing use of L-tryptophan in the elderly with use in other age groups.

Other medicines—Although certain medicines should not be used together at all, in other cases two different medicines may be used together even if an interaction might occur. In these cases, your doctor may want to change the dose, or other precautions may be necessary. When you are taking L-tryptophan, it is especially important that your doctor and pharmacist know if you are taking any of the following:

- Lithium (e.g., Eskalith) or
- Monoamine oxidase (MAO) inhibitors (furazolidone [e.g., Furoxone], isocarboxazid [e.g., Marplan], phenelzine [e.g., Nardil], procarbazine [e.g., Matulane], selegiline [e.g., Eldepryl], tranylcypromine [e.g., Parnate])—Using these medicines with L-tryptophan may increase the chance of side effects

Other medical problems—The presence of other medical problems may affect the use of L-tryptophan. Make sure you tell your doctor if you have any other medical problems, especially:

- Achlohydria or malabsorption (digestion problems)—L-tryptophan may cause breathing problems in patients with certain types of digestion problems
- Bladder cancer—L-tryptophan may increase the risk of bladder cancer
- Cataracts—L-tryptophan may cause cataracts
- Diabetes mellitus (sugar diabetes)—L-tryptophan may cause diabetes in patients with a family history of diabetes

Proper Use of This Medicine

Take with a low-protein, carbohydrate-rich meal or snack to prevent an upset stomach.

Dosing—The dose of L-tryptophan will be different for different patients. *Follow your doctor's orders or the directions on the label.* The following information includes only the average doses of L-tryptophan. *If your dose is different, do not change it* unless your doctor tells you to do so.

The number of capsules or tablets that you take depends on the strength of the medicine. Also, *the number of doses you take each day, the time allowed between doses, and the length of time you take the medicine depend on the medical problem for which you are taking L-tryptophan.*

- For *oral* dosage forms (capsules or tablets):
  —For mental depression:
    - Adults—8 to 12 grams per day, given in 3 to 4 equally divided doses
    - Children—Use and dose must be determined by your doctor.

Missed dose—If you miss a dose of this medicine, it is not necessary to make up the missed dose. Skip the missed dose and continue with your next scheduled dose. Do not double doses.

Storage—To store this medicine:

- Keep out of the reach of children.
- Store away from heat and direct light.
- Do not store the capsule or tablet form of this medicine in the bathroom, near the kitchen sink, or in other damp places. Heat or moisture may cause the medicine to break down.
- Do not keep outdated medicine or medicine no longer needed. Be sure that any discarded medicine is out of the reach of children.

Precautions While Using This Medicine

It is important that your doctor check your progress at regular visits, to allow dosage adjustments and help reduce any side effects.

This medicine may cause some people to become drowsy, dizzy, or less alert than they are normally. *Make sure you know how you react to this medicine before you drive, use machines, or do anything else that could be dangerous if you are dizzy or are not alert.*

This medicine may cause dryness of the mouth. Using sugarless candy or gum, ice, or a saliva substitute may be helpful. Check with your physician or dentist if dry mouth continues for more than 2 weeks.

Avoid excessive exposure to ultraviolet light to reduce the chance of cataract formation.

Side Effects of This Medicine

Along with its needed effects, a medicine may cause some unwanted effects. Although not all of these side effects may occur, if they do occur they may need medical attention.

Symptoms of overdose

> *Get emergency help immediately if any of the following symptoms of overdose occur*
> Agitation; confusion; diarrhea; fever; overactive reflexes; poor coordination; restlessness; shivering; sweating; talking or acting with excitement you cannot control; trembling or shaking; twitching; vomiting

Other side effects may occur that usually do not need medical attention. These side effects may go away during treatment as your body adjusts to the medicine. However, check with your doctor if any of the following side effects continue or are bothersome:

> Dizziness; drowsiness; dry mouth; headache; loss of appetite; nausea

Other side effects not listed above may also occur in some patients. If you notice any other effects, check with your doctor.

Developed: 09/07/2000

LYME DISEASE VACCINE   Systemic

Commonly used brand name(s):

In the U.S.—
   LYMErix

Anther commonly used name is Lyme disease vaccine (recombinant OspA).

Description

Lyme disease vaccine is an active immunizing agent used to prevent infection by Lyme disease bacteria. It works by causing your body to produce its own protection (antibodies) against the bacteria.

Lyme disease causes rash, fever, weakness, and joint and muscle pain. The disease is caused by bacteria passed to humans by the bite of infected ticks.

The risk of getting tick-borne infections can be lessened by such precautions as wearing long-sleeved shirts and long pants, tucking pants into socks, treating clothing with tick repellent, and checking for and removing attached ticks.

This medicine is available only with your doctor's prescription, in the following dosage form(s):

Parenteral
- Injection (U.S.)

Before Using This Medicine

In deciding to use a medicine, the risks of taking the medicine must be weighed against the good it will do. This is a decision you and your doctor will make. For Lyme disease vaccine, the following should be considered:

Allergies—Tell your doctor if you have ever had any unusual or allergic reaction to Lyme disease vaccine. Also tell your health care professional if you are allergic to any other substances, such as preservatives.

Pregnancy—Studies on effects in pregnancy have not been done in either humans or animals.

Breast-feeding—This vaccine has not been reported to cause problems in nursing babies.

Children—Lyme disease vaccine has not been tested in persons younger than 15 years of age. Use is not recommended in infants and children.

Teenagers—Lyme disease vaccine is not recommended for use in persons younger than 15 years of age.

Older adults—Many medicines have not been studied specifically in older people. Therefore, it may not be known whether they work exactly as they do in younger adults. Although there is no specific information comparing use of Lyme disease vaccine in the elderly with use in other age groups, this vaccine is not expected to cause different side effects or problems in older people than it does in younger adults.

Other medicines—Although certain medicines should not be used together at all, in other cases two different medicines may be used together even if an interaction might occur. In these cases, your doctor may want to change the dose, or other precautions may be necessary. Tell your health care professional if you are taking any other prescription or nonprescription (over-the-counter [OTC]) medicine.

Other medical problems—The presence of other medical problems may affect the use of Lyme disease vaccine. Make sure you tell your doctor if you have any other medical problems.

Proper Use of This Medicine

Dosing—The following information includes only the average doses of Lyme disease vaccine.

- For *injection* dosage form:
  —For prevention of Lyme disease:
  - Adults and adolescents 15 years of age and older—One dose injected into the arm muscle during the first office visit, then one month and twelve months after the first dose, for a total of three doses.

Side Effects of This Medicine

Along with its needed effects, a medicine may cause some unwanted effects. Although not all of these side effects may occur, if they do occur they may need medical attention.

Check with your doctor as soon as possible if any of the following side effects occur:
More common
    Numbness; tingling; unusual tiredness or weakness
Less common
    Bone pain; chills; cough; fever; muscle aches; runny or stuffy nose; shivering; skin rash, itching, redness, swelling, or other sign of irritation not present before vaccination; sneezing; sore throat; sweating
Rare
    Headache, severe

Other side effects may occur that usually do not need medical attention. However, check with your doctor if any of the following side effects continue or are bothersome:
More common
    Back pain; pain in joints and/or muscles
Less common
    Depression; diarrhea; dizziness; feeling unusually cold

Other side effects not listed above may also occur in some patients. If you notice any other side effects, check with your doctor.

Developed: 03/08/99

LYPRESSIN   Systemic

Commonly used brand name(s):

In the U.S.—
    Diapid

Description

Lypressin (lye-PRESS-in) is a hormone used to prevent or control the frequent urination, increased thirst, and loss of water associated with diabetes insipidus (water diabetes).

Lypressin is available only with your doctor's prescription, in the following dosage form:

Nasal
- Nasal spray (U.S.)

Before Using This Medicine

In deciding to use a medicine, the risks of taking the medicine must be weighed against the good it will do. This is a decision you and your doctor will make. For lypressin, the following should be considered:

Allergies—Tell your doctor if you have ever had any unusual or allergic reaction to lypressin or vasopressin. Also tell

your health care professional if you are allergic to any other substances, such as foods, preservatives, or dyes.

Pregnancy—Studies on the effects in pregnancy have not been done in either humans or animals.

Breast-feeding—It is not known whether lypressin passes into breast milk. However, this medicine has not been reported to cause problems in nursing babies.

Children—Although there is no specific information comparing use of lypressin in children with use in other age groups, this medicine is not expected to cause different side effects or problems in children than it does in adults.

Older adults—Many medicines have not been studied specifically in older people. Therefore, it may not be known whether they work exactly the same way they do in younger adults or if they cause different side effects or problems in older people. There is no specific information comparing use of lypressin in the elderly with use in other age groups.

Other medicines—Although certain medicines should not be used together at all, in other cases two different medicines may be used together even if an interaction might occur. In these cases, your doctor may want to change the dose, or other precautions may be necessary. Tell your health care professional if you are taking any other prescription or nonprescription (over-the-counter [OTC]) medicine.

Other medical problems—The presence of other medical problems may affect the use of lypressin. Make sure you tell your doctor if you have any other medical problems, especially:

- Hay fever or other allergies or
- Infection of ears, lungs, nose, or throat or
- Stuffy nose—May prevent nasal lypressin from being absorbed into the bloodstream, through the lining of the nose
- High blood pressure—Lypressin may increase blood pressure

Proper Use of This Medicine

Use this medicine only as directed. Do not use more of it and do not use it more often than your doctor ordered. To do so may increase the chance of unwanted effects.

To use:

- Blow nose gently. Hold the bottle in an upright position. With head upright, spray the medicine into each nostril by squeezing the bottle quickly and firmly. Do not lie down when spraying this medicine.

Rinse the tip of the bottle with hot water, taking care not to suck water into the bottle, and dry with a clean tissue. Replace the cap right after use.

Dosing—The dose of lypressin will be different for different patients. *Follow your doctor's orders or the directions on the label.* The following information includes only the average doses of lypressin. *If your dose is different, do not change it* unless your doctor tells you to do so.

- For *nasal* dosage forms:
  —Adults: One or two sprays in each nostril four times a day.
  —Children six weeks of age and older: One or two sprays in each nostril four times a day.
  —Children less than six weeks of age: Use is generally not recommended.

Missed dose—If you miss a dose of this medicine, use it as soon as possible. However, if it is almost time for your next dose, skip the missed dose and go back to your regular dosing schedule. Do not double doses.

Storage—To store this medicine:
- Keep out of the reach of children.
- Store away from heat and direct light.
- Do not store in the bathroom, near the kitchen sink, or in other damp places. Heat or moisture may cause the medicine to break down.
- Keep the medicine from freezing.
- Do not keep outdated medicine or medicine no longer needed. Be sure that any discarded medicine is out of the reach of children.

Side Effects of This Medicine

Along with its needed effects, a medicine may cause some unwanted effects. Although not all of these effects may occur, if they do occur they may need medical attention.

Check with your doctor immediately if any of the following side effects occur since they may be signs or symptoms of too much fluid in the body or overdose:
  Coma; confusion; convulsions (seizures); drowsiness; headache (continuing); problems with urination; weight gain

Check with your doctor as soon as possible if any of the following side effects occur:
  Rare
    Cough (continuing); feeling of tightness in chest; shortness of breath or troubled breathing

Other side effects may occur that usually do not need medical attention. These side effects may go away during treatment as your body adjusts to the medicine. However, check with your doctor if any of the following side effects continue or are bothersome:
  Less common or rare
    Abdominal or stomach cramps; headache; heartburn; increased bowel movements; irritation or pain in the eye; itching, irritation, or sores inside nose; runny or stuffy nose

Other side effects not listed above may also occur in some patients. If you notice any other effects, check with your doctor.

Revised: 07/01/93

MAFENIDE   Topical†

Commonly used brand name(s):

In the U.S.—
  Sulfamylon

†Not commercially available in Canada.

Description

Mafenide (MA-fe-nide), a sulfa medicine, is used to prevent and treat bacterial or fungus infections. It works by preventing growth of the fungus or bacteria.

Mafenide cream is applied to the skin and/or burned area(s) to prevent and treat bacterial or fungus infections that may occur in burns.

Other medicines are used along with this medicine for burns. Patients with severe burns or burns over a large area of the body must be treated in a hospital.

This medicine is available only with your doctor's prescription, in the following dosage form:

Topical
- Cream (U.S.)

Before Using This Medicine

In deciding to use a medicine, the risks of taking the medicine must be weighed against the good it will do. This is a decision you and your doctor will make. For mafenide, the following should be considered:

Allergies—Tell your doctor if you have ever had any unusual or allergic reaction to mafenide, acetazolamide (e.g., Diamox), oral antidiabetics (diabetes medicine you take by mouth), dichlorphenamide (e.g., Daranide), furosemide (e.g., Lasix), methazolamide (e.g., Neptazane), other sulfa medicines, or thiazide diuretics (water pills). Also tell your health care professional if you are allergic to any other substances, such as preservatives or dyes.

Pregnancy—Studies on effects in pregnancy have not been done in either humans or animals. However, use is not recommended in women during their child-bearing years unless the burn area covers more than 20% of the total body surface. In addition, sulfa medicines may increase the chance of liver problems in newborn infants and should not be used near the due date of the pregnancy.

Breast-feeding—Mafenide, when used on skin and/or burns, is absorbed into the mother's body. It is not known whether this medicine passes into breast milk. Sulfa medicines given by mouth do pass into the breast milk, and may cause liver problems, anemia (iron-poor blood), and other unwanted effects in nursing babies, especially those with glucose-6-phosphate dehydrogenase deficiency (lack of G6PD enzyme). Be sure you have discussed the risks and benefits of mafenide with your doctor.

Children—Use of mafenide is not recommended in premature or newborn infants up to 2 months of age. Sulfa medicines may cause liver problems in these infants.

Older adults—Many medicines have not been tested in older people. Therefore, it may not be known whether they work exactly the same way they do in younger adults or if they cause different side effects or problems in older people. There is no specific information comparing use of mafenide in the elderly with use in other age groups.

Other medicines—Although certain medicines should not be used together at all, in other cases two different medicines may be used together even if an interaction might occur. In these cases, your doctor may want to change the dose, or other precautions may be necessary. Tell your health care professional if you are using any other prescription or nonprescription (over-the-counter [OTC]) medicine.

Other medical problems—The presence of other medical problems may affect the use of mafenide. Make sure you tell your doctor if you have any other medical problems, especially:
- Blood problems—Use of mafenide may make the condition worse

- Glucose-6-phosphate dehydrogenase deficiency (lack of G6PD enzyme)—Use of mafenide in persons with this condition may result in hemolytic anemia
- Kidney problems or
- Lung problems or
- Metabolic acidosis—Use of mafenide in persons with any of these conditions may increase the risk of a side effect called metabolic acidosis

Proper Use of This Medicine

To use:
- Before applying this medicine, cleanse the affected area(s). Remove dead or burned skin and other debris.
- Wear a sterile glove to apply this medicine. Apply a thin layer (about 1/16 inch) of mafenide to the affected area(s). Keep the affected area(s) covered with the medicine at all times.
- If this medicine is rubbed off the affected area(s) by moving around or if it is washed off during bathing, showering, or the use of a whirlpool bath, reapply the medicine.
- After this medicine has been applied, the treated area(s) may be covered with a dressing or left uncovered as desired.

To help clear up your skin and/or burn infection completely, *keep using mafenide for the full time of treatment*. You should keep using this medicine until the burn area has healed or is ready for skin grafting. *Do not miss any doses*.

Dosing—The dose of topical mafenide will be different for different patients. *Follow your doctor's orders or the directions on the label*. The following information includes only the average doses of topical mafenide. *If your dose is different, do not change it* unless your doctor tells you to do so.
- For *topical* dosage form (cream):
  - For bacterial or fungus infection:
    - Adults and children 2 months of age and over—Use one or two times a day.
    - Infants and children up to 2 months of age—Use is not recommended.

Missed dose—If you miss a dose of this medicine, apply it as soon as possible. However, if it is almost time for your next dose, skip the missed dose and go back to your regular dosing schedule.

Storage—To store this medicine:
- Keep out of the reach of children.
- Store away from heat and direct light.
- Keep the medicine from freezing.
- Do not keep outdated medicine or medicine no longer needed. Be sure that any discarded medicine is out of the reach of children.

Precautions While Using This Medicine

It is important that your doctor check your progress at regular visits.

If your skin infection or burn does not improve within a few days or if your more serious burns or burns over larger areas do not improve within a few weeks, or if they become worse, check with your doctor.

Side Effects of This Medicine

Along with its needed effects, a medicine may cause some unwanted effects. Although not all of these side effects may occur, if they do occur they may need medical attention.

Check with your doctor immediately if any of the following side effects occur:

> *Less common*
> > Itching; skin rash or redness; swelling of face or skin; wheezing or troubled breathing
>
> *Rare*
> > Bleeding or oozing of skin; drowsiness; fast, deep breathing; nausea

Other side effects may occur that usually do not need medical attention. These side effects may go away during treatment as your body adjusts to the medicine. However, check with your doctor if any of the following side effects continue or are bothersome:

> *More common*
> > Pain or burning feeling on treated area(s)

Other side effects not listed above may also occur in some patients. If you notice any other effects, check with your doctor.

Revised: 04/22/94

MAGNESIUM SUPPLEMENTS
Systemic

Commonly used brand name(s):

In the U.S.—

Almora[4]	Mag-Tab SR[6]
Chloromag[1]	Magtrate[4]
Citroma[2]	Maox[7]
Concentrated Phillips' Milk of Magnesia[5]	MGP[4]
Mag-200[7]	Phillips' Chewable Tablets[5]
Mag-L-100[1]	Phillips' Milk of Magnesia[5]
Magonate[4]	Slow-Mag[1]
Mag-Ox 400[7]	Uro-Mag[7]

In Canada—

Citro-Mag[2]	Magnesium-Rougier[3]
Mag 2[8]	Phillips' Magnesia Tablets[5]
Maglucate[4]	Phillips' Milk of Magnesia[5]

Note: For quick reference, the following magnesium supplements are numbered to match the corresponding brand names.

This information applies to the following:
1. Magnesium Chloride (mag-NEE-zhum KLOR-ide) †‡
2. Magnesium Citrate (mag-NEE-zhum SIH-trayt) ‡
3. Magnesium Gluceptate (mag-NEE-zhum gloo-SEP-tate) *
4. Magnesium Gluconate (mag-NEE-zhum GLOO-ko-nate) ‡
5. Magnesium Hydroxide †† (mag-NEE-zhum hye-DROX-ide)‡
6. Magnesium Lactate (mag-NEE-zhumLAK-tate) †
7. Magnesium Oxide (mag-NEE-zhum OX-ide) ‡§
8. Magnesium Pidolate (mag-NEE-zhum PID-o-late) *
9. Magnesium Sulfate (mag-NEE-zhum SUL-fate) ‡§

---

*Not commercially available in the U.S.
†Not commercially available in Canada.
‡Generic name product may be available in the U.S.
§Generic name product may be available in Canada.
†† See Antacids (Oral) for antacid use of magnesium hydroxide and magnesium oxide.

Description

Magnesium is used as a dietary supplement for individuals who are deficient in magnesium. Although a balanced diet usually supplies all the magnesium a person needs, magnesium supplements may be needed by patients who have lost magnesium because of illness or treatment with certain medicines.

Lack of magnesium may lead to irritability, muscle weakness, and irregular heartbeat.

Injectable magnesium is given only by or under the supervision of a health care professional. Some oral magnesium preparations are available only with a prescription. Others are available without a prescription.

Magnesium supplements are available in the following dosage forms:

> *Oral*
> > Magnesium Chloride
> > - Tablets (U.S.)
> > - Enteric-coated tablets (U.S.)
> > - Extended-release tablets (U.S.)
> >
> > Magnesium Citrate
> > - Oral solution (U.S. and Canada)
> >
> > Magnesium Gluceptate
> > - Oral solution (Canada)
> >
> > Magnesium Gluconate
> > - Oral solution (U.S.)
> > - Tablets (U.S. and Canada)
> >
> > Magnesium Hydroxide
> > - Tablets (U.S.)
> > - Chewable tablets (U.S. and Canada)
> > - Oral solution (U.S. and Canada)
> >
> > Magnesium Lactate
> > - Extended-release tablets (U.S.)
> >
> > Magnesium Oxide
> > - Capsules (U.S.)
> > - Tablets (U.S. and Canada)
> >
> > Magnesium Pidolate
> > - Powder for oral solution (Canada)
> >
> > Magnesium Sulfate
> > - Crystals (U.S.)
>
> *Parenteral*
> > Magnesium Chloride
> > - Injection (U.S.)
> >
> > Magnesium Sulfate
> > - Injection (U.S. and Canada)

Importance of Diet

For good health, it is important that you eat a balanced and varied diet. Follow carefully any diet program your health care professional may recommend. For your specific dietary vitamin and/or mineral needs, ask your health care professional for a list of appropriate foods. If you think that you are not getting enough vitamins and/or minerals in your diet, you may choose to take a dietary supplement.

The best dietary sources of magnesium include green leafy vegetables, nuts, peas, beans, and cereal grains in which the germ or outer layers have not been removed. Hard water has been found to contain more magnesium than soft water. A diet high in fat may cause less magnesium to be absorbed. Cooking may decrease the magnesium content of food.

The daily amount of magnesium needed is defined in several different ways.

> *For U.S.—*
> - Recommended Dietary Allowances (RDAs) are the amount of vitamins and minerals needed to provide for adequate nutrition in most healthy persons. RDAs for a given nutrient may vary depending on a person's age, sex, and physical condition (e.g., pregnancy).

- Daily Values (DVs) are used on food and dietary supplement labels to indicate the percent of the recommended daily amount of each nutrient that a serving provides. DV replaces the previous designation of United States Recommended Daily Allowances (US-RDAs).

For Canada—

- Recommended Nutrient Intakes (RNIs) are used to determine the amounts of vitamins, minerals, and protein needed to provide adequate nutrition and lessen the risk of chronic disease.

Normal daily recommended intakes in milligrams (mg) for magnesium are generally defined as follows:

Persons	U.S. (mg)	Canada (mg)
Infants and children		
Birth to 3 years of age	40–80	20–50
4 to 6 years of age	120	65
7 to 10 years of age	170	100–135
Adolescent and adult males	270–400	130–250
Adolescent and adult females	280–300	135–210
Pregnant females	320	195–245
Breast-feeding females	340–355	245–265

Before Using This Dietary Supplement

If you are taking this dietary supplement without a prescription, carefully read and follow any precautions on the label. For magnesium supplements, the following should be considered:

Allergies—Tell your health care professional if you have ever had any unusual or allergic reaction to magnesium. Also tell your health care professional if you are allergic to any other substances, such as foods, preservatives, or dyes.

Pregnancy—It is especially important that you are receiving enough vitamins and minerals when you become pregnant and that you continue to receive the right amount of vitamins and minerals throughout your pregnancy. The healthy growth and development of the fetus depend on a steady supply of nutrients from the mother. However, taking large amounts of dietary supplements during pregnancy may be harmful to the mother and/or fetus and should be avoided.

Breast-feeding—It is especially important that you receive the right amount of vitamins and minerals so that your baby will also get the vitamins and minerals needed to grow properly. However, taking large amounts of a dietary supplement while breast-feeding may be harmful to the mother and/or baby and should be avoided.

Children—Problems in children have not been reported with intake of normal daily recommended amounts.

Older adults—Problems in older adults have not been reported with intake of normal daily recommended amounts.

Studies have shown that older adults may have lower blood levels of magnesium than younger adults. Your health care professional may recommend that you take a magnesium supplement.

Medicines or other dietary supplements—Although certain medicines or other dietary supplements should not be used together at all, in other cases they may be used together even if an interaction might occur. In these cases, your health care professional may want to change the dose, or other precautions may be necessary. When you are taking magnesium, it is especially important that your health care professional know if you are taking any of the following:

- Cellulose sodium phosphate—Use with magnesium supplements may prevent cellulose sodium phosphate from working properly; magnesium supplements should be taken at least 1 hour before or after cellulose sodium phosphate

- Magnesium-containing preparations, other, including magnesium enemas—Use with magnesium supplements may cause high blood levels of magnesium, which may increase the chance of side effects

- Sodium polystyrene sulfonate—Use with magnesium supplements may cause the magnesium supplement to be less effective

- Tetracyclines, oral—Use with magnesium supplements may prevent the tetracycline from working properly; magnesium supplements should be taken at least 1 to 3 hours before or after oral tetracycline

Other medical problems—The presence of other medical problems may affect the use of magnesium. Make sure you tell your health care professional if you have any other medical problems, especially:

- Heart disease—Magnesium supplements may make this condition worse

- Kidney problems—Magnesium supplements may increase the risk of hypermagnesemia (too much magnesium in the blood), which could cause serious side effects; your health care professional may need to change your dose

Proper Use of This Dietary Supplement

Dosing—The amount of magnesium needed to meet normal daily recommended intakes will be different for different patients. The following information includes only the average amounts of magnesium.

- For *oral* dosage form (capsules, chewable tablets, crystals for oral solution, extended-release tablets, enteric-coated tablets, powder for oral solution, tablets, oral solution):
  - To prevent deficiency, the amount taken by mouth is based on normal daily recommended intakes (Note that the normal daily recommended intakes are expressed as an actual amount of magnesium. The salt form [e.g., magnesium chloride, magnesium gluconate, etc.] has a different strength.):

  For the U.S.
  - Adult and teenage males—270 to 400 milligrams (mg) per day.
  - Adult and teenage females—280 to 300 mg per day.
  - Pregnant females—320 mg per day.
  - Breast-feeding females—340 to 355 mg per day.
  - Children 7 to 10 years of age—170 mg per day.
  - Children 4 to 6 years of age—120 mg per day.
  - Children birth to 3 years of age—40 to 80 mg per day.

  For Canada
  - Adult and teenage males—130 to 250 mg per day.
  - Adult and teenage females—135 to 210 mg per day.
  - Pregnant females—195 to 245 mg per day.
  - Breast-feeding females—245 to 265 mg per day.

- Children 7 to 10 years of age—100 to 135 mg per day.
- Children 4 to 6 years of age—65 mg per day.
- Children birth to 3 years of age—20 to 50 mg per day.
  —To treat deficiency:
  - Adults, teenagers, and children—Treatment dose is determined by prescriber for each individual based on severity of deficiency.

Magnesium supplements should be taken with meals. Taking magnesium supplements on an empty stomach may cause diarrhea.

For individuals taking the *extended-release form* of this dietary supplement:
- Swallow the tablets whole. Do not chew or suck on the tablet.
- Some tablets may be broken or crushed and sprinkled on applesauce or other soft food. However, check with your health care professional first, since this should not be done for most tablets.

For individuals taking the *powder form* of this dietary supplement:
- Pour powder into a glass.
- Add water and stir.

Missed dose—If you miss taking your magnesium supplement for one or more days there is no cause for concern, since it takes some time for your body to become seriously low in magnesium. However, if your health care professional has recommended that you take magnesium, try to remember to take it as directed every day.

Storage—To store this dietary supplement:
- Keep out of the reach of children.
- Store away from heat and direct light.
- Do not store in the bathroom, near the kitchen sink, or in other damp places. Heat or moisture may cause the dietary supplement to break down.
- Keep the dietary supplement from freezing. Do not refrigerate.
- Do not keep dietary supplements that are outdated or are no longer needed. Be sure that any discarded dietary supplement is out of the reach of children.

Side Effects of This Dietary Supplement

Along with its needed effects, a dietary supplement may cause some unwanted effects. Although not all of these side effects may occur, if they do occur they may need medical attention.

Check with your health care professional immediately if any of the following side effects occur:
Rare (with injectable magnesium only)
    Dizziness or fainting; flushing; irritation and pain at injection site—for intramuscular administration only; muscle paralysis; troubled breathing
Symptoms of overdose (rare in individuals with normal kidney function)
    Blurred or double vision; coma; dizziness or fainting; drowsiness (severe); increased or decreased urination; slow heartbeat; troubled breathing

Other side effects may occur that usually do not need medical attention. These side effects may go away during treatment as your body adjusts to the medicine. However, check with

your health care professional if the following side effect continues or is bothersome:
Less common (with oral magnesium)
    Diarrhea

Other side effects not listed above may also occur in some individuals. If you notice any other effects, check with your health care professional.

Revised: 07/11/95

MAGNETIC RESONANCE IMAGING CONTRAST AGENTS   Diagnostic

This information applies to the following medicines:
1. Gadodiamide (gad-oh-DYE-a-mide)
2. Gadopentetate (gad-o-PEN-te-tate) †
3. Gadoteridol (gad-oh-TER-i-dol) †
4. Gadoversetamide (gad-oh-ver-SET-a-mide) †

†Not commercially available in Canada.

Description

MRI (magnetic resonance imaging) contrast agents (also called paramagnetic agents) are used to help provide a clear picture during MRI. MRI is a special kind of diagnostic procedure. It uses magnets and computers to create images or "pictures" of certain areas inside the body. Unlike x-rays, it does not involve ionizing radiation.

MRI contrast agents are given by injection before or during MRI to help diagnose problems or diseases of the brain or the spine. In addition, gadopentetate is used to help diagnose problems in other parts of the body, such as the bones and joints, breast, liver, soft tissues, and uterus. Gadoversetamide is also used to help diagnose problems in the liver.

MRI contrast agents may also be used to diagnose other conditions as determined by your doctor.

MRI contrast agents are injected into a vein. The doses of these agents will be different for different patients depending on the weight of the person.

These agents are to be used only by or under the supervision of a doctor.

Before Having This Test

In deciding to use a diagnostic test, any risks of the test must be weighed against the good it will do. This is a decision you and your doctor will make. Also, test results may be affected by other things. For MRI contrast agents, the following should be considered:

Allergies—Tell your doctor if you have ever had any unusual or allergic reaction to contrast agents such as gadodiamide, gadopentetate, gadoteridol, or gadoversetamide. Also, tell your doctor if you are allergic to any other substances, such as foods, preservatives, or dyes.

Pregnancy—Studies have not been done in pregnant women. However, in animal studies, MRI contrast agents caused a delay in development of the animal fetus, increased the risk of losing the fetus, and caused birth defects and other side effects in the offspring when these agents were given to the mother in doses many times the human dose. Also, it is not known yet what effect the magnetic field used in MRI might have on the development of the fetus. Be sure you have discussed this with your doctor.

Breast-feeding—It is not known what amount of MRI contrast agents passes into the breast milk. However, your doctor may want you to stop breast-feeding for some time after you receive an MRI contrast agent. Be sure you have discussed this with your doctor.

Children—Although there is no specific information comparing use of MRI contrast agents in children with use in other age groups, these agents are not expected to cause different side effects or problems in children than they do in adults.

Older adults—These contrast agents have been tested and have not been shown to cause different side effects or problems in older people than they do in younger adults.

Other medical problems—The presence of other medical problems may affect the use of MRI contrast agents. Make sure you tell your doctor if you have any other medical problems, especially:

- Allergies or asthma (history of)—If you have a history of allergies or asthma, you may be at greater risk of having an allergic reaction to the contrast agent
- Anemia or
- Low blood pressure—MRI contrast agents may make these conditions worse
- Epilepsy—There may be an increased chance of seizures
- Heart disease—There may be an increased chance of developing an irregular heart beat
- Kidney disease (severe)—Kidney disease can cause the MRI agent to stay in the body longer than usual, which may increase the chance of side effects
- Sickle cell disease—There may be a greater risk of blockage of the blood vessels in patients with this condition

Your doctor may have special instructions for you to get ready for your test, depending on the type of test you are having. If you do not understand the instructions you receive or if you have not received any instructions, check with your doctor ahead of time.

Side Effects of This Medicine

Along with their needed effects, MRI contrast agents may cause some unwanted effects. Although not all of these side effects may occur, if they do occur they may need medical attention.

Less common or rare

Black, tarry stools; chest pain; confusion; convulsions (seizures); cough; decreased, increased, or painful urination; dizziness; drowsiness; fainting; fast or irregular heartbeat; hot, painful, swollen skin; itching, watery eyes; skin rash or hives; spitting or coughing up blood; swelling of face; thickening of tongue; throat spasm; unusual bleeding or bruising; unusual tiredness or weakness (severe); wheezing, tightness in chest, or troubled breathing

Other side effects may occur that usually do not need medical attention. These side effects may go away as your body adjusts to this agent. However, check with your doctor if any of the following side effects continue or are bothersome:

More common

Changes in taste; coldness at the place of injection; headache; nausea; unusual warmth and flushing of skin

Less common or rare

Abdominal pain or discomfort; agitation; anxiety; back pain; burning, tingling, or prickly sensation; change in appetite; change in sense of hearing or smell; diarrhea or constipation; dryness of mouth; fever; increased muscle tone; increased salivation; gas, bloating, flatulence; increased watering of mouth; joint pain; muscle pain or spasm; nosebleeds; pain and/or burning sensation at place of injection; pale skin; redness, pain, or swelling of eye; ringing or buzzing in ears; seeing, hearing, or smelling things that are not there; sore throat; stomach pain or upset; stuffy, runny nose or sneezing; swelling of face, hands, lower legs, or feet; thirst; tremor; twisting or other unusual body movements; vision disturbances; vomiting; weakness or tiredness

Not all of the side effects listed above have been reported for each of these agents, but they have been reported for at least one of them. There are some similarities among these agents, so many of the above side effects may occur with any of them.

Other side effects not listed above may also occur in some patients. If you notice any other effects, check with your doctor.

Revised: 03/20/00

MAGNETIC RESONANCE IMAGING CONTRAST AGENTS, IRON-CONTAINING   Diagnostic†

This information applies to the following diagnostic agent:
1. Ferumoxides (fer-yoo-MOX-ides) †

†Not commercially available in Canada.

Description

Iron-containing MRI (magnetic resonance imaging) contrast agents (also called superparamagnetic agents) are used to help provide a clear picture during MRI. MRI is a special kind of diagnostic procedure. It uses magnets and computers to create images or "pictures" of certain areas inside the body. Unlike x-rays, it does not involve ionizing radiation.

Ferumoxides, an iron-containing contrast agent, is given by injection before MRI to help find and diagnose tumors of the liver.

The dose of ferumoxides will be different for different patients according to body weight.

Ferumoxides is to be used only by or under the supervision of a doctor.

Before Having This Test

In deciding to use a diagnostic test, any risks of the test must be weighed against the good it will do. This is a decision you and your doctor will make. Also, test results may be affected by other things. For MRI contrast agents, the following should be considered:

Allergies—Tell your doctor if you have ever had any unusual or allergic reaction to contrast agents or to injectable preparations of iron. Also, tell your doctor if you are allergic to any other substances, such as foods, preservatives, or dyes.

Pregnancy—Studies with ferumoxides have not been done in pregnant women. However, in animal studies, ferumoxides caused birth defects in the offspring when given to the mother in doses many times larger than the human dose. Also, it is not yet known what effect the magnetic field used in MRI might have on the development of the fetus. Be sure you have discussed this with your doctor.

Breast-feeding—It is not known whether ferumoxides passes into the breast milk. However, your doctor may want you to stop breast-feeding for some time after you receive an MRI contrast agent. Be sure you have discussed this with your doctor.

Children—There is no specific information comparing use of MRI contrast agents in children with use in other age groups.

Older adults—Ferumoxides has been used in tests in older adults and has not been shown to cause different side effects or problems in older people than it does in younger adults.

Other medical problems—The presence of other medical problems may affect the use of MRI contrast agents. Make sure you tell your doctor if you have any other medical problems, especially:

- Allergies or asthma (history of) or
- Immunity problems—If you have a history of allergies or asthma or have a decreased natural immunity, you may be at greater risk of having an allergic reaction to the contrast agent

Preparation for This Test

Your doctor may have special instructions for you to get ready for your test, depending on the type of test you are having. If you do not understand the instructions you receive or if you have not received any instructions, check with your doctor ahead of time.

Side Effects of This Medicine

Along with their needed effects, MRI contrast agents may cause some unwanted effects. Although not all of these side effects may occur, if they do occur they may need medical attention.

Less common or rare
Back, leg or groin pain (severe); itching, watery eyes; skin rash or hives; swelling of face; thickening of tongue; unusual tiredness or weakness (severe); wheezing, tightness in chest, or troubled breathing

Other side effects may occur that usually do not need medical attention. These side effects may go away as your body adjusts to this agent. However, check with your doctor if any of the following side effects continue or are bothersome:

Less common
Brown discoloration of skin; nausea; unusual warmth and flushing of skin

Other side effects not listed above may also occur in some patients. If you notice any other effects, check with your doctor.

Developed: 10/22/97

MALATHION   Topical

Commonly used brand name(s):
In the U.S.—
   Ovide

Description

Malathion (mal-a-THYE-on) belongs to the group of medicines known as pediculicides (medicines that kill lice).

Malathion is applied to the hair and scalp to treat head lice infections. It acts by killing both the lice and their eggs.

This medicine is available only with your doctor's prescription, in the following dosage form:

Topical
   • Lotion (U.S.)

Before Using This Medicine

In deciding to use a medicine, the risks of taking the medicine must be weighed against the good it will do. This is a decision you and your doctor will make. For malathion, the following should be considered:

Allergies—Tell your doctor if you have ever had any unusual or allergic reaction to malathion. Also tell your health care professional if you are allergic to any other substances, such as preservatives or dyes.

Pregnancy—Malathion may be absorbed through the skin. Although it has not been studied in pregnant women, malathion has not been shown to cause birth defects or other problems in animal studies.

Breast-feeding—Malathion may be absorbed through the mother's skin. It is not known whether malathion passes into the breast milk. Although most medicines pass into breast milk in small amounts, many of them may be used safely while breast-feeding. Mothers who are using this medicine and who wish to breast-feed should discuss this with their doctor.

Children—This medicine has been tested in children 6 years of age and older and, in effective doses, has not been shown to cause different side effects or problems than it does in adults. There is no specific information comparing use of malathion in children less than 6 years of age with use in other age groups.

Older adults—Many medicines have not been studied specifically in older people. Therefore, it may not be known whether they work exactly the same way they do in younger adults or if they cause different side effects or problems in older people. There is no specific information comparing use of malathion in the elderly with use in other age groups.

Other medicines—Although certain medicines should not be used together at all, in other cases two different medicines may be used together even if an interaction might occur. In these cases, your doctor may want to change the dose, or other precautions may be necessary. When you are using malathion, it is especially important that your health care professional know if you are using any of the following:

- Antimyasthenics (ambenonium, neostigmine, pyridostigmine) or
- Demecarium, echothiophate, or isoflurophate eye medicine—Use of malathion with these medicines may increase the chance of side effects

Other medical problems—The presence of other medical problems may affect the use of malathion. Make sure you

tell your doctor if you have any other medical problems, especially:

- Anemia (severe) or
- Brain surgery, recent, or
- Liver disease or
- Malnutrition—These conditions may increase the chance of some side effects of malathion

- Asthma or
- Epilepsy or other seizure disorders or
- Heart disease or
- Myasthenia gravis or other nerve/muscle disease or
- Parkinson's disease or
- Stomach ulcer or other stomach or intestinal problems—Use of malathion may make the condition worse

Proper Use of This Medicine

Malathion is a poison. Keep it away from the mouth because it is harmful if swallowed.

Use this medicine only as directed by your doctor. Do not use more of it, do not use it more often, and do not use it for a longer time than your doctor ordered. To do so may increase the chance of absorption through the skin and the chance of malathion poisoning.

To use:

- Apply malathion by sprinkling on dry hair and rubbing in until the hair and scalp are thoroughly moistened.
- Immediately after using this medicine, wash your hands to remove any medicine that may be on them.
- Allow the hair to dry naturally. Use no heat (as from a hair dryer) and leave the hair uncovered.
- After the medicine has been allowed to remain on the hair and scalp for 8 to 12 hours, *wash the hair with a nonmedicated shampoo and then rinse thoroughly*.
- After rinsing, use a fine-toothed comb to remove the dead lice and eggs from the hair.

Keep this medicine away from the eyes. If you should accidentally get some in your eyes, flush them thoroughly with water at once.

This medicine is flammable. Do not use near heat, near open flame, or while smoking.

Head lice can be easily transferred from one person to another by direct contact with clothing, hats, scarves, bedding, towels, washcloths, hairbrushes and combs, or hairs from infected persons. Therefore, *all household members of your family should be examined for head lice and receive treatment if they are found to be infected.* If you have any questions about this, check with your doctor.

Dosing—The dose of malathion will be different for different patients. *Follow your doctor's orders or the directions on the label.* The following information includes only the average doses of malathion. *If your dose is different, do not change it* unless your doctor tells your to do so.

- For *lotion* dosage form:
  —For head lice infestations:
    - Adults and children 6 years of age and older—Apply to the hair and scalp one time. Treatment may be repeated after seven to nine days if necessary.
    - Children up to 6 years of age—Use and dose must be determined by your doctor.

Storage—To store this medicine:
- Keep out of the reach of children.

- Flammable. Keep away from heat and open flame.
- Store away from heat and direct light.
- Keep the medicine from freezing.
- Do not keep outdated medicine or medicine no longer needed. Be sure that any discarded medicine is out of the reach of children.

Precautions While Using This Medicine

To prevent reinfection or the spreading of the infection to other people, good health habits are also required. These include the following:

- Wash all clothing, bedding, towels, and washcloths in very hot water or dry-clean them.
- Wash all hairbrushes and combs in very hot soapy water and do not share them with other people.
- Clean the house or room by thorough vacuuming.

If you have any questions about this, check with your doctor.

Breathing in even small amounts of carbamate- or organophosphate-type insecticides or pesticides (for example, carbaryl [Sevin], demeton [Systox], diazinon, malathion, parathion, ronnel [Trolene]) may add to the effects of this medicine. Farmers, gardeners, residents of communities undergoing insecticide or pesticide spraying or dusting, workers in plants manufacturing such products, or other persons exposed to such poisons should protect themselves by wearing a mask over the nose and mouth, changing clothes frequently, and washing hands often while using this medicine.

Side Effects of This Medicine

Along with its needed effects, a medicine may cause some unwanted effects. Although not all of these side effects may occur, if they do occur they may need medical attention.

Check with your doctor as soon as possible if any of the following side effects occur:
Rare
Skin rash

When malathion is applied to the skin in recommended doses, symptoms of poisoning have not been reported. However, the chance may exist, especially if the skin is broken. *Symptoms of malathion poisoning* include:
Abdominal or stomach cramps; anxiety or restlessness; clumsiness or unsteadiness; confusion or mental depression; convulsions (seizures); diarrhea; difficult or labored breathing; dizziness; drowsiness; increased sweating; increased watering of mouth or eyes; loss of bowel or bladder control; muscle twitching of eyelids, face, and neck; pinpoint pupils; slow heartbeat; trembling; unusual weakness

Other side effects may occur that usually do not need medical attention. These side effects may go away during treatment as your body adjusts to the medicine. However, check with your doctor if either of the following side effects continues or is bothersome:
Less common or rare
Redness, pain, swelling of eye, eyelid, inner lining of eyelid; burning, dry or itching eyes, discharge, excessive tearing; stinging or irritation of scalp

Other side effects not listed above may also occur in some patients. If you notice any other effects, check with your doctor.

Revised: 2/4/00

MANGAFODIPIR Systemic

Commonly used brand name(s):

In the U.S.—
Teslascan

Description

Mangafodipir (man-ga-FOE-di-peer) is an MRI (magnetic resonance imaging) contrast agent (also known as paramagnetic agents). MRI agents are used to help provide a clear picture during MRI. MRI is a special kind of diagnostic procedure. It uses magnets and computers to create images or "pictures" of certain areas inside the body. Unlike x-rays, it does not involve ionizing radiation.

Mangafodipir is given by injection before MRI to help diagnose problems in the liver.

Mangafodipir is injected into a vein. The dose of this agent will be different for different patients depending on the body weight of the person.

This medicine is to be used only by or under the supervision of a doctor. It is available in the following dosage form:

Parenteral
  • Injection (U.S.)

Before Having This Test

In deciding to use a diagnostic test, any risks of the test must be weighed against the good it will do. This is a decision you and your doctor will make. Also, test results may be affected by other things. For mangafodipir, the following should be considered:

Allergies—Tell your doctor if you have ever had any unusual or allergic reaction to mangafodipir or other contrast agents, or to manganese. Also tell your health care professional if you are allergic to any other substances, such as foods, preservatives, or dyes.

Pregnancy—Studies have not been done in pregnant women. However, in animal studies, mangafodipir caused birth defects and other problems (such as decreased weight) in the fetus. In addition, manganese, which is part of mangafodipir, may cause nerve problems.

Breast-feeding—It is not known whether mangafodipir passes into breast milk. However, your doctor may want you to stop breast-feeding for some time after you receive it. Be sure you have discussed this with your doctor.

Children—Studies on this medicine have been done only in adult patients, and there is no specific information comparing use of mangafodipir in children under 12 years of age with use in other age groups.

Teenagers—Although there is no specific information comparing use of mangafodipir in teenagers with use in other age groups, it is not expected to cause different side effects or problems in teenagers than it does in adults.

Older adults—Many medicines have not been studied specifically in older people. Therefore, it may not be known whether they work exactly the same way they do in younger adults or if they cause different side effects or problems in older people. There is no specific information comparing use of mangafodipir in the elderly with use in other age groups.

Other medical problems—The presence of other medical problems may affect the use of mangafodipir. Make sure you tell your doctor if you have any other medical problems, especially:

  • Allergies (history of) or
  • Immune system problems (history of)—Possible increased risk of having an allergic reaction to mangafodipir
  • Nausea or vomiting or
  • Other stomach problems such as reflux (acid backing up from the stomach)—This medicine commonly causes nausea and vomiting, which could cause more problems

Side Effects of This Medicine

Along with its needed effects, a medicine may cause some unwanted effects. Although not all of these side effects may occur, if they do occur they may need medical attention.

Check with your doctor as soon as possible if any of the following side effects occur:
Rare
  Chest pain; irregular heartbeat; itching; shortness of breath; skin rash or hives; swelling of face

Other side effects may occur that usually do not need medical attention. These side effects may go away during treatment as your body adjusts to the medicine. However, check with your doctor if any of the following side effects continue or are bothersome:
More common
  Nausea and/or vomiting; redness at place of injection; warmth at place of injection
Less common
  Abdominal or stomach pain; coldness at place of injection; feeling of pressure at place of injection; dizziness; headache; pain at place of injection

Other side effects not listed above may also occur in some patients. If you notice any other effects, check with your doctor.

Developed: 08/24/98

MANGANESE SUPPLEMENTS Systemic

This information applies to the following:
  1. Manganese Chloride (MAN-ga-nees KLOR-ide) †‡
  2. Manganese Sulfate (MAN-ga-nees SUL-fate) †

†Not commercially available in Canada.
‡Generic name product may be available in the U.S.

Description

Manganese supplements are used to prevent or treat manganese deficiency.

The body needs manganese for normal growth and health. For patients who are unable to get enough manganese in their regular diet or who have a need for more manganese, manganese supplements may be necessary. Manganese helps your body break down fats, carbohydrates, and proteins. It does so as part of several enzymes.

Manganese deficiency has not been reported in humans. Lack of manganese in animals has been found to cause improper formation of bone and cartilage, may decrease the body's ability to use sugar properly, and may cause growth problems.

Injectable manganese supplements are given by or under the supervision of a health care professional.

Manganese supplements are available in the following dosage forms:

Oral
    Manganese is available orally as part of a multivitamin/ mineral combination.

Parenteral
    Manganese Chloride
      • Injection (U.S.)
    Manganese Sulfate
      • Injection (U.S.)

Importance of Diet

For good health, it is important that you eat a balanced and varied diet. Follow carefully any diet program your health care professional may recommend. For your specific dietary vitamin and/or mineral needs, ask your health care professional for a list of appropriate foods. If you think that you are not getting enough vitamins and/or minerals in your diet, you may choose to take a dietary supplement.

Manganese is found in whole grains, cereal products, lettuce, dry beans, and peas.

The daily amount of manganese needed is defined in several different ways.

For U.S.—
• Recommended Dietary Allowances (RDAs) are the amount of vitamins and minerals needed to provide for adequate nutrition in most healthy persons. RDAs for a given nutrient may vary depending on a person's age, sex, and physical condition (e.g., pregnancy).
• Daily Values (DVs) are used on food and dietary supplement labels to indicate the percent of the recommended daily amount of each nutrient that a serving provides. DV replaces the previous designation of United States Recommended Daily Allowances (US-RDAs).

For Canada—
• Recommended Nutrient Intakes (RNIs) are used to determine the amounts of vitamins, minerals, and protein needed to provide adequate nutrition and lessen the risk of chronic disease.

Because a lack of manganese is rare, there is no RDA or RNI for it. The following daily intakes are thought to be plenty for most individuals:

• Infants and children—
    Birth to 3 years of age: 0.3 to 1.5 milligrams (mg).
    4 to 6 years of age: 1.5 to 2 mg.
    7 to 10 years of age: 2 to 3 mg.
• Adolescents and adults—2 to 5 mg.

Before Using This Dietary Supplement

If you are taking this dietary supplement without a prescription, carefully read and follow any precautions on the label. For manganese, the following should be considered:

Allergies—Tell your health care professional if you have ever had any unusual or allergic reaction to manganese. Also tell your health care professional if you are allergic to any other substances, such as foods, preservatives, or dyes.

Pregnancy—It is especially important that you are receiving enough vitamins and minerals when you become pregnant and that you continue to receive the right amount of vitamins and minerals throughout your pregnancy. The healthy growth and development of the fetus depend on a steady supply of nutrients from the mother. However, taking large amounts of a dietary supplement in pregnancy may be harmful to the mother and/or fetus and should be avoided.

Breast-feeding—It is important that you receive the right amounts of vitamins and minerals so that your baby will also get the vitamins and minerals needed to grow properly. However, taking large amounts of a dietary supplement while breast-feeding may be harmful to the mother and/or baby and should be avoided.

Children—Problems in children have not been reported with intake of normal daily recommended amounts.

Older adults—Problems in older adults have not been reported with intake of normal daily recommended amounts.

Medicines or other dietary supplements—Although certain medicines or dietary supplements should not be used together at all, in other cases they may be used together even if an interaction might occur. In these cases, your health care professional may want to change the dose, or other precautions may be necessary. Tell your health care professional if you are taking any other dietary supplement or any prescription or nonprescription (over-the-counter [OTC]) medicines.

Other medical problems—The presence of other medical problems may affect the use of manganese. Make sure you tell your health care professional if you have any other medical problems, especially:

• Biliary disease or
• Liver disease—Taking manganese supplements may cause high blood levels of manganese, and dosage of manganese may have to be changed

Proper Use of This Dietary Supplement

Dosing—The amount of manganese needed to meet normal daily recommended intakes will be different for different individuals. The following information includes only the average amounts of manganese.

• For *oral* dosage form (as part of a multivitamin/mineral supplement):
  —To prevent deficiency, the amount taken by mouth is based on normal daily recommended intakes:
    • Adults and teenagers—2 to 5 milligrams (mg) per day.
    • Children 7 to 10 years of age—2 to 3 mg per day.
    • Children 4 to 6 years of age—1.5 to 2 mg per day.
    • Children birth to 3 years of age—0.3 to 1.5 mg per day.
  —To treat deficiency:
    • Adults, teenagers, and children—Treatment dose is determined by prescriber for each individual based on severity of deficiency.

Missed dose—If you miss taking manganese supplements for one or more days there is no cause for concern, since it takes some time for your body to become seriously low in manganese. However, if your health care professional has recommended that you take manganese, try to remember to take it as directed every day.

Storage—To store this dietary supplement:
• Keep out of the reach of children.

- Store away from heat and direct light.
- Do not store in the bathroom, near the kitchen sink, or in other damp places. Heat or moisture may cause the dietary supplement to break down.
- Keep the dietary supplement from freezing. Do not refrigerate.
- Do not keep outdated dietary supplements or those no longer needed. Be sure that any discarded dietary supplement is out of the reach of children.

Side Effects of This Dietary Supplement

No side effects or toxic effects have been reported for manganese. However, check with your health care professional if you notice any unusual effects while you are taking it.

Revised: 02/01/92
Interim revision: 08/07/92; 08/15/94; 04/25/95

MAPROTILINE   Systemic

Commonly used brand name(s):

In the U.S.—
  Ludiomil
  Generic name product may be available.

In Canada—
  Ludiomil

Description

Maprotiline (ma-PROE-ti-leen) is used to relieve mental depression, including anxiety that sometimes occurs with depression.

Maprotiline is available only with your doctor's prescription, in the following dosage form:

  Oral
  • Tablets (U.S. and Canada)

Before Using This Medicine

In deciding to use a medicine, the risks of taking the medicine must be weighed against the good it will do. This is a decision you and your doctor will make. For maprotiline, the following should be considered:

Allergies—Tell your doctor if you have ever had any unusual or allergic reaction to maprotiline or tricyclic antidepressants. Also tell your health care professional if you are allergic to any other substances, such as foods, preservatives, or dyes.

Pregnancy—Maprotiline has not been studied in pregnant women. However, this medicine has not been shown to cause birth defects or other problems in animal studies.

Breast-feeding—Maprotiline passes into the breast milk. However, this medicine has not been reported to cause problems in nursing babies.

Children—Studies on this medicine have been done only in adult patients, and there is no specific information comparing use of maprotiline in children with use in other age groups.

Older adults—Drowsiness, dizziness or lightheadedness; confusion; vision problems; dryness of mouth; constipation; and difficulty in urinating may be especially likely to occur in elderly patients, who are usually more sensitive than younger adults to the effects of maprotiline.

Other medicines—Although certain medicines should not be used together at all, in other cases two different medicines may be used together even if an interaction might occur. In these cases, your doctor may want to change the dose, or other precautions may be necessary. When you are taking maprotiline, it is especially important that your health care professional know if you are taking any of the following:

- Amphetamines or
- Appetite suppressants (diet pills) or
- Medicine for asthma or other breathing problems or
- Medicine for colds, sinus problems, or hay fever or other allergies (including nose drops or sprays)—Using these medicines with maprotiline may cause serious unwanted effects on your heart and blood pressure
- Central nervous system (CNS) depressants (medicines that cause drowsiness)—Taking these medicines with maprotiline may increase the CNS depressant effects
- Monoamine oxidase (MAO) inhibitors (furazolidone [e.g., Furoxone], isocarboxazid [e.g., Marplan], phenelzine [e.g., Nardil], procarbazine [e.g., Matulane], selegiline [e.g., Eldepryl], tranylcypromine [e.g., Parnate])—Taking maprotiline while you are taking or within 2 weeks of taking monoamine oxidase (MAO) inhibitors may cause very serious side effects, such as sudden high body temperature, extremely high blood pressure, and severe convulsions; at least 14 days should be allowed between stopping treatment with one medicine and starting treatment with the other

Other medical problems—The presence of other medical problems may affect the use of maprotiline. Make sure you tell your doctor if you have any other medical problems, especially:

- Alcohol abuse or
- Seizure disorders (including epilepsy)—The risk of seizures may be increased
- Asthma or
- Difficult urination or
- Enlarged prostate or
- Glaucoma or
- Mental illness (severe) or
- Stomach or intestinal problems—Maprotiline may make the condition worse
- Heart or blood vessel disease or
- Overactive thyroid—Serious effects on your heart may occur
- Liver disease—Higher blood levels of maprotiline may occur, increasing the chance of side effects

Proper Use of This Medicine

Take this medicine only as directed by your doctor to benefit your condition as much as possible. Do not take more of it, do not take it more often, and do not take it for a longer time than your doctor ordered.

Sometimes this medicine must be taken for up to two or three weeks before you begin to feel better. Your doctor should check your progress at regular visits.

Dosing—The dose of maprotiline will be different for different patients. *Follow your doctor's orders or the directions on the label.* The following information includes only the average doses of maprotiline. *If your dose is different, do not change it* unless your doctor tells you to do so.

The number of tablets that you take depends on the strength of the medicine. Also, *the number of doses you take each day, the time allowed between doses, and the length of time you take the medicine depend on the medical problem for which you are taking maprotiline.*

- For *oral* dosage form (tablets):
  - —For depression:
    - Adults—At first, 25 milligrams (mg) taken one to three times a day. Your doctor may increase your dose as needed. However, the dose is usually not more than 150 mg a day, unless you are in the hospital. Some hospitalized patients may need higher doses.
    - Children—Use and dose must be determined by your doctor.

Missed dose—If you miss a dose of this medicine and your dosing schedule is:

- One dose a day at bedtime—Do not take the missed dose in the morning since it may cause disturbing side effects during waking hours. Instead, check with your doctor.
- More than one dose a day—Take the missed dose as soon as possible. Then go back to your regular dosing schedule. However, if it is almost time for your next dose, skip the missed dose and go back to your regular dosing schedule. Do not double doses. If you have any questions about this, check with your doctor.

Storage—To store this medicine:

- Keep out of the reach of children.
- Store away from heat and direct light.
- Do not store in the bathroom, near the kitchen sink, or in other damp places. Heat or moisture may cause the medicine to break down.
- Do not keep outdated medicine or medicine no longer needed. Be sure that any discarded medicine is out of the reach of children.

Precautions While Using This Medicine

It is very important that your doctor check your progress at regular visits. This will allow your dosage to be changed if necessary and will help to reduce side effects.

This medicine will add to the effects of alcohol and other CNS depressants (medicines that slow down the nervous system, possibly causing drowsiness). Some examples of CNS depressants are antihistamines or medicine for hay fever, other allergies, or colds; sedatives, tranquilizers, or sleeping medicine; prescription pain medicine or narcotics; barbiturates; medicine for seizures; or anesthetics, including some dental anesthetics. *Check with your doctor before taking any of the above while you are using this medicine.*

This medicine may cause blurred vision, especially during the first few weeks of treatment. It may also cause some people to become drowsy or less alert than they are normally. *If these effects occur, do not drive, use machines, or do anything else that could be dangerous if you are not alert or able to see well.*

Dizziness, lightheadedness, or fainting may occur, especially when you get up from a lying or sitting position. Getting up slowly may help. If this problem continues or gets worse, check with your doctor.

Maprotiline may cause dryness of the mouth. For temporary relief, use sugarless gum or candy, melt bits of ice in your mouth, or use a saliva substitute. However, if your mouth continues to feel dry for more than 2 weeks, check with your medical doctor or dentist. Continuing dryness of the mouth may increase the chance of dental disease, including tooth decay, gum disease, and fungus infections.

Before having any kind of surgery, dental treatment, or emergency treatment, tell the medical doctor or dentist in charge that you are using this medicine. Taking maprotiline together with medicines that are used during surgery or dental or emergency treatments may increase the CNS depressant effects.

Do not stop taking this medicine without first checking with your doctor. Your doctor may want you to reduce gradually the amount you are taking before stopping completely. This will allow your body to adjust properly and will reduce the possibility of unwanted effects.

Side Effects of This Medicine

Along with its needed effects, a medicine may cause some unwanted effects. Although not all of these side effects may occur, if they do occur they may need medical attention.

Check with your doctor as soon as possible if any of the following side effects occur:

More common
  Skin rash, redness, swelling, or itching

Less common
  Constipation (severe); nausea or vomiting; shakiness or trembling; seizures (convulsions); unusual excitement; weight loss

Rare
  Breast enlargement—in males and females; confusion (especially in the elderly); difficulty in urinating; fainting; hallucinations (seeing, hearing, or feeling things that are not there); inappropriate secretion of milk—in females; irregular heartbeat (pounding, racing, skipping); sore throat and fever; swelling of testicles; yellow eyes or skin

Symptoms of overdose
  Convulsions (seizures); dizziness (severe); drowsiness (severe); fast or irregular heartbeat; fever; muscle stiffness or weakness (severe); restlessness or agitation; trouble in breathing; vomiting

Other side effects may occur that usually do not need medical attention. These side effects may go away during treatment as your body adjusts to the medicine. However, check with your doctor if any of the following side effects continue or are bothersome:

More common
  Blurred vision; decreased sexual ability; dizziness or lightheadedness (especially in the elderly); drowsiness; dryness of mouth; headache; increased or decreased sexual drive; tiredness or weakness

Less common
  Constipation (mild); diarrhea; heartburn; increased appetite and weight gain; increased sensitivity of skin to sunlight; increased sweating; trouble in sleeping; weight loss

After you stop taking this medicine, your body will need time to adjust. This usually takes about 3 to 10 days. Continue to follow the precautions listed above during this period of time.

Other side effects not listed above may also occur in some patients. If you notice any other effects, check with your doctor.

Additional Information

Once a medicine has been approved for marketing for a certain use, experience may show that it is also useful for other medical problems. Although this use is not included in product labeling, maprotiline is used in certain patients with the following medical condition:

- Chronic neurogenic pain (a certain type of pain that is continuing)

Other than the above information, there is no additional information relating to proper use, precautions, or side effects for these uses.

Revised: 08/29/94

MASOPROCOL   Topical†

†Not commercially available in Canada.

Description

Masoprocol (ma-SOE-pro-kole) is applied to the skin to treat a condition called actinic keratoses, which can become cancerous if not treated.

This medicine was withdrawn from the U.S. market in June 1996.

Before Using This Medicine

In deciding to use a medicine, the risks of using the medicine must be weighed against the good it will do. This is a decision you and your doctor will make. For topical masoprocol, the following should be considered:

Allergies—Tell your doctor if you have ever had any unusual or allergic reaction to masoprocol. Also tell your health care professional if you are allergic to any other substances, such as sulfites or other preservatives or dyes. Masoprocol for use on the skin contains sulfites.

Pregnancy—Tell your doctor if you are pregnant or if you intend to become pregnant. Although masoprocol applied to the skin has not been shown to cause problems in humans, some of it is absorbed through the skin. Be sure that you have discussed this with your doctor before using this medicine.

Breast-feeding—Although masoprocol applied to the skin has not been shown to cause problems in nursing babies, some of it is absorbed through the skin.

Children—There is no specific information comparing use of masoprocol on the skin in children with use in other age groups.

Older adults—Many medicines have not been studied specifically in older people. Therefore, it may not be known whether they work exactly the same way they do in younger adults or if they cause different side effects or problems in older people. Although there is no specific information comparing use of masoprocol on the skin in the elderly with use in other age groups, this medicine is not expected to cause different side effects or problems in older people than it does in younger adults.

Proper Use of This Medicine

Keep using this medicine for the full time of treatment. However, *do not use this medicine more often or for a longer time than your doctor ordered*. Apply enough medicine each time to cover the entire affected area with a thin layer.

After washing the area with mild soap and water and drying carefully, use your fingertips to apply the medicine in a thin layer to your skin and rub it in gently.

Make sure you *wash your hands immediately after applying the cream*, to prevent any of the medicine from accidentally getting in your eyes or mouth.

Masoprocol commonly causes redness, soreness, swelling, itching, dryness, and flaking of affected skin. This effect will go away about 2 weeks after you stop using the medicine. However, do not stop using this medicine without first checking with your doctor. If this reaction occurs, check with your doctor.

Dosing—The dose of masoprocol will be different for different patients. *Follow your doctor's orders or the directions on the label*. The following information includes only the average dose of masoprocol. *If your dose is different, do not change it* unless your doctor tells you to do so.

- Adults—Use the 10% cream on the affected areas of skin two times a day.
- Children—Use and dose must be determined by your doctor.

Missed dose—If you miss a dose of this medicine, apply it as soon as possible. However, if more than a few hours have passed, skip the missed dose and go back to your regular dosing schedule. If you miss more than one dose, check with your doctor.

Storage—To store this medicine:
- Keep out of the reach of children.
- Store away from heat and direct light.
- Do not store in the bathroom, near the kitchen sink, or in other damp places. Heat or moisture may cause the medicine to break down.
- Do not keep outdated medicine or medicine no longer needed. Be sure that any discarded medicine is out of the reach of children.

Precautions While Using This Medicine

It is very important that your doctor check your progress at regular visits to make sure that this medicine is working properly and to check for unwanted effects.

Apply this medicine very carefully when using it on your face. Avoid getting any in your eyes, nose, or mouth.

This preparation contains sulfites as a preservative. Sulfites may cause an allergic reaction in some people. Signs of an allergic reaction to sulfites include bluish discoloration of skin, severe dizziness or feeling faint, or wheezing or trouble in breathing. *If any of these signs occur, check with your doctor immediately.*

Side Effects of This Medicine

Along with its needed effects, a medicine may cause some unwanted effects. Although not all of these side effects may occur, if they do occur they may need medical attention.

Stop using this medicine and check with your doctor immediately if the following side effects occur:

More common
Redness and swelling of normal skin

Check with your doctor immediately if the following side effect occurs:

Less common
Blistering or oozing where medicine is applied

Signs and symptoms of allergic reaction to sulfites
Bluish discoloration of skin; dizziness (severe) or feeling faint; wheezing or trouble in breathing

Check with your doctor as soon as possible if the following side effects occur:

More common
Redness, soreness, swelling, itching, dryness, and flaking of skin where medicine is applied

Other side effects may occur that usually do not need medical attention. These side effects may go away during treatment as your body adjusts to the medicine. However, check with your doctor if any of the following side effects continue, worsen, or are bothersome:

More common
Burning feeling where medicine is applied

Less common
Leathery feeling to skin; skin roughness; wrinkles

Other side effects not listed above may also occur in some patients. If you notice any other effects, check with your doctor.

Developed: 07/31/1995
Revised: 10/13/2000

MEASLES AND RUBELLA VIRUS VACCINE LIVE   Systemic†

Commonly used brand name(s):

In the U.S.—
M-R-VAX II

†Not commercially available in Canada.

Description

Measles and rubella (MEE-zills and rue-BELL-a) virus vaccine live is an active immunizing agent used to prevent infection by the measles and rubella viruses. It works by causing your body to produce its own protection (antibodies) against the viruses.

Measles (also known as coughing measles, hard measles, morbilli, red measles, rubeola, and 10-day measles) is an infection that is easily spread from one person to another. Infection with measles can cause serious problems, such as pneumonia, ear infections, sinus problems, convulsions (seizures), brain damage, and possibly death. The risk of serious complications and death is greater for adults and infants than for children and teenagers.

Rubella (also known as German measles) is a serious infection that causes miscarriages, stillbirths, or birth defects in unborn babies when pregnant women get the disease.

While immunization against measles and rubella is recommended for all persons 12 months of age and older, it is es-

pecially important for women of childbearing age and persons traveling outside the U.S.

If measles and rubella vaccine is to be given to a child, the child should be at least 12 months of age. This is to make sure the measles vaccine is effective. In a younger child, antibodies from the mother may prevent the vaccine from working.

This vaccine should be administered only by or under the supervision of your doctor or other health care professional. It is available in the following dosage form:

Parenteral
• Injection (U.S.)

Before Receiving This Vaccine

In deciding to use a medicine, the risks of taking the medicine must be weighed against the good it will do. This is a decision you and your doctor will make. For measles and rubella vaccine, the following should be considered:

Allergies—Tell your doctor if you have ever had any unusual or allergic reaction to measles and rubella vaccine, to the antibiotic neomycin, or to gelatin. Also tell your health care professional if you are allergic to any other substances, such as preservatives.

Pregnancy—Tell your doctor if you are pregnant or if you may become pregnant within 3 months after receiving this vaccine. Although adequate studies have not been done in either humans or animals, and problems have not been shown to occur, use of measles and rubella vaccine during pregnancy, or becoming pregnant within 3 months after receiving the measles and rubella vaccine, is not recommended. Because the natural measles infection has been shown to increase the chance of birth defects and other problems, it is thought that the live virus vaccine might cause similar problems. Rubella vaccine crosses the placenta. However, the Centers for Disease Control and Prevention monitored over 200 women who received the vaccine within 3 months before or after becoming pregnant, and those women gave birth to normal babies.

Breast-feeding—Rubella vaccine virus passes into breast milk. However, this vaccine has not been reported to cause problems in nursing babies.

Children—Use of this vaccine is not recommended for infants younger than 12 months of age, unless the risk of measles infection is high. Waiting until children are at least 12 months of age is important because antibodies that infants receive from their mothers before birth may interfere with the effectiveness of the vaccine. In addition, there may be special reasons why children between 6 months and 12 months of age also may require measles vaccination.

Other medicines—Although certain medicines should not be used together at all, in other cases two different medicines may be used together even if an interaction might occur. In these cases, your doctor may want to change the dose, or other precautions may be necessary. Before you receive measles and rubella vaccine, it is especially important that your health care professional know if you have received any of the following:

• Cancer medicines or
• X-ray treatment—May reduce the useful effect of the vaccine

Other medical problems—The presence of other medical problems may affect the use of measles and rubella vaccine. Make sure you tell your doctor if you have any other medical problems, especially:

- Immune deficiency condition (or family history of)—Condition may increase the chance and severity of side effects of the vaccine and/or may decrease the useful effects of the vaccine
- Severe illness with fever—The symptoms of the condition may be confused with the possible side effects of the vaccine

Proper Use of This Vaccine

Dosing—The following information includes only the average dose of measles and rubella vaccine.

- For *injection* dosage form:
  - —For prevention of measles and rubella:
    - Adults and children 12 months of age and older—One dose injected under the skin.
    - Children up to 12 months of age—Use is not recommended.

Precautions After Receiving This Vaccine

Do not become pregnant for 3 months after receiving measles and rubella vaccine without first checking with your doctor. There may be a chance that this vaccine can cause birth defects.

Tell your doctor that you have received this vaccine:

- If you are to receive a tuberculin skin test within 4 to 6 weeks after receiving this vaccine. The results of the test may be affected by this vaccine.
- If you are to receive blood products or immune globulins within 14 days of receiving this vaccine.
- If you are to receive this vaccine within 3 to 11 months of receiving blood products or immune globulins

Side Effects of This Vaccine

Along with its needed effects, a vaccine may cause some unwanted effects. Although not all of these side effects may occur, if they do occur they may need medical attention.

Get emergency help immediately if any of the following side effects occur:

Symptoms of allergic reaction—rare
Difficulty in breathing or swallowing; hives; itching, especially of feet or hands; reddening of skin, especially around ears; swelling of eyes, face, or inside of nose; unusual tiredness or weakness (sudden and severe)

Check with your doctor as soon as possible if any of the following side effects occur:

More common
Fever over 103 °F (39.4 °C)

Less common
Pain or tenderness of eyes

Rare
Bruising or purple spots on skin; confusion; convulsions (seizures); double vision; headache (severe or continuing); irritability; pain, numbness, or tingling of hands, arms, legs, or feet; stiff neck; vomiting

Other side effects may occur that usually do not need medical attention. However, check with your doctor if any of the following side effects continue or are bothersome:

More common
Burning or stinging at place of injection; fever between 100 and 103 °F (37.7 and 39.4 °C); skin rash; swelling of glands in neck

Less common
Aches or pain in joints; headache (mild); itching, swelling, redness, tenderness, or hard lump at place of injection; nausea; runny nose; sore throat; vague feeling of bodily discomfort

The above side effects (especially aches or pain in joints) are more likely to occur in adults, particularly women.

Other side effects not listed above may also occur in some patients. If you notice any other effects, check with your doctor.

Developed: 04/29/97

MEASLES VIRUS VACCINE LIVE
Systemic

Commonly used brand name(s):

In the U.S.—
Attenuvax

Description

Measles (MEE-zills) Virus Vaccine Live is an immunizing agent used to prevent infection by the measles virus. It works by causing your body to produce its own protection (antibodies) against the virus. This vaccine does not protect you against German measles (Rubella). A separate immunization is needed for that type of measles.

Measles (also known as coughing measles, hard measles, morbilli, red measles, rubeola, and ten-day measles) is an infection that is easily spread from one person to another. Infection with measles can lead to serious problems, such as pneumonia, ear infections, sinus problems, convulsions (seizures), brain damage, and possibly death. The risk of serious complications and death is greater for adults and infants than for children and teenagers.

Immunization against measles is recommended for everyone 12 to 15 months of age and older. In addition, there may be special reasons why children from 6 months of age up to 12 months of age may also require measles vaccine.

Immunization against measles is usually not recommended for infants up to 12 months of age, unless the risk of their getting a measles infection is high. This is because antibodies they received from their mothers before birth may interfere with the effectiveness of the vaccine. Children who were immunized against measles before 12 months of age should be immunized twice again.

You can be considered to be immune to measles only if you received two doses of measles vaccine starting on or after your first birthday and have the medical record to prove it, if you have a doctor's diagnosis of a previous measles infection, or if you have had a blood test showing immunity to measles.

This vaccine is to be administered only by or under the supervision of your doctor or other health care professional. It is available in the following dosage form:

Parenteral
- Injection (U.S. and Canada)

Before Receiving This Vaccine

In deciding to use a medicine, the risks of taking the medicine must be weighed against the good it will do. This is a decision you and your doctor will make. For measles vaccine, the following should be considered:

Allergies—Tell your doctor if you have ever had any unusual or allergic reaction to measles vaccine or to any form of the antibiotic neomycin. Also, tell your health care professional if you are allergic to any other substances, such as gelatin.

Pregnancy—Although studies on effects in pregnancy have not been done in humans and problems have not been shown to occur, use of measles vaccine during pregnancy, or becoming pregnant within 3 months after receiving measles vaccine, is not recommended.

Breast-feeding—Measles vaccine virus may pass into breast milk. However, this vaccine has not been reported to cause problems in nursing babies.

Children—Measles vaccine usually is not recommended for infants up to 12 months of age. In special cases, such as children traveling outside the U.S. or children living in high-risk areas, measles vaccine may be given to children as young as 6 months of age.

Other medicines—Although certain medicines should not be used together at all, in other cases two different medicines may be used together even if an interaction might occur. In these cases, your doctor may want to change the dose, or other precautions may be necessary. Before you receive measles vaccine, it is especially important that your health care professional knows if you have received any of the following:

- Treatment with x-rays or cancer medicines—Treatment may increase the action of the vaccine, causing an increase in vaccine side effects, or treatment may interfere with the useful effect of the vaccine

Other medical problems—The presence of other medical problems may affect the use of measles vaccine. Make sure you tell your doctor if you have any other medical problems, especially:

- Immune deficiency condition (or family history of)—Condition may increase the chance and severity of side effects of the vaccine and/or may decrease the useful effects of the vaccine

- Severe illness with fever—The symptoms of the condition may be confused with the possible side effects of the vaccine

Proper Use of This Vaccine

Dosing—The dose of measles vaccine will be different for different patients. The following information includes only the average doses of measles vaccine.

- For *injection* dosage form:
  —For prevention of measles:
    - Adults and children 12 months of age and older—One dose injected under the skin, followed by a second dose at least one month later.

Precautions After Receiving This Vaccine

Do not become pregnant for 3 months after receiving measles vaccine without first checking with your doctor.

Tell your doctor that you have received this vaccine:

- If you are to receive a tuberculin skin test within 4 to 6 weeks after receiving this vaccine. The results of the test may be affected by this vaccine.
- If you are to receive this vaccine within 2 weeks before or 3 to 11 months after receiving blood transfusions or other blood products.
- If you are to receive this vaccine 2 weeks before or 3 to 11 months after receiving gamma globulin or other immune globulins.

Side Effects of This Vaccine

Along with its needed effects, a vaccine may cause some unwanted effects. Although not all of these side effects may occur, if they do occur they may need medical attention.

Get emergency help immediately if any of the following side effects occur:
Symptoms of allergic reaction
> Difficulty in breathing or swallowing; hives; itching, especially of feet or hands; reddening of skin, especially around ears; swelling of eyes, face, or inside of nose; unusual tiredness or weakness (sudden and severe)

Check with your doctor as soon as possible if any of the following side effects occur:
More common
> Fever over 103 °F (39.4 °C)
Rare
> Bruising or purple spots on skin; confusion; convulsions (seizures); double vision; headache (severe or continuing); irritability; stiff neck; swelling, blistering or pain at place of injection; swelling of glands in neck; vomiting

Other side effects may occur that usually do not need medical attention. However, check with your doctor if any of the following side effects continue or are bothersome:
More common
> Burning or stinging at place of injection; fever of 100 °F (37.7 °C) or less
Less common
> Fever between 100 and 103 °F (37.7 and 39.4 °C); itching, swelling, redness, tenderness, or hard lump at place of injection; skin rash

Fever or skin rash may occur from 5 to 12 days after vaccination and usually lasts several days.

Other side effects not listed above may also occur in some patients. If you notice any other effects, check with your doctor.

Revised: 07/23/97

MEASLES, MUMPS, AND RUBELLA VIRUS VACCINE LIVE   Systemic

Commonly used brand name(s):

In the U.S.—
M-M-R II

In Canada—
M-M-R II

Description

Measles, mumps, and rubella (MEE-zills and rue-BELL-a) virus vaccine live is an active immunizing agent used to prevent infection by the measles, mumps, and rubella viruses. It works by causing your body to produce its own protection (antibodies) against the virus.

Measles (also known as coughing measles, hard measles, morbilli, red measles, rubeola, and 10-day measles) is an infection that is easily spread from one person to another. Infection with measles can cause serious problems, such as stomach problems, pneumonia, ear infections, sinus problems, convulsions (seizures), brain damage, and possibly death. The risk of serious complications and death is greater for adults and infants than for children and teenagers.

Mumps is an infection that can cause serious problems, such as encephalitis and meningitis, which affect the brain. In addition, adolescent boys and men are very susceptible to a condition called orchitis, which causes pain and swelling in the testicles and scrotum and, in rare cases, sterility. Also, mumps infection can cause spontaneous abortion (miscarriage) in women during the first 3 months of pregnancy.

Rubella (also known as German measles) is a serious infection that causes miscarriages, stillbirths, or birth defects in unborn babies when pregnant women get the disease.

While immunization against measles, mumps, and rubella is recommended for all persons 12 months of age and older, it is especially important for women of childbearing age and persons traveling outside the U.S.

If measles, mumps, and rubella vaccine is to be given to a child, the child should be at least 12 months of age. This is to make sure the measles vaccine is effective. In a younger child, antibodies from the mother may interfere with the effectiveness of the vaccine.

This vaccine should be administered only by or under the supervision of your doctor or other health care professional. It is available in the following dosage form:

Parenteral
- Injection (U.S. and Canada)

Before Receiving This Vaccine

In deciding to use a medicine, the risks of taking the medicine must be weighed against the good it will do. This is a decision you and your doctor will make. For measles, mumps, and rubella vaccine, the following should be considered:

Allergies—Tell your doctor if you have ever had any unusual or allergic reaction to measles, mumps, and rubella vaccine, to the antibiotic neomycin, to gelatin, or to eggs. Also tell your health care professional if you are allergic to any other substances, such as preservatives.

Pregnancy—Tell your doctor if you are pregnant or if you may become pregnant within 3 months after receiving this vaccine. Although adequate studies have not been done in either humans or animals and problems have not been shown to occur, use of measles, mumps, and rubella vaccine during pregnancy, or becoming pregnant within 3 months after receiving the measles, mumps, and rubella vaccine, is not recommended. Because the natural measles infection has been shown to increase the chance of birth defects and other problems, it is thought that the live virus vaccine may cause similar problems. Mumps vaccine may infect the placenta, although the vaccine has not been shown to infect the fetus or to cause

birth defects. Rubella vaccine crosses the placenta. However, the Centers for Disease Control observed more than 200 women who received the vaccine within 3 months before or after becoming pregnant and those women gave birth to normal babies.

Breast-feeding—Mothers who are receiving measles, mumps, and rubella vaccine and who wish to breast-feed should discuss this with their doctors, because rubella vaccine virus may pass into the breast milk and may cause mild rubella infection in nursing babies. However, studies have not shown that this infection causes any serious problems.

Children—Use is not recommended for infants younger than 12 months of age, unless the risk of measles infection is high. Waiting until children are at least 12 months of age is important because antibodies that infants receive from their mothers before birth may interfere with the effectiveness of the vaccine. There may be special reasons why children between 6 months and 12 months of age also may require measles vaccination.

Other medicines—Although certain medicines should not be used together at all, in other cases two different medicines may be used together even if an interaction might occur. In these cases, your doctor may want to change the dose, or other precautions may be necessary. Before you receive measles, mumps, and rubella vaccine, it is especially important that your health care professional know if you have received any of the following:
- Cancer medicines or
- Radiation therapy—May reduce the useful effect of the vaccine

Other medical problems—The presence of other medical problems may affect the use of measles, mumps, and rubella vaccine. Make sure you tell your doctor if you have any other medical problems, especially:
- Immune deficiency condition (or family history of)—Condition may increase the chance of developing side effects and the severity of side effects of the vaccine and/or may decrease the useful effects of the vaccine
- Severe illness with fever—The symptoms of the condition may be confused with the possible side effects of the vaccine

Proper Use of This Vaccine

Dosing—The dose of measles, mumps, and rubella vaccine will be different for different patients. The following information includes only the average dose of measles, mumps, and rubella vaccine.
- For *injection* dosage form:
  —For prevention of measles, mumps, and rubella:
    - Adults and children 12 months of age and older—One dose injected under the skin.
    - Children up to 12 months of age—Use is not recommended.

Precautions After Receiving This Vaccine

Do not become pregnant for 3 months after receiving measles, mumps, and rubella vaccine. There is a chance that this vaccine may cause birth defects.

Tell your doctor that you have received this vaccine:
- If you are to receive a tuberculin skin test within 8 weeks after receiving this vaccine. The results of the test may be affected by this vaccine.

- If you are to receive any other live virus vaccines within 1 month after receiving this vaccine.
- If you are to receive blood transfusions or other blood products within 2 weeks after receiving this vaccine.
- If you are to receive gamma globulin or other globulins within 2 weeks after receiving this vaccine.

Side Effects of This Vaccine

Along with its needed effects, a vaccine may cause some unwanted effects. Although not all of these side effects may occur, if they do occur they may need medical attention.

Get emergency help immediately if any of the following side effects occur:
  Symptoms of allergic reaction
    Difficulty in breathing or swallowing; hives; itching, especially of feet or hands; reddening of skin, especially around ears; swelling of eyes, face, or inside of nose; unusual tiredness or weakness (sudden and severe)

Check with your doctor as soon as possible if any of the following side effects occur:
  More common
    Fever higher than 103 °F (39.4 °C)
  Less common
    Pain or tenderness of eyes
  Rare
    Bruising or purple spots on skin; confusion; convulsions (seizures); double vision; headache (severe or continuing); irritability; pain, numbness, or tingling of hands, arms, legs, or feet; pain, tenderness, or swelling in testicles and scrotum; stiff neck; vomiting

Other side effects may occur that usually do not need medical attention. However, check with your doctor if any of the following side effects continue or are bothersome:
  More common
    Burning or stinging at place of injection; fever between 100 and 103 °F (37.7 and 39.4 °C); skin rash; swelling of glands in neck
  Less common
    Aches or pain in joints; headache (mild); itching, swelling, redness, tenderness, or hard lump at place of injection; nausea; runny nose; sore throat; vague feeling of bodily discomfort

The above side effects (especially aches or pain in joints) are more likely to occur in adults, particularly women.

Other side effects not listed above also may occur in some patients. If you notice any other effects, check with your doctor.

Revised: 04/15/99

MEBENDAZOLE   Systemic

Commonly used brand name(s):
In the U.S.—
  Vermox
  Generic name product may be available.

In Canada—
  Vermox

Description

Mebendazole (me-BEN-da-zole) belongs to the family of medicines called anthelmintics (ant-hel-MIN-tiks). Anthelmintics are medicines used in the treatment of worm infections.

Mebendazole is used to treat:
- Common roundworms (ascariasis);
- Hookworm infections (uncinariasis);
- Pinworms (enterobiasis; oxyuriasis);
- Whipworms (trichuriasis); and
- More than one worm infection at a time.

This medicine may also be used for other worm infections as determined by your doctor.

Mebendazole works by keeping the worm from absorbing sugar (glucose). This gradually causes loss of energy and death of the worm.

Mebendazole is available only with your doctor's prescription, in the following dosage form:
  Oral
    • Chewable tablets (U.S. and Canada)

Before Using This Medicine

In deciding to use a medicine, the risks of taking the medicine must be weighed against the good it will do. This is a decision you and your doctor will make. For mebendazole, the following should be considered:

Allergies—Tell your doctor if you have ever had any unusual or allergic reaction to mebendazole. Also tell your health care professional if you are allergic to any other substances, such as foods, preservatives, or dyes.

Pregnancy—Mebendazole is not recommended for use during pregnancy. It has been shown to cause birth defects and other problems in rats given a single dose, which was several times the usual human dose. However, mebendazole did not cause birth defects or other problems in women who took this medicine during the first 3 months of pregnancy. Be sure you have discussed this with your doctor.

Breast-feeding—It is not known whether mebendazole passes into the breast milk. Although most medicines pass into breast milk in small amounts, many of them may be used safely while breast-feeding. Mothers who are taking this medicine and who wish to breast-feed should discuss this with their doctor.

Children—This medicine has been tested in a limited number of children 2 years of age or older and, in effective doses, has not been shown to cause different side effects or problems in children than it does in adults.

Older adults—Many medicines have not been studied specifically in older people. Therefore, it may not be known whether they work exactly the same way they do in younger adults or if they cause different side effects or problems in older people. There is no specific information comparing use of mebendazole in the elderly with use in other age groups.

Other medicines—Although certain medicines should not be used together at all, in other cases two different medicines may be used together even if an interaction might occur. In these cases, your doctor may want to change the dose, or other precautions may be necessary. Tell your health care professional if you are taking any prescription or nonprescription (over-the-counter [OTC]) medicine.

Other medical problems—The presence of other medical problems may affect the use of mebendazole. Make sure

you tell your doctor if you have any other medical problems, especially:

- Crohn's disease or
- Liver disease or
- Ulcerative colitis—Patients with these diseases may have an increased chance of side effects from mebendazole

---

Proper Use of This Medicine

Mebendazole usually comes with patient directions. Read them carefully before using this medicine.

No special preparations or other steps (for example, special diets, fasting, other medicines, laxatives, or enemas) are necessary before, during, or immediately after taking mebendazole.

Mebendazole tablets may be chewed, swallowed whole, or crushed and mixed with food.

For patients taking *mebendazole for hookworms, round-worms, or whipworms:*

- To help clear up your infection completely, *take this medicine exactly as directed by your doctor for the full time of treatment.* In some patients a second course of this medicine may be required to clear up the infection completely. *Do not miss any doses.*

For patients taking *mebendazole for pinworms:*

- To help clear up your infection completely, *take this medicine exactly as directed by your doctor.* A second course of this medicine is usually required to clear up the infection completely.
- Pinworms may be easily passed from one person to another, especially in a household. Therefore, all household members may have to be treated at the same time. This helps to prevent infection or reinfection of other household members. Also, all household members may have to be treated again in 2 to 3 weeks to clear up the infection completely.

For patients taking mebendazole for infections in which *high doses* are needed:

- *Mebendazole is best taken with meals, especially fatty ones (for example, meals that include whole milk or ice cream).* This helps to clear up the infection by helping your body absorb the medicine better. *However, if you are on a low-fat diet, check with your doctor.*

Dosing— The dose of mebendazole will be different for different patients. *Follow your doctor's orders or the directions on the label.* The following information includes only the average doses of mebendazole. *If your dose is different, do not change it* unless your doctor tells you to do so.

The number of doses you take each day, the time allowed between doses, and the length of time you take the medicine depend on the medical problem for which you are taking mebendazole.

- For *oral* dosage form (chewable tablets):
  —For common roundworms, hookworms, and whipworms:
  - Adults and children 2 years of age and over—100 milligrams (mg) two times a day, morning and evening, for three days. Treatment may need to be repeated in two to three weeks.
  - Children up to 2 years of age—Use and dose must be determined by your doctor.

—For pinworms:
- Adults and children 2 years of age and over—100 mg once a day for one day. Treatment may need to be repeated in two to three weeks.
- Children up to 2 years of age—Use and dose must be determined by your doctor.

—For more than one worm infection at a time:
- Adults and children 2 years of age and over—100 mg two times a day, morning and evening, for three days.
- Children up to 2 years of age—Use and dose must be determined by your doctor.

Missed dose— If you miss a dose of this medicine, take it as soon as possible. However, if it is almost time for your next dose, skip the missed dose and go back to your regular dosing schedule. Do not double doses.

Storage— To store this medicine:
- Keep out of the reach of children.
- Store away from heat and direct light.
- Do not store in the bathroom, near the kitchen sink, or in other damp places. Heat or moisture may cause the medicine to break down.
- Do not keep outdated medicine or medicine no longer needed. Be sure that any discarded medicine is out of the reach of children.

Precautions While Using This Medicine

It is important that your doctor check your progress at regular visits, especially in infections in which high doses are needed. This is to make sure that the infection is cleared up completely and to allow your doctor to check for any unwanted effects.

If your symptoms do not improve within a few days, or if they become worse, check with your doctor.

For patients taking *mebendazole for pinworms:*

- In some patients, pinworms may return after treatment with mebendazole. Washing (not shaking) all bedding and nightclothes (pajamas) after treatment may help to prevent this.
- Some doctors may also recommend other measures to help keep your infection from returning. If you have any questions about this, check with your doctor.

For patients taking *mebendazole for hookworms or whipworms:*

- In hookworm and whipworm infections anemia may occur. Therefore, your doctor may want you to take iron supplements to help clear up the anemia. If so, it is important to take iron every day while you are being treated for hookworms or whipworms; do not miss any doses. Your doctor may also want you to keep taking iron supplements for up to 6 months after you stop taking mebendazole. If you have any questions about this, check with your doctor.

Side Effects of This Medicine

Along with its needed effects, a medicine may cause some unwanted effects. Although not all of these side effects may occur, if they do occur they may need medical attention.

Check with your doctor as soon as possible if any of the following side effects occur:
Rare
  Fever; skin rash or itching; sore throat and fever; unusual tiredness and weakness

Other side effects may occur that usually do not need medical attention. These side effects may go away during treatment as your body adjusts to the medicine. However, check with your doctor if any of the following side effects continue or are bothersome:

Less common
> Abdominal or stomach pain or upset; diarrhea; nausea or vomiting

Rare
> Dizziness; hair loss; headache

Other side effects not listed above may also occur in some patients. If you notice any other effects, check with your doctor.

Revised: 08/01/95

MECAMYLAMINE   Systemic†

Commonly used brand name(s):

In the U.S.—
> Inversine

> †Not commercially available in Canada.

Description

Mecamylamine (mek-a-MILL-a-meen) belongs to the general class of medicines called antihypertensives. It is used to treat high blood pressure (hypertension).

High blood pressure adds to the workload of the heart and arteries. If it continues for a long time, the heart and arteries may not function properly. This can damage the blood vessels of the brain, heart, and kidneys, resulting in a stroke, heart failure, or kidney failure. High blood pressure may also increase the risk of heart attacks. These problems may be less likely to occur if blood pressure is controlled.

Mecamylamine works by controlling impulses along certain nerve pathways. As a result, it relaxes blood vessels so that blood passes through them more easily. This helps to lower blood pressure.

Mecamylamine is available only with your doctor's prescription, in the following dosage form:

Oral
- Tablets (U.S.)

Before Using This Medicine

In deciding to use a medicine, the risks of taking the medicine must be weighed against the good it will do. This is a decision you and your doctor will make. For mecamylamine, the following should be considered:

Allergies— Tell your doctor if you have ever had any unusual or allergic reaction to mecamylamine. Also tell your health care professional if you are allergic to any other substances, such as foods, preservatives, or dyes.

Pregnancy— Studies on effects in pregnancy have not been done in either humans or animals. However, in general, use of this medicine during pregnancy is not recommended because pregnant women may be more sensitive to its effects. In addition, mecamylamine may cause bowel problems in the unborn baby.

Breast-feeding— It is not known whether mecamylamine passes into breast milk. However, this medicine has not been reported to cause problems in nursing babies.

Children— Studies on this medicine have been done only in adult patients, and there is no specific information comparing use of mecamylamine in children with use in other age groups.

Older adults— Dizziness or lightheadedness may be more likely to occur in the elderly, who are more sensitive to the effects of mecamylamine.

Other medicines— Although certain medicines should not be used together at all, in many cases two different medicines may be used together even if an interaction might occur. In these cases, changes in dose or other precautions may be necessary. When taking mecamylamine it is especially important that your health care professional know if you are taking any of the following:

- Antibiotics or
- Sulfonamides (sulfa medicine)—Patients with chronic pyelonephritis being treated with these medications should not be treated with mecamylamine
- Antimyasthenics (ambenonium [e.g., Mytelase], neostigmine [e.g., Prostigmin], pyridostigmine [e.g., Mestinon])—Effects of these medicines may be decreased by mecamylamine
- Urinary alkalizers (medicine that makes the urine less acid, such as acetazolamide [e.g., Diamox], calcium- and/or magnesium-containing antacids, dichlorphenamide [e.g., Daranide], methazolamide [e.g., Neptazane], potassium or sodium citrate and/or citric acid, sodium bicarbonate [baking soda])—Effects of mecamylamine may be increased because these medicines cause it to be removed more slowly from the body

Other medical problems— The presence of other medical problems may affect the use of mecamylamine. Make sure you tell your doctor if you have any other medical problems, especially:

- Bladder or prostate problems—Mecamylamine may interfere with urination
- Bowel problems—Patients with bowel problems who take mecamylamine may be at inceased risk for serious bowel side effects of mecamylamine
- Diarrhea or
- Fever or infection or
- Nausea or vomiting—Effects of mecamylamine on blood pressure may be increased
- Glaucoma—Mecamylamine may make this condition worse
- Heart or blood vessel disease or
- Heart attack or stroke (recent)—Lowering of blood pressure by mecamylamine may make problems resulting from these conditions worse
- Kidney disease—Effects of mecamylamine may be increased because of slower removal of mecamylamine from the body

Proper Use of This Medicine

In addition to the use of the medicine your doctor has prescribed, treatment for your high blood pressure may include weight control and care in the types of foods you eat, especially foods high in sodium. Your doctor will tell you which of these are most important for you. You should check with your doctor before changing your diet.

Many patients who have high blood pressure will not notice any signs of the problem. In fact, many may feel normal. *It is very important that you take your medicine exactly as directed and that you keep your appointments with your doctor* even if you feel well.

Remember that this medicine will not cure your high blood pressure but it does help control it. Therefore, you must continue to take it as directed if you expect to lower your blood pressure and keep it down. *You may have to take high blood pressure medicine for the rest of your life.* If high blood pressure is not treated, it can cause serious problems such as heart failure, blood vessel disease, stroke, or kidney disease.

To help you remember to take your medicine, try to get into the habit of taking it at the same time each day.

Dosing—The dose of mecamylamine will be different for different patients. *Follow your doctor's orders or the directions on the label.* The following information includes only the average doses of mecamylamine. *If your dose is different, do not change it* unless your doctor tells you to do so:

- For *oral* dosage forms (tablets):
  —Adults: 2.5 milligrams two times a day to 25 milligrams three times a day.

Missed dose—If you miss a dose of this medicine, take it as soon as possible. Then go back to your regular dosing schedule. *If you miss two or more doses in a row, check with your doctor right away.* If your body goes without this medicine for too long, your blood pressure may go up to a dangerously high level.

Storage—To store this medicine:
- Keep out of the reach of children.
- Store away from heat and direct light.
- Do not store in the bathroom, near the kitchen sink, or in other damp places. Heat or moisture may cause the medicine to break down.
- Do not keep outdated medicine or medicine no longer needed. Be sure that any discarded medicine is out of the reach of children.

Precautions While Using This Medicine

It is important that your doctor check your progress at regular visits to make sure that this medicine is working properly.

Check with your doctor before you stop taking this medicine. Your doctor may want you to reduce gradually the amount you are taking before stopping completely.

Make sure that you have enough medicine on hand to last through weekends, holidays, or vacations. You should not miss taking any doses. You may want to ask your doctor for another written prescription for mecamylamine to carry in your wallet or purse. You can then have it filled if you run out of medicine when you are away from home.

Do not take other medicines unless they have been discussed with your doctor. This especially includes over-the-counter (nonprescription) medicines for appetite control, asthma, colds, cough, hay fever, or sinus problems, since they may tend to increase your blood pressure.

Dizziness, lightheadedness, or fainting may occur, especially when you get up from a lying or sitting position. This is more likely to occur in the morning. *Getting up slowly may help.* When you get up from lying down, sit on the edge of the bed with your feet dangling for one or two minutes.

Then stand up slowly. If you feel dizzy, sit or lie down. If the problem continues or gets worse, check with your doctor.

The dizziness, lightheadedness, or fainting is also more likely to occur if you drink alcohol, stand for a long time, exercise, or if the weather is hot. *While you are taking this medicine, be careful to limit the amount of alcohol you drink. Also, use extra care during exercise or hot weather or if you must stand for a long time.*

Sodium bicarbonate (commonly known as baking soda) may cause you to get a greater than normal effect from this medicine. To prevent problems, check with your health care professional before using an antacid or medicine for heartburn since some of these contain sodium bicarbonate.

Tell your doctor if you get a fever or infection since that may change the amount of medicine you have to take.

Mecamylamine may cause dryness of the mouth, nose, and throat. For temporary relief of mouth dryness, use sugarless candy or gum, melt bits of ice in your mouth, or use a saliva substitute. However, if your mouth continues to feel dry for more than 2 weeks, check with your medical doctor or dentist. Continuing dryness of the mouth may increase the chance of dental disease, including tooth decay, gum disease, and fungus infections.

Before having any kind of surgery (including dental surgery) or emergency treatment, tell the medical doctor or dentist in charge that you are taking this medicine.

Side Effects of This Medicine

Along with its needed effects, a medicine may cause some unwanted effects. Although not all of these side effects may occur, if they do occur they may need medical attention.

Check with your doctor as soon as possible if any of the following side effects occur:
More common
   Dizziness or lightheadedness, especially when getting up from a lying or sitting position

Less common
   Difficult urination

Rare
   Bloating and frequent loose stools; confusion or excitement; constipation (severe); convulsions (seizures); mental depression; shortness of breath; trembling; uncontrolled movements of face, hands, arms, or legs

Other side effects may occur that usually do not need medical attention. These side effects may go away during treatment as your body adjusts to the medicine. However, check with your doctor if any of the following side effects continue or are bothersome:
More common
   Constipation; drowsiness; unusual tiredness

Less common or rare
   Blurred vision; decreased sexual ability or interest in sex; dryness of mouth; enlarged pupils; loss of appetite; nausea and vomiting; weakness

Other side effects not listed above may also occur in some patients. If you notice any other effects, check with your doctor.

Revised: 01/20/93

MECHLORETHAMINE   Systemic

Commonly used brand name(s):

In the U.S.—
Mustargen

In Canada—
Mustargen

Other commonly used names are chlormethine and nitrogen mustard.

Description

Mechlorethamine (me-klor-ETH-a-meen) belongs to the group of medicines called alkylating agents. It is used to treat some kinds of cancer as well as some noncancerous conditions.

Mechlorethamine interferes with the growth of cancer cells, which are eventually destroyed. Since the growth of normal body cells may also be affected by mechlorethamine, other effects will also occur. Some of these may be serious and must be reported to your doctor. Other effects, like hair loss, may not be serious but may cause concern. Some effects may not occur for months or years after the medicine is used.

Before you begin treatment with mechlorethamine, you and your doctor should talk about the good this medicine will do as well as the risks of using it.

Mechlorethamine is to be administered only by or under the immediate supervision of your doctor. It is available in the following dosage form:

Parenteral
• Injection (U.S. and Canada)

Before Using This Medicine

In deciding to use a medicine, the risks of taking the medicine must be weighed against the good it will do. This is a decision you and your doctor will make. For mechlorethamine, the following should be considered:

Allergies—Tell your doctor if you have ever had any unusual or allergic reaction to mechlorethamine, including a reaction if it was applied to the skin.

Pregnancy—Tell your doctor if you are pregnant or if you intend to have children. This medicine may cause birth defects if either the male or female is receiving it at the time of conception or if it is used during pregnancy. In addition, many cancer medicines may cause sterility which could be permanent. Sterility has been reported with mechlorethamine and the possibility should be kept in mind.

Be sure that you have discussed this with your doctor before receiving this medicine. It is best to use some kind of birth control while you are receiving mechlorethamine. Tell your doctor right away if you think you have become pregnant while receiving mechlorethamine.

Breast-feeding—Tell your doctor if you are breast-feeding or if you intend to breast-feed during treatment with this medicine. Because mechlorethamine may cause serious side effects, breast-feeding is generally not recommended while you are receiving it.

Children—Although there is no specific information comparing use of mechlorethamine in children with use in other age groups, it is not expected to cause different side effects or problems in children than it does in adults.

Older adults—Many medicines have not been studied specifically in older people. Therefore, it may not be known whether they work exactly the same way they do in younger adults or if they cause different side effects or problems in older people. There is no specific information comparing use of mechlorethamine in the elderly with use in other age groups.

Other medicines—Although certain medicines should not be used together at all, in other cases two different medicines may be used together even if an interaction might occur. In these cases, your doctor may want to change the dose, or other precautions may be necessary. When you are receiving mechlorethamine, it is especially important that your health care professional know if you are taking any of the following:

• Amphotericin B by injection (e.g., Fungizone) or
• Antithyroid agents (medicine for overactive thyroid) or
• Azathioprine (e.g., Imuran) or
• Chloramphenicol (e.g., Chloromycetin) or
• Colchicine or
• Flucytosine (e.g., Ancobon) or
• Ganciclovir (e.g., Cytovene) or
• Interferon (e.g., Intron A, Roferon-A) or
• Plicamycin (e.g., Mithracin) or
• Zidovudine (e.g., AZT, Retrovir) or
• If you have ever been treated with radiation or cancer medicines—Mechlorethamine may increase the effects of these medicines or radiation therapy on the blood

• Probenecid (e.g., Benemid) or
• Sulfinpyrazone (e.g., Anturane)—Mechlorethamine may raise the concentration of uric acid in the blood. Since these medicines are used to lower uric acid levels, they may not be as effective in patients receiving mechlorethamine

Other medical problems—The presence of other medical problems may affect the use of mechlorethamine. Make sure you tell your doctor if you have any other medical problems, especially:

• Chickenpox (including recent exposure) or
• Herpes zoster (shingles)—Risk of severe disease affecting other parts of the body

• Gout or
• Kidney stones—Mechlorethamine may increase levels of uric acid in the body, which can cause gout and kidney stones

• Infection—Mechlorethamine may decrease your body's ability to fight infection

Proper Use of This Medicine

Mechlorethamine is sometimes given together with certain other medicines. If you are using a combination of medicines, it is important that you receive each one at the proper time. If you are taking some of these medicines by mouth, ask your health care professional to help you plan a way to take them at the right times.

While you are using this medicine, your doctor may want you to drink extra fluids so that you will pass more urine. This will help prevent kidney problems and keep your kidneys working well.

Mechlorethamine often causes nausea and vomiting, which usually last only 8 to 24 hours. It is very important that you continue to receive the medicine, even if you begin to feel ill. Ask your health care professional for ways to lessen these effects.

Dosing—The dose of mechlorethamine will be different for different patients. The dose that is used may depend on a number of things, including what the medicine is being used for, the patient's weight, and whether or not other medicines are also being taken. *If you are receiving mechlorethamine at home, follow your doctor's orders or the directions on the label.* If you have any questions about the proper dose of mechlorethamine, ask your doctor.

Precautions While Using This Medicine

It is very important that your doctor check your progress at regular visits to make sure that this medicine is working properly and to check for unwanted effects.

While you are being treated with mechlorethamine, and after you stop treatment with it, *do not have any immunizations (vaccinations) without your doctor's approval.* Mechlorethamine may lower your body's resistance and there is a chance you might get the infection the immunization is meant to prevent. In addition, other persons living in your household should not take oral polio vaccine since there is a chance they could pass the polio virus on to you. Also, avoid persons who have taken oral polio vaccine. Do not get close to them, and do not stay in the same room with them for very long. If you cannot take these precautions, you should consider wearing a protective face mask that covers the nose and mouth.

Mechlorethamine can temporarily lower the number of white blood cells in your blood, increasing the chance of getting an infection. It can also lower the number of platelets, which are necessary for proper blood clotting. If this occurs, there are certain precautions you can take, especially when your blood count is low, to reduce the risk of infection or bleeding:

- If you can, avoid people with infections. *Check with your doctor immediately* if you think you are getting an infection or if you get a fever or chills, cough or hoarseness, lower back or side pain, or painful or difficult urination.
- *Check with your doctor immediately* if you notice any unusual bleeding or bruising; black, tarry stools; blood in urine or stools; or pinpoint red spots on your skin.
- Be careful when using a regular toothbrush, dental floss, or toothpick. Your medical doctor, dentist, or nurse may recommend other ways to clean your teeth and gums. Check with your medical doctor before having any dental work done.
- Do not touch your eyes or the inside of your nose unless you have just washed your hands and have not touched anything else in the meantime.
- Be careful not to cut yourself when you are using sharp objects such as a safety razor or fingernail or toenail cutters.
- Avoid contact sports or other situations where bruising or injury could occur.

If mechlorethamine accidentally seeps out of the vein into which it is injected, it may damage some tissues and cause scarring. *Tell the health care professional right away if you notice redness, pain, or swelling at the place of injection.*

Side Effects of This Medicine

Along with its needed effects, a medicine may cause some unwanted effects. Although not all of these side effects may occur, if they do occur they may need medical attention.

Also, because of the way cancer medicines act on the body, there is a chance that they might cause other effects that may not occur until months or years after these medicines are used. These delayed effects may include certain types of cancer. Discuss these possible effects with your doctor.

Check with your doctor or nurse immediately if any of the following side effects occur:
> *Less common*
>> Black, tarry stools; blood in urine or stools; cough or hoarseness; fever or chills; lower back or side pain; pain or redness at place of injection; painful or difficult urination; pinpoint red spots on skin; unusual bleeding or bruising

> *Rare*
>> Shortness of breath, itching, or wheezing

Check with your health care professional as soon as possible if any of the following side effects occur:
> *More common*
>> Missing menstrual periods; painful rash

> *Less common*
>> Dizziness; joint pain; loss of hearing; ringing in ears; swelling of feet or lower legs

> *Rare*
>> Numbness, tingling, or burning of fingers, toes, or face; sores in mouth and on lips; yellow eyes or skin

Other side effects may occur that usually do not need medical attention. These side effects may go away during treatment as your body adjusts to the medicine. Also, your health care professional may be able to tell you about ways to prevent or reduce some of these side effects. Check with your health care professional if any of the following side effects continue or are bothersome or if you have any questions about them:
> *More common*
>> Nausea and vomiting (usually lasts only 8 to 24 hours)

> *Less common*
>> Confusion; diarrhea; drowsiness; headache; loss of appetite; metallic taste; weakness

This medicine may cause a temporary loss of hair in some people. After treatment with mechlorethamine has ended, normal hair growth should return.

After you stop receiving mechlorethamine, it may still produce some side effects that need attention. During this period of time, check with your doctor if you notice any of the following side effects:
> Black, tarry stools; blood in urine or stools; cough or hoarseness; fever or chills; lower back or side pain; painful or difficult urination; pinpoint red spots on skin; unusual bleeding or bruising

Other side effects not listed above may also occur in some patients. If you notice any other effects, check with your doctor.

Additional Information

Once a medicine has been approved for marketing for a certain use, experience may show that it is also useful for other medical problems. Although these uses are not included in product labeling, mechlorethamine is used in certain patients with the following medical conditions:

- Cancer of the lymph system (part of the immune system) that affects the skin

Other than the above information, there is no additional information relating to proper use, precautions, or side effects for these uses.

Revised: 08/14/2000

MECLIZINE/BUCLIZINE/CYCLIZINE
Systemic

Commonly used brand name(s):

In the U.S.—
Antivert[3]	Dramamine II[3]
Antivert/25[3]	Marezine[2]
Antivert/50[3]	Meclicot[3]
Bonine[3]	Medivert[3]

In Canada—
Bonamine[3]
Marzine[2]

Note: For quick reference, the following medicines are numbered to match the corresponding brand names.

This information applies to the following medicines:
1. Buclizine (BYOO-kli-zeen) *†
2. Cyclizine (SYE-kli-zeen)
3. Meclizine (MEK-li-zeen) ‡

*Not commercially available in the U.S.
†Not commercially available in Canada.
‡Generic name product may be available in the U.S.

Description

Buclizine, cyclizine, and meclizine are used to prevent and treat nausea, vomiting, and dizziness associated with motion sickness, and vertigo (dizziness caused by other medical problems).

Some of these preparations are available only with your doctor's prescription. Others are available without a prescription; however, your doctor may have special instructions on the proper dose of the medicine for your medical condition. They are available in the following dosage forms:

Oral
Buclizine
• Chewable tablets
Cyclizine
• Tablets (U.S.)
Meclizine
• Tablets (U.S.)
• Chewable tablets (U.S. and Canada)

Parenteral
Cyclizine
• Injection (Canada)

Before Using This Medicine

If you are taking this medicine without a prescription, carefully read and follow any precautions on the label. For buclizine, cyclizine, and meclizine, the following should be considered:

Allergies—Tell your doctor if you have ever had any unusual or allergic reaction to buclizine, cyclizine, or meclizine. Also tell your health care professional if you are allergic to any other substances, such as foods, preservatives, or dyes.

Pregnancy—These medicines have not been shown to cause birth defects or other problems in humans. However, studies in animals have shown that buclizine, cyclizine, and meclizine given in doses many times the usual human dose cause birth defects, such as cleft palate.

Breast-feeding—Although these medicines may pass into breast milk, they have not been reported to cause problems in nursing babies. However, since these medicines tend to decrease the secretions of the body, it is possible that the flow of breast milk may be reduced in some patients.

Children—There is no specific information comparing use of buclizine, cyclizine, and meclizine in children with use in other age groups. However, children may be especially sensitive to the anticholinergic effects (e.g., dryness of mouth, nose, and throat) of these medicines.

Older adults—There is no specific information comparing use of buclizine, cyclizine, and meclizine in the elderly with use in other age groups. Many medicines have not been studied specifically in older people. Therefore, it may not be known whether they work exactly the same way they do in younger adults. However, older people may be especially sensitive to the anticholinergic effects (e.g., constipation; difficult urination; dryness of mouth, nose, and throat) of these medicines.

Other medicines—Although certain medicines should not be used together at all, in other cases two different medicines may be used together even if an interaction might occur. In these cases, your doctor may want to change the dose, or other precautions may be necessary. When you are taking buclizine, cyclizine, or meclizine, it is especially important that your health care professional know if you are taking the following:
- Central nervous system (CNS) depressants, other (medicines that make you drowsy or less alert) or
- Tricyclic antidepressants (medicine for depression)—Use with buclizine, cyclizine, or meclizine may increase the side effects of either medicine

Other medical problems—The presence of other medical problems may affect the use of buclizine, cyclizine, or meclizine. Make sure you tell your doctor if you have any other medical problems, especially:
- Asthma, bronchitis, emphysema, or other chronic lung disease—Cyclizine or meclizine may cause serious breathing problems in patients who have any of these conditions
- Enlarged prostate or
- Glaucoma or
- Intestinal blockage or
- Urinary tract blockage—Buclizine, cyclizine, or meclizine may make these conditions worse
- Heart failure—Cyclizine may make the condition worse

Proper Use of This Medicine

This medicine is used to relieve or prevent the symptoms of motion sickness or vertigo (dizziness caused by other medical problems). Take it only as directed. Do not take more of it or take it more often than stated on the label or ordered by your doctor. To do so may increase the chance of side effects.

Dosing—The dose of buclizine, cyclizine, or meclizine will be different for different patients. *Follow your doctor's orders or the directions on the label.* The following information includes only the average doses of buclizine, cyclizine, or meclizine. *If your dose is different, do not change it* unless your doctor tells you to do so.

For buclizine
- For *oral* dosage form (chewable tablets):
  —To prevent motion sickness:
    - Adults and teenagers—The usual dose is 50 milligrams (mg) thirty minutes before travel. The dose may be repeated every four to six hours if needed. Not more than 150 mg should be taken in one day.
    - Children—Dose must be determined by your doctor.

For cyclizine
- For *oral* dosage form (tablets):
  —To prevent and treat motion sickness:
    - Adults and teenagers—The usual dose is 50 milligrams (mg) thirty minutes before travel. The dose may be repeated every four to six hours if needed. Not more than 200 mg should be taken in one day.
    - Children 6 to 12 years of age—The usual dose is 25 mg thirty minutes before travel. The dose may be repeated every six to eight hours if needed. Not more than 75 mg should be taken in one day.
    - Children up to 6 years of age—Use and dose must be determined by your doctor.
- For *injection* dosage form:
  —To prevent and treat motion sickness:
    - Adults and teenagers—The usual dose is 50 mg injected into a muscle every four to six hours as needed.
    - Children—Dose is based on body weight and must be determined by your doctor. The usual dose is 1 mg per kilogram (0.45 mg per pound) of body weight injected into a muscle three times a day as needed.

For meclizine
- For *oral* dosage forms (tablets and chewable tablets):
  —To prevent and treat motion sickness:
    - Adults and children 12 years of age or older—The usual dose is 25 to 50 milligrams (mg) one hour before travel. The dose may be repeated every twenty-four hours as needed.
    - Children up to 12 years of age—Use and dose must be determined by your doctor.
  —To prevent and treat vertigo (dizziness):
    - Adults and children 12 years of age or older—The usual dose is 25 to 100 mg a day as needed, divided into smaller doses.
    - Children up to 12 years of age—Use and dose must be determined by your doctor.

Missed dose—If you must take this medicine regularly and you miss a dose, take the missed dose as soon as possible. However, if it is almost time for your next dose, skip the missed dose and go back to your regular dosing schedule. Do not double doses.

Storage—To store this medicine:
- Keep out of the reach of children.
- Store away from heat and direct light.
- Do not store the tablets in the bathroom, near the kitchen sink, or in other damp places. Heat or moisture may cause the medicine to break down.
- Do not keep outdated medicine or medicine no longer needed. Be sure that any discarded medicine is out of the reach of children.

Precautions While Using This Medicine

Tell the doctor in charge that you are taking this medicine before you have any skin tests for allergies. The results of the test may be affected by this medicine.

Buclizine, cyclizine, or meclizine will add to the effects of alcohol and other CNS depressants (medicines that make you drowsy or less alert). Some examples of CNS depressants are antihistamines or medicine for hay fever, other allergies, or colds; sedatives, tranquilizers, or sleeping medicine; prescription pain medicine or narcotics; barbiturates; medicine for seizures; muscle relaxants; or anesthetics, including some dental anesthetics. *Check with your doctor before taking any of the above while you are using this medicine.*

This medicine may cause some people to become drowsy or less alert than they are normally. *Make sure you know how you react to this medicine before you drive, use machines, or do anything else that could be dangerous if you are not alert.*

Buclizine, cyclizine, and meclizine may cause dryness of the mouth. For temporary relief use sugarless candy or gum, melt bits of ice in your mouth, or use a saliva substitute. However, if your mouth continues to feel dry for more than 2 weeks, check with your medical doctor or dentist. Continuing dryness of the mouth may increase the chance of dental disease, including tooth decay, gum disease, and fungus infections.

Side Effects of This Medicine

Along with its needed effects, a medicine may cause some unwanted effects. The following side effects may go away during treatment as your body adjusts to the medicine; however, check with your doctor if they continue or are bothersome:

More common
   Drowsiness
Less common or rare
   Blurred or double vision; constipation; diarrhea; difficult or painful urination; dizziness; dryness of mouth, nose, and throat; fast heartbeat; headache; loss of appetite; nervousness, restlessness, or trouble in sleeping; skin rash; upset stomach

Not all of the side effects listed above have been reported for each of these medicines, but they have been reported for at least one of them. Buclizine, cyclizine, and meclizine are similar, so any of the above side effects may occur with any of these medicines.

Other side effects not listed above may also occur in some patients. If you notice any other effects, check with your doctor.

Additional Information

Once a medicine has been approved for marketing for a certain use, experience may show that it is also useful for other medical problems. Although these uses are not included in product labeling, some of these medicines are used in certain patients to prevent the following medical conditions:
- Nausea and vomiting following surgery
- Nausea and vomiting following cancer radiation treatment

Other than the above information, there is no additional information relating to proper use, precautions, or side effects for these uses.

Revised: 02/24/99

MEDROXYPROGESTERONE AND ESTRADIOL Systemic— INTRODUCTORY VERSION

Commonly used brand name(s):

In the U.S.—
Lunelle

Description

Contraceptives are designed to prevent pregnancy. The combination of medroxyprogesterone (me-DROX-ee-proe-JES-ter-rone) and estradiol (es-tra-DYE-ole) are two types of hormones that work by stopping a women's egg from fully developing each month. The egg can no longer accept sperm and fertilization is prevented. Although contraceptives have other effects that help prevent a pregnancy from occurring, this is the main action

This medicine is available only with your doctor's prescription, in the following dosage forms:

Parenteral
- Injection (U.S.)

Before Using This Medicine

In deciding to use a medicine, the risks of taking the medicine must be weighed against the good it will do. If you are using injectable contraceptives you should understand how their benefits and risks compare to those of other birth control methods. This is a decision you, your sexual partner, and your doctor will make. For medroxyprogesterone and estradiol combination, the following should be considered:

Allergies—Tell your doctor if you have ever had any unusual or allergic reaction to progesterones or estrogens. Also tell your health care professional if you are allergic to any other substances, such as foods, preservatives, or dyes.

Pregnancy—Contraceptives are not recommended for use during pregnancy and should be discontinued if you become pregnant or if you think that you are pregnant. In rare cases when oral contraceptives have been taken early in a pregnancy, problems in the fetus have not occurred.

Breast-feeding—It is not known whether monthly injectable contraceptives pass into breast milk, but oral contraceptives do pass into the breast milk and can change the content or lower the amount of breast milk. Injectable contraceptives may be used by women who are breast-feeding and they may begin their contraceptive six weeks after having their baby.

Teenagers—This medicine can be used for birth control in teenage females and is not expected to cause different side effects or problems than it does in adults. Some teenagers may need extra information on the importance of taking this medication exactly as prescribed.

Other medicines—Although certain medicines should not be used together at all, in other cases two different medicines may be used together even if an interaction might occur. In these cases, your doctor may want to change the dose, or other precautions may be necessary. When you are taking medroxyprogesterone and estradiol, it is especially important that your health care professional know if you are taking any of the following:

- Aminoglutethamide (e.g., Cytadren)—These medicines may decrease the effectiveness of the contraceptive

- Carbamazepine (e.g., Tegretol) or
- Phenobarbital (e.g., Luminal) or
- Phenytoin (e.g., Dilantin)—These medicines may increase the removal of medroxyprogesterone and estradiol from the body, resulting in a decrease in the ability to protect against pregnancy.

- Rifampin (e.g., Rifadin)—These medicines may increase the removal of medroxyprogesterone and estradiol from the body, resulting in a decrease in the ability to protect against pregnancy

Other medical problems—The presence of other medical problems may affect the use of medroxyprogesterone and estradiol. Make sure you tell your doctor if you have any other medical problems, especially:

- Abnormal changes in menstrual or uterine bleeding
- Blood clots (or history of) or
- Gallbladder disease or gallstones (or history of) or
- Heart or circulation problems or
- High blood cholesterol or
- High blood pressure (hypertension) or
- Liver disease (or history of) or
- Mental problems—Combination contraceptives may make these conditions worse or, rarely, cause them to occur again.

- Cancer, including breast cancer—Contraceptives may worsen some cancers, especially when breast, cervical, or uterine cancers already exist. Use of monthly injectable contraceptives is not recommended if you have any of these conditions. If you have a family history of breast disease, injectable contraceptives may still be a good choice but you may need to be tested more often

- Diabetes mellitus (sugar diabetes)—Use of combination contraceptives may cause an increase, usually only a small increase, in your blood sugar and usually does not affect the amount of diabetes medicine that you take.

- Migraine headaches—Combination contraceptives may cause fluid build-up and may cause these conditions to become worse; however, some people have fewer migraine headaches when they use contraceptives

Proper Use of This Medicine

Dosing—To make monthly injectable contraceptives as safe and reliable as possible, you should understand how and when to take them and what effects may be expected. *Follow your doctor's orders.*

- For *injection* dosage form:
  —For contraception
    - Adults—0.5 milliliters (mL) injected into a muscle in the upper arm, upper thigh or in the buttocks every 28 to 30 days.

Missed dose—If you miss having your next injection by day 33 your doctor will want to rule out pregnancy before the medicine is given to you again. Another method of birth control should be used until your period begins or until your doctor determines that you are not pregnant, and you are able to have the medicine again.

Precautions While Using This Medicine

It is very important that your health care professional check your progress at regular visits to make sure this medicine does not cause unwanted effects. These physical exams will usually be every 12 months, but you need to visit your doctor every 28 to 30 days to get your injection.

This medicine does not protect a woman from sexually transmitted diseases (STDs), including human immunodeficiency virus (HIV), or acquired immunodeficiency syndrome (AIDS).

Side Effects of This Medicine

Along with its needed effects, a medicine may cause some unwanted effects. Although not all of these side effects may occur, if they do occur they may need medical attention.

Check with your doctor immediately if any of the following side effects occur:

More common

Bloating or swelling of face, hands, lower legs and/or feet; cough; difficulty swallowing; dizziness; fast heartbeat; hives; itching; loss of appetite and nausea; puffiness or swelling of the eyelids or around the eyes, face, lips or tongue; rapid weight gain; shortness of breath; tightness in chest; unusual tiredness or weakness; vomiting blood; wheezing; yellow eyes or skin

Symptoms of overdose

More common

Nausea; menstrual irregularities; vaginal bleeding; vomiting

Other side effects may occur that usually do not need medical attention. These side effects may go away during treatment as your body adjusts to the medicine. Also, your health care professional may be able to tell you about ways to prevent or reduce some of these side effects. Check with your health care professional if any of the following side effects continue or are bothersome or if you have any questions about them:

More common

Abdominal pain or enlarged abdomen; absent or missed menstrual periods; acne; allergic rash; brown, blotchy spots on skin; decreased sex drive; depression; hair loss/thinning of hair; headache; increased amount of menstrual bleeding, or normal bleeding that comes earlier; lack or loss of strength; nervousness; quick to react or overact emotionally; rapidly changing moods; stopping of menstrual bleeding over several months; vaginal yeast infection; weight change

---

Developed: 01/24/2001

MEFLOQUINE   Systemic

Commonly used brand name(s):

In the U.S.—
Lariam

In Canada—
Lariam

Description

Mefloquine (ME-floe-kwin) belongs to a group of medicines called antimalarials. It is used to prevent or treat malaria, a red blood cell infection transmitted by the bite of a mosquito.

Malaria transmission occurs in large areas of Central and South America, Hispaniola, sub-Saharan Africa, the Indian subcontinent, Southeast Asia, the Middle East, and Oceania. Country-specific information on malaria can be obtained from the Centers for Disease Control and Prevention (CDC), or from the CDC's web site at *http://www.cdc.gov/travel*.

This medicine may cause some serious side effects. Therefore, it is usually used only to prevent the symptoms of malaria or to treat serious malaria infections in areas where it is known that other medicines may not work.

Mefloquine is available only with your doctor's prescription, in the following dosage form:

Oral
• Tablets (U.S. and Canada)

Before Using This Medicine

In deciding to use a medicine, the risks of taking the medicine must be weighed against the good it will do. This is a decision you and your doctor will make. For mefloquine, the following should be considered:

Allergies—Tell your doctor if you have ever had any unusual or allergic reaction to mefloquine, quinidine (e.g., Quinidex), quinine, or any related medicines. Also tell your health care professional if you are allergic to any other substances, such as foods, preservatives, or dyes.

Pregnancy—It is best if pregnant women can avoid traveling to areas where there is a chance of getting malaria. However, if travel is necessary, mefloquine may be used for women traveling to areas where the parasite is resistant to chloroquine. Pregnant women are advised to report to their doctor any side effects following the use of mefloquine.

Breast-feeding—Mefloquine passes into the breast milk in small amounts. However, the amount in breast milk is not enough to prevent the infant from getting malaria.

Children—Children should avoid traveling to areas where there is a chance of getting malaria, unless they can take effective antimalarial medicines such as mefloquine.

Older adults—Many medicines have not been studied specifically in older people. Therefore, it may not be known whether they work exactly the same way they do in younger adults or if they cause different side effects or problems in older people. There is no specific information comparing use of mefloquine in the elderly with use in other age groups.

Other medicines—Although certain medicines should not be used together at all, in other cases two different medicines may be used together even if an interaction might occur. In these cases, your doctor may want to change the dose, or other precautions may be necessary. When you are taking mefloquine, it is especially important that your health care professional know if you are taking any of the following:
• Halofantrine (e.g., Halfan)
• Quinidine (e.g., Quinidex) or
• Quinine or
• Verapamil (e.g., Calan)—Use of these medicines together with mefloquine may result in slow heartbeat and other heart problems; also, an increased chance of convulsions (seizures) may occur when quinine is taken together with mefloquine
• Chloroquine (e.g., Aralen)—Use of chloroquine with mefloquine may increase the chance of convulsions (seizures)
• Divalproex (e.g., Depakote) or

- Valproic acid (e.g., Depakene)—Use of these medicines together with mefloquine may result in low blood levels of valproic acid and an increased chance of convulsions (seizures)

Other medical problems—The presence of other medical problems may affect the use of mefloquine. Make sure you tell your doctor if you have any other medical problems, especially:

- Convulsions (seizures), history of or
- Epilepsy or
- Heart block or
- Heart rhythm disturbance or
- Psychiatric (mental) disorders, history of—Mefloquine may make these conditions worse

Proper Use of This Medicine

Mefloquine is best taken with a full glass (8 ounces) of water and with food, unless otherwise directed by your doctor.

For patients taking *mefloquine* to *prevent the symptoms of malaria:*

- Your doctor will want you to start taking this medicine 1 to 2 weeks before you travel to an area where there is a chance of getting malaria. This will help you to see how you react to the medicine. Also, it will allow time for your doctor to prescribe another medicine for you if you have a reaction to this medicine.
- *Also, you should keep taking this medicine while you are in the area where malaria is present and for 4 weeks after you leave the area.* No medicine will protect you completely from malaria. However, to protect you as completely as possible, *it is important that you keep taking this medicine for the full time your doctor ordered.* Also, if fever or "flu-like" symptoms develop during your travels or within 2 to 3 months after you leave the area, *check with your doctor immediately.*
- This medicine works best when you take it on a regular schedule. For example, if you are to take it once a week, it is best to take it on the same day each week. *Do not miss any doses.* If you have any questions about this, check with your health care professional.

For patients taking *mefloquine* to *treat malaria:*

- To help clear up your infection completely, *take this medicine exactly as directed by your doctor.*

Dosing—The dose of mefloquine will be different for different patients. *Follow your doctor's orders or the directions on the label.* The following information includes only the average doses of mefloquine. *If your dose is different, do not change it* unless your doctor tells you to do so.

The number of doses you take each day, the time allowed between doses, and the length of time you take the medicine depend on whether you are using mefloquine to prevent or to treat malaria.

- For *oral* dosage form (tablets):
  —For prevention of malaria:
  - Adults and children weighing over 45 kilograms (kg) (99 pounds)—250 milligrams (mg) (1 tablet) one to two weeks before traveling to an area where malaria occurs. Then 250 mg once a week while staying in the area and every week for four weeks after leaving the area.
  - Children—Dose is based on body weight and must be determined by your doctor.

    —Children weighing up to 15 kg (33 pounds): 5 mg per kg of body weight one to two weeks before traveling to an area where malaria occurs.
    —Children weighing 15 to 19 kg (33 to 43 pounds): 62.5 mg (¼ tablet) one to two weeks before traveling to an area where malaria occurs. Then 62.5 mg once a week while staying in the area where malaria occurs and every week for four weeks after leaving the area.
    —Children weighing 20 to 30 kg (44 to 66 pounds): 125 mg (½ tablet) one to two weeks before traveling to an area where malaria occurs. Then 125 mg once a week while staying in the area and every week for four weeks after leaving the area.
    —Children weighing 31 to 45 kg (67 to 99 pounds): 187.5 mg (¾ tablet) one to two weeks before traveling to an area where malaria occurs. Then 187.5 mg once a week while staying in the area and every week for four weeks after leaving the area.
  —For treatment of malaria:
  - Adults—1250 mg as a single dose.
  - Children—Dose is based on body weight and must be determined by your doctor. The usual dose is 20 to 25 mg per kg (9 to 11 mg per pound) of body weight as a single dose.

Missed dose—If you miss a dose of this medicine, take it as soon as possible. This will help to keep you taking your medicine on a regular schedule. However, if it is almost time for your next dose, skip the missed dose and go back to your regular dosing schedule. Do not double doses.

Storage—To store this medicine:

- Keep out of the reach of children.
- Store away from heat and direct light.
- Do not store in the bathroom, near the kitchen sink, or in other damp places. Heat or moisture may cause the medicine to break down.
- Do not keep outdated medicine or medicine no longer needed. Be sure that any discarded medicine is out of the reach of children.

Precautions While Using This Medicine

Mefloquine may cause vision problems. It may also cause some people to become dizzy or lightheaded or to have hallucinations (seeing, hearing, or feeling things that are not there). *Make sure you know how you react to this medicine before you drive, use machines, or do anything else that could be dangerous if you are dizzy or are not alert or able to see well.* This is especially important for people whose jobs require fine coordination. If these reactions are especially bothersome, check with your doctor.

Malaria is spread by the bite of certain kinds of infected female mosquitoes. If you are living in, or will be traveling to, an area where there is a chance of getting malaria, the following mosquito-control measures will help to prevent infection:

- If possible, sleep under mosquito netting, preferably netting coated or soaked with pyrethrum, to avoid being bitten by malaria-carrying mosquitoes.
- Remain in air-conditioned rooms to reduce contact with mosquitoes

- Wear long-sleeved shirts or blouses and long trousers to protect your arms and legs, especially from dusk through dawn when mosquitoes are out.
- Apply mosquito repellant, preferably one containing DEET, to uncovered areas of the skin from dusk through dawn when mosquitoes are out.
- Using a pyrethrum-containing flying insect spray to kill mosquitoes in living and sleeping quarters during evening and nighttime hours.

If you are taking quinidine (e.g., Quinidex) or quinine, talk to your doctor before you take mefloquine. While you are taking mefloquine, take mefloquine at least 12 hours after the last dose of quinidine or quinine. Taking mefloquine and either of these medicines at the same time may result in a greater chance of serious side effects.

For patients taking *mefloquine* to *treat malaria:*
- If your symptoms do not improve within a few days, or if they become worse, check with your doctor.

Side Effects of This Medicine

Along with its needed effects, a medicine may cause some unwanted effects. Although not all of these side effects may occur, if they do occur they may need medical attention.

Check with your doctor immediately if any of the following side effects occur:
Less common
   Abnormal dreams; dizziness; forgetfulness; severe or continuing headache; mental depression; mood or mental changes; trouble in sleeping; unusual tiredness or weakness
Rare
   Aching joints and muscles; anxiety; black, tarry stools; blistering, loosening, peeling, or redness of the skin; chills, fever, and/or sore throat; confusion; convulsions (seizures); cough or hoarseness; depression; hallucinations (seeing, hearing, or feeling things that are not there); irregular heartbeat; irritability; lower back or side pain; painful or difficult urination; pinpoint red spots on skin; psychotic symptoms, such as mood or mental changes, mental depression, and/or restlessness; red or irritated eye; shortness of breath and/or wheezing; sores, ulcers, and/or white spots in mouth or on lips; stiff neck; swelling of ankles, feet, and/or lower legs; unusual bleeding or bruising; vomiting

Other side effects may occur that usually do not need medical attention. These side effects may go away during treatment as your body adjusts to the medicine. However, check with your doctor if any of the following side effects continue or are bothersome:
More common
   Diarrhea; nausea; stomach pain
Less common
   Loss of appetite

Mefloquine very rarely may cause partial loss of hair. After treatment with mefloquine has ended, normal hair growth should return.

Other side effects not listed above may also occur in some patients. If you notice any other effects, check with your doctor.

Revised: 01/24/2001

MELOXICAM   Systemic

Commonly used brand name(s):

In the U.S.—
   Mobic

Description

Meloxicam (mel-OX-i-kam) is a nonsteroidal anti-inflammatory drug (NSAID) used to relieve some symptoms of arthritis, such as inflammation, swelling, stiffness, and joint pain. However, this medicine does not cure arthritis and will help you only as long as you continue to take it.

This medicine is available only with your doctor's prescription, in the following dosage forms:
Oral
   - Tablets (U.S.)

Before Using This Medicine

In deciding to use a medicine, the risks of taking the medicine must be weighed against the good it will do. This is a decision you and your doctor will make. For meloxicam, the following should be considered:

Allergies—Tell your doctor if you have ever had any unusual or allergic reaction to meloxicam, aspirin, or other nonsteroidal anti-inflammatory drugs. Also tell your doctor and pharmacist if you are allergic to any other substances, such as foods, preservatives, or dyes.

Pregnancy—Meloxicam has not been studied in pregnant women. However, studies in animals have shown that meloxicam causes birth defects. Before taking this medicine, make sure your doctor knows if you are pregnant or if you may become pregnant.

Breast-feeding—Studies to determine if meloxicam passes into human breast milk have not been done. However, meloxicam has been found in the milk of rats. Meloxicam may cause unwanted effects in nursing babies. It may be necessary for you to take another medicine or stop breast-feeding during treatment. Be sure you have discussed the risks and benefits of the medicine with your doctor.

Children—Meloxicam has been studied only in adult patients, and there is no specific information comparing use of meloxicam in children with use in other age groups.

Older adults—This medicine has been tested and has not been shown to cause different side effects or problems in older people than it does in younger adults.

Other medicines—Although certain medicines should not be used together at all, in other cases two different medicines may be used together even if an interaction might occur. In these cases, your doctor may want to change the dose, or other precautions may be necessary. When you are taking meloxicam, it is especially important that your doctor and pharmacist know if you are taking any of the following:
- Aspirin—Use of aspirin with meloxicam may cause stomach or intestinal bleeding
- Lithium (e.g., Lithane)—When you take meloxicam, your dose of lithium may need to be changed because higher blood levels of lithium may occur

Other medical problems—The presence of other medical problems may affect the use of meloxicam. Make sure

you tell your doctor if you have any other medical problems, especially:

- Alcohol abuse or
- Bleeding problems or
- Stomach ulcer or other stomach problems or
- Tobacco (or recent history of)—The chance of side effects may be increased

- Anemia or
- Asthma or
- Dehydration or
- Fluid retention (swelling of feet or lower legs) or
- Heart disease or
- High blood pressure or
- Kidney disease or
- Liver disease—Meloxicam may make these conditions worse

- Aspirin triad (asthma, nasal polyps, and aspirin intolerance) or
- Previous allergic or anaphylactic response to aspirin or other nonsteroidal anti-inflammatory drugs—Use of meloxicam may cause a serious allergic reaction

Proper Use of This Medicine

For safe and effective use of this medicine, do not take more of it, do not take it more often, and do not take it for a longer time than ordered by your health care professional. Taking too much of this medicine may increase the chance of unwanted side effects.

Dosing—The dose of meloxicam will be different for different patients. *Follow your doctor's orders or the directions on the label.* The following information includes only the average dose of meloxicam. *If your dose is different, do not change it* unless your doctor tells you to do so.

- For *oral* dosage form (tablets):
  —For symptoms of osteoarthritis:
    - Adults—7.5 milligrams (mg) once a day
    - Children—Use must be determined by your doctor

Missed dose—If you miss a dose of this medicine, take the missed dose as soon as possible. However, if you do not remember the missed dose until the next day, skip the missed dose and go back to your regular dosing schedule. Do not double doses.

Storage—To store this medicine:

- Keep out of the reach of children.
- Do not store in the bathroom, near the kitchen sink, or in other damp places. Heat or moisture may cause the medicine to break down.
- Do not refrigerate or freeze.
- Do not keep outdated medicine or medicine no longer needed. Ask your health care professional how you should dispose of any medicine you do not use. Be sure that any discarded medicine is out of the reach of children.

Precautions While Using This Medicine

If you will be taking this medicine for a long time, *it is very important that your doctor check you at regular visits* for any blood problems that may be caused by this medicine.

Stomach problems may be more likely to occur if you drink alcoholic beverages while being treated with this medicine. Therefore, *do not regularly drink alcoholic beverages while taking this medicine, unless otherwise directed by your doctor.*

Taking two or more of the nonsteroidal anti-inflammatory drugs together on a regular basis may increase the chance of unwanted effects. Also, taking acetaminophen, aspirin or other salicylates, or ketorolac (e.g., Toradol) regularly while you are taking a nonsteroidal anti-inflammatory drug may increase the chance of unwanted effects. The risk will depend on how much of each medicine you take every day, and on how long you take the medicines together. If your health care professional directs you to take these medicines together on a regular basis, follow his or her directions carefully. However, *do not take acetaminophen or aspirin or other salicylates together with this medicine for more than a few days, and do not take any ketorolac (e.g., Toradol) while taking this medicine, unless your doctor has directed you to do so and is following your progress.*

Serious side effects can occur during treatment with this medicine. Sometimes serious side effects can occur without warning. However, possible warning signs often occur, including severe stomach pain, black tarry stools, and/or vomiting of blood or material that looks like coffee grounds; skin rash; swelling of face, fingers, feet and/or lower legs. *Stop taking this medicine and check with your doctor immediately if you notice any of these warning signs.*

If you notice signs of liver toxicity including nausea, unusual tiredness, itching of the skin, stomach pain or fever,

stop taking this medicine and check with your doctor immediately if you notice any of these warning signs.

Meloxicam may cause a serious type of allergic reaction called anaphylaxis. Although this is rare, it may occur often in patients who are allergic to aspirin or other nonsteroidal anti-inflammatory drugs. *Anaphylaxis requires immediate medical attention.* The most serious signs of this reaction are very fast or irregular breathing, gasping for breath, wheezing, or fainting. Other signs may include changes in skin color of face; very fast but irregular heartbeat or pulse; hive-like swellings on the skin; puffiness or swelling of the eyelids or around the eyes. If these effects occur, get emergency help at once. Ask someone to drive you to the nearest hospital emergency room. Call an ambulance, lie down, cover yourself to keep warm, and prop your feet higher than your head. Stay in that position until help arrives.

Side Effects of This Medicine

Along with its needed effects, a medicine may cause some unwanted effects. Although not all of these side effects may occur, if they do occur they may need medical attention.

Check with your doctor immediately if any of the following side effects occur:

Rare

Bloody or black, tarry stools; difficulty swallowing; puffiness or swelling of the eyelids or around the eyes, face, lips or tongue; severe stomach pain; shortness of breath; tightness in chest; vomiting of blood or material that looks like coffee grounds; wheezing

Symptoms of overdose

Get emergency help immediately if any of the following symptoms of overdose occur

Bloody or black tarry stools; blue lips, fingernails or skin; blurred vision; confusion; convulsions (seizures); dark urine; decreased urine output; difficulty breathing; difficulty swallowing; dizziness; fever with or without chills; pain in chest, upper stomach, or throat; pounding in ears; skin rash; slow or fast heartbeat; swelling around eyes, face, lips, or tongue; shortness of breath; severe stomach pain; unusual tiredness or weakness; tightness in chest; vomiting of blood or material that looks like coffee grounds; weight gain (rapid); wheezing; yellow eyes or skin

Other side effects may occur that usually do not need medical attention. These side effects may go away during treatment as your body adjusts to the medicine. However, check with your doctor if any of the following side effects continue or are bothersome.

More common
Diarrhea; gas; heartburn; indigestion

Less common or rare
Abdominal pain; anxiety; confusion; constipation; nausea and/or vomiting; nervousness; sleepiness

Other side effects not listed above may also occur in some patients. If you notice any other effects, check with your doctor.

Developed: 06/08/2000

MELPHALAN   Systemic

Commonly used brand name(s):

In the U.S.—
Alkeran

In Canada—
Alkeran

Other commonly used names are L-PAM and phenylalanine mustard.

Description

Melphalan (MEL-fa-lan) belongs to the group of medicines called alkylating agents. It is used to treat cancer of the ovaries and a certain type of cancer in the bone marrow.

Melphalan interferes with the growth of cancer cells, which are eventually destroyed. Since the growth of normal body cells may also be affected by melphalan, other effects will also occur. Some of these may be serious and must be reported to your doctor. Other effects may not be serious but may cause concern. Some effects may not occur for months or years after the medicine is used.

Before you begin treatment with melphalan, you and your doctor should talk about the good this medicine will do as well as the risks of using it.

Melphalan is available only with your doctor's prescription, in the following dosage form:

Oral
• Tablets (U.S. and Canada)
Parenteral
• Injection (U.S. and Canada)

Before Using This Medicine

In deciding to use a medicine, the risks of taking the medicine must be weighed against the good it will do. This is a decision you and your doctor will make. For melphalan, the following should be considered:

Allergies—Tell your doctor if you have ever had any unusual or allergic reaction to melphalan or chlorambucil.

Pregnancy—Tell your doctor if you are pregnant or if you intend to have children. There is a chance that this medicine may cause birth defects if either the male or female is taking it at the time of conception or if it is taken during pregnancy. In addition, many cancer medicines may cause sterility which could be permanent. Sterility has been reported with melphalan and the possibility should be kept in mind.

Be sure that you have discussed this with your doctor before taking this medicine. It is best to use some kind of birth control while you are taking melphalan. Tell your doctor right away if you think you have become pregnant while taking melphalan.

Breast-feeding—Tell your doctor if you are breast-feeding or if you intend to breast-feed during treatment with this medicine. Because melphalan may cause serious side effects, breast-feeding is not recommended while you are taking it.

Children—Although there is no specific information comparing use of melphalan in children with use in other age groups, this medicine is not expected to cause different side effects or problems in children than it does in adults.

Older adults—Many medicines have not been studied specifically in older people. Therefore, it may not be known whether they work exactly the same way they do in younger adults or if they cause different side effects or problems in older people. There is no specific information comparing the use of melphalan in the elderly with use in other age groups.

Other medicines—Although certain medicines should not be used together at all, in other cases two different medicines may be used together even if an interaction might occur. In these cases, your doctor may want to change the dose, or other precautions may be necessary. When you are taking melphalan, it is especially important that your health care professional know if you are taking any of the following:

• Amphotericin B by injection (e.g., Fungizone) or
• Antithyroid agents (medicine for overactive thyroid) or
• Azathioprine (e.g., Imuran) or
• Chloramphenicol (e.g., Chloromycetin) or
• Colchicine or
• Flucytosine (e.g., Ancobon) or
• Ganciclovir (e.g., Cytovene) or
• Interferon (e.g., Intron A, Roferon-A) or
• Plicamycin (e.g., Mithracin) or
• Zidovudine (e.g., AZT, Retrovir) or
• If you have been treated with x-rays or cancer medicines within 3 to 4 weeks—Melphalan may increase the effects of these medicines or radiation therapy on the blood

• Probenecid (e.g., Benemid) or
• Sulfinpyrazone (e.g., Anturane)—Melphalan may raise the concentration of uric acid in the blood, which these medicines are used to lower

Other medical problems—The presence of other medical problems may affect the use of melphalan. Make sure you tell your doctor if you have any other medical problems, especially:

• Chickenpox (including recent exposure) or
• Herpes zoster (shingles)—Risk of severe disease affecting other parts of the body

• Gout (history of) or
• Kidney stones (history of)—Melphalan may increase levels of a chemical called uric acid in the body, which can cause gout or kidney stones

- Infection—Melphalan decreases your body's ability to fight infection
- Kidney disease—Risk of toxic effects on the blood may be increased

Proper Use of This Medicine

Take melphalan only as directed by your doctor. Do not take more or less of it, do not take it more often, and do not take it for a longer time than your doctor ordered. The exact amount of medicine you need has been carefully worked out. Taking too much may increase the chance of side effects, while taking too little may not improve your condition.

Melphalan is sometimes given together with certain other medicines. If you are using a combination of medicines, it is important that you receive each one at the proper time. If you are taking some of these medicines by mouth, ask your health care professional to help you plan a way to remember to take your medicine at the right times.

While you are using melphalan, your doctor may want you to drink extra fluids so that you will pass more urine. This will help prevent kidney problems and keep your kidneys working well.

This medicine may cause nausea, vomiting, and loss of appetite. However, it is very important that you continue to receive the medicine, even if you begin to feel ill. Ask your health care professional for ways to lessen these effects.

If you vomit shortly after taking a dose of melphalan, check with your doctor. You will be told whether to take the dose again or to wait until the next scheduled dose.

Dosing—The dose of melphalan will be different for different patients. The dose that is used may depend on a number of things, including what the medicine is being used for, the patient's weight, whether the medicine is being given by mouth or by injection, and whether or not other medicines are also being taken. *If you are taking or receiving melphalan at home, follow your doctor's orders or the directions on the label.* If you have any questions about the proper dose of melphalan, ask your doctor.

Missed dose—If you miss a dose of this medicine, do not take the missed dose at all and do not double the next one. Instead, go back to your regular dosing schedule and check with your doctor.

Storage—To store this medicine:

- Keep out of the reach of children.
- Store in the original glass container away from heat and direct light.
- Do not store in the bathroom, near the kitchen sink, or in other damp places. Heat or moisture may cause the medicine to break down.
- Do not keep outdated medicine or medicine no longer needed. Be sure that any discarded medicine is out of the reach of children.

Precautions While Using This Medicine

It is very important that your doctor check your progress at regular visits to make sure that this medicine is working properly and to check for unwanted effects.

While you are being treated with melphalan, and after you stop treatment with it, *do not have any immunizations (vaccinations) without your doctor's approval.* Melphalan may lower your body's resistance and there is a chance you might get the infection the immunization is meant to prevent. In ad-

dition, other persons living in your household should not take or should not have taken oral polio vaccine within the last several months since there is a chance they could pass the polio virus on to you. Also, avoid other persons who have taken oral polio vaccine. Do not get close to them and do not stay in the same room with them for very long. If you cannot take these precautions, you should consider wearing a protective face mask that covers the nose and mouth.

Melphalan can lower the number of white blood cells in your blood temporarily, increasing the chance of getting an infection. It can also lower the number of platelets, which are necessary for proper blood clotting. If this occurs, there are certain precautions you can take, especially when your blood count is low, to reduce the risk of infection or bleeding:

- If you can, avoid people with infections. *Check with your doctor immediately* if you think you are getting an infection or if you get a fever or chills, cough or hoarseness, lower back or side pain, or painful or difficult urination.
- *Check with your doctor immediately* if you notice any unusual bleeding or bruising; black, tarry stools; blood in urine or stools; or pinpoint red spots on your skin.
- Be careful when using a regular toothbrush, dental floss, or toothpick. Your medical doctor, dentist, or nurse may recommend other ways to clean your teeth and gums. Check with your medical doctor before having any dental work done.
- Do not touch your eyes or the inside of your nose unless you have just washed your hands and have not touched anything else in the meantime.
- Be careful not to cut yourself when you are using sharp objects such as a safety razor or fingernail or toenail cutters.
- Avoid contact sports or other situations where bruising or injury could occur.

Side Effects of This Medicine

Along with their needed effects, medicines like melphalan can sometimes cause unwanted effects such as blood problems and other side effects. These and others are described below. Also, because of the way these medicines act on the body, there is a chance that they might cause other unwanted effects that may not occur until months or years after the medicine is used. These delayed effects may include certain types of cancer, such as leukemia. Discuss these possible effects with your doctor.

Although not all of these side effects may occur, if they do occur they may need medical attention.

Check with your doctor immediately if any of the following side effects occur:

Less common

Black, tarry stools; blood in urine or stools; cough or hoarseness, accompanied by fever or chills; fast or irregular heart beat; fever or chills; lower back or side pain, accompanied by fever or chills; painful or difficult urination, accompanied by fever or chills; pinpoint red spots on skin; redness and/or soreness at the infusion site; shortness of breath; skin rash or itching (sudden); troubled breathing; unusual bleeding or bruising

Check with your doctor as soon as possible if any of the following side effects occur:

Less common or rare

Diarrhea; difficulty swallowing; joint pain; redness and/

or soreness in arm or leg; sores in mouth and on lips; swelling of feet or lower legs

Other side effects may occur that usually do not need medical attention. These side effects may go away during treatment as your body adjusts to the medicine. Also, your health care professional may be able to tell you about ways to prevent or reduce some of these side effects. Check with your health care professional if the following side effects continue or are bothersome or if you have any questions about them:

Less common
    Nausea and vomiting

After you stop taking melphalan, it may still produce some side effects that need attention. During this period of time, check with your doctor if you notice any of the following side effects:

    Black, tarry stools; blood in urine or stools; cough or hoarseness, accompanied by fever or chills; fever or chills; lower back or side pain, accompanied by fever or chills; painful or difficult urination, accompanied by fever or chills; pinpoint red spots on skin; unusual bleeding or bruising

Other side effects not listed above may also occur in some patients. If you notice any other effects, check with your doctor.

Additional Information

Once a medicine has been approved for marketing for a certain use, experience may show that it is also useful for other medical problems. Although these uses are not included in product labeling, melphalan is used in certain patients with the following conditions:

- Cancer of the breast
- Waldenström's macroglobulinemia (a certain type of cancer of the blood)
- Cancer of the blood and lymph system
- Cancer of the endometrium
- Malignant melanoma (a type of skin cancer that has spread to other parts of the body)

Other than the above information, there is no additional information relating to the proper use, precautions, or side effects of this medicine for these uses.

Revised: 06/14/99

MENOTROPINS Systemic

Commonly used brand name(s):

In the U.S.—
    Humegon
    Pergonal

In Canada—
    Humegon
    Pergonal

Other commonly used names are human menopausal gonadotropins (hMG), human gonadotropins, and menotrophin.

Description

Menotropins (men-oh-TROE-pins) are a mixture of follicle-stimulating hormone (FSH) and luteinizing hormone (LH) that are naturally produced by the pituitary gland.

Use in females—FSH is primarily responsible for stimulating growth of the ovarian follicle, which includes the developing egg, the cells surrounding the egg that produce the hormones needed to support a pregnancy, and the fluid around the egg. As the follicle grows, an increasing amount of the hormone estrogen is produced by the cells in the follicle and released into the bloodstream. Estrogen causes the endometrium (lining of the uterus) to thicken before ovulation occurs. The higher blood levels of estrogen will also tell the hypothalamus and pituitary gland to slow the production and release of FSH.

LH also helps to increase the amount of estrogen produced by the follicle cells. However, its main function is to cause ovulation. The sharp rise in the blood level of LH that triggers ovulation is called the LH surge. After ovulation, the group of hormone-producing follicle cells become the corpus luteum, which will produce estrogen and large amounts of another hormone, progesterone. Progesterone causes the endometrium to mature so that it can support implantation of the fertilized egg or embryo. If implantation of a fertilized egg does not occur, the levels of estrogen and progesterone decrease, the endometrium sloughs off, and menstruation occurs.

Menotropins are usually given in combination with human chorionic gonadotropin (hCG). The actions of hCG are almost the same as those of LH. It is given to simulate the natural LH surge. This results in ovulation at an expected time.

Many women choosing treatment with menotropins have already tried clomiphene (e.g., Serophene) and have not been able to conceive yet. Menotropins may also be used to cause the ovary to produce several follicles, which can then be harvested for use in gamete intrafallopian transfer (GIFT) or in vitro fertilization (IVF).

Use in males—Menotropins are used to stimulate the production of sperm in some forms of male infertility.

Menotropins are to be given only by or under the supervision of your doctor. It is available in the following dosage form:

Parenteral
    • Injection (U.S. and Canada)

Before Using This Medicine

In deciding to use a medicine, the risks of receiving the medicine must be weighed against the good it will do. This is a decision you and your doctor will make. For menotropins, the following should be considered:

Allergies—Tell your doctor if you have ever had any unusual or allergic reaction to menotropins. Also tell your health care professional if you are allergic to any other substances, such as foods, preservatives, or dyes.

Pregnancy—If you become pregnant as a result of using this medicine, there is an increased chance of a multiple pregnancy.

Other medicines—Although certain medicines should not be used together at all, in other cases two different medicines may be used together even if an interaction might occur. In these cases, your doctor may want to change the dose, or other precautions may be necessary. Tell your health care professional if you are taking any other prescription or nonprescription (over-the-counter [OTC]) medicine.

Other medical problems—The presence of other medical problems may affect the use of menotropins. Make sure you tell your doctor if you have any other medical problems, especially:

- Cyst on ovary—Menotropins can cause further growth of cysts on the ovary

- Unusual vaginal bleeding—Some irregular vaginal bleeding is a sign that the endometrium is growing too rapidly, possibly of endometrial cancer, or some hormone imbalances; the increases in estrogen production caused by menotropins can make these problems worse. If a hormonal imbalance is present, it should be treated before beginning menotropins therapy

Proper Use of This Medicine

Dosing—The dose of menotropins will be different for different patients. *Follow your doctor's orders or the directions on the label.* The following information includes only the average doses of menotropins. *If your dose is different, do not change it* unless your doctor tells you to do so.

- For *injection* dosage form:
  —For causing ovulation to help in becoming pregnant:
  - Adults—75 Units of FSH and 75 Units of LH injected into a muscle once a day for seven or more days. Usually your doctor will give you another medicine called human chorionic gonadotropin (hCG) the day after the last dose of menotropins.
  —For help in becoming pregnant while using other pregnancy-promoting methods (assisted reproductive technology [ART]):
  - Adults—150 Units of FSH and 150 Units of LH injected into a muscle once a day for seven or more days. Usually your doctor will give you another medicine called human chorionic gonadotropin (hCG) the day after the last dose of menotropins.
  —For producing sperm:
  - Adults—75 Units of FSH and 75 Units of LH injected into a muscle three times a week for four or more months. Usually your doctor will give you another medicine called chorionic gonadotropin before and during treatment with menotropins. If needed, your doctor may increase your dose to 150 Units of FSH and 150 Units of LH three times a week after four months.

Precautions While Using This Medicine

It is very important that your doctor check your progress at regular visits to make sure that the medicine is working properly and to check for unwanted effects. Your doctor will likely want to watch the development of the ovarian follicle(s) by measuring the amount of estrogen in your bloodstream and by checking the size of the follicle(s) with ultrasound examinations.

For females only:
- If your doctor has asked you to record your basal body temperatures (BBTs) daily, make sure that you do this every day. It is important that intercourse take place around the time of ovulation to give you the best chance of becoming pregnant. *Follow your doctor's instructions carefully.*

Side Effects of This Medicine

Along with its needed effects, a medicine may cause some unwanted effects. Although not all of these side effects may occur, if they do occur they may need medical attention.

Check with your doctor as soon as possible if any of the following side effects occur:
For females only
  More common
    Bloating (mild); pain, swelling, or irritation at place of injection; rash at place of injection or on body; stomach or pelvic pain

  Less common or rare
    Abdominal or stomach pain (severe); bloating (moderate to severe); decreased amount of urine; feeling of indigestion; nausea, vomiting, or diarrhea (continuing or severe); pelvic pain (severe); shortness of breath; swelling of the lower legs; weight gain (rapid)

For males only
  More common
    Dizziness; fainting; headache; irregular heartbeat; loss of appetite; more frequent nosebleeds; shortness of breath

Other side effects may occur that usually do not need medical attention. These side effects may go away during treatment as your body adjusts to the medicine. However, check with your doctor if the following side effect continues or is bothersome:
For males only
  Less common
    Enlargement of breasts

After you stop using this medicine, your body may need time to adjust. The length of time this takes depends on the amount of medicine you were using and how long you used it. During this period of time check with your doctor if you notice any of the following side effects:
For females only
    Abdominal or stomach pain (severe); bloating (moderate to severe); decreased amount of urine; feeling of indigestion; nausea, vomiting, or diarrhea (continuing or severe); pelvic pain (severe); shortness of breath; weight gain (rapid)

Other side effects not listed above may also occur in some patients. If you notice any other effects, check with your doctor.

Revised: 07/07/92
Interim revision: 06/30/94; 08/04/97

MEPROBAMATE AND ASPIRIN
Systemic

Commonly used brand name(s):

In the U.S.—

Epromate-M	Meprogesic
Equagesic	Meprogesic Q
Heptogesic	Micrainin

Generic name product may be available.

In Canada—
Equagesic‡

‡In Canada, Equagesic also contains ethoheptazine citrate

Description

Meprobamate (me-proe-BA-mate) and aspirin (AS-pir-in) combination is used to relieve pain, anxiety, and tension in certain disorders or diseases.

This medicine is available only with your doctor's prescription, in the following dosage form:

Oral
- Tablets (U.S. and Canada)

Before Using This Medicine

In deciding to use a medicine, the risks of taking the medicine must be weighed against the good it will do. This is a decision you and your doctor will make. For meprobamate and aspirin combination, the following should be considered:

Allergies—Tell your doctor if you have ever had any unusual or allergic reaction to meprobamate or to medicines like meprobamate such as carbromal, carisoprodol, mebutamate, or tybamate, or to aspirin or other salicylates, including methyl salicylate (oil of wintergreen), or to any of the following medicines:

    Diclofenac (e.g., Voltaren)
    Diflunisal (e.g., Dolobid)
    Etodolac (e.g., Lodine)
    Fenoprofen (e.g., Nalfon)
    Floctafenine (e.g., Idarac)
    Flurbiprofen, oral (e.g., Ansaid)
    Ibuprofen (e.g., Motrin)
    Indomethacin (e.g., Indocin)
    Ketoprofen (e.g., Orudis)
    Ketorolac (e.g., Toradol)
    Meclofenamate (e.g., Meclomen)
    Mefenamic acid (e.g., Ponstel)
    Naproxen (e.g., Naprosyn)
    Oxyphenbutazone (e.g., Tandearil)
    Phenylbutazone (e.g., Butazolidin)
    Piroxicam (e.g., Feldene)
    Sulindac (e.g., Clinoril)
    Suprofen (e.g., Suprol)
    Tiaprofenic acid (e.g., Surgam)
    Tolmetin (e.g., Tolectin)
    Zomepirac (e.g., Zomax)

Also tell your health care professional if you are allergic to any other substances, such as foods, preservatives, or dyes.

Pregnancy—Meprobamate (contained in this combination medicine) has been reported to increase the chance of birth defects if taken during the first 3 months of pregnancy.

Studies in humans have not shown that aspirin (contained in this combination medicine) causes birth defects. However, studies in animals have shown that aspirin causes birth defects. Some reports have suggested that too much use of aspirin late in pregnancy may cause a decrease in the newborn's weight and possible death of the fetus or newborn infant. However, the mothers in these reports had been taking much larger amounts of aspirin than are usually recommended. Studies of mothers taking aspirin in the doses that are usually recommended did not show these unwanted effects. However, regular use of aspirin late in pregnancy may cause unwanted effects on the heart or blood flow in the fetus or in the newborn infant. Also, use of aspirin during the last 2 weeks of pregnancy may cause bleeding problems in the fetus before or during delivery or in the newborn infant. In addition, too much use of aspirin during the last 3 months of pregnancy may increase the length of pregnancy, prolong labor, cause other problems during delivery, or cause severe bleeding in the mother before, during, or after delivery.

Breast-feeding—Meprobamate (contained in this combination medicine) passes into the breast milk and may cause drowsiness in babies of mothers taking this medicine. Although aspirin (contained in this combination medicine) passes into the breast milk, it has not been shown to cause problems in nursing babies.

Children—*Do not give a medicine containing aspirin to a child with a fever or other symptoms of a virus infection, especially flu or chickenpox, without first discussing this with your child's doctor.* This is very important because aspirin may cause a serious illness called Reye's syndrome in children with fever caused by a virus infection, especially flu or chickenpox. Children who do not have a virus infection may also be more sensitive to the effects of aspirin (contained in this combination medicine), especially if they have a fever or have lost large amounts of body fluid because of vomiting, diarrhea, or sweating. This may increase the chance of side effects during treatment.

Teenagers—*Teenagers with fever or other symptoms of a virus infection, especially flu or chickenpox, should check with a doctor before taking this medicine.* The aspirin in this combination medicine may cause a serious illness called Reye's syndrome in teenagers with fever caused by a virus infection, especially flu or chickenpox.

Older adults—Elderly people may be especially sensitive to the effects of meprobamate and aspirin. This may increase the chance of side effects during treatment.

Other medicines—Although certain medicines should not be used together at all, in other cases two different medicines may be used together even if an interaction might occur. In these cases, your doctor may want to change the dose, or other precautions may be necessary. When you are taking meprobamate and aspirin combination, it is especially important that your health care professional know if you are taking any of the following:

- Anticoagulants (blood thinners) or
- Carbenicillin by injection (e.g., Geopen) or
- Cefamandole (e.g., Mandol) or
- Cefoperazone (e.g., Cefobid) or
- Cefotetan (e.g., Cefotan) or
- Dipyridamole (e.g., Persantine) or
- Divalproex (e.g., Depakote) or
- Heparin or
- Inflammation or pain medicine, except narcotics, or
- Moxalactam (e.g., Moxam) or
- Pentoxifylline (e.g., Trental) or
- Plicamycin (e.g., Mithracin) or
- Ticarcillin (e.g., Ticar) or
- Valproic acid (e.g., Depakene)—Taking these medicines together with aspirin may increase the chance of bleeding

- Antidiabetics, oral (diabetes medicine you take by mouth)—Aspirin may increase the effects of the antidiabetic medicine; a change in dose may be needed if meprobamate and aspirin combination is taken regularly

- Central nervous system (CNS) depressants (medicine that causes drowsiness) or
- Tricyclic antidepressants (medicine for depression)—Taking these medicines with meprobamate and aspirin combination may increase the CNS depressant effects

- Methotrexate (e.g., Mexate)—The chance of serious side effects may be increased
- Probenecid (e.g., Benemid)—Aspirin may keep probenecid from working properly in the treatment of gout
- Sulfinpyrazone (e.g., Anturane)—Aspirin may keep sulfinpyrazone from working properly in the treatment of gout; also, there may be an increased chance of bleeding
- Urinary alkalizers (medicine that makes the urine less acid, such as acetazolamide [e.g., Diamox], calcium- and/or magnesium-containing antacids, dichlorphenamide [e.g., Daranide], methazolamide [e.g., Neptazane], potassium or sodium citrate and/or citric acid, sodium bicarbonate [baking soda])—These medicines may make aspirin less effective by causing it to be removed from the body more quickly
- Vancomycin (e.g., Vancocin)—Hearing loss may occur and may lead to deafness

Other medical problems—The presence of other medical problems may affect the use of meprobamate and aspirin combination. Make sure you tell your doctor if you have any other medical problems, especially:

- Alcohol abuse (or history of) or
- Drug abuse or dependence (or history of)—Dependence on meprobamate may develop
- Anemia or
- Stomach ulcer or other stomach problems—Aspirin may make your condition worse
- Asthma, allergies, and nasal polyps (history of) or
- Kidney disease or
- Liver disease—The chance of side effects may be increased.
- Epilepsy—The risk of seizures may be increased
- Gout—Aspirin may make this condition worse and may also lessen the effects of some medicines used to treat gout
- Hemophilia or other bleeding problems—The chance of bleeding may be increased by aspirin
- Porphyria—Meprobamate may make the condition worse

Proper Use of This Medicine

Take this medicine with food or a full glass (8 ounces) of water to lessen stomach irritation.

Do not take this medicine if it has a strong vinegar-like odor. This odor means the aspirin in it is breaking down. If you have any questions about this, check with your health care professional.

Take this medicine only as directed by your doctor. Do not take more of it, do not take it more often, and do not take it for a longer time than your doctor ordered. If too much meprobamate is taken, it may become habit-forming. Also, taking too much aspirin may cause stomach problems or lead to medical problems because of an overdose.

Dosing—The dose of meprobamate and aspirin combination will be different for different patients. *Follow your doctor's orders or the directions on the label.* The following information includes only the average doses of meprobamate and aspirin combination. *If your dose is different, do not change it* unless your doctor tells you to do so:

- Adults—Oral, 1 or 2 tablets three or four times a day, as needed.
- Children up to 12 years of age: Use is not recommended.

Storage—To store this medicine:

- Keep this medicine out of the reach of children. Overdose of meprobamate is very dangerous in children.
- Store away from heat and direct light.
- Do not store in the bathroom, near the kitchen sink, or in other damp places. Heat or moisture may cause the medicine to break down.
- Do not keep outdated medicine or medicine no longer needed. Be sure that any discarded medicine is out of the reach of children.

Precautions While Using This Medicine

If you will be taking this medicine regularly for a long time:
- Your doctor should check your progress at regular visits.
- Check with your doctor at least every 4 months to make sure you need to continue taking this medicine.

If you will be taking this medicine in large doses or for a long time, do not stop taking it without first checking with your doctor. Your doctor may want you to reduce gradually the amount you are taking before stopping completely.

Check the labels of all nonprescription (over-the-counter [OTC]) and prescription medicines you now take. If any contain aspirin or other salicylates (including bismuth subsalicylate [e.g., Pepto-Bismol]), be especially careful. Taking or using any of these medicines while taking this combination medicine containing aspirin may lead to overdose. If you have any questions about this, check with your health care professional.

This medicine will add to the effects of alcohol and other CNS depressants (medicines that slow down the nervous system, possibly causing drowsiness). Some examples of CNS depressants are antihistamines or medicine for hay fever, other allergies, or colds; sedatives, tranquilizers, or sleeping medicine; prescription pain medicine or narcotics; barbiturates; medicine for seizures; muscle relaxants; or anesthetics, including some dental anesthetics. *Check with your doctor before taking any of the above while you are taking this medicine.*

Stomach problems may be more likely to occur if you drink alcoholic beverages while being treated with this medicine, especially if you are taking the medicine in high doses or for a long time. Check with your doctor if you have any questions about this.

Too much use of this medicine together with certain other medicines may increase the chance of stomach problems. Therefore, do not regularly take this medicine together with any of the following medicines, unless directed to do so by your medical doctor or dentist:

  Acetaminophen (e.g., Tylenol)
  Diclofenac (e.g., Voltaren)
  Diflunisal (e.g., Dolobid)
  Etodolac (e.g., Lodine)
  Fenoprofen (e.g., Nalfon)
  Floctafenine (e.g., Idarac)
  Flurbiprofen (oral) (e.g., Ansaid)
  Ibuprofen (e.g., Motrin)
  Indomethacin (e.g., Indocin)
  Ketoprofen (e.g., Orudis)
  Ketorolac (e.g., Toradol)
  Meclofenamate (e.g., Meclomen)

Mefenamic acid (e.g., Ponstel)
Naproxen (e.g., Naprosyn)
Phenylbutazone (e.g., Butazolidin)
Piroxicam (e.g., Feldene)
Sulindac (e.g., Clinoril)
Tiaprofenic acid (e.g., Surgam)
Tolmetin (e.g., Tolectin)

If you are taking a laxative containing cellulose, do not take it within 2 hours of taking this medicine. Taking these medicines close together may make this medicine less effective by preventing the aspirin (contained in this combination medicine) from being absorbed by your body.

For diabetic patients:

- False urine sugar test results may occur if you take 8 or more 325-mg (5-grain) doses of aspirin (contained in this combination medicine) every day for several days in a row. Smaller doses or occasional use of aspirin usually will not affect urine sugar tests. If you have any questions about this, check with your doctor, especially if your diabetes is not well controlled.

Before you have any medical tests, tell the medical doctor in charge that you are taking this medicine. The results of some tests, such as the metyrapone test and the phentolamine test, may be affected by this medicine.

If you plan to have surgery, including dental surgery, do not take aspirin (contained in this combination medicine) for 5 days before the surgery, unless otherwise directed by your medical doctor or dentist. Taking aspirin during this time may cause bleeding problems.

If you think you or someone else may have taken an overdose of this medicine, get emergency help at once. Taking an overdose of this medicine or taking alcohol or other CNS depressants with it may lead to unconsciousness and possibly death. Some signs of an overdose are continuing ringing or buzzing in ears; any hearing loss; severe confusion, drowsiness, or weakness; shortness of breath or slow or troubled breathing; staggering; and slow heartbeat.

This medicine may cause some people to become dizzy, lightheaded, drowsy, or less alert than they are normally. *Make sure you know how you react to this medicine before you drive, use machines, or do anything else that could be dangerous if you are dizzy or are not alert.*

Meprobamate (contained in this combination medicine) may cause dryness of the mouth. For temporary relief, use sugarless candy or gum, melt bits of ice in your mouth, or use a saliva substitute. However, if your mouth continues to feel dry for more than 2 weeks, check with your medical doctor or dentist. Continuing dryness of the mouth may increase the chance of dental disease, including tooth decay, gum disease, and fungus infections.

Side Effects of This Medicine

Along with its needed effects, a medicine may cause some unwanted effects. Although not all of these side effects may occur, if they do occur they may need medical attention.

Check with your doctor immediately if any of the following side effects occur:
Rare
Wheezing, shortness of breath, troubled breathing, or tightness in chest
Symptoms of overdose
Any loss of hearing; bloody urine; confusion (severe);

convulsions (seizures); diarrhea (severe or continuing); dizziness or lightheadedness (continuing); drowsiness (severe); fast or deep breathing; hallucinations (seeing, hearing, or feeling things that are not there); headache (severe or continuing); increased sweating; nausea or vomiting (continuing); nervousness or excitement (severe); ringing or buzzing in ears (continuing); slow heartbeat; slurred speech; staggering; stomach pain (severe or continuing); unexplained fever; unusual or uncontrolled flapping movements of the hands, especially in elderly patients; unusual thirst; vision problems; weakness (severe)

Symptoms of overdose in children
Changes in behavior; drowsiness or tiredness (severe); fast or deep breathing

Also, check with your doctor as soon as possible if any of the following side effects occur:
Rare
Bloody or black, tarry stools; confusion; skin rash, hives, or itching; sore throat and fever; unusual bleeding or bruising; unusual excitement; unusual tiredness or weakness; vomiting of blood or material that looks like coffee grounds

Other side effects may occur that usually do not need medical attention. These side effects may go away during treatment as your body adjusts to the medicine. However, check with your doctor if any of the following side effects continue or are bothersome:
More common
Drowsiness; heartburn or indigestion; nausea with or without vomiting; stomach pain (mild)
Less common
Blurred vision or change in near or distant vision; dizziness or lightheadedness; headache

After you stop using this medicine, your body may need time to adjust. The length of time this takes depends on the amount of medicine you were using and how long you used it. During this period of time check with your doctor if you notice any of the following side effects:
Clumsiness or unsteadiness; confusion; convulsions (seizures); hallucinations (seeing, hearing, or feeling things that are not there); increased dreaming; muscle twitching; nausea or vomiting; nervousness or restlessness; nightmares; trembling; trouble in sleeping

Other side effects not listed above may also occur in some patients. If you notice any other effects, check with your doctor.

Revised: 01/13/93

MEQUINOL AND TRETINOIN
Topical†

Commonly used brand name(s):

In the U.S.—
Solagé

†Not commercially available in Canada.

Description

Mequinol and Tretinoin (MEC-kwin-all and TRET-i-noyn) is used to treat areas of the skin that have become darker after repeated exposure to the sun. These areas are called solar lentigines, or age or liver spots.

Mequinol and tretinoin is available only with your doctor's prescription, in the following dosage form:

Topical
- Topical solution (U.S.)

Before Using This Medicine

In deciding to use a medicine, the risks of using the medicine must be weighed against the good it will do. This is a decision you and your doctor will make. For mequinol and tretinoin, the following should be considered:

Allergies—Tell your doctor if you have ever had any unusual or allergic reaction to acitretin, etretinate, isotretinoin, mequinol, tretinoin, or vitamin A preparations. Also tell your health care professional if you are allergic to any other substances, such as preservatives or dyes.

Pregnancy—Mequinol and tretinoin has not been studied in pregnant women. Topical mequinol and tretinoin is not recommended during pregnancy. Topical mequinol and tretinoin may cause fetal harm. Before using this medicine, make sure your doctor knows if you are pregnant or if you may become pregnant.

Breast-feeding—It is not known whether mequinol and tretinoin passes into the breast milk. Mothers who are using this medicine and who wish to breast-feed should discuss this with their doctors.

Children—Studies on this medicine have been done only in adult patients, and there is no specific information comparing use of this medicine in children with use in other age groups. Mequinol and tretinoin should not be used in children.

Older adults—This medicine has been tested and has not been shown to cause different side effects or problems in older people than it does in younger adults.

Other medicines—Although certain medicines should not be used together at all, in other cases two different medicines may be used together even if an interaction might occur. In these cases, your doctor may want to change the dose, or other precautions may be necessary. Tell your health care professional if you are using any other topical prescription or nonprescription (over-the-counter [OTC]) medicine that is to be applied to the same area of the skin. When you are using topical mequinol and tretinoin, it is especially important that your health care professional know if you are taking any of the following:

- Fluoroquinolones (ciprofloxacin [e.g., Cipro], enoxacin [e.g., Penetrex], grepafloxacin [e.g., Raxar], levofloxacin [e.g., Levaquin], lomefloxacin [e.g., Maxaquin], norfloxacin [e.g., Noroxin], ofloxacin [e.g., Floxin], sparfloxacin [e.g., Zagam]) or
- Phenothiazines (chlorpromazine [e.g., Thorazine], fluphenazine [e.g., Prolixin], mezoridazine [e.g., Serentil], perphenazine [e.g., Trilafon], prochlorperazine [e.g., Compazine], thioridazine [e.g., Mellaril], trifluoperazine [e.g., Stelazine], triflupromazine [e.g., Vesprin]) or
- Sulfonamides (sulfa medicine) or
- Tetracyclines (medicine for infection) or
- Thiazide diuretics (water pills)—These medicines may cause your skin to become more sensitive to light

Other medical problems—The presence of other medical problems may affect the use of mequinol and tretinoin topical solution. Make sure you tell your doctor if you have any other medical problems, especially:

- Eczema or
- Frequent exposure to sunlight or sunlamps or
- Sunburn—Use of this medicine may cause or increase the irritation associated with these conditions
- Vitiligo (or a family history of this condition)—Use of this medicine may cause lightening of areas of the skin that have not been treated

Proper Use of This Medicine

It is very important that you use this medicine only as directed. Do not use more of it, do not use it more often, and do not use it for a longer time than your doctor ordered. To do so may cause irritation of the skin.

Do not apply this medicine to windburned or sunburned skin or on open wounds.

Do not use this medicine in or around the eyes or lips, or inside of the nose. Spread the medicine away from these areas when applying. If the medicine accidentally gets on these areas, wash with water at once.

This medicine usually comes with patient directions. Read them carefully before using the medicine.

To use this medicine:
- Using the applicator tip, apply enough mequinol and tretinoin solution to cover the affected areas. Apply only enough medicine to make the lesion appear moist. Avoid areas of normally colored skin.
- You should not shower or bathe for at least 6 hours after applying the medicine.
- Cosmetics may be applied 30 minutes after application of the medicine.

Dosing—*Follow your doctor's orders or the directions on the label.* The following information includes usual dose of topical mequinol and tretinoin. *If your dose is different, do not change it* unless your doctor tells you to do so.

- For *topical* dosage form (solution):
  —For age or liver spots:
  - Adults—Apply to the affected areas of the skin twice daily, morning and evening, at least 8 hours apart.
  - Children—Use is not recommended.

Missed dose—If you miss a dose of this medicine, skip the missed dose and go back to your regular dosing schedule. Do not double doses.

Storage—To store this medicine:
- Keep out of the reach of children.
- Store away from heat and direct light. The product is flammable and should be kept away from fire or excessive heat.
- Keep the medicine from freezing.
- Do not keep outdated medicine or medicine no longer needed. Be sure that any discarded medicine is out of the reach of children.

Precautions While Using This Medicine

You may notice redness, stinging, burning or irritation when you first start using this medicine. It may take up to 6 months before you notice full beneficial effects, even if you use the medicine every day. Check with your health care professional at any time skin irritation becomes severe or if your age spots get darker in color.

Unless your doctor tells you otherwise, *it is especially important to avoid using the following skin products on the same area as mequinol and tretinoin topical solution:*

- Hair products that are irritating, such as permanents or hair removal products
- Skin products that cause sensitivity to the sun, such as those containing spices or limes
- Skin products containing a large amount of alcohol, such as astringents, shaving creams, or after-shave lotions
- Skin products that are too drying or abrasive, such as some cosmetics, soaps, or skin cleansers

Using these products along with mequinol and tretinoin may cause mild to severe irritation of the skin. Check with your doctor before using other topical medicines.

Avoid overexposing the treated areas to sunlight, wind, or cold weather. The skin will be more prone to sunburn, dryness, or irritation. *Do not use a sunlamp.*

Regularly use sunscreen or sunblocking lotions with a sun protection factor (SPF) of at least 15. Also, wear protective clothing and hats, and apply creams, lotions, or moisturizers often.

Check with your doctor any time your skin becomes too dry and irritated. Your health care professional can help you choose the right skin products for you to reduce skin dryness and irritation and may include:

- Taking part in an ongoing program to avoid further damage to your skin from the sun. The program should stress staying out of the sun when possible and wearing proper clothing or hats to protect your skin from sunlight.
- Regular use of oil-based creams or lotions to help to reduce skin irritation or dryness caused by the use of mequinol and tretinoin topical solution.

Side Effects of This Medicine

In some animal studies, mequinol and tretinoin has been shown to cause skin tumors to develop faster when the treated area is exposed to ultraviolet light (sunlight or artificial sunlight from a sunlamp). Other studies have not shown the same result and more studies need to be done. It is not known if mequinol and tretinoin topical solution causes skin tumors to develop faster in humans.

Along with its needed effects, a medicine may cause some unwanted effects. Although not all of these side effects may occur, if they do occur they may need medical attention.

Check with your doctor as soon as possible if any of the following side effects occur:

More common
  Burning feeling or stinging skin (severe); itching (severe); peeling of skin (severe); redness of skin (severe)

Less common
  Allergic reaction; large blisters on the skin

Other side effects may occur that usually do not need medical attention. These side effects may go away during treatment as your body adjusts to the medicine. However, check with your doctor if any of the following side effects continue or are bothersome:

More common
  Burning feeling, stinging, or tingling of skin (mild)— lasting for a short time after first applying the medicine; itching (mild); chapping or slight peeling of skin

(mild); lightening of skin around treated area; lightening of skin on treated area; redness of skin (mild); skin irritation; unusually warm skin (mild)

Less common
  Crusting of skin; dry skin; skin rash

Other side effects not listed above may also occur in some patients. If you notice any other effects, check with your doctor.

Developed: 04/26/00

MERCAPTOPURINE   Systemic

Commonly used brand name(s):

In the U.S.—
  Purinethol

In Canada—
  Purinethol
Another commonly used name is 6-MP.

Description

Mercaptopurine (mer-kap-toe-PYOOR-een) belongs to the group of medicines known as antimetabolites. It is used to treat some kinds of cancer.

Mercaptopurine interferes with the growth of cancer cells, which are eventually destroyed. Since the growth of normal body cells may also be affected by mercaptopurine, other effects will also occur. Some of these may be serious and must be reported to your doctor. Other effects may not be serious but may cause concern. Some effects may not occur for months or years after the medicine is used.

Before you begin treatment with mercaptopurine, you and your doctor should talk about the good this medicine will do as well as the risks of using it.

Mercaptopurine may also be used for other conditions as determined by your doctor.

Mercaptopurine is available only with your doctor's prescription, in the following dosage form:

Oral
  - Tablets (U.S. and Canada)

Before Using This Medicine

In deciding to use a medicine, the risks of taking the medicine must be weighed against the good it will do. This is a decision you and your doctor will make. For mercaptopurine, the following should be considered:

Allergies—Tell your doctor if you have ever had any unusual or allergic reaction to mercaptopurine.

Pregnancy—Tell your doctor if you are pregnant or if you intend to have children. There is a chance that this medicine may cause birth defects if either the male or female is taking it at the time of conception or if it is taken during pregnancy. However, studies have not been done in humans. Mercaptopurine has been shown to cause damage to the fetus in rats and increases the risk of miscarriage or premature births in humans. In addition, many cancer medicines may cause sterility which could be permanent. Although this has not been reported with this medicine, the possibility should be kept in mind.

Be sure that you have discussed this with your doctor before taking this medicine. It is best to use some kind of birth control while you are taking mercaptopurine. Tell your doctor right away if you think you have become pregnant while taking mercaptopurine.

Breast-feeding—Tell your doctor if you are breast-feeding or if you intend to breast-feed during treatment with this medicine. Because mercaptopurine may cause serious side effects, breast-feeding is generally not recommended while you are taking it.

Children—Although there is no specific information comparing use of mercaptopurine in children with use in other age groups, it is not expected to cause different side effects or problems in children than it does in adults.

Older adults—Many medicines have not been studied specifically in older people. Therefore, it may not be known whether they work exactly the same way they do in younger adults or if they cause different side effects or problems in older people. There is no specific information comparing use of mercaptopurine in the elderly with use in other age groups.

Other medicines—Although certain medicines should not be used together at all, in other cases two different medicines may be used together even if an interaction might occur. In these cases, your doctor may want to change the dose, or other precautions may be necessary. When you are taking mercaptopurine, it is especially important that your health care professional know if you are taking any of the following:

- Acetaminophen (e.g., Tylenol) (with long-term, high-dose use) or
- Amiodarone (e.g., Cordarone) or
- Anabolic steroids (nandrolone [e.g., Anabolin], oxandrolone [e.g., Anavar], oxymetholone [e.g., Anadrol], stanozolol [e.g., Winstrol]) or
- Androgens (male hormones) or
- Anti-infectives by mouth or by injection (medicine for infection) or
- Antithyroid agents (medicine for overactive thyroid) or
- Carbamazepine (e.g., Tegretol) or
- Chloroquine (e.g., Aralen) or
- Dantrolene (e.g., Dantrium) or
- Disulfiram (e.g., Antabuse) or
- Divalproex (e.g., Depakote) or
- Estrogens (female hormones) or
- Etretinate (e.g., Tegison) or
- Gold salts (medicine for arthritis) or
- Hydroxychloroquine (e.g., Plaquenil) or
- Methyldopa (e.g., Aldomet) or
- Naltrexone (e.g., Trexan) (with long-term, high-dose use) or
- Oral contraceptives (birth control pills) containing estrogen or
- Phenothiazines (acetophenazine [e.g., Tindal], chlorpromazine [e.g., Thorazine], fluphenazine [e.g., Prolixin], mesoridazine [e.g., Serentil], perphenazine [e.g., Trilafon], prochlorperazine [e.g., Compazine], promazine [e.g., Sparine], promethazine [e.g., Phenergan], thioridazine [e.g., Mellaril], trifluoperazine [e.g., Stelazine], triflupromazine [e.g., Vesprin], trimeprazine [e.g., Temaril]) or
- Phenytoin (e.g., Dilantin) or
- Plicamycin (e.g., Mithracin) or
- Valproic acid (e.g., Depakene)—Risk of unwanted effects on the liver may be increased

- Azathioprine (e.g., Imuran) or
- Corticosteroids (cortisone-like medicine) or
- Cyclosporine (e.g., Sandimmune) or
- Muromonab-CD3 (monoclonal antibody) (e.g., Orthoclone OKT3)—There may be an increased risk of infection and development of cancer because mercaptopurine reduces the body's immunity

- Allopurinol (e.g., Zyloprim)—Effects of mercaptopurine may be increased because allopurinol blocks its removal from the body

- Amphotericin B by injection (e.g., Fungizone) or
- Antithyroid agents (medicine for overactive thyroid) or
- Azathioprine (e.g., Imuran) or
- Chloramphenicol (e.g., Chloromycetin) or
- Colchicine or
- Flucytosine (e.g., Ancobon) or
- Ganciclovir (e.g., Cytovene) or
- Interferon (e.g., Intron A, Roferon-A) or
- Plicamycin (e.g., Mithracin) or
- Zidovudine (e.g., AZT, Retrovir) or
- If you have ever been treated with radiation or cancer medicines—Mercaptopurine may increase the effects of these medicines or radiation therapy on the blood

- Probenecid (e.g., Benemid) or
- Sulfinpyrazone (e.g., Anturane)—Mercaptopurine may raise the concentration of uric acid in the blood. Since these medicines are used to lower uric acid levels, they may not be as effective in patients taking mercaptopurine

Other medical problems—The presence of other medical problems may affect the use of mercaptopurine. Make sure you tell your doctor if you have any other medical problems, especially:

- Chickenpox (including recent exposure) or
- Herpes zoster (shingles)—Risk of severe disease affecting other parts of the body

- Gout (history of) or
- Kidney stones (history of)—Mercaptopurine may increase levels of uric acid in the body, which can cause gout or kidney stones

- Infection—Mercaptopurine may decrease your body's ability to fight infection

- Kidney disease or
- Liver disease—Effects of mercaptopurine may be increased because of slower removal from the body

Proper Use of This Medicine

Use this medicine only as directed by your doctor. Do not use more or less of it, and do not use it more often than your doctor ordered. The exact amount of medicine you need has been carefully worked out. Taking too much may increase the chance of side effects, while taking too little may not improve your condition.

Mercaptopurine is often given together with certain other medicines. If you are using a combination of medicines, make sure that you take each one at the right time and do not mix them. Ask your health care professional to help you plan a way to remember to take your medicines at the right times.

While you are using mercaptopurine, your doctor may want you to drink extra fluids so that you will pass more urine. This will help prevent kidney problems and keep your kidneys working well.

If you vomit shortly after taking a dose of mercaptopurine, check with your doctor. You will be told whether to take the dose again or to wait until the next scheduled dose.

Dosing—The dose of mercaptopurine will be different for different patients. The dose that is used may depend on a number of things, including what the medicine is being used for, the patient's weight, and whether or not other medicines are also being taken. *If you are taking mercaptopurine at home, follow your doctor's orders or the directions on the label*. If you have any questions about the proper dose of mercaptopurine, ask your doctor.

Missed dose—If you miss a dose of this medicine, do not take the missed dose at all and do not double the next one. Instead, go back to your regular dosing schedule and check with your doctor.

Storage—To store this medicine:
- Keep out of the reach of children.
- Store away from heat and direct light.
- Do not store in the bathroom, near the kitchen sink, or in other damp places. Heat or moisture may cause the medicine to break down.
- Do not keep outdated medicine or medicine no longer needed. Be sure that any discarded medicine is out of the reach of children.

Precautions While Using This Medicine

It is very important that your doctor check your progress at regular visits to make sure that this medicine is working properly and to check for unwanted effects.

Avoid alcoholic beverages until you have discussed their use with your doctor. Alcohol may increase the harmful effects of this medicine.

While you are being treated with mercaptopurine, and after you stop treatment with it, *do not have any immunizations (vaccinations) without your doctor's approval*. Mercaptopurine may lower your body's resistance and there is a chance you might get the infection the immunization is meant to prevent. In addition, other persons living in your household should not take oral polio vaccine since there is a chance they could pass the polio virus on to you. Also, avoid persons who have taken oral polio vaccine. Do not get close to them and do not stay in the same room with them for very long. If you cannot take these precautions, you should consider wearing a protective face mask that covers the nose and mouth.

Mercaptopurine can temporarily lower the number of white blood cells in your blood, increasing the chance of getting an infection. It can also lower the number of platelets, which are necessary for proper blood clotting. If this occurs, there are certain precautions you can take, especially when your blood count is low, to reduce the risk of infection or bleeding:
- If you can, avoid people with infections. *Check with your doctor immediately* if you think you are getting an infection or if you get a fever or chills, cough or hoarseness, lower back or side pain, or painful or difficult urination.
- *Check with your doctor immediately* if you notice any unusual bleeding or bruising; black, tarry stools; blood in urine or stools; or pinpoint red spots on your skin.
- Be careful when using a regular toothbrush, dental floss, or toothpick. Your medical doctor, dentist, or nurse may recommend other ways to clean your teeth and gums. Check with your medical doctor before having any dental work done.

- Do not touch your eyes or the inside of your nose unless you have just washed your hands and have not touched anything else in the meantime.
- Be careful not to cut yourself when you are using sharp objects such as a safety razor or fingernail or toenail cutters.
- Avoid contact sports or other situations where bruising or injury could occur.

Tell the doctor in charge that you are taking this medicine before you have any medical tests. The results of tests for the amount of sugar or uric acid in the blood measured by a machine called a sequential multiple analyzer (SMA) may be affected by this medicine.

Side Effects of This Medicine

Along with its needed effects, a medicine may cause some unwanted effects. Although not all of these side effects may occur, if they do occur they may need medical attention.

Also, because of the way cancer medicines act on the body, there is a chance that they might cause other unwanted effects that may not occur until months or years after the medicine is used. These delayed effects may include certain types of cancer. Discuss these possible effects with your doctor.

Check with your doctor immediately if any of the following side effects occur:
> *Less common*
>> Black, tarry stools; blood in urine or stools; cough or hoarseness; fever or chills; lower back or side pain; painful or difficult urination; pinpoint red spots on skin; unusual bleeding or bruising

Check with your doctor as soon as possible if any of the following side effects occur:
> *More common*
>> Unusual tiredness or weakness; yellow eyes or skin
>
> *Less common*
>> Joint pain; loss of appetite; nausea and vomiting; swelling of feet or lower legs
>
> *Rare*
>> Sores in mouth and on lips

Other side effects may occur that usually do not need medical attention. These side effects may go away during treatment as your body adjusts to the medicine. Also, your health care professional may be able to tell you about ways to prevent or reduce some of these side effects. Check with your health care professional if any of the following side effects continue or are bothersome or if you have any questions about them:
> *Less common*
>> Darkening of skin; diarrhea; headache; skin rash and itching; weakness

After you stop taking mercaptopurine, it may still produce some side effects that need attention. During this period of time, check with your doctor if you notice any of the following side effects:
> Black, tarry stools; blood in urine or stools; cough or hoarseness; fever or chills; lower back or side pain; painful or difficult urination; pinpoint red spots on skin; unusual bleeding or bruising; yellow eyes or skin

Other side effects not listed above may also occur in some patients. If you notice any other effects, check with your doctor.

Revised: 06/21/94

MESALAMINE   Oral

Commonly used brand name(s):

In the U.S.—
　　Asacol
　　Pentasa

In Canada—
　　Asacol   Pentasa
　　Mesasal   Salofalk

Other commonly used names are: 5-aminosalicylic acid, 5-ASA, and mesalazine.

Description

Mesalamine (me-SAL-a-meen) is used to treat inflammatory bowel disease, such as ulcerative colitis. It works inside the bowel by helping to reduce the inflammation and other symptoms of the disease.

Mesalamine is available only with your doctor's prescription. It is available in the following dosage forms:

Oral
- Extended-release capsules (U.S. and Canada)
- Delayed-release tablets (U.S. and Canada)
- Extended-release tablets (Canada)

Before Using This Medicine

In deciding to use a medicine, the risks of taking the medicine must be weighed against the good it will do. This is a decision you and your doctor will make. For mesalamine, the following should be considered:

Allergies—Tell your doctor if you have ever had any unusual or allergic reaction to mesalamine, olsalazine, sulfasalazine, or any salicylates (for example, aspirin). Also tell your health care professional if you are allergic to any other substances, such as foods, preservatives, or dyes.

Pregnancy—Mesalamine has not been studied in pregnant women. However, mesalamine has not been shown to cause birth defects or other problems in animal studies.

Breast-feeding—Mesalamine may pass into the breast milk. However, this medicine has not been reported to cause problems in nursing babies.

Children—Studies on this medicine have been done only in adult patients, and there is no specific information comparing use of mesalamine in children with use in other age groups.

Older adults—Many medicines have not been studied specifically in older people. Therefore, it may not be known whether they work exactly the same way they do in younger adults or if they cause different side effects or problems in older people. There is no information comparing use of mesalamine in the elderly with use in other age groups.

Other medicines—Although certain medicines should not be used together at all, in other cases two different medicines may be used together even if an interaction might occur. In these cases, your doctor may want to change the dose, or other precautions may be necessary. Tell your health care professional if you are using any other prescription or nonprescription (over-the-counter [OTC]) medicine.

Other medical problems—The presence of other medical problems may affect the use of mesalamine. Make sure you tell your doctor if you have any other medical problems, especially:

- Kidney disease—The use of mesalamine may cause further damage to the kidneys
- Narrowing of the tube where food passes out of the stomach—May delay release of mesalamine into the body

Proper Use of This Medicine

Swallow the capsule or tablet whole. Do not break, crush, or chew it before swallowing.

Take this medicine before meals and at bedtime with a full glass (8 ounces) of water, unless otherwise directed by your doctor.

Keep taking this medicine for the full time of treatment, even if you begin to feel better after a few days. Do not miss any doses.

Do not change to another brand without checking with your doctor. The doses are different for different brands. If you refill your medicine and it looks different, check with your pharmacist.

Dosing—The dose of mesalamine will be different for different patients. *Follow your doctor's orders or the directions on the label.* The following information includes only the average doses of mesalamine. *If your dose is different, do not change it* unless your doctor tells you to do so.

The number of capsules or tablets that you take depends on the brand and strength of the medicine.

- For inflammatory bowel disease:
  - —For *long-acting oral* dosage form (extended-release capsules or tablets):
    - Adults—*For Pentasa:* 1 gram four times a day for up to eight weeks.
    - Children—Use and dose must be determined by your doctor.
  - —For *long-acting oral* dosage form (delayed-release tablets):
    - Adults—
      - —For *Asacol:* 800 milligrams (mg) three times a day for six weeks. For maintenance treatment of ulcerative colitis, 1600 mg a day, divided into smaller doses that are taken at separate times.
      - —For *Mesasal:* A total of 1.5 to 3 grams a day, divided into smaller doses that are taken at separate times.
      - —For *Salofalk:* 1 gram three or four times a day.
    - Children—Use and dose must be determined by your doctor.

Missed dose—If you miss a dose of this medicine, take it as soon as possible. However, if it is almost time for your next dose, skip the missed dose and go back to your regular dosing schedule. Do not double doses.

Storage—To store this medicine:
- Keep out of the reach of children.
- Store away from heat and direct light.
- Do not store in the bathroom, near the kitchen sink, or in other damp places. Heat or moisture may cause the medicine to break down.
- Keep the medicine from freezing. Do not refrigerate.
- Do not keep outdated medicine or medicine no longer needed. Be sure that any discarded medicine is out of the reach of children.

Precautions While Using This Medicine

It is important that your doctor check your progress at regular visits.

For patients taking the capsule form of this medicine:

- You may sometimes notice what looks like small beads in your stool. These are just the empty shells that are left after the medicine has been absorbed into your body.

For patients taking the tablet form of this medicine:

- You may sometimes notice what looks like a tablet in your stool. This is just the empty shell that is left after the medicine has been absorbed into your body.

Side Effects of This Medicine

Along with its needed effects, a medicine may cause some unwanted effects. Although not all of these side effects may occur, if they do occur they may need medical attention.

Stop taking this medicine and check with your doctor immediately if any of the following side effects occur:

Less common

Abdominal or stomach cramps or pain (severe); bloody diarrhea; fever; headache (severe); skin rash and itching

Rare

Anxiety; back or stomach pain (severe); blue or pale skin; chest pain, possibly moving to the left arm, neck, or shoulder; chills; fast heartbeat; nausea or vomiting; shortness of breath; swelling of the stomach; unusual tiredness or weakness; yellow eyes or skin

Symptoms of overdose

Confusion; diarrhea (severe or continuing); dizziness or lightheadedness; drowsiness (severe); fast or deep breathing; headache (severe or continuing); hearing loss or ringing or buzzing in ears (continuing); nausea or vomiting (continuing)

Other side effects may occur that usually do not need medical attention. These side effects may go away during treatment as your body adjusts to the medicine. However, check with your doctor if any of the following side effects continue or are bothersome:

More common

Abdominal or stomach cramps or pain (mild); diarrhea (mild); dizziness; headache (mild); runny or stuffy nose or sneezing

Less common

Acne; back or joint pain; gas or flatulence; indigestion; loss of appetite; loss of hair

Other side effects not listed above may also occur in some patients. If you notice any other effects, check with your doctor.

Additional Information

Once a medicine has been approved for marketing for a certain use, experience may show that it is also useful for other medical problems. Although this use is not included in product labeling, mesalamine may be used to treat mild or moderate Crohn's disease and help prevent it from occurring again.

Other than the above information, there is no additional information relating to proper use, precautions, or side effects for this use.

Developed: 03/17/95
Interim revision: 08/14/98

METFORMIN Systemic

Commonly used brand name(s):

In the U.S.—
Glucophage
Glucophage XR

In Canada—

Apo-Metformin	Glycon
Gen-Metformin	Novo-Metformin
Glucophage	Nu-Metformin

Description

Metformin (met-FOR-min) is used to treat a type of diabetes mellitus (sugar diabetes) called type 2 diabetes. With this type of diabetes, insulin produced by the pancreas is not able to get sugar into the cells of the body where it can work properly. Using metformin alone, with a type of oral antidiabetic medicine called a sulfonylurea, or with insulin will help to lower blood sugar when it is too high and help restore the way you use food to make energy.

Many people can control type 2 diabetes with diet alone or diet and exercise. Following a specially planned diet and exercising will always be important when you have diabetes, even when you are taking medicines. To work properly, the amount of metformin you take must be balanced against the amount and type of food you eat and the amount of exercise you do. If you change your diet, your exercise, or both, you will want to test your blood sugar to find out if it is too low. Your health care professional will teach you what to do if this happens.

At some point, this medicine may stop working as well and your blood glucose will increase. You will need to know if this happens and what to do. Instead of taking more of this medicine, your doctor may want you to change to another antidiabetic medicine. If that does not lower your blood sugar, your doctor may have you stop taking the medicine and begin receiving insulin injections instead.

Metformin does not help patients who have insulin-dependent or type 1 diabetes because they cannot produce insulin from their pancreas gland. Their blood glucose is best controlled by insulin injections.

Metformin is available only with your doctor's prescription, in the following dosage form:

Oral
- Tablets (U.S. and Canada)

Before Using This Medicine

In deciding to use a medicine, the risks of taking the medicine must be weighed against the good it will do. This is a decision you and your doctor will make. For metformin, the following should be considered:

Allergies—Tell your doctor if you have ever had any unusual or allergic reaction to metformin. Also tell your health

care professional if you are allergic to any other substances, such as foods, preservatives, or dyes.

Pregnancy—Metformin has not been shown to cause birth defects or other problems in humans. However, metformin is not used during pregnancy. Instead, your doctor may want to control your blood sugar by diet or by a combination of diet and insulin. It is especially important for your health and your baby's health that your blood sugar be closely controlled. Close control of your blood sugar can reduce the chance of your baby gaining too much weight, having birth defects, or having high or low blood sugar. Be sure to tell your doctor if you plan to become pregnant or if you think you are pregnant.

Breast-feeding—It is not known whether metformin passes into human breast milk. Although most medicines pass into breast milk in small amounts, many of them may be used safely while breast-feeding. Mothers who are taking this medicine and who wish to breast-feed should discuss this with their doctor.

Children—Metformin tablets have been tested in children older than 10 years old and, in effective doses, have not been shown to cause different side effects or problems than it does in adults.

Studies with metformin *extended-release tablets* have been done only in adult patients, and there is no specific information comparing use of this medicine in children with use in other age groups.

Teenagers—Metformin tablets have been tested in teenagers older than 17 years and, in effective doses, have not been shown to cause different side effects or problems than it does in adults.

Studies with metformin *extended-release tablets* have not been done in patients younger than 17–years-old.

Older adults—Use in older adults is similar to use in adults of younger age. However, if you have blood vessel disorders or kidney problems, your health care professional may adjust your dose or tell you to stop taking this medicine, if necessary.

Other medicines—Although certain medicines should not be used together at all, in other cases two different medicines may be used together even if an interaction might occur. In these cases, your doctor may want to change the dose, or other precautions may be necessary. *Do not take any other medicine unless prescribed or approved by your doctor*. When you are taking metformin, it is especially important that your health care professional know if you are taking any of the following:

- Alcohol—Small amounts of alcohol taken with meals do not usually cause a problem; however, either larger amounts of alcohol taken for a long time or a large amount of alcohol taken in one sitting without food can increase the effect of metformin. This can keep the blood sugar low for a longer period of time than normal

- Amiloride (e.g., Midamor) or
- Calcium channel blocking agents (amlodipine [e.g., Norvasc], bepridil [e.g., Bepadin], diltiazem [e.g., Cardizem], felodipine [e.g., Plendil], flunarizine [e.g., Sibelium], isradipine [e.g., DynaCirc], nicardipine [e.g., Cardene], nifedipine [e.g., Procardia], nimodipine [e.g., Nimotop], verapamil [e.g., Calan]) or
- Cimetidine (e.g., Tagamet) or
- Digoxin (heart medicine) or
- Furosemide (e.g., Lasix) or
- Morphine (e.g., M S Contin) or

- Procainamide (e.g., Pronestyl) or
- Quinidine (e.g., Quinidex) or
- Quinine (malaria medicine) or
- Ranitidine (e.g., Zantac) or
- Triamterene (e.g., Dyrenium) or
- Trimethoprim (e.g., Proloprim) or
- Vancomycin (e.g., Vancocin)—Use with metformin may cause high blood levels of metformin, which may increase the chance of low blood sugar or side effects

Other medical problems—The presence of other medical problems may affect the use of metformin. Make sure you tell your doctor if you have any other medical problems, especially:

- Acid in the blood (ketoacidosis or lactic acidosis) or
- Burns (severe) or
- Dehydration or
- Diarrhea (severe) or
- Female hormone changes for some women (e.g., during puberty, pregnancy, or menstruation) or
- Fever, high or
- Infection (severe) or
- Injury (severe) or
- Ketones in the urine or
- Mental stress (severe) or
- Overactive adrenal gland (not properly controlled) or
- Problems with intestines (severe) or
- Slow stomach emptying or
- Surgery (major) or
- Vomiting or
- Any other condition that causes problems with eating or absorbing food or
- Any other condition in which blood sugar changes rapidly—Metformin in many cases will be replaced with insulin by your doctor, possibly only for a short time. Use of insulin is best to help control diabetes mellitus in patients with these conditions that without warning cause quick changes in the blood sugar.

- Heart or blood vessel disorders or
- Kidney disease or kidney problems or
- Liver disease (or history of)—Lactic acidosis can occur in these conditions and chances of it occurring are even greater with use of metformin

- Kidney, heart, or other problems that require medical tests or examinations that use certain medicines called contrast agents, with x-rays—Metformin should be stopped before medical exams or diagnostic tests that might cause less urine output than usual. Passing unusually low amounts of urine may increase the chance of a build-up of metformin and unwanted effects. Metformin may be restarted 48 hours after the exams or tests if kidney function is tested and found to be normal

- Overactive thyroid (not properly controlled) or
- Underactive thyroid (not properly controlled)—Until the thyroid condition is controlled, it may change the amount or type of antidiabetic medicine you need

- Underactive adrenal gland (not properly controlled) or
- Underactive pituitary gland (not properly controlled) or
- Undernourished condition or
- Weakened physical condition or
- Any other condition that causes low blood sugar—Patients who have any of these conditions may be more likely to develop low blood sugar, which can affect the dose of metformin you need and increase the need for blood sugar testing

Proper Use of This Medicine

Use this medicine as directed even if you feel well and do not notice any signs of high blood sugar. Do not take more of this medicine and do not take it more often than your doctor ordered. To do so may increase the chance of serious side effects. Remember that this medicine will not cure your diabetes, but it does help control it. Therefore, you must continue to take it as directed if you expect to lower your blood sugar and keep it low. *You may have to take an antidiabetic medicine for the rest of your life.* If high blood sugar is not treated, it can cause serious problems, such as heart failure, blood vessel disease, eye disease, or kidney disease.

Your doctor will give you instructions about diet, exercise, how to test your blood sugar, and how to adjust your dose when you are sick.

- Blood sugar tests: Testing for blood sugar is the best way to tell whether your diabetes is being controlled properly. Blood sugar testing helps you and your health care team adjust your antidiabetic medicine dose, meal plan, and exercise schedule.
- Diet: The daily number of calories in your meal plan should be adjusted by your doctor or a registered dietitian to help you reach and maintain a healthy body weight. In addition, regular meals and snacks are arranged to meet the energy needs of your body at different times of the day. *It is very important that you carefully follow your meal plan.*
- Exercise: Ask your doctor what kind of exercise to do, the best time to do it, and how much you should do each day.
- Fluid (water) replacement: It is important to replace the water or fluid that your body uses. Tell your doctor if you have less urine output than usual or severe diarrhea that lasts for more than 1 day.
- On sick days:
  - When you become sick with a cold, fever, or the flu, you need to take your usual dose of metformin, even if you feel too ill to eat. This is especially true if you have nausea, vomiting, or diarrhea. Infection usually increases your need to produce more insulin. Sometimes you may need to be switched from metformin to insulin for a short period of time while you are sick to properly control blood sugar. *Call your doctor for specific instructions, especially if severe or prolonged vomiting occurs.*
  - Continue taking your metformin and try to stay on your regular meal plan. If you have trouble eating solid food, drink fruit juices, nondiet soft drinks, or clear soups, or eat small amounts of bland foods. A dietitian or your health care professional can give you a list of foods and the amounts to use for sick days.
  - Test your blood sugar and check your urine for ketones. If ketones are present, call your doctor at once. Even when you start feeling better, let your doctor know how you are doing.

Dosing—The dose of metformin will be different for different patients. *Follow your doctor's orders or the directions on the label.* The following information includes only the average doses of metformin. *If your dose is different, do not change it* unless your doctor tells you to do so.

The number of tablets that you take depends on the strength of the medicine. Also, *the number of doses you take each day, the time allowed between doses, and the length of time you take the medicine depend on the amount of sugar in your blood or urine.*

- For *oral* dosage form (tablets):
  - For type 2 diabetes:
  - For patients taking metformin tablets
  - Adults:
    - Metformin alone: At first, 500 milligrams (mg) two times a day taken with the morning and evening meals. Or, 850 mg a day taken with the morning meal. Then, your doctor may increase your dose a little at a time every week or every other week if needed. Later, your doctor may want you to take 500 or 850 mg two to three times a day with meals.
    - Metformin with a sulfonylurea: Your doctor will determine the dose of each medicine.
    - Metformin with insulin: At first, 500 mg a day. Then, your doctor may increase your dose by 500 mg every week if needed.
  - Children up to 10 years of age—Use and dose must be determined by your doctor.
  - Children 10 years of age and over—At first, 500 milligrams (mg) with your morning meal and 500 mg with your evening meal. Then, your doctor may increase your dose a little at a time every week if needed.
  - For patients taking metformin *extended-release tablets*
  - Adults and teenagers:
    - Metformin alone: At first, 500 milligrams (mg) once daily with the evening meal. Then, your doctor may increase your dose a little at a time every week if needed. If you need more medicine, your doctor may tell you to take more than one dose a day.
    - Metformin with a sulfonylurea: Your doctor will determine the dose of each medicine.
    - Metformin with insulin: At first, 500 mg a day. Then, your doctor may increase your dose by 500 mg every week if needed.
  - Children up to 17 years of age—Use and dose must be determined by your doctor.

Missed dose—If you miss a dose of this medicine, take it as soon as possible. However, if it is almost time for your next dose, skip the missed dose and go back to your regular dosing schedule. Do not double doses.

Storage—To store this medicine:
- Keep out of the reach of children.
- Store away from heat and direct light.
- Keep the medicine from freezing. Do not refrigerate.
- Do not keep outdated medicine or medicine no longer needed. Be sure that any discarded medicine is out of the reach of children.

Precautions While Using This Medicine

Your doctor will want to check your progress at regular visits, especially during the first few weeks that you take this medicine.

It is very important to follow carefully any instructions from your health care team about:
- Alcohol—Drinking alcohol may cause very low blood sugar. Discuss this with your health care team.
- Other medicines—Do not take other medicines unless they have been discussed with your doctor. This espe-

cially includes nonprescription medicines such as aspirin, and medicines for appetite control, asthma, colds, cough, hay fever, or sinus problems.

- Counseling—Other family members need to learn how to prevent side effects or help with side effects if they occur. Counseling on birth control and pregnancy may be needed because of the problems that can occur in pregnancy for patients with diabetes.
- Travel—Carry a recent prescription and your medical history. Be prepared for an emergency as you would normally. Make allowances for changing time zones, but keep your meal times as close as possible to your usual meal times.

In case of emergency—There may be a time when you need emergency help for a problem caused by your diabetes. You need to be prepared for these emergencies. It is a good idea to:

- Wear a medical identification (I.D.) bracelet or neck chain at all times. Also, carry an I.D. card in your wallet or purse that says that you have diabetes and a list of all of your medicines.
- Have a glucagon kit available in case severe low blood sugar occurs. Check and replace any expired kits regularly.
- Keep some kind of quick-acting sugar handy to treat low blood sugar.

If you are scheduled to have surgery or medical tests that involve x-rays, you should tell your doctor that you are taking metformin. Your doctor will instruct you to stop taking metformin until at least 2 days after the surgery or medical tests. During this time, if your blood sugar cannot be controlled by diet and exercise, you may be advised to take insulin.

Too much metformin, under certain conditions, can cause lactic acidosis. *Symptoms of lactic acidosis are severe and quick to appear* and usually occur when other health problems not related to the medicine are present and are very severe, such as a heart attack or kidney failure. Symptoms include diarrhea, fast and shallow breathing, severe muscle pain or cramping, unusual sleepiness, and unusual tiredness or weakness.

If symptoms of lactic acidosis occur, you should check your blood sugar and get immediate emergency medical help. Also, tell your doctor if severe vomiting occurs.

Too much metformin also can cause low blood sugar (hypoglycemia) when it is used under certain conditions. *Symptoms of low blood sugar must be treated before they lead to unconsciousness (passing out).* Different people may feel different symptoms of low blood sugar. *It is important that you learn which symptoms of low blood sugar you usually have so that you can treat it quickly and call someone on your health care team right away when you need advice.*

- Symptoms of low blood sugar can include: anxious feeling, behavior change similar to being drunk, blurred vision, cold sweats, confusion, cool pale skin, difficulty in concentrating, drowsiness, excessive hunger, fast heartbeat, headache, nausea, nervousness, nightmares, restless sleep, shakiness, slurred speech, and unusual tiredness or weakness.
- The symptoms of low blood sugar may develop quickly and may result from:
  —delaying or missing a scheduled meal or snack.
  —exercising more than usual.
  —drinking a large amount of alcohol.

  —taking certain medicines.
  —if also using insulin or a sulfonylurea, using too much of these medicines.
  —sickness (especially with vomiting or diarrhea).
- *Know what to do if symptoms of low blood sugar occur.* Eating some form of quick-acting sugar when symptoms of low blood sugar first appear will usually prevent them from getting worse.
- Good ways to increase your blood sugar include:
  —Using glucagon injections in emergency situations such as unconsciousness. Have a glucagon kit available and know how to prepare and use it. Members of your household also should know how and when to use it.
  —Eating glucose tablets or gel or sugar cubes (6 one-half–inch size). Or drinking fruit juice or nondiet soft drink (4 to 6 ounces [one-half cup]), corn syrup or honey (1 tablespoon), or table sugar (dissolved in water).
  - Do not use chocolate. The sugar in chocolate may not enter into your blood stream fast enough. This is because the fat in chocolate slows down the sugar entering into the blood stream.
  - If a meal is not scheduled for an hour or more, you should also eat a light snack, such as crackers or half a sandwich.

High blood sugar (hyperglycemia) is another problem related to uncontrolled diabetes. Symptoms of mild high blood sugar appear more slowly than those of low blood sugar.

- *Check with your health care team as soon as possible if you notice any of the following symptoms:* Blurred vision, drowsiness, dry mouth, increased frequency and volume of urination, loss of appetite, nausea or vomiting, stomachache, tiredness, or unusual thirst.
- *Get emergency help right away if you notice any of the following symptoms:* Flushed dry skin, fruit-like breath odor, ketones in urine, passing out, or troubled breathing (rapid and deep). If high blood sugar is not treated, severe hyperglycemia can occur, leading to ketoacidosis (diabetic coma) and death.
- *It is important to recognize what can cause the loss of blood glucose control.* Calling your doctor early may be important to prevent problems from developing when the following occur. High blood sugar symptoms may occur if you:
  —have a fever or an infection.
  —are using insulin, sulfonylurea, or metformin and do not take enough of these medicines or skip a dose.
  —do not exercise as much as usual.
  —take certain medicines to treat conditions other than diabetes that change the amount of sugar in your blood.
  —overeat or do not follow your meal plan.
- Know what to do if high blood sugar occurs. Your doctor may recommend changes in your antidiabetic medicine dose(s) or meal plan to avoid high blood sugar. Symptoms of high blood sugar must be corrected before they progress to more serious conditions. Check with your doctor often to make sure you are controlling your blood sugar, *but do not change your dose without checking with your doctor.* Your doctor might discuss the following with you:
  —Delaying a meal if your blood glucose is over 200 mg/dL to allow time for your blood sugar to go down. An extra dose of metformin or an injection of

insulin may be needed if your blood sugar does not come down shortly.

—Not exercising if your blood glucose is over 240 mg/dL and reporting this to your doctor immediately.

—Being hospitalized if ketoacidosis or diabetic coma occurs.

Side Effects of This Medicine

Along with its needed effects, a medicine may cause some unwanted effects. Although not all of these side effects may occur, if they do occur they may need medical attention.

Check with your doctor immediately if the following side effect occurs:
> *Rare*
>> Lactic acidosis (quick and severe), including diarrhea, fast shallow breathing, muscle pain or cramping, unusual sleepiness, unusual tiredness or weakness

Check with your doctor as soon as possible if the following side effect occurs:
> *Rare*
>> Low blood sugar (mild), including anxious feeling, behavior change similar to being drunk, blurred vision, cold sweats, confusion, cool pale skin, difficulty in concentrating, drowsiness, excessive hunger, fast heartbeat, headache, nausea, nervousness, nightmares, restless sleep, shakiness, slurred speech

Other side effects may occur that usually do not need medical attention. These side effects may go away during treatment as your body adjusts to the medicine. However, check with your doctor if any of the following side effects continue or are bothersome:
> *More common*
>> Loss of appetite; metallic taste in mouth; passing of gas; stomachache; vomiting; weight loss

Other side effects not listed above may also occur in some patients. If you notice any other effects, check with your doctor.

Revised: 03/28/2001

METHENAMINE   Systemic

Commonly used brand name(s):

In the U.S.—
> Hiprex
> Mandelamine
> Urex
> Generic name product may be available.

In Canada—
> Hip-Rex
> Mandelamine

Description

Methenamine (meth-EN-a-meen) belongs to the family of medicines called anti-infectives. It is used to help prevent and treat infections of the urinary tract. Methenamine is available only with your doctor's prescription, in the following dosage forms:
> *Oral*
> • Enteric-coated tablets (U.S.)
> • Granules for oral solution (U.S.)
> • Oral suspension (U.S.)
> • Tablets (U.S. and Canada)

Before Using This Medicine

In deciding to use a medicine, the risks of taking the medicine must be weighed against the good it will do. This is a decision you and your doctor will make. For methenamine, the following should be considered:

Allergies—Tell your doctor if you have ever had any unusual or allergic reaction to methenamine. Also tell your health care professional if you are allergic to any other substances, such as foods, preservatives, or dyes.

Pregnancy—Methenamine has not been studied in either humans or animals. However, individual case reports on the use of methenamine during pregnancy have not shown that this medicine causes birth defects or other problems in humans.

Breast-feeding—Methenamine passes into the breast milk. However, methenamine has not been reported to cause problems in nursing babies.

Children—Although there is no special information comparing use of methenamine in children with use in other age groups, this medicine is not expected to cause different side effects or problems in children than it does in adults.

Older adults—Many medicines have not been studied specifically in older people. Therefore, it may not be known whether they work exactly the same way they do in younger adults or if they cause different side effects or problems in older people. There is no specific information comparing use of methenamine in the elderly with use in other age groups.

Other medicines—Although certain medicines should not be used together at all, in other cases two different medicines may be used together even if an interaction might occur. In these cases, your doctor may want to change the dose, or other precautions may be necessary. When you are taking methenamine, it is especially important that your health care professional knows if you are taking any of the following:
> • Sulfamethizole (use of methenamine with this medicine may damage your kidneys)
> • Thiazide diuretics (water pills) or
> • Urinary alkalizers (medicine that makes the urine less acid, such as acetazolamide [e.g., Diamox], calcium- and/or magnesium-containing antacids, dichlorphenamide [e.g., Daranide], methazolamide [e.g., Neptazane], potassium or sodium citrate and/or citric acid, sodium bicarbonate [baking soda])—Use of methenamine with any of these medicines may decrease the effectiveness of methenamine

Other medical problems—The presence of other medical problems may affect the use of methenamine. Make sure you tell your doctor if you have any other medical problems, especially:
> • Dehydration (severe) or
> • Kidney disease (severe)—Patients with severe kidney disease who take methenamine may have an increase in side effects that affect the kidneys

> • Liver disease (severe)—Patients with severe liver disease who take methenamine may have an increase in symptoms of their liver disease

Proper Use of This Medicine

Before you start taking this medicine, check your urine with phenaphthazine paper or another test to see if it is acid. *Your urine must be acidic (pH 5.5 or below) for this medicine to work properly.* If you have any questions about this, check with your health care professional.

The following changes in your diet may help make your urine more acid; however, check with your doctor first if you are on a special diet (for example, for diabetes). Avoid most fruits (especially citrus fruits and juices), milk and other dairy products, and other foods that make the urine less acid. Also, avoid antacids unless otherwise directed by your doctor. Eating more protein and foods such as cranberries (especially cranberry juice with vitamin C added), plums, or prunes may also help. If your urine is still not acid enough, check with your doctor.

If this medicine causes nausea or upset stomach, it may be taken after meals and at bedtime.

For patients taking the *dry granule form of this medicine:*
- Dissolve the contents of each packet in 2 to 4 ounces of cold water immediately before taking. Stir well. Be sure to drink all the liquid to get the full dose of medicine.

For patients taking the *oral liquid form of this medicine:*
- Use a specially marked measuring spoon or other device to measure each dose accurately. The average household teaspoon may not hold the right amount of liquid.

For patients taking the *enteric-coated tablet form of this medicine:*
- Swallow tablets whole. Do not break, crush, or take if chipped.

To help clear up your infection completely, *keep taking this medicine for the full time of treatment,* even if you begin to feel better after a few days. *Do not miss any doses.*

Dosing—The dose of methenamine will be different for different patients. *Follow your doctor's orders or the directions on the label.* The following information includes only the average doses of methenamine. *If your dose is different, do not change it* unless your doctor tells you to do so.

The number of tablets or teaspoonfuls of solution or suspension that you take depends on the strength of the medicine.
- For the treatment of urinary tract infections:
  —For *oral* dosage form (methenamine hippurate tablets):
  - Adults and children 12 years of age and over—1 gram two times a day. Take in the morning and the evening.
  - Children up to 6 years of age—Use and dose must be determined by your doctor.
  - Children 6 to 12 years of age—500 milligrams (mg) to 1 gram two times a day. Take in the morning and the evening.
  —For *oral* dosage form (methenamine mandelate enteric-coated tablets, regular tablets, solution, and suspension):
  - Adults and children 12 years of age and over—1 gram four times a day. Take after meals and at bedtime.
  - Children up to 6 years of age—Dose is based on body weight. The usual dose is 18.3 mg per kilogram (kg) (8.3 mg per pound) of body weight four times a day. Take after meals and at bedtime.
  - Children 6 to 12 years of age—500 mg four times a day. Take after meals and at bedtime.

Missed dose—If you miss a dose of this medicine, take it as soon as possible. However, if it is almost time for your next dose, skip the missed dose and go back to your regular dosing schedule. Do not double doses.

Storage—To store this medicine:
- Keep out of the reach of children.
- Store away from heat and direct light.
- Do not store the dry granule or tablet form of this medicine in the bathroom, near the kitchen sink, or in other damp places. Heat or moisture may cause the medicine to break down.
- Keep the oral liquid form of this medicine from freezing.
- Do not keep outdated medicine or medicine no longer needed. Be sure that any discarded medicine is out of the reach of children.

Precautions While Using This Medicine

If your symptoms do not improve within a few days, or if they become worse, check with your doctor.

Side Effects of This Medicine

Along with its needed effects, a medicine may cause some unwanted effects. Although not all of these side effects may occur, if they do occur they may need medical attention.

Check with your doctor immediately if any of the following side effects occur:
Less common
   Skin rash
Rare
   Blood in urine; lower back pain; pain or burning while urinating

Other side effects may occur that usually do not need medical attention. These side effects may go away during treatment as your body adjusts to the medicine. However, check with your doctor if any of the following side effects continue or are bothersome:
Less common
   Nausea and vomiting

Other side effects not listed above may also occur in some patients. If you notice any other effects, check with your doctor.

Revised: 03/28/00

METHOTREXATE—For Cancer
Systemic

Commonly used brand name(s):

In the U.S.—
   Generic name product may be available.

In Canada—
   Generic name product may be available.

Another commonly used name is amethopterin.

Description

Methotrexate (meth-o-TREX-ate) belongs to the group of medicines known as antimetabolites. It is used to treat cancer of the breast, head and neck, lung, blood, bone, and lymph, and tumors in the uterus. It may also be used to treat other kinds of cancer, as determined by your doctor.

Methotrexate blocks an enzyme needed by the cell to live. This interferes with the growth of cancer cells, which are eventually destroyed. Since the growth of normal body cells may also be affected by methotrexate, other effects will also occur. Some of these may be serious and must be reported to your doctor. Other effects, like hair loss, may not be serious but may cause concern. Some effects may not occur for months or years after the medicine is used.

Before you begin treatment with methotrexate, you and your doctor should talk about the good this medicine will do as well as the risks of using it.

Methotrexate is available only with your doctor's prescription, in the following dosage forms:

Oral
- Tablets (U.S. and Canada)

Parenteral
- Injection (U.S. and Canada)

Before Using This Medicine

In deciding to use a medicine, the risks of taking the medicine must be weighed against the good it will do. This is a decision you and your doctor will make. For methotrexate, the following should be considered:

Allergies—Tell your doctor if you have ever had any unusual or allergic reaction to methotrexate.

Pregnancy—Tell your doctor if you are pregnant or if you intend to have children. There is a good chance that this medicine may cause birth defects if either the male or female is taking it at the time of conception or if it is taken during pregnancy. Methotrexate may cause harm or even death of the fetus. In addition, many cancer medicines may cause sterility, which could be permanent. Although sterility is probably rare with this medicine, the possibility should be kept in mind.

Be sure that you have discussed this with your doctor before taking this medicine. It is best to use some kind of birth control while you are taking methotrexate. Tell your doctor right away if you think you have become pregnant while taking methotrexate.

Breast-feeding—Tell your doctor if you are breast-feeding or if you intend to breast-feed during treatment with this medicine. Because methotrexate may cause serious side effects, breast-feeding is generally not recommended while you are taking it.

Children—Newborns and other infants may be more sensitive to the effects of methotrexate. However, in other children it is not expected to cause different side effects or problems than it does in adults.

Older adults—Side effects may be more likely to occur in the elderly, who are usually more sensitive to the effects of methotrexate.

Other medicines—Although certain medicines should not be used together at all, in other cases two different medicines may be used together even if an interaction might occur. In these cases, your doctor may want to change the dose, or other precautions may be necessary. When you are taking methotrexate, it is especially important that your health care professional know if you are taking any other prescription or nonprescription (over-the-counter [OTC]) medicine. They should also be told if you have ever been treated with x-rays or cancer medicines or if you drink alcohol.

Other medical problems—The presence of other medical problems may affect the use of methotrexate. Make sure you tell your doctor if you have any other medical problems, especially:

- Alcohol abuse (or history of)—Increased risk of unwanted effects on the liver
- Chickenpox (including recent exposure) or
- Herpes zoster (shingles)—Risk of severe disease affecting other parts of the body
- Colitis
- Disease of the immune system
- Gout (history of) or
- Kidney stones (or history of)—Methotrexate may increase levels of a chemical called uric acid in the body, which can cause gout or kidney stones
- Infection—Methotrexate can reduce immunity to infection
- Intestine blockage or
- Kidney disease or
- Liver disease—Effects may be increased because of slower removal of methotrexate from the body
- Mouth sores or inflammation or
- Stomach ulcer—May be worsened

Proper Use of This Medicine

Take this medicine only as directed by your doctor. Do not take more or less of it, and do not take it more often than your doctor ordered. The exact amount of medicine you need has been carefully worked out. Taking too much may increase the chance of side effects, while taking too little may not improve your condition.

Methotrexate is often given together with certain other medicines. If you are using a combination of medicines, make sure that you take each one at the proper time and do not mix them. Ask your health care professional to help you plan a way to remember to take your medicines at the right times.

While you are using methotrexate, your doctor may want you to drink extra fluids so that you will pass more urine. This will help the drug to pass from the body, and will prevent kidney problems and keep your kidneys working well.

Methotrexate commonly causes nausea and vomiting. Even if you begin to feel ill, *do not stop using this medicine without first checking with your doctor*. Ask your health care professional for ways to lessen these effects.

If you vomit shortly after taking a dose of methotrexate, check with your doctor. You will be told whether to take the dose again or to wait until the next scheduled dose.

Dosing—The dose of methotrexate will be different for different patients. The dose that is used may depend on a number of things, including what the medicine is being used for, the patient's size, whether the medicine is being given by mouth or by injection, and whether or not other medicines are also being taken. *If you are taking or receiving methotrexate at home, follow your doctor's orders or the directions on the label.* If you have any questions about the proper dose of methotrexate, ask your doctor.

Missed dose—If you miss a dose of this medicine, do not take the missed dose at all and do not double the next one. Instead, go back to your regular dosing schedule and check with your doctor.

Storage—To store this medicine:
- Keep out of the reach of children.

- Store away from heat and direct light.
- Do not store in the bathroom, near the kitchen sink, or in other damp places. Heat or moisture may cause the medicine to break down.
- Do not keep outdated medicine or medicine no longer needed. Be sure that any discarded medicine is out of the reach of children.

Precautions While Using This Medicine

It is very important that your doctor check your progress at regular visits to make sure that this medicine is working properly and to check for unwanted effects.

Do not drink alcohol while using this medicine. Alcohol can increase the chance of liver problems.

Some patients who take methotrexate may become more sensitive to sunlight than they are normally. When you first begin taking methotrexate, avoid too much sun and do not use a sunlamp until you see how you react to the sun, especially if you tend to burn easily. In case of a severe burn, check with your doctor.

Do not take medicine for inflammation or pain (aspirin or other salicylates, diclofenac, diflunisal, fenoprofen, ibuprofen, indomethacin, ketoprofen, meclofenamate, mefenamic acid, naproxen, phenylbutazone, piroxicam, sulindac, suprofen, tolmetin) without first checking with your doctor. These medicines may increase the effects of methotrexate, which could be harmful.

While you are being treated with methotrexate, and after you stop treatment with it, *do not have any immunizations (vaccinations) without your doctor's approval.* Methotrexate may lower your body's resistance and there is a chance you might get the infection the immunization is meant to prevent. In addition, other persons living in your household should not take oral polio vaccine since there is a chance they could pass the polio virus on to you. Also, avoid other persons who have taken oral polio vaccine within the last several months. Do not get close to them, and do not stay in the same room with them for very long. If you cannot take these precautions, you should consider wearing a protective face mask that covers the nose and mouth.

Methotrexate can lower the number of white blood cells in your blood temporarily, increasing the chance of getting an infection. It can also lower the number of platelets, which are necessary for proper blood clotting. If this occurs, there are certain precautions you can take, especially when your blood count is low, to reduce the risk of infection or bleeding:

- If you can, avoid people with infections. *Check with your doctor immediately* if you think you are getting an infection or if you get a fever or chills, cough or hoarseness, lower back or side pain, or painful or difficult urination.
- *Check with your doctor immediately* if you notice any unusual bleeding or bruising; black, tarry stools; blood in urine or stools; or pinpoint red spots on your skin.
- Be careful when using a regular toothbrush, dental floss, or toothpick. Your medical doctor, dentist, or nurse may recommend other ways to clean your teeth and gums. Check with your medical doctor before having any dental work done.
- Do not touch your eyes or the inside of your nose unless you have just washed your hands and have not touched anything else in the meantime.

- Be careful not to cut yourself when you are using sharp objects such as a safety razor or fingernail or toenail cutters.
- Avoid contact sports or other situations where bruising or injury could occur.

Side Effects of This Medicine

Along with their needed effects, medicines like methotrexate can sometimes cause unwanted effects such as blood problems, kidney problems, stomach or liver problems, loss of hair, and other side effects. These and others are described below. Also, because of the way these medicines act on the body, there is a chance that they might cause other unwanted effects that may not occur until months or years after the medicine is used. These delayed effects may include certain types of cancer, such as leukemia. Discuss these possible effects with your doctor.

Although not all of these side effects may occur, if they do occur they may need medical attention.

Check with your doctor immediately if any of the following side effects occur:
  More common
    Black, tarry stools; blood in urine or stools; bloody vomit; diarrhea; joint pain; reddening of skin; stomach pain; swelling of feet or lower legs
  Less common
    Blurred vision; confusion; convulsions (seizures); cough; pinpoint red spots on skin; shortness of breath; unusual bleeding or bruising

Check with your doctor as soon as possible if any of the following side effects occur:
  More common
    Sores in mouth and on lips
  Less common
    Back pain; cough or hoarseness accompanied by fever or chills; dark urine; dizziness; drowsiness; fever or chills; headache; lower back or side pain accompanied by fever or chills; painful or difficult urination accompanied by fever or chills; unusual tiredness or weakness; yellow eyes or skin

Other side effects may occur that usually do not need medical attention. These side effects may go away during treatment as your body adjusts to the medicine. Also, your health care professional may be able to tell you about ways to prevent or reduce some of these side effects. Check with your health care professional if any of the following side effects continue or are bothersome or if you have any questions about them:
  More common
    Loss of appetite; nausea or vomiting
  Less common
    Acne; boils; pale skin; skin rash or itching

This medicine may cause a temporary loss of hair in some people. After treatment with methotrexate has ended, normal hair growth should return.

After you stop using methotrexate, it may still produce some side effects that need attention. During this period of time, check with your doctor as soon as possible if you notice any of the following side effects:
    Back pain; blurred vision; confusion; convulsions (seizures); dizziness; drowsiness; fever; headache; unusual tiredness or weakness

Other side effects not listed above may also occur in some patients. If you notice any other effects, check with your doctor.

Additional Information

Once a medicine has been approved for marketing for a certain use, experience may show that it is also useful for other medical problems. Although these uses are not included in product labeling, methotrexate is used in certain patients with the following medical conditions:

- Acute nonlymphocytic leukemia (a type of cancer of the blood and lymph system)
- Cancer in the membranes that cover and protect the brain and spinal cord (the meninges)
- Cancer of the bladder
- Cancer of the brain (lymphoma)
- Cancer of the cervix
- Cancer of colon and rectum
- Cancer of the esophagus
- Cancer of the ovaries
- Cancer of the pancreas
- Cancer of the penis
- Cancers of the soft tissues of the body, including the muscles, connective tissues (tendons), vessels that carry blood or lymph, or fat
- Cancer of the stomach
- Hodgkin's lymphoma (a cancer of the lymph system, a part of the body's immune system)

Other than the above information, there is no additional information relating to proper use, precautions, or side effects for these uses.

Revised: 08/01/2000

METHOTREXATE—For Noncancerous Conditions
Systemic

Commonly used brand name(s):

In the U.S.—

Folex	Methotrexate LPF
Folex PFS	Rheumatrex

Generic name product may be available.

In Canada—

Rheumatrex

Another commonly used name is amethopterin.

Description

Methotrexate (meth-o-TREX-ate) belongs to the group of medicines known as antimetabolites. It is used to treat psoriasis and rheumatoid arthritis. It may also be used for other conditions as determined by your doctor.

Methotrexate blocks an enzyme needed by the cell to live. This interferes with the growth of certain cells, such as skin cells in psoriasis that are growing rapidly. Since the growth of normal body cells may also be affected by methotrexate, other effects will also occur. Some of these may be serious and must be reported to your doctor. Other effects, like hair loss, may not be serious but may cause concern. Some ef-

fects may not occur for months or years after the medicine is used.

Before you begin treatment with methotrexate, you and your doctor should talk about the good this medicine will do as well as the risks of using it.

Methotrexate is available only with your doctor's prescription, in the following dosage forms:

Oral
- Tablets (U.S. and Canada)

Parenteral
- Injection (U.S. and Canada)

Before Using This Medicine

In deciding to use a medicine, the risks of taking the medicine must be weighed against the good it will do. This is a decision you and your doctor will make. For methotrexate, the following should be considered:

Allergies—Tell your doctor if you have ever had any unusual or allergic reaction to methotrexate.

Pregnancy—There is a good chance that this medicine may cause birth defects if either the male or female is taking it at the time of conception or if it is taken during pregnancy. Methotrexate may cause harm or even death of the fetus. In addition, this medicine may rarely cause temporary sterility.

Methotrexate is not recommended during pregnancy. Be sure that you have discussed this with your doctor before taking this medicine. It is best to use some kind of birth control while you are taking methotrexate. Tell your doctor right away if you think you have become pregnant while taking methotrexate.

Breast-feeding—Tell your doctor if you are breast-feeding or if you intend to breast-feed during treatment with this medicine. Because methotrexate may cause serious side effects, breast-feeding is generally not recommended while you are taking it.

Children—Newborns and other infants may be more sensitive to the effects of methotrexate. However, in other children it is not expected to cause different side effects or problems than it does in adults.

Older adults—Side effects may be more likely to occur in the elderly, who are usually more sensitive to the effects of methotrexate.

Other medicines—Although certain medicines should not be used together at all, in other cases two different medicines may be used together even if an interaction might occur. In these cases, your doctor may want to change the dose, or other precautions may be necessary. When you are taking methotrexate, it is especially important that your health care professional know if you are taking any other prescription or nonprescription (over-the-counter [OTC]) medicine. They should also be told if you have ever been treated with x-rays or cancer medicines or if you drink alcohol.

Other medical problems—The presence of other medical problems may affect the use of methotrexate. Make sure you tell your doctor if you have any other medical problems, especially:

- Alcohol abuse (or history of)—Increased risk of unwanted effects on the liver
- Chickenpox (including recent exposure) or
- Herpes zoster (shingles)—Risk of severe disease affecting other parts of the body
- Colitis

- Disease of the immune system
- Folate deficiency—May increase the chance of side effects
- Infection—Methotrexate can reduce immunity to infection
- Intestine blockage or
- Kidney disease or
- Liver disease—Effects may be increased because of slower removal of methotrexate from the body
- Mouth sores or inflammation or
- Stomach ulcer—May be worsened

Proper Use of This Medicine

Take this medicine only as directed by your doctor. Do not take more or less of it, and do not take it more often than your doctor ordered. The exact amount of medicine you need has been carefully worked out. Taking too much may increase the chance of side effects, while taking too little may not improve your condition.

Methotrexate may cause nausea. Even if you begin to feel ill, *do not stop using this medicine without first checking with your doctor*. Ask your health care professional for ways to lessen these effects. If you begin vomiting, check with your doctor.

If you vomit shortly after taking a dose of methotrexate, check with your doctor. You will be told whether to take the dose again or to wait until the next scheduled dose.

Dosing—The dose of methotrexate will be different for different patients. *Follow your doctor's orders or the directions on the label*. The following information includes only the average doses of methotrexate. *If your dose is different, do not change it* unless your doctor tells you to do so.

The number of tablets that you take or doses of injection that you use depends on the strength of the medicine. Also, *the number of doses you take each day, the time allowed between doses, and the length of time you take the medicine depend on the medical problem for which you are taking methotrexate.*

- For *oral* dosage form (tablets):
  —For psoriasis:
    - Adults—2.5 to 5 milligrams (mg) every twelve hours for three doses once a week, or 10 to 25 mg once a week. Your doctor may increase the dose as needed.
    - Children—Dose must be determined by your doctor.
  —For rheumatoid arthritis:
    - Adult—2.5 to 5 mg every twelve hours for three doses once a week, or 7.5 mg once a week. Your doctor may increase the dose as needed.
    - Children—Dose must be determined by your doctor.
- For *injection* dosage form:
  —For psoriasis:
    - Adults—To start, 10 mg injected into a muscle or vein once a week. Your doctor may increase the dose as needed.
    - Children—Dose must be determined by your doctor.

Missed dose—If you miss a dose of this medicine, do not take the missed dose at all and do not double the next one.

Instead, go back to your regular dosing schedule and check with your doctor.

Storage—To store this medicine:
- Keep out of the reach of children.
- Store away from heat and direct light.
- Do not store in the bathroom, near the kitchen sink, or in other damp places. Heat or moisture may cause the medicine to break down.
- Do not keep outdated medicine or medicine no longer needed. Be sure that any discarded medicine is out of the reach of children.

Precautions While Using This Medicine

It is very important that your doctor check your progress at regular visits to make sure that this medicine is working properly and to check for unwanted effects.

Do not drink alcohol while using this medicine. Alcohol can increase the chance of liver problems.

Some patients who take methotrexate may become more sensitive to sunlight than they are normally. When you first begin taking methotrexate, avoid too much sun and do not use a sunlamp until you see how you react to the sun, especially if you tend to burn easily. In case of a severe burn, check with your doctor. This is especially important if you are taking this medicine for psoriasis because sunlight can make the psoriasis worse.

Do not take medicine for inflammation or pain (aspirin or other salicylates, diclofenac, diflunisal, fenoprofen, ibuprofen, indomethacin, ketoprofen, meclofenamate, mefenamic acid, naproxen, phenylbutazone, piroxicam, sulindac, suprofen, tolmetin) without first checking with your doctor. These medicines may increase the effects of methotrexate, which could be harmful.

While you are being treated with methotrexate, and after you stop treatment with it, *do not have any immunizations (vaccinations) without your doctor's approval*. Methotrexate may lower your body's resistance and there is a chance you might get the infection the immunization is meant to prevent. In addition, other persons living in your household should not take or should not have recently taken oral polio vaccine since there is a chance they could pass the polio virus on to you. Also, avoid other persons who have taken oral polio vaccine. Do not get close to them, and do not stay in the same room with them for very long. If you cannot take these precautions, you should consider wearing a protective face mask that covers the nose and mouth.

Methotrexate can lower the number of white blood cells in your blood temporarily, increasing the chance of getting an infection. It can also lower the number of platelets, which are necessary for proper blood clotting. If this occurs, there are certain precautions you can take, especially when your blood count is low, to reduce the risk of infection or bleeding:

- If you can, avoid people with infections. *Check with your doctor immediately* if you think you are getting an infection or if you get a fever or chills, cough or hoarseness, lower back or side pain, or painful or difficult urination.
- *Check with your doctor immediately* if you notice any unusual bleeding or bruising; black, tarry stools; blood in urine or stools; or pinpoint red spots on your skin.
- Be careful when using a regular toothbrush, dental floss, or toothpick. Your medical doctor, dentist, or nurse may recommend other ways to clean your teeth and gums.

Check with your medical doctor before having any dental work done.

- Do not touch your eyes or the inside of your nose unless you have just washed your hands and have not touched anything else in the meantime.
- Be careful not to cut yourself when you are using sharp objects such as a safety razor or fingernail or toenail cutters.
- Avoid contact sports or other situations where bruising or injury could occur.

Side Effects of This Medicine

Along with their needed effects, medicines like methotrexate can sometimes cause unwanted effects such as blood problems, kidney problems, stomach or liver problems, loss of hair, and other side effects. These and others are described below. Also, because of the way these medicines act on the body, there is a chance that they might cause other unwanted effects that may not occur until months or years after the medicine is used. These delayed effects may include certain types of cancer, such as leukemia. Discuss these possible effects with your doctor.

Although not all of these side effects may occur, if they do occur they may need medical attention.

Check with your doctor immediately if any of the following side effects occur:
Less common
Diarrhea; reddening of skin; sores in mouth and on lips; stomach pain
Rare
Black, tarry stools; blood in urine or stools; blurred vision; chest pain; convulsions (seizures); cough or hoarseness; dead or loose skin layers; fever or chills; lower back or side pain; painful or difficult urination; painful peeling of skin patches; pinpoint red spots on skin; red blisters, ulcers on the lip, mouth, eye, nasal passages, and genital area; reddening of the skin with or without hair loss; shortness of breath; sloughing of skin, muscle and bone; unusual bleeding or bruising

Check with your doctor as soon as possible if any of the following side effects occur:
Rare
Back pain; dark urine; dizziness; drowsiness; headache; unusual tiredness or weakness; yellow eyes or skin

Other side effects may occur that usually do not need medical attention. These side effects may go away during treatment as your body adjusts to the medicine. Also, your health care professional may be able to tell you about ways to prevent or reduce some of these side effects. Check with your health care professional if any of the following side effects continue or are bothersome or if you have any questions about them:
Less common or rare
Acne; boils; loss of appetite; nausea or vomiting; pale skin; skin rash or itching

This medicine may cause a temporary loss of hair in some people. After treatment with methotrexate has ended, normal hair growth should return.

Other side effects not listed above may also occur in some patients. If you notice any other effects, check with your doctor.

Additional Information

Once a medicine has been approved for marketing for a certain use, experience may show that it is also useful for other medical problems. Although these uses are not included in product labeling, methotrexate is used in certain patients with the following medical conditions:
- Psoriatic arthritis
- Systemic dermatomyositis
- Seronegative arthritides

Other than the above information, there is no additional information relating to proper use, precautions, or side effects for these uses.

Revised: 01/27/2000

METHOXSALEN   Extracorporeal-Systemic

Commonly used brand name(s):

In the U.S.—
Uvadex

Description

Methoxsalen (meth-OX-a-len) belongs to the group of medicines called psoralens. It is used along with ultraviolet light (found in sunlight and some special lamps) to treat the white blood cells from your blood in a process called photopheresis. The treated white blood cells are returned to your body to control skin problems associated with cutaneous T-cell lymphoma, a cancer of the lymph system.

Methoxsalen is to be administered only by or under the supervision of your doctor or other health care professional. It is available in the following dosage form:

Extracorporeal
- Sterile solution (U.S.)

Before Using This Medicine

Methoxsalen is a very strong medicine that increases the skin's sensitivity to sunlight. In addition to causing serious sunburns, if precautions are not properly taken, it has been reported to increase the chance of skin cancer and cataracts. Too much sunlight can also cause premature aging of the skin. In deciding to use a medicine, the risks of using the medicine must be weighed against the good it will do. This is a decision you and your doctor wil make. For methoxsalen, the following should be considered:

Allergies—Tell your doctor if you have ever had any unusual or allergic reaction to psoralens. Also tell your health care professional if you are allergic to any other substances, such as foods, preservatives, or dyes.

Diet—Eating certain foods while you are receiving methoxsalen treatment may increase your skin's sensitivity to sunlight. To help prevent this, avoid eating limes, figs, parsley, parsnips, mustard, carrots, and celery while you are being treated with this medicine.

Pregnancy—It is best to avoid pregnancy during treatment with this medicine. Studies in animals have found that methoxsalen causes birth defects and death of the fetus. Be sure you have discussed this with your doctor before starting treatments with this medicine. Also, tell your doctor right away if you think you have become pregnant while receiving this medicine.

Breast-feeding—It is not known whether methoxsalen passes into breast milk. Mothers who are receiving this medicine and who wish to breast-feed should discuss this with their doctor.

Children—Studies on this medicine have been done only in adult patients, and there is no specific information comparing use of methoxsalen in children with use in other age groups.

Older adults—Many medicines have not been studied specifically in older people. Therefore, it may not be known whether they work exactly the same way they do in younger adults or if they cause different side effects or problems in older people. There is no specific information comparing use of methoxsalen in the elderly with use in other age groups.

Other medicines—Although certain medicines should not be used together at all, in other cases two different medicines may be used together even if an interaction might occur. In these cases, your medical doctor may want to change the dose, or other precautions may be necessary. When you are receiving methoxsalen, it is especially important that your health care professional know if you are taking any of the following:

- Anthralin (eg, Drithocreme) or
- Bacteriostatic soaps or
- Certain organic dyes (such as methylene blue, methyl orange, rose bengal, and toluidine blue) or
- Coal tar or medicine made from coal tar (eg, Alphosyl) or
- Griseofulvin (eg, Fulvicin-U/F) or
- Nalidixic acid (eg, NegGram) or
- Phenothiazines (acetophenazine [eg, Tindel], chlorpromazine [eg, Thorazine], fluphenazine [eg, Prolixin], mesoridazine [eg, Serentil], methotrimeprazine [eg, Nozinan], pericyazine [eg, Neuleptil], perphenazine [eg, Trilafon], pipotiazine [eg, Piportil L$_4$], prochlorperazine [eg, Compazine], promazine [eg, Primazine], thiopropazate [eg, Dartal], thioproperazine [eg, Majeptil], thioridazine [eg, Mellaril], trifluoperazine [eg, Stelazine], triflupromazine [eg, Vesprin]) or
- Sulfonamides (sulfa medicine) or
- Tetracyclines (medicine for infection) or
- Thiazide diuretics (water pills)—May increase sensitivity to light

Other medical problems—The presence of other medical problems may affect the use of methoxsalen. Make sure you tell your doctor if you have any other medical problems, especially:

- Albinism (pigment lacking in the skin, hair, and eyes, or eyes only) or
- Erythropoietic protoporphyria or
- Lupus erythematosus or
- Porphyria cutanea tarda or
- Skin cancer or
- Variegate porphyria or
- Xeroderma pigmentosum—Methoxsalen treatment may make condition worse

- Eye problems, such as cataracts or loss of the lens of the eye—Methoxsalen and light treatment may make these conditions worse or may cause damage to the eye

Precautions While Using This Medicine

Your doctor should check your progress at regular visits to make sure this treatment is working and that it does not cause unwanted effects. You also should have regular eye examinations.

This medicine increases the sensitivity of your skin to sunlight and also may cause premature aging of the skin. Therefore, *exposure to the sun, even through window glass or on a cloudy day, could cause a serious burn*. If you must go out during the daylight hours:

- *After each treatment, cover your skin with protective clothing for at least 24 hours*. In addition, use a sun block product that has a skin protection factor (SPF) of at least 15 on those areas of your body that cannot be covered. If you have any questions about this, check with your health care professional.

For 24 hours after your methoxsalen treatment, your eyes should be protected during daylight hours with special wraparound sunglasses that totally block or absorb ultraviolet light (ordinary sunglasses are not adequate). This is to prevent cataracts. Your doctor will tell you what kind of sunglasses to use. These glasses should be worn even in indirect light, such as light coming through a window, or on a cloudy day.

Side Effects of This Medicine

Along with its needed effects, a medicine may cause some unwanted effects. Although not all of these side effects may occur, if they do occur they may need medical attention.

Check with your doctor immediately if any of the following side effects occur:

Rare
    Fever; irregular heartbeat; redness or pain at catheter site

Symptoms of overdose
    Blistering and peeling of skin; reddened, sore skin

Other side effects may occur that usually do not need medical attention. These side effects may go away during treatment as your body adjusts to the medicine. However, check with your doctor if the following side effect continues or is bothersome:

    Reddening of skin, slight

Treatment with this medicine usually causes a slight reddening of your skin 24 to 48 hours after the treatment. This is an expected effect and is no cause for concern. However, check with your doctor right away if your skin becomes sore and red or blistered.

There is an increased risk of developing skin cancer after use of methoxsalen. You should check your body regularly and show your doctor any skin sores that do not heal, new skin growths, or skin growths that have changed in the way they look or feel.

Premature aging of the skin may occur as a result of prolonged methoxsalen therapy. This effect is permanent and is similar to what happens when a person sunbathes for long periods of time.

Other side effects not listed above may also occur in some patients. If you notice any other effects, check with your doctor.

Developed: 9/17/99

METHOXSALEN Systemic

Commonly used brand name(s):

In the U.S.—
  8-MOP
  Oxsoralen-Ultra

In Canada—
  Oxsoralen
  Ultra MOP
  Oxsoralen-Ultra

Description

Methoxsalen (meth-OX-a-len) belongs to the group of medicines called psoralens. It is used along with ultraviolet light (found in sunlight and some special lamps) in a treatment called PUVA to treat vitiligo, a disease in which skin color is lost, and psoriasis, a skin condition associated with red and scaly patches.

Methoxsalen is also used with ultraviolet light in the treatment of white blood cells. This treatment is called photopheresis and is used to treat the skin problems associated with mycosis fungoides, which is a type of lymphoma.

Methoxsalen may also be used for other conditions as determined by your doctor.

This medicine is available only with your doctor's prescription, in the following dosage forms:

  Oral
  • Hard gelatin capsules (U.S. and Canada)
  • Soft gelatin capsules (U.S. and Canada)

Before Using This Medicine

Methoxsalen is a very strong medicine that increases the skin's sensitivity to sunlight. In addition to causing serious sunburns if not properly used, it has been reported to increase the chance of skin cancer and cataracts. Also, like too much sunlight, PUVA can cause premature aging of the skin. Therefore, methoxsalen should be used only as directed and it should *not* be used simply for suntanning. Before using this medicine, be sure that you have discussed its use with your doctor.

In deciding to use a medicine, the risks of using the medicine must be weighed against the good it will do. This is a decision you and your doctor will make. For methoxsalen, the following should be considered:

Allergies—Tell your doctor if you have ever had any unusual or allergic reaction to methoxsalen. Also tell your health care professional if you are allergic to any other substances, such as foods, preservatives, or dyes.

Diet—Eating certain foods while you are taking methoxsalen may increase your skin's sensitivity to sunlight. To help prevent this, avoid eating limes, figs, parsley, parsnips, mustard, carrots, and celery while you are being treated with this medicine.

Pregnancy—Studies on effects in pregnancy have not been done in either humans or animals.

Breast-feeding—It is not known whether methoxsalen passes into breast milk. Although most medicines pass into breast milk in small amounts, many of them may be used safely while breast-feeding. Mothers who are using this medicine and who wish to breast-feed should discuss this with their doctor.

Children—Some of the side effects are more likely to occur in children up to 12 years of age, since these children may be more sensitive to the effects of methoxsalen.

Older adults—Many medicines have not been studied specifically in older people. Therefore, it may not be known whether they work exactly the same way they do in younger adults or if they cause different side effects or problems in older people. There is no specific information comparing use of methoxsalen in the elderly with use in other age groups.

Other medicines—Although certain medicines should not be used together at all, in other cases two different medicines may be used together even if an interaction might occur. In these cases, your doctor may want to change the dose, or other precautions may be necessary. When you are using methoxsalen, it is especially important that your health care professional know if you are using the following:

  • Arsenicals or recent treatment with x-rays, or cancer medicines or plans to have x-rays in the near future— Arsenicals, x-rays and cancer medicines increase the chance of side effects from treatment with PUVA

Other medical problems—The presence of other medical problems may affect the use of methoxsalen. Make sure you tell your doctor if you have any other medical problems, especially:

  • Allergy to sunlight (or family history of) or
  • Infection or
  • Lupus erythematosus or
  • Porphyria or
  • Skin cancer (history of) or
  • Skin conditions (other) or
  • Stomach problems—Use of PUVA may make the condition worse
  • Eye problems, such as cataracts or loss of the lens of the eye—The light treatment may make the condition worse or may cause damage to the eye
  • Heart or blood vessel disease (severe)—The heat or prolonged standing associated with each light treatment may make the condition worse
  • Liver disease—Condition may cause increased blood levels of the medicine and cause an increase in side effects

Proper Use of This Medicine

Methoxsalen usually comes with patient directions. Read them carefully before using this medicine.

This medicine may take 6 to 8 weeks to really help your condition. *Do not increase the amount of methoxsalen you are taking or spend extra time in the sunlight or under an ultraviolet lamp.* This will not make the medicine act any more quickly and may result in a serious burn.

If this medicine upsets your stomach:

  • Patients taking the hard gelatin capsules may take them with food or milk.
  • Patients taking the soft gelatin capsules may take them with low-fat food or low-fat milk.

Dosing—The dose of methoxsalen will be different for different patients. *Follow your doctor's orders or the directions on the label.* The following information includes only the average doses of methoxsalen. *If your dose is different, do not change it* unless your doctor tells you to do so.

The number of capsules that you take depends on the strength of the medicine. Also, *the number of doses you take each day, the time allowed between doses, and the length of time you take the medicine depend on the medical problem for which you are taking methoxsalen.*

- For *oral* dosage form (hard gelatin capsule):
  - —For treating mycosis fungoides and psoriasis:
    - Adults and children 12 years of age and over—Dose is based on body weight and must be determined by your doctor. However, the usual dose is 0.6 mg per kilogram (kg) (0.27 mg per pound) of body weight taken two hours before UVA exposure. This treatment (methoxsalen and UVA) is given two or three times a week with the treatment spaced at least forty-eight hours apart.
    - Children up to 12 years of age—Dose must be determined by your doctor.
  - —For vitiligo:
    - Adults and children 12 years of age and over—20 milligrams (mg) per day taken two to four hours before ultraviolet light A (UVA) exposure. This treatment (methoxsalen and UVA) is given two or three times a week with the treatment spaced at least forty-eight hours apart.
    - Children up to 12 years of age—Dose must be determined by your doctor.
- For *oral* dosage form (soft gelatin capsule):
  - —For psoriasis:
    - Adults and children 12 years of age and over—Dose is based on body weight and must be determined by your doctor. The usual dose is 0.4 mg per kg (0.18 mg per pound) of body weight taken one and one-half to two hours before UVA exposure. This treatment (methoxsalen and UVA) is given two or three times a week, with the treatment spaced at least forty-eight hours apart.
    - Children up to 12 years of age—Dose must be determined by your doctor.

Missed dose—If you are late in taking, or miss taking, a dose of this medicine, notify your doctor so your light treatment can be rescheduled. Remember that exposure to sunlight or ultraviolet light must take place a certain number of hours *after* you take the medicine or it will not work. For patients taking the hard gelatin capsules, this is 2 to 4 hours. For patients taking the soft gelatin capsules, this is 1½ to 2 hours. If you have any questions about this, check with your doctor.

Storage—To store this medicine:
- Keep out of the reach of children.
- Store away from heat and direct light.
- Do not store in the bathroom, near the kitchen sink, or in other damp places. Heat or moisture may cause the medicine to break down.
- Do not keep outdated medicine or medicine no longer needed. Be sure that any discarded medicine is out of the reach of children.

Precautions While Using This Medicine

Your doctor should check your progress at regular visits to make sure this medicine is working and that it does not cause unwanted effects. Eye examinations should be included.

This medicine increases the sensitivity of your skin and lips to sunlight. Therefore, *exposure to the sun, even through window glass or on a cloudy day, could cause a serious burn.* If you must go out during the daylight hours:
- *Before each treatment, cover your skin for at least 24 hours* by wearing protective clothing, such as long-

sleeved shirts, full-length slacks, wide-brimmed hat, and gloves. In addition, *protect your lips with a special sun block lipstick that has a skin protection factor (SPF) of at least 15.* Check with your doctor before using sun block products on other parts of your body before a treatment, since sun block products should not be used on the areas of your skin that are to be treated.
- *After each treatment, cover your skin for at least 8 hours* by wearing protective clothing. In addition, use a sun block product that has a skin protection factor (SPF) of at least 15 on your lips and on those areas of your body that cannot be covered.

If you have any questions about this, check with your health care professional.

Your skin may continue to be sensitive to sunlight for some time after treatment with this medicine. Use extra caution for at least 48 hours following each treatment if you plan to spend any time in the sun. In addition, do not sunbathe anytime during your course of treatment with methoxsalen.

For 24 hours after you take each dose of methoxsalen, your eyes should be protected during daylight hours with special wraparound sunglasses that totally block or absorb ultraviolet light (ordinary sunglasses are not adequate). This is to prevent cataracts. Your doctor will tell you what kind of sunglasses to use. These glasses should be worn even in indirect light, such as light coming through window glass or on a cloudy day.

This medicine may cause your skin to become dry or itchy. *However, check with your doctor before applying anything to your skin to treat this problem.*

Side Effects of This Medicine

Along with its needed effects, a medicine may cause some unwanted effects. Although not all of these side effects may occur, if they do occur they may need medical attention.

Check with your doctor immediately if you think you have taken an overdose or if any of the following side effects occur, since they may indicate a serious burn:

Blistering and peeling of skin; reddened, sore skin; swelling (especially of feet or lower legs)

Other side effects may occur that usually do not need medical attention. These side effects may go away during treatment as your body adjusts to the medicine. However, check with your doctor if any of the following side effects continue for more than 48 hours or are bothersome:

More common
Itching of skin; nausea

Less common
Dizziness; headache; mental depression; nervousness; trouble in sleeping

Treatment with this medicine usually causes a slight reddening of your skin 24 to 48 hours after the treatment. This is an expected effect and is no cause for concern. However, check with your doctor right away if your skin becomes sore and red or blistered.

There is an increased risk of developing skin cancer after use of methoxsalen. You should check your body regularly and show your doctor any skin sores that do not heal, new skin growths, and skin growths that have changed in the way they look or feel.

Premature aging of the skin may occur as a result of prolonged methoxsalen therapy. This effect is permanent and is similar to what happens when a person sunbathes for long periods of time.

Other side effects not listed above may also occur in some patients. If you notice any other effects, check with your doctor.

Additional Information

Once a medicine has been approved for marketing for a certain use, experience may show that it is also useful for other medical problems. Although these uses are not included in the product labeling, methoxsalen is used in certain patients with the following medical conditions:

- Alopecia areata
- Atopic dermatitis
- Eczema
- Lichen planus
- Skin that is abnormally sensitive to sunlight

Other than the above information, there is no additional information relating to proper use, precautions, or side effects for these uses.

Revised: 06/24/94
Interim revision: 07/08/98

METHOXSALEN   Topical

Commonly used brand name(s):

In the U.S.—
Oxsoralen Lotion

In Canada—
Oxsoralen Lotion
UltraMOP Lotion

Description

Methoxsalen (meth-OX-a-len) belongs to the group of medicines called psoralens. It is used along with ultraviolet light (found in sunlight and some special lamps) in a treatment called psoralen plus ultraviolet light A (PUVA) to treat vitiligo, a disease in which skin color is lost. Methoxsalen may also be used for other conditions as determined by your doctor.

Methoxsalen is available only with a prescription and is to be administered by or under the direct supervision of your doctor, in the following dosage form:

Topical
- Topical solution (U.S. and Canada)

Before Using This Medicine

Methoxsalen is a very strong medicine that increases the skin's sensitivity to sunlight. In addition to causing serious sunburns if not properly used, it has been reported to increase the chance of skin cancer. Also, like too much sunlight, PUVA can cause premature aging of the skin. Therefore, methoxsalen should be used only as directed and should *not* be used simply for suntanning. Before using this medicine, be sure that you have discussed its use with your doctor.

In deciding to use a medicine, the risks of using the medicine must be weighed against the good it will do. This is a decision you and your doctor will make. For topical methoxsalen, the following should be considered:

Allergies—Tell your doctor if you have ever had any unusual or allergic reaction to methoxsalen. Also tell your health care professional if you are allergic to any other substances, such as foods, preservatives, or dyes.

Diet—Eating certain foods while you are using methoxsalen may increase your skin's sensitivity to sunlight. To help prevent this, avoid eating limes, figs, parsley, parsnips, mustard, carrots, and celery while you are being treated with this medicine.

Pregnancy—Studies on effects in pregnancy have not been done in either humans or animals.

Breast-feeding—It is not known whether methoxsalen passes into breast milk. Although most medicines pass into breast milk in small amounts, many of them may be used safely while breast-feeding. Mothers who are taking this medicine and who wish to breast-feed should discuss this with their doctor.

Children—Studies on this medicine have been done only in adult patients, and there is no specific information comparing use of methoxsalen in children up to 12 years of age with use in other age groups.

Older adults—Many medicines have not been studied specifically in older people. Therefore, it may not be known whether they work exactly the same way they do in younger adults or if they cause different side effects or problems in older people. There is no specific information comparing use of topical methoxsalen in the elderly with use in other age groups.

Other medicines—Although certain medicines should not be used together at all, in other cases two different medicines may be used together even if an interaction might occur. In these cases, your doctor may want to change the dose, or other precautions may be necessary. When you are using topical methoxsalen, it is especially important that your health care professional know if you are receiving the following:

- Recent treatment with x-rays or cancer medicines or plans to have x-rays in the near future—Increases the chance of side effects from treatment with PUVA

Other medical problems—The presence of other medical problems may affect the use of topical methoxsalen. Make sure you tell your doctor if you have any other medical problems, especially:

- Allergy to sunlight (or family history of) or
- Infection or
- Lupus erythematosus or
- Porphyria or
- Skin cancer (history of) or
- Skin conditions (other)—Use of PUVA may make the condition worse

- Heart or blood vessel disease (severe)—The heat or prolonged standing associated with each light treatment may make the condition worse

Proper Use of This Medicine

Use this medicine only under the direct supervision of your doctor.

After UVA exposure, wash the treated area of skin with soap and water. Then use a sunscreen or wear protective clothing to protect the area.

Dosing—Follow your doctor's directions in using this medicine. The following information includes only the average

doses of methoxsalen. *If your dose is different, do not change it* unless your doctor tells you to do so.
- For *topical solution* dosage form:
  —For vitiligo:
    - Adults and children 12 years of age and over—Apply to the affected area of the skin and allow to dry for one to two minutes, then apply again within two to two and one-half hours before UVA exposure.
    - Children under 12 years of age—Use and dose must be determined by your doctor.

Precautions While Using This Medicine

It is important that you visit your doctor as directed for treatments and to have your progress checked.

This medicine increases the sensitivity of the treated areas of your skin to sunlight. Therefore, *exposure to the sun, even through window glass or on a cloudy day, could cause a serious burn.* After each light treatment, thoroughly wash the treated areas of your skin. Also, if you must go out during daylight hours, cover the treated areas of your skin for at least 12 to 48 hours following treatment by wearing protective clothing or a sun block product that has a skin protection factor (SPF) of at least 15. Some patients may require a product with a higher SPF number, especially if they have a fair complexion. If you have any questions about this, check with your health care professional.

The treated areas of your skin may continue to be sensitive to sunlight for some time after treatment with this medicine. Use extra caution for at least 72 hours following each treatment if you plan to spend any time in the sun. In addition, do not sunbathe anytime during your course of treatment with methoxsalen.

This medicine may cause your skin to become dry or itchy. *However, check with your doctor before applying anything to your skin to treat this problem.*

Side Effects of This Medicine

Along with its needed effects, a medicine may cause some unwanted effects. Although not all of these side effects may occur, if they do occur they may need medical attention.

Check with your doctor immediately if any of the following side effects occur, since they may indicate a serious burn:
   Blistering and peeling of skin; reddened, sore skin; swelling, especially of the feet or lower legs

There is an increased risk of developing skin cancer after use of methoxsalen. You should check the treated areas of your body regularly and show your doctor any skin sores that do not heal, new skin growths, and skin growths that have changed in the way they look or feel.

Premature aging of the skin may occur as a result of prolonged methoxsalen therapy. This effect is permanent and is similar to the result of sunbathing for long periods of time.

Other side effects not listed above may also occur in some patients. If you notice any other effects, check with your doctor.

Additional Information

Once a medicine has been approved for marketing for a certain use, experience may show that it is also useful for other medical problems. Although these uses are not included in product labeling, topical methoxsalen is used in certain patients with the following medical conditions:
- Alopecia areata
- Eczema
- Inflammatory dermatoses
- Lichen planus
- Mycosis fungoides
- Need to increase tolerance of skin to sunlight
- Psoriasis

Other than the above information, there is no additional information relating to proper use, precautions, or side effects for these uses.

Revised: 05/26/94

METHYLDOPA   Systemic

Commonly used brand name(s):

In the U.S.—
   Aldomet
   Generic name product may be available.

In Canada—
   Aldomet   Dopamet
   Apo-Methyldopa   Novomedopa
   Nu-Medopa

Description

Methyldopa (meth-ill-DOE-pa) belongs to the general class of medicines called antihypertensives. It is used to treat high blood pressure (hypertension).

High blood pressure adds to the work load of the heart and arteries. If it continues for a long time, the heart and arteries may not function properly. This can damage the blood vessels of the brain, heart, and kidneys, resulting in a stroke, heart failure, or kidney failure. High blood pressure may also increase the risk of heart attacks. These problems may be less likely to occur if blood pressure is controlled.

Methyldopa works by controlling impulses along certain nerve pathways. As a result, it relaxes blood vessels so that blood passes through them more easily. This helps to lower blood pressure.

Methyldopa is available only with your doctor's prescription, in the following dosage forms:

Oral
- Oral suspension (U.S.)
- Tablets (U.S. and Canada)

Parenteral
- Injection (U.S. and Canada)

Before Using This Medicine

In deciding to use a medicine, the risks of taking the medicine must be weighed against the good it will do. This is a decision you and your doctor will make. For methyldopa, the following should be considered:

Allergies—Tell your doctor if you have ever had any unusual or allergic reaction to methyldopa. Also tell your health care professional if you are allergic to any other substances, such as foods, sulfites or other preservatives, or dyes. Some methyldopa products may contain sulfites. Your health care professional can help you avoid products that may cause a problem.

Pregnancy—Methyldopa has not been studied in pregnant women in the first and second trimesters (the first 6 months of pregnancy). However, studies in pregnant women during the third trimester (the last 3 months of pregnancy) have not shown that methyldopa causes birth defects or other problems.

Breast-feeding—Although methyldopa passes into breast milk, it has not been reported to cause problems in nursing babies.

Children—Although there is no specific information comparing use of methyldopa in children with use in other age groups, this medicine is not expected to cause different side effects or problems in children than it does in adults.

Older adults—Dizziness or lightheadedness and drowsiness may be more likely to occur in the elderly, who are more sensitive to the effects of methyldopa.

Other medicines—Although certain medicines should not be used together at all, in other cases two different medicines may be used together even if an interaction might occur. In these cases, your doctor may want to change the dose, or other precautions may be necessary. When you are taking methyldopa, it is especially important that your health care professional know if you are taking any of the following:

- Monoamine oxidase (MAO) inhibitors (furazolidone [e.g., Furoxone], isocarboxazid [e.g., Marplan], phenelzine [e.g., Nardil], procarbazine [e.g., Matulane], selegiline [e.g., Eldepryl], tranylcypromine [e.g., Parnate])—Taking methyldopa while you are taking or within 2 weeks of taking MAO inhibitors may cause nervousness in patients receiving MAO inhibitors; headache, severe high blood pressure, and hallucinations have been reported

Other medical problems—The presence of other medical problems may affect the use of methyldopa. Make sure you tell your doctor if you have any other medical problems, especially:

- Angina (chest pain) or
- Parkinson's disease—Methyldopa may make these conditions worse
- Kidney disease or
- Liver disease—Effects of methyldopa may be increased because of slower removal from the body
- Mental depression (history of)—Methyldopa can cause mental depression
- Pheochromocytoma—Methyldopa may interfere with tests for the condition; in addition, there have been reports of increased blood pressure
- If you have taken methyldopa in the past and developed liver problems

Proper Use of This Medicine

In addition to the use of the medicine your doctor has prescribed, treatment for your high blood pressure may include weight control and care in the types of foods you eat, especially foods high in sodium. Your doctor will tell you which of these are most important for you. You should check with your doctor before changing your diet.

Many patients who have high blood pressure will not notice any signs of the problem. In fact, many may feel normal. It is very important that you *take your medicine exactly as directed* and that you keep your appointments with your doctor even if you feel well.

Remember that methyldopa will not cure your high blood pressure but it does help control it. Therefore, you must continue to take it as directed if you expect to lower your blood pressure and keep it down. *You may have to take high blood pressure medicine for the rest of your life*. If high blood pressure is not treated, it can cause serious problems such as heart failure, blood vessel disease, stroke, or kidney disease.

To help you remember to take your medicine, try to get into the habit of taking it at the same time each day.

Dosing—The dose of methyldopa will be different for different patients. *Follow your doctor's orders or the directions on the label*. The following information includes only the average doses of methyldopa. *If your dose is different, do not change it* unless your doctor tells you to do so.

The number of tablets or teaspoonfuls of suspension that you take depends on the strength of the medicine.

- For *oral* dosage form (suspension or tablets):
  —For high blood pressure:
    - Adults—250 milligrams (mg) to 2 grams a day. This is divided into two to four doses.
    - Children—Dose is based on body weight or size and must be determined by your doctor. The usual dose is 10 mg per kilogram (kg) (4.5 mg per pound) of body weight a day. This is divided into two to four doses. Your doctor may increase the dose as needed.
- For *injection* dosage form:
  —For high blood pressure:
    - Adults—250 to 500 mg mixed in 100 milliliters (mL) of solution (5% dextrose) and slowly injected into a vein every six hours as needed.
    - Children—Dose is based on body weight and must be determined by your doctor. The usual dose is 20 to 40 mg per kg (9.1 to 18.2 mg per pound) of body weight. This is mixed in a solution (5% dextrose) and slowly injected into a vein every six hours as needed.

Missed dose—If you miss a dose of this medicine, take it as soon as possible. However, if it is almost time for your next dose, skip the missed dose and go back to your regular dosing schedule. Do not double doses.

Storage—To store this medicine:

- Keep out of the reach of children.
- Store away from heat and direct light.
- Do not store in the bathroom, near the kitchen sink, or in other damp places. Heat or moisture may cause the medicine to break down.
- Keep the oral liquid form of this medicine from freezing.
- Do not keep outdated medicine or medicine no longer needed. Be sure that any discarded medicine is out of the reach of children.

Precautions While Using This Medicine

It is important that your doctor check your progress at regular visits to make sure that this medicine is working properly.

Do not take other medicines unless they have been discussed with your doctor. This especially includes over-the-counter (nonprescription) medicines for appetite control, asthma, colds, cough, hay fever, or sinus problems, since they may tend to increase your blood pressure.

If you have a fever and there seems to be no reason for it, check with your doctor. This is especially important during the first few weeks you take methyldopa, since fever may be a sign of a serious reaction to this medicine.

Before having any kind of surgery (including dental surgery) or emergency treatment, make sure the medical doctor or dentist in charge knows that you are taking this medicine.

Methyldopa may cause some people to become drowsy or less alert than they are normally. This is more likely to happen when you begin to take it or when you increase the amount of medicine you are taking. *Make sure you know how you react to this medicine before you drive, use machines, or do anything else that could be dangerous if you are not alert.*

Dizziness, lightheadedness, or fainting may occur, especially when you get up from a lying or sitting position. Getting up slowly may help, but if the problem continues or gets worse, check with your doctor.

Methyldopa may cause dryness of the mouth. For temporary relief, use sugarless candy or gum, melt bits of ice in your mouth, or use a saliva substitute. However, if your mouth continues to feel dry for more than 2 weeks, check with your medical doctor or dentist. Continuing dryness of the mouth may increase the chance of dental disease, including tooth decay, gum disease, and fungus infections.

Tell the doctor in charge that you are taking this medicine before you have any medical tests. The results of some tests may be affected by this medicine.

Side Effects of This Medicine

Along with its needed effects, a medicine may cause some unwanted effects. Although not all of these side effects may occur, if they do occur they may need medical attention.

Check with your doctor immediately if the following side effect occurs:
> *Less common*
>> Fever, shortly after starting to take this medicine

Check with your doctor as soon as possible if any of the following side effects occur:
> *More common*
>> Swelling of feet or lower legs
> *Less common*
>> Mental depression or anxiety; nightmares or unusually vivid dreams
> *Rare*
>> Dark or amber urine; diarrhea or stomach cramps (severe or continuing); fever, chills, troubled breathing, and fast heartbeat; general feeling of discomfort or illness or weakness; joint pain; pale stools; skin rash or itching; stomach pain (severe) with nausea and vomiting; tiredness or weakness after having taken this medicine for several weeks (continuing); yellow eyes or skin

Other side effects may occur that usually do not need medical attention. These side effects may go away during treatment as your body adjusts to the medicine. However, check with your doctor if any of the following side effects continue or are bothersome:
> *More common*
>> Drowsiness; dryness of mouth; headache

> *Less common*
>> Decreased sexual ability or interest in sex; diarrhea; dizziness or lightheadedness when getting up from a lying or sitting position; nausea or vomiting; numbness, tingling, pain, or weakness in hands or feet; slow heartbeat; stuffy nose; swelling of breasts or unusual milk production

Other side effects not listed above may also occur in some patients. If you notice any other effects, check with your doctor.

Revised: 07/22/96

METHYLDOPA AND THIAZIDE DIURETICS   Systemic

Commonly used brand name(s):

In the U.S.—
Aldoclor[1]
Aldoril[2]

In Canada—
Aldoril[2]
PMS Dopazide[2]
Supres[1]

Note: For quick reference, the following medicines are numbered to match the corresponding brand names.

This information applies to the following medicines:
1. Methyldopa and Chlorothiazide (meth-il-DOE-pa and klor-oh-THYE-a-zide) ‡
2. Methyldopa and Hydrochlorothiazide (meth-il-DOE-pa and hye-droe-klor-oh-THYE-a-zide) ‡

‡Generic name product may be available in the U.S.

Description

Combinations of methyldopa and a thiazide diuretic (chlorothiazide or hydrochlorothiazide) are used to treat high blood pressure (hypertension).

High blood pressure adds to the workload of the heart and arteries. If it continues for a long time, the heart and arteries may not function properly. This can damage the blood vessels of the brain, heart, and kidneys, resulting in a stroke, heart failure, or kidney failure. High blood pressure may also increase the risk of heart attacks. These problems may be less likely to occur if blood pressure is controlled.

Methyldopa works by controlling nerve impulses along certain nerve pathways. As a result, it relaxes blood vessels so that blood passes through them more easily. Thiazide diuretics help reduce the amount of water in the body by increasing the flow of urine. These actions help to lower blood pressure.

This medicine is available only with your doctor's prescription, in the following dosage forms:
> *Oral*
>> Methyldopa and Chlorothiazide
>> • Tablets (U.S. and Canada)
>> Methyldopa and Hydrochlorothiazide
>> • Tablets (U.S. and Canada)

Before Using This Medicine

In deciding to use a medicine, the risks of taking the medicine must be weighed against the good it will do. This is a decision

you and your doctor will make. For methyldopa and thiazide diuretics, the following should be considered:

Allergies—Tell your doctor if you have ever had any unusual or allergic reaction to methyldopa, sulfonamides (sulfa drugs), bumetanide, furosemide, indapamide, acetazolamide, dichlorphenamide, methazolamide, or thiazide diuretics (water pills). Also tell your health care professional if you are allergic to any other substances, such as foods, sulfites or other preservatives, or dyes.

Pregnancy—Studies in humans have not shown that methyldopa causes birth defects or other problems. However, when thiazide diuretics are used during pregnancy, they may cause side effects including jaundice, blood problems, and low potassium in the newborn infant. Thiazide diuretics have not been shown to cause birth defects.

Breast-feeding—This medicine passes into breast milk. Thiazide diuretics may decrease the flow of breast milk. Therefore, you should avoid use of thiazide diuretics during the first month of breast-feeding.

Children—Although there is no specific information comparing use of this medicine in children with use in other age groups, it is not expected to cause different side effects or problems in children than it does in adults.

Older adults—Dizziness or light-headedness, drowsiness, or signs of too much potassium loss may be more likely to occur in the elderly, who are more sensitive to the effects of methyldopa and thiazide diuretics.

Other medicines—Although certain medicines should not be used together at all, in other cases two different medicines may be used together even if an interaction might occur. In these cases, your doctor may want to change the dose, or other precautions may be necessary. When you are taking methyldopa and thiazide diuretics, it is especially important that your health care professional know if you are taking any of the following:

- Digitalis glycosides (heart medicine)—Thiazide diuretics may cause low potassium in the blood, which can lead to symptoms of digitalis toxicity

- Lithium (e.g., Lithane)—Risk of lithium overdose, even at usual doses, may be increased

- Monoamine oxidase (MAO) inhibitors (furazolidone [e.g., Furoxone], isocarboxazid [e.g., Marplan], phenelzine [e.g., Nardil], procarbazine [e.g., Matulane], selegiline [e.g., Eldepryl], tranylcypromine [e.g., Parnate])—Taking methyldopa while you are taking or within 2 weeks of taking MAO inhibitors may cause nervousness; headache, severe high blood pressure, and hallucinations have been reported

Other medical problems—The presence of other medical problems may affect the use of methyldopa and thiazide diuretics. Make sure you tell your doctor if you have any other medical problems, especially:

- Angina (chest pain)—Methyldopa may worsen the condition

- Diabetes mellitus (sugar diabetes)—Thiazide diuretics may change the amount of diabetes medicine needed

- Gout (history of)—Thiazide diuretics may increase the amount of uric acid in the blood, which can lead to gout

- High cholesterol—Thiazide diuretics may raise cholesterol levels

- Kidney disease—Effects of methyldopa and thiazide diuretics may be increased because of slower removal from the body. If severe, thiazide diuretics may not work

- Liver disease—Effects of methyldopa may be increased because of slower removal from the body. If thiazide diuretics cause loss of too much water from the body, liver disease can become much worse

- Lupus erythematosus (history of)—Thiazide diuretics may worsen the condition

- Mental depression (history of)—Methyldopa can cause mental depression

- Pancreatitis (inflammation of the pancreas)

- Parkinson's disease—Methyldopa may worsen the condition

- Pheochromocytoma—Methyldopa may interfere with tests for the condition; in addition, there have been reports of increased blood pressure

- If you have taken methyldopa in the past and developed liver problems

Proper Use of This Medicine

In addition to the use of the medicine your doctor has prescribed, appropriate treatment for your high blood pressure may include weight control and care in the types of foods you eat, especially foods high in sodium. Your doctor will tell you which factors are most important for you. You should check with your doctor before changing your diet.

Many patients who have high blood pressure will not notice any signs of the problem. In fact, many may feel normal. It is very important *that you take your medicine exactly as directed* and that you keep your appointments with your doctor even if you feel well.

Remember that this medicine will not cure your high blood pressure but it does help control it. Therefore, you must continue to take it as directed if you expect to lower your blood pressure and keep it down. *You may have to take high blood pressure medicine for the rest of your life*. If high blood pressure is not treated, it can cause serious problems such as heart failure, blood vessel disease, stroke, or kidney disease.

This medicine may cause you to have an unusual feeling of tiredness when you begin to take it. You may also notice an increase in the amount of urine or in your frequency of urination. After taking the medicine for a while, these effects should lessen. In general, to keep the increase in urine from affecting your sleep:

- If you are to take a single dose a day, take it in the morning after breakfast.
- If you are to take more than one dose a day, take the last dose no later than 6 p.m., unless otherwise directed by your doctor.

However, it is best to plan your dose or doses according to a schedule that will least affect your personal activities and sleep. Ask your health care professional to help you plan the best time to take this medicine.

To help you remember to take your medicine, try to get into the habit of taking it at the same time each day.

Dosing—The dose of methyldopa and thiazide diuretic combinations will be different for different patients. *Follow your doctor's orders or the directions on the label*. The following information includes only the average doses of methyldopa and thiazide diuretic combinations. *If your dose is different, do not change it* unless your doctor tells you to do so:

For methyldopa and chlorothiazide
- For *oral* dosage form (tablets):
  - —Adults: Two to four tablets a day, taken as a single dose or in divided doses.
  - —Children: Dose must be determined by your doctor.

For methyldopa and hydrochlorothiazide
- For *oral* dosage form (tablets):
  - —Adults: Two to four tablets a day, taken as a single dose or in divided doses.
  - —Children: Dose must be determined by your doctor.

Missed dose—If you miss a dose of this medicine, take it as soon as possible. However, if it is almost time for your next dose, skip the missed dose and go back to your regular dosing schedule. Do not double doses.

Storage—To store this medicine:
- Keep out of the reach of children.
- Store away from heat and direct light.
- Do not store in the bathroom, near the kitchen sink, or in other damp places. Heat or moisture may cause the medicine to break down.
- Do not keep outdated medicine or medicine no longer needed. Be sure that any discarded medicine is out of the reach of children.

Precautions While Using This Medicine

It is important that your doctor check your progress at regular visits to make sure that this medicine is working properly.

Do not take other medicines unless they have been discussed with your doctor. This especially includes over-the-counter (nonprescription) medicines for appetite control, asthma, colds, cough, hay fever, or sinus problems, since they may tend to increase your blood pressure.

This medicine may cause a loss of potassium from your body:
- To help prevent this, your doctor may want you to:
  - —eat or drink foods that have a high potassium content (for example, orange or other citrus fruit juices), or
  - —take a potassium supplement, or
  - —take another medicine to help prevent the loss of the potassium in the first place.
- It is very important to follow these directions. Also, it is important not to change your diet on your own. This is more important if you are already on a special diet (as for diabetes), or if you are taking a potassium supplement or a medicine to reduce potassium loss. Extra potassium may not be necessary and, in some cases, too much potassium could be harmful.

Check with your doctor if you become sick and have severe or continuing vomiting or diarrhea. These problems may cause you to lose additional water and potassium.

Before having any kind of surgery (including dental surgery) or emergency treatment, tell the medical doctor or dentist in charge that you are taking this medicine.

If you have a fever and there seems to be no reason for it, check with your doctor. This is especially important during the first few weeks you take this medicine since fever may be a sign of a serious reaction to methyldopa.

This medicine may cause some people to become drowsy or less alert than they are normally. This is more likely to happen when you begin to take it or when you increase the amount of medicine you are taking. *Make sure you know how you react to this medicine before you drive, use machines, or do anything else that could be dangerous if you are not alert.*

Dizziness, light-headedness, or fainting may occur, especially when you get up from a lying or sitting position. Getting up slowly may help, but if the problem continues or gets worse, check with your doctor.

The dizziness, light-headedness, or fainting is also more likely to occur if you drink alcohol, stand for long periods of time, exercise, or if the weather is hot. Drinking alcoholic beverages may also make the drowsiness worse. *While you are taking this medicine, be careful in the amount of alcohol you drink.* Also, use extra care during exercise or hot weather or if you must stand for long periods of time.

For *diabetic patients:*
- This medicine may raise blood sugar levels. While you are using this medicine, be especially careful in testing for sugar in your urine. If you have any questions about this, check with your doctor.

This medicine may cause dryness of the mouth. For temporary relief, use sugarless candy or gum, melt bits of ice in your mouth, or use a saliva substitute. However, if your mouth continues to feel dry for more than 2 weeks, check with your medical doctor or dentist. Continuing dryness of the mouth may increase the chance of dental disease, including tooth decay, gum disease, and fungus infections.

Thiazide diuretics may cause your skin to be more sensitive to sunlight than it is normally. Exposure to sunlight, even for brief periods of time, may cause a skin rash, itching, redness or other discoloration of the skin, or a severe sunburn. When you begin taking this medicine:
- Stay out of direct sunlight, especially between the hours of 10:00 a.m. and 3:00 p.m., if possible.
- Wear protective clothing, including a hat. Also, wear sunglasses.
- Apply a sun block product that has a skin protection factor (SPF) of at least 15. Some patients may require a product with a higher SPF number, especially if they have a fair complexion. If you have any questions about this, check with your health care professional.
- Apply a sun block lipstick that has an SPF of at least 15 to protect your lips.
- Do not use a sunlamp or tanning bed or booth.

If you have a severe reaction from the sun, check with your doctor.

Before you have any medical tests, tell the doctor in charge that you are taking this medicine. The results of some tests may be affected by this medicine.

Side Effects of This Medicine

Along with its needed effects, a medicine may cause some unwanted effects. Although not all of these side effects may occur, if they do occur they may need medical attention.

Check with your doctor immediately if the following side effect occurs:
  Rare
    Unexplained fever shortly after starting to take this medicine

Check with your doctor as soon as possible if any of the following side effects occur, especially since some of them may mean that your body is losing too much potassium:
> *Signs and symptoms of too much potassium loss*
>> Dry mouth; increased thirst; irregular heartbeats; muscle cramps or pain; nausea or vomiting; unusual tiredness or weakness; weak pulse

> *Less common*
>> Mental depression or anxiety; nightmares or unusually vivid dreams

> *Rare*
>> Cough or hoarseness; dark or amber urine; diarrhea or stomach cramps (severe or continuing); fever, chills, troubled breathing, and fast heartbeat; general feeling of discomfort or illness or weakness; joint pain; lower back or side pain; painful or difficult urination; pale stools; skin rash, hives, or itching; stomach pain (severe) with nausea and vomiting; tiredness or weakness after having taken this medicine for several weeks (continuing); yellow eyes or skin

Other side effects may occur that usually do not need medical attention. These side effects may go away during treatment as your body adjusts to the medicine. However, check with your doctor if any of the following side effects continue or are bothersome:
> *More common*
>> Dizziness or light-headedness when getting up from a lying or sitting position; drowsiness; dryness of mouth; headache

> *Less common*
>> Decreased sexual ability or interest in sex; diarrhea; increased sensitivity of skin to sunlight (skin rash, itching, redness or other discoloration of skin or severe sunburn after exposure to sunlight); loss of appetite; numbness, tingling, pain, or weakness in hands or feet; slow heartbeat; stuffy nose; swelling of breasts or unusual milk production

Other side effects not listed above may also occur in some patients. If you notice any other effects, check with your doctor.

Revised: 08/28/2000

METHYLENE BLUE   Systemic

Commonly used brand name(s):

In the U.S.—
> Urolene Blue
> Generic name product may be available.

Other commonly used names are aniline violet, methylthionine chloride, and tetramethylthionine chloride.

Description

Methylene (METH-i-leen) blue is used to treat a condition called methemoglobinemia. This condition occurs when the blood cannot deliver oxygen where it is needed in the body. Methylene blue is also used as a dye to stain certain parts of the body before or during surgery.

Oral
> • Tablets (U.S.)
Parenteral
> • Injection (U.S. and Canada)

Before Using This Medicine

In deciding to use a medicine, the risks of taking the medicine must be weighed against the good it will do. This is a decision you and your doctor will make. For methylene blue, the following should be considered:

Allergies—Tell your doctor if you have ever had any unusual or allergic reaction to methylene blue. Also tell your health care professional if you are allergic to any other substances, such as foods, preservatives, or dyes.

Pregnancy—Studies on effects in pregnancy have not been done in either humans or animals.

Breast-feeding—It is not known whether methylene blue passes into breast milk. Although most medicines pass into breast milk in small amounts, many of them may be used safely while breast-feeding. Mothers who are taking this medicine and who wish to breast-feed should discuss this with their doctor.

Children—Babies are especially sensitive to the effects of methylene blue. This may increase the chance of side effects during treatment.

Older adults—Many medicines have not been studied specifically in older people. Therefore, it may not be known whether they work exactly the same way they do in younger adults. Although there is no specific information comparing the use of methylene blue in the elderly with use in other age groups, this medicine is not expected to cause different side effects or problems in older people than it does in younger adults.

Other medicines—Although certain medicines should not be used together at all, in other cases two different medicines may be used together even if an interaction might occur. In these cases, your doctor may want to change the dose, or other precautions may be necessary. Tell your health care professional if you are taking any other prescription or nonprescription (over-the-counter [OTC]) medicine.

Other medical problems—The presence of other medical problems may affect the use of methylene blue. Make sure you tell your doctor if you have any other medical problems, especially:
> • Glucose-6-phosphate dehydrogenase (G6PD) deficiency—Methylene blue may cause anemia or make methemoglobinemia worse
> • Kidney disease—In patients with kidney disease methylene blue may accumulate in the body; smaller doses of this medicine may be needed
> • Methemoglobinemia to treat cyanide toxicity—Methylene blue may make cyanide toxicity worse by increasing the amount of cyanide in the blood

Proper Use of This Medicine

For patients taking the *tablet* form of this medicine:
> • Take tablets after meals with a full glass (8 ounces) of water.

Take this medicine only as directed. Do not take more of it and do not take it more often than recommended on the label unless directed by your doctor. To do so may increase the chance of side effects.

Dosing—The dose of methylene blue will be different for different patients. *Follow your doctor's orders or the directions on the label.* The following information includes only the average doses of methylene blue. *If your dose is different, do not change it* unless your doctor tells you to do so.

- For *oral* dosage form (tablets):
  —For methemoglobinemia:
  - Adults and children—100 to 300 milligrams (mg) a day.
- For *injection* dosage form:
  —For methemoglobinemia:
  - Adults and children—Dose is based on body weight or size and must be determined by your doctor. The dose is usually 1 to 2 mg per kilogram (kg) (0.45 to 0.9 mg per pound) of body weight, or 25 to 50 mg per square meter of body surface area, injected into a vein over a period of five minutes. A second dose may be given after one hour, if needed.

Missed dose—If you miss a dose of this medicine, take it as soon as possible. However, if it is almost time for your next dose, skip the missed dose and go back to your regular dosing schedule. Do not double doses.

Storage—To store this medicine:
- Keep out of the reach of children.
- Store away from heat and direct light.
- Do not store in the bathroom, near the kitchen sink, or in other damp places. Heat or moisture may cause the medicine to break down.
- Keep the medicine from freezing. Do not refrigerate.
- Do not keep outdated medicine or medicine no longer needed. Be sure that any discarded medicine is out of the reach of children.

Precautions While Using This Medicine

Before you have any medical tests, tell the doctor in charge that you are taking this medicine. The results of some tests may be affected by this medicine.

Side Effects of This Medicine

Along with its needed effects, a medicine may cause some unwanted effects. Although not all of these side effects may occur, if they do occur they may need medical attention.

Check with your doctor immediately if any of the following side effects occur:
Symptoms of overdose
   Anxiety; back pain; bluish fingernails, lips, or skin; chest pain; chills; confusion; difficulty in breathing; dizziness; headache; leg pain; nausea and vomiting; severe sweating; stomach pain; trembling; unusual tiredness or weakness

Other side effects may occur that usually do not need medical attention. These side effects may go away during treatment as your body adjusts to the medicine. However, check with your doctor if any of the following side effects continue or are bothersome:
More common
   Greenish blue to blue discoloration of urine and stools

Less common
   Diarrhea; nausea and vomiting; painful urination or increased need to urinate (with tablet form)

Other side effects not listed above may also occur in some patients. If you notice any other effects, check with your doctor.

Developed: 05/27/94

METHYLPHENIDATE   Systemic

Commonly used brand name(s):

In the U.S.—
   Concerta
   Ritalin
   Ritalin-SR
   Generic name product may be available.

In Canada—

PMS-Methylphenidate	Ritalin
Riphenidate	Ritalin SR

Description

Methylphenidate (meth-il-FEN-i-date) belongs to the group of medicines called central nervous system (CNS) stimulants. It is used to treat attention-deficit hyperactivity disorder (ADHD), narcolepsy (uncontrollable desire for sleep or sudden attacks of deep sleep), and other conditions as determined by the doctor.

Methylphenidate works in the treatment of ADHD by increasing attention and decreasing restlessness in children and adults who are overactive, cannot concentrate for very long or are easily distracted, and are impulsive. This medicine is used as part of a total treatment program that also includes social, educational, and psychological treatment.

This medicine is available only with a doctor's prescription. Prescriptions cannot be refilled. A new written prescription must be obtained from your doctor each time you or your child needs this medicine.

Methylphenidate is available in the following dosage forms:
Oral
- Tablets (U.S. and Canada)
- Extended-release tablets (U.S. and Canada)

Before Using This Medicine

In deciding to use a medicine, the risks of taking the medicine must be weighed against the good it will do. This is a decision you and your doctor will make. For methylphenidate, the following should be considered:

Allergies—Tell your doctor if you have ever had any unusual or allergic reaction to methylphenidate. Also tell your health care professional if you are allergic to any other substances, such as foods, preservatives, or dyes.

Pregnancy—Studies on effects in pregnancy have not been done in either humans or animals.

Breast-feeding—It is not known whether methylphenidate passes into breast milk. Although most medicines pass into breast milk in small amounts, many of them may be used safely while breast-feeding. Mothers who are taking this medicine and who wish to breast-feed should discuss this with the doctor.

Children—Loss of appetite, trouble in sleeping, stomach pain, fast heartbeat, and weight loss may be especially likely to occur in children, who are usually more sensitive than adults to the effects of methylphenidate. Some children who used medicines like methylphenidate for a long time grew more slowly than expected. It is not known whether long-term use of methylphenidate causes slowed growth. The doctor should regularly measure the height and weight of children who are taking methylphenidate. Some doctors recommend stopping treatment with methylphenidate during times when the child is not under stress, such as on weekends.

Older adults—Many medicines have not been studied specifically in older people. Therefore, it may not be known whether they work exactly the same way they do in younger adults or if they cause different side effects or problems in older people. There is no specific information comparing use of methylphenidate in the elderly with use in other age groups.

Other medicines—Although certain medicines should not be used together at all, in other cases two different medicines may be used together even if an interaction might occur. In these cases, your doctor may want to change the dose, or other precautions may be necessary. When you are taking methylphenidate, it is especially important that your health care professional know if you are taking any of the following:

- Amantadine (e.g., Symmetrel) or
- Amphetamines or
- Appetite suppressants (diet pills) or
- Bupropion (e.g., Wellbutrin, Zyban) or
- Caffeine (e.g., NoDoz) or
- Chlophedianol (e.g., Ulone) or
- Cocaine or
- Medicine for asthma or other breathing problems or
- Medicine for colds, sinus problems, hay fever or other allergies (including nose drops or sprays) or
- Nabilone (e.g., Cesamet) or
- Pemoline (e.g., Cylert)—Using these medicines with methylphenidate may cause severe nervousness, irritability, trouble in sleeping, or possibly irregular heartbeat or seizures

- Monoamine oxidase (MAO) inhibitors (furazolidone [e.g., Furoxone], isocarboxazid [e.g., Marplan], phenelzine [e.g., Nardil], procarbazine [e.g., Matulane], selegiline [e.g., Eldepryl], tranylcypromine [e.g., Parnate])—Taking methylphenidate while you are taking or less than 2 weeks after taking an MAO inhibitor may cause sudden extremely high blood pressure and severe convulsions; at least 14 days should be allowed between stopping treatment with an MAO inhibitor and starting treatment with methylphenidate

- Pimozide (e.g., Orap)—Pimozide is not used to treat tics that are caused by medicines. Before tics are treated with pimozide, the doctor should find out if the tics are caused by methylphenidate

Other medical problems—The presence of other medical problems may affect the use of methylphenidate. Make sure you tell your doctor if you have any other medical problems, especially:

- Alcohol abuse (or history of) or
- Drug abuse or dependence (or history of)—Dependence on methylphenidate may be more likely to develop

- Epilepsy or other seizure disorders—The risk of having convulsions (seizures) may be increased
- Gilles de la Tourette's disorder (or family history of) or
- Glaucoma or
- High blood pressure or
- Psychosis or
- Severe anxiety, agitation, tension, or depression or
- Tics (other than Tourette's disorder)—Methylphenidate may make the condition worse

Proper Use of This Medicine

Take this medicine only as directed by your doctor. Do not take more of it, do not take it more often, and do not take it for a longer time than your doctor ordered. If too much is taken, it may become habit-forming.

Take this medicine with or after a meal or a snack.

To help prevent trouble in sleeping, take the last dose of the short-acting tablets before 6 p.m., unless otherwise directed by your doctor.

If you think this medicine is not working properly after you have taken it for several weeks, *do not increase the dose.* Instead, check with your doctor.

If you are taking the long-acting form of this medicine:

- These tablets are to be swallowed whole. Do not break, crush, or chew before swallowing.
- If you are taking Concerta brand of methylphenidate extended-release tablets, you may sometimes notice what looks like a tablet in your stool. This is just the empty shell that is left after the medicine has been absorbed into your body.

Dosing—The dose of methylphenidate will be different for different patients. *Follow your doctor's orders or the directions on the label.* The following information includes only the average doses of methylphenidate. *If your dose is different, do not change it* unless your doctor tells you to do so.

The number of tablets that you take depends on the strength of the medicine. Also, *the number of doses you take each day, the time allowed between doses, and the length of time you take the medicine depend on the medical problem for which you are using methylphenidate.*

- For attention-deficit hyperactivity disorder:
  —For *short-acting oral* dosage form (tablets):
  - Adults and teenagers—5 to 20 milligrams (mg) two or three times a day, taken with or after meals.
  - Children 6 years of age and older—To start, 5 mg two times a day, taken with or after breakfast and lunch. If needed, your doctor may increase the dose once a week by 5 to 10 mg a day until symptoms improve or a maximum dose is reached.
  - Children up to 6 years of age—The dose must be determined by the doctor.
  —For *long-acting oral* dosage form (extended-release tablets):
  - Adults, teenagers, and children—The dose must be determined by the doctor.
- For narcolepsy:
  —For *short-acting oral* dosage form (tablets):
  - Adults and teenagers—5 to 20 mg two or three times a day, taken with or after meals.
  —For *long-acting oral* dosage form (extended-release tablets):
  - Adults and teenagers—The dose must be determined by the doctor.

Missed dose—If you miss a dose of this medicine, take it as soon as possible. Then take any remaining doses for that day at regularly spaced intervals. Do not double doses.

Storage—To store this medicine:

- Keep out of the reach of children.
- Store away from heat and direct light.
- Do not store in the bathroom, near the kitchen sink, or in other damp places. Heat or moisture may cause the medicine to break down.
- Do not keep outdated medicine or medicine no longer needed. Be sure that any discarded medicine is out of the reach of children.

Precautions While Using This Medicine

Your doctor should check your progress at regular visits and make sure that this medicine does not cause unwanted effects, such as high blood pressure.

Methylphenidate may cause dizziness, drowsiness, or changes in vision. Do not drive a car, ride a bicycle, operate machinery, or do other things that might be dangerous until you know how this medicine affects you.

If you take this medicine in large doses and/or for a long time, *do not stop taking it without first checking with your doctor*. Your doctor may want you to reduce gradually the amount you are taking before you stop completely. This is to help reduce unwanted effects.

If you think you may have become mentally or physically dependent on this medicine, check with your doctor. Some signs of dependence on methylphenidate are:

- A strong desire or need to continue taking the medicine.
- A need to increase the dose to receive the effects of the medicine.
- Withdrawal side effects (for example, mental depression, unusual behavior, or unusual tiredness or weakness) occurring after the medicine is stopped.

Side Effects of This Medicine

Along with its needed effects, a medicine may cause some unwanted effects. Although not all of these side effects may occur, if they do occur they may need medical attention.

Check with your doctor as soon as possible if any of the following side effects occur:

More common
Fast heartbeat; increased blood pressure

Less common
Chest pain; fever; joint pain; skin rash or hives; uncontrolled movements of the body

Rare
Black, tarry stools; blood in urine or stools; blurred vision or other changes in vision; convulsions (seizures); muscle cramps; pinpoint red spots on skin; uncontrolled vocal outbursts and/or tics (uncontrolled and repeated body movements); unusual bleeding or bruising

With long-term use or at high doses
Changes in mood; confusion; delusions (false beliefs); depersonalization (feeling that self or surroundings are not real); hallucinations (seeing, hearing, or feeling things that are not there); weight loss

Symptoms of overdose
Agitation; confusion (severe); convulsions (seizures); dryness of mouth or mucous membranes; false sense of well-being; fast, pounding, or irregular heartbeat; fever; hallucinations (seeing, hearing, or feeling things that are not there); headache (severe); increased blood pressure; increased sweating; large pupils; muscle twitching; overactive reflexes; trembling or shaking; vomiting

Other side effects may occur that usually do not need medical attention. These side effects may go away during treatment as your body adjusts to the medicine. However, check with your doctor if any of the following side effects continue or are bothersome:

More common
Loss of appetite; nervousness; trouble in sleeping

Less common
Dizziness; drowsiness; headache; nausea; stomach pain

After you stop using this medicine, your body may need time to adjust. The length of time this takes depends on the amount of medicine you were using and how long you used it. During this period of time check with your doctor if you notice any of the following side effects:

Mental depression (severe); unusual behavior; unusual tiredness or weakness

Other side effects not listed above may also occur in some patients. If you notice any other effects, check with your doctor.

Additional Information

Once a medicine has been approved for marketing for a certain use, experience may show that it is also useful for other medical problems. Although not specifically included in product labeling, methylphenidate may be used in certain patients with the following condition:

- Depressive disorder secondary to physical illness in patients who cannot take antidepressant medicines.

Other than the above information, there is no additional information relating to proper use, precautions, or side effects for this use.

Revised: 04/02/2001

METHYPRYLON   Systemic†

†Not commercially available in Canada.

Description

Methyprylon (meth-i-PRYE-lon) is used to treat insomnia (trouble in sleeping). However, it has generally been replaced by other medicines for the treatment of insomnia. If methyprylon is used regularly (for example, every day) to help produce sleep, it may not be effective for more than 1 week.

Note: This medicine was withdrawn from the U.S. market in June 1965 and the Canadian market in September 1990.

Before Using This Medicine

In deciding to use a medicine, the risks of taking the medicine must be weighed against the good it will do. This is a decision you and your doctor will make. For methyprylon, the following should be considered:

Allergies—Tell your doctor if you have ever had any unusual or allergic reaction to methyprylon. Also tell your health care professional if you are allergic to any other substances, such as foods, preservatives, or dyes.

Pregnancy—Methyprylon has not been studied in pregnant women. However, it has not been shown to cause birth defects or other problems in animal studies.

Breast-feeding—It is not known whether methyprylon passes into the breast milk. However, this medicine has not been reported to cause problems in nursing babies.

Children—Studies on this medicine have been done only in adult patients and there is no specific information about its use in children.

Older adults—Elderly people may be especially sensitive to the effects of methyprylon. This may increase the chance of side effects during treatment.

Other medicines—Although certain medicines should not be used together at all, in other cases two different medicines may be used together even if an interaction might occur. In these cases, your doctor may want to change the dose, or other precautions may be necessary. When you are taking methyprylon, it is especially important that your health care professional know if you are taking any of the following:

- Central nervous system (CNS) depressants, other— Using these medicines with methyprylon may increase the CNS and other depressant effects

Other medical problems—The presence of other medical problems may affect the use of methyprylon. Make sure you tell your doctor if you have any other medical problems, especially:

- Kidney disease or
- Liver disease—Higher blood levels of methyprylon may occur, increasing the chance of side effects
- Porphyria—Methyprylon may make the condition worse

Proper Use of This Medicine

Take this medicine only as directed by your doctor. Do not take more of it, do not take it more often, and do not take it for a longer time than your doctor ordered. If too much is taken, it may become habit-forming.

Storage—To store this medicine:

- Keep out of the reach of children. Overdose of methyprylon is especially dangerous in children.
- Store away from heat and direct light.
- Do not store in the bathroom, near the kitchen sink, or in other damp places. Heat or moisture may cause the medicine to break down.
- Do not keep outdated medicine or medicine no longer needed. Be sure that any discarded medicine is out of the reach of children.

Precautions While Using This Medicine

If you will be taking this medicine regularly for a long time:

- Your doctor should check your progress at regular visits.

- Do not stop taking it without first checking with your doctor. Your doctor may want you to reduce gradually the amount you are taking before stopping completely.

This medicine will add to the effects of alcohol and other CNS depressants (medicines that slow down the nervous system, possibly causing drowsiness). Some examples of CNS depressants are antihistamines or medicine for hay fever, other allergies, or colds; sedatives, tranquilizers, or sleeping medicine; prescription pain medicine or narcotics; barbiturates; medicine for seizures; muscle relaxants; or anesthetics, including some dental anesthetics. *Check with your doctor before taking any of the above while you are taking this medicine.*

If you think you or someone else may have taken an overdose of this medicine, get emergency help at once. Taking an overdose of methyprylon or taking alcohol or other CNS depressants with methyprylon may lead to unconsciousness and possibly death. Some signs of an overdose are confusion, fast heartbeat, severe weakness, shortness of breath or slow or troubled breathing, and staggering.

This medicine may cause some people to become dizzy, drowsy, or less alert than they are normally. Even if taken at bedtime, it may cause some people to feel drowsy or less alert on arising. *Make sure you know how you react to this medicine before you drive, use machines, or do anything else that could be dangerous if you are dizzy or are not alert.*

Side Effects of This Medicine

Along with its needed effects, a medicine may cause some unwanted effects. Although not all of these side effects may occur, if they do occur they may need medical attention.

Check with your doctor as soon as possible if any of the following side effects occur:

Less common
Skin rash; unusual excitement

Rare
Fever (unexplained); mental depression; ulcers or sores in mouth or throat (continuing); unusual bleeding or bruising

Symptoms of overdose
Confusion; drowsiness (severe); fast heartbeat; shortness of breath or slow or troubled breathing; staggering; swelling of feet or lower legs; weakness (severe)

Other side effects may occur that usually do not need medical attention. These side effects may go away during treatment as your body adjusts to the medicine. However, check with your doctor if any of the following side effects continue or are bothersome:

More common
Dizziness; drowsiness (daytime) (mild); headache

Less common or rare
Blurred or double vision; clumsiness or unsteadiness; constipation; diarrhea; nausea; unusual weakness; vomiting

After you stop using this medicine, your body may need time to adjust. The length of time this takes depends on the amount of medicine you were using and how long you used it. During this period of time check with your doctor if you notice any of the following side effects:

Confusion; convulsions (seizures); hallucinations (seeing, hearing, or feeling things that are not there); increased dreaming; increased sweating; nausea or vomiting; nightmares; restlessness or nervousness; stomach cramps; trembling; trouble in sleeping; unusual weakness

Other side effects not listed above may also occur in some patients. If you notice any other effects, check with your doctor.

Revised: 10/13/2000

METHYSERGIDE   Systemic

Commonly used brand name(s):

In the U.S.—
Sansert

In Canada—
Sansert

Description

Methysergide (meth-i-SER-jide) belongs to the group of medicines known as ergot alkaloids. It is used to prevent migraine headaches and some kinds of throbbing headaches. It is not used to treat an attack once it has started. The exact way methysergide acts on the body is not known.

This medicine is available only with your doctor's prescription, in the following dosage form:

Oral
  • Tablets (U.S. and Canada)

Before Using This Medicine

In deciding to use a medicine, the risks of taking the medicine must be weighed against the good it will do. This is a decision you and your doctor will make. For methysergide, the following should be considered:

Allergies—Tell your doctor if you have ever had any unusual or allergic reaction to methysergide or to other ergot medicines. Also tell your health care professional if you are allergic to any other substances, such as foods, preservatives, or dyes.

Pregnancy—Methysergide is not recommended during pregnancy. Before taking this medicine, make sure your doctor knows if you are pregnant or if you may become pregnant.

Breast-feeding—This medicine passes into the breast milk and may cause unwanted effects such as vomiting, diarrhea, weak pulse, unstable blood pressure, and convulsions (seizures) in nursing babies.

Children—Methysergide can cause serious side effects in any patient. Therefore, it is especially important that you discuss with the child's doctor the good that this medicine may do as well as the risks of using it.

Older adults—Elderly people are especially sensitive to the effects of methysergide. This may increase the chance of side effects during treatment.

Other medicines—Although certain medicines should not be used together at all, in other cases two different medicines may be used together even if an interaction might occur. In these cases, your doctor may want to change the dose, or other precautions may be necessary. When you are taking methysergide, it is important that your health care professional know if you are using any other prescription or nonprescription (over-the-counter [OTC]) medicine, or if you smoke.

Other medical problems—The presence of other medical problems may affect the use of methysergide. Make sure you tell your doctor if you have any other medical problems, especially:

  • Arthritis or
  • Heart or blood vessel disease or
  • Infection or
  • Itching (severe) or
  • Kidney disease or
  • Liver disease or
  • Lung disease—The chance of serious side effects may be increased

  • High blood pressure or
  • Stomach ulcer—Methysergide can make your condition worse

Proper Use of This Medicine

Take this medicine only as directed by your doctor. If the amount you are to take does not prevent your headaches from occurring as often as before, do not take more than your doctor ordered. Instead, check with your doctor. Taking too much of this medicine or taking it too frequently may cause serious effects such as nausea and vomiting; cold, painful hands or feet; or even gangrene.

If this medicine upsets your stomach, it may be taken with meals or milk. If stomach upset continues or is severe, check with your doctor.

Dosing—The dose of methysergide will be different for different patients. *Follow your doctor's orders or the directions on the label.* The following information includes only the average doses of methysergide. *If your dose is different, do not change it* unless your doctor tells you to do so.

  • For *oral* dosage form (tablets):
    —For preventing migraine and other throbbing headaches:
      • Adults—2 milligrams (mg) (one tablet) two to four times a day.
      • Children—Use is not recommended.

Missed dose—If you miss a dose of this medicine, skip the missed dose and go back to your regular dosing schedule. Do not double doses.

Storage—To store this medicine:
  • Keep out of the reach of children.
  • Store away from heat and direct light.
  • Do not store in the bathroom, near the kitchen sink, or in other damp places. Heat or moisture may cause the medicine to break down.
  • Do not keep outdated medicine or medicine no longer needed. Be sure that any discarded medicine is out of the reach of children.

Precautions While Using This Medicine

If you have been taking this medicine regularly, *do not stop taking it without first checking with your doctor.* Your doctor may want you to reduce gradually the amount you are using before stopping completely. If you stop taking it suddenly, your headaches may return or worsen.

Your doctor will tell you how long you should take this medicine. Usually it is not taken for longer than 6 months at a time. *If the doctor tells you to stop taking the medicine for a while, do not continue to take it.* If your body does not get a rest from the medicine, it can have harmful effects.

This medicine may cause some people to become dizzy, lightheaded, drowsy, or less alert than they are normally. Even if taken at bedtime, it may cause some people to feel drowsy or less alert on arising. *Make sure you know how you react to this medicine before you drive, use machines, or do anything else that could be dangerous if you are dizzy or are not alert.*

If dizziness occurs, get up slowly after lying or sitting down. If the problem continues or gets worse, check with your doctor.

Since drinking alcoholic beverages may make headaches worse, it is best to avoid alcohol while you are suffering from them. If you have any questions about this, check with your doctor.

Since smoking may increase some of the harmful effects of this medicine, it is best to avoid smoking while you are using it. If you have any questions about this, check with your doctor.

This medicine may make you more sensitive to cold temperatures, especially if you have blood circulation problems. It tends to decrease blood circulation in the skin, fingers, and toes. Dress warmly during cold weather and be careful during prolonged exposure to cold, such as in winter sports. This is especially important for elderly people, who are more likely than younger adults to already have problems with their circulation.

Check with your doctor if a serious infection or illness of any kind occurs while you are taking methysergide, since an infection may make you more sensitive to the medicine's effects.

Side Effects of This Medicine

Along with its needed effects, a medicine may cause some unwanted effects. Although not all of these side effects may occur, if they do occur they may need medical attention.

Check with your doctor immediately if any of the following side effects occur:

  Chest pain or tightness in chest; convulsions (seizures); difficult or painful urination; dizziness (severe); fever or chills; increase or decrease (large) in the amount of urine; leg cramps; pain in arms, legs, groin, lower back, or side; pale or cold hands or feet; shortness of breath or difficult breathing; swelling of hands, ankles, feet, or lower legs

Check with your doctor as soon as possible if the following side effects occur:

  More common
  Abdominal or stomach pain; itching; numbness and tingling of fingers, toes, or face; weakness in the legs

  Less common or rare
  Changes in vision; clumsiness or unsteadiness; cough or hoarseness; excitement or difficulty in thinking; fast or slow heartbeat; feeling of being outside the body; hallucinations (seeing, hearing, or feeling things that are not there); loss of appetite or weight loss; mental depression; nightmares; raised red spots on skin; redness or flushing of face; skin rash; unusual weight gain

Other side effects may occur that usually do not need medical attention. These side effects may go away during treatment as your body adjusts to the medicine. However, check with your doctor if any of the following side effects continue or are bothersome:

  More common
  Diarrhea; dizziness or lightheadedness, especially when you get up from a lying or sitting position; drowsiness; nausea or vomiting

  Less common or rare
  Constipation; hair loss; heartburn; trouble in sleeping

After you stop using this medicine, your body may need time to adjust. The length of time this takes depends on the amount of medicine you were using and how long you used it. During this time check with your doctor if your headaches begin again or worsen.

Other side effects not listed above may also occur in some patients. If you notice any other effects, check with your doctor.

Revised: 05/29/97
Interim revision: 08/17/94

METOCLOPRAMIDE   Systemic

Commonly used brand name(s):

In the U.S.—
  Octamide
  Metoclopramide Intensol
  Reglan
  Generic name product may be available.

In Canada—
  Apo-Metoclop   PMS-Metoclopramide
  Maxeran   Reglan

Description

Metoclopramide (met-oh-kloe-PRA-mide) is a medicine that increases the movements or contractions of the stomach and intestines. When given by injection, it is used to help diagnose certain problems of the stomach and/or intestines. It is also used by injection to prevent the nausea and vomiting that may occur after treatment with anticancer medicines. Another medicine may be used with metoclopramide to prevent side effects that may occur when metoclopramide is used with anticancer medicines.

When taken by mouth, metoclopramide is used to treat the symptoms of a certain type of stomach problem called diabetic gastroparesis. It relieves symptoms such as nausea, vomiting, continued feeling of fullness after meals, and loss of appetite. Metoclopramide is also used, for a short time, to treat symptoms such as heartburn in patients who suffer esophageal injury from a backward flow of gastric acid into the esophagus.

Metoclopramide may also be used for other conditions as determined by your doctor.

Metoclopramide is available only with your doctor's prescription. It is available in the following dosage forms:

Oral
- Tablets (U.S. and Canada)
- Oral Concentrate (U.S.)
- Oral Solution (U.S. and Canada)

Parenteral
- Injection (U.S. and Canada)

Before Using This Medicine

In deciding to use a medicine, the risks of taking the medicine must be weighed against the good it will do. This is a decision you and your doctor will make. For metoclopramide, the following should be considered:

Allergies—Tell your doctor if you have ever had any unusual or allergic reaction to metoclopramide, procaine, or procainamide. Also tell your health care professional if you are allergic to any other substances, such as foods, preservatives, or dyes.

Pregnancy—Not enough studies have been done in humans to determine metoclopramide's safety during pregnancy. However, metoclopramide has not been shown to cause birth defects or other problems in animal studies.

Breast-feeding—Metoclopramide passes into the breast milk and may cause unwanted effects in nursing babies. Be sure you have discussed the risks and benefits of the medicine with your doctor.

Children—Muscle spasms, especially of jaw, neck, and back, and tic-like (jerky) movements of head and face may be especially likely to occur in children, who are usually more sensitive than adults to the effects of metoclopramide. Premature and full-term infants may develop blood problems if given high doses of metoclopramide.

Older adults—Shuffling walk and trembling and shaking of hands may be especially likely to occur in elderly patients after they have taken metoclopramide over a long time.

Other medicines—Although certain medicines should not be used together at all, in other cases two different medicines may be used together even if an interaction might occur. In these cases, your doctor may want to change the dose, or other precautions may be necessary. When you are taking metoclopramide, it is especially important that your health care professional know if you are taking the following:

- Central nervous system (CNS) depressants (medicine that causes drowsiness)—Use with metoclopramide may cause severe drowsiness

Other medical problems—The presence of other medical problems may affect the use of metoclopramide. Make sure you tell your doctor if you have any other medical problems, especially:

- Abdominal or stomach bleeding or
- Asthma or
- High blood pressure or
- Intestinal blockage or
- Mental depression or
- Parkinson's disease—Metoclopramide may make these conditions worse
- Epilepsy—Metoclopramide may increase the risk of having a seizure

- Kidney disease (severe)—Higher blood levels of metoclopramide may result, possibly increasing the chance of side effects

Proper Use of This Medicine

Take this medicine 30 minutes before meals and at bedtime, unless otherwise directed by your doctor.

Take metoclopramide only as directed. Do not take more of it, do not take it more often, and do not take it for a longer time than your doctor ordered. To do so may increase the chance of side effects.

To take *metoclopramide oral concentrate:* This medicine should be mixed with another liquid, such as water, juices, soda or soda-like beverages, or with a semi-solid food, such as applesauce or pudding.

Dosing—The dose of metoclopramide will be different for different patients. *Follow your doctor's orders or the directions on the label.* The following information includes only the average doses of metoclopramide. *If your dose is different, do not change it* unless your doctor tells you to do so.

The number of tablets or teaspoonfuls of solution that you take depends on the strength of the medicine. Also, *the number of doses you take each day, the time allowed between doses, and the length of time you take the medicine depend on the medical problem for which you are taking metoclopramide.*

- For *oral* dosage forms (concentrate, solution, or tablets):
  - To treat the symptoms of a stomach problem called diabetic gastroparesis:
    - Adults and teenagers—10 milligrams (mg) thirty minutes before symptoms are likely to begin or before each meal and at bedtime. The dose may be taken up to four times a day. However, most people usually will not take more than 500 micrograms (mcg) per kilogram (kg) (227 mcg per pound) of body weight a day.
    - Children—Dose must be determined by your doctor.
  - For heartburn:
    - Adults and teenagers—10 to 15 mg thirty minutes before symptoms are likely to begin or before each meal and at bedtime. The dose may be taken up to four times a day. However, most people usually will not take more than 500 mcg per kg (227 mcg per pound) of body weight a day.
    - Children—Dose must be determined by your doctor.
  - To increase movements or contractions of the stomach and intestines:
    - Children 5 to 14 years of age—2.5 to 5 mg three times a day, thirty minutes before meals.

- For *injection* dosage form:
  - To increase movements or contractions of the stomach and intestine:
    - Adults and teenagers—10 mg injected into a vein.
    - Children—Dose is based on body weight and must be determined by your doctor. The usual dose is 1 mg per kilogram (kg) (0.45 mg per

pound) of body weight injected into a vein. Your doctor may repeat this dose after sixty minutes if needed.

—To prevent nausea and vomiting caused by anti-cancer medicines:

- Adults and teenagers—Dose is based on body weight and must be determined by your doctor. The usual dose is 1 to 2 mg per kg (0.45 to 0.9 mg per pound) of body weight, injected slowly into a vein, thirty minutes before you take your anti-cancer medicine. Your doctor may repeat this dose every two or three hours if needed. Some people may need a larger dose to start.
- Children—1 mg per kg (0.45 mg per pound) of body weight injected into a vein. Your doctor may repeat this dose after sixty minutes if needed.

—To prevent vomiting after surgery:

- Adults and teenagers—10 to 20 mg injected into a muscle near the end of surgery.
- Children—Dose must be determined by your doctor.

Missed dose—If you miss a dose of this medicine, take it as soon as possible. However, if it is almost time for your next dose, skip the missed dose and go back to your regular dosing schedule. Do not double doses.

Storage—To store this medicine:

- Keep out of the reach of children.
- Store away from heat and direct light.
- Do not store the tablet form of this medicine in the bathroom, near the kitchen sink, or in other damp places. Heat or moisture may cause the medicine to break down.
- Keep the concentrate and solution forms of this medicine from freezing.
- Do not keep outdated medicine or medicine no longer needed. Be sure that any discarded medicine is out of the reach of children.

Precautions While Using This Medicine

This medicine will add to the effects of alcohol and other CNS depressants (medicines that cause drowsiness). Some examples of CNS depressants are antihistamines or medicine for hay fever, other allergies, or colds; sedatives, tranquilizers, or sleeping medicine; prescription pain medicine or narcotics; barbiturates; medicine for seizures; muscle relaxants; or anesthetics, including some dental anesthetics. *Check with your doctor before taking any of the above while you are using this medicine.*

This medicine may cause some people to become dizzy, lightheaded, drowsy, or less alert than they are normally. *Make sure you know how you react to this medicine before you drive, use machines, or do anything else that could be dangerous if you are dizzy or are not alert.*

Side Effects of This Medicine

Along with its needed effects, a medicine may cause some unwanted effects. Although not all of these side effects may occur, if they do occur they may need medical attention.

Check with your doctor as soon as possible if any of the following side effects occur:

Rare

Chills; difficulty in speaking or swallowing; dizziness or fainting; fast or irregular heartbeat; fever; general feeling of tiredness or weakness; headache (severe or continuing); inability to move eyes; increase in blood pressure; lip smacking or puckering; loss of balance control; mask-like face; muscle spasms of face, neck, and back; puffing of cheeks; rapid or worm-like movements of tongue; shuffling walk; sore throat; stiffness of arms or legs; trembling and shaking of hands and fingers; tic-like or twitching movements; twisting movements of body; uncontrolled chewing movements; uncontrolled movements of arms and legs; weakness of arms and legs

With high doses—may occur within minutes of receiving a dose of metoclopramide and last for 2 to 24 hours

Aching or discomfort in lower legs; panic-like sensation; sensation of crawling in legs; unusual nervousness, restlessness, or irritability

Symptoms of overdose—may also occur rarely with usual doses, especially in children and young adults, and with high doses used to treat the nausea and vomiting caused by anticancer medicines

Confusion; convulsions (seizures); drowsiness (severe)

Other side effects may occur that usually do not need medical attention. These side effects may go away during treatment as your body adjusts to the medicine. However, check with your doctor if any of the following side effects continue or are bothersome:

More common

Diarrhea—with high doses; drowsiness; restlessness

Less common or rare

Breast tenderness and swelling; changes in menstruation; constipation; increased flow of breast milk; mental depression; nausea; skin rash; trouble in sleeping; unusual dryness of mouth; unusual irritability

Other side effects not listed above may also occur in some patients. If you notice any other effects, check with your doctor.

Additional Information

Once a medicine has been approved for marketing for a certain use, experience may show that it is also useful for other medical problems. Although these uses are not included in product labeling, metoclopramide is used in certain patients with the following medical conditions:

- Failure of the stomach to empty its contents
- Nausea and vomiting caused by other medicines
- Persistent hiccups
- Prevention of aspirating fluid into the lungs during surgery
- Vascular headaches

Other than the above information, there is no additional information relating to proper use, precautions, or side effects for these uses.

Revised: 08/12/98

METRONIDAZOLE   Systemic

Commonly used brand name(s):

In the U.S.—

Flagyl	Flagyl I.V. RTU
Flagyl 375	Metric 21
Flagyl ER	Metro I.V.
Flagyl I.V.	Protostat

Generic name product may be available.

In Canada—

Apo-Metronidazole	Novonidazol
Flagyl	Trikacide

Description

Metronidazole (me-troe-NI-da-zole) is used to treat infections. It may also be used for other problems as determined by your doctor. It will not work for colds, flu, or other virus infections.

Metronidazole is available only with your doctor's prescription, in the following dosage forms:

Oral
- Capsules (U.S. and Canada)
- Tablets (U.S. and Canada)

Parenteral
- Injection (U.S. and Canada)

Before Using This Medicine

In deciding to use a medicine, the risks of taking the medicine must be weighed against the good it will do. This is a decision you and your doctor will make. For metronidazole, the following should be considered:

Allergies—Tell your doctor if you have ever had any unusual or allergic reaction to metronidazole. Also tell your health care professional if you are allergic to any other substances, such as foods, preservatives, or dyes.

Pregnancy—Studies have not been done in humans. Metronidazole has not been shown to cause birth defects in animal studies; however, use is not recommended during the first trimester of pregnancy.

Breast-feeding—Use is not recommended in nursing mothers since metronidazole passes into the breast milk and may cause unwanted effects in the baby. However, in some infections your doctor may want you to stop breast-feeding and take this medicine for a short time. During this time the breast milk should be squeezed out or sucked out with a breast pump and thrown away. One or two days after you finish taking this medicine, you may go back to breast-feeding.

Children—Metronidazole has been used in children and, in effective doses, has not been shown to cause different side effects or problems in children than it does in adults.

Older adults—Many medicines have not been studied specifically in older people. Therefore, it may not be known whether they work exactly the same way they do in younger adults or if they cause different side effects or problems in older people. There is no specific information comparing use of metronidazole in the elderly with use in other age groups.

Other medicines—Although certain medicines should not be used together at all, in other cases two different medicines may be used together even if an interaction might occur. In these cases, your doctor may want to change the

dose, or other precautions may be necessary. When you are taking metronidazole, it is especially important that your health care professional knows if you are taking any of the following:

- Anticoagulants (blood thinners)—Patients taking anticoagulants with metronidazole may have an increased chance of bleeding
- Disulfiram (e.g., Antabuse)—Patients taking disulfiram with metronidazole may have an increase in side effects affecting the central nervous system
- Lithium —Patients taking lithium with metronidazole may have an increased chance of experiencing lithium toxicity

Other medical problems—The presence of other medical problems may affect the use of metronidazole. Make sure you tell your doctor if you have any other medical problems, especially:

- Blood disease or a history of blood disease—Metronidazole may make the condition worse
- Central nervous system (CNS) disease, including epilepsy—Metronidazole may increase the chance of seizures (convulsions) or other CNS side effects
- Heart disease—Metronidazole by injection may make heart disease worse
- Liver disease, severe—Patients with severe liver disease may have an increase in side effects
- Oral thrush or vaginal yeast infection—Metronidazole may make yeast infections worse.

Proper Use of This Medicine

If this medicine upsets your stomach, it may be taken with meals or a snack. If stomach upset (nausea, vomiting, stomach pain, or diarrhea) continues, check with your doctor. If you are taking the extended–release formulation, you should try to take it an hour before or two hours after your meal.

To help clear up your infection completely, *keep taking this medicine for the full time of treatment*, even if you begin to feel better after a few days. If you stop taking this medicine too soon, your symptoms may return.

In some kinds of infections, this medicine works best when there is a constant amount in the blood. *To help keep the amount constant, do not miss any doses. Also, it is best to take the doses at evenly spaced times, day and night.* For example, if you are to take 4 doses a day, the doses should be spaced about 6 hours apart. If this interferes with your sleep or other daily activities, or if you need help in planning the best times to take your medicine, check with your health care professional.

Dosing—The dose of metronidazole will be different for different patients. *Follow your doctor's orders or the directions on the label.* The following information includes only the average doses of metronidazole. *If your dose is different, do not change it* unless your doctor tells you to do so.

The number of capsules or tablets that you take depends on the strength of the medicine. Also, *the number of doses you take each day, the time allowed between doses, and the length of time you take the medicine depend on the medical problem for which you are taking metronidazole.*

- For *oral* dosage forms (capsules, tablets):
  - —For bacterial infections:
    - Adults and teenagers—Dose is based on body weight. The usual dose is 7.5 milligrams (mg) per kilogram (kg) (3.4 mg per pound) of body weight, up to a maximum dose of 1 gram, every six hours for at least seven days.
    - Children—Dose is based on body weight. The usual dose is 7.5 mg per kg (3.4 mg per pound) of body weight every six hours; or 10 mg per kg (4.5 mg per pound) every eight hours.
  - —For amebiasis infections:
    - Adults and teenagers—500 to 750 mg three times a day for five to ten days.
    - Children—Dose is based on body weight. The usual dose is 11.6 to 16.7 mg per kg (5.3 to 7.6 mg per pound) of body weight three times a day for ten days.
  - —For trichomoniasis infections:
    - Adults and teenagers—A single dose of 2 grams; or 1 gram two times a day for one day; or 250 mg three times a day for seven days.
    - Children—Dose is based on body weight. The usual dose is 5 mg per kg (2.3 mg per pound) of body weight three times a day for seven days.
- For *oral* dosage form (extended release tablets):
  - —For bacterial vaginosis:
    - Adults and teenagers—750 mg once a day for seven days.
    - Children—Use and dose must be determined by your doctor.
- For *injection* dosage form:
  - —For bacterial infections:
    - Adults and children over 1 month of age—Dose is based on body weight. The usual dose is 15 mg per kg (6.8 mg per pound) of body weight one time to start, then 7.5 mg per kg (3.4 mg per pound) of body weight injected into a vein every six hours for at least seven days.
    - Preterm infants—Dose is based on body weight. The usual dose is 15 mg per kg (6.8 mg per pound) of body weight one time to start, then 7.5 mg per kg (3.4 mg per pound) of body weight, injected into a vein, every twelve hours starting forty-eight hours after the first dose.
    - Full-term infants—Dose is based on body weight. The usual dose is 15 mg per kg (6.8 mg per pound) of body weight one time to start, then 7.5 mg per kg (3.4 mg per pound) of body weight, injected into a vein, every twelve hours starting twenty-four hours after the first dose.
  - —For treatment before and during bowel surgery:
    - Adults and teenagers—Dose is based on body weight. The usual dose is 15 mg per kg (6.8 mg per pound), injected into a vein, one hour before surgery, then 7.5 mg per kg (3.4 mg per pound) of body weight, injected into a vein, six hours and twelve hours after the first dose.
    - Children—Use and dose must be determined by your doctor.

Missed dose—If you miss a dose of this medicine, take it as soon as possible. This will help to keep a constant amount of medicine in the blood. However, if it is almost time for your next dose, skip the missed dose and go back to your regular dosing schedule. Do not double doses.

Storage—To store this medicine:
- Keep out of the reach of children.
- Store away from heat and direct light.
- Do not store the capsule or tablet form of this medicine in the bathroom, near the kitchen sink, or in other damp places. Heat or moisture may cause the medicine to break down.
- Do not keep outdated medicine or medicine no longer needed. Be sure that any discarded medicine is out of the reach of children.

Precautions While Using This Medicine

If your symptoms do not improve within a few days, or if they become worse, check with your doctor.

Drinking alcoholic beverages while taking this medicine may cause stomach pain, nausea, vomiting, headache, or flushing or redness of the face. Other alcohol-containing preparations (for example, elixirs, cough syrups, tonics) may also cause problems. These problems may last for at least a day after you stop taking metronidazole. Also, this medicine may cause alcoholic beverages to taste different. Therefore, *you should not drink alcoholic beverages or take other alcohol-containing preparations while you are taking this medicine and for at least 3 days after stopping it.*

Metronidazole may cause dryness of the mouth, an unpleasant or sharp metallic taste, and a change in taste sensation. For temporary relief of dry mouth, use sugarless candy or gum, melt bits of ice in your mouth, or use a saliva substitute. However, if your mouth continues to feel dry for more than 2 weeks, check with your medical doctor or dentist. Continuing dryness of the mouth may increase the chance of dental disease, including tooth decay, gum disease, and fungus infections.

This medicine may also cause some people to become dizzy or lightheaded. *Make sure you know how you react to this medicine before you drive, use machines, or do anything else that could be dangerous if you are dizzy or are not alert.* If these reactions are especially bothersome, check with your doctor.

If you are taking this medicine for trichomoniasis (an infection of the sex organs in males and females), your doctor may want to treat your sexual partner at the same time you are being treated, even if he or she has no symptoms. Also, it may be desirable to use a condom (prophylactic) during intercourse. These measures will help keep you from getting the infection back again from your partner. If you have any questions about this, check with your doctor.

Side Effects of This Medicine

Along with its needed effects, a medicine may cause some unwanted effects. Although not all of these side effects may occur, if they do occur they may need medical attention.

Check with your doctor immediately if any of the following side effects occur:
  Less common
    Numbness, tingling, pain, or weakness in hands or feet
  Rare
    Convulsions (seizures)

Also, check with your doctor as soon as possible if any of the following side effects occur:
  Less common
    Any vaginal irritation, discharge, or dryness not present

before use of this medicine; black, tarry stools; blood in urine or stools; clumsiness or unsteadiness; frequent or painful urination; inability to control urine flow; mood or other mental changes; nausea and vomiting; pinpoint red spots on skin; sense of pelvic pressure; skin rash, hives, redness, or itching; sore throat and fever; stomach and back pain (severe); unusual bleeding or bruising

For injection form

Pain, tenderness, redness, or swelling over vein in which the medicine is given

Other side effects may occur that usually do not need medical attention. These side effects may go away during treatment as your body adjusts to the medicine. However, check with your doctor if any of the following side effects continue or are bothersome:

More common

Diarrhea; dizziness or light-headedness; headache; loss of appetite; nausea or vomiting; stomach pain or cramps

Less common or rare

Change in taste sensation; dryness of mouth; unpleasant or sharp metallic taste

In some patients metronidazole may cause dark urine. This is only temporary and will go away when you stop taking this medicine.

Other side effects not listed above may also occur in some patients. If you notice any other effects, check with your doctor.

Additional Information

Once a medicine has been approved for marketing for a certain use, experience may show that it is also useful for other medical problems. Although these uses are not included in product labeling, metronidazole is used in certain patients with the following medical conditions:

- Antibiotic-associated colitis
- Balantidiasis
- Dental infections
- Gastritis or ulcer due to *Helicobacter pylori*
- Giardiasis
- Inflammatory bowel disease

For patients taking this medicine for *giardiasis:*

- After treatment, it is important that your doctor check whether or not the infection in your intestinal tract has been cleared up completely.

Other than the above information, there is no additional information relating to proper use, precautions, or side effects for this use.

Revised: 04/06/2001

METRONIDAZOLE   Topical

Commonly used brand name(s):

In the U.S.—
MetroCream
MetroGel
MetroLotion

In Canada—
MetroCream
MetroGel

Description

Topical metronidazole (me-troe-NI-da-zole) is applied to the skin in adults to help control rosacea (roe-ZAY-she-ah), also known as acne rosacea and "adult acne." This medicine helps to reduce the redness of the skin and the number of pimples, usually found on the face, in patients with rosacea.

Topical metronidazole is available only with your doctor's prescription, in the following dosage forms:

Topical
- Cream (U.S. and Canada)
- Gel (U.S. and Canada)
- Lotion (U.S.)

Before Using This Medicine

In deciding to use a medicine, the risks of taking the medicine must be weighed against the good it will do. This is a decision you and your doctor will make. For topical metronidazole, the following should be considered:

Allergies—Tell your doctor if you have ever had any unusual or allergic reaction to metronidazole, clotrimazole, or tioconazole. Also tell your health care professional if you are allergic to any other substances, such as preservatives or dyes.

Pregnancy—Topical metronidazole has not been studied in pregnant women. However, metronidazole given by mouth (e.g., Flagyl) has not been shown to cause birth defects or other problems in animal studies.

Breast-feeding—Topical metronidazole is absorbed into the mother's body only in small amounts. The small amounts of this medicine that are absorbed are unlikely to cause serious problems in nursing babies.

Children—Rosacea is usually considered an adult disease. Therefore, topical metronidazole is not generally used in children.

Older adults—Many medicines have not been studied specifically in older people. Therefore, it may not be known whether they work exactly the same way they do in younger adults or if they cause different side effects or problems in older people. There is no specific information comparing use of topical metronidazole in the elderly with use in other age groups.

Other medicines—Although certain medicines should not be used together at all, in other cases two different medicines may be used together even if an interaction might occur. In these cases, your doctor may want to change the dose, or other precautions may be necessary. Tell your health care professional if you are using any other topical prescription or nonprescription (over-the-counter [OTC]) medicine that is to be applied to the same area of the skin.

Other medical problems—The presence of other medical problems may affect the use of topical metronidazole. Make sure you tell your doctor if you have any other medical problems, especially:

- Blood disease or a history of blood disease—Metronidazole may make the condition worse

Proper Use of This Medicine

Do not use this medicine in or near the eyes. Watering of the eyes may occur when the medicine is used too close to the eyes.

If this medicine does get into your eyes, wash them out immediately, but carefully, with large amounts of cool tap water. If your eyes still burn or are painful, check with your doctor.

Before applying this medicine, thoroughly wash the affected area(s) with a mild, nonirritating cleanser, rinse well, and gently pat dry.

To use:
- After washing the affected area(s), apply this medicine with your fingertips.
- Apply and rub in a thin film of medicine, using enough to cover the affected area(s) lightly. *You should apply the medicine to the whole area usually affected by rosacea, not just to the pimples themselves.*
- Wash the medicine off your hands.

To help keep your rosacea under control, *keep using this medicine for the full time of treatment.* You may have to continue using this medicine every day for 9 weeks or longer. *Do not miss any doses.*

Dosing—The dose of topical metronidazole will be different for different patients. *Follow your doctor's orders or the directions on the label.* The following information includes only the average doses of topical metronidazole. *If your dose is different, do not change it* unless your doctor tells you to do so.
- For *topical* dosage forms (cream, gel, and lotion):
  —For rosacea:
    - Adults—Apply to the affected area(s) of skin two times a day, morning and evening, for nine weeks.
    - Children—Use and dose must be determined by your doctor.

Missed dose—If you miss a dose of this medicine, apply it as soon as possible. However, if it is almost time for your next dose, skip the missed dose and go back to your regular dosing schedule.

Storage—To store this medicine:
- Keep out of the reach of children.
- Store away from heat and direct light.
- Keep the medicine from freezing.
- Do not keep outdated medicine or medicine no longer needed. Be sure that any discarded medicine is out of the reach of children.

Precautions While Using This Medicine

If your rosacea does not improve within 3 weeks, or if it becomes worse, check with your doctor. However, treatment of rosacea may take up to 9 weeks or longer before you see full improvement.

Stinging or burning of the skin may be expected after this medicine is applied. These effects may last up to a few minutes or more. If irritation continues, check with your doctor. You may have to use the medicine less often or stop using it altogether. Follow your doctor's directions.

You may continue to use cosmetics (make-up) while you are using this medicine for rosacea. However, it is best to use only "oil-free" cosmetics. Also, it is best not to use cosmetics too heavily or too often. They may make your rosacea worse. If you have any questions about this, check with your doctor.

Side Effects of This Medicine

Along with its needed effects, a medicine may cause some unwanted effects. The following side effects may go away during treatment as your body adjusts to the medicine. However, check with your doctor if any of these effects continue or are bothersome:

Less common
Dry skin; redness or other signs of skin irritation not present before use of this medicine; stinging or burning of the skin; watering of eyes

Rare
Metallic taste in the mouth; nausea; tingling or numbness of arms, legs, hands, or feet

Other side effects not listed above may also occur in some patients. If you notice any other effects, check with your doctor.

Revised: 12/22/99

METRONIDAZOLE   Vaginal

Commonly used brand name(s):

In the U.S.—
MetroGel-Vaginal

In Canada—
Flagyl
Nidagel

Description

Metronidazole (me-troe-NI-da-zole) is used to treat certain vaginal infections. It works by killing bacteria. This medicine will not work for vaginal fungus or yeast infections.

Metronidazole is available only with your doctor's prescription, in the following dosage forms:

Vaginal
- Cream (Canada)
- Gel (U.S. and Canada)
- Tablets (Canada)

Before Using This Medicine

In deciding whether to use a medicine, the risks of using the medicine must be weighed against the good it will do. This is a decision you and your doctor will make. For vaginal metronidazole, the following should be considered:

Allergies—Tell your doctor if you have ever had any unusual or allergic reaction to metronidazole. Also tell your health care professional if you are allergic to any other substances, such as foods, preservatives, or dyes.

Pregnancy—Vaginal metronidazole has not been studied in pregnant women. Metronidazole given by mouth (e.g., Flagyl) has not been shown to cause birth defects. Before taking this medicine, make sure your doctor knows if you are pregnant or if you may become pregnant.

Breast-feeding—Use is not recommended in nursing mothers since metronidazole passes into breast milk and may cause unwanted effects in the baby. In addition, metronidazole may change the taste of your breast milk. Your doctor may want you to stop breast-feeding and use this medicine for a short time. During this time the breast milk should be pumped or drawn out with a breast pump and thrown away. Two days after you finish using this medicine, you may go back to breast-feeding.

Children—Studies on these medicines have been done only in adult patients, and there is no specific information comparing use of vaginal metronidazole in children with use in other age groups.

Older adults—Many medicines have not been studied specifically in older people. Therefore, it may not be known whether they work exactly the same way they do in younger adults or if they cause different side effects or problems in older people. There is no specific information comparing use of metronidazole in the elderly with use in other age groups.

Other medicines—Although certain medicines should not be used together at all, in other cases two different medicines may be used together even if an interaction might occur. In these cases, your doctor may want to change the dose, or other precautions may be necessary. When you are using vaginal metronidazole it is especially important that your health care professional know if you are taking any of the following:

- Alcohol or alcohol-containing medicines (e.g., NyQuil, Geritol)—Metronidazole can cause serious side effects such as abdominal cramping, flushing, headache, nausea, or vomiting when it is used with alcohol
- Anticoagulants (blood thinners)—Taking metronidazole may increase the effects of anticoagulants, changing the amount you need to take
- Disulfiram (e.g., Antabuse)—Severe confusion or mental problems can occur if metronidazole is used together with disulfiram or if it is used up to 2 weeks after disulfiram treatment has been stopped

Other medical problems—The presence of other medical problems may affect the use of vaginal metronidazole. Make sure you tell your doctor if you have any other medical problems, especially:

- Central nervous system (CNS) disease, including epilepsy—Metronidazole may increase the chance of seizures (convulsions) or other side effects
- Liver disease, severe—Patients with severe liver disease may have an increase in side effects
- Low white blood cell count (or history of)—Metronidazole may make the condition worse

Proper Use of This Medicine

Wash your hands before and after using the medicine. Also, keep the medicine out of your eyes.

If this medicine does get into your eyes, wash them out immediately, but carefully, with large amounts of tap water. If your eyes still burn or are painful, check with your doctor.

Vaginal metronidazole products usually come with patient directions. Read them carefully before using this medicine.

Use vaginal metronidazole exactly as directed by your doctor.
- *To fill the applicator*
  —For cream or gel dosage forms:
    - Break the metal seal at the opening of the tube by using the point on the top of the cap.
    - Screw the applicator onto the tube.
    - Squeeze the medicine into the applicator slowly until it is full.

- Remove the applicator from the tube. Replace the cap on the tube.
  —For vaginal tablet dosage form:
    - Place the vaginal tablet into the applicator. Wet the vaginal tablet with water for a few seconds.
- *To insert vaginal metronidazole using the applicator*
  —For all dosage forms:
    - Relax while lying on your back with your knees bent.
    - Hold the full applicator in one hand. Insert it slowly into the vagina. Stop before it becomes uncomfortable.
    - Slowly press the plunger until it stops.
    - Withdraw the applicator. The medicine will be left behind in the vagina.
- *To care for the applicator*
  —For all dosage forms:
    - Clean the applicator after use by pulling the plunger out of the applicator and washing both parts completely in warm soapy water.
    - Rinse well.
    - After drying the applicator, replace the plunger.

To help clear up your infection completely, *it is very important that you keep using this medicine for the full time of treatment*, even if your symptoms begin to clear up after a few days. If you stop using this medicine too soon, your symptoms may return. *Do not miss any doses*. Also, *continue using this medicine even if your menstrual period starts during the time of treatment.*

Dosing—The dose of vaginal metronidazole will be different for different patients. The following information includes only the average doses of vaginal metronidazole. *If your dose is different, do not change it* unless your doctor tells you to do so.
- *For vaginal cream* dosage form:
  —For bacterial vaginosis or trichomoniasis:
    - Adults and teenagers—One applicatorful (500 milligrams [mg]), inserted into the vagina. Use the medicine one or two times a day for ten or twenty days.
    - Children—Use and dose must be determined by your doctor.
- *For vaginal gel* dosage form:
  —For bacterial vaginosis:
    - Adults and teenagers—One applicatorful (37.5 mg), inserted into the vagina one or two times a day for five days.
    - Children—Use and dose must be determined by your doctor.
- *For vaginal tablets* dosage form:
  —For bacterial vaginosis or trichomoniasis:
    - Adults and teenagers—One 500-mg tablet, inserted high into the vagina. Use the medicine once a day in the evening for ten or twenty days.
    - Children—Use and dose must be determined by your doctor.

Missed dose—If you miss a dose of this medicine, use it as soon as possible. However, if it is almost time for your next dose, skip the missed dose and go back to your regular dosing schedule.

Storage—To store this medicine:
- Keep out of the reach of children.
- Store away from heat and direct light.

- Do not store the vaginal tablets in the bathroom, near the kitchen sink, or in other damp places. Heat or moisture may cause the medicine to break down.
- Keep this medicine from freezing.
- Do not keep outdated medicine or medicine no longer needed. Be sure that any discarded medicine is out of the reach of children.

Precautions While Using This Medicine

If your symptoms do not improve within a few days, or if they become worse, check with your doctor.

It is important that you visit your doctor after you have used all your medicine to make sure that the infection is gone.

Drinking alcoholic beverages while using this medicine may cause stomach pain, nausea, vomiting, headache, or flushing or redness of the face. Alcohol-containing medicines (for example, elixirs, cough syrups, tonics) may also cause problems. The chance of these problems occurring may continue for at least a day after you stop using metronidazole. Therefore, *you should not drink alcoholic beverages or take other alcohol-containing medicines while you are using this medicine and for at least a day after stopping it.*

This medicine may cause some people to become dizzy or lightheaded. *Make sure you know how you react to this medicine before you drive, use machines, or do anything else that could be dangerous if you are dizzy or are not alert.* If these reactions are especially bothersome, check with your doctor.

Vaginal medicines usually leak out of the vagina during treatment. To keep the medicine from getting on your clothing, wear a minipad or sanitary napkin. *Do not use tampons* (like those used for menstrual periods) since they may soak up the medicine.

To help clear up your infection completely and to help make sure it does not return, good health habits are also required.

- Wear cotton panties (or panties or pantyhose with cotton crotches) instead of synthetic (for example, nylon or rayon) panties.
- Wear only freshly washed panties daily.

Do not have sexual intercourse while you are using this medicine. Having sexual intercourse may reduce the strength of the medicine. This may cause the medicine to not work as well. Also, oils in the cream and vaginal tablets (but not the vaginal gel) may damage latex (rubber) contraceptive devices, such as cervical caps, condoms, or diaphragms, causing them to leak, wear out sooner, or not work properly.

Many vaginal infections (for example, trichomoniasis) are spread by having sexual intercourse. You can give the infection to your sexual partner, and he can give the infection back to you later. Your partner may also need to be treated for some infections. *Until you are sure that the infection is completely cleared up after your treatment with this medicine, your partner should wear a condom during sexual intercourse.* If you have any questions about this, check with your health care professional.

Side Effects of This Medicine

Along with its needed effects, a medicine may cause some unwanted effects. Although not all of these side effects may occur, if they do occur they may need medical attention.

Check with your doctor as soon as possible if any of the following side effects occur:
More common
Itching in the vagina; pain during sexual intercourse; thick, white vaginal discharge with no odor or with a mild odor
Less common
Abdominal or stomach cramping or pain; burning or irritation of penis of sexual partner; burning on urination or need to urinate more often; itching, stinging or redness of the genital area

Other side effects may occur that usually do not need medical attention. These side effects may go away during treatment as your body adjusts to the medicine. However, check with your doctor if any of the following side effects continue or are bothersome:
Less common
Diarrhea; dizziness or lightheadedness; dryness of mouth; headache; feeling of a furry tongue; loss of appetite; metallic taste or other change in taste sensation; nausea; vomiting

Metronidazole may cause your urine to become dark. This is harmless and will go away when you stop using this medicine.

After you stop using this medicine, your body may need time to adjust. The length of time this takes depends on the amount of medicine you were using and how long you used it. During this period of time check with your doctor if you notice any of the following side effects:
Any vaginal or genital irritation or itching; pain during sexual intercourse; thick, white vaginal discharge not present before treatment, with no odor or with a mild odor

Other side effects not listed above may also occur in some patients. If you notice any other effects, check with your doctor.

Revised: 08/13/98

METYROSINE   Systemic†

Commonly used brand name(s):
In the U.S.—
Demser

†Not commercially available in Canada.

Description

Metyrosine (me-TYE-roe-seen) belongs to the general class of medicines called antihypertensives. It is used to treat high blood pressure (hypertension) caused by a disease called pheochromocytoma (a noncancerous tumor of the adrenal gland).

Metyrosine reduces the amount of certain chemicals in the body. When these chemicals are present in large amounts, they cause high blood pressure.

Metyrosine is available only with your doctor's prescription, in the following dosage form:
Oral
- Capsules (U.S.)

Before Using This Medicine

In deciding to use a medicine, the risks of taking the medicine must be weighed against the good it will do. This is a decision you and your doctor will make. For metyrosine, the following should be considered:

Allergies—Tell your doctor if you have ever had any unusual or allergic reaction to metyrosine. Also tell your health care professional if you are allergic to any other substances, such as foods, sulfites or other preservatives, or dyes.

Pregnancy—Studies on effects in pregnancy have not been done in either humans or animals.

Breast-feeding—It is not known whether metyrosine passes into breast milk. However, this medicine has not been reported to cause problems in nursing babies.

Children—Studies on this medicine have been done only in adult patients, and there is no specific information comparing use of metyrosine in children with use in other age groups.

Older adults—Many medicines have not been studied specifically in older people. Therefore, it may not be known whether they work exactly the same way they do in younger adults or if they cause different side effects or problems in older people. There is no specific information comparing use of metyrosine in the elderly with use in other age groups.

Other medicines—Although certain medicines should not be used together at all, in other cases two different medicines may be used together even if an interaction might occur. In these cases, your doctor may want to change the dose, or other precautions may be necessary. Tell your health care professional if you are taking any other prescription or nonprescription (over-the-counter [OTC]) medicine.

Other medical problems—The presence of other medical problems may affect the use of metyrosine. Make sure you tell your doctor if you have any other medical problems, especially:
- Kidney disease or
- Liver disease—Effects of metyrosine may be increased because of slower removal from the body
- Mental depression (or history of) or
- Parkinson's disease—Metyrosine may make these conditions worse

Proper Use of This Medicine

Take this medicine only as directed by your doctor. Do not take more or less of it than your doctor ordered.

To help you remember to take your medicine, try to get into the habit of taking it at the same times each day.

Dosing—The dose of metyrosine will be different for different patients. *Follow your doctor's orders or the directions on the label*. The following information includes only the average doses of metyrosine. *If your dose is different, do not change it* unless your doctor tells you to do so:
- For *oral* dosage forms (capsules):
  —Adults and children 12 years of age and older: 1000 milligrams to 3000 milligrams (1 to 3 grams) a day, divided into four doses.

Missed dose—If you miss a dose of this medicine, take it as soon as possible. However, if it is almost time for your next dose, skip the missed dose and go back to your regular dosing schedule. Do not double doses.

Storage—To store this medicine:
- Keep out of the reach of children.
- Store away from heat and direct light.
- Do not store in the bathroom, near the kitchen sink, or in other damp places. Heat or moisture may cause the medicine to break down.
- Do not keep outdated medicine or medicine no longer needed. Be sure that any discarded medicine is out of the reach of children.

Precautions While Using This Medicine

It is important that your doctor check your progress at regular visits to make sure that this medicine is working properly and to check for unwanted effects.

While taking this medicine, it is important that you drink plenty of fluids and urinate often. This will help prevent kidney problems and keep your kidneys working well. If you have any questions about how much you should drink, check with your doctor.

This medicine will add to the effects of alcohol and other CNS depressants (medicines that slow down the nervous system, possibly causing drowsiness). Some examples of CNS depressants are antihistamines or medicine for hay fever, other allergies, or colds; sedatives, tranquilizers, or sleeping medicine; prescription pain medicine or narcotics; barbiturates; medicine for seizures; tricyclic antidepressants (medicine for depression); muscle relaxants; or anesthetics, including some dental anesthetics. *Check with your doctor before taking any of the above while you are taking this medicine.*

Before having any kind of surgery (including dental surgery), tell the medical doctor or dentist in charge that you are taking this medicine.

This medicine may cause most people to become drowsy or less alert than they are normally. *Make sure you know how you react to this medicine before you drive, use machines, or do anything else that could be dangerous if you are not alert.*

Side Effects of This Medicine

Along with its needed effects, a medicine may cause some unwanted effects. Although not all of these side effects may occur, if they do occur they may need medical attention.

Check with your doctor as soon as possible if any of the following side effects occur:

More common
  Diarrhea; drooling; trembling and shaking of hands and fingers; trouble in speaking

Less common
  Anxiety; confusion; hallucinations (seeing, hearing, or feeling things that are not there); mental depression

Rare
  Black, tarry stools; blood in urine or stools; unusual bleeding or bruising; muscle spasms, especially of neck and back; painful urination; pinpoint red spots on skin; restlessness; shortness of breath; shuffling walk; skin rash and itching; swelling of feet or lower legs; tic-like (jerky) movements of head, face, mouth, and neck; unusual tiredness or weakness

Other side effects may occur that usually do not need medical attention. These side effects may go away during treatment as your body adjusts to the medicine. However, check with

your doctor if any of the following side effects continue or are bothersome:

More common
Drowsiness

Less common
Decreased sexual ability in men; dryness of mouth; nausea, vomiting, or stomach pain; stuffy nose; swelling of breasts or unusual milk production

After you stop taking this medicine, it may still produce some side effects that need attention. During this period of time check with your doctor if you notice the following side effect:

More common
Diarrhea

Also, after you stop taking this medicine, you may have feelings of increased energy or you may have trouble sleeping. However, these effects should last only for two or three days.

Other side effects not listed above may also occur in some patients. If you notice any other effects, check with your doctor.

Revised: 01/20/93

MEXILETINE   Systemic

Commonly used brand name(s):

In the U.S.—
Mexitil

In Canada—
Mexitil

Description

Mexiletine (MEX-i-le-teen) belongs to the group of medicines known as antiarrhythmics. It is used to correct irregular heartbeats to a normal rhythm.

Mexiletine produces its helpful effects by slowing nerve impulses in the heart and making the heart tissue less sensitive.

Mexiletine is available only with your doctor's prescription, in the following dosage form:

Oral
• Capsules (U.S. and Canada)

Before Using This Medicine

In deciding to use a medicine, the risks of taking the medicine must be weighed against the good it will do. This is a decision you and your doctor will make. For mexiletine, the following should be considered:

Allergies—Tell your doctor if you have ever had any unusual or allergic reaction to mexiletine, lidocaine, or tocainide. Also tell your health care professional if you are allergic to any other substance, such as foods, preservatives, or dyes.

Pregnancy—Mexiletine has not been studied in pregnant women. However, studies in animals have shown that mexiletine causes a decrease in successful pregnancies but no birth defects. Before taking this medicine, make sure your doctor knows if you are pregnant or if you may become pregnant.

Breast-feeding—Mexiletine passes into breast milk. Because this medicine may cause serious side effects, breast-feeding is generally not recommended while you are receiving it. Be sure you have discussed this with your doctor before taking mexiletine.

Children—Studies on this medicine have been done only in adult patients, and there is no specific information comparing use of mexiletine in children with use in other age groups.

Older adults—Many medicines have not been studied specifically in older people. Therefore, it may not be known whether they work exactly the same way they do in younger adults or if they cause different side effects or problems in older people. There is no specific information comparing use of mexiletine in the elderly with use in other age groups.

Other medicines—Although certain medicines should not be used together at all, in other cases two different medicines may be used together even if an interaction might occur. In these cases, your doctor may want to change the dose, or other precautions may be necessary. Tell your health care professional if you are taking any other prescription or nonprescription (over-the-counter [OTC]) medicine.

Smoking—Smoking may decrease the effects of mexiletine.

Other medical problems—The presence of other medical problems may affect the use of mexiletine. Make sure you tell your doctor if you have any other medical problems, especially:

• Congestive heart failure or
• Low blood pressure—Mexiletine may make these conditions worse

• Heart attack (severe) or
• Liver disease—Effects may last longer because of slower removal of mexiletine from the body

• Seizures (history of)—Mexiletine can cause seizures

Proper Use of This Medicine

Take mexiletine exactly as directed by your doctor, even though you may feel well. Do not take more medicine than ordered.

To lessen the possibility of stomach upset, mexiletine should be taken with food or immediately after meals or with milk or an antacid.

This medicine works best when there is a constant amount in the blood. *To help keep this amount constant, do not miss any doses. Also it is best to take the doses at evenly spaced times day and night*. For example, if you are to take 3 doses a day, the doses should be spaced about 8 hours apart. If this interferes with your sleep or other daily activities, or if you need help in planning the best times to take your medicine, check with your health care professional.

Dosing—The dose of mexiletine will be different for different patients. *Follow your doctor's orders or the directions on the label*. The following information includes only the average dose of mexiletine. *If your dose is different, do not change it* unless your doctor tells you to do so.

The number of capsules that you take depends on the strength of the medicine.

• For *oral* dosage form (capsules):
—For irregular heartbeat (arrhythmias):
• Adults—At first, 200 milligrams (mg) every eight hours. Then, your doctor may raise or lower your dose as needed.

- Children—Use and dose must be determined by your doctor.

Missed dose—If you miss a dose of this medicine and remember within 4 hours, take it as soon as possible. Then go back to your regular dosing schedule. However, if you do not remember until later, skip the missed dose and go back to your regular dosing schedule. Do not double doses.

Storage—To store this medicine:

- Keep out of the reach of children.
- Store away from heat and direct light.
- Do not store in the bathroom, near the kitchen sink, or in other damp places. Heat or moisture may cause the medicine to break down.
- Do not keep outdated medicine or medicine no longer needed. Be sure that any discarded medicine is out of the reach of children.

Precautions While Using This Medicine

It is important that your doctor check your progress at regular visits to make sure the medicine is working properly. This will allow for changes to be made in the amount of medicine you are taking, if necessary.

Your doctor may want you to carry a medical identification card or bracelet stating that you are using this medicine.

Before having any kind of surgery (including dental surgery) or emergency treatment, tell the medical doctor or dentist in charge that you are taking this medicine.

Mexiletine may cause some people to become dizzy, lightheaded, or less alert than they are normally. *Make sure you know how you react to this medicine before you drive, use machines, or do anything else that could be dangerous if you are dizzy or are not alert.*

Side Effects of This Medicine

Along with its needed effects, a medicine may cause some unwanted effects. Although not all of these side effects may occur, if they do occur they may need medical attention.

Check with your doctor as soon as possible if any of the following side effects occur:
Less common
Chest pain; fast or irregular heartbeat; shortness of breath
Rare
Convulsions (seizures); fever or chills; unusual bleeding or bruising

Other side effects may occur that usually do not need medical attention. These side effects may go away during treatment as your body adjusts to the medicine. However, check with your doctor if any of the following side effects continue or are bothersome:
More common
Dizziness or lightheadedness; heartburn; nausea and vomiting; nervousness; trembling or shaking of the hands; unsteadiness or difficulty in walking
Less common
Blurred vision; confusion; constipation or diarrhea; headache; numbness or tingling of fingers and toes; ringing in the ears; skin rash; slurred speech; trouble in sleeping; unusual tiredness or weakness

Other side effects not listed above may also occur in some patients. If you notice any other effects, check with your doctor.

Revised: 10/06/92
Interim revision: 07/14/94

MIBEFRADIL   Systemic†—INTRODUCTORY VERSION

†Not commercially available in Canada.

Description

Mibefradil (mi-be-FRA-dil) belongs to a group of medicines called calcium channel blocking agents, or, more commonly, calcium channel blockers.

Calcium channel blocking agents affect the movement of calcium into the cells of the heart and blood vessels. As a result, they relax blood vessels and increase the supply of blood and oxygen to the heart while reducing its workload.

Mibefradil is used to treat high blood pressure (hypertension). High blood pressure adds to the workload of the heart and arteries. If it continues for a long time, the heart and arteries may not function properly. This can damage the blood vessels of the brain, heart, and kidneys, resulting in a stroke, heart failure, or kidney failure. High blood pressure may also increase the risk of heart attacks. These problems may be less likely to occur if blood pressure is controlled.

Mibefradil is also used to treat recurring chest pain (angina pectoris). Angina occurs when the vessels that carry blood to the heart become narrowed and blocked, reducing the supply of blood and oxygen to the heart. As a result, chest tightness and/or a pressing or squeezing pain can occur. Mibefradil is thought to reduce angina by increasing the supply of blood and oxygen to the heart.

Mibefradil may also be used for other conditions as determined by your doctor.

The medicine was withdrawn from the U.S. market in May 1998.

Before Using This Medicine

In deciding to use a medicine, the risks of taking the medicine must be weighed against the good it will do. This is a decision you and your doctor will make. For mibefradil, the following should be considered:

Allergies—Tell your doctor if you have ever had any unusual or allergic reaction to mibefradil. Also tell your health care professional if you are allergic to any other substances, such as foods, preservatives, or dyes.

Pregnancy—Mibefradil has not been studied in pregnant women. However, studies in animals have shown that large doses of mibefradil can cause heart defects in rat fetuses. Before taking this medicine, make sure your doctor knows if you are pregnant or may become pregnant.

Breast-feeding—It is not known if mibefradil passes into breast milk, however, it passes into the milk of lactating rats. Newborn babies have been reported to be sensitive to other calcium channel blocking agents. Be sure you have discussed the risks and benefits of this medicine with your doctor.

Children—Although there is no specific information comparing use of mibefradil in children with use in other age groups, it is not expected to cause different side effects or problems in children than it does in adults.

Older adults—Elderly people may be more sensitive to the heart rate slowing effects of mibefradil.

Other medicines—Although certain medicines should not be used together at all, in other cases two different medicines may be used together even if an interaction might occur. In these cases, your doctor may want to change the dose, or other precautions may be necessary. When you are taking mibefradil, it is especially important that your health care professional know if you are taking any of the following:

- Astemizole (e.g., Hismanal) or
- Cisapride (e.g., Propulsid) or
- Terfenadine (e.g., Seldane)—These medicines should not be used with mibefradil because unwanted effects of these medicines on the heart may be increased

- Atorvastatin (e.g., Lipitor) or
- Cerivastatin (e.g., Baycol) or
- Lovastatin (e.g., Mevacor) or
- Simvastatin (e.g., Zocor)—These medicines should not be used with mibefradil because unwanted effects of these medicines, such as muscle aches or cramps (rhabdomyolysis), may be increased and may lead to development of kidney problems

- Beta-adrenergic blocking agents (acebutolol [e.g., Sectral], atenolol [e.g., Tenormin], betaxolol [e.g., Kerlone], carteolol [e.g., Cartrol], carvedilol, [e.g., Coreg], labetalol [e.g., Normodyne], metoprolol [e.g., Lopressor], nadolol [e.g., Corgard], oxprenolol [e.g., Trasicor], penbutolol [e.g., Levatol], pindolol [e.g., Visken], propranolol [e.g., Inderal], sotalol [e.g., Sotacor], timolol [e.g., Blocadren]) or
- Digitalis glycosides (e.g., Lanoxin) or
- Diltiazem (e.g., Cardizem) or
- Verapamil (e.g., Calan)—Effects to slow the heart rate may be increased

- Cyclosporine (e.g., Sandimmune) or
- Desipramine (e.g., Norpramin) or
- Imipramine (e.g., Tofranil) or
- Tacrolimus (e.g., Prograf)—Effects of these medicines may be increased if they are used with mibefradil

- Flecainide (e.g., Tambocor) or
- Propafenone (e.g., Rythmol)—Unwanted effects of these medicines on the heart may be increased

Other medical problems—The presence of other medical problems may affect the use of mibefradil. Make sure you tell your doctor if you have any other medical problems, especially:

- Heart rhythm or heart rate problems—Mibefradil can worsen these conditions

Proper Use of This Medicine

Take this medicine exactly as directed. This medicine works best if you take it at the same time each day; however, do not take more of this medicine and do not take it more often than your doctor ordered. Do not miss any doses.

Swallow the tablet whole, without crushing or chewing it.

For patients taking this medicine *for high blood pressure:*

- In addition to the use of the medicine your doctor has prescribed, appropriate treatment for your high blood pressure may include weight control and care in the types of food you eat, especially foods high in sodium (salt). Your doctor will tell you which factors are most important for you. You should check with your doctor before changing your diet.
- Many patients who have high blood pressure will not notice any signs of the problem. In fact, many may feel normal. It is very important that you *take your medicine exactly as directed* and that you keep your appointments with your doctor even if you feel well.
- Remember that this medicine will not cure your high blood pressure but it does help control it. Therefore, you must continue to take it as directed if you expect to lower your blood pressure and keep it down. *You may have to take high blood pressure medicine for the rest of your life*. If high blood pressure is not treated, it can cause serious problems such as heart failure, blood vessel disease, stroke, or kidney disease.

Dosing—The dose of mibefradil will be different for different patients. *Follow your doctor's orders or the directions on the label.* The following information includes only the average doses of mibefradil. *If your dose is different, do not change it* unless your doctor tells you to do so.

The number of tablets that you take depends on the strength of the medicine. Also, *the number of doses you take each day, the time allowed between doses, and the length of time you take the medicine depend on the medical problem for which you are taking mibefradil.*

- For *oral* dosage form (tablets):
  —For angina (chest pain):
  - Adults—50 milligrams (mg) once a day to start. Your doctor may increase your dose.
  - Children—Use and dose must be determined by your doctor.
  —For high blood pressure:
  - Adults—50 mg once a day to start. Your doctor may increase your dose.
  - Children—Use and dose must be determined by your doctor.

Missed dose—If you miss a dose of this medicine, take it as soon as possible. However, if it is almost time for your next dose, skip the missed dose and go back to your regular dosing schedule. Do not double doses.

Storage—To store this medicine:
- Keep out of the reach of children.
- Store away from heat and direct light.
- Do not store in the bathroom, near the kitchen sink, or in other damp places. Heat or moisture may cause the medicine to break down.
- Do not keep outdated medicine or medicine no longer needed. Be sure that any discarded medicine is out of the reach of children.

Precautions While Using This Medicine

It is important that your doctor check your progress at regular visits. This will allow your doctor to make sure the medicine is working properly and to change the dosage if needed.

If you have been using this medicine regularly for several weeks, do not suddenly stop using it. Stopping suddenly may bring on your previous problem. Check with your doctor for the best way to reduce gradually the amount you are taking before stopping completely.

For patients taking this medicine for *chest pain:*
- Chest pain resulting from exercise or physical exertion is usually reduced or prevented by this medicine. This may tempt you to be overly active. *Make sure you discuss with your doctor a safe amount of exercise for your medical problem.*

For patients taking this medicine *for high blood pressure:*
- *Do not take other medicines unless you have discussed them with your doctor.*

This medicine may cause some people to become dizzy, drowsy, lightheaded, or to faint. Make sure you know how you react to this medicine before you drive, use machines, or do anything else that could be dangerous if you are dizzy or are not alert. If unusual tiredness or fainting occurs, check with your doctor.

This medicine may cause problems in an unborn or newborn child. Check with your doctor if you become pregnant, are planning to become pregnant, or are breast-feeding.

Side Effects of This Medicine

Along with its needed effects, a medicine may cause some unwanted effects. Although not all of these side effects may occur, if they do occur they may need medical attention.

Check with your doctor as soon as possible if any of the following side effects occur:

Less common
> Dizziness, lightheadedness or fainting, recurring (sudden); slow heart rate; swelling of the legs; unusual tiredness

Rare
> Chest pain

Other side effects may occur that usually do not need medical attention. These side effects may go away during treatment as your body adjusts to the medicine. However, check with your doctor if any of the following side effects continue or are bothersome:

More common
> Abdominal pain; belching, heartburn, or stomach discomfort; flushing; headache; nausea or vomiting; pounding heartbeat; stomach pain; stuffy nose

Other side effects not listed above may also occur in some patients. If you notice any other effects, check with your doctor.

Developed: 04/14/1998
Revised: 10/13/2000

MICONAZOLE   Topical

Commonly used brand name(s):

In the U.S.—
> Micatin
> Monistat-Derm
> Zeasorb-AF
> Generic name product may be available.

In Canada—
> Micatin
> Monistat-Derm

Description

Miconazole (mi-KON-a-zole) belongs to the group of medicines called antifungals. Topical miconazole is used to treat some types of fungus infections.

Some of these preparations may be available without a prescription; however, your doctor may have special instructions on the proper use of these medicines for your medical problem. Others are available only with your doctor's prescription.

Topical miconazole is available in the following dosage forms:

Topical
- Aerosol powder (U.S.)
- Aerosol solution (U.S.)
- Cream (U.S. and Canada)
- Lotion (U.S. and Canada)
- Powder (U.S.)

Before Using This Medicine

If you are using this medicine without a prescription, carefully read and follow any precautions on the label. For miconazole, the following should be considered:

Allergies—Tell your doctor if you have ever had any unusual or allergic reaction to miconazole. Also, tell your health care professional if you are allergic to any other substances, such as preservatives or dyes.

Pregnancy—Miconazole topical preparations have not been shown to cause birth defects or other problems in humans.

Breast-feeding—Miconazole topical preparations have not been reported to cause problems in nursing babies.

Children—Although there is no specific information comparing use of topical miconazole in children with use in other age groups, this medicine is not expected to cause different side effects or problems in children than it does in adults.

Older adults—Many medicines have not been studied specifically in older people. Therefore, it may not be known whether they work exactly the same way they do in younger adults. Although there is no specific information comparing use of topical miconazole in the elderly with use in other age groups, this medicine is not expected to cause different side effects or problems in older people than it does in younger adults.

Other medicines—Although certain medicines should not be used together at all, in other cases two different medicines may be used together even if an interaction might occur. In these cases, your doctor may want to change the dose, or other precautions may be necessary. Tell your health care professional if you are using any other topical prescription or nonprescription (over-the-counter [OTC]) medicine that is to be applied to the same area of the skin.

Proper Use of This Medicine

Keep this medicine away from the eyes.

Apply enough miconazole to cover the affected area, and rub in gently.

To use the *aerosol powder form* of miconazole:
- Shake well before using.
- From a distance of 6 to 10 inches, spray the powder on the affected areas. If it is used on the feet, spray it between the toes, on the feet, and in the socks and shoes.
- Do not inhale the powder.
- Do not use near heat, near open flame, or while smoking.

To use the *aerosol solution form* of miconazole:
- Shake well before using.
- From a distance of 4 to 6 inches, spray the solution on the affected areas. If it is used on the feet, spray it between the toes and on the feet.
- Do not inhale the vapors from the spray.
- Do not use near heat, near open flame, or while smoking.

To use the *powder form* of miconazole:
- If the powder is used on the feet, sprinkle it between the toes, on the feet, and in the socks and shoes.

When miconazole is used to treat certain types of fungus infections of the skin, an occlusive dressing (airtight covering, such as kitchen plastic wrap) should *not* be applied over this medicine. To do so may cause irritation of the skin. *Do not apply an occlusive dressing over this medicine unless you have been directed to do so by your doctor.*

To help clear up your infection completely, *keep using this medicine for the full time of treatment*, even if your condition has improved. *Do not miss any doses.*

Dosing—The dose of topical miconazole will be different for different patients. *Follow your doctor's orders or the directions on the label.* The following information includes only the average doses of topical miconazole. *If your dose is different, do not change it* unless your doctor tells you to do so.
- For *aerosol powder, aerosol solution, cream*, and *powder* dosage forms:
  —For fungus infections:
    - Adults and children—Apply to the affected area(s) of the skin two times a day, morning and evening.
- For *cream* and *lotion* dosage forms:
  —For sun fungus:
    - Adults and children—Apply to the affected area(s) of the skin once a day.

Missed dose—If you miss a dose of this medicine, apply it as soon as possible. However, if it is almost time for your next dose, skip the missed dose and go back to your regular dosing schedule.

Storage—To store this medicine:
- Keep out of the reach of children.
- Store away from heat and direct light.
- Do not store the powder form of this medicine in the bathroom, near the kitchen sink, or in other damp places. Heat or moisture may cause the medicine to break down.
- Keep the cream, lotion, and aerosol solution forms of this medicine from freezing.
- Do not puncture, break, or burn the aerosol powder or aerosol solution container.
- Do not keep outdated medicine or medicine no longer needed. Be sure that any discarded medicine is out of the reach of children.

Precautions While Using This Medicine

If your skin problem does not improve within 4 weeks, or if it becomes worse, check with your health care professional.

Side Effects of This Medicine

Along with its needed effects, a medicine may cause some unwanted effects. Although not all of these side effects may occur, if they do occur they may need medical attention.

Check with your doctor as soon as possible if any of the following side effects occur:
    Blistering, burning, redness, skin rash, or other sign of skin irritation not present before use of this medicine

Other side effects not listed above may also occur in some patients. If you notice any other effects, check with your doctor.

Revised: 07/25/94

MIDAZOLAM   Systemic

Commonly used brand name(s):

In the U.S.—
    Versed

In Canada—
    Versed

Description

Midazolam (MID-ay-zoe-lam) is used to produce sleepiness or drowsiness and to relieve anxiety before surgery or certain procedures. It is also used to produce loss of consciousness before and during surgery. Midazolam is used sometimes in patients in intensive care units in hospitals to cause unconsciousness. This may allow the patients to withstand the stress of being in the intensive care unit and help the patients cooperate when a machine must be used to assist them with breathing.

Midazolam is given only by or under the immediate supervision of a doctor trained to use this medicine. If you will be receiving midazolam during surgery, your doctor or anesthesiologist will give you the medicine and closely follow your progress.

Midazolam is available in the following dosage forms:
    Oral
    - Oral solution (U.S.)
    Parenteral
    - Injection (U.S. and Canada)

Before Using This Medicine

In deciding to use a medicine, the risks of taking the medicine must be weighed against the good it will do. This is a decision you and your doctor will make. For midazolam, the following should be considered:

Allergies—Tell your doctor if you have ever had any unusual or allergic reaction to midazolam or other benzodiazepines (such as alprazolam [e.g., Xanax], bromazepam [e.g., Lectopam], chlordiazepoxide [e.g., Librium], clonazepam [e.g., Klonopin], clorazepate [e.g., Tranxene], diazepam [e.g., Valium], estazolam [e.g., ProSom], flurazepam [e.g., Dalmane], halazepam [e.g., Paxipam], ketazolam [e.g., Loftran], lorazepam [e.g., Ativan], nitrazepam [e.g., Mogadon], oxazepam [e.g., Serax], prazepam [e.g., Centrax], quazepam [e.g., Doral], temazepam [e.g., Restoril], triazolam [e.g., Halcion]). Also, tell your health care professional if you are allergic to any other substances, such as foods, preservatives, or dyes.

Pregnancy—Midazolam is not recommended for use during pregnancy because it may cause birth defects. Other benzodiazepines, such as chlordiazepoxide (e.g., Librium) and diazepam (e.g., Valium) that are related chemically and in action to midazolam, have been reported to increase the chance of birth defects when used during the first 3 months of pregnancy. Also, use of midazolam during pregnancy, especially during the last few days, may cause drowsiness, slow heartbeat, shortness of breath, or troubled breathing in the newborn infant. In addition, receiving midazolam just before or during labor may cause weakness in the newborn infant.

Breast-feeding—Midazolam passes into human breast milk. Because newborn babies may be especially sensitive to the effects of midazolam, you should discuss breast-feeding with your physician if you are going to receive midazolam. It may be advisable to stop breast-feeding for a short period of time after receiving midazolam.

Children—Newborn babies may be especially sensitive to the effects of midazolam. This may increase the chance of side effects during the use of this medicine. Also, time to complete recovery after midazolam is given may be longer in very ill newborn babies.

Older adults—Elderly people are especially sensitive to the effects of midazolam. This may increase the chance of side effects during the use of this medicine. Also, time to complete recovery after midazolam is given may be slower in the elderly than in younger adults.

Other medicines—Although certain medicines should not be used together at all, in other cases two different medicines may be used together even if an interaction might occur. In these cases, your doctor may want to change the dose, or other precautions may be necessary. When you are receiving midazolam, it is especially important that your health care professional know if you are taking any of the following:

- Central nervous system (CNS) depressants (medicines that cause drowsiness) or alcohol—The CNS depressant and other effects of alcohol, other medicines, or midazolam may be increased; also, the effects of midazolam may last longer
- Saquinavir (e.g., Fortovase, Invirase)—Saquinavir may interfere with the removal of midazolam from the body, which could lead to serious side effects

Other medical problems—The presence of other medical problems may affect the use of midazolam. Make sure you tell your doctor if you have any other medical problems, especially:

- Heart disease or
- Kidney disease or
- Liver disease or
- Obesity (overweight)—The effects of midazolam may last longer
- Lung disease or

- Myasthenia gravis or other muscle and nerve disease—Midazolam may make the condition worse

Proper Use of This Medicine

Dosing—The dose of midazolam will be different for different patients. Your doctor will decide on the right amount for you. The dose will depend on:

- Your age;
- Your weight;
- Your general physical condition;
- The kind of surgery or other procedure you are having; and
- Other medicines you are taking or will receive before and during the procedure.

Precautions After Receiving This Medicine

For patients going home within 24 hours after receiving midazolam:

- Midazolam may cause some people to feel drowsy, tired, or weak for 1 or 2 days after it has been given. It may also cause problems with coordination and one's ability to think. Therefore, *do not drive, use machines, or do anything else that could be dangerous if you are not alert* until the effects of the medicine have disappeared or until the day after you receive midazolam, whichever period of time is longer.
- *Do not drink alcoholic beverages or take other CNS depressants (medicines that slow down the nervous system, possibly causing drowsiness) for about 24 hours after you have received midazolam, unless otherwise directed by your doctor.* To do so may add to the effects of the medicine. Some examples of CNS depressants are antihistamines or medicine for hay fever, other allergies, or colds; other sedatives, tranquilizers, or sleeping medicine; prescription pain medicine or narcotics; medicine for seizures; and muscle relaxants.

Side Effects of This Medicine

Along with its needed effects, a medicine may cause some unwanted effects. While you are receiving midazolam your doctor will monitor you closely for the side effects of midazolam, for example, breathing problems and confusion.

Some side effects may occur that usually do not need medical attention. Most side effects will go away as the effects of midazolam wear off.

However, check with your doctor if any side effects continue or are bothersome.

Revised: 05/09/2001

MIDODRINE   Systemic

Commonly used brand name(s):

In the U.S.—
ProAmatine

Description

Midodrine (MI-doe-dreen) is a medicine used to treat low blood pressure (hypotension). It works by stimulating nerve endings in blood vessels, causing the blood vessels to tighten. As a result, blood pressure is increased.

This medicine is available only with your doctor's prescription, in the following dosage form:

Oral
- Tablets (U.S.)

Before Using This Medicine

In deciding to use a medicine, the risks of taking the medicine must be weighed against the good it will do. This is a decision you and your doctor will make. For midodrine, the following should be considered:

Allergies—Tell your doctor if you have ever had any unusual or allergic reaction to midodrine. Also tell your health care professional if you are allergic to any other substances, such as foods, preservatives, or dyes.

Pregnancy—Midodrine has not been studied in pregnant women. However, studies in animals have shown that large doses of midodrine can cause reduced body weight in rat fetuses and decreased survival in rabbit fetuses. Before taking this medicine, make sure your doctor knows if you are pregnant or may become pregnant.

Breast-feeding—It is not known if midodrine passes into breast milk. However, it has not been reported to cause problems in nursing babies.

Children—This medicine has been tested in a limited number of children 6 months to 12 years of age. In effective doses, the medicine has not been shown to cause different side effects or problems than it does in adults.

Older adults—This medicine has been tested and has not been shown to cause different side effects or problems in older people than it dose in younger adults.

Other medicines—Although certain medicines should not be used together at all, in other cases two different medicines may be used together even if an interaction might occur. In these cases, your doctor may want to change the dose, or other precautions may be necessary. When you are taking midodrine, it is especially important that your health care professional know if you are taking any of the following:

- Digitalis glycosides (e.g., Lanoxin)—Effects on the heart may be increased

- Steroids that cause sodium retention, such as fludrocortisone (e.g., Florinef) or

- Vasoconstricting medication, such as dihydroergotamine (e.g., Migranal), and ephedrine, phenylephrine, phenylpropanolamine, or pseudoephedrine (ingredients in many cough/cold combination products)—Effects on blood pressure may be increased

Other medical problems—The presence of other medical problems may affect the use of midodrine. Make sure you tell your doctor if you have any other medical problems, especially:

- Heart disease, severe or
- Hypertension (high blood pressure) or
- Overactive thyroid or
- Visual problems—Effects of midodrine on blood pressure may aggravate these problems

- Kidney disease or
- Liver disease—Effects of midodrine may be increased because of slower removal of the medicine from the body

- Urinary retention—Effects of midodrine on the bladder may aggravate this condition

Proper Use of This Medicine

The last dose of midodrine should not be taken after the evening meal or less than 3 to 4 hours before bedtime because high blood pressure upon lying down (supine hypertension) can occur, which can cause blurred vision, headaches, and pounding in the ears while lying down after taking this medicine.

Also, midodrine should not be taken if you will be lying down for any length of time.

Dosing—The dose of midodrine will be different for different patients. *Follow your doctor's orders or the directions on the label.* The following information includes only the average doses of midodrine. *If your dose is different, do not change it* unless your doctor tells you to do so.

The number of tablets that you take depends on the strength of the medicine. Also, *the number of doses you take each day, the time allowed between doses, and the length of time you take the medicine depend on the medical problem for which you are taking midodrine.*

- For *oral* dosage form (tablets):
  —Low blood pressure (hypotension):
  - Adults—10 milligrams (mg) three times a day in approximately four-hour intervals during the daytime hours: shortly before or upon rising in the morning, at midday, and in the late afternoon (not later than six p.m.). Your doctor may increase your dose if needed.
  - Children—Use and dose must be determined by your doctor.

Missed dose—If you miss a dose of this medicine, take it as soon as possible. However, if it is almost time for your next dose, skip the missed dose and go back to your regular dosing schedule. Do not double doses.

Storage—To store this medicine:
- Keep out of the reach of children.
- Store away from heat and direct light.
- Do not store in the bathroom, near the kitchen sink, or in other damp places. Heat or moisture may cause the medicine to break down.
- Do not keep outdated medicine or medicine no longer needed. Be sure that any discarded medicine is out of the reach of children.

Precautions While Using This Medicine

Do not take other medicines unless they have been discussed with your doctor. This especially includes over-the-counter (nonprescription) medicines for appetite control, asthma, colds, cough, hayfever, or sinus problems, since they may tend to increase your blood pressure.

Side Effects of This Medicine

Along with its needed effects, a medicine may cause some unwanted effects. Although not all of these side effects may occur, if they do occur they may need medical attention.

Check with your doctor as soon as possible if any of the following side effects occur:

More common

Blurred vision, cardiac awareness, headache, and/or pounding in the ears

Rare

Fainting; increased dizziness; slow pulse

Other side effects may occur that usually do not need medical attention. These side effects may go away during treatment as your body adjusts to the medicine. However, check with your doctor if any of the following side effects continue or are bothersome:

More common

Burning, itching, or prickling of the scalp; chills; goose-bumps; urinary frequency, retention, or urgency

Less common

Anxiety or nervousness; confusion; dry mouth; flushing; headache or feeling of pressure in the head; skin rash

Rare

Backache; canker sores; dizziness; drowsiness; dry skin; leg cramps; pain or sensitivity of skin to touch; stomach problems such as gas, heartburn, or nausea; trouble in sleeping; trouble seeing; weakness

Other side effects not listed above may also occur in some patients. If you notice any other effects, check with your doctor.

Additional Information

Once a medicine has been approved for marketing for a certain use, experience may show that it is also useful for other medical problems. Although not specifically included in product labeling, midodrine is used in certain patients with the following medical conditions:

* Low blood pressure (hypotension) caused by kidney dialysis
* Low blood pressure caused by certain medicines used to treat mental illness
* Low blood pressure in children with an infection

Other than the above information, there is no additional information related to proper use, precautions, or side effects for these uses.

Developed: 08/10/98
Revised: 01/30/2001

MIFEPRISTONE Systemic— INTRODUCTORY VERSION

Commonly used brand name(s):

In the U.S.—

Mifeprex

Other commonly used names are
RU 486

Description

Mifepristone (mif-i-PRIS-tone) is used to end a pregnancy that is less than 49 days' in duration. It works by stopping the supply of hormones that maintains the interior of the uterus. Without these hormones, the uterus cannot support the pregnancy and the contents of the uterus are expelled.

This medicine is available only with your doctor's prescription, in the following dosage form:

Oral

* Tablets (U.S.)

Before Using This Medicine

In deciding to use a medicine, the risks of taking the medicine must be weighed against the good it will do. This is a decision you and your doctor will make. For mifepristone, the following should be considered:

Allergies—Tell your doctor if you have ever had any unusual or allergic reaction to mifepristone, misoprostol or any other prostaglandins.

Pregnancy—Mifepristone is used to terminate an early pregnancy. Fetal deformities may result if a pregnancy is allowed to continue following a failed attempt at medical termination.

Breast-feeding—It is unknown whether mifepristone is distributed in the breast milk.

Other medicines—Although certain medicines should not be used together at all, in other cases two different medicines may be used together even if an interaction might occur. In these cases, your doctor may want to change the dose, or other precautions may be necessary. When you are taking mifepristone, it is especially important that your doctor and pharmacist know if you are taking any of the following:

* Carbamazepine (e.g., Tegretol) or
* Dexamethasone (e.g., Decadron) or
* Phenobarbital (e.g., Luminal) or
* Phenytoin (e.g., Dilantin) or
* Rifampin (e.g., Rifadin) or
* St. John's Wort—May decrease the concentration of mifepristone in the blood

* Erythromycin (e.g., E-Mycin) or
* Grapefruit juice or
* Itraconazole (e.g., Sporanox) or
* Ketoconazole (e.g., Nizoral)—May increase the concentration of mifepristone in the blood

* Anticoagulants, such as warfarin (e.g., Coumadin)—May increase the risk of bleeding

* Corticosteroids (cortisone-like medicine)—Mifepristone may not work as well

Other medical problems—The presence of other medical problems may affect the use of mifepristone. Make sure you tell your doctor if you have any other medical problems, especially:

* Bleeding problems—May cause excessive vaginal bleeding

* Adrenal failure—Mifepristone may not work appropriately

* Ectopic pregnancy or
* Lower abdominal mass—Mifepristone will not terminate an ectopic pregnancy

* An intrauterine device (IUD) that is still in the uterus—Must be removed before mifepristone therapy is started

* Porphyria, inherited
* Anemia, severe or

- Poor blood circulation or
- Inability of blood to clot properly—Mifepristone causes heavy bleeding in a small portion of users, this may be intensified in patients with bleeding disorders

Proper Use of This Medicine

Dosing—
- To terminate a pregnancy of 49 days or less duration:
  —For *oral* dosage form (tablets):
  - Adults—600 milligrams (mg) (three 200 mg tablets) as a single oral dose followed two days later by 400 micrograms (mcg) (two 200 mcg tablets) of misoprostol as a single oral dose as needed.

Precautions While Using This Medicine

You must have 3 visits to your physicians office during the treatment procedure. It is **extremely important** that you attend all three visits.

Check with your physician if the vaginal bleeding becomes severe or seems to last longer than expected.

You may need to have a surgical procedure to stop excessive vaginal bleeding or to terminate a pregnancy that was not terminated with the medical treatment procedure.

Side Effects of This Medicine

Along with its needed effects, a medicine may cause some unwanted effects. Although not all of these side effects may occur, if they do occur they may need medical attention.

Check with your doctor as soon as possible if any of the following side effects occur:
Less common
Excessively heavy vaginal bleeding; unusual tiredness or weakness

Other side effects may occur that usually do not need medical attention. These side effects may go away during treatment as your body adjusts to the medicine. However, check with your doctor if any of the following side effects continue or are bothersome.
More common
Abdominal pain or uterine cramping; back pain; diarrhea; dizziness; headache; nausea or vomiting
Less common
Acid or sour stomach; anxiety; belching; cough; fainting or light-headedness when getting up from a lying or sitting position; fever; flu-like symptoms; headache; heartburn; increased clear or white vaginal discharge; indigestion; itching of the vagina or genital area; lack or loss of strength; pain during sexual intercourse; pain or tenderness around eyes and cheekbones; pale skin; shaking chills; shortness of breath or troubled breathing; sleeplessness or trouble sleeping; stomach discomfort, upset, or pain; tightness of chest or wheezing; troubled breathing, exertional; unusual bleeding or bruising; stuffy or runny nose

Other side effects not listed above may also occur in some patients. If you notice any other effects, check with your doctor.

Developed: 10/13/2000

MIGLITOL   Systemic—INTRODUCTORY VERSION

Commonly used brand name(s):

In the U.S.—
Glyset

Description

Miglitol (MIG-le-tall) is used to treat high blood sugar levels that are caused by a type of diabetes mellitus or sugar diabetes called type 2 diabetes. Normally, after you eat, your pancreas releases insulin to help your body store excess sugar for later use. This process occurs during normal digestion of food. In type 2 diabetes, your body does not work properly to store the excess sugar and the sugar remains in your bloodstream. Having high blood sugar can lead to serious health problems in the future. Proper diet is the first step in managing type 2 diabetes but often medicines are needed to help your body. Miglitol is a medicine that slows the digestion of sugars so your body has time to store extra sugar. Sometimes another medicine called sulfonylurea can be used in combination with miglitol to help your body store more sugar.

This medicine is available only with your doctor's prescription, in the following dosage form:

Oral
- Tablets (U.S.)

Before Using This Medicine

In deciding to use a medicine, the risks of taking the medicine must be weighed against the good it will do. This is a decision you and your doctor will make. For miglitol, the following should be considered:

Allergies—Tell your doctor if you have ever had any unusual or allergic reaction to miglitol. Also, tell your health care professional if you are allergic to any other substances, such as foods, preservatives, or dyes.

Pregnancy—Miglitol has not been studied in pregnant women. However, studies in animals have shown that miglitol causes birth defects or other problems. Before taking this medicine, make sure your doctor knows if you are pregnant or if you may become pregnant.

Breast-feeding—Although a very small amount of this medicine passes into human breast milk, it has not been shown to cause problems in nursing babies. Miglitol is not recommended for a nursing woman. Mothers who are taking this medicine and who wish to breast-feed should discuss this with their doctor.

Children—Studies on this medicine have been done only in adult patients, and there is no specific information comparing use of miglitol in children with use in other age groups.

Older adults—This medicine has been tested and has not been shown to cause different side effects or problems in older people than it does in younger adults.

Other medicines—Although certain medicines should not be used together at all, in other cases two different medicines may be used together even if an interaction might occur. In these cases, your doctor may want to change the dose, or other precautions may be necessary. When you are

taking miglitol, it is especially important that your health care professional know if you are taking any of the following:

- Digestive enzymes (e.g., Pancrease, Viokase, etc.) or
- Activated charcoal (e.g., Insta-Char, Liqui-Char)—Miglitol may not work as well when taken with these medicines
- Propranolol (e.g., Inderal) or
- Ranitidine (e.g., Zantac)—These medicines may not work as well when taken with miglitol.

Other medical problems—The presence of other medical problems may affect the use of miglitol. Make sure you tell your doctor if you have any other medical problems, especially:

- Digestion problems or
- Inflammatory bowel disease or
- Intestinal blockage or
- Other intestinal problems—Miglitol should not be used
- Kidney disease—Higher levels of miglitol may result and a smaller dose may be needed

Proper Use of This Medicine

Follow carefully the special meal plan you doctor gave you. This is the most important part of controlling your condition, and is necessary if the medicine is to work properly. Also, exercise regularly and test for sugar in your blood or urine as directed.

For this medicine to work properly it should be taken with the first bite of each main meal.

Dosing—The dose of miglitol will be different for different patients. *Follow your doctor's orders or the directions on the label.* The following information includes only the average doses of miglitol. *If your dose is different, do not change it* unless your doctor tells you to do so.

- For *oral* dosage form (tablets):
  —For type 2 diabetes:
  - Adults—At first the dose is 25 milligrams (mg) three times a day, at the start (with the first bite) of each main meal. After four to eight weeks, your doctor may increase your dose to 50 mg three times a day. Then, after an additional twelve weeks, if necessary, your doctor may increase your dose to 100 mg three times a day.
  - Children—Use and dose must be determined by your doctor.

Missed dose—If meal completed without having taken medication: Skipping missed dose; taking next dose with next meal; not doubling doses

Storage—To store this medicine:

- Keep out of the reach of children.
- Do not store in the bathroom, near the kitchen sink, or in other damp places. Heat or moisture may cause the medicine to break down.
- Keep the medicine from freezing. Do not refrigerate.
- Do not keep outdated medicine or medicine no longer needed. Ask your health care professional how you should dispose of any medicine you do not use. Be sure that any discarded medicine is out of the reach of children.

Precautions While Using This Medicine

Your doctor will want to check your progress at regular visits, especially during the first few weeks that you take this medicine.

It is very important to follow carefully any instructions from your health care team about:

- Alcohol—Drinking alcohol may cause severe low blood sugar. Discuss this with your health care team.
- Other medicines—Do not take other medicines during the time you are taking miglitol unless they have been discussed with your doctor. This especially includes nonprescription medicines such as aspirin, and medicines for appetite control, asthma, colds, cough, hay fever, or sinus problems.
- Counseling—Other family members need to learn how to prevent side effects or help with side effects if they occur. Also, patients with diabetes may need special counseling about diabetes medicine dosing changes that might occur because of lifestyle changes, such as changes in exercise and diet. Furthermore, counseling on contraception and pregnancy may be needed because of the problems that can occur in patients with diabetes during pregnancy.
- Travel—Keep a recent prescription and your medical history with you. Be prepared for an emergency as you would normally. Make allowances for changing time zones and keep your meal times as close as possible to your usual meal times.

In case of emergency—There may be a time when you need emergency help for a problem caused by your diabetes. You need to be prepared for these emergencies. It is a good idea to wear a medical identification (ID) bracelet or neck chain at all times. Also, carry an ID card in your wallet or purse that says that you have diabetes and a list of all your medicines.

Symptoms of hypoglycemia (low blood sugar) include anxiety; behavior change similar to being drunk; blurred vision; cold sweats; confusion; cool, pale skin; difficulty in thinking; drowsiness; excessive hunger; fast heartbeat; headache (continuing); nausea; nervousness; nightmares; restless sleep; shakiness; slurred speech; or unusual tiredness or weakness.

Miglitol does not cause low blood sugar. However, it can occur if you delay or miss a meal or snack, drink alcohol, exercise more than usual, cannot eat because of nausea or vomiting, or take miglitol with another type of diabetes medicine. *Symptoms of low blood sugar must be treated before they lead to unconsciousness (passing out).* Different people feel different symptoms of low blood sugar. *It is important that you learn which symptoms of low blood sugar you usually have so that you can treat it quickly.*

If symptoms of low blood sugar occur, *eat glucose tablets or gel or honey, or drink fruit juice to relieve the symptoms. Table sugar (sucrose) or regular (nondiet) soft drinks will not work.* Also, check your blood for low blood sugar. *Glucagon is used in emergency situations when severe symptoms such as seizures (convulsions) or unconsciousness occur.* Have a glucagon kit available, along with a syringe or needle, and know how to use it. Members of your household also should know how to use it.

Symptoms of hyperglycemia (high blood sugar) include blurred vision; drowsiness; dry mouth; flushed, dry skin; fruit-like breath odor; increased urination; ketones in urine; loss of appetite; stomachache, nausea, or vomiting; tiredness; troubled breathing (rapid and deep); unconsciousness; or unusual thirst.

High blood sugar may occur if you do not exercise as much as usual, have a fever or infection, do not take enough or skip a dose of your diabetes medicine, or overeat or do not follow your meal plan.

If symptoms of high blood sugar occur, *check your blood sugar level and then call your health care professional for instructions.*

Side Effects of This Medicine

Other side effects may occur that usually do not need medical attention. These side effects may go away during treatment as your body adjusts to the medicine. However, check with your health care professional if any of the following side effects continue or are bothersome:

More common
>Bloated full feeling; excess air or gas in stomach or intestines; increase in bowel movements; loose stools; passing gas; soft stools; stomach or abdomen pain

Less common
>Skin rash

Other side effects not listed above may also occur in some patients. If you notice any other effects, check with your doctor.

Developed: 11/09/2000

MINOXIDIL   Systemic

Commonly used brand name(s):

In the U.S.—
>Loniten
>Generic name product may be available.

In Canada—
>Loniten

Description

Minoxidil (mi-NOX-i-dill) belongs to the general class of medicines called antihypertensives. It is used to treat high blood pressure (hypertension).

High blood pressure adds to the workload of the heart and arteries. If it continues for a long time, the heart and arteries may not function properly. This can damage the blood vessels of the brain, heart, and kidneys, resulting in a stroke, heart failure, or kidney failure. High blood pressure may also increase the risk of heart attacks. These problems may be less likely to occur if blood pressure is controlled.

Minoxidil works by relaxing blood vessels so that blood passes through them more easily. This helps to lower blood pressure.

Minoxidil has other effects that could be bothersome for some patients. These include increased hair growth, weight gain, fast heartbeat, and chest pain. Before you take this medicine, be sure that you have discussed the use of it with your doctor.

Minoxidil is being applied to the scalp in liquid form by some balding men to stimulate hair growth. However, improper use of liquids made from minoxidil tablets can result in minoxidil being absorbed into the body, where it may cause unwanted effects on the heart and blood vessels.

Minoxidil is available only with your doctor's prescription, in the following dosage form:

Oral
>• Tablets (U.S. and Canada)

Before Using This Medicine

In deciding to use a medicine, the risks of taking the medicine must be weighed against the good it will do. This is a decision you and your doctor will make. For minoxidil, the following should be considered:

Allergies—Tell your doctor if you have ever had any unusual or allergic reaction to minoxidil. Also tell your health care professional if you are allergic to any other substances, such as foods, preservatives, or dyes.

Pregnancy—Minoxidil has not been studied in pregnant women. However, there have been reports of babies born with extra thick or dark hair on their bodies after the mothers took minoxidil during pregnancy. Discuss this possible effect with your doctor.

Studies in rats found a decreased rate of conception, and studies in rabbits at 5 times the human dose have shown a decrease in successful pregnancies. Minoxidil did not cause birth defects in rats or rabbits.

Breast-feeding—Although minoxidil passes into breast milk, it has not been reported to cause problems in nursing babies.

Children—Although there is no specific information comparing use of minoxidil in children with use in other age groups, this medicine is not expected to cause different side effects or problems in children than it does in adults.

Older adults—Elderly patients may be more sensitive to the effects of minoxidil. In addition, minoxidil may reduce tolerance to cold temperatures in elderly patients.

Other medicines—Although certain medicines should not be used together at all, in other cases two different medicines may be used together even if an interaction might occur. In these cases, your doctor may want to change the dose, or other precautions may be necessary. When taking minoxidil it is especially important that your health care professional know if you are taking any of the following:

>• Guanethidine (e.g., Ismelin) or
>• Nitrates (medicine for angina)—Severe lowered blood pressure may occur

Other medical problems—The presence of other medical problems may affect the use of minoxidil. Make sure you tell your doctor if you have any other medical problems, especially:

>• Angina (chest pain)—Minoxidil may make this condition worse

>• Heart attack or stroke (recent)—Lowering blood pressure may make problems resulting from heart attack or stroke worse

>• Heart or blood vessel disease—Minoxidil can cause fluid buildup, which can cause problems

>• Kidney disease—Effects may be increased because of slower removal of minoxidil from the body

>• Pheochromocytoma—Minoxidil may cause the tumor to be more active

Proper Use of This Medicine

In addition to the use of the medicine your doctor has prescribed, treatment for your high blood pressure may include weight control and care in the types of foods you eat, especially foods high in sodium. Your doctor will tell you which of these are most important for you. You should check with your doctor before changing your diet.

Many patients who have high blood pressure will not notice any signs of the problem. In fact, many may feel normal. It is very important that you *take your medicine exactly as directed* and that you keep your appointments with your doctor even if you feel well.

Remember that minoxidil will not cure your high blood pressure but it does help control it. Therefore, you must continue to take it as directed if you expect to lower your blood pressure and keep it down. *You may have to take high blood pressure medicine for the rest of your life.* If high blood pressure is not treated, it can cause serious problems such as heart failure, blood vessel disease, stroke, or kidney disease.

To help you remember to take your medicine, try to get into the habit of taking it at the same time each day.

This medicine is usually given together with certain other medicines. If you are using a combination of drugs, make sure that you take each medicine at the proper time and do not mix them. Ask your health care professional to help you plan a way to remember to take your medicines at the right time.

Dosing—The dose of minoxidil will be different for different patients. *Follow your doctor's orders or the directions on the label.* The following information includes only the average doses of minoxidil. *If your dose is different, do not change it* unless your doctor tells you to do so:

- For *oral* dosage forms (tablets):
  —Adults and children over 12 years of age: 5 to 40 milligrams taken as a single dose or in divided doses.
  —Children up to 12 years of age: 200 micrograms to 1 milligram per kilogram of body weight a day to be taken as a single dose or in divided doses.

Missed dose—If you miss a dose of this medicine and remember it within a few hours, take it when you remember. However, if you do not remember until the next day, skip the missed dose and go back to your regular dosing schedule. Do not double doses.

Storage—To store this medicine:

- Keep out of the reach of children.
- Store away from heat and direct light.
- Do not store in the bathroom, near the kitchen sink, or in other damp places. Heat or moisture may cause the medicine to break down.
- Do not keep outdated medicine or medicine no longer needed. Be sure that any discarded medicine is out of the reach of children.

Precautions While Using This Medicine

It is important that your doctor check your progress at regular visits to make sure that this medicine is working properly.

Ask your doctor about checking your pulse rate before and after taking minoxidil. Then, while you are taking this medicine, *check your pulse regularly while you are resting.* If it increases by 20 beats or more a minute, check with your doctor right away.

While you are taking minoxidil, *weigh yourself every day.* A weight gain of 2 to 3 pounds (about 1 kg) in an adult is normal and should be lost with continued treatment. However, if you suddenly gain 5 pounds (2 kg) or more (for a child, 2 pounds [1 kg] or more) or if you notice swelling of your feet or lower legs, check with your doctor right away.

Do not take other medicines unless they have been discussed with your doctor. This especially includes over-the-counter (nonprescription) medicines for appetite control, asthma, colds, cough, hay fever, or sinus problems, since they may tend to increase your blood pressure.

Side Effects of This Medicine

Along with its needed effects, a medicine may cause some unwanted effects. Although not all of these side effects may occur, if they do occur they may need medical attention.

Check with your doctor immediately if any of the following side effects occur:
> *More common*
> Fast or irregular heartbeat; weight gain (rapid) of more than 5 pounds (2 pounds in children)

> *Less common*
> Chest pain; shortness of breath

Check with your doctor as soon as possible if any of the following side effects occur:
> *More common*
> Bloating; flushing or redness of skin; swelling of feet or lower legs

> *Less common*
> Numbness or tingling of hands, feet, or face

> *Rare*
> Skin rash and itching

Other side effects may occur that usually do not need medical attention. These side effects may go away during treatment as your body adjusts to the medicine. However, check with your doctor if any of the following side effects continue or are bothersome:
> *More common*
> Increase in hair growth, usually on face, arms, and back

> *Less common or rare*
> Breast tenderness in males and females; headache

This medicine causes a temporary increase in hair growth in most people. Hair may grow longer and darker in both men and women. This may first be noticed on the face several weeks after you start taking minoxidil. Later, new hair growth may be noticed on the back, arms, legs, and scalp. Talk to your doctor about shaving or using a hair remover during this time. After treatment with minoxidil has ended, the hair will stop growing, although it may take several months for the new hair growth to go away.

Other side effects not listed above may also occur in some patients. If you notice any other effects, check with your doctor.

Revised: 05/26/93

MINOXIDIL   Topical

Commonly used brand name(s):

In the U.S.—
Rogaine Extra Strength For Men	Rogaine For Men
	Rogaine For Women

Generic name product may be available.

In Canada—
Apo-Gain	Minoxigaine
Gen-Minoxidil	Rogaine

Description

Minoxidil (mi-NOX-i-dil) applied to the scalp is used to stimulate hair growth in adult men and women with a certain type of baldness. The exact way that this medicine works is not known.

If hair growth is going to occur with the use of minoxidil, it usually occurs after the medicine has been used for several months and lasts only as long as the medicine continues to be used. Hair loss will begin again within a few months after minoxidil treatment is stopped.

In the U.S., this medicine is available without a prescription. In Canada, this medicine is available only with your doctor's prescription. It is available in the following dosage form:

Topical
- Topical solution (U.S. and Canada)

Before Using This Medicine

In deciding to use a medicine, the risks of using the medicine must be weighed against the good it will do. This is a decision you and your doctor will make. For topical minoxidil, the following should be considered:

Allergies—Tell your doctor if you have ever had any unusual or allergic reaction to minoxidil or propylene glycol (non-active product in medicine). Also tell your health care professional if you are allergic to any other substances, such as preservatives or dyes.

Pregnancy—Topical minoxidil has not been studied in pregnant women. However, some studies in animals have shown that minoxidil, when given by mouth, causes problems during pregnancy, although the studies have not shown that the medicine causes birth defects. Before using this medicine, make sure your doctor knows if you are pregnant or if you may become pregnant.

Breast-feeding—It is not known whether topical minoxidil passes into breast milk. However, minoxidil, taken by mouth, does pass into breast milk. Minoxidil is not recommended during breast-feeding, because it may cause problems in nursing babies.

Children—Studies of this medicine have been done only in adult patients, and there is no specific information comparing use of topical minoxidil in children up to 18 years of age with use in other age groups. Use in infants and children is not recommended. If you think your child has hair loss, discuss it with the doctor.

Older adults—This medicine has been tested in a limited number of older patients up to 65 years of age and has not been shown to cause different side effects or problems in this age group than it does in younger adults. However, studies have shown that the medicine works best in younger patients who have a short history of hair loss. Minoxidil has not been studied in patients older than 65 years of age.

Other medicines—Although certain medicines should not be used together at all, in other cases two different medicines may be used together even if an interaction might occur. In these cases, your doctor may want to change the dose, or other precautions may be necessary. When you are using topical minoxidil, it is especially important that your health care professional know if you are taking any other prescription or nonprescription (over-the-counter [OTC]) medicine or if you are using any of the following on your scalp:

- Corticosteroids (cortisone-like medicines) or
- Petrolatum (e.g., Vaseline) or
- Tretinoin (e.g., Retin-A)—Use of these products on your scalp may cause too much topical minoxidil to be absorbed into the body and may increase the chance of side effects

Other medical problems—The presence of other medical problems may affect the use of topical minoxidil. Make sure you tell your doctor if you have any other medical problems, especially:

- Any other skin problems or an irritation or a sunburn on the scalp—The condition may cause too much topical minoxidil to be absorbed into the body and may increase the chance of side effects
- Heart disease or
- Hypertension (high blood pressure)—Topical minoxidil has not been studied in patients who have these conditions, but more serious problems may develop for these patients if they use more medicine than is recommended over a large area and too much minoxidil is absorbed into the body

Proper Use of This Medicine

This medicine usually comes with patient instructions. It is important that you read the instructions carefully.

It is very important that you use this medicine only as directed. Do not use more of it and do not use it more often than your doctor ordered. To do so may increase the chance of it being absorbed through the skin. For the same reason, do not apply minoxidil to other parts of your body. Absorption into the body may affect the heart and blood vessels and cause unwanted effects.

Do not use any other skin products on the same skin area on which you use minoxidil. Hair coloring, hair permanents, and hair relaxers may be used during minoxidil therapy as long as the scalp is washed just before applying the hair coloring, permanent, or relaxer. Minoxidil should not be used 24 hours before and after the hair treatment procedure. *Be sure to not double your doses of minoxidil to make up for any missed doses.*

To apply minoxidil solution:
- Make sure your hair and scalp are completely dry before applying this medicine.
- Apply the amount prescribed to the area of the scalp being treated, beginning in the center of the area. Follow your doctor's instructions on how to apply the solution, using the applicator provided.
- Do not shampoo your hair for 4 hours after applying minoxidil.
- Immediately after using this medicine, wash your hands to remove any medicine that may be on them.
- Do not use a hairdryer to dry the scalp after you apply minoxidil solution. Blowing with a hairdryer on the scalp may make the treatment less effective.
- Allow the minoxidil to completely dry for 2 to 4 hours after applying it, including before going to bed. Minoxidil can stain clothing, hats, or bed linen if your hair or scalp is not fully dry after using the medicine.
- Avoid transferring the medicine while wet to other parts of the body. This can occur if the medicine gets on your pillowcase or bed linens or if your hands are not washed after applying minoxidil.

If your scalp becomes abraded, irritated, or sunburned, check with your doctor before applying minoxidil.

Keep this medicine away from the eyes, nose, and mouth. If you should accidentally get some in your eyes, nose, or mouth, flush the area thoroughly with cool tap water. *If you are using the pump spray, be careful not to breathe in the spray.*

Dosing—The dose of topical minoxidil will be different for different patients. *Follow your doctor's orders or the directions on the label.* The following information includes only the average dose of topical minoxidil. *If your dose is different, do not change it* unless your doctor tells you to do so.

- For *topical solution* dosage form:
  - For hair growth:
    - Adults up to 65 years of age—Apply 1 milliliter to the scalp two times a day.
    - Adults 65 years of age and older—Use and dose must be determined by the doctor.
    - Infants—Use is not recommended.
    - Children up to 18 years of age—Use and dose must be determined by the doctor.

Missed dose—If you miss a dose of this medicine, go back to your regular dosing schedule. Do not double doses.

Storage—To store this medicine:
- Keep out of the reach of children.
- Store away from heat and direct light.
- Keep the medicine from freezing.
- Do not keep outdated medicine or medicine no longer needed. Be sure that any discarded medicine is out of the reach of children.

Precautions While Using This Medicine

It is important that your doctor check your progress at regular visits to make sure that this medicine is working properly and to check for unwanted effects.

Tell your doctor if you notice continued itching, redness, or burning of your scalp after you apply minoxidil. If the itching, redness, or burning is severe, wash the medicine off and check with your doctor before using it again.

Hair loss may continue for 2 weeks after you start using minoxidil. Tell your doctor if your hair loss continues after 2 weeks. Also, tell your doctor if your hair growth does not increase after using minoxidil for 4 months.

Side Effects of This Medicine

Along with its needed effects, a medicine may cause some unwanted effects. Although not all of these side effects may occur, if they do occur they may need medical attention.

Check with your doctor as soon as possible if any of the following side effects occur:

Less common
  Itching or skin rash (continued)

Rare
  Acne at site of application; burning of scalp; increased hair loss; inflammation or soreness at root of hair; reddened skin; swelling of face

Signs and symptoms of too much medicine being absorbed into the body—Rare
  Blurred vision or other changes in vision; chest pain; decrease of sexual ability or desire; fast or irregular heartbeat; flushing; headache; lightheadedness; numbness or tingling of hands, feet, or face; swelling of face, hands, feet, or lower legs; weight gain (rapid)

Other side effects not listed above may also occur in some patients. If you notice any other effects, check with your doctor.

Revised: 07/20/98

MIRTAZAPINE   Systemic

Commonly used brand name(s):

In the U.S.—
  Remeron
  Remeron SolTab

Description

Mirtazapine (mir-TAZ-a-peen) is used to treat mental depression.

This medicine is available only with your doctor's prescription, in the following dosage form(s):

Oral
- Oral Disintegrating Tablets (U.S.)
- Tablets (U.S.)

Before Using This Medicine

In deciding to use a medicine, the risks of taking the medicine must be weighed against the good it will do. This is a decision you and your doctor will make. For mirtazapine, the following should be considered:

Allergies—Tell your doctor if you have ever had any unusual or allergic reaction to mirtazapine. Also tell your health care professional if you are allergic to any other substances, such as foods, preservatives, or dyes.

Pregnancy—Mirtazapine has not been studied in pregnant women. However, this medicine has been shown to cause death of the fetus in animals given doses many times higher than the usual human dose. Mirtazapine has not been shown to cause birth defects in animals.

Breast-feeding—It is not known whether mirtazapine passes into breast milk. Although most medicines pass into breast milk in small amounts, many of them may be used safely while breast-feeding. Mothers who are taking this medicine and who wish to breast-feed should discuss this with their doctor.

Children—Studies on this medicine have been done only in adult patients, and there is no specific information comparing use of mirtazapine in children with use in other age groups.

Older adults—This medicine has been tested and has not been shown to cause different side effects or problems in older people than it does in younger adults. However, it is removed from the body more slowly in older people.

Other medicines—Although certain medicines should not be used together at all, in other cases two different medicines may be used together even if an interaction might occur. In these cases, your doctor may want to change the dose, or other precautions may be necessary. When you are taking mirtazapine, it is especially important that your health care professional know if you are taking any of the following:

- Alcohol or

- Central nervous system (CNS) depressants (medicines that cause drowsiness) or
- Tricyclic antidepressants (amitriptyline [e.g., Elavil], amoxapine [e.g., Asendin], clomipramine [e.g., Anafranil], desipramine [e.g., Pertofrane], doxepin [e.g., Sinequan], imipramine [e.g., Tofranil], nortriptyline [e.g., Aventyl], protriptyline [e.g., Vivactil], trimipramine [e.g., Surmontil])—Using these medicines with mirtazapine may increase the CNS depressant effects
- Monoamine oxidase (MAO) inhibitors (furazolidone [e.g., Furoxone], phenelzine [e.g., Nardil], procarbazine [e.g., Matulane], selegiline [e.g., Eldepryl], tranylcypromine [e.g., Parnate])—*Do not take mirtazapine while you are taking, or within 2 weeks of taking, an MAO inhibitor* or you may develop confusion, agitation, restlessness, stomach or intestinal symptoms, sudden high body temperature, extremely high blood pressure, and severe convulsions; at least 14 days should be allowed between stopping treatment with one medicine and starting treatment with the other

Other medical problems— The presence of other medical problems may affect the use of mirtazapine. Make sure you tell your doctor if you have any other medical problems, especially:

- Convulsions (seizures) (history of)—Mirtazapine has been reported to cause seizures rarely
- Dehydration or
- Heart disease or
- Stroke (history of)—Mirtazapine may make the condition worse by causing low blood pressure (hypotension)
- Kidney disease—Effects of mirtazapine may be increased because of slower removal from the body
- Liver disease—Mirtazapine may cause liver problems; also, effects of mirtazapine may be increased because of slower removal from the body
- Mania (a type of mental illness) (or history of)—Mirtazapine may cause this problem to recur
- Phenylketonuria (PKU)—The oral disintegrating tablets may contain aspartame, which can make your condition worse

Proper Use of This Medicine

Take this medicine only as directed by your doctor in order to improve your condition as much as possible. Do not take more of it and do not take it more often than your doctor ordered.

Mirtazapine may be taken with or without food, on a full or empty stomach. If your doctor tells you to take it a certain way, follow your doctor's instructions.

For patients using the *oral disintegrating tablet* form of this medicine:

- Make sure your hands are dry.
- Do not push the tablet through the foil backing of the package. Instead, gently peel back the foil backing and remove the tablet.
- Immediately place the tablet on top of the tongue.
- The tablet will dissolve in seconds, and you may swallow it with your saliva. You do not need to drink water or other liquid to swallow the tablet.

Dosing— The dose of mirtazapine will be different for different patients. *Follow your doctor's orders or the directions on the label*. The following information includes only the average doses of mirtazapine. *If your dose is different, do not change it* unless your doctor tells you to do so.

The number of tablets that you take depends on the strength of the medicine.

- For *oral* dosage form (tablets and oral disintergrating tablets):
  —For mental depression:
  - Adults—At first, 15 milligrams (mg) once a day, preferably in the evening just before you go to sleep. Your doctor may increase the dose if necessary. However, the dose usually is not more than 45 mg a day.
  - Children—Use and dose must be determined by your doctor.

Missed dose— If you miss a dose of this medicine, take it as soon as possible if you remember it the same day. However, if you don't remember until the next day, skip the missed dose and return to your regular dosing schedule. Do not double doses.

Storage— To store this medicine:
- Keep out of the reach of children.
- Store away from heat and direct light.
- Do not store in the bathroom, near the kitchen sink, or in other damp places. Heat or moisture may cause the medicine to break down.
- Do not keep outdated medicine or medicine no longer needed. Be sure that any discarded medicine is out of the reach of children.

Precautions While Using This Medicine

It is important that your doctor check your progress at regular visits, to allow for changes in your dose and to help reduce any side effects.

Do not take mirtazapine with monoamine oxidase (MAO) inhibitors (e.g., furazolidone, phenelzine, procarbazine, selegiline, or tranylcypromine) or sooner than 14 days after stopping an MAO inhibitor. Do not take an MAO inhibitor sooner than 14 days after stopping mirtazapine. To do so may increase the chance of serious side effects.

This medicine may add to the effects of alcohol and other CNS depressants (medicines that make you drowsy or less alert). Some examples of CNS depressants are antihistamines or medicine for hay fever, other allergies, or colds; sedatives, tranquilizers, or sleeping medicine; prescription pain medicine or narcotics; barbiturates; medicine for seizures; muscle relaxants; or anesthetics, including some dental anesthetics. *Check with your doctor before taking any of the above while you are taking this medicine.*

Check with your doctor immediately if you develop fever, chills, sore throat, or sores in the mouth. These may be signs of a very serious blood problem that has occurred rarely in patients taking mirtazapine.

Mirtazapine may cause drowsiness or trouble in thinking. *Make sure you know how you react to this medicine before you drive, use machines, or do other jobs that require you to be alert and clearheaded.*

Dizziness, light-headedness, or fainting may occur, especially when you get up from a lying or sitting position. Getting up slowly may help. If this problem continues or gets worse, check with your doctor.

This medicine may cause dryness of the mouth. For temporary relief, use sugarless gum or candy, melt bits of ice in your mouth, or use a saliva substitute. However, if your mouth feels dry for more than 2 weeks, check with your medical doctor or dentist. Continuing dryness of the mouth may increase the chance of dental disease, including tooth decay, gum disease, and fungus infections.

Side Effects of This Medicine

Along with its needed effects, a medicine may cause some unwanted effects. Although not all of these side effects may occur, if they do occur they may need medical attention.

Check with your doctor immediately if any of the following side effects occur:

Rare
> Convulsions (seizures); mouth sores; sore throat, chills, or fever

Also, check with your doctor as soon as possible if any of the following side effects occur:

Less common
> Decreased or increased movement; mood or mental changes, including abnormal thinking, agitation, anxiety, confusion, and feelings of not caring; shortness of breath; skin rash; swelling

Rare
> Decreased sexual ability; menstrual pain; missing periods; mood or mental changes, including anger, feelings of being outside the body, hallucinations (seeing, hearing, or feeling things that are not there), mood swings, and unusual excitement

Other side effects may occur that usually do not need medical attention. These side effects may go away during treatment as your body adjusts to the medicine. However, check with your doctor if any of the following side effects continue or are bothersome:

More common
> Constipation; dizziness; drowsiness; dryness of mouth; increased appetite; weight gain

Less common
> Abdominal pain; abnormal dreams; back pain; dizziness or fainting when getting up suddenly from a lying or sitting position; increased need to urinate; increased sensitivity to touch; increased thirst; low blood pressure; muscle pain; nausea; sense of constant movement of self or surroundings; trembling or shaking; vomiting; weakness

Other side effects not listed above may also occur in some patients. If you notice any other effects, check with your doctor.

Developed: 03/20/1998
Revised: 02/14/2001

MISOPROSTOL   Systemic

Commonly used brand name(s):

In the U.S.—
> Cytotec

In Canada—
> Cytotec

Description

Misoprostol (mye-soe-PROST-ole) is taken to prevent stomach ulcers in patients taking anti-inflammatory drugs, including aspirin. Misoprostol may also be used for other conditions as determined by your doctor.

Misoprostol helps the stomach protect itself against acid damage. It also decreases the amount of acid produced by the stomach.

This medicine is available only with your doctor's prescription, in the following dosage form:

Oral
> • Tablets (U.S. and Canada)

Before Using This Medicine

In deciding to use a medicine, the risks of taking the medicine must be weighed against the good it will do. This is a decision you and your doctor will make. For misoprostol, the following should be considered:

Allergies—Tell your doctor if you have ever had any unusual or allergic reaction to misoprostol. Also tell your health care professional if you are allergic to any other substances, such as foods, preservatives, or dyes.

Pregnancy—*Misoprostol must not be used during pregnancy.* It has been shown to cause contractions and bleeding of the uterus. Misoprostol may also cause miscarriage.

Before starting to take this medicine you must have had a negative pregnancy test within the previous 2 weeks. Also, you must start taking misoprostol only on the second or third day of your next normal menstrual period. In addition, it will be necessary that you use an effective form of birth control while taking this medicine. Be sure that you have discussed this with your doctor before taking this medicine.

Breast-feeding—It is not known whether misoprostol passes into breast milk. However, misoprostol is not recommended for use during breast-feeding because it may cause diarrhea in nursing babies.

Children—Studies on this medicine have been done only in adult patients, and there is no specific information comparing use of misoprostol in children with use in other age groups.

Older adults—This medicine has been tested and has not been shown to cause different side effects or problems in older people than it does in younger adults.

Other medicines—Although certain medicines should not be used together at all, in other cases two different medicines may be used together even if an interaction might occur. In these cases, your doctor may want to change the dose, or other precautions may be necessary. Tell your health care professional if you are taking any other prescription or nonprescription (over-the-counter [OTC]) medicine.

Other medical problems—The presence of other medical problems may affect the use of misoprostol. Make sure you tell your doctor if you have any other medical problems, especially:

> • Blood vessel disease—Medicines similar to misoprostol have been shown to make this condition worse

> • Epilepsy (uncontrolled)—Medicines similar to misoprostol have been shown to cause convulsions (seizures)

- Inflammatory bowel disease—Misoprostol may worsen diarrhea, which could lead to dehydration

Proper Use of This Medicine

Misoprostol is best taken with or after meals and at bedtime, unless otherwise directed by your doctor. To help prevent loose stools, diarrhea, and abdominal cramping, always take this medicine with food or milk.

Dosing—The dose of misoprostol will be different for different patients. *Follow your doctor's orders or the directions on the label.* The following information includes only the average doses of misoprostol. *If your dose is different, do not change it* unless your doctor tells you to do so.

- To prevent stomach ulcers in patients taking anti-inflammatory medicines including aspirin:
  —For *oral* dosage form (tablets):
  - Adults—200 micrograms (mcg) four times a day, with or after meals and at bedtime. Or, your dose may be 400 mcg two times a day with the last dose taken at bedtime. Your doctor may reduce the dose to 100 mcg if you are sensitive to high doses.
  - Children and teenagers—Dose must be determined by your doctor.

Missed dose—If you miss a dose of this medicine, take it as soon as possible. However, if it is almost time for your next dose, skip the missed dose and go back to your regular dosing schedule. Do not double doses.

Storage—To store this medicine:

- Keep out of the reach of children.
- Store away from heat and direct light.
- Do not store in the bathroom, near the kitchen sink, or in other damp places. Heat or moisture may cause the medicine to break down.
- Do not keep outdated medicine or medicine no longer needed. Be sure that any discarded medicine is out of the reach of children.

Precautions While Using This Medicine

Misoprostol may cause miscarriage if taken during pregnancy. Therefore, if you suspect that you may have become pregnant, stop taking this medicine immediately and check with your doctor.

This medicine may cause diarrhea, stomach cramps, or nausea in some people. These effects will usually disappear within a few days as your body adjusts to the medicine. However, check with your doctor if the diarrhea, cramps, or nausea is severe and/or does not stop after a week. Your doctor may have to lower the dose of misoprostol you are taking.

Side Effects of This Medicine

Along with its needed effects, a medicine may cause some unwanted effects. Some side effects may occur that usually do not need medical attention. These side effects may go away during treatment as your body adjusts to the medicine. However, check with your doctor if any of the following side effects continue or are bothersome:

More common
  Abdominal or stomach pain (mild); diarrhea

Less common or rare
  Bleeding from vagina; constipation; cramps in lower abdomen or stomach area; gas; headache; heartburn, indigestion, or acid stomach; nausea and/or vomiting

Symptoms of overdose
  Abdominal pain; convulsions (seizures); diarrhea; drowsiness; fast or pounding heartbeat; fever; low blood pressure; slow heartbeat; tremor; troubled breathing

Other side effects not listed above may also occur in some patients. If you notice any other effects, check with your doctor.

Revised: 01/29/2001

MITOMYCIN Systemic

Commonly used brand name(s):

In the U.S.—
  Mutamycin

In Canada—
  Mutamycin

Description

Mitomycin (mye-toe-MYE-sin) belongs to the group of medicines known as antineoplastics. It is used to treat some kinds of cancer.

Mitomycin interferes with the growth of cancer cells, which are eventually destroyed. Since the growth of normal body cells may also be affected by mitomycin, other effects will also occur. Some of these may be serious and must be reported to your doctor. Other effects, like hair loss, may not be serious but may cause concern. Some effects may not occur for months or years after the medicine is used.

Before you begin treatment with mitomycin, you and your doctor should talk about the good this medicine will do as well as the risks of using it.

Mitomycin is to be administered only by or under the immediate supervision of your doctor. It is available in the following dosage form:

Parenteral
  - Injection (U.S. and Canada)

Before Using This Medicine

In deciding to use a medicine, the risks of taking the medicine must be weighed against the good it will do. This is a decision you and your doctor will make. For mitomycin, the following should be considered:

Allergies—Tell your doctor if you have ever had any unusual or allergic reaction to mitomycin.

Pregnancy—Tell your doctor if you are pregnant or if you intend to have children. There is a chance that this medicine may cause birth defects if either the male or female is taking it at the time of conception or if it is taken during pregnancy. Studies have shown that mitomycin causes birth defects in animals. In addition, many cancer medicines may cause sterility which could be permanent. Although sterility has not been reported with this medicine, the possibility should be kept in mind.

Be sure that you have discussed this with your doctor before taking this medicine. It is best to use some kind of birth control while you are receiving mitomycin. Tell your doctor right away if you think you have become pregnant while receiving mitomycin.

Breast-feeding—Tell your doctor if you are breast-feeding or if you intend to breast-feed during treatment with this medicine. Because mitomycin may cause serious side effects, breast-feeding is generally not recommended while you are receiving it.

Children—Although there is no specific information comparing use of mitomycin in children with use in other age groups, it is not expected to cause different side effects or problems in children than it does in adults.

Older adults—Many medicines have not been studied specifically in older people. Therefore, it may not be known whether they work exactly the same way they do in younger adults or if they cause different side effects or problems in older people. There is no specific information comparing use of mitomycin in the elderly with use in other age groups.

Other medicines—Although certain medicines should not be used together at all, in other cases two different medicines may be used together even if an interaction might occur. In these cases, your doctor may want to change the dose, or other precautions may be necessary. When you are receiving mitomycin, it is especially important that your health care professional know if you are taking any of the following:
- Amphotericin B by injection (e.g., Fungizone) or
- Antithyroid agents (medicine for overactive thyroid) or
- Azathioprine (e.g., Imuran) or
- Chloramphenicol (e.g., Chloromycetin) or
- Colchicine or
- Flucytosine (e.g., Ancobon) or
- Ganciclovir (e.g., Cytovene) or
- Interferon (e.g., Intron A, Roferon-A) or
- Plicamycin (e.g., Mithracin) or
- Zidovudine (e.g., AZT, Retrovir) or
- If you have ever been treated with radiation or cancer medicines—Mitomycin may increase the effects of these medicines or radiation therapy on the blood

Other medical problems—The presence of other medical problems may affect the use of mitomycin. Make sure you tell your doctor if you have any other medical problems, especially:
- Bleeding problems
- Chickenpox (including recent exposure) or
- Herpes zoster (shingles)—Risk of severe disease affecting other parts of the body
- Infection—Mitomycin may decrease your body's ability to fight infection
- Kidney disease—May be worsened

Proper Use of This Medicine

Mitomycin is usually given together with certain other medicines. If you are using a combination of medicines, it is important that you receive each one at the proper time. If you are taking some of these medicines by mouth, ask your health care professional to help you plan a way to remember to take them at the right times.

This medicine often causes nausea, vomiting, and loss of appetite. However, it is very important that you continue to receive the medicine, even if you begin to feel ill. Ask your health care professional for ways to lessen these effects.

Dosing—The dose of mitomycin will be different for different patients. The dose that is used may depend on a number of things, including what the medicine is being used for, the patient's size, and whether or not other medicines are also being taken. *If you are receiving mitomycin at home, follow your doctor's orders or the directions on the label.* If you have any questions about the proper dose of mitomycin, ask your doctor.

Precautions While Using This Medicine

It is very important that your doctor check your progress at regular visits to make sure that this medicine is working properly and to check for unwanted effects.

While you are being treated with mitomycin, and after you stop treatment with it, *do not have any immunizations (vaccinations) without your doctor's approval*. Mitomycin may lower your body's resistance and there is a chance you might get the infection the immunization is meant to prevent. In addition, other persons living in your household should not take oral polio vaccine since there is a chance they could pass the polio virus on to you. Also, avoid persons who have taken oral polio vaccine. Do not get close to them, and do not stay in the same room with them for very long. If you cannot take these precautions, you should consider wearing a protective face mask that covers the nose and mouth.

Mitomycin can temporarily lower the number of white blood cells in your blood, increasing the chance of getting an infection. It can also lower the number of platelets, which are necessary for proper blood clotting. If this occurs, there are certain precautions you can take, especially when your blood count is low, to reduce the risk of infection or bleeding:
- If you can, avoid people with infections. *Check with your doctor immediately* if you think you are getting an infection or if you get a fever or chills, cough or hoarseness, lower back or side pain, or painful or difficult urination.
- *Check with your doctor immediately* if you notice any unusual bleeding or bruising; black, tarry stools; blood in urine or stools; or pinpoint red spots on your skin.
- Be careful when using a regular toothbrush, dental floss, or toothpick. Your medical doctor, dentist, or nurse may recommend other ways to clean your teeth and gums. Check with your medical doctor before having any dental work done.
- Do not touch your eyes or the inside of your nose unless you have just washed your hands and have not touched anything else in the meantime.
- Be careful not to cut yourself when you are using sharp objects such as a safety razor or fingernail or toenail cutters.
- Avoid contact sports or other situations where bruising or injury could occur.

If mitomycin accidentally seeps out of the vein into which it is injected, it may damage the skin and cause scarring. In some patients, this may occur weeks or even months after this medicine is given. *Tell the doctor or nurse right away if you notice redness, pain, or swelling at the place of injection or anywhere else on your skin.*

Side Effects of This Medicine

Along with its needed effects, a medicine may cause some unwanted effects. Although not all of these side effects may occur, if they do occur they may need medical attention.

Also, because of the way cancer medicines act on the body, there is a chance that they might cause other unwanted effects that may not occur until months or years after the medicine is used. These delayed effects may include certain types of cancer. Discuss these possible effects with your doctor.

Check with your doctor or nurse immediately if any of the following side effects occur:

Less common
> Black, tarry stools; blood in urine or stools; cough or hoarseness; fever or chills; lower back or side pain; painful or difficult urination; pinpoint red spots on skin; unusual bleeding or bruising

Rare
> Redness or pain, especially at place of injection

Check with your doctor as soon as possible if any of the following side effects occur:

Less common
> Cough; decreased urination; shortness of breath; sores in mouth and on lips; swelling of feet or lower legs

Rare
> Bloody vomit

Other side effects may occur that usually do not need medical attention. These side effects may go away during treatment as your body adjusts to the medicine. Also, your health care professional may be able to tell you about ways to prevent or reduce some of these side effects. Check with your doctor if any of the following side effects continue or are bothersome or if you have any questions about them:

More common
> Loss of appetite; nausea and vomiting

Less common
> Numbness or tingling in fingers and toes; purple-colored bands on nails; skin rash; unusual tiredness or weakness

Mitomycin sometimes causes a temporary loss of hair. After treatment has ended, normal hair growth should return.

After you stop receiving mitomycin, it may still produce some side effects that need attention. During this period of time, *check with your doctor immediately* if you notice the following:

> Blood in urine

Also, check with your doctor if you notice any of the following:
> Black, tarry stools; blood in stools; cough or hoarseness; decreased urination; fever or chills; lower back or side pain; painful or difficult urination; pinpoint red spots on skin; red or painful skin; shortness of breath; swelling of feet or lower legs; unusual bleeding or bruising

Other side effects not listed above may also occur in some patients. If you notice any other effects, check with your doctor.

Revised: 07/05/94

MITOTANE Systemic

Commonly used brand name(s):

In the U.S.—
 Lysodren

In Canada—
 Lysodren

Description

Mitotane (MYE-toe-tane) is a medicine that acts on a part of the body called the adrenal cortex. It is used to treat some kinds of cancer that affect the adrenal cortex. Also, it is sometimes used when the adrenal cortex is overactive without being cancerous.

Mitotane reduces the amounts of adrenocorticoids (cortisone-like hormones) produced by the adrenal cortex. These steroids are important for various functions of the body, including growth. However, too much of these steroids can cause problems.

Mitotane is available only with your doctor's prescription, in the following dosage form:

Oral
 • Tablets (U.S. and Canada)

Before Using This Medicine

In deciding to use a medicine, the risks of taking the medicine must be weighed against the good it will do. This is a decision you and your doctor will make. For mitotane, the following should be considered:

Allergies—Tell your doctor if you have ever had any unusual or allergic reaction to mitotane. Also tell your health care professional if you are allergic to any other substance, such as foods, preservatives, or dyes.

Pregnancy—Mitotane has not been shown to cause problems in humans.

Breast-feeding—Although it is not known whether mitotane passes into the breast milk, it has not been reported to cause problems in nursing babies.

Children—Although there is no specific information about the use of mitotane in children, it is not expected to cause different side effects or problems in children than it does in adults.

Older adults—Many medicines have not been tested in older people. Therefore, it may not be known whether they work exactly the same way they do in younger adults or if they cause different side effects or problems in older people. There is no specific information about the use of mitotane in the elderly.

Other medicines—Although certain medicines should not be used together at all, in other cases two different medicines may be used together even if an interaction might occur. In these cases, your doctor may want to change the dose, or other precautions may be necessary. When you are taking mitotane, it is especially important that your health care professional know if you are taking any of the following:
 • Central nervous system (CNS) depressants—CNS depressant effects may be increased

Other medical problems—The presence of other medical problems may affect the use of mitotane. Make sure you tell your doctor if you have any other medical problems, especially:
 • Infection
 • Liver disease—Effects may be increased because of slower removal of mitotane from the body

Proper Use of This Medicine

Take mitotane only as directed by your doctor. Do not take more or less of it, and do not take it more often than your doctor ordered.

Do not stop taking this medicine without first checking with your doctor. To do so may increase the chance of unwanted effects.

Dosing—The dose of mitotane will be different for different patients. The dose that is used may depend on a number of things, including what the medicine is being used for and whether or not other medicines are also being taken. *If you are taking mitotane at home, follow your doctor's orders or the directions on the label*. If you have any questions about the proper dose of mitotane, ask your doctor.

Missed dose—If you miss a dose of this medicine, take the missed dose as soon as you remember it. However, if it is almost time for the next dose, skip the missed dose and do not double the next one. Instead, go back to your regular dosing schedule and check with your doctor.

Storage—To store this medicine:
- Keep out of the reach of children.
- Store away from heat and direct light.
- Do not store in the bathroom, near the kitchen sink, or in other damp places. Heat or moisture may cause the medicine to break down.
- Do not keep outdated medicine or medicine no longer needed. Be sure that any discarded medicine is out of the reach of children.

Precautions While Using This Medicine

It is very important that your doctor check your progress at regular visits to make sure this medicine is working properly and to check for unwanted effects.

Your doctor may want you to carry an identification card stating that you are taking this medicine.

This medicine will add to the effects of alcohol and other CNS depressants (medicines that slow down the nervous system, possibly causing drowsiness). Some examples of CNS depressants are antihistamines or medicine for hay fever, other allergies, or colds; sedatives, tranquilizers, or sleeping medicine; prescription pain medicine or narcotics; barbiturates; medicine for seizures; tricyclic antidepressants (medicine for depression); muscle relaxants; or anesthetics, including some dental anesthetics. *Check with your doctor before taking any of the above while you are using this medicine.*

This medicine may cause some people to become dizzy, drowsy, or less alert than they are normally. *Make sure you know how you react to this medicine before you drive, use machines, or do anything else that could be dangerous if you are dizzy or are not alert.*

Check with your doctor right away if you get an injury, infection, or illness of any kind. This medicine may weaken your body's defenses against infection or inflammation.

Side Effects of This Medicine

Along with its needed effects, a medicine may cause some unwanted effects. Although not all of these side effects may occur, if they do occur they may need medical attention.

Check with your doctor as soon as possible if any of the following side effects occur:
More common
    Darkening of skin; diarrhea; dizziness; drowsiness; loss of appetite; mental depression; nausea and vomiting; skin rash; unusual tiredness
Less common
    Blood in urine; blurred vision; double vision

Rare
    Shortness of breath; wheezing

Other side effects may occur that usually do not need medical attention. These side effects may go away during treatment as your body adjusts to the medicine. However, check with your health care professional if any of the following side effects continue or are bothersome:
Less common
    Aching muscles; dizziness or lightheadedness when getting up from a lying or sitting position; fever; flushing or redness of skin; muscle twitching

Other side effects not listed above may also occur in some patients. If you notice any other effects, check with your doctor.

Revised: 08/90
Interim revision: 06/30/94

MITOXANTRONE   Systemic

Commonly used brand name(s):

In the U.S.—
    Novantrone

In Canada—
    Novantrone

Description

Mitoxantrone (mye-toe-ZAN-trone) belongs to the general group of medicines known as antineoplastics. It is used to treat some kinds of cancer. It is also used to treat some forms of multiple sclerosis (MS). This medicine will not cure MS, but may extend the time between relapses.

Mitoxantrone seems to interfere with the growth of cancer cells, which are eventually destroyed. Since the growth of normal body cells may also be affected by mitoxantrone, other effects will also occur. Some of these may be serious and must be reported to your doctor. Other effects, like hair loss, may not be serious but may cause concern. Some effects may not occur for months or years after the medicine is used.

Before you begin treatment with mitoxantrone, you and your doctor should talk about the good this medicine will do as well as the risks of using it.

Mitoxantrone is to be administered only by or under the immediate supervision of your doctor. It is available in the following dosage form:
Parenteral
- Injection (U.S. and Canada)

Before Using This Medicine

In deciding to use a medicine, the risks of taking the medicine must be weighed against the good it will do. This is a decision you and your doctor will make. For mitoxantrone, the following should be considered:

Allergies—Tell your health care professional if you have ever had any unusual or allergic reaction to mitoxantrone.

Pregnancy—Tell your doctor if you are pregnant or if you intend to have children. There is a chance that this medicine may cause birth defects if either the male or female is receiving it at the time of conception or if it is taken during pregnancy. Mitoxantrone has been reported to cause low birth weight and slow growth of the kidney in rats and premature birth in rabbits. In addition, many cancer medicines may cause sterility, which could be permanent. Although sterility has not been reported with this medicine, the possibility should be kept in mind.

Be sure that you have discussed this with your doctor before receiving this medicine. It is best to use some kind of birth control while you are receiving mitoxantrone. Tell your doctor right away if you think you have become pregnant while receiving mitoxantrone.

Breast-feeding—Tell your doctor if you are breast-feeding or if you intend to breast-feed during treatment with this medicine. It is not known whether mitoxantrone passes into breast milk. However, because mitoxantrone may cause serious side effects, breast-feeding is generally not recommended while you are receiving it.

Children—There is no specific information comparing use of mitoxantrone in children with use in other age groups.

Older adults—Many medicines have not been studied specifically in older people. Therefore, it may not be known whether they work exactly the same way they do in younger adults or if they cause different side effects or problems in older people. There is no specific information comparing use of mitoxantrone in the elderly with use in other age groups.

Other medicines—Although certain medicines should not be used together at all, in other cases two different medicines may be used together even if an interaction might occur. In these cases, your doctor may want to change the dose, or other precautions may be necessary. When you are receiving mitoxantrone, it is especially important that your health care professional know if you are taking any of the following:

- Amphotericin B by injection (e.g., Fungizone) or
- Antithyroid agents (medicine for overactive thyroid) or
- Azathioprine (e.g., Imuran) or
- Chloramphenicol (e.g., Chloromycetin) or
- Colchicine or
- Flucytosine (e.g., Ancobon) or
- Ganciclovir (e.g., Cytovene) or
- Interferon (e.g., Intron A, Roferon-A) or
- Plicamycin (e.g., Mithracin) or
- Zidovudine (e.g., AZT, Retrovir) or
- If you have been treated with radiation or cancer medicines—Mitoxantrone may increase the effects of these medicines or radiation on the blood

- Probenecid (e.g., Benemid) or
- Sulfinpyrazone (e.g., Anturane)—Mitoxantrone may increase the concentration of uric acid in the blood. Since these medicines are used to lower uric acid levels, they may not work as well in patients receiving mitoxantrone

Other medical problems—The presence of other medical problems may affect the use of mitoxantrone. Make sure you tell your doctor if you have any other medical problems, especially:

- Chickenpox (including recent exposure) or
- Herpes zoster (shingles)—Risk of severe disease affecting other parts of the body

- Gout (history of) or
- Kidney stones—Mitoxantrone may increase levels of uric acid in the body, which can cause gout or kidney stones

- Heart disease—Risk of heart problems caused by mitoxantrone may be increased

- Infection—Mitoxantrone may decrease your body's ability to fight infection

- Liver disease—Effects of mitoxantrone may be increased because of slower removal from the body

Proper Use of This Medicine

Mitoxantrone is sometimes given together with certain other medicines. If you are using a combination of medicines, it is important that you receive each one at the proper time. If you are taking some of these medicines by mouth, ask your health care professional to help you plan a way to take them at the right times.

While you are receiving mitoxantrone, your doctor may want you to drink extra fluids so that you will pass more urine. This will help prevent kidney problems and keep your kidneys working well.

Mitoxantrone often causes nausea and vomiting. However, it is very important that you continue to receive the medicine, even if your stomach is upset. Ask your health care professional for ways to lessen these effects.

Dosing—The dose of mitoxantrone will be different for different patients. The dose that is used may depend on a number of things, including what the medicine is being used for, the patient's size, and whether or not other medicines are also being taken. *If you are receiving mitoxantrone at home, follow your doctor's orders or the directions on the label.* If you have any questions about the proper dose of mitoxantrone, ask your doctor.

Precautions While Using This Medicine

It is very important that your doctor check your progress at regular visits to make sure that this medicine is working properly and to check for unwanted effects.

While you are being treated with mitoxantrone, and after you stop treatment with it, *do not have any immunizations (vaccinations) without your doctor's approval*. Mitoxantrone may lower your body's resistance and there is a chance you might get the infection the immunization is meant to prevent. In addition, other persons living in your household should not take oral polio vaccine since there is a chance they could pass the polio virus on to you. Also, avoid persons who have taken oral polio vaccine. Do not get close to them and do not stay in the same room with them for very long. If you cannot take these precautions, you should consider wearing a protective face mask that covers the nose and mouth.

Mitoxantrone can temporarily lower the number of white blood cells in your blood, increasing the chance of getting an infection. It can also lower the number of platelets, which are necessary for proper blood clotting. If this occurs, there are certain precautions you can take, especially when your blood count is low, to reduce the risk of infection or bleeding:

- If you can, avoid people with infections. *Check with your doctor immediately* if you think you are getting an infection or if you get a fever or chills, cough or hoarseness, lower back or side pain, or painful or difficult urination.
- *Check with your doctor immediately* if you notice any unusual bleeding or bruising; black, tarry stools; blood in urine or stools; or pinpoint red spots on your skin.
- Be careful when using a regular toothbrush, dental floss, or toothpick. Your medical doctor, dentist, or nurse may

recommend other ways to clean your teeth and gums. Check with your medical doctor before having any dental work done.

- Do not touch your eyes or the inside of your nose unless you have just washed your hands and have not touched anything else in the meantime.
- Be careful not to cut yourself when you are using sharp objects such as a safety razor or fingernail or toenail cutters.
- Avoid contact sports or other situations where bruising or injury could occur.

Side Effects of This Medicine

Along with its needed effects, a medicine may cause some unwanted effects. Although not all of these side effects may occur, if they do occur they may need medical attention.

Also, because of the way cancer medicines act on the body, there is a chance that they might cause other unwanted effects that may not occur until months or years after the medicine is used. These delayed effects may include certain types of cancer, such as leukemia. Discuss these possible effects with your doctor.

Check with your doctor or nurse immediately if any of the following side effects occur:

More common
Black, tarry stools; cough or shortness of breath

Less common
Blood in urine or stools; fast or irregular heartbeat; fever or chills; lower back or side pain; painful or difficult urination; pinpoint red spots on skin; swelling of feet and lower legs; unusual bleeding or bruising

Check with your health care professional as soon as possible if any of the following side effects occur:

More common
Sores in mouth and on lips; stomach pain

Less common
Decrease in urination; seizures; sore, red eyes; yellow eyes or skin

Rare
Blue skin at place of injection; pain or redness at place of injection; skin rash

Other side effects may occur that usually do not need medical attention. These side effects may go away during treatment as your body adjusts to the medicine. Also, your health care professional may be able to tell you about ways to prevent or reduce some of these side effects. Check with your health care professional if any of the following side effects continue or are bothersome:

More common
Body aches or pains; congestion; constipation; diarrhea; dryness or soreness of throat; headache; irregular menstrual periods; longer or heavier menstrual periods; nausea and vomiting; oral bleeding; runny nose; sneezing; stuffy nose; tender, swollen glands in neck

Mitoxantrone may cause the urine to turn a blue-green color. It may also cause the whites of the eyes to turn a blue color. These effects are normal and last for only 1 or 2 days after each dose is given.

This medicine often causes a temporary loss of hair. After treatment with mitoxantrone has ended, normal hair growth should return.

Other side effects not listed above may also occur in some patients. If you notice any other effects, check with your health care professional.

Revised: 12/28/94

MOCLOBEMIDE   Systemic

Commonly used brand name(s):

In Canada—
Manerix

Another commonly used name is RO 11–1163.

Description

Moclobemide (moe-KLOE-be-mide) is a monoamine oxidase (MAO) inhibitor used to relieve certain types of mental depression. It works by blocking the action of a chemical substance known as monoamine oxidase (MAO) in the nervous system.

Although this medicine is very effective for certain patients, it may also cause some unwanted reactions if not taken in the right way. It is very important to avoid certain beverages and medicines while you are being treated with an MAO inhibitor. Your doctor may provide a list as a reminder of which products you should avoid.

This medicine is available only with your doctor's prescription, in the following dosage forms:

Oral
Moclobemide
- Tablets (Canada)

Before Using This Medicine

In deciding to use a medicine, the risks of taking the medicine must be weighed against the good it will do. This is a decision you and your doctor will make. For moclobemide, the following should be considered:

Allergies—Tell your doctor if you have ever had any unusual or allergic reaction to moclobemide or monoamine oxidase inhibitors. Also tell your doctor and pharmacist if you are allergic to any other substances, such as foods, preservatives, or dyes.

Diet—
- Ask your doctor about any changes you should make to your diet.
- Do not drink excessive amounts of alcohol while you are taking this medicine.

Pregnancy—Studies of moclobemide use in pregnant women have not been done. In some animal studies, weight gain was decreased in pregnant females or their offspring after high doses of moclobemide. Before taking this medicine, make sure your doctor knows if you are pregnant or if you may become pregnant.

Breast-feeding—Small quantities of moclobemide pass into the breast milk. Moclobemide is not recommended during breast-feeding, because it may cause unwanted effects in nursing babies.

Children—Studies on moclobemide have been done only in adult patients, and there is no specific information comparing use of moclobemide in children with use in other age groups.

Older adults — Older adults are especially sensitive to the effects of moclobemide. This may increase the chance of side effects during treatment. Dizziness or lightheadedness may be especially likely to occur in elderly patients, who are usually more sensitive than younger adults to these effects.

Other medicines — Although certain medicines should not be used together at all, in other cases two different medicines may be used together even if an interaction might occur. In these cases, your doctor may want to change the dose, or other precautions may be necessary. When you are taking moclobemide, it is especially important that your doctor and pharmacist know if you are taking any of the following:

- Amphetamines or
- Appetite suppressants (diet pills) or
- Dextromethorphan or
- Medicine for asthma or other breathing problems
- Medicines for colds, sinus problems, or hay fever or other allergies (including nose drops or sprays) or
- Meperidine (e.g., Demerol) or
- Selective serotonin reuptake inhibitor antidepressants (fluvoxamine [e.g., Luvox], fluoxetine [e.g., Prozac], paroxetine [e.g., Paxil], sertraline [e.g., Zoloft]) or
- Tricyclic antidepressants (amitriptyline [e.g., Elavil], amoxapine [e.g., Asendin], clomipramine [e.g., Anafranil], desipramine [e.g., Norpramin], doxepin [e.g., Sinequan], imipramine [e.g., Tofranil], nortriptyline [e.g., Aventyl], protriptyline [e.g., Vivactil], trimipramine [e.g., Surmontil]—Using these medicines together may increase the chance of serious side effects
- Cimetidine (e.g., Tagamet)—May increase the effect of moclobemide; moclobemide doses may need to be lowered by approximately 50% in patients using cimetidine
- Monoamine oxidase (MAO) inhibitors (furazolidone [e.g., Furoxone], isocarboxazid [e.g., Marplan], phenelzine [e.g., Nardil], procarbazine [e.g., Matulane], selegiline [e.g., Eldepryl], tranylcypromine [e.g., Parnate])—Taking moclobemide while you are taking or within 2 weeks of taking monoamine oxidase (MAO) inhibitors may cause very serious side effects, such as sudden high body temperature, extremely high blood pressure, and severe convulsions; at least 14 days should be allowed between stopping treatment with one medicine and starting treatment with the other

Other medical problems — The presence of other medical problems may affect the use of moclobemide. Make sure you tell your doctor if you have any other medical problems, especially:

- Hypertension—Moclobemide may make the problem worse
- Liver disease—Effects of moclobemide may be increased because of slower removal of the medicine from the body; your doctor may need to change your dose

Proper Use of This Medicine

Sometimes this medicine must be taken for several weeks before you begin to feel better. Your doctor should check your progress at regular visits, especially during the first few months of treatment, to make sure that this medicine is working properly and to check for unwanted effects.

Take this medicine only as directed by your doctor. Do not take more of it, do not take it more often, and do not take it for a longer time than your doctor ordered.

Moclobemide should be taken after a meal. However, if your doctor tells you to take the medicine a certain way, take it exactly as directed.

Dosing — The dose of moclobemide will be different for different patients. *Follow your doctor's orders or the directions on the label.* The following information includes only the average doses of moclobemide. *If your dose is different, do not change it* unless your doctor tells you to do so.

The number of tablets that you take depends on the strength of the medicine. Also, *the number of doses you take each day, the time allowed between doses, and the length of time you take the medicine depend on the medical problem for which you are taking moclobemide.*

- For *oral* dosage form (tablets):
  - For treatment of depression:
    - Adults—At first, 150 milligrams (mg), two times a day. Your doctor may increase your dose as needed, but the total daily dose is usually not more than 600 mg.
    - Children—Use and dose must be determined by your doctor.

Missed dose — If you miss a dose of this medicine, take it as soon as possible. However, if it is almost time for your next dose, skip the missed dose and go back to your regular dosing schedule. Do not double doses.

Storage — To store this medicine:

- Keep out of the reach of children. Overdose of moclobemide is very dangerous in young children.
- Store away from heat and direct light.
- Do not store in the bathroom, near the kitchen sink, or in other damp places. Heat or moisture may cause the medicine to break down.
- Do not keep outdated medicine or medicine no longer needed. Be sure that any discarded medicine is out of the reach of children.

Precautions While Using This Medicine

When taken with certain drinks or other medicines, moclobemide and other monoamine oxidase inhibitors can cause very dangerous reactions such as sudden high blood pressure (also called hypertensive crisis). To avoid such reactions, *obey the following rules of caution:*

- Do not drink excessive amounts of alcohol.
- Do not take any other medicine unless approved or prescribed by your doctor. This especially includes nonprescription (over-the-counter [OTC]) medicine, such as that for colds (including nose drops or sprays), cough, hay fever, and appetite control; "keep awake" products; or products that make you sleepy.

Check with your doctor immediately if you experience any combination of the following symptoms: severe throbbing headache which starts at the back of the head and radiates forward, stiff neck, fast or racing heartbeat, pounding or irregular heartbeat, or slow heartbeat. These may be symptoms of a serious side effect that should have a doctor's attention.

Do not stop taking this medicine without first checking with your doctor. Your doctor may want you to reduce gradually the amount you are using before stopping completely.

Dizziness, lightheadedness, or fainting may occur, especially when you get up from a lying or sitting position. *Getting up slowly may help.* When you get up from lying down, sit on the edge of the bed with your feet dangling for 1 or 2 minutes. Then stand up slowly. If the problem continues or gets worse, check with your doctor.

This medicine may cause blurred vision or make some people drowsy or less alert than they are normally. *Make sure you know how you react to this medicine before you drive, use machines, or do anything else that could be dangerous if you are unable to see well or are not alert.*

Before having any kind of surgery, dental treatment, or emergency treatment, tell the medical doctor or dentist in charge that you are using this medicine or have used it within the past 2 weeks. Taking moclobemide together with medicines that are used during surgery or dental or emergency treatments may increase the risk of serious side effects.

After you stop using this medicine, you must continue to exercise caution for at least 1 to 2 weeks concerning drink and other medicine, since these things may continue to react with moclobemide.

Side Effects of This Medicine

Along with its needed effects, a medicine may cause some unwanted effects. Although not all of these side effects may occur, if they do occur they may need medical attention.

Stop taking this medicine and check with your doctor immediately if any combination of the following side effects occur:

Fast or racing heartbeat; pounding or irregular heartbeat; neck stiffness; severe throbbing headache which starts at the back of the head and radiates forward; slow heartbeat

Check with your doctor as soon as possible if any of the following side effects occur:

More common

Mild to moderate headache, or pressure in head

Less common

Anxiety; blurred vision or other changes in vision; dizziness, faintness, or lightheadedness, especially when getting up from a sitting or lying position; fast or racing heartbeat; high blood pressure; irritability; nervousness; pounding or irregular heartbeat; restlessness; unusual tiredness or weakness

Rare

Aggressive behavior; bleeding gums; burning, prickling, or tingling sensations; chest pain; confusion; increased depression, or other mood and mental changes; difficulty in speaking; fast, slow, or irregular heart beat; feeling of something in the eye; general feeling of illness; headache (severe); increase in urination; increased sensitivity of eyes to light; irregular or prolonged menstrual periods; irritation or soreness of mouth; itching, redness, and swelling of eye; loss of balance control; loss of interest in self or surroundings; memory problems; pain or straining to pass urine or stool; painful urination; restlessness or desire to keep moving; ringing or noise in ears; seeing, hearing, or feeling something things that are not there; skin rash, hives, or itching; stomach pain or burning; slow heartbeat; troubled breathing; twisting movements of body; uncontrolled movements, especially of face, neck, and back

Symptoms of overdose

Get emergency help immediately if any of the following symptoms of overdose occur

Agitation; confusion; convulsions (seizures); de-

creased reflexes; extreme drowsiness; high blood pressure; loss of memory; nausea; slurred speech; vomiting

Other side effects may occur that usually do not need medical attention. These side effects may go away during treatment as your body adjusts to the medicine. However, check with your doctor if any of the following side effects continue or are bothersome.

More common

Dryness of mouth; trembling or shaking of arms or legs

Less common or rare

Abdominal or stomach pain or discomfort; change in your sense of taste; constipation; diarrhea; dizziness; drowsiness; feeling of warmth of the face, neck, arms, and occasionally upper chest; heartburn or indigestion; increased or decreased appetite; increased sweating; joint or muscle pain; nightmares; trouble sleeping.

Other side effects not listed above may also occur in some patients. If you notice any other effects, check with your doctor.

Developed: 05/17/2000

MODAFINIL   Systemic

Commonly used brand name(s):

In the U.S.—
Provigil

Description

Modafinil (moe-DAF-i-nil) is used to help people who have narcolepsy to stay awake during the day. Modafinil does not cure narcolepsy and will only work as long as you continue to take it.

This medicine is available only with your doctor's prescription, in the following dosage form:

Oral
• Tablets (U.S.)

Before Using This Medicine

In deciding to use a medicine, the risks of taking the medicine must be weighed against the good it will do. This is a decision you and your doctor will make. For modafinil, the following should be considered:

Allergies—Tell your doctor if you have ever had any unusual or allergic reaction to modafinil or any other central nervous system stimulating medicine, such as methylphenidate (e.g., Ritalin) or dextroamphetamine (e.g., Dexedrine). Also tell your health care professional if you are allergic to any other substances, such as foods, preservatives, or dyes.

Pregnancy—Birth-control medicines, such as birth-control pills or implants, may not work properly while you are using modafinil and for 1 month after you stop using modafinil. If you do not use a different type of birth control during this time, such as condoms, you are more likely to become pregnant. If you are using a medicine for birth control, discuss this with your doctor. Modafinil has not been studied in pregnant women. However, studies in animals suggest that modafinil may cause birth defects and fewer successful pregnancies.

Before taking this medicine, make sure your doctor knows if you are pregnant or if you may become pregnant.

Breast-feeding—It is not known whether modafinil passes into the breast milk. Although most medicines pass into breast milk in small amounts, many of them may be used safely while breast-feeding. Mothers who are taking modafinil and who wish to breast-feed should discuss this with their doctor.

Children—Studies on this medicine have been done only in adult patients, and there is no specific information comparing use of modafinil in children with use in other age groups.

Older adults—Many medicines have not been studied specifically in older people. Therefore, it may not be known whether they work exactly the same way they do in younger adults. Although there is no specific information comparing use of modafinil in the elderly with use in other age groups, this medicine has been used in a few elderly patients and was not shown to cause different side effects or problems in older people than it does in younger adults.

Other medicines—Although certain medicines should not be used together at all, in other cases two different medicines may be used together even if an interaction might occur. In these cases, your doctor may want to change the dose, or other precautions may be necessary. When you are taking modafinil, it is especially important that your health care professional know if you are taking any of the following:

- Amantadine (e.g., Symmetrel) or
- Amphetamines or
- Appetite suppressants (diet pills) or
- Bupropion (e.g., Wellbutrin, Zyban) or
- Caffeine (e.g., NoDoz) or
- Chlophedianol (e.g., Ulone) or
- Cocaine or
- Medicine for asthma or other breathing problems or
- Medicine for colds, sinus problems, or hay fever or other allergies (including nose drops or sprays) or
- Methylphenidate (e.g., Ritalin) or
- Nabilone (e.g., Cesamet) or
- Pemoline (e.g., Cylert)—These medicines may add to the central nervous system (CNS) stimulating effects of modafinil, such as irritability, nervousness, trembling or shaking, or trouble in sleeping at night

- Cyclosporine (e.g., Sandimmune) or
- Diazepam (e.g., Valium) or
- Mephenytoin (e.g., Mesantoin) or
- Phenytoin (e.g., Dilantin) or
- Propranolol (e.g., Inderal) or
- Theophylline (e.g., Slo-Bid Gyrocaps, Theo-Dur) or
- Warfarin (e.g., Coumadin)—Higher or lower blood levels of these medicines may occur. This increases the chance that unwanted effects will occur or that these medicines will not work properly. Your doctor may need to adjust your dose of these medicines

- Monoamine oxidase (MAO) inhibitors (furazolidone [e.g., Furoxone], isocarboxazid [e.g., Marplan], phenelzine [e.g., Nardil], procarbazine [e.g., Matulane], selegiline [e.g., Eldepryl], tranylcypromine [e.g., Parnate])—These medicines can cause very serious problems when they are used with certain other medicines. It is not known if they will cause any problems when they are used with modafinil

- Steroid contraceptives (birth control medicines, including birth control pills and implants [e.g., Norplant])—Birth control medicines may not work properly while you are taking modafinil and for 1 month after you stop taking modafinil. It is important that you use another method of birth control to avoid pregnancy during and for 1 month after modafinil therapy. Discuss this with your doctor

- Tricyclic antidepressants (amitriptyline [e.g., Elavil], amoxapine [e.g., Asendin], clomipramine [e.g., Anafranil], desipramine [e.g., Pertofrane], doxepin [e.g., Sinequan], imipramine [e.g., Tofranil], nortriptyline [e.g., Aventyl], protriptyline [e.g., Vivactil], trimipramine [e.g., Surmontil])—Higher blood levels of these medicines may occur, increasing the chance that unwanted effects will occur

Other medical problems—The presence of other medical problems may affect the use of modafinil. Make sure you tell your doctor if you have any other medical problems, especially:

- Heart disease or
- Heart attack, recent or
- High blood pressure—It is not known how modafinil will affect these conditions

- Heart problems during the use of other central nervous system (CNS) stimulating medicines, history of—Similar problems may occur when you use modafinil

- Kidney disease, severe—Higher blood levels of a breakdown product of modafinil may occur. It is not known if this will cause any problems

- Liver disease, severe—Higher blood levels of modafinil may occur, increasing the chance of having unwanted effects. You will probably receive a lower dose than a patient without liver disease

- Severe mental illness, history of—Modafinil may cause the illness to return

Proper Use of This Medicine

Take this medicine only as directed by your doctor. Do not take more of it, do not take it more often, and do not take it for a longer time than your doctor ordered. If too much is taken, it may become habit-forming.

Dosing—The dose of modafinil will be different for different patients. *Follow your doctor's orders or the directions on the label.* The following information includes only the average dose of modafinil. *If your dose is different, do not change it* unless your doctor tells you to do so.

The number of tablets that you take depends on the strength of the medicine.

- For *oral* dosage form (tablets):
  —For narcolepsy:
  - Adults—Usually 200 milligrams (mg) a day, taken as a single dose in the morning.
  - Children—Use and dose must be determined by your doctor.

Missed dose—If you miss a dose of modafinil and you remember it before 12:00 noon the same day, take the missed dose as soon as possible. If you do not remember until later, skip the missed dose so that this medicine will not make it difficult for you to sleep that night. Go back to your regular dosing schedule. Do not double doses.

Storage—To store this medicine:

- Keep out of the reach of children.
- Store away from heat and direct light.
- Do not store in the bathroom, near the kitchen sink, or in other damp places. Heat or moisture may cause the medicine to break down.

• Do not keep outdated medicine or medicine no longer needed. Be sure that any discarded medicine is out of the reach of children.

Precautions While Using This Medicine

Your doctor should check your progress at regular visits to make sure that this medicine is working properly.

If you think modafinil is not working properly after you have taken it for a few weeks, *do not increase the dose*. Instead, check with your doctor.

If you are using a medicine for birth control, such as birth control pills or implants, it may not work properly while you are taking modafinil and for 1 month after stopping modafinil. Another form of birth control should be used during this time.

Modafinil may cause some people to feel dizzy, to have changes in thinking, to have difficulty controlling movements, or to have blurred vision. *Make sure you know how you react to this medicine before you drive, use machines, or do anything else that could be dangerous.*

If you have been taking this medicine for a long time or in large doses and *you think you may have become mentally or physically dependent on it*, check with your doctor. Some signs of dependence on modafinil are:

• a strong desire or need to continue taking the medicine.
• a need to increase the dose to receive the effects of the medicine.
• withdrawal side effects when you stop taking the medicine.

If you have been taking this medicine in large doses or for a long time, *do not stop taking it without first checking with your doctor*. Your doctor may want you to reduce gradually the amount you are taking before you stop completely.

Side Effects of This Medicine

Along with its needed effects, a medicine may cause some unwanted effects. Although not all of these side effects may occur, if they do occur they may need medical attention.

Check with your doctor as soon as possible if any of the following side effects occur:

Less common
Blurred vision or other vision changes; chills or fever; clumsiness or unsteadiness; confusion; dizziness or fainting; increased thirst and increased urination; mental depression; problems with memory; rapidly changing moods; shortness of breath; sore throat; trouble in urinating; uncontrolled movements of the face, mouth, or tongue

Symptoms of overdose—may be more severe than side effects seen with regular doses or several symptoms may occur together
Agitation or excitement; fast or pounding heartbeat; increased blood pressure; trouble in sleeping

Other side effects may occur that usually do not need medical attention. These side effects may go away during treatment as your body adjusts to the medicine. However, check with your doctor if any of the following side effects continue or are bothersome:

More common
Anxiety; headache; nausea; nervousness; trouble in sleeping

Less common
Decrease in appetite; diarrhea; dryness of mouth; dry-

ness of skin; flushing or redness of skin; muscle stiffness; stuffy or runny nose; tingling, burning, or prickling sensations in the skin; trembling or shaking; vomiting

After you stop using this medicine, your body may need time to adjust. The length of time this takes depends on the amount of medicine you were using and how long you used it. During this period of time check with your doctor if you have any disturbing or uncomfortable side effects.

Other side effects not listed above may also occur in some patients. If you notice any other effects, check with your doctor.

Developed: 03/10/99

MOLINDONE   Systemic†

Commonly used brand name(s):

In the U.S.—
Moban
Moban Concentrate

†Not commercially available in Canada.

Description

Molindone (moe-LIN-done) is used to treat nervous, mental, and emotional conditions.

Molindone is available only with your doctor's prescription, in the following dosage forms:

Oral
• Solution (U.S.)
• Tablets (U.S.)

Before Using This Medicine

In deciding to use a medicine, the risks of taking the medicine must be weighed against the good it will do. This is a decision you and your doctor will make. For molindone, the following should be considered:

Allergies—Tell your doctor if you have ever had any unusual or allergic reaction to molindone, phenothiazines, thioxanthenes, haloperidol, or loxapine. Also tell your health care professional if you are allergic to any other substances, such as foods, preservatives, or dyes.

Pregnancy—Molindone has not been shown to cause birth defects or other problems in humans. However, studies in mice have shown a slight decrease in successful pregnancies.

Breast-feeding—It is not known if molindone passes into breast milk.

Children—Studies on this medicine have been done only in adult patients, and there is no specific information comparing use of molindone in children with use in other age groups.

Older adults—Elderly patients are usually more sensitive than younger adults to the effects of molindone. Constipation, dizziness or lightheadedness, drowsiness, dryness of mouth, trembling of the hands and fingers, and symptoms of tardive dyskinesia (such as rapid, worm-like movements of the tongue or any other uncontrolled movements of the mouth, tongue, or jaw, and/or arms and legs) are especially likely to occur in elderly patients.

Other medicines—Although certain medicines should not be used together at all, in other cases 2 different medicines may be used together even if an interaction might occur. In these cases, your doctor may want to change the dose, or other precautions may be necessary. When you are taking molindone, it is especially important that your health care professional know if you are taking any of the following:

- Amoxapine (e.g., Asendin) or
- Methyldopa (e.g., Aldomet) or
- Metoclopramide (e.g., Reglan) or
- Metyrosine (e.g., Demser) or
- Other antipsychotics (medicine for mental illness) or
- Pemoline (e.g., Cylert) or
- Pimozide (e.g., Orap) or
- Promethazine (e.g., Phenergan) or
- Rauwolfia alkaloids (alseroxylon [e.g., Rauwiloid], deserpidine [e.g., Harmonyl], rauwolfia serpentina [e.g., Raudixin], reserpine [e.g., Serpasil]) or
- Trimeprazine (e.g., Temaril)—Taking these medicines with molindone may increase the chance and seriousness of some side effects
- Central nervous system (CNS) depressants (medicine that causes drowsiness) or
- Tricyclic antidepressants (medicine for depression)—Taking these medicines with molindone may increase the CNS depressant effects
- Lithium (e.g., Eskalith, Lithane)—The chance of serious side effects may be increased

Other medical problems—The presence of other medical problems may affect the use of molindone. Make sure you tell your doctor if you have any other medical problems, especially:

- Brain tumor or
- Intestinal blockage—Molindone may interfere with the diagnosis of these conditions
- Difficult urination or
- Enlarged prostate or
- Glaucoma or
- Liver disease or
- Parkinson's disease—Molindone may make the condition worse

Proper Use of This Medicine

Molindone should be taken with food or a full glass (8 ounces) of water or milk to reduce stomach irritation.

The liquid form of molindone may be taken undiluted or mixed with milk, water, fruit juice, or carbonated beverages.

Take this medicine only as directed by your doctor. Do not take more of it, do not take it more often, and do not take it for a longer time than your doctor ordered. To do so may increase the chance of side effects.

Sometimes this medicine must be taken for several weeks before its full effect is reached in the treatment of certain mental and emotional conditions.

Dosing—The dose of molindone will be different for different patients. *Follow your doctor's orders or the directions on the label.* The following information includes only the average doses of molindone. *If your dose is different, do not change it* unless your doctor tells you to do so.

The number of tablets or amount of solution that you take depends on the strength of the medicine. Also, *the number*

of doses you take each day, the time allowed between doses, and the length of time you take the medicine depend on the medical problem for which you are using molindone.

- For *oral* dosage forms (solution or tablets):
  - —Adults: To start, 50 to 75 milligrams a day, taken in smaller doses three or four times during the day. For maintenance, the dose you take will depend on your condition and may be from 15 to 225 milligrams a day, taken in smaller doses three or four times during the day.
  - —Children up to 12 years of age: The dose must be determined by the doctor.

Missed dose—If you miss a dose of this medicine, take it as soon as possible. However, if it is within 2 hours of your next dose, skip the missed dose and go back to your regular dosing schedule. Do not double doses.

Storage—To store this medicine:

- Keep out of the reach of children.
- Store away from heat and direct light.
- Do not store the tablets in the bathroom, near the kitchen sink, or in other damp places. Heat or moisture may cause the medicine to break down.
- Keep the liquid form of this medicine from freezing.
- Do not keep outdated medicine or medicine no longer needed. Be sure that any discarded medicine is out of the reach of children.

Precautions While Using This Medicine

Your doctor should check your progress at regular visits. This will allow the dosage of the medicine to be adjusted when necessary and also will reduce the possibility of side effects.

Do not stop taking this medicine without first checking with your doctor. Your doctor may want you to reduce gradually the amount you are taking before stopping completely.

Do not take molindone within 1 or 2 hours of taking antacids or medicine for diarrhea. Taking them too close together may make molindone less effective.

This medicine will add to the effects of alcohol and other CNS depressants (medicines that slow down the nervous system, possibly causing drowsiness). Some examples of CNS depressants are antihistamines or medicine for hay fever, other allergies, or colds; sedatives, tranquilizers, or sleeping medicine; prescription pain medicine or narcotics; barbiturates; medicine for seizures; muscle relaxants; or anesthetics, including some dental anesthetics. *Check with your doctor before taking any of the above while you are using this medicine.*

Molindone may cause some people to become drowsy or less alert than they are normally, especially during the first few weeks the medicine is being taken. Even if you take this medicine only at bedtime, you may feel drowsy or less alert on arising. *Make sure you know how you react to this medicine before you drive, use machines, or do anything else that could be dangerous if you are not alert.*

Dizziness or lightheadedness may occur, especially when you get up from a lying or sitting position. Getting up slowly may help. If the problem continues or gets worse, check with your doctor.

These medicines may make you sweat less, causing your body temperature to increase. *Use extra care not to become overheated during exercise or hot weather while you are taking this medicine, since overheating may result in heat stroke.* Also, hot baths or saunas may make you feel dizzy or faint while you are taking this medicine.

Molindone may cause dryness of the mouth. For temporary relief, use sugarless candy or gum, melt bits of ice in your mouth, or use a saliva substitute. However, if your mouth continues to feel dry for more than 2 weeks, check with your medical doctor or dentist. Continuing dryness of the mouth may increase the chance of dental disease, including tooth decay, gum disease, and fungus infection.

Side Effects of This Medicine

Along with its needed effects, molindone can sometimes cause serious side effects. Tardive dyskinesia (a movement disorder) may occur and may not go away after you stop using the medicine. Symptoms of tardive dyskinesia include fine, worm-like movements of the tongue, or other uncontrolled movements of the mouth, tongue, cheeks, jaw, or arms and legs. Other serious but rare side effects may also occur. These include severe muscle stiffness, fever, unusual tiredness or weakness, fast heartbeat, difficult breathing, increased sweating, loss of bladder control, and seizures (neuroleptic malignant syndrome). *You and your doctor should discuss the good this medicine will do as well as the risks of taking it.*

Stop taking molindone and get emergency help immediately if any of the following side effects occur:
Rare
   Convulsions (seizures); difficult or fast breathing; fast heartbeat or irregular pulse; fever (high); high or low (irregular) blood pressure; increased sweating; loss of bladder control; muscle stiffness (severe); unusually pale skin; unusual tiredness or weakness

Also, check with your doctor as soon as possible if any of the following side effects occur:
More common
   Difficulty in talking or swallowing; inability to move eyes; lip smacking or puckering; loss of balance control; mask-like face; muscle spasms, especially of the neck and back; puffing of cheeks; rapid or worm-like movements of tongue; restlessness or need to keep moving (severe); shuffling walk; stiffness of arms and legs; trembling and shaking of hands; twisting movements of body; uncontrolled movements of arms and legs; unusual chewing movements

Less common
   Mental depression
Rare
   Confusion; hot, dry skin, or lack of sweating; muscle weakness; skin rash; yellow eyes or skin

Other side effects may occur that usually do not need medical attention. These side effects may go away during treatment as your body adjusts to the medicine. However, check with your doctor if any of the following side effects continue or are bothersome:
More common
   Blurred vision; constipation; decreased sweating; difficult urination; dizziness or lightheadedness, especially when getting up suddenly from a lying or sitting position; drowsiness; dryness of mouth; headache; nausea; stuffy nose

Less common
   Changes in menstrual periods; decreased sexual ability; false sense of well-being; swelling of breasts; unusual secretion of milk

Some side effects may occur after you have stopped taking this medicine. Check with your doctor as soon as possible if you notice any of the following effects:
   Lip smacking or puckering; puffing of cheeks; rapid or worm-like movements of tongue; uncontrolled chewing movements; uncontrolled movements of arms and legs

Other side effects not listed above may also occur in some patients. If you notice any other effects, check with your doctor.

Revised: 03/19/93

MOLYBDENUM SUPPLEMENTS
Systemic†

Commonly used brand name(s):

In the U.S.—
   Molypen
   Generic name product may be available.

†Not commercially available in Canada.

Description

The body needs molybdenum (moh-LIB-den-um) for normal growth and health. For patients who are unable to get enough molybdenum in their regular diet or who have a need for more molybdenum, molybdenum supplements may be necessary. They are generally taken by mouth in multivitamin/mineral products but some patients may have to receive them by injection. Molybdenum is part of certain enzymes that are important for several body functions.

A deficiency of molybdenum is rare. However, if the body does not get enough molybdenum, certain enzymes needed by the body are affected. This may lead to a build up of unwanted substances in some people.

Injectable molybdenum is administered only by or under the supervision of your health care professional. Molybdenum is available in the following dosage forms:
Oral
   Molybdenum is available orally as part of a multivitamin/mineral combination.
Parenteral
   • Injection (U.S.)

Importance of Diet

For good health, it is important that you eat a balanced and varied diet. Follow carefully any diet program your health care professional may recommend. For your specific dietary vitamin and/or mineral needs, ask your health care professional for a list of appropriate foods. If you think that you are not getting enough vitamins and/or minerals in your diet, you may choose to take a dietary supplement.

The amount of molybdenum in foods depends on the soil in which the food is grown. Some soils have more molybdenum than others. Peas, beans, cereal products, leafy vegetables, and low-fat milk are good sources of molybdenum.

The daily amount of molybdenum needed is defined in several different ways.

For U.S.—
- Recommended Dietary Allowances (RDAs) are the amount of vitamins and minerals needed to provide for adequate nutrition in most healthy persons. RDAs for a given nutrient may vary depending on a person's age, sex, and physical condition (e.g., pregnancy).
- Daily Values (DVs) are used on food and dietary supplement labels to indicate the percent of the recommended daily amount of each nutrient that a serving provides. DV replaces the previous designation of United States Recommended Daily Allowances (USRDAs).

For Canada—
- Recommended Nutrient Intakes (RNIs) are used to determine the amounts of vitamins, minerals, and protein needed to provide adequate nutrition and lessen the risk of chronic disease.

Because a lack of molybdenum is rare, there is no RDA or RNI for it. The following daily intakes are thought to be plenty for most individuals:
- Infants and children—
  Birth to 3 years of age: 15 to 50 micrograms (mcg).
  4 to 6 years of age: 30 to 75 mcg.
  7 to 10 years of age: 50 to 150 mcg.
- Adolescents and adults—75 to 250 mcg.

Before Using This Dietary Supplement

If you are taking this dietary supplement without a prescription, carefully read and follow any precautions on the label. For molybdenum, the following should be considered:

Allergies—Tell your health care professional if you have ever had any unusual or allergic reaction to molybdenum. Also tell your health care professional if you are allergic to any other substances, such as foods, preservatives, or dyes.

Pregnancy—It is especially important that you are receiving enough vitamins and minerals when you become pregnant and that you continue to receive the right amount of vitamins and minerals throughout your pregnancy. The healthy growth and development of the fetus depend on a steady supply of nutrients from the mother. However, taking large amounts of a dietary supplement in pregnancy may be harmful to the mother and/or fetus and should be avoided.

Breast-feeding—It is important that you receive the right amounts of vitamins and minerals so that your baby will also get the vitamins and minerals needed to grow properly. However, taking large amounts of a dietary supplement while breast-feeding may be harmful to the mother and/or baby and should be avoided.

Children—Problems in children have not been reported with intake of normal daily recommended amounts.

Older adults—Problems in older adults have not been reported with intake of normal daily recommended amounts.

Medicines or other dietary supplements—Although certain medicines or dietary supplements should not be used together at all, in other cases they may be used together even if an interaction might occur. In these cases, your health care professional may want to change the dose, or other precautions may be necessary. Tell your health care professional if you are taking any other dietary supplement or any prescription or nonprescription (over-the-counter [OTC]) medicine.

Other medical problems—The presence of other medical problems may affect the use of molybdenum. Make sure you tell your health care professional if you have any other medical problems, especially:
- Copper deficiency—Molybdenum may make this condition worse
- Kidney diease or
- Liver disease—These conditions may cause higher blood levels of molybdenum, which may increase the chance of unwanted effects

Proper Use of This Dietary Supplement

Molybdenum is available orally only as part of a multivitamin/mineral product.

Dosing—The amount of molybdenum needed to meet normal daily recommended intakes will be different for different individuals. The following information includes only the average amounts of molybdenum.
- For *oral* dosage form (as part of a multivitamin/mineral supplement):
  —To prevent deficiency, the amount taken by mouth is based on normal daily recommended intakes:
    - Adults and teenagers—75 to 250 micrograms (mcg) per day.
    - Children 7 to 10 years of age—50 to 150 mcg per day.
    - Children 4 to 6 years of age—30 to 75 mcg per day.
    - Children birth to 3 years of age—15 to 150 mcg per day.
  —To treat deficiency:
    - Adults, teenagers, and children—Treatment dose is determined by prescriber for each individual based on severity of deficiency.

Missed dose—If you miss taking your multivitamin containing molybdenum for one or more days there is no cause for concern, since it takes some time for your body to become seriously low in molybdenum. However, if your health care professional has recommended that you take molybdenum, try to remember to take it as directed every day.

Storage—To store this dietary supplement:
- Keep out of the reach of children.
- Store away from heat and direct light.
- Do not store in the bathroom, near the kitchen sink, or in other damp places. Heat or moisture may cause the dietary supplement to break down.
- Keep the dietary supplement from freezing. Do not refrigerate.
- Do not keep outdated dietary supplements or those no longer needed. Be sure that any discarded dietary supplement is out of the reach of children.

Precautions While Using This Dietary Supplement

Large amounts of molybdenum may cause your body to lose copper. Your health care professional may recommend that you take a copper supplement while on molybdenum therapy.

Side Effects of This Dietary Supplement

Along with its needed effects, a dietary supplement may cause some unwanted effects. Although oral molybdenum supplements have not been reported to cause any side effects, *check with your health care professional immediately* if any of the following side effects occur:

Symptoms of overdose

Joint pain; side, lower back, or stomach pain; swelling of feet or lower legs

Note: Reported rarely in individuals consuming foods grown in soil containing a high content of molybdenum.

Other side effects not listed above may also occur in some individuals. If you notice any other effects, check with your health care professional.

Revised: 4/25/95

MONOCTANOIN   Local†

Commonly used brand name(s):

In the U.S.—
Moctanin

Another commonly used name is monooctanoin.

†Not commercially available in Canada.

Description

Monoctanoin (mon-OCK-ta-noyn) is used to dissolve cholesterol gallstones. Gallstones, which are found in the gallbladder or bile duct, sometimes remain in the bile duct even after the gallbladder has been removed by surgery. These stones may be too large to pass out of the body on their own. A catheter or tube is used to put the solution of monoctanoin into the bile duct where it will come in contact with the gallstone or gallstones and dissolve them. This process continues for 2 to 10 days.

Monoctanoin is administered only by or under the supervision of your doctor. It is available in the following dosage form:

Local
• Irrigation (U.S.)

Before Using This Medicine

In deciding to use a medicine, the risks of taking the medicine must be weighed against the good it will do. This is a decision you and your doctor will make. For monoctanoin, the following should be considered:

Allergies—Tell your doctor if you have ever had any unusual or allergic reaction to monoctanoin or any vegetable oils. Also, tell your doctor if you are allergic to any other substances, such as foods, preservatives, or dyes.

Pregnancy—Studies on effects in pregnancy have not been done in either humans or animals.

Breast-feeding—It is not known whether monoctanoin passes into the breast milk. However, this medicine has not been reported to cause problems in nursing babies.

Children—Studies on this medicine have been done only in adult patients, and there is no specific information comparing use of monoctanoin in children with use in other age groups.

Older adults—Many medicines have not been studied specifically in older people. Therefore, it may not be known whether they work exactly the same way they do in younger adults or if they cause different side effects or problems in older people. There is no specific information comparing use of monoctanoin in the elderly with use in other age groups.

Other medical problems—The presence of other medical problems may affect the use of monoctanoin. Make sure you tell your doctor if you have any other medical problems, especially:

• Bile duct blockage—The chance of serious side effects may be increased

• Biliary tract problems (other) or
• Jaundice or
• Pancreatitis (inflammation of the pancreas)—Monoctanoin may make these conditions worse

• Duodenal ulcer (recent) or
• Intestinal problems—Monoctanoin may make these conditions worse and may increase the chance of bleeding

• Liver disease (severe)—Unwanted effects may occur if the liver is not working properly

Proper Use of This Medicine

Dosing—The dose of monoctanoin will be different for different patients. The following information includes only the average doses of monoctanoin.

• For *irrigation* dosage form:
—For gallstone disease:
• Adults and teenagers—The usual dose is 3 to 5 milliliters (mL) per hour given through a catheter or tube. The dose is given over a period of 2 to 10 days.
• Children—Use and dose must be determined by your doctor.

Side Effects of This Medicine

Along with its needed effects, a medicine may cause some unwanted effects. Although not all of these side effects appear very often, when they do occur they may require medical attention.

Check with your doctor as soon as possible if any of the following side effects occur:

Less common or rare

Abdominal or stomach pain (severe); back pain (severe); chills, fever, or sore throat; drowsiness (severe); nausea (continuing); shortness of breath (severe)

Other side effects may occur that usually do not need medical attention. These side effects may go away during treatment as your body adjusts to the medicine. However, check with your doctor if any of the following side effects continue or are bothersome:

More common

Abdominal or stomach pain (mild) or burning sensation

Less common or rare

Back pain (mild); diarrhea; flushing or redness of face; loss of appetite; metallic taste; nausea or vomiting

Other side effects not listed above may also occur in some patients. If you notice any other effects, check with your doctor.

Revised: 07/20/95

MONTELUKAST Systemic

Commonly used brand name(s):

In the U.S.—
   Singulair

Description

Montelukast (mon-te-LOO-kast) is used in mild to moderate asthma to decrease the symptoms of asthma and the number of acute asthma attacks. However, this medicine should not be used to relieve an asthma attack that has already started.

This medicine is available only with your doctor's prescription, in the following dosage form:

   Oral
- Tablets (U.S.)
- Chewable tablets (U.S.)

Before Using This Medicine

In deciding to use a medicine, the risks of taking the medicine must be weighed against the good it will do. This is a decision you and your doctor will make. For montelukast, the following should be considered:

Allergies—Tell your doctor if you have ever had any unusual or allergic reaction to montelukast. Also tell your health care professional if you are allergic to any other substances, such as foods, preservatives, or dyes.

Pregnancy—Montelukast has not been studied in pregnant women. However, it has been studied in animals and has not been found to cause birth defects or other problems.

Breast-feeding—It is not known whether montelukast passes into breast milk in humans. However, it does pass into breast milk in animals. Although most medicines pass into breast milk in small amounts, many of them may be used safely while breast-feeding. Mothers who are using this medicine and who wish to breast-feed should discuss this with their doctor.

Children—No information is available regarding use of montelukast in children younger than 6 years of age. The chewable tablet contains aspartame, which has phenylalanine as a component. Children who have phenylketonuria should be aware that each chewable tablet contains 0.842 mg of phenylalanine.

Older adults—Many medicines have not been studied specifically in older people. Therefore, it may not be known whether they work exactly the same way they do in younger adults. There is no specific information comparing use of montelukast in the elderly with its use in other age groups. However, it has been used in some elderly patients and no differences in effectiveness or side effects were seen from those that occurred in younger adults.

Other medicines—Although certain medicines should not be used together at all, in other cases two different medicines may be used together even if an interaction might occur. In these cases, your doctor may want to change the dose, or other precautions may be necessary. Tell your health care professional if you are taking or using any other prescription or nonprescription (over-the-counter [OTC]) medicine.

Other medical problems—The presence of other medical problems may affect the use of montelukast. Make sure you tell your doctor if you have any other medical problems, especially:

- Liver disease—Effects of montelukast may be increased because of slower removal from the body

Proper Use of This Medicine

Montelukast is used to prevent asthma attacks. It is not used to relieve an attack that has already started. For relief of an asthma attack that has already started, you should use another medicine. If you do not have another medicine to use for an attack or if you have any questions about this, check with your health care professional.

Dosing—The dose of montelukast will be different for different patients. *Follow your doctor's orders or the directions on the label.* The following information includes only the average doses of montelukast. *If your dose is different, do not change it* unless your doctor tells you to do so.

The number of tablets that you take depends on the strength of the medicine.

- For asthma:
  —For *tablets* dosage form:
  - Adults and children 15 years of age and over—10 milligrams (mg) once a day in the evening.
  —For *chewable tablets* dosage form:
  - Children 6 to 15 years of age—5 mg once a day in the evening.
  - Children younger than 6 years of age—Use and dose must be determined by your doctor.

Missed dose—If you miss a dose of this medicine, take it as soon as you remember. However, if it is almost time for the next dose, skip the missed dose and go back to your regular dosing schedule. Do not double doses.

Storage—To store this medicine:
- Keep out of the reach of children.
- Store away from heat and direct light.
- Do not store in the bathroom, near the kitchen sink, or in other damp places. Heat or moisture may cause the medicine to break down.
- Do not keep outdated medicine or medicine no longer needed. Be sure that any discarded medicine is out of the reach of children.

Precautions While Using This Medicine

To work properly, montelukast must be taken every day at the same time, even if your asthma seems better.

Do not stop taking montelukast, even if your asthma seems better, unless you are told to do so by your doctor.

Check with your doctor if your symptoms do not improve or if your asthma gets worse.

You may be taking other medicines for asthma along with montelukast. *Do not stop taking or reduce the dose of the other medicines, even if your asthma seems better, unless you are told to do so by your doctor.*

Side Effects of This Medicine

Along with its needed effects, a medicine may cause some unwanted effects. Although not all of these side effects may occur, if they do occur they may need medical attention.

Check with your doctor as soon as possible if the following side effect occurs:

Rare
  Pus in the urine

Other side effects may occur that usually do not need medical attention. These side effects may go away during treatment as your body adjusts to the medicine. However, check with your doctor if any of the following side effects continue or are bothersome:

More common
  Headache

Less common
  Abdominal or stomach pain; cough; dental pain; dizziness; fever; heartburn; skin rash; stuffy nose; weakness or unusual tiredness

Other side effects not listed above may also occur in some patients. If you notice any other effects, check with your doctor.

Developed: 08/12/98
Interim revision: 02/17/99

MORICIZINE   Systemic†

Commonly used brand name(s):

In the U.S.—
  Ethmozine

†Not commercially available in Canada.

Description

Moricizine (mor-IH-siz-een) belongs to the group of medicines known as antiarrhythmics. It is used to correct irregular or rapid heartbeats to a normal rhythm by making the heart tissue less sensitive.

There is a chance that moricizine may cause new or make worse existing heart rhythm problems when it is used. Since other antiarrhythmic medicines have been shown to cause severe problems in some patients, moricizine is only used to treat serious heart rhythm problems. Discuss this possible effect with your doctor.

This medicine is available only with your doctor's prescription, in the following dosage form:

Oral
  • Tablets (U.S.)

Before Using This Medicine

In deciding to use a medicine, the risks of taking the medicine must be weighed against the good it will do. This is a decision you and your doctor will make. For moricizine, the following should be considered:

Allergies—Tell your doctor if you have ever had any unusual or allergic reaction to moricizine. Also tell your health care professional if you are allergic to any other substances, such as foods, preservatives, or dyes.

Pregnancy—Moricizine has not been studied in pregnant women. However, this medicine has not been shown to cause birth defects or other problems in animal studies, although it affected weight gain in some animals. Before taking moricizine, make sure your doctor knows if you are pregnant or if you may become pregnant.

Breast-feeding—Moricizine passes into the milk of some animals and may also pass into the milk of humans. However, this medicine has not been reported to cause problems in nursing babies.

Children—Studies on this medicine have been done only in adult patients, and there is no specific information comparing use of moricizine in children with use in other age groups.

Older adults—Many medicines have not been studied specifically in older people. Therefore, it may not be known whether they work exactly the same way they do in younger adults or if they cause different side effects or problems in older people. There is no specific information comparing use of moricizine in the elderly with use in other age groups, although the risk of some unwanted effects may be increased.

Other medicines—Although certain medicines should not be used together at all, in other cases two different medicines may be used together even if an interaction might occur. In these cases, your doctor may want to change the dose, or other precautions may be necessary. Tell your health care professional if you are taking any other prescription or nonprescription (over-the-counter [OTC]) medicine.

Other medical problems—The presence of other medical problems may affect the use of moricizine. Make sure you tell your doctor if you have any other medical problems, especially:

  • Kidney disease or
  • Liver disease—Effects may be increased because of slower removal of moricizine from the body

  • Heart disease or
  • Recent heart attack or
  • If you have a pacemaker—Risk of irregular heartbeats may be increased

Proper Use of This Medicine

Take moricizine exactly as directed by your doctor, even though you may feel well. Do not take more or less of it than your doctor ordered.

This medicine works best when there is a constant amount in the blood. *To help keep the amount constant, do not miss any doses. Also, it is best to take each dose at evenly spaced times day and night*. For example, if you are to take 3 doses a day, doses should be spaced about 8 hours apart. If you need help in planning the best times to take your medicine, check with your health care professional.

Dosing—The dose of moricizine will be different for different patients. *Follow your doctor's orders or the directions on the label*. The following information includes only the average doses of moricizine. *If your dose is different, do not change it* unless your doctor tells you to do so.

The number of tablets that you take depends on the strength of the medicine.

- For *oral* dosage form (tablets):
  —For irregular heartbeat (arrhythmias):
    • Adults—600 to 900 milligrams (mg) a day. This is divided into three doses and taken every eight hours.
    • Children—Use and dose must be determined by your doctor.

Missed dose—If you miss a dose of moricizine and remember within 4 hours, take it as soon as possible. However, if you do not remember until later, skip the missed dose and go back to your regular dosing schedule. Do not double doses.

Storage—To store this medicine:
- Keep out of the reach of children.
- Store away from heat and direct light.
- Do not store in the bathroom, near the kitchen sink, or in other damp places. Heat or moisture may cause the medicine to break down.
- Do not keep outdated medicine or medicine no longer needed. Be sure that any discarded medicine is out of the reach of children.

Precautions While Using This Medicine

It is important that your doctor check your progress at regular visits to make sure the medicine is working properly. This will allow changes to be made in the amount of medicine you are taking, if necessary.

Your doctor may want you to carry a medical identification card or bracelet stating that you are using this medicine.

Before having any kind of surgery (including dental surgery) or emergency treatment, tell the medical doctor or dentist in charge that you are taking this medicine.

Moricizine may cause some people to become dizzy or lightheaded. Make sure you know how you react to this medicine before you drive, use machines, or do anything else that could be dangerous if you are dizzy.

Side Effects of This Medicine

Along with its needed effects, a medicine may cause some unwanted effects. Although not all of these side effects may occur, if they do occur they may need medical attention.

Check with your doctor as soon as possible if any of the following side effects occur:
Less common
  Chest pain; fast or irregular heartbeat; shortness of breath; swelling of feet or lower legs
Rare
  Fever (sudden, high)

Other side effects may occur that usually do not need medical attention. These side effects may go away during treatment as your body adjusts to the medicine. However, check with your doctor if any of the following side effects continue or are bothersome:
More common
  Dizziness
Less common
  Blurred vision; diarrhea; dryness of mouth; headache; nausea or vomiting; nervousness; numbness or tingling in arms or legs or around mouth; pain in arms or legs; stomach pain; trouble in sleeping; unusual tiredness or weakness

Other side effects not listed above may also occur in some patients. If you notice any other effects, check with your doctor.

Revised: 09/27/92
Interim revision: 06/30/94

MUPIROCIN   Topical

Commonly used brand name(s):

In the U.S.—
  Bactroban

In Canada—
  Bactroban

Other commonly used names are pseudomonic acid and pseudomonic acid A.

Description

Mupirocin (myoo-PEER-oh-sin) is used to treat bacterial infections. It works by killing bacteria or preventing their growth.

Mupirocin ointment is applied to the skin to treat impetigo. It may also be used for other bacterial skin infections as determined by your doctor.

Mupirocin cream is applied to the skin to treat secondarily infected traumatic skin lesions.

Mupirocin is available in the U.S. only with your doctor's prescription. It is available in Canada without a prescription; however, your doctor may have special instructions on the proper use of this medicine for your medical problem. Mupirocin is available in the following dosage form:

Topical
  • Ointment (U.S. and Canada)
  • Cream (U.S.)

Before Using This Medicine

In deciding to use a medicine, the risks of taking the medicine must be weighed against the good it will do. This is a decision you and your doctor will make. For topical mupirocin, the following should be considered:

Allergies—Tell your doctor if you have ever had any unusual or allergic reaction to mupirocin. Also tell your health care professional if you are allergic to any other substances, such as preservatives or dyes.

Pregnancy—Topical mupirocin has not been studied in pregnant women. However, this medication has not been shown to cause birth defects or other problems in animal studies.

Breast-feeding—It is not known whether topical mupirocin passes into the breast milk. However, this medicine is unlikely to pass into the breast milk in large amounts, since very little mupirocin is absorbed into the mother's body when applied to the skin.

Children—Safety and effectiveness of mupirocin cream have not been established in children up to 3 months of age.

Safety and effectiveness of mupirocin ointment have not been established in children up to 2 months of age.

Older adults—No overall difference in safety and efficacy were observed in patients over 65 years of age.

Other medicines—Although certain medicines should not be used together at all, in other cases two different medicines may be used together even if an interaction might occur. In these cases, your doctor may want to change the dose, or other precautions may be necessary. Tell your health care professional if you are using any other prescription or nonprescription (over-the-counter [OTC]) medicine that is to be applied to the same area of skin.

Proper Use of This Medicine

Do not use this medicine in the eyes.

To use:
- Before applying this medicine, wash the affected area(s) with soap and water, and dry thoroughly. Then apply a small amount to the affected area(s) and rub in gently.
- After applying this medicine, the treated area(s) may be covered with a gauze dressing if desired.

To help clear up your skin infection completely, keep using mupirocin for the full time of treatment, even if your symptoms have disappeared. *Do not miss any doses.*

Dosing—*Follow your doctor's orders or the directions on the label.* The following information includes only the average dose of mupirocin. *If your dose is different, do not change it* unless your doctor tells you to do so.

- For *ointment* dosage form:
  —Impetigo:
  - Adults and children 2 months of age and older— Apply three times a day.
  - Children under 2 months of age—Use and dose must be determined by your doctor.

- For *cream* dosage form:
  —Secondarily infected traumatic skin lesions
  - Adults and children 3 months of age and older— Apply three times a day, for 10 days.
  - Children under 3 months of age—Use and dose must be determined by your doctor.

Missed dose—If you miss a dose of this medicine, apply it as soon as possible. However, if it is almost time for your next dose, skip the missed dose and go back to your regular dosing schedule.

Storage—To store this medicine:
- Keep out of the reach of children.
- Store away from heat and direct light.
- Keep the medicine from freezing.
- Do not keep outdated medicine or medicine no longer needed. Be sure that any discarded medicine is out of the reach of children.

Precautions While Using This Medicine

If your skin infection does not improve within 3 to 5 days, or if it becomes worse, check with your health care professional.

Side Effects of This Medicine

Along with its needed effects, a medicine may cause some unwanted effects. The following side effects may go away during treatment as your body adjusts to the medicine.

However, check with your doctor if any of these effects continue or are bothersome:
Less common
    Dry skin; skin burning, itching, pain, rash, redness, stinging, or swelling; headache; nausea

Other side effects not listed above may also occur in some patients. If you notice any other effects, check with your doctor.
Rare
    Abdominal pain; dizziness; secondary wound infection; sores on mouth and on lips

Revised: 06/11/2001

MUROMONAB-CD3   Systemic

Commonly used brand name(s):

In the U.S.—
    Orthoclone OKT3

In Canada—
    Orthoclone OKT3

Description

Muromonab-CD3 (myoo-roe-MOE-nab cee-dee-three) is a monoclonal antibody. It is used to reduce the body's natural immunity in patients who receive organ (for example, kidney) transplants.

When a patient receives an organ transplant, the body's white blood cells will try to get rid of (reject) the transplanted organ. Muromonab-CD3 works by preventing the white blood cells from doing this.

The effect of muromonab-CD3 on the white blood cells may also reduce the body's ability to fight infections. Before you begin treatment, you and your doctor should talk about the good this medicine will do as well as the risks of using it.

Muromonab-CD3 is to be administered only by or under the immediate supervision of your doctor. It is available in the following dosage form:

Parenteral
- Injection (U.S. and Canada)

Before Using This Medicine

In deciding to use a medicine, the risks of taking the medicine must be weighed against the good it will do. This is a decision you and your doctor will make. For muromonab-CD3, the following should be considered:

Allergies—Tell your doctor if you have ever had any unusual or allergic reaction to muromonab-CD3 or to rodents (such as mice or rats). Muromonab-CD3 is grown in a mouse cell culture. Also tell your health care professional if you are allergic to any other substance, such as preservatives.

Pregnancy—Studies have not been done in either humans or animals. Muromonab-CD3 may cross the placenta, but it is not known whether it causes harmful effects on the fetus. Before receiving this medicine, make sure your doctor knows if you are pregnant or if you may become pregnant.

Breast-feeding—It is not known whether muromonab-CD3 passes into breast milk. Muromonab-CD3 has not been reported to cause problems in nursing babies. However, it may be necessary for you to stop breast-feeding during treatment. Be sure you have discussed the risks and benefits of the medicine with your doctor.

Children—There is no specific information comparing use of muromonab-CD3 in children with use in other age groups. However, children are more likely to get dehydrated from the diarrhea and vomiting that may be caused by this medicine.

Older adults—Many medicines have not been studied specifically in older people. Therefore, it may not be known whether they work exactly the same way they do in younger adults or if they cause different side effects or problems in older people. There is no specific information comparing use of muromonab-CD3 in the elderly with use in other age groups.

Other medicines—Although certain medicines should not be used together at all, in other cases two different medicines may be used together even if an interaction might occur. In these cases, your doctor may want to change the dose, or other precautions may be necessary. When you are receiving muromonab-CD3, it is especially important that your health care professional know if you are taking any of the following:

- Azathioprine (e.g., Imuran) or
- Chlorambucil (e.g., Leukeran) or
- Corticosteroids (cortisone-like medicine) or
- Cyclophosphamide (e.g., Cytoxan) or
- Cyclosporine (e.g., Sandimmune) or
- Cytarabine (e.g., Cytosar-U) or
- Mercaptopurine (e.g., Purinethol) or
- Tacrolimus (e.g., Prograf)—There may be an increased risk of infection and development of cancer because muromonab-CD3 reduces the body's ability to fight them

Other medical problems—The presence of other medical problems may affect the use of muromonab-CD3. Make sure you tell your doctor if you have any other medical problems, especially:

- Angina (chest pain) or
- Circulation problems or
- Convulsions (seizures) or
- Heart attack (recent) or
- Heart problems, other, or
- Kidney problems or
- Lung problems or
- Nervous system problems—Increased risk of serious unwanted effects from muromonab-CD3

- Blood clots (history of)—Risk of blood clots in transplanted organ or blood vessels

- Chickenpox (including recent exposure) or
- Herpes zoster (shingles)—Risk of severe disease affecting other parts of the body

- Infection—Muromonab-CD3 decreases your body's ability to fight infection

Proper Use of This Medicine

Dosing—The dose of muromonab-CD3 may be different for different patients. Muromonab-CD3 is usually given by a doctor or nurse in the hospital. The following information includes only the average doses of muromonab-CD3:

- For *injection* dosage form:
  - To prevent organ transplant rejection:
    - Adults—5 milligrams (mg) injected into a vein once a day.
    - Children less than 12 years of age—Dose is based on body weight and must be determined by your doctor.

Precautions While Using This Medicine

It is very important that your doctor check your progress at regular visits to make sure that this medicine is working properly and to check for unwanted effects.

While you are being treated with muromonab-CD3 and after you stop treatment with it, *do not have any immunizations (vaccinations) without your doctor's approval.* Muromonab-CD3 may lower your body's resistance. For some immunizations, there is a chance you might get the infection the immunization is meant to prevent. For other immunizations, it may be especially important to receive the immunization to prevent a disease. In addition, other persons living in your house should not take oral polio vaccine since there is a chance they could pass the polio virus on to you. Also, avoid persons who have recently taken oral polio vaccine. Do not get close to them and do not stay in the same room with them for very long. If you cannot take these precautions, you should consider wearing a protective face mask that covers the nose and mouth.

Treatment with muromonab-CD3 may also increase the chance of getting other infections. If you can, avoid people with colds or other infections. If you think you are getting a cold or other infection, check with your doctor.

This medicine commonly causes chest pain, dizziness, fever and chills, shortness of breath, stomach upset, and trembling within a few hours after the first dose. These effects should be less after the second dose. However, *check with your doctor or nurse immediately* if you have chest pain, rapid or irregular heartbeat, shortness of breath or wheezing, or swelling of the face or throat after any dose.

Side Effects of This Medicine

Along with its needed effects, a medicine may cause some unwanted effects.

Because of the way that muromonab-CD3 acts on the body, there is a chance that it may cause effects that may not occur until years after the medicine is used. These delayed effects may include certain types of cancer, such as lymphomas and skin cancers. Discuss these possible effects with your doctor.

Although not all of the following side effects may occur, if they do occur, they may need medical attention.

Check with your doctor or nurse immediately if the following side effects occur:
Less common
   Chest pain; rapid or irregular heartbeat; shortness of breath or wheezing; swelling of face or throat

Check with your doctor as soon as possible if any of the following side effects occur:
More common
   Diarrhea; dizziness or faintness; fever and chills; general feeling of discomfort or illness; headache; muscle or joint pain; nausea and vomiting

Less common or rare
   Confusion; black, tarry stools; blood in urine or stools; convulsions (seizures); cough or hoarseness; hallucinations (seeing, hearing, or feeling things that are not there); itching or tingling; loss of hearing or vision; lower back or side pain; painful or difficult urination; pinpoint red spots on skin; skin rash; sores, ulcers, or white spots on the lips or in the mouth; stiff neck; swollen or painful glands; tight-

ness in the chest; trembling and shaking of hands; troubled breathing; unusual sensitivity of eyes to light; unusual bleeding or bruising; unusual tiredness; weakness

After you stop using this medicine, it may still produce some side effects that need medical attention. During this period of time check with your doctor if you notice the following side effects:

Fever and chills

Other side effects not listed above may also occur in some patients. If you notice any other effects, check with your doctor.

Revised: 06/01/99

MYCOPHENOLATE   Systemic

Commonly used brand name(s):

In the U.S.—
CellCept

Description

Mycophenolate (mye-koe-FEN-oh-late) belongs to a group of medicines known as immunosuppressive agents. It is used to lower the body's natural immunity in patients who receive organ transplants.

When a patient receives an organ transplant, the body's white blood cells will try to get rid of (reject) the transplanted organ. Mycophenolate works by preventing the white blood cells from getting rid of the transplanted organ.

This medicine is available only with your doctor's prescription, in the following dosage form(s):

Oral
• Capsules (U.S.)
• Tablets (U.S.)

Parenteral
• Injection (U.S.)

Before Using This Medicine

In deciding to use a medicine, the risks of taking the medicine must be weighed against the good it will do. This is a decision you and your doctor will make. For mycophenolate, the following should be considered:

Allergies—Tell your doctor if you have ever had any unusual or allergic reaction to mycophenolate. Also tell your health care professional if you are allergic to any other substances, such as food preservatives or dyes.

Pregnancy—Mycophenolate has not been studied in pregnant women. However, mycophenolate causes birth defects in animals, and it may cause birth defects in people too. If you are taking mycophenolate, you should use two forms of reliable birth control before beginning treatment with mycophenolate, while being treated with mycophenolate, and for at least 6 weeks after discontinuing mycophenolate.

Breast-feeding—It is not known whether mycophenolate passes into breast milk. Although most medicines pass into breast milk in small amounts, many of them can be used safely while breast-feeding. Mothers who are taking this med-

icine and who wish to breast-feed should discuss this with their doctor.

Children—Although there is no specific information comparing the use of mycophenolate in children with use in other age groups, this medicine is not expected to cause different side effects or problems in children than it does in adults.

Older adults—Many medicines have not been studied specifically in older people. Therefore, it may not be known whether they work exactly the same way they do in younger adults or if they cause different side effects or problems in older people. There is no specific information comparing use of mycophenolate in the elderly with use in other age groups.

Dental—The effects of mycophenolate may cause increased infections and delayed healing. Dental work, whenever possible, should be completed prior to beginning this medicine.

Other medicines—Although certain medicines should not be used together at all, in other cases two different medicines may be used together even if an interaction might occur. In these cases, your doctor may want to change the dose, or other precautions may be necessary. When you are taking mycophenolate, it is especially important that your health care professional know if you are taking any of the following:

• Antithymocyte globulin (e.g., Atgam) or
• Azathioprine (e.g., Imuran) or
• Chlorambucil (e.g., Leukeran) or
• Corticosteroids, glucocorticoid (e.g., Cortef, Decadron, Deltasone, Medrol) or
• Cyclophosphamide (e.g., Cytoxan) or
• Cyclosporine (e.g., Neoral, Sandimmune) or
• Mercaptopurine (e.g., Purinethol) or
• Muromonab-CD3 (e.g., Orthoclone OKT3) or
• Tacrolimus (e.g., Prograf)—There may be an increased chance of developing certain kinds of cancers and infections because of increased suppression of your immune system

Other medical problems—The presence of other medical problems may affect the use of mycophenolate. Make sure you tell your doctor if you have any other medical problems, especially:

• Delayed kidney function following kidney transplantation or
• Kidney problems, severe—Reduced elimination of mycophenolate and increased chance of developing fever and chills, cough or hoarseness, lower back or side pain, painful or difficult urination

• Digestive system disease, active—Risk of bleeding from the stomach

Proper Use of This Medicine

This medicine should be taken on an empty stomach.

Take this medicine only as directed by your doctor. Do not take more or less of it and do not take it more often than your doctor ordered. Taking too much may increase the chance of side effects, while taking too little may lead to rejection of your transplanted organ.

To help you remember to take your medicine, try to get into the habit of taking it at the same time each day.

Do not stop taking this medicine without first checking with your doctor. Your physician will use the results of tests and your physical examination to decide how long you should take this medicine.

The capsules or tablets of mycophenolate should be swallowed whole. The tablets should not be crushed and the capsules should not be opened because it is important that other people not be exposed to mycophenolate powder.

Dosing—*Follow your doctor's orders or the directions on the label*. The following information includes only the average doses of mycophenolate. *If your dose is different, do not change it* unless your doctor tells you to do so.

The number of capsules or tablets that you take depends on the strength of the medicine.

- For *oral* dosage form (capsules or tablets):
  —For prevention of rejection of transplanted heart:
  - Adults—1.5 grams (six capsules or three tablets) two times a day.
  —For prevention of rejection of transplanted kidney:
  - Adults—1 gram (four capsules or two tablets) two times a day.
  — For prevention of rejection of transplanted liver:
  - Adults—1.5 grams (six capsules or three tablets) two times a day.

- For *injection* dosage form:
  —For prevention of rejection of transplanted heart:
  - Adults—1.5 grams two times a day.
  —For prevention of rejection of transplanted kidney:
  - Adults—1 gram two times a day.
  — For prevention of rejection of transplanted liver:
  - Adults—1 gram two times a day.

Missed dose—If you miss a dose of mycophenolate and remember it within a few hours, take the missed dose as soon as you remember. However, if it is almost time for the next dose, skip the missed dose, go back to your regular dosing schedule, and check with your doctor. Do not double doses.

Storage—To store this medicine:
- Keep out of the reach of children.
- Store away from heat and direct light.
- Do not store in the bathroom, near the kitchen sink, or in other damp places. Heat or moisture may cause the medicine to break down.
- Do not keep outdated medicine or medicine no longer needed. Be sure that any discarded medicine is out of the reach of children.

Precautions While Using This Medicine

It is very important that your doctor check your progress at regular visits. Your doctor will want to do laboratory tests to make sure that mycophenolate is working properly and to check for unwanted effects.

While you are taking mycophenolate, it is important to maintain good dental hygiene and see a dentist regularly for teeth cleaning.

Treatment with mycophenolate may increase the chance of getting other infections. If you can, avoid contact with people with colds or other infections. If you think you are getting a cold or other infection, check with your doctor.

Side Effects of This Medicine

Along with its needed effects, a medicine may cause some unwanted effects. Although not all of these side effects may occur, if they do occur they may need medical attention.

Check with your doctor as soon as possible if any of the following side effects occur:
More common
  Blood in the urine; chest pain; cough or hoarseness; fever or chills; increased cough; lower back or side pain; painful or difficult urination; shortness of breath; swelling of feet or lower legs
Less common
  Abdominal pain; black, tarry stools; bloody vomit; enlarged gums; irregular heartbeat; joint pain; muscle pain; pinpoint red spots on the skin; red, inflamed, bleeding gums; sores inside mouth; trembling or shaking of hands or feet; unusual bleeding or bruising; white patches on the mouth, tongue, or throat

Other side effects may occur that usually do not need medical attention. These side effects may go away during treatment as your body adjusts to the medicine. However, check with your doctor if any of the following side effects continue or are bothersome:
More common
  Constipation; diarrhea; headache; heartburn; nausea; stomach pain; vomiting; weakness
Less common
  Acne; dizziness; skin rash; trouble in sleeping

Other side effects not listed above may also occur in some patients. If you notice any other effects, check with your doctor.

Revised: 12/20/2000

NABILONE   Systemic

Commonly used brand name(s):

In Canada—
  Cesamet

Description

Nabilone (NA-bi-lone) is chemically related to marijuana. It is used to prevent the nausea and vomiting that may occur after treatment with cancer medicines. It is used only when other kinds of medicine for nausea and vomiting do not work.

Nabilone is available only with your doctor's prescription. Prescriptions cannot be refilled and you must obtain a new prescription from your doctor each time you need this medicine. Nabilone is available in the following dosage form:

Oral
- Capsules (Canada)

Before Using This Medicine

In deciding to use a medicine, the risks of taking the medicine must be weighed against the good it will do. This is a decision you and your doctor will make. For nabilone, the following should be considered:

Allergies—Tell your doctor if you have ever had any unusual or allergic reaction to nabilone or marijuana products. Also tell your health care professional if you are allergic to any other substances, such as foods, preservatives, or dyes.

Pregnancy—Studies have not been done in pregnant women. However, studies in animals have shown a decrease in successful pregnancies and a decrease in the number of live babies born, when nabilone was given in doses many times the usual human dose.

Breast-feeding—It is not known whether nabilone passes into the breast milk. However, nabilone is not recommended during breast-feeding because other medicines similar to nabilone that pass into the breast milk have been shown to cause unwanted effects in the nursing baby.

Children—Studies on this medicine have been done only in adult patients, and there is no specific information comparing use of nabilone in children with use in other age groups.

Older adults—Fast or pounding heartbeat, feeling faint or lightheaded, and unusual tiredness or weakness may be especially likely to occur in elderly patients, who are usually more sensitive than younger adults to the effects of nabilone. Also, the effects this medicine may have on the mind may be of special concern in the elderly. Therefore, older people should be watched closely while taking this medicine.

Other medicines—Although certain medicines should not be used together at all, in other cases two different medicines may be used together even if an interaction might occur. In these cases, your doctor may want to change the dose, or other precautions may be necessary. When you are taking nabilone, it is especially important that your health care professional know if you are taking any of the following:

- Central nervous system (CNS) depressants (medicine that causes drowsiness) or
- Tricyclic antidepressants (medicine for depression)—Taking these medicines with nabilone may increase the CNS-depressant effects

Other medical problems—The presence of other medical problems may affect the use of nabilone. Make sure you tell your doctor if you have any other medical problems, especially:

- Alcohol abuse (or history of) or
- Drug abuse or dependence (or history of)—Dependence on nabilone may develop

- Emotional problems or
- Heart disease or
- Low blood pressure or
- Manic or depressive states or
- Mental illness (severe) or
- Schizophrenia—Nabilone may make the condition worse

- Liver disease (severe)—Higher blood levels of nabilone may occur, increasing the chance of side effects

Proper Use of This Medicine

Take this medicine only as directed by your doctor. Do not take more of it, do not take it more often, and do not take it for a longer time than your doctor ordered. If too much is taken, it may lead to other medical problems because of an overdose.

Dosing—The dose of nabilone will be different for different patients. *Follow your doctor's orders or the directions on the label*. The following information includes only the average doses of nabilone. *If your dose is different, do not change it* unless your doctor tells you to do so.

- For *oral* dosage forms (capsules):
  - —For nausea and vomiting caused by cancer medicines:
    - Adults and teenagers—Usually 1 or 2 milligrams (mg) twice a day. Your doctor will tell you how and when to take this medicine while you are taking your cancer medicine.
    - Children—Use and dose must be determined by your doctor.

Missed dose—If you miss a dose of this medicine, take it as soon as you remember. However, if it is almost time for your next dose, skip the missed dose and go back to your regular dosing schedule. *Do not double doses.*

Storage—To store this medicine:

- Keep out of the reach of children.
- Store away from heat and direct light.
- Do not store this medicine in the bathroom, near the kitchen sink, or in other damp places. Heat or moisture may cause the medicine to break down.
- Do not keep outdated medicine or medicine no longer needed. Be sure that any discarded medicine is out of the reach of children.

Precautions While Using This Medicine

Nabilone will add to the effects of alcohol and other central nervous system (CNS) depressants (medicines that make you feel drowsy or less alert). Some examples of CNS depressants are antihistamines or medicine for hay fever, other allergies, or colds; sedatives, tranquilizers, or sleeping medicine; prescription pain medicines, including other narcotics; barbiturates; medicine for seizures; muscle relaxants; or anesthetics, including some dental anesthetics. *Check with your doctor before taking any of the above while you are taking this medicine.*

If you think you or someone else may have taken an overdose, get emergency help at once. Taking an overdose of this medicine or taking alcohol or CNS depressants with this medicine may cause severe mental effects. Symptoms of overdose include changes in mood; confusion; difficulty in breathing; hallucinations (seeing, hearing, or feeling things that are not there); nervousness or anxiety (severe); and fast or pounding heartbeat.

This medicine may cause some people to become drowsy, dizzy, or lightheaded, or to feel a false sense of well-being. *Make sure you know how you react to this medicine before you drive, use machines, or do anything else that could be dangerous if you are dizzy or are not alert and clearheaded.*

Dizziness, lightheadedness, or fainting may occur, especially when you get up suddenly from a lying or sitting position. Getting up slowly may help lessen this problem.

Nabilone may cause dryness of the mouth. For temporary relief, use sugarless candy or gum, melt bits of ice in your mouth, or use a saliva substitute. However, if your mouth continues to feel dry for more than 2 weeks, check with your medical doctor or dentist. Continuing dryness of the mouth may increase the chance of dental disease, including tooth decay, gum disease, and fungus infections.

Side Effects of This Medicine

Along with its needed effects, a medicine may cause some unwanted effects. Although not all of these side effects may occur, if they do occur they may need medical attention.

Check with your doctor as soon as possible if any of the following side effects occur:

Changes in mood; confusion; convulsions (seizures); delusions; dizziness or fainting; fast or pounding heartbeat; hallucinations (seeing, hearing, or feeling things that are not there); mental depression; nervousness or anxiety; unusual tiredness or weakness (severe)

Symptoms of overdose

Difficulty in breathing; hallucinations (seeing, hearing, or feeling things that are not there); mental changes (severe); nervousness or anxiety (severe)

Other side effects may occur that usually do not need medical attention. These side effects may go away during treatment as your body adjusts to the medicine. However, check with your doctor if any of the following side effects continue or are bothersome:

More common

Clumsiness or unsteadiness; drowsiness; dryness of mouth; false sense of well-being; headache

Less common or rare

Blurred vision or any changes in vision; dizziness or lightheadedness, especially when getting up from a lying or sitting position—more common with high doses; loss of appetite

Other side effects not listed above may also occur in some patients. If you notice any other effects, check with your doctor.

Revised: 01/29/99

NADROPARIN Systemic—INTRODUCTORY VERSION

Commonly used brand name(s):

In Canada—
Fraxiparine
Fraxiparine Forte

Description

Nadroparin (na-dro-PA-rin) is used to prevent and treat deep vein thrombosis, a condition in which harmful blood clots form in the blood vessels of the legs. These blood clots can travel to the lungs and can become lodged in the blood vessels of the lungs, causing a condition called pulmonary embolism. Nadroparin is used for several days after surgery, while you are unable to walk. Nadroparin also is used to prevent blood clots from forming during hemodialysis.

This medicine is available only with your doctor's prescription, in the following dosage form:

Parenteral
• Injection (Canada)

Before Using This Medicine

In deciding to use a medicine, the risks of using the medicine must be weighed against the good it will do. This is a decision you and your doctor will make. For nadroparin, the following should be considered:

Allergies—Tell your doctor if you have ever had any unusual or allergic reaction to nadroparin. Also tell your health care professional if you are allergic to any other substances, such as foods, preservatives, or dyes.

Pregnancy—Nadroparin has not been shown to cause birth defects or other problems in humans or animals. However, before taking this medicine, make sure your doctor knows if you are pregnant or if you may become pregnant.

Breast-feeding—It is not known whether nadroparin passes into breast milk. However, mothers receiving nadroparin should avoid breast-feeding.

Children—Studies on this medicine have been done only in adult patients and there is no specific information comparing use of nadroparin in children with use in other age groups.

Older adults—This medicine has been tested and has not been shown to cause different side effects or problems in older people than it does in younger adults.

Other medicines—Although certain medicines should not be used together at all, in other cases two different medicines may be used together even if an interaction might occur. In these cases, your doctor may want to change the dose, or other precautions may be necessary. When you are taking nadroparin, it is especially important that your health care professional know if you are taking any of the following:

• Abciximab (e.g., ReoPro) or
• Anagrelide (e.g., Agrylin) or
• Calcium channel blocking agents (bepridil [e.g., Vascor], diltiazem [e.g., Cardizem], felodipine [e.g., Plendil], flunarizine [e.g., Sibelium], nicardipine [e.g., Cardene], nifedipine [e.g., Procardia], nimodipine [e.g., Nimotop], verapamil [e.g., Calan]) or
• Clopidogril (e.g., Plavix) or
• Dipyridamole (e.g., Persantine) or
• Divalproex (e.g., Depakote) or
• Epoprostenol (e.g., Flolan) or
• Eptifibatide (e.g., Integrilin) or
• Inflammation or pain medicine, except narcotics or
• Mezlocillin (e.g., Mezlin) or
• Pentoxifylline (e.g., Trental) or
• Piperacillin (e.g., Pipracil) or
• Plicamycin (e.g., Mithracin) or
• Sulfinpyrazone (e.g., Anturane) or
• Ticarcillin (e.g., Ticar) or
• Ticlopidine (e.g., Ticlid) or
• Tirofiban (e.g., Aggrastat) or
• Valproic acid (e.g., Depakene)—Using any of these medicines together with nadroparin may increase the risk of bleeding

Other medical problems—The presence of other medical problems may affect the use of nadroparin. Make sure you tell your doctor if you have any other medical problems, especially:

• Abortion (risk of) or
• Bleeding problems or
• Eye problems caused by diabetes or high blood pressure or
• Heart infection or
• High blood pressure or
• Injury or surgery involving the brain, ears, eyes, or spinal cord or

- Liver disease or
- Low blood platelet count or
- Stomach or intestinal ulcer or
- Stroke—The risk of bleeding may be increased

- Kidney disease—Nadroparin is removed from the body by the kidneys; patients with kidney disease may need to receive a lower dose of nadroparin

Proper Use of This Medicine

If you are using nadroparin at home, your health care professional will teach you how to inject yourself with the medicine. *Be sure to follow the directions carefully. Check with your health care professional if you have any problems using the medicine.*

Put used syringes in a puncture-resistant, disposable container or dispose of them as directed by your health care professional.

Dosing—The dose of nadroparin will be different for different patients. *Follow your doctor's orders or the directions on the label.* The following information includes only the average doses of nadroparin. *If your dose is different, do not change it* unless your doctor tells you to do so.

The number of milliliters (mL) of nadroparin that you take depends on the strength of the medicine. Also, *the number of doses you take each day, the time allowed between doses, and the length of time you take the medicine depend on the medical problem for which you are taking nadroparin:*

- For *injection* dosage form:
  —For unstable angina or certain types of heart attacks:
    - Adults: The dose is based on body weight. It is usually 86 anti-factor Xa International Units (IU) per kilogram (kg) (39.1 anti-factor Xa IU per pound) of body weight injected under the skin every twelve hours for six days.
    - Children: Use and dose must be determined by your doctor.
  —For prevention of deep vein thrombosis (blood clots in the legs) or pulmonary embolism (blood clots in the lungs) after general surgery:
    - Adults: The dose is usually 2850 anti-factor Xa IU injected under the skin once a day beginning two to four hours before surgery and continuing for at least seven days.
    - Children: Use and dose must be determined by your doctor.
  —For prevention of deep vein thrombosis or pulmonary embolism after hip replacement surgery:
    - Adults: The dose is usually 38 anti-factor Xa IU per kg (17.3 anti-factor Xa IU per pound) of body weight injected under the skin twelve hours before surgery, twelve hours after surgery, and once a day for the first three days after surgery. Then, the dose is 57 anti-factor Xa IU per kg (26 anti-factor Xa IU per pound) of body weight injected under the skin once a day from the fourth through the tenth days after surgery.
    - Children: Use and dose must be determined by your doctor.
  —For treatment of deep vein thrombosis:
    - Adults:
      —Patients weighing less than 40 kg (88 pounds) or more than 100 kg (220 pounds): Dose must be determined by your doctor.
      —Patients weighing 40 to 100 kg (88 to 220 pounds): The dose is usually 171 anti-factor Xa IU per kg (77.7 anti-factor Xa IU per pound) of body weight injected under the skin once a day. Or, the dose may be 86 anti-factor Xa IU per kg (39.1 anti-factor Xa IU per pound) of body weight injected under the skin two times a day.
    - Children: Use and dose must be determined by your doctor.
  —For prevention of blood clots during hemodialysis (kidney dialysis):
    - Adults: The dose is usually 65 anti-factor Xa IU per kg (29.5 anti-factor Xa IU per pound) of body weight injected into an artery at the start of each dialysis session.
    - Children: Use and dose must be determined by your doctor.

Storage—To store this medicine:
- Keep out of the reach of children.
- Keep the medicine from freezing. Do not refrigerate.
- Do not keep outdated medicine or medicine no longer needed. Ask your health care professional how you should dispose of any medicine you do not use. Be sure that any discarded medicine is out of the reach of children.

Precautions While Using This Medicine

Tell all of your medical doctors and dentists that you are using this medicine.

Side Effects of This Medicine

Along with its needed effects, a medicine may cause some unwanted effects. Although not all of these side effects may occur, if they do occur they may need medical attention.

Stop using this medicine and check with your doctor immediately if any of the following side effects occur:
  More common
    Deep, dark purple bruise, pain, or swelling at place of injection

  Rare
    Back pain; black, tarry stools; bleeding from the mouth or gums; blood in the urine; blue-green to black skin discoloration; bluish discoloration, flushing, or redness of skin; burning, pricking, tickling, or tingling sensation; coughing; difficulty in swallowing; dizziness or feeling faint; fever; hives; itching; leg weakness; nosebleed; numbness; paralysis; problems with bladder or bowel function; redness or sloughing of skin at place of injection; skin rash; small purple or red spots in the mouth, on the gums, or on the skin; swelling of eyelids, face, or lips; tightness in chest, troubled breathing, and/or wheezing; vomiting of blood or coffee ground-like material

Other side effects not listed above may also occur in some patients. If you notice any other effects, check with your doctor.

Developed: 03/21/01

NAFARELIN   Systemic

Commonly used brand name(s):

In the U.S.—
Synarel

In Canada—
Synarel

Description

Nafarelin (NAF-a-re-lin) is a hormone similar to the one normally released from the hypothalamus gland in the brain. It is used in the treatment of:

- Endometriosis, a painful condition caused by extra tissue similar to the lining of the uterus growing inside and outside of the uterus.
- Central precocious puberty (CPP), puberty developing too early in boys and girls.

Nafarelin works by decreasing the amount of estrogen and testosterone in the blood.

When given regularly to boys and girls, this medicine helps to prevent them from continuing to develop the sexual features associated with puberty, slowing down the development of breasts in girls and the development of genital areas in boys and girls. This medicine delays puberty in a child only as long as the child continues to take it.

Nafarelin prevents the growth of tissue associated with endometriosis in adult women during treatment and for 6 months after treatment is discontinued. Reducing the amount of estrogen in the body is one way of treating endometriosis.

Suppressing estrogen can thin the bones or slow their growth. This is a problem for adult women whose bones are no longer growing like the bones of children. Slowing the growth of bones is a positive effect for girls and boys whose bones grow too fast when puberty begins too early. This is why nafarelin is used only for up to 6 months in adult women treated for endometriosis, but often is used for a longer time in girls and boys with pubertal problems. Boys and girls may benefit by adding inches to their adult height when nafarelin causes their bones to grow at a proper rate.

Nafarelin is available only with your doctor's prescription, in the following dosage form:

Nasal
- Solution (U.S. and Canada)

Before Using This Medicine

In deciding to use a medicine, the risks of taking the medicine must be weighed against the good it will do. This is a decision you and your doctor will make. For nafarelin, the following should be considered:

Allergies—Tell your doctor if you have ever had any unusual or allergic reaction to nafarelin or to gonadotropin-releasing hormone-like medicines. Also tell your health care professional if you are allergic to any other substances, such as foods, preservatives, or dyes.

Pregnancy—Nafarelin use is not recommended during pregnancy. Nafarelin has not been studied in pregnant women. It has been shown to cause problems in animals, such as low birth weights and a slight decrease in the number of successful pregnancies.

For treatment of endometriosis—Stop taking this medicine immediately and check with your doctor if you suspect that you may have become pregnant.

Breast-feeding—It is not known whether nafarelin passes into the breast milk. However, use of nafarelin is not recommended during breast-feeding because it may cause unwanted effects in nursing babies.

Children—Studies of this medicine for treatment of endometriosis have been done only in adult patients, and there is no specific information comparing use of nafarelin to treat this condition in children younger than 18 years of age with use in other age groups. Endometriosis is not likely to occur before puberty.

When used to treat a child for central precocious puberty, nafarelin will stop having an effect soon after the child stops using it, and puberty will advance normally. It is not known if nafarelin causes:

- Changes in boys' and girls' future abilities to have babies after having used nafarelin around the time of puberty. Their chances of having children later are thought to be normal.
- Problems in the ovaries, such as cysts or a larger than normal ovary. Nafarelin stimulates the ovaries in adult women and has caused these problems in the ovary. It is not known whether nafarelin can also have these effects in younger girls treated for central precocious puberty.

It is especially important that you discuss with the child's doctor the good that this medicine may do as well as the risks of using it.

Other medicines—Although certain medicines should not be used together at all, in other cases two different medicines may be used together even if an interaction might occur. In these cases, your doctor may want to change the dose, or other precautions may be necessary. When you are taking nafarelin, it is especially important that your health care professional know if you are taking the following:

- Nasal decongestant sprays—It is not known whether nasal decongestant sprays can decrease the amount of nafarelin that enters the bloodstream through the lining of the nose. For this reason, you should wait at least 2 hours after using nafarelin before you use a nasal decongestant spray

Other medical problems—The presence of other medical problems may affect the use of nafarelin. Make sure you tell your doctor if you have any other medical problems, especially:

- Bleeding from the vagina (abnormal or of unknown cause)—For adult women treated for endometriosis or girls treated for central precocious puberty, using nafarelin when the reason for vaginal bleeding is not known may make it harder for the doctor to find the cause of the problem, and may cause a delay in treatment of the condition
- Other conditions that increase the chances of developing thinning bones or osteoporosis (brittle bones)—If you are an adult female being treated for endometriosis, it is important that your doctor know if you already have an increased risk of osteoporosis. Some things that can increase your risk for having osteoporosis include cigarette smoking, alcohol abuse, and a family history of osteoporosis or easily broken bones. Some medicines, such as corticosteroids (cortisone-like medicines) or an-

ticonvulsants (seizure medicine), can also cause thinning of the bones when used for a long time

Proper Use of This Medicine

You will be given a fact sheet with your prescription for nafarelin that explains how to use the pump spray bottle. If you have any questions about using the pump spray, ask your health care professional.

To use *nafarelin spray:*

- Before you use each new bottle of nafarelin, the spray pump needs to be started. To do this, point the bottle away from you and pump the bottle firmly about seven times. A spray should come out by the seventh time you pump the spray bottle. *This only needs to be done once for each new bottle of nafarelin.* Be careful not to breathe in this spray. You could inhale extra doses of nafarelin, since the medicine is dissolved in the spray.
- Before you take your daily doses of nafarelin, blow your nose gently. Hold your head forward a little. Put the spray tip into one nostril. Aim the tip toward the back and outside of your nostril. You do not need to put the tip too far into your nose.
- Close your other nostril off by pressing on the outside of your nose with a finger. Then, sniff in the spray as you pump the bottle once.
- Take the spray bottle out of your nose. Tilt your head back for 30 seconds, to let the spray get onto the back of your nose.
- Repeat these steps for each dose of medicine.
- Each time you use the spray bottle, wipe off the tip with a clean tissue or cloth. Keep the blue safety clip and plastic cap on the bottle when you are not using it.
- Every 3 or 4 days you should clean the tip of the spray bottle. To do this, hold the bottle sideways. Rinse the tip with warm water, while wiping the tip with your finger or a soft cloth for about 15 seconds. Dry the tip with a soft cloth or tissue. Replace the cap right after use. Be careful not to get water into the bottle, since this could dilute the medicine.

It is important to avoid sneezing when spraying and immediately after using the medicine. If you sneeze, the medicine may not be absorbed as well.

Use this medicine only as directed by your doctor. Do not use more or less of it, and do not use it more often than your doctor ordered. The exact amount of medicine you need has been carefully worked out. Using too much may increase the chance of side effects, while using too little may not improve your condition.

Many boys and girls who have central precocious puberty will not feel sick or will not understand the importance of taking the medicine regularly. It is very important that the medicine is used exactly as directed and that the proper amount is used at the proper time. It works best when there is a constant amount in the blood. To help keep the amount constant, nafarelin must be given on a regular schedule.

Dosing—The dose of nafarelin will be different for different patients. *Follow your doctor's orders or the directions on the label.* The following information includes only the average dose of nafarelin. *If your dose is different, do not change it* unless your doctor tells you to do so.

- For *nasal solution* dosage form:
  - For treating central precocious puberty:
    - Children—800 micrograms (mcg) (two sprays into each nostril) two times a day, once in the morning

and once in the evening. This provides a total daily dose of eight sprays or 1600 mcg a day. Sometimes a larger dose may be needed. 1800 mcg a day is provided by using three sprays in alternating nostrils three times a day to provide a total of nine sprays a day.
  - For treating endometriosis:
    - Adults—200 mcg (one spray) inhaled into one nostril in the morning and one spray inhaled into the other nostril in the evening, for six months. Begin your treatment on Day 2, 3, or 4 of your menstrual period.

Missed dose—If you miss a dose of this medicine, take it as soon as possible. However, if you do not remember until the next day, skip the missed dose and go back to your regular dosing schedule. Do not double doses.

Storage—To store this medicine:

- Keep out of the reach of children.
- The bottle should be stored standing upright, with the tip up.
- Store away from heat and direct light.
- Keep the medicine from freezing. Do not refrigerate.
- Do not keep outdated medicine or medicine no longer needed. Be sure that any discarded medicine is out of the reach of children.

Precautions While Using This Medicine

All scheduled visits to the doctor should be kept, even if the medicine seems to be working properly and you feel well. This is especially important for children using the medicine for treatment of central precocious puberty, even if their condition improves. Their progress still must be checked by the doctor when they are no longer using the medicine.

For children treated for central precocious puberty—Tell the doctor if nafarelin does not stop puberty from progessing within 6 to 8 weeks. You may notice puberty progressing in your child for the first few weeks of therapy, but you should see signs that puberty is stopping within 4 weeks after your child begins nafarelin therapy.

For adult women treated for endometriosis—

- During the time you are receiving nafarelin, your menstrual period may not be regular or you may not have a menstrual period at all. This is to be expected when being treated with this medicine. If regular menstrual periods do not begin within 2 to 3 months after you stop using this medicine, check with your health care professional.
- To prevent pregnancy if you are sexually active during the time you are using nafarelin, you should use birth control methods that do not contain hormones, such as condoms or a diaphragm or a cervical cap with a spermicide. If you have any questions about this, check with your health care professional.
- Use a water-based vaginal lubricant product if dryness of the vagina causes problems, such as pain during sexual intercourse. Make sure the lubricant you choose can be used with a latex birth control device if you are using one. Some lubricants contain oils, which can break down the latex rubber of condoms, a cervical cap, or a diaphragm, and cause them to rip or tear.
- *If you suspect you are pregnant, stop using this medicine and check with your doctor immediately.* There is a chance that nafarelin could cause problems to the unborn baby if taken during a pregnancy.

Side Effects of This Medicine

In the first few weeks of therapy, you may notice puberty progressing in your child, including vaginal bleeding and breast enlargement in girls. Within 4 weeks after nafarelin has had time to begin working properly, you should see signs in boys and girls that puberty is stopping. However, pubic hair may continue to show or grow in either boys or girls.

Along with its needed effects, a medicine may cause some unwanted effects. Although not all of these side effects may occur, if they do occur they may need medical attention.

Check with your doctor as soon as possible if any of the following side effects occur:

More common
For adults (female)
Breast enlargement; light vaginal bleeding between regular menstrual periods called spotting; longer or heavier menstrual periods; vaginal bleeding between regular menstrual periods called breakthrough bleeding
For children (male)
Body odor; growth of pubic hair
For children (female)
Body odor; breast enlargement; growth of pubic hair; light vaginal bleeding between regular menstrual periods called spotting; longer or heavier menstrual periods; vaginal bleeding between regular menstrual periods called breakthrough bleeding
Less common or rare
For adults (female)
Allergic reaction (shortness of breath, chest pain, hives); fast or irregular heartbeat; numbness or tingling of hands or feet; pain in eyes or joints; patchy brown or dark brown discoloration of skin; pelvic bloating or tenderness; unexpected or excess milk flow from breasts; unusual tiredness or weakness
For children (male and female)
Allergic reaction (shortness of breath, chest pain, hives)

Other side effects may occur that usually do not need medical attention. Some of these side effects may go away during treatment as your body adjusts to the medicine. However, check with your doctor if any of the following side effects continue or are bothersome:

More common
For adults (female)
Acne; dandruff; hot flashes; increase or decrease in sexual desire; increased hair growth, often abnormally distributed; mood swings; muscle pain; oily skin; pain during sexual intercourse; rapid weight gain; reduced breast size; stopping of menstrual periods; swelling of feet or lower legs; vaginal dryness
For children (male)
Acne; dandruff; mood swings; oily skin
For children (female)
Acne; dandruff; hot flashes; mood swings; oily skin
Less common or rare
For adults (female)
Breast pain; headache (mild and transient); irritated or runny nose; mental depression (mild and transient); skin rash

For children (male)
Irritated or runny nose
For children (female)
Irritated or runny nose; white or brownish vaginal discharge

Other side effects not listed above may also occur in some patients. If you notice any other effects, check with your doctor.

Revised: 05/27/98

NAPHAZOLINE   Ophthalmic

Commonly used brand name(s):

In the U.S.—

Ak-Con	Muro's Opcon
Albalon	Nafazair
Allerest	Naphcon
Allergy Drops	Naphcon Forte
Clear Eyes Lubricating Eye Redness Reliever	Ocu-Zoline Sterile Ophthalmic Solution
Comfort Eye Drops	VasoClear
Degest 2	VasoClear A
Estivin II	Vasocon Regular
I-Naphline	

Generic name product may be available.

In Canada—

Ak-Con	Naphcon Forte
Albalon Liquifilm	Vasocon

Description

Naphazoline (naf-AZ-oh-leen) is used to relieve redness due to minor eye irritations, such as those caused by colds, dust, wind, smog, pollen, swimming, or wearing contact lenses.

Some of these preparations are available only with your doctor's prescription. Others are available without a prescription; however, your doctor may have special instructions on the proper use of this medicine for your medical problem.

Naphazoline is available in the following dosage form:

Ophthalmic
• Ophthalmic solution (eye drops) (U.S. and Canada)

Before Using This Medicine

If you are using this medicine without a prescription, carefully read and follow any precautions on the label. For ophthalmic naphazoline, the following should be considered:

Allergies—Tell your doctor if you have ever had any unusual or allergic reaction to naphazoline. Also tell your health care professional if you are allergic to any other substances, such as preservatives.

Pregnancy—This medicine may be absorbed into the body. However, studies on effects in pregnancy have not been done in either humans or animals.

Breast-feeding—Naphazoline may be absorbed into the mother's body. However, this medicine has not been reported to cause problems in nursing babies.

Children—Use by infants and children is not recommended, since they are especially sensitive to the effects of naphazoline.

Older adults—Many medicines have not been studied specifically in older people. Therefore, it may not be known whether they work exactly the same way they do in younger adults or if they cause different side effects or problems in older people. There is no specific information comparing use of naphazoline in the elderly with use in other age groups.

Other medicines—Although certain medicines should not be used together at all, in other cases two different medicines may be used together even if an interaction might occur. In these cases, your doctor may want to change the dose, or other precautions may be necessary. Tell your health care professional if you are using any other prescription or nonprescription (over-the-counter [OTC]) medicine.

Other medical problems—The presence of other medical problems may affect the use of ophthalmic naphazoline. Make sure you tell your doctor if you have any other medical problems, especially:

- Diabetes mellitus (sugar diabetes) or
- Heart disease or
- High blood pressure or
- Overactive thyroid—Use of ophthalmic naphazoline may make the condition worse
- Eye disease, infection, or injury—The symptoms of the condition may be confused with possible side effects of ophthalmic naphazoline

Proper Use of This Medicine

Do not use naphazoline ophthalmic solution if it becomes cloudy or changes color.

Naphazoline should not be used in infants and children. It may cause severe slowing down of the central nervous system (CNS), which may lead to unconsciousness. It may also cause a severe decrease in body temperature.

Use this medicine only as directed. Do not use more of it, do not use it more often, and do not use it for more than 72 hours, unless otherwise directed by your doctor. To do so may make your eye redness and irritation worse and may also increase the chance of side effects.

To use:

- First, wash your hands. With the middle finger, apply pressure to the inside corner of the eye (and continue to apply pressure for 1 or 2 minutes after the medicine has been placed in the eye). Tilt the head back and with the index finger of the same hand, pull the lower eyelid away from the eye to form a pouch. Drop the medicine into the pouch and gently close the eyes. Do not blink. Keep the eyes closed for 1 or 2 minutes to allow the medicine to be absorbed.
- To keep the medicine as germ-free as possible, do not touch the applicator tip to any surface (including the eye). Also, keep the container tightly closed.

Dosing—The dose of ophthalmic naphazoline will be different for different patients. *Follow your doctor's orders or the directions on the label.* The following information includes only the average doses of ophthalmic naphazoline. *If your dose is different, do not change it* unless your doctor tells you to do so.

- For *ophthalmic solution (eye drop)* dosage form:
  —For eye redness:
    - Adults—Use one drop not more often than every four hours.
    - Children—Use is not recommended.

Storage—To store this medicine:

- Keep out of the reach of children.
- Store away from heat and direct light.
- Keep the medicine from freezing.
- Do not keep outdated medicine or medicine no longer needed. Be sure that any discarded medicine is out of the reach of children.

Precautions While Using This Medicine

If eye pain or change in vision occurs or if redness or irritation of the eye continues, gets worse, or lasts for more than 72 hours, stop using the medicine and check with your doctor.

Side Effects of This Medicine

Along with its needed effects, a medicine may cause some unwanted effects. Although not all of these side effects may occur, if they do occur they may need medical attention.

When this medicine is used for short periods of time at recommended doses, side effects usually are rare. However, check with your doctor as soon as possible if any of the following occur:

With overuse or long-term use
　　Increase in eye irritation

Symptoms of too much medicine being absorbed into the body
　　Dizziness; headache; increased sweating; nausea; nervousness; weakness

Symptoms of overdose
　　Decrease in body temperature; drowsiness; slow heartbeat; weakness (severe)

Other side effects may occur that usually do not need medical attention. These side effects may go away during treatment as your body adjusts to the medicine. However, check with your health care professional if either of the following side effects continues or is bothersome:

Less common or rare
　　Blurred vision; large pupils

Other side effects not listed above may also occur in some patients. If you notice any other effects, check with your health care professional.

Revised: 05/14/92
Interim revision: 02/24/94

NARATRIPTAN   Systemic

Commonly used brand name(s):

In the U.S.—
　　Amerge

Description

Naratriptan (NAR-a-trip-tan) is used to treat severe migraine headaches. Many people find that their headaches go away completely after they take naratriptan. Other people find that their headaches are much less painful, and that they are able to go back to their normal activities even though their headaches are not completely gone. Naratriptan often relieves symptoms that occur together with a migraine headache, such as nausea, vomiting, sensitivity to light, and sensitivity to sound.

Naratriptan is not an ordinary pain reliever. It should not be used to relieve any kind of pain other than migraine headaches.

Naratriptan may cause serious side effects in some people, especially people who have heart or blood vessel disease. Be sure that you discuss with your doctor the risks of using this medicine as well as the good that it can do.

Naratriptan is available only with your doctor's prescription, in the following dosage form:

Oral
- Tablets (U.S.)

Before Using This Medicine

In deciding to use a medicine, the risks of taking the medicine must be weighed against the good it will do. This is a decision you and your doctor will make. For naratriptan, the following should be considered:

Allergies—Tell your doctor if you have ever had any unusual or allergic reaction to naratriptan. Also tell your health care professional if you are allergic to any other substances, such as foods, preservatives, or dyes.

Pregnancy—Naratriptan has not been studied in pregnant women. However, in some animal studies, naratriptan caused harmful effects to the fetus. These unwanted effects usually occurred when naratriptan was given in amounts that were large enough to cause harmful effects in the mother.

Breast-feeding—Although most medicines pass into breast milk in small amounts, many of them may be used safely while breast-feeding. Mothers who are taking this medicine and who wish to breast-feed should discuss this with their doctor.

Children—There is no specific information comparing use of naratriptan in children with use in other age groups.

Teenagers—This medicine has been tested in a limited number of children 12 years of age or older. In effective doses, the medicine has not been shown to cause different side effects or problems than it does in adults.

Older adults—Although there is no specific information comparing the use of naratriptan in the elderly with use in other age groups, use of this medicine is not recommended in older adults.

Other medicines—Although certain medicines should not be used together at all, in other cases two different medicines may be used together even if an interaction might occur. In these cases, your doctor may want to change the dose, or other precautions may be necessary. Tell your health care professional if you are taking any other prescription or nonprescription (over-the-counter [OTC]) medicine, especially other prescription medicine for migraine headaches or depression.

Other medical problems—The presence of other medical problems may affect the use of naratriptan. Make sure you tell your doctor if you have any other medical problems, especially:
- Angina (chest pain) or
- Heart or blood vessel disease or
- High blood pressure or
- Kidney disease or
- Liver disease or

- Stroke (history of)—The chance of side effects may be increased. Heart or blood vessel disease and high blood pressure sometimes do not cause any symptoms, so some people do not know that they have these problems. Before deciding whether you should use naratriptan, your doctor may need to do some tests to make sure that you do not have any of these conditions.

Proper Use of This Medicine

Do not use naratriptan for a headache that is different from your usual migraines. Instead, check with your doctor.

To relieve your migraine as soon as possible, use naratriptan as soon as the headache pain begins. Even if you get warning signals of a coming migraine (an aura), you should wait until the headache pain starts before using naratriptan.

Lying down in a quiet, dark room for a while after you use this medicine may help relieve your migraine.

Ask your doctor ahead of time about any other medicine you may take if naratriptan does not work. *After you take the other medicine, check with your doctor as soon as possible.* Headaches that are not relieved by naratriptan are sometimes caused by conditions that need other treatment.

If you feel much better after a dose of naratriptan, but your headache comes back or gets worse after a while, you may use more naratriptan. However, *use this medicine only as directed by your doctor. Do not use more of it, and do not use it more often, than directed.* Using too much naratriptan may increase the chance of side effects.

Your doctor may direct you to take another medicine to help prevent headaches. *It is important that you follow your doctor's directions, even if your headaches continue to occur.* Headache-preventing medicines may take several weeks to start working. Even after they do start working, your headaches may not go away completely. However, your headaches should occur less often, and they should be less severe and easier to relieve. This can reduce the amount of naratriptan or other pain medicines that you need. If you do not notice any improvement after several weeks of headache-preventing treatment, check with your doctor.

Dosing—The dose of naratriptan will be different for different patients. *Follow your doctor's orders or the directions on the label.* The following information includes only the average doses of naratriptan. *If your dose is different, do not change it* unless your doctor tells you to do so.
- For *oral* dosage form (tablets):
  —For migraine headaches:
    - Adults—1 or 2.5 mg as a single dose. If the migraine comes back after being relieved, another dose may be taken four hours after the last dose. *Do not take more than 5 mg in any twenty-four-hour period* (one day). Patients with kidney or liver disease should take less than 2.5 mg as a single dose once daily and should not exceed 2.5 mg in a twenty-four-hour period.
    - Children—Use and dose must be determined by your doctor.

Storage—To store this medicine:
- Keep out of the reach of children since overdose is especially dangerous in children.
- Store away from heat and direct light.

- Do not store tablets in the bathroom, near the kitchen sink, or in other damp places. Heat or moisture may cause the medicine to break down.
- Do not keep outdated medicine or medicine no longer needed. Be sure that any discarded medicine is out of the reach of children.

Precautions While Using This Medicine

Drinking alcoholic beverages can make headaches worse or cause new headaches to occur. People who suffer from severe headaches should probably avoid alcoholic beverages, especially during a headache.

Some people feel drowsy or dizzy during or after a migraine, or after taking naratriptan to relieve a migraine. As long as you are feeling drowsy or dizzy, *do not drive, use machines, or do anything else that could be dangerous if you are dizzy or are not alert.*

Side Effects of This Medicine

Along with its needed effects, a medicine may cause some unwanted effects. Although not all of these side effects may occur, if they do occur they may need medical attention.

Stop using this medicine and check with your doctor immediately if any of the following side effects occur:

More common

Chest pain (severe); heaviness, tightness, or pressure in chest, throat, and/or neck; sensation of burning, warmth, heat, numbness, tightness, or tingling

Less common or rare

Convulsions (seizures); irregular heartbeat; slow heartbeat

Other side effects may occur that usually do not need medical attention. Some of the following effects, such as nausea, vomiting, drowsiness, dizziness, and general feeling of illness or tiredness, often occur during or after a migraine, even when naratriptan has not been used. However, check with your doctor if any of the following side effects continue or are bothersome:

More common

Dizziness; drowsiness; increased tiredness; nausea and/or vomiting

Less common or rare

Acne; anxiety; blurred vision; bone or skeletal pain; change in taste sensation; chills and/or fever; confusion; constipation; diarrhea; difficulty sleeping; eye problems; fainting; fluid imbalance; increased thirst; itching of the skin; joint pain; mood or mental changes; muscle or joint stiffness, tightness, or rigidity; muscle pain or spasms; pounding heartbeat; restlessness; skin rash; stomach discomfort and/or pain; sudden large increase in frequency and amount of urine; trembling or shaking of hands or feet; unusual tiredness or weakness

Other side effects not listed above may also occur in some patients. If you notice any other effects, check with your doctor.

Developed: 07/07/98

NARCOTIC ANALGESICS AND ACETAMINOPHEN   Systemic

Commonly used brand name(s):

In the U.S.—

Allay[4]	Panacet 5/500[4]
Anexsia 5/500[4]	Panlor[4]
Anexsia 7.5/650[4]	Percocet 2.5/325[5]
Anolor DH 5[4]	Percocet 5/325[5]
Bancap-HC[4]	Percocet 7.5/500[5]
Capital with Codeine[1]	Percocet 10/650[5]
Co-Gesic[4]	Phenaphen with Codeine No.3[1]
Darvocet-N 50[7]	
Darvocet-N 100[7]	Phenaphen with Codeine No.4[1]
DHCplus[3]	
Dolacet[4]	Polygesic[4]
Dolagesic[4]	Propacet 100[7]
Duocet[4]	Pyregesic-C[1]
E-Lor[7]	Roxicet[5]
Endocet[5]	Roxicet 5/500[5]
EZ III[1]	Roxilox[5]
Hycomed[4]	Stagesic[4]
Hyco-Pap[4]	Talacen[6]
Hydrocet[4]	T-Gesic[4]
Hydrogesic[4]	Tylenol with Codeine Elixir[1]
HY-PHEN[4]	Tylenol with Codeine No.2[1]
Lorcet 10/650[4]	Tylenol with Codeine No.3[1]
Lorcet-HD[4]	Tylenol with Codeine No.4[1]
Lorcet Plus[4]	Tylox[5]
Lortab[4]	Ugesic[4]
Lortab 2.5/500[4]	Vanacet[4]
Lortab 5/500[4]	Vendone[4]
Lortab 7.5/500[4]	Vicodin[4]
Lortab 10/500[4]	Vicodin ES[4]
Margesic #3[1]	Wygesic[7]
Margesic-H[4]	Zydone[4]
Oncet[4]	

In Canada—

Acet-2[2]	Novo-Gesic C8[2]
Acet-3[2]	Novo-Gesic C15[2]
Acet Codeine 30[1]	Novo-Gesic C30[2]
Acet Codeine 60[1]	Oxycocet[5]
Atasol-8[2]	Percocet[5]
Atasol-15[2]	Percocet-Demi[5]
Atasol-30[2]	PMS-Acetaminophen with Codeine[1]
Cetaphen with Codeine[2]	
Cetaphen Extra-Strength with Codeine[2]	Roxicet[5]
	Triatec-8[2]
Cotabs[2]	Triatec-30[1]
Empracet-30[1]	Triatec-8 Strong[2]
Empracet-60[1]	Tylenol with Codeine Elixir[1]
Emtec-30[1]	Tylenol with Codeine No.1[2]
Endocet[5]	Tylenol with Codeine No.2[2]
Exdol-8[2]	Tylenol with Codeine No.3[2]
Lenoltec with Codeine No.1[2]	Tylenol with Codeine No.4[1]
Lenoltec with Codeine No.2[2]	Tylenol with Codeine No.1 Forte[2]
Lenoltec with Codeine No.3[2]	
Lenoltec with Codeine No.4[1]	

Other commonly used names are:

APAP with codeine
Co-codAPAP
Co-hycodAPAP
Co-oxycodAPAP
Co-proxAPAP
Drocode, acetaminophen, and caffeine
Hydrocodone with APAP
Oxycodone with APAP
Propoxyphene with APAP

Note: For quick reference, the following narcotic analgesics and acetaminophen combinations are numbered to match the corresponding brand names.

This information applies to the following medicines:

1. Acetaminophen and Codeine (a-seat-a-MIN-oh-fen and KOE-deen) ‡§
2. Acetaminophen, Codeine, and Caffeine (a-seat-a-MIN-oh-fen, KOE-deen, and kaf-EEN) *§
3. Dihydrocodeine, Acetaminophen, and Caffeine (dye-hye-droe-KOE-deen, a-seat-a-MIN-oh-fen, and kaf-EEN) †
4. Hydrocodone and Acetaminophen (hye-droe-KOE-done and a-seat-a-MIN-oh-fen) †‡
5. Oxycodone and Acetaminophen (ox-i-KOE-done and a-seat-a-MIN-oh-fen) ‡
6. Pentazocine and Acetaminophen (pen-TAZ-oh-seen and a-seat-a-MIN-oh-fen) †
7. Propoxyphene and Acetaminophen (proe-POX-i-feen and a-seat-a-MIN-oh-fen) †‡

Note: In Canada, *Phenaphen with Codeine* is different from the product with that name in the U.S. The Canadian product contains phenobarbital, ASA, and codeine.

---

*Not commercially available in the U.S.
†Not commercially available in Canada.
‡Generic name product may be available in the U.S.
§Generic name product may be available in Canada.

Description

Combination medicines containing narcotic analgesics (nar-KOT-ik an-al-JEE-zicks) and acetaminophen (a-seat-a-MIN-oh-fen) are used to relieve pain. A narcotic analgesic and acetaminophen used together may provide better pain relief than either medicine used alone. In some cases, relief of pain may come at lower doses of each medicine.

Narcotic analgesics act in the central nervous system (CNS) to relieve pain. Many of their side effects are also caused by actions in the CNS. When narcotics are used for a long time, your body may get used to them so that larger amounts are needed to relieve pain. This is called tolerance to the medicine. Also, when narcotics are used for a long time or in large doses, they may become habit-forming (causing mental or physical dependence). Physical dependence may lead to withdrawal symptoms when you stop taking the medicine.

Acetaminophen does not become habit-forming when taken for a long time or in large doses, but it may cause other unwanted effects, including liver damage, if too much is taken.

In the U.S., these medicines are available only with your medical doctor's or dentist's prescription. In Canada, some acetaminophen, codeine, and caffeine combinations are available without a prescription.

These medicines are available in the following dosage forms:

Oral

Acetaminophen and Codeine
- Capsules (U.S.)
- Oral solution (U.S. and Canada)
- Oral suspension (U.S.)
- Tablets (U.S. and Canada)

Acetaminophen, Codeine, and Caffeine
- Tablets (Canada)

Dihydrocodeine, Acetaminophen, and Caffeine
- Capsules (U.S.)

Hydrocodone and Acetaminophen
- Capsules (U.S.)
- Oral solution (U.S.)
- Tablets (U.S.)

Oxycodone and Acetaminophen
- Capsules (U.S.)
- Oral solution (U.S.)
- Tablets (U.S. and Canada)

Pentazocine and Acetaminophen
- Tablets (U.S.)

Propoxyphene and Acetaminophen
- Tablets (U.S.)

Before Using This Medicine

In deciding to use a medicine, the risks of taking the medicine must be weighed against the good it will do. This is a decision you and your doctor will make. For narcotic analgesic and acetaminophen combinations, the following should be considered:

Allergies—Tell your doctor if you have ever had any unusual or allergic reaction to acetaminophen or to a narcotic analgesic. Also tell your health care professional if you are allergic to any other substances, such as foods, preservatives, or dyes.

Pregnancy—

- *For acetaminophen:* Although studies on birth defects with acetaminophen have not been done in pregnant women, it has not been reported to cause birth defects or other problems.
- *For narcotic analgesics:* Although studies on birth defects with narcotic analgesics have not been done in pregnant women, they have not been reported to cause birth defects. However, hydrocodone caused birth defects in animal studies when very large doses were used. Codeine did not cause birth defects in animals, but it caused slower development of bones and other toxic or harmful effects in the fetus. Pentazocine and propoxyphene did not cause birth defects in animals. There is no information about whether dihydrocodeine or oxycodone causes birth defects in animals. Too much use of a narcotic during pregnancy may cause the fetus to become dependent on the medicine. This may lead to withdrawal side effects in the newborn baby. Also, some of these medicines may cause breathing problems in the newborn baby if taken just before or during delivery.
- *For caffeine:* Studies in humans have not shown that caffeine (contained in some of these combination medicines) causes birth defects. However, studies in animals have shown that caffeine causes birth defects when given in very large doses (amounts equal to those present in 12 to 24 cups of coffee a day).

Breast-feeding—Acetaminophen, codeine, and propoxyphene pass into the breast milk. It is not known whether other narcotic analgesics pass into the breast milk. However, these medicines have not been reported to cause problems in nursing babies.

Children—Breathing problems may be especially likely to occur when narcotic analgesics are given to children younger than 2 years of age. These children are usually more sensitive than adults to the effects of narcotic analgesics. Also, unusual excitement or restlessness may be more likely to occur in children receiving these medicines.

Acetaminophen has been tested in children and has not been shown to cause different side effects or problems in children than it does in adults.

Older adults—Elderly people are especially sensitive to the effects of narcotic analgesics. This may increase the chance of side effects, especially breathing problems, during treatment.

Acetaminophen has been tested and has not been shown to cause different side effects or problems in older people than it does in younger adults.

Other medicines—Although certain medicines should not be used together at all, in other cases two different medicines may be used together even if an interaction might occur. In these cases, your doctor may want to change the dose, or other precautions may be necessary. When you are taking a narcotic analgesic and acetaminophen combination, it is especially important that your health care professional know if you are taking any of the following:

- Carbamazepine (e.g., Tegretol)—Propoxyphene may increase the blood levels of carbamazepine, which increases the chance of serious side effects

- Central nervous system (CNS) depressants or
- Monoamine oxidase (MAO) inhibitors (furazolidone [e.g., Furoxone], isocarboxazid [e.g., Marplan], pargyline [e.g., Eutonyl], phenelzine [e.g., Nardil], procarbazine [e.g., Matulane], tranylcypromine [e.g., Parnate]) (taken currently or within the past 2 weeks) or
- Tricyclic antidepressants (amitriptyline [e.g., Elavil], amoxapine [e.g., Asendin], clomipramine [e.g., Anafranil], desipramine [e.g., Pertofrane], doxepin [e.g., Sinequan], imipramine [e.g., Tofranil], nortriptyline [e.g., Aventyl], protriptyline [e.g., Vivactil], trimipramine [e.g., Surmontil])—Taking these medicines together with a narcotic analgesic may increase the chance of serious side effects

- Naltrexone (e.g., Trexan)—Naltrexone keeps narcotic analgesics from working to relieve pain; people taking naltrexone should take pain relievers that do not contain a narcotic

- Zidovudine (e.g., AZT, Retrovir)—Acetaminophen may increase the blood levels of zidovudine, which increases the chance of serious side effects

Other medical problems—The presence of other medical problems may affect the use of narcotic analgesic and acetaminophen combinations. Make sure you tell your doctor if you have any other medical problems, especially:

- Alcohol and/or other drug abuse, or history of, or
- Brain disease or head injury or
- Colitis or
- Convulsions (seizures), history of, or
- Emotional problems or mental illness or
- Emphysema, asthma, or other chronic lung disease or
- Hepatitis or other liver disease or
- Kidney disease or
- Underactive thyroid—The chance of serious side effects may be increased

- Enlarged prostate or problems with urination or
- Gallbladder disease or gallstones—Some of the effects of narcotic analgesics may be especially serious in people with these medical problems

- Heart disease—Caffeine (present in some of these combination medicines) can make some kinds of heart disease worse

Proper Use of This Medicine

Take this medicine only as directed by your medical doctor or dentist. Do not take more of it, do not take it more often, and do not take it for a longer time than your medical doctor or dentist ordered. This is especially important for young children and elderly patients, who may be more sensitive than other people to the effects of narcotic analgesics. If too much of a narcotic analgesic is taken, it may become habit-forming (causing mental or physical dependence) or lead to medical problems because of an overdose. Taking too much acetaminophen may cause liver damage.

If you think that this medicine is not working properly after you have been taking it for a few weeks, *do not increase the dose.* Instead, check with your medical doctor or dentist.

Dosing—The dose of these medicines will be different for different patients. *Follow your doctor's orders or the directions on the label.* The following information includes only the average doses of these medicines. *If your dose is different, do not change it* unless your doctor tells you to do so.

The number of capsules or tablets or teaspoonfuls of solution or suspension that you take depends on the strength of the medicine.

For acetaminophen and codeine
- For *oral capsule or tablet* dosage form:
  —For pain:
    - Adults—1 or 2 capsules or tablets containing acetaminophen with 15 or 30 milligrams (mg) of codeine, or 1 capsule or tablet containing acetaminophen with 60 mg of codeine, every four hours as needed.
    - Children—Dose must be determined by the doctor, depending on the age of the child. Most young children will receive the oral solution or suspension, rather than tablets or capsules.
- For *oral solution or suspension* dosage form:
  —For pain:
    - Adults—1 tablespoonful (3 teaspoonfuls) every four hours as needed.
    - Children younger than 3 years of age—Dose must be determined by your doctor.
    - Children 3 to 7 years of age—1 teaspoonful three or four times a day as needed.
    - Children 7 to 12 years of age—2 teaspoonfuls three or four times a day as needed.

For acetaminophen, codeine, and caffeine
- For *oral tablet* dosage form:
  —For pain:
    - Adults—1 or 2 tablets every four hours as needed.
    - Children—Dose must be determined by your doctor.

For dihydrocodeine, acetaminophen, and caffeine
- For *oral capsule* dosage form:
  —For pain:
    - Adults—2 capsules every four hours.
    - Children—Dose must be determined by your doctor.

For hydrocodone and acetaminophen
- For *oral capsule* dosage form:
  —For pain:
    - Adults—1 capsule every four to six hours as needed.

- Children—Dose must be determined by your doctor.
- For *oral solution* dosage form:
  —For pain:
  - Adults—1 to 3 teaspoonfuls every four to six hours as needed.
  - Children—Dose must be determined by your doctor.
- For *oral tablet* dosage form:
  —For pain:
  - Adults—1 or 2 tablets containing acetaminophen with 2.5 milligrams (mg) of hydrocodone, or 1 tablet containing acetaminophen with 5, 7.5, or 10 mg of hydrocodone, every four to six hours as needed.
  - Children—Dose must be determined by your doctor.

For oxycodone and acetaminophen
- For *oral capsule or tablet* dosage form:
  —For pain:
  - Adults—1 to 2 capsules or tablets every four to six hours as needed.
  - Children—Dose must be determined by your doctor.
- For *oral solution* dosage form:
  —For pain:
  - Adults—1 teaspoonful every four to six hours as needed.
  - Children—Dose must be determined by your doctor.

For pentazocine and acetaminophen
- For *oral tablet* dosage form:
  —For pain:
  - Adults—1 tablet every four hours.
  - Children—Dose must be determined by your doctor.

For propoxyphene and acetaminophen
- For *oral tablet* dosage form:
  —For pain:
  - Adults—1 or 2 tablets, depending on the strength, every four hours as needed.
  - Children—Dose must be determined by your doctor.

Missed dose—If your medical doctor or dentist has ordered you to take this medicine according to a regular schedule and you miss a dose, take it as soon as you remember. However, if it is almost time for your next dose, skip the missed dose and go back to your regular dosing schedule. *Do not double doses.*

Storage—To store this medicine:
- Keep out of the reach of children. Overdose is very dangerous in young children.
- Store away from heat and direct light.
- Do not store tablets or capsules in the bathroom, near the kitchen sink, or in other damp places. Heat or moisture may cause the medicine to break down.
- Keep the liquid forms of this medicine from freezing.
- Do not keep outdated medicine or medicine no longer needed. Be sure that any discarded medicine is out of the reach of children.

Precautions While Using This Medicine

If you will be taking this medicine for a long time (for example, for several months at a time), or in high doses, your doctor should check your progress at regular visits.

Check the labels of all nonprescription (over-the-counter [OTC]) and prescription medicines you now take. If any contain acetaminophen or a narcotic be especially careful, since taking them while taking this medicine may lead to overdose. If you have any questions about this, check with your medical doctor, dentist, or pharmacist.

The narcotic analgesic in this medicine will add to the effects of alcohol and other CNS depressants (medicines that slow down the nervous system, possibly causing drowsiness). Some examples of CNS depressants are antihistamines or medicine for hay fever, other allergies, or colds; sedatives, tranquilizers, or sleeping medicine; other prescription pain medicine or narcotics; barbiturates; medicine for seizures; muscle relaxants; or anesthetics, including some dental anesthetics. Also, there may be a greater risk of liver damage if you drink three or more alcoholic beverages while you are taking acetaminophen. *Do not drink alcoholic beverages, and check with your medical doctor or dentist before taking any of the medicines listed above, while you are using this medicine.*

Too much use of the acetaminophen in this combination medicine together with certain other medicines may increase the chance of unwanted effects. The risk will depend on how much of each medicine you take every day, and on how long you take the medicines together. If your doctor directs you to take these medicines together on a regular basis, follow his or her directions carefully. However, do not take this medicine together with any of the following medicines for more than a few days, unless your doctor has directed you to do so and is following your progress:

    Aspirin or other salicylates
    Diclofenac (e.g., Voltaren)
    Diflunisal (e.g., Dolobid)
    Etodolac (e.g., Lodine)
    Fenoprofen (e.g., Nalfon)
    Floctafenine (e.g., Idarac)
    Flurbiprofen, oral (e.g., Ansaid)
    Ibuprofen (e.g., Motrin)
    Indomethacin (e.g., Indocin)
    Ketoprofen (e.g., Orudis)
    Ketorolac (e.g., Toradol)
    Meclofenamate (e.g., Meclomen)
    Mefenamic acid (e.g., Ponstel)
    Nabumetone (e.g., Relafen)
    Naproxen (e.g., Naprosyn)
    Oxaprozin (e.g., Daypro)
    Phenylbutazone (e.g., Butazolidin)
    Piroxicam (e.g., Feldene)
    Sulindac (e.g., Clinoril)
    Tenoxicam (e.g., Mobiflex)
    Tiaprofenic acid (e.g., Surgam)
    Tolmetin (e.g., Tolectin)

This medicine may cause some people to become drowsy, dizzy, or lightheaded, or to feel a false sense of well-being. *Make sure you know how you react to this medicine before you drive, use machines, or do anything else that could be dangerous if you are dizzy or are not alert and clearheaded.*

Dizziness, lightheadedness, or fainting may occur, especially when you get up suddenly from a lying or sitting position. Getting up slowly may help lessen this problem.

Nausea or vomiting may occur, especially after the first couple of doses. This effect may go away if you lie down for a while. However, if nausea or vomiting continues, check with your medical doctor or dentist. Lying down for a while may also help relieve some other side effects, such as dizziness or lightheadedness, that may occur.

Before having any kind of surgery (including dental surgery) or emergency treatment, tell the medical doctor or dentist in charge that you are taking this medicine.

Narcotic analgesics may cause dryness of the mouth. For temporary relief, use sugarless candy or gum, melt bits of ice in your mouth, or use a saliva substitute. However, if dry mouth continues for more than 2 weeks, check with your dentist. Continuing dryness of the mouth may increase the chance of dental disease, including tooth decay, gum disease, and fungus infections.

If you have been taking this medicine regularly for several weeks or more, *do not suddenly stop taking it without first checking with your doctor.* Your doctor may want you to reduce gradually the amount you are taking before stopping completely, to lessen the chance of withdrawal side effects. This will depend on which of these medicines you have been taking, and the amount you have been taking every day.

If you think you or someone else may have taken an overdose of this medicine, get emergency help at once. Taking an overdose of this medicine or taking alcohol or CNS depressants with this medicine may lead to unconsciousness or death. Signs of overdose of narcotics include convulsions (seizures), confusion, severe nervousness or restlessness, severe dizziness, severe drowsiness, shortness of breath or troubled breathing, and severe weakness. Signs of severe acetaminophen overdose may not occur until several days after the overdose is taken.

Side Effects of This Medicine

Along with its needed effects, a medicine may cause some unwanted effects. Although not all of these side effects may occur, if they do occur they may need medical attention.

Get emergency help immediately if any of the following symptoms of overdose occur:
>Cold, clammy skin; confusion (severe); convulsions (seizures); diarrhea; dizziness (severe); drowsiness (severe); increased sweating; low blood pressure; nausea or vomiting (continuing); nervousness or restlessness (severe); pinpoint pupils of eyes; shortness of breath or unusually slow or troubled breathing; slow heartbeat; stomach cramps or pain; weakness (severe)

Also, check with your doctor as soon as possible if any of the following side effects occur:
>*Less common or rare*
>>Black, tarry stools; bloody or cloudy urine; confusion; dark urine; difficult or painful urination; fast, slow, or pounding heartbeat; frequent urge to urinate; hallucinations (seeing, hearing, or feeling things that are not there); increased sweating; irregular breathing or wheezing; mental depression; pain in lower back and/or side (severe and/or sharp); pale stools; pinpoint red spots on skin; redness or flushing of face; ringing or buzzing in ears; skin rash, hives, or itching; sore throat and fever; sudden decrease in amount of urine; swelling of face; trembling or un-

controlled muscle movements; unusual bleeding or bruising; unusual excitement (especially in children); yellow eyes or skin

Other side effects may occur that usually do not need medical attention. These side effects may go away during treatment as your body adjusts to the medicine. However, check with your medical doctor or dentist if any of the following side effects continue or are bothersome:
>*More common*
>>Dizziness, lightheadedness, or feeling faint; drowsiness; nausea or vomiting; unusual tiredness or weakness
>*Less common or rare*
>>Blurred or double vision or other changes in vision; constipation (more common with long-term use and with codeine or meperidine); dry mouth; false sense of well-being; general feeling of discomfort or illness; headache; loss of appetite; nervousness or restlessness; nightmares or unusual dreams; trouble in sleeping

Although not all of the side effects listed above have been reported for all of these combination medicines, they have been reported for at least one of them. However, since all of the narcotic analgesics are very similar, any of the above side effects may occur with any of these medicines.

After you stop using this medicine, your body may need time to adjust. The length of time this takes depends on which of these medicines you were taking, the amount of medicine you were using, and how long you used it. During this time check with your doctor if you notice any of the following side effects:
>Body aches; diarrhea; fast heartbeat; fever, runny nose, or sneezing; gooseflesh; increased sweating; increased yawning; loss of appetite; nausea or vomiting; nervousness, restlessness, or irritability; shivering or trembling; stomach cramps; trouble in sleeping; weakness

Other side effects not listed above may also occur in some patients. If you notice any other effects, check with your doctor.

Revised: 05/21/2001

NARCOTIC ANALGESICS AND ASPIRIN   Systemic

Commonly used brand name(s):

In the U.S.—

Damason-P[5]	PC-Cap[9]
Darvon Compound-65[9]	Percodan[6]
Empirin with Codeine No.3[2]	Percodan-Demi[6]
Empirin with Codeine No.4[2]	Propoxyphene Compound-65[9]
Endodan[6]	Roxiprin[6]
Lortab ASA[5]	Synalgos-DC[1]
Panasal 5/500[5]	Talwin Compound[7]

In Canada—

Anacin with Codeine[3]	Oxycodan[6]
C2 Buffered with Codeine[4]	Percodan[6]
C2 with Codeine[3]	Percodan-Demi[6]
Darvon-N Compound[9]	692[9]
Darvon-N with A.S.A.[8]	222[3]
Endodan[6]	282[3]
Novo-AC and C[3]	292[3]

Other commonly used names are:
A.C.&C
AC and C
Co-codaprin
dihydrocodeine compound
drocode and aspirin
propoxyphene hydrochloride compound

Note: For quick reference, the following narcotic analgesics and aspirin combinations are numbered to match the corresponding brand names.

This information applies to the following medicines:

1. Aspirin, Caffeine, and Dihydrocodeine (AS-pir-in kaf-EEN and dye-hye-droe-KOE-deen) †
2. Aspirin and Codeine (AS-pir-in and KOE-deen) †‡
3. Aspirin, Codeine, and Caffeine # (AS-pir-in KOE-deen and kaf-EEN) *§
4. Aspirin, Codeine, and Caffeine, Buffered #*
5. Hydrocodone and Aspirin (hye-droe-KOE-done and AS-pir-in)†
6. Oxycodone and Aspirin # (ox-i-KOE-done and AS-pir-in) ‡
7. Pentazocine and Aspirin (pen-TAZ-oh-seen and AS-pir-in) †
8. Propoxyphene and Aspirin # (proe-POX-i-feen and AS-pir-in) *
9. Propoxyphene, Aspirin, and Caffeine # (proe-POX-i-feen AS-pir-in and kaf-EEN) ‡

---

*Not commercially available in the U.S.
†Not commercially available in Canada.
‡Generic name product may be available in the U.S.
§Generic name product may be available in Canada.
#In Canada, *Aspirin* is a brand name. Acetylsalicylic acid is the generic name in Canada. ASA, a synonym for acetylsalicylic acid, is the term that commonly appears on Canadian product labels.

Description

Combination medicines containing narcotic analgesics (nar-KOT-ik an-al-JEE-zicks) and aspirin (AS-pir-in) are used to relieve pain. A narcotic analgesic and aspirin used together may provide better pain relief than either medicine used alone. In some cases, relief of pain may come at lower doses of each medicine.

Narcotic analgesics act in the central nervous system (CNS) to relieve pain. Many of their side effects are also caused by actions in the CNS. When narcotics are used for a long time, your body may get used to them so that larger amounts are needed to relieve pain. This is called tolerance to the medicine. Also, when narcotics are used for a long time or in large doses, they may become habit-forming (causing mental or physical dependence). Physical dependence may lead to withdrawal symptoms when you stop taking the medicine.

Aspirin does not become habit-forming when taken for a long time or in large doses, but it may cause other unwanted effects if too much is taken.

In the U.S., these medicines are available only with your medical doctor's or dentist's prescription. In Canada, some strengths of aspirin, codeine, and caffeine combination are available without a prescription.

These medicines are available in the following dosage forms:

Oral
Aspirin, Caffeine, and Dihydrocodeine
• Capsules (U.S.)
Aspirin and Codeine
• Tablets (U.S.)
Aspirin, Codeine, and Caffeine
• Tablets (Canada)
Aspirin, Codeine, and Caffeine, Buffered
• Tablets (Canada)
Hydrocodone and Aspirin
• Tablets (U.S.)
Oxycodone and Aspirin
• Tablets (U.S. and Canada)
Pentazocine and Aspirin
• Tablets (U.S.)
Propoxyphene and Aspirin
• Capsules (Canada)
Propoxyphene, Aspirin, and Caffeine
• Capsules (U.S. and Canada)
• Tablets (Canada)

Before Using This Medicine

In deciding to use a medicine, the risks of taking the medicine must be weighed against the good it will do. This is a decision you and your doctor will make. For narcotic analgesic and aspirin combinations, the following should be considered:

Allergies—Tell your doctor if you have ever had any unusual or allergic reaction to a narcotic analgesic, aspirin or other salicylates, including methyl salicylate (oil of wintergreen), or any of the following medicines:

Diclofenac (e.g., Voltaren)
Diflunisal (e.g., Dolobid)
Etodolac (e.g., Lodine)
Fenoprofen (e.g., Nalfon)
Floctafenine (e.g., Idarac)
Flurbiprofen, oral (e.g., Ansaid)
Ibuprofen (e.g., Motrin)
Indomethacin (e.g., Indocin)
Ketoprofen (e.g., Orudis)
Ketorolac (e.g., Toradol)
Meclofenamate (e.g., Meclomen)
Mefenamic acid (e.g., Ponstel)
Nabumetone (e.g., Relafen)
Naproxen (e.g., Naprosyn)
Oxaprozin (e.g., Daypro)
Oxyphenbutazone (e.g., Tandearil)
Phenylbutazone (e.g., Butazolidin)
Piroxicam (e.g., Feldene)
Sulindac (e.g., Clinoril)
Suprofen (e.g., Suprol)
Tenoxicam (e.g., Mobiflex)
Tiaprofenic acid (e.g., Surgam)
Tolmetin (e.g., Tolectin)
Zomepirac (e.g., Zomax)

Also tell your health care professional if you are allergic to any other substances, such as foods, preservatives, or dyes.

Pregnancy—

• *For aspirin:* Studies in humans have not shown that aspirin causes birth defects. However, studies in animals have shown that aspirin causes birth defects. Some reports have suggested that too much use of aspirin late in pregnancy may cause a decrease in the newborn's weight and possible death of the fetus or newborn baby. However, the mothers in these reports had been taking much larger amounts of aspirin than are usually recommended. Studies of mothers taking aspirin in the doses that are usually recommended did not show these effects. However, regular use of aspirin late in pregnancy may cause unwanted effects on the heart or blood flow in the fetus or in the newborn baby. Also, use of aspirin during the last 2 weeks of pregnancy may cause bleeding problems in the fetus before or during delivery or in the newborn baby. Too much use of aspirin during the last 3 months of pregnancy may increase the length of pregnancy, prolong labor, cause other problems during delivery, or cause severe bleeding in the mother before, during, or after delivery. *Do not take aspirin during the last 3 months of pregnancy unless it has been ordered by your doctor.*

- *For narcotic analgesics:* Although studies on birth defects with narcotic analgesics have not been done in pregnant women, they have not been reported to cause birth defects. However, hydrocodone caused birth defects in animal studies when given in very large doses. Codeine did not cause birth defects in animals, but it caused slower development of bones and other toxic or harmful effects on the fetus. Pentazocine and propoxyphene did not cause birth defects in animals. There is no information about whether dihydrocodeine or oxycodone causes birth defects in animals. Too much use of a narcotic during pregnancy may cause the fetus to become dependent on the medicine. This may lead to withdrawal side effects in the newborn baby. Also, some of these medicines may cause breathing problems in the newborn baby if taken just before or during delivery.
- *For caffeine:* Studies in humans have not shown that caffeine (contained in some of these combination medicines) causes birth defects. However, studies in animals have shown that caffeine causes birth defects when given in very large doses (amounts equal to those present in 12 to 24 cups of coffee a day).

Breast-feeding—These combination medicines have not been reported to cause problems in nursing babies. However, aspirin, caffeine, codeine, and propoxyphene pass into the breast milk. It is not known whether dihydrocodeine, hydrocodone, oxycodone, or pentazocine passes into the breast milk.

Children—*Do not give a medicine containing aspirin to a child or a teenager with a fever or other symptoms of a virus infection, especially flu or chickenpox, without first discussing its use with your child's doctor.* This is very important because aspirin may cause a serious illness called Reye's syndrome in children with fever caused by a virus infection, especially flu or chickenpox. Children who do not have a virus infection may also be more sensitive to the effects of aspirin, especially if they have a fever or have lost large amounts of body fluid because of vomiting, diarrhea, or sweating. This may increase the chance of side effects during treatment.

The narcotic analgesic in this combination medicine can cause breathing problems, especially in children younger than 2 years of age. These children are usually more sensitive than adults to the effects of narcotic analgesics. Also, unusual excitement or restlessness may be more likely to occur in children receiving these medicines.

Older adults—Elderly people are especially sensitive to the effects of aspirin and of narcotic analgesics. This may increase the chance of side effects, especially breathing problems caused by narcotic analgesics, during treatment.

Other medicines—Although certain medicines should not be used together at all, in other cases two different medicines may be used together even if an interaction might occur. In these cases, your doctor may want to change the dose, or other precautions may be necessary. When you are taking a narcotic analgesic and aspirin combination, it is especially important that your health care professional know if you are taking any of the following:

- Anticoagulants (blood thinners) or
- Carbenicillin by injection (e.g., Geopen) or

- Cefamandole (e.g., Mandol) or
- Cefoperazone (e.g., Cefobid) or
- Cefotetan (e.g., Cefotan) or
- Dipyridamole (e.g., Persantine) or
- Divalproex (e.g., Depakote) or
- Heparin or
- Medicine for inflammation or pain, except narcotics, or
- Pentoxifylline (e.g., Trental) or
- Plicamycin (e.g., Mithracin) or
- Ticarcillin (e.g., Ticar) or
- Valproic acid (e.g., Depakene)—Taking these medicines together with aspirin may increase the chance of bleeding

- Antidiabetics, oral (diabetes medicine you take by mouth)—Aspirin may increase the effects of the antidiabetic medicine; a change in the dose of the antidiabetic medicine may be needed if aspirin is taken regularly

- Carbamazepine (e.g., Tegretol)—Propoxyphene can increase the blood levels of carbamazepine, which increases the chance of serious side effects

- Central nervous system (CNS) depressants or
- Diarrhea medicine or
- Methotrexate (e.g., Mexate) or
- Tricyclic antidepressants (amitriptyline [e.g., Elavil], amoxapine [e.g., Asendin], clomipramine [e.g., Anafranil], desipramine [e.g., Pertofrane], doxepin [e.g., Sinequan], imipramine [e.g., Tofranil], nortriptyline [e.g., Aventyl], protriptyline [e.g., Vivactil], trimipramine [e.g., Surmontil]) or
- Vancomycin (e.g., Vancocin)—The chance of side effects may be increased

- Naltrexone (e.g., Trexan)—Naltrexone keeps narcotic analgesics from working to relieve pain; people taking naltrexone should use pain relievers that do not contain a narcotic

- Probenecid (e.g., Benemid) or
- Sulfinpyrazone (e.g., Anturane)—Aspirin can keep these medicines from working as well for treating gout; also, use of sulfinpyrazone and aspirin together may increase the chance of bleeding

- Urinary alkalizers (medicine that makes the urine less acid, such as acetazolamide [e.g., Diamox], calcium-and/or magnesium-containing antacids, dichlorphenamide [e.g., Daranide], methazolamide [e.g., Neptazane], potassium or sodium citrate and/or citric acid, sodium bicarbonate [baking soda])—These medicines may make aspirin less effective by causing it to be removed from the body more quickly

- Zidovudine (e.g., AZT, Retrovir)—Higher blood levels of zidovudine and an increased chance of serious side effects may occur

Other medical problems—The presence of other medical problems may affect the use of narcotic analgesic and aspirin combinations. Make sure you tell your doctor if you have any other medical problems, especially:

- Alcohol and/or other drug abuse, or history of, or
- Asthma, allergies, and nasal polyps (history of) or
- Brain disease or head injury or
- Colitis or
- Convulsions (seizures), history of, or
- Emotional problems or mental illness or
- Emphysema or other chronic lung disease or
- Kidney disease or
- Liver disease or

                                                                **

- Underactive thyroid—The chance of serious side effects may be increased

- Anemia or
- Overactive thyroid or
- Stomach ulcer or other stomach problems—Aspirin may make these conditions worse

- Enlarged prostate or problems with urination or
- Gallbladder disease or gallstones—Narcotic analgesics have side effects that may be dangerous if these medical problems are present

- Gout—Aspirin can make this condition worse and can also lessen the effects of some medicines used to treat gout

- Heart disease—Large amounts of aspirin and caffeine (present in some of these combination medicines) can make some kinds of heart disease worse

- Hemophilia or other bleeding problems or
- Vitamin K deficiency—Aspirin increases the chance of serious bleeding

Proper Use of This Medicine

Take this medicine with food or a full glass (8 ounces) of water to lessen stomach irritation.

Do not take this medicine if it has a strong vinegar-like odor. This odor means the aspirin in it is breaking down. If you have any questions about this, check with your health care professional.

Take this medicine only as directed by your medical doctor or dentist. Do not take more of it, do not take it more often, and do not take it for a longer time than your medical doctor or dentist ordered. This is especially important for children and elderly patients, who are usually more sensitive to the effects of these medicines. If too much of a narcotic analgesic is taken, it may become habit-forming (causing mental or physical dependence) or lead to medical problems because of an overdose. Also, taking too much aspirin may cause stomach problems or lead to medical problems because of an overdose.

If you think that this medicine is not working as well after you have been taking it for a few weeks, *do not increase the dose.* Instead, check with your medical doctor or dentist.

Dosing—The dose of these medicines will be different for different patients. *Follow your doctor's orders or the directions on the label.* The following information includes only the average doses of these medicines. *If your dose is different, do not change it* unless your doctor tells you to do so.

The number of capsules or tablets that you take depends on the strength of the medicine and on the amount of pain you are having.

For aspirin, caffeine, and dihydrocodeine
- For *oral* dosage form (capsules):
    —For pain:
    - Adults—2 capsules every four hours as needed.
    - Children—Dose must be determined by your doctor.

For aspirin and codeine
- For *oral* dosage form (tablets):
    —For pain:
    - Adults—1 or 2 tablets every four hours as needed.
    - Children—Dose must be determined by your doctor.

For aspirin, codeine, and caffeine
- For *oral* dosage form (tablets):
    —For pain:
    - Adults—1 or 2 tablets every four hours as needed.
    - Children—Dose must be determined by your doctor.

For buffered aspirin, codeine, and caffeine
- For *oral* dosage form (tablets):
    —For pain:
    - Adults—1 or 2 tablets every four hours as needed.
    - Children—Dose must be determined by your doctor.

For hydrocodone and aspirin
- For *oral* dosage form (tablets):
    —For pain:
    - Adults—1 or 2 tablets every four to six hours as needed.
    - Children—Dose must be determined by your doctor.

For oxycodone and aspirin
- For *oral* dosage form (tablets):
    —For pain:
    - Adults—1 or 2 half-strength tablets, or 1 full-strength tablet, every four to six hours as needed.
    - Children up to 6 years of age—Use is not recommended.
    - Children 6 to 12 years of age—One-quarter of a half-strength tablet every six hours as needed.
    - Children 12 years of age and older—One-half of a half-strength tablet every six hours as needed.

For pentazocine and aspirin
- For *oral* dosage form (tablets):
    —For pain:
    - Adults—2 tablets three or four times a day as needed.
    - Children—Dose must be determined by your doctor.

For propoxyphene and aspirin
- For *oral* dosage form (capsules):
    —For pain:
    - Adults—1 capsule every four hours as needed.
    - Children—Dose must be determined by your doctor.

For propoxyphene, aspirin, and caffeine
- For *oral* dosage form (capsules or tablets):
    —For pain:
    - Adults—1 capsule or tablet every four hours as needed.
    - Children—Dose must be determined by your doctor.

Missed dose—If your medical doctor or dentist has ordered you to take this medicine according to a regular schedule and you miss a dose, take it as soon as you remember. However, if it is almost time for your next dose, skip the missed dose and go back to your regular dosing schedule. *Do not double doses.*

Storage—To store this medicine:
- Keep out of the reach of children. Overdose is very dangerous in young children.
- Store away from heat and direct light.
- Do not store this medicine in the bathroom, near the kitchen sink, or in other damp places. Heat or moisture may cause the medicine to break down.

- Do not keep outdated medicine or medicine no longer needed. Be sure that any discarded medicine is out of the reach of children.

Precautions While Using This Medicine

If you will be taking this medicine for a long time (for example, for several months at a time), your doctor should check your progress at regular visits.

Check the labels of all nonprescription (over-the-counter [OTC]) and prescription medicines you now take. If any contain a narcotic, aspirin, or other salicylates, check with your health care professional. Taking them together with this medicine may cause an overdose.

This medicine will add to the effects of alcohol and other CNS depressants (medicines that slow down the nervous system, possibly causing drowsiness). Some examples of CNS depressants are antihistamines or medicine for hay fever, other allergies, or colds; sedatives, tranquilizers, or sleeping medicine; other prescription pain medicine or narcotics; barbiturates; medicine for seizures; muscle relaxants; or anesthetics, including some dental anesthetics. Also, stomach problems may be more likely to occur if you drink alcoholic beverages while you are taking aspirin. *Do not drink alcoholic beverages, and check with your medical doctor or dentist before taking any of the medicines listed above, while you are using this medicine.*

Taking acetaminophen or certain other medicines together with the aspirin in this combination medicine may increase the chance of unwanted effects. The risk will depend on how much of each medicine you take every day, and on how long you take the medicines together. If your medical doctor or dentist directs you to take these medicines together on a regular basis, follow his or her directions carefully. However, do not take acetaminophen or any of the following medicines together with this combination medicine for more than a few days, unless your medical doctor or dentist has directed you to do so and is following your progress:

- Diclofenac (e.g., Voltaren)
- Diflunisal (e.g., Dolobid)
- Etodolac (e.g., Lodine)
- Fenoprofen (e.g., Nalfon)
- Floctafenine (e.g., Idarac)
- Flurbiprofen, oral (e.g., Ansaid)
- Ibuprofen (e.g., Motrin)
- Indomethacin (e.g., Indocin)
- Ketoprofen (e.g., Orudis)
- Ketorolac (e.g., Toradol)
- Meclofenamate (e.g., Meclomen)
- Mefenamic acid (e.g., Ponstel)
- Nabumetone (e.g., Relafen)
- Naproxen (e.g., Naprosyn)
- Oxaprozin (e.g., Daypro)
- Phenylbutazone (e.g., Butazolidin)
- Piroxicam (e.g., Feldene)
- Sulindac (e.g., Clinoril)
- Tenoxicam (e.g., Mobiflex)
- Tiaprofenic acid (e.g., Surgam)
- Tolmetin (e.g., Tolectin)

This medicine may cause some people to become drowsy, dizzy, or lightheaded, or to feel a false sense of well-being. *Make sure you know how you react to this medicine before you drive, use machines, or do anything else that could be dangerous if you are dizzy or are not alert and clearheaded.*

Dizziness, lightheadedness, or fainting may occur, especially when you get up suddenly from a lying or sitting position. Getting up slowly may help lessen this problem.

Nausea or vomiting may occur, especially after the first couple of doses. This effect may go away if you lie down for a while. However, if nausea or vomiting continues, check with your doctor. Lying down for a while may also help some other side effects, such as dizziness or lightheadedness.

Before having any kind of surgery (including dental surgery) or emergency treatment, tell the medical doctor or dentist in charge that you are taking this medicine.

Do not take this medicine for 5 days before any surgery, including dental surgery, unless otherwise directed by your medical doctor or dentist. Taking aspirin during this time may cause bleeding problems.

For patients taking the *buffered aspirin, codeine, and caffeine* combination (C2 Buffered with Codeine):

- This product contains antacids that can keep many other medicines, especially some medicines used to treat infections, from working properly. This problem can be prevented by not taking the 2 medicines too close together. Ask your pharmacist how long you should wait between taking any other medicine and the buffered aspirin, codeine, and caffeine combination.

For *diabetic patients:*

- False urine sugar test results may occur if you are regularly taking 8 or more 325-mg (5-grain) or 5 or more 500-mg doses of aspirin a day. Smaller amounts or occasional use of aspirin usually will not affect urine sugar tests. If you have any questions about this, check with your health care professional, especially if your diabetes is not well controlled.

Narcotic analgesics may cause dryness of the mouth. For temporary relief, use sugarless candy or gum, melt bits of ice in your mouth, or use a saliva substitute. However, if dry mouth continues for more than 2 weeks, check with your dentist. Continuing dryness of the mouth may increase the chance of dental disease, including tooth decay, gum disease, and fungus infections.

If you have been taking this medicine regularly for several weeks or more, *do not suddenly stop using it without first checking with your doctor.* Depending on which of these medicines you have been taking, and the amount you have been taking every day, your doctor may want you to reduce gradually the amount you are taking before stopping completely, to lessen the chance of withdrawal side effects.

If you think you or someone else may have taken an overdose of this medicine, get emergency help at once. Taking an overdose of this medicine or taking alcohol or CNS depressants with this medicine may lead to unconsciousness or death. Signs of overdose of this medicine include convulsions (seizures); hearing loss; confusion; ringing or buzzing in the ears; severe excitement, nervousness, or restlessness; severe dizziness, severe drowsiness, shortness of breath or troubled breathing, and severe weakness.

Side Effects of This Medicine

Along with its needed effects, a medicine may cause some unwanted effects. Although not all of these side effects may occur, if they do occur they may need medical attention.

Get emergency help immediately if any of the following symptoms of overdose occur:

Any loss of hearing; bloody urine; cold, clammy skin; confusion (severe); convulsions (seizures); diarrhea (severe or continuing); dizziness or lightheadedness (severe); drowsiness (severe); excitement, nervousness, or restlessness (severe); fever; hallucinations (seeing, hearing, or feeling things that are not there); headache (severe or continuing); increased sweating; increased thirst; low blood pressure; nausea or vomiting (severe or continuing); pinpoint pupils of eyes; ringing or buzzing in the ears; shortness of breath or unusually slow or troubled breathing; slow heartbeat; stomach pain (severe or continuing); uncontrollable flapping movements of the hands (especially in elderly patients); vision problems; weakness (severe)

Also, check with your doctor as soon as possible if any of the following side effects occur:

Less common or rare

Bloody or black, tarry stools; confusion; dark urine; fast, slow, or pounding heartbeat; increased sweating (more common with hydrocodone); irregular breathing; mental depression; pale stools; redness or flushing of face (more common with hydrocodone); skin rash, hives, or itching; stomach pain (severe); swelling of face; tightness in chest or wheezing; trembling or uncontrolled muscle movements; unusual excitement (especially in children); unusual tiredness or weakness; vomiting of blood or material that looks like coffee grounds; yellow eyes or skin

Other side effects may occur that usually do not need medical attention. These side effects may go away during treatment as your body adjusts to the medicine. However, check with your doctor if any of the following side effects continue or are bothersome:

More common

Dizziness, lightheadedness, or feeling faint; drowsiness; heartburn or indigestion; nausea or vomiting; stomach pain (mild)

Less common or rare

Blurred or double vision or other changes in vision; constipation (more common with long-term use and with codeine); difficult, painful, or decreased urination; dryness of mouth; false sense of well-being; frequent urge to urinate; general feeling of discomfort or illness; headache; loss of appetite; nervousness or restlessness; nightmares or unusual dreams; trouble in sleeping; unusual tiredness; unusual weakness

Although not all of the side effects listed above have been reported for all of these medicines, they have been reported for at least one of them. However, since all of the narcotic analgesics are very similar, any of the above side effects may occur with any of these medicines.

After you stop using this medicine, your body may need time to adjust. The length of time this takes depends on which of these medicines you were taking, the amount of medicine you were using, and how long you used it. During this period of time check with your doctor if you notice any of the following side effects:

Body aches; diarrhea; fever, runny nose, or sneezing; gooseflesh; increased sweating; increased yawning; loss of appetite; nausea or vomiting; nervousness, rest-

lessness, or irritability; shivering or trembling; stomach cramps; trouble in sleeping; weakness

Other side effects not listed above may also occur in some patients. If you notice any other effects, check with your medical doctor or dentist.

Revised: 07/05/95

NARCOTIC ANALGESICS—For Pain Relief   Systemic

Commonly used brand name(s):

In the U.S.—

Astramorph PF[10]	MS/L Concentrate[10]
Buprenex[2]	MS/S[10]
Cotanal-65[16]	Nubain[11]
Darvon[16]	Numorphan[14]
Darvon-N[16]	OMS Concentrate[10]
Demerol[8]	Oramorph SR[10]
Dilaudid[6]	OxyContin[13]
Dilaudid-5[6]	PP-Cap[16]
Dilaudid-HP[6]	Rescudose[10]
Dolophine[9]	RMS Uniserts[10]
Duramorph[10]	Roxanol[10]
Hydrostat IR[6]	Roxanol 100[10]
Kadian[10]	Roxanol UD[10]
Levo-Dromoran[7]	Roxicodone[13]
Methadose[9]	Roxicodone Intensol[13]
M S Contin[10]	Stadol[3]
MSIR[10]	Talwin[15]
MS/L[10]	Talwin-Nx[15]

In Canada—

Darvon-N[16]	M S Contin[10]
Demerol[8]	MS`IR[10]
Dilaudid[6]	Nubain[11]
Dilaudid-HP[6]	Numorphan[14]
Epimorph[10]	Oramorph SR[10]
Hycodan #[5]	OxyContin SR[13]
Kadian[10]	Pantopon[12]
Leritine[1]	Paveral[4]
Levo-Dromoran[7]	PMS-Hydromorphone[6]
M-Eslon[10]	PMS-Hydromorphone Syrup[6]
Morphine Extra-Forte[10]	Robidone[5]
Morphine Forte[10]	642[16]
Morphine H.P.[10]	Statex[10]
Morphitec[10]	Statex Drops[10]
M.O.S.[10]	Supeudol[13]
M.O.S.-S.R.[10]	Talwin[15]

Other commonly used names are: dextropropoxyphene[16], dihydromorphinone[6], levorphan[7], papaveretum[12], pethidine[8].

Note: For quick reference, the following narcotic analgesics are numbered to match the corresponding brand names.

This information applies to the following medicines:

1. Anileridine (an-i-LER-i-deen) *
2. Buprenorphine (byoo-pre-NOR-feen)
3. Butorphanol (byoo-TOR-fa-nole) †
4. Codeine (KOE-deen) ‡§
5. Hydrocodone (hye-droe-KOE-done) *
6. Hydromorphone (hye-droe-MOR-fone) ‡
7. Levorphanol (lee-VOR-fa-nole) ‡
8. Meperidine (me-PER-i-deen) ‡§
9. Methadone (METH-a-done) **‡
10. Morphine (MOR-feen) ‡§
11. Nalbuphine (NAL-byoo-feen) ‡
12. Opium Injection (OH-pee-um) *

13. Oxycodone (ox-i-KOE-done)
14. Oxymorphone (ox-i-MOR-fone)
15. Pentazocine (pen-TAZ-oh-seen)
16. Propoxyphene (proe-POX-i-feen) ‡

This information does *not* apply to Opium Tincture or Paregoric.

---

*Not commercially available in the U.S.
†Not commercially available in Canada.
‡Generic name product may be available in the U.S.
§Generic name product may be available in Canada.
#For Canadian product only. In the U.S., *Hycodan* also contains homatropine; in Canada, *Hycodan* contains only hydrocodone.
**In Canada, methadone is available only through doctors who have received special approval to prescribe it for treating drug addicts.

Description

Narcotic (nar-KOT-ik) analgesics (an-al-JEE-zicks) are used to relieve pain. Some of these medicines are also used just before or during an operation to help the anesthetic work better. Codeine and hydrocodone are also used to relieve coughing. Methadone is also used to help some people control their dependence on heroin or other narcotics. Narcotic analgesics may also be used for other conditions as determined by your doctor.

Narcotic analgesics act in the central nervous system (CNS) to relieve pain. Some of their side effects are also caused by actions in the CNS.

If a narcotic is used for a long time, it may become habit-forming (causing mental or physical dependence). Physical dependence may lead to withdrawal side effects when you stop taking the medicine.

These medicines are available only with your medical doctor's or dentist's prescription. For some of them, prescriptions cannot be refilled and you must obtain a new prescription from your medical doctor or dentist each time you need the medicine. In addition, other rules and regulations may apply when methadone is used to treat narcotic dependence.

These medicines are available in the following dosage forms:

Oral
Anileridine
  • Tablets (Canada)
Codeine
  • Oral solution (U.S. and Canada)
  • Tablets (U.S. and Canada)
Hydrocodone
  • Syrup (Canada)
  • Tablets (Canada)
Hydromorphone
  • Oral solution (U.S. and Canada)
  • Tablets (U.S. and Canada)
Levorphanol
  • Tablets (U.S. and Canada)
Meperidine
  • Syrup (U.S.)
  • Tablets (U.S. and Canada)
Methadone
  • Oral concentrate (U.S.)
  • Oral solution (U.S.)
  • Tablets (U.S.)
  • Dispersible tablets (U.S.)
Morphine
  • Capsules (U.S.)
  • Extended-release capsules (U.S. and Canada)
  • Oral solution (U.S. and Canada)
  • Syrup (Canada)
  • Tablets (U.S. and Canada)
  • Extended-release tablets (U.S. and Canada)
Oxycodone
  • Oral solution (U.S.)
  • Tablets (U.S. and Canada)
  • Extended-release tablets (U.S. and Canada)
Pentazocine
  • Tablets (Canada)
Pentazocine and Naloxone
  • Tablets (U.S.)
Propoxyphene
  • Capsules (U.S. and Canada)
  • Oral suspension (U.S.)
  • Tablets (U.S. and Canada)

Parenteral
Buprenorphine
  • Injection (U.S.)
Butorphanol
  • Injection (U.S.)
Codeine
  • Injection (U.S. and Canada)
Hydromorphone
  • Injection (U.S. and Canada)
Levorphanol
  • Injection (U.S. and Canada)
Meperidine
  • Injection (U.S. and Canada)
Methadone
  • Injection (U.S.)
Morphine
  • Injection (U.S. and Canada)
Nalbuphine
  • Injection (U.S. and Canada)
Opium
  • Injection (Canada)
Oxymorphone
  • Injection (U.S. and Canada)
Pentazocine
  • Injection (U.S. and Canada)

Rectal
Hydromorphone
  • Suppositories (U.S. and Canada)
Morphine
  • Suppositories (U.S. and Canada)
Oxycodone
  • Suppositories (Canada)
Oxymorphone
  • Suppositories (U.S. and Canada)

Before Using This Medicine

In deciding to use a medicine, the risks of taking the medicine must be weighed against the good it will do. This is a decision you and your doctor will make. For narcotic analgesics, the following should be considered:

Allergies—Tell your doctor if you have ever had any unusual or allergic reaction to any of the narcotic analgesics. Also tell your health care professional if you are allergic to any other substances, such as foods, preservatives, or dyes.

Pregnancy—Although studies on birth defects with narcotic analgesics have not been done in pregnant women,

---

© 2002 MICROMEDEX Thomson Healthcare

these medicines have not been reported to cause birth defects. However, hydrocodone, hydromorphone, and morphine caused birth defects in animals when given in very large doses. Buprenorphine and codeine did not cause birth defects in animal studies, but they caused other unwanted effects. Butorphanol, nalbuphine, pentazocine, and propoxyphene did not cause birth defects in animals. There is no information about whether other narcotic analgesics cause birth defects in animals.

Too much use of a narcotic during pregnancy may cause the baby to become dependent on the medicine. This may lead to withdrawal side effects after birth. Also, some of these medicines may cause breathing problems in the newborn infant if taken just before delivery.

Breast-feeding—Most narcotic analgesics have not been reported to cause problems in nursing babies. However, when the mother is taking large amounts of methadone (in a methadone maintenance program), the nursing baby may become dependent on the medicine. Also, butorphanol, codeine, meperidine, morphine, opium, and propoxyphene pass into the breast milk.

Children—Breathing problems may be especially likely to occur in children younger than 2 years of age. These children are usually more sensitive than adults to the effects of narcotic analgesics. Also, unusual excitement or restlessness may be more likely to occur in children receiving these medicines.

Older adults—Elderly people are especially sensitive to the effects of narcotic analgesics. This may increase the chance of side effects, especially breathing problems, during treatment.

Other medicines—Although certain medicines should not be used together at all, in other cases two different medicines may be used together even if an interaction might occur. In these cases, your doctor may want to change the dose, or other precautions may be necessary. When you are taking a narcotic analgesic, it is especially important that your health care professional know if you are taking any of the following:

- Carbamazepine (e.g., Tegretol)—Propoxyphene may increase the blood levels of carbamazepine, which increases the chance of serious side effects

- Central nervous system (CNS) depressants or
- Monoamine oxidase (MAO) inhibitors (furazolidone [e.g., Furoxone], isocarboxazid [e.g., Marplan], pargyline [e.g., Eutonyl], phenelzine [e.g., Nardil], procarbazine [e.g., Matulane], tranylcypromine [e.g., Parnate] (taken currently or within the past 2 weeks) or
- Tricyclic antidepressants (amitriptyline [e.g., Elavil], amoxapine [e.g., Asendin], clomipramine [e.g., Anafranil], desipramine [e.g., Pertofrane], doxepin [e.g., Sinequan], imipramine [e.g., Tofranil], nortriptyline [e.g., Aventyl], protriptyline [e.g., Vivactil], trimipramine [e.g., Surmontil])—The chance of side effects may be increased; the combination of meperidine (e.g., Demerol) and MAO inhibitors is especially dangerous

- Naltrexone (e.g., Trexan)—Narcotics will not be effective in people taking naltrexone

- Rifampin (e.g., Rifadin)—Rifampin decreases the effects of methadone and may cause withdrawal symptoms in people who are dependent on methadone

- Zidovudine (e.g., AZT, Retrovir)—Morphine may increase the blood levels of zidovudine and increase the chance of serious side effects

Other medical problems—The presence of other medical problems may affect the use of narcotic analgesics. Make sure you tell your doctor if you have any other medical problems, especially:

- Alcohol abuse, or history of, or
- Drug dependence, especially narcotic abuse, or history of, or
- Emotional problems—The chance of side effects may be increased; also, withdrawal symptoms may occur if a narcotic you are dependent on is replaced by buprenorphine, butorphanol, nalbuphine, or pentazocine

- Brain disease or head injury or
- Emphysema, asthma, or other chronic lung disease or
- Enlarged prostate or problems with urination or
- Gallbladder disease or gallstones—Some of the side effects of narcotic analgesics can be dangerous if these conditions are present

- Colitis or
- Heart disease or
- Kidney disease or
- Liver disease or
- Underactive thyroid—The chance of side effects may be increased

- Convulsions (seizures), history of—Some of the narcotic analgesics can cause convulsions

Proper Use of This Medicine

Some narcotic analgesics given by injection may be given at home to patients who do not need to be in the hospital. If you are using an injection form of this medicine at home, *make sure you clearly understand and carefully follow your doctor's instructions.*

To take the *syrup form of meperidine:*
- Unless otherwise directed by your medical doctor or dentist, *take this medicine mixed with a half glass (4 ounces) of water* to lessen the numbing effect of the medicine on your mouth and throat.

To take the *oral liquid forms of methadone:*
- *This medicine may have to be mixed with water or another liquid before you take it.* Read the label carefully for directions. If you have any questions about this, check with your health care professional.

To take the *dispersible tablet form of methadone:*
- *These tablets must be stirred into water or fruit juice just before each dose is taken. Read the label carefully for directions.* If you have any questions about this, check with your health care professional.

To take *oral liquid forms of morphine:*
- This medicine may be mixed with a glass of fruit juice just before you take it, if desired, to improve the taste.

To take *long-acting morphine tablets:*
- *These tablets must be swallowed whole.* Do not break, crush, or chew them before swallowing.

To use *suppositories:*
- If the suppository is too soft to insert, chill it in the refrigerator for 30 minutes or run cold water over it before removing the foil wrapper.

• To insert the suppository: First remove the foil wrapper and moisten the suppository with cold water. Lie down on your side and use your finger to push the suppository well up into the rectum.

Take this medicine only as directed by your medical doctor or dentist. Do not take more of it, do not take it more often, and do not take it for a longer time than your medical doctor or dentist ordered. This is especially important for young children and elderly patients, who are especially sensitive to the effects of narcotic analgesics. If too much is taken, the medicine may become habit-forming (causing mental or physical dependence) or lead to medical problems because of an overdose.

If you think this medicine is not working properly after you have been taking it for a few weeks, *do not increase the dose.* Instead, check with your doctor.

Dosing—The dose of these medicines will be different for different patients. *Follow your doctor's orders or the directions on the label.* The following information includes only the average doses of these medicines. *If your dose is different, do not change it* unless your doctor tells you to do so.

The number of capsules or tablets or teaspoonfuls of oral solution or syrup that you take, or the amount of injection that you are directed to use, depends on the strength of the medicine. Also, *the number of doses you take each day, the time allowed between doses, and the length of time you take the medicine depend on the narcotic you are taking, whether or not you are taking a long-acting form of the medicine, and the reason you are taking the medicine.*

For anileridine
• For *oral* dosage form:
  —For pain
  • Adults and teenagers—25 to 50 milligrams (mg) every 6 hours as needed.
  • Children up to 13 years of age—Dose must be determined by your doctor.

For buprenorphine
• For *injection* dosage form:
  —For pain:
  • Adults and teenagers—0.3 milligrams (mg), injected into a muscle or a vein every six hours as needed.
  • Children up to 2 years of age—Dose must be determined by your doctor.
  • Children 2 to 12 years of age—0.002 to 0.006 mg per kilogram (kg) (0.0008 to 0.0024 mg per pound) of body weight, injected into a muscle or a vein every four to six hours as needed.

For butorphanol
• For *injection* dosage form:
  —For pain:
  • Adults—1 to 4 milligrams (mg) (usually 2 mg), injected into a muscle every three or four hours as needed. Some people may receive 0.5 to 2 mg (usually 1 mg) injected into a vein every three or four hours as needed.
  • Children and teenagers—Dose must be determined by your doctor.

For codeine
• For *oral* dosage forms (oral solution or tablets):
  —For pain:
  • Adults—15 to 60 milligrams (mg) (usually 30 mg) every three to six hours as needed.
  • Children—0.5 mg per kilogram (kg) (0.2 mg per pound) of body weight every four to six hours as needed. Young children will probably take the oral solution, rather than tablets. Small doses may need to be measured by a special dropper instead of a teaspoon.
  —For cough:
  • Adults—10 to 20 mg every four to six hours.
  • Children up to 2 years of age—Use is not recommended.
  • Children 2 years of age—3 mg every four to six hours, up to a maximum of 12 mg a day. Children this young will probably take the oral solution, rather than tablets. Small doses may need to be measured by a special dropper instead of a teaspoon.
  • Children 3 years of age—3.5 mg every four to six hours, up to a maximum of 14 mg a day. Children this young will probably take the oral solution, rather than tablets. Small doses may need to be measured by a special dropper instead of a teaspoon.
  • Children 4 years of age—4 mg every four to six hours, up to a maximum of 16 mg a day. Children this young will probably take the oral solution, rather than tablets. Small doses may need to be measured by a special dropper instead of a teaspoon.
  • Children 5 years of age—4.5 mg every four to six hours, up to a maximum of 18 mg a day. Children this young will probably take the oral solution, rather than tablets. Small doses may need to be measured by a special dropper instead of a teaspoon.
  • Children 6 to 12 years of age—5 to 10 mg every four to six hours, up to a maximum of 60 mg a day.
• For *injection* dosage form:
  —For pain:
  • Adults—15 to 60 mg (usually 30 mg), injected into a muscle or a vein or under the skin every four to six hours as needed.
  • Children—0.5 mg per kg (0.2 mg per pound) of body weight, injected into a muscle or under the skin every four to six hours as needed.

For hydrocodone
• For *oral* dosage form (syrup or tablets):
  —For pain:
  • Adults—5 to 10 milligrams (mg) every four to six hours as needed.
  • Children—0.15 mg per kilogram (kg) (0.06 mg per pound) of body weight every six hours as needed.
  —For cough:
  • Adults—5 mg every four to six hours as needed.
  • Children—Dose must be determined by your doctor.

For hydromorphone
• For *oral* dosage form (oral solution or tablets):
  —For pain:
  • Adults—2 or 2.5 milligrams (mg) every three to six hours as needed.

- Children—Dose must be determined by your doctor.
- For *injection* dosage form:
  —For pain:
  - Adults—1 or 2 mg, injected into a muscle or under the skin every three to six hours as needed. Some people may receive 0.5 mg, injected slowly into a vein every three hours as needed.
  - Children—Dose must be determined by your doctor.
- For *rectal suppository* dosage form:
  —For pain:
  - Adults—3 mg every four to eight hours as needed.
  - Children—Dose must be determined by your doctor.

For levorphanol
- For *oral* dosage form (tablets):
  —For pain:
  - Adults—2 milligrams (mg). Some people with severe pain may need 3 or 4 mg.
  - Children—Dose must be determined by your doctor.
- For *injection* dosage form:
  —For pain:
  - Adults—2 mg, injected under the skin or into a vein. Some people may need 3 mg.
  - Children—Dose must be determined by your doctor.

For meperidine
- For *oral* dosage form (syrup or tablets):
  —For pain:
  - Adults—50 to 150 milligrams (mg) (usually 100 mg) every three or four hours as needed.
  - Children—1.1 to 1.76 mg per kilogram (kg) (0.44 to 0.8 mg per pound) of body weight, up to a maximum of 100 mg, every three or four hours as needed. Young children will probably take the syrup, rather than tablets. Small doses may need to be measured by a special dropper instead of a teaspoon.
- For *injection* dosage form:
  —For pain:
  - Adults—50 to 150 milligrams (mg) (usually 100 mg), injected into a muscle or under the skin every three or four hours as needed. The medicine may also be injected continuously into a vein at a rate of 15 to 35 mg an hour.
  - Children—1.1 to 1.76 mg per kg (0.44 to 0.8 mg per pound) of body weight, up to a maximum of 100 mg, injected into a muscle or under the skin every three or four hours as needed.

For methadone
- For *oral solution* dosage form:
  —For pain:
  - Adults—5 to 20 mg every four to eight hours.
  - Children—Dose must be determined by your doctor.
  —For narcotic addiction:
  - Adults 18 years of age or older—
    —For detoxification: At first, 15 to 40 mg once a day. Your doctor will gradually decrease the dose you take every day until you do not need the medicine any more.
    —For maintenance: Dose must be determined by the needs of the individual patient, up to a maximum of 120 mg a day.
  - Children up to 18 years of age—Special conditions must be met before methadone can be used for narcotic addiction in patients younger than 18 years of age. Use and dose must be determined by your doctor.
- For *oral tablet* dosage form:
  —For pain:
  - Adults—2.5 to 10 mg every three or four hours as needed.
  - Children—Dose must be determined by your doctor.
  —For narcotic addiction:
  - Adults 18 years of age or older—
    —For detoxification: At first, 15 to 40 mg once a day. Your doctor will gradually decrease the dose you take every day until you do not need the medicine any more.
    —For maintenance: Dose must be determined by the needs of the individual patient, up to a maximum of 120 mg a day.
  - Children up to 18 years of age—Special conditions must be met before methadone can be used for narcotic addiction in patients younger than 18 years of age. Use and dose must be determined by your doctor.
- For *injection* dosage form:
  —For pain:
  - Adults—2.5 to 10 mg, injected into a muscle or under the skin, every three or four hours as needed.
  - Children—Dose must be determined by your doctor.
  —For narcotic addiction:
  - Adults 18 years of age and older—For detoxification only, in patients unable to take medicine by mouth: At first, 15 to 40 mg a day. Your doctor will gradually decrease the dose you receive every day until you do not need the medicine any more.
  - Children younger than 18 years of age—Use and dose must be determined by your doctor.

For morphine
- For *short-acting oral* dosage forms (capsules, oral solution, syrup, or tablets):
  —For severe, chronic pain (severe pain that lasts a long time):
  - Adults—At first, 10 to 30 milligrams (mg) every four hours. Your doctor will then adjust the dose according to your individual needs. If you have already been taking other narcotics to relieve severe, chronic pain, your starting dose will depend on the amount of other narcotic you were taking every day.
  - Children—Dose must be determined by your doctor.
- For *long-acting oral* dosage forms (extended-release capsules or tablets):
  —For severe, chronic pain (severe pain that lasts a long time):
  - Adults—Long-acting forms of morphine are usually used for patients who have already been receiving narcotics to relieve pain. The starting dose will depend on the amount of narcotic you have

been receiving every day. Your doctor will then adjust the dose according to your individual needs. To be helpful, these medicines need to be taken two times a day at regularly scheduled times. Some people may need to take a short-acting form of morphine if breakthrough pain occurs between doses of the long-acting medicine.
- Children—Dose must be determined by your doctor.

- For *injection* dosage form:
  —For pain:
  - Adults—5 to 20 mg (usually 10 mg), injected into a muscle or under the skin every four hours as needed. Some people may receive 4 to 10 mg, injected slowly into a vein. Morphine may also be injected continuously into a vein or under the skin at a rate that depends on the needs of the patient. This medicine may also be injected into the spinal area. The dose will depend on where and how the medicine is injected into the spinal area and on the needs of the patient.
  - Children—0.1 to 0.2 mg per kg (0.04 or 0.09 mg per pound) of body weight, up to a maximum of 15 mg, injected under the skin every four hours as needed. Some patients may receive 0.05 to 0.1 mg per kg (0.02 to 0.04 mg per pound) of body weight, injected slowly into a vein.

- For *rectal suppository* dosage form:
  —For pain:
  - Adults—10 to 30 mg every four to six hours as needed.
  - Children—Dose must be determined by your doctor.

For nalbuphine
- For *injection* dosage form:
  —For pain:
  - Adults—10 milligrams (mg) every three to six hours as needed, injected into a muscle or a vein or under the skin.
  - Children—Dose must be determined by your doctor.

For opium
- For *injection* dosage form:
  —For pain:
  - Adults—5 to 20 milligrams (mg), injected into a muscle or under the skin every four to five hours as needed.
  - Children—Dose must be determined by your doctor.

For oxycodone
- For *oral* dosage form (oral solution or tablets):
  —For pain:
  - Adults—5–15 milligrams (mg) every 4–6 hours as needed.
  - Children—Dose must be determined by your doctor. Children up to 6 years of age will probably take the oral solution, rather than tablets. Small doses may need to be measured by a special dropper instead of a teaspoon.

- For *long-acting oral* dosage form (extended-release tablets):
  —For pain:
  - Adults—Your doctor will determine the dose according to your individual needs. To be helpful,

these medicines need to be taken two times a day at regularly scheduled times.
- Children—Use and dose must be determined by your doctor.

- For *rectal suppository* dosage form:
  —For pain:
  - Adults—10 to 40 mg three or four times a day.
  - Children—Dose must be determined by your doctor.

For oxymorphone
- For *injection* dosage form:
  —For pain:
  - Adults—1 to 1.5 milligrams (mg), injected into a muscle or under the skin every three to six hours as needed. Some patients may receive 0.5 mg, injected into a vein.
  - Children—Dose must be determined by your doctor.

- For *rectal suppository* dosage form:
  —For pain:
  - Adults—5 mg every four to six hours as needed.
  - Children—Dose must be determined by your doctor.

For pentazocine
- For *oral* dosage form (tablets):
  —For pain:
  - Adults—50 mg every three to four hours as needed. Some patients may need 100 mg every three to four hours. The usual maximum dose is 600 mg a day.
  - Children—Dose must be determined by your doctor.

- For *injection* dosage form:
  —For pain:
  - Adults—30 mg, injected into a muscle or a vein or under the skin every three to four hours as needed.
  - Children—Dose must be determined by your doctor.

For propoxyphene
- For *oral* dosage form (capsules, oral suspension, or tablets):
  —For pain:
  - Adults—Propoxyphene comes in two different forms, propoxyphene hydrochloride and propoxyphene napsylate. 100 mg of propoxyphene napsylate provides the same amount of pain relief as 65 mg of propoxyphene hydrochloride. The dose of propoxyphene hydrochloride is 65 milligrams (mg) every four hours as needed, up to a maximum of 390 mg a day. The dose of propoxyphene napsylate is 100 mg every four hours as needed, up to a maximum of 600 mg a day.
  - Children—Dose must be determined by your doctor.

Missed dose—If your medical doctor or dentist has ordered you to take this medicine according to a regular schedule and you miss a dose, take it as soon as you remember. However, if it is almost time for your next dose, skip the missed dose and go back to your regular dosing schedule. *Do not double doses.*

Storage—To store this medicine:
- Keep out of the reach of children. Overdose is very dangerous in young children.

- Store away from heat and direct light.
- Do not store tablets or capsules in the bathroom, near the kitchen sink, or in other damp places. Heat or moisture may cause the medicine to break down.
- Store hydromorphone, oxycodone, or oxymorphone suppositories in the refrigerator.
- Keep liquid (including injections) and suppository forms of the medicine from freezing.
- Do not keep outdated medicine or medicine no longer needed. Be sure that any discarded medicine is out of the reach of children.

Precautions While Using This Medicine

If you will be taking this medicine for a long time (for example, for several months at a time), your doctor should check your progress at regular visits.

Narcotic analgesics will add to the effects of alcohol and other CNS depressants (medicines that slow down the nervous system, possibly causing drowsiness). Some examples of CNS depressants are antihistamines or medicine for hay fever, other allergies, or colds; sedatives, tranquilizers, or sleeping medicine; other prescription pain medicines including other narcotics; barbiturates; medicine for seizures; muscle relaxants; or anesthetics, including some dental anesthetics. *Do not drink alcoholic beverages, and check with your medical doctor or dentist before taking any of the medicines listed above, while you are using this medicine.*

This medicine may cause some people to become drowsy, dizzy, or lightheaded, or to feel a false sense of well-being. *Make sure you know how you react to this medicine before you drive, use machines, or do anything else that could be dangerous if you are dizzy or are not alert and clearheaded.*

Dizziness, light-headedness, or fainting may occur, especially when you get up suddenly from a lying or sitting position. Getting up slowly may help lessen this problem.

Nausea or vomiting may occur, especially after the first couple of doses. This effect may go away if you lie down for a while. However, if nausea or vomiting continues, check with your medical doctor or dentist. Lying down for a while may also help relieve some other side effects, such as dizziness or light-headedness, that may occur.

Before having any kind of surgery (including dental surgery) or emergency treatment, tell the medical doctor or dentist in charge that you are taking this medicine.

Narcotic analgesics may cause dryness of the mouth. For temporary relief, use sugarless candy or gum, melt bits of ice in your mouth, or use a saliva substitute. However, if dry mouth continues for more than 2 weeks, check with your dentist. Continuing dryness of the mouth may increase the chance of dental disease, including tooth decay, gum disease, and fungus infections.

If you have been taking this medicine regularly for several weeks or more, *do not suddenly stop using it without first checking with your doctor*. Your doctor may want you to reduce gradually the amount you are taking before stopping completely, in order to lessen the chance of withdrawal side effects.

If you think you or someone else may have taken an overdose, get emergency help at once. Taking an overdose of this medicine or taking alcohol or CNS depressants with this medicine may lead to unconsciousness or death. Signs of overdose include convulsions (seizures), confusion, severe nervousness or restlessness, severe dizziness, severe drowsiness, slow or troubled breathing, and severe weakness.

Side Effects of This Medicine

Along with its needed effects, a medicine may cause some unwanted effects. Although not all of these side effects may occur, if they do occur they may need medical attention.

Get emergency help immediately if any of the following symptoms of overdose occur:

Cold, clammy skin; confusion; convulsions (seizures); dizziness (severe); drowsiness (severe); low blood pressure; nervousness or restlessness (severe); pinpoint pupils of eyes; slow heartbeat; slow or troubled breathing; weakness (severe)

Also, check with your doctor as soon as possible if any of the following side effects occur:

Less common or rare

Dark urine (for propoxyphene only); fast, slow, or pounding heartbeat; feelings of unreality; hallucinations (seeing, hearing, or feeling things that are not there); hives, itching, or skin rash; increased sweating (more common with hydrocodone, meperidine, and methadone); irregular breathing; mental depression or other mood or mental changes; pale stools (for propoxyphene only); redness or flushing of face (more common with hydrocodone, meperidine, and methadone); ringing or buzzing in the ears; shortness of breath, wheezing, or troubled breathing; swelling of face; trembling or uncontrolled muscle movements; unusual excitement or restlessness (especially in children); yellow eyes or skin (for propoxyphene only)

Other side effects may occur that usually do not need medical attention. These side effects may go away during treatment as your body adjusts to the medicine. However, check with your doctor if any of the following side effects continue or are bothersome:

More common

Dizziness, light-headedness, or feeling faint; drowsiness; nausea or vomiting

Less common or rare

Blurred or double vision or other changes in vision; constipation (more common with long-term use and with codeine); decrease in amount of urine; difficult or painful urination; dry mouth; false sense of well-being; frequent urge to urinate; general feeling of discomfort or illness; headache; loss of appetite; nervousness or restlessness; nightmares or unusual dreams; redness, swelling, pain, or burning at place of injection; stomach cramps or pain; trouble in sleeping; unusual tiredness or weakness

After you stop using this medicine, your body may need time to adjust. The length of time this takes depends on the amount of medicine you were using and how long you used it. During this period of time check with your doctor if you notice any of the following side effects:

Body aches; diarrhea; fast heartbeat; fever, runny nose, or sneezing; gooseflesh; increased sweating; increased yawning; loss of appetite; nausea or vomiting; nervousness, restlessness, or irritability; shivering or trembling; stomach cramps; trouble in sleeping; unusually large pupils of eyes; weakness

Other side effects not listed above may also occur in some patients. If you notice any other effects, check with your doctor.

Additional Information

Once a medicine has been approved for marketing for a certain use, experience may show that it is also useful for other medical problems. Although not specifically included in product labeling, morphine by injection is used in certain pediatric patients with the following medical conditions:

- Pain, during mechanical ventilation, neonatal
- Pain, postoperative, neonatal

Other than the above information, there is no additional information relating to proper use, precautions, or side effects for these uses.

Revised: 05/21/2001

NARCOTIC ANALGESICS—For Surgery and Obstetrics Systemic

Commonly used brand name(s):

In the U.S.—

Alfenta[1]	Nubain[7]
Astramorph[6]	Stadol[3]
Astramorph PF[6]	Sublimaze[4]
Buprenex[2]	Sufenta[9]
Demerol[5]	Ultiva[8]
Duramorph[6]	

In Canada—

Alfenta[1]	Stadol[3]
Demerol[5]	Sufenta[9]
Epimorph[6]	Ultiva[8]
Nubain[7]	

Another commonly used name for meperidine is pethidine.

Note: For quick reference, the following narcotic analgesics are numbered to match the corresponding brand names.

This information applies to the following medicines:

1. Alfentanil (al-FEN-ta-nil)
2. Buprenorphine (byoo-pre-NOR-feen)
3. Butorphanol (byoo-TOR-fa-nole)
4. Fentanyl (FEN-ta-nil) ‡§
5. Meperidine (me-PER-i-deen) ‡§
6. Morphine (MOR-feen) ‡§
7. Nalbuphine (NAL-byoo-feen) ‡
8. Remifentanil (rem-i-FEN-ta-nil) ‡
9. Sufentanil (soo-FEN-ta-nil) ‡

‡Generic name product may be available in the U.S.
§Generic name product may be available in Canada.

Description

Narcotic analgesics (nar-KOT-ik an-al-JEE-zicks) are given to relieve pain before and during surgery (including dental surgery) or during labor and delivery. These medicines may also be given before or together with an anesthetic (either a general anesthetic or a local anesthetic), even when the patient is not in pain, to help the anesthetic work better.

When a narcotic analgesic is used for surgery or obstetrics (labor and delivery), it will be given by or under the immediate supervision of a medical doctor or dentist, or by a specially trained nurse, in the doctor's office or in a hospital.

The following information applies only to these special uses of narcotic analgesics. If you are taking or receiving a narcotic analgesic to relieve pain after surgery, or for any other reason, ask your health care professional for additional information about the medicine and its use.

These medicines are available in the following dosage forms:

Parenteral

Alfentanil
- Injection (U.S. and Canada)

Buprenorphine
- Injection (U.S. and Canada)

Butorphanol
- Injection (U.S. and Canada)

Fentanyl
- Injection (U.S. and Canada)

Meperidine
- Injection (U.S. and Canada)

Morphine
- Injection (U.S. and Canada)

Nalbuphine
- Injection (U.S. and Canada)

Remifentanil
- Injection (U.S. and Canada)

Sufentanil
- Injection (U.S. and Canada)

Before Receiving This Medicine

In deciding to use a medicine, the risks of using the medicine must be weighed against the good it will do. This is a decision you and your doctor will make. For narcotic analgesics, the following should be considered:

Allergies—Tell your doctor if you have ever had any unusual or allergic reaction to a narcotic analgesic. Also tell your health care professional if you are allergic to any other substances, such as foods, preservatives, or dyes.

Pregnancy—Although studies on birth defects have not been done in pregnant women, these medicines have not been reported to cause birth defects. However, in animal studies, many narcotics have caused birth defects or other unwanted effects when they were given for a long time in amounts that were large enough to cause harmful effects in the mother.

Use of a narcotic during labor and delivery sometimes causes drowsiness or breathing problems in the newborn baby. If this happens, your health care professional can give the baby another medicine that will overcome these effects. Narcotics are usually not used during the delivery of a premature baby.

Breast-feeding—Some narcotics have been shown to pass into the breast milk. However, these medicines have not been reported to cause problems in nursing babies.

Children—Children younger than 2 years of age may be especially sensitive to the effects of narcotic analgesics. This may increase the chance of side effects.

Older adults—Elderly people are especially sensitive to the effects of narcotic analgesics. This may increase the chance of side effects.

Other medicines—Although certain medicines should not be used together at all, in other cases two different medicines may be used together even if an interaction might occur. In these cases, it may be necessary to change the dose, or other precautions may be necessary. It is very important that you tell the person in charge if you are taking:

- Any other medicine, prescription or nonprescription (over-the-counter [OTC]), or
- "Street" drugs, such as amphetamines ("uppers"), barbiturates ("downers"), cocaine (including "crack"), marijuana, phencyclidine (PCP, "angel dust"), and heroin or other narcotics—Serious side effects may occur if anyone gives you an anesthetic without knowing that you have taken another medicine

- Benzodiazepines or
- Central nervous system (CNS) depressants (medicine that causes drowsiness)—The CNS depressant and other effects of either these medicines or the narcotic analgesics may be increased

- Buprenorphine or similar medicines—The narcotic analgesics may not work if you are taking buprenorphine or other similar medicines

- Cimetidine or
- Erythromycin—Increased chance of side effects with some narcotic analgesics

- Naltrexone—The narcotic analgesics will not work if you are taking naltrexone

Other medical problems—The presence of other medical problems may affect the use of narcotic analgesics. Make sure you tell your doctor if you have *any* other medical problems, especially:
- Abdominal problems or
- Brain tumor or
- Head injury or
- Gallbladder disease or
- Heart disease or
- Kidney disease or
- Liver disease or
- Lung disease or
- Prostate disease or
- Thyroid disease or
- Urinary tract disease—Narcotic analgesics may make these conditions or the symptoms of these conditions worse

Proper Use of This Medicine

Dosing—The dose of narcotic analgesic will be different for different patients. Your health care professional will decide on the right amount for you, depending on:
- Your age;
- Your general physical condition;
- The reason you are receiving the narcotic analgesic; and
- Other medicines you are taking or will receive before or after the narcotic analgesic is given.

Precautions After Receiving This Medicine

For patients going home within a few hours after surgery:
- Narcotic analgesics and other medicines that may be given with them during surgery may cause some people to feel drowsy, tired, or weak for up to a few days after they have been given. Therefore, for at least 24 hours (or longer if necessary) after receiving this medicine, *do not drive, use machines, or do anything else that could be dangerous if you are dizzy or are not alert.*
- Unless otherwise directed by your medical doctor or dentist, *do not drink alcoholic beverages or take other CNS depressants (medicines that slow down the nervous system, possibly causing drowsiness) for about 24 hours after you have received this medicine.* To do so may add to the effects of the narcotic analgesic. Some examples of CNS depressants are antihistamines or medicine for hay fever, other allergies, or colds; sedatives, tranquilizers, or sleeping medicine; prescription pain medicine or narcotics; barbiturates; medicine for seizures; and muscle relaxants.

Side Effects of This Medicine

Along with its needed effects, a medicine may cause some unwanted effects. Before you leave the hospital or doctor's office, your health care professional will closely follow the effects of this medicine. However, some effects may continue, or may not be noticed until later.

Check with your medical doctor or dentist as soon as possible if any of the following side effects occur:
  More common
   Dizziness, light-headedness, or feeling faint; drowsiness; nausea or vomiting; unusual tiredness or weakness
  Less common or rare
   Blurred or double vision or other vision problems; confusion; constipation; convulsions (seizures); difficult or painful urination; mental depression; shortness of breath, trouble in breathing, tightness in the chest, or wheezing; skin rash, hives, or itching; unusual excitement

Other side effects not listed above may also occur in some patients. If you notice any other effects, check with your doctor.

Additional Information

Once a medicine has been approved for marketing for a certain use, experience may show that it is also useful for other medical problems. Although not specifically included in product labeling, fentanyl by injection is used in certain pediatric patients with the following medical conditions:
- Pain, during surgery, neonatal

Other than the above information, there is no additional information relating to proper use, precautions, or side effects for these uses.

Revised: 02/14/2001

NATAMYCIN   Ophthalmic†

Commonly used brand name(s):
In the U.S.—
  Natacyn
Another commonly used name is pimaricin.

†Not commercially available in Canada.

Description

Natamycin (na-ta-MYE-sin) belongs to the group of medicines called antifungals. It is used to treat some types of fungus infections of the eye.

Natamycin is available only with your doctor's prescription, in the following dosage form:

Ophthalmic
- Ophthalmic suspension (eye drops) (U.S.)

Before Using This Medicine

In deciding to use a medicine, the risks of taking the medicine must be weighed against the good it will do. This is a decision you and your doctor will make. For ophthalmic natamycin, the following should be considered:

Allergies—Tell your doctor if you have ever had any unusual or allergic reaction to natamycin. Also tell your health care professional if you are allergic to any other substances, such as preservatives.

Pregnancy—Studies on effects in pregnancy have not been done in either humans or animals.

Breast-feeding—It is not known whether natamycin passes into breast milk. Although most medicines pass into breast milk in small amounts, many of them may be used safely while breast-feeding. Mothers who are using this medicine and who wish to breast-feed should discuss this with their doctor.

Children—Studies on this medicine have been done only in adult patients, and there is no specific information comparing use of natamycin in children with use in other age groups.

Older adults—Many medicines have not been studied specifically in older people. Therefore, it may not be known whether they work exactly the same way they do in younger adults. Although there is no specific information comparing use of natamycin in the elderly with use in other age groups, this medicine is not expected to cause different side effects or problems in older people than it does in younger adults.

Proper Use of This Medicine

The bottle is only partially full to provide proper drop control. To use:
- First, wash your hands. Tilt the head back and, pressing your finger gently on the skin just beneath the lower eyelid, pull the lower eyelid away from the eye to make a space. Drop the medicine into this space. Let go of the eyelid and gently close the eyes. Do not blink. Keep the eyes closed for 1 or 2 minutes to allow the medicine to come into contact with the infection.
- If you think you did not get the drop of medicine into your eye properly, use another drop.
- To keep the medicine as germ-free as possible, do not touch the applicator tip to any surface (including the eye). Also, keep the container tightly closed.

To help clear up your eye infection completely, *keep using this medicine for the full time of treatment*, even if your condition has improved. *Do not miss any doses.*

Dosing—The dose of ophthalmic natamycin will be different for different patients. *Follow your doctor's orders or the directions on the label.* The following information includes only the average doses of ophthalmic natamycin. *If your dose is different, do not change it* unless your doctor tells you to do so.
- For fungus infection of the eye:
  —For *eye drops* dosage form:
  - Adults—Use one drop in the eye every four to six hours. For more serious infections, your doctor may tell you to use one drop in the eye every one or two hours for three or four days, then one drop six to eight times a day thereafter.
  - Children—Use and dose must be determined by your doctor.

Missed dose—If you miss a dose of this medicine, apply it as soon as possible. Then go back to your regular dosing schedule.

Storage—To store this medicine:
- Keep out of the reach of children.
- Store away from heat and direct light.
- Keep the medicine from freezing.
- Do not keep outdated medicine or medicine no longer needed. Be sure that any discarded medicine is out of the reach of children.

Precautions While Using This Medicine

Your doctor should check your progress at regular visits. For some eye infections, these visits may be as often as several times a week.

If your symptoms do not improve within 7 to 10 days, or if they become worse, check with your doctor.

Side Effects of This Medicine

Along with its needed effects, a medicine may cause some unwanted effects. Although not all of these side effects may occur, if they do occur they may need medical attention.

Check with your doctor as soon as possible if any of the following side effects occur:

Eye irritation, redness, or swelling not present before use of this medicine

Other side effects not listed above may also occur in some patients. If you notice any other effects, check with your doctor.

Revised: 05/16/94

NATEGLINIDE   Systemic—INTRODUCTORY VERSION

Commonly used brand name(s):

In the U.S.—
Starlix

Description

Nateglinide (na-TEG-li-nide) is used to treat a type of diabetes mellitus (sugar diabetes) called type 2 diabetes. With this type of diabetes, insulin produced by the pancreas is not able to get sugar into the cells of the body where it can work properly. Using nateglinide alone, or with another type of oral antidiabetic medicine called metformin, will help to lower blood sugar when it is too high and help restore the way you use food to make energy.

Many people can control type 2 diabetes with diet alone or with diet and exercise. Following a specially planned diet and exercising will always be important when you have diabetes, even when you are taking medicines. To work properly, the amount of nateglinide you take must be balanced against the amount and type of food you eat and the amount of exercise you do. If you change your diet, your exercise, or both, you will want to test your blood sugar to find out if it is too low. Your health care professional will teach you what to do if this happens.

Nateglinide does not help patients who have insulin-dependent or type 1 diabetes because they cannot produce insulin from their pancreas gland. Their blood glucose is best controlled by insulin injections.

Nateglinide does not help patients who have already been treated with other antidiabetic medicines for a long time.

Nateglinide may be used together with metformin, but should not take the place of metformin.

Nateglinide is available only with your doctor's prescription, in the following dosage form:

Oral
- Tablets (U.S.)

Before Using This Medicine

In deciding to use a medicine, the risks of taking the medicine must be weighed against the good it will do. This is a decision you and your doctor will make. For nateglinide, the following should be considered:

Allergies—Tell your doctor if you have ever had any unusual or allergic reaction to nateglinide. Also tell your health care professional if you are allergic to any other substances, such as foods, preservatives, or dyes.

Pregnancy—Nateglinide has not been studied in pregnant women. However, studies in animals have shown that nateglinide causes birth defects. Before taking this medicine, make sure your doctor knows if you are pregnant or if you may become pregnant.

Breast-feeding—It is not known whether nateglinide passes into human breast milk. However, nateglinide is not recommended during breast-feeding, because it may cause unwanted effects in nursing babies

Children—Studies on this medicine have been done only in adult patients, and there is no specific information comparing use of nateglinide in children with use in other age groups.

Older adults—This medicine has been tested and has not been shown to cause different side effects or problems in older people than it does in younger adults. However, the first signs of low blood sugar are not easily seen or do not occur at all in older patients. This may increase the chance of low blood sugar developing during treatment.

Other medicines—Although certain medicines should not be used together at all, in other cases two different medicines may be used together even if an interaction might occur. In these cases, your doctor may want to change the dose, or other precautions may be necessary. When you are taking nateglinide, it is especially important that your health care professional know if you are taking any of the following:

- Beta-adrenergic blocking agents (acebutolol [e.g., Sectral], atenolol [e.g., Tenormin], betaxolol [e.g., Kerlone], bisoprolol [e.g., Zebeta], carteolol [e.g., Cartrol], labetalol [e.g., Trandate], metoprolol [e.g., Lopressor], nadolol [e.g., Corgard], oxprenolol [e.g., Trasicor], penbutolol [e.g., Levatol], pindolol [e.g., Visken], propranolol [e.g., Inderal], sotalol [e.g., Betapace], timolol [e.g., Blocadren])—These medicines can hide some of the symptoms of low blood sugar; because of this, a person with

diabetes might not recognize that he or she has low blood sugar and might not take immediate steps to treat it

Other medical problems—The presence of other medical problems may affect the use of nateglinide. Make sure you tell your doctor if you have any other medical problems, especially:

- Ketones in the blood (diabetic ketoacidosis) or
- Type 1 (insulin-dependent) diabetes—Insulin is needed to control diabetes in patients with these conditions
- Nervous system disorder (autonomic neuropathy)—Patients with this condition might not be able to detect the symptoms of low blood sugar and might not take immediate steps to treat it

Proper Use of This Medicine

Follow carefully the special meal plan that your doctor gave you. This is the most important part of controlling your condition and is necessary if the medicine is to work properly. Also, exercise regularly and test for sugar in your blood or urine as directed.

This medicine is usually taken between 1 and 30 minutes before a meal. *If you skip the meal, also skip the scheduled dose of nateglinide.*

Use this medicine as directed even if you feel well and do not notice any signs of high blood sugar. Remember that this medicine will not cure your diabetes, but it does help to control it. You must to continue to take it as directed if you expect to lower your blood sugar and keep it low. You may have to take an antidiabetic medicine for the rest of your life. If high blood sugar is not treated, it can cause serious problems, such as blood vessel disease, eye disease, heart failure, or kidney disease.

Dosing—The dose of nateglinide will be different for different patients. *Follow your doctor's orders or the directions on the label.* The following information includes only the average doses of nateglinide. *If your dose is different, do not change it* unless your doctor tells you to do so.

The number of tablets that you take depends on the strength of the medicine. Also, *the number of doses you take each day, the time allowed between doses, and the length of time you take the medicine depend on the amount of sugar in your blood or urine.*

- For *oral* dosage form (tablets):
  - For type 2 diabetes:
    - Adults—60 to 120 mg three times a day taken between one and thirty minutes before meals.
    - Children—Use and dose must be determined by your doctor.

Missed dose—If you miss a dose of this medicine, take it as soon as possible. However, if it is almost time for your next dose, skip the missed dose and go back to your regular dosing schedule. Do not double doses.

Storage—To store this medicine:
- Keep out of the reach of children.
- Do not store in the bathroom, near the kitchen sink, or in other damp places. Heat or moisture may cause the medicine to break down.
- Keep the medicine from freezing. Do not refrigerate.
- Do not keep outdated medicine or medicine no longer needed. Ask your health care professional how you should dispose of any medicine you do not use. Be sure

that any discarded medicine is out of the reach of children.

Precautions While Using This Medicine

Your doctor will want to check your progress at regular visits, especially during the first few weeks that you take this medicine.

It is very important to follow carefully any instructions from your health care team about:

- Alcohol—Drinking alcohol may cause severe low blood sugar. Discuss this with your health care team.
- Other medicines—Do not take other medicines during the time you are taking nateglinide unless they have been discussed with your doctor. This especially includes nonprescription medicines for appetite control, asthma, colds, cough, hay fever, pain relief, or sinus problems.
- Counseling—Other family members need to learn how to prevent side effects or help with side effects if they occur. Also, patients with diabetes may need special counseling about diabetes medicine dosing changes that might occur because of lifestyle changes, such as changes in exercise and diet. Furthermore, counseling on contraception and pregnancy may be needed because of the problems that can occur in patients with diabetes during pregnancy.
- Travel—Keep a recent prescription and your medical history with you. Be prepared for an emergency as you would normally. Make allowances for changing time zones and keep your meal times as close as possible to your usual meal times.

In case of emergency—There may be a time when you need emergency help for a problem caused by your diabetes. You need to be prepared for these emergencies. It is a good idea to wear a medical identification (ID) bracelet or neck chain at all times. Also, carry an ID card in your wallet or purse that says that you have diabetes and a list of all of your medicines.

Too much nateglinide can cause low blood sugar (hypoglycemia). Low blood sugar also can occur if you use nateglinide with another antidiabetic medicine, delay or miss a meal or snack, exercise more than usual, drink alcohol, or cannot eat because of nausea or vomiting. *Symptoms of low blood sugar must be treated before they lead to unconsciousness (passing out).* Different people may feel different symptoms of low blood sugar. *It is important that you learn which symptoms of low blood sugar you usually have so that you can treat it quickly.*

Symptoms of low blood sugar include anxiety; behavior change similar to being drunk; blurred vision; cold sweats; confusion; cool, pale skin; difficulty in thinking; drowsiness; excessive hunger; fast heartbeat; headache (continuing); nausea; nervousness; nightmares; restless sleep; shakiness; slurred speech; or unusual tiredness or weakness.

If symptoms of low blood sugar occur, eat glucose tablets or gel, corn syrup, honey, or sugar cubes; or drink fruit juice, nondiet soft drink, or sugar dissolved in water to relieve the symptoms. Also, check your blood for low blood sugar. *Get to a doctor or a hospital right away if the symptoms do not improve. Someone should call for emergency help immediately if severe symptoms such as convulsions (seizures) or unconsciousness occur.* Food or drink should not be forced because the patient could choke from not swallowing correctly.

Hyperglycemia (high blood sugar) may occur if you do not take enough or skip a dose of your antidiabetic medicine, overeat or do not follow your meal plan, have a fever or infection, or do not exercise as much as usual.

Symptoms of high blood sugar include blurred vision; drowsiness; dry mouth; flushed, dry skin; fruit-like breath odor; increased urination; ketones in urine; loss of appetite; stomachache, nausea, or vomiting; tiredness; troubled breathing (rapid and deep); unconsciousness; or unusual thirst.

If symptoms of high blood sugar occur, *check your blood sugar level and then call your doctor for instructions.*

Side Effects of This Medicine

Along with its needed effects, a medicine may cause some unwanted effects. Although not all of these side effects may occur, if they do occur they may need medical attention.

Check with your doctor immediately if any of the following side effects occur:

Less common
Convulsions (seizures); unconsciousness

Check with your doctor as soon as possible if any of the following side effects occur:

Less common
Low blood sugar, including anxious feeling, behavior change similar to being drunk, blurred vision, cold sweats, confusion, cool pale skin, difficulty in thinking, drowsiness, excessive hunger, fast heartbeat, headache, nausea, nervousness, nightmares, restless sleep, shakiness, slurred speech, or unusual tiredness or weakness

Other side effects may occur that usually do not need medical attention. These side effects may go away during treatment as your body adjusts to the medicine. However, check with your doctor if any of the following side effects continue or are bothersome.

More common
Cough; runny or stuffy nose; sore throat

Less common
Abdominal or stomach pain; back pain; chills; dizziness; pain in joints or muscles; sneezing; swelling in joints

Other side effects not listed above may also occur in some patients. If you notice any other effects, check with your doctor.

Developed: 05/29/2001

NEDOCROMIL   Inhalation

Commonly used brand name(s):

In the U.S.—
Tilade

In Canada—
Tilade

Description

Nedocromil (ne-DOK-roe-mil) is used to prevent the symptoms of asthma. When it is used regularly, nedocromil lessens the number and severity of asthma attacks by reducing inflammation in the lungs. Nedocromil is also used just before exposure to conditions or substances (for example, allergens, chemicals, cold air, or air pollutants) that cause reactions, to prevent bronchospasm (wheezing or difficulty in breathing). In addition, nedocromil is used to prevent bronchospasm following exercise. This medicine will not help an asthma or bronchospasm attack that has already started.

Nedocromil may be used alone or with other asthma medicines, such as bronchodilators (medicines that open up narrowed breathing passages) and corticosteroids (cortisone-like medicines).

Nedocromil works by acting on certain inflammatory cells in the lungs to prevent them from releasing substances that cause asthma symptoms and/or bronchospasm.

This medicine is available only with your doctor's prescription, in the following dosage form:

Inhalation
  • Inhalation aerosol (U.S. and Canada)

Before Using This Medicine

In deciding to use a medicine, the risks of using the medicine must be weighed against the good it will do. This is a decision you and your doctor will make. For nedocromil, the following should be considered:

Allergies—Tell your doctor if you have ever had any unusual or allergic reaction to nedocromil or to any other inhalation aerosol medicine.

Pregnancy—Nedocromil has not been studied in pregnant women. However, nedocromil has not been shown to cause birth defects or other problems in animal studies.

Breast-feeding—It is not known whether nedocromil passes into breast milk. Although most medicines pass into breast milk in small amounts, many of them may be used safely while breast-feeding. Mothers who are using this medicine and who wish to breast-feed should discuss this with their doctor.

Children—Nedocromil has been tested in children 6 years of age and older. In effective doses, it is not expected to cause different side effects or problems in children than it does in adults.

Older adults—Many medicines have not been studied specifically in older people. Therefore, it may not be known whether they work the same way they do in younger adults. Although there is no specific information comparing use of nedocromil in the elderly with use in other age groups, it is not expected to cause different side effects or problems in older people than it does in younger adults.

Proper Use of This Medicine

Nedocromil is used to help prevent symptoms of asthma or bronchospasm (wheezing or difficulty in breathing). When this medicine is used regularly, it decreases the number and severity of asthma attacks. Nedocromil will not relieve an asthma or bronchospasm attack that has already started.

Nedocromil inhalation aerosol usually comes with patient directions. Read them carefully before using this medicine. If you do not understand the directions or if you are not sure how to use the inhaler, ask your health care professional to show you what to do. Also, ask your health care professional to check regularly how you use the inhaler to make sure you are using it properly.

The nedocromil aerosol canister provides 104 inhalations for the inhaler that is available in the U.S. or 112 inhalations for the Canadian inhaler. You should keep a record of the number of inhalations you use so you will know when the canister is almost empty. This canister, unlike other aerosol canisters, cannot be floated in water to test its fullness.

When you use the inhaler for the first time, or if you have not used it for more than seven days, the inhaler may not deliver the right amount of medicine with the first puff. Therefore, before using the inhaler, prime it to make sure it provides the correct dose.

To prime the inhaler:
  • Insert the metal canister firmly into the clean mouthpiece according to the manufacturer's instructions. Check to make sure the canister is placed properly into the mouthpiece.
  • Take the cover off the mouthpiece and shake the inhaler well.
  • Hold the canister well away from you against a light background, and press the top of the canister, spraying the medicine one time into the air. Repeat this two more times for a total of three sprays. If the inhaler is working properly, a fine mist will be sprayed from the mouthpiece.

To use the inhaler:
  • Using your thumb and one or two fingers, hold the inhaler upright with the mouthpiece end down and pointing toward you.
  • Take the cover off the mouthpiece. Check the mouthpiece for any foreign objects. Do not use the inhaler with any other mouthpieces.
  • Gently shake the inhaler three or four times.
  • Hold the mouthpiece away from your mouth and breathe out slowly and completely to the end of a normal breath.
  • Use the inhalation method recommended by your doctor.
    —Open-mouth method: Place the mouthpiece about 1 to 2 inches (2 fingerwidths) in front of your widely opened mouth. Make sure the inhaler is aimed into your mouth so the spray does not hit the roof of your mouth or your tongue. Close your eyes just before spraying to keep the spray out of your eyes.
    —Closed-mouth method: Place the mouthpiece in your mouth between your teeth and over your tongue with your lips closed tightly around it. Make sure your tongue or teeth are not blocking the opening.
  • Tilt your head back a little. Start to breathe in slowly and deeply through your mouth and, at the same time, press the top of the canister once to get one puff of medicine. Continue to breathe in slowly for 3 to 4 seconds until you have taken a full breath. It is important to press down on the canister and breathe in slowly at the same time so the medicine is pulled into your lungs. This step may be difficult at first. If you are using the closed-mouth method and you see a fine mist coming from your mouth or nose, the inhaler is not being used correctly.
  • Hold your breath as long as you can for up to 10 seconds (count slowly to 10). This gives the medicine time to get into your airways and lungs.
  • Take the mouthpiece away from your mouth and breathe out slowly.
  • If your doctor has told you to inhale more than one puff of medicine at each dose, wait 1 minute between puffs. Then, gently shake the inhaler again, and take the second puff following exactly the same steps you used for the first puff. Breathe in only one puff at a time.

- If your doctor has told you to use an inhaled bronchodilator before using nedocromil, you should wait at least 2 minutes after using the bronchodilator before using nedocromil. This allows the nedocromil to get deeper into your lungs.
- When you are finished, wipe off the mouthpiece and replace the cover to keep the mouthpiece clean and free of foreign objects.
- Keep track of the number of sprays you have used by noting each one on the chart provided with the inhaler. The inhaler should be discarded once 104 sprays have been used. Even though the inhaler may not be empty after 104 sprays, the dose may be inaccurate so you may not receive the correct amount of medicine.

Your doctor may want you to use a spacer device with the inhaler. A spacer makes the inhaler easier to use. It allows more of the medicine to reach your lungs and helps make sure that less of it stays in your mouth and throat.

To use a spacer device with the inhaler:

- Attach the spacer to the inhaler according to the manufacturer's directions. There are different types of spacers available, but the method of breathing remains the same with most spacers.
- Gently shake the inhaler and spacer three or four times.
- Hold the mouthpiece of the spacer away from your mouth and breathe out slowly to the end of a normal breath.
- Place the mouthpiece into your mouth between your teeth and over your tongue with your lips closed around it.
- Press down on the canister top once to release one puff of medicine into the spacer. Then, within one or two seconds, begin to breathe in slowly and deeply through your mouth for 5 to 10 seconds. Count the seconds while inhaling. Do not breathe in through your nose.
- Hold your breath as long as you can for up to 10 seconds (count slowly to ten).
- Breathe out slowly. Do not remove the mouthpiece from your mouth. Breathe in and out slowly two or three times to make sure the spacer device is emptied.
- If your doctor has told you to take more than one puff of medicine at each dose, wait a minute between puffs. Then, gently shake the inhaler and spacer again and take the second puff, following exactly the same steps you used for the first puff.
- When you have finished, remove the spacer device from the inhaler and replace the cover of the mouthpiece.

To clean the inhaler:

- Clean the inhaler often to prevent build-up of medicine and blocking of the mouthpiece. The mouthpiece can be washed every day and should be washed at least twice a week.
- Remove the metal canister from the inhaler and set it aside. Do not get the canister wet.
- Wash the mouthpiece in hot water.
- Shake off the excess water and let the mouthpiece air dry completely before replacing the metal canister and cover.

For patients using nedocromil regularly (for example, every day):

- *In order for nedocromil to work properly, it must be inhaled every day in regularly spaced doses as ordered by your doctor.*

- Usually about 2 to 4 weeks may pass before you begin to feel the full effects of this medicine.

Missed dose—If you are using nedocromil regularly and you miss a dose of this medicine, take it as soon as possible. Then take any remaining doses for that day at regularly spaced times.

Dosing—The dose of nedocromil will be different for different patients. *Follow your doctor's orders or the directions on the label. Do not use more of it and do not use it more often than recommended on the label, unless otherwise directed by your doctor.* The following information includes only the average doses of nedocromil. *If your dose is different, do not change it* unless your doctor tells you to do so:

- For *inhalation* dosage form (inhalation aerosol):
  —For prevention of asthma symptoms:
  - Adults and children 6 years of age or older—3.5 or 4 milligrams (mg) (2 puffs) two to four times a day at regularly spaced times.
  - Children up to 6 years of age—Use and dose must be determined by the doctor.
  —For prevention of bronchospasm caused by exercise or a substance:
  - Adults and children 12 years of age or older—4 mg (2 puffs) as a single dose up to thirty minutes before exercise or exposure to any condition or substance that may cause an attack.
  - Children up to 12 years of age—Use and dose must be determined by the doctor.

Storage—To store this medicine:

- Keep out of the reach of children.
- Store away from heat and direct sunlight.
- Keep the medicine from freezing.
- Do not puncture, break, or burn the aerosol container, even if it is empty.
- Do not keep outdated medicine or medicine no longer needed. Be sure that any discarded medicine is out of the reach of children.
- Always keep the dust cover on the mouthpiece when the inhaler is not in use.
- Store container at room temperature before use for best results.

Precautions While Using This Medicine

If your symptoms do not improve within 2 to 4 weeks, check with your doctor. Also, check with your doctor if your condition becomes worse.

You may also be taking a corticosteroid or a bronchodilator for asthma along with this medicine. *Do not stop taking the corticosteroid or bronchodilator even if your asthma seems better, unless you are told to do so by your doctor.*

Throat irritation and/or an unpleasant taste may occur after you use this medicine. Gargling and rinsing the mouth after each dose may help prevent these effects.

Side Effects of This Medicine

Along with its needed effects, a medicine may cause some unwanted effects. Although not all of these side effects may occur, if they do occur they may need medical attention.

Check with your doctor as soon as possible if any of the following side effects occur:

Less common
Abdominal pain; increased wheezing, tightness in chest, or difficulty in breathing

Rare
Pain, stiffness, or swelling of joints; signs of infection, such as fever, sore throat, body aches, or chills

Other side effects may occur that usually do not need medical attention. These side effects may go away during treatment as your body adjusts to the medicine. However, check with your doctor if any of the following side effects continue or are bothersome:

Less common or rare
Cough; headache; nausea or vomiting; runny or stuffy nose; sensation of warmth; throat irritation; tremor

After you use nedocromil inhalation aerosol, you may notice an unpleasant taste. This may be expected and will usually go away after a while.

Other side effects not listed above may also occur in some patients. If you notice any other effects, check with your doctor.

Revised: 08/13/98

NEDOCROMIL   Ophthalmic†

Commonly used brand name(s):

In the U.S.—
Alocril

†Not commercially available in Canada.

Description

Nedocromil (ne-DOK-roe-mil) is used to treat the itching in your eyes that happens with allergies.

Nedocromil works by acting on certain inflammatory cells to prevent them from releasing substances that cause allergic symptom.

This medicine is available only with your doctor's prescription, in the following dosage forms:

Topical
• Ophthalmic solution (U.S.)

Before Using This Medicine

In deciding to use a medicine, the risks of using the medicine must be weighed against the good it will do. This is a decision you and your doctor will make. For nedocromil, the following should be considered:

Allergies—Tell your doctor if you have ever had any unusual or allergic reaction to nedocromil. Also tell your doctor and pharmacist if you are allergic to any other substances.

Pregnancy—Nedocromil has not been studied in pregnant women. However, nedocromil has not been shown to cause birth defects or other problems in animal studies.

Breast-feeding—It is not known whether nedocromil passes into breast milk. Although most medicines pass into breast milk in small amounts, many of them may be used safely while breast-feeding. Mothers who are using this med-icine and who wish to breast-feed should discuss this with their doctor.

Children—Nedocromil has been tested in children 3 years of age and older. In effective doses, it is not expected to cause different side effects or problems in children than it does in adults.

Older adults—No differences in safety or effectiveness have been observed between elderly and younger patients.

Proper Use of This Medicine

Dosing—*Nedocromil is used to help treat the itching that occurs with allergic conjunctivitis.* To use the ophthalmic solution *(eye drops)* form of this medicine:

• First, wash your hands. Tilt the head back and, pressing your finger gently on the skin just beneath the lower eyelid, pull the lower eyelid away from the eye to make a space. Drop the medicine into this space. Let go of the eyelid and gently close the eyes. Blink a few times to make sure the eye is covered with the medicine.
• To keep the medicine as germ-free as possible, do not touch the applicator tip to any surface (including the eye). Also, keep the container tightly closed.

Missed dose—If you miss a dose of this medicine, take it as soon as possible. However, if it is almost time for your next dose, skip the missed dose and go back to your regular dosing schedule. Do not double doses.

Storage—To store this medicine:

• Keep out of the reach of children.
• Do not keep outdated medicine or medicine no longer needed. Ask your health care professional how you should dispose of any medicine you do not use. Be sure that any discarded medicine is out of the reach of children.

Precautions While Using This Medicine

You should avoid wearing your contact lenses while your eyes are itching from your allergies.

Side Effects of This Medicine

The side effects that may occur usually do not need medical attention. These side effects may go away during treatment as your body adjusts to the medicine. However, check with your doctor if any of the following side effects continue or are bothersome.

More common
Blurred vision; change in color vision; cough; difficulty breathing; noisy breathing; shortness of breath, tightness in chest, or wheezing; difficulty seeing at night; dry or itching eyes; headache; increased sensitivity of eyes to sunlight; redness, pain, or swelling of eye, eyelid, or inner lining of the eye; runny or stuffy nose; sneezing; stinging, irritation or burning of your eyes; unpleasant taste; unusual watering of eyes or discharge

Other side effects not listed above may also occur in some patients. If you notice any other effects, check with your doctor.

Developed: 03/28/2000
Revised: 08/07/2000

NEFAZODONE   Systemic

Commonly used brand name(s):

In the U.S.—
Serzone

In Canada—
Serzone

Description

Nefazodone (nef-AY-zoe-done) is used to treat mental depression.

This medicine is available only with your doctor's prescription, in the following dosage form:

Oral
- Tablets (U.S. and Canada)

Before Using This Medicine

In deciding to use a medicine, the risks of taking the medicine must be weighed against the good it will do. This is a decision you and your doctor will make. For nefazodone, the following should be considered:

Allergies—Tell your doctor if you have ever had any unusual or allergic reaction to nefazodone or trazodone. Also tell your health care professional if you are allergic to any other substances, such as foods, preservatives, or dyes.

Pregnancy—Studies have not been done in pregnant women. However, studies in animals have shown that nefazodone causes a decrease in the number of successful pregnancies, as well as a decrease in the weight of offspring, when given in doses several times higher than the human dose. Before taking this medicine, make sure your doctor knows if you are pregnant or if you may become pregnant.

Breast-feeding—It is not known whether nefazodone passes into human breast milk. Mothers who are using this medicine and who wish to breast-feed should discuss this with their doctor.

Children—Studies on nefazodone have been done only in adult patients, and there is no specific information comparing use of this medicine in children up to 18 years of age with use in other age groups.

Older adults—The relationship of age to the effects of nefazodone has not been systematically studied in older people. However, blood levels of nefazodone have been found to be higher in older patients. An older adult may require a lower dose of nefazodone than a younger adult.

Other medicines—Although certain medicines should not be used together at all, in other cases two different medicines may be used together even if an interaction might occur. In these cases, your doctor may want to change the dose, or other precautions may be necessary. When you are taking nefazodone, it is especially important that your health care professional know if you are taking any of the following:

- Alprazolam (e.g., Xanax) or
- Triazolam (e.g., Halcion)—Use with nefazodone may result in increased blood levels of these medicines and, therefore, increased effects. Your doctor may want to reduce the dose of these medicines if they are used at the same time as nefazodone. An older adult should not receive both triazolam and nefazodone

- Astemizole (e.g., Hismanal) or
- Cisapride (e.g., Propulsid) or

- Terfenadine (e.g., Seldane)—*Do not use these medicines with nefazodone* or you may develop a very serious change in heart rhythm

- Monoamine oxidase (MAO) inhibitors (furazolidone [e.g., Furoxone], phenelzine [e.g., Nardil], procarbazine [e.g., Matulane], selegiline [e.g., Eldepryl], tranylcypromine [e.g., Parnate])—*Do not take nefazodone while you are taking an MAO inhibitor* or you may develop confusion, agitation, restlessness, stomach or intestinal problems, sudden high body temperature, extremely high blood pressure, and/or severe convulsions; at least 14 days should pass between stopping treatment with an MAO inhibitor and starting treatment with nefazodone and at least 7 days should pass between stopping treatment with nefazodone and starting treatment with an MAO inhibitor

Other medical problems—The presence of other medical problems may affect the use of nefazodone. Make sure you tell your doctor if you have any other medical problems, especially:

- Convulsions (seizures) (history of)—The risk of seizures may be increased

- Dehydration or
- Hypovolemia (low blood volume)—May increase the chance that low blood pressure (hypotension) will occur

- Heart disease or
- Stroke (or history of)—Nefazodone may make these conditions worse by causing low blood pressure (hypotension)

- Liver disease—Use of nefazodone may result in increased blood levels of the medicine; your doctor may want to reduce your dose of nefazodone

- Mania (a type of mental illness) (history of)—Nefazodone may cause this problem to recur

Proper Use of This Medicine

Take this medicine only as directed by your doctor. Do not take more or less of it and do not take it more or less often than your doctor ordered.

Sometimes this medicine must be taken for several weeks before you begin to feel better.

Dosing—The dose of nefazodone will be different for different patients. *Follow your doctor's orders or the directions on the label*. The following information includes only the average doses of nefazodone. *If your dose is different, do not change it* unless your doctor tells you to do so.

The number of tablets that you take depends on the strength of the medicine.

- For *oral* dosage form (tablets):
  —For mental depression:
  - Adults (18 years of age and older)—To start, 100 to 200 milligrams (mg) a day, divided into two doses. Your doctor may increase the dose if needed.
  - Older adults—To start, 100 mg a day, divided into two doses. Your doctor may increase the dose if needed.
  - Children up to 18 years of age—Use and dose must be determined by the doctor.

Missed dose—If you miss a dose of this medicine, take it as soon as possible. However, if it is almost time for your

next dose, skip the missed dose and go back to your regular dosing schedule. Do not double doses.

Storage—To store this medicine:

- Keep out of the reach of children.
- Store away from heat and direct light.
- Do not store in the bathroom, near the kitchen sink, or in other damp places. Heat or moisture may cause the medicine to break down.
- Do not keep outdated medicine or medicine no longer needed. Be sure that any discarded medicine is out of the reach of children.

Precautions While Using This Medicine

It is important that your doctor check your progress at regular visits to allow dosage adjustments and to help reduce side effects.

Do not take astemizole, cisapride, or terfenadine while you are taking nefazodone. If you do, you may develop a very serious change in the rhythm of your heartbeat.

Do not take a monoamine oxidase (MAO) inhibitor (furazolidone, phenelzine, procarbazine, selegiline, tranylcypromine) while you are taking or less than 7 days after taking nefazodone. Do not take nefazodone less than 14 days after taking an MAO inhibitor. If you do, you may develop convulsions (seizures), extremely high fever, or other serious unwanted effects.

This medicine may add to the effects of alcohol and other central nervous system (CNS) depressants (medicines that make you drowsy or less alert). Some examples of CNS depressants are antihistamines or medicine for hay fever, other allergies, or colds; sedatives, tranquilizers, or sleeping medicine; prescription pain medicine or narcotics; barbiturates; medicine for seizures; muscle relaxants; or anesthetics, including some dental anesthetics. *Check with your doctor before taking any of the above while you are using this medicine.*

This medicine may cause some people to become dizzy or drowsy, or to have blurred vision or other vision changes. *Make sure you know how you react to this medicine before you drive, use machines, or do other jobs that require you to be alert and able to see well.*

Dizziness, lightheadedness, or fainting may occur, especially when you get up from a lying or sitting position. Getting up slowly may help. If this problem continues or gets worse, check with your doctor.

This medicine may cause dryness of the mouth. For temporary relief, use sugarless gum or candy, melt bits of ice in your mouth, or use a saliva substitute. *However, if your mouth feels dry for more than 2 weeks, check with your medical doctor or dentist.* Continuing dryness of the mouth may increase the chance of dental disease, including tooth decay, gum disease, and fungus infections.

Side Effects of This Medicine

Along with its needed effects, a medicine may cause some unwanted effects. Although not all of these side effects may occur, if they do occur they may need medical attention.

Check with your doctor as soon as possible if any of the following side effects occur:

More common
    Blurred vision or other changes in vision; clumsiness or

unsteadiness; lightheadedness or fainting; ringing in the ears; skin rash or itching

Less common
    Diarrhea; eye pain; nausea; shortness of breath, tightness in chest, or wheezing; stomach pain; troubled breathing

Rare
    Asthma; bleeding from the rectum; bloody or black, tarry stools; change in sexual desire or performance; chest pain; double vision; dryness of eye; ear pain; fainting; fast heartbeat; fever, chills, or sore throat; hallucinations (seeing, hearing, or feeling things that are not there); hives; increased sense of hearing; increased sensitivity to sun; irritation or soreness of mouth; joint or muscle pain or stiffness; kidney stones; large pupils of eyes; lower back, side, or stomach pain; menstrual changes; mood or mental changes; nerve pain or twitching; pelvic pain; problems in speaking; problems with urination; prolonged, painful, inappropriate penile erection; red or irritated eyes; sensitivity of eyes to light; swelling of face; swollen glands; talking, feeling, and acting with excitement and activity you cannot control; unusual bleeding or bruising; unusual feeling of well-being; unusual tiredness or weakness; vomiting of blood or material that looks like coffee grounds

Other side effects may occur that usually do not need medical attention. These side effects may go away during treatment as your body adjusts to the medicine. However, check with your doctor if any of the following side effects continue or are bothersome:

More common
    Abnormal dreams; agitation; confusion; constipation; diarrhea; dizziness; drowsiness; dryness of mouth; flushing or feeling of warmth; headache; heartburn; increased appetite; increased cough; memory problems; nausea; swelling of arms or legs; tingling, burning, or prickly sensations; tremor; trouble in sleeping; vomiting

Less common or rare
    Breast pain; increased thirst; loss of strength or energy; muscle weakness

Other side effects not listed above may also occur in some patients. If you notice any other effects, check with your doctor.

Developed: 03/06/1998
Revised: 05/17/2001

NELFINAVIR   Systemic

Commonly used brand name(s):

In the U.S.—
    Viracept

Description

Nelfinavir (nel-FIN-a-veer) is used, usually in combination with other medicines, in the treatment of the infection caused by the human immunodeficiency virus (HIV). HIV is the virus that causes acquired immune deficiency syndrome (AIDS).

Nelfinavir will not cure or prevent HIV infection or AIDS; however, it helps keep HIV from reproducing and appears to slow down the destruction of the immune system. This may help delay the development of problems usually related to AIDS or HIV disease. Nelfinavir will not keep you from spreading HIV to other people. People who receive this medicine may continue to have other problems usually related to AIDS or HIV disease.

This medicine is available only with your doctor's prescription, in the following dosage forms:

Oral
- Oral powder (U.S.)
- Tablets (U.S.)

Before Using This Medicine

In deciding to use a medicine, the risks of taking the medicine must be weighed against the good it will do. This is a decision you and your doctor will make. For nelfinavir, the following should be considered:

Allergies—Tell your doctor if you have ever had any unusual or allergic reaction to nelfinavir. Also tell your health care professional if you are allergic to any other substances, such as foods, preservatives, or dyes.

Pregnancy—Studies have not been done in humans. However, nelfinavir has not been reported to cause birth defects or other problems in animal studies.

Breast-feeding—It is not known whether nelfinavir passes into breast milk. However, breast-feeding is usually not recommended in AIDS patients because of the risk of passing the AIDS virus on to the nursing infant.

Children—This medicine has been tested in children between 2 and 13 years of age and, in effective doses, has not been reported to cause different side effects or problems in children than it does in adults.

Older adults—Many medicines have not been studied specifically in older people. Therefore, it may not be known whether they work exactly the same way they do in younger adults. There is no specific information comparing use of nelfinavir in the elderly with use in other age groups.

Other medicines—Although certain medicines should not be used together at all, in other cases two different medicines may be used together even if an interaction might occur. In these cases, your doctor may want to change the dose, or other precautions may be necessary. When you are taking nelfinavir, it is especially important that your health care professional know if you are taking any of the following:
- Amiodarone (e.g., Cordarone) or
- Astemizole (e.g., Hismanal) or
- Cisapride (e.g., Propulsid) or
- Ergot medicines (dihydroergotamine [e.g., D.H.E. 45], ergoloid mesylates [e.g., Hydergine], ergonovine [e.g., Ergotrate], methylergonovine [e.g., Methergine], methysergide [e.g., Sansert]) or
- Midazolam (e.g., Versed) or
- Quinidine (e.g., Quinidex) or
- Terfenadine (e.g., Seldane) or
- Triazolam (e.g., Halcion)—There is a possibility that nelfinavir may interfere with the removal of these medicines from the body, which could lead to serious side effects
- Oral contraceptives (birth control pills)—Nelfinavir may cause these medicines to be less effective

- Rifabutin (e.g., Mycobutin)—Use of this medicine with nelfinavir may increase the amount of rifabutin and decrease the amount of nelfinavir in the body
- Rifampin (e.g., Rifadin)—Use of this medicine with nelfinavir may decrease the amount of nelfinavir in the body

Other medical problems—The presence of other medical problems may affect the use of nelfinavir. Make sure you tell your doctor if you have any other medical problems, especially:
- Liver disease—Effects of nelfinavir may be increased because of slower removal from the body
- Phenylketonuria (a metabolic problem)—The oral powder form of nelfinavir contains phenylalanine, which may not be broken down properly in people with this condition

Proper Use of This Medicine

Nelfinavir works best if it is taken with food.

Take this medicine exactly as directed by your doctor. Do not take it more often, and do not take it for a longer time than your doctor ordered. Also, do not stop taking this medicine without checking with your doctor first.

Keep taking nelfinavir for the full time of treatment, even if you begin to feel better.

This medicine works best when there is a constant amount in the blood. *To help keep the amount constant, do not miss any doses. Also, it is best to take the doses at evenly spaced times, day and night.* For example, if you are to take three doses a day, the doses should be spaced about 8 hours apart. If you need help in planning the best times to take your medicine, check with your health care professional.

Only take medicine that your doctor has prescribed specially for you. Do not share your medicine with others.

Dosing—The dose of nelfinavir will be different for different patients. *Follow your doctor's orders or the directions on the label.* The following information includes only the average doses of nelfinavir. *If your dose is different, do not change it* unless your doctor tells you to do so.
- For *oral* dosage form (oral powder):
  —For treatment of HIV infection:
    - Children 2 to 13 years of age—Dose is based on body weight and must be determined by your doctor. The usual dose is 20 to 30 milligrams (mg) per kilogram (kg) (9 to 13.6 mg per pound) of body weight three times a day with food.
    - Children less than 2 years of age—Use and dose must be determined by your doctor.
- For *oral* dosage form (tablets):
  —For treatment of HIV infection:
    - Adults and teenagers—750 mg three times a day with food.
    - Children 2 to 13 years of age—Dose is based on body weight and must be determined by your doctor. The usual dose is 20 to 30 mg per kg (9 to 13.6 mg per pound) of body weight three times a day with food.
    - Children less than 2 years of age—Use and dose must be determined by your doctor.

Missed dose—If you miss a dose of this medicine, take it as soon as you remember. However, if it is almost time for

your next dose, skip the missed dose and go back to your regular dosing schedule. Do not double doses.

Storage—To store this medicine:

- Keep out of the reach of children.
- Store away from heat and direct light.
- Do not store in the bathroom, near the kitchen sink, or in other damp places. Heat or moisture may cause the medicine to break down.
- Do not keep outdated medicine or medicine no longer needed. Be sure that any discarded medicine is out of the reach of children.

Precautions While Using This Medicine

Do not take any other medicines without checking with your doctor first. To do so may increase the chance of side effects from nelfinavir.

Nelvinavir should be taken at least 2 hours before or 1 hour after taking didanosine.

This medicine may decrease the effects of some oral contraceptives (birth control pills). *To avoid unwanted pregnancy, it is a good idea to use some additional contraceptive measures while being treated with nelfinavir.*

It is very important that your doctor check your progress at regular visits to make sure this medicine is working properly and check for unwanted effects, especially increases in blood sugar.

Side Effects of This Medicine

Along with its needed effects, a medicine may cause some unwanted effects. Although not all of these side effects may occur, if they do occur they may need medical attention.

Check with your doctor as soon as possible if any of the following side effects occur:

> Confusion; dehydration; dry or itchy skin; fatigue; fruity mouth odor; increased hunger; increased thirst; increased urination; nausea; vomiting; weight loss

Other side effects may occur that usually do not need medical attention. These side effects may go away during treatment as your body adjusts to the medicine. However, check with your doctor if any of the following side effects continue or are bothersome:

> *More common*
> Diarrhea
> *Less common*
> Intestinal gas; skin rash

Other side effects not listed above may also occur in some patients. If you notice any other effects, check with your doctor.

Developed: 08/05/98

NEOMYCIN   Topical†

Commonly used brand name(s):

In the U.S.—
Myciguent
Generic name product may be available.

In Canada—
Myciguent

†Not commercially available in Canada.

Description

Neomycin (nee-oh-MYE-sin) belongs to the family of medicines called antibiotics. Neomycin topical preparations are used to help prevent infections of the skin. This medicine may be used for other problems as determined by your doctor.

Neomycin topical preparations are available without a prescription; however, your doctor may have special instructions on the proper use of topical neomycin for your medical problem.

Topical neomycin is available in the following dosage forms:

> *Topical*
> - Cream (U.S.)
> - Ointment (U.S.)

Before Using This Medicine

In deciding to use a medicine, the risks of using the medicine must be weighed against the good it will do. This is a decision you and your doctor will make. For topical neomycin, the following should be considered:

Allergies—Tell your doctor if you have ever had any unusual or allergic reaction to this medicine or to any related antibiotic, such as amikacin (e.g., Amikin), gentamicin (e.g., Garamycin), kanamycin (e.g., Kantrex), neomycin by mouth or by injection (e.g., Mycifradin), netilmicin (e.g., Netromycin), streptomycin, or tobramycin (e.g., Nebcin). Also tell your health care professional if you are allergic to any other substances, such as preservatives or dyes.

Pregnancy—Neomycin topical preparations have not been shown to cause birth defects or other problems in humans.

Breast-feeding—Neomycin topical preparations have not been reported to cause problems in nursing babies.

Children—Studies on this medicine have been done only in adult patients, and there is no specific information comparing use of topical neomycin in children with use in other age groups.

Older adults—Many medicines have not been studied specifically in older people. Therefore, it may not be known whether they work exactly the same way they do in younger adults or if they cause different side effects or problems in older people. There is no specific information comparing use of topical neomycin in the elderly with use in other age groups.

Other medicines—Although certain medicines should not be used together at all, in other cases two different medicines may be used together even if an interaction might occur. In these cases, your doctor may want to change the dose, or other precautions may be necessary. Tell your health care professional if you are using any other topical prescription or nonprescription (over-the-counter [OTC]) medicine that is to be applied to the same area of the skin.

Proper Use of This Medicine

If you are using this medicine without a prescription, do not use it to treat deep wounds, puncture wounds, serious burns, or raw areas without first checking with your health care professional.

Do not use this medicine in the eyes.

Before applying this medicine, wash the affected area with soap and water, and dry thoroughly.

For patients using the *cream form* of this medicine:
- Apply a generous amount of cream to the affected area, and rub in gently until the cream disappears.

For patients using the *ointment form* of this medicine:
- Apply a generous amount of ointment to the affected area, and rub in gently.

After this medicine is applied, the treated area may be covered with a gauze dressing if desired.

To help clear up your infection completely, *keep using this medicine for the full time of treatment*, even if your symptoms have disappeared. *Do not miss any doses*.

Dosing—The dose of topical neomycin will be different for different patients. *Follow your doctor's orders or the directions on the label*. The following information includes only the average dose of topical neomycin. *If your dose is different, do not change it* unless your doctor tells you to do so.
- For *topical* dosage forms (cream or ointment):
  —For minor bacterial skin infections:
    - Adults and children—Apply to the affected area(s) of the skin one to three times a day.

Missed dose—If you miss a dose of this medicine, apply it as soon as possible. However, if it is almost time for your next dose, skip the missed dose and go back to your regular dosing schedule.

Storage—To store this medicine:
- Keep out of the reach of children.
- Store away from heat and direct light.
- Keep the medicine from freezing.
- Do not keep outdated medicine or medicine no longer needed. Be sure that any discarded medicine is out of the reach of children.

Precautions While Using This Medicine

If your skin problem does not improve within 1 week, or if it becomes worse, check with your health care professional.

Side Effects of This Medicine

Along with its needed effects, a medicine may cause some unwanted effects. Although not all of these side effects may occur, if they do occur they may need medical attention.

Check with your doctor immediately if any of the following side effects occur:
  More common
    Itching, rash, redness, swelling, or other sign of skin irritation not present before use of this medicine
  Rare
    Any loss of hearing

Other side effects not listed above may also occur in some patients. If you notice any other effects, check with your doctor.

Revised: 08/04/2000

NEOMYCIN AND POLYMYXIN B
Topical†

Commonly used brand name(s):

In the U.S.—
Neosporin Cream‡

‡In Canada, Neosporin cream also contains gramicidin.
†Not commercially available in Canada.

Description

Neomycin and polymyxin B (nee-oh-MYE-sin and pol-i-MIX-in bee) combination is used to prevent bacterial infections. It works by killing bacteria.

Neomycin and polymyxin B cream is applied to the skin to prevent minor bacterial skin infections. It may also be used for other problems as determined by your doctor.

This medicine is available without a prescription; however, your doctor may have special instructions on the proper use of this medicine for your medical problem.

Neomycin and polymyxin B combination is available in the following dosage form:
  Topical
  - Cream (U.S.)

Before Using This Medicine

If you are using this medicine without a prescription, carefully read and follow any precautions on the label. For neomycin and polymyxin B topical preparations, the following should be considered:

Allergies—Tell your doctor if you have ever had any unusual or allergic reaction to neomycin and polymyxin B combination or to any related antibiotic: Amikacin (e.g., Amikin), colistimethate (e.g., Coly-Mycin M), colistin (e.g., Coly-Mycin S), gentamicin (e.g., Garamycin), kanamycin (e.g., Kantrex), neomycin by mouth or by injection (e.g., Mycifradin), netilmicin (e.g., Netromycin), paromomycin (e.g., Humatin), polymyxin B by injection (e.g., Aerosporin), streptomycin, or tobramycin (e.g., Nebcin). Also, tell your health care professional if you are allergic to any other substances, such as preservatives or dyes.

Pregnancy—Neomycin and polymyxin B topical preparations have not been shown to cause birth defects or other problems in humans.

Breast-feeding—Neomycin and polymyxin B topical preparations have not been reported to cause problems in nursing babies.

Children—Although there is no specific information comparing use of neomycin and polymyxin B combination in children with use in other age groups, this medicine is not expected to cause different side effects or problems in children than it does in adults.

Older adults—Many medicines have not been studied specifically in older people. Therefore, it may not be known whether they work exactly the same way they do in younger adults or if they cause different side effects or problems in older people. There is no specific information comparing use of neomycin and polymyxin B combination in the elderly with use in other age groups.

Other medicines—Although certain medicines should not be used together at all, in other cases two different medicines may be used together even if an interaction might occur. In these cases, your doctor may want to change the dose, or other precautions may be necessary. Tell your health care professional if you are using any other topical prescription or nonprescription (over-the-counter [OTC]) medicine that is to be applied to the same area of the skin.

Proper Use of This Medicine

If you are using this medicine without a prescription, *do not use it to treat deep wounds, puncture wounds, animal bites, serious burns, or raw areas* without first checking with your health care professional.

Do not use this medicine in the eyes.

To use:

- Before applying this medicine, wash the affected area(s) with soap and water, and dry thoroughly.
- Apply a small amount of this medicine to the affected area(s) and rub in gently.
- After applying this medicine, the treated area(s) may be covered with a gauze dressing if desired.

Do not use this medicine for longer than 1 week or on large areas of the skin, unless otherwise directed by your doctor. To do so may increase the chance of side effects.

To help clear up your skin infection completely, *keep using this medicine for the full time of treatment*, even if your symptoms have disappeared. *Do not miss any doses.*

Dosing—The dose of neomycin and polymyxin B combination will be different for different patients. *Follow your doctor's orders or the directions on the label*. The following information includes only the average dose of neomycin and polymyxin B combination. *If your dose is different, do not change it* unless your doctor tells you to do so.

- For *topical* dosage form (cream):
    —For prevention of minor bacterial infections:
    - Adults and children 2 years of age and older— Apply to the affected area(s) of the skin one to three times a day.
    - Children up to 2 years of age—Use and dose must be determined by your doctor.

Missed dose—If you miss a dose of this medicine, apply it as soon as possible. However, if it is almost time for your next dose, skip the missed dose and go back to your regular dosing schedule.

Storage—To store this medicine:

- Keep out of the reach of children.
- Store away from heat and direct light.
- Keep the medicine from freezing.
- Do not keep outdated medicine or medicine no longer needed. Be sure that any discarded medicine is out of the reach of children.

Precautions While Using This Medicine

If your skin infection does not improve within 1 week, or if it becomes worse, check with your health care professional.

Side Effects of This Medicine

Along with its needed effects, a medicine may cause some unwanted effects. Although not all of these side effects may occur, if they do occur they may need medical attention.

Check with your doctor immediately if any of the following side effects occur:

More common

Itching, pain, skin rash, swelling, redness, or other sign of skin irritation not present before use of this medicine

Rare

Loss of hearing

Other side effects not listed above may also occur in some patients. If you notice any other effects, check with your doctor.

Revised: 06/09/94

NEOMYCIN, POLYMYXIN B, AND BACITRACIN   Ophthalmic

Commonly used brand name(s):

In the U.S.—

Ak-Spore Ophthalmic Ointment	Ocusporin
Neocidin Ophthalmic Ointment	Ocutricin Ophthalmic Ointment
Neosporin Ophthalmic Ointment	Ophthalmic
Neotal	Spectro-Sporin
Ocu-Spor-B	Triple Antibiotic

Generic name product may be available.

In Canada—

Neosporin Ophthalmic Ointment

Description

Neomycin, polymyxin B, and bacitracin (nee-oh-MYE-sin, pol-i-MIX-in bee, and bass-i-TRAY-sin) combination antibiotic medicine is used to treat infections of the eye.

Neomycin, polymyxin B, and bacitracin combination is available only with your doctor's prescription, in the following dosage form:

Ophthalmic

- Ophthalmic ointment (U.S. and Canada)

Before Using This Medicine

In deciding to use a medicine, the risks of using the medicine must be weighed against the good it will do. This is a decision you and your doctor will make. For neomycin, polymyxin B, and bacitracin ophthalmic combination, the following should be considered:

Allergies—Tell your doctor if you have ever had any unusual or allergic reaction to this medicine or to any related antibiotic, such as amikacin (e.g., Amikin), colistimethate (e.g., Coly-Mycin M), colistin (e.g., Coly-Mycin S), gentamicin (e.g., Garamycin), kanamycin (e.g., Kantrex), netilmicin (e.g., Netromycin), paromomycin (e.g., Humatin), streptomycin, or tobramycin (e.g., Nebcin). Also tell your health care professional if you are allergic to any other substances, such as preservatives or dyes.

Pregnancy—Neomycin, polymyxin B, and bacitracin ophthalmic combination has not been shown to cause birth defects or other problems in humans.

Breast-feeding—Neomycin, polymyxin B, and bacitracin ophthalmic combination has not been reported to cause problems in nursing babies.

Children—Studies on this medicine have been done only in adult patients, and there is no specific information comparing use of neomycin, polymyxin B, and bacitracin combination in children with use in other age groups.

Older adults—Many medicines have not been studied specifically in older people. Therefore, it may not be known whether they work exactly the same way they do in younger adults or if they cause different side effects or problems in older people. There is no specific information comparing use of neomycin, polymyxin B, and bacitracin combination in the elderly with use in other age groups.

Proper Use of This Medicine

To use:

- First, wash your hands. Tilt the head back and, pressing your finger gently on the skin just beneath the lower eyelid, pull the lower eyelid away from the eye to make a space. Squeeze a thin strip of ointment into this space. A 1-cm (approximately ⅓-inch) strip of ointment is usually enough, unless you have been told by your doctor to use a different amount. Let go of the eyelid and gently close the eyes. Keep the eyes closed for 1 or 2 minutes to allow the medicine to come into contact with the infection.
- To keep the medicine as germ-free as possible, do not touch the applicator tip to any surface (including the eye). After using neomycin, polymyxin B, and bacitracin eye ointment, wipe the tip of the ointment tube with a clean tissue and keep the tube tightly closed.

To help clear up your infection completely, *keep using this medicine for the full time of treatment*, even if your symptoms have disappeared. *Do not miss any doses.*

Dosing—The dose of neomycin, polymyxin B, and bacitracin ophthalmic combination will be different for different patients. *Follow your doctor's orders or the directions on the label.* The following information includes only the average dose of neomycin, polymyxin B, and bacitracin ophthalmic combination. *If your dose is different, do not change it* unless your doctor tells you to do so.

- For eye infections:
  —For *eye ointment* dosage forms:
  - Adults and children—Use a thin strip of ointment in the eyes every three or four hours for seven to ten days.

Missed dose—If you miss a dose of this medicine, apply it as soon as possible. However, if it is almost time for your next dose, skip the missed dose and go back to your regular dosing schedule.

Storage—To store this medicine:

- Keep out of the reach of children.
- Store away from heat and direct light.
- Keep the medicine from freezing.

- Do not keep outdated medicine or medicine no longer needed. Be sure that any discarded medicine is out of the reach of children.

Precautions While Using This Medicine

If your symptoms do not improve within a few days, or if they become worse, check with your doctor.

Side Effects of This Medicine

Along with its needed effects, a medicine may cause some unwanted effects. Although not all of these side effects may occur, if they do occur they may need medical attention.

Check with your doctor immediately if any of the following side effects occur:

More common

Itching, rash, redness, swelling, or other sign of irritation not present before use of this medicine

After application, eye ointments usually cause your vision to blur for a few minutes.

Other side effects not listed above may also occur in some patients. If you notice any other effects, check with your doctor.

Revised: 05/16/94
Interim revision: 05/24/95

NEOMYCIN, POLYMYXIN B, AND BACITRACIN   Topical

Commonly used brand name(s):

In the U.S.—

Bactine First Aid Antibiotic
Foille
Mycitracin

Neosporin Maximum Strength Ointment
Neosporin Ointment
Topisporin

Generic name product may be available.

Description

Neomycin, Polymyxin B, and Bacitracin (nee-oh-MYE-sin, pol-i-MIX-in bee, and bass-i-TRAY-sin) is a combination antibiotic medicine used to help prevent infections of the skin.

Neomycin, polymyxin B, and bacitracin combination is available without a prescription; however, your doctor may have special instructions on the proper use of this medicine for your medical problem.

Topical neomycin, polymyxin B, and bacitracin combination is available in the following dosage form:

Topical
- Ointment (U.S. and Canada)

Before Using This Medicine

If you are using this medicine without a prescription, carefully read and follow any precautions on the label. For topical neomycin, polymyxin B, and bacitracin combination, the following should be considered:

Allergies—Tell your doctor if you have ever had any unusual or allergic reaction to this medicine or to any related antibiotic, such as amikacin (e.g., Amikin), colistimethate (e.g., Coly-Mycin M), colistin (e.g., Coly-Mycin S), gentamicin (e.g., Garamycin), kanamycin (e.g., Kantrex), neomycin by mouth or by injection (e.g., Mycifradin), netilmicin (e.g., Netromycin), paromomycin (e.g., Humatin), polymyxin B by injection (e.g., Aerosporin), streptomycin, or tobramycin (e.g., Nebcin). Also tell your health care professional if you are allergic to any other substances, such as preservatives or dyes.

Pregnancy—Neomycin, polymyxin B, and bacitracin topical preparations have not been studied in pregnant women. However, this medicine has not been shown to cause birth defects or other problems in humans.

Breast-feeding—It is not known whether topical neomycin, polymyxin B, and bacitracin combination passes into breast milk. However, this medicine has not been reported to cause problems in nursing babies.

Children—Studies on this medicine have been done only in adult patients, and there is no specific information comparing use of topical neomycin, polymyxin B, and bacitracin combination in children with use in other age groups.

Older adults—Many medicines have not been studied specifically in older people. Therefore, it may not be known whether they work exactly the same way they do in younger adults or if they cause different side effects or problems in older people. There is no specific information comparing use of topical neomycin, polymyxin B, and bacitracin combination in the elderly with use in other age groups.

Other medicines—Although certain medicines should not be used together at all, in other cases two different medicines may be used together even if an interaction might occur. In these cases, your doctor may want to change the dose, or other precautions may be necessary. Tell your health care professional if you are using any other prescription or nonprescription (over-the-counter [OTC]) medicine.

Proper Use of This Medicine

If you are using this medicine without a prescription, do not use it to treat deep wounds, puncture wounds, serious burns, or raw areas without first checking with your health care professional.

Do not use this medicine in the eyes.

Before applying this medicine, wash the affected area with soap and water, and dry thoroughly.

After applying this medicine, the treated area may be covered with a gauze dressing if desired.

To help clear up your infection completely, *keep using this medicine for the full time of treatment,* even if your symptoms have disappeared. *Do not miss any doses.*

Dosing—The dose of topical neomycin, polymyxin B, and bacitracin combination will be different for different patients. *Follow your doctor's orders or the directions on the label.* The following information includes only the average doses of topical neomycin, polymyxin B, and bacitracin combination. *If your dose is different, do not change it* unless your doctor tells you to do so.

- For *topical* dosage form (ointment):
  —For prevention of minor bacterial infections:
    - Adults and children—Apply to the affected area(s) of the skin two to five times a day.

Missed dose—If you miss a dose of this medicine, apply it as soon as possible. However, if it is almost time for your next dose, skip the missed dose and go back to your regular dosing schedule.

Storage—To store this medicine:
- Keep out of the reach of children.
- Store away from heat and direct light.
- Keep the medicine from freezing.
- Do not keep outdated medicine or medicine no longer needed. Be sure that any discarded medicine is out of the reach of children.

Precautions While Using This Medicine

If your skin problem does not improve within 1 week, or if it becomes worse, check with your health care professional.

Side Effects of This Medicine

Along with its needed effects, a medicine may cause some unwanted effects. Although not all of these side effects may occur, if they do occur they may need medical attention.

Check with your doctor immediately if any of the following side effects occur:
  More common
    Itching, skin rash, redness, swelling, or other sign of irritation not present before use of this medicine

  Rare
    Any loss of hearing

Other side effects not listed above may also occur in some patients. If you notice any other effects, check with your doctor.

Revised: 07/25/94

NEOMYCIN, POLYMYXIN B, AND GRAMICIDIN   Ophthalmic

Commonly used brand name(s):

In the U.S.—

Ak-Spore Ophthalmic Solution	Ocutricin Ophthalmic Solution
Neocidin Ophthalmic Solution	P.N. Ophthalmic
Neosporin Ophthalmic Solution	Tribiotic
Ocu-Spor-G	Tri-Ophthalmic
	Triple Antibiotic

Generic name product may be available.

In Canada—
Neosporin Ophthalmic Solution

Description

Neomycin, polymyxin B, and gramicidin (nee-oh-MYE-sin, pol-i-MIX-in bee, and gram-i-SYE-din) is a combination antibiotic medicine used to treat infections of the eye.

Neomycin, polymyxin B, and gramicidin combination is available only with your doctor's prescription, in the following dosage form:

Ophthalmic
- Ophthalmic solution (eye drops) (U.S. and Canada)

Before Using This Medicine

In deciding to use a medicine, the risks of taking the medicine must be weighed against the good it will do. This is a decision you and your doctor will make. For neomycin, polymyxin B, and gramicidin ophthalmic drops, the following should be considered:

Allergies—Tell your doctor if you have ever had any unusual or allergic reaction to this medicine or to any related antibiotic, such as amikacin (e.g., Amikin), colistimethate (e.g., Coly-Mycin M), colistin (e.g., Coly-Mycin S), gentamicin (e.g., Garamycin), kanamycin (e.g., Kantrex), netilmicin (e.g., Netromycin), paromomycin (e.g., Humatin), streptomycin, or tobramycin (e.g., Nebcin). Also tell your health care professional if you are allergic to any other substances, such as preservatives.

Pregnancy—Neomycin, polymyxin B, and gramicidin combination has not been shown to cause birth defects or other problems in humans.

Breast-feeding—Neomycin, polymyxin B, and gramicidin combination has not been reported to cause problems in nursing babies.

Children—Studies on this medicine have been done only in adult patients, and there is no specific information comparing use of this combination in children with use in other age groups.

Older adults—Many medicines have not been studied specifically in older people. Therefore, it may not be known whether they work exactly the same way they do in younger adults or if they cause different side effects or problems in older people. There is no specific information comparing use of neomycin, polymyxin B, and gramicidin combination in the elderly with use in other age groups.

Proper Use of This Medicine

The bottle is only partially full to provide proper drop control.

To use:

- First, wash your hands. Tilt the head back and, pressing your finger gently on the skin just beneath the lower eyelid, pull the lower eyelid away from the eye to make a space. Drop the medicine into this space. Let go of the eyelid and gently close the eyes. Do not blink. Keep the eyes closed for 1 or 2 minutes to allow the medicine to come into contact with the infection.
- If you think you did not get the drop of medicine into your eye properly, use another drop.
- To keep the medicine as germ-free as possible, do not touch the applicator tip or dropper to any surface (including the eye). Also, keep the container tightly closed.

To help clear up your infection completely, *keep using this medicine for the full time of treatment*, even if your symptoms have disappeared. *Do not miss any doses.*

Dosing—The dose of neomycin, polymyxin B, and gramicidin ophthalmic combination will be different for different patients. *Follow your doctor's orders or the directions on the label.* The following information includes only the average doses of neomycin, polymyxin B, and gramicidin ophthalmic combination. *If your dose is different*, do not change it unless your doctor tells you to do so.

- For eye infections:
  —For *eye drops* dosage form:
    - Adults and children—Use one drop in the eye two to four times a day for seven to ten days. If you

have a more serious infection, your doctor may want you to use one drop in the eye every fifteen to thirty minutes at first. Then your doctor may have you use the medicine less often.

Missed dose—If you miss a dose of this medicine, apply it as soon as possible. However, if it is almost time for your next dose, skip the missed dose and go back to your regular dosing schedule.

Storage—To store this medicine:

- Keep out of the reach of children.
- Store away from heat and direct light.
- Keep the medicine from freezing.
- Do not keep outdated medicine or medicine no longer needed. Be sure that any discarded medicine is out of the reach of children.

Precautions While Using This Medicine

If your symptoms do not improve within a few days, or if they become worse, check with your doctor.

Side Effects of This Medicine

Along with its needed effects, a medicine may cause some unwanted effects. Although not all of these side effects may occur, if they do occur they may need medical attention.

Check with your doctor immediately if any of the following side effects occur:

> *More common*
>> Itching, rash, redness, swelling, or other sign of irritation in or around the eye not present before use of this medicine

Other side effects may occur that usually do not need medical attention. These side effects may go away during treatment as your body adjusts to the medicine. However, check with your doctor if either of the following side effects continues or is bothersome:

> *Less common*
>> Burning or stinging sensation in the eye

Other side effects not listed above may also occur in some patients. If you notice any other effects, check with your doctor.

Revised: 06/21/94
Interim revision: 10/16/98

NEOMYCIN, POLYMYXIN B, AND HYDROCORTISONE   Ophthalmic

Commonly used brand name(s):

In the U.S.—
Ak-Spore H.C. Ophthalmic Suspension	Cortisporin Ophthalmic Suspension

Generic name product may be available.

In Canada—
Cortisporin Eye/Ear Suspension

Description

Neomycin, polymyxin B, and hydrocortisone (nee-oh-MYE-sin, pol-i-MIX-in bee, and hye-droe-KOR-ti-sone) is a combination antibiotic and cortisone-like medicine. It is used to treat infections of the eye and to help provide relief from redness, irritation, and discomfort of certain eye problems.

Neomycin, polymyxin B, and hydrocortisone combination is available only with your doctor's prescription, in the following dosage form:

Ophthalmic
- Ophthalmic suspension (eye drops) (U.S. and Canada)

Before Using This Medicine

In deciding to use a medicine, the risks of using the medicine must be weighed against the good it will do. This is a decision you and your doctor will make. For neomycin, polymyxin B, and hydrocortisone ophthalmic drops, the following should be considered:

Allergies—Tell your doctor if you have ever had any unusual or allergic reaction to this medicine or to any related antibiotic, such as amikacin (e.g., Amikin), colistimethate (e.g., Coly-Mycin M), colistin (e.g., Coly-Mycin S), gentamicin (e.g., Garamycin), kanamycin (e.g., Kantrex), netilmicin (e.g., Netromycin), paromomycin (e.g., Humatin), streptomycin, or tobramycin (e.g., Nebcin). Also tell your health care professional if you are allergic to any other substances, such as preservatives.

Pregnancy—Neomycin, polymyxin B, and hydrocortisone ophthalmic preparations have not been studied in pregnant women. However, studies in animals have shown that topical corticosteroids cause birth defects. Before using this medicine, make sure your doctor knows if you are pregnant or if you may become pregnant.

Breast-feeding—Neomycin, polymyxin B, and hydrocortisone ophthalmic drops have not been reported to cause problems in nursing babies.

Children—Studies on this medicine have been done only in adult patients, and there is no specific information comparing use in children with use in other age groups.

Older adults—Many medicines have not been studied specifically in older people. Therefore, it may not be known whether they work exactly the same way they do in younger adults or if they cause different side effects or problems in older people. There is no specific information comparing use of ophthalmic neomycin, polymyxin B, and hydrocortisone combination in the elderly with use in other age groups.

Other medical problems—The presence of other medical problems may affect the use of neomycin, polymyxin B, and hydrocortisone ophthalmic drops. Make sure you tell your doctor if you have any other medical problems, especially:
- Any other eye infection or condition or
- Glaucoma—Use of neomycin, polymyxin B, and hydrocortisone ophthalmic drops may make the condition worse
- Cataract surgery, recent—Use of neomycin, polymyxin B, and hydrocortisone ophthalmic drops may delay healing or cause other problems

Proper Use of This Medicine

The bottle is only partially full to provide proper drop control.

To use:
- First, wash your hands. Then tilt the head back and pull the lower eyelid away from the eye to form a pouch. Drop the medicine into the pouch and gently close the eyes.

Do not blink. Keep the eyes closed for 1 or 2 minutes to allow the medicine to come into contact with the infection.
- If you think you did not get the drop of medicine into your eye properly, use another drop.
- To keep the medicine as germ-free as possible, do not touch the applicator tip to any surface (including the eye). Also, keep the container tightly closed.

To help clear up your infection completely, *keep using this medicine for the full time of treatment*, even if your symptoms have disappeared. *Do not miss any doses.*

Dosing—The dose of ophthalmic neomycin, polymyxin B, and hydrocortisone combination will be different for different patients. *Follow your doctor's orders or the directions on the label*. The following information includes only the average doses of ophthalmic neomycin, polymyxin B, and hydrocortisone combination. *If your dose is different, do not change it* unless your doctor tells you to do so.

The number of doses you use each day, the time allowed between doses, and the length of time you use the medicine depend on the medical problem for which you are using ophthalmic neomycin, polymyxin B, and hydrocortisone combination.
- For eye infection:
  —For *ophthalmic suspension* dosage forms:
    - Adults—One drop every three or four hours.
    - Children—Use and dose must be determined by your doctor.

Missed dose—If you miss a dose of this medicine, apply it as soon as possible. However, if it is almost time for your next dose, skip the missed dose and go back to your regular dosing schedule.

Do not use any leftover medicine for future eye problems without checking with your doctor first. This medicine should not be used on many different kinds of infection.

Storage—To store this medicine:
- Keep out of the reach of children.
- Store away from heat and direct light.
- Keep the medicine from freezing.
- Do not keep outdated medicine or medicine no longer needed. Be sure that any discarded medicine is out of the reach of children.

Precautions While Using This Medicine

If you will be using this medicine for more than 10 days, your doctor should check your eyes at regular visits.

If your symptoms do not improve within a few days, or if they become worse, check with your doctor.

Side Effects of This Medicine

Along with its needed effects, a medicine may cause some unwanted effects. Although not all of these side effects may occur, if they do occur they may need medical attention.

Stop using this medicine and get emergency help immediately if any of the following side effects occur:

Rare
 Fainting; lightheadedness (sudden and severe); shortness of breath or trouble breathing (severe); swelling around face

Check with your doctor immediately if any of the following side effects occur:

More common

Itching, rash, redness, swelling, or other sign of irritation not present before use of this medicine

Rare

Blurred vision or other change in vision; delayed healing of eye infection

Other side effects may occur that usually do not need medical attention. These side effects may go away during treatment as your body adjusts to the medicine. However, check with your doctor if either of the following side effects continues or is bothersome:

Less common

Burning or stinging when applying medicine

Other side effects not listed above may also occur in some patients. If you notice any other effects, check with your doctor.

Revised: 06/11/99

NEOMYCIN, POLYMYXIN B, AND HYDROCORTISONE   Otic

Commonly used brand name(s):

In the U.S.—

AK-Spore HC Otic	Masporin Otic
Antibiotic Ear	Octicair
Cortatrigen Ear	Octigen
Cortatrigen Modified Ear	Otic-Care
Drops	Otic-Care Ear
Cort-Biotic	Otimar
Cortisporin	Otisan
Cortomycin	Otocidin
Drotic	Otocort
Ear-Eze	Pediotic
LazerSporin-C	UAD Otic

Generic name product may be available.

In Canada—
Cortisporin

Description

Neomycin, polymyxin B, and hydrocortisone (nee-oh-MYE-sin, pol-i-MIX-in bee, and hye-droe-KOR-ti-sone) is a combination antibiotic and cortisone-like medicine. It is used to treat infections of the ear canal and to help provide relief from redness, irritation, and discomfort of certain ear problems.

Neomycin, polymyxin B, and hydrocortisone preparation is available only with your doctor's prescription, in the following dosage forms:

Otic
- Solution (U.S. and Canada)
- Suspension (U.S. and Canada)

Before Using This Medicine

In deciding to use a medicine, the risks of using the medicine must be weighed against the good it will do. This is a decision you and your doctor will make. For neomycin, polymyxin B, and hydrocortisone otic preparations, the following should be considered:

Allergies—Tell your doctor if you have ever had any unusual or allergic reaction to this medicine or to any related antibiotic, such as amikacin (e.g., Amikin), colistimethate (e.g., Coly-Mycin M), colistin (e.g., Coly-Mycin S), gentamicin (e.g., Garamycin), kanamycin (e.g., Kantrex), neomycin by mouth or by injection (e.g., Mycifradin), netilmicin (e.g., Netromycin), paromomycin (e.g., Humatin), polymyxin B by injection (e.g., Aerosporin), streptomycin, or tobramycin (e.g., Nebcin). Also tell your health care professional if you are allergic to any other substances, such as preservatives or dyes.

Pregnancy—Neomycin, polymyxin B, and hydrocortisone otic preparations have not been studied in pregnant women. However, studies in animals have shown that topical corticosteroids (such as hydrocortisone) cause birth defects. Before using this medicine, make sure your doctor knows if you are pregnant or if you may become pregnant.

Breast-feeding—Neomycin, polymyxin B, and hydrocortisone otic preparations have not been reported to cause problems in nursing babies.

Children—Although there is no specific information comparing use of otic neomycin, polymyxin B, and hydrocortisone preparation in children with use in other age groups, this preparation is not expected to cause different side effects or problems in children than it does in adults.

Older adults—Many medicines have not been studied specifically in older people. Therefore, it may not be known whether they work exactly the same way they do in younger adults. Although there is no specific information comparing use of otic neomycin, polymyxin B, and hydrocortisone preparation in the elderly with use in other age groups, this preparation is not expected to cause different side effects or problems in older people than it does in younger adults.

Other medicines—Although certain medicines should not be used together at all, in other cases two different medicines may be used together even if an interaction might occur. In these cases, your doctor may want to change the dose, or other precautions may be necessary. Tell your health care professional if you are using any other otic (for the ear) prescription or nonprescription (over-the-counter [OTC] medicine).

Other medical problems—The presence of other medical problems may affect the use of neomycin, polymyxin B, and hydrocortisone otic preparations. Make sure you tell your doctor if you have any other medical problems, especially:

- Any other ear infection or condition (including punctured eardrum)—Use of neomycin, polymyxin B, and hydrocortisone otic preparations may make the condition worse

Proper Use of This Medicine

You may warm the ear drops to body temperature (37 °C or 98.6 °F), but no higher, by holding the bottle in your hand for a few minutes before using the medicine. If the medicine gets too warm, it may break down and not work at all.

To use:

- Lie down or tilt the head so that the infected ear faces up. Gently pull the earlobe up and back for adults (down and back for children) to straighten the ear canal. Drop the medicine into the ear canal. Keep the ear facing up for about 5 minutes to allow the medicine to coat the ear canal. (For young children and other patients who cannot stay still for 5 minutes, try to keep the ear facing up for at least 1 or 2 minutes.) Your doctor may have inserted a gauze or cotton wick into your ear and may want you to keep the wick moistened with this medicine. Your doctor also may have other directions for you, such as how long you should keep the wick in your ear or when you should return to your doctor to have the wick replaced. If you have any questions about this, check with your doctor.

- To keep the medicine as germ-free as possible, do not touch the dropper to any surface (including the ear). Also, keep the container tightly closed.

To help clear up your infection completely, *keep using this medicine for the full time of treatment*, even if your symptoms have disappeared. *Do not miss any doses.*

Dosing—The dose of neomycin, polymyxin B, and hydrocortisone otic preparation will be different for different patients. *Follow your doctor's orders or the directions on the label*. The following information includes only the average doses of neomycin, polymyxin B, and hydrocortisone otic preparation. *If your dose is different, do not change it* unless your doctor tells you to do so.

- For *otic (ear drops)* dosage forms:
  —For ear canal infection:
    - Adults—Use four drops in the ear three or four times a day.
    - Children—Use three drops in the ear three or four times a day.
  —For mastoid cavity infection:
    - Adults—Use four to ten drops in the ear every six to eight hours.
    - Children—Use four or five drops in the ear every six to eight hours.

Missed dose—If you miss a dose of this medicine, apply it as soon as possible. However, if it is almost time for your next dose, skip the missed dose and go back to your regular dosing schedule.

Do not use this medicine for more than 10 days unless otherwise directed by your doctor.

Storage—To store this medicine:

- Keep out of the reach of children.
- Store away from heat and direct light.
- Keep the medicine from freezing.
- Do not keep outdated medicine or medicine no longer needed. Be sure that any discarded medicine is out of the reach of children.

Precautions While Using This Medicine

If your symptoms do not improve within 1 week, or if they become worse, check with your doctor.

Side Effects of This Medicine

Along with its needed effects, a medicine may cause some unwanted effects. Although not all of these side effects may occur, if they do occur they may need medical attention.

Check with your doctor immediately if any of the following side effects occur:

More common
   Itching, skin rash, redness, swelling, or other sign of irritation in or around the ear not present before use of this medicine

Other side effects not listed above may also occur in some patients. If you notice any other effects, check with your doctor.

Revised: 06/21/94
Interim revision: 06/02/95

NEVIRAPINE   Systemic

Commonly used brand name(s):

In the U.S.—
   Viramune

In Canada—
   Viramune

Description

Nevirapine (ne-VYE-ra-peen) is used, alone or in combination with other medicines, in the treatment of the infection caused by the human immunodeficiency virus (HIV). HIV is the virus that causes acquired immune deficiency syndrome (AIDS).

Nevirapine will not cure or prevent HIV infection or AIDS; however, it helps keep HIV from reproducing and appears to slow down the destruction of the immune system. This may help delay the development of problems usually related to AIDS or HIV disease. Nevirapine will not keep you from spreading HIV to other people. People who receive this medicine may continue to have other problems usually related to AIDS or HIV disease.

This medicine is available only with your doctor's prescription, in the following dosage form:

Oral
- Oral suspension (U.S.)
- Tablets (U.S. and Canada)

Before Using This Medicine

In deciding to use a medicine, the risks of taking the medicine must be weighed against the good it will do. This is a decision you and your doctor will make. For nevirapine, the following should be considered:

Allergies—Tell your doctor if you have ever had any unusual or allergic reaction to nevirapine. Also tell your health care professional if you are allergic to any other substances, such as foods, preservatives, or dyes.

Pregnancy—Nevirapine has not been studied in pregnant women. However, studies in animals at high doses have found that it causes decreased body weight of infant animals. Nevirapine did not cause birth defects in animals.

Breast-feeding—Nevirapine passes into human breast milk. Breast-feeding is usually not recommended in HIV positive or AIDS patients because of the risk of passing the AIDS virus on to the nursing infant.

Children—Granulocytopenia may be more likely to occur in children, who are usually more sensitive than adults to this effect of nevirapine.

Older adults—Many medicines have not been studied specifically in older people. Therefore, it may not be known whether they work exactly the same way they do in younger adults. There is no specific information comparing use of nevirapine in the elderly with use in other age groups.

Other medicines—Although certain medicines should not be used together at all, in other cases two different medicines may be used together even if an interaction might occur. In these cases, your doctor may want to change the dose, or other precautions may be necessary. When you are taking nevirapine, it is especially important that your health care professional know if you are taking any of the following:

- Indinavir (e.g., Crixivan) or
- Ketoconazole (e.g., Nizoral) or
- Oral contraceptives (birth control pills) containing estrogen or
- Saquinavir (e.g., Fortovase; Invirase)—Nevirapine may decrease the amount of these medicines in the body and cause them to be less effective
- Methadone (e.g., Diskets, Dolophine)—Methadone levels may be reduced when taking nevirapine and could lead to narcotic withdrawal syndrome
- Rifabutin (e.g., Mycobutin) or
- Rifampin (e.g., Rifadin)—These medicines may decrease the amount of nevirapine in the body
- St. John's wort—Medicines with this ingredient decrease the amount of nevirapine in the body and possibly lead to a loss of therapeutic response

Other medical problems—The presence of other medical problems may affect the use of nevirapine. Make sure you tell your doctor if you have any other medical problems, especially:

- Kidney disease—Nevirapine may be removed more slowly from the body
- Liver disease—Nevirapine has been reported to cause unwanted and sometimes serious effects in the liver

Proper Use of This Medicine

Nevirapine may be taken with or without food.

Take this medicine exactly as directed by your doctor. Do not take it more often, and do not take it for a longer time than your doctor ordered. Also, do not stop taking this medicine without checking with your doctor first.

Keep taking nevirapine for the full time of treatment, even if you begin to feel better.

This medicine works best when there is a constant amount in the blood. *To help keep the amount constant, do not miss any doses. Also, it is best to take the doses at evenly spaced times, day and night.* For example, if you are to take one dose a day, try to take it at the same time each day. If you are taking two doses a day, the doses should be spaced about 12 hours apart. If you need help in planning the best times to take your medicine, check with your health care professional.

Only take medicine that your doctor has prescribed specially for you. Do not share your medicine with others.

Dosing—The dose of nevirapine will be different for different patients. *Follow your doctor's orders or the directions on the label.* The following information includes only

the average doses of nevirapine. *If your dose is different, do not change it* unless your doctor tells you to do so.

- For *oral* dosage form (suspension or tablets):
  —For treatment of HIV infection:
  - Adults—200 milligrams (mg) once a day for two weeks, followed by 200 mg two times a day, in combination with other medicines.
  - Children 8 years of age and older—Dose is based on body weight and must be determined by your doctor. The usual dose is 4 mg per kilogram (kg) (1.8 mg per pound) of body weight once a day for two weeks, followed by 4 mg per kg (1.8 mg per pound) of body weight two times a day, in combination with other medicines. Total daily dose should not exceed 400 mg.
  - Children 2 months to 8 years of age—Dose is based on body weight and must be determined by your doctor. The usual dose is 4 mg per kilogram (kg) (1.8 mg per pound) of body weight once a day for two weeks, followed by 7 mg per kg (3.2 mg per pound) of body weight two times a day, in combination with other medicines. Total daily dose should not exceed 400 mg.
  - Infants up to 2 months of age—Use and dose must be determined by your doctor.

Missed dose—If you miss a dose of this medicine, take it as soon as you remember. However, if it is almost time for your next dose, skip the missed dose and go back to your regular dosing schedule. Do not double doses.

Storage—To store this medicine:

- Keep out of the reach of children.
- Store away from heat and direct light. The oral suspension form of this medicine does not need to be refrigerated.
- Do not store in the bathroom, near the kitchen sink, or in other damp places. Heat or moisture may cause the medicine to break down.
- Do not keep outdated medicine or medicine no longer needed. Be sure that any discarded medicine is out of the reach of children.

Precautions While Using This Medicine

Do not take any other medicines without checking with your doctor first. To do so may increase the chance of side effects from nevirapine or other medicines.

It is very important that your doctor check your progress at regular visits to make sure this medicine is working properly and check for unwanted effects.

This medicine may decrease the effects of some oral contraceptives (birth control pills). *To avoid unwanted pregnancy, it is a good idea to use some additional contraceptive measures while being treated with nevirapine.*

Side Effects of This Medicine

Along with its needed effects, a medicine may cause some unwanted effects. Although not all of these side effects may occur, if they do occur they may need medical attention.

Check with your doctor as soon as possible if any of the following side effects occur:

More common
  Chills, fever, or sore throat; skin rash

Chills, fever, and sore throat are more commonly seen in children.

Less common
> Abdominal or stomach pain; clay-colored stools; dark urine; diarrhea; dizziness; headache; itching; loss of appetite; nausea; rash; sores or ulcers in the mouth; unpleasant breath odor; unusual tiredness or weakness; vomiting of blood; yellow skin or eyes

Other side effects not listed above may also occur in some patients. If you notice any other effects, check with your doctor.

Developed: 08/04/1998
Revised: 01/03/2001

NIACIN (VITAMIN B₃)   Systemic

Commonly used brand name(s):

In the U.S.—

Endur-Acin[1]	Nico-400[1]
Nia-Bid[1]	Nicobid Temples[1]
Niac[1]	Nicolar[1]
Niacels[1]	Nicotinex Elixir[1]
Niacor[1]	Slo-Niacin[1]

In Canada—
Novo-Niacin[1]

Other commonly used names are:

Nicotinamide[2]
Nicotinic acid[1]
Vitamin B₃ [2]

Note: For quick reference, the following products are numbered to match the corresponding brand names.

This information applies to the following products:
1. Niacin (nye-a-SIN) ‡§
2. Niacinamide (nye-a-SIN-a-mide) ‡§

‡Generic name product may be available in the U.S.
§Generic name product may be available in Canada.

Description

Vitamins (VYE-ta-mins) are compounds that you *must* have for growth and health. They are needed in small amounts only and are usually available in the foods that you eat. Niacin and niacinamide are necessary for many normal functions of the body, including normal tissue metabolism. They may have other effects as well.

Lack of niacin may lead to a condition called pellagra. Pellagra causes diarrhea, stomach problems, skin problems, sores in the mouth, anemia (weak blood), and mental problems. Your health care professional may treat this by prescribing niacin for you.

Some conditions may increase your need for niacin. These include:
- Cancer
- Diabetes mellitus (sugar diabetes)
- Diarrhea (prolonged)
- Fever (prolonged)
- Hartnup disease
- Infection (prolonged)
- Intestinal problems
- Liver disease
- Mouth or throat sores
- Overactive thyroid
- Pancreas disease
- Stomach ulcer
- Stress (prolonged)
- Surgical removal of stomach

Increased need for niacin should be determined by your health care professional.

Claims that niacin is effective for treatment of acne, alcoholism, unwanted effects of drug abuse, leprosy, motion sickness, muscle problems, poor circulation, and mental problems, and for prevention of heart attacks, have not been proven. Many of these treatments involve large and expensive amounts of vitamins.

Injectable niacin and niacinamide are given by or under the supervision of a health care professional. Other forms of niacin and niacinamide are available without a prescription.

Niacin and niacinamide are available in the following dosage forms:

Oral
Niacin
- Extended-release capsules (U.S.)
- Solution (U.S.)
- Tablets (U.S. and Canada)
- Extended-release tablets (U.S. and Canada)
Niacinamide
- Tablets (U.S. and Canada)

Parenteral
Niacin
- Injection (U.S.)
Niacinamide
- Injection (U.S.)

Importance of Diet

For good health, it is important that you eat a balanced and varied diet. Follow carefully any diet program your health care professional may recommend. For your specific dietary vitamin and/or mineral needs, ask your health care professional for a list of appropriate foods. If you think that you are not getting enough vitamins and/or minerals in your diet, you may choose to take a dietary supplement.

Niacin is found in meats, eggs, and milk and dairy products. Little niacin is lost from foods during ordinary cooking.

Vitamins alone will not take the place of a good diet and will not provide energy. Your body also needs other substances found in food such as protein, minerals, carbohydrates, and fat. Vitamins themselves often cannot work without the presence of other foods.

The daily amount of niacin needed is defined in several different ways.

For U.S.—
- Recommended Dietary Allowances (RDAs) are the amount of vitamins and minerals needed to provide for adequate nutrition in most healthy persons. RDAs for a given nutrient may vary depending on a person's age, sex, and physical condition (e.g., pregnancy).
- Daily Values (DVs) are used on food and dietary supplement labels to indicate the percent of the recommended daily amount of each nutrient that a serving provides. DV replaces the previous designation of

United States Recommended Daily Allowances (USRDAs).

For Canada—
- Recommended Nutrient Intakes (RNIs) are used to determine the amounts of vitamins, minerals, and protein needed to provide adequate nutrition and lessen the risk of chronic disease.

Normal daily recommended intakes in milligrams (mg) for niacin are generally defined as follows:

Persons	U.S. (mg)	Canada (mg)
Infants and children		
Birth to 3 years of age	5–9	4–9
4 to 6 years of age	12	13
7 to 10 years of age	13	14–18
Adolescent and adult males	15–20	14–23
Adolescent and adult females	13–15	14–16
Pregnant females	17	14–16
Breast-feeding females	20	14–16

Before Using This Dietary Supplement

If you are taking this dietary supplement without a prescription, carefully read and follow any precautions on the label. For niacin or niacinamide, the following should be considered:

Allergies—Tell your health care professional if you have ever had any unusual or allergic reaction to niacin or niacinamide. Also tell your health care professional if you are allergic to any other substances, such as foods, preservatives, or dyes.

Pregnancy—It is especially important that you are receiving enough vitamins when you become pregnant and that you continue to receive the right amount of vitamins throughout your pregnancy. The healthy growth and development of the fetus depend on a steady supply of nutrients from the mother. However, taking large amounts of a dietary supplement in pregnancy may be harmful to the mother and/or fetus and should be avoided.

Breast-feeding—It is especially important that you receive the right amounts of vitamins so that your baby will also get the vitamins needed to grow properly. However, taking large amounts of a dietary supplement while breast-feeding may be harmful to the mother and/or baby and should be avoided.

Children—Problems in children have not been reported with intake of normal daily recommended amounts.

Older adults—Problems in older adults have not been reported with intake of normal daily recommended amounts.

Medicines or other dietary supplements—Although certain medicines or dietary supplements should not be used together at all, in other cases they may be used together even if an interaction might occur. In these cases, your health care professional may want to change the dose, or other precautions may be necessary. Tell your health care professional if you are using any other dietary supplement or any prescription or nonprescription (over-the-counter [OTC]) medicine.

Other medical problems—The presence of other medical problems may affect the use of niacin or niacinamide. Make sure you tell your health care professional if you have any other medical problems, especially:
- Bleeding problems or
- Diabetes mellitus (sugar diabetes) or
- Glaucoma or
- Gout or
- Liver disease or
- Low blood pressure or
- Stomach ulcer—Niacin or niacinamide may make these conditions worse

Proper Use of This Dietary Supplement

Dosing—The amount of niacin and niacinamide needed to meet normal daily recommended intakes will be different for different individuals. The following information includes only the average amounts of niacin and niacinamide.

For niacin
- For *oral* dosage form (capsules, extended-release capsules and tablets, tablets, oral solution):
  —To prevent deficiency, the amount taken by mouth is based on normal daily recommended intakes:
  For the U.S.
    - Adult and teenage males—15 to 20 milligrams (mg) per day.
    - Adult and teenage females—13 to 15 mg per day.
    - Pregnant females—17 mg per day.
    - Breast-feeding females—20 mg per day.
    - Children 7 to 10 years of age—13 mg per day.
    - Children 4 to 6 years of age—12 mg per day.
    - Children birth to 3 years of age—5 to 9 mg per day.
  For Canada
    - Adult and teenage males—14 to 23 mg per day.
    - Adult and teenage females—14 to 16 mg per day.
    - Pregnant females—14 to 16 mg per day.
    - Breast-feeding females—14 to 16 mg per day.
    - Children 7 to 10 years of age—14 to 18 mg per day.
    - Children 4 to 6 years of age—13 mg per day.
    - Children birth to 3 years of age—4 to 9 mg per day.
  —To treat deficiency:
    - Adults, teenagers, and children—Treatment dose is determined by prescriber for each individual based on the severity of deficiency.

For niacinamide
- For *oral* dosage form (tablets):
  —To prevent deficiency, the amount taken by mouth is based on normal daily recommended intakes:
  For the U.S.
    - Adult and teenage males—15 to 20 milligrams (mg) per day.
    - Adult and teenage females—13 to 15 mg per day.
    - Pregnant females—17 mg per day.
    - Breast-feeding females—20 mg per day.
    - Children 7 to 10 years of age—13 mg per day.
    - Children 4 to 6 years of age—12 mg per day.
    - Children birth to 3 years of age—5 to 9 mg per day.
  For Canada
    - Adult and teenage males—14 to 23 mg per day.
    - Adult and teenage females—14 to 16 mg per day.
    - Pregnant females—14 to 16 mg per day.
    - Breast-feeding females—14 to 16 mg per day.
    - Children 7 to 10 years of age—14 to 18 mg per day.
    - Children 4 to 6 years of age—13 mg per day.

- Children birth to 3 years of age—4 to 9 mg per day.
  —To treat deficiency:
  - Adults, teenagers, and children—Treatment dose is determined by prescriber for each individual based on the severity of deficiency.

If this dietary supplement upsets your stomach, it may be taken with meals or milk. If stomach upset (nausea or diarrhea) continues, check with your health care professional.

For individuals taking the *extended-release capsule form* of this dietary supplement:

- Swallow the capsule whole. Do not crush, break, or chew before swallowing. However, if the capsule is too large to swallow, you may mix the contents of the capsule with jam or jelly and swallow without chewing.

For individuals taking the *extended-release tablet form* of this dietary supplement:

- Swallow the tablet whole. If the tablet is scored, it may be broken, but not crushed or chewed, before being swallowed.

Missed dose—If you miss taking a vitamin for one or more days there is no cause for concern, since it takes some time for your body to become seriously low in vitamins. However, if your health care professional has recommended that you take this vitamin, try to remember to take it as directed every day.

Storage—To store this dietary supplement:

- Keep out of the reach of children.
- Store away from heat and direct light.
- Do not store in the bathroom, near the kitchen sink, or in other damp places. Heat or moisture may cause the dietary supplement to break down.
- Keep the liquid form of this dietary supplement from freezing.
- Do not keep outdated dietary supplements or those no longer needed. Be sure that any discarded dietary supplement is out of the reach of children.

Precautions While Using This Dietary Supplement

This dietary supplement may cause you to feel dizzy or faint, especially when you get up from a lying or sitting position. Getting up slowly may help. This effect should lessen after a week or two as your body gets used to the dietary supplement. However, if the problem continues or gets worse, check with your health care professional.

Side Effects of This Dietary Supplement

Along with its needed effects, a dietary supplement may cause some unwanted effects. Although not all of these side effects may occur, if they do occur they may need medical attention.

Check with your health care professional immediately if any of the following side effects occur:

With injection only
Skin rash or itching; wheezing

With prolonged use of extended-release niacin
Darkening of urine; light gray-colored stools; loss of appetite; severe stomach pain; yellow eyes or skin

Other side effects may occur that usually do not need medical attention. These side effects may go away during treatment as your body adjusts to the dietary supplement. However, check with your health care professional if any of the following side effects continue or are bothersome:

Less common—with niacin only
Feeling of warmth; flushing or redness of skin, especially on face and neck; headache

With high doses
Diarrhea; dizziness or faintness; dryness of skin; fever; frequent urination; itching of skin; joint pain; muscle aching or cramping; nausea or vomiting; side, lower back, or stomach pain; swelling of feet or lower legs; unusual thirst; unusual tiredness or weakness; unusually fast, slow, or irregular heartbeat

Other side effects not listed above may also occur in some individuals. If you notice any other effects, check with your health care professional.

Revised: 05/26/95

NIACIN—For High Cholesterol
Systemic

Commonly used brand name(s):

In the U.S.—

Endur-Acin	Nico-400
Nia-Bid	Nicobid Tempules
Niac	Nicolar
Niacels	Nicotinex Elixir
Niacor	Slo-Niacin

Generic name product may be available.

In Canada—
Novo-Niacin

Other commonly used names are nicotinic acid or vitamin B₃.

Description

Niacin (NYE-a-sin) is used to help lower high cholesterol and fat levels in the blood. This may help prevent medical problems caused by cholesterol and fat clogging the blood vessels.

Some strengths of niacin are available only with your doctor's prescription. Others are available without a prescription, since niacin is also a vitamin. However, it is best to take it only under your doctor's direction so that you can be sure you are taking the correct dose.

Niacin for use in the treatment of high cholesterol is available in the following dosage forms:

Oral
- Extended-release capsules (U.S.)
- Solution (U.S.)
- Tablets (U.S. and Canada)
- Extended-release tablets (U.S. and Canada)

Before Using This Medicine

If you are taking this medicine without a prescription, carefully read and follow any precautions on the label. For niacin, the following should be considered:

Allergies—Tell your doctor if you have ever had any unusual or allergic reaction to niacin. Also tell your health care professional if you are allergic to any other substances, such as foods, preservatives, or dyes.

Diet—Before prescribing medicine for your condition, your doctor will probably try to control your condition by prescribing a personal diet for you. Such a diet may be low in fats, sugars, and/or cholesterol. Many people are able to control their condition by carefully following their doctor's orders for proper diet and exercise. *Medicine is prescribed only when additional help is needed* and is effective only when a schedule of diet and exercise is properly followed.

Also, this medicine is less effective if you are greatly overweight. It may be very important for you to go on a reducing diet. However, check with your doctor before going on any diet.

Make certain your health care professional knows if you are on any special diet, such as a low-sodium or low-sugar diet.

Pregnancy—Studies have not been done in either humans or animals.

Breast-feeding—Niacin has not been reported to cause problems in nursing babies.

Children—There is no specific information comparing the use of niacin for high cholesterol in children with use in other age groups. However, use is not recommended in children under 2 years of age since cholesterol is needed for normal development.

Older adults—Many medicines have not been studied specifically in older people. Therefore, it may not be known whether they work exactly the same way they do in younger adults or if they cause different side effects or problems in older people. Although there is no specific information comparing the use of niacin for high cholesterol in the elderly with use in other age groups, it is not expected to cause different side effects or problems in older people than in younger adults.

Other medicines—Although certain medicines should not be used together at all, in other cases two different medicines may be used together even if an interaction might occur. In these cases, your doctor may want to change the dose, or other precautions may be necessary. Tell your health care professional if you are using any other prescription or nonprescription (over-the-counter [OTC]) medicine.

Other medical problems—The presence of other medical problems may affect the use of niacin. Make sure you tell your doctor if you have any other medical problems, especially:

- Bleeding problems or
- Diabetes mellitus (sugar diabetes) or
- Glaucoma or
- Gout or
- Liver disease or
- Low blood pressure or
- Stomach ulcer—Niacin may make these conditions worse

Proper Use of This Medicine

Use this medicine only as directed by your doctor. Do not use more or less of it, do not use it more often, and do not use it for a longer time than your doctor ordered. To do so may increase the chance of unwanted effects.

Remember that niacin will not cure your condition but it does help control it. Therefore, you must continue to take it as directed if you expect to keep your cholesterol levels down.

Follow carefully the special diet your doctor gave you. This is the most important part of controlling your condition, and is necessary if the medicine is to work properly.

If this medicine upsets your stomach, it may be taken with meals or milk. If stomach upset (nausea or diarrhea) continues, check with your doctor.

For patients taking the *extended-release capsule form* of this medicine:

- Swallow the capsule whole. Do not crush, break, or chew before swallowing. However, if the capsule is too large to swallow, you may mix the contents of the capsule with jam or jelly and swallow without chewing.

For patients taking the *extended-release tablet form* of this medicine:

- Swallow the tablet whole. If the tablet is scored, it may be broken, but not crushed or chewed, before being swallowed.

Dosing—The dose of niacin will be different for different patients. *Follow your doctor's orders or the directions on the label*. The following information includes only the average doses of niacin. *If your dose is different, do not change it* unless your doctor tells you to do so.

The number of capsules or tablets or teaspoonfuls of solution that you take depends on the strength of the medicine.

- For *oral* dosage form (extended-release capsules, extended-release tablets, oral solution, or regular tablets):
  —For treatment of high cholesterol:
  - Adults and teenagers—1 to 2 grams three times a day.
  - Children—Use and dose must be determined by your doctor.

Missed dose—If you miss a dose of this medicine, take it as soon as possible. However, if it is almost time for your next dose, skip the missed dose and go back to your regular dosing schedule. Do not double doses.

Storage—To store this medicine:

- Keep out of the reach of children.
- Store away from heat and direct light.
- Do not store in the bathroom, near the kitchen sink, or in other damp places. Heat or moisture may cause the medicine to break down.
- Keep the liquid form of this medicine from freezing.
- Do not keep outdated medicine or medicine no longer needed. Be sure that any discarded medicine is out of the reach of children.

Precautions While Using This Medicine

It is very important that your doctor check your progress at regular visits. This will allow your doctor to see if the medicine is working properly to lower your cholesterol and triglyceride (fat) levels and if you should continue to take it.

Do not stop taking niacin without first checking with your doctor. When you stop taking this medicine, your blood cholesterol levels may increase again. Your doctor may want you to follow a special diet to help prevent this from happening.

This medicine may cause you to feel dizzy or faint, especially when you get up from a lying or sitting position. Getting up slowly may help. This effect should lessen after a week or two as your body gets used to the medicine. However, if the problem continues or gets worse, check with your doctor.

Side Effects of This Medicine

Along with its needed effects, a medicine may cause some unwanted effects. Although not all of these side effects may occur, if they do occur they may need medical attention. *Check with your doctor immediately* if any of the following side effects occur:

Less common
With prolonged use of extended-release niacin
Darkening of urine; light gray-colored stools; loss of appetite; severe stomach pain; yellow eyes or skin

Other side effects may occur that usually do not need medical attention. These side effects may go away during treatment as your body adjusts to the medicine. However, check with your doctor if any of the following side effects continue or are bothersome:

Less common
Feeling of warmth; flushing or redness of skin, especially on face and neck; headache
With high doses
Diarrhea; dizziness or faintness; dryness of skin; fever; frequent urination; itching of skin; joint pain; muscle aching or cramping; nausea or vomiting; side, lower back, or stomach pain; swelling of feet or lower legs; unusual thirst; unusual tiredness or weakness; unusually fast, slow, or irregular heartbeat

Other side effects not listed above may also occur in some patients. If you notice any other effects, check with your health care professional.

Revised: 11/09/91
Interim revision: 08/10/94

NICOTINE Inhalation-Systemic

Commonly used brand name(s):

In the U.S.—
Nicotrol Inhaler

Description

Nicotine (NIK-oh-teen), in an inhaler, is used to help you stop smoking. It is used for up to 6 months as part of a stop-smoking program. This program may include counseling, education, specific behavior change techniques, or support groups.

With the inhaler, nicotine is inhaled through the mouth and is absorbed in the mouth and throat, but not in the lungs. Eight to ten puffs on the inhaler provide about the same amount of nicotine as one puff on an average cigarette. This nicotine takes the place of the nicotine that you would otherwise get from smoking. In this way, the withdrawal effects of not smoking are less severe. Then, as your body adjusts to not smoking, the use of the nicotine inhaler is decreased gradually over several weeks. Finally, use is stopped altogether.

This medicine is available only with your doctor's prescription, in the following dosage form:

Inhalation
• Cartridges for inhalation (U.S.)

Before Using This Medicine

In deciding to use a medicine, the risks of using the medicine must be weighed against the good it will do. This is a decision you and your doctor will make. For nicotine, the following should be considered:

Allergies—Tell your doctor if you have ever had any unusual or allergic reaction to nicotine or to menthol. Also tell your health care professional if you are allergic to any other substances, such as foods, preservatives, or dyes.

Pregnancy—Nicotine, whether from smoking or from the inhaler, is not recommended during pregnancy. Studies in animals have shown that nicotine can cause harmful effects in the fetus.

Breast-feeding—Nicotine passes into breast milk and may cause unwanted effects in the baby. It may be necessary for you to stop breast-feeding during treatment.

Children—Small amounts of nicotine can cause poisoning in children. Even used nicotine inhaler cartridges contain enough nicotine to cause serious harm in children. Also, the cartridges are small enough that they can cause choking if they are swallowed.

Older adults—This medicine has been tested in a limited number of patients 60 years of age or older and has not been shown to cause different side effects or problems in older people than it does in younger adults.

Other medicines—Although certain medicines should not be used together at all, in other cases two different medicines may be used together even if an interaction might occur. In these cases, your doctor may want to change the dose, or other precautions may be necessary. When you are using the nicotine inhaler, it is especially important that your health care professional know if you are taking any of the following medicines:

• Theophylline (e.g., Theo-Dur) or
• Tricyclic antidepressants (amitriptyline [e.g., Elavil], amoxapine [e.g., Asendin], clomipramine [e.g., Anafranil], desipramine [e.g., Norpramin], doxepin [e.g., Sinequan], imipramine [e.g., Tofranil], nortriptyline [e.g., Aventyl], protriptyline [e.g., Vivactil], trimipramine [e.g., Surmontil])—Stopping smoking may change the effects of these medicines; the amount of medicine you need to take may change

Other medical problems—The presence of other medical problems may affect the use of nicotine. Make sure you tell your doctor if you have any other medical problems, especially:

• Asthma or other breathing problems or
• Heart or blood vessel disease or
• High blood pressure or
• Liver disease or
• Overactive thyroid or
• Pheochromocytoma or
• Stomach ulcer or
• Type 1 diabetes mellitus (sugar diabetes)—Nicotine may make the condition worse

Proper Use of This Medicine

The nicotine inhaler usually comes with patient directions. *Read the directions carefully before using this medicine.*

The nicotine inhaler should be used at or above room temperature (60 °F [16 °C]). Cold temperatures decrease the amount of nicotine you inhale.

It is important to participate in a stop-smoking program during treatment. This may make it easier for you to stop smoking.

To decrease the risk of becoming dependent on the nicotine inhaler, your doctor may instruct you to stop treatment gradually. This may be done by keeping track of, and steadily reducing, use of the nicotine inhaler or by setting a planned date for stopping use of the inhaler.

Dosing—The dose of nicotine will be different for different patients. *Follow your doctor's orders or the directions on the label.* The following information includes only the average doses of nicotine. *If your dose is different, do not change it* unless your doctor tells you to do so.

- For cartridge for inhalation dosage form:
  —To help you stop smoking:
  - Adults and older teenagers—At first, the dose is 6 to 16 cartridges per day for up to twelve weeks. Then the dose is gradually reduced over a period of up to twelve weeks.
  - Children—Use and dose must be determined by your doctor.

Storage—To store this medicine:

- Keep out of the reach of children.
- Store away from heat and direct light.
- Do not store in the bathroom, near the kitchen sink, or in other damp places. Heat or moisture may cause the medicine to break down.
- Do not keep outdated medicine or medicine no longer needed. Be sure that any discarded medicine is out of the reach of children.

Precautions While Using This Medicine

Do not smoke during treatment with the nicotine inhaler because of the risk of nicotine overdose.

Do not use the nicotine inhaler for longer than 6 months if you have stopped smoking because continuing use of nicotine in any form can be harmful and addictive.

Nicotine should not be used in pregnancy. If there is a possibility you might become pregnant, you may want to use some type of birth control. If you think you may have become pregnant, stop taking this medicine immediately and check with your doctor.

Nicotine products must be kept out of the reach of children and pets. Even used nicotine inhaler cartridges contain enough nicotine to cause serious harm in children. If a child chews on or swallows a cartridge, contact your doctor or poison control center at once.

Side Effects of This Medicine

Along with its needed effects, a medicine may cause some unwanted effects. Although not all of these side effects may occur, if they do occur they may need medical attention.

Check with your doctor as soon as possible if any of the following side effects occur:

Less common
Fast or irregular heartbeat; fever with or without chills; headache; nausea with or without vomiting; runny nose; shortness of breath, tightness in chest, trouble in breathing, or wheezing; skin rash, itching, or hives; tearing of eyes

Symptoms of overdose
Abdominal or stomach pain; cold sweat; confusion; convulsions (seizures); disturbed hearing and vision; drooling; extreme exhaustion; pale skin; slow heartbeat; tremors

Other side effects may occur that usually do not need medical attention. These side effects may go away during treatment as your body adjusts to the medicine. However, check with your doctor if any of the following side effects continue or are bothersome:

More common
Coughing; indigestion; mouth and throat irritation; stuffy nose

Less common
Anxiety; back pain; change in taste; diarrhea; dizziness; feeling of burning, numbness, tightness, tingling, warmth or heat; feelings of drug dependence; flu-like symptoms; general pain; hiccups; mental depression; pain in jaw and neck; pain in muscles; passing of gas; problems with teeth; trouble in sleeping; unusual tiredness or weakness

Other side effects not listed above may also occur in some patients. If you notice any other effects, check with your doctor.

Developed: 07/06/98

NICOTINE   Nasal

Commonly used brand name(s):

In the U.S.—
Nicotrol NS

Description

Nicotine (NIK-oh-teen) in a nasal spray is used to help you stop smoking. It is used for up to 3 months as part of a stop-smoking program. This program may include counseling, education, or psychological support.

With the nasal spray, nicotine is inhaled through your nose and passes into your blood stream. This nicotine takes the place of the nicotine you would otherwise get from smoking. In this way, the withdrawal effects of not smoking are less severe. Then, as your body adjusts to not smoking, the use of nicotine nasal spray is decreased gradually over several weeks. Finally, use is stopped altogether.

This medicine is available only with your doctor's prescription, in the following dosage form:

Nasal
- Nasal spray (U.S.)

Before Using This Medicine

In deciding to use a medicine, the risks of using the medicine must be weighed against the good it will do. This is a decision you and your doctor will make. For nicotine, the following should be considered:

Allergies—Tell your doctor if you have ever had any unusual or allergic reaction to nicotine. Also tell your health care professional if you are allergic to any other substances, such as foods, preservatives, or dyes.

Pregnancy—Nicotine, whether from smoking or from the nasal spray, is not recommended during pregnancy. Studies in animals have shown that nicotine can cause harmful effects in the fetus.

Breast-feeding—Nicotine passes into breast milk and may cause unwanted effects in the baby. It may be necessary for you to stop breast-feeding during treatment.

Children—Small amounts of nicotine can cause poisoning in children.

Older adults—This medicine has been tested in a limited number of patients 60 years of age or older and has not been shown to cause different side effects or problems in older people than it does in younger adults.

Other medicines—Although certain medicines should not be used together at all, in other cases two different medicines may be used together even if an interaction might occur. In these cases, your doctor may want to change the dose, or other precautions may be necessary. When you are using nicotine nasal spray, it is especially important that your health care professional know if you are taking any of the following medicines:

- Beta-adrenergic blocking agents (acebutolol [e.g., Sectral], atenolol [e.g., Tenormin], betaxolol [e.g., Kerlone], bisoprolol [e.g., Zebeta], carteolol [e.g., Cartrol], labetalol [e.g., Trandate], metoprolol [e.g., Lopressor], nadolol [e.g., Corgard], oxprenolol [e.g., Trasicor], penbutolol [e.g., Levatol], pindolol [e.g., Visken], propranolol [e.g., Inderal], sotalol [e.g., Betapace], timolol [e.g., Blocadren]) or
- Insulin or
- Theophylline (e.g., Theo-Dur)—Stopping smoking may increase the effects of these medicines; the amount of medicine you need may change

Other medical problems—The presence of other medical problems may affect the use of nicotine. Make sure you tell your doctor if you have any other medical problems, especially:

- Allergies or
- Heart or blood vessel disease or
- High blood pressure or
- Liver disease or
- Nose polyps or
- Overactive thyroid or
- Pheochromocytoma or
- Sinus problems or
- Stomach ulcer or
- Type 1 diabetes (sugar diabetes)—Nicotine may make the condition worse
- Common cold or
- Stuffy nose—Nicotine nasal spray may not work properly

Proper Use of This Medicine

Nicotine nasal spray usually comes with patient directions. *Read the directions carefully before using this medicine.*

It is important to participate in a stop-smoking program during treatment. To do so may make it easier for you to stop smoking.

Use of nicotine nasal spray may be gradually reduced by using only one half of a dose at a time or skipping doses by not using the spray every hour. You may also keep track of the number of doses and use fewer each day, or set a date to stop using nicotine nasal spray.

Dosing—The dose of nicotine will be different for different patients. *Follow your doctor's orders or the directions on*

the label. The following information includes only the average doses of nicotine. *If your dose is different, do not change it* unless your doctor tells you to do so.

- For the nasal spray dosage form:
  —To help you stop smoking:
    - Adults—At first, the dose is 1 or 2 sprays into each nostril every hour. The dose should then be adjusted based on the number of cigarettes you smoked each day before beginning treatment with the nasal spray and the side effects the nasal spray causes.
    - Children—Use and dose must be determined by your doctor.

Storage—To store this medicine:

- Keep out of the reach of children.
- Store away from heat and direct light.
- Do not store in the bathroom, near the kitchen sink, or in other damp places. Heat or moisture may cause the medicine to break down.
- Keep the medicine from freezing. Do not refrigerate.
- Do not keep outdated medicine or medicine no longer needed. Be sure that any discarded medicine is out of the reach of children.

Precautions While Using This Medicine

Nicotine nasal spray should not be used by people who do not smoke because they can become addicted to nicotine.

During the first week of use, you may have a hot, peppery feeling in the back of your throat or nose; coughing; runny nose; sneezing; or watery eyes. *Do not stop using this medicine. If you continue to use nicotine nasal spray regularly, you should adjust to these effects. If these effects do not lessen after 1 week, check with your doctor.*

Avoid contact with the skin, mouth, eyes, and ears. If even a small amount of nicotine nasal spray comes into contact with the skin, mouth, eyes, or ears, the affected area should be immediately rinsed with water only.

Do not use nicotine nasal spray for longer than 3 months. To do so may result in physical dependence on the nicotine.

Nicotine should not be used in pregnancy. If there is a possibility you might become pregnant, you may want to use some type of birth control. If you think you may have become pregnant, stop using this medicine immediately and check with your doctor.

Nicotine products must be kept out of the reach of children and pets. Even very small amounts of nicotine may cause poisoning in children. If a child uses nicotine nasal spray, contact your doctor or poison control center at once.

Side Effects of This Medicine

Along with its needed effects, a medicine may cause some unwanted effects. Although not all of these side effects may occur, if they do occur they may need medical attention.

Check with your doctor as soon as possible if any of the following side effects occur:

More common
    Feelings of dependence; joint pain; shortness of breath; swelling of gums, mouth, or tongue; tightness in chest; tingling in arms, legs, hands, or feet

Less common
    Burning, tingling, or prickly sensations in nose, mouth, or head; confusion; difficulty in swallowing; dryness or pain in throat; fast or irregular heartbeat; muscle

pain; nasal blister or sore; numbness of nose or mouth

Rare

Blood-containing blisters on skin; difficulty in speaking; loss of memory; migraine headache; skin rash; swelling of feet or lower legs; wheezing

Symptoms of overdose

Cold sweat; convulsions (seizures); disturbed hearing and vision; dizziness; drooling; pale skin; slow heartbeat; tremors; vomiting; unusual tiredness or weakness

Other side effects may occur that usually do not need medical attention. These side effects may go away during treatment as your body adjusts to the medicine. However, check with your doctor if any of the following side effects continue or are bothersome:

More common

Back pain; constipation; cough; headache; hot, peppery feeling in the back of the throat or nose; indigestion; nausea; runny nose; sneezing; watery eyes

Less common

Abdominal or stomach pain; acne; change in sense of smell or taste; dryness, burning, itching, or irritation of the eyes; earache; flushing of face; passing of gas; hoarseness; itching; menstrual problems; nosebleed; sinus problems; soreness of teeth and gums; stuffy nose

Rare

Changes in vision; diarrhea; dryness of mouth; hiccups; increased amount of sputum

Other side effects not listed above may also occur in some patients. If you notice any other effects, check with your doctor.

Developed: 08/05/98

NICOTINE Systemic

Commonly used brand name(s):

In the U.S.—

Habitrol	Nicotrol
NicoDerm CQ	Prostep
Nicorette	

Generic name product may be available.

In Canada—

Habitrol	Nicorette Plus
Nicoderm	Nicotrol
Nicorette	Prostep

Description

Nicotine (NIK-o-teen), in a flavored chewing gum or a skin patch, is used to help you stop smoking. It is used for up to 12 weeks as part of a stop-smoking program. This program may include education, counseling, and psychological support.

As you chew nicotine gum, nicotine passes through the lining of your mouth and into your blood stream. When you wear a nicotine patch, nicotine passes through your skin into your blood stream. This nicotine takes the place of nicotine that you would otherwise get from smoking. In this way, the withdrawal effects of not smoking are less severe. Then, as your body adjusts to not smoking, the use of the nicotine gum is decreased gradually until use is stopped altogether. For most brands of patches, the strength of the patch you use will be decreased over a few weeks until use is stopped. If you are using the brand of patch that is available in only one strength, use is stopped after the treatment period indicated on the label.

Children, pregnant women, and nonsmokers should not use nicotine gum or patches because of harmful effects.

Nicotine gum is available without a prescription. Some nicotine patches are available without a prescription; others require a doctor's prescription. Nicotine is available in the following dosage forms:

Oral

• Chewing gum (U.S. and Canada)

Topical

• Transdermal (stick-on) skin patch (U.S. and Canada)

Before Using This Medicine

If you are using this medicine without a prescription, carefully read and follow any precautions on the label. For nicotine gum and patches, the following should be considered:

Allergies—Tell your doctor if you have ever had any unusual or allergic reaction to nicotine. Also tell your health care professional if you are allergic to any other substances, such as foods, preservatives, or dyes. If you plan to use the nicotine patches, tell your doctor if you have ever had a rash or irritation from adhesive tape or bandages.

Pregnancy—Nicotine, whether from smoking or from the gum or patches, is not recommended during pregnancy. Studies in humans show that miscarriages have occurred in pregnant women using nicotine replacement products. In addition, studies in animals have shown that nicotine can cause harmful effects in the fetus.

Breast-feeding—Nicotine passes into breast milk. It may be necessary for you to stop breast-feeding during treatment.

Children—Small amounts of nicotine can cause serious harm in children. Even nicotine patches that have been used still contain enough nicotine to cause problems in children.

Teenagers—Although there is no specific information comparing use of nicotine in teenagers with use in other age groups, this medicine is not expected to cause different side effects or problems in nicotine-dependent teenagers than it does in adults.

Older adults—Nicotine gum and patches have been used in a limited number of patients 60 years of age or older, and have not been shown to cause different side effects or problems in older people than in younger adults.

Other medicines—Although certain medicines should not be used together at all, in other cases two different medicines may be used together even if an interaction might occur. In these cases, your doctor may want to change the dose, or other precautions may be necessary. When you are using nicotine gum or patches, it is especially important that your health care professional know if you are taking any of the following:

• Aminophylline (e.g., Phyllocontin) or
• Insulin or
• Labetalol (e.g., Trandate) or
• Oxtriphylline (e.g., Choledyl) or
• Prazosin (e.g., Minipress) or

- Propoxyphene (e.g., Darvon) or
- Propranolol (e.g., Inderal) or
- Theophylline (e.g., Slo-Phyllin, Theo-Dur)—Stopping smoking may increase the effects of these medicines; the amount of medicine you need to take may change

- Isoproterenol (e.g., Isuprel) or
- Phenylephrine (e.g., Neo-Synephrine)—Stopping smoking may decrease the effects of these medicines; the amount of medicine you need to take may change

Other medical problems— The presence of other medical problems may affect the use of nicotine gum or patches. Make sure you tell your doctor if you have any other medical problems, especially:

- Dental problems (with gum only) or
- Diabetes, type 1 (sugar diabetes) or
- Heart or blood vessel disease or
- High blood pressure or
- Inflammation of mouth or throat (with gum only) or
- Irritated skin (with patches only) or
- Overactive thyroid or
- Pheochromocytoma (PCC) or
- Stomach ulcer or
- Stroke, recent or
- Temporomandibular (jaw) joint disorder (TMJ) (with gum only)—Nicotine may make the condition worse

Proper Use of This Medicine

For patients using the *chewing gum:*
- Nicotine gum usually comes with patient directions. *Read the directions carefully before using this medicine.*
- *Use nicotine gum exactly as directed on the label.* Remember that it is also important to participate in a stop-smoking program during treatment. This may make it easier for you to stop smoking.
- *When you feel the urge to smoke, chew one piece of gum very slowly* until you taste it or feel a slight tingling in your mouth. Stop chewing, and place ("park") the chewing gum between your cheek and gum until the taste or tingling is almost gone. Then chew slowly until you taste it again. Continue chewing and stopping ("parking") in this way for about 30 minutes in order to get the full dose of nicotine.
- *Do not chew too fast*, do not chew more than one piece at a time, and do not chew more than one piece of gum within an hour. To do so may cause unpleasant side effects or an overdose. Also, slower chewing will reduce the possibility of belching.
- *You should not drink acidic beverages, such as citrus fruit juices, coffee, soft drinks, or tea within 15 minutes before or while chewing a piece of gum.* The acid will prevent the nicotine from being released from the gum.
- As your urge to smoke becomes less frequent, *gradually reduce the number of pieces of gum you chew each day* until you are chewing three to six pieces a day. This may be possible within 2 to 3 months.
- *Remember to carry nicotine gum with you at all times* in case you feel the sudden urge to smoke. One cigarette may be enough to start you on the smoking habit again.
- Using hard sugarless candy between doses of gum may help to relieve any nicotine cravings you may have between doses of gum.

For patients using the *transdermal system (skin patch):*
- Nicotine patches usually come with patient instructions. *Read them carefully before using this medicine. Nicotine patches will work only if applied correctly.*
- *Remember that it is also important to participate in a stop-smoking program during treatment.* This may make it easier for you to stop smoking.
- *Do not remove the patch from its sealed pouch until you are ready to put it on your skin.* The patch may not work as well if it is unwrapped too soon.
- *Do not try to trim or cut the adhesive patch to adjust the dosage.* Check with your doctor if you think the medicine is not working as it should.
- Apply the patch to a clean, dry area of skin on your upper arm, chest, or back. Choose an area that is not very oily, has little or no hair, and is free of scars, cuts, burns, or any other skin irritations.
- Press the patch firmly in place with the palm of your hand for about 10 seconds. Make sure there is good contact with your skin, especially around the edges of the patch.
- The patch should stay in place even when you are showering, bathing, or swimming. Apply a new patch if one falls off.
- *Rinse your hands with plain water after you have finished applying the patch to your skin.* Nicotine on your hands could get into your eyes and nose and cause stinging, redness, or more serious problems. *Using soap to wash your hands will increase the amount of nicotine that passes through your skin.*
- After 16 or 24 hours, depending on which product you are using, remove the patch. Choose a different place on your skin to apply the next patch. *Do not put a new patch in the same place for at least 1 week. Do not leave the patch on for more than 24 hours.* It will not work as well after that time and it may irritate your skin.
- After removing a used patch, fold the patch in half with the sticky sides together. Place the folded, used patch in its protective pouch or in aluminum foil. Make sure to dispose of it out of the reach of children and pets.
- Try to change the patch at the same time each day. If you want to change the time when you put on your patch, just remove the patch you are wearing and put on a new patch. After that, apply a fresh patch at the new time each day.
- Nicotine patches should be removed from the skin during strenuous exercise. If a patch is left on, too much nicotine may pass through your skin into your blood stream.
- If you are using a 24-hour patch and begin having unusual dreams or disturbed sleep, you may take the patch off before going to bed and put a new one on after you wake up the next morning.

Dosing— The dose of nicotine will be different for different patients. *Follow your doctor's orders or the directions on the label.* The following information includes only the average doses of nicotine. *If your dose is different, do not change it* unless your doctor tells you to do so.

- For the *oral* dosage form (chewing gum):
    —To help you stop smoking:
    - Adults and teenagers—The usual dose is one piece of chewing gum every one to two hours for six weeks, one piece of chewing gum every two to four hours for three weeks, then one piece of chewing gum every four to eight hours for three

weeks. You should not chew more than 24 pieces of gum a day.

- Children—Use and dose must be determined by your doctor.

- For the *transdermal* (stick-on) skin patch:
  —To help you stop smoking:
    - Adults and teenagers—The dose you receive will be based on your body weight, how often you have the urge to smoke, and the brand and strength of the patch you use. This dose will be provided on the package label if the medicine was purchased over-the-counter (OTC) or by your doctor if you had to have a prescription to get the medicine.
    - Children—Use and dose must be determined by your doctor.

Storage—To store this medicine:

- Keep out of the reach of children because even small doses of nicotine can cause serious harm in children.
- Store away from heat and direct light.
- Do not store in the bathroom, near the kitchen sink, or in other damp places. Heat or moisture may cause the medicine to break down.
- Do not keep outdated medicine or medicine no longer needed. Be sure that any discarded medicine is out of the reach of children and pets.

Precautions While Using This Medicine

Do not smoke during treatment with nicotine gum or patches because of the risk of nicotine overdose.

Nicotine should not be used in pregnancy. If there is a possibility you might become pregnant, you may want to use some type of birth control. If you think you may have become pregnant, stop using this medicine immediately and check with your doctor.

Nicotine products must be kept out of the reach of children and pets. Even nicotine patches that have been used still contain enough nicotine to cause problems in children. If a child chews or swallows one or more pieces of nicotine gum, contact your doctor or poison control center at once. If a child puts on a nicotine patch or plays with a patch that is out of the sealed pouch, take it away from the child and contact your doctor or poison control center at once.

For patients using the *chewing gum:*

- *Do not chew more than 24 pieces of gum a day.* Chewing too many pieces may be harmful because of the risk of overdose.
- *Do not use nicotine gum for longer than 6 months.* To do so may result in physical dependence on the nicotine. If you feel the need to continue using the gum after 6 months, contact your doctor.
- *If the gum sticks to your dental work, stop using it and check with your medical doctor or dentist.* Dentures or other dental work may be damaged because nicotine gum is stickier and harder to chew than ordinary gum.

For patients using the *transdermal system (skin patch):*

- Mild itching, burning, or tingling may occur when the patch is first applied, and should go away within 24 hours. After a patch is removed, the skin underneath it may be red. It should not remain red for more than a day. *If you get a skin rash from the patch, or if the skin becomes swollen or very red, call your doctor.* Do not put on a new patch. If you become allergic to the nicotine in the patch, you could get sick from using cigarettes or other products that contain nicotine.
- *Do not use nicotine patches for longer than 12 weeks* if you have stopped smoking. If you feel the need to continue using nicotine patches after 12 weeks, contact your doctor.

Side Effects of This Medicine

Along with its needed effects, a medicine may cause some unwanted effects. Although not all of these side effects may occur, if they do occur they may need medical attention.

Check with your doctor as soon as possible if any of the following side effects occur:

More common
> Injury or irritation to mouth, teeth, or dental work—with chewing gum only

Less common
> High blood pressure

Rare
> Fast or irregular heartbeat; hives, itching, rash, redness, or swelling of skin

Symptoms of overdose (may occur in the following order)
> Nausea and/or vomiting; increased watering of mouth (severe); abdominal or stomach pain (severe); diarrhea (severe); pale skin; cold sweat; headache (severe); dizziness (severe); disturbed hearing and vision; tremor; confusion; weakness (severe); extreme exhaustion; fainting; low blood pressure; difficulty in breathing (severe); fast, weak, or irregular heartbeat; convulsions (seizures)

Other side effects may occur that usually do not need medical attention. These side effects may go away during treatment as your body adjusts to the medicine. However, check with your doctor if any of the following side effects continue or are bothersome:

More common
> Belching—with chewing gum only; headache (mild); increased appetite; increased watering of mouth (mild)—with chewing gum only; jaw muscle ache—with chewing gum only; redness, itching, and/or burning at site of application of patch—usually stops within 24 hours; sore mouth or throat—with chewing gum only

Less common or rare
> Abdominal or stomach pain (mild); change in sense of taste; constipation; coughing (increased); diarrhea; dizziness or lightheadedness (mild); drowsiness; dryness of mouth; hiccups—with chewing gum only; hoarseness—with chewing gum only; indigestion (mild); loss of appetite; menstrual pain; muscle or joint pain; nausea or vomiting (mild); passing of gas; sweating (increased); trouble in sleeping or unusual dreams; unusual irritability or nervousness

Other side effects not listed above may also occur in some patients. If you notice any other effects, check with your doctor.

Revised: 01/28/99

NISOLDIPINE   Systemic

Commonly used brand name(s):

In the U.S.—
Sular

Description

Nisoldipine (NYE-sole-di-peen) is a calcium channel blocking agent used to treat high blood pressure. Nisoldipine affects the movement of calcium into the cells of the heart and blood vessels. It relaxes blood vessels and increases the supply of blood and oxygen to the heart while reducing the heart's workload.

High blood pressure adds to the workload of the heart and arteries. If it continues for a long time, the heart and arteries may not function properly. This can damage the blood vessels of the brain, heart, and kidneys, resulting in a stroke, heart failure, or kidney failure. High blood pressure may also increase the risk of heart attacks. These problems may be less likely to occur if blood pressure is controlled.

This medicine is available only with your doctor's prescription, in the following dosage form:

Oral
  • Extended-release tablets (U.S.)

Before Using This Medicine

In deciding to use a medicine, the risks of taking the medicine must be weighed against the good it will do. This is a decision you and your doctor will make. For nisoldipine, the following should be considered:

Allergies—Tell your doctor if you have ever had any unusual or allergic reaction to nisoldipine or any other dihydropyridine-type calcium channel blocking agent. Also tell your health care professional if you are allergic to any other substances, such as foods, preservatives, or dyes.

Pregnancy—Nisoldipine has not been studied in pregnant women. However, studies in animals have shown that, at very high doses, nisoldipine may cause fetal death. Before taking this medicine, make sure your doctor knows if you are pregnant or if you may become pregnant.

Breast-feeding—It is not known whether nisoldipine passes into breast milk. Mothers who are taking this medicine and who wish to breast-feed should discuss this with their doctor.

Children—Studies on this medicine have been done only in adult patients, and there is no specific information comparing use of nisoldipine in children with use in other age groups.

Older adults—Elderly people may have higher blood levels of nisoldipine, which may increase the chance of side effects during treatment.

Other medicines—Although certain medicines should not be used together at all, in other cases two different medicines may be used together even if an interaction might occur. In these cases, your doctor may want to change the dose, or other precautions may be necessary. Tell your health care professional if you are using any other prescription or nonprescription (over-the-counter [OTC]) medicine.

Other medical problems—The presence of other medical problems may affect the use of nisoldipine. Make sure you tell your doctor if you have any other medical problems, especially:

  • Blood vessel disease (coronary artery disease)—Nisoldipine may cause chest pain or a heart attack
  • Congestive heart failure—Nisoldipine may make this condition worse
  • Liver disease—Higher blood levels of nisoldipine may result and a smaller dose may be needed

Proper Use of This Medicine

Take this medicine exactly as directed even if you feel well. Do not take more of this medicine and do not take it more often than your doctor ordered. This medicine works best if there is a constant amount in the blood. To keep blood levels constant, take this medicine at the same time each day and do not miss any doses.

Swallow the tablet whole, without breaking, crushing, or chewing it.

Nisoldipine should not be taken with a high-fat meal or with grapefruit juice or other grapefruit products because these may increase the levels of nisoldipine in the body.

Dosing—The dose of nisoldipine will be different for different patients. *Follow your doctor's orders or the directions on the label.* The following information includes only the average doses of nisoldipine. *If your dose is different, do not change it* unless your doctor tells you to do so.

The number of tablets that you take depends on the strength of the medicine.

  • For *oral* dosage form (tablets):
    —For high blood pressure:
      • Adults—10 to 20 mg once a day. Your doctor may increase your dose if needed.
      • Children—Use and dose must be determined by your doctor.

Missed dose—If you miss a dose of this medicine, take it as soon as possible. However, if it is almost time for your next dose, skip the missed dose and go back to your regular dosing schedule. Do not double doses.

Storage—To store this medicine:
  • Keep out of the reach of children.
  • Store away from heat and direct light.
  • Do not store in the bathroom, near the kitchen sink, or in other damp places. Heat or moisture may cause the medicine to break down.
  • Do not keep outdated medicine or medicine no longer needed. Be sure that any discarded medicine is out of the reach of children.

Precautions While Using This Medicine

It is important that your doctor check your progress at regular visits. This will allow your doctor to make sure the medicine is working properly and to change the dosage if needed.

This medicine may cause dizziness, lightheadedness, or fainting. Make sure you know how you react to this medicine before you drive, use machines, or do anything else that could be dangerous if you experience these effects.

Side Effects of This Medicine

Along with its needed effects, a medicine may cause some unwanted effects. Although not all of these side effects may occur, if they do occur they may need medical attention.

Check with your doctor as soon as possible if any of the following side effects occur:

More common
Swelling of ankles, feet, or lower legs

Less common
Chest pain; dizziness, lightheadedness, or fainting; rash

Rare
A reaction which may include swelling of the arms, face, legs, lips, tongue, and/or throat; shortness of breath; fast heart rate; chest tightness; dizziness, lightheadedness, or fainting; and/or skin rash

Other side effects may occur that usually do not need medical attention. These side effects may go away during treatment as your body adjusts to the medicine. However, check with your doctor if any of the following side effects continue or are bothersome:

More common
Headache

Less common
Dizziness; hoarseness and/or sore throat; heartbeat sensations; stuffy nose

Other side effects not listed above may also occur in some patients. If you notice any other effects, check with your doctor.

Developed: 01/04/99

NITRATES—Lingual Aerosol
Systemic†

This information applies to nitroglycerin oral spray.
Commonly used brand name(s):

In the U.S.—
Nitrolingual
Another commonly used name is glyceryl trinitrate.

†Not commercially available in Canada.

Description

Nitrates (NYE-trates) are used to treat the symptoms of angina (chest pain). Depending on the type of dosage form and how it is taken, nitrates are used to treat angina in three ways:

- to relieve an attack that is occurring by using the medicine when the attack begins;
- to prevent attacks from occurring by using the medicine just before an attack is expected to occur; or
- to reduce the number of attacks that occur by using the medicine regularly on a long-term basis.

When used as a lingual (in the mouth) spray, nitroglycerin is used either to relieve the pain of angina attacks or to prevent an expected angina attack.

Nitroglycerin works by relaxing blood vessels and increasing the supply of blood and oxygen to the heart while reducing its work load.

Nitroglycerin as discussed here is available only with your doctor's prescription, in the following dosage form:

Oral
- Lingual aerosol (U.S.)

Before Using This Medicine

In deciding to use a medicine, the risks of taking the medicine must be weighed against the good it will do. This is a decision you and your doctor will make. For nitroglycerin lingual aerosol, the following should be considered:

Allergies—Tell your doctor if you have ever had any unusual or allergic reaction to nitrates or nitrites. Also tell your health care professional if you are allergic to any other substances, such as certain foods, preservatives, or dyes.

Pregnancy—Studies on effects in pregnancy have not been done in either humans or animals.

Breast-feeding—It is not known whether this medicine passes into breast milk. Although most medicines pass into breast milk in small amounts, many of them may be used safely while breast-feeding. Mothers who are taking this medicine and who wish to breast-feed should discuss this with their doctor.

Children—Studies on this medicine have been done only in adult patients, and there is no specific information comparing use of nitroglycerin in children with use in other age groups.

Older adults—Dizziness or lightheadedness may be more likely to occur in the elderly, who may be more sensitive to the effects of nitrates.

Other medicines—Although certain medicines should not be used together at all, in other cases two different medicines may be used together even if an interaction might occur. In these cases, your doctor may want to change the dose, or other precautions may be necessary. When you are taking nitroglycerin, it is especially important that your health care professional know if you are taking any of the following:

- Antihypertensives (high blood pressure medicine) or
- Other heart medicine or
- Sildenafil—May increase the effects of nitroglycerin on blood pressure

Other medical problems—The presence of other medical problems may affect the use of nitroglycerin. Make sure you tell your doctor if you have any other medical problems, especially:

- Anemia (severe)
- Glaucoma—May be worsened by nitroglycerin
- Head injury (recent) or
- Stroke (recent)—Nitroglycerin may increase pressure in the brain, which can make problems worse
- Heart attack (recent)—Nitroglycerin may lower blood pressure, which can aggravate problems associated with heart attack
- Kidney disease or
- Liver disease—Effects may be increased because of slower removal of nitroglycerin from the body
- Overactive thyroid

Proper Use of This Medicine

Use nitroglycerin spray exactly as directed by your doctor. It will work only if used correctly.

This medicine usually comes with patient instructions. Read them carefully before you actually need to use it. Then, if you need the medicine quickly, you will know how to use it.

To use nitroglycerin lingual spray:
- Remove the plastic cover. *Do not shake the container.*
- Hold the container upright. With the container held close to your mouth, press the button to spray onto or under your tongue. *Do not inhale the spray.*
- Release the button and close your mouth. Avoid swallowing immediately after using the spray.

For patients using nitroglycerin oral spray *to relieve the pain of an angina attack:*
- *When you begin to feel an attack of angina starting (chest pains or a tightness or squeezing in the chest), sit down. Then use 1 or 2 sprays as directed by your doctor.* This medicine works best when you are standing or sitting. However, since you may become dizzy, lightheaded, or faint soon after using a spray, it is safer to sit rather than stand while the medicine is working. If you become dizzy or faint while sitting, take several deep breaths and bend forward with your head between your knees.
- Remain calm and you should feel better in a few minutes.
- *This medicine usually gives relief in less than 5 minutes.* However, if the pain is not relieved, use a second spray. If the pain continues for another 5 minutes, a third spray may be used. *If you still have the chest pains after a total of 3 sprays in a 15-minute period, contact your doctor or go to a hospital emergency room immediately.*

For patients using nitroglycerin oral spray *to prevent an expected angina attack:*
- You may prevent anginal chest pains for up to 1 hour by using a spray 5 to 10 minutes before expected emotional stress or physical exertion that in the past seemed to bring on an attack.

Dosing—The dose of nitroglycerin lingual spray will be different for different patients. *Follow your doctor's orders or the directions on the label.* The following information includes only the average doses of nitroglycerin lingual spray. *If your dose is different, do not change it* unless your doctor tells you to do so.
- For *oral* dosage form (lingual spray):
  —For chest pain:
    - Adults—One or two sprays on or under the tongue. The dose may be repeated every five minutes as needed. If the chest pain is not relieved after a total of three sprays in a fifteen-minute period, call your doctor or go to the emergency room right away.

Storage—To store this medicine
- Keep out of the reach of children.
- Store away from heat and direct light.
- Keep the medicine from freezing.
- Do not puncture, break, or burn the aerosol container, even after it is empty.
- Do not keep outdated medicine or medicine no longer needed. Be sure that any discarded medicine is out of the reach of children.

Precautions While Using This Medicine

Do not take sildenafil (e.g., Viagra) if you are taking this medicine. When sildenafil is taken with nitrates, the combination can lower blood pressure and cause dizziness, lightheadedness, or fainting. *In some case, sildenafil taken with nitrates has caused death.*

If you have been using this medicine regularly for several weeks, do not suddenly stop using it. Stopping suddenly may bring on attacks of angina. Check with your doctor for the best way to reduce gradually the amount you are using before stopping completely.

Dizziness, lightheadedness, or faintness may occur, especially when you get up quickly from a lying or sitting position. Getting up slowly may help. If you feel dizzy, sit or lie down.

The dizziness, lightheadedness, or fainting is also more likely to occur if you drink alcohol, stand for long periods of time, exercise, or if the weather is hot. *While you are taking this medicine, be careful to limit the amount of alcohol you drink. Also, use extra care during exercise or hot weather or if you must stand for long periods of time.*

After using a dose of this medicine you may get a headache that lasts for a short time. This is a common side effect, which should become less noticeable after you have used the medicine for a while. If this effect continues or if the headaches are severe, check with your doctor.

Side Effects of This Medicine

Along with its needed effects, a medicine may cause some unwanted effects. Although not all of these side effects may occur, if they do occur they may need medical attention.

Check with your doctor as soon as possible if any of the following side effects occur:
Rare
  Blurred vision; dryness of mouth; headache (severe or prolonged); skin rash
Signs and symptoms of overdose (in the order in which they may occur)
  Bluish-colored lips, fingernails, or palms of hands; dizziness (extreme) or fainting; feeling of extreme pressure in head; shortness of breath; unusual tiredness or weakness; weak and fast heartbeat; fever; convulsions (seizures)

Other side effects may occur that usually do not need medical attention. These side effects may go away during treatment as your body adjusts to the medicine. However, check with your doctor if any of the following side effects continue or are bothersome:
More common
  Dizziness or lightheadedness, especially when getting up from a lying or sitting position; fast pulse; flushing of face and neck; headache; nausea or vomiting; restlessness

Other side effects not listed above may also occur in some patients. If you notice any other effects, check with your doctor.

Revised: 10/06/93
Interim revision: 08/21/98

NITRATES —Oral   Systemic

Commonly used brand name(s):

In the U.S.—

Dilatrate-SR[1]	Nitrocot[3]
IMDUR[2]	Nitroglyn E-R[3]
ISDN[1]	Nitro-par[3]
ISMO[2]	Nitro-time[3]
Isordil Tembids[1]	Nitrong[3]
Isordil Titradose[1]	Sorbitrate[1]
Monoket[2]	

In Canada—

Apo-ISDN[1]	IMDUR[2]
Cedocard-SR[1]	ISMO[2]
Coradur[1]	Isordil Titradose[1]
Coronex[1]	Nitrong SR[3]

Another commonly used name is:

Glyceryl trinitrate

Note: For quick reference, the following nitrates are numbered to match the corresponding brand names.

This information applies to the following medicines:
1. Isosorbide Dinitrate (eye-soe-SOR-bide dye-NYE-trate) ‡§
2. Isosorbide Mononitrate (eye-soe-SOR-bide mon-oh-NYE-trate)
3. Nitroglycerin (nye-troe-GLI-ser-in) ‡

Note: This information does *not* apply to amyl nitrite or mannitol hexanitrate.

---

‡Generic name product may be available in the U.S.
§Generic name product may be available in Canada.

Description

Nitrates (NYE-trates) are used to treat the symptoms of angina (chest pain). Depending on the type of dosage form and how it is taken, nitrates are used to treat angina in three ways:

- to relieve an attack that is occurring by using the medicine when the attack begins;
- to prevent attacks from occurring by using the medicine just before an attack is expected to occur; or
- to reduce the number of attacks that occur by using the medicine regularly on a long-term basis.

When taken orally and swallowed, nitrates are used to reduce the number of angina attacks that occur. They do not act fast enough to relieve the pain of an angina attack.

Nitrates work by relaxing blood vessels and increasing the supply of blood and oxygen to the heart while reducing its work load.

Nitrates may also be used for other conditions as determined by your doctor.

The nitrates discussed here are available only with your doctor's prescription, in the following dosage forms:

Oral
Isosorbide dinitrate
- Extended-release capsules (U.S.)
- Tablets (U.S. and Canada)
- Chewable tablets (U.S.)
- Extended-release tablets (U.S. and Canada)
Isosorbide mononitrate
- Extended-release tablets (U.S.)
- Tablets (U.S.)
Nitroglycerin
- Extended-release capsules (U.S.)
- Extended-release tablets (U.S. and Canada)

Before Using This Medicine

In deciding to use a medicine, the risks of taking the medicine must be weighed against the good it will do. This is a decision you and your doctor will make. For nitrates, the following should be considered:

Allergies—Tell your doctor if you have ever had any unusual or allergic reaction to nitrates or nitrites. Also tell your health care professional if you are allergic to any other substances, such as certain foods, preservatives, or dyes.

Pregnancy—Nitrates have not been studied in pregnant women. However, studies in rabbits given large doses of isosorbide dinitrate have shown adverse effects on the fetus. Before taking these medicines, make sure your doctor knows if you are pregnant or if you may become pregnant.

Breast-feeding—It is not known whether these medicines pass into breast milk. Although most medicines pass into breast milk in small amounts, many of them may be used safely while breast-feeding. Mothers who are taking these medicines and who wish to breast-feed should discuss this with their doctor.

Children—Studies on these medicines have been done only in adult patients, and there is no specific information comparing use of nitrates in children with use in other age groups.

Older adults—Dizziness or lightheadedness may be more likely to occur in the elderly, who may be more sensitive to the effects of nitrates.

Other medicines—Although certain medicines should not be used together at all, in other cases two different medicines may be used together even if an interaction might occur. In these cases, your doctor may want to change the dose, or other precautions may be necessary. When you are taking nitrates, it is especially important that your health care professional know if you are taking any of the following:

- Antihypertensives (high blood pressure medicine) or
- Other heart medicine or
- Sildenafil—May increase the effects of nitrates on blood pressure

Other medical problems—The presence of other medical problems may affect the use of nitrates. Make sure you tell your doctor if you have any other medical problems, especially:

- Anemia (severe)
- Glaucoma—May be worsened by nitrates
- Head injury (recent) or
- Stroke (recent)—Nitrates may increase pressure in the brain, which can make problems worse
- Heart attack (recent)—Nitrates may lower blood pressure, which can aggravate problems associated with heart attack
- Kidney disease or
- Liver disease—Effects may be increased because of slower removal of nitroglycerin from the body
- Overactive thyroid

Proper Use of This Medicine

Take this medicine exactly as directed by your doctor. It will work only if taken correctly.

This form of nitrate is used to reduce the number of angina attacks. In most cases, it will not relieve an attack

---

that has already started because it works too slowly (the extended-release form releases medicine gradually over a 6-hour period to provide its effect for 8 to 10 hours). Check with your doctor if you need a fast-acting medicine to relieve the pain of an angina attack.

Take this medicine with a full glass (8 ounces) of water on an empty stomach. If taken either 1 hour before or 2 hours after meals, it will start working sooner.

Extended-release capsules and tablets are not to be broken, crushed, or chewed before they are swallowed. If broken up, they will not release the medicine properly.

Dosing—The dose of nitrates will be different for different patients. *Follow your doctor's orders or the directions on the label.* The following information includes only the average doses of nitrates. *If your dose is different, do not change it* unless your doctor tells you to do so.

The number of capsules or tablets that you take depends on the strength of the medicine. Also, *the number of doses you take each day, the time allowed between doses, and the length of time you take the medicine depend on the medical problem for which you are taking nitrates.*

For isosorbide dinitrate
- For angina (chest pain):
  —For *regular (short-acting) oral* dosage forms (capsules or tablets):
    - Adults—5 to 40 mg four times a day.
    - Children—Dose must be determined by your doctor.
  —For *long-acting oral* dosage forms (extended-release capsules or tablets):
    - Adults—20 to 80 mg every eight to twelve hours.
    - Children—Dose must be determined by your doctor.

For isosorbide mononitrate
- For angina (chest pain):
  —For *regular (short-acting) oral* dosage form (tablets):
    - Adults—20 mg two times a day. The two doses should be taken seven hours apart.
    - Children—Use and dose must be determined by your doctor.
  —For *long-acting oral* dosage forms (extended-release tablets):
    - Adults—30 to 240 mg once a day.
    - Children—Use and dose must be determined by your doctor.

For nitroglycerin
- For angina (chest pain):
  —For *long-acting oral* dosage forms (capsules or tablets):
    - Adults—2.5 to 9.0 mg every eight to twelve hours.
    - Children—Dose must be determined by your doctor.

Missed dose—If you are taking this medicine regularly and you miss a dose, take it as soon as possible. However, if the next scheduled dose is within 2 hours (or within 6 hours for extended-release capsules or tablets), skip the missed dose and go back to your regular dosing schedule. Do not double doses.

Storage—To store this medicine:
- Keep out of the reach of children.
- Store away from heat and direct light.
- Do not store in the bathroom, near the kitchen sink, or in other damp places. Heat or moisture may cause the medicine to break down.
- Do not keep outdated medicine or medicine no longer needed. Be sure that any discarded medicine is out of the reach of children.

Precautions While Using This Medicine

Do not take sildenafil (e.g., Viagra) if you are taking this medicine. When sildenafil is taken with nitrates, the combination can lower blood pressure and cause dizziness, lightheadedness, or fainting. *In some case, sildenafil taken with nitrates has caused death.*

If you have been taking this medicine regularly for several weeks or more, do not suddenly stop using it. Stopping suddenly may bring on attacks of angina. Check with your doctor for the best way to reduce gradually the amount you are taking before stopping completely.

Dizziness, lightheadedness, or faintness may occur, especially when you get up quickly from a lying or sitting position. Getting up slowly may help. If you feel dizzy, sit or lie down.

The dizziness, lightheadedness, or fainting is also more likely to occur if you drink alcohol, stand for long periods of time, exercise, or if the weather is hot. *While you are taking this medicine, be careful to limit the amount of alcohol you drink. Also, use extra care during exercise or hot weather or if you must stand for long periods of time.*

After taking a dose of this medicine you may get a headache that lasts for a short time. This is a common side effect, which should become less noticeable after you have taken the medicine for a while. If this effect continues, or if the headaches are severe, check with your doctor.

For patients taking the *extended-release dosage forms of isosorbide dinitrate:*
- Partially dissolved tablets have been found in the stools of a few patients taking the extended-release tablets. Be alert to this possibility, especially if you have frequent bowel movements, diarrhea, or digestive problems. Notify your doctor if any such tablets are discovered. The tablets must be properly digested to provide the correct dose of medicine.

Side Effects of This Medicine

Along with its needed effects, a medicine may cause some unwanted effects. Although not all of these side effects may occur, if they do occur they may need medical attention.

Check with your doctor as soon as possible if any of the following side effects occur:
Rare
  Blurred vision; dryness of mouth; headache (severe or prolonged); skin rash
Signs and symptoms of overdose (in the order in which they may occur)
  Bluish-colored lips, fingernails, or palms of hands; dizziness (extreme) or fainting; feeling of extreme pressure in head; shortness of breath; unusual tiredness or weakness; weak and fast heartbeat; fever; convulsions (seizures)

Other side effects may occur that usually do not need medical attention. These side effects may go away during treatment as your body adjusts to the medicine. However, check with

your doctor if any of the following side effects continue or are bothersome:

   More common
      Dizziness or lightheadedness, especially when getting up from a lying or sitting position; fast pulse; flushing of face and neck; headache; nausea or vomiting; restlessness

Other side effects not listed above may also occur in some patients. If you notice any other effects, check with your doctor.

Revised: 08/17/98

NITRATES —Sublingual, Chewable, or Buccal   Systemic

Commonly used brand name(s):

In the U.S.—

Isordil[1]	Nitrostat[2]
Nitrogard[2]	Sorbitrate[1]

In Canada—

Apo-ISDN[1]	Isordil[1]
Coronex[1]	Nitrostat[2]

Another commonly used name is:
   Glyceryl trinitrate

Note: For quick reference, the following nitrates are numbered to match the corresponding brand names.

This information applies to the following medicines:
1. Isosorbide Dinitrate (eye-soe-SOR-bide dye-NYE-trate) ‡§
2. Nitroglycerin (nye-troe-GLI-ser-in) ‡§

Note: This information does *not* apply to amylnitrite.

---

‡Generic name product may be available in the U.S.
§Generic name product may be available in Canada.

Description

Nitrates (NYE-trates) are used to treat the symptoms of angina (chest pain). Depending on the type of dosage form and how it is taken, nitrates are used to treat angina in three ways:
* to relieve an attack that is occurring by using the medicine when the attack begins;
* to prevent attacks from occurring by using the medicine just before an attack is expected to occur; or
* to reduce the number of attacks that occur by using the medicine regularly on a long-term basis.

Nitrates are available in different forms. Sublingual nitrates are generally placed under the tongue where they dissolve and are absorbed through the lining of the mouth. Some can also be used buccally, being placed under the lip or in the cheek. The chewable dosage forms, after being chewed and held in the mouth before swallowing, are absorbed in the same way. *It is important to remember that each dosage form is different and that the specific directions for each type must be followed if the medicine is to work properly.*

Nitrates that are used *to relieve the pain* of an angina attack include:
* sublingual nitroglycerin;
* buccal nitroglycerin;
* sublingual isosorbide dinitrate; and
* chewable isosorbide dinitrate.

Those that can be used *to prevent expected attacks* of angina include:
* sublingual nitroglycerin;
* buccal nitroglycerin;
* sublingual isosorbide dinitrate; and
* chewable isosorbide dinitrate.

Products that are used regularly on a long-term basis *to reduce the number of attacks* that occur include:
* buccal nitroglycerin;
* chewable isosorbide dinitrate; and
* sublingual isosorbide dinitrate.

Nitrates work by relaxing blood vessels and increasing the supply of blood and oxygen to the heart while reducing its work load.

Nitrates may also be used for other conditions as determined by your doctor.

The nitrates discussed here are available only with your doctor's prescription, in the following dosage forms:

   Buccal
   Nitroglycerin
      • Extended-release tablets (U.S. and Canada)
   Chewable
   Isosorbide dinitrate
      • Tablets (U.S.)
   Sublingual
   Isosorbide dinitrate
      • Tablets (U.S. and Canada)
   Nitroglycerin
      • Tablets (U.S. and Canada)

Before Using This Medicine

In deciding to use a medicine, the risks of taking the medicine must be weighed against the good it will do. This is a decision you and your doctor will make. For nitrates, the following should be considered:

Allergies—Tell your doctor if you have ever had any unusual or allergic reaction to nitrates or nitrites. Also tell your health care professional if you are allergic to any other substances, such as certain foods, preservatives, or dyes.

Pregnancy—Nitrates have not been studied in pregnant women. However, studies in rabbits given large doses of isosorbide dinitrate have shown adverse effects on the fetus. Before taking these medicines, make sure your doctor knows if you are pregnant or if you may become pregnant.

Breast-feeding—It is not known whether these medicines pass into breast milk. Although most medicines pass into breast milk in small amounts, many of them may be used safely while breast-feeding. Mothers who are taking these medicines and who wish to breast-feed should discuss this with their doctor.

Children—Studies on these medicines have been done only in adult patients, and there is no specific information comparing use of nitrates in children with use in other age groups.

Older adults—Dizziness or lightheadedness may be more likely to occur in the elderly, who may be more sensitive to the effects of nitrates.

Other medicines—Although certain medicines should not be used together at all, in other cases two different medicines may be used together even if an interaction might occur. In these cases, your doctor may want to change the

dose, or other precautions may be necessary. When you are taking nitrates, it is especially important that your health care professional know if you are taking any of the following:

- Antihypertensives (high blood pressure medicine) or
- Other heart medicine or
- Sildenafil—May increase the effects of nitrates on blood pressure

Other medical problems—The presence of other medical problems may affect the use of nitrates. Make sure you tell your doctor if you have any other medical problems, especially:

- Anemia (severe)
- Glaucoma—May be worsened by nitrates
- Head injury (recent) or
- Stroke (recent)—Nitrates may increase pressure in the brain, which can make problems worse
- Heart attack (recent)—Nitrates may lower blood pressure, which can aggravate problems associated with heart attack
- Kidney disease or
- Liver disease—Effects may be increased because of slower removal of nitroglycerin from the body
- Overactive thyroid

Proper Use of This Medicine

Take this medicine exactly as directed by your doctor. It will work only if taken correctly.

Sublingual tablets should not be chewed, crushed, or swallowed. They work much faster when absorbed through the lining of the mouth. Place the tablet under the tongue, between the lip and gum, or between the cheek and gum and let it dissolve there. Do not eat, drink, smoke, or use chewing tobacco while a tablet is dissolving.

Buccal extended-release tablets should not be chewed, crushed, or swallowed. They are designed to release a dose of nitroglycerin over a period of hours, not all at once.

- Allow the tablet to dissolve slowly in place between the upper lip and gum (above the front teeth), or between the cheek and upper gum. If food or drink is to be taken during the 3 to 5 hours when the tablet is dissolving, place the tablet between the *upper* lip and gum, above the front teeth. If you have dentures, you may place the tablet anywhere between the cheek and gum.
- Touching the tablet with your tongue or drinking hot liquids may cause the tablet to dissolve faster.
- Do not go to sleep while a tablet is dissolving because it could slip down your throat and cause choking.
- If you accidentally swallow the tablet, replace it with another one.
- Do not use chewing tobacco while a tablet is in place.

Chewable tablets must be chewed well and held in the mouth for about 2 minutes before you swallow them. This will allow the medicine to be absorbed through the lining of the mouth.

For patients using *nitroglycerin or isosorbide dinitrate to relieve the pain of an angina attack:*

- *When you begin to feel an attack of angina starting (chest pains or a tightness or squeezing in the chest), sit down. Then place a tablet in your mouth, either sublingually or buccally, or chew a chewable tablet.* This medicine works best when you are standing or sitting. However, since you may become dizzy, light-headed, or faint soon after using a tablet, it is safer to sit rather than stand while the medicine is working. If you become dizzy or faint while sitting, take several deep breaths and bend forward with your head between your knees.
- Remain calm and you should feel better in a few minutes.
- *This medicine usually gives relief in 1 to 5 minutes.* However, if the pain is not relieved, and you are using:
  - Sublingual tablets, either sublingually or buccally: Use a second tablet. If the pain continues for another 5 minutes, a third tablet may be used. *If you still have the chest pains after a total of 3 tablets in a 15-minute period, contact your doctor or go to a hospital emergency room immediately.*
  - Buccal extended-release tablets: *Use a sublingual (under the tongue) nitroglycerin tablet and check with your doctor.* Do not use another buccal tablet since the effects of a buccal tablet last for several hours.

For patients using *nitroglycerin or isosorbide dinitrate to prevent an expected angina attack:*

- You may prevent anginal chest pains for up to 1 hour (6 hours for the extended-release nitroglycerin tablet) by using a buccal or sublingual tablet or chewing a chewable tablet 5 to 10 minutes before expected emotional stress or physical exertion that in the past seemed to bring on an attack.

For patients using *isosorbide dinitrate or extended-release buccal nitroglycerin regularly on a long-term basis to reduce the number of angina attacks that occur:*

- Chewable or sublingual isosorbide dinitrate and buccal extended-release nitroglycerin tablets can be used either to prevent angina attacks or to help relieve an attack that has already started.

Dosing—The dose of nitrates will be different for different patients. *Follow your doctor's orders or the directions on the label.* The following information includes only the average doses of nitrates. *If your dose is different, do not change it* unless your doctor tells you to do so.

For isosorbide dinitrate
- For angina (chest pain):
  - For *chewable* dosage form (tablets):
    - Adults—5 mg every two to three hours, chewed well and held in mouth for one or two minutes.
    - Children—Dose must be determined by your doctor.
  - For *sublingual* dosage form (tablets):
    - Adults—2.5 to 5 mg every two to three hours.
    - Children—Dose must be determined by your doctor.

For nitroglycerin
- For angina (chest pain):
  - For *buccal* dosage form (extended-release tablets):
    - Adults—1 mg every five hours while awake. Your doctor may increase your dose.
    - Children—Dose must be determined by your doctor.
  - For *sublingual* dosage form (tablets):
    - Adults—300 to 600 micrograms (mcg) (0.3 to 0.6 mg) every five minutes. If you still have chest pain after a total of three tablets in fifteen minutes, call your doctor or go to the emergency room right away.

• Children—Dose must be determined by your doctor.

Missed dose—For patients using isosorbide dinitrate or extended-release buccal nitroglycerin regularly on a long-term basis to reduce the number of angina attacks that occur:

• If you miss a dose of this medicine, use it as soon as possible. However, if the next scheduled dose is within 2 hours, skip the missed dose and go back to your regular dosing schedule. Do not double doses.

Stability and proper storage—*For sublingual nitroglycerin*

• Sublingual nitroglycerin tablets may lose some of their strength if they are exposed to air, heat, or moisture for long periods of time. However, if you screw the cap on tightly after each use and you properly store the bottle, the tablets should retain their strength until the expiration date on the bottle.
• Some people think they should test the strength of their sublingual nitroglycerin tablets by looking for a tingling or burning sensation, a feeling of warmth or flushing, or a headache after a tablet has been dissolved under the tongue. This kind of testing is not completely reliable since some patients may be unable to detect these effects. In addition, newer, stabilized sublingual nitroglycerin tablets are less likely to produce these detectable effects.
• To help keep the nitroglycerin tablets at full strength:
  —keep the medicine in the original glass, screw-cap bottle. For patients who wish to carry a small number of tablets with them for emergency use, a specially designed container is available. However, only containers specifically labeled as suitable for use with nitroglycerin sublingual tablets should be used.
  —remove the cotton plug that comes in the bottle and *do not* put it back.
  —*put the cap on the bottle quickly and tightly after each use.*
  —to select a tablet for use, pour several into the bottle cap, take one, and pour the others back into the bottle. Try not to hold them in the palm of your hand because they may pick up moisture and crumble.
  —do not keep other medicines in the same bottle with the nitroglycerin since they will weaken the nitroglycerin effect.
  —keep the medicine handy at all times but try not to carry the bottle close to the body. Medicine may lose strength because of body warmth. Instead, carry the tightly closed bottle in your purse or the pocket of a jacket or other loose-fitting clothing whenever possible.
  —store the bottle of nitroglycerin tablets in a cool, dry place. Storage at average room temperature away from direct heat or direct sunlight is best. Do not store in the refrigerator or in a bathroom medicine cabinet because the moisture usually present in these areas may cause the tablets to crumble if the container is not tightly closed. Do not keep the tablets in your automobile glove compartment.
• Keep out of the reach of children.
• Do not keep outdated medicine or medicine no longer needed. Be sure that any discarded medicine is out of the reach of children.

For isosorbide dinitrate and buccal extended-release nitroglycerin

• These forms of nitrates are more stable than sublingual nitroglycerin.
• Keep out of the reach of children.
• Store away from heat and direct light.
• Do not store in the bathroom, near the kitchen sink, or in other damp places. Heat or moisture may cause the medicine to break down.
• Do not keep outdated medicine or medicine no longer needed. Be sure that any discarded medicine is out of the reach of children.

Precautions While Using This Medicine

Do not take sildenafil (e.g., Viagra) if you are taking this medicine. When sildenafil is taken with nitrates, the combination can lower blood pressure and cause dizziness, lightheadedness, or fainting. *In some case, sildenafil taken with nitrates has caused death.*

If you have been taking this medicine regularly for several weeks, do not suddenly stop using it. Stopping suddenly may bring on attacks of angina. Check with your doctor for the best way to reduce gradually the amount you are taking before stopping completely.

Dizziness, lightheadedness, or faintness may occur, especially when you get up quickly from a lying or sitting position. Getting up slowly may help. If you feel dizzy, sit or lie down.

The dizziness, lightheadedness, or fainting is also more likely to occur if you drink alcohol, stand for long periods of time, exercise, or if the weather is hot. *While you are taking this medicine, be careful to limit the amount of alcohol you drink. Also, use extra care during exercise or hot weather or if you must stand for long periods of time.*

After taking a dose of this medicine you may get a headache that lasts for a short time. This is a common side effect, which should become less noticeable after you have taken the medicine for a while. If this effect continues or if the headaches are severe, check with your doctor.

Side Effects of This Medicine

Along with its needed effects, a medicine may cause some unwanted effects. Although not all of these side effects may occur, if they do occur they may need medical attention.

Check with your doctor as soon as possible if any of the following side effects occur:
Rare
  Blurred vision; dryness of mouth; headache (severe or prolonged); skin rash
Signs and symptoms of overdose (in the order in which they may occur)
  Bluish-colored lips, fingernails, or palms of hands; dizziness (extreme) or fainting; feeling of extreme pressure in head; shortness of breath; unusual tiredness or weakness; weak and fast heartbeat; fever; convulsions (seizures)

Other side effects may occur that usually do not need medical attention. These side effects may go away during treatment as your body adjusts to the medicine. However, check with

your doctor if any of the following side effects continue or are bothersome:

More common

> Dizziness or lightheadedness, especially when getting up from a lying or sitting position; fast pulse; flushing of face and neck; headache; nausea or vomiting; restlessness

Other side effects not listed above may also occur in some patients. If you notice any other effects, check with your doctor.

Revised: 08/18/98

NITRATES —Topical   Systemic

Commonly used brand name(s):

In the U.S.—

Deponit[2]	Nitro-Dur[2]
Minitran[2]	Nitrol[1]
Nitro-Bid[1]	Transderm-Nitro[2]
Nitrodisc[2]	

In Canada—

Minitran[2]	Nitrol[1]
Nitro-Dur[2]	Transderm-Nitro[2]

Another commonly used name for nitroglycerin is glyceryl trinitrate.

Note: For quick reference, the following nitrates are numbered to match the corresponding brand names.

This information applies to the following medicines:
1. Nitroglycerin Ointment‡
2. Nitroglycerin Transdermal Patches‡

‡Generic name product may be available in the U.S.

Description

Nitrates (NYE-trates) are used to treat the symptoms of angina (chest pain). Depending on the type of dosage form and how it is taken, nitrates are used to treat angina in three ways:
- to relieve an attack that is occurring by using the medicine when the attack begins;
- to prevent attacks from occurring by using the medicine just before an attack is expected to occur; or
- to reduce the number of attacks that occur by using the medicine regularly on a long-term basis.

When applied to the skin, nitrates are used to reduce the number of angina attacks that occur. The only nitrate available for this purpose is topical nitroglycerin (nye-troe-GLI-ser-in).

Topical nitroglycerin is absorbed through the skin. It works by relaxing blood vessels and increasing the supply of blood and oxygen to the heart while reducing its work load. This helps prevent future angina attacks from occurring.

Topical nitroglycerin may also be used for other conditions as determined by your doctor.

Nitroglycerin as discussed here is available only with your doctor's prescription, in the following dosage forms:

Topical
- Ointment (U.S. and Canada)
- Transdermal (stick-on) patch (U.S. and Canada)

Before Using This Medicine

In deciding to use a medicine, the risks of taking the medicine must be weighed against the good it will do. This is a decision you and your doctor will make. For nitroglycerin applied to the skin, the following should be considered:

Allergies—Tell your doctor if you have ever had any unusual or allergic reaction to nitrates or nitrites. Also tell your health care professional if you are allergic to any other substances, such as certain foods, preservatives, or dyes.

Pregnancy—Nitrates have not been studied in pregnant women. Before taking these medicines, make sure your doctor knows if you are pregnant or if you may become pregnant.

Breast-feeding—It is not known whether this medicine passes into breast milk. Although most medicines pass into breast milk in small amounts, many of them may be used safely while breast-feeding. Mothers who are taking these medicines and who wish to breast-feed should discuss this with their doctor.

Children—Studies on these medicines have been done only in adult patients, and there is no specific information comparing use of nitrates in children with use in other age groups.

Older adults—Dizziness or lightheadedness may be more likely to occur in the elderly, who may be more sensitive to the effects of nitrates.

Other medicines—Although certain medicines should not be used together at all, in other cases two different medicines may be used together even if an interaction might occur. In these cases, your doctor may want to change the dose, or other precautions may be necessary. When you are using nitroglycerin, it is especially important that your health care professional know if you are taking any of the following:
- Antihypertensives (high blood pressure medicine) or
- Other heart medicine or
- Sildenafil—May increase the effects of nitroglycerin on blood pressure

Other medical problems—The presence of other medical problems may affect the use of nitroglycerin. Make sure you tell your doctor if you have any other medical problems, especially:
- Anemia (severe)
- Glaucoma—May be worsened by nitroglycerin
- Head injury (recent) or
- Stroke (recent)—Nitroglycerin may increase pressure in the brain, which can make problems worse
- Heart attack (recent)—Nitroglycerin may lower blood pressure, which can aggravate problems associated with heart attack
- Kidney disease or
- Liver disease—Effects may be increased because of slower removal of nitroglycerin from the body
- Overactive thyroid

Proper Use of This Medicine

Use nitroglycerin exactly as directed by your doctor. It will work only if applied correctly.

The ointment and transdermal forms of nitroglycerin are used to reduce the number of angina attacks. They will not relieve an attack that has already started because they work too slowly. Check with your doctor if you need a fast-acting medicine to relieve the pain of an angina attack.

This medicine usually comes with patient instructions. Read them carefully before using this medicine.

For patients using the *ointment* form of this medicine:

- Before applying a new dose of ointment, remove any ointment remaining on the skin from a previous dose. This will allow the fresh ointment to release the nitroglycerin properly.
- This medicine comes with dose-measuring papers. Use them to measure the length of ointment squeezed from the tube and to apply the ointment to the skin. *Do not rub or massage the ointment into the skin; just spread in a thin, even layer, covering an area of the same size each time it is applied.*
- Apply the ointment to skin that has little or no hair.
- Apply each dose of ointment to a different area of skin to prevent irritation or other skin problems.
- If your doctor has ordered an occlusive dressing (airtight covering, such as kitchen plastic wrap) to be applied over this medicine, make sure you know how to apply it. Since occlusive dressings increase the amount of medicine absorbed through the skin and the possibility of side effects, use them only as directed. If you have any questions about this, check with your health care professional.

For patients using the *transdermal (stick-on patch) system:*

- Do not try to trim or cut the adhesive patch to adjust the dosage. Check with your doctor if you think the medicine is not working as it should.
- Apply the patch to a clean, dry skin area with little or no hair and free of scars, cuts, or irritation. Remove the previous patch before applying a new one.
- Apply a new patch if the first one becomes loose or falls off.
- Apply each dose to a different area of skin to prevent skin irritation or other problems.

Dosing—The dose of nitroglycerin will be different for different patients. *Follow your doctor's orders or the directions on the label*. The following information includes only the average doses of nitrates. *If your dose is different, do not change it* unless your doctor tells you to do so.

For nitroglycerin

- For angina (chest pain):
  —For *ointment* dosage form:
    - Adults—15 to 30 milligrams (mg) (about one to two inches of ointment squeezed from tube) every six to eight hours.
    - Children—Use and dose must be determined by your doctor.
  —For *transdermal system (skin patch)* dosage form:
    - Adults—Apply one transdermal dosage system (skin patch) to intact skin once a day. The patch is usually left on for 12 to 14 hours a day and then taken off. Follow your doctor's instructions for when to put on and take off the skin patch.
    - Children—Use and dose must be determined by your doctor.

Missed dose—

- For patients using the *ointment* form of this medicine: If you miss a dose of this medicine, apply it as soon as

possible unless the next scheduled dose is within 2 hours. Then go back to your regular dosing schedule. Do not increase the amount used.

- For patients using the *transdermal (stick-on patch) system:* If you miss a dose of this medicine, apply it as soon as possible. Then go back to your regular dosing schedule.

Storage—

- To store the *ointment* form of this medicine:
  —Keep out of the reach of children.
  —Store the tube of nitroglycerin ointment in a cool place and keep it tightly closed.
  —Do not keep outdated medicine or medicine no longer needed. Be sure that any discarded medicine is out of the reach of children.
- To store the *transdermal (stick-on patch) system:*
  —Keep out of the reach of children.
  —Store away from heat and direct light.
  —Do not store in the bathroom, near the kitchen sink, or in other damp places. Heat or moisture may cause the medicine to break down.
  —Do not keep outdated medicine or medicine no longer needed. Be sure that any discarded medicine is out of the reach of children.

Precautions While Using This Medicine

Do not take sildenafil (e.g., Viagra) if you are taking this medicine. When sildenafil is taken with nitrates, the combination can lower blood pressure and cause dizziness, lightheadedness, or fainting. *In some case, sildenafil taken with nitrates has caused death.*

If you have been using nitroglycerin regularly for several weeks or more, do not suddenly stop using it. Stopping suddenly may bring on attacks of angina. Check with your doctor for the best way to reduce gradually the amount you are using before stopping completely.

Dizziness, lightheadedness, or faintness may occur, especially when you get up quickly from a lying or sitting position. Getting up slowly may help. If you feel dizzy, sit or lie down.

The dizziness, lightheadedness, or fainting is also more likely to occur if you drink alcohol, stand for long periods of time, exercise, or if the weather is hot. *While you are taking this medicine, be careful to limit the amount of alcohol you drink. Also, use extra care during exercise or hot weather or if you must stand for long periods of time.*

After using a dose of this medicine you may get a headache that lasts for a short time. This is a common side effect, which should become less noticeable after you have used the medicine for a while. If this effect continues, or if the headaches are severe, check with your doctor.

Side Effects of This Medicine

Along with its needed effects, a medicine may cause some unwanted effects. Although not all of these side effects may occur, if they do occur they may need medical attention.

Check with your doctor as soon as possible if any of the following side effects occur:

Rare

Blurred vision; dryness of mouth; headache (severe or prolonged)

Signs and symptoms of overdose (in the order in which they may occur)

Bluish-colored lips, fingernails, or palms of hands; dizziness (extreme) or fainting; feeling of extreme pressure in head; shortness of breath; unusual tiredness or weakness; weak and fast heartbeat; fever; convulsions (seizures)

Other side effects may occur that usually do not need medical attention. These side effects may go away during treatment as your body adjusts to the medicine. However, check with your doctor if any of the following side effects continue or are bothersome:

More common

Dizziness or lightheadedness, especially when getting up from a lying or sitting position; fast pulse; flushing of face and neck; headache; nausea or vomiting; restlessness

Less common

Sore, reddened skin

Other side effects not listed above may also occur in some patients. If you notice any other effects, check with your doctor.

Revised: 08/21/98

NITROFURANTOIN   Systemic

Commonly used brand name(s):

In the U.S.—

Furadantin
Macrobid
Macrodantin
Generic name product may be available.

In Canada—

Apo-Nitrofurantoin   Macrodantin
Macrobid   Novo-Furantoin

Description

Nitrofurantoin (nye-troe-fyoor-AN-toyn) belongs to the family of medicines called anti-infectives. It is used to treat infections of the urinary tract. It may also be used for other conditions as determined by your doctor.

Nitrofurantoin is available only with your doctor's prescription, in the following dosage forms:

Oral

- Capsules (U.S. and Canada)
- Extended-release Capsules (U.S. and Canada)
- Oral Suspension (U.S.)
- Tablets (U.S. and Canada)

Before Using This Medicine

In deciding to use a medicine, the risks of taking the medicine must be weighed against the good it will do. This is a decision you and your doctor will make. For nitrofurantoin, the following should be considered:

Allergies—Tell your doctor if you have ever had any unusual or allergic reaction to nitrofurantoin or to any related medicines such as furazolidone (e.g., Furoxone) or nitrofur-azone (e.g., Furacin). Also tell your health care professional if you are allergic to any other substances, such as foods, preservatives, or dyes.

Pregnancy—Nitrofurantoin should not be used if you are within a week or 2 of your delivery date or during labor and delivery. It may cause problems in the infant. Studies in animals have shown some problems when given in doses many times the human dose. Before taking this medicine, make sure your doctor knows if you are pregnant or if you may become pregnant.

Breast-feeding—Nitrofurantoin passes into the breast milk in small amounts and may cause problems in nursing babies, especially those with glucose-6-phosphate dehydrogenase (G6PD) deficiency. It may be necessary for you to take another medicine or to stop breast-feeding during treatment. Be sure you have discussed the risks and benefits of the medicine with your doctor.

Children—This medicine has been tested in children 1 month of age and older and, in effective doses, has not been shown to cause different side effects or problems in children than it does in adults. However, infants up to 1 month of age should not be given this medicine because they are especially sensitive to the effects of nitrofurantoin.

Older adults—Elderly people may be more sensitive to the effects of nitrofurantoin. This may increase the chance of side effects during treatment.

Other medicines—Although certain medicines should not be used together at all, in other cases two different medicines may be used together even if an interaction might occur. In these cases, your doctor may want to change the dose, or other precautions may be necessary. When you are taking nitrofurantoin, it is especially important that your health care professional know if you are taking any of the following:

- Acetohydroxamic acid (e.g., Lithostat) or
- Antidiabetics, oral (diabetes medicine you take by mouth) or
- Dapsone or
- Furazolidone (e.g., Furoxone) or
- Methyldopa (e.g., Aldomet) or
- Primaquine or
- Procainamide (e.g., Pronestyl) or
- Quinidine (e.g., Quinidex) or
- Sulfonamides (sulfa medicine) or
- Sulfoxone (e.g., Diasone) or
- Vitamin K (e.g., AquaMEPHYTON, Synkayvite)—Patients who take nitrofurantoin with any of these medicines may have an increase in side effects affecting the blood

- Carbamazepine (e.g., Tegretol) or
- Chloroquine (e.g., Aralen) or
- Cisplatin (e.g., Platinol) or
- Cytarabine (e.g., Cytosar-U) or
- Diphtheria, tetanus, and pertussis (DTP) vaccine or
- Disulfiram (e.g., Antabuse) or
- Ethotoin (e.g., Peganone) or
- Hydroxychloroquine (e.g., Plaquenil) or
- Lindane, topical (e.g., Kwell) or
- Lithium (e.g., Lithane) or
- Mephenytoin (e.g., Mesantoin) or
- Mexiletine (e.g., Mexitil) or
- Other anti-infectives by mouth or by injection (medicine for infection) or
- Pemoline (e.g., Cylert) or

- Phenytoin (e.g., Dilantin) or
- Pyridoxine (e.g., Hexa-Betalin) (with long-term, high-dose use) or
- Vincristine (e.g., Oncovin)—Patients who take nitrofurantoin with any of these medicines, or who have received a DTP vaccine within the last 30 days or are going to receive a DTP vaccine may have an increase in side effects affecting the nervous system
- Probenecid (e.g., Benemid) or
- Sulfinpyrazone (e.g., Anturane)—Patients who take nitrofurantoin with either of these medicines may have an increase in side effects
- Quinine (e.g., Quinamm)—Patients who take nitrofurantoin with quinine may have an increase in side effects affecting the blood and the nervous system

Other medical problems—The presence of other medical problems may affect the use of nitrofurantoin. Make sure you tell your doctor if you have any other medical problems, especially:

- Anemia or
- Diabetes mellitus or
- Lung disease or
- Nerve damage or
- Other serious illness or
- Vitamin B deficiency—These conditions may increase the chance for side effects
- Glucose-6-phosphate dehydrogenase (G6PD) deficiency—Nitrofurantoin may cause anemia in patients with G6PD deficiency
- Kidney disease (other than infection)—The chance of side effects of this medicine may be increased and the medicine may be less effective in patients with kidney disease

Proper Use of This Medicine

Do not give this medicine to infants up to 1 month of age.

Nitrofurantoin is best taken with food or milk. This may lessen stomach upset and help your body to better absorb the medicine.

For patients taking the *oral liquid form of this medicine:*

- Shake the oral liquid forcefully before each dose to help make it pour more smoothly and to be sure the medicine is evenly mixed.
- Use a specially marked measuring spoon or other device to measure each dose accurately. The average household teaspoon may not hold the right amount of liquid.
- Nitrofurantoin may be mixed with water, milk, fruit juices, or infants' formulas. If it is mixed with any of these liquids, take the medicine immediately after mixing. Be sure to drink all the liquid in order to get the full dose of medicine.

For patients taking the *extended-release capsule* form of this medicine:

- Swallow the capsules whole.
- Do not open, crush, or chew the capsules before swallowing them.

To help clear up your infection completely, *keep taking this medicine for the full time of treatment*, even if you begin to feel better after a few days. *Do not miss any doses.*

Dosing—The dose of nitrofurantoin will be different for different patients. *Follow your doctor's orders or the direc-*

tions on the label. The following information includes only the average doses of nitrofurantoin. *If your dose is different, do not change it* unless your doctor tells you to do so.

- For the *capsule, oral suspension, and tablet* dosage forms:
  —For the *prevention* of urinary tract infection:
  - Adults and adolescents—50 to 100 mg once a day at bedtime.
  - Children 1 month of age and older—Dose is based on body weight and must be determined by your doctor.
  - Children up to 1 month of age—Use is not recommended.
  —For the *treatment* of urinary tract infection:
  - Adults and adolescents—50 to 100 mg every six hours.
  - Children 1 month of age and older—Dose is based on body weight and must be determined by your doctor.
  - Children up to 1 month of age—Use is not recommended.
- For the *extended-release capsule* dosage form:
  —Adults and children 12 years of age and older: 100 mg every twelve hours for seven days.
  —Children up to 12 years of age: Dose must be determined by the doctor.

Missed dose—If you do miss a dose of this medicine, take it as soon as possible. However, if it is almost time for your next dose, skip the missed dose and go back to your regular dosing schedule. Do not double doses.

Storage—To store this medicine:

- Keep out of the reach of children.
- Store away from heat and direct light.
- Do not store the capsule or tablet form of this medicine in the bathroom, near the kitchen sink, or in other damp places. Heat or moisture may cause the medicine to break down.
- Keep the oral liquid form of this medicine from freezing.
- Do not keep outdated medicine or medicine no longer needed. Be sure that any discarded medicine is out of the reach of children.

Precautions While Using This Medicine

It is important that your doctor check your progress at regular visits if you will be taking this medicine for a long time.

If your symptoms do not improve within a few days, or if they become worse, check with your doctor.

For *diabetic patients:*

- *This medicine may cause false test results with some urine sugar tests.* Check with your doctor before changing your diet or the dosage of your diabetes medicine.

Side Effects of This Medicine

Along with its needed effects, a medicine may cause some unwanted effects. Although not all of these side effects may occur, if they do occur they may need medical attention.

Check with your doctor immediately if any of the following side effects occur:
   More common
      Changes in facial skin color; chest pain; chills; cough;

fever; general feeling of discomfort or illness; hives; hoarseness; itching; joint or muscle pain; shortness of breath; skin rash; sudden trouble in swallowing or breathing; swelling of face, mouth, hands, or feet; troubled breathing

Less common

Black, tarry stools; blood in urine or stools; burning, numbness, tingling, or painful sensations; dizziness; drowsiness; headache; pinpoint red spots on skin; sore throat; unusual bleeding or bruising; unusual tiredness or weakness; weakness in arms, hands, legs, or feet

Rare

Abdominal or stomach pain; blistering, peeling, or loosening of skin and mucous membranes; bluish color of skin; blurred vision or loss of vision, with or without eye pain; bulging fontanel in infants; confusion; darkening of urine; diarrhea, watery and severe, which may also be bloody; loss of appetite; mental depression; mood or mental changes; nausea or vomiting; pale skin; pale stools; red skin lesions, often with a purple center; red, thickened, or scaly skin; skin rash; sores, ulcers, or white spots on lips or in mouth; swollen or painful glands; unpleasant breath odor; visual changes; vomiting of blood; wheezing or tightness in chest; yellow eyes or skin

Other side effects may occur that usually do not need medical attention. These side effects may go away during treatment as your body adjusts to the medicine. However, check with your doctor if any of the following side effects continue or are bothersome:

More common

Diarrhea; gas

After you stop using this medicine, your body may need time to adjust. The length of time this takes depends on the amount of medicine you were using and how long you used it. During this period of time *check with your doctor immediately* if you notice any of the following side effects:

Abdominal or stomach cramps or pain, severe; diarrhea, watery and severe, which may also be bloody; fever

This medicine may cause the urine to become rust-yellow to brown. This side effect does not require medical attention.

Nitrofurantoin may cause a temporary loss of hair in some people.

Other side effects not listed above may also occur in some patients. If you notice any other effects, check with your doctor.

Revised: 06/14/99

NITROFURAZONE   Topical

Commonly used brand name(s):

In the U.S.—

Furacin Cream
Furacin Soluble Dressing
Furacin Topical Solution

Description

Nitrofurazone (nye-tro-FYOOR-a-zone) is used to treat burns that have become infected. It is also used to treat skin infections due to skin grafts. It works by killing bacteria or preventing their growth.

Nitrofurazone may be applied directly to the skin or placed on a gauze pad that will cover the skin.

This medicine is available only with your doctor's prescription, in the following dosage form(s):

Topical
- Cream (U.S.)
- Soluble Dressing (U.S.)
- Solution (U.S.)

Before Using This Medicine

In deciding to use a medicine, the risks of using the medicine must be weighed against the good it will do. This is a decision you and your doctor will make. For nitrofurazone, the following should be considered:

Allergies—Tell your doctor if you have ever had any unusual or allergic reaction to nitrofurazone. Also tell your health care professional if you are allergic to any other substances, such as preservatives or dyes.

Pregnancy—Topical nitrofurazone has not been studied in pregnant women. Nitrofurazone given to rabbits in oral doses thirty times greater than the human dose produced a slight increase in the number of stillbirths.

Breast-feeding—It is not known whether topical nitrofurazone passes into breast milk. Although most medicines pass into breast milk in small amounts, many of them may be used safely while breast-feeding. Mothers who are using this medicine and who wish to breast-feed should discuss this with their doctor.

Children—Studies on this medicine have been done only in adult patients, and there is no specific information comparing use of nitrofurazone in children with use in other age groups.

Older adults—Many medicines have not been studied specifically in older people. Therefore, it may not be known whether they work exactly the same way they do in younger adults or if they cause different side effects or problems in older people. There is no specific information comparing use of nitrofurazone in the elderly with use in other age groups.

Other medicines—Although certain medicines should not be used together at all, in other cases two different medicines may be used together even if an interaction might occur. In these cases, your doctor may want to change the dose, or other precautions may be necessary. Tell your health care professional if you are using any other prescription or nonprescription (over-the-counter [OTC]) medicine that is to be applied to the same area of the skin.

Other medical problems—The presence of other medical problems may affect the use of nitrofurazone. Make sure you tell your doctor if you have any other medical problems, especially:

- Kidney disease—Certain ingredients (polyethylene glycols) in the topical solution and the soluble dressing may be absorbed through the skin and may not be eliminated from the body normally in patients with kidney function impairment, which may increase the chance of side effects. Nitrofurazone cream does not contain polyethylene glycol.

Proper Use of This Medicine

Apply sufficient medication to affected area or place medication on gauze and cover the affected area.

Dosing—The dose of nitrofurazone will be different for different patients. *Follow your doctor's orders or the directions on the label.* The following information includes only the average doses of nitrofurazone. *If your dose is different, do not change it* unless your doctor tells you to do so.

- For *cream* dosage form:
  —Burns or skin infections:
  - Adults—Apply directly to the lesion, or place on gauze that will cover the lesion, once daily or every few days, depending on the usual dressing technique of the affected area.
  - Children—Use and dose must be determined by your doctor.
- For *soluble dressing* dosage form:
  —Burns or skin infections:
  - Adults—Apply directly to the lesion or place on gauze that will cover the lesion, depending on the usual dressing technique of the affected area.
  - Children—Use and dose must be determined by your doctor.
- For *topical solution* dosage form:
  —Burns:
  - Adults—Apply directly to the burn.
  - Children—Use and dose must be determined by your doctor.

Missed dose—If you miss a dose of this medicine, apply it as soon as possible. However, if it is almost time for your next dose, skip the missed dose and go back to your regular dosing schedule.

Storage—To store this medicine:
- Keep out of the reach of children.
- Store away from excessive heat.
- Do not store in the bathroom, near the kitchen sink, or in other damp places. Heat or moisture may cause the medicine to break down.
- Keep the medicine away from direct sunlight or strong fluorescent lighting.
- Keep away from alkaline materials, such as soap and ammonia.
- Do not keep outdated medicine or medicine no longer needed. Be sure that any discarded medicine is out of the reach of children.

Precautions While Using This Medicine

If your burn or skin infection does not improve, or if it becomes worse, check with your health care professional.

Side Effects of This Medicine

Along with its needed effects, a medicine may cause some unwanted effects. Although not all of these side effects may occur, if they do occur they may need medical attention.

Check with your doctor as soon as possible if any of the following side effects occur:
Less common
  Itching; rash; swelling

Other side effects not listed above may also occur in some patients. If you notice any other effects, check with your doctor.

Developed: 5/4/99

NORFLOXACIN   Ophthalmic

Commonly used brand name(s):

In the U.S.—
  Chibroxin

In Canada—
  Noroxin

Description

Norfloxacin (nor-FLOX-a-sin) is an antibiotic. The ophthalmic preparation is used to treat infections of the eye.

Norfloxacin is available only with your doctor's prescription, in the following dosage form:

Ophthalmic
- Ophthalmic solution (eye drops) (U.S. and Canada)

Before Using This Medicine

In deciding to use a medicine, the risks of taking the medicine must be weighed against the good it will do. This is a decision you and your doctor will make. For ophthalmic norfloxacin, the following should be considered:

Allergies—Tell your doctor if you have ever had any unusual or allergic reaction to norfloxacin or to any related medicines, such as cinoxacin (e.g., Cinobac), ciprofloxacin (e.g., Cipro or Ciloxan), enoxacin (e.g., Penetrax), lomefloxacin (e.g., Maxaquin), nalidixic acid (e.g., NegGram), or ofloxacin (e.g., Floxin or Ocuflox). Also tell your health care professional if you are allergic to any other substances, such as foods, preservatives, or dyes.

Pregnancy—Studies have not been done in humans. However, norfloxacin taken by mouth can cause bone problems in young animals. Since it is not known whether ophthalmic norfloxacin can cause bone problems in infants, use is not recommended during pregnancy.

Breast-feeding—It is not known whether ophthalmic norfloxacin passes into the breast milk. Low doses of norfloxacin taken by mouth do not pass into breast milk, but other related medicines do. Also, norfloxacin taken by mouth can cause bone problems in young animals. Since it is not known whether ophthalmic norfloxacin can cause bone problems in infants, use is not recommended in nursing mothers.

Children—Use is not recommended in infants and children up to 1 year of age. Norfloxacin taken by mouth has been shown to cause bone problems in young animals. It is not known whether ophthalmic norfloxacin can cause bone problems in infants. In children 1 year of age and older, this medicine is not expected to cause different side effects or problems than it does in adults.

Older adults—Many medicines have not been studied specifically in older people. Therefore, it may not be known whether they work exactly the same way they do in younger adults. Although there is no specific information comparing use of ophthalmic norfloxacin in the elderly with use in other age groups, this medicine is not expected to cause different side effects or problems in older people than it does in younger adults.

Other medicines—Although certain medicines should not be used together at all, in other cases two different medicines may be used together even if an interaction might occur. In these cases, your doctor may want to change the dose, or other precautions may be necessary. Tell your health care professional if you are taking or using any prescription or nonprescription (over-the-counter [OTC]) medicine.

Proper Use of This Medicine

To use:
- First, wash your hands. Tilt the head back and with the index finger of one hand, press gently on the skin just beneath the lower eyelid and pull the lower eyelid away from the eye to make a space. Drop the medicine into this space. Let go of the eyelid and gently close the eyes. Do not blink. Keep the eyes closed for 1 or 2 minutes, to allow the medicine to come into contact with the infection.
- If you think you did not get the drop of medicine into your eye properly, use another drop.
- To keep the medicine as germ-free as possible, do not touch the applicator tip to any surface (including the eye). Also, keep the container tightly closed.

Dosing—The dose of ophthalmic norfloxacin will be different for different patients. *Follow your doctor's orders or the directions on the label.* The following information includes only the average doses of ophthalmic norfloxacin. *If your dose is different, do not change it* unless your doctor tells you to do so:
- For infants and children up to 1 year of age: Use is not recommended.
- For adults and children 1 year of age and over: Place 1 drop in each eye four times a day for 7 days.

To help clear up your infection completely, *keep using this medicine for the full time of treatment,* even if your symptoms begin to clear up after a few days. If you stop using this medicine too soon, your symptoms may return. *Do not miss any doses.*

Missed dose—If you do miss a dose of this medicine, apply it as soon as possible. However, if it is almost time for your next dose, skip the missed dose and go back to your regular dosing schedule.

Storage—To store this medicine:
- Keep out of the reach of children.
- Store away from heat and direct light.
- Keep the medicine from freezing.
- Do not keep outdated medicine or medicine no longer needed. Be sure that any discarded medicine is out of the reach of children.

Precautions While Using This Medicine

If your symptoms do not improve within a few days, or if they become worse, check with your doctor.

This medicine may cause your eyes to become more sensitive to light than they are normally. Wearing sunglasses and avoiding too much exposure to bright light may help lessen the discomfort.

Side Effects of This Medicine

Along with its needed effects, a medicine may cause some unwanted effects. Although not all of these side effects may occur, if they do occur they may need medical attention.

Check with your doctor immediately if any of the following side effects occur:
Rare
Skin rash or other sign of allergic reaction

Other side effects may occur that usually do not need medical attention. These side effects may go away during treatment as your body adjusts to the medicine. However, check with your doctor if any of the following side effects continue or are bothersome:
More common
Burning or other eye discomfort
Less common
Bitter taste following use in the eye; increased sensitivity of eye to light; redness of the lining of the eyelids; swelling of the membrane covering the white part of the eye

Other side effects not listed above may also occur in some patients. If you notice any other effects, check with your doctor.

Revised: 12/22/93

NYLIDRIN   Systemic

Commonly used brand name(s):

In Canada—
Arlidin
Arlidin Forte
PMS Nylidrin

Description

Nylidrin (NYE-li-drin) belongs to the group of medicines called vasodilators. Vasodilators increase the size of blood vessels. Nylidrin is used to treat problems due to poor blood circulation.

Nylidrin is available only with your doctor's prescription, in the following dosage form:
Oral
- Tablets (Canada)

Before Using This Medicine

In deciding to use a medicine, the risks of taking the medicine must be weighed against the good it will do. This is a decision you and your doctor will make. For nylidrin, the following should be considered:

Allergies—Tell your doctor if you have ever had any unusual or allergic reaction to nylidrin. Also tell your health care professional if you are allergic to any other substances, such as foods, preservatives, or dyes.

Pregnancy—Studies on effects in pregnancy have have not been done in either humans or animals.

Breast-feeding—It is not known whether nylidrin passes into breast milk. Although most medicines pass into breast milk in small amounts, many of them may be used safely while breast-feeding. Mothers who are taking this medicine and who wish to breast-feed should discuss this with their doctor.

Older adults—Many medicines have not been studied specifically in older people. Therefore, it may not be known whether they work exactly the same way they do in younger adults or if they cause different side effects or problems in older people. There is no specific information comparing use of nylidrin in the elderly with use in other age groups. However, nylidrin may reduce tolerance to cold temperatures in elderly patients.

Other medicines—Although certain medicines should not be used together at all, in other cases two different medicines may be used together even if an interaction might occur. In these cases, your doctor may want to change the dose, or other precautions may be necessary. Tell your health care professional if you are taking any other prescription or nonprescription (over-the-counter [OTC]) medicine, or if you smoke.

Other medical problems—The presence of other medical problems may affect the use of nylidrin. Make sure you tell your doctor if you have any other medical problems, especially:

- Angina (chest pain) or
- Fast heartbeat or
- Heart attack (recent) or other heart disease or
- Overactive thyroid gland or
- Stomach ulcer—Nylidrin may make these conditions worse

Proper Use of This Medicine

Nylidrin may cause you to have a fast or pounding heartbeat. To keep this from affecting your sleep, do not take the last dose of the day at bedtime. Instead, it is best to plan your dose or doses according to a schedule that will least affect your sleep. Ask your health care professional to help you plan the best time to take this medicine.

Dosing—The dose of nylidrin will be different for different patients. *Follow your doctor's orders or the directions on the label.* The following information includes only the average doses of nylidrin. *If your dose is different, do not change it* unless your doctor tells you to do so:

- For *oral* dosage form (tablets):
  —Adults: 3 to 12 milligrams (mg) three or four times a day.

Missed dose—If you miss a dose of this medicine, take the missed dose as soon as you remember. However, if it is almost time for the next dose, skip the missed dose and go back to your regular dosing schedule. Do not double doses.

Storage—To store this medicine:

- Keep out of the reach of children.
- Store away from heat and direct light.
- Do not store in the bathroom, near the kitchen sink, or in other damp places. Heat or moisture may cause the medicine to break down.
- Do not keep outdated medicine or medicine no longer needed. Be sure that any discarded medicine is out of the reach of children.

Precautions While Using This Medicine

It may take some time for this medicine to work. If you feel that the medicine is not working, do not stop taking it on your own. Instead, check with your doctor.

The helpful effects of this medicine may be decreased if you smoke. If you have any questions about this, check with your doctor.

Side Effects of This Medicine

Along with its needed effects, a medicine may cause some unwanted effects. Although not all of these side effects may occur, if they do occur they may need medical attention.

Check with your doctor as soon as possible if any of the following side effects occur:

Less common
  Dizziness; fast or irregular heartbeat; weakness or tiredness (continuing)
Signs and symptoms of overdose
  Blurred vision; chest pain; decrease in urination or inability to urinate; fever; metallic taste

Other side effects may occur that usually do not need medical attention. These side effects may go away during treatment as your body adjusts to the medicine. However, check with your doctor if any of the following side effects continue or are bothersome:

Less common
  Chilliness; flushing or redness of face; headache; nausea and vomiting; nervousness; trembling

Other side effects not listed above may also occur in some patients. If you notice any other effects, check with your doctor.

Revised: 05/14/93

NYSTATIN   Oral

Commonly used brand name(s):

In the U.S.—
  Mycostatin
  Nilstat
  Nystex
  Generic name product may be available.

In Canada—
  Mycostatin   Nilstat
  Nadostine   PMS Nystatin

Description

Nystatin (nye-STAT-in) belongs to the group of medicines called antifungals. The dry powder, lozenge (pastille), and liquid forms of this medicine are used to treat fungus infections in the mouth.

Nystatin is available only with your doctor's prescription, in the following dosage forms:

Oral
- Lozenges (Pastilles) (U.S.)
- Oral suspension (U.S. and Canada)
- Powder for oral suspension (U.S. and Canada)
- Tablets (U.S. and Canada)

Before Using This Medicine

In deciding to use a medicine, the risks of taking the medicine must be weighed against the good it will do. This is a decision you and your doctor will make. For nystatin, the following should be considered:

Allergies—Tell your doctor if you have ever had any unusual or allergic reaction to nystatin. Also tell your health care professional if you are allergic to any other substances, such as foods, preservatives, or dyes.

Pregnancy—Studies in humans have not shown that oral nystatin causes birth defects or other problems.

Breast-feeding—Oral nystatin has not been reported to cause problems in nursing babies.

Children—This medicine has been tested in children and has not been reported to cause different side effects or problems in children than it does in adults. However, since children up to 5 years of age may be too young to use the lozenges (pastilles) or tablets safely, the oral suspension dosage form is best for this age group.

Older adults—Many medicines have not been studied specifically in older people. Therefore, it may not be known whether they work exactly the same way they do in younger adults or if they cause different side effects or problems in older people. There is no specific information comparing use of oral nystatin in the elderly with use in other age groups.

Proper Use of This Medicine

For patients taking the *dry powder form of nystatin:*
- Add about 1/8 teaspoonful of dry powder to about 4 ounces of water immediately before taking. Stir well.
- After it is mixed, take this medicine by dividing the whole amount (4 ounces) into several portions. Hold each portion of the medicine in your mouth or swish it around in your mouth for as long as possible, gargle, and swallow. Be sure to use all the liquid to get the full dose of medicine.

For patients taking the *lozenge (pastille) form of nystatin:*
- Nystatin lozenges (pastilles) should be held in the mouth and allowed to dissolve slowly and completely. This may take 15 to 30 minutes. Also, the saliva should be swallowed during this time. *Do not chew or swallow the lozenges whole.*
- *Do not give nystatin lozenges (pastilles) to infants or children up to 5 years of age.* They may be too young to use the lozenges safely.

For patients taking the *oral liquid form of nystatin:*
- This medicine is to be taken by mouth even if it comes in a dropper bottle. If it does come in a dropper bottle, use the specially marked dropper to measure each dose accurately.
- Take this medicine by placing one-half of the dose in each side of your mouth. Hold the medicine in your mouth or swish it around in your mouth for as long as possible, then gargle and swallow.

Patients with full or partial dentures may need to soak their dentures nightly in nystatin for oral suspension to eliminate the fungus from the dentures. In rare cases when this does not eliminate the fungus, it may be necessary to have new dentures made.

To help clear up your infection completely, *keep taking this medicine for the full time of treatment*, even if your condition has improved. *Do not miss any doses.*

Dosing—The dose of nystatin will be different for different patients. *Follow your doctor's orders or the directions on the label.* The following information includes only the average doses of nystatin. *If your dose is different, do not change it* unless your doctor tells you to do so.

The number of lozenges, tablets, or milliliters (mL) of suspension that you take depends on the strength of the medicine. Also, *the number of doses you take each day, the time allowed between doses, and the length of time you take the medicine depend on the medical problem for which you are taking nystatin.*
- For the *lozenge (pastille) and tablet* dosage forms:
  - Adults and children 5 years of age and older: 1 or 2 lozenges or tablets three to five times a day for up to fourteen days.
  - Children up to 5 years of age: Children this young may not be able to use the lozenges or tablets safely. The oral suspension is better for this age group.
- For the *suspension* dosage form:
  - Adults and children 5 years of age and older: 4 to 6 milliliters (mL) (about 1 teaspoonful) four times a day.
  - For older infants: 2 mL four times a day.
  - For premature and low-birth-weight infants: 1 mL four times a day.

Missed dose—If you do miss a dose of this medicine, take it as soon as possible. However, if it is almost time for your next dose, skip the missed dose and go back to your regular dosing schedule. Do not double doses.

Storage—To store this medicine:
- Keep out of the reach of children.
- Store away from heat and direct light.
- Do not store the tablet or dry powder form of this medicine in the bathroom, near the kitchen sink, or in other damp places. Heat or moisture may cause the medicine to break down.
- Store the lozenge (pastille) form in the refrigerator. Heat will cause this medicine to break down.
- Keep the oral liquid form of this medicine from freezing.
- Do not keep outdated medicine or medicine no longer needed. Be sure that any discarded medicine is out of the reach of children.

Side Effects of This Medicine

Along with its needed effects, a medicine may cause some unwanted effects. The following side effects may go away during treatment as your body adjusts to the medicine. However, check with your doctor if any of the following side effects continue or are bothersome:

Less common
    Diarrhea; nausea or vomiting; stomach pain

Other side effects not listed above may also occur in some patients. If you notice any other effects, check with your doctor.

Additional Information

Once a medicine has been approved for marketing for a certain use, experience may show that it is also useful for other

medical problems. Although this use is not included in product labeling, nystatin is used in certain patients with the following medical condition:

- Candidiasis, oral (fungus infection of the mouth) (prevention)

Other than the above information, there is no additional information relating to proper use, precautions, or side effects for this use.

Revised: 01/19/93

NYSTATIN   Topical

Commonly used brand name(s):

In the U.S.—
Mycostatin
Nilstat
Nystex

Nystop
Pedi-Dri

Generic name product may be available.

In Canada—
Mycostatin
Nadostine

Nilstat
Nyaderm

Description

Nystatin (nye-STA-tin) belongs to the group of medicines called antifungals. Topical nystatin is used to treat some types of fungus infections of the skin.

Nystatin is available in the U.S. only with your doctor's prescription. It is available in Canada without a prescription; however, your doctor may have special instructions on the proper use of this medicine for your medical problem. Nystatin is available in the following dosage forms:

Topical
- Cream (U.S. and Canada)
- Ointment (U.S. and Canada)
- Topical powder (U.S. and Canada)

Before Using This Medicine

In deciding to use a medicine, the risks of using the medicine must be weighed against the good it will do. This is a decision you and your doctor will make. For nystatin, the following should be considered:

Allergies—Tell your doctor if you have ever had any unusual or allergic reaction to nystatin. Also tell your health care professional if you are allergic to any other substances, such as preservatives or dyes.

Pregnancy—Nystatin topical preparations have not been shown to cause birth defects or other problems in humans.

Breast-feeding—It is not known whether nystatin passes into breast milk. Although most medicines pass into breast milk in small amounts, many of them may be used safely while breast-feeding. Mothers who are using this medicine and who wish to breast-feed should discuss this with their doctor.

Children—Although there is no specific information comparing use of topical nystatin in children with use in other age groups, this medicine is not expected to cause different side effects or problems in children than it does in adults.

Older adults—Many medicines have not been studied specifically in older people. Therefore, it may not be known whether they work exactly the same way they do in younger adults or if they cause different side effects or problems in older people. There is no specific information comparing use of topical nystatin in the elderly with use in other age groups.

Other medicines—Although certain medicines should not be used together at all, in other cases two different medicines may be used together even if an interaction might occur. In these cases, your doctor may want to change the dose, or other precautions may be necessary. Tell your health care professional if you are using any other topical prescription or nonprescription (over-the-counter [OTC]) medicine that is to be applied to the same area of the skin.

Proper Use of This Medicine

Topical nystatin should not be used in the eyes.

Apply enough nystatin to cover the affected area.

For patients using the *powder form* of this medicine on the feet:

- Sprinkle the powder between the toes, on the feet, and in socks and shoes.

The use of any kind of occlusive dressing (airtight covering, such as kitchen plastic wrap) over this medicine may increase the chance of irritation. Therefore, *do not bandage, wrap, or apply any occlusive dressing over this medicine* unless directed to do so by your doctor. When using this medicine on the diaper area of children, *avoid tight-fitting diapers and plastic pants.*

To help clear up your infection completely, *keep using this medicine for the full time of treatment*, even if your condition has improved. *Do not miss any doses.*

Dosing—The dose of topical nystatin will be different for different patients. *Follow your doctor's orders or the directions on the label*. The following information includes only the average dose of topical nystatin. *If your dose is different, do not change it* unless your doctor tells you to do so.

- For *topical* dosage forms (cream or ointment):
  —For fungus infections:
    - Adults and children—Apply to the affected area(s) of the skin two times a day.
- For *topical* dosage form (powder):
  —For fungus infections:
    - Adults and children—Apply to the affected area(s) of the skin two or three times a day.

Missed dose—If you miss a dose of this medicine, apply it as soon as possible. Then go back to your regular dosing schedule.

Storage—To store this medicine:

- Keep out of the reach of children.
- Store away from heat and direct light.
- Do not store the powder form of this medicine in the bathroom, near the kitchen sink, or in other damp places. Heat or moisture may cause the medicine to break down.
- Keep the cream and ointment forms of this medicine from freezing.
- Do not keep outdated medicine or medicine no longer needed. Be sure that any discarded medicine is out of the reach of children.

Side Effects of This Medicine

Along with its needed effects, a medicine may cause some unwanted effects. Although not all of these side effects may occur, if they do occur they may need medical attention.

Check with your doctor as soon as possible if the following side effect occurs:

Skin irritation not present before use of this medicine

Other side effects not listed above may also occur in some patients. If you notice any other effects, check with your doctor.

Revised: 3/1/99

NYSTATIN   Vaginal

Commonly used brand name(s):

In the U.S.—

Generic name product may be available.

In Canada—

Mycostatin	Nilstat
Nadostine	Nyaderm

Description

Nystatin (nye-STAT-in) belongs to the group of medicines called antifungals. Vaginal nystatin is used to treat fungus infections of the vagina. Nystatin vaginal cream or tablets may also be used for other problems as determined by your doctor.

Nystatin is available only with your doctor's prescription, in the following dosage forms:

Vaginal
- Cream (Canada)
- Tablets (U.S. and Canada)

Before Using This Medicine

In deciding to use a medicine, the risks of taking the medicine must be weighed against the good it will do. This is a decision you and your doctor will make. For nystatin, the following should be considered:

Allergies—Tell your doctor if you have ever had any unusual or allergic reaction to nystatin. Also tell your health care professional if you are allergic to any other substances, such as foods, preservatives, or dyes.

Pregnancy—Studies have not been done in animals. However, nystatin vaginal tablets have not been shown to cause birth defects or other problems in humans.

Breast-feeding—It is not known whether nystatin passes into breast milk. However, this medicine has not been reported to cause problems in nursing babies.

Children—Studies on this medicine have been done only in adults, and there is no specific information comparing use of vaginal nystatin in children with use in other age groups.

Older adults—Many medicines have not been studied specifically in older people. Therefore, it may not be known whether they work exactly the same way they do in younger adults or if they cause different side effects or problems in older people. There is no specific information comparing the use of vaginal nystatin in the elderly with use in other age groups.

Other medicines—Although certain medicines should not be used together at all, in other cases two different medicines may be used together even if an interaction might occur. In these cases, your doctor may want to change the dose, or other precautions may be necessary. Tell your health care professional if you are using any other vaginal prescription or nonprescription (over-the-counter [OTC]) medicine.

Proper Use of This Medicine

Nystatin usually comes with patient directions. Read them carefully before using this medicine.

This medicine is usually inserted into the vagina with an applicator. However, if you are pregnant, check with your doctor before using the applicator to insert the vaginal tablet.

To help clear up your infection completely, *keep using this medicine for the full time of treatment,* even if your condition has improved. Also, keep using this medicine even if you begin to menstruate during the time of treatment. *Do not miss any doses.*

Dosing—The dose of nystatin will be different for different patients. *Follow your doctor's orders or the directions on the label.* The following information includes only the average doses of nystatin. *If your dose is different, do not change it* unless your doctor tells you to do so.

- For treating fungus (yeast) infections:
  —For *vaginal cream* dosage form:
  - Adults and teenagers—One 100,000-unit applicatorful inserted into the vagina one or two times a day for two weeks. Or, your doctor may want you to insert one 500,000-unit applicatorful into the vagina once a day.
  - Children—Dose must be determined by your doctor.
  —For *vaginal tablet* dosage form:
  - Adults and teenagers—One 100,000-unit tablet inserted into the vagina one or two times a day for two weeks.
  - Children—Dose must be determined by your doctor.

Missed dose—If you do miss a dose of this medicine, insert it as soon as possible. However, if it is almost time for your next dose, skip the missed dose and go back to your regular dosing schedule.

Storage—To store this medicine:
- Keep out of the reach of children.
- Store away from heat and direct light.
- Do not store in the bathroom, near the kitchen sink, or in other damp places. Heat or moisture may cause the medicine to break down.
- Do not keep outdated medicine or medicine no longer needed. Be sure that any discarded medicine is out of the reach of children.

Precautions While Using This Medicine

To help cure the infection and to help prevent reinfection, good health habits are required.
- Wear cotton panties (or panties or pantyhose with cotton crotches) instead of synthetic (for example, nylon, rayon) underclothes.
- Wear freshly laundered underclothes.

If you have any questions about this, check with your health care professional.

If you have any questions about douching or intercourse during the time of treatment with nystatin, check with your doctor.

Since there may be some vaginal drainage while you are using this medicine, a sanitary napkin may be worn to protect your clothing.

Side Effects of This Medicine

Along with its needed effects, a medicine may cause some unwanted effects. Although not all of these side effects may occur, if they do occur they may need medical attention.

Check with your doctor as soon as possible if the following side effect occurs:
Rare
    Vaginal burning or itching not present before use of this medicine

Other side effects not listed above may also occur in some patients. If you notice any other effects, check with your doctor.

Revised: 08/11/98

OCTREOTIDE   Systemic

Commonly used brand name(s):
In the U.S.—
    Sandostatin
    Sandostatin LAR Depot
In Canada—
    Sandostatin

Description

Octreotide (ok-TREE-oh-tide) is used to treat the severe diarrhea and other symptoms that occur with certain intestinal tumors. It does not cure the tumor but it helps the patient live a more normal life.

Also, this medicine is used to treat a condition called acromegaly, which is caused by too much growth hormone in the body. Too much growth hormone produced in adults causes the hands, feet, and parts of the face to become large, thick, and bulky. Other problems such as arthritis also can develop. Octreotide works by reducing the amount of growth hormone that the body produces.

Octreotide may also be used for other medical conditions as determined by your doctor.

Octreotide is available only with your doctor's prescription, in the following dosage form:
Parenteral
    • Injection (U.S. and Canada)

Before Using This Medicine

In deciding to use a medicine, the risks of using the medicine must be weighed against the good it will do. This is a decision you and your doctor will make. For octreotide, the following should be considered:

Allergies—Tell your doctor if you have ever had any unusual or allergic reaction to octreotide. Also tell your health care professional if you are allergic to any other substances, such as foods, preservatives, or dyes.

Pregnancy—Studies have not been done in humans. However, studies in rats and rabbits have not shown that octreotide causes birth defects or other problems, even when given in doses much larger than the human dose.

Breast-feeding—It is not known whether octreotide passes into breast milk. Although most medicines pass into breast milk in small amounts, many of them may be used safely while breast-feeding. Mothers who are taking this medicine and who wish to breast-feed should discuss this with their doctor.

Children—The short-acting form of this medicine has been tested in a limited number of children as young as 1 month of age and has not been shown to cause different side effects or problems than it does in adults.

Studies on the long-acting form of this medicine have been done only in adult patients, and there is no specific information comparing its use in children with use in other age groups.

Older adults—This medicine has been used in persons up to 83 years of age and has not been shown to cause different side effects or problems in older people than it does in younger adults.

Other medicines—Although certain medicines should not be used together at all, in other cases two different medicines may be used together even if an interaction might occur. In these cases, your doctor may want to change the dose, or other precautions may be necessary. When you are taking octreotide, it is especially important that your health care professional know if you are taking any of the following:
    • Antidiabetic agents, sulfonylurea (diabetes medicine you take by mouth) or
    • Diazoxide (e.g., Proglycem) or
    • Glucagon or
    • Insulin—Octreotide may cause high or low blood sugar; your doctor may need to change the dose of your diabetes medicine
    • Growth hormone—Octreotide may cause high or low blood sugar; your doctor may need to change the dose of this medicine

Other medical problems—The presence of other medical problems may affect the use of octreotide. Make sure you tell your doctor if you have any other medical problems, especially:
    • Diabetes mellitus (sugar diabetes)—Octreotide may cause high or low blood sugar; your doctor may need to change the dose of your diabetes medicine
    • Gallbladder disease or gallstones (or history of)—This medicine may increase the chance of having gallstones
    • Kidney disease (severe)—If you have this condition, octreotide may remain in the body longer than normal; your doctor may need to change the dose of your medicine

Proper Use of This Medicine

To control the symptoms of your medical problem, this medicine must be taken as ordered by your doctor. *Make sure that you understand exactly how to take this medicine.*

Octreotide is packaged in a kit containing an ampul opener, alcohol swabs, ampuls of the medicine, and, in some kits, a vial of diluent to mix with the medicine. *Directions on how to prepare and inject the medicine are in the package. Read the directions carefully* and ask your health care professional for additional explanation, if necessary.

It is important to follow any instructions from your doctor about the careful selection and rotation of injection sites on your body. This will help to prevent skin problems, such as irritation.

Some patients may feel pain, stinging, tingling, or burning sensations at the place where they inject the medicine. These sensations usually last only a few moments and may be eased by rubbing the spot after the injection. Injecting the medicine after it has been warmed to room temperature rather than cold from the refrigerator may reduce the discomfort. The medicine should be taken from the refrigerator 20 to 60 minutes before it is to be used. However, do not use heat to warm it faster because heat can destroy the medicine.

Put used needles and syringes in a puncture-resistant disposable container or dispose of them as directed by your health care professional. *Do not reuse needles and syringes.*

Dosing—The dose of octreotide will be different for different patients. *Follow your doctor's orders or the directions on the label.* The following information includes only the average doses of octreotide. *If your dose is different, do not change it* unless your doctor tells you to do so.

- For long-acting *injection* dosage form:
  —For treating the severe diarrhea that occurs with certain types of intestinal tumors:
    - Adults and teenagers—At first, 20 milligrams (mg) injected into the gluteal muscle once every four weeks for two months. Then, the dose will be adjusted by your doctor, based on your response to the medicine.
    - Children—Use and dose must be determined by your doctor.
  —For treating acromegaly:
    - Adults—At first, 20 mg injected into the gluteal muscle once every four weeks for three months. Then, the dose will be adjusted by your doctor, based on your response to the medicine.
- For short-acting *injection* dosage form:
  —For treating the severe diarrhea that occurs with certain types of intestinal tumors:
    - Adults and teenagers—At first, 50 micrograms (mcg) injected under the skin two or three times a day. Then, the dose is slowly increased. Some people may need doses as high as 600 mcg a day for the first two weeks. Thereafter, the dose is usually between 50 and 1500 mcg per day.
    - Children—The dose is based on body weight and must be determined by your doctor. The usual dose is 1 to 10 mcg per kilogram (kg) (0.45 to 4.5 mcg per pound) of body weight a day, injected under the skin.
  —For treating acromegaly:
    - Adults—At first, 50 mcg injected under the skin or into a vein three times a day. Then, the dose is slowly increased to 100 to 200 mcg three times a day. Higher doses may be needed, as determined by your doctor.

Missed dose—If you miss a dose of the long-acting form of this medicine, contact your doctor.

If you miss a dose of the short-acting form of this medicine, use it as soon as you remember it. However, if it is almost time for the next dose, skip the missed dose and go back to your regular dosing schedule. Do not double doses. Although you will not be harmed by forgetting a dose, the symptoms that you are trying to control (for example, diarrhea) may reappear. To be able to control your symptoms, your doses should be evenly spaced over a period of 24 hours. If you have any questions about this, check with your health care professional.

Storage—To store this medicine:
- Keep out of the reach of children.
- Store the ampuls of octreotide in the refrigerator until they are to be used. Ampuls of the short-acting form of octreotide may be kept at room temperature for 14 days when they are protected from light. If the ampuls are not protected from light, problems with the solution can develop much sooner.
- Do not keep outdated medicine or medicine no longer needed. Be sure that any discarded medicine and syringes are out of the reach of children.

Precautions While Using This Medicine

It is very important that your doctor check your progress at regular visits to make sure that this medicine is working properly and to check for unwanted effects.

Side Effects of This Medicine

Along with its needed effects, a medicine may cause some unwanted effects. Although not all of these side effects may occur, if they do occur they may need medical attention.

Check with your doctor immediately if any of the following side effects occur:
  Less common or rare
    Convulsions (seizures); unconsciousness

Also check with your doctor as soon as possible if any of the following side effects occur:
  More common
    Irregular heartbeat; slow heartbeat
  Less common or rare
    Hyperglycemia (high blood sugar), including blurred vision, drowsiness, dry mouth, flushed dry skin, fruit-like breath odor, increased urination (frequency and volume), ketones in urine, loss of appetite, nausea, stomachache, tiredness, troubled breathing (rapid and deep), unusual thirst, or vomiting; hypoglycemia (low blood sugar), including anxious feeling, behavior change similar to drunkenness, blurred vision, cold sweats, confusion, cool pale skin, difficulty in concentrating, drowsiness, excessive hunger, fast heartbeat, headache, nausea, nervousness, nightmares, restless sleep, shakiness, slurred speech, or unusual tiredness or weakness; inflammation of the pancreas gland, including abdominal or stomach pain or bloating, nausea, or vomiting

Other side effects may occur that usually do not need medical attention. These side effects may go away during treatment as your body adjusts to the medicine. However, check with

your doctor if any of the following side effects continue or are bothersome:

More common
Constipation; diarrhea; pain, stinging, tingling, or burning sensation at place of injection, with redness and swelling; passing of gas

Less common or rare
Dizziness or light-headedness; fever; hair loss; redness or flushing of face; swelling of feet or lower legs

Other side effects not listed above may also occur in some patients. If you notice any other effects, check with your doctor.

Additional Information

Once a medicine has been approved for marketing for a certain use, experience may show that it is also useful for other medical problems. Although these uses are not included in product labeling, octreotide is used in certain patients with the following medical conditions:

- Acquired immunodeficiency syndrome (AIDS)-related diarrhea
- Chemotherapy-induced diarrhea
- Insulin-producing tumors of the pancreas

Other than the above information, there is no additional information relating to proper use, precautions, or side effects for these uses.

Revised: 02/16/2001

OFLOXACIN   Ophthalmic

Commonly used brand name(s):

In the U.S.—
Ocuflox

In Canada—
Ocuflox

Description

Ofloxacin (oh-FLOKS-a-sin) is an antibiotic used to treat bacterial infections of the eye, such as conjunctivitis and corneal ulcers.

Ofloxacin is available only with your doctor's prescription, in the following dosage form:

Ophthalmic
- Ophthalmic solution (eye drops) (U.S. and Canada)

Before Using This Medicine

In deciding to use a medicine, the risks of using the medicine must be weighed against the good it will do. This is a decision you and your doctor will make. For ophthalmic ofloxacin, the following should be considered:

Allergies—Tell your doctor if you have ever had any unusual or allergic reaction to ophthalmic or systemic ofloxacin (e.g., Floxin) or any related medicines, such as cinoxacin (e.g., Cinobac), ciprofloxacin (e.g., Ciloxan or Cipro), enoxacin (e.g., Penetrax), lomefloxacin (e.g., Maxaquin), nalidixic acid (e.g., NegGram), or norfloxacin (e.g., Chibroxin or Noroxin). Also tell your health care professional if you are allergic to any other substances, such as foods, preservatives, or dyes.

Pregnancy—Ophthalmic ofloxacin has not been studied in pregnant women. However, studies in animals that were given very high doses of ofloxacin by mouth have shown that ofloxacin can cause birth defects or other problems. Before taking this medicine, make sure your doctor knows if you are pregnant or if you may become pregnant.

Breast-feeding—It is not known whether ophthalmic ofloxacin passes into breast milk. However, ofloxacin given by mouth does pass into breast milk. Although most medicines pass into breast milk in small amounts, many of them may be used safely while breast-feeding. Mothers who are using this medicine and who wish to breast-feed should discuss this with their doctor.

Children—Use is not recommended in infants up to 1 year of age. In children 1 year of age and older, this medicine is not expected to cause different side effects or problems than it does in adults.

Older adults—Many medicines have not been studied specifically in older people. Therefore, it may not be known whether they work exactly the same way they do in younger adults or if they cause different side effects or problems in older people. There is no specific information comparing use of ophthalmic ofloxacin in the elderly with use in other age groups.

Other medicines—Although certain medicines should not be used together at all, in other cases two different medicines may be used together even if an interaction might occur. In these cases, your doctor may want to change the dose, or other precautions may be necessary. Tell your health care professional if you are using any other prescription or nonprescription (over-the-counter [OTC]) medicine that is to be used in the eye.

Proper Use of This Medicine

To use:
- First, wash your hands. Tilt the head back and with the index finger of one hand, press gently on the skin just beneath the lower eyelid and pull the lower eyelid away from the eye to make a space. Drop the medicine into this space. Let go of the eyelid and gently close the eyes. Do not blink. Keep the eyes closed for 1 to 2 minutes, to allow the medicine to come into contact with the infection.
- If you think you did not get the drop of medicine into your eyes properly, use another drop.
- To keep the medicine as germ-free as possible, do not touch the applicator tip to any surface (including the eye). Also, keep the container tightly closed.

To help clear up your eye infection completely, *keep using ophthalmic ofloxacin for the full time of treatment*, even if your symptoms have disappeared. *Do not miss any doses.*

Dosing—The dose of ophthalmic ofloxacin will be different for different patients. *Follow your doctor's orders or the directions on the label.* The following information includes only the average doses of ophthalmic ofloxacin. *If your dose is different, do not change it* unless your doctor tells you to do so.

- For *ophthalmic (eye drops)* dosage form:
  —For conjunctivitis:
   - Adults and children 1 year of age and older—Use 1 drop in the affected eye every two to four hours,

while you are awake, for two days. Then, use 1 drop in each eye four times a day for up to five more days.

- Infants up to 1 year of age—Use and dose must be determined by your doctor.

—For bacterial corneal ulcers:

- Adults and children 1 year of age and older—Use 1 drop in the affected eye every thirty minutes while you are awake and 1 drop four to six hours after you go to bed, for two days. Then use 1 drop every hour while you are awake for up to seven more days. After the seventh, eighth, or ninth day, as instructed by your doctor, use 1 drop four times a day until your doctor determines that the treatment is complete.
- Infants up to 1 year of age—Use and dose must be determined by your doctor.

Missed dose—If you miss a dose of this medicine, use it as soon as possible. However, if it is almost time for your next dose, skip the missed dose and go back to your regular dosing schedule.

Storage—To store this medicine:

- Keep out of the reach of children.
- Store away from heat and direct light.
- Keep the medicine from freezing. Do not refrigerate.
- Do not keep outdated medicine or medicine no longer needed. Be sure that any discarded medicine is out of the reach of children.

Precautions While Using This Medicine

If your eye infection does not improve within 7 days, or if it becomes worse, check with your doctor.

Discontinue using these eye drops immediately and contact your physician at the first sign of a rash or an allergic reaction.

This medicine may cause your eyes to become more sensitive to light than they are normally. Wearing sunglasses and avoiding too much exposure to bright light may help lessen the discomfort.

Side Effects of This Medicine

Along with its needed effects, a medicine may cause some unwanted effects. Although not all of these side effects may occur, if they do occur they may need medical attention.

Check with your doctor immediately if any of the following side effects occur:

Rare
Puffiness or swelling of eyes; signs of an allergic reaction, such as hives, itching, rash, swelling of face or lips, tightness in chest, troubled breathing, or wheezing

Check with your doctor as soon as possible if the following side effect occurs:

Rare
Dizziness

Other side effects may occur that usually do not need medical attention. These side effects may go away during treatment as your body adjusts to the medicine. However, check with your doctor if any of the following side effects continue or are bothersome:

More common
Burning of eye

Less common
Blurred vision; eye pain; feeling of something in the eye; increased sensitivity of eye to light; redness, irritation, or itching of eye, eyelid, or inner lining of eyelid; stinging, tearing, or dryness of eye

Other side effects not listed above may also occur in some patients. If you notice any other effects, check with your doctor.

Developed: 12/21/93
Revised: 09/22/98

OFLOXACIN   Otic

Commonly used brand name(s):

In the U.S.—
Floxin Otic

Description

Ofloxacin (oh-FLOX-a-sin) belongs to the family of medicines called antibiotics. Ofloxacin otic solution is used to treat infections of the ear canal. It also is used to treat infections of the middle ear in patients with nonintact tympanic membranes (holes or tubes in the eardrums).

This medicine is available only with your doctor's prescription, in the following dosage form:

Otic
- Otic solution (eardrops) (U.S.)

Before Using This Medicine

In deciding to use a medicine, the risks of using the medicine must be weighed against the good it will do. This is a decision you and your doctor will make. For ofloxacin otic preparations, the following should be considered:

Allergies—Tell your doctor if you have ever had any unusual or allergic reaction to any medicine containing ofloxacin (including tablets, injections, eye drops, and eardrops) or to any related antibiotics such as cinoxacin (e.g., Cinobac), ciprofloxacin (e.g., Ciloxan or Cipro), enoxacin (e.g., Penetrax), levofloxacin (e.g., Levaquin), lomefloxacin (e.g., Maxaquin), nalidixic acid (e.g., NegGram), norfloxacin (e.g., Chibroxin or Noroxin), or trovafloxacin/alatrofloxacin (e.g., Trovan). Also tell your health care professional if you are allergic to any other substances, such as foods, preservatives, or dyes.

Pregnancy—Otic ofloxacin has not been studied in pregnant women. Studies in animals that were given high doses of ofloxacin by mouth have shown that ofloxacin can cause birth defects or other problems. However, ofloxacin has not been shown to cause birth defects or other problems when given in doses comparable to the amount of ofloxacin that is found in the eardrops. Before you use this medicine, make sure your doctor knows if you are pregnant or if you may become pregnant.

Breast-feeding—It is not known whether otic ofloxacin passes into breast milk. However, ofloxacin given by mouth does pass into breast milk. Because there is a potential for serious adverse reactions from ofloxacin in nursing babies, mothers who are using this medicine and who wish to breast-feed should discuss this with their doctor.

Children—Use is not recommended in infants younger than 1 year of age.

Older adults—Many medicines have not been studied specifically in older people. Therefore, it may not be known whether they work exactly the same way they do in younger adults or if they cause different side effects or problems in older people. There is no specific information comparing use of otic ofloxacin in the elderly with use in other age groups.

Other medicines—Although certain medicines should not be used together at all, in other cases two different medicines may be used together even if an interaction might occur. In these cases, your doctor may want to change the dose, or other precautions may be necessary. Tell your health care professional if you are taking or using any other prescription or nonprescription (over-the-counter [OTC]) medicine.

Proper Use of This Medicine

Ofloxacin eardrops comes with patient information and instructions (Medication Guide). *Be sure to read these instructions before using the eardrops.* If you have any questions, check with your doctor or health care professional.

To use:

- Hold the bottle in your hands for 1 or 2 minutes to warm up the solution before putting it in your ear. Otherwise, putting cold solution in your ear could cause you to become dizzy.
- Wash your hands with soap and water.
- Gently clean any discharge that can be removed easily from the outer ear, *but do not insert any object or swab into the ear canal.*
- If you are using the eardrops for a middle ear infection— Drop the medicine into the ear canal. Then, gently press the tragus of the ear (see the diagram in the Medication Guide) four times in a pumping motion. This will allow the drops to pass through the hole or tube in the eardrum and into the middle ear.
- If you are using the eardrops for an ear canal infection— Gently pull the outer ear up and back for adults (down and back for children) to straighten the ear canal. This will allow the eardrops to flow down into the ear canal.
- Keep the ear facing up for about 5 minutes to allow the medicine to come into contact with the infection.
- If both ears are being treated, turn over after 5 minutes, and repeat the application for the other ear.
- *To keep the medicine as germ-free as possible, do not touch the applicator tip to any surface (including the ear).* Also, keep the container tightly closed.

To help clear up your infection completely, *keep using this medicine for the full time of treatment*, even if your symptoms have disappeared. *Do not miss any doses.*

Dosing—The dose of ofloxacin otic will be different for different patients. *Follow your doctor's orders or the directions on the label.* The following information includes only the average doses of ofloxacin otic. *If your dose is different, do not change it* unless your doctor tells you to do so.

- For *eardrops* dosage form:
  —For ear infections:
    - Adults and teenagers (12 years of age and older)—Place 10 drops in each affected ear two times a day for ten to fourteen days, depending on the infection.
    - Children 1 to 12 years of age—Place 5 drops in each affected ear two times a day for ten days.
    - Children younger than 1 year of age—Use and dose must be determined by your doctor.

Missed dose—If you miss a dose of this medicine, use it as soon as possible. However, if it is almost time for your next dose, skip the missed dose and go back to your regular dosing schedule.

Storage—To store this medicine:

- Keep out of the reach of children.
- Store away from heat and direct light.
- Keep the medicine from freezing.
- Do not keep outdated medicine or medicine no longer needed. Be sure that any discarded medicine is out of the reach of children.

Precautions While Using This Medicine

If your symptoms do not improve within a few days, or if they become worse, check with your doctor.

Oral and systemic ofloxacin and other similar antibiotics have sometimes caused a severe allergic reaction. It is not known if otic ofloxacin may cause this reaction. However, *stop using this medicine and check with your doctor immediately if you notice skin rash or itching, shortness of breath, or swelling of the face or neck.*

Side Effects of This Medicine

Along with its needed effects, a medicine may cause some unwanted effects. Although not all of these side effects may occur, if they do occur they may need medical attention.

Check with your doctor immediately if any of the following side effects occur:
> *Less common*
>> Burning, itching, redness, skin rash, swelling, or other sign of irritation not present before use of this medicine

Also, check with your doctor as soon as possible if any of the following side effects occur:
> *Less common*
>> Dizziness
>
> *Rare*
>> Bleeding from the ear; fast heartbeat; fever; headache; ringing in the ear; runny or stuffy nose; sore throat

Other side effects may occur that usually do not need medical attention. These side effects may go away during treatment as your body adjusts to the medicine. However, check with your doctor if any of the following side effects continue or are bothersome:
> *Less common*
>> Change in taste; earache; numbness or tingling

Other side effects not listed above may also occur in some patients. If you notice any other effects, check with your doctor.

Developed: 08/14/98
Interim revision: 08/27/98

OLANZAPINE Systemic

Commonly used brand name(s):

In the U.S.—
   Zyprexa

Description

Olanzapine (oh-LAN-za-peen) is used to treat psychotic mental disorders, such as schizophrenia.

This medicine is available only with your doctor's prescription, in the following dosage form:

   Oral
   • Tablets (U.S.)

Before Using This Medicine

In deciding to use a medicine, the risks of taking the medicine must be weighed against the good it will do. This is a decision you and your doctor will make. For olanzapine, the following should be considered:

Allergies—Tell your doctor if you have ever had any unusual or allergic reaction to olanzapine. Also tell your health care professional if you are allergic to any other substances, such as foods, preservatives, or dyes.

Pregnancy—Olanzapine has not been studied in pregnant women. A few women have become pregnant during treatment with this medicine; some pregnancies were normal and some resulted in miscarriages. Olanzapine crosses the placenta in animals and has been shown to cause a decrease in the number of successful births.

Breast-feeding—It is not known whether olanzapine passes into human breast milk. However, it does pass into the milk of animals. In general, breast-feeding is not recommended during treatment with olanzapine.

Children—Studies on this medicine have been done only in adult patients, and there is no specific information comparing use of olanzapine in children up to 18 years of age with use in other age groups.

Older adults—This medicine has been tested and has not been shown to cause different side effects or problems in older people than it does in younger adults. However, it is removed from the body more slowly in older people.

Other medicines—Although certain medicines should not be used together at all, in other cases two different medicines may be used together even if an interaction might occur. In these cases, your doctor may want to change the dose, or other precautions may be necessary. *Many different medicines can increase the chance that you will develop unwanted effects while taking olanzapine. These effects include liver problems, heat stroke, drowsiness, constipation, and dizziness or fainting when getting up from a lying or sitting position.* When you are taking olanzapine, it is especially important that your health care professional know if you are taking any other prescription or nonprescription (over-the-counter [OTC]) medicine.

Other medical problems—The presence of other medical problems may affect the use of olanzapine. Make sure you tell your doctor if you have any other medical problems, especially:
   • Alzheimer's disease—Risk of pneumonia and convulsions (seizures) may be increased

   • Breast cancer (or history of)—Certain types of breast cancer may be worsened
   • Convulsions (seizures) (existing or history of)—Olanzapine has been reported to cause seizures rarely
   • Dehydration—Increased risk of heat stroke because olanzapine affects the body's ability to cool itself
   • Enlarged prostate or
   • Glaucoma, narrow-angle or
   • Paralytic ileus (severe intestinal problem) (history of)—May be worsened
   • Heart or blood vessel disease, including previous heart attack or
   • Poor circulation to the brain—Low blood pressure may be worsened or may make these conditions worse
   • Liver disease—Olanzapine can cause liver problems

Proper Use of This Medicine

Take this medicine only as directed by your doctor in order to improve your condition as much as possible. Do not take more of it and do not take it more often than your doctor ordered.

Olanzapine may be taken with or without food, on a full or an empty stomach. If your doctor tells you to take it a certain way, follow your doctor's instructions.

Dosing—The dose of olanzapine will be different for different patients. *Follow your doctor's orders or the directions on the label.* The following information includes only the average doses of olanzapine. *If your dose is different, do not change it* unless your doctor tells you to do so.

The number of tablets that you take depends on the strength of the medicine.
   • For *oral* dosage form (tablets):
      —For treatment of psychotic disorders:
         • Adults—At first, 5 to 10 milligrams (mg) once a day. This dose may be changed to a higher or lower dose by your doctor as needed.
         • Children up to 18 years of age—Use and dose must be determined by your doctor.

Missed dose—If you miss a dose of this medicine, take it as soon as possible if you remember it the same day. However, if you don't remember until the next day, skip the missed dose and return to your regular dosing schedule. Do not double doses.

Storage—To store this medicine:
   • Keep out of the reach of children.
   • Store away from heat and direct light.
   • Do not store in the bathroom, near the kitchen sink, or in other damp places. Heat or moisture may cause the medicine to break down.
   • Do not keep outdated medicine or medicine no longer needed. Be sure that any discarded medicine is out of the reach of children.

Precautions While Using This Medicine

It is important that your doctor check your progress at regular visits, to allow for changes in your dose and help reduce any side effects.

This medicine may add to the effects of alcohol and other central nervous system (CNS) depressants (medicines that make you drowsy or less alert). Some examples of CNS depressants are antihistamines or medicine for hay fever, other allergies, or colds; sedatives, tranquilizers, or sleeping medicine; prescription pain medicine or narcotics; barbiturates; medicine for seizures; muscle relaxants; or anesthetics, including some dental anesthetics. *Check with your doctor before taking any CNS depressants while you are taking this medicine.*

Olanzapine may cause drowsiness, trouble in thinking, trouble in controlling movements, or trouble in seeing clearly. *Make sure you know how you react to this medicine before you drive, use machines, or do other jobs that require you to be alert, well-coordinated, or able to think or see well.*

Dizziness, lightheadedness, or fainting may occur, especially when you get up from a lying or sitting position. Getting up slowly may help. If this problem continues or gets worse, check with your doctor.

This medicine may make it more difficult for your body to cool itself down. *Use care not to become overheated during exercise or hot weather* since overheating may result in heat stroke.

Olanzapine may cause dryness of the mouth. For temporary relief, use sugarless gum or candy, melt bits of ice in your mouth, or use a saliva substitute. However, if your mouth feels dry for more than 2 weeks, check with your medical doctor or dentist. Continuing dryness of the mouth may increase the chance of dental disease, including tooth decay, gum disease, and fungus infections.

Side Effects of This Medicine

Along with its needed effects, a medicine may cause some unwanted effects. Although not all of these side effects may occur, if they do occur they may need medical attention.

Check with your doctor as soon as possible if any of the following side effects occur:

More common
> Agitation; behavior problems; difficulty in speaking or swallowing; restlessness or need to keep moving; stiffness of arms or legs; trembling or shaking of hands and fingers

Less common
> Chest pain; fever; flu-like symptoms; inability to move eyes; lip smacking or puckering; mood or mental changes, such as anger, anxiety, giddiness, loss of memory, or nervousness; muscle spasms of face, neck, and back; puffing of cheeks; rapid or worm-like movements of tongue; swelling of feet or ankles; twitching movements; uncontrolled chewing movements; uncontrolled movements of arms and legs

Rare
> Changes in menstrual period; confusion; mental or physical sluggishness; skin rash; swelling of face; trouble in breathing

Other side effects may occur that usually do not need medical attention. These side effects may go away during treatment as your body adjusts to the medicine. However, check with your doctor if any of the following side effects continue or are bothersome:

More common
> Constipation; dizziness; dizziness or fainting when getting up suddenly from a lying or sitting position; drowsiness; dryness of mouth; headache; runny nose; vision problems; weakness; weight gain

Less common or rare
> Abdominal pain; awareness of heartbeat; decrease in sexual desire; double vision; fast heartbeat; increased appetite; increased cough; increased sensitivity of skin to sunlight; joint pain; low blood pressure; nausea; sore throat; stuttering; thirst; tightness of muscles; trouble in controlling urine; trouble in sleeping; vomiting; watering of mouth; weight loss

Other side effects not listed above may also occur in some patients. If you notice any other effects, check with your doctor.

Developed: 03/13/98

OLOPATADINE   Ophthalmic

Commonly used brand name(s):

In the U.S.—
> Patanol

Description

Olopatadine (oh-loe-pa-TA-deen) ophthalmic (eye) solution is used to temporarily prevent itching of the eye caused by a condition known as allergic conjunctivitis. It works by acting on certain cells, called mast cells, to prevent them from releasing substances that cause the allergic reaction.

This medicine is available only with your doctor's prescription, in the following dosage form:

Ophthalmic
> • Ophthalmic solution (eye drops) (U.S.)

Before Using This Medicine

In deciding to use a medicine, the risks of using the medicine must be weighed against the good it will do. This is a decision you and your doctor will make. For olopatadine, the following should be considered:

Allergies—Tell your doctor if you have ever had any unusual or allergic reaction to olopatadine. Also tell your health care professional if you are allergic to any other substances, such as certain preservatives.

Pregnancy—Olopatadine has not been studied in pregnant women. However, studies in animals have found that this medicine given in extremely high doses results in a decreased number of live births; it has not been found to cause birth defects. Before using this medicine, make sure your doctor knows if you are pregnant or if you may become pregnant.

Breast-feeding—It is not known whether olopatadine passes into human breast milk. However, it does pass into the milk of animals with nursing young. Discuss with your doctor whether or not to breast-feed while using this medicine.

Children—Studies on this medicine have been done only in adult patients, and there is no specific information comparing use of olopatadine in children up to 3 years of age with use in other age groups.

Older adults—Many medicines have not been studied specifically in older people. Therefore, it may not be known whether they work exactly the same way they do in younger adults or if they cause different side effects or problems in older people. There is no specific information comparing use of olopatadine in the elderly with use in other age groups.

Other medicines—Although certain medicines should not be used together at all, in other cases two different medicines may be used together even if an interaction might occur. In these cases, your doctor may want to change the dose, or other precautions may be necessary. Tell your health care professional if you are taking or using any other prescription or nonprescription (over-the-counter [OTC]) medicine.

Proper Use of This Medicine

If you wear contact lenses: Take out your contact lenses before using olopatadine eye drops. Wait at least 15 minutes after putting the eye drops in before you put your contact lenses back in.

To use the *eye drops:*

- First, wash your hands. Tilt your head back and, pressing your finger gently on the skin just beneath the lower eyelid, pull the lower eyelid away from the eye to make a space. Drop the medicine into this space. Let go of the eyelid and gently close the eyes. Do not blink. Keep the eyes closed for 1 or 2 minutes to allow the medicine to be absorbed by the eye.
- If you think you did not get the drop of medicine into your eye properly, use another drop.
- *To keep the medicine as germ-free as possible, do not touch the applicator tip to any surface (including the eye).* Also, keep the container tightly closed.

Dosing—The dose of ophthalmic olopatadine will be different for different patients. *Follow your doctor's orders or the directions on the label.* The following information includes only the average doses of ophthalmic olopatadine. *If your dose is different, do not change it* unless your doctor tells you to do so.

- For *ophthalmic* dosage form (eye drops):
  —For treatment of allergic conjunctivitis:
  - Adults and children 3 years of age and older— Use one drop in each affected eye two times a day, with each dose being at least six to eight hours apart.
  - Children up to 3 years of age—Use and dose must be determined by your doctor.

Missed dose—If you miss a dose of this medicine, use it as soon as possible. However, if it is almost time for the next dose, skip the missed dose and go back to your regular dosing schedule. Do not double doses.

Storage—To store this medicine:

- Keep out of the reach of children.
- Store away from heat and direct light.
- Keep the medicine from freezing.
- Do not keep outdated medicine or medicine no longer needed. Be sure that any discarded medicine is out of the reach of children.

Precautions While Using This Medicine

If your symptoms do not improve or if your condition becomes worse, check with your doctor.

Side Effects of This Medicine

Along with its needed effects, a medicine may cause some unwanted effects. Although not all of these side effects may occur, if they do occur they may need medical attention.

The following side effects usually do not need medical attention. These side effects may go away during treatment as your body adjusts to the medicine. However, check with your doctor if any of the following side effects continue or are bothersome:

More common
  Headache
Less common
  Burning, dryness, itching, or stinging of the eye; change in taste; eye irritation or pain; feeling of something in the eye; redness of eye or inside of eyelid; runny or stuffy nose; sore throat; swelling of eyelid; unusual tiredness or weakness

Other side effects not listed above may also occur in some patients. If you notice any other effects, check with your doctor.

Developed: 08/13/98

OLSALAZINE   Oral

Commonly used brand name(s):

In the U.S.—
  Dipentum

In Canada—
  Dipentum

Other commonly used names are azodisal sodium and sodium azodisalicylate.

Description

Olsalazine (ole-SAL-a-zeen) is used in patients who have had ulcerative colitis to prevent the condition from occurring again. It works inside the bowel by helping to reduce inflammation and other symptoms of the disease.

Olsalazine is available only with your doctor's prescription, in the following dosage form:

Oral
- Capsules (U.S. and Canada)

Before Using This Medicine

In deciding to use a medicine, the risks of taking the medicine must be weighed against the good it will do. This is a decision you and your doctor will make. For olsalazine, the following should be considered:

Allergies—Tell your doctor if you have ever had any unusual or allergic reaction to olsalazine, mesalamine, sulfasalazine, or any salicylates (for example, aspirin). Also tell your health care professional if you are allergic to any other substances, such as foods, preservatives, or dyes.

Pregnancy—Olsalazine has not been studied in pregnant women. However, studies in rats have shown that olsalazine causes birth defects and other problems at doses 5 to 20 times the human dose. Before taking this medicine, make sure your doctor knows if you are pregnant or if you may become pregnant.

Breast-feeding—It is not known whether olsalazine passes into human breast milk. However, olsalazine has been shown to cause unwanted effects, such as slowed growth, in the pups of rats given olsalazine while nursing. It may be necessary for you to take another medicine or to stop breast-feeding during treatment. Be sure you have discussed the risks and benefits of the medicine with your doctor.

Children—Studies on this medicine have been done only in adult patients, and there is no specific information comparing use of olsalazine in children with use in other age groups.

Older adults—Many medicines have not been studied specifically in older people. Therefore, it may not be known whether they work exactly the same way they do in younger adults. Although there is no specific information comparing use of olsalazine in the elderly with use in other age groups, this medicine is not expected to cause different side effects or problems in older people than it does in younger adults.

Other medicines—Although certain medicines should not be used together at all, in other cases two different medicines may be used together even if an interaction might occur. In these cases, your doctor may want to change the dose, or other precautions may be necessary. Tell your health care professional if you are using any other prescription or nonprescription (over-the-counter [OTC]) medicine.

Other medical problems—The presence of other medical problems may affect the use of olsalazine. Make sure you tell your doctor if you have any other medical problems, especially:

- Kidney disease—The use of olsalazine may cause further damage to the kidneys

Proper Use of This Medicine

Olsalazine is best taken with food, to lessen stomach upset. If stomach or intestinal problems continue or are bothersome, check with your doctor.

Keep taking this medicine for the full time of treatment, even if you begin to feel better after a few days. *Do not miss any doses.*

Dosing—The dose of olsalazine will be different for different patients. *Follow your doctor's orders or the directions on the label.* The following information includes only the average doses of olsalazine. *If your dose is different, do not change it* unless your doctor tells you to do so.

- For *oral* dosage form (capsules):
  - To prevent ulcerative colitis from occurring again:
    - Adults and teenagers—500 milligrams (mg) two times a day.
    - Children—Use and dose must be determined by your doctor.

Missed dose—If you miss a dose of this medicine, take it as soon as possible. However, if it is almost time for your next dose, skip the missed dose and go back to your regular dosing schedule. Do not double doses.

Storage—To store this medicine:

- Keep out of the reach of children.
- Store away from heat and direct light.
- Do not store this medicine in the bathroom, near the kitchen sink, or in other damp places. Heat or moisture may cause the medicine to break down.

- Do not keep outdated medicine or medicine no longer needed. Be sure that any discarded medicine is out of the reach of children.

Precautions While Using This Medicine

It is very important that your doctor check your progress at regular visits, especially if you will be taking olsalazine for a long time.

Side Effects of This Medicine

Along with its needed effects, a medicine may cause some unwanted effects. Although not all of these side effects may occur, if they do occur they may need medical attention.

Check with your doctor as soon as possible if any of the following side effects occur:
> *Rare*
>> Back or stomach pain (severe); bloody diarrhea; fast heartbeat; fever; nausea or vomiting; skin rash; swelling of the stomach; yellow eyes or skin

Other side effects may occur that usually do not need medical attention. These side effects may go away during treatment as your body adjusts to the medicine. However, check with your doctor if any of the following side effects continue or are bothersome:
> *More common*
>> Abdominal or stomach pain or upset; diarrhea; loss of appetite
> *Less common*
>> Aching joints and muscles; acne; anxiety or depression; dizziness or drowsiness; headache; trouble in sleeping

Other side effects not listed above may also occur in some patients. If you notice any other effects, check with your doctor.

Additional Information

Once a medicine has been approved for marketing for a certain use, experience may show that it is also useful for other medical problems. Although this use is not included in product labeling, olsalazine may be used in certain patients to treat mild or moderate ulcerative colitis.

Other than the above information, there is no additional information relating to proper use, precautions, or side effects for this use.

Revised: 03/15/95

OMEPRAZOLE   Systemic

Commonly used brand name(s):

In the U.S.—
  Prilosec

In Canada—
  Losec

Description

Omeprazole (o-MEP-ra-zole) is used to treat certain conditions in which there is too much acid in the stomach. It is used to treat gastric and duodenal ulcers and gastroesophageal reflux disease, a condition in which the acid in the stomach washes back up into the esophagus. Sometimes omeprazole is used in combination with antibiotics to treat ulcers associated with infection caused by the *H. pylori* bacteria (germ).

Omeprazole is also used to treat Zollinger-Ellison disease, a condition in which the stomach produces too much acid.

Omeprazole is also used to treat dyspepsia, a condition that causes sour stomach, belching, heart burn, or indigestion.

Omeprazole works by decreasing the amount of acid produced by the stomach.

This medicine is available only with your doctor's prescription.

Oral
- Delayed-release capsules (U.S.)
- Delayed-release tablets (Canada)

Before Using This Medicine

In deciding to use a medicine, the risks of taking the medicine must be weighed against the good it will do. This is a decision you and your doctor will make. For omeprazole, the following should be considered:

Allergies—Tell your doctor if you have ever had any unusual or allergic reaction to omeprazole. Also tell your health care professional if you are allergic to any other substances, such as foods, preservatives, or dyes.

Pregnancy—Studies have not been done in humans. However, studies in animals have shown that omeprazole may cause harm to the fetus.

Breast-feeding—Omeprazole may pass into the breast milk. Since this medicine has been shown to cause unwanted effects, such as tumors and cancer in animals, it may be necessary for you to take another medicine or to stop breast-feeding during treatment. Be sure you have discussed the risks and benefits of the medicine with your doctor.

Children—There is no specific information comparing the use of omeprazole in children with use in other age groups.

Older adults—Many medicines have not been studied specifically in older people. Therefore, it may not be known whether they work exactly the same way they do in younger adults or if they cause different side effects or problems in older people. There is no specific information comparing use of omeprazole in the elderly with use in other age groups.

Other medicines—Although certain medicines should not be used together at all, in other cases two different medicines may be used together even if an interaction might occur. In these cases, your doctor may want to change the dose, or other precautions may be necessary. When you are taking omeprazole, it is especially important that your health care professional know if you are taking any of the following:
- Anticoagulants (blood thinners) or
- Diazepam (e.g., Valium) or
- Phenytoin (e.g., Dilantin)—Use with omeprazole may cause high blood levels of these medicines, which may increase the chance of side effects

Other medical problems—The presence of other medical problems may affect the use of omeprazole. Make sure you tell your doctor if you have any other medical problems, especially:
- Liver disease or a history of liver disease—This condition may cause omeprazole to build up in the body

Proper Use of This Medicine

Take omeprazole *capsules* immediately before a meal, preferably in the morning. Omeprazole *tablets* may be taken with food or on an empty stomach.

It may take several days before this medicine begins to relieve stomach pain. To help relieve this pain, antacids may be taken with omeprazole, unless your doctor has told you not to use them.

Swallow the *capsule* and *tablet* forms of omeprazole whole. Do not open the capsule. Do not crush, break, or chew the capsule or the tablet.

Take this medicine for the full time of treatment, even if you begin to feel better. Also, keep your appointments with your doctor for check-ups so that your doctor will be better able to tell you when to stop taking this medicine.

Dosing—The dose of omeprazole will be different for different patients. *Follow your doctor's orders or the directions on the label*. The following information includes only the average doses of omeprazole. *If your dose is different, do not change it* unless your doctor tells you to do so.
- For *oral* dosage forms (capsules, tablets):
  —To treat dyspepsia:
  - Adults—20 milligrams (mg) taken once a day for four weeks. Patients may respond adequately to 10 mg once daily, so individual dose adjustment may be considered.
  - Children—Use and dose must be determined by your doctor.
  —To treat gastroesophageal reflux disease (GERD):
  - Adults—20 milligrams (mg) taken once a day for four to eight weeks. Or your doctor may tell you to take 40 mg a day for certain conditions. Also, your doctor may want you to take omeprazole for more than eight weeks for certain conditions.
  - Children—Use and dose must be determined by your doctor.
  —To treat conditions in which the stomach produces too much acid:
  - Adults—60 mg taken once a day. Your doctor may change the dose as needed. Your treatment may be continued for as long as it is needed.
  - Children—Use and dose must be determined by your doctor.
  —To treat duodenal ulcers:
  - Adults—20 mg taken once a day. Or your doctor may tell you to take 40 mg a day for certain conditions.
  - Children—Use and dose must be determined by your doctor.
  —To treat gastric ulcers:
  - Adults—40 mg taken once a day for four to eight weeks.
  - Children—Use and dose must be determined by your doctor.
  —To treat ulcers related to infection with *H. pylori*:
  - Adults—40 mg once a day, taken along with clarithromycin 500 mg three times a day, for the first fourteen days. For days 15 through 28, omeprazole 20 mg taken once a day.
  - Children—Use and dose must be determined by your doctor.

Missed dose—If you miss a dose of this medicine, take it as soon as possible. However, if it is almost time for your next dose, skip the missed dose and go back to your regular dosing schedule. Do not double doses.

Storage—To store this medicine:

- Keep out of the reach of children.
- Store away from heat and direct light.
- Do not store in the bathroom, near the kitchen sink, or in other damp places. Heat or moisture may cause the medicine to break down.
- Do not keep outdated medicine or medicine no longer needed. Be sure that any discarded medicine is out of the reach of children.

Precautions While Using This Medicine

It is important that your doctor check your progress at regular visits. If your condition does not improve, or if it becomes worse, check with your doctor.

Side Effects of This Medicine

Along with its needed effects, a medicine may cause some unwanted effects. Although not all of these side effects may occur, if they do occur they may need medical attention.

Check with your doctor as soon as possible if any of the following side effects occur:

Rare

Back, leg, or stomach pain; bleeding or crusting sores on lips; blisters; bloody or cloudy urine; chills; continuing ulcers or sores in mouth; difficult, burning, or painful urination; fever; frequent urge to urinate; general feeling of discomfort or illness; joint pain; loss of appetite; muscle aches or cramps; pain; red or irritated eyes; redness, tenderness, itching, burning, or peeling of skin; skin rash or itching; sore throat; sores, ulcers, or white spots on lips, in mouth, or on genitals; unusual bleeding or bruising; unusual tiredness or weakness

Symptoms of overdose

Blurred vision; confusion; drowsiness; dryness of mouth; fast or irregular heartbeat; flushing; general feeling of discomfort or illness; headache; increased sweating; nausea

Other side effects may occur that usually do not need medical attention. These side effects may go away during treatment as your body adjusts to the medicine. However, check with your doctor if any of the following side effects continue or are bothersome:

More common

Abdominal or stomach pain

Less common

Back pain; chest pain; constipation; diarrhea or loose stools; dizziness; gas; headache; heartburn; muscle pain; nausea and vomiting; skin rash or itching; unusual drowsiness; unusual tiredness

Other side effects not listed above may also occur in some patients. If you notice any other effects, check with your doctor.

Revised: 02/05/2001

ONDANSETRON   Systemic

Commonly used brand name(s):

In the U.S.—
Zofran
Zofran ODT

In Canada—
Zofran

Description

Ondansetron (on-DAN-se-tron) is used to treat or prevent the nausea and vomiting that may occur after therapy with anticancer medicines (chemotherapy) or radiation, or after surgery.

Ondansetron is available only with your doctor's prescription, in the following dosage forms:

Oral

- Oral Solution (U.S. and Canada)
- Oral Disintegrating Tablets (U.S.)
- Tablets (U.S. and Canada)

Parenteral

- Injection (U.S. and Canada)

Before Using This Medicine

In deciding to use a medicine, the risks of taking the medicine must be weighed against the good it will do. This is a decision you and your doctor will make. For ondansetron, the following should be considered:

Allergies—Tell your doctor if you have ever had any unusual or allergic reaction to ondansetron, granisetron, or dolasetron. Also tell your health care professional if you are allergic to any other substances, such as foods, preservatives, or dyes.

Pregnancy—Ondansetron has not been studied in pregnant women. However, this medicine has not been shown to cause birth defects or other problems in animal studies.

Breast-feeding—It is not known whether ondansetron passes into the breast milk. Although most medicines pass into breast milk in small amounts, many of them may be used safely while breast-feeding. Mothers who are taking this medicine and who wish to breast-feed should discuss this with their doctor.

Children—This medicine has been tested in a limited number of children with cancer 4 years of age or older and after surgery in children 2 to 12 years of age. In effective doses, the medicine has not been shown to cause different side effects or problems than it does in adults.

Older adults—This medicine has been tested in a limited number of cancer patients 65 years of age or older and has not been shown to cause different side effects or problems in older people than it does in younger adults.

Other medicines—Although certain medicines should not be used together at all, in other cases two different medicines may be used together even if an interaction might occur. In these cases, your doctor may want to change the dose, or other precautions may be necessary. Tell your health care professional if you are taking any other prescription or nonprescription (over-the-counter [OTC]) medicine.

Other medical problems—The presence of other medical problems may affect the use of ondansetron. Make sure

you tell your doctor if you have any other medical problems, especially:

- Abdominal surgery—Use of ondansetron may cover up stomach problems
- Liver disease—Patients with liver disease may have an increased chance of side effects
- Phenylketonuria (PKU)—The oral disintegrating tablets may contain aspartame, which can make your condition worse

Proper Use of This Medicine

If you vomit within 30 minutes after taking this medicine, take the same amount of medicine again. If vomiting continues, check with your doctor.

For patients using the *oral disintegrating tablet* form of this medicine:

- Make sure your hands are dry.
- Do not push the tablet through the foil backing of the package. Instead, gently peel back the foil backing and remove the tablet.
- Immediately place the tablet on top of the tongue.
- The tablet will dissolve in seconds, and you may swallow it with your saliva. You do not need to drink water or other liquid to swallow the tablet.

Dosing—The dose of ondansetron will be different for different patients. *Follow your doctor's orders or the directions on the label*. The following information includes only average doses of ondansetron. *If your dose is different, do not change it* unless your doctor tells you to do so.

- For *oral* dosage forms (solution, oral disintegrating tablets, and tablets):
  —For prevention of nausea and vomiting after anticancer medicine:
    - Adults and children 12 years of age and older—At first, the dose is 8 milligrams (mg) taken thirty minutes before the anticancer medicine is given. The 8-mg dose is taken again eight hours after the first dose. Then, the dose is 8 mg every twelve hours for one to two days.
    - Children 4 to 12 years of age—At first, the dose is 4 mg taken thirty minutes before the anticancer medicine is given. The 4-mg dose is taken again four and eight hours after the first dose. Then, the dose is 4 mg every eight hours for one to two days.
    - Children up to 4 years of age—Dose must be determined by your doctor.
  —For prevention of nausea and vomiting after surgery:
    - Adults—Dose is usually 16 mg one hour before anesthesia (medicine to put you to sleep before surgery).
    - Children—Dose must be determined by your doctor.
  —For prevention of nausea and vomiting after radiation treatment:
    - Adults—At first, the dose is 8 mg taken one to two hours before radiation treatment. Then, the dose is 8 mg every eight hours.
    - Children—Dose must be determined by your doctor.
- For *injection* dosage form:
  —For prevention of nausea and vomiting after anticancer medicine:
    - Adults—Dose is usually 32 mg injected into a vein, over a period of fifteen minutes, beginning

thirty minutes before the anticancer medicine is given. Or, if the dose is based on body weight, it is usually 150 micrograms (mcg) per kilogram (kg) (68 mcg per pound) of body weight. This dose is injected into a vein over a period of fifteen minutes, beginning thirty minutes before the anticancer medicine is given. It is injected again four and eight hours after the first dose.

- Children 4 to 18 years of age—Dose is based on body weight and must be determined by your doctor. It is usually 150 mcg per kg (68 mcg per pound) of body weight, injected into a vein over a period of fifteen minutes, beginning thirty minutes before the anticancer medicine is given. The dose is given again four and eight hours after the first dose.
- Children up to 4 years of age—Dose must be determined by your doctor.
—For prevention of nausea and vomiting after surgery:
- Adults—Dose is usually 4 mg injected into a vein over a period of thirty seconds to five minutes. It is given just before anesthesia (medicine to put you to sleep before surgery) or after surgery if nausea and vomiting begin.
- Children 2 to 12 years of age—Dose is based on body weight and must be determined by your doctor. It is usually 150 mcg per kg (68 mcg per pound) of body weight for children weighing 40 kg or less (88 pounds or less), or 4 mg for children weighing over 40 kg (over 88 pounds). The dose is injected into a vein over a period of thirty seconds to five minutes. It is given just before anesthesia or after surgery if nausea and vomiting begin.
- Children up to 2 years of age—Dose must be determined by your doctor.

Missed dose—If you miss a dose of this medicine, and you do not feel nauseated, skip the missed dose and go back to your regular dosing schedule. If you miss a dose of this medicine, and you feel nauseated or you vomit, take the missed dose as soon as possible.

Storage—To store this medicine:

- Keep out of the reach of children.
- Store away from heat and direct light.
- Do not store in the bathroom, near the kitchen sink, or in other damp places. Heat or moisture may cause the medicine to break down.
- Keep the medicine from freezing.
- Do not keep outdated medicine or medicine no longer needed. Be sure that any discarded medicine is out of the reach of children.

Side Effects of This Medicine

Along with its needed effects, a medicine may cause some unwanted effects. Although not all of these side effects may occur, if they do occur they may need medical attention.

Check with your doctor immediately if any of the following side effects occur:

Rare

Chest pain; pain, redness, or burning at place of injection; shortness of breath; skin rash, hives, and/or itching; tightness in chest; troubled breathing; wheezing

Other side effects may occur that usually do not need medical attention. These side effects may go away during treatment as your body adjusts to the medicine. However, check with your doctor if any of the following side effects continue or are bothersome:

More common
Constipation; diarrhea; fever; headache

Less common
Abdominal pain or stomach cramps; burning, tingling, or prickling sensations; dizziness or lightheadedness; drowsiness; dryness of mouth; feeling cold; itching; unusual tiredness or weakness

Other side effects not listed above may also occur in some patients. If you notice any other effects, check with your doctor.

Revised: 05/22/2001

OPIUM PREPARATIONS   Systemic

Other commonly used names are camphorated opium tincture and laudanum.

Note: For quick reference, the following opium preparations are numbered to match the corresponding brand names.

This information applies to the following medicines:
1. Opium Tincture (OH-pee-um TINK-tur)
2. Paregoric (par-e-GOR-ik)

Description

Opium preparations are used along with other measures to treat severe diarrhea. These medicines belong to the group of medicines called narcotics. If too much of a narcotic is taken, it may become habit-forming, causing mental or physical dependence. Physical dependence may lead to withdrawal side effects when you stop taking the medicine.

Opium preparations are available only with your doctor's prescription, in the following dosage forms:

Oral
Opium Tincture
• Oral liquid (U.S. and Canada)
Paregoric
• Oral liquid (U.S. and Canada)

Before Using This Medicine

In deciding to use a medicine, the risks of taking the medicine must be weighed against the good it will do. This is a decision you and your doctor will make. For opium preparations, the following should be considered:

Allergies — Tell your doctor if you have ever had any unusual or allergic reaction to morphine, codeine, or papaverine. Also tell your health care professional if you are allergic to any other substances, such as foods, preservatives, or dyes.

Pregnancy — Opium preparations have not been studied in pregnant women. However, morphine (contained in these medicines) has caused birth defects in animals when given in very large doses.

Regular use of opium preparations during pregnancy may cause the fetus to become dependent on the medicine. This may lead to withdrawal side effects in the newborn baby. Also, these medicines may cause breathing problems in the newborn baby, especially if they are taken just before delivery.

Breast-feeding — Opium preparations have not been reported to cause problems in nursing babies.

Children — Breathing problems may be especially likely to occur in children up to 2 years of age, who are usually more sensitive than adults to the effects of opium preparations.

Older adults — Breathing problems may be especially likely to occur in elderly patients, who are usually more sensitive than younger adults to the effects of opium preparations.

Other medicines — Although certain medicines should not be used together at all, in other cases two different medicines may be used together even if an interaction might occur. In these cases, your doctor may want to change the dose, or other precautions may be necessary. When you are taking an opium preparation, it is especially important that your health care professional know if you are taking any of the following:

• Anticholinergics (medicine for abdominal or stomach spasms or cramps) or
• Central nervous system (CNS) depressants, especially other narcotics, or
• Other diarrhea medicine or
• Tricyclic antidepressants (amitriptyline [e.g., Elavil], amoxapine [e.g., Asendin], clomipramine [e.g., Anafranil], desipramine [e.g., Pertofrane], doxepin [e.g., Sinequan], imipramine [e.g., Tofranil], nortriptyline [e.g., Aventyl], protriptyline [e.g., Vivactil], trimipramine [e.g., Surmontil])—The chance of side effects is increased

• Naltrexone (e.g., Trexan)—Naltrexone blocks the effects of opium preparations and makes them less effective in treating diarrhea

Other medical problems — The presence of other medical problems may affect the use of opium preparations. Make sure you tell your doctor if you have any other medical problems, especially:

• Alcohol or other drug abuse (or history of) or
• Colitis or
• Heart disease or
• Kidney disease or
• Liver disease or
• Underactive thyroid—The chance of side effects may be increased

• Brain disease or head injury or
• Emphysema, asthma, bronchitis, or other chronic lung disease or
• Enlarged prostate or problems with urination or
• Gallbladder disease or gallstones—Some of the side effects of opium preparations can be dangerous if these conditions are present

• Convulsions (seizures), history of—Opium can rarely cause convulsions

Proper Use of This Medicine

This medicine is to be taken by mouth even if it comes in a dropper bottle. The amount you should take is to be measured with the special dropper provided with your prescription and diluted with water just before you take each dose. This will cause the medicine to turn milky in color, but it will still work.

If your prescription does not come in a dropper bottle and the directions on the bottle say to take it by the teaspoonful, it is not necessary to dilute it before using.

If this medicine upsets your stomach, your doctor may want you to take it with food.

Take this medicine only as directed by your doctor. Do not take more of it, do not take it more often, and do not take it for a longer time than your doctor ordered. This is especially important for young children and for elderly patients, who are especially sensitive to the effects of opium preparations. If too much is taken, this medicine may become habit-forming (causing mental or physical dependence) or lead to problems because of an overdose.

Dosing—The dose of these medicines will be different for different patients. *Follow your doctor's orders or the directions on the label.* The following information includes only the average doses of these medicines. *If your dose is different, do not change it* unless your doctor tells you to do so.

For opium tincture (laudanum)
  • For *oral liquid* dosage form (drops):
    —For diarrhea:
      • Adults—5 to 16 drops of liquid, measured with the dropper in the bottle and mixed with a little water, four times a day until diarrhea is controlled.
      • Children—Dose must be determined by your doctor.

For paregoric
  • For *oral liquid* dosage form:
    —For diarrhea:
      • Adults—1 or 2 teaspoonfuls one to four times a day until diarrhea is controlled. Use a measuring spoon to measure the dose. An ordinary household teaspoon that is used at the table may not hold the right amount of medicine.
      • Children 2 years of age and older—0.25 to 0.5 milliliters (mL) (4 to 8 drops) per kilogram weight, mixed with a little water, one to four times a day until diarrhea is controlled. This amount of medicine must be measured with a dropper or a special measuring device that can be used for very small amounts of liquid. If you did not receive a dropper or measuring device with the medicine, check with your pharmacist.

Missed dose—If you miss a dose of this medicine, take it as soon as you remember. However, if it is almost time for your next dose, skip the missed dose and go back to your regular dosing schedule. *Do not double doses.*

Storage—To store this medicine:
  • Keep out of the reach of children. Overdose is very dangerous in young children.
  • Store away from heat and direct light.
  • Keep the container for this medicine tightly closed to prevent the alcohol from evaporating and the medicine from becoming stronger.
  • Do not store this medicine in the refrigerator or allow the medicine to freeze. If it does get cold and you notice any solid particles in it, throw it away.
  • Do not keep outdated medicine or medicine no longer needed. Be sure that any discarded medicine is out of the reach of children.

Precautions While Using This Medicine

Check with your doctor if your diarrhea does not stop after 1 or 2 days or if you develop a fever.

This medicine will add to the effects of alcohol and other CNS depressants (medicines that slow down the nervous system, possibly causing drowsiness). Some examples of CNS depressants are antihistamines or medicine for hay fever, other allergies, or colds; sedatives, tranquilizers, or sleeping medicine; prescription pain medicine or other narcotics; barbiturates; medicine for seizures; muscle relaxants; or anesthetics, including some dental anesthetics. *Do not drink alcoholic beverages, and check with your doctor before taking any of the medicines listed above, while you are taking this medicine.*

This medicine may cause some people to become drowsy, dizzy, lightheaded, or less alert than they are normally. Even if taken at bedtime, it may cause some people to feel drowsy or less alert on arising. *Make sure you know how you react to this medicine before you drive, use machines, or do anything else that could be dangerous if you are dizzy or are not alert.*

Dizziness, lightheadedness, or fainting may be especially likely to occur when you get up suddenly from a lying or sitting position. Getting up slowly may help lessen this problem. If you feel very dizzy, lightheaded, or faint after taking this medicine, lying down for a while may help.

If you have been taking this medicine regularly for several weeks or more, *do not stop using it without first checking with your doctor.* Your doctor may want you to reduce gradually the amount you are using before stopping completely, to lessen the chance of withdrawal side effects.

If you think you or someone else may have taken an overdose, get emergency help at once. Taking an overdose of this medicine or taking alcohol or other CNS depressants with this medicine may lead to unconsciousness and possibly death. Signs of overdose include convulsions (seizures), confusion, severe nervousness or restlessness, severe dizziness, severe drowsiness, slow or irregular breathing, and severe weakness.

Side Effects of This Medicine

Along with its needed effects, a medicine may cause some unwanted effects. Although not all of these side effects may occur, if they do occur they may need medical attention.

Get emergency help immediately if any of the following symptoms of overdose occur:
  Cold, clammy skin; confusion; convulsions (seizures); dizziness (severe); drowsiness (severe); low blood pressure; nervousness or restlessness (severe); pinpoint pupils of eyes; slow heartbeat; slow or irregular breathing; weakness (severe)

Also, *check with your doctor immediately* if any of the following side effects are severe and occur suddenly since they may indicate a more severe and dangerous problem with your bowels:
  Rare
    Bloating; constipation; loss of appetite; nausea or vomiting; stomach cramps or pain

In addition, check with your doctor as soon as possible if any of the following side effects occur:

© 2002 MICROMEDEX Thomson Healthcare

Rare
> Fast heartbeat; increased sweating; mental depression; redness or flushing of face; shortness of breath, wheezing, or troubled breathing; skin rash, hives, or itching; slow heartbeat

Other side effects may occur that usually do not need medical attention. These side effects may go away during treatment as your body adjusts to the medicine. However, check with your doctor if any of the following side effects continue or are bothersome:

More common with large doses
> Difficult or painful urination; dizziness, lightheadedness, or feeling faint; drowsiness; frequent urge to urinate; nervousness or restlessness; unusual decrease in amount of urine; unusual tiredness or weakness

After you stop using this medicine, your body may need time to adjust. The length of time this takes depends on the amount of medicine you were using and how long you used it. During this period of time check with your doctor if you notice any of the following side effects:
> Body aches; diarrhea; fever, runny nose, or sneezing; gooseflesh; increased sweating; increased yawning; loss of appetite; nausea or vomiting; nervousness, restlessness, or irritability; shivering or trembling; stomach cramps; trouble in sleeping; unusually large pupils of eyes; weakness (severe)

Other side effects not listed above may also occur in some patients. If you notice any other effects, check with your doctor.

Revised: 6/15/2000

OPRELVEKIN   Systemic

Commonly used brand name(s):

In the U.S.—
> Neumega

Other commonly used names are interleukin-11, recombinant; and rIL-11.

Description

Oprelvekin (oh-PREL-ve-kin) is a synthetic (man-made) version of a substance called interleukin-11. Naturally occurring interleukin-11 is produced by bone marrow cells in the body and helps to make platelets, which are necessary for proper clotting of blood. Oprelvekin is used to help prevent low platelet counts caused by treatment with some cancer medicines.

This medicine is available only with your doctor's prescription, in the following dosage form(s):

Parenteral
• Injection (U.S.)

Before Using This Medicine

In deciding to use a medicine, the risks of taking the medicine must be weighed against the good it will do. This is a decision you and your doctor will make. For oprelvekin, the following should be considered:

Allergies—Tell your doctor if you have ever had any unusual or allergic reaction to oprelvekin. Also tell your health care professional if you are allergic to any other substances, such as foods, preservatives, or dyes.

Pregnancy—Oprelvekin has not been studied in pregnant women. However, in rats and rabbits this medicine was found to cause harmful effects on the fetus, including miscarriages and poor growth. It has not been found to cause birth defects in animals.

Breast-feeding—It is not known whether oprelvekin passes into breast milk. Discuss with your doctor whether or not you should breast-feed during treatment with this medicine.

Children—Oprelvekin has caused joint and tendon problems in animals and there is a possibility it could also cause these effects in children receiving it. Discuss these possible effects with your doctor.

Older adults—This medicine has been tested and has not been shown to cause different side effects or problems in older people than it does in younger adults.

Other medicines—Although certain medicines should not be used together at all, in other cases two different medicines may be used together even if an interaction might occur. In these cases, your doctor may want to change the dose, or other precautions may be necessary. Tell your health care professional if you are taking any other prescription or nonprescription (over-the-counter [OTC]) medicine.

Other medical problems—The presence of other medical problems may affect the use of oprelvekin. Make sure you tell your doctor if you have any other medical problems, especially:
• Congestive heart failure—May be worsened because oprelvekin causes the body to retain water
• Atrial arrhythmias (heart rhythm problems)—This medicine may cause heart rhythm problems
• Fluid build-up in the abdomen or lungs—May be worsened by oprelvekin

Proper Use of This Medicine

If you are injecting this medicine yourself, each package of oprelvekin will contain a patient instruction sheet. Read this sheet carefully and make sure you understand:
• How to prepare the injection.
• Proper use of disposable syringes.
• How to give the injection.
• How long the injection is stable.
If you have any questions about any of this, check with your health care professional.

This medicine works best if it is given at the same time every day.

Dosing—The dose of oprelvekin will be different for different patients. The dose that is used may depend on a number of things, including the patient's body weight. *If you are receiving oprelvekin at home, follow your doctor's orders or the directions on the label.* If you have any questions about the proper dose of oprelvekin, ask your doctor.

Missed dose—If you miss a dose of this medicine, skip the missed dose and give the next dose at the usual time.

Storage—To store this medicine:
- Keep out of the reach of children.
- Store in the refrigerator.
- Keep the medicine from freezing.
- Do not keep outdated medicine or medicine no longer needed. Ask your health care professional how you should dispose of any medicine you do not use. Be sure that any discarded medicine is out of the reach of children.

Precautions While Using This Medicine

It is very important that your doctor check your progress at regular visits to make sure that this medicine is working properly and to check for unwanted effects.

Side Effects of This Medicine

Along with its needed effects, a medicine may cause some unwanted effects. Although not all of these side effects may occur, if they do occur they may need medical attention.

The side effects listed below include only those that might be caused by oprelvekin. To find out about other side effects that may be caused by the cancer medicines you are also receiving, see the information about those medicines.

Check with your doctor as soon as possible if any of the following side effects occur:

More common
   Fast heartbeat; irregular heartbeat; shortness of breath; sore mouth or tongue; swelling of feet or lower legs; white patches in mouth and/or on tongue

Less common
   Bloody eye; blurred vision; severe redness and peeling of skin

This medicine may also cause the following side effect that your doctor will watch for:

More common
   Heart rhythm problems

Other side effects may occur that usually do not need medical attention. These side effects may go away during treatment as your body adjusts to the medicine. However, check with your doctor if any of the following side effects continue or are bothersome:

More common
   Red eyes; weakness

Less common
   Numbness or tingling of hands or feet; skin discoloration; skin rash at place of injection

Other side effects not listed above may also occur in some patients. If you notice any other effects, check with your doctor.

Developed: 04/23/98

ORLISTAT   Oral—Local

Commonly used brand name(s):

In the U.S.—
Xenical

Description

Orlistat (OR-li-stat) is used as an aid to help you lose weight. The medicine prevents the digestion of some of the fat you eat. Fats that are not digested cannot be absorbed and therefore do not contribute calories. To give the greatest weight loss, orlistat must be used with a weight-reduction diet.

Orlistat is available only with your doctor's prescription, in the following dosage form(s):

Oral
   - Capsules (U.S.)

Before Using This Medicine

In deciding to use a medicine, the risks of taking the medicine must be weighed against the good it will do. This is a decision you and your doctor will make. For orlistat, the following should be considered:

Allergies—Tell your doctor if you have ever had any unusual or allergic reaction to orlistat. Also tell your health care professional if you are allergic to any other substances, such as foods, preservatives, or dyes.

Diet—When using orlistat, your diet should contain no more than 30% of calories as fat. More fat in your diet will increase the side effects of this medicine. Your diet should be nutritionally balanced, and your daily intake of fat, carbohydrates, and protein should be distributed over three main meals.

Pregnancy—Orlistat has not been studied in pregnant women. However, orlistat may decrease the amount of certain vitamins that your body can absorb from the food you eat. Make sure you have discussed with your doctor the use of this medication during pregnancy.

Breast-feeding—It is not known whether orlistat passes into breast milk. Although most medicines pass into breast milk in small amounts, many of them may be used safely while breast-feeding. Mothers who are taking this medicine and who wish to breast-feed should discuss this with their doctor.

Children—Studies on this medicine have been done only in adult patients, and there is no specific information comparing use of orlistat in children with use in other age groups.

Older adults—There is no specific information comparing use of orlistat in the elderly with use in younger adults. However, this medicine is not expected to cause different side effects or problems in older people than it does in younger adults.

Other medicines—Although certain medicines should not be used together at all, in other cases two different medicines may be used together even if an interaction might occur. In these cases, your doctor may want to change the dose, or other precautions may be necessary. When you are taking orlistat, it is especially important that your health care professional know if you are taking the following:

   - Warfarin—Orlistat may decrease the absorption of vitamin K and may change your bleeding time

Other medical problems—The presence of other medical problems may affect the use of orlistat. Make sure you tell your doctor if you have any other medical problems, especially:
   - Kidney stones or
   - Gallbladder problems—Orlistat may make the condition worse

Proper Use of This Medicine

Orlistat prevents the absorption of some of the fat you eat. Therefore, you should take it during the meal or within 1 hour of eating. If you occasionally miss a meal or eat a meal that contains no fat, you should skip the dose of orlistat.

Because orlistat may decrease the amount of some vitamins that your body can absorb from food, you will need to take a multivitamin supplement once a day. Take the vitamin supplement at least 2 hours before or after taking orlistat.

Dosing—The dose of orlistat will be different for different patients. *Follow your doctor's orders or the directions on the label.* The following information includes only the average doses of orlistat. *If your dose is different, do not change it* unless your doctor tells you to do so.

- For *oral* dosage form (capsules):
  —For treatment of obesity:
    - Adults—120 milligrams (mg) three times a day with meals containing fat.
    - Children—Use and dose must be determined by your doctor.

Missed dose—If you miss a dose of orlistat after a fat-containing meal, skip that dose. Wait until your next meal, and take the medicine on your regular schedule. *Do not double doses.*

Storage—To store this medicine:
- Keep out of the reach of children.
- Store away from heat and direct light.
- Keep the medicine from freezing. Do not refrigerate.
- Do not keep outdated medicine or medicine no longer needed. Be sure that any discarded medicine is out of the reach of children.

Precautions While Using This Medicine

It is very important that your doctor check your progress at regular visits to make sure that this medicine is working properly and to check for unwanted effects.

For patients with diabetes: Weight loss may result in an improvement in your condition, and your doctor may need to change your dose of oral diabetes medicine or insulin.

Side Effects of This Medicine

Along with its needed effects, a medicine may cause some unwanted effects. Although not all of these side effects may occur, if they do occur they may need medical attention. Check with your doctor as soon as possible if any of the following side effects occur:

More common
> Bodyache; chills; cough; fever; headache; nasal congestion; runny nose; sneezing; sore throat

Less common
> Tightness in chest; tooth or gum problems; troubled breathing; wheezing

Rare
> Bloody or cloudy urine; change in hearing; contagious diarrhea; difficult or painful urination; earache; frequent urge to urinate; pain in ear

Other side effects may occur that usually do not need medical attention. These side effects may go away during treatment as your body adjusts to the medicine. However, check with your doctor if any of the following side effects continue or are bothersome:

More common
> Gas with leaky bowel movements; inability to hold bowel movement; increases in bowel movements; oily bowel movements; oily spotting of underclothes

Less common
> Anxiety; back pain; menstrual changes; rectal pain or discomfort

After you stop using this medicine, your body may need time to adjust. Side effects caused by orlistat usually disappear within 2 to 3 days after stopping it.

Other side effects not listed above may also occur in some patients. If you notice any other effects, check with your doctor.

Developed: 11/22/99

ORPHENADRINE   Systemic

Commonly used brand name(s):

In the U.S.—
Banflex	Norflex
Flexoject	Orfro
Myolin	Orphenate
Myotrol	

Generic name product may be available.

In Canada—
Disipal
Norflex

Description

Orphenadrine (or-FEN-a-dreen) is used to help relax certain muscles in your body and relieve the stiffness, pain, and discomfort caused by strains, sprains, or other injury to your muscles. One form of orphenadrine is also used to relieve trembling caused by Parkinson's disease. However, this medicine does not take the place of rest, exercise or physical therapy, or other treatment that your doctor may recommend for your medical problem.

Orphenadrine acts in the central nervous system (CNS) to produce its muscle relaxant effects. Orphenadrine also has other actions (anticholinergic) that produce its helpful effects in Parkinson's disease. Orphenadrine's CNS and anticholinergic actions may also be responsible for some of its side effects.

In the U.S., this medicine is available only with your doctor's prescription. In Canada, it may be available without a prescription. It is available in the following dosage forms:

Oral
- Tablets (Canada)
- Extended-release tablets (U.S. and Canada)

Parenteral
- Injection (U.S. and Canada)

Before Using This Medicine

In deciding to use a medicine, the risks of taking the medicine must be weighed against the good it will do. This is a decision

you and your doctor will make. For orphenadrine, the following should be considered:

Allergies—Tell your doctor if you have ever had any unusual or allergic reaction to orphenadrine. Also tell your health care professional if you are allergic to any other substances, such as foods, preservatives, or dyes.

Pregnancy—Orphenadrine has not been reported to cause birth defects or other problems in humans.

Breast-feeding—It is not known whether orphenadrine passes into the breast milk. However, orphenadrine has not been reported to cause problems in nursing babies.

Children—Studies on this medicine have been done only in adult patients, and there is no specific information comparing use of orphenadrine in children with use in other age groups.

Older adults—Many medicines have not been tested in older people. Therefore, it may not be known whether they work exactly the same way they do in younger adults or if they cause different side effects or problems in older people. There is no specific information about the use of orphenadrine in the elderly.

Other medicines—Although certain medicines should not be used together at all, in other cases two different medicines may be used together even if an interaction might occur. In these cases, your doctor may want to change the dose, or other precautions may be necessary. When you are taking orphenadrine, it is especially important that your health care professional knows if you are taking any of the following:

- Alcohol or
- Central nervous system (CNS) depressants or
- Tricyclic antidepressants (amitriptyline [e.g., Elavil], amoxapine [e.g., Asendin], clomipramine [e.g., Anafranil], desipramine [e.g., Pertofrane], doxepin [e.g., Sinequan], imipramine [e.g., Tofranil], nortriptyline [e.g., Aventyl], protriptyline [e.g., Vivactil], trimipramine [e.g., Surmontil])—The chance of side effects may be increased

Other medical problems—The presence of other medical problems may affect the use of orphenadrine. Make sure you tell your doctor if you have any other medical problems, especially:

- Disease of the digestive tract, especially esophagus disease, stomach ulcer, or intestinal blockage, or
- Enlarged prostate or
- Fast or irregular heartbeat or
- Glaucoma or
- Myasthenia gravis or
- Urinary tract blockage—Orphenadrine has side effects that may be harmful to people with these conditions

- Heart disease or
- Kidney disease or
- Liver disease—The chance of side effects may be increased

Proper Use of This Medicine

Dosing—The dose of orphenadrine will be different for different patients. *Follow your doctor's orders or the directions on the label*. The following information includes only the average doses of orphenadrine. *If your dose is different, do not change it* unless your doctor tells you to do so.

- For *extended-release tablet* dosage form:
  —For relaxing stiff, sore muscles:
  - Adults and teenagers—100 milligrams (mg) two times a day, in the morning and evening.
  - Children—Use and dose must be determined by your doctor.
- For *oral tablet* dosage form:
  —For relaxing stiff, sore muscles and for Parkinson's disease:
  - Adults—50 mg three times a day.
  - Children—Dose must be determined by your doctor.
- For *injection* dosage form:
  —For relaxing stiff, sore muscles:
  - Adults—60 mg, injected into a muscle or a vein, every twelve hours as needed.
  - Children—Use and dose must be determined by your doctor.

Missed dose—If you miss a dose of this medicine and remember within an hour or so of the missed dose, take it right away. But if you do not remember until later, skip the missed dose and go back to your regular dosing schedule. Do not double doses.

Storage—To store this medicine:
- Keep out of the reach of children.
- Store away from heat and direct light.
- Do not store this medicine in the bathroom, near the kitchen sink, or in other damp places. Heat or moisture may cause the medicine to break down.
- Do not keep outdated medicine or medicine no longer needed. Be sure that any discarded medicine is out of the reach of children.

Precautions While Using This Medicine

If you will be taking this medicine for a long time (for example, more than a few weeks), your doctor should check your progress at regular visits.

This medicine may add to the effects of alcohol and other CNS depressants (medicines that slow down the nervous system, possibly causing drowsiness). Some examples of CNS depressants are antihistamines or medicine for hay fever, other allergies, or colds; sedatives, tranquilizers, or sleeping medicine; prescription pain medicine or narcotics; barbiturates; medicine for seizures; other muscle relaxants; or anesthetics, including some dental anesthetics. *Do not drink alcoholic beverages, and check with your doctor before taking any of the medicines listed above, while you are using this medicine.*

This medicine may cause some people to have blurred vision or to become drowsy, dizzy, lightheaded, faint, or less alert than they are normally. It may also cause muscle weakness in some people. *Make sure you know how you react to this medicine before you drive, use machines, or do anything else that could be dangerous if you are dizzy or are not alert and able to see well.*

Orphenadrine may cause dryness of the mouth. For temporary relief, use sugarless candy or gum, melt bits of ice in your mouth, or use a saliva substitute. However, if dry mouth continues for more than 2 weeks, check with your dentist. Continuing dryness of the mouth may increase the chance of dental disease, including tooth decay, gum disease, and fungus infections.

Side Effects of This Medicine

Along with its needed effects, a medicine may cause some unwanted effects. Although not all of these side effects may occur, if they do occur they may need medical attention.

Check with your doctor as soon as possible if any of the following side effects occur:

Less common

Decreased urination; eye pain; fainting; fast or pounding heartbeat

Rare

Hallucinations (seeing, hearing, or feeling things that are not there); shortness of breath, troubled breathing, tightness in chest, and/or wheezing; skin rash, hives, itching, or redness; sores, ulcers, or white spots on lips or in mouth; swollen and/or painful glands; unusual bruising or bleeding; unusual tiredness or weakness

Other side effects may occur that usually do not need medical attention. These side effects may go away during treatment as your body adjusts to the medicine. However, check with your doctor if any of the following side effects continue or are bothersome:

More common

Dryness of mouth

Less common or rare

Abdominal or stomach cramps or pain; blurred or double vision or other vision problems; confusion; constipation; difficult urination; dizziness or lightheadedness; drowsiness; excitement, irritability, nervousness, or restlessness; headache; muscle weakness; nausea or vomiting; trembling; unusually large pupils of eyes

Other side effects not listed above may also occur in some patients. If you notice any other effects, check with your doctor.

Revised: 08/11/95

ORPHENADRINE AND ASPIRIN
Systemic

Commonly used brand name(s):

In the U.S.—

Norgesic   Orphenagesic
Norgesic Forte   Orphenagesic Forte

In Canada—

‡Norgesic
Norgesic Forte

‡In Canada, *Aspirin* is a brand name. Acetylsalicylic acid is the generic name in Canada. ASA, a synonym for acetylsalicylic acid, is the term that commonly appears on Canadian product labels.

Description

Orphenadrine and aspirin (or-FEN-a-dreen and AS-pir-in) combination is used to help relax certain muscles in your body and relieve the pain and discomfort caused by strains, sprains, or other injury to your muscles. However, this medicine does not take the place of rest, exercise, or other treatment that your doctor may recommend for your medical problem.

Orphenadrine acts in the central nervous system (CNS) to produce its muscle relaxant effects. Actions in the CNS may also be responsible for some of its side effects. Orphenadrine also has other actions (antimuscarinic) that may be responsible for some of its side effects.

This combination medicine also contains caffeine (kaf-EEN).

In the U.S., this combination medicine is available only with your doctor's prescription. In Canada, it is available without a prescription.

These medicines are available in the following dosage forms:

Oral
• Tablets (U.S. and Canada)

Before Using This Medicine

In deciding to use a medicine, the risks of taking the medicine must be weighed against the good it will do. This is a decision you and your doctor will make. For orphenadrine and aspirin combination, the following should be considered:

Allergies—Tell your doctor if you have ever had any unusual or allergic reaction to orphenadrine, caffeine, aspirin or other salicylates including methyl salicylate (oil of wintergreen), or to any of the following medicines:

Diclofenac (e.g., Voltaren)
Diflunisal (e.g., Dolobid)
Etodolac (e.g., Lodine)
Fenoprofen (e.g., Nalfon)
Floctafenine (e.g., Idarac)
Flurbiprofen, oral (e.g., Ansaid)
Ibuprofen (e.g., Motrin)
Indomethacin (e.g., Indocin)
Ketoprofen (e.g., Orudis)
Ketorolac (e.g., Toradol)
Meclofenamate (e.g., Meclomen)
Mefenamic acid (e.g., Ponstel)
Nabumetone (e.g., Relafen)
Naproxen (e.g., Naprosyn)
Oxaprozin (e.g., Daypro)
Oxyphenbutazone (e.g., Tandearil)
Phenylbutazone (e.g., Butazolidin)
Piroxicam (e.g., Feldene)
Sulindac (e.g., Clinoril)
Suprofen (e.g., Suprol)
Tenoxicam (e.g., Mobiflex)
Tiaprofenic acid (e.g., Surgam)
Tolmetin (e.g., Tolectin)
Zomepirac (e.g., Zomax)

Also tell your health care professional if you are allergic to any other substances, such as foods, preservatives, or dyes.

Pregnancy—

• *For aspirin:* Studies in humans have not shown that aspirin causes birth defects. However, aspirin has caused birth defects in animal studies. Some reports have suggested that too much use of aspirin late in pregnancy may cause a decrease in the newborn's weight and possible death of the fetus or newborn baby. However, the mothers in these reports had been taking much larger amounts of aspirin than are usually recommended. Studies of mothers taking aspirin in the doses that are usually recommended did not show these unwanted effects. Regular use of aspirin late in pregnancy may cause unwanted effects on the heart or blood flow in the fetus or in the newborn baby. Also, use of aspirin during the last 2 weeks of pregnancy may cause bleeding problems in the fetus before or during delivery or in the newborn baby. In addition, too much use of aspirin during the last 3 months of pregnancy may increase the length of pregnancy, prolong labor, cause other problems during delivery, or cause severe bleeding in the mother before, during, or after delivery. *Do not take aspirin during the last 3 months of pregnancy unless it has been ordered by your doctor.*

- *For orphenadrine:* Orphenadrine has not been reported to cause birth defects or other problems in humans.

Breast-feeding—This medicine has not been shown to cause problems in nursing babies. However, aspirin passes into the breast milk. Also, caffeine passes into the breast milk in small amounts. It is not known whether orphenadrine passes into the breast milk.

Children—*Do not give a medicine containing aspirin to a child or a teenager with a fever or other symptoms of a virus infection, especially flu or chickenpox, without first discussing its use with your child's doctor.* This is very important because aspirin may cause a serious illness called Reye's syndrome in children with fever caused by a virus infection, especially flu or chickenpox. Children who do not have a virus infection may also be more sensitive to the effects of aspirin, especially if they have a fever or have lost large amounts of body fluid because of vomiting, diarrhea, or sweating. This may increase the chance of side effects during treatment.

There is no specific information about the use of orphenadrine in children.

Older adults—Elderly people are especially sensitive to the effects of aspirin. This may increase the chance of side effects during treatment.

There is no specific information about the use of orphenadrine in the elderly.

Other medicines—Although certain medicines should not be used together at all, in other cases two different medicines may be used together even if an interaction might occur. In these cases, your doctor may want to change the dose, or other precautions may be necessary. When you are taking orphenadrine and aspirin combination, it is especially important that your health care professional know if you are taking any of the following:

- Anticoagulants (blood thinners) or
- Carbenicillin by injection (e.g., Geopen) or
- Cefamandole (e.g., Mandol) or
- Cefoperazone (e.g., Cefobid) or
- Cefotetan (e.g., Cefotan) or
- Dipyridamole (e.g., Persantine) or
- Divalproex (e.g., Depakote) or
- Heparin or
- Medicine for inflammation or pain, except narcotics, or
- Moxalactam (e.g., Moxam) or
- Pentoxifylline (e.g., Trental) or

- Plicamycin (e.g., Mithracin) or
- Ticarcillin (e.g., Ticar) or
- Valproic acid (e.g., Depakene)—Taking these medicines together with aspirin may increase the chance of bleeding

- Anticholinergics (medicine for abdominal or stomach spasms or cramps) or
- Central nervous system (CNS) depressants or
- Methotrexate (e.g., Mexate) or
- Tricyclic antidepressants (amitriptyline [e.g., Elavil], amoxapine [e.g., Asendin], clomipramine [e.g., Anafranil], desipramine [e.g., Pertofrane], doxepin [e.g., Sinequan], imipramine [e.g., Tofranil], nortriptyline [e.g., Aventyl], protriptyline [e.g., Vivactil], trimipramine [e.g., Surmontil]) or
- Vancomycin (e.g., Vancocin)—The chance of side effects may be increased

- Antidiabetics, oral (diabetes medicine you take by mouth)—Aspirin may increase the effects of the antidiabetic medicine; a change in dose may be needed if aspirin is taken regularly

- Probenecid (e.g., Benemid) or
- Sulfinpyrazone (e.g., Anturane)—Aspirin can keep these medicines from working properly for treating gout; also, taking aspirin together with sulfinpyrazone may increase the chance of bleeding

- Urinary alkalizers (medicine that makes the urine less acid, such as acetazolamide [e.g., Diamox], dichlorphenamide [e.g., Daranide], methazolamide [e.g., Neptazane], potassium or sodium citrate and/or citric acid)—These medicines may make aspirin less effective by causing it to be removed from the body more quickly

- Zidovudine (e.g., AZT; Retrovir)—Aspirin may increase the blood levels of zidovudine, which increases the chance of serious side effects

Other medical problems—The presence of other medical problems may affect the use of orphenadrine and aspirin combination. Make sure you tell your doctor if you have any other medical problems, especially:

- Anemia or
- Overactive thyroid or
- Stomach ulcer or other stomach problems—Aspirin may make your condition worse

- Asthma, allergies, and nasal polyps, history of or
- Glucose-6-phosphate dehydrogenase (G6PD) deficiency or
- Kidney disease or
- Liver disease—The chance of side effects may be increased

- Disease of the digestive tract, especially esophagus disease or intestinal blockage, or
- Enlarged prostate or
- Fast or irregular heartbeat or
- Glaucoma or
- Myasthenia gravis or
- Urinary tract blockage—Orphenadrine has side effects that may be harmful to people with these conditions

- Gout—Aspirin can make this condition worse and can also lessen the effects of some medicines used to treat gout

- Heart disease—The chance of some side effects may be increased. Also, the caffeine present in this combination medicine can make your condition worse

- Hemophilia or other bleeding problems or
- Vitamin K deficiency—Aspirin may increase the chance of bleeding

Proper Use of This Medicine

Take this medicine with food or a full glass (8 ounces) of water to lessen stomach irritation.

Do not take this medicine if it has a strong vinegar-like odor. This odor means the aspirin in it is breaking down. If you have any questions about this, check with your health care professional.

Do not take more of this medicine than your doctor ordered to lessen the chance of side effects or overdose.

Dosing—The dose of orphenadrine and aspirin combination medicine will be different for different people. *Follow your doctor's orders or the directions on the label*. The following information includes only the average doses of the combination medicine. *If your dose is different, do not change it* unless your doctor tells you to do so.
- For *oral* dosage forms (tablets):
  —For muscle pain and stiffness:
    - Adults and teenagers—One or two tablets containing 25 milligrams (mg) of orphenadrine and 385 mg of aspirin, or one-half or one tablet containing 50 mg of orphenadrine and 770 mg of aspirin, three or four times a day.
    - Children—Dose must be determined by your doctor.

Missed dose—If you miss a dose of this medicine and remember within an hour or so of the missed dose, take it right away. But if you do not remember until later, skip the missed dose and go back to your regular dosing schedule. Do not double doses.

Storage—To store this medicine:
- Keep out of the reach of children. Overdose of aspirin is especially dangerous in young children.
- Store away from heat and direct light.
- Do not store this medicine in the bathroom, near the kitchen sink, or in other damp places. Heat or moisture may cause the medicine to break down.
- Do not keep outdated medicine or medicine no longer needed. Be sure that any discarded medicine is out of the reach of children.

Precautions While Using This Medicine

If you will be taking this medicine for a long time (for example, more than a few weeks), your doctor should check your progress at regular visits.

Check the labels of all nonprescription (over-the-counter [OTC]) and prescription medicines you now take. If any contain orphenadrine or aspirin or other salicylates be especially careful, since taking them while taking this medicine may lead to overdose. If you have any questions about this, check with your health care professional.

Too much use of acetaminophen or certain other medicines together with the aspirin in this combination medicine may increase the chance of unwanted effects. The risk depends on how much of each medicine you take every day, and on

how long you take the medicines together. If your doctor directs you to take these medicines together on a regular basis, follow his or her directions carefully. However, do not take acetaminophen or any of the following medicines together with this combination medicine for more than a few days, unless your doctor has directed you to do so and is following your progress:
  Diclofenac (e.g., Voltaren)
  Diflunisal (e.g., Dolobid)
  Etodolac (e.g., Lodine)
  Fenoprofen (e.g., Nalfon)
  Floctafenine (e.g., Idarac)
  Flurbiprofen, oral (e.g., Ansaid)
  Ibuprofen (e.g., Motrin)
  Indomethacin (e.g., Indocin)
  Ketoprofen (e.g., Orudis)
  Ketorolac (e.g., Toradol)
  Meclofenamate (e.g., Meclomen)
  Mefenamic acid (e.g., Ponstel)
  Nabumetone (e.g., Relafen)
  Naproxen (e.g., Naprosyn)
  Oxaprozin (e.g., Daypro)
  Phenylbutazone (e.g., Butazolidin)
  Piroxicam (e.g., Feldene)
  Sulindac (e.g., Clinoril)
  Tenoxicam (e.g., Mobiflex)
  Tiaprofenic acid (e.g., Surgam)
  Tolmetin (e.g., Tolectin)

For *diabetic patients:*
- The aspirin in this combination medicine may cause false urine sugar test results if you are regularly taking 6 or more of the regular-strength tablets or 3 or more of the double-strength tablets of this medicine a day. Smaller doses or occasional use of aspirin usually will not affect urine sugar tests. If you have any questions about this, check with your health care professional especially if your diabetes is not well controlled.

Do not take this medicine for 5 days before any surgery, including dental surgery, unless otherwise directed by your medical doctor or dentist. Taking aspirin during this time may cause bleeding problems.

The orphenadrine in this combination medicine may add to the effects of alcohol and other CNS depressants (medicines that slow down the nervous system, possibly causing drowsiness). Some examples of CNS depressants are antihistamines or medicine for hay fever, other allergies, or colds; sedatives, tranquilizers, or sleeping medicine; prescription pain medicine or narcotics; barbiturates; medicine for seizures; other muscle relaxants; or anesthetics, including some dental anesthetics. Also, stomach problems may be more likely to occur if you drink alcoholic beverages while you are taking aspirin. *Do not drink alcoholic beverages, and check with your doctor before taking any of the medicines listed above, while you are using this medicine.*

This medicine may cause some people to have blurred vision or to become drowsy, dizzy, lightheaded, faint, or less alert than they are normally. *Make sure you know how you react to this medicine before you drive, use machines, or do anything else that could be dangerous if you are dizzy or are not alert.*

Dryness of the mouth may occur while you are taking this medicine. For temporary relief, use sugarless candy or gum, melt bits of ice in your mouth, or use a saliva substitute. However, if dry mouth continues for more than 2 weeks, check with your dentist. Continuing dryness of the mouth may increase the chance of dental disease, including tooth decay, gum disease, and fungus infections.

If you think that you or someone else may have taken an overdose of this medicine, get emergency help at once. Taking an overdose of this medicine may cause unconsciousness or death. Signs of overdose include convulsions (seizures), hearing loss, confusion, ringing or buzzing in the ears, severe drowsiness or tiredness, severe excitement or nervousness, and fast or deep breathing.

Side Effects of This Medicine

Along with its needed effects, a medicine may cause some unwanted effects. Although not all of these side effects may occur, if they do occur they may need medical attention.

Get emergency help immediately if any of the following symptoms of overdose occur:
> Any loss of hearing; bloody urine; confusion; convulsions (seizures); diarrhea; dizziness or lightheadedness (severe); drowsiness (severe); excitement or nervousness (severe); fast or deep breathing; hallucinations (seeing, hearing, or feeling things that are not there); headache (severe or continuing); increased sweating; nausea or vomiting (severe or continuing); ringing or buzzing in the ears (continuing); uncontrollable flapping movements of the hands, especially in elderly patients; unexplained fever; unusual thirst; vision problems

Symptoms of overdose in children
> Changes in behavior; drowsiness or tiredness (severe); fast or deep breathing

Also, check with your doctor as soon as possible if any of the following side effects occur:
Less common or rare
> Abdominal or stomach pain, cramping, or burning (severe); bloody or black, tarry stools; decreased urination; eye pain; fainting; fast or pounding heartbeat; shortness of breath, troubled breathing, tightness in chest, or wheezing; skin rash, hives, itching, or redness; sores, ulcers, or white spots on lips or in mouth; swollen and/or painful glands; unusual bleeding or bruising; unusual tiredness or weakness; vomiting of blood or material that looks like coffee grounds

Other side effects may occur that usually do not need medical attention. These side effects may go away during treatment as your body adjusts to the medicine. However, check with your doctor if any of the following side effects continue or are bothersome:
More common
> Abdominal or stomach cramps, pain, or discomfort (mild to moderate); dryness of mouth; heartburn or indigestion; nausea or vomiting (mild)

Less common
> Blurred or double vision or other vision problems; confusion; constipation; difficult urination; dizziness or lightheadedness; drowsiness; excitement, nervousness, or restlessness; headache; muscle weakness; trembling; unusually large pupils of eyes

Other side effects not listed above may also occur in some patients. If you notice any other effects, check with your doctor.

Revised: 08/11/94

OSELTAMIVIR   Systemic

Commonly used brand name(s):

In the U.S.—
> Tamiflu

In Canada—
> Tamiflu

Description

Oseltamivir (Oh−sel−TAM−i−veer) belongs to the family of medicines called antivirals, which are used to treat infections caused by viruses. Oseltamivir is used in the treatment of the infection caused by the flu virus (influenza A and influenza B). Oseltamivir may reduce flu symptoms (weakness, headache, fever, cough, and sore throat) by 1 day. Oseltamivir has also been shown to prevent influenza infection if you have come into close contact with someone who has the flu.

If you receive the flu vaccine every year, continue to do so.

Oseltamivir is available only with your doctor's prescription in the following dosage form:

Oral
> - Capsules (U.S. and Canada)
> - Oral suspension (U.S.)

Before Using This Medicine

In deciding to use a medicine, the risks of taking the medicine must be weighed against the good it will do. This is a decision you and your doctor will make. For oseltamivir, the following should be considered:

Allergies—Tell your doctor if you have ever had any unusual or allergic reaction to oseltamivir. Also tell your health care professional if you are allergic to any other substances, such as foods, preservatives, or dyes.

Pregnancy—Oseltamivir has not been studied in pregnant women. However, studies in animals have shown that oseltamivir causes problems. Before taking this medicine, make sure your doctor knows if you are pregnant or if you may become pregnant.

Breast-feeding—It is not known whether oseltamivir passes into human breast milk. Although most medicines pass into breast milk in small amounts, many of them may be used safely while breast-feeding. Mothers who are using this medicine and who wish to breast-feed should discuss this with their doctor.

Children—This medicine has not been tested in children younger than 1 year of age.

Older adults—This medicine has been tested in older adults and has not been shown to cause different side effects or problems in older adults than it does in younger adults.

Other medicines—Although certain medicines should not be used together at all, in other cases two different medicines may be used together even if an interaction might occur. In these cases, your doctor may want to change the dose, or other precautions may be necessary. When you are taking oseltamivir it is especially important that your doctor and pharmacist know if you are taking any of the following:
> - Probenecid (e.g., Benemid)—Co-administration may result in higher blood levels of the active metabolite of oseltamivir

Other medical problems—The presence of other medical problems may affect the use of oseltamivir. Make sure to tell your doctor if you have any other medical problems, especially:

- Kidney disease
- Heart disease
- Illnesses caused by viruses other than influenza Type A or B
- Liver disease
- Lung disease
- Serious medical problems that may require admission to a hospital

Proper Use of This Medicine

Talk to your doctor about the possibility of getting a flu shot if you have not had one yet. Patient information about oseltamivir is available. Read this information carefully.

For patients taking oseltamivir for treatment of the flu: This medicine works best if taken within 2 days of having flu symptoms (weakness, headache, fever, cough, and sore throat). Oseltamivir capsules may be taken with meals or on an empty stomach. Taking oseltamivir with food may lessen the possibility of stomach upset. This medicine should be taken for 5 days. *Continue taking this medicine for the full time of treatment* even if you begin to feel better after a few days. This will help to clear up your infection completely. If you stop taking this medicine too soon, your symptoms may return.

For patients taking oseltamivir for prevention of the flu after exposure: The medicine should be taken within 2 days of being exposed to the flu. Oseltamivir capsules may be taken with meals or on an empty stomach. Taking oseltamivir with food may lessen the possibility of stomach upset. This medicine should be taken for at least 7 days.

For patients taking the *oral suspension form* of this medicine:

- This medicine is to be taken only by mouth. Use the specially marked measuring device that is given to you with the medicine to measure each dose accurately. The average household spoon may not hold the right amount of liquid.
- Do not use after the expiration date on the label. The medicine may not work properly after that date. If you have any questions about this, check with your pharmacist.

Dosing—The dose of oseltamivir will be different for different patients. *Follow your doctor's orders or the directions on the label.* The following information includes only the average doses of oseltamivir. If your dose is different, do not change it unless your doctor tells you to do so.

- For *oral* dosage forms (capsules and oral suspension):
  —For treatment of the flu:
  - Adults: 75 milligrams (mg) two times a day for five days.
  - Children 1 year of age or older: Dose is based on body weight and must be determined by your doctor. It is usually between 30 and 75 mg two times a day for five days.
  - Children up to 1 year of age: Use and dose must be determined by your doctor.
  —For prevention of the flu:
  - Adults and teenagers 13 years of age or older: 75 mg once a day for at least seven days.
  - Children up to 13 years of age: Use and dose must be determined by your doctor.

Missed dose—This medicine works best when there is a constant amount in the body. To help keep the amount constant, do not miss any doses. If you miss a dose, take as soon as possible, except if it is near the next dose (within 2 hours). Then go back to your regular dosing schedule. Do not double doses. If you have missed several doses, inform your doctor and follow the advice given to you.

Storage—To store this medicine:

- Keep out of the reach of children.
- Do not store the capsules in the bathroom, near the kitchen sink, or in other damp places. Heat or moisture may cause the medicine to break down.
- Store the oral suspension at room temperature or in the refrigerator. However, keep the medicine from freezing.
- Do not keep outdated medicine or medicine no longer needed. Be sure that any discarded medicine is out of the reach of children.

Precautions While Using This Medicine

If your symptoms do not improve after you finish taking the medicine, or if they become worse, check with your doctor.

Side Effects of This Medicine

Along with its needed effects, a medicine may cause some unwanted effects. Although not all of these side effects may occur, if they do occur they may need medical attention.

Stop using this medicine and get emergency help immediately if either of the following side effects occur:
Less common
Phlegm producing cough or wheezing

Other side effects may occur that usually do not need medical attention. These side effects may go away during treatment as your body adjusts to the medicine. However, check with your doctor if any of the following side effects continue or are bothersome:

More common
Diarrhea; nausea; vomiting
Less common
Abdominal or stomach pain; bloody nose or unexplained nosebleeds (occurs mainly in children); burning, dry or itching eyes, redness, pain, swelling of eye or eyelid, or excessive tearing (occurs mainly in children); cough; dizziness; ear disorder (occurs mainly in children); fatigue; headache; trouble in sleeping

Other side effects not listed above may also occur in some patients. If you notice any other effects, check with your doctor.

Developed: 01/13/2000
Revised: 01/10/2001

OXAMNIQUINE   Systemic†

Other countries—
May be available in other countries.

†Not commercially available in Canada.

Description

Oxamniquine (ox-AM-ni-kwin) is used to treat a certain kind of worm infection (blood fluke), also known as snail fever, Manson's schistosomiasis (shis-toe-soe-MYE-a-siss), or bilharziasis (bil-har-ZYE-a-siss). It will not work for other kinds of worm infections (for example, pinworms or roundworms).

Oxamniquine is available only with your doctor's prescription, in the following dosage form:

Oral
- Capsules

Before Using This Medicine

In deciding to use a medicine, the risks of taking the medicine must be weighed against the good it will do. This is a decision you and your doctor will make. For oxamniquine, the following should be considered:

Allergies—Tell your doctor if you have ever had any unusual or allergic reaction to oxamniquine. Also tell your health care professional if you are allergic to any other substances, such as foods, preservatives, or dyes.

Pregnancy—Studies have not been done in humans. Studies in animals have shown that oxamniquine may harm the unborn animal when it is given in high doses. However, there have been no reports of problems with the pregnancies or babies of pregnant women who took oxamniquine.

Breast-feeding—It is not known whether oxamniquine passes into the breast milk. However, this medicine has not been reported to cause problems in nursing babies.

Children—This medicine has been used in children, and, in effective doses, has not been shown to cause different side effects or problems in children than it does in adults.

Older adults—Many medicines have not been studied specifically in older people. Therefore, it may not be known whether they work exactly the same way they do in younger adults or if they cause different side effects or problems in older people. There is no specific information comparing use of oxamniquine in the elderly with use in other age groups.

Other medicines—Although certain medicines should not be used together at all, in other cases two different medicines may be used together even if an interaction might occur. In these cases, your doctor may want to change the dose, or other precautions may be necessary. Tell your health care professional if you are taking any other prescription or nonprescription (over-the-counter [OTC]) medicine.

Other medical problems—The presence of other medical problems may affect the use of oxamniquine. Make sure you tell your doctor if you have any other medical problems, especially:
- History of epilepsy or other medical problems that cause convulsions—Patients with a history of epilepsy may be more likely to have side effects

Proper Use of This Medicine

No special preparations (for example, special diets, fasting, other medicines, laxatives, or enemas) are necessary before, during, or immediately after taking oxamniquine.

Take this medicine after meals to lessen the chance of side effects such as stomach upset, drowsiness, or dizziness, unless otherwise directed by your doctor.

To help clear up your infection completely, *take this medicine exactly as directed by your doctor for the full time of treatment. Do not miss any doses.*

Dosing—The dose of oxamniquine will be different for different patients. *Follow your doctor's orders or the directions on the label.* The following information includes only the average doses of oxamniquine. *If your dose is different, do not change it* unless your doctor tells you to do so.
- For *oral* dosage form (capsules):
  —For East, North, or South African snail fever:
  - Adults and children—Dose is based on body weight and must be determined by your doctor. The usual dose is 15 milligrams (mg) per kilogram (kg) (6.8 mg per pound) of body weight two times a day for one, two, or three days.
  —For West African and Western Hemisphere snail fever:
  - Adults and children weighing 30 kg (66 pounds) and over—Dose is based on body weight and must be determined by your doctor. The usual dose is 15 mg per kg (6.8 mg per pound) of body weight as a single dose.
  - Children weighing up to 30 kg (66 pounds)—Dose is based on body weight and must be determined by your doctor. The usual dose is 10 mg per kg (4.5 mg per pound) of body weight taken twice a day, two to eight hours apart.

Missed dose—If you miss a dose of this medicine, take it as soon as possible. However, if it is almost time for your next dose, skip the missed dose and go back to your regular dosing schedule. Do not double doses.

Storage—To store this medicine:
- Keep out of the reach of children.
- Store away from heat and direct light.
- Do not store in the bathroom, near the kitchen sink, or in other damp places. Heat or moisture may cause the medicine to break down.
- Do not keep outdated medicine or medicine no longer needed. Be sure that any discarded medicine is out of the reach of children.

Precautions While Using This Medicine

It is important that your doctor check your progress at regular visits.

If your symptoms do not improve after you take this medicine for the full time of treatment, or if they become worse, check with your doctor.

This medicine may cause some people to become dizzy, drowsy, or less alert than they are normally. *Make sure you know how you react to this medicine before you drive, use machines, or do anything else that could be dangerous if you are dizzy or are not alert.* If these reactions are especially bothersome, check with your doctor.

Side Effects of This Medicine

Along with its needed effects, a medicine may cause some unwanted effects. Although not all of these side effects may occur, if they do occur they may need medical attention.

Check with your doctor immediately if any of the following side effects occur:
Rare
  Convulsions (seizures); fever; hallucinations (seeing,

hearing, or feeling things that are not there); skin rash or hives

Other side effects may occur that usually do not need medical attention. These side effects may go away during treatment as your body adjusts to the medicine. However, check with your doctor if any of the following side effects continue or are bothersome:

More common
Dizziness; drowsiness; headache

Less common
Abdominal or stomach pain; diarrhea; loss of appetite; nausea or vomiting

This medicine may cause the urine to turn reddish orange. This side effect does not require medical attention.

Other side effects not listed above may also occur in some patients. If you notice any other effects, check with your doctor.

Revised: 06/11/99

OXCARBAZEPINE   Systemic

Commonly used brand name(s):

In the U.S.—
Trileptal
Another commonly used name is GP 47680

Description

Oxcarbazepine (oks-kar-BAZ-e-peen) is used to control some types of seizures in the treatment of epilepsy. This medicine cannot cure epilepsy and will only work to control seizures for as long as you continue to take it.

This medicine is available only with your doctor's prescription, in the following dosage form

Oral
• Tablets (U.S.)

Before Using This Medicine

In deciding to use a medicine, the risks of taking the medicine must be weighed against the good it will do. This is a decision you and your doctor will make. For oxcarbazepine, the following should be considered:

Allergies—Tell your doctor if you have ever had any unusual or allergic reaction to oxcarbazepine or carbamazepine. Also tell your doctor and pharmacist if you are allergic to any other substances, such as foods, preservatives, or dyes.

Pregnancy—Oxcarbazepine has not been studied in pregnant women. However, oxcarbazepine is closely related to carbamazepine, a drug known for causing birth defects in humans. Before taking this medicine, make sure that your doctor knows if you are pregnant or if you may become pregnant.

Breast-feeding—Oxcarbazepine is known to pass into breast milk and may cause unwanted effects in nursing infants. It may be necessary for you to take another medicine or to stop breast-feeding during treatment. Be sure you have discussed the risks and benefits of the medicine with your doctor.

Children—This medicine has been tested in children 4 years of age and older, and in effective doses, has not been shown to cause different side effects or problems than in adults.

Other medicines—Although certain medicines should not be used together at all, in other cases two different medicines may be used together even if an interaction might occur. In these cases, your doctor may want to change the dose, or other precautions may be necessary. When you are taking oxcarbazepine, it is especially important that your doctor and pharmacist know if you are taking any of the following:

• Carbamazepine (e.g., Tegretol) or
• Phenobarbital or
• Phenytoin (e.g., Dilantin) or
• Valproic acid (e.g., Depakote)—Blood levels of oxcarbazepine may be decreased, causing a decrease in effectiveness and a possible increase in seizure frequency
• Felodipine (e.g., Plendil) or
• Verapamil (e.g., Calan)—The effect of these medicines may be decreased.
• Oral contraceptives (birth control pills containing estrogen)—The effectiveness of these medicines may be decreased

Other medical problems—The presence of other medical problems may affect the use of oxcarbazepine. Make sure you tell your doctor if you have any other medical problems, especially:

• Kidney disease or
• Prior hypersensitivity reaction to carbamazepine or
• Hyponatremia (condition in which your body has too little sodium)

Proper Use of This Medicine

Take this medicine only as directed by your doctor. Do not take more or less of it, and do not take more or less often than your doctor ordered.

Do not suddenly stop taking this medicine without first checking with your doctor. To keep your seizures under control, it is usually best to gradually reduce the amount of oxcarbazepine you are taking before stopping completely.

Dosing—The dose of oxcarbazepine will be different for different patients. *Follow your doctor's orders or the directions on the label.* The following information includes only the average doses of oxcarbazepine. *If your dose is different, do not change it* unless your doctor tells you to do so.

• For *oral* dosage form (tablets):
  —For epilepsy:
    • Adults and teenagers 17 years of age and older—At first, 300 milligrams (mg) two times a day. Your doctor may increase your dose as needed. However, the dose is usually not more than 2400 mg a day.
    • Children 4 to 16 years of age—Dose is based on body weight. The usual dose is 8 to 10 mg per kg (3.7 to 4.5 mg per pound) of body weight. The doctor may need to adjust the dose based on your response to the medicine.
    • Children up to 4 years of age—Use and dose must be determined by your doctor.

Missed dose—If you miss a dose of this medicine, take it as soon as possible. However, if it is almost time for your next dose, skip the missed dose and go back to your regular dosing schedule. Check with your doctor if you miss two or more doses. Do not double doses.

Storage—To store this medicine:
- Keep out of the reach of children.
- Do not store in the bathroom, near the kitchen sink, or in other damp places. Heat or moisture may cause the medicine to break down.
- Do not keep outdated medicine or medicine no longer needed. Ask your health care professional how you should dispose of any medicine you do not use. Be sure that any discarded medicine is out of the reach of children.

Precautions While Using This Medicine

Your doctor should check your progress at regular visits. This is to make sure the medicine is working for you and to allow the dosage to be changed if needed.

If your symptoms do not improve within a few days or if they become worse, check with your doctor.

Do not take other medicines unless they have been discussed with your doctor. This medicine will add to the effects of alcohol and other CNS depressants (medicines that make you drowsy or less alert). Some examples of CNS depressants are antihistamines or medicines for hay fever, other allergies or colds; sedatives, tranquilizers, or sleeping medicine; prescription pain medicine or narcotics; and other medicines for seizures.

This medicine may cause some people to become drowsy, dizzy, or less alert than they are normally. *Make sure you know how you react to this medicine before you drive, use machines, or do anything else that could be dangerous if you are dizzy or are not alert.*

Oral contraceptives (birth control pills) containing estrogen or progestin, contraceptive progestin injections (e.g., Depo-Provera), and implant contraceptive forms of progestin (e.g., Norplant) may not work properly if you take them while you are taking oxcarbazepine. Unplanned pregnancies may occur. You should use a different or additional means of birth control while you are taking oxcarbazepine. If you have any questions about this, check with your health care professional.

Dizziness, lightheadedness, or fainting may occur, especially when you get up from a lying or sitting position. Getting up slowly may help. If the problem continues or gets worse, check with your doctor.

Do not stop taking this medicine without first checking with your doctor. Stopping the medicine suddenly may cause your seizures to return or to occur more often. Your doctor may want you to gradually reduce the amount of oxcarbazepine you are taking before stopping completely.

Side Effects of This Medicine

Along with its needed effects, a medicine may cause some unwanted effects. Although not all of these side effects may occur, if they do occur they may need medical attention.

Check with your doctor as soon as possible if any of the following side effects occur:

More common
Change in vision; change in walking or balance; clumsiness or unsteadiness; cough, fever, sneezing, or sore throat; crying; dizziness; double vision; false sense of well-being; feeling of constant movement of self or surroundings; mental depression; sensation of spinning; uncontrolled back-and-forth and/or rolling eye movements

Less common
Agitation; awkwardness; bloody or cloudy urine; blurred vision; bruising; confusion; congestion; convulsions (seizures); decreased urination; difficulty in focusing eyes; disorientation; faintness or light-headedness when getting up from a lying or sitting position; fast or irregular heartbeat; frequent falls; frequent urge to urinate; general feeling of illness; headache; hoarseness; increased thirst; itching of the vagina, with or without white vaginal discharge; loss of consciousness; memory loss; muscle cramps; pain or burning while urinating; pain or tenderness around eyes or cheekbones; poor control in body movements—for example, when reaching or stepping; problems with coordination; shaking or trembling of arms, legs, hands, and feet; shortness of breath; skin rash; stuffy or runny nose; tightness in chest; trouble in walking; troubled breathing; unusual feelings; unusual tiredness or weakness; wheezing

Rare
Anxiety; bleeding or crusting sores on lips; burning feeling in chest or stomach; chest pain; chills; decreased response to stimulation; hives or itching; irritability; joint pain; muscle pain or weakness; nervousness; purple spots on skin; rectal bleeding; redness, blistering, peeling, or loosening of skin; restlessness; sores, ulcers, or white spots in mouth or on lips; stomach upset; swelling of legs; swollen glands

Other side effects may occur that usually do not need medical attention. These side effects may go away during treatment as your body adjusts to the medicine. However, check with your doctor if any of the following side effects continue or are bothersome.

More common
Abdominal pain; burning feeling in chest or stomach; nausea and vomiting; runny or stuffy nose; sleepiness or unusual drowsiness

Less common
Acid or sour stomach; acne; back pain; belching; bloody nose; blurred vision; change in your sense of taste; constipation; diarrhea; difficulty in speaking; dryness of mouth; feeling of warmth and redness of face, neck, arms, and occasionally chest; heartburn; increased sweating; increased urination; nervousness; trouble in sleeping

Other side effects not listed above may also occur in some patients. If you notice any other effects, check with your doctor.

Developed: 05/11/2000

OXYBUTYNIN Systemic

Commonly used brand name(s):

In the U.S.—
Ditropan
Generic name product may be available.

In Canada—
Ditropan

Description

Oxybutynin (ox-i-BYOO-ti-nin) belongs to the group of medicines called antispasmodics. It helps decrease muscle spasms of the bladder and the frequent urge to urinate caused by these spasms.

Oxybutynin is available only with your doctor's prescription, in the following dosage forms:

Oral
- Syrup (U.S. and Canada)
- Tablets (U.S. and Canada)

Before Using This Medicine

In deciding to use a medicine, the risks of taking the medicine must be weighed against the good it will do. This is a decision you and your doctor will make. For oxybutynin, the following should be considered:

Allergies—Tell your doctor if you have ever had any unusual or allergic reaction to oxybutynin. Also tell your health care professional if you are allergic to any other substances, such as foods, preservatives, or dyes.

Pregnancy—Oxybutynin has not been studied in pregnant women. However, it has not been shown to cause birth defects or other problems in animal studies.

Breast-feeding—Oxybutynin has not been reported to cause problems in nursing babies. However, since this medicine tends to decrease the secretions of the body, it is possible that the flow of breast milk may be reduced in some patients.

Children—There is no specific information about the use of oxybutynin in children under 5 years of age. In older children, oxybutynin is not expected to cause different side effects or problems than it does in adults.

Older adults—Elderly people are especially sensitive to the effects of oxybutynin. This may increase the chance of side effects during treatment.

Other medicines—Although certain medicines should not be used together at all, in other cases two different medicines may be used together even if an interaction might occur. In these cases, your doctor may want to change the dose, or other precautions may be necessary. When you are taking oxybutynin, it is especially important that your health care professional know if you are taking any of the following:
- Amantadine (e.g., Symmetrel) or
- Anticholinergics (medicine for abdominal or stomach spasms or cramps) or
- Antidepressants (medicine for depression) or
- Antidyskinetics (medicine for Parkinson's disease or other conditions affecting control of muscles) or
- Antihistamines or
- Antipsychotics (medicine for mental illness) or
- Buclizine (e.g., Bucladin) or
- Carbamazepine (e.g., Tegretol) or
- Cyclizine (e.g., Marezine) or
- Cyclobenzaprine (e.g., Flexeril) or
- Disopyramide (e.g., Norpace) or
- Flavoxate (e.g., Urispas) or
- Ipratropium (e.g., Atrovent) or
- Meclizine (e.g., Antivert) or
- Methylphenidate (e.g., Ritalin) or
- Orphenadrine (e.g., Norflex) or
- Procainamide (e.g., Pronestyl) or
- Promethazine (e.g., Phenergan) or
- Quinidine (e.g., Quinidex) or
- Trimeprazine (e.g., Temaril)—Taking oxybutynin with these medicines may increase the effects of either medicine

Other medical problems—The presence of other medical problems may affect the use of oxybutynin. Make sure you tell your doctor if you have any other medical problems, especially:
- Bleeding (severe)—Oxybutynin may increase heart rate, which may make this condition worse
- Colitis (severe) or
- Dryness of mouth (severe and continuing) or
- Enlarged prostate or
- Glaucoma or
- Heart disease or
- Hiatal hernia or
- High blood pressure (hypertension) or
- Intestinal blockage or other intestinal or stomach problems or
- Myasthenia gravis or
- Toxemia of pregnancy or
- Urinary tract blockage or problems with urination—Oxybutynin may make these conditions worse
- Kidney disease or
- Liver disease—Higher blood levels of oxybutynin may occur, which increases the chance of side effects
- Overactive thyroid—Oxybutynin may further increase heart rate

Proper Use of This Medicine

This medicine is usually taken with water on an empty stomach. However, your doctor may want you to take it with food or milk to lessen stomach upset.

Take this medicine only as directed. Do not take more of it, do not take it more often, and do not take it for a longer time than your doctor ordered. To do so may increase the chance of side effects.

Dosing—The dose of oxybutynin will be different for different patients. *Follow your doctor's orders or the directions on the label.* The following information includes only the average doses of oxybutynin. *If your dose is different, do not change it* unless your doctor tells you to do so.
- For *oral* dosage forms (syrup or tablets):
  —For treatment of bladder problems:
  - Adults and children 12 years of age and over—5 milligrams (mg) two or three times a day.
  - Children up to 5 years of age—Use and dose have not been determined.
  - Children 5 to 12 years of age—5 mg two or three times a day. The dose is usually not more than 15 mg a day.

Missed dose—If you miss a dose of this medicine, take it as soon as possible. However, if it is almost time for your

next dose, skip the missed dose and go back to your regular dosing schedule. Do not double doses.

Storage—To store this medicine:

- Keep out of the reach of children.
- Store away from heat and direct light.
- Do not store the tablet form of this medicine in the bathroom, near the kitchen sink, or in other damp places. Heat or moisture may cause the medicine to break down.
- Keep the syrup form of this medicine from freezing.
- Do not keep outdated medicine or medicine no longer needed. Be sure that any discarded medicine is out of the reach of children.

Precautions While Using This Medicine

This medicine will add to the effects of alcohol and other CNS depressants (medicines that slow down the nervous system, possibly causing drowsiness). Some examples of CNS depressants are antihistamines or medicine for hay fever, other allergies, or colds; sedatives, tranquilizers, or sleeping medicine; prescription pain medicine or narcotics; barbiturates; medicine for seizures; muscle relaxants; or anesthetics, including some dental anesthetics. *Check with your doctor before taking any of the above while you are using this medicine.*

This medicine may cause your eyes to become more sensitive to light than they are normally. Wearing sunglasses and avoiding too much exposure to bright light may help lessen the discomfort.

This medicine may cause some people to become drowsy or have blurred vision. *Make sure you know how you react to this medicine before you drive, use machines, or do anything else that could be dangerous if you are not alert or able to see well.*

Oxybutynin may make you sweat less, causing your body temperature to increase. *Use extra care not to become overheated during exercise or hot weather while you are taking this medicine,* since overheating may result in heat stroke. Also, hot baths or saunas may make you feel dizzy or faint while you are taking this medicine.

Your mouth, nose, and throat may feel very dry while you are taking this medicine. For temporary relief of mouth dryness, use sugarless candy or gum, melt bits of ice in your mouth, or use a saliva substitute. However, if your mouth continues to feel dry for more than 2 weeks, check with your medical doctor or dentist. Continuing dryness of the mouth may increase the chance of dental disease, including tooth decay, gum disease, and fungus infections.

Side Effects of This Medicine

Along with its needed effects, a medicine may cause some unwanted effects. Although not all of these side effects may occur, if they do occur they may need medical attention.

Check with your doctor as soon as possible if any of the following side effects occur:

Rare

Eye pain; skin rash or hives

Symptoms of overdose

Clumsiness or unsteadiness; confusion; dizziness; drowsiness (severe); fast heartbeat; fever; flushing or redness of face; hallucinations (seeing, hearing, or feeling things that are not there); shortness of breath or troubled breathing; unusual excitement, nervousness, restlessness, or irritability

Other side effects may occur that usually do not need medical attention. These side effects may go away during treatment as your body adjusts to the medicine. However, check with your doctor if any of the following side effects continue or are bothersome:

More common

Constipation; decreased sweating; drowsiness; dryness of mouth, nose, and throat

Less common or rare

Blurred vision; decreased flow of breast milk; decreased sexual ability; difficult urination; difficulty in swallowing; headache; increased sensitivity of eyes to light; nausea or vomiting; trouble in sleeping; unusual tiredness or weakness

Other side effects not listed above may also occur in some patients. If you notice any other effects, check with your doctor.

Revised: 06/16/93

OXYMETAZOLINE   Nasal

Commonly used brand name(s):

In the U.S.—

Afrin Cherry 12 Hour Nasal Spray

Afrin Extra Moisturizing 12 Hour Nasal Spray

Afrin Original 12 Hour Nasal Spray

Afrin Original 12 Hour Nose Drops

Afrin Sinus 12 Hour Nasal Spray

Afrin Original 12 Hour Pump Mist

Dristan 12-Hr Nasal Spray

Duramist Plus Up To 12 Hour Nasal Decongestant Spray

Duration 12 Hour Nasal Spray

Genasal Nasal Spray Up to 12 Hour Relief

Nasal Relief 12 Hour Nasal Spray

Neo-Synephrine 12 Hour Extra Moisturizing Spray

Neo-Synephrine 12 Hour Spray

Nostrilla 12 Hour Nasal Decongestant

Twice-A-Day Extra Moisturizing 12 Hour Nasal Spray

Twice-A-Day Soothing 12 Hour Nasal Spray

Vicks Sinex 12-Hour Nasal Spray

Vicks Sinex 12-Hour Ultra Fine Mist for Sinus Relief

4-Way 12-Hour Nasal Spray

Generic name product may be available.

In Canada—

Dristan Long Lasting Nasal Mist

Dristan Long Lasting Mentholated Nasal Spray

Drixoral Nasal Solution

Description

Oxymetazoline (ox-i-met-AZ-oh-leen) is used for the temporary relief of nasal (of the nose) congestion or stuffiness caused by hay fever or other allergies, colds, or sinus trouble.

This medicine may also be used for other conditions as determined by your doctor.

This medicine is available without a prescription; however, your doctor may have special instructions on the proper use or dose for your medical condition.

Oxymetazoline is available in the following dosage forms:

Nasal
- Nasal drops (U.S.)
- Nasal spray (U.S. and Canada)

Before Using This Medicine

If you are using this medicine without a prescription, carefully read and follow any precautions on the label. For oxymetazoline, the following should be considered:

Allergies—Tell your doctor if you have ever had any unusual or allergic reaction to oxymetazoline or any other nasal decongestant. Also tell your health care professional if you are allergic to any other substances, such as foods, preservatives, or dyes.

Pregnancy—Oxymetazoline has not been studied in pregnant women. Before using this medicine, make sure your doctor knows if you are pregnant or if you may become pregnant.

Breast-feeding—Oxymetazoline may be absorbed into the body. However, oxymetazoline has not been reported to cause problems in nursing babies.

Children—Children may be especially sensitive to the effects of oxymetazoline. This may increase the chance of side effects during treatment.

Older adults—Many medicines have not been tested in older people. Therefore, it may not be known whether they work exactly the same way they do in younger adults or if they cause different side effects or problems in older people. There is no specific information about the use of oxymetazoline in the elderly.

Other medicines—Although certain medicines should not be used together at all, in other cases two different medicines may be used together even if an interaction might occur. In these cases, your doctor may want to change the dose, or other precautions may be necessary. When you are using oxymetazoline, it is especially important that your health care professional know if you are taking any other prescription, including the following, or nonprescription (over-the-counter [OTC]) medicine.

- Maprotiline or
- Monoamine oxidase (MAO) inhibitors (furazolidone [e.g., Furoxone], phenelzine [e.g., Nardil], procarbazine [e.g., Matulane], selegiline [e.g., Eldepryl], tranylcypromine [e.g., Parnate]) or
- Tricyclic antidepressants (amitriptyline [e.g., Elavil], amoxapine [e.g., Asendin], clomipramine [e.g., Anafranil], desipramine [e.g., Norpramin], doxepin [e.g., Sinequan], imipramine [e.g., Tofranil], nortriptyline [e.g., Aventyl, Pamelor], protriptyline [e.g., Vivactil], trimipramine [e.g., Surmontil])—Taking oxymetazoline while you are taking maprotiline, tricyclic antidepressants, MAO inhibitors or within 2 weeks of taking MAO inhibitors may cause constriction of blood vessels

Other medical problems—The presence of other medical problems may affect the use of oxymetazoline. Make sure you tell your doctor if you have any other medical problems, especially:

- Diabetes mellitus (sugar diabetes)
- Dry membranes in nose
- Enlarged prostate—Difficulty urinating may worsen
- Glaucoma

- Heart or blood vessel disease or
- High blood pressure—Oxymetazoline may make the condition worse

- Overactive thyroid

Proper Use of This Medicine

To use the *nose drops:*
- Blow your nose gently. Tilt the head back while standing or sitting up, or lie down on a bed and hang the head over the side. Place the drops into each nostril and keep the head tilted back for a few minutes to allow the medicine to spread throughout the nose.
- Rinse the dropper with hot water and dry with a clean tissue. Replace the cap right after use.
- To avoid spreading the infection, do not use the container for more than one person.

To use the *nose spray:*
- Blow your nose gently. With the head upright, spray the medicine into each nostril. Sniff briskly while squeezing the bottle quickly and firmly. For best results, spray once into each nostril, wait 3 to 5 minutes to allow the medicine to work, then blow the nose gently and thoroughly. Repeat until the complete dose is used.
- Rinse the tip of the spray bottle with hot water, taking care not to suck water into the bottle, and dry with a clean tissue. Replace the cap right after use.
- To avoid spreading the infection, do not use the container for more than one person.

Use this medicine only as directed. Do not use more of it, do not use it more often, and do not use it for longer than 3 days without first checking with your doctor. To do so may make your runny or stuffy nose worse and may also increase the chance of side effects.

Dosing—The dose of oxymetazoline will be different for different patients. *Follow your doctor's orders or the directions on the label.* The following information includes only the average doses of oxymetazoline. *If your dose is different, do not change it* unless your doctor tells you to do so.

- For *nasal* dosage form (nose drops or spray):
  —For nasal congestion or stuffiness:
    - Adults and children 6 years of age and older— Use 2 or 3 drops or sprays of 0.05% solution in each nostril every ten to twelve hours. Do not use more than two times in twenty four hours.
    - Children up to 6 years of age—Use and dose must be determined by your doctor.

Missed dose—If you are using this medicine on a regular schedule and you miss a dose, use it right away if you remember within an hour or so of the missed dose. However, if you do not remember until later, skip the missed dose and go back to your regular dosing schedule. Do not double doses.

Storage—To store this medicine:
- Keep out of the reach of children.
- Store away from heat and direct light, at room temperature.
- Keep the medicine from freezing.
- Do not keep outdated medicine or medicine no longer needed. Be sure that any discarded medicine is out of the reach of children.

Side Effects of This Medicine

Along with its needed effects, a medicine may cause some unwanted effects. Although not all of these side effects may occur, if they do occur they may need medical attention.

When this medicine is used for short periods of time at low doses, side effects usually are rare. However, check with your doctor as soon as possible if any of the following occur:

Increase in runny or stuffy nose

Symptoms of too much medicine being absorbed into the body

Blurred vision; fast, irregular, or pounding heartbeat; headache, dizziness, drowsiness, or lightheadedness; high blood pressure; nervousness; trembling; trouble in sleeping; weakness.

The above side effects are more likely to occur in children because there is a greater chance in children that too much of this medicine may be absorbed into the body.

Other side effects may occur that usually do not need medical attention. These side effects may go away during treatment as your body adjusts to the medicine. However, check with your health care professional if any of the following side effects continue or are bothersome:

Burning, dryness, or stinging inside of nose; increase in nasal discharge; sneezing

Other side effects not listed above may also occur in some patients. If you notice any other effects, check with your health care professional.

Revised: 6/14/2000

OXYMETAZOLINE Ophthalmic

Commonly used brand name(s):

In the U.S.—
Visine L.R.

In Canada—
OcuClear

Description

Oxymetazoline (ox-i-met-AZ-oh-leen) is used to relieve redness due to minor eye irritations, such as those caused by colds, dust, wind, smog, pollen, swimming, or wearing contact lenses.

Oxymetazoline is available without a prescription; however, your doctor may have special instructions on the proper use of this medicine for your medical condition.

Oxymetazoline is available in the following dosage form:

Ophthalmic
• Ophthalmic solution (eye drops) (U.S. and Canada)

Before Using This Medicine

If you are taking this medicine without a prescription, carefully read and follow any precautions on the label. For ophthalmic oxymetazoline, the following should be considered:

Allergies—Tell your doctor if you have ever had any unusual or allergic reaction to oxymetazoline or to any other decongestant used in the eye. Also tell your health care provider if you are allergic to any other substances, such as preservatives.

Pregnancy—Ophthalmic oxymetazoline may be absorbed into the body. However, studies on effects in pregnancy have not been done in either humans or animals.

Breast-feeding—Oxymetazoline may be absorbed into the body. However, oxymetazoline has not been shown to cause problems in nursing babies.

Children—Check with your doctor before using oxymetazoline eye drops in children up to 6 years of age. Eye redness in children can occur with illnesses, such as allergies, fevers, colds, and measles, that may require medical attention.

Older adults—Many medicines have not been studied specifically in older people. Therefore, it may not be known whether they work exactly the same way they do in younger adults or if they cause different side effects or problems in older people. There is no specific information comparing use of oxymetazoline in the elderly with use in other age groups.

Other medicines—Although certain medicines should not be used together at all, in other cases two different medicines may be used together even if an interaction might occur. In these cases, your doctor may want to change the dose, or other precautions may be necessary. Tell your health care provider if you are using any other prescription or non-prescription (over-the-counter [OTC]) medicine.

Other medical problems—The presence of other medical problems may affect the use of ophthalmic oxymetazoline. Make sure you tell your doctor if you have any other medical problems, especially:

• Eye disease, infection, or injury—This medicine may mask the symptoms of these conditions
• Heart or blood vessel disease or
• High blood pressure or
• Overactive thyroid—If absorbed into the body, this medicine may cause side effects that may make the medical problem worse
• Use of soft contact lenses—Because of the preservative in this medicine, some eye conditions may get worse if this medicine is used on top of soft contact lenses

Proper Use of This Medicine

Do not use oxymetazoline ophthalmic solution if it becomes cloudy or changes color.

To use:

• First, wash your hands. With the middle finger, apply pressure to the inside corner of the eye (and continue to apply pressure for 1 or 2 minutes after the medicine has been placed in the eye). Tilt the head back and with the index finger of the same hand, pull the lower eyelid away from the eye to form a pouch. Drop the medicine into the pouch and gently close the eyes. Do not blink. Keep the eyes closed for 1 or 2 minutes to allow the medicine to be absorbed.
• To keep the medicine as germ-free as possible, do not touch the applicator tip to any surface (including the eye). Also, keep the container tightly closed.

Use this medicine only as directed. Do not use more of it, do not use it more often, and do not use it for more than 72 hours, unless otherwise directed by your doctor. To do so may make your eye irritation worse and may also increase the chance of side effects.

Dosing—The dose of ophthalmic oxymetazoline will be different for different patients. *Follow your doctor's orders or the directions on the label.* The following information includes only the average doses of ophthalmic oxymetazoline. *If your dose is different, do not change it* unless your doctor tells you to do so.

- For *ophthalmic solution (eye drops)* dosage form:
  —For eye redness:
  - Adults and children 6 years of age and older— Use 1 drop in the eye every six hours.
  - Children up to 6 years of age—Use and dose must be determined by your doctor.

Storage—To store this medicine:

- Keep out of the reach of children.
- Store away from heat and direct light.
- Keep the medicine from freezing.
- Do not keep outdated medicine or medicine no longer needed. Be sure that any discarded medicine is out of the reach of children.

Precautions While Using This Medicine

If eye pain or change in vision occurs or if redness or irritation of the eye continues, gets worse, or lasts for more than 72 hours, stop using the medicine and check with your doctor.

Side Effects of This Medicine

Along with its needed effects, a medicine may cause some unwanted effects. Although not all of these side effects may occur, if they do occur they may need medical attention.

When this medicine is used for short periods of time at low doses, side effects usually are rare.

Check with your doctor as soon as possible if any of the following side effects occur:

With overuse or long-term use
  Increase in irritation or redness of eyes

Symptoms of too much medicine being absorbed into the body
  Fast, irregular, or pounding heartbeat; headache or lightheadedness; nervousness; trembling; trouble in sleeping

Other side effects not listed above may also occur in some patients. If you notice any other effects, check with your doctor.

Revised: 08/13/98

OXYTOCIN   Systemic

Commonly used brand name(s):

In the U.S.—
Pitocin
Syntocinon
Generic name product may be available.

In Canada—
Syntocinon

Description

Oxytocin (ox-i-TOE-sin) is a hormone used to help start or continue labor and to control bleeding after delivery. It is also sometimes used to help milk secretion in breast-feeding.

Oxytocin may also be used for other conditions as determined by your doctor.

In general, oxytocin should not be used to start labor unless there are specific medical reasons. Be sure you have discussed this with your doctor before receiving this medicine.

Oxytocin is available only with your doctor's prescription, in the following dosage forms:

Nasal
- Solution (U.S. and Canada)

Parenteral
- Injection (U.S. and Canada)

Before Using This Medicine

In deciding to use a medicine, the risks of taking the medicine must be weighed against the good it will do. This is a decision you and your doctor will make. For oxytocin, the following should be considered:

Allergies—Tell your doctor if you have ever had any unusual or allergic reaction to oxytocin. Also tell your health care professional if you are allergic to any other substances, such as foods, preservatives, or dyes.

Breast-feeding—Although very small amounts of this medicine pass into breast milk, it has not been reported to cause problems in nursing babies.

Other medicines—Although certain medicines should not be used together at all, in other cases two different medicines may be used together even if an interaction might occur. In these cases, your doctor may want to change the dose, or other precautions may be necessary. Tell your health care professional if you are taking any other prescription or nonprescription (over-the-counter [OTC]) medicine.

Other medical problems—The presence of other medical problems may affect the use of oxytocin. Make sure you tell your doctor if you have any other medical problems, especially:

- Heart disease
- Hypertension
- Kidney disease

Proper Use of This Medicine

For patients using the *nasal spray* form of this medicine:

- This medicine usually comes with directions for use. Read them carefully before using.

Dosing—The dose of oxytocin will be different for different patients. *Follow your doctor's orders.* The following information includes only the average doses of oxytocin.

- For *nasal* dosage form:
  —For increasing milk production in breast feeding:
  - Adults—One spray into one or both nostrils two or three minutes before nursing or pumping milk from breasts.
- For *injection* dosage form:
  —For helping to start or continue labor:
  - Adults—At first, 0.5 to 2 milliunits per minute

slowly injected into a vein. Then, your doctor may increase the dose every fifteen to sixty minutes as needed.

—For treating incomplete abortion, causing abortion, or controlling bleeding after an abortion:
  • Adults—10 units injected slowly into a vein.
—For helping to control bleeding after delivery:
  • Adults—10 units injected into a muscle or slowly into a vein.

Storage—To store this medicine:
  • Keep out of the reach of children.
  • Store away from heat and direct light.
  • Protect the medicine from freezing.
  • Do not keep outdated medicine or medicine no longer needed. Be sure that any discarded medicine is out of the reach of children.

Precautions While Using This Medicine

Oxytocin nasal spray may not help milk secretion in some breast-feeding women. Call your doctor if this medicine is not working.

Side Effects of This Medicine

Oxytocin can be very useful for helping labor. However, there are certain risks with using it. Oxytocin causes contractions of the uterus. In women who are unusually sensitive to its effects, these contractions may become too strong. In rare cases, this may lead to tearing of the uterus. Also, if contractions are too strong, the supply of blood and oxygen to the fetus may be decreased.

Oxytocin has been reported to cause irregular heartbeat and increase bleeding after delivery in some women. It has also been reported to cause jaundice in some newborn infants.

Along with its needed effects, a medicine may cause some unwanted effects. Although not all of these side effects may occur, if they do occur they may need medical attention:

Rare (with use of injection)
  Confusion; convulsions (seizures); difficulty in breathing; dizziness; fast or irregular heartbeat; headache (continuing or severe); hives; pelvic or abdominal pain (severe); skin rash or itching; vaginal bleeding (increased or continuing); weakness; weight gain (rapid)

Rare (with use of nasal spray)
  Convulsions (seizures); mental disturbances; unexpected bleeding or contractions of the uterus

Other side effects may occur that usually do not need medical attention. However, check with your doctor if any of the following side effects continue or are bothersome:

Rare (with use of injection)
  Nausea; vomiting

Rare (with use of nasal spray)
  Nasal irritation; runny nose; tearing of the eyes

Other side effects not listed above may also occur in some patients. If you notice any other effects, check with your doctor.

Additional Information

Once a medicine has been approved for marketing for a certain use, experience may show that it is also useful for other medical problems. Although this use is not included in product labeling, oxytocin is used in certain patients for the following:
  • Testing the ability of the placenta to support a pregnancy

Other than the above information, there is no additional information relating to proper use, precautions, or side effects for this use.

Revised: 07/14/93
Interim revision: 06/30/94

PACLITAXEL   Systemic

Commonly used brand name(s):

In the U.S.—
  Taxol

In Canada—
  Taxol

Description

Paclitaxel (PAK-li-tax-el) belongs to the group of medicines called antineoplastics. It is used to treat cancer of the ovaries, breast, certain types of lung cancer, and a cancer of the skin and mucous membranes more commonly found in patients with acquired immunodeficiency syndrome (AIDS). It may also be used to treat other kinds of cancer, as determined by your doctor.

Paclitaxel interferes with the growth of cancer cells, which are eventually destroyed. Since the growth of normal body cells may also be affected by paclitaxel, other effects will also occur. Some of these may be serious and must be reported to your doctor. Other effects may not be serious but may cause concern. Some effects may not occur until months or years after the medicine is used.

Before you begin treatment with paclitaxel, you and your doctor should talk about the good this medicine will do as well as the risks of using it.

Paclitaxel is to be administered only by or under the immediate supervision of your doctor. It is available in the following dosage form:

Parenteral
  • Injection (U.S. and Canada)

Before Using This Medicine

In deciding to use a medicine, the risks of taking the medicine must be weighed against the good it will do. This is a decision you and your doctor will make. For paclitaxel, the following should be considered:

Allergies—Tell your doctor if you have ever had any unusual or allergic reaction to paclitaxel.

Pregnancy—Tell your doctor if you are pregnant or if you intend to become pregnant. Studies in rats and rabbits have shown that paclitaxel causes miscarriages and deaths of the fetus, as well as problems in the mother.

Be sure that you have discussed this with your doctor before taking this medicine. It is best to use some kind of birth control while you are receiving paclitaxel. Tell your doctor right away if you think you have become pregnant while receiving paclitaxel.

Breast-feeding—It is not known whether paclitaxel passes into breast milk. However, because this medicine may cause serious side effects, breast-feeding is generally not recommended while you are receiving it.

Children—There is no specific information comparing use of paclitaxel in children with use in other age groups.

Older adults—This medicine has been tested in a limited number of patients and has not been shown to cause different side effects or problems in older people than it does in younger adults.

Other medicines—Although certain medicines should not be used together at all, in other cases two different medicines may be used together even if an interaction might occur. In these cases, your doctor may want to change the dose, or other precautions may be necessary. When you are receiving paclitaxel, it is especially important that your health care professional know if you are taking any of the following:

- Amphotericin B by injection (e.g., Fungizone) or
- Antithyroid agents (medicine for overactive thyroid) or
- Azathioprine (e.g., Imuran) or
- Chloramphenicol (e.g., Chloromycetin) or
- Colchicine or
- Flucytosine (e.g., Ancobon) or
- Ganciclovir (e.g., Cytovene) or
- Interferon (e.g., Intron A, Roferon-A) or
- Plicamycin (e.g., Mithracin) or
- Zidovudine (e.g., AZT, Retrovir) or
- If you have ever been treated with x-rays or cancer medicines—Paclitaxel may increase the effects of these medicines or radiation therapy on the blood

Other medical problems—The presence of other medical problems may affect the use of paclitaxel. Make sure you tell your doctor if you have any other medical problems, especially:

- Chickenpox (including recent exposure) or
- Herpes zoster (shingles)—Risk of severe disease affecting other parts of the body

- Heart rhythm problems—May be made worse by paclitaxel

- Infection—Paclitaxel may decrease your body's ability to fight infection

Proper Use of This Medicine

This medicine often causes nausea and vomiting, which is usually mild. However, it is very important that you continue to receive the medicine even if you begin to feel ill. Ask your health care professional for ways to lessen these effects.

Dosing—The dose of paclitaxel will be different for different patients. The dose that is used may depend on a number of things, including what the medicine is being used for, the patient's size, and whether or not other medicines are also being taken. *If you are receiving paclitaxel at home, follow your doctor's orders or the directions on the label.* If you have any questions about the proper dose of paclitaxel, ask your doctor.

Precautions While Using This Medicine

It is very important that your doctor check your progress at regular visits to make sure that this medicine is working properly and to check for unwanted effects.

While you are being treated with paclitaxel, and after you stop treatment with it, *do not have any immunizations (vaccinations) without your doctor's approval.* Paclitaxel may lower your body's resistance and there is a chance you might get the infection the immunization is meant to prevent. In addition, other persons living in your household should not take oral polio vaccine since there is a chance they could pass the polio virus on to you. Also, avoid persons who have taken oral polio vaccine within the last several months. Do not get close to them and do not stay in the same room with them for very long. If you cannot take these precautions, you should consider wearing a protective face mask that covers the nose and mouth.

Paclitaxel can temporarily lower the number of white blood cells in your blood, increasing the chance of getting an infection. It can also lower the number of platelets, which are necessary for proper blood clotting. If this occurs, there are certain precautions you can take, especially when your blood count is low, to reduce the risk of infection or bleeding:

- If you can, avoid people with infections. *Check with your doctor immediately* if you think you are getting an infection or if you get a fever or chills, cough or hoarseness, lower back or side pain, or painful or difficult urination.
- *Check with your doctor immediately* if you notice any unusual bleeding or bruising; black, tarry stools; blood in urine or stools; or pinpoint red spots on your skin.
- Be careful when using a regular toothbrush, dental floss, or toothpick. Your medical doctor, dentist, or nurse may recommend other ways to clean your teeth and gums. Check with your medical doctor before having any dental work done.
- Do not touch your eyes or the inside of your nose unless you have just washed your hands and have not touched anything else in the meantime.
- Be careful not to cut yourself when you are using sharp objects such as a safety razor or fingernail or toenail cutters.
- Avoid contact sports or other situations where bruising or injury could occur.

Side Effects of This Medicine

Along with its needed effects, a medicine may cause some unwanted effects. Some side effects will have signs or symptoms that you can see or feel. Your doctor may watch for others by doing certain tests.

Also, because of the way these medicines act on the body, there is a chance that they might cause other unwanted effects that may not occur until months or years after the medicine is used. These delayed effects may include certain types of cancer. Discuss these possible effects with your doctor.

Check with your doctor immediately if any of the following side effects occur:
Less common
    Black, tarry stools; blood in urine or stools; pinpoint red spots on skin; unusual bleeding or bruising

Rare
    Shortness of breath (severe); skin reaction (severe)

Check with your doctor as soon as possible if any of the following side effects occur:

More common

Cough or hoarseness accompanied by fever or chills; fever or chills; flushing of face; lower back or side pain accompanied by fever or chills; painful or difficult urination accompanied by fever or chills; shortness of breath; skin rash or itching

Rare

Pain or redness at place of injection; sores in mouth and on lips (usually get better within 7 days after treatment)

This medicine may also cause the following side effects that your doctor will watch out for:

More common

Anemia; low platelet count in blood; low white blood cell count

Less common

Effects on liver; low blood pressure; slow heartbeat

Other side effects may occur that usually do not need medical attention. These side effects may go away during treatment as your body adjusts to the medicine. Also, your health care professional may be able to tell you about ways to prevent or reduce some of these side effects. Check with your health care professional if any of the following side effects continue or are bothersome or if you have any questions about them:

More common

Diarrhea; nausea and vomiting; numbness, burning, or tingling in hands or feet; pain in joints or muscles, especially in arms or legs (begins 2 to 3 days after treatment and may last up to 5 days)

This medicine usually causes a temporary and total loss of hair (including eyebrows, eyelashes, and pubic hair) about 2 to 3 weeks after treatment begins. After treatment with paclitaxel has ended, normal hair growth should return.

Other side effects not listed above may also occur in some patients. If you notice any other effects, check with your doctor.

Additional Information

Once a medicine has been approved for marketing for a certain use, experience may show that it is also useful for other medical problems. Although these uses are not included in product labeling, paclitaxel is used in certain patients with the following medical conditions:

- Cancer of the bladder
- Cancer of the cervix
- Cancer of the endometrium
- Cancer of the esophagus
- Cancers of the head and neck
- Small cell lung cancer (a certain type found in the tissues of the lungs)
- Cancer of the stomach
- Cancer of the prostate
- Cancer of the testes
- Cancer of unknown primary site

Other than the above information, there is no additional information relating to proper use, precautions, or side effects for these uses.

Revised: 04/13/2001

PALIVIZUMAB   Systemic

Commonly used brand name(s):

In the U.S.—
Synagis

Description

Palivizumab (pal-i-VI-zu-mab) belongs to a group of medicines known as immunizing agents. Palivizumab is used to prevent infection caused by respiratory syncytial virus (RSV). This medicine works by giving your body the antibodies it needs to protect it against RSV infection.

RSV infection can cause serious problems that affect the lungs, such as pneumonia and bronchitis, and in severe cases even can cause death. These problems are more likely to occur in infants and children younger than 6 months of age with chronic lung disease and breathing problems and in babies who were premature.

Palivizumab is used to prevent serious lower respiratory tract infection caused by the RSV.

Onset of RSV activity usually occurs in November and continues through April, but it may begin earlier or continue later in certain communities. A good way to help prevent RSV infection is to receive palivizumab before the start of the RSV season.

Palivizumab is to be administered only by or under the supervision of your doctor or other health care professional. It is available in the following dosage form:

Parenteral
- Injection (U.S.)

Before Using This Medicine

In deciding to use a medicine, the risks of taking the medicine must be weighed against the good it will do. This is a decision you and your doctor will make. For palivizumab, the following should be considered:

Allergies—Tell your doctor if you have ever had any unusual or allergic reaction to palivizumab. Also tell your health care professional if you are allergic to any other substances, such as foods, preservatives, or dyes.

Pregnancy—Studies on effects in pregnancy have not been done in either humans or animals.

Breast-feeding—It is not known whether palivizumab passes into breast milk. However, this medicine has not been reported to cause problems in nursing babies.

Children—Studies on this medicine have been done only in children, and it has been shown to be effective in children with breathing problems and those with a history of premature birth.

Older adults—Studies on this medicine have been done only in infants and children, and there is no specific information about its use in older patients.

Other medicines—Although certain medicines should not be used together at all, in other cases two different medicines may be used together even if an interaction might occur. In these cases, your doctor may want to change the dose, or other precautions may be necessary. Tell your health care professional if you are taking any other prescription or nonprescription (over-the-counter [OTC]) medicine.

Other medical problems—The presence of other medical problems may affect the use of palivizumab. Make sure you tell your doctor if you have any other medical problems, especially:

- Hypersensitivity to palivizumab

Proper Use of This Medicine

Dosing—The dose of palivizumab will be different for different patients. Doses are based on body weight. If you have any questions about the proper dose of palivizumab, ask your doctor.

Side Effects of This Medicine

Along with its needed effects, a medicine may cause some unwanted effects. Although not all of these side effects may occur, if they do occur they may need medical attention.

Check with your doctor as soon as possible if any of the following side effects occur:

More common
Difficulty in breathing; ringing or buzzing in the ears; runny nose; skin rash

Other side effects not listed above may also occur in some patients. If you notice any other effects, check with your doctor.

Developed: 08/11/98

PAMIDRONATE   Systemic

Commonly used brand name(s):

In the U.S.—
Aredia

In Canada—
Aredia

Another commonly used name is APD.

Description

Pamidronate (pa-mi-DROE-nate) is used to treat hypercalcemia (too much calcium in the blood) that may occur with some types of cancer. It is also used to treat Paget's disease of bone and to treat bone metastases (spread of cancer).

This medicine is to be administered only by or under the supervision of your doctor. It is available in the following dosage form:

Parenteral
- Injection (U.S. and Canada)

Before Receiving This Medicine

In deciding to use a medicine, the risks of receiving the medicine must be weighed against the good it will do. This is a decision you and your doctor will make. For pamidronate, the following should be considered:

Allergies—Tell your doctor if you have ever had any unusual or allergic reaction to pamidronate or etidronate. Also tell your health care professional if you are allergic to any other substances, such as foods, preservatives, or dyes.

Pregnancy—Studies have not been done in humans. However, studies in rats given higher doses of oral pamidronate have shown that the medicine may decrease fertility, increase the length of pregnancy, and cause death of the baby rat.

Breast-feeding—It is not known if pamidronate passes into breast milk.

Children—Studies on this medicine have been done only in adult patients, and there is no specific information comparing use of pamidronate in children with use in other age groups.

Older adults—When pamidronate is given along with a large amount of fluids, older people tend to retain (keep) the excess fluid.

Other medicines—Although certain medicines should not be used together at all, in other cases two different medicines may be used together even if an interaction might occur. In these cases, your doctor may want to change the dose, or other precautions may be necessary. When you are receiving pamidronate, it is especially important that your health care professional know if you are taking any of the following:

- Calcium-containing preparations or
- Vitamin D-containing preparations—Use with pamidronate may keep pamidronate from working properly

Other medical problems—The presence of other medical problems may affect the use of pamidronate. Make sure you tell your doctor if you have any other medical problems, especially:

- Heart problems—The increased amount of fluid may make this condition worse
- Kidney problems—Pamidronate may build up in the bloodstream, which may increase the chance of unwanted effects

Proper Use of This Medicine

Dosing—The dose of pamidronate will be different for different patients. *Follow your doctor's orders.* The following information includes only the average doses of pamidronate.

- For *injection* dosage form:
  —For treating hypercalcemia (too much calcium in the blood):
  - Adults: 30 to 90 milligrams (mg) in a solution to be injected over 4 to 24 hours into a vein.
  - Children: Use and dose must be determined by your doctor.
  —For treating Paget's disease of bone:
  - Adults: Dose and frequency must be determined by your doctor. The usual dose is 30 mg daily injected over 4 hours into a vein for 3 days. Your doctor may repeat this dose.
  - Children: Use and dose must be determined by your doctor.
  —For treating bone metastases:
  - Adults—90 mg in a solution to be injected over 2 to 4 hours into a vein. Your dose may be given every three to four weeks or once a month.
  - Children—Use and dose must be determined by your doctor.

Precautions While Receiving This Medicine

It is important that your doctor check your progress at regular visits after you have received pamidronate. If your condition has improved, your progress must still be checked. The results of laboratory tests or the occurrence of certain symptoms will tell your doctor if your condition is coming back and a second treatment is needed.

For patients using this medicine for *hypercalcemia (too much calcium in the blood):*

- Your doctor may want you to follow a low-calcium diet. If you have any questions about this, check with your doctor.

Side Effects of This Medicine

Along with its needed effects, a medicine may cause some unwanted effects. Although not all of these side effects may occur, if they do occur they may need medical attention.

Check with your doctor as soon as possible if any of the following side effects occur:

More common

Abdominal cramps; chills; confusion; fever; muscle spasms; sore throat

Note: Abdominal cramps, confusion, and muscle spasms are less common when pamidronate is given in doses of 60 mg or less.

Other side effects may occur that usually do not need medical attention. These side effects may go away during treatment as your body adjusts to the medicine. However, check with your doctor if any of the following side effects continue or are bothersome:

More common—at higher doses

Nausea; pain and swelling at place of injection

Less common

Muscle stiffness

Other side effects not listed above may also occur in some patients. If you notice any other effects, check with your doctor.

Developed: 06/02/93
Revised: 08/18/97

PANCRELIPASE   Systemic

Commonly used brand name(s):

In the U.S.—

Cotazym	Pancrease MT 4
Cotazym-S	Pancrease MT 10
Creon 5	Pancrease MT 16
Creon 10	Pancrease MT 20
Creon 20	Panokase
Enzymase-16	Protilase
Ilozyme	Ultrase MT 12
Ku-Zyme HP	Ultrase MT 20
Pancoate	Viokase
Pancrease	Zymase

Generic name product may be available.

In Canada—

Cotazym	Pancrease
Cotazym-65 B	Pancrease MT 4
Cotazym E.C.S. 8	Pancrease MT 10
Cotazym E.C.S. 20	Pancrease MT 16

Another commonly used name is lipancreatin.

Description

Pancrelipase (pan-kre-LI-pase) is used to help digestion in certain conditions in which the pancreas is not working properly. It may also be used for other conditions as determined by your doctor.

Pancrelipase contains the enzymes needed for the digestion of proteins, starches, and fats.

Pancrelipase is available only with your doctor's prescription, in the following dosage forms:

Oral
- Capsules (U.S. and Canada)
- Delayed-release capsules (U.S. and Canada)
- Powder (U.S.)
- Tablets (U.S.)

Before Using This Medicine

In deciding to use a medicine, the risks of taking the medicine must be weighed against the good it will do. This is a decision you and your doctor will make. For pancrelipase, the following should be considered:

Allergies—Tell your doctor if you have ever had any unusual or allergic reaction to pancrelipase, pancreatin, or pork products. Also tell your health care professional if you are allergic to any other substances, such as foods, preservatives, or dyes.

Pregnancy—Studies have not been done in either humans or animals.

Breast-feeding—Pancrelipase has not been reported to cause problems in nursing babies.

Children—This medicine has been tested in children 6 months of age or older and has not been shown to cause different side effects or problems than it does in adults.

Older adults—Many medicines have not been studied specifically in older people. Therefore, it may not be known whether they work exactly the same way they do in younger adults. Although there is no specific information comparing use of pancrelipase in the elderly with use in other age groups, this medicine is not expected to cause different side effects or problems in older people than it does in younger adults.

Other medicines—Although certain medicines should not be used together at all, in other cases two different medicines may be used together even if an interaction might occur. In these cases, your doctor may want to change the dose, or other precautions may be necessary. Tell your health care professional if you are taking any other prescription or nonprescription (over-the-counter [OTC]) medicine.

Other medical problems—The presence of other medical problems may affect the use of pancrelipase. Make sure you tell your doctor if you have any other medical problems, especially:

- Pancreatitis (sudden, severe inflammation of the pancreas)—Pancrelipase may make this condition worse

Proper Use of This Medicine

Take this medicine before or with meals and snacks, unless otherwise directed by your doctor.

When prescribing this medicine for your condition, your doctor may also prescribe a personal diet for you. Follow carefully the special diet your doctor gave you. This is most important and necessary for the medicine to work properly and to avoid indigestion. It is important to drink plenty of water while you are on this medicine.

For patients taking the *tablet form* of this medicine:

- *Swallow the tablets quickly with some liquid, without chewing,* to avoid mouth irritation.

For patients taking the *capsules containing the enteric-coated spheres:*

- Swallow the capsule whole.
- Do not crush, break, or chew before swallowing.
- When given to children, the capsule may be opened and sprinkled on a small amount of liquid or soft food that can be swallowed without chewing, such as applesauce or gelatin. However, it should not be mixed with alkaline foods, such as milk and ice cream, which may reduce its effect.

Dosing—The dose of pancrelipase will be different for different patients. *Follow your doctor's orders or the directions on the label.* The following information includes only the average doses of pancrelipase. *If your dose is different, do not change it* unless your doctor tells you to do so.

- To help digestion:
  —For *oral* dosage form (capsules):
  - Older adults, adults, and teenagers—One to three capsules before or with meals and snacks. Your doctor may change your dose if needed.
  - Children—The contents of one to three capsules sprinkled on food at each meal. Your doctor may change your dose if needed.
  —For *oral* dosage form (delayed-release capsules):
  - Older adults, adults, and teenagers—One to four capsules before or with meals and snacks. Your doctor will decide what your dose should be at first. Your doctor may change your dose if needed.
  - Children over 6 years old—The contents of one to four capsules with meals. Your doctor will decide what dose to start with. Your doctor may change your dose if needed. You should take the contents of the capsules with a liquid or a small amount of a soft food that you do not have to chew. You should eat the food with the medicine in it right away and follow that with a glass of water or juice.
  - Children under 6 years old—The contents of one to two capsules with meals. Your doctor will decide what dose to start with. Your doctor may change your dose if needed. You should take the contents of the capsules with a liquid or a small amount of a soft food that you do not have to chew. You should eat the food with the medicine in it right away and follow that with a glass of water or juice.
  —For *oral* dosage form (powder):
  - Older adults, adults, and teenagers—1/4 teaspoonful (0.7 gram) with meals and snacks. Your doctor may change your dose if needed.
  - Children—1/4 teaspoonful with meals. Your doctor may change your dose if needed.
  —For *oral* dosage form (tablets):
  - Older adults, adults, and teenagers—One to three tablets before or with meals and snacks. Your doctor may change your dose if needed.
  - Children—One to two tablets with meals.

Missed dose—If you miss a dose of this medicine, take it as soon as possible. However, if it is almost time for your next dose, skip the missed dose and go back to your regular dosing schedule. Do not double doses.

Storage—To store this medicine:

- Keep out of the reach of children.
- Store away from heat and direct light.
- Do not store the capsule, powder, or tablet form of this medicine in the bathroom, near the kitchen sink, or in other damp places. Heat or moisture may cause the medicine to break down.
- Do not keep outdated medicine or medicine no longer needed. Be sure that any discarded medicine is out of the reach of children.

Precautions While Using This Medicine

Your doctor may recommend that you take pancrelipase with another medicine, such as certain antacids or anti-ulcer medicines. However, antacids that contain calcium carbonate and/or magnesium hydroxate may not let the pancrelipase work properly and should be avoided.

Do not change brands or dosage forms of pancrelipase without first checking with your doctor. Different products may not work in the same way. If you refill your medicine and it looks different, check with your pharmacist.

For patients taking the *capsules containing the powder:*

- If the capsules are opened to mix with food, be careful not to breathe in the powder. To do so may cause harmful effects such as stuffy nose, shortness of breath, troubled breathing, wheezing, or tightness in chest.

For patients taking the *powder form* of this medicine:

- Avoid breathing in the powder. To do so may cause harmful effects such as stuffy nose, shortness of breath, troubled breathing, wheezing, or tightness in chest.

Side Effects of This Medicine

Along with its needed effects, a medicine may cause some unwanted effects. Although not all of these side effects may occur, if they do occur they may need medical attention.

Check with your doctor as soon as possible if any of the following side effects occur:

Rare
  Skin rash or hives

With high doses
  Diarrhea; intestinal blockage; nausea; stomach cramps or pain

With very high doses
  Blood in urine; joint pain; swelling of feet or lower legs

With powder dosage form or powder from opened capsules—if breathed in
  Shortness of breath; stuffy nose; tightness in chest; troubled breathing; wheezing

With tablets—if held in mouth
  Irritation of the mouth

Other side effects not listed above may also occur in some patients. If you notice any other effects, check with your doctor.

Revised: 03/28/2001

PANTOPRAZOLE   Systemic

Commonly used brand name(s):

In the U.S.—
 Protonix
In Canada—
 Pantoloc

Description

Pantoprazole (pan-TOE-pra-zole) is used to treat certain conditions in which there is too much acid in the stomach. It is used to treat duodenal and gastric ulcers and gastroesophageal reflux disease (GERD), a condition in which the acid in the stomach washes back up into the esophagus.

Pantoprazole works by decreasing the amount of acid produced by the stomach.

This medicine is available only with your doctor's prescription.

 Oral
 • Delayed-release tablets (U.S. and Canada)
 Parenteral
 • Injection (U.S.)

Before Using This Medicine

In deciding to use a medicine, the risks of taking the medicine must be weighed against the good it will do. This is a decision you and your doctor will make. For pantoprazole, the following should be considered:

Allergies—Tell your doctor if you have ever had any unusual or allergic reaction to pantoprazole. Also tell your health care professional if you are allergic to any other substances, such as foods, preservatives, or dyes.

Pregnancy—Pantoprazole has not been studied in pregnant women. However, studies in animals have shown that pantoprazole causes problems. Before taking this medicine, make sure your doctor knows if you are pregnant or if you may become pregnant.

Breast-feeding—It is not known whether pantoprazole passes into human breast milk. Since this medicine has been shown to cause unwanted effects in animals, it may be necessary for you to take another medicine or to stop breast-feeding during treatment. Be sure you have discussed the risks and benefits of the medicine with your doctor.

Children—Studies on this medicine have been done only in adult patients, and there is no specific information comparing the use of pantoprazole in children with use in other age groups.

Older adults—This medicine has been tested and has not been shown to cause different side effects or problems in older people than it does in younger adults.

Other medicines—Although certain medicines should not be used together at all, in other cases two different medicines may be used together even if an interaction might occur. In these cases, your doctor may want to change the dose, or other precautions may be necessary. Tell your health care professional if you are taking any other prescription or nonprescription (over-the-counter [OTC]) medicine.

Other medical problems—The presence of other medical problems may affect the use of pantoprazole. Make sure you tell your doctor if you have any other medical problems, especially:

• Liver disease—This condition may cause pantoprazole to build up in the body

Proper Use of This Medicine

Take pantoprazole tablets immediately before a meal, preferably in the morning. Pantoprazole tablets may be taken with food or on an empty stomach.

Swallow the tablet whole. Do not crush, break, or chew the tablet.

It may take several days before this medicine begins to relieve stomach pain. To help relieve this pain, antacids may be taken with pantoprazole, unless your doctor has told you not to use them.

Take this medicine for the full time of treatment, even if you begin to feel better. Also, keep your appointments with your doctor for check-ups so that your doctor will be better able to tell you when to stop taking this medicine.

Dosing—The dose of pantoprazole will be different for different patients. *Follow your doctor's orders or the directions on the label.* The following information includes only the average doses of pantoprazole. *If your dose is different, do not change it* unless your doctor tells you to do so.

• For *oral* dosage form (delayed-release tablets):
 —To treat gastroesophageal reflux disease (GERD):
  • Adults—40 milligrams (mg) once a day, preferably in the morning for up to eight weeks. Your doctor may advise you to continue taking the medicine for an additional eight weeks if your condition does not improve after the first eight weeks.
  • Children—Use and dose must be determined by your doctor.
 —To treat gastric ulcers:
  • Adults—40 mg once a day, preferably in the morning for four weeks.
  • Children—Use and dose must be determined by your doctor.
 —To treat duodenal ulcers:
  • Adults—40 mg once a day, preferably in the morning for two weeks.
  • Children—Use and dose must be determined by your doctor.
• For *injection* dosage form:
 —To treat GERD:
  • Adults—40 mg injected into a vein once a day for seven to ten days.
  • Children—Use and dose must be determined by your doctor.

Missed dose—If you miss a dose of this medicine, take it as soon as possible. However, if it is almost time for your next dose, skip the missed dose and go back to your regular dosing schedule. Do not double doses.

Storage—To store this medicine:
• Keep out of the reach of children.
• Store away from heat and direct light.
• Do not store in the bathroom, near the kitchen sink, or in other damp places. Heat or moisture may cause the medicine to break down.
• Do not keep outdated medicine or medicine no longer needed. Be sure that any discarded medicine is out of the reach of children.

Precautions While Using This Medicine

It is important that your doctor check your progress at regular visits. If your condition does not improve, or if it becomes worse, check with your doctor.

Side Effects of This Medicine

Along with its needed effects, a medicine may cause some unwanted effects. Although not all of these side effects may occur, if they do occur they may need medical attention.

Check with your doctor as soon as possible if any of the following side effects occur:

Less common or rare
Abdominal or stomach pain; blistering, loosening, peeling, or redness of skin; bull's eye-like rash on skin; changes in facial skin color; chest pain; diarrhea; difficulty in speaking; difficulty in urinating; discoloration, itching, numbness, pain, or redness at place of injection; fast or irregular breathing; increased frequency and volume of urination; infection; large, hive-like swellings on eyelids, face, lips, mouth, and/or tongue; loosening and/or stripping off of top layer of skin; loss of appetite; loss of vision (sudden); nausea; painful urination; pain in joints or muscles; puffiness or swelling of the eyelids or around the eyes; shortness of breath, troubled breathing, tightness in chest, and/or wheezing; skin rash, hives, and itching; skin tenderness with burning; unusual tiredness or weakness; unusual thirst; vomiting; yellow eyes or skin

Other side effects may occur that usually do not need medical attention. These side effects may go away during treatment as your body adjusts to the medicine. However, check with your doctor if any of the following side effects continue or are bothersome.

More common
Headache

Less common or rare
Aching, fullness, or tension in sinuses; anxiety; back pain; belching; blurred vision; chills; confusion; constipation; cough; difficulty in moving; dizziness; drooling; feeling of constant movement of self or surroundings; flatulence; hoarseness; indigestion; loss of energy or strength; migraine headache; muscle rigidness or stiffness; neck pain; pain; rectal problems; ringing or buzzing in the ears; runny or stuffy nose; sensation of spinning; sneezing; sore throat; trouble in sleeping

Other side effects not listed above may also occur in some patients. If you notice any other effects, check with your doctor.

Developed: 04/03/2000
Revised: 05/25/2001

PAROXETINE   Systemic

Commonly used brand name(s):
In the U.S.—
Paxil

In Canada—
Paxil

Description

Paroxetine (pa-ROX-uh-teen) is used to treat mental depression, obsessive-compulsive disorder, panic disorder, and social anxiety disorder (also known as social phobia).

Paroxetine belongs to a group of medicines known as selective serotonin reuptake inhibitors (SSRIs). These medicines are thought to work by increasing the activity of the chemical serotonin in the brain.

This medicine is available only with your doctor's prescription, in the following dosage forms:
Oral
- Extended-release Tablets (U.S.)
- Oral Suspension (U.S.)
- Tablets (U.S. and Canada)

Before Using This Medicine

In deciding to use a medicine, the risks of taking the medicine must be weighed against the good it will do. This is a decision you and your doctor will make. For paroxetine, the following should be considered:

Allergies—Tell your doctor if you have ever had any unusual or allergic reaction to paroxetine. Also tell your health care professional if you are allergic to any other substances, such as foods, preservatives, or dyes.

Pregnancy—One study looked at the babies of 97 women who took paroxetine either at the beginning of pregnancy or through the entire pregnancy. This study found no harmful effects of paroxetine on the babies. However, more study is needed to be sure that paroxetine is safe to use during pregnancy. Before taking this medicine, make sure your doctor knows if you are pregnant or if you may become pregnant.

Breast-feeding—Paroxetine passes into the breast milk. However, the effects of this medicine in nursing babies are not known.

Children—Studies on this medicine have been done only in adult patients, and there is no specific information comparing use of paroxetine in children with use in other age groups.

Older adults—In studies that have included elderly people, paroxetine did not cause different side effects or problems in older people than it did in younger adults. However, paroxetine may be removed from the body more slowly in elderly people. An older adult may need a lower dose than a younger adult.

Other medicines—Although certain medicines should not be used together at all, in other cases two different medicines may be used together even if an interaction might occur. In these cases, your doctor may want to change the dose, or other precautions may be necessary. When you are taking paroxetine, it is especially important that your health care professional know if you are taking any of the following:
- Astemizole (e.g., Hismanal)—Taking astemizole while you are using paroxetine may lead to a serious change in the rhythm of your heartbeat
- Buspirone (e.g., BuSpar) or
- Bromocriptine (e.g., Parlodel) or
- Dextromethorphan (cough medicine) or
- Levodopa (e.g., Sinemet) or
- Lithium (e.g., Eskalith) or
- Meperidine (e.g., Demerol) or
- Nefazodone (e.g., Serzone) or

- Pentazocine (e.g., Talwin) or
- Selective serotonin reuptake inhibitors, other (citalopram [e.g., Celexa], fluoxetine [e.g., Prozac], fluvoxamine [e.g., Luvox], sertraline [Zoloft]) or
- Street drugs (LSD, MDMA [e.g., ecstasy], marijuana) or
- Sumatriptan (e.g., Imitrex) or
- Tramadol (e.g., Ultram) or
- Trazodone (e.g., Desyrel) or
- Tryptophan or
- Venlafaxine (e.g., Effexor)—Using these medicines with paroxetine may increase the chance of developing a rare, but very serious, unwanted effect known as the serotonin syndrome. This syndrome may cause confusion, diarrhea, fever, poor coordination, restlessness, shivering, sweating, talking or acting with excitement you cannot control, trembling or shaking, or twitching. If you develop these symptoms, contact your doctor as soon as possible. Using tryptophan with paroxetine is not recommended

- Moclobemide (e.g., Manerex)—The risk of developing serious unwanted effects, including the serotonin syndrome, is increased. Use of moclobemide with paroxetine is not recommended. Also, it is recommended that 3 to 7 days be allowed between stopping treatment with moclobemide and starting treatment with paroxetine, and that 2 weeks be allowed between stopping treatment with paroxetine and starting treatment with moclobemide

- Monoamine oxidase (MAO) inhibitors (furazolidone [e.g., Furoxone], phenelzine [e.g., Nardil], procarbazine [e.g., Matulane], selegiline [e.g., Eldepryl], tranylcypromine [e.g., Parnate])—*Do not take paroxetine while you are taking or within 2 weeks of taking an MAO inhibitor*, or you may develop confusion, agitation, restlessness, stomach or intestinal symptoms, sudden high body temperature, extremely high blood pressure, severe convulsions, or the serotonin syndrome. At least 14 days should be allowed between stopping treatment with one medicine (paroxetine or the MAO inhibitor) and starting treatment with the other

- Tricyclic antidepressants (amitriptyline [e.g., Elavil], amoxapine [e.g., Asendin], clomipramine [e.g., Anafranil], desipramine [e.g., Pertofrane], doxepin [e.g., Sinequan], imipramine [e.g., Tofranil], nortriptyline [e.g., Aventyl], protriptyline [e.g., Vivactil], trimipramine [e.g., Surmontil])—Taking a tricyclic antidepressant together with paroxetine may increase the risk of side effects. Your doctor may need to adjust the dose of either medicine or check blood levels of the tricyclic antidepressant. Also, taking paroxetine with amitriptyline, clomipramine, or imipramine may increase the chance that the serotonin syndrome will develop

- Warfarin (e.g., Coumadin)—Taking this medicine together with paroxetine may cause bleeding problems; your doctor may need to adjust the dosage of either medicine

Other medical problems—The presence of other medical problems may affect the use of paroxetine. Make sure you tell your doctor if you have any other medical problems, especially:

- Brain disease or damage or
- Mental retardation or
- Seizures (history of)—The risk of seizures may be increased

- Kidney disease, severe, or
- Liver disease, severe—Higher blood levels of paroxetine may occur, increasing the chance of side effects
- Mania (history of)—The condition may be activated

Proper Use of This Medicine

Take this medicine only as directed by your doctor to benefit your condition as much as possible. Do not take more of it, do not take it more often, and do not take it for a longer time than your doctor ordered.

Paroxetine may be taken with or without food or on a full or empty stomach. However, if your doctor tells you to take the medicine a certain way, take it exactly as directed.

You may have to take paroxetine for several weeks before you begin to feel better. Your doctor should check your progress at regular visits during this time. Also, if you are taking paroxetine for depression, you will probably need to continue taking it for at least 6 months to help prevent the depression from returning.

If you are taking the oral suspension form of paroxetine, shake the bottle well before measuring each dose. Use a small measuring cup or a measuring spoon to measure each dose. The teaspoons and tablespoons that are used for serving and eating food do not measure exact amounts.

If you are taking the extended-release tablet form of this medicine, swallow the tablet whole. Do not crush, break, or chew before swallowing.

Dosing—The dose of paroxetine will be different for different patients. *Follow your doctor's orders or the directions on the label.* The following information includes only the average doses of paroxetine. *If your dose is different, do not change it* unless your doctor tells you to do so.

- For *oral suspension* dosage form:
  —For treatment of depression:
    - Adults—At first, 20 milligrams (mg) (10 milliliters [mL]) once a day, usually taken in the morning. Your doctor may increase your dose if needed. However, the dose usually is not more than 50 mg (25 mL) a day.
    - Children—Use and dose must be determined by your doctor.
    - Older adults—At first, 10 mg (5 mL) once a day, usually taken in the morning. Your doctor may increase your dose if needed. However, the dose usually is not more than 40 mg (20 mL) a day.
  —For treatment of obsessive-compulsive disorder:
    - Adults—At first, 20 milligrams (mg) (10 milliliters [mL]) once a day, usually taken in the morning. Your doctor may increase your dose if needed. However, the dose usually is not more than 60 mg (30 mL) a day.
    - Children—Use and dose must be determined by your doctor.
    - Older adults—At first, 10 mg (5 mL) once a day, usually taken in the morning. Your doctor may increase your dose if needed. However, the dose usually is not more than 40 mg (20 mL) a day.
  —For treatment of panic disorder:
    - Adults—At first, 10 milligrams (mg) (5 milliliters [mL]) once a day, usually taken in the morning. Your doctor may increase your dose if needed. However, the dose usually is not more than 60 mg (30 mL) a day.

- Children—Use and dose must be determined by your doctor.
- Older adults—At first, 10 mg (5 mL) once a day, usually taken in the morning. Your doctor may increase your dose if needed. However, the dose usually is not more than 40 mg (20 mL) a day.
—For treatment of social anxiety disorder:
  - Adults—At first, 20 milligrams (mg) (10 milliliters [mL]) once a day, usually taken in the morning. Your doctor may increase your dose if needed. However, the dose usually is not not more than 60 mg (30 mL) a day.
  - Children—Use and dose must be determined by your doctor.
  - Older adults—At first, 10 mg once a day, usually taken in the morning. Your doctor may increase your dose if needed. However, the dose usually is not more than 40 mg a day.

- For *oral tablet* dosage form:
—For treatment of depression:
  - Adults—At first, 20 milligrams (mg) once a day, usually taken in the morning. Your doctor may increase your dose if needed. However, the dose usually is not more than 50 mg a day.
  - Children—Use and dose must be determined by your doctor.
  - Older adults—At first, 10 mg once a day, usually taken in the morning. Your doctor may increase your dose if needed. However, the dose usually is not more than 40 mg a day.
—For treatment of obsessive-compulsive disorder:
  - Adults—At first, 20 milligrams (mg) once a day, usually taken in the morning. Your doctor may increase your dose if needed. However, the dose usually is not more than 60 mg a day.
  - Children—Use and dose must be determined by your doctor.
  - Older adults—At first, 10 mg once a day, usually taken in the morning. Your doctor may increase your dose if needed. However, the dose usually is not more than 40 mg a day.
—For treatment of panic disorder:
  - Adults—At first, 10 milligrams (mg) once a day, usually taken in the morning. Your doctor may increase your dose if needed. However, the dose usually is not more than 60 mg a day.
  - Children—Use and dose must be determined by your doctor.
  - Older adults—At first, 10 mg once a day, usually taken in the morning. Your doctor may increase your dose if needed. However, the dose usually is not more than 40 mg a day.
—For treatment of social anxiety disorder:
  - Adults—At first, 20 milligrams (mg) once a day, usually taken in the morning. Your doctor may increase your dose if needed. However, the dose usually is not more than 60 mg a day.
  - Children—Use and dose must be determined by your doctor.
  - Older adults—At first, 10 mg once a day, usually taken in the morning. Your doctor may increase your dose if needed. However, the dose usually is not more than 40 mg a day.

- For *oral extended-release tablet* dosage form:
—For treatment of depression:
  - Adults—At first, 25 milligrams (mg) once a day, usually taken in the morning. Your doctor may increase your dose if needed. However, the dose usually is not more than 62.5 mg a day.
  - Children—Use and dose must be determined by your doctor.
  - Older adults—At first, 12.5 mg once a day, usually taken in the morning. Your doctor may increase your dose if needed. However, the dose usually is not more than 50 mg a day.

Missed dose—If you miss a dose of this medicine, take it as soon as possible. However, if it is almost time for your next dose, skip the missed dose and go back to your regular dosing schedule. Do not double doses.

Storage—To store this medicine:
- Keep out of the reach of children.
- Store away from heat and direct light.
- Do not store the tablet form of this medicine in the bathroom, near the kitchen sink, or in other damp places. Heat or moisture may cause the medicine to break down.
- Keep the oral suspension form of this medicine from freezing.
- Do not keep outdated medicine or medicine no longer needed. Be sure that any discarded medicine is out of the reach of children.

Precautions While Using This Medicine

It is important that your doctor check your progress at regular visits, to allow for changes in your dose and to help reduce any side effects.

Do not stop taking this medicine without first checking with your doctor. Your doctor may want you to reduce gradually the amount you are taking before stopping completely. This is to decrease the chance of having discontinuation symptoms such as agitation, confusion, diarrhea, dizziness or lightheadedness, headache, increased sweating, muscle pain, nausea, restlessness, runny nose, trouble in sleeping, trembling or shaking, unusual tiredness or weakness, vision changes, or vomiting.

Do not take paroxetine if you have taken a monoamine oxidase (MAO) inhibitor (furazolidone, phenelzine, procarbazine, selegiline, tranylcypromine) in the past 2 weeks. Do not start taking an MAO inhibitor within 2 weeks of stopping paroxetine. If you do, you may develop confusion, agitation, restlessness, stomach or intestinal symptoms, sudden high body temperature, extremely high blood pressure, severe convulsions, or the serotonin syndrome.

Paroxetine has not been shown to add to the effects of alcohol. However, use of alcohol is not recommended in patients who are taking paroxetine.

Paroxetine may cause some people to become drowsy or have blurred vision. *Make sure you know how you react to this medicine before you drive, use machines, or do anything else that could be dangerous if you are not alert or able to see clearly.*

Side Effects of This Medicine

Along with its needed effects, a medicine may cause some unwanted effects. One rare but serious unwanted effect that may occur with paroxetine use is the serotonin syndrome. This syndrome (group of symptoms) is more likely to occur shortly after the dose of paroxetine is increased.

Although not all of these side effects may occur, if they do occur they may need medical attention.

Check with your doctor as soon as possible if any of the following side effects occur:

Less common
Agitation; fast or irregular heartbeat; muscle pain or weakness; skin rash

Rare
Absence of or decrease in body movements; difficulty in speaking; inability to move eyes; incomplete, sudden, or unusual body or facial movements; low blood sodium (confusion, convulsions [seizures], drowsiness, dryness of mouth, increased thirst, lack of energy); red or purple patches on skin; serotonin syndrome (confusion, diarrhea, fever, poor coordination, restlessness, shivering, sweating, talking and acting with excitement you cannot control, trembling or shaking, twitching); talking, feeling, and acting with excitement and activity you cannot control

Symptoms of overdose
Dizziness; drowsiness; dryness of mouth; flushing of face; irritability; large pupils; nausea; racing heartbeat; trembling or shaking; vomiting

Other side effects may occur that usually do not need medical attention. These side effects may go away during treatment as your body adjusts to the medicine. However, check with your doctor if any of the following side effects continue or are bothersome:

More common
Constipation; decreased sexual ability; diarrhea; dizziness; drowsiness; dryness of mouth; headache; increased sweating; nausea; problems in urinating; trembling or shaking; trouble in sleeping; unusual tiredness or weakness; vomiting

Less common
Anxiety or nervousness; blurred vision; change in sense of taste; decreased or increased appetite; decreased sexual desire; tingling, burning, or prickling sensations; weight loss or gain

After you stop using this medicine, your body may need time to adjust. The length of time this takes depends on the amount of medicine you were using and how long you used it. During this period of time check with your doctor if you notice any of the following side effects:

Agitation, confusion, or restlessness; diarrhea; dizziness or light-headedness; headache; increased sweating; muscle pain; nausea or vomiting; runny nose; trembling or shaking; trouble in sleeping; unusual tiredness or weakness; vision changes

Other side effects not listed above may also occur in some patients. If you notice any other effects, check with your doctor.

Revised: 11/02/1999

PEGASPARGASE   Systemic†

Commonly used brand name(s):

In the U.S.—
Oncaspar

Another commonly used name is PEG-L-asparaginase.

†Not commercially available in Canada.

Description

Pegaspargase (peg-AS-par-jase) belongs to the general group of medicines known as antineoplastics. It is used to treat some kinds of cancer.

Pegaspargase seems to interfere with the growth of cancer cells, which are eventually destroyed. Since the growth of normal body cells also may be affected by pegaspargase, other effects also occur. Some of these effects may be serious and must be reported to your doctor.

Before you begin treatment with pegaspargase, you and your doctor should talk about the good this medicine will do as well as the risks of using it.

Pegaspargase is to be administered only by or under the immediate supervision of your doctor. It is available in the following dosage form:

Parenteral
• Injection (U.S.)

Before Receiving This Medicine

In deciding to use a medicine, the risks of taking the medicine must be weighed against the good it will do. This is a decision you and your doctor will make. For pegaspargase, the following should be considered:

Allergies—Tell your doctor if you have ever had any unusual or allergic reaction to pegaspargase.

Pregnancy—Pegaspargase has not been studied in pregnant women or animals; however, many cancer medicines may cause sterility that could be permanent. Although sterility has not been reported with pegaspargase, the possibility of this effect in humans should be kept in mind. Cancer medicines may also cause birth defects; therefore, use during pregnancy is not recommended.

Be sure you have discussed this with your doctor before receiving this medicine. It is best to use some kind of birth control while you are receiving pegaspargase. Tell your doctor right away if you think you have become pregnant while receiving pegaspargase.

Breast-feeding—Because pegaspargase may cause serious side effects, breast-feeding is generally not recommended while you are receiving it.

Children—Infants up to 1 year of age—Safety and efficacy have not been established.

Children 1 year of age and older—This medicine has been studied in children 1 year of age and older and has not been shown to cause different side effects or problems than it does in adults. In fact, the side effects of this medicine seem to be less severe in children than in adults.

Older adults—There is no specific information comparing the use of pegaspargase in the elderly with use in other age groups. Safety and efficacy of pegaspargase in the elderly have not been established.

Other medicines—Although certain medicines should not be used together at all, in other cases two different medicines may be used together even if an interaction might occur. In these cases, your doctor may want to change the dose, or other precautions may be necessary. When you are taking pegaspargase, it is especially important that your health care professional know if you are taking any of the following:

- Aspirin or
- Dipyridamole (e.g., Persantine) or
- Heparin or
- Inflammation or pain medicine, except narcotics or
- Warfarin (e.g., Coumadin)—Using any of these medicines together with pegaspargase may increase the risk of bleeding

- Amphotericin B by injection (e.g., Fungizone) or
- Antithyroid agents (medicine for overactive thyroid) or
- Azathioprine (e.g., Imuran) or
- Chloramphenicol (e.g., Chloromycetin) or
- Colchicine or
- Cyclophosphamide (e.g., Cytoxan) or
- Flucytosine (e.g., Ancobon) or
- Ganciclovir (e.g., Cytovene) or
- Interferon (e.g., Intron A, Roferon-A) or
- Mercaptopurine (e.g., Purinethol) or
- Methotrexate (e.g., Mexate) or
- Plicamycin (e.g., Mithracin) or
- Zidovudine (e.g., AZT, Retrovir) or
- If you have ever been treated with radiation or cancer medicines—Pegaspargase may increase the effects of these medicines or radiation therapy on the blood

Other medical problems—The presence of other medical problems may affect the use of pegaspargase. Make sure you tell your doctor if you have any other medical problems, especially:

- Anticoagulant therapy (treatment with blood thinners) or
- Bleeding problems—The chance of bleeding may be increased
- Chickenpox (including recent exposure) or
- Herpes zoster (shingles)—Risk of severe disease affecting other parts of the body
- Diabetes mellitus (sugar diabetes)—The chance of side effects may be increased
- Infection—Pegaspargase can decrease your body's ability to fight infection
- Liver disease—Effects of pegaspargase may be increased because of slower removal of this medicine from the body
- Pancreatitis—The chance of side effects may be increased

Proper Use of This Medicine

Pegaspargase sometimes is given together with certain other medicines. If you are using a combination of medicines, it is important that you receive each one at the proper time. If you are taking some of these medicines by mouth, ask your health care professional to help you plan a way to take them at the right times.

While you are receiving pegaspargase, your doctor may want you to drink extra fluids so that you will pass more urine. This will help prevent kidney problems and keep your kidneys working well.

This medicine often causes nausea and vomiting. However, it is very important that you continue to receive the medicine, even if you begin to feel ill. Ask your health care professional for ways to lessen these effects, especially if they are severe.

Dosing—The dose of pegaspargase will be different for different patients. The dose that is used may depend on a number of things, including what the medicine is used for, the patient's size, and whether or not other medicines are also being taken. *If you are receiving pegaspargase at home, follow your doctor's orders or the directions on the label.* If you have any questions about the proper dose of pegaspargase, ask your doctor.

Precautions While Using This Medicine

It is very important that your doctor check your progress at regular visits to make sure that this medicine is working properly and to check for unwanted effects.

While you are being treated with pegaspargase, and after you stop treatment with it, *do not have any immunizations (vaccinations) without your doctor's approval.* Pegaspargase may lower your body's resistance and there is a chance you might get the infection the immunization is meant to prevent. In addition, other persons living in your household should not take oral poliovirus vaccine, since there is a chance they could pass the poliovirus on to you. Also, avoid persons who have taken oral poliovirus vaccine. Do not get close to them, and do not stay in the same room with them for long. If you cannot take these precautions, you should consider wearing a protective face mask that covers the nose and the mouth.

Pegaspargase can temporarily lower the number of white blood cells in your blood, increasing the chance of getting infection. It can also lower the number of platelets, which are necessary for proper blood clotting. If this occurs, there are certain precautions you can take, especially when your blood count is low, to reduce the risk of infection or bleeding:

- If you can, avoid people with infection. *Check with your doctor immediately* if you think you are getting an infection or if you get a fever or chills, cough or hoarseness, lower back or side pain, or have painful or difficult urination.
- *Check with your doctor immediately* if you notice any unusual bleeding or bruising; black tarry stools; blood in urine or stools; or pinpoint red spots on your skin.
- Be careful when using a regular toothbrush, dental floss, or toothpick. Your medical doctor, dentist, or nurse may recommend other ways to clean your teeth and gums. Check with your medical doctor before having any dental work done.
- Do not touch your eyes or the inside of your nose unless you have just washed your hands and have not touched anything else in the meantime.
- Be careful not to cut yourself when you are using sharp objects such as safety razor or fingernail or toenail cutters.
- Avoid contact sports or other situations where bruising or injury can occur.

If pegaspargase accidentally seeps out of the vein into which it is injected, it may damage some tissue and cause scarring. *Tell the doctor or nurse right away if you notice redness, pain, or swelling at the place of injection.*

Side Effects of This Medicine

Along with its needed effects, a medicine may cause some unwanted effects. Although not all of these side effects may occur, if they do occur they may need medical attention.

Check with your doctor as soon as possible if any of the following side effects occur:

More common
Abdominal or stomach pain; blurry vision; constipation; dry mouth and skin; fatigue; increased hunger or thirst; increased need to urinate; nausea; skin rash; unexplained weight loss; vomiting

Less common
Difficulty in breathing or swallowing; hives; itching, especially of hands and feet; reddening of the skin, especially around ears; swelling of eyes, face, or inside of nose; unusual tiredness or weakness (sudden and severe)

Rare
Black, tarry stools; blood in urine; cough or hoarseness; fever or chills; lower back or side pain; painful or difficult urination; pinpoint red spots on skin; unusual bleeding or bruising

Other side effects may occur that usually do not need medical attention. These side effects may go away during treatment as your body adjusts to the medicine. However, check with your doctor if any of the following side effects continue or are bothersome:

More common
General feeling of discomfort or illness

Less common
Anxiety; behavior change similar to drunkenness; blurred vision; cold sweats; confusion; convulsions (seizures); cool pale skin; difficulty in concentrating; drowsiness; fast heartbeat; headache; lack of appetite; nervousness; nightmares; pain at place of injection; pain in joints or muscles; restless sleep; shakiness; severe or unusual tiredness or weakness; slurred speech

After you stop using this medicine, your body may need time to adjust. The length of time this takes depends on the amount of medicine you were using and how long you used it. During this period of time check with your doctor if you notice any other side effects not listed above.

Developed: 07/01/98

PEMIROLAST   Ophthalmic†

Commonly used brand name(s):

In the U.S.—
Alamast

†Not commercially available in Canada.

Description

Pemirolast (pe-MEER-oh-last) is used to treat the itching in your eyes that happens with allergies.

Pemirolast works by preventing certain types of inflammatory cells from releasing irritating substances that cause allergic symptoms.

This medicine is available only with your doctor's prescription, in the following dosage forms:

Topical
• Ophthalmic solution (U.S.)

Before Using This Medicine

In deciding to use a medicine, the risks of using the medicine must be weighed against the good it will do. This is a decision you and your doctor will make. For pemirolast, the following should be considered:

Allergies—Tell your doctor if you have ever had any unusual or allergic reaction to pemirolast. Also tell your doctor and pharmacist if you are allergic to any other substances, such as foods, preservatives, or dyes.

Pregnancy—Pemirolast has not been shown to cause birth defects or other problems in humans. However, in rats given 20,000 to 30,000 times the human dose of pemirolast, there was an increase in the number of fetal bone and heart deformities as well as an increased number of fetal implantation losses.

Breast-feeding—It is not known whether pemirolast passes into human breast milk. Although most medicines pass into breast milk in small amounts, many of them may be used safely while breast feeding. Mothers who are taking this medicine and who wish to breast-feed should discuss this with their doctor.

Children—This medicine has been tested in children 3 years of age and older and, in effective doses, has not been shown to cause different side effects or problems than it does in adults.

Older adults—There is no specific information available comparing the use of pemirolast in the elderly with use in other age groups.

Other medical problems—The presence of other medical problems may affect the use of pemirolast. Make sure you tell your doctor if you have any other medical problems, especially:
• Contact lens-related irritation—Pemirolast should not be used to treat this condition

Proper Use of This Medicine

Pemirolast is used to help treat the itching that often occurs with allergic conjunctivitis.
• To use the *eye drops* form of this medicine:
  —First, wash your hands. Then tilt the head back and, pressing your finger gently on the skin just beneath the lower eyelid, pull the lower eyelid away from the eye to make a space. Drop the medicine into this space. Let go of the eyelid and gently close the eyes. Blink a few times to make sure the eye is covered with the medicine.
  —*To keep the medicine as germ-free as possible, do not touch the applicator tip to any surface (including the eye). Also, keep the container tightly closed. Serious damage to the eye and possible loss of vision may result from using contaminated eye drops.*

Dosing—*Use this medicine only as directed.* Do not use more of it and do not use it more often than your doctor ordered.

Follow your doctor's orders or the directions on the label. The following information includes only the average dose of ophthalmic pemirolast. *If your dose is different, do not change it* unless your doctor tells you to do so.

- For *ophthalmic* dosage form (eye drops):
  —For eye allergies:
    - Adults and children 3 years of age and older—Use one to two drops in each affected eye four times a day.
    - Children up to 3 years of age—Use and dose must be determined by your doctor.

Missed dose—If you miss a dose of this medicine, apply it as soon as possible. However, if it is almost time for your next dose, skip the missed dose and go back to your regular dosing schedule. Do not double doses.

Storage—To store this medicine:
- Keep out of the reach of children.
- Keep the medicine from freezing. Do not refrigerate.
- Do not keep outdated medicine or medicine no longer needed. Ask your health care professional how you should dispose of any medicine you do not use. Be sure that any discarded medicine is out of the reach of children.

Precautions While Using This Medicine

You should avoid wearing contact lenses when your eyes are red and irritated from your allergies.

For patients who continue to wear contact lenses and whose eyes are not red, be certain to wait at least 10 minutes after applying pemirolast to your eyes before replacing any contact lenses normally worn.

Side Effects of This Medicine

Along with its needed effects, a medicine may cause some unwanted effects. Although not all of these side effects may occur, if they do occur they may need medical attention.

Check with your doctor as soon as possible if any of the following side effects occur:
Less common
  Cough (mucus-producing); headache (severe); stomach pain and cramping; pain and tenderness around eyes and cheekbones; painful menstrual bleeding; runny or stuffy nose; tightness in chest; troubled breathing

Other side effects may occur that usually do not need medical attention. These side effects may go away during treatment as your body adjusts to the medicine. However, check with your doctor if any of the following side effects continue or are bothersome.
More common
  Chills; cough; fever; sneezing; sore throat
Less common
  Back pain; burning feeling in eye; eyelid swelling; eye dryness; foreign body feeling in eye; general feeling of eye discomfort; increased itching of the eye; redness of the eye

Other side effects not listed above may also occur in some patients. If you notice any other effects, check with your doctor.

Developed: 04/26/2000

PEMOLINE   Systemic

Commonly used brand name(s):

In the U.S.—
    Cylert
    Cylert Chewable

In Canada—
    Cylert

Description

Pemoline (PEM-oh-leen) belongs to the group of medicines called central nervous system (CNS) stimulants. It is used to treat children with attention-deficit hyperactivity disorder (ADHD).

Pemoline increases attention and decreases restlessness in children who are overactive, cannot concentrate for very long or are easily distracted, and are emotionally unstable. This medicine is used as part of a total treatment program that also includes social, educational, and psychological treatment.

Rarely, pemoline has caused serious liver problems. You and your doctor should talk about the good this medicine will do as well as the risks of using it. In addition, you will be asked to sign an informed consent form stating that you understand and agree to accept the risk of liver problems.

Pemoline is available only with your doctor's prescription, in the following dosage forms:
Oral
  - Tablets (U.S. Available in Canada only through a special access program).
  - Chewable tablets (U.S.)

Before Using This Medicine

In deciding to use a medicine, the risks of taking the medicine must be weighed against the good it will do. This is a decision you and your doctor will make. For pemoline, the following should be considered:

Allergies—Tell your doctor if you have ever had any unusual or allergic reaction to pemoline. Also tell your health care professional if you are allergic to any other substances, such as foods, preservatives, or dyes.

Pregnancy—Pemoline has not been shown to cause birth defects or other problems in humans. However, studies in animals given large doses of pemoline have shown that pemoline causes an increase in stillbirths and decreased survival of the offspring after birth.

Breast-feeding—It is not known whether pemoline passes into breast milk.

Children—Slowed growth rate in children who received medicines like pemoline for a long period of time has been reported. Some doctors recommend medicine-free periods during treatment with pemoline to help prevent slowed growth.

Pemoline may make behavior worse in children with serious mental illness.

Other medicines—Although certain medicines should not be used together at all, in other cases two different medicines may be used together even if an interaction might occur. In these cases, your doctor may want to change the dose, or other precautions may be necessary. When you are taking pemoline, it is especially important that your health care professional know if you are taking any of the following:

- Amantadine (e.g., Symmetrel) or
- Amphetamines or
- Appetite suppressants (diet pills) or
- Caffeine (e.g., NoDoz) or
- Chlophedianol (e.g., Ulone) or
- Cocaine or
- Medicine for asthma or other breathing problems or
- Medicine for colds, sinus problems, hay fever or other allergies (including nose drops or sprays) or
- Methylphenidate (e.g., Ritalin) or
- Nabilone (e.g., Cesamet)—Using these medicines with pemoline may cause severe nervousness, irritability, trouble in sleeping, or possibly irregular heartbeat or seizures
- Anticonvulsants (medicine to control seizures)—Pemoline may increase the chance of having seizures; your doctor may change the dose of your anticonvulsant medicine
- Monoamine oxidase (MAO) inhibitors (furazolidone [e.g., Furoxone], isocarboxazid [e.g., Marplan], phenelzine [e.g., Nardil], procarbazine [e.g., Matulane], selegiline [e.g., Eldepryl], tranylcypromine [e.g., Parnate])—*Taking pemoline while you are taking or within 2 weeks of taking an MAO inhibitor may result in sudden extremely high blood pressure or fever, irregular heartbeat, or seizures*

Other medical problems—The presence of other medical problems may affect the use of pemoline. Make sure you tell your doctor if you have any other medical problems, especially:

- Drug abuse or dependence (or history of)—Dependence on pemoline may develop
- Gilles de la Tourette's syndrome or other tics or
- Liver disease or
- Mental illness (severe)—Pemoline may make the condition worse
- Kidney disease—Higher blood levels of pemoline may occur, increasing the chance of side effects

Proper Use of This Medicine

For patients taking the *chewable tablet form* of this medicine:

- These tablets must be chewed before swallowing. Do not swallow whole.

Sometimes this medicine must be taken for 3 to 4 weeks before improvement is noticed.

Take pemoline only as directed by your doctor. Do not take more of it, do not take it more often, and do not take it for a longer time than your doctor ordered. If too much is taken, it may become habit-forming.

Dosing—The dose of pemoline will be different for different patients. *Follow your doctor's orders or the directions on the label.* The following information includes only the average doses of pemoline. *If your dose is different, do not change it* unless your doctor tells you to do so.

The number of tablets that you take depends on the strength of the medicine.

- For *oral* or *chewable* dosage forms (tablets):
  —Children 6 years of age and over: To start, 37.5 milligrams (mg) every morning. Your doctor may increase your dose if needed. However, the dose is usually not more than 112.5 mg a day.
  —Children up to 6 years of age: Use and dose must be determined by the doctor.

Missed dose—If you miss a dose of this medicine, take it as soon as possible and go back to your regular dosing schedule. If you do not remember the missed dose until the next day, skip the missed dose and go back to your regular dosing schedule. Do not double doses.

Storage—To store this medicine:

- Keep out of the reach of children.
- Store away from heat and direct light.
- Do not store in the bathroom, near the kitchen sink, or in other damp places. Heat or moisture may cause the medicine to break down.
- Do not keep outdated medicine or medicine no longer needed. Be sure that any discarded medicine is out of the reach of children.

Precautions While Using This Medicine

Your doctor should check your progress at regular visits to make sure that this medicine does not cause unwanted effects. In addition, you must have your blood tested every other week to see if this medicine is affecting your liver.

Dark urine or yellow eyes or skin may be a sign of a serious unwanted effect on your liver. *Check with your doctor immediately if you develop dark urine or yellow eyes or skin.*

This medicine may cause some people to become dizzy or less alert than they are normally. *Make sure you know how you react to this medicine before you ride a bicycle or do anything else that could be dangerous if you are dizzy or are not alert.*

If you have been using this medicine for a long time and you think you may have become mentally or physically dependent on it, check with your doctor. Some signs of dependence on pemoline are:

- a strong desire or need to continue taking the medicine.
- a need to increase the dose to receive the effects of the medicine.
- withdrawal side effects (for example, mental depression, unusual behavior, or unusual tiredness or weakness) occurring after the medicine is stopped.

If you take this medicine in large doses for a long time, do not stop taking it without first checking with your doctor. Your doctor may want you to reduce gradually the amount you are taking before stopping completely.

Side Effects of This Medicine

Along with its needed effects, a medicine may cause some unwanted effects. Some side effects will have signs or symptoms that you can see or feel. Your doctor may watch for others by doing certain tests.

Pemoline may cause some serious side effects, including liver problems. Also, medicines like pemoline, when used for a long time, have been reported to slow the growth rate of children. Some doctors recommend medicine-free periods during treatment with pemoline. Pemoline may also cause unwanted effects on behavior in children with severe mental illness.

Although not all of these side effects may occur, if they do occur they may need medical attention.

Check with your doctor immediately if either of the following side effects occurs:

Rare

Dark urine; yellow eyes or skin

Check with your doctor as soon as possible if any of the following side effects occur:

Rare

Convulsions (seizures); hallucinations (seeing, hearing, or feeling things that are not there); nausea and vomiting; shortness of breath, troubled breathing, wheezing, or tightness in chest; skin rash; sores, ulcers, or white spots on lips or in mouth; swollen or painful glands; uncontrolled movements of eyes, tongue, lips, face, arms, or legs; unusual bleeding or bruising; unusual tiredness; vocal sounds you cannot control

Symptoms of overdose

Agitation; confusion; convulsions (seizures)—may be followed by coma; false sense of well-being; fast heartbeat; hallucinations (seeing, hearing, or feeling things that are not there); headache (severe); high blood pressure; high fever; large pupils; muscle trembling or twitching; restlessness; sweating; vomiting

This medicine may also cause the following side effects that your doctor will watch for:

Rare

Liver problems; slow growth in children

Other side effects may occur that usually do not need medical attention. These side effects may go away during treatment as your body adjusts to the medicine. However, check with your doctor if any of the following side effects continue or are bothersome:

More common

Loss of appetite; trouble in sleeping; weight loss

Less common

Dizziness; drowsiness; headache; increased irritability; mental depression; stomachache

After you stop using this medicine, your body may need time to adjust. The length of time this takes depends on the amount of medicine you were using and how long you used it. During this period of time check with your doctor if you notice any of the following side effects:

Abdominal pain; convulsions (seizures); headache; mental depression; nausea; unusual behavior; unusual tiredness or weakness; vomiting

Other side effects not listed above may also occur in some patients. If you notice any other effects, check with your doctor.

Revised: 08/08/2000

PENCICLOVIR   Topical

Commonly used brand name(s):

In the U.S.—
Denavir

Description

Penciclovir (pen-SYE-kloe-veer) belongs to the family of medicines called antivirals. Antivirals are used to treat infections caused by viruses. Usually they work for only one kind or group of virus infections.

Topical penciclovir is used to treat the symptoms of herpes simplex virus infections around the mouth (cold sores). Although topical penciclovir will not cure herpes simplex, it may help relieve the pain and discomfort and may help the sores heal faster.

This medicine is available only with your doctor's prescription, in the following dosage form:

Topical
• Cream (U.S.)

Before Using This Medicine

In deciding to use a medicine, the risks of using the medicine must be weighed against the good it will do. This is a decision you and your doctor will make. For topical penciclovir, the following should be considered:

Allergies—Tell your doctor if you have ever had any unusual or allergic reaction to penciclovir. Also tell your health care professional if you are allergic to any other substances, such as preservatives or dyes.

Pregnancy—Topical penciclovir has not been studied in pregnant women. However, this medicine has not been shown to cause birth defects or other problems in animal studies.

Breast-feeding—It is not known whether topical penciclovir passes into the breast milk. However, it does pass into the milk in animals when given orally. Although most medicines pass into breast milk in small amounts, many of them may be used safely while breast-feeding. Mothers who are taking this medicine and who wish to breast-feed should discuss this with their doctor.

Children—There is no specific information comparing the use of topical penciclovir in children with use in other age groups.

Older adults—Many medicines have not been studied specifically in older people. Therefore, it may not be known whether they work exactly the same way they do in younger adults. There is no specific information comparing use of penciclovir in the elderly with use in other age groups. However, this medicine has been used in some older patients and has not been found to cause different side effects or other problems than it does in younger adults.

Other medicines—Although certain medicines should not be used together at all, in other cases two different medicines may be used together even if an interaction might occur. In these cases, your doctor may want to change the dose, or other precautions may be necessary. Tell your health care professional if you are using any other prescription or nonprescription (over-the-counter [OTC]) medicine.

Other medical problems—The presence of other medical problems may affect the use of topical penciclovir. Make

sure you tell your doctor if you have any other medical problems, especially:

- Immune system problems—It is not known if this medicine will work properly in patients with these problems

Proper Use of This Medicine

This medicine should only be used on the lips or face.

Penciclovir is best used as soon as possible after the symptoms of herpes infection (for example, pain, burning, or blisters) begin to appear.

Do not use this medicine in or near the eyes.

Do not use this medicine inside the mouth or nose or on other internal parts of the body.

Dosing—The dose of topical penciclovir will be different for different patients. *Follow your doctor's orders or the directions on the label.* The following information includes only the average doses of topical penciclovir. *If your dose is different, do not change it* unless your doctor tells you to do so.

- For *topical* dosage form (cream):
  —For herpes simplex infection (cold sores):
  - Adults—Apply to the affected area(s) of the skin every two hours, while awake, for four days.
  - Children—Use and dose must be determined by your doctor.

Missed dose—If you miss a dose of this medicine, apply it as soon as you remember. However, if it is almost time for your next dose, skip the missed dose and go back to your regular dosing schedule. Do not double doses.

Storage—To store this medicine:

- Keep out of the reach of children.
- Store away from heat and direct light.
- Keep the medicine from freezing.
- Do not keep outdated medicine or medicine no longer needed. Be sure that any discarded medicine is out of the reach of children.

Side Effects of This Medicine

Along with its needed effects, a medicine may cause some unwanted effects. Although not all of these side effects may occur, if they do occur they may need medical attention.

Check with your doctor as soon as possible if any of the following side effects occur:
Rare
Mild pain, burning, or stinging

Other side effects may occur that usually do not need medical attention. These side effects may go away during treatment as your body adjusts to the medicine. However, check with your doctor if any of the following side effects continue or are bothersome:
More common
Headache
Less common
Change in sense of taste; decreased sensitivity of skin, particularly to touch; redness of the skin; skin rash

Other side effects not listed above may also occur in some patients. If you notice any other effects, check with your doctor.

Developed: 08/12/98

PENICILLINS   Systemic

Commonly used brand name(s):

In the U.S.—

Amoxil[1]	Pfizerpen[12]
Bactocill[11]	Pfizerpen-AS[12]
Beepen-VK[13]	Pipracil[14]
Betapen-VK[13]	Polycillin[2]
Bicillin L-A[12]	Polycillin-N[2]
Cloxapen[5]	Polymox[1]
Crysticillin 300 A.S.[12]	Principen[2]
Dynapen[6]	Prostaphlin[11]
Dycill[6]	Spectrobid[3]
Geocillin[4]	Staphcillin[8]
Geopen[4]	Tegopen[5]
Ledercillin VK[13]	Ticar[17]
Mezlin[9]	Totacillin[2]
Nafcil[10]	Totacillin-N[2]
Nallpen[10]	Trimox[1]
Omnipen[2]	Unipen[10]
Omnipen-N[2]	V-Cillin K[13]
Pathocil[6]	Veetids[13]
Pentids[12]	Wycillin[12]
Pen Vee K[13]	Wymox[1]
Permapen[12]	

In Canada—

Amoxil[1]	Nu-Amoxi[1]
Ampicin[2]	Nu-Ampi[2]
Apo-Amoxi[1]	Nu-Cloxi[5]
Apo-Ampi[2]	Nu-Pen-VK[13]
Apo-Cloxi[5]	Orbenin[5]
Apo-Pen VK[13]	Penbritin[2]
Ayercillin[12]	Penglobe[3]
Bicillin L-A[12]	Pen-Vee[13]
Fluclox[7]	Pipracil[14]
Geopen Oral[4]	Pondocillin[15]
Ledercillin VK[13]	PVF[13]
Megacillin[12]	PVF K[13]
Nadopen-V[13]	Pyopen[4]
Nadopen-V 200[13]	Selexid[16]
Nadopen-V 400[13]	Tegopen[5]
Novamoxin[1]	Ticar[17]
Novo-Ampicillin[2]	Unipen[10]
Novo-Cloxin[5]	V-Cillin K[13]
Novo-Pen-VK[13]	Wycillin[12]

Note: For quick reference, the following penicillins are numbered to match the corresponding brand names.

This information applies to the following medicines:
1. Amoxicillin (a-mox-i-SILL-in) ‡
2. Ampicillin (am-pi-SILL-in) ‡
3. Bacampicillin (ba-kam-pi-SILL-in)
4. Carbenicillin (kar-ben-i-SILL-in)
5. Cloxacillin (klox-a-SILL-in) ‡
6. Dicloxacillin (dye-klox-a-SILL-in) †‡
7. Flucloxacillin (floo-klox-a-SILL-in) *
8. Methicillin (meth-i-SILL-in) †
9. Mezlocillin (mez-loe-SILL-in) †
10. Nafcillin (naf-SILL-in) ‡
11. Oxacillin (ox-a-SILL-in) †‡
12. Penicillin G (pen-i-SILL-in G) §
13. Penicillin V (pen-i-SILL-in V) ‡
14. Piperacillin (pi-PER-a-sill-in)
15. Pivampicillin (piv-am-pi-SILL-in) *
16. Pivmecillinam (piv-me-SILL-in-am) *
17. Ticarcillin (tye-kar-SILL-in)

*Not commercially available in the U.S.
†Not commercially available in Canada.
‡Generic name product may be available in the U.S.
§Generic name product may be available in Canada.

Description

Penicillins are used to treat infections caused by bacteria. They work by killing the bacteria or preventing their growth.

There are several different kinds of penicillins. Each is used to treat different kinds of infections. One kind of penicillin usually may not be used in place of another. In addition, penicillins are used to treat bacterial infections in many different parts of the body. They are sometimes given with other antibacterial medicines (antibiotics). Some of the penicillins may also be used for other problems as determined by your doctor. However, none of the penicillins will work for colds, flu, or other virus infections.

Penicillins are available only with your doctor's prescription, in the following dosage forms:

Oral
Amoxicillin
- Capsules (U.S. and Canada)
- Oral suspension (U.S. and Canada)
- Tablets (U.S.)
- Chewable tablets (U.S. and Canada)

Ampicillin
- Capsules (U.S. and Canada)
- Oral suspension (U.S. and Canada)

Bacampicillin
- Oral suspension (U.S.)
- Tablets (U.S. and Canada)

Carbenicillin
- Tablets (U.S. and Canada)

Cloxacillin
- Capsules (U.S. and Canada)
- Oral solution (U.S. and Canada)

Dicloxacillin
- Capsules (U.S.)
- Oral suspension (U.S.)

Flucloxacillin
- Capsules (Canada)
- Oral suspension (Canada)

Nafcillin
- Capsules (U.S.)
- Tablets (U.S.)

Oxacillin
- Capsules (U.S.)
- Oral solution (U.S.)

Penicillin G Benzathine
- Oral suspension (Canada)

Penicillin G Potassium
- Oral solution (U.S.)
- Tablets (U.S. and Canada)

Penicillin V Benzathine
- Oral suspension (Canada)

Penicillin V Potassium
- Oral solution (U.S. and Canada)
- Tablets (U.S. and Canada)

Pivampicillin
- Oral suspension (Canada)
- Tablets (Canada)

Pivmecillinam
- Tablets (Canada)

Parenteral
Ampicillin
- Injection (U.S. and Canada)

Carbenicillin
- Injection (U.S. and Canada)

Cloxacillin
- Injection (Canada)

Methicillin
- Injection (U.S.)

Mezlocillin
- Injection (U.S.)

Nafcillin
- Injection (U.S. and Canada)

Oxacillin
- Injection (U.S.)

Penicillin G Benzathine
- Injection (U.S. and Canada)

Penicillin G Potassium
- Injection (U.S. and Canada)

Penicillin G Procaine
- Injection (U.S. and Canada)

Penicillin G Sodium
- Injection (U.S. and Canada)

Piperacillin
- Injection (U.S. and Canada)

Ticarcillin
- Injection (U.S. and Canada)

Before Using This Medicine

In deciding to use a medicine, the risks of taking the medicine must be weighed against the good it will do. This is a decision you and your doctor will make. For penicillins, the following should be considered:

Allergies—Tell your doctor if you have ever had any unusual or allergic reaction to any of the penicillins or cephalosporins. Also tell your health care professional if you are allergic to any other substances, such as foods, preservatives, or dyes, or procaine (e.g., Novocain) or other ester-type anesthetics (medicines that cause numbing) if you are receiving penicillin G procaine.

Diet—Make certain your health care professional knows if you are on a low-sodium (low-salt) diet. Some of these medicines contain enough sodium to cause problems in some people.

Pregnancy—Penicillins have not been studied in pregnant women. However, penicillins have been widely used in pregnant women and have not been shown to cause birth defects or other problems in animal studies.

Breast-feeding—Penicillins pass into the breast milk. Even though only small amounts may pass into breast milk, allergic reactions, diarrhea, fungus infections, and skin rash may occur in nursing babies.

Children—Many penicillins have been used in children and, in effective doses, are not expected to cause different side effects or problems in children than they do in adults.

Some strengths of the chewable tablets of amoxicillin contain aspartame, which is changed by the body to phenylalanine, a substance that is harmful to patients with phenylketonuria.

Older adults—Penicillins have been used in the elderly and have not been shown to cause different side effects or problems in older people than they do in younger adults.

Other medicines—Although certain medicines should not be used together at all, in other cases two different medicines may be used together even if an interaction might occur. In these cases, your doctor may want to change the dose, or other precautions may be necessary. When you are taking a penicillin, it is especially important that your health care professional know if you are taking any of the following:

- Acetaminophen (e.g., Tylenol) (with long-term, high-dose use) or
- Amiodarone (e.g., Cordarone) or
- Anabolic steroids (nandrolone [e.g., Anabolin], oxandrolone [e.g., Anavar], oxymetholone [e.g., Anadrol], stanozolol [e.g., Winstrol]) or
- Androgens (male hormones) or
- Antithyroid agents (medicine for overactive thyroid) or
- Carmustine (e.g., BiCNU) or
- Chloroquine (e.g., Aralen) or
- Dantrolene (e.g., Dantrium) or
- Daunorubicin (e.g., Cerubidine) or
- Disulfiram (e.g., Antabuse) or
- Divalproex (e.g., Depakote) or
- Estrogens (female hormones) or
- Etretinate (e.g., Tegison) or
- Gold salts (medicine for arthritis) or
- Hydroxychloroquine (e.g., Plaquenil) or
- Mercaptopurine (e.g., Purinethol) or
- Methotrexate (e.g., Mexate) or
- Methyldopa (e.g., Aldomet) or
- Naltrexone (e.g., Trexan) (with long-term, high-dose use) or
- Oral contraceptives (birth control pills) containing estrogen or
- Other anti-infectives by mouth or by injection (medicine for infection) or
- Phenothiazines (acetophenazine [e.g., Tindal], chlorpromazine [e.g., Thorazine], fluphenazine [e.g., Prolixin], mesoridazine [e.g., Serentil], perphenazine [e.g., Trilafon], prochlorperazine [e.g., Compazine], promazine [e.g., Sparine], promethazine [e.g., Phenergan], thioridazine [e.g., Mellaril], trifluoperazine [e.g., Stelazine], triflupromazine [e.g., Vesprin], trimeprazine [e.g., Temaril]) or
- Plicamycin (e.g., Mithracin) or
- Valproic acid (e.g., Depakene)—These medicines may increase the chance of liver damage if taken with cloxacillin, dicloxacillin, flucloxacillin, mezlocillin, nafcillin, oxacillin, or piperacillin

- Amiloride (e.g., Midamor) or
- Benazepril (e.g., Lotensin) or
- Captopril (e.g., Capoten) or
- Enalapril (e.g., Vasotec) or
- Fosinopril (e.g., Monopril) or
- Lisinopril (e.g., Prinivil, Zestril) or
- Potassium-containing medicine or
- Quinapril (e.g., Accupril) or
- Ramipril (e.g., Altace) or
- Spironolactone (e.g., Aldactone) or
- Triamterene (e.g., Dyrenium)—Use of these medicines with penicillin G by injection may cause an increase in side effects

- Anticoagulants (blood thinners) or
- Dipyridamole (e.g., Persantine) or
- Divalproex (e.g., Depakote) or
- Heparin (e.g., Panheprin) or
- Inflammation or pain medicine (except narcotics) or
- Pentoxifylline (e.g., Trental) or
- Plicamycin (e.g., Mithracin) or
- Sulfinpyrazone (e.g., Anturane) or
- Valproic acid (e.g., Depakene)—Use of these medicines with high doses of carbenicillin, piperacillin, or ticarcillin may increase the chance of bleeding

- Cloramphenicol (e.g., Chloromycetin) or
- Erythromycins (e.g., E.E.S., E-Mycin, ERYC) or
- Sulfonamides (e.g., Gantanol, Gantrisin) or
- Tetracyclines (e.g., Achromycin, Minocin, Vibramycin)—Use of these medicines with penicillins may prevent the penicillin from working properly
- Cholestyramine (e.g., Questran) or
- Colestipol (e.g., Colestid)—Use of these medicines with oral penicillin G may prevent penicillin G from working properly
- Oral contraceptives (birth control pills) containing estrogen—Use of ampicillin, amoxicillin, or penicillin V with estrogen-containing oral contraceptives may prevent oral contraceptives from working properly, increasing the chance of pregnancy
- Methotrexate (e.g., Mexate)—Use of methotrexate with penicillins may increase the chance of side effects of methotrexate
- Probenecid (e.g., Benemid)—Probenecid causes penicillins to build up in the blood. This may increase the chance of side effects. However, your doctor may want to give you probenecid with a penicillin to treat some infections

Other medical problems—The presence of other medical problems may affect the use of penicillins. Make sure you tell your doctor if you have any other medical problems, especially:

- Allergy, general (such as asthma, eczema, hay fever, hives), history of—Patients with a history of general allergies may be more likely to have a severe reaction to penicillins
- Bleeding problems, history of—Patients with a history of bleeding problems may be more likely to have bleeding when receiving carbenicillin, piperacillin, or ticarcillin
- Congestive heart failure (CHF) or
- High blood pressure—Large doses of carbenicillin or ticarcillin may make these conditions worse, because these medicines contain a large amount of salt
- Cystic fibrosis—Patients with cystic fibrosis may have an increased chance of fever and skin rash when receiving piperacillin
- Kidney disease—Patients with kidney disease may have an increased chance of side effects
- Mononucleosis ("mono")—Patients with mononucleosis may have an increased chance of skin rash when receiving ampicillin, bacampicillin, or pivampicillin
- Phenylketonuria—Some strengths of the amoxicillin chewable tablets contain aspartame, which is changed by the body to phenylalanine, a substance that is harmful to patients with phenylketonuria.
- Stomach or intestinal disease, history of (especially colitis, including colitis caused by antibiotics)—Patients with a history of stomach or intestinal disease may be more likely to develop colitis while taking penicillins

Proper Use of This Medicine

Penicillins (except bacampicillin tablets, amoxicillin, penicillin V, pivampicillin, and pivmecillinam) are best taken with a full glass (8 ounces) of water on an empty stomach (either 1 hour before or 2 hours after meals) unless otherwise directed by your doctor.

For patients taking *amoxicillin, penicillin V, pivampicillin, and pivmecillinam:*
- Amoxicillin, penicillin V, pivampicillin, and pivmecillinam may be taken on a full or empty stomach.
- The *liquid form of amoxicillin* may also be taken by itself or mixed with formulas, milk, fruit juice, water, ginger ale, or other cold drinks. If mixed with other liquids, take immediately after mixing. Be sure to drink all the liquid to get the full dose of medicine.

For patients taking *bacampicillin:*
- The liquid form of this medicine is best taken with a full glass (8 ounces) of water on an empty stomach (either 1 hour before or 2 hours after meals) unless otherwise directed by your doctor.
- The tablet form of this medicine may be taken on a full or empty stomach.

For patients taking *penicillin G by mouth:*
- Do not drink acidic fruit juices (for example, orange or grapefruit juice) or other acidic beverages within 1 hour of taking penicillin G since this may keep the medicine from working properly.

For patients taking the *oral liquid form of penicillins:*
- This medicine is to be taken by mouth even if it comes in a dropper bottle. If this medicine does not come in a dropper bottle, use a specially marked measuring spoon or other device to measure each dose accurately. The average household teaspoon may not hold the right amount of liquid.
- Do not use after the expiration date on the label. The medicine may not work properly after that date. If you have any questions about this, check with your pharmacist.

For patients taking the *chewable tablet form of amoxicillin:*
- Tablets should be chewed or crushed before they are swallowed.

To help clear up your infection completely, *keep taking this medicine for the full time of treatment,* even if you begin to feel better after a few days. *If you have a "strep" infection, you should keep taking this medicine for at least 10 days. This is especially important in "strep" infections. Serious heart problems could develop later* if your infection is not cleared up completely. Also, if you stop taking this medicine too soon, your symptoms may return.

This medicine works best when there is a constant amount in the blood or urine. *To help keep the amount constant, do not miss any doses. Also, it is best to take the doses at evenly spaced times, day and night.* For example, if you are to take four doses a day, the doses should be spaced about 6 hours apart. If this interferes with your sleep or other daily activities, or if you need help in planning the best times to take your medicine, check with your health care professional.

Dosing—The dose of these medicines will be different for different patients. *Follow your doctor's orders or the directions on the label.* The following information includes only the average doses of these medicines. *If your dose is different, do not change it* unless your doctor tells you to do so.

The number of tablets or teaspoonfuls of suspension that you take depends on the strength of the medicine. Also, *the number of doses you take each day, the time allowed between doses, and the length of time you take the medicine depend on the medical problem for which you are taking a penicillin.*

For amoxicillin
- For bacterial infections:
  —For *oral* dosage forms (capsules, oral suspension, tablets, and chewable tablets):
  - Adults, teenagers, and children weighing more than 40 kilograms (kg) (88 pounds)—250 to 500 milligrams (mg) every eight hours or 500 to 875 mg every twelve hours, depending on the type and severity of the infection.
  - Neonates and infants up to 3 months of age—Dose is based on body weight and must be determined by your doctor. The usual dose is 15 mg per kg (6.8 mg per pound) of body weight or less every twelve hours.
  - Infants 3 months of age and older and children weighing up to 40 kg (88 lbs.)—Dose is based on body weight and must be determined by your doctor. The usual dose is 6.7 to 13.3 mg per kg (3 to 6 mg per pound) of body weight every eight hours or 12.5 to 22.5 mg per kg (5.7 to 10.2 mg per pound) of body weight every twelve hours.
- For duodenal ulcers (associated with *Helicobacter pylori* bacterial infection):
  —For *oral* dosage forms (capsules, oral suspension, tablets, and chewable tablets):
  - For triple medicine therapy—
    - Adults: 1000 mg twice a day every twelve hours for fourteen days, along with the two other medicines, clarithromycin and lansoprazole, as directed by your doctor.
    - Teenagers and children: Use and dose must be determined by your doctor.
  - For dual medicine therapy—
    - Adults: 1000 mg three times a day every eight hours for fourteen days, along with the other medicine, lansoprazole, as directed by your doctor.
    - Teenagers and children: Use and dose must be determined by your doctor.

For ampicillin
- For bacterial infections:
  —For *oral* dosage forms (capsules and oral suspension):
  - Adults, teenagers, and children weighing more than 20 kilograms (kg) (44 pounds)—250 to 500 milligrams (mg) every six hours.
  - Infants and children weighing up to 20 kg (44 pounds)—Dose is based on body weight and must be determined by your doctor. The usual dose is 12.5 to 25 mg per kg (5.7 to 11.4 mg per pound) of body weight every six hours; or 16.7 to 33.3 mg per kg (7.6 to 15 mg per pound) of body weight every eight hours.
  —For *injection* dosage form:
  - Adults, teenagers, and children weighing more than 20 kg (44 pounds)—250 to 500 mg, injected into a vein or muscle every three to six hours.
  - Infants and children weighing up to 20 kg (44 pounds)—Dose is based on body weight and must be determined by your doctor. The usual dose is 12.5 mg per kg (5.7 mg per pound) of body weight, injected into a vein or muscle every six hours.

For bacampicillin
- For bacterial infections:
  - —For *oral* dosage forms (oral suspension and tablets):
    - Adults, teenagers, and children weighing more than 25 kilograms (kg) (55 pounds)—400 to 800 milligrams (mg) every twelve hours.
    - Children weighing up to 25 kg (55 pounds)—Bacampicillin tablets are not recommended for use in children weighing up to 25 kg (55 pounds). The dose of the oral suspension is based on body weight and must be determined by your doctor. The usual dose is 12.5 to 25 mg per kg (5.7 to 11.4 mg per pound) of body weight every twelve hours.

For carbenicillin
- For bacterial infections:
  - —For *oral* dosage form (tablets):
    - Adults and teenagers—500 milligrams (mg) to 1 gram every six hours.
    - Children—Dose must be determined by your doctor.
  - —For *injection* dosage form:
    - Adults and teenagers—Dose is based on body weight and must be determined by your doctor. The usual dose is 50 to 83.3 mg per kilogram (kg) (22.8 to 37.9 mg per pound) of body weight, injected into a vein or muscle every four hours.
    - Older infants and children—Dose is based on body weight and must be determined by your doctor. The usual dose is 16.7 to 75 mg per kg (7.6 to 34 mg per pound) of body weight, injected into a vein or muscle every four to six hours.

For cloxacillin
- For bacterial infections:
  - —For *oral* dosage form (capsules and oral solution):
    - Adults, teenagers, and children weighing more than 20 kilograms (kg) (44 pounds)—250 to 500 milligrams (mg) every six hours.
    - Infants and children weighing up to 20 kg (44 pounds)—Dose is based on body weight and must be determined by your doctor. The usual dose is 6.25 to 12.5 mg per kg (2.8 to 5.7 mg per pound) of body weight every six hours.
  - —For *injection* dosage form:
    - Adults, teenagers, and children weighing more than 20 kg—250 to 500 mg, injected into a vein every six hours.
    - Infants and children weighing up to 20 kg (44 pounds)—Dose is based on body weight and must be determined by your doctor. The usual dose is 6.25 to 12.5 mg per kg (2.8 to 5.7 mg per pound) of body weight, injected into a vein every six hours.

For dicloxacillin
- For bacterial infections:
  - —For *oral* dosage form (capsules and oral suspension):
    - Adults, teenagers, and children weighing more than 40 kilograms (kg) (88 pounds)—125 to 250 milligrams (mg) every six hours.
    - Infants and children weighing up to 40 kg (88 pounds)—Dose is based on body weight and must be determined by your doctor. The usual

dose is 3.1 to 6.2 mg per kg (1.4 to 2.8 mg per pound) of body weight every six hours.

For flucloxacillin
- For bacterial infections:
  - —For *oral* dosage form (capsules and oral suspension):
    - Adults, teenagers, and children more than 12 years of age and weighing more than 40 kilograms (kg) (88 pounds)—250 to 500 milligrams (mg) every six hours.
    - Children less than 12 years of age and weighing up to 40 kg (88 pounds)—125 to 250 mg every six hours; or 6.25 to 12.5 mg per kg (2.8 to 5.7 mg per pound) of body weight every six hours.
    - Infants up to 6 months of age—Dose is based on body weight and must be determined by your doctor. The usual dose is 6.25 mg per kg (2.8 mg per pound) of body weight every six hours.

For methicillin
- For bacterial infections:
  - —For *injection* dosage form:
    - Adults, teenagers, and children weighing more than 40 kilograms (kg) (88 pounds)—1 gram injected into a muscle every four to six hours; or 1 gram injected into a vein every six hours.
    - Children weighing up to 40 kg (88 pounds)—Dose is based on body weight and must be determined by your doctor. The usual dose is 25 milligrams (mg) per kg (11.4 mg per pound) of body weight, injected into a vein or muscle every six hours.

For mezlocillin
- For bacterial infections:
  - —For *injection* dosage form:
    - Adults and teenagers—Dose is based on body weight and must be determined by your doctor. The usual dose is 33.3 to 87.5 milligrams (mg) per kilogram (kg) (15.1 to 39.8 mg per pound) of body weight, injected into a vein or muscle every four to six hours; or 3 to 4 grams every four to six hours.
    - Infants over 1 month of age and children up to 12 years of age—Dose is based on body weight and must be determined by your doctor. The usual dose is 50 mg per kg (22.7 mg per pound) of body weight, injected into a vein or muscle every four hours.

For nafcillin
- For bacterial infections:
  - —For *oral* dosage form (capsules and tablets):
    - Adults and teenagers—250 milligrams (mg) to 1 gram every four to six hours.
    - Older infants and children—Dose is based on body weight and must be determined by your doctor. The usual dose is 6.25 to 12.5 mg per kilogram (kg) (2.8 to 5.7 mg per pound) of body weight every six hours.
    - Newborns—Dose is based on body weight and must be determined by your doctor. The usual dose is 10 mg per kg (4.5 mg per pound) of body weight every six to eight hours.
  - —For *injection* dosage form:
    - Adults and teenagers—500 mg to 2 grams injected into a vein or muscle every four to six hours.
    - Infants and children—Dose is based on body weight and must be determined by your doctor.

The usual dose is 10 to 25 mg per kg (4.5 to 11.4 mg per pound) of body weight, injected into a muscle every twelve hours; or 10 to 40 mg per kg (4.5 to 18.2 mg per pound) of body weight, injected into a vein every four to eight hours.

For oxacillin
- For bacterial infections:
  —For *oral* dosage form (capsules and oral solution):
  - Adults, teenagers, and children weighing more than 40 kilograms (kg) (88 pounds)—500 milligrams (mg) to 1 gram every four to six hours.
  - Children weighing up to 40 kg (88 pounds)—Dose is based on body weight and must be determined by your doctor. The usual dose is 12.5 to 25 mg per kg (5.7 to 11.4 mg per pound) of body weight every six hours.
  —For *injection* dosage form:
  - Adults, teenagers, and children weighing more than 40 kg (88 pounds)—250 mg to 1 gram injected into a vein or muscle every four to six hours.
  - Children weighing up to 40 kg (88 pounds)—Dose is based on body weight and must be determined by your doctor. The usual dose is 12.5 to 25 mg per kg (5.7 to 11.4 mg per pound) of body weight, injected into a vein or muscle every four to six hours.
  - Premature infants and newborns—Dose is based on body weight and must be determined by your doctor. The usual dose is 6.25 mg per kg (2.8 mg per pound) of body weight, injected into a vein or muscle every six hours.

For penicillin G
- For bacterial infections:
  —For *oral* dosage form (oral solution, oral suspension, and tablets):
  - Adults and teenagers—200,000 to 500,000 Units (125 to 312 milligrams [mg]) every four to six hours.
  - Infants and children less than 12 years of age—Dose is based on body weight and must be determined by your doctor. The usual dose is 4167 to 30,000 Units per kilogram (kg) (189 to 13,636 Units per pound) of body weight every four to eight hours.
  —For *benzathine injection* dosage form:
  - Adults and teenagers—1,200,000 to 2,400,000 Units injected into a muscle as a single dose.
  - Infants and children—300,000 to 1,200,000 Units injected into a muscle as a single dose; or 50,000 Units per kg (22,727 Units per pound) of body weight injected into a muscle as a single dose.
  —For *injection* dosage forms (potassium and sodium salts):
  - Adults and teenagers—1,000,000 to 5,000,000 Units, injected into a vein or muscle every four to six hours.
  - Older infants and children—Dose is based on body weight and must be determined by your doctor. The usual dose is 8333 to 25,000 Units per kg (3788 to 11,363 Units per pound) of body weight, injected into a vein or muscle every four to six hours.
  - Premature infants and newborns—Dose is based on body weight and must be determined by your

doctor. The usual dose is 30,000 Units per kg (13,636 Units per pound) of body weight, injected into a vein or muscle every twelve hours.
  —For *procaine injection* dosage form:
  - Adults and teenagers—600,000 to 1,200,000 Units injected into a muscle once a day.
  - Children—Dose is based on body weight and must be determined by your doctor. The usual dose is 50,000 Units per kg (22,727 Units per pound) of body weight, injected into a muscle once a day.

For penicillin V
- For bacterial infections:
  —For the *benzathine salt oral* dosage form (oral solution):
  - Adults and teenagers—200,000 to 500,000 Units every six to eight hours.
  - Children—100,000 to 250,000 Units every six to eight hours.
  —For the *potassium salt oral* dosage forms (oral solution, oral suspension, and tablets):
  - Adults and teenagers—125 to 500 milligrams (mg) every six to eight hours.
  - Children—Dose is based on body weight and must be determined by your doctor. The usual dose is 2.5 to 16.7 mg per kilogram (kg) (1.1 to 7.6 mg per pound) of body weight every four to eight hours.

For piperacillin
- For bacterial infections:
  —For *injection* dosage form:
  - Adults and teenagers—3 to 4 grams, injected into a vein or muscle every four to six hours.
  - Infants and children—Dose must be determined by your doctor.

For pivampicillin
- For bacterial infections:
  —For *oral* dosage form (oral suspension):
  - Adults, teenagers, and children 10 years of age and older—525 to 1050 milligrams (mg) two times a day.
  - Children 7 to 10 years of age—350 mg two times a day.
  - Children 4 to 6 years of age—262.5 mg two times a day.
  - Children 1 to 3 years of age—175 mg two times a day.
  - Infants 3 to 12 months of age—Dose is based on body weight and must be determined by your doctor. The usual dose is 20 to 30 mg per kilogram (kg) (9.1 to 13.6 mg per pound) of body weight two times a day.
  —For *oral* dosage form (tablets):
  - Adults, teenagers, and children 10 years of age and older—500 mg to 1 gram two times a day.
  - Children up to 10 years of age—Dose must be determined by your doctor.

For pivmecillinam
- For bacterial infections:
  —For *oral* dosage form (tablets):
  - Adults, teenagers, and children weighing more than 40 kilograms (kg) (88 pounds)—200 milligrams (mg) two to four times a day for three days.

- Children up to 40 kg (88 pounds)—Dose must be determined by your doctor.

For ticarcillin
- For bacterial infections:
  —For *injection* dosage form:
    - Adults, teenagers, and children weighing more than 40 kilograms (kg) (88 pounds)—3 grams injected into a vein every four hours; or 4 grams injected into a vein every six hours.
    - Children up to 40 kg (88 pounds)—Dose is based on body weight and must be determined by your doctor. The usual dose is 33.3 to 75 milligrams (mg) per kg (15 to 34 mg per pound) of body weight, injected into a vein every four to six hours.

Missed dose—If you miss a dose of this medicine, take it as soon as possible. This will help to keep a constant amount of medicine in the blood or urine. However, if it is almost time for your next dose, skip the missed dose and go back to your regular dosing schedule. Do not double doses.

Storage—To store this medicine:
- Keep out of the reach of children.
- Store away from heat and direct light.
- Do not store the capsule or tablet form of penicillins in the bathroom, near the kitchen sink, or in other damp places. Heat or moisture may cause the medicine to break down.
- Store the oral liquid form of penicillins in the refrigerator because heat will cause this medicine to break down. However, keep the medicine from freezing. Follow the directions on the label.
- Do not keep outdated medicine or medicine no longer needed. Be sure that any discarded medicine is out of the reach of children.

Precautions While Using This Medicine

If your symptoms do not improve within a few days, or if they become worse, check with your doctor.

Penicillins may cause diarrhea in some patients.
- *Check with your doctor if severe diarrhea occurs.* Severe diarrhea may be a sign of a serious side effect. *Do not take any diarrhea medicine without first checking with your doctor.* Diarrhea medicines may make your diarrhea worse or make it last longer.
- For mild diarrhea, diarrhea medicine containing kaolin or attapulgite (e.g., Kaopectate tablets, Diasorb) may be taken. However, other kinds of diarrhea medicine should not be taken. They may make your diarrhea worse or make it last longer.
- If you have any questions about this or if mild diarrhea continues or gets worse, check with your health care professional.

Oral contraceptives (birth control pills) containing estrogen may not work properly if you take them while you are taking ampicillin, amoxicillin, or penicillin V. Unplanned pregnancies may occur. You should use a different or additional means of birth control while you are taking any of these penicillins. If you have any questions about this, check with your health care professional.

For *diabetic patients:*
- *Penicillins may cause false test results with some urine sugar tests.* Check with your doctor before changing your diet or the dosage of your diabetes medicine.

Before you have any medical tests, tell the doctor in charge that you are taking this medicine. The results of some tests may be affected by this medicine.

Side Effects of This Medicine

Along with its needed effects, a medicine may cause some unwanted effects. Although not all of these side effects may occur, if they do occur they may need medical attention.

Stop taking this medicine and get emergency help immediately if any of the following side effects occur:
  Less common
    Fast or irregular breathing; fever; joint pain; lightheadedness or fainting (sudden); puffiness or swelling around the face; red, scaly skin; shortness of breath; skin rash, hives, itching

In addition to the side effects mentioned above, *check with your doctor immediately* if any of the following side effects occur:
  Rare
    Abdominal or stomach cramps and pain (severe); abdominal tenderness; convulsions (seizures); decreased amount of urine; diarrhea (watery and severe), which may also be bloody; mental depression; nausea and vomiting; pain at place of injection; sore throat and fever; unusual bleeding or bruising; yellow eyes or skin
  Note: Some of the above side effects (severe abdominal or stomach cramps and pain, and watery and severe diarrhea, which may also be bloody) may also occur up to several weeks after you stop taking any of these medicines.

  Rare—For penicillin G procaine only
    Agitation or combativeness; anxiety; confusion; fear of impending death; feeling, hearing, or seeing things that are not real

Other side effects may occur that usually do not need medical attention. These side effects may go away during treatment as your body adjusts to the medicine. However, check with your doctor if any of the following side effects continue or are bothersome:
  More common
    Diarrhea (mild); headache; sore mouth or tongue; vaginal itching and discharge; white patches in the mouth and/or on the tongue

Other side effects not listed above may also occur in some patients. If you notice any other effects, check with your doctor.

Additional Information

Once a medicine has been approved for marketing for a certain use, experience may show that it is also useful for other medical problems. Although these uses are not included in product labeling, penicillins are used in certain patients with the following medical conditions:
- Chlamydia infections in pregnant women—Amoxicillin and ampicillin
- Gas gangrene—Penicillin G
- *Helicobacter pylori*-associated gastritis or peptic ulcer disease—Amoxicillin

- Leptospirosis—Ampicillin and penicillin G
- Lyme disease—Amoxicillin and penicillin V
- Typhoid fever—Amoxicillin and ampicillin

Other than the above information, there is no additional information relating to proper use, precautions, or side effects for these uses.

Revised: 06/11/99

PENICILLINS AND BETA-LACTAMASE INHIBITORS   Systemic

Commonly used brand name(s):

In the U.S.—
Augmentin[1]   Unasyn[2]
Timentin[4]   Zosyn[3]

In Canada—
Clavulin-250[1]   Clavulin-500F[1]
Clavulin-125F[1]   Tazocin[3]
Clavulin-250F[1]   Timentin[4]

Note: For quick reference, the following penicillins and beta-lactamase inhibitors are numbered to match the corresponding brand names.

This information applies to the following medicines:
1. Amoxicillin and Clavulanate (a-mox-i-SILL-in and klav-yoo-LAN-ate)
2. Ampicillin and Sulbactam (am-pi-SILL-in and sul-BAK-tam) †
3. Piperacillin and Tazobactam (pi-PER-a-sill-in and ta-zoe-BAK-tam)
4. Ticarcillin and Clavulanate (tye-kar-SILL-in and klav-yoo-LAN-ate)

†Not commercially available in Canada.

Description

Penicillins and beta-lactamase inhibitors are used to treat infections caused by bacteria. They work by killing the bacteria or preventing their growth. The beta-lactamase inhibitor is added to the penicillin to protect the penicillin from certain substances (enzymes) that will destroy the penicillin before it can kill the bacteria.

There are several different kinds of penicillins. Each is used to treat different kinds of infections. One kind of penicillin usually may not be used in place of another. In addition, penicillins are used to treat bacterial infections in many different parts of the body. They are sometimes given with other antibacterial medicines. Some of the penicillins may also be used for other problems as determined by your doctor. However, none of the penicillins will work for colds, flu, or other virus infections.

Penicillins are available only with your doctor's prescription, in the following dosage forms:

Oral
Amoxicillin and Clavulanate
- Oral suspension (U.S. and Canada)
- Tablets (U.S. and Canada)
- Chewable tablets (U.S.)

Parenteral
Ampicillin and Sulbactam
- Injection (U.S.)

Piperacillin and Tazobactam
- Injection (U.S. and Canada)
Ticarcillin and Clavulanate
- Injection (U.S. and Canada)

Before Using This Medicine

In deciding to use a medicine, the risks of taking the medicine must be weighed against the good it will do. This is a decision you and your doctor will make. For penicillins, the following should be considered:

Allergies—Tell your doctor if you have ever had any unusual or allergic reaction to any of the penicillins, cephalosporins, or beta-lactamase inhibitors. Also tell your health care professional if you are allergic to any other substances, such as foods, preservatives, or dyes.

Diet—Tell your doctor if you are on a low-sodium (low-salt) diet. Some of these medicines contain enough sodium to cause problems in some people.

Pregnancy—Penicillins and beta-lactamase inhibitors have not been studied in pregnant women. However, penicillins have not been shown to cause birth defects or other problems in animal studies.

Breast-feeding—Penicillins and sulbactam, a beta-lactamase inhibitor, pass into the breast milk. Even though only small amounts may pass into breast milk, allergic reactions, diarrhea, fungus infections, and skin rash may occur in nursing babies.

Children—Penicillins and beta-lactamase inhibitors have been used in children and, in effective doses, are not expected to cause different side effects or problems in children than they do in adults.

Some strengths of the chewable tablets and oral suspensions of amoxicillin and clavulanate combination contain aspartame, which is changed by the body to phenylalanine, a substance that is harmful to patients with phenylketonuria.

Older adults—Penicillins and beta-lactamase inhibitors have been used in the elderly and have not been shown to cause different side effects or problems in older people than they do in younger adults.

Other medicines—Although certain medicines should not be used together at all, in other cases two different medicines may be used together even if an interaction might occur. In these cases, your doctor may want to change the dose, or other precautions may be necessary. When you are taking a penicillin and beta-lactamase inhibitor combination, it is especially important that your health care professional know if you are taking any of the following:

- Anticoagulants (blood thinners) or
- Dipyridamole (e.g., Persantine) or
- Divalproex (e.g., Depakote) or
- Heparin (e.g., Panheprin) or
- Inflammation or pain medicine (except narcotics) or
- Pentoxifylline (e.g., Trental) or
- Plicamycin (e.g., Mithracin) or
- Sulfinpyrazone (e.g., Anturane) or
- Valproic acid (e.g., Depakene)—Use of these medicines with piperacillin and tazobactam combination or with ticarcillin and clavulanate combination may increase the chance of bleeding

- Oral contraceptives (birth control pills)—Use of penicillins and beta-lactamase inhibitors may prevent oral contraceptives from working properly, increasing the chance for pregnancy

- Probenecid (e.g., Benemid)—Probenecid causes penicillins, sulbactam, and tazobactam to build up in the blood. This may increase the chance of side effects. However, your doctor may want to give you probenecid with a penicillin and beta-lactamase inhibitor combination to treat some infections

Other medical problems—The presence of other medical problems may affect the use of penicillin and beta-lactamase inhibitor combinations. Make sure you tell your doctor if you have any other medical problems, especially:

- Allergies or a history of allergies, such as asthma, eczema, hay fever, or hives—Patients with a history of allergies may be more likely to have a severe allergic reaction to a penicillin and beta-lactamase inhibitor combination
- Bleeding problems, history of—Patients with a history of bleeding problems may be more likely to have bleeding when receiving piperacillin and tazobactam combination or ticarcillin and clavulanate combination
- Congestive heart failure (CHF) or
- High blood pressure—Large doses of ticarcillin and clavulanate combination may make these conditions worse, because this medicine contains a large amount of salt
- Cystic fibrosis—Patients with cystic fibrosis may have an increased chance of fever and skin rash when receiving piperacillin and tazobactam combination
- Kidney disease—Patients with kidney disease may have an increased chance of side effects
- Liver disease (active or a history of)—Penicillins and beta-lactamase inhibitor combinations may cause this condition to recur or become worse
- Mononucleosis ("mono")—Patients with mononucleosis may have an increased chance of skin rash when receiving ampicillin and sulbactam combination
- Phenylketonuria—Some strengths of the amoxicillin and clavulanate combination chewable tablets and oral suspension contain aspartame, which is changed by the body to phenylalanine.
- Stomach or intestinal disease, history of (especially colitis, including colitis caused by antibiotics)—Patients with a history of stomach or intestinal disease may be more likely to develop colitis while taking penicillins and beta-lactamase inhibitors

Proper Use of This Medicine

Amoxicillin and clavulanate combination may be taken on a full or empty stomach. Taking amoxicillin and clavulanate combination with food may decrease the chance of diarrhea, nausea, and vomiting.

For patients taking the *oral liquid form of amoxicillin and clavulanate combination:*

- Use a specially marked measuring spoon or other device to measure each dose accurately. The average household teaspoon may not hold the right amount of liquid.
- Do not use after the expiration date on the label. The medicine may not work properly after that date. If you have any questions about this, check with your pharmacist.

For patients taking the *chewable tablet form of amoxicillin and clavulanate combination:*

- Tablets should be chewed or crushed before they are swallowed.

To help clear up your infection completely, *keep taking this medicine for the full time of treatment*, even if you begin to feel better after a few days.

This medicine works best when there is a constant amount in the blood or urine. *To help keep the amount constant, do not miss any doses. Also, it is best to take the doses at evenly spaced times, day and night.* For example, if you are to take four doses a day, the doses should be spaced about 6 hours apart. If this interferes with your sleep or other daily activities, or if you need help in planning the best times to take your medicine, check with your health care professional.

Dosing—The dose of these medicines will be different for different patients. *Follow your doctor's orders or the directions on the label.* The following information includes only the average doses of these medicines. *If your dose is different, do not change it* unless your doctor tells you to do so.

The number of tablets or teaspoonfuls of suspension that you take depends on the strength of the medicine. Also, *the number of doses you take each day, the time allowed between doses, and the length of time you take the medicine depend on the medical problem for which you are taking a penicillin and beta-lactamase inhibitor combination.*

For amoxicillin and clavulanate combination

- For bacterial infections:
  —For *oral* dosage forms (chewable tablets and suspension):
  - Adults, teenagers, and children weighing more than 40 kilograms (kg) (88 pounds)—250 to 500 milligrams (mg) of amoxicillin, in combination with 125 mg of clavulanate, every eight hours or 500 to 875 mg of amoxicillin, in combination with 125 mg of clavulanate, every twelve hours.
  - Neonates and infants up to 12 weeks (3 months) of age—Dose is based on body weight and must be determined by your doctor. The usual dose is 15 mg of amoxicillin per kg (6.8 mg per pound) of body weight every twelve hours.
  - Infants 3 months of age and older and children weighing up to 40 kg (88 pounds)—6.7 to 22.5 mg of amoxicillin per kg (3 to 10.2 mg per pound) of body weight, in combination with 1.7 to 3.2 mg of clavulanate per kg (0.8 to 1.5 mg per pound) of body weight, every eight or twelve hours.
  —For *oral* dosage form (tablets):
  - Adults, teenagers, and children weighing more than 40 kg (88 pounds)—250 to 500 mg of amoxicillin, in combination with 125 mg of clavulanate, every eight hours or 500 to 875 mg of amoxicillin, in combination with 125 mg of clavulanate, every twelve hours.
  - Infants and children weighing up to 40 kg (88 pounds)—The amoxicillin and clavulanate combination tablets are too strong for children weighing less than 40 kg (88 pounds). The chewable tablets or oral suspension are used in these children.

For ampicillin and sulbactam combination
- For bacterial infections:
  —For *injection* dosage form:
    - Adults and teenagers—1 to 2 grams of ampicillin, in combination with 500 milligrams (mg) to 1 gram of sulbactam, injected into a vein or a muscle every six hours.
    - Children 1 to 12 years of age—Dose must be determined by your doctor.
    - Children up to 1 year of age—Use and dose must be determined by your doctor.

For piperacillin and tazobactam combination
- For bacterial infections:
  —For *injection* dosage form:
    - Adults and teenagers—3 to 4 grams of piperacillin, in combination with 0.375 to 0.5 grams of tazobactam, injected into a vein every six to eight hours for seven to ten days.
    - Children up to 12 years of age—Dose must be determined by your doctor.

For ticarcillin and clavulanate combination
- For bacterial infections:
  —For *injection* dosage form:
    - Adults and teenagers weighing 60 kilograms (kg) (132 pounds) or more—3 grams of ticarcillin, in combination with 100 milligrams (mg) of clavulanate, injected into a vein every four to six hours.
    - Adults and teenagers weighing less than 60 kg (132 pounds)—50 mg of ticarcillin per kg (22.7 mg per pound) of body weight, in combination with 1.7 mg of clavulanate per kg (0.8 mg per pound) of body weight, injected into a vein every four to six hours.
    - Infants and children 1 month to 12 years of age—50 mg of ticarcillin per kg (22.7 mg per pound) of body weight, in combination with 1.7 mg of clavulanate per kg (0.8 mg per pound) of body weight, injected into a vein every four to six hours.
    - Infants up to 1 month of age—Use and dose must be determined by your doctor.

Missed dose—If you miss a dose of this medicine, take it as soon as possible. This will help to keep a constant amount of medicine in the blood or urine. However, if it is almost time for your next dose, skip the missed dose and go back to your regular dosing schedule. Do not double doses.

Storage—To store this medicine:
- Keep out of the reach of children.
- Store away from heat and direct light.
- Do not store tablets in the bathroom, near the kitchen sink, or in other damp places. Heat or moisture may cause the medicine to break down.
- Store the oral liquid form of penicillins in the refrigerator because heat will cause this medicine to break down. However, keep the medicine from freezing. Follow the directions on the label.
- Do not keep outdated medicine or medicine no longer needed. Be sure that any discarded medicine is out of the reach of children.

Precautions While Using This Medicine

If your symptoms do not improve within a few days, or if they become worse, check with your doctor.

Penicillins may cause diarrhea in some patients.
- *Check with your doctor if severe diarrhea occurs.* Severe diarrhea may be a sign of a serious side effect. *Do not take any diarrhea medicine.* Diarrhea medicines may make your diarrhea worse or make it last longer.
- For mild diarrhea, diarrhea medicine containing kaolin or attapulgite (e.g., Kaopectate tablets, Diasorb) may be taken. However, other kinds of diarrhea medicine should not be taken. They may make your diarrhea worse or make it last longer.
- If you have any questions about this or if mild diarrhea continues or gets worse, check with your health care professional.

For *patients with diabetes:*
- *Penicillin and beta-lactamase inhibitor combinations may cause false test results with some urine sugar tests.* Check with your doctor before changing your diet or the dosage of your diabetes medicine.

Before you have any medical tests, tell the doctor in charge that you are taking this medicine. The results of some tests may be affected by this medicine.

Side Effects of This Medicine

Along with its needed effects, a medicine may cause some unwanted effects. Although not all of these side effects may occur, if they do occur they may need medical attention.

Stop taking this medicine and get emergency help immediately if any of the following side effects occur:
  Less common
    Cough; fast or irregular breathing; fever; joint pain; lightheadedness or fainting (sudden); pain, redness, or swelling at site of injection; puffiness or swelling around the face; red, irritated eyes; shortness of breath; skin rash, hives, itching; sore mouth or tongue; unusual tiredness or weakness; vaginal itching and discharge; white patches in mouth and/or on tongue

In addition to the side effects mentioned above, *check with your doctor immediately* if any of the following side effects occur:
  Rare
    Abdominal or stomach cramps and pain (severe); blistering, peeling, or loosening of skin and mucous membranes; chest pain; cloudy urine; convulsions (seizures); diarrhea (watery and severe), which may also be bloody; general feeling of illness or discomfort; nausea or vomiting; redness, soreness, or swelling of tongue; red skin lesions, often with a purple center; sore throat; swelling of face, fingers, lower legs, or feet; trouble in urinating; unusual bleeding or bruising; weight gain; yellow eyes or skin

  Note: Some of the above side effects (severe abdominal or stomach cramps and pain, and watery and severe diarrhea, which may also be bloody) may also occur up to several weeks after you stop taking any of these medicines.

Other side effects may occur that usually do not need medical attention. These side effects may go away during treatment as your body adjusts to the medicine. However, check with

your doctor if any of the following side effects continue or are bothersome:

More common
Diarrhea (mild); gas; headache; stomach pain; swelling of abdomen

Less common or rare
Chills; nosebleed; long-lasting muscle relaxation (with piperacillin and tazobactam combination); unusual tiredness or weakness

Other side effects not listed above may also occur in some patients. If you notice any other effects, check with your doctor.

Additional Information

Once a medicine has been approved for marketing for a certain use, experience may show that it is also useful for other medical problems. Although these uses are not included in product labeling, penicillins and beta-lactamase inhibitor combinations are used in certain patients with the following medical conditions:

Amoxicillin and clavulanate combination
• Bronchitis
• Chancroid

Ampicillin and sulbactam combination
• Gonorrhea

Ticarcillin and clavulanate combination
• Certain surgeries, such as colorectal surgery, abdominal hysterectomy, and high-risk cesarean section: This medicine is sometimes used to prevent infection from these surgical procedures.

Other than the above information, there is no additional information relating to proper use, precautions, or side effects for these uses.

Revised: 12/12/2000

PENTAMIDINE Systemic

Commonly used brand name(s):

In the U.S.—
Pentam 300
Generic name product may be available.

In Canada—
Pentacarinat

Description

Pentamidine (pen-TAM-i-deen) is used to treat *Pneumocystis carinii* (noo-moe-SISS-tis) pneumonia (PCP), a very serious kind of pneumonia. This kind of pneumonia occurs commonly in patients whose immune system is not working normally, such as cancer patients, transplant patients, and patients with acquired immune deficiency syndrome (AIDS). In addition, your doctor may prescribe pentamidine for some other medical problems caused by protozoa. This medicine may also be used for other conditions as determined by your doctor.

Pentamidine may cause some serious side effects. Before you begin treatment with pentamidine, you and your doctor should talk about the good this medicine will do as well as the risks of using it.

Pentamidine is to be administered only by or under the immediate supervision of your doctor. It is available in the following dosage form:

Parenteral
• Injection (U.S. and Canada)

Before Receiving This Medicine

In deciding to use a medicine, the risks of taking the medicine must be weighed against the good it will do. This is a decision you and your doctor will make. For pentamidine, the following should be considered:

Allergies—Tell your doctor if you have ever had any unusual or allergic reaction to pentamidine. Also tell your health care professional if you are allergic to any other substances, such as foods, preservatives, or dyes.

Diet—Make certain your health care professional knows if you are on a low-sodium, low-sugar, or any other special diet. Since most medicines contain more than their active ingredient, some products may have to be avoided.

Pregnancy—Pentamidine has not been studied in pregnant women. However, studies in rabbits have shown an increase in miscarriages and bone defects in the fetus.

Breast-feeding—It is not known whether pentamidine passes into breast milk. However, because of the risk of side effects in the newborn, breast-feeding is not recommended during treatment with this medicine.

Children—Although pentamidine has not been widely used in children, this medicine is not expected to cause different side effects or problems in children than it does in adults.

Older adults—Many medicines have not been studied specifically in older people. Therefore, it may not be known whether they work exactly the same way they do in younger adults or if they cause different side effects or problems in older people. There is no specific information comparing use of pentamidine in the elderly with use in other age groups.

Other medicines—Although certain medicines should not be used together at all, in other cases two different medicines may be used together even if an interaction might occur. In these cases, your doctor may want to change the dose, or other precautions may be necessary. When you are receiving pentamidine, it is especially important that your health care professional know if you are taking any of the following:

• Amphotericin B by injection (e.g., Fungizone) or
• Antithyroid agents (medicine for overactive thyroid) or
• Azathioprine (e.g., Imuran) or
• Chloramphenicol (e.g., Chloromycetin) or
• Colchicine or
• Cyclophosphamide (e.g., Cytoxan) or
• Flucytosine (e.g., Ancobon) or
• Ganciclovir (e.g., Cytovene) or
• Interferon (e.g., Intron A, Roferon-A) or
• Mercaptopurine (e.g., Purinethol) or
• X-ray treatment or
• Zidovudine (e.g., AZT, Retrovir) or
• If you have ever been treated with x-rays or cancer medicine—When taken with pentamidine, these medicines may increase the chance of damage to your blood cells

- Carmustine (e.g., BiCNU) or
- Cisplatin (e.g., Platinol) or
- Combination pain medicine containing acetaminophen and aspirin (e.g., Excedrin) or other salicylates (with large amounts taken regularly) or
- Cyclosporine (e.g., Sandimmune) or
- Deferoxamine (e.g., Desferal) (with long-term use) or
- Foscarnet (e.g., Foscavir) or
- Gold salts (medicine for arthritis) or
- Inflammation or pain medicine (except narcotics) or
- Lithium (e.g., Lithane) or
- Other anti-infectives by mouth or by injection (medicine for infection) or
- Penicillamine (e.g., Cuprimine) or
- Streptozocin (e.g., Zanosar) or
- Tiopronin (e.g., Thiola)—When taken with pentamidine, these medicines may increase the chance of kidney damage
- Didanosine (e.g., ddI, Videx)—When taken with pentamidine, didanosine may increase the chance of pancreatitis (inflammation of the pancreas)
- Methotrexate (e.g., Mexate) or
- Plicamycin (e.g., Mithracin)—When taken with pentamidine, these medicines may increase the chance of damage to your blood cells and your kidneys

Other medical problems— The presence of other medical problems may affect the use of pentamidine. Make sure you tell your doctor if you have any other medical problems, especially:

- Anemia or
- Bleeding disorders (history of) or
- Heart disease or
- Hypotension (low blood pressure) or
- Kidney disease or
- Liver disease—Pentamidine may make these conditions worse
- Diabetes mellitus (sugar diabetes) or
- Hypoglycemia (low blood sugar)—Pentamidine may increase or decrease blood sugar levels and may disturb control of sugar diabetes

Proper Use of This Medicine

To help clear up your infection completely, *pentamidine must be given for the full time of treatment*, even if you begin to feel better after a few days. Also, this medicine works best when there is a constant amount in the blood. To help keep the amount constant, pentamidine must be given on a regular schedule.

Dosing— The dose of pentamidine will be different for different patients. *Follow your doctor's orders or the directions on the label*. The following information includes only the average doses of pentamidine. *If your dose is different, do not change it* unless your doctor tells you to do so.

- For *injection* dosage form:
  - —For *Pneumocystis carinii* pneumonia (PCP):
    - Adults and children—Dose is based on body weight and must be determined by your doctor. The usual dose is 4 milligrams (mg) per kilogram (kg) (1.8 mg per pound) of body weight given once a day for fourteen to twenty-one days. This dose is injected slowly into a vein over a one- to two-hour period of time.

Precautions While Using This Medicine

Some patients may develop sudden, severe low blood pressure after a dose of pentamidine. Therefore, you should be lying down while you are receiving this medicine. Also, your doctor may want to check your blood pressure while you are receiving a pentamidine injection and several times after the dose has been given until your blood pressure is stable.

Pentamidine can lower the number of white blood cells in your blood, increasing the chance of your getting certain infections. It can also lower the number of platelets, which are necessary for proper blood clotting. If these problems occur, there are certain precautions you can take to reduce the risk of infection or bleeding:

- *Check with your doctor immediately* if you think you are getting a cold or any other infection.
- *Check with your doctor immediately* if you notice any unusual bleeding or bruising.
- Be careful when using regular toothbrushes, dental floss, or toothpicks. Your medical doctor, dentist, or nurse may recommend other ways to clean your teeth and gums. Check with your health care professional before having any dental work done.
- Avoid using a safety razor. Use an electric shaver instead. Also, be careful when using fingernail or toenail cutters.

Side Effects of This Medicine

Pentamidine may cause some serious side effects, including heart problems, low blood pressure, low or high blood sugar, and other blood problems. *You and your doctor should discuss the good this medicine will do as well as the risks of receiving it.*

Along with its needed effects, a medicine may cause some unwanted effects. Although not all of these side effects may occur, if they do occur they may need medical attention.

Check with your health care professional immediately if any of the following side effects occur:

More common
> Decrease in urination; sore throat and fever; unusual bleeding or bruising

Signs of diabetes mellitus or high blood sugar
> Drowsiness; flushed, dry skin; fruit-like breath odor; increased thirst; increased urination; loss of appetite

Signs of low blood sugar
> Anxiety; chills; cold sweats; cool, pale skin; headache; increased hunger; nausea; nervousness; shakiness

Signs of low blood pressure
> Blurred vision; confusion; dizziness; fainting or lightheadedness; unusual tiredness or weakness

Signs of diabetes mellitus or high blood sugar, or signs of low blood sugar may also occur up to several months after you stop receiving this medicine.

Less common
> Fast or irregular pulse; fever; nausea and vomiting; pain in upper abdomen; pain, redness, and/or hardness at place of injection; skin rash, redness, or itching

Other side effects may occur that usually do not need medical attention. These side effects may go away during treatment

as your body adjusts to the medicine. However, check with your doctor if any of the following side effects continue or are bothersome:

More common
Diarrhea; loss of appetite; nausea and vomiting

Stomach problems, such as nausea and vomiting, or loss of appetite, are common minor side effects seen in pentamidine treatment. However, if you have these problems, and at the same time have sharp pain in the upper abdomen, or an unusual decrease in the amount of urine, check with your doctor immediately.

Pentamidine may also cause an unpleasant metallic taste. This side effect is to be expected and does not require medical attention.

Other side effects not listed above may also occur in some patients. If you notice any other effects, check with your doctor.

Additional Information

Once a medicine has been approved for marketing for a certain use, experience may show that it is also useful for other medical problems. Although these uses are not included in product labeling, pentamidine is used in certain patients with the following medical conditions:

- Leishmaniasis, cutaneous
- Leishmaniasis, visceral (kala-azar)
- Trypanosomiasis, African (African sleeping sickness)

If you are living in or will be traveling to an area where there is a chance of getting kala-azar or African sleeping sickness, the following measures will help to prevent reinfection with either disease:

- If possible, sleep under fine-mesh netting to avoid being bitten by sandflies (which carry kala-azar) or tsetse flies (which carry African sleeping sickness).
- Wear long-sleeved shirts or blouses and long trousers to protect your arms and legs, especially at dusk or during evening hours when sandflies are out. Since tsetse flies can bite through thin clothing, it is best to wear clothing made from fairly heavy material to protect arms and legs.
- Apply insect repellant to uncovered areas of the skin when sandflies or tsetse flies are out.

Other than the above information, there is no additional information relating to proper use, precautions, or side effects for these uses.

Revised: 05/27/94
Interim revision: 04/24/95

PENTOXIFYLLINE   Systemic

Commonly used brand name(s):

In the U.S.—
Trental
Generic name product may be available.

In Canada—
Trental
Another commonly used name is oxypentifylline.

Description

Pentoxifylline (pen-tox-IF-i-lin) improves the flow of blood through blood vessels. It is used to reduce leg pain caused by poor blood circulation. Pentoxifylline makes it possible to walk farther before having to rest because of leg cramps.

Pentoxifylline is available only with your doctor's prescription, in the following dosage form:

Oral
- Extended-release tablets (U.S. and Canada)

Before Using This Medicine

In deciding to use a medicine, the risks of taking the medicine must be weighed against the good it will do. This is a decision you and your doctor will make. For pentoxifylline, the following should be considered:

Allergies—Tell your doctor if you have ever had any unusual or allergic reaction to pentoxifylline or to other xanthines such as aminophylline, caffeine, dyphylline, ethylenediamine (contained in aminophylline), oxtriphylline, theobromine, or theophylline. Also tell your health care professional if you are allergic to any other substances, such as foods, preservatives, or dyes.

Pregnancy—Pentoxifylline has not been studied in pregnant women. Studies in animals have not shown that it causes birth defects. However, at very high doses it has caused other harmful effects. Before taking this medicine, make sure your doctor knows if you are pregnant or if you may become pregnant.

Breast-feeding—Pentoxifylline passes into breast milk. The medicine has not been reported to cause problems in nursing babies. However, pentoxifylline has caused noncancerous tumors in animals when given for a long time in doses much larger than those used in humans. Therefore, your doctor may not want you to breast-feed while taking it. Be sure that you discuss the risks and benefits of this medicine with your doctor.

Children—Studies on this medicine have been done only in adult patients, and there is no specific information comparing use of pentoxifylline in children with use in other age groups.

Older adults—Side effects may be more likely to occur in the elderly, who are usually more sensitive than younger adults to the effects of pentoxifylline.

Other medicines—Although certain medicines should not be used together at all, in other cases two different medicines may be used together even if an interaction might occur. In these cases, your doctor may want to change the dose, or other precautions may be necessary. When you are taking pentoxifylline, it is important that your health care professional know if you are taking any other prescription or nonprescription (over-the-counter [OTC]) medicine, or if you smoke tobacco.

Other medical problems—The presence of other medical problems may affect the use of pentoxifylline. Make sure you tell your doctor if you have any other medical problems, especially:

- Any condition in which there is a risk of bleeding (e.g., recent stroke)—Pentoxifylline may make the condition worse
- Kidney disease or

• Liver disease—The chance of side effects may be increased

Proper Use of This Medicine

Swallow the tablet whole. Do not crush, break, or chew it before swallowing.

Pentoxifylline should be taken with meals to lessen the chance of stomach upset. Taking an antacid with the medicine may also help.

Dosing—The dose of pentoxifylline will be different for different patients. *Follow your doctor's orders or the directions on the label.* The following information includes only the average doses of pentoxifylline. *If your dose is different, do not change it* unless your doctor tells you to do so.

• For *oral* dosage form (extended-release tablets):
  —For peripheral vascular disease (circulation problems):
    • Adults—400 milligrams (mg) two to three times a day, taken with meals.
    • Children—Use must be determined by your doctor.

Missed dose—If you miss a dose of this medicine, take it as soon as possible. However, if it is almost time for your next dose, skip the missed dose and go back to your regular dosing schedule. Do not double doses.

Storage—To store this medicine:
• Keep out of the reach of children.
• Store away from heat and direct light.
• Do not store in the bathroom, near the kitchen sink, or in other damp places. Heat or moisture may cause the medicine to break down.
• Do not keep outdated medicine or medicine no longer needed. Be sure that any discarded medicine is out of the reach of children.

Precautions While Using This Medicine

It may take several weeks for this medicine to work. If you feel that pentoxifylline is not working, do not stop taking it on your own. Instead, check with your doctor.

Smoking tobacco may worsen your condition since nicotine may further narrow your blood vessels. Therefore, it is best to avoid smoking.

Side Effects of This Medicine

Along with its needed effects, a medicine may cause some unwanted effects. Although not all of these side effects may occur, if they do occur they may need medical attention.

Check with your doctor as soon as possible if any of the following side effects occur:
Rare
    Chest pain; irregular heartbeat
Signs and symptoms of overdose (in the order in which they may occur)
    Drowsiness; flushing; faintness; unusual excitement; convulsions (seizures)

Other side effects may occur that usually do not need medical attention. These side effects may go away during treatment as your body adjusts to the medicine. However, check with

your doctor if any of the following side effects continue or are bothersome:
Less common
    Dizziness; headache; nausea or vomiting; stomach discomfort

Other side effects not listed above may also occur in some patients. If you notice any other effects, check with your doctor.

Revised: 07/13/93
Interim revision: 08/05/97

PERGOLIDE   Systemic

Commonly used brand name(s):

In the U.S.—
    Permax
In Canada—
    Permax

Description

Pergolide (PER-go-lide) belongs to the group of medicines known as ergot alkaloids. It is used with levodopa or with carbidopa and levodopa combination to treat people who have Parkinson's disease. It works by stimulating certain parts of the central nervous system (CNS) that are involved in this disease.

Pergolide is available only with your doctor's prescription, in the following dosage form:
Oral
    • Tablets (U.S. and Canada)

Before Using This Medicine

In deciding to use a medicine, the risks of taking the medicine must be weighed against the good it will do. This is a decision you and your doctor will make. For pergolide, the following should be considered:

Allergies—Tell your doctor if you have ever had any unusual or allergic reaction to pergolide or other ergot medicines such as ergotamine. Also tell your health care professional if you are allergic to any other substances, such as foods, preservatives, or dyes.

Pregnancy—Studies have not been done in pregnant women. However, pergolide has not been shown to cause birth defects or other problems in animal studies.

Breast-feeding—This medicine may stop milk from being produced.

Children—Studies on this medicine have been done only in adult patients, and there is no specific information about its use in children.

Older adults—This medicine has been tested and has not been shown to cause different side effects or problems in older people than it does in younger adults.

Other medicines—Although certain medicines should not be used together at all, in other cases 2 different medicines may be used together even if an interaction might occur. In these cases, your doctor may want to change the dose, or other precautions may be necessary. When you are taking pergolide, it is especially important that your health care professional know if you are taking any other prescription or nonprescription (over-the-counter [OTC]) medicine.

Other medical problems—The presence of other medical problems may affect the use of pergolide. Make sure you tell your doctor if you have any other medical problems, especially:

- Heart disease or
- Mental problems (history of)—Pergolide may make the condition worse

Proper Use of This Medicine

If pergolide upsets your stomach, it may be taken with meals. If stomach upset continues, check with your doctor.

Dosing—The dose of pergolide will be different for different patients. *Follow your doctor's orders or the directions on the label.* The following information includes only the average doses of pergolide. *If your dose is different, do not change it* unless your doctor tells you to do so.

The number of tablets that you take depends on the strength of the medicine. Also, *the number of doses you take each day, the time allowed between doses, and the length of time you take the medicine depend on the medical problem for which you are taking pergolide.*

- For *oral* dosage form (tablets):
  - Adults: 50 micrograms a day for the first two days. The dose may be increased every three days as needed. However, the usual dose is not more than 5000 micrograms.

Missed dose—If you miss a dose of this medicine, take it as soon as you remember it. However, if it is almost time for your next dose, skip the missed dose and go back to your regular dosing schedule. Do not double doses.

Storage—To store this medicine:

- Keep out of the reach of children.
- Store away from heat and direct light.
- Do not store in the bathroom, near the kitchen sink, or in other damp places. Heat or moisture may cause the medicine to break down.
- Do not keep outdated medicine or medicine no longer needed. Be sure that any discarded medicine is out of the reach of children.

Precautions While Using This Medicine

It is important that your doctor check your progress at regular visits, to make sure that this medicine is working and to check for unwanted effects.

This medicine may cause some people to become drowsy, dizzy, or less alert than they are normally. *Make sure you know how you react to this medicine before you drive, use machines, or do anything else that could be dangerous if you are dizzy or are not alert.*

Dizziness, lightheadedness, or fainting may occur after the first doses of pergolide, especially when you get up from a lying or sitting position. Getting up slowly may help. Taking the first dose at bedtime or when you are able to lie down may also lessen problems. If the problem continues or gets worse, check with your doctor.

Pergolide may cause dryness of the mouth. For temporary relief, use sugarless candy or gum, melt bits of ice in your mouth, or use a saliva substitute. However, if your mouth continues to feel dry for more than 2 weeks, check with your medical doctor or dentist. Continuing dryness of the mouth may increase the chance of dental disease, including tooth decay, gum disease, and fungus infections.

It may take several weeks for pergolide to work. Do not stop taking this medicine or reduce the amount you are taking without first checking with your doctor.

Side Effects of This Medicine

Along with its needed effects, a medicine may cause some unwanted effects. Although not all of these side effects may occur, if they do occur they may need medical attention.

Check with your doctor immediately if any of the following side effects occur:
Rare
Chest pain (severe); convulsions (seizures); difficulty in breathing; fainting; fast heartbeat or irregular pulse; headache (severe or continuing); high fever; high or low (irregular) blood pressure; increased sweating; loss of bladder control; nausea and vomiting (continuing or severe); nervousness; severe muscle stiffness; sudden weakness; unexplained shortness of breath; unusual tiredness or weakness; unusually pale skin; vision changes, such as blurred vision or temporary blindness

Also, check with your doctor as soon as possible if any of the following side effects occur:
More common
Anxiety; bloody or cloudy urine; confusion; difficult or painful urination; frequent urge to urinate; hallucinations (seeing, hearing, or feeling things that are not there); uncontrolled movements of the body, such as the face, tongue, arms, hands, head, and upper body

Less common
Dizziness; headache; swelling in hands and legs
Rare
Abdominal pain or pressure; chills; cough; decreased flow of urine; fever; pain in side or lower back

Other side effects may occur that usually do not need medical attention. These side effects may go away during treatment as your body adjusts to the medicine. However, check with your doctor if any of the following side effects continue or are bothersome:
More common
Chest congestion; constipation; dizziness or lightheadedness, especially when getting up from a lying or sitting position; drowsiness; heartburn; lower back pain; muscle pain; nausea; runny or stuffy nose; trouble in sleeping; weakness

Less common
Diarrhea; dryness of mouth; loss of appetite; swelling of the face; vomiting

Other side effects not listed above may also occur in some patients. If you notice any other effects, check with your doctor.

Revised: 09/30/1999

PERMETHRIN   Topical

Commonly used brand name(s):

In the U.S.—
    Acticin Cream
    Elimite Cream
    Nix Cream Rinse

In Canada—
    Nix Cream Rinse

Description

Permethrin (per-METH-rin) 1% lotion is used to treat head lice infections. It acts by destroying both the lice and their eggs. The 5% cream is used to treat scabies infections by destroying the mites which cause scabies.

This medicine is available in the following dosage form:

Topical
- Cream (U.S.)
- Lotion (U.S. and Canada)

Before Using This Medicine

If you are using this medicine without a prescription, carefully read any precautions on the label. For topical permethrin, the following should be considered:

Allergies—Tell your doctor if you have ever had any unusual or allergic reaction to permethrin; to other synthetic pyrethroids, such as those found in household insecticides; to pyrethrins or chrysanthemums; or to veterinary insecticides containing permethrin. Also tell your health care professional if you are allergic to any other substances, such as preservatives or dyes.

Pregnancy—Permethrin has not been studied in pregnant women. However, this medication has not been shown to cause birth defects or other problems in animal studies.

Breast-feeding—It is not known whether permethrin passes into the breast milk. However, animal studies have shown that permethrin can cause tumors. Be sure you have discussed the risks and benefits of the medicine with your doctor.

Children—Studies on this medicine have been done only in adult patients, and there is no specific information comparing use of topical permethrin in children with use in other age groups.

Older adults—Many medicines have not been studied specifically in older people. Therefore, it may not be known whether they work exactly the same way they do in younger adults or if they cause different side effects or problems in older people. There is no specific information comparing use of topical permethrin in the elderly with use in other age groups.

Other medicines—Although certain medicines should not be used together at all, in other cases two different medicines may be used together even if an interaction might occur. In these cases, your doctor may want to change the dose, or other precautions may be necessary. Tell your health care professional if you are using any other prescription or nonprescription (over-the-counter [OTC]) medicine that is to be applied to the hair, scalp, or skin.

Other medical problems—The presence of other medical problems may affect the use of topical permethrin. Make sure you tell your doctor if you have other medical problems, especially:
- Severe inflammation of the scalp—Use of permethrin may make the condition worse

Proper Use of This Medicine

Keep this medicine away from the eyes. If you accidentally get some in your eyes, flush them thoroughly with water at once.

Permethrin lotion which is used to treat lice, comes in a container that holds only one treatment. Use as much of the medicine as you need and discard any remaining lotion properly.

For the treatment of head lice (1% lotion):

- Shampoo the hair and scalp using regular shampoo.
- Thoroughly rinse and towel dry the hair and scalp.
- Allow hair to air dry for a few minutes.
- Shake the permethrin lotion well before applying.
- Thoroughly wet the hair and scalp with the permethrin lotion. Be sure to cover the areas behind the ears and on the back of the neck also. Allow the lotion to remain in place for 10 minutes.
- Then, rinse the hair and scalp thoroughly and dry with a clean towel.
- When the hair is dry, you may want to comb the hair with a fine-toothed comb to remove any remaining nits (eggs) or nit shells.

Head lice can be easily transferred from one person to another by direct contact with clothing, hats, scarves, bedding, towels, washcloths, hairbrushes and combs, or hairs from infected persons. Therefore, *all members of your household should be examined for head lice and should receive treatment if they are found to be infected*. If you have any questions about this, check with your doctor.

For the treatment of scabies (5% cream):

- Read package directions carefully before using.
- Thoroughly wash and dry skin.
- Massage the cream into the skin from the head to the soles of the feet, paying special attention to creases in the skin, hands, feet, between fingers and toes, underarms, and groin.
- Scabies rarely infests the scalp of adults, although the hairline, neck, side of the head, and forehead may be infested in older people and in infants. Infants should be treated on the scalp, side of the head, and forehead.
- Leave the permethrin cream on the skin for 8 to 14 hours.
- Wash off by taking a shower or bath.
- Change into clean clothes.
- After treatment, itching may continue for up to 4 weeks.

Dosing—*Follow your doctor's orders or the directions on the label.* The following information includes only the average dose of permethrin. *If your dose is different, do not change it* unless your doctor tells you to do so.

- For *topical* dosage forms (cream and lotion):
  —For head lice:
  - Adults and children 2 years of age and older— Apply to the hair and scalp one time.
  - Children up to 2 years of age—Use and dose must be determined by your doctor.

  —For scabies:
  - Adults and children 2 months of age and older— Apply to the skin one time.

- Children up to 2 months of age—Use and dose must be determined by your doctor.

Storage—To store this medicine:
- Keep out of the reach of children.
- Store away from heat and direct light.
- Keep this medicine from freezing. Do not refrigerate.
- Do not keep outdated medicine or medicine no longer needed. Be sure that any discarded medicine is out of the reach of children.

Precautions While Using This Medicine

To prevent reinfection or spreading of the infection to other people, good health habits are required. These include the following:

- Machine wash all clothing (including hats, scarves, and coats), bedding, towels, and washcloths in very hot water and dry them by using the hot cycle of a dryer for at least 20 minutes. Clothing or bedding that cannot be washed should be dry cleaned or sealed in an airtight plastic bag for 2 weeks.
- Shampoo all wigs and hairpieces.
- Wash all hairbrushes and combs in very hot soapy water (above 130 °F) for 5 to 10 minutes and do not share them with other people.
- Clean the house or room by thoroughly vacuuming upholstered furniture, rugs, and floors.
- Wash all toys in very hot soapy water (above 130 °F) for 5 to 10 minutes or seal in an airtight plastic bag for 2 weeks. This is especially important for stuffed toys used on the bed.

Side Effects of This Medicine

Along with its needed effects, a medicine may cause some unwanted effects. Although not all of these side effects may occur, if they do occur they may need medical attention.

Check with your doctor if any of the following side effects continue or are bothersome:
Less common or rare
  Burning, itching, numbness, rash, redness, stinging, swelling, or tingling of the scalp

Other side effects not listed above may also occur in some patients. If you notice any other effects, check with your doctor.

Revised: 05/02/2000

PHENAZOPYRIDINE   Systemic

Commonly used brand name(s):

In the U.S.—

Azo-Standard	Pyridiate
Baridium	Pyridium
Eridium	Urodine
Geridium	Urogesic
Phenazodine	Viridium

Generic name product may be available.

In Canada—
Phenazo
Pyridium

Description

Phenazopyridine (fen-az-oh-PEER-i-deen) is used to relieve the pain, burning, and discomfort caused by infection or irritation of the urinary tract. It is not an antibiotic and will not cure the infection itself.

In the U.S., phenazopyridine is available only with your doctor's prescription. In Canada, it is available without a prescription. It is available in the following dosage form:

Oral
- Tablets (U.S. and Canada)

Before Using This Medicine

In deciding to use a medicine, the risks of taking the medicine must be weighed against the good it will do. This is a decision you and your doctor will make. For phenazopyridine, the following should be considered:

Allergies—Tell your doctor if you have ever had any unusual or allergic reaction to phenazopyridine. Also tell your health care professional if you are allergic to any other substances, such as foods, preservatives, or dyes.

Pregnancy—Phenazopyridine has not been studied in pregnant women. However, phenazopyridine has not been shown to cause birth defects in animal studies.

Breast-feeding—It is not known whether phenazopyridine passes into the breast milk. However, phenazopyridine has not been reported to cause problems in nursing babies.

Children—Although there is no specific information comparing use of phenazopyridine in children with use in other age groups, it is not expected to cause different side effects or problems in children than it does in adults.

Older adults—Many medicines have not been studied specifically in older people. Therefore, it may not be known whether they work exactly the same way they do in younger adults. Although there is no specific information comparing use of phenazopyridine in the elderly with use in other age groups, this medicine is not expected to cause different side effects or problems in older people than it does in younger adults.

Other medicines—Although certain medicines should not be used together at all, in other cases two different medicines may be used together even if an interaction might occur. In these cases, your doctor may want to change the dose, or other precautions may be necessary. Tell your health care professional if you are taking any other prescription or nonprescription (over-the-counter [OTC]) medicine.

Other medical problems—The presence of other medical problems may affect the use of phenazopyridine. Make sure you tell your doctor if you have any other medical problems, especially:
- Glucose-6-phosphate dehydrogenase (G6PD) deficiency or
- Hepatitis or
- Kidney disease—The chance of side effects may be increased.

Proper Use of This Medicine

This medicine is best taken with food or after eating a meal or a snack to lessen stomach upset.

Do not use any leftover medicine for future urinary tract problems without first checking with your doctor. An infection may require additional medicine.

Dosing—The dose of phenazopyridine will be different for different patients. *Follow your doctor's orders or the directions on the label.* The following information includes only the average doses of phenazopyridine. *If your dose is different, do not change it* unless your doctor tells you to do so.

- For *oral* dosage form (tablets):
  —For relieving pain, burning, and discomfort in the urinary tract:
  - Adults and teenagers—200 milligrams (mg) three times a day.
  - Children—The dose is based on body weight and must be determined by your doctor. The usual dose is 4 mg per kilogram (kg) (about 1.8 mg per pound) of body weight three times a day.

Missed dose—If you miss a dose of this medicine, take it as soon as you remember. However, if it is almost time for your next dose, skip the missed dose and go back to your regular dosing schedule. Do not double doses.

Storage—To store this medicine:
- Keep out of the reach of children.
- Store away from heat and direct light.
- Do not store this medicine in the bathroom, near the kitchen sink, or in other damp places. Heat or moisture may cause the medicine to break down.
- Do not keep outdated medicine or medicine no longer needed. Be sure that any discarded medicine is out of the reach of children.

Precautions While Using This Medicine

Check with your doctor if symptoms such as bloody urine, difficult or painful urination, frequent urge to urinate, or sudden decrease in the amount of urine appear or become worse while you are taking this medicine.

Phenazopyridine causes the urine to turn reddish orange. This is to be expected while you are using it. This effect is harmless and will go away after you stop taking the medicine. Also, the medicine may stain clothing.

For *patients who wear soft contact lenses:*
- It is best not to wear soft contact lenses while being treated with this medicine. Phenazopyridine may cause discoloration or staining of contact lenses. It may not be possible to remove the stain.

For *diabetic patients:*
- This medicine may cause false test results with urine sugar tests and urine ketone tests. If you have any questions about this, check with your health care professional, especially if your diabetes is not well controlled.

Before you have any medical tests, tell the person in charge that you are taking this medicine. The results of some tests may be affected by this medicine.

Side Effects of This Medicine

Along with its needed effects, a medicine may cause some unwanted effects. Although not all of these side effects may occur, if they do occur they may need medical attention.

Check with your doctor as soon as possible if any of the following side effects occur:
  Rare
    Blue or blue-purple color of skin; fever and confusion; shortness of breath, tightness in chest, wheezing, or troubled breathing; skin rash; sudden decrease in the amount of urine; swelling of face, fingers, feet, and/or lower legs; unusual tiredness or weakness; weight gain; yellow eyes or skin

Other side effects may occur that usually do not need medical attention. These side effects may go away during treatment as your body adjusts to the medicine. However, check with your doctor if any of the following side effects continue or are bothersome:
  Less common or rare
    Dizziness; headache; indigestion; itching of the skin; stomach cramps or pain

Other side effects not listed above may also occur in some patients. If you notice any other effects, check with your doctor.

Revised: 12/17/99

PHENOTHIAZINES   Systemic

Commonly used brand name(s):

In the U.S.—

Chlorpromazine Hydrochloride Intensol[1]	Prolixin Decanoate[2]
	Prolixin Enanthate[2]
Compazine[8]	Serentil[3]
Compazine Spansule[8]	Serentil Concentrate[3]
Mellaril[11]	Stelazine[12]
Mellaril Concentrate[11]	Stelazine Concentrate[12]
Mellaril-S[11]	Thorazine[1]
Permitil[2]	Thorazine Spansule[1]
Permitil Concentrate[2]	Trilafon[6]
Prolixin[2]	Trilafon Concentrate[6]
Prolixin Concentrate[2]	Vesprin[13]

In Canada—

Apo-Fluphenazine[2]	Novo-Trifluzine[12]
Apo-Perphenazine[6]	Novo-Ridazine[11]
Apo-Thioridazine[11]	Nozinan[4]
Apo-Trifluoperazine[12]	Nozinan Liquid[4]
Chlorpromanyl-20[1]	Nozinan Oral Drops[4]
Chlorpromanyl-40[1]	Nu-Prochlor[8]
Largactil[1]	Piportil L₄[7]
Largactil Liquid[1]	PMS Fluphenazine[2]
Largactil Oral Drops[1]	PMS Perphenazine[6]
Majeptil[10]	PMS Prochlorperazine[8]
Mellaril[11]	PMS Thioridazine[11]
Modecate[2]	PMS Trifluoperazine[12]
Modecate Concentrate[2]	Serentil[3]
Moditen Enanthate[2]	Stelazine[12]
Moditen HCl[2]	Stemetil[8]
Neuleptil[5]	Stemetil Liquid[8]
Novo-Chlorpromazine[1]	

Note: For quick reference, the following phenothiazines are numbered to match the corresponding brand names.

This information applies to the following medicines:
1. Chlorpromazine (klor-PROE-ma-zeen) ‡§
2. Fluphenazine (floo-FEN-a-zeen) ‡§
3. Mesoridazine (mez-oh-RID-a-zeen)
4. Methotrimeprazine (meth-oh-trye-MEP-ra-zeen) *

5. Pericyazine (pair-ee-SYE-a-zeen) *
6. Perphenazine (per-FEN-a-zeen) ‡§
7. Pipotiazine (pip-oh-TYE-a-zeen) *
8. Prochlorperazine (proe-klor-PAIR-a-zeen) ‡§
9. Promazine (PROE-ma-zeen) *§
10. Thioproperazine (thye-oh-proe-PAIR-a-zeen) *
11. Thioridazine (thye-oh-RID-a-zeen) ‡
12. Trifluoperazine (trye-floo-oh-PAIR-a-zeen) ‡§
13. Triflupromazine (trye-floo-PROE-ma-zeen) †

Note: This information does *not* apply to Ethopropazine, Promethazine, Propiomazine, and Trimeprazine.

---

*Not commercially available in the U.S.
†Not commercially available in Canada.
‡Generic name product may be available in the U.S.
§Generic name product may be available in Canada.

Description

Phenothiazines (FEE-noe-THYE-a-zeens) are used to treat serious mental and emotional disorders, including schizophrenia and other psychotic disorders. Some are used also to control agitation in certain patients, severe nausea and vomiting, severe hiccups, and moderate to severe pain in some hospitalized patients. Chlorpromazine is used also in the treatment of certain types of porphyria, and with other medicines in the treatment of tetanus. Phenothiazines may also be used for other conditions as determined by your doctor.

Phenothiazines may cause unwanted, unattractive, and uncontrolled face or body movements that may not go away when you stop taking the medicine. They may also cause other serious unwanted effects. You and your doctor should talk about the good this medicine will do as well as the risks of using it. Also, your doctor should look for early signs of these effects at regular visits. Your doctor may be able to stop or decrease some unwanted effects, if they do occur, by changing your dose or by making other changes in your treatment.

Phenothiazines are available only with your doctor's prescription in the following dosage forms:

Oral
Chlorpromazine
  • Extended-release capsules (U.S.)
  • Oral concentrate (U.S. and Canada)
  • Syrup (U.S. and Canada)
  • Tablets (U.S. and Canada)
Fluphenazine
  • Elixir (U.S. and Canada)
  • Oral solution (U.S.)
  • Tablets (U.S. and Canada)
Mesoridazine
  • Oral solution (U.S.)
  • Tablets (U.S. and Canada)
Methotrimeprazine
  • Oral solution (Canada)
  • Tablets (Canada)
Pericyazine
  • Capsules (Canada)
  • Oral solution (Canada)
Perphenazine
  • Oral solution (U.S. and Canada)
  • Tablets (U.S. and Canada)
Prochlorperazine
  • Extended-release capsules (U.S.)
  • Oral solution (U.S. and Canada)
  • Tablets (U.S. and Canada)
Thioproperazine
  • Tablets (Canada)
Thioridazine
  • Oral solution (U.S. and Canada)
  • Oral suspension (U.S. and Canada)
  • Tablets (U.S. and Canada)
Trifluoperazine
  • Syrup (U.S. and Canada)
  • Tablets (U.S. and Canada)
Parenteral
Chlorpromazine
  • Injection (U.S. and Canada)
Fluphenazine
  • Injection (U.S. and Canada)
Mesoridazine
  • Injection (U.S.)
Methotrimeprazine
  • Injection (Canada)
Perphenazine
  • Injection (U.S.)
Pipotiazine
  • Injection (Canada)
Prochlorperazine
  • Injection (U.S. and Canada)
Promazine
  • Injection (Canada)
Trifluoperazine
  • Injection (U.S.)
Triflupromazine
  • Injection (U.S.)
Rectal
Chlorpromazine
  • Suppositories (U.S. and Canada)
Prochlorperazine
  • Suppositories (U.S. and Canada)

Before Using This Medicine

In deciding to use a medicine, the risks of taking the medicine must be weighed against the good it will do. This is a decision you and your doctor will make. For phenothiazines, the following should be considered:

Allergies — Tell your doctor if you have ever had any unusual or allergic reaction to phenothiazines. Also tell your health care professional if you are allergic to any other substances, such as foods, preservatives, or dyes. Some of the phenothiazine dosage forms contain parabens, sulfites, or tartrazine.

Pregnancy — Although studies have not been done in pregnant women, some side effects, such as jaundice and movement disorders, have occurred in a few newborns whose mothers received phenothiazines during pregnancy. Studies in animals have shown that, when given to the mother during pregnancy, these medicines can decrease the number of successful pregnancies and cause problems with bone development in the offspring. Before taking this medicine, make sure your doctor knows if you are pregnant or if you may become pregnant.

Breast-feeding — Phenothiazines pass into breast milk and may cause drowsiness or unusual muscle movements in the nursing baby. It may be necessary for you to take a different medicine or to stop breast-feeding during treatment. Be sure you have discussed the risks and benefits of the medicine with your doctor.

Children—Certain side effects, such as muscle spasms of the face, neck, and back, tic-like or twitching movements, inability to move the eyes, twisting of the body, or weakness of the arms and legs, are more likely to occur in children, especially those with severe illness or dehydration. Children are usually more sensitive than adults to the effects of phenothiazines.

Older adults—Constipation, trouble urinating, dryness of mouth, confusion, problems with memory, dizziness or fainting, drowsiness, trembling of the hands and fingers, and problems with muscle movement, such as decreased or unusual movements, are especially likely to occur in elderly patients, who are usually more sensitive than younger adults to the effects of phenothiazines.

Other medicines—Although certain medicines should not be used together at all, in other cases two different medicines may be used together even if an interaction might occur. In these cases, your doctor may want to change the dose, or other precautions may be necessary. When you are taking phenothiazines, it is especially important that your health care professional know if you are taking any of the following:

- Amantadine (e.g., Symmetrel) or
- Antihypertensives (high blood pressure medicine) or
- Bromocriptine (e.g., Parlodel) or
- Deferoxamine (e.g., Desferal) or
- Diuretics (water pills) or
- Levobunolol (e.g., Betagan) or
- Medicine for heart disease or
- Metipranolol (e.g., OptiPranolol) or
- Nabilone (e.g., Cesamet) (with high doses) or
- Narcotic pain medicine or
- Pentamidine (e.g., Pentam)—Severe low blood pressure may occur

- Antidepressants (medicine for depression)—The risk of developing serious side effects, including severe constipation, low blood pressure, severe drowsiness, unusual body or facial movements, and changes in heart rhythm, may be increased

- Antipsychotics, other (medicine for mental illness) or
- Promethazine (e.g., Phenergan) or
- Trimeprazine (e.g., Temaril)—Severe low blood pressure or unusual body or facial movements may occur

- Antithyroid agents (medicine for overactive thyroid)—The risk of developing serious blood problems may be increased

- Astemizole (e.g., Hismanal) or
- Cisapride (e.g., Propulsid) or
- Disopyramide (e.g., Norpace) or
- Erythromycin (e.g., E.E.S., EryPed) or
- Probucol (e.g., Lorelco) or
- Procainamide (e.g., Procan SR) or
- Quinidine (e.g., Duraquin)—Serious changes in heart rhythm may occur

- Central nervous system (CNS) depressants (medicines that cause drowsiness)—Severe drowsiness and trouble in breathing may occur

- Epinephrine (e.g., Adrenalin)—Severe low blood pressure and fast heartbeat may occur

- Levodopa (e.g., Dopar)—Phenothiazines may prevent levodopa from working properly in the treatment of Parkinson's disease

- Lithium (e.g., Lithane, Lithizine, Lithobid)—Some unwanted effects, such as decreased or unusual body or facial movements, may be increased. The blood levels of the phenothiazine and/or lithium may be changed, so the medicines may not work properly. Your doctor may need to change your dose of either or both medicines

- Metoclopramide (e.g., Reglan) or
- Metyrosine (e.g., Demser) or
- Pemoline (e.g., Cylert) or
- Rauwolfia alkaloids (deserpidine [e.g., Harmonyl], rauwolfia serpentina [e.g., Raudixin], reserpine [e.g., Serpasil])—Taking these medicines with phenothiazines may increase the chance of having decreased or unusual body or facial movements or may make the movement problems worse

- Pimozide (e.g., Orap)—Serious changes in heart rhythm, severe low blood pressure, or unusual body or facial movements may occur

Other medical problems—The presence of other medical problems may affect the use of phenothiazines. Make sure you tell your doctor if you have any other medical problems, especially:

- Alcohol abuse—Certain unwanted effects, such as heatstroke and liver disease, may be more likely to occur

- Blood disease or
- Breast cancer or
- Difficult urination or
- Glaucoma or
- Heart or blood vessel disease or
- Parkinson's disease or
- Seizure disorders, or history of or
- Stomach ulcers—Phenothiazines may make the condition worse

- Brain damage or
- Blood vessel disease in the brain—Serious increase in body temperature may occur

- Enlarged prostate—Difficulty in urinating may occur or may become more severe

- Liver disease—Phenothiazines may make the condition worse. Higher blood levels of phenothiazines may occur, increasing the chance of having unwanted effects

- Lung disease—Difficulty in breathing may become more severe. Decrease in cough reflex caused by phenothiazines may increase the risk of developing complications, such as pneumonia

- Pheochromocytoma or
- Kidney disease—Severe low blood pressure may occur

- Reye's syndrome—The risk that the phenothiazine will have unwanted effects on the liver may be increased

Proper Use of This Medicine

For patients taking this medicine *by mouth:*

- This medicine may be taken with food or a full glass (8 ounces) of water or milk to reduce stomach irritation.
- *If your medicine comes in a dropper bottle*, measure each dose with the special dropper provided with your prescription and dilute it in a small glass (4 ounces) of orange or grapefruit juice or water just before taking it.

- If you are taking the *extended-release capsule form* of this medicine, each dose should be swallowed whole. *Do not break, crush, or chew before swallowing.*

For patients using the *suppository form* of this medicine:

- If the suppository is too soft to insert, chill it in the refrigerator for 30 minutes or run cold water over it before removing the foil wrapper.
- To insert the suppository: First remove the foil wrapper and moisten the suppository with cold water. Lie down on your side and use your finger to push the suppository well up into the rectum.

Do not take more or less of this medicine and do not take it more or less often than your doctor ordered. Not taking more than your doctor ordered is particularly important for children or elderly patients, since they may react very strongly to this medicine.

This medicine must be taken for several weeks before its full effect is reached when it is used to treat mental and emotional conditions.

Dosing—The dose of phenothiazines will be different for different patients. *Follow your doctor's orders or the directions on the label.* The following information includes only the average doses of phenothiazines. *If your dose is different, do not change it* unless your doctor tells you to do so.

The number of capsules, tablets, or teaspoonfuls of elixir, solution, suspension, or syrup that you take, or the number of injections you receive or suppositories that you use, depends on the strength of the medicine. Also, *the number of doses you use each day, the time allowed between doses, and the length of time you take the medicine depend on the medical problem for which you are taking phenothiazines.*

For chlorpromazine

- For *oral extended-release capsule* dosage form:
  —For mental or emotional disorders:
    - Adults—30 to 300 milligrams (mg) one to three times a day. Your doctor may increase your dose if needed.
    - Children—This dosage form is not recommended for use in children.
- For *oral concentrate, syrup, or tablet* dosage forms:
  —For mental or emotional disorders:
    - Adults and teenagers—At first, 10 to 25 mg two to four times a day. Your doctor may increase your dose if needed.
    - Children up to 6 months of age—Dose must be determined by your doctor.
    - Children 6 months to 12 years of age—Dose is based on body weight or size, and must be determined by your doctor. The usual dose is 0.55 mg per kilogram (kg) (0.25 mg per pound) of body weight, every four to six hours.
  —For nausea and vomiting:
    - Adults and teenagers—10 to 25 mg every four to six hours as needed.
    - Children up to 6 months of age—Dose must be determined by your doctor.
    - Children 6 months to 12 years of age—Dose is based on body weight or size, and must be determined by your doctor. The usual dose is 0.55 mg per kg (0.25 mg per pound) of body weight, every four to six hours.

—For sedation before surgery:
- Adults and teenagers—25 to 50 mg two to three hours before surgery.
- Children—Dose is based on body weight or size, and must be determined by your doctor. The usual dose is 0.55 mg per kg (0.25 mg per pound) of body weight, two to three hours before surgery.

—For treatment of hiccups:
- Adults and teenagers—25 to 50 mg three or four times a day. If hiccups remain after two to three days of oral treatment, treatment by injection may be needed.
- Children—Dose must be determined by your doctor.

—For porphyria:
- Adults and teenagers—25 to 50 mg three or four times a day.
- Children—Dose must be determined by your doctor.

- For *injection* dosage form:
  —For severe mental or emotional disorders:
    - Adults—At first, 25 to 50 mg, injected into a muscle. The dose may be repeated in one hour, and every three to twelve hours thereafter. Your doctor may increase your dose if needed.
    - Children up to 6 months of age—Dose must be determined by your doctor.
    - Children 6 months to 12 years of age—Dose is based on body weight or size and must be determined by your doctor. The usual dose is 0.55 mg per kg (0.25 mg per pound) of body weight, injected into a muscle every six to eight hours as needed.
  —For nausea and vomiting:
    - Adults—At first, 25 mg injected into a muscle. If needed, doses of 25 to 50 mg may be given every three to four hours.
    - Children up to 6 months of age—Dose must be determined by your doctor.
    - Children 6 months to 12 years of age—Dose is based on body weight or size and must be determined by your doctor. The usual dose is 0.55 mg per kg (0.25 mg per pound) of body weight, injected into a muscle every six to eight hours as needed.
  —For nausea and vomiting during surgery:
    - Adults—At first, 12.5 mg injected into a muscle. The dose may be repeated if needed. Or up to 25 mg may be diluted and injected slowly into a vein.
    - Children up to 6 months of age—Dose must be determined by your doctor.
    - Children 6 months to 12 years of age—Dose is based on body weight or size and must be determined by your doctor. The usual dose is 0.275 mg per kg (0.125 mg per pound) of body weight injected into a muscle or diluted and injected slowly into a vein.
  —For sedation before surgery:
    - Adults—12.5 to 25 mg, injected into a muscle one to two hours before surgery.
    - Children up to 6 months of age—Dose must be determined by your doctor.
    - Children 6 months to 12 years of age—Dose is based on body weight and must be determined by

your doctor. The usual dose is 0.55 mg per kg (0.25 mg per pound) of body weight, injected into a muscle one to two hours before surgery.

—For treatment of hiccups:

* Adults—25 to 50 mg, injected into a muscle three or four times a day. If hiccups remain after treatment by injection into muscle, 25 to 50 mg may be diluted and injected slowly into a vein.
* Children—Dose must be determined by your doctor.

—For porphyria:

* Adults—25 mg injected into a muscle every six to eight hours.
* Children—Dose must be determined by your doctor.

—For tetanus:

* Adults—25 to 50 mg, injected into a muscle three or four times a day. Or 25 to 50 mg, diluted and injected slowly into a vein. Your doctor may increase your dose if needed.
* Children up to 6 months of age—Dose must be determined by your doctor.
* Children 6 months to 12 years of age—Dose is based on body weight and must be determined by your doctor. The usual dose is 0.55 mg per kg (0.25 mg per pound) of body weight, injected into a muscle every six to eight hours or diluted and injected slowly into a vein.

* For *rectal* dosage form (suppositories):

—For nausea and vomiting:

* Adults and teenagers—50 to 100 mg, inserted into the rectum every six to eight hours as needed.
* Children up to 6 months of age—Dose must be determined by your doctor.
* Children 6 months to 12 years of age—Dose is based on body weight and must be determined by your doctor. The usual dose is 1 mg per kg (0.45 mg per pound) of body weight, inserted into the rectum every six to eight hours as needed.

For fluphenazine

* For *oral* dosage form (elixir, solution, or tablets):

—For mental or emotional disorders:

* Adults—At first, a total of 2.5 to 10 milligrams (mg) a day, taken in smaller doses every six to eight hours during the day. Your doctor may increase your dose if needed. However, the dose usually is not more than 20 mg a day.
* Children—0.25 to 0.75 mg one to four times a day.
* Older adults—1 to 2.5 mg a day. Your doctor may increase your dose if needed.

* For *long-acting decanoate injection* dosage form:

—For mental or emotional disorders:

* Adults—At first, 12.5 to 25 mg, injected into a muscle or under the skin every one to three weeks. Your doctor may increase your dose if needed. However, the dose usually is not more than 100 mg.
* Children 5 to 12 years of age—3.125 to 12.5 mg, injected into a muscle or under the skin every one to three weeks.
* Children 12 years of age and older—At first, 6.25 to 18.75 mg, injected into a muscle or under the skin once a week. Your doctor may increase your dose if needed. However, the dose usually is not more than 25 mg every one to three weeks.

* For *long-acting enanthate injection* dosage form:

—For mental or emotional disorders:

* Adults and teenagers—At first, 25 mg, injected into a muscle or under the skin every two weeks. Your doctor may adjust your dose if needed. However, the dose usually is not more than 100 mg.
* Children up to 12 years of age—Dose must be determined by your doctor.

* For *short-acting hydrochloride injection* dosage form:

—For mental or emotional disorders:

* Adults and teenagers—At first, 1.25 mg, injected into a muscle. Your doctor may repeat and increase your dose if needed. However, the dose usually is not more than 10 mg a day.
* Children up to 12 years of age—Dose must be determined by your doctor.
* Older adults—1 to 2.5 mg a day, injected into a muscle. Your doctor may increase your dose if needed.

For mesoridazine

* For *oral* dosage form (solution or tablets):

—For mental or emotional disorders:

* Adults and teenagers—A total of 30 to 150 milligrams (mg) a day, taken in smaller doses two or three times during the day.
* Children up to 12 years of age—Dose must be determined by your doctor.

* For *injection* dosage form:

—For mental or emotional disorders:

* Adults and teenagers—25 mg injected into a muscle. The dose may be repeated in thirty to sixty minutes if needed.
* Children up to 12 years of age—Dose must be determined by your doctor.

For methotrimeprazine

* For *oral* dosage form (solution or tablets):

—For mental or emotional disorders:

* Adults and teenagers—At first, a total of 50 to 75 milligrams (mg) a day, taken in smaller doses two or three times a day with meals. Your doctor may increase your dose if needed.
* Children—Dose is based on body weight and must be determined by your doctor. At first, the usual dose is a total of 0.25 mg per kilogram (kg) (0.11 mg per pound) of body weight a day, taken in smaller doses two or three times a day with meals. Your doctor may increase your dose if needed.

—For pain:

* Adults and teenagers—For moderate pain, at first a total of 6 to 25 mg a day, taken in smaller doses three times a day with meals. For severe pain, at first a total of 50 to 75 mg a day, taken in smaller doses two or three times a day with meals. Your doctor may increase your dose if needed.
* Children—Dose is based on body weight and must be determined by your doctor. At first, the usual dose is a total of 0.25 mg per kg (0.11 mg per pound) of body weight a day, taken in smaller doses two or three times a day with meals. Your doctor may increase your dose if needed. However, the dose usually is not more than 40 mg a day.

—For sedation:

* Adults and teenagers—At first, a total of 6 to 25 mg a day, taken in smaller doses three times a

day with meals. Your doctor may increase your dose if needed.
- Children—Dose is based on body weight and must be determined by your doctor. At first, the usual dose is a total of 0.25 mg per kg (0.11 mg per pound) of body weight a day, taken in smaller doses two or three times a day with meals. Your doctor may increase your dose if needed. However, the dose usually is not more than 40 mg a day.

- For *injection* dosage form:
—For mental or emotional disorders:
  - Adults and teenagers—At first, 10 to 20 mg, injected into a muscle every four to six hours. Your doctor may increase your dose if needed.
  - Children—Dose is based on body weight and must be determined by your doctor. The usual dose is a total of 0.062 to 0.125 mg per kg (0.028 to 0.057 mg per pound) of body weight a day, injected into a muscle in one dose or in a few smaller doses.
—For pain:
  - Adults and teenagers—At first, 2.5 to 20 mg, injected into a muscle. Your doctor may repeat or increase your dose if needed.
  - Children—Dose is based on body weight and must be determined by your doctor. The usual dose is a total of 0.062 to 0.125 mg per kg (0.028 to 0.057 mg per pound) of body weight a day, injected into a muscle in one dose or in a few smaller doses.
  - Older adults—At first, 5 to 10 mg injected into a muscle every four to six hours. Your doctor may increase your dose if needed.
—For sedation before surgery:
  - Adults and teenagers—2 to 20 mg, injected into a muscle forty-five minutes to three hours before surgery.
  - Children—Dose must be determined by your doctor.

For pericyazine
- For *oral* dosage form (capsules or solution):
—For mental or emotional disorders:
  - Adults—At first, 5 milligrams (mg) taken in the morning, and 10 mg taken in the evening. Your doctor may change your dose if needed. However, the dose usually is not more than 20 mg taken in the morning and 40 mg taken in the evening.
  - Children up to 5 years of age—Dose must be determined by your doctor.
  - Children 5 years of age and older—2.5 to 10 mg taken in the morning, and 5 to 30 mg taken in the evening.
  - Older adults—At first, 5 mg a day. Your doctor may increase your dose if needed. However, the dose usually is not more than 30 mg a day.

For perphenazine
- For *oral solution* dosage form:
—For mental or emotional disorders in hospitalized patients:
  - Adults and teenagers—8 to 16 milligrams (mg) two to four times a day.
  - Children up to 12 years of age—Dose must be determined by your doctor.

- For *oral tablet* dosage form:
—For mental or emotional disorders:
  - Adults and teenagers—4 to 16 mg two to four times a day.
  - Children up to 12 years of age—Dose must be determined by your doctor.
—For nausea and vomiting:
  - Adults and teenagers—A total of 8 to 16 mg a day, taken in smaller doses during the day. Your doctor will lower your dose as soon as possible.
  - Children up to 12 years of age—Dose must be determined by your doctor.

- For *injection* dosage form:
—For mental or emotional disorders:
  - Adults and teenagers—5 to 10 mg injected into a muscle every six hours.
  - Children up to 12 years of age—Dose must be determined by your doctor.
—For nausea and vomiting:
  - Adults and teenagers—At first, 5 to 10 mg injected into a muscle, or 5 mg diluted and injected slowly into a vein. Your doctor may adjust your dose if needed.
  - Children up to 12 years of age—Dose must be determined by your doctor.

For pipotiazine
- For *injection* dosage form:
—For mental or emotional disorders:
  - Adults and teenagers—At first, 50 to 100 milligrams (mg) injected into a muscle every two to three weeks. Your doctor may increase your dose if needed. However, the dose usually is not more than 150 mg every four weeks.
  - Children up to 12 years of age—Dose must be determined by your doctor.

For prochlorperazine
- For *oral extended-release capsule* dosage form:
—For mental or emotional disorders:
  - Adults and teenagers—Dose must be determined by your doctor.
  - Children—This dosage form is not recommended for use in children.
—For nausea and vomiting:
  - Adults and teenagers—At first, 15 mg taken once a day in the morning, or 10 mg taken every twelve hours. Your doctor may increase your dose if needed. However, the dose usually is not more than 40 mg a day.
  - Children—This dosage form is not recommended for use in children.

- For *oral* dosage form (solution or tablets):
—For mental or emotional disorders:
  - Adults and teenagers—At first, 5 to 10 milligrams (mg) three or four times a day. Your doctor may increase your dose if needed. However, the dose usually is not more than 150 mg a day.
  - Children up to 2 years of age—Dose must be determined by your doctor.
  - Children 2 to 12 years of age—2.5 mg two or three times a day. Your doctor may increase your dose if needed. However, for children 2 through 5 years of age, the dose usually is not more than 20 mg a day. For children 6 to 12 years of age, the dose usually is not more than 25 mg a day.

—For nausea and vomiting:
  - Adults and teenagers—5 to 10 mg three or four times a day.
  - Children—Dose is based on body weight and must be determined by your doctor. The usual dose is 2.5 mg taken one to three times a day.

- For *injection* dosage form:
  —For mental or emotional disorders:
  - Adults and teenagers—At first, 10 to 20 mg injected into a muscle. The dose may be repeated if needed. Later, the dose is usually 10 to 20 mg every four to six hours. However, the dose usually is not more than 200 mg a day.
  - Children up to 2 years of age—Dose must be determined by your doctor.
  - Children 2 to 12 years of age—Dose is based on body weight and must be determined by your doctor. The usual dose is 0.132 mg per kilogram (kg) (0.06 mg per pound) of body weight, injected into a muscle. However, the dose for children 2 through 5 years of age usually is not more than 20 mg a day. The dose for children 6 to 12 years of age usually is not more than 25 mg a day.
  —For nausea and vomiting:
  - Adults and teenagers—5 to 10 mg, injected into a muscle every three to four hours as needed. Or 2.5 to 10 mg injected slowly into a vein. The dose usually is not more than 40 mg a day.
  - Children up to 2 years of age—Dose must be determined by your doctor.
  - Children 2 to 12 years of age—Dose is based on body weight and must be determined by your doctor. The usual dose is 0.132 mg per kg (0.06 mg per pound) of body weight, injected into a muscle. However, the dose for children 2 through 5 years of age usually is not more than 20 mg a day. The dose for children 6 to 12 years of age usually is not more than 25 mg a day.
  —For nausea and vomiting in surgery:
  - Adults and teenagers—5 to 10 mg, injected into a muscle or injected slowly into a vein. The dose may be repeated if needed. However, the total dose usually is not more than 40 mg a day.
  - Children—Dose must be determined by your doctor.

- For *rectal* dosage form (suppositories):
  —For mental or emotional disorders:
  - Adults and teenagers—10 mg inserted into the rectum three or four times a day. Your doctor may increase your dose if needed.
  - Children 2 to 12 years of age—2.5 mg inserted into the rectum two or three times a day. Your doctor may increase your dose if needed. However, for children 2 through 5 years of age, the dose usually is not more than 20 mg a day. For children 6 to 12 years of age, the dose usually is not more than 25 mg a day.
  —For nausea and vomiting:
  - Adults and teenagers—25 mg inserted into the rectum two times a day.
  - Children up to 2 years of age—Dose must be determined by your doctor.
  - Children 2 to 12 years of age—Dose is based on body weight and must be determined by your doctor. The usual dose is 2.5 mg inserted into the rectum one to three times a day.

For promazine
- For *injection* dosage form:
  —For mental or emotional disorders:
  - Adults—At first, 50 to 150 mg, injected into a muscle or, in hospitalized patients, diluted and injected into a vein. Later, 10 to 200 mg, injected into a muscle every four to six hours.
  - Children up to 12 years of age—Dose must be determined by your doctor.
  - Children 12 years of age and older—10 to 25 mg, injected into a muscle, every four to six hours.

For thioproperazine
- For *oral* dosage form (tablets):
  —For mental or emotional disorders:
  - Adults and teenagers—At first, 5 milligrams (mg) a day. Your doctor may increase your dose if needed.
  - Children 3 through 10 years of age—Dose must be determined by your doctor.
  - Children 11 years of age and older—At first, a total of 1 to 3 mg a day taken all at one time in a single dose each day or divided and taken in smaller doses several times during the day. Your doctor may increase your dose if needed.

For thioridazine
- For *oral* dosage form (suspension, solution, or tablets):
  —For mental or emotional disorders:
  - Adults and teenagers—At first, 50 to 100 milligrams (mg) one to three times a day. Your doctor may adjust your dose if needed. However, the dose usually is not more than 800 mg a day.
  - Children up to 2 years of age—Dose must be determined by your doctor.
  - Children 2 to 12 years of age—At first, 10 to 25 mg two or three times a day. Your doctor may adjust your dose, if needed, based on body weight or size.

For trifluoperazine
- For *oral* dosage form (syrup or tablets):
  —For mental or emotional disorders:
  - Adults and teenagers—At first, 2 to 5 milligrams (mg) one or two times a day. Your doctor may increase your dose if needed. However, the dose usually is not more than 40 mg a day.
  - Children up to 6 years of age—Dose must be determined by your doctor.
  - Children 6 to 12 years of age—At first, 1 mg one or two times a day. Your doctor may increase your dose if needed.

- For *injection* dosage form:
  —For mental or emotional disorders:
  - Adults and teenagers—1 to 2 mg, injected into a muscle every four to six hours as needed. However, the dose usually is not more than 10 mg a day.
  - Children up to 6 years of age—Dose must be determined by your doctor.
  - Children 6 to 12 years of age—1 mg injected into a muscle one or two times a day.

For triflupromazine
- For *injection* dosage form:
  —For mental or emotional disorders:
  - Adults and teenagers—60 milligrams (mg) injected into a muscle as needed. However, the dose usually is not more than 150 mg a day.

- Children up to 2½ years of age—Dose must be determined by your doctor.
- Children 2½ years of age and older—Dose is based on body weight and must be determined by your doctor. The usual dose is 0.2 to 0.25 mg per kilogram (kg) (0.09 to 0.11 mg per pound) of body weight, injected into a muscle. However, the dose usually is not more than 10 mg a day.

—For nausea and vomiting:

- Adults and teenagers—5 to 15 mg injected into a muscle every four hours, as needed. However, the dose usually is not more than 60 mg a day injected into a muscle. Or 1 mg injected into a vein, the dose being repeated as needed. However, the dose usually is not more than 3 mg a day injected into a vein.
- Children up to 2½ years of age—Dose must be determined by your doctor.
- Children 2½ years of age and older—Dose is based on body weight and must be determined by your doctor. The usual dose is 0.2 to 0.25 mg per kg (0.09 to 0.11 mg per pound) of body weight, injected into a muscle. However, the dose usually is not more than 10 mg a day.

Missed dose—If you miss a dose of this medicine and your dosing schedule is:

- One dose a day—Take the missed dose as soon as possible. Then go back to your regular dosing schedule. However, if you do not remember the missed dose until the next day, skip it and go back to your regular dosing schedule. Do not double doses.
- More than one dose a day—If you remember within an hour or so of the missed dose, take it right away. However, if you do not remember until later, skip the missed dose and go back to your regular dosing schedule. Do not double doses.

If you have any questions about this, check with your doctor.

Storage—To store this medicine:

- Keep out of the reach of children.
- Store away from heat and direct light.
- Do not store the capsule or tablet form of this medicine in the bathroom, near the kitchen sink, or in other damp places. Heat or moisture may cause the medicine to break down.
- Keep the liquid form of this medicine from freezing.
- Do not keep outdated medicine or medicine no longer needed. Be sure that any discarded medicine is out of the reach of children.

Precautions While Using This Medicine

Your doctor should check your progress at regular visits, especially during the first few months of treatment with this medicine. This will allow your dosage to be changed if necessary to meet your needs.

Do not stop taking this medicine without first checking with your doctor. Your doctor may want you to reduce gradually the amount you are taking before stopping completely. This is to prevent side effects and to keep your condition from becoming worse.

Do not take this medicine within 2 hours of taking antacids or medicine for diarrhea. Taking these products too close together may make this medicine less effective.

This medicine will add to the effects of alcohol and other central nervous system (CNS) depressants (medicines that slow down the nervous system, possibly causing drowsiness). Some examples of CNS depressants are antihistamines or medicine for hay fever, other allergies, or colds; sedatives, tranquilizers, or sleeping medicine; prescription pain medicine or narcotics; barbiturates; medicine for seizures; muscle relaxants; or anesthetics, including some dental anesthetics. *Check with your doctor before taking any of the above while you are using this medicine.*

Before using any prescription or over-the-counter (OTC) medicine for colds or allergies, check with your doctor. These medicines may increase the chance of developing heatstroke or other unwanted effects, such as dizziness, dry mouth, blurred vision, and constipation, while you are taking a phenothiazine.

Before you have any medical tests, tell the medical doctor in charge that you are taking this medicine. The results of some tests (such as electrocardiogram [ECG or EKG] readings, the gonadorelin test, the metyrapone test, tests for phenylketonuria, and urine bilirubin tests) may be affected by this medicine.

Before having any kind of surgery, dental treatment, or emergency treatment, tell the medical doctor or dentist in charge that you are using this medicine. Taking phenothiazines together with medicines that are used during surgery, dental treatments, or emergency treatments may increase CNS depression or cause low blood pressure.

This medicine may cause some people to become drowsy or less alert than they are normally. Even if this medicine is taken only at bedtime, it may cause some people to feel drowsy or less alert on arising. *Make sure you know how you react to this medicine before you drive, use machines, or do anything else that could be dangerous if you are not alert.*

Phenothiazines may cause blurred vision, difficulty in reading, or other changes in vision, especially during the first few weeks of treatment. Do not drive, use machines, or do anything else that could be dangerous if you are not able to see well. *If the problem continues or gets worse, check with your doctor.*

Dizziness, lightheadedness, or fainting may occur, especially when you get up from a lying or sitting position. Getting up slowly may help. If the problem continues or gets worse, check with your doctor.

This medicine may make you sweat less, causing your body temperature to increase. *Use extra care not to become overheated during exercise or hot weather while you are taking this medicine,* since overheating may result in heatstroke. Also, hot baths or saunas may make you feel dizzy or faint while you are taking this medicine.

This medicine also may make you more sensitive to cold temperatures. Dress warmly during cold weather. Be careful during prolonged exposure to cold, such as in winter sports or swimming in cold water.

Phenothiazines may cause dryness of the mouth. For temporary relief, use sugarless candy or gum, melt bits of ice in your mouth, or use a saliva substitute. However, if your mouth continues to feel dry for more than 2 weeks, check with your medical doctor or dentist. Continuing dryness of the mouth may increase the chance of dental disease, including tooth decay, gum disease, and fungus infections.

Phenothiazines may cause your skin to be more sensitive to sunlight than it is normally. Exposure to sunlight, even for brief periods of time, may cause a skin rash, itching, redness or other discoloration of the skin, or a severe sunburn. When you begin taking this medicine:

- Stay out of direct sunlight, especially between the hours of 10:00 a.m. and 3:00 p.m., if possible.
- Wear protective clothing, including a hat. Also, wear sunglasses.
- Apply a sunblock product that has a skin protection factor (SPF) of at least 15. You may require a product with a higher SPF number, especially if you have a fair complexion. If you have any questions about this, check with your health care professional.
- Apply a sunblock lipstick that has an SPF of at least 15 to protect your lips.
- Do not use a sunlamp or tanning bed or booth.

If you have a severe reaction from the sun, check with your doctor.

Phenothiazines may cause your eyes to be more sensitive to sunlight than they are normally. Exposure to sunlight over a period of time (several months to years) may cause blurred vision, change in color vision, or difficulty in seeing at night. When you go out during the daylight hours, even on cloudy days, wear sunglasses that block ultraviolet (UV) light. Ordinary sunglasses may not protect your eyes. If you have any questions about the kind of sunglasses to wear, check with your medical doctor or eye doctor.

If you are taking a liquid form of this medicine, avoid getting it on your skin or clothing because it may cause a skin rash or other irritation.

If you are receiving this medicine by injection:

- The effects of the long-acting injection form of this medicine may last for 6 to 12 weeks. *The precautions and side effects information for this medicine applies during this time.*

Side Effects of This Medicine

Along with their needed effects, phenothiazines can sometimes cause serious unwanted effects. Tardive dyskinesia or tardive dystonia (muscle movement disorders) may occur and may not go away after you stop using the medicine. Signs of tardive dyskinesia or tardive dystonia include worm-like movements of the tongue, or other uncontrolled movements of the mouth, tongue, cheeks, jaw, body, arms, or legs. Another possible serious unwanted effect is the neuroleptic malignant syndrome (NMS). Signs and symptoms of NMS include severe muscle stiffness, fever, fast heartbeat, difficult breathing, increased sweating, and loss of bladder control. *You and your doctor should discuss the good this medicine will do as well as the risks of taking it.*

Stop taking this medicine and check with your doctor immediately if any of the following side effects occur:

Rare—Symptoms of neuroleptic malignant syndrome
    Confusion (severe) or coma; difficult or fast breathing; drooling; fast heartbeat; fever; high or low (irregular) blood pressure; increased sweating; loss of bladder control; muscle stiffness (severe); trembling or shaking; trouble in speaking or swallowing

Check with your doctor immediately if any of the following side effects occur:

More common
    Inability to move eyes; increased blinking or spasms of eyelid; lip smacking or puckering; muscle spasms of face, neck, body, arms, or legs causing unusual postures or unusual expressions on face; puffing of

cheeks; rapid or worm-like movements of tongue; sticking out of tongue; tic-like or twitching movements; trouble in breathing, speaking, or swallowing; uncontrolled chewing movements; uncontrolled movements of arms or legs; uncontrolled twisting movements of neck, trunk, arms, or legs

Rare
    Irregular or slow heart rate; recurrent fainting

Also, check with your doctor as soon as possible if any of the following side effects occur:

More common
    Blurred vision, change in color vision, or difficulty in seeing at night; fainting; loss of balance control; mask-like face; restlessness or need to keep moving; shuffling walk; stiffness of arms or legs; trembling and shaking of hands and fingers

Less common
    Difficulty in urinating; skin rash; sunburn (severe)

Rare
    Abdominal or stomach pains; aching muscles and joints; agitation, bizarre dreams, excitement, or trouble in sleeping; bleeding or bruising (unusual); chest pain; clumsiness; confusion (mild); constipation (severe); convulsions (seizures); dark urine; fever and chills; hair loss; headaches; hot, dry skin or lack of sweating; itchy skin (severe); muscle weakness; nausea, vomiting, or diarrhea; pain in joints; prolonged, painful, inappropriate erection of the penis; redness of hands; shivering; skin discoloration (tan or blue-gray); sore throat and fever; sores in mouth; unusual bleeding or bruising; unusual tiredness or weakness; yellow eyes or skin

Phenothiazines may cause your urine to be dark. In most cases, this is not a sign of a serious problem. However, if your urine does become dark, discuss it with your doctor.

Other side effects may occur that usually do not need medical attention. These side effects may go away during treatment as your body adjusts to the medicine. However, check with your doctor if any of the following side effects continue or are bothersome:

More common
    Constipation (mild); decreased sweating; dizziness; drowsiness; dryness of mouth; nasal congestion

Less common
    Changes in menstrual period; decreased sexual ability; increased sensitivity of eyes to light; rough or "fuzzy" tongue; secretion of milk (unusual); swelling or pain in breasts; watering of mouth; weight gain (unusual)

After you stop using this medicine, your body may need time to adjust. The length of time this takes depends on the amount of medicine you were using and how long you used it. During this time, check with your doctor if you notice dizziness, nausea and vomiting, stomach pain, trembling of the fingers and hands, or any of the following signs of tardive dyskinesia or tardive dystonia:

    Inability to move eyes; lip smacking or puckering; muscle spasms of face, neck, body, arms, or legs, causing unusual body positions or unusual expressions on face; puffing of cheeks; rapid or worm-like movements of tongue; sticking out of tongue; tic-like or twitching movements; trouble in breathing, speaking, or swallowing; uncontrolled chewing movements; uncontrolled twisting or other movements of neck, trunk, arms, or legs

Although not all of the side effects listed above have been reported for all of the phenothiazines, they have been reported for at least one of them. However, since all of the phenothiazines are very similar, any of the above side effects may occur with any of these medicines.

Other side effects not listed above may also occur in some patients. If you notice any other effects, check with your doctor.

Additional Information

Once a medicine has been approved for marketing for a certain use, experience may show that it also is useful for other medical problems. Although these uses are not included in product labeling, phenothiazines are used in certain patients with the following medical conditions:

- Chronic neurogenic pain (certain continuing pain conditions)
- Huntington's chorea (hereditary movement disorder)

Other than the above information, there is no additional information relating to proper use, precautions, or side effects for these uses.

Revised: 08/15/2000

PHENOXYBENZAMINE   Systemic

Commonly used brand name(s):

In the U.S.—
    Dibenzyline

Description

Phenoxybenzamine (fen-ox-ee-BEN-za-meen) belongs to the general class of medicines called antihypertensives. It is used to treat high blood pressure (hypertension) due to a disease called pheochromocytoma.

Phenoxybenzamine blocks the effects of certain chemicals in the body. When these chemicals are present in large amounts, they cause high blood pressure.

Phenoxybenzamine may also be used for other conditions as determined by your doctor.

Phenoxybenzamine is available only with your doctor's prescription, in the following dosage form:

Oral
- Capsules (U.S.)

Before Using This Medicine

In deciding to use a medicine, the risks of taking the medicine must be weighed against the good it will do. This is a decision you and your doctor will make. For phenoxybenzamine, the following should be considered:

Allergies—Tell your doctor if you have ever had any unusual or allergic reaction to phenoxybenzamine. Also, tell your health care professional if you are allergic to any other substances, such as foods, preservatives, or dyes.

Pregnancy—Phenoxybenzamine has not been studied in pregnant women or animals. Make sure your doctor knows if you are pregnant or if you may become pregnant before taking phenoxybenzamine.

Breast-feeding—It is not known whether phenoxybenzamine passes into breast milk. However, this medicine has not been reported to cause problems in nursing babies.

Children—Although there is no specific information about the use of phenoxybenzamine in children, it is not expected to cause different side effects or problems in children than it does in adults.

Older adults—Dizziness or lightheadedness may be more likely to occur in the elderly, who are more sensitive to the effects of phenoxybenzamine. In addition, phenoxybenzamine may reduce tolerance to cold temperatures in elderly patients.

Other medicines—Although certain medicines should not be used together at all, in other cases two different medicines may be used together even if an interaction might occur. In these cases, your doctor may want to change the dose, or other precautions may be necessary. Tell your health care professional if you are taking any other prescription or nonprescription (over-the-counter [OTC]) medicine.

Other medical problems—The presence of other medical problems may affect the use of phenoxybenzamine. Make sure you tell your doctor if you have any other medical problems, especially:

- Angina (chest pain) or
- Heart or blood vessel disease—Some kinds may be worsened by phenoxybenzamine
- Kidney disease—Effects may be increased
- Lung infection—Symptoms such as stuffy nose may be worsened
- Recent heart attack or stroke—Lowering blood pressure may make problems resulting from stroke or heart attack worse

Proper Use of This Medicine

To help you remember to take your medicine, try to get into the habit of taking it at the same time each day.

Dosing—The dose of phenoxybenzamine will be different for different patients. *Follow your doctor's orders or the directions on the label*. The following information includes only the average doses of phenoxybenzamine. *If your dose is different, do not change it* unless your doctor tells you to do so.

- For *oral* dosage form (capsules):
    —For high blood pressure caused by pheochromocytoma:
    - Adults—At first, 10 milligrams (mg) two times a day. Then, your doctor may increase your dose to 20 to 40 mg two or three times a day.
    - Children—Dose is based on body weight and must be determined by your doctor. The usual starting dose is 0.2 mg per kilogram (kg) (0.09 mg per pound) of body weight taken once a day. Then, your doctor may increase your dose to 0.4 to 1.2 mg per kg (0.18 to 0.55 mg per pound) of body weight a day. This is divided into three or four doses.

Missed dose—If you miss a dose of this medicine, take it as soon as you remember. However, if it is almost time for

your next dose, skip the missed dose and go back to your regular dosing schedule. Do not double doses.

Storage—To store this medicine:

- Keep out of the reach of children.
- Store away from heat and direct light.
- Do not store in the bathroom, near the kitchen sink, or in other damp places. Heat or moisture may cause the medicine to break down.
- Do not keep outdated medicine or medicine no longer needed. Be sure that any discarded medicine is out of the reach of children.

Precautions While Using This Medicine

It is important that your doctor check your progress at regular visits to make sure that this medicine is working properly and to check for unwanted effects.

Do not take other medicines unless they have been discussed with your doctor. This especially includes over-the-counter (nonprescription) medicines for appetite control, asthma, colds, cough, hay fever, or sinus problems, since they may interfere with the effects of this medicine.

Phenoxybenzamine may cause some people to become dizzy, drowsy, or less alert than they are normally. This is more likely to happen when you begin to take it or when you increase the amount of medicine you are taking. *Make sure you know how you react to this medicine before you drive, use machines, or do anything else that could be dangerous if you are dizzy or not alert.*

Dizziness, lightheadedness, or fainting may occur, especially when you get up from a lying or sitting position. Getting up slowly may help, but if the problem continues or gets worse, check with your doctor.

The dizziness, lightheadedness, or fainting is also more likely to occur if you drink alcohol, stand for a long time, exercise, or if the weather is hot. *While you are taking this medicine, be careful in the amount of alcohol you drink. Also, use extra care during exercise or hot weather or if you must stand for a long time.*

Before having any kind of surgery (including dental surgery) or emergency treatment, *tell the medical doctor or dentist in charge that you are using this medicine.*

Phenoxybenzamine may cause dryness of the mouth, nose, and throat. For temporary relief of mouth dryness, use sugarless candy or gum, melt bits of ice in your mouth, or use a saliva substitute. However, if dry mouth continues for more than 2 weeks, check with your medical doctor or dentist. Continuing dryness of the mouth may increase the chance of dental disease, including tooth decay, gum disease, and fungus infections.

Side Effects of This Medicine

In rats and mice, phenoxybenzamine has been found to increase the risk of development of malignant tumors. It is not known if phenoxybenzamine increases the chance of tumors in humans.

Along with its needed effects, a medicine may cause some unwanted effects. The following side effects may go away as your body adjusts to the medicine. However, check with your doctor if any of these effects continue or are bothersome:

More common
   Dizziness or lightheadedness, especially when getting

up from a lying or sitting position; fast heartbeat; pinpoint pupils; stuffy nose

Less common
   Confusion; drowsiness; dryness of mouth; headache; lack of energy; sexual problems in males; unusual tiredness or weakness

Other side effects not listed above may also occur in some patients. If you notice any other effects, check with your doctor.

Additional Information

Once a medicine has been approved for marketing for a certain use, experience may show that it is also useful for other medical problems. Although this use is not included in product labeling, phenoxybenzamine is used in certain patients with the following medical condition:

- Benign prostatic hypertrophy

Other than the above information, there is no additional information relating to proper use, precautions, or side effects for this use.

Revised: 09/20/92
Interim revision: 07/20/94

PHENYLEPHRINE   Nasal

Commonly used brand name(s):

In the U.S.—

Alconefrin Nasal Drops 12	Neo-Synephrine Nasal Spray
Alconefrin Nasal Drops 25	Neo-Synephrine Pediatric
Alconefrin Nasal Drops 50	Nasal Drops
Alconefrin Nasal Spray 25	Nostril Spray Pump
Doktors	Nostril Spray Pump Mild
Duration	Rhinall
Neo-Synephrine Nasal Drops	Vicks Sinex
Neo-Synephrine Nasal Jelly	

Generic name product may be available.

In Canada—
Neo-Synephrine Nasal Drops
Neo-Synephrine Nasal Spray

Description

Phenylephrine (fen-ill-EF-rin) is used for the temporary relief of congestion or stuffiness in the nose caused by hay fever or other allergies, colds, or sinus trouble. It may also be used in ear infections to relieve congestion.

This medicine may also be used for other conditions as determined by your doctor.

This medicine is available without a prescription; however, your doctor may have special instructions on the proper use or dose for your medical condition.

Phenylephrine is available in the following dosage forms:

Nasal
- Nasal jelly (U.S.)
- Nasal drops (U.S. and Canada)
- Nasal spray (U.S. and Canada)

Before Using This Medicine

If you are using this medicine without a prescription, carefully read and follow any precautions on the label. For nasal phenylephrine, the following should be considered:

Allergies—Tell your doctor if you have ever had any unusual or allergic reaction to phenylephrine or to any other nasal decongestant. Also tell your health care professional if you are allergic to any other substances, such as foods, preservatives, or dyes.

Pregnancy—Nasal phenylephrine may be absorbed into the body. However, nasal phenylephrine has not been shown to cause birth defects or other problems in humans.

Breast-feeding—Nasal phenylephrine may be absorbed into the body. However, it is not known whether phenylephrine passes into the breast milk. This medicine has not been reported to cause problems in nursing babies.

Children—Children may be especially sensitive to the effects of nasal phenylephrine. This may increase the chance of side effects during treatment.

Older adults—Many medicines have not been studied specifically in older people. Therefore, it may not be known whether they work exactly the same way they do in younger adults or if they cause different side effects or problems in older people. There is no specific information comparing use of nasal phenylephrine in the elderly with use in other age groups.

Other medicines—Although certain medicines should not be used together at all, in other cases two different medicines may be used together even if an interaction might occur. In these cases, your doctor may want to change the dose, or other precautions may be necessary. Tell your health care professional if you are using any other prescription or nonprescription (over-the-counter [OTC]) medicine.

Other medical problems—The presence of other medical problems may affect the use of nasal phenylephrine. Make sure you tell your doctor if you have any other medical problems, especially:
- Diabetes mellitus (sugar diabetes) or
- Heart or blood vessel disease or
- High blood pressure or
- Overactive thyroid—Nasal phenylephrine may make the condition worse

Proper Use of This Medicine

To use the *nose drops:*
- Blow your nose gently. Tilt the head back while standing or sitting up, or lie down on a bed and hang head over the side. Place the drops into each nostril and keep the head tilted back for a few minutes to allow the medicine to spread throughout the nose.
- Rinse the dropper with hot water and dry with a clean tissue. Replace the cap right after use.
- To avoid spreading the infection, do not use the container for more than one person.

To use the *nose spray:*
- Blow your nose gently. With the head upright, spray the medicine into each nostril. Sniff briskly while squeezing the bottle quickly and firmly. For best results, spray once or twice into each nostril and wait 3 to 5 minutes to allow the medicine to work. Then, blow your nose gently and thoroughly. Repeat until the complete dose is used.
- Rinse the tip of the spray bottle with hot water, taking care not to suck water into the bottle, and dry with a clean tissue. Replace the cap right after use.
- To avoid spreading the infection, do not use the container for more than one person.

To use the *nose jelly:*
- Blow your nose gently. Wash your hands before applying the medicine. With your finger, place a small amount of jelly (about the size of a pea) up each nostril. Sniff it well back into the nose.
- Wipe the tip of the tube with a clean, damp tissue and replace the cap right after use.

Use this medicine only as directed. Do not use more of it, do not use it more often, and do not use it for longer than 3 days without first checking with your doctor. To do so may make your runny or stuffy nose worse and may also increase the chance of side effects.

Dosing—The dose of nasal phenylephrine will be different for different patients. *Follow your doctor's orders or the directions on the label.* The following information includes only the average doses of nasal phenylephrine. *If your dose is different, do not change it* unless your doctor tells you to do so.
- For stuffy nose:
  —For *nose jelly* dosage form:
  - Adults—Use a small amount in the nose every three or four hours as needed.
  - Children—Use is not recommended.
  —For *nose drops* dosage form:
  - Adults and children 12 years of age and older—Use two or three drops of a 0.25 to 0.5% solution in the nose every four hours as needed.
  - Children 6 to 12 years of age—Use two or three drops of a 0.25% solution in the nose every four hours as needed.
  - Children 2 to 6 years of age—Use two or three drops of a 0.125 or 0.16% solution in the nose every four hours as needed.
  - Children up to 2 years of age—Use and dose must be determined by your doctor.
  —For *nose spray* dosage form:
  - Adults and children 12 years of age and older—Use two or three sprays of a 0.25 to 0.5% solution in the nose every four hours as needed.
  - Children 6 to 12 years of age—Use two or three sprays of a 0.25% solution in the nose every four hours as needed.
  - Children up to 6 years of age—Use and dose must be determined by your doctor.

Missed dose—If you are using this medicine on a regular schedule and you miss a dose, use it right away if you remember within an hour or so of the missed dose. However, if you do not remember until later, skip the missed dose and go back to your regular dosing schedule. Do not double doses.

Storage—To store this medicine:
- Keep out of the reach of children.
- Store away from heat and direct light.
- Keep the medicine from freezing.
- Do not keep outdated medicine or medicine no longer needed. Be sure that any discarded medicine is out of the reach of children.

Side Effects of This Medicine

Along with its needed effects, a medicine may cause some unwanted effects. Although not all of these side effects may occur, if they do occur they may need medical attention.

When this medicine is used for short periods of time at low doses, side effects usually are rare. However, check with your doctor as soon as possible if any of the following occur:

Increase in runny or stuffy nose

Symptoms of too much medicine being absorbed into the body

Fast, irregular, or pounding heartbeat; headache or dizziness; increased sweating; nervousness; paleness; trembling; trouble in sleeping

Note: The above side effects are more likely to occur in children because there is a greater chance that too much of this medicine may be absorbed into the body.

Other side effects may occur that usually do not need medical attention. These side effects may go away during treatment as your body adjusts to the medicine. However, check with your health care professional if any of the following side effects continue or are bothersome:

Burning, dryness, or stinging of inside of nose

Other side effects not listed above may also occur in some patients. If you notice any other effects, check with your health care professional.

Revised: 05/16/94

PHENYLPROPANOLAMINE
Systemic†

Commonly used brand name(s):

In the U.S.—

Acutrim 16 Hour	Propagest
Acutrim Late Day	Thinz Back to Nature
Acutrim II Maximum Strength	Thinz-Span
Dexatrim Caffeine-Free	Unitrol Diet Plan Maximum
Extended Duration	Strength
Dexatrim Caffeine-Free	
Maximum Strength Caplets	

Generic name product may be available.

Another commonly used name is PPA

Note: In November 2000, the Food and Drug Administration (FDA) issued a public health warning regarding phenylpropanolamine (PPA) due to the risk of hemorrhagic stroke. The FDA, supported by results of a research program, requested that manufacturers voluntarily discontinue marketing products that contain PPA and that consumers work with their healthcare providers to select alternative products.

†Not commercially available in Canada.

Description

Phenylpropanolamine (fen-ill-proe-pa-NOLE-a-meen), commonly known as PPA, is used as a nasal decongestant or as an appetite suppressant. It acts on many different parts of the body. PPA produces effects that may be helpful or harmful. This depends on a patient's individual condition and response and the amount of medicine taken.

Phenylpropanolamine clears nasal congestion (stuffy nose) by narrowing or constricting the blood vessels. However, this same action may cause an increase in blood pressure in patients who have hypertension (high blood pressure).

Phenylpropanolamine also decreases appetite. However, the way PPA and similar medicines do this is unclear. Stimulation of the central nervous system (CNS) may be a major reason. Phenylpropanolamine in combination with dieting, exercise, and changes in eating habits can help obese patients lose weight. However, this appetite-reducing effect is only temporary, and is useful only for the first few weeks of dieting until new eating habits are established.

Phenylpropanolamine has caused serious side effects (even death) when too much was taken.

There are a number of products on the market that contain only phenylpropanolamine. Other products contain PPA along with added ingredients. The information that follows is for PPA alone. There may be additional information for the combination products. Read the label of the product you are using. If you have questions or if you want more information about the other ingredients, check with your health care professional.

Some preparations containing PPA are available only with your doctor's prescription. Others are available without a prescription; however, your doctor may have special instructions on the proper use of this medicine.

Phenylpropanolamine is available in the following dosage forms:

Oral
- Capsules (U.S.)
- Extended-release capsules (U.S.)
- Tablets (U.S.)
- Extended-release tablets (U.S.)

Before Using This Medicine

If you are taking this medicine without a prescription, carefully read and follow any precautions on the label. For phenylpropanolamine, the following should be considered:

Allergies—Tell your doctor if you have ever had any unusual or allergic reaction to phenylpropanolamine or to amphetamine, dextroamphetamine, ephedrine, epinephrine, isoproterenol, metaproterenol, methamphetamine, norepinephrine, phenylephrine, pseudoephedrine, or terbutaline. Also tell your health care professional if you are allergic to any other substances, such as foods, preservatives, or dyes.

Pregnancy—Phenylpropanolamine has not been shown to cause birth defects in humans. However, women who take phenylpropanolamine in the weeks following delivery may be more likely to suffer mental or mood changes.

Breast-feeding—Phenylpropanolamine has not been reported to cause problems in nursing babies.

Children—Mental changes may be more likely to occur in young children taking phenylpropanolamine than in adults. Phenylpropanolamine should not be used for weight control in children under the age of 12 years. Children 12 to 18 years old should not take phenylpropanolamine for weight control unless its use is ordered and supervised by a doctor.

Older adults—Many medicines have not been studied specifically in older people. Therefore, it may not be known whether they work exactly the same way they do in younger adults or if they cause different side effects or problems in older people. There is no specific information comparing use of phenylpropanolamine in the elderly with use in other age groups.

Other medicines—Although certain medicines should not be used together at all, in other cases two different medicines may be used together even if an interaction might occur. In these cases, your doctor may want to change the dose, or other precautions may be necessary. When you are taking phenylpropanolamine, it is especially important that your health care professional know if you are taking any of the following:
- Amantadine (e.g., Symmetrel) or
- Amphetamines or
- Caffeine (e.g., NoDoz) or
- Chlophedianol (e.g., Ulone) or
- Cocaine or
- Medicine for asthma or other breathing problems or
- Methylphenidate (e.g., Ritalin) or
- Nabilone (e.g., Cesamet) or
- Other appetite suppressants (diet pills) or
- Other medicine for colds, sinus problems, or hay fever or other allergies (including nose drops or sprays) or
- Pemoline (e.g., Cylert)—Using these medicines while taking phenylpropanolamine may cause severe nervousness, irritability, trouble in sleeping, or possibly irregular heartbeat or seizures
- Beta-adrenergic blocking agents (acebutolol [e.g., Sectral], atenolol [e.g., Tenormin], betaxolol [e.g., Kerlone], carteolol [e.g., Cartrol], labetalol [e.g., Normodyne], metoprolol [e.g., Lopressor], nadolol [e.g., Corgard], oxprenolol [e.g., Trasicor], penbutolol [e.g., Levatol], pindolol [e.g., Visken], propranolol [e.g., Inderal], sotalol [e.g., Sotacor], timolol [e.g., Blocadren])—Taking these medicines with phenylpropanolamine may cause serious high blood pressure (hypertension) and other effects on the heart ·
- Digitalis glycosides (heart medicine)—Changes in the rhythm of your heart may occur
- Monoamine oxidase (MAO) inhibitors (furazolidone [e.g., Furoxone], phenelzine [e.g., Nardil], procarbazine [e.g., Matulane], selegiline [e.g., Eldepryl], tranylcypromine [e.g., Parnate])—Taking phenylpropanolamine while you are taking or within 2 weeks of taking MAO inhibitors may cause sudden high body temperature, extremely high blood pressure, and severe convulsions; at least 14 days should be allowed between stopping treatment with one medicine and starting treatment with the other
- Rauwolfia alkaloids (alseroxylon [e.g., Rauwiloid], deserpidine [e.g., Harmonyl], rauwolfia serpentina [e.g., Raudixin], reserpine [e.g., Serpasil])—Phenylpropanolamine may not work properly when taken with rauwolfia alkaloids

Other medical problems—The presence of other medical problems may affect the use of phenylpropanolamine. Make sure you tell your doctor if you have any other medical problems, especially:
- Diabetes mellitus (sugar diabetes)—Use of phenylpropanolamine may cause an increase in blood glucose levels

- Enlarged prostate or
- Glaucoma or
- High blood pressure—Use of phenylpropanolamine may make the condition worse
- Heart disease or blood vessel disease (including a history of heart attack or stroke) or
- Overactive thyroid—Serious effects on the heart may occur
- Mental illness, history of—Use of phenylpropanolamine may cause the mental illness to return

Proper Use of This Medicine

For patients taking an *extended-release form* of this medicine:
- Swallow the capsule or tablet whole. Do not crush, break, or chew before swallowing.
- Take with a full glass (at least 8 ounces) of water.
- If taking only one dose of this medicine a day, take it in the morning around 10 a.m.

Take phenylpropanolamine (PPA) only as directed. Do not take more of it, do not take it more often, and do not take it for a longer time than directed. To do so may increase the chance of side effects.

For patients taking this medicine *as an appetite suppressant:*
- *Do not take this medicine for longer than a few weeks without your doctor's permission.*

If PPA causes trouble in sleeping, take the last dose for each day a few hours before bedtime.

Dosing—The dose of phenylpropanolamine will be different for different patients. *Follow your doctor's orders or the directions on the label.* The following information includes only the average doses of phenylpropanolamine. *If your dose is different, do not change it* unless your doctor tells you to do so.

The number of capsules or tablets that you take depends on the strength of the medicine. Also, *the number of doses you take each day, the time allowed between doses, and the length of time you take the medicine depend on the medical problem for which you are taking phenylpropanolamine.*
- For appetite control:
  —For *oral* dosage forms (capsules and tablets):
    - Adults—25 mg three times a day. Do not take more than 75 mg in twenty-four hours.
    - Children 12 to 18 years of age—Use and dose must be determined by your doctor.
    - Children up to 12 years of age—Use is not recommended.
  —For *long-acting* dosage forms (extended-release capsules and tablets):
    - Adults—75 mg taken once a day in the morning around 10 a.m.
    - Children 12 to 18 years of age—Use and dose must be determined by your doctor.
    - Children up to 12 years of age—Use is not recommended.
- For stuffy nose:
  —For *oral* dosage forms (capsules and tablets):
    - Adults and children 12 to 18 years of age—25 mg every four hours as needed. Do not take more than 150 mg in twenty-four hours.

- Children 6 to 12 years of age—12.5 mg every four hours as needed. Do not take more than 75 mg in twenty-four hours.
- Children 2 to 6 years of age—6.25 mg every four hours as needed. Do not take more than 37.5 mg in twenty-four hours.
- Children up to 2 years of age—Use and dose must be determined by your doctor.

—For *long-acting* dosage forms (extended-release capsules and tablets):

- Adults—75 mg every twelve hours.
- Children—Use and dose must be determined by your doctor.

Missed dose—For patients taking phenylpropanolamine *for nasal congestion:* If you miss a dose, take it as soon as possible. However, if it is within 2 hours (or 12 hours for extended-release forms) of your next dose, skip the missed dose and go back to your regular dosing schedule. Do not double doses.

Storage—To store this medicine

- Keep out of the reach of children.
- Store away from heat and direct light.
- Do not store in the bathroom, near the kitchen sink, or in other damp places. Heat or moisture may cause the medicine to break down.
- Do not keep outdated medicine or medicine no longer needed. Be sure that any discarded medicine is out of the reach of children.

Precautions While Using This Medicine

Do not drink large amounts of caffeine-containing beverages, such as coffee, tea, or colas while you are taking this medicine. To do so may cause unwanted effects.

This medicine may cause some people to become dizzy. *Make sure you know how you react to this medicine before you drive, use machines, or do anything else that could be dangerous if you are dizzy or not alert.*

For patients taking this medicine *for nasal congestion:*

- *If cold symptoms do not improve within 7 days or if you also have a high fever, check with your doctor. These signs may mean that you have other medical problems.*

Side Effects of This Medicine

Along with its needed effects, a medicine may cause some unwanted effects. Although not all of these side effects may occur, if they do occur they may need medical attention.

Check with your doctor as soon as possible if any of the following side effects occur:
Rare
   Headache (severe); increased blood pressure; painful or difficult urination; tightness in chest
Early symptoms of overdose
   Abdominal or stomach pain; fast, pounding, or irregular heartbeat; headache (severe); increased sweating not caused by exercise; nausea and vomiting (severe); nervousness (severe); restlessness (severe)
Late symptoms of overdose
   Confusion; convulsions (seizures); fast breathing; fast and irregular pulse; hallucinations (seeing, hearing,

or feeling things that are not there); hostile behavior; muscle trembling

Other side effects may occur that usually do not need medical attention. These side effects may go away during treatment as your body adjusts to the medicine. However, check with your doctor if any of the following side effects continue or are bothersome:
Less common—more common with high doses
   Dizziness; dryness of nose or mouth; false sense of well-being; headache (mild); nausea (mild); nervousness (mild); restlessness (mild); trouble in sleeping

Other side effects not listed above may also occur in some patients. If you notice any other effects, check with your doctor.

Additional Information

Once a medicine has been approved for marketing for a certain use, experience may show that it is also useful for other medical problems. Although this use is not included in product labeling, phenylpropanolamine is used in certain patients with the following medical condition:

- Urinary stress incontinence (loss of bladder control when you cough, sneeze, or laugh)

Other than the above information, there is no additional information relating to proper use, precautions, or side effects for this use.

Revised: 12/12/2000

PHOSPHATES   Systemic

Commonly used brand name(s):

In the U.S.—

K-Phos M. F.[2]
K-Phos Neutral[2]
K-Phos No. 2[2]
K-Phos Original[1]

Neutra-Phos[2]
Neutra-Phos-K[1]
Uro-KP-Neutral[2]

In Canada—
Uro-KP-Neutral[2]

Note: For quick reference, the following phosphates are numbered to match the corresponding brand names.

This information applies to the following medicines:
1. Potassium Phosphates (poe-TASS-ee-um FOS-fates) ‡§
2. Potassium and Sodium Phosphates (poe-TASS-ee-um and SOE-dee-um FOS-fates) ‡§
3. Sodium Phosphates (SOE-dee-um FOS-fates) †‡

†Not commercially available in Canada.
‡Generic name product may be available in the U.S.
§Generic name product may be available in Canada.

Description

Phosphates are used as dietary supplements for patients who are unable to get enough phosphorus in their regular diet, usually because of certain illnesses or diseases. Phosphate is the drug form (salt) of phosphorus. Some phosphates are used to make the urine more acid, which helps treat certain urinary tract infections. Some phosphates are used to prevent the formation of calcium stones in the urinary tract.

Injectable phosphates are to be administered only by or under the supervision of your health care professional. Some of these oral preparations are available only with a prescription. Others are available without a prescription; however, your health care professional may have special instructions on the proper dose of this medicine for your medical condition. You should take phosphates only under the supervision of your health care professional.

Phosphates are available in the following dosage forms:

Oral
Potassium Phosphates
- Capsules for solution (U.S.)
- Powder for solution (U.S.)
- Tablets for solution (U.S.)

Potassium and Sodium Phosphates
- Capsules for solution (U.S.)
- Powder for solution (U.S.)
- Tablets for solution (U.S. and Canada)

Parenteral
Potassium Phosphates
- Injection (U.S. and Canada)

Sodium Phosphates
- Injection (U.S.)

Importance of Diet

For good health, it is important that you eat a balanced and varied diet. Follow carefully any diet program your health care professional may recommend. For your specific dietary vitamin and/or mineral needs, ask your health care professional for a list of appropriate foods. If you think that you are not getting enough vitamins and/or minerals in your diet, you may choose to take a dietary supplement.

The best dietary sources of phosphorus include dairy products, meat, poultry, fish, and cereal products.

The daily amount of phosphorus needed is defined in several different ways.

For U.S.—
- Recommended Dietary Allowances (RDAs) are the amount of vitamins and minerals needed to provide for adequate nutrition in most healthy persons. RDAs for a given nutrient may vary depending on a person's age, sex, and physical condition (e.g., pregnancy).
- Daily Values (DVs) are used on food and dietary supplement labels to indicate the percent of the recommended daily amount of each nutrient that a serving provides. DV replaces the previous designation of United States Recommended Daily Allowances (USRDAs).

For Canada—
- Recommended Nutrient Intakes (RNIs) are used to determine the amounts of vitamins, minerals, and protein needed to provide adequate nutrition and lessen the risk of chronic disease.

Normal daily recommended intakes for phosphorus are generally defined as follows:

Persons	U.S. (mg)	Canada (mg)
Infants and children		
Birth to 3 years of age	300–800	150–350
4 to 6 years of age	800	400
7 to 10 years of age	800	500–800
Adolescent and adult males	800–1200	700–1000
Adolescent and adult females	800–1200	800–850
Pregnant females	1200	1050
Breast-feeding females	1200	1050

Before Using This Medicine

In deciding to use a medicine, the risks of taking the medicine must be weighed against the good it will do. This is a decision you and your health care professional will make. For phosphates the following should be considered:

Allergies—Tell your health care professional if you have ever had any unusual or allergic reaction to potassium, sodium, or phosphates. Also, tell your health care professional if you are allergic to any other substances, such as foods, preservatives, or dyes.

Pregnancy—It is especially important that you are receiving enough vitamins and minerals when you become pregnant and that you continue to receive the right amount of vitamins and minerals throughout your pregnancy. The healthy growth and development of the fetus depend on a steady supply of nutrients from the mother. However, taking large amounts of a dietary supplement in pregnancy may be harmful to the mother and/or fetus and should be avoided.

Breast-feeding—It is especially important that you receive the right amount of vitamins and minerals so that your baby will also get the vitamins and minerals needed to grow properly. However, taking large amounts of a dietary supplement while breast-feeding may be harmful to the mother and/or baby and should be avoided.

Children—Problems in children have not been reported with intake of normal daily recommended amounts. However, use of enemas that contain phosphates in children has resulted in high blood levels of phosphorus.

Older adults—Problems in older adults have not been reported with intake of normal daily recommended amounts.

Other medicines—Although certain medicines should not be used together at all, in other cases two different medicines may be used together even if an interaction might occur. In these cases, your health care professional may want to change the dose, or other precautions may be necessary. When you are taking phosphates, it is especially important that your health care professional know if you are taking any of the following:

- Amiloride (e.g., Midamor) or
- Angiotensin-converting enzyme (ACE) inhibitors (benazepril [e.g., Lotensin], captopril [e.g., Capoten], enalapril [e.g., Vasotec], fosinopril [e.g., Monopril], lisinopril [e.g., Zestril, Prinivil], quinapril [e.g., Accupril], ramipril [e.g., Altace]) or
- Cyclosporine or
- Digitalis glycosides (heart medicine) or
- Heparin (e.g., Panheprin), with long-term use, or
- Medicine for inflammation or pain (except narcotics) or
- Other potassium-containing medicine or
- Salt substitutes, low-salt foods, or milk or

- Spironolactone (e.g., Aldactone) or
- Triamterene (e.g., Dyrenium)—Use with potassium-containing phosphates may increase the risk of hyperkalemia (too much potassium in the blood), possibly leading to serious side effects

- Antacids—Use with phosphates may prevent the phosphate from working properly

- Calcium-containing medicine, including antacids and calcium supplements—Use with phosphates may prevent the phosphate from working properly; calcium deposits may form in tissues

- Corticosteroids (cortisone-like medicine)—Use with sodium-containing phosphates may increase the risk of swelling

- Phosphate-containing medications, other, including phosphate enemas—Use with sodium or potassium phophates may cause high blood levels of phosphorus which may increase the chance of side effects

- Sodium-containing medicines (other)—Use with sodium phosphates may cause your body to retain (keep) water

Other medical problems—The presence of other medical problems may affect the use of phosphates. Make sure you tell your health care professional if you have any other medical problems, especially:

- Burns, severe or
- Heart disease or
- Pancreatitis (inflammation of the pancreas) or
- Rickets or
- Softening of bones or
- Underactive parathyroid glands—Sodium- or potassium-containing phosphates may make these conditions worse

- Dehydration or
- Underactive adrenal glands—Potassium-containing phosphates may increase the risk of hyperkalemia (too much potassium in the blood)

- Edema (swelling in feet or lower legs or fluid in lungs) or
- High blood pressure or
- Liver disease or
- Toxemia of pregnancy—Sodium-containing phosphates may make these conditions worse

- High blood levels of phosphate (hyperphosphatemia)—Use of phosphates may make this condition worse

- Infected kidney stones—Phosphates may make this condition worse

- Kidney disease—Sodium-containing phosphates may make this condition worse; potassium-containing phosphates may increase the risk of hyperkalemia (too much potassium in the blood)

- Myotonia congenita—Potassium-containing phosphates may increase the risk of hyperkalemia (too much potassium in the blood), and make this condition worse

Proper Use of This Medicine

For patients taking the *tablet form* of this medicine:
- *Do not swallow the tablet.* Before taking, dissolve the tablet in ¾ to 1 glass (6 to 8 ounces) of water. Let the tablet soak in water for 2 to 5 minutes and then stir until completely dissolved.

For patients using the *capsule form* of this medicine:
- *Do not swallow the capsule.* Before taking, mix the contents of 1 capsule in one-third glass (about 2½ ounces) of water or juice or the contents of 2 capsules in two-thirds glass (about 5 ounces) of water and stir well until dissolved.

For patients using the *powder form* of this medicine:
- Add the entire contents of 1 bottle (2¼ ounces) to enough warm water to make 1 gallon of solution *or* the contents of one packet to enough warm water to make 1/3 of a glass (about 2.5 ounces) of solution. Shake the container for 2 or 3 minutes or until all the powder is dissolved.
- Do not dilute solution further.
- This solution may be chilled to improve the flavor; do not allow it to freeze.
- Discard unused solution after 60 days.

Take this medicine immediately after meals or with food to lessen possible stomach upset or laxative action.

To help prevent kidney stones, *drink at least a full glass (8 ounces) of water every hour during waking hours*, unless otherwise directed by your health care professional.

Take this medicine only as directed. Do not take more of it and do not take it more often than recommended on the label, unless otherwise directed by your health care professional.

Dosing—The dose of these single or combination medicines will be different for different patients. *Follow your health care professional's orders or the directions on the label.* The following information includes only the average doses of these medicines. *If your dose is different, do not change it* unless your health care professional tells you to do so.

The number of teaspoonfuls or ounces of prepared solution that you drink depends on the equivalent amount of phosphorus contained in the product. Also, *the number of doses you take each day, the time allowed between doses, and the length of time you take the medicine depend on the medical problem for which you are taking the single or combination medicine.*

For potassium phosphates
- For *tablets for oral solution* dosage form:
  —To replace phosphorus lost by the body or to make the urine more acid or to prevent the formation of kidney stones in the urinary tract:
    - Adults and teenagers—The equivalent of 228 milligrams (mg) of phosphorus (2 tablets) dissolved in six to eight ounces of water four times a day, with meals and at bedtime.
  —To replace phosphorus lost by the body:
    - Children over 4 years of age—The equivalent of 228 mg of phosphorus (2 tablets) dissolved in six to eight ounces of water four times a day, with meals and at bedtime.
    - Children up to 4 years of age—The dose must be determined by your doctor.

- For *capsules for oral solution* dosage form:
  —To replace phosphorus lost by the body:
    - Adults, teenagers, and children over 4 years of age—The equivalent of 250 mg of phosphorus (contents of 1 capsule) dissolved in two and one-half ounces of water or juice four times a day, after meals and at bedtime.

- Children up to 4 years of age—Dose must be determined by your doctor.
- For *powder for oral solution* dosage form:
  —To replace phosphorus lost by the body:
  - Adults, teenagers, and children over 4 years of age—The equivalent of 250 mg of phosphorus dissolved in two and one-half ounces of water four times a day, after meals and at bedtime.
  - Children up to 4 years of age—Dose must be determined by your doctor.

For potassium and sodium phosphates
- For *tablets for oral solution* dosage form:
  —To replace phosphorus lost by the body or to make the urine more acid or to prevent the fomation of kidney stones in the urinary tract:
  - Adults and teenagers—The equivalent of 250 milligrams (mg) of phosphorus dissolved in eight ounces of water four times a day, after meals and at bedtime.
  —To replace phosphorus lost by the body:
  - Children over 4 years of age—The equivalent of 250 mg of phosphorus dissolved in eight ounces of water four times a day, after meals and at bedtime.
  - Children up to 4 years of age—Dose must be determined by your doctor.
- For *capsules for oral solution* dosage form:
  —To replace phosphorus lost by the body:
  - Adults, teenagers, and children over 4 years of age—The equivalent of 250 mg of phosphorus (the contents of 1 capsule) dissolved in two and one-half ounces of water or juice four times a day, after meals and at bedtime.
  - Children up to 4 years of age—Dose must be determined by your doctor.
- For *powder for oral solution* dosage form:
  —To replace phosphorus lost by the body:
  - Adults, teenagers, and children over 4 years of age—The equivalent of 250 mg of phosphorus dissolved in two and one-half ounces of water four times a day, after meals and at bedtime.
  - Children up to 4 years of age—Dose must be determined by your doctor.
- For *tablets for oral solution* dosage form:
  —To replace phosphorus lost by the body:
  - Adults, teenagers, and children over 4 years of age—The equivalent of 250 mg of phosphorus (1 tablet) dissolved in eight ounces of water four times a day.
  - Children up to 4 years of age—Dose must be determined by your doctor.

Missed dose—If you miss a dose of this medicine, take it as soon as possible. However, if it is within 1 or 2 hours of your next dose, skip the missed dose and go back to your regular dosing schedule. Do not double doses.

Storage—To store this medicine:
- Keep out of the reach of children.
- Store away from heat and direct light.
- Do not store the capsule, tablet, or powder form of this medicine in the bathroom, near the kitchen sink, or in other damp places. Heat or moisture may cause the medicine to break down.
- Keep the liquid form of this medicine from freezing.
- Do not keep outdated medicine or medicine no longer needed. Be sure that any discarded medicine is out of the reach of children.

Precautions While Using This Medicine

Your health care professional should check your progress at regular visits to make sure that this medicine does not cause unwanted effects.

Do not take iron supplements within 1 to 2 hours of taking this medicine. To do so may keep the iron from working properly.

For patients taking potassium phosphate-containing medicines:
- Check with your health care professional before starting any strenuous physical exercise, especially if you are out of condition and are taking other medication. Exercise and certain medicines may increase the amount of potassium in the blood.

For patients on a *potassium-restricted diet:*
- This medicine may contain a large amount of potassium. If you have any questions about this, check with your health care professional.
- Do not use salt substitutes and low-salt milk unless told to do so by your health care professional. They may contain potassium.

For patients on a sodium-restricted diet:
- This medicine may contain a large amount of sodium. If you have any questions about this, check with your health care professional.

Side Effects of This Medicine

Along with its needed effects, a medicine may cause some unwanted effects. Although not all of these side effects may occur, if they do occur they may need medical attention.

Check with your health care professional as soon as possible if any of the following side effects occur:
  Less common or rare
    Confusion; convulsions (seizures); decrease in amount of urine or in frequency of urination; fast, slow, or irregular heartbeat; headache or dizziness; increased thirst; muscle cramps; numbness, tingling, pain, or weakness in hands or feet; numbness or tingling around lips; shortness of breath or troubled breathing; swelling of feet or lower legs; tremor; unexplained anxiety; unusual tiredness or weakness; weakness or heaviness of legs; weight gain

Other side effects may occur that usually do not need medical attention. These side effects may go away during treatment as your body adjusts to the medicine. However, check with your health care professional if any of the following side effects continue or are bothersome:
    Diarrhea; nausea or vomiting; stomach pain

Other side effects not listed above may also occur in some patients. If you notice any other effects, check with your health care professional.

Revised: 08/18/2000

PHYSOSTIGMINE   Ophthalmic†

Commonly used brand name(s):

In the U.S.—
    Eserine Salicylate
    Eserine Sulfate
    Isopto Eserine
    Generic name product may be available.

†Not commercially available in Canada.

Description

Physostigmine (fi-zoe-STIG-meen) is used to treat certain types of glaucoma.

This medicine is available only with your doctor's prescription, in the following dosage forms:

Ophthalmic
- Ophthalmic ointment (U.S.)
- Ophthalmic solution (eye drops) (U.S.)

Before Using This Medicine

In deciding to use a medicine, the risks of taking the medicine must be weighed against the good it will do. This is a decision you and your doctor will make. For physostigmine, the following should be considered:

Allergies—Tell your doctor if you have ever had any unusual or allergic reaction to physostigmine. Also tell your health care professional if you are allergic to any other substances, such as preservatives.

Pregnancy—Ophthalmic physostigmine may be absorbed into the body. However, studies on effects in pregnancy have not been done in either humans or animals.

Breast-feeding—Ophthalmic physostigmine may be absorbed into the mother's body. However, physostigmine has not been reported to cause problems in nursing babies.

Children—Although there is no specific information comparing use of this medicine in children with use in other age groups, it is not expected to cause different side effects or problems in children than it does in adults.

Older adults—Many medicines have not been studied specifically in older people. Therefore, it may not be known whether they work exactly the same way they do in younger adults or if they cause different side effects or problems in older people. Although there is no specific information comparing use of physostigmine in the elderly with use in other age groups, it is not expected to cause different side effects or problems in older people than it does in younger adults.

Other medicines—Although certain medicines should not be used together at all, in other cases two different medicines may be used together even if an interaction might occur. In these cases, your doctor may want to change the dose, or other precautions may be necessary. Tell your health care professional if you are using any other prescription or nonprescription (over-the-counter [OTC]) medicine.

Other medical problems—The presence of other medical problems may affect the use of physostigmine. Make sure you tell your doctor if you have any other medical problems, especially:
- Eye disease or problems (other)—Physostigmine may make the condition worse

Proper Use of This Medicine

To use the *ophthalmic solution (eye drops) form* of this medicine:
- Do not use if the solution becomes discolored.
- First, wash your hands. With the middle finger, apply pressure to the inside corner of the eye (and continue to apply pressure for 1 or 2 minutes after the medicine has been placed in the eye). Tilt the head back and with the index finger of the same hand, pull the lower eyelid away from the eye to form a pouch. Drop the medicine into the pouch and gently close the eyes. Do not blink. Keep the eyes closed for 1 or 2 minutes to allow the medicine to be absorbed.
- Immediately after using the eye drops, wash your hands to remove any medicine that may be on them.
- To keep the medicine as germ-free as possible, do not touch the applicator tip to any surface (including the eye). Also, keep the container tightly closed.

To use the *ointment form* of this medicine:
- First, wash your hands. Pull the lower eyelid away from the eye to form a pouch. Squeeze a thin strip of ointment into the pouch. A 1-cm (approximately 1/3-inch) strip of ointment is usually enough unless otherwise directed by your doctor. Gently close the eyes and keep them closed for 1 or 2 minutes to allow the medicine to be absorbed.
- Immediately after using the eye ointment, wash your hands to remove any medicine that may be on them.
- To keep the medicine as germ-free as possible, do not touch the applicator tip to any surface (including the eye). After using the eye ointment, wipe the tip of the ointment tube with a clean tissue and keep the tube tightly closed.

Use this medicine only as directed. Do not use more of it and do not use it more often than your doctor ordered. To do so may increase the chance of too much medicine being absorbed into the body and the chance of side effects.

Dosing—The dose of ophthalmic physostigmine will be different for different patients. *Follow your doctor's orders or the directions on the label*. The following information includes only the average doses of ophthalmic physostigmine. *If your dose is different, do not change it* unless your doctor tells you to do so.

The number of doses you use each day, the time allowed between doses, and the length of time you use the medicine depend on the medical problem for which you are using ophthalmic physostigmine.
- For glaucoma:
  —For *ophthalmic ointment* dosage form:
  - Adults and children—Use in each eye one to three times a day.
  —For *ophthalmic solution (eye drops)* dosage form:
  - Adults and children—One drop in each eye up to four times a day.

Missed dose—If you miss a dose of this medicine and your dosing schedule is:
- One dose a day—Apply the missed dose as soon as possible. However, if you do not remember the missed dose until the next day, skip the missed dose and go back to your regular dosing schedule. Do not double doses.
- More than one dose a day—Apply the missed dose as soon as possible. However, if it is almost time for your

next dose, skip the missed dose and go back to your regular dosing schedule. Do not double doses.

Storage—To store this medicine:
- Keep out of the reach of children.
- Store away from heat and direct light.
- Keep the medicine from freezing.
- Do not keep outdated medicine or medicine no longer needed. Be sure that any discarded medicine is out of the reach of children.

Precautions While Using This Medicine

Your doctor should check your eye pressure at regular visits.

For a short time after you apply this medicine, your vision may be blurred or there may be a change in your near or distant vision, especially at night. *Make sure your vision is clear before you drive, use machines, or do anything else that could be dangerous if you are not able to see well.*

Side Effects of This Medicine

Along with its needed effects, a medicine may cause some unwanted effects. Although not all of these side effects may occur, if they do occur they may need medical attention.

Check with your doctor as soon as possible if any of the following side effects occur:

Symptoms of too much medicine being absorbed into the body
Increased sweating; loss of bladder control; muscle weakness; nausea, vomiting, diarrhea, or stomach cramps or pain; shortness of breath, tightness in chest, or wheezing; slow or irregular heartbeat; unusual tiredness or weakness; watering of mouth

Other side effects may occur that usually do not need medical attention. These side effects may go away during treatment as your body adjusts to the medicine. However, check with your doctor if any of the following side effects continue or are bothersome:

More common
Blurred vision or change in near or distant vision; eye pain

Less common
Burning, redness, stinging, or other eye irritation; headache or browache; twitching of eyelids; watering of eyes

Other side effects not listed above may also occur in some patients. If you notice any other effects, check with your doctor.

Revised: 07/01/93

PILOCARPINE   Ophthalmic

Commonly used brand name(s):

In the U.S.—

Adsorbocarpine	Pilagan
Akarpine	Pilocar
Isopto Carpine	Pilopine HS
Ocu-Carpine	Piloptic-½
Ocusert Pilo-20	Piloptic-1
Ocusert Pilo-40	Piloptic-2

Piloptic-3	Piloptic-6
Piloptic-4	Pilostat

Generic name product may be available.

In Canada—

Isopto Carpine	Pilopine HS
Minims Pilocarpine	Pilostat
Miocarpine	P.V. Carpine Liquifilm
Ocusert Pilo-20	Spersacarpine
Ocusert Pilo-40	

Description

Pilocarpine (pye-loe-KAR-peen) is used to treat glaucoma and other eye conditions.

This medicine is available only with your doctor's prescription, in the following dosage forms:

Ophthalmic
- Ocular system (eye insert) (U.S. and Canada)
- Ophthalmic gel (eye gel) (U.S. and Canada)
- Ophthalmic solution (eye drops) (U.S. and Canada)

Before Using This Medicine

In deciding to use a medicine, the risks of taking the medicine must be weighed against the good it will do. This is a decision you and your doctor will make. For pilocarpine, the following should be considered:

Allergies—Tell your doctor if you have ever had any unusual or allergic reaction to pilocarpine. Also tell your health care professional if you are allergic to any other substances, such as preservatives.

Pregnancy—Ophthalmic pilocarpine may be absorbed into the body. However, studies on effects in pregnancy have not been done in either humans or animals.

Breast-feeding—Ophthalmic pilocarpine may be absorbed into the body. However, it is not known whether pilocarpine passes into the breast milk. Although most medicines pass into breast milk in small amounts, many of them may be used safely while breast-feeding. Mothers who are using this medicine and who wish to breast-feed should discuss this with their doctor.

Children—Although there is no specific information comparing use of this medicine in children with use in other age groups, pilocarpine is not expected to cause different side effects or problems in children than it does in adults.

Older adults—Many medicines have not been studied specifically in older people. Therefore, it may not be known whether they work exactly the same way they do in younger adults or if they cause different side effects or problems in older people. Although there is no specific information comparing use of pilocarpine in the elderly with use in other age groups, this medicine is not expected to cause different side effects or problems in older people than it does in younger adults.

Other medicines—Although certain medicines should not be used together at all, in other cases two different medicines may be used together even if an interaction might occur. In these cases, your doctor may want to change the dose, or other precautions may be necessary. Tell your health care professional if you are using any other prescription or nonprescription (over-the-counter [OTC]) medicine.

Other medical problems—The presence of other medical problems may affect the use of pilocarpine. Make sure

you tell your doctor if you have any other medical problems, especially:

- Asthma or
- Eye disease or problems (other)—Pilocarpine may make the condition worse

Proper Use of This Medicine

To use the *eye drop form* of pilocarpine:

- First, wash your hands. Tilt the head back and, pressing your finger gently on the skin just beneath the lower eyelid, pull the lower eyelid away from the eye to make a space. Drop the medicine into this space. Let go of the eyelid and gently close the eyes. Do not blink. Keep the eyes closed and apply pressure to the inner corner of the eye with your finger for 1 or 2 minutes to allow the medicine to be absorbed by the eye.
- Immediately after using the eye drops, wash your hands to remove any medicine that may be on them.
- To keep the medicine as germ-free as possible, do not touch the applicator tip to any surface (including the eye). Also, keep the container tightly closed.

To use the *eye gel form* of pilocarpine:

- First, wash your hands. Tilt the head back and, pressing your finger gently on the skin just beneath the lower eyelid, pull the lower eyelid away from the eye to make a space. Squeeze a thin strip of gel into this space. A 1½-cm (approximately ½-inch) strip of gel is usually enough, unless you have been told by your doctor to use a different amount. Let go of the eyelid and gently close the eyes. Keep the eyes closed for 1 or 2 minutes to allow the medicine to be absorbed by the eye.
- Immediately after using the eye gel, wash your hands to remove any medicine that may be on them.
- To keep the medicine as germ-free as possible, do not touch the applicator tip to any surface (including the eye). After using the eye gel, wipe the tip of the gel tube with a clean tissue and keep the tube tightly closed.

To use the *eye insert form* of pilocarpine:

- This medicine usually comes with patient directions. Read them carefully before using this medicine.
- If you think this medicine unit may be damaged, do not use it. If you have any questions about this, check with your health care professional.
- If the unit seems to be releasing too much medicine into your eye, remove it and replace with a new unit. If you have any questions about this, check with your doctor.

Use this medicine only as directed. Do not use more of it and do not use it more often than your doctor ordered. To do so may increase the chance of too much medicine being absorbed into the body and the chance of side effects.

Dosing—The dose of ophthalmic pilocarpine will be different for different patients. *Follow the doctor's orders or the directions on the label.* The following information includes only the average doses of ophthalmic pilocarpine. *If your dose is different, do not change it unless your doctor tells you to do so.*

The number of doses you use each day, the time allowed between doses, and the length of time you use the medicine depend on the medical problem for which you are using ophthalmic pilocarpine.

- For *eye drop* dosage form:
  —For chronic glaucoma:
  - Adults and children—One drop one to four times a day.

  —For acute angle-closure glaucoma:
  - Adults and children—One drop every five to ten minutes for three to six doses. Then one drop every one to three hours until eye pressure is reduced.

- For *eye gel* dosage form:
  —For glaucoma:
  - Adults and teenagers—Use once a day at bedtime.
  - Children—Use and dose must be determined by your doctor.

- For *eye insert* dosage form:
  —For glaucoma:
  - Adults and children—Insert one ocular system every seven days.
  - Infants—Use and dose must be determined by your doctor.

Missed dose—

- For patients using the *eye drop form* of pilocarpine: If you miss a dose of this medicine, use it as soon as possible. However, if it is almost time for your next dose, skip the missed dose and go back to your regular dosing schedule. Do not double doses.
- For patients using the *eye gel form* of pilocarpine: If you miss a dose of this medicine, use it as soon as possible. However, if you do not remember the missed dose until the next day, skip the missed dose and go back to your regular dosing schedule. Do not double doses.
- For patients using the *eye insert form* of pilocarpine: If you forget to replace the eye insert at the proper time, replace it as soon as possible. Then go back to your regular dosing schedule.

Storage—To store this medicine:

- Keep out of the reach of children.
- Store away from heat and direct light.
- Store the eye system form of this medicine in the refrigerator. However, keep the medicine from freezing.
- Store the 5-gram size of the gel form of this medicine in the refrigerator. Store the 3.5-gram size at room temperature. Also, keep both sizes of the gel form of this medicine from freezing.
- Keep the solution form of this medicine from freezing.
- Do not keep outdated medicine or medicine no longer needed. Be sure that any discarded medicine is out of the reach of children.

Precautions While Using This Medicine

Your doctor should check your eye pressure at regular visits.

For patients using the *eye drop or gel form* of this medicine:

- For a short time after you use this medicine, your vision may be blurred or there may be a change in your near or far vision, especially at night. *Make sure your vision is clear before you drive, use machines, or do anything else that could be dangerous if you are not able to see well.*

For patients using the *eye insert form* of this medicine:

- For the first several hours after you insert this unit in the eye, your vision may be blurred or there may be a change in your near or far vision, especially at night. Therefore, insert this unit in the eye at bedtime, unless otherwise directed by your doctor. If this unit is inserted in the eye at any other time of the day, *make sure your vision is clear before you drive, use machines, or do anything else that could be dangerous if you are not able to see well.*

Side Effects of This Medicine

Along with its needed effects, a medicine may cause some unwanted effects. Although not all of these side effects may occur, if they do occur they may need medical attention.

Check with your doctor as soon as possible if any of the following side effects occur:

Symptoms of too much medicine being absorbed into the body

Increased sweating; muscle tremors; nausea, vomiting, or diarrhea; troubled breathing or wheezing; watering of mouth

Less common or rare

Eye pain

Other side effects may occur that usually do not need medical attention. These side effects may go away during treatment as your body adjusts to the medicine. However, check with your doctor if any of the following side effects continue or are bothersome:

More common

Blurred vision or change in near or far vision; decrease in night vision

Less common

Eye irritation; headache or browache

Other side effects not listed above may also occur in some patients. If you notice any other effects, check with your doctor.

Revised: 06/21/95

PIMOZIDE　Systemic

Commonly used brand name(s):

In the U.S.—
Orap

In Canada—
Orap

Description

Pimozide (PIM-oh-zide) is used to treat the symptoms of Tourette's syndrome. It is meant only for patients with severe symptoms who cannot take or have not been helped by other medicine.

Pimozide works in the central nervous system to help control the vocal outbursts and uncontrolled, repeated movements of the body (tics) that interfere with normal life. It will not completely cure the tics, but will help to reduce their number and severity.

Pimozide may also be used for other conditions as determined by your doctor.

This medicine is available only with your doctor's prescription, in the following dosage form:

Oral
- Tablets (U.S. and Canada)

Before Using This Medicine

In deciding to use a medicine, the risks of taking the medicine must be weighed against the good it will do. This is a decision you and your doctor will make. For pimozide, the following should be considered:

Allergies—Tell your doctor if you have ever had any unusual or allergic reaction to pimozide, haloperidol, or other medicines used to treat mental illness. Also tell your health care professional if you are allergic to any other substances, such as foods, preservatives, or dyes.

Diet—*It is very important that you do not take pimozide with grapefruit juice*. Studies have shown that taking pimozide with grapefruit juice may cause heart rhythm problems.

Pregnancy—Studies in rats and rabbits given more than the highest recommended human dose of pimozide have shown fewer pregnancies, slowed development of the fetus, and toxic effects in the mother and fetus.

Breast-feeding—It is not known whether pimozide passes into breast milk.

Children—Children are especially sensitive to the effects of pimozide. This may increase the chance of side effects during treatment. Pimozide usually is not used in children for any condition other than Tourette's syndrome.

Older adults—Constipation, dizziness or fainting, drowsiness, dryness of mouth, and trembling of the hands and fingers, and symptoms of tardive dyskinesia (such as rapid, worm-like movements of the tongue or any other uncontrolled movements of the mouth, tongue, or jaw, and/or arms and legs) may be especially likely to occur in the elderly, who are usually more sensitive than younger adults to the effects of pimozide.

Other medicines—Although certain medicines should not be used together at all, in other cases two different medicines may be used together even if an interaction might occur. In these cases, your doctor may want to change the dose, or other precautions may be necessary. When you are taking pimozide, it is especially important that your health care professional know if you are taking any of the following:

- Amoxapine (e.g., Asendin) or
- Antipsychotics (medicine for mental illness) or
- Metoclopramide (e.g., Reglan) or
- Metyrosine (e.g., Demser) or
- Paroxetine (e.g., Paxil) or
- Promethazine (e.g., Phenergan) or
- Rauwolfia alkaloids (deserpidine [e.g., Harmonyl], rauwolfia serpentina [e.g., Raudixin], reserpine [e.g., Serpalan]) or
- Tacrine (e.g., Cognex)—Taking these medicines with pimozide may increase the chance of developing unusual movements

- Amphetamines or
- Methylphenidate (e.g., Ritalin) or
- Pemoline (e.g., Cylert)—These medicines may cause tics and pimozide is not used to treat tics caused by other medicines

- Anticholinergics (medicine for abdominal or stomach spasms or cramps)—Taking these medicines with pimozide may increase the chance of certain side effects, such as dryness of mouth, constipation, and unusual excitement

- Azithromycin (e.g., Zithromax) or

- Clarithromycin (e.g., Biaxin) or
- Dirithromycin (e.g., Dynabac) or
- Disopyramide (e.g., Norpace) or
- Erythromycin (e.g., Erybid) or
- Indinavir (e.g., Crixivan) or
- Itraconazole (e.g., Sporanox) or
- Ketoconazole (e.g., Nizoral) or
- Maprotiline (e.g., Ludiomil) or
- Nefazodone (e.g., Serzone) or
- Nelfinavir (e.g., Viracept) or
- Phenothiazines (chlorpromazine [e.g., Thorazine], fluphenazine [e.g., Prolixin], mesoridazine [e.g., Serentil], methotrimeprazine [e.g., Nozinan], pericyazine [e.g., Neuleptil], perphenazine [e.g., Trilafon], pipotiazine [e.g., Piportil L $_4$], prochlorperazine [e.g., Compazine], promazine [e.g., Sparine], thiopropazate [e.g., Dartal], thioproperazine [e.g., Majeptil], thioridazine [e.g., Mellaril], trifluoperazine [e.g., Stelazine], triflupromazine [e.g., Vesprin]) or
- Probucol (e.g., Lorelco) or
- Procainamide (e.g., Pronestyl) or
- Quinidine (e.g., Quinidex) or
- Ritonavir (e.g., Norvir) or
- Saquinavir (e.g., Invirase) or
- Tricyclic antidepressants (amitriptyline [e.g., Elavil], amoxapine [e.g., Asendin], clomipramine [e.g., Anafranil], desipramine [e.g., Pertofrane], doxepin [e.g., Sinequan], imipramine [e.g., Tofranil], nortriptyline [e.g., Aventyl], protriptyline [e.g., Vivactil], trimipramine [e.g., Surmontil])
- Troleandomycin (e.g., Tao) or
- Zileuton (e.g., Zyflo)— *Do not take any of these medicines while you are taking pimozide.* Taking these medicines with pimozide may increase the chance of developing serious changes in the rhythm of your heart
- Central nervous system (CNS) depressants (medicines that cause drowsiness)—Using these medicines with pimozide may increase the CNS depressant effects

Other medical problems— The presence of other medical problems may affect the use of pimozide. Make sure you tell your doctor if you have any other medical problems, especially:

- Breast cancer (history of) or
- Glaucoma, narrow angle or
- Heart disease or
- Intestinal blockage or
- Urinary tract blockage or difficult urination—Pimozide may make the condition worse
- Kidney disease or
- Liver disease—Higher blood levels of pimozide may occur, increasing the chance of side effects
- Low blood potassium—Pimozide may increase the chance of developing serious changes in heart rhythm
- Seizures, history of—Pimozide may increase the chance of having seizures
- Tics other than those caused by Tourette's syndrome—Pimozide should not be used because of the risk of serious side effects

Proper Use of This Medicine

Use pimozide only as directed by your doctor. Do not use more of it, do not use it more often, and do not use it for a longer time than your doctor ordered. To do so may increase the chance of side effects.

Dosing— The dose of pimozide will be different for different patients. *Follow your doctor's orders or the directions on the label.* The following information includes only the average doses of pimozide. *If your dose is different, do not change it* unless your doctor tells you to do so.

The number of tablets that you take depends on the strength of the medicine. Also, *the number of doses you take each day, the time allowed between doses, and the length of time you take the medicine depend on the medical problem for which you are using pimozide.*

- For *oral* dosage form (tablets):
  —For Tourette's syndrome:
  - Adults—To start, 1 to 2 milligrams (mg) a day. Your doctor may increase your dose if needed. However, the dose is usually not more than 10 mg a day.
  - Children up to 12 years of age—Dose must be determined by the doctor.
  - Children 12 years of age and older—To start, 0.05 mg per kilogram (0.023 mg per pound) of body weight a day. Your doctor may increase your dose if needed. However, the dose is usually not more than 10 mg a day.

Missed dose— If you miss a dose of this medicine, skip the missed dose and go back to your regular dosing schedule. Do not double doses.

Storage— To store this medicine:

- Keep out of the reach of children.
- Store away from heat and direct light.
- Do not store in the bathroom, near the kitchen sink, or in other damp places. Heat or moisture may cause the medicine to break down.
- Do not keep outdated medicine or medicine no longer needed. Be sure that any discarded medicine is out of the reach of children.

Precautions While Using This Medicine

Your doctor should check your progress at regular visits, especially during the first few months of treatment with this medicine. The amount of pimozide you take may be changed often to meet the needs of your condition and to help avoid unwanted effects.

Do not take azithromycin, clarithromycin, dirithromycin, disopyramide, erythromycin, indinavir, itraconazole, ketoconazole, maprotiline, nefazodone, nelfinavir, phenothiazines, probucol, procainamide, quinidine, ritonavir, saquinavir, tricyclic antidepressants, troleandomycin, or zileuton while you are taking pimozide, or you may develop a very serious irregular heartbeat.

Do not suddenly stop taking this medicine without first checking with your doctor. Your doctor may want you to reduce gradually the amount you are taking before stopping completely. This will allow your body time to adjust and help to avoid worsening of your medical condition.

This medicine will add to the effects of alcohol and other CNS depressants (medicines that slow down the nervous system, possibly causing drowsiness). Some examples of CNS depressants are antihistamines or medicine for hay fever, other allergies, or colds; sedatives, tranquilizers, or sleeping medicine; prescription pain medicine or narcotics; barbiturates; medicine for seizures; muscle relaxants; or anesthetics, including some dental anesthetics. *Check with your doctor before taking any of the above while you are using this medicine.*

This medicine may cause some people to become drowsy or less alert or to have blurred vision or muscle stiffness, especially as the amount of medicine is increased. Even if you take pimozide at bedtime, you may feel drowsy or less alert on arising. *Make sure you know how you react to this medicine before you drive, use machines, or do anything else that could be dangerous if you are not alert or able to see well or if you do not have good muscle control.*

Although not a problem for many patients, dizziness, lightheadedness, or fainting may occur when you get up from a sitting or lying position. Getting up slowly may help. If the problem continues or gets worse, check with your doctor.

Before having any kind of surgery, dental treatment, or emergency treatment, tell the medical doctor or dentist in charge that you are using this medicine. Taking pimozide together with medicines that are used during surgery or dental or emergency treatment may increase the CNS depressant effects.

Pimozide may cause dryness of the mouth. For temporary relief, use sugarless gum or candy, melt bits of ice in your mouth, or use a saliva substitute. However, if your mouth continues to feel dry for more than 2 weeks, check with your medical doctor or dentist. Continuing dryness of the mouth may increase the chance of dental disease, including tooth decay, gum disease, and fungus infections.

Side Effects of This Medicine

Along with its needed effects, pimozide can sometimes cause serious unwanted effects. Tardive dyskinesia (a movement disorder) may occur and may not go away after you stop using the medicine. Signs of tardive dyskinesia include fine, worm-like movements of the tongue, or other uncontrolled movements of the mouth, tongue, cheeks, jaw, or arms and legs. Other serious but rare side effects, such as abnormal heart rhythm or the neuroleptic malignant syndrome, may also occur. *You and your doctor should discuss the good this medicine will do as well as the risks of taking it.*

Stop taking pimozide and get emergency help immediately if any of the following side effects occur:
  Rare—Signs of the neuroleptic malignant syndrome (usually two or more occur together)
    Convulsions (seizures); difficult or unusually fast breathing; fast heartbeat or irregular pulse; fever (high); high or low (irregular) blood pressure; increased sweating; loss of bladder control; muscle stiffness (severe)
  Symptoms of overdose
    Coma; convulsions (seizures); dizziness (severe); muscle trembling, jerking, or stiffness (severe); troubled breathing (severe); uncontrolled movements (severe)

Check with your doctor as soon as possible if any of the following side effects occur:
  More common
    Difficulty in speaking; dizziness or fainting; fast or irregular heartbeat; loss of balance control; lack of facial expression; mood or behavior changes; restlessness or need to keep moving; shuffling walk; slowed movements; stiffness of arms and legs; swelling or soreness of breasts (less common in males); trembling and shaking of fingers and hands; unusual secretion of milk (rare in males)
  Less common or rare
    Difficulty in swallowing; inability to move eyes; in-

creased blinking or spasms of eyelid; lip smacking or puckering; menstrual changes; muscle spasms, especially of the face, neck, or back; puffing of cheeks; rapid or worm-like movements of tongue; skin rash and itching; sore throat and fever; swelling of face; uncontrolled chewing movements; uncontrolled movements of neck, trunk, arms, or legs, including twisting movements; unusual bleeding or bruising; unusual facial expressions or body positions; yellow eyes or skin

Other side effects may occur that usually do not need medical attention. These side effects may go away during treatment as your body adjusts to the medicine. However, check with your doctor if any of the following side effects continue or are bothersome:
  More common
    Blurred vision or other vision problems; constipation; dizziness, lightheadedness, or fainting when getting up from a lying or sitting position; drowsiness; dryness of mouth; skin discoloration
  Less common
    Decreased sexual ability; diarrhea; headache; loss of appetite and weight; mental depression; nausea and vomiting; tiredness or weakness

After you stop using pimozide, it may still produce some side effects that need attention. During this period of time, check with your doctor as soon as possible if you notice any of the following side effects:
  Lip smacking or puckering; puffing of cheeks; rapid or worm-like movements of the tongue; uncontrolled chewing movements; uncontrolled movements of the arms and legs

Other side effects not listed above may also occur in some patients. If you notice any other effects, check with your doctor.

Additional Information

Once a medicine has been approved for marketing for a certain use, experience may show that it is also useful for other medical problems. Although this use is not included in product labeling, pimozide is used in certain patients with the following medical condition:
  • Psychotic disorders, such as schizophrenia

Other than the above information, there is no additional information relating to proper use, precautions, or side effects for this use.

Revised: 01/6/2000

PIOGLITAZONE   Systemic

Commonly used brand name(s):
In the U.S.—
  Actos

Description

Pioglitazone (pye-oh-GLI-ta-zone) is used to treat a certain type of diabetes mellitus (sugar diabetes) called type 2 diabetes. It may be used alone, with insulin, or with metformin or another type of oral diabetes medicine called a sulfonylurea.

This medicine is available only with your doctor's prescription, in the following dosage form:

Oral
- Tablets (U.S. and Canada)

Before Using This Medicine

In deciding to use a medicine, the risks of taking the medicine must be weighed against the good it will do. This is a decision you and your doctor will make. For pioglitazone, the following should be considered:

Allergies—Tell your doctor if you have ever had any unusual or allergic reaction to pioglitazone. Also tell your health care professional if you are allergic to any other substances, such as foods, preservatives, or dyes.

Pregnancy—Pioglitazone has not been studied in pregnant women. However, it is easier during pregnancy to control your blood sugar by using injections of insulin, rather than by taking pioglitazone. Close control of your blood sugar can reduce the chance of your baby gaining too much weight, having birth defects, or having high blood sugar before birth. Be sure to tell your doctor if you plan to become pregnant or you think you are pregnant.

Breast-feeding—It is not known whether pioglitazone passes into the breast milk of humans. However, pioglitazone is not recommended during breast-feeding.

Children—Studies on this medicine have been done only in adult patients, and there is no specific information comparing use of pioglitazone in children with use in other age groups.

Older adults—This medicine has been tested in a limited number of patients 65 years of age or older and has not been shown to cause different side effects or problems in older people than it does in younger adults.

Other medicines—Although certain medicines should not be used together at all, in other cases two different medicines may be used together even if an interaction might occur. In these cases, your doctor may want to change the dose, or other precautions may be necessary. When you are taking pioglitazone, it is especially important that your health care professional know if you are taking the following:
- Ketoconazole—Use of this medicine with pioglitazone may decrease the effect of pioglitazone

Other medical problems—The presence of other medical problems may affect the use of pioglitazone. Make sure you tell your doctor if you have any other medical problems, especially
- Diabetic ketoacidosis (ketones in the blood) or
- Type 1 diabetes—Insulin is needed to control these conditions
- Heart disease or
- Liver disease—Pioglitazone may make these conditions worse

Proper Use of This Medicine

Follow carefully the special meal plan your doctor gave you. This is the most important part of controlling your condition, and is necessary if the medicine is to work properly. Also, exercise regularly and test for sugar in your blood or urine as directed.

Pioglitazone may be taken with or without food.

Dosing—The dose of pioglitazone will be different for different patients. *Follow your doctor's orders or the directions on the label. If your dose is different, do not change it* unless your doctor tells you to do so.
- For *oral* dosage form (tablets):
  —For type 2 diabetes:
  - Pioglitazone alone:
    —Adults: At first, the dose is 15 or 30 milligrams (mg) once daily with or without meals. Your doctor may later increase your dose up to 45 mg once daily.
    —Children: Use and dose must be determined by your doctor.
  - Pioglitazone with insulin:
    —Adults: At first, the dose is 15 or 30 mg once daily with or without meals.
    —Children: Use and dose must be determined by your doctor.
  - Pioglitazone with metformin:
    —Adults: At first, the dose is 15 or 30 mg once daily with or without meals.
    —Children: Use and dose must be determined by your doctor.
  - Pioglitazone with a sulfonylurea:
    —Adults: At first, the dose is 15 or 30 mg once daily with or without meals.
    —Children: Use and dose must be determined by your doctor.

Missed dose—If you miss a dose of this medicine, take it as soon as you remember. However, if you do not remember it until it is time for your next dose, skip the missed dose and go back to your regular dosing schedule. Do not double doses.

Storage—To store this medicine:
- Keep out of the reach of children.
- Do not store in the bathroom, near the kitchen sink, or in other damp places. Heat or moisture may cause the medicine to break down.
- Store away from heat and direct light.
- Do not keep outdated medicine or medicine no longer needed. Ask your health care professional how you should dispose of any medicine you do not use. Be sure that any discarded medicine is out of the reach of children.

Precautions While Using This Medicine

If you experience abdominal or stomach pain, dark urine, loss of appetite, nausea or vomiting, unusual tiredness or weakness, or yellow eyes or skin, check with your doctor immediately. These may be symptoms of liver problems.

It is very important that your doctor check your progress at regular visits to make sure that this medicine is working properly and to check for unwanted effects

It is very important to follow carefully any instructions from your health care team about
- Alcohol—Drinking alcohol may cause severe low blood sugar. Discuss this with your health care team.
- Other medicines—Do not take other medicines during the time you are taking pioglitazone unless they have been discussed with your doctor. This especially includes nonprescription medicines such as aspirin, and medicines for appetite control, asthma, colds, cough, hay fever, or sinus problems.

- Counseling—Other family members need to learn how to prevent side effects or help with side effects if they occur. Also, diabetic patients may need special counseling about diabetes medicine dosing changes that might occur because of lifestyle changes, such as changes in exercise and diet. Furthermore, counseling on contraception and pregnancy may be needed because of the problems that can occur during pregnancy in patients with diabetes.
- Travel—Keep a recent prescription and your medical history with you. Be prepared for an emergency as you would normally. Make allowances for changing time zones and keep your meal times as close as possible to your usual meal times.
- *In case of emergency* —There may be a time when you need emergency help for a problem caused by your diabetes. You need to be prepared for these emergencies. It is a good idea to wear a medical identification (ID) bracelet or neck chain at all times. Also, carry an ID card in your wallet or purse that says that you have diabetes and a list of all of your medicines.
- *This medicine does not cause hypoglycemia (low blood sugar). However, low blood sugar can occur* when you take pioglitazone with other medicines that can lower blood sugar, such as insulin, metformin, or a sulfonylurea. Low blood sugar also can occur if you delay or miss a meal or snack, exercise more than usual, drink alcohol, or cannot eat because of nausea or vomiting.
- *Symptoms of low blood sugar include* anxiety; behavior change similar to being drunk; blurred vision; cold sweats; confusion; cool, pale skin; difficulty in thinking; drowsiness; excessive hunger; fast heartbeat; headache (continuing); nausea; nervousness; nightmares; restless sleep; shakiness; slurred speech; or unusual tiredness or weakness.
- If symptoms of low blood sugar occur, *eat glucose tablets or gel, corn syrup, honey, or sugar cubes; or drink fruit juice, nondiet soft drink, or sugar dissolved in water to relieve the symptoms.* Also, check your blood for low blood sugar. *Glucagon is used in emergency situations when severe symptoms such as seizures (convulsions) or unconsciousness occur.* Have a glucagon kit available, along with a syringe and needle, and know how to use it. Members of your family also should know how to use it.

Hyperglycemia (high blood sugar) may occur if you do not take enough or skip a dose of your antidiabetic medicine, overeat or do not follow your meal plan, have a fever or infection, or do not exercise as much as usual.

Symptoms of high blood sugar include blurred vision; drowsiness; dry mouth; flushed, dry skin; fruit-like breath odor; increased urination (frequency and amount); ketones in urine; loss of appetite; stomachache, nausea, or vomiting; tiredness; troubled breathing (rapid and deep); unconsciousness; or unusual thirst.

If symptoms of high blood sugar occur, *check your blood sugar level and then call your doctor for instructions.*

Side Effects of This Medicine

Along with its needed effects, a medicine may cause some unwanted effects. Although not all of these side effects may occur, if they do occur they may need medical attention.

Check with your doctor as soon as possible if any of the following side effects occur:
More common
Problems with teeth
Less common
Swelling of feet or lower legs

Other side effects may occur that usually do not need medical attention. These side effects may go away during treatment as your body adjusts to the medicine. However, check with your doctor if any of the following side effects continue or are bothersome:
More common
Cough; fever; headache; muscle soreness; runny or stuffy nose; sore throat

Other side effects not listed above may also occur in some patients. If you notice any other effects, check with your doctor.

Developed: 1/20/2000
Revised: 2/1/2001

PLICAMYCIN   Systemic†

Commonly used brand name(s):

In the U.S.—
Mithracin

Another commonly used name is mithramycin.

†Not commercially available in Canada.

Description

Plicamycin (plye-ka-MYE-sin) belongs to the group of medicines known as antineoplastics. It may be used to treat certain types of cancer. It is also used to treat hypercalcemia or hypercalciuria (too much calcium in the blood or urine) that may occur with some types of cancer.

Plicamycin may also be used for other conditions as determined by your doctor.

Plicamycin is to be administered by or under the immediate care of your doctor. It is available only with a prescription, in the following dosage form:

Parenteral
- Injection (U.S.)

Before Receiving This Medicine

Plicamycin is a very strong medicine. In addition to its helpful effects in treating your medical problem, it has side effects that could be very serious. Before you receive this medicine, be sure that you have discussed its use with your doctor.

In deciding to use a medicine, the risks of taking the medicine must be weighed against the good it will do. This is a decision you and your doctor will make. For plicamycin, the following should be considered:

Allergies—Tell your doctor if you have ever had any unusual or allergic reaction to plicamycin. Also tell your health care professional if you are allergic to any other substances, such as foods, preservatives, or dyes.

Pregnancy—Plicamycin is not recommended for use during pregnancy. There is a possibility that it may be harmful to the fetus.

Breast-feeding—It is not known whether plicamycin passes into the breast milk.

Children—Studies on this medicine have not been done in children; however, plicamycin can cause serious side effects in any patient. Therefore, it is especially important that you discuss with the child's doctor the good that this medicine may do as well as the risks of using it.

Older adults—Many medicines have not been studied specifically in older people. Therefore, it may not be known whether they work exactly the same way they do in younger adults or if they cause different side effects or problems in older people. There is no specific information comparing use of plicamycin in the elderly with use in other age groups.

Other medicines—Although certain medicines should not be used together at all, in other cases two different medicines may be used together even if an interaction might occur. In these cases, your doctor may want to change the dose, or other precautions may be necessary. Tell your health care professional if you are taking *any* other medicines or are having x-ray treatments.

Other medical problems—The presence of other medical problems may affect the use of plicamycin. Make sure you tell your doctor if you have any other medical problems, especially:

- Bleeding problems—Use of plicamycin may increase the risk of bleeding

- Blood disease or
- Kidney disease or
- Liver disease—Use of plicamycin may make these conditions worse

- Chickenpox (including recent exposure) or
- Herpes zoster (shingles)—Use of plicamycin may make your reaction to either of these conditions worse

Proper Use of This Medicine

Plicamycin sometimes causes nausea, vomiting, and loss of appetite. However, it is very important that you continue to receive the medicine, even if you begin to feel ill. If you have any questions about this, check with your doctor.

Dosing—The dose of plicamycin will be different for different patients. The dose is based on body weight and will be determined by your doctor. *Follow your doctor's orders.* The following information includes only the average doses of plicamycin.

- For *injection* dosage form:
  —To treat cancer:
  - Adults and children—The dose that is used may depend on a number of things, including what the medicine is being used for, the patient's weight, and whether or not other medicines are also being taken. *If you are receiving plicamycin at home, follow your doctor's orders or the directions on the label.* If you have any questions about the proper dose of plicamycin, ask your doctor.
  —To treat hypercalcemia or hypercalciuria (too much calcium in the blood or urine):
  - Adults—The dose is based on body weight and must be determined by your doctor. At first, the usual dose is 15 to 25 micrograms (mcg) per kg

(6.8 to 11.4 mcg per pound) of body weight a day, injected slowly into a vein. The dose is given over a period of four to six hours once a day for three to four days. Your doctor may repeat the treatment if needed.
- Children—Dose must be determined by your doctor.

Precautions After Receiving This Medicine

It is very important that your doctor check your progress daily while you are receiving plicamycin to make sure that this medicine does not cause unwanted effects.

Your doctor may want you to follow a low-calcium, low-vitamin D diet. If you have any questions about this, check with your doctor.

Do not take aspirin or large amounts of any other preparations containing aspirin, other salicylates, or acetaminophen without first checking with your doctor. These medicines may increase the effects of plicamycin.

While you are being treated with plicamycin, and after you stop treatment with it, *do not have any immunizations (vaccinations) without your doctor's approval.* Plicamycin may lower your body's resistance and there is a chance you might get the infection the immunization is meant to prevent. In addition, other persons living in your household should not take or have recently taken oral polio vaccine since there is a chance they could pass the polio virus on to you. Also, avoid other persons who have taken oral polio vaccine. Do not get close to them, and do not stay in the same room with them for very long. If you cannot take these precautions, you should consider wearing a protective face mask that covers the nose and mouth.

Plicamycin can lower the number of white blood cells in your blood temporarily, increasing the chance of getting an infection. It can also lower the number of platelets, which are necessary for proper blood clotting. If this occurs, there are certain precautions your doctor may ask you to take, especially when your blood count is low, to reduce the risk of infection or bleeding:

- If you can, avoid people with infections. *Check with your doctor immediately* if you think you are getting an infection or if you get a fever or chills.
- *Check with your doctor immediately* if you notice any unusual bleeding or bruising.
- Be careful when using a regular toothbrush, dental floss, or toothpick. Your medical doctor, dentist, or nurse may recommend other ways to clean your teeth and gums. Check with your medical doctor before having any dental work done.
- Do not touch your eyes or the inside of your nose unless you have just washed your hands and have not touched anything else in the meantime.
- Be careful not to cut yourself when you are using sharp objects such as a safety razor or fingernail or toenail cutters.
- Avoid contact sports or other situations where bruising or injury could occur.

Side Effects of This Medicine

Along with its needed effects, a medicine may cause some unwanted effects. Although not all of these side effects may occur, if they do occur they may need medical attention.

Check with your doctor or nurse immediately if any of the following side effects occur:

Less common
Muscle and abdominal cramps

Symptoms of overdose
Bloody or black, tarry stools; flushing or redness or swelling of face; nosebleed; skin rash or small red spots on skin; sore throat and fever; unusual bleeding or bruising; vomiting of blood; yellow eyes or skin

Other side effects may occur that usually do not need medical attention. These side effects may go away during treatment as your body adjusts to the medicine. However, check with your doctor if any of the following side effects continue or are bothersome:

More common
Diarrhea; irritation or soreness of mouth; loss of appetite; nausea or vomiting—may occur 1 to 2 hours after the injection is started and continue for 12 to 24 hours

Less common
Drowsiness; fever; headache; mental depression; pain, redness, soreness, or swelling at place of injection; unusual tiredness or weakness

After you stop using plicamycin, it may still produce some side effects that need attention. During this period of time check with your doctor if you notice any of the following side effects:
Bloody or black, tarry stools; nosebleed; sore throat and fever; unusual bleeding or bruising; vomiting of blood

Other side effects not listed above may also occur in some patients. If you notice any other effects, check with your doctor.

Additional Information

Once a medicine has been approved for marketing for a certain use, experience may show that it is also useful for other medical problems. Although this use is not included in product labeling, plicamycin is used in certain patients with the following medical condition:

- Paget's disease of the bone

Other than the above information, there is no additional information relating to proper use, precautions, or side effects for these uses.

Revised: 09/14/92
Interim revision: 08/02/94

PNEUMOCOCCAL CONJUGATE VACCINE   Systemic

Commonly used brand name(s):

In the U.S.—
Prevnar

Description

Pneumococcal (NEU-mo-KOK-al) conjugate vaccine is an active immunizing agent used to prevent infection by pneu-mococcal bacteria. It works by causing your body to produce its own protection (antibodies) against the disease.

Pneumococcal infection can cause serious problems, such as pneumonia, which affects the lungs; meningitis, which affects the brain; and bacteremia, which is a severe infection in the blood. Pneumococcal infection is also an important cause of ear infections in children.

Unless otherwise contraindicated, immunization against pneumococcal disease is recommended for infants and young children.

Immunization requires 1 to 4 doses of the vaccine, depending on the age at the first dose. This vaccine can be given at the same time as other routine vaccinations.

This vaccine is to be administered only by or under the supervision of your doctor or other health care professional. It is available in the following dosage form:

Parenteral
- Injection (U.S.)

Before Receiving This Vaccine

In deciding to use a medicine, the risks of taking the medicine must be weighed against the good it will do. This is a decision you and your doctor will make. For pneumococcal conjugate vaccine, the following should be considered:

Allergies—Tell your doctor if your child has ever had any unusual or allergic reaction to pneumococcal vaccine, diphtheria toxoid, or latex. Also tell your doctor and pharmacist if your child is allergic to any other substances, such as preservatives.

Pregnancy—Studies on effects in pregnancy have not been done in either humans or animals. This vaccine is not recommended for use in pregnant women.

Breast-feeding—It is not known whether pneumococcal vaccine passes into breast milk.

Children—This vaccine is generally well tolerated and effective in infants. The safety and effectiveness in infants below 6 weeks of age has not been established.

Older adults—This vaccine is not recommended for use in adult populations.

Other medicines—Although certain medicines should not be used together at all, in other cases two different medicines may be used together even if an interaction might occur. In these cases, your doctor may want to change the dose, or other precautions may be necessary. Tell your health care professional if your child is receiving any other prescription or nonprescription (over-the-counter [OTC]) medicine.

Proper Use of This Medicine

Dosing—The number of injections your child will receive for protection from pneumococcal infection will depend on your child's age at the first dose:

- Children 6 weeks to 6 months of age—4 doses
- Children 7 to 11 months of age—3 doses
- Children 12 to 23 months of age—2 doses
- Children 2 years through 9 years of age—1 dose
- Children older than 9 years of age—Use of this vaccine is not recommended in this age group.

Your doctor will tell you when your child should receive the next dose.

Precautions While Using This Medicine

If your child has more than one doctor, be sure they all know that your child has received pneumococcal conjugated vaccine so that they can put the information into your child's medical records.

Side Effects of This Medicine

Along with its needed effects, a medicine may cause some unwanted effects. Although not all of these side effects may occur, if they do occur they may need medical attention.

Get emergency help immediately if any of the following side effects occur:

Symptoms of allergic reaction
Difficulty in breathing or swallowing; hives; itching, especially of feet or hands; reddening of skin, especially around ears; swelling of eyes, face, or inside of nose; unusual tiredness or weakness (sudden and severe)

Check with your doctor as soon as possible if the following side effects occur:

Less common
Fever over 39 °C (102.2 °F)

Rare
Collapse or shock-like state; convulsions

Other side effects may occur that usually do not need medical attention. These side effects may go away during treatment as your body adjusts to the medicine. However, check with your doctor if any of the following side effects continue or are bothersome.

More common
Decreased appetite; diarrhea; drowsiness; fever of less than 39 °C (102.2 °F); irritability; redness, soreness, hard lump, swelling, or pain at injection site; restless sleep; vomiting

Less common
Skin rash or hives

Other side effects not listed above may also occur in some patients. If you notice any other effects, check with your doctor.

Developed: 5/5/2000

PNEUMOCOCCAL VACCINE POLYVALENT   Systemic

Commonly used brand name(s):

In the U.S.—
Pneumovax 23
Pnu-Imune 23

In Canada—
Pneumovax 23

Description

Pneumococcal (NEU-mo-KOK-al) vaccine polyvalent is an active immunizing agent used to prevent infection by pneumococcal bacteria. It works by causing your body to produce its own protection (antibodies) against the disease.

The following information applies only to the polyvalent 23 pneumococcal vaccine. Other polyvalent pneumococcal vaccines may be available in countries other than the U.S.

Pneumococcal infection can cause serious problems, such as pneumonia, which affects the lungs; meningitis, which affects the brain; bacteremia, which is a severe infection in the blood; and possibly death. These problems are more likely to occur in older adults and persons with certain diseases or conditions that make them more susceptible to a pneumococcal infection or more apt to develop serious problems from a pneumococcal infection.

Unless otherwise contraindicated, immunization against pneumococcal disease is recommended for all adults and children 2 years of age and older, especially:

- Older adults, especially those 65 years of age and older.
- Adults and children 2 to 64 years of age with chronic illnesses.
- Adults and children 2 to 64 years of age with sickle cell disease, those with spleen problems or without spleens, and those who are to have their spleens removed.
- Adults and children 2 to 64 years of age who are at increased risk for pneumococcal disease because of other illness (e.g., heart disease, lung disease, diabetes, alcoholism, and liver disease).
- Adults and children 2 to 64 years of age who are living in special environments or social settings (e.g., Alaskan Natives and certain American Indian populations) and residents of nursing homes and other long-term-care facilities.
- Adults and children 2 to 64 years of age with decreased disease-fighting ability (e.g., those with human immunodeficiency virus (HIV) infection, organ or bone marrow transplantations, and cancer).

Immunization against pneumococcal infection is not recommended for infants and children younger than 2 years of age, because these persons cannot produce enough antibodies to the vaccine to protect them against a pneumococcal infection.

Pneumococcal vaccine usually is given only once to each person. Additional injections are not given, except in special cases, because of the possibility of more frequent and more severe side effects.

This vaccine is to be administered only by or under the supervision of your doctor or other health care professional. It is available in the following dosage form:

Parenteral
- Injection (U.S. and Canada)

Before Receiving This Vaccine

In deciding to use a medicine, the risks of taking the medicine must be weighed against the good it will do. This is a decision you and your doctor will make. For pneumococcal vaccine, the following should be considered:

Allergies—Tell your doctor if you have ever had any unusual or allergic reaction to pneumococcal vaccine. Also tell your health care professional if you are allergic to any other substances, such as preservatives (especially thimerosal).

Pregnancy—Studies on effects in pregnancy have not been done in either humans or animals. However, if the vaccine is needed, it should be given after the first 3 months of pregnancy and only to women who have certain diseases or conditions that make them more susceptible to a pneumococcal infection or more likely to develop serious problems from a pneumococcal infection.

Breast-feeding—It is not known whether pneumococcal vaccine passes into breast milk. Although most medicines pass into breast milk in small amounts, many of them may be used safely while breast-feeding. Mothers who are receiving this vaccine and who wish to breast-feed should discuss this with their doctor.

Children—Use of pneumococcal vaccine is not recommended in infants and children younger than 2 years of age. In children 2 years of age and older, this vaccine is not expected to cause different side effects or problems than it does in adults.

Older adults—Many medicines have not been studied specifically in older people. Therefore, it may not be known whether they work exactly the same way they do in younger adults. Although there is no specific information comparing use of pneumococcal vaccine in the elderly with use in other age groups, this vaccine is not expected to cause different side effects or problems in older people than it does in younger adults.

Other medicines—Although certain medicines should not be used together at all, in other cases two different medicines may be used together even if an interaction might occur. In these cases, your doctor may want to change the dose, or other precautions may be necessary. Tell your health care professional if you are taking any other prescription or nonprescription (over-the-counter [OTC]) medicine.

Other medical problems—The presence of other medical problems may affect the use of pneumococcal vaccine. Make sure you tell your doctor if you have any other medical problems, especially:

- Severe illness with fever—The symptoms of the illness may be confused with possible side effects of the vaccine
- Previous severe reaction to the vaccine or
- Thrombocytopenic purpura (blood disorder)—Use of pneumococcal vaccine may make the condition worse

Proper Use of This Vaccine

Dosing—The dose of pneumococcal vaccine will be different for different patients. The following information includes only the average doses of pneumococcal vaccine.

- For *injection* dosage form:
  —For prevention of pneumococcal pneumonia:
    - Adults and children 2 years of age and older— One dose injected under the skin or into a muscle.
    - Children up to 2 years of age—Use is not recommended.

Precautions After Receiving This Vaccine

If you have more than one doctor, be sure they all know that you have received pneumococcal vaccine polyvalent 23 so that they can put the information into your medical records. This vaccine usually is given only once to each person, except in special cases.

Side Effects of This Vaccine

Along with its needed effects, a medicine may cause some unwanted effects. Although not all of these side effects may occur, if they do occur they may need medical attention.

Get emergency help immediately if any of the following side effects occur:
Symptoms of allergic reaction
Difficulty in breathing or swallowing; hives; itching, es-

pecially of feet or hands; reddening of skin, especially around ears; swelling of eyes, face, or inside of nose; unusual tiredness or weakness (sudden and severe)

Check with your doctor as soon as possible if the following side effect occurs:
Rare
Fever over 102.2 °F (39 °C)

Other side effects may occur that usually do not need medical attention. However, check with your doctor if any of the following side effects continue or are bothersome:
More common
Redness, soreness, hard lump, swelling, or pain at place of injection
Less common or rare
Aches or pain in joints or muscles; fever of 101 °F (38.3 °C) or less; skin rash; swollen glands; unusual tiredness or weakness; vague feeling of bodily discomfort

Side effects may be more common and more severe if this is not the first time you have received pneumococcal vaccine. Check with your doctor as soon as possible if you do have a severe reaction. Other side effects not listed above may also occur in some patients. If you notice any other effects, check with your doctor.

Revised: 02/02/99

PODOFILOX   Topical

Commonly used brand name(s):

In the U.S.—
Condylox

Another commonly used name is podophyllotoxin.

Description

Podofilox (po-do-FIL-ox) is used to remove certain types of warts on the outside skin of the genital areas (penis or vulva). The gel is used also to treat warts between the genitals and the rectum, the solution is not. Neither the gel nor the solution is used to treat warts that occur inside the rectum, vagina, or urine passageways inside the penis (male) or the vulva (female). Podofilox works by destroying the skin of the wart.

This medicine is available only with your doctor's prescription, in the following dosage form(s):

Topical
- Gel (U.S.)
- Solution (U.S.)

Before Using This Medicine

In deciding to use a medicine, the risks of using the medicine must be weighed against the good it will do. This is a decision you and your doctor will make. For podofilox, the following should be considered:

Allergies—Tell your doctor if you have ever had any unusual or allergic reaction to podofilox. Also tell your health care professional if you are allergic to any other substances, such as foods, preservatives, or dyes.

Pregnancy—Podofilox has not been studied in pregnant women. However, studies in rats have shown that podofilox causes problems during pregnancy when injected at high doses. Topical podofilox may be absorbed into the skin at certain doses. Before using this medicine, make sure your doctor knows if you are pregnant or if you may become pregnant.

Breast-feeding—It is not known whether topical podofilox passes into breast milk. Although most medicines pass into breast milk in small amounts, many of them may be used safely while breast-feeding. Mothers who are using this medicine and who wish to breast-feed should discuss this with their doctor.

Children—Studies of this medicine have been done only in adult patients, and there is no specific information comparing use of podofilox in children with use in other age groups.

Older adults—Many medicines have not been studied specifically in older people. Therefore, it may not be known whether they work exactly the same way they do in younger adults or if they cause different side effects or problems in older people. There is no specific information comparing use of podofilox in the elderly with use in other age groups.

Other medicines—Although certain medicines should not be used together at all, in other cases two different medicines may be used together even if an interaction might occur. In these cases, your doctor may want to change the dose, or other precautions may be necessary. Tell your doctor and pharmacist if you are using any other prescription or nonprescription (over-the-counter [OTC]) medicine.

Proper Use of This Medicine

A paper with information for the patient will be given to you with your filled prescription and will provide many details concerning the use of podofilox. *Read this paper carefully* and ask your health care professional if you need additional information.

Also, *keep podofilox away from the eyes and mucous membranes*, such as the inside of the penis, rectum, or vagina. This medicine may cause severe irritation. If you get this medicine in your eyes or on one of these areas, immediately flush the area with water for 15 minutes.

Use podofilox only as directed, no more than 3 days a week and no more than 4 treatment cycles. Do not use more of it, do not use it more often, and do not use it for a longer time than your doctor ordered. To do so may increase the chances that this medicine is absorbed into the body and that side effects could occur.

Do not apply the medicine to any other wart until you discuss it with your doctor. The total dose of podofilox used on all warts should not exceed that which would cover an area measuring 1.6 square inches (10 square centimeters), about the size of a dollar coin.

To use:
- To apply the solution, use the applicators that come with the solution or a cotton-tipped applicator. To apply the gel, use a cotton-tipped applicator or your finger. *Never reuse an applicator or dip a used applicator into the bottle.*
- *Apply podofilox only to the wart(s) discussed with your doctor.*
- Podofilox can cause severe irritation of normal skin. *If*

you get medicine on normal skin, wash it off immediately.
- *Make sure the treated area is dry* before allowing the treated skin to come in contact with normal, untreated skin.
- Immediately after applying this medicine, wash your hands to remove any medicine. Properly discard used applicator(s).

Dosing—The dose of podofilox will be different for different patients. *Follow your doctor's orders or the directions on the label.* The following information includes only the average doses of podofilox. *If your dose is different, do not change it* unless your doctor tells you to do so.

- For *topical* dosage form (gel):
  —For warts on penis or vulva (genitals) or on skin between genitals and rectum:
    - Adults—Apply to the wart(s) two times a day for three days in a row using an applicator tip or finger. Skip four days by not applying any medicine for four days in a row. If the wart can still be seen, this application cycle may be repeated each week for up to four weeks, until the wart is gone. No more than 0.5 grams of gel should be used each day of treatment.
    - Children—Use and dose must be determined by the doctor.
- For *topical* dosage form (solution):
  —For warts on penis or vulva (genitals) only:
    - Adults—Apply to the wart(s) two times a day (every twelve hours) for three days in a row using applicator tip. Skip four days by not applying any medicine for four days in a row. If the wart can still be seen, this application cycle may be repeated each week for up to four weeks, until the wart is gone. No more than 0.5 milliliters of solution should be used each day of treatment.
    - Children—Use and dose must be determined by the doctor.

Missed dose—If you miss a dose of this medicine, apply it as soon as possible. Then go back to your regular dosing schedule.

Storage—To store this medicine:
- Keep out of the reach of children.
- Store away from heat and direct light.
- Keep top tightly closed.
- Do not keep outdated medicine or medicine no longer needed. Be sure that any discarded medicine is out of the reach of children.

Precautions While Using This Medicine

Podofilox may not be able to prevent previously healed warts from reappearing or stop new warts from growing.

This medicine contains alcohol and therefore may be flammable. *Do not use near heat, near open flame, or while smoking.*

Side Effects of This Medicine

Along with its needed effects, a medicine may cause some unwanted effects. Although not all of these side effects may occur, if they do occur they may need medical attention.

Check with your doctor as soon as possible if any of the following side effects occur:

More common

Bad odor (solution only); bleeding of treated skin; blistering, crusting, or scabbing of treated skin; bloody urine (solution only); burning feeling of treated skin; dizziness (solution only); headache (gel only); itching of treated skin; pain during sexual intercourse (solution only); pain of treated skin; problems with foreskin of penis (solution only); redness or swelling of treated skin; scarring of treated skin (solution only); skin ulcers of treated skin; vomiting (solution only)

Symptoms of overdose—in order of occurrence

Nausea; vomiting; diarrhea; chills; fever; sore throat; unusual bleeding or bruising; oral ulcers

Other side effects may occur that usually do not need medical attention. These side effects may go away during treatment as your body adjusts to the medicine. However, check with your doctor if any of the following side effects continue or are bothersome:

More common

Dryness of treated skin; peeling of treated skin; soreness or tenderness of treated skin; stinging or tingling of treated skin; trouble in sleeping (solution only)

Less common

Changes in color of treated skin (gel only); skin rash (gel only)

Other side effects not listed above may also occur in some patients. If you notice any other effects, check with your doctor.

Developed: 06/27/98

POLYETHYLENE GLYCOL AND ELECTROLYTES   Local

Commonly used brand name(s):

In the U.S.—

Co-Lav	Go-Evac
Colovage	GoLYTELY
Colyte	NuLYTELY
Colyte-flavored	NuLYTELY, Cherry Flavor
Colyte with Flavor Packs	OCL

In Canada—

Colyte	Peglyte
GoLYTELY	PEG-3350 & Electrolytes
Klean-Prep	

Description

The polyethylene glycol (pol-ee-ETH-i-leen GLYE-col) (PEG) and electrolytes solution is used to clean the colon (large bowel or lower intestine) before certain tests or surgery of the colon. The PEG-electrolyte solution is usually taken by mouth. However, sometimes it is given in the hospital through a nasogastric tube (a tube inserted through the nose).

The PEG-electrolyte solution acts like a laxative. It causes liquid stools or mild diarrhea. In this way, it flushes all solid material from the colon, so the doctor can have a clear view of the colon.

The PEG-electrolyte solution is available only with your doctor's prescription. It is available in the following dosage forms:

Oral
- Oral solution (U.S. and Canada)
- Powder for oral solution (U.S. and Canada)

Before Using This Medicine

In deciding to use a medicine, the risks of taking the medicine must be weighed against the good it will do. This is a decision you and your doctor will make. For the PEG-electrolyte solution, the following should be considered:

Allergies—Tell your doctor if you have ever had any unusual or allergic reaction to PEG. Also tell your health care professional if you are allergic to any other substances, such as foods, preservatives, or dyes.

Pregnancy—Studies on effects in pregnancy have not been done in either humans or animals. Before taking the PEG-electrolyte solution or having a colon examination, make sure your doctor knows if you are pregnant.

Breast-feeding—It is not known whether PEG-electrolyte solution passes into breast milk. Although most medicines pass into breast milk in small amounts, many of them may be used safely while breast-feeding. Mothers who are taking this medicine and who wish to breast-feed should discuss this with their doctor.

Children—Although there is no specific information comparing use of PEG-electrolyte solution in children with use in other age groups, this medicine is not expected to cause different side effects or problems in children than it does in adults.

Older adults—This medicine has been tested and has not been shown to cause different side effects or problems in older people than it does in younger adults.

Other medicines—Although certain medicines should not be used together at all, in other cases two different medicines may be used together even if an interaction might occur. In these cases, your doctor may want to change the dose, or other precautions may be necessary. Tell your health care professional if you are taking any of the following:

- Any other oral medicines—Any medicines taken within 1 hour of the PEG-electrolyte solution may be flushed from the body and not have an effect

Other medical problems—The presence of other medical problems may affect the use of PEG-electrolyte solution. Make sure you tell your doctor if you have any other medical problems, especially:

- Blockage or obstruction of the intestine or
- Paralytic ileus or
- Perforated bowel or
- Toxic colitis or
- Toxic megacolon—PEG-electrolyte solution may make these conditions worse; in some cases the colon may rip open or tear

---

Proper Use of This Medicine

Your doctor may have special instructions for you, depending on the type of test you are going to have. If you have not received such instructions or if you do not understand them, check with your doctor in advance.

Take the PEG-electrolyte solution exactly as directed. Otherwise, the test you are going to have may not work and may have to be done again.

It will take close to 3 hours to drink all of the PEG-electrolyte solution. The first bowel movement may start an hour or so after you start drinking the solution. *Continue drinking all the solution to get the best results*, unless otherwise directed by your doctor.

Do not eat anything for at least 3 hours before taking the PEG-electrolyte solution. If you do so, the colon may not get completely clean. If you are drinking the PEG-electrolyte solution the evening before the test, you may drink clear liquids (e.g., water, ginger ale, decaffeinated cola, decaffeinated tea, broth, gelatin) up until the time of the test. However, check first with your doctor.

For patients *using the powder form of this medicine:*

- *The powder must be mixed with water before it is used.* Add lukewarm water to the fill mark on the bottle.
- *Shake well* until all the ingredients are dissolved.
- Do not add any other ingredients, such as flavoring, to the solution.
- After you mix the solution, you must use it within 48 hours.

Dosing—*Follow your doctor's orders or the directions on the label.* The following information includes only the usual amount taken of PEG-electrolyte solution. *If your dose is different, do not change it* unless your doctor tells you to do so:

- For cleaning the colon:
  —For *oral* dosage forms (oral solution and powder for oral solution):
    - Adults and teenagers—Drink one full glass (8 ounces) of the PEG-electrolyte solution *rapidly* every ten minutes. If you sip small amounts of the solution, it will not work as well.
    - Children—The amount of PEG-electrolyte solution taken is based on body weight and must be determined by your doctor. It is usually 25 to 40 milliliters (mL) per kilogram (kg) (11.3 to 18.2 mL per pound) of body weight per hour.

Storage—To store this medicine:

- Keep out of the reach of children.
- Store away from heat and direct light.
- Store the solution in the refrigerator to improve the taste. However, keep the medicine from freezing.
- Do not keep any leftover solution. Be sure that any discarded medicine is out of the reach of children.

Side Effects of This Medicine

Along with its needed effects, a medicine may cause some unwanted effects. Although not all of these side effects may occur, if they do occur they may need medical attention.

Check with your doctor as soon as possible if the following side effect occurs:

Rare
    Skin rash

Other side effects may occur that usually do not need medical attention. These side effects may go away as your body adjusts to the medicine. However, check with your health care professional if any of the following side effects continue or are bothersome:

More common
    Bloating; nausea
Less common
    Abdominal or stomach cramps; irritation of the anus; vomiting

Other side effects not listed above may also occur in some patients. If you notice any other effects, check with your health care professional.

Revised: 09/29/2000

POTASSIUM SUPPLEMENTS
Systemic

Commonly used brand name(s):

In the U.S.—

Cena-K[5]	Klor-Con Powder[5]
Effer-K[4]	Klor-Con/25 Powder[5]
Gen-K[5]	Klorvess[3]
Glu-K[6]	Klorvess Effervescent
K-8[5]	Granules[3]
K+ 10[5]	Klorvess 10% Liquid[5]
Kaochlor 10%[5]	Klotrix[5]
Kaochlor S-F 10%[5]	K-Lyte[2]
Kaon[6]	K-Lyte/Cl[3]
Kaon-Cl[5]	K-Lyte/Cl 50[3]
Kaon-Cl-10[5]	K-Lyte/Cl Powder[5]
Kaon-Cl 20% Liquid[5]	K-Lyte DS[4]
Kato[5]	K-Norm[5]
Kay Ciel[5]	Kolyum[7]
Kaylixir[6]	K-Sol[5]
K+ Care[5]	K-Tab[5]
K+ Care ET[2]	K-Vescent[2]
K-Dur[5]	Micro-K[5]
K-Electrolyte[2]	Micro-K 10[5]
K-G Elixir[6]	Micro-K LS[5]
K-Ide[2]	Potasalan[5]
K-Lease[5]	Rum-K[5]
K-Lor[5]	Slow-K[5]
Klor-Con 8[5]	Ten-K[5]
Klor-Con 10[5]	Tri-K[9]
Klor-Con/EF[2]	Twin-K[8]

In Canada—

Apo-K[5]	K-Lyte[2]
K-10[5]	K-Lyte/Cl[5]
Kalium Durules[5]	K-Med 900[5]
Kaochlor-10[5]	Micro-K[5]
Kaochlor-20[5]	Micro-K 10[5]
Kaon[6]	Neo-K[3]
KCL 5%[5]	Potassium-Rougier[6]
K-Dur[5]	Potassium-Sandoz[3]
K-Long[5]	Roychlor-10%[5]
K-Lor[5]	Slow-K[5]

Another commonly used name for trikates is potassium triplex.

Note: For quick reference, the following potassium supplements are numbered to match the corresponding brand names.

This information applies to the following:
1. Potassium Acetate (poe-TAS-ee-um AS-a-tate) †‡
2. Potassium Bicarbonate (poe-TAS-ee-um bi-KAR-bo-nate) ‡
3. Potassium Bicarbonate and Potassium Chloride (poe-TAS-ee-um bi-KAR-bo-nate and poe-TAS-ee-um KLOR-ide)
4. Potassium Bicarbonate and Potassium Citrate (poe-TAS-ee-um bi-KAR-bo-nate and poe-TAS-ee-um SIH-trayt) †
5. Potassium Chloride (poe-TAS-ee-um KLOR-ide) ‡§
6. Potassium Gluconate (poe-TAS-ee-um GLOO-ko-nate) ‡

7. Potassium Gluconate and Potassium Chloride (poe-TAS-ee-um GLOO-ko-nate and poe-TAS-ee-um KLOR-ide) †
8. Potassium Gluconate and Potassium Citrate (poe-TAS-ee-um GLOO-ko-nate and poe-TAS-ee-um SIH-trayt) †
9. Trikates (TRI-kates) †

†Not commercially available in Canada.
‡Generic name product may be available in the U.S.
§Generic name product may be available in Canada.

Description

Potassium is needed to maintain good health. Although a balanced diet usually supplies all the potassium a person needs, potassium supplements may be needed by patients who do not have enough potassium in their regular diet or have lost too much potassium because of illness or treatment with certain medicines.

There is no evidence that potassium supplements are useful in the treatment of high blood pressure.

Lack of potassium may cause muscle weakness, irregular heartbeat, mood changes, or nausea and vomiting.

Injectable potassium is administered only by or under the supervision of your doctor. Some forms of oral potassium may be available in stores without a prescription. Since too much potassium may cause health problems, you should take potassium supplements only if directed by your doctor. Potassium supplements are available with your doctor's prescription in the following dosage forms:

Oral
Potassium Bicarbonate
  • Tablets for solution (U.S. and Canada)
Potassium Bicarbonate and Potassium Chloride
  • Powder for solution (U.S. and Canada)
  • Tablets for solution (U.S. and Canada)
Potassium Bicarbonate and Potassium Citrate
  • Tablets for solution (U.S.)
Potassium Chloride
  • Extended-release capsules (U.S. and Canada)
  • Solution (U.S. and Canada)
  • Powder for solution (U.S. and Canada)
  • Powder for suspension (U.S.)
  • Extended-release tablets (U.S. and Canada)
Potassium Gluconate
  • Elixir (U.S. and Canada)
  • Tablets (U.S.)
Potassium Gluconate and Potassium Chloride
  • Solution (U.S.)
  • Powder for solution (U.S.)
Potassium Gluconate and Potassium Citrate
  • Solution (U.S.)
Trikates
  • Solution (U.S.)
Parenteral
Potassium Acetate
  • Injection (U.S.)
Potassium Chloride
  • Concentrate for injection (U.S. and Canada)

Importance of Diet

For good health, it is important that you eat a balanced and varied diet. Follow carefully any diet program your health care professional may recommend. For your specific dietary vitamin and/or mineral needs, ask your health care professional for a list of appropriate foods.

The following table includes some potassium-rich foods.

Food (amount)	Milligrams of potassium	Milliequivalents of potassium
Acorn squash, cooked (1 cup)	896	23
Potato with skin, baked (1 long)	844	22
Spinach, cooked (1 cup)	838	21
Lentils, cooked (1 cup)	731	19
Kidney beans, cooked (1 cup)	713	18
Split peas, cooked (1 cup)	710	18
White navy beans, cooked (1 cup)	669	17
Butternut squash, cooked (1 cup)	583	15
Watermelon (1/16)	560	14
Raisins (½ cup)	553	14
Yogurt, low-fat, plain (1 cup)	531	14
Orange juice, frozen (1 cup)	503	13
Brussel sprouts, cooked (1 cup)	494	13
Zucchini, cooked, sliced (1 cup)	456	12
Banana (medium)	451	12
Collards, frozen, cooked (1 cup)	427	11
Cantaloupe (¼)	412	11
Milk, low-fat 1% (1 cup)	348	9
Broccoli, frozen, cooked (1 cup)	332	9

The daily amount of potassium needed is defined in several different ways.

For U.S.—
  • Recommended Dietary Allowances (RDAs) are the amount of vitamins and minerals needed to provide for adequate nutrition in most healthy persons. RDAs for a given nutrient may vary depending on a person's age, sex, and physical condition (e.g., pregnancy).
  • Daily Values (DVs) are used on food and dietary supplement labels to indicate the percent of the recommended daily amount of each nutrient that a serving provides. DV replaces the previous designation of United States Recommended Daily Allowances (USRDAs).
For Canada—
  • Recommended Nutrient Intakes (RNIs) are used to determine the amounts of vitamins, minerals, and protein needed to provide adequate nutrition and lessen the risk of chronic disease.

Because lack of potassium is rare, there is no RDA or RNI for this mineral. However, it is thought that 1600 to 2000 mg (40 to 50 milliequivalents [mEq]) per day for adults is adequate.

Remember:
  • The total amount of potassium that you get every day includes what you get from food *and* what you may take as a supplement. Read the labels of processed foods. Many foods now have added potassium.
  • Your total intake of potassium should not be greater than the recommended amounts, unless ordered by your doctor. In some cases, too much potassium may cause muscle weakness, confusion, irregular heartbeat, or difficult breathing.

Before Using This Medicine

In deciding to use a medicine, the risks of taking the medicine must be weighed against the good it will do. This is a decision you and your doctor will make. For potassium supplements, the following should be considered:

Allergies—Tell your doctor if you have ever had any unusual or allergic reaction to potassium preparations. Also tell your doctor and pharmacist if you are allergic to any other substances, such as foods, preservatives, or dyes.

Pregnancy—Potassium supplements have not been shown to cause problems in humans.

Breast-feeding—Potassium supplements pass into breast milk. However, this medicine has not been reported to cause problems in nursing babies.

Children—Although there is no specific information comparing use of potassium supplements in children with use in other age groups, they are not expected to cause different side effects or problems in children than they do in adults.

Older adults—Many medicines have not been studied specifically in older people. Therefore, it may not be known whether they work exactly the same way they do in younger adults. Although there is no specific information comparing use of potassium supplements in the elderly with use in other age groups, they are not expected to cause different side effects or problems in older people than they do in younger adults.

Older adults may be at a greater risk of developing high blood levels of potassium (hyperkalemia).

Other medicines—Although certain medicines should not be used together at all, in other cases two different medicines may be used together even if an interaction might occur. In these cases, your doctor may want to change the dose, or other precautions may be necessary. When you are taking potassium supplements, it is especially important that your doctor and pharmacist know if you are taking any of the following:

- Amantadine (e.g., Symmetrel) or
- Anticholinergics (medicine for abdominal or stomach spasms or cramps) or
- Antidepressants (medicine for depression) or
- Antidyskinetics (medicine for Parkinson's disease or other conditions affecting control of muscles) or
- Antihistamines or
- Antipsychotic medicine (medicine for mental illness) or
- Buclizine (e.g., Bucladin) or
- Carbamazepine (e.g., Tegretol) or
- Cyclizine (e.g., Marezine) or
- Cyclobenzaprine (e.g., Flexeril) or
- Disopyramide (e.g., Norpace) or
- Flavoxate (e.g., Urispas) or
- Ipratropium (e.g., Atrovent) or
- Meclizine (e.g., Antivert) or
- Methylphenidate (e.g., Ritalin) or
- Orphenadrine (e.g., Norflex) or
- Oxybutynin (e.g., Ditropan) or
- Procainamide (e.g., Pronestyl) or
- Promethazine (e.g., Phenergan) or
- Quinidine (e.g., Quinidex) or
- Trimeprazine (e.g., Temaril)—Use with potassium supplements may cause or worsen certain stomach or intestine problems
- Angiotensin-converting enzyme (ACE) inhibitors (benazepril [e.g., Lotensin], captopril [e.g., Capoten], enalapril [e.g., Vasotec], fosinopril [e.g., Monotril], lisinopril [e.g., Prinivil, Zestril], quinapril [e.g., Accupril], ramipril [e.g., Altace]) or
- Amiloride (e.g., Midamor) or
- Beta-adrenergic blocking agents (acebutolol [e.g., Sectral], atenolol [e.g., Tenormin], betaxolol [e.g., Kerlone], carteolol [e.g., Cartrol], labetalol [e.g., Normodyne], metoprolol [e.g., Lopressor], nadolol [e.g., Corgard], ox-

prenolol [e.g., Trasicor], penbutolol [e.g., Levatol], pindolol [e.g., Visken], propranolol [e.g., Inderal], sotalol [e.g., Sotacor], timolol [e.g., Blocadren]) or
- Heparin (e.g., Panheprin) or
- Inflammation or pain medicine (except narcotics) or
- Potassium-containing medicines (other) or
- Salt substitutes, low-salt foods, or milk or
- Spironolactone (e.g., Aldactone) or
- Triamterene (e.g., Dyrenium)—Use with potassium supplements may further increase potassium blood levels, which may cause or worsen heart problems
- Digitalis glycosides (heart medicine)—Use with potassium supplements may make heart problems worse
- Thiazide diuretics (water pills)—If you have been taking a potassium supplement and a thiazide diuretic together, stopping the thiazide diuretic may cause hyperkalemia (high blood levels of potassium)

Other medical problems—The presence of other medical problems may affect the use of potassium supplements. Make sure you tell your doctor if you have any other medical problems, especially:

- Addison's disease (underactive adrenal glands) or
- Dehydration (excessive loss of body water, continuing or severe)
- Diabetes mellitus (sugar diabetes) or
- Kidney disease—Potassium supplements may increase the risk of hyperkalemia (high blood levels of potassium), which may worsen or cause heart problems in patients with these conditions
- Diarrhea (continuing or severe)—The loss of fluid in combination with potassium supplements may cause kidney problems, which may increase the risk of hyperkalemia (high blood levels of potassium)
- Heart disease—Potassium supplements may make this condition worse
- Intestinal or esophageal blockage—Potassium supplements may damage the intestines
- Stomach ulcer—Potassium supplements may make this condition worse

Proper Use of This Medicine

For patients taking the *liquid form* of this medicine:
- This medicine *must be diluted* in at least one-half glass (4 ounces) of cold water or juice to reduce its possible stomach-irritating or laxative effect.
- If you are on a salt (sodium)-restricted diet, check with your doctor before using tomato juice to dilute your medicine. Tomato juice has a high salt content.

For patients taking the *soluble granule, soluble powder, or soluble tablet form* of this medicine:
- This medicine must be completely dissolved in at least one-half glass (4 ounces) of cold water or juice to reduce its possible stomach-irritating or laxative effect.
- Allow any "fizzing" to stop before taking the dissolved medicine.
- If you are on a salt (sodium)-restricted diet, check with your doctor before using tomato juice to dilute your medicine. Tomato juice has a high salt content.

For patients taking the *extended-release tablet form* of this medicine:
- Swallow the tablets whole with a full (8-ounce) glass of water. Do not chew or suck on the tablet.

- Some tablets may be broken or crushed and sprinkled on applesauce or other soft food. However, check with your doctor or pharmacist first, since this should not be done for most tablets.
- If you have trouble swallowing tablets or if they seem to stick in your throat, check with your doctor. When this medicine is not properly released, it can cause irritation that may lead to ulcers.

For patients taking the *extended-release capsule form* of this medicine:

- Do not crush or chew the capsule. Swallow the capsule whole with a full (8-ounce) glass of water.
- Some capsules may be opened and the contents sprinkled on applesauce or other soft food. However, check with your doctor or pharmacist first, since this should not be done for most capsules.

Take this medicine immediately after meals or with food to lessen possible stomach upset or laxative action.

Take this medicine only as directed by your doctor. Do not take more of it, do not take it more often, and do not take it for a longer time than your doctor ordered. *This is especially important if you are also taking both diuretics (water pills) and digitalis medicines for your heart.*

Dosing—The dose of these single or combination medicines will be different for different patients. *Follow your doctor's orders or the directions on the label.* The following information includes only the average dose of these medicines. *If your dose is different, do not change it* unless your doctor tells you to do so.

The number of ounces of solution that you drink, or the number of tablets or capsules you take, depends on the strength of the medicine. Also, *the number of doses you take each day, the time allowed between doses, and the length of time you take the medicine depend on the medical problem for which you are taking the single or combination medicine.*

For potassium bicarbonate
- For *oral* dosage form (tablets for solution):
  —To prevent potassium loss or replace potassium lost by the body:
    - Adults and teenagers—25 to 50 milliequivalents (mEq) dissolved in one-half to one glass of cold water, taken one or two times a day. Your doctor may change the dose if needed. However, most people will not take more than 100 mEq a day.
    - Children—Dose must be determined by your doctor.

For potassium bicarbonate and potassium chloride
- For *oral* dosage form (granules for solution):
  —To prevent potassium loss or replace potassium lost by the body:
    - Adults and teenagers—20 milliequivalents (mEq) dissolved in one-half to one glass of cold water, taken one or two times a day. Your doctor may change the dose if needed. However, most people will not take more than 100 mEq a day.
    - Children—Dose must be determined by your doctor.
- For *oral* dosage form (tablets for solution):
  —To prevent potassium loss or replace potassium lost by the body:
    - Adults and teenagers—20, 25, or 50 mEq dissolved in one-half to one glass of cold water, taken one or two times a day. Your doctor may change

the dose if needed. However, most people will not take more than 100 mEq a day.
    - Children—Dose must be determined by your doctor.

For potassium bicarbonate and potassium citrate
- For *oral* dosage form (tablets for solution):
  —To prevent potassium loss or replace potassium lost by the body:
    - Adults and teenagers—25 or 50 milliequivalents (mEq) dissolved in one-half to one glass of cold water, taken one or two times a day. Your doctor may change the dose if needed. However, most people will not take more than 100 mEq a day.
    - Children—Dose must be determined by your doctor.

For potassium chloride
- For *oral* dosage form (extended-release capsules):
  —To replace potassium lost by the body:
    - Adults and teenagers—40 to 100 milliequivalents (mEq) a day, divided into two or three smaller doses during the day. Your doctor may change the dose if needed. However, most people will not take more than 100 mEq a day.
  —To prevent potassium loss:
    - Adults and teenagers—16 to 24 mEq a day, divided into two or three smaller doses during the day. Your doctor may change the dose if needed. However, most people will not take more than 100 mEq a day.
    - Children—Dose must be determined by your doctor.
- For *oral* dosage form (liquid for solution):
  —To prevent potassium loss or replace potassium lost by the body:
    - Adults and teenagers—20 mEq mixed into one-half glass of cold water or juice, taken one to four times a day. Your doctor may change the dose if needed. However, most people will not take more than 100 mEq a day.
    - Children—Dose is based on body weight and must be determined by your doctor. The usual dose is 1 to 3 mEq of potassium per kilogram (kg) (0.45 to 1.36 mEq per pound) of body weight taken in smaller doses during the day. The solution should be well mixed in water or juice.
- For *oral* dosage form (powder for solution):
  —To prevent potassium loss or replace potassium lost by the body:
    - Adults and teenagers—15 to 25 mEq dissolved in four to six ounces of cold water, taken two or four times a day. Your doctor may change the dose if needed. However, most people will not take more than 100 mEq a day.
    - Children—Dose is based on body weight and must be determined by your doctor. The usual dose is 1 to 3 mEq per kg (0.45 to 1.36 mEq per pound) of body weight taken in smaller doses during the day. The solution should be mixed into water or juice.
- For *oral* dosage form (powder for suspension):
  —To prevent potassium loss or replace potassium lost by the body:
    - Adults and teenagers—20 mEq dissolved in two to six ounces of cold water, taken one to five times a day. Your doctor may change the dose if

needed. However, most people will not take more than 100 mEq a day.
  - Children—Dose must be determined by your doctor.

- For *oral* dosage form (extended-release tablets):
  —To prevent potassium loss or replace potassium lost by the body:
  - Adults and teenagers—6.7 to 20 mEq taken three times a day. However, most people will not take more than 100 mEq a day.
  - Children—Dose must be determined by your doctor.

For potassium gluconate
- For *oral* dosage form (liquid for solution):
  —To prevent potassium loss or replace potassium lost by the body:
  - Adults and teenagers—20 milliequivalents (mEq) mixed into one-half glass of cold water or juice, taken two to four times a day. Your doctor may change the dose if needed. However, most people will not take more than 100 mEq a day.
  - Children—Dose is based on body weight and must be determined by your doctor. The usual dose is 2 to 3 mEq per kilogram (kg) (0.9 to 1.36 mEq per pound) of body weight a day, taken in smaller doses during the day. The solution should be completely mixed into water or juice.

- For *oral* dosage form (tablets):
  —To prevent potassium loss or replace potassium lost by the body:
  - Adults and teenagers—5 to 10 mEq taken two to four times a day. However, most people will not take more than 100 mEq a day.
  - Children—Dose must be determined by your doctor.

For potassium gluconate and potassium chloride
- For *oral* dosage form (liquid for solution):
  —To prevent potassium loss or replace potassium lost by the body:
  - Adults and teenagers—20 milliequivalents (mEq) diluted in 2 tablespoonfuls or more of cold water or juice, taken two to four times a day. Your doctor may change the dose if needed. However, most people will not take more than 100 mEq a day.
  - Children—Dose is based on body weight and must be determined by your doctor. The usual dose is 2 to 3 mEq per kilogram (kg) (0.9 to 1.36 mEq per pound) of body weight taken in smaller doses during the day. The solution should be well mixed into water or juice.

- For *oral* dosage form (powder for solution):
  —To prevent potassium loss or replace potassium lost by the body:
  - Adults and teenagers—20 mEq mixed in 2 table-spoonfuls or more of cold water or juice taken two to four times a day. Your doctor may change the dose if needed. However, most people will not take more than 100 mEq a day.
  - Children—Dose is base on body weight and must be determined by your doctor. The usual dose is 2 to 3 mEq per kg (0.9 to 1.36 mEq per pound) of body weight taken in smaller doses during the day. The solution should be well mixed into water or juice.

For potassium gluconate and potassium citrate
- For *oral* dosage form (liquid for solution):
  —To prevent potassium loss or replace potassium lost by the body:
  - Adults and teenagers—20 milliequivalents (mEq) mixed into one-half glass of cold water or juice, taken two to four times a day. Your doctor may change the dose if needed. However, most people will not take more than 100 mEq a day.
  - Children—Dose is based on body weight and must be determined by your doctor. The usual dose is 2 to 3 mEq per kg (0.9 to 1.36 mEq per pound) of body weight taken in smaller doses during the day. The solution should be well mixed into water or juice.

For trikates
- For *oral* dosage form (liquid for solution):
  —To prevent potassium loss or replace potassium lost by the body:
  - Adults and teenagers—15 milliequivalents (mEq) mixed into one-half glass of cold water or juice, taken three or four times a day. Your doctor may change the dose if needed. However, most people will not take more than 100 mEq a day.
  - Children—Dose is based on body weight and must be determined by your doctor. The usual dose is 2 to 3 mEq per kilogram (kg) (0.9 to 1.36 mEq per pound) of body weight taken in smaller doses during the day. The solution should be well mixed into water or juice.

Missed dose—If you miss a dose of this medicine and remember within 2 hours, take the missed dose right away with food or liquids. Then go back to your regular dosing schedule. However, if you do not remember until later, skip the missed dose and go back to your regular dosing schedule. Do not double doses.

Storage—To store this medicine:
- Keep out of the reach of children.
- Store away from heat and direct light.
- Do not store in the bathroom, near the kitchen sink, or in other damp places. Heat or moisture may cause the medicine to break down.
- Keep the liquid form of this medicine from freezing.
- Do not keep outdated medicine or medicine no longer needed. Be sure that any discarded medicine is out of the reach of children.

Precautions While Using This Medicine

Your doctor should check your progress at regular visits to make sure the medicine is working properly and that possible side effects are avoided. Laboratory tests may be necessary.

Do not use salt substitutes, eat low-sodium foods, especially some breads and canned foods, or drink low-sodium milk unless you are told to do so by your doctor, since these products may contain potassium. It is important to read the labels carefully on all low-sodium food products.

Check with your doctor before starting any physical exercise program, especially if you are out of condition and are taking any other medicine. Exercise and certain medicines may increase the amount of potassium in the blood.

Check with your doctor at once if you notice blackish stools or other signs of stomach or intestinal bleeding.

This medicine may cause such a condition to become worse, especially when taken in tablet form.

Side Effects of This Medicine

Along with its needed effects, a medicine may cause some unwanted effects. Although not all of these side effects may occur, if they do occur they may need medical attention.

Stop taking this medicine and check with your doctor immediately if any of the following side effects occur:
  Less common
    Confusion; irregular or slow heartbeat; numbness or tingling in hands, feet, or lips; shortness of breath or difficult breathing; unexplained anxiety; unusual tiredness or weakness; weakness or heaviness of legs

Also, check with your doctor if any of the following side effects occur:
  Rare
    Abdominal or stomach pain, cramping, or soreness (continuing); chest or throat pain, especially when swallowing; stools with signs of blood (red or black color)

Other side effects may occur that usually do not need medical attention. These side effects may go away during treatment as your body adjusts to the medicine. However, check with your doctor if any of the following side effects continue or are bothersome:
  More common
    Diarrhea; nausea; stomach pain, discomfort, or gas (mild); vomiting

Sometimes you may see what appears to be a whole tablet in the stool after taking certain extended-release potassium chloride tablets. This is to be expected. Your body has absorbed the potassium from the tablet and the shell is then expelled.

Other side effects not listed above may also occur in some patients. If you notice any other effects, check with your doctor.

Revised: 07/16/92
Interim revision: 07/11/95

PRAMIPEXOLE Systemic

Commonly used brand name(s):

In the U.S.—
  Mirapex
In Canada—
  Mirapex

Description

Pramipexole (pra-mi-PEX-ole) is used to treat Parkinson's disease. It may be used alone, or in combination with levodopa or other medicines to treat this disease.

This medicine is available only with your doctor's prescription, in the following dosage form(s):

  Oral
  • Tablets (U.S. and Canada)

Before Using This Medicine

In deciding to use a medicine, the risks of taking the medicine must be weighed against the good it will do. This is a decision you and your doctor will make. For pramipexole, the following should be considered:

Allergies—Tell your doctor if you have ever had any unusual or allergic reaction to pramipexole. Also tell your health care professional if you are allergic to any other substances, such as foods, preservatives, or dyes.

Pregnancy—Pramipexole has not been studied in pregnant women. However, studies in pregnant animals have shown that pramipexole may interfere with the pregnancy when the mother is given doses many times higher than the human dose. Before taking this medicine, make sure your doctor knows if you are pregnant or if you may become pregnant.

Breast-feeding—It is not known whether pramipexole passes into breast milk. Because of the possibility of serious unwanted effects in the nursing infant, it is important that you discuss the use of this medicine with your doctor if you wish to breast-feed.

Children—Studies on this medicine have been done only in adult patients, and there is no specific information comparing use of pramipexole in children with use in other age groups.

Older adults—Hallucinations (seeing, hearing, or feeling things that are not there) may be especially likely to occur in elderly patients, who are usually more sensitive than younger adults to the effects of pramipexole.

Other medicines—Although certain medicines should not be used together at all, in other cases two different medicines may be used together even if an interaction might occur. In these cases, your doctor may want to change the dose, or other precautions may be necessary. When you are taking pramipexole, it is especially important that your health care professional know if you are taking any of the following:
  • Carbidopa and levodopa combination (e.g., Sinemet) or
  • Levodopa (e.g., Dopar, Larodopa)—Pramipexole may cause an increase in the side effects of levodopa; your doctor may need to adjust your dosage

Other medical problems—The presence of other medical problems may affect the use of pramipexole. Make sure you tell your doctor if you have any other medical problems, especially:
  • Eye problems, especially with the retina—Animal studies have shown that problems with the retina may occur; it is not certain if this may occur in humans
  • Hallucinations (seeing, hearing, or feeling things that are not there) or
  • Hypotension (low blood pressure) or
  • Postural hypotension (dizziness, lightheadedness, or fainting, especially when getting up from a lying or sitting position)—Pramipexole may make these conditions worse
  • Kidney problems—Higher blood levels of pramipexole may result, and cause an increase in side effects

Proper Use of This Medicine

Take this medicine every day exactly as directed by your doctor in order to improve your condition as much as possible. Do not take more of it or less of it, and do not take it more or less often than your doctor ordered.

Dosing—The dose of pramipexole will be different for different patients. *Follow your doctor's orders or the directions on the label.* The following information includes only the average doses of pramipexole. *If your dose is different, do not change it* unless your doctor tells you to do so.

The number of tablets that you take depends on the strength of the medicine. Also, *the number of doses you take each day, the time allowed between doses, and the length of time you take the medicine depend on your medical condition.*

- For *oral* dosage form (tablets):
  —For Parkinson's disease:
  - Adults—At first, 0.125 milligrams (mg) three times a day. Your doctor will increase your dose gradually as needed and tolerated. However, the dose usually is not more than 4.5 mg a day.
  - Children—Use and dose must be determined by your doctor.

Missed dose—If you miss a dose of this medicine, take it as soon as possible. However, if it is almost time for your next dose, skip the missed dose and go back to your regular dosing schedule. Do not double doses.

Storage—To store this medicine:
- Keep out of the reach of children.
- Store away from heat and direct light.
- Do not store in the bathroom, near the kitchen sink, or in other damp places. Heat or moisture may cause the medicine to break down.
- Keep the medicine from freezing. Do not refrigerate.
- Do not keep outdated medicine or medicine no longer needed. Be sure that any discarded medicine is out of the reach of children.

Precautions While Using This Medicine

It is important that your doctor check your progress at regular visits. This is necessary to allow dose adjustments and to reduce any unwanted effects.

Do not stop taking this medicine without first checking with your doctor. Your doctor may want you to reduce gradually the amount you are taking before stopping completely.

This medicine may cause some people to become drowsy, dizzy or lightheaded, or to have vision problems, weakness, or problems with coordination. *Make sure you know how you react to this medicine before you drive, use machines, or do anything else that could be dangerous if you are not alert, well-coordinated, or able to think or see well.*

Patients receiving this medicine have reported falling asleep while engaged in daily living activities, including the operation of motor vehicles. Some patients have further reported that they were fully alert just prior to falling asleep and had no warning signs such as excessive drowsiness.

Dizziness, lightheadedness, or fainting may occur, especially when you get up from a lying or sitting position. These symptoms are more likely to occur when you begin taking this medicine, or when the dose is increased. Getting up slowly may help. If you should have this problem, check with your doctor.

Hallucinations (seeing, hearing, or feeling things that are not there) may occur in some patients. This is more common with elderly patients.

Side Effects of This Medicine

Along with its needed effects, a medicine may cause some unwanted effects. Although not all of these side effects may occur, if they do occur they may need medical attention.

Check with your doctor as soon as possible if any of the following side effects occur:
More common
  Dizziness, lightheadedness, or fainting, especially when standing up; drowsiness; hallucinations (seeing, hearing, or feeling things that are not there); nausea; trouble in sleeping; twitching, twisting, or other unusual body movements; unusual tiredness or weakness
Less common
  Confusion; cough; difficulty in swallowing; double vision or other changes in vision; falling asleep without warning; fearfulness, suspiciousness, or other mental changes; fever; frequent urination; memory loss; muscle or joint pain; muscle weakness; restlessness or need to keep moving; shortness of breath; swelling of body; tightness in chest; troubled breathing; wheezing; writhing, twisting, or other unusual body movements
Rare
  Abnormal thinking; anxiety; bloody or cloudy urine; chest pain; difficult, burning, or painful urination; dizziness; frequent urge to urinate; loss of bladder control; mood or mental changes; swelling of arms or legs

Other side effects may occur that usually do not need medical attention. These side effects may go away during treatment as your body adjusts to the medicine. However, check with your doctor if any of the following side effects continue or are bothersome:
More common
  Constipation; dryness of mouth; headache; heartburn, indigestion, or acid stomach
Less common
  Abnormal dreams; decreased sexual drive or ability; general feeling of discomfort or illness; increased cough; increased sweating; itching; joint pain; loss of appetite; runny nose; skin problems, such as rash or itching; weight loss

Other side effects not listed above may also occur in some patients. If you notice any other effects, check with your doctor.

Developed: 06/14/99
Revised: 09/30/99

PRAZOSIN   Systemic

Commonly used brand name(s):

In the U.S.—
  Minipress
  Generic name product may be available.

In Canada—
Minipress

Description

Prazosin (PRA-zoe-sin) belongs to the general class of medicines called antihypertensives. It is used to treat high blood pressure (hypertension).

High blood pressure adds to the work load of the heart and arteries. If it continues for a long time, the heart and arteries may not function properly. This can damage the blood vessels of the brain, heart, and kidneys, resulting in a stroke, heart failure, or kidney failure. High blood pressure may also increase the risk of heart attacks. These problems may be less likely to occur if blood pressure is controlled.

Prazosin works by relaxing blood vessels so that blood passes through them more easily. This helps to lower blood pressure.

Prazosin may also be used for other conditions as determined by your doctor.

Prazosin is available only with your doctor's prescription, in the following dosage forms:

Oral
- Capsules (U.S.)
- Tablets (Canada)

Before Using This Medicine

In deciding to use a medicine, the risks of taking the medicine must be weighed against the good it will do. This is a decision you and your doctor will make. For prazosin, the following should be considered:

Allergies—Tell your doctor if you have ever had any unusual or allergic reaction to prazosin, doxazosin, or terazosin. Also tell your health care professional if you are allergic to any other substance, such as foods, preservatives, or dyes.

Pregnancy—Limited use of prazosin to control high blood pressure in pregnant women has not shown that prazosin causes birth defects or other problems. Studies in animals given many times the highest recommended human dose of prazosin also have not shown that prazosin causes birth defects. However, in rats given many times the highest recommended human dose, lower birth weights were seen.

Breast-feeding—Prazosin passes into breast milk in small amounts. However, it has not been reported to cause problems in nursing babies.

Children—Studies on this medicine have been done only in adult patients, and there is no specific information comparing use of prazosin in children with use in other age groups.

Older adults—Dizziness, lightheadedness, or fainting (especially when getting up from a lying or sitting position) may be more likely to occur in the elderly, who are more sensitive to the effects of prazosin. In addition, prazosin may reduce tolerance to cold temperatures in elderly patients.

Other medicines—Although certain medicines should not be used together at all, in other cases two different medicines may be used together even if an interaction might occur. In these cases, your doctor may want to change the dose, or other precautions may be necessary. Tell your health care professional if you are taking any other prescription or nonprescription (over-the-counter [OTC]) medicine.

Other medical problems—The presence of other medical problems may affect the use of prazosin. Make sure you tell your doctor if you have any other medical problems, especially:
- Angina (chest pain) or
- Heart disease (severe)—Prazosin may make these conditions worse
- Kidney disease—Possible increased sensitivity to the effects of prazosin

---

Proper Use of This Medicine

For patients *taking this medicine for high blood pressure:*
- In addition to the use of the medicine your doctor has prescribed, treatment for your high blood pressure may include weight control and care in the types of foods you eat, especially foods high in sodium. Your doctor will tell you which of these are most important for you. You should check with your doctor before changing your diet.
- Many patients who have high blood pressure will not notice any signs of the problem. In fact, many may feel normal. It is very important that you *take your medicine exactly as directed* and that you keep your appointments with your doctor even if you feel well.
- Remember that prazosin will not cure your high blood pressure but it does help control it. Therefore, you must continue to take it as directed if you expect to lower your blood pressure and keep it down. *You may have to take high blood pressure medicine for the rest of your life.* If high blood pressure is not treated, it can cause serious problems such as heart failure, blood vessel disease, stroke, or kidney disease.

To help you remember to take your medicine, try to get into the habit of taking it at the same time each day.

Dosing—The dose of prazosin will be different for different patients. *Follow your doctor's orders or the directions on the label.* The following information includes only the average doses of prazosin. *If your dose is different, do not change it* unless your doctor tells you to do so.

The number of capsules or tablets that you take depends on the strength of the medicine.
- For *oral* dosage form (capsules or tablets):
  —For high blood pressure:
    - Adults—At first, 0.5 or 1 milligram (mg) two or three times a day. Then, your doctor will slowly increase your dose to 6 to 15 mg a day. This is divided into two or three doses.
    - Children—Dose is based on body weight and must be determined by your doctor. The usual dose is 50 to 400 micrograms (mcg) (0.05 to 0.4 mg) per kilogram of body weight (22.73 to 181.2 mcg per pound [0.023 to 0.18 mg per pound]) a day. This is divided into two or three doses.

Missed dose—If you miss a dose of this medicine, take it as soon as possible. However, if it is almost time for your next dose, skip the missed dose and go back to your regular dosing schedule. Do not double doses.

Storage—To store this medicine:
- Keep out of the reach of children.
- Store away from heat and direct light.
- Do not store in the bathroom, near the kitchen sink, or in other damp places. Heat or moisture may cause the medicine to break down.

• Do not keep outdated medicine or medicine no longer needed. Be sure that any discarded medicine is out of the reach of children.

Precautions While Using This Medicine

It is important that your doctor check your progress at regular visits to make sure that this medicine is working properly.

For patients *taking this medicine for high blood pressure:*
• *Do not take other medicines unless they have been discussed with your doctor.* This especially includes over-the-counter (nonprescription) medicines for appetite control, asthma, colds, cough, hay fever, or sinus problems, since they may tend to make prazosin less effective.

Dizziness, lightheadedness, or sudden fainting may occur after you take this medicine, especially when you get up from a lying or sitting position. These effects are more likely to occur when you take the first dose of this medicine. Taking the first dose at bedtime may prevent problems. However, *be especially careful if you need to get up during the night.* These effects may also occur with any doses you take after the first dose. Getting up slowly may help lessen this problem. *If you feel dizzy, lie down so that you do not faint.* Then sit for a few moments before standing to prevent the dizziness from returning.

The dizziness, lightheadedness, or fainting is more likely to occur if you drink alcohol, stand for a long time, exercise, or if the weather is hot. *While you are taking this medicine, be careful to limit the amount of alcohol you drink. Also, use extra care during exercise or hot weather or if you must stand for a long time.*

Prazosin may cause some people to become drowsy or less alert than they are normally. *Make sure you know how you react to this medicine before you drive, use machines, or do anything else that could be dangerous if you are dizzy, drowsy, or are not alert.* After you have taken several doses of this medicine, these effects should lessen.

Side Effects of This Medicine

Along with its needed effects, a medicine may cause some unwanted effects. Although not all of these side effects may occur, if they do occur they may need medical attention.

Check with your doctor as soon as possible if any of the following side effects occur:
More common
Dizziness or lightheadedness, especially when getting up from a lying or sitting position; fainting (sudden)
Less common
Loss of bladder control; pounding heartbeat; swelling of feet or lower legs
Rare
Chest pain; painful inappropriate erection of penis (continuing); shortness of breath

Other side effects may occur that usually do not need medical attention. These side effects may go away during treatment as your body adjusts to the medicine. However, check with your doctor if any of the following side effects continue or are bothersome:
More common
Drowsiness; headache; lack of energy
Less common
Dryness of mouth; nervousness; unusual tiredness or weakness

Rare
Frequent urge to urinate; nausea

Other side effects not listed above may also occur in some patients. If you notice any other effects, check with your doctor.

Additional Information

Once a medicine has been approved for marketing for a certain use, experience may show that it is also useful for other medical problems. Although these uses are not included in product labeling, prazosin is used in certain patients with the following medical conditions:
• Congestive heart failure
• Ergot alkaloid poisoning
• Pheochromocytoma
• Raynaud's disease
• Benign enlargement of the prostate

For patients taking this medicine for *benign enlargement of the prostate:*
• Prazosin will not shrink the size of your prostate, but it does help to relieve the symptoms.

Other than the above information, there is no additional information relating to proper use, precautions, or side effects for these uses.

Revised: 08/02/94

PRIMAQUINE   Systemic

Description

Primaquine (PRIM-a-kween) belongs to the group of medicines called antiprotozoals. It is used in the treatment of malaria, a red blood cell infection transmitted by the bite of a mosquito.

Malaria transmission occurs in large areas of Central and South America, Hispaniola, sub-Saharan Africa, the Indian subcontinent, Southeast Asia, the Middle East, and Oceania. Country-specific information on malaria can be obtained from the Centers for Disease Control and Prevention (CDC), or from the CDC's web site at *http://www.cdc.gov/travel/yellowbk*

Primaquine is available only with your doctor's prescription, in the following dosage form:
Oral
• Tablets (U.S. and Canada)

Before Using This Medicine

In deciding to use a medicine, the risks of taking the medicine must be weighed against the good it will do. This is a decision you and your doctor will make. For primaquine, the following should be considered:

Allergies—Tell your doctor if you have ever had any unusual or allergic reaction to primaquine or iodoquinol (e.g., Yodoxin). Also tell your health care professional if you are allergic to any other substances, such as foods, preservatives, or dyes.

Pregnancy—Primaquine is not recommended for use during pregnancy.

Breast-feeding—It is not known if primaquine is distributed into breast milk. However, primaquine has not been reported to cause problems in nursing babies.

Children—Children should avoid traveling to areas where there is a chance of getting malaria, unless they can take effective antimalarial medicines such as primaquine.

Older adults—Many medicines have not been studied specifically in older people. Therefore, it may not be known whether they work exactly the same way they do in younger adults or if they cause different side effects or problems in older people. There is no specific information comparing use of primaquine in the elderly with use in other age groups.

Other medicines—Although certain medicines should not be used together at all, in other cases two different medicines may be used together even if an interaction might occur. In these cases, your doctor may want to change the dose, or other precautions may be necessary. When you are taking primaquine it is especially important that your health care professional know if you are taking any of the following:

- Acetohydroxamic acid (e.g., Lithostat) or
- Antidiabetics, oral (diabetes medicine you take by mouth) or
- Dapsone or
- Furazolidone (e.g., Furoxone) or
- Methyldopa (e.g., Aldomet) or
- Nitrofurantoin (e.g., Furadantin) or
- Procainamide (e.g., Pronestyl) or
- Quinacrine (e.g., Atabrine) or
- Quinidine (e.g., Quinidex) or
- Quinine (e.g., Quinamm) or
- Sulfonamides (sulfa medicine) or
- Sulfoxone (e.g., Diasone) or
- Vitamin K (e.g., AquaMEPHYTON, Synkayvite)—Taking these medicines with primaquine may increase the chance of side effects affecting the blood

Other medical problems—The presence of other medical problems may affect the use of primaquine. Make sure you tell your doctor if you have any other medical problems, especially:

- Family or personal history of favism or hemolytic anemia or
- Glucose-6-phosphate dehydrogenase (G6PD) deficiency or
- Nicotinamide adenine dinucleotide (NADH) methemoglobin reductase deficiency—Patients with any of these medical problems who take primaquine may have an increased chance of side effects affecting the blood

Proper Use of This Medicine

If this medicine upsets your stomach, it may be taken with meals or with antacids. If stomach upset (nausea, vomiting, or stomach pain) continues, check with your doctor.

If you are taking primaquine for malaria, *keep taking it for the full time of treatment* to help prevent or completely clear up the infection. *Do not miss any doses.*

Dosing—The dose of primaquine will be different for different patients. *Follow your doctor's orders or the directions on the label.* The following information includes only the average doses of primaquine. *If your dose is different, do not change it* unless your doctor tells you to do so.

The number of tablets that you take depends on the strength of the medicine. Also, *the number of doses you take each day, the time allowed between doses, and the length of time you take the medicine depend on the medical problem for which you are taking primaquine.*

- For the *treatment of malaria:*
  —Adults and older children: 15 mg once a day for fourteen days.
  —Younger children: Dose is based on body weight and must be determined by the doctor.

Missed dose—If you do miss a dose of this medicine, take it as soon as possible. However, if it is almost time for your next dose, skip the missed dose and go back to your regular dosing schedule. Do not double doses.

Storage—To store this medicine:
- Keep out of the reach of children.
- Store away from heat and direct light.
- Do not store in the bathroom, near the kitchen sink, or in other damp places. Heat or moisture may cause the medicine to break down.
- Do not keep outdated medicine or medicine no longer needed. Be sure that any discarded medicine is out of the reach of children.

Precautions While Using This Medicine

Your doctor should check your progress at regular visits to make sure that primaquine is not causing blood problems.

Side Effects of This Medicine

Along with its needed effects, a medicine may cause some unwanted effects. Although not all of these side effects may occur, if they do occur they may need medical attention.

Check with your doctor immediately if any of the following side effects occur:
More common
  Back, leg, or stomach pains; dark urine; fever; loss of appetite; pale skin; unusual tiredness or weakness
Less common
  Bluish fingernails, lips, or skin; difficulty breathing; dizziness or lightheadedness
Rare
  Sore throat and fever

Other side effects may occur that usually do not need medical attention. These side effects may go away during treatment as your body adjusts to the medicine. However, check with your doctor if any of the following side effects continue or are bothersome:
More common
  Cramps; nausea or vomiting

Other side effects not listed above may also occur in some patients. If you notice any other effects, check with your doctor.

Additional Information

Once a medicine has been approved for marketing for a certain use, experience may show that it is also useful for other medical problems. Although this use is not included in product labeling, primaquine is used in certain patients with the following medical condition:

- *Pneumocystis carinii* pneumonia (PCP)

Other than the above information, there is no additional information relating to proper use, precautions, or side effects for this use.

Revised: 05/18/99

PRIMIDONE   Systemic

Commonly used brand name(s):

In the U.S.—
  Myidone
  Mysoline

In Canada—
  Apo-Primidone   PMS Primidone
  Mysoline   Sertan

  Generic name product may be available in U.S. and Canada.

Description

Primidone (PRYE-mih-done) belongs to the group of medicines called anticonvulsants. It is used in the treatment of epilepsy to manage certain types of seizures. Primidone may be used alone or in combination with other anticonvulsants. It acts by controlling nerve impulses in the brain.

Primidone is available only with your doctor's prescription, in the following dosage forms:

Oral
  • Suspension (U.S.)
  • Tablets (U.S. and Canada)
  • Chewable tablets (Canada)

Before Using This Medicine

In deciding to use a medicine, the risks of taking the medicine must be weighed against the good it will do. This is a decision you and your doctor will make. For primidone, the following should be considered:

Allergies—Tell your doctor if you have ever had any unusual or allergic reaction to primidone or to any barbiturate medicine (for example, amobarbital, butabarbital, pentobarbital, phenobarbital, secobarbital). Also tell your health care professional if you are allergic to any other substances, such as foods, preservatives, or dyes.

Pregnancy—Although most mothers who take medicine for seizure control deliver normal babies, there are reports of increased birth defects when these medicines are used during pregnancy. Newborns whose mothers were taking primidone during pregnancy have been reported to have bleeding problems. It is not definitely known if any of these medicines are the cause of such problems.

Breast-feeding—Primidone passes into the breast milk and may cause unusual drowsiness in nursing babies. It may be necessary for you to take another medicine or to stop breast-feeding during treatment. Be sure you have discussed the risks and benefits of the medicine with your doctor.

Children—Unusual excitement or restlessness may occur in children, who are usually more sensitive than adults to these effects of primidone.

Older adults—Unusual excitement or restlessness may occur in elderly patients, who are usually more sensitive than younger adults to these effects of primidone.

Other medicines—Although certain medicines should not be used together at all, in other cases 2 different medicines may be used together even if an interaction might occur. In these cases, your doctor may want to change the dose, or other precautions may be necessary. When you are taking primidone it is especially important that your health care professional know if you are taking any of the following:
  • Adrenocorticoids (cortisone-like medicines) or

  • Anticoagulants (blood thinners)—Use with primidone may decrease the effects of these medications, and the amount of medicine you need to take may change
  • Central nervous system (CNS) depressants (medicine that causes drowsiness)—Using these medicines with primidone may increase the CNS and other depressant effects
  • Oral contraceptives (birth control pills) containing estrogen—Primidone may decrease the effectiveness of these oral contraceptives, and you may need to change to a different type of birth control
  • Other anticonvulsants (seizure medicine)—A change in the pattern of seizures may occur; close monitoring of blood levels of both medications is recommended. Use of valproic acid with primidone may cause increased CNS depression and other serious side effects
  • Monoamine oxidase (MAO) inhibitors (furazolidone [e.g., Furoxone], isocarboxazid [e.g., Marplan], phenelzine [e.g., Nardil], procarbazine [e.g., Matulane], selegiline [e.g., Eldepryl], tranylcypromine [e.g., Parnate])—Taking primidone while you are taking or within 2 weeks of taking monoamine oxidase (MAO) inhibitors may prolong the effects of primidone and may change the pattern of seizures

Other medical problems—The presence of other medical problems may affect the use of primidone. Make sure you tell your doctor if you have any other medical problems, especially:
  • Asthma, emphysema, or chronic lung disease—Primidone may cause serious problems in breathing

  • Hyperactivity (in children) or
  • Kidney disease or
  • Liver disease—Primidone may make the condition worse

  • Porphyria—Primidone should not be used when this medical problem exists because it may make the condition worse

Proper Use of This Medicine

Take primidone every day in regularly spaced doses as ordered by your doctor. This will provide the proper amount of medicine needed to prevent seizures.

Dosing—The dose of primidone will be different for different patients. *Follow your doctor's orders or the directions on the label.* The following information includes only the average doses of primidone. *If your dose is different, do not change it* unless your doctor tells you to do so.

The number of tablets or teaspoonfuls of suspension that you take depends on the strength of the medicine. Also, *the number of doses you take each day, the time allowed between doses, and the length of time you take the medicine depend on your special needs.*
  • For *oral* dosage forms (chewable tablets, tablets or suspension):
    —For epilepsy:
      • Adults, teenagers, and children 8 years of age or older—At first, 100 or 125 milligrams (mg) once a day at bedtime. Your doctor may increase your dose if needed. However, the dose is usually not more than 2000 mg a day.
      • Children up to 8 years of age—At first, 50 mg once a day at bedtime. Your doctor may increase your dose if needed.

All rights reserved

Missed dose—If you miss a dose of this medicine, take it as soon as possible. However, if it is within an hour of your next dose, skip the missed dose and go back to your regular dosing schedule. Do not double doses.

Storage—To store this medicine:

- Keep out of the reach of children.
- Store away from heat and direct light.
- Do not store the tablet form of this medicine in the bathroom, near the kitchen sink, or in other damp places. Heat or moisture may cause the medicine to break down.
- Keep the liquid form of this medicine from freezing.
- Do not keep outdated medicine or medicine no longer needed. Be sure that any discarded medicine is out of the reach of children.

Precautions While Using This Medicine

It is very important that your doctor check your progress at regular visits, especially during the first few months of treatment with primidone. This will allow your doctor to adjust the amount of medicine you are taking to meet your needs.

If you have been taking primidone regularly for several weeks, you should not suddenly stop taking it. Your doctor may want you to reduce gradually the amount you are taking before stopping completely.

Before you have any medical tests, tell the medical doctor in charge that you are taking this medicine. The results of some tests (such as the metyrapone and phentolamine tests) may be affected by this medicine.

Before having any kind of surgery, dental treatment, or emergency treatment, tell the medical doctor or dentist in charge that you are using this medicine.

This medicine will add to the effects of alcohol and other CNS depressants (medicines that cause drowsiness). Some examples of CNS depressants are antihistamines or medicine for hay fever, other allergies, or colds; sedatives, tranquilizers, or sleeping medicine; prescription pain medicine or narcotics; barbiturates; medicine for seizures; muscle relaxants; or anesthetics, including some dental anesthetics. *Check with your doctor before taking any of the above while you are using this medicine.*

Primidone may cause some people to become dizzy, lightheaded, drowsy, or less alert than they are normally. Even if taken at bedtime, it may cause some people to feel drowsy or less alert on arising. *Make sure you know how you react to this medicine before you drive, use machines, or do anything else that could be dangerous if you are dizzy or are not alert.*

Oral contraceptives (birth control pills) containing estrogen may not work properly if you take them while you are taking primidone. Unplanned pregnancies may occur. You should use a different or additional means of birth control while you are taking primidone. If you have any questions about this, check with your health care professional.

Side Effects of This Medicine

Along with its needed effects, a medicine may cause some unwanted effects. Although not all of these side effects may occur, if they do occur they may need medical attention.

Check with your doctor if any of the following side effects occur:

Less common
  Unusual excitement or restlessness (especially in children and in the elderly)

Rare
  Skin rash; unusual tiredness or weakness

Symptoms of overdose
  Confusion; continuous, uncontrolled back-and-forth and/or rolling eye movements; double vision; shortness of breath or troubled breathing

Other side effects may occur that usually do not need medical attention. These side effects may go away during treatment as your body adjusts to the medicine. However, check with your doctor if any of the following side effects continue or are bothersome:

More common
  Clumsiness or unsteadiness; dizziness

Less common
  Decreased sexual ability; drowsiness; loss of appetite; mood or mental changes; nausea or vomiting

Other side effects not listed above may also occur in some patients. If you notice any other effects, check with your doctor.

Additional Information

Once a medicine has been approved for marketing for a certain use, experience may show that it is also useful for other medical problems. Although this use is not included in product labeling, primidone is used in certain patients with the following medical conditions:

- Essential tremor

Other than the above information, there is no additional information relating to proper use, precautions, or side effects for these uses.

Revised: 01/27/92
Interim revision: 08/16/94

PROBENECID   Systemic

Commonly used brand name(s):

In the U.S.—
  Benemid
  Probalan
  Generic name product may be available.

In Canada—
  Benemid
  Benuryl

Description

Probenecid (proe-BEN-e-sid) is used in the treatment of chronic gout or gouty arthritis. These conditions are caused by too much uric acid in the blood. The medicine works by removing the extra uric acid from the body. Probenecid does not cure gout, but after you have been taking it for a few months it will help prevent gout attacks. This medicine will help prevent gout attacks only as long as you continue to take it.

Probenecid is also used to prevent or treat other medical problems that may occur if too much uric acid is present in the body.

Probenecid is sometimes used with certain kinds of antibiotics to make them more effective in the treatment of infections.

Probenecid is available only with your doctor's prescription, in the following dosage form:

Oral
- Tablets (U.S. and Canada)

Before Using This Medicine

In deciding to use a medicine, the risks of taking the medicine must be weighed against the good it will do. This is a decision you and your doctor will make. For probenecid, the following should be considered:

Allergies—Tell your doctor if you have ever had any unusual or allergic reaction to probenecid. Also tell your health care professional if you are allergic to any other substances, such as foods, preservatives, or dyes.

Pregnancy—Probenecid has not been shown to cause birth defects or other problems in humans.

Breast-feeding—Probenecid has not been reported to cause problems in nursing babies.

Children—Probenecid has been tested in children 2 to 14 years of age for use together with antibiotics. It has not been shown to cause different side effects or problems than it does in adults. Studies on the effects of probenecid in patients with gout have been done only in adults. Gout is very rare in children.

Older adults—Many medicines have not been studied specifically in older people. Therefore, it may not be known whether they work exactly the same way they do in younger adults. There is no specific information comparing use of probenecid in the elderly with use in other age groups.

Other medicines—Although certain medicines should not be used together at all, in other cases two different medicines may be used together even if an interaction might occur. In these cases, your doctor may want to change the dose, or other precautions may be necessary. When you are taking probenecid, it is especially important that your health care professional know if you are taking any of the following:

- Antineoplastics (cancer medicine)—The chance of serious side effects may be increased

- Aspirin or other salicylates—These medicines may keep probenecid from working properly for treating gout, depending on the amount of aspirin or other salicylate that you take and how often you take it

- Heparin—Probenecid may increase the effects of heparin, which increases the chance of side effects

- Indomethacin (e.g., Indocin) or
- Ketoprofen (e.g., Orudis) or
- Methotrexate (e.g., Mexate)—Probenecid may increase the blood levels of these medicines, which increases the chance of side effects

- Medicine for infection, including tuberculosis or virus infection—Probenecid may increase the blood levels of many of these medicines. In some cases, this is a desired effect and probenecid may be used to help the other medicine work better. However, the chance of side effects is sometimes also increased

- Nitrofurantoin (e.g., Furadantin)—Probenecid may keep nitrofurantoin from working properly

- Zidovudine (e.g., AZT, Retrovir)—Probenecid increases the blood level of zidovudine and may allow lower doses of zidovudine to be used. However, the chance of side effects is also increased

Other medical problems—The presence of other medical problems may affect the use of probenecid. Make sure you tell your doctor if you have any other medical problems, especially:

- Blood disease or
- Cancer being treated by antineoplastics (cancer medicine) or radiation (x-rays) or
- Kidney disease or stones (or history of) or
- Stomach ulcer (history of)—The chance of side effects may be increased

Proper Use of This Medicine

If probenecid upsets your stomach, it may be taken with food. If this does not work, an antacid may be taken. If stomach upset (nausea, vomiting, or loss of appetite) continues, check with your doctor.

For patients taking probenecid *for gout:*

- After you begin to take probenecid, gout attacks may continue to occur for a while. However, if you take this medicine regularly as directed by your doctor, the attacks will gradually become less frequent and less painful than before. After you have been taking probenecid for several months, they may stop completely.

- This medicine will help prevent gout attacks but it will not relieve an attack that has already started. *Even if you take another medicine for gout attacks, continue to take this medicine also.* If you have any questions about this, check with your doctor.

For patients taking probenecid *for gout or to help remove uric acid from the body:*

- When you first begin taking probenecid, the amount of uric acid in the kidneys is greatly increased. This may cause kidney stones or other kidney problems in some people. To help prevent this, your doctor may want you to drink at least 10 to 12 full glasses (8 ounces each) of fluids each day, or to take another medicine to make your urine less acid. It is important that you follow your doctor's instructions very carefully.

Dosing—The dose of probenecid will be different for different patients. *Follow your doctor's orders or the directions on the label.* The following information includes only the average doses of probenecid. *If your dose is different, do not change it* unless your doctor tells you to do so.

- *For treating gout or removing uric acid from the body:*
  —Adults: 250 mg (one-half of a 500-mg tablet) two times a day for about one week, then 500 mg (one tablet) two times a day for a few weeks. After this, the dose will depend on the amount of uric acid in your blood or urine. Most people need 2, 3, or 4 tablets a day, but some people may need higher doses.
  —Children: It is not likely that probenecid will be needed to treat gout or to remove uric acid from the body in children. If a child needs this medicine, however, the dose would have to be determined by the doctor.

• *For helping antibiotics work better:*
—Adults: The amount of probenecid will depend on the condition being treated. Sometimes, only one dose of 2 tablets is needed. Other times, the dose will be 1 tablet four times a day.
—Children: The dose will have to be determined by the doctor. It depends on the child's weight, as well as on the condition being treated. Older children and teenagers may need the same amount as adults.

Missed dose—If you are taking probenecid regularly and you miss a dose, take the missed dose as soon as possible. However, if you do not remember until it is almost time for the next dose, skip the missed dose and go back to your regular dosing schedule. Do not double doses.

Storage—To store this medicine:
• Keep out of the reach of children.
• Store away from heat and direct light.
• Do not store this medicine in the bathroom, near the kitchen sink, or in other damp places. Heat or moisture may cause the medicine to break down.
• Do not keep outdated medicine or medicine no longer needed. Be sure that any discarded medicine is out of the reach of children.

Precautions While Using This Medicine

If you will be taking probenecid for more than a few weeks, your doctor should check your progress at regular visits.

Before you have any medical tests, tell the person in charge that you are taking this medicine. The results of some tests may be affected by probenecid.

For *diabetic patients:*
• Probenecid may cause false test results with copper sulfate urine sugar tests (Clinitest®), but not with glucose enzymatic urine sugar tests (Clinistix®). If you have any questions about this, check with your health care professional.

For patients taking probenecid *for gout or to help remove uric acid from the body:*
• Taking aspirin or other salicylates may lessen the effects of probenecid. This will depend on the dose of aspirin or other salicylate that you take, and on how often you take it. Also, drinking too much alcohol may increase the amount of uric acid in the blood and lessen the effects of this medicine. Therefore, *do not take aspirin or other salicylates or drink alcoholic beverages while taking this medicine,* unless you have first checked with your doctor.

Side Effects of This Medicine

Along with its needed effects, a medicine may cause some unwanted effects. Although not all of these side effects may occur, if they do occur they may need medical attention.

The following side effects may mean that you are having an allergic reaction to this medicine. *Check with your doctor immediately* if any of the following side effects occur:
Rare
Fast or irregular breathing; puffiness or swellings of the eyelids or around the eyes; shortness of breath, troubled breathing, tightness in chest, or wheezing; changes in the skin color of the face occurring together with any of the other side effects listed here; or skin rash, hives, or itching occurring together with any of the other side effects listed here

Also, check with your doctor as soon as possible if any of the following side effects occur:
Less common
Bloody urine; difficult or painful urination; lower back or side pain (especially if severe or sharp); skin rash, hives, or itching (occurring without other signs of an allergic reaction)

Rare
Cloudy urine; cough or hoarseness; fast or irregular breathing; fever; pain in back and/or ribs; sores, ulcers, or white spots on lips or in mouth; sore throat and fever with or without chills; sudden decrease in the amount of urine; swelling of face, fingers, feet, and/or lower legs; swollen and/or painful glands; unusual bleeding or bruising; unusual tiredness or weakness; yellow eyes or skin; weight gain

Other side effects may occur that usually do not need medical attention. These side effects may go away during treatment as your body adjusts to the medicine. However, check with your doctor if any of the following side effects continue or are bothersome:
More common
Headache; joint pain, redness, or swelling; loss of appetite; nausea or vomiting (mild)

Less common
Dizziness; flushing or redness of face (occurring without any signs of an allergic reaction); frequent urge to urinate; sore gums

Other side effects not listed above may also occur in some patients. If you notice any other effects, check with your doctor.

Interim revision: 01/01/00

PROBENECID AND COLCHICINE
Systemic

Commonly used brand name(s):

In the U.S.—
ColBenemid
Col-Probenecid
Proben-C
Generic name product may be available.

Description

Probenecid and colchicine (proe-BEN-e-sid and KOL-chi-seen) combination is used to treat gout or gouty arthritis.

The probenecid in this medicine helps to prevent gout attacks by removing extra uric acid from the body. The colchicine in this medicine also helps to prevent gout attacks. Although colchicine may also be used to relieve an attack of gout, this requires more colchicine than this combination medicine contains. Probenecid and colchicine combination does not cure gout. This medicine will help prevent gout attacks only as long as you continue to take it.

Probenecid and colchicine combination is available only with your doctor's prescription, in the following dosage form:

Oral
  • Tablets (U.S.)

Before Using This Medicine

In deciding to use a medicine, the risks of taking the medicine must be weighed against the good it will do. This is a decision you and your doctor will make. For probenecid and colchicine combination, the following should be considered:

Allergies—Tell your doctor if you have ever had any unusual or allergic reaction to probenecid or to colchicine. Also tell your health care professional if you are allergic to any other substances, such as foods, preservatives, or dyes.

Pregnancy—Probenecid has not been shown to cause birth defects or other problems in humans. Although studies with colchicine have not been done in pregnant women, some reports have suggested that use of colchicine during pregnancy can cause harm to the fetus. Also, studies in animals have shown that colchicine causes birth defects. Therefore, do not begin taking this medicine during pregnancy, and do not become pregnant while taking it, unless you have first discussed this problem with your doctor. Also, check with your doctor immediately if you suspect that you have become pregnant while taking this medicine.

Breast-feeding—This medicine has not been reported to cause problems in nursing babies.

Children—Studies on this combination medicine have been done only in adult patients, and there is no specific information about its use in children.

Older adults—Elderly people are especially sensitive to the effects of colchicine. This may increase the chance of side effects during treatment.

There is no specific information comparing use of probenecid in the elderly with use in other age groups.

Other medicines—Although certain medicines should not be used together at all, in other cases two different medicines may be used together even if an interaction might occur. In these cases, your doctor may want to change the dose, or other precautions may be necessary. When you are taking probenecid and colchicine combination, it is especially important that your health care professional know if you are taking any of the following:
  • Amphotericin B by injection (e.g., Fungizone) or
  • Antineoplastics (cancer medicine) or
  • Antithyroid agents (medicine for overactive thyroid) or
  • Azathioprine (e.g., Imuran) or
  • Cyclophosphamide (e.g., Cytoxan) or
  • Flucytosine (e.g., Ancobon) or
  • Ganciclovir (e.g., Cytovene) or
  • Interferon (e.g., Intron A, Roferon-A) or
  • Mercaptopurine (e.g., Purinethol) or
  • Methotrexate (e.g., Mexate) or
  • Phenylbutazone (e.g., Butazolidin) or
  • Plicamycin (e.g., Mithracin) or
  • Zidovudine (e.g., AZT, Retrovir)—Taking any of these medicines together with colchicine may increase the chance of serious side effects. Also, the chance of serious side effects may be increased when antineoplastics (cancer medicine), methotrexate, phenylbutazone, or zidovudine are taken together with probenecid

  • Aspirin or other salicylates, including bismuth subsalicylate (e.g., Pepto-Bismol)—These medicines may keep probenecid from working properly for treating gout, depending on the amount of aspirin or other salicylate that you take and how often you take it
  • Heparin—Probenecid may increase the effects of heparin, which increases the chance of side effects
  • Indomethacin (e.g., Indocin) or
  • Ketoprofen (e.g., Orudis)—Probenecid may increase the blood levels of these medicines, which increases the chance of side effects
  • Medicine for infection, including tuberculosis or virus infection—Probenecid may increase the blood levels of many of these medicines, which may increase the chance of side effects. Also, the chance of serious side effects may be increased when some of these medicines are taken together with colchicine
  • Nitrofurantoin (e.g., Furadantin)—Probenecid may keep nitrofurantoin from working properly

Other medical problems—The presence of other medical problems may affect the use of probenecid and colchicine combination. Make sure you tell your doctor if you have any other medical problems, especially:
  • Alcohol abuse or
  • Blood disease or
  • Cancer being treated by antineoplastics (cancer medicine) or radiation (x-rays) or
  • Heart disease (severe) or
  • Intestinal disease (severe) or
  • Kidney disease or stones (or history of) or
  • Liver disease or
  • Stomach ulcer or other stomach problems (or history of)—The chance of serious side effects may be increased

Proper Use of This Medicine

If this medicine upsets your stomach, it may be taken with food. If this does not work, an antacid may be taken. If stomach upset (nausea, vomiting, loss of appetite, or stomach pain) continues, check with your doctor.

Take this medicine only as directed by your doctor. Do not take more of it and do not take it more often than your doctor ordered. The colchicine in this combination medicine may cause serious side effects if too much is taken.

After you begin to take this medicine, gout attacks may continue to occur for a while. However, if you take this medicine regularly as directed by your doctor, the attacks will gradually become less frequent and less painful than before. After you have been taking this medicine for several months, they may stop completely.

This medicine will help prevent gout attacks but it will not relieve an attack that has already started. *Even if you take another medicine for gout attacks, continue to take this medicine also.*

When you first begin taking this medicine, the amount of uric acid in the kidneys is greatly increased. This may cause kidney stones or other kidney problems in some people. To help prevent this, your doctor may want you to drink at least 10 to 12 full glasses (8 ounces each) of fluids each day, or to take another medicine to make your urine less acid. It is important that you follow your doctor's instructions very carefully.

Dosing—The dose of probenecid and colchicine combination will be different for different patients. *Follow your doctor's orders or the directions on the label.* The following information includes only the average doses of this medicine. *If your dose is different, do not change it* unless your doctor tells you to do so.

- For *oral* dosage form (tablets):
  —For preventing gout attacks:
    - Adults—One tablet a day for one week, then one tablet twice a day. If you are still having a lot of gout attacks a month after you start taking two tablets a day, your doctor may direct you to increase the dose.
    - Children—Dose must be determined by your doctor.

Missed dose—If you miss a dose of this medicine, take it as soon as possible. However, if it is almost time for your next dose, skip the missed dose and go back to your regular dosing schedule. Do not double doses.

Storage—To store this medicine:

- Keep out of the reach of children.
- Store away from heat and direct light.
- Do not store this medicine in the bathroom, near the kitchen sink, or in other damp places. Heat or moisture may cause the medicine to break down.
- Do not keep outdated medicine or medicine no longer needed. Be sure that any discarded medicine is out of the reach of children.

Precautions While Using This Medicine

Your doctor should check your progress at regular visits while you are taking this medicine.

Before you have any medical tests, tell the person in charge that you are taking this medicine. The results of some tests may be affected by probenecid or by colchicine.

For *diabetic patients:*

- The probenecid in this combination medicine may cause false test results with copper sulfate urine sugar tests (e.g., Clinitest®), but not with glucose enzymatic urine sugar tests (e.g., Clinistix®). If you have any questions about this, check with your health care professional.

Taking aspirin or other salicylates may lessen the effects of the probenecid in this combination medicine. This will depend on the dose of aspirin or other salicylate that you take, and on how often you take it. Also, drinking large amounts of alcoholic beverages may increase the chance of stomach problems and may increase the amount of uric acid in your blood. *Therefore, do not take aspirin or other salicylates or drink alcoholic beverages while you are taking this medicine,* unless you have first checked with your doctor.

For patients taking 4 tablets or more of this medicine a day:

- *Stop taking this medicine immediately and check with your doctor as soon as possible if severe diarrhea, nausea or vomiting, or stomach pain occurs while you are taking this medicine.*

Side Effects of This Medicine

Along with its needed effects, a medicine may cause some unwanted effects. Although not all of these side effects may occur, if they do occur they may need medical attention.

The following side effects may mean that you are having an allergic reaction to this medicine. *Check with your doctor immediately* if any of the following side effects occur:
Rare
  Fast or irregular breathing; puffiness or swelling of the eyelids or around the eyes; shortness of breath, troubled breathing, tightness in chest, or wheezing; changes in the skin color of the face occurring together with any of the other side effects listed here; or skin rash, hives, or itching occurring together with any of the other side effects listed here

Also check with your doctor immediately if any of the following side effects occur:
Symptoms of overdose
  Bloody urine; burning feeling in stomach, throat, or skin; convulsions (seizures); diarrhea (severe or bloody); fever; mood or mental changes; muscle weakness (severe); nausea or vomiting (severe and continuing); sudden decrease in amount of urine; troubled or difficult breathing

Also, check with your doctor as soon as possible if any of the following side effects occur:
Less common
  Difficult or painful urination; lower back or side pain (especially if severe or sharp); skin rash, hives, or itching (occurring without other signs of an allergic reaction)
Rare
  Black or tarry stools; cloudy urine; cough or hoarseness; fast or irregular breathing; numbness, tingling, pain, or weakness in hands or feet; pinpoint red spots on skin; sores, ulcers, or white spots on lips or in mouth; sore throat, fever, and chills; sudden decrease in the amount of urine; swelling of face, fingers, feet, and/or lower legs; swollen and/or painful glands; unusual bleeding or bruising; unusual tiredness or weakness; yellow eyes or skin; weight gain

Other side effects may occur that usually do not need medical attention. These side effects may go away during treatment as your body adjusts to the medicine. However, check with your doctor if any of the following side effects continue or are bothersome:
More common
  Diarrhea (mild); headache; loss of appetite; nausea or vomiting (mild); stomach pain
Less common
  Dizziness; flushing or redness of face (occurring without any signs of an allergic reaction); frequent urge to urinate; sore gums; unusual loss of hair

Other side effects not listed above may also occur in some patients. If you notice any other effects, check with your doctor.

Revised: 09/09/92
Interim revision: 08/27/94

PROBUCOL   Systemic

Commonly used brand name(s):

In Canada—
Lorelco

Other—
Bifenabid
Lesterol
Lurselle
Panesclerina
Superlipid

Description

Probucol (PROE-byoo-kole) is used to lower levels of cholesterol (a fat-like substance) in the blood. This may help prevent medical problems caused by cholesterol clogging the blood vessels.

Probucol is available only with your doctor's prescription, in the following dosage form:

Oral
- Tablets (Canada)

Before Using This Medicine

In deciding to use a medicine, the risks of taking the medicine must be weighed against the good it will do. This is a decision you and your doctor will make. For probucol, the following should be considered:

Allergies—Tell your doctor if you have ever had any unusual or allergic reaction to probucol. Also tell your health care professional if you are allergic to any other substances, such as foods, preservatives, or dyes.

Diet—Before prescribing medicine for your condition, your doctor will probably try to control your condition by prescribing a personal diet for you. Such a diet may be low in fats, sugars, and/or cholesterol. Many people are able to control their condition by carefully following their doctor's orders for proper diet and exercise. Medicine is prescribed only when additional help is needed and is effective only when a schedule of diet and exercise is properly followed.

Also, this medicine is less effective if you are greatly overweight. It may be very important for you to go on a reducing diet. However, check with your doctor before going on any diet.

Make certain your health care professional knows if you are on a low-sodium, low-sugar, or any other special diet.

Pregnancy—Probucol has not been studied in pregnant women. However, it has not been shown to cause birth defects or other problems in rats or rabbits.

Breast-feeding—It is not known whether probucol passes into the breast milk. However, this medicine is not recommended for use during breast-feeding because it may cause unwanted effects in nursing babies.

Children—There is no specific information about the use of probucol in children. However, use is not recommended in children under 2 years of age since cholesterol is needed for normal development.

Older adults—Many medicines have not been studied specifically in older people. Therefore, it may not be known whether they work exactly the same way they do in younger adults or if they cause different side effects or problems in older people. There is no specific information comparing use of probucol in the elderly with use in other age groups.

Other medicines—Although certain medicines should not be used together at all, in other cases two different medicines may be used together even if an interaction might occur. In these cases, your doctor may want to change the dose, or other precautions may be necessary. Tell your health care professional if you are taking any other prescription or nonprescription (over-the-counter [OTC]) medicine.

Other medical problems—The presence of other medical problems may affect the use of probucol. Make sure you tell your doctor if you have any other medical problems, especially:

- Gallbladder disease or gallstones or
- Heart disease—Probucol may make these conditions worse
- Liver disease—Higher blood levels of probucol may result, which may increase the chance of side effects

Proper Use of This Medicine

Many patients who have high cholesterol levels will not notice any signs of the problem. In fact, many may feel normal. *Take this medicine exactly as directed by your doctor, even though you may feel well.* Try not to miss any doses and do not take more medicine than your doctor ordered.

Remember that this medicine will not cure your condition but it does help control it. Therefore, you must continue to take it as directed if you expect to keep your cholesterol levels down.

Follow carefully the special diet your doctor gave you. This is the most important part of controlling your condition, and is necessary if the medicine is to work properly.

This medicine works better when taken with meals.

Dosing—The dose of probucol will be different for different patients. *Follow your doctor's orders or the directions on the label.* The following information includes only the average doses of probucol. *If your dose is different, do not change it* unless your doctor tells you to do so:

- The number of tablets that you take depends on the strength of the medicine.
- For *oral* dosage form (tablets):
  —Adults: 500 milligrams two times a day taken with the morning and evening meals.
  —Children:
    - Up to 2 years of age—Use is not recommended.
    - 2 years of age and over—Dose must be determined by your doctor.

Missed dose—If you miss a dose of this medicine, take it as soon as possible. However, if it is almost time for your next dose, skip the missed dose and go back to your regular dosing schedule. Do not double doses.

Storage—To store this medicine:
- Keep out of the reach of children.
- Store away from heat and direct light.
- Do not store in the bathroom, near the kitchen sink, or in other damp places. Heat or moisture may cause the medicine to break down.
- Do not keep outdated medicine or medicine no longer needed. Be sure that any discarded medicine is out of the reach of children.

Precautions While Using This Medicine

It is very important that your doctor check your progress at regular visits. This will allow your doctor to see if the medicine is working properly to lower your cholesterol levels and to decide if you should continue to take it.

Do not stop taking this medicine without first checking with your doctor. When you stop taking this medicine, your blood fat levels may increase again. Your doctor may want you to follow a special diet to help prevent this.

Side Effects of This Medicine

Along with its needed effects, a medicine may cause some unwanted effects. Although not all of these side effects may occur, if they do occur they may need medical attention.

Check with your doctor as soon as possible if any of the following side effects occur:

More common
Dizziness or fainting; fast or irregular heartbeat

Rare
Swellings on face, hands, or feet, or in mouth; unusual bleeding or bruising; unusual tiredness or weakness

Other side effects may occur that usually do not need medical attention. These side effects may go away during treatment as your body adjusts to the medicine. However, check with your doctor if any of the following side effects continue or are bothersome:

More common
Bloating; diarrhea; nausea and vomiting; stomach pain

Less common
Headache; numbness or tingling of fingers, toes, or face

Other side effects not listed above may also occur in some patients. If you notice any other effects, check with your doctor.

Revised: 08/18/97

PROCAINAMIDE   Systemic

Commonly used brand name(s):

In the U.S.—
Procan SR   Pronestyl
Promine   Pronestyl-SR
Generic name product may be available.

In Canada—
Procan SR   Pronestyl-SR
Pronestyl

Description

Procainamide (proe-KANE-a-mide) is used to correct irregular heartbeats to a normal rhythm and to slow an overactive heart. This allows the heart to work more efficiently. Procainamide produces its beneficial effects by slowing nerve impulses in the heart and reducing sensitivity of heart tissues.

Procainamide is available only with your doctor's prescription, in the following dosage forms:

Oral
• Capsules (U.S. and Canada)
• Tablets (U.S.)
• Extended-release tablets (U.S. and Canada)
Parenteral
• Injection (U.S. and Canada)

Before Using This Medicine

In deciding to use a medicine, the risks of taking the medicine must be weighed against the good it will do. This is a decision you and your doctor will make. For procainamide, the following should be considered:

Allergies— Tell your doctor if you have ever had any unusual or allergic reaction to procainamide, procaine, or any other "caine-type" medicine. Also tell your health care professional if you are allergic to any other substance, such as foods, preservatives, or dyes.

Pregnancy— Procainamide has not been studied in pregnant women. However, it has been used in some pregnant women and has not been shown to cause problems. Before taking this medicine, make sure your doctor knows if you are pregnant or if you may become pregnant.

Breast-feeding— Procainamide passes into breast milk.

Children— Procainamide has been used in a limited number of children. In effective doses, the medicine has not been shown to cause different side effects or problems than it does in adults.

Older adults— Dizziness or lightheadedness is more likely to occur in the elderly, who are usually more sensitive to the effects of this medicine.

Other medicines— Although certain medicines should not be used together at all, in other cases two different medicines may be used together even if an interaction might occur. In these cases, your doctor may want to change the dose, or other precautions may be necessary. When you are taking procainamide, it is especially important that your health care professional know if you are taking any of the following:

• Antiarrhythmics (medicines for heart rhythm problems), other—Effects on the heart may be increased

• Antihypertensives (high blood pressure medicine)—Effects on blood pressure may be increased

• Antimyasthenics (ambenonium [e.g., Mytelase], neostigmine [e.g., Prostigmin], pyridostigmine [e.g., Mestinon])—Effects may be blocked by procainamide

• Pimozide (e.g., Orap)—May increase the risk of heart rhythm problems

Other medical problems— The presence of other medical problems may affect the use of procainamide. Make sure you tell your doctor if you have any other medical problems, especially:

• Asthma—Possible allergic reaction

• Kidney disease or
• Liver disease—Effects may be increased because of slower removal of procainamide from the body

• Lupus erythematosus (history of)—Procainamide may cause the condition to become active

• Myasthenia gravis—Procainamide may increase muscle weakness

Proper Use of This Medicine

Take procainamide exactly as directed by your doctor, even though you may feel well. Do not take more medicine than ordered.

Procainamide should be taken with a glass of water on an empty stomach 1 hour before or 2 hours after meals so that it will be absorbed more quickly. However, to lessen stomach upset, your doctor may want you to take the medicine with food or milk.

For patients taking the *extended-release tablets:*
• Swallow the tablet whole without breaking, crushing, or chewing it.

This medicine works best when there is a constant amount in the blood. *To help keep the amount constant, do not miss any doses. Also, it is best to take the doses at evenly spaced times day and night.* For example, if you are to take 6 doses a day, the doses should be spaced about 4 hours apart. If this interferes with your sleep or other daily activities, or if you need help in planning the best times to take your medicine, check with your health care professional.

Dosing—The dose of procainamide will be different for different patients. *Follow your doctor's orders or the directions on the label.* The following information includes only the average doses of procainamide. *If your dose is different, do not change it* unless your doctor tells you to do so.

The number of capsules or tablets that you take depends on the strength of the medicine.
• For *regular (short-acting) oral* dosage forms (capsules or tablets):
  —For atrial arrhythmias (fast or irregular heartbeat):
   • Adults—500 milligrams (mg) to 1000 mg (1 gram) every four to six hours.
   • Children—12.5 mg per kilogram (5.68 mg per pound) of body weight four times a day.
  —For ventricular arrhythmias (fast or irregular heartbeat):
   • Adults—50 mg per kilogram (22.73 mg per pound) of body weight per day divided into eight doses taken every three hours.
   • Children—12.5 mg per kilogram (5.68 mg per pound) of body weight four times a day.
• For *long-acting oral* dosage form (extended-release tablets):
  —For atrial arrhythmias (fast or irregular heartbeat):
   • Adults—1000 mg (1 gram) every six hours.
   • Children—Use is not recommended.
  —For ventricular arrhythmias (fast or irregular heartbeat):
   • Adults—50 mg per kilogram (22.73 mg per pound) of body weight per day divided into four doses taken every six hours.
• For *injection* dosage form:
  —For arrhythmias (fast or irregular heartbeat):
   • Adults—
    —*First few doses:* May be given intramuscularly (into the muscle) at 50 mg per kilogram (22.73 mg per pound) of body weight per day in divided doses every three hours; or may be given intravenously (into the vein) by slowly injecting 100 mg (mixed in fluid) every five minutes or infusing 500 to 600 mg (mixed in fluid) over a twenty-five to thirty minute period.
    —*Doses after the first few doses:* 2 to 6 mg (mixed in fluid) per minute infused into the vein.
   • Children—Dose must be determined by your doctor.

Missed dose—If you miss a dose of this medicine and remember within 2 hours (4 hours if you are taking the long-acting tablets), take it as soon as possible. However, if you do not remember until later, skip the missed dose and go back to your regular dosing schedule. Do not double doses.

Storage—To store this medicine:
• Keep out of the reach of children.
• Store away from heat and direct light.
• Do not store in the bathroom, refrigerator, near the kitchen sink, or in other damp places. Moisture usually present in these areas may cause the medicine to break down. Keep the container tightly closed and store in a dry place.
• Do not keep outdated medicine or medicine no longer needed. Be sure that any discarded medicine is out of the reach of children.

Precautions While Using This Medicine

It is important that your doctor check your progress at regular visits to make sure the medicine is working properly. This will allow necessary changes in the amount of medicine you are taking, which also may help reduce side effects.

Do not stop taking this medicine without first checking with your doctor. Stopping it suddenly may cause a serious change in the activity of your heart. Your doctor may want you to reduce gradually the amount you are taking before stopping completely.

Before having any kind of surgery (including dental surgery) or emergency treatment, tell the medical doctor or dentist in charge that you are taking this medicine.

Your doctor may want you to carry a medical identification card or bracelet stating that you are taking this medicine.

Dizziness or lightheadedness may occur, especially in elderly patients and when large doses are used. *Elderly patients should use extra care to avoid falling. Make sure you know how you react to this medicine before you drive, use machines, or do anything else that could be dangerous if you are dizzy or are not alert.*

Tell the doctor in charge that you are taking this medicine before you have any medical tests. The results of some tests may be affected by this medicine.

Side Effects of This Medicine

Along with its needed effects, a medicine may cause some unwanted effects. Although not all of these side effects may occur, if they do occur they may need medical attention.

Check with your doctor as soon as possible if any of the following side effects occur:
Less common
 Fever and chills; joint pain or swelling; pains with breathing; skin rash or itching

Rare
> Confusion; fever or sore mouth, gums, or throat; hallucinations (seeing, hearing, or feeling things that are not there); mental depression; unusual bleeding or bruising; unusual tiredness or weakness

Signs and symptoms of overdose
> Confusion; decrease in urination; dizziness (severe) or fainting; drowsiness; fast or irregular heartbeat; nausea and vomiting

Other side effects may occur that usually do not need medical attention. These side effects may go away during treatment as your body adjusts to the medicine. However, check with your doctor if any of the following side effects continue or are bothersome:

More common
> Diarrhea; loss of appetite

Less common
> Dizziness or lightheadedness

The medicine in the extended-release tablets is contained in a special wax form (matrix). The medicine is slowly released, after which the wax matrix passes out of the body. Sometimes it may be seen in the stool. This is normal and is no cause for concern.

Other side effects not listed above may also occur in some patients. If you notice any other effects, check with your doctor.

Revised: 08/04/93

PROCARBAZINE   Systemic

Commonly used brand name(s):

In the U.S.—
Matulane

In Canada—
Natulan

Description

Procarbazine (pro-KAR-ba-zeen) belongs to the group of medicines known as alkylating agents. It is used to treat some kinds of cancer.

Procarbazine is thought to interfere with the growth of cancer cells which are eventually destroyed. It also blocks the action of a chemical substance in the central nervous system called monoamine oxidase (MAO), but this is probably not related to its effect against cancer. Since the growth of normal body cells may also be affected by procarbazine, other effects will also occur. Some of these may be serious and must be reported to your doctor. Other effects, like hair loss, may not be serious but may cause concern. Some effects may not occur for months or years after the medicine is used.

Before you begin treatment with procarbazine, you and your doctor should talk about the good this medicine will do as well as the risks of using it.

Procarbazine is available only with your doctor's prescription, in the following dosage form:

Oral
- Capsules (U.S. and Canada)

Before Using This Medicine

In deciding to use a medicine, the risks of taking the medicine must be weighed against the good it will do. This is a decision you and your doctor will make. For procarbazine, the following should be considered:

Allergies—Tell your doctor if you have ever had any unusual or allergic reaction to procarbazine.

Pregnancy—Tell your doctor if you are pregnant or if you intend to have children. This medicine may cause birth defects or premature birth if either the male or female is taking it at the time of conception or if it is taken during pregnancy. Procarbazine causes birth defects frequently in animals. In addition, many cancer medicines may cause sterility which could be permanent. Although sterility has not been reported with this medicine, procarbazine does affect production of sperm and the possibility should be kept in mind.

Be sure that you have discussed this with your doctor before taking this medicine. It is best to use some kind of birth control while you are taking procarbazine. Tell your doctor right away if you think you have become pregnant while taking procarbazine.

Breast-feeding—Tell your doctor if you are breast-feeding or if you intend to breast-feed during treatment with this medicine. Because procarbazine may cause serious side effects, breast-feeding is generally not recommended while you are taking it.

Children—Although there is no specific information about the use of procarbazine in children, it is not expected to cause different side effects or problems in children than it does in adults.

Older adults—Side effects may be more likely to occur in elderly patients, who are usually more sensitive to the effects of procarbazine.

Other medicines—Although certain medicines should not be used together at all, in other cases two different medicines may be used together even if an interaction might occur. In these cases, your doctor may want to change the dose, or other precautions may be necessary. When you are taking procarbazine, it is especially important that your health care professional know if you are taking any of the following:
- Amantadine (e.g., Symmetrel) or
- Anticholinergics (medicine to help reduce stomach acid and for abdominal or stomach spasms or cramps) or
- Antidiabetics, oral (diabetes medicine you take by mouth) or
- Antidyskinetics (medicine for Parkinson's disease or other conditions affecting control of muscles) or
- Antihistamines or
- Antipsychotics (medicine for mental illness) or
- Buclizine (e.g., Bucladin) or
- Central nervous system (CNS) depressants or
- Cyclizine (e.g., Marezine) or
- Disopyramide (e.g., Norpace) or
- Flavoxate (e.g., Urispas) or
- Insulin or
- Ipratropium (e.g., Atrovent) or
- Meclizine (e.g., Antivert) or
- Orphenadrine (e.g., Norflex) or
- Oxybutynin (e.g., Ditropen) or
- Procainamide (e.g., Pronestyl) or
- Promethazine (e.g., Phenergan) or

- Quinidine (e.g., Quinidex) or
- Trimeprazine (e.g., Temaril)—Effects of these medicines may be increased by procarbazine

- Amphetamines or
- Appetite suppressants (diet pills) or
- Dextromethorphan (e.g., Delsym) or
- Levodopa (e.g., Dopar) or
- Medicine for asthma or other breathing problems or
- Medicine for colds, sinus problems, or hay fever or other allergies (including nose drops or sprays) or
- Methyldopa (e.g., Aldomet) or
- Methylphenidate (e.g., Ritalin) or
- Narcotic pain medicine—Taking any of these medicines while you are taking or within 2 weeks of taking procarbazine may cause a severe high blood pressure reaction

- Amphotericin B by injection (e.g., Fungizone) or
- Antithyroid agents (medicine for overactive thyroid) or
- Azathioprine (e.g., Imuran) or
- Chloramphenicol (e.g., Chloromycetin) or
- Colchicine or
- Flucytosine (e.g., Ancobon) or
- Interferon (e.g., Intron A, Roferon-A) or
- Plicamycin (e.g., Mithracin) or
- Zidovudine (e.g., Retrovir) or
- If you have ever been treated with x-rays or cancer medicines—Procarbazine may increase the effects of these medicines or radiation therapy on the blood

- Buspirone (e.g., BuSpar)—Risk of increased blood pressure

- Carbamazepine (e.g., Tegretol) or
- Cyclobenzaprine (e.g., Flexeril) or
- Maprotiline (e.g., Ludiomil) or
- Monoamine oxidase (MAO) inhibitors (furazolidone [e.g., Furoxone], isocarboxazid [e.g., Marplan], pargyline [e.g., Eutonyl], phenelzine [e.g., Nardil], procarbazine [e.g., Matulane], tranylcypromine [e.g., Parnate]) or
- Tricyclic antidepressants (amitriptyline [e.g., Elavil], amoxapine [e.g., Asendin], clomipramine [e.g., Anafranil], desipramine [e.g., Pertofrane], doxepin [e.g., Sinequan], imipramine [e.g., Tofranil], nortriptyline [e.g., Aventyl], protriptyline [e.g., Vivactil], trimipramine [e.g., Surmontil])—Taking procarbazine while you are taking or within 2 weeks of taking any of these medicines may cause a severe high blood pressure reaction

- Cocaine—Use of cocaine while you are taking or within 2 weeks of taking procarbazine may cause a severe high blood pressure reaction

- Fluoxetine (e.g., Prozac)—Taking this medicine while you are taking or within 2 weeks of taking procarbazine may cause a severe high blood pressure reaction or may lead to confusion, agitation, restlessness, and stomach problems

- Guanadrel (e.g., Hylorel) or
- Guanethidine (e.g., Ismelin) or
- Rauwolfia alkaloids (alseroxylon [e.g., Rauwiloid], deserpidine [e.g., Harmonyl], rauwolfia serpentina [e.g., Raudixin], reserpine [e.g., Serpasil])—Taking these medicines while you are taking or within 1 week of taking procarbazine may cause a severe high blood pressure reaction

Other medical problems—The presence of other medical problems may affect the use of procarbazine. Make sure you tell your doctor if you have any other medical problems, especially:

- Alcoholism
- Angina (chest pain) or
- Heart or blood vessel disease or
- Heart attack or stroke (recent)—Lowered blood pressure caused by procarbazine may make problems associated with some of these conditions worse

- Chickenpox (including recent exposure) or
- Herpes zoster (shingles)—Risk of severe disease affecting other parts of the body
- Diabetes mellitus (sugar diabetes)—Procarbazine may change the amount of diabetes medicine needed
- Epilepsy—Procarbazine may change the seizures
- Headaches (severe or frequent)—You may not realize when a severe headache is caused by a dangerous reaction to procarbazine
- Infection—Procarbazine can reduce immunity to infection
- Kidney disease—Effects may be increased because of slower removal of procarbazine from the body
- Liver disease—Procarbazine can cause severe liver disease to become much worse
- Mental illness (or history of)—Some cases of mental illness may be worsened
- Overactive thyroid—Increased risk of dangerous reaction to procarbazine
- Parkinson's disease—May be worsened
- Pheochromocytoma—Blood pressure may be affected

Proper Use of This Medicine

Use this medicine only as directed by your doctor. Do not use more or less of it and do not use it more often than your doctor ordered. The exact amount of medicine you need has been carefully worked out. Taking too much may increase the chance of side effects while taking too little may not improve your condition.

Procarbazine is sometimes given together with certain other medicines. If you are using a combination of medicines, make sure that you take each one at the right time and do not mix them. Ask your health care professional to help you plan a way to take your medicines at the right times.

Procarbazine commonly causes nausea and vomiting. Even if you begin to feel ill, *do not stop using this medicine without first checking with your doctor.* Ask your health care professional for ways to lessen these effects.

If you vomit shortly after taking a dose of procarbazine, check with your doctor. You will be told whether to take the dose again or to wait until the next scheduled dose.

Dosing—The dose of procarbazine will be different for different patients. The dose that is used may depend on a number of things, including what the medicine is being used for, the patient's weight, and whether or not other medicines are also being taken. *If you are taking procarbazine at home, follow your doctor's orders or the directions on the label.* If you have any questions about the proper dose of procarbazine, ask your doctor.

Missed dose—If you miss a dose of this medicine and you remember it within a few hours, take it as soon as you remember it. However, if several hours have passed or if it is almost time for the next dose, skip the missed dose and go back to your regular dosing schedule and check with your doctor. Do not double doses.

Storage—To store this medicine:

- Keep out of the reach of children.
- Store away from heat and direct light.
- Do not store in the bathroom, near the kitchen sink, or in other damp places. Heat or moisture may cause the medicine to break down.
- Do not keep outdated medicine or medicine no longer needed. Be sure that any discarded medicine is out of the reach of children.

Precautions While Using This Medicine

It is very important that your doctor check your progress at regular visits to make sure that this medicine is working properly and to check for unwanted effects.

Check with your doctor or hospital emergency room immediately if severe headache, stiff neck, chest pains, fast heartbeat, or nausea and vomiting occur while you are taking this medicine. These may be symptoms of a serious high blood pressure reaction that should have a doctor's attention.

When taken with certain foods, drinks, or other medicines, procarbazine can cause very dangerous reactions such as sudden high blood pressure. To avoid such reactions, *obey the following rules of caution:*

- Do not eat foods that have a high tyramine content (most common in foods that are aged or fermented to increase their flavor), such as cheeses, yeast or meat extracts, fava or broad bean pods, smoked or pickled meat, poultry, or fish, fermented sausage (bologna, pepperoni, salami, and summer sausage) or other unfresh meat, or any overripe fruit. If a list of these foods and beverages is not given to you, ask your health care professional to provide one.
- Do not drink alcoholic beverages or alcohol-free or reduced-alcohol beer or wine.
- Do not eat or drink large amounts of caffeine-containing food or beverages, such as chocolate, coffee, tea, or cola.
- Do not take any other medicine unless approved or prescribed by your doctor. This especially includes over-the-counter (OTC) or nonprescription medicine such as that for colds (including nose drops or sprays), cough, asthma, hay fever, appetite control; "keep awake" products; or products that make you sleepy.

After you stop using this medicine you must continue to obey the rules of caution concerning food, drink, and other medication for at least 2 weeks since procarbazine may continue to react with certain foods or other medicines for up to 14 days after you stop taking it.

This medicine will add to the effects of alcohol and other CNS depressants (medicines that slow down the nervous system, possibly causing drowsiness). Some examples of CNS depressants are antihistamines or medicine for hay fever, other allergies, or colds; sedatives, tranquilizers, or sleeping medicine; prescription pain medicine or narcotics; barbiturates; medicine for seizures; muscle relaxants; or anesthetics, including some dental anesthetics. *Check with your doctor before taking any of the above while you are using this medicine.*

This medicine may cause some people to become drowsy or less alert than they are normally. Make sure you know how you react to this medicine before you drive, use machines, or do anything else that could be dangerous if you are not alert.

While you are being treated with procarbazine, and after you stop treatment with it, *do not have any immunizations (vaccinations) without your doctor's approval.* Procarbazine may lower your body's resistance and there is a chance you might get the infection the immunization is meant to prevent. In addition, other persons living in your household should not take or should not have recently taken oral polio vaccine since there is a chance they could pass the polio virus on to you. Also, avoid persons who have taken oral polio vaccine. Do not get close to them and do not stay in the same room with them for very long. If you cannot take these precautions, you should consider wearing a protective face mask that covers the nose and mouth.

Procarbazine can lower the number of white blood cells in your blood temporarily, increasing the chance of getting an infection. It can also lower the number of platelets, which are necessary for proper blood clotting. If this occurs, there are certain precautions you can take, especially when your blood count is low, to reduce the risk of infection or bleeding:

- If you can, avoid people with infections. *Check with your doctor immediately* if you think you are getting an infection or if you get a fever or chills, cough or hoarseness, lower back or side pain, or painful or difficult urination.
- *Check with your doctor immediately* if you notice any unusual bleeding or bruising; black, tarry stools; blood in urine or stools; or pinpoint red spots on your skin.
- Be careful when using a regular toothbrush, dental floss, or toothpick. Your medical doctor, dentist, or nurse may recommend other ways to clean your teeth and gums. Check with your medical doctor before having any dental work done.
- Do not touch your eyes or the inside of your nose unless you have just washed your hands and have not touched anything else in the meantime.
- Be careful not to cut yourself when you are using sharp objects such as a safety razor or fingernail or toenail cutters.
- Avoid contact sports or other situations where bruising or injury could occur.

For *diabetic patients:*

- Procarbazine may affect blood sugar levels. While you are using this medicine, be especially careful in testing for sugar in your blood or urine.

If you are going to have surgery (including dental surgery) or emergency treatment tell the medical doctor or dentist in charge that you are using this medicine or have used it within the past 2 weeks.

Your doctor may want you to carry an identification card stating that you are using this medicine.

Side Effects of This Medicine

Along with their needed effects, medicines like procarbazine can sometimes cause unwanted effects such as blood problems, loss of hair, high blood pressure reactions, and other side effects. These and others are described below. Also, because of the way these medicines act on the body, there is a chance that they might cause other unwanted effects that may not occur until months or years after the medicine is used. These delayed effects may include certain types of cancer, such as leukemia. Discuss these possible effects with your doctor.

Although not all of these side effects may occur, if they do occur they may need medical attention.

Stop taking this medicine and check with your doctor immediately if the following side effects occur. If your doctor is not available, go to the nearest hospital emergency room.

Rare

Chest pain (severe); enlarged pupils of eyes; fast or slow heartbeat; headache (severe); increased sensitivity of eyes to light; increased sweating (possibly with fever or cold, clammy skin); stiff or sore neck

Check with your doctor immediately if any of the following side effects occur:

Less common

Black, tarry stools; blood in urine or stools; bloody vomit; cough or hoarseness; fever or chills; lower back or side pain; painful or difficult urination; pinpoint red spots on skin; unusual bleeding or bruising

Check with your doctor as soon as possible if any of the following side effects occur:

More common

Confusion; convulsions (seizures); cough; hallucinations (seeing, hearing, or feeling things that are not there); missing menstrual periods; shortness of breath; thickening of bronchial secretions; tiredness or weakness (continuing)

Less common

Diarrhea; sores in mouth and on lips; tingling or numbness of fingers or toes; unsteadiness or awkwardness; yellow eyes or skin

Rare

Fainting; skin rash, hives, or itching; wheezing

Other side effects may occur that usually do not need medical attention. These side effects may go away during treatment as your body adjusts to the medicine. Also, your health care professional may be able to tell you about ways to prevent or reduce some of these side effects. Check with your health care professional if any of the following side effects continue or are bothersome or if you have any questions about them:

More common

Drowsiness; muscle or joint pain; muscle twitching; nausea and vomiting; nervousness; nightmares; trouble in sleeping; unusual tiredness or weakness

Less common

Constipation; darkening of skin; difficulty in swallowing; dizziness or lightheadedness when getting up from a lying or sitting position; dry mouth; feeling of warmth and redness in face; headache; loss of appetite; mental depression

This medicine may cause a temporary loss of hair in some people. After treatment with procarbazine has ended, normal hair growth should return.

Other side effects not listed above may also occur in some patients. If you notice any other effects, check with your doctor.

Revised: 06/30/94

PROGESTERONE INTRAUTERINE DEVICE (IUD)†

Commonly used brand name(s):

In the U.S.—
Progestasert

†Not commercially available in Canada.

Description

A progesterone intrauterine device (proe-JES-ter-one IN-tra-YOU-ta-rin de-VICE) (also called an IUD) is inserted by a health care professional into a woman's uterus as a contraceptive (birth control method).

The progesterone IUD works by causing changes in the uterus that help to prevent pregnancy. The fertilization of the woman's egg with her partner's sperm is less likely with an IUD in place, but it can occur. Even so, the IUD makes it harder for the fertilized egg to become attached to the uterus walls, making it hard to become pregnant. The hormone, progesterone, released from the IUD is believed to improve the effects of the device. After the IUD is removed, most women trying to become pregnant can become pregnant.

Studies have shown that pregnancy can occur in up to 2 of each 100 women using a progesterone IUD during the first year of use. Other birth control methods such as not having intercourse, taking birth control pills (the Pill), or having surgery to become sterile are as effective or more effective. Methods that do not work as well include using condoms, diaphragms, vaginal sponges, or spermicides. Discuss with your health care professional what your options are for birth control and the risks and benefits of each method.

IUDs do not protect a woman from sexually transmitted diseases (STDs), including human immunodeficiency virus (HIV) or acquired immunodeficiency syndrome (AIDS). The use of latex (rubber) condoms or abstinence (not having intercourse) is recommended for protection from these diseases.

Your lifestyle will determine how safe and reliable the progesterone IUD will be for you. Problems that may occur with use of an IUD are far less likely to occur in women who have a long-term relationship with one sexual partner. Also, it is important that your sexual partner not have any other sexual partners. If you or your partner has more than one sexual partner it increases *your* chance of getting an infection in the vagina. If an infection is present in the vagina or uterus when the IUD is in the uterus it may make an infection more serious. *If your lifestyle changes while you are using an IUD or you get or are exposed to a sexually transmitted disease, call your health care professional.*

Progesterone IUDs are available only from your doctor or other authorized health care professional in the following form:

Intrauterine
• Progesterone Intrauterine Device (U.S.)

Before Receiving This Device

In deciding whether to use a progesterone IUD as a method of birth control, you need to consider the risks of using it as well as the good it can do. This is a decision you, your sexual partner, and your health care professional will make. For progesterone IUDs, the following should be considered:

Pregnancy—IUD use is not recommended during pregnancy or if you plan to become pregnant in the near future. It is also not recommended in women who have had a pregnancy develop outside of the uterus (ectopic pregnancy).

There is a rare chance that a woman can become pregnant with the IUD in the uterus. If this happens, it is recommended that the IUD be removed or that the pregnancy be ended within the first 3 months. If the pregnancy continues, removing the IUD decreases the chance of a problem developing. However, whether the IUD is removed or not, some problems can occur. Some of these problems include miscarriage, premature labor and delivery, infection, and, very rarely, death of the mother.

Your health care professional will help you decide on the proper time to begin using an IUD after delivering a baby. Sometimes problems can occur if you start using the IUD too soon after delivery. These problems include having the IUD move out of place or having it press into the walls of the uterus or the cervix (opening to the uterus). These problems may harm the cervix or uterus, causing pain or unusual uterine bleeding. *Call your health care professional immediately* if you have any problems.

Breast-feeding—The progesterone IUD has not been shown to cause problems in nursing babies and its use is recommended for those women needing contraception while breast-feeding.

Teenagers—Sexually active teenagers are strongly encouraged to use a contraceptive method that protects them against sexually transmitted diseases (STDs).

Teenagers who have not had children usually have more side effects than teenagers or adults who have had children. In teenagers who have not had children, the IUD may move out of place. This may harm the uterus or cervix. Abdominal pain and increased menstrual bleeding also are more common in teenagers than in women who are older and have had children.

Other medical problems—The presence of other medical problems may affect the use of progesterone IUDs. Make sure you tell your health care professional if you have any other medical problems, especially:

- Abnormal uterus—May decrease the IUD's ability to prevent pregnancy or may increase the chance of problems, such as the IUD moving out of the uterus or pressing through the cervix or uterus

- Acquired immunodeficiency syndrome (AIDS), autoimmune diseases, treatable cancer, suspected or known cancer of the uterus or cervix, or any other condition that may decrease the ability of the body to fight infection—These conditions may increase the chance of a vaginal infection occurring with the use of an IUD

- Blood disorders or
- Uterine bleeding problems, especially heavy bleeding during periods or bleeding between periods—At the time of insertion, use of a progesterone IUD can make uterine bleeding worse, although this lessens with continued use. Also, heavy uterine bleeding may cause the IUD to move out of place

- Diabetes, insulin-dependent or

- Heart defect—If an infection occurs during use of an IUD, the infection may become worse and/or be harder to treat in these patients

- Ectopic pregnancy (pregnancy not in the uterus), history of—The chance of an ectopic pregnancy may be increased if contraception fails during IUD use

- Fainting (history of) or
- Slow heartbeat (history of)—The chance of problems may be increased when, or soon after, the IUD is inserted

- Infection in the vagina or uterus or
- Recent infected abortion or
- Sexually transmitted disease in the last 12 months—Use of an IUD may make an infection worse

- Surgery involving the uterus or fallopian tubes—Certain surgeries of the uterus or the fallopian tubes may increase the chance of problems if an IUD is present in the uterus. Also, if contraception fails, the chance of an ectopic pregnancy may be higher

Proper Use of This Device

IUDs come with patient information. *You must understand this information.* You should keep a copy for reference. *Be sure you understand possible problems with the progesterone IUD, especially side effects, risks, and warning signs of trouble.*

Spermicides such as contraceptive foams or creams are not needed to prevent pregnancy with a properly placed progesterone IUD.

It is important that you check for the IUD threads every month (if not more often) especially after each menstrual period. Feeling the IUD threads near the cervix lets you know that the progesterone IUD is still in place.

To check for the IUD threads:
- Wash your hands thoroughly.
- Squat and, using your middle finger, find the cervix high in the vagina.
- The IUD threads should hang down from the cervix.
- *Do not pull on the threads.*

Dosing—*Follow your health care professional's orders to schedule the proper time to remove and replace your progesterone IUD, usually at 12 months.* You and your health care professional may choose to replace it sooner or begin a new method of birth control.

- For preventing pregnancy:
  —For progesterone dosage form:
  - Adults and teenagers—One device inserted into the vagina by a health care professional and replaced within 12 months of use.

Precautions While Using This Device

It is very important to keep all medical appointments with your health care professional during the first year of IUD use. This will allow the health care professional to make sure that the device is still in place and working properly.

Check with your medical doctor if you plan to have surgery of the uterus or fallopian tubes. Your doctor may remove your IUD before the surgery or help you choose another type of treatment.

Tell your doctor immediately if you think that the IUD has moved out of place. Do not try to put the IUD back into place inside the uterus. Do not try to remove the IUD.

Although IUDs are very reliable, there is a rare chance that the IUD may fail to protect some people from becoming pregnant. Very rarely a pregnancy can occur outside of the uterus; this is called an ectopic pregnancy. It can be hard to tell if an ectopic pregnancy has occurred. Unlike a normal pregnancy in the uterus, which stops the menstrual period, some people can still have a menstrual period with an ectopic pregnancy. These women may not think they are pregnant.

Notify your doctor immediately if you feel many of the following changes that can occur with a pregnancy: Enlarged or tender breasts, lack of or unusual menstrual period, lower abdominal pain or cramping (possibly severe), sore abdomen, unusual tiredness or weakness, unusual uterine bleeding (in some cases, very heavy).

If you think you are pregnant or if you miss a period while you are using the IUD, tell your health care professional. Until your doctor is able to see you, use another birth control method, such as condoms, to prevent pregnancy just in case you are not pregnant.

Also, notify your doctor and use another birth control method, such as condoms, if:

- you have unusual uterine bleeding;
- you are exposed to or get a sexually transmitted disease (STD);
- you feel the tip of the IUD at the cervix or you or your partner feels pain during sexual intercourse;
- you cannot find the threads from the IUD or think that the thread length is different;
- you or your sexual partner's lifestyle changes and one or both of you have more than one sexual partner;
- you have unusual or severe lower abdominal pain or cramping, possibly with a fever; or
- you develop vaginal discharge or sores in the vaginal area.

You can use other products in the vagina, such as tampons or condoms, while you are using a progesterone IUD.

After you stop using this device, you may become pregnant. The contraceptive effect of a progesterone IUD is usually reversible. If you stop using an IUD and still do not want to become pregnant, you should begin using another contraceptive method immediately to prevent pregnancy.

Side Effects of This Device

Along with its needed effects, a progesterone IUD may cause some unwanted effects. Although not all of these side effects may occur, if any do occur they may need medical attention.

Get emergency help immediately if any of the following side effects occur:

Rare
> Abdominal pain or cramping (severe); faintness, dizziness, or sharp pain at time of IUD insertion; uterine bleeding (heavy or unexpected)

Check with your health care professional immediately if any of the following side effects occur:

More common
> Abdominal pain or cramping on insertion (continuing); unusual spotting or uterine bleeding between periods; unusual uterine bleeding on insertion (continuing)

Rare
> Abdominal pain, continuous (dull or aching), fever, odorous vaginal discharge, unusual tiredness or weakness, and any unusual uterine bleeding

Other side effects not listed above may also occur in some patients. If you notice any other effects, check with your health care professional.

Developed: 12/04/95

PROGESTINS—For Contraceptive Use   Systemic

Commonly used brand name(s):

In the U.S.—

Depo-Provera Contraceptive Injection[2]	Nor-QD[3]
	Ovrette[4]
Micronor[3]	Plan B[1]
NORPLANT System[1]	

In Canada—

Depo-Provera[2]	NORPLANT System[1]
Micronor[3]	

Another commonly used name is norethisterone[3].

Note: For quick reference, the following progestins are numbered to match the corresponding brand names.

This information applies to the following medicines
1. Levonorgestrel (LEE-voe-nor-jes-trel)
2. Medroxyprogesterone (me-DROX-ee-proe-JES-te-rone)
3. Norethindrone (nor-eth-IN-drone)
4. Norgestrel (nor-JES-trel) †

†Not commercially available in Canada.

Description

Progestins (proe-JES-tins) are hormones.

The low-dose progestins for contraception are used to prevent pregnancy. Other names for progestin-only oral contraceptives are minipills and progestin-only pills (POPs). Progestins can prevent fertilization by preventing a woman's egg from fully developing.

Also, progestins cause changes at the opening of the uterus, such as thickening of the cervical mucus. This makes it hard for the partner's sperm to reach the egg. The fertilization of the woman's egg with her partner's sperm is less likely to occur while she is taking, receiving, or using a progestin, but it can occur. Even so, the progestins make it harder for the fertilized egg to become attached to the walls of the uterus, making it difficult to become pregnant.

No contraceptive method is 100 percent effective. *Studies show that fewer than 1 of each 100 women become pregnant during the first year of use when correctly receiving the injection on time or receiving the levonorgestrel implants. Fewer than 10 of each 100 women correctly taking progestins by mouth for contraception become pregnant during the first year of use.* Methods that do not work as well include using condoms, diaphragms, or spermicides. Discuss with your health care professional what your options are for birth control.

Progestins are available only with your doctor's prescription, in the following dosage forms:

Oral
Levonorgestrel
- Tablets (U.S.)
Norethindrone
- Tablets (U.S. and Canada)
Norgestrel
- Tablets (U.S.)

Subdermal
Levonorgestrel
- Implants (U.S. and Canada)

Parenteral
Medroxyprogesterone
- Injection (U.S. and Canada)

Before Using This Medicine

In deciding to use a medicine, the risks of taking the medicine must be weighed against the good it will do. If you are using progestins for contraception you should understand how their benefits and risks compare to those of other birth control methods. This is a decision you, your sexual partner, and your doctor will make. For progestins, the following should be considered:

Allergies—Tell your doctor if you have ever had any unusual or allergic reaction to progestins. Also tell your health care professional if you are allergic to any other substances, such as foods, preservatives, or dyes.

Diet—Make certain your health care professional knows if you are on any special diet, such as a low-sodium or low-sugar diet.

Pregnancy—Use of progestin-only contraceptives during pregnancy is not recommended. Doctors should be told if pregnancy is suspected. When accidently used during pregnancy, progestins used for contraception have not caused problems.

Breast-feeding—Although progestins pass into the breast milk, the low doses of progestins used for contraception have not been shown to cause problems in nursing babies. Progestins used for contraception are recommended for nursing mothers when contraception is desired.

Teenagers—Progestins have been used by teenagers and have not been shown to cause different side effects or problems than they do in adults. You must take progestin-only oral contraceptives every day in order for them to work. Progestins do not protect against sexually transmitted diseases, a risk factor for teenagers.

Older adults—This medicine has been tested and has not been shown to cause different side effects or problems in older people than it does in younger adults.

Other medicines—Although certain medicines should not be used together at all, in other cases two different medicines may be used together even if an interaction might occur. In these cases, your doctor may want to change the dose, or other precautions may be necessary. When you are taking a progestin, it is especially important that your health care professional know if you are taking any of the following:
- Aminoglutethimide (e.g., Cytadren) or
- Carbamazepine (e.g., Tegretol) or
- Phenobarbital or
- Phenytoin (e.g., Dilantin) or
- Rifabutin (e.g., Mycobutin) or

- Rifampin (e.g., Rifadin, Rimactane)—These medicines may decrease the effects of progestins and increase your chance of pregnancy, so use of a second form of birth control is recommended

Other medical problems—The presence of other medical problems may affect the use of progestins. Make sure you tell your doctor if you have any other medical problems, especially:
- Asthma or
- Epilepsy (or history of) or
- Heart or circulation problems or
- Kidney disease (severe) or
- Migraine headaches—Progestins may cause fluid build-up and may cause these conditions to become worse
- Bleeding problems, undiagnosed, such as blood in urine or changes in vaginal bleeding—May make diagnosis of these problems more difficult
- Breast disease (such as breast lumps or cysts) (history of)—May make this condition worse in certain types of diseases that do not react in a positive way to progestins
- Central nervous system (CNS) disorders, such as mental depression (or history of) or
- High blood cholesterol—Effects of progestins may cause these conditions or may make these conditions worse
- Diabetes mellitus (sugar diabetes)—May cause a mild increase in your blood sugar and a need to change the amount of medicine you take for diabetes
- Liver disease—Effects of some progestins may be increased and may worsen this condition
- Other conditions that increase the chances for osteoporosis (brittle bones)—Since it is possible that certain doses of progestins may cause temporary thinning of the bones by changing your hormone balance, it is important that your doctor know if you have an increased risk of osteoporosis. Some things that can increase your risk for having osteoporosis include cigarette smoking, abusing alcohol, taking or drinking large amounts of caffeine, and having a family history of osteoporosis or easily broken bones. Some medicines, such as glucocorticoids (cortisone-like medicines) or anticonvulsants (seizure medicine), can also cause thinning of the bones. However, it is thought that progestins can help protect against osteoporosis in postmenopausal women

Proper Use of This Medicine

To make the use of a progestin as safe and reliable as possible, you should understand how and when to take it and what effects may be expected. Progestins for contraception usually come with patient directions. Read them carefully before taking or using this medicine.

Progestins do not protect a woman from sexually transmitted diseases (STDs), including human immunodeficiency virus (HIV), or acquired immunodeficiency syndrome (AIDS). The use of latex (rubber) condoms or abstinence is recommended for protection from these diseases.

Take this medicine only as directed by your doctor. Do not take more of it and do not take it for a longer time than your doctor ordered. To do so may increase the chance of side effects. Try to take the medicine at the same time each day to reduce the possibility of side effects and to allow it to work better.

When using the levonorgestrel subdermal dosage form:
- For insertion:
  —Six implants are inserted under the skin of your upper arm by a health care professional. This usually takes about 15 minutes. No pain should be felt from the insertion process because you will receive a small injection from your doctor of a medicine that will numb your arm.
- For care of insertion site:
  —Keep the gauze wrap on for 24 hours after the insertion. Then, you should remove it. The sterile strips of tape should be left over the area for 3 days.
  —Be careful not to bump the site or get that area wet for at least 3 days after the procedure. Do not do any heavy lifting for 24 hours. Swelling and bruising are common for a few days.
- For contraceptive protection:
  —Full protection from pregnancy begins within 24 hours, if the insertion is done within 7 days of the beginning of your menstrual period. Otherwise, use another birth control method for the rest of your first cycle. Protection using implants lasts for 5 years or until removal, whichever comes first.
- For removal:
  —The implants need to be removed after 5 years. However, you may have them removed by a health care professional at any time before that.
  —If you want to continue using this form of birth control after 5 years, your health care professional may insert new implants in the same area where the old ones were or into the other arm.
  —After a local injection numbs the area on your arm, removal of the medication usually takes 20 minutes or longer. If the implants are hard to remove, your health care professional may want you to return another day to complete the removal process.
  —Keep a gauze wrap on for 24 hours after the removal. The sterile strips of tape underneath the gauze wrap should be left over the area for 3 days. Be careful not to bump the site or get that area wet until the area is healed.

When using levonorgestrel tablet dosage form for emergency contraception:
- The tablets may be taken at any time during the menstrual cycle.

When using medroxyprogesterone injection dosage form for contraception:
- Your injection is given by a health care professional every 3 months (13 weeks).
- To stop using medroxyprogesterone injection for contraception, simply do not have another injection.
- Full protection from pregnancy begins immediately if you receive the first injection within the first 5 days of your menstrual period or within 5 days after delivering a baby if you will not be breast-feeding. If you are going to breast-feed, you may have to wait for 6 weeks from your delivery date before receiving your first injection. If you follow this schedule, you do not need to use another form of birth control. Protection from that one injection ends at 3 months (13 weeks). You will need another injection every 3 months (13 weeks) to have full protection from becoming pregnant. However, if the injection is given later than 5 days from the first day of your last menstrual period, you will need to use another method of birth control as directed by your doctor.

When using an oral progestin dosage form:
- Take a tablet every 24 hours each day of the year. Taking the medicine at the same time each day helps to reduce the possibility of side effects and makes it work as expected. Taking your tablet 3 hours late is the same as missing a dose and can cause the medicine to not work properly.
- Keep the tablets in the container in which you received them to help you to keep track of your dosage schedule.
- When switching from estrogen and progestin oral contraceptives, you should take the first dose of the progestin-only contraceptive the next day after the last active pill of the estrogen and progestin oral contraceptive has been taken. This means you will not take the last 7 days (placebo or nonactive pills) of a 28-day cycle of the estrogen and progestin oral contraceptive pack. You will begin a new pack of progestin-only birth control pills on the 22nd day.
- Also, when switching, full protection from pregnancy begins after 48 hours if the first dose of the progestin-only contraceptive is taken on the first day of the menstrual period. If the birth control is begun on other days, full protection may begin 3 weeks after you begin taking the medicine for the first time. You should *use a second method of birth control for at least the first 3 weeks to ensure full protection.* You are not fully protected if you miss pills. The chances of your getting pregnant are greater with each pill that is missed.

Dosing—*Follow your doctor's orders or the directions on the label.* Also, follow your health care professional's orders to schedule the proper time to remove the implants or receive an injection of progestins for contraception. You and your health care professional may choose to replace the implants sooner or begin a new method of birth control. The following information includes only the average doses of these medicines. *If your dose is different, do not change it* unless your doctor tells you to do so.

For levonorgestrel
- For *subdermal* dosage form (implants):
  —For preventing pregnancy:
    - Adults and teenagers—Six implants (a total dose of 216 milligrams [mg]) inserted under the skin of the upper arm in a fan-like pattern. From this total dose, about 30 mcg is released every day for 5 years.
- For *oral* dosage form (tablet):
  —For emergency contraception for preventing pregnancy:
    - Adults and teenagers—The first dose of 0.75 milligram (mg) should be taken as soon as possible within 72 hours of intercourse. The second dose must be taken 12 hours later.

For medroxyprogesterone
- For *injection* dosage form:
  —For preventing pregnancy:
    - Adults and teenagers—150 milligrams injected into a muscle in the upper arm or in the buttocks every three months (13 weeks).

For norethindrone
- For *oral* dosage form (tablets):
  —For preventing pregnancy:
    - Adults and teenagers—0.35 milligrams (mg) every 24 hours, beginning on the first day of your menstrual cycle whether menstrual bleeding begins or not. The first day of your menstrual cycle

can be figured out by counting 28 days from the first day of your last menstrual cycle.

For norgestrel
- For *oral* dosage form (tablets):
  —For preventing pregnancy:
    - Adults and teenagers—75 micrograms (mcg) every 24 hours, beginning on the first day of your menstrual cycle whether menstrual bleeding occurs or not. The first day of your menstrual cycle can be figured out by counting 28 days from the first day of your last menstrual cycle.

Missed dose—

- For *oral* dosage form (tablets): When you miss 1 day's dose of oral tablets or are 3 hours or more late in taking your dose, many doctors recommend that you take the missed dose immediately, continue your normal schedule, and use another method of contraception for 2 days. This is different from what is done after a person misses a dose of birth control tablets that contain more than one hormone.
- For *injection* dosage form: If you miss having your next injection and it has been longer than 13 weeks since your last injection, your doctor may want you to stop receiving the medicine. Use another method of birth control until your period begins or until your doctor determines that you are not pregnant.
- If your doctor has other directions, follow that advice. *Any time you miss a menstrual period within 45 days after a missed or delayed dose you will need to be tested for a possible pregnancy.*

Storage—To store this medicine:

- Keep out of the reach of children.
- Store away from heat. Light will fade some tablet colors but will not change the tablets' effect.
- Do not store in the bathroom, near the kitchen sink, or in other damp places. Heat or moisture may cause the medicine to break down.
- Keep the medicine from freezing. Do not refrigerate.
- Keep the injectable form of this medicine from freezing.
- Do not keep outdated medicine or medicine no longer needed. Be sure that any discarded medicine is out of the reach of children.

Precautions While Using This Medicine

It is very important that your health care professional check your progress at regular visits. This will allow your dosage to be adjusted to your changing needs, and will allow any unwanted effects to be detected. These visits are usually every 12 months when you are taking progestins by mouth for birth control.

- If you are receiving the medroxyprogesterone injection for contraception, a physical exam is needed only every 12 months, but you need an injection every 3 months (13 weeks).
- If you are using the levonorgestrel implants, your doctor will want to check the area where they were placed within 30 days after they are put into or removed from your arm. After that, a visit every 12 months usually is all that is needed.

Progestins may cause some people to become dizzy. Make sure you know how you react to this medicine before you drive, use machines, or do anything else that could be dangerous if you are not alert.

Vaginal bleeding of various amounts may occur between your regular menstrual periods during the first 3 months of use. This is not unusual and does not mean you should stop the medicine. This is sometimes called spotting when the bleeding is slight, or breakthrough bleeding when it is heavier. If this occurs, continue on your regular dosing schedule. *Check with your doctor:*
- If vaginal bleeding continues for an unusually long time.
- If your menstrual period has not started within 45 days of your last period.

Missed menstrual periods may occur. *If you suspect a pregnancy, you should call your doctor immediately.*

If you are scheduled for any laboratory tests, tell your health care professional that you are taking a progestin. Progestins can change certain test results.

The following medicines might reduce the effectiveness of progestins for contraception:
    Aminoglutethimide (e.g., Cytadren)
    Carbamazepine (e.g., Tegretol)
    Phenobarbital
    Phenytoin (e.g., Dilantin)
    Rifabutin (e.g., Mycobutin)
    Rifampin (e.g., Rifadin)
Sometimes your doctor may use these medicines with progestins for contraception but will give you special directions to follow to make sure your progestin is working properly. *Use a second method of birth control* while using these medicines that reduce the effectiveness of progestins for contraception. If you are using medroxyprogesterone injection for contraception, continue using a back-up method of birth control until you have your next injection, even if those medicines that affect contraceptives are discontinued. If you are using the oral tablets or implants, continue using a back-up method of birth control for a full cycle (or 4 weeks), even if those medicines that affect contraceptives are discontinued.

If you vomit your oral progestin-only contraceptive for any reason within hours of taking it, do not take another dose. Return to your regular dosing schedule and use an additional back-up method of birth control for 48 hours.

If you are receiving levonorgestrel tablets for emergency contraception and vomiting occurs within 1 hour of taking either dose of the medicine, contact your physician to discuss whether the dose should be repeated.

Side Effects of This Medicine

Along with its needed effects, a medicine may cause some unwanted effects. Although not all of these side effects may occur, if they do occur they may need medical attention.

Check with your doctor as soon as possible if any of the following side effects occur:
More common
    Changes in uterine bleeding (increased amounts of menstrual bleeding occurring at regular monthly periods; lighter uterine bleeding between menstrual periods; heavier uterine bleeding between regular monthly periods; or stopping of menstrual periods)

Less common
    Mental depression; skin rash; unexpected or increased flow of breast milk

Other side effects may occur that usually do not need medical attention. These side effects may go away during treatment as your body adjusts to the medicine. However, check with

your doctor if any of the following side effects continue or are bothersome:

More common
> Abdominal pain or cramping; diarrhea; dizziness; fatigue; mild headache; mood changes; nausea; nervousness; pain or irritation at place of injection or place where implants were inserted; swelling of face, ankles, or feet; unusual tiredness or weakness; vomiting; weight gain

Less common
> Acne; breast pain or tenderness; brown spots on exposed skin, possibly long-lasting; hot flashes; loss or gain of body, facial, or scalp hair; loss of sexual desire; trouble in sleeping

Not all of the side effects listed above have been reported for each of these medicines, but they have been reported for at least one of them. All of the progestins are similar, so any of the above side effects may occur with any of these medicines.

After you stop using this medicine, your body may need time to adjust. The length of time this takes depends on the amount of medicine you were using and how long you used it. During this period of time check with your doctor if you notice any of the following side effects:

> Delayed return to fertility; stopping of menstrual periods; unusual menstrual bleeding (continuing)

Other side effects not listed above may also occur in some patients. If you notice any other effects, check with your doctor.

Revised: 01/04/00

PROGESTINS—For Noncontraceptive Use   Systemic

Commonly used brand name(s):

In the U.S.—

Amen[3]	Hy/Gestrone[1]
Aygestin[5]	Hylutin[1]
Crinone[6]	Megace[4]
Curretab[3]	Prodrox[1]
Cycrin[3]	Prometrium[6]
Depo-Provera[3]	Pro-Span[1]
Gesterol 50[6]	Provera[3]
Gesterol LA 250[1]	

In Canada—

Alti-MPA[3]	Norlutate[5]
Apo-Megestrol[4]	Novo-Medrone[3]
Colprone[2]	PMS-Progesterone[6]
Depo-Provera[3]	Prometrium[6]
Gen-Medroxy[3]	Provera[3]
Megace[4]	Provera Pak[3]
Megace OS[4]	

Another commonly used name is norethisterone[5].

Note: For quick reference, the following progestins are numbered to match the corresponding brand names.

This information applies to the following medicines
1. Hydroxyprogesterone (hye-drox-ee-proe-JES-te-rone) †‡
2. Medrogestone (me-droe-JES-tone) *
3. Medroxyprogesterone (me-DROX-ee-proe-JES-te-rone) ‡
4. Megestrol (me-JES-trole) ‡
5. Norethindrone (nor-eth-IN-drone)
6. Progesterone (proe-JES-ter-one) ‡

*Not commercially available in the U.S.
†Not commercially available in Canada.
‡Generic name product may be available in the U.S.

Description

Progestins (proe-JES-tins) are hormones. They are used by both men and women for different purposes.

Progestins are prescribed for several reasons:
- To properly regulate the menstrual cycle and treat unusual stopping of the menstrual periods (amenorrhea). Progestins work by causing changes in the uterus. After the amount of progestins in the blood drops, the lining of the uterus begins to come off and vaginal bleeding occurs (menstrual period). Progestins help other hormones start and stop the menstrual cycle.
- To help a pregnancy occur during egg donor or infertility procedures in women who do not produce enough progesterone. Also, progesterone is given to help maintain a pregnancy when not enough of it is made by the body.
- To prevent estrogen from thickening the lining of the uterus (endometrial hyperplasia) in women around menopause who are being treated with estrogen for ovarian hormone therapy (OHT). OHT is also called hormone replacement therapy (HRT) and estrogen replacement therapy (ERT).
- To treat a condition called endometriosis or unusual and heavy bleeding of the uterus (dysfunctional uterine bleeding) by starting or stopping the menstrual cycle.
- To help treat cancer of the breast, kidney, or uterus. Progestins help change the cancer cell's ability to react to other hormones and proteins that cause tumor growth. In this way, progestins can stop the growth of a tumor.
- To test the body's production of certain hormones such as estrogen.
- To treat loss of appetite and severe weight or muscle loss in patients with acquired immunodeficiency syndrome (AIDS) or cancer by causing certain proteins to be produced that cause increased appetite and weight gain.

Progestins may also be used for other conditions as determined by your doctor.

Depending on how much and which progestin you use or take, a progestin can have different effects. For instance, high doses of progesterone are necessary for some women to continue a pregnancy while other progestins in low doses can prevent a pregnancy from occurring. Other effects include causing weight gain, increasing body temperature, developing the milk-producing glands for breast-feeding, and relaxing the uterus to maintain a pregnancy.

Progestins can help other hormones work properly. Progestins may help to prevent anemia (low iron in blood), too much menstrual blood loss, and cancer of the uterus.

Progestins are available only with your doctor's prescription, in the following dosage forms:

Oral
Medrogestone
- Tablets (Canada)
Medroxyprogesterone
- Tablets (U.S. and Canada)
Megestrol
- Oral suspension (U.S. and Canada)
- Tablets (U.S. and Canada)

Norethindrone
- Tablets (U.S. and Canada)

Progesterone
- Capsules (U.S. and Canada)

Parenteral

Hydroxyprogesterone
- Injection (U.S.)

Medroxyprogesterone
- Injection (U.S. and Canada)

Progesterone
- Injection (U.S. and Canada)

Vaginal

Progesterone
- Gel (U.S.)
- Suppositories

Before Using This Medicine

In deciding to use a medicine, the risks of taking the medicine must be weighed against the good it will do. This is a decision you and your health care professional will make. For progestins, the following should be considered:

Allergies—Tell your doctor if you have ever had any unusual reaction to progestins. If using progesterone capsules or injection, tell your doctor if you are allergic to peanuts. Also tell your health care professional if you are allergic to any other substances, such as foods, preservatives, or dyes.

Diet—Make certain your health care professional knows if you are on any special diet, such as a low-sodium or low-sugar diet.

Pregnancy—Progesterone, a natural hormone that the body makes during pregnancy, has not caused problems. In fact, it is sometimes used in women to treat a certain type of infertility and to aid in egg donor or infertility procedures.

Other progestins have not been studied in pregnant women. Be sure to tell your doctor if you become pregnant while using any of the progestins. It is best to use some kind of birth control method while you are receiving progestins in high doses. High doses of progestins are not recommended for use during pregnancy since there have been some reports that they may cause birth defects in the genitals (sex organs) of a male fetus. Also, some of these progestins may cause male-like changes in a female fetus and female-like changes in a male fetus, but these problems usually can be reversed. Low doses of progestins, such as those doses used for contraception, have not caused major problems when used accidentally during pregnancy.

Breast-feeding—Although progestins pass into the breast milk, they have not been shown to cause problems in nursing babies. However, progestins may change the quality or amount (increase or decrease) of the mother's breast milk. It may be necessary for you to take another medicine or to stop breast-feeding during treatment. Be sure you have discussed the risks and benefits of the medicine with your doctor.

Children—Although there is no specific information comparing use of progestins in children with use in other age groups, this medicine is not expected to cause different side effects or problems in children than it does in adults.

Teenagers—Although there is no specific information comparing use of progestins in teenagers with use in other age groups, this medicine is not expected to cause different side effects or problems in teenagers than it does in adults.

Older adults—This medicine has been tested and has not been shown to cause different side effects or problems in older people than it does in younger adults.

Other medicines—Although certain medicines should not be used together at all, in other cases two different medicines may be used together even if an interaction might occur. In these cases, your doctor may want to change the dose, or other precautions may be necessary. When you are taking a progestin, it is especially important that your health care professional know if you are taking any of the following:
- Aminoglutethimide (e.g., Cytadren) or
- Carbamazepine (e.g., Tegretol) or
- Phenobarbital or
- Phenytoin (e.g., Dilantin) or
- Rifabutin (e.g., Mycobutin) or
- Rifampin (e.g., Rifadin, Rimactane)—These medicines may decrease the effects of progestins

Other medical problems—The presence of other medical problems may affect the use of progestins. Make sure you tell your doctor if you have any other medical problems, especially:
- Asthma or
- Epilepsy (or history of) or
- Heart or circulation problems or
- Kidney disease (severe) or
- Migraine headaches—Progestins may cause fluid build-up and may cause these conditions to become worse
- Bleeding problems, undiagnosed, such as blood in urine or changes in vaginal bleeding—May make diagnosis of these problems more difficult
- Blood clots (or history of) or
- Stroke (or history of) or
- Varicose veins—May have greater chance of causing blood clots if these conditions are already present when high doses of progestins are taken
- Breast disease (such as breast lumps or cysts) (history of)—May make this condition worse in certain types of diseases that do not react in a positive way to progestins
- Central nervous system (CNS) disorders, such as mental depression (or history of) or
- High blood cholesterol—Effects of progestins may cause these conditions, or may make these conditions worse
- Diabetes mellitus (sugar diabetes)—May cause an increase in your blood sugar and a change in the amount of medicine you take for diabetes; progestins in high doses are more likely to cause this problem
- Liver disease—Effects of progestins may be increased and may make this condition worse
- Other conditions that increase the chances for osteoporosis (brittle bones)—Since it is possible that certain doses of progestins may cause temporary thinning of the bones by changing your hormone balance, it is important that your doctor know if you have an increased risk of osteoporosis. Some things that can increase your risk for having osteoporosis include cigarette smoking, abusing alcohol, taking or drinking large amounts of caffeine, and having a family history of osteoporosis or easily broken bones. Some medicines, such as glucocorticoids (cortisone-like medicines) or anticonvulsants (seizure medicine), can also cause thinning of the bones. However, it is thought that progestins can help protect against osteoporosis in postmenopausal women

Proper Use of This Medicine

To make the use of a progestin as safe and reliable as possible, you should understand how and when to take it and what effects may be expected. Progestins usually come with patient directions. Read them carefully before taking or using this medicine.

Take this medicine only as directed by your doctor. Do not take more of it and do not take it for a longer time than your doctor ordered. To do so may increase the chance of side effects. Try to take the medicine at the same time each day to reduce the possibility of side effects and to allow it to work better.

Progestins are often given together with certain medicines. If you are using a combination of medicines, make sure that you take each one at the proper time and do not mix them. Ask your health care professional to help you plan a way to remember to take your medicines at the right times.

Dosing—The dose of these medicines will be different for different patients. *Follow your doctor's orders or the directions on the label.* The following information includes only the average doses of these medicines. *If your dose is different, do not change it* unless your doctor tells you to do so.

The number of tablets, injections, or suppositories that you take, receive, or use depends on the strength of the medicine. Also, *the number of doses you take or use each day, the time allowed between doses, and the length of time you take or use the medicine depend on the medical problem for which you are taking progestins.*

For hydroxyprogesterone
- For *injection* dosage form:
  —For controlling unusual and heavy bleeding of the uterus (dysfunctional uterine bleeding) or treating unusual stopping of menstrual periods (amenorrhea):
    - Adults and teenagers—375 milligrams (mg) injected into a muscle as a single dose.
  —For preparing the uterus for the menstrual period:
    - Adults and teenagers—125 to 250 mg injected into a muscle as a single dose on Day 10 of the menstrual cycle (counting from the first day of the last menstrual cycle). May be repeated every seven days if needed.

For medrogestone
- For *oral* dosage form (tablets):
  —For preparing the uterus for the menstrual period, controlling unusual and heavy bleeding of the uterus (dysfunctional uterine bleeding), preventing estrogen from thickening the lining of the uterus (endometrial hyperplasia) when taking estrogen for ovarian hormone therapy in postmenopausal women, or treating unusual stopping of menstrual periods (amenorrhea):
    - Adults and teenagers—5 to 10 milligrams (mg) a day for ten to fourteen days each month as directed by your doctor.

For medroxyprogesterone
- For *oral* dosage form (tablets):
  —For controlling unusual and heavy bleeding of the uterus (dysfunctional uterine bleeding) or treating unusual stopping of menstrual periods (amenorrhea):
    - Adults and teenagers—5 to 10 milligrams (mg) a day for five to ten days as directed by your doctor.
  —For preparing the uterus for the menstrual period:
    - Adults and teenagers—10 mg daily for five or ten days as directed by your doctor.
  —For preventing estrogen from thickening the lining of the uterus (endometrial hyperplasia) when taking estrogen for ovarian hormone therapy in postmenopausal women:
    - Adults—When taking estrogen each day on Days 1 through 25: Oral, 5 to 10 mg of medroxyprogesterone daily for ten to fourteen or more days each month as directed by your doctor. Or, your doctor may want you to take 2.5 or 5 mg a day without stopping. Your doctor will help decide the number of tablets that is best for you and when to take them.

- For *injection* dosage form:
  —For treating cancer of the kidneys or uterus:
    - Adults and teenagers—At first, 400 to 1000 milligrams (mg) injected into a muscle as a single dose once a week. Then, your doctor may lower your dose to 400 mg or more once a month.

For megestrol
- For *oral* dosage form (suspension):
  —For treating loss of appetite (anorexia), muscles (cachexia), or weight caused by acquired immunodeficiency syndrome (AIDS):
    - Adults and teenagers—800 milligrams (mg) a day for the first month. Then your doctor may want you to take 400 or 800 mg a day for three more months.

- For *oral* dosage form (tablets):
  —For treating cancer of the breast:
    - Adults and teenagers—160 mg a day as a single dose or in divided doses for two or more months.
  —For treating cancer of the uterus:
    - Adults and teenagers—40 to 320 mg a day for two or more months.
  —For treating loss of appetite (anorexia), muscles (cachexia), or weight caused by cancer:
    - Adults and teenagers—400 to 800 milligrams (mg) a day.

For norethindrone
- For *oral* dosage form (tablets):
  —For controlling unusual and heavy bleeding of the uterus (dysfunctional uterine bleeding) or treating unusual stopping of menstrual periods (amenorrhea):
    - Adults and teenagers—2.5 to 10 milligrams (mg) a day from Day 5 through Day 25 (counting from the first day of the last menstrual cycle). Or, your doctor may want you to take the medicine only for five to ten days as directed.
  —For treating endometriosis:
    - Adults and teenagers—At first, 5 mg a day for two weeks. Then, your doctor may increase your dose slowly up to 15 mg a day for six to nine months. Let your doctor know if your menstrual period starts. Your doctor may want you to take more of the medicine or may want you to stop taking the medicine for a short period of time.

For progesterone
- For *oral* dosage form (capsules):
  - —For preventing estrogen from thickening the lining of the uterus (endometrial hyperplasia) when taking estrogen for ovarian hormone therapy in postmenopausal women:
    - Adults—200 mg a day at bedtime during the last fourteen days of estrogen treatment each month. Although other schedules are possible, usually treatment begins either on Day 8 through Day 21 of a twenty-eight–day cycle or on Day 12 through Day 25 of a thirty-day cycle. Your doctor may ask you not to take progestins or estrogens for the last five to seven days of each month. Sometimes your doctor may increase your dose to 100 mg in the morning to be taken 2 hours after breakfast and 200 mg to be taken at bedtime.
  - —For treating unusual stopping of menstrual periods (amenorrhea):
    - Adults—400 mg a day in the evening for ten days.
- For *vaginal* dosage form (gel):
  - —For treating unusual stopping of menstrual periods (amenorrhea):
    - Adults and teenagers—45 mg (one applicatorful of 4% gel) once every other day for up to six doses. Dose may be increased to 90 mg (one applicatorful of 8% gel) once every other day for up to six doses if needed.
  - —For use with infertility procedures:
    - Adults and teenagers—90 mg (one applicatorful of 8% gel) one or two times a day. If pregnancy occurs, treatment can continue for up to ten to twelve weeks.
- For *injection* dosage form:
  - —For controlling unusual and heavy bleeding of the uterus (dysfunctional uterine bleeding) or treating unusual stopping of menstrual periods (amenorrhea):
    - Adults and teenagers—5 to 10 milligrams (mg) a day injected into a muscle for six to ten days. Or, your doctor may want you to receive 100 or 150 mg injected into a muscle as a single dose. Sometimes your doctor may want you first to take another hormone called estrogen. If your menstrual period starts, your doctor will want you to stop taking the medicine.
- For *suppositories* dosage form (vaginal):
  - —For maintaining a pregnancy (at ovulation and at the beginning of pregnancy):
    - Adults and teenagers—25 mg to 100 mg (one suppository) inserted into the vagina one or two times a day beginning near the time of ovulation. Your doctor may want you to receive the medicine for up to eleven weeks.

Missed dose—For all progestins, except for progesterone capsules for postmenopausal women: If you miss a dose of this medicine, take the missed dose as soon as possible. However, if it is almost time for your next dose, skip the missed dose and go back to your regular dosing schedule. Do not double doses.

For progesterone capsules for postmenopausal women: If you miss a dose of 200 mg of progesterone capsules at bedtime, take 100 mg in the morning then go back to your regular dosing schedule. If you take 300 mg of progesterone a day

and you miss your morning and evening doses, you should not take the missed dose. Return to your regular dosing schedule.

Storage—To store this medicine:
- Keep out of the reach of children.
- Store away from heat.
- Do not store in the bathroom, near the kitchen sink, or in any other damp places. Heat or moisture may cause the medicine to break down.
- Keep the injectable form of this medicine from freezing.
- Do not keep outdated medicine or medicine no longer needed. Be sure that any discarded medicine is out of the reach of children.

Precautions While Using This Medicine

It is very important that your doctor check your progress at regular visits. This will allow your dosage to be adjusted to your changing needs, and will allow any unwanted effects to be detected. These visits will usually be every 6 to 12 months, but some doctors require them more often.

Progestins may cause some people to become dizzy. For oral or vaginal progesterone, dizziness or drowsiness may occur 1 to 4 hours after taking or using it. Make sure you know how you react to this medicine before you drive, use machines, or do anything else that could be dangerous if you are not alert.

Unusual or unexpected vaginal bleeding of various amounts may occur between your regular menstrual periods during the first 3 months of use. This is sometimes called spotting when slight, or breakthrough menstrual bleeding when heavier. If this should occur, continue on your regular dosing schedule. *Check with your doctor:*
- If unusual or unexpected vaginal bleeding continues for an unusually long time.
- If your menstrual period has not started within 45 days of your last period.

Missed menstrual periods may occur. *If you suspect a pregnancy, you should stop taking this medicine immediately and call your doctor.* Your doctor will let you know if you should continue taking the progestin.

If you are scheduled for any laboratory tests, tell your health care professional that you are taking a progestin. Progestins can change certain test results.

In some patients, tenderness, swelling, or bleeding of the gums may occur. Brushing and flossing your teeth carefully and regularly and massaging your gums may help prevent this. See your dentist regularly to have your teeth cleaned. Check with your medical doctor or dentist if you have any questions about how to take care of your teeth and gums, or if you notice any tenderness, swelling, or bleeding of your gums.

You will need to use a birth control method while taking progestins for noncontraceptive use if you are fertile and sexually active.

If you are using vaginal progesterone, avoid using other vaginal products for 6 hours before and for 6 hours after inserting the vaginal dose of progesterone.

Side Effects of This Medicine

Along with their needed effects, progestins used in high doses sometimes cause some unwanted effects such as blood clots, heart attacks, and strokes, or problems of the liver and eyes. Although these effects are rare, some of them can be very serious and cause death. It is not clear if these problems are due to the progestin. They may be caused by the disease or condition for which progestins are being used.

The following side effects may be caused by blood clots. Although not all of these side effects may occur, if they do occur they need immediate medical attention. *Get emergency help immediately* if any of the following side effects occur:

Rare
> *Symptoms of blood clotting problems, usually severe or sudden,* such as headache or migraine; loss of or change in speech, coordination, or vision; numbness of or pain in chest, arm, or leg; unexplained shortness of breath

Also, check with your doctor as soon as possible if any of the following side effects occur:

More common
> Changes in vaginal bleeding (increased amounts of menstrual bleeding occurring at regular monthly periods, lighter vaginal bleeding between menstrual periods, heavier vaginal bleeding between regular monthly periods, or stopping of menstrual periods); symptoms of blood sugar problems (dry mouth, frequent urination, loss of appetite, or unusual thirst)

Less common
> Mental depression; skin rash; unexpected or increased flow of breast milk

Rare
> *For megestrol—During chronic treatment*
>> Backache; dizziness; filling or rounding out of the face; irritability; mental depression; unusual decrease in sexual desire or ability in men; nausea or vomiting; unusual tiredness or weakness

Other side effects may occur that usually do not need medical attention. These side effects may go away during treatment as your body adjusts to the medicine. However, check with your doctor if any of the following side effects continue or are bothersome:

More common
> Abdominal pain or cramping; bloating or swelling of ankles or feet; blood pressure increase (mild); dizziness; drowsiness (progesterone only); headache (mild); mood changes; nervousness; pain or irritation at place of injection site; swelling of face, ankles, or feet; unusual or rapid weight gain

Less common
> Acne; breast pain or tenderness; brown spots on exposed skin, possibly long-lasting; hot flashes; loss or gain of body, facial, or scalp hair; loss of sexual desire; trouble in sleeping

Not all of the side effects listed above have been reported for each of these medicines, but they have been reported for at least one of them. All of the progestins are similar, so any of the above side effects may occur with any of these medicines.

After you stop using this medicine, your body may need time to adjust. The length of time this takes depends on the amount of medicine you were using and how long you used it. During this period of time check with your doctor if you notice the following side effect:

> Delayed return to fertility; stopping of menstrual periods; unusual menstrual bleeding (continuing)

For megestrol
> Dizziness; nausea or vomiting; unusual tiredness or weakness

Other side effects not listed above may also occur in some patients. If you notice any other effects, check with your doctor.

Additional Information

Once a medicine has been approved for marketing for a certain use, experience may show that it is also useful for other medical problems. Although these uses are not included in product labeling, progestins are used in certain patients with the following medical conditions:

- Carcinoma of the prostate
- Corpus luteum insufficiency
- Endometrial hyperplasia
- Polycystic ovary syndrome
- Precocious puberty

Other than the above information, there is no additional information relating to proper use, precautions, or side effects for these uses.

Revised: 06/29/98

PROPAFENONE   Systemic

Commonly used brand name(s):

In the U.S.—
> Rythmol

In Canada—
> Rythmol

Description

Propafenone (proe-pa-FEEN-none) belongs to the group of medicines known as antiarrhythmics. It is used to treat abnormal heart rhythms.

Propafenone produces its helpful effects by slowing nerve impulses in the heart and making the heart tissue less sensitive.

There is a chance that propafenone may cause new heart rhythm problems or make worse those that already exist. Since similar medicines have been shown to cause severe problems in some patients, propafenone is only used to treat serious heart rhythm problems. Discuss this possible effect with your doctor.

This medicine is available only with your doctor's prescription, in the following dosage form:

Oral
> • Tablets (U.S. and Canada)

Before Using This Medicine

In deciding to use a medicine, the risks of taking the medicine must be weighed against the good it will do. This is a decision you and your doctor will make. For propafenone, the following should be considered:

Allergies—Tell your doctor if you have ever had any unusual or allergic reaction to propafenone. Also tell your health care professional if you are allergic to any other substances, such as foods, preservatives, or dyes.

Pregnancy—Propafenone has not been studied in pregnant women. Although this medicine has not been shown to cause birth defects in animal studies, it has been shown to reduce fertility in monkeys, dogs, and rabbits. In addition, in rats it caused decreased growth in the infant and deaths of mothers and infants. Before taking propafenone, make sure your doctor knows if you are pregnant or if you may become pregnant.

Breast-feeding—Propafenone passes into breast milk. Because of the potential for problems in the nursing infant, propafenone is generally not recommended in mothers who are breast-feeding.

Children—Propafenone can cause serious side effects in any patient. Therefore, it is especially important that you discuss with the child's doctor the good that this medicine may do as well as the risks of using it.

Older adults—Many medicines have not been studied specifically in older people. Therefore, it may not be known whether they work exactly the same way they do in younger adults or if they cause different side effects or problems in older people. There is no specific information comparing use of propafenone in the elderly with use in other age groups.

Other medicines—Although certain medicines should not be used together at all, in other cases two different medicines may be used together even if an interaction might occur. In these cases, your doctor may want to change the dose, or other precautions may be necessary. When you are taking propafenone it is especially important that your health care professional know if you are taking either of the following:

- Digoxin (e.g., Lanoxin) or
- Warfarin (e.g., Coumadin)—Effects of these medicines may be increased when used with propafenone

Other medical problems—The presence of other medical problems may affect the use of propafenone. Make sure you tell your doctor if you have any other medical problems, especially:

- Asthma or
- Bronchitis or
- Emphysema—Propafenone can increase trouble in breathing
- Bradycardia (unusually slow heartbeat)—There is a risk of further decreased heart function
- Congestive heart failure or other heart disease or
- Myasthenia gravis or
- Severe low blood pressure—Propafenone may make these conditions worse
- Electrolyte (i.e., potassium) disorders—Propafenone may worsen heart rhythm problems
- Kidney disease or
- Liver disease—Effects of propafenone may be increased because of slower removal from the body
- If you have a pacemaker—Propafenone may interfere with the pacemaker and require more careful follow-up by the doctor

Proper Use of This Medicine

Take propafenone exactly as directed by your doctor. Do not take more or less of this medicine, and do not take it more often than your doctor ordered.

This medicine works best when there is a constant amount in the blood. *To help keep the amount constant, do not miss any doses. Also, it is best to take each dose at evenly spaced times day and night.* For example, if you are to take 3 doses a day, doses should be spaced about 8 hours apart. If you need help in planning the best times to take your medicine, check with your health care professional.

Dosing—The dose of propafenone will be different for different patients. *Follow your doctor's orders or the directions on the label.* The following information includes only the average doses of propafenone. *If your dose is different, do not change it* unless your doctor tells you to do so:

- The number of tablets that you take depends on the strength of the medicine.
- For *oral* dosage forms (tablets):
  —Adults: 150 milligrams every eight hours. Your doctor may increase your dose if needed.
  —Children: Use and dose must be determined by your doctor.

Missed dose—If you miss a dose of propafenone and remember within 4 hours, take it as soon as possible. However, if you do not remember until later, skip the missed dose and go back to your regular dosing schedule. Do not double doses.

Storage—To store this medicine:

- Keep out of the reach of children.
- Store away from heat and direct light.
- Do not store in the bathroom, near the kitchen sink, or in other damp places. Heat or moisture may cause the medicine to break down.
- Do not keep outdated medicine or medicine no longer needed. Be sure that any discarded medicine is out of the reach of children.

Precautions While Using This Medicine

It is important that your doctor check your progress at regular visits to make sure the medicine is working properly. This will allow changes to be made in the amount of medicine you are taking, if necessary.

Your doctor may want you to carry a medical identification card or bracelet stating that you are using this medicine.

Before having any kind of surgery (including dental surgery) or emergency treatment, tell the medical doctor or dentist in charge that you are taking this medicine.

Propafenone may cause some people to become dizzy or lightheaded. Make sure you know how you react to this medicine before you drive, use machines, or do anything else that could be dangerous if you are dizzy.

Side Effects of This Medicine

Along with its needed effects, a medicine may cause some unwanted effects. Although not all of these side effects may occur, if they do occur they may need medical attention.

Check with your doctor as soon as possible if any of the following side effects occur:
Less common
    Chest pain; shortness of breath; fast, irregular, or slow heartbeat, dizziness, and/or fainting; swelling of feet or lower legs; weight gain
Rare
    Chills, fever, and weakness; joint pain; trembling or shaking

Other side effects may occur that usually do not need medical attention. These side effects may go away during treatment

as your body adjusts to the medicine. However, check with your doctor if any of the following side effects continue or are bothersome:

More common
   Change in taste or bitter or metallic taste

Less common
   Blurred vision; constipation or diarrhea; dryness of mouth; headache; nausea and/or vomiting; skin rash; unusual tiredness or weakness

Other side effects not listed above may also occur in some patients. If you notice any other effects, check with your doctor.

Revised: 02/26/99

PSEUDOEPHEDRINE   Systemic

Commonly used brand name(s):

In the U.S.—
Cenafed
Chlor-Trimeton Non-Drowsy
   Decongestant 4 Hour
Decofed
Dimetapp Decongestant
Dimetapp Decongestant
   Pediatric Drops
Drixoral Nasal Decongestant
Efidac/24
Genaphed
Myfedrine
PediaCare Infants' Oral
   Decongestant Drops

Pseudo 60's
Sudafed
Sudafed Children's Nasal
   Decongestant Liquid
   Medication
Sudafed 12 Hour
Triaminic AM Decongestant
   Formula
Triaminic Infant Oral
   Decongestant Drops

In Canada—
Balminil Decongestant Syrup
Benylin Decongestant
Drixoral N.D.
Eltor 120
Maxenal
Robidrine

Sudafed Decongestant
Sudafed Decongestant Extra
   Strength
Sudafed Decongestant 12
   Hour

Generic name product may be available in the U.S. and Canada.

Description

Pseudoephedrine (soo-doe-e-FED-rin) is used to relieve nasal or sinus congestion caused by the common cold, sinusitis, and hay fever and other respiratory allergies. It is also used to relieve ear congestion caused by ear inflammation or infection.

Some of these preparations are available only with your doctor's prescription. Others are available without a prescription; however, your doctor may have special instructions on the proper dose of pseudoephedrine for your medical condition.

Pseudoephedrine is available in the following dosage forms:

Oral
   • Capsules (U.S. and Canada)
   • Extended-release capsules (Canada)
   • Oral solution (U.S.)
   • Syrup (U.S. and Canada)
   • Tablets (U.S. and Canada)
   • Extended-release tablets (U.S. and Canada)

Before Using This Medicine

If you are taking this medicine without a prescription, carefully read and follow any precautions on the label. For pseudoephedrine, the following should be considered:

Allergies—Tell your doctor if you have ever had any unusual or allergic reaction to pseudoephedrine or similar medicines, such as albuterol, amphetamines, ephedrine, epinephrine, isoproterenol, metaproterenol, norepinephrine, phenylephrine, phenylpropanolamine, or terbutaline. Also tell your health care professional if you are allergic to any other substances, such as foods, preservatives, or dyes.

Pregnancy—Studies on birth defects have not been done in humans. Pseudoephedrine has not been shown to cause birth defects in animal studies. However, studies in animals have shown that pseudoephedrine causes a reduction in average weight, length, and rate of bone formation in the animal fetus.

Breast-feeding—Pseudoephedrine passes into breast milk and may cause unwanted effects in nursing babies (especially newborn and premature babies).

Children—Pseudoephedrine may be more likely to cause side effects in infants, especially newborn and premature infants, than in older children and adults.

Older adults—Many medicines have not been studied specifically in older people. Therefore, it may not be known whether they work exactly the same way they do in younger adults or if they cause different side effects or problems in older people. There is no specific information comparing use of pseudoephedrine in the elderly with use in other age groups.

Other medicines—Although certain medicines should not be used together at all, in other cases two different medicines may be used together even if an interaction might occur. In these cases, your doctor may want to change the dose, or other precautions may be necessary. When you are taking pseudoephedrine, it is especially important that your health care professional know if you are taking any of the following:

• Beta-blockers (acebutolol [e.g., Sectral], atenolol [e.g., Tenormin], betaxolol [e.g., Kerlone], bisoprolol [e.g., Zebeta], carteolol [e.g., Cartrol], labetalol [e.g., Normodyne], metoprolol [e.g., Lopressor], nadolol [e.g., Corgard], oxprenolol [e.g., Trasicor], penbutolol [e.g., Levatol], pindolol [e.g., Visken], propranolol [e.g., Inderal], sotalol [e.g., Sotacor], timolol [e.g., Blocadren])—Pseudoephedrine may decrease the effect of these medicines; also, taking pseudoephedrine with beta-blockers may increase the chance of side effects

• Cocaine—Using cocaine with pseudoephedrine may increase the effects of either one of these medicines on the heart and increase the chance of side effects

• Monoamine oxidase (MAO) inhibitors (furazolidone [e.g., Furoxone], isocarboxazid [e.g., Marplan], phenelzine [e.g., Nardil], procarbazine [e.g., Matulane], selegiline [e.g., Eldepryl], tranylcypromine [e.g., Parnate])—Taking pseudoephedrine while you are taking or within 2 weeks of taking monoamine oxidase (MAO) inhibitors may increase the chance of serious side effects

Other medical problems—The presence of other medical problems may affect the use of pseudoephedrine. Make

sure you tell your doctor if you have any other medical problems, especially:

- Diabetes mellitus (sugar diabetes)—Use of pseudoephedrine may cause an increase in blood glucose levels
- Enlarged prostate or
- Glaucoma, or a predisposition to glaucoma or
- Heart disease or blood vessel disease or
- High blood pressure—Pseudoephedrine may make the condition worse
- Overactive thyroid—Use of pseudoephedrine may make the condition worse

Proper Use of This Medicine

For patients taking *pseudoephedrine extended-release capsules:*

- Swallow the capsule whole. However, if the capsule is too large to swallow, you may mix the contents of the capsule with jam or jelly and swallow without chewing.
- Do not crush or chew before swallowing.

For patients taking *pseudoephedrine extended-release tablets:*

- Swallow the tablet whole.
- Do not break, crush, or chew before swallowing.

To help prevent trouble in sleeping, *take the last dose of pseudoephedrine for each day a few hours before bedtime.* If you have any questions about this, check with your doctor.

Take this medicine only as directed. Do not take more of it, do not take it more often, and do not take it for a longer period of time than recommended on the label (usually 7 days), unless otherwise directed by your doctor. To do so may increase the chance of side effects.

Dosing—The dose of pseudoephedrine will be different for different patients. *Follow your doctor's orders or the directions on the label.* The following information includes only the average doses of pseudoephedrine. *If your dose is different, do not change it* unless your doctor tells you to do so.

The number of capsules, tablets, or teaspoonfuls of solution or syrup that you take each day depends on the strength of the medicine. Also, the time between doses depends on whether you are taking a short-acting or long-acting form of pseudoephedrine.

- For nasal or sinus congestion:
    —For *regular (short-acting) oral* dosage form (capsules, oral solution, syrup, or tablets):
    - Adults and children 12 years of age and older—60 milligrams (mg) every four to six hours. Do not take more than 240 mg in twenty-four hours.
    - Children 6 to 12 years of age—30 mg every four to six hours. Do not take more than 120 mg in twenty-four hours.
    - Children 2 to 6 years of age—15 mg every four to six hours. Do not take more than 60 mg in twenty-four hours.
    - Children 4 months to 2 years of age—Dose must be determined by your doctor
    - Children up to 4 months of age—Use and dose must be determined by your doctor.
    —For *long-acting oral* dosage form (extended-release capsules or extended-release tablets):
    - Adults and children 12 years of age and older—120 mg every 12 hours, or 240 mg every 24 hours.
    - Do not take more than 240 mg in twenty-four hours.
    - Children up to 12 years of age—Use is not recommended.

Missed dose—If you miss a dose of this medicine and you remember within an hour or so of the missed dose, take it right away. However, if you do not remember until later, skip the missed dose and go back to your regular dosing schedule. Do not double doses.

Storage—To store this medicine:

- Keep out of the reach of children.
- Store away from heat and direct light.
- Do not store the capsule or tablet form of this medicine in the bathroom, near the kitchen sink, or in other damp places. Heat or moisture may cause the medicine to break down.
- Keep the liquid form of this medicine from freezing.
- Do not keep outdated medicine or medicine no longer needed. Be sure that any discarded medicine is out of the reach of children.

Precautions While Using This Medicine

If symptoms do not improve within 7 days or if you also have a high fever, check with your doctor since these signs may mean that you have other medical problems.

Side Effects of This Medicine

Along with its needed effects, a medicine may cause some unwanted effects. Although not all of these side effects may occur, if they do occur they may need medical attention.

Check with your doctor as soon as possible if any of the following side effects occur:

Rare—more common with high doses
    Convulsions (seizures); hallucinations (seeing, hearing, or feeling things that are not there); irregular or slow heartbeat; shortness of breath or troubled breathing

Symptoms of overdose
    Convulsions (seizures); fast breathing; hallucinations (seeing, hearing, or feeling things that are not there); increase in blood pressure; irregular heartbeat (continuing); shortness of breath or troubled breathing (severe or continuing); slow or fast heartbeat (severe or continuing); unusual nervousness, restlessness, or excitement

Other side effects may occur that usually do not need medical attention. These side effects may go away during treatment as your body adjusts to the medicine. However, check with your health care professional if any of the following side effects continue or are bothersome:

More common
    Nervousness; restlessness; trouble in sleeping

Less common
    Difficult or painful urination; dizziness or lightheadedness; fast or pounding heartbeat; headache; increased sweating; nausea or vomiting; trembling; unusual paleness; weakness

Other side effects not listed above may also occur in some patients. If you notice any other effects, check with your health care professional.

Revised: 12/14/98

PYRETHRINS AND PIPERONYL BUTOXIDE   Topical

Commonly used brand name(s):

In the U.S.—

A-200 Gel Concentrate	Pyrinyl
A-200 Shampoo Concentrate	R & C
Barc	Rid
Blue	Tisit
Licetrol	Tisit Blue
Pronto Lice Killing Shampoo	Tisit Shampoo
Kit	Triple X

In Canada—
  R & C

Description

Medicine containing pyrethrins (pye-REE-thrins) is used to treat head, body, and pubic lice infections. This medicine is absorbed by the lice and destroys them by acting on their nervous systems. It does not affect humans in this way. The piperonyl butoxide (pye-PEER-i-nil byoo-TOX-ide) is included to make the pyrethrins more effective in killing the lice. This combination medicine is known as a pediculicide (pe-DIK-yoo-li-side).

This medicine is available without a prescription; however, your doctor may have special instructions on the proper use of this medicine for your medical condition.

Pyrethrins and piperonyl butoxide combination medicine is available in the following dosage forms:

Topical
  • Gel (U.S.)
  • Solution shampoo (U.S. and Canada)
  • Topical solution (U.S.)

Before Using This Medicine

If you are using this medicine without a prescription, carefully read and follow any precautions on the label. For pyrethrins and piperonyl butoxide combination, the following should be considered:

Allergies—Tell your doctor if you have ever had any unusual or allergic reaction to pyrethrins, piperonyl butoxide, ragweed, chrysanthemum plants, or kerosene or other petroleum products. Also tell your health care professional if you are allergic to any other substances, such as preservatives or dyes.

Pregnancy—Pyrethrins and piperonyl butoxide may be absorbed through the skin. However, this medicine has not been shown to cause birth defects or other problems in humans when used on the skin.

Breast-feeding—Pyrethrins and piperonyl butoxide combination may be absorbed through the mother's skin. It is not known whether pyrethrins and piperonyl butoxide combination passes into the breast milk. Although most medicines pass into breast milk in small amounts, many of them may be used safely while breast-feeding. Mothers who are using this medicine and who wish to breast-feed should discuss this with their doctor.

Children—Although there is no specific information comparing use of pyrethrins and piperonyl butoxide combination in children with use in other age groups, this medicine is not expected to cause different side effects or problems in children than it does in adults.

Older adults—Many medicines have not been studied specifically in older people. Therefore, it may not be known whether they work exactly the same way they do in younger adults. Although there is no specific information comparing use of pyrethrins and piperonyl butoxide combination medicine in the elderly with use in other age groups, this medicine is not expected to cause different side effects or problems in older people than it does in younger adults.

Other medical problems—The presence of other medical problems may affect the use of pyrethrins and piperonyl butoxide combination. Make sure you tell your doctor if you have any other medical problems, especially:

  • Inflammation of the skin (severe)—Use of pyrethrins and piperonyl butoxide combination may make the condition worse

Proper Use of This Medicine

Pyrethrins and piperonyl butoxide combination medicine usually comes with patient directions. Read them carefully before using this medicine.

Use this medicine only as directed. Do not use more of it and do not use it more often than recommended on the label. To do so may increase the chance of absorption through the skin and the chance of side effects.

Keep pyrethrins and piperonyl butoxide combination medicine away from the mouth and do not inhale it. This medicine is harmful if swallowed or inhaled.

To lessen the chance of inhaling this medicine, apply it in a well-ventilated room (for example, one with free flowing air or with a fan turned on).

Keep this medicine away from the eyes and other mucous membranes, such as the inside of the nose, mouth, or vagina, because it may cause irritation. If you accidentally get some in your eyes, flush them thoroughly with water at once.

Do not apply this medicine to the eyelashes or eyebrows. If they become infected with lice, check with your doctor.

To use the *gel or solution form* of this medicine:
  • Apply enough medicine to thoroughly wet the dry hair and scalp or skin. Allow the medicine to remain on the affected areas for exactly 10 minutes.
  • Then, thoroughly wash the affected areas with warm water and soap or regular shampoo. Rinse thoroughly and dry with a clean towel.

To use the *shampoo form* of this medicine:
  • Apply enough medicine to thoroughly wet the dry hair and scalp or skin. Allow the medicine to remain on the affected areas for exactly 10 minutes.
  • Then use a small amount of water and work shampoo into the hair and scalp or skin until a lather forms. Rinse thoroughly and dry with a clean towel.

After rinsing and drying, use a nit removal comb (special fine-toothed comb, usually included with this medicine) to remove the dead lice and eggs (nits) from hair.

Immediately after using this medicine, wash your hands to remove any medicine that may be on them.

This medicine should be used again in 7 to 10 days after the first treatment in order to kill any newly hatched lice.

Lice can easily move from one person to another by close body contact. This can happen also by direct contact with such things as clothing, hats, scarves, bedding, towels, washcloths, hairbrushes and combs, or the hair of infected persons. Therefore, *all members of your household should be examined for lice and receive treatment if they are found to be infected.*

To use this medicine for *pubic (crab) lice:*
- Your sexual partner may also need to be treated, since the infection may spread to persons in close contact. If your partner is not being treated or if you have any questions about this, check with your doctor.

Dosing—The dose of pyrethrins and piperonyl butoxide combination will be different for different patients. *Follow your doctor's orders or the directions on the label.* The following information includes only the average doses of pyrethrins and piperonyl butoxide combination. *If your dose is different, do not change it* unless your doctor tells you to do so.
- For *topical* dosage forms (gel, solution shampoo, and topical solution):
  —For head, body, or pubic lice:
  - Adults and children—Use one time, then repeat one time in seven to ten days.

Storage—To store this medicine:
- Keep out of the reach of children.
- Store away from heat and direct light.
- Keep the medicine from freezing.
- Do not keep outdated medicine or medicine no longer needed. Be sure that any discarded medicine is out of the reach of children.

Precautions While Using This Medicine

To prevent reinfection or spreading of the infection to other people, good health habits are also required. These include the following:
- For *head lice*
  —Machine wash all clothing (including hats, scarves, and coats), bedding, towels, and washcloths in very hot water and dry them by using the hot cycle of a dryer for at least 20 minutes. Clothing or bedding that cannot be washed should be dry-cleaned or sealed in a plastic bag for 2 weeks.
  —Shampoo all wigs and hairpieces.
  —Wash all hairbrushes and combs in very hot soapy water (above 130 °F) for 5 to 10 minutes and do not share them with other people.
  —Clean the house or room by thoroughly vacuuming upholstered furniture, rugs, and floors.
- For *body lice*
  —Machine wash all clothing, bedding, towels, and washcloths in very hot water and dry them by using the hot cycle of a dryer for at least 20 minutes. Clothing or bedding that cannot be washed should be dry-cleaned or sealed in a plastic bag for 2 weeks.
  —Clean the house or room by thoroughly vacuuming upholstered furniture, rugs, and floors.
- For *pubic lice*
  —Machine wash all clothing (especially underwear), bedding, towels, and washcloths in very hot water and dry them by using the hot cycle of a dryer for at least 20 minutes. Clothing or bedding that cannot be

washed should be dry-cleaned or sealed in a plastic bag for 2 weeks.
—Scrub toilet seats frequently.

Side Effects of This Medicine

Along with its needed effects, a medicine may cause some unwanted effects. Although not all of these side effects may occur, if they do occur they may need medical attention.

Check with your doctor as soon as possible if any of the following side effects occur:
Less common or rare
  Skin irritation not present before use of this medicine; skin rash or infection; sneezing (sudden attacks of); stuffy or runny nose; wheezing or difficulty in breathing

Other side effects not listed above may also occur in some patients. If you notice any other effects, check with your health care professional.

Revised: 07/26/93
Interim revision: 02/18/94

PYRIDOXINE (VITAMIN B₆)
Systemic

Commonly used brand name(s):

In the U.S.—
Beesix	Pyri
Doxine	Rodex
Nestrex	Vitabee 6

Generic name product may be available.

Description

Vitamins (VYE-ta-mins) are compounds that you *must* have for growth and health. They are needed in small amounts only and are usually available in the foods that you eat. Pyridoxine (peer-i-DOX-een) (vitamin B₆) is necessary for normal breakdown of proteins, carbohydrates, and fats.

Some conditions may increase your need for pyridoxine. These include:
- Alcoholism
- Burns
- Diarrhea
- Dialysis
- Heart disease
- Intestinal problems
- Liver disease
- Overactive thyroid
- Stress, long-term illness, or serious injury
- Surgical removal of stomach

In addition, infants receiving unfortified formulas such as evaporated milk may need additional pyridoxine.

Increased need for pyridoxine should be determined by your health care professional.

Lack of pyridoxine may lead to anemia (weak blood), nerve damage, seizures, skin problems, and sores in the mouth.

Your doctor may treat these problems by prescribing pyridoxine for you.

Claims that pyridoxine is effective for treatment of acne and other skin problems, alcohol intoxication, asthma, hemorrhoids, kidney stones, mental problems, migraine headaches, morning sickness, and menstrual problems, or to stimulate appetite or milk production have not been proven.

Injectable pyridoxine is given by or under the supervision of a health care professional. Other forms of pyridoxine are available without a prescription.

Pyridoxine is available in the following dosage forms:

Oral
- Extended-release capsules (U.S.)
- Tablets (U.S. and Canada)
- Extended-release tablets (U.S.)

Parenteral
- Injection (U.S. and Canada)

Importance of Diet

For good health, it is important that you eat a balanced and varied diet. Follow carefully any diet program your health care professional may recommend. For your specific dietary vitamin and/or mineral needs, ask your health care professional for a list of appropriate foods. If you think that you are not getting enough vitamins and/or minerals in your diet, you may choose to take a dietary supplement.

Pyridoxine is found in various foods, including meats, bananas, lima beans, egg yolks, peanuts, and whole-grain cereals. Pyridoxine is not lost from food during ordinary cooking, although some other forms of vitamin B₆ are.

Vitamins alone will not take the place of a good diet and will not provide energy. Your body also needs other substances found in food such as protein, minerals, carbohydrates, and fat. Vitamins themselves often cannot work without the presence of other foods.

The daily amount of pyridoxine needed is defined in several different ways.

For U.S.—
- Recommended Dietary Allowances (RDAs) are the amount of vitamins and minerals needed to provide for adequate nutrition in most healthy persons. RDAs for a given nutrient may vary depending on a person's age, sex, and physical condition (e.g., pregnancy).
- Daily Values (DVs) are used on food and dietary supplement labels to indicate the percent of the recommended daily amount of each nutrient that a serving provides. DV replaces the previous designation of United States Recommended Daily Allowances (USRDAs).

For Canada—
- Recommended Nutrient Intakes (RNIs) are used to determine the amounts of vitamins, minerals, and protein needed to provide adequate nutrition and lessen the risk of chronic disease.

Normal daily recommended intakes for pyridoxine are generally defined as follows:
- Infants and children—
  Birth to 3 years of age: 0.3 to 1 milligram (mg).
  4 to 6 years of age: 1.1 mg.
  7 to 10 years of age: 1.4 mg.
- Adolescent and adult males—1.7 to 2 mg.
- Adolescent and adult females—1.4 to 1.6 mg.

- Pregnant females—2.2 mg.
- Breast-feeding females—2.1 mg.

Before Using This Dietary Supplement

If you are taking this dietary supplement without a prescription, carefully read and follow any precautions on the label. For pyridoxine, the following should be considered:

Allergies—Tell your health care professional if you have ever had any unusual or allergic reaction to pyridoxine. Also tell your health care professional if you are allergic to any other substances, such as foods, preservatives, or dyes.

Pregnancy—It is especially important that you are receiving enough vitamins when you become pregnant and that you continue to receive the right amount of vitamins throughout your pregnancy. The healthy growth and development of the fetus depend on a steady supply of nutrients from the mother. However, excessive doses of pyridoxine taken during pregnancy may cause the infant to become dependent on pyridoxine.

Breast-feeding—It is especially important that you receive the right amounts of vitamins so that your baby will also get the vitamins needed to grow properly. You should also check with your health care professional if you are giving your baby an unfortified formula. In that case, the baby must get the vitamins needed some other way. However, taking large amounts of a dietary supplement while breast-feeding may be harmful to the mother and/or baby and should be avoided.

Children—Problems in children have not been reported with intake of normal daily recommended amounts.

Older adults—Problems in older adults have not been reported with intake of normal daily recommended amounts.

Medicines or other dietary supplements—Although certain medicines or dietary supplements should not be used together at all, in other cases they may be used together even if an interaction might occur. In these cases, your health care professional may want to change the dose, or other precautions may be necessary. When you are taking pyridoxine, it is especially important that your health care professional know if you are taking the following:
- Levodopa (e.g., Larodopa)—Use with pyridoxine may prevent the levodopa from working properly

Proper Use of This Dietary Supplement

Dosing—The amount of pyridoxine needed to meet normal daily recommended intakes will be different for different individuals. The following information includes only the average amounts of pyridoxine.

- For *oral* dosage forms (capsules, tablets, oral solution):
  —To prevent deficiency, the amount taken by mouth is based on normal daily recommended intakes:
  - Adult and teenage males—1.7 to 2 milligrams (mg) per day.
  - Adult and teenage females—1.4 to 1.6 mg per day.
  - Pregnant females—2.2 mg per day.
  - Breast-feeding females—2.1 mg per day.
  - Children 7 to 10 years of age—1.4 mg per day.
  - Children 4 to 6 years of age—1.1 mg per day.
  - Children birth to 3 years of age—0.3 to 1 mg per day.

—To treat deficiency:
- Adults, teenagers, and children—Treatment dose is determined by prescriber for each individual based on the severity of deficiency.

To use the *extended-release capsule form* of this dietary supplement:
- Swallow the capsule whole.
- Do not crush, break, or chew before swallowing.
- If the capsule is too large to swallow, you may mix the contents of the capsule with jam or jelly and swallow without chewing.

To use the *extended-release tablet form* of this dietary supplement:
- Swallow the tablet whole.
- Do not crush, break, or chew before swallowing.

Missed dose—If you miss taking a vitamin for 1 or more days there is no cause for concern, since it takes some time for your body to become seriously low in vitamins. However, if your health care professional has recommended that you take this vitamin, try to remember to take it as directed every day.

Storage—To store this dietary supplement:
- Keep out of the reach of children.
- Store away from heat and direct light.
- Do not store the capsule or tablet form of this medicine in the bathroom, near the kitchen sink, or in other damp places. Heat or moisture may cause the dietary supplement to break down.
- Do not keep outdated dietary supplements or those no longer needed. Be sure that any discarded medicine is out of the reach of children.

Side Effects of This Dietary Supplement

Along with its needed effects, a dietary supplement may cause some unwanted effects. Although pyridoxine does not usually cause any side effects at usual doses, check with your health care professional as soon as possible if you notice either of the following side effects:

With large doses
Clumsiness; numbness of hands or feet

Also check with your health care professional if you notice any other unusual effects while you are taking pyridoxine.

Revised: 05/01/95

QUETIAPINE   Systemic

Commonly used brand name(s):

In the U.S.—
Seroquel

Description

Quetiapine (kwe-TYE-a-peen) is used to treat psychotic disorders, such as schizophrenia.

Quetiapine is available only with your doctor's prescription, in the following dosage form:

Oral
- Tablets (U.S. and Canada)

Before Using This Medicine

In deciding to use a medicine, the risks of taking the medicine must be weighed against the good it will do. This is a decision you and your doctor will make. For quetiapine, the following should be considered:

Allergies—Tell your doctor if you have ever had any unusual or allergic reaction to quetiapine. Also tell your health care professional if you are allergic to any other substances, such as foods, preservatives, or dyes.

Pregnancy—Quetiapine has not been studied in pregnant women. However, studies in rats and rabbits have shown that quetiapine at doses higher than the highest human dose causes reduced weight and other problems in the fetus. Before taking this medicine, make sure your doctor knows if you are pregnant or if you may become pregnant.

Breast-feeding—Quetiapine has been shown to pass into the milk of animals. It is not known whether this medicine passes into breast milk. However, quetiapine is not recommended for use during breast-feeding, because it may cause unwanted effects in nursing babies. Be sure you have discussed the risks and benefits of the medicine with your doctor.

Children—Studies on this medicine have been done only in adult patients, and there is no specific information comparing use of quetiapine in children with use in other age groups.

Older adults—This medicine has been tested in a limited number of patients 65 years of age or older and has not been shown to cause different side effects or problems in older people than it does in younger adults. However, quetiapine may be removed from the body more slowly in older adults, so an older adult may receive a lower dose than a younger adult.

Other medicines—Although certain medicines should not be used together at all, in other cases two different medicines may be used together even if an interaction might occur. In these cases, your doctor may want to change the dose, or other precautions may be necessary. When you are taking quetiapine, it is especially important that your health care professional know if you are taking any of the following:

- Alcohol (with chronic use) or
- Barbiturates or
- Carbamazepine (e.g., Tegretol) or
- Griseofulvin (e.g., Fulvicin) or
- Phenylbutazone (e.g., Butazolidin) or
- Phenytoin (e.g., Dilantin) or
- Primidone (e.g., Mysoline) or
- Rifampin (e.g., Rifadin) or
- Saquinavir (e.g., Invirase) or
- Troglitazone (e.g., Rezulin)—These medicines may cause lower blood levels of quetiapine; the dose of quetiapine may need to be changed if one of these medicines is started or stopped during treatment with quetiapine
- Central nervous system (CNS) depressants (medicines that cause drowsiness) or
- Tricyclic antidepressants (medicine for depression)—Quetiapine may increase the CNS depressant effects of these medicines, such as drowsiness
- Clarithromycin (e.g., Biaxin) or
- Diltiazem (e.g., Cardizem) or
- Erythromycin (e.g., E-Mycin, E.E.S.) or

- Fluconazole (e.g., Diflucan) or
- Itraconazole (e.g., Sporanox) or
- Ketoconazole (e.g., Nizoral) or
- Nefazodone (e.g., Serzone) or
- Verapamil (e.g., Calan)—These medicines may cause higher blood levels of quetiapine, increasing the chance of side effects

Other medical problems—The presence of other medical problems may affect the use of quetiapine. Make sure you tell your doctor if you have any other medical problems, especially:

- Alzheimer's disease—Quetiapine may cause problems with swallowing, which may increase the chance of pneumonia; also, the chance of seizures may be increased
- Breast cancer, or history of or
- Underactive thyroid—Quetiapine may make these conditions worse
- Dehydration—Decreased blood pressure caused by quetiapine may be more severe; chance of developing heatstroke may be increased
- Heart disease or
- Stroke, or history of—Decreased blood pressure caused by quetiapine may be more severe or may make these conditions worse
- Kidney disease (severe) or
- Liver disease—Higher blood levels of quetiapine may occur, increasing the chance of side effects; the dose may need to be changed
- Seizures, or history of—Chance of seizures may be increased

Proper Use of This Medicine

Take this medicine only as directed by your doctor to benefit your condition as much as possible. Do not take more or less of it and do not take it more or less often than your doctor ordered.

Quetiapine may be taken with or without food on a full or empty stomach. However, if your doctor tells you to take it a certain way, take it as directed.

Dosing—The dose of quetiapine will be different for different patients. *Follow your doctor's orders or the directions on the label.* The following information includes only the average doses of quetiapine. *If your dose is different, do not change it* unless your doctor tells you to do so.

The number of tablets that you take depends on the strength of the medicine. Also, *the number of doses you take each day, the time allowed between doses, and the length of time you take the medicine depend on the medical problem for which you are taking quetiapine.*

- For *oral* dosage form (tablets):
  —For schizophrenia:
  - Adults—At first, 25 milligrams (mg) two times a day. The dose usually is increased to 300 to 400 mg a day, which is divided and given in two or three doses a day. Your doctor may increase your dose further, if needed. However, the dose usually is not more than 800 mg a day.
  - Children—Use and dose must be determined by the doctor.

Missed dose—If you miss a dose of quetiapine, take it as soon as possible. However, if it is almost time for your next dose, skip the missed dose and go back to your regular dosing schedule. Do not double doses.

Storage—To store this medicine:
- Keep out of the reach of children.
- Store away from heat and direct light.
- Do not store in the bathroom, near the kitchen sink, or in other damp places. Heat or moisture may cause the medicine to break down.
- Do not keep outdated medicine or medicine no longer needed. Be sure that any discarded medicine is out of the reach of children.

Precautions While Using This Medicine

Your doctor should check your progress at regular visits, especially during the first few months of treatment with this medicine. This will allow your dosage to be changed if necessary to meet your needs.

This medicine may add to the effects of alcohol and other CNS depressants (medicines that make you drowsy or less alert). Some examples of CNS depressants are antihistamines or medicine for hay fever, other allergies, or colds; sedatives, tranquilizers, or sleeping medicine; prescription pain medicine or narcotics; barbiturates; medicine for seizures; muscle relaxants; or anesthetics, including some dental anesthetics. *Check with your doctor before taking any of the above while you are using quetiapine.*

Quetiapine may cause drowsiness, especially during the first week of use. *Make sure you know how you react to this medicine before you drive, use machines, or do anything else that could be dangerous if you are not alert.*

Dizziness, lightheadedness, or fainting may occur, especially when you get up from a lying or sitting position. Getting up slowly may help. If the problem continues or gets worse, check with your doctor.

Quetiapine may make it more difficult for your body to cool down. *Use extra care not to become overheated and to drink plenty of fluids during exercise or hot weather while you are taking this medicine.* Overheating may result in heatstroke.

Side Effects of This Medicine

Along with its needed effects, quetiapine can sometimes cause serious side effects. Some side effects will have signs or symptoms that you can see or feel. Your doctor may watch for others, such as changes in the lenses of the eyes, by doing certain tests. Tardive dyskinesia (a movement disorder) may occur and may not go away after you stop using the medicine. Signs of tardive dyskinesia include fine, worm-like movements of the tongue, or other uncontrolled movements of the mouth, tongue, cheeks, jaw, or arms and legs. Another serious but rare side effect that may occur is the neuroleptic malignant syndrome (NMS). *You and your doctor should discuss the good this medicine will do as well as the risks of taking it.*

Stop taking this medicine and get emergency help immediately if the following side effects occur:
  Rare—Symptoms of NMS; two or more occur together; most of these effects do not require emergency medical attention if they occur alone
    Convulsions (seizures); difficult or unusually fast breathing; fast heartbeat or irregular pulse; high fever; high or low (irregular) blood pressure; in-

creased sweating; loss of bladder control; severe muscle stiffness; unusually pale skin; unusual tiredness or weakness

Check with your doctor as soon as possible if any of the following side effects occur:

Less common
> Dizziness, lightheadedness, or fainting, especially when getting up from a lying or sitting position; fever, chills, muscle aches, or sore throat; loss of balance control; mask-like face; shuffling walk; skin rash; slowed movements; stiffness of arms or legs; swelling of feet or lower legs; trembling and shaking of hands and fingers; trouble in breathing, speaking, or swallowing

Rare
> Fainting; fast, pounding, or irregular heartbeat; menstrual changes; unusual secretion of milk (in females)

Rare—Symptoms of underactive thyroid; usually two or more occur together; these effects do not require medical attention if they occur alone unless they continue or are bothersome
> Dry, puffy skin; loss of appetite; tiredness; weight gain

Symptoms of overdose—May be similar to side effects seen at normal doses but may be more severe or two or more may occur together
> Drowsiness; fast, slow, or irregular heartbeat; low blood pressure; weakness

Other side effects may occur that usually do not need medical attention. These side effects may go away during treatment as your body adjusts to the medicine. However, check with your doctor if any of the following side effects continue or are bothersome:

More common
> Constipation; drowsiness; dry mouth; increased weight; indigestion

Less common
> Abdominal pain; abnormal vision; decrease in appetite; decreased strength and energy; feeling of fast or irregular heartbeat; headache; increased muscle tone; increased sweating; stuffy or runny nose

Other side effects not listed above may also occur in some patients. If you notice any other effects, check with your doctor.

Developed: 02/17/98
Revised: 06/14/2000

QUINIDINE Systemic

Commonly used brand name(s):

In the U.S.—

Cardioquin	Quinidex Extentabs
Quinaglute Dura-tabs	Quin-Release

In Canada—

Apo-Quinidine	Quinaglute Dura-tabs
Biquin Durules	Quinate
Cardioquin	Quinidex Extentabs
Novoquinidin	

Generic name product may be available in the U.S. and Canada.

Description

Quinidine (KWIN-i-deen) is used to treat abnormal heart rhythms. It is also used to treat malaria.

Do not confuse this medicine with *quinine*, which, although related, has different medical uses.

Quinidine is available only with your doctor's prescription, in the following dosage forms:

Oral
- Tablets (U.S. and Canada)
- Extended-release tablets (U.S. and Canada)

Parenteral
- Injection (U.S. and Canada)

Before Using This Medicine

In deciding to use a medicine, the risks of taking the medicine must be weighed against the good it will do. This is a decision you and your doctor will make. For quinidine, the following should be considered:

Allergies—Tell your doctor if you have ever had any unusual or allergic reaction to quinidine or quinine. Also tell your health care professional if you are allergic to any other substances, such as foods, preservatives, or dyes.

Pregnancy—Studies on effects in pregnancy have not been done in either humans or animals. However, quinidine has been used during pregnancy and, although serious side effects are uncommon, it has been shown to cause mild uterine contractions, premature labor, and blood problems in the neonate.

Breast-feeding—Quinidine passes into breast milk and, because of the potential for problems in the nursing infant, it is generally not recommended in mothers who are breast-feeding.

Children—Quinidine has not been widely studied in children; however, it is used in children to treat abnormal heart rhythms and to treat malaria. Children may be able to take higher doses than adults and may have fewer side effects (such as vomiting, loss of appetite, and diarrhea) than adults.

Older adults—Many medicines have not been studied specifically in older people. Therefore, it may not be known whether they work exactly the same way they do in younger adults. Although there is no specific information comparing use of quinidine in the elderly with use in other age groups, this medicine is not expected to cause different side effects or problems in older people than it does in younger adults. However, quinidine may remain in the bodies of older adults longer than it does in younger adults, which may increase the risk of side effects and which may require lower doses.

Other medicines—Although certain medicines should not be used together at all, in other cases two different medicines may be used together even if an interaction might occur. In these cases, your doctor may want to change the dose, or other precautions may be necessary. When you are taking quinidine, it is especially important that your health care professional know if you are taking any of the following:

- Amiodarone—Effects may be increased because levels of quinidine in the body may be increased

- Digitalis medicines (heart medicine)—Effects may be increased because levels of digitalis in the body may be increased

- Antidepressants, tricyclic, such as amitriptyline (e.g., Elavil), clomipramine (e.g., Anafranil), desipramine (e.g., Norpramin), doxepin (e.g., Sinequan), imipramine (e.g., Tofranil), and nortriptyline (e.g., Pamelor) or
- Astemizole (e.g., Hismanal) or
- Chloroquine (e.g., Aralen) or
- Clarithromycin (e.g., Biaxin) or
- Cisapride (e.g., Propulsid) or
- Diphenhydramine (e.g., Benadryl) or
- Erythromycin (e.g., Erythrocin, Erytab) or
- Fludrocortisone (e.g., Florinef) or
- Halofantrine (e.g., Halfan) or
- Haloperidol (e.g., Haldol) or
- Indapamide (e.g., Lozol) or
- Maprotiline (e.g., Ludiomil) or
- Mefloquine (e.g., Lariam) or
- Other heart medicine, including bepridil (e.g., Vascor), beta-adrenergic blocking agents such as propranolol (e.g., Inderal), diltiazem (e.g., Cardizem), disopyramide (e.g. Norpace), encainide (e.g., Encaid), flecainide (e.g., Tambocor), ibutilide (e.g., Corvert), lidocaine (e.g., Xylocaine), procainamide (e.g., Procanbid), propafenone (e.g., Rythmol), sotalol (e.g., Betapace, Sotacor), tocainide (e.g., Tonocard), and verapamil (e.g., Calan, Isoptin) or
- Pentamidine (e.g., NebuPent, Pentam) or
- Phenothiazines (e.g., chlorpromazine [e.g., Thorazine], perphenazine [e.g., Trilafon], prochlorperazine [e.g., Compazine], thioridazine [e.g., Mellaril]) or
- Pimozide (e.g., Orap) or
- Risperidone (e.g., Risperdal) or
- Sparfloxacin (e.g., Zagam) or
- Tamoxifen (e.g., Nolvadex) or
- Thiothixene (e.g., Navane) or
- Trimethoprim and sulfamethoxazole combination (e.g., Bactrim, Septra)—Effects on the heart may be increased

- Urinary alkalizers (medicine that makes the urine less acid, such as acetazolamide [e.g., Diamox], dichlorphenamide [e.g., Daranide], methazolamide [e.g., Neptazane], and sodium bicarbonate [baking soda])—Effects may be increased because levels of quinidine in the body may be increased

Other medical problems—The presence of other medical problems may affect the use of quinidine. Make sure you tell your doctor if you have any other medical problems, especially:

- Electrolyte disorders—Quinidine may worsen heart rhythm problems

- Heart disease or
- Myasthenia gravis—Quinidine may make these conditions worse

- Kidney disease or
- Liver disease—Effects may be increased because of slower removal of quinidine from the body

Proper Use of This Medicine

Take this medicine exactly as directed. Do not take more of this medicine and do not take it more often than your doctor ordered. Do not miss any doses.

Taking quinidine with food may help lessen stomach upset.

For patients taking the *extended-release tablet* form of this medicine:

- Quinidex Extentabs or Biquin Durules—Swallow the tablets whole; do not break, crush, or chew before swallowing. Note that Biquin Durules may sometimes appear as a whole tablet in the stool; this tablet is just the empty shell that is left after the medicine has been absorbed into the body.
- Quinaglute Duratabs or Quin-Release—These tablets may be broken in half; however, they should not be crushed or chewed before swallowing.

Dosing—The dose of quinidine will be different for different patients. *Follow your doctor's orders or the directions on the label.* The following information includes only the average doses of quinidine. *If your dose is different, do not change it* unless your doctor tells you to do so.

The number of tablets that you take depends on the strength of the medicine. Also, *the number of doses you take each day, the time allowed between doses, and the length of time you take the medicine depend on the medical problem for which you are taking quinidine.*

- For *regular (short-acting) oral* dosage form (tablets):
  —For abnormal heart rhythm:
  - Adults—200 to 650 milligrams (mg) three or four times a day.
  - Children—30 to 40 mg per kilogram (kg) (13.6 to 18.2 mg per pound) of body weight per day. Your doctor may increase the dose if needed.

- For *long-acting oral* dosage form (tablets):
  —For abnormal heart rhythm:
  - Adults—300 to 660 mg every eight to twelve hours.
  - Children—30 to 40 mg per kilogram (kg) (13.6 to 18.2 mg per pound) of body weight per day. Your doctor may increase the dose if needed.

- For *injection* dosage form:
  —For abnormal heart rhythm:
  - Adults—190 to 380 mg injected into the muscle every two to four hours. Or, up to 0.25 mg per kg (0.11 mg per pound) of body weight per minute in a solution injected into a vein.
  - Children—Dose must be determined by your doctor.
  —For malaria:
  - Adults—10 mg per kg (4.54 mg per pound) of body weight in a solution injected slowly into a vein over one to two hours. Then, 0.02 mg per kg (0.009 mg per pound) of body weight per minute is given. Or, 24 mg per kg (10.91 mg per pound) of body weight in a solution injected slowly into a vein over a four-hour period. Then, eight hours after the first dose, 12 mg per kg (5.45 mg per pound) of body weight, injected slowly into a vein over a four-hour period, and repeated every eight hours.
  - Children—Dose must be determined by your doctor.

Missed dose—If you miss a dose of this medicine and remember within 2 hours of the missed dose, take it as soon as possible. However, if you do not remember until later, skip the missed dose and go back to your regular dosing schedule. Do not double doses.

Storage—To store this medicine:

- Keep out of the reach of children.
- Store away from heat and direct light.
- Do not store in the bathroom, near the kitchen sink, or in other damp places. Heat or moisture may cause the medicine to break down.
- Do not keep outdated medicine or medicine no longer needed. Be sure that any discarded medicine is out of the reach of children.

Precautions While Using This Medicine

It is very important that your doctor check your progress at regular visits to make sure that the quinidine is working properly and does not cause unwanted effects.

Do not stop taking this medicine without first checking with your doctor, to avoid possible worsening of your condition.

Before having any kind of surgery (including dental surgery) or emergency treatment, tell the medical doctor or dentist in charge that you are taking this medicine.

Dizziness or lightheadedness may occur with this medicine, especially when you get up from a lying or sitting position. Getting up slowly may help.

Fainting may occur with this medicine. Do not drive or do anything else that could be dangerous if fainting occurs.

Check with your doctor immediately if you faint or experience other side effects with this medicine.

Your doctor may want you to carry a medical identification card or bracelet stating that you are using this medicine.

Side Effects of This Medicine

Along with its needed effects, a medicine may cause some unwanted effects. Although not all of these side effects may occur, if they do occur they may need medical attention.

Check with your doctor immediately if any of the following side effects occur:

Less common
 Abdominal pain and/or yellow eyes or skin; blurred and/or double vision, confusion, delirium, disturbed color perception, headache, noises or ringing in the ear, and/or visual intolerance of light; dizziness or lightheadedness; fainting; fever

Rare
 Chest pain, fever, general discomfort, joint pain, joint swelling, muscle pain, and/or skin rash; nosebleeds or bleeding gums; unusual tiredness or weakness and/or pale skin

Other side effects may occur that usually do not need medical attention. These side effects may go away during treatment as your body adjusts to the medicine. However, check with your doctor if any of the following side effects continue or are bothersome:

More common
 Diarrhea; loss of appetite; muscle weakness; nausea or vomiting

Other side effects not listed above may also occur in some patients. If you notice any other effects, check with your doctor.

Revised: 5/26/99

QUININE Systemic

Description

Quinine (KWYE-nine) is used to treat malaria. This medicine usually is given with one or more other medicines for malaria.

Quinine may also be used for other problems as determined by your doctor. Do not confuse quinine with *quinidine*, a different medicine that is used for heart problems.

Quinine is available only with your doctor's prescription in the following dosage forms:

Oral
 - Capsules (U.S. and Canada)
 - Tablets (U.S.)

Before Using This Medicine

In deciding to use a medicine, the risks of taking the medicine must be weighed against the good it will do. This is a decision you and your doctor will make. For quinine, the following should be considered:

Allergies—Tell your doctor if you have ever had any unusual or allergic reaction to quinine, quinidine (e.g., Quinidex), or to dietary items that contain quinine, such as tonic water or bitter lemon. Also tell your health care professional if you are allergic to any other substances, such as foods, preservatives, or dyes.

Pregnancy—Quinine has been used for the treatment of malaria in pregnant women. Treatment is important because if a pregnant woman gets malaria, there is an increased chance of premature births, stillbirths, and abortion. However, quinine has been shown to cause birth defects in rabbits and guinea pigs and has also been shown to cause rare birth defects, stillbirths, and other problems in humans. In addition, quinine has been shown to cause miscarriage when taken in large amounts.

Breast-feeding—Quinine passes into the breast milk in small amounts. However, this medicine has not been reported to cause problems in nursing babies.

Children—This medicine has been used to treat malaria in children and, in effective doses, has not been shown to cause different side effects or problems in children than it does in adults.

Older adults—Many medicines have not been studied specifically in older people. Therefore, it may not be known whether they work exactly the same way they do in younger adults or if they cause different side effects or problems in older people. There is no specific information comparing use of quinine in the elderly with use in other age groups.

Other medicines—Although certain medicines should not be used together at all, in other cases two different medicines may be used together even if an interaction might occur. In these cases, your doctor may want to change the dose, or other precautions may be necessary. When you are taking quinine, it is especially important that your health care professional know if you are taking the following:

- Mefloquine (e.g., Lariam)—Use of mefloquine with quinine may increase the chance of side effects

Other medical problems—The presence of other medical problems may affect the use of quinine. Make sure you tell your doctor if you have any other medical problems, especially:

- Blackwater fever, history of, or
- Glucose-6-phosphate dehydrogenase (G6PD) deficiency or
- Purpura, or history of (purplish or brownish-red discoloration of skin)—Patients with a history of blackwater fever, G6PD deficiency, or purpura may have an increased risk of side effects affecting the blood
- Heart disease—Quinine can cause side effects affecting the heart, usually at higher doses
- Hypoglycemia—Quinine may cause low blood sugar
- Myasthenia gravis—Quinine may increase muscle weakness in patients with myasthenia gravis

Proper Use of This Medicine

Take this medicine only as directed. Do not take more of it, do not take it more often, and do not take it for a longer time than recommended on the label, unless otherwise directed by your doctor. To do so may increase the chance of side effects.

Take this medicine with or after meals to lessen possible stomach upset, unless otherwise directed by your doctor. If you are to take this medicine at bedtime, take it with a snack or with a glass of water, milk, or other beverage.

For patients *taking quinine for malaria:*

- To help clear up your infection completely, *keep taking this medicine for the full time of treatment*, even if you begin to feel better after a few days. If you stop taking this medicine too soon, your symptoms may return. *Do not miss any doses.*

Dosing—The dose of quinine will be different for different patients. *Follow your doctor's orders or the directions on the label*. The following information includes only the average dose of quinine. *If your dose is different, do not change it* unless your doctor tells you to do so.

The number of capsules or tablets that you take depends on the strength of the medicine. Also, *the number of doses you take each day, the time allowed between doses, and the length of time you take the medicine depend on the medical problem for which you are taking quinine.*

- For treatment of *malaria:*
  —Adults and teenagers: 600 to 650 mg every eight hours for at least three days. This medicine must be taken with other medicine to treat malaria.
  —Children: Dose must be determined by the doctor.

Missed dose—If you do miss a dose of this medicine, take it as soon as possible. However, if it is almost time for your next dose, skip the missed dose and go back to your regular dosing schedule. Do not double doses.

Storage—To store this medicine:

- Keep out of the reach of children.
- Store away from heat and direct light.
- Do not store in the bathroom, near the kitchen sink, or in other damp places. Heat or moisture may cause the medicine to break down.
- Do not keep outdated medicine or medicine no longer needed. Be sure that any discarded medicine is out of the reach of children.

Precautions While Using This Medicine

Quinine may cause blurred vision or a change in color vision. *Make sure you know how you react to this medicine before you drive, use machines, or do anything else that could be dangerous if you are not able to see well.* If these reactions are especially bothersome, check with your doctor.

Side Effects of This Medicine

Along with its needed effects, a medicine may cause some unwanted effects. Although not all of these side effects may occur, if they do occur they may need medical attention.

Check with your doctor immediately if any of the following side effects occur:
  More common
    Abdominal or stomach cramps or pain; diarrhea; nausea; vomiting
  Less common
    Anxiety; behavior change, similar to drunkenness; black, tarry stools; blood in urine or stools; blurred vision; cold sweats; confusion; convulsions (seizures) or coma; cool pale skin; cough or hoarseness; difficulty in concentrating; drowsiness; excessive hunger; fast heartbeat; fever or chills; headache; lower back or side pain; nervousness; nightmares; painful or difficult urination; pinpoint red spots on skin; restless sleep; shakiness; slurred speech; sore throat; unusual bleeding or bruising; unusual tiredness or weakness
  Rare
    Difficulty in breathing and/or swallowing; disturbed color perception; double vision; hives; increased sweating; muscle aches; night blindness; reddening of the skin, especially around ears; ringing or buzzing in ears; swelling of eyes, face, or inside of nose
  Signs and symptoms of overdose
    Blindness; chest pain; dizziness; double vision; fainting; lightheadedness; rapid or irregular heartbeat; sleepiness

Other side effects may occur that usually do not need medical attention. These side effects may go away during treatment as your body adjusts to the medicine. However, check with your doctor if any of the following side effects occur or progress after you stop taking this medicine:
  Blurred vision or change in vision

Other side effects not listed above may also occur in some patients. If you notice any other effects, check with your doctor.

Additional Information

Once a medicine has been approved for marketing for a certain use, experience may show that it is also useful for other medical problems. Although these uses are not included in product labeling, quinine is used in certain patients with the following medical conditions:

- Babesiosis (infection caused by parasites)
- Nighttime leg cramps

Other than the above information, there is no additional information relating to proper use, precautions, or side effects for these uses.

Revised: 05/24/99

QUINUPRISTIN AND DALFOPRISTIN Systemic†

Commonly used brand name(s):

In the U.S.—
Synercid

†Not commercially available in Canada.

Description

Quinupristin (qui-NYOO-pris-tin) and dalfopristin (dal-FOE-pris-tin) belong to the family of medicine called antibiotics. Antibiotics are medicines used in the treatment of infections caused by bacteria. They work by killing bacteria or preventing their growth. Quinupristin and dalfopristin will not work for colds, flu, or other virus infections.

Quinupristin and dalfopristin injection is used to treat infection of the skin or the blood. It may also be used for other conditions as determined by your doctor. It is given by injection and is used mainly for serious infection for which other medicine may not work.

Quinupristin and dalfopristin injection is available only with your doctor's prescription, in the following dosage form:

Parenteral
  • Injection (U.S.)

Before Using This Medicine

In deciding to use a medicine, the risks of taking the medicine must be weighed against the good it will do. This is a decision you and your doctor will make. For quinupristin and dalfopristin, the following should be considered:

Allergies—Tell your doctor if you have ever had any unusual or allergic reaction to quinupristin or dalfopristin. Also tell your health care professional if you are allergic to any other substances, such as foods, preservatives, or dyes.

Pregnancy—Quinupristin and dalfopristin have not been studied in pregnant women. However, they have not been shown to cause birth defects or other problems in animal studies.

Breast-feeding—It is not known whether quinupristin and dalfopristin pass into breast milk. Although most medicines pass into breast milk in small amounts, many of them may be used safely while breast-feeding. Mothers who are taking this medicine and who wish to breast-feed should discuss this with their doctor.

Children—Studies on this medicine have been done only in adult patients, and there is no specific information comparing use of quinupristin and dalfopristin in children under 16 years old with use in other age groups.

Older adults—In studies of patients 65 years or older, quinupristin and dalfopristin have not been shown to cause different side effects or problems than they do in younger adults.

Other medicines—Although certain medicines should not be used together at all, in other cases two different medicines may be used together even if an interaction might occur. In these cases, your doctor may want to change the dose, or other precautions may be necessary. When you are receiving quinupristin and dalfopristin it is especially important that you tell your doctor if you are taking any of the following:

  • Cyclosporine (e.g., Sandimmune) or
  • Midazolam (e.g., Versed) or
  • Nifedipine (e.g., Adalat) or
  • Terfenadine (e.g., Seldane)—Use of these medicine with quinupristin and dalfopristin may increase their effects because of slower removal of the medicine from the body.

Other medical problems—The presence of other medical problems may affect the use of quinupristin and dalfopristin. Make sure you tell your doctor if you have any other medical problems, especially:

  • Liver disease—Liver disease may increase blood levels of this medicine, increasing the chance of side effects

Proper Use of This Medicine

Some medicine given by injection may sometimes be given at home to patients who do not need to be in the hospital. If you are using this medicine at home, make sure you clearly understand and carefully follow your doctor's instructions.

To help clear up your infection completely, *this medicine must be given for the full time of treatment*, even if you begin to feel better after a few days. Also, it works best when there is a constant amount in the blood. To help keep the amount constant, quinupristin and dalfopristin must be given on a regular schedule.

Dosing—The dose of quinupristin and dalfopristin will be different for different patients. The dose that is used may depend on a number of things, including what the medicine is being used for, the patient's size, and whether or not other medicines are also being taken. *If you are receiving quinupristin and dalfopristin at home, follow your doctor's orders or the directions on the label.*

Side Effects of This Medicine

Along with its needed effects, a medicine may cause some unwanted effects. Although not all of these side effects may occur, if they do occur they may need medical attention.

Check with your doctor as soon as possible if any of the following side effects occur:
More common
  Swelling, redness, or pain at the injection area
Less common
  Joint pain; muscle pain; redness, burning sensation, or pain under the skin usually in the area of injection
Rare
  Chest pain; fast heartbeat; blood in urine; redness, burning sensation, or pain in vagina; severe bloody diarrhea; skin rash with red patches; hives

Other side effects not listed above may also occur in some patients. If you notice any other effects, check with your doctor.

Developed: 12/20/99

RABEPRAZOLE Systemic

Commonly used brand name(s):

In the U.S.—
AcipHex

Description

Rabeprazole (ra-BE-pray-zole) is used to treat certain conditions in which there is too much acid in the stomach. It is used to treat duodenal ulcers and gastroesophageal reflux disease (GERD), a condition in which the acid in the stomach washes back up into the esophagus. Rabeprazole is also used to treat Zollinger-Ellison disease, a condition in which the stomach produces too much acid.

Rabeprazole works by decreasing the amount of acid produced by the stomach.

This medicine is available only with your doctor's prescription.

Oral
- Delayed-release tablet (U.S.)

Before Using This Medicine

In deciding to use a medicine, the risks of taking the medicine must be weighed against the good it will do. This is a decision you and your doctor will make. For rabeprazole, the following should be considered:

Allergies—Tell your doctor if you have ever had any unusual or allergic reaction to rabeprazole. Also tell your health care professional if you are allergic to any other substances, such as foods, preservatives, or dyes.

Pregnancy—Studies have not been done in humans. However, studies in animals have not been shown that rabeprazole causes harm to the fetus.

Breast-feeding—Rabeprazole may pass into the breast milk. Since this medicine has been shown to cause a decrease in body weight gain in animal studies, it may be necessary for you to take another medicine or to stop breast-feeding during treatment. Be sure you discussed the risks and benefits of the medicine with your doctor.

Children—There is no specific information comparing the use of rabeprazole in children with use in other age groups.

Older adults—In studies done to date that have included older adults, rabeprazole did not cause different side effects or problems than it did in younger adults.

Other medicines—Although certain medicines should not be used together at all, in other cases two different medicines may be used together even if an interaction might occur. In these cases, your doctor may want to change the dose, or other precautions may be necessary. When you are taking rabeprazole, it is especially important that your health care professional know if you are taking any of the following:
- Digoxin (e.g., Lanoxin)—Rabeprazole may increase the amount of digoxin in the blood.
- Ketoconazole (e.g., Nizoral tablets)—Rabeprazole may decrease the amount of ketoconazole absorbed into the body.

Other medical problems—
- Liver disease—May increase chance of side effects
- Stomach infection—May make the condition worse

Proper Use of This Medicine

Swallow the tablet whole. Do not crush, chew, or split the tablet. Take this medicine for the full time of treatment, even if you begin to feel better. Also, keep your appointments with your doctor for check-ups so that your doctor will be better able to tell you when to stop taking this medicine.

Dosing—The dose of rabeprazole will be different for different patients. *Follow your doctor's orders or the directions on the label.* The following information includes only the average doses of rabeprazole. *If your dose is different, do not change it* unless your doctor tells you to do so.

The number of doses you take each day and the length of time you take the medicine depend on the medical problem for which you are taking rabeprazole
- For *oral* dosage form (delayed-release tablet):
  —To treat gastroesophageal reflux disease (GERD):
  - Adults—20 mg once a day for 4 to 8 weeks.
  - Children up to 18 years of age—Use and dose must be determined by your doctor
  —To prevent gastroesophageal reflux disease (GERD):
  - Adults—20 mg once a day.
  - Children up to 18 years of age—Use and dose must be determined by your doctor
  —To treat duodenal ulcers:
  - Adults—20 mg once a day after the morning meal for up to 4 weeks.
  - Children up to 18 years of age—Use and dose must be determined by your doctor.
  —To treat conditions in which the stomach produces too much acid:
  - Adults—At first, 60 mg once a day. Your doctor may increase your dose if needed.
  - Children up to 18 years of age—Use and dose must be determined by your doctor.

Missed dose—If you miss a dose of this medicine, take it as soon as possible. However, if it is almost time for your next dose, skip the missed dose and go back to your regular dosing schedule. Do not double doses.

Storage—To store this medicine:
- Keep out of the reach of children.
- Store away from heat and direct light.
- Do not store in the bathroom, near the kitchen sink, or in other damp places. Heat or moisture may cause the medicine to break down.
- Do not keep outdated medicine or medicine no longer needed. Ask your health care professional how you should dispose of any medicine you do not use. Be sure that any discarded medicine is out of the reach of children.

Precautions While Using This Medicine

It is very important that your doctor check your progress at regular visits to make sure that this medicine is working properly and to check for unwanted effects. If your condition does not improve, or it it becomes worse, discuss this with your doctor.

Side Effects of This Medicine

Along with its needed effects, a medicine may cause some unwanted effects. Although not all of these side effects may occur, if they do occur they may need medical attention.

Check with your doctor as soon as possible if any of the following side effects occur:

Rare

Breathing interruptions; bloody urine; convulsions (seizures); chills, fever, or sore throat; continuing ulcers or sores in mouth; unusual bleeding or bruising; unusual tiredness or weakness; yellow eyes or skin

Other side effects may occur that usually do not need medical attention. These side effects may go away during treatment as your body adjusts to the medicine. However, check with your doctor if any of the following side effects continue or are bothersome:

More common

Headache

Less common or rare

Constipation; diarrhea; dizziness; feeling weak; gas; heartburn; itchy skin; nausea and vomiting; numbness, tingling, pain, or weakness in hands or feet; sleepiness; stomach pain

Other side effects not listed above may also occur in some patients. If you notice any other effects, check with your doctor.

Developed: 12/2/99

RADIOPHARMACEUTICALS
Diagnostic

This information applies to the following medicines when used for diagnosis:

1. Ammonia N 13 (a-MOE-nya)
2. Cyanocobalamin Co 57 (sye-an-oh-koe-BAL-a-min)
3. Ferrous Citrate Fe 59 (FER-us SI-trate)
4. Fludeoxyglucose F 18 (flu-dee-ox-ee-GLOO-kose)
5. Gallium Citrate Ga 67 (GAL-ee-um)
6. Indium In 111 Oxyquinoline (IN-dee-um ox-i-KWIN-oh-leen)
7. Indium In 111 Pentetate (PEN-te-tate)
8. Indium In 111 Pentetreotide (pen-te-TREE-oh-tide)
9. Indium In 111 Satumomab Pendetide (sa-TYOO-mo-mab)
10. Iobenguane, Radioiodinated (eye-oh-BEN-gwane)
11. Iodohippurate Sodium I 123 (eye-oh-doe-HIP-yoor-ate SOE-dee-um)
12. Iodohippurate Sodium I 131 (eye-oh-doe-HIP-yoor-ate SOE-dee-um)
13. Iofetaminel 123 (eye-oh-FET-a-meen)
14. Iothalamate Sodium I 125 (eye-oh-thal-A-mate)
15. Krypton Kr 81m (KRIP-tonn)
16. Methionine C 11 (me-THYE-oh-neen)
17. Radioiodinated Albumin (ray-dee-oh-EYE-oh-din-nay-ted al-BYOO-min)
18. Rubidium Rb 82 (roo-BID-ee-um)
19. Sodium Chromate Cr 51 (KROE-mate)
20. Sodium Fluoride F 18 (FLOR-ide) *†
21. Sodium Iodide I 123 (EYE-oh-dyed)
22. Sodium Iodide I 131 (EYE-oh-dyed)
23. Sodium Pertechnetate Tc 99m (per-TEK-ne-tate)
24. Technetium Tc 99m Albumin (tek-NEE-see-um al-BYOO-min)
25. Technetium Tc 99m Albumin Aggregated
26. Technetium Tc 99m Albumin Colloid
27. Technetium Tc 99m Arcitumomab
28. Technetium Tc 99m Bicisate (bye-SIS-ate)
29. Technetium Tc 99m Disofenin (DYE-so-fen-in)
30. Technetium Tc 99m Exametazime (ex-a-MET-a-zeem)
31. Technetium Tc 99m Gluceptate (gloo-SEP-tate)

32. Technetium Tc 99m Lidofenin (lye-doe-FEN-in)
33. Technetium Tc 99m Mebrofenin (ME-bro-fen-in)
34. Technetium Tc 99m Medronate (ME-droe-nate)
35. Technetium Tc 99m Mertiatide (meer-TYE-a-tide)
36. Technetium Tc 99m Nofetumomab Merpentan†
37. Technetium Tc 99m Oxidronate (OX-i-dron-ate)
38. Technetium Tc 99m Pentetate (PEN-te-tate)
39. Technetium Tc 99m Pyrophosphate (peer-oh-FOS-fate)
40. Technetium Tc 99m (Pyro- and trimeta-) Phosphates
41. Technetium Tc 99m Sestamibi (SES-ta-mi-bi)
42. Technetium Tc 99m Succimer (SUX-sim-mer)
43. Technetium Tc 99m Sulfur Colloid
44. Technetium Tc 99m Teboroxime (te-boe-ROX-eem)
45. Technetium Tc 99m Tetrofosmin (te-troe-FOS-min) †
46. Thallous Chloride Tl 201 (THA-luss KLOR-ide)
47. Xenon Xe 127 (ZEE-non)
48. Xenon Xe 133

*Not commercially available in the U.S.
†Not commercially available in Canada.

Description

Radiopharmaceuticals (ray-dee-oh-far-ma-SOO-ti-kals) are agents used to diagnose certain medical problems or treat certain diseases. They may be given to the patient in several different ways. For example, they may be given by mouth, given by injection, or placed into the eye or into the bladder.

These radiopharmaceuticals are used in the diagnosis of:

- Abscess and infection—Gallium Citrate Ga 67, Indium In 111 Oxyquinoline
- Biliary tract blockage—Technetium Tc 99m Disofenin, Technetium Tc 99m Lidofenin, Technetium Tc 99m Mebrofenin
- Blood volume studies—Radioiodinated Albumin, Sodium Chromate Cr 51
- Blood vessel diseases—Sodium Pertechnetate Tc 99m
- Blood vessel diseases of the brain—Ammonia N 13, Iofetamine I 123, Technetium Tc 99m Bicisate, Technetium Tc 99m Exametazime, Xenon Xe 133
- Bone diseases—Sodium Fluoride F 18, Technetium Tc 99m Medronate, Technetium Tc 99m Oxidronate, Technetium Tc 99m Pyrophosphate, Technetium Tc 99m (Pyro- and trimeta-) Phosphates
- Bone marrow diseases—Sodium Chromate Cr 51, Technetium Tc 99m Albumin Colloid, Technetium Tc 99m Sulfur Colloid
- Brain diseases and tumors—Fludeoxyglucose F 18, Indium In 111 Pentetreotide, Iofetamine I 123, Sodium Pertechnetate Tc 99m, Technetium Tc 99m Exametazime, Technetium Tc 99m Gluceptate, Technetium Tc 99m Pentetate
- Cancer; tumors—Fludeoxyglucose F 18, Gallium Citrate Ga 67, Indium In 111 Pentetreotide, Indium In 111 Satumomab Pendetide, Methionine C 11, Radioiodinated Iobenguane, Sodium Fluoride F 18, Technetium Tc 99m Arcitumomab, Technetium Tc 99m Nofetumomab Merpentan
- Colorectal disease—Technetium Tc 99m Arcitumomab
- Disorders of iron metabolism and absorption—Ferrous Citrate Fe 59
- Heart disease—Ammonia N 13, Fludeoxyglucose F 18, Rubidium Rb 82, Sodium Pertechnetate Tc 99m, Technetium Tc 99m Albumin, Technetium Tc 99m Sestamibi, Technetium Tc 99m Teboroxime, Technetium Tc 99m Tetrofosmin, Thallous Chloride Tl 201
- Heart muscle damage (infarct)—Ammonia N 13, Fludeoxyglucose F 18, Rubidium Rb 82, Technetium Tc 99m Pyrophosphate, Technetium Tc 99m (Pyro- and

trimeta-) Phosphates, Technetium Tc 99m Sestamibi, Technetium Tc 99m Teboroxime, Technetium Tc 99m Tetrofosmin, Thallous Chloride Tl 201

- Impaired flow of cerebrospinal fluid in brain—Indium In 111 Pentetate
- Kidney diseases—Iodohippurate Sodium I 123, Iodohippurate Sodium I 131, Iothalamate Sodium I 125, Technetium Tc 99m Gluceptate, Technetium Tc 99m Mertiatide, Technetium Tc 99m Pentetate, Technetium Tc 99m Succimer
- Liver diseases—Ammonia N 13, Fludeoxyglucose F 18, Technetium Tc 99m Albumin Colloid, Technetium Tc 99m Disofenin, Technetium Tc 99m Lidofenin, Technetium Tc 99m Mebrofenin, Technetium Tc 99m Sulfur Colloid
- Lung diseases—Krypton Kr 81m, Technetium Tc 99m Albumin Aggregated, Technetium Tc 99m Pentetate, Xenon Xe 127, Xenon Xe 133
- Parathyroid diseases; parathyroid cancer—Technetium Tc 99m Sestamibi, Thallous Chloride Tl 201
- Pernicious anemia; improper absorption of vitamin B_{12} from intestines—Cyanocobalamin Co 57
- Red blood cell diseases—Sodium Chromate Cr 51
- Salivary gland diseases—Sodium Pertechnetate Tc 99m
- Spleen diseases—Sodium Chromate Cr 51, Technetium Tc 99m Albumin Colloid, Technetium Tc 99m Sulfur Colloid
- Stomach and intestinal bleeding—Sodium Chromate Cr 51, Sodium Pertechnetate Tc 99m, Technetium Tc 99m (Pyro- and trimeta-) Phosphates, Technetium Tc 99m Sulfur Colloid
- Stomach problems—Technetium Tc 99m Sulfur Colloid
- Tear duct blockage—Sodium Pertechnetate Tc 99m
- Thyroid diseases; thyroid cancer—Fludeoxyglucose F 18, Indium In 111 Pentetreotide, Radioiodinated Iobenguane, Sodium Iodide I 123, Sodium Iodide I 131, Sodium Pertechnetate Tc 99m, Technetium Tc 99m Sestamibi
- Urinary bladder diseases—Sodium Pertechnetate Tc 99m

Radiopharmaceuticals are radioactive agents. However, when small amounts are used, the radiation your body receives from them is very low and is considered safe. When larger amounts of these agents are given to treat disease, there may be different effects on the body.

When radiopharmaceuticals are used to help diagnose medical problems, only small amounts are given to the patient. The radiopharmaceutical then passes through, or is taken up by, an organ of the body (which organ depends on what radiopharmaceutical is used and how it has been given). Then the radioactivity is detected, and pictures are produced, by special imaging equipment. These pictures allow the nuclear medicine doctor to study how the organ is working and to detect cancer or tumors that may be present in the organ.

Some radiopharmaceuticals are used in larger amounts to treat certain kinds of cancer and other diseases. In those cases, the radioactive agent is taken up in the cancerous area and destroys the affected tissue. *The information that follows applies only to radiopharmaceuticals when used in small amounts to diagnose medical problems.*

The dosages of radiopharmaceuticals that are used to diagnose medical problems will be different for different patients and depend on the type of test. The amount of radioactivity of a radiopharmaceutical is expressed in units called becquerels or curies. Radiopharmaceutical dosages given may be as small as 0.185 megabecquerels (5 microcuries) or as high as 1295 megabecquerels (35 millicuries). The radiation received from these dosages may be about the same as, or even less than, the radiation received from an x-ray study of the same organ.

Radiopharmaceuticals are to be given only by or under the direct supervision of a doctor with specialized training in nuclear medicine.

Before Having This Test

In deciding to use a diagnostic test, any risks of the test must be weighed against the good it will do. This is a decision you and your doctor will make. Also, test results may be affected by other things. For radiopharmaceuticals, the following should be considered:

Allergies—If you will be receiving albumin in the form of radioiodinated albumin, technetium Tc 99m albumin aggregated, technetium Tc 99m albumin colloid, or technetium Tc 99m albumin for your test, tell your doctor if you have ever had any unusual or allergic reaction to products containing human serum albumin. Also tell your doctor if you are allergic to any other substance, such as foods, preservatives, or dyes.

Pregnancy—Radiopharmaceuticals usually are not recommended for use during pregnancy. This is to avoid exposing the fetus to radiation. Some radiopharmaceuticals may be used for diagnostic tests in pregnant women, but it is necessary to inform your doctor if you are pregnant so the doctor may reduce the radiation dose to the baby. This is especially important with radiopharmaceuticals that contain radioactive iodine, which can go to the baby's thyroid gland and, in high enough amounts, may cause thyroid damage. Be sure you have discussed this with your doctor.

Breast-feeding—Some radiopharmaceuticals pass into the breast milk and may expose the baby to radiation. If you must receive a radiopharmaceutical, it may be necessary for you to stop breast-feeding for some time after receiving it. Be sure you have discussed this with your doctor.

Children—For most radiopharmaceuticals, the amount of radiation used for a diagnostic test is very low and considered safe. However, be sure you have discussed with your doctor the benefit versus the risk of exposing your child to radiation.

Older adults—Many medicines have not been studied specifically in older people. Therefore, it may not be known whether they work exactly the same way they do in younger adults or if they cause different side effects or problems in older people. Although there is no specific information comparing use of most radiopharmaceuticals in the elderly with use in other age groups, problems would not be expected to occur. However, it is a good idea to check with your doctor if you notice any unusual effects after receiving a radiopharmaceutical.

Other medicines—Although certain medicines should not be used together at all, in other cases two different medicines may be used together even if an interaction might occur. In these cases, your doctor may want to change the dose, or other precautions may be necessary. When you are going to receive a radiopharmaceutical, it is especially important that your doctor know if you are taking any other prescription or nonprescription (over-the-counter [OTC]) medicine.

In addition, if you will be receiving radioactive iodine (sodium iodide I 123, sodium iodide I 131) or sodium pertechnetate Tc 99m for a thyroid test, it is especially important that your doctor know if you have been taking iodine through other medicine or foods. For example, the results of your test may be affected if:

- You are taking iodine-containing medicines, including certain multivitamins and cough syrups.
- You eat large amounts of iodine-containing foods, such as iodized salt, seafood, cabbage, kale, rape (turnip-like vegetable), or turnips.
- You have had an x-ray test recently for which you were given a special dye that contained iodine.

Other medical problems—The presence of other medical problems may affect the use of radiopharmaceuticals. Make sure you tell your doctor if you have any other medical problems.

The nuclear medicine doctor may have special instructions for you in preparation for your test. For example, before some tests you must fast for several hours, or the results of the test may be affected. For other tests you should drink plenty of liquids. If you do not understand the instructions you receive or if you have not received any instructions, check with the nuclear medicine doctor in advance.

Precautions After Having This Test

There are usually no special precautions to observe for radiopharmaceuticals when they are used in small amounts for diagnosis.

Some radiopharmaceuticals may accumulate in your bladder. Therefore, to increase the flow of urine and lessen the amount of radiation to your bladder, your doctor may instruct you to drink plenty of liquids and urinate often after certain tests.

For patients receiving *radioactive iodine (iodohippurate sodium I 123, iodohippurate sodium I 131, iofetamine I 123, iothalamate I 125, radioiodinated albumin, or radioiodinated iobenguane):*

- Make sure your doctor knows if you are planning to have any future thyroid tests. Even after several weeks, the results of the thyroid test may be affected by the iodine solution that may be given before the radiopharmaceutical.

Side Effects of This Medicine

Along with its needed effects, a medicine may cause some unwanted effects. When radiopharmaceuticals are used in very small doses to study an organ of the body, side effects are rare and usually involve an allergic reaction. These effects may occur almost immediately or a few minutes after the radiopharmaceutical is given. It may be helpful to note the time when you first notice any side effect. Your doctor, nuclear medicine physician and/or technologist, or nurse will be prepared to give you immediate medical attention if needed.

Check with your doctor or nurse immediately if any of the following side effects occur:
   Rare
      Chills; difficulty breathing; drowsiness (severe); fainting; fast heartbeat; fever; flushing or redness of skin; headache (severe); nausea or vomiting; skin rash, hives, or itching; stomach pain; swelling of throat, hands, or feet

Other side effects not listed above may also occur in some patients. If you notice any other effects, note the time when they start and check with your doctor.

Revised: 08/18/98

RALOXIFENE   Systemic

Commonly used brand name(s):

In the U.S.—
   Evista

Description

Raloxifene (ral-OX-i-feen) is used to help prevent and treat thinning of the bones (osteoporosis) only in postmenopausal women.

It works like an estrogen to stop the bone loss that can develop in women after menopause, but it does not increase the bone density as much as daily 0.625 mg doses of conjugated estrogens. Raloxifene will not treat hot flashes of menopause and may cause hot flashes to occur. Also, raloxifene does not stimulate the breast or uterus as estrogen does.

Raloxifene lowers the blood concentrations of total and low-density lipoprotein (LDL) cholesterol, the bad cholesterols, but it does not increase concentrations of high-density lipoprotein (HDL) cholesterol, the good cholesterol, in your blood.

This medicine is available only with your doctor's prescription, in the following dosage form(s):
   Oral
      - Tablets (U.S.)

Before Using This Medicine

In deciding to use a medicine, the risks of taking the medicine must be weighed against the good it will do. This is a decision you and your doctor will make. For raloxifene, the following should be considered:

Allergies—Tell your doctor if you have ever had any unusual or allergic reaction to raloxifene. Also tell your health care professional if you are allergic to any other substances, such as foods, preservatives, or dyes.

Pregnancy—Raloxifene is not recommended during pregnancy. Presently, raloxifene is to be used in postmenopausal women only. It has been shown to cause serious birth defects or other problems in animals. Be sure you have discussed this with your doctor.

Breast-feeding—It is not known whether raloxifene passes into breast milk. However, raloxifene is not recommended during breast-feeding because it may cause unwanted effects in nursing babies. Presently, raloxifene is to be used in postmenopausal women only.

Older adults—This medicine has been tested only in women past menopause and has not been shown to cause different side effects or problems in elderly people than it does in adults who have just gone through menopause.

Other medicines—Although certain medicines should not be used together at all, in other cases two different medicines may be used together even if an interaction might occur. In these cases, your doctor may want to change the

dose, or other precautions may be necessary. When you are taking raloxifene, it is especially important that your health care professional know if you are taking any of the following:

- Cholestyramine (e.g., Questran)—Cholestyramine can significantly reduce the absorption of raloxifene
- Estrogens, injection (e.g., Premarin) or
- Estrogens, oral (e.g., Premarin, Estrace, Estratab) or
- Estrogens, transdermal (e.g., Climara, Estrace, Vivelle)—Raloxifene should not be used with estrogens
- Warfarin (e.g., Coumadin)—Raloxifene may decrease the effect of warfarin, and the dose of warfarin may need to be adjusted when adding or stopping raloxifene

Other medical problems—The presence of other medical problems may affect the use of raloxifene. Make sure you tell your doctor if you have any other medical problems, especially:

- Blood clot formation, active or history of, including deep vein thrombosis, pulmonary embolism, and retinal embolism—Raloxifene may slightly increase the chances of these conditions and, if they are already present, cause them to worsen
- Cancer or tumors or
- Congestive heart failure or
- Any other condition that increases the risk of blood clots—Taking raloxifene while having one of these conditions may worsen the chance that blood clots can form
- Liver disease—This condition may cause higher concentrations of raloxifene in the blood

Proper Use of This Medicine

A paper with information for the patient will be given to you with your filled prescription, and will provide many details concerning the use of raloxifene. *Read this paper carefully* and ask your health care professional if you need additional information or explanation.

Many patients trying to prevent or treat bone loss will not notice any signs of the problem. In fact, many may feel normal. *It is very important that you take your medicine exactly as directed.*

Dosing—The dose of raloxifene will be different for different patients. *Follow your doctor's orders or the directions on the label.* The following information includes only the average dose of raloxifene. *If your dose is different, do not change it* unless your doctor tells you to do so.

- For *oral* dosage form (tablets):
  —For preventing bone loss:
   - Adults—60 mg once a day, with or without meals.
  —For treating bone loss:
   - Adults—60 mg once a day, with or without meals.

Missed dose—If you miss a dose of this medicine, skip the missed dose and go back to your regular dosing schedule. Do not double doses. If you have any questions about this, check with your doctor.

Storage—To store this medicine:

- Keep out of the reach of children.
- Store away from heat and direct light.
- Do not store in the bathroom, near the kitchen sink, or in other damp places. Heat or moisture may cause the medicine to break down.
- Do not keep outdated medicine or medicine no longer needed. Be sure that any discarded medicine is out of the reach of children.

Precautions While Using This Medicine

It is very important that you keep your appointments with your doctor even if you feel well.

Before you have any kind of surgery, tell the medical doctor in charge that you are using this medicine. Discuss discontinuing use of raloxifene 3 days before you think you will have a long period of inactivity, sitting, or bed rest, such as after having surgery or going on a long trip. The doctor may have you start the medicine again after you are back on your feet and fully mobile. If you are going on a trip and stay on raloxifene, you should walk regularly or move about when possible. Remaining still for long periods may cause blood clots for some people, and raloxifene may rarely worsen their condition.

If you are able to become pregnant, stop using the medicine immediately if you think you have become pregnant and check with your doctor. Raloxifene is recommended for women who are past menopause.

Raloxifene does not act like an estrogen to stimulate the uterus or breast. *If you experience vaginal bleeding, breast pain or enlargement, or swelling of hands or feet while on raloxifene, you should report it to your doctor.*

Other ways that may be used with raloxifene to help prevent or treat bone loss are taking calcium plus vitamin D supplements and getting weight-bearing exercise. You may want to discuss these options with your doctor.

Side Effects of This Medicine

Along with its needed effects, a medicine may cause some unwanted effects. Although not all of these side effects may occur, if they do occur they may need medical attention.

Stop taking this medicine and get emergency help immediately if any of the following side effects occur:
   Rare
   Coughing blood; headache or migraine headache; loss of or change in speech, coordination, or vision; pain or numbness in chest, arm, or leg; shortness of breath (unexplained)

Check with your doctor as soon as possible if any of the following side effects occur:
   More common
   Bloody or cloudy urine; chest pain; difficult, burning, or painful urination; fever; frequent urge to urinate; infection, including body aches or pain, congestion in throat, cough, dryness or soreness of throat, and loss of voice; runny nose; leg cramping; skin rash; swelling of hands, ankles, or feet; vaginal itching

   Less common
   Abdominal pain (severe); aching body pains; congestion in lungs; diarrhea; difficulty in breathing; hoarseness; loss of appetite; nausea; trouble in swallowing; weakness

Other side effects may occur that usually do not need medical attention. These side effects may go away during treatment as your body adjusts to the medicine. However, check with your doctor if any of the following side effects continue or are bothersome:
   More common
   Hot flashes, including sudden sweating and feelings of warmth (especially common during the first 6 months of treatment); increased white vaginal discharge; joint or muscle pain; mental depression;

problems of stomach or intestines, including passing of gas, upset stomach, or vomiting; swollen joints; trouble in sleeping; weight gain (unexplained)

Other side effects not listed above may also occur in some patients. If you notice any other effects, check with your doctor.

Developed: 03/26/98
Interim revision: 12/14/99

RALTITREXED—For Colorectal Cancer Systemic—INTRODUCTORY VERSION

Commonly used brand name(s):

In Canada—
Tomudex

Description

Raltitrexed (ral-ti-TREX-ed) belongs to a group of medicines known as antimetabolites. It is used to treat cancer of the colon and rectum. It may also be used to treat other kinds of cancer, as determined by your doctor.

Raltitrexed blocks an enzyme needed by the cell to live. This interferes with the growth of cancer cells, which are eventually destroyed. Since the growth of normal body cells may also be affected by raltitrexed, other effects will also occur. Some of these may be serious and must be reported to your doctor. Other effects, like hair loss, may not be serious but may cause concern.

Before you begin treatment with raltitrexed, you and your doctor should talk about the good this medicine will do as well as the risks of using it.

Raltitrexed is to be administered only by or under the immediate supervision of your doctor. It is available in the following dosage form:

Parenteral
- Injection (Canada)

Before Using This Medicine

In deciding to use a medicine, the risks of taking the medicine must be weighed against the good it will do. This is a decision you and your doctor will make. For raltitrexed, the following should be considered:

Allergies—Tell your doctor if you have ever had any unusual or allergic reaction to raltitrexed.

Pregnancy—Tell your doctor if you are pregnant or if you intend to have children. There is a chance that this medicine may cause birth defects if either the male or female is taking it at the time of conception or if it is taken during pregnancy. Raltitrexed causes toxic or harmful effects in rats. In addition, many cancer medicines may cause sterility which could be permanent. Although sterility has not been reported with this medicine, the possibility should be kept in mind.

Be sure that you have discussed this with your doctor before receiving this medicine. It is best to use some kind of birth control while you are receiving raltitrexed. Tell your doctor right away if you think you have become pregnant while receiving raltitrexed. Because raltitrexed may cause serious side effects, pregnancy is generally not recommended while you are taking it.

Breast-feeding—Tell your doctor if you are breast-feeding or if you intend to breast-feed during treatment with this medicine. Because raltitrexed may cause serious side effects, breast-feeding is generally not recommended while you are taking it.

Children—Studies on this medicine have been done only in adult patients, and there is no specific information comparing use of raltitrexed in children with use in other age groups.

Older adults—Elderly people are especially sensitive to the effects of raltitrexed. Raltitrexed may be more likely to cause side effects such as cracked lips, diarrhea, difficulty in swallowing, sores, ulcers, or white spots on the lips, tongue, or inside the mouth in elderly patients.

Other medicines—Although certain medicines should not be used together at all, in other cases two different medicines may be used together even if an interaction might occur. In these cases, your doctor may want to change the dose, or other precautions may be necessary. When you are receiving raltitrexed, it is especially important that your doctor and pharmacist know if you are taking any of the following:

- Amphotericin B by injection (e.g., Fungizone) or
- Antithyroid agents (medicine for overactive thyroid) or
- Azathioprine (e.g., Imuran) or
- Chloramphenicol (e.g., Chloromycetin) or
- Colchicine or
- Flucytosine (e.g., Ancobon) or
- Ganciclovir (e.g., Cytovene) or
- Interferon (e.g., Intron A, Roferon-A) or
- Mercaptopurine (e.g., Purinethol) or
- Methotrexate (e.g., Rheumatrex) or
- Plicamycin (e.g., Mithracin) or
- Zidovudine (e.g., AZT, Retrovir) or
- If you have ever been treated with radiation or cancer medicines—Raltitrexed may increase the effects of these medicines or radiation therapy on the blood
- Folic acid or
- Leucovorin (e.g., Wellcovorin) or
- Vitamin preparations containing folic or folinic acid—May interfere with the effectiveness of raltitrexed

Other medical problems—The presence of other medical problems may affect the use of raltitrexed. Make sure you tell your doctor if you have any other medical problems, especially:

- Chickenpox (including recent exposure) or
- Herpes zoster (shingles)—Risk of severe disease affecting other parts of the body

- Infection—Raltitrexed can decrease your body's ability to fight infection

- Kidney disease or
- Liver disease—Effects of raltitrexed may be increased because of slower removal from the body; your doctor may need to change your dose

Proper Use of This Medicine

This medicine is sometimes given together with certain other medicines. If you are using a combination of medicines, it is important that you receive each one at the proper time. If you are taking some of these medicines by mouth, ask your health care professional to help you plan a way to take them at the right times.

This medicine usually causes nausea and vomiting that may be severe. However, it is very important that you continue to receive the medicine, even if you begin to feel ill. Ask your health care professional for ways to lessen these effects, especially if they are severe.

Dosing—The dose of raltitrexed will be different for different patients. The dose that is used may depend on a number of things, including what the medicine is being used for, the patient's size, and whether or not other medicines are also being taken. If you have any questions about the proper dose of raltitrexed, ask your doctor.

- For *parenteral* dosage form (injection):
  —For colorectal cancer
  - Adults—3 milligrams (mg) per square meter of body surface area given over a 15 minute period. The dose may be repeated every 3 weeks.
  - Children—Use and dose must be determined by your doctor.

Missed dose—If you have any questions about this, check with your doctor.

Precautions While Using This Medicine

It is very important that your doctor check your progress at regular visits to make sure that this medicine is working properly and to check for unwanted effects.

This medicine may cause some people to feel unusually tired or ill. *Make sure you know how you react to this medicine before you drive, use machines, or do anything else that could be dangerous if you are less alert.*

While you are being treated with raltitrexed, and after you stop treatment with it, *do not have any immunizations (vaccinations) without your doctor's approval.* Raltitrexed may lower your body's resistance and there is a chance you might get the infection the immunization is meant to prevent. In addition, other persons living in your household should not take oral polio vaccine since there is a chance they could pass the polio virus on to you. Also, avoid persons who have taken oral polio vaccine within the last several months. Do not get close to them and do not stay in the same room with them for very long. If you cannot take these precautions, you should consider wearing a protective face mask that covers the nose and mouth.

Raltitrexed can temporarily lower the number of white blood cells in your blood, increasing the chance of getting an infection. It can also lower the number of platelets, which are necessary for proper blood clotting. If this occurs, there are certain precautions you can take, especially when your blood count is low, to reduce the risk of infection or bleeding:

- If you can, avoid people with infections. *Check with your doctor immediately* if you think you are getting an infection or if you get a fever or chills, cough or hoarseness, lower back or side pain, or painful or difficult urination.
- *Check with your doctor immediately* if you notice any unusual bleeding or bruising; black, tarry stools; blood in urine or stools; or pinpoint red spots on your skin.
- Be careful when using a regular toothbrush, dental floss, or toothpick. Your medical doctor, dentist, or nurse may recommend other ways to clean your teeth and gums. Check with your medical doctor before having any dental work done.

- Do not touch your eyes or the inside of your nose unless you have just washed your hands and have not touched anything else in the meantime.
- Be careful not to cut yourself when you are using sharp objects such as a safety razor or fingernail or toenail cutters.
- Avoid contact sports or other situations where bruising or injury could occur.

Side Effects of This Medicine

Along with its needed effects, a medicine may cause some unwanted effects. Although not all of these side effects may occur, if they do occur they may need medical attention.

Check with your doctor immediately if any of the following side effects occur:
More common
  Pale skin, troubled breathing, unusual bleeding or bruising, unusual tiredness or weakness; black, tarry stools, chest pain, chills, cough, fever, painful or difficult urination, shortness of breath, sore throat, sores, ulcers, or white spots on lips or in mouth, swollen glands; increase in bowel movements, loose stools, soft stools

Less common
  Dizziness, fainting, fast, slow, or irregular heartbeat, decreased urine output, dilated neck veins, extreme fatigue, irregular breathing, swelling of face, fingers, feet, or lower legs, tightness in chest, weight gain, wheezing

Other side effects may occur that usually do not need medical attention. These side effects may go away during treatment as your body adjusts to the medicine. However, check with your doctor if any of the following side effects continue or are bothersome.
More common
  Stomach or abdomen pain; loss of appetite, weight loss; constipation; nausea and vomiting; lack or loss of strength; general feeling of discomfort or illness, headache, joint pain, muscle aches and pains, runny nose, shivering, sweating, trouble sleeping; rash

Less common
  Bloating or swelling of face, arms, hands, lower legs, or feet, rapid weight gain, tingling of hands or feet

Other side effects may occur that usually do not need medical attention. These side effects may go away during treatment as your body adjusts to the medicine. Also, your health care professional may be able to tell you about ways to prevent or reduce some of these side effects. Check with your health care professional if any of the following side effects continue or are bothersome or if you have any questions about them:
More common
  Hair loss, thinning of hair

Less common
  Change in taste, bad unusual or unpleasant (after) taste

After you stop receiving raltitrexed, it may still produce some side effects that need attention. During this period of time check with your doctor if you notice any of the following side effects:
  Black, tarry stools, blood in urine or stools, cough or hoarseness, fever or chills, lower back or side pain,

---

© 2002 MICROMEDEX Thomson Healthcare

painful or difficult urination, pinpoint red spots on skin, unusual bleeding or bruising

Other side effects not listed above may also occur in some patients. If you notice any other effects, check with your doctor.

Developed: 08/08/2000

RANITIDINE BISMUTH CITRATE
Systemic

Commonly used brand name(s):

In Canada—
   Pylorid

Description

Ranitidine bismuth citrate (ra-NI-ti-deen BIS-muth SI-trayt) is used to treat active duodenal ulcers associated with infection caused by the *H. pylori* organism. It is used in combination with an antibiotic called clarithromycin. Ranitidine bismuth citrate should not be taken alone for the treatment of ulcers.

This medicine is available only with your doctor's prescription, in the following dosage form:

   Oral
   • Tablet (Canada)

Before Using This Medicine

In deciding to use a medicine, the risks of taking the medicine must be weighed against the good it will do. This is a decision you and your doctor will make. For ranitidine bismuth citrate, the following should be considered:

Allergies—Tell your doctor if you have ever had any unusual or allergic reaction to ranitidine bismuth citrate. Also tell your health care professional if you are allergic to any other substances, such as foods, preservatives, or dyes.

Pregnancy—Studies have not been done in pregnant women. A few women who became pregnant during studies of ranitidine bismuth citrate delivered normal infants; one woman with a history of problems during pregnancy delivered an infant with a birth defect. However, it is not known if this defect was caused by the medicine. Studies in pregnant animals have not shown that ranitidine bismuth citrate causes harmful effects in the offspring. Before taking this medicine, make sure your doctor knows if you are pregnant or if you may become pregnant.

Breast-feeding—It is not known whether ranitidine bismuth citrate passes into breast milk. Although most medicines pass into breast milk in small amounts, many of them may be used safely while breast-feeding. Mothers who are taking this medicine and who wish to breast-feed should discuss this with their doctor.

Children—Studies on this medicine have been done only in adult patients, and there is no specific information comparing use of ranitidine bismuth citrate in children with use in other age groups.

Older adults—In studies done to date that have included older adults, ranitidine bismuth citrate has not been shown to cause different side effects or problems in older people than it does in younger adults.

Other medicines—Although certain medicines should not be used together at all, in other cases two different medicines may be used together even if an interaction might occur. In these cases, your doctor may want to change the dose, or other precautions may be necessary. When you are taking ranitidine bismuth citrate, it is especially important that your health care professional know if you are taking any other prescription or nonprescription (over-the-counter [OTC]) medicines.

Other medical problems—The presence of other medical problems may affect the use of ranitidine bismuth citrate. Make sure you tell your doctor if you have any other medical problems, especially:

• Acute porphyria, history of—Ranitidine bismuth citrate may make the condition worse
• Kidney disease—Higher blood levels of ranitidine bismuth citrate may result and increase the chance of side effects

Proper Use of This Medicine

Take this medicine for the full time of treatment, even if you begin to feel better. It is important to see your doctor regularly to determine if the combination of ranitidine bismuth citrate and clarithromycin is working properly to cure the infection causing your ulcer.

Dosing—The dose of ranitidine bismuth citrate will be different for different patients. *Follow your doctor's orders or the directions on the label.* The following information includes only the average doses of ranitidine bismuth citrate. *If your dose is different, do not change it* unless your doctor tells you to do so.

• For *oral* dosage form (tablet):
   —For duodenal ulcers:
      • Adults—400 milligrams (mg) two times a day for four weeks, taken together with clarithromycin 500 mg three times a day or 250 mg four times a day for the first two weeks.
      • Children—Use and dose must be determined by your physician.

Missed dose—If you miss a dose of this medicine, take it as soon as possible. However, if it is almost time for your next dose, skip the missed dose and go back to your regular dosing schedule. Do not double doses.

Storage—To store this medicine:
• Keep out of the reach of children.
• Store away from heat and direct light.
• Do not store in the bathroom, near the kitchen sink, or in other damp places. Heat or moisture may cause the medicine to break down.
• Do not keep outdated medicine or medicine no longer needed. Be sure that any discarded medicine is out of the reach of children.

Precautions While Using This Medicine

This medicine may cause *dizziness, lightheadedness, or fainting, especially when you get up from a lying or sitting position.* These symptoms are more likely to occur when you begin taking this medicine. Getting up slowly may help. If you should have this problem, check with your doctor.

The results of dipstick tests for protein in the urine may be affected by this medicine. While you are taking ranitidine bismuth citrate, testing with sulfosalicylic acid is recommended.

Side Effects of This Medicine

Along with its needed effects, a medicine may cause some unwanted effects. Although not all of these side effects may occur, if they do occur they may need medical attention.

Check with your doctor as soon as possible if any of the following side effects occur:

More common
　Diarrhea; headache

Less common
　Dizziness; itching; nausea; trouble in sleeping; vomiting

Rare
　Constipation; fast heartbeat; skin rash; stomach pain; sudden faintness or weakness; swelling of face; troubled breathing or wheezing

Other side effects may occur that usually do not need medical attention. These side effects may go away during treatment as your body adjusts to the medicine. However, check with your doctor if any of the following side effects continue or are bothersome:

More common
　Change in sense of taste

Less common
　Darkening of tongue and/or stools; hair loss or thinning of hair

Other side effects not listed above may also occur in some patients. If you notice any other effects, check with your doctor.

Developed: 03/19/98
Revised: 6/12/2000

RAUWOLFIA ALKALOIDS　Systemic

Commonly used brand name(s):

In the U.S.—

Harmonyl[1]	Rauverid[2]
Raudixin[2]	Serpalan[3]
Rauval[2]	Wolfina[2]

In Canada—
Novoreserpine[3]
Reserfia[3]
Serpasil[3]

Note: For quick reference, the following rauwolfia alkaloids are numbered to match the corresponding brand names.

This information applies to the following medicines:
1. Deserpidine (de-SER-pi-deen) †
2. Rauwolfia Serpentina (rah-WOOL-fee-a ser-pen-TEE-na) †‡
3. Reserpine (re-SER-peen) ‡

†Not commercially available in Canada.
‡Generic name product may be available in the U.S.

Description

Rauwolfia alkaloids belong to the general class of medicines called antihypertensives. They are used to treat high blood pressure (hypertension).

High blood pressure adds to the workload of the heart and arteries. If it continues for a long time, the heart and arteries may not function properly. This can damage the blood vessels of the brain, heart, and kidneys, resulting in a stroke, heart failure, or kidney failure. High blood pressure may also increase the risk of heart attacks. These problems may be less likely to occur if blood pressure is controlled.

Rauwolfia alkaloids work by controlling nerve impulses along certain nerve pathways. As a result, they act on the heart and blood vessels to lower blood pressure.

Rauwolfia alkaloids may also be used to treat other conditions as determined by your doctor.

These medicines are available only with your doctor's prescription, in the following dosage forms:

Oral
　Deserpidine
　　• Tablets (U.S.)
　Rauwolfia Serpentina
　　• Tablets (U.S.)
　Reserpine
　　• Tablets (U.S. and Canada)

Before Using This Medicine

In deciding to use a medicine, the risks of taking the medicine must be weighed against the good it will do. This is a decision you and your doctor will make. For rauwolfia alkaloids, the following should be considered:

Allergies—Tell your doctor if you have ever had any unusual or allergic reaction to rauwolfia alkaloids. Also tell your health care professional if you are allergic to any other substance, such as foods, preservatives, or dyes.

Pregnancy—Rauwolfia alkaloids have not been studied in pregnant women. However, too much use of rauwolfia alkaloids during pregnancy may cause unwanted effects (difficult breathing, low temperature, loss of appetite) in the baby. In rats, use of rauwolfia alkaloids during pregnancy causes birth defects and in guinea pigs decreases newborn survival rates. Before taking this medicine, make sure your doctor knows if you are pregnant or if you may become pregnant.

Breast-feeding—Rauwolfia alkaloids pass into breast milk and may cause unwanted effects (difficult breathing, low temperature, loss of appetite) in infants of mothers taking large doses of this medicine. Be sure you have discussed this with your doctor before taking this medicine.

Children—Although there is no specific information comparing use of rauwolfia alkaloids in children with use in other age groups, rauwolfia alkaloids are not expected to cause different side effects or problems in children than they do in adults.

Older adults—Many medicines have not been studied specifically in older people. Therefore, it may not be known whether they work exactly the same way they do in younger adults. Although there is no specific information comparing use of rauwolfia alkaloids in the elderly with use in other age groups, dizziness or drowsiness may be more likely to occur in the elderly, who are more sensitive to the effects of rauwolfia alkaloids.

Other medicines—Although certain medicines should not be used together at all, in other cases two different medicines may be used together even if an interaction might occur. In these cases, your doctor may want to change the dose, or other precautions may be necessary. When you are taking rauwolfia alkaloids, it is especially important that your health care professional know if you are taking any of the following:

- Monoamine oxidase (MAO) inhibitors (furazolidone [e.g., Furoxone], isocarboxazid [e.g., Marplan], phenelzine [e.g., Nardil], procarbazine [e.g., Matulane], selegiline [e.g., Eldepryl], tranylcypromine [e.g., Parnate])—Taking a rauwolfia alkaloid while you are taking or within 2 weeks of taking MAO inhibitors may increase the risk of central nervous system depression or may cause a severe high blood pressure reaction

Other medical problems—The presence of other medical problems may affect the use of rauwolfia alkaloids. Make sure you tell your doctor if you have any other medical problems, especially:

- Allergies or other breathing problems such as asthma—Rauwolfia alkaloids can cause breathing problems

- Epilepsy

- Gallstones or
- Stomach ulcer or
- Ulcerative colitis—Rauwolfia alkaloids increase activity of the stomach, which may make the condition worse

- Heart disease—Rauwolfia alkaloids can cause heart rhythm problems or slow heartbeat

- Kidney disease—Some patients may not do well when blood pressure is lowered by rauwolfia alkaloids

- Mental depression (or history of)—Rauwolfia alkaloids cause mental depression

- Parkinson's disease—Rauwolfia alkaloids can cause parkinsonism-like effects

- Pheochromocytoma

Proper Use of This Medicine

For patients taking this medicine *for high blood pressure:*

- In addition to the use of the medicine your doctor has prescribed, treatment for your high blood pressure may include weight control and care in the types of foods you eat, especially foods high in sodium. Your doctor will tell you which of these are most important for you. You should check with your doctor before changing your diet.

- Many patients who have high blood pressure will not notice any signs of the problem. In fact, many may feel normal. It is very important that you *take your medicine exactly as directed* and that you keep your appointments with your doctor even if you feel well.

- Remember that this medicine will not cure your high blood pressure but it does help control it. Therefore, you must continue to take it as directed if you expect to lower your blood pressure and keep it down. *You may have to take high blood pressure medicine for the rest of your life.* If high blood pressure is not treated, it can cause serious problems such as heart failure, blood vessel disease, stroke, or kidney disease.

To help you remember to take your medicine, try to get into the habit of taking it at the same time each day.

This medicine is sometimes given together with certain other medicines. If you are using a combination of drugs, make sure that you take each medicine at the proper time and do not mix them. Ask your health care professional to help you plan a way to remember to take your medicines at the right times.

If this medicine upsets your stomach, it may be taken with meals or milk. If stomach upset (nausea, vomiting, stomach cramps or pain) continues or gets worse, check with your doctor.

Dosing—The dose of these medicines will be different for different patients. *Follow your doctor's orders or the directions on the label.* The following information includes only the average doses of these medicines. *If your dose is different, do not change it* unless your doctor tells you to do so.

The number of tablets that you take depends on the strength of the medicine.

For deserpidine
- For *oral* dosage form (tablets):
  —For high blood pressure:
    - Adults—250 to 500 micrograms (mcg) a day. This may be taken as a single dose or divided into two doses.
    - Children—Dose must be determined by your doctor.

For rauwolfia serpentina
- For *oral* dosage form (tablets):
  —For high blood pressure:
    - Adults—50 to 200 milligrams (mg) a day. This may be taken as a single dose or divided into two doses.
    - Children—Dose must be determined by your doctor.

For reserpine
- For *oral* dosage form (tablets):
  —For high blood pressure:
    - Adults—100 to 250 micrograms (mcg) a day.
    - Children—Dose is based on body weight and must be determined by your doctor. The usual dose is 5 to 20 mcg per kilogram (kg) (2.27 to 9.1 mcg per pound) of body weight a day. This may be taken as a single dose or divided into two doses.

Missed dose—If you miss a dose of this medicine, do not take the missed dose at all and do not double the next one. Instead, go back to your regular dosing schedule.

Storage—To store this medicine:
- Keep out of the reach of children.
- Store away from heat and direct light.
- Do not store in the bathroom, near the kitchen sink, or in other damp places. Heat or moisture may cause the medicine to break down.
- Do not keep outdated medicine or medicine no longer needed. Be sure that any discarded medicine is out of the reach of children.

Precautions While Using This Medicine

It is important that your doctor check your progress at regular visits to make sure that this medicine is working properly.

For patients taking this medicine *for high blood pressure:*

- *Do not take other medicines unless they have been discussed with your doctor.* This especially includes over-the-counter (nonprescription) medicines for appetite control, asthma, colds, cough, hay fever, or sinus problems, since they may tend to increase your blood pressure.

Before having any kind of surgery (including dental surgery) or emergency treatment, *tell the medical doctor or dentist in charge that you are taking this medicine.*

In some patients, this medicine may cause mental depression. *Tell your doctor right away:*

- if you or anyone else notices unusual changes in your mood.
- if you start having early-morning sleeplessness or unusually vivid dreams or nightmares.

This medicine will add to the effects of alcohol and other CNS depressants (medicines that slow down the nervous system, possibly causing drowsiness). Some examples of CNS depressants are antihistamines or medicine for hay fever, other allergies, or colds; sedatives, tranquilizers, or sleeping medicine; prescription pain medicine or narcotics; barbiturates; medicine for seizures; muscle relaxants; or anesthetics, including some dental anesthetics. *Check with your doctor before taking any of the above while you are using this medicine.*

This medicine may cause some people to become drowsy or less alert than they are normally. This is more likely to happen when you begin to take it or when you increase the amount of medicine you are taking. *Make sure you know how you react to this medicine before you drive, use machines, or do anything else that could be dangerous if you are not alert.*

This medicine may cause dryness of the mouth. For temporary relief, use sugarless candy or gum, melt bits of ice in your mouth, or use a saliva substitute. However, if dry mouth continues for more than 2 weeks, check with your medical doctor or dentist. Continuing dryness of the mouth may increase the chance of dental disease, including tooth decay, gum disease, and fungus infections.

This medicine often causes stuffiness in the nose. However, do not use nasal decongestant medicines without first checking with your health care professional.

Side Effects of This Medicine

Suggestions that rauwolfia alkaloids may increase the risk of breast cancer occurring later have not been proven. However, rats and mice given 100 to 300 times the human dose had an increased number of tumors.

Along with its needed effects, a medicine may cause some unwanted effects. Although not all of these side effects may occur, if they do occur they may need medical attention.

Check with your doctor immediately if any of the following side effects occur:

Less common
> Drowsiness or faintness; impotence or decreased sexual interest; lack of energy or weakness; mental depression or inability to concentrate; nervousness or anxiety; vivid dreams or nightmares or early-morning sleeplessness

Check with your doctor as soon as possible if any of the following side effects occur:

More common
> Dizziness

Less common
> Black, tarry stools; bloody vomit; chest pain; headache; irregular heartbeat; shortness of breath; slow heartbeat; stomach cramps or pain

Rare
> Painful or difficult urination; skin rash or itching; stiffness; trembling and shaking of hands and fingers; unusual bleeding or bruising

Signs and symptoms of overdose
> Dizziness or drowsiness (severe); flushing of skin; pinpoint pupils of eyes; slow pulse

Other side effects may occur that usually do not need medical attention. These side effects may go away during treatment as your body adjusts to the medicine. However, check with your doctor if any of the following side effects continue or are bothersome:

More common
> Diarrhea; dryness of mouth; loss of appetite; nausea and vomiting; stuffy nose

Less common
> Swelling of feet and lower legs

After you stop using this medicine, it may still produce some side effects that need attention. During this period of time *check with your doctor immediately* if you notice any of the following side effects:

> Drowsiness or faintness; impotence or decreased sexual interest; irregular or slow heartbeat; lack of energy or weakness; mental depression or inability to concentrate; nervousness or anxiety; vivid dreams or nightmares or early-morning sleeplessness

Other side effects not listed above may also occur in some patients. If you notice any other effects, check with your doctor.

Additional Information

Once a medicine has been approved for marketing for a certain use, experience may show that it is also useful for other medical problems. Although this use is not included in product labeling, reserpine is used in certain patients with the following medical condition:

- Raynaud's disease

Other than the above information, there is no additional information relating to proper use, precautions, or side effects for this use.

Revised: 07/28/92
Interim revision: 07/20/94

REPAGLINIDE   Systemic

Commonly used brand name(s):

In the U.S.—
> Prandin

Description

Repaglinide (re-PAG-lin-ide) is used to treat a certain type of diabetes mellitus (sugar diabetes) called type 2 diabetes. When you have type 2 diabetes, insulin is still being produced by your pancreas. Sometimes the amount of insulin you produce may not be enough or your body may not be using it properly and you may still need more. Repaglinide works by causing your pancreas to release more insulin into the blood stream. Repaglinide may be used alone or with another oral diabetes medicine called metformin.

This medicine is available only with your doctor's prescription, in the following dosage form:

Oral
- Tablets (U.S.)

Before Using This Medicine

In deciding to use a medicine, the risks of taking the medicine must be weighed against the good it will do. This is a decision you and your doctor will make. For repaglinide, the following should be considered:

Allergies—Tell your doctor if you have ever had any unusual or allergic reaction to repaglinide. Also tell your health care professional if you are allergic to any other substances, such as foods, preservatives, or dyes.

Pregnancy—Repaglinide has not been studied in pregnant women. However, it is easier during pregnancy to control your blood sugar by using injections of insulin, rather than by taking repaglinide. Close control of your blood sugar can reduce the chance of your baby gaining too much weight, having birth defects, or having high blood sugar before birth. Be sure to tell your doctor if you plan to become pregnant or if you think you are pregnant.

Breast-feeding—It is not known whether repaglinide passes into human breast milk. However, it has been shown to cause unwanted effects in nursing animals. It may be necessary for you to take another medicine or to stop breast-feeding during treatment. Be sure you have discussed the risks and benefits of the medicine with your doctor.

Children—Studies on this medicine have been done only in adult patients, and there is no specific information comparing use of repaglinide in children with use in other age groups.

Older adults—This medicine has been tested in a limited number of patients 65 years of age or older and has not been shown to cause different side effects or problems in older people than it does in younger adults. However, the first signs of low blood sugar are not easily seen or do not occur at all in older patients. This may increase the chance of low blood sugar developing during treatment.

Other medicines—Although certain medicines should not be used together at all, in other cases two different medicines may be used together even if an interaction might occur. In these cases, your doctor may want to change the dose, or other precautions may be necessary. When you are taking repaglinide, it is especially important that your health care professional know if you are taking any of the following:

- Beta-adrenergic blocking agents (acebutolol [e.g., Sectral], atenolol [e.g., Tenormin], betaxolol [e.g., Kerlone], bisoprolol [e.g., Zebeta], carteolol [e.g., Cartrol], labetalol [e.g., Trandate], metoprolol [e.g., Lopressor], na-

dolol [e.g., Corgard], oxprenolol [e.g., Trasicor], penbutolol [e.g., Levatol], pindolol [e.g., Visken], propranolol [e.g., Inderal], sotalol [e.g., Betapace], timolol [e.g., Blocadren])—These medicines may increase the chance that high or low blood sugar can occur; also, they can hide symptoms of low blood sugar (such as fast heartbeat). Because of this, a person with diabetes might not recognize that he or she has low blood sugar and might not take immediate steps to treat it

Other medical problems—The presence of other medical problems may affect the use of repaglinide. Make sure you tell your doctor if you have any other medical problems, especially:

- Infection or
- Ketones in the blood (diabetic ketoacidosis) or
- Surgery or
- Trauma or
- Type 1 (insulin-dependent) diabetes or
- Unusual stress—Insulin may be needed to control diabetes in patients with these conditions

- Kidney disease or
- Liver disease—Higher blood levels of repaglinide may occur; this may change the amount of medicine you need

- Underactive adrenal gland or
- Underactive pituitary gland or
- Undernourished condition or
- Weakened physical condition—Patients with these conditions may be more likely to develop low blood sugar while taking repaglinide

Proper Use of This Medicine

Follow carefully the special meal plan your doctor gave you. This is the most important part of controlling your condition, and is necessary if the medicine is to work properly. Also, exercise regularly and test for sugar in your blood or urine as directed.

This medicine usually is taken 15 minutes before a meal but may be taken up to 30 minutes before a meal.

Dosing—The dose of repaglinide will be different for different patients. *Follow your doctor's orders or the directions on the label.* The following information includes only the average doses of repaglinide. *If your dose is different, do not change it* unless your doctor tells you to do so.

- For *oral* dosage form (tablets):
  - —For type 2 diabetes:
    - Adults:
      - —For patients who have never taken medicine to lower their blood sugar or who have a glycosylated hemoglobin (hemoglobin A_{1c}) measurement that is less than 8%: At first the dose is 0.5 milligram (mg) fifteen to thirty minutes before each meal. The dose may then be adjusted by your doctor based on your fasting blood sugar level.
      - —For patients who have taken medicine to lower their blood sugar and who have a hemoglobin A_{1c} measurement that is higher than 8%: At first the dose is 1 or 2 mg fifteen to thirty minutes before each meal. The dose may then be adjusted by your doctor based on your fasting blood sugar level.

- Children: Use and dose must be determined by your doctor.

Missed dose—You should skip a dose of repaglinide if a meal is skipped and add a dose of repaglinide if you eat an extra meal.

Storage—To store this medicine:

- Keep out of the reach of children.
- Store away from heat and direct light.
- Do not store in the bathroom, near the kitchen sink, or in other damp places. Heat or moisture may cause the medicine to break down.
- Do not keep outdated medicine or medicine no longer needed. Be sure that any discarded medicine is out of the reach of children.

Precautions While Using This Medicine

Your doctor will want to check your progress at regular visits, especially during the first few weeks you take this medicine.

It is very important to follow carefully any instructions from your health care team about:

- Alcohol—Drinking alcohol may cause severe low blood sugar. Discuss this with your health care team.
- Other medicines—Do not take other medicines during the time you are taking repaglinide unless they have been discussed with your doctor. This especially includes nonprescription medicines such as aspirin, and medicines for appetite control, asthma, colds, cough, hay fever, or sinus problems.
- Counseling—Other family members need to learn how to prevent side effects or help with side effects if they occur. Also, patients with diabetes may need special counseling about diabetes medicine dosing changes that might occur because of lifestyle changes, such as changes in exercise and diet. Furthermore, counseling on contraception and pregnancy may be needed because of the problems that can occur in patients with diabetes during pregnancy.
- Travel—Keep a recent prescription and your medical history with you. Be prepared for an emergency as you would normally. Make allowances for changing time zones and keep your meal times as close as possible to your usual meal times.

In case of emergency—There may be a time when you need emergency help for a problem caused by your diabetes. You need to be prepared for these emergencies. It is a good idea to wear a medical identification (ID) bracelet or neck chain at all times. Also, carry an ID card in your wallet or purse that says that you have diabetes and a list of all of your medicines.

Too much repaglinide can cause low blood sugar (hypoglycemia). Low blood sugar also can occur if you use repaglinide with another antidiabetic medicine, delay or miss a meal or snack, exercise more than usual, drink alcohol, or cannot eat because of nausea or vomiting. *Symptoms of low blood sugar must be treated before they lead to unconsciousness (passing out).* Different people may feel different symptoms of low blood sugar. *It is important that you learn which symptoms of low blood sugar you usually have so that you can treat it quickly.*

Symptoms of low blood sugar include anxiety; behavior change similar to being drunk; blurred vision; cold sweats; confusion; cool, pale skin; difficulty in thinking; drowsiness; excessive hunger; fast heartbeat; headache (continuing); nausea; nervousness; nightmares; restless sleep; shakiness; slurred speech; or unusual tiredness or weakness.

If symptoms of low blood sugar occur, *eat glucose tablets or gel, corn syrup, honey, or sugar cubes; or drink fruit juice, nondiet soft drink, or sugar dissolved in water to relieve the symptoms.* Also, check your blood for low blood sugar. *Get to a doctor or a hospital right away if the symptoms do not improve. Someone should call for emergency help immediately if severe symptoms such as convulsions (seizures) or unconsciousness occur.* Food or drink should not be forced because the patient could choke from not swallowing correctly.

Hyperglycemia (high blood sugar) may occur if you do not take enough or skip a dose of your antidiabetic medicine, overeat or do not follow your meal plan, have a fever or infection, or do not exercise as much as usual.

Symptoms of high blood sugar include blurred vision; drowsiness; dry mouth; flushed, dry skin; fruit-like breath odor; increased urination; ketones in urine; loss of appetite; stomachache, nausea, or vomiting; tiredness; troubled breathing (rapid and deep); unconsciousness; or unusual thirst.

If symptoms of high blood sugar occur, *check your blood sugar level and then call your doctor for instructions.*

Side Effects of This Medicine

Along with its needed effects, a medicine may cause some unwanted effects. Although not all of these side effects may occur, if they do occur they may need medical attention.

Check with your doctor immediately if any of the following side effects occur:

More common

Convulsions (seizures); unconsciousness

Check with your doctor as soon as possible if any of the following side effects occur:

More common

Cough; fever; low blood sugar, including anxious feeling, behavior change similar to being drunk, blurred vision, cold sweats, confusion, cool pale skin, difficulty in thinking, drowsiness, excessive hunger, fast heartbeat, headache, nausea, nervousness, nightmares, restless sleep, shakiness, slurred speech, or unusual tiredness or weakness; pain in the chest; runny or stuffy nose; shortness of breath; sinus congestion with pain; sneezing; sore throat

Less common

Bloody or cloudy urine; burning, painful, or difficult urination; chest pain; chills; frequent urge to urinate; problems with teeth; skin rash, itching, or hives; tearing of eyes; tightness in chest; trouble in breathing; vomiting; wheezing

Rare

Black, tarry stools; blood in stools; fast or irregular heartbeat; hoarseness; lower back or side pain; pinpoint red spots on skin; unusual bleeding or bruising

Other side effects may occur that usually do not need medical attention. These side effects may go away during treatment as your body adjusts to the medicine. However, check with your doctor if any of the following side effects continue or are bothersome:

More common
> Back pain; diarrhea; joint pain

Less common
> Constipation; feeling of burning, numbness, tightness, tingling, warmth, or heat; indigestion

Other side effects not listed above may also occur in some patients. If you notice any other effects, check with your doctor.

Developed: 07/30/98

RESPIRATORY SYNCYTIAL VIRUS IMMUNE GLOBULIN INTRAVENOUS
Systemic

Commonly used brand name(s):

In the U.S.—
> RespiGam

In Canada—
> RespiGam

Another commonly used name is RSV-IGIV.

Description

Respiratory syncytial virus immune globulin intravenous (res-pi-ra-TOR-e SIN-sish-al VI-ras im-MUNE GLOB-yoo-lin IN-tra-ve-nas) (RSV-IGIV) belongs to a group of medicines known as immunizing agents. RSV-IGIV is used to prevent infection caused by respiratory syncytial virus (RSV). RSV-IGIV works by giving your body the antibodies it needs to protect it against RSV infection.

RSV infection can cause serious problems, such as pneumonia and bronchitis, which affect the lungs; and in severe cases, even death. These problems are more likely to occur in infants and young children less than 6 months of age with chronic lung disease, those born with heart problems, and those with a history of premature birth.

Onset of RSV activity usually occurs in November and continues through April or early May, with peak activity occurring from late January through mid-February. A good way to help prevent RSV infection is to get RSV-IGIV before the start of the RSV season.

RSV-IGIV is used to prevent serious lower respiratory tract infection caused by the respiratory syncytial virus (RSV) in children less than 24 months of age with breathing problems or a history of premature birth.

RSV-IGIV is to be administered only by or under the supervision of your doctor or other health care professional. It is available in the following dosage form:

Parenteral
- Injection (U.S. and Canada)

Before Receiving This Medicine

In deciding to use a medicine, the risks of taking the medicine must be weighed against the good it will do. This is a decision you and your doctor will make. For respiratory syncytial virus immune globulin intravenous (RSV-IGIV), the following should be considered:

Allergies—Tell your doctor if you have ever had any unusual or allergic reaction to intramuscular or intravenous immune globulins. Also tell your health care professional if you are allergic to any other substances, such as foods, preservatives, or dyes.

Diet—Make certain your health care professional knows if you are on any special diet, such as low-sodium or low-sugar diet.

Pregnancy—Studies on effects in pregnancy have not been done in either humans or animals.

Breast-feeding—It is not known whether RSV-IGIV passes into breast milk. However, this medicine has not been reported to cause problems in nursing babies.

Children—Children 24 months of age and older: Use is not recommended. Use is not recommended in children born with chronic heart disease. Also, too much fluid in the body is more likely to occur in infants and children with underlying lung disease.

Older adults—RSV-IGIV has been tested only in infants and young children less than 24 months of age and there is no specific information about its use in older patients.

Other medicines—Although certain medicines should not be used together at all, in other cases two different medicines may be used together even if an interaction might occur. In these cases, your doctor may want to change the dose, or other precautions may be necessary. Tell your health care professional if you are using any other prescription or nonprescription (over-the-counter [OTC]) medicine.

Other medical problems—The presence of other medical problems may affect the use of RSV-IGIV. Make sure you tell your doctor if you have any other medical problems, especially:
- Allergic reaction to human immunoglobulins or
- Immunoglobulin A (IgA) deficiencies—RSV-IGIV may cause severe reactions

Proper Use of This Medicine

Dosing—The dose of respiratory syncytial virus immune globulin intravenous (RSV-IGIV) will be different for different patients. Doses are based on body weight. The following information includes only the average doses of RSV-IGIV.
- For *injection* dosage form:
  - For preventing respiratory syncytial virus (RSV) infection:
    - Adults and children 24 months of age and older—Use is not recommended.
    - Infants and children younger than 24 months of age—750 milligrams (mg) per kilogram (kg) (340.9 mg per pound) of body weight injected into a vein once a month for five months.

Side Effects of This Medicine

Along with its needed effects, a medicine may cause some unwanted effects. Although not all of these side effects may occur, if they do occur they may need medical attention.

Get emergency help immediately if any of the following side effects occur:

Rare
> Difficulty in breathing and swallowing; hives; itching, es-

pecially of feet and hands; reddening of skin, especially around ears; swelling of eyes, face, or inside of nose; unusual tiredness or weakness, sudden and severe; fever of 39.2 °C (102.6 °F) or higher; increased heart rate; vomiting

Other side effects not listed above may also occur in some patients. If you notice any other effects, check with your doctor.

Developed: 07/29/98

RH$_o$ (D) IMMUNE GLOBULIN
Systemic

Commonly used brand name(s):

In the U.S.—

Gamulin Rh	Mini-Gamulin Rh
HypRho-D Full Dose	RhoGAM
HypRho-D Mini-Dose	WinRho SDF
MICRhoGAM	

In Canada—
HypRho-D Full Dose
WinRho SD

Other commonly used names are anti-D gammaglobulin; anti-D (Rh$_o$) immunoglobulin; anti-Rh immunoglobulin; anti-Rh$_o$ (D); D(Rh$_o$) immune globulin; RhD immune globulin; Rh immune globulin; Rh-IG; and Rh$_o$ (D) immune human globulin.

Description

Rh$_o$ (D) immune globulin is used to prevent your body from interacting with any of your baby's blood that may get into your blood system while you are pregnant or during the delivery of your baby. If your blood type is Rh$_o$ (D) negative and your baby's blood type is Rh$_o$ (D) positive, your body may produce a defense (antibodies) against Rh$_o$ (D) positive blood. These antibodies usually will not cause a problem if this is your first pregnancy, unless you have had a blood transfusion in the past and have already developed these antibodies. However, if you have other Rh$_o$ (D) positive babies in the future, these antibodies may try to destroy the blood of the future babies. If this occurs, it is a very serious condition. Babies born with this condition may need to have their blood replaced.

Rh$_o$ (D) immune globulin can be used to treat immume thrombocytopenic purpura, a type of blood disorder. This medicine may be helpful to prevent excessive bleeding.

Rh$_o$ (D) immune globulin may also be used if you have recently received a transfusion that contained Rh$_o$ (D) positive blood and your blood type is Rh$_o$ (D) negative.

Rh$_o$ (D) immune globulin is to be administered only by or under the supervision of your doctor or other health care professional. It is available in the following dosage form:

Parenteral
• Injection (U.S. and Canada)

Before Using This Medicine

In deciding to use a medicine, the risks of using the medicine must be weighed against the good it will do. This is a decision you and your doctor will make. For Rh$_o$ (D) immune globulin, the following should be considered:

Allergies—Tell your doctor if you have ever had any unusual or allergic reaction to Rh$_o$ (D) immune globulin, any other kind of human immune globulin, or to thimerosal. Also tell your health care professional if you are allergic to any other substances, such as foods, preservatives, or dyes.

Pregnancy—Studies on effects in pregnancy have not been done in either humans or animals. However, this medicine has been used in pregnant women and has not been shown to cause birth defects or other problems.

Breast-feeding—Rh$_o$ (D) immune globulin has not been reported to cause problems in nursing babies.

Children—Studies on this medicine have been done only in adult patients and there is no specific information comparing use of Rh$_o$ (D) immune globulin in children with use in other age groups.

Other medical problems—The presence of other medical problems may affect the use of Rh$_o$ (D) immune globulin. Make sure you tell your doctor if you have any other medical problems, especially:

• Immunoglobulin A (IgA) deficiencies—Rh$_o$ (D) immune globulin may cause an allergic reaction to occur
• Rh$_o$ (D) positive patients with immune thrombocytopenic purpura, ITP (a type of blood disorder)—Should be monitored for anemia and kidney problems

Proper Use of This Medicine

Dosing—The dose of Rh$_o$ (D) immune globulin will be different for different patients. The following information includes only the average dose of Rh$_o$ (D) immune globulin.

• For *injection* dosage form:
—To prevent your body from producing antibodies against Rh$_o$ (D) positive blood:
• Adults and children—One or more injections, depending on how much Rh$_o$ (D) positive blood has gotten into your blood system. The medicine may be used during your pregnancy, within 72 hours after your baby is born, at the end of an incomplete pregnancy (abortion, miscarriage), or after a transfusion. The medicine is usually injected into a muscle, although it may be injected into a vein.
—To help prevent excessive bleeding in patients with immune thrombocytopenic purpura, ITP (a type of blood disorder):
• Adults and children—One or more injections, depending on factors in your blood. The medicine is injected into a vein.

Side Effects of This Medicine

Along with its needed effects, a medicine may cause some unwanted effects. Although not all of these side effects may occur, if they do occur they may need medical attention. Check with your doctor if any of the following side effects occur:

Rare
Bloody urine; decreased frequency of urination or amount of urine; increased blood pressure; increased thirst; loss of appetite; lower back pain; nausea or vomiting; pale skin; swelling of face, fingers, or lower legs; troubled breathing; unusual bleeding or bruising; unusual tiredness or weakness; weight gain

The following side effects may occur and usually do not need medical attention. However, check with your doctor if either of the following side effects continue or are bothersome:

Less common
Fever; soreness at the place of injection

Other side effects not listed above may also occur in some patients. If you notice any other effects, check with your doctor.

Developed: 08/31/94
Revised: 04/05/00

RIBAVIRIN   Systemic

Commonly used brand name(s):

In the U.S.—
Virazole

In Canada—
Virazole

Other—
Virazid

Another commonly used name is tribavirin.

Description

Ribavirin (rye-ba-VYE-rin) is used to treat severe virus pneumonia in infants and young children. It is given by oral inhalation (breathing in the medicine as a fine mist through the mouth), using a special nebulizer (sprayer) attached to an oxygen hood or tent or face mask.

This medicine may also be used for other virus infections as determined by your doctor. However, it will not work for certain viruses, such as the common cold.

Ribavirin is to be administered only by or under the immediate supervision of your doctor, in the following dosage form:

Inhalation
• For inhalation solution (U.S. and Canada)

Before Receiving This Medicine

In deciding to use a medicine, the risks of taking the medicine must be weighed against the good it will do. This is a decision you and your doctor will make. For ribavirin, the following should be considered:

Allergies—Tell your doctor if you or your child has ever had any unusual or allergic reaction to ribavirin for inhalation. Also tell your health care professional if you or your child is allergic to any other substances, such as foods, preservatives, or dyes.

Pregnancy—Ribavirin for inhalation is not usually prescribed for teenagers or adults. However, women who are pregnant or may become pregnant may be exposed to ribavirin that is given off in the air if they spend time at the patient's bedside while ribavirin is being given. Although studies have not been done in humans, ribavirin has been shown to cause birth defects and other problems in certain animal studies. Be sure you have discussed this with your doctor.

Breast-feeding—Ribavirin for inhalation is not usually prescribed for teenagers or adults. However, ribavirin passes into the breast milk of animals and has been shown to cause problems in nursing animals and their young.

Children—This medicine has been tested in children, and, when used as it should be and in effective doses, has not been shown to cause serious side effects or problems.

Older adults—Ribavirin for inhalation is not usually prescribed for use in elderly patients.

Proper Use of This Medicine

To help clear up your infection completely, *ribavirin must be given for the full time of treatment*, even if you or your child begins to feel better after a few days. Also, this medicine works best when there is a constant amount in the lungs. To help keep the amount constant, ribavirin must be given on a regular or continuous schedule.

Dosing—The dose of ribavirin will be different for different patients. *Follow your doctor's orders or the directions.* The following information includes only the average doses of ribavirin. *If your dose is different, do not change it* unless your doctor tells you to do so.

• For the *inhalation* dosage form:
 —For treatment of respiratory syncytial virus (RSV) infection:
  • Adults and teenagers—Dose has not been determined since this medicine is not usually prescribed for teenagers or adults.
  • Infants and children—Dose must be determined by the doctor.

Side Effects of This Medicine

Along with its needed effects, a medicine may cause some unwanted effects. The following side effects may go away during treatment as your body adjusts to the medicine. However, check with your doctor if any of the following side effects continue or are bothersome:

Rare
Headache; itching, redness, or swelling of eyes; skin rash or irritation

Other side effects not listed above may also occur in some patients. If you notice any other effects, check with your doctor.

Additional Information

Once a medicine has been approved for marketing for a certain use, experience may show that it is also useful for other medical problems. Although these uses are not included in product labeling, ribavirin is used in certain patients with the following medical conditions:

• Influenza A and B (given by aerosol inhalation)
• Lassa fever (either given orally or by injection)

For patients taking this medicine by mouth or injection for *Lassa fever:*

• *Check with your doctor immediately* if any of the following side effects occur:

More common
Unusual tiredness and weakness

• Other side effects may occur that usually do not need medical attention. The following side effects may go away during treatment as your body adjusts to the medicine. However, check with your doctor if any of the following side effects continue or are bothersome:

Less common
Headache; loss of appetite; nausea; trouble in sleeping; unusual tiredness or weakness

© 2002 **MICROMEDEX** Thomson Healthcare

Other than the above information, there is no additional information relating to proper use, precautions, or side effects for these uses.

Revised: 02/23/93
Interim revision: 06/08/94

RIBAVIRIN AND INTERFERON ALFA-2B, RECOMBINANT Systemic

Commonly used brand name(s):

In the U.S.—
Rebetron

In Canada—
Rebetron

Description

Ribavirin and interferon alfa-2b (rye-ba-VYE-rin and in-ter-FEER-on AL-fa) combination is used to treat a viral liver infection known as hepatitis C infection. Ribavirin is taken by mouth and interferon alfa-2b is administered beneath the skin (subcutaneously). Ribavirin is used to treat virus infections. Interferons are substances naturally produced by cells in the body to help fight infections and tumors. Interferon alfa-2b is a synthetic (man-made) version of these substances. Interferon alfa-2b is used to treat a variety of tumors and viruses including the hepatitis C virus.

Ribavirin is available for oral administration. Interferon alfa-2b is available only as an injectable form.

Before Using This Medicine

In deciding to use a medicine, the risks of taking the medicine must be weighed against the good it will do. This is a decision you and your doctor will make. For ribavirin and interferon alfa-2b combination, the following should be considered:

Allergies—Tell your doctor if you have ever had any unusual or allergic reaction to alpha interferons or ribavirin.

Pregnancy—Ribavirin should not be used while pregnant, if you plan on becoming pregnant, or by men whose female partners are pregnant.

Breast-feeding—It is not known whether ribavirin or interferon alfa-2b passes into breast milk. However, because these medicines may cause serious side effects, breast-feeding may not be recommended while you are receiving them. Discuss with your doctor whether or not you should breast-feed while you are receiving this combination medicine.

Children—Studies on this combination medicine have been done only in adult patients and there is no specific information comparing use of ribavirin and recombinant interferon alfa-2b combination in children younger than 18 years of age with use in other age group.

Older adults—Many medicines have not been studied specifically in older people. Therefore, it may not be known whether they work exactly the same way they do in younger adults or if they cause different side effects or problems in older people. There is no specific information comparing use of ribavirin and interferon alfa-2b combination medicine in the elderly with use in other age group.

Other medicines—Although certain medicines should not be used together at all, in other cases two different medicines may be used together even if an interaction might occur. In these cases, your doctor may want to change the dose, or other precautions may be necessary. Tell your health care professional if you are taking any other prescription or nonprescription (over-the-counter [OTC]) medicine.

Other medical problems—The presence of other medical problems may affect the use of ribavirin and interferon alfa-2b. Make sure you tell your doctor if you have any other medical problems, especially:

- Anemia, severe or
- Autoimmune hepatitis or
- Bleeding disorders—May worsen with ribavirin and /or recombinant interferon alfa-2b
- Diabetes (increased sugar in blood)—May increase the risk of developing eye problems
- Heart disease—May worsen with ribavirin and/or recombinant interferon alfa-2b
- Hepatitis B or human immunodeficiency virus infection or
- Hepatitis C which has worsened or
- Hepatitis C which did not get better when treated with interferon alone—Safety and effectiveness in these conditions are unknown.
- High blood pressure—May increase the risk of developing eye problems
- Kidney problems—May worsen with ribavirin and/or recombinant interferon alfa-2b
- Liver or other organ transplant—Safety and effectiveness in these conditions are unknown.
- Lung problems—May worsen with ribavirin and /or recombinant interferon alfa-2b
- Mental problems (or history of)—May result in depression, aggressive, violent and suicidal behavior
- Problem with immune system or
- Psoriasis (inflammatory skin problem) or
- Thyroid problem—May worsen with ribavirin and /or recombinant interferon alfa-2b
- Virus infections, other—Use of ribavirin alone is not recommended

Proper Use of This Medicine

If you are injecting interferon alfa-2b yourself, *use it exactly as directed by your doctor*. Do not use more or less of it, and do not use it more often than your doctor ordered. The exact amount of medicine you need has been carefully worked out. Using too much will increase the risk of side effects, while using too little may not improve your condition.

Interferon alfa-2b often cause unusual tiredness. This effect is less likely to cause problems if you inject this medicine at bedtime. Also, your doctor may want you to drink extra fluids, especially during the early phase of treatment.

Dosing—The dose of ribavirin and interferon alfa-2b will be different for different patients. The dose that is used may depend on a number of things, including the patient's size and laboratory test. *If you are receiving interferon alfa-2b at home, follow your doctor's orders or the directions* on the label. If you have any questions about the proper dose of interferons alfa-2b, ask your doctor.

Missed dose—If you miss a dose of ribavirin or interferon alfa-2b, do not inject the missed dose at all and do not double the next one. Check with your doctor for further instructions.

Storage—To store this medicine:
- Keep out of the reach of children.
- Store in the refrigerator.
- Keep the medicine from freezing.
- Do not keep outdated medicine or medicine no longer needed. Ask your health care professional how you should dispose of any medicine you do not use. Be sure that any discarded medicine is out of the reach of children.

Precautions While Using This Medicine

It is very important that your doctor check your progress at regular visits to make sure that this medicine is working properly and to check for unwanted effects.

This medicine may cause some people to become unusually tired or dizzy, or less alert than they are normally. *Make sure you know how you react to this medicine before you drive, use machines, or do anything else that could be dangerous if you are dizzy or if you are not alert.*

This medicine may make you feel very sad, depressed or very angry. *Call your doctor if you feel you cannot cope or you feel like you want to hurt yourself or someone else.*

Interferon alfa-2b commonly causes a flu-like reaction, with aching muscles, fever and chills, and headache. To prevent problems from your temperature going too high, your doctor may ask you to take medicine for pain and fever such as acetaminophen (e.g., Anacin 3, Tylenol) before each dose of interferon alfa-2b. You may also need to take it after a dose to bring your temperature down. *Follow your doctor's instructions carefully about taking your temperature, and how much and when to take the medicine such as acetaminophen.*

Women of childbearing potential should use two reliable forms of effective contraception.

Alpha interferon can lower the number of white blood cells in your blood temporarily, increasing the chance of getting an infection. It can also lower the number of platelets, which are necessary for proper blood clotting. If this occurs, there are certain precautions you can take, especially when your blood count is low, to reduce the risk of infection or bleeding:
- If you can, avoid being close to people with infections. *Check with your doctor immediately* if you think you are getting an infection or if you get a fever or chills, cough or hoarseness, lower back or side pain, or have painful or difficult urination.
- *Check with your doctor immediately* if you notice any unusual bleeding or bruising; black, tarry stools; blood in urine or stools; or pinpoint red spots on your skin.
- Be careful when using a regular toothbrush, dental floss, or toothpick. Your medical doctor, dentist, or nurse may recommend other ways to clean your teeth and gums. Check with your medical doctor before having any dental work done
- Do not touch your eyes or the inside of your nose unless you have just washed your hands and have not touched anything else in the meantime.

- Be careful not to cut yourself when you are using sharp objects such as a safety razor or fingernail or toenail cutters.
- Avoid contact sports or other situations where bruising or injury could occur.

Side Effects of This Medicine

Along with its needed effects, a medicine may cause some unwanted effects. Although not all of these side effects may occur, if they do occur they may need medical attention.

Check with your doctor as soon as possible if any of the following side effects occur:
More common
　　Chest pain; mood changes; trouble breathing; unusual tiredness or weakness
Rare
　　Thoughts of suicide, attempts at suicide, changes in behavior

Other side effects may occur that usually do not need medical attention. These side effects may go away during treatment as your body adjusts to the medicine. However, check with your doctor if any of the following side effects continue or are bothersome:
More common
　　Dizziness; fatigue; fever; headache; impaired concentration; impaired taste; influenza-like symptoms such as unusual tiredness or weakness; irritability; red itchy skin; large swing in moods; loss of appetite; muscle or joint pain; nausea, vomiting, or upset stomach; nervousness; Redness and warm feeling at the site of injection; shaking; temporary thinning of hair; stuffy nose; trouble sleeping

Other side effects not listed above may also occur in some patients. If you notice any other effects, check with your doctor.

Developed: 10/5/99

RIBOFLAVIN (VITAMIN B₂)
Systemic

Description

Vitamins (VYE-ta-mins) are compounds that you *must* have for growth and health. They are needed in small amounts only and are usually available in the foods that you eat. Riboflavin (RYE-boe-flay-vin) (vitamin B₂) is needed to help break down carbohydrates, proteins, and fats. It also makes it possible for oxygen to be used by your body.

Lack of riboflavin may lead to itching and burning eyes, sensitivity of eyes to light, sore tongue, itching and peeling skin on the nose and scrotum, and sores in the mouth. Your doctor may treat this condition by prescribing riboflavin for you.

Some conditions may increase your need for riboflavin. These include:
- Alcoholism
- Burns

- Cancer
- Diarrhea (continuing)
- Fever (continuing)
- Illness (continuing)
- Infection
- Intestinal diseases
- Liver disease
- Overactive thyroid
- Serious injury
- Stress (continuing)
- Surgical removal of stomach

In addition, riboflavin may be given to infants with high blood levels of bilirubin (hyperbilirubinemia).

Increased need for riboflavin should be determined by your health care professional.

Claims that riboflavin is effective for treatment of acne, some kinds of anemia (weak blood), migraine headaches, and muscle cramps have not been proven.

Oral forms of riboflavin are available without a prescription. If you take more than you need, it will simply be lost from your body.

Riboflavin is available in the following dosage form:

Oral
- Tablets (U.S. and Canada)

Importance of Diet

For good health, it is important that you eat a balanced and varied diet. Follow carefully any diet program your health care professional may recommend. For your specific dietary vitamin and/or mineral needs, ask your health care professional for a list of appropriate foods. If you think that you are not getting enough vitamins and/or minerals in your diet, you may choose to take a dietary supplement.

Riboflavin is found in various foods, including milk and dairy products, fish, meats, green leafy vegetables, and whole grain and enriched cereals and bread. It is best to eat fresh fruits and vegetables whenever possible since they contain the most vitamins. Food processing may destroy some of the vitamins, although little riboflavin is lost from foods during ordinary cooking.

Vitamins alone will not take the place of a good diet and will not provide energy. Your body also needs other substances found in food such as protein, minerals, carbohydrates, and fat. Vitamins themselves often cannot work without the presence of other foods.

The daily amount of riboflavin needed is defined in several different ways.

For U.S.—
- Recommended Dietary Allowances (RDAs) are the amount of vitamins and minerals needed to provide for adequate nutrition in most healthy persons. RDAs for a given nutrient may vary depending on a person's age, sex, and physical condition (e.g., pregnancy).
- Daily Values (DVs) are used on food and dietary supplement labels to indicate the percent of the recommended daily amount of each nutrient that a serving provides. DV replaces the previous designation of United States Recommended Daily Allowances (USRDAs).

For Canada—
- Recommended Nutrient Intakes (RNIs) are used to determine the amounts of vitamins, minerals, and

protein needed to provide adequate nutrition and lessen the risk of chronic disease.

Normal daily recommended intakes for riboflavin are generally defined as follows:

Persons	U.S. (mg)	Canada (mg)
Infants and children		
Birth to 3 years of age	0.4–0.8	0.3–0.7
4 to 6 years of age	1.1	0.9
7 to 10 years of age	1.2	1–1.3
Adolescent and adult males	1.4–1.8	1–1.6
Adolescent and adult females	1.2–1.3	1–1.1
Pregnant females	1.6	1.1–1.4
Breast-feeding females	1.7–1.8	1.4–1.5

Before Using This Dietary Supplement

If you are taking this dietary supplement without a prescription, carefully read and follow any precautions on the label. For riboflavin, the following should be considered:

Allergies—Tell your health care professional if you are allergic to any substances, such as foods, preservatives, or dyes.

Pregnancy—It is especially important that you are receiving enough vitamins when you become pregnant and that you continue to receive the right amounts of vitamins throughout your pregnancy. The healthy growth and development of the fetus depend on a steady supply of nutrients from the mother. However, taking large amounts of a dietary supplement in pregnancy may be harmful to the mother and/or fetus and should be avoided.

Breast-feeding—It is especially important that you receive the right amounts of vitamins so that your baby will also get the vitamins needed to grow properly. However, taking large amounts of a dietary supplement while breast-feeding may be harmful to the mother and/or baby and should be avoided.

Children—Problems in children have not been reported with intake of normal daily recommended amounts.

Older adults—Problems in older adults have not been reported with intake of normal daily recommended amounts.

Other medicines or dietary supplements—Although certain medicines or dietary supplements should not be used together at all, in other cases two different medicines or dietary supplements may be used together even if an interaction might occur. In these cases, your health care professional may want to change the dose, or other precautions may be necessary. Tell your health care professional if you are taking any other dietary supplements or prescription or nonprescription (over-the-counter [OTC]) medicine.

Proper Use of This Dietary Supplement

Dosing—The amount of riboflavin needed to meet normal daily recommended intakes will be different for different patients. The following information includes only the average amounts of riboflavin.

- For *oral* dosage form (tablets):
  —To prevent deficiency, the amount taken by mouth is based on normal daily recommended intakes:
  For the U.S.
  - Adults and teenage males—1.4 to 1.8 milligrams (mg) per day.

- Adults and teenage females—1.2 to 1.3 mg per day.
- Pregnant females—1.6 mg per day.
- Breast-feeding females—1.7 to 1.8 mg per day.
- Children 7 to 10 years of age—1.2 mg per day.
- Children 4 to 6 years of age—1.1 mg per day.
- Children birth to 3 years of age—0.4 to 0.8 mg per day.

For Canada
- Adults and teenage males—1 to 1.6 mg per day.
- Adults and teenage females—1 to 1.1 mg per day.
- Pregnant females—1.1 to 1.4 mg per day.
- Breast-feeding females—1.4 to 1.5 mg per day.
- Children 7 to 10 years of age—1 to 1.3 mg per day.
- Children 4 to 6 years of age—0.9 mg per day.
- Children birth to 3 years of age—0.3 to 0.7 mg per day.

—To treat deficiency:
  - Adults and teenagers—Treatment dose is determined by prescriber for each individual based on the severity of deficiency.

Missed dose—If you miss taking a vitamin for 1 or more days there is no cause for concern, since it takes some time for your body to become seriously low in vitamins. However, if your health care professional has recommended that you take this vitamin, try to remember to take it as directed every day.

Storage—To store this dietary supplement:
- Keep out of the reach of children.
- Store away from heat and direct light.
- Do not store in the bathroom, near the kitchen sink, or in other damp places. Heat or moisture may cause the dietary supplement to break down.
- Do not keep outdated dietary supplements or those no longer needed. Be sure that any discarded dietary supplement is out of the reach of children.

Side Effects of This Dietary Supplement

Along with its needed effects, a dietary supplement may cause some unwanted effects. Riboflavin may cause urine to have a more yellow color than normal, especially if large doses are taken. This is to be expected and is no cause for alarm. Usually, however, riboflavin does not cause any side effects. Check with your health care professional if you notice any other unusual effects while you are using it.

Revised: 05/01/95

RIFABUTIN Systemic

Commonly used brand name(s):

In the U.S.—
Mycobutin

In Canada—
Mycobutin

Description

Rifabutin (rif-a-BUE-tin) is used to help prevent *Mycobacterium avium* complex (MAC) disease from causing disease throughout the body in patients with advanced human immunodeficiency virus (HIV) infection. MAC is an infection caused by two similar bacteria, *Mycobacterium avium* and *Mycobacterium intracellulare*. *Mycobacterium avium* is more common in patients with HIV infection. MAC also may occur in other patients whose immune system is not working properly. Symptoms of MAC in people with acquired immunodeficiency syndrome (AIDS) include fever, night sweats, chills, weight loss, and weakness. Rifabutin will not work for colds, flu, or most other infections.

Rifabutin is available only with your doctor's prescription, in the following dosage form:

Oral
- Capsules (U.S. and Canada)

Before Using This Medicine

In deciding to use a medicine, the risks of taking the medicine must be weighed against the good it will do. This is a decision you and your doctor will make. For rifabutin, the following should be considered:

Allergies—Tell your doctor if you have ever had any unusual or allergic reaction to rifabutin or rifampin. Also tell your health care professional if you are allergic to any other substances, such as foods, preservatives, or dyes.

Pregnancy—Rifabutin has not been studied in pregnant women. However, studies in animals have shown that rifabutin causes birth defects. Before you take this medicine, make sure your doctor knows if you are pregnant or if you may become pregnant.

Breast-feeding—It is not known whether rifabutin passes into the breast milk. However, if your baby does not have the AIDS virus, there is a chance that you could pass the virus to your baby by breast-feeding. Talk to your doctor first if you are thinking about breast-feeding your baby.

Children—Studies on this medicine have only been done in adult patients, and there is no specific information comparing use of rifabutin in children with use in other age groups. However, studies are being done to determine the best dose for children.

Older adults—Many medicines have not been studied specifically in older people. Therefore, it may not be known whether they work exactly the same way they do in younger adults. Although there is no specific information comparing use of rifabutin in the elderly with use in other age groups, this medicine is not expected to cause different side effects or problems in older people than it does in younger adults.

Other medicines—Although certain medicines should not be used together at all, in other cases two different medicines may be used together even if an interaction might occur. In these cases, your doctor may want to change the dose, or other precautions may be necessary. When you are taking rifabutin, it is especially important that your health care professional know if you are taking any of the following:
- Amprenavir (e.g. Agenerase) or
- Delavirdine (e.g., Rescriptor) or
- Efavirenz (e.g., Sustiva) or
- Indinavir (e.g., Crixivan) or
- Nelfinavir (e.g., Viracept) or

- Nevirapine (e.g., Viramune) or
- Ritonavir (e.g., Norvir) or
- Saquinavir (e.g., Fortovase, Invirase) or
- Zidovudine (e.g., AZT, Retrovir)—Use of rifabutin with these medicines may lower the amount of these medicines in the blood

- Oral contraceptives (birth control pills) containing estrogen—Use of rifabutin with these birth control pills may increase the chance of pregnancy occurring

Other medical problems—The presence of other medical problems may affect the use of rifabutin. Make sure you tell your doctor if you have any other medical problems.

Proper Use of This Medicine

Rifabutin may be taken on an empty stomach (either 1 hour before or 2 hours after a meal). However, if this medicine upsets your stomach, you may want to take it with food.

For *patients unable to swallow capsules:*

- The contents of the capsules may be mixed with applesauce. Be sure to take all the food to get the full dose of medicine.

To help prevent MAC disease, *it is very important that you keep taking this medicine for the full time of treatment.* You may have to take it every day for many months. *It is important that you do not miss any doses.*

Dosing—The dose of rifabutin may be different for different patients. *Follow your doctor's orders or the directions on the label.* The following information includes only the average doses of rifabutin. *If your dose is different, do not change it* unless your doctor tells you to do so.

- For *oral* dosage forms (capsules):
  - —For the prevention of *Mycobacterium avium* complex (MAC):
    - Adults and teenagers—300 milligrams (mg) once a day, or 150 mg two times a day.
    - Children—Use and dose must be determined by your doctor.

Missed dose—If you miss a dose of this medicine, take it as soon as possible. However, if it is almost time for your next dose, skip the missed dose and go back to your regular dosing schedule. Do not double doses. *If this medicine is taken on an irregular schedule, side effects may occur more often and may be more serious than usual.* If you have any questions about this, check with your health care professional.

Storage—To store this medicine:

- Keep out of the reach of children.
- Store away from heat and direct light.
- Do not store in the bathroom, near the kitchen sink, or in other damp places. Heat or moisture may cause the medicine to break down.
- Do not keep outdated medicine or medicine no longer needed. Be sure that any discarded medicine is out of the reach of children.

Precautions While Using This Medicine

It is very important that your doctor check your progress at regular visits.

Rifabutin will cause your urine, stool, saliva, skin, sputum, sweat, and tears to turn reddish-orange to reddish-brown.

This is to be expected while you are taking this medicine. This effect may cause soft contact lenses to become permanently discolored. Standard cleaning solutions may not take out all the discoloration. Therefore, *it is best not to wear soft contact lenses while taking this medicine*. Hard contact lenses are not discolored by rifabutin. If you have any questions about this, check with your doctor.

Be careful when using a regular toothbrush, dental floss, or toothpick. Your medical doctor, dentist, or nurse may recommend other ways to clean your teeth and gums. Check with your medical doctor before having any dental work done.

Side Effects of This Medicine

Along with its needed effects, a medicine may cause some unwanted effects. Although not all of these side effects may occur, if they do occur they may need medical attention.

Check with your doctor immediately if any of the following side effects occur:
More common
Diarrhea; fever; heartburn; indigestion; loss of appetite; nausea; skin itching and/or rash; sore throat; sour stomach; vomiting

Less common
Loss of strength or energy

Rare
Bruising or purple spots on skin; change in taste; eye pain; joint pain; loss of vision; muscle pain; yellow skin

Other side effects may occur that usually do not need medical attention. These side effects may go away during treatment as your body adjusts to the medicine. However, check with your doctor if any of the following side effects continue or are bothersome:
More common
Headche; trouble in sleeping

This medicine commonly causes reddish-orange to reddish-brown discoloration of urine, stools, saliva, skin, sputum, sweat, and tears. This side effect usually does not need medical attention. However, tears that have been discolored by this medicine may also discolor soft contact lenses (see *Precautions While Using This Medicine*).

Other side effects not listed above may also occur in some patients. If you notice any other effects, check with your doctor.

Additional Information

Once a medicine has been approved for marketing for a certain use, experience may show that it is also useful for other medical problems. Although these uses are not included in product labeling, rifabutin is used in certain patients with the following medical condition:

- Treatment of tuberculosis in patients with human immunodeficiency virus (HIV) infection

Other than the above information, there is no additional information relating proper use, precautions, or side effects of this use.

Revised: 06/02/99

RIFAMPIN Systemic

Commonly used brand name(s):

In the U.S.—
 Rifadin
 Rifadin IV
 Rimactane

In Canada—
 Rifadin
 Rimactane
 Rofact

Generic name product may also be available inthe U.S.

Another commonly used name is rifampicin.

Description

Rifampin (rif-AM-pin) is used to treat certain bacterial infections.

Rifampin is used with other medicines to treat tuberculosis (TB). Rifampin is also taken by itself by patients who may carry meningitis bacteria in their nose and throat (without feeling sick) and may spread these bacteria to others. This medicine may also be used for other problems as determined by your doctor. However, rifampin will not work for colds, flu, or other virus infections.

To help clear up your tuberculosis (TB) completely, you must keep taking this medicine for the full time of treatment, even if you begin to feel better. This is very important. It is also important that you do not miss any doses.

Rifampin is available only with your doctor's prescription, in the following dosage forms:

 Oral
 • Capsules (U.S. and Canada)
 • Suspension (U.S. and Canada)
 Parenteral
 • Injection (U.S.)

Before Using This Medicine

In deciding to use a medicine, the risks of taking the medicine must be weighed against the good it will do. This is a decision you and your doctor will make. For rifampin, the following should be considered:

Allergies—Tell your doctor if you have ever had any unusual or allergic reaction to rifampin. Also tell your health care professional if you are allergic to any other substances, such as foods, preservatives, or dyes.

Pregnancy—Pregnant women with tuberculosis (TB) should be treated with TB medicines, including rifampin. Rifampin can rarely cause bleeding in newborn babies and mothers when taken during the last weeks of pregnancy. Studies in rats and mice have shown that rifampin given in high doses causes birth defects, usually backbone problems (spina bifida) and cleft palate.

Breast-feeding—Rifampin passes into the breast milk. However, rifampin has not been reported to cause problems in nursing babies.

Children—This medicine has been tested in children and, in effective doses, has not been shown to cause different side effects or problems in children than it does in adults.

Older adults—Many medicines have not been studied specifically in older people. Therefore, it may not be known whether they work exactly the same way they do in younger

adults. Although there is no specific information comparing use of rifampin in the elderly with use in other age groups, this medicine is not expected to cause different side effects or problems in older people than it does in younger adults.

Other medicines—Although certain medicines should not be used together at all, in other cases two different medicines may be used together even if an interaction might occur. In these cases, your doctor may want to change the dose, or other precautions may be necessary. When you are taking rifampin, it is especially important that your health care professional know if you are taking any of the following:

 • Acetaminophen (e.g., Tylenol) (with long-term, high-dose use) or
 • Amiodarone (e.g., Cordarone) or
 • Anabolic steroids (nandrolone [e.g., Anabolin], oxandrolone [e.g., Anavar], oxymetholone [e.g., Anadrol], stanozolol [e.g., Winstrol]) or
 • Androgens (male hormones) or
 • Antithyroid agents (medicine for overactive thyroid) or
 • Carbamazepine (e.g., Tegretol) or
 • Carmustine (e.g., BiCNU) or
 • Chloroquine (e.g., Aralen) or
 • Dantrolene (e.g., Dantrium) or
 • Daunorubicin (e.g., Cerubidine) or
 • Disulfiram (e.g., Antabuse) or
 • Divalproex (e.g., Depakote) or
 • Etretinate (e.g., Tegison) or
 • Gold salts (medicine for arthritis) or
 • Hydroxychloroquine (e.g., Plaquenil) or
 • Isoniazid (e.g., INH, Nydrazid) or
 • Mercaptopurine (e.g., Purinethol) or
 • Methotrexate (e.g., Mexate) or
 • Methyldopa (e.g., Aldomet) or
 • Naltrexone (e.g., Trexan) (with long-term, high-dose use) or
 • Phenothiazines (acetophenazine [e.g., Tindal], chlorpromazine [e.g., Thorazine], fluphenazine [e.g., Prolixin], mesoridazine [e.g., Serentil], perphenazine [e.g., Trilafon], prochlorperazine [e.g., Compazine], promazine [e.g., Sparine], promethazine [e.g., Phenergan], thioridazine [e.g., Mellaril], trifluoperazine [e.g., Stelazine], triflupromazine [e.g., Vesprin], trimeprazine [e.g., Temaril]) or
 • Plicamycin (e.g., Mithracin) or
 • Valproic acid (e.g., Depakene)—These medicines may increase the chance of liver damage if taken with rifampin

 • Anticoagulants (blood thinners) or
 • Aminophylline (e.g., Somophyllin) or
 • Amprenavir (e.g. Agenerase) or
 • Antidiabetics, oral (diabetes medicine you take by mouth), or
 • Chloramphenicol or
 • Corticosteroids (cortisone-like medicine) or
 • Delavirdine (e.g., Rescriptor) or
 • Digitalis glycosides (heart medicine) or
 • Disopyramide (e.g., Norpace) or
 • Efavirenz (e.g., Sustiva) or
 • Fluconazole (e.g., Diflucan) or
 • Indinavir (e.g., Crixivan) or
 • Itraconazole (e.g., Sporanox) or
 • Ketoconazole (e.g., Nizoral) or
 • Methadone (e.g., Dolophine) or
 • Mexiletine (e.g., Mexitil) or
 • Nelfinavir (e.g., Viracept) or

- Nevirapine (e.g., Viramune) or
- Oxtriphylline (e.g., Choledyl) or
- Quinidine (e.g., Quinidex) or
- Ritonavir (e.g., Norvir) or
- Saquinavir (e.g., Fortovase, Invirase) or
- Theophylline (e.g., Theo-Dur, Somophyllin-T) or
- Tocainide (e.g., Tonocard) or
- Verapamil (e.g., Calan)—Rifampin may decrease the effects of these medicines

- Estramustine (e.g., EMCYT) or
- Estrogens (female hormones) or
- Oral contraceptives (birth control pills) containing estrogen or
- Phenytoin (e.g., Dilantin)—Rifampin may decrease the effects of these medicines. If you are taking oral contraceptives, this may increase the chance of pregnancy. These medicines may also increase the chance of liver damage if taken with rifampin

Other medical problems—The presence of other medical problems may affect the use of rifampin. Make sure you tell your doctor if you have any other medical problems, especially:

- Alcohol abuse (or history of) or
- Liver disease—There may be an increased chance of side effects affecting the liver in patients with a history of alcohol abuse or liver disease

Proper Use of This Medicine

Rifampin is best taken with a full glass (8 ounces) of water on an empty stomach (either 1 hour before or 2 hours after a meal). However, if this medicine upsets your stomach, your doctor may want you to take it with food.

For *patients unable to swallow capsules:*

- Contents of the capsules may be mixed with applesauce or jelly. Be sure to take all the food to get the full dose of medicine.
- Your pharmacist can prepare an oral liquid form of this medicine if needed. The liquid form may be kept at room temperature or in the refrigerator. Follow the directions on the label. Shake the bottle well before using. Do not use after the expiration date on the label. The medicine may not work properly after that date. In addition, use a specially marked measuring spoon or other device to measure each dose accurately. The average household teaspoon may not hold the right amount of liquid.

To help clear up your tuberculosis (TB) infection completely, it is very important that you keep taking this medicine for the full time of treatment, even if you begin to feel better after a few weeks. You may have to take it every day for as long as 1 to 2 years or more. *It is important that you do not miss any doses.*

Dosing—The dose of rifampin will be different for different patients. *Follow your doctor's orders or the directions on the label.* The following information includes only the average doses of rifampin. *If your dose is different, do not change it* unless your doctor tells you to do so.

The number of capsules that you take depends on the strength of the medicine. Also, *the number of doses you take each day, the time allowed between doses, and the length of time you take the medicine depend on the medical problem for which you are taking rifampin.*

- For *oral* dosage form (capsules) and *injection* dosage form:
  —For the treatment of tuberculosis (TB):
  - Adults and older children—600 milligrams (mg) once a day. Your doctor may instruct you to take 600 mg two times a week or three times a week. Rifampin must be taken with other medicines to treat tuberculosis.
  - Infants and children—Dose is based on body weight and will be determined by your doctor. Rifampin is usually taken once a day. Your doctor may instruct you to take rifampin two times a week or three times a week. Rifampin must be taken with other medicines to treat tuberculosis.
  —For the treatment of patients in contact with the meningitis bacteria:
  - Adults and older children—600 mg once a day for four days.
  - Infants and children—Dose is based on body weight and will be determined by your doctor.

Missed dose—If you miss a dose of this medicine, take it as soon as possible. However, if it is almost time for your next dose, skip the missed dose and go back to your regular dosing schedule. Do not double doses. *If this medicine is taken on an irregular schedule, side effects may occur more often and may be more serious than usual.* If you have any questions about this, check with your health care professional.

Storage—To store the capsule form of this medicine:
- Keep out of the reach of children.
- Store away from heat and direct light.
- Do not store in the bathroom, near the kitchen sink, or in other damp places. Heat or moisture may cause the medicine to break down.
- Do not keep outdated medicine or medicine no longer needed. Be sure that any discarded medicine is out of the reach of children.

Precautions While Using This Medicine

It is very important that your doctor check your progress at regular visits.

If your symptoms do not improve within 2 to 3 weeks, or if they become worse, check with your doctor.

Oral contraceptives (birth control pills) containing estrogen may not work properly if you take them while you are taking rifampin. Unplanned pregnancies may occur. You should use a different means of birth control while you are taking rifampin. If you have any questions about this, check with your health care professional.

Liver problems may be more likely to occur if you drink alcoholic beverages regularly while you are taking this medicine. Also, the regular use of alcohol may keep this medicine from working properly. Therefore, *you should not drink alcoholic beverages while you are taking this medicine.*

If this medicine causes you to feel very tired or very weak or causes a loss of appetite, nausea, or vomiting, stop taking it and check with your doctor immediately. These may be early warning signs of more serious problems that could develop later.

Rifampin will cause the urine, stool, saliva, sputum, sweat, and tears to turn reddish-orange to reddish-brown. This is to be expected while you are taking this medicine. This effect may cause soft contact lenses to become permanently discolored. Standard cleaning solutions may not take out all the discoloration. Therefore, *it is best not to wear soft contact lenses while taking this medicine.* This condition will return to normal once you stop taking this medicine. Hard contact lenses are not discolored by rifampin. If you have any questions about this, check with your doctor.

Rifampin can lower the number of white blood cells in your blood temporarily, increasing the chance of getting an infection. It can also lower the number of platelets, which are necessary for proper blood clotting. These problems may result in a greater chance of getting certain infections, slow healing, and bleeding of the gums. Be careful when using a regular toothbrush, dental floss, or a toothpick. Dental work should be delayed until your blood counts have returned to normal. Check with your medical doctor or dentist if you have any questions about proper oral hygiene (mouth care) during treatment.

Before you have any medical tests, tell the doctor in charge that you are taking this medicine. The results of some tests may be affected by this medicine.

Side Effects of This Medicine

Along with its needed effects, a medicine may cause some unwanted effects. Although not all of these side effects may occur, if they do occur they may need medical attention.

Check with your doctor immediately if any of the following side effects occur:

Less common
    Chills; difficult breathing; dizziness; fever; headache; itching; muscle and bone pain; shivering; skin rash and redness

Rare
    Bloody or cloudy urine; greatly decreased frequency of urination or amount of urine; loss of appetite; nausea or vomiting; sore throat; unusual bleeding or bruising; unusual tiredness or weakness; yellow eyes or skin

Signs and symptoms of overdose
    Itching over the whole body; mental changes; reddish-orange color of skin, mouth, and eyeballs; swelling around the eyes or the whole face

Other side effects may occur that usually do not need medical attention. These side effects may go away during treatment as your body adjusts to the medicine. However, check with your doctor if any of the following side effects continue or are bothersome:

More common
    Diarrhea; stomach cramps

Less common
    Sores on mouth or tongue

This medicine commonly causes reddish-orange to reddish-brown discoloration of urine, stool, saliva, sputum, sweat, and tears. This side effect does not usually need medical attention.

Other side effects not listed above may also occur in some patients. If you notice any other effects, check with your doctor.

Additional Information

Once a medicine has been approved for marketing for a certain use, experience may show that it is also useful for other medical problems. Although these uses are not included in product labeling, rifampin is used in certain patients with the following medical conditions:

- Atypical mycobacterial infections, such as *Mycobacterium avium* complex (MAC)
- Leprosy (Hansen's disease)
- Prevention of *Haemophilus influenzae* infection
- Treatment of serious staphylococcal (bacterial) infections

Other than the above information, there is no additional information relating to proper use, precautions, or side effects for these uses.

Developed: 08/12/1998
Revised: 09/13/2000

RIFAMPIN AND ISONIAZID
Systemic†

Commonly used brand name(s):
In the U.S.—
    Rifamate
Another commonly used name is rifampicin and isoniazid.

†Not commercially available in Canada.

Description

Rifampin and isoniazid (rif-AM-pin and eye-soe-NYE-a-zid) is a combination antibiotic and anti-infective medicine. This combination medication is used to treat tuberculosis (TB). It may be taken alone or with one or more other medicines for TB.

To help clear up your tuberculosis (TB) infection completely, you must keep taking this medicine for the full time of treatment, even if you begin to feel better. This is very important. It is also important that you do not miss any doses.

Rifampin and isoniazid combination is available only with your doctor's prescription, in the following dosage form:

Oral
    • Capsules (U.S.)

Before Using This Medicine

In deciding to use a medicine, the risks of taking the medicine must be weighed against the good it will do. This is a decision you and your doctor will make. For rifampin and isoniazid combination, the following should be considered:

Allergies—Tell your doctor if you have ever had any unusual or allergic reaction to ethionamide (e.g., Trecator-SC), pyrazinamide, niacin (e.g., Nicobid, nicotinic acid), rifampin (e.g., Rifadin), rifabutin (e.g., Mycobutin), or isoniazid (e.g., INH, Nydrazid). Also tell your health care professional if you are allergic to any other substances, such as foods, preservatives, or dyes.

Pregnancy—Pregnant women with tuberculosis (TB) should be treated with TB medicines, including isoniazid and rifampin. Rifampin and isoniazid combination has not been shown to cause birth defects or other problems in humans. However, rifampin rarely caused bleeding in newborn babies and mothers when it was taken during the last weeks of pregnancy. Also, studies in rats and mice have shown that rifampin given in high doses causes birth defects, usually backbone problems (spina bifida) and cleft palate.

Breast-feeding—Rifampin and isoniazid both pass into the breast milk. However, rifampin and isoniazid have not been reported to cause problems in nursing babies.

Children—Rifampin and isoniazid combination is not recommended for use in children.

Older adults—Liver problems are more likely to occur in patients over 50 years of age who are taking isoniazid-containing medicines.

Other medicines—Although certain medicines should not be used together at all, in other cases two different medicines may be used together even if an interaction might occur. In these cases, your doctor may want to change the dose, or other precautions may be necessary. When you are taking rifampin and isoniazid combination, it is especially important that your health care professional know if you are taking any of the following:

- Acetaminophen (e.g., Tylenol) (with long-term, high-dose use) or
- Alfentanil (e.g., Alfenta) or
- Amiodarone (e.g., Cordarone) or
- Anabolic steroids (nandrolone [e.g., Anabolin], oxandrolone [e.g., Anavar], oxymetholone [e.g., Anadrol], stanozolol [e.g., Winstrol]) or
- Androgens (male hormones) or
- Antithyroid agents (medicine for overactive thyroid) or
- Carbamazepine (e.g., Tegretol) or
- Carmustine (e.g., BiCNU) or
- Chloroquine (e.g., Aralen) or
- Dantrolene (e.g., Dantrium) or
- Daunorubicin (e.g., Cerubidine) or
- Disulfiram (e.g., Antabuse) or
- Divalproex (e.g., Depakote) or
- Etretinate (e.g., Tegison) or
- Gold salts (medicine for arthritis) or
- Hydroxychloroquine (e.g., Plaquenil) or
- Mercaptopurine (e.g., Purinethol) or
- Methyldopa (e.g., Aldomet) or
- Naltrexone (e.g., Trexan) (with long-term, high-dose use) or
- Phenothiazines (acetophenazine [e.g., Tindal], chlorpromazine [e.g., Thorazine], fluphenazine [e.g., Prolixin], mesoridazine [e.g., Serentil], perphenazine [e.g., Trilafon], prochlorperazine [e.g., Compazine], promazine [e.g., Sparine], promethazine [e.g., Phenergan], thioridazine [e.g., Mellaril], trifluoperazine [e.g., Stelazine], triflupromazine [e.g., Vesprin], trimeprazine [e.g., Temaril]) or
- Plicamycin (e.g., Mithracin) or
- Valproic acid (e.g., Depakene)—These medicines may increase the chance of liver damage if taken with rifampin and isoniazid combination

- Aminophylline (e.g., Somophyllin) or
- Anticoagulants (blood thinners) or
- Antidiabetics, oral (diabetes medicine you take by mouth) or
- Chloramphenicol or
- Corticosteroids (cortisone-like medicine) or
- Digitalis glycosides (heart medicine) or
- Disopyramide (e.g., Norpace) or
- Estramustine (e.g., EMCYT) or
- Fluconazole (e.g., Diflucan) or

- Human immunodeficiency virus (HIV) protease inhibitors (medicines for the treatment of HIV infection) or
- Itraconazole (e.g., Sporanox) or
- Ketoconazole (e.g., Nizoral) or
- Methadone (e.g., Dolophine) or
- Methotrexate (e.g., Mexate) or
- Mexiletine (e.g., Mexitil) or
- Oxtriphylline (e.g., Choledyl) or
- Quinidine (e.g., Quinidex) or
- Theophylline (e.g., Theo-Dur, Somophyllin-T) or
- Tocainide (e.g., Tonocard) or
- Verapamil (e.g., Calan)—Rifampin and isoniazid combination may decrease the effects of these medicines

- Disulfiram (e.g., Antabuse)—This medicine may increase the chance of liver damage and side effects, such as dizziness, lack of coordination, irritability, and inability to sleep

- Estrogens (female hormones) or
- Oral contraceptives (birth control pills) containing estrogen or
- Phenytoin (e.g., Dilantin)—Rifampin and isoniazid combination may decrease the effects of these medicines. If you are taking oral contraceptives, this may increase the chance of pregnancy. These medicines may also increase the chance of liver damage if taken with rifampin and isoniazid combination

Other medical problems—The presence of other medical problems may affect the use of rifampin and isoniazid combination. Make sure you tell your doctor if you have any other medical problems, especially:

- Alcohol abuse (or history of) or
- Liver disease—There may be an increased chance of getting hepatitis if you take this medicine and drink alcohol daily
- Convulsive disorders such as seizures or epilepsy—Rifampin and isoniazid combination may increase the frequency of seizures (convulsions) in some patients
- Kidney disease (severe)—There may be an increased chance of side effects in patients with severe kidney disease

---

Proper Use of This Medicine

If this medicine upsets your stomach, take it with food. Antacids may also help. However, do not take aluminum-containing antacids within 1 hour of the time you take rifampin and isoniazid combination. They may keep this medicine from working properly.

To help clear up your tuberculosis (TB) completely, it is very important that you keep taking this medicine for the full time of treatment, even if you begin to feel better after a few weeks. You may have to take it every day for as long as 1 to 2 years or more. *It is important that you do not miss any doses.*

Your doctor may also want you to take pyridoxine (e.g., HexaBetalin, vitamin B$_6$) every day to help prevent or lessen some of the side effects of isoniazid. If it is needed, *it is very important to take pyridoxine every day along with this medicine. Do not miss any doses.*

Dosing—The dose of rifampin and isoniazid combination will be different for different patients. *Follow your doctor's orders or the directions on the label.* The following information includes only the average doses of rifampin and isoniazid combination. *If your dose is different, do not change it* unless your doctor tells you to do so.

- For the *oral* dosage form (capsules):
  —For the treatment of tuberculosis:
  - Adults and older children—600 milligrams (mg) of rifampin and 300 mg of isoniazid once a day.
  - Children—This combination medicine is not recommended for use in children.

Missed dose—If you do miss a dose of this medicine, take it as soon as possible. However, if it is almost time for your next dose, skip the missed dose and go back to your regular dosing schedule. Do not double doses. *If rifampin and isoniazid combination is taken on an irregular schedule, side effects may occur more often and may be more serious than usual.* If you have any questions about this, check with your health care professional.

Storage—To store this medicine:

- Keep out of the reach of children.
- Store away from heat and direct light.
- Do not store in the bathroom, near the kitchen sink, or in other damp places. Heat or moisture may cause the medicine to break down.
- Do not keep outdated medicine or medicine no longer needed. Be sure that any discarded medicine is out of the reach of children.

Precautions While Using This Medicine

It is very important that your doctor check your progress at regular visits. In addition, you should check with your doctor immediately if blurred vision or loss of vision, with or without eye pain, occurs during treatment. He or she may want you to have your eyes checked by an ophthalmologist (eye doctor).

If your symptoms do not improve within 2 to 3 weeks, or if they become worse, check with your doctor.

Oral contraceptives (birth control pills) containing estrogen may not work properly if you take them while you are taking rifampin and isoniazid combination. Unplanned pregnancies may occur. You should use a different means of birth control while you are taking this medicine. If you have any questions about this, check with your health care professional.

Liver problems may be more likely to occur if you drink alcoholic beverages regularly while you are taking this medicine. Also, the regular use of alcohol may keep this medicine from working properly. Therefore, *you should strictly limit the amount of alcoholic beverages you drink while you are taking this medicine.*

Certain foods such as cheese (Swiss or Cheshire) or fish (tuna, skipjack, or Sardinella) may rarely cause reactions in some patients taking isoniazid-containing medicines. Check with your doctor if redness or itching of the skin, hot feeling, fast or pounding heartbeat, sweating, chills or clammy feeling, headache, or lightheadedness occurs after eating these foods while you are taking this medicine.

This medicine will cause the urine, stool, saliva, sputum, sweat, and tears to turn reddish-orange to reddish-brown. This is to be expected while you are taking this medicine. This effect may cause soft contact lenses to become permanently discolored. Standard cleaning solutions may not take out all the discoloration. Therefore, *it is best not to wear soft contact lenses while taking this medicine.* This condition will

return to normal once you stop taking this medicine. Hard contact lenses are not discolored by this medicine. If you have any questions about this, check with your doctor.

If this medicine causes you to feel very tired or very weak; or causes clumsiness; unsteadiness; a loss of appetite; nausea; numbness, tingling, burning, or pain in the hands and feet; or vomiting, stop taking it and check with your doctor immediately. These may be early warning symptoms of more serious liver or nerve problems that could develop later.

Rifampin and isoniazid combination may cause blood problems. These problems may result in a greater chance of certain infections, slow healing, and bleeding of the gums. Therefore, you should be careful when using regular toothbrushes, dental floss, and toothpicks. Dental work should be delayed until your blood counts have returned to normal. Check with your medical doctor or dentist if you have any questions about proper oral hygiene (mouth care) during treatment.

Side Effects of This Medicine

Along with its needed effects, a medicine may cause some unwanted effects. Although not all of these side effects may occur, if they do occur they may need medical attention.

Check with your doctor immediately if any of the following side effects occur:

More common
> Clumsiness or unsteadiness; dark urine; loss of appetite; nausea and vomiting; numbness, tingling, burning, or pain in hands and feet; unusual tiredness or weakness; yellow eyes or skin

Less common
> Chills; difficult breathing; dizziness; fever; headache; itching; muscle and bone pain; shivering; skin rash and redness

Rare
> Bloody or cloudy urine; blurred vision or loss of vision, with or without eye pain; convulsions (seizures); depression; greatly decreased frequency of urination or amount of urine; mood or mental changes; sore throat; unusual bleeding or bruising

Other side effects may occur that usually do not need medical attention. These side effects may go away during treatment as your body adjusts to the medicine. However, check with your doctor if any of the following side effects continue or are bothersome:

More common
> Diarrhea; stomach pain or upset

Less common
> Sore mouth or tongue

This medicine commonly causes reddish-orange to reddish-brown discoloration of urine, stool, saliva, sputum, sweat, and tears. This side effect does not usually require medical attention.

Dark urine and yellowing of the eyes or skin (signs of liver problems) are more likely to occur in patients 50 years of age and older.

Other side effects not listed above may also occur in some patients. If you notice any other effects, check with your doctor.

Revised: 08/15/97

RIFAPENTINE   Systemic†

Commonly used brand name(s):

In the U.S.—
   Priftin

†Not commercially available in Canada.

Description

Rifapentine (RIF-a-pen-teen) is used with other medicines to treat tuberculosis.

To help clear up your tuberculosis completely, you must keep taking this medicine for the full time of treatment, even if you begin to feel better. This is very important. It is also important that you do not miss any doses.

Rifapentine is available only with your doctor's prescription, in the following dosage form:

   Oral
   • Tablets (U.S.)

Before Using This Medicine

In deciding to use a medicine, the risks of taking the medicine must be weighed against the good it will do. This is a decision you and your doctor will make. For rifapentine, the following should be considered:

Allergies—Tell your doctor if you have ever had any unusual or allergic reaction to rifabutin (e.g., Mycobutin), rifampin (e.g., Rifadin), or rifapentine. Also tell your health care professional if you are allergic to any other substances, such as foods, preservatives, or dyes.

Pregnancy—Use of rifapentine during the last few weeks of pregnancy may rarely result in bleeding in the mother and newborn.

Breast-feeding—It is not known whether rifapentine passes into the breast milk.

Children—Safety and efficacy have not been established in infants and children younger than 12 years of age. For children 12 years of age and older, rifapentine is not expected to cause different side effects or problems than it does in adults.

Older adults—Rifapentine is not expected to cause different side effects or problems in older people than it does in younger adults.

Other medicines—Although certain medicines should not be used together at all, in other cases two different medicines may be used together even if an interaction might occur. In these cases, your doctor may want to change the dose, or other precautions may be necessary. When you are taking rifapentine, it is especially important that your health care professional know if you are taking any of the following:

   • Alcohol—Alcohol may increase the chance of liver damage if taken with rifapentine

   • Antidiabetic agents, oral (diabetes medicine you take by mouth) or
   • Chloramphenicol (e.g., Chloromycetin) or
   • Ciprofloxacin (e.g., Cipro) or
   • Clarithromycin (e.g., Biaxin) or
   • Corticosteroids (cortisone-like medicine) or
   • Delavirdine (e.g., Rescriptor) or

   • Digitalis glycosides (heart medicine) or
   • Diltiazem (e.g., Cardizem) or
   • Disopyramide (e.g., Norpace) or
   • Doxycycline (e.g., Vibramycin) or
   • Estrogen-containing oral contraceptives (birth control pills) or
   • Fluconazole (e.g., Diflucan) or
   • Human immunodeficiency virus (HIV) protease inhibitors (medicines for the treatment of HIV infection) or
   • Itraconazole (e.g., Sporanox) or
   • Ketoconazole (e.g., Nizoral) or
   • Methadone (e.g., Dolophine) or
   • Mexiletine (e.g., Mexitil) or
   • Nifedipine (e.g., Procardia) or
   • Phenytoin (e.g., Dilantin) or
   • Quinidine (e.g., Quinidex) or
   • Theophylline (e.g., Theo-dur) or
   • Tocainide (e.g., Tonocard) or
   • Verapamil (e.g., Calan) or
   • Warfarin (e.g., Coumadin) or
   • Zidovudine (e.g., AZT, Retrovir)—Rifapentine may decrease the effects of these medicines. If you are taking oral contraceptives, this may increase the chance of pregnancy.

Other medical problems—The presence of other medical problems may affect the use of rifapentine. Make sure you tell your doctor if you have any other medical problems, especially:

   • Alcohol abuse (or history of) or
   • Liver disease—There may be an increased chance of side effects affecting the liver in patients with a history of alcohol abuse or liver disease

Proper Use of This Medicine

The treatment of tuberculosis may take months or years to complete. *It is very important that you comply with the full course of therapy.*

Dosing—The dose of rifapentine will be different for different patients. *Follow your doctor's orders or the directions on the label.* The following information includes only the average doses of rifapentine. *If your dose is different, do not change it* unless your doctor tells you to do so.

   • For *oral* dosage form (tablets):
      —For the treatment of tuberculosis (TB):
         • Adults and children 12 years of age and older—600 milligrams (mg) twice a week with an interval of not less than three days (seventy-two hours) between doses. Rifapentine must be taken with other medicines to treat tuberculosis.
         • Infants and children up to 12 years of age—Use and dose must be determined by your doctor.

Missed dose—If you do miss a dose of this medicine, take it as soon as possible. However, if it is almost time for your next dose, skip the missed dose and go back to your regular dosing schedule. Do not double doses. *If this medicine is taken on an irregular schedule, side effects may occur more often and may be more serious than usual.* If you have any questions about this, check with your health care professional.

Storage—To store this medicine:
   • Keep out of the reach of children.
   • Store away from heat and direct light.

- Do not store in the bathroom, near the kitchen sink, or in other damp places. Heat or moisture may cause the medicine to break down.
- Do not keep outdated medicine or medicine no longer needed. Be sure that any discarded medicine is out of the reach of children.

Precautions While Using This Medicine

It is very important that your doctor check your progress at regular visits.

If your symptoms do not improve within 2 to 3 weeks, or if they become worse, check with your doctor.

If this medicine causes you to feel very tired or very weak or causes a loss of appetite, nausea, or vomiting, stop taking it and check with your doctor immediately. These may be early warning signs of more serious problems that could develop later.

Oral contraceptives (birth control pills) may not work properly if you take them while you are taking rifapentine. Unplanned pregnancies may occur. You should use a different means of birth control while you are taking rifapentine. If you have any questions about this, check with your health care professional.

Liver problems may be more likely to occur if you drink alcoholic beverages regularly while you are taking this medicine. Also, the regular use of alcohol may keep this medicine from working properly. Therefore, *you should not drink alcoholic beverages while you are taking this medicine.*

Rifapentine will cause the urine, stools, saliva, sputum, sweat, and tears to turn reddish-orange to reddish-brown. This is to be expected while you are taking this medicine. This effect may cause soft contact lenses to become permanently discolored. Standard cleaning solutions may not take out all the discoloration. Therefore, *it is best not to wear soft contact lenses while taking this medicine.* Hard contact lenses are not discolored by rifapentine. If you have any question about this, check with your doctor.

Rifapentine can lower the number of white blood cells in your blood temporarily, increasing the chance of getting infection. It can also lower the number of platelets, which are necessary for proper blood clotting. These problems may result in a greater chance of getting certain infections, slow healing, and bleeding of the gums. Be careful when using a regular toothbrush, dental floss, or a toothpick. Dental work should be delayed until your blood counts have returned to normal. Check with your medical doctor or dentist if you have any questions about proper oral hygiene (mouth care) during treatment.

Before you have any medical tests, tell the doctor in charge that you are taking this medicine.

Side Effects of This Medicine

Along with its needed effects, a medicine may cause some unwanted effects. Although not all of these side effects may occur, if they do occur they may need medical attention.

Check with your doctor as soon as possible if any of the following side effects occur:
More common
Blood in urine; joint pain; lower back or side pain; swelling of feet or lower legs
Less common
Aggressive reaction; black, tarry stools; blood in stools; nausea; pinpoint red spots on skin; severe abdominal or stomach pain; sore throat and fever; unusual bleeding or bruising; unusual tiredness or weakness; yellow eyes or skin; vomiting
Rare
Diarrhea; dizziness; severe or continuing headaches; increase in blood pressure

Other side effects may occur that usually do not need medical attention. These side effects may go away during treatment as your body adjusts to the medicine. However, check with your doctor if any of the following side effects continue or are bothersome:
Less common
Acne; constipation; loss of appetite

This medicine commonly causes reddish-orange to reddish-brown discoloration of urine, stools, saliva, sputum, sweat, and tears. This side effect does not usually need medical attention.

Other side effects not listed above may also occur in some patients. If you notice any other effects, check with your doctor.

Developed: 01/08/99

RILUZOLE Systemic†

Commonly used brand name(s):

In the U.S.—
Rilutek

†Not commercially available in Canada.

Description

Riluzole (RIL-yoo-zole) is used to treat patients with amyotrophic lateral sclerosis (ALS), also known as Lou Gehrig's disease. Riluzole is not a cure for ALS, but it may extend survival in the early stages of the disease, and/or may extend the time until a tracheostomy may be needed.

Riluzole is available only with your doctor's prescription, in the following dosage form:
Oral
- Tablets (U.S.)

Before Using This Medicine

In deciding to use a medicine, the risks of taking the medicine must be weighed against the good it will do. This is a decision you and your doctor will make. For riluzole, the following should be considered:

Allergies—Tell your doctor if you have ever had any unusual or allergic reaction to riluzole. Also tell your health care professional if you are allergic to any other substances, such as foods, preservatives, or dyes.

Pregnancy—Studies with riluzole have not been done in pregnant women. Some unwanted effects have been reported in animal studies. Before taking this medicine, make sure your doctor knows if you are pregnant or if you may become pregnant.

Breast-feeding—Riluzole has been shown to pass into the milk of nursing animals. It may also pass into human milk and may cause unwanted effects in nursing babies. It may be necessary for you to stop breast-feeding during treatment. Be sure you have discussed the risks and benefits of the medicine with your doctor.

Children—Studies on this medicine have been done only in adult patients, and there is no specific information comparing use of riluzole in children with use in other age groups.

Older adults—Many medicines have not been studied specifically in older people. Therefore, it may not be known whether they work exactly the same way they do in younger adults. Although there is no specific information comparing use of riluzole in the elderly with use in other age groups, this medicine has been used in elderly patients and is not expected to cause different side effects or problems in older people than it does in younger adults.

Other medicines—Although certain medicines should not be used together at all, in other cases two different medicines may be used together even if an interaction might occur. In these cases, your doctor may want to change the dose, or other precautions may be necessary. Tell your doctor and pharmacist if you are taking any other prescription or nonprescription (over-the-counter [OTC]) medicine.

Other medical problems—The presence of other medical problems may affect the use of riluzole. Make sure you tell your doctor if you have any other medical problems, especially:
- Kidney disease or
- Liver disease—Higher blood levels of riluzole may occur, increasing the chance of side effects

Proper Use of This Medicine

Riluzole should be taken on a regular basis and at the same time of the day (for example, in the morning and the evening).

Riluzole should be taken on an empty stomach. Take this medicine at least one hour before meals or two hours after meals.

Dosing—The dose of riluzole will be different for different patients. *Follow your doctor's orders or the directions on the label.* The following information includes only the average doses of riluzole. *If your dose is different, do not change it* unless your doctor tells you to do so.
- For *oral* dosage form (tablets):
  —For ALS:
    - Adults—Oral, 50 milligrams (mg) every twelve hours.
    - Children up to 18 years of age—Use and dose must be determined by your doctor.

Missed dose—If you miss a dose of this medicine, skip the missed dose and go back to your regular dosing schedule. Do not double doses.

Storage—To store this medicine:
- Keep out of the reach of children.
- Store away from heat and bright light.
- Do not store in the bathroom, near the kitchen sink, or in other damp places. Heat or moisture may cause the medicine to break down.
- Do not keep outdated medicine or medicine no longer needed. Be sure that any discarded medicine is out of the reach of children.

Precautions While Using This Medicine

If you become ill with a fever, report this to your doctor promptly. Fever may be a sign of infection.

This medicine may cause dizziness or drowsiness. *Make sure you know how you react to this medicine before you drive, use machines, or do anything else that could be dangerous if you are dizzy or are not alert.*

Avoid drinking alcoholic beverages. It is not known if drinking alcohol while taking riluzole may cause liver problems.

Side Effects of This Medicine

Along with its needed effects, a medicine may cause some unwanted effects. Although not all of these side effects may occur, if they do occur they may need medical attention.

Check with your doctor as soon as possible if any of the following side effects occur:
More common
   Diarrhea; nausea; vomiting; worsening of some symptoms of ALS, including spasticity and tiredness or weakness

Less common
   Difficulty in breathing; increased cough; pneumonia

Rare
   Bloody or cloudy urine, frequent urge to urinate, or painful or difficult urination; convulsions (seizures); fast or pounding heartbeat; fever, chills, or continuing sores in mouth; hypertension (high blood pressure); increased thirst, irregular heartbeat, mood or mental changes, or muscle cramps, pain, or weakness; lack of coordination; lack of energy; mental depression; pain, tenderness, bluish color, or swelling of foot or leg; redness, scaling, or peeling of the skin; swelling of eyelids, mouth, lips, tongue, and/or throat; swelling of face; trouble in swallowing; yellow eyes or skin

Other side effects may occur that usually do not need medical attention. These side effects may go away during treatment as your body adjusts to the medicine. However, check with your doctor if any of the following side effects continue or are bothersome:
More common
   Abdominal pain or gas; dizziness; drowsiness; loss of appetite; numbness or tingling around the mouth

Less common
   Back or muscle pain or stiffness; constipation; general feeling of discomfort or illness; hair loss; headache; irritation or soreness of mouth; runny nose; skin rash or itching; trouble in sleeping

This medicine may also cause the following side effect that your doctor will watch for:
More common
   Liver problems

Other side effects not listed above may also occur in some patients. If you notice any other effects, check with your doctor.

Developed: 07/30/96

RIMANTADINE Systemic†

Commonly used brand name(s):

In the U.S.—
Flumadine

†Not commercially available in Canada.

Description

Rimantadine (ri-MAN-ta-deen) is an antiviral. It is used to prevent or treat certain influenza (flu) infections (type A). It may be given alone or along with flu shots. Rimantadine will not work for colds, other types of flu, or other virus infections.

Rimantadine is available only with your doctor's prescription, in the following dosage forms:

Oral
- Syrup (U.S.)
- Tablets (U.S.)

Before Using This Medicine

In deciding to use a medicine, the risks of taking the medicine must be weighed against the good it will do. This is a decision you and your doctor will make. For rimantadine, the following should be considered:

Allergies—Tell your doctor if you have ever had any unusual or allergic reaction to rimantadine or amantadine. Also tell your health care professional if you are allergic to any other substances, such as foods, preservatives, or dyes.

Pregnancy—Studies have not been done in humans. However, studies in some animals have shown that rimantadine is harmful to the fetus and causes birth defects.

Breast-feeding—It is not known if rimantadine passes into breast milk. Although most medicines pass into breast milk in small amounts, many of them may be used safely while breast-feeding. Mothers who are taking this medicine and who wish to breast-feed should discuss this with their doctor.

Children—This medicine has been tested in children over one year of age and has not been shown to cause different side effects or problems in these children than it does in adults. There is no specific information comparing the use of rimantadine in children under one year of age with use in other age groups.

Older adults—Elderly people are especially sensitive to the effects of rimantadine. Difficulty in sleeping, difficulty in concentrating, dizziness, headache, nervousness, and weakness may be especially likely to occur. Stomach pain, nausea, vomiting, and loss of appetite may also occur.

Other medicines—Although certain medicines should not be used together at all, in other cases two different medicines may be used together even if an interaction might occur. In these cases, your doctor may want to change the dose, or other precautions may be necessary. Tell your health care professional if you are taking any other prescription or nonprescription (over-the-counter [OTC]) medicine.

Other medical problems—The presence of other medical problems may affect the use of rimantadine. Make sure you tell your doctor if you have any other medical problems, especially:

- Epilepsy or other seizures (history of)—Rimantadine may increase the frequency of convulsions (seizures) in patients with a seizure disorder
- Kidney disease—Rimantadine is removed from the body by the kidneys; patients with severe kidney disease will need to receive a lower dose of rimantadine
- Liver disease—Patients with severe liver disease may need to receive a lower dose of rimantadine

Proper Use of This Medicine

Talk to your doctor about the *possibility of getting a flu shot* if you have not had one yet.

This medicine is *best taken before exposure, or as soon as possible after exposure*, to people who have the flu.

To help keep yourself from getting the flu, *keep taking this medicine for the full time of treatment.*

If you already have the flu, *continue taking this medicine for the full time of treatment even if you begin to feel better after a few days.* This will help to clear up your infection completely. If you stop taking this medicine too soon, your symptoms may return. This medicine should be taken for at least 5 to 7 days.

This medicine works best when there is a constant amount in the blood. *To help keep the amount constant, do not miss any doses. Also, it is best to take the doses at evenly spaced times day and night.*

If you are using the oral liquid form of rimantadine, use a specially marked measuring spoon or other device to measure each dose accurately. The average household teaspoon may not hold the right amount of liquid.

Dosing—The dose of rimantadine will be different for different patients. *Follow your doctor's orders or the directions on the label.* The following information includes only the average doses of rimantadine. Your dose may be different if you have kidney disease or liver disease. *If your dose is different, do not change it* unless your doctor tells you to do so.

- For *oral* dosage forms (syrup, tablets):
  —For the prevention or treatment of flu:
  - Elderly adults—100 milligrams (mg) once a day.
  - Adults and children 10 years of age and older—100 mg two times a day.
  - Children up to 10 years of age—5 mg per kilogram (2.3 mg per pound) of body weight once a day. Children in this age group should not receive more than 150 mg a day.

Missed dose—If you do miss a dose of this medicine, take it as soon as possible. This will help to keep a constant amount of medicine in the blood. However, if it is almost time for your next dose, skip the missed dose and go back to your regular dosing schedule. Do not double doses.

Storage—To store this medicine:
- Keep out of the reach of children.
- Store away from heat and direct light.
- Keep the syrup form of this medicine from freezing.
- Do not keep outdated medicine or medicine no longer needed. Be sure that any discarded medicine is out of the reach of children.

Precautions While Using This Medicine

This medicine may cause some people to become dizzy or confused, or to have trouble concentrating. *Make sure you know how you react to this medicine before you drive, use machines, or do anything else that could be dangerous if you are dizzy or confused.* If these reactions are especially bothersome, check with your doctor.

If your symptoms do not improve within a few days, or if they become worse, check with your doctor.

Side Effects of This Medicine

Along with its needed effects, a medicine may cause some unwanted effects. Although not all of these side effects may occur, if they do occur they may need medical attention.

Side effects may occur that usually do not need medical attention. These side effects may go away during treatment as your body adjusts to the medicine. However, check with your doctor if any of the following side effects continue or are bothersome:

> *Less common*
> Difficulty in concentrating; dizziness; dryness of mouth; headache; loss of appetite; nausea; nervousness; stomach pain; trouble in sleeping; unusual tiredness; vomiting

Other side effects not listed above may also occur in some patients. If you notice any other effects, check with your doctor.

Developed: 03/29/94

RIMEXOLONE   Ophthalmic

Commonly used brand name(s):

In the U.S.—
Vexol

Description

Rimexolone (ri-MEX-oh-lone) belongs to the group of medicines known as corticosteroids (cortisone-like medicines). It is used to treat inflammation of the eye, which may occur following eye surgery or with certain eye problems.

This medicine is available only with your doctor's prescription, in the following dosage form:

> *Ophthalmic*
> • Eye drops (U.S.)

Before Using This Medicine

In deciding to use a medicine, the risks of using the medicine must be weighed against the good it will do. This is a decision you and your doctor will make. For ophthalmic rimexolone, the following should be considered:

Allergies—Tell your doctor if you have ever had any unusual or allergic reaction to rimexolone or other corticosteroids. Also tell your health care professional if you are allergic to any other substances, such as foods, preservatives, or dyes.

Pregnancy—Ophthalmic rimexolone has not been studied in pregnant women. However, rimexolone has been shown to cause birth defects and other unwanted effects in the animal fetus when injected into pregnant animals.

Breast-feeding—It is not known whether enough rimexolone is absorbed from the eye to get into breast milk. Discuss with your physician whether or not to breast-feed while using this medicine.

Children—Studies on this medicine have been done only in adult patients, and there is no specific information comparing use of rimexolone in children with use in other age groups.

Older adults—Many medicines have not been studied specifically in older people. Therefore, it may not be known whether they work exactly the same way they do in younger adults or if they cause different side effects or problems in older people. There is no specific information comparing use of rimexolone in the elderly with use in other age groups.

Other medical problems—The presence of other medical problems may affect the use of ophthalmic rimexolone. Make sure you tell your doctor if you have any other medical problems, especially:

> • Certain eye diseases that cause the cornea to get thin— Use of ophthalmic rimexolone could cause a hole to form (perforation)

> • Fungus infection of the eye or
> • Herpes infection of the eye or
> • Virus infection of the eye or
> • Yeast infection of the eye or
> • Any other eye infection—Ophthalmic rimexolone may make existing infections worse or cause new infections

Proper Use of This Medicine

Shake the container very well before applying the eye drops.

To use:
> • First, wash your hands. Tilt your head back and, pressing your finger gently on the skin just beneath the lower eyelid, pull the lower eyelid away from the eye to make a space. Drop the medicine into this space. Let go of the eyelid and gently close the eyes. Do not blink. Keep the eyes closed and apply pressure to the inner corner of the eye with your finger for 1 or 2 minutes to allow the medicine to be absorbed by the eye.
> • If you think you did not get the drop of medicine into your eye properly, use another drop.
> • *To keep the medicine as germ-free as possible, do not touch the applicator tip to any surface (including the eye).* Also, keep the container tightly closed.

Dosing—The dose of ophthalmic rimexolone will be different for different patients. *Follow your doctor's orders or the directions on the label.* The following information includes only the average doses of ophthalmic rimexolone. *If your dose is different, do not change it* unless your doctor tells you to do so.

> • For *ophthalmic* dosage form (eye drops):
> —For inflammation after surgery:
> • Adults—Use one or two drops in the affected eye four times a day beginning twenty-four hours after surgery and continuing throughout the first two weeks after surgery.
> • Children—Use and dose must be determined by your doctor.

—For anterior uveitis (inflammation in the iris of the eye):

- Adults—Use one or two drops in the affected eye every hour, while awake, for the first week. Then use one drop in the affected eye every two hours, while awake, for the second week. Then gradually decrease the number of times the medicine is used each day according to your physician's instructions.
- Children—Use and dose must be determined by your doctor.

Missed dose—If you miss a dose of this medicine, use it as soon as possible. However, if it is almost time for your next dose, skip the missed dose and go back to your regular dosing schedule.

Storage—To store this medicine:

- Keep out of the reach of children.
- Store away from heat and direct light.
- Keep the medicine from freezing.
- Do not keep outdated medicine or medicine no longer needed. Be sure that any discarded medicine is out of the reach of children.

Precautions While Using This Medicine

An ophthalmologist (eye doctor) should examine your eyes at regular visits while you are using this medicine.

Side Effects of This Medicine

Along with its needed effects, a medicine may cause some unwanted effects. Although not all of these side effects may occur, if they do occur they may need medical attention.

Check with your doctor as soon as possible if any of the following side effects occur:

Less common or rare
Blurred vision or other change in vision; eye discharge, discomfort, dryness, or tearing; eye redness, irritation, or pain; feeling of something in the eye; itching; sore throat; stuffy or runny nose; swelling of the lining of the eyelids

Other side effects may occur that usually do not need medical attention. These side effects may go away during treatment as your body adjusts to the medicine. However, check with your doctor if any of the following side effects continue or are bothersome:

Less common or rare
Browache; change in taste; crusting in corner of eye; dizziness, lightheadedness, or faintness; headache; increased sensitivity of eyes to light; sticky sensation of eyelids; unusual tiredness or weakness

Other side effects not listed above may also occur in some patients. If you notice any other effects, check with your doctor.

Developed: 08/14/98

RISEDRONATE   Systemic

Commonly used brand name(s):

In the U.S.—
Actonel

In Canada—
Actonel

Description

Risedronate (ris-ED-roe-nate) is used to prevent and treat osteoporosis (thinning of bone) in women after menopause. It may also be used in men and women to prevent and treat osteoporosis caused by long-term use of corticosteroids (cortisone-like medicine). Risedronate is also used to treat Paget's disease of the bone.

This medicine is available only with your doctor's prescription, in the following dosage form:

Oral
- Tablets (U.S.)
- Tablets (Canada)

Before Using This Medicine

In deciding to use a medicine, the risks of taking the medicine must be weighed against the good it will do. This is a decision you and your doctor will make. For risedronate, the following should be considered:

Allergies—Tell your doctor if you have ever had any unusual or allergic reaction to risedronate. Also tell your health care professional if you are allergic to any other substances, such as foods, preservatives, or dyes.

Pregnancy—Studies have not been done in pregnant women. However, studies in animals given large doses of risedronate have shown that this medicine causes decreased weight gain, cleft palate, and deformed bones in the fetus, and, in some cases, death of the fetus.

Breast-feeding—It is not known whether risedronate passes into milk. However, it does pass into the milk in animals. Discuss with your doctor whether or not to breast-feed while you are being treated with this medicine.

Children—There is no specific information comparing use of risedronate in children with use in other age groups.

Older adults—Risedronate has been tested in elderly patients and has not been found to cause different side effects or problems in older people than it does in younger adults.

Other medicines—Although certain medicines should not be used together at all, in other cases two different medicines may be used together even if an interaction might occur. In these cases, your doctor may want to change the dose, or other precautions may be necessary. When you are taking risedronate, it is especially important that your health care professional know if you are taking any of the following:

- Antacids containing calcium or
- Mineral supplements containing calcium—These medicines may decrease the amount of risedronate that is absorbed into the body

Other medical problems—The presence of other medical problems may affect the use of risedronate. Make sure you tell your doctor if you have any other medical problems, especially:

- Digestive system problems, including trouble swallowing, inflammation of the esophagus, or ulcer—Risedronate may make these conditions worse

- Kidney problems—Effects of risedronate may be increased because of slower removal from the body

Proper Use of This Medicine

Take risedronate with a full glass (6 to 8 ounces) of plain water on an empty stomach. It should be taken in the morning at least 30 minutes before any food, beverage, or other medicines. Food and beverages will decrease the amount of risedronate absorbed by the body. Waiting longer than 30 minutes will allow more of the drug to be absorbed. Medicines such as antacids that contain calcium or calcium supplements also will decrease the absorption of risedronate.

Do not lie down for 30 minutes after taking risedronate. This will help risedronate reach your stomach faster. It also will help prevent irritation to your esophagus.

It is important that you eat a well-balanced diet with adequate amounts of calcium and vitamin D (found in milk or other dairy products). However, do not take any foods, beverages, or calcium supplements within 30 minutes or longer before taking the risedronate. To do so may keep this medicine from working properly.

Dosing—The dose of risedronate will be different for different patients. *Follow your doctor's orders or the directions on the label.* The following information includes only the average doses of risedronate. *If your dose is different, do not change it* unless your doctor tells you to do so.

- For *oral* dosage form (tablets):
  —For prevention and treatment of postmenopausal and corticosteroid-induced osteoporosis:
  - Adults—5 milligrams (mg) daily at least 30 minutes before the first food or drink of the day other than water.
  - Children—Use and dose must be determined by your doctor.
  —For Paget's disease of the bone:
  - Adults—30 mg a day for two months. Your doctor may tell you to repeat this dose.
  - Children—Use and dose must be determined by your doctor.

Missed dose—If you miss a dose of this medicine, do not take it later in the day. Resume your usual schedule the next morning. Do not double doses.

Storage—To store this medicine:
- Keep out of the reach of children.
- Store away from heat and direct light.
- Do not store in the bathroom, near the kitchen sink, or in other damp places. Heat or moisture may cause the medicine to break down.
- Do not keep outdated medicine or medicine no longer needed. Be sure that any discarded medicine is out of the reach of children.

Precautions While Using This Medicine

It is important that your doctor check your progress at regular visits to make sure this medicine is working properly and watch for unwanted effects.

Side Effects of This Medicine

Along with its needed effects, a medicine may cause some unwanted effects. Although not all of these side effects may occur, if they do occur they may need medical attention.

Check with your doctor as soon as possible if any of the following side effects occur:
More common
Abdominal or stomach pain; skin rash

Less common
Abdominal or stomach pain (severe); belching; bone pain; cramping of stomach
Rare
Red, sore eyes

Other side effects may occur that usually do not need medical attention. These side effects may go away during treatment as your body adjusts to the medicine. However, check with your doctor if any of the following side effects continue or are bothersome:
More common
Diarrhea; headache; joint pain
Less common
Blurred vision or change in vision; chest pain; constipation; cough; dizziness; dry eyes; fever; general feeling of discomfort or illness; headache; leg cramps; nausea; ringing in the ears; swelling of feet or lower legs; weakness

Other side effects not listed above may also occur in some patients. If you notice any other effects, check with your doctor.

Developed: 08/12/1998
Revised: 08/16/2000

RISPERIDONE   Systemic

Commonly used brand name(s):

In the U.S.—
Risperdal

In Canada—
Risperdal

Description

Risperidone (ris-PER-i-done) is used to treat the symptoms of psychotic disorders, such as schizophrenia.

Risperidone is available only with your doctor's prescription, in the following dosage forms:
Oral
- Oral solution (U.S. and Canada)
- Tablets (U.S. and Canada)

Before Using This Medicine

In deciding to use a medicine, the risks of taking the medicine must be weighed against the good it will do. This is a decision you and your doctor will make. For risperidone, the following should be considered:

Allergies—Tell your doctor if you have ever had any unusual or allergic reaction to risperidone. Also tell your health care professional if you are allergic to any other substances, such as foods, preservatives, or dyes.

Pregnancy—Studies with risperidone have not been done in pregnant women. One baby whose mother took risperidone during pregnancy was born with a serious brain problem. However, it is not known whether this problem was caused by risperidone. Some unwanted effects have been reported in animal studies, but the risk to human babies is not clear. Before taking this medicine, make sure your doctor knows if you are pregnant or if you may become pregnant.

Breast-feeding—Risperidone has been shown to pass into the milk of nursing animals. It may also pass into human milk and may cause unwanted effects, such as behavior changes, in nursing babies. It may be necessary for you to take another medicine or to stop breast-feeding during treatment. Be sure you have discussed the risks and benefits of the medicine with your doctor.

Children—Studies on this medicine have been done only in adult patients, and there is no specific information comparing use of risperidone in children with use in other age groups.

Older adults—Elderly people may be especially sensitive to the effects of risperidone. This may increase the chance of having side effects during treatment.

Other medicines—Although certain medicines should not be used together at all, in other cases two different medicines may be used together even if an interaction might occur. In these cases, your doctor may want to change the dose, or other precautions may be necessary. When you are taking risperidone, it is especially important that your health care professional know if you are taking any of the following:

- Antihypertensives (high blood pressure medicine) or
- Central nervous system (CNS) depressants (medicine that makes you drowsy or less alert) or
- Tricyclic antidepressants (amitriptyline [e.g., Elavil], amoxapine [e.g., Asendin], clomipramine [e.g., Anafranil], desipramine [e.g., Pertofrane], doxepin [e.g., Sinequan], imipramine [e.g., Tofranil], nortriptyline [e.g., Aventyl], protriptyline [e.g., Vivactil], trimipramine [e.g., Surmontil])—Risperidone may add to the effects of these medicines, causing unwanted effects such as increased drowsiness or low blood pressure

- Bromocriptine (e.g., Parlodel) or
- Levodopa (e.g., Dopar, Larodopa) or
- Pergolide (e.g., Permax)—Risperidone may interfere with the effects of these medicines so that they do not work properly

- Carbamazepine (e.g., Epitol, Tegretol) or
- Clozapine (e.g., Clozaril)—These medicines may affect the blood levels of risperidone so that risperidone does not work properly or causes unwanted effects. Your doctor may need to change your dose of risperidone

Other medical problems—The presence of other medical problems may affect the use of risperidone. Make sure you tell your doctor if you have any other medical problems, especially:

- Breast cancer or
- Heart or blood vessel problems, including stroke or
- Parkinson's disease—Risperidone may make these conditions worse

- Epilepsy or other seizure disorders—Risperidone may increase the risk of having seizures

- Kidney disease or
- Liver disease—Higher blood levels of risperidone may occur, increasing the chance of side effects

Proper Use of This Medicine

Take this medicine only as directed by your doctor to benefit your condition as much as possible. Do not take more or less of it, do not take it more or less often, and do not take it for a longer or shorter time than your doctor ordered.

Dosing—The dose of risperidone will be different for different patients. *Follow your doctor's orders or the direc-*

tions on the label. The following information includes only the average doses of risperidone. *If your dose is different, do not change it* unless your doctor tells you to do so.

- For symptoms of psychotic disorder:
  —For *oral solution* dosage form—
  - Adults—At first, 1 milligram (mg) [1 milliliter (mL)] two times a day. Your doctor may increase your dose as needed. However, the dose usually is not more than 16 mg (16 mL) a day.
  - Children younger than 18 years of age—Use and dose must be determined by the doctor.
  - Older adults—At first, 0.5 mg (0.5 mL) two times a day. Your doctor may increase your dose as needed. However, the dose usually is not more than 3 mg (3 mL) a day.
  —For *oral tablet* dosage form—
  - Adults—At first, 1 milligram (mg) two times a day. Your doctor may increase your dose as needed. However, the dose usually is not more than 16 mg a day.
  - Children younger than 18 years of age—Use and dose must be determined by the doctor.
  - Older adults—At first, 0.5 mg two times a day. Your doctor may increase your dose as needed. However, the dose usually is not more than 3 mg a day.

For patients taking the *oral solution* form of risperidone:

- Measure the dose with the measuring device provided with your medicine. Stir the dose into a small glass (3 to 4 ounces) of water, coffee, orange juice, or low-fat milk just before taking it. Do not mix this medicine with cola or tea.
- Rinse the empty measuring device with water and place it back in its storage case. Put the plastic cap back on the bottle of medicine.

Missed dose—If you miss a dose of this medicine, take it as soon as possible. However, if it is almost time for your next dose, skip the missed dose and go back to your regular dosing schedule. Do not double doses.

Storage—To store this medicine:

- Keep out of the reach of children.
- Store away from heat and direct light.
- Do not store the tablet form of this medicine in the bathroom, near the kitchen sink, or in other damp places. Heat or moisture may cause the medicine to break down.
- Keep the solution form of this medicine from freezing.
- Do not keep outdated medicine or medicine no longer needed. Be sure that any discarded medicine is out of the reach of children.

Precautions While Using This Medicine

Your doctor should check your progress at regular visits, especially during the first few months of treatment with this medicine. This will allow the dosage to be changed if necessary to meet your needs.

Do not stop taking this medicine without first checking with your doctor. Your doctor may want you to reduce gradually the amount you are taking before stopping completely. This is to prevent side effects and to keep your condition from becoming worse.

This medicine may add to the effects of alcohol and other CNS depressants (medicine that makes you drowsy or less alert). Some examples of CNS depressants are antihistamines or medicine for hay fever, other allergies, or colds; sedatives, tranquilizers, or sleeping medicine; prescription pain medicine or narcotics; barbiturates; medicine for seizures; muscle relaxants; or anesthetics, including some dental anesthetics. *Check with your doctor before taking any of the above while you are using this medicine.*

Before having any kind of surgery, dental treatment, or emergency treatment, tell the medical doctor or dentist in charge that you are using this medicine. Taking risperidone together with medicines that are used during surgery, dental, or emergency treatments may increase the CNS depressant effects.

This medicine may cause blurred vision, dizziness, or drowsiness. *Make sure you know how you react to this medicine before you drive, use machines, or do anything else that could be dangerous if you are not alert or able to see clearly.*

Dizziness, lightheadedness, or fainting may occur, especially when you get up from a lying or sitting position. Getting up slowly may help. If the problem continues or gets worse, check with your doctor.

Risperidone may cause your skin to be more sensitive to sunlight than it is normally. Exposure to sunlight, even for brief periods of time, may cause a skin rash, itching, redness or other discoloration of the skin, or a severe sunburn. When you begin taking this medicine:

- Stay out of direct sunlight, especially between the hours of 10:00 a.m. and 3:00 p.m., if possible.
- Wear protective clothing, including a hat. Also, wear sunglasses.
- Apply a sun block product that has a skin protection factor (SPF) of at least 15. You may require a product with a higher SPF number, especially if you have a fair complexion. If you have any questions about this, check with your health care professional.
- Apply a sun block lipstick that has an SPF of at least 15 to protect your lips.
- Do not use a sunlamp or tanning bed or booth.

If you have a severe reaction from the sun, check with your doctor.

This medicine may make it more difficult for your body to keep a constant temperature. Use extra care not to become overheated during exercise or hot weather while you are taking this medicine, since overheating may result in heatstroke. Hot baths or saunas may make you feel dizzy or faint while you are taking this medicine. Also, use extra care not to become too cold while you are taking risperidone. If you become too cold, you may feel drowsy, confused, or clumsy.

Side Effects of This Medicine

Along with its needed effects, risperidone can sometimes cause serious side effects. Tardive dyskinesia (a movement disorder) may occur and may not go away after you stop using the medicine. Signs of tardive dyskinesia include fine, worm-like movements of the tongue, or other uncontrolled movements of the mouth, tongue, cheeks, jaw, or arms and legs. Other serious but rare side effects may also occur. These include neuroleptic malignant syndrome (NMS), which may cause severe muscle stiffness, fever, severe tiredness or weakness, fast heartbeat, difficult breathing, increased sweating, loss of bladder control, or seizures. *You and your doctor should discuss the good this medicine will do as well as the risks of taking it.*

Stop taking risperidone and get emergency help immediately if any of the following side effects occur:
  Rare
    Convulsions (seizures); difficult or fast breathing; fast heartbeat or irregular pulse; fever (high); high or low blood pressure; increased sweating; loss of bladder control; muscle stiffness (severe); unusually pale skin; unusual tiredness or weakness (severe)

Check with your doctor immediately if any of the following side effects occur:
  More common
    Difficulty in speaking or swallowing; inability to move eyes; muscle spasms of face, neck, and back; twisting movements of body

  Rare
    High body temperature (dizziness; fast, shallow breathing; fast, weak heartbeat; headache; muscle cramps; pale, clammy skin; increased thirst); lip smacking or puckering; low body temperature (confusion, drowsiness, poor coordination, shivering); prolonged, painful, inappropriate erection of the penis; puffing of cheeks; rapid or worm-like movements of tongue; uncontrolled chewing movements; uncontrolled movements of arms and legs

Check with your doctor as soon as possible if any of the following side effects occur:
  More common
    Anxiety or nervousness; changes in vision, including blurred vision; decreased sexual desire or performance; loss of balance control; mask-like face; menstrual changes; mood or mental changes, including aggressive behavior, agitation, difficulty in concentration, and memory problems; problems in urination or increase in amount of urine; restlessness or need to keep moving (severe); shuffling walk; skin rash or itching; stiffness or weakness of arms or legs; tic-like or twitching movements; trembling and shaking of fingers and hands; trouble in sleeping

  Less common
    Back pain; chest pain; seborrhea (skin condition that may include dandruff and oily skin); unusual secretion of milk

  Rare
    Extreme thirst; increased blinking or spasms of eyelid; loss of appetite; talking, feeling, and acting with excitement and activity that cannot be controlled; uncontrolled twisting movements of neck, trunk, arms, or legs; unusual bleeding or bruising; unusual facial expressions or body positions

Other side effects may occur that usually do not need medical attention. These side effects may go away during treatment as your body adjusts to the medicine. However, check with your doctor if any of the following side effects continue or are bothersome:
  More common
    Constipation; coughing; diarrhea; drowsiness; dryness of mouth; headache; heartburn; increased dream activity; increased length of sleep; nausea; sore throat; stuffy or runny nose; unusual tiredness or weakness; weight gain

  Less common
    Darkening of skin color; dry skin; increased sensitivity

of the skin to sun; increased watering of mouth; joint pain; stomach pain; vomiting; weight loss

Some side effects, such as uncontrolled movements of the mouth, tongue, and jaw, or uncontrolled movements of arms and legs, may occur after you have stopped taking this medicine. If you notice any of these effects, check with your doctor as soon as possible.

Other side effects not listed above may also occur in some patients. If you notice any other effects, check with your doctor.

Developed: 08/15/95
Revised: 08/07/98

RITODRINE   Systemic

Commonly used brand name(s):

In the U.S.—
Yutopar
Generic name product may be available.

In Canada—
Yutopar
Yutopar S.R.

Description

Ritodrine (RI-toe-dreen) is used to stop premature labor. It is available only with your doctor's prescription and is to be administered only by or under the supervision of your doctor.

Ritodrine is available in the following dosage forms:

Oral
- Extended-release capsules (Canada)
- Tablets (Canada)

Parenteral
- Injection (U.S. and Canada)

Before Using This Medicine

In deciding to use a medicine, the risks of taking the medicine must be weighed against the good it will do. This is a decision you and your doctor will make. For ritodrine, the following should be considered:

Allergies—Tell your doctor if you have ever had any unusual or allergic reaction to ritodrine or sulfites. Also tell your health care professional if you are allergic to any other substances, such as foods, preservatives, or dyes.

Other medicines—Although certain medicines should not be used together at all, in other cases two different medicines may be used together even if an interaction might occur. In these cases, your doctor may want to change the dose, or other precautions may be necessary. When you are taking or receiving ritodrine, it is especially important that your health care professional know if you are taking any of the following:

- Beta-adrenergic blocking agents (acebutolol [e.g., Sectral], atenolol [e.g., Tenormin], betaxolol [e.g., Kerlone], bisoprolol [e.g., Zebeta], carteolol [e.g., Cartrol], labetalol [e.g., Normodyne], metoprolol [e.g., Lopressor], nadolol [e.g., Corgard], oxprenolol [e.g., Trasicor], penbutolol [e.g., Levatol], pindolol [e.g., Visken], propranolol [e.g., Inderal], sotalol [e.g., Sotacor], timolol [e.g., Blo-

cadren])—Ritodrine may be less effective if it is used with any of these medicines

- Corticosteroids (cortisone-like medicines)—These medicines are often given together to the mother to help her baby's lungs develop. If you are taking corticosteroids, your dose may need to be changed if ritodrine is also taken or injected. Sometimes the combination of these medicines increases the chance of side effects occurring in the mother.

- Medicine for asthma or breathing problems—Because these products have some effects that are similar to those of ritodrine, the chance of side effects developing is increased when these medicines are used with ritodrine

Other medical problems—The presence of other medical problems may affect the use of ritodrine. Make sure you tell your doctor if you have any other medical problems, especially:

- Diabetes mellitus (sugar diabetes)—Ritodrine may make this condition worse

- Heart or blood vessel disease or
- Overactive thyroid, uncontrolled—Use of ritodrine may cause serious effects of the heart, including irregular heartbeat

- High blood pressure (hypertension), uncontrolled, or
- Migraine headaches (or history of)—Ritodrine may make these conditions worse. Rarely, use of ritodrine during a migraine headache may cause problems with blood circulation in the brain

Proper Use of This Medicine

Dosing—The dose of ritodrine will be different for different women. *Follow your doctor's orders or the directions on the label.* The following information includes only the average doses of ritodrine. *If your dose is different, do not change it* unless your doctor tells you to do so. The injection form of this medicine will be given to you by your health care professional.

- For *oral* dosage form (extended-release capsules):
  —Adults: In the first twenty-four hours after the doctor stops your intravenous ritodrine, your dose may be as high as 40 milligrams (mg) every eight hours. After that, the dose is usually 40 mg taken every eight to twelve hours. Your doctor may want you to take oral ritodrine up until it is time for you to deliver your baby or until your 37th week of pregnancy.
- For *oral* dosage form (tablets):
  —Adults: In the first twenty-four hours after the doctor stops your intravenous ritodrine, your dose may be as high as 10 mg every two hours. After that, the dose is usually 10 to 20 mg every four to six hours. Your doctor may want you to take oral ritodrine up until it is time for you to deliver your baby or until your 37th week of pregnancy.
- For *injection* dosage form:
  —Adults: 50 to 350 micrograms per minute, injected into a vein.

Missed dose—If you miss an oral dose of this medicine and remember within an hour or so of the missed dose, take it right away. However, if you do not remember until later, skip the missed dose and go back to your regular dosing schedule. Do not double doses.

Storage—To store this medicine:
- Keep out of the reach of children.
- Store away from heat and direct light.
- Do not store in the bathroom, near the kitchen sink, or in other damp places. Heat or moisture may cause the medicine to break down.
- Do not keep outdated medicine or medicine no longer needed. Be sure that any discarded medicine is out of the reach of children.

Precautions While Using This Medicine

Check with your doctor right away if your contractions begin again or your water breaks.

Do not take other medicines unless they have been discussed with your doctor. This especially includes over-the-counter (nonprescription) medicines for appetite control, asthma, colds, cough, hay fever, or sinus problems since they may increase the unwanted effects of this medicine.

Side Effects of This Medicine

Along with its needed effects, a medicine may cause some unwanted effects. Although not all of these side effects may occur, if they do occur they may need medical attention.

Tell your health care professional immediately if either of the following side effects occurs while you are receiving this medicine:

More common
> Chest pain or tightness; shortness of breath—rare with oral form

Check with your health care professional as soon as possible if the following side effects occur:

More common
> Blurred vision; dizziness or lightheadedness; drowsiness; dry mouth; flushed and dry skin; fast or irregular heartbeat—rare with oral form; fruit-like breath odor; increased urination; loss of appetite; nausea; severe pounding or racing heartbeat—rare with oral form; sleepiness; stomachache; tiredness; troubled breathing (rapid and deep); unusual thirst; vomiting

Rare
> Sore throat or fever; yellow eyes or skin

Symptoms of overdose
> Fast or irregular heartbeat (severe); nausea or vomiting (severe); nervousness or trembling (severe); shortness of breath (severe)

Other side effects may occur that usually do not need medical attention. These side effects may go away during treatment as your body adjusts to the medicine. However, check with your doctor if any of the following side effects continue or are bothersome:

More common
> Headache; reddened skin; trembling

Less common or rare
> Anxiety; emotional upset; jitteriness, nervousness, or restlessness; skin rash

After you stop using this medicine, your body may need time to adjust. The length of time this takes depends on the amount of medicine you were using and how long you used it. During this period of time check with your doctor if you notice the following side effect:
> Shortness of breath

Other side effects not listed above may also occur in some patients. If you notice any other effects, check with your doctor.

Revised: 06/28/96

RITONAVIR   Systemic

Commonly used brand name(s):

In the U.S.—
> Norvir

Description

Ritonavir (ri-TOE-na-veer) is used, alone or in combination with other medicines, in the treatment of the infection caused by the human immunodeficiency virus (HIV). HIV is the virus that causes acquired immune deficiency syndrome (AIDS).

Ritonavir will not cure or prevent HIV infection or AIDS; however, it helps keep HIV from reproducing and appears to slow down the destruction of the immune system. This may help delay the development of problems usually related to AIDS or HIV disease. Ritonavir will not keep you from spreading HIV to other people. People who receive this medicine may continue to have other problems usually related to AIDS or HIV disease.

This medicine is available only with your doctor's prescription, in the following dosage forms:

Oral
- Capsules (U.S.)
- Oral solution (U.S.)

Before Using This Medicine

In deciding to use a medicine, the risks of taking the medicine must be weighed against the good it will do. This is a decision you and your doctor will make. For ritonavir, the following should be considered:

Allergies—Tell your doctor if you have ever had any unusual or allergic reaction to ritonavir. Also tell your health care professional if you are allergic to any other substances, such as foods, preservatives, or dyes.

Pregnancy—Studies have not been done in humans. However, in animal studies, ritonavir has been found to cause reduced weight and delayed growth in the infants. Ritonavir did not cause birth defects in animal studies.

Breast-feeding—It is not known whether ritonavir passes into breast milk. However, breast-feeding is usually not recommended in AIDS patients because of the risk of passing the AIDS virus on to the infant.

Children—This medicine has been tested in a limited number of children 2 years of age and older. In effective doses, the medicine has not been shown to cause different side effects or problems than it does in adults.

Older adults—Many medicines have not been studied specifically in older people. Therefore, it may not be known whether they work exactly the same way they do in younger adults. There is no specific information comparing use of ritonavir in the elderly with use in other age groups.

Other medicines—Although certain medicines should not be used together at all, in other cases two different medicines may be used together even if an interaction might occur. In these cases, your doctor may want to change the dose, or other precautions may be necessary. When you are taking ritonavir, it is especially important that your health care professional know if you are taking any of the following:

- Amiodarone (e.g., Cordarone) or
- Astemizole (e.g., Hismanal) or
- Bepridil (e.g., Bepadin) or
- Bupropion (e.g., Wellbutrin) or
- Cisapride (e.g., Propulsid) or
- Clozapine (e.g., Clozaril) or
- Dihydroergotamine (e.g., D.H.E. 45) or
- Encainide (e.g., Enkaid) or
- Ergotamine or
- Flecainide (e.g., Tambocor) or
- Meperidine (e.g., Demerol) or
- Pimozide (e.g., Orap) or
- Piroxicam (e.g., Feldene) or
- Propafenone (e.g., Rythmol) or
- Quinidine (e.g., Quinidex) or
- Rifabutin (e.g., Mycobutin) or
- Terfenadine (e.g., Seldane)—There is a possibility that ritonavir may interfere with the removal of these medicines from the body, which could lead to serious side effects
- Clarithromycin (e.g., Biaxin)—Use with ritonavir may increase the amount of clarithromycin in the body, which could lead to increased side effects
- Clorazepate (e.g., Tranxene) or
- Diazepam (e.g., Valium) or
- Estazolam (e.g., ProSom) or
- Flurazepam (e.g., Dalmane) or
- Midazolam (e.g., Versed) or
- Triazolam (e.g., Halcion) or
- Zolpidem (e.g., Ambien)—There is a possibility that ritonavir may interfere with the removal of these medicines from the body, which could lead to serious side effects
- Oral contraceptives (birth control pills) containing estrogen—Ritonavir may cause these medicines to be less effective
- Theophylline (e.g., Theo-Dur)—Ritonavir may decrease the amount of theophylline in the body, so that it is less effective

Other medical problems—The presence of other medical problems may affect the use of ritonavir. Make sure you tell your doctor if you have any other medical problems, especially:

- Hemophilia—Possible increased risk of bleeding
- Liver disease—Effects of ritonavir may be increased because of slower removal from the body

Proper Use of This Medicine

It is important that ritonavir be be taken with food.

Take this medicine exactly as directed by your doctor. Do not take it more often, and do not take it for a longer time than your doctor ordered. Also, do not stop taking this medicine without checking with your doctor first.

Keep taking ritonavir for the full time of treatment, even if you begin to feel better.

This medicine works best when there is a constant amount in the blood. *To help keep the amount constant, do not miss any doses. Also, it is best to take the doses at evenly spaced times, day and night.* For example, if you are to take two doses a day, the doses should be spaced about 12 hours apart. If you need help in planning the best times to take your medicine, check with your health care professional.

Only take medicine that your doctor has prescribed specially for you. Do not share your medicine with others.

Dosing—The dose of ritonavir will be different for different patients. *Follow your doctor's orders or the directions on the label.* The following information includes only the average doses of ritonavir. *If your dose is different, do not change it* unless your doctor tells you to do so.

- For *oral* dosage form (capsules):
  —For treatment of HIV infection:
    - Adults—600 milligrams (mg) two times a day.
    - Children—This oral dosage form is usually not used for children. Please refer to oral solution dosage form.

- For *oral* dosage form (oral solution):
  —For treatment of HIV infection:
    - Adults—600 milligrams (mg) two times a day.
    - Children 2 years of age and older—Dose is based on body size and must be determined by your doctor.
    - Children less than 2 years of age—Use and dose must be determined by your doctor.

Missed dose—If you miss a dose of this medicine, take it as soon as you remember. However, if it is almost time for your next dose, skip the missed dose and go back to your regular dosing schedule. Do not double doses.

Storage—To store this medicine:

- Keep out of the reach of children.
- Store the capsule form of this medicine in the refrigerator. The oral solution form should not be refrigerated; it should be stored at room temperature.
- Do not store in the bathroom, near the kitchen sink, or in other damp places. Heat or moisture may cause the medicine to break down.
- Do not keep outdated medicine or medicine no longer needed. Be sure that any discarded medicine is out of the reach of children.

Precautions While Using This Medicine

Do not take any other medicines without checking with your doctor first. To do so may increase the chance of side effects from ritonavir or the other medicines.

It is very important that your doctor check your progress at regular visits to make sure this medicine is working properly and check for unwanted effects, especially increases in blood sugar.

This medicine may decrease the effects of some oral contraceptives (birth control pills). *To avoid unwanted pregnancy, it is a good idea to use some additional contraceptive measures while being treated with ritonavir.*

Side Effects of This Medicine

Along with its needed effects, a medicine may cause some unwanted effects. Although not all of these side effects may occur, if they do occur they may need medical attention.

Check with your doctor as soon as possible if any of the following side effects occur:

Less common
Numbness or tingling feeling around the mouth; numbness or tingling feeling in the hands or feet

Rare
Confusion; dehydration; dry or itchy skin; fatigue; fruity mouth odor; increased hunger; increased thirst; increased urination; nausea; vomiting; weight loss

Other side effects may occur that usually do not need medical attention. These side effects may go away during treatment as your body adjusts to the medicine. However, check with your doctor if any of the following side effects continue or are bothersome:

More common
Change in sense of taste; diarrhea; loss of appetite; stomach pain; weakness

Less common
Dizziness; headache; sleepiness

Other side effects not listed above may also occur in some patients. If you notice any other effects, check with your doctor.

Developed: 08/04/98

RITUXIMAB Systemic

Commonly used brand name(s):

In the U.S.—
Rituxan

Description

Rituximab (ri-TUX-i-mab) is a monoclonal antibody. It is used to treat a type of cancer called non-Hodgkin's lymphoma.

Rituximab is to be administered only by or under the immediate supervision of your doctor. It is available in the following dosage form:

Parenteral
• Injection (U.S.)

Before Using This Medicine

In deciding to use a medicine, the risks of taking the medicine must be weighed against the good it will do. This is a decision you and your doctor will make. For rituximab, the following should be considered:

Allergies—Tell your doctor if you have ever had any unusual reaction to rituximab or to mouse proteins.

Pregnancy—Studies on effects in pregnancy have not been done in either humans or animals. However, rituximab is related to immunoglobulin, which affects the baby's ability to fight infection and which does cross the placenta. Women who are able to bear children should use some kind of birth control during treatment with rituximab and for up to 12 months after treatment has ended. Before receiving this medicine, make sure your doctor knows if you are pregnant or if you may become pregnant.

Tell your doctor right away if you think you have become pregnant while receiving rituximab.

Breast-feeding—It is not known whether rituximab passes into the breast milk. However, because of the possibility of serious effects, breast-feeding is not recommended while you are receiving this medicine and for a while after you stop receiving it. Discuss with your doctor the proper time to begin breast-feeding after treatment with rituximab.

Children—Studies on this medicine have been done only in adult patients, and there is no specific information comparing use of rituximab in children with use in other age groups.

Other medicines—Although certain medicines should not be used together at all, in other cases two different medicines may be used together even if an interaction might occur. In these cases, your doctor may want to change the dose, or other precautions may be necessary. Tell your health care professional if you are taking any other prescription or nonprescription (over-the-counter [OTC]) medicine.

Other medical problems—The presence of other medical problems may affect the use of rituximab. Make sure you tell your doctor if you have any other medical problems, especially heart problems (angina; arrhythmias) or sensitivity or a previous severe allergic reaction to rituximab or to mouse proteins.

Proper Use of This Medicine

Dosing—The dose of rituximab will be different for different patients. The dose that is used may depend on a number of things, including your size. Rituximab is usually given by a doctor or nurse in the hospital or an outpatient clinic. If you have any questions about the proper dose of rituximab, ask your doctor.

Side Effects of This Medicine

Along with its needed effects, a medicine may cause some unwanted effects. Although not all of these side effects may occur, if they do occur they may need medical attention.

Check with your doctor as soon as possible if any of the following side effects occur:

More common
Dizziness; feeling of swelling of tongue or throat; fever and chills; flushing of face; headache; itching; nausea; runny nose; shortness of breath; skin rash; unusual tiredness; vomiting

Less common
Black, tarry stools; blood in urine or stools; fever or chills with cough or hoarseness, lower back or side pain, or painful or difficult urination; pain at place of injection; pinpoint red spots on skin; red, itchy lining of eye; swelling of feet or lower legs; unusual bleeding or bruising; unusual weakness

Rare
Chest pain; irregular heartbeat

This medicine may also cause the following side effects that your doctor will watch for:

Less common
Anemia; hypertension (high blood pressure); low white blood cell count

Other side effects may occur that usually do not need medical attention. These side effects may go away during treatment as your body adjusts to the medicine. However, check with your doctor if any of the following side effects continue or are bothersome:

Less common

Abdominal or stomach pain; agitation or anxiety; back pain; change in taste; diarrhea; dry eyes; general feeling of discomfort or illness; heartburn; increased cough; joint pain; loss of appetite; muscle pain; nervousness; numbness or tingling of hands or feet; sore throat; swelling of stomach; trouble in sleeping

After you stop using this medicine, it may still produce some side effects that need attention. During this period of time *check with your doctor immediately* if you notice any of the following:

Black, tarry stools; blood in urine or stools; fever or chills with cough or hoarseness, lower back or side pain, or painful or difficult urination; pinpoint red spots on skin; unusual bleeding or bruising; unusual tiredness or weakness

Other side effects not listed above may also occur in some patients. If you notice any other effects, check with your doctor.

Developed: 03/23/98

RIVASTIGMINE Systemic— INTRODUCTORY VERSION

Commonly used brand name(s):

In the U.S.—
Exelon

In Canada—
Exelon

Description

Rivastigmine (riv-a-STIG-meen) is used to treat the symptoms of mild to moderate Alzheimer's disease. Rivastigmine will not cure Alzheimer's disease, and it will not stop the disease from getting worse. However, rivastigmine can improve thinking ability in some patients with Alzheimer's disease.

In Alzheimer's disease, many chemical changes take place in the brain. One of the earliest and biggest changes is that there is less of a chemical called acetylcholine (ACh). ACh helps the brain to work properly. Rivastigmine slows the breakdown of ACh, so it can build up and have a greater effect. However, as Alzheimer's disease gets worse, there will be less and less ACh, so rivastigmine may not work as well.

This medicine is available only with your doctor's prescription, in the following dosage forms:

Oral
• Capsules (U.S. and Canada)

Before Using This Medicine

In deciding to use a medicine, the risks of taking the medicine must be weighed against the good it will do. This is a decision you and your doctor will make. For rivastigmine the following should be considered:

Allergies—Tell your doctor if you have ever had any unusual or allergic reaction to rivastigmine or to other medications. Also tell your health care professional if you are allergic to any other substances, such as foods, preservatives, or dyes.

Pregnancy—Rivastigmine has not been studied in pregnant women. However, rivastigmine has not been shown to cause birth defects or other problems in animal studies.

Breast-feeding—It is not known whether rivastigmine passes into human breast milk. However, use of rivastigmine is not recommended in nursing mothers.

Children—Studies on this medicine have been done only in adult patients, and there is no specific information comparing use of rivastigmine in children with use in other age groups.

Older adults—Studies on rivastigmine have been done only in middle-aged and older patients. Information on the effects of rivastigmine is based on these patients.

Other medicines—Although certain medicines should not be used together at all, in other cases two different medicines may be used together even if an interaction might occur. In these cases, your doctor may want to change the dose, or other precautions may be necessary. When you are taking rivastigmine, it is especially important that your doctor and pharmacist know if you are taking any of the following:

• Inflammation or pain medicine, except narcotics—Stomach irritation may be increased

• Neuromuscular blocking agents (medicines used in surgery to relax muscles)—Rivastigmine may increase the effects of these medicines; your doctor may change the dose of rivastigmine before you have surgery

Other medical problems—The presence of other medical problems may affect the use of rivastigmine. Make sure you tell your doctor if you have any other medical problems, especially:

• Asthma (or history of) or
• Blockage in the intestines or stomach, or
• Heart problems, including slow heartbeat or hypotension (low blood pressure), or
• Stomach ulcer (or history of) or
• Urinary tract blockage or difficult urination—Rivastigmine may make these conditions worse

• Epilepsy or history of seizures or
• Diabetes, hormone, or thyroid problems that are poorly controlled—Rivastigmine may cause seizures

Proper Use of This Medicine

Take this medicine only as directed by your doctor. Do not take more or less of it, and do not take it more or less often than your doctor ordered. Taking too much may increase the chance of side effects, while taking too little may not improve your condition.

Rivastigmine is best taken with food.

Rivastigmine seems to work best when it is taken at regularly spaced times, usually two times a day, in the morning and evening.

Dosing—The dose of rivastigmine will be different for different patients. *Follow your doctor's orders or the direc-*

tions on the label. The following information includes only the average doses of rivastigmine. *If your dose is different, do not change it* unless your doctor tells you to do so.

- For *oral* dosage form (capsules):
  - —For treatment of Alzheimer's disease:
    - Adults—To start, 1.5 milligrams (mg) twice a day. Your doctor may increase your dose gradually if you are doing well on this medicine. However, the dose is usually not more than 6 mg twice a day.

Missed dose— If you miss a dose of this medicine, take it as soon as possible. However, if you do not remember within a few hours, skip the missed dose and go back to your regular dosing schedule. Do not double doses. Do not take your morning and evening doses close together.

Storage—To store this medicine:

- Keep out of the reach of children.
- Do not store in the bathroom, near the kitchen sink, or in other damp places. Heat or moisture may cause the medicine to break down.
- Store away from heat and direct light.
- Do not keep outdated medicine or medicine no longer needed. Ask your health care professional how you should dispose of any medicine you do not use. Be sure that any discarded medicine is out of the reach of children.

Precautions While Using This Medicine

It is very important that your doctor check your progress at regular visits.

Tell your doctor if your symptoms get worse, or if you notice any new symptoms.

Before you have any kind of surgery, dental treatment, or emergency treatment, tell the doctor medical doctor or dentist in charge that you are taking this medicine. Taking rivastigmine together with medicines that are sometimes used during surgery or dental or emergency treatments may increase the effects of these medicines.

Rivastigmine may cause some people to become dizzy, clumsy, or unsteady. *Make sure you know how you react to this medicine before you drive, use machines, or do anything else that could be dangerous if you are dizzy or are not alert.*

Rivastigmine causes a large number of patients to have problems with their stomachs and intestines. Tell your doctor about any nausea, vomiting, stomach pain or loss of appetite.

Do not stop taking this medicine or decrease your dose without first checking with your doctor. Stopping this medicine suddenly or decreasing the dose by a large amount may cause mental or behavior changes.

If you think you or someone else may have taken an overdose of rivastigmine, get emergency help at once. Taking an overdose of rivastigmine may lead to convulsions (seizures) or shock. Some signs of shock are large pupils, irregular breathing, and fast weak pulse. Other signs of an overdose are severe nausea and vomiting, increasing muscle weakness, greatly increased sweating, and greatly increased watering of the mouth.

Side Effects of This Medicine

Along with its needed effects, a medicine may cause some unwanted effects. Although not all of these side effects may occur, if they do occur they may need medical attention.

Check with your doctor as soon as possible if any of the following side effects occur.

More common
    Diarrhea; indigestion; loss of appetite; loss of strength; nausea and vomiting; weight loss

Less common
    High blood pressure; fainting

Rare
    Aggression; convulsions (seizures); trembling and shaking of hands and fingers; trouble in urinating

Symptoms of overdose
    Seizures; fast weak pulse; greatly increased sweating; greatly increased watering of mouth; irregular breathing; increasing muscle weakness; large pupils; low blood pressure; nausea; slow heartbeat; vomiting (severe)

Other side effects may occur that usually do not need medical attention. These side effects may go away during treatment as your body adjusts to the medicine. However, check with your doctor if any of the following side effects continue or are bothersome.

More common
    Abdominal or stomach pain or cramping; bloated full feeling; confusion; constipation; mental depression; dizziness; fatigue; headache; seeing, hearing, or feeling things that are not there; trouble in sleeping

Less common
    General feeling of discomfort or illness; increased sweating; runny nose

Other side effects not listed above may also occur in some patients. If you notice any other effects, check with your doctor.

Developed: 08/07/2000
Revised: 03/05/2001

RIZATRIPTAN   Systemic

Commonly used brand name(s):

In the U.S.—
    Maxalt
    Maxalt-MLT

Description

Rizatriptan (rye-za-TRIP-tan) is used to treat severe migraine headaches. Many people find that their headaches go away completely after they take rizatriptan. Other people find that their headaches are much less painful, and that they are able to go back to their normal activities even though their headaches are not completely gone.

Rizatriptan is not an ordinary pain reliever. It should not be used to relieve any kind of pain other than migraine headaches.

Rizatriptan may cause serious side effects in some people, especially people who have heart or blood vessel disease. Be sure that you discuss with your doctor the risks of using this medicine as well as the good that it can do.

This medicine is available only with your doctor's prescription, in the following dosage form(s):

Oral
- Tablets (U.S.)
- Orally disintegrating tablets (U.S.)

Before Using This Medicine

In deciding to use a medicine, the risks of taking the medicine must be weighed against the good it will do. This is a decision you and your doctor will make. For rizatriptan, the following should be considered:

Allergies—Tell your doctor if you have ever had any unusual or allergic reaction to rizatriptan or aspartame. Also tell your health care professional if you are allergic to any other substances, such as foods, preservatives, or dyes.

Pregnancy—Rizatriptan has not been studied in pregnant women. However, in some animal studies, rizatriptan caused harmful effects to the fetus. These unwanted effects usually occurred when rizatriptan was given in amounts that were large enough to cause harmful effects in the mother. Rizatriptan crosses the placenta in animals.

Breast-feeding—It is not known whether rizatriptan passes into human breast milk. However, it has been shown to pass into the milk of nursing animals.

Children—There is no specific information comparing use of rizatriptan in children with use in other age groups.

Older adults—Rizatriptan has been tested in elderly patients and has not been shown to cause different side effects or problems in older people than it does in younger adults.

Other medicines—Although certain medicines should not be used together at all, in other cases two different medicines may be used together even if an interaction might occur. In these cases, your doctor may want to change the dose, or other precautions may be necessary. When you are taking rizatriptan, it is especially important that your health care professional know if you are taking any of the following:

- Dihydroergotamine
- Ergotamine
- Methysergide
- Other 5-hydroxytryptamine agonists (naratriptan [e.g., Amerge], sumatriptan [e.g., Imitrex], zolmitriptan [e.g., Zomig])—Taking these medications with rizatriptan may increase the effects of rizatriptan
- Monoamine oxidase inhibitors (isocarboxazid [e.g., Marplan], phenelzine [e.g., Nardil], procarbazine [e.g., Matulane], selegiline [e.g., Eldepryl])—Taking rizatriptan while you are taking or within 2 weeks of taking MAO inhibitors may cause sudden high body temperature, extremely high blood pressure, and severe convulsions; at least 14 days should be allowed between stopping treatment with one medicine and starting treatment with the other.

Other medical problems—The presence of other medical problems may affect the use of rizatriptan. Make sure you tell your doctor if you have any other medical problems, especially:

- Angina (chest pain) or
- Heart or blood vessel disease or
- High blood pressure (uncontrolled) or
- Kidney disease or
- Liver disease—The chance of side effects may be increased. Heart or blood vessel disease and high blood pressure sometimes do not cause any symptoms, so some people do not know that they have these problems. Before deciding whether you should use rizatriptan, your doctor may need to do some tests to make sure that you do not have any of these conditions

Proper Use of This Medicine

Take this medicine exactly as directed by your doctor. It will work only if taken correctly.

Do not use rizatriptan for a headache that is different from your usual migraines. Instead, check with your doctor.

To relieve your migraine as soon as possible, use rizatriptan as soon as the headache pain begins. Even if you get warning signals of a coming migraine (an aura), you should wait until the headache pain starts before using rizatriptan.

Lying down in a quiet, dark room for a while after you use this medicine may help relieve your migraine.

Ask your doctor ahead of time about any other medicine you may take if rizatriptan does not work. *After you take the other medicine, check with your doctor as soon as possible.* Headaches that are not relieved by rizatriptan are sometimes caused by conditions that need other treatment.

If you feel much better after a dose of rizatriptan, but your headache comes back or gets worse after a while, you may use more rizatriptan. However, *use this medicine only as directed by your doctor. Do not use more of it, and do not use it more often, than directed.* Using too much rizatriptan may increase the chance of side effects.

Your doctor may direct you to take another medicine to help prevent headaches. *It is important that you follow your doctor's directions, even if your headaches continue to occur.* Headache-preventing medicines may take several weeks to start working. Even after they do start working, your headaches may not go away completely. However, your headaches should occur less often, and they should be less severe and easier to relieve. This can reduce the amount of rizatriptan or other pain medicines that you need. If you do not notice any improvement after several weeks of headache-preventing treatment, check with your doctor.

Dosing—The dose of rizatriptan will be different for different patients. *Follow your doctor's orders or the directions on the label.* The following information includes only the average doses of rizatriptan. *If your dose is different, do not change it* unless your doctor tells you to do so.

- For *oral* dosage form (tablets and orally disintegrating tablets):
  —For migraine headaches:
    - Adults—5 or 10 mg as a single dose. If the migraine comes back after being relieved, another dose may be taken two hours after the last dose.
    - Children—Use and dose must be determined by your doctor.

Storage—To store this medicine:
- Keep out of the reach of children.
- Store away from heat and direct light.
- Do not store in the bathroom, near the kitchen sink, or in other damp places. Heat or moisture may cause the medicine to break down.
- Do not keep outdated medicine or medicine no longer needed. Be sure that any discarded medicine is out of the reach of children.

Precautions While Using This Medicine

Drinking alcoholic beverages can make headaches worse or cause new headaches to occur. People who suffer from severe headaches should probably avoid alcoholic beverages, especially during a headache.

Some people feel drowsy or dizzy during or after a migraine, or after taking rizatriptan to relieve a migraine. As long as you are feeling drowsy or dizzy, *do not drive, use machines, or do anything else that could be dangerous if you are dizzy or are not alert.*

Side Effects of This Medicine

Along with its needed effects, a medicine may cause some unwanted effects. Although not all of these side effects may occur, if they do occur they may need medical attention.

Check with your doctor as soon as possible if any of the following side effects occur:

More common
Chest pain; heaviness, tightness, or pressure in chest and/or neck; pounding heartbeat; sensation of burning, warmth, heat, numbness, tightness, or tingling; shortness of breath

Less common
Increased heartbeat; irregular heartbeat; slow heartbeat

Symptoms of overdose
Dizziness; fainting; headache, severe or continuing; sleepiness; slow heartbeat; vomiting

Other side effects may occur that usually do not need medical attention. These side effects may go away during treatment as your body adjusts to the medicine. However, check with your doctor if any of the following side effects continue or are bothersome:

More common
Dizziness; dry mouth; hot flashes; nausea and/or vomiting; sleepiness; unusual tiredness or muscle weakness

Less common
Agitation; anxiety; blurred vision; chills; confusion; constipation; depression; diarrhea; difficulty swallowing; dry eyes; eye irritation; feeling of constant movement of self or surroundings; gas; headache; heartburn; heat sensitivity; inability to sleep; increased sweating; increased thirst; irritability; itching of the skin; muscle or joint stiffness, tightness, or rigidity; muscle pain or spasms; ringing or buzzing in ears; sudden large increase in frequency or quantity of urine; trembling of hands or feet; unusual feeling of well-being; warm and/or cold sensations

Other side effects not listed above may also occur in some patients. If you notice any other effects, check with your doctor.

Developed: 11/11/98

ROFECOXIB   Systemic

Commonly used brand name(s):

In the U.S.—
Vioxx

Description

Rofecoxib (roe-fe-COKS-ib) is used to relieve some symptoms caused by arthritis, such as inflammation, swelling, stiffness, and joint pain. However, this medicine does not cure arthritis and will help you only as long as you continue to take it.

Rofecoxib is also used to relieve other kinds of pain, such as menstrual cramps, and pain following surgery.

This medicine is available only with your doctor's prescription, in the following dosage form(s):

Oral
- Oral suspension (U.S.)
- Tablets (U.S.)

Before Using This Medicine

In deciding to use a medicine, the risks of taking the medicine must be weighed against the good it will do. This is a decision you and your doctor will make. For rofecoxib, the following should be considered:

Allergies—Tell your doctor if you have ever had any unusual or allergic reaction to rofecoxib. Also tell your health care professional if you are allergic to any other substances, such as foods, preservatives, or dyes.

Pregnancy—Rofecoxib has not been studied in pregnant women. However, there is a chance that this medicine may cause unwanted effects on the heart or blood flow of the fetus or newborn baby if it is taken regularly during the last few months of pregnancy. Studies in animals have shown that rofecoxib has caused birth defects of the spine. Before taking this medicine, make sure your doctor knows if you are pregnant or if you may become pregnant.

Breast-feeding—It is not known whether rofecoxib passes into breast milk. However, rofecoxib may cause unwanted effects in nursing babies. It may be necessary for you to take another medicine or stop breast-feeding during treatment. Be sure you have discussed the risks and benefits of the medicine with your doctor.

Children—Studies on this medicine have been done only in adult patients, and there is no specific information comparing the use of rofecoxib in children with use in older age groups.

Older adults—This medicine has been tested in a limited number of elderly patients 65 years of age and older and has not been shown to cause different side effects or problems in older people than it does in younger adults.

Other medicines—Although certain medicines should not be used together at all, in other cases two different medicines may be used together even if an interaction might occur. In these cases, your doctor may want to change the dose, or other precautions may be necessary. When you are taking rofecoxib, it is especially important that your health care professional know if you are taking any of the following:

- Aspirin—The chance of serious side effects may be increased

- Lithium (e.g., Lithane)—Higher blood levels of lithium and an increased chance of side effects may occur

- Rifampin—Lower blood levels of rofecoxib may occur

Other medical problems—The presence of other medical problems may affect the use of rofecoxib. Make sure you tell your doctor if you have any other medical problems, especially:

- Alcohol abuse or
- Bleeding problems or
- Stomach ulcer or other stomach or intestinal problems
- Tobacco use (or recent history of)—The chance of side effects may be increased

- Anemia or
- Asthma or
- Dehydration or
- Fluid retention (swelling of feet or lower legs) or
- Heart disease or
- High blood pressure or
- Kidney disease or
- Liver disease—Rofecoxib may make these conditions worse

Proper Use of This Medicine

For safe and effective use of this medicine, do not take more of it, do not take it more often, and do not take it for a longer time than ordered by your health care professional. Taking too much of this medicine may increase the chance of unwanted effects.

Dosing—The dose of rofecoxib will be different for different patients. *Follow your doctor's orders or the directions on the label.* The following information includes only the average doses of rofecoxib. *If your dose is different, do not change it* unless your doctor tells you to do so.

The number of tablets or teaspoonfuls of suspension that you take depends on the strength of the medicine. Also, *the number of doses you take each day, the time allowed between doses, and the length of time you take the medicine depend on the medical problem for which you are taking rofecoxib.*

- For *oral* dosage form (suspension, tablets):
  - —For osteoarthritis:
    - Adults—12.5 to 25 milligrams (mg) once a day.
    - Children—Use and dose must be determined by your doctor.
  - —Pain or menstrual cramps:
    - Adults—50 mg to start and 50 mg daily as needed for up to five days.
    - Children—Use and dose must be determined by your doctor.

Missed dose—If your health care professional has ordered you to take this medicine according to a regular schedule, and you miss a dose, take it as soon as possible. However, if it is almost time for your next dose, skip the missed dose and go back to your regular dosing schedule. Do not double doses.

Storage—To store this medicine:
- Keep out of the reach of children.
- Store away from heat and direct light.
- Do not store in the bathroom, near the kitchen sink, or in other damp places. Heat or moisture may cause the medicine to break down.
- Keep the medicine from freezing. Do not refrigerate.
- Do not keep outdated medicine or medicine no longer needed. Be sure that any discarded medicine is out of the reach of children.

Precautions While Using This Medicine

If you will be taking this medicine for a long time, your doctor should check your progress at regular visits.

Stomach problems may be more likely to occur if you drink alcoholic beverages while being treated with this medicine. Therefore, *do not regularly drink alcoholic beverages while taking this medicine, unless otherwise directed by your doctor*.

Taking two or more of the nonsteroidal anti-inflammatory drugs together on a regular basis may increase the chance of unwanted effects. Also, taking acetaminophen, aspirin or other salicylates, or ketorolac (e.g., Toradol) regularly while you are taking a nonsteroidal anti-inflammatory drug may increase the chance of unwanted effects. The risk will depend on how much of each medicine you take every day, and on how long you take the medicines together. If your health care professional directs you to take these medicines together on a regular basis, follow his or her directions carefully. However, *do not take acetaminophen or aspirin or other salicylates together with this medicine for more than a few days, and do not take any ketorolac (e.g., Toradol) while taking this medicine, unless your doctor has directed you to do so and is following your progress*.

Serious side effects can occur during treatment with this medicine. Sometimes serious side effects can occur without warning. However, possible warning signs often occur, including severe stomach pain, black tarry stools, and/or vomiting of blood or material that looks like coffee grounds; skin rash; swelling of the face, fingers, feet, and/or lower legs. *Stop taking this medicine and check with your doctor immediately if you notice any of these warning signs.*

Rofecoxib may cause a serious type of allergic reaction called anaphylaxis. Although this is rare, it may occur often in patients who are allergic to aspirin or other nonsteroidal anti-inflammatory drugs. *Anaphylaxis requires immediate medical attention.* The most serious signs of this reaction are very fast or irregular breathing, gasping for breath, wheezing, or fainting. Other signs may include changes in skin color of the face; very fast but irregular heartbeat or pulse; hive-like swellings on the skin; puffiness or swellings of the eyelids or around the eyes. If these effects occur, get emergency help at once. Ask someone to drive you to the nearest hospital emergency room. Call an ambulance, lie down, cover yourself to keep warm, and prop your feet higher than your head. Stay in that position until help arrives.

Side Effects of This Medicine

Along with its needed effects, a medicine may cause some unwanted effects. Although not all of these side effects may occur, if they do occur they may need medical attention.

Check with your doctor as soon as possible if any of the following side effects occur:
> *More common*
>> Congestion in chest; cough; fever; sneezing; sore throat
>
> *Less common or rare*
>> Bloody or black, tarry stools; chills; burning feeling in chest or stomach; hives; loss of appetite; muscle aches and pain; prolonged or severe vomiting; shortness of breath; skin rash; tenderness in the stomach area; unusual weight gain; vomiting of blood or material that looks like coffee grounds

Other side effects may occur that usually do not need medical attention. These side effects may go away during treatment as your body adjusts to the medicine. However, check with

your doctor if any of the following side effects continue or are bothersome:

> *More common*
> Back pain; diarrhea; dizziness; headache; heartburn; loss of energy or weakness; nausea; stuffy or runny nose; swelling of legs and feet

> *Less common or rare*
> Blurred vision; constipation

Other side effects not listed above may also occur in some patients. If you notice any other effects, check with your doctor.

Developed: 06/14/99

ROPINIROLE   Systemic

Commonly used brand name(s):

In the U.S.—
   Requip

In Canada—
   Requip

Description

Ropinirole (ro-PIN-a-rol) is used alone or with other medicines to treat Parkinson's disease.

This medicine is available only with your doctor's prescription, in the following dosage form:

> *Oral*
> • Tablets (U.S. and Canada)

Before Using This Medicine

In deciding to use a medicine, the risks of taking the medicine must be weighed against the good it will do. This is a decision you and your doctor will make. For ropinirole, the following should be considered:

Allergies—Tell your doctor if you have ever had any unusual or allergic reaction to ropinirole. Also tell your health care professional if you are allergic to any other substances, such as foods, preservatives, or dyes.

Pregnancy—Ropinirole has not been studied in pregnant women. However, studies in pregnant animals have shown that ropinirole may cause birth defects in the offspring when the mother is given doses many times higher than the human dose. Before taking this medicine, make sure your doctor knows if you are pregnant or if you may become pregnant.

Breast-feeding—It is not known whether ropinirole passes into breast milk. Because of the possibility of serious unwanted effects in the nursing infant, it is important that you discuss the use of this medicine with your doctor if you wish to breast-feed.

Children—Studies on this medicine have been done only in adult patients, and there is no specific information comparing use of ropinirole in children with use in other age groups.

Older adults—Hallucinations (seeing, hearing, or feeling things that are not there) may be especially likely to occur in elderly patients, who are usually more sensitive than younger adults to the effects of ropinirole.

Other medicines—Although certain medicines should not be used together at all, in other cases two different medicines may be used together even if an interaction might occur. In these cases, your doctor may want to change the dose, or other precautions may be necessary. When you are taking ropinirole, it is especially important that your health care professional know if you are taking any of the following:

> • Carbidopa and levodopa combinations (e.g., Sinemet) or
> • Levodopa (e.g., Dopar, Larodopa)—Ropinirole may cause an increase in the side effects of levodopa; your doctor may need to adjust your dosage

Other medical problems—The presence of other medical problems may affect the use of ropinirole. Make sure you tell your doctor if you have any other medical problems, especially:

> • Eye problems, especially with the retina—Animal studies have shown that problems with the retina may occur; it is not certain if this may occur in humans
> • Hallucinations (seeing, hearing, or feeling things that are not there) or
> • Hypotension (low blood pressure) or
> • Postural hypotension (dizziness, lightheadedness, or fainting when getting up from a lying or sitting position)—Ropinirole may make these conditions worse
> • Liver problems—Higher blood levels of ropinirole may result, and cause an increase in side effects
> • Lung problems resulting from treatment with some other Parkinson's disease medicines—Ropinirole may cause the condition to recur

---

Proper Use of This Medicine

Take this medicine every day exactly as ordered by your doctor in order to improve your condition as much as possible. Do not take more of it or less of it, and do not take it more or less often than your doctor ordered.

This medicine may be taken with or without food, or on an empty or full stomach. Taking this medicine with food may reduce nausea.

Dosing—The dose of ropinirole will be different for different patients. *Follow your doctor's orders or the directions on the label.* The following information includes only the average doses of ropinirole. *If your dose is different, do not change it* unless your doctor tells you to do so.

The number of tablets that you take depends on the strength of the medicine. Also, *the number of doses you take each day, the time allowed between doses, and the length of time you take the medicine depend on the medical problem for which you are taking ropinirole.*

> • For *oral* dosage form (tablets):
> —For Parkinson's disease:
> • Adults—At first, 0.25 milligrams (mg) three times a day. Your doctor will increase your dose as needed and tolerated. However, the dose is usually not more than 24 mg a day.
> • Children—Use and dose must be determined by the doctor.

Missed dose—If you miss a dose of this medicine, take it as soon as possible. However, if it is almost time for your next dose, skip the missed dose and go back to your regular dosing schedule. Do not double doses.

Storage—To store this medicine:

> • Keep out of the reach of children.

- Store away from heat and direct light.
- Do not store in the bathroom, near the kitchen sink, or in other damp places. Heat or moisture may cause the medicine to break down.
- Keep the medicine from freezing. Do not refrigerate.
- Do not keep outdated medicine or medicine no longer needed. Be sure that any discarded medicine is out of the reach of children.

Precautions While Using This Medicine

It is important that your doctor check your progress at regular visits. This is necessary to allow dose adjustments and to reduce any unwanted effects.

Do not stop taking this medicine without first checking with your doctor. Your doctor may want you to reduce gradually the amount you are taking before stopping completely.

This medicine may cause some people to become drowsy, dizzy or lightheaded, to be less alert than they are normally, or to have vision problems, weakness, or problems with co-ordination. *Make sure you know how you react to this medicine before you drive, use machines, or do anything else that could be dangerous if you are not alert, well-coordinated, or able to think or see well.* People taking this medicine have reported falling asleep without warning during activities of daily living, including driving which sometimes resulted in accidents. This may happen as late as one year after taking the medicine.

Dizziness, lightheadedness, or fainting may occur, especially when you get up from a lying or sitting position. These symptoms are more likely to occur when you begin taking this medicine, or when the dose is increased. Getting up slowly may help. If you should have this problem, check with your doctor.

Hallucinations (seeing, hearing, or feeling things that are not there) may occur in some patients. This is more common with elderly patients.

Side Effects of This Medicine

Along with its needed effects, a medicine may cause some unwanted effects. Although not all of these side effects may occur, if they do occur they may need medical attention.

Check with your doctor as soon as possible if any of the following side effects occur:

More common
   Confusion; dizziness; drowsiness; falling; lightheadedness or fainting, especially when standing up; nausea; seeing, hearing, or feeling things that are not there (hallucinations); swelling of legs; twisting, twitching, or other unusual body movements; unusual tiredness or weakness; worsening of parkinsonism

Less common
   Abdominal pain; blood in urine; burning, pain, or difficulty in urinating; chest pain; cough; double vision or other eye or vision problems; fast heartbeat; high or low blood pressure; irregular or pounding heartbeat; loss of memory; mental depression; pain; pain in arms or legs; shortness of breath; sore throat; tightness in chest; tingling, numbness, or prickly feelings; trouble in concentrating; troubled breathing; vomiting; wheezing

Rare
   Anxiety or nervousness; buzzing or ringing in ears; chills; cough; fever; headache; joint pain; loss of

bladder control; muscle cramps, pain, or spasms; nasal congestion; runny nose; sneezing; trouble in swallowing

Symptoms of overdose
   Agitation; chest pain; confusion; dizziness or lightheadedness, especially when standing up; drowsiness; grogginess; increase in unusual body movements, especially of the face or mouth; nausea; vomiting

Other side effects may occur that usually do not need medical attention. These side effects may go away during treatment as your body adjusts to the medicine. However, check with your doctor if any of the following side effects continue or are bothersome:

Less common
   Abnormal dreams; constipation; decrease in sexual desire or performance; diarrhea; dryness of mouth; flushing; general feeling of discomfort or illness; headache; heartburn or gas; hot flashes; increased sweating; loss of appetite; tremor; weight loss; yawning

Other side effects not listed above may also occur in some patients. If you notice any other effects, check with your doctor.

Developed: 02/24/98
Revised: 04/25/00

ROSIGLITAZONE   Systemic

Commonly used brand name(s):

In the U.S.—
   Avandia

In Canada—
   Avandia

Description

Rosiglitazone (ROS-e-glit-a-zone) is used to treat a certain type of diabetes mellitus (sugar diabetes) called type 2 diabetes. It may be used alone or with another type of oral diabetes medicine, such as metformin or a sulfonylurea.

This medicine is available only with your doctor's prescription, in the following dosage form:

Oral
   • Tablets (U.S. and Canada)

Before Using This Medicine

In deciding to use a medicine, the risks of taking the medicine must be weighed against the good it will do. This is a decision you and your doctor will make. For rosiglitazone, the following should be considered:

Allergies—Tell your doctor if you have ever had any unusual or allergic reaction to rosiglitazone. Also tell your health care professional if you are allergic to any other substances, such as foods, preservatives, or dyes.

Pregnancy—Rosiglitazone has not been studied in pregnant women. However, it is easier during pregnancy to control your blood sugar by using injections of insulin, rather than by taking rosiglitazone. Close control of your blood sugar can reduce the chance of your baby gaining too much weight, having birth defects, or having high blood sugar before birth.

Be sure to tell your doctor if you plan to become pregnant or you think you are pregnant.

Breast-feeding—It is not known whether rosiglitazone passes into the breast milk of humans. However, rosiglitazone is not recommended during breast-feeding.

Children—Studies on this medicine have been done only in adult patients, and there is no specific information comparing use of rosiglitazone in children with use in other age groups.

Older adults—This medicine has been tested in a limited number of patients 65 years of age or older and has not been shown to cause different side effects or problems in older people than it does in younger adults.

Other medical problems—The presence of other medical problems may affect the use of rosiglitazone. Make sure you tell your doctor if you have any other medical problems, especially:

- Diabetic ketoacidosis (ketones in the blood) or
- Type 1 diabetes–Insulin is needed to control these conditions
- Heart disease or
- Liver disease–Rosiglitazone may make these conditions worse

Proper Use of This Medicine

Follow carefully the special meal plan your doctor gave you. This is the most important part of controlling your condition, and is necessary if the medicine is to work properly. Also, exercise regularly and test for sugar in your blood or urine as directed.

Rosiglitazone may be taken with or without food.

Dosing—The dose of rosiglitazone will be different for different patients. *Follow your doctor's orders or the directions on the label. If your dose is different, do not change it* unless your doctor tells you to do so.

- For *oral* dosage form (tablets):
  —For type 2 diabetes:
  - Rosiglitazone alone:
    —Adults—At first, the dose is 4 milligrams (mg) once a day or 2 mg twice a day. After 12 weeks, the dose may be increased to 8 mg once a day or 4 mg twice a day
    —Children: Use and dose must be determined by your doctor.
  - Rosiglitazone with metformin:
    —Adults—At first, the dose is 4 mg once a day or 2 mg twice a day. After 12 weeks, the dose may be increased to 8 mg once a day or 4 mg twice a day.
    —Children: Use and dose must be determined by your doctor.
  - Rosiglitazone with a sulfonylurea:
    —Adults—4 mg once a day or 2 mg twice a day. Any changes in the dose will be determined by your doctor.
    —Children: Use and dose must be determined by your doctor.

Missed dose—If you miss a dose of this medicine, take it as soon as you remember. However, if you do not remember it until it is time for your next dose, skip the missed dose and go back to your regular dosing schedule. Do not double doses.

Storage—To store this medicine:

- Keep out of the reach of children.
- Store away from heat and direct light.
- Do not keep outdated medicine or medicine no longer needed. Ask your health care professional how you should dispose of any medicine you do not use. Be sure that any discarded medicine is out of the reach of children.

Precautions While Using This Medicine

If you experience abdominal or stomach pain, dark urine, loss of appetite, nausea or vomiting, unusual tiredness or weakness, or yellow eyes or skin, check with your doctor immediately. These may be symptoms of liver problems.

It is very important that your doctor check your progress at regular visits to make sure that this medicine is working properly and to check for unwanted effects

It is very important to follow carefully any instructions from your health care team about

- Alcohol—Drinking alcohol may cause severe low blood sugar. Discuss this with your health care team.
- Other medicines—Do not take other medicines during the time you are taking rosiglitazone unless they have been discussed with your doctor. This especially includes nonprescription medicines such as aspirin, and medicines for appetite control, asthma, colds, cough, hay fever, or sinus problems.
- Counseling—Other family members need to learn how to prevent side effects or help with side effects if they occur. Also, diabetic patients may need special counseling about diabetes medicine dosing changes that might occur because of lifestyle changes, such as changes in exercise and diet. Furthermore, counseling on contraception and pregnancy may be needed because of the problems that can occur in patients with diabetes during pregnancy.
- Travel—Keep a recent prescription and your medical history with you. Be prepared for an emergency as you would normally. Make allowances for changing time zones and keep your meal times as close as possible to your usual meal times.
- *In case of emergency*—There may be a time when you need emergency help for a problem caused by your diabetes. You need to be prepared for these emergencies. It is a good idea to wear a medical identification (ID) bracelet or neck chain at all times. Also, carry an ID card in your wallet or purse that says that you have diabetes and a list of all of your medicines.
- *This medicine does not cause hypoglycemia (low blood sugar). However, low blood sugar can occur* if you delay or miss a meal or snack, exercise more than usual, drink alcohol, or cannot eat because of nausea or vomiting.
- *Symptoms of low blood sugar include* anxiety; behavior change similar to being drunk; blurred vision; cold sweats; confusion; cool, pale skin; difficulty in thinking; drowsiness; excessive hunger; fast heartbeat; headache (continuing); nausea; nervousness; nightmares; restless sleep; shakiness; slurred speech; or unusual tiredness or weakness.
- If symptoms of low blood sugar occur, *eat glucose tablets or gel, corn syrup, honey, or sugar cubes; or drink fruit juice, nondiet soft drink, or sugar dissolved in water to relieve the symptoms.* Also, check

your blood for low blood sugar. *Glucagon is used in emergency situations when severe symptoms such as seizures (convulsions) or unconsciousness occur* Have a glucagon kit available, along with a syringe and needle, and know how to use it. Members of your family also should know how to use it.

Hyperglycemia (high blood sugar) may occur if you do not take enough or skip a dose of your antidiabetic medicine, overeat or do not follow your meal plan, have a fever or infection, or do not exercise as much as usual.

Symptoms of high blood sugar include blurred vision; drowsiness; dry mouth; flushed, dry skin; fruit-like breath odor; increased urination; ketones in urine; loss of appetite; stomachache, nausea, or vomiting; tiredness; troubled breathing (rapid and deep); unconsciousness; or unusual thirst.

If symptoms of high blood sugar occur, *check your blood sugar level and then call your doctor for instructions*

Side Effects of This Medicine

Along with its needed effects, a medicine may cause some unwanted effects. Although not all of these side effects may occur, if they do occur they may need medical attention.

Check with your doctor as soon as possible if any of the following side effects occur
More common
Fever, runny or stuffy nose; swelling of feet or lower legs

Other side effects may occur that usually do not need medical attention. These side effects may go away during treatment as your body adjusts to the medicine. However, check with your doctor if any of the following side effects continue or are bothersome:
More common
Back pain; headache
Less common
Dizziness or lightheadedness

Other side effects not listed above may also occur in some patients. If you notice any other effects, check with your doctor.

Developed: 1/20/2000
Revised: 9/14/2000

ROTAVIRUS VACCINE LIVE ORAL
Systemic†—INTRODUCTORY VERSION

†Not commercially available in Canada.

Description

Rotavirus (ROE-ta-VYE-rus) vaccine live oral is an immunizing agent used to prevent infection by the rotavirus. It works by causing your body to produce its own protection (antibodies) against the virus.

Rotavirus infection is the single most important cause of diarrhea and vomiting in infants and young children both in developed and developing countries. If untreated, severe rota-

viral diarrhea in infants can rapidly become life-threatening. The risk of serious complications and death from rotaviral infection is greater for infants and younger children than for adults.

Immunization against rotavirus infection is recommended for infants 2 to 6 months of age. The first dose of rotavirus vaccine live oral may be administered at as early as 6 weeks of age.

This vaccine is to be administered only by or under the supervision of your doctor or other health care professional.

The medicine was withdrawn from the U.S. market in October 1999.

Before Receiving This Vaccine

In deciding to use a medicine, the risks of taking the medicine must be weighed against the good it will do. This is a decision you and your doctor will make. For rotavirus vaccine live oral, the following should be considered:

Allergies—Tell your doctor if your child has ever had any unusual or allergic reaction to rotavirus vaccine live oral, aminoglycosides, or amphotericin B. Also tell your health care professional if your child is allergic to any other substances, such as foods, preservatives, or dyes.

Pregnancy—Studies on the effects of rotavirus vaccine live oral on pregnancy have not been done in either humans or animals. Use is not recommended in persons older than 6 months of age.

Breast-feeding—Rotavirus vaccine live oral has not been reported to cause problems in nursing babies.

Children—Use is not recommended in children older than 6 months of age.

Older adults—Rotavirus vaccine live oral has been tested only in infants and there is no specific information about its use in older patients. Use is not recommended in persons older than 6 months of age.

Other medicines—Although certain medicines should not be used together at all, in other cases two different medicines may be used together even if an interaction might occur. In these cases, your doctor may want to change the dose, or other precautions may be necessary. Tell your health care professional if your child is using any other prescription or nonprescription (over-the-counter [OTC]) medicine.

Other medical problems—The presence of other medical problems may affect the use of rotavirus vaccine live oral. Make sure you tell your doctor if your child has any other medical problems, especially:

• Diarrhea or
• Vomiting—The condition may reduce the useful effect of the vaccine

• Fever—The symptoms of the condition may be confused with possible side effects of the vaccine

• Immune deficiency conditions (or family history of)—The condition may increase the chance of side effects of the vaccine

Proper Use of This Vaccine

Dosing—The following information includes only the average doses of rotavirus vaccine live oral.

- For *oral* dosage form (oral solution):
  —For prevention of rotavirus infection:
  - Adults, children and infants older than 6 months of age—Use is not recommended.
  - Infants 2 to 6 months of age—One dose is given at 2 months of age, a second dose is given at 4 months of age, and a third dose is given at 6 months of age.

Side Effects of This Vaccine

Along with its needed effects, a medicine may cause some unwanted effects. Although not all of these side effects may occur, if they do occur they may need medical attention.

Check with your doctor as soon as possible if any of the following side effects occur:

More common
   Fever of 100.4 to 102.2 °F (38 to 39 °C)
Rare
   Fever of 102.2 °F (39 °C) or more

Other side effects may occur that usually do not need medical attention. These side effects may go away during treatment as your body adjusts to the medicine. However, check with your doctor if any of the following side effects continue or are bothersome:

More common
   Decreased activity; decreased appetite; irritability
Less common
   Abdominal cramping

Other side effects not listed above may also occur in some patients. If you notice any other effects, check with your doctor.

Developed: 05/24/1999
Revised: 10/13/2000

SALICYLATES   Systemic

Commonly used brand name(s):

In the U.S.—

Acuprin 81[1]
Amigesic[8]
Anacin Caplets[2]
Anacin Maximum Strength[2]
Anacin Tablets[2]
Anaflex 750[8]
Arthritis Pain Ascriptin[3]
Arthritis Pain Formula[3]
Arthritis Strength Bufferin[3]
Arthropan[5]
Aspergum[1]
Aspirin Regimen Bayer Adult Low Dose[1]
Aspirin Regimen Bayer Regular Strength Caplets[1]
Aspir-Low[1]
Aspirtab[1]
Aspirtab-Max[1]
Backache Caplets[7]
Bayer Children's Aspirin[1]
Bayer Select Maximum Strength Backache Pain Relief Formula[7]
Bufferin Caplets[3]
Bufferin Tablets[3]
Buffex[3]
Buffinol[3]
Buffinol Extra[3]
Cama Arthritis Pain Reliever[3]
CMT[6]
Cope[4]
Disalcid[8]
Doan's Regular Strength Tablets[7]
Easprin[1]
Ecotrin Caplets[1]
Ecotrin Tablets[1]
Empirin[1]
Extended-release Bayer 8-Hour[1]
Extra Strength Bayer Arthritis Pain Formula Caplets[1]
Extra Strength Bayer Aspirin Caplets[1]
Extra Strength Bayer Aspirin Tablets[1]
Extra Strength Bayer Plus Caplets[3]
Gensan[2]
Genuine Bayer Aspirin Caplets[1]
Genuine Bayer Aspirin Tablets[1]
Halfprin[1]
Healthprin Adult Low Strength[1]
Healthprin Full Strength[1]
Healthprin Half-Dose[1]
Magan[7]
Magnaprin[3]
Marthritic[8]
Maximum Strength Arthritis Foundation Safety Coated Aspirin[1]
Maximum Strength Ascriptin[3]
Maximum Strength Doan's Analgesic Caplets[7]
Mobidin[7]
Mono-Gesic[8]
Norwich Aspirin[1]
P-A-C Revised Formula[2]
Regular Strength Ascriptin[3]
Salflex[8]
Salsitab[8]
Sloprin[1]
St. Joseph Adult Chewable Aspirin[1]
Tricosal[6]
Trilisate[6]
ZORprin[1]

In Canada—

Anacin[2]
Anacin Extra Strength[2]
Antidol[2]
Apo-Asa[1]
Apo-ASEN[1]
Arco Pain Tablet[2]
Arthrisin[1]
Artria S.R[1]
Aspergum[1]
Aspirin Caplets[1]
Aspirin Children's Tablets[1]
Aspirin, Coated[1]
Aspirin Plus Stomach Guard Extra Strength[3]
Aspirin Plus Stomach Guard Regular Strength[3]
Aspirin Tablets[1]
Astone[2]
Astrin[1]
Bufferin Caplets[3]
Bufferin Extra Strength Caplets[3]
Calmine[2]
C2[2]
C2 Buffered[4]
Coryphen[1]
Disalcid[8]
Doan's Backache Pills[7]
Dodd's Extra Strength[9]
Dodd's Pills[9]
Dolomine[2]
Entrophen Caplets[1]
Entrophen Extra Strength[1]
Entrophen 15 Maximum Strength Tablets[1]
Entrophen 10 Super Strength Caplets[1]
Entrophen Tablets[1]
Gin Pain Pills[9]
Headache Tablet[1]
Herbopyrine[2]
Instantine[2]
Kalmex[2]
Nervine[2]
Novasen[1]
Novasen Sp.C[1]
Pain Aid[2]
PMS-ASA[1]
Sero-Gesic[7]
217 Strong[2]
217[2]
Tri-Buffered ASA[3]
Trilisate[6]

Other commonly used names are:

acetylsalicylic acid
ASA
choline magnesium trisalicylate
salicylsalicylic acid

Note: For quick reference, the following salicylates are numbered to match the corresponding brand names.

This information applies to the following medicines:
1. Aspirin (AS-pir-in) ‡§
2. Aspirin and Caffeine (AS-pir-in and KAF-een) ‡
3. Buffered Aspirin**‡
4. Buffered Aspirin and Caffeine
5. Choline Salicylate (KOE-leen sa-LI-si-late) †
6. Choline and Magnesium Salicylates (KOE-leen and mag-NEE-zhum sa-LI-si-lates) ‡
7. Magnesium Salicylate (mag-NEE-zhum sa-LI-si-late)
8. Salsalate (SAL-sa-late) ‡
9. Sodium Salicylate (SOE-dee-um sa-LI-si-late) ‡

†Not commercially available in Canada.
‡Generic name product may be available in the U.S.
§Generic name product may be available in Canada.
**Some of the buffered aspirin products may be identified on the label as Aspirin (ASA), Alumina, and Magnesia or as Aspirin, Alumina, and Magnesium Oxide.

Description

Salicylates are used to relieve pain and reduce fever. Most salicylates are also used to relieve some symptoms caused by arthritis (rheumatism), such as swelling, stiffness, and joint pain. However, they do not cure arthritis and will help you only as long as you continue to take them.

Aspirin may also be used to lessen the chance of heart attack, stroke, or other problems that may occur when a blood vessel is blocked by blood clots. Aspirin helps prevent dangerous blood clots from forming. However, this effect of aspirin may increase the chance of serious bleeding in some people. Therefore, aspirin should be used for this purpose only when your doctor decides, after studying your medical condition and history, that the danger of blood clots is greater than the risk of bleeding. *Do not take aspirin to prevent blood clots or a heart attack unless it has been ordered by your doctor.*

Salicylates may also be used for other conditions as determined by your doctor.

The caffeine present in some of these products may provide additional relief of headache pain or faster pain relief.

Some salicylates are available only with your medical doctor's or dentist's prescription. Others are available without a prescription; however, your medical doctor or dentist may have special instructions on the proper dose of these medicines for your medical condition.

These medicines are available in the following dosage forms:

Oral
  Aspirin
  • Tablets (U.S. and Canada)
  • Chewable tablets (U.S. and Canada)
  • Chewing gum tablets (U.S. and Canada)
  • Delayed-release (enteric-coated) tablets (U.S. and Canada)
  • Extended-release tablets (U.S. and Canada)
  Aspirin and Caffeine
  • Capsules (Canada)
  • Tablets (U.S. and Canada)
  Buffered Aspirin
  • Tablets (U.S. and Canada)
  Buffered Aspirin and Caffeine
  • Tablets (U.S. and Canada)
  Choline Salicylate
  • Oral solution (U.S.)
  Choline and Magnesium Salicylates
  • Oral solution (U.S.)
  • Tablets (U.S. and Canada)
  Magnesium Salicylate
  • Tablets (U.S. and Canada)
  Salsalate
  • Capsules (U.S.)
  • Tablets (U.S. and Canada)
  Sodium Salicylate
  • Tablets (Canada)
  • Delayed-release (enteric-coated) tablets (U.S.)

Rectal
  Aspirin
  • Suppositories (U.S. and Canada)

Before Using This Medicine

If you are taking this medicine without a prescription, carefully read and follow any precautions on the label. For salicylates, the following should be considered:

Allergies—Tell your doctor if you have ever had any unusual or allergic reaction to aspirin or other salicylates, including methyl salicylate (oil of wintergreen), or to any of the following medicines:

  Diclofenac (e.g., Voltaren)
  Diflunisal (e.g., Dolobid)
  Etodolac (e.g., Lodine)
  Fenoprofen (e.g., Nalfon)
  Floctafenine (e.g., Idarac)
  Flurbiprofen, oral (e.g., Ansaid)
  Ibuprofen (e.g., Motrin)
  Indomethacin (e.g., Indocin)
  Ketoprofen (e.g., Orudis)
  Ketorolac (e.g., Toradol)
  Meclofenamate (e.g., Meclomen)
  Mefenamic acid (e.g., Ponstel)
  Nabumetone (e.g., Relafen)
  Naproxen (e.g., Naprosyn)
  Oxaprozin (e.g., Daypro)
  Oxyphenbutazone (e.g., Tandearil)
  Phenylbutazone (e.g., Butazolidin)
  Piroxicam (e.g., Feldene)
  Sulindac (e.g., Clinoril)
  Suprofen (e.g., Suprol)
  Tenoxicam (e.g., Mobiflex)
  Tiaprofenic acid (e.g., Surgam)
  Tolmetin (e.g., Tolectin)
  Zomepirac (e.g., Zomax)

Also tell your health care professional if you are allergic to any other substances, such as foods, preservatives, or dyes.

Diet—Make certain your health care professional knows if you are on a low-sodium diet. Regular use of large amounts of sodium salicylate (as for arthritis) can add a large amount of sodium to your diet. Sodium salicylate contains 46 mg of sodium in each 325-mg tablet and 92 mg of sodium in each 650-mg tablet.

Pregnancy—Salicylates have not been shown to cause birth defects in humans. Studies on birth defects in humans have been done with aspirin but not with other salicylates. However, salicylates caused birth defects in animal studies.

Some reports have suggested that too much use of aspirin late in pregnancy may cause a decrease in the newborn's weight and possible death of the fetus or newborn infant. However, the mothers in these reports had been taking much larger amounts of aspirin than are usually recommended. Studies of mothers taking aspirin in the doses that are usually recommended did not show these unwanted effects. However, there is a chance that regular use of salicylates late in pregnancy may cause unwanted effects on the heart or blood flow in the fetus or in the newborn infant.

Use of salicylates, especially aspirin, during the last 2 weeks of pregnancy may cause bleeding problems in the fetus before or during delivery or in the newborn infant. Also, too much use of salicylates during the last 3 months of pregnancy may increase the length of pregnancy, prolong labor, cause other problems during delivery, or cause severe bleeding in the mother before, during, or after delivery. *Do not take aspirin during the last 3 months of pregnancy unless it has been ordered by your doctor.*

Studies in humans have not shown that caffeine (present in some aspirin products) causes birth defects. However, studies in animals have shown that caffeine causes birth defects when given in very large doses (amounts equal to those present in 12 to 24 cups of coffee a day).

Breast-feeding—Salicylates pass into the breast milk. Although salicylates have not been reported to cause problems in nursing babies, it is possible that problems may occur if large amounts are taken regularly, as for arthritis (rheumatism).

Caffeine passes into the breast milk in small amounts.

Children—*Do not give aspirin or other salicylates to a child or a teenager with a fever or other symptoms of a virus infection, especially flu or chickenpox, without first discussing its use with your child's doctor.* This is very important because salicylates may cause a serious illness called Reye's syndrome in children and teenagers with fever caused by a virus infection, especially flu or chickenpox.

Some children may need to take aspirin or another salicylate regularly (as for arthritis). However, your child's doctor may want to stop the medicine for a while if a fever or other symptoms of a virus infection occur. Discuss this with your child's doctor, so that you will know ahead of time what to do if your child gets sick.

Children who do not have a virus infection may also be more sensitive to the effects of salicylates, especially if they have a fever or have lost large amounts of body fluid because of vomiting, diarrhea, or sweating. This may increase the chance of side effects during treatment.

Older adults—Elderly people are especially sensitive to the effects of salicylates. This may increase the chance of side effects during treatment.

Other medicines—Although certain medicines should not be used together at all, in other cases two different medicines may be used together even if an interaction might occur. In these cases, your doctor may want to change the dose, or other precautions may be necessary. When you are taking a salicylate, it is especially important that your health care professional know if you are taking any of the following:
- Anticoagulants (blood thinners) or
- Carbenicillin by injection (e.g., Geopen) or
- Cefamandole (e.g., Mandol) or
- Cefoperazone (e.g., Cefobid) or
- Cefotetan (e.g., Cefotan) or
- Dipyridamole (e.g., Persantine) or
- Divalproex (e.g., Depakote) or
- Heparin or
- Inflammation or pain medicine, except narcotics, or
- Pentoxifylline (e.g., Trental) or
- Plicamycin (e.g., Mithracin) or
- Ticarcillin (e.g., Ticar) or
- Valproic acid (e.g., Depakene)—Taking these medicines together with a salicylate, especially aspirin, may increase the chance of bleeding
- Antidiabetics, oral (diabetes medicine you take by mouth)—Salicylates may increase the effects of the antidiabetic medicine; a change in dose may be needed if a salicylate is taken regularly
- Ciprofloxacin (e.g., Cipro) or
- Enoxacin (e.g., Penetrex) or
- Itraconazole (e.g., Sporanox) or
- Ketoconazole (e.g., Nizoral) or
- Lomefloxacin (e.g., Maxaquin) or
- Norfloxacin (e.g., Noroxin) or
- Ofloxacin (e.g., Floxin) or
- Tetracyclines (medicine for infection), taken by mouth—Buffered aspirin, choline and magnesium salicylates, and magnesium salicylate may keep these medicines from working properly if taken too close to them
- Methotrexate (e.g., Mexate) or
- Vancomycin (e.g., Vancocin)—The chance of serious side effects may be increased
- Probenecid (e.g., Benemid)—Salicylates can keep probenecid from working properly for treating gout
- Sulfinpyrazone (e.g., Anturane)—Salicylates can keep sulfinpyrazone from working properly for treating gout; also, taking a salicylate, especially aspirin, with sulfinpyrazone may increase the chance of bleeding
- Urinary alkalizers (medicine that makes the urine less acid, such as acetazolamide [e.g., Diamox], calcium- and/or magnesium-containing antacids, dichlorphenamide [e.g., Daranide], methazolamide [e.g., Neptazane], potassium or sodium citrate and/or citric acid, sodium bicarbonate [baking soda])—These medicines may make the salicylate less effective by causing it to be removed from the body more quickly

Other medical problems—The presence of other medical problems may affect the use of salicylates. Make sure you tell your doctor if you have any other medical problems, especially:
- Anemia or
- Overactive thyroid or
- Stomach ulcer or other stomach problems—Salicylates may make your condition worse
- Asthma, allergies, and nasal polyps (history of) or
- Glucose-6-phosphate dehydrogenase (G6PD) deficiency or
- High blood pressure (hypertension) or
- Kidney disease or
- Liver disease—The chance of side effects may be increased.
- Gout—Salicylates can make this condition worse and can also lessen the effects of some medicines used to treat gout
- Heart disease—The chance of some side effects may be increased. Also, the caffeine present in some aspirin products can make some kinds of heart disease worse
- Hemophilia or other bleeding problems—The chance of bleeding may be increased, especially with aspirin

Proper Use of This Medicine

Take this medicine after meals or with food (except for enteric-coated capsules or tablets and aspirin suppositories) to lessen stomach irritation.

Take tablet or capsule forms of this medicine with a full glass (8 ounces) of water. Also, do not lie down for about 15 to 30 minutes after swallowing the medicine. This helps to prevent irritation that may lead to trouble in swallowing.

For patients taking *aspirin (including buffered aspirin and/ or products containing caffeine):*

- *Do not use any product that contains aspirin if it has a strong, vinegar-like odor.* This odor means the medicine is breaking down. If you have any questions about this, check with your health care professional.
- If you are to take any medicine that contains aspirin within 7 days after having your tonsils removed, a tooth pulled, or other dental or mouth surgery, be sure to swallow the aspirin whole. Do not chew aspirin during this time.
- Do not place any medicine that contains aspirin directly on a tooth or gum surface. This may cause a burn.
- There are several different forms of aspirin or buffered aspirin tablets. If you are using:
  - —*chewable aspirin tablets*, they may be chewed, dissolved in liquid, crushed, or swallowed whole.
  - —*delayed-release (enteric-coated) aspirin tablets*, they must be swallowed whole. Do not crush them or break them up before taking.
  - —*extended-release (long-acting) aspirin tablets*, check with your pharmacist as to how they should be taken. Some may be broken up (but must not be crushed) before swallowing if you cannot swallow them whole. Others should not be broken up and must be swallowed whole.

To use *aspirin suppositories:*

- If the suppository is too soft to insert, chill it in the refrigerator for 30 minutes or run cold water over it before removing the foil wrapper.
- To insert the suppository: First remove the foil wrapper and moisten the suppository with cold water. Lie down on your side and use your finger to push the suppository well up into the rectum.

To take *choline and magnesium salicylates (e.g., Trilisate) oral solution:*

- The liquid may be mixed with fruit juice just before taking.
- Drink a full glass (8 ounces) of water after taking the medicine.

To take *enteric-coated sodium salicylate tablets:*

- The tablets must be swallowed whole. Do not crush them or break them up before taking.

Unless otherwise directed by your medical doctor or dentist:

- Do not take more of this medicine than recommended on the label, to lessen the chance of side effects.
- Children up to 12 years of age should not take this medicine more than 5 times a day.

When used for arthritis (rheumatism), this medicine must be taken regularly as ordered by your doctor in order for it to help you. Up to 2 to 3 weeks or longer may pass before you feel the full effects of this medicine.

Dosing—The dose of these medicines will be different for different patients. *Follow your doctor's orders or the directions on the label.* The following information includes only the average doses of these medicines. *If your dose is different, do not change it* unless your doctor tells you to do so.

The number of capsules or tablets or teaspoonfuls of solution that you take depends on the strength of the medicine. Also, *the number of doses you take each day, the time allowed between doses, and the length of time you take the medicine depend on whether you are taking a long-acting or* a short-acting form of the medicine and the medical problem for which you are taking the salicylate.

For aspirin

- For *short-acting tablet, chewable tablet, and delayed-release (enteric-coated) tablet oral* dosage forms:
  - —For pain or fever:
    - Adults and teenagers—325 to 500 milligrams (mg) every three or four hours, 650 mg every four to six hours, or 1000 mg every six hours as needed.
    - Children up to 2 years of age—Dose must be determined by your doctor.
    - Children 2 to 4 years of age—160 mg every four hours as needed.
    - Children 4 to 6 years of age—240 mg every four hours as needed.
    - Children 6 to 9 years of age—320 to 325 mg every four hours as needed.
    - Children 9 to 11 years of age—320 to 400 mg every four hours as needed.
    - Children 11 to 12 years of age—320 to 480 mg every four hours as needed.
  - —For arthritis:
    - Adults and teenagers—A total of 3600 to 5400 mg a day, divided into several smaller doses.
    - Children—A total of 80 to 100 mg per kilogram (kg) (32 to 40 mg per pound) of body weight a day, divided into several smaller doses.
  - —For preventing a heart attack, stroke, or other problems caused by blood clots:
    - Adults—Most people will take 81, 162.5, or 325 mg a day or 325 mg every other day. Some people taking aspirin to prevent a stroke may need as much as 1000 mg a day.
    - Children—Use and dose must be determined by your doctor.
- For *chewing gum tablet* dosage form:
  - —For pain:
    - Adults and teenagers—2 tablets every four hours as needed.
    - Children up to 3 years of age—Dose must be determined by your doctor.
    - Children 3 to 6 years of age—1 tablet (227 mg) up to three times a day.
    - Children 6 to 12 years of age—1 or 2 tablets (227 mg each) up to four times a day.
- For *long-acting oral* dosage forms (extended-release tablets):
  - —For pain:
    - Adults and teenagers—1 or 2 tablets twice a day.
    - Children—The long-acting aspirin tablets are too strong for use in children.
  - —For arthritis:
    - Adults and teenagers—1 or 2 tablets twice a day, at first. Your doctor will then adjust your dose as needed.
    - Children—The long-acting aspirin tablets are too strong for use in children.
- For *rectal* dosage form (suppositories):
  - —For pain or fever:
    - Adults and teenagers—325 to 650 mg every four hours as needed.
    - Children up to 2 years of age—Dose must be determined by your doctor.

- Children 2 to 4 years of age—160 mg every four hours as needed.
- Children 4 to 6 years of age—240 mg every four hours as needed.
- Children 6 to 9 years of age—325 mg every four hours as needed.
- Children 9 to 11 years of age—325 to 400 mg every four hours as needed.
- Children 11 to 12 years of age—325 to 480 mg every four hours as needed.

—For arthritis:
- Adults and teenagers—A total of 3600 to 5400 mg a day, divided into several smaller doses.
- Children—A total of 80 to 100 mg per kilogram (kg) (32 to 40 mg per pound) of body weight a day, divided into several smaller doses.

For aspirin and caffeine
- For *oral capsule* dosage form:
  —For pain or fever:
  - Adults and teenagers—325 to 500 milligrams (mg) of aspirin every three or four hours, 650 mg of aspirin every four to six hours, or 1000 mg of aspirin every six hours as needed.
  - Children up to 6 years of age—Aspirin and caffeine capsules are too strong for use in children up to 6 years of age.
  - Children 6 to 9 years of age—325 mg every four hours as needed.
  - Children 9 to 12 years of age—325 to 400 mg every four hours as needed.

  —For arthritis:
  - Adults and teenagers—A total of 3600 to 5400 mg of aspirin a day, divided into several smaller doses.
  - Children—A total of 80 to 100 mg per kilogram (kg) (32 to 40 mg per pound) of body weight a day, divided into several smaller doses.

  —For preventing a heart attack, stroke, or other problems caused by blood clots:
  - Adults—325 mg a day or every other day. People who take smaller doses of aspirin will have to use a different product. Some people taking aspirin to prevent a stroke may need as much as 1000 mg a day.
  - Children—Use and dose must be determined by your doctor.

- For *oral tablet* dosage form:
  —For pain or fever:
  - Adults and teenagers—325 to 500 mg of aspirin every three or four hours, 650 mg of aspirin every four to six hours, or 1000 mg of aspirin every six hours as needed.
  - Children up to 9 years of age—Aspirin and caffeine tablets are too strong for use in children up to 9 years of age.
  - Children 9 to 12 years of age—325 to 400 mg every four hours as needed.

  —For arthritis:
  - Adults and teenagers—A total of 3600 to 5400 mg of aspirin a day, divided into several smaller doses.
  - Children—A total of 80 to 100 mg per kg (32 to 40 mg per pound) of body weight a day, divided into several smaller doses.

—For preventing a heart attack, stroke, or other problems caused by blood clots:
- Adults—325 mg a day or every other day. People who take smaller doses of aspirin will have to use a different product. Some people taking aspirin to prevent a stroke may need as much as 1000 mg a day.
- Children—Use and dose must be determined by your doctor.

For buffered aspirin
- For *oral* dosage form (tablets):
  —For pain or fever:
  - Adults and teenagers—325 to 500 milligrams (mg) of aspirin every three or four hours, 650 mg of aspirin every four to six hours, or 1000 mg of aspirin every six hours as needed.
  - Children up to 2 years of age—Dose must be determined by your doctor.
  - Children 2 to 4 years of age—One-half of a 325-mg tablet every four hours as needed.
  - Children 4 to 6 years of age—Three-fourths of a 325-mg tablet every four hours as needed.
  - Children 6 to 9 years of age—One 325-mg tablet every four hours as needed.
  - Children 9 to 11 years of age—One or one and one-fourth 325-mg tablets every four hours as needed.
  - Children 11 to 12 years of age—One or one and one-half 325-mg tablets every four hours as needed.

  —For arthritis:
  - Adults and teenagers—A total of 3600 to 5400 mg of aspirin a day, divided into several smaller doses.
  - Children—A total of 80 to 100 mg per kilogram (kg) (32 to 40 mg per pound) of body weight a day, divided into several smaller doses.

  —For preventing a heart attack, stroke, or other problems caused by blood clots:
  - Adults—325 mg a day or every other day. People who take smaller doses of aspirin will have to use a different product. Some people taking aspirin to prevent a stroke may need as much as 1000 mg a day.
  - Children—Use and dose must be determined by your doctor.

For buffered aspirin and caffeine
- For *oral* dosage form (tablets):
  —For pain or fever:
  - Adults and teenagers—325 or 421 milligrams (mg) of aspirin every three or four hours, 650 mg of aspirin every four to six hours, or 842 mg of aspirin every six hours as needed.
  - Children up to 2 years of age—Dose must be determined by your doctor.
  - Children 2 to 4 years of age—One-half of a 325-mg tablet every four hours as needed.
  - Children 4 to 6 years of age—Three-fourths of a 325-mg tablet every four hours as needed.
  - Children 6 to 9 years of age—One 325-mg or 421-mg tablet every four hours as needed.
  - Children 9 to 11 years of age—One or one and one-fourth 325-mg tablets every four hours as needed.

- Children 11 to 12 years of age—One or one and one-half 325-mg tablets, or one 421-mg tablet, every four hours as needed.

—For arthritis:

- Adults and teenagers—A total of 3600 to 5400 mg of aspirin a day, divided into several smaller doses.
- Children—A total of 80 to 100 mg per kilogram (kg) (32 to 40 mg per pound) of body weight a day, divided into several smaller doses.

—For preventing a heart attack, stroke, or other problems caused by blood clots:

- Adults—162.5 or 325 mg (one-half or one 325-mg tablet) a day or 325 mg every other day. People who need smaller doses of aspirin will have to use a different product. Some people taking aspirin to prevent a stroke may need as much as 1000 mg a day.
- Children—Use and dose must be determined by your doctor.

For *choline salicylate*

- For *oral* dosage form (oral solution):

  —For pain or fever:

  - Adults and teenagers—One-half or three-fourths of a teaspoonful every three hours, one-half or one teaspoonful every four hours, or one or one and one-half teaspoonfuls every six hours as needed.
  - Children up to 2 years of age—Dose must be determined by your doctor.
  - Children 2 to 4 years of age—1.25 milliliters (mL) (one-fourth of a teaspoonful) every four hours as needed. This amount should be measured by a special dropper or measuring spoon.
  - Children 4 to 6 years of age—1.66 mL every four hours as needed. This amount should be measured by a special dropper or measuring spoon.
  - Children 6 to 11 years of age—2.5 mL (one-half of a teaspoonful) every four hours as needed. This amount should be measured by a special measuring spoon.
  - Children 11 to 12 years of age—2.5 to 3.75 mL (one-half to three-fourths of a teaspoonful) every four hours as needed. This amount should be measured by a special measuring spoon.

  —For arthritis:

  - Adults—A total of five and one-half to eight teaspoonfuls a day, divided into several smaller doses.
  - Children—A total of 0.6 to 0.7 mL per kilogram (kg) (0.25 to 0.28 mL per pound) of body weight a day, divided into several smaller doses.

For *choline and magnesium salicylates*

- For *oral* dosage forms (oral solution or tablets):

  —For pain or fever:

  - Adults and teenagers—A total of 2000 to 3000 milligrams (mg) a day, divided into two or three doses.
  - Children weighing up to 37 kilograms (kg) (about 89 pounds)—A total of 50 mg per kg (20 mg per pound) of body weight a day, divided into two doses.
  - Children weighing more than 37 kg (90 pounds or more)—2200 mg a day, divided into two doses.

—For inflammation or arthritis:

- Adults and teenagers—A total of 3000 mg a day, divided into two or three doses, to start. Your doctor will then adjust your dose as needed.
- Children weighing up to 37 kg (about 89 pounds)—A total of 50 mg per kg (20 mg per pound) of body weight a day, divided into two doses.
- Children weighing more than 37 kg (90 pounds or more)—2200 mg a day, divided into two doses.

For *magnesium salicylate*

- For *oral* dosage form (tablets):

  —For pain:

  - Adults and teenagers—2 regular-strength tablets every four hours, up to a maximum of 12 tablets a day, or 2 extra-strength tablets every eight hours, up to a maximum of 8 tablets a day.
  - Children—Dose must be determined by your doctor.

For *salsalate*

- For *oral* dosage forms (capsules or tablets):

  —For arthritis:

  - Adults and teenagers—500 to 1000 milligrams (mg) two or three times a day, to start. Your doctor will then adjust your dose as needed.
  - Children—Dose must be determined by your doctor.

For *sodium salicylate*

- For *oral* dosage forms (tablets or delayed-release [enteric-coated] tablets):

  —For pain or fever:

  - Adults and teenagers—325 or 650 milligrams (mg) every four hours as needed.
  - Children up to 6 years of age—This medicine is too strong for use in children younger than 6 years of age.
  - Children 6 years of age and older—325 mg every four hours as needed.

  —For arthritis:

  - Adults and teenagers—A total of 3600 to 5400 mg a day, divided into several smaller doses.
  - Children—A total of 80 to 100 mg per kilogram (kg) (32 to 40 mg per pound) of body weight a day, divided into several smaller doses.

Missed dose—If your medical doctor or dentist has ordered you to take this medicine according to a regular schedule and you miss a dose, take it as soon as you remember. However, if it is almost time for your next dose, skip the missed dose and go back to your regular dosing schedule. Do not double doses.

Storage—To store this medicine:

- Keep out of the reach of children. Overdose is very dangerous in young children.
- Store away from heat and direct light.
- Do not store tablets or capsules in the bathroom, near the kitchen sink, or in other damp places. Heat or moisture may cause the medicine to break down.
- Keep liquid forms of this medicine from freezing.
- Store aspirin suppositories in a cool place. It is usually best to keep them in the refrigerator, but keep them from freezing.

• Do not keep outdated medicine or medicine no longer needed. Be sure that any discarded medicine is out of the reach of children.

Precautions While Using This Medicine

Check the labels of all nonprescription (over-the-counter [OTC]) and prescription medicines you now take. If any contain aspirin or other salicylates (including bismuth subsalicylate [e.g., Pepto-Bismol] or any shampoo or skin medicine that contains salicylic acid or any other salicylate), check with your health care professional. Taking or using them together with this medicine may cause an overdose.

If you will be taking salicylates for a long time (more than 5 days in a row for children or 10 days in a row for adults) or in large amounts, *your doctor should check your progress at regular visits.*

Check with your medical doctor or dentist:

• If you are taking this medicine to relieve pain and the pain lasts for more than 10 days (5 days for children) or if the pain gets worse, if new symptoms occur, or if redness or swelling is present. These could be signs of a serious condition that needs medical or dental treatment.
• If you are taking this medicine to bring down a fever, and the fever lasts for more than 3 days or returns, if the fever gets worse, if new symptoms occur, or if redness or swelling is present. These could be signs of a serious condition that needs treatment.
• If you are taking this medicine for a sore throat, and the sore throat is very painful, lasts for more than 2 days, or occurs together with or is followed by fever, headache, skin rash, nausea, or vomiting.
• If you are taking this medicine regularly, as for arthritis (rheumatism), and you notice a ringing or buzzing in your ears or severe or continuing headaches. These are often the first signs that too much salicylate is being taken. Your doctor may want to change the amount of medicine you are taking every day.

For patients taking *aspirin to lessen the chance of heart attack, stroke, or other problems caused by blood clots:*

• *Take only the amount of aspirin ordered by your doctor.* If you need a medicine to relieve pain, a fever, or arthritis, your doctor may not want you to take extra aspirin. It is a good idea to discuss this with your doctor, so that you will know ahead of time what medicine to take.
• *Do not stop taking this medicine for any reason without first checking with the doctor who directed you to take it.*

Taking certain other medicines together with a salicylate may increase the chance of unwanted effects. The risk will depend on how much of each medicine you take every day, and on how long you take the medicines together. If your doctor directs you to take these medicines together on a regular basis, follow his or her directions carefully. However, *do not take any of the following medicines together with a salicylate for more than a few days, unless your doctor has directed you to do so and is following your progress:*

Acetaminophen (e.g., Tylenol)
Diclofenac (e.g., Voltaren)
Diflunisal (e.g., Dolobid)

Etodolac (e.g., Lodine)
Fenoprofen (e.g., Nalfon)
Floctafenine (e.g., Idarac)
Flurbiprofen, oral (e.g., Ansaid)
Ibuprofen (e.g., Motrin)
Indomethacin (e.g., Indocin)
Ketoprofen (e.g., Orudis)
Ketorolac (e.g., Toradol)
Meclofenamate (e.g., Meclomen)
Mefenamic acid (e.g., Ponstel)
Nabumetone (e.g., Relafen)
Naproxen (e.g., Naprosyn)
Oxaprozin (e.g., Daypro)
Phenylbutazone (e.g., Butazolidin)
Piroxicam (e.g., Feldene)
Sulindac (e.g., Clinoril)
Tenoxicam (e.g., Mobiflex)
Tiaprofenic acid (e.g., Surgam)
Tolmetin (e.g., Tolectin)

For *diabetic patients:*

• False urine sugar test results may occur if you are regularly taking large amounts of salicylates, such as:
—*Aspirin:* 8 or more 325-mg (5-grain), or 4 or more 500-mg or 650-mg (10-grain), or 3 or more 800-mg (or higher strength), doses a day.
—*Buffered aspirin* or
—*Sodium salicylate:* 8 or more 325-mg (5-grain), or 4 or more 500-mg or 650-mg (10-grain), doses a day.
—*Choline salicylate:* 4 or more teaspoonfuls (each teaspoonful containing 870 mg) a day.
—*Choline and magnesium salicylates:* 5 or more 500-mg tablets or teaspoonfuls, 4 or more 750-mg tablets, or 2 or more 1000-mg tablets, a day.
—*Magnesium salicylate:* 7 or more regular-strength, or 4 or more extra-strength, tablets a day.
—*Salsalate:* 4 or more 500-mg doses, or 3 or more 750-mg doses, a day.
• Smaller doses or occasional use of salicylates usually will not affect urine sugar tests. However, check with your health care professional (especially if your diabetes is not well-controlled) if:
—you are not sure how much salicylate you are taking every day.
—you notice any change in your urine sugar test results.
—you have any other questions about this possible problem.

Do not take aspirin for 5 days before any surgery, including dental surgery, unless otherwise directed by your medical doctor or dentist. Taking aspirin during this time may cause bleeding problems.

For patients taking *buffered aspirin, choline and magnesium salicylates (e.g., Trilisate), or magnesium salicylate (e.g., Doan's):*

• Buffered aspirin, choline and magnesium salicylates, or magnesium salicylate can keep many other medicines, especially some medicines used to treat infections, from working properly. This problem can be prevented by not taking the 2 medicines too close together. Ask your health care professional how long you should wait between taking a medicine for infection and taking buffered

---

© 2002 MICROMEDEX Thomson Healthcare

aspirin, choline and magnesium salicylates, or magnesium salicylate.

If you are taking a laxative containing cellulose, take the salicylate at least 2 hours before or after you take the laxative. Taking these medicines too close together may lessen the effects of the salicylate.

For patients taking this medicine by mouth:

- Stomach problems may be more likely to occur if you drink alcoholic beverages while being treated with this medicine, especially if you are taking it in high doses or for a long time. Check with your doctor if you have any questions about this.

For patients using *aspirin suppositories:*

- Aspirin suppositories may cause irritation of the rectum. Check with your doctor if this occurs.

Salicylates may interfere with the results of some medical tests. Before you have any medical tests, tell the doctor in charge if you have taken any of these medicines within the past week. If possible, it is best to check with the doctor first, to find out whether the medicine may be taken during the week before the test.

For patients taking one of the products that contain *caffeine:*

- Caffeine may interfere with the result of a test that uses adenosine (e.g., Adenocard) or dipyridamole (e.g., Persantine) to help find out how well your blood is flowing through certain blood vessels. Therefore, you should not have any caffeine for at least 8 to 12 hours before the test.

If you think that you or anyone else may have taken an overdose, get emergency help at once. Taking an overdose of these medicines may cause unconsciousness or death. Signs of overdose include convulsions (seizures), hearing loss, confusion, ringing or buzzing in the ears, severe drowsiness or tiredness, severe excitement or nervousness, and fast or deep breathing.

Side Effects of This Medicine

Along with its needed effects, a medicine may cause some unwanted effects. When this medicine is used for short periods of time at low doses, side effects usually are rare. Although not all of the following side effects may occur, if they do occur they may need medical attention.

Get emergency help immediately if any of the following side effects occur:

Any loss of hearing; bloody urine; confusion; convulsions (seizures); diarrhea (severe or continuing); difficulty in swallowing; dizziness, lightheadedness, or feeling faint (severe); drowsiness (severe); excitement or nervousness (severe); fast or deep breathing; flushing, redness, or other change in skin color; hallucinations (seeing, hearing, or feeling things that are not there); increased sweating; increased thirst; nausea or vomiting (severe or continuing); shortness of breath, troubled breathing, tightness in chest, or wheezing; stomach pain (severe or continuing); swelling of eyelids, face, or lips; unexplained fever; uncontrollable flapping movements of the hands (especially in elderly patients); vision problems

Symptoms of overdose in children

Changes in behavior; drowsiness or tiredness (severe); fast or deep breathing

Also, check with your doctor as soon as possible if any of the following side effects occur:

Less common or rare

Abdominal or stomach pain, cramping, or burning (severe); bloody or black, tarry stools; headache (severe or continuing); ringing or buzzing in ears (continuing); skin rash, hives, or itching; unusual tiredness or weakness; vomiting of blood or material that looks like coffee grounds

Other side effects may occur that usually do not need medical attention. These side effects may go away during treatment as your body adjusts to the medicine. However, check with your health care professional if any of the following side effects continue or are bothersome:

More common

Abdominal or stomach cramps, pain, or discomfort (mild to moderate); heartburn or indigestion; nausea or vomiting

Less common

Trouble in sleeping, nervousness, or jitters (only for products containing caffeine)

Other side effects not listed above may also occur in some patients. If you notice any other effects, check with your doctor.

Revised: 8/90
Interim revision: 07/25/95

SAQUINAVIR   Systemic

Commonly used brand name(s):

In the U.S.—
Fortovase
Invirase

Description

Saquinavir (sa-KWIN-a-veer) is used, usually in combination with other medicines, in the treatment of the infection caused by the human immunodeficiency virus (HIV). HIV is the virus that causes acquired immune deficiency syndrome (AIDS).

Saquinavir will not cure or prevent HIV infection or AIDS; however, it helps keep HIV from reproducing and appears to slow down the destruction of the immune system. This may help delay the development of problems usually related to AIDS or HIV disease. Saquinavir will not keep you from spreading HIV to other people. People who receive this medicine may continue to have other problems usually related to AIDS or HIV disease.

This medicine is available only with your doctor's prescription, in the following dosage forms:

Oral
- Capsules (U.S.)
- Soft gelatin capsules (U.S.)

Before Using This Medicine

In deciding to use a medicine, the risks of taking the medicine must be weighed against the good it will do. This is a decision

you and your doctor will make. For saquinavir, the following should be considered:

Allergies—Tell your doctor if you have ever had any unusual or allergic reaction to saquinavir. Also tell your health care professional if you are allergic to any other substances, such as foods, preservatives, or dyes.

Pregnancy—Studies have not been done in humans. However, saquinavir has not been reported to cause birth defects or other problems in animal studies.

Breast-feeding—It is not known whether saquinavir passes into breast milk. However, breast-feeding is usually not recommended in AIDS patients because of the risk of passing the AIDS virus on to the infant.

Children—There is no specific information comparing use of saquinavir in children with use in other age groups.

Older adults—Many medicines have not been studied specifically in older people. Therefore, it may not be known whether they work exactly the same way they do in younger adults. There is no specific information comparing use of saquinavir in the elderly with use in other age groups.

Other medicines—Although certain medicines should not be used together at all, in other cases two different medicines may be used together even if an interaction might occur. In these cases, your doctor may want to change the dose, or other precautions may be necessary. When you are taking saquinavir, it is especially important that your health care professional know if you are taking any of the following:

- Astemizole (e.g., Hismanal) or
- Cisapride (e.g., Propulsid) or
- Ergot medicines (dihydroergotamine [e.g., D.H.E. 45], ergoloid mesylates [e.g., Hydergine], ergotamine [e.g., Ergotrate], methylergonovine [e.g., Methergine], methysergide [e.g., Sansert]) or
- Midazolam (e.g., Versed) or
- Terfenadine (e.g., Seldane) or
- Triazolam (e.g., Halcion)—There is a possibility that saquinavir may interfere with the removal of these medicines from the body, which could lead to serious side effects

- Calcium channel blocking agents (bepridil [e.g., Bepadin], diltiazem [e.g., Cardizem], felodipine [e.g., Plendil], flunarizine [e.g., Sibelium], isradipine [e.g., DynaCirc], nicardipine [e.g., Cardene], nifedipine [e.g., Procardia], nimodipine [e.g., Nimotop], verapamil [e.g., Calan]) or
- Quinidine (e.g., Quinidex)—There is a possibility that saquinavir may interfere with the removal of these medicines from the body, which could lead to increased side effects

- Carbamazepine (e.g., Tegretol) or
- Dexamethasone (e.g., Decadron) or
- Phenobarbital (e.g., Luminal) or
- Phenytoin (e.g., Dilantin) or
- Rifabutin (e.g., Mycobutin) or
- Rifampin (e.g., Rifadin)—These medicines may decrease the amount of saquinavir in the body

- Delavirdine (e.g., Rescriptor) or
- Ritonavir (e.g., Norvir)—This medicine may increase the amount of saquinavir in the body, which could lead to increased side effects

Other medical problems—The presence of other medical problems may affect the use of saquinavir. Make sure you tell your doctor if you have any other medical problems, especially:

- Hemophilia—Possible increased risk of bleeding

- Liver disease—Effects of saquinavir may be increased because of slower removal of the medicine from the body; also saquinavir has been reported to cause unwanted effects on the liver

Proper Use of This Medicine

It is important that this medicine be taken with food in order to work properly. *Take saquinavir with a meal or within 2 hours after a meal.*

Take this medicine exactly as directed by your doctor. Do not take it more often, and do not take it for a longer time than your doctor ordered. Also, do not stop taking this medicine without checking with your doctor first.

Keep taking saquinavir for the full time of treatment, even if you begin to feel better.

This medicine works best when there is a constant amount in the blood. *To help keep the amount constant, do not miss any doses. Also, it is best to take the doses at evenly spaced times, day and night.* For example, if you are to take three doses a day, the doses should be spaced about 8 hours apart. If you need help in planning the best times to take your medicine, check with your health care professional.

Only take medicine that your doctor has prescribed specially for you. Do not share your medicine with others.

Dosing—The dose of saquinavir will be different for different patients. *Follow your doctor's orders or the directions on the label.* The following information includes only the average doses of saquinavir. *If your dose is different, do not change it* unless your doctor tells you to do so.

- For *oral* dosage form (capsules [brand name *Invirase*]):
  —For treatment of HIV infection:
  - Adults—600 milligrams (mg) three times a day, in combination with other medicines for HIV infection.
  - Children up to 16 years of age—Use and dose must be determined by your doctor.

- For *oral* dosage form (soft gelatin capsules [brand name *Fortovase*]):
  —For treatment of HIV infection:
  - Adults—1200 mg three times a day, in combination with other medicines for HIV infection.
  - Children up to 16 years of age—Use and dose must be determined by your doctor.

Missed dose—If you miss a dose of this medicine, take it as soon as you remember. However, if it is almost time for your next dose, skip the missed dose and go back to your regular dosing schedule. Do not double doses.

Storage—To store this medicine:

- Keep out of the reach of children.
- Store away from heat and direct light.
- Store the soft gelatin capsule form (*Fortovase*) in the refrigerator. The *Invirase* capsules do not need to be refrigerated.
- Do not store in the bathroom, near the kitchen sink, or in other damp places. Heat or moisture may cause the medicine to break down.
- Do not keep outdated medicine or medicine no longer needed. Be sure that any discarded medicine is out of the reach of children.

Precautions While Using This Medicine

Do not take any other medicines without checking with your doctor first. To do so may increase the chance of side effects from saquinavir or other medicines.

It is very important that your doctor check your progress at regular visits to make sure this medicine is working properly and to check for unwanted effects, especially increases in blood sugar.

Side Effects of This Medicine

Along with its needed effects, a medicine may cause some unwanted effects. Although not all of these side effects may occur, if they do occur they may need medical attention.

Check with your doctor as soon as possible if any of the following side effects occur:

Rare
   Burning or prickling sensation; confusion; dehydration; dry or itchy skin; fruity mouth odor; increased hunger; increased thirst; increased urination; nausea; skin rash; unusual tiredness; vomiting; weight loss

Other side effects may occur that usually do not need medical attention. These side effects may go away during treatment as your body adjusts to the medicine. However, check with your doctor if any of the following side effects continue or are bothersome:

Less common or rare
   Abdominal pain; diarrhea; headache; mouth ulcers; weakness

Other side effects not listed above may also occur in some patients. If you notice any other effects, check with your doctor.

Developed: 08/05/98

SELEGILINE   Systemic

Commonly used brand name(s):

In the U.S.—
   Carbex
   Eldepryl
   Generic name product may be available.

In Canada—

Apo-Selegiline	Nu-Selegiline
Eldepryl	SD Deprenyl
Gen-Selegiline	Selegiline-5
Novo-Selegiline	

Other commonly used names are deprenil and deprenyl.

Description

Selegiline (seh-LEDGE-ah-leen) is used in combination with levodopa or levodopa and carbidopa combination to treat Parkinson's disease, sometimes called shaking palsy or paralysis agitans. This medicine works to increase and extend the effects of levodopa, and may help to slow the progress of Parkinson's disease.

Selegiline is available only with your doctor's prescription, in the following dosage form:

Oral
   • Capsules (U.S.)
   • Tablets (U.S. and Canada)

Before Using This Medicine

In deciding to use a medicine, the risks of taking the medicine must be weighed against the good it will do. This is a decision you and your doctor will make. For selegiline, the following should be considered:

Allergies—Tell your doctor if you have ever had any unusual or allergic reaction to selegiline. Also tell your health care professional if you are allergic to any other substances, such as foods, preservatives, or dyes.

Pregnancy—Selegiline has not been studied in pregnant women. However, this medicine has not been shown to cause birth defects or other problems in animal studies.

Breast-feeding—It is not known whether selegiline passes into the breast milk.

Children—Studies on this medicine have been done only in adult patients and there is no specific information about its use in children. Therefore, be sure to discuss with your doctor the use of this medicine in children.

Older adults—In studies done to date that included elderly people, selegiline did not cause different side effects or problems in older people than it did in younger adults.

Other medicines—Although certain medicines should not be used together at all, in other cases 2 different medicines may be used together even if an interaction might occur. In these cases, your doctor may want to change the dose, or other precautions may be necessary. When you are taking selegiline, it is especially important that your health care professional know if you are taking any of the following:

   • Antidepressants, tricyclic (amitriptyline [e.g., Elavil], amoxapine [e.g., Asendin], clomipramine [e.g., Anafranil], desipramine [e.g., Norpramin], doxepin [e.g., Sinequan], imipramine [e.g., Tofranil], nortriptyline [e.g., Pamelor], protriptyline [e.g., Vivactil], trimipramine [e.g., Surmontil]) or
   • Fluoxetine (e.g., Prozac) or
   • Fluvoxamine (e.g., Luvox) or
   • Meperidine (e.g., Demerol) or
   • Nefazodone (e.g., Serzone) or
   • Paroxetine (e.g., Paxil) or
   • Sertraline (e.g., Zoloft) or
   • Venlafaxine (e.g., Effexor)—Using these medicines together may increase the chance of serious side effects

Other medical problems—The presence of other medical problems may affect the use of selegiline. Make sure you tell your doctor if you have any other medical problems, especially:

   • Stomach ulcer (history of)—Selegiline may make the condition worse

Proper Use of This Medicine

Take this medicine only as directed by your doctor. Do not take more of it, do not take it more often, and do not take it for a longer time than your doctor ordered.

Dosing—The dose of selegiline will be different for different patients. Your doctor will determine the proper dose of selegiline for you. *Follow your doctor's orders or the directions on the label.*

For the treatment of Parkinson's disease, the usual dose of selegiline is 5 mg two times a day, taken with breakfast and lunch. Some patients may need less than this.

Missed dose—If you miss a dose of this medicine, take it as soon as possible. However, if you do not remember the missed dose until late afternoon or evening, skip the missed dose and go back to your regular dosing schedule. Do not double doses.

Storage—To store this medicine:
- Keep out of the reach of children.
- Store away from heat and direct light.
- Do not store in the bathroom, near the kitchen sink, or in other damp places. Heat or moisture may cause the medicine to break down.
- Do not keep outdated medicine or medicine no longer needed. Be sure that any discarded medicine is out of the reach of children.

Precautions While Using This Medicine

When selegiline is taken at doses of 10 mg or less per day for the treatment of Parkinson's disease, there are no restrictions on food or beverages you eat or drink. However, the chance exists that dangerous reactions, such as sudden high blood pressure, may occur if doses higher than those used for Parkinson's disease are taken with certain foods, beverages, or other medicines. These foods, beverages, and medicines include:

- Foods that have a high tyramine content (most common in foods that are aged or fermented to increase their flavor), such as cheeses; fava or broad bean pods; yeast or meat extracts; smoked or pickled meat, poultry, or fish; fermented sausage (bologna, pepperoni, salami, summer sausage) or other fermented meat; sauerkraut; or any overripe fruit. If a list of these foods and beverages is not given to you, ask your health care professional to provide one.
- Alcoholic beverages or alcohol-free or reduced-alcohol beer and wine.
- Large amounts of caffeine-containing food or beverages such as coffee, tea, cola, or chocolate.
- Any other medicine unless approved or prescribed by your doctor. This especially includes nonprescription (over-the-counter [OTC]) medicine, such as that for colds (including nose drops or sprays), cough, asthma, hay fever, and appetite control; "keep awake" products; or products that make you sleepy.

Also, for at least 2 weeks after you stop taking this medicine, these foods, beverages, and other medicines may continue to react with selegiline if it was taken in doses higher than those usually used for Parkinson's disease.

Check with your doctor or hospital emergency room immediately if severe headache, stiff neck, chest pains, fast heartbeat, or nausea and vomiting occur while you are taking this medicine. These may be symptoms of a serious side effect that should have a doctor's attention.

Dizziness, lightheadedness, or fainting may occur, especially when you get up from a lying or sitting position. Getting up slowly may help. If the problem continues or gets worse, check with your doctor.

Selegiline may cause dryness of the mouth. For temporary relief, use sugarless candy or gum, melt bits of ice in your mouth, or use a saliva substitute. However, if your mouth continues to feel dry for more than 2 weeks, check with your medical doctor or dentist. Continuing dryness of the mouth may increase the chance of dental disease, including tooth decay, gum disease, and fungus infections.

Side Effects of This Medicine

When you start taking selegiline in addition to levodopa or carbidopa and levodopa combination, you may experience an increase in side effects. If this occurs, your doctor may gradually reduce the amount of levodopa or carbidopa and levodopa combination you take.

Along with its needed effects, a medicine may cause some unwanted effects. Although not all of these side effects may occur, if they do occur they may need medical attention.

Stop taking this medicine and get emergency help immediately if any of the following side effects occur:
Symptoms of unusually high blood pressure (caused by reaction of higher than usual doses of selegiline with restricted foods or medicines)
Chest pain (severe); enlarged pupils; fast or slow heartbeat; headache (severe); increased sensitivity of eyes to light; increased sweating (possibly with fever or cold, clammy skin); nausea and vomiting (severe); stiff or sore neck

Check with your doctor as soon as possible if any of the following side effects occur:
More common
Increase in unusual movements of body; mood or other mental changes

Less common or rare
Bloody or black, tarry stools; difficult or frequent urination; difficulty in breathing; difficulty in speaking; dizziness or lightheadedness, especially when getting up from a lying or sitting position; hallucinations (seeing, hearing, or feeling things that are not there); irregular heartbeat; lip smacking or puckering; loss of balance control; puffing of cheeks; rapid or wormlike movements of tongue; restlessness or desire to keep moving; severe stomach pain; swelling of feet or lower legs; tightness in chest; twisting movements of body; uncontrolled chewing movements; uncontrolled movements of face, neck, back, arms or legs; vomiting of blood or material that looks like coffee grounds; wheezing

Symptoms of overdose
Agitation or irritability; chest pain; convulsions (seizures); difficulty opening mouth or lockjaw; dizziness (severe) or fainting; fast or irregular pulse (continuing); high fever; high or low blood pressure; increased sweating (possibly with fever or cold, clammy skin); severe spasm where the head and heels are bent backward and the body arched forward; troubled breathing

Other side effects may occur that usually do not need medical attention. These side effects may go away during treatment as your body adjusts to the medicine. However, check with your doctor if any of the following side effects continue or are bothersome:
More common
Abdominal or stomach pain; dizziness or feeling faint; dryness of mouth; nausea; trouble in sleeping; vomiting

Less common or rare

Anxiety; back or leg pain; blurred or double vision; body ache; burning of lips, mouth, or throat; chills; constipation; diarrhea; drowsiness; headache; heartburn; high or low blood pressure; inability to move; frequent urge to urinate; increased sensitivity of skin to light; increased sweating; irritability (temporary); loss of appetite; memory problems; muscle cramps; nervousness; numbness of fingers or toes; pounding or fast heartbeat; red, raised, or itchy skin; restlessness; ringing or buzzing in ears; slow or difficult urination; slowed movements; taste changes; uncontrolled closing of eyelids; unusual feeling of well-being; unusual tiredness or weakness; unusual weight loss

With doses higher than 10 mg a day

Clenching, gnashing, or grinding teeth; sudden jerky movements of body

Other side effects not listed above may also occur in some patients. If you notice any other effects, check with your doctor.

Revised: 09/30/92
Interim revision: 03/28/95; 08/21/96; 01/21/98

SELENIUM SUPPLEMENTS
Systemic

Commonly used brand name(s):

In the U.S.—
Sele-Pak[1]
Selepen[1]

Note: For quick reference, the following selenium supplements are numbered to match the corresponding brand names.

This information applies to the following:
1. Selenious Acid (se-LEE-nee-us as-id) †‡
2. Selenium (se-LEE-nee-um) ‡§

---

†Not commercially available in Canada.
‡Generic name product may be available in the U.S.
§Generic name product may be available in Canada.

Description

Selenium supplements are used to prevent or treat selenium deficiency.

The body needs selenium for normal growth and health. Selenium is needed for certain enzymes that help with normal body functions.

Lack of selenium may lead to changes in fingernails, muscle weakness, and heart problems.

Selenium deficiency in the United States is rare. Patients receiving total parenteral nutrition (TPN) for long periods of time may need selenium. Selenium deficiency is a problem in areas of the world where the soil contains little selenium.

Although selenium is being used to prevent certain types of cancer, there is not enough information to show that this is effective.

Injectable selenium is given by or under the supervision of a health care professional. Other forms of selenium are available without a prescription.

Selenium supplements are available as part of a multivitamin/mineral complex or alone in the following dosage forms:

Oral
Selenium
• Tablets (U.S. and Canada)

Parenteral
Selenious Acid
• Injection (U.S.)

Importance of Diet

For good health, it is important that you eat a balanced and varied diet. Follow carefully any diet program your health care professional may recommend. For your specific dietary vitamin and/or mineral needs, ask your health care professional for a list of appropriate foods. If you think that you are not getting enough vitamins and/or minerals in your diet, you may choose to take a dietary supplement.

Selenium is found in seafood, liver, lean red meat, and grains grown in soil that is rich in selenium.

The daily amount of selenium needed is defined in several different ways.

For U.S.—
• Recommended Dietary Allowances (RDAs) are the amount of vitamins and minerals needed to provide for adequate nutrition in most healthy persons. RDAs for a given nutrient may vary depending on a person's age, sex, and physical condition (e.g., pregnancy).
• Daily Values (DVs) are used on food and dietary supplement labels to indicate the percent of the recommended daily amount of each nutrient that a serving provides. DV replaces the previous designation of United States Recommended Daily Allowances (USRDAs).

For Canada—
• Recommended Nutrient Intakes (RNIs) are used to determine the amounts of vitamins, minerals, and protein needed to provide adequate nutrition and lessen the risk of chronic disease.

Normal daily recommended intakes for selenium are generally defined as follows:
• Infants and children—
Birth to 3 years of age: 10 to 20 micrograms (mcg) per day.
4 to 6 years of age: 20 mcg per day.
7 to 10 years of age: 30 mcg per day.
• Adolescent and adult males—40 to 70 mcg per day.
• Adolescent and adult females—45 to 55 mcg per day.
• Pregnant females—65 mcg per day.
• Breast-feeding females—75 mcg per day.

Before Using This Dietary Supplement

If you are taking this dietary supplement without a prescription, carefully read and follow any precautions on the label. For selenium supplements, the following should be considered:

Allergies—Tell your health care professional if you have ever had any unusual or allergic reaction to selenious acid or selenium. Also tell your health care professional if you are allergic to any other substances, such as foods, preservatives, or dyes.

Pregnancy—It is especially important that you are receiving enough vitamins and minerals when you become pregnant and that you continue to receive the right amount of vitamins and minerals throughout your pregnancy. The healthy growth and development of the fetus depend on a steady supply of nutrients from the mother. However, taking large amounts of a dietary supplement in pregnancy may be harmful to the mother and/or fetus and should be avoided.

Studies in animals have shown that selenium causes birth defects when given in large doses.

Breast-feeding— It is important that you receive the right amounts of vitamins and minerals so that your baby will also get the vitamins and minerals needed to grow properly. However, taking large amounts of a dietary supplement while breast-feeding may be harmful to the mother and/or baby and should be avoided.

Children— Problems in children have not been reported with intake of normal daily recommended amounts.

Older adults— Problems in older adults have not been reported with intake of normal daily recommended amounts.

Medicines or dietary supplements— Although certain medicines should not be used together at all, in other cases medicines or dietary supplements may be used together even if an interaction might occur. In these cases, your doctor may want to change the dose, or other precautions may be necessary. Tell your health care professional if you are taking any other dietary supplement or any nonprescription (over-the-counter [OTC]) or prescription medicine.

Other medical problems— The presence of other medical problems may affect the use of selenium supplements. Make sure you tell your health care professional if you have any other medical problems, especially:
- Kidney problems or
- Stomach problems—These conditions may cause higher blood levels of selenium, which may increase the chance of unwanted effects

Proper Use of This Dietary Supplement

Dosing— The amount of selenium needed to meet normal daily recommended intakes will be different for different patients. The following information includes only the average amounts of selenium.
- For *oral* dosage form (tablets):
  —To prevent deficiency, the amount taken by mouth is based on normal daily recommended intakes:
  - Adult and teenage males—40 to 70 micrograms (mcg) per day.
  - Adult and teenage females—45 to 55 mcg per day.
  - Pregnant females—65 mcg per day.
  - Breast-feeding females—75 mcg per day.
  - Children 7 to 10 years of age—30 mcg per day.
  - Children 4 to 6 years of age—20 mcg per day.
  - Children birth to 3 years of age—10 to 20 mcg per day.
  —To treat deficiency:
  - Adults, teenagers, and children—Treatment dose is determined by prescriber for each individual based on severity of deficiency.

Missed dose— If you miss taking selenium supplements for one or more days there is no cause for concern, since it takes some time for your body to become seriously low in selenium. However, if your health care professional has recommended that you take selenium, try to remember to take it as directed every day.

Storage— To store this dietary supplement:
- Keep out of the reach of children.
- Store away from heat and direct light.
- Do not store in the bathroom, near the kitchen sink, or in other damp places. Heat or moisture may cause the dietary supplement to break down.
- Keep the dietary supplement from freezing. Do not refrigerate.
- Do not keep outdated dietary supplement or those no longer needed. Be sure that any discarded dietary supplement is out of the reach of children.

Side Effects of This Dietary Supplement

Along with its needed effects, a dietary supplement may cause some unwanted effects. Although selenium supplements have not been reported to cause any side effects, check with your health care professional immediately if any of the following side effects occur as a result of an overdose:

Symptoms of overdose
  Diarrhea; fingernail weakening; garlic odor of breath and sweat; hair loss; irritability; itching of skin; metallic taste; nausea and vomiting; unusual tiredness and weakness

Other side effects not listed above may also occur in some individuals. If you notice any other effects, check with your health care professional.

Revised: 04/16/92
Interim revision: 06/06/92; 08/15/94; 05/01/95

SERMORELIN   Systemic

Commonly used brand name(s):

In the U.S.—
  Geref

Description

Sermorelin (ser-moe-REL-in) is a synthetic (man-made) version of a naturally occurring substance that causes release of growth hormone from the pituitary gland. Growth hormone is naturally produced by the pituitary gland and is necessary for growth in children. In children who fail to grow normally because their bodies are not producing enough growth hormone, this medicine may be used to increase the amount of growth hormone produced by the pituitary gland.

This medicine is available only with your doctor's prescription, in the following dosage form:

Parenteral
  - Injection (U.S.)

Before Using This Medicine

In deciding to use a medicine, the risks of using the medicine must be weighed against the good it will do. This is a decision you and your doctor will make. For sermorelin, the following should be considered:

Allergies— Tell your doctor if you have ever had any unusual or allergic reaction to sermorelin. Also tell your health care professional if you are allergic to any other substances, such as foods, preservatives, or dyes.

Pregnancy—Sermorelin has not been studied in pregnant women. However, studies in animals have shown that sermorelin causes minor birth defects. Before taking this medicine, make sure your doctor knows if you are pregnant or if you may become pregnant.

Other medicines—Although certain medicines should not be used together at all, in other cases two different medicines may be used together even if an interaction might occur. In these cases, your doctor may want to change the dose, or other precautions may be necessary. When you are taking sermorelin, it is especially important that your health care professional know if you are taking any of the following:

- Corticosteroids (cortisone-like medicines)—These medicines can interfere with the effects of sermorelin

Other medical problems—The presence of other medical problems may affect the use of sermorelin. Make sure you tell your doctor if you have any other medical problems, especially:

- Underactive thyroid—This condition can interfere with the effects of sermorelin

Proper Use of This Medicine

If you are injecting this medicine yourself, *use it exactly as directed by your doctor*. Do not use more or less of it, and do not use it more often than your doctor ordered. The exact amount of medicine needed has been carefully worked out. Using too much will increase the risk of side effects, while using too little may not improve the condition.

Each package of sermorelin contains a patient instruction sheet. Read this sheet carefully and make sure you understand:

- How to prepare the injection.
- Proper use of disposable syringes and needles, including safe handling and disposal.
- How to give the injection.
- How long the injection is safe to use.

It is best to use a different place on the body for each injection (for example, abdomen, hip, thigh, or upper arm). To help you remember to do this, you may want to keep a record of the date and location for each injection.

Dosing—The dose of sermorelin will be different for different patients. *Follow your doctor's orders or the directions on the label*. The following information includes only the average doses of sermorelin. *If your dose is different, do not change it* unless your doctor tells you to do so.

- For *parenteral* dosage form (injection):
  —For stimulating growth:
    - Children—Dose is based on body weight and must be determined by your doctor. It is usually 0.03 milligrams (mg) per kilogram (kg) (0.014 mg per pound) of body weight injected under the skin once a day at bedtime.

Storage—To store this medicine:

- Keep out of the reach of children.
- Store in the refrigerator.
- Do not keep outdated medicine or medicine no longer needed. Be sure that any discarded medicine is out of the reach of children.

Precautions While Using This Medicine

It is very important that your doctor check your progress at regular visits.

Side Effects of This Medicine

Along with its needed effects, a medicine may cause some unwanted effects. Although not all of these side effects may occur, if they do occur they may need medical attention.

Check with your doctor as soon as possible if any of the following side effects occur:

More common
  Pain, redness, or swelling at the place of injection
Rare
  Itching; trouble in swallowing

Other side effects may occur that usually do not need medical attention. These side effects may go away during treatment as your body adjusts to the medicine. However, check with your doctor if any of the following side effects continue or are bothersome:

Rare
  Dizziness; flushing; headache; sleepiness; trouble sitting still

Other side effects not listed above may also occur in some patients. If you notice any other effects, check with your doctor.

Developed: 06/17/98

SERTRALINE   Systemic

Commonly used brand name(s):

In the U.S.—
  Zoloft

In Canada—
  Zoloft

Description

Sertraline (SER-tra-leen) is used to treat mental depression, obsessive-compulsive disorder, and panic disorder.

Sertraline belongs to a group of medicines known as selective serotonin reuptake inhibitors (SSRIs). These medicines are thought to work by increasing the activity of the chemical serotonin in the brain.

This medicine is available only with your doctor's prescription, in the following dosage forms:

Oral
- Capsules (Canada)
- Tablets (U.S.)
- Oral Concentrate (U.S.)

Before Using This Medicine

In deciding to use a medicine, the risks of taking the medicine must be weighed against the good it will do. This is a decision you and your doctor will make. For sertraline, the following should be considered:

Allergies—Tell your doctor if you have ever had any unusual or allergic reaction to sertraline. Also tell your health care professional if you are allergic to any other substances, such as foods, preservatives, dyes, or latex. The dispenser dropper for sertraline oral concentrate contains dry natural rubber.

Pregnancy—One study looked at the babies of 147 women who took sertraline either at the beginning of pregnancy or through the entire pregnancy. This study found no harmful effects of sertraline on the babies. However, more study is needed to be sure that sertraline is safe to use during pregnancy. Before taking this medicine, make sure your doctor knows if you are pregnant or if you may become pregnant.

Breast-feeding—Sertraline passes into breast milk. No problems have been reported in nursing babies, but the long-term effects are not known.

Children—Sertraline has been tested in children 6 to 17 years of age with obsessive-compulsive disorder. In effective doses, this medicine has not been shown to cause different side effects or problems than it does in adults. However, sertraline can cause a decrease in appetite and children who take this medicine for a long time should have their growth and body weight measured by the doctor at regular visits.

Older adults—In studies done to date that have included elderly people, sertraline did not cause different side effects or problems in older people than it did in younger adults. However, this medicine may be removed from the body more slowly in older adults. An older adult may receive a lower dose of sertraline than a younger adult, especially when first starting treatment.

Other medicines—Although certain medicines should not be used together at all, in other cases two different medicines may be used together even if an interaction might occur. In these cases, your doctor may want to change the dose, or other precautions may be necessary. When you are taking sertraline, it is especially important that your health care professional know if you are taking any of the following:

- Astemizole (e.g., Hismanal) or
- Terfenadine (e.g., Seldane)—Taking these medicines while you are taking sertraline may lead to a serious change in the rhythm of your heartbeat

- Buspirone (e.g., BuSpar) or
- Bromocriptine (e.g., Parlodel) or
- Dextromethorphan (cough medicine) or
- Levodopa (e.g., Sinemet) or
- Lithium (e.g., Eskalith) or
- Meperidine (e.g., Demerol) or
- Nefazodone (e.g., Serzone) or
- Pentazocine (e.g., Talwin) or
- Selective serotonin reuptake inhibitors, other (citalopram [e.g., Celexa], fluoxetine [e.g., Prozac], fluvoxamine [e.g., Luvox], paroxetine [e.g., Paxil]) or
- Street drugs (LSD, MDMA [e.g., ecstasy], marijuana) or
- Sumatriptan (e.g., Imitrex) or
- Tramadol (e.g., Ultram) or
- Trazodone (e.g., Desyrel) or
- Tryptophan or
- Venlafaxine (e.g., Effexor)—Using these medicines with sertraline may increase the chance of developing a rare, but very serious, unwanted effect known as the serotonin syndrome. This syndrome may cause confusion, diarrhea, fever, poor coordination, restlessness, shivering, sweating, talking or acting with excitement you cannot control, trembling or shaking, or twitching. If you develop these symptoms, contact your doctor as soon as possible

- Digitoxin (e.g., Crystodigin) or
- Warfarin (e.g., Coumadin)—Higher or lower blood levels of these medicines or sertraline may occur, which may increase the chance of having unwanted effects. Your doctor may need to change the dose of either these medicines or sertraline

- Disulfiram (e.g., Antabuse)—Disulfiram will react with the alcohol in sertraline oral concentrate and may cause serious problems

- Moclobemide (e.g., Manerex)—The risk of developing serious unwanted effects, including the serotonin syndrome, is increased. Use of moclobemide with sertraline is not recommended. Also, it is recommended that 3 to 7 days be allowed between stopping treatment with moclobemide and starting treatment with sertraline, and it is recommended that 2 weeks be allowed between stopping treatment with sertraline and starting treatment with moclobemide

- Monoamine oxidase (MAO) inhibitors (furazolidone [e.g., Furoxone], phenelzine [e.g., Nardil], procarbazine [e.g., Matulane], selegiline [e.g., Eldepryl], tranylcypromine [e.g., Parnate])—*Do not take sertraline while you are taking or within 2 weeks of taking an MAO inhibitor*. If you do, you may develop confusion, agitation, restlessness, stomach or intestinal symptoms, sudden high body temperature, extremely high blood pressure, severe convulsions, or the serotonin syndrome. At least 14 days should be allowed between stopping treatment with one medicine (sertraline or the MAO inhibitor) and starting treatment with the other

- Tricyclic antidepressants (amitriptyline [e.g., Elavil], amoxapine [e.g., Asendin], clomipramine [e.g., Anafranil], desipramine [e.g., Pertofrane], doxepin [e.g., Sinequan], imipramine [e.g., Tofranil], nortriptyline [e.g., Aventyl], protriptyline [e.g., Vivactil], trimipramine [e.g., Surmontil])—Higher blood levels of these medicines may occur, which may increase the chance of developing unwanted effects. Your doctor may check the blood level of the tricyclic antidepressant, and may change the dose of either these medicines or sertraline. Also, taking sertraline with amitriptyline, clomipramine, or imipramine may increase the chance of developing the serotonin syndrome

Other medical problems—The presence of other medical problems may affect the use of sertraline. Make sure you tell your doctor if you have any other medical problems, especially:

- Brain disease or damage or
- Mental retardation or
- Seizure disorders (history of)—The risk of seizures may be increased

- Kidney disease—It is not known whether the chance of side effects will be increased

- Liver disease—Higher blood levels of sertraline may occur, increasing the chance of side effects. Your doctor may want you to take a lower dose or to take your doses less often than a person without liver disease

- Mania (history of)—May be activated

- Weight loss—Sertraline may cause weight loss. This weight loss is usually small, but if a large weight loss occurs, it may be harmful in some patients

Proper Use of This Medicine

Take this medicine only as directed by your doctor, to benefit your condition as much as possible. Do not take more of it, do not take it more often, and do not take it for a longer time than your doctor ordered.

Sertraline may be taken with or without food on a full or empty stomach. If your doctor tells you to take it a certain way, follow your doctor's instructions.

If you are taking the oral concentrate, mix it with 4 ounces of water, ginger ale, lemon-lime soda, lemonade or orange juice. Take it right away after mixing.

You may have to take sertraline for 4 weeks or longer before you begin to feel better. Your doctor should check your progress at regular visits during this time. Also, if you are taking this medicine for depression, you may need to keep taking it for 6 months or longer to help prevent the return of the depression.

Dosing—The dose of sertraline will be different for different patients. *Follow your doctor's orders or the directions on the label.* The following information includes only the average doses of sertraline. *If your dose is different, do not change it* unless your doctor tells you to do so.

Also, *the number of capsules or tablets that you take depends on the strength of the medicine and the medical problem for which you are taking sertraline.*

- For *oral* dosage forms (capsules, oral solution or tablets):
  - —Adults:
    - For mental depression or obsessive-compulsive disorder: To start, usually 50 milligrams (mg) once a day, taken either in the morning or evening. Your doctor may increase your dose gradually if needed. However, the dose usually is not more than 200 mg a day.
    - For panic disorder or posttraumatic stress disorder: To start, usually 25 mg once a day, taken either in the morning or evening. Your doctor may increase your dose gradually if needed. However, the dose usually is not more than 200 mg a day.
  - —Children:
    - For mental depression, posttraumatic stress disorder, or panic disorder: Use and dose must be determined by the doctor.
    - For obsessive-compulsive disorder:
      - —Children younger than 6 years old: Use and dose must be determined by the doctor.
      - —Children 6 to 12 years old: To start, usually 25 mg once a day, taken either in the morning or evening. Your doctor may increase your dose gradually if needed. However, the dose usually is not more than 200 mg a day.
      - —Children 13 to 17 years old: To start, usually 50 mg once a day, taken either in the morning or evening. Your doctor may increase your dose gradually if needed. However, the dose usually is not more than 200 mg a day.
  - —Older adults:
    - For mental depression, obsessive-compulsive disorder, or panic disorder (using capsules or tablets): To start, usually 12.5 to 25 mg once a day, taken either in the morning or evening. Your doctor may increase your dose gradually if needed.

Missed dose—Because sertraline may be given to different patients at different times of the day, you and your doctor should discuss what to do about any missed doses.

Storage—To store this medicine:
- Keep out of the reach of children.
- Store away from heat and direct light.
- Do not store in the bathroom, near the kitchen sink, or in other damp places. Heat or moisture may cause the medicine to break down.
- Do not keep outdated medicine or medicine no longer needed. Be sure that any discarded medicine is out of the reach of children.

Precautions While Using This Medicine

It is important that your doctor check your progress at regular visits, to allow for changes in your dose and to help reduce any side effects.

Do not take sertraline with or within 14 days of taking an MAO inhibitor (furazolidone, phenelzine, procarbazine, selegiline, tranylcypromine). Do not take an MAO inhibitor within 14 days of taking sertraline. If you do, you may develop extremely high blood pressure or convulsions (seizures).

Avoid drinking alcoholic beverages while taking sertraline.

This medicine may cause some people to become drowsy, to have trouble thinking, or to have problems with movement. *Make sure you know how you react to sertraline before you drive, use machines, or do anything else that could be dangerous if you are not alert or well-coordinated.*

Do not stop taking this medicine without first checking with your doctor. Your doctor may want you to reduce gradually the amount you are taking before stopping completely. This is to decrease the chance of having discontinuation symptoms such as agitation, anxiety, dizziness, feeling of constant movement of self or surroundings, headache, increased sweating, nausea, trembling or shaking, trouble in sleeping or walking, or unusual tiredness.

Side Effects of This Medicine

Along with its needed effects, a medicine may cause some unwanted effects. Although not all of these side effects may occur, if they do occur they may need medical attention. One rare, but very serious, effect that may occur is the serotonin syndrome. This syndrome (group of symptoms) is more likely to occur shortly after an increase in sertraline dose.

Check with your doctor as soon as possible if any of the following side effects occur:

More common
    Decreased sexual desire or ability

Less common or rare
    Breast tenderness or enlargement; fast or irregular heartbeat; fast talking and excited feelings or actions that are out of control; fever; inability to sit still; low blood sodium (confusion, convulsions [seizures], drowsiness, dryness of mouth, increased thirst, lack of energy); nose bleeds; red or purple

spots on skin; restlessness; serotonin syndrome (diarrhea, fever, increased sweating, mood or behavior changes, overactive reflexes, racing heartbeat, restlessness, shivering or shaking); skin rash, hives, or itching; unusual or sudden body or facial movements or postures; unusual secretion of milk (in females)

Symptoms of overdose—may be more severe than side effects occurring at regular doses or several may occur together

Anxiety; drowsiness; nausea; serotonin syndrome (diarrhea, fever, increased sweating, mood or behavior changes, overactive reflexes, racing heartbeat, restlessness, shivering or shaking); unusually fast heartbeat; unusually large pupils; vomiting

Other side effects may occur that usually do not need medical attention. These side effects may go away during treatment as your body adjusts to the medicine. However, check with your doctor if any of the following side effects continue or are bothersome:

More common

Decreased appetite or weight loss; diarrhea or loose stools; dizziness; drowsiness; dryness of mouth; headache; increased sweating; nausea; stomach or abdominal cramps, gas, or pain; tiredness or weakness; trembling or shaking; trouble in sleeping

Less common

Agitation, anxiety, or nervousness; changes in vision, including blurred vision; constipation; flushing or redness of skin, with feeling of warmth or heat; increased appetite; vomiting

After you stop taking sertraline, your body may need time to adjust. The length of time this takes depends on the amount of medicine you were using and how long you used it. During this period of time, check with your doctor if you notice any of the following side effects:

Agitation; anxiety; dizziness; feeling of constant movement of self or surroundings; headache; increased sweating; nausea; trembling or shaking; trouble in sleeping; trouble in walking; unusual tiredness

Other side effects not listed above may also occur in some patients. If you notice any other effects, check with your doctor.

Revised: 06/12/01

SEVELAMER   Oral

Commonly used brand name(s):

In the U.S.—
Renagel

Description

Sevelamer (se-VEL-a-mer) is used to treat hyperphosphatemia (too much phosphate in the blood) in patients with kidney disease who are on dialysis.

This medicine is available only with your doctor's prescription, in the following dosage form:

Oral
- Capsules (U.S.)
- Tablets (U.S.)

Before Using This Medicine

In deciding to use a medicine, the risks of taking the medicine must be weighed against the good it will do. This is a decision you and your doctor will make. For sevelamer, the following should be considered:

Allergies—Tell your doctor if you have ever had any unusual or allergic reaction to sevelamer. Also tell your health care professional if you are allergic to any other substances, such as foods, preservatives, or dyes.

Pregnancy—Studies have not been done in humans. Studies in animals have found that sevelamer may affect development of bones, possibly by reducing the amount of vitamin D absorbed into the body. It is not known if sevelamer affects the absorption of vitamins in pregnant women; however, sevelamer did not affect the levels of vitamins in the blood in humans who were taking multivitamins. Before taking this medicine, make sure your doctor knows if you are pregnant or if you may become pregnant.

Breast-feeding—Sevelamer has not been reported to cause problems in nursing babies.

Children—Studies on this medicine have been done only in adult patients, and there is no specific information comparing use of sevelamer in children with use in other age groups.

Older adults—Many medicines have not been studied specifically in older people. Therefore, it may not be known whether they work exactly the same way they do in younger adults. Although there is no specific information comparing use of sevelamer in the elderly with use in other age groups, this medicine has been used in elderly patients and is not expected to cause different side effects or problems in older people than it does in younger adults.

Other medicines—Although certain medicines should not be used together at all, in other cases two different medicines may be used together even if an interaction might occur. In these cases, your doctor may want to change the dose, or other precautions may be necessary. When you are taking sevelamer, it is especially important that your health care professional know if you are taking *any* other prescription or nonprescription (over-the-counter [OTC]) medicine.

Other medical problems—The presence of other medical problems may affect the use of sevelamer. Make sure you tell your doctor if you have any other medical problems, especially:

- Bowel obstruction (blockage) or other disorders affecting the gastrointestinal tract or
- Difficulty in swallowing or
- Major surgery on the gastrointestinal tract—Use of sevelamer may cause problems in these conditions
- Hypophosphatemia—Use of sevelamer may make this condition worse

Proper Use of This Medicine

Take this medicine with meals.

Take this medicine only as directed by your doctor. Do not take more or less of it, and do not take it more often than your doctor ordered.

Swallow the capsule whole. Do not break or chew the capsule before swallowing.

Do not open up the capsules before taking them. The medicine inside may swell if it comes in contact with water.

Follow carefully any diet program your doctor may recommend.

Dosing—The dose of sevelamer will be different for different patients. *Follow your doctor's orders or the directions on the label.* The following information includes only the average doses of sevelamer. *If your dose is different, do not change it* unless your doctor tells you to do so.

- For *oral* dosage form (capsules):
  —For high phosphorus levels in the blood:
  - Adults not taking a phosphate binder—The first dose is usually between 2 and 4 capsules three times a day, with each meal, depending on how high your blood phosphorus level is. After that, your doctor may change the dose, again depending on your blood phosphorus levels.
  - Adults switching from calcium acetate to sevelamer— The first dose of sevelamer is generally between 2 and 5 capsules three times a day, with each meal, depending on how many tablets of calcium acetate you are currently taking. After that the doctor may change the dose, depending on your blood phosphorus levels.
  - Children—Use and dose must be determined by your doctor.

- For *oral* dosage forms (tablets)
  —For high phosphorus levels in the blood:
  - Adults not taking a phosphate binder—The first dose is usually between 1 and 4 tablets three times a day, with each meal, depending on how high your blood phosphorus level is. After that, your doctor may change the dose, depending on your blood phosphorus levels.
  - Adults switching from calcium acetate to sevelamer— The first dose of sevelamer is generally between 1 and 5 tablets three times a day, with each meal, depending on how many tablets of calcium acetate you are currently taking. After that the doctor may change the dose, depending on your blood phosphorus levels.
  - Children—Use and dose must be determined by your doctor.

Missed dose—If you miss a dose of this medicine, take it as soon as you remember. However, if it is almost time for the next dose, skip the missed dose and go back to your regular dosing schedule. Do not double doses.

Storage—To store this medicine:
- Keep out of the reach of children.
- Store away from heat and direct light.
- Do not store in the bathroom, near the kitchen sink, or in other damp places. Heat or moisture may cause the medicine to break down.
- Do not keep outdated medicine or medicine no longer needed. Be sure that any discarded medicine is out of the reach of children.

Side Effects of This Medicine

Along with its needed effects, a medicine may cause some unwanted effects. The following side effects may go away during treatment as your body adjusts to the medicine. How-

ever, check with your doctor if any of the following side effects continue or are bothersome:

Less common
   Bloating or gas; constipation; diarrhea; heartburn; nausea or vomiting

Other side effects not listed above may also occur in some patients. If you notice any other effects, check with your doctor.

Developed: 06/08/1999
Revised: 01/16/2001

SIBUTRAMINE   Systemic†

Commonly used brand name(s):

In the U.S.—
   Meridia

†Not commercially available in Canada.

Description

Sibutramine (si-BYOO-tra-meen) is used together with a reduced-calorie diet to help you lose weight and to help keep the lost weight from returning. Sibutramine is thought to work by increasing the activity of certain chemicals, called norepinephrine and serotonin, in the brain. This medicine is approved for use only in people who are very overweight.

This medicine is available only with your doctor's prescription, in the following dosage form:

Oral
   - Capsules (U.S.)

Before Using This Medicine

In deciding to use a medicine, the risks of taking the medicine must be weighed against the good it will do. This is a decision you and your doctor will make. For sibutramine, the following should be considered:

Allergies—Tell your doctor if you have ever had any unusual or allergic reaction to sibutramine. Also tell your health care professional if you are allergic to any other substances, such as foods, preservatives, or dyes.

Diet—You must follow a reduced-calorie diet while taking sibutramine in order to lose weight and keep the lost weight from returning.

Pregnancy—Sibutramine has not been studied in pregnant women. However, studies in animals have shown that sibutramine causes birth defects when used in doses many times higher than the usual human dose. Before taking this medicine, make sure your doctor knows if you are pregnant or if you may become pregnant.

Breast-feeding—It is not known whether sibutramine passes into breast milk. Although most medicines pass into breast milk in small amounts, many of them may be used safely while breast-feeding. A mother who is taking this medicine and who wishes to breast-feed should discuss this with her doctor.

Children—Studies on this medicine have been done only in adult patients, and there is no specific information com-

paring use of sibutramine in children with use in other age groups.

Older adults—Many medicines have not been studied specifically in older people. Therefore, it may not be known whether they work exactly the same way they do in younger adults. Although there is no specific information comparing use of sibutramine in the elderly with use in other age groups, this medicine is not expected to cause different side effects or problems in older people than it does in younger adults.

Other medicines—Although certain medicines should not be used together at all, in other cases two different medicines may be used together even if an interaction might occur. In these cases, your doctor may want to change the dose, or other precautions may be necessary. When you are taking sibutramine, it is especially important that your health care professional know if you are taking any of the following:

- Appetite suppressants, other (benzphetamine [e.g., Didrex], diethylpropion [e.g., Tenuate], mazindol [e.g., Sanorex], phendimetrazine [e.g., Phendiet], phentermine [e.g., Ionamin])—The effects of using sibutramine in combination with another appetite suppressant are not known

- Bromocriptine (e.g., Parlodel) or
- Buspirone (e.g., BuSpar) or
- Certain tricyclic antidepressants (amitriptyline [e.g., Elavil], clomipramine [e.g., Anafranil], imipramine [e.g., Tofranil]) or
- Dextromethorphan (cough medicine) or
- Levodopa (e.g., Sinemet) or
- Lithium (e.g., Eskalith) or
- Meperidine (e.g., Demerol) or
- Nefazodone (e.g., Serzone) or
- Pentazocine (e.g., Talwin) or
- Selective serotonin reuptake inhibitors (citalopram [e.g., Celexa], fluoxetine [e.g., Prozac], fluvoxamine [e.g., Luvox], paroxetine [e.g., Paxil], sertraline [e.g., Zoloft]) or
- Street drugs (LSD, MDMA [e.g., ecstasy], marijuana) or
- Sumatriptan (e.g., Imitrex) or
- Tramadol (e.g., Ultram) or
- Trazodone (e.g., Desyrel) or
- Tryptophan or
- Venlafaxine (e.g., Effexor)—Using these medicines with sibutramine may increase the chance of developing a rare, but very serious, unwanted effect known as the serotonin syndrome. Symptoms of this syndrome include confusion, diarrhea, fever, poor coordination, restlessness, shivering, sweating, talking or acting with excitement you cannot control, trembling or shaking, or twitching. If you develop these symptoms, contact your doctor as soon as possible

- Moclobemide (e.g., Manerex)—Taking moclobemide and sibutramine together or less than 3 days apart may increase the chance of developing serious unwanted effects, including the serotonin syndrome, and is not recommended

- Monoamine oxidase (MAO) inhibitors (furazolidone [e.g., Furoxone], phenelzine [e.g., Nardil], procarbazine [e.g., Matulane], selegiline [e.g., Eldepryl], tranylcypromine [e.g., Parnate])— *Do not take sibutramine while you are taking or within 2 weeks of taking an MAO inhibitor, and do not take an MAO inhibitor within 2 weeks of taking sibutramine.* If you do, you may develop severe seizures, extremely high blood pressure, or the serotonin syndrome. Allow at least 2 weeks to pass between taking one of these medicines (sibutramine or an MAO inhibitor) and taking the other

Other medical problems—The presence of other medical problems may affect the use of sibutramine. Make sure you tell your doctor if you have any other medical problems, especially:

- Anorexia nervosa (an eating disorder) or
- Glaucoma, narrow angle or
- High blood pressure (or history of)—Sibutramine may make these conditions worse

- Brain disease or damage, or mental retardation or
- Seizures (history of)—Sibutramine may increase the chance of having seizures

- Gallstones (or history of)—Weight loss may make this condition worse

- Heart disease (or history of) or
- Stroke (or history of)—Increased blood pressure or heart rate caused by sibutramine may make these conditions worse

- Kidney disease (severe) or
- Liver disease (severe)—Higher blood levels of sibutramine may occur, increasing the chance of having unwanted effects

Proper Use of This Medicine

Take this medicine only as directed. Do not take more of it, do not take it more often, and do not take it for a longer time than directed by your doctor. To do so may increase the chance of developing unwanted effects, such as high blood pressure.

Follow a reduced-calorie diet while taking sibutramine, as directed by your doctor.

Sibutramine may be taken with or without food, on a full or empty stomach. However, if your doctor tells you to take it in a certain way, take it as directed.

Dosing—The dose of sibutramine will be different for different patients. *Follow your doctor's orders or the directions on the label.* The following information includes only the average doses of sibutramine. *If your dose is different, do not change it* unless your doctor tells you to do so.

The number of capsules that you take depends on the strength of the medicine.

- For *oral* dosage form (capsules):
  —For weight loss:
    - Adults—At first, 10 milligrams (mg) one time a day, usually in the morning. Your doctor may increase or decrease your dose if needed. However, the dose is usually not more than 15 mg a day.
    - Children—Use and dose must be determined by the doctor.

Missed dose—If you miss a dose of sibutramine and you remember it within 2 to 3 hours, take it as soon as possible. If you do not remember the missed dose until later, skip the missed dose and return to your regular dosing schedule. Do not double doses.

Storage—To store this medicine:

- Keep out of the reach of children.
- Store away from heat and direct light.
- Do not store in the bathroom, near the kitchen sink, or in other damp places. Heat or moisture may cause the medicine to break down.

- Do not keep outdated medicine or medicine no longer needed. Be sure that any discarded medicine is out of the reach of children.

Precautions While Using This Medicine

It is important that your doctor check your progress at regular visits. Sibutramine may increase blood pressure or heart rate and your doctor will check for these effects. Your doctor may need to adjust your dose.

If sibutramine does not seem to be working well, do not increase your dosage. Check with your doctor.

Do not take sibutramine while you are taking or within 2 weeks of taking a monoamine oxidase (MAO) inhibitor, such as furazolidone (e.g., Furoxone), phenelzine (e.g., Nardil), procarbazine (e.g., Matulane), selegiline (e.g., Elde-pryl), or tranylcypromine (e.g., Parnate). *Do not take an MAO inhibitor within 2 weeks of taking sibutramine.* To do so may cause severe seizures, extremely high blood pressure, or a life-threatening adverse effect called the serotonin syndrome.

Do not drink excess alcohol while taking sibutramine.

Notify your doctor as soon as possible if you develop a skin rash, hives, or other allergic symptoms.

Sibutramine may cause dizziness, drowsiness, or poor judgment. *Be sure you know how you react to this medicine before you drive, operate machinery, or do other things that could be dangerous if you are not alert and able to think clearly.*

Sibutramine may cause dryness of the mouth. For temporary relief, use sugarless candy or gum, melt bits of ice in your mouth, or use a saliva substitute. However, if your mouth continues to feel dry for more than 2 weeks, check with your medical doctor or dentist. Continuing dryness of the mouth may increase the chance of dental disease, including tooth decay, gum disease, and fungus infections.

Side Effects of This Medicine

Along with its needed effects, a medicine may cause some unwanted effects. Some of these effects, such as high blood pressure, may not have signs or symptoms that you can see or feel. While you are taking sibutramine, your doctor will check your blood pressure and heart rate at regular visits.

Although not all of these side effects may occur, if they do occur they may need medical attention.

Check with your doctor as soon as possible if any of the following side effects occur:

Less common
Achiness; chills; fast or irregular heartbeat; increased blood pressure; mental depression; painful menstruation; swelling of body or of feet and ankles

Rare
Bruising or red spots or patches on skin; convulsions (seizures); excessive bleeding following injury; headache (severe); rapidly changing moods; skin rash; weight gain (unusual)

Other side effects may occur that usually do not need medical attention. These side effects may go away during treatment as your body adjusts to the medicine. However, check with your doctor if any of the following side effects continue or are bothersome:

More common
Anxiety; constipation; dizziness; dryness of mouth; headache; irritability or unusual impatience; nervousness; stuffy or runny nose; trouble in sleeping

Less common
Abdominal pain; back pain; burning, itching, prickling, or tingling of skin; change in sense of taste; diarrhea; drowsiness; increase in appetite; increased sweating; increased thirst; indigestion; nausea; unusual warmth or flushing of skin

Other side effects not listed above may also occur in some patients. If you notice any other effects, check with your doctor.

Developed: 04/26/99

SILDENAFIL   Systemic

Commonly used brand name(s):

In the U.S.—
Viagra

In Canada—
Viagra

Description

Sildenafil (sil-DEN-a-fil) belongs to a group of medicines that delay the enzymes called phosphodiesterases from working too quickly. The penis is one of the areas where these enzymes work. Sildenafil is used to treat men who have erectile dysfunction (also called sexual impotence).

By controlling the enzyme phosphodiesterase, sildenafil helps to maintain an erection that is produced when the penis is stroked. Without physical action to the penis, such as that occurring during sexual intercourse, sildenafil will not work to cause an erection.

This medicine is available only with your doctor's prescription, in the following dosage form(s):

Oral
- Tablets (U.S.)

Before Using This Medicine

In deciding to use a medicine, the risks of taking the medicine must be weighed against the good it will do. This is a decision you and your doctor will make. For sildenafil, the following should be considered:

Allergies—Tell your doctor if you have ever had any unusual or allergic reaction to sildenafil. Also tell your health care professional if you are allergic to any other substances, such as foods, preservatives, or dyes.

Pregnancy—Sildenafil is not indicated for use in women. Sildenafil has not been studied in pregnant women. However, sildenafil has not been shown to cause birth defects or other problems in animal studies.

Breast-feeding—It is not known whether sildenafil passes into breast milk. Sildenafil is not indicated for use in women.

Older adults—Elderly people are especially sensitive to the effects of sildenafil, which may increase their chance of having side effects. Patients 65 years of age and older are started on a low dose, 25 mg, of sildenafil. The dose may be increased by a doctor as needed and tolerated.

Other medicines—Although certain medicines should not be used together at all, in other cases two different medicines may be used together even if an interaction might occur. In these cases, your doctor may want to change the dose, or other precautions may be necessary. When you are taking sildenafil, it is especially important that your health care professional know if you are taking any of the following:

- Cimetidine (e.g., Tagamet)
- Erythromycin (e.g., E.E.S. or Ery-Tab)
- Itraconazole (e.g., Sporanox)
- Ketaconazole (e.g., Nizoral)
- Mibefradil (e.g., Posicor)
- Ritonavir (e.g., Norvir)
- Saquinavir (e.g., Fortovase or Invirase)—These medicines may increase the unwanted effects of sildenafil, unless lower starting doses of sildenafil are used

- Nitrates, such as nitroglycerin (e.g., Nitrostat or Transderm-Nitro)—Sildenafil increases the lowering of blood pressure by nitrates too much and their use together is not recommended

Other medical problems—The presence of other medical problems may affect the use of sildenafil. Make sure you tell your doctor if you have any other medical problems, especially:

- Arrhythmias (irregular heartbeat) or
- Coronary artery disease or
- Heart attack, history of (within the last 6 months) or
- High blood pressure or
- Low blood pressure or
- Stroke, history of (within the last 6 months)—Chance of problems occurring may be increased

- Abnormal penis, including curved penis and birth defects of the penis—Chance of problems occurring may be increased

- Bleeding problems or
- Retinitis pigmentosa—Chance of problems occurring may be increased. It is not known if the medicine is safe for use in these patients

- Conditions causing thickened blood or slower blood flow, including leukemia; multiple myeloma (tumors of the bone marrow); or polycythemia, sickle cell disease, and thrombocythemia (blood problems) or
- Priapism (history of)—Although sildenafil does not cause priapism (erection lasting longer than 6 hours), patients with these conditions have an increased risk of priapism and it could occur while using sildenafil

- Heart or blood disease—Sexual activity increases the heart rate and blood flow and can increase the chance of problems occurring for some patients who use any type of medicine, including sildenafil, that increases sexual ability

- Kidney problems (severe) or
- Liver problems (severe)—Chance of problems occurring may be increased. Lower starting doses may be used and doses increased as needed and as tolerated

Proper Use of This Medicine

Special patient directions come with sildenafil. *Read the directions carefully before using the medicine.*

This medicine usually begins to work within 30 minutes after taking it. It continues to work for up to 4 hours, although its action is usually less after 2 hours.

Dosing—The dose of sildenafil will be different for different patients. *Follow your doctor's orders or the directions on the label.* The following information includes only the average doses of sildenafil. *If your dose is different, do not change it* unless your doctor tells you to do so.

- For *oral* dosage form (tablets):
  —For treatment of erectile dysfunction:
    - Adults up to 65 years of age—50 mg as a single dose no more than once a day, 1 hour before sexual intercourse. Alternatively, the medicine may be taken 30 minutes to 4 hours before sexual intercourse. If needed, your doctor may increase your daily dose to 100 mg or decrease your daily dose to 25 mg.
    - Adults 65 years of age and older—25 mg as a single dose no more than once a day, 1 hour before sexual intercourse. Alternatively, the medicine may be taken 30 minutes to 4 hours before sexual intercourse. If needed, your doctor may increase your daily dose.
    - If you are taking protease inhibitors, such as for the treatment of HIV, your doctor may recommend a 25 mg dose and may limit you to a maximum single dose of 25 mg of Viagra in a 48 hour period

Storage—To store this medicine:
- Keep out of the reach of children.
- Store away from heat and direct light.
- Do not store in the bathroom, near the kitchen sink, or in other damp places. Heat or moisture may cause the medicine to break down.
- Keep the medicine from freezing. Do not refrigerate.
- Do not keep outdated medicine or medicine no longer needed. Be sure that any discarded medicine is out of the reach of children.

Precautions While Using This Medicine

Sildenafil has not been studied with other medicines used for treatment of erectile dysfunction. Presently, using them together is not recommended.

Use sildenafil exactly as directed by your doctor. Do not use more of it and do not use it more often than your doctor ordered. If too much is used, the chance of side effects is increased.

If you experience a prolonged or painful erection for 4 hours or more, contact your doctor immediately. This condition may require prompt medical treatment to prevent tissue damage of the penis and possible permanent impotence.

Side Effects of This Medicine

Along with its needed effects, a medicine may cause some unwanted effects. Although not all of these side effects may occur, if they do occur they may need medical attention.

Less common
> Abnormal vision, including blurred vision, seeing shades of colors differently than before, or sensitivity to light; bladder pain; cloudy or bloody urine; dizziness; increased frequency of urination; pain on urination

Rare
> Bleeding of the eye; convulsions (seizures); decreased vision or other changes in vision; double vision; prolonged, painful, or inappropriate erection of penis;

redness, burning, or swelling of the eye; vision loss, temporary

Note: The following rare side effects have not been completely established as being caused by sildenafil

Blood sugar problems (more likely with patients with diabetes mellitus), such as anxiety, behavior change similar to drunkenness, blurred vision, cold sweats, confusion, cool and pale skin, difficulty in concentrating, drowsiness, excessive hunger, fast heartbeat, headache, nausea, nervousness, nightmares, restless sleep, shakiness, slurred speech, and unusual tiredness or weakness; bone pain; breast enlargement; chest pain; chills; confusion; convulsions (seizures); deafness; decrease in amount of urine or in frequency of urination; dizziness or lightheadedness, especially when getting up from a lying or sitting position; dry eyes; dry mouth; dryness, redness, scaling, or peeling of the skin; eye pain; fainting or faintness; fast, irregular, or pounding heartbeat; feeling of something in the eye; groups of skin lesions with swelling; headache (severe or continuing); heart failure; hives; increase in size of pupil; increased sweating; increased thirst; itching of skin; low blood pressure; lower back or side pain; migraine headache; nausea (severe or continuing); nervousness; numbness of hands; painful, swollen joints; redness, itching, or tearing of eyes; shortness of breath or troubled breathing; skin paleness; skin rash; skin ulcers; sore throat and fever or chills; sudden weakness; swelling of face, hands, feet, or lower legs; twitching of muscles; unusual tiredness or weakness; unusual feeling of burning or stinging of skin

Other side effects may occur that usually do not need medical attention. These side effects may go away during treatment as your body adjusts to the medicine. However, check with your doctor if any of the following side effects continue or are bothersome:

More common

Flushing; headache; nasal congestion; stomach discomfort following meals

Less common

Diarrhea

Rare

Anxiety

Note: The following rare side effects have not been completely established as being caused by sildenafil

Abdominal pain; abnormal dreams; aches or pains of muscles; clumsiness or unsteadiness; cough; diarrhea or stomach cramps (severe or continuing); difficulty in swallowing; ear pain; increased amount of saliva; increased skin sensitivity; lack of coordination; loss of bladder control; mental depression; nausea; numbness or tingling of hands, legs, or feet; rectal bleeding; redness or irritation of the tongue; redness, soreness, swelling, or bleeding of gums; ringing or buzzing in ears; sensation of motion, usually whirling, either of

one's self or of one's surroundings; sexual problems in men (continuing), including failure to experience a sexual orgasm; sleepiness; sores in mouth and on lips; tense muscles; tightness of chest or wheezing; trembling and shaking; trouble in sleeping; vomiting; waking to urinate at night; worsening of asthma

Other side effects not listed above may also occur in some patients. If you notice any other effects, check with your doctor.

Developed: 05/28/98
Revised: 2/15/00

SILVER SULFADIAZINE   Topical

Commonly used brand name(s):

In the U.S.—

Silvadene	SSD AF
SSD	Thermazene

In Canada—
Flamazine

Description

Silver sulfadiazine (SILL-ver sul-fa-DYE-a-zeen), a sulfa medicine, is used to prevent and treat bacterial or fungus infections. It works by killing the fungus or bacteria.

Silver sulfadiazine cream is applied to the skin and/or burned area(s) to prevent and treat bacterial or fungus infections that may occur in burns. This medicine may also be used for other problems as determined by your doctor.

Other medicines are used along with this medicine for burns. Patients with severe burns or burns over a large area of the body must be treated in a hospital.

Silver sulfadiazine is available only with your doctor's prescription, in the following dosage form:

Topical
• Cream (U.S. and Canada)

Before Using This Medicine

In deciding to use a medicine, the risks of using the medicine must be weighed against the good it will do. This is a decision you and your doctor will make. For silver sulfadiazine, the following should be considered:

Allergies—Tell your doctor if you have ever had any unusual or allergic reaction to silver sulfadiazine or to any of the following medicines:

• Acetazolamide (e.g., Diamox)
• Antidiabetics, oral (diabetes medicine you take by mouth)
• Dichlorphenamide (e.g., Daranide)
• Furosemide (e.g., Lasix)
• Methazolamide (e.g., Neptazane)
• Sulfonamides, other (sulfa medicine)
• Thiazide diuretics (water pills)

Also tell your health care professional if you are allergic to any other substances, such as preservatives or dyes.

Pregnancy—Studies have not been done in humans. However, sulfa medicines may increase the chance of liver problems in newborn infants. Silver sulfadiazine has not been shown to cause birth defects or other problems in studies in rabbits treated with 3 to 10 times the usual amount of silver sulfadiazine.

Breast-feeding—It is not known whether silver sulfadiazine applied to the skin and/or burns passes into the breast milk. However, silver sulfadiazine may be absorbed into the body when used on skin and/or burns. Sulfa medicines given by mouth do pass into the breast milk. They may cause liver problems, anemia (iron-poor blood), and other unwanted effects in nursing babies, especially those with glucose-6-phosphate dehydrogenase deficiency (lack of G6PD enzyme). Therefore, caution is recommended when using this medicine in nursing women.

Children—Use is not recommended in premature or newborn infants up to 2 months of age. Sulfa medicines may cause liver problems in these infants. Although there is no specific information comparing use of silver sulfadiazine in older infants and children with use in other age groups, this medicine is not expected to cause different side effects or problems in older infants and children than it does in adults.

Older adults—Many medicines have not been studied specifically in older people. Therefore, it may not be known whether they work exactly the same way they do in younger adults or if they cause different side effects or problems in older people. There is no specific information comparing use of silver sulfadiazine in the elderly with use in other age groups.

Other medicines—Although certain medicines should not be used together at all, in other cases two different medicines may be used together even if an interaction might occur. In these cases, your doctor may want to change the dose, or other precautions may be necessary. When you are taking silver sulfadiazine, it is especially important that your health care professional know if you are taking any of the following:

- Cimetidine—May increase the risk of leukopenia (low white blood cell counts)

- Collagenase (e.g., Santyl) or
- Papain (e.g., Panafil) or
- Sutilains (e.g., Travase)—Silver sulfadiazine may prevent these enzymes from working properly

Other medical problems—The presence of other medical problems may affect the use of silver sulfadiazine. Make sure you tell your doctor if you have any other medical problems, especially:

- Blood problems or
- Glucose-6-phosphate dehydrogenase deficiency (lack of G6PD enzyme)—Use of this medicine may cause blood problems or make them worse

- Kidney disease or
- Liver disease—In persons with these conditions, use may result in higher blood levels of this medicine; a smaller dose may be needed

- Porphyria—Use of this medicine may result in a severe attack of porphyria

Proper Use of This Medicine

This medicine should not be used on premature or newborn infants up to 2 months of age, unless otherwise directed by your doctor. It may cause liver problems in these infants.

To use:
- Before applying this medicine, cleanse the affected area(s). Remove dead or burned skin and other debris.
- Wear a sterile glove to apply this medicine. Apply a thin layer (about 1/16 inch) of silver sulfadiazine to the affected area(s). Keep the affected area(s) covered with the medicine at all times.
- If this medicine is rubbed off the affected area(s) by moving around or if it is washed off during bathing, showering, or the use of a whirlpool bath, reapply the medicine.
- After this medicine has been applied, the treated area(s) may be covered with a dressing or left uncovered as desired.

To help clear up your skin and/or burn infection completely, *keep using silver sulfadiazine for the full time of treatment*. You should keep using this medicine until the burned area has healed or is ready for skin grafting. *Do not miss any doses.*

Dosing—The dose of silver sulfadiazine will be different for different patients. *Follow your doctor's orders or the directions on the label.* The following information includes only the average doses of silver sulfadiazine. *If your dose is different, do not change it* unless your doctor tells you to do so.

- For *topical* dosage form (cream):
  —For burn wound infections:
    - Adults and children 2 months of age and older— Use one or two times a day.
    - Premature and newborn infants up to 2 months of age—Use and dose must be determined by the doctor.

Missed dose—If you miss a dose of this medicine, apply it as soon as possible. However, if it is almost time for your next dose, skip the missed dose and go back to your regular dosing schedule.

Storage—To store this medicine:
- Keep out of the reach of children.
- Store away from heat and direct light.
- Keep the medicine from freezing.
- Do not keep outdated medicine or medicine no longer needed. Be sure that any discarded medicine is out of the reach of children.

Precautions While Using This Medicine

It is important that your doctor check your progress at regular visits.

If your skin infection or burn does not improve within a few days or weeks (for more serious burns or burns over larger areas), or if it becomes worse, check with your doctor.

This medicine may rarely stain skin brownish gray.

Side Effects of This Medicine

Along with its needed effects, a medicine may cause some unwanted effects. Although not all of these side effects may occur, if they do occur they may need medical attention.

Check with your doctor as soon as possible if the following side effect occurs:
Rare
Blistering, peeling or loosening of skin; bloody or cloudy

urine; chills or fever; cough; decreased amount of urine or less frequent urination; increased sensitivity of skin to sunlight, especially in patients with burns on large areas; intense itching of burn wounds; pain at site of application; painful or difficult urination; red skin lesions, often with a purple center; shortness of breath; sore throat; sores, ulcers or white spots on lips or in mouth; swollen glands; unusual bleeding or bruising; unusual tiredness or weakness

Other side effects may occur that usually do not need medical attention. These side effects may go away during treatment as your body adjusts to the medicine. However, check with your doctor if any of the following side effects continue or are bothersome:

More common
   Burning feeling on treated area(s)
Less common or rare
   Brownish-gray skin discoloration; itching or skin rash

Other side effects not listed above may also occur in some patients. If you notice any other effects, check with your doctor.

Revised: 03/17/00

SIMETHICONE Oral

Commonly used brand name(s):

In the U.S.—

Extra Strength Maalox Anti-Gas	Gas-X Extra Strength
Flatulex	Genasyme
Gas Relief	Maalox Anti-Gas
Gas-X	Maximum Strength Gas Relief
Maximum Strength Mylanta Gas Relief	Mylanta Gas Relief
Maximum Strength Phazyme	Mylicon Drops
My Baby Gas Relief Drops	Phazyme
Mylanta Gas	Phazyme-95

Generic name product may be available.

In Canada—

Extra Strength Maalox GRF Gas Relief Formula	Ovol-40
Baby's Own Infant Drops	Ovol-80
Maalox GRF Gas Relief Formula	Ovol-160
Ovol	Phazyme Drops
	Phazyme-95
	Phazyme-125

Description

Simethicone (si-METH-i-kone) is used to relieve the painful symptoms of too much gas in the stomach and intestines.

Simethicone may also be used for other conditions as determined by your doctor.

Simethicone is available without a prescription; however, your doctor may have special instructions on the proper use and dose for your medical problem. It is available in the following dosage forms:

Oral
- Capsules (U.S. and Canada)
- Oral suspension (U.S. and Canada)
- Tablets (U.S.)
- Chewable tablets (U.S. and Canada)

Before Using This Medicine

In deciding to use a medicine, the risks of taking the medicine must be weighed against the good it will do. This is a decision you and your doctor will make. For simethicone, the following should be considered:

Allergies—Tell your doctor if you have ever had any unusual or allergic reaction to simethicone. Also tell your health care professional if you are allergic to any other substances, such as foods, preservatives, or dyes.

Diet—Avoid foods that seem to increase gas. Chew food thoroughly and slowly. Reduce air swallowing by avoiding fizzy, carbonated drinks. Do not smoke before meals. Develop regular bowel habits and exercise regularly. Make certain your health care professional knows if you are on a low-sodium, low-sugar, or any other special diet. Most medicines contain more than their active ingredient.

Pregnancy—Simethicone is not absorbed into the body and is not likely to cause problems.

Breast-feeding—Simethicone has not been reported to cause problems in nursing babies.

Children—This medicine has been tested in children and, in effective doses, has not been shown to cause different side effects or problems than it does in adults.

Older adults—Many medicines have not been studied specifically in older people. Therefore, it may not be known whether they work exactly the same way they do in younger adults. There is no specific information comparing use of simethicone in the elderly with use in other age groups.

Proper Use of This Medicine

For effective use of simethicone:
- Follow your doctor's instructions if this medicine was prescribed.
- Follow the manufacturer's package directions if you are treating yourself.

Take this medicine after meals and at bedtime for best results.

For patients taking the *chewable tablet* form of this medicine:
- It is important that you chew the tablets thoroughly before you swallow them. This is to allow the medicine to work faster and more completely.

For patients taking the *oral liquid* form of this medicine:
- This medicine is to be taken by mouth even if it comes in a dropper bottle. The amount you should take is to be measured with the specially marked dropper or measuring spoon.

Dosing—The dose of simethicone will be different for different patients. *Follow your doctor's orders or the directions on the label.* The following information includes only the average doses of simethicone. *If your dose is different, do not change it* unless your doctor tells you to do so.
- For symptoms of too much gas:
  —For *oral* dosage forms (capsules or tablets):
    - Adults and teenagers—Usual dose is 60 to 125 milligrams (mg) four times a day, after meals and at bedtime. The dose should not be more than 500 mg in twenty-four hours.
    - Children—Dose must be determined by the doctor.

—For *oral* dosage form (chewable tablets):
- Adults and teenagers—Usual dose is 40 to 125 mg four times a day, after meals and at bedtime or the dose may be 150 mg three times a day, after meals. The dose should not be more than 500 mg in twenty-four hours.
- Children—Dose must be determined by the doctor.

—For *oral* dosage form (suspension):
- Adults and teenagers—Usual dose is 40 to 95 mg four times a day, after meals and at bedtime. The dose should not be more than 500 mg in twenty-four hours.
- Children—Dose must be determined by the doctor.

Missed dose—If you must take this medicine regularly and you miss a dose, take it as soon as possible. However, if it is almost time for your next dose, skip the missed dose and go back to your regular dosing schedule. Do not double doses.

Storage—To store this medicine:
- Keep out of the reach of children.
- Store away from heat and direct light.
- Do not store the capsule or tablet form of this medicine in the bathroom, near the kitchen sink, or in other damp places. Heat or moisture may cause the medicine to break down.
- Keep the liquid form of this medicine from freezing.
- Do not keep outdated medicine or medicine no longer needed. Be sure that any discarded medicine is out of the reach of children.

Side Effects of This Medicine

There have not been any common or important side effects reported with this medicine. However, if you notice any side effects, check with your doctor.

Additional Information

Once a medicine has been approved for marketing for a certain use, experience may show that it is also useful for other medical problems. Although these uses are not included in product labeling, simethicone is used in certain patients before the following tests:
- Before a gastroscopy
- Before a radiography of the bowel

Other than the above information, there is no additional information relating to proper use, precautions, or side effects for these uses.

Revised: 06/16/93
Interim revision: 06/21/95; 08/14/98

SIROLIMUS   Systemic

rapamycinCommonly used brand name(s):

In the U.S.—
  Rapamune

Description

Sirolimus (sir-OH-li-mus) belongs to a group of medicines known as immunosuppressive agents. It is used to lower the body's natural immunity in patients who receive kidney transplants.

When a patient receives an organ transplant, the body's white blood cells will try to get rid of (reject) the transplanted organ. Sirolimus works by preventing the white blood cells from getting rid of the transplanted organ.

Sirolimus is a very strong medicine. It can cause side effects that can be very serious, such as kidney problems. It may also reduce the body's ability to fight infections. You and your doctor should talk about the good this medicine will do as well as the risks of using it.

Sirolimus is available only with your doctor's prescription, in the following dosage forms:

Oral
- Oral Solution (U.S.)
- Tablets (U.S.)

Before Using This Medicine

In deciding to use a medicine, the risks of taking the medicine must be weighed against the good it will do. This is a decision you and your doctor will make. For sirolimus, the following should be considered:

Allergies— Tell your doctor if you have ever had any unusual or allergic reaction to sirolimus. Also tell your health care professional if you are allergic to any other substances, such as foods, preservatives, or dyes.

Pregnancy— Sirolimus has not been studied in pregnant women. However, studies in animals have shown that sirolimus causes problems in the fetus. It is very important that an effective form of birth control be used before starting sirolimus therapy, during sirolimus therapy, and for 12 weeks after sirolimus therapy has stopped.

Breast-feeding—It is not known whether sirolimus passes into human breast milk. However, because this medicine may cause serious side effects, breast-feeding may not be recommended while you are receiving it. Discuss with your doctor whether or not you should breast-feed while you are receiving sirolimus.

Other medicines—Although certain medicines should not be used together at all, in other cases two different medicines may be used together even if an interaction might occur. In these cases, your doctor may want to change the dose, or other precautions may be necessary. When you are taking sirolimus, it is especially important that your health care professional knows if you are taking any of the following:
- Cyclosporine (e.g. Neoral or Sandimmune) or
- Diltiazem (e.g. Cardizem) or
- Ketoconazole (e.g. Nizoral)—May increase the effects of sirolimus by increasing the amount of this medicine in the body
- Rifampin (e.g. Rifadin)—May decrease the effects of sirolimus by decreasing the amount of sirolimus in the body

Other medical problems—The presence of other medical problems may affect the use of sirolimus. Make sure you tell your doctor if you have any other medical problems, especially:
- Cancer or

- Hyperlipidemia (high amount of cholesterol and fats in the blood)—Sirolimus can make these conditions worse
- Chickenpox (including recent exposure) or
- Herpes zoster (shingles)—Risk of severe disease affecting other parts of the body
- Infection—Sirolimus decreases the body's ability to fight infection
- Liver disease—A lower dose of sirolimus may be needed in patients with this condition

Proper Use of This Medicine

This medicine usually comes with patient information or directions. Read them carefully and make sure you understand them before taking this medicine. If you have any questions, ask your health care professional.

Take this medicine only as directed by your doctor. Do not use more or less of it, and do not use it more often than your doctor ordered. The exact amount of medicine you need has been carefully worked out. Using too much will increase the risk of side effects, while using too little may lead to rejection of your transplanted kidney.

To help you remember to take your medicine, try to get into the habit of taking it at the same time each day. This will help sirolimus work better by keeping a constant amount in the blood.

Absorption of this medicine may be changed if you change your diet. This medicine should be taken consistently with respect to meals. You should not change the type or amount of food you eat unless you discuss it with your health care professional.

Do not stop taking this medicine without first checking with your doctor. You may have to take this medicine for the rest of your life to prevent your body from rejecting the transplant.

Sirolimus usually is used along with a corticosteroid (cortisone-like medicine) and cyclosporine (another immunosuppressive agent). Sirolimus should be taken 4 hours after cyclosporine modified oral solution (*Neoral, SangCya*) or cyclosporine modified capsules (*Neoral*). If you have any questions about this, ask your health care professional.

Mix sirolimus oral solution with at least 2 ounces (¼ cup, 60 milliliters [mL]) of water or orange juice in a glass or plastic container. Stir the mixture well and drink it immediately. Then, rinse the container with at least 4 ounces (½ cup, 120 mL) of additional water or orange juice, stir it well, and drink it to make sure that all of the medicine is taken.

Dosing—The dose of sirolimus will be different for different patients. *Follow your doctor's orders or the directions on the label.* The following information includes only the average doses of sirolimus. *If your dose is different, do not change it unless your doctor tells you to do so.* If you have any questions about the proper dose of sirolimus, ask your doctor.

- For *oral* dosage form (oral solution or tablets):
  —Adults and children 13 years of age and older weighing 88 pounds (40 kilograms) or more: The usual dose is 2 milligrams (mg) a day after an initial one-time dose of 6 mg.
  —For children 13 years of age and older who weigh less than 88 pounds (40 kilograms): The dose is based on body size. It is usually 1 mg per square meter of body surface area once a day after an initial one-time dose of 3 mg per square meter of body surface area.
  —For children up to 13 years of age: Use and dose must be determined by your doctor.

Missed dose—If you miss a dose of sirolimus and remember it within 12 hours, take the missed dose as soon as you remember. However, if it is almost time for the next dose, skip the missed dose, go back to your regular dosing schedule, and check with your doctor. Do not double doses.

Storage—To store this medicine:
- Keep out of the reach of children.
- Store the oral liquid form in the refrigerator.
- Store tablets at room temperature.
- Protect from exposure to light.
- Keep the medicine from freezing.
- Do not keep outdated medicine or medicine no longer needed. Ask your health care professional how you should dispose of any medicine you do not use. Be sure that any discarded medicine is out of the reach of children.

Precautions While Using This Medicine

It is very important that your doctor check your progress at regular visits to make sure that this medicine is working properly and to check for unwanted effects.

While you are taking sirolimus, it is important to maintain good dental hygiene and see a dentist regularly for teeth cleaning.

Raw oysters or other shellfish may contain bacteria that can cause serious illness and possibly death. This is more likely to be a problem if these foods are eaten by patients with certain medical conditions. Even eating oysters from "clean" water or good restaurants does not guarantee that the oysters do not contain the bacteria. Eating raw shellfish is not a problem for most healthy people; however, patients with the following conditions may be at greater risk: cancer, immune disorders, organ transplantation, long-term corticosteroid use (as for asthma, arthritis, or organ transplantation), liver disease (including viral hepatitis), excess alcohol intake (2 to 3 drinks or more per day), diabetes, stomach problems (including stomach surgery and low stomach acid), and hemochromatosis (an iron disorder). *Do not eat raw oysters or other shellfish while you are taking sirolimus. Be sure oysters and shellfish are fully cooked.*

While you are being treated with sirolimus, and after you stop treatment with it, *it is important to see your doctor about the immunizations (vaccinations) you should receive. Do not get any immunizations without your doctor's approval.* Sirolimus may lower your body's resistance and there is a chance you might get the infection the immunization is meant to prevent. In addition, other persons living in your household should not take or have recently taken oral polio vaccine since there is a chance they could pass the polio virus on to you. Also, avoid other persons who have taken the oral polio vaccine. Do not get close to them, and do not stay in the same room with them for very long. If you cannot take these precautions, you should consider wearing a protective face mask that covers the nose and mouth.

Treatment with sirolimus may also increase the chance of getting other infections. If you can, avoid people with colds or other infections. If you think you are getting a cold or other infection, check with your doctor.

Grapefruits and grapefruit juice may increase the effects of sirolimus by increasing the amount of this medicine in your body. *You should not eat grapefruit or drink grapefruit juice while you taking this medicine.*

Side Effects of This Medicine

Along with its needed effects, a medicine may cause some unwanted effects. Although not all of these side effects may occur, if they do occur they may need medical attention.

Also, because of the way sirolimus acts on the body, there is a chance that it may cause effects that may not occur until years after the medicine is used. These delayed effects may include certain types of cancer, such as lymphoma.

Check with your doctor or nurse immediately if any of the following side effects occur:
  More common
    Chest pain; black, tarry stools; general feeling of illness; shortness of breath; swollen glands; weight loss, unusual; yellow skin and eyes

Check with your doctor as soon as possible if any of the following side effects occur:
  More common
    Abdominal pain; anxiousness, unexplained; bloody or cloudy urine; bone pain; chills; confusion; convulsions (seizures); cough; decreased urge to urinate; fast, slow, or irregular heartbeat; fever; frequent urge to urinate; increased thirst; loss of appetite; lower back or side pain; mood changes; muscle pain or cramps; nausea or vomiting; numbness or tingling around lips, hands, or feet; painful or difficult urination; rash; sore throat; sores or white spots on lips or in mouth; swelling of hands, ankles, feet, or lower legs; swollen glands; trouble breathing; unusual bleeding or bruising; unusual tiredness or weakness; weakness or heaviness of legs
  Less common
    Skin ulcer or sores
  Rare
    Weight gain, unusual

Other side effects may occur that usually do not need medical attention. These side effects may go away during treatment as your body adjusts to the medicine. However, check with your doctor if any of the following side effects continue or are bothersome:
  More common
    Acne; constipation; diarrhea; difficulty in moving; headache; loss of energy or weakness; muscle pain or stiffness; pain; shaking or trembling; trouble in sleeping
  Less common
    Nosebleed; swelling of the face

Other side effects not listed above may also occur in some patients. If you notice any other effects, check with your doctor.

Developed: 04/20/00
Revised: 03/21/01

SKELETAL MUSCLE RELAXANTS
Systemic

Commonly used brand name(s):

In the U.S.—

Carbacot[5]	Robaxin[5]
EZE-DS[3]	Robaxin-750[5]
Maolate[2]	Skelaxin[4]
Paraflex[3]	Skelex[5]
Parafon Forte DSC[3]	Soma[1]
Relaxazone[3]	Strifon Forte DSC[3]
Remular[3]	Vanadom[1]
Remular-S[3]	

In Canada—

Robaxin[5]	Soma[1]
Robaxin-750[5]	

Note: For quick reference, the following skeletal muscle relaxants are numbered to match the corresponding brand names.

This information applies to the following medicines:
  1. Carisoprodol (kar-eye-soe-PROE-dole) ‡
  2. Chlorphenesin (klor-FEN-e-sin) †
  3. Chlorzoxazone (klor-ZOX-a-zone) †‡
  4. Metaxalone (me-TAX-a-lone) †
  5. Methocarbamol (meth-oh-KAR-ba-mole) ‡

This information does *not* apply to Baclofen, Cyclobenzaprine, Dantrolene, Diazepam, or Orphenadrine.

†Not commercially available in Canada.
‡Generic name product may be available in the U.S.

Description

Skeletal muscle relaxants are used to relax certain muscles in your body and relieve the stiffness, pain, and discomfort caused by strains, sprains, or other injury to your muscles. However, these medicines do not take the place of rest, exercise or physical therapy, or other treatment that your doctor may recommend for your medical problem. Methocarbamol also has been used to relieve some of the muscle problems caused by tetanus.

Skeletal muscle relaxants act in the central nervous system (CNS) to produce their muscle relaxant effects. Their actions in the CNS may also produce some of their side effects.

In the U.S., these medicines are available only with your doctor's prescription. In Canada, some of these medicines are available without a prescription.

These medicines are available in the following dosage forms:

Oral
  Carisoprodol
    • Tablets (U.S. and Canada)
  Chlorphenesin
    • Tablets (U.S.)
  Chlorzoxazone
    • Tablets (U.S.)
  Metaxalone
    • Tablets (U.S.)
  Methocarbamol
    • Tablets (U.S. and Canada)

Parenteral
  Methocarbamol
    • Injection (U.S. and Canada)

Before Using This Medicine

In deciding to use a medicine, the risks of taking the medicine must be weighed against the good it will do. This is a decision you and your doctor will make. For the skeletal muscle relaxants, the following should be considered:

Allergies—Tell your doctor if you have ever had any unusual or allergic reaction to any of the skeletal muscle relaxants or to carbromal, mebutamate, meprobamate (e.g., Equanil), or tybamate. Also tell your health care professional if you are allergic to any other substances, such as foods, preservatives, or dyes.

Pregnancy—Although skeletal muscle relaxants have not been shown to cause birth defects or other problems, studies on birth defects have not been done in pregnant women. Studies in animals with metaxalone have not shown that it causes birth defects.

Breast-feeding—Carisoprodol passes into the breast milk and may cause drowsiness or stomach upset in nursing babies. It is not known whether chlorphenesin, chlorzoxazone, metaxalone, or methocarbamol passes into the breast milk. However, these medicines have not been reported to cause problems in nursing babies.

Children—Studies with the skeletal muscle relaxants have been done only in adult patients, and there is no specific information comparing use of these medicines in children with use in other age groups. However, carisoprodol and chlorzoxazone have been used in children. They have not been reported to cause different side effects or problems in children than they do in adults.

Older adults—Many medicines have not been tested in older people. Therefore, it may not be known whether they work exactly the same way they do in younger adults or if they cause different side effects or problems in older people. There is no specific information about the use of skeletal muscle relaxants in the elderly.

Other medicines—Although certain medicines should not be used together at all, in other cases two different medicines may be used together even if an interaction might occur. In these cases, your doctor may want to change the dose, or other precautions may be necessary. When you are taking a skeletal muscle relaxant, it is especially important that your health care professional know if you are taking any of the following:

- Alcohol or
- Central nervous system (CNS) depressants or
- Tricyclic antidepressants (amitriptyline [e.g., Elavil], amoxapine [e.g., Asendin], clomipramine [e.g., Anafranil], desipramine [e.g., Pertofrane], doxepin [e.g., Sinequan], imipramine [e.g., Tofranil], nortriptyline [e.g., Aventyl], protriptyline [e.g., Vivactil], trimipramine [e.g., Surmontil])—The chance of side effects may be increased

Other medical problems—The presence of other medical problems may affect the use of a skeletal muscle relaxant. Make sure you tell your doctor if you have any other medical problems, especially:

- Allergies, history of, or
- Blood disease caused by an allergy or reaction to any other medicine, history of, or

- Drug abuse or dependence, or history of, or
- Kidney disease or
- Liver disease or
- Porphyria—Depending on which of the skeletal muscle relaxants you take, the chance of side effects may be increased; your doctor can choose a muscle relaxant that is less likely to cause problems

- Epilepsy—Convulsions may be more likely to occur if methocarbamol is given by injection

Proper Use of This Medicine

Chlorzoxazone, metaxalone, or methocarbamol tablets may be crushed and mixed with a little food or liquid if needed to make the tablets easier to swallow.

Dosing—The dose of these medicines will be different for different patients. *Follow your doctor's orders or the directions on the label*. The following information includes only the average doses of these medicines. *If your dose is different, do not change it* unless your doctor tells you to do so.

For carisoprodol
- For *oral* dosage form (tablets):
  —For relaxing stiff, sore muscles:
    - Adults and teenagers—350 milligrams (mg) four times a day.
    - Children up to 5 years of age—Dose must be determined by your doctor.
    - Children 5 to 12 years of age—6.25 mg per kilogram (2.5 mg per pound) of body weight four times a day.

For chlorphenesin
- For *oral* dosage form (tablets):
  —For relaxing stiff, sore muscles:
    - Adults and teenagers—800 milligrams (mg) three times a day, at first. Your doctor may decrease your dose after you begin to feel better.
    - Children—Use and dose must be determined by your doctor.

For chlorzoxazone
- For *oral* dosage form (tablets):
  —For relaxing stiff, sore muscles:
    - Adults and teenagers—500 milligrams (mg) three or four times a day.
    - Children—125 to 500 mg three or four times a day, depending on the child's size and weight.

For metaxalone
- For *oral* dosage form (tablets):
  —For relaxing stiff, sore muscles:
    - Adults and teenagers—800 milligrams (mg) three or four times a day.
    - Children—Use and dose must be determined by your doctor.

For methocarbamol
- For *oral* dosage form (tablets):
  —For relaxing stiff, sore muscles:
    - Adults and teenagers—1500 milligrams (mg) four times a day, at first. Your doctor may decrease your dose after you begin to feel better.
    - Children—Use and dose must be determined by your doctor.

- For *injection* dosage form:
  —For relaxing stiff, sore muscles:
    - Adults and teenagers—1 to 3 grams a day, injected into a muscle or a vein. This total daily dose may be divided into smaller amounts that are given several times a day, especially when the medicine is injected into a muscle.
    - Children—Use and dose must be determined by your doctor.

Missed dose—If you miss a dose of this medicine and remember within an hour or so of the missed dose, take it right away. But if you do not remember until later, skip the missed dose and go back to your regular dosing schedule. Do not double doses.

Storage—To store this medicine:

- Keep out of the reach of children.
- Store away from heat and direct light.
- Do not store this medicine in the bathroom, near the kitchen sink, or in other damp places. Heat or moisture may cause the medicine to break down.
- Do not keep outdated medicine or medicine no longer needed. Be sure that any discarded medicine is out of the reach of children.

Precautions While Using This Medicine

If you will be taking this medicine for a long time (for example, more than a few weeks), your doctor should check your progress at regular visits.

This medicine will add to the effects of alcohol and other CNS depressants (medicines that slow down the nervous system, possibly causing drowsiness). Some examples of CNS depressants are antihistamines or medicine for hay fever, other allergies, or colds; sedatives, tranquilizers, or sleeping medicine; prescription pain medicine or narcotics; barbiturates; medicine for seizures; other muscle relaxants; or anesthetics, including some dental anesthetics. *Do not drink alcoholic beverages, and check with your doctor before taking any of the medicines listed above, while you are using this medicine.*

Skeletal muscle relaxants may cause blurred vision or clumsiness or unsteadiness in some people. They may also cause some people to feel drowsy, dizzy, lightheaded, faint, or less alert than they are normally. *Make sure you know how you react to this medicine before you drive, use machines, or do anything else that could be dangerous if you are dizzy or are not alert, well-coordinated, and able to see well.*

For *diabetic patients:*

- Metaxalone (e.g., Skelaxin) may cause false test results with one type of test for sugar in your urine. If your urine sugar test shows an unusually large amount of sugar, or if you have any questions about this, check with your health care professional. This is especially important if your diabetes is not well controlled.

Side Effects of This Medicine

Along with its needed effects, a medicine may cause some unwanted effects. Although not all of these side effects may occur, if they do occur they may need medical attention.

Check with your doctor as soon as possible if any of the following side effects occur:

Less common

Fainting; fast heartbeat; fever; hive-like swellings (large) on face, eyelids, mouth, lips, and/or tongue; mental depression; shortness of breath, troubled breathing, tightness in chest, and/or wheezing; skin rash, hives, itching, or redness; slow heartbeat (methocarbamol injection only); stinging or burning of eyes; stuffy nose and red or bloodshot eyes

Rare

Blood in urine; bloody or black, tarry stools; convulsions (seizures) (methocarbamol injection only); cough or hoarseness; fast or irregular breathing; lower back or side pain; muscle cramps or pain (not present before treatment or more painful than before treatment); painful or difficult urination; pain, tenderness, heat, redness, or swelling over a blood vessel (vein) in arm or leg (methocarbamol injection only); pinpoint red spots on skin; puffiness or swelling of the eyelids or around the eyes; sores, ulcers, or white spots on lips or in mouth; sore throat and fever with or without chills; swollen and/or painful glands; unusual bruising or bleeding; unusual tiredness or weakness; vomiting of blood or material that looks like coffee grounds; yellow eyes or skin

Other side effects may occur that usually do not need medical attention. These side effects may go away during treatment as your body adjusts to the medicine. However, check with your doctor if any of the following side effects continue or are bothersome:

More common

Blurred or double vision or any change in vision; dizziness or lightheadedness; drowsiness

Less common or rare

Abdominal or stomach cramps or pain; clumsiness or unsteadiness; confusion; constipation; diarrhea; excitement, nervousness, restlessness, or irritability; flushing or redness of face; headache; heartburn; hiccups; muscle weakness; nausea or vomiting; pain or peeling of skin at place of injection (methocarbamol only); trembling; trouble in sleeping; uncontrolled movements of eyes (methocarbamol injection only)

Although not all of the side effects listed above have been reported for all of these medicines, they have been reported for at least one of them. However, since all of these skeletal muscle relaxants have similar effects, it is possible that any of the above side effects may occur with any of these medicines.

In addition to the other side effects listed above, chlorzoxazone may cause your urine to turn orange or reddish purple. Methocarbamol may cause your urine to turn black, brown, or green. This effect is harmless and will go away when you stop taking the medicine. However, if you have any questions about this, check with your doctor.

Other side effects not listed above may also occur in some patients. If you notice any other effects, check with your doctor.

Revised: 08/11/95

SODIUM BICARBONATE   Systemic

Commonly used brand name(s):

In the U.S.—
Arm and Hammer
Pure Baking Soda
Bell/ans

Citrocarbonate
Soda Mint

Generic name product may be available.

In Canada—
Citrocarbonate

Description

Sodium bicarbonate (SOE-dee-um bye-KAR-boe-nate), also known as baking soda, is used to relieve heartburn, sour stomach, or acid indigestion by neutralizing excess stomach acid. When used for this purpose, it is said to belong to the group of medicines called antacids. It may be used to treat the symptoms of stomach or duodenal ulcers. Sodium bicarbonate is also used to make the blood and urine more alkaline in certain conditions.

Antacids should not be given to young children (up to 6 years of age) unless prescribed by their doctor. Since children cannot usually describe their symptoms very well, a doctor should check the child before giving this medicine. The child may have a condition that needs other treatment. If so, antacids will not help and may even cause unwanted effects or make the condition worse.

Sodium bicarbonate for oral use is available without a prescription; however, your doctor may have special instructions on the proper use and dose for your medical problem. Sodium bicarbonate is available in the following dosage forms:

Oral
- Effervescent powder (U.S. and Canada)
- Oral powder (U.S. and Canada)
- Tablets (U.S. and Canada)

Parenteral
- Injection (U.S. and Canada)

Before Using This Medicine

If you are taking this medicine without a prescription, carefully read and follow any precautions on the label. For sodium bicarbonate, the following should be considered:

Allergies—Tell your doctor if you have ever had any unusual or allergic reaction to sodium bicarbonate. Also tell your health care professional if you are allergic to any other substances, such as foods, preservatives, or dyes.

Pregnancy—Sodium bicarbonate is absorbed by the body and although it has not been shown to cause problems, the chance always exists. In addition, medicines containing sodium should usually be avoided if you tend to retain (keep) body water.

Breast-feeding—It is not known whether sodium bicarbonate passes into the breast milk. However, this medicine has not been reported to cause problems in nursing babies.

Children—Antacids should not be given to young children (up to 6 years of age) unless prescribed by a physician. This medicine may not help and may even worsen some conditions, so make sure that your child's problem should be treated with this medicine before you use it.

Older adults—Many medicines have not been studied specifically in older people. Therefore, it may not be known whether they work exactly the same way they do in younger adults or if they cause different side effects or problems in older people. There is no specific information comparing use of sodium bicarbonate in the elderly with use in other age groups.

Other medicines—Although certain medicines should not be used together at all, in other cases two different medicines may be used together even if an interaction might occur. In these cases, your doctor may want to change the dose, or other precautions may be necessary. When you are taking sodium bicarbonate, it is especially important that your health care professional know if you are taking any of the following:

- Ketoconazole (e.g., Nizoral) or
- Tetracyclines (medicine for infection) taken by mouth— Use with sodium bicarbonate may result in lower blood levels of these medicines, possibly decreasing their effectiveness
- Mecamylamine (e.g., Inversine)—Use with sodium bicarbonate may increase the effects of mecamylamine
- Methenamine (e.g., Mandelamine)—Use with sodium bicarbonate may reduce the effects of methenamine

Other medical problems—The presence of other medical problems may affect the use of sodium bicarbonate. Make sure you tell your doctor if you have any other medical problems, especially:

- Appendicitis or
- Intestinal or rectal bleeding—Oral forms of sodium bicarbonate may make these conditions worse
- Edema (swelling of feet or lower legs) or
- Heart disease or
- High blood pressure (hypertension) or
- Kidney disease or
- Liver disease or
- Problems with urination or
- Toxemia of pregnancy—Sodium bicarbonate may cause the body to retain (keep) water, which may make these conditions worse

Proper Use of This Medicine

For safe and effective use of sodium bicarbonate:
- Follow your doctor's instructions if this medicine was prescribed.
- Follow the manufacturer's package directions if you are treating yourself.

For patients *taking this medicine for a stomach ulcer:*
- *Take it exactly as directed and for the full time of treatment as ordered by your doctor*, to obtain maximum relief of your symptoms.
- Take it 1 and 3 hours after meals and at bedtime for best results, unless otherwise directed by your doctor.

Dosing—The dose of sodium bicarbonate will be different for different patients. *Follow your doctor's orders or the directions on the label.* The following information includes only the average doses of this medicine. *If your dose is different, do not change it* unless your doctor tells you to do so.

The number of teaspoonfuls of powder or of tablets you take depends on the strength of the medicine. *Also, the number of doses you take each day, the time allowed between doses, and the length of time you take the medicine depends on the medical problem for which you are taking sodium bicarbonate.*

- For *sodium bicarbonate* effervescent powder:
  —To relieve heartburn or sour stomach:
    - Adults and teenagers—3.9 to 10 grams (1 to 2½ teaspoonfuls) in a glass of cold water after meals. However, the dose is usually not more than 19.5 grams (5 teaspoonfuls) a day.
    - Children up to 6 years of age—Dose must be determined by your doctor.
    - Children 6 to 12 years of age—1 to 1.9 grams (¼ to ½ teaspoonful) in a glass of cold water after meals.
- For *sodium bicarbonate* powder:
  —To relieve heartburn or sour stomach:
    - Adults and teenagers—One-half teaspoonful in a glass of water every two hours. Your doctor may change the dose if needed.
    - Children—Dose must be determined by your doctor.
  —To make the urine more alkaline (less acidic):
    - Adults and teenagers—One teaspoonful in a glass of water every four hours. Your doctor may change the dose if needed. However, the dose is usually not more than 4 teaspoonfuls a day.
    - Children—Dose must be determined by your doctor.
- For *sodium bicarbonate* tablets:
  —To relieve heartburn or sour stomach:
    - Adults and teenagers—325 milligrams (mg) to 2 grams one to four times a day.
    - Children up to 6 years of age—Dose must be determined by your doctor.
    - Children 6 to 12 years of age—The dose is 520 mg. The dose may be repeated in thirty minutes.
  —To make the urine more alkaline (less acidic):
    - Adults and teenagers—At first, four grams, then 1 to 2 grams every four hours. However, the dose is usually not more than 16 grams a day.
    - Children—The dose is based on body weight and must be determined by your doctor. The usual dose is 23 to 230 mg per kilogram (kg) (10.5 to 105 mg per pound) of body weight a day. Your doctor may change the dose if needed.

Missed dose—If you must take this medicine regularly and you miss a dose, take it as soon as possible. However, if it is almost time for your next dose, skip the missed dose and go back to your regular dosing schedule. Do not double doses.

Storage—To store this medicine:
- Keep out of the reach of children.
- Store away from heat and direct light.
- Do not store the powder or tablet form of this medicine in the bathroom, near the kitchen sink, or in other damp places. Heat or moisture may cause the medicine to break down.
- Do not keep outdated medicine or medicine no longer needed. Be sure that any discarded medicine is out of the reach of children.

Precautions While Using This Medicine

If this medicine has been ordered by your doctor and if you will be taking it regularly for a long time, your doctor should check your progress at regular visits. This is to make sure the medicine does not cause unwanted effects.

Do not take sodium bicarbonate:
- *Within 1 to 2 hours of taking other medicine by mouth.* To do so may keep the other medicine from working properly.
- *For a long period of time.* To do so may increase the chance of side effects.

For patients on a *sodium-restricted diet:*
- This medicine contains a large amount of sodium. If you have any questions about this, check with your health care professional.

For patients *taking this medicine as an antacid:*
- *Do not take this medicine if you have any signs of appendicitis* (such as stomach or lower abdominal pain, cramping, bloating, soreness, nausea, or vomiting). Instead, check with your doctor as soon as possible.
- *Do not take this medicine with large amounts of milk or milk products.* To do so may increase the chance of side effects.
- *Do not take sodium bicarbonate for more than 2 weeks* or if the problem comes back often. Instead, check with your doctor. Antacids should be used only for occasional relief, unless otherwise directed by your doctor.

Side Effects of This Medicine

Along with its needed effects, a medicine may cause some unwanted effects. Although the following side effects occur very rarely when this medicine is taken as recommended, they may be more likely to occur if it is taken:
- In large doses.
- For a long time.
- By patients with kidney disease.

Check with your doctor as soon as possible if any of the following side effects occur:
  Frequent urge to urinate; headache (continuing); loss of appetite (continuing); mood or mental changes; muscle pain or twitching; nausea or vomiting; nervousness or restlessness; slow breathing; swelling of feet or lower legs; unpleasant taste; unusual tiredness or weakness

Other side effects may occur that usually do not need medical attention. These side effects may go away during treatment as your body adjusts to the medicine. However, check with your doctor if any of the following side effects continue or are bothersome:
Less common
  Increased thirst; stomach cramps

Other side effects not listed above may also occur in some patients. If you notice any other effects, check with your doctor.

Revised: 02/03/92
Interim revision: 08/10/94

SODIUM FLUORIDE   Systemic

Commonly used brand name(s):

In the U.S.—

Fluoritab	Luride Lozi-Tabs
Fluorodex	Luride-SF Lozi-Tabs
Flura	Pediaflor
Flura-Drops	Pharmaflur
Flura-Loz	Pharmaflur 1.1
Karidium	Pharmaflur df
Luride	Phos-Flur

Generic name product may be available.

In Canada—

Flozenges	Karidium
Fluor-A-Day	PDF
Fluoritabs	Pedi-Dent
Fluorosol	Solu-Flur

Description

Fluoride (FLURE-ide) has been found to be helpful in reducing the number of cavities in the teeth. It is usually present naturally in drinking water. However, some areas of the country do not have a high enough level in the water to prevent cavities. To make up for this, extra fluorides may be added to the diet. Some children may require both dietary fluorides and topical fluoride treatments by the dentist. Use of a fluoride toothpaste or rinse may be helpful as well.

Taking fluorides does not replace good dental habits. These include eating a good diet, brushing and flossing teeth often, and having regular dental checkups.

Fluoride may also be used for other conditions as determined by your health care professional.

This medicine is available only with a prescription, in the following dosage forms:

Oral
- Lozenges (U.S. and Canada)
- Oral solution (U.S. and Canada)
- Tablets (U.S. and Canada)
- Chewable tablets (U.S. and Canada)

Importance of Diet

For good health, it is important that you eat a balanced and varied diet. Follow carefully any diet program your health care professional may recommend. For your specific dietary vitamin and/or mineral needs, ask your health care professional for a list of appropriate foods. If you think that you are not getting enough vitamins and/or minerals in your diet, you may choose to take a dietary supplement.

People get needed fluoride from fish, including the bones, tea, and drinking water that has fluoride added to it. Food that is cooked in water containing fluoride or in Teflon-coated pans also provides fluoride. However, foods cooked in aluminum pans provide less fluoride.

The daily amount of fluoride needed is defined in several different ways.

For U.S.—
- Recommended Dietary Allowances (RDAs) are the amount of vitamins and minerals needed to provide for adequate nutrition in most healthy persons. RDAs for a given nutrient may vary depending on a person's age, sex, and physical condition (e.g., pregnancy).

- Daily Values (DVs) are used on food and dietary supplement labels to indicate the percent of the recommended daily amount of each nutrient that a serving provides. DV replaces the previous designation of United States Recommended Daily Allowances (USRDAs).

For Canada—
- Recommended Nutrient Intakes (RNIs) are used to determine the amounts of vitamins, minerals, and protein needed to provide adequate nutrition and lessen the risk of chronic disease.

There is no RDA or RNI for fluoride. Daily recommended intakes for fluoride are generally defined as follows:
- Infants and children—
  Birth to 3 years of age: 0.1 to 1.5 milligrams (mg).
  4 to 6 years of age: 1 to 2.5 mg.
  7 to 10 years of age: 1.5 to 2.5 mg.
- Adolescents and adults—1.5 to 4 mg.

Remember:
- The total amount of fluoride you get every day includes what you get from the foods and beverages that you eat and what you may take as a supplement.
- This total amount *should not* be greater than the above recommendations, unless ordered by your health care professional. Taking too much fluoride can cause serious problems to the teeth and bones.

Before Using This Medicine

In deciding to use a medicine, the risks of taking the medicine must be weighed against the good it will do. This is a decision you and your health care professional will make. For sodium fluoride, the following should be considered:

Allergies—Tell your health care professional if you are allergic to any other substances, such as foods, preservatives, or dyes.

Pregnancy—It is especially important that you are receiving enough vitamins and minerals when you become pregnant and that you continue to receive the right amount of vitamins and minerals throughout your pregnancy. The healthy growth and development of the fetus depend on a steady supply of nutrients from the mother. However, taking large amounts of a dietary supplement in pregnancy may be harmful to the mother and/or fetus and should be avoided. Sodium fluoride occurs naturally in water and has not been shown to cause problems in infants of mothers who drank fluoridated water or took appropriate doses of supplements.

Breast-feeding—It is especially important that you receive the right amounts of vitamins and minerals so that your baby will also get the vitamins and minerals needed to grow properly. However, taking large amounts of a dietary supplement while breast-feeding may be harmful to the mother and/or baby and should be avoided. Small amounts of sodium fluoride pass into breast milk.

Children—Problems in children have not been reported with intake of normal daily recommended amounts. Doses of sodium fluoride that are too large or are taken for a long time may cause bone problems and teeth discoloration in children.

Older adults—Problems in older adults have not been reported with intake of normal daily recommended amounts. Older people are more likely to have joint pain, kidney problems, or stomach ulcers which may be made worse by taking large doses of sodium fluoride. You should check with your health care professional.

Other medicines—Although certain medicines or dietary supplements should not be used together at all, in other cases they may be used together even if an interaction might occur. In these cases, your health care professional may want to change the dose, or other precautions may be necessary. Tell your health care professional if you are taking/using any other prescription or nonprescription (over-the-counter [OTC]) medicine.

Other medical problems—The presence of other medical problems may affect the use of sodium fluoride. Make sure you tell your health care professional if you have any other medical problems, especially:

- Brown, white, or black discoloration of teeth or
- Joint pain or
- Kidney problems (severe) or
- Stomach ulcer—Sodium fluoride may make these conditions worse

Proper Use of This Medicine

Take this medicine only as directed by your health care professional. Do not take more of it and do not take it more often than ordered. Taking too much fluoride over a period of time may cause unwanted effects.

For individuals taking the *chewable tablet form* of this medicine:

- Tablets should be chewed or crushed before they are swallowed.
- This medicine works best if it is taken at bedtime, after the teeth have been thoroughly brushed. Do not eat or drink for at least 15 minutes after taking sodium fluoride.

For individuals taking the *oral liquid form* of this medicine:

- This medicine is to be taken by mouth even though it comes in a dropper bottle. The amount to be taken is to be measured with the specially marked dropper.
- *Always store this medicine in the original plastic container.* Fluoride will affect glass and should not be stored in glass containers.
- This medicine may be dropped directly into the mouth or mixed with cereal, fruit juice, or other food. However, if this medicine is mixed with foods or beverages that contain calcium, the amount of sodium fluoride that is absorbed may be reduced.

Dosing—The dose of sodium fluoride will be different for different individuals. *Follow your health care professional's orders or the directions on the label.* The following information includes only the average doses of sodium fluoride. *If your dose is different, do not change it* unless your health care professional tells you to do so.

The amount of solution or the number of lozenges or tablets you take depends on the strength of the medicine. Also, *the number of doses you take each day, the time allowed between doses, and the length of time you take the medicine depend on the medical problem for which you are taking sodium fluoride.*

- For *oral* dosage form (lozenges, solution, tablets, or chewable tablets):
  —To prevent cavities in the teeth (where there is not enough fluoride in the water):
    • Children—Dose is based on the amount of fluoride in drinking water in your area. Dose is also

based on the child's age and must be determined by your health care professional.

Missed dose—If you miss a dose of this medicine, take it as soon as you remember. However, if it is almost time for the next dose, skip the missed dose and go back to your regular dosing schedule. Do not double doses. If you have any questions about this, check with your health care professional.

Storage—To store this medicine:

- Keep out of the reach of children, since overdose is especially dangerous in children.
- Store away from heat and direct light.
- Do not store in the bathroom, near the kitchen sink, or in other damp places. Heat or moisture may cause the medicine to break down.
- Protect the oral liquid from freezing.
- Do not keep outdated medicine or medicine no longer needed. Be sure that any discarded medicine is out of the reach of children.

Precautions While Using This Medicine

The level of fluoride present in the water is different in different parts of the U.S. If you move to another area, check with a health care professional in the new area as soon as possible to see if this medicine is still needed or if the dose needs to be changed. Also, check with your health care professional if you change infant feeding habits (e.g., breast-feeding to infant formula), drinking water (e.g., city water to nonfluoridated bottled water), or filtration (e.g., tap water to filtered tap water).

Do not take calcium supplements or aluminum hydroxide-containing products and sodium fluoride at the same time. It is best to space doses of these two products 2 hours apart, to get the full benefit from each medicine.

Inform your health care professional as soon as possible if you notice white, brown, or black spots on the teeth. These are signs of too much fluoride in children when it is given during periods of tooth development.

Side Effects of This Medicine

Along with its needed effects, a medicine may cause some unwanted effects. Although not all of these side effects may occur, if they do occur they may need medical attention.

Check with your health care professional as soon as possible if any of the following side effects occur:
    Sores in mouth and on lips (rare)

Sodium fluoride in drinking water or taken as a supplement does not usually cause any side effects. However, *taking an overdose of fluoride may cause serious problems.*

Stop taking this medicine and check with your health care professional immediately if any of the following side effects occur, as they may be symptoms of severe overdose:
    Black, tarry stools; bloody vomit; diarrhea; drowsiness; faintness; increased watering of mouth; nausea or vomiting; shallow breathing; stomach cramps or pain; tremors; unusual excitement; watery eyes; weakness

Check with your health care professional as soon as possible if the following side effects occur, as some may be early symptoms of possible chronic overdose:
    Pain and aching of bones; stiffness; white, brown, or black discoloration of teeth—occur only during periods of tooth development in children

Other side effects not listed above may also occur in some individuals. If you notice any other effects, check with your health care professional.

Revised: 07/17/92
Interim revision: 08/07/95

SPECTINOMYCIN   Systemic

Commonly used brand name(s):

In the U.S.—
Trobicin

In Canada—
Trobicin

Description

Spectinomycin (spek-ti-noe-MYE-sin) is used to treat most types of gonorrhea. It is given by injection into a muscle. It is sometimes given with other medicines for gonorrhea and related infections.

Spectinomycin may be used in patients who are allergic to penicillins, cephalosporins, or probenecid (e.g., Benemid). This medicine is also used to treat recent sexual partners of patients who have gonorrhea. However, spectinomycin will not work for gonorrhea of the throat, syphilis, colds, flu, or other virus infections.

Spectinomycin is available only with your doctor's prescription, in the following dosage form:

Parenteral
• Injection (U.S. and Canada)

Before Receiving This Medicine

In deciding to use a medicine, the risks of taking the medicine must be weighed against the good it will do. This is a decision you and your doctor will make. For spectinomycin, the following should be considered:

Allergies—Tell your doctor if you have ever had any unusual or allergic reaction to spectinomycin. Also tell your health care professional if you are allergic to any other substances, such as foods, preservatives, or dyes.

Pregnancy—Studies have not been done in humans. However, spectinomycin has been recommended for the treatment of gonorrhea and related infections in pregnant patients who are allergic to penicillins, cephalosporins, or probenecid (e.g., Benemid). In addition, studies in animals have not shown that spectinomycin causes birth defects or other problems.

Breast-feeding—It is not known if spectinomycin passes into breast milk. However, spectinomycin has not been reported to cause problems in nursing babies.

Children—This medicine has been used in a limited number of children. In effective doses, the medicine has not been shown to cause different side effects or problems than it does in adults. However, use in infants is not recommended.

Older adults—Many medicines have not been studied specifically in older people. Therefore, it may not be known whether they work exactly the same way they do in younger adults. Although there is no specific information comparing use of spectinomycin in the elderly with use in other age groups, this medicine is not expected to cause different side effects or problems in older people than it does in younger adults.

Other medicines—Although certain medicines should not be used together at all, in other cases two different medicines may be used together even if an interaction might occur. In these cases, your doctor may want to change the dose, or other precautions may be necessary. Tell your health care professional if you are taking any other prescription or nonprescription (over-the-counter [OTC]) medicine.

Proper Use of This Medicine

Spectinomycin is given by injection into a muscle. To help clear up your gonorrhea completely, usually only one dose is needed. However, in some infections a second dose of this medicine may be required.

Gonorrhea and related infections are spread by having sex with an infected partner. Therefore, it may be desirable that the male sexual partner wear a condom (prophylactic) during intercourse to prevent infection. Also, it may be necessary for your partner to be treated at the same time you are being treated. This will help to avoid passing the infection back and forth.

Dosing—The dose of spectinomycin will be different for different patients. The following information includes only the average doses of spectinomycin.
• For *cervical, rectal, or urethral gonorrhea:*
  —Adults and children 45 kilograms of body weight (99 pounds) and over: 2 grams injected into a muscle as a single dose.
  —Children up to 45 kilograms of body weight (99 pounds): 40 milligrams per kilogram of body weight injected into a muscle as a single dose.
  —Infants: Use is not recommended.

Precautions After Receiving This Medicine

If your symptoms do not improve within a few days, or if they become worse, check with your doctor.

This medicine may cause some people to become dizzy. *Make sure you know how you react to this medicine before you drive, use machines, or do anything else that could be dangerous if you are dizzy.* If this reaction is especially bothersome, check with your doctor.

Side Effects of This Medicine

Along with its needed effects, a medicine may cause some unwanted effects. Although not all of these side effects may occur, if they do occur they may need medical attention.

Check with your doctor as soon as possible if any of the following side effects occur:
Rare
  Chills or fever; itching or redness of the skin

Other side effects may occur that usually do not need medical attention. These side effects may go away during treatment as your body adjusts to the medicine. However, check with your doctor if any of these effects continue or are bothersome:
Less common
  Dizziness; nausea and vomiting; pain at the place of injection; stomach cramps

Other side effects not listed above may also occur in some patients. If you notice any other effects, check with your doctor.

Revised: 02/23/93

SPERMICIDES   Vaginal

Commonly used brand name(s):

In the U.S.—

Advantage 24[2]	Koromex Cream[3]
Because[2]	Koromex Crystal Clear Gel[2]
Conceptrol Contraceptive	Koromex Foam[2]
Inserts[2]	Koromex Jelly[2]
Conceptrol Gel[2]	K-Y Plus[2]
Delfen[2]	Ortho-Creme[2]
Emko[2]	Ortho-Gynol[3]
Emko Pre-Fil[2]	Ramses Crystal Clear Gel[2]
Encare[2]	Semicid[2]
Gynol II Extra Strength	Shur-Seal[2]
Contraceptive Jelly[2]	VCF[2]
Gynol II Original Formula	
Contraceptive Jelly[2]	

In Canada—

Advantage 24[2]	Ortho-Gynol[3]
Delfen[2]	Pharmatex[1]
Emko[2]	Ramses Contraceptive Foam[2]
Encare[2]	

Note: For quick reference, the following spermicides are numbered to match the corresponding brand names.

This information applies to the following medicines
1. Benzalkonium Chloride (benz-al-KOE-nee-um KLOR-ide) *
2. Nonoxynol 9 (no-NOX-i-nole nine)
3. Octoxynol 9 (awk-TOX-i-nole nine)

*Not commercially available in the U.S.

Description

Vaginal spermicides are a type of contraceptive (birth control). These products are inserted into the vagina *before* any genital contact occurs or sexual intercourse begins. They work by damaging and killing sperm in the vagina. Therefore, the sperm are not able to travel from the vagina into the uterus and fallopian tubes, where fertilization usually takes place.

Vaginal spermicides when used alone are much less effective in preventing pregnancy than birth control pills or the IUD or spermicides used with another form of birth control, such as cervical caps, condoms, or diaphragms. *Studies have shown that when spermicides are used alone, pregnancy usually occurs in 21 of each 100 women during the first year of spermicide use.* The number of pregnancies is reduced when spermicides are used with another method, especially the condom. Discuss with a doctor what your options are for birth control and the risks and benefits of each method.

Laboratory studies have shown that nonoxynol 9 kills or stops the growth of the AIDS virus (HIV) and herpes simplex I and II viruses. It was also shown to be effective against other types of organisms that cause gonorrhea, chlamydia, syphilis, trichomoniasis, and other sexually transmitted diseases (venereal disease, VD, STDs). Benzalkonium chloride also killed the AIDS virus in laboratory studies. Although this has *not* been proven in *human* studies, some scientists *believe* that if spermicides are put into the vagina or on the inside and outside of a latex (rubber) condom, they *may* kill these germs before they are able to come in contact with the vagina or rectum (lower bowel).

The most effective way to protect yourself against STDs (such as AIDS) is by abstinence (not having sexual intercourse) or by having one partner who you can be sure is not already infected or is not going to get an STD. However, if either of these methods is not likely or possible, using latex (rubber) condoms with a spermicide is the best way of protecting yourself.

The use of a spermicide is recommended even when you are using nonbarrier methods of birth control such as birth control pills (the Pill) or intrauterine devices (IUDs), since these do not offer any protection from STDs.

The safety of using spermicides in the rectum (lower bowel), anus, or rectal area is not known. However, no side effects or problems have been reported that are different from those reported for use in the vagina.

Vaginal spermicides are available without a prescription, in the following dosage forms:

Vaginal
Benzalkonium chloride
• Suppositories (Canada)
Nonoxynol 9
• Cream (U.S. and Canada)
• Film (U.S.)
• Foam (U.S. and Canada)
• Gel (U.S. and Canada)
• Jelly (U.S.)
• Suppositories (U.S. and Canada)
Octoxynol 9
• Cream (U.S.)
• Jelly (U.S. and Canada)

Before Using This Medicine

In deciding to use vaginal spermicides, the risks of using them must be weighed against the good they will do. This is a decision you and possibly your doctor will make. The following information may help you in making your decision:

Allergies—If you have ever had any unusual or allergic reaction to benzalkonium chloride, nonoxynol 9, or octoxynol 9, it is best to check with your doctor before using vaginal spermicides.

Pregnancy—Many studies have shown that the use of vaginal spermicides does not increase the risk of birth defects or miscarriage.

Breast-feeding—It is not known if vaginal spermicides pass into breast milk in humans. However, their use has not been reported to cause problems in nursing babies.

Teenagers—These products have been used by teenagers and have not been shown to cause different side effects or problems than they do in adults. However, some younger users may need extra counseling and information on the importance of using spermicides exactly as they are supposed to be used so they will work properly.

Other medicines—If you are using this medicine without a prescription, carefully read and follow any precautions on the label. For spermicides, the following should be considered:

• Salicylates used on the skin (e.g., some types of ointments for muscle aches) or

- Sulfonamides (sulfa medicine) for use in the vagina or
- Chemicals or substances such as aluminum, citrate, cotton dressings, hydrogen peroxide, iodides, lanolin, nitrates, permanganates, some forms of silver, soaps, detergents, or tartrates—Benzalkonium chloride may not work if it comes in direct contact with these as well as many other chemicals

- Vaginal douches and rectal or vaginal cleansing products—For spermicides to work properly to prevent pregnancy, they must stay in contact with the sperm in the vagina for at least 6 or 8 hours (depending upon which brand of spermicide you use) after sexual intercourse. *Vaginal douching is not necessary after use of these medicines.* Douching too soon (even with just water) may stop the spermicide from working. Also, washing or rinsing the vaginal or rectal area may also make the spermicide ineffective in helping to prevent sexually transmitted diseases

Other medical problems—The presence of certain medical problems may affect the use of vaginal spermicides. Since in some cases spermicides should not be used, check with your doctor if you have any of the following:

- Allergies, irritations, or infections of the genitals—Using vaginal spermicides may cause moderate to severe irritation in these conditions. Also, benzalkonium suppositories may be less effective in women with vaginal infections

- Conditions or medical problems where it is important that pregnancy does not occur—Vaginal spermicides when used alone are much less effective than birth control pills or the IUD or spermicides used with another form of birth control such as cervical caps, condoms, or diaphragms. Discuss with your doctor what your options are for birth control and the risks and benefits of each method

- Recent childbirth or abortion or
- Toxic shock syndrome (history of)—Cervical caps or diaphragms should not be used in these cases because there is an increased chance of developing toxic shock syndrome

- Sores on the genitals (sex organs) or
- Irritation of the vagina—It is not known whether spermicides can cause breaks in the skin that could increase the chances of getting a sexually transmitted disease, especially AIDS. Discuss this with a doctor if you have any questions

If you develop any medical problem or begin using any new medicine (prescription or nonprescription) while you are using this medicine, you may want to check with your doctor.

Proper Use of This Medicine

Make sure you carefully read and follow the directions that come with each spermicide product. Each product may have different directions for using the product. The directions tell you how much to use, how long you must wait before having intercourse, and how long you must leave it in the vagina after intercourse.

Vaginal douching is not needed or advised after using these medicines. When using a spermicide, douching within 6 to 8 hours after the last sexual intercourse (even with just water) may stop the spermicide from working properly. Also, washing or rinsing the vaginal or rectal area may wash the spermicide away before it has had time to work properly.

Cervical caps and diaphragms are not recommended for use during your menstrual period because of an increased chance of developing toxic shock syndrome. Your doctor may advise you to use condoms with a spermicide instead during your menstrual periods when protection is needed.

For proper use of spermicide when used alone:
- Follow directions carefully to make sure the spermicide is properly placed in the vagina. The spermicide should be inserted deep into the vagina, directly on the cervix (opening to the uterus).
- Use the correct amount, according to the product directions.
- Use another dose for *each* act of intercourse.
- After you have applied or inserted the spermicide, wait the correct amount of time before having intercourse so that the spermicide can begin to work.
- If you do not have intercourse within half an hour, read the product directions to see if you need to apply more spermicide.

For proper use of spermicide with cervical caps, condoms, or diaphragms:
- *Make sure the directions for the spermicide you choose state that it is safe for use with latex cervical caps, condoms, or diaphragms.* If the directions do not say the spermicide is safe to use with latex products, the spermicide may cause cervical caps, condoms, or diaphragms to weaken and leak or cause condoms to break during intercourse.
- If there is a leak or break during intercourse, it may be a good idea for the female partner to immediately place more spermicide in the vagina.
- *If you need an extra lubricant, make sure it is a water-based product safe for use with cervical caps, condoms, or diaphragms.* Spermicides, especially gels and jellies, provide some lubrication during sexual intercourse.
- Oil-based products such as hand, face, or body cream; petroleum jelly; cooking oils or shortenings; or baby oil should *not* be used because they weaken the latex rubber. (Even some products that easily rinse away with water are oil-based and should not be used.) Use of oil-based products increases the chances of the condom breaking during sexual intercourse. These products can also cause the rubber in cervical caps or diaphragms to break down faster and wear out sooner.

For patients using spermicides with a cervical cap:
- *To be most effective at preventing pregnancy, the cervical cap must always be used with a spermicide.* Both must be used every time you have sexual intercourse.
- Before inserting the cervical cap, inspect it for holes, tears, or cracks. If there are holes or defects, the cervical cap will not work effectively, even with a spermicide. It must be replaced.
- Before you put the cervical cap over the cervix (opening to the uterus), a spermicide cream, foam, gel, or jelly should be put into the cup of the cervical cap. Follow the manufacturer's directions on how long before sexual intercourse you may apply the spermicide. Fill the cervical cap one-third full with spermicide.
- To insert the cervical cap, squeeze the rim between your thumb and forefinger so that it is narrow enough to fit into the vagina. While in a comfortable position, push the cervical cap as deeply into the vagina as it will go. Re-

lease the rim and press it into place around the cervix with your finger. The rim should be round again and be directly on the cervix. The cervical cap is held onto the cervix by suction.

- Some doctors may recommend that you put more spermicide into the vagina each time you repeat sexual intercourse using a cervical cap. You should also check to make sure the cervical cap is in the proper position on the cervix before and after each time you have intercourse. You may wear the cervical cap for up to 48 hours (2 days).
- *Do not remove the cervical cap if it has been less than 8 hours since the last time you had sexual intercourse.* For the cervical cap to be most effective at preventing pregnancy, it must remain in the vagina for at least 8 hours after sexual intercourse.
- To remove the cervical cap, use 1 or 2 fingers to push the rim away from the cervix. This will break the suction seal with the cervix. Then gently pull the cervical cap out of the vagina. *Call your doctor if you have trouble removing the cervical cap.*

For patients using spermicides with condoms:

- Condoms do not have to be used with spermicides, but the spermicide may provide a back-up birth control method in case the condom breaks or leaks.
- Spread some spermicide on the outside of the condom, after it is unrolled over the penis. It is even more important that the female partner also use a spermicide inside the vagina.
- Each time you repeat intercourse, a new condom must be used. *Condoms should never be reused.* Spermicide should also be applied to the outside of the new condom. The female partner must also put more spermicide in the vagina each time she has intercourse.

For patients using spermicides with a diaphragm:

- *To be most effective at preventing pregnancy, diaphragms must always be used with a spermicide.* Some women may choose to insert a diaphragm every night, to avoid the chance of unprotected sexual intercourse and unplanned pregnancy happening.
- Inspect the diaphragm for holes by holding it up to a light. If there are holes or defects, the diaphragm will not work effectively, even with a spermicide. It must be replaced.
- Before you put the diaphragm over the cervix (opening to the uterus), a spermicide cream, foam, gel, or jelly should be put into the cup of the diaphragm. Follow the manufacturer's directions on how much spermicide to use and how long before sexual intercourse you may apply the spermicide. Also, spread some spermicide all around the rim of the diaphragm that will be touching the cervix. Some doctors also advise spreading more spermicide on the outside of the cup of the diaphragm.
- To insert the diaphragm, squeeze the rim between your thumb and forefinger so that it is narrow enough to fit into the vagina. While in a comfortable position, push the diaphragm as deeply into the vagina as it will go. (Some women use a special applicator that makes it easier to insert the diaphragm.) Release the rim. The diaphragm rim should be round again and be directly on the cervix.
- Each time you repeat sexual intercourse, you should put more spermicide into the vagina. *Do not remove the diaphragm if it has been less than 6 or 8 hours (depending upon which brand of spermicide you use) since the last sexual intercourse.* For the diaphragm to be most effective at preventing pregnancy, it must

remain in the vagina for at least 6 or 8 hours (depending upon which brand of spermicide you use) after sexual intercourse. Be careful not to move the diaphragm out of place while you are applying more spermicide.

- Do not wear the diaphragm for more than 24 hours, since doing so increases the risk of getting toxic shock syndrome or a urinary tract (bladder) infection.
- To remove the diaphragm, hook one finger over the rim nearest the front. Pull the diaphragm downward and out of the vagina. *Call your doctor if you have trouble removing the diaphragm.*

Dosing—*Follow your doctor's orders or the directions on the label.* The following information includes the usual way that spermicides are used.

For benzalkonium chloride

- For preventing pregnancy:
  —For *vaginal suppositories* dosage form:
  - Adults and teenagers:
    —For use alone: One suppository inserted into the vagina at least ten minutes but not longer than four hours before each time you have sexual intercourse.
    —For use with a diaphragm: After the diaphragm with spermicide has been placed into the vagina, insert one suppository at least ten minutes, but not longer than four hours, before each time you have sexual intercourse. Also, insert another suppository before sexual intercourse if six hours have passed since you inserted the diaphragm.

For nonoxynol 9

- For preventing pregnancy:
  —For *vaginal cream* dosage form:
  - Adults and teenagers:
    —For use alone: One applicatorful of a 5% cream inserted into the vagina just before each time you have sexual intercourse.
    —For use with a diaphragm: One applicatorful of a 2 or 5% cream inserted into the cup of the diaphragm. Spread more spermicide along the rim of the diaphragm. Insert the diaphragm into the vagina just before, but not longer than six hours before, sexual intercourse. Also, insert one applicatorful just before each time you have intercourse or if six hours have passed since you inserted the diaphragm.

  —For *vaginal film* dosage form:
  - Adults and teenagers—One film inserted into the vagina from five to fifteen minutes (but not longer than one and one-half hours) before each time you have sexual intercourse.

  —For *vaginal foam* dosage form:
  - Adults and teenagers:
    —For use alone: One applicatorful inserted into the vagina just before, but not longer than one hour before, each time you have sexual intercourse.
    —For use with a diaphragm: One applicatorful inserted into either the vagina or into the cup of the diaphragm, depending on the product. Spread more spermicide along the rim of the diaphragm. Insert the diaphragm into the vagina just before, but not longer than one hour before, sexual intercourse. Also, insert another applicatorful into the vagina just before,

but not longer than one hour before, each time you have sexual intercourse.

—For *vaginal gel* dosage form:
  • Adults and teenagers:
    —For use alone: One applicatorful of a 3.5, 4, or 5% gel inserted into the vagina before each time you have sexual intercourse. The 3.5% gel may be used up to twenty-four hours before each act of intercourse. The 4% gel may be used up to one hour before each act of intercourse. The 5% gel must used just before intercourse.
    —For use with a diaphragm: One or two teaspoonfuls (depending on the product) or the contents of one packet of gel is placed into the cup of the diaphragm. Spread more spermicide along the rim of the diaphragm. Insert the diaphragm into the vagina just before, or up to six hours before, sexual intercourse. Also, insert another applicatorful or the contents of one packet into the vagina before each time you have sexual intercourse or if six hours have passed since you inserted the diaphragm.

—For *vaginal jelly* dosage form:
  • Adults and teenagers:
    —For use alone: One applicatorful of 2.2 or 3% jelly inserted into the vagina just before each time you have sexual intercourse. The contraceptive effect of the 2.2 or 3% jelly will last one hour.
    —For use with a diaphragm: One applicatorful or two teaspoonfuls of jelly (depending on the product) placed into the cup of the diaphragm. Spread more spermicide along the rim of the diaphragm. Insert the diaphragm into the vagina just before, but not longer than six hours before, sexual intercourse. Also, insert another applicatorful before each time you have sexual intercourse or if six hours have passed since you inserted the diaphragm.

—For *vaginal suppositories* dosage form:
  • Adults and teenagers:
    —For use alone: One suppository inserted into the vagina from ten to fifteen minutes (depending on the product) before, but not longer than one hour before, each time you have sexual intercourse.
  • Adults and teenagers:
    —For use with a diaphragm: After the diaphragm with spermicide has been placed into the vagina, insert one suppository into the vagina from ten to fifteen minutes (depending on the product) before, but not longer than one hour before, sexual intercourse. Also, insert another suppository before each time you have sexual intercourse or if six hours have passed since you have inserted the diaphragm.

For octoxynol 9
  • For preventing pregnancy:
    —For *vaginal cream* dosage form:
      • Adults and teenagers:
        —For use with a diaphragm: Two teaspoonfuls placed into the cup of the diaphragm. Spread more spermicide along the rim of the dia-

phragm. Insert the diaphragm into the vagina just before, but not longer than six hours before, sexual intercourse. Also, insert one applicatorful of the vaginal cream just before each time you have sexual intercourse or if six hours have passed since you inserted the diaphragm.

—For *vaginal jelly* dosage form:
  • Adults and teenagers:
    —For use with a diaphragm: One applicatorful placed into the cup of the diaphragm. Spread more spermicide along the rim of the diaphragm. Insert the diaphragm into the vagina just before, but not longer than six hours before, sexual intercourse. Also, insert another applicatorful just before each time you have sexual intercourse or if six hours have passed since you inserted the diaphragm.

Storage—To store this medicine:
  • Keep out of the reach of children.
  • Store away from heat and direct light.
  • Do not store in the bathroom, near the kitchen sink, or in other damp places. Heat or moisture may cause the medicine to break down.
  • Do not refrigerate.
  • Do not keep outdated products or products no longer needed. Be sure that any discarded products are out of the reach of children.

Precautions While Using This Medicine

During use of spermicides, either partner may feel burning, stinging, warmth, itching, or other irritation of the skin, sex organs, anus, or rectum. Using a weaker strength of vaginal spermicide or one with different ingredients may be necessary. If you are using benzalkonium chloride suppositories, it may help to wet them before they are inserted into the vagina. If any of these effects continue after you have changed products, you may have an allergy to these products or an infection, and should contact a doctor as soon as possible.

Side Effects of This Medicine

Along with its needed effects, a medicine may cause some unwanted effects. Although not all of these side effects may occur, if they do occur they may need medical attention.

Check with a doctor *immediately* if any of the following side effects occur:
  Rare
    Signs of toxic shock syndrome—for cervical caps or diaphragms
      Chills; confusion; dizziness; fever; lightheadedness; muscle aches; sunburn-like skin rash that is followed by peeling of the skin; unusual redness of the inside of the nose, mouth, throat, vagina, or insides of the eyelids

Also, check with a doctor as soon as possible if any of the following side effects occur:
  Rare
    For females and males
      Skin rash, redness, irritation, or itching that does not subside or go away within a short period of time
    For females only
      Cloudy or bloody urine; increased frequency of urination; pain in the bladder or lower abdomen;

pain on urination; thick, white, or curd-like vaginal discharge—with use of cervical caps or diaphragms only; vaginal irritation, redness, rash, dryness, or whitish discharge

Other side effects may occur that usually do not need medical attention. However, check with a doctor if any of the following side effects continue or are bothersome:

Less common
Vaginal discharge (temporary)—for creams, foams, and suppositories; vaginal dryness or odor

Other side effects not listed above may also occur in some people. If you notice any other effects, check with your doctor.

Revised: 07/28/93
Interim revision: 06/30/94; 08/16/97

SPIRAMYCIN Systemic

Commonly used brand name(s):

In Canada—
Rovamycine

Other—
Provamicina
Rovamycina
Rovamycine
Rovamycine 250
Rovamycine 500
Spiramycine Coquelusédal

Description

Spiramycin (speer-a-MYE-sin) is used to treat many kinds of infections. It is often used to treat toxoplasmosis in pregnant women since this medicine decreases the chance that the unborn baby will get the infection. This medicine may also be used for other problems as determined by your doctor. It will not work for colds, flu, or other virus infections.

Spiramycin is available only with your doctor's prescription, in the following dosage forms:

Oral
Spiramycin
• Capsules (Canada)
• Tablets (France, Germany, Italy, Mexico, Spain)

Parenteral
Spiramycin Adipate
• Injection (France)

Rectal
Spiramycin Adipate
• Suppository (France)

Before Using This Medicine

In deciding to use a medicine, the risks of taking the medicine must be weighed against the good it will do. This is a decision you and your doctor will make. For spiramycin, the following should be considered:

Allergies—Tell your doctor if you have ever had any unusual or allergic reaction to spiramycin, or any related medicines, such as erythromycin, azithromycin, clarithromycin, troleandomycin, dirithromycin, or josamycin. Also tell your health care professional if you are allergic to any other substances, such as foods, preservatives, or dyes.

Pregnancy—Spiramycin is used to treat toxoplasmosis in pregnant women since this medicine decreases the chance that the unborn baby will get the infection. If the unborn baby is already infected with toxoplasmosis, spiramycin does not treat the infection. This medicine has not been found to cause birth defects or other problems in humans.

Breast-feeding—Spiramycin passes into the breast milk. However, spiramycin has not been shown to cause problems in nursing babies to date.

Children—This medicine has been tested in children and, in effective doses, has not been shown to cause different side effects or problems in children than it does in adults.

Older adults—Many medicines have not been studied specifically in older people. Therefore, it may not be known whether they work exactly the same way they do in younger adults or if they cause different side effects or problems in older people. There is no specific information comparing use of spiramycin in the elderly with use in other age groups.

Other medicines—Although certain medicines should not be used together at all, in other cases two different medicines may be used together even if an interaction might occur. In these cases, your doctor may want to change the dose, or other precautions may be necessary. Tell your health care professional if you are taking any other prescription or nonprescription (over-the-counter [OTC]) medicine.

Other medical problems—The presence of other medical problems may affect the use of spiramycin. Make sure you tell your doctor if you have any other medical problems, especially:
• Liver disease or
• Obstruction of the bile ducts—Liver disease or obstruction of the bile ducts may increase the chance of side effects

Proper Use of This Medicine

Spiramycin is *best taken on an empty stomach.*

To help clear up your infection completely, *keep taking this medicine for the full time of treatment,* even if you begin to feel better after a few days. If you stop taking this medicine too soon, your symptoms may return.

This medicine works best when there is a constant amount in the blood. *To help keep the amount constant, do not miss any doses. Also, it is best to take the doses at evenly spaced times day and night.* If this interferes with your sleep or other daily activities, or if you need help in planning the best times to take your medicine, check with your health care professional.

For patients using *spiramycin suppositories:*
• First remove the foil wrapper and moisten the suppository with cold water. Lie down on your side and use your finger to push the suppository well up into the rectum.

Dosing—The dose of spiramycin will be different for different patients. *Follow your doctor's orders or the directions on the label.* The following information includes only the average doses of spiramycin. *If your dose is different, do not change it* unless your doctor tells you to do so.

The number of capsules or tablets that you take or the number of suppositories that you use depends on the strength of the medicine. Also, *the number of doses you take each day, the time allowed between doses, and the length of time you take the medicine depend on the medical problem for which you are taking spiramycin.*

- For *oral* dosage forms (capsules or tablets):
  —For treatment of infections:
  - Adults and teenagers—1 to 2 grams (3,000,000 to 6,000,000 International Units [IU]) two times a day, or 500 mg to 1 gram (1,500,000 to 3,000,000 IU) three times a day. For severe infections, the dose is 2 to 2.5 grams (6,000,000 to 7,500,000 IU) two times a day.
  - Children weighing 20 kilograms (kg) (44 pounds) or more—Dose is based on body weight. The usual dose is 25 mg (75,000 IU) per kg (11.4 mg per pound) of body weight two times a day, or 17 mg (51,000 IU) per kg (7.7 mg per pound) of body weight three times a day.
- For *injection* dosage form:
  —For treatment of infections:
  - Adults and teenagers—500 mg (1,500,000 IU) injected slowly into a vein every eight hours. For severe infections, the dose is 1 gram (3,000,000 IU) injected slowly into a vein every eight hours.
  - Children—Use and dose must be determined by your doctor.
- For *rectal* dosage form (suppository):
  —For treatment of infections:
  - Adults and children 12 years of age and over—Two or three 750 mg (1,950,000 IU) suppositories per day.
  - Children up to 12 years of age—Two or three 500 mg (1,300,000 IU) suppositories per day.
  - Newborns—Dose is based on body weight. The usual dose is one 250 mg (650,000 IU) suppository per 5 kg (250 mg suppository per 11 pounds) of body weight once a day.

Missed dose—If you miss a dose of this medicine, take it as soon as possible. This will help to keep a constant amount of medicine in the blood. However, if it is almost time for your next dose, skip the missed dose and go back to your regular dosing schedule. Do not double doses.

Storage—To store this medicine:
- Keep out of the reach of children.
- Store away from heat and direct light.
- Do not store the tablet form of spiramycin in the bathroom, near the kitchen sink, or in other damp places. Heat or moisture may cause the medicine to break down.
- Do not keep outdated medicine or medicine no longer needed. Be sure that any discarded medicine is out of the reach of children.

Precautions While Using This Medicine

If your symptoms do not improve within a few days, or if they become worse, check with your doctor.

Side Effects of This Medicine

Along with its needed effects, a medicine may cause some unwanted effects. Although not all of these side effects may occur, if they do occur they may need medical attention.

Check with your doctor immediately if any of the following side effects occur:
Less common
Skin rash and itching; unusual bleeding or bruising

Rare—with spiramycin injection only
Pain at site of injection

Rare
Bloody stools; chest pain; fever; heartburn; irregular heartbeat; nausea; recurrent fainting; stomach pain and tenderness; vomiting; yellow eyes or skin

Other side effects may occur that usually do not need medical attention. These side effects may go away during treatment as your body adjusts to the medicine. However, check with your doctor if the following side effect continues or is bothersome:
Less common
Diarrhea

Other side effects not listed above may also occur in some patients. If you notice any other effects, check with your doctor.

Developed: 05/28/96

STAVUDINE   Systemic

Commonly used brand name(s):

In the U.S.—
Zerit

In Canada—
Zerit

Another commonly used name is d4T.

Description

Stavudine (STAV-yoo-deen) (also known as d4T) is used in the treatment of the infection caused by the human immunodeficiency virus (HIV). HIV is the virus responsible for acquired immune deficiency syndrome (AIDS).

Stavudine (d4T) will not cure or prevent HIV infection or AIDS; however, it helps to keep HIV from reproducing and appears to slow down the destruction of the immune system. This may help delay the development of problems usually related to AIDS or HIV disease. Stavudine will not keep you from spreading HIV to other people. People who receive this medicine may continue to have the problems usually related to AIDS or HIV disease.

Stavudine may cause some serious side effects, including peripheral neuropathy. Symptoms of peripheral neuropathy include tingling, burning, numbness, and pain in the hands or feet. *Check with your doctor if any new health problems or symptoms occur while you are taking stavudine.*

Stavudine is available only with your doctor's prescription, in the following dosage form:
Oral
- Capsules (U.S. and Canada)
- Oral solution (U.S.)

Before Using This Medicine

In deciding to use a medicine, the risks of taking the medicine must be weighed against the good it will do. This is a decision you and your doctor will make. For stavudine, the following should be considered:

Allergies—Tell your doctor if you have ever had any unusual or allergic reaction to stavudine. Also tell your health care professional if you are allergic to any other substances, such as foods, preservatives, or dyes.

Pregnancy—

Note: The combination of stavudine and didanosine should be used with caution during pregnancy.

Stavudine has not been studied in pregnant women. However, studies in animals have shown that stavudine causes birth defects when given in very high doses. Before taking this medicine, make sure your doctor knows if you are pregnant or if you may become pregnant.

Breast-feeding—It is not known whether stavudine passes into the breast milk. However, if your baby does not already have the AIDS virus, there is a chance that you could pass it to your baby by breast-feeding. Talk to your doctor first if you are thinking about breast-feeding your baby.

Children—This medicine has been tested in a limited number of children 5 weeks of age and older. In effective doses, this medicine has not been shown to cause different side effects or problems in children than it does in adults.

Older adults—Stavudine has not been studied specifically in older people. Therefore, it is not known whether it causes different side effects or problems in the elderly than it does in younger adults.

Other medicines—Although certain medicines should not be used together at all, in other cases two different medicines may be used together even if an interaction might occur. In these cases, your doctor may want to change the dose, or other precautions may be necessary. When you are taking stavudine, it is especially important that your health care professional know if you are taking any of the following:

- Chloramphenicol (e.g., Chloromycetin) or
- Cisplatin (e.g., Platinol) or
- Dapsone (e.g., Avlosulfon) or
- Didanosine (e.g., ddI, Videx) or
- Ethambutol (e.g., Myambutol) or
- Ethionamide (e.g., Trecator-SC) or
- Hydralazine (e.g., Apresoline) or
- Isoniazid (e.g., Nydrazid) or
- Lithium (e.g., Eskalith, Lithobid) or
- Metronidazole (e.g., Flagyl) or
- Nitrofurantoin (e.g., Macrodantin) or
- Phenytoin (e.g., Dilantin) or
- Vincristine (e.g., Oncovin) or
- Zalcitabine (e.g., ddC, HIVID)—Use of these medicines with stavudine may increase the chance of peripheral neuropathy (tingling, burning, numbness, or pain in your hands or feet)

- Didanosine (e.g., ddI, Videx) or
- Hydroxyurea (e.g., Hydrea)—Use of these medicines with stavudine may increase the chance of liver toxicity or pancreatitis

- Zidovudine (e.g., Retrovir)—May prevent stavudine from working effectively; using stavudine and zidovudine at the same time is not recommended

Other medical problems—The presence of other medical problems may affect the use of stavudine. Make sure you tell your doctor if you have any other medical problems, especially:

- Alcohol abuse, active or a history of, or
- Liver disease—Stavudine may make liver disease worse in patients with liver disease, active alcohol abuse, or a history of alcohol abuse
- Kidney disease—Patients with kidney disease may have an increased chance of side effects

- Peripheral neuropathy—Stavudine may make this condition worse

Proper Use of This Medicine

Take this medicine exactly as directed by your doctor. Do not take more of it, do not take it more often, and do not take it for a longer time than your doctor ordered. Also, do not stop taking this medicine without checking with your doctor first.

Keep taking stavudine for the full time of treatment, even if you begin to feel better.

This medicine works best when there is a constant amount in the blood. *To help keep the amount constant, do not miss any doses.* If you need help in planning the best times to take your medicine, check with your health care professional.

Only take medicine that your doctor has prescribed specifically for you. Do not share your medicine with others.

Dosing—The dose of stavudine will be different for different patients. *Follow your doctor's orders or the directions on the label.* The following information includes only the average doses of stavudine. Your dose may be different if you have kidney disease. *If your dose is different, do not change it* unless your doctor tells you to do so:

- For *oral* dosage forms (capsules, oral solution):
  —For treatment of HIV infection:
    - Adults and teenagers weighing 60 kilograms (kg) (132 pounds) or more—40 milligrams (mg) every twelve hours.
    - Adults and teenagers weighing up to 60 kg (132 pounds)—30 mg every twelve hours.
    - Children weighing 30 kg (66 pounds) or more—30 mg every twelve hours.
    - Children weighing up to 30 kg (66 pounds)—1 mg per kg (0.45 mg per pound) of body weight, every twelve hours.

Missed dose—If you miss a dose of this medicine, take it as soon as possible. However, if it is almost time for your next dose, skip the missed dose and go back to your regular dosing schedule. Do not double doses.

Storage—To store this medicine:

- Keep out of the reach of children.
- Store away from heat and direct light.
- Store the oral solution form in the refrigerator. However, keep the medicine from freezing.
- Do not store the capsules in the bathroom, near the kitchen sink, or in other damp places. Heat or moisture may cause the medicine to break down.
- Do not keep outdated medicine or medicine no longer needed. Be sure that any discarded medicine is out of the reach of children.

Precautions While Using This Medicine

It is very important that your doctor check your progress at regular visits.

Do not take any other medicines without checking with your doctor first. To do so may increase the chance of side effects from stavudine.

HIV may be acquired from or spread to other people through infected body fluids, including blood, vaginal fluid, or semen. *If you are infected, it is best to avoid any sexual activity involving an exchange of body fluids with other people. If you do have sex, always wear (or have your partner wear) a condom ("rubber").* Only use condoms made of latex, and *use them every time you have vaginal, anal, or oral sex.* The use of a spermicide (such as nonoxynol-9) may also help prevent transmission of HIV if it is not irritating to the vagina, rectum, or mouth. Spermicides have been shown to kill HIV in lab tests. Do not use oil-based jelly, cold cream, baby oil, or shortening as a lubricant—these products can cause the condom to break. Lubricants without oil, such as *K-Y Jelly,* are recommended. Women may wish to carry their own condoms. Birth control pills and diaphragms will help protect against pregnancy, but they will not prevent someone from giving or getting the AIDS virus. *If you inject drugs,* get help to stop. *Do not share needles or equipment with anyone.* In some cities, more than half of the drug users are infected, and sharing even 1 needle or syringe can spread the virus. If you have any questions about this, check with your health care professional.

Side Effects of This Medicine

Along with its needed effects, a medicine may cause some unwanted effects. Although not all of these side effects may occur, if they do occur they may need medical attention.

Check with your doctor immediately if any of the following side effects occur:
   More common
      Tingling, burning, numbness, or pain in the hands or feet
   Less common
      Fever; joint pain; muscle pain; skin rash
   Rare
      Nausea and vomiting; stomach pain (severe); unusual tiredness or weakness

Other side effects may occur that usually do not need medical attention. These side effects may go away during treatment as your body adjusts to the medicine. However, check with your doctor if any of the following side effects continue or are bothersome:
   More common
      Chills with fever; weight loss
   Less common
      Diarrhea; difficulty in sleeping; headache; lack of strength or energy; loss of appetite; stomach pain (mild)

Other side effects not listed above may also occur in some patients. If you notice any other effects, check with your doctor.

Developed: 11/28/1994
Revised: 02/06/2001

STREPTOZOCIN   Systemic

Commonly used brand name(s):

In the U.S.—
   Zanosar

In Canada—
   Zanosar

Description

Streptozocin (strep-toe-ZOE-sin) belongs to the group of medicines known as alkylating agents. It is used to treat cancer of the pancreas.

Streptozocin seems to interfere with the growth of cancer cells, which are eventually destroyed. It also directly affects the way the pancreas works. Since the growth of normal body cells may also be affected by streptozocin, other effects will also occur. Some of these may be serious and must be reported to your doctor. Other effects may not be serious but may cause concern. Some effects may not occur for months or years after the medicine is used.

Before you begin treatment with streptozocin, you and your doctor should talk about the good this medicine will do as well as the risks of using it.

Streptozocin is to be given only by or under the immediate supervision of your doctor. It is available in the following dosage form:
   Parenteral
      • Injection (U.S. and Canada)

Before Using This Medicine

In deciding to use a medicine, the risks of taking the medicine must be weighed against the good it will do. This is a decision you and your doctor will make. For streptozocin, the following should be considered:

Allergies—Tell your doctor if you have ever had any unusual or allergic reaction to streptozocin.

Pregnancy—Tell your doctor if you are pregnant or if you intend to have children. There is a chance that this medicine may cause birth defects if either the male or the female is receiving it at the time of conception or if it is taken during pregnancy. Studies in rats and rabbits have shown that streptozocin causes birth defects or miscarriage. In addition, many cancer medicines may cause sterility which could be permanent. Although this has not been reported with this medicine, the possibility should be kept in mind.

Be sure that you have discussed this with your doctor before receiving this medicine. It is best to use some kind of birth control while you are receiving streptozocin. Tell your doctor right away if you think you have become pregnant while receiving streptozocin.

Breast-feeding—Tell your doctor if you are breast-feeding or if you intend to breast-feed during treatment with this medicine. Because streptozocin may cause serious side effects, breast-feeding is generally not recommended while you are receiving it.

Children—There is no specific information comparing use of streptozocin in children with use in other age groups.

Older adults—Many medicines have not been studied specifically in older people. Therefore, it may not be known whether they work exactly the same way they do in younger adults or if they cause different side effects or problems in older people. There is no specific information comparing use of streptozocin in the elderly with use in other age groups.

Other medicines—Although certain medicines should not be used together at all, in other cases two different medicines may be used together even if an interaction might occur. In these cases, your doctor may want to change the dose, or other precautions may be necessary. When you are receiving streptozocin, it is especially important that your health care professional know if you are taking any of the following:

- Anti-infectives by mouth or by injection (medicine for infection) or
- Carmustine (e.g., BiCNU) or
- Cisplatin (e.g., Platinol) or
- Combination pain medicine containing acetaminophen and aspirin (e.g., Excedrin) or other salicylates (with large amounts taken regularly) or
- Cyclosporine (e.g., Sandimmune) or
- Deferoxamine (e.g., Desferal) (with long-term use) or
- Gold salts (medicine for arthritis) or
- Inflammation or pain medicine except narcotics or
- Lithium (e.g., Lithane) or
- Methotrexate (e.g., Mexate) or
- Penicillamine (e.g., Cuprimine) or
- Plicamycin (e.g., Mithracin) or
- Tiopronin (e.g., Thiola)—Increased risk of harmful effects on the kidney
- Phenytoin (e.g., Dilantin)—May interfere with the effects of streptozocin

Other medical problems—The presence of other medical problems may affect the use of streptozocin. Make sure you tell your doctor if you have any other medical problems, especially:

- Chickenpox (including recent exposure) or
- Herpes zoster (shingles)—Risk of severe disease affecting other parts of the body
- Diabetes mellitus (sugar diabetes)—May be worsened
- Infection—Streptozocin can decrease your body's ability to fight infection
- Kidney disease or
- Liver disease—Effects of streptozocin may be increased because of slower removal from the body

Proper Use of This Medicine

While you are receiving streptozocin, your doctor may want you to drink extra fluids so that you will pass more urine. This will help prevent kidney problems and keep your kidneys working well.

This medicine usually causes nausea and vomiting, which may be severe. However, it is very important that you continue to receive the medicine, even if you begin to feel ill. Ask your health care professional for ways to lessen these effects.

Dosing—The dose of streptozocin will be different for different patients. The dose that is used may depend on a number of things, including what the medicine is being used for, the patient's size, and whether or not other medicines are also being taken. *If you are receiving streptozocin at home, follow your doctor's orders or the directions on the label.* If you have any questions about the proper dose of streptozocin, ask your doctor.

Precautions While Using This Medicine

It is very important that your doctor check your progress at regular visits to make sure that this medicine is working properly and to check for any unwanted effects.

While you are being treated with streptozocin, and after you stop treatment with it, *do not have any immunizations (vaccinations) without your doctor's approval.* Streptozocin may lower your body's resistance and there is a chance you might get the infection the immunization is meant to prevent.

In addition, other people living in your household should not take oral polio vaccine since there is a chance they could pass the polio virus on to you. Also, avoid persons who have recently taken oral polio vaccine. Do not get close to them and do not stay in the same room with them for very long. If you cannot take these precautions, you should consider wearing a protective face mask that covers the nose and mouth.

If streptozocin accidentally seeps out of the vein into which it is injected, it may damage some tissues and cause scarring. *Tell the health care professional right away if you notice redness, pain, or swelling at the place of injection.*

Side Effects of This Medicine

Along with their needed effects, medicines like streptozocin can sometimes cause unwanted effects such as kidney problems and other side effects. These and others are described below. Also, because of the way these medicines act on the body, there is a chance that they might cause other unwanted effects that may not occur until months or years after the medicine is used. These delayed effects may include certain types of cancer, such as leukemia. Streptozocin has been shown to cause tumors (some cancerous) in animals. Discuss these possible effects with your doctor.

Although not all of these side effects may occur, if they do occur they may need medical attention.

Check with your health care professional immediately if any of the following side effects occur shortly after the medicine is given:
Less common
   Anxiety, nervousness, or shakiness; chills, cold sweats, or cool, pale skin; drowsiness or unusual tiredness or weakness; fast pulse; headache; pain or redness at place of injection; unusual hunger

Check with your doctor immediately if the following side effects occur any time while you are being treated with this medicine:
Rare
   Black, tarry stools; blood in urine or stools; cough or hoarseness; fever or chills; lower back or side pain; painful or difficult urination; pinpoint red spots on skin; unusual bleeding or bruising

Check with your health care professional as soon as possible if any of the following side effects occur:
More common
   Swelling of feet or lower legs; unusual decrease in urination

Other side effects may occur that usually do not need medical attention. These side effects may go away during treatment as your body adjusts to the medicine. Also, your health care professional may be able to tell you about ways to prevent or reduce some of these side effects. Check with your health care professional if any of the following side effects continue or are bothersome or if you have any questions about them:
More common
   Nausea and vomiting (usually occurs within 2 to 4 hours after receiving dose and may be severe)
Less common
   Diarrhea

After you stop receiving streptozocin, your body may need time to adjust. The length of time this takes depends on the amount of medicine you were using and how long you used it. During this period of time, check with your doctor if you notice either of the following side effects:

More common
>   Decrease in urination; swelling of feet or lower legs

Other side effects not listed above may also occur in some patients. If you notice any other effects, check with your doctor.

Revised: 08/26/92
Interim revision: 06/30/94

SUCCIMER   Systemic†

Commonly used brand name(s):

In the U.S.—
>   Chemet

Other commonly used names are dimercaptosuccinic acid and DMSA.

†Not commercially available in Canada.

Description

Succimer (SUKS-si-mer) is used in the treatment of acute lead poisoning to remove excess lead from the body, especially in small children.

Succimer combines with lead in the blood stream. The combination of lead and succimer is then removed from the body by the kidneys. By removing the excess lead, the medicine lessens damage to various organs and tissues of the body.

Oral
- Capsules (U.S.)

Before Using This Medicine

In deciding to use a medicine, the risks of taking the medicine must be weighed against the good it will do. This is a decision you and your doctor will make. For succimer, the following should be considered:

Allergies—Tell your doctor if you have ever had any unusual or allergic reaction to succimer. Also, tell your health care professional if you are allergic to any other substances, such as foods, preservatives, or dyes.

Pregnancy—Succimer has not been studied in pregnant women. However, some studies in animals have shown that succimer causes birth defects. Before taking this medicine, make sure your doctor knows if you are pregnant or if you may become pregnant.

Breast-feeding—It is not known whether succimer passes into breast milk. However, breast-feeding is not recommended while taking succimer.

Children—This medicine has been tested in children over the age of 1 year and, in effective doses, has not been shown to cause different side effects or problems than it does in adults.

Older adults—Many medicines have not been studied specifically in older people. Therefore, it may not be known whether they work exactly the same way they do in younger adults or if they cause different side effects or problems in

older people. There is no specific information comparing use of succimer in the elderly with use in other age groups.

Other medical problems—The presence of other medical problems may affect the use of succimer. Make sure you tell your doctor if you have any other medical problems, especially:

- Dehydration—Before and while taking succimer, you must drink plenty of fluids and urinate regularly
- Kidney disease—The combination of lead and succimer may not be removed from the body as quickly as it normally would
- Liver disease—This condition may be made worse; your doctor should perform liver function tests regularly while you are taking succimer

Proper Use of This Medicine

Children who have too much lead in their bodies should be removed from the lead-containing environment (for example, home, school, or other areas where the child has been exposed to lead) until the lead has been removed from the environment. If this is not possible, the environment should be made as safe as possible for the child.

Your doctor may want to put your child in the hospital while he or she is receiving succimer. This will allow the doctor to check your child's condition while the lead can be removed from the child's environment.

When opening your bottle of succimer, you may notice an unpleasant odor. However, this is a normal odor for these capsules and does not affect how the medicine works.

If the capsules cannot be swallowed, the contents of the capsule may be sprinkled on food and eaten immediately. The contents may also be given on a spoon and followed by a fruit drink.

It is important to drink plenty of fluids while taking succimer.

Dosing—The dose of succimer will be different for different patients. *Follow your doctor's orders or the directions on the label.*

- For the *oral* dosage form (capsules):
  —For treatment of lead poisoning:
  - For adults and children 12 years of age or older—Dose is based on body weight. The usual dose is 10 milligrams (mg) of succimer per kilogram (kg) (4.5 mg per pound) of body weight every eight hours for five days.
  - For children 1 to 11 years of age—Dose is based on body weight. The usual dose is 10 mg of succimer per kg (4.5 mg per pound) of body weight every eight hours for five days. The same dose is then given every twelve hours for the next fourteen days, for a total of nineteen days of therapy.
  - For children up to 1 year of age—Use and dose must be determined by your doctor.

Missed dose—If you miss a dose of this medicine, take it as soon as possible. However, if it is almost time for your next dose, skip the missed dose and go back to your regular dosing schedule. Do not double doses.

Storage—To store this medicine:
- Keep out of the reach of children.
- Store away from heat and direct light.

- Do not store in the bathroom, near the kitchen sink, or in other damp places. Heat or moisture may cause the medicine to break down.
- Keep the medicine from freezing. Do not refrigerate.
- Do not keep outdated medicine or medicine no longer needed. Be sure that any discarded medicine is out of the reach of children.

Precautions While Using This Medicine

It is important that your doctor check your progress at regular visits to make sure that this medicine is working properly and to prevent unwanted effects. Certain blood and urine tests must be done regularly to determine how long you need to take succimer.

If you think you are getting an infection or if you get a fever or chills, contact your doctor as soon as possible. You will need certain tests. Based on the results of the tests, your doctor may advise you to temporarily stop taking succimer to prevent serious side effects from occurring.

Side Effects of This Medicine

Along with its needed effects, a medicine may cause some unwanted effects. Although not all of these side effects may occur, if they do occur they may need medical attention.

Check with your doctor as soon as possible if either of the following side effects occurs:
Less common
Chills; fever

Other side effects may occur that usually do not need medical attention. These side effects may go away during treatment as your body adjusts to the medicine. However, check with your doctor if any of the following side effects continue or are bothersome:
More common
Diarrhea; loose stools; loss of appetite; nausea and vomiting; skin rash

Succimer may cause your urine, sweat, and feces to have an unpleasant odor.

Other side effects not listed above may also occur in some patients. If you notice any other effects, check with your doctor.

Revised: 06/10/99

SUCRALFATE   Oral

Commonly used brand name(s):

In the U.S.—
Carafate
Generic name product may be available.

In Canada—
Apo-sucralfate
Sulcrate
Sulcrate Suspension Plus

Description

Sucralfate (soo-KRAL-fate) is used to treat and prevent duodenal ulcers. This medicine may also be used for other conditions as determined by your doctor.

Sucralfate works by forming a "barrier" or "coating" over the ulcer. This protects the ulcer from the acid of the stomach, allowing it to heal. Sucralfate contains an aluminum salt.

This medicine is available only with your doctor's prescription, in the following dosage form:
Oral
- Oral suspension (U.S. and Canada)
- Tablets (U.S. and Canada)

Before Using This Medicine

In deciding to use a medicine, the risks of taking the medicine must be weighed against the good it will do. This is a decision you and your doctor will make. For sucralfate, the following should be considered:

Allergies—Tell your doctor if you have ever had any unusual or allergic reaction to sucralfate. Also, tell your health care professional if you are allergic to any other substances, such as foods, preservatives, or dyes.

Pregnancy—Studies have not been done in humans. However, sucralfate has not been shown to cause birth defects or other problems in animal studies.

Breast-feeding—Sucralfate has not been shown to cause problems in nursing babies.

Children—This medicine has been tested in a limited number of children. In effective doses, the medicine has not been shown to cause different side effects or problems than it does in adults.

Older adults—Many medicines have not been studied specifically in older people. Therefore, it may not be known whether they work exactly the same way they do in younger adults. Although there is no specific information comparing the use of sucralfate in the elderly with use in other age groups, this medicine is not expected to cause different side effects or problems in older people than it does in younger adults.

Other medicines—Although certain medicines should not be used together at all, in other cases two different medicines may be used together even if an interaction might occur. In these cases, your doctor may want to change the dose, or other precautions may be necessary. When you are taking sucralfate, it is especially important that your health care professional know if you are taking the following:
- Ciprofloxacin or
- Digoxin or
- Norfloxacin or
- Ofloxacin or
- Phenytoin or
- Theophylline—Sucralfate may prevent these medicines from working properly

Other medical problems—The presence of other medical problems may affect the use of sucralfate. Make sure you tell your doctor if you have any other medical problems, especially:
- Gastrointestinal tract obstruction disease—Sucralfate may bind with other foods and drugs and cause obstruction of the gastrointestinal tract

- Kidney failure—Use may lead to a toxic increase of aluminum blood levels

Proper Use of This Medicine

Sucralfate is best taken with water on an empty stomach 1 hour before meals and at bedtime, unless otherwise directed by your doctor.

Take this medicine for the full time of treatment, even if you begin to feel better. Also, it is important that you keep your doctor's appointments for check-ups so that your doctor will be better able to tell you when to stop taking this medicine.

Dosing—The dose of sucralfate will be different for different patients. *Follow your doctor's orders or the directions on the label*. The following information includes only the average doses of sucralfate. *If your dose is different, do not change it* unless your doctor tells you to do so.

The number of tablets or teaspoonfuls of suspension that you take depends on the strength of the medicine. Also, *the number of doses you take each day, the time allowed between doses, and the length of time you take the medicine depend on the medical problem for which you are taking sucralfate.*

- For *oral* dosage form (suspension):
  - —To treat duodenal ulcers:
    - Adults and teenagers—One gram four times a day, one hour before each meal and at bedtime. Some people may take two grams two times a day, when they wake up and at bedtime on an empty stomach.
    - Children—Dose must be determined by your doctor.
- For *oral* dosage form (tablets):
  - —To treat duodenal ulcers:
    - Adults and teenagers—One gram four times a day, one hour before each meal and at bedtime.
    - Children—Dose must be determined by your doctor.
  - —To prevent duodenal ulcers:
    - Adults and teenagers—One gram two times a day on an empty stomach.
    - Children—Dose must be determined by your doctor.

Missed dose—If you miss a dose of this medicine, take it as soon as possible. However, if it is almost time for your next dose, skip the missed dose and go back to your regular dosing schedule. Do not double doses.

Storage—To store this medicine:
- Keep out of the reach of children.
- Store away from heat and direct light.
- Do not store in the bathroom, near the kitchen sink, or in other damp places. Heat or moisture may cause the medicine to break down.
- Keep the liquid form of this medicine from freezing. Do not refrigerate.
- Do not keep outdated medicine or medicine no longer needed. Be sure that any discarded medicine is out of the reach of children.

Precautions While Using This Medicine

Antacids may be taken with sucralfate to help relieve any stomach pain, unless your doctor has told you not to use them. *However, antacids should not be taken within 30 minutes before or after sucralfate.* Taking these medicines too close together may keep sucralfate from working properly.

Side Effects of This Medicine

Along with its needed effects, a medicine may cause some unwanted effects. Some side effects may occur that usually do not need medical attention. These side effects may go away during treatment as your body adjusts to the medicine.

Check with your doctor immediately if any of the following side effects occur:
Signs of aluminum toxicity
Drowsiness; convulsions (seizures)

Check with your doctor as soon as possible if any of the following side effects continue or are bothersome:
More common
Constipation
Less common or rare
Backache; diarrhea; dizziness or lightheadedness; dryness of mouth; indigestion; nausea; skin rash, hives, or itching; stomach cramps or pain

Other side effects not listed above may also occur in some patients. If you notice any other effects, check with your doctor.

Additional Information

Once a medicine has been approved for marketing for a certain use, experience may show that it is also useful for other medical problems. Although these uses are not included in product labeling, sucralfate is used in certain patients with the following medical conditions:
- Gastric ulcers
- Gastroesophageal reflux disease (a condition in which stomach acid washes back into the esophagus)
- Stomach or intestinal ulcers resulting from stress or trauma damage or from damage caused by medication used to treat rheumatoid arthritis

Other than the above information, there is no additional information relating to proper use, precautions, or side effects for these uses.

Revised: 03/24/92
Interim revision: 08/17/94; 07/26/96; 03/24/98

SULFAPYRIDINE   Systemic

Commonly used brand name(s):

In Canada—
Dagenan
Generic name product may be available.

Description

Sulfapyridine (sul-fa-PEER-i-deen) is a sulfa medicine. It is used to help control dermatitis herpetiformis (Duhring's disease), a skin problem. It may also be used for other problems as determined by your doctor. However, this medicine will not work for any kind of infection as other sulfa medicines do.

This medicine may cause some serious side effects. *Before using this medicine, be sure to talk to your doctor about these problems, as well as the good this medicine will do.*

Sulfapyridine is available only with your doctor's prescription, in the following dosage form:

Oral
- Tablets (U.S. and Canada)

Before Using This Medicine

In deciding to use a medicine, the risks of taking the medicine must be weighed against the good it will do. This is a decision you and your doctor will make. For sulfapyridine, the following should be considered:

Allergies—Tell your doctor if you have ever had any unusual or allergic reaction to sulfa medicines, furosemide (e.g., Lasix) or thiazide diuretics (water pills), oral antidiabetics (diabetes medicine you take by mouth), glaucoma medicine you take by mouth (acetazolamide [e.g., Diamox], dichlorphenamide [e.g., Daranide], methazolamide [e.g., Neptazane]), or pyrimethamine (e.g., Daraprim). Also tell your health care professional if you are allergic to any other substances, such as foods, preservatives, or dyes.

Pregnancy—Studies have not been done in humans. Studies in rats and mice have shown that some sulfa medicines, given by mouth in high doses, cause birth defects, including cleft palate and bone problems. In addition, sulfa medicines may cause liver problems in newborn infants. Therefore, use is not recommended during pregnancy.

Breast-feeding—Sulfapyridine passes into the breast milk. This medicine may cause liver problems in nursing babies. In addition, it may cause blood problems in nursing babies with glucose-6-phosphate dehydrogenase (G6PD) deficiency (lack of G6PD enzyme). Therefore, use is not recommended in nursing women.

Children—Use of this medicine is not recommended since dermatitis herpetiformis usually does not occur in children.

Older adults—Many medicines have not been studied specifically in older people. Therefore, it may not be known whether they work exactly the same way they do in younger adults or if they cause different side effects or problems in older people. There is no specific information comparing the use of sulfapyridine in the elderly with use in other age groups.

Other medicines—Although certain medicines should not be used together at all, in other cases two different medicines may be used together even if an interaction might occur. In these cases, your doctor may want to change the dose, or other precautions may be necessary. When you are taking sulfapyridine, it is especially important that your health care professional know if you are taking any of the following:

- Acetaminophen (e.g., Tylenol) (with long-term, high-dose use) or
- Amiodarone (e.g., Cordarone) or
- Anabolic steroids (nandrolone [e.g., Anabolin], oxandrolone [e.g., Anavar], oxymetholone [e.g., Anadrol], stanozolol [e.g., Winstrol]) or
- Androgens (male hormones) or
- Antithyroid agents (medicine for overactive thyroid) or
- Carbamazepine (e.g., Tegretol) or
- Carmustine (e.g., BiCNU) or
- Chloroquine (e.g., Aralen) or
- Dantrolene (e.g., Dantrium) or
- Daunorubicin (e.g., Cerubidine) or
- Disulfiram (e.g., Antabuse) or
- Divalproex (e.g., Depakote) or
- Estrogens (female hormones) or
- Etretinate (e.g., Tegison) or
- Gold salts (medicine for arthritis) or
- Hydroxychloroquine (e.g., Plaquenil) or
- Mercaptopurine (e.g., Purinethol) or
- Naltrexone (e.g., Trexan) (with long-term, high-dose use) or
- Oral contraceptives (birth control pills) containing estrogen or
- Other anti-infectives by mouth or by injection (medicine for infection) or
- Phenothiazines (acetophenazine [e.g., Tindal], chlorpromazine [e.g., Thorazine], fluphenazine [e.g., Prolixin], mesoridazine [e.g., Serentil], perphenazine [e.g., Trilafon], prochlorperazine [e.g., Compazine], promazine [e.g., Sparine], promethazine [e.g., Phenergan], thioridazine [e.g., Mellaril], trifluoperazine [e.g., Stelazine], triflupromazine [e.g., Vesprin], trimeprazine [e.g., Temaril]) or
- Plicamycin (e.g., Mithracin) or
- Valproic acid (e.g., Depakene)—Use of sulfapyridine with these medicines may increase the chance of side effects affecting the liver

- Acetohydroxamic acid (e.g., Lithostat) or
- Dapsone or
- Furazolidone (e.g., Furoxone) or
- Nitrofurantoin (e.g., Furadantin) or
- Primaquine or
- Procainamide (e.g., Pronestyl) or
- Quinidine (e.g., Quinidex) or
- Quinine (e.g., Quinamm) or
- Sulfoxone (e.g., Diasone) or
- Vitamin K (e.g., AquaMEPHYTON, Synkayvite)—Use of sulfapyridine with these medicines may increase the chance of side effects affecting the blood

- Anticoagulants (blood thinners) or
- Ethotoin (e.g., Peganone) or
- Mephenytoin (e.g., Mesantoin)—Use of sulfapyridine with these medicines may increase the chance of side effects of these medicines

- Antidiabetics, oral (diabetes medicine you take by mouth)—Use of oral antidiabetics with sulfapyridine may increase the chance of side effects affecting the blood and/or the side effects or oral antidiabetics

- Methotrexate (e.g., Mexate)—Use of methotrexate with sulfapyridine may increase the chance of side effects affecting the liver and/or the side effects of methotrexate

- Methyldopa (e.g., Aldomet)—Use of methyldopa with sulfapyridine may increase the chance of side effects affecting the liver and/or the blood

- Phenytoin (e.g., Dilantin)—Use of phenytoin with sulfapyridine may increase the chance of side effects affecting the liver and/or the side effects of phenytoin

Other medical problems—The presence of other medical problems may affect the use of sulfapyridine. Make sure you tell your doctor if you have any other medical problems, especially:

- Blood problems or

- Glucose-6-phosphate dehydrogenase deficiency (lack of G6PD enzyme)—Patients with these problems may have an increase in side effects affecting the blood
- Kidney disease or
- Liver disease—Patients with kidney disease or liver disease may have an increased chance of side effects
- Porphyria—Use of sulfapyridine may cause an attack of porphyria

---

Proper Use of This Medicine

Each dose of sulfapyridine should be taken with a full glass (8 ounces) of water. Several additional glasses of water should be taken every day, unless otherwise directed by your doctor. Drinking extra water will help to prevent some unwanted effects (e.g., kidney stones) of the sulfa medicine.

For patients taking sulfapyridine *for dermatitis herpetiformis:*

- Your doctor may want you to follow a strict, gluten-free diet.
- You may have to use this medicine regularly for 6 months to a year before you can reduce the dose of sulfapyridine or stop it altogether. If you have any questions about this, check with your doctor.

Dosing—The dose of sulfapyridine will be different for different patients. *Follow your doctor's orders or the directions on the label.* The following information includes only the average doses of sulfapyridine. Your dose may be different if you have kidney disease. *If your dose is different, do not change it* unless your doctor tells you to do so.

- For *dermatitis herpetiformis:*
  —Adults and adolescents: 250 milligrams to 1 gram four times a day until improvement occurs. After improvement has occurred, the dose should then be reduced by 250 to 500 milligrams every three days until there are no symptoms; that dose should be taken once daily.
  —Children: Use is not recommended, because children usually do not get this condition.

Missed dose—For patients taking sulfapyridine *for dermatitis herpetiformis:* You may skip a missed dose if this does not make your symptoms return or get worse. If your symptoms do return or get worse, take the missed dose as soon as possible. Then go back to your regular dosing schedule.

Storage—To store this medicine:

- Keep out of the reach of children.
- Store away from heat and direct light.
- Do not store in the bathroom, near the kitchen sink, or in other damp places. Heat or moisture may cause the medicine to break down.
- Do not keep outdated medicine or medicine no longer needed. Be sure that any discarded medicine is out of the reach of children.

Precautions While Using This Medicine

It is very important that your doctor check your progress at regular visits. This medicine may cause blood problems, especially if it is taken for a long time.

If your symptoms do not improve within a few days, or if they become worse, check with your doctor.

Sulfapyridine may cause blood problems. These problems may result in a greater chance of certain infections, slow healing, and bleeding of the gums. Therefore, you should be careful when using regular toothbrushes, dental floss, and toothpicks. Dental work should be delayed until your blood counts have returned to normal. Check with your medical doctor or dentist if you have any questions about proper oral hygiene (mouth care) during treatment.

Sulfapyridine may cause your skin to be more sensitive to sunlight than it is normally. Exposure to sunlight, even for brief periods of time, may cause a skin rash, itching, redness or other discoloration of the skin, or a severe sunburn. When you begin taking this medicine:

- Stay out of direct sunlight, especially between the hours of 10:00 A.M. and 3:00 P.M., if possible.
- Wear protective clothing, including a hat. Also, wear sunglasses.
- Apply a sun block product that has a skin protection factor (SPF) of at least 15. Some patients may require a product with a higher SPF number, especially if they have a fair complexion. If you have any questions about this, check with your health care professional.
- Apply a sun block lipstick that has an SPF of at least 15 to protect your lips.
- Do not use a sunlamp or tanning bed or booth.

You may still be more sensitive to sunlight or sunlamps for many months after stopping this medicine. *If you have a severe reaction from the sun, check with your doctor.*

Tell the doctor in charge that you are taking this medicine before you have any medical tests. The results of the bentiromide (e.g., Chymex) test for pancreas function are affected by this medicine.

Side Effects of This Medicine

Along with its needed effects, a medicine may cause some unwanted effects. Although not all of these side effects may occur, if they do occur they may need medical attention.

Check with your doctor immediately if any of the following side effects occur:
  More common
    Fever; headache (continuing); itching; skin rash
  Less common
    Aching of joints and muscles; difficulty in swallowing; pale skin; redness, blistering, peeling, or loosening of skin; sore throat; unusual bleeding or bruising; unusual tiredness or weakness; yellow eyes or skin
  Rare
    Blood in urine; lower back pain; pain or burning while urinating; swelling of front part of neck

Also, check with your doctor as soon as possible if the following side effect occurs:
  More common
    Increased sensitivity of skin to sunlight

Other side effects may occur that usually do not need medical attention. These side effects may go away during treatment as your body adjusts to the medicine. However, check with your doctor if any of the following side effects continue or are bothersome:
  More common
    Diarrhea; loss of appetite; nausea or vomiting

Other side effects not listed above may also occur in some patients. If you notice any other effects, check with your doctor.

Additional Information

Once a medicine has been approved for marketing for a certain use, experience may show that it is also useful for other medical problems. Although these uses are not included in product labeling, sulfapyridine is used in certain patients with the following medical conditions:

- Pemphigoid
- Pyoderma gangrenosum
- Subcorneal pustular dermatitis

Other than the above information, there is no additional information relating to proper use, precautions, or side effects for these uses.

Revised: 02/01/93

SULFASALAZINE   Systemic

Commonly used brand name(s):

In the U.S.—
Azulfidine
Azulfidine EN-Tabs

Generic name product may be available.

In Canada—

Alti-Sulfasalazine	Salazopyrin EN-Tabs
PMS-Sulfasalazine	S.A.S.-500
PMS-Sulfasalazine E.C.	S.A.S. Enteric-500
Salazopyrin	

Other commonly used names are salazosulfapyridine, salicylazosulfapyridine, and sulphasalazine.

Description

Sulfasalazine (sul-fa-SAL-a-zeen), a sulfa medicine, is used to prevent and treat inflammatory bowel disease, such as ulcerative colitis. It works inside the bowel by helping to reduce the inflammation and other symptoms of the disease. Sulfasalazine is sometimes given with other medicines to treat inflammatory bowel disease.

Sulfasalazine is also used to treat rheumatoid arthritis in patients who have not been helped by or who cannot tolerate other medicines for rheumatoid arthritis.

Sulfasalazine is available only with your doctor's prescription, in the following dosage forms:

Oral
- Tablets (U.S. and Canada)
- Enteric-coated tablets (U.S. and Canada)

Rectal
- Enema (Canada)

Before Using This Medicine

In deciding to use a medicine, the risks of taking the medicine must be weighed against the good it will do. This is a decision you and your doctor will make. For sulfasalazine, the following should be considered:

Allergies—Tell your doctor if you have ever had any unusual or allergic reaction to any of the sulfa medicines, furosemide (e.g., Lasix) or thiazide diuretics (water pills), oral antidiabetics (diabetes medicine you take by mouth), glaucoma medicine you take by mouth (for example, acetazolamide [e.g., Diamox], dichlorphenamide [e.g., Daranide], methazolamide [e.g., Neptazane]), or salicylates (for example, aspirin). Also tell your health care professional if you are allergic to any other substances, such as foods, preservatives, or dyes.

Pregnancy—Sulfasalazine has not been studied in pregnant women. However, reports on women who took sulfasalazine during pregnancy have not shown that it causes birth defects or other problems. In addition, sulfasalazine has not been shown to cause birth defects in studies in rats and rabbits given doses of up to 6 times the human dose.

Breast-feeding—Sulfa medicines pass into the breast milk in small amounts and have been shown to cause unwanted effects in nursing babies with glucose-6-phosphate dehydrogenase (G6PD) deficiency. It may be necessary for you to take another medicine or to stop breast-feeding during treatment. Be sure you have discussed the risks and benefits of the medicine with your doctor.

Children—Sulfasalazine should not be used in children up to 2 years of age because it may cause brain problems. However, sulfasalazine has not been shown to cause different side effects or problems in children over the age of 2 years than it does in adults.

Older adults—This medicine has been tested and has not been shown to cause different side effects or problems in older people than it does in younger adults.

Other medicines—Although certain medicines should not be used together at all, in other cases two different medicines may be used together even if an interaction might occur. In these cases, your doctor may want to change the dose, or other precautions may be necessary. When you are taking sulfasalazine, it is especially important that your health care professional know if you are taking any of the following:

- Acetaminophen (e.g., Tylenol) (with long-term, high-dose use) or
- Amiodarone (e.g., Cordarone) or
- Anabolic steroids (nandrolone [e.g., Anabolin], oxandrolone [e.g., Anavar], oxymetholone [e.g., Anadrol], stanozolol [e.g., Winstrol]) or
- Androgens (male hormones) or
- Carbamazepine (e.g., Tegretol) or
- Carmustine (e.g., BiCNU) or
- Dantrolene (e.g., Dantrium) or
- Daunorubicin (e.g., Cerubidine) or
- Disulfiram (e.g., Antabuse) or
- Divalproex (e.g., Depakote) or
- Estrogens (female hormones) or
- Ethionamide (e.g., Trecator-SC) or
- Etretinate (e.g., Tegison) or
- Fat emulsions, intravenous (e.g., Intralipid) (with prolonged use) or
- Fluconazole (e.g., Diflucan) or
- Gold salts (medicine for arthritis) or
- Inflammation or pain medicine, except narcotics or
- Iron (with overdose) or
- Labetalol (e.g., Normodyne) or
- Lovastatin (e.g., Mevacor) or
- Mercaptopurine (e.g., Purinethol) or
- Methimazole (e.g., Tapazole) or
- Naltrexone (e.g., ReVia) (with long-term, high-dose use) or

- Niacin (with high doses, sustained release, and antihyperlipidemic use) or
- Nitrofurans or
- Other anti-infectives by mouth or by injection (medicine for infection) or
- Phenothiazines (acetophenazine [e.g., Tindal], chlorpromazine [e.g., Thorazine], fluphenazine [e.g., Prolixin], mesoridazine [e.g., Serentil], perphenazine [e.g., Trilafon], prochlorperazine [e.g., Compazine], promazine [e.g., Sparine], promethazine [e.g., Phenergan], thioridazine [e.g., Mellaril], trifluoperazine [e.g., Stelazine], triflupromazine [e.g., Vesprin], trimeprazine [e.g., Temaril]) or
- Plicamycin (e.g., Mithracin) or
- Pravastatin (e.g., Pravachol) or
- Propylthiouracil (e.g., Propyl-Thyracil) or
- Simvastatin (e.g., Zocor) or
- Troleandomycin or
- Valproic acid (e.g., Depakene) or
- Vitamin A (with chronic overdose)—Use of sulfasalazine with these medicines may increase the chance of side effects affecting the liver

- Acetohydroxamic acid (e.g., Lithostat) or
- Dapsone or
- Furazolidone (e.g., Furoxone) or
- Menadiol (e.g., Synkavite) or
- Nitrofurantoin (e.g., Furadantin) or
- Primaquine or
- Procainamide (e.g., Pronestyl) or
- Quinidine (e.g., Quinidex) or
- Quinine (e.g., Quinamm) or
- Sulfoxone (e.g., Diasone)—Use of sulfasalazine with these medicines may increase the chance of side effects affecting the blood

- Anticoagulants (blood thinners) or
- Ethotoin (e.g., Peganone) or
- Mephenytoin (e.g., Mesantoin)—Use of sulfasalazine with these medicines may increase the chance of side effects of these medicines

- Antidiabetics, oral (diabetes medicine you take by mouth)—Use of oral antidiabetics with sulfasalazine may increase the chance of side effects affecting the blood and/or increase the side effects of oral antidiabetics

- Methotrexate (e.g., Mexate)—Use of methotrexate with sulfasalazine may increase the chance of side effects affecting the liver and/or increase the side effects of methotrexate

- Methyldopa (e.g., Aldomet)—Use of methyldopa with sulfasalazine may increase the chance of side effects affecting the liver and/or the blood

- Phenytoin (e.g., Dilantin)—Use of phenytoin with sulfasalazine may increase the chance of side effects affecting the liver and/or increase the side effects of phenytoin

Other medical problems—The presence of other medical problems may affect the use of sulfasalazine. Make sure you tell your doctor if you have any other medical problems, especially:

- Allergies, severe or
- Asthma, bronchial—The risk of an allergic reaction to sulfasalazine may be increased
- Blood problems or

- Glucose-6-phosphate dehydrogenase deficiency (lack of G6PD enzyme)—Patients with these problems may have an increase in side effects affecting the blood
- Intestinal blockage—Sulfasalazine will not reach the site of action in the bowel
- Kidney disease or
- Liver disease—Patients with kidney disease or liver disease may have an increased chance of side effects
- Porphyria—Use of sulfasalazine may cause an attack of porphyria
- Urinary blockage—Sulfasalazine may not be eliminated properly, causing an increased risk of side effects

Proper Use of This Medicine

Do not give sulfasalazine to infants and children up to 2 years of age, unless otherwise directed by your doctor. It may cause brain problems.

Sulfasalazine is best taken right after meals or with food to lessen stomach upset. If stomach upset continues or is bothersome, check with your doctor.

Each dose of sulfasalazine should also be taken with a full glass (8 ounces) of water. Several additional glasses of water should be taken every day, unless otherwise directed by your doctor. Drinking extra water will help to prevent some unwanted effects of the sulfa medicine.

For patients taking the *enteric-coated tablet* form of this medicine:

- Swallow tablets whole. Do not break or crush.

Keep taking this medicine for the full time of treatment, even if you begin to feel better after a few days. *Do not miss any doses.*

Dosing—The dose of sulfasalazine will be different for different patients. *Follow your doctor's orders or the directions on the label.* The following information includes only the average doses of sulfasalazine. *If your dose is different, do not change it* unless your doctor tells you to do so.

The number of tablets that you take depends on the strength of the medicine. Also, *the number of doses you take each day, the time allowed between doses, and the length of time you take the medicine depend on the medical problem for which you are taking sulfasalazine.*

- For prevention or treatment of inflammatory bowel disease:
  —For *oral* dosage forms (tablets, enteric-coated tablets):
  - Adults and teenagers—To start, 500 milligrams (mg) to 1000 mg (1 gram) every six to eight hours. Your doctor may then decrease the dose to 500 mg every six hours. Later, your doctor may change your dose as needed.
  - Children 2 years of age and over—Dose is based on body weight and must be determined by your doctor.
    —To start, the dose is usually:
    - 6.7 to 10 mg per kilogram (kg) (3.05 to 4.55 mg per pound) of body weight every four hours or
    - 10 to 15 mg per kg (4.55 to 6.82 mg per pound) of body weight every six hours or
    - 13.3 to 20 mg per kg (6.05 to 9.09 mg per pound) of body weight every eight hours.

—Then, the dose is usually 7.5 mg per kg (3.41 mg per pound) of body weight every six hours.
- Infants and children up to 2 years of age—Use is not recommended.

—For *rectal* dosage form (enema):
- Adults and teenagers—3 grams (1 unit), used rectally as directed, every night.
- Children 2 years of age and over—Dose must be determined by your doctor.
- Infants and children up to 2 years of age—Use is not recommended.

- For treatment of rheumatoid arthritis:
For *oral* dosage forms (tablets, enteric-coated tablets):
- Adults and teenagers—To start, 500 mg to 1000 mg (1 gram) daily. Your doctor may increase your dose as needed, but the dose is generally not more than 3000 mg (3 grams) a day.
- Children 2 years of age and over—Dose must be determined by your doctor.
- Infants and children up to 2 years of age—Use is not recommended.

Missed dose—If you do miss a dose of this medicine, take it as soon as possible. However, if it is almost time for your next dose, skip the missed dose and go back to your regular dosing schedule. Do not double doses.

Storage—To store this medicine:
- Keep out of the reach of children.
- Store away from heat and direct light.
- Do not store the tablet form of this medicine in the bathroom, near the kitchen sink, or in other damp places. Heat or moisture may cause the medicine to break down.
- Keep the enema form of this medicine from freezing.
- Do not keep outdated medicine or medicine no longer needed. Be sure that any discarded medicine is out of the reach of children.

Precautions While Using This Medicine

It is very important that your doctor check your progress at regular visits. This medicine may cause blood problems, especially if it is taken for a long time.

If your symptoms (including diarrhea) do not improve within 1 or 2 months, or if they become worse, check with your doctor.

Sulfasalazine may cause blood problems. These problems may result in a greater chance of certain infections, slow healing, and bleeding of the gums. Therefore, you should be careful when using regular toothbrushes, dental floss, and toothpicks. Dental work should be delayed until your blood counts have returned to normal. Check with your medical doctor or dentist if you have any questions about proper oral hygiene (mouth care) during treatment.

Sulfasalazine may cause your skin to be more sensitive to sunlight than it is normally. Exposure to sunlight, even for brief periods of time, may cause a skin rash, itching, redness or other discoloration of the skin, or a severe sunburn. When you begin taking this medicine:
- Stay out of direct sunlight, especially between the hours of 10:00 a.m. and 3:00 p.m., if possible.
- Wear protective clothing, including a hat. Also, wear sunglasses.

- Apply a sun block product that has a skin protection factor (SPF) of at least 15. Some patients may require a product with a higher SPF number, especially if they have a fair complexion. If you have any questions about this, check with your health care professional.
- Apply a sun block lipstick that has an SPF of at least 15 to protect your lips.
- Do not use a sunlamp or tanning bed or booth.

If you have a severe reaction from the sun, check with your doctor.

This medicine may also cause some people to become dizzy. *Make sure you know how you react to this medicine before you drive, use machines, or do anything else that could be dangerous if you are dizzy.* If this reaction is especially bothersome, check with your doctor.

Before you have any medical tests, tell the doctor in charge that you are taking this medicine. The results of the bentiromide (e.g., Chymex) test for pancreas function are affected by this medicine.

Side Effects of This Medicine

Along with its needed effects, a medicine may cause some unwanted effects. Although not all of these side effects may occur, if they do occur they may need medical attention.

Check with your doctor immediately if any of the following side effects occur:
More common
Aching of joints; headache (continuing); itching; skin rash
Less common or rare
Aching of joints and muscles; back, leg, or stomach pains; bloody diarrhea; bluish fingernails, lips, or skin; chest pain; cough; difficult breathing; difficulty in swallowing; fever, chills, or sore throat; general feeling of discomfort or illness; loss of appetite; pale skin; redness, blistering, peeling, or loosening of skin; unusual bleeding or bruising; unusual tiredness or weakness; yellow eyes or skin

Also, check with your doctor as soon as possible if the following side effect occurs:
More common
Increased sensitivity of skin to sunlight

Other side effects may occur that usually do not need medical attention. These side effects may go away during treatment as your body adjusts to the medicine. However, check with your doctor if any of the following side effects continue or are bothersome:
More common
Abdominal or stomach pain or upset; diarrhea; loss of appetite; nausea or vomiting

In some patients this medicine may also cause the urine or skin to become orange-yellow. This side effect does not need medical attention.

Other side effects not listed above may also occur in some patients. If you notice any other effects, check with your doctor.

Additional Information

Once a medicine has been approved for marketing for a certain use, experience may show that it is also useful for other medical problems. Although these uses are not included in product labeling, sulfasalazine is used in certain patients with the following medical conditions:

- Ankylosing spondylitis

Other than the above information, there is no additional information relating to proper use, precautions, or side effects for these uses.

Revised: 08/11/98

SULFONAMIDES   Ophthalmic

Commonly used brand name(s):

In the U.S.—

Ak-Sulf[1]	Sodium Sulamyd[1]
Bleph-10[1]	Spectro-Sulf[1]
Cetamide[1]	Steri-Units Sulfacetamide[1]
Gantrisin[2]	Sulf-10[1]
Isopto-Cetamide[1]	Sulfair[1]
I-Sulfacet[1]	Sulfair 10[1]
Ocu-Sul-10[1]	Sulfair 15[1]
Ocu-Sul-15[1]	Sulfair Forte[1]
Ocu-Sul-30[1]	Sulfamide[1]
Ocusulf-10[1]	Sulten-10[1]
Ophthacet[1]	

In Canada—

Ak-Sulf[1]	Isopto-Cetamide[1]
Bleph-10[1]	Sodium Sulamyd[1]
Cetamide[1]	Sulfex[1]

Another commonly used name for sulfisoxazole is sulfafurazole[2].

Note: For quick reference, the following sulfonamides are numbered to match the corresponding brand names.

This information applies to the following medicines:
1. Sulfacetamide (sul-fa-SEE-ta-mide) ‡
2. Sulfisoxazole (sul-fi-SOX-a-zole)

‡Generic name product may be available in the U.S.

Description

Sulfonamides (sul-FON-a-mides), or sulfa medicines, belong to the family of medicines called anti-infectives. Sulfonamide ophthalmic preparations are used to treat infections of the eye.

Sulfonamides are available only with your doctor's prescription, in the following dosage forms:

Ophthalmic
Sulfacetamide
- Ophthalmic ointment (U.S. and Canada)
- Ophthalmic solution (eye drops) (U.S. and Canada)
Sulfisoxazole
- Ophthalmic ointment (U.S.)
- Ophthalmic solution (eye drops) (U.S.)

Before Using This Medicine

In deciding to use a medicine, the risks of using the medicine must be weighed against the good it will do. This is a decision you and your doctor will make. For sulfonamide ophthalmic preparations, the following should be considered:

Allergies—Tell your doctor if you have ever had any unusual or allergic reaction to any of the sulfa medicines; furosemide (e.g., Lasix) or thiazide diuretics (water pills); oral an-

tidiabetics (diabetes medicine you take by mouth); or glaucoma medicine you take by mouth (for example, acetazolamide [e.g., Diamox], dichlorphenamide [e.g., Daranide], or methazolamide [e.g., Neptazane]). Also tell your health care professional if you are allergic to any other substances, such as preservatives.

Pregnancy—Sulfonamide ophthalmic preparations have not been shown to cause birth defects or other problems in humans.

Breast-feeding—Sulfonamide ophthalmic preparations have not been reported to cause problems in nursing babies.

Children—Studies on sulfonamide ophthalmic preparations have been done only in adult patients, and there is no specific information comparing use in children with use in other age groups.

Older adults—Many medicines have not been studied specifically in older people. Therefore, it may not be known whether they work exactly the same way they do in younger adults or if they cause different side effects or problems in older people. There is no specific information comparing use of sulfonamides in the elderly with use in other age groups.

Other medicines—Although certain medicines should not be used together at all, in other cases two different medicines may be used together even if an interaction might occur. In these cases, your doctor may want to change the dose, or other precautions may be necessary. When you are taking sulfonamide ophthalmic preparations, it is especially important that your health care professional know if you are using any of the following:

- Silver preparations, such as silver nitrate or mild silver protein for the eye—Sulfonamide ophthalmic preparations should not be used with silver ophthalmic preparations, since a chemical reaction may occur.

Proper Use of This Medicine

For patients using the *eye drop form* of sulfonamides:
- The bottle is only partially full to provide proper drop control.
- To use:
  —First, wash your hands. Then tilt the head back and pull the lower eyelid away from the eye to form a pouch. Drop the medicine into the pouch and gently close the eyes. Do not blink. Keep the eyes closed for 1 or 2 minutes to allow the medicine to come into contact with the infection.
  —If you think you did not get the drop of medicine into your eye properly, use another drop.
  —To keep the medicine as germ-free as possible, do not touch the applicator tip to any surface (including the eye). Also, keep the container tightly closed.

For patients using the *eye ointment form* of sulfonamides:
- To use:
  —First, wash your hands. Then pull the lower eyelid away from the eye to form a pouch. Squeeze a thin strip of ointment into the pouch. A 1.25- to 2.5-cm (approximately ½- to 1-inch) strip of ointment is usually enough unless otherwise directed by your doctor. Gently close the eyes and keep them closed for 1 or 2 minutes to allow the medicine to come into contact with the infection.
  —To keep the medicine as germ-free as possible, do not touch the applicator tip to any surface (including the eye). After using sulfonamides eye ointment,

wipe the tip of the ointment tube with a clean tissue and keep the tube tightly closed.

To help clear up your infection completely, *keep using this medicine for the full time of treatment*, even if your symptoms have disappeared. *Do not miss any doses.*

Dosing—The dose of ophthalmic sulfonamides will be different for different patients. *Follow your doctor's orders or the directions on the label*. The following information includes only the average doses of ophthalmic sulfonamides. *If your dose is different, do not change it* unless your doctor tells you to do so.

The number of doses you use each day, the time allowed between doses, and the length of time you use the medicine depend on the medical problem for which you are using ophthalmic sulfonamides.

For sulfacetamide
- For eye infections:
  —For *ophthalmic* dosage forms (ointment):
  - Adults and adolescents—Use four times a day and at bedtime.
  - Children—Use and dose must be determined by your doctor.
  —For *ophthalmic* dosage forms (solution):
  - Adults and adolescents—One drop every one to three hours during the day and less often during the night.
  - Children—Use and dose must be determined by your doctor.

For sulfisoxazole
- For eye infections:
  —For *ophthalmic* dosage forms (ointment):
  - Adults and children—Use one to three times a day and at bedtime.
  —For *ophthalmic* dosage forms (solution):
  - Adults and adolescents—One drop three or more times a day.
  - Children—
    —Infants up to 2 months of age: Use and dose must be determined by your doctor.
    —Infants and children 2 months of age and older: One drop three or more times a day.

Missed dose—If you miss a dose of this medicine, apply it as soon as possible. However, if it is almost time for your next dose, skip the missed dose and go back to your regular dosing schedule.

Storage—To store this medicine:
- Keep out of the reach of children.
- Store away from heat and direct light.
- Keep sulfacetamide eye drops in a cool place. Keep all dosage forms of these medicines from freezing.
- Do not keep outdated medicine or medicine no longer needed. Be sure that any discarded medicine is out of the reach of children.

Precautions While Using This Medicine

After application, eye ointments usually cause your vision to blur for a few minutes.

After application of this medicine to the eye, occasional stinging or burning may be expected.

If your symptoms do not improve within a few days, or if they become worse, check with your doctor.

Side Effects of This Medicine

Along with its needed effects, a medicine may cause some unwanted effects. Although not all of these side effects may occur, if they do occur they may need medical attention.

Check with your doctor as soon as possible if any of the following side effects occur:
> *More common*
>> Itching, redness, swelling, or other sign of irritation not present before use of this medicine

Other side effects not listed above may also occur in some patients. If you notice any other effects, check with your doctor.

Revised: 07/01/93

SULFONAMIDES   Systemic

Commonly used brand name(s):

In the U.S.—
  Gantanol[3]
  Gantrisin[4]
  Thiosulfil Forte[2]

In Canada—
  Apo-Sulfamethoxazole[3]
  Apo-Sulfisoxazole[4]
  Novo-Soxazole[4]

Note: For quick reference, the following sulfonamides are numbered to match the corresponding brand names.

This information applies to the following medicines:
1. Sulfadiazine (sul-fa-DYE-a-zeen) ‡§
2. Sulfamethizole (sul-fa-METH-a-zole) †
3. Sulfamethoxazole (sul-fa-meth-OX-a-zole) §
4. Sulfisoxazole (sul-fi-SOX-a-zole) ‡

†Not commercially available in Canada.
‡Generic name product may be available in the U.S.
§Generic name product may be available in Canada.

Description

Sulfonamides (sul-FON-a-mides) or sulfa medicines are used to treat infections. They will not work for colds, flu, or other virus infections.

Sulfonamides are available only with your doctor's prescription, in the following dosage forms:
> *Oral*
>> Sulfadiazine
>> - Tablets (U.S. and Canada)
>> Sulfamethizole
>> - Tablets (U.S.)
>> Sulfamethoxazole
>> - Tablets (U.S. and Canada)
>> Sulfisoxazole
>> - Oral suspension (U.S.)
>> - Syrup (U.S.)
>> - Tablets (U.S. and Canada)

Before Using This Medicine

In deciding to use a medicine, the risks of taking the medicine must be weighed against the good it will do. This is a decision

you and your doctor will make. For sulfonamides, the following should be considered:

Allergies—Tell your doctor if you have ever had any unusual or allergic reaction to sulfa medicines, furosemide (e.g., Lasix) or thiazide diuretics (water pills), oral antidiabetics (diabetes medicine you take by mouth), glaucoma medicine you take by mouth (for example, acetazolamide [e.g., Diamox], dichlorphenamide [e.g., Daranide], or methazolamide [e.g., Neptazane]). Also tell your health care professional if you are allergic to any other substances, such as foods, preservatives, or dyes.

Pregnancy—Studies have not been done in pregnant women. However, studies in mice, rats, and rabbits have shown that some sulfonamides cause birth defects, including cleft palate and bone problems. Sulfonamides are not recommended for use at the time of labor and delivery. These medicines may cause unwanted effects in the baby.

Breast-feeding—Sulfonamides pass into the breast milk. This medicine is not recommended for use during breast-feeding. It may cause liver problems, anemia, and other unwanted effects in nursing babies, especially those with glucose-6-phosphate dehydrogenase (G6PD) deficiency.

Children—Sulfonamides should not be given to infants under 2 months of age unless directed by the child's doctor, because they may cause unwanted effects.

Older adults—Elderly people are especially sensitive to the effects of sulfonamides. Severe skin problems and blood problems may be more likely to occur in the elderly. These problems may also be more likely to occur in patients who are taking diuretics (water pills) along with this medicine.

Other medicines—Although certain medicines should not be used together at all, in other cases two different medicines may be used together even if an interaction might occur. In these cases, your doctor may want to change the dose, or other precautions may be necessary. When you are taking sulfonamides, it is especially important that your health care professional knows if you are taking any of the following:

- Acetaminophen (e.g., Tylenol) (with long-term, high-dose use) or
- Amiodarone (e.g., Cordarone) or
- Anabolic steroids (nandrolone [e.g., Anabolin], oxandrolone [e.g., Anavar], oxymetholone [e.g., Anadrol], stanozolol [e.g., Winstrol]) or
- Androgens (male hormones) or
- Antithyroid agents (medicine for overactive thyroid) or
- Carbamazepine (e.g., Tegretol) or
- Carmustine (e.g., BiCNU) or
- Chloroquine (e.g., Aralen) or
- Dantrolene (e.g., Dantrium) or
- Daunorubicin (e.g., Cerubidine) or
- Disulfiram (e.g., Antabuse) or
- Divalproex (e.g., Depakote) or
- Estrogens (female hormones) or
- Etretinate (e.g., Tegison) or
- Gold salts (medicine for arthritis) or
- Hydroxychloroquine (e.g., Plaquenil) or
- Mercaptopurine (e.g., Purinethol) or
- Naltrexone (e.g., Trexan) (with long-term, high-dose use) or
- Oral contraceptives (birth control pills) containing estrogens or
- Other anti-infectives by mouth or by injection (medicine for infection) or

- Phenothiazines (acetophenazine [e.g., Tindal], chlorpromazine [e.g., Thorazine], fluphenazine [e.g., Prolixin], mesoridazine [e.g., Serentil], perphenazine [e.g., Trilafon], prochlorperazine [e.g., Compazine], promazine [e.g., Sparine], promethazine [e.g., Phenergan], thioridazine [e.g., Mellaril], trifluoperazine [e.g., Stelazine], triflupromazine [e.g., Vesprin], trimeprazine [e.g., Temaril]) or
- Plicamycin (e.g., Mithracin) or
- Valproic acid (e.g., Depakene)—Use of sulfonamides with these medicines may increase the chance of side effects affecting the liver

- Acetohydroxamic acid (e.g., Lithostat) or
- Dapsone or
- Furazolidone (e.g., Furoxone) or
- Nitrofurantoin (e.g., Furadantin) or
- Primaquine or
- Procainamide (e.g., Pronestyl) or
- Quinidine (e.g., Quinidex) or
- Quinine (e.g., Quinamm) or
- Sulfoxone (e.g., Diasone) or
- Vitamin K (e.g., AquaMEPHYTON, Synkayvite)—Use of sulfonamides with these medicines may increase the chance of side effects affecting the blood

- Anticoagulants (blood thinners) or
- Ethotoin (e.g., Peganone) or
- Mephenytoin (e.g., Mesantoin)—Use of sulfonamides with these medicines may increase the chance of side effects of these medicines

- Antidiabetics, oral (diabetes medicine you take by mouth)—Use of oral antidiabetics with sulfonamides may increase the chance of side effects affecting the blood and/or the side effects of oral antidiabetics

- Methenamine (e.g., Mandelamine)—Use of this medicine with sulfonamides may increase the chance of side effects of sulfonamides

- Methotrexate (e.g., Mexate) or
- Phenytoin (e.g., Dilantin)—Use of these medicines with sulfonamides may increase the chance of side effects affecting the liver and/or the side effects of these medicines

- Methyldopa (e.g., Aldomet)—Use of methyldopa with sulfonamides may increase the chance of side effects affecting the liver and/or the blood

Other medical problems—The presence of other medical problems may affect the use of sulfonamides. Make sure you tell your doctor if you have any other medical problems, especially:

- Anemia or other blood problems or
- Glucose-6-phosphate dehydrogenase (G6PD) deficiency—Patients with these problems may have an increase in side effects affecting the blood

- Kidney disease or
- Liver disease—Patients with kidney and/or liver disease may have an increased chance of side effects

- Porphyria—This medicine may bring on an attack of porphyria

Proper Use of This Medicine

Sulfonamides should not be given to infants less than 2 months of age unless directed by the patient's doctor because sulfonamides may cause serious unwanted effects.

Sulfonamides are best taken with a full glass (8 ounces) of water. Several additional glasses of water should be taken every day, unless otherwise directed by your doctor. Drinking extra water will help to prevent some unwanted effects of sulfonamides.

For patients taking the *oral liquid form* of this medicine:

- Use a specially marked measuring spoon or other device to measure each dose accurately. The average household teaspoon may not hold the right amount of liquid.

To help clear up your infection completely, *keep taking this medicine for the full time of treatment*, even if you begin to feel better after a few days. If you stop taking this medicine too soon, your symptoms may return.

This medicine works best when there is a constant amount in the blood or urine. *To help keep the amount constant, do not miss any doses. Also, it is best to take the doses at evenly spaced times day and night.* If you need help in planning the best times to take your medicine, check with your health care professional.

Dosing—The dose of these medicines will be different for different patients. *Follow your doctor's orders or the directions on the label.* The following information includes only the average doses of these medicines. *If your dose is different, do not change it* unless your doctor tells you to do so.

For sulfadiazine
- For *tablet* dosage form:
  —For bacterial or protozoal infections:
  - Adults and teenagers—2 to 4 grams for the first dose, then 2 to 4 grams every four to six hours.
  - Children up to 2 months of age—Use is not recommended.
  - Children 2 months of age and older—Dose is based on body weight. The usual dose is 75 milligrams (mg) per kilogram (kg) (34 mg per pound) of body weight for the first dose, then 37.5 mg per kg (17 mg per pound) of body weight every six hours, or 25 mg per kg (11.4 mg per pound) of body weight every four hours.

For sulfamethizole
- For *tablet* dosage form:
  —For bacterial infections:
  - Adults and teenagers—500 milligrams (mg) to 1 gram every six to eight hours.
  - Children up to 2 months of age—Use is not recommended.
  - Children 2 months of age and older—Dose is based on body weight. The usual dose is 7.5 to 11.25 mg per kilogram (kg) (3.4 to 5.1 mg per pound) of body weight every six hours.

For sulfamethoxazole
- For *tablet* dosage form:
  —For bacterial or protozoal infections:
  - Adults and teenagers—2 to 4 grams for the first dose, then 1 to 2 grams every eight to twelve hours.
  - Children up to 2 months of age—Use and dose must be determined by your doctor.
  - Children 2 months of age and older—Dose is based on body weight. The usual dose is 50 to 60 milligrams (mg) per kilogram (kg) (22.7 to 27.3 mg per pound) of body weight for the first dose, then

25 to 30 mg per kg (11.4 to 13.6 mg per pound) of body weight every twelve hours.

For sulfisoxazole
- For *suspension, syrup, or tablet* dosage forms:
  —For bacterial or protozoal infections:
  - Adults and teenagers—2 to 4 grams for the first dose, then 750 milligrams (mg) to 1.5 grams every four hours; or 1 to 2 grams every six hours.
  - Children up to 2 months of age—Use and dose must be determined by your doctor.
  - Children 2 months of age and older—Dose is based on body weight. The usual dose is 75 mg per kilogram (kg) (34 mg per pound) of body weight for the first dose, then 25 mg per kg (11.4 mg per pound) of body weight every four hours, or 37.5 mg per kg (17 mg per pound) of body weight every six hours.

Missed dose—If you miss a dose of this medicine, take it as soon as possible. This will help to keep a constant amount of medicine in the blood or urine. However, if it is almost time for your next dose, skip the missed dose and go back to your regular dosing schedule. Do not double doses.

Storage—To store this medicine:
- Keep out of the reach of children.
- Store away from heat and direct light.
- Do not store the tablet form of this medicine in the bathroom, near the kitchen sink, or in other damp places. Heat or moisture may cause the medicine to break down.
- Keep the oral liquid forms of this medicine from freezing.
- Do not keep outdated medicine or medicine no longer needed. Be sure that any discarded medicine is out of the reach of children.

Precautions While Using This Medicine

It is very important that your doctor check your progress at regular visits. This medicine may cause blood problems, especially if it is taken for a long time.

If your symptoms do not improve within a few days, or if they become worse, check with your doctor.

Sulfonamides may cause blood problems. These problems may result in a greater chance of certain infections, slow healing, and bleeding of the gums. Therefore, you should be careful when using regular toothbrushes, dental floss, and toothpicks. Dental work should be delayed until your blood counts have returned to normal. Check with your medical doctor or dentist if you have any questions about proper oral hygiene (mouth care) during treatment.

Sulfonamides may cause your skin to be more sensitive to sunlight than it is normally. Exposure to sunlight, even for brief periods of time, may cause a skin rash, itching, redness or other discoloration of the skin, or a severe sunburn. When you begin taking this medicine:

- Stay out of direct sunlight, especially between the hours of 10:00 a.m. and 3:00 p.m., if possible.
- Wear protective clothing, including a hat. Also, wear sunglasses.
- Apply a sun block product that has a skin protection factor (SPF) of at least 15. Some patients may require a product with a higher SPF number, especially if they have a fair complexion. If you have any questions about this, check with your health care professional.

- Apply a sun block lipstick that has an SPF of at least 15 to protect your lips.
- Do not use a sunlamp or tanning bed or booth.

If you have a severe reaction from the sun, check with your doctor.

This medicine may also cause some people to become dizzy. *Make sure you know how you react to this medicine before you drive, use machines, or do anything else that could be dangerous if you are dizzy or are not alert.* If this reaction is especially bothersome, check with your doctor.

Side Effects of This Medicine

Along with its needed effects, a medicine may cause some unwanted effects. Although not all of these side effects may occur, if they do occur they may need medical attention.

Check with your doctor immediately if any of the following side effects occur:

More common
   Itching; skin rash

Less common
   Aching of joints and muscles; difficulty in swallowing; pale skin; redness, blistering, peeling, or loosening of skin; sore throat and fever; unusual bleeding or bruising; unusual tiredness or weakness; yellow eyes or skin

Rare
   Abdominal or stomach cramps and pain (severe); abdominal tenderness; blood in urine; diarrhea (watery and severe), which may also be bloody; greatly increased or decreased frequency of urination or amount of urine; increased thirst; lower back pain; mood or mental changes; pain or burning while urinating; swelling of front part of neck

   Note: Some of the above side effects (severe abdominal or stomach cramps and pain, and watery and severe diarrhea, which may also be bloody) may also occur up to several weeks after you stop taking any of these medicines.

Also, check with your doctor as soon as possible if the following side effect occurs:

More common
   Increased sensitivity of skin to sunlight

Other side effects may occur that usually do not need medical attention. These side effects may go away during treatment as your body adjusts to the medicine. However, check with your doctor if any of the following side effects continue or are bothersome:

More common
   Diarrhea; dizziness; headache; loss of appetite; nausea or vomiting; tiredness

Other side effects not listed above may also occur in some patients. If you notice any other effects, check with your doctor.

Revised: 08/25/95

SULFONAMIDES   Vaginal

Commonly used brand name(s):

In the U.S.—
   AVC[1]
   Sultrin[2]
   Trysul[2]

In Canada—
   AVC[1]
   Sultrin[2]

Another commonly used name is sulfathiazole, sulfacetamide, and sulfabenzamide[2].

Note: For quick reference, the following vaginal sulfonamides are numbered to match the corresponding brand names.

This information applies to the following medicines
   1. Sulfanilamide (sul-fa-NILL-a-mide) ‡
   2. Triple Sulfa (TRI-pel SUL-fa) ‡

‡Generic name product may be available in the U.S.

Description

Sulfonamides (sul-FON-a-mides), or sulfa medicines, are used to treat bacterial infections. They work by killing bacteria or preventing their growth.

Vaginal sulfonamides are used to treat bacterial infections. These medicines may also be used for other problems as determined by your doctor.

Vaginal sulfonamides are available only with your doctor's prescription, in the following dosage forms:

Vaginal
   Sulfanilamide
   - Cream (U.S. and Canada)
   - Suppositories (U.S.)
   Triple Sulfa
   - Cream (U.S. and Canada)
   - Tablets (U.S.)

Before Using This Medicine

In deciding to use a medicine, the risks of using the medicine must be weighed against the good it will do. This is a decision you and your doctor will make. For vaginal sulfonamides, the following should be considered:

Allergies—Tell your doctor if you have ever had any unusual or allergic reaction to any of the sulfa medicines, furosemide (e.g., Lasix) or thiazide diuretics (water pills), oral antidiabetics (diabetes medicine you take by mouth), or glaucoma medicine you take by mouth (for example, acetazolamide [e.g., Diamox], dichlorphenamide [e.g., Daranide], or methazolamide [e.g., Neptazane]). Also tell your health care professional if you are allergic to any other substances, such as foods, preservatives, or dyes, including to parabens, lanolin, or peanut oil.

Pregnancy—Studies have not been done in humans. However, vaginal sulfonamides are absorbed through the vagina into the bloodstream and appear in the bloodstream of the fetus. Studies in rats and mice given high doses by mouth have shown that certain sulfonamides cause birth defects.

Breast-feeding—Vaginal sulfonamides are absorbed through the vagina into the bloodstream and pass into the breast milk. Use is not recommended in nursing mothers. Vaginal sulfonamides may cause liver problems in nursing babies. These medicines may also cause anemia in nursing babies with glucose-6-phosphate dehydrogenase (G6PD) deficiency.

Children—Studies on this medicine have been done only in adult patients and there is no specific information comparing the use of vaginal sulfonamides in children with use in other age groups.

Older adults—Many medicines have not been studied specifically in older people. Therefore, it may not be known whether they work exactly the same way they do in younger adults or if they cause different side effects or problems in older people. There is no specific information comparing the use of vaginal sulfonamides in the elderly with use in other age groups.

Other medicines—Although certain medicines should not be used together at all, in other cases two different medicines may be used together even if an interaction might occur. In these cases, your doctor may want to change the dose, or other precautions may be necessary. Tell your health care professional if you are taking or using any other prescription or nonprescription (over-the-counter [OTC]) medicine.

Other medical problems—The presence of other medical problems may affect the use of vaginal sulfonamides. Make sure you tell your doctor if you have any other medical problems, especially:

- Glucose-6-phosphate dehydrogenase (G6PD) deficiency—Anemia (a blood problem) can occur if sulfonamides are used

- Kidney disease

- Porphyria—Sulfonamides can cause porphyria attacks

Proper Use of This Medicine

Vaginal sulfonamides usually come with patient directions. Read them carefully before using this medicine.

This medicine is usually inserted into the vagina with an applicator. However, if you are pregnant, check with your doctor before using the applicator.

To help clear up your infection completely, *it is very important that you keep using this medicine for the full time of treatment*, even if your symptoms begin to clear up after a few days. If you stop using this medicine too soon, your symptoms may return. *Do not miss any doses*. Also, *do not stop using this medicine if your menstrual period starts during the time of treatment*.

Dosing—The dose of these medicines will be different for different patients. *Follow your doctor's orders or the directions on the label*. The following information includes only the average doses of these medicines. *If your dose is different, do not change it* unless your doctor tells you to do so.

For sulfanilamide
- For *vaginal cream* dosage form:
  —For bacterial infections:
    - Adults and teenagers—One applicatorful (approximately 6 grams) inserted into the vagina one or two times a day for thirty days.
    - Children—Use and dose must be determined by your doctor.

- For *vaginal suppositories* dosage form:
  —For bacterial infections:
    - Adults and teenagers—One suppository inserted into the vagina one or two times a day for thirty days.
    - Children—Use and dose must be determined by your doctor.

For triple sulfa
- For *vaginal cream* dosage form:
  —For bacterial infections:
    - Adults and teenagers—At first, one applicatorful (approximately 4 to 5 grams) inserted into the vagina two times a day for four to six days. Then, your doctor may lower your dose to one-half to one-quarter applicatorful two times a day. Use when you wake up and just before you go to bed.
    - Children—Use and dose must be determined by your doctor.

- For *vaginal tablets* dosage form:
  —For bacterial infections:
    - Adults and teenagers—One tablet inserted into the vagina two times a day for ten days.
    - Children—Use and dose must be determined by your doctor.

Missed dose—If you miss a dose of this medicine, insert it as soon as possible. However, if it is almost time for your next dose, skip the missed dose and go back to your regular dosing schedule.

Storage—To store this medicine:
- Keep out of the reach of children.
- Store away from heat and direct light.
- Do not store the vaginal tablet or vaginal suppository form of this medicine in the bathroom, near the kitchen sink, or in other damp places. Heat or moisture may cause the medicine to break down.
- Keep the vaginal cream and vaginal suppository forms of this medicine from freezing.
- Do not keep outdated medicine or medicine no longer needed. Be sure that any discarded medicine is out of the reach of children.

Precautions While Using This Medicine

If your symptoms do not improve within a few days, or if they become worse, check with your doctor.

Vaginal medicines usually will slowly work their way out of the vagina during treatment. To keep the medicine from soiling or staining your clothing, a sanitary napkin may be worn. Minipads, clean paper tissues, or paper diapers may also be used. However, the use of tampons is not recommended since they may soak up too much of the medicine. In addition, tampons may be more likely to slip out of the vagina if you use them during treatment with this medicine.

To help clear up your infection completely and to help make sure it does not return, good health habits are also required.

- Wear cotton panties (or panties or pantyhose with cotton crotches) instead of synthetic (for example, nylon or rayon) underclothes.
- Wear only freshly washed underclothes.

If you have any questions about this, check with your health care professional.

Many vaginal infections are spread by sexual intercourse. The male sexual partner may carry the fungus or other organism in his reproductive tract. Therefore, it may be desirable that your partner wear a condom (prophylactic) during intercourse to keep the infection from returning. Also, it may be necessary for your partner to be treated at the same time you are being treated to avoid passing the infection back and forth. In addition, *do not stop using this medicine if you have intercourse during treatment*.

Some patients who use vaginal medicines may prefer to use a douche for cleansing purposes before inserting the next dose of medicine. Some doctors recommend a vinegar and water or other douche. However, others do not recommend douching at all. If you do use a douche, *do not overfill the vagina with douche solution*. To do so may force the solution up into the uterus (womb) and may cause inflammation or infection. Also, *do not douche if you are pregnant since this may harm the fetus*. If you have any questions about this or which douche products are best for you, check with your health care professional.

Side Effects of This Medicine

Studies in rats have shown that long-term use of sulfonamides may cause cancer of the thyroid gland. In addition, studies in rats have shown that sulfonamides may increase the chance of goiters (noncancerous tumors of the thyroid gland).

Along with its needed effects, a medicine may cause some unwanted effects. Although not all of these side effects may occur, if they do occur they may need medical attention.

Check with your doctor immediately if any of the following side effects occur:

Less common
 Itching, burning, skin rash, redness, swelling, or other sign of irritation not present before use of this medicine

Rare
 Burning at site of application

Other side effects may occur that usually do not need medical attention. These side effects may go away during treatment as your body adjusts to the medicine. However, check with your doctor if either of the following side effects continues or is bothersome:

Less common or rare
 Rash or irritation of penis of sexual partner

Other side effects not listed above may also occur in some patients. If you notice any other effects, check with your doctor.

Revised: 08/13/98

SULFONAMIDES AND PHENAZOPYRIDINE Systemic

Commonly used brand name(s):

In the U.S.—
 Azo Gantanol[1]   Azo-Sulfisoxazole[2]
 Azo Gantrisin[2]   Azo-Truxazole[2]
 Azo-Sulfamethoxazole[1] Sul-Azo[2]

Note: For quick reference, the following sulfonamides and phenazopyridine combinations are numbered to match the corresponding brand names.

This information applies to the following medicines:
1. Sulfamethoxazole and Phenazopyridine (sul-fa-meth-OX-a-zole and fen-az-oh-PEER-i-deen) †‡
2. Sulfisoxazole and Phenazopyridine (sul-fi-SOX-a-zole and fen-az-oh-PEER-i-deen) ‡

---

†Not commercially available in Canada.
‡Generic name product may be available in the U.S.

Description

Sulfonamides and phenazopyridine, combination products containing a sulfa medicine and a urinary pain reliever, are used to treat infections of the urinary tract and to help relieve the pain, burning, and irritation of these infections.

Sulfonamides and phenazopyridine combinations are available only with your doctor's prescription, in the following dosage forms:

Oral
 Sulfamethoxazole and Phenazopyridine
  • Tablets (U.S.)
 Sulfisoxazole and Phenazopyridine
  • Tablets (U.S. and Canada)

Before Using This Medicine

In deciding to use a medicine, the risks of taking the medicine must be weighed against the good it will do. This is a decision you and your doctor will make. For sulfonamides and phenazopyridine, the following should be considered:

Allergies—Tell your doctor if you have ever had any unusual or allergic reaction to any of the sulfa medicines, furosemide (e.g., Lasix) or thiazide diuretics (water pills), oral antidiabetics (diabetes medicine you take by mouth), glaucoma medicine you take by mouth (for example, acetazolamide [e.g., Diamox], dichlorphenamide [e.g., Daranide], methazolamide [e.g., Neptazane]), or phenazopyridine (e.g., Pyridium). Also tell your health care professional if you are allergic to any other substances, such as foods, preservatives, or dyes.

Pregnancy—Studies have not been done in humans. Studies in mice, rats, and rabbits have shown that some sulfonamides cause birth defects, including cleft palate and bone problems. In addition, sulfa medicines may cause liver problems in newborn infants. Therefore, use is not recommended during pregnancy. Phenazopyridine has not been shown to cause birth defects in animal studies.

Breast-feeding—Sulfonamides pass into the breast milk. This medicine is not recommended for use during breast-feeding. It may cause liver problems, anemia, and other unwanted effects in nursing babies, especially those with glucose-6-phosphate dehydrogenase (G6PD) deficiency.

Children—This medicine has been tested in a limited number of children 12 years of age or older. In effective doses, the medicine has not been shown to cause different side effects or problems in children than it does in adults.

Older adults—Elderly people are especially sensitive to the effects of sulfonamides. Severe skin problems and blood problems may be more likely to occur in the elderly. These problems may also be more likely to occur in patients who are taking diuretics (water pills) along with this medicine.

Other medicines—Although certain medicines should not be used together at all, in other cases two different medicines may be used together even if an interaction might occur. In these cases, your doctor may want to change the dose, or other precautions may be necessary. When you are taking sulfonamides and phenazopyridine, it is especially important that your health care professional know if you are taking any of the following:

- Acetaminophen (e.g., Tylenol) (with long-term, high-dose use) or
- Amiodarone (e.g., Cordarone) or
- Anabolic steroids (nandrolone [e.g., Anabolin], oxandrolone [e.g., Anavar], oxymetholone [e.g., Anadrol], stanozolol [e.g., Winstrol]) or
- Androgens (male hormones) or
- Antithyroid agents (medicine for overactive thyroid) or
- Carbamazepine (e.g., Tegretol) or
- Carmustine (e.g., BiCNU) or
- Chloroquine (e.g., Aralen) or
- Dantrolene (e.g., Dantrium) or
- Daunorubicin (e.g., Cerubidine) or
- Disulfiram (e.g., Antabuse) or
- Divalproex (e.g., Depakote) or
- Estrogens (female hormones) or
- Etretinate (e.g., Tegison) or
- Gold salts (medicine for arthritis) or
- Hydroxychloroquine (e.g., Plaquenil) or
- Mercaptopurine (e.g., Purinethol) or
- Naltrexone (e.g., Trexan) (with long-term, high-dose use) or
- Oral contraceptives (birth control pills) containing estrogen or
- Other anti-infectives by mouth or by injection (medicine for infection) or
- Phenothiazines (acetophenazine [e.g., Tindal], chlorpromazine [e.g., Thorazine], fluphenazine [e.g., Prolixin], mesoridazine [e.g., Serentil], perphenazine [e.g., Trilafon], prochlorperazine [e.g., Compazine], promazine [e.g., Sparine], promethazine [e.g., Phenergan], thioridazine [e.g., Mellaril], trifluoperazine [e.g., Stelazine], triflupromazine [e.g., Vesprin], trimeprazine [e.g., Temaril]) or
- Plicamycin (e.g., Mithracin) or
- Valproic acid (e.g., Depakene)—Use of sulfonamides and phenazopyridine combination with these medicines may increase the chance of side effects affecting the liver
- Acetohydroxamic acid (e.g., Lithostat) or
- Dapsone or
- Furazolidone (e.g., Furoxone) or
- Nitrofurantoin (e.g., Furadantin) or
- Primaquine or
- Procainamide (e.g., Pronestyl) or
- Quinidine (e.g., Quinidex) or
- Quinine (e.g., Quinamm) or
- Sulfoxone (e.g., Diasone) or
- Vitamin K (e.g., AquaMEPHYTON, Synkayvite)—Use of sulfonamides and phenazopyridine combination with these medicines may increase the chance of side effects affecting the blood
- Anticoagulants (blood thinners) or
- Ethotoin (e.g., Peganone) or
- Heparin or

- Mephenytoin (e.g., Mesantoin)—Use of sulfonamides and phenazopyridine combination with these medicines may increase the chance of side effects of these medicines
- Antidiabetics, oral (diabetes medicine you take by mouth)—Use of oral antidiabetics with sulfonamides and phenazopyridine combination may increase the chance of side effects affecting the blood and/or the side effects of oral antidiabetics
- Methenamine (e.g., Mandelamine) or
- Methenamine-containing medicines (e.g., Urised)—Use of these medicines with sulfonamides and phenazopyridine combination may increase the chance of side effects of the sulfonamides
- Methotrexate (e.g., Mexate)—Use of methotrexate with sulfonamides and phenazopyridine combination may increase the chance of side effects affecting the liver and/or the side effects of methotrexate
- Methyldopa (e.g., Aldomet)—Use of methyldopa with sulfonamides and phenazopyridine combination may increase the chance of side effects affecting the liver and/or the blood
- Phenytoin (e.g., Dilantin)—Use of phenytoin with sulfonamides and phenazopyridine combination may increase the chance of side effects affecting the liver and/or the side effects of phenytoin

Other medical problems—The presence of other medical problems may affect the use of sulfonamides and phenazopyridine. Make sure you tell your doctor if you have any other medical problems, especially:

- Anemia or other blood problems or
- Glucose-6-phosphate dehydrogenase deficiency (lack of G6PD enzyme)—Patients with these problems may have an increase in side effects affecting the blood
- Hepatitis or other liver disease or
- Kidney disease—Patients with kidney disease or liver disease may have an increased chance of side effects
- Porphyria—Use of sulfonamides may bring on an attack of porphyria

Proper Use of This Medicine

Sulfonamides and phenazopyridine combinations are best taken with a full glass (8 ounces) of water. Several additional glasses of water should be taken every day, unless otherwise directed by your doctor. Drinking extra water will help to prevent some unwanted effects (e.g., kidney stones) of the sulfonamide. This medicine may be taken with meals or following meals if it upsets your stomach.

To help clear up your infection completely, *keep taking this medicine for the full time of treatment,* even if you begin to feel better after a few days. If you stop taking this medicine too soon, your symptoms may return.

This medicine works best when there is a constant amount in the urine. *To help keep the amount constant, do not miss any doses. Also, it is best to take the doses at evenly spaced times, day and night.* For example, if you are to take 4 doses a day, the doses should be spaced about 6 hours apart. If this interferes with your sleep or other daily activities, or if you need help in planning the best times to take your medicine, check with your health care professional.

Dosing—The dose of sulfonamides and phenazopyridine combination may be different for different patients. *Follow* *your doctor's orders or the directions on the label.* The following information includes only the average doses of sulfonamides and phenazopyridine combination. Your dose may be different if you have kidney disease. *If your dose is different, do not change it* unless your doctor tells you to do so.

- For *sulfamethoxazole and phenazopyridine combination:*
  —Adults and children 12 years of age and older: 2 grams of sulfamethoxazole and 400 mg of phenazopyridine for the first dose, then 1 gram of sulfamethoxazole and 200 mg of phenazopyridine every twelve hours for up to two days.
  —Children up to 12 years of age: This medication is not recommended.
- For *sulfisoxazole and phenazopyridine combination:*
  —Adults and children 12 years of age and older: 2 to 3 grams of sulfisoxazole and 200 to 300 mg of phenazopyridine for the first dose, then 1 gram of sulfisoxazole and 100 mg of phenazopyridine every twelve hours for up to two days.
  —Children up to 12 years of age: This medication is not recommended.

Missed dose—If you miss a dose of this medicine, take it as soon as possible. This will help to keep a constant amount of medicine in the urine. However, if it is almost time for your next dose, skip the missed dose and go back to your regular dosing schedule. Do not double doses.

Storage—To store this medicine:
- Keep out of the reach of children.
- Store away from heat and direct light.
- Do not store in the bathroom, near the kitchen sink, or in other damp places. Heat or moisture may cause the medicine to break down.
- Do not keep outdated medicine or medicine no longer needed. Be sure that any discarded medicine is out of the reach of children.

Precautions While Using This Medicine

If your symptoms do not improve within a few days, or if they become worse, check with your doctor.

Sulfonamides may cause blood problems. These problems may result in a greater chance of certain infections, slow healing, and bleeding of the gums. Therefore, you should be careful when using regular toothbrushes, dental floss, and toothpicks. Dental work should be delayed until your blood counts have returned to normal. Check with your medical doctor or dentist if you have any questions about proper oral hygiene (mouth care) during treatment.

Sulfonamides may cause your skin to be more sensitive to sunlight than it is normally. Exposure to sunlight, even for brief periods of time, may cause a skin rash, itching, redness or other discoloration of the skin, or a severe sunburn. When you begin taking this medicine:
- Stay out of direct sunlight, especially between the hours of 10:00 a.m. and 3:00 p.m., if possible.
- Wear protective clothing, including a hat. Also, wear sunglasses.
- Apply a sun block product that has a skin protection factor (SPF) of at least 15. Some patients may require a product with a higher SPF number, especially if they have a fair complexion. If you have any questions about this, check with your health care professional.

- Apply a sun block lipstick that has an SPF of at least 15 to protect your lips.
- Do not use a sunlamp or tanning bed or booth.

If you have a severe reaction, check with your doctor.

This medicine may also cause some people to become dizzy. *Make sure you know how you react to this medicine before you drive, use machines, or do anything else that could be dangerous if you are dizzy or are not alert.* If this reaction is especially bothersome, check with your doctor.

This medicine causes the urine to turn reddish orange. This is to be expected while you are using this medicine and is not harmful. Also, the medicine may stain clothing. If you have any questions about removing the stain, check with your health care professional.

For diabetic patients:
- *This medicine may cause false test results with some urine sugar tests and urine ketone tests.* Check with your doctor before changing your diet or the dosage of your diabetes medicine.

Side Effects of This Medicine

Along with its needed effects, a medicine may cause some unwanted effects. Although not all of these side effects may occur, if they do occur they may need medical attention.

Check with your doctor immediately if any of the following side effects occur:

More common
  Itching; skin rash

Less common
  Aching of joints and muscles; blue or blue-purple discoloration of skin; difficulty in swallowing; pale skin; redness, blistering, peeling, or loosening of skin; shortness of breath; sore throat and fever; unusual bleeding or bruising; unusual tiredness or weakness; yellow eyes or skin

Rare
  Blood in urine; greatly increased or decreased frequency of urination or amount of urine; increased thirst; lower back pain; pain or burning while urinating; swelling of front part of neck

In addition to the side effects listed above, check with your doctor as soon as possible if the following side effect occurs:
More common
  Increased sensitivity of skin to sunlight

Other side effects may occur that usually do not need medical attention. These side effects may go away during treatment as your body adjusts to the medicine. However, check with your doctor if any of the following side effects continue or are bothersome:
More common
  Diarrhea; dizziness; headache; loss of appetite; nausea or vomiting; tiredness

Less common
  Indigestion; stomach cramps or pain

This medicine causes the urine to become reddish orange. This side effect does not require medical attention.

Other side effects not listed above may also occur in some patients. If you notice any other effects, check with your doctor.

Revised: 02/01/93

SULFONAMIDES AND TRIMETHOPRIM   Systemic

Commonly used brand name(s):

In the U.S.—

Bactrim[2]	Septra DS[2]
Bactrim DS[2]	Septra I.V.[2]
Bactrim I.V.[2]	Septra Suspension[2]
Bactrim Pediatric[2]	Septra Grape Suspension[2]
Cofatrim Forte[2]	Sulfatrim[2]
Cotrim[2]	Sulfatrim-DS[2]
Cotrim DS[2]	Sulfatrim Pediatric[2]
Cotrim Pediatric[2]	Sulfatrim S/S[2]
Septra[2]	Sulfatrim Suspension[2]

In Canada—

Apo-Sulfatrim[2]	Novo-Trimel D.S.[2]
Apo-Sulfatrim DS[2]	Nu-Cotrimox[2]
Bactrim[2]	Nu-Cotrimox DS[2]
Bactrim DS[2]	Roubac[2]
Coptin[1]	Septra[2]
Coptin 1[1]	Septra DS[2]
Novo-Trimel[2]	

Other commonly used names are:

Cotrimazine
Cotrimoxazole
SMZ-TMP

Note: For quick reference, the following sulfonamide and trimethoprim combinations are numbered to match the corresponding brand names.

This information applies to the following medicines:
1. Sulfadiazine and Trimethoprim (sul-fa-DYE-a-zeen and trye-METH-oh-prim) *
2. Sulfamethoxazole and Trimethoprim (sul-fa-meth-OX-a-zole and trye-METH-oh-prim) ‡

---

*Not commercially available in the U.S.
‡Generic name product may be available in the U.S.

Description

Sulfonamide (sul-FON-ah-mide) and trimethoprim combinations are used to prevent and treat infections. Sulfadiazine and trimethoprim combination is used to treat urinary tract infections. Sulfamethoxazole and trimethoprim combination is used to treat infections, such as bronchitis, middle ear infection, urinary tract infection, and traveler's diarrhea. It is also used for the prevention and treatment of *Pneumocystis carinii* pneumonia (PCP). These medicines will not work for colds, flu, or other virus infections. They may also be used for other conditions as determined by your doctor.

Sulfonamide and trimethoprim combinations are available only with your doctor's prescription, in the following dosage forms:

Oral
Sulfadiazine and Trimethoprim
  • Oral suspension (Canada)
  • Tablets (Canada)
Sulfamethoxazole and Trimethoprim
  • Oral suspension (U.S. and Canada)
  • Tablets (U.S. and Canada)

Parenteral
Sulfamethoxazole and Trimethoprim
  • Injection (U.S. and Canada)

Before Using This Medicine

In deciding to use a medicine, the risks of taking the medicine must be weighed against the good it will do. This is a decision you and your doctor will make. For sulfonamide and trimethoprim combinations, the following should be considered:

Allergies—Tell your doctor if you have ever had any unusual or allergic reaction to sulfa medicines, furosemide (e.g., Lasix) or thiazide diuretics (water pills), oral antidiabetics (diabetes medicine you take by mouth), glaucoma medicine you take by mouth (for example, acetazolamide [e.g., Diamox], dichlorphenamide [e.g., Daranide], methazolamide [e.g., Neptazane]), or trimethoprim (e.g., Trimpex). Also tell your health care professional if you are allergic to any other substances, such as foods, preservatives (e.g., sulfites), or dyes.

Pregnancy—Sulfamethoxazole and trimethoprim combination has not been reported to cause birth defects or other problems in humans. However, studies in mice, rats, and rabbits have shown that some sulfonamides cause birth defects, including cleft palate and bone problems. Studies in rabbits have also shown that trimethoprim causes birth defects, as well as a decrease in the number of successful pregnancies. Sulfonamides are not recommended for use at the time of labor and delivery because these medicines may cause unwanted effects in the baby.

Breast-feeding—Sulfonamides and trimethoprim pass into the breast milk. These medicines are not recommended for use during breast-feeding. They may cause liver problems, anemia, and other unwanted effects in nursing babies, especially those with glucose-6-phosphate dehydrogenase (G6PD) deficiency.

Children—Sulfadiazine and trimethoprim combination should not be given to infants less than 3 months of age. Sulfamethoxazole and trimethoprim combination should not be given to infants less than 2 months of age unless directed by the child's doctor. These combinations may cause unwanted effects. In special situations, sulfamethoxazole and trimethoprim combination may be given to infants less than 2 months of age.

Older adults—Elderly people are especially sensitive to the effects of sulfonamide and trimethoprim combinations. Severe skin problems and blood problems may be more likely to occur in the elderly. These problems may also be more likely to occur in patients who are taking diuretics (water pills) along with this medicine.

Other medicines—Although certain medicines should not be used together at all, in other cases two different medicines may be used together even if an interaction might occur. In these cases, your doctor may want to change the dose, or other precautions may be necessary. When you are taking sulfonamide and trimethoprim combinations, it is especially important that your health care professional know if you are taking any of the following:
  • Acetaminophen (e.g., Tylenol) (with long-term, high-dose use) or
  • Amiodarone (e.g., Cordarone) or
  • Anabolic steroids (nandrolone [e.g., Anabolin], oxandrolone [e.g., Anavar], oxymetholone [e.g., Anadrol], stanozolol [e.g., Winstrol]) or
  • Androgens (male hormones) or
  • Antithyroid agents (medicine for overactive thyroid) or
  • Carbamazepine (e.g., Tegretol) or

- Carmustine (e.g., BiCNU) or
- Chloroquine (e.g., Aralen) or
- Dantrolene (e.g., Dantrium) or
- Daunorubicin (e.g., Cerubidine) or
- Disulfiram (e.g., Antabuse) or
- Divalproex (e.g., Depakote) or
- Estrogens (female hormones) or
- Etretinate (e.g., Tegison) or
- Gold salts (medicine for arthritis) or
- Mercaptopurine (e.g., Purinethol) or
- Naltrexone (e.g., Trexan) (with long-term, high-dose use) or
- Oral contraceptives (birth control pills) containing estrogens or
- Other anti-infectives by mouth or by injection (medicine for infection) or
- Phenothiazines (acetophenazine [e.g., Tindal], chlorpromazine [e.g., Thorazine], fluphenazine [e.g., Prolixin], mesoridazine [e.g., Serentil], perphenazine [e.g., Trilafon], prochlorperazine [e.g., Compazine], promazine [e.g., Sparine], promethazine [e.g., Phenergan], thioridazine [e.g., Mellaril], trifluoperazine [e.g., Stelazine], triflupromazine [e.g., Vesprin], trimeprazine [e.g., Temaril]) or
- Plicamycin (e.g., Mithracin) or
- Valproic acid (e.g., Depakene)—Use of sulfonamide and trimethoprim combinations with these medicines may increase the chance of side effects affecting the liver

- Acetohydroxamic acid (e.g., Lithostat) or
- Furazolidone (e.g., Furoxone) or
- Nitrofurantoin (e.g., Furadantin) or
- Primaquine or
- Procainamide (e.g., Pronestyl) or
- Quinidine (e.g., Quinidex) or
- Quinine (e.g., Quinamm) or
- Sulfoxone (e.g., Diasone)—Use of sulfonamide and trimethoprim combinations with these medicines may increase the chance of side effects affecting the blood

- Anticoagulants (blood thinners) or
- Digoxin (e.g., Lanoxin)
- Ethotoin (e.g., Peganone) or
- Mephenytoin (e.g., Mesantoin) or
- Methotrexate (e.g., Mexate) or
- Phenytoin (e.g., Dilantin)—Use of sulfonamide and trimethoprim combinations with these medicines may increase the chance of side effects of these medicines

- Antidiabetics, oral (diabetes medicine you take by mouth)—Use of oral antidiabetics with sulfonamide and trimethoprim combinations may increase the chance of side effects affecting the blood and/or the side effects of the oral antidiabetics

- Methenamine (e.g., Mandelamine)—Use of methenamine with sulfonamide and trimethoprim combinations may increase the chance of side effects of the sulfonamide

- Methyldopa (e.g., Aldomet)—Use of methyldopa with sulfonamide and trimethoprim combinations may increase the chance of side effects affecting the liver and/or the blood

Other medical problems—The presence of other medical problems may affect the use of sulfonamide and trimethoprim combinations. Make sure you tell your doctor if you have any other medical problems, especially:

- Anemia or other blood problems or
- Glucose-6-phosphate dehydrogenase (G6PD) deficiency—Patients with these problems may have an increase in side effects affecting the blood

- Kidney disease or
- Liver disease—Patients with kidney and/or liver disease may have an increased chance of side effects

- Porphyria—This medicine may bring on an attack of porphyria

---

Proper Use of This Medicine

Sulfadiazine and trimethoprim combination should not be given to infants less than 3 months of age, and sulfamethoxazole and trimethoprim combination should not be given to infants less than 2 months of age unless directed by the child's doctor. These medicines may cause unwanted effects in the baby. In special situations, sulfamethoxazole and trimethoprim combination may be given to infants less than 2 months of age.

Sulfonamide and trimethoprim combinations are best taken with a full glass (8 ounces) of water. Several additional glasses of water should be taken every day, unless otherwise directed by your doctor. Drinking extra water will help to prevent some unwanted effects of sulfonamides.

For patients taking the *oral liquid form* of this medicine:
- Use a specially marked measuring spoon or other device to measure each dose accurately. The average household teaspoon may not hold the right amount of liquid.

To help clear up your infection completely, *keep taking this medicine for the full time of treatment,* even if you begin to feel better after a few days. If you stop taking this medicine too soon, your symptoms may return.

This medicine works best when there is a constant amount in the blood or urine. *To help keep the amount constant, do not miss any doses. Also, it is best to take the doses at evenly spaced times day and night.* If you need help in planning the best times to take your medicine, check with your health care professional.

Dosing—The dose of these medicines will be different for different patients. *Follow your doctor's orders or the directions on the label.* The following information includes only the average doses of these medicines. *If your dose is different, do not change it* unless your doctor tells you to do so.

The number of tablets or teaspoonfuls of suspension that you take depends on the strength of the medicine. Also, *the number of doses you take each day, the time allowed between doses, and the length of time you take the medicine depend on the medical problem for which you are taking sulfonamide and trimethoprim combinations.*

For sulfadiazine and trimethoprim combination
- For *oral* dosage forms (suspension, tablets):
  —For bacterial infections:
  - Adults and teenagers—820 milligrams (mg) of sulfadiazine and 180 mg of trimethoprim once a day.
  - Infants less than 3 months of age—Use is not recommended.

- Infants 3 months of age and older and children up to 12 years of age—Dose is based on body weight. The usual dose is 7 mg of sulfadiazine and 1.5 mg of trimethoprim per kilogram (kg) (3.2 mg of sulfadiazine and 0.7 mg of trimethoprim per pound) of body weight every twelve hours.

For sulfamethoxazole and trimethoprim combination
- For *oral* dosage forms (suspension, tablets):
  —For bacterial infections:
  - Adults and children 40 kilograms (kg) of body weight (88 pounds) and over—800 milligrams (mg) of sulfamethoxazole and 160 mg of trimethoprim every twelve hours.
  - Infants less than 2 months of age—Use is not recommended.
  - Infants 2 months of age and older and children up to 40 kg of weight (88 pounds)—Dose is based on body weight. The usual dose is 20 to 30 mg of sulfamethoxazole and 4 to 6 mg of trimethoprim per kg (9.1 to 13.6 mg of sulfamethoxazole and 1.8 to 2.7 mg of trimethoprim per pound) of body weight every twelve hours.
  —For the treatment of *Pneumocystis carinii* pneumonia (PCP):
  - Adults and children older than 2 months—Dose is based on body weight. The usual dose is 18.75 to 25 mg of sulfamethoxazole and 3.75 to 5 mg of trimethoprim per kg (8.5 to 11.4 mg of sulfamethoxazole and 1.7 to 2.3 mg of trimethoprim per pound) of body weight every six hours.
  —For the prevention of *Pneumocystis carinii* pneumonia (PCP):
  - Adults and teenagers—800 mg of sulfamethoxazole and 160 mg of trimethoprim once a day.
  - Infants and children 4 weeks of age and older—Dose is based on body size and must be determined by your doctor. There are several dosing regimens available that your doctor may choose from. One dosing regimen is 375 mg of sulfamethoxazole and 75 mg of trimethoprim per square meter of body surface two times a day, three times a week on consecutive days (e.g., Monday, Tuesday, Wednesday).
- For *injection* dosage form:
  —For bacterial infections:
  - Adults and children older than 2 months—The usual total daily dose is 40 to 50 mg of sulfamethoxazole and 8 to 10 mg of trimethoprim per kg (18.2 to 22.7 mg of sulfamethoxazole and 3.6 to 4.5 mg of trimethoprim per pound) of body weight. This total daily dose may be divided up and injected into a vein every six, eight, or twelve hours.
  - Infants less than 2 months of age—Use is not recommended.
  —For the treatment of *Pneumocystis carinii* pneumonia (PCP):
  - Adults and children older than 2 months—The usual dose is 18.75 to 25 mg of sulfamethoxazole and 3.75 to 5 mg of trimethoprim per kg (8.5 to 11.4 mg of sulfamethoxazole and 1.7 to 2.3 mg of trimethoprim per pound) of body weight. This is injected into a vein every six hours.
  - Infants less than 2 months of age—Use is not recommended.

Missed dose—If you miss a dose of this medicine, take it as soon as possible. This will help to keep a constant amount of medicine in the blood or urine. However, if it is almost time for your next dose, skip the missed dose and go back to your regular dosing schedule. Do not double doses.

Storage—To store this medicine:
- Keep out of the reach of children.
- Store away from heat and direct light.
- Do not store the tablet form of this medicine in the bathroom, near the kitchen sink, or in other damp places. Heat or moisture may cause the medicine to break down.
- Keep the oral liquid form of this medicine from freezing.
- Do not keep outdated medicine or medicine no longer needed. Be sure that any discarded medicine is out of the reach of children.

Precautions While Using This Medicine

It is very important that your doctor check your progress at regular visits. This medicine may cause blood problems, especially if it is taken for a long time.

If your symptoms do not improve within a few days, or if they become worse, check with your doctor.

Sulfonamide and trimethoprim combinations may cause blood problems. These problems may result in a greater chance of certain infections, slow healing, and bleeding of the gums. Therefore, you should be careful when using regular toothbrushes, dental floss, and toothpicks. Dental work should be delayed until your blood counts have returned to normal. Check with your medical doctor or dentist if you have any questions about proper oral hygiene (mouth care) during treatment.

Sulfonamide and trimethoprim combinations may cause your skin to be more sensitive to sunlight than it is normally. Exposure to sunlight, even for brief periods of time, may cause a skin rash, itching, redness or other discoloration of the skin, or a severe sunburn. When you begin taking this medicine:
- Stay out of direct sunlight, especially between the hours of 10:00 a.m. and 3:00 p.m., if possible.
- Wear protective clothing, including a hat and sunglasses.
- Apply a sun block product that has a skin protection factor (SPF) of at least 15. Some patients may require a product with a higher SPF number, especially if they have a fair complexion. If you have any questions about this, check with your health care professional.
- Apply a sun block lipstick that has an SPF of at least 15 to protect your lips.
- Do not use a sunlamp or tanning bed or booth.

If you have a severe reaction from the sun, check with your doctor.

This medicine may also cause some people to become dizzy. *Make sure you know how you react to this medicine before you drive, use machines, or do anything else that could be dangerous if you are dizzy or are not alert.* If this reaction is especially bothersome, check with your doctor.

Side Effects of This Medicine

Along with its needed effects, a medicine may cause some unwanted effects. Although not all of these side effects may occur, if they do occur they may need medical attention.

Check with your doctor immediately if any of the following side effects occur:

More common
  Itching; skin rash

Less common
  Aching of joints and muscles; difficulty in swallowing; pale skin; redness, blistering, peeling, or loosening of skin; sore throat and fever; unusual bleeding or bruising; unusual tiredness or weakness; yellow eyes or skin

Rare
  Abdominal or stomach cramps and pain (severe); abdominal or stomach tenderness; anxiety; blood in urine; bluish fingernails, lips, or skin; confusion; diarrhea (watery and severe), which may also be bloody; difficult breathing; drowsiness; fever; general feeling of illness; greatly increased or decreased frequency of urination or amount of urine; hallucinations; headache, severe; increased thirst; lower back pain; mental depression; muscle pain or weakness; nausea; nervousness; pain at site of injection; pain or burning while urinating; seizures (convulsions); stiff neck and/or back; swelling of front part of neck

  Note: Some of the above side effects (severe abdominal or stomach cramps and pain, and watery and severe diarrhea, which may also be bloody) may also occur up to several weeks after you stop using any of these medicines.

Also, check with your doctor as soon as possible if the following side effect occurs:

More common
  Increased sensitivity of skin to sunlight

Other side effects may occur that usually do not need medical attention. These side effects may go away during treatment as your body adjusts to the medicine. However, check with your doctor if any of the following side effects continue or are bothersome:

More common
  Diarrhea; dizziness; headache; loss of appetite; mouth sores or swelling of the tongue; nausea or vomiting; tiredness

Other side effects not listed above may also occur in some patients. If you notice any other effects, check with your doctor.

Additional Information

Once a medicine has been approved for marketing for a certain use, experience may show that it is also useful for other medical problems. Although these uses are not included in product labeling, sulfamethoxazole and trimethoprim combination is used in certain patients for the following medical conditions:

• Bile infections
• Bone and joint infections
• HIV-related infections in Africa
• Sexually transmitted diseases, such as gonorrhea
• Sinus infections
• Toxoplasmosis (prevention of)
• Urinary tract infections (prevention of)
• Whipple's disease

Other than the above information, there is no additional information relating to proper use, precautions, or side effects for these uses.

Revised: 08/08/2000

SUMATRIPTAN   Systemic

Commonly used brand name(s):

In the U.S.—
  Imitrex

In Canada—
  Imitrex

Description

Sumatriptan (soo-ma-TRIP-tan) is used to treat severe migraine headaches. Many people find that their headaches go away completely after they take sumatriptan. Other people find that their headaches are much less painful, and that they are able to go back to their normal activities even though their headaches are not completely gone. Sumatriptan often relieves other symptoms that occur together with a migraine headache, such as nausea, vomiting, sensitivity to light, and sensitivity to sound.

Sumatriptan is not an ordinary pain reliever. It will not relieve any kind of pain other than migraine headaches. This medicine is usually used for people whose headaches are not relieved by acetaminophen, aspirin, or other pain relievers.

Sumatriptan injection is also used to treat cluster headaches.

Sumatriptan has caused serious side effects in some people, especially people who have heart or blood vessel disease. Be sure that you discuss with your doctor the risks of using this medicine as well as the good that it can do.

Sumatriptan is available only with your doctor's prescription, in the following dosage forms:

Nasal
  • Nasal spray (U.S. and Canada)
Oral
  • Tablets (U.S. and Canada)
Parenteral
  • Injection (U.S. and Canada)

Before Using This Medicine

In deciding to use a medicine, the risks of using the medicine must be weighed against the good it will do. This is a decision you and your doctor will make. For sumatriptan, the following should be considered:

Allergies—Tell your doctor if you have ever had any unusual or allergic reaction to sumatriptan. Also tell your health care professional if you are allergic to any other substances, such as foods, preservatives, or dyes.

Pregnancy—Sumatriptan has not been studied in pregnant women. However, in some animal studies, sumatriptan caused harmful effects to the fetus. These unwanted effects usually occurred when sumatriptan was given in amounts that were large enough to cause harmful effects in the mother.

Breast-feeding—Sumatriptan passes into human breast milk. Breast-feeding mothers should discuss the risks and benefits of this medicine with their doctors.

Children—Studies on this medicine have been done only in patients 18 years of age or older, and there is no specific information comparing use of sumatriptan in children with use in other age groups.

Older adults—This medicine has been tested in a limited number of patients between 60 and 65 years of age. It did not cause different side effects or problems in these patients than it did in younger adults. However, there is no specific information comparing use of sumatriptan in patients older than 65 years of age with use in younger adults.

Other medicines—Although certain medicines should not be used together at all, in other cases two different medicines may be used together even if an interaction might occur. In these cases, your doctor may want to change the dose, or other precautions may be necessary. Tell your health care professional if you are taking any other prescription or nonprescription (over-the-counter [OTC]) medicine, especially other prescription medicine for migraine headaches, or if you smoke tobacco.

When you are taking sumatriptan, it is especially important that your health care professional know if you are taking the following:

- Monoamine oxidase (MAO) inhibitors (furazolidone [e.g., Furoxone]; isocarboxazid [e.g., Marplan], phenelzine [e.g., Nardil], procarbazine [e.g., Matulane], selegiline [e.g., Eldepryl], tranylcypromine [e.g., Parnate])—Taking sumatriptan while you are taking or within 2 weeks of taking MAO inhibitors may cause sudden high body temperature, extremely high blood pressure and severe convulsions; at least 14 days should be allowed between stopping treatment with one medicine and starting treatment with the other.

Other medical problems—The presence of other medical problems may affect the use of sumatriptan. Make sure you tell your doctor if you have any other medical problems, especially:

- Angina (chest pain) or
- Fast or irregular heartbeat or
- Heart or blood vessel disease or
- High blood pressure or
- Kidney disease or
- Liver disease or
- Stroke (history of)—The chance of side effects may be increased. Heart or blood vessel disease and high blood pressure sometimes do not cause any symptoms, so some people do not know that they have these problems. Before deciding whether you should use sumatriptan, your doctor may need to do some tests to make sure that you do not have any of these conditions.

Proper Use of This Medicine

Do not use sumatriptan for a headache that is different from your usual migraines. Instead, check with your doctor.

To relieve your migraine as soon as possible, use sumatriptan as soon as the headache pain begins. Even if you get warning signals of a coming migraine (an aura), you should wait until the headache pain starts before using sumatriptan. Using sumatriptan during the aura probably will not prevent the headache from occurring. However, even if you do not use su-

matriptan until your migraine has been present for several hours, the medicine will still work.

Lying down in a quiet, dark room for a while after you use this medicine may help relieve your migraine.

If you are not much better in 1 or 2 hours after an injection of sumatriptan, or in 2 to 4 hours after a tablet is taken, *do not use any more of this medicine for the same migraine*. A migraine that is not relieved by the first dose of sumatriptan probably will not be relieved by a second dose, either. Ask your doctor ahead of time about other medicine to be taken if sumatriptan does not work. After taking the other medicine, check with your doctor as soon as possible. Headaches that are not relieved by sumatriptan are sometimes caused by conditions that need other treatment. However, even if sumatriptan does not relieve one migraine, it may still relieve the next one.

If you feel much better after a dose of sumatriptan, but your headache comes back or gets worse after a while, you may use more sumatriptan. However, *use this medicine only as directed by your doctor. Do not use more of it, and do not use it more often, than directed.* Using too much sumatriptan may increase the chance of side effects.

Your doctor may direct you to take another medicine to help prevent headaches. *It is important that you follow your doctor's directions, even if your headaches continue to occur.* Headache-preventing medicines may take several weeks to start working. Even after they do start working, your headaches may not go away completely. However, your headaches should occur less often, and they should be less severe and easier to relieve. This can reduce the amount of sumatriptan or pain relievers that you need. If you do not notice any improvement after several weeks of headache-preventing treatment, check with your doctor.

For patients taking *sumatriptan tablets:*

- Sumatriptan tablets are to be swallowed whole with a full glass of water. *Do not break, crush, or chew the tablets before swallowing them.*

For patients using *sumatriptan injection:*

- This medicine comes with patient directions. *Read them carefully before using the medicine,* and check with your health care professional if you have any questions.
- Your health care professional will teach you how to inject yourself with the medicine. *Be sure to follow the directions carefully. Check with your health care professional if you have any problems using the medicine.*
- After you have finished injecting the medicine, be sure to follow the precautions in the patient directions about safely discarding the empty cartridge and the needle. Always return the empty cartridge and needle to their container before discarding them. Do not throw away the autoinjector unit, because refills are available.

For patients using *sumatriptan nasal solution:*

- This medicine comes with patient directions. *Read them carefully before using the medicine,* and check with your health care professional if you have any questions.

Dosing—The dose of sumatriptan will be different for different patients. *Follow your doctor's orders or the directions on the label.* The following information includes only the average doses of sumatriptan. *If your dose is different, do not change it* unless your doctor tells you to do so.

- For *nasal* dosage form (nasal solution):
  —For migraine headaches:
    - Adults—5 milligrams (mg) or 10 mg (1 or 2 sprays into each nostril) or 20 mg (1 spray into one nostril). If pain is not relieved, another spray (5 mg, 10 mg, or 20 mg) should not be used for the same migraine attack. Another spray (5 mg, 10 mg, or 20 mg) may be used for a migraine that occurs at a later time as long as it has been at least two hours since the last spray. *Do not use more than 40 mg in a twenty-four-hour period (one day).*
    - Children—Use and dose must be determined by your doctor.

- For *oral* dosage form (tablets):
  —For migraine headaches:
    - Adults—25 to 100 mg as a single dose. If the migraine comes back after being relieved, another dose may be taken two hours after the last dose. *Do not take more than 300 mg in any twenty-four-hour period.* If you are taking the tablets after using an injection, do not take more than 200 mg in a twenty-four-hour period.
    - Children—Use and dose must be determined by your doctor.

- For *parenteral* dosage form (injection):
  —For migraine or cluster headaches:
    - Adults—One 6-mg injection. One more 6-mg dose may be injected, if necessary, if the migraine comes back after being relieved. However, the second injection should not be given any sooner than one hour after the first one. *Do not use more than two 6-mg injections in a twenty-four-hour period (one day).* However, some people may be directed to use no more than two 6-mg doses in a forty-eight-hour period (two days).
    - Children—Use and dose must be determined by your doctor.

Storage—To store this medicine:
- Keep out of the reach of children since overdose is especially dangerous in children.
- Store away from heat and direct light.
- Do not store tablets in the bathroom, near the kitchen sink, or in other damp places. Heat or moisture may cause the medicine to break down.
- Keep the injection and nasal solution forms of sumatriptan from freezing.
- Do not keep outdated medicine or medicine no longer needed. Be sure that any discarded medicine is out of the reach of children.

Precautions While Using This Medicine

Check with your doctor if you have used sumatriptan for three headaches, and have not had good relief. Also, check with your doctor if your migraine headaches are worse, or if they are occurring more often, than before you started using sumatriptan.

Drinking alcoholic beverages can make headaches worse or cause new headaches to occur. People who suffer from severe headaches should probably avoid alcoholic beverages, especially during a headache.

Some people feel drowsy or dizzy during or after a migraine, or after taking sumatriptan to relieve a migraine. As long as you are feeling drowsy or dizzy, *do not drive, use machines, or do anything else that could be dangerous if you are dizzy or are not alert.*

Side Effects of This Medicine

Along with its needed effects, a medicine may cause some unwanted effects. Most side effects of sumatriptan are milder and occur less often with the tablets than with the injection. Although not all of these side effects may occur, if they do occur they may need medical attention.

Stop using this medicine and check with your doctor immediately if any of the following side effects occur:
  Rare
    Chest pain (severe); changes in skin color on face; convulsions (seizures); fast or irregular breathing; puffiness or swelling of eyelids, area around the eyes, face, or lips; shortness of breath, troubled breathing, or wheezing

Check with your doctor right away if any of the following side effects continue for more than 1 hour. Even if they go away in less than 1 hour, *check with your doctor before using any more sumatriptan if any of the following side effects occur:*
  Less common
    Chest pain (mild); heaviness, tightness, or pressure in chest and/or neck

Also check with your doctor as soon as possible if any of the following side effects occur:
  Less common
    Difficulty in swallowing; pounding heartbeat; skin rash, hives, itching, or bumps on skin

Other side effects may occur that usually do not need medical attention. Some of the following effects, such as nausea, vomiting, drowsiness, dizziness, and general feeling of illness or tiredness, often occur during or after a migraine, even when sumatriptan has not been used. Most of the side effects caused by sumatriptan go away within a short time (less than 1 hour after an injection or 2 hours after a tablet). However, check with your doctor if any of the following side effects continue or are bothersome:
  More common
    Burning, discharge, pain, and/or soreness in the nose; burning, pain, or redness at place of injection; change in sense of taste; discomfort in jaw, mouth, tongue, throat, nose, or sinuses; dizziness; drowsiness; feeling of burning, warmth, heat, numbness, tightness, or tingling; feeling cold, "strange," or weak; flushing; lightheadedness; muscle aches, cramps, or stiffness; nausea or vomiting
  Less common or rare
    Anxiety; general feeling of illness or tiredness; vision changes

Other side effects not listed above may also occur in some patients. If you notice any other effects, check with your doctor.

Revised: 3/30/98

TACRINE Systemic†

Commonly used brand name(s):

In the U.S.—
Cognex

Other commonly used names are THA and tetrahydroaminoacridine.

---

†Not commercially available in Canada.

Description

Tacrine (TAK-reen) is used to treat the symptoms of mild to moderate Alzheimer's disease. Tacrine will not cure Alzheimer's disease, and it will not stop the disease from getting worse. However, tacrine can improve thinking ability in some patients with Alzheimer's disease.

In Alzheimer's disease, many chemical changes take place in the brain. One of the earliest and biggest changes is that there is less of a chemical messenger called acetylcholine (ACh). ACh helps the brain to work properly. Tacrine slows the breakdown of ACh, so it can build up and have a greater effect. However, as Alzheimer's disease gets worse, there will be less and less ACh, so tacrine may not work as well.

Tacrine may cause liver problems. While taking this medicine, you must have blood tests regularly to see if the medicine is affecting your liver.

This medicine is available only with your doctor's prescription, in the following dosage form:

Oral
- Capsules (U.S.)

Before Using This Medicine

In deciding to use a medicine, the risks of taking the medicine must be weighed against the good it will do. This is a decision you and your doctor will make. For tacrine the following should be considered:

Allergies—Tell your doctor if you have ever had any unusual or allergic reaction to tacrine or to wound antiseptics (e.g., Akrinol, Panflavin, Monacrin). Also tell your health care professional if you are allergic to any other substances, such as foods, preservatives, or dyes.

Pregnancy—Studies on effects in pregnancy have not been done in either humans or animals.

Breast-feeding—It is not known whether tacrine passes into breast milk. However, use of tacrine is not recommended in nursing mothers.

Children—Studies on this medicine have been done only in adult patients, and there is no specific information comparing use of tacrine in children with use in other age groups.

Older adults—Studies on tacrine have been done only in middle-aged and older patients. Information on the effects of tacrine is based on these patients.

Other medicines—Although certain medicines should not be used together at all, in other cases two different medicines may be used together even if an interaction might occur. In these cases, your doctor may want to change the dose, or other precautions may be necessary. When you are taking tacrine, it is especially important that your health care professional know if you are taking any of the following:

- Cimetidine (e.g., Tagamet)—Cimetidine may cause higher blood levels of tacrine, which may increase the chance of side effects
- Inflammation or pain medicine, except narcotics—Stomach irritation may be increased
- Neuromuscular blocking agents (medicines used in surgery to relax muscles)—Tacrine may increase the effects of these medicines; your doctor may change the dose of tacrine before you have surgery
- Smoking tobacco—Smoking may cause lower blood levels of tacrine, which may decrease the effects of tacrine; if you smoke, your doctor may need to change the dose of tacrine
- Theophylline (e.g., Theo-Dur, Uniphyl)—Tacrine may cause higher blood levels of theophylline, which may increase the chance of side effects; your doctor may need to change the dose of theophylline

Other medical problems—The presence of other medical problems may affect the use of tacrine. Make sure you tell your doctor if you have any other medical problems, especially:

- Asthma (or history of) or
- Heart problems, including slow heartbeat or hypotension (low blood pressure), or
- Intestinal blockage or
- Liver disease (or history of) or
- Parkinson's disease or
- Stomach ulcer (or history of) or
- Urinary tract blockage or difficult urination—Tacrine may make these conditions worse
- Brain disease, other, or
- Epilepsy or history of seizures or
- Head injury with loss of consciousness—Tacrine may cause seizures

---

Proper Use of This Medicine

Take this medicine only as directed by your doctor. Do not take more or less of it, and do not take it more or less often than your doctor ordered. Taking too much may increase the chance of side effects, while taking too little may not improve your condition.

Tacrine is best taken on an empty stomach (1 hour before or 2 hours after meals). However, if this medicine upsets your stomach, your doctor may want you to take it with food.

Tacrine seems to work best when it is taken at regularly spaced times, usually four times a day.

Dosing—The dose of tacrine will be different for different patients. *Follow your doctor's orders or the directions on the label*. The following information includes only the average doses of tacrine. *If your dose is different, do not change it unless your doctor tells you to do so*.

- For *oral* dosage form (capsules):
  - For treatment of Alzheimer's disease:
    - Adults—To start, 10 milligrams (mg) four times a day. Your doctor may increase your dose gradually if you are doing well on this medicine and your liver tests are normal. However, the dose is usually not more than 40 mg four times a day.

Missed dose—If you miss a dose of this medicine, take it as soon as possible. However, if it is within 2 hours of your

---

next dose, skip the missed dose and go back to your regular dosing schedule. Do not double doses.

Storage—To store this medicine:

- Keep out of the reach of children.
- Store away from heat and direct light.
- Do not store in the bathroom, near the kitchen sink, or in other damp places. Heat or moisture may cause the medicine to break down.
- Do not keep outdated medicine or medicine no longer needed. Be sure that any discarded medicine is out of the reach of children.

Precautions While Using This Medicine

It is important that your doctor check your progress at regular visits. Also, you must have your blood tested every other week for at least the first 4 to 16 weeks when you start using tacrine to see if this medicine is affecting your liver. If all of the blood tests are normal, you will still need regular testing, but then your doctor may decide to do the tests less often.

Tell your doctor if your symptoms get worse, or if you notice any new symptoms.

Before you have any kind of surgery, dental treatment, or emergency treatment, tell the medical doctor or dentist in charge that you are taking this medicine. Taking tacrine together with medicines that are sometimes used during surgery or dental or emergency treatments may increase the effects of these medicines.

Tacrine may cause some people to become dizzy, clumsy, or unsteady. Make sure you know how you react to this medicine before you do anything that could be dangerous if you are dizzy, clumsy, or unsteady.

Do not stop taking this medicine or decrease your dose without first checking with your doctor. Stopping this medicine suddenly or decreasing the dose by a large amount may cause mental or behavior changes.

If you think you or someone else may have taken an overdose of tacrine, get emergency help at once. Taking an overdose of tacrine may lead to seizures or shock. Some signs of shock are large pupils, irregular breathing, and fast weak pulse. Other signs of an overdose are severe nausea and vomiting, increasing muscle weakness, greatly increased sweating, and greatly increased watering of the mouth.

Side Effects of This Medicine

Along with its needed effects, a medicine may cause some unwanted effects. Some side effects will have signs or symptoms that you can see or feel. Your doctor may watch for others by doing certain tests

Tacrine may cause some serious side effects, including liver problems. You and your doctor should discuss the good this medicine will do as well as the risks of receiving it.

Check with your doctor as soon as possible if any of the following side effects occur:

More common
　　Clumsiness or unsteadiness; diarrhea; loss of appetite; nausea; vomiting

Less common
　　Fainting; fast or pounding heartbeat; fever; high or low blood pressure; skin rash; slow heartbeat

Rare
　　Aggression, irritability, or nervousness; change in stool color; convulsions (seizures); cough, tightness in chest, troubled breathing, or wheezing; stiffness of arms or legs, slow movement, or trembling and shaking of hands and fingers; trouble in urinating; yellow eyes or skin

Symptoms of overdose
　　Convulsions (seizures); greatly increased sweating; greatly increased watering of mouth; increasing muscle weakness; low blood pressure; nausea (severe); shock (fast weak pulse, irregular breathing, large pupils); slow heartbeat; vomiting (severe)

This medicine may also cause the following side effect that your doctor will watch for:

More common
　　Liver problems

Other side effects may occur that usually do not need medical attention. These side effects may go away during treatment as your body adjusts to the medicine. However, check with your doctor if any of the following side effects continue or are bothersome:

More common
　　Abdominal or stomach pain or cramping; dizziness; headache; indigestion; muscle aches or pain

Less common
　　Belching; fast breathing; flushing of skin; general feeling of discomfort or illness; increased sweating; increased urination; increased watering of eyes; increased watering of mouth; runny nose; swelling of feet or lower legs; trouble in sleeping

Other side effects not listed above may also occur in some patients. If you notice any other effects, check with your doctor.

Developed: 08/05/94
Revised: 11/19/98

TACROLIMUS   Systemic

Commonly used brand name(s):

In the U.S.—
　　Prograf

In Canada—
　　Prograf

Description

Tacrolimus (ta-KROE-li-mus) belongs to a group of medicines known as immunosuppressive agents. It is used to lower the body's natural immunity in patients who receive organ (for example, kidney, liver, pancreas, lung, and heart) transplants.

When a patient receives an organ transplant, the body's white blood cells will try to get rid of (reject) the transplanted organ. Tacrolimus works by preventing the white blood cells from getting rid of the transplanted organ.

Tacrolimus may also be used for other indications, as determined by your doctor.

Tacrolimus is a very strong medicine. It can cause side effects that can be very serious, such as kidney problems. It may also reduce the body's ability to fight infections. You and your doctor should talk about the good this medicine will do as well as the risks of using it.

Tacrolimus is available only with your doctor's prescription, in the following dosage forms:

Oral
- Capsules (U.S. and Canada)

Parenteral
- Injection (U.S. and Canada)

Before Using This Medicine

In deciding to use a medicine, the risks of taking the medicine must be weighed against the good it will do. This is a decision you and your doctor will make. For tacrolimus, the following should be considered:

Allergies—Tell your health care professional if you have ever had any unusual or allergic reaction to tacrolimus. Also, if you will be receiving this medicine by injection, tell your health care professional if you are allergic to any other substances, such as castor oil.

Pregnancy—Some women have become pregnant and had babies while receiving tacrolimus after an organ transplantation. Some of the newborn babies had temporary kidney problems after birth. Some babies were born prematurely.

Breast-feeding—Tacrolimus passes into breast milk. There is a chance that it causes the same side effects in the baby that it does in the mother. It may be necessary for you to stop breast-feeding during treatment.

Children—This medicine does not cause different types of side effects or problems in children than it does in adults, although some side effects may occur more or less often than they do in adult patients.

Older adults—There is no specific information comparing the use of tacrolimus in the elderly with the use in other age groups. Tacrolimus is not expected to cause different side effects or problems in older people than it does in younger adults. However, older patients may need lower doses of tacrolimus.

Dental—The effects of tacrolimus may cause increased infections and delayed healing. Dental work, whenever possible, should be completed prior to beginning this medicine.

Other medicines—Although certain medicines should not be used together at all, in other cases two different medicines may be used together even if an interaction might occur. In these cases, your doctor may want to change the dose, or other precautions may be necessary. When you are taking tacrolimus, it is especially important that your health care professional knows if you are taking any of the following:

- Amiloride or
- Spironolactone (e.g., Aldactone) or
- Triamterene (e.g., Dyrenium)—Since both tacrolimus and these medicines increase the amount of potassium in the body, potassium levels could become too high
- Cyclosporine (e.g., Neoral)—May increase the effects of tacrolimus by increasing the amount of this medicine in the body; may cause kidney problems
- Danazol (e.g., Danocrine) or
- Erythromycin (medicine for infection) or

- Fluconazole (e.g., Diflucan) or
- Itraconazole (e.g., Sporanox) or
- Ketoconazole (e.g., Nizoral)—May increase the effects of tacrolimus by increasing the amount of this medicine in the body
- Rifampin (e.g., Rifadin)—May decrease the effects of tacrolimus by decreasing the amount of this medicine in the body

Other medical problems—The presence of other medical problems may affect the use of tacrolimus. Make sure you tell your doctor if you have any other medical problems, especially:

- Cancer—Tacrolimus can make this condition worse
- Chickenpox (including recent exposure) or
- Herpes zoster (shingles)—Risk of severe disease affecting other parts of the body
- Diabetes mellitus (sugar diabetes)—Tacrolimus can increase the amount of sugar in the blood
- Hepatitis or
- Kidney disease or
- Liver disease, other—Tacrolimus can have harmful effects on the kidney in patients with these conditions; a lower dose of tacrolimus may be needed in patients with these conditions
- Hyperkalemia (high amount of potassium in the blood) or
- Nervous system problems—Tacrolimus can make these conditions worse
- Infection—Tacrolimus decreases the body's ability to fight infection

Proper Use of This Medicine

Take this medicine only as directed by your doctor. Do not take more or less of it and do not take it more often than your doctor ordered. The exact amount of medicine you need has been carefully worked out. Taking too much may increase the chance of side effects, while taking too little may lead to rejection of your transplanted organ.

To help you remember to take your medicine, try to get into the habit of taking it at the same time each day. This will also help tacrolimus work better by keeping a constant amount in the blood.

Absorption of this medicine may be changed if you change your diet. This medicine should be taken consistently with respect to meals. You should not change the type or amount of food you eat unless you discuss it with your health care professional.

Do not stop taking this medicine without first checking with your doctor. You may have to take medicine for the rest of your life to prevent your body from rejecting the transplant.

Dosing—The dose of tacrolimus will be different for different patients. *Follow your doctor's orders or the directions on the label.* The following information includes only the average doses of tacrolimus. *If your dose is different, do not change it* unless your doctor tells you to do so.

The number of capsules that you take depends on the strength of the medicine in the capsule and the dose prescribed by your doctor. Also, *the number of doses you take each day, the time allowed between doses, and the length of time you take the medicine depend on the medical problem for which you are taking tacrolimus.*

- For *oral* dosage form (capsules):
  —Adults, teenagers, or children—Dose is based on body weight. The usual dose is 0.1 to 0.3 milligrams (mg) per kilogram (kg) (0.045 to 0.14 mg per pound) of body weight a day.
- For *injection* dosage form:
  —Adults, teenagers, or children—Dose is based on body weight. The usual dose is 0.01 to 0.05 mg per kg (0.0045 to 0.0227 mg per pound) of body weight a day.

Missed dose—If you miss a dose of tacrolimus and remember it within 12 hours, take the missed dose as soon as you remember. However, if it is almost time for the next dose, skip the missed dose, go back to your regular dosing schedule, and check with your doctor. Do not double doses.

Storage—To store this medicine:

- Keep out of the reach of children.
- Store away from heat and direct light.
- Do not store in the bathroom, near the kitchen sink, or in other damp places.
- Do not keep outdated medicine or medicine no longer needed. Be sure that any discarded medicine is out of reach of children.

Precautions While Using This Medicine

It is very important that your doctor check your progress at regular visits. Your doctor will want to do laboratory tests to make sure that tacrolimus is working properly and to check for unwanted effects.

While you are taking tacrolimus, it is important to maintain good dental hygiene and see a dentist regularly for teeth cleaning.

Raw oysters or other shellfish may contain bacteria that can cause serious illness, and possibly death. This is more likely to be a problem if these foods are eaten by patients with certain medical conditions. Even eating oysters from "clean" water or good restaurants does not guarantee that the oysters do not contain the bacteria. Symptoms of this infection include sudden chills, fever, nausea, vomiting, blood poisoning, and sometimes death. Eating raw shellfish is not a problem for most healthy people; however, patients with the following conditions may be at greater risk: cancer, immune disorders, organ transplantation, long-term corticosteroid use (as for asthma, arthritis, or organ transplantation), liver disease (including viral hepatitis), excess alcohol intake (2 to 3 drinks or more per day), diabetes, stomach problems (including previous stomach surgery and low stomach acid), and hemochromatosis (an iron disorder). *Do not eat raw oysters or other shellfish while you are taking tacrolimus. Be sure oysters and shellfish are fully cooked.*

While you are being treated with tacrolimus, and after you stop treatment with it, *it is important to see your doctor about the immunizations (vaccinations) you should receive. Do not get any immunizations without your doctor's approval.* Tacrolimus lowers your body's resistance. For some immunizations, there is a chance you might get the infection the immunization is meant to prevent. For other immunizations, it may be especially important to receive the immunization to prevent a disease. In addition, other persons living in your house should not take oral poliovirus vaccine since there is a chance they could pass the poliovirus on to you. Also, avoid persons who have recently taken oral poliovirus vaccine. Do not get close to them, and do not stay in the same room with them for very long. If you cannot take these precautions, you should consider wearing a protective face mask that covers the nose and mouth.

Treatment with tacrolimus may also increase the chance of getting other infections. If you can, avoid people with colds or other infections. If you think you are getting a cold or other infection, check with your doctor.

Tacrolimus is not available in all countries. *If you are traveling to another country, be sure you will have a supply of your medicine.*

Grapefruits and grapefruit juice may increase the effects of tacrolimus by increasing the amount of this medicine in the body. *You should not eat grapefruit or drink grapefruit juice while you are taking this medicine.*

Side Effects of This Medicine

Along with its needed effects, a medicine may cause some unwanted effects. Some side effects will have signs or symptoms that you can see or feel. Your doctor will watch for others by doing certain tests.

Also, because of the way tacrolimus acts on the body, there is a chance that it may cause effects that may not occur until years after the medicine is used. These delayed effects may include certain types of cancer, such as lymphomas or skin cancers.

Check with your doctor or nurse immediately if any of the following side effects occur:

More common
Abdominal pain; abnormal dreams; agitation; anxiety; chills; confusion; convulsions (seizures); diarrhea; dizziness; fever and sore throat; flu-like symptoms; frequent urination; hallucinations (seeing or hearing things that are not there); headache; infection; itching; loss of appetite; loss of energy or weakness; mental depression; muscle trembling or twitching; nausea; nervousness; pale skin; shortness of breath; skin rash; swelling of feet or lower legs; tingling; trembling and shaking of hands; trouble in sleeping; unusual bleeding or bruising; unusual tiredness or weakness; vomiting

Less common
Blurred vision; chest pain; increased sensitivity to pain; muscle cramps; numbness or pain in legs; ringing in ears; sweating

Rare
Flushing of face or neck; general feeling of discomfort or illness; weight loss; wheezing

This medicine may also cause the following side effects that your doctor will watch for:

More common
Hyperkalemia (too much potassium in the blood); hypomagnesemia (not enough magnesium in the blood); kidney problems

Less common
Hyperlipidemia (high cholesterol); hypertension (high blood pressure)

Other side effects not listed above may also occur in some patients. If you notice any other effects, check with your doctor.

Additional Information

Once a medicine has been approved for marketing for a certain use, experience may show that it is also useful for other medical problems. Although not specifically included in the product labeling, tacrolimus is used in certain patients with the following medical conditions:

- Bone marrow transplantation
- Uveitis, severe, refractory (an eye condition)

For patients receiving bone marrow transplantation, tacrolimus may work by preventing the cells from the transplanted bone marrow from attacking the cells of the patient. The dose of tacrolimus for patients receiving bone marrow transplantation is based on body weight. The usual dose is 0.12 to 0.3 mg per kg (0.05 to 0.14 mg per pound) of body weight a day for patients taking tacrolimus by mouth, and 0.04 to 0.1 mg per kg (0.018 to 0.045 mg per pound) of body weight a day for patients receiving tacrolimus by injection.

The dose of tacrolimus for patients with severe, refractory uveitis is based on body weight. For severe, refractory uveitis, the usual dose is 0.1 to 0.15 mg per kg (0.045 to 0.068 mg per pound) of body weight a day.

Other than the above information, there is no additional information relating to proper use, precautions, or side effects for these uses.

Developed: 08/14/97

TACROLIMUS Topical— INTRODUCTORY VERSION

Commonly used brand name(s):

In the U.S.—
  Protopic

Description

Tacrolimus (ta-KROE-li-mus) ointment is used for moderate to severe atopic dematitis. This is a skin condition where there is itching, redness and inflammation, much like an allergic reaction. Tacrolimus helps to suppress these symptoms which are a reaction caused by the body's immune system. It can be used for short-term or long-term intermittent treatment. It is often used when other types of treatment are not working or not tolerated by the patient.

Tacrolimus is available only with your doctor's prescription, in the following dosage forms:

Topical
  - Ointment (U.S)

Before Using This Medicine

In deciding to use a medicine, the risks of using tacrolimus ointment must be weighed against the good it will do. This is a decision you and your doctor will make. For tacrolimus ointment, the following should be considered:

Allergies—Tell your doctor if you have ever had any unusual or allergic reaction to tacrolimus. Also tell your doctor and pharmacist if you are allergic to any other substances, such as foods, preservatives, or dyes.

Pregnancy—Tacrolimus ointment has not been studied in pregnant women. However, studies in animals have shown that tacrolimus taken orally causes birth defects. Tacrolimus taken orally has been associated with kidney problems and high potassium concentrations in the blood of newborn infants. Before taking this medicine, make sure your doctor knows if you are pregnant or if you may become pregnant.

Breast-feeding—Tacrolimus applied as a topical ointment may pass into the breast milk, and may cause unwanted effects in nursing babies. It may be necessary for you to take another medicine or to stop breast-feeding during treatment. Be sure you have discussed the risks and benefits of the medicine with your doctor.

Children—Some side effects may occur more or less often in children than they do in adult patients. This medicine has not been tested in children under 2 years of age.

Older adults—Tacrolimus ointment has been tested and has not been shown to cause different side effects or problems in older people than it does in younger adults.

Other medicines—Although certain medicines should not be used together at all, in other cases two different medicines may be used together even if an interaction might occur. In these cases, your doctor may want to change the dose, or other precautions may be necessary. Tell your health care professional if you are taking any other prescription or nonprescription (over-the-counter [OTC]) medicine.

Other medical problems—The presence of other medical problems may affect the use of tacrolimus ointment. Make sure you tell your doctor if you have any other medical problems, especially:

- Eczema herpeticum or
- Herpes simplex virus infection or
- Varicella zoster virus infection—Increased risk may be associated with these conditions
- Erythroderma, generalized—Safety is unknown
- Netherton's syndrome—May cause too much of the tacrolimus to be absorbed into the body

Proper Use of This Medicine

Infections in the affected areas should be treated before starting treatment with tacrolimus ointment.

Dry skin completely before applying tacrolimus ointment.

Wash hand thoroughly after applying tacrolimus ointment, if hands are not any area for treatment.

Dosing—The dose of tacrolimus ointment will be different for different patients. *Follow your doctor's orders or the directions on the label*. The following information includes only the average doses of tacrolimus ointment. *If your dose is different, do not change it* unless your doctor tells you to do so.

- For *ointment* dosage form
  —For atopic dermatitis:
    - Adults—Apply 0.03% or 0.1% ointment to skin that is clean and dry two times a day. Do not cover the area with a bandage that sticks to the skin. Continue to treat for 1 week after symptoms are gone.
    - Children over 2 years old—Apply 0.03% ointment to skin that is clean and dry two times a day. Do

not cover the area with a bandage that sticks to the skin. Continue to treat for 1 week after symptoms are gone.

Missed dose—If you miss a dose of this medicine, use it as soon as possible. However, if it is almost time for your next dose, skip the missed dose and go back to your regular dosing schedule. Do not double doses.

Storage—To store this medicine:
- Keep out of the reach of children.
- Keep the medicine from freezing. Do not refrigerate.
- Keep out of direct sunlight.
- Do not keep outdated medicine or medicine no longer needed. Ask your health care professional how you should dispose of any medicine you do not use. Be sure that any discarded medicine is out of the reach of children.

Precautions While Using This Medicine

It is very important that your doctor check your progress at regular visits. Your doctor will want to make sure the tacrolimus ointment is working properly and to check for unwanted effects.

Report any adverse reactions or side effects to your doctor.

Use this medicine only for the condition for which it was prescribed by your doctor.

Tacrolimus ointment may cause your skin to be more sensitive to sunlight than it is normally. Exposure to sunlight, even for brief periods of time, may cause your symptoms to be worse or cause severe sunburn. When you begin taking this medicine:
- Stay out of direct sunlight, especially between the hours of 10:00 a.m. and 3:00 p.m., if possible.
- Wear protective clothing, including a hat. Also, wear sunglasses.
- Apply a sun block product that has a skin protection factor (SPF) of at least 15. Some patients may require a product with a higher SPF number, especially if they have a fair complexion. If you have any questions about this, check with your health care professional.
- Apply a sun block lipstick that has an SPF of at least 15 to protect your lips.
- Do not use a sunlamp or tanning bed or booth.

If you have a severe reaction from the sun, check with your doctor.

Side Effects of This Medicine

Other side effects may occur that usually do not need medical attention. These side effects may go away during treatment as your body adjusts to the medicine. However, check with your doctor if any of the following side effects continue or are bothersome.

More common

Cough; loss of appetite; general aches and pains; sneezing; weakness; earache—in children; ringing or buzzing in the ears—in children; skin burning; itching skin; headache; fever

Less common

Watery eyes; troubled breathing or wheezing; severe skin rash or hives; flushing; chills; runny nose; increased sensitivity to sunlight; joint pain; swollen glands; acne; alcohol intolerance; lack or loss of

strength; back pain; coughing up cloudy mucus; redness in eye; pain in eye; swelling of eye, eyelid, or inner lining of eyelid; burning to eyes; dry or itching eyes; discharge from eyes; excessive tearing; diarrhea—in children; cyst; painful menstruation; acid or sour stomach; belching; heartburn; indigestion; stomach discomfort, upset, or pain; skin blisters; burning; pain in hairy areas; pus at root of hair; chickenpox—in children; swollen and/or painful glands; increased skin sensitivity; muscle aches or pain; stuffy nose; skin tingling or redness; pain or tenderness around eyes and cheekbones; tightness of chest

Rare

Abdominal pain; accidental injury; dry skin; face swelling; blisters on lips, nose, or genitals; sleeplessness; nausea; swelling of hands, lower legs, and feet; dry or sore throat; accumulation of pus; red thickened or scaly skin; unusual bruising; chest pain; sunburn; vomiting; weakness

Other side effects not listed above may also occur in some patients. If you notice any other effects, check with your doctor.

Developed: 05/24/2001

TAMOXIFEN   Systemic

Commonly used brand name(s):

In the U.S.—
Nolvadex
Generic name product may be available.

In Canada—

Apo-Tamox	Novo-Tamoxifen
Gen-Tamoxifen	Tamofen
Nolvadex	Tamone
Nolvadex-D	

Description

Tamoxifen (ta-MOX-i-fen) is a medicine that blocks the effects of the estrogen hormone in the body. It is used to treat breast cancer in women or men. It may also be used to treat other kinds of cancer, as determined by your doctor.

Tamoxifen also may be used to reduce the risk of developing breast cancer in women who have a high risk of developing breast cancer. Women at high risk for developing breast cancer are at least 35 years of age and have a combination of risk factors that make their chance of developing breast cancer 1.67% or more over the next 5 years. Your doctor will help to determine your risk of developing breast cancer.

The following are risk factors that may increase your chance of developing breast cancer:
- If you have close family members (mother, sister, or daughter) with breast cancer
- If you have ever had a breast biopsy or if high-risk changes in your breast(s) have been found from a breast biopsy
- If you have never been pregnant or if your first pregnancy occurred at a late age
- If your first menstrual period occurred at an early age

The exact way that tamoxifen works against cancer is not known, but it may be related to the way it blocks the effects of estrogen on the body.

Before you begin treatment with tamoxifen, you and your doctor should talk about the good this medicine will do as well as the risks of using it.

Tamoxifen is available only with your doctor's prescription, in the following dosage form:

Oral
- Tablets (U.S. and Canada)

Before Using This Medicine

In deciding to use a medicine, the risks of taking the medicine must be weighed against the good it will do. This is a decision you and your doctor will make. For tamoxifen, the following should be considered:

Allergies—Tell your doctor if you have ever had any unusual or allergic reaction to tamoxifen.

Pregnancy—Tell your doctor if you are pregnant or if you intend to become pregnant. Tamoxifen should not used to reduce the risk of breast cancer if you are pregnant of if you intend to become pregnant. Tamoxifen use in women has been shown to cause miscarriages, birth defects, death of the fetus, and vaginal bleeding. Studies in rats and rabbits have shown that tamoxifen causes miscarriages, death of the fetus, and slowed learning. Studies in animals also have shown that tamoxifen may cause some of the same problems as those caused by an estrogen called diethylstilbestrol (DES). DES causes genital tract problems and, rarely, an increased risk of cancer of the cervix or vagina in daughters of women who took it during their pregnancy; it is not known whether tamoxifen causes these same problems.

Be sure that you have discussed this with your doctor before taking this medicine. It is best to use some kind of birth control while you are taking tamoxifen and for about 2 months after you stop taking it. However, do not use oral contraceptives ("the Pill") since they may interfere with this medicine. Tell your doctor right away if you think you have become pregnant while taking tamoxifen.

Breast-feeding—Because this medicine may cause serious side effects, breast-feeding is generally not recommended while you are taking it.

Older adults—Many medicines have not been studied specifically in older people. Therefore, it may not be known whether they work exactly the same way they do in younger adults. Although there is no specific information comparing use of tamoxifen in the elderly with use in other age groups, this medicine is not expected to cause different side effects or problems in older people than it does in younger adults.

Other medicines—Although certain medicines should not be used together at all, in other cases two different medicines may be used together even if an interaction might occur. In these cases, your doctor may want to change the dose, or other precautions may be necessary. Tell your health care professional if you are taking any other prescription or nonprescription (over-the-counter [OTC]) medicine. If you are taking tamoxifen to reduce the risk of breast cancer, it is especially important that your health care professional know if you are taking the following:

- Anticoagulant, coumarin-type (blood thinners)—Tamoxifen may cause blood clots

Other medical problems—The presence of other medical problems may affect the use of tamoxifen. Make sure you tell your doctor if you have any other medical problems, especially:

- Cataracts or other eye problems—Tamoxifen may also cause these problems
- High cholesterol levels in the blood—Tamoxifen can increase cholesterol levels
- Blood problems—Tamoxifen may cause certain blood problems

When used for reducing the risk for developing breast cancer in high-risk women
- Blood clots (or history of) or
- Pulmonary embolism (or history of)—Tamoxifen may cause these problems

Proper Use of This Medicine

Use this medicine only as directed by your doctor. Do not use more or less of it, and do not use it more often than your doctor ordered. The exact amount of medicine you need has been carefully worked out. Taking too much may increase the chance of side effects, while taking too little may not improve your condition.

Tamoxifen sometimes causes mild nausea and vomiting. However, it may have to be taken for several weeks or months to be effective. Even if you begin to feel ill, *do not stop using this medicine without first checking with your doctor*. Ask your health care professional for ways to lessen these effects.

If you vomit shortly after taking a dose of tamoxifen, check with your doctor. You will be told whether to take the dose again or to wait until the next scheduled dose.

Dosing—The dose of tamoxifen will be different for different patients. *Follow your doctor's orders or the directions on the label*. The following information includes only the average doses of tamoxifen. *If your dose is different, do not change it* unless your doctor tells you to do so.

- For *oral* dosage form (tablets)
  —For breast cancer in women or men:
    - Adults—10 to 20 milligrams (mg) two times a day, in the morning and evening.
  —For reducing the risk of developing breast cancer in high-risk women:
    - Adults—20 milligrams (mg) a day, for five years
  —For reducing the risk of developing invasive breast cancer in women with ductal carcinoma in situ:
    - Adults—20 milligrams (mg) a day, for five years

Missed dose—If you miss a dose of this medicine, do not take the missed dose at all and do not double the next one. Instead, go back to your regular dosing schedule and check with your doctor.

Storage—To store this medicine:
- Keep out of the reach of children.
- Store away from heat and direct light.
- Do not store in the bathroom, near the kitchen sink, or in other damp places. Heat or moisture may cause the medicine to break down.
- Do not keep outdated medicine or medicine no longer needed. Be sure that any discarded medicine is out of the reach of children.

Precautions While Using This Medicine

It is very important that your doctor check your progress at regular visits to make sure that this medicine is working properly and to check for unwanted effects.

For women: Tamoxifen may make you more fertile. It is best to use some type of birth control while you are taking it. However, do not use oral contraceptives ("the Pill") since they may change the effects of tamoxifen. Tell your doctor right away if you think you have become pregnant while taking this medicine.

Side Effects of This Medicine

Along with its needed effects, a medicine may cause some unwanted effects. Some side effects will have signs or symptoms that you can see or feel. Your doctor will watch for others by doing certain tests.

Also, because of the way this medicine acts on the body, there is a chance that it might cause other unwanted effects that may not occur until months or years after the medicine is used. Tamoxifen has been reported to increase the chance of cancer of the uterus (womb) in some women taking it. It also causes liver cancer in rats. In addition, tamoxifen has been reported to cause cataracts and other eye problems. Discuss these possible effects with your doctor.

Check with your doctor as soon as possible if any of the following side effects occur:
> *For both females and males*
>> *Less common or rare*
>>> Blistering, peeling, or loosening of skin and mucous membranes; blurred vision; confusion; pain or swelling in legs; shortness of breath; weakness or sleepiness; yellow eyes or skin

> *For females only*
>> *Less common or rare*
>>> Change in vaginal discharge; pain or feeling of pressure in pelvis; vaginal bleeding

This medicine may also cause the following side effect that your doctor will watch for:
> *For both females and males*
>> *Less common or rare*
>>> Cataracts in the eyes or other eye problems; liver problems

Other side effects may occur that usually do not need medical attention. These side effects may go away during treatment as your body adjusts to the medicine. Also, your health care professional may be able to tell you about ways to prevent or reduce some of these side effects. Check with your health care professional if any of the following side effects continue or are bothersome or if you have any questions about them:
> *For both females and males*
>> *Less common*
>>> Bone pain; hair thinning or partial hair loss; headache; nausea and/or vomiting (mild); skin rash or dryness

> *For females only*
>> *More common*
>>> Hot flashes; weight gain

>> *Less common*
>>> Changes in menstrual period; itching in genital area; vaginal discharge

> *For males only*
>> *Less common*
>>> Impotence or decreased sexual interest

Other side effects not listed above may also occur in some patients. If you notice any other effects, check with your doctor.

Additional Information

Once a medicine has been approved for marketing for a certain use, experience may show that it is also useful for other medical problems. Although these uses are not included in product labeling, tamoxifen is used in certain patients with the following medical conditions:
- Malignant melanoma (a certain type of skin cancer)
- Cancer of the endometrium (lining of the uterus)

Other than the above information, there is no additional information relating to proper use, precautions, or side effects for these uses.

Revised: 11/20/00

TAMSULOSIN   Systemic

Commonly used brand name(s):

In the U.S.—
Flomax

Description

Tamsulosin (tam-SOO-loh-sin) is used to treat the signs and symptoms of benign enlargement of the prostate (benign prostatic hyperplasia or BPH). Benign enlargement of the prostate is a problem that can occur in men as they get older. The prostate gland is located below the bladder. As the prostate gland enlarges, certain muscles in the gland may become tight and get in the way of the tube that drains urine from the bladder. This can cause problems in urinating, such as a need to urinate often, a weak stream when urinating, or a feeling of not being able to empty the bladder completely.

Tamsulosin helps relax the muscles in the prostate and the opening of the bladder. This may help increase the flow of urine and/or decrease the symptoms. However, tamsulosin will not shrink the prostate. The prostate may continue to get larger. This may cause the symptoms to become worse over time. Therefore, even though tamsulosin may lessen the problems caused by enlarged prostate now, surgery still may be needed in the future.

This medicine is available only with your doctor's prescription, in the following dosage form:
> *Oral*
>> • Capsules (U.S.)

Before Using This Medicine

In deciding to use a medicine, the risks of taking the medicine must be weighed against the good it will do. This is a decision you and your doctor will make. For tamsulosin, the following should be considered:

Allergies—Tell your doctor if you have ever had any unusual or allergic reaction to tamsulosin. Also tell your health

care professional if you are allergic to any other substances, such as foods, preservatives, or dyes.

Other medicines—Although certain medicines should not be used together at all, in other cases two different medicines may be used together even if an interaction might occur. In these cases, your doctor may want to change the dose, or other precautions may be necessary. When you are taking tamsulosin, it is especially important that your health care professional know if you are taking any of the following:

- Doxazosin (e.g., Cardura) or
- Phentolamine or
- Prazosin (e.g., Minipress) or
- Terazosin (e.g., Hytrin)—Effects of these medicines or tamsulosin may be increased
- Warfarin (e.g., Coumadin)—These medicines should be used together with caution

Proper Use of This Medicine

To help you remember to take your medicine, try to get into the habit of taking it at the same time each day. Take it approximately 30 minutes after the same meal each day.

Swallow the capsules whole. Do not crush, chew, or open them, unless otherwise directed by your doctor.

Dosing—The dose of tamsulosin will be different for different patients. *Follow your doctor's orders or the directions on the label*. The following information includes only the average doses of tamsulosin. *If your dose is different, do not change it* unless your doctor tells you to do so.

- For *oral* dosage form (capsules):
  —For benign enlargement of the prostate:
  - Adults—At first, 0.4 milligram (mg) once a day, about thirty minutes after the same meal each day. Your doctor may increase the dose if necessary.

Missed dose—If you miss a dose of this medicine, skip the missed dose and go back to your regular dosing schedule. Do not double doses.

Storage—To store this medicine:

- Keep out of the reach of children.
- Store away from heat and direct light.
- Do not store in the bathroom, near the kitchen sink, or in other damp places. Heat or moisture may cause the medicine to break down.
- Do not keep outdated medicine or medicine no longer needed. Be sure that any discarded medicine is out of the reach of children.

Precautions While Using This Medicine

It is important that your doctor check your progress at regular visits to make sure that this medicine is working properly.

Dizziness, lightheadedness, or fainting may occur after you take this medicine, especially when you get up from a lying or sitting position. Getting up slowly may help lessen this problem. *If you feel dizzy, lie down so that you do not faint*. Then sit for a few moments before standing to prevent the dizziness from returning.

Because tamsulosin may cause some people to become dizzy, *make sure you know how you react to this medicine before you drive, use machines, or do anything else that could be dangerous if you are dizzy*.

Side Effects of This Medicine

Along with its needed effects, a medicine may cause some unwanted effects. Although not all of these side effects may occur, if they do occur they may need medical attention.

The following side effects may go away during treatment as your body adjusts to the medicine. However, check with your doctor if any of the following side effects continue or are bothersome:

More common
    Abnormal ejaculation; back pain; diarrhea; dizziness; headache; stuffy or runny nose; unusual weakness

Less common
    Chest pain; decreased sexual drive or performance; difficulty in sleeping; fainting or lightheadedness, especially when getting up from a lying or sitting position; drowsiness; nausea

Other side effects not listed above may also occur in some patients. If you notice any other effects, check with your doctor.

Developed: 03/02/98

TAZAROTENE   Topical

Commonly used brand name(s):

In the U.S.—
   Tazorac

Description

Tazarotene (ta-ZAR-oh-teen) is used to treat acne on the face and and to treat psoriasis.

It works to help clear acne on the face partly by keeping skin pores clear. It works in the treatment of psoriasis by making the skin less red and reducing the number and size of lesions of the skin.

This medicine is available only with your doctor's prescription, in the following dosage form(s):

Topical
- Gel (U.S.)
- Cream (U.S.)

Before Using This Medicine

In deciding to use a medicine, the risks of using the medicine must be weighed against the good it will do. This is a decision you and your doctor will make. For tazarotene, the following should be considered:

Allergies—Tell your doctor if you have ever had any unusual or allergic reaction to vitamin A or retinoid medicines, such as acitretin, etretinate, isotretinoin, and tretinoin. Also tell your health care professional if you are allergic to any other substances, such as foods, preservatives, or dyes.

Pregnancy—Tazarotene is not recommended during pregnancy. It has been shown to cause serious birth defects and problems in animals. Be sure you have discussed this with your doctor.

Breast-feeding—It is not known whether tazarotene passes into breast milk. However, tazarotene is not recommended during breast-feeding because it may cause unwanted effects in nursing babies.

Children—Studies of this medicine have been done only in adult patients, and there is no specific information comparing use of tazarotene in children up to 12 years of age (gel) and up to 18 years of age (cream) with use in other age groups.

Older adults—Many medicines have not been studied specifically in older people. Therefore, it may not be known whether or not they work in exactly the same way they do in younger adults or if they cause different side effects or problems in older people. There is no specific information comparing the use of tazarotene in the elderly with use in other age groups.

Other medicines—Although certain medicines should not be used together at all, in other cases two different medicines may be used together even if an interaction might occur. In these cases, your doctor may want to change the dose, or other precautions may be necessary. Tell your doctor or pharmacist if you are using any other prescription or nonprescription (over-the-counter [OTC]) medicine.

Other medical problems—The presence of other medical problems may affect the use of tazarotene. Make sure you tell your doctor if you have any other medical problems, especially:

- Eczema—Tazarotene may cause skin irritation and may worsen this condition

Proper Use of This Medicine

It is very important that you use this medicine only as directed. Do not use more of it, do not use it more often, and do not use it for a longer time than your doctor ordered. To do so may cause irritation of the skin.

Read the patient information that will come with your medicine.

For acne—Before applying tazarotene to acne areas of the skin, wash the skin with a mild soap or cleanser and warm water, then gently pat dry. Wait at least 20 to 30 minutes before applying this medicine.

For acne or psoriasis—*Do not use this medicine in or around the eyes or lips, or inside of the nose.* Spread the medicine away from these areas when applying.

Do not apply this medicine to windburned or sunburned skin or on open wounds.

When using tazarotene, apply medicine to dry skin. If skin has just been washed and dried, *wait at least 20 to 30 minutes before applying this medicine.* Applying to wet or damp skin may cause skin irritation.

Apply a thin layer of this medicine only to lesions of psoriasis on the body or areas on face prone to developing acne. Rub medicine in gently and well. Wash medicine off skin areas not intended to be treated.

After applying the medicine, wash your hands to remove any medicine that might remain on them.

Dosing—The dose of tazarotene will be different for different patients. *Follow your doctor's orders or the directions on the label.* The following information includes only the average doses of tazarotene. *If your dose is different, do not change it* unless your doctor tells you to do so.

For *topical* dosage form (gel):
—For acne:
- Adults and children 12 years of age and older— Apply 0.1% tazarotene to clean, dry affected areas of the face once a day, usually in the evening or at bedtime.
- Children up to 12 years of age—Use and dose must be determined by the doctor.

—For psoriasis:
- Adults and children 12 years of age and older— Apply 0.05% or 0.1% tazarotene to dry affected areas of the body once a day, usually in the evening or at bedtime. Do not treat a larger area of the skin than your doctor tells you to treat.
- Children up to 12 years of age—Use and dose must be determined by the doctor.

For *topical* dosage form (cream):
—For psoriasis:
- Adults and children 18 years of age and older— Apply 0.05% or 0.1% tazarotene to dry affected areas of the body once a day, usually in the evening or at bedtime. Do not treat a larger area of the skin than your doctor tells you to treat.
- Children up to 18 years of age—Use and dose must be determined by the doctor.

Missed dose—If you miss a dose of this medicine, skip the missed dose and go back to your regular dosing schedule. Do not double doses.

Storage—To store this medicine:
- Keep out of the reach of children.
- Store away from heat and direct light.
- Keep the medicine from freezing.
- Do not keep outdated medicine or medicine no longer needed. Be sure that any discarded medicine is out of the reach of children.

Precautions While Using This Medicine

If you think that you may be pregnant, stop using the medicine immediately and check with your doctor.

If you are using this medicine to treat acne of the face, your condition may seem to worsen at first before it begins to improve in about 4 weeks. Check with your doctor if your condition does not improve within 8 to 12 weeks.

If your are using this medicine to treat psoriasis, scaly patches on skin may begin to improve in about 1 to 4 weeks but redness may take longer to improve. Check with your doctor if your condition becomes worse.

Do not cover the treated area with a bandage.

When using tazarotene, do not use skin products such as abrasive soaps or cleansers; alcohol-containing products; cosmetics or soaps that dry the skin; hair products that are irritating, such as permanents or hair removal products; skin products containing spices, limes, or other ingredients that may make the skin more sensitive to the sun; *or other topical medicine for the skin on the same area as tazarotene,* unless otherwise directed. To do so may cause severe irritation of the skin.

Ask your doctor before taking vitamin A supplements by mouth while using this medicine.

During treatment with this medicine, avoid exposing the treated areas to sunlight when possible, since the skin may be more likely to become sunburned. Do not use a sunlamp.

Some people who use this medicine may become more sensitive to wind or cold weather, as well as to sunlight. Avoiding exposure to these conditions by using sunscreen products with a sun protection factor (SPF) of 15 or more and wearing protective clothing will help protect your skin against becoming too dry, irritated, or sunburned.

Side Effects of This Medicine

It is likely that your skin may become irritated with normal use of this medicine. You should not stop using tazarotene unless your skin becomes too red, dry, puffy, or otherwise irritated. If severe irritation occurs, contact your doctor.

Along with its needed effects, a medicine may cause some unwanted effects. Although not all of these side effects may occur, if they do occur they may need medical attention.

Check with your doctor as soon as possible if any of the following side effects occur:

More common
> Burning or stinging of the skin (severe); changes in color of treated skin; deep grooves or lines in skin; dryness, itching, peeling, or redness of the skin (severe); pain or swelling of treated skin; skin rash (in patients with psoriasis only)

Other side effects may occur that usually do not need medical attention. These side effects may go away during treatment as your body adjusts to the medicine. However, check with your doctor if any of the following side effects continue or are bothersome:

More common
> Burning or stinging after application; dryness, itching, peeling, or redness of the skin (mild)

Other side effects not listed above may also occur in some patients. If you notice any other effects, check with your doctor.

Developed: 11/14/97
Revised: 03/05/2001

TELMISARTAN   Systemic

Commonly used brand name(s):

In the U.S.—
Micardis

In Canada—
Micardis

Description

Telmisartan (tel-mi-SAR-tan) belongs to the class of medicines called angiotensin II inhibitors. It is used to treat high blood pressure (hypertension).

High blood pressure adds to the workload of the heart and arteries. If it continues for a long time, the heart and arteries may not function properly. This can damage the blood vessels of the brain, heart, and kidneys, resulting in a stroke, heart failure, or kidney failure. High blood pressure may also increase the risk of heart attacks. These problems may be less likely to occur if blood pressure is controlled.

Telmisartan works by blocking the action of a substance in the body that causes blood vessels to tighten. As a result, telmisartan relaxes blood vessels. This lowers blood pressure.

This medicine is available only with your doctor's prescription, in the following dosage form:

Oral
> • Tablets (U.S. and Canada)

Before Using This Medicine

In deciding to use a medicine, the risks of taking the medicine must be weighed against the good it will do. This is a decision you and your doctor will make. For telmisartan, the following should be considered:

Allergies—Tell your doctor if you have ever had any unusual or allergic reaction to telmisartan. Also tell your health care professional if you are allergic to any other substances, such as foods, preservatives, or dyes.

Pregnancy—Use of telmisartan during pregnancy, especially during the second and third trimesters (after the first 3 months) can cause low blood pressure, severe kidney failure, or possibly death in the newborn. *Therefore, it is important that you check with your doctor immediately if you think that you may have become pregnant.* Be sure that you have discussed this with your doctor before taking this medicine.

Breast-feeding—It is not known whether telmisartan passes into breast milk. However, telmisartan passes into the milk of lactating rats. Because this medicine may cause serious side effects, breast-feeding is generally not recommended while you are taking it.

Children—Studies on this medicine have been done only in adult patients, and there is no specific information comparing use of telmisartan in children with use in other age groups.

Older adults—This medicine has been tested in patients 65 years of age or older and has not been shown to cause different side effects or problems in older people than it does in younger adults.

Racial differences—Black patients may have a smaller response to the blood pressure-lowering effects of telmisartan.

Other medicines—Although certain medicines should not be used together at all, in other cases two different medicines may be used together even if an interaction might occur. In these cases, your doctor may want to change the dose, or other precautions may be necessary. It is important that your health care professional know if you are taking any other medicines.

Other medical problems—The presence of other medical problems may affect the use of telmisartan. Make sure you tell your doctor if you have any other medical problems, especially:

• Aortic valve damage—Risk of decreased blood flow through the heart

• Congestive heart failure (severe)—Lowering of blood pressure by telmisartan may make this condition worse

• Dehydration (fluid and electrolyte loss due to excessive perspiration, vomiting, diarrhea, prolonged diuretic therapy, dialysis, or dietary salt restriction)—Blood pressure-lowering effects of telmisartan may be increased

- Kidney disease—Effects of telmisartan may make this condition worse
- Liver disease, severe—Blood levels of telmisartan may be higher in patients with this condition

Proper Use of This Medicine

Take this medicine only as directed by your doctor. Do not take more of it and do not take it more often than your doctor ordered. This medicine also works best when there is a constant amount in the blood. *To help keep the amount constant, do not miss any doses. Also, it is best to take the doses at the same time each day.*

Dosing—The dose of telmisartan will be different for different patients. *Follow your doctor's orders or the directions on the label.* The following information includes only the average doses of telmisartan. *If your dose is different, do not change it* unless your doctor tells you to do so.

The number of tablets that you take depends on the strength of the medicine.

- For *oral* dosage form (tablets):
  —For high blood pressure:
  - Adults—40 milligrams (mg) once a day. Your doctor may increase your dose if needed.
  - Children—Use and dose must be determined by your doctor.

Missed dose—If you miss a dose of this medicine, take it as soon as possible. However, if it is almost time for your next dose, skip the missed dose and go back to your regular dosing schedule. Do not double doses.

Storage—To store this medicine:

- Keep out of the reach of children.
- Store away from heat and direct light.
- Do not store in the bathroom, near the kitchen sink, or in other damp places. Heat or moisture may cause the medicine to break down.
- Do not keep outdated medicine or medicine no longer needed. Be sure that any discarded medicine is out of the reach of children.

Precautions While Using This Medicine

It is important that your doctor check your progress at regular visits to make sure that this medicine is working properly and to check for unwanted effects.

Check with your doctor immediately if you think that you may be pregnant. Telmisartan may cause birth defects or other problems in the baby if taken during pregnancy.

Do not take other medicines unless they have been discussed with your doctor. This especially includes over-the-counter (nonprescription) medicines for appetite control, asthma, colds, cough, hay fever, or sinus problems, since they may increase your blood pressure.

Dizziness or lightheadedness may occur, especially if you have been taking a diuretic (water pill). Make sure you know how you react to this medicine before you drive, use machines, or do anything else that could be dangerous if you experience these effects.

Check with your doctor right away if you become sick while taking this medicine, especially with severe or continuing nausea and vomiting or diarrhea. These conditions may cause you to lose too much water and lead to low blood pressure.

Dizziness, lightheadedness, or fainting also may occur if you exercise or if the weather is hot. Heavy sweating can cause loss of too much water and result in low blood pressure. Use extra care during exercise or hot weather.

Side Effects of This Medicine

Along with its needed effects, a medicine may cause some unwanted effects. Although not all of these side effects may occur, if they do occur they may need medical attention.

Check with your doctor as soon as possible if any of the following side effects occur:
> *Rare*
>> Changes in vision; dizziness, lightheadedness, or fainting; fast heartbeat; large hives

Other side effects may occur that usually do not need medical attention. These side effects may go away during treatment as your body adjusts to the medicine. However, check with your doctor if any of the following side effects continue or are bothersome:
> *Less common*
>> Abdominal pain; back pain; bloating or gas; changes in appetite; coughing, ear congestion or pain, fever, head congestion, nasal congestion, runny nose, sneezing, and/or sore throat; diarrhea; dry mouth; general tiredness or weakness; headache; heartburn; increased sweating; muscle pain or spasm; nausea; nervousness; painful urination or changes in urinary frequency; skin rash; swelling in hands, lower legs, and feet

Other side effects not listed above may also occur in some patients. If you notice any other effects, check with your doctor.

Developed: 01/04/99
Revised: 10/25/99

TEMOZOLOMIDE   Systemic

Commonly used brand name(s):

In the U.S.—
Temodar

In Canada—
Temodal

Description

Temozolomide (tem-oh-ZOHL-oh-mide) belongs to the general group of medicines known as antineoplastics. It is used to treat a specific type of cancer of the brain in adults whose tumors have returned.

Temozolomide seems to interfere with the growth of cancer cells, which are then eventually destroyed by the body. Since the growth of normal body cells may also be affected by temozolomide, other effects will also occur. Some of these may be serious and must be reported to your doctor.

Before you begin treatment with temozolomide, you and your doctor should talk about the good this medicine will do as well as the risks of using it.

Temozolomide is to be administered only by or under the immediate supervision of your doctor. It is available in the following dosage form:

Oral
- Capsules (U.S. and Canada)

Before Using This Medicine

In deciding to use a medicine, the risks of taking the medicine must be weighed against the good it will do. This is a decision you and your doctor will make. For temozolomide, the following should be considered:

Allergies—Tell your doctor if you have ever had any unusual or allergic reaction to dacarbazine or temozolomide. Also tell your health care professional if you are allergic to any other substances, such as foods, preservatives, or dyes.

Pregnancy—There is a chance that this medicine may cause birth defects if it is taken at the time of conception or if it is taken during pregnancy. You should wait for 6 months after the treatment is finished before becoming pregnant. Studies in rats and rabbits have shown that temozolomide causes birth defects in the fetus and other problems (including miscarriages).

Be sure that you have discussed these possible effects with your doctor before taking this medicine. Before taking temozolomide, make sure your doctor knows if you are pregnant or if you may become pregnant. It is best to use some kind of birth control while you are taking temozolomide. Tell your doctor right away if you think you have become pregnant while taking temozolomide.

If you are a man taking temozolomide you should be very careful not to father a child up to 6 months after treatment. Use a good form of birth control. Treatment with temozolomide may make you sterile. You may want to save and freeze your sperm before you start treatment with temozolomide in case this happens.

Breast-feeding—It is not known whether temozolomide passes into human breast milk. However, temozolomide is not recommended during breast-feeding because it may cause unwanted effects in nursing babies.

Children—Studies on this medicine have been done only in adult patients, and there is no specific information comparing the use of temozolomide in children with use in other age groups.

Older adults—Elderly patients may be more sensitive to the effects of temozolomide. Blood problems such as low platelet (the cell that helps blood to clot) counts and low white blood cell (the cell that helps fight off infections) counts may be especially likely to occur in patients 70 years of age or older.

Other medicines—Although certain medicines should not be used together at all, in other cases two different medicines may be used together even if an interaction might occur. In these cases, your doctor may want to change the dose, or other precautions may be necessary. When you are taking temozolomide it is especially important that your health care professional knows if you are taking any of the following:
- Acyclovir (e.g., Zovirax) or
- Anticonvulsants (seizure medicine) or
- Antidiabetics, oral (diabetes medicine taken by mouth) or
- Anti-infectives by mouth or by injection (medicine for infection) or

- Antipsychotics (medicine for mental illness) or
- Captopril (e.g., Capoten) or
- Enalapril (e.g., Vasotec) or
- Flecainide (e.g., Tambocor) or
- Imipenem or
- Inflammation or pain medicine, except narcotics or
- Lisinopril (e.g., Prinivil, Zestril) or
- Maprotiline (e.g., Ludiomil) or
- Penicillamine (e.g., Cuprimine) or
- Pimozide (e.g., Orap) or
- Procainamide (e.g., Pronestyl) or
- Promethazine (e.g., Phenergan) or
- Ramipril (e.g., Altace) or
- Sulfasalazine (e.g., Azulfidine) or
- Tiopronin (e.g., Thiola) or
- Tocainide (e.g., Tonocard) or
- Tricyclic antidepressants (medicine for depression) or
- Trimeprazine (e.g., Temaril)—Concurrent use of these agents with temozolomide may cause blood disorders
- Alpha Interferons (e.g., Intron A, Roferon-A) or
- Amphotericin B by injection (e.g., Fungizone) or
- Antineoplastics, other (cancer medicine) or
- Antithyroid agents (medicine for overactive thyroid) or
- Azathioprine (e.g., Imuran) or
- Chloramphenicol (e.g., Chloromycetin) or
- Colchicine or
- Flucytosine (e.g., Ancoban) or
- Ganciclovir (e.g., Cytovene) or
- Zidovudine (e.g., AZT, Retrovir)—Concurrent use of these agents with temozolomide increases the risk of infection

- If you have ever been treated with radiation or cancer medicines—Temozolomide may increase the effects that these medicines or radiation therapy may have on the blood

Other medical problems—The presence of other medical problems may affect the use of temozolomide. Make sure you tell your doctor if you have any other medical problems, especially:
- Bone marrow depression, existing or
- Infection—There may be an increased risk of infections or worsening infections because of the body's reduced ability to fight them
- Chickenpox (including recent exposure) or
- Herpes zoster (shingles)—Risk of severe disease affecting other parts of the body
- Kidney disease or
- Liver disease—Temozolomide should be used with caution

Proper Use of This Medicine

Take this medicine only as directed. Do not take more or less of it and do not take it for a longer time than directed. To do so may increase the chance of unwanted side effects. This is especially important for elderly patients, who may be more sensitive to the effects of this medicine.

Temozolomide often causes nausea and vomiting. However, *it is very important that you continue to take the medicine, even if you begin to feel ill.* Taking the medicine on an empty stomach or at bedtime may help to lessen the nausea. Ask your health care professional for other ways to help lessen these effects.

Temozolomide should be taken at the same time each day in relation to meals.

*Temozolomide capsules should be swallowed whole with
a full glass of water. The capsules should not be chewed,
crushed or broken open.* If the capsules are opened accidentally, do not allow the powder to come into contact with
your skin or into your mouth or nose. Be careful not to inhale
the contents of the capsule.

Dosing—The dose of temozolomide will be different for
different patients. The dose that is used will depend on a
number of things, including the patient's body size and various laboratory test results. *If you are taking temozolomide
at home, follow your doctor's orders or the directions on
the label.* If you have any questions about the proper dose
of temozolomide, ask your doctor.

Missed dose—If you miss a dose of this medicine, do not
double the next one. Check with your doctor for further instructions.

Storage—To store this medicine:
- Keep out of the reach of children.
- Store away from heat and direct light.
- Do not store in the bathroom, near the kitchen sink, or
  in other damp places. Heat or moisture may cause the
  medicine to break down.
- Do not keep outdated medicine or medicine no longer
  needed. Ask your health care professional how you
  should dispose of any medicine you do not use. Be sure
  that any discarded medicine is out of the reach of children.

Precautions While Using This Medicine

*It is very important that your doctor check your progress
at regular visits* to make sure that this medicine is working
properly and to check for unwanted effects.

While you are being treated with temozolomide, and after you
stop treatment with it, *do not have any immunizations (vaccinations) without your doctor's approval.* Temozolomide
may lower your body's resistance, and there is a chance you
might get the infection that the immunization is meant to prevent. In addition, other persons living in your household
should not take oral polio vaccine, since there is a chance
they could pass the polio virus on to you. Also, avoid persons
who have taken oral polio vaccine within the last several
months. Do not get close to them, and do not stay in the room
with them for very long. If you cannot take these precautions,
you should consider wearing a protective face mask that
covers the nose and mouth.

Temozolomide can temporarily lower the number of white
blood cells in your blood, increasing the chance of getting an
infection. It can also lower the number of platelets, which are
necessary for proper blood clotting. If this occurs, there are
certain precautions you can take, especially when your blood
count is low, to reduce the risk of infection or bleeding:
- If you can, avoid people with infections. *Check with
  your doctor immediately* if you think you are getting an
  infection or if you get a fever or chills, cough or hoarseness, lower back or side pain, or painful or difficult urination.
- *Check with your doctor immediately* if you notice any
  unusual bleeding or bruising; black, tarry stools; blood
  in urine or stools; or pinpoint red spots on your skin.
- Be careful when using a regular toothbrush, dental floss,
  or toothpick. Your medical doctor, dentist, or nurse may
  recommend other ways to clean your teeth and gums.
  Check with your medical doctor before having any dental
  work done.

- Do not touch your eyes or the inside of your nose unless
  you have just washed your hands and have not touched
  anything else in the meantime.
- Be careful not to cut yourself when you are using sharp
  objects such as a safety razor or fingernail or toenail
  cutters.
- Avoid contact sports or other situations where bruising
  or injury could occur.

Side Effects of This Medicine

Along with its needed effects, temozolomide may cause some
unwanted effects. Although not all of these side effects may
occur, if they do occur they may need medical attention.

Check with your doctor or nurse immediately if any of the
following side effects occur:
Less common or rare
   Amnesia; black, tarry stools; blood in urine or stools;
   convulsions (seizures); cough or hoarseness; fever
   or chills; infection; lower back or side pain; muscle
   weakness or paralysis on one or both sides of the
   body; painful or difficult urination; pinpoint red spots
   on skin; swelling of feet or lower legs; unusual
   bleeding or bruising

Other side effects may occur that usually do not need medical
attention. These side effects may go away during treatment
as your body adjusts to the medicine. However, check with
your doctor if any of the following side effects continue or are
bothersome:
More common
   Constipation; headache; nausea and vomiting; unusual
   tiredness or weakness
Less common or rare
   Abdominal or stomach pain; anxiety; blurred or double
   vision; breast pain (in females); burning or prickling
   feeling on the skin; confusion; diarrhea; difficulty in
   speaking; dizziness; drowsiness; loss of appetite;
   loss of muscle coordination; mental depression;
   muscle pain; runny or stuffy nose; skin rash or
   itching; sore throat; trouble in sleeping; unusual
   weight gain; urinary incontinence or increased urge
   to urinate

Other side effects not listed above may also occur in some
patients. If you notice any other effects, check with your
doctor.

Developed: 11/29/1999
Revised: 03/06/2001

TENECTEPLASE   Systemic

Commonly used brand name(s):
In the U.S.—
   TNKase
Another commonly used name is TNK, TNK-tPA, TNK-tissue plas-
minogen activator

Description

Tenecteplase (TEN-neck-te-place) is used to dissolve blood
clots that have formed in the blood vessels of the heart and
seriously lessen the flow of blood in the heart. This medicine
is used to improve survival after a heart attack.

Tenecteplase is to be administered only by or under the immediate supervision of your doctor, it is available in the following dosage forms:

Parenteral
- Injection (U.S.)

Before Receiving This Medicine

In deciding to use a medicine, the risks of using the medicine must be weighed against the good it will do. This is a decision you and your doctor will make. For tenecteplase, the following should be considered:

Allergies—Tell your doctor if you have ever had any unusual or allergic reaction to tenecteplase. Also tell your doctor and pharmacist if you are allergic to any other substances.

Pregnancy—Tenecteplase has not been studied in pregnant women. However, studies in rabbits have shown that multiple intravenous administrations of tenecteplase cause maternal and embryo toxicity, but no fetal abnormalities have been observed. Tenecteplase does not cause maternal and embryo toxicity in rabbits after a single intravenous administration. Before taking this medicine, make sure your doctor knows if you are pregnant or if you have recently had a baby.

The most common adverse effect of tenecteplase therapy is bleeding, and pregnancy can increase this risk.

Breast-feeding—It is not known whether tenecteplase passes into breast milk. Although most medicines pass into breast milk in small amounts, many of them may be used safely while breast-feeding. Mothers who have been given this medicine and who wish to breast-feed should discuss this with their doctor.

Children—Studies on this medicine have been done only in adult patients, and there is no specific information comparing use of tenecteplase in children with use in other age groups.

Older adults—The need for treatment with tenecteplase may be increased in elderly patients with blood clots. However, the chance of bleeding may also be increased. It is especially important that you discuss the use of this medicine with your doctor.

Other medicines—Although certain medicines should not be used together at all, in other cases two different medicines may be used together even if an interaction might occur. In these cases, your doctor may want to change the dose, or other precautions may be necessary. Before you receive tenecteplase, it is especially important that your doctor know if you are taking any of the following:

- Anticoagulants (blood thinners) or
- Aspirin or
- Clopidogrel (e.g., Plavix) or
- Dipyridamole (e.g., Persantine) or
- Heparin or
- Ticlopidine (e.g., Ticlid) or
- Warfarin (e.g., Coumadin)—The chance of bleeding may be increased

Other medical problems—Other medical problems or recent childbirth. The presence of other medical problems or recent delivery of a child may affect the use of tenecteplase. Make sure you tell your doctor if you have any other medical problems, especially:

- Blood disease, bleeding problems, or a history of bleeding in any part of the body or

- Brain disease or tumor or
- Heart or blood vessel disease, including irregular heartbeat or
- High blood pressure or
- Liver disease or
- Stroke—The chance of bleeding may be increased

- Infection—Chance of spreading the infection into the blood stream

Also, tell your doctor if you have recently had any of the following conditions:

- Falls or blow to the body or head or any other injury or
- Injections into a blood vessel or
- Placement of any tube into the body or
- Surgery of any kind, including dental surgery—The chance of serious bleeding may be increased

If you have recently had a baby, use of this medicine may cause serious bleeding.

Proper Use of This Medicine

Dosing—The dose of tenecteplase will be different for different patients. The dose you receive will depend on your body weight.

Precautions While Using This Medicine

Tenecteplase can cause bleeding that usually is not serious. However, serious bleeding may occur in some people. *To help prevent serious bleeding, carefully follow any instructions given by your health care professional. Also, move around and be handled as little as possible, and do not get out of bed on your own, unless your health care professional tells you it is all right to do so.*

Do not take other medicines unless they have been discussed with your doctor. This especially includes nonprescription medicines, such as aspirin.

Side Effects of This Medicine

Along with its needed effects, a medicine may cause some unwanted effects. Although not all of these side effects may occur, if they do occur they may need medical attention.

Check with your doctor immediately if any of the following side effects occur:
More common
  Bleeding or bruising of any kind, especially around the place of injection; collection of blood under skin

Less common or rare
  Abdominal or stomach pain or swelling; back pain or backaches; blood in throat; blood in urine; bloody or black, tarry stools; constipation; cough; coughing up blood; difficulty swallowing; dizziness; fast, slow or irregular breathing; fast, slow or irregular heartbeat; headaches; hives; nosebleeds; shortness of breath and/or wheezing; skin rash, hives or itching; swelling of eyes, face, lips, or tongue; tightness in chest; unusual tiredness or weakness; vomiting of blood or material that looks like coffee grounds; wheezing

Other side effects may occur that usually do not need medical attention. These side effects may go away during treatment as your body adjusts to the medicine. However, check with your doctor if any of the following side effects continue or are bothersome.

Less common
    Bloody nose; unexplained nosebleeds

Developed: 07/28/2000

TENIPOSIDE Systemic

Commonly used brand name(s):

In the U.S.—
    Vumon

In Canada—
    Vumon

Another commonly used name is VM-26.

Description

Teniposide (ten-i-POE-side) belongs to the group of medicines called antineoplastics. Teniposide injection is used along with other medicines to treat acute lymphoblastic leukemia (ALL), non-Hodgkin's lymphoma (NHL), and neuroblastoma.

Teniposide interferes with the growth of cancer cells, which are eventually destroyed. Since the growth of normal body cells may also be affected by teniposide, other effects will also occur. Some of these may be serious and must be reported to your doctor. Other effects may not be serious but may cause concern.

Teniposide is to be administered only by or under the immediate supervision of your doctor. It is available in the following dosage form:

Parenteral
    • Injection (U.S. and Canada)

Before Using This Medicine

In deciding to use a medicine, the risks of using the medicine must be weighed against the good it will do. This is a decision you and your doctor will make. For teniposide, the following should be considered:

Allergies—Tell your doctor if you have ever had any unusual or allergic reaction to teniposide. Also tell your health care professional if you are allergic to any other substances, such as castor oil.

Pregnancy—Teniposide has not been studied in pregnant women. However, studies in animals have shown that teniposide causes slower development or death of the fetus and birth defects, such as defects of the spine or ribs, deformed extremities, being born without eyes, and a defect or absence of breast-bone. Be sure that you have discussed this with your doctor. Tell your doctor right away if you think you have become pregnant while receiving teniposide.

Breast-feeding—It is not known if teniposide passes into the breast milk. However, due to the potential for serious side effects, if you are breast-feeding or plan to breast-feed while receiving this medicine, be sure that you have discussed this with your doctor.

Children—Children with Down syndrome may be more sensitive to the effects of this medicine compared to other children. Your doctor may decide to start treatment with this medicine at a lower dose.

Older adults—Many medicines have not been studied specifically in older people. Therefore, it may not be known whether they work exactly the same way they do in younger adults or if they cause different side effects or problems in older people. There is no specific information comparing use of teniposide in the elderly with use in other age groups.

Other medicines—Although certain medicines should not be used together at all, in other cases two different medicines may be used together even if an interaction might occur. In these cases, your doctor may want to change the dose, or other precautions may be necessary. When you are taking teniposide, it is especially important that your health care professional know if you are taking any of the following:

• Acyclovir (e.g., Zovirax) or
• Anticonvulsants (seizure medicine) or
• Antidiabetics, oral (diabetes medicine taken by mouth) or
• Anti-infectives by mouth or by injection (medicine for infection) or
• Antipsychotics (medicine for mental illness) or
• Captopril (e.g., Capoten) or
• Carbamazepine (e.g., Tegretol)
• Enalapril (e.g., Vasotec) or
• Flecainide (e.g., Tambocor) or
• Gold salts (medicine for arthritis) or
• Imipenem or
• Inflammation or pain medicine, except narcotics or
• Lisinopril (e.g., Prinivil, Zestril) or
• Maprotiline (e.g., Ludiomil) or
• Penicillamine (e.g., Cuprimine) or
• Pimozide (e.g., Orap) or
• Procainamide (e.g., Pronestyl) or
• Promethazine (e.g., Phenergan) or
• Ramipril (e.g., Altace) or
• Sulfasalazine (e.g., Azulfidine) or
• Tiopronin (e.g., Thiola) or
• Tocainide (e.g., Tonocard) or
• Tricyclic antidepressants (medicine for depression) or
• Trimeprazine (e.g., Temaril)—Concurrent use of these agents with teniposide may cause blood disorders

• Alpha interferons (e.g., Intron A, Roferon-A) or
• Amphotericin B by injection (e.g., Fungizone) or
• Antineoplastics, other (cancer medicine) or
• Antithyroid agents (medicine for overactive thyroid) or
• Azathioprine (e.g., Imuran) or
• Chloramphenicol (e.g., Chloromycetin) or
• Colchicine or
• Cyclophosphamide (e.g. Cytoxan) or
• Flucytosine (e.g. Ancoban) or
• Ganciclovir (e.g., Cytovene) or
• Mercaptopurine (e.g., Purinethol) or
• Plicamycin (e.g., Mithracin) or
• Zidovudine (e.g., AZT, Retrovir)—Concurrent use of these agents with teniposide increases the risk of infection

• Sodium salicylate or
• Sulfamethizole (e.g., Thiosulfil Forte) or
• Tolbutamide (e.g., Orinase)—Taking these medicines while receiving teniposide may cause the level of teniposide in the body to be higher than usual, which may increase the chance of unwanted effects

• If you have ever been treated with radiation or cancer medicines—Teniposide may increase the effects of these medicines or radiation therapy on the blood

Other medical problems—The presence of other medical problems may affect the use of teniposide. Make sure you tell your doctor if you have any other medical problems, especially:

- Blood disorders due to bone marrow depression or
- Infection—There may be an increased risk of infections or worsening infections because of the body's reduced ability to fight them
- Chickenpox (including recent exposure) or
- Herpes zoster (shingles)—Risk of severe disease affecting other parts of the body
- Down syndrome—Patients who have this condition may be more sensitive to this medicine
- Hypoalbuminemia or
- Kidney disease or
- Liver disease—These conditions may cause the level of teniposide in the body to be higher than usual, which may increase the chance of unwanted effects

Proper Use of This Medicine

Teniposide often causes nausea and vomiting, which usually are not severe. However, it is very important that you continue to receive the medicine, even if you begin to feel ill. Ask your doctor, nurse, or pharmacist for ways to lessen these effects.

Dosing—The dose of teniposide will be different for different patients. The dose that is used may depend on a number of things, including the patient's weight, other medical conditions, and whether or not other medicines are also being taken. Because this medicine can cause very serious side effects, your doctor will be watching your dose very carefully and may change it as needed. If you have any questions about the proper dose of teniposide, ask your doctor.

Precautions While Using This Medicine

It is very important that your doctor check your progress at regular visits to make sure that teniposide is working properly and to check for unwanted effects.

It is important to tell your doctor or nurse right away if redness, pain, swelling, or a lump under the skin occurs in the area where the injection is given.

While you are being treated with teniposide, and after you stop treatment, *do not have any immunizations (vaccinations) without your doctor's approval.* Teniposide may lower your body's resistance, and there is a chance you might get the infection the immunization is meant to prevent. In addition, other persons living in your household should not take oral polio vaccine, since there is a chance they could pass the polio virus on to you. Also, avoid persons who have taken oral polio vaccine within the last several months. Do not get close to them, and do not stay in the same room with them for very long. If you cannot take these precautions, you should consider wearing a protective face mask that covers the nose and mouth.

Teniposide can temporarily lower the number of white blood cells in your blood, increasing the chance of getting an infection. It can also lower the number of platelets, which are necessary for proper blood clotting. If this occurs, there are certain precautions you can take, especially when your blood count is low, to reduce the risk of infection or bleeding:

- If you can, avoid people with infections. *Check with*

your doctor immediately if you think you are getting an infection or if you get a fever or chills, cough or hoarseness, lower back or side pain, or painful or difficult urination.
- *Check with your doctor immediately* if you notice any unusual bleeding or bruising; black, tarry stools; blood in urine or stools; or pinpoint red spots on your skin.
- Be careful when using a regular toothbrush, dental floss, or toothpick. Your medical doctor, dentist, or nurse may recommend other ways to clean your teeth and gums. Check with your medical doctor before having any dental work done.
- Do not touch your eyes or the inside of your nose unless you have just washed your hands and have not touched anything else in the meantime.
- Be careful not to cut yourself when you are using sharp objects such as a safety razor or fingernail or toenail cutters.
- Avoid contact sports or other situations where bruising or injury could occur.

Side Effects of This Medicine

Along with its needed effects, a medicine may cause some unwanted effects. Although not all of these side effects may occur, if they do occur they may need medical attention.

Check with your doctor immediately if any of the following side effects occur:
  More common
    Black, tarry stools; blood in urine or stools; chills; cough or hoarseness; fever; hives; lower back or side pain; painful or difficult urination; pinpoint red spots on skin; shortness of breath; tightness in chest, or wheezing; troubled breathing; unusual bleeding or bruising

Check with your doctor as soon as possible if any of the following side effects occur:
  More common
    Flushing of face; sores in mouth or on lips; unusually fast heartbeat; unusual tiredness

  Less common
    Skin rash

  Rare
    Decreased urination; swelling of face, fingers, feet, or lower legs; yellow eyes or skin

Other side effects may occur that usually do not need medical attention. These side effects may go away during treatment as your body adjusts to the medicine. However, check with your doctor if any of the following side effects continue or are bothersome:
  More common
    Diarrhea; nausea and vomiting

This medicine often causes a temporary loss of hair. After treatment with teniposide has ended, normal hair growth should return.

Other side effects not listed above may also occur in some patients. If you notice any other effects, check with your doctor, nurse, or pharmacist.

Developed: 08/13/98
Revised: 05/25/00

TERAZOSIN   Systemic

Commonly used brand name(s):

In the U.S.—
　Hytrin

In Canada—
　Hytrin

Description

Terazosin (ter-AY-zoe-sin) is used to treat high blood pressure (hypertension).

High blood pressure adds to the work load of the heart and arteries. If it continues for a long time, the heart and arteries may not function properly. This can damage the blood vessels of the brain, heart, and kidneys, resulting in a stroke, heart failure, or kidney failure. High blood pressure may also increase the risk of heart attacks. These problems may be less likely to occur if blood pressure is controlled.

Terazosin helps to lower blood pressure by relaxing blood vessels so that blood passes through them more easily.

Terazosin is also used to treat benign enlargement of the prostate (benign prostatic hyperplasia [BPH]). Benign enlargement of the prostate is a problem that can occur in men as they get older. The prostate gland is located below the bladder. As the prostate gland enlarges, certain muscles in the gland may become tight and get in the way of the tube that drains urine from the bladder. This can cause problems in urinating, such as a need to urinate often, a weak stream when urinating, or a feeling of not being able to empty the bladder completely.

Terazosin helps relax the muscles in the prostate and the opening of the bladder. This may help increase the flow of urine and/or decrease the symptoms. However, terazosin will not help shrink the prostate. The prostate may continue to grow. This may cause the symptoms to become worse over time. Therefore, even though terazosin may lessen the problems caused by enlarged prostate now, surgery still may be needed in the future.

Terazosin is available only with your doctor's prescription, in the following dosage form:

　Oral
　　• Tablets (U.S. and Canada)

Before Using This Medicine

In deciding to use a medicine, the risks of taking the medicine must be weighed against the good it will do. This is a decision you and your doctor will make. For terazosin, the following should be considered:

Allergies—Tell your doctor if you have ever had any unusual or allergic reaction to terazosin, prazosin, or doxazosin. Also tell your health care professional if you are allergic to any other substances, such as foods, preservatives, or dyes.

Pregnancy—Studies have not been done in humans. Studies in animals given many times the highest recommended human dose have not shown that terazosin causes birth defects. However, these studies have shown a decrease in successful pregnancies.

Breast-feeding—It is not known whether terazosin passes into breast milk. Although most medicines pass into breast milk in small amounts, many of them may be used safely while breast-feeding. Mothers who are taking this medicine and who wish to breast-feed should discuss this with their doctor.

Children—Studies on this medicine have been done only in adult patients, and there is no specific information comparing use of terazosin in children with use in other age groups.

Older adults—Dizziness, lightheadedness, or fainting (especially when getting up from a lying or sitting position) may be more likely to occur in the elderly, who are more sensitive to the effects of terazosin.

Other medicines—Although certain medicines should not be used together at all, in other cases two different medicines may be used together even if an interaction might occur. In these cases, your doctor may want to change the dose, or other precautions may be necessary. Tell your health care professional if you are taking any other prescription or nonprescription (over-the-counter [OTC]) medicine.

Other medical problems—The presence of other medical problems may affect the use of terazosin. Make sure you tell your doctor if you have any other medical problems, especially:

　• Angina (chest pain)—Terazosin may make this condition worse

　• Heart disease (severe)—Terazosin may make this condition worse

　• Kidney disease—Possible increased sensitivity to the effects of terazosin

Proper Use of This Medicine

For patients *taking this medicine for high blood pressure:*

　• In addition to the use of the medicine your doctor has prescribed, treatment for your high blood pressure may include weight control and care in the types of foods you eat, especially foods high in sodium. Your doctor will tell you which of these are most important for you. You should check with your doctor before changing your diet.

　• Many patients who have high blood pressure will not notice any signs of the problem. In fact, many may feel normal. It is very important that you *take your medicine exactly as directed* and that you keep your appointments with your doctor even if you feel well.

　• Remember that terazosin will not cure your high blood pressure but it does help control it. Therefore, you must continue to take it as directed if you expect to lower your blood pressure and keep it down. *You may have to take high blood pressure medicine for the rest of your life.* If high blood pressure is not treated, it can cause serious problems such as heart failure, blood vessel disease, stroke, or kidney disease.

For patients *taking this medicine for benign enlargement of the prostate:*

　• Remember that terazosin will not shrink the size of your prostate but it does help to relieve the symptoms.

　• It may take up to 6 weeks before your symptoms get better.

To help you remember to take your medicine, try to get into the habit of taking it at the same time each day.

Dosing—The dose of terazosin will be different for different patients. *Follow your doctor's orders or the directions on the label.* The following information includes only the average doses of terazosin. *If your dose is different, do not change it* unless your doctor tells you to do so.

The number of tablets that you take depends on the strength of the medicine.

- For *oral* dosage form (tablets):
  - —For benign enlargement of the prostate:
    - Adults—At first, 1 milligram (mg) taken at bedtime. Then, 5 to 10 mg once a day.
  - —For high blood pressure:
    - Adults—At first, 1 mg taken at bedtime. Then, 1 to 5 mg once a day.
    - Children—Use and dose must be determined by your doctor.

Missed dose—If you miss a dose of this medicine, take it as soon as possible the same day. However, if you do not remember the missed dose until the next day, skip the missed dose and go back to your regular dosing schedule. Do not double doses.

Storage—To store this medicine:
- Keep out of the reach of children.
- Store away from heat and direct light.
- Do not store in the bathroom, near the kitchen sink, or in other damp places. Heat or moisture may cause the medicine to break down.
- Do not keep outdated medicine or medicine no longer needed. Be sure that any discarded medicine is out of the reach of children.

Precautions While Using This Medicine

It is important that your doctor check your progress at regular visits to make sure that this medicine is working properly.

For patients *taking this medicine for high blood pressure:*
- *Do not take other medicines unless they have been discussed with your doctor.* This especially includes over-the-counter (nonprescription) medicines for appetite control, asthma, colds, cough, hay fever, or sinus problems, since they may tend to increase your blood pressure.

Dizziness, lightheadedness, or sudden fainting may occur after you take this medicine, especially when you get up from a lying or sitting position. These effects are more likely to occur when you take the first dose of this medicine. Taking the first dose at bedtime may prevent problems. However, *be especially careful if you need to get up during the night.* These effects may also occur with any doses you take after the first dose. Getting up slowly may help lessen this problem. *If you feel dizzy, lie down so that you do not faint.* Then sit for a few moments before standing to prevent the dizziness from returning.

The dizziness, lightheadedness, or fainting is more likely to occur if you drink alcohol, stand for long periods of time, exercise, or if the weather is hot. *While you are taking this medicine, be careful to limit the amount of alcohol you drink. Also, use extra care during exercise or hot weather or if you must stand for long periods of time.*

Terazosin may cause some people to become drowsy or less alert than they are normally. *Make sure you know how you react to this medicine before you drive, use machines, or do anything else that could be dangerous if you are dizzy, drowsy, or are not alert.* After you have taken several doses of this medicine, these effects should lessen.

Side Effects of This Medicine

Along with its needed effects, a medicine may cause some unwanted effects. Although not all of these side effects may occur, if they do occur they may need medical attention.

Check with your doctor as soon as possible if any of the following side effects occur:

More common
  Dizziness

Less common
  Chest pain; dizziness or lightheadedness when getting up from a lying or sitting position; fainting (sudden); fast or irregular heartbeat; pounding heartbeat; shortness of breath; swelling of feet or lower legs

Rare
  Weight gain

Other side effects may occur that usually do not need medical attention. These side effects may go away during treatment as your body adjusts to the medicine. However, check with your doctor if any of the following side effects continue or are bothersome:

More common
  Headache; unusual tiredness or weakness

Less common
  Back or joint pain; blurred vision; drowsiness; nausea and vomiting; stuffy nose

Other side effects not listed above may also occur in some patients. If you notice any other effects, check with your doctor.

Revised: 06/26/92
Interim revision: 07/08/94

TERBINAFINE   Systemic

Commonly used brand name(s):

In the U.S.—
  Lamisil

In Canada—
  Lamisil

Description

Terbinafine (ter-BIN-a-feen) belongs to the group of medicines called antifungals. It is used to treat fungus infections of the scalp, body, groin (jock itch), feet (athlete's foot), fingernails, and toenails.

Terbinafine is available only with your doctor's prescription, in the following dosage form:

Oral
- Tablets (U.S. and Canada)

Before Using This Medicine

In deciding to use a medicine, the risks of taking the medicine must be weighed against the good it will do. This is a decision you and your doctor will make. For terbinafine, the following should be considered:

Allergies—Tell your doctor if you have ever had any unusual or allergic reaction to terbinafine. Also tell your health

care professional if you are allergic to any other substances, such as foods, preservatives, or dyes.

Pregnancy—Terbinafine has not been studied in pregnant women. Before taking any medicine, make sure your doctor knows if you are pregnant or if you may become pregnant.

Breast-feeding—Terbinafine passes into breast milk. Mothers who are taking this medicine and wish to breast-feed should discuss this with their doctor.

Children—Studies on this medicine have been done only in adult patients, and there is no specific information comparing use of terbinafine in children with use in other age groups.

Older adults—Many medicines have not been studied specifically in older people. Therefore, it may not be known whether they work exactly the same way they do in younger adults or if they cause different side effects or problems in older people. There is no specific information comparing use of terbinafine in the elderly with use in other age groups.

Other medicines—Although certain medicines should not be used together at all, in other cases two different medicines may be used together even if an interaction might occur. In these cases, your doctor may want to change the dose, or other precautions may be necessary. When you are taking terbinafine, it is especially important that your health care professional know if you are taking any of the following:

- Acetaminophen (e.g., Tylenol) (with long-term, high-dose use) or
- Amiodarone (e.g., Cordarone) or
- Anabolic steroids (nandrolone [e.g., Anabolin], oxandrolone [e.g., Anavar], oxymetholone [e.g., Anadrol], stanozolol [e.g., Winstrol]) or
- Androgens (male hormones) or
- Antithyroid agents (medicine for overactive thyroid) or
- Carmustine (e.g., BiCNU) or
- Chloroquine (e.g., Aralen) or
- Dantrolene (e.g., Dantrium) or
- Daunorubicin (e.g., Cerubidine) or
- Estrogens (female hormones) or
- Etretinate (e.g., Tegison) or
- Gold salts (medicine for arthritis) or
- Hydroxychloroquine (e.g., Plaquenil) or
- Mercaptopurine (e.g., Purinethol) or
- Methotrexate (e.g., Mexate) or
- Methyldopa (e.g., Aldomet) or
- Naltrexone (e.g., Trexan) (with long-term, high-dose use) or
- Other anti-infectives by mouth or by injection (medicine for infection) or
- Phenothiazines (acetophenazine [e.g., Tindal], chlorpromazine [e.g., Thorazine], fluphenazine [e.g., Prolixin], mesoridazine [e.g., Serentil], perphenazine [e.g., Trilafon], prochlorperazine [e.g., Compazine], promazine [e.g., Sparine], promethazine [e.g., Phenergan], thioridazine [e.g., Mellaril], trifluoperazine [e.g., Stelazine], triflupromazine [e.g., Vesprin], trimeprazine [e.g., Temaril]) or
- Plicamycin (e.g., Mithracin)—Use of these medicines with terbinafine may increase the chance of side effects affecting the liver

- Azole antifungals (fluconazole [e.g., Diflucan], itraconazole [e.g., Sporanox], ketoconazole [e.g., Nizoral]) or
- Chloramphenicol (e.g., Chloromycetin) or
- Cimetidine (e.g., Tagamet) or
- Clarithromycin (e.g., Biaxin) or
- Diltiazem (e.g., Cardizem) or

- Erythromycins (e.g., EES, E-Mycin) or
- Isoniazid (e.g., INH, Nydrazid) or
- Quinine (e.g., Quinamm) or
- Ranitidine (e.g., Zantac) or
- Verapamil (e.g., Calan)—Use of these medicines with terbinafine may increase the chance of side effects of terbinafine

- Carbamazepine (e.g., Tegretol) or
- Corticosteroids (cortisone-like medicine) or
- Griseofulvin (e.g., Fulvicin, Grisovin) or
- Phenobarbital (e.g., Luminal) or
- Phenylbutazone (e.g., Butazolidin) or
- Primidone (e.g., Mysoline) or
- Rifampin (e.g., Rifadin)—Use of these medicines with terbinafine may prevent terbinafine from working properly

- Disulfiram (e.g., Antabuse) or
- Divalproex (e.g., Depakote) or
- Oral contraceptives (birth control pills) containing estrogen or
- Valproic acid (e.g., Depakene)—Use of these medicines with terbinafine may increase the chance of side effects of terbinafine, especially those affecting the liver

- Phenytoin (e.g., Dilantin)—Use of this medicine with terbinafine may prevent terbinafine from working properly and may increase the chance of side effects affecting the liver

Other medical problems—The presence of other medical problems may affect the use of terbinafine. Make sure you tell your doctor if you have any other medical problems, especially:

- Alcohol abuse (or history of) or—Problems with alcohol may increase the chance of side effects caused by terbinafine
- Kidney disease or
- Liver disease, active or chronic—These conditions may increase the chance of side effects caused by terbinafine. Terbinafine is not recommended for patients with liver or kidney problems

---

Proper Use of This Medicine

Terbinafine may be taken with food or on an empty stomach.

To help clear up your infection completely, *it is very important that you keep taking this medicine for the full time of treatment,* even if your symptoms begin to clear up or you begin to feel better after a few days. Since fungus infections may be very slow to clear up, you may need to take this medicine for several weeks or months. If you stop taking this medicine too soon, your symptoms may return.

This medicine works best when there is a constant amount in the blood. *To help keep the amount constant, do not miss any doses. Also, it is best to take the doses at the same times every day.* If you need help in planning the best time to take your medicine, check with your health care professional.

Dosing—The dose of terbinafine may be different for different patients. *Follow your doctor's orders or the directions on the label.* The following information includes only the average doses of terbinafine. Your dose may be different if you have kidney or liver disease. *If your dose is different, do not change it* unless your doctor tells you to do so.

The number of tablets that you take depends on the strength of the medicine. Also, *the length of time you take the med-*

icine depends on the medical problem for which you are taking terbinafine.

- For *oral* dosage form (tablets):
  - —For onychomycosis (fungus infections of the fingernails or toenails):
    - Adults and teenagers—250 milligrams (mg) once a day for six to twelve weeks.
    - Children—Use and dose must be determined by the doctor.
  - —For tinea corporis (ringworm of the body):
    - Adults and teenagers—250 mg once a day for two to four weeks.
    - Children—Use and dose must be determined by the doctor.
  - —For tinea cruris (ringworm of the groin; jock itch):
    - Adults and teenagers—250 mg once a day for two to four weeks.
    - Children—Use and dose must be determined by the doctor.
  - —For tinea pedis (ringworm of the foot; athlete's foot):
    - Adults and teenagers—250 mg once a day for two to six weeks.
    - Children—Use and dose must be determined by the doctor.

Missed dose—If you miss a dose of this medicine, take it as soon as possible. This will help to keep a constant amount of medicine in the blood. However, if it is almost time for your next dose, skip the missed dose and go back to your regular dosing schedule. Do not double doses.

Storage—To store this medicine:
- Keep out of the reach of children.
- Store away from heat and direct light.
- Do not store this medicine in the bathroom, near the kitchen sink, or in other damp places. Heat or moisture may cause the medicine to break down.
- Do not keep outdated medicine or medicine no longer needed. Be sure that any discarded medicine is out of the reach of children.

Precautions While Using This Medicine

It is important that your doctor check your progress at regular visits. This will allow your doctor to check for any unwanted effects.

If your symptoms do not improve within a few weeks (or months for onychomycosis), or if they become worse, check with your doctor.

Liver problems may be more likely to occur if you drink alcoholic beverages while you are taking this medicine. Therefore, you should not drink alcoholic beverages while you are taking this medicine.

It is important that you check with your doctor immediately if you persistently experience any discomforts of liver disease (e.g., nausea or vomiting, lack of appetite, general feeling of tiredness or weakness, stomach pain, yellow eyes or skin, dark urine, or pale stools).

Side Effects of This Medicine

Along with its needed effects, a medicine may cause some unwanted effects. Although not all of these effects may occur, if they do occur they may need medical attention.

Check with your doctor immediately if any of the following side effects occur:

Less common
  Skin rash or itching

Rare
  Aching joints and muscles; dark urine; difficulty in swallowing; fever, chills, or sore throat; loss of appetite; pale skin; pale stools; redness, blistering, peeling, or loosening of skin; unusual bleeding or bruising; unusual tiredness or weakness; yellow skin or eyes; continuing headache; stomach pain or vomiting; general feeling of tiredness or weakness

Other side effects may occur that usually do not need medical attention. These side effects may go away during treatment as your body adjusts to the medicine. However, check with your doctor if any of the following side effects continue or are bothersome:

More common
  Diarrhea; nausea and vomiting; stomach pain (mild)

Less common
  Change of taste or loss of taste

Other side effects not listed above may also occur in some patients. If you notice any other effects, check with your doctor.

Developed: 06/22/95
Revised: 06/27/2001

TERBINAFINE   Topical

Commonly used brand name(s):

In the U.S.—
  Lamisil

In Canada—
  Lamisil

Description

Terbinafine (TER-bin-a-feen) is used to treat infections caused by a fungus. It works by killing the fungus or preventing its growth.

Terbinafine is applied to the skin to treat:
- ringworm of the body (tinea corporis);
- ringworm of the foot (interdigital and plantar tinea pedis; athlete's foot);
- ringworm of the groin (tinea cruris; jock itch);
- tinea versicolor (sometimes called "sun fungus"); and
- yeast infection of the skin (cutaneous candidiasis).

Terbinafine is available only with your doctor's prescription, in the following dosage form:

Topical
- Cream (U.S. and Canada)
- Solution (Pump Spray) (U.S.)

Before Using This Medicine

In deciding to use a medicine, the risks of using the medicine must be weighed against the good it will do. This is a decision you and your doctor will make. For terbinafine, the following should be considered:

Allergies—Tell your doctor if you have ever had any unusual or allergic reaction to terbinafine. Also tell your health care professional if you are allergic to any other substances, such as foods, preservatives, or dyes.

Pregnancy—Terbinafine has not been studied in pregnant women. However, terbinafine has not been shown to cause birth defects or other problems in animal studies.

Breast-feeding—Oral terbinafine passes into breast milk. It is not known whether topical terbinafine passes into breast milk. Although most medicines pass into breast milk in small amounts, many of them may be used safely while breast-feeding. Mothers who are using this medicine and who wish to breast-feed should discuss this with their doctor. Nursing mothers should not apply topical terbinafine to the breasts.

Children—Studies on this medicine have been done only in adult patients, and there is no specific information comparing use of terbinafine in children under the age of 12 with use in other age groups.

Older adults—Many medicines have not been studied specifically in older people. Therefore, it may not be known whether they work exactly the same way they do in younger adults. Although there is no specific information comparing use of terbinafine in the elderly with use in other age groups, this medicine is not expected to cause different side effects or problems in older people than it does in younger adults.

Other medicines—Although certain medicines should not be used together at all, in other cases two different medicines may be used together even if an interaction might occur. In these cases, your doctor may want to change the dose, or other precautions may be necessary. Tell your health care professional if you are using any other topical prescription or nonprescription (over-the-counter [OTC]) medicine that is to be applied to the same area of the skin.

Other medical problems—The presence of other medical problems may affect the use of terbinafine. Make sure you tell your doctor if you have any other medical problems, especially:
- Fungus infection of the nails—condition may decrease the effect of terbinafine when this medicine is used to treat a type of ringworm of the foot (plantar tinea pedis)

Proper Use of This Medicine

Apply enough terbinafine cream to cover the affected and surrounding skin areas and rub in gently.

Apply enough terbinafine solution to wet and cover the affected and surrounding skin areas. Allow it to dry.

Keep this medicine away from the eyes, nose, mouth, and other mucous membranes. The solution may be especially irritating to the eyes.

Terbinafine spray solution contains alcohol and should not be applied to the face.

Do not apply an occlusive dressing (airtight covering, such as a tight bandage or plastic kitchen wrap) over this medicine unless you have been directed to do so by your doctor.

Dosing—The dose of terbinafine will be different for different patients. *Follow your doctor's orders or the directions on the label.* The following information includes only the average doses of terbinafine. *If your dose is different, do not change it* unless your doctor tells you to do so.

The number of doses you use each day, the time allowed between doses, and the length of time you use the medicine depend on the medical problem for which you are using terbinafine.
- For *topical* dosage form (cream):
  —For cutaneous candidiasis:
    - Adults—Use one or two times a day for seven to fourteen days.

- Children—Use and dose must be determined by your doctor.
  —For tinea corporis or tinea cruris:
    - Adults and children 12 years of age and older—Use one or two times a day for seven to twenty-eight days.
    - Infants and children younger than 12 years of age—Use and dose must be determined by your doctor.
  —For tinea pedis (interdigital):
    - Adults and children 12 years of age and older—Use two times a day for seven to twenty-eight days.
    - Infants and children younger than 12 years of age—Use and dose must be determined by your doctor.
  —For tinea pedis (plantar):
    - Adults and children 12 years of age and older—Use two times a day for fourteen days.
    - Infants and children younger than 12 years of age—Use and dose must be determined by your doctor.
  —For tinea versicolor:
    - Adults—Use one or two times a day for fourteen days.
    - Children—Use and dose must be determined by your doctor.
- For *topical* dosage form (spray solution):
  —For tinea corporis or tinea cruris:
    - Adults—Use once a day for seven days.
    - Children—Use and dose must be determined by your doctor.
  —For tinea pedis or tinea versicolor:
    - Adults—Use two times a day for seven days.
    - Children—Use and dose must be determined by your doctor.

To help clear up your infection completely, it *is very important that you keep using terbinafine for the full time of treatment,* even if your symptoms begin to clear up after a few days. Since fungus infections may be very slow to clear up, you may have to continue using this medicine every day for several weeks or more. If you stop using this medicine too soon, your symptoms may return. *Do not miss any doses.*

Missed dose—If you do miss a dose of this medicine, apply it as soon as possible. However, if it is almost time for your next dose, skip the missed dose and go back to your regular dosing schedule.

Storage—To store this medicine:
- Keep out of the reach of children.
- Store away from heat and direct light.
- Keep the medicine from freezing.
- Do not keep outdated medicine or medicine no longer needed. Be sure that any discarded medicine is out of the reach of children.

Precautions While Using This Medicine

Discontinue using this medicine and check with your doctor if increased irritation or possible sensitization (redness, itching, burning, blistering, swelling, or oozing) occurs while using the medication.

If your skin problem does not improve within 4 to 7 weeks, or if it becomes worse, check with your doctor.

To help clear up your infection completely and to help make sure it does not return, good health habits are also needed. The following measures will help reduce chafing and irritation and will also help keep the area cool and dry.

- *For patients using terbinafine for ringworm of the body:*
  - —Carefully dry yourself after bathing.
  - —Avoid too much heat and humidity if possible. Try to keep moisture from building up on affected areas of the body.
  - —Wear well-ventilated, loose-fitting clothing.
  - —Use a bland, absorbent powder (for example, talcum powder) once or twice a day. Be sure to use the powder after terbinafine cream or solution has been applied and has disappeared into the skin.
- *For patients using terbinafine for ringworm of the groin:*
  - —Avoid wearing underwear that is tight-fitting or made from synthetic (man-made) materials (for example, rayon or nylon). Instead, wear loose-fitting, cotton underwear.
  - —Use a bland, absorbent powder (for example, talcum powder) on the skin. It is best to use the powder between the times you use terbinafine.
- *For patients using terbinafine for ringworm of the foot:*
  - —Carefully dry the feet, especially between the toes, after bathing.
  - —Avoid wearing socks made from wool or synthetic materials (for example, rayon or nylon). Instead, wear clean, cotton socks and change them daily or more often if the feet sweat a lot.
  - —Wear sandals or well-ventilated shoes (for example, shoes with holes).
  - —Use a bland, absorbent powder (for example, talcum powder) between the toes, on the feet, and in socks and shoes once or twice a day. It is best to use the powder between the times you use terbinafine.

If you have any questions about these measures, check with your health care professional.

Side Effects of This Medicine

Along with its needed effects, a medicine may cause some unwanted effects. Although not all of these side effects may occur, if they do occur they may need medical attention.

Check with your health care professional as soon as possible if any of the following side effects occur:

Rare

Dryness; redness; itching; burning; peeling; rash; stinging; tingling; or other signs of skin irritation not present before use of this medicine

Other side effects not listed above may also occur in some patients. If you notice any other effects, check with your doctor.

Revised: 03/04/99

TERIPARATIDE   Systemic†

†Not commercially available in Canada.

Description

Teriparatide (terr-ih-PAR-a-tyd) is synthetic human parathyroid hormone used by injection as a test to help diagnose problems of the parathyroid gland. This test determines whether you have hypoparathyroidism or a type of pseudo-hypoparathyroidism.

How this test is done: Before the medicine is given, at least three blood and urine samples will be collected and tested. The dose of teriparatide, which is based on body weight, is injected into an arm vein over a 10-minute period. Then more blood and urine samples are collected and tested. Teriparatide causes changes in the amounts of certain chemicals in the urine. These changes will help determine which hypoparathyroid problem you have.

This product was withdrawn from the U.S. market in January 1997.

Before Having This Test

In deciding to use a diagnostic test, any risks of the test must be weighed against the good it will do. This is a decision you and your doctor will make. For teriparatide, the following should be considered:

Allergies—Tell your doctor if you have ever had any unusual or allergic reaction to peptides, gelatin, or teriparatide. Also tell your health care professional if you are allergic to any other substances, such as foods, preservatives, or dyes.

Pregnancy—Teriparatide has not been shown to cause birth defects or other problems in humans.

Breast-feeding—It is not known whether teriparatide passes into the breast milk. However, teriparatide is not recommended during breast-feeding, because it may cause unwanted effects in nursing babies.

Children—This medicine has not been shown to cause different side effects or problems in children over 3 years of age than it does in adults.

Older adults—Many medicines have not been studied specifically in older people. Therefore, it may not be known whether they work exactly the same way they do in younger adults. Although there is no specific information comparing use of teriparatide in the elderly with use in other age groups, this medicine is not expected to cause different side effects or problems in older people than it does in younger adults.

Other medicines—Although certain medicines should not be used together at all, in other cases two different medicines may be used together even if an interaction might occur. In these cases, your doctor may want to change the dose, or other precautions may be necessary. Tell your health care professional if you are taking any other prescription or nonprescription (over-the-counter [OTC]) medicine.

Preparation for This Test

Follow your doctor's instructions carefully. Otherwise, this test may not work well and may have to be done again.

Unless otherwise directed by your doctor:

- Do not eat or drink anything but water after 8:00 p.m. the night before the test. Food may affect the test results.
- Starting about 2½ hours before the test, drink about 6 or 7 ounces of water every 30 minutes until the test is

finished. This is to be sure there is enough urine for testing.

Side Effects of This Medicine

Along with its needed effects, a medicine may cause some unwanted effects. Check with your doctor as soon as possible if any of the following side effects occur:

Symptoms of overdose

Constipation; headache; loss of appetite; muscle weakness

Other side effects may occur that usually do not need medical attention. These side effects may go away after the test as your body adjusts to the medicine. However, check with your doctor if any of the following side effects continue or are bothersome:

Rare

Abdominal or stomach cramps; diarrhea; metallic taste; nausea; pain at the place of injection during or following injection; tingling feeling in hands and feet; urge for bowel movement

Other side effects not listed above may also occur in some patients. If you notice any other effects, check with your doctor.

Revised: 10/16/2000

TETANUS IMMUNE GLOBULIN
Systemic

Commonly used brand name(s):

In the U.S.—
BayTet
Generic name product may be available.

Another commonly used name is TIG.

Description

Tetanus immune globulin (TET-n-us im-MUNE GLOB-yoo-lin) is used to prevent tetanus infection (also known as lockjaw). Tetanus is a serious illness that causes convulsions (seizures) and severe muscle spasms that can be strong enough to cause bone fractures of the spine. Tetanus causes death in 30 to 40 percent of cases.

In recent years, two thirds of all tetanus cases have been in persons 50 years of age and older. A tetanus infection in the past does not make you immune to tetanus in the future.

Tetanus immune globulin works by giving your body the antibodies it needs to protect it against tetanus infection. This is called passive protection. This passive protection lasts long enough to protect your body until your body can produce its own antibodies against tetanus.

Tetanus immune globulin is to be administered only by or under the supervision of your doctor or other health care professional. It is available in the following dosage form:

Parenteral
- Injection (U.S. and Canada)

Before Receiving This Medicine

In deciding to use a medicine, the risks of using the medicine must be weighed against the good it will do. This is a decision you and your doctor will make. For tetanus immune globulin, the following should be considered:

Allergies—Tell your doctor if you have ever had any unusual or allergic reaction to tetanus immune globulin.

Pregnancy—Studies on effects in pregnancy have not been done in either humans or animals. However, there is no reason to suspect that tetanus immune globulin causes problems in pregnant women.

Breast-feeding—Tetanus immune globulin has not been reported to cause problems in nursing babies.

Children—Although there is no specific information comparing use of tetanus immune globulin in children with use in other age groups, this medicine is not expected to cause different side effects or problems in children than it does in adults.

Older adults—Many medicines have not been studied specifically in older people. Therefore, it may not be known whether they work exactly the same way they do in younger adults or if they cause different side effects or problems in older people. There is no specific information comparing use of tetanus immune globulin in the elderly with use in other age groups. However, there is no evidence that the effects of tetanus immune globulin in older adults differ from those in younger persons.

Other medical problems—The presence of other medical problems may affect the use of tetanus immune globulin. Make sure you tell your doctor if you have any other medical problems.

Proper Use of This Medicine

Dosing—The dose of tetanus immune globulin will be different for different patients. The following information includes only the average dose of tetanus immune globulin.
- For *injection* dosage form:
  —For preventing tetanus infection:
  - Adults and children—250 units injected into a muscle.

Side Effects of This Medicine

Along with its needed effects, a medicine may cause some unwanted effects. Although not all of these side effects may occur, if they do occur they may need medical attention.

Check with your doctor immediately if any of the following side effects occur:

Rare

Difficulty in breathing or swallowing; hives; itching, especially of soles or palms; reddening of skin, especially around ears; swelling of eyes, face, or inside of nose; unusual tiredness or weakness, sudden and severe

Other side effects not listed above may also occur in some patients. If you notice any other effects, check with your doctor.

Developed: 06/27/97

TETANUS TOXOID   Systemic

Description

Tetanus (TET-n-us) Toxoid is used to prevent tetanus (also known as lockjaw). Tetanus is a serious illness that causes convulsions (seizures) and severe muscle spasms that can be strong enough to cause bone fractures of the spine. Tetanus causes death in 30 to 40 percent of cases.

Immunization against tetanus is recommended for all infants 6 to 8 weeks of age and older, all children, and all adults. Immunization against tetanus consists first of a series of either 3 or 4 injections, depending on which type of tetanus toxoid you receive. In addition, it is very important that you get a booster injection every 10 years for the rest of your life. Also, if you get a wound that is unclean or hard to clean, you may need an emergency booster injection if it has been more than 5 years since your last booster. In recent years, two-thirds of all tetanus cases have been in persons 50 years of age and older. A tetanus infection in the past does not make you immune to tetanus in the future.

This vaccine is to be administered only by or under the supervision of your doctor or other health care professional. It is available in the following dosage form:

Parenteral
- Injection (U.S. and Canada)

Before Receiving This Vaccine

In deciding to receive this vaccine, the risks of receiving the vaccine must be weighed against the good it will do. This is a decision you and your doctor will make. For tetanus toxoid, the following should be considered:

Allergies—Tell your doctor if you have ever had any unusual or allergic reaction to tetanus toxoid. Also tell your health care professional if you are allergic to any other substances, such as preservatives (especially thimerosal).

Pregnancy—This vaccine has not been shown to cause birth defects or other problems in humans. Vaccination of a pregnant woman can prevent her newborn baby from getting tetanus at birth.

Breast-feeding—Tetanus toxoid has not been reported to cause problems in nursing babies.

Children—Use is not recommended for infants up to 6 weeks of age. For infants and children 6 weeks of age and older, tetanus toxoid is not expected to cause different side effects or problems than it does in adults.

Older adults—This vaccine is not expected to cause different side effects or problems in older people than it does in younger adults. However, the vaccine may be slightly less effective in older persons than in younger adults.

Other medicines—Although certain medicines should not be used together at all, in other cases two different medicines may be used together even if an interaction might occur. In these cases, your doctor may want to change the dose, or other precautions may be necessary. Before you receive tetanus toxoid, it is especially important that your health care professional know if you are using any prescription or nonprescription (over-the-counter [OTC]) medicine.

Other medical problems—The presence of other medical problems may affect the use of tetanus toxoid. Make sure you tell your doctor if you have any other medical problems, especially:

- A severe reaction or a fever greater than 103 °F (39.4 °C) following a previous dose of tetanus toxoid—May increase the chance of side effects with future doses of tetanus toxoid; be sure your doctor knows about this before you receive the next dose of tetanus toxoid

- Bronchitis, pneumonia, or other illness involving lungs or bronchial tubes, or

- Severe illness with fever—Possible side effects from tetanus toxoid may be confused with the symptoms of the condition

Proper Use of This Vaccine

Dosing—The dose of tetanus toxoid will be different for different patients. The following information includes only the average doses of tetanus toxoid.

- For *injection* dosage forms:
  - For prevention of tetanus (lockjaw):
    - Adults, children, and infants 6 weeks of age and older—One dose is given at your first visit, then a second dose is given four to eight weeks later. Depending on the product given, you may receive a third dose four to eight weeks after the second dose, and a fourth dose six to twelve months after that; or you may receive a third dose six to twelve months after the second dose. Everyone should receive a booster dose every ten years. The doses are injected under the skin or into a muscle. In addition, if you get a wound that is unclean or hard to clean, you may need an emergency booster injection if it has been more than 5 years since your last booster dose.

Side Effects of This Vaccine

Along with its needed effects, a vaccine may cause some unwanted effects. Although not all of these side effects may occur, if they do occur they may need medical attention.

Get emergency help immediately if any of the following side effects occur:
Symptoms of allergic reaction
Difficulty in breathing or swallowing; hives; itching, especially of feet or hands; reddening of skin, especially around ears; swelling of eyes, face, or inside of nose; unusual tiredness or weakness (sudden and severe)

Check with your doctor as soon as possible if any of the following side effects occur:
Rare
Confusion; convulsions (seizures); fever over 103 °F (39.4 °C); headache (severe or continuing); sleepiness (excessive); swelling, blistering, or pain at place of injection (severe or continuing); swelling of glands in armpit; unusual irritability; vomiting (severe or continuing)

Other side effects may occur that usually do not need medical attention. However, check with your doctor if any of the following side effects continue or are bothersome:
More common
Redness or hard lump at place of injection

Less common
> Chills, fever, irritability, or unusual tiredness; pain, tenderness, itching, or swelling at place of injection; skin rash

Other side effects not listed above may also occur in some patients. If you notice any other effects, check with your doctor.

Revised: 07/12/94

TETRACYCLINE PERIODONTAL FIBERS   Dental†

Commonly used brand name(s):

In the U.S.—
Actisite

†Not commercially available in Canada.

Description

Tetracycline periodontal fibers (tet-ra-SYE-kleen pare-ee-o-DON-tal FI-bers) are used to help treat periodontal disease (a disease of your gums). Periodontal disease is caused by bacteria growing beneath the gum line. Tetracycline works by keeping the number of bacteria from growing. Lowering the amount of bacteria helps to reduce inflammation and swelling in your mouth, and the amount of bleeding around the teeth. Tetracycline fibers are placed in the inflamed mouth areas by your dentist after he or she has thoroughly cleaned your teeth.

Tetracycline periodontal fibers are available only from your dentist, in the following dosage form:

Dental
* Periodontal fibers (U.S.)

Before Using This Medicine

In deciding to use a medicine, the risks of using the medicine must be weighed against the good it will do. This is a decision you and your dentist will make. For tetracycline periodontal fibers, the following should be considered:

Allergies—Tell your dentist if you have ever had any unusual or allergic reaction to tetracycline or any other tetracycline medicine (such as doxycycline, demeclocycline, oxytetracycline, or minocycline). Also tell your dentist if you are allergic to any other substances, such as foods, preservatives, or dyes.

Pregnancy—Studies on the effects in pregnancy have not been done in either humans or animals.

Breast-feeding—It is not known whether the tetracycline from tetracycline periodontal fibers passes into the breast milk.

Children—Studies on this medicine have been done only in adult patients, and there is no specific information comparing use of this medicine in children with use in other age groups.

Older adults—Many medicines have not been studied specifically in older people. Therefore, it may not be known whether they work exactly the same way they do in younger adults or if they cause different side effects or problems in older people. There is no specific information comparing use of this medicine in the elderly with use in other age groups.

Proper Use of This Medicine

When tetracycline periodontal fibers are in place in your mouth, *try to avoid any actions that may knock the fibers loose*. For example:
* Do not chew hard, crusty, or sticky foods, or chewing gum.
* Do not brush or floss near any treated areas, but continue to clean the other teeth.
* Do not use a dental spray device (e.g., Water-Pik).
* Do not probe or pick at the fibers with your tongue, toothpicks, or fingers.

Dosing—The amount of tetracycline periodontal fibers that will be put in your gums will be determined by your dentist. The number of teeth that need treatment and the depth of the pockets in your gums will determine the amount of fiber that is used.

Precautions While Using This Medicine

Check with your dentist right away if the fibers become loose or fall out before your next dental visit.

Check with your dentist right away if you have pain or swelling or other problems in the treated areas.

It is very important that your dentist check your progress and remove the tetracycline periodontal fibers after ten days. Do not miss any dental appointments.

Side Effects of This Medicine

Along with its needed effects, a medicine may cause some unwanted effects. Although not all of these side effects may occur, if they do occur they may need medical attention.

Check with your dentist immediately if any of the following side effects occur:
> *Rare*
> > Gum redness, swelling, and pain in the areas of treatment; tongue pain and redness

Other side effects may occur that usually do not need medical attention. These side effects may go away during treatment as your body adjusts to the medicine. However, check with your dentist if any of the following side effects continue or are bothersome:
> *More common*
> > Discomfort in the area where the fibers have been placed; redness in the area where the fibers were removed
> *Rare*
> > Sore throat; staining of the tongue; white patches on tongue or in mouth

Other side effects not listed above may also occur in some patients. If you notice any other effects, check with your dentist.

Developed: 12/15/94
Revised: 06/11/99

TETRACYCLINES   Ophthalmic†

Other countries—
May be available in other countries.

This information applies to the following medicines:
1. Chlortetracycline (klor-te-tra-SYE-kleen) *†
2. Tetracycline (te-tra-SYE-kleen) *†

*Not commercially available in the U.S.
†Not commercially available in Canada.

Description

Tetracyclines belong to the family of medicines called antibiotics. Tetracycline ophthalmic preparations are used to treat infections of the eye. They may also be used along with other medicines that are taken by mouth for infections of the eye.

Tetracyclines are available only with your doctor's prescription, in the following dosage forms:

Ophthalmic
  Chlortetracycline
    • Ophthalmic ointment
  Tetracycline
    • Ophthalmic ointment

Before Using This Medicine

In deciding to use a medicine, the risks of using the medicine must be weighed against the good it will do. This is a decision you and your doctor will make. For tetracycline ophthalmic preparations, the following should be considered:

Allergies—Tell your doctor if you have ever had any unusual or allergic reaction to tetracycline or chlortetracycline or to any related antibiotics, such as demeclocycline (e.g., Declomycin), doxycycline (e.g., Vibramycin), methacycline (e.g., Rondomycin), minocycline (e.g., Minocin), or oxytetracycline (e.g., Terramycin). Also tell your health care professional if you are allergic to any other substances, such as preservatives.

Pregnancy—Tetracycline ophthalmic preparations have not been shown to cause birth defects or other problems in humans.

Breast-feeding—Tetracycline ophthalmic preparations have not been reported to cause problems in nursing babies.

Children—Although there is no specific information comparing use of ophthalmic tetracyclines in children with use in other age groups, they are not expected to cause different side effects or problems in children than they do in adults.

Older adults—Many medicines have not been studied specifically in older people. Therefore, it may not be known whether they work exactly the same way they do in younger adults or if they cause different side effects or problems in older people. There is no specific information comparing use of tetracyclines in the elderly with use in other age groups.

Other medicines—Although certain medicines should not be used together at all, in other cases two different medicines may be used together even if an interaction might occur. In these cases, your doctor may want to change the dose, or other precautions may be necessary. Tell your health care professional if you are using any other prescription or nonprescription (over-the-counter [OTC]) medicine that is to be used in the eye.

Proper Use of This Medicine

For patients using the *eye ointment form* of tetracyclines:
- To use:
  —First, wash your hands. Then pull the lower eyelid away from the eye to form a pouch. Squeeze a thin strip of ointment into the pouch. A 1-cm (approximately ⅓-inch) strip of ointment is usually enough unless otherwise directed by your doctor. Gently close the eyes and keep them closed for 1 or 2 minutes to allow the medicine to come into contact with the infection.
  —To keep the medicine as germ-free as possible, do not touch the applicator tip to any surface (including the eye). After using tetracyclines eye ointment, wipe the tip of the ointment tube with a clean tissue and keep the tube tightly closed.

To help clear up your infection completely, *keep using this medicine for the full time of treatment*, even if your symptoms have disappeared. *Do not miss any doses.*

Dosing—The dose of ophthalmic tetracyclines will be different for different patients. *Follow your doctor's orders or the directions on the label*. The following information includes only the average doses of ophthalmic tetracyclines. *If your dose is different, do not change it* unless your doctor tells you to do so.

The number of doses you use each day, the time allowed between doses, and the length of time you use the medicine depend on the medical problem for which you are using ophthalmic tetracyclines.

- For eye infections:
  —For *ophthalmic ointment* dosage forms:
    • Adults and children—Use every two to four hours.

Missed dose—If you miss a dose of this medicine, apply it as soon as possible. However, if it is almost time for your next application, skip the missed dose and go back to your regular dosing schedule.

Storage—To store this medicine:
- Keep out of the reach of children.
- Store away from heat and direct light.
- Keep the medicine from freezing.
- Do not keep outdated medicine or medicine no longer needed. Be sure that any discarded medicine is out of the reach of children.

Precautions While Using This Medicine

After application, this medicine usually causes your vision to blur for a few minutes.

If your symptoms do not improve within a few days, or if they become worse, check with your doctor.

Side Effects of This Medicine

There have not been any common or important side effects reported with this medicine. However, if you notice any unusual effects, check with your doctor.

Revised: 06/09/99

TETRACYCLINES Systemic

Commonly used brand name(s):

In the U.S.—

Achromycin V[5]	Monodox[2]
Declomycin[1]	Terramycin[4]
Doryx[2]	Vibramycin[2]
Dynacin[3]	Vibra-Tabs[2]
Minocin[3]	

In Canada—

Alti-Doxycycline[2]	Minocin[3]
Alti-Minocycline[3]	Novo-Doxylin[2]
Apo-Doxy[2]	Novo-Minocycline[3]
Apo-Doxy-Tabs[2]	Novo-Tetra[5]
Apo-Minocycline[3]	Nu-Doxycycline[2]
Apo-Tetra[5]	Nu-Tetra[5]
Declomycin[1]	Vibramycin[2]
Doxycin[2]	Vibra-Tabs[2]
Doxytec[2]	Vibra-Tabs C-Pak[2]
Gen-Minocycline[3]	

Note: For quick reference, the following tetracyclines are numbered to match the corresponding brand names.

This information applies to the following medicines:
1. Demeclocycline (dem-e-kloe-SYE-kleen)
2. Doxycycline (dox-i-SYE-kleen) ‡
3. Minocycline (mi-noe-SYE-kleen) ‡
4. Oxytetracycline (ox-i-tet-ra-SYE-kleen) †‡
5. Tetracycline (tet-ra-SYE-kleen) ‡

---

†Not commercially available in Canada.
‡Generic name product may be available in the U.S.

Description

Tetracyclines are used to treat infections and to help control acne. Demeclocycline, doxycycline, and minocycline also may be used for other problems as determined by your doctor. Tetracyclines will not work for colds, flu, or other virus infections.

Tetracyclines are available only with your doctor's prescription, in the following dosage forms:

Oral
Demeclocycline
- Tablets (U.S. and Canada)
Doxycycline
- Capsules (U.S. and Canada)
- Delayed-release capsules (U.S.)
- Oral suspension (U.S.)
- Tablets (U.S. and Canada)
Minocycline
- Capsules (U.S. and Canada)
- Oral suspension (U.S.)
Oxytetracycline
- Capsules (U.S.)
Tetracycline
- Capsules (U.S. and Canada)
- Oral suspension (Canada)

Parenteral
Doxycycline
- Injection (U.S.)
Minocycline
- Injection (U.S.)
Oxytetracycline
- Injection (U.S.)

Before Using This Medicine

In deciding to use a medicine, the risks of taking the medicine must be weighed against the good it will do. This is a decision you and your doctor will make. For tetracyclines, the following should be considered:

Allergies—Tell your doctor if you have ever had any unusual or allergic reaction to any of the tetracyclines or combination medicines containing a tetracycline. Also tell your health care professional if you are allergic to any other substances, such as foods, preservatives, or dyes. In addition, if you are going to be given oxytetracycline by injection, tell your doctor if you have ever had an unusual or allergic reaction to "caine-type" anesthetics (e.g., lidocaine).

Pregnancy—Use is not recommended during the last half of pregnancy. If tetracyclines are taken during that time, they may cause the unborn infant's teeth to become discolored and may slow down the growth of the infant's teeth and bones. In addition, liver problems may occur in pregnant women, especially those receiving high doses by injection into a vein.

Breast-feeding—Use is not recommended since tetracyclines pass into breast milk. They may cause the nursing baby's teeth to become discolored and may slow down the growth of the baby's teeth and bones. They may also increase the sensitivity of nursing babies' skin to sunlight and cause fungus infections of the mouth and vagina. In addition, minocycline may cause dizziness, light-headedness, or unsteadiness in nursing babies.

Children—Tetracyclines may cause permanent discoloration of teeth and slow down the growth of bones. These medicines should not be given to children 8 years of age and younger unless directed by the child's doctor.

Older adults—Many medicines have not been studied specifically in older people. Therefore, it may not be known whether they work exactly the same way they do in younger adults or if they cause different side effects or problems in older people. There is no specific information comparing use of tetracyclines in the elderly with use in other age groups.

Other medicines—Although certain medicines should not be used together at all, in other cases two different medicines may be used together even if an interaction might occur. In these cases, your doctor may want to change the dose, or other precautions may be necessary. When you are taking tetracyclines, it is especially important that your health care professional know if you are taking any of the following:
- Antacids or
- Calcium supplements such as calcium carbonate or
- Cholestyramine (e.g., Questran) or
- Choline and magnesium salicylates (e.g., Trilisate) or
- Colestipol (e.g., Colestid) or
- Iron-containing medicine or
- Laxatives (magnesium-containing) or
- Magnesium salicylate (e.g., Magan)—Use of these medicines with tetracyclines may decrease the effect of tetracyclines
- Oral contraceptives (birth control pills) containing estrogen—Use of birth control pills with tetracyclines may decrease the effect of the birth control pills and increase the chance of unwanted pregnancy
- Penicillins—Use of tetracyclines with penicillins may decrease the effect of penicillins

Other medical problems—The presence of other medical problems may affect the use of tetracyclines. Make sure you tell your doctor if you have any other medical problems, especially:

- Diabetes insipidus (water diabetes)—Demeclocycline may make the condition worse
- Kidney disease (does not apply to doxycycline or minocycline)—Patients with kidney disease may have an increased chance of side effects
- Liver disease—Patients with liver disease may have an increased chance of side effects if they use doxycycline or minocycline

Proper Use of This Medicine

Do not give tetracyclines to infants or children 8 years of age and younger unless directed by your doctor. Tetracyclines may cause permanently discolored teeth and other problems in patients in these age groups.

Tetracyclines should be taken with a full glass (8 ounces) of water to prevent irritation of the esophagus (tube between the throat and stomach) or stomach. In addition, most tetracyclines (except doxycycline and minocycline) are best taken on an empty stomach (either 1 hour before or 2 hours after meals). However, if this medicine upsets your stomach, your doctor may want you to take it with food.

Do not take milk, milk formulas, or other dairy products within 1 to 2 hours of the time you take tetracyclines (except doxycycline and minocycline) by mouth. They may keep this medicine from working properly.

If this medicine has changed color or tastes or looks different, has become outdated (old), or has been stored incorrectly (too warm or too damp area or place), do not use it. To do so may cause *serious side effects*. Throw away the medicine. If you have any questions about this, check with your health care professional.

For patients taking the *oral liquid form* of this medicine:

- Use a specially marked measuring spoon or other device to measure each dose accurately. The average household teaspoon may not hold the right amount of liquid.
- Do not use after the expiration date on the label since the medicine may not work properly after that date. Check with your pharmacist if you have any questions about this.

For patients taking *doxycycline* or *minocycline:*

- These medicines may be taken with food or milk if they upset your stomach.
- Swallow the capsule (with enteric-coated pellets) form of doxycycline whole. Do not break or crush it.

To help clear up your infection completely, *keep taking this medicine for the full time of treatment*, even if you begin to feel better after a few days. If you stop taking this medicine too soon, your symptoms may return.

This medicine works best when there is a constant amount in the blood or urine. *To help keep the amount constant, do not miss any doses. Also, it is best to take the doses at evenly spaced times day and night.* For example, if you are to take four doses a day, the doses should be spaced about 6 hours apart. If this interferes with your sleep or other daily activities, or if you need help in planning the best times to take your medicine, check with your health care professional.

Dosing—The dose of these medicines will be different for different patients. *Follow your doctor's orders or the di-*

rections on the label. The following information includes only the average doses of these medicines. *If your dose is different, do not change it* unless your doctor tells you to do so.

The number of capsules, tablets, or teaspoonfuls of suspension that you take depends on the strength of the medicine. Also, *the number of doses you take each day, the time allowed between doses, and the length of time you take the medicine depend on the medical problem for which you are taking a tetracycline.*

For demeclocycline

- For *oral* dosage form (tablets):
  —For bacterial or protozoal infections:
    - Adults and teenagers—150 milligrams (mg) every six hours; or 300 mg every twelve hours. Gonorrhea is treated with 600 mg on the first day, then 300 mg every twelve hours for four days.
    - Children older than 8 years of age—Dose is based on body weight. The usual dose is 1.65 to 3.3 mg per kilogram (kg) (0.8 to 1.5 mg per pound) of body weight every six hours; or 3.3 to 6.6 mg per kg (1.5 to 3 mg per pound) of body weight every twelve hours.
    - Infants and children 8 years of age and younger—Tetracyclines usually are not used in young children because tetracyclines can permanently stain teeth.

For doxycycline

- For *oral* dosage forms (capsules, suspension, and tablets):
  —For bacterial or protozoal infections:
    - Adults and children older than 8 years of age who weigh more than 45 kilograms (kg) (99 pounds)—100 milligrams (mg) every twelve hours the first day, then 100 mg once a day or 50 to 100 mg every twelve hours.
    - Children older than 8 years of age who weigh 45 kg (99 pounds) or less—Dose is based on body weight. The usual dose is 2.2 mg per kg (1 mg per pound) of body weight two times a day on the first day, then 2.2 to 4.4 mg per kg (1 to 2 mg per pound) of body weight once a day or 1.1 to 2.2 mg per kg (0.5 to 1 mg per pound) of body weight twice a day.
    - Infants and children 8 years of age and younger—Tetracyclines are usually not used in young children because tetracyclines can permanently stain teeth.
  —For the prevention of malaria:
    - Adults and teenagers—100 mg once a day. You should take the first dose one or two days before travel to an area where malaria may occur, and continue taking the medicine every day throughout travel and for four weeks after you leave the malarious area.
    - Children older than 8 years of age—Dose is based on body weight. The usual dose is 2 mg per kg (0.9 mg per pound) of body weight once a day. You should take the first dose one or two days before travel to an area where malaria may occur, and continue taking the medicine every day throughout travel and for four weeks after you leave the malarious area.
    - Infants and children 8 years of age and younger—Tetracyclines are usually not used in young chil-

dren because tetracyclines can permanently stain teeth.

- For *injection* dosage form:
  - —For bacterial or protozoal infections:
    - Adults and children older than 8 years of age who weigh more than 45 kg of body weight (99 pounds)—200 mg injected slowly into a vein once a day; or 100 mg injected slowly into a vein every twelve hours the first day, then 100 to 200 mg injected slowly into a vein once a day or 50 to 100 mg injected slowly into a vein every twelve hours.
    - Children older than 8 years of age who weigh 45 kg of body weight (99 pounds) or less—Dose is based on body weight. The usual dose is 4.4 mg per kg (2 mg per pound) of body weight injected slowly into a vein once the first day, or 2.2 mg per kg (1 mg per pound) of body weight injected slowly into a vein every twelve hours the first day; then 2.2 to 4.4 mg per kg (1 to 2 mg per pound) of body weight once a day, or 1.1 to 2.2 per kg (0.5 to 1 mg per pound) of body weight every twelve hours.
    - Infants and children 8 years of age and younger— Tetracyclines are usually not used in young children because tetracyclines can permanently stain teeth.

For minocycline
- For *oral* dosage forms (capsules and suspension):
  - —For bacterial or protozoal infections:
    - Adults and teenagers—200 milligrams (mg) at first, then 100 mg every twelve hours; or 100 to 200 mg at first, then 50 mg every six hours.
    - Children older than 8 years of age—Dose is based on body weight. The usual dose is 4 mg per kilogram (kg) (1.8 mg per pound) of body weight at first, then 2 mg per kg (0.9 mg per pound) of body weight every twelve hours.
    - Infants and children 8 years of age and younger— Tetracyclines are usually not used in young children because tetracyclines can permanently stain teeth.

- For *injection* dosage form:
  - —For bacterial or protozoal infections:
    - Adults and teenagers—200 mg at first, then 100 mg every twelve hours, injected slowly into a vein.
    - Children older than 8 years of age—Dose is based on body weight. The usual dose is 4 mg per kg (1.8 mg per pound) of body weight at first, then 2 mg per kg (0.9 mg per pound) of body weight every twelve hours, injected slowly into a vein.
    - Infants and children 8 years of age and younger— Tetracyclines are usually not used in young children because tetracyclines can permanently stain teeth.

For oxytetracycline
- For *oral* dosage form (capsules):
  - —For bacterial or protozoal infections:
    - Adults and teenagers—250 to 500 milligrams (mg) every six hours.
    - Children older than 8 years of age—Dose is based on body weight. The usual dose is 6.25 to 12.5 mg per kilogram (kg) (2.8 to 5.7 mg per pound) of body weight every six hours.

- Infants and children 8 years of age and younger— Tetracyclines are usually not used in young children because tetracyclines can permanently stain teeth.

- For *injection* dosage form (muscle injection):
  - —For bacterial or protozoal infections:
    - Adults and teenagers—100 mg every eight hours; or 150 mg every twelve hours; or 250 mg once a day, injected into a muscle.
    - Children older than 8 years of age—Dose is based on body weight. The usual dose is 5 to 8.3 mg per kg (2.3 to 3.8 mg per pound) of body weight every eight hours; or 7.5 to 12.5 mg per kg (3.4 to 5.7 mg per pound) of body weight every twelve hours, injected into a muscle.
    - Infants and children 8 years of age and younger— Tetracyclines are usually not used in young children because tetracyclines can permanently stain teeth.

For tetracycline
- For *oral* dosage forms (capsules and suspension):
  - —For bacterial or protozoal infections:
    - Adults and teenagers—250 to 500 milligrams (mg) every six hours; or 500 mg to 1 gram every twelve hours. Gonorrhea is treated with 1.5 grams as the first dose, then 500 mg every six hours for four days.
    - Children older than 8 years of age—Dose is based on body weight. The usual dose is 6.25 to 12.5 mg per kilogram (kg) (2.8 to 5.7 mg per pound) of body weight every six hours; or 12.5 to 25 mg per kg (5.7 to 11.4 mg per pound) of body weight every twelve hours.
    - Infants and children 8 years of age and younger— Tetracyclines are usually not used in young children because tetracyclines can permanently stain teeth.

Missed dose—If you miss a dose of this medicine, take it as soon as possible. This will help to keep a constant amount of medicine in the blood or urine. However, if it is almost time for your next dose, skip the missed dose and go back to your regular dosing schedule. Do not double doses.

Storage—To store this medicine:
- Keep out of the reach of children.
- Store away from heat and direct light.
- Do not store the capsule or tablet form of this medicine in the bathroom, near the kitchen sink, or in other damp places. Heat or moisture may cause the medicine to break down.
- Keep the oral liquid forms of this medicine from freezing.
- Do not keep outdated medicine or medicine no longer needed. Be sure that any discarded medicine is out of the reach of children.

Precautions While Using This Medicine

If your symptoms do not improve within a few days (or a few weeks or months for acne patients), or if they become worse, check with your doctor.

Oral contraceptives (birth control pills) containing estrogen may not work properly if you take them while you are taking tetracyclines. Unplanned pregnancies may occur. You should use a different or additional means of birth control while you are taking tetracyclines. If you have any questions about this, check with your health care professional.

Before having surgery (including dental surgery) with a general anesthetic, tell the medical doctor or dentist in charge that you are taking a tetracycline. This does not apply to doxycycline, however.

Tetracyclines may cause your skin to be more sensitive to sunlight than it is normally. Exposure to sunlight, even for brief periods of time, may cause a skin rash, itching, redness or other discoloration of the skin, or a severe sunburn. When you begin taking this medicine:

- Stay out of direct sunlight, especially between the hours of 10:00 a.m. and 3:00 p.m., if possible.
- Wear protective clothing, including a hat. Also, wear sunglasses.
- Apply a sun block product that has a skin protection factor (SPF) of at least 15. Some patients may require a product with a higher SPF number, especially if they have a fair complexion. If you have any questions about this, check with your health care professional.
- Apply a sun block lipstick that has an SPF of at least 15 to protect your lips.
- Do not use a sunlamp or tanning bed or booth.

You may still be more sensitive to sunlight or sunlamps for 2 weeks to several months or more after stopping this medicine. *If you have a severe reaction, check with your doctor.*

For patients taking *minocycline:*

- Minocycline may also cause some people to become dizzy, lightheaded, or unsteady. *Make sure you know how you react to this medicine before you drive, use machines, or do anything else that could be dangerous if you are dizzy or are not alert.* If these reactions are especially bothersome, check with your doctor.

Side Effects of This Medicine

Along with its needed effects, a medicine may cause some unwanted effects. In some infants and children, tetracyclines may cause the teeth to become discolored. Even though this may not happen right away, check with your doctor as soon as possible if you notice this effect or if you have any questions about it.

For all tetracyclines
  More common
    Increased sensitivity of skin to sunlight (rare with minocycline)
  Rare
    Abdominal pain; bulging fontanel (soft spot on head) of infants; headache; loss of appetite; nausea and vomiting; visual changes; yellowing skin
For demeclocycline only
  Less common
    Greatly increased frequency of urination or amount of urine; increased thirst; unusual tiredness or weakness
For minocycline only
  Less common
    Pigmentation (darker color or discoloration) of skin and mucous membranes

Other side effects may occur that usually do not need medical attention. These side effects may go away during treatment as your body adjusts to the medicine. However, check with your doctor if any of the following side effects continue or are bothersome:

For all tetracyclines
  More common
    Cramps or burning of the stomach; diarrhea
  Less common
    Itching of the rectal or genital (sex organ) areas; sore mouth or tongue
For minocycline only
  More common
    Dizziness, light-headedness, or unsteadiness

In some patients tetracyclines may cause the tongue to become darkened or discolored. This effect is only temporary and will go away when you stop taking this medicine.

Other side effects not listed above may also occur in some patients. If you notice any other effects, check with your doctor.

Additional Information

Once a medicine has been approved for marketing for a certain use, experience may show that it is also useful for other medical problems. Although these uses are not included in product labeling, tetracyclines are used in certain patients with the following medical conditions:

- Gonococcal arthritis
- Leprosy (for minocycline)
- Lyme disease (for doxycycline and tetracycline)
- Malaria treatment (for doxycycline and tetracycline)
- Nocardiosis (a type of bacterial infection) (for doxycycline and minocycline)
- Ocular rosacea (a type of eye infection) (for doxycycline and tetracycline)
- Pneumothorax (a pocket of air in the space surrounding the lungs) (for doxycycline and tetracycline)
- Rheumatoid arthritis (for minocycline)
- Shigellosis (a type of intestinal infection) (for doxycycline and tetracycline)
- Syndrome of inappropriate antidiuretic hormone (SIADH) (for demeclocycline)

For patients taking this medicine for *SIADH:*

- Some doctors may prescribe demeclocycline for certain patients who retain (keep) more body water than usual. Although demeclocycline works like a diuretic (water pill) in these patients, it will not work that way in other patients who may need a diuretic.

Other than the above information, there is no additional information relating to proper use, precautions, or side effects for these uses.

Revised: 05/14/2001

THALIDOMIDE   Systemic†

Commonly used brand name(s):

In the U.S.—
  THALOMID

†Not commercially available in Canada.

Description

Thalidomide (tha-LI-doe-mide) is used to treat and prevent erythema nodosum leprosum (ENL), a painful skin disease associated with leprosy. This medicine may also be used for other problems as determined by your doctor.

Thalidomide is available only from your doctor. It has not been widely available since the early 1960s because it was found to cause birth defects. However, under special conditions, your doctor may decide that this medicine will be useful for your treatment.

This medicine is available only with your doctor's prescription, in the following dosage form:

Oral
- Capsules (U.S.)

Before Using This Medicine

In deciding to use a medicine, the risks of taking the medicine must be weighed against the good it will do. This is a decision you and your doctor will make. For thalidomide, the following should be considered:

Allergies—Tell your doctor if you have ever had any unusual or allergic reaction to thalidomide. Also tell your health care professional if you are allergic to any other substances, such as foods, preservatives, or dyes.

Pregnancy—Thalidomide must not be used by pregnant women. If this medicine is taken early in pregnancy (within the first 8 weeks [2 months]), your baby may be born with serious birth defects. Before taking this medicine, make sure your doctor knows if you are pregnant or if you may become pregnant.

Breast-feeding—It is not known if thalidomide passes into breast milk. Be sure you have discussed the risks and benefits of using this medicine with your doctor.

Children—A small number of children have been safely treated with thalidomide. Be sure to discuss with your child's doctor the use of this medicine in children.

Older adults—Many medicines have not been studied specifically in older people. Therefore, it may not be known whether they work exactly the same way they do in younger adults or if they cause different side effects or problems in older people. There is no specific information comparing use of thalidomide in the elderly with use in other age groups.

Other medicines—Although certain medicines should not be used together at all, in other cases two different medicines may be used together even if an interaction might occur. In these cases, your doctor may want to change the dose, or other precautions may be necessary. When you are taking thalidomide, it is especially important that your health care professional know if you are taking any of the following:

- Alcohol or
- Barbiturates or
- Central nervous system (CNS) depressants (medicine that causes drowsiness) or
- Chlorpromazine (e.g., Thorazine) or
- Reserpine (e.g., Serpalan) or
- Tricyclic antidepressants (medicine for depression)—Use of these medicines with thalidomide may make you more drowsy
- Chloramphenicol (e.g., Chloromycetin) or
- Cisplatin (e.g., Platinol) or
- Dapsone (e.g., Avlosulfon) or
- Didanosine (e.g., Videx) or
- Ethambutol (e.g., Myambutol) or
- Ethionamide (e.g., Trecator-SC) or
- Hydralazine (e.g., Apresoline) or
- Isoniazid (e.g., Nydrazid) or
- Lithium (e.g., Eskalith, Lithobid) or
- Metronidazole (e.g., Flagyl) or
- Nitrofurantoin (e.g., Furadantin, Macrodantin) or
- Nitrous oxide or
- Phenytoin (e.g., Dilantin) or
- Stavudine (e.g., d4T, Zerit) or
- Vincristine (e.g., Oncovin) or
- Zalcitabine (e.g., HIVID)—Use of these medicines with thalidomide may increase the chance of peripheral neuropathy (tingling, burning, numbness, or pain in your hands or feet) or may make it worse

- Carbamazepine (e.g., Tegretol) or
- Griseofulvin (e.g., Grifulvin V) or
- Human immunodeficiency virus (HIV)–protease inhibitors (indinavir [e.g., Crixivan], nelfinavir [e.g., Viracept], ritonavir [e.g., Norvir], saquinavir [e.g., Fortovase, Invirase]) or
- Rifabutin (e.g., Mycobutin) or
- Rifampin (e.g., Rifadin)—Use of these medicines with certain birth control agents may keep the birth control agents from working properly; effective birth control is required for women taking thalidomide who are able to bear children

Other medical problems—The presence of other medical problems may affect the use of thalidomide. Make sure you tell your doctor if you have any other medical problems, especially:

- Decreased white blood cell counts or
- Peripheral neuropathy—Thalidomide may make these conditions worse

Proper Use of This Medicine

Take this medicine exactly as directed by your doctor. Do not take more of it, do not take it more often, and do not take it for a longer time than your doctor ordered. Also, do not stop taking this medicine without checking with your doctor first.

Only take medicine that your doctor has prescribed specifically for you. *Do not share your medicine with others.*

Dosing—The dose of thalidomide will be different for different patients. *Follow your doctor's orders or the directions on the label.* The following information includes only the average doses of thalidomide. *If your dose is different, do not change it* unless your doctor tells you to do so:

- For *oral* dosage form (capsules):
  —For erythema nodosum leprosum (ENL):
    - Adults and teenagers—100 to 400 mg once a day until the condition improves. Then, the dose may be decreased as determined by your doctor.
    - Children—Use and dose must be determined by your doctor.

Missed dose—If you miss a dose of this medicine, take it as soon as possible. However, if it is almost time for your next dose, skip the missed dose and go back to your regular dosing schedule. Do not double doses.

Storage—To store this medicine:
- Keep out of the reach of children.
- Store away from heat and direct light.

- Do not store in the bathroom, near the kitchen sink, or in other damp places. Heat or moisture may cause the medicine to break down.
- Do not keep outdated medicine or medicine no longer needed. Be sure that any discarded medicine is out of the reach of children.

Precautions While Using This Medicine

This medicine will add to the effects of alcohol and other CNS depressants (medicines that may make you drowsy or less alert). Some examples of CNS depressants are antihistamines or medicine for hay fever, other allergies, or colds; sedatives, tranquilizers, or sleeping medicine; prescription pain medicine or narcotics; barbiturates; medicine for seizures; muscle relaxants; or anesthetics, including some dental anesthetics. *Check with your doctor before taking any of these while you are using thalidomide.*

For women of childbearing age: If you are able to bear children, *you must have a pregnancy test within 24 hours before starting thalidomide treatment, once a week during the first month of treatment, and every 2 to 4 weeks after that. Also, you must not have heterosexual sexual intercourse, or you must use two effective birth control methods at the same time for at least 1 month before starting thalidomide treatment, during treatment, and for at least 1 month after you stop taking thalidomide.*

It is very important that your doctor check you at regular visits for any nerve problems that may be caused by this medicine. *If you notice any symptoms of peripheral neuropathy (tingling, burning, numbness, or pain in the hands or feet), stop taking this medicine and call your doctor right away.*

Side Effects of This Medicine

Along with its needed effects, a medicine may cause other unwanted effects. Although not all of these side effects may occur, if they do occur they may need medical attention.

Check with your doctor immediately if any of the following side effects occur:
  More common
      Muscle weakness; tingling, burning, numbness, or pain in the hands, arms, feet, or legs
  Rare
      Blood in urine; decreased urination; fever, alone or with chills and sore throat; irregular heartbeat; low blood pressure; skin rash

Other side effects may occur that usually do not need medical attention. These side effects may go away during treatment as your body adjusts to the medicine. However, check with your doctor if any of the following side effects continue or are bothersome:
  More common
      Constipation; diarrhea; dizziness; drowsiness; nausea; stomach pain
  Less common
      Dryness of mouth; dry skin; headache; increased appetite; mood changes; swelling in the legs

Other side effects not listed above may also occur in some patients. If you notice any other effects, check with your doctor.

Additional Information

Once a medicine has been approved for marketing for a certain use, experience may show that it is also useful for other medical problems. Although these uses are not included in product labeling, thalidomide is used in certain patients with the following medical conditions:

- Multiple myeloma (certain type of cancer of the blood)

Other than the above information, there is no additional information relating to proper use, precautions, or side effects for these uses.

Revised: 08/08/2000

THIABENDAZOLE   Systemic†

Commonly used brand name(s):

In the U.S.—
    Mintezol

†Not commercially available in Canada.

Description

Thiabendazole (thye-a-BEN-da-zole) belongs to the family of medicines called anthelmintics (ant-hel-MIN-tiks). Anthelmintics are medicines used in the treatment of worm infections.

Thiabendazole is used to treat:
- creeping eruption (cutaneous larva migrans);
- pork worms (trichinosis);
- threadworms (strongyloidiasis); and
- visceral larva migrans (toxocariasis).

This medicine may also be used for other worm infections as determined by your doctor.

Thiabendazole is available only with your doctor's prescription, in the following dosage forms:

Oral
    - Chewable tablets (U.S.)
    - Oral suspension (U.S.)

Before Using This Medicine

In deciding to use a medicine, the risks of taking the medicine must be weighed against the good it will do. This is a decision you and your doctor will make. For thiabendazole, the following should be considered:

Allergies—Tell your doctor if you have ever had any unusual or allergic reaction to thiabendazole. Also tell your health care professional if you are allergic to any other substances, such as foods, preservatives, or dyes.

Pregnancy—Studies have not been done in humans. In addition, thiabendazole has not been shown to cause birth defects or other problems in studies in rabbits, rats, and mice given 2½ to 15 times the usual human dose. However, another study in mice given 10 times the usual human dose has shown that thiabendazole causes cleft palate (a split in the roof of the mouth) and bone defects.

Breast-feeding—It is not known whether thiabendazole passes into human breast milk. However, this medicine has not been reported to cause problems in nursing babies.

Children—This medicine has been tested in children over 13.6 kg of body weight (30 pounds). In effective doses, it has not been reported to cause different side effects or problems in children than it does in adults.

Older adults—Many medicines have not been studied specifically in older people. Therefore, it may not be known whether they work exactly the same way they do in younger adults or if they cause different side effects or problems in older people. There is no specific information comparing use of thiabendazole in the elderly with use in other age groups.

Other medicines—Although certain medicines should not be used together at all, in other cases two different medicines may be used together even if an interaction might occur. In these cases, your doctor may want to change the dose, or other precautions may be necessary. When you are taking thiabendazole, it is especially important that your health care professional know if you are taking any of the following:

- Theophylline—Patients taking thiabendazole and theophylline together may have an increased chance of theophylline side effects

Other medical problems—The presence of other medical problems may affect the use of thiabendazole. Make sure you tell your doctor if you have any other medical problems, especially:

- Kidney disease or
- Liver disease—Patients with kidney and/or liver disease may have an increased chance of side effects

Proper Use of This Medicine

No special preparations (for example, special diets, fasting, other medicines, laxatives, or enemas) are necessary before, during, or immediately after treatment with thiabendazole.

Thiabendazole is best taken after meals (breakfast and evening meal). This helps to prevent some common side effects such as nausea, vomiting, dizziness, or loss of appetite.

Doctors may also prescribe a corticosteroid (a cortisone-like medicine) for certain patients with *pork worms (trichinosis)*, especially for those with severe symptoms. This is to help reduce the inflammation caused by the pork worm larvae. If your doctor prescribes these 2 medicines together, it is important to take the corticosteroid along with thiabendazole. Take them exactly as directed by your doctor. Do not miss any doses.

For patients taking the *oral liquid form* of thiabendazole:

- Use a specially marked measuring spoon or other device to measure each dose accurately. The average household teaspoon may not hold the right amount of liquid.

For patients taking the *chewable tablet form* of thiabendazole:

- Tablets should be chewed or crushed before they are swallowed.

To help clear up your infection completely, *take this medicine exactly as directed by your doctor for the full time of treatment*. In some patients a second course of this medicine may be required to clear up the infection completely. *Do not miss any doses.*

Dosing—The dose of thiabendazole will be different for different patients. *Follow your doctor's orders or the directions on the label*. The following information includes only the average doses of thiabendazole. *If your dose is different, do not change it* unless your doctor tells you to do so.

The number of tablets or teaspoonfuls of suspension that you take depends on the strength of the medicine. Also, *the number of doses you take each day, the time allowed between doses, and the length of time you take the medicine depend on the medical problem for which you are taking thiabendazole.*

- For *oral* dosage forms (oral suspension or tablets):
    —Adults and children over 13.6 kilograms (30 pounds) of body weight:
- For *cutaneous larva migrans* and *strongyloidiasis:* Dose is based on body weight and will be determined by your doctor. The dose is taken two times a day for two days.
- For *trichinosis:* Dose is based on body weight and will be determined by your doctor. The dose is taken two times a day for two to four days.
- For *visceral larva migrans:* Dose is based on body weight and will be determined by your doctor. The dose is taken two times a day for five to seven days.
    —Children up to 13.6 kilograms (30 pounds) of body weight: Dose must be determined by the doctor.

Missed dose—If you do miss a dose of this medicine, take it as soon as possible. However, if it is almost time for your next dose, skip the missed dose and go back to your regular dosing schedule. Do not double doses.

Storage—To store this medicine:

- Keep out of the reach of children.
- Store away from heat and direct light.
- Do not store the chewable tablet form of this medicine in the bathroom, near the kitchen sink, or in other damp places. Heat or moisture may cause the medicine to break down.
- Keep the oral liquid form of this medicine from freezing.
- Do not keep outdated medicine or medicine no longer needed. Be sure that any discarded medicine is out of the reach of children.

Precautions While Using This Medicine

It is important that your doctor check your progress at regular visits. This is to make sure that the infection is cleared up completely.

Thiabendazole may cause blurred vision or yellow vision. It may also cause some people to become dizzy, drowsy, or less alert than they are normally. *Make sure you know how you react to this medicine before you drive, use machines, or do anything else that could be dangerous if you are dizzy or are not alert or able to see well.* If these reactions are especially bothersome, check with your doctor.

Good health habits are required to help prevent reinfection. These include the following:

- For creeping eruption (cutaneous larva migrans) or visceral larva migrans (toxocariasis):
    —Keep dogs and cats off beaches and bathing areas.
    —Treat household pets for worms (deworm) regularly.
    —Cover children's sandboxes when not being used. These measures help to prevent contamination of the sand or soil by worm larvae from the animals'

wastes. This helps to keep children from picking up the larvae when they put their hands in their mouths after touching contaminated sand or soil.

- For pork worms (trichinosis):
  —Cook all pork, pork-containing products, and game at not less than 140 °F (60 °C) until well done (not pink in the center) before eating. This will kill any trichinosis larvae that may be in the meat.

Side Effects of This Medicine

Along with its needed effects, a medicine may cause some unwanted effects. Although not all of these side effects may occur, if they do occur they may need medical attention.

Check with your doctor immediately if any of the following side effects occur:

More common
Confusion; diarrhea (severe); hallucinations (seeing, hearing, and feeling things that are not there); irritability; loss of appetite; nausea and vomiting (severe); numbness or tingling in the hands or feet

Less common
Skin rash or itching

In addition to the side effects mentioned above, check with your doctor as soon as possible if any of the following side effects occur:

Rare
Aching of joints and muscles; blurred or yellow vision; chills; convulsions (seizures); dark urine; fever; lower back pain; pain or burning while urinating; pale stools; redness, blistering, peeling, or loosening of skin; unusual feeling in the eyes; unusual tiredness or weakness; yellow eyes and skin

Other side effects may occur that usually do not need medical attention. These side effects may go away during treatment as your body adjusts to the medicine. However, check with your doctor if any of the following side effects continue or are bothersome:

More common
Dizziness; drowsiness; dryness of eyes and mouth; headache; ringing or buzzing in the ears

This medicine may cause the urine to have an asparagus-like or other unusual odor while you are taking it and for about 24 hours after you stop taking it. This side effect does not need medical attention.

Other side effects not listed above may also occur in some patients. If you notice any other effects, check with your doctor.

Additional Information

Once a medicine has been approved for marketing for a certain use, experience may show that it is also useful for other medical problems. Although these uses are not included in product labeling, thiabendazole is used in certain patients with the following medical conditions:

- Capillariasis
- Dracunculiasis
- Trichostrongyliasis

Other than the above information, there is no additional information relating to proper use, precautions, or side effects for these uses.

Revised: 02/01/93

THIAMINE (VITAMIN B₁)   Systemic

Commonly used brand name(s):

In the U.S.—
  Biamine
  Generic name product may be available.

In Canada—
  Betaxin
  Bewon
  Generic name product may be available.

Description

Vitamins (VYE-ta-mins) are compounds that you *must* have for growth and health. They are needed in small amounts only and are usually available in the foods that you eat. Thiamine (THYE-a-min) (vitamin B₁) is needed for the breakdown of carbohydrates.

Some conditions may increase your need for thiamine. These include:

- Alcoholism
- Burns
- Diarrhea (continuing)
- Fever (continuing)
- Illness (continuing)
- Intestinal disease
- Liver disease
- Overactive thyroid
- Stress (continuing)
- Surgical removal of stomach

Also, the following groups of people may have a deficiency of thiamine:

- Patients using an artificial kidney (on hemodialysis)
- Individuals who do heavy manual labor on a daily basis

Increased need for thiamine should be determined by your health care professional.

Lack of thiamine may lead to a condition called beriberi. Signs of beriberi include loss of appetite, constipation, muscle weakness, pain or tingling in arms or legs, and possible swelling of feet or lower legs. In addition, if severe, lack of thiamine may cause mental depression, memory problems, weakness, shortness of breath, and fast heartbeat. Your health care professional may treat this by prescribing thiamine for you.

Thiamine may also be used for other conditions as determined by your health care professional.

Claims that thiamine is effective for treatment of skin problems, chronic diarrhea, tiredness, mental problems, multiple sclerosis, nerve problems, and ulcerative colitis (a disease of the intestines), or as an insect repellant or to stimulate appetite have not been proven.

Injectable thiamine is administered only by or under the supervision of your health care professional. Other forms of thiamine are available without a prescription.

Thiamine is available in the following dosage forms:

Oral
- Elixir (Canada)
- Tablets (U.S. and Canada)

Parenteral
- Injection (U.S. and Canada)

Importance of Diet

For good health, it is important that you eat a balanced and varied diet. Follow carefully any diet program your health care professional may recommend. For your specific dietary vitamin and/or mineral needs, ask your health care professional for a list of appropriate foods. If you think that you are not getting enough vitamins and/or minerals in your diet, you may choose to take a dietary supplement.

Thiamine is found in various foods, including cereals (whole-grain and enriched), peas, beans, nuts, and meats (especially pork and beef). Some thiamine in foods is lost with cooking.

Vitamins alone will not take the place of a good diet and will not provide energy. Your body also needs other substances found in food such as protein, minerals, carbohydrates, and fat. Vitamins themselves often cannot work without the presence of other foods.

The daily amount of thiamine needed is defined in several different ways.

For U.S.—
- Recommended Dietary Allowances (RDAs) are the amount of vitamins and minerals needed to provide for adequate nutrition in most healthy persons. RDAs for a given nutrient may vary depending on a person's age, sex, and physical condition (e.g., pregnancy).
- Daily Values (DVs) are used on food and dietary supplement labels to indicate the percent of the recommended daily amount of each nutrient that a serving provides. DV replaces the previous designation of United States Recommended Daily Allowances (USRDAs).

For Canada—
- Recommended Nutrient Intakes (RNIs) are used to determine the amounts of vitamins, minerals, and protein needed to provide adequate nutrition and lessen the risk of chronic disease.

Normal daily recommended intakes in milligrams (mg) for thiamine are generally defined as follows:

Persons	U.S. (mg)	Canada (mg)
Infants and children		
Birth to 3 years of age	0.3–0.7	0.3–0.6
4 to 6 years of age	0.9	0.7
7 to 10 years of age	1	0.8–1
Adolescent and adult males	1.2–1.5	0.8–1.3
Adolescent and adult females	1–1.1	0.8–0.9
Pregnant females	1.5	0.9–1
Breast-feeding females	1.6	1–1.2

Before Using This Dietary Supplement

If you are taking this dietary supplement without a prescription, carefully read and follow any precautions on the label. For thiamine, the following should be considered:

Allergies—Tell your health care professional if you have ever had any unusual or allergic reaction to thiamine. Also tell your health care professional if you are allergic to any other substances, such as foods, preservatives, or dyes.

Pregnancy—It is especially important that you are receiving enough vitamins when you become pregnant and that you continue to receive the right amount of vitamins throughout your pregnancy. The healthy growth and development of the fetus depend on a steady supply of nutrients from the mother. However, taking large amounts of a dietary supplement in pregnancy may be harmful to the mother and/or fetus and should be avoided.

Breast-feeding—It is especially important that you receive the right amounts of vitamins so that your baby will also get the vitamins needed to grow properly. However, taking large amounts of a dietary supplement while breast-feeding may be harmful to the mother and/or baby and should be avoided.

Children—Problems in children have not been reported with intake of normal daily recommended amounts.

Older adults—Problems in older adults have not been reported with intake of normal daily recommended amounts. Studies have shown that older adults may have lower blood levels of thiamine than younger adults. Your health care professional may recommend that you take a vitamin supplement that contains thiamine.

Medicines or other dietary supplements—Although certain medicines or dietary supplements should not be used together at all, in other cases they may be used together even if an interaction might occur. In these cases, your health care professional may want to change the dose, or other precautions may be necessary. Tell your health care professional if you are taking any other dietary supplement or prescription or nonprescription (over-the-counter [OTC]) medicine.

Proper Use of This Dietary Supplement

Dosing—The amount of thiamine needed to meet normal daily recommended intakes will be different for different individuals. The following information includes only the average amounts of thiamine.

- For *oral* dosage forms (tablets, oral solution):
  —To prevent deficiency, the amount taken by mouth is based on normal daily recommended intakes:

For the U.S.
- Adult and teenage males—1.2 to 1.5 milligrams (mg) per day.
- Adult and teenage females—1 to 1.1 mg per day.
- Pregnant females—1.5 mg per day.
- Breast-feeding females—1.6 mg per day.
- Children 7 to 10 years of age—1 mg per day.
- Children 4 to 6 years of age—0.9 mg per day.
- Children birth to 3 years of age—0.3 to 0.7 mg per day.

For Canada
- Adult and teenage males—0.8 to 1.3 mg per day.
- Adult and teenage females—0.8 to 0.9 mg per day.
- Pregnant females—0.9 to 1 mg per day.
- Breast-feeding females—1 to 1.2 mg per day.
- Children 7 to 10 years of age—0.8 to 1 mg per day.
- Children 4 to 6 years of age—0.7 mg per day.
- Children birth to 3 years of age—0.3 to 0.6 mg per day.

—To treat deficiency:
- Adults and teenagers—Treatment dose is determined by prescriber for each individual based on the severity of deficiency. The following dosage has been established: Beriberi—Oral, 5 to 10 mg three times a day.

- Children—Treatment dose is determined by prescriber for each individual based on the severity of deficiency. The following dosage has been established: Beriberi—Oral, 10 a day.

Missed dose—If you miss taking a vitamin for 1 or more days there is no cause for concern, since it takes some time for your body to become seriously low in vitamins. However, if your health care professional has recommended that you take this vitamin, try to remember to take it as directed every day.

Storage—To store this dietary supplement:
- Keep out of the reach of children.
- Store away from heat and direct light.
- Do not store in the bathroom, near the kitchen sink, or in other damp places. Heat or moisture may cause the dietary supplement to break down.
- Keep the oral liquid form of this dietary supplement from freezing.
- Do not keep outdated dietary supplements or those no longer needed. Be sure that any discarded dietary supplement is out of the reach of children.

Side Effects of This Dietary Supplement

Along with its needed effects, a dietary supplement may cause some unwanted effects. Although not all of these side effects may occur, if they do occur they may need medical attention.

Check with your health care professional immediately if any of the following side effects occur:
    Rare—Soon after receiving injection only
        Coughing; difficulty in swallowing; hives; itching of skin; swelling of face, lips, or eyelids; wheezing or difficulty in breathing

Other side effects not listed above may also occur in some individuals. If you notice any other effects, check with your health care professional.

Additional Information

Once a medicine or dietary supplement has been approved for marketing for a certain use, experience may show that it is also useful for other medical problems. Although this use is not included in product labeling, thiamine is used in certain patients with the following medical conditions:

- Enzyme deficiency diseases such as encephalomyelopathy, maple syrup urine disease, pyruvate carboxylase, and hyperalaninemia

Other than the above information, there is no additional information relating to proper use, precautions, or side effects for these uses.

Revised: 06/24/92
Interim revision: 07/29/94; 05/26/95

THIOTEPA   Systemic

Description

Thiotepa (thye-oh-TEP-a) belongs to the group of medicines called alkylating agents. It is used to treat some kinds of cancer.

Thiotepa interferes with the growth of cancer cells, which are eventually destroyed. Since the growth of normal body cells may also be affected by thiotepa, other effects will also occur. Some of these may be serious and must be reported to your doctor. Other effects, like hair loss, may not be serious but may cause concern. Some effects do not occur for months or years after the medicine is used.

Before you begin treatment with thiotepa, you and your doctor should talk about the good this medicine will do as well as the risks of using it.

Thiotepa is to be administered only by or under the immediate supervision of your doctor. It is available in the following dosage form:

Parenteral
- Injection (U.S. and Canada)

Before Using This Medicine

In deciding to use a medicine, the risks of taking the medicine must be weighed against the good it will do. This is a decision you and your doctor will make. For thiotepa, the following should be considered:

Allergies—Tell your doctor if you have ever had any unusual or allergic reaction to thiotepa.

Pregnancy—Tell your doctor if you are pregnant or if you intend to have children. There is a chance that this medicine may cause birth defects if either the male or female is using it at the time of conception or if it is used during pregnancy. Studies have shown that thiotepa causes birth defects in humans. In addition, many cancer medicines may cause sterility which could be permanent. Although this is uncommon with this medicine, the possibility should be kept in mind.

Be sure that you have discussed this with your doctor before using this medicine. It is best to use some kind of birth control while you are receiving thiotepa. Tell your doctor right away if you think you have become pregnant while receiving thiotepa.

Breast-feeding—Tell your doctor if you intend to breast-feed. Because this medicine may cause serious side effects, breast-feeding is generally not recommended while you are receiving it. It is not known whether thiotepa passes into the breast milk.

Children—There is no specific information about the use of thiotepa in children.

Older adults—Many medicines have not been tested in older people. Therefore, it may not be known whether they work exactly the same way they do in younger adults or if they cause different side effects or problems in older people. There is no specific information about the use of thiotepa in the elderly.

Other medicines—Although certain medicines should not be used together at all, in other cases two different medicines may be used together even if an interaction might occur. In these cases, your doctor may want to change the dose, or other precautions may be necessary. When you are receiving thiotepa, it is especially important that your health care professional know if you are taking any of the following:

- Antithyroid agents (medicine for overactive thyroid) or
- Azathioprine (e.g., Imuran) or
- Chloramphenicol (e.g., Chloromycetin) or
- Colchicine or
- Flucytosine (e.g., Ancobon) or
- Interferon (e.g., Intron A, Roferon-A) or

- Plicamycin (e.g., Mithracin) or
- Zidovudine (e.g., Retrovir) or
- If you have ever been treated with x-rays or cancer medicines—Thiotepa may increase the effects of these medicines or radiation therapy on the blood

- Probenecid (e.g., Benemid) or
- Sulfinpyrazone (e.g., Anturane)—Thiotepa may increase the concentration of uric acid in the blood, which these medicines are used to lower

Other medical problems—The presence of other medical problems may affect the use of thiotepa. Make sure you tell your doctor if you have any other medical problems, especially:

- Chickenpox (including recent exposure) or
- Herpes zoster (shingles)—Risk of severe disease affecting other parts of the body

- Gout (history of) or
- Kidney stones (history of)—Thiotepa may increase levels of uric acid in the body, which can cause gout or kidney stones

- Infection—Thiotepa can reduce immunity to infection

- Kidney disease or
- Liver disease—Effects may be increased because of slower removal of thiotepa from the body

Proper Use of This Medicine

While you are using thiotepa, your doctor may want you to drink extra fluids so that you will pass more urine. This will help prevent kidney problems and keep your kidneys working well.

Thiotepa sometimes causes nausea, vomiting, and loss of appetite. However, it is very important that you continue to receive the medicine, even if you begin to feel ill. Ask your health care professional for ways to lessen these effects.

Dosing—The dose of thiotepa will be different for different patients. The dose that is used may depend on a number of things, including what the medicine is being used for, the patient's weight, and whether or not other medicines are also being taken. *If you are receiving thiotepa at home, follow your doctor's orders or the directions on the label.* If you have any questions about the proper dose of thiotepa, ask your doctor.

Precautions While Using This Medicine

It is very important that your doctor check your progress at regular visits to make sure that this medicine is working properly and to check for unwanted effects.

Before having any kind of surgery, including dental surgery, make sure the medical doctor or dentist in charge knows that you are taking this medicine.

While you are being treated with thiotepa, and after you stop treatment with it, *do not have any immunizations (vaccinations) without your doctor's approval.* Thiotepa may lower your body's resistance and there is a chance you might get the infection the immunization is meant to prevent. Other people living in your household should not take or should not have recently taken oral polio vaccine since there is a chance they could pass the polio virus on to you. Also, avoid other persons who have taken oral polio vaccine. Do not get close to them and do not stay in the same room with them for very long. If you cannot take these precautions, you should consider wearing a protective face mask that covers the nose and mouth.

Thiotepa can lower the number of white blood cells in your blood temporarily, increasing the chance of getting an infection. It can also lower the number of platelets, which are necessary for proper blood clotting. If this occurs, there are certain precautions you can take, especially when your blood count is low, to reduce the risk of infection or bleeding:

- If you can, avoid people with infections. *Check with your doctor immediately* if you think you are getting an infection or if you get a fever or chills, cough or hoarseness, lower back or side pain, or painful or difficult urination.
- *Check with your doctor immediately* if you notice any unusual bleeding or bruising; black, tarry stools; blood in urine or stools; pinpoint red spots on your skin.
- Be careful when using a regular toothbrush, dental floss, or toothpick. Your medical doctor, dentist, or nurse may recommend other ways to clean your teeth and gums. Check with your medical doctor before having any dental work done.
- Do not touch your eyes or the inside of your nose unless you have just washed your hands and have not touched anything else in the meantime.
- Be careful not to cut yourself when you are using sharp objects such as a safety razor or fingernail or toenail cutters.
- Avoid contact sports or other situations where bruising or injury could occur.

Side Effects of This Medicine

Along with their needed effects, medicines like thiotepa can sometimes cause unwanted effects such as blood problems, loss of hair, and other side effects. These and others are described below. Also, because of the way these medicines act on the body, there is a chance that they might cause other unwanted effects that may not occur until months or years after the medicine is used. These delayed effects may include certain types of cancer, such as leukemia. Discuss these possible effects with your doctor.

Although not all of these side effects may occur, if they do occur they may need medical attention.

Check with your doctor or nurse immediately if any of the following side effects occur:
Less common
   Black, tarry stools; blood in urine or stools; cough or hoarseness; fever or chills; lower back or side pain; painful or difficult urination; pinpoint red spots on skin; unusual bleeding or bruising

Rare
   Skin rash; tightness of throat; wheezing

Check with your health care professional as soon as possible if any of the following side effects occur:
Less common
   Joint pain; pain at place of injection or instillation; swelling of feet or lower legs

Rare
   Sores in mouth and on lips

Other side effects may occur that usually do not need medical attention. These side effects may go away during treatment as your body adjusts to the medicine. Also, your health care professional may be able to tell you about ways to prevent or reduce some of these side effects. Check with your health care professional if any of the following side effects continue or are bothersome or if you have any questions about them:

Less common

Dizziness; hives; loss of appetite; missing menstrual periods; nausea and vomiting

This medicine may cause a temporary loss of hair in some people. After treatment with thiotepa has ended, normal hair growth should return.

After you stop receiving thiotepa, it may still produce some side effects that need attention. During this period of time, check with your doctor if you notice any of the following:

Black, tarry stools; blood in urine or stools; cough or hoarseness; fever or chills; lower back or side pain; painful or difficult urination; pinpoint red spots on skin; unusual bleeding or bruising

Other side effects not listed above may also occur in some patients. If you notice any other effects, check with your doctor.

Additional Information

Once a medicine has been approved for marketing for a certain use, experience may show that it is also useful for other medical problems. Although these uses are not included in product labeling, thiotepa is used in certain patients with the following medical conditions:

• Cancer in the membranes that cover and protect the brain and spinal cord (the meninges)

Other than the above information, there is no additional information relating to proper use, precautions, or side effects for these uses.

Revised: 08/14/2000

THIOXANTHENES   Systemic

Commonly used brand name(s):

In the U.S.—
Navane[3]
Taractan[1]
Thiothixene HCl Intensol[3]

In Canada—
Fluanxol[2]
Fluanxol Depot[2]
Navane[3]

Note: For quick reference, the following thioxanthenes are numbered to match the corresponding brand names.

This information applies to the following medicines:
1. Chlorprothixene (klor-proe-THIX-een) †
2. Flupenthixol (floo-pen-THIX-ole) *
3. Thiothixene (thye-oh-THIX-een) ‡

*Not commercially available in the U.S.
†Not commercially available in Canada.
‡Generic name product may be available in the U.S.

Description

This medicine belongs to the family of medicines known as thioxanthenes (thye-oh-ZAN-theens). It is used in the treatment of nervous, mental, and emotional conditions. Improve-

ment in such conditions is thought to result from the effect of the medicine on nerve pathways in specific areas of the brain.

Thioxanthene medicines are available only with your doctor's prescription, in the following dosage forms:

Oral
Chlorprothixene
• Suspension (U.S.)
• Tablets (U.S.)
Flupenthixol
• Tablets (Canada)
Thiothixene
• Capsules (U.S. and Canada)
• Solution (U.S.)

Parenteral
Chlorprothixene
• Injection (U.S.)
Flupenthixol
• Injection (Canada)
Thiothixene
• Injection (U.S.)

Before Using This Medicine

In deciding to use a medicine, the risks of taking the medicine must be weighed against the good it will do. This is a decision you and your doctor will make. For thioxanthenes, the following should be considered:

Allergies—Tell your doctor if you have ever had any unusual or allergic reaction to thioxanthene or to phenothiazine medicines. Also tell your health care professional if you are allergic to any other substances, such as foods, preservatives, or dyes.

Pregnancy—Studies have not been done in pregnant women. Although animal studies have not shown that thioxanthenes cause birth defects, the studies have shown that these medicines cause a decrease in fertility and fewer successful pregnancies.

Breast-feeding—It is not known if thioxanthenes pass into the breast milk. However, similar medicines for nervous, mental, or emotional conditions do pass into breast milk and may cause drowsiness and increase the risk of other problems in the nursing baby. Be sure you have discussed the risks and benefits of this medicine with your doctor.

Children—Certain side effects, such as muscle spasms of the face, neck, and back, tic-like or twitching movements, inability to move the eyes, twisting of the body, or weakness of the arms and legs, are more likely to occur in children, who are usually more sensitive than adults to the side effects of thioxanthenes.

Older adults—Constipation, dizziness or fainting, drowsiness, dryness of mouth, trembling of the hands and fingers, and symptoms of tardive dyskinesia (such as rapid, worm-like movements of the tongue or any other uncontrolled movements of the mouth, tongue, or jaw, and/or arms and legs) are especially likely to occur in elderly patients, who are usually more sensitive than younger adults to the effects of thioxanthenes.

Other medicines—Although certain medicines should not be used together at all, in other cases 2 different medicines may be used together even if an interaction might occur. In these cases, your doctor may want to change the dose, or other precautions may be necessary. When you are taking thioxanthenes, it is especially important that your health care professional know if you are taking any of the following:

- Amoxapine (e.g., Asendin) or
- Methyldopa (e.g., Aldomet) or
- Metoclopramide (e.g., Reglan) or
- Metyrosine (e.g., Demser) or
- Other antipsychotics (medicine for mental illness) or
- Pemoline (e.g., Cylert) or
- Pimozide (e.g., Orap) or
- Promethazine (e.g., Phenergan) or
- Rauwolfia alkaloids (alseroxylon [e.g., Rauwiloid], deserpidine [e.g., Harmonyl], rauwolfia serpentina [e.g., Raudixin], reserpine [e.g., Serpasil]) or
- Trimeprazine (e.g., Temaril)—Taking these medicines with thioxanthenes may increase the chance and severity of certain side effects
- Central nervous system (CNS) depressants (medicine that causes drowsiness) or
- Tricyclic antidepressants (medicine for depression)—Taking these medicines with thioxanthenes may add to the CNS depressant effects
- Epinephrine (e.g., Adrenalin)—Severe low blood pressure (hypotension) and fast heartbeat may occur if epinephrine is used with thioxanthenes
- Levodopa (e.g., Sinemet)—Thioxanthenes may keep levodopa from working properly in the treatment of Parkinson's disease
- Quinidine (e.g., Quinidex)—Unwanted effects on your heart may occur

Other medical problems—The presence of other medical problems may affect the use of thioxanthenes. Make sure you tell your doctor if you have any other medical problems, especially:

- Alcohol abuse—Drinking alcohol will add to the central nervous system (CNS) depressant effects of thioxanthenes
- Blood disease or
- Enlarged prostate or
- Glaucoma or
- Heart or blood vessel disease or
- Lung disease or
- Parkinson's disease or
- Stomach ulcers or
- Urination problems—Thioxanthenes may make the condition worse
- Liver disease—Higher blood levels of thioxanthenes may occur, increasing the chance of side effects
- Reye's syndrome—The risk of liver problems may be increased
- Seizure disorders—The risk of seizures may be increased

Proper Use of This Medicine

This medicine may be taken with food or a full glass (8 ounces) of water or milk to reduce stomach irritation.

For patients taking *thiothixene oral solution:*

- This medicine must be diluted before you take it. Just before taking, measure the dose with the specially marked dropper. Mix the medicine with a full glass of water, milk, tomato or fruit juice, soup, or carbonated beverage.

Do not take more of this medicine or take it more often than your doctor ordered. This is particularly important when this medicine is given to children, since they may react very strongly to its effects.

Sometimes this medicine must be taken for several weeks before its full effect is reached.

Dosing—The dose of these medicines will be different for different patients. *Follow your doctor's orders or the directions on the label.* The following information includes only the average doses of these medicines. *If your dose is different, do not change it* unless your doctor tells you to do so.

The number of capsules or tablets or the amount of liquid that you take depends on the strength of the medicine. Also, the number of doses you take each day, the time allowed between doses, and the length of time you take the medicine depend on the medical problem for which you are taking thioxanthenes.

For chlorprothixene
- For treatment of psychosis:
  —*Oral* dosage forms (suspension or tablets):
  - Adults and teenagers—25 to 50 milligrams (mg) three or four times a day.
  - Children 6 to 12 years of age—10 to 25 mg three or four times a day.
  - Children up to 6 years of age—Use and dose must be determined by your doctor.
  —*Injection* dosage form:
  - Adults and teenagers—25 to 50 mg, injected into a muscle, three or four times a day.
  - Children up to 12 years of age—Use and dose must be determined by your doctor.

For flupenthixol
- For treatment of psychosis:
  —*Oral* dosage form (tablets):
  - Adults—To start, 1 milligram (mg) three times a day. Your doctor may increase your dose if needed, depending on your condition.
  - Children—Use and dose must be determined by your doctor.
  —*Long-acting injection* dosage form:
  - Adults—To start, 20 to 40 milligrams (mg) injected into a muscle. Your doctor will determine whether your dose needs to be changed, depending on your condition.
  - Children—Use and dose must be determined by your doctor.

For thiothixene
- For treatment of psychosis:
  —*Oral* dosage forms (capsules and solution):
  - Adults and teenagers—To start, 2 milligrams (mg) three times a day, or 5 mg two times a day. Your doctor may increase your dose if needed. However, the dose is usually not more than 60 mg a day.
  - Children up to 12 years of age—Use and dose must be determined by your doctor.
  —*Injection* dosage form:
  - Adults and teenagers—4 milligrams (mg), injected into a muscle, two to four times a day. Your doctor may increase your dose if needed. However, the dose is usually not more than 30 mg a day.
  - Children up to 12 years of age—Use and dose must be determined by your doctor.

Missed dose—If you miss a dose of this medicine, take it as soon as possible. However, if it is within 2 hours of your next dose, skip the missed dose and go back to your regular dosing schedule. Do not double doses.

Storage—To store this medicine:
- Keep out of the reach of children.
- Store away from heat and direct light.
- Do not store the capsule or tablet form of this medicine in the bathroom, near the kitchen sink, or in other damp places. Heat or moisture may cause the medicine to break down.
- Keep the liquid form of this medicine from freezing.
- Do not keep outdated medicine or medicine no longer needed. Be sure that any discarded medicine is out of the reach of children.

Precautions While Using This Medicine

Your doctor should check your progress at regular visits. This will allow the dosage of the medicine to be adjusted when necessary and also will reduce the possibility of side effects.

Do not stop taking this medicine without first checking with your doctor. Your doctor may want you to gradually reduce the amount you are taking before stopping completely. This is to prevent side effects and to prevent your condition from becoming worse.

This medicine will add to the effects of alcohol and other CNS depressants (medicines that slow down the nervous system, possibly causing drowsiness). Some examples of CNS depressants are antihistamines or medicine for hay fever, other allergies, or colds; sedatives, tranquilizers, or sleeping medicine; prescription pain medicine or narcotics; barbiturates; medicine for seizures; muscle relaxants; or anesthetics, including some dental anesthetics. *Check with your doctor before taking any such depressants while you are using this medicine.*

Do not take this medicine within an hour of taking antacids or medicine for diarrhea. Taking them too close together may make this medicine less effective.

Before having any kind of surgery, dental treatment, or emergency treatment, tell the medical doctor or dentist in charge that you are using this medicine. Taking thioxanthenes together with medicines that are used during surgery or dental or emergency treatments may increase the CNS depressant effects.

This medicine may cause some people to become drowsy or less alert than they are normally, especially during the first few weeks the medicine is being taken. Even if you take this medicine only at bedtime, you may feel drowsy or less alert on arising. *Make sure you know how you react to this medicine before you drive, use machines, or do anything else that could be dangerous if you are not alert.*

Dizziness, lightheadedness, or fainting may occur while you are taking this medicine, especially when you get up from a lying or sitting position. Getting up slowly may help. If the problem continues or gets worse, check with your doctor.

This medicine may make you sweat less, causing your body temperature to increase. *Use extra care not to become overheated during exercise or hot weather while you are taking this medicine,* since overheating may result in heat stroke. Also, hot baths or saunas may make you feel dizzy or faint while you are taking this medicine.

Thioxanthenes may cause your skin to be more sensitive to sunlight than it is normally. Exposure to sunlight, even for brief periods of time, may cause a skin rash, itching, redness or other discoloration of the skin, or a severe sunburn. When you begin taking this medicine:
- Stay out of direct sunlight, especially between the hours of 10:00 a.m. and 3:00 p.m., if possible.
- Wear protective clothing, including a hat. Also, wear sunglasses.
- Apply a sun block product that has a skin protection factor (SPF) of at least 15. Some patients may require a product with a higher SPF number, especially if they have a fair complexion. If you have any questions about this, check with your health care professional.
- Apply a sun block lipstick that has an SPF of at least 15 to protect your lips.
- Do not use a sunlamp or tanning bed or booth.

If you have a severe reaction from the sun, check with your doctor.

This medicine may cause dryness of the mouth. For temporary relief, use sugarless gum or candy, melt bits of ice in your mouth, or use a saliva substitute. However, if your mouth continues to feel dry for more than 2 weeks, check with your medical doctor or dentist. Continuing dryness of the mouth may increase the chance of dental disease, including tooth decay, gum disease, and fungus infections.

If you are taking a liquid form of this medicine, *try to avoid spilling it on your skin or clothing.* Skin rash and irritation have been caused by similar medicines.

If you are receiving this medicine by injection:
- The effects of the long-acting injection form of this medicine may last for up to 3 weeks. *The precautions and side effects information for this medicine applies during this period of time.*

Side Effects of This Medicine

Along with their needed effects, thioxanthenes can sometimes cause serious side effects. Tardive dyskinesia (a movement disorder) may occur and may not go away after you stop using the medicine. Signs of tardive dyskinesia include fine, worm-like movements of the tongue, or other uncontrolled movements of the mouth, tongue, cheeks, jaw, or arms and legs. Other serious but rare side effects may also occur. Some of these side effects, including severe muscle stiffness, fever, unusual tiredness or weakness, fast heartbeat, difficult breathing, increased sweating, loss of bladder control, and seizures, may be the sign of a condition called neuroleptic malignant syndrome. *You and your doctor should discuss the good this medicine will do as well as the risks of taking it.*

Although not all of these side effects may occur, if they do occur they may need medical attention.

Stop taking this medicine and get emergency help immediately if any of the following side effects occur:
Rare
    Convulsions (seizures); difficulty in breathing; fast heartbeat; high fever; high or low (irregular) blood pressure; increased sweating; loss of bladder control; muscle stiffness (severe); unusually pale skin; unusual tiredness

Also, check with your doctor as soon as possible if any of the following side effects occur:

More common

Difficulty in talking or swallowing; inability to move eyes; lip smacking or puckering; loss of balance control; mask-like face; muscle spasms, especially of the neck and back; puffing of cheeks; rapid or worm-like movements of tongue; restlessness or need to keep moving (severe); shuffling walk; stiffness of arms and legs; trembling and shaking of fingers and hands; twisting movements of body; uncontrolled chewing movements; uncontrolled movements of the arms and legs

Less common

Blurred vision or other eye problems; difficult urination; fainting; skin discoloration; skin rash

Rare

Hot, dry skin or lack of sweating; increased blinking or spasms of eyelid; muscle weakness; sore throat and fever; uncontrolled twisting movements of neck, trunk, arms, or legs; unusual bleeding or bruising; unusual facial expressions or body positions; yellow eyes or skin

Symptoms of overdose

Difficulty in breathing (severe); dizziness (severe); drowsiness (severe); muscle trembling, jerking, stiffness, or uncontrolled movements (severe); small pupils; unusual excitement; unusual tiredness or weakness (severe)

Other side effects may occur that usually do not need medical attention. These side effects may go away during treatment as your body adjusts to the medicine. However, check with your doctor if any of the following side effects continue or are bothersome:

More common

Constipation; decreased sweating; dizziness, lightheadedness, or fainting; drowsiness (mild); dryness of mouth; increased appetite and weight; increased sensitivity of skin to sunlight (skin rash, itching, redness or other discoloration of skin, or severe sunburn); stuffy nose

Less common

Changes in menstrual period; decreased sexual ability; swelling of breasts (in males and females); unusual secretion of milk

After you stop taking this medicine your body may need time to adjust, especially if you took this medicine in high doses or for a long time. If you stop taking it too quickly, the following withdrawal effects may occur and should be reported to your doctor:

Dizziness; nausea and vomiting; stomach pain; trembling of fingers and hands; uncontrolled, continuing movements of mouth, tongue, or jaw

Although not all of the side effects listed above have been reported for all thioxanthenes, they have been reported for at least one of them. However, since these medicines are very similar, any of the above side effects may occur with any of them.

Other side effects not listed above may also occur in some patients. If you notice any other effects, check with your doctor.

Revised: 06/17/93

THROMBOLYTIC AGENTS
Systemic

Commonly used brand name(s):

In the U.S.—

Abbokinase[5]	Eminase[2]
Abbokinase Open-Cath[5]	Retavase[3]
Activase[1]	Streptase[4]

In Canada—

Abbokinase[5]	Eminase[2]
Abbokinase Open-Cath[5]	Streptase[4]
Activase rt-PA[1]	

Other commonly used names are: Anisoylated plasminogen-streptokinase activator complex[2], APSAC[2], tissue-type plasminogen activator (recombinant)[1], t-PA[1], and rt-PA[1].

Note: For quick reference, the following thrombolytic agents are numbered to match the corresponding brand names.

This information applies to the following medicines:
1. Alteplase, Recombinant (AL-te-plase)
2. Anistreplase (a-NISS-tre-place)
3. Reteplase, Recombinant (RE-te-plays) †
4. Streptokinase (strep-toe-KIN-ace)
5. Urokinase (yoor-oh-KIN-ace)

†Not commercially available in Canada.

Description

Thrombolytic agents are used to dissolve blood clots that have formed in certain blood vessels. These medicines are usually used when a blood clot seriously lessens the flow of blood to certain parts of the body.

Thrombolytic agents are also used to dissolve blood clots that form in tubes that are placed into the body. The tubes allow treatments (such as dialysis or injections into a vein) to be given over a long period of time.

These medicines are to be given only by or under the direct supervision of a doctor.

These medicines are available in the following dosage forms:

Parenteral

Alteplase, Recombinant
- Injection (U.S. and Canada)

Anistreplase
- Injection (U.S. and Canada)

Reteplase, Recombinant
- Injection (U.S.)

Streptokinase
- Injection (U.S. and Canada)

Urokinase
- Injection (U.S. and Canada)

Note: Recently, the Food and Drug Administration (FDA) revealed that certain manufacturing practices in the production of urokinase may increase the risk of infectious disease from the use of urokinase. Although there have been no reports of disease caused by the use of urokinase, the FDA recommends that urokinase be used only when other thrombolytic agents are not acceptable. It may be necessary for you to take another medicine instead of urokinase. Be sure you have discussed the risks and benefits of urokinase with your doctor.

Before Receiving This Medicine

In deciding to use a medicine, the risks of using the medicine must be weighed against the good it will do. This is a decision you and your doctor will make. For thrombolytic agents, the following should be considered:

Allergies—Tell your doctor if you have ever had any unusual or allergic reaction to alteplase, anistreplase, streptokinase, or urokinase. Also tell your health care professional if you are allergic to any other substances, such as foods, preservatives, or dyes.

Pregnancy—Tell your doctor if you are pregnant or if you have recently had a baby.

There is a slight chance that use of a thrombolytic agent during the first five months of pregnancy may cause a miscarriage. However, both streptokinase and urokinase have been used in pregnant women and have not been reported to cause this problem. Also, studies in pregnant women (for streptokinase) and studies in animals (for urokinase) have not shown that these medicines cause either miscarriage or harm to the fetus (including birth defects). Studies on birth defects with alteplase and anistreplase have not been done in either pregnant women or animals.

Breast-feeding—It is not known whether thrombolytic agents pass into the breast milk. Although most medicines pass into breast milk in small amounts, many of them may be used safely while breast-feeding. Mothers who are taking any of these medicines and who wish to breast-feed should discuss this with their doctor.

Children—Studies on these medicines have been done only in adult patients, and there is no specific information comparing the use of thrombolytic agents in children with use in other age groups. However, streptokinase has occasionally been used in children to dissolve blood clots in certain blood vessels. Bleeding may be more likely to occur in children, who are usually more sensitive than adults to the effects of streptokinase.

Older adults—The need for treatment with a thrombolytic agent (instead of other kinds of treatment) may be increased in elderly patients with blood clots. However, the chance of bleeding may also be increased. It is especially important that you discuss the use of this medicine with your doctor.

Other medicines—Although certain medicines should not be used together at all, in other cases two different medicines may be used together even if an interaction might occur. In these cases, your doctor may want to change the dose, or other precautions may be necessary. Before you receive a thrombolytic agent, it is especially important that your doctor know if you are taking any of the following:

- Anticoagulants (blood thinners) or
- Aspirin or
- Cefamandole (e.g., Mandol) or
- Cefoperazone (e.g., Cefobid) or
- Cefotetan (e.g., Cefotan) or
- Divalproex (e.g., Depakote) or
- Enoxaparin (e.g., Lovenox) or
- Heparin or
- Indomethacin (e.g., Indocin) or
- Inflammation or pain medicine (except narcotics) or
- Phenylbutazone (e.g., Butazolidin) or
- Plicamycin (e.g., Mithracin) or
- Sulfinpyrazone (e.g., Anturane) or
- Ticlopidine (e.g., Ticlid) or

- Valproic acid (e.g., Depakene)—The chance of bleeding may be increased

Also, tell your doctor if you have had an injection of anistreplase or streptokinase within the past year. If you have, these medicines may not work properly if they are given to you again. Your doctor may decide to use alteplase or urokinase instead.

Other medical problems—The presence of other medical problems or recent delivery of a child may affect the use of thrombolytic agents. Make sure you tell your doctor if you have any other medical problems, especially:

- Allergic reaction to streptokinase or anistreplase (or history of)—Increased risk of an allergic reaction
- Blood disease, bleeding problems, or a history of bleeding in any part of the body or
- Brain disease or tumor or
- Heart or blood vessel disease, including irregular heartbeat or
- High blood pressure or
- Liver disease (severe) or
- Stroke, especially with seizure (or history of)—The chance of serious bleeding may be increased
- Streptococcal ("strep") infection (recent)—Anistreplase or streptokinase may not work properly after a streptococcal infection; your doctor may decide to use a different thrombolytic agent

Also, tell your doctor if you have recently had any of the following conditions:

- Falls or blows to the body or head or any other injury or
- Injections into a blood vessel or
- Placement of any tube into the body or
- Surgery, including dental surgery—The chance of serious bleeding may be increased

If you have recently had a baby, use of these medicines may cause serious bleeding.

Proper Use of This Medicine

Dosing—The dose of these medicines will be different for different patients. The dose you receive will depend on the medicine you receive and will be based on the condition for which you are receiving the medicine. In some cases, the dose will also depend on your body weight.

Precautions While Using This Medicine

Thrombolytic agents can cause bleeding that usually is not serious. However, serious bleeding may occur in some people. *To help prevent serious bleeding, carefully follow any instructions given by your health care professional. Also, move around as little as possible, and do not get out of bed on your own, unless your health care professional tells you it is all right to do so.*

Side Effects of This Medicine

Along with its needed effects, a medicine may cause some unwanted effects. Although not all of these side effects may occur, if they do occur they may need medical attention.

Tell your health care professional immediately if any of the following side effects occur:
  More common
    Bleeding or oozing from cuts, gums, wounds, or around the place of injection; fever; low blood pressure

Less common or rare

Bruising; changes in facial skin color; confusion; double vision; fast or irregular breathing; flushing or redness of skin; headache (mild); muscle pain (mild); nausea; shortness of breath, troubled breathing, tightness in chest, and/or wheezing; skin rash, hives, or itching; swelling of eyes, face, lips, or tongue; trouble in speaking; weakness in arms or legs

Symptoms of bleeding inside the body

Abdominal or stomach pain or swelling; back pain or backaches; blood in urine; bloody or black, tarry stools; constipation; coughing up blood; dizziness; headaches (sudden, severe, or continuing); joint pain, stiffness, or swelling; muscle pain or stiffness (severe or continuing); nosebleeds; unexpected or unusually heavy bleeding from vagina; vomiting of blood or material that looks like coffee grounds

Other side effects not listed above may also occur in some patients. If you notice any other effects, check with your doctor.

Revised: 02/08/00

THYROID HORMONES Systemic

Commonly used brand name(s):

In the U.S.—

Armour Thyroid[5]	Thyrar[5]
Cytomel[2]	Thyroid Strong[5]
Levo-T[1]	Thyrolar[3]
Levothroid[1]	Triostat[2]
Levoxyl[1]	Westhroid[5]
Synthroid[1]	

In Canada—

Cytomel[2]	PMS-Levothyroxine Sodium[1]
Eltroxin[1]	Synthroid[1]

Note: For quick reference, the following thyroid hormones are numbered to match the corresponding brand names.

This information applies to the following medicines:

1. Levothyroxine (lee-voe-thye-ROX-een) ‡
2. Liothyronine (lye-oh-THYE-roe-neen) ‡
3. Liotrix (LYE-oh-trix) †
4. Thyroglobulin (thye-roe-GLOB-yoo-lin) *†
5. Thyroid (THYE-roid) ‡§

Note: This information does *not* apply to Thyrotropin.

*Not commercially available in the U.S.
†Not commercially available in Canada.
‡Generic name product may be available in the U.S.
§Generic name product may be available in Canada.

Description

Thyroid medicines belong to the general group of medicines called hormones. They are used when the thyroid gland does not produce enough hormone. They are also used to help decrease the size of enlarged thyroid glands (known as goiter) and to treat thyroid cancer.

These medicines are available only with your doctor's prescription, in the following dosage forms:

Oral

Levothyroxine
 • Tablets (U.S. and Canada)

Liothyronine
 • Tablets (U.S. and Canada)

Liotrix
 • Tablets (U.S.)

Thyroglobulin
 • Tablets

Thyroid
 • Tablets (U.S. and Canada)

Parenteral

Levothyroxine
 • Injection (U.S. and Canada)

Liothyronine
 • Injection (U.S.)

Before Using This Medicine

In deciding to use a medicine, the risks of taking the medicine must be weighed against the good it will do. This is a decision you and your doctor will make. For thyroid hormones, the following should be considered:

Allergies—Tell your doctor if you have ever had any unusual or allergic reaction to thyroid hormones. Also tell your health care professional if you are allergic to any other substances, such as foods, preservatives, or dyes.

Pregnancy—Use of proper amounts of thyroid hormone during pregnancy has not been shown to cause birth defects or other problems. However, your doctor may want you to change your dose while you are pregnant. This will make regular visits to your doctor important.

Breast-feeding—Use of proper amounts of thyroid hormones by mothers has not been shown to cause problems in nursing babies.

Children—Thyroid hormones have been tested in children and have not been shown to cause different side effects or problems in children than they do in adults.

Older adults—This medicine has been tested and has not been shown to cause different side effects or problems in older people than it does in younger adults. However, a different dose may be needed in the elderly. Therefore, it is important to take the medicine only as directed by the doctor.

Other medicines—Although certain medicines should not be used together at all, in other cases two different medicines may be used together even if an interaction might occur. In these cases, your doctor may want to change the dose, or other precautions may be necessary. When you are taking thyroid hormones, it is especially important that your health care professional know if you are taking any of the following:

• Amphetamines

• Anticoagulants (blood thinners)

• Appetite suppressants (diet pills)

• Cholestyramine (e.g., Questran)

• Colestipol (e.g., Colestid)

• Medicine for asthma or other breathing problems

• Medicine for colds, sinus problems, or hay fever or other allergies (including nose drops or sprays)

Other medical problems—The presence of other medical problems may affect the use of thyroid hormones. Make sure you tell your doctor if you have any other medical problems especially:

- Diabetes mellitus (sugar diabetes)
- Hardening of the arteries
- Heart disease
- High blood pressure
- Overactive thyroid (history of)
- Underactive adrenal gland
- Underactive pituitary gland

Proper Use of This Medicine

Use this medicine only as directed by your doctor. Do not use more or less of it, and do not use it more often than your doctor ordered. Your doctor has prescribed the exact amount your body needs and if you take different amounts, you may experience symptoms of an overactive or underactive thyroid. Take it at the same time each day to make sure it always has the same effect.

If your condition is due to a lack of thyroid hormone, you may have to take this medicine for the rest of your life. It is very important that you *do not stop taking this medicine without first checking with your doctor*.

Dosing—The dose of these medicines will be different for different patients. *Follow your doctor's orders or the directions on the label*. The following information includes only the average doses of these medicines. *If your dose is different, do not change it* unless your doctor tells you to do so.

The number of tablets that you take depends on the strength of the medicine. The amount of thyroid hormone that you need to take every day depends on the results of your thyroid tests. However, treatment is usually started with lower doses that are increased a little at a time until you are taking the full amount. This helps prevent side effects.

For levothyroxine
- For *oral* dosage form (tablets):
  —For replacing the thyroid hormone:
    - Adults and teenagers—At first, 0.0125 to 0.05 milligrams (mg) once a day. Then, your doctor may increase your dose a little at a time to 0.075 to 0.125 mg a day. The dose is usually no higher than 0.15 mg once a day.
    - Children less than 6 months of age—The dose is based on body weight and must be determined by your doctor. The usual dose is 0.025 to 0.05 mg once a day.
    - Children 6 months to 12 months of age—The dose is based on body weight and must be determined by your doctor. The usual dose is 0.05 to 0.075 mg once a day.
    - Children 1 to 5 years of age—The dose is based on body weight and must be determined by your doctor. The usual dose is 0.075 to 0.1 mg once a day.
    - Children 6 to 10 years of age—The dose is based on body weight and must be determined by your doctor. The usual dose is 0.1 to 0.15 mg once a day.
    - Children over 10 years of age—The dose is based on body weight and must be determined by your doctor. The usual dose is 0.15 to 0.2 mg once a day.

- For *injection* dosage form:
  —For replacing the thyroid hormone:
    - Adults and teenagers—50 to 100 micrograms (mcg) injected into a muscle or into a vein once a day. People with very serious conditions caused by too little thyroid hormone may need higher doses.
    - Children less than 6 months of age—The dose is based on body weight and must be determined by your doctor. The usual dose is 0.019 to 0.038 mg once a day.
    - Children 6 months to 12 months of age—The dose is based on body weight and must be determined by your doctor. The usual dose is 0.038 to 0.056 mg once a day.
    - Children 1 to 5 years of age—The dose is based on body weight and must be determined by your doctor. The usual dose is 0.056 to 0.075 mg once a day.
    - Children 6 to 10 years of age—The dose is based on body weight and must be determined by your doctor. The usual dose is 0.075 to 0.113 mg once a day.
    - Children over 10 years of age—The dose is based on body weight and must be determined by your doctor. The usual dose is 0.113 to 0.15 mg once a day.

For liothyronine sodium
- For *oral* dosage form (tablets):
  —For replacing the thyroid hormone:
    - Adults and teenagers—At first, 25 micrograms (mcg) a day. Some patients with very serious conditions caused by too little thyroid hormone may need to take only 2.5 to 5 mcg a day at first. Also, some patients with heart disease or the elderly may need lower doses at first. Then, your doctor may increase your dose a little at a time to up to 50 mcg a day if needed. Your doctor may want you to divide your dose into smaller amounts that are taken two or more times a day.
  —For treating a large thyroid gland (goiter):
    - Adults—At first, 5 mcg a day. Some patients with heart disease or the elderly may need lower doses at first. Then, your doctor may increase your dose a little at a time to 50 to 100 mcg a day.

- For *injection* dosage form:
  —For replacing the thyroid hormone in very serious conditions (myxedema coma):
    - Adults—At first, 10 to 50 mcg injected into a vein every four to twelve hours. Then, your doctor may want to adjust your dose depending on your condition.
    - Children—Use and dose must be determined by your doctor.

For liotrix (levothyroxine and liothyronine combination)
- For *oral* dosage form (tablets):
  —For replacing the thyroid hormone:
    - Adults, teenagers, and children—At first, 50 micrograms (mcg) of levothyroxine and 12.5 mcg of liothyronine once a day. Some people with very serious conditions caused by too little thyroid hormone may need only 12.5 mcg of levothyroxine and 3.1 mcg of liothyronine once a day. Also, some elderly patients may need lower doses at

first. Then, your doctor may want to increase your dose a little at a time to up to 100 mcg of levothyroxine and 25 mcg of liothyronine.

For thyroglobulin
- For *oral* dosage form (tablets):
  —For replacing the thyroid hormone:
  - Adults, teenagers, and children—At first, 32 milligrams (mg) a day. Some people with very serious conditions caused by too little thyroid hormone may need to take only 16 to 32 mg a day at first. Then, the doctor may want you to increase your dose a little at a time to 65 to 160 mg a day.

For thyroid
- For *oral* dosage form (tablets):
  —For replacing thyroid hormone:
  - Adults, teenagers, and children—60 milligrams (mg) a day. Some people with very serious conditions caused by too little thyroid hormone may need to take only 15 mg a day at first. Also, some elderly patients may need lower doses at first. Then, your doctor may want you to increase your dose a little at a time to 60 to 120 mg a day.

Missed dose—If you miss a dose of this medicine, take it as soon as possible. However, if it is almost time for your next dose, skip the missed dose and go back to your regular dosing schedule. Do not double doses. If you miss 2 or more doses in a row or if you have any questions about this, check with your doctor.

Storage—To store this medicine:
- Keep out of the reach of children.
- Store away from heat and direct light.
- Do not store in the bathroom, near the kitchen sink, or in other damp places. Heat or moisture may cause the medicine to break down.
- Do not keep outdated medicine or medicine no longer needed. Be sure that any discarded medicine is out of the reach of children.

Precautions While Using This Medicine

It is very important that your doctor check your progress at regular visits, to make sure that this medicine is working properly.

If you have certain kinds of heart disease, this medicine may cause chest pain or shortness of breath when you exert yourself. If these occur, do not overdo exercise or physical work. If you have any questions about this, check with your doctor.

Before having any kind of surgery (including dental surgery) or emergency treatment, *tell the medical doctor or dentist in charge that you are taking this medicine.*

Do not take any other medicine unless prescribed by your doctor. Some medicines may increase or decrease the effects of thyroid on your body and cause problems in controlling your condition. Also, thyroid hormones may change the effects of other medicines.

Side Effects of This Medicine

Along with its needed effects, a medicine may cause some unwanted effects. Although not all of these side effects may occur, if they do occur they may need medical attention.

Check with your doctor as soon as possible if any of the following side effects occur since they may indicate an overdose or an allergic reaction:

Less common or rare
  Headache (severe) in children; skin rash or hives
Signs and symptoms of overdose
  Chest pain; confusion; fast or irregular heartbeat; mood swings; muscle weakness; psychosis; restlessness (extreme); yellow eyes or skin; shortness of breath

For patients taking this medicine for underactive thyroid:
- This medicine usually takes several weeks to have a noticeable effect on your condition. Until it begins to work, you may experience no change in your symptoms. Check with your doctor if the following symptoms continue:
  Clumsiness; coldness; constipation; dry, puffy skin; listlessness; muscle aches; sleepiness; tiredness; weakness; weight gain

Other effects may occur if the dose of the medicine is not exactly right. These side effects will go away when the dose is corrected. Check with your doctor if any of the following symptoms occur:
  Changes in appetite; changes in menstrual periods; diarrhea; fever; hand tremors; headache; increased sensitivity to heat; irritability; leg cramps; nervousness; sweating; trouble in sleeping; vomiting; weight loss

Other side effects not listed above may also occur in some patients. If you notice any other effects, check with your doctor.

Revised: 06/21/2000

TIAGABINE   Systemic

Commonly used brand name(s):

In the U.S.—
  Gabitril

Description

Tiagabine (tye-AG-a-been) is used to help control some types of seizures in the treatment of epilepsy. This medicine cannot cure epilepsy and will only work to control seizures for as long as you continue to take it.

Tiagabine is available only with your doctor's prescription, in the following dosage form:

Oral
- Tablets (U.S.)

Before Using This Medicine

In deciding to use a medicine, the risks of taking the medicine must be weighed against the good it will do. This is a decision you and your doctor will make. For tiagabine, the following should be considered:

Allergies—Tell your doctor if you have ever had any unusual or allergic reaction to tiagabine. Also tell your health care professional if you are allergic to any other substances, such as foods, preservatives, or dyes.

Pregnancy—Tiagabine has not been studied in pregnant women. However, studies in pregnant animals have shown that tiagabine may cause harmful effects in the fetus when given to the mother in doses greater than the usual human dose. Before taking this medicine, make sure your doctor knows if you are pregnant or if you may become pregnant.

Breast-feeding—It is not known whether tiagabine passes into breast milk. Although most medicines pass into breast milk in small amounts, many of them may be used safely while breast-feeding. Mothers who are taking this medicine and who wish to breast-feed should discuss this with their doctor.

Children—Although there is no specific information comparing use of tiagabine in children younger than 12 years of age with use in other age groups, this medicine is not expected to cause different side effects or problems in children than it does in adults.

Older adults—Many medicines have not been studied specifically in older people. Therefore, it may not be known whether they work exactly the same way they do in younger adults. Although there is no specific information comparing use of tiagabine in the elderly with use in other age groups, this medicine is not expected to cause different side effects or problems in older people than it does in younger adults.

Other medicines—Although certain medicines should not be used together at all, in other cases two different medicines may be used together even if an interaction might occur. In these cases, your doctor may want to change the dose, or other precautions may be necessary. When you are taking tiagabine, it is especially important that your health care professional know if you are taking any of the following:

- Carbamazepine (e.g., Tegretol) or
- Phenobarbital or
- Phenytoin (e.g., Dilantin) or
- Primidone (e.g., Mysoline)—Lower blood levels of tiagabine may occur, so tiagabine may not work properly; your doctor may need to adjust your dosage

Other medical problems—The presence of other medical problems may affect the use of tiagabine. Make sure you tell your doctor if you have any other medical problems, especially:

- Liver problems—Higher blood levels of tiagabine may result, leading to an increase in the chance of side effects
- Status epilepticus—Tiagabine may cause the condition to recur

Proper Use of This Medicine

Take this medicine only as directed by your doctor, to help your condition as much as possible. Do not take more or less of it, and do not take it more or less often than your doctor ordered.

Tiagabine should be taken with food or on a full stomach.

Dosing—The dose of tiagabine will be different for different patients. *Follow your doctor's orders or the directions on the label.* The following information includes only the average doses of tiagabine. *If your dose is different, do not change it unless your doctor tells you to do so.*

The number of tablets that you take depends on the strength of the medicine. Also, *the number of doses you take each day, the time allowed between doses, and the length of time you take the medicine depend on the medical problem for which you are taking tiagabine.*

- For *oral* dosage form (tablets):
  - For epilepsy:
    - Adults and teenagers 12 years of age and older— At first, 4 milligrams (mg) once a day. Your doctor may increase your dose slowly as needed and tolerated. However, the dose usually is not greater than 56 mg a day.
    - Children up to 12 years of age—Use and dose must be determined by the doctor.

Missed dose—If you miss a dose of this medicine, take it as soon as possible. However, if it is almost time for your next dose, skip the missed dose and go back to your regular dosing schedule. Do not double doses.

Storage—To store this medicine:

- Keep out of the reach of children.
- Store away from heat and direct light.
- Do not store in the bathroom, near the kitchen sink, or in other damp places. Heat or moisture may cause the medicine to break down.
- Keep the medicine from freezing. Do not refrigerate.
- Do not keep outdated medicine or medicine no longer needed. Be sure that any discarded medicine is out of the reach of children.

Precautions While Using This Medicine

Tiagabine may cause dizziness, drowsiness, trouble in thinking, trouble with motor skills, or vision problems. *Make sure you know how you react to this medicine before you drive, use machines, or do anything else that could be dangerous if you are not alert, well-coordinated, or able to think or see well.*

This medicine will add to the effects of alcohol and other CNS depressants (medicines that make you drowsy or less alert). Some examples of CNS depressants are antihistamines or medicine for hay fever, other allergies, or colds; sedatives, tranquilizers, or sleeping medicine; prescription pain medicine or narcotics; barbiturates; other medicines for seizures; muscle relaxants; or anesthetics, including some dental anesthetics. Check with your medical doctor or dentist before taking any of the above while you are taking tiagabine.

Do not stop taking tiagabine without first checking with your doctor. Stopping the medicine suddenly may cause your seizures to return or to occur more often. Your doctor may want you to gradually reduce the amount you are taking before stopping completely.

Side Effects of This Medicine

Along with its needed effects, a medicine may cause some unwanted effects. Although not all of these side effects may occur, if they do occur they may need medical attention.

Check with your doctor as soon as possible if any of the following side effects occur:

More common

Blue or purple spots on skin; difficulty in concentrating or paying attention

Less common

Burning, numbness, or tingling sensations; clumsiness or unsteadiness; confusion; itching; mental depression; speech or language problems

Rare
> Agitation; bloody or cloudy urine; burning, pain, or difficulty in urinating; frequent urge to urinate; generalized weakness; hostility; memory problems; quick to react or overreact emotionally; rash; uncontrolled back-and-forth and/or rolling eye movements; walking in unusual manner

Symptoms of overdose
> Agitation (severe); clumsiness or unsteadiness (severe); coma; confusion (severe); drowsiness (severe); increase in seizures; mental depression; severe muscle twitching or jerking; sluggishness; speech problems (severe); weakness

Other side effects may occur that usually do not need medical attention. These side effects may go away during treatment as your body adjusts to the medicine. However, check with your doctor if any of the following side effects continue or are bothersome:

More common
> Chills; diarrhea; dizziness; drowsiness; fever; headache; muscle aches or pain; nervousness; sore throat; tremor; unusual tiredness or weakness; vomiting

Less common
> Abdominal pain; flushing; impaired vision; increased appetite; increased cough; mouth ulcers; muscle weakness; nausea; pain; trouble in sleeping

Other side effects not listed above may also occur in some patients. If you notice any other effects, check with your doctor.

Developed: 02/26/98

TICLOPIDINE   Systemic

Commonly used brand name(s):

In the U.S.—
> Ticlid

In Canada—
> Ticlid

Description

Ticlopidine (tye-KLOE-pi-deen) is used to lessen the chance of having a stroke. It is given to people who have already had a stroke and to people with certain medical problems that may lead to a stroke. Because ticlopidine can cause serious side effects, especially during the first 3 months of treatment, it is used mostly for people who cannot take aspirin to prevent strokes.

A stroke may occur when blood flow to the brain is interrupted by a blood clot. Ticlopidine reduces the chance that a harmful blood clot will form, by preventing certain cells in the blood from clumping together. This effect of ticlopidine may also increase the chance of serious bleeding in some people.

This medicine is available only with a doctor's prescription in the following dosage form:

Oral
> • Tablets (U.S. and Canada)

Before Using This Medicine

In deciding to use a medicine, the risks of taking the medicine must be weighed against the good it will do. This is a decision you and your doctor will make. For ticlopidine, the following should be considered:

Allergies—Tell your doctor if you have ever had any unusual or allergic reaction to ticlopidine. Also tell your health care professional if you are allergic to any other substances, such as foods, preservatives, or dyes.

Pregnancy—Studies with ticlopidine have not been done in pregnant women. This medicine did not cause birth defects in animal studies. However, it caused other unwanted effects in animal studies when it was given in amounts that were large enough to cause harmful effects in the mother.

Breast-feeding—It is not known whether ticlopidine passes into the breast milk.

Children—There is no specific information comparing use of ticlopidine in children with use in other age groups.

Older adults—This medicine has been tested and has not been shown to cause different side effects or problems in older people than it does in younger adults.

Other medicines—Although certain medicines should not be used together at all, in other cases two different medicines may be used together even if an interaction might occur. In these cases, your doctor may want to change the dose, or other precautions may be necessary. When you are taking ticlopidine, it is especially important that your health care professional know if you are taking any of the following:

• Anticoagulants (blood thinners) or
• Aspirin or
• Carbenicillin by injection (e.g., Geopen) or
• Dipyridamole (e.g., Persantine) or
• Divalproex (e.g., Depakote) or
• Heparin (e.g., Hepalean, Liquaemin) or
• Inflammation or pain medicine, except narcotics, or
• Pentoxifylline (e.g., Trental) or
• Plicamycin (e.g., Mithracin) or
• Sulfinpyrazone (e.g., Anturane) or
• Ticarcillin (e.g., Ticar) or
• Valproic acid (e.g., Depakene)—The chance of serious bleeding may be increased

• Phenytoin (e.g., Dilantin)—Ticlopidine may increase the amount of phenytoin in the blood and increase the chance of side effects from phenytoin

Other medical problems—The presence of other medical problems may affect the use of ticlopidine. Make sure you tell your doctor if you have any other medical problems, especially:

• Blood clotting problems, such as hemophilia and von Willebrand's disease, or
• Liver disease (severe) or
• Stomach ulcers—The chance of serious bleeding may be increased

• Blood disease—The chance of serious side effects may be increased

• Kidney disease (severe)—Ticlopidine is removed from the body more slowly when the kidneys are not working properly. This may increase the chance of side effects

Also, tell your doctor if you have ever had a problem called thrombotic thrombocytopenic purpura (TTP). This problem could reoccur if you take ticlopidine.

Proper Use of This Medicine

Ticlopidine should be taken with food. This increases the amount of medicine that is absorbed into the body. It may also lessen the chance of stomach upset.

Take this medicine only as directed by your doctor. Ticlopidine will not work properly if you take less of it than directed. Taking more ticlopidine than directed may increase the chance of serious side effects without increasing the helpful effects.

Dosing—*Follow your doctor's orders or the directions on the label.* The following dose was used, and found effective, in studies. However, some people may need a different dose. *If your dose is different, do not change it* unless your doctor tells you to do so:

- For *oral* dosage form (tablets):
  - —For prevention of strokes:
    - Adults—1 tablet (250 mg) two times a day, with food.
    - Children—It is not likely that ticlopidine would be used to help prevent strokes in children. If a child needs this medicine, however, the dose would have to be determined by the doctor.

Missed dose—If you miss a dose of this medicine, take it as soon as possible. However, if it is almost time for your next dose, skip the missed dose and go back to your regular dosing schedule. Do not double doses.

Storage—To store this medicine:

- Keep out of the reach of children.
- Store away from heat and direct light.
- Do not store in the bathroom, near the kitchen sink, or in other damp places. Heat or moisture may cause the medicine to break down.
- Do not keep outdated medicine or medicine no longer needed. Be sure that any discarded medicine is out of the reach of children.

Precautions While Using This Medicine

It is very important that blood tests be done before treatment is started with ticlopidine, and repeated every 2 weeks for the first 3 months of treatment with ticlopidine. The tests are needed to find out whether certain side effects are occurring. Finding these side effects early helps to prevent them from becoming serious. Your doctor will arrange for the blood tests to be done. *Be sure that you do not miss any appointments for these tests.* You will probably not need to have your blood tested so often after the first 3 months of treatment, because the side effects are less likely to occur after that time.

Tell all medical doctors, dentists, nurses, and pharmacists you go to that you are taking this medicine. Ticlopidine may increase the risk of serious bleeding during an operation or some kinds of dental work. Therefore, treatment may have to be stopped about 10 days to 2 weeks before the operation or dental work is done.

Ticlopidine may cause serious bleeding, especially after an injury. Sometimes, bleeding inside the body can occur without your knowing about it. Ask your doctor whether there are certain activities you should avoid while taking this medicine (for example, sports that can cause injuries). *Also, check with*

your doctor immediately if you are injured while being treated with this medicine.

Check with your doctor immediately if you notice any of the following side effects:

- Bruising or bleeding, especially bleeding that is hard to stop. Bleeding inside the body sometimes appears as bloody or black, tarry stools, or faintness. Also, bleeding may occur from the gums when brushing or flossing teeth.
- Any sign of infection, such as fever, chills, or sore throat.
- Sores, ulcers, or white spots in the mouth.
- Dark or bloody urine, difficulty in speaking, fever, pale color of skin, pinpoint red spots on skin, convulsions (seizures), weakness, or yellow eyes or skin.

After you stop taking ticlopidine, the chance of bleeding may continue for 1 or 2 weeks. During this period of time, continue to follow the same precautions that you followed while you were taking the medicine.

Side Effects of This Medicine

Along with its needed effects, a medicine may cause some unwanted effects. Although not all of these side effects may occur, if they do occur they may need medical attention.

Check with your doctor immediately if any of the following side effects occur:
> *Less common or rare*
>> Abdominal or stomach pain (severe) or swelling; back pain; blistering, peeling, or loosening of the skin or lips or mucous membranes (moist lining of many body cavities, including the mouth, lips, inside of nose, anus, and vagina); blood in eyes; bloody or black tarry stools; bruising or purple areas on skin; change in mental status; convulsions (seizures); coughing up blood; dark or bloody urine; decreased alertness; dizziness; fever, chills, or sore throat; headache (severe or continuing); joint pain or swelling; nosebleeds; pale color of skin; paralysis or problems with coordination; pinpoint red spots on skin; red lesions on the skin, often with a purple center; red, thickened, or scaly skin; sores, ulcers, or white spots in mouth; stammering or other difficulty in speaking; unusually heavy bleeding or oozing from cuts or wounds; unusually heavy or unexpected menstrual bleeding; vomiting of blood or material that looks like coffee grounds; weakness; yellow eyes or skin

Also, check with your doctor as soon as possible if any of the following side effects occur:
> *More common*
>> Skin rash

> *Less common or rare*
>> General feeling of discomfort or illness; hives or itching of skin; ringing or buzzing in ears

Other side effects may occur that usually do not need medical attention. These side effects may go away during treatment as your body adjusts to the medicine. However, check with your doctor if any of the following side effects continue or are bothersome:

More common
    Abdominal or stomach pain (mild); diarrhea; indigestion; nausea
Less common
    Bloating or gas; dizziness; vomiting

Other side effects not listed above may also occur in some patients. If you notice any other effects, check with your doctor.

Revised: 07/26/96
Interim revision: 08/05/97; 5/17/99

TILUDRONATE   Systemic

Commonly used brand name(s):

In the U.S.—
    Skelid

Description

Tiludronate (tye-LOO-droh-nate) is used to treat Paget's disease of the bone.

This medicine is available only with your doctor's prescription, in the following dosage form:

Oral
  • Tablets (U.S.)

Before Using This Medicine

In deciding to use a medicine, the risks of taking the medicine must be weighed against the good it will do. This is a decision you and your doctor will make. For tiludronate, the following should be considered:

Allergies—Tell your doctor if you have ever had any unusual or allergic reaction to tiludronate. Also tell your health care professional if you are allergic to any other substances, such as foods, preservatives, or dyes.

Pregnancy—Studies have not been done in pregnant women. However, studies in rabbits given large doses of tiludronate have shown that this medicine causes deformed bones in the fetus. In rats, tiludronate caused prolonged labor and, in some cases, death of the fetus or mother.

Breast-feeding—It is not known whether tiludronate passes into breast milk.

Children—Studies on this medicine have been done only in adult patients, and there is no specific information comparing use of tiludronate in children with use in other age groups.

Older adults—Tiludronate has been tested in elderly patients and has not been found to cause different side effects or problems in older people than it does in younger adults.

Other medicines—Although certain medicines should not be used together at all, in other cases two different medicines may be used together even if an interaction might occur. In these cases, your doctor may want to change the dose, or other precautions may be necessary. When you are taking tiludronate, it is especially important that your health care professional know if you are taking any of the following:

  • Antacids containing magnesium or aluminum or
  • Aspirin or other salicylates or salicylate-containing medicines or
  • Mineral supplements containing calcium, iron, magnesium, or aluminum—These medicines may decrease the effects of tiludronate and should be taken at least 2 hours before or after taking tiludronate

Other medical problems—The presence of other medical problems may affect the use of tiludronate. Make sure you tell your doctor if you have any other medical problems, especially:

  • Hypocalcemia (low calcium levels in the blood)
  • Overactive parathyroid gland or
  • Vitamin D deficiency—Tiludronate may make these conditions worse

  • Kidney disease—Effects may be increased because of slower removal of tiludronate from the body

  • Stomach or intestine problems, including trouble swallowing, inflammation of the esophagus, or ulcer—Tiludronate may make these conditions worse

Proper Use of This Medicine

Take tiludronate with a full glass (6 to 8 ounces) of plain water on an empty stomach.

It is important that you eat a well-balanced diet with an adequate amount of calcium and vitamin D (found in milk or other dairy products). However, do not take any beverages (including mineral water), dietary supplements, food, or other medicines at least 2 hours before or after taking the tiludronate. To do so may keep this medicine from working properly.

Dosing—The dose of tiludronate will be different for different patients. *Follow your doctor's orders or the directions on the label.* The following information includes only the average doses of tiludronate. *If your dose is different, do not change it* unless your doctor tells you to do so.

  • For *oral* dosage form (tablets):
    —For treating Paget's disease of the bone:
      • Adults and teenagers—400 milligrams (mg) a day for at least three months.
      • Children—Use and dose must be determined by your doctor.

Missed dose—If you miss a dose of this medicine, take it as soon as possible. However, if it is almost time for the next dose, skip the missed dose and go back to your regular dosing schedule. Do not double doses.

Storage—To store this medicine:

  • Keep out of the reach of children.
  • Store away from heat and direct light.
  • Do not store in the bathroom, near the kitchen sink, or in other damp places. Heat or moisture may cause the medicine to break down.
  • Do not keep outdated medicine or medicine no longer needed. Be sure that any discarded medicine is out of the reach of children.

Side Effects of This Medicine

Along with its needed effects, a medicine may cause some unwanted effects. Although not all of these side effects may occur, if they do occur they may need medical attention.

Check with your doctor as soon as possible if any of the following side effects occur:

More common
Cough; fever; head congestion; hoarseness or other voice changes; nasal congestion; runny nose; sneezing; sore throat

Less common
Blurred or decreased vision; chest pain; eye pain; headache; swelling of face, feet, or lower legs; unusual weight gain

Other side effects may occur that usually do not need medical attention. These side effects may go away during treatment as your body adjusts to the medicine. However, check with your doctor if any of the following side effects continue or are bothersome:

More common
Back pain; body pain (general); diarrhea; nausea; upset stomach

Less common
Dizziness; joint pain; muscle pain; pain in throat; red or irritated eyes; skin rash; stomach gas; vomiting

Other side effects not listed above may also occur in some patients. If you notice any other effects, check with your doctor.

Developed: 03/23/98

TINZAPARIN Systemic— INTRODUCTORY VERSION

Commonly used brand name(s):

In the U.S.—
Innohep

In Canada—
Innohep

Description

Tinzaparin (tin-ZA-pa-rin) is used for the prevention and/or treatment of deep venous thrombosis, a condition in which harmful blood clots form in the blood vessels of the legs. These blood clots can travel to the lungs and can become lodged in the blood vessels of the lungs, causing a condition called pulmonary embolism. Tinzaparin is used for several days after surgery, while you are unable to walk. It is during this time that blood clots are most likely to form. Tinzaparin also may be used for other conditions as determined by your doctor.

This medicine is available only with your doctor's prescription, in the following dosage forms:

Parenteral
• Injection (U.S. and Canada)

Before Using This Medicine

In deciding to use a medicine, the risks of taking the medicine must be weighed against the good it will do. This is a decision you and your doctor will make. For tinzaparin, the following should be considered:

Allergies—Tell your doctor if you have ever had any unusual or allergic reaction to tinzaparin. Also tell your doctor and pharmacist if you are allergic to any other substances, such as foods, especially pork or pork products, preservatives, or dyes.

Pregnancy—Tinzaparin has not been studied in pregnant women. However, tinzaparin has not been shown to cause birth defects or other problems in animal studies.

Breast-feeding—It is not known whether tinzaparin passes into breast milk. Breast-feeding is not recommended while taking this medicine. Mothers who are taking this medicine and who wish to breast-feed should discuss this with their doctor.

Children—Studies on this medicine have been done only in adult patients, and there is no specific information comparing use of tinzaparin in children with use in other age groups.

Older adults—This medicine has been tested and has not been shown to cause different side effects or problems in older people than it does in younger adults.

Other medicines—Although certain medicines should not be used together at all, in other cases two different medicines may be used together even if an interaction might occur. In these cases, your doctor may want to change the dose, or other precautions may be necessary. When you are using tinzaparin, it is especially important that your doctor and pharmacist know if you are taking any of the following:

• Aspirin or
• Inflammation or pain medicine, except narcotics—Using any of these medicines together with tinzaparin may increase the risk of bleeding

Other medical problems—The presence of other medical problems may affect the use of tinzaparin. Make sure you tell your doctor if you have any other medical problems, especially:

• Blood disease or bleeding problems or
• Eye problems caused by diabetes or high blood pressure or
• Heart infection or
• High blood pressure (hypertension) or
• Kidney disease or
• Liver disease or
• Stomach or intestinal ulcer (active) or
• Stroke—The risk of bleeding may be increased

Also, tell your doctor if you have received tinzaparin or heparin before and had a reaction to either of them called thrombocytopenia (a low platelet count in the blood), or if new blood clots formed while you were receiving the medicine.

In addition, *tell your doctor if you have recently had medical surgery*. This may increase the risk of serious bleeding when you are taking tinzaparin.

Proper Use of This Medicine

If you are using tinzaparin at home, your health care professional will teach you how to inject yourself with the medicine. *Be sure to follow the directions carefully. Check with your health care professional if you have any problems using the medicine.*

Put used syringes in a puncture-resistant, disposable container, or dispose of them as directed by your health care professional.

Dosing—The dose of tinzaparin will be different for different patients. *Follow your doctor's orders or the directions on the label*. The following information includes only the average doses of tinzaparin. *If your dose is different, do not change it* unless your doctor tells you to do so.

- For *injection* dosage form:
  —For prevention of deep venous thrombosis (leg clots) due to surgery:
  Adults
  - General surgery—3500 International Units (IU) 2 hours before surgery then 3500 IU once daily for seven to ten days.
  - Hip surgery—50 International Units (IU) per kilogram (kg) of body weight 2 hours before surgery then 50 IU per kg of body weight once daily for seven to ten days, or 75 IU per kg of body weight given after surgery once daily for seven to ten days.
  - Knee surgery—75 International Units (IU) per kilogram (kg) of body weight given after surgery once daily for seven to ten days.
  - Children—Use and dose must be determined by your doctor.
  —For treatment of deep venous thrombosis (leg clots) with or without pulmonary embolism (lung clots):
  - Adults—175 International Units (IU) per kilogram (kg) of body weight once daily for six to seven days.
  - Children—Use and dose must be determined by your doctor.

Missed dose—If you miss a dose of this medicine, discuss this with your physician.

Storage—To store this medicine:
- Keep out of the reach of children.
- Store away from heat and direct light.
- Keep the medicine from freezing. Do not refrigerate.
- Do not keep outdated medicine or medicine no longer needed. Be sure that any discarded medicine is out of the reach of children.

Precautions While Using This Medicine

Tell all your medical doctors and dentists that you are using this medicine.

Check with your doctor immediately if you notice any of the following side effects:
- Bruising or bleeding, especially bleeding that is hard to stop. (Bleeding inside the body sometimes appears as bloody or black, tarry stools or causes faintness.)
- Back pain; burning, pricking, tickling, or tingling sensation; leg weakness; numbness; paralysis; or problems with bowel or bladder function.

Side Effects of This Medicine

Along with its needed effects, a medicine may cause some unwanted effects. Although not all of these side effects may occur, if they do occur they may need medical attention.

Check with your doctor immediately if any of the following side effects occur:
More common
  Deep, dark purple bruise, pain, or swelling at place of injection

Less common
  Bladder pain; bleeding gums; blood in urine; bloody or cloudy urine; blurred vision; chest pain; chest tightness; chills; confusion; cough; coughing up blood; difficulty in breathing or swallowing; dizziness; faintness, or lightheadedness when getting up from a lying or sitting position suddenly; fast, slow, or irregular heartbeat; fever; frequent urge to urinate; headache; increased menstrual flow or vaginal bleeding; lower back pain or side pain; nosebleeds; pain or burning while urinating; painful or difficult urination; pale skin; palpitations; paralysis; pounding in the ears; prolonged bleeding from cuts; red or dark brown urine; red or black, tarry stools; severe or continuing dull nervousness; shortness of breath; skin rash; sore throat; sores, ulcers, or white spots on lips or in mouth; sweating; swollen glands; troubled breathing, exertional; unexplained pain, swelling, or discomfort, especially in the chest, abdomen, joints, or muscles; unusual bleeding or bruising; unusual tiredness or weakness; vomiting of blood or coffee ground-like material

Rare
  Blue-green to black skin discoloration; bowel/bladder dysfunction; hives; itching; leg weakness; numbness; pain, redness, or sloughing of skin at place of injection; paresthesia; puffiness or swelling of the eyelids or around the eyes, face, lips or tongue; wheezing

Other side effects may occur that usually do not need medical attention. These side effects may go away during treatment as your body adjusts to the medicine. However, check with your doctor if any of the following side effects continue or are bothersome.
Less common or rare
  Constipation; nausea and vomiting; prolonged, painful, inappropriate erection of the penis; trouble in sleeping

Other side effects not listed above may also occur in some patients. If you notice any other effects, check with your doctor.

Developed: 08/11/2000

TIOCONAZOLE   Topical

Commonly used brand name(s):

In Canada—
Trosyd AF cream
Trosyd J cream

Description

Tioconazole (tye-o-KON-a-zole) belongs to the family of medicines called antifungals, which are used to treat infections caused by a fungus or yeast. They work by killing the fungus or yeast or preventing its growth.

Tioconazole cream is applied to the skin to treat:

- ringworm of the body (tinea corporis);
- ringworm of the foot (tinea pedis; athlete's foot);
- ringworm of the groin (tinea cruris; jock itch);
- tinea versicolor (sometimes called "sun fungus"); and
- yeast infection of the skin (cutaneous candidiasis).

Tioconazole is available in the following dosage forms:

Topical
- Cream (Canada)

Before Using This Medicine

In deciding to use a medicine, the risks of using the medicine must be weighed against the good it will do. This is a decision you and your doctor will make. For topical tioconazole, the following should be considered:

Allergies—Tell your doctor if you have ever had any unusual or allergic reaction to tioconazole, ketoconazole, miconazole, or another imidazole antifungal medicine. Also tell your doctor and pharmacist if you are allergic to any other substances, such as preservatives or dyes.

Pregnancy—Topical tioconazole has not been studied in pregnant women. When used vaginally during various stages in pregnancy, tioconazole has not been shown to cause birth defects or other problems in humans. However, studies in animals showed an increased number of stillbirths and delays in development when rats were given tioconazole by mouth or injection. Before using this medicine, make sure your doctor knows if you are pregnant or if you may become pregnant.

Breast-feeding—It is not known whether topical tioconazole passes into the breast milk. Although most medicines pass into breast milk in small amounts, many of them may be used safely while breast-feeding. Mothers who are taking this medicine and who wish to breast-feed should discuss this with their doctor.

Children—Although there is no specific information comparing use of this medicine in children with use in other age groups, this medicine is not expected to cause different side effects or problems in children than it does in adults.

Older adults—Many medicines have not been studied specifically in older people. Therefore, it may not be known whether they work exactly the same way they do in younger adults. Although there is no specific information comparing use of tioconazole in the elderly with use in other age groups, this medicine is not expected to cause different side effects or problems in older people than it does in younger adults.

Other medicines—Although certain medicines should not be used together at all, in other cases two different medicines may be used together even if an interaction might occur. In these cases, your doctor may want to change the dose, or other precautions may be necessary. Tell your health care professional if you are using any other topical prescription or nonprescription (over the counter [OTC]) medicine that is to be applied to the same area of the skin.

Proper Use of This Medicine

Apply enough tioconazole to cover the affected and surrounding skin areas, and rub in gently.

Keep this medicine away from the eyes.

Do not apply an occlusive dressing (airtight covering, such as kitchen plastic wrap) over this medicine unless you have been directed to do so by your doctor. To do so may cause irritation of the skin.

To help clear up your infection completely, *it is very important that you keep using tioconazole for the full time of treatment,* even if your symptoms begin to clear up after a few days. Since fungus infections may be very slow to clear up, you may have to continue using this medicine every day for several weeks or more. If you stop using this medicine too soon, your symptoms may return. *Do not miss any doses.*

Dosing—The dose of topical tioconazole will be different for different patients. *Follow your doctor's orders or the directions on the label.* The following information includes only the average doses of tioconazole. *If your dose is different, do not change it* unless your doctor tells you to do so.

The number of doses you use each day, the time allowed between doses, and the length of time you use the medicine depend on the medical problem for which you are using topical tioconazole.

- For *topical cream* dosage form:
  —For ringworm of the body or yeast infection of the skin:
  - Adults—Use two times a day for 2 to 4 weeks.
  - Children—Dose must be determined by your doctor.
  —For ringworm of the foot:
  - Adults—Use two times a day for up to 6 weeks.
  - Children—Dose must be determined by your doctor.
  —For ringworm of the groin:
  - Adults—Use two times a day for up to 2 weeks.
  - Children—Dose must be determined by your doctor.
  —For tinea versicolor ("sun fungus"):
  - Adults—Use two times a day for 1 to 4 weeks.
  - Children—Dose must be determined by your doctor.

Missed dose—If you miss a dose of this medicine, apply it as soon as possible. However, if it is almost time for your next dose, skip the missed dose and go back to your regular dosing schedule.

Storage—To store this medicine:
- Keep out of the reach of children.
- Store away from heat and direct light.
- Keep the medicine from freezing. Do not refrigerate.
- Do not keep outdated medicine or medicine no longer needed. Ask your health care professional how you should dispose of any medicine you do not use. Be sure that any discarded medicine is out of the reach of children.

Precautions While Using This Medicine

If your skin problem does not improve within:

- 2 weeks for ringworm of the body or yeast infection of the skin, tinea versicolor, or ringworm of the groin;
- 4 to 6 weeks for ringworm of the foot;

or if it becomes worse, check with your doctor.

To help clear up your infection completely and to help make sure it does not return, good health habits are also required. The following measures will help reduce chaffing and irritation and will also help keep the area cool and dry:

- For patients using tioconazole for *ringworm of the groin (tinea cruris; jock itch):*
  —Avoid wearing underwear that is tight-fitting or made from synthetic materials (for example, rayon or nylon). Instead, wear loose-fitting, cotton underwear.
- For patients using tioconazole for *ringworm of the foot (tinea pedis; athlete's foot):*
  —Carefully dry the feet, especially between the toes, after bathing.
  —Avoid wearing socks made from wool or synthetic materials (for example, rayon or nylon). Instead wear clean, cotton socks and change them daily or more often if the feet sweat a lot.
  —Wear sandals or other well-ventilated shoes.
- For patients using tioconazole for *ringworm of the body (tinea corporis):*
  —Carefully dry yourself after bathing.
  —Avoid too much heat and humidity if possible.
  —Wear well-ventilated, loose-fitting clothing.

If you have any questions about these measures, check with your health care professional.

Side Effects of This Medicine

Along with its needed effects, a medicine may cause some unwanted effects. Although not all of these side effects may occur, if they do occur they may need medical attention.

Check with your doctor as soon as possible if any of the following side effects occur:

Less common
Burning; itching; redness; skin rash; swelling; or other signs of skin irritation not present before use of this medicine

Other side effects not listed above may also occur in some patients. If you notice any other effects, check with your doctor.

Developed: 06/12/2000

TIZANIDINE   Systemic†

Commonly used brand name(s):

In the U.S.—
Zanaflex

†Not commercially available in Canada.

Description

Tizanidine (tye-ZAN-i-dine) is used to help relax certain muscles in your body. It relieves the spasms, cramping, and tight-ness of muscles caused by medical problems such as multiple sclerosis or certain injuries to the spine. Tizanidine does not cure these problems, but it may allow other treatment, such as physical therapy, to be more helpful in improving your condition.

Tizanidine acts on the central nervous system (CNS) to produce its muscle relaxant effects. Its actions on the CNS may also cause some of the medicine's side effects.

This medicine is available only with your doctor's prescription, in the following dosage form:

Oral
- Tablets (U.S.)

Before Using This Medicine

In deciding to use a medicine, the risks of taking the medicine must be weighed against the good it will do. This is a decision you and your doctor will make. For tizanidine, the following should be considered:

Allergies—Tell your doctor if you have ever had any unusual or allergic reaction to tizanidine. Also tell your health care professional if you are allergic to any other substances, such as foods, preservatives, or dyes.

Pregnancy—Tizanidine has not been studied in pregnant women. However, studies in animals have shown that tizanidine causes birth defects and other pregnancy problems. Before taking this medicine, make sure your doctor knows if you are pregnant or if you become pregnant.

Breast-feeding—Tizanidine may pass into the breast milk. However, this medicine has not been reported to cause problems in nursing babies.

Children—Studies on this medicine have been done only in adult patients, and there is no specific information comparing use of tizanidine in children with use in other age groups.

Older adults—Studies in older adults show that tizanidine stays in the body a little longer than it does in younger adults. Your doctor will consider this when deciding on your dose.

Other medicines—Although certain medicines should not be used together at all, in other cases two different medicines may be used together even if an interaction might occur. In these cases, your doctor may want to change the dose, or other precautions may be necessary. When you are taking tizanidine, it is especially important that your health care professional know if you are taking any of the following:

- Antihypertensives (high blood pressure medicine)—Severe low blood pressure may occur
- Oral contraceptives (birth control pills)—The chance of side effects may be increased
- Phenytoin—Tizanidine may increase the blood levels of phenytoin, which increases the chance of serious side effects

Other medical problems—The presence of other medical problems may affect the use of tizanidine. Make sure you tell your doctor if you have any other medical problems, especially:

- Kidney disease or
- Liver disease—The chance of side effects may be increased; higher blood levels of tizanidine may result and a smaller dose may be needed

Proper Use of This Medicine

Take this medicine only as directed. Do not take more of it and do not take it more often than recommended on the label, unless otherwise directed by your doctor. To do so may increase the chance of side effects.

Dosing—The dose of tizanidine will be different for different patients. *Follow your doctor's orders or the directions on the label.* The following information includes only the average doses of tizanidine. *If your dose is different, do not change it* unless your doctor tells you to do so.
- For *oral* dosage form (tablets):
  —For muscle relaxation:
  - Adults—The dose is 8 milligrams (mg) every six to eight hours as needed. No more than 36 mg should be taken within a twenty-four-hour period.
  - Children—Use and dose must be determined by your doctor.

Missed dose—If you miss a dose of this medicine, and you remember within an hour or so of the missed dose, take it as soon as you remember. However, if you do not remember until later, skip the missed dose and go back to your regular dosing schedule. Do not double doses.

Storage—To store this medicine:
- Keep out of the reach of children.
- Store away from heat and direct light.
- Do not store in the bathroom, near the kitchen sink, or in other damp places. Heat or moisture may cause the medicine to break down.
- Do not keep outdated medicine or medicine no longer needed. Be sure that any discarded medicine is out of the reach of children.

Precautions While Using This Medicine

Your doctor should check your progress at regular visits, especially during the first few weeks of treatment with this medicine. During this time the amount of medicine you are taking may have to be changed often to meet your individual needs.

Do not suddenly stop taking this medicine. Unwanted effects may occur if the medicine is stopped suddenly. Check with your doctor for the best way to reduce gradually the amount you are taking before stopping completely.

This medicine will add to the effects of alcohol and other CNS depressants (medicines that make you drowsy or less alert). Some examples of CNS depressants are antihistamines or medicine for hay fever, other allergies, or colds; sedatives, tranquilizers, or sleeping medicine; prescription pain medicine or narcotics; barbiturates; medicine for seizures; other muscle relaxants; or anesthetics, including some dental anesthetics. *Check with your doctor before taking any of the above while you are using tizanidine.*

This medicine may cause dizziness, drowsiness, lightheadedness, clumsiness or unsteadiness, or vision problems in some people. *Make sure you know how you react to this medicine before you drive, use machines, or do anything else that could be dangerous if you are not alert, well-coordinated, and able to see well.*

Tizanidine may cause dryness of the mouth. For temporary relief, use sugarless candy or gum, melt bits of ice in your mouth, or use a saliva substitute. However, if dry mouth continues for more than 2 weeks, check with your medical doctor or dentist. Continuing dryness of the mouth may increase the chance of dental disease, including tooth decay, gum disease, and fungus infections.

Dizziness, lightheadedness, or fainting may occur when you get up suddenly from a lying or sitting position. Getting up slowly may help lessen this problem.

Side Effects of This Medicine

Along with its needed effects, a medicine may cause some unwanted effects. Although not all of these side effects may occur, if they do occur they may need medical attention.

Check with your doctor as soon as possible if any of the following side effects occur:
More common
Fever; loss of appetite; nausea and/or vomiting; nervousness; pain or burning while urinating; sores on the skin; tingling, burning, or prickling sensations; yellow eyes or skin

Less common
Black, tarry stools; bloody vomit; blurred vision; chills or sore throat; coldness; convulsions (seizures); cough; dry, puffy skin; eye pain; fainting; irregular heartbeat; kidney stones; seeing things that are not there; unusual tiredness or weakness; weight gain

Other side effects may occur that usually do not need medical attention. These side effects may go away during treatment as your body adjusts to the medicine. However, check with your doctor if any of the following side effects continue or are bothersome:
More common
Anxiety; back pain; constipation; depression; diarrhea; difficulty in speaking; dizziness or lightheadedness, especially when getting up from a lying or sitting position; drowsiness; dry mouth; heartburn; increased sweating; increased muscle spasms or tone; muscle weakness; pain or burning in throat; runny nose; skin rash; sleepiness; stomach pain; uncontrolled movements of the body

Less common
Difficulty swallowing; dry skin; joint or muscle pain or stiffness; loss of hair; migraine headache; mood changes; neck pain; swelling of feet or lower legs; swollen area that feels warm and tender; trembling or shaking; unusual feeling of well-being; weight loss

Other side effects not listed above may also occur in some patients. If you notice any other effects, check with your doctor.

Developed: 08/12/97

TOBRAMYCIN   Ophthalmic

Commonly used brand name(s):

In the U.S.—
AKTob
Tobrex
Generic name product may be available.

In Canada—
Tobrex

Description

Ophthalmic tobramycin (toe-bra-MYE-sin) is used in the eye to treat bacterial infections of the eye. Tobramycin works by killing bacteria.

Ophthalmic tobramycin may be used alone or with other medicines for eye infections. Either the drops or the ointment form of this medicine may be used alone during the day. In addition, both forms may be used together, with the drops being used during the day and the ointment at night.

Tobramycin ophthalmic preparations are available only with your doctor's prescription, in the following dosage forms:

Ophthalmic
- Ophthalmic ointment (U.S. and Canada)
- Ophthalmic solution (eye drops) (U.S. and Canada)

Before Using This Medicine

In deciding to use a medicine, the risks of using the medicine must be weighed against the good it will do. This is a decision you and your doctor will make. For ophthalmic tobramycin, the following should be considered:

Allergies—Tell your doctor if you have ever had any unusual or allergic reaction to ophthalmic tobramycin or to any related medicines, such as amikacin (e.g., Amikin), gentamicin (e.g., Garamycin), kanamycin (e.g., Kantrex), neomycin (e.g., Mycifradin), netilmicin (e.g., Netromycin), streptomycin, or tobramycin by injection (e.g., Nebcin). Also tell your health care professional if you are allergic to any other substances, such as preservatives.

Pregnancy—Studies have not been done in humans. However, tobramycin ophthalmic preparations have not been shown to cause birth defects or other problems in animals even when given at high doses.

Breast-feeding—Tobramycin ophthalmic preparations may be absorbed into the eye. However, tobramycin is unlikely to pass into the breast milk in large amounts and little would be absorbed by the infant. Therefore, this medicine is unlikely to cause serious problems in nursing babies.

Children—This medicine has been tested in children and, in effective doses, has not been shown to cause different side effects or problems than it does in adults.

Older adults—Many medicines have not been studied specifically in older people. Therefore, it may not be known whether they work exactly the same way they do in younger adults or if they cause different side effects or problems in older people. There is no specific information comparing use of ophthalmic tobramycin in the elderly with use in other age groups.

Other medicines—Although certain medicines should not be used together at all, in other cases two different medicines may be used together even if an interaction might occur. In these cases, your doctor may want to change the dose, or other precautions may be necessary. Tell your health care professional if you are using any other prescription or nonprescription (over-the-counter [OTC]) medicine that is to be used in the eye.

Proper Use of This Medicine

For patients using tobramycin *ophthalmic solution (eye drops):*
- The bottle is only partially full to provide proper drop control.

- To use:
  - First, wash your hands. Tilt the head back and with the index finger of one hand, press gently on the skin just beneath the lower eyelid and pull the lower eyelid away from the eye to make a space. Drop the medicine into this space. Let go of the eyelid and gently close the eyes. Do not blink. Keep the eyes closed for 1 or 2 minutes, to allow the medicine to come into contact with the infection.
  - If you think you did not get the drop of medicine into your eye properly, use another drop.
  - To keep the medicine as germ-free as possible, do not touch the applicator tip to any surface (including the eye). Also, keep the container tightly closed.
- If your doctor ordered two different ophthalmic solutions to be used together, wait at least 5 minutes between the times you apply the medicines. This will help to keep the second medicine from "washing out" the first one.

For patients using tobramycin *ophthalmic ointment (eye ointment):*
- To use:
  - First, wash your hands. Tilt the head back and with the index finger of one hand, press gently on the skin just beneath the lower eyelid and pull the lower eyelid away from the eye to make a space. Squeeze a thin strip of ointment into this space. A 1.25-cm (approximately ½-inch) strip of ointment usually is enough, unless you have been told by your doctor to use a different amount. Let go of the eyelid and gently close the eyes and keep them closed for 1 or 2 minutes, to allow the medicine to come into contact with the infection.
  - To keep the medicine as germ-free as possible, do not touch the applicator tip to any surface (including the eye). After using tobramycin eye ointment, wipe the tip of the ointment tube with a clean tissue and keep the tube tightly closed.

To help clear up your eye infection completely, *keep using tobramycin for the full time of treatment,* even if your symptoms have disappeared. *Do not miss any doses.*

Dosing—The dose of ophthalmic tobramycin will be different for different patients. *Follow your doctor's orders or the directions on the label.* The following information includes only the average dose of ophthalmic tobramycin. *If your dose is different, do not change it* unless your doctor tells you to do so.

The number of doses you use each day, the time allowed between doses, and the length of time you use the medicine depend on the medical problem for which you are using ophthalmic tobramycin.

- For *ophthalmic ointment* dosage forms:
  - For mild to moderate infections:
    - Adults and children—Use every eight to twelve hours.
  - For severe infections:
    - Adults and children—Use every three to four hours until improvement occurs.

- For *ophthalmic solution (eye drops)* dosage forms:
  - For mild to moderate infections:
    - Adults and children—One drop every four hours.
  - For severe infections:
    - Adults and children—One drop every hour until improvement occurs.

Missed dose—If you miss a dose of this medicine, use it as soon as possible. However, if it is almost time for your next dose, skip the missed dose and go back to your regular dosing schedule.

Storage—To store this medicine:

- Keep out of the reach of children.
- Store away from heat and direct light.
- Keep the medicine from freezing.
- Do not keep outdated medicine or medicine no longer needed. Be sure that any discarded medicine is out of the reach of children.

Precautions While Using This Medicine

If your eye infection does not improve within a few days, or if it becomes worse, check with your doctor.

Side Effects of This Medicine

Along with its needed effects, a medicine may cause some unwanted effects. Although not all of these side effects may occur, if they do occur they may need medical attention.

Check with your doctor immediately if any of the following side effects occur:

Less common
>   Itching, redness, swelling, or other sign of eye or eyelid irritation not present before use of this medicine

Symptoms of overdose
>   Increased watering of the eyes; itching, redness, or swelling of the eyes or eyelids; painful irritation of the clear front part of the eye

Other side effects may occur that usually do not need medical attention. These side effects may go away during treatment as your body adjusts to the medicine. However, check with your doctor if either of the following side effects continues or is bothersome:

Less common
>   Burning or stinging of the eyes

Eye ointments usually cause your vision to blur for a few minutes after application.

Other side effects not listed above may also occur in some patients. If you notice any other effects, check with your doctor.

Revised: 3/2/99

TOCAINIDE   Systemic

Commonly used brand name(s):

In the U.S.—
>   Tonocard

In Canada—
>   Tonocard

Description

Tocainide (toe-KAY-nide) belongs to the group of medicines known as antiarrhythmics. It is used to correct irregular heart-beats to a normal rhythm.

Tocainide produces its helpful effects by slowing nerve impulses in the heart and making the heart tissue less sensitive.

Tocainide is available only with your doctor's prescription, in the following dosage form:

Oral
- Tablets (U.S. and Canada)

Before Using This Medicine

In deciding to use a medicine, the risks of taking the medicine must be weighed against the good it will do. This is a decision you and your doctor will make. For tocainide, the following should be considered:

Allergies—Tell your doctor if you have ever had any unusual or allergic reaction to tocainide or anesthetics. Also tell your health care professional if you are allergic to any other substances, such as foods, preservatives, or dyes.

Pregnancy—Tocainide has not been shown to cause birth defects or other problems in humans. Studies in animals have shown that high doses of tocainide may increase the possibility of death in the animal fetus.

Breast-feeding—Tocainide may pass into breast milk. Mothers who are taking this medicine and who wish to breast-feed should discuss this with their doctor.

Children—Studies on this medicine have been done only in adult patients and there is no specific information comparing use of tocainide in children with use in other age groups.

Older adults—Dizziness or lightheadedness may be more likely to occur in the elderly, who are usually more sensitive to the effects of tocainide.

Other medicines—Although certain medicines should not be used together at all, in other cases two different medicines may be used together even if an interaction might occur. In these cases, your doctor may want to change the dose, or other precautions may be necessary. Tell your health care professional if you are taking any other prescription or nonprescription (over-the-counter [OTC]) medicine.

Other medical problems—The presence of other medical problems may affect the use of tocainide. Make sure you tell your doctor if you have any other medical problems, especially:

- Congestive heart failure—Tocainide may make this condition worse
- Kidney disease or
- Liver disease—Effects may be increased because of slower removal of tocainide from the body

Proper Use of This Medicine

Take tocainide exactly as directed by your doctor, even though you may feel well. Do not take more medicine than ordered.

If tocainide upsets your stomach, your doctor may advise you to take it with food or milk.

This medicine works best when there is a constant amount in the blood. *To help keep the amount constant, do not miss any doses. Also, it is best to take the doses at evenly spaced times day and night.* For example, if you are to take 3 doses a day, the doses should be spaced about 8 hours apart. If this interferes with your sleep or other daily activities, or if you need help in planning the best times to take your medicine, check with your health care professional.

Dosing—The dose of tocainide will be different for different patients. *Follow your doctor's orders or the directions on the label.* The following information includes only the average doses of tocainide. *If your dose is different, do not change it* unless your doctor tells you to do so.

The number of tablets that you take depends on the strength of the medicine.

- For *oral* dosage form (tablets):
  —For irregular heartbeat:
  - Adults—At first, 400 milligrams (mg) every eight hours. Then, your doctor may increase your dose up to 600 mg three times a day.
  - Children—Use and dose must be determined by your doctor.

Missed dose—If you miss a dose of tocainide and remember within 4 hours, take it as soon as possible. Then go back to your regular dosing schedule. However, if you do not remember until later, skip the missed dose and go back to your regular dosing schedule. Do not double doses.

Storage—To store this medicine:

- Keep out of the reach of children.
- Store away from heat and direct light.
- Do not store in the bathroom, near the kitchen sink, or in other damp places. Heat or moisture may cause the medicine to break down.
- Do not keep outdated medicine or medicine no longer needed. Be sure that any discarded medicine is out of the reach of children.

Precautions While Using This Medicine

It is important that your doctor check your progress at regular visits to make sure the medicine is working properly. This will allow changes to be made in the amount of medicine you are taking, if necessary.

Your doctor may want you to carry a medical identification card or bracelet stating that you are using this medicine.

Tocainide may cause some people to become dizzy, lightheaded, or less alert than they are normally. *Make sure you know how you react to this medicine before you drive, use machines, or do anything else that could be dangerous if you are dizzy or are not alert.*

Before having any kind of surgery (including dental surgery) or emergency treatment, tell the medical doctor or dentist in charge that you are taking this medicine.

Side Effects of This Medicine

Along with its needed effects, a medicine may cause some unwanted effects. Although not all of these side effects may occur, if they do occur they may need medical attention.

Check with your doctor as soon as possible if any of the following side effects occur:

Less common
  Trembling or shaking
Rare
  Blisters on skin; cough or shortness of breath; fever or chills; irregular heartbeats; peeling or scaling of skin; skin rash (severe); sores in mouth; unusual bleeding or bruising

Other side effects may occur that usually do not need medical attention. These side effects may go away during treatment as your body adjusts to the medicine. However, check with your doctor if any of the following side effects continue or are bothersome:

More common
  Dizziness or lightheadedness; loss of appetite; nausea

Less common
  Blurred vision; confusion; headache; nervousness; numbness or tingling of fingers and toes; skin rash; sweating; vomiting

Other side effects not listed above may also occur in some patients. If you notice any other effects, check with your doctor.

Revised: 08/21/96

TOLCAPONE   Systemic

Commonly used brand name(s):

In the U.S.—
  Tasmar

Description

Tolcapone (TOLE-ka-pone) is used in combination with levodopa and carbidopa for the treatment of the symptoms of Parkinson's disease.

This medicine is available only with your doctor's prescription, in the following dosage form(s):

Oral
- Tablets (U.S.)

Before Using This Medicine

In deciding to use a medicine, the risks of taking the medicine must be weighed against the good it will do. This is a decision you and your doctor will make. For tolcapone, the following should be considered:

Allergies—Tell your doctor if you have ever had any unusual or allergic reaction to tolcapone. Also tell your health care professional if you are allergic to any other substances, such as foods, preservatives, or dyes.

Pregnancy—Tolcapone has not been studied in pregnant women. However, studies in animals have shown that tolcapone causes birth defects and other problems. Before taking this medicine, make sure your doctor knows if you are pregnant or if you may become pregnant.

Breast-feeding—It is not known whether tolcapone passes into breast milk. However, because of the risk of unwanted effects in nursing babies, make sure your doctor knows if you are breast-feeding or planning to breast-feed.

Children—Studies on this medicine have been done only in adult patients. There is no identified potential use of tolcapone in children.

Older adults—The risk of hallucinations (seeing, hearing, or feeling things that are not there) may be increased in patients older than 75 years of age.

Other medicines—Although certain medicines should not be used together at all, in other cases two different medicines may be used together even if an interaction might occur. In these cases, your doctor may want to change the dose, or other precautions may be necessary. Tell your doctor and pharmacist if you are taking any other prescription or nonprescription (over-the-counter [OTC]) medicine.

Other medical problems—The presence of other medical problems may affect the use of tolcapone. Make sure you

tell your doctor if you have any other medical problems, especially:

- Hallucinations (seeing, hearing, or feeling things that are not there)—Condition may become worse
- Kidney problems, severe—Elimination of tolcapone may be decreased, which increases the risk of unwanted effects
- Liver problems—Chance of serious unwanted effects may be increased
- Low blood pressure or
- Orthostatic or postural low blood pressure (dizziness or lightheadedness when getting up suddenly from a sitting or lying position)—Condition may become worse

Proper Use of This Medicine

Take this medicine only as directed by your doctor, to help your condition as much as possible. Do not take more or less of it, and do not take it more or less often than your doctor ordered.

Dosing—The dose of tolcapone will be different for different patients. *Follow your doctor's orders or the directions on the label*. The following information includes only the average doses of tolcapone. *If your dose is different, do not change it* unless your doctor tells you to do so.

The number of tablets that you take depends on the strength of the medicine. Also, *the number of doses you take each day, the time allowed between doses, and the length of time you take the medicine depend on your medical condition.*

- For *oral* dosage form (tablets):
  —For Parkinson's disease:
  - Adults—100 milligrams (mg) three times a day, taken in addition to levodopa and carbidopa.
  - Children—Use and dose must be determined by your doctor.

Missed dose—If you miss a dose of this medicine, take it as soon as possible. However, if it is almost time for your next dose, skip the missed dose and go back to your regular dosing schedule. Do not double doses.

Storage—To store this medicine:

- Keep out of the reach of children.
- Store away from heat and direct light.
- Do not store in the bathroom, near the kitchen sink, or in other damp places. Heat or moisture may cause the medicine to break down.
- Keep the medicine from freezing. Do not refrigerate.
- Do not keep outdated medicine or medicine no longer needed. Be sure that any discarded medicine is out of the reach of children.

Precautions While Using This Medicine

It is important that your doctor check your progress at regular visits. Tolcapone may have serious effects on your liver. You must have regular blood tests done to make sure this medicine is not affecting your liver.

Because tolcapone may have serious effects on your liver, you should watch for any signs of these effects. Signs include dark urine; itching; light-colored stools; loss of appetite; nausea (continuing); tenderness in upper right part of abdomen; unusual drowsiness, dullness, or feeling sluggish; unusual tiredness or weakness; or yellow eyes or skin. *If you notice any of these signs, contact your doctor.*

Do not stop taking tolcapone without first checking with your doctor. Your doctor may want you to gradually reduce the amount you are taking before stopping completely.

Tolcapone may cause dizziness or lightheadedness, drowsiness, weakness, or trouble in thinking or concentrating. *Make sure you know how you react to this medicine before you drive, use machines, or do anything else that could be dangerous if you are not alert, well-coordinated, or able to think clearly.*

Dizziness, lightheadedness, or fainting may occur, especially when you get up from a lying or sitting position. Getting up slowly may help. If you should have this problem, check with your doctor.

Hallucinations (seeing, hearing, or feeling things that are not there) may occur in some patients. This is more common in elderly patients.

Tolcapone causes the urine to turn bright yellow. This is to be expected while you are taking it. This effect is harmless and will go away after you stop taking the medicine.

Side Effects of This Medicine

Along with its needed effects, a medicine may cause some unwanted effects. Although not all of these side effects may occur, if they do occur they may need medical attention.

Check with your doctor immediately if any of the following side effects occur:

Rare

Dark urine; itching; light-colored stools; loss of appetite; nausea (continuing); tenderness in upper right part of abdomen; unusual drowsiness, dullness, or feeling sluggish; unusual tiredness or weakness; yellow eyes or skin

Check with your doctor as soon as possible if any of the following side effects occur:

More common

Abdominal pain; cough; diarrhea; dizziness; dizziness or lightheadedness when getting up from a lying or sitting position; drowsiness; fainting; fever; hallucinations (seeing, hearing, or feeling things that are not there); headache; nasal congestion (stuffy nose); nausea; runny nose; sneezing; sore throat; trouble in sleeping; twitching, twisting, or other unusual body movements; vomiting

Less common

Blood in urine; chest pain; chills; confusion; falling; general feeling of discomfort or illness; hyperactivity; loss of balance control; muscle pain; troubled breathing

Rare

Agitation; bloody or cloudy urine; burning of feet; burning, prickling, or tingling sensations; chest discomfort; difficult or painful urination; difficulty in thinking or concentrating; frequent urge to urinate; irritability; joint pain, redness, or swelling; low blood pressure; muscle cramps; neck pain; stiffness

Other side effects may occur that usually do not need medical attention. These side effects may go away during treatment as your body adjusts to the medicine. However, check with your doctor if any of the following side effects continue or are bothersome:

More common

Constipation; dryness of mouth; excessive dreaming; increased sweating

Less common
    Heartburn; gas

After you stop using this medicine, your body may need time to adjust. The length of time this takes depends on the amount of medicine you were using and how long you used it. During this period of time, check with your doctor if you notice that the following side effects occur together:
    Confusion; fever; muscle rigidity

Other side effects not listed above may also occur in some patients. If you notice any other effects, check with your doctor.

Developed: 05/15/98
Interim revision: 12/21/98

TOLTERODINE   Systemic

Commonly used brand name(s):

In the U.S.—
    Detrol

Description

Tolterodine (TOLE-tear-oh-deen) is used to treat bladder problems such as frequent need to urinate or loss of control of urinary function.

This medicine is available only with your doctor's prescription, in the following dosage form:

Oral
    • Tablets (U.S.)

Before Using This Medicine

In deciding to use a medicine, the risks of taking tolterodine must be weighed against the good it will do. This is a decision you and your doctor will make. For tolterodine, the following should be considered:

Allergies—Tell your doctor if you have ever had any unusual or allergic reaction to tolterodine. Also tell your health care professional if you are allergic to any other substances, such as foods, preservatives, or dyes.

Pregnancy—Tolterodine has not been shown to cause birth defects in humans. However, studies in animals have shown that tolterodine causes death of the embryo, a decrease in the weight of the fetus, and other problems in the fetus. Before taking this medicine, make sure your doctor knows if you are pregnant or may become pregnant.

Breast-feeding—It is not known whether tolterodine passes into breast milk. However, tolterodine does pass into the milk of animals and has caused a short-term loss of weight of the offspring. Mothers who are taking this medicine and who wish to breast-feed should discuss this with their doctor.

Children—Studies on this medicine have been done only in adult patients, and there is no specific information comparing use of tolterodine in children with use in other age groups.

Older adults—This medicine has been tested and has not been shown to cause different side effects or problems in older people than is does in younger adults.

Other medicines—Although certain medicines should not be used together at all, in other cases two different medicines may be used together even if an interaction might occur. In these cases, your doctor may want to change the dose, or other precautions may be necessary. Tell your health care professional if you are taking any other prescription or nonprescription (over-the-counter [OTC]) medicine.

Other medical problems—The presence of other medical problems may affect the use of tolterodine. Make sure you tell your doctor if you have any other medical problems, especially:

• Glaucoma or
• Stomach problems or
• Urinary retention—Tolterodine may make these conditions worse
• Liver problems—A lower dose of tolterodine may be necessary

Proper Use of This Medicine

Take this medicine only as directed. Do not take more of it, do not take it more often, and do not take it for a longer time than your doctor ordered. To do so may increase the chance of side effects.

Dosing—The dose of tolterodine will be different for different patients. *Follow your doctor's orders or the directions on the label.* The following information includes only the average doses of tolterodine. *If your dose is different, do not change it* unless your doctor tells you to do so.

• For *oral* dosage form (tablets):
    —To treat bladder problems:
        • Adults—1 to 2 milligrams (mg) two times a day. Your doctor may change your dose.
        • Children—Use and dose must be determined by your doctor.

Missed dose—If you miss a dose of this medicine, take it as soon as possible. However, if it is almost time for your next dose, skip the missed dose and go back to your regular dosing schedule. Do not double doses.

Storage—To store this medicine:

• Keep out of the reach of children.
• Store away from heat and direct light.
• Do not store in the bathroom, near the kitchen sink, or in other damp places. Heat or moisture may cause the medicine to break down.
• Keep the medicine from freezing. Do not refrigerate.
• Do not keep outdated medicine or medicine no longer needed. Be sure that any discarded medicine is out of the reach of children.

Precautions While Using This Medicine

This medicine may cause some people to have vision problems. *Make sure your vision is clear before you drive or do anything else that could be dangerous if you are not able to see well.*

This medicine, especially in high doses, may cause some people to become dizzy or drowsy. *Make sure you know how you react to this medicine before you drive, use machines, or do anything else that could be dangerous if you are dizzy or are not alert.*

This medicine may cause dryness of the mouth, nose, and throat. For temporary relief of mouth dryness, use sugarless candy or gum, melt bits of ice in your mouth, or use a saliva substitute. However, if your mouth continues to feel dry for more than 2 weeks, check with your medical doctor or dentist. Continuing dryness of the mouth may increase the chance of dental disease, including tooth decay, gum disease, and fungus infections.

Side Effects of This Medicine

Along with its needed effects, a medicine may cause some unwanted effects. Although not all of these side effects may occur, if they do occur they may need medical attention.

Check with your doctor as soon as possible if any of the following side effects occur:

More common

Abnormal vision, including difficulty adjusting to distances; bloody or cloudy urine; difficult, burning, or painful urination; frequent urge to urinate

Other side effects may occur that usually do not need medical attention. These side effects may go away during treatment as your body adjusts to the medicine. However, check with your doctor if any of the following side effects continue or are bothersome:

More common

Abdominal pain; chest pain; constipation; diarrhea; dizziness; drowsiness; dry eyes; dry mouth; fatigue; headache; joint pain; nausea; upset stomach

Less common

Difficult urination

Other side effects not listed above may also occur in some patients. If you notice any other effects, check with your doctor.

Developed: 08/13/98

TOPIRAMATE   Systemic†

Commonly used brand name(s):

In the U.S.—

Topamax

†Not commercially available in Canada.

Description

Topiramate (toe-PYRE-a-mate) is used to help control some types of seizures in the treatment of epilepsy. This medicine cannot cure epilepsy and will only work to help control seizures for as long as you continue to take it.

This medicine is available only with your doctor's prescription, in the following dosage form:

Oral

• Tablets (U.S.)
• Capsules (U.S.)

Before Using This Medicine

In deciding to use a medicine, the risks of taking topiramate must be weighed against the good it will do. This is a decision you and your doctor will make. For topiramate, the following should be considered:

Allergies—Tell your doctor if you have ever had any unusual or allergic reaction to topiramate. Also tell your health care professional if you are allergic to any other substances, such as foods, preservatives, or dyes.

Pregnancy—Topiramate has not been studied in pregnant women. However, studies in pregnant animals have shown that topiramate may cause birth defects in the offspring, as well as adverse effects in the mother, when given in doses many times higher than the human dose. Before taking this medicine, make sure your doctor knows if you are pregnant or if you may become pregnant.

Breast-feeding—It is not known whether topiramate passes into breast milk. Although most medicines pass into breast milk in small amounts, many of them may be used safely while breast-feeding. Mothers who are taking this medicine and who wish to breast-feed should discuss this with their doctor.

Children—Although there is no specific information comparing the use of topiramate in children with use in other age groups, this medicine is not expected to cause different side effects or problems in children than it does in adults.

Older adults—In studies done to date that have included adults older than 60 years of age, topiramate has not been shown to cause different side effects or problems in older people than it does in younger adults.

Other medicines—Although certain medicines should not be used together at all, in other cases two different medicines may be used together even if an interaction might occur. In these cases, your doctor may want to change the dose, or other precautions may be necessary. When you are taking topiramate, it is especially important that your health care professional know if you are taking any of the following:

• Acetazolamide (e.g., Diamox) or
• Dichlorphenamide (e.g., Daranide)—Taking these medicines with topiramate may increase the chance of getting kidney stones
• Carbamazepine (e.g., Tegretol)—Blood levels of topiramate may be decreased. Your doctor may need to adjust the dosage of either or both medicines
• Oral contraceptives (birth control pills) containing estrogen—Topiramate may decrease the effects of these medicines; contraceptive failure may result; additional birth control measures may be needed to decrease the risk of pregnancy
• Phenytoin (e.g., Dilantin)—Blood levels of topiramate may be decreased. Your doctor may need to adjust the dosage of either or both medicines
• Valproic acid (e.g., Depakene, Depakote)—Blood levels of topiramate and/or valproic acid may be decreased. Your doctor may need to adjust the dosage of either or both medicines

Other medical problems—The presence of other medical problems may affect the use of topiramate. Make sure you tell your doctor if you have any other medical problems, especially:

• History of kidney stones—Risk of having kidney stones again may be increased

• Kidney problems or
• Liver problems—Higher blood levels of topiramate may result and increase the chance of side effects

Proper Use of This Medicine

Take this medicine every day exactly as ordered by your doctor in order to improve your condition as much as possible. Do not take more or less of it, and do not take it more or less often than your doctor ordered.

Topiramate may be taken with or without food, on a full or an empty stomach. Swallow the tablets whole, without breaking, crushing, or chewing them. The bitter taste may be more noticeable if the tablets are held in the mouth or chewed.The capsules may be swallowed whole, or the contents of the capsule may be opened and the contents sprinkled on a small amount (teaspoonful) of soft food (such as applesauce, custard, ice cream, oatmeal, pudding, or yogurt) and swallowed immediately without chewing

Dosing—The dose of topiramate will be different for different patients. *Follow your doctor's orders or the directions on the label.* The following information includes only the average doses of topiramate. *If your dose is different, do not change it* unless your doctor tells you to do so.

The number of tablets that you take depends on the strength of the medicine. Also, *the number of doses you take each day, the time allowed between doses, and the length of time you take the medicine depend on the medical problem for which you are taking topiramate.*

- For *oral* dosage form (tablets or capsules):
  —As an anticonvulsant:
  - Adults—At first, 50 milligrams (mg) a day for the first week. Your doctor may increase your dose gradually every week if needed and tolerated, but the usual dose is not greater than 400 mg a day.
  - Children (age 2 to 16 years)—At first, 25 milligrams (mg) nightly for the first week. Your doctor may increase your dose gradually every 1 or 2 weeks to be taken in two divided doses.

Missed dose—If you miss a dose of this medicine, take it as soon as possible. However, if it is almost time for your next dose, skip the missed dose and go back to your regular dosing schedule. Do not double doses.

Storage—To store this medicine:
- Keep out of the reach of children.
- Store away from heat and direct light.
- Do not store in the bathroom, near the kitchen sink, or in other damp places. Heat or moisture may cause the medicine to break down.
- Keep the medicine from freezing. Do not refrigerate.
- Do not keep outdated medicine or medicine no longer needed. Be sure that any discarded medicine is out of the reach of children.

Precautions While Using This Medicine

This medicine may cause some people to have blurred vision, double vision, clumsiness or unsteadiness, or to become dizzy, drowsy, or have trouble in thinking. *Make sure you know how you react to this medicine before you drive, use machines, or do anything else that could be dangerous if you are not alert, well-coordinated, or able to think or see well.*

Oral contraceptives (birth control pills) containing estrogen may not work properly if you take them while you are taking topiramate. Unplanned pregnancies may occur. You should use a different or additional means of birth control while you are using topiramate. If you have any questions about this, check with your doctor or pharmacist.

It is important that you *drink plenty of fluids every day* during therapy with topiramate to help prevent kidney stones from forming.

Side Effects of This Medicine

Along with its needed effects, a medicine may cause some unwanted effects. Although not all of these side effects may occur, if they do occur they may need medical attention.

Check with your doctor as soon as possible if any of the following side effects occur:

More common
Burning, prickling, or tingling sensations; clumsiness or unsteadiness; confusion; continuous, uncontrolled back-and-forth or rolling eye movements; dizziness; double vision or other vision problems; drowsiness; generalized slowing of mental and physical activity; memory problems; menstrual changes; menstrual pain; nervousness; speech or language problems; trouble in concentrating or paying attention; unusual tiredness or weakness

Less common
Abdominal pain; fever, chills, or sore throat; lessening of sensations or perception; loss of appetite; mood or mental changes, including aggression, agitation, apathy, irritability, and mental depression; red, irritated, or bleeding gums; weight loss

Rare
Blood in urine; decrease in sexual performance or desire; difficult or painful urination; eye pain; frequent urination; hearing loss; itching; loss of bladder control; lower back or side pain; nosebleeds; pale skin; red or irritated eyes; ringing or buzzing in ears; skin rash; swelling; troubled breathing

Other side effects may occur that usually do not need medical attention. These side effects may go away during treatment as your body adjusts to the medicine. However, check with your doctor if any of the following side effects continue or are bothersome:

More common
Breast pain in women; nausea; tremors

Less common
Back pain; chest pain; constipation; heartburn; hot flushes; increased sweating; leg pain

Topiramate may cause a change in your sense of taste.

Other side effects not listed above may also occur in some patients. If you notice any other effects, check with your doctor.

Developed: 03/03/98
Revised: 1/18/00

TOPOTECAN   Systemic

Commonly used brand name(s):

In the U.S.—
Hycamtin

In Canada—
Hycamtin

Description

Topotecan (toe-poe-TEE-kan) belongs to the group of medicines known as antineoplastics. It is used to treat cancer of the ovaries and certain types of lung cancer.

Topotecan interferes with the growth of cancer cells, which are eventually destroyed. Since the growth of normal cells may also be affected by the medicine, other effects may also occur. Some of these may be serious and must be reported to your doctor. Other effects, like hair loss, may not be serious but may cause concern. Some effects may occur after treatment with topotecan has been stopped.

This medicine is available only with your doctor's prescription, in the following dosage form(s):

Parenteral
- Injection (U.S. and Canada)

Before Using This Medicine

In deciding to use a medicine, the risks of using the medicine must be weighed against the good it will do. This is a decision you and your doctor will make. For topotecan, the following should be considered:

Allergies—Tell your doctor if you have ever had any unusual or allergic reaction to topotecan. Also tell your health care professional if you are allergic to any other substances.

Pregnancy—Tell your doctor if you are pregnant. Studies in rats and rabbits have shown that topotecan causes birth defects and deaths of the fetus, as well as problems in the mother.

Be sure that you have discussed this with your doctor before starting treatment with this medicine. It is best to use birth control while you are receiving topotecan. Also, tell your doctor right away if you think you have become pregnant during treatment.

Breast-feeding—It is not known whether topotecan passes into breast milk. However, because this medicine may cause serious side effects, breast-feeding is generally not recommended while you are receiving it.

Children—Topotecan has been studied in a limited number of children. One study showed that seriously low blood counts may be more likely to occur in children than in adults.

Older adults—This medicine has been tested in elderly patients and has not been shown to cause different side effects or problems in older people than it does in younger adults.

Other medicines—Although certain medicines should not be used together at all, in other cases two different medicines may be used together even if an interaction might occur. In these cases, your doctor may want to change the dose, or other precautions may be necessary. When you are taking topotecan, it is especially important that your health care professional know if you are taking any of the following:

- Amphotericin B by injection (e.g., Fungizone) or
- Antithyroid agents (medicine for overactive thyroid) or
- Azathioprine (e.g., Imuran) or
- Chloramphenicol (e.g., Chloromycetin) or
- Colchicine or
- Flucytosine (e.g., Ancobon) or
- Ganciclovir (e.g., Cytovene) or
- Interferon (e.g., Intron A, Roferon-A) or
- Plicamycin (e.g., Mithracin) or

- Zidovudine (e.g., AZT, Retrovir) or
- If you have ever been treated with radiation or other cancer medicines—The risk of seriously low blood counts may be increased

- Azathioprine (e.g., Imuran) or
- Chlorambucil (e.g., Leukeran) or
- Corticosteroids (cortisone-like medicine) or
- Cyclosporine (e.g., Sandimmune) or
- Mercaptopurine (e.g., Purinethol) or
- Muromonab-CD3 (monoclonal antibody) (e.g., Orthoclone OKT3) or
- Tacrolimus (e.g., Prograf)—There may be an increased risk of infection because topotecan decreases your body's ability to fight it

Other medical problems—The presence of other medical problems may affect the use of topotecan. Make sure you tell your doctor if you have any other medical problems, especially:

- Chickenpox (including recent exposure) or
- Herpes zoster (shingles)—Topotecan may cause these conditions to get worse and spread to other parts of your body

- Infection—Topotecan may decrease your body's ability to fight an infection

- Kidney disease—Higher blood levels of topotecan can occur, which increases the risk of serious side effects

Proper Use of This Medicine

Topotecan often causes nausea and vomiting. *It is very important that you continue to receive the medicine* even if it makes you feel ill. Ask your health care professional for ways to lessen these effects.

Dosing—The dose of topotecan will be different for different patients. The dose that is used may depend on a number of things, including the patient's size and whether or not other treatments are also being given. *If you are receiving topotecan at home, follow your doctor's orders or the directions on the label*. If you have any questions about the proper dose of this medicine, ask your doctor.

Precautions While Using This Medicine

It is very important that your doctor check your progress at regular visits to make sure that this medicine is working properly and to check for unwanted effects. Some of the side effects of this medicine do not have any symptoms and must be found with a blood test.

While you are being treated with topotecan, and after you stop treatment with it, *do not have any immunizations (vaccinations) without your doctor's approval*. Topotecan may lower your body's resistance, and there is a chance you might get the infection the immunization is meant to prevent. In addition, other persons living in your household should not take oral polio vaccine, since there is a chance they could pass the polio virus on to you. Also, avoid persons who have taken oral polio vaccine within the past several months. Do not get close to them and do not stay in the same room with them for very long. If you cannot take these precautions, you should consider wearing a protective face mask that covers the nose and mouth.

Topotecan can temporarily lower the number of white blood cells in your blood, increasing the chance of getting an infection. It can also lower the number of platelets, which are needed for proper blood clotting. If this occurs, there are certain precautions you can take, especially when your blood count is low, to reduce the risk of infection or bleeding:

- If you can, avoid people with infections. *Check with your doctor immediately* if you think you are getting an infection or if you get a fever or chills, cough or hoarseness, lower back or side pain, or painful or difficult urination.
- *Check with your doctor immediately* if you notice any unusual bleeding or bruising; black, tarry stools; blood in urine or stools; or pinpoint red spots on your skin.
- Be careful when using a regular toothbrush, dental floss, or toothpick. Your medical doctor, dentist, or nurse may recommend other ways to clean your teeth and gums. Also, check with your medical doctor before having any dental work done.
- Do not touch your eyes or the inside of your nose unless you have just washed your hands and have not touched anything else in the meantime.
- Be careful not to cut yourself when you are using sharp objects such as a safety razor or fingernail or toenail cutters.
- Avoid contact sports or other situations where bruising or injury could occur.

Side Effects of This Medicine

Along with its needed effects, a medicine may cause some unwanted effects. Although not all of these side effects may occur, if they do occur they may need medical attention.

Check with your doctor immediately if any of the following side effects occur:

More common
> Black, tarry stools; blood in urine or stools; cough or hoarseness (accompanied by fever or chills); fever or chills; lower back or side pain (accompanied by fever or chills); painful or difficult urination (accompanied by fever or chills); pinpoint red spots on skin; shortness of breath or troubled breathing; unusual bleeding or bruising

Rare
> Fast or irregular breathing; large, hive-like swellings on the face, eyelids, mouth, lips, and/or tongue; puffiness or swelling of the eyelids or around the eyes; tightness in chest or wheezing

Also check with your doctor as soon as possible if any of the following side effects occur:

More common
> Unusual tiredness or weakness

Rare
> Changes in the skin color of the face; skin rash, hives, and/or itching

Some of the above side effects may occur, or continue to occur, after treatment with topotecan has ended. Check with your doctor if you notice any of them after you stop receiving the medicine.

Other side effects may occur that usually do not need medical attention. These side effects may go away during treatment as your body adjusts to the medicine. However, check with your doctor if any of the following side effects continue or are bothersome:

More common
> Abdominal or stomach pain; burning or tingling in hands or feet; constipation; diarrhea; fatigue; headache; loss of appetite; muscle weakness; nausea or vomiting; sores, ulcers, or white spots on lips or tongue or inside the mouth

Topotecan sometimes causes bruising or redness at the place of injection. Check with your doctor or nurse if these effects are especially bothersome.

Topotecan may also cause a temporary loss of hair in some people. After treatment with topotecan has ended, normal hair growth should return.

Other side effects not listed above may also occur in some patients. If you notice any other effects, check with your doctor.

Additional Information

Once a medicine has been approved for marketing for a certain use, experience may show that it is also useful for other medical problems. Although these uses are not included in product labeling, topotecan is used in certain patients with the following medical conditions:

- Chronic myelomonocytic leukemia (CMML)
- Myelodysplastic syndrome (MDS)

Other than the above information, there is no additional information relating to proper use, precautions, or side effects for these uses.

Revised: 01/24/2001

TOREMIFENE Systemic

Commonly used brand name(s):

In the U.S.—
Fareston

Description

Toremifene (TOR-em-i-feen) is a medicine that blocks the effects of the estrogen hormone in the body. It is used to treat breast cancer in women.

The exact way that toremifene works against cancer is not known but it may be related to the way it blocks the effects of estrogen in the body.

Before you begin treatment with toremifene, you and your doctor should talk about the good this medicine will do as well as the risks of using it.

Toremifene is available only with your doctor's prescription, in the following dosage form:

Oral
- Tablets (U.S.)

Before Using This Medicine

In deciding to use a medicine, the risks of taking [using] the medicine must be weighed against the good it will do. This is a decision you and your doctor will make. For toremifene, the following should be considered:

Allergies—Tell your doctor if you have ever had any unusual or allergic reaction to toremifene.

Pregnancy—Tell your doctor if you are pregnant or if you intend to become pregnant. Studies in rats and rabbits have shown that toremifene causes miscarriages, birth defects, and death of the fetus. Studies in animals have also shown that toremifene may cause some of the same problems as an estrogen called diethylstilbestrol (DES). DES causes genital tract problems and, rarely, an increased risk of cancer of the cervix or vagina in daughters of women who took it during their pregnancy; it is not known whether toremifene causes these same problems.

Tell your doctor right away if you think you have become pregnant while taking toremifene.

Other medicines—Although certain medicines should not be used together at all, in other cases two different medicines may be used together even if an interaction might occur. In these cases, your doctor may want to change the dose, or other precautions may be necessary. When you are taking toremifene, it is especially important that your health care professional know if you are taking any of the following:

- Anticoagulants, coumarin-type (blood thinners)—Use with this medicine may increase the amount of time it takes blood to clot

- Carbamazepine (e.g., Tegretol) or
- Phenobarbital or
- Phenytoin (e.g., Dilantin)—These medicines may decrease blood levels of toremifene, which could make it less effective

Other medical problems—The presence of other medical problems may affect the use of toremifene. Make sure you tell your doctor if you have any other medical problems, especially:

- Blood clots (history of)—Use of toremifene is usually not recommended

- Unusual growth of the lining of the uterus (womb)—Long-term use of toremifene is usually not recommended

Proper Use of This Medicine

Dosing—The dose of toremifene will be different for different patients. *Follow your doctor's orders or the directions on the label.* The following information includes only the average doses of toremifene. *If your dose is different, do not change it* unless your doctor tells you to do so.

- For *oral* dosage form (tablets):
  —For breast cancer:
    • Adults—60 milligrams (mg) once a day.

Storage—To store this medicine:
- Keep out of the reach of children.
- Store away from heat and direct light.
- Do not store in the bathroom, near the kitchen sink, or in other damp places. Heat or moisture may cause the medicine to break down.
- Do not keep outdated medicine or medicine no longer needed. Be sure that any discarded medicine is out of the reach of children.

Side Effects of This Medicine

Along with its needed effects, a medicine may cause some unwanted effects. Some side effects will have signs or symptoms that you can see or feel. Your doctor will watch for others by doing certain tests.

Also, because of the way this medicine acts on the body, there is a chance that it might cause other unwanted effects that may not occur until months or years after the medicine

is used. Some patients who have used toremifene have developed cancer of the uterus (womb), although it is not known for sure if it was caused by the medicine. Discuss this possible effect with your doctor.

Check with your doctor as soon as possible if any of the following side effects occur:

Less common
    Blurred vision; change in vaginal discharge; changes in vision; confusion; increased urination; loss of appetite; pain or feeling of pressure in pelvis; unusual tiredness; vaginal bleeding

Rare
    Chest pain; pain or swelling of feet or legs; shortness of breath

This medicine may also cause the following side effect(s) that your doctor will watch for:

Less common
    Liver problems

Other side effects may occur that usually do not need medical attention. These side effects may go away during treatment as your body adjusts to the medicine. However, check with your doctor if any of the following side effects continue or are bothersome:

More common
    Nausea; sudden sweating and feelings of warmth

Less common
    Bone pain; dizziness; dry eyes; vomiting

Other side effects not listed above may also occur in some patients. If you notice any other effects, check with your doctor.

Developed: 03/23/98

TORSEMIDE   Systemic†

Commonly used brand name(s):

In the U.S.—
    Demadex

†Not commercially available in Canada.

Description

Torsemide (TORE-se-mide) belongs to the group of medicines called loop diuretics. Torsemide is given to help reduce the amount of water in the body in certain conditions, such as congestive heart failure, severe liver disease (cirrhosis), or kidney disease. It works by acting on the kidneys to increase the flow of urine.

Torsemide is also used to treat high blood pressure (hypertension). High blood pressure adds to the work load of the heart and arteries. If it continues for a long time, the heart and arteries may not function properly. This can damage the blood vessels of the brain, heart, and kidneys, resulting in a stroke, heart failure, or kidney failure. High blood pressure may also increase the risk of heart attacks. These problems may be less likely to occur if blood pressure is controlled.

Torsemide is available only with your doctor's prescription, in the following dosage forms:

Oral
- Tablets (U.S.)

Parenteral
- Injection (U.S.)

Before Using This Medicine

In deciding to use a medicine, the risks of taking the medicine must be weighed against the good it will do. This is a decision you and your doctor will make. For torsemide, the following should be considered:

Allergies—Tell your doctor if you have ever had any unusual or allergic reaction to bumetanide, ethacrynic acid, furosemide, sulfonamides (sulfa drugs), or thiazide diuretics (water pills). Also, tell your health care professional if you are allergic to any other substances, such as foods, preservatives, or dyes.

Pregnancy—Studies have not been done in pregnant women. In general, diuretics are not useful for normal swelling of feet and hands that occurs during pregnancy. Diuretics should not be taken during pregnancy unless recommended by your doctor.

Breast-feeding—It is not known whether torsemide passes into breast milk. Although most medicines pass into breast milk in small amounts, many of them may be used safely while breast-feeding. Mothers who are taking this medicine and who wish to breast-feed should discuss this with their doctor.

Children—Studies on this medicine have been done only in adult patients, and there is no specific information comparing use of torsemide in children with use in other age groups.

Older adults—Many medicines have not been studied specifically in older people. Therefore, it may not be known whether they work exactly the same way they do in younger adults. Although there is no specific information comparing use of torsemide in the elderly with use in other age groups, this medicine is not expected to cause different side effects or problems in older people than it does in younger adults.

Other medicines—Although certain medicines should not be used together at all, in other cases two different medicines may be used together even if an interaction might occur. In these cases, your doctor may want to change the dose, or other precautions may be necessary. When you are taking torsemide, it is especially important that your health care professional know if you are taking any of the following:
- Acetazolamide (e.g., Diamox) or
- Alcohol or
- Amphotericin B by injection (e.g., Fungizone) or
- Azlocillin (e.g., Azlin) or
- Capreomycin (e.g., Capastat) or
- Carbenicillin by injection (e.g., Geopen) or
- Corticosteroids (cortisone-like medicine) or
- Corticotropin (ACTH) or
- Dichlorphenamide (e.g., Daranide) or
- Diuretics (water pills) or
- Insulin or
- Laxatives (with overdose or chronic misuse) or
- Methazolamide (e.g., Neptazane) or
- Mezlocillin (e.g., Mezlin) or
- Piperacillin (e.g., Pipracil) or
- Salicylates or
- Sodium bicarbonate (e.g., baking soda) or
- Ticarcillin (e.g., Ticar) or

- Ticarcillin and clavulanate (e.g., Timentin) or
- Vitamin B$_{12}$ (e.g., AlphaRedisol, Rubramin-PC) (when used in megaloblastic anemia) or
- Vitamin D—Use of these medicines with torsemide may increase the chance of potassium loss

- Aldesleukin (e.g., Proleukin) or
- Anti-infectives by mouth or by injection (medicine for infection) or
- Carmustine (e.g., BiCNU) or
- Cisplatin (e.g., Platinol) or
- Combination pain medicine containing acetaminophen and aspirin (e.g., Excedrin) or other salicylates (with large amounts taken regularly) or
- Cyclosporine (e.g., Sandimmune) or
- Deferoxamine (e.g., Desferal) (with long-term use) or
- Gold salts (medicine for arthritis) or
- Inflammation or pain medicine, except narcotics, or
- Methotrexate (e.g., Mexate) or
- Penicillamine (e.g., Cuprimine) or
- Pentamidine (e.g., Pentam 300) or
- Plicamycin (e.g., Mithracin) or
- Streptozocin (e.g., Zanosar) or
- Tiopronin (e.g., Thiola)—Use of these medicines with torsemide may increase the chance of kidney damage

- Anticoagulants (blood thinners)—Torsemide may decrease the effects of these medicines

- Lithium (e.g., Lithane)—Use of lithium with torsemide may increase the chance of kidney damage; also, the chance of side effects of lithium may be increased

Other medical problems—The presence of other medical problems may affect the use of torsemide. Make sure you tell your doctor if you have any other medical problems, especially:
- Diabetes mellitus (sugar diabetes)—Torsemide may increase the amount of sugar in the blood
- Gout or
- Hearing problems—Torsemide may make these conditions worse
- Heart attack (recent)—Use of torsemide after a recent heart attack may make this condition worse
- Kidney disease (severe) or
- Liver disease—Higher blood levels of torsemide may occur, which may increase the chance of side effects

Proper Use of This Medicine

This medicine may cause you to have an unusual feeling of tiredness when you begin to take it. You may also notice an increase in the amount of urine or in your frequency of urination. After you have taken the medicine for a while, these effects should lessen.

It is best to plan your dose or doses according to a schedule that will least affect your personal activities and sleep. Ask your health care professional to help you plan the best time to take this medicine.

To help you remember to take your medicine, try to get into the habit of taking it at the same time each day.

For patients taking this medicine for *high blood pressure:*
- In addition to the use of the medicine your doctor has prescribed, treatment for your high blood pressure may include weight control and care in the types of foods you eat, especially foods high in sodium. Your doctor will tell

you which of these are most important for you. You should check with your doctor before changing your diet.

- Many patients who have high blood pressure will not notice any signs of the problem. In fact, many may feel normal. It is very important that you *take your medicine exactly as directed* and that you keep your appointments with your doctor even if you feel well.
- Remember that this medicine will not cure your high blood pressure but it does help control it. Therefore, you must continue to take it as directed if you expect to lower your blood pressure and keep it down. *You may have to take high blood pressure medicine for the rest of your life.* If high blood pressure is not treated, it can cause serious problems, such as heart failure, blood vessel disease, stroke, or kidney disease.

Dosing—The dose of torsemide will be different for different patients. *Follow your doctor's orders or the directions on the label.* The following information includes only the average doses of torsemide. *If your dose is different, do not change it* unless your doctor tells you to do so.

The number of tablets that you take depends on the strength of the medicine. Also, *the length of time you take the medicine depends on the medical problem for which you are taking torsemide.*

- For *oral* dosage form (tablets):
  —For lowering the amount of water in the body:
  - Adults—Dose is usually 5 to 20 milligrams (mg) once a day. However, your doctor may increase your dose as needed.
  - Children—Use and dose must be determined by your doctor.
  —For high blood pressure:
  - Adults—5 to 10 mg once a day.
  - Children—Use and dose must be determined by your doctor.
- For *injection* dosage form:
  —For lowering the amount of water in the body:
  - Adults—Dose is usually 5 to 20 mg injected into a vein once a day. However, your doctor may increase your dose as needed.
  - Children—Use and dose must be determined by your doctor.

Missed dose—If you miss a dose of this medicine, take it as soon as possible. However, if it is almost time for your next dose, skip the missed dose and go back to your regular dosing schedule. Do not double doses.

Storage—To store this medicine:
- Keep out of the reach of children.
- Store away from heat and direct light.
- Do not store in the bathroom, near the kitchen sink, or in other damp places. Heat or moisture may cause the medicine to break down.
- Keep the medicine from freezing. Do not refrigerate.
- Do not keep outdated medicine or medicine no longer needed. Be sure that any discarded medicine is out of the reach of children.

Precautions While Using This Medicine

It is important that your doctor check your progress at regular visits to make sure that this medicine is working properly.

This medicine may cause a loss of potassium from your body:

- To help prevent this, your doctor may want you to:
  —eat or drink foods that have a high potassium content (for example, orange or other citrus fruit juices), or
  —take a potassium supplement, or
  —take another medicine to help prevent the loss of the potassium in the first place.
- It is very important to follow these directions. Also, it is important not to change your diet on your own. This is more important if you are already on a special diet (as for diabetes) or if you are taking a potassium supplement or a medicine to reduce potassium loss. Extra potassium may not be necessary and, in some cases, too much potassium could be harmful.

To prevent the loss of too much water and potassium, tell your doctor if you become sick, especially with severe or continuing nausea and vomiting or diarrhea.

Before having any kind of surgery (including dental surgery) or emergency treatment, make sure the medical doctor or dentist in charge knows that you are taking this medicine.

Dizziness, lightheadedness, or fainting may occur, especially when you get up from a lying or sitting position. This is more likely to occur in the morning. *Getting up slowly may help.* When you get up from lying down, sit on the edge of the bed with your feet dangling for 1 or 2 minutes. Then stand up slowly. If the problem continues or gets worse, check with your doctor.

The dizziness, lightheadedness, or fainting is also more likely to occur if you drink alcohol, stand for long periods of time, or exercise, or if the weather is hot. *While you are taking this medicine, be careful to limit the amount of alcohol you drink. Also, use extra care during exercise or hot weather or if you must stand for long periods of time.*

For *diabetic patients:*

- This medicine may affect blood sugar levels. While you are using this medicine, be especially careful in testing for sugar in your blood or urine.

For patients taking this medicine for *high blood pressure:*

- *Do not take other medicines unless they have been discussed with your doctor.* This especially includes over-the-counter (nonprescription) medicines for appetite control, asthma, colds, cough, hay fever, or sinus problems, since they may tend to increase your blood pressure.

Side Effects of This Medicine

Along with its needed effects, a medicine may cause some unwanted effects. Although not all of these side effects may occur, if they do occur they may need medical attention.

Check with your doctor as soon as possible if any of the following side effects occur:

Less common

Dryness of mouth; fast or irregular heartbeat; increased thirst; mood or mental changes; muscle pain or cramps; nausea or vomiting; unusual tiredness or weakness

Rare

Black, tarry stools; dizziness when getting up from a sitting or lying position; ringing or buzzing in the ears or any hearing loss; skin rash

Other side effects may occur that usually do not need medical attention. These side effects may go away during treatment as your body adjusts to the medicine. However, check with

your doctor if any of the following side effects continue or are bothersome:

More common
Constipation; dizziness; headache; stomach upset

Developed: 02/15/95
Interim revision: 08/01/95

TRAMADOL   Systemic†

Commonly used brand name(s):

In the U.S.—
Ultram

†Not commercially available in Canada.

Description

Tramadol (TRA-ma-dole) is used to relieve pain, including pain after surgery. The effects of tramadol are similar to those of narcotic analgesics. Although tramadol is not a narcotic, it may become habit-forming, causing mental or physical dependence.

Tramadol is available only with your doctor's prescription, in the following dosage form:

Oral
• Tablets (U.S.)

Before Using This Medicine

In deciding to use a medicine, the risks of taking the medicine must be weighed against the good it will do. This is a decision you and your doctor will make. For tramadol, the following should be considered:

Allergies—Tell your doctor if you have ever had any unusual or allergic reaction to tramadol or narcotic analgesics. Also tell your health care professional if you are allergic to any other substances, such as foods, preservatives, or dyes.

Pregnancy—Although studies on birth defects have not been done in pregnant women, tramadol has not been reported to cause birth defects. In animal studies, there were drug-related birth defects observed. Studies done in animals given very high (toxic) doses resulted in lower than normal birth weights and some deaths in the fetuses and birth defects in some of the newborns.

Breast-feeding—Tramadol passes into breast milk and may cause unwanted effects in nursing babies. It may be necessary for you to take another medicine or to stop breast-feeding during treatment. Be sure you have discussed the risks and benefits of the medicine with your doctor.

Children—There is no specific information on the relationship of age to the effects of tramadol in patients less than 16 years of age.

Older adults—Studies in older adults show that tramadol stays in the body a little longer than it does in younger adults. Your doctor will consider this when deciding on your doses.

Other medicines—Although certain medicines should not be used together at all, in other cases two different medicines may be used together even if an interaction might occur. In these cases, your doctor may want to change the

dose, or other precautions may be necessary. When you are taking tramadol, it is especially important that your health care provider know if you are taking any of the following:

• Carbamazepine (e.g., Tegretol)—May decrease the effects of tramadol by decreasing the amount of medicine in the body
• Central nervous system (CNS) depressants (medicines that cause drowsiness)—Using these medicines with tramadol may increase the chance of serious side effects or increase the risk of convulsions (seizures)
• Monoamine oxidase (MAO) inhibitors (furazolidone [e.g., Furoxone], isocarboxazid [e.g., Marplan], phenelzine [e.g., Nardil], procarbazine [e.g., Matulane], selegiline [e.g., Eldepryl], tranylcypromine [e.g., Parnate])—The chance of convulsions (seizures) may be increased

Other medical problems—The presence of other medical problems may affect the use of tramadol. Make sure you tell your doctor if you have any other medical problems, especially:

• Abdominal or stomach conditions (severe)—Tramadol may hide signs of other medical conditions
• Alcohol or drug abuse, or history of—May increase the serious side effects of tramadol
• Head injury—Tramadol can hide signs of other medical conditions
• Kidney disease or
• Liver disease—The chance of side effects may be increased
• Seizures—The chance of convulsions (seizures) may be increased

Proper Use of This Medicine

If you think that this medicine is not working as well after you have been taking it for a few weeks, *do not increase the dose.* Instead, check with your medical doctor or dentist.

Dosing—The dose of tramadol will be different for different patients. *Follow your doctor's orders or the directions on the label.* The following information includes only the average doses of tramadol. *If your dose is different, do not change it* unless your doctor tells you to do so.

The number of doses you take each day, the time allowed between doses, and the length of time you take the medicine depend on the medical problem for which you are taking tramadol.

Take this medicine only as directed. Do not take more of it, do not take it more often, and do not take it for a longer time than your doctor ordered. Using too much of this medicine increases the chance of unwanted effects.

• For pain:
—For *oral* dosage form (tablets):
• Adults—One to two 50-milligram (mg) tablets every six hours as needed. Your doctor may want you to take 2 tablets for the first dose if you are having severe pain. This helps the medicine start working a little faster.
• Children up to 16 years of age—Use and dose must be determined by your doctor.

Missed dose—If your medical doctor or dentist has directed you to take this medicine according to a regular schedule and you miss a dose of this medicine, take it as soon as possible. However, if it is almost time for your next dose, skip the missed dose and go back to your regular dosing schedule. Do not double doses.

Storage—To store this medicine:

- Keep out of the reach of children.
- Store away from heat and direct light.
- Do not store tramadol tablets in the bathroom, near the kitchen sink, or in other damp places. Heat or moisture may cause the medicine to break down.
- Do not keep outdated medicine or medicine no longer needed. Be sure that any discarded medicine is out of the reach of children.

Precautions While Using This Medicine

This medicine will add to the effects of alcohol and other CNS depressants (medicine that causes drowsiness). Some examples of CNS depressants are antihistamines or medicine for hay fever, other allergies, or colds; sedatives, tranquilizers, or sleeping medicine; prescription pain medicine or narcotics; barbiturates; medicine for seizures; muscle relaxants; or anesthetics, including some dental anesthetics. *Do not drink alcoholic beverages, and check with your medical doctor or dentist before taking any of the medicines listed above while you are using this medicine.*

This medicine may cause some people to become drowsy, dizzy, or lightheaded. *Make sure you know how you react to this medicine before you drive, use machines, or do anything else that could be dangerous if you are dizzy or are not alert.*

Dizziness, lightheadedness, or fainting may occur, especially when you get up suddenly from a lying or sitting position. Getting up slowly may help lessen this problem.

Nausea or vomiting may occur, especially after the first couple of doses. This effect may go away if you lie down for awhile. However, if nausea or vomiting continues, check with your medical doctor or dentist. Lying down for a while may also help relieve some other side effects, such as dizziness or lightheadedness, that may occur.

Before having any kind of surgery (including dental surgery) or emergency treatment, tell the medical doctor or dentist in charge that you are taking this medicine. Taking tramadol together with medicines that are used during surgery or dental or emergency treatments may cause increased side effects.

If you think you or someone else may have taken an overdose of tramadol, get emergency help at once. Signs of an overdose include convulsions (seizures) and pinpoint pupils of the eyes.

Side Effects of This Medicine

Along with its needed effects, a medicine may cause some unwanted effects. Although not all of these side effects may occur, if they do occur they may need medical attention.

Get emergency help immediately if any of the following symptoms of overdose occur:

Convulsions (seizures); difficulty in breathing; pinpointed pupils of the eyes

Also, check with your doctor as soon as possible if any of the following side effects occur:

Less common or rare

Blisters under the skin; blurred vision; change in walking and balance; convulsions (seizures); difficult urination; dizziness or lightheadedness when getting up from a lying or sitting position; fainting; fast heartbeat; frequent urge to urinate; loss of memory; numbness, tingling, pain, or weakness in hands or feet; seeing, hearing, or feeling things that are not there; severe redness, swelling, and itching of the skin; shortness of breath; trembling and shaking of hands or feet; trouble performing routine tasks

Other side effects may occur that usually do not need medical attention. These side effects may go away during treatment as your body adjusts to the medicine. However, check with your doctor if any of the following side effects continue or are bothersome:

More common

Abdominal or stomach pain; agitation; anxiety; constipation; diarrhea; dizziness; drowsiness; dry mouth; headache; heartburn; itching of the skin; loss of appetite; loss of strength or weakness; nausea; nervousness; skin rash; sweating; unusual feeling of excitement; vomiting

Less common

Confusion; depression; excessive gas; flushing or redness of the skin; general feeling of bodily discomfort; hot flashes; trouble in sleeping

After you stop using this medicine, your body may need time to adjust. The length of time this takes depends on the amount of medicine you were using and how long you used it. During this period of time check with your doctor if you notice any of the following side effects:

Anxiety; body aches; diarrhea; fast heartbeat; fever, runny nose, or sneezing; gooseflesh; high blood pressure; increased sweating; increased yawning; loss of appetite; nausea or vomiting; nervousness, restlessness or irritability; shivering or trembling; stomach cramps; trouble in sleeping; unusually large pupils; weakness

Other side effects not listed above may also occur in some patients. If you notice any other effects, check with your doctor.

Developed: 07/15/96
Revised: 10/15/98

TRANDOLAPRIL AND VERAPAMIL
Systemic

Commonly used brand name(s):

In the U.S.—
Tarka

Description

Trandolapril (tran-DOHL-a-pril) and verapamil (ver-AP-a-mil) combination belongs to the class of medicines called high blood pressure medicines (antihypertensives). It is used to treat high blood pressure (hypertension).

High blood pressure adds to the workload of the heart and arteries. If it continues for a long time, the heart and arteries may not function properly. This can damage the blood vessels of the brain, heart, and kidneys, resulting in a stroke, heart failure, or kidney failure. High blood pressure may also increase the risk of heart attacks. These problems may be less likely to occur if blood pressure is controlled.

The exact way in which this medicine works is not known. Trandolapril is a type of medicine known as an angiotensin-converting enzyme (ACE) inhibitor. It blocks an enzyme in the body that is necessary in producing a substance that causes blood vessels to tighten. Verapamil is a type of medicine known as a calcium channel blocker. Calcium channel blocking agents affect the movement of calcium into the cells of the heart and blood vessels. The actions of both medicines relax blood vessels, lower blood pressure, and increase the supply of blood and oxygen to the heart.

This medicine is available only with your doctor's prescription, in the following dosage form:

> *Oral*
> * Extended-release tablets (U.S.)

Before Using This Medicine

In deciding to use a medicine, the risks of taking the medicine must be weighed against the good it will do. This is a decision you and your doctor will make. For trandolapril and verapamil combination, the following should be considered:

Allergies—Tell your doctor if you have ever had any unusual or allergic reaction to trandolapril or to any other ACE inhibitor (benazepril, captopril, enalapril, fosinopril, lisinopril, moexipril, quinapril, or ramipril) or to verapamil. Also tell your health care professional if you are allergic to any other substances, such as foods, preservatives, or dyes.

Pregnancy—Studies with this combination medicine have not been done in pregnant women. However, use of any of the ACE inhibitors during pregnancy, especially in the second and third trimesters (after the first 3 months) can cause low blood pressure, kidney failure, an underdeveloped skull, or even death in newborns. *Therefore, it is important that you check with your doctor immediately if you think that you may be pregnant.* Be sure that you have discussed this with your doctor before taking this combination medicine.

Breast-feeding—Verapamil passes into breast milk. It is not known whether trandolapril passes into breast milk; however, it does pass into the milk of lactating rats. Breast-feeding is not recommended in women who are taking this combination medicine.

Children—Studies on this medicine have been done only in adult patients, and there is no specific information comparing use of trandolapril and verapamil in children with use in other age groups.

Older adults—Although this medicine has not been shown to cause different side effects or problems in older people than it does in younger adults, blood levels of trandolapril and verapamil may be increased in the elderly. Elderly people also may be more sensitive to the effects of this medicine.

Other medicines—Although certain medicines should not be used together at all, in other cases two different medicines may be used together even if an interaction might occur. In these cases, your doctor may want to change the dose, or other precautions may be necessary. When you are taking this medicine, it is especially important that your health care professional know if you are taking any of the following:

* Beta-blockers (acebutolol [e.g., Sectral], atenolol [e.g., Tenormin], betaxolol [e.g., Kerlone], bisoprolol [e.g., Zebeta], carteolol [e.g., Cartrol], carvedilol [e.g., Coreg], labetalol [e.g., Normodyne], metoprolol [e.g., Lopressor], nadolol [e.g., Corgard], oxprenolol [e.g., Trasicor], penbutolol [e.g., Levatol], pindolol [e.g., Visken], propranolol [e.g., Inderal], sotalol [e.g., Sotacor], timolol [e.g., Blocadren])—Effects of these medicines and verapamil on the heart may be increased

* Digitalis glycosides (heart medicine [e.g., Lanoxin])—Effects of these medicines may be increased

* Disopyramide (e.g., Norpace)—Effects of verapamil on the heart may be increased

* Diuretics (water pills)—May increse the blood pressure–lowering effects

* Potassium-containing medicines or supplements or
* Salt substitutes that contain potassium—Use of these substances with ACE inhibitors may result in an unusually high potassium level in the blood, which can lead to irregular heart rhythm and other problems

Also, tell your health care professional if you are using any of the following medicines in the eye:
* Betaxolol (e.g., Betoptic) or
* Carteolol (e.g., Ocupress) or
* Levobunolol (e.g., Betagan) or
* Metipranolol (e.g., OptiPranolol) or
* Timolol (e.g., Timoptic)—Effects on the heart may be increased

Other medical problems—The presence of other medical problems may affect the use of this medicine. Make sure you tell your doctor if you have any other medical problems, especially:

* Bee-sting allergy treatments or
* Dialysis treatments—Increased risk of serious allergic reaction occurring

* Dehydration—Lowering effects on blood pressure may be increased

* Diabetes mellitus (sugar diabetes)—Increased risk of potassium levels in the body becoming too high

* Duchenne's muscular dystrophy—Verapamil may make this condition worse

* Heart disease or
* Hypotension (low blood pressure)—Further lowering of blood pressure may make problems resulting from these conditions worse

* Kidney disease or
* Liver disease—Effects may be increased because of slower removal of the medicine from the body

* Scleroderma or
* Systemic lupus erythematosus (SLE) (or history of)—Increased risk of blood problems with ACE inhibitors

* Previous reaction to any ACE inhibitor involving hoarseness; swelling of face, mouth, hands, or feet; or sudden trouble in breathing—Reaction is more likely to occur again with ACE inhibitors

Proper Use of This Medicine

Take this medicine exactly as directed by your doctor, at the same time each day. Do not take more of it and do not take it more often than directed.

Swallow the tablets whole, without breaking, crushing, or chewing them.

Take this medicine with food or milk.

Dosing—The dose of this medicine will be different for different patients. *Follow your doctor's orders or the directions on the label.* The following information includes only the average doses of this medicine. *If your dose is different, do not change it* unless your doctor tells you to do so.

The number of tablets that you take depends on the strength of the medicine. Also, *the number of doses you take each day, the time allowed between doses, and the length of time you take the medicine depend on the medical problem for which you are taking it.*

* For *oral* dosage form (extended-release tablets):
  —For high blood pressure:
    * Adults—1 or 2 tablets a day.
    * Children—Use and dose must be determined by your doctor.

Missed dose—If you miss a dose of this medicine, take it as soon as possible. However, if it is almost time for your next dose, skip the missed dose and go back to your regular dosing schedule. Do not double doses.

Storage—To store this medicine:
* Keep out of the reach of children.
* Store away from heat and direct light.
* Do not store in the bathroom, near the kitchen sink, or in other damp places. Heat or moisture may cause the medicine to break down.
* Do not keep outdated medicine or medicine no longer needed. Be sure that any discarded medicine is out of the reach of children.

Precautions While Using This Medicine

It is very important that your doctor check your progress at regular visits. This will allow your doctor to make sure the medicine is working properly, to check for unwanted effects, and to change the dosage if needed.

If you think that you may have become pregnant, check with your doctor immediately. Use of this medicine, especially during the second and third trimesters (after the first 3 months) of pregnancy, may cause serious injury or even death to the unborn child.

Do not take any other medicines, especially potassium supplements, or salt substitutes that contain potassium unless approved or prescribed by your doctor.

Dizziness, lightheadedness, or fainting may occur after the first dose, especially if you have been taking a diuretic (water pill). Make sure you know how you react to the medicine before you drive, use machines, or do other things that could be dangerous if you experience these effects.

Check with your doctor if you notice any signs of fever, sore throat, or chills. These could be symptoms of an infection resulting from low white blood cell counts.

Check with your doctor immediately if you notice difficult breathing or swelling of the face, arms, or legs. These could be symptoms of a serious allergic reaction.

Check with your doctor if you become sick while taking this medicine, especially with severe or continuing vomiting or diarrhea. These conditions may cause you to lose too much water, possibly resulting in low blood pressure.

Dizziness, lightheadedness, or fainting may also occur if you exercise or if the weather is hot. Heavy sweating can cause loss of too much water which can result in low blood pressure. Use extra care during exercise or hot weather.

Before having any kind of surgery (including dental surgery) or emergency treatment, tell the medical doctor or dentist in charge that you are taking this medicine.

Side Effects of This Medicine

Along with its needed effects, a medicine may cause some unwanted effects. Although not all of these side effects may occur, if they do occur they may need medical attention.

Check with your doctor immediately if any of the following side effects occur:
Rare
  Swelling of face, mouth, hands, or feet; trouble in swallowing or breathing (sudden) accompanied by hoarseness

Check with your doctor as soon as possible if any of the following side effects occur:
Rare
  Chest pain; cough (with mucus); dark urine, yellow eyes or skin, or pain in right side; lightheadedness or fainting; fever, chills, or sore throat; general feeling of discomfort or illness; shortness of breath; slow heartbeat; wheezing
Signs and symptoms of too much potassium in the body
  Confusion; irregular heartbeat; nervousness; numbness or tingling in hands, feet, or lips; weakness or heaviness of legs

Other side effects may occur that usually do not need medical attention. These side effects may go away during treatment as your body adjusts to the medicine. However, check with your doctor if any of the following side effects continue or are bothersome:
Less common or rare
  Constipation; cough (dry, continuing); diarrhea; dizziness; itching; joint pain or pain in arms or legs; nausea; unusual tiredness

Other side effects not listed above may also occur in some patients. If you notice any other effects, check with your doctor.

Developed: 08/10/98

TRASTUZUMAB   Systemic

Commonly used brand name(s):

In the U.S.—
  Herceptin

Description

Trastuzumab (tras-TOO-ze-mab) is a monoclonal antibody. It is used to treat breast cancer that has spread to other parts of the body. Trastuzumab may prevent the growth of some breast tumors that produce extra amounts of a certain substance known as the HER2 protein. Trastuzumab should be used only in certain patients whose breast tumors have been shown to produce extra amounts of this protein.

Trastuzumab is to be administered only by or under the immediate supervision of your doctor. It is available in the following dosage form:

Parenteral
- Injection (U.S.)

Before Using This Medicine

In deciding to use a medicine, the risks of taking the medicine must be weighed against the good it will do. This is a decision you and your doctor will make. For trastuzumab, the following should be considered:

Allergies—Tell your doctor if you have ever had any unusual or allergic reaction to trastuzumab or to mouse proteins. Also tell your health care professional if you are allergic to any other substances, such as foods, preservatives, or dyes.

Pregnancy—Trastuzumab has not been studied in pregnant women. However, this medicine was found to cross the placenta in monkeys but did not cause harmful effects in the fetus.

Breast-feeding—It is not known whether trastuzumab passes into the breast milk. However, breast-feeding is not recommended while you are receiving this medicine and for a while after you stop receiving it.

Children—Studies on this medicine have been done only in adult patients, and there is no specific information comparing use of trastuzumab in children with use in other age groups.

Older adults—There is no specific information comparing the use of trastuzumab in the elderly with use in other age groups. However, certain heart problems may be more likely to occur in the elderly, who may be more sensitive to the effects of trastuzumab.

Other medicines—Although certain medicines should not be used together at all, in other cases two different medicines may be used together even if an interaction might occur. In these cases, your doctor may want to change the dose, or other precautions may be necessary. Tell your health care professional if you are taking any other prescription or nonprescription (over-the-counter [OTC]) medicine.

Other medical problems—The presence of other medical problems may affect the use of trastuzumab. Make sure you tell your doctor if you have any other medical problems, especially:

- Heart disease—Risk of heart problems caused by trastuzumab may be increased
- Lung disease—Risk of lung problems caused by trastuzumab may be increased

Proper Use of This Medicine

Dosing—The dose of trastuzumab will be different for different patients. The dose that is used may depend on a number of things, including your size. Trastuzumab usually is given by a doctor or nurse in the hospital or outpatient clinic. If you have any questions about the proper dose of trastuzumab, ask your doctor.

Precautions While Using This Medicine

It is very important that your doctor check your progress at regular visits to make sure that this medicine is working properly and to check for any unwanted effects.

Side Effects of This Medicine

Along with its needed effects, a medicine may cause some unwanted effects. Although not all of these side effects may occur, if they do occur they may need medical attention.

Check with your doctor immediately if any of the following side effects occur *during or after the administration of trastuzumab:*

More common
   Dizziness; fever or chills; headache; nausea or vomiting; shortness of breath; skin rash; weakness

Rare
   Tightness in chest; troubled breathing; wheezing

Check with your doctor as soon as possible if any of the following side effects occur:

Less common
   Fast or irregular heartbeat; increased cough; swelling of feet or lower legs

Rare
   Blue lips and fingernails; blurred vision; chest pain; confusion; Cough or hoarseness, accompanied by fever or chills; faintness or light-headedness when getting up from a lying or sitting position; increased sweating; itching; large, hive-like swelling on face, eyelids, lips, tongue, throat, hands, feet, or sex organs; lower back or side pain, accompanied by fever or chills; painful or difficult urination, accompanied by fever or chills; pale skin; redness of skin; unusual tiredness or weakness

Other side effects may occur that usually do not need medical attention. These side effects may go away during treatment as your body adjusts to the medicine. However, check with your doctor if any of the following side effects continue or are bothersome:

More common
   Diarrhea; pain

Less common
   Loss of appetite; numbness or tingling of hands or feet; runny nose; trouble in sleeping

Other side effects not listed above may also occur in some patients. If you notice any other effects, check with your doctor.

Developed: 12/11/98
Revised: 07/24/2000

TRAZODONE   Systemic

Commonly used brand name(s):

In the U.S.—
   Desyrel
   Generic name product may be available.

In Canada—
   Desyrel

Description

Trazodone (TRAZ-oh-done) belongs to the group of medicines known as antidepressants or "mood elevators." It is used to relieve mental depression and depression that sometimes occurs with anxiety.

Trazodone is available only with your doctor's prescription, in the following dosage form:

Oral
- Tablets (U.S. and Canada)

Before Using This Medicine

In deciding to use a medicine, the risks of taking the medicine must be weighed against the good it will do. This is a decision you and your doctor will make. For trazodone, the following should be considered:

Allergies—Tell your doctor if you have ever had any unusual or allergic reaction to trazodone. Also tell your health care professional if you are allergic to any other substances, such as foods, preservatives, or dyes.

Pregnancy—Studies have not been done in pregnant women. However, studies in animals have shown that trazodone causes birth defects and a decrease in the number of successful pregnancies when given in doses many times larger than human doses.

Breast-feeding—Trazodone passes into breast milk.

Children—Studies on this medicine have been done only in adult patients, and there is no specific information comparing use of trazodone in children with use in other age groups.

Older adults—Drowsiness, dizziness, confusion, vision problems, dryness of mouth, and constipation may be more likely to occur in the elderly, who are usually more sensitive to the effects of trazodone.

Other medicines—Although certain medicines should not be used together at all, in other cases two different medicines may be used together even if an interaction might occur. In these cases, your doctor may want to change the dose, or other precautions may be necessary. When you are taking trazodone, it is especially important that your health care professional know if you are taking any of the following:

- Antihypertensives (high blood pressure medicine)—Taking these medicines with trazodone may result in low blood pressure (hypotension); the amount of medicine you need to take may change
- Central nervous system (CNS) depressants (medicine that causes drowsiness) or
- Tricyclic antidepressants (medicine for depression)—Taking these medicines with trazodone may add to the CNS depressant effects

Other medical problems—The presence of other medical problems may affect the use of trazodone. Make sure you tell your doctor if you have any other medical problems, especially:

- Alcohol abuse (or history of)—Drinking alcohol with trazodone will increase the central nervous system (CNS) depressant effects
- Heart disease—Trazodone may make the condition worse
- Kidney disease or
- Liver disease—Higher blood levels of trazodone may occur, increasing the chance of side effects

Proper Use of This Medicine

To lessen stomach upset and to reduce dizziness and light-headedness, take this medicine with or shortly after a meal or light snack, even for a daily bedtime dose, unless your doctor has told you to take it on an empty stomach.

Take trazodone only as directed by your doctor, to benefit your condition as much as possible.

Sometimes trazodone must be taken for up to 4 weeks before you begin to feel better, although most people notice improvement within 2 weeks.

Dosing—The dose of trazodone will be different for different patients. *Follow your doctor's orders or the directions on the label.* The following information includes only the average doses of trazodone. *If your dose is different, do not change it* unless your doctor tells you to do so:

- Adults—Oral, to start, 50 milligrams per dose taken three times a day, or 75 milligrams per dose taken two times a day. Your doctor may increase your dose if needed.
- Children 6 to 18 years of age—Oral. Your doctor will tell you what dose to take based on your body weight.
- Children up to 6 years of age—Dose must be determined by the doctor.
- Elderly patients—Oral, to start, 25 milligrams per dose taken three times a day. Your doctor may increase your dose if needed.

Missed dose—If you miss a dose of this medicine, take it as soon as possible. However, if it is within 4 hours of your next dose, skip the missed dose and go back to your regular dosing schedule. Do not double doses.

Storage—To store this medicine:
- Keep out of the reach of children.
- Store away from heat and direct light.
- Do not store in the bathroom, near the kitchen sink, or in other damp places. Heat or moisture may cause the medicine to break down.
- Do not keep outdated medicine or medicine no longer needed. Be sure that any discarded medicine is out of the reach of children.

Precautions While Using This Medicine

It is very important that your doctor check your progress at regular visits. This will allow your doctor to check the medicine's effects and to change the dose if needed.

Do not stop taking this medicine without first checking with your doctor. To prevent a possible return of your medical problem, your doctor may want you to reduce gradually the amount of medicine you are using before you stop completely.

Before having any kind of surgery, dental treatment, or emergency treatment, tell the medical doctor or dentist in charge that you are using this medicine. Taking trazodone together with medicines that are used during surgery or dental or emergency treatments may increase the CNS depressant effects.

This medicine will add to the effects of alcohol and other CNS depressants (medicines that slow down the nervous system, possibly causing drowsiness). Some examples of CNS depressants are antihistamines or medicine for hay fever, other allergies, or colds; sedatives, tranquilizers, or sleeping medicine; prescription pain medicine or narcotics; barbiturates; medicine for seizures; muscle relaxants; or anesthetics, including some dental anesthetics. *Check with your doctor before taking any of the above while you are using this medicine.*

This medicine may cause some people to become drowsy or less alert than they are normally. *Make sure you know how you react to this medicine before you drive, use machines, or do anything else that could be dangerous if you are not alert.*

Dizziness, lightheadedness, or fainting may occur, especially when you get up from a lying or sitting position. Getting up slowly may help. If this problem continues or gets worse, check with your doctor.

Trazodone may cause dryness of the mouth. For temporary relief, use sugarless gum or candy, melt bits of ice in your mouth, or use a saliva substitute. However, if your mouth continues to feel dry for more than 2 weeks, check with your medical doctor or dentist. Continuing dryness of the mouth may increase the chance of dental disease, including tooth decay, gum disease, and fungus infections.

Side Effects of This Medicine

Along with its needed effects, a medicine may cause some unwanted effects. Although not all of these side effects may occur, if they do occur they may need medical attention.

Stop taking this medicine and check with your doctor immediately if the following side effect occurs:
> *Rare*
>> Painful, inappropriate erection of the penis, continuing

Also, check with your doctor as soon as possible if any of the following side effects occur:
> *Less common*
>> Confusion; fainting; muscle tremors
> *Rare*
>> Fast or slow heartbeat; skin rash; unusual excitement
> *Symptoms of overdose*
>> Drowsiness; loss of muscle coordination; nausea and vomiting

Other side effects may occur that usually do not need medical attention. These side effects may go away during treatment as your body adjusts to the medicine. However, check with your doctor if any of the following side effects continue or are bothersome:
> *More common*
>> Dizziness or lightheadedness; drowsiness; dryness of mouth (usually mild); headache; nausea and vomiting; unpleasant taste
> *Less common*
>> Blurred vision; constipation; diarrhea; muscle aches or pains; unusual tiredness or weakness

Other side effects not listed above may also occur in some patients. If you notice any other effects, check with your doctor.

Revised: 12/16/99

TRETINOIN   Systemic

Commonly used brand name(s):

In the U.S.—
Vesanoid

Description

Tretinoin (TRET-i-noyn) belongs to the group of medicines known as retinoids (RET-i-noyds). It is used to treat a form of leukemia (acute promyelocytic leukemia [APL]).

Tretinoin has side effects that can be very serious. Be sure that you discuss with your doctor the good that this medicine can do as well as the risks of taking it.

This medicine is available only with your doctor's prescription, in the following dosage form(s):

> *Oral*
> • Capsules (U.S.)

Before Using This Medicine

In deciding to use a medicine, the risks of taking the medicine must be weighed against the good it will do. This is a decision you and your doctor will make. For tretinoin, the following should be considered:

Allergies—Tell your doctor if you have ever had any unusual or allergic reaction to tretinoin or to acitretin, etretinate, isotretinoin, or vitamin A preparations. Also tell your health care professional if you are allergic to any other substances, such as foods, preservatives, or dyes.

Pregnancy—*Tretinoin must not be taken during pregnancy because there is a very high risk of causing severe birth defects in the infant. In addition, tretinoin must not be taken if there is a chance that you may become pregnant during treatment or within 1 month after treatment is ended.* Women who are able to have children, and even some women who have started the menopause, must have a pregnancy test done within 1 week before starting tretinoin, to make sure they are not pregnant. The pregnancy test must be repeated once a month during treatment. *During treatment with tretinoin, and for a month after treatment is over, you must use two effective forms of birth control at the same time.* If you have any questions about what kinds of birth control to use, check with your health care professional. *Be sure that you have discussed this information with your doctor. You will be asked to sign an informed consent form stating that you have received and understand the above information.*

Breast-feeding—It is not known whether tretinoin passes into the breast milk. However, because this medicine can cause serious side effects, women should stop breast-feeding before starting treatment.

Children—Studies in a limited number of children between 1 and 16 years of age have shown that children may be especially sensitive to the effects of this medicine, and may be more likely than adults to experience severe headaches and some other side effects during treatment.

Older adults—Many medicines have not been studied specifically in older people. Therefore, it may not be known whether they work exactly the same way they do in younger adults or if they cause different side effects or problems in older people. There is no specific information comparing use of tretinoin in the elderly with use in other age groups.

Other medicines—Although certain medicines should not be used together at all, in other cases two different medicines may be used together even if an interaction might occur. In these cases, your doctor may want to change the dose, or other precautions may be necessary. When you are

taking tretinoin, it is especially important that your health care professional know if you are taking any of the following:

- Corticosteroids (cortisone-like medicine) or
- Cimetidine (e.g., Tagamet) or
- Cyclosporine (e.g., Sandimmune) or
- Diltiazem (e.g., Cardizem) or
- Erythromycin (e.g., E-Mycin, Ilotycin) or
- Ketoconazole (e.g., Nizoral) or
- Pentobarbital (e.g., Nembutal) or
- Phenobarbital (e.g., Luminal) or
- Rifampin (e.g., Rifadin) or
- Verapamil (e.g., Calan)—These medicines may increase or decrease the metabolism (breakdown) of tretinoin, leading to higher-than-usual or lower-than-usual amounts of tretinoin in the body

Proper Use of This Medicine

It is very important that you take tretinoin only as directed by your doctor. Do not take more of it, do not take it more often, and do not take it for a longer time than your doctor ordered. To do so may increase the chance of side effects.

Dosing—The dose of tretinoin will be different for different patients. *Follow your doctor's orders or the directions on the label.* The following information includes only the average dose of tretinoin. *If your dose is different, do not change it* unless your doctor tells you to do so.

- For *oral* dosage form (capsules):
  —For acute promyelocytic leukemia (APL):
    - Adults—Dose is based on body size and must be determined by your doctor. The usual dose is 45 milligrams (mg) for each square meter of body surface area a day, given in two equally divided doses.
    - Children—The dose will be determined by your doctor.

Missed dose—If you miss a dose of this medicine, take it as soon as possible. However, if it is almost time for your next dose, *check with your health care professional* to find out how much medicine to take for the next dose.

Storage—To store this medicine:

- Keep out of the reach of children.
- Store away from heat and direct light.
- Do not store in the bathroom, near the kitchen sink, or in other damp places. Heat or moisture may cause the medicine to break down.
- Do not keep outdated medicine or medicine no longer needed. Be sure that any discarded medicine is out of the reach of children.

Precautions While Using This Medicine

Your doctor should check your progress at regular visits to make sure that the medicine is working properly and to check for unwanted effects.

Tretinoin causes fever, headache, tiredness, and weakness in most people who take it. *It is very important that you continue taking the medicine even if it makes you feel ill.* Your health care professional may be able to suggest ways to relieve some of these effects. However, if you develop a very severe headache or a headache that occurs together with nausea, vomiting, or vision problems, *check with your doctor right away.*

Tretinoin sometimes causes a severe reaction that affects the lungs at first, but can later spread to other parts of the body. Signs of this reaction include breathing problems, bone pain, chest pain, and fever. *Check with your doctor right away if any of these effects occur during treatment.*

Side Effects of This Medicine

Along with its needed effects, a medicine may cause some unwanted effects. Although not all of these side effects may occur, if they do occur they may need medical attention.

Check with your doctor immediately if any of the following side effects occur:

More common
Bone pain; discomfort or pain in chest; fever; shortness of breath, troubled breathing, tightness in chest, or wheezing; weight gain (occurring together with any of the other symptoms listed before)

Less common
Convulsions (seizures); difficulty in speaking, slow speech, or inability to speak; feeling of heaviness in chest; headache (severe); inability to move arms, legs, or muscles of the face; nausea and vomiting (occurring together with a headache); pain in back or left arm; vision problems (occurring together with a headache)

Also, check with your doctor as soon as possible if any of the following side effects occur:

More common
Any change in vision (not occurring with a headache); coughing, sneezing, sore throat, and stuffy or runny nose; cracked lips; crusting, redness, pain, or sores in mouth or nose; decreased urination; earache or feeling of fullness in the ear; increase or decrease in blood pressure; irregular heartbeat; mental depression; pain and swelling in leg or foot; skin rash; swelling of abdomen (stomach area); swelling of face, fingers, hands, feet, or lower legs

Less common
Cramping or pain in stomach (severe); difficult or painful urination; drowsiness (very severe and continuing); hallucinations (seeing, hearing, or feeling things that are not there); hearing loss; heartburn, indigestion, or nausea (severe and continuing); mood, mental, or personality changes; pain in lower back or side; swollen area that feels sore and tender; yellow eyes or skin

Other side effects may occur that usually do not need medical attention. These side effects may go away during treatment as your body adjusts to the medicine. However, check with your doctor if any of the following side effects continue or are bothersome:

More common
Anxiety; burning, crawling, or tingling feeling in the skin; confusion; constipation; diarrhea; dizziness; dryness of skin, mouth, or nose; flushing; general feeling of discomfort or illness; hair loss; headache (mild and not occurring together with other side effects); indigestion; itching of skin; loss of appetite; muscle pain; nausea and vomiting (not occurring together with a headache); shivering; trouble sleeping; weight loss

Less common
Anxiety and restlessness (occurring together); clumsi-

ness or unsteadiness when walking; forgetfulness; frequent urination; trembling, sometimes with a flapping movement; weakness in legs

Other side effects not listed above may also occur in some patients. If you notice any other effects, check with your doctor.

Developed: 08/14/98

TRETINOIN   Topical

Commonly used brand name(s):

In the U.S.—
Avita
Renova

Retin-A
Retin-A MICRO

In Canada—
Renova
Retin-A
Retisol-A
Stieva-A

Stieva-A Forte
Vitamin A Acid
Vitinoin

Other commonly used names are retinoic acid and vitamin A acid.

Description

Tretinoin (TRET-i-noyn) is used to treat acne. It works partly by keeping skin pores clear.

One of the tretinoin creams is used to treat fine wrinkles, dark spots, or rough skin on the face caused by damaging rays of the sun. It works by lightening the skin, replacing older skin with newer skin, and by slowing down the way the body removes skin cells that may have been harmed by the sun. Tretinoin works best when used within a skin care program that includes protecting the treated skin from the sun. However, it does not completely or permanently erase these skin problems or greatly improve more obvious changes in the skin, such as deep wrinkles caused by sun or the natural aging process.

Tretinoin may also be used to treat other skin diseases as determined by your doctor.

Tretinoin is available only with your doctor's prescription, in the following dosage forms:

Topical
- Cream (U.S. and Canada)
- Gel (U.S. and Canada)
- Topical solution (U.S. and Canada)

Before Using This Medicine

In deciding to use a medicine, the risks of using the medicine must be weighed against the good it will do. This is a decision you and your doctor will make. For tretinoin, the following should be considered:

Allergies—Tell your doctor if you have ever had any unusual or allergic reaction to acitretin, etretinate, isotretinoin, tretinoin, or vitamin A preparations. Also tell your health care professional if you are allergic to any other substances, such as preservatives or dyes.

Pregnancy—Tretinoin has not been studied in pregnant women. Topical tretinoin is not recommended during pregnancy. Topical tretinoin has been shown to cause delayed bone development in some animal fetuses. Before using this

medicine, make sure your doctor knows if you are pregnant or if you may become pregnant.

Breast-feeding—It is not known whether tretinoin passes into the breast milk. Mothers who are using this medicine and who wish to breast-feed should discuss this with their doctors.

Children—Studies on this medicine have been done only in adult patients, and there is no specific information comparing use of this medicine in children with use in other age groups. Children are unlikely to have skin problems due to the sun. In older children treated for acne, tretinoin is not expected to cause different side effects or problems than it does in other age groups.

Older adults—Many medicines have not been studied specifically in older people. Therefore, it may not be known whether they work exactly the same way they do in younger adults or if they cause different side effects or problems in older people. There is no specific information comparing use of tretinoin in patients 50 years of age and older with use in other age groups.

Other medicines—Although certain medicines should not be used together at all, in other cases two different medicines may be used together even if an interaction might occur. In these cases, your doctor may want to change the dose, or other precautions may be necessary. Tell your health care professional if you are using any other topical prescription or nonprescription (over-the-counter [OTC]) medicine that is to be applied to the same area of the skin. When you are using topical tretinoin, it is especially important that your health care professional know if you are taking any of the following:

- Acitretin (e.g., Soriatane)
- Etretinate (e.g., Tegison)
- Tretinoin, oral (e.g., Vesanoid)—May increase chance of getting severe dryness or redness of skin

Other medical problems—The presence of other medical problems may affect the use of tretinoin. Make sure you tell your doctor if you have any other medical problems, especially:

- Dermatitis, seborrheic or
- Eczema or
- Sunburn—Use of this medicine may cause or increase the irritation associated with these problems

Proper Use of This Medicine

It is very important that you use this medicine only as directed. Do not use more of it, do not use it more often, and do not use it for a longer time than your doctor ordered. To do so may cause irritation of the skin.

Do not apply this medicine to windburned or sunburned skin or on open wounds.

Do not use this medicine in or around the eyes or lips, or inside of the nose. Spread the medicine away from these areas when applying. If the medicine accidentally gets on these areas, wash with water at once.

This medicine usually comes with patient directions. Read them carefully before using the medicine.

Before applying tretinoin, wash the skin with a mild soap or cleanser and warm water by using the tips of your fingers. Then gently pat dry. Do not scrub your face with a sponge or washcloth. *Wait 20 to 30 minutes before applying this medicine to make sure the skin is completely dry.* Applying tretinoin to wet skin can irritate the skin.

To use the *cream or gel form* of this medicine:
- Apply just enough medicine to very lightly cover the affected areas, and rub in gently but well. A pea-sized amount is enough to cover the whole face.

To use the *solution form* of this medicine:
- Using your fingertips, a gauze pad, or a cotton swab, apply enough tretinoin solution to cover the affected areas. If you use a gauze pad or a cotton swab for applying the medicine, avoid getting it too wet. This will help prevent the medicine from running into areas not intended for treatment.

After applying the medicine, wash your hands to remove any medicine that might remain on them.

Dosing—The dose of topical tretinoin will be different for different patients. *Follow your doctor's orders or the directions on the label.* The following information includes only the average dose of topical tretinoin. *If your dose is different, do not change it* unless your doctor tells you to do so.

- For *topical* dosage forms (cream, gel, or solution):
  —For acne:
    - Adults and teenagers—Apply to the affected area(s) of the skin once a day, at bedtime.
- For *cream* dosage form (brand name *Renova* only):
  —For fine wrinkles, dark spots, or rough skin caused by the sun:
    - Adults up to 50 years of age—Apply to the affected area(s) of the skin once a day, at bedtime.
    - Adults 50 years of age and older—Use and dose must be determined by your doctor.

Missed dose—If you miss a dose of this medicine, skip the missed dose and go back to your regular dosing schedule. Do not double doses.

Storage—To store this medicine:
- Keep out of the reach of children.
- Store away from heat and direct light. The gel product is flammable and should be kept away from fire or excessive heat.
- Keep the medicine from freezing.
- Do not keep outdated medicine or medicine no longer needed. Be sure that any discarded medicine is out of the reach of children.

Precautions While Using This Medicine

During the first 3 weeks you are using tretinoin, your skin may become irritated. Also, your acne may seem to get worse before it gets better. It may take longer than 12 weeks before you notice full improvement of your acne, even if you use the medicine every day. Check with your health care professional at any time skin irritation becomes severe or if your acne does not improve within 8 to 12 weeks.

You should avoid washing the skin treated with tretinoin for at least 1 hour after applying it.

Avoid using any topical medicine on the same area within 1 hour before or after using tretinoin. Otherwise, tretinoin may not work properly or skin irritation might occur.

Unless your doctor tells you otherwise, it is especially important to avoid using the following skin products on the same area as tretinoin:

- Any other topical acne product or skin product containing a peeling agent (such as benzoyl peroxide, resorcinol, salicylic acid, or sulfur)
- Hair products that are irritating, such as permanents or hair removal products
- Skin products that cause sensitivity to the sun, such as those containing spices or limes
- Skin products containing a large amount of alcohol, such as astringents, shaving creams, or after-shave lotions
- Skin products that are too drying or abrasive, such as some cosmetics, soaps, or skin cleansers

Using these products along with tretinoin may cause mild to severe irritation of the skin. Although skin irritation can occur, some doctors sometimes allow benzoyl peroxide to be used with tretinoin to treat acne. Usually tretinoin is applied at night so that it does not cause a problem with any other topical products that you might use during the day. Check with your doctor before using topical medicines with tretinoin.

During the first 6 months of use, *avoid overexposing the treated areas to sunlight, wind, or cold weather.* The skin will be more prone to sunburn, dryness, or irritation, especially during the first 2 or 3 weeks. However, you should not stop using this medicine unless the skin irritation becomes too severe. *Do not use a sunlamp.*

To help tretinoin work properly, regularly use sunscreen or sunblocking lotions with a sun protection factor (SPF) of at least 15. Also, wear protective clothing and hats, and apply creams, lotions, or moisturizers often.

Check with your doctor at any time your skin becomes too dry and irritated. Your health care professional can help you choose the right skin products for you to reduce skin dryness and irritation and may include the following:

- For patients using tretinoin for the treatment of acne:
  —Regular use of water-based creams or lotions helps to reduce skin irritation or dryness that may be caused by the use of tretinoin.
- For patients using tretinoin for the treatment of fine wrinkling, dark spots, and rough skin caused by the sun:
  —This medicine should be used as *part of an ongoing program to avoid further damage* to your skin from the sun. This program includes staying out of the sun when possible or wearing proper clothing or hats to protect your skin from sunlight.
  —Regular use of oil-based creams or lotions helps to reduce skin irritation or dryness caused by the use of tretinoin.

Side Effects of This Medicine

In some animal studies, tretinoin has been shown to cause skin tumors to develop faster when the treated area is exposed to ultraviolet light (sunlight or artificial sunlight from a sunlamp). Other studies have not shown the same result and more studies need to be done. It is not known if tretinoin causes skin tumors to develop faster in humans.

Along with its needed effects, a medicine may cause some unwanted effects. Although not all of these side effects may occur, if they do occur they may need medical attention.

Check with your doctor as soon as possible if any of the following side effects occur:
More common
  Burning feeling or stinging skin (severe); lightening of skin of treated area, unexpected; peeling of skin (se-

vere); redness of skin (severe); unusual dryness of skin (severe)

Rare
Darkening of treated skin

Other side effects may occur that usually do not need medical attention. These side effects may go away during treatment as your body adjusts to the medicine. However, check with your doctor if any of the following side effects continue or are bothersome:

More common
Burning feeling, stinging, or tingling of skin (mild)—lasting for a short time after first applying the medicine; chapping or slight peeling of skin (mild); redness of skin (mild); unusual dryness of skin (mild); unusually warm skin (mild)

The side effects will go away after you stop using tretinoin. On the rare chance that your skin color changes, this effect may last for several months before your skin color returns to normal.

Other side effects not listed above may also occur in some patients. If you notice any other effects, check with your doctor.

Additional Information

Once a medicine has been approved for marketing for a certain use, experience may show that it is also useful for other medical problems. Although this use is not included in product labeling, tretinoin is used in certain patients with the following medical conditions:

- Keratosis follicularis (skin disorder of small, red bumps)
- Verruca plana (flat warts)

Other than the above information, there is no additional information relating to its proper use, precautions, or side effects for these uses.

Revised: 08/21/97
Interim revision: 04/24/98

TRIFLURIDINE   Ophthalmic

Commonly used brand name(s):

In the U.S.—
Viroptic

In Canada—
Viroptic

Another commonly used name is trifluorothymidine.

Description

Trifluridine (trye-FLURE-i-deen) ophthalmic preparations are used to treat virus infections of the eye.

Trifluridine is available only with your doctor's prescription, in the following dosage form:

Ophthalmic
- Ophthalmic solution (eye drops) (U.S. and Canada)

Before Using This Medicine

In deciding to use a medicine, the risks of using the medicine must be weighed against the good it will do. This is a decision you and your doctor will make. For trifluridine, the following should be considered:

Allergies—Tell your doctor if you have ever had any unusual or allergic reaction to trifluridine. Also tell your health care professional if you are allergic to any other substances, such as preservatives.

Pregnancy—Studies have not been done in humans. When injected into developing chick embryos, trifluridine has been shown to cause birth defects. However, studies in rats and rabbits have not shown that trifluridine causes birth defects, although it did cause delayed bone formation in rats and rabbits and death in unborn rabbits.

Breast-feeding—It is unlikely that trifluridine, used in the eyes, is absorbed into the mother's body and passes into the breast milk. In addition, trifluridine has not been reported to cause problems in nursing babies.

Children—Although there is no specific information comparing the use of trifluridine in children with use in other age groups, it is not expected to cause different side effects or problems in children than it does in adults.

Older adults—Many medicines have not been studied specifically in older people. Therefore, it may not be known whether they work exactly the same way they do in younger adults or if they cause different side effects or problems in older people. There is no specific information comparing the use of trifluridine in the elderly with use in other age groups.

Other medicines—Although certain medicines should not be used together at all, in other cases two different medicines may be used together even if an interaction might occur. In these cases, your doctor may want to change the dose, or other precautions may be necessary. Tell your health care professional if you are using any other prescription or nonprescription (over-the-counter [OTC]) medicine that is to be used in the eye.

Proper Use of This Medicine

The bottle is only partially full to provide proper drop control.

To use:
- First, wash your hands. Then tilt the head back and pull the lower eyelid away from the eye to form a pouch. Drop the medicine into the pouch and gently close the eyes. Do not blink. Keep the eyes closed for 1 or 2 minutes to allow the medicine to come into contact with the infection.
- If you think you did not get the drop of medicine into your eye properly, use another drop.
- To keep the medicine as germ-free as possible, do not touch the applicator tip to any surface (including the eye). Also, keep the container tightly closed.

Do not use this medicine more often or for a longer time than your doctor ordered. To do so may cause problems in the eyes. If you have any questions about this, check with your doctor.

To help clear up your infection completely, *keep using this medicine for the full time of treatment*, even if your symptoms have disappeared. *Do not miss any doses.*

Dosing—The dose of ophthalmic trifluridine will be different for different patients. *Follow your doctor's orders or the directions on the label.* The following information includes only the average doses of ophthalmic trifluridine. *If your dose is different, do not change it unless your doctor tells you to do so.*

The number of doses you use each day, the time allowed between doses, and the length of time you use the medicine depend on the medical problem for which you are using ophthalmic trifluridine.

- For *ophthalmic solution* dosage forms:
  - —For viral eye infection:
    - Adults and children 6 years of age and older— One drop every two hours while you are awake. After healing has occurred, the dose may be reduced for seven more days to one drop every four hours (at least 5 doses a day) while you are awake.
    - Children up to 6 years of age—Use and dose must be determined by your doctor.

Missed dose—If you miss a dose of this medicine, apply it as soon as possible. However, if it is almost time for your next dose, skip the missed dose and go back to your regular dosing schedule.

Storage—To store this medicine:

- Keep out of the reach of children.
- Store in the refrigerator because heat will cause this medicine to break down. However, keep the medicine from freezing. Follow the directions on the label.
- Do not keep outdated medicine or medicine no longer needed. Be sure that any discarded medicine is out of the reach of children.

Precautions While Using This Medicine

It is very important that you keep your appointment with your doctor. If your symptoms become worse, check with your doctor sooner.

Side Effects of This Medicine

Along with its needed effects, a medicine may cause some unwanted effects. Although not all of these side effects may occur, if they do occur they may need medical attention.

Check with your doctor as soon as possible if any of the following side effects occur:

Rare
> Blurred vision or other change in vision; dryness of eye; irritation of eye; itching, redness, swelling, or other sign of irritation not present before use of this medicine

Other side effects may occur that usually do not need medical attention. These side effects may go away during treatment as your body adjusts to the medicine. However, check with your doctor if either of the following side effects continues or is bothersome:

More common
> Burning or stinging

Other side effects not listed above may also occur in some patients. If you notice any other effects, check with your doctor.

Revised: 03/29/00

TRILOSTANE   Systemic†

†Not commercially available in Canada.

Description

Trilostane (TRYE-loe-stane) is used in the treatment of Cushing's syndrome. It is normally used in short-term treatment until permanent therapy is possible.

In Cushing's syndrome, the adrenal gland overproduces steroids. Although steroids are important for various functions of the body, too much can cause problems. Trilostane reduces the amount of steroids produced by the adrenal gland.

This product was withdrawn from the U.S. market in April 1994.

Before Using This Medicine

In deciding to use a medicine, the risks of taking the medicine must be weighed against the good it will do. This is a decision you and your doctor will make. For trilostane, the following should be considered:

Allergies—Tell your doctor if you have ever had any unusual or allergic reaction to trilostane. Also tell your health care professional if you are allergic to any other substance, such as foods, preservatives, or dyes.

Pregnancy—Use of trilostane is not recommended during pregnancy. It has been shown to cause serious problems, including miscarriage, in humans. Trilostane has also been shown to cause birth defects in animals.

Breast-feeding—It is not known whether trilostane passes into breast milk. However, this medicine has not been reported to cause problems in nursing babies.

Children—There is no specific information about the use of trilostane in children.

Older adults—Many medicines have not been tested in older people. Therefore, it may not be known whether they work exactly the same way they do in younger adults or if they cause different side effects or problems in older people. There is no specific information about the use of trilostane in the elderly.

Other medicines—Although certain medicines should not be used together at all, in other cases two different medicines may be used together even if an interaction might occur. In these cases, your doctor may want to change the dose, or other precautions may be necessary. When you are taking trilostane, it is especially important that your health care professional know if you are taking any other prescription or nonprescription (over-the-counter [OTC]) medicine.

Other medical problems—The presence of other medical problems may affect the use of trilostane. Make sure you tell your doctor if you have any other medical problems, especially:

- Infection or
- Injury (recent serious)—Trilostane may weaken the body's normal defenses
- Kidney disease
- Liver disease

Proper Use of This Medicine

Take trilostane only as directed by your doctor. Do not take more or less of it, and do not take it more often than your doctor ordered.

Dosing—The dose of trilostane will be different for different patients. *Follow your doctor's orders or the directions on* *the label*. The following information includes only the average doses of trilostane. *If your dose is different, do not change it* unless your doctor tells you to do so.

- For *oral* dosage form (capsules):
  - —For Cushing's syndrome:
    - Adults—To start, 30 milligrams (mg) four times a day. Your doctor may increase the dose every three to four days as needed. However, the dose is usually not more than 90 mg four times a day.
    - Children—Dose must be determined by your doctor.

Missed dose—If you miss a dose of this medicine, take it as soon as possible. However, if it is almost time for your next dose, skip the missed dose and go back to your regular dosing schedule. Do not double doses.

Storage—To store this medicine:
- Keep out of the reach of children.
- Store away from heat and direct light.
- Do not store in the bathroom, near the kitchen sink, or in other damp places. Heat or moisture may cause the medicine to break down.
- Do not keep outdated medicine or medicine no longer needed. Be sure that any discarded medicine is out of the reach of children.

Precautions While Using This Medicine

It is very important that your doctor check your progress at regular visits to make sure that trilostane is working properly and does not cause unwanted effects.

Check with your doctor right away if you get an injury, infection, or illness of any kind. This medicine may weaken your body's normal defenses.

Before having any kind of surgery (including dental surgery) or emergency treatment, tell the medical doctor or dentist in charge that you are taking trilostane.

Your doctor may want you to carry a medical identification card or wear a bracelet stating that you are taking this medicine.

Side Effects of This Medicine

Along with its needed effects, a medicine may cause some unwanted effects. Although not all of these side effects may occur, if they do occur they may need medical attention.

Check with your doctor as soon as possible if any of the following side effects occur:
Rare
    Darkening of skin; drowsiness or tiredness; loss of appetite; mental depression; skin rash; vomiting

Other side effects may occur that usually do not need medical attention. These side effects may go away during treatment as your body adjusts to the medicine. However, check with your health care professional if any of the following side effects continue or are bothersome:
More common
    Diarrhea; stomach pain or cramps
Less common
    Aching muscles; belching or bloating; burning mouth or nose; dizziness or lightheadedness; fever; flushing; headache; increase in salivation; nausea; watery eyes

Other side effects not listed above may also occur in some patients. If you notice any other effects, check with your doctor.

Revised: 10/16/2000

TRIMETREXATE   Systemic

Commonly used brand name(s):
In the U.S.—
    Neutrexin
In Canada—
    Neutrexin

Description

Trimetrexate (tri-me-TREX-ate) is used, together with leucovorin (loo-koe-VOR-in), to treat *Pneumocystis carinii* (noo-moe-SISS-tis) pneumonia (PCP), a very serious kind of pneumonia. This kind of pneumonia occurs commonly in patients whose immune system is not working normally, such as cancer patients, transplant patients, and patients with acquired immune deficiency syndrome (AIDS).

Trimetrexate may cause some serious, even life-threatening, side effects. To prevent these effects, *you must take another medicine, leucovorin, together with trimetrexate* and for 3 days after you stop receiving trimetrexate. Before you begin treatment with trimetrexate, you and your doctor should talk about the good this medicine will do as well as the risks of using it.

Trimetrexate is to be administered only by or under the immediate supervision of your doctor. It is available in the following dosage form:
Parenteral
    • Injection (U.S. and Canada)

Before Receiving This Medicine

In deciding to use a medicine, the risks of using the medicine must be weighed against the good it will do. This is a decision you and your doctor will make. For trimetrexate, the following should be considered:

Allergies—Tell your doctor if you have ever had any unusual or allergic reaction to trimetrexate, methotrexate, or leucovorin. Also tell your health care professional if you are allergic to any other substances, such as foods, preservatives, or dyes.

Pregnancy—Use of trimetrexate during pregnancy should be avoided whenever possible since trimetrexate has caused birth defects and death of the fetus in animal studies. The use of birth control is recommended during trimetrexate therapy. Tell your doctor immediately if you think you may be pregnant or if you need advice about birth control.

Breast-feeding—It is not known if trimetrexate passes into breast milk. However, breast-feeding should be stopped during treatment with this medicine because trimetrexate may cause serious unwanted effects in nursing babies.

Children—This medicine has been tested in a limited number of children younger than 18 years of age. Trimetrexate can cause serious side effects in any patient. However, in effective doses, this medicine did not cause different side effects or problems in the few children who received it than it does in adults.

Older adults—Many medicines have not been studied specifically in older people. Therefore, it may not be known whether they work exactly the same way they do in younger adults or if they cause different side effects or problems in older people. There is no specific information comparing use of trimetrexate in the elderly with use in other age groups.

Other medicines—Although certain medicines should not be used together at all, in other cases two different medicines may be used together even if an interaction might occur. In these cases, your doctor may want to change the dose, or other precautions may be necessary. When you are taking trimetrexate, it is especially important that your health care professional know if you are taking any of the following:

- Acetaminophen (e.g., Tylenol) (with long-term, high-dose use) or
- Amiodarone (e.g., Cordarone) or
- Anabolic steroids (nandrolone [e.g., Anabolin], oxandrolone [e.g., Anavar], oxymetholone [e.g., Anadrol], stanozolol [e.g., Winstrol]) or
- Androgens (male hormones) or
- Carbamazepine (e.g., Tegretol) or
- Chloroquine (e.g., Aralen) or
- Dantrolene (e.g., Dantrium) or
- Daunorubicin (e.g., Cerubidine) or
- Estrogens (female hormones) or
- Etretinate (e.g., Tegison) or
- Hydroxychloroquine (e.g., Plaquenil) or
- Methyldopa (e.g., Aldomet) or
- Naltrexone (e.g., Trexan) (with long-term, high-dose use) or
- Phenothiazines (acetophenazine [e.g., Tindal], chlorpromazine [e.g., Thorazine], fluphenazine [e.g., Prolixin], mesoridazine [e.g., Serentil], perphenazine [e.g., Trilafon], prochlorperazine [e.g., Compazine], promazine [e.g., Sparine], promethazine [e.g., Phenergan], thioridazine [e.g., Mellaril], trifluoperazine [e.g., Stelazine], triflupromazine [e.g., Vesprin], trimeprazine [e.g., Temaril]) or
- Phenytoin (e.g., Dilantin)—Use of these medicines while you are taking trimetrexate may decrease the breakdown of trimetrexate in the liver and increase the chance of trimetrexate side effects

- Alcohol or
- Cimetidine (e.g., Tagamet) or
- Diltiazem (e.g., Cardizem) or
- Erythromycins (medicine for infection) or
- Isoniazid (e.g., INH, Nydrazid) or
- Quinine (e.g., Quinamm) or
- Ranitidine (e.g., Zantac) or
- Verapamil (e.g., Calan)—Use of these medicines with trimetrexate may increase the chance of trimetrexate side effects

- Amphotericin B by injection (e.g., Fungizone) or
- Antineoplastics (cancer medicine) or
- Azathioprine (e.g., Imuran) or
- Colchicine or
- Cyclophosphamide (e.g., Cytoxan) or
- Flucytosine (e.g., Ancobon) or
- Ganciclovir (e.g., Cytovene) or
- Interferon (e.g., Intron A, Roferon-A) or
- Zidovudine (e.g., AZT, Retrovir)—Receiving trimetrexate while you are using these medicines may make side effects affecting the blood worse

- Cisplatin (e.g., Platinol) or
- Combination pain medicine containing acetaminophen and aspirin (e.g., Excedrin) or other salicylates (with large amounts taken regularly) or
- Cyclosporine (e.g., Sandimmune) or
- Deferoxamine (e.g., Desferal) (with long-term use) or
- Foscarnet (e.g., Foscavir) or
- Inflammation or pain medicine (except narcotics) or
- Lithium (e.g., Lithane) or
- Penicillamine (e.g., Cuprimine) or
- Streptozocin (e.g., Zanosar) or
- Tiopronin (e.g., Thiola)—Use of these medicines while you are taking trimetrexate may decrease the elimination of trimetrexate through the kidneys and increase the chance of trimetrexate toxicity

- Antithyroid agents (medicine for overactive thyroid) or
- Carmustine (e.g., BiCNU) or
- Chloramphenicol (e.g., Chloromycetin) or
- Disulfiram (e.g., Antabuse) or
- Divalproex (e.g., Depakote) or
- Gold salts (medicine for arthritis) or
- Mercaptopurine (e.g., Purinethol) or
- Methotrexate (e.g., Mexate) or
- Oral contraceptives (birth control pills) containing estrogen or
- Other anti-infectives (medicine for infection) by mouth or by injection or
- Plicamycin (e.g., Mithracin) or
- Valproic acid (e.g., Depakene)—Use of these medicines with trimetrexate may increase the chance of side effects from trimetrexate

Other medical problems—The presence of other medical problems may affect the use of trimetrexate. Make sure you tell your doctor if you have any other medical problems, especially:

- Anemia or
- Low platelet count or
- Low white blood cell count—Trimetrexate may make any blood diseases that you have worse

- Kidney disease or
- Liver disease—Kidney or liver disease may increase the chance of side effects from trimetrexate

---

Proper Use of This Medicine

When you take *leucovorin:*

- *Leucovorin must be taken with trimetrexate* to help prevent very serious, possibly life-threatening, unwanted side effects. Leucovorin should be taken during trimetrexate treatment and for 3 days after trimetrexate is stopped.
- *Take oral leucovorin exactly as directed by your doctor.* Do not take more of it, do not take it more often, and do not take it for a longer time than your doctor ordered. Also, do not stop taking this medicine without checking with your doctor first.
- Oral leucovorin works best when there is a constant amount in the blood. *To help keep the amount constant, do not miss any doses.* If you need help in planning the best times to take your medicine, check with your health care professional.
- If you vomit shortly after taking an oral dose of leucovorin, check with your doctor. You will be told whether to take the dose again or to wait until the next scheduled dose.

Dosing—The doses of trimetrexate and of leucovorin will be different for different patients. *Follow your doctor's orders or the directions on the label.* The following information includes only the average doses of trimetrexate and leucovorin. *If your doses are different, do not change them* unless your doctor tells you to do so.

For trimetrexate
- For the treatment of *Pneumocystis carinii* pneumonia:
  —For *injection* dosage form:
    - Adults—45 milligrams per square meter of body surface area (mg/m²) injected into a vein once a day for twenty-one days. Your doctor will check your blood counts and may change your dose based on these counts.
    - Children and teenagers—Use and dose must be determined by your doctor.

For leucovorin
- For the prevention of serious side effects of trimetrexate in the treatment of *Pneumocystis carinii* pneumonia:
  —For the *oral or injection* dosage forms:
    - Adults—20 milligrams per square meter of body surface area (mg/m²) taken by mouth or injected into a vein every six hours for twenty-four days. Your doctor will check your blood counts and may change your dose based on these counts.
    - Children and teenagers—Use and dose must be determined by your doctor.

Missed dose—If you miss a dose of leucovorin, take it as soon as possible. This will help to keep a constant amount of medicine in the blood. However, if it is almost time for your next dose, skip the missed dose and go back to your regular dosing schedule. Do not double doses.

Storage—To store leucovorin:
- Keep out of the reach of children.
- Store away from heat and direct light.
- Do not store in the bathroom, near the kitchen sink, or in other damp places. Heat or moisture may cause the medicine to break down.
- Do not keep outdated medicine or medicine no longer needed. Be sure that any discarded medicine is out of the reach of children.

Precautions While Receiving This Medicine

If your symptoms do not improve within a few days, or if they become worse, check with your doctor.

It is very important that your doctor check your progress at regular visits to make sure that this medicine is working properly and to check for unwanted effects.

Trimetrexate can lower the number of white blood cells in your blood temporarily, increasing your chance of getting an infection. It can also lower the number of platelets, which are necessary for proper blood clotting. If this occurs, there are certain precautions you can take, especially when your blood count is low, to reduce the risk of infection or bleeding:
- If you can, avoid people with infections. *Check with your doctor immediately* if you think you are getting an infection or if you get a fever or chills, cough or hoarseness, lower back or side pain, or painful or difficult urination.
- *Check with your doctor immediately* if you notice any unusual bleeding or bruising; black, tarry stools; blood in urine or stools; or pinpoint red spots on your skin.

- Be careful when using a regular toothbrush, dental floss, or toothpick. Your medical doctor, dentist, or nurse may recommend other ways to clean your teeth and gums. Check with your medical doctor before having any dental work done.
- Be careful not to cut yourself when you are using sharp objects such as a safety razor or fingernail or toenail cutters.

Side Effects of This Medicine

Along with its needed effects, a medicine may cause some unwanted effects. Although not all of these side effects may occur, if they do occur they may need medical attention.

Check with your doctor immediately if any of the following side effects occur:
More common
    Fever and sore throat
Less common
    Black, tarry stools; blood in urine or stools; fever; mouth sores or ulcers; pinpoint red spots on skin; skin rash and itching; unusual bleeding or bruising; unusual tiredness or weakness

Other side effects may occur that usually do not need medical attention. These side effects may go away during treatment as your body adjusts to the medicine. However, check with your doctor if any of the following side effects continue or are bothersome:
Less common
    Confusion; nausea and vomiting; stomach pain

Other side effects not listed above may also occur in some patients. If you notice any other effects, check with your doctor.

Additional Information

Once a medicine has been approved for marketing for a certain use, experience may show that it is also useful for other medical problems. Although this use is not included in product labeling, trimetrexate is used in certain patients with the following medical condition:
- Cancer of the colon

Other than the above information, there is no additional information relating to proper use, precautions, or side effects for this use.

Revised: 03/16/99

TRIPTORELIN Systemic—INTRODUCTORY VERSION

Commonly used brand name(s):

In the U.S.—
    Trelstar Depot

Description

Triptorelin (TRIP-toe-rel-in) is similar to a hormone normally released from the hypothalamus gland.

When given regularly to men, triptorelin decreases testosterone levels. Reducing the amount of testosterone in the body is one way of treating cancer of the prostate.

Triptorelin is to be given only under the supervision of your doctor. It is to be injected into a muscle and is available in the following dosage form:

Parenteral
- Injection (U.S.)

Before Using This Medicine

In deciding to use a medicine, the risks of taking the medicine must be weighed against the good it will do. This is a decision you and your doctor will make. For triptorelin, the following should be considered:

Allergies—Tell your doctor if you have ever had any unusual or allergic reaction to triptorelin, other luteinizing hormone releasing hormone (LHRH) products or LHRH itself. Also tell your health care provider if you are allergic to any other substances, such as preservatives.

Pregnancy—Triptorelin use is not recommended during pregnancy. In animals, it has been shown to cause harm to the fetus or problems in the mother. Be sure you have discussed this with your doctor.

Breast-feeding—It is not known whether triptorelin passes into breast milk. However, triptorelin is not recommended during breast-feeding, because it may cause unwanted effects in nursing babies.

Children—Studies on this medicine have been done only in adult patients, and there is no specific information comparing use of triptorelin in children with use in other age groups.

Older adults—Many medicines have not been tested in older people. Therefore, it may not be known whether they work exactly the same way they do in younger adults. Although there is no specific information comparing use of triptorelin in the elderly with use in other age groups, it has been used mostly in elderly patients and is not expected to cause different side effects or problems in older people than it does in younger adults.

Other medicines—Although certain medicines should not be used together at all, in other cases two different medicines may be used together even if an interaction might occur. In these cases, your doctor may want to change the dose, or other precautions may be necessary. Tell your health care professional if you are taking any other prescription or nonprescription (over-the-counter [OTC]) medicine.

Other medical problems—The presence of other medical problems may affect the use of triptorelin. Make sure you tell your doctor if you have any other medical problems, especially:
- Cancer that has spread to the backbone or
- Problems in passing urine—Conditions may get worse for a short time after treatment with triptorelin is started

Proper Use of This Medicine

Triptorelin sometimes causes unwanted effects such as hot flashes or decreased sexual ability. It may also cause a temporary increase in pain or difficulty in urinating. However, it is very important that you continue to use the medicine. *Do not stop using this medicine without first checking with your doctor.*

Dosing—The dose of triptorelin will be different for different patients. *Follow your doctor's orders or the directions on the label.* The following information includes only the average doses of triptorelin. *If your dose is different, do not change it* unless your doctor tells you to do so.
- For *long-acting (1-month)* injection dosage forms:
  —For *cancer of the prostate:*
    - Adults—3.75 milligrams (mg) injected into a muscle once a month.

Missed dose—If you miss a dose of this medicine, receive it as soon as possible and then go back to your regular dosing schedule.

Storage—To store this medicine:
- Keep out of the reach of children.
- Store away from heat and direct light.
- Keep the medicine from freezing.
- Do not keep outdated medicine or medicine no longer needed. Dispose of used syringes properly in the container provided. Be sure that any discarded medicine is out of the reach of children.

Precautions While Using This Medicine

It is very important that your doctor check your progress at regular visits to make sure that this medicine is working properly and to check for unwanted effects.

Side Effects of This Medicine

Along with its needed effects, a medicine may cause some unwanted effects. Although not all of these side effects may occur, if they do occur they may need medical attention.

Check with your doctor as soon as possible if any of the following side effects occur:
Less common
    Bladder pain; bloody or cloudy urine; decrease in urine volume or frequency of urination; difficulty in passing urine; frequent urge to urinate; high blood pressure; lower back or side pain; painful urination; pale skin; troubled breathing; unusual bleeding or bruising; unusual tiredness or weakness

Other side effects may occur that usually do not need medical attention. These side effects may go away during treatment as your body adjusts to the medicine. However, check with your doctor if any of the following side effects continue or are bothersome.
More common
    Decreased interest in sexual intercourse; feeling of warmth or redness of the face, neck, arms and occasionally, upper chest; headache; inability to have or keep an erection; loss in sexual ability, desire, drive, or performance; sudden sweating

Less common
    Crying; diarrhea; dizziness; injection site pain; itching; leg pain; mental depression; paranoia; rapidly changing moods; trouble sleeping or getting to sleep; vomiting

Other side effects not listed above may also occur in some patients. If you notice any other effects, check with your doctor.

Developed: 11/10/2000

TROGLITAZONE Systemic—INTRODUCTORY VERSION

Description

Troglitazone (TROE-glit-a-zone) is used to treat a certain type of diabetes mellitus (sugar diabetes) called type 2 diabetes. It may be used with insulin, or with a type of oral diabetes medicine called a sulfonylurea, or with a sulfonylurea and metformin.

This medicine was withdrawn from the U.S. market in March 2000.

Before Using This Medicine

In deciding to use a medicine, the risks of taking the medicine must be weighed against the good it will do. This is a decision you and your doctor will make. For troglitazone, the following should be considered:

Allergies—Tell your doctor if you have ever had any unusual or allergic reaction to troglitazone. Also tell your health care professional if you are allergic to any other substances, such as foods, preservatives, or dyes.

Pregnancy—Troglitazone has not been studied in pregnant women. However, it is easier during pregnancy to control your blood sugar by using injections of insulin, rather than by taking troglitazone. Close control of your blood sugar can reduce the chance of your baby gaining too much weight, having birth defects, or having high blood sugar before birth. Be sure to tell your doctor if you plan to become pregnant or you think you are pregnant.

Breast-feeding—It is not known whether troglitazone passes into the breast milk of humans. However, troglitazone is not recommended during breast-feeding.

Children—Studies on this medicine have been done only in adult patients, and there is no specific information comparing use of troglitazone in children with use in other age groups.

Older adults—This medicine has been tested in a limited number of patients 65 years of age or older and has not been shown to cause different side effects or problems in older people than it does in younger adults.

Other medicines—Although certain medicines should not be used together at all, in other cases two different medicines may be used together even if an interaction might occur. In these cases, your doctor may want to change the dose, or other precautions may be necessary. When you are taking troglitazone, it is especially important that your health care professional know if you are taking any of the following:

- Cholestyramine (e.g., Questran)—Use of this medicine with troglitazone may decrease the effects of troglitazone; these medicines should not be used together
- Oral contraceptives (birth control pills) containing estrogen or norethindrone—Use of troglitazone with oral contraceptives may prevent oral contraceptives from working properly, increasing the chance of pregnancy
- Terfenadine (e.g., Seldane)—Use of troglitazone with terfenadine may decrease the effects of terfenadine; these medicines should not be used together

Other medical problems—The presence of other medical problems may affect the use of troglitazone. Make sure you tell your doctor if you have any other medical problems, especially:

- Diabetic ketoacidosis (ketones in the blood) or
- Type 1 diabetes—Insulin is needed to control these conditions

- Heart disease or
- Liver disease—Troglitazone may make these conditions worse

Proper Use of This Medicine

Follow carefully the special meal plan your doctor gave you. This is the most important part of controlling your condition, and is necessary if the medicine is to work properly. Also, exercise regularly and test for sugar in your blood or urine as directed.

This medicine should be taken with a meal.

Dosing—The dose of troglitazone will be different for different patients. *Follow your doctor's orders or the directions on the label.* The following information includes only the average doses of troglitazone. *If your dose is different, do not change it* unless your doctor tells you to do so.

- For *oral* dosage form (tablets):
  - For type 2 diabetes:
    - Troglitazone with insulin:
      - Adults: At first, the dose is 200 mg once a day with a meal. After two to four weeks, the dose may be increased to 400 mg once a day with a meal.
      - Children: Use and dose must be determined by your doctor.
    - Troglitazone with a sulfonylurea:
      - Adults: At first, the dose is 200 mg once a day with a meal. After two to four weeks the dose may be increased, if needed.
      - Children: Use and dose must be determined by your doctor.
    - Troglitazone with a sulfonylurea and metformin:
      - Adults: The dose is 400 mg once a day with a meal.
      - Children: Use and dose must be determined by your doctor.

Missed dose—If you miss a dose of this medicine, and you remember it the same day, take it with the next meal. However, if you do not remember it until the next day, skip the missed dose and go back to your regular dosing schedule. Do not double doses.

Storage—To store this medicine:

- Keep out of the reach of children.
- Store away from heat and direct light.
- Do not store in the bathroom, near the kitchen sink, or in other damp places. Heat or moisture may cause the medicine to break down.
- Do not keep outdated medicine or medicine no longer needed. Be sure that any discarded medicine is out of the reach of children.

Precautions While Using This Medicine

If you experience abdominal or stomach pain, dark urine, loss of appetite, nausea or vomiting, unusual tiredness or weakness, or yellow eyes or skin, check with your doctor immediately. These may be symptoms of liver problems.

Your doctor will want to check your progress at regular visits, especially during the first year you take this medicine. *Your doctor will need to check on a regular basis to make sure your liver is working properly.*

It is very important to follow carefully any instructions from your health care team about:

- Alcohol—Drinking alcohol may cause severe low blood sugar. Discuss this with your health care team.
- Other medicines—Do not take other medicines during the time you are taking troglitazone unless they have been discussed with your doctor. This especially includes nonprescription medicines such as aspirin, and medicines for appetite control, asthma, colds, cough, hay fever, or sinus problems.
- Counseling—Other family members need to learn how to prevent side effects or help with side effects if they occur. Also, diabetic patients may need special counseling about diabetes medicine dosing changes that might occur because of lifestyle changes, such as changes in exercise and diet. Furthermore, counseling on contraception and pregnancy may be needed because of the problems that can occur in patients with diabetes during pregnancy.
- Travel—Keep a recent prescription and your medical history with you. Be prepared for an emergency as you would normally. Make allowances for changing time zones and keep your meal times as close as possible to your usual meal times.

In case of emergency—There may be a time when you need emergency help for a problem caused by your diabetes. You need to be prepared for these emergencies. It is a good idea to wear a medical identification (ID) bracelet or neck chain at all times. Also, carry an ID card in your wallet or purse that says that you have diabetes and a list of all of your medicines.

This medicine does not cause hypoglycemia (low blood sugar). However, low blood sugar can occur when troglitazone is taken with other medicines, such as insulin or sulfonylureas, that can lower blood sugar. Low blood sugar can also occur if you delay or miss a meal or snack, exercise more than usual, drink alcohol, or cannot eat because of nausea or vomiting.

Symptoms of low blood sugar include anxiety; behavior change similar to being drunk; blurred vision; cold sweats; confusion; cool, pale skin; difficulty in thinking; drowsiness; excessive hunger; fast heartbeat; headache (continuing); nausea; nervousness; nightmares; restless sleep; shakiness; slurred speech; or unusual tiredness or weakness.

If symptoms of low blood sugar occur, *eat glucose tablets or gel, corn syrup, honey, or sugar cubes; or drink fruit juice, nondiet soft drink, or sugar dissolved in water to relieve the symptoms.* Also, check your blood for low blood sugar. *Glucagon is used in emergency situations when severe symptoms such as seizures (convulsions) or unconsciousness occur.* Have a glucagon kit available, along with a syringe and needle, and know how to use it. Members of your family also should know how to use it.

Hyperglycemia (high blood sugar) may occur if you do not take enough or skip a dose of your antidiabetic medicine, overeat or do not follow your meal plan, have a fever or infection, or do not exercise as much as usual.

Symptoms of high blood sugar include blurred vision; drowsiness; dry mouth; flushed, dry skin; fruit-like breath odor; increased urination (frequency and amount); ketones in urine; loss of appetite; stomachache, nausea, or vomiting; tiredness; troubled breathing (rapid and deep); unconsciousness; or unusual thirst.

If symptoms of high blood sugar occur, *check your blood sugar level and then call your doctor for instructions.*

Side Effects of This Medicine

Along with its needed effects, a medicine may cause some unwanted effects. Although not all of these side effects may occur, if they do occur they may need medical attention.

Check with your doctor immediately if either of the following side effects occur:

Rare
Yellow eyes or skin

Check with your doctor as soon as possible if any of the following side effects occur:

More common
Back pain; infection; pain

Less common
Painful or increased urination; swelling of feet or lower legs

Other side effects may occur that usually do not need medical attention. These side effects may go away during treatment as your body adjusts to the medicine. However, check with your doctor if any of the following side effects continue or are bothersome:

More common
Dizziness; headache; nausea; unusual tiredness or weakness

Less common
Diarrhea; sore throat; stuffy nose

Other side effects not listed above may also occur in some patients. If you notice any other effects, check with your doctor.

Developed: 02/18/1998
Revised: 10/16/2000

TROVAFLOXACIN   Systemic

Commonly used brand name(s):

In the U.S.—
Trovan

This information applies to the following medicines
1. Alatrofloxacin (a-lat-roe-FLOX-a-sin)
2. Trovafloxacin (TRO-va-flox-a-sin)

Description

Alatrofloxacin and trovafloxacin are used to treat very serious bacterial infections in many different parts of the body. They work by killing bacteria or preventing their growth. However, these medicines will not work for colds, flu, or other virus infections.

Liver failure has been reported rarely with the use of alatrofloxacin and trovafloxacin. Because of the risk of liver problems, these medicines are used only to treat serious bacterial infections, such as those that are life-threatening or when there is a risk of losing a limb. Because of this, treatment usually is started in the hospital or in another in-patient health care facility.

These medicines are available only with your doctor's prescription, in the following dosage forms:

Oral
Trovafloxacin
- Tablets (U.S.)

Parenteral
Alatrofloxacin
- Injection (U.S.)

Before Using This Medicine

In deciding to use a medicine, the risks of taking the medicine must be weighed against the good it will do. This is a decision you and your doctor will make. For alatrofloxacin or trovafloxacin, the following should be considered:

Allergies—Tell your doctor if you have ever had any unusual or allergic reaction to alatrofloxacin, trovafloxacin, any of the fluoroquinolones, or any related medicines, such as cinoxacin (e.g., Cinobac) or nalidixic acid (e.g., NegGram). Also tell your health care professional if you are allergic to any other substances, such as foods, preservatives, or dyes.

Pregnancy—Studies have not been done in humans. However, use is not recommended during pregnancy since alatrofloxacin and trovafloxacin have been reported to cause bone development problems in young animals.

Breast-feeding—Alatrofloxacin and trovafloxacin pass into breast milk. Since alatrofloxacin and trovafloxacin have been reported to cause bone development problems in young animals, breast-feeding is not recommended during treatment with either of these medicines.

Children—Use is not recommended for infants or children since alatrofloxacin and trovafloxacin have been shown to cause bone development problems in young animals.

Teenagers—Use is not recommended for teenagers up to 18 years of age since alatrofloxacin and trovafloxacin have been shown to cause bone development problems in young animals.

Older adults—Alatrofloxacin and trovafloxacin have been tested in and, in effective doses, have not been shown to cause different side effects or problems in older people than they do in younger adults.

Other medicines—Although certain medicines should not be used together at all, in other cases two different medicines may be used together even if an interaction might occur. In these cases, your doctor may want to change the dose, or other precautions may be necessary. When you are taking alatrofloxacin or trovafloxacin, it is especially important that your health care professional know if you are taking any of the following:

- Antacids that contain aluminum or magnesium or
- Citric acid buffered with sodium citrate (e.g., Bicitra) or
- Iron supplements or other vitamins or
- Morphine (injection dosage form) or
- Sucralfate—Antacids, citric acid buffered with sodium citrate, iron or vitamins, intravenous morphine, or sucralfate may keep trovafloxacin tablets from working properly

Other medical problems—The presence of other medical problems may affect the use of alatrofloxacin or trovafloxacin. Make sure you tell your doctor if you have any other medical problems, especially:

- Brain or spinal cord disease, including hardening of the arteries in the brain, or epilepsy or other problems that may cause seizures—Alatrofloxacin or trovafloxacin may cause nervous system side effects

- Liver disease—Patients with liver disease may have an increased chance of side effects

Proper Use of This Medicine

Do not take alatrofloxacin or trovafloxacin if you are pregnant. Do not give alatrofloxacin or trovafloxacin to infants, children, or teenagers unless otherwise specified by your doctor. These medicines have been shown to cause bone development problems in young animals.

Trovafloxacin tablets may be taken with or without meals.

If you are taking alatrofloxacin injection, use it exactly as directed by your doctor. If you have any questions, ask your health care professional.

To help clear up your infection completely, *keep taking alatrofloxacin or trovafloxacin for the full time of treatment*, even if you begin to feel better after a few days. If you stop taking this medicine too soon, your symptoms may return.

Alatrofloxacin and trovafloxacin work best when there is a constant amount in the blood or urine. *To help keep the amount constant, do not miss any doses. Also, it is best to take the doses at evenly spaced times, day and night.* For example, if you are to take one dose a day, that dose should be taken about the same time every day. If this interferes with your sleep or other daily activities, or if you need help in planning the best time to take your medicine, check with your health care professional.

Dosing—The doses of alatrofloxacin or trovafloxacin will be different for different patients. *Follow your doctor's orders or the directions on the label.* The following information includes only the average doses of these medicines. Your dose may be different if you have liver disease. *If your dose is different, do not change it* unless your doctor tells you to do so.

If you are taking trovafloxacin tablets, the number of tablets that you take depends on the strength of the medicine. Also, *the number of doses you take each day, the time allowed between doses, and the length of time you take the medicine depend on the medical problem for which you are taking trovafloxacin.* In general, the Food and Drug Administration (FDA) recommends that treatment with trovafloxacin not go beyond 14 days. Longer treatment may increase the chance of liver problems.

- For *oral* dosage form (trovafloxacin tablets):
  —For treatment of bacterial infections:
  - Adults—100 or 200 milligrams (mg) once every twenty-four hours for three days to several weeks, depending on the medical problem being treated. Gonorrhea is treated with a single oral dose of 100 mg.
  - Children up to 18 years of age—This medicine is not recommended for infants, children, or teenagers.

—For prevention of infection in surgical patients:
- Adults—200 milligrams one-half to four hours before the start of surgery.
- Children up to 18 years of age—This medicine is not recommended for infants, children, or teenagers.
- For *injection* dosage form (alatrofloxacin injection):
  —For treatment of bacterial infections:
  - Adults—200 to 300 milligrams (mg) injected slowly into a vein over a period of sixty minutes, once every twenty-four hours for up to fourteen days, depending on the medical problem being treated.
  - Children up to 18 years of age—This medicine is not recommended for infants, children, or teenagers.
  —For prevention of infection in surgical patients:
  - Adults—200 milligrams injected slowly into a vein over a period of sixty minutes, one half to four hours before the start of surgery.
  - Children up to 18 years of age—This medicine is not recommended for infants, children, or teenagers.

Missed dose—If you are taking trovafloxacin tablets and you miss a dose of this medicine, take it as soon as possible if remembered the same day. This will help to keep a constant amount of medicine in the blood or urine. However, if you do miss a dose on one day, skip the missed dose and go back to your regular dosing schedule. Do not double doses.

Storage—To store this medicine:
- Keep out of the reach of children.
- Store away from heat and direct light.
- Do not store in the bathroom, near the kitchen sink, or in other damp places. Heat or moisture may cause the medicine to break down.
- Do not keep outdated medicine or medicine no longer needed. Be sure that any discarded medicine is out of the reach of children.

Precautions While Using This Medicine

Alatrofloxacin and trovafloxacin may cause liver problems, including liver failure, at any time during treatment in a small number of people who are treated with these medicines. *Check with your doctor immediately if you notice that your urine has become dark or your skin or eyes are yellow in color or if you experience loss of appetite, nausea or vomiting, severe abdominal pain, or unusual tiredness or weakness.* These may be possible signs or symptoms of a liver problem.

If you are taking aluminum- or magnesium-containing antacids, citric acid buffered with sodium citrate (e.g., Bicitra), iron supplements or vitamins, intravenous morphine, or sucralfate, do not take them at the same time that you take trovafloxacin tablets. It is best to take these medicines at least 2 hours before or 2 hours after taking trovafloxacin. These medicines may keep trovafloxacin tablets from working properly.

Some people who take alatrofloxacin or trovafloxacin may become more sensitive to sunlight than they are normally. Exposure to sunlight, even for brief periods of time, may cause severe sunburn or skin rash, redness, itching, or discoloration. When you begin taking this medicine:

Stay out of direct sunlight, especially between the hours of 10:00 a.m. and 3:00 p.m., if possible.

Apply a sun block product that has a skin protection factor (SPF) of at least 15. Some patients may require a product with a higher SPF number, especially if they have a fair complexion. If you have any questions about this, check with your health care professional.

Do not use a sunlamp or tanning bed or booth.

If you have a severe reaction from the sun, check with your doctor.

Alatrofloxacin or trovafloxacin may cause some people to become dizzy, lightheaded, or less alert than they are normally. *Make sure you know how you react to this medicine before you drive, use machines, or do anything else that could be dangerous if you are dizzy or are not alert.* If these reactions are especially bothersome, check with your doctor.

Side Effects of This Medicine

Along with its needed effects, a medicine may cause some unwanted effects. Although not all of these side effects may occur, if they do occur they may need medical attention.

Check with your doctor as soon as possible if any of the following side effects occur:

Rare

Abdominal or stomach cramps and pain (severe); abdominal tenderness; agitation; confusion; dark urine; diarrhea (watery and severe, which may also be bloody); difficulty in breathing or swallowing; fever; hallucinations (seeing, hearing, or feeling things that are not there); loss of appetite; nausea or vomiting; pain at place of injection; pain in calves that spreads to heels; rapid heartbeat; shakiness or tremors; shortness of breath; skin rash, itching, or redness; swelling of face, throat, or tongue; swelling of calves or lower legs; unusual tiredness or weakness; yellow eyes or skin

Note: Some of the above side effects may also occur up to several weeks after you stop taking this medicine.

Other side effects may occur that usually do not need medical attention. These side effects may go away during treatment as your body adjusts to the medicine. However, check with your doctor if any of the following side effects continue or are bothersome:

More common

Diarrhea (mild); dizziness or lightheadedness; headache; vaginal pain and discharge

Less common or rare

Increased sensitivity of skin to sunlight

Other side effects not listed above may also occur in some patients. If you notice any other effects, check with your doctor.

Developed: 02/25/98
Interim revision: 06/10/99; 06/16/99

UNOPROSTONE Ophthalmic—
INTRODUCTORY VERSION

Commonly used brand name(s):

In the U.S.—
Rescula

Description

Unoprostone (yoo-noh-PROST-ohn) is used to treat increased pressure in the eye caused by open-angle glaucoma. It is also used to treat a condition called ocular hypertension (hypertension of the eye).

This medicine is available only with your doctor's prescription, in the following dosage form:

Ophthalmic
* Ophthalmic solution (eye drops) (U.S.)

Before Using This Medicine

In deciding to use a medicine, the risks of using the medicine must be weighed against the good it will do. This is a decision you and your doctor will make. For unoprostone, the following should be considered:

Allergies—Tell your doctor if you have ever had any unusual or allergic reaction to unoprostone. Also tell your health care professional if you are allergic to any other substances, such as benzalkonium chloride.

Pregnancy—Unoprostone has not been studied in pregnant women. However, studies in animals have shown that unoprostone given by injection causes increases in the number of miscarriages. Before using this medicine, make sure your doctor knows if you are pregnant or if you may become pregnant.

Breast-feeding—It is not known whether unoprostone passes into human breast milk. However, it has been shown to pass into the milk of nursing animals.

Children—Studies on this medicine have been done only in adult patients and there is no specific information comparing use of ophthalmic unoprostone in children with use in other age groups.

Older adults—This medicine has been tested and has not been shown to cause different side effects or problems in older people than it does in younger adults.

Proper Use of This Medicine

To use the eye drops:
* First, wash your hands. Tilt the head back and, pressing your finger gently on the skin just beneath the lower eyelid, pull the lower eyelid away from the eye to make a space. Drop the medicine into this space. Let go of the eyelid and gently close the eyes. Do not blink. Keep the eyes closed and apply pressure to the inner corner of the eye with your finger for 1 or 2 minutes to allow the medicine to be absorbed by the eye.
* To keep this medicine as germ-free as possible, do not touch the applicator tip to any surface (including the eye). Also, keep the container tightly closed.

Use this medicine only as directed. Do not use more of it and do not use it more often than your doctor ordered. To do so may increase the chance of too much medicine being absorbed into the body and the chance of side effects.

If you wear contact lenses: These eye drops contain a preservative that could be absorbed by the contact lenses. *Wait at least 15 minutes after putting these drops in before you put in your contact lenses.*

If your doctor ordered two different eye drops to be used together, wait at least 5 minutes between the times you apply the medicines.

Dosing—The dose of unoprostone will be different for different patients. *Follow your doctor's orders or the directions on the label.* The following information includes only the average doses of unoprostone. *If your dose is different, do not change it* unless your doctor tells you to do so.
* For *ophthalmic* dosage form (eye drops):
  —For glaucoma or hypertension of the eye:
  * Adults—Use one drop in the affected eye or eyes two times a day.
  * Children—Use and dose must be determined by your doctor.

Missed dose—If you miss a dose of this medicine, use it as soon as possible. However, if it is almost time for your next dose, skip the missed dose and go back to your regular dosing schedule. Do not double doses.

Storage—To store this medicine:
* Keep out of the reach of children.
* Store away from heat and direct light.
* Keep the medicine from freezing. Do not refrigerate.
* Do not keep outdated medicine or medicine no longer needed. Ask your health care professional how you should dispose of any medicine you do not use. Be sure that any discarded medicine is out of the reach of children.

Precautions While Using This Medicine

It is very important that your doctor check your progress at regular visits to make sure that this medicine is working and to check for unwanted effects.

Contact your doctor immediately if you are having eye surgery, you experience trauma to your eye, or you develop an eye infection to determine if you should continue to use your present container of eye drops.

This medicine may cause some people to have blurred vision for a short time. *Make sure you know how you react to this medicine before you drive, use machines, or do anything else that could be dangerous if you cannot see properly.*

Ophthalmic unoprostone may cause your eyes to become more sensitive to light than they are normally. Wearing sunglasses and avoiding too much exposure to bright light may help lessen the discomfort.

Side Effects of This Medicine

Along with its needed effects, a medicine may cause some unwanted effects. Although not all of these side effects may occur, if they do occur they may need medical attention.

Check with your doctor as soon as possible if any of the following side effects occur:
Less common
Blood in the whites of the eyes; blurred vision or eye pain; eye irritation or redness
Rare
Blindness; color blindness; decreased vision or other changes in vision

Other side effects may occur that usually do not need medical attention. These side effects may go away during treatment as your body adjusts to the medicine. However, check with your doctor if any of the following side effects continue or are bothersome:

More common
Abnormal tearing of eyes; burning or stinging of eyes; chills; cough; diarrhea; double vision; dry eyes; fever; general feeling of discomfort or illness; headache; itching of eyes; joint pain; loss of appetite; muscle aches and pains; nausea; runny nose; shivering; sore throat; sweating; trouble sleeping; unusual tiredness or weakness; vomiting

Less common or rare
Discharge from eye; inflammation of the eye; redness, pain, swelling of eye, eyelid, or inner lining of eyelid; sensitivity to light

Other side effects may occur that usually do not need medical attention. These side effects may go away during treatment as your body adjusts to the medicine. Also, your health care professional may be able to tell you about ways to prevent or reduce some of these side effects. Check with your health care professional if any of the following side effects continue or are bothersome or if you have any questions about them:

More common
Feeling of having something in the eye; increased or decreased length of eyelashes

Less common or rare
Change in the color of the iris or eyelid; increase in number of eyelashes; difficulty seeing at night; increased sensitivity of eyes to sunlight

Other side effects not listed above may also occur in some patients. If you notice any other effects, check with your doctor.

Developed: 10/10/2000

VALACYCLOVIR   Systemic

Commonly used brand name(s):

In the U.S.—
Valtrex

In Canada—
Valtrex

Description

Valacyclovir (val-ay-SYE-kloe-veer) is used to treat the symptoms of herpes zoster (also known as shingles), a herpes virus infection of the skin; it is also used to treat and prevent genital herpes infections. In your body, valacyclovir becomes the anti-herpes medicine, acyclovir. Although valacyclovir will not cure shingles or genital herpes, it does help relieve the pain and discomfort and helps the sores heal faster.

Valacyclovir is available only with your doctor's prescription, in the following dosage form:

Oral
• Tablets (U.S. and Canada)

Before Using This Medicine

In deciding to use a medicine, the risks of taking the medicine must be weighed against the good it will do. This is a decision you and your doctor will make. For valacyclovir, the following should be considered:

Allergies—Tell your doctor if you have ever had any unusual or allergic reaction to valacyclovir or acyclovir. Also tell your health care professional if you are allergic to any other substances, such as foods, sulfites or other preservatives, or dyes.

Pregnancy—Adequate and well-controlled studies in humans have not been done with valacyclovir or acyclovir. However, acyclovir has been used in pregnant women and has not been reported to cause birth defects or other problems.

Breast-feeding—It is not known whether valacyclovir passes into breast milk. However, acyclovir does pass into breast milk but has not been reported to cause problems in nursing babies.

Children—Studies on this medicine have been done only in adult patients. There is no specific information comparing use of valacyclovir in children with use in other age groups.

Older adults—Valacyclovir has been used in elderly patients and has not been shown to cause different side effects or problems in older people than it does in younger adults. Elderly patients are at a high risk for dehydration and should drink plenty of fluids.

Other medicines—Although certain medicines should not be used together at all, in other cases two different medicines may be used together even if an interaction might occur. In these cases, your doctor may want to change your dose or other precautions may be necessary. Tell your health care professional if you are taking any other prescription or nonprescription (over-the-counter [OTC]) medicine.

Other medical problems—The presence of other medical problems may affect the use of valacyclovir. Make sure you tell your doctor if you have any other medical problems, especially:

• Advanced human immunodeficiency virus (HIV) infection or
• Bone marrow transplantation or
• Kidney transplantation—Patients with these medical problems may have an increased risk of severe side effects

• Kidney disease—Kidney disease may increase blood levels of this medicine, increasing the chance of side effects

Proper Use of This Medicine

Valacyclovir works best *if it is used within 48 hours after the first symptoms of shingles or genital herpes* (for example, pain, burning, or blisters) *begin to appear.* For recurrent outbreaks of genital herpes, valacyclovir works best if it is used within 24 hours after the symptoms begin to appear.

Valacyclovir may be taken with meals.

Keep taking valacyclovir for the full time of treatment, even if your symptoms begin to clear up after a few days. *Do not miss any doses.* However, *do not use this medicine more often or for a longer time than your doctor ordered.*

Dosing—The dose of valacyclovir will be different for different patients. *Follow your doctor's orders or the directions on the label.* The following information includes only the average doses of valacyclovir. Your dose may be different if you have kidney disease. *If your dose is different, do not change it* unless your doctor tells you to do so.

- For *oral* dosage form (tablets):
  - —For treatment of genital herpes, first outbreak:
    - Adults—1 gram two times a day for ten days.
    - Children—Use and dose must be determined by your doctor.
  - —For treatment of genital herpes, recurrent outbreaks:
    - Adults—500 milligrams (mg) two times a day for five days.
    - Children—Use and dose must be determined by your doctor.
  - —To prevent recurrent outbreaks of genital herpes:
    - Adults—500 mg or 1 gram once a day.
    - Children—Use and dose must be determined by your doctor.
  - —For treatment of shingles:
    - Adults—1 gram three times a day for seven days.
    - Children—Use and dose must be determined by your doctor.

Missed dose—If you miss a dose of this medicine, take it as soon as possible. However, if it is almost time for your next dose, skip the missed dose and go back to your regular dosing schedule. Do not double doses.

Storage—To store this medicine:
- Keep out of the reach of children.
- Store away from heat and direct light.
- Do not store the tablets in the bathroom, near the kitchen sink, or in other damp places. Heat or moisture may cause the medicine to break down.
- Do not keep outdated medicine or medicine no longer needed. Be sure that any discarded medicine is out of the reach of children.

Precautions While Using This Medicine

If your symptoms do not improve within a few days, or if they become worse, check with your doctor.

The areas affected by genital herpes or shingles should be kept as clean and dry as possible. Also, wear loose-fitting clothing to avoid irritating the sores (blisters).

Side Effects of This Medicine

Along with its needed effects, a medicine may cause some unwanted effects. Although not all of these side effects may occur, if they do they may need medical attention.

Check with your doctor as soon as possible if the following side effect occurs:

Less common
Painful menstruation, including abdominal cramps, diarrhea, or nausea

Rare
Black, tarry stools; chest pain; chills; cough; decreased frequency/output of urine; fever; flu-like symptoms; headache; lower back/side pain; reduced mental alertness; shortness of breath; unusual tiredness; yellow eyes or skin

Frequency not determined
Back, leg or stomach pains; changes in behavior, es-

pecially in interactions with other people; difficulty breathing or swallowing; fast, pounding, or irregular heartbeat; high blood pressure; itching; lightheadedness when getting up from a lying or sitting position; redness of skin; seeing, hearing, or feeling things that are not there; skin rash; swelling or puffiness of face, hands, legs, or feet; wheezing

Symptoms of overdose with intravenous acyclovir Because the information on valacyclovir overdose is limited, information on intravenous acyclovir overdose is provided. In the body, valacyclovir is converted into acyclovir.
Anxiety; convulsions (seizures); decrease in urine output; decreased frequency of urination; dry mouth; hallucinations (seeing, hearing, or feeling things that are not there); irritability; loss of consciousness; lower back/side pain; nervousness; restlessness-

Other side effects may occur that usually do not need medical attention. These side effects may go away during treatment as your body adjusts to the medicine. However, check with your doctor if any of these side effects continue or are bothersome:

More common
Headache; nausea

Less common
Constipation; diarrhea; dizziness; joint pain; loss of appetite; stomach pain; unusual tiredness or weakness; vomiting

Frequency not determined
Anxiety; dry mouth; irritability; mood or mental changes; nervousness; restlessness

Other side effects not listed above may also occur in some patients. If you notice any other effects, check with your doctor.

Developed: 05/28/96
Revised: 06/20/2000

VALPROIC ACID   Systemic

Commonly used brand name(s):

In the U.S.—
Depacon[2]
Depakene[3]
Depakote[1]
Depakote Sprinkle[1]

In Canada—
Alti-Valproic[3]
Depakene[3]
Deproic[3]
Dom-Valproic[3]
Epival[1]
Med Valproic[3]
Novo-Valproic[3]
Nu-Valproic[3]
Penta-Valproic[3]
pms-Valproic Acid[3]
pms-Valproic Acid E.C.[3]

Note: For quick reference, the following medicines are numbered to match the corresponding brand names.

This information applies to the following medicines:
1. Divalproex (dye-VAL-pro-ex)
2. Valproate Sodium (val-PRO-ate SO-dee-um) †
3. Valproic Acid (val-PRO-ic acid) ‡

---

†Not commercially available in Canada.
‡Generic name product may be available in the U.S.

Description

Valproic acid, valproate sodium, and divalproex belong to the group of medicines called anticonvulsants. They are used to control certain types of seizures in the treatment of epilepsy. Valproic acid, valproate sodium, and divalproex may be used alone or with other seizure medicine. Divalproex is also used to treat the manic phase of bipolar disorder (manic-depressive illness), and to help prevent migraine headaches.

Divalproex and valproate sodium form valproic acid in the body. Therefore, the following information applies to all of these medicines.

These medicines are available only with your doctor's prescription, in the following dosage forms:

Oral
Divalproex
- Delayed-release capsules (U.S.)
- Delayed-release tablets (U.S. and Canada)
Valproic Acid
- Capsules (U.S. and Canada)
- Syrup (U.S. and Canada)

Parenteral
Valproate Sodium
- Injection (U.S.)

Before Using This Medicine

In deciding to use a medicine, the risks of taking the medicine must be weighed against the good it will do. This is a decision you and your doctor will make. For valproic acid, valproate sodium, and divalproex, the following should be considered:

Allergies—Tell your doctor if you have ever had any unusual or allergic reaction to valproic acid, valproate sodium, or divalproex. Also tell your health care professional if you are allergic to any other substances, such as foods, preservatives, or dyes.

Pregnancy—Valproic acid, valproate sodium, and divalproex have been reported to cause birth defects when taken by the mother during the first 3 months of pregnancy. Also, animal studies have shown that valproic acid, valproate sodium, and divalproex cause birth defects when taken in doses several times greater than doses used in humans. However, these medicines may be necessary to control seizures in some pregnant patients. Be sure you have discussed this with your doctor.

Breast-feeding—Valproic acid, valproate sodium, and divalproex pass into the breast milk, but their effect on the nursing baby is not known. It may be necessary for you to take another medicine or to stop breast-feeding during treatment with valproic acid, valproate sodium, or divalproex. Be sure you have discussed the risks and benefits of this medicine with your doctor.

Children—Abdominal or stomach cramps, nausea or vomiting, tiredness or weakness, and yellow eyes or skin may be especially likely to occur in children, who are usually more sensitive to the effects of these medicines. Children up to 2 years of age, those taking more than one medicine for seizure control, and children with certain other medical problems may be more likely to develop serious side effects.

Older adults—Elderly people are especially sensitive to the effects of these medicines. This may increase the chance of side effects during treatment. The dose of this medicine may be lower for older adults.

Other medicines—Although certain medicines should not be used together at all, in other cases two different medicines may be used together even if an interaction might occur. In these cases, your doctor may want to change the dose, or other precautions may be necessary. When you are taking valproic acid, valproate sodium, or divalproex, it is especially important that your health care professional knows if you are taking any of the following:

- Acetaminophen (e.g., Tylenol) (with long-term, high-dose use) or
- Amiodarone (e.g., Cordarone) or
- Anabolic steroids (nandrolone [e.g., Anabolin], oxandrolone [e.g., Anavar], oxymetholone [e.g., Anadrol], stanozolol [e.g., Winstrol]) or
- Androgens (male hormones) or
- Barbiturates or
- Carbamazepine (e.g., Tegretol) or
- Carmustine (e.g., BiCNU) or
- Dantrolene (e.g., Dantrium) or
- Daunorubicin (e.g., Cerubidine) or
- Disulfiram (e.g., Antabuse) or
- Estrogens (female hormones) or
- Etretinate (e.g., Tegison) or
- Gold salts (medicine for arthritis) or
- Mercaptopurine (e.g., Purinethol) or
- Methotrexate (e.g., Mexate) or
- Methyldopa (e.g., Aldomet) or
- Naltrexone (e.g., Trexan) (with long-term, high-dose use) or
- Phenothiazines (acetophenazine [e.g., Tindal], chlorpromazine [e.g., Thorazine], fluphenazine [e.g., Prolixin], mesoridazine [e.g., Serentil], perphenazine [e.g., Trilafon], prochlorperazine [e.g., Compazine], promazine [e.g., Sparine], promethazine [e.g., Phenergan], thioridazine [e.g., Mellaril], trifluoperazine [e.g., Stelazine], triflupromazine [e.g., Vesprin], trimeprazine [e.g., Temaril]) or
- Plicamycin (e.g., Mithracin)—There is an increased risk of serious side effects to the liver

- Central nervous system (CNS) depressants (medicines that cause drowsiness) or
- Tricyclic antidepressants (medicine for depression)—There may be an increase in CNS depressant effects

- Carbenicillin by injection (e.g., Geopen) or
- Dipyridamole (e.g., Persantine) or
- Inflammation or pain medicine, except narcotics, or
- Pentoxifylline (e.g., Trental) or
- Sulfinpyrazone (e.g., Anturane) or
- Ticarcillin (e.g., Ticar)—Valproic acid, valproate sodium, or divalproex may increase the chance of bleeding because of decreased blood clotting ability; the potential of aspirin, medicine for inflammation or pain, or sulfinpyrazone to cause stomach ulcer and bleeding may also increase the chance of bleeding in patients taking valproic acid, valproate sodium, or divalproex

- Heparin—There is an increased risk of side effects that may cause bleeding

- Mefloquine—The amount of valproic acid, valproate sodium, or divalproex that you need to take may change

- Other anticonvulsants (medicine for seizures)—There is an increased risk of seizures or other unwanted effects

Other medical problems—The presence of other medical problems may affect the use of these medicines. Make

sure you tell your doctor if you have any other medical problems, especially:

- Blood disease or
- Brain disease or
- Kidney disease—There is an increased risk of serious side effects
- Liver disease—Valproic acid, valproate sodium, or divalproex may make the condition worse

Proper Use of This Medicine

For patients taking the *capsule form* of valproic acid:
- Swallow the capsule whole without chewing, crushing, or breaking. This is to prevent irritation of the mouth or throat.

For patients taking the *delayed-release capsule form* of divalproex:
- Swallow the capsule whole, or sprinkle the contents on a small amount of soft food, such as applesauce or pudding, and swallow without chewing.

For patients taking the *delayed-release tablet form* of divalproex:
- Swallow the tablet whole without chewing, breaking, or crushing. This is to prevent damage to the special coating that helps lessen irritation of the stomach.

For patients taking the *syrup form* of valproic acid:
- The syrup may be mixed with any liquid or added to food for a better taste.

For patients taking the oral dosage forms of valproic acid and divalproex:
- These medicines may be taken with meals or snacks to reduce stomach upset.

This medicine must be taken exactly as directed by your doctor to prevent seizures and lessen the possibility of side effects.

Dosing—The dose of valproic acid, valproate sodium, or divalproex will be different for different patients. *Follow your doctor's orders or the directions on the label.* The following information includes only the average doses of valproic acid, valproate sodium, or divalproex. *If your dose is different, do not change it* unless your doctor tells you to do so.

The number of capsules or tablets or teaspoonfuls of syrup that you take or the number of injections you receive depends on the strength of the medicine. Also, *the number of doses you take each day, the time allowed between doses, and the length of time you take the medicine depend on the medical problem for which you are using valproic acid, valproate sodium, or divalproex.*

- If valproic acid or divalproex is the only medicine you are taking for seizures:
  —Adults and adolescents: Dose is based on body weight. The usual dose is 5 to 15 milligrams (mg) per kilogram (kg) (2.3 to 6.9 mg per pound) of body weight to start. Your doctor may increase your dose gradually every week by 5 to 10 mg per kg of body weight if needed. However, the dose is usually not more than 60 mg per kg of body weight a day. If the total dose a day is greater than 250 mg, it is usually divided into smaller doses and taken two or more times during the day.
  —Children 1 to 12 years of age: Dose is based on body weight. The usual dose is 15 to 45 mg per kg (6.9

to 20.7 mg per pound) of body weight to start. The doctor may increase the dose gradually every week by 5 to 10 mg per kg of body weight if needed.

- If you are taking more than one medicine for seizures:
  —Adults and adolescents: Dose is based on body weight. The usual dose is 10 to 30 mg per kg (4.6 to 13.8 mg per pound) of body weight to start. Your doctor may increase your dose gradually every week by 5 to 10 mg per kg of body weight if needed. If the total dose a day is greater than 250 mg, it is usually divided into smaller doses and taken two or more times during the day.
  —Children 1 to 12 years of age: Dose is based on body weight. The usual dose is 30 to 100 mg per kg (13.8 to 45.5 mg per pound) of body weight.
- If you are using valproate sodium for seizures because you temporarily cannot take oral medication:
  —Adults, adolescents, and children: Dose is based on body weight, and will be determined by your doctor. The dose is injected into a vein.
- If you are taking divalproex for treatment of mania:
  —Adults: At first, 750 mg a day, usually divided into smaller doses and taken two or more times during the day. Your doctor may increase your dose if needed.
  —Children: Use and dose must be determined by your doctor.
- If you are taking divalproex for prevention of migraine headaches:
  —Adults: At first, 250 mg two times a day. Your doctor may increase your dose if needed. However, the dose is usually not more than 1000 mg a day.
  —Children: Use and dose must be determined by your doctor.

Missed dose—If you miss a dose of this medicine, and your dosing schedule is:

- One dose a day—Take the missed dose as soon as possible. However, if you do not remember until the next day, skip the missed dose and go back to your regular dosing schedule. Do not double doses.
- Two or more doses a day—If you remember within 6 hours of the missed dose, take it right away. Then take the rest of the doses for that day at equally spaced times. Do not double doses.

If you have any questions about this, check with your doctor.

Storage—To store this medicine:

- Keep out of the reach of children.
- Store away from heat and direct light.
- Do not store the capsule or tablet form of this medicine in the bathroom, near the kitchen sink, or in other damp places. Heat or moisture may cause the medicine to break down.
- Keep the syrup form of this medicine from freezing.
- Do not keep outdated medicine or medicine no longer needed. Be sure that any discarded medicine is out of the reach of children.

Precautions While Using This Medicine

Your doctor should check your progress at regular visits, especially for the first few months that you take this medicine. This is necessary to allow dose adjustments and to reduce any unwanted effects.

Do not stop taking this medicine without first checking with your doctor. Your doctor may want you to gradually reduce the amount you are taking before stopping completely.

Before you have any medical tests, tell the doctor in charge that you are taking this medicine. The results of the metyrapone and thyroid function tests may be affected by this medicine.

Before having any kind of surgery, dental treatment, or emergency treatment, tell the medical doctor or dentist in charge that you are taking this medicine. Valproic acid, valproate sodium, or divalproex may change the time it takes your blood to clot, which may increase the chance of bleeding. Also, taking valproic acid, valproate sodium, or divalproex together with medicines that are used during surgery or dental or emergency treatments may increase the CNS depressant effects.

Valproic acid, valproate sodium, and divalproex will add to the effects of alcohol and other CNS depressants (medicines that make you drowsy or less alert). Some examples of CNS depressants are antihistamines or medicine for hay fever, other allergies, or colds; sedatives, tranquilizers, or sleeping medicine; prescription pain medicine or narcotics; barbiturates; medicine for seizures; muscle relaxants; or anesthetics, including some dental anesthetics. *Check with your doctor before taking any of the above while you are using this medicine.*

For diabetic patients:
- This medicine may interfere with urine tests for ketones and give false-positive results.

Your doctor may want you to carry a medical identification card or bracelet stating that you are taking this medicine.

This medicine may cause some people to become drowsy or less alert than they are normally. *Make sure you know how you react to this medicine before you drive, use machines, or do anything else that could be dangerous if you are drowsy or not alert.*

Side Effects of This Medicine

Along with its needed effects, a medicine may cause some unwanted effects. Although not all of these side effects may occur, if they do occur they may need medical attention.

Check with your doctor as soon as possible if any of the following side effects occur:

Less common
 Abdominal or stomach cramps (severe); behavioral, mood, or mental changes; continuous, uncontrolled back-and-forth and/or rolling eye movements; double vision; increase in seizures; loss of appetite; nausea or vomiting (continuing); spots before eyes; swelling of face; tiredness and weakness; unusual bleeding or bruising; yellow eyes or skin

Other side effects may occur that usually do not need medical attention. These side effects may go away during treatment as your body adjusts to the medicine. However, check with your doctor if any of the following side effects continue or are bothersome:

More common
 Abdominal or stomach cramps (mild); change in menstrual periods; diarrhea; hair loss; indigestion; loss of appetite; nausea and vomiting; trembling of hands and arms; unusual weight loss or gain

Less common or rare
 Clumsiness or unsteadiness; constipation; dizziness; drowsiness; headache; skin rash; unusual excitement, restlessness, or irritability

Other side effects not listed above may also occur in some patients. If you notice any other effects, check with your doctor.

Revised: 08/15/97
Interim revision: 08/14/98

VALRUBICIN   Mucosal-Local

Commonly used brand name(s):

In the U.S.—
 Valstar

Description

Valrubicin (val-ROO-bi-sin) is used as a solution that is run through a tube (instilled through a catheter) into the bladder to treat bladder cancer.

Valrubicin is to be administered only by or under the immediate supervision of your doctor. It is available in the following dosage form(s):

Mucosal-Local
- Bladder instillation (U.S.)

Before Using This Medicine

In deciding to use a medicine, the risks of using the medicine must be weighed against the good it will do. This is a decision you and your doctor will make. For valrubicin, the following should be considered:

Allergies—Tell your doctor if you have ever had any unusual or allergic reaction to valrubicin or to similar medicines (daunorubicin, doxorubicin, epirubicin). Also tell your health care professional if you are allergic to any other substances, such as foods, preservatives, or dyes.

Pregnancy—Valrubicin has not been studied in humans but has been found to cause birth defects and other problems in animals. Make sure your doctor knows if you are pregnant or if you intend to have children (for women and men).

Breast-feeding—It is not known whether valrubicin instilled into the bladder passes into breast milk. However, because of the possible harmful effects if it gets into the milk, breast-feeding is not recommended during treatment with this medicine.

Children—Studies on this medicine have been done only in adult patients, and there is no specific information comparing use of valrubicin in children with use in other age groups.

Older adults—Many medicines have not been studied specifically in older people. Therefore, it may not be known whether they work exactly the same way they do in younger adults. Although there is no specific information comparing the use of valrubicin in the elderly with use in other age groups, this medicine has been used mostly in patients older than 60 years of age and is not expected to cause different side effects or problems in older people than it does in younger adults.

Other medicines—Although certain medicines should not be used together at all, in other cases two different medicines may be used together even if an interaction might occur. In these cases, your doctor may want to change the dose, or other precautions may be necessary. Tell your doctor or pharmacist if you are using any other prescription or nonprescription (over-the-counter [OTC]) medicine.

Other medical problems—The presence of other medical problems may affect the use of valrubicin. Make sure you tell your doctor if you have any other medical problems, especially:

- Bladder irritation or other bladder problems—Increased risk of unwanted effects
- Small bladder—Possible trouble in being able to hold all of the solution
- Urinary tract infection

Proper Use of This Medicine

Your doctor may ask you to empty your bladder completely before the solution is instilled into it (unless a tube is used to drain the bladder).

Follow your doctor's instructions carefully about how long to hold the solution in your bladder:

- The solution should be held in your bladder for 2 hours. If you think you cannot hold it, tell your health care professional.

It is important that you drink extra fluids after each treatment with valrubicin so that you will pass more urine.

Dosing—The dose of valrubicin may be different for different patients. If you have any questions about the proper dose of valrubicin, ask your doctor.

- For *bladder instillation* dosage form (solution):
  —For bladder cancer:
    - Adults—800 milligrams (mg) (75 milliters [mL]) instilled into the bladder once a week for six weeks.

Precautions While Using This Medicine

Valrubicin commonly causes the urine to turn red for about 24 hours after it is given. This is normal and is no cause for concern. However, tell your doctor if you continue to pass red urine for longer than 24 hours.

Side Effects of This Medicine

Along with its needed effects, a medicine may cause some unwanted effects. The following side effects may go away during treatment as your body adjusts to the medicine. However, check with your doctor if any of the following side effects continue or are bothersome:

More common
  Blood in urine; loss of bladder control; painful or difficult urination; red color in urine; strong urge to urinate; unusually frequent urination

Less common
  Increased urination at night; local burning sensation

Rare
  Frequent urge to defecate; itching; loss of sense of taste

Other side effects not listed above may also occur in some patients. If you notice any other effects, check with your doctor.

Developed: 4/12/99

VALSARTAN   Systemic

Commonly used brand name(s):

In the U.S.—
  Diovan

In Canada—
  Diovan

Description

Valsartan (val-SAR-tan) belongs to the class of medicines called angiotensin II inhibitors. It is used to treat high blood pressure (hypertension).

High blood pressure adds to the workload of the heart and arteries. If it continues for a long time, the heart and arteries may not function properly. This can damage the blood vessels of the brain, heart, and kidneys, resulting in a stroke, heart failure, or kidney failure. High blood pressure may also increase the risk of heart attacks. These problems may be less likely to occur if blood pressure is controlled.

Valsartan works by blocking the action of a substance in the body that causes blood vessels to tighten. As a result, valsartan relaxes blood vessels. This lowers blood pressure.

This medicine is available only with your doctor's prescription, in the following dosage form(s):

Oral
  - Capsules (U.S. and Canada)

Before Using This Medicine

In deciding to use a medicine, the risks of taking the medicine must be weighed against the good it will do. This is a decision you and your doctor will make. For valsartan, the following should be considered:

Allergies—Tell your doctor if you have ever had any unusual or allergic reaction to valsartan. Also tell your health care professional if you are allergic to any other substances, such as foods, preservatives, or dyes.

Pregnancy—Use of valsartan during pregnancy, especially during the second and third trimesters (after the first 3 months) can cause low blood pressure, severe kidney failure, or even death in the newborn. *Therefore, it is important that you check with your doctor immediately if you think that you may have become pregnant.* Be sure that you have discussed this with your doctor before taking this medicine.

Breast-feeding—It is not known whether valsartan passes into breast milk. However, valsartan passes into the milk of lactating rats. Because this medicine may cause serious side effects, breast-feeding is generally not recommended while you are taking it.

Children—Studies on this medicine have been done only in adult patients, and there is no specific information comparing use of valsartan in children with use in other age groups.

Older adults—This medicine has been tested in patients 65 years of age or older and has not been shown to cause different side effects or problems in older people than it does in younger adults. However, blood levels of valsartan and the time it takes for it to be eliminated from the body are increased in the elderly. Additionally, elderly patients may be more sensitive to its effects.

Other medicines—Although certain medicines should not be used together at all, in other cases two different medicines may be used together even if an interaction might occur. In these cases, your doctor may want to change the dose, or other precautions may be necessary. When you are taking valsartan, it is especially important that your health care professional know if you are taking any of the following:

- Diuretics (water pills)—Effects on blood pressure may be increased
- Potassium-sparing medicines, potassium supplements, or potassium-containing salt substitutes—May increase blood potassium levels

Other medical problems—The presence of other medical problems may affect the use of valsartan. Make sure you tell your doctor if you have any other medical problems, especially:

- Dehydration—Blood pressure–lowering effects of valsartan may be increased.
- Kidney disease—Effects of valsartan may make this condition worse.
- Liver disease—Effects of valsartan may be increased because of slower removal of medicine from the body.

Proper Use of This Medicine

Take this medicine only as directed by your doctor. Do not take more of it and do not take it more often than your doctor ordered. This medicine also works best when there is a constant amount in the blood. *To help keep the amount constant, do not miss any doses. Also, it is best to take the doses at the same time each day.*

Valsartan may be taken with or without food

Dosing—The dose of valsartan will be different for different patients. *Follow your doctor's orders or the directions on the label.* The following information includes only the average doses of valsartan. *If your dose is different, do not change it* unless your doctor tells you to do so.

The number of capsules that you take depends on the strength of the medicine.

- For *oral* dosage form (capsules):
  —For high blood pressure:
  - Adults—80 milligrams (mg) once a day. Your doctor may increase your dose as needed.
  - Children—Use and dose must be determined by your doctor.

Missed dose—If you miss a dose of this medicine, take it as soon as possible. However, if it is almost time for your next dose, skip the missed dose and go back to your regular dosing schedule. Do not double doses.

Storage—To store this medicine:

- Keep out of the reach of children.
- Store away from heat and direct light.
- Do not store in the bathroom, near the kitchen sink, or in other damp places. Heat or moisture may cause the medicine to break down.

- Do not keep outdated medicine or medicine no longer needed. Be sure that any discarded medicine is out of the reach of children.

Precautions While Using This Medicine

It is important that your doctor check your progress at regular visits to make sure that this medicine is working properly and to check for unwanted effects.

Check with your doctor immediately if you think that you may be pregnant. Valsartan may cause birth defects or other problems in the baby if taken during pregnancy.

Do not take other medicines unless they have been discussed with your doctor. This especially includes over-the-counter (nonprescription) medicines for appetite control, asthma, colds, cough, hay fever, or sinus problems, since they may tend to increase your blood pressure.

Dizziness or lightheadedness may occur, especially if you have been taking a diuretic (water pill). Make sure you know how you react to this medicine before you drive, use machines, or do anything else that could be dangerous if you experience these effects.

Check with your doctor right away if you become sick while taking this medicine, especially with severe or continuing nausea and vomiting or diarrhea. These conditions may cause you to lose too much water and lead to low blood pressure.

Dizziness, lightheadedness, or fainting may also occur if you exercise or if the weather is hot. Heavy sweating can cause loss of too much water and result in low blood pressure. Use extra care during exercise or hot weather.

Side Effects of This Medicine

Along with its needed effects, a medicine may cause some unwanted effects. Although not all of these side effects may occur, if they do occur they may need medical attention.

Check with your doctor immediately if any of the following side effects occur:
  Rare
    Chills, fever, or sore throat; swelling of face, mouth, hands, or feet; trouble in swallowing or breathing (sudden)

Check with your doctor as soon as possible if any of the following side effects occur:
  Rare
    Dizziness, lightheadedness, or fainting; hoarseness

Other side effects may occur that usually do not need medical attention. These side effects may go away during treatment as your body adjusts to the medicine. However, check with your doctor if any of the following side effects continue or are bothersome:
  Less common
    Abdominal pain; back pain; cold or flu-like symptoms; coughing; diarrhea; difficulty in moving; headache; muscle pain or stiffness; pain, swelling, or redness in joints; unusual tiredness

Other side effects not listed above may also occur in some patients. If you notice any other effects, check with your doctor.

Developed: 08/10/1998
Revised: 09/06/2000

VALSARTAN AND HYDROCHLOROTHIAZIDE
Systemic

Commonly used brand name(s):

In the U.S.—
Diovan HCT

Description

Valsartan (val-SAR-tan) and Hydrochlorothiazide (hye-droe-klor-oh-THYE-a-zide)

This combination medicine belongs to the class of medicines called high blood pressure medicines (antihypertensives). It is used to treat high blood pressure (hypertension).

High blood pressure adds to the workload of the heart and arteries. If it continues for a long time, the heart and arteries may not function properly. This can damage the blood vessels of the brain, heart, and kidneys, resulting in a stroke, heart failure, or kidney failure. High blood pressure may also increase the risk of heart attacks. These problems may be less likely to occur if blood pressure is controlled.

Valsartan works by blocking a substance in the body that causes blood vessels to tighten. As a result, valsartan relaxes blood vessels. This lowers blood pressure and increases the supply of blood and oxygen to the heart. Hydrochlorothiazide helps reduce the amount of salt and water in the body by acting on the kidneys to increase the flow of urine; this also helps to lower blood pressure.

This combination may also be used for other conditions as determined by your doctor.

This medicine is available only with your doctor's prescription, in the following dosage form(s):

Oral
- Tablets (U.S.)

Before Using This Medicine

In deciding to use a medicine, the risks of taking the medicine must be weighed against the good it will do. This is a decision you and your doctor will make. For valsartan and hydrochlorothiazide, the following should be considered:

Allergies—Tell your doctor if you have ever had any unusual or allergic reaction to valsartan, sulfonamides (sulfa drugs), bumetanide, furosemide, acetazolamide, dichlorphenamide, or methazolamide or to hydrochlorothiazide or any of the other thiazide diuretics (water pills). Also tell your health care professional if you are allergic to any other substances, such as foods, sulfites or other preservatives, or dyes.

Pregnancy—Use of valsartan during pregnancy, especially after the first three months, can cause low blood pressure, kidney failure, too much potassium, or death in newborns. Additionally, when hydrochlorothiazide is used during pregnancy, it may cause jaundice, blood problems, and other side effects in the newborn baby. *Therefore, it is important that you check with your doctor immediately if you think that you may be pregnant.*

Breast-feeding—It is not known whether valsartan passes into breast milk. However, it does pass into the milk of lactating rats. Hydrochlorothiazide does pass into breast milk. Be sure that you discuss this with your doctor if you decide to breast feed while taking these medicines.

Children—Studies on this medicine have been done only in adult patients, and there is no specific information comparing use of valsartan and hydrochlorothiazide combination in children with use in other age groups.

Older adults—Elderly patients may be more sensitive than younger adults to the effects of this medicine.

Other medicines—Although certain medicines should not be used together at all, in other cases two different medicines may be used together even if an interaction might occur. In these cases, your doctor may want to change the dose, or other precautions may be necessary. Tell your health care professional if you are taking any other prescription or nonprescription (over-the-counter [OTC]) medicine.

Other medical problems—The presence of other medical problems may affect the use of valsartan and hydrochlorothiazide. Make sure you tell your doctor if you have any other medical problems, especially:

- Diabetes mellitus (sugar diabetes)—Hydrochlorothiazide may raise blood sugar levels

- Fluid or electrolyte (e.g., potassium, chloride, sodium) imbalance (due to excessive perspiration, vomiting, diarrhea, etc.)—The side effects of valsartan and hydrochlorothiazide may be increased

- Gout—Hydrochlorothiazide may increase the amount of uric acid in the body, which may activate or aggravate this condition

- Heart failure, severe—Lowering of blood pressure by these medicines may make this condition worse

- Kidney disease or
- Liver disease—These conditions may be aggravated by valsartan and hydrochlorothiazide

Proper Use of This Medicine

This medicine works best if there is a constant amount in the blood. To help keep this amount constant, *do not miss any doses and take the medicine at the same time each day.*

In addition to the use of the medicine your doctor has prescribed, treatment for your high blood pressure may include weight control and care in the types of foods you eat, especially foods high in sodium. Your doctor will tell you which of these is most important for you. You should check with your doctor before changing your diet.

Many patients who have high blood pressure will not notice any signs of the problem. In fact, many may feel normal. It is very important that you *take your medicine exactly as directed* and that you keep your appointments with your doctor even if you feel well.

Remember that this medicine will not cure your high blood pressure but it does help control it. Therefore, you must continue to take it as directed if you expect to lower your blood pressure and keep it down. *You may have to take high blood pressure medicine for the rest of your life.* If high blood pressure is not treated, it can cause serious problems such as heart failure, blood vessel disease, stroke, or kidney disease.

Dosing—The dose of these medicines will be different for different patients. *Follow your doctor's orders or the directions on the label.* The following information includes only the average doses of this medicine. *If your dose is different, do not change it* unless your doctor tells you to do so.

The number of tablets that you take depends on the strength of the medicine. Also, *the number of doses you take each day, the time allowed between doses, and the length of time you take the medicine depend on the medical problem for which you are taking valsartan and hydrochlorothiazide.*

- For *oral* dosage form (tablets):
  - —For high blood pressure:
    - Adults—1 tablet once a day. Your doctor may increase your dose if needed.
    - Children—Use and dose must be determined by your doctor.

Missed dose—If you miss a dose of this medicine, take it as soon as possible. However, if it is almost time for your next dose, skip the missed dose and go back to your regular dosing schedule. Do not double doses.

Storage—To store this medicine:
- Keep out of the reach of children.
- Store away from heat and direct light.
- Do not store in the bathroom, near the kitchen sink, or in other damp places. Heat or moisture may cause the medicine to break down.
- Keep the medicine from freezing. Do not refrigerate.
- Do not keep outdated medicine or medicine no longer needed. Be sure that any discarded medicine is out of the reach of children.

Precautions While Using This Medicine

It is important that your doctor check your progress at regular visits to make sure that this medicine is working properly and to check for unwanted effects.

Check with your doctor immediately if you think that you may be pregnant. Valsartan and hydrochlorothiazide may cause birth defects or other problems in the baby if taken during pregnancy.

Check with your doctor immediately if lightheadedness or fainting occurs while you are taking this medicine. A dosage adjustment or change in medication may be necessary.

For *diabetic patients:*
- Hydrochlorothiazide may raise blood sugar levels. Check with your doctor if any changes in your blood sugar levels occur.

Do not take other medicines unless they have been discussed with your doctor. This especially includes potassium supplements or salt substitutes that contain potassium, since they may alter your blood potassium levels, or over-the-counter (nonprescription) medicines for appetite control, asthma, colds, cough, hay fever, or sinus problems, since they may tend to increase your blood pressure.

Dizziness, lightheadedness, or fainting may occur with this medicine. Make sure you know how you react to this medicine before you drive, use machines, or do anything else that could be dangerous if you experience these effects.

Check with your doctor right away if you become sick while taking this medicine, especially with severe or continuing nausea and vomiting or diarrhea. These conditions may cause you to lose too much water and lead to low blood pressure.

Dizziness, lightheadedness, or fainting may also occur if you exercise or if the weather is hot. Heavy sweating can cause loss of too much water and result in low blood pressure. Use extra care during exercise or hot weather.

Before having any kind of surgery (including dental surgery) or emergency treatment, tell the medical doctor or dentist in charge that you are taking this medicine.

Avoid alcoholic beverages until you have discussed their use with your doctor. Alcohol may make the low blood pressure effect worse and/or increase the possibility of dizziness or fainting.

Hydrochlorothiazide may cause your skin to be more sensitive to sunlight than it is normally. Be sure to wear protective clothing and a hat or apply a product to the skin that prevents sunburn before going outside.

Side Effects of This Medicine

Along with its needed effects, a medicine may cause some unwanted effects. Although not all of these side effects may occur, if they do occur they may need medical attention.

Check with your doctor immediately if any of the following side effects occur:

Rare

Itching, pain, redness, or swelling of eye or eyelid, watering of eyes, troubled breathing or wheezing, severe skin rash or hives, and flushing; chills, fever, and sore throat; bloating or pain of the stomach, fever, nausea, and vomiting; fainting; yellow eyes or skin

Symptoms of fluid and electrolyte imbalance

Confusion; convulsions (seizures); dizziness or lightheadedness; diminished urine output; drowsiness or sluggishness; dry mouth; fast heartbeat; muscle cramps or pain; muscle fatigue; nausea and vomiting; restlessness; thirst; weakness

Check with your doctor as soon as possible if any of the following side effects occur:

Less common

Cold or flu-like symptoms; dizziness; fatigue; sore throat, difficulty swallowing, tender or swollen lymph nodes in the neck

Rare

Abdominal pain; rash; sudden occurrence of joint pain, usually in the ankle, knee, or great toe; joint stiffness, or swelling

Other side effects may occur that usually do not need medical attention. These side effects may go away during treatment as your body adjusts to the medicine. However, check with your doctor if any of the following side effects continue or are bothersome:

Less common

Cough; diarrhea (mild); headache

Rare

Anxiety; heartbeat sensations; redness of face or neck; increased sensitivity to sunlight; reduced sexual performance or drive; increased sweating

Other side effects not listed above may also occur in some patients. If you notice any other effects, check with your doctor.

Developed: 09/02/98

VANCOMYCIN   Systemic

Commonly used brand name(s):

In the U.S.—
Vancocin
Generic name product may be available.

In Canada—
Vancocin

Description

Vancomycin (van-koe-MYE-sin) belongs to the family of medicines called antibiotics. Antibiotics are medicines used in the treatment of infections caused by bacteria. They work by killing bacteria or preventing their growth. Vancomycin will not work for colds, flu, or other virus infections.

Vancomycin is used to treat infections in many different parts of the body. It is sometimes given with other antibiotics. Vancomycin also is used in patients with heart valve disease (e.g., rheumatic fever) or prosthetic (artificial) heart valves who are allergic to penicillin. Under certain circumstances, this medicine also may be used to prevent endocarditis (inflammation of the lining of the heart) in these patients who are having dental work done or surgery on the upper respiratory tract (for example, nose or throat). Vancomycin also may be used for other conditions as determined by your doctor.

Vancomycin given by injection is used mainly for serious infections for which other medicines may not work. However, this medicine may cause some serious side effects, including damage to your hearing and kidneys. These side effects may be more likely to occur in elderly patients. You and your doctor should talk about the good this medicine will do as well as the risks associated with receiving it.

Vancomycin is available only with your doctor's prescription, in the following dosage form:

Parenteral
• Injection (U.S. and Canada)

Before Receiving This Medicine

In deciding to use a medicine, the risks of taking the medicine must be weighed against the good it will do. This is a decision you and your doctor will make. For vancomycin, the following should be considered:

Allergies—Tell your doctor if you have ever had any unusual or allergic reaction to vancomycin. Also tell your health care professional if you are allergic to any other substances, such as foods, preservatives, or dyes.

Pregnancy—Vancomycin has not been reported to cause hearing loss or kidney damage in the infants of women given vancomycin during their second or third trimester of pregnancy.

Breast-feeding—Vancomycin passes into breast milk. However, this medicine has not been reported to cause problems in nursing babies.

Children—Vancomycin can cause serious side effects in any patient. Therefore, it is especially important that you discuss with the child's doctor the good that this medicine will do as well as the risks of using it.

Older adults—Elderly people may be especially sensitive to the effects of vancomycin. This may increase the chance of hearing loss or kidney damage.

Other medicines—Although certain medicines should not be used together at all, in other cases two different medicines may be used together even if an interaction might occur. In these cases, your doctor may want to change the dose, or other precautions may be necessary. When you are receiving vancomycin, it is especially important that your health care professional know if you are taking any of the following:

• Aminoglycosides by injection (amikacin [e.g., Amikin], gentamicin [e.g., Garamycin], kanamycin [e.g., Kantrex], netilmicin [e.g., Netromycin], streptomycin, tobramycin [e.g., Nebcin]) or
• Amphotericin B by injection (e.g., Fungizone) or
• Bacitracin by injection or
• Bumetanide by injection (e.g., Bumex) or
• Capreomycin (e.g., Capastat) or
• Cisplatin (e.g., Platinol) or
• Cyclosporine (e.g., Sandimmune) or
• Ethacrynic acid by injection (e.g., Edecrin) or
• Furosemide by injection (e.g., Lasix) or
• Paromomycin (e.g., Humatin) or
• Polymyxins, especially colistimethate (e.g., Coly-Mycin M) and polymyxin B (e.g., Aerosporin) or
• Streptozocin (e.g., Zanosar) or
• Vecuronium (e.g., Norcuron)—Use of these medicines with vancomycin may increase the chance of side effects

• Dexamethasone (e.g., Dalalone L.A., Decadrol, Decadron)—Use of dexamethasone with vancomycin may keep vancomycin from working properly

Other medical problems—The presence of other medical problems may affect the use of vancomycin. Make sure you tell your doctor if you have any other medical problems, especially:

• Kidney disease or
• Loss of hearing, or deafness, history of—Patients with kidney disease or a history of hearing loss or deafness may have an increased chance of side effects

Proper Use of This Medicine

Some medicines given by injection may sometimes be given at home to patients who do not need to be in the hospital for the full time of treatment. If you are receiving this medicine at home, *make sure you clearly understand and carefully follow your doctor's instructions.*

To help clear up your infection completely, *vancomycin must be given for the full time of treatment,* even if you begin to feel better after a few days. Also, this medicine works best when there is a constant amount in the blood. To help keep the amount constant, vancomycin must be given on a regular schedule.

Dosing—The dose of vancomycin will be different for different patients. *Follow your doctor's orders or the directions on the label.* The following information includes only the average doses of vancomycin. *If your dose is different, do not change it* unless your doctor tells you to do so.

• For *injection* dosage form:
  —For treatment of bacterial infections:
    • Adults and teenagers—7.5 mg per kg (3.4 mg per pound) of body weight, or 500 mg, injected into a vein every six hours; or 15 mg per kg (6.8 mg per pound) of body weight, or 1 gram, injected into a vein every twelve hours.

- Children 1 month to 12 years of age—10 mg per kg (4.5 mg per pound) of body weight injected into a vein every six hours; or 20 mg per kg (9.1 mg per pound) of body weight injected into a vein every twelve hours.
- Infants 1 week to 1 month of age—15 mg per kg (6.8 mg per pound) of body weight injected into a vein at first, then 10 mg per kg (4.5 mg per pound) of body weight injected into a vein every eight hours.
- Newborns up to 1 week of age—15 mg per kg (6.8 mg per pound) of body weight injected into a vein at first, then 10 mg per kg (4.5 mg per pound) of body weight injected into a vein every twelve hours.

Side Effects of This Medicine

Along with its needed effects, a medicine may cause some unwanted effects. Although not all of these side effects may occur, if they do occur they may need medical attention.

Check with your health care professional immediately if any of the following side effects occur:

Less common
Change in the frequency of urination or amount of urine; chills; coughing; difficulty in breathing; drowsiness; fever; increased thirst; loss of appetite; nausea or vomiting; sore throat; weakness

Rare
Abdominal tenderness; abnormal bleeding or bruising; large blisters on arms, legs, hands, feet, or upper body; loss of hearing; ringing or buzzing or a feeling of fullness in the ears; severe abdominal or stomach cramps and pain; watery and severe diarrhea, which may also be bloody

Note: Some of the above side effects also may occur up to several weeks after you stop receiving this medicine.

Symptoms of "red man syndrome"—Less common
Chills or fever; fainting; fast heartbeat; hives; itching; low blood pressure; nausea or vomiting; rash or redness of the face, base of neck, upper body, back, and arms

Note: Symptoms of the "red man syndrome" are more common when vancomycin is given by direct or rapid injection.

The above side effects, except the "red man syndrome," are more likely to occur in the elderly, who are usually more sensitive to the effects of vancomycin.

Other side effects not listed above may also occur in some patients. If you notice any other effects, check with your doctor.

Revised: 06/15/99

VENLAFAXINE   Systemic

Commonly used brand name(s):

In the U.S.—
Effexor
Effexor XR

In Canada—
Effexor
Effexor XR

Description

Venlafaxine (ven-la-FAX-een) is used to treat mental depression. It is also used to treat certain anxiety disorders or to relieve the symptoms of anxiety. However, it usually is not used for anxiety or tension caused by the stress of everyday life.

This medicine is available only with your doctor's prescription, in the following dosage forms:

Oral
- Extended-release capsules (U.S. and Canada)
- Tablets (U.S. and Canada)

Before Using This Medicine

In deciding to use a medicine, the risks of taking the medicine must be weighed against the good it will do. This is a decision you and your doctor will make. For venlafaxine, the following should be considered:

Allergies—Tell your doctor if you have ever had any unusual or allergic reaction to venlafaxine. Also tell your health care professional if you are allergic to any other substances, such as foods, preservatives, or dyes.

Pregnancy—Studies have not been done in pregnant women. However, when pregnant rats were given venlafaxine in doses much larger than the usual human dose, some of their pups died before or soon after birth. Before taking this medicine, make sure your doctor knows if you are pregnant or if you may become pregnant.

Breast-feeding—This medicine passes into breast milk and may cause unwanted effects. It may be necessary for you to take another medicine or to stop breast-feeding during treatment. Be sure you have discussed the risks and benefits of this medicine with your doctor.

Children—Studies on this medicine have been done only in adult patients, and there is no specific information comparing use of venlafaxine in children with use in other age groups.

Older adults—In studies done to date that have included elderly people, venlafaxine did not cause different side effects or problems in older people than it did in younger adults.

Other medicines—Although certain medicines should not be used together at all, in other cases two different medicines may be used together even if an interaction might occur. In these cases, your doctor may want to change the dose, or other precautions may be necessary. When you are taking venlafaxine, it is especially important that your health care professional know if you are taking the following:

- Buspirone (e.g., BuSpar) or
- Bromocriptine (e.g., Parlodel) or
- Certain tricyclic antidepressants (amitriptyline [e.g., Elavil], clomipramine [e.g., Anafranil], or imipramine [e.g., Tofranil]) or
- Dextromethorphan (cough medicine) or
- Levodopa (e.g., Sinemet) or
- Lithium (e.g., Eskalith) or
- Meperidine (e.g., Demerol) or
- Nefazodone (e.g., Serzone) or
- Pentazocine (e.g., Talwin) or
- Selective serotonin reuptake inhibitors (fluoxetine [e.g., Prozac], fluvoxamine [e.g., Luvox], paroxetine [e.g., Paxil], sertraline [e.g., Zoloft]) or
- Street drugs (LSD, MDMA [e.g., ecstasy], marijuana) or
- Sumatriptan (e.g., Imitrex) or

- Tramadol (e.g., Ultram) or
- Trazodone (e.g., Desyrel) or
- Tryptophan—Using these medicines with venlafaxine may increase the chance of developing a rare, but very serious, unwanted effect known as the serotonin syndrome; symptoms of this syndrome include confusion, diarrhea, fever, poor coordination, restlessness, shivering, sweating, talking or acting with excitement you cannot control, trembling or shaking, or twitching; if you experience these symptoms contact your doctor as soon as possible

- Moclobemide (e.g., Manerex)—Taking moclobemide and venlafaxine together or less than 3 days apart may increase the chance of developing serious unwanted effects, including the serotonin syndrome, and is not recommended

- Monoamine oxidase (MAO) inhibitors (furazolidone [e.g., Furoxone], phenelzine [e.g., Nardil], isocarboxazid [e.g., Marplan] procarbazine [e.g., Matulane], selegiline [e.g., Eldepryl], tranylcypromine [e.g., Parnate])—*Do not take venlafaxine while you are taking or within 2 weeks of taking an MAO inhibitor*; if you do, you may develop confusion, agitation, restlessness, stomach or intestinal symptoms, sudden high body temperature, extremely high blood pressure, and severe convulsions; at least 14 days should be allowed between stopping treatment with an MAO inhibitor and starting treatment with venlafaxine, and at least 7 days should be allowed between stopping treatment with venlafaxine and starting treatment with an MAO inhibitor

Other medical problems—The presence of other medical problems may affect the use of venlafaxine. Make sure you tell your doctor if you have any other medical problems, especially:

- Brain disease or damage, or mental retardation or
- Seizures (history of)—The risk of seizures may be increased

- Heart disease or
- High or low blood pressure—Venlafaxine may make these conditions worse

- Kidney disease or
- Liver disease—Higher blood levels of venlafaxine may occur, increasing the chance of side effects; your doctor may need to adjust your venlafaxine dose

- Mania (history of)—The risk of developing mania may be increased

- Weight loss—Venlafaxine may cause weight loss; this weight loss is usually small, but if a large weight loss occurs, it may be harmful in some patients

Proper Use of This Medicine

Take this medicine only as directed by your doctor to benefit your condition as much as possible. Do not take more of it, do not take it more often, and do not take it for a longer time than your doctor ordered.

You may have to take venlafaxine for 4 weeks or longer before you begin to feel better. Also, you will probably need to keep taking this medicine for at least 6 months, even if you feel better, to help prevent your depression from returning. Your doctor should check your progress at regular visits during this time.

Venlafaxine should be taken with food or on a full stomach to lessen the chance of stomach upset. However, if your doctor tells you to take the medicine a certain way, take it exactly as directed.

If you are taking the extended-release capsule dosage form, swallow the capsule whole with fluid; do not break, crush, chew, or place the capsule in liquid.

Dosing—The dose of venlafaxine will be different for different patients. *Follow your doctor's orders or the directions on the label.* The following information includes only the average doses of venlafaxine. *If your dose is different, do not change it* unless your doctor tells you to do so.

The number of capsules or tablets that you take depends on the strength of the medicine. Also, *the number of doses you take each day, the time allowed between doses, and the length of time you take the medicine depend on your special needs.*

- For mental depression:
  —For *oral extended-release capsule* dosage form:
    - Adults—At first, 75 milligrams (mg) a day, taken in one dose in the morning or evening. Your doctor may increase your dose if needed. However, the dose is usually not more than 225 mg a day.
    - Children—Use and dose must be determined by your doctor.
  —For *oral tablet* dosage form:
    - Adults—At first, a total of 75 mg a day, taken in smaller doses two or three times during the day. Your doctor may increase your dose if needed. However, the dose is usually not more than 375 mg a day.
    - Children up to 18 years of age—Use and dose must be determined by your doctor.

- For anxiety
  —For *oral extended-release capsule* dosage form:
    - Adults—At first, 75 mg a day, taken in one dose in the morning or evening. Your doctor may increase your dose if needed. However, the dose is usually not more than 225 mg per day.
    - Children—Use and dose must be determined by your doctor.

Missed dose—*If you are taking the tablet form of venlafaxine and you miss a dose*, take it as soon as possible. However, if it is within 2 hours of your next dose, skip the missed dose and go back to your regular dosing schedule. Do not double doses.

If you are taking the extended-release capsule form of venlafaxine and you miss a dose, take it as soon as possible. However, if you do not remember the missed dose until the next day, skip the missed dose and go back to your regular dosing schedule. Do not double doses.

Storage—To store this medicine:
- Keep out of the reach of children.
- Store away from heat and direct light.
- Do not store in the bathroom, near the kitchen sink, or in other damp places. Heat or moisture may cause the medicine to break down.
- Do not keep outdated medicine or medicine no longer needed. Be sure that any discarded medicine is out of the reach of children.

Precautions While Using This Medicine

It is important that your doctor check your progress at regular visits, to allow for changes in your dose and to help reduce any side effects.

Tell your doctor right away if you develop any allergic reactions, such as skin rash or hives, while taking venlafaxine.

Do not stop taking this medicine without first checking with your doctor. Your doctor may want you to reduce gradually the amount you are taking before stopping completely. This is to decrease the chance of side effects.

It is not known how venlafaxine will interact with alcohol and other central nervous system (CNS) depressants (medicines that may make you drowsy or less alert). Some examples of CNS depressants are antihistamines or medicine for hay fever, other allergies, or colds; sedatives, tranquilizers, or sleeping medicine; prescription pain medicine or narcotics; barbiturates; medicine for seizures; muscle relaxants; or anesthetics, including some dental anesthetics. Check with your doctor before taking any of the above while you are using this medicine.

Venlafaxine may cause some people to become drowsy or have blurred vision. *Make sure you know how you react to this medicine before you drive, use machines, or do anything else that could be dangerous if you are not alert or able to see clearly.*

Dizziness, lightheadedness, or fainting may occur, especially when you get up from a lying or sitting position. Getting up slowly may help. If this problem continues or gets worse, check with your doctor.

Side Effects of This Medicine

Along with its needed effects, a medicine may cause some unwanted effects. Although not all of these side effects may occur, if they do occur they may need medical attention.

Check with your doctor as soon as possible if any of the following side effects occur:

More common
> Changes in vision, such as blurred vision; decrease in sexual desire or ability; headache

Less common
> Chest pain; fast or irregular heartbeat; mood or mental changes; ringing or buzzing in ears

Rare
> Convulsions (seizures); itching or skin rash; lightheadedness or fainting, especially when getting up suddenly from a sitting or lying position; lockjaw; menstrual changes; problems in urinating or in holding urine; swelling; talking, feeling, and acting with excitement and activity you cannot control; trouble in breathing

Symptoms of overdose
> Agitation; convulsions (seizures); drowsiness; extreme tiredness or weakness; fast heartbeat; tingling, burning, or prickling sensations; trembling or shaking

This medicine may also cause the following side effect that your doctor will watch for:

More common
> High blood pressure

Other side effects may occur that usually do not need medical attention. These side effects may go away during treatment as your body adjusts to the medicine. However, check with your doctor if any of the following side effects continue or are bothersome:

More common
> Abnormal dreams; anxiety or nervousness; chills; constipation; diarrhea; dizziness; drowsiness; dryness of mouth; heartburn; increased sweating; loss of appetite; nausea; stuffy or runny nose; stomach pain or gas; tingling, burning, or prickly sensations; trembling or shaking; trouble in sleeping; unusual tiredness or weakness; vomiting; weight loss

Less common
> Change in sense of taste; muscle tension; yawning

After you stop using this medicine, your body may need time to adjust. The length of time this takes depends on the amount of medicine you were using and how long you used it. During this period of time check with your doctor if you notice any of the following side effects:

> Changes in dreaming; dizziness; dryness of mouth; headache; increased sweating; nausea; nervousness; trouble in sleeping; unusual tiredness or weakness

Other side effects not listed above may also occur in some patients. If you notice any other effects, check with your doctor.

Developed: 05/24/95
Revised: 11/4/99

VERTEPORFIN   Systemic

Commonly used brand name(s):

In the U.S.—
> Visudyne

In Canada—
> Visudyne

Another commonly used name is benzoporphyrin derivative.

Description

Verteporfin (ver-te-POR-fin) is used together with a special laser light, to treat abnormal blood vessel formation in a part of the eye which, if left untreated, can lead to a loss of eyesight.

This medicine is to be administered only by or under the immediate supervision of your doctor. It is available in the following dosage forms:

Parenteral
> • Injection (U.S. and Canada)

Before Using This Medicine

In deciding to use a medicine, the risks of using the medicine must be weighed against the good it will do. This is a decision you and your doctor will make. For verteporfin, the following should be considered:

Allergies—Tell your doctor if you have ever had any unusual or allergic reaction to verteporfin. Also, tell your health care professional if you are allergic to any other substances, such as foods or preservatives.

Pregnancy—Verteporfin has not been studied in pregnant women. However, it has caused harm to the fetus in animals.

Before using this medicine, make sure your doctor knows if you are pregnant or if you may become pregnant.

Breast-feeding—It is not known whether verteporfin passes into breast milk. Although most medicines pass into breast milk in small amounts, many of them may be used safely while breast-feeding. Mothers who are taking this medicine and who wish to breast-feed should discuss this with their doctor.

Children—Studies on this medicine have been done only in adult patients, and there is no specific information comparing use of verteporfin in children with use in other age groups.

Older adults—Studies show that the effects of verteporfin are less in patients 75 years of age or older.

Other medicines—Although certain medicines should not be used together at all, in other cases two different medicines may be used together even if an interaction might occur. In these cases, your doctor may want to change the dose or other precautions may be necessary. When you are using verteporfin, it is especially important that your health care professional know if you are taking any of the following:
- Calcium channel blocking agents (medicine class for blood pressure) or
- Polymyxin B (antibiotic in eye preparations) or
- Radiation therapy—Use of these medicines with verteporfin may increase the effects of verteporfin

- Alcohol or
- Anti-oxidant vitamins and minerals (e.g., Beta-carotene) or
- Dimethyl sulfoxide (e.g., DMSO, Rimso-50) or
- Medications that decrease blood clotting and blood vessel constriction—The effects of verteporfin may be decreased

- Antidiabetics, oral (diabetes medicine you take by mouth) or
- Griseofulvin (e.g., Fulvicin, Gris-PEG) or
- Phenothiazines (antipsychotic medications) or
- Sulfonamides (sulfa medicine) or
- Tetracyclines (medicine for infection) or
- Thiazide diuretics (water pills)—Use with verteporfin may increase the sensitivity of skin to light

Other medical problems—The presence of other medical problems may affect the use of verteporfin. Make sure you tell your doctor if you have any other medical problems, especially:
- Liver function impairment
- Porphyria—Sensitivity to light may be increased
- Previous reaction to verteporfin—Reaction is more likely to occur again

Proper Use of This Medicine

Treatment with verteporfin and laser light occurs in two steps. First, the verteporfin is injected into your body. Second, 15 minutes later, a laser light is directed at the affected eye.

Dosing—The dose of verteporfin will be different for different patients depending on your body surface area. *Laser light treatment must follow verteporfin injection 15 minutes after the start of the injection.* The laser light treatment lasts 83 seconds. If you have any questions about the proper dose of verteporfin, ask your doctor.

Precautions After Receiving This Medicine

For 5 days after you receive an injection of verteporfin, your eyes will be extra sensitive to light, including sunlight and bright indoor lights. Certain types of sunglasses can help protect your eyes during this time. *Check with your doctor about which sunglasses to use.*

For 5 days after you receive an injection of verteporfin, your skin will be extra sensitive to sunlight and to very bright indoor lights, such as tanning lamps, bright halogen lighting and lights in dental offices or operating rooms. *Do not expose your skin to direct sunlight or to bright indoor lights during this time.* Sunscreens will *not* protect your skin from a severe reaction to light (blistering, burning, and swelling of the skin). However, exposure to normal amounts of indoor light (for example, daylight or light from lamps with shades) will help clear up the verteporfin remaining in your skin. Therefore, *do not protect your skin from normal amounts of indoor light.* If you have any questions about whether the light in your home is too bright, check with your doctor or nurse. *If you do have a severe reaction to light, call your doctor immediately.*

Side Effects of This Medicine

Along with its needed effects, a medicine may cause some unwanted effects. Although not all of these side effects may occur, if they do occur they may need medical attention.

Check with your doctor immediately if any of the following side effects occur:
More common
   Blurred vision or other change in vision
Less common
   Decrease in vision, may be severe; dizziness; dull nervousness; eye pain; fainting; fast, slow, or irregular heartbeat; itching, redness, or other irritation of eye; pale skin; pounding in the ears; troubled breathing on exertion; unusual bleeding or bruising; unusual tiredness or weakness

Other side effects may occur that usually do not need medical attention. These side effects may go away after treatment as your body eliminates the medicine. However, check with your doctor if any of the following side effects continue or are bothersome:
More common
   Bleeding, blistering, burning, coldness, discoloration of skin, feeling of pressure, infection, itching, numbness, pain, rash, redness, scarring, stinging, swelling, tenderness, tingling, ulceration, and/or warmth at the injection site; headache
Less common
   Back pain (during infusion of verteporfin); chills; cloudy urine; constipation; cough; decreased hearing; decreased sensitivity to touch; diarrhea; difficult or painful urination; difficulty in moving; double vision; dry eyes; feeling of constant movement of self or surroundings; fever; general feeling of discomfort or illness; hoarseness; increased sensitivity of skin to sunlight; joint pain; light headedness; loss of appetite; loss of strength or energy; muscle pain or stiffness; nausea; pain, swelling, or redness in joints; pelvic discomfort; redness or other discoloration of skin; runny nose; severe sunburn; shivering; skin

rash; sore throat; sweating; tearing; tender, swollen glands in neck; throat congestion; trouble in sleeping; trouble in swallowing; trouble sleeping; varicose veins; voice changes; vomiting

Other side effects not listed above may also occur in some patients. If you notice any other effects, check with your doctor.

Developed: 07/07/2000
Revised: 08/17/2000

VIDARABINE   Ophthalmic

Commonly used brand name(s):

In the U.S.—
   Vira-A

In Canada—
   Vira-A

Other commonly used names are arabinoside and ara-A.

Description

Vidarabine (vye-DARE-a-been) ophthalmic preparations are used to treat virus infections of the eye.

Vidarabine is available only with your doctor's prescription, in the following dosage form:

Ophthalmic
   • Ophthalmic ointment (U.S. and Canada)

Before Using This Medicine

In deciding to use a medicine, the risks of using the medicine must be weighed against the good it will do. This is a decision you and your doctor will make. For vidarabine, the following should be considered:

Allergies—Tell your doctor if you have ever had any un-usual or allergic reaction to vidarabine. Also tell your health care professional if you are allergic to any other substances, such as preservatives.

Pregnancy—Studies have not been done in humans. Studies in rats and rabbits have shown that vidarabine, given by injection, causes birth defects. In addition, studies in rab-bits have shown that vidarabine, applied as a 10% ointment to the skin, may cause birth defects or other problems. How-ever, these doses are much higher than those used in the eyes of humans. Therefore, the chance that vidarabine oph-thalmic ointment would cause birth defects or other problems in humans is very small.

Breast-feeding—It is not known whether vidarabine, ap-plied to the eyes, is absorbed into the body and passes into the breast milk. Although most medicines pass into breast milk in small amounts, many of them may be used safely while breast-feeding. Mothers who are taking this medicine and who wish to breast-feed should discuss this with their doctor.

Children—Although there is no specific information com-paring use of vidarabine in children with use in other age groups, it is not expected to cause different side effects or problems in children than it does in adults.

Older adults—Many medicines have not been studied specifically in older people. Therefore, it may not be known whether they work exactly the same way they do in younger adults or if they cause different side effects or problems in older people. There is no specific information comparing use of vidarabine in the elderly with use in other age groups.

Other medicines—Although certain medicines should not be used together at all, in other cases two different med-icines may be used together even if an interaction might occur. In these cases, your doctor may want to change the dose, or other precautions may be necessary. Tell your health care professional if you are using any other prescription or nonprescription (over-the-counter [OTC]) medicine in your eyes.

Proper Use of This Medicine

To use:
   • First, wash your hands. Then pull the lower eyelid away from the eye to form a pouch. Squeeze a thin strip of ointment into the pouch. A 1.25-cm (approximately ½-inch) strip of ointment is usually enough unless other-wise directed by your doctor. Gently close the eyes and keep them closed for 1 or 2 minutes to allow the medi-cine to come into contact with the infection.
   • To keep the medicine as germ-free as possible, do not touch the applicator tip to any surface (including the eye). After using vidarabine eye ointment, wipe the tip of the ointment tube with a clean tissue and keep the tube tightly closed.

Do not use this medicine more often or for a longer time than your doctor ordered. To do so may cause problems in the eyes. If you have any questions about this, check with your doctor.

To help clear up your infection completely, *keep using this medicine for the full time of treatment*, even if your symp-toms have disappeared. *Do not miss any doses.*

Dosing—The dose of ophthalmic vidarabine will be dif-ferent for different patients. *Follow your doctor's orders or the directions on the label.* The following information in-cludes only the average doses of ophthalmic vidarabine. *If your dose is different, do not change it* unless your doctor tells you to do so.

The number of doses you use each day, the time allowed between doses, and the length of time you use the medi-cine depend on the medical problem for which you are using ophthalmic vidarabine.

   • For *ophthalmic ointment* dosage forms:
      —For virus eye infection:
         • Adults and children—Use in each eye every three hours (five times a day). After healing has oc-curred, the dose may be reduced to two times a day for seven days more.

Missed dose—If you miss a dose of this medicine, apply it as soon as possible. However, if it is almost time for your next dose, skip the missed dose and go back to your regular dosing schedule.

Storage—To store this medicine:
   • Keep out of the reach of children.
   • Store away from heat and direct light.
   • Keep the medicine from freezing.
   • Do not keep outdated medicine or medicine no longer needed. Be sure that any discarded medicine is out of the reach of children.

Precautions While Using This Medicine

After application, eye ointments usually cause your vision to blur for a few minutes.

It is very important that you keep your appointments with your doctor. If your symptoms become worse, check with your doctor sooner.

This medicine may cause your eyes to become more sensitive to light than they are normally. Wearing sunglasses and avoiding too much exposure to bright light may help lessen the discomfort.

Side Effects of This Medicine

Along with its needed effects, a medicine may cause some unwanted effects. Although not all of these side effects may occur, if they do occur they may need medical attention.

Check with your doctor as soon as possible if any of the following side effects occur:
> Increased sensitivity of eyes to light; itching, redness, swelling, pain, burning, or other sign of irritation not present before use of this medicine

Other side effects may occur that usually do not need medical attention. These side effects may go away during treatment as your body adjusts to the medicine. However, check with your doctor if either of the following side effects continues or is bothersome:
> Excess flow of tears; feeling of something in the eye

Other side effects not listed above may also occur in some patients. If you notice any other effects, check with your doctor.

Revised: 07/01/93

VIGABATRIN Systemic— INTRODUCTORY VERSION

Commonly used brand name(s):

In Canada—
> Sabril

Description

Vigabatrin (VYE–gab–a–trin) increases the amount of the brain chemical GABA. It is thought that epileptic seizures are the result of low levels of GABA. By increasing the amount of GABA, vigabatrin reduces the likelihood of an epileptic seizure.

This medicine is available only with your doctor's prescription, in the following dosage forms:

Oral
> • Powder (Canada)
> • Tablets (Canada)

Before Using This Medicine

In deciding to use a medicine, the risks of taking vigabatrin must be weighed against the good it will do. This is a decision you and your doctor will make. For vigabatrin, the following should be considered:

Allergies—Tell your doctor if you have ever had any unusual or allergic reaction to vigabatrin. Also tell your health care provider if you are allergic to any other substances, such as foods, preservatives, or dyes.

Pregnancy—Studies have not been done in pregnant women. However, studies in rabbits have shown that vigabatrin causes birth defects. Before taking this medicine, make sure your doctor knows if you are pregnant or if you may become pregnant.

Breast-feeding—It is not known if vigabatrin passes into breast milk. Because of the risk of unwanted effects in the nursing infant, breast-feeding is not recommended.

Children—This medicine has been tested in children and, in effective doses, has not been shown to cause different problems than it does in adults.

Older adults—Many medicines have not been studied specifically in older people. Therefore, it may not be known whether they work exactly the same way they do in younger adults or if they cause different side effects or problems in older people. There is no specific information comparing use of vigabatrin in the elderly with use in other age groups.

Other medicines—Although certain medicines should not be used together at all, in other cases two different medicines may be used together even if an interaction might occur. In these cases, your doctor may want to change the dose, or other precautions may be necessary. Tell your health care professional if you are using any other prescription or nonprescription (over-the-counter [OTC]) medicine.

Other medical problems—The presence of other medical problems may affect the use of vigabatrin. Make sure you tell your doctor if you have any other medical problems, especially:
> • Mental illness—Patients with a history of emotional or behavioral disturbances may be more likely to have an episode following vigabatrin therapy.
>
> • Kidney disease—Vigabatrin is removed from the body by the kidney; slower removal from the body may increase the chance of side effects

Proper Use of This Medicine

Dosing—The dose of vigabatrin will be different for different patients. *Follow your doctor's orders or the directions on the label*. The following information includes only the average doses of vigabatrin. *If your dose is different, do not change it* unless your doctor tells you to do so.

> • For *oral* dosage form (powder):
> > —For epilepsy
> > > • Adults—To start, 1000 milligrams (mg) a day. The doctor may need to adjust the dose depending on your response to the medicine. However, the dose is usually not more than 4000 mg a day.
> > > • Children—The dose is based on body weight and will be determined by your doctor. To start, 40 milligrams (mg) per kilogram (kg) (18.2 mg per pound) of body weight per day. Your doctor may increase your dose as needed. However, the dose is usually not more than 100 mg per kg (45.5 mg per pound) of body weight a day, taken in two smaller doses.

—For infantile spasms
- Children—The dose is based on body weight and will be determined by your doctor. The usual dose is 50 to 100 mg per kg (22.7 to 45.5 mg per pound) of body weight per day, given in smaller doses twice a day. The doctor may need to adjust the dose based on your response to the medicine.

- For *oral* dosage form (tablets):
  —For epilepsy
  - Adults—To start, 1000 milligrams (mg) a day. The doctor may need to adjust the dose depending on your response to the medicine. However, the dose is usually not more than 4000 mg a day.
  - Children—The dose is based on body weight and will be determined by your doctor. To start, 40 mg per kg (18.2 mg per pound) of body weight a day. Your doctor may increase your dose as needed. However, the dose is usually not more than 100 mg per kg (45.5 mg per pound) of body weight a day, taken in two smaller doses.

Missed dose—If you miss a dose of this medicine, take it as soon as possible. However, if it is almost time for your next dose, skip the missed dose and go back to your regular dosing schedule. Do not double doses.

Storage—To store this medicine:
- Keep out of the reach of children.
- Store away from heat and direct light.
- Do not store in the bathroom, near the kitchen sink, or in other damp places. Heat or moisture may cause the medicine to break down.
- Do not keep outdated medicine or medicine no longer needed. Ask your health care professional how you should dispose of any medicine you do not use. Be sure that any discarded medicine is out of the reach of children.

Precautions While Using This Medicine

It is important that you visit your physician.

If you will be taking this medicine for a long time, *it is very important that your eye doctor check you approximately every 3 months* for any visual problems.

If your symptoms do not improve or if they become worse, check with your doctor.

Do not take other medicines unless they have been discussed with your doctor.

This medicine may cause some people to become drowsy, dizzy, or less alert than they are normally. *Make sure you know how you react to this medicine before you drive, use machines, or do anything else that could be dangerous if you are dizzy, drowsy, or not alert.*

Do not suddenly stop taking this medicine without first checking with your doctor. Your doctor may want to reduce your dose gradually. Stopping this medicine suddenly may cause seizures.

Side Effects of This Medicine

Along with its needed effects, a medicine may cause some unwanted effects. Although not all of these side effects may occur, if they do occur they may need medical attention.

Check with your doctor immediately if any of the following side effects occur:
More common
Amnesia; blurred vision; blue-yellow color blindness; decreased vision or other vision changes; eye pain; increase in seizures
Less common or rare
Uncontrolled rolling eye movements
Symptoms of overdose
Get emergency help immediately if any of the following symptoms of overdose occur
Mood or mental changes

Other side effects may occur that usually do not need medical attention. These side effects may go away during treatment as your body adjusts to the medicine. However, check with your doctor if any of the following side effects continue or are bothersome.
More common
abnormal coordination; agitation; anxiety; clumsiness,; confusion; constipation; mental depression; diarrhea; dizziness; drowsiness; double vision or seeing double; fatigue; hyperactivity; increased movement; joint pain; burning, tingling, or prickly sensations; shakiness; sleepiness or unusual drowsiness; trembling; tremor; unsteadiness
Less common
Aggression; concentration impaired; headache; increased saliva; insomnia; muscle weakness; nausea; speech disorder; thinking abnormal; vomiting; weight gain

Other side effects not listed above may also occur in some patients. If you notice any other effects, check with your doctor.

Developed: 03/05/2001

VINBLASTINE   Systemic

Commonly used brand name(s):

In the U.S.—
Velban
Generic name product may be available.

In Canada—
Velbe

Description

Vinblastine (vin-BLAS-teen) belongs to the group of medicines known as antineoplastic agents. It is used to treat certain kinds of cancer, including lymphoma and cancer of the breast or testicles, as well as some noncancerous conditions.

Vinblastine interferes with the growth of cancer cells, which are eventually destroyed. Since the growth of normal body cells may also be affected by vinblastine, other effects will also occur. Some of these may be serious and must be reported to your doctor. Other effects, such as hair loss, may not be serious but may cause concern. Some effects do not occur until months or years after the medicine is used.

Before you begin treatment with vinblastine, you and your doctor should talk about the good this medicine will do as well as the risks of using it.

Vinblastine is to be administered only by or under the immediate supervision of your doctor. It is available in the following dosage form:

Parenteral
- Injection (U.S. and Canada)

Before Using This Medicine

In deciding to use a medicine, the risks of taking the medicine must be weighed against the good it will do. This is a decision you and your doctor will make. For vinblastine, the following should be considered:

Allergies—Tell your doctor if you have ever had any unusual or allergic reaction to vinblastine.

Pregnancy—Tell your doctor if you are pregnant or if you intend to have children. This medicine may cause birth defects if either the male or female is taking it at the time of conception or if it is taken during pregnancy. In addition, many cancer medicines may cause sterility which could be permanent. Although sterility has not been reported with this medicine, vinblastine may interfere with production of sperm and the possibility should be kept in mind.

Be sure that you have discussed this with your doctor before receiving this medicine. It is best to use some kind of birth control while you are receiving vinblastine. Tell your doctor right away if you think you have become pregnant while receiving vinblastine.

Breast-feeding—Tell your doctor if you are breast-feeding or if you intend to breast-feed during treatment with this medicine. Because vinblastine may cause serious side effects, breast-feeding is generally not recommended while you are receiving it.

Children—This medicine has been tested in children and has not been shown to cause different side effects or problems than it does in adults.

Older adults—Many medicines have not been tested in older people. Therefore, it may not be known whether they work exactly the same way they do in younger adults or if they cause different side effects or problems in older people. There is no specific information about the use of vinblastine in the elderly.

Other medicines—Although certain medicines should not be used together at all, in other cases two different medicines may be used together even if an interaction might occur. In these cases, your doctor may want to change the dose, or other precautions may be necessary. When you are receiving vinblastine, it is especially important that your health care professional know if you are taking any of the following:
- Amphotericin B by injection (e.g., Fungizone) or
- Antithyroid agents (medicine for overactive thyroid) or
- Azathioprine (e.g., Imuran) or
- Chloramphenicol (e.g., Chloromycetin) or
- Colchicine or
- Flucytosine (e.g., Ancobon) or
- Ganciclovir (e.g., Cytovene) or
- Interferon (e.g., Intron A, Roferon-A) or
- Plicamycin (e.g., Mithracin) or
- Zidovudine (e.g., Retrovir) or

- If you have ever been treated with x-rays or cancer medicines—Vinblastine may increase the effects of these medicines or radiation therapy on the blood
- Probenecid (e.g., Benemid) or
- Sulfinpyrazone (e.g., Anturane)—Vinblastine may increase the concentration of uric acid in the blood. Since probenecid and sulfinpyrazone are used to lower uric acid levels, they may not be as effective in patients taking vinblastine

Other medical problems—The presence of other medical problems may affect the use of vinblastine. Make sure you tell your doctor if you have any other medical problems, especially:
- Chickenpox (including recent exposure) or
- Herpes zoster (shingles)—Risk of severe disease affecting other parts of the body
- Gout (history of) or
- Kidney stones (history of)—Vinblastine may increase levels of uric acid in the body, which can cause gout or kidney stones
- Infection—Vinblastine may decrease your body's ability to fight infection
- Liver disease—Effects may be increased because of slower removal of vinblastine from the body

Proper Use of This Medicine

Vinblastine is sometimes given together with certain other medicines. If you are using a combination of medicines, it is important that you receive each one at the proper time. If you are taking some of these medicines by mouth, ask your health care professional to help you plan a way to take them at the right times.

While you are using this medicine, your doctor may want you to drink extra fluids so that you will pass more urine. This will help prevent kidney problems and keep your kidneys working well.

Vinblastine sometimes causes nausea and vomiting. However, it is very important that you continue to receive the medicine, even if you begin to feel ill. Ask your health care professional for ways to lessen these effects.

Dosing—The dose of vinblastine will be different for different patients. The dose that is used may depend on a number of things, including what the medicine is being used for, the patient's weight or size, and whether or not other medicines are also being taken. *If you are receiving vinblastine at home, follow your doctor's orders or the directions on the label.* If you have any questions about the proper dose of vinblastine, ask your doctor.

Precautions While Using This Medicine

It is very important that your doctor check your progress at regular visits to make sure that this medicine is working properly and to check for unwanted effects.

While you are being treated with vinblastine, and after you stop treatment with it, *do not have any immunizations (vaccinations) without your doctor's approval.* Vinblastine may lower your body's resistance and there is a chance you might get the infection the immunization is meant to prevent. Other people living in your household should not take oral polio vaccine since there is a chance they could pass the polio virus on to you. Also, avoid persons who have taken oral polio vaccine within the past several months. Do not get close to them, and do not stay in the same room with them for very long. If you cannot take these precautions, you should consider wearing a protective face mask that covers the nose and mouth.

Vinblastine can temporarily lower the number of white blood cells in your blood, increasing the chance of getting an infection. It can also lower the number of platelets, which are necessary for proper blood clotting. If this occurs, there are certain precautions you can take, especially when your blood count is low, to reduce the risk of infection or bleeding:

- If you can, avoid people with infections. *Check with your doctor immediately* if you think you are getting an infection or if you get a fever or chills, cough or hoarseness, lower back or side pain, or painful or difficult urination.
- *Check with your doctor immediately* if you notice any unusual bleeding or bruising; black, tarry stools; blood in urine or stools; or pinpoint red spots on your skin.
- Be careful when using a regular toothbrush, dental floss, or toothpick. Your medical doctor, dentist, or nurse may recommend other ways to clean your teeth and gums. Check with your medical doctor before having any dental work done.
- Do not touch your eyes or the inside of your nose unless you have just washed your hands and have not touched anything else in the meantime.
- Be careful not to cut yourself when you are using sharp objects such as a safety razor or fingernail or toenail cutters.
- Avoid contact sports or other situations where bruising or injury could occur.

If vinblastine accidentally seeps out of the vein into which it is injected, it may damage the skin and cause some scarring. *Tell the doctor or nurse right away if you notice redness, pain, or swelling at the place of injection.*

Side Effects of This Medicine

Along with their needed effects, medicines like vinblastine can sometimes cause unwanted effects such as blood problems, loss of hair, and other side effects. These and other effects are described below. Also, because of the way these medicines act on the body, there is a chance that they might cause other unwanted effects that may not occur until months or years after the medicine is used. These delayed effects may include certain types of cancer, such as leukemia. Discuss these possible effects with your doctor.

Although not all of these side effects may occur, if they do occur they may need medical attention.

Check with your doctor or nurse immediately if any of the following side effects occur:

More frequent

Cough or hoarseness accompanied by fever or chills; fever or chills; lower back or side pain accompanied by fever or chills; painful or difficult urination accompanied by fever or chills

Less common

Blood in urine or stools; pain or redness at place of injection; pinpoint red spots on skin; unusual bleeding or bruising

Rare

Black, tarry stools

Check with your health care professional as soon as possible if any of the following side effects occur:

Less common

Joint pain; sores in mouth and on lips; swelling of feet or lower legs

Rare

Difficulty in walking; dizziness; double vision; drooping eyelids; headache; jaw pain; mental depression; numbness or tingling in fingers and toes; pain in fingers and toes; pain in testicles; weakness

Other side effects may occur that usually do not need medical attention. These side effects may go away during treatment as your body adjusts to the medicine. Also, your health care professional may be able to tell you about ways to prevent or reduce some of these side effects. Check with your health care professional if any of the following side effects continue or are bothersome or if you have any questions about them:

Less common

Bone or muscle pain; nausea and vomiting

This medicine often causes a temporary loss of hair. After treatment with vinblastine has ended, or sometimes even during treatment, normal hair growth should return.

Other side effects not listed above may also occur in some patients. If you notice any other effects, check with your doctor.

Additional Information

Once a medicine has been approved for marketing for a certain use, experience may show that it is also useful for other medical problems. Although these uses are not included in product labeling, vinblastine is used in certain patients with the following medical conditions:

- Cancer of the bladder
- Cancer of the kidneys
- Cancer of the lungs
- Cancer of the prostate
- Germ cell ovarian tumors (a certain type of cancer of the ovaries)
- Malignant melanoma

Other than the above information, there is no additional information relating to proper use, precautions, or side effects for these uses.

Revised: 07/19/2000

VINCRISTINE   Systemic

Commonly used brand name(s):

In the U.S.—
Oncovin
Vincasar PFS
Vincrex

In Canada—
Oncovin

Description

Vincristine (vin-KRIS-teen) belongs to the group of medicines known as antineoplastic agents. It is used to treat some kinds of cancer as well as some noncancerous conditions.

Vincristine interferes with the growth of cancer cells, which are eventually destroyed. Since the growth of normal body cells may also be affected by vincristine, other effects will also occur. Some of these may be serious and must be reported to your doctor. Other effects, such as hair loss, may not be serious but may cause concern. Some effects may not occur for months or years after the medicine is used.

Before you begin treatment with vincristine, you and your doctor should talk about the good this medicine will do as well as the risks of using it.

Vincristine is to be administered only by or under the immediate supervision of your doctor. It is available in the following dosage form:

Parenteral
- Injection (U.S. and Canada)

Before Using This Medicine

In deciding to use a medicine, the risks of taking the medicine must be weighed against the good it will do. This is a decision you and your doctor will make. For vincristine, the following should be considered:

Allergies—Tell your doctor if you have ever had any unusual or allergic reaction to vincristine. Also tell your health care professional if you are allergic to any other substances, such as foods, preservatives, or dyes.

Pregnancy—Tell your doctor if you are pregnant or if you intend to have children. There is a chance that this medicine may cause birth defects if either the male or female is taking it at the time of conception or if it is taken during pregnancy. Vincristine causes birth defects and death of the fetus in animals. In addition, many cancer medicines may cause sterility, which could be permanent. Although sterility has not been reported with this medicine, the possibility should be kept in mind.

Be sure that you have discussed this with your doctor before receiving this medicine. It is best to use some kind of birth control while you are receiving vincristine. Tell your doctor right away if you think you have become pregnant while receiving vincristine.

Breast-feeding—Tell your doctor if you are breast-feeding or if you intend to breast-feed during treatment with this medicine. Because vincristine may cause serious side effects, breast-feeding is generally not recommended while you are receiving it.

Children—This medicine has been tested in children and has not been shown to cause different side effects or problems than it does in adults.

Older adults—Nervous system effects may be more likely to occur in the elderly, who are usually more sensitive to the effects of vincristine.

Other medicines—Although certain medicines should not be used together at all, in other cases two different medicines may be used together even if an interaction might occur. In these cases, your doctor may want to change the dose, or other precautions may be necessary. When you are receiving vincristine, it is especially important that your health care professional know if you are taking any of the following:
- Probenecid (e.g., Benemid) or
- Sulfinpyrazone (e.g., Anturane)—Vincristine may increase the concentration of uric acid in the blood, which these medicines are used to lower

- If you have ever been treated with x-rays or cancer medicines—Vincristine may increase the effects of these medicines or radiation therapy on the blood

Other medical problems—The presence of other medical problems may affect the use of vincristine. Make sure you tell your doctor if you have any other medical problems, especially:
- Chickenpox (including recent exposure) or
- Herpes zoster (shingles)—Risk of severe disease affecting other parts of the body
- Gout (history of) or
- Kidney stones (history of)—Vincristine may increase levels of uric acid in the body, which can cause gout or kidney stones
- Infection—Vincristine can reduce immunity to infection
- Liver disease—Effects may be increased because of slower removal of vincristine from the body
- Nerve or muscle disease—May be worsened

Proper Use of This Medicine

Vincristine is often given together with certain other medicines. If you are using a combination of medicines, it is important that you receive each one at the proper time. If you are taking some of these medicines by mouth, ask your health care professional to help you plan a way to take them at the right times.

While you are using this medicine, it may be necessary to drink extra fluids so that you will pass more urine. This will help prevent kidney problems and keep your kidneys working well. Ask your doctor if this is necessary for you.

This medicine sometimes causes nausea and vomiting. However, it is very important that you continue to receive the medicine, even if you begin to feel ill. Ask your health care professional for ways to lessen these effects.

Vincristine frequently causes constipation and stomach cramps. Your doctor may want you to take a laxative. However, do not decide to take these medicines on your own without first checking with your doctor.

Dosing—The dose of vincristine will be different for different patients. The dose that is used may depend on a number of things, including what the medicine is being used for, the patient's weight or size, and whether or not other medicines are also being taken. *If you are receiving vincristine at home, follow your doctor's orders or the directions on the label.* If you have any questions about the proper dose of vincristine, ask your doctor.

Precautions While Using This Medicine

It is very important that your doctor check your progress at regular visits to make sure that vincristine is working properly and to check for unwanted effects.

While you are being treated with vincristine, and after you stop treatment with it, *do not have any immunizations (vaccinations) without your doctor's approval.* Vincristine may lower your body's resistance and there is a chance you might get the infection the immunization is meant to prevent. Other people living in your household should not take or should not have recently taken oral polio vaccine since there is a chance they could pass the polio virus on to you. Also, avoid other persons who have taken oral polio vaccine. Do not get close to them, and do not stay in the same room with them for very long. If you cannot take these precautions, you should consider wearing a protective face mask that covers the nose and mouth.

If vincristine accidentally seeps out of the vein into which it is injected, it may damage some tissues and cause scarring. *Tell the doctor or nurse right away if you notice redness, pain, or swelling at the place of injection.*

Side Effects of This Medicine

Along with their needed effects, medicines like vincristine can sometimes cause unwanted effects such as blood problems, nervous system problems, loss of hair, and other side effects. These and others are described below. Also, because of the way these medicines act on the body, there is a chance that they might cause other unwanted effects that may not occur until months or years after the medicine is used. Discuss these possible effects with your doctor.

Although not all of these side effects may occur, if they do occur they may need medical attention. *Check with your doctor or nurse immediately* if any of the following side effects occur:

Less common
>   Pain or redness at place of injection

Rare
>   Black, tarry stools; blood in urine or stools; cough or hoarseness; fever or chills; pinpoint red spots on skin; unusual bleeding or bruising

Check with your health care professional as soon as possible if any of the following side effects occur:

More common
>   Blurred or double vision; constipation; difficulty in walking; drooping eyelids; headache; jaw pain; joint pain; lower back or side pain; numbness or tingling in fingers and toes; pain in fingers and toes; pain in testicles; stomach cramps; swelling of feet or lower legs; weakness

Less common
>   Agitation; bed-wetting; confusion; convulsions (seizures); decrease or increase in urination; dizziness or lightheadedness when getting up from a lying or sitting position; hallucinations (seeing, hearing, or feeling things that are not there); lack of sweating; loss of appetite; mental depression; painful or difficult urination; trouble in sleeping; unconsciousness

Rare
>   Sores in mouth and on lips

Other side effects may occur that usually do not need medical attention. These side effects may go away during treatment as your body adjusts to the medicine. Also, your health care professional may be able to tell you about ways to prevent or reduce some of these side effects. Check with your health care professional if any of the following side effects continue or are bothersome or if you have any questions about them:

Less common
>   Bloating; diarrhea; loss of weight; nausea and vomiting; skin rash

Other side effects may occur that usually do not need medical attention. This medicine often causes a temporary loss of hair. After treatment with vincristine has ended, or sometimes even during treatment, normal hair growth should return.

Other side effects not listed above may also occur in some patients. If you notice any other effects, check with your doctor.

Revised: 03/06/2001

VINDESINE   Systemic

Commonly used brand name(s):

In Canada—
>   Eldisine®

Other commonly used names are desacetyl vinblastine amide sulfate and vincaleukoblastine.

Description

Vindesine (VIN-de-seen) belongs to the group of medicines known as antineoplastic agents. It is used to treat some kinds of cancer, including leukemia and lung cancer.

Vindesine interferes with the growth of cancer cells, which are eventually destroyed. Since the growth of normal body cells may also be affected by vindesine, other effects will also occur. Some of these may be serious and must be reported to your doctor. Other effects, such as hair loss, may not be serious but may cause concern.

Before you begin treatment with vindesine, you and your doctor should talk about the good this medicine will do as well as the risks of using it.

This medicine is available only with your doctor's prescription, in the following dosage form:

Parenteral
>   • Injection (Canada)

Before Using This Medicine

In deciding to use a medicine, the risks of taking the medicine must be weighed against the good it will do. This is a decision you and your doctor will make. For vindesine, the following should be considered:

Allergies—Tell your doctor if you have ever had any unusual or allergic reaction to vindesine.

Pregnancy—Vindesine has not been studied in pregnant women.

Before receiving vindesine make sure your doctor knows if you are pregnant or if you may become pregnant. It is best to use some kind of birth control while you are receiving vindesine. Tell your doctor right away if you think you have become pregnant while receiving vindesine.

Breast-feeding—It is not known whether vindesine passes into the breast milk. However, vindesine is not recommended during breast-feeding, because it may cause unwanted effects in nursing babies.

Children—Although there is no specific information comparing use of vindesine in children with use in other age groups, this medicine is not expected to cause different side effects or problems in children than it does in adults.

Older adults—Many medicines have not been studied specifically in older people. Therefore, it may not be known whether they work exactly the same way they do in younger adults or if they cause different side effects or problems in

older people. There is no specific information comparing use of vindesine in the elderly with use in other age groups.

Other medicines—Although certain medicines should not be used together at all, in other cases two different medicines may be used together even if an interaction might occur. In these cases, your doctor may want to change the dose, or other precautions may be necessary. When you are taking vindesine, it is especially important that your doctor or pharmacist know if you are taking any of the following:

- Acyclovir (e.g., Zovirax) or
- Anticonvulsants (seizure medicine) or
- Antidiabetics, oral (diabetes medicine taken by mouth) or
- Anti-infectives by mouth or by injection (medicine for infection) or
- Antipsychotics (medicine for mental illness) or
- Captopril (e.g., Capoten) or
- Carbamazepine (e.g., Tegretol) or
- Enalapril (e.g., Vasotec) or
- Flecainide (e.g., Tambocor) or
- Gold salts (medicine for arthritis) or
- Imipenem or
- Inflammation or pain medicine, except narcotics or
- Lisinopril (e.g., Prinivil, Zestril) or
- Maprotiline (e.g., Ludiomil) or
- Penicillamine (e.g., Cuprimine) or
- Pimozide (e.g., Orap) or
- Procainamide (e.g., Pronestyl) or
- Promethazine (e.g., Phenergan) or
- Ramipril (e.g., Altace) or
- Sulfasalazine (e.g., Azulfidine) or
- Tiopronin (e.g., Thiola) or
- Tocainide (e.g., Tonocard) or
- Tricyclic antidepressants (medicine for depression) or
- Trimeprazine (e.g., Temaril)—Concurrent use of these agents with vindesine may cause blood disorders

- Alpha interferons (e.g., Intron A, Roferon-A) or
- Amphotericin B by injection (e.g., Fungizone) or
- Antineoplastics, other (cancer medicine) or
- Antithyroid agents (medicine for overactive thyroid) or
- Azathioprine (e.g., Imuran) or
- Chloramphenicol (e.g., Chloromycetin) or
- Colchicine or
- Cyclophosphamide (e.g., Cytoxan) or
- Flucytosine (e.g., Ancoban) or
- Ganciclovir (e.g., Cytovene) or
- Mercaptopurine (e.g., Purinethol)
- Methotrexate (e.g., Rheumatrex) or
- Plicamycin (e.g., Mithracin) or
- Zidovudine (e.g., AZT, Retrovir)—Concurrent use of these agents with vindesine increases the risk of infection

- Anti-infectives by mouth or by injection (medicine for infection)
- Carbamazepine (e.g., Tegretol) or
- Chloroquine (e.g., Aralen) or
- Cisplatin (e.g., Platinol) or
- Cytarabine (e.g., Cytosar-U) or
- Diptheria, tetanus, and pertussis (DTP) vaccine (recent, within 30 days of vindesine therapy)
- Disulfiram (e.g., Antabuse) or
- Ethotoin (e.g., Peganone) or
- Hydroxychloroquine (e.g., Plaquenil) or
- Lindane, topical (e.g., Kwell) or
- Lithium (e.g., Lithane) or

- Mephenytoin (e.g., Mesantoin) or
- Mexilitene (e.g., Mexitil) or
- Pemoline (e.g., Cylert) or
- Pyridoxine (e.g., Hexa-Betalin) (with long-term, high-dose use) or
- Quinine (e.g., Quinamm)—Concurrent use of these agents with vindesine increases the risk of neurotoxicity
- Phenytoin (e.g., Dilantin)—Concurrent use of this agent with vindesine increases the risk of seizures

- If you have ever been treated with radiation or cancer medicines—Vindesine may increase the effects of these medicines or radiation therapy on the blood

Other medical problems—The presence of other medical problems may affect the use of vindesine. Make sure you tell your doctor if you have any other medical problems, especially:

- Charcot-Marie-Tooth syndrome, demyelinating form— May cause increased neuropathic effects
- Drug-induced blood disorders—May worsen
- Infection—There may be an increased risk of infections or worsening infections because of the body's reduced ability to fight them
- Chickenpox (including recent exposure) or
- Herpes zoster (shingles)—Risk of severe disease affecting other parts of the body
- Liver disease—Effects of vindesine may increase because of slower removal from the body
- Nerve or muscle disease—May worsen

Proper Use of This Medicine

This medicine sometimes causes nausea and vomiting. However, it is very important that you continue to receive the medicine, even if you begin to feel ill. Ask your doctor, nurse, or pharmacist for ways to lessen these effects.

Vindesine frequently causes constipation and stomach cramps. Your doctor may want you to take a laxative. However, do not decide to take these medicines on your own without first checking with your doctor.

Dosing—The dose of vindesine will be different for different patients. The dose that is used may depend on a number of things, including what the medicine is being used for, the patient's body size, and whether or not other medicines are also being taken. *If you are taking or receiving vindesine at home, follow your doctor's orders or the directions on the label.* If you have any questions about the proper dose of vindesine, ask your doctor.

Precautions While Using This Medicine

It is very important that your doctor check your progress at regular visits to make sure that vindesine is working properly and to check for unwanted effects.

While you are being treated with vindesine, and after you stop treatment with it, *do not have any immunizations (vaccinations) without your doctor's approval.* Vindesine may lower your body's resistance and there is a chance you might get the infection the immunization is meant to prevent. Other people living in your household should not take or should not have recently taken oral polio vaccine since there is a chance they could pass the polio virus on to you. Also, avoid other persons who have taken oral polio vaccine. Do not get close to them, and do not stay in the same room with them for very long. If you cannot take these precautions, you should consider wearing a protective face mask that covers the nose and mouth.

Vindesine can temporarily lower the number of white blood cells in your blood, increasing the chance of getting an infection. It can also lower the number of platelets, which are necessary for proper blood clotting. If this occurs, there are certain precautions you can take, especially when your blood count is low, to reduce the risk of infection or bleeding:

- If you can, avoid people with infections. *Check with your doctor immediately* if you think you are getting an infection or if you get a fever or chills, cough or hoarseness, lower back or side pain, or painful or difficult urination.
- *Check with your doctor immediately* if you notice any unusual bleeding or bruising; black, tarry stools; blood in urine or stools; or pinpoint red spots on your skin.
- Be careful when using a regular toothbrush, dental floss, or toothpick. Your medical doctor, dentist, or nurse may recommend other ways to clean your teeth and gums. Check with your medical doctor before having any dental work done.
- Do not touch your eyes or the inside of your nose unless you have just washed your hands and have not touched anything else in the meantime.
- Be careful not to cut yourself when you are using sharp objects such as a safety razor or fingernail or toenail cutters.
- Avoid contact sports or other situations where bruising or injury could occur.

If vindesine accidentally seeps out of the vein into which it is injected, it may damage some tissues and cause scarring. *Tell the doctor or nurse right away if you notice redness, pain, or swelling at the place of injection.*

Side Effects of This Medicine

Along with its needed effects, a medicine may cause some unwanted effects. Although not all of these side effects may occur, if they do occur they may need medical attention.

Check with your doctor or nurse immediately if any of the following side effects occur:

More common
Black, tarry stools; chest pain; chills; cough; fever; painful or difficult urination; shortness of breath; sore throat; sores, ulcers, or white spots on lips or in mouth; swollen glands

Less common or rare
Blindness; blurred or double vision; convulsions (seizures); difficulty in walking; drooping eyelids; headache; jaw pain; numbness or tingling in fingers and toes; pain in fingers and toes; pain in testicles; unusual bleeding or bruising; unusual tiredness or weakness

Symptoms of overdose
Get emergency help immediately if any of the following symptoms of overdose occur
Abnormal drowsiness; Agitation; confusion; dazed feeling; decreased urine output; depression; dizziness; headache; hostility; irritability; muscle twitching; nausea; rapid weight gain; seizures; swelling of face, ankles, or hands

Other side effects may occur that usually do not need medical attention. These side effects may go away during treatment as your body adjusts to the medicine. However, check with your doctor if any of the following side effects continue or are bothersome.

Less common or rare
Constipation; general feeling of discomfort or illness; increase in bowel movements; loose stools; loss of appetite; muscle or bone pain; nausea and vomiting; skin rash; soft stools; weight loss

This medicine often causes a temporary loss of hair. After treatment with vindesine has ended, normal hair growth should return.

Other side effects not listed above may also occur in some patients. If you notice any other effects, check with your doctor.

Developed: 05/25/00

VINORELBINE   Systemic

Commonly used brand name(s):

In the U.S.—
Navelbine

In Canada—
Navelbine

Description

Vinorelbine (vi-NOR-el-been) belongs to the general group of medicines known as antineoplastics. It is used to treat some kinds of lung cancer. It may also be used to treat other kinds of cancer, as determined by your doctor.

Vinorelbine interferes with the growth of cancer cells, which are eventually destroyed. Since the growth of normal cells also may be affected by vinorelbine, other effects will occur. Some of these may be serious and must be reported to your doctor. Other effects, such as hair loss, may not be serious but may cause concern. Some effects may not occur until months or years after the medicine is used.

Before you begin treatment with vinorelbine, you and your doctor should talk about the good this medicine will do as well as the risks of using it.

Vinorelbine is to be administered only by or under the immediate supervision of your doctor. It is available in the following dosage form:

Parenteral
- Injection (U.S. and Canada)

Before Receiving This Medicine

In deciding to use a medicine, the risks of receiving the medicine must be weighed against the good it will do. This is a decision you and your doctor will make. For vinorelbine, the following should be considered:

Allergies—Tell your doctor if you have ever had any unusual or allergic reaction to vinorelbine.

Pregnancy—Tell your doctor if you are pregnant or if you intend to have children. This medicine may cause birth defects if either the male or female is receiving it at the time of conception or if it is taken during pregnancy. In addition, many cancer medicines may cause sterility, which could be permanent. Although decreased fertility has been reported only in male rats with this medicine, the possibility of an effect in human males and females should be kept in mind.

Be sure that you have discussed this with your doctor before receiving this medicine. It is best to use some kind of birth control while you are receiving vinorelbine. Tell your doctor right away if you think you have become pregnant while receiving vinorelbine.

Breast-feeding—Tell your doctor if you are breast-feeding or if you intend to breast-feed during treatment with this medicine. Because vinorelbine may cause serious side effects in nursing babies, breast-feeding is generally not recommended while you are receiving this medicine.

Children—There is no specific information comparing use of vinorelbine in children with use in other age groups. Safety and efficacy of vinorelbine in children have not been established.

Older adults—Vinorelbine has been studied in the elderly. Although patients older than 65 years of age have shown a slight increase in side effects compared with patients younger than 65 years of age, the overall safety and efficacy of vinorelbine are not different for older people.

Other medicines—Although certain medicines should not be used together at all, in other cases two different medicines may be used together even if an interaction might occur. In these cases, your doctor may want to change the dose, or other precautions may be necessary. When you are taking vinorelbine, it is especially important that your health care professional know if you are taking any of the following:

- Amphotericin B by injection (e.g., Fungizone) or
- Antithyroid agents (medicine for overactive thyroid) or
- Azathioprine (e.g., Imuran) or
- Chloramphenicol (e.g., Chloromycetin) or
- Colchicine or
- Cyclophosphamide (e.g., Cytoxan) or
- Flucytosine (e.g., Ancobon) or
- Ganciclovir (e.g., Cytovene) or
- Interferon (e.g., Intron A, Roferon-A) or
- Mercaptopurine (e.g., Purinethol) or
- Methotrexate (e.g., Mexate) or
- Mitomycin (e.g., Mutamycin) or
- Paclitaxel (e.g., Taxol) or
- Plicamycin (e.g., Mithracin) or
- Zidovudine (e.g., Retrovir) or
- If you have ever been treated with x-rays or cancer medicines—Vinorelbine may increase the effects of these medicines or radiation therapy on the blood

Other medical problems—The presence of other medical problems may affect the use of vinorelbine. Make sure you tell your doctor if you have any other medical problems, especially:

- Chickenpox (including recent exposure) or
- Herpes zoster (shingles)—Risk of severe disease affecting other parts of the body
- Infection—Vinorelbine may decrease your body's ability to fight infections

Proper Use of This Medicine

Vinorelbine is sometimes given together with certain other medicines. If you are using a combination of medicines, it is important that you receive each one at the proper time. If you are taking some of these medicines by mouth, ask your health care professional to help you plan a way to take them at the right times.

While you are receiving vinorelbine, your doctor may want you to drink extra fluids so that you will pass more urine. This will help prevent kidney problems and keep your kidneys working well.

This medicine often causes nausea and vomiting. However, it is very important that you continue to receive it, even if you begin to feel ill. Ask your health care professional for ways to lessen these effects.

Dosing—The dose of vinorelbine will be different for different patients. The dose that is used may depend on a number of things, including what the medicine is being used for, the patient's size, and whether or not other medicines are also being taken. *If you are receiving vinorelbine at home, follow your doctor's orders or the directions on the label.* If you have any question about the proper dose of vinorelbine, ask your doctor.

Precautions While Using This Medicine

It is very important that your doctor check your progress at regular visits to make sure that this medicine is working properly and to check for unwanted effects.

While you are being treated with vinorelbine, and after you stop treatment with it, *do not have any immunizations (vaccinations) without your doctor's approval.* Vinorelbine may lower your body's resistance and there is a chance you might get the infection the immunization is meant to prevent. In addition, other persons living in your household should not take oral poliovirus vaccine, since there is a chance they could pass the poliovirus on to you. Also, avoid persons who have taken oral poliovirus vaccine within the last several months. Do not get close to them, and do not stay in the same room with them for very long. If you cannot take these precautions, you should consider wearing a protective face mask that covers the nose and the mouth.

Vinorelbine can temporarily lower the number of white blood cells in your blood, increasing the chance of getting an infection. It can also lower the number of platelets, which are necessary for proper blood clotting. If this occurs, there are certain precautions you can take, especially when your blood count is low, to reduce the risk of infection or bleeding:

- If you can, avoid people with infection. *Check with your doctor immediately* if you think you are getting an infection or if you get a fever or chills, cough or hoarseness, lower back or side pain, or have painful or difficult urination.
- *Check with your doctor immediately* if you notice any unusual bleeding or bruising; black, tarry stools; blood in urine or stools; or pinpoint red spots on your skin.
- Do not touch your eyes or the inside of your nose, unless you have just washed your hands and have not touched anything else in the meantime.
- Be careful not to cut yourself when you are using sharp objects, such as a safety razor or fingernail or toenail cutters.
- Avoid contact sports or other situations where bruising or injury can occur.

If vinorelbine accidentally seeps out of the vein into which it is injected, it may damage some tissue and cause scarring. *Tell the doctor or nurse right away if you notice redness, pain, or swelling at the place of injection.*

Be careful when using a regular toothbrush, dental floss, or toothpick. Your medical doctor, dentist, or nurse may recommend other ways to clean your teeth and gums. Check with your medical doctor before having any dental work done.

Side Effects of This Medicine

Along with its needed effects, a medicine may cause some unwanted effects. Although not all of these side effects may occur, if they do occur they may need medical attention.

Check with your doctor or nurse immediately if any of the following side effects occur:

More common
   Cough or hoarseness, accompanied by fever or chills; fever or chills; lower back or side pain, accompanied by fever or chills; painful or difficult urination, accompanied by fever or chills; redness, increased warmth, pain, or discoloration of vein at place of injection; sore throat, accompanied by fever or chills

Less common
   Chest pain; shortness of breath; sores in mouth and on lips

Rare
   Black, tarry stools; bloating; blood in urine or stools; chills; darkened urine; fast heartbeat; fever; indigestion; loss of appetite; nausea; painful urination; pains in stomach; pinpoint red spots on skin; skin rash; unusual bleeding or bruising; vomiting; yellow eyes or skin

Check with your doctor as soon as possible if any of the following side effects occur:

More common
   Loss of strength and energy; unusual tiredness or weakness

Less common
   Numbness or tingling in fingers and toes

Symptoms of overdose
   Chest pain; cough or hoarseness, accompanied by fever or chills; fever or chills; heartburn; lower back or side pain, accompanied by fever or chills; mild abdominal pain and constipation; numbness or tingling in fingers and toes; painful or difficult urination, accompanied by fever or chills; sore throat, accompanied by fever or chills; unusual bleeding or bruising; unusual tiredness or weakness; vomiting

Other side effects may occur that usually do not need medical attention. These side effects may go away during treatment as your body adjusts to the medicine. However, check with your doctor if any of the following side effects continue or are bothersome:

More common
   Constipation; loss of appetite; nausea and vomiting

Less common
   Diarrhea; jaw pain; joint or muscle pain

Other side effects not listed above may also occur in some patients. If you notice any other effects, check with your doctor.

Additional Information

Once a medicine has been approved for marketing for a certain use, experience may show that it is also useful for other medical problems. Although this use is not included in product labeling, vinorelbine is used in certain patients with the following medical condition:

- Breast cancer
- Cervical cancer
- Ovarian cancer (epithelial)

Other than the above information, there is no additional information relating to proper use, precautions, or side effects for this use.

Developed: 07/01/1998
Revised: 11/20/2000

VITAMIN A   Systemic

Commonly used brand name(s):

In the U.S.—
   Aquasol A
   Generic name product may be available.

In Canada—
   Aquasol A

Another commonly used name is retinol.

Description

Vitamins (VYE-ta-mins) are compounds that you *must* have for growth and health. They are needed in small amounts only and are usually available in the foods that you eat. Vitamin A is needed for night vision and for growth of skin, bones, and male and female reproductive organs. In pregnant women vitamin A is necessary for the growth of a healthy fetus.

Lack of vitamin A may lead to a rare condition called night blindness (problems seeing in the dark), as well as dry eyes, eye infections, skin problems, and slowed growth. Your health care professional may treat these problems by prescribing vitamin A for you.

Some conditions may increase your need for vitamin A. These include:
- Diarrhea
- Eye diseases
- Intestine diseases
- Infections (continuing or chronic)
- Measles
- Pancreas disease
- Stomach removal
- Stress (continuing)

In addition, infants receiving unfortified formula may need vitamin A supplements.

Vitamin A absorption will be decreased in any condition in which fat is poorly absorbed.

Increased need for vitamin A should be determined by your health care professional.

Claims that vitamin A is effective for treatment of conditions such as acne or lung diseases, or for treatment of eye problems, wounds, or dry or wrinkled skin not caused by lack of vitamin A have not been proven. Although vitamin A is being used to prevent certain types of cancer, some experts feel there is not enough information to show that this is effective, particularly in well-nourished individuals.

Injectable vitamin A is given by or under the supervision of a health care professional. Other forms of vitamin A are available without a prescription.

Vitamin A is available in the following dosage forms:

Oral
- Capsules (U.S. and Canada)
- Oral solution (U.S.)
- Tablets (U.S.)

Parenteral
- Injection (U.S.)

Importance of Diet

For good health, it is important that you eat a balanced and varied diet. Follow carefully any diet program your health care professional may recommend. For your specific dietary vitamin and/or mineral needs, ask your health care professional for a list of appropriate foods. If you think that you are not getting enough vitamins and/or minerals in your diet, you may choose to take a dietary supplement.

Vitamin A is found in various foods including yellow-orange fruits and vegetables; dark green, leafy vegetables; vitamin A-fortified milk; liver; and margarine. Vitamin A comes in two different forms, retinols and beta-carotene. Retinols are found in foods that come from animals (meat, milk, eggs). The form of vitamin A found in plants is called beta-carotene (which is converted to vitamin A in the body). Food processing may destroy some of the vitamins. For example, freezing may reduce the amount of vitamin A in foods.

Vitamins alone will not take the place of a good diet and will not provide energy. Your body needs other substances found in food, such as protein, minerals, carbohydrates, and fat. Vitamins themselves often cannot work without the presence of other foods. For example, small amounts of fat are needed so that vitamin A can be absorbed into the body.

The daily amount of vitamin A needed is defined in several different ways.

For U.S.—
- Recommended Dietary Allowances (RDAs) are the amount of vitamins and minerals needed to provide for adequate nutrition in most healthy persons. RDAs for a given nutrient may vary depending on a person's age, sex, and physical condition (e.g., pregnancy).
- Daily Values (DVs) are used on food and dietary supplement labels to indicate the percent of the recommended daily amount of each nutrient that a serving provides. DV replaces the previous designation of United States Recommended Daily Allowances (USRDAs).
- Normal daily recommended intakes in the United States for vitamin A are generally defined according to age or condition and to the form of vitamin A as follows:

Age or Condition	Form of Vitamin A		
	RE or mcg of Retinol	Amount in Units as Retinol	Amount in Units as a Combination of Retinol and Beta-carotene*
Infants and children			
Birth to 3 years	375–400	1250–1330	1875–2000
4 to 6 years	500	1665	2500
7 to 10 years	700	2330	3500
Teenage and adult males	1000	3330	5000
Teenage and adult females	800	2665	4000
Pregnant females	800	2665	4000
Breast-feeding females	1200–1300	4000–4330	6000–6500

*Based on 1980 Recommended Dietary Allowances (RDAs) for vitamin A in the diet that is a combination of retinol and beta-carotene.

For Canada—
- Recommended Nutrient Intakes (RNIs) are used to determine the amounts of vitamins, minerals, and protein needed to provide adequate nutrition and lessen the risk of chronic disease.
- Normal daily recommended intakes in Canada for vitamin A are generally defined according to age or condition and to the form of vitamin A as follows:

Age or Condition	Form of Vitamin A		
	RE or mcg of Retinol	Amount in Units as Retinol	Amount in Units as a Combination of Retinol and Beta-carotene*
Infants and children			
Birth to 3 years	400	1330	2000
4 to 6 years	500	1665	2500
7 to 10 years	700–800	2330–2665	3500
Teenage and adult males	1000	3330	5000
Teenage and adult females	800	2665	4000
Pregnant females	900	2665–3000	4000–4500
Breast-feeding females	1200	4000	6000

*Based on 1980 U.S. Recommended Dietary Allowances (RDAs) for vitamin A in the diet that is a combination of retinol and beta-carotene.

In the past, the RDA and RNI for vitamin A have been expressed in Units. This term Units has been replaced by retinol equivalents (RE) or micrograms (mcg) of retinol, with 1 RE equal to 1 mcg of retinol. This was done to better describe the two forms of vitamin A, retinol and beta-carotene. One RE of vitamin A is equal to 3.33 Units of retinol and 10 Units of beta-carotene. Some products available have not changed their labels and continue to be labeled in Units.

Before Using This Dietary Supplement

If you are taking this dietary supplement without a prescription, carefully read and follow any precautions on the label. For vitamin A, the following should be considered:

Allergies—Tell your health care professional if you have ever had any unusual or allergic reaction to vitamin A. Also tell your health care professional if you are allergic to any other substances, such as foods, preservatives, or dyes.

Pregnancy—It is especially important that you are receiving enough vitamins when you become pregnant and that you continue to receive the right amount of vitamins throughout your pregnancy. The healthy growth and development of the fetus depend on a steady supply of nutrients from the mother.

However, taking too much vitamin A (more than 1800 RE [6000 Units]) during pregnancy can also cause harmful effects such as birth defects or slow or reduced growth in the child.

Breast-feeding—It is especially important that you receive the right amounts of vitamins so that your baby will also get the vitamins needed to grow properly. However, taking large amounts of a dietary supplement while breast-feeding may be harmful to the mother and/or baby and should be avoided.

Children—Problems in children have not been reported with intake of normal daily recommended amounts. However, side effects from high doses and/or prolonged use of vitamin A are more likely to occur in young children than adults.

Older adults—Problems in older adults have not been reported with intake of normal daily recommended amounts. However, some studies have shown that the elderly may be at risk of high blood levels of vitamin A with long-term use.

Dental—High doses and/or prolonged use of vitamin A may cause bleeding from the gums; dry or sore mouth; or drying, cracking, or peeling of the lips.

Medicines or other dietary supplements—Although certain medicines or dietary supplements should not be used together at all, in other cases they may be used together even if an interaction might occur. In these cases, your health care professional may want to change the dose, or other precautions may be necessary. When you are taking vitamin A, it is especially important that your health care professional know if you are taking any of the following:

- Etretinate or
- Isotretinoin (e.g., Accutane)—Use with vitamin A may cause high blood levels of vitamin A, which may increase the chance of side effects

Other medical problems—The presence of other medical problems may affect the use of vitamin A. Make sure you tell your health care professional if you have any other medical problems, especially:

- Alcohol abuse (or history of) or
- Liver disease—Vitamin A use may make liver problems worse

- Kidney disease—May cause high blood levels of vitamin A, which may increase the chance of side effects

Proper Use of This Dietary Supplement

Dosing—The amount of vitamin A needed to meet normal daily recommended intakes will be different for different individuals. The following information includes only the average amounts of vitamin A. The combination of retinol and beta-carotene in the diet is based on 1980 U.S. Recommended Dietary Allowances (RDAs).

- For *oral* dosage form (capsules, tablets, oral solution):
  —To prevent deficiency, the amount taken by mouth is based on normal daily recommended intakes:

  For the U.S.
  - Adult and teenage males—1000 retinol equivalents (RE) (3330 Units of retinol or 5000 Units as a combination of retinol and beta-carotene) per day.
  - Adult and teenage females—800 RE (2665 Units of retinol or 4000 Units as a combination of retinol and beta-carotene) per day.
  - Pregnant females—800 RE (2665 Units of retinol or 4000 Units as a combination of retinol and beta-carotene) per day.
  - Breast-feeding females—1200 to 1300 RE (4000 to 4330 Units of retinol or 6000 to 6500 Units as a combination of retinol and beta-carotene) per day.
  - Children 7 to 10 years of age—700 RE (2330 Units of retinol or 3500 Units as a combination of retinol and beta-carotene) per day.
  - Children 4 to 6 years of age—500 RE (1665 Units of retinol or 2500 Units as a combination of retinol and beta-carotene) per day.
  - Children birth to 3 years of age—375 to 400 RE (1250 to 1330 Units of retinol or 1875 to 2000

Units as a combination of retinol and beta-carotene) per day.

For Canada
- Adult and teenage males—1000 RE (3330 Units of retinol or 5000 Units as a combination of retinol and beta-carotene) per day.
- Adult and teenage females—800 RE (2665 Units of retinol or 4000 Units as a combination of retinol and beta-carotene) per day.
- Pregnant females—900 RE (2665 to 3000 Units of retinol or 4000 to 4500 Units as a combination of retinol and beta-carotene) per day.
- Breast-feeding females—1200 RE (4000 Units of retinol or 6000 Units as a combination of retinol and beta-carotene) per day.
- Children 7 to 10 years of age—700 to 800 RE (2330 to 2665 Units of retinol or 3500 Units as a combination of retinol and beta-carotene) per day.
- Children 4 to 6 years of age—500 RE (1665 Units of retinol or 2500 Units as a combination of retinol and beta-carotene) per day.
- Children birth to 3 years of age—400 RE (1330 Units or 2000 Units as a combination of retinol and beta-carotene) per day.

—To treat deficiency:
- Adults and teenagers—Treatment dose is determined by prescriber for each individual based on severity of deficiency. The following dose has been determined for xerophthalmia (eye disease): Oral, 7500 to 15,000 RE (25,000 to 50,000 Units) a day.
- Children—Treatment dose is determined by prescriber for each individual based of severity of deficiency. The following doses have been determined:
  —For measles—
  - Children 6 months to 1 year of age: Oral, 30,000 RE (100,000 Units) as a single dose.
  - For children 1 year of age and older: Oral, 60,000 RE (200,000 Units) as a single dose.
  —Xerophthalmia (eye disease)—
  - Children 6 months to 1 year of age: Oral, 30,000 RE (100,000 Units) as a single dose, the same dose being repeated the next day and again at 4 weeks.
  - Children 1 year of age and older: Oral, 60,000 RE (200,000 Units) as a single dose, the same dose being repeated the next day and again at 4 weeks.
  - Note: Vitamin A is used in measles and xerophthalmia only when vitamin A deficiency is a problem as determined by your health care professional. Vitamin A deficiency occurs in malnutrition or in certain disease states.

Missed dose—If you miss taking a vitamin for one or more days there is no cause for concern, since it takes some time for your body to become seriously low in vitamins. However, if your health care professional has recommended that you take this vitamin, try to remember to take it as directed every day.

For individuals taking the *oral liquid form* of vitamin A:
- This preparation is to be taken by mouth even though it comes in a dropper bottle.
- This dietary supplement may be dropped directly into the mouth or mixed with cereal, fruit juice, or other food.

Storage—To store this dietary supplement:

- Keep out of the reach of children.
- Store away from heat and direct light.
- Do not store in the bathroom, near the kitchen sink or in other damp places. Heat or moisture may cause the dietary supplement to break down.
- Keep the oral liquid form of this dietary supplement from freezing.
- Do not keep outdated dietary supplements or those no longer needed. Be sure that any discarded dietary supplement is out of the reach of children.

Precautions While Using This Dietary Supplement

Vitamin A is stored in the body; therefore, when you take more than the body needs, it will build up in the body. This may lead to poisoning and even death. Problems are more likely to occur in:

- Adults taking 7500 RE (25,000 Units) a day for 8 months in a row, or 450,000 RE (1,500,000 Units) all at once; or
- Children taking 5400 RE (18,000 Units) to 15,000 RE (50,000 Units) a day for several months in a row, or 22,500 RE (75,000 Units) to 105,100 RE (350,000 Units) all at once.
- Pregnant women taking more than 1800 RE (6000 Units) a day.

Remember that the total amount of vitamin A you get every day includes what you get from foods that you eat and what you take as a supplement.

Side Effects of This Dietary Supplement

Along with its needed effects, a dietary supplement may cause some unwanted effects. Vitamin A does not usually cause any side effects at normal recommended doses.

However, taking large amounts of vitamin A over a period of time may cause some unwanted effects that can be serious. Check with your health care professional immediately if any of the following side effects occur, since they may be signs of sudden overdose:

Bleeding from gums or sore mouth; bulging soft spot on head (in babies); confusion or unusual excitement; diarrhea; dizziness or drowsiness; double vision; headache (severe); irritability (severe); peeling of skin, especially on lips and palms; vomiting (severe)

Check with your health care professional as soon as possible if any of the following side effects occur, since they may also be signs of gradual overdose:

Bone or joint pain; convulsions (seizures); drying or cracking of skin or lips; dry mouth; fever; general feeling of discomfort or illness or weakness; headache; increased sensitivity of skin to sunlight; increase in frequency of urination, especially at night, or in amount of urine; irritability; loss of appetite; loss of hair; stomach pain; unusual tiredness; vomiting; yellow-orange patches on soles of feet, palms of hands, or skin around nose and lips

Other side effects not listed above may also occur in some individuals. If you notice any other effects, check with your health care professional.

Revised: 07/29/94
Interim revision: 05/26/95

VITAMIN B₁₂   Systemic

Commonly used brand name(s):

In the U.S.—

Alphamin[2]	Hydroxy-Cobal[2]
Cobex[1]	LA-12[2]
Cobolin-M[1]	Neuroforte-R[1]
Crystamine[1]	Nascobal[1]
Crysti-12[1]	Primabalt[1]
Cyanoject[1]	Rubramin PC[1]
Cyomin[1]	Shovite[1]
Hydrobexan[2]	Vibal[1]
Hydro-Cobex[2]	Vibal LA[2]
Hydro-Crysti-12[2]	Vitabee 12[1]

In Canada—

Anacobin[1]
Bedoz[1]

Note: For quick reference, the following supplements are numbered to match the corresponding brand names.

This information applies to the following:

1. Cyanocobalamin (sye-an-oh-koe-BAL-a-min) ‡§
2. Hydroxocobalamin (hye-drox-oh-koe-BAL-a-min) †‡

†Not commercially available in Canada.
‡Generic name product may be available in the U.S.
§Generic name product may be available in Canada.

Description

Vitamins (VYE-ta-mins) are compounds that you *must* have for growth and health. They are needed in small amounts only and are usually available in the foods that you eat. Vitamin B₁₂ is necessary for healthy blood. Cyanocobalamin and hydroxocobalamin are man-made forms of vitamin B₁₂.

Some people have a medical problem called pernicious anemia in which vitamin B₁₂ is not absorbed from the intestine. Others may have a badly diseased intestine or have had a large part of their stomach or intestine removed, so that vitamin B₁₂ cannot be absorbed. These people need to receive vitamin B₁₂ by injection.

Some conditions may increase your need for vitamin B₁₂. These include:

- Alcoholism
- Anemia, hemolytic
- Fever (continuing)
- Genetic disorders such as homocystinuria and/or methylmalonic aciduria
- Intestine diseases
- Infections (continuing or chronic)
- Kidney disease
- Liver disease
- Pancreas disease
- Stomach disease
- Stress (continuing)
- Thyroid disease
- Worm infections

In addition, persons that are strict vegetarians or have macrobiotic diets may need vitamin B₁₂ supplements.

Increased need for vitamin B₁₂ should be determined by your health care professional.

Lack of vitamin B₁₂ may lead to anemia (weak blood), stomach problems, and nerve damage. Your health care professional may treat this by prescribing vitamin B₁₂ for you.

Claims that vitamin B₁₂ is effective for treatment of various conditions such as aging, allergies, eye problems, slow growth, poor appetite or malnutrition, skin problems, tiredness, mental problems, sterility, thyroid disease, and nerve diseases have not been proven. Many of these treatments involve large and expensive amounts of vitamins.

Injectable vitamin B_{12} is given by or under the supervision of a health care professional. Some strengths of oral vitamin B_{12} are available only with your health care professional's prescription. Others are available without a prescription.

Vitamin B_{12} is available in the following dosage forms:

Nasal
Cyanocobalamin
- Nasal gel (U.S.)

Oral
Cyanocobalamin
- Extended-release tablets (U.S.)
- Tablets (U.S. and Canada)

Parenteral
Cyanocobalamin
- Injection (U.S. and Canada)
Hydroxocobalamin
- Injection (U.S.)

Importance of Diet

For good health, it is important that you eat a balanced and varied diet. Follow carefully any diet program your health care professional may recommend. For your specific dietary vitamin and/or mineral needs, ask your health care professional for a list of appropriate foods. If you think that you are not getting enough vitamins and/or minerals in your diet, you may choose to take a dietary supplement.

Vitamin B_{12} is found in various foods, including fish, egg yolk, milk, and fermented cheeses. It is *not* found in any vegetables. Ordinary cooking probably does not destroy the vitamin B_{12} in food.

Vitamins alone will not take the place of a good diet and will not provide energy. Your body also needs other substances found in food, such as protein, minerals, carbohydrates, and fat. Vitamins themselves often cannot work without the presence of other foods.

The daily amount of vitamin B_{12} needed is defined in several different ways.

For U.S.—
- Recommended Dietary Allowances (RDAs) are the amount of vitamins and minerals needed to provide for adequate nutrition in most healthy persons. RDAs for a given nutrient may vary depending on a person's age, sex, and physical condition (e.g., pregnancy).
- Daily Values (DVs) are used on food and dietary supplement labels to indicate the percent of the recommended daily amount of each nutrient that a serving provides. DV replaces the previous designation of United States Recommended Daily Allowances (USRDAs).

For Canada—
- Recommended Nutrient Intakes (RNIs) are used to determine the amounts of vitamins, minerals, and protein needed to provide adequate nutrition and lessen the risk of chronic disease.

Normal daily recommended intakes in micrograms (mcg) for vitamin B_{12} are generally defined as follows:

Persons	U.S. (mcg)	Canada (mcg)
Infants and children		
Birth to 3 years of age	0.3–0.7	0.3–0.4
4 to 6 years of age	1	0.5
7 to 10 years of age	1.4	0.8–1
Adolescent and adult males	2	1–2
Adolescent and adult females	2	1–2
Pregnant females	2.2	2–3
Breast-feeding females	2.6	1.5–2.5

Before Using This Dietary Supplement

If you are taking this dietary supplement without a prescription, carefully read and follow any precautions on the label. For vitamin B_{12}, the following should be considered:

Allergies—Tell your health care professional if you have ever had any unusual or allergic reaction to vitamin B_{12}. Also, tell your health care professional if you are allergic to any other substances, such as foods, preservatives, or dyes.

Pregnancy—It is especially important that you are receiving enough vitamins when you become pregnant and that you continue to receive the right amount of vitamins throughout your pregnancy. Healthy fetal growth and development depend on a steady supply of nutrients from mother to fetus. However, taking large amounts of a dietary supplement in pregnancy may be harmful to the mother and/or fetus and should be avoided.

You may need vitamin B_{12} supplements if you are a strict vegetarian (vegan-vegetarian). Too little vitamin B_{12} can cause harmful effects such as anemia or nervous system injury.

Breast-feeding—It is especially important that you receive the right amounts of vitamins so that your baby will also get the vitamins needed to grow properly. If you are a strict vegetarian, your baby may not be getting the vitamin B_{12} needed. However, taking large amounts of a dietary supplement while breast-feeding may be harmful to the mother and/or baby and should be avoided.

Children—Problems in children have not been reported with intake of normal daily recommended amounts.

Older adults—Problems in older adults have not been reported with intake of normal daily recommended amounts.

Medicines or other dietary supplements—Although certain medicines or dietary supplements should not be used together at all, in other cases they may be used together even if an interaction might occur. In these cases, your health care professional may want to change the dose, or other precautions may be necessary. Tell your health care professional if you are taking any other dietary supplement or any prescription or nonprescription (over-the-counter [OTC]) medicine.

Other medical problems—The presence of other medical problems may affect the use of vitamin B_{12}. Make sure you tell your health care professional if you have any other medical problems, especially:
- Leber's disease (an eye disease)—Vitamin B_{12} may make this condition worse

Proper Use of This Dietary Supplement

Dosing—If you are taking vitamin B_{12} intranasal gel:
- Take it *at least one hour before or one hour after hot foods or liquids.*

- Check with your doctor for *follow-up blood tests every 3 to 6 months.*

The amount of vitamin B$_{12}$ needed to meet normal daily recommended intakes will be different for different individuals. The following information includes only the average amounts of vitamin B$_{12}$.

- For *nasal* dosage form (intranasal gel):
  - —To prevent deficiency, you are given this dosage form only if you have received vitamin B$_{12}$ by injection into the muscle and are in remission state.
    - Adults—500 mcg (0.5 mg) into the nostrils once a week.
- For *oral* dosage form (tablets or extended-release tablets):
  - —To prevent deficiency, the amount taken by mouth is based on normal daily recommended intakes:

  For the U.S.
    - Adults and teenagers—2 micrograms (mcg) per day.
    - Pregnant females—2.2 mcg per day.
    - Breast-feeding females—2.6 mcg per day.
    - Children 7 to 10 years of age—1.4 mcg per day.
    - Children 4 to 6 years of age—1 mcg per day.
    - Children birth to 3 years of age—0.3 to 0.7 mcg per day.

  For Canada
    - Adults and teenagers—1 to 2 mcg per day.
    - Pregnant females—2 to 3 mcg per day.
    - Breast-feeding females—1.5 to 2.5 mcg per day.
    - Children 7 to 10 years of age—0.8 to 1 mcg per day.
    - Children 4 to 6 years of age—0.5 mcg per day.
    - Children birth to 3 years of age—0.3 to 0.4 mcg per day.
  - —To treat deficiency:
    - Adults, teenagers, and children—Treatment dose is determined by prescriber for each individual based on the severity of deficiency.

For patients receiving vitamin B$_{12}$ by injection for pernicious anemia or if part of the stomach or intestine has been removed:

- You will have to receive treatment for the rest of your life. You must continue to receive vitamin B$_{12}$ even if you feel well, in order to prevent future problems.

Missed dose—If you miss taking a vitamin for one or more days there is no cause for concern, since it takes some time for your body to become seriously low in vitamins. However, if your health care professional has recommended that you take this vitamin, try to remember to take it as directed.

Storage—To store this dietary supplement:
- Keep out of the reach of children.
- Store away from heat and direct light.
- Do not store in the bathroom, near the kitchen sink, or in other damp places. Heat or moisture may cause the dietary supplement to break down.
- Do not keep outdated dietary supplement or those no longer needed. Be sure that any discarded dietary supplement is out of the reach of children.

Side Effects of This Dietary Supplement

Along with its needed effects, a dietary supplement may cause some unwanted effects. Cyanocobalamin or hydroxocobalamin does not usually cause any side effects.

However, check with your health care professional immediately if any of the following side effects occur:
  Rare—soon after receiving injection only
    Skin rash or itching; wheezing

Check with your health care professional as soon as possible if either of the following side effects continues or is bothersome:
  Less common
    Diarrhea; itching of skin

Other side effects not listed above may also occur in some individuals. If you notice any other effects, check with your health care professional.

Revised: 06/23/2000

VITAMIN D AND RELATED COMPOUNDS   Systemic

Commonly used brand name(s):

In the U.S.—

Calciferol[6]	Drisdol[6]
Calciferol Drops[6]	Drisdol Drops[6]
Calcijex[3]	Hectorol[5]
Calderol[2]	Hytakerol[4]
DHT[4]	Rocaltrol[3]
DHT Intensol[4]	Zemplar[7]

In Canada—

Calciferol[6]	One-Alpha[1]
Calcijex[3]	Ostoforte[6]
Drisdol[6]	Radiostol Forte[6]
Hytakerol[4]	Rocaltrol[3]

Note: For quick reference, the following vitamin D and related compounds are numbered to match the corresponding brand names.

This information applies to the following:
  1. Alfacalcidol (al-fa-KAL-si-dol) *
  2. Calcifediol (kal-si-fe-DYE-ole) †
  3. Calcitriol (kal-si-TRYE-ole)
  4. Dihydrotachysterol (dye-hye-droh-tak-ISS-ter-ole)
  5. Doxercalciferol (docks-er-kal-SIF-e-role) ‡
  6. Ergocalciferol (er-goe-kal-SIF-e-role) ‡§
  7. Paricalcitol (par-i-KAL-si-trole) ‡§

*Not commercially available in the U.S.
†Not commercially available in Canada.
‡Generic name product may be available in the U.S.
§Generic name product may be available in Canada.

Description

Vitamins (VYE-ta-mins) are compounds that you *must* have for growth and health. They are needed in small amounts only and are available in the foods that you eat. Vitamin D is necessary for strong bones and teeth.

Lack of vitamin D may lead to a condition called rickets, especially in children, in which bones and teeth are weak. In adults it may cause a condition called osteomalacia, in which calcium is lost from bones so that they become weak. Your doctor may treat these problems by prescribing vitamin D for you. Vitamin D is also sometimes used to treat other diseases in which calcium is not used properly by the body.

Ergocalciferol is the form of vitamin D used in vitamin supplements.

Some conditions may increase your need for vitamin D. These include:

- Alcoholism
- Intestine diseases
- Kidney disease
- Liver disease
- Overactivity of the parathyroid glands with kidney failure
- Pancreas disease
- Surgical removal of stomach

In addition, individuals and breast-fed infants who lack exposure to sunlight, as well as dark-skinned individuals, may be more likely to have a vitamin D deficiency. Increased need for vitamin D should be determined by your health care professional.

Alfacalcidol, calcifediol, calcitriol, and dihydrotachysterol are forms of vitamin D used to treat hypocalcemia (not enough calcium in the blood). Alfacalcidol, calcifediol, and calcitriol are also used to treat certain types of bone disease that may occur with kidney disease in patients who are undergoing kidney dialysis.

Claims that vitamin D is effective for treatment of arthritis and prevention of nearsightedness or nerve problems have not been proven. Some psoriasis patients may benefit from vitamin D supplements; however, controlled studies have not been performed.

Injectable vitamin D is given by or under the supervision of a health care professional. Some strengths of ergocalciferol and all strengths of alfacalcidol, calcifediol, calcitriol, and dihydrotachysterol are available only with your doctor's prescription. Other strengths of ergocalciferol are available without a prescription. However, it may be a good idea to check with your health care professional before taking vitamin D on your own. *Taking large amounts over long periods may cause serious unwanted effects.*

Vitamin D and related compounds are available in the following dosage forms:

Oral
Alfacalcidol
- Capsules (Canada)
- Oral solution (Canada)
- Oral drops (Canada)
Calcifediol
- Capsules (U.S.)
Calcitriol
- Capsules (U.S. and Canada)
- Oral solution (Canada)
Dihydrotachysterol
- Capsules (U.S. and Canada)
- Oral solution (U.S.)
- Tablets (U.S.)
Doxercalciferol
- Capsules (U.S.)
Ergocalciferol
- Capsules (U.S. and Canada)
- Oral solution (U.S. and Canada)
- Tablets (U.S. and Canada)

Parenteral
Alfacalcidol
- Injection (Canada)
Calcitriol
- Injection (U.S. and Canada)

Ergocalciferol
- Injection (U.S. and Canada)
Paricalcitol
- Injection (U.S.)

Importance of Diet

For good health, it is important that you eat a balanced and varied diet. Follow carefully any diet program your health care professional may recommend. For your specific dietary vitamin and/or mineral needs, ask your health care professional for a list of appropriate foods. If you think that you are not getting enough vitamins and/or minerals in your diet, you may choose to take a dietary supplement.

Vitamin D is found naturally only in fish and fish-liver oils. However, it is also found in milk (vitamin D-fortified). Cooking does not affect the vitamin D in foods. Vitamin D is sometimes called the "sunshine vitamin" since it is made in your skin when you are exposed to sunlight. If you eat a balanced diet and get outside in the sunshine at least 1.5 to 2 hours a week, you should be getting all the vitamin D you need.

Vitamins alone will not take the place of a good diet and will not provide energy. Your body also needs other substances found in food such as protein, minerals, carbohydrates, and fat. Vitamins themselves often cannot work without the presence of other foods. For example, fat is needed so that vitamin D can be absorbed into the body.

The daily amount of vitamin D needed is defined in several different ways.

For U.S.—
- Recommended Dietary Allowances (RDAs) are the amount of vitamins and minerals needed to provide for adequate nutrition in most healthy persons. RDAs for a given nutrient may vary depending on a person's age, sex, and physical condition (e.g., pregnancy).
- Daily Values (DVs) are used on food and dietary supplement labels to indicate the percent of the recommended daily amount of each nutrient that a serving provides. DV replaces the previous designation of United States Recommended Daily Allowances (USRDAs).

For Canada—
- Recommended Nutrient Intakes (RNIs) are used to determine the amounts of vitamins, minerals, and protein needed to provide adequate nutrition and lessen the risk of chronic disease.

In the past, the RDA and RNI for vitamin D have been expressed in Units (U). This term has been replaced by micrograms (mcg) of vitamin D.

Normal daily recommended intakes in mcg and Units are generally defined as follows:

Persons	U.S.		Canada	
	(mcg)	Units	(mcg)	Units
Infants and children				
Birth to 3 years of age	7.5–10	300–400	5–10	200–400
4 to 6 years of age	10	400	5	200
7 to 10 years of age	10	400	2.5–5	100–200
Adolescents and adults	5–10	200–400	2.5–5	100–200
Pregnant and breast-feeding females	10	400	5–7.5	200–300

Remember:
- The total amount of each vitamin that you get every day includes what you get from the foods that you eat *and* what you may take as a supplement.
- Your total amount should not be greater than the RDA or RNI, unless ordered by your doctor. *Taking too much vitamin D over a period of time may cause harmful effects.*

Before Using This Dietary Supplement

If you are taking this dietary supplement without a prescription, carefully read and follow any precautions on the label. For vitamin D and related compounds, the following should be considered:

Allergies—Tell your health care professional if you have ever had any unusual or allergic reaction to alfacalcidol, calcifediol, calcitriol, dihydrotachysterol, doxercalciferol, ergocalciferol, or paricalcitol. Also, tell your health care professional if you are allergic to any other substances, such as foods, preservatives, or dyes.

Pregnancy—It is especially important that you are receiving enough vitamin D when you become pregnant and that you continue to receive the right amounts of vitamins throughout your pregnancy. The healthy growth and development of the fetus depend on a steady supply of nutrients from the mother.

You may need vitamin D supplements if you are a strict vegetarian (vegan-vegetarian) and/or have little exposure to sunlight and do not drink vitamin D-fortified milk.

Taking too much alfacalcidol, calcifediol, calcitriol, dihydrotachysterol, or ergocalciferol can also be harmful to the fetus. Taking more than your health care professional has recommended can cause your baby to be more sensitive than usual to its effects, can cause problems with a gland called the parathyroid, and can cause a defect in the baby's heart.

Doxercalciferol or paricalcitol have not been studied in pregnant women. However, studies in animals have shown that paricalcitol causes problems in newborns. Before taking this medicine, make sure your doctor knows if you are pregnant or if you may become pregnant.

Breast-feeding—It is especially important that you receive the right amounts of vitamins so that your baby will also get the vitamins needed to grow properly. Infants who are totally breast-fed and have little exposure to the sun may require vitamin D supplementation. However, taking large amounts of a dietary supplement while breast-feeding may be harmful to the mother and/or baby and should be avoided.

Only small amounts of alfacalcidol, calcifediol, calcitriol, or dihydrotachysterol pass into breast milk and these amounts have not been reported to cause problems in nursing babies.

It is not known whether doxercalciferol or paricalcitol passes into breast milk. Be sure you have discussed the risks and benefits of the supplement with your doctor.

Children—Problems in children have not been reported with intake of normal daily recommended amounts. Some studies have shown that infants who are totally breast-fed, especially with dark-skinned mothers, and have little exposure to sunlight may be at risk of vitamin D deficiency. Your health care professional may prescribe a vitamin/mineral supplement that contains vitamin D. Some infants may be sensitive to even small amounts of alfacalcidol, calcifediol, calcitriol, dihydrotachysterol, or ergocalciferol. Also, children

may show slowed growth when receiving large doses of alfacalcidol, calcifediol, calcitriol, dihydrotachysterol, or ergocalciferol for a long time.

Studies on doxercalciferol or paricalcitol have been done only in adult patients, and there is no specific information comparing the use of doxercalciferol or paricalcitol in children with use in other age groups.

Older adults—Problems in older adults have not been reported with intake of normal daily recommended amounts. Studies have shown that older adults may have lower blood levels of vitamin D than younger adults, especially those who have little exposure to sunlight. Your health care professional may recommend that you take a vitamin supplement that contains vitamin D.

Medicines or other dietary supplements—Although certain medicines or dietary supplements should not be used together at all, in other cases they may be used together even if an interaction might occur. In these cases, your health care professional may want to change the dose, or other precautions may be necessary. When you are taking vitamin D and related compounds, it is especially important that your health care professional know if you are taking any of the following:

- Antacids containing magnesium—Use of these products with any vitamin D–related compound may result in high blood levels of magnesium, especially in patients with kidney disease
- Calcium-containing preparations or
- Thiazide diuretics (water pills)—Use of these preparations with vitamin D may cause high blood levels of calcium and increase the chance of side effects
- Vitamin D and related compounds, other—Use of vitamin D with a related compound may cause high blood levels of vitamin D and increase the chance of side effects.

Other medical problems—The presence of other medical problems may affect the use of vitamin D and related compounds. Make sure you tell your health care professional if you have any other medical problems, especially:

- Heart or blood vessel disease—Alfacalcidol, calcifediol, calcitriol, or dihydrotachysterol may cause hypercalcemia (high blood levels of calcium), which may make these conditions worse
- Kidney disease—High blood levels of alfacalcidol, calcifediol, calcitriol, dihydrotachysterol, or ergocalciferol may result, which may increase the chance of side effects
- Sarcoidosis—May increase sensitivity to alfacalcidol, calcifediol, calcitriol, dihydrotachysterol, or ergocalciferol and increase the chance of side effects

Proper Use of This Dietary Supplement

For use as a dietary supplement:
- *Do not take more than the recommended daily amount.* Vitamin D is stored in the body, and taking too much over a period of time can cause poisoning and even death.

If you have any questions about this, check with your health care professional.

For individuals taking the *oral liquid form* of this dietary supplement:

- This preparation should be taken by mouth even though it comes in a dropper bottle.
- This dietary supplement may be dropped directly into the mouth or mixed with cereal, fruit juice, or other food.

While you are taking alfacalcidol, calcifediol, calcitriol, dihydrotachysterol, doxercalciferol or paricalcitol, your health care professional may want you to follow a special diet or take a calcium supplement. Be sure to follow instructions carefully. If you are already taking a calcium supplement or any medicine containing calcium, make sure your health care professional knows.

Dosing—The dose of these vitamin D and related compounds will be different for different patients. *Follow your doctor's orders or the directions on the label.* The following information includes only the average doses of these medicines. *If your dose is different, do not change it* unless your health care professional tells you to do so.

The number of milliliters (mL) of solution that you take, or the number of capsules or tablets you take, depends on the strength of the medicine. Also, *the number of doses you take each day, the time allowed between doses, and the length of time you take the medicine depend on the medical problem for which you are taking the combination medicine.*

For alfacalcidol
- To treat bone disease in kidney patients undergoing kidney dialysis:
  —For *oral* dosage form (capsules):
  - Adults and teenagers—At first, 1 microgram (mcg) a day. Your doctor may change your dose if needed. However, most people will take not more than 3 mcg a day.
  —For *oral* dosage form (drops):
  - Adults and teenagers—At first, 1 microgram (mcg) a day. Your doctor may change your dose if needed. However, most people will take not more than 3 mcg a day.
  —For *oral* dosage form (solution):
  - Adults and teenagers—At first, 1 mcg a day. Your doctor may change your dose if needed. However, most people will take not more than 3 mcg a day.
  —For *parenteral* dosage form (injection):
  - Adults and teenagers—At first, 1 mcg a day. Your doctor may change your dose if needed. However, most people will take not more than 12 mcg a week.
- To treat diseases in which calcium is not used properly by the body
  —For *oral* dosage form (capsules):
  - Adults and teenagers—At first, 0.25 microgram (mcg) a day. Your doctor may change your dose if needed. However, most people will take not more than 1 mcg a day.
  —For *oral* dosage form (drops):
  - Adults and teenagers—At first, 0.25 microgram (mcg) a day. Your doctor may change your dose if needed. However, most people will take not more than 1 mcg a day.
  —For *oral* dosage form (solution):
  - Adults and teenagers—At first, 0.25 mcg a day. Your doctor may change your dose if needed.

However, most people will take not more than 1 mcg a day.

For calcifediol
- To treat diseases in which calcium is not used properly by the body or to treat bone disease in kidney patients undergoing kidney dialysis:
  —For *oral* dosage form (capsules):
  - Adults, teenagers, and children over 10 years of age—At first, 300 to 350 micrograms (mcg) a week, taken in divided doses either once a day or every other day. Your doctor may change your dose if needed.
  - Children up to 2 years of age—20 to 50 mcg a day.
  - Children 2 to 10 years of age—50 mcg a day.

For calcitriol
- To treat diseases in which calcium is not used properly by the body or to treat bone disease in kidney patients undergoing kidney dialysis:
  —For *oral* dosage form (capsules and solution):
  - Adults, teenagers, and children—At first, 0.25 micrograms (mcg) a day. Your doctor may change your dose if needed.
  —For *injection* dosage form:
  - Adults and teenagers—At first, 0.5 mcg injected into a vein three times a week. Your doctor may change your dose if needed.
  - Children—Use and dose must be determined by your doctor.

For dihydrotachysterol
- To treat diseases in which calcium is not used properly by the body:
  —For *oral* dosage forms (capsules, solution, or tablets):
  - Adults and teenagers—At first, 100 micrograms (mcg) to 2.5 milligrams (mg) a day. Your doctor may change your dose if needed.
  - Children—At first, 1 to 5 mg a day. Your doctor may change your dose if needed.

For doxercalciferol
- To treat an overactive parathyroid gland in patients with kidney failure:
  —For *oral* dosage form (capsules):
  - Adults: 10 micrograms (mcg) three times weekly at dialysis. The doctor may change your dose if needed.
  - Children: Use and dose must be determined by your doctor.

For ergocalciferol
- For *oral* dosage forms (capsules, tablets, oral solution):
  —The amount of vitamin D to meet normal daily recommended intakes will be different for different individuals. The following information includes only the average amounts of vitamin D.
  —To prevent deficiency, the amount taken by mouth is based on normal daily recommended intakes:
  For the U.S.
  - Adults and teenagers: 5 to 10 micrograms (mcg) (200 to 400 Units) per day.
  - Pregnant and breast-feeding females: 10 mcg (400 Units) per day.
  - Children 4 to 10 years of age: 10 mcg (400 Units) per day.

- Children birth to 3 years of age: 7.5 to 10 mcg (300 to 400 Units) per day.

For Canada

- Adults and teenagers: 2.5 to 5 mcg (100 to 200 Units) per day.
- Pregnant and breast-feeding females: 5 to 7.5 mcg (200 to 300 Units) per day.
- Children 7 to 10 years of age: 2.5 to 5 mcg (100 to 200 Units) per day.
- Children 4 to 6 years of age: 5 mcg (200 Units) per day.
- Children birth to 3 years of age: 5 to 10 mcg (200 to 400 Units) per day.

—To treat deficiency:

- Adults, teenagers, and children: Treatment dose is determined by prescriber for each individual based on severity of deficiency.

—To treat diseases in which calcium and phosphate are not used properly by the body:

- Adults and teenagers: At first, 1000 to 500,000 Units a day. The doctor may change your dose if needed.
- Children: At first, 1000 to 200,000 Units a day. The doctor may change your dose if needed.

For paricalcitol

- To treat an overactive parathyroid gland in patients with kidney failure:

—For *injection* dosage form:

- Adults: 0.04 to 0.1 micrograms (mcg) per kg no more than every other day during dialysis. The doctor may change your dose if needed.
- Children: Use and dose must be determined by your doctor.

Missed dose—

- *For use as a dietary supplement:* If you miss taking a dietary supplement for one or more days there is no cause for concern, since it takes some time for your body to become seriously low in vitamins. However, if your health care professional has recommended that you take this dietary supplement, try to remember to take it as directed every day.
- If you are taking this medicine for a reason other than as a dietary supplement and you miss a dose and your dosing schedule is:

—One dose every other day: Take the missed dose as soon as possible if you remember it on the day it should be taken. However, if you do not remember the missed dose until the next day, take it at that time. Then skip a day and start your dosing schedule again. Do not double doses.

—One dose a day: Take the missed dose as soon as possible. Then go back to your regular dosing schedule. However, if you do not remember the missed dose until the next day, skip the missed dose and go back to your regular dosing schedule. Do not double doses.

—More than one dose a day: Take the missed dose as soon as possible. Then go back to your regular dosing schedule. However, if it is almost time for your next dose, skip the missed dose and go back to your regular dosing schedule. Do not double doses.

If you have any questions about this, check with your health care professional.

Storage—To store this dietary supplement:

- Keep out of the reach of children.
- Store away from heat and direct light.
- Do not store in the bathroom, near the kitchen sink, or in other damp places. Heat or moisture may cause the dietary supplement to break down.
- Keep the oral liquid form of the dietary supplement from freezing.
- Do not keep outdated dietary supplements or those no longer needed. Be sure that any discarded dietary supplement is out of the reach of children.

Precautions While Using This Dietary Supplement

For individuals taking vitamin D *without a prescription:*

- Vitamin D is stored in the body; therefore, when you take more than the body needs, it will build up in the body. This may lead to poisoning. Problems are more likely to occur in:

  —Adults taking 20,000 to 80,000 Units a day and more for several weeks or months.

  —Children taking 2,000 to 4,000 Units a day for several months.

- Remember that the total amount of vitamin D you get every day includes what you get from foods that you eat and what you take as a supplement.

If you are taking this medicine for a reason other than as a dietary supplement, *your doctor should check your progress at regular visits* to make sure that it does not cause unwanted effects.

Do not take any nonprescription (over-the-counter [OTC]) medicine or dietary supplement that contains calcium, phosphorus, or vitamin D while you are taking any of these dietary supplements unless you have been told to do so by your health care professional. The extra calcium, phosphorus, or vitamin D may increase the chance of side effects.

Do not take antacids or other medicines containing magnesium while you are taking any of these medicines. Taking these medicines together may cause unwanted effects.

Side Effects of This Dietary Supplement

Along with its needed effects, a dietary supplement may cause some unwanted effects. Alfacalcidol, calcifediol, calcitriol, dihydrotachysterol, and ergocalciferol do not usually cause any side effects when taken as directed. However, *taking large amounts over a period of time may cause some unwanted effects that can be serious.*

Check with your doctor immediately if any of the following effects occur:

Late symptoms of severe overdose

High blood pressure; high fever; irregular heartbeat; stomach pain (severe)

Check with your health care professional as soon as possible if any of the following effects occur:

Early symptoms of overdose

Bone pain; constipation (especially in children or adolescents); diarrhea; drowsiness; dryness of mouth; headache (continuing); increased thirst; increase in frequency of urination, especially at night, or in amount of urine; irregular heartbeat; itching skin; loss of appetite; metallic taste; muscle pain; nausea or vomiting (especially in children or adolescents); unusual tiredness or weakness

Late symptoms of overdose

Bone pain; calcium deposits (hard lumps) in tissues outside of the bone; cloudy urine; drowsiness; increased sensitivity of eyes to light or irritation of eyes; itching of skin; loss of appetite; loss of sex drive; mood or mental changes; muscle pain; nausea or vomiting; protein in the urine; redness or discharge of the eye, eyelid, or lining of the eyelid; runny nose; weight loss

Other side effects not listed above may also occur in some individuals. If you notice any other effects, check with your health care professional.

Revised: 03/28/2001

VITAMIN E   Systemic

Commonly used brand name(s):

In the U.S.—

Amino-Opti-E	E-400 I.U. in a Water Soluble
Aquasol E	Base
E-Complex-600	E-Vitamin Succinate
E-200 I.U. Softgels	Liqui-E
E-1000 I.U. Softgels	Pheryl-E
	Vita Plus E

Generic name product may be available.

In Canada—

Aquasol E
Webber Vitamin E

Another commonly used name is alpha tocopherol.

Description

Vitamins (VYE-ta-mins) are compounds that you *must* have for growth and health. They are needed in only small amounts and are available in the foods that you eat. Vitamin E prevents a chemical reaction called oxidation, which can sometimes result in harmful effects in your body. It is also important for the proper function of nerves and muscles.

Some conditions may increase your need for vitamin E. These include:

- Intestine disease
- Liver disease
- Pancreas disease
- Surgical removal of stomach

Increased need for vitamin E should be determined by your health care professional.

Infants who are receiving a formula that is not fortified with vitamin E may be likely to have a vitamin E deficiency. Also, diets high in polyunsaturated fatty acids may increase your need for vitamin E.

Claims that vitamin E is effective for treatment of cancer and for prevention or treatment of acne, aging, loss of hair, bee stings, liver spots on the hands, bursitis, diaper rash, frostbite, stomach ulcer, heart attacks, labor pains, certain blood diseases, miscarriage, muscular dystrophy, poor posture, sexual impotence, sterility, infertility, menopause, sunburn, and lung damage from air pollution have not been proven.

Although vitamin E is being used to prevent certain types of cancer, there is not enough information to show that this is effective.

Lack of vitamin E is extremely rare, except in people who have a disease in which it is not absorbed into the body.

Vitamin E is available without a prescription in the following dosage forms:

Oral

- Capsules (U.S. and Canada)
- Oral solution (U.S. and Canada)
- Tablets (U.S.)
- Chewable tablets (U.S.)

Importance of Diet

For good health, it is important that you eat a balanced and varied diet. Follow carefully any diet program your health care professional may recommend. For your specific dietary vitamin and/or mineral needs, ask your health care professional for a list of appropriate foods. If you think that you are not getting enough vitamins and/or minerals in your diet, you may choose to take a dietary supplement.

Vitamin E is found in various foods including vegetable oils (corn, cottonseed, soybean, safflower), wheat germ, whole-grain cereals, and green leafy vegetables. Cooking and storage may destroy some of the vitamin E in foods.

Vitamin supplements alone will not take the place of a good diet and will not provide energy. Your body also needs other substances found in food such as protein, minerals, carbohydrates, and fat. Vitamins themselves often cannot work without the presence of other foods. For example, small amounts of fat are needed so that vitamin E can be absorbed into the body.

The daily amount of vitamin E needed is defined in several different ways.

For U.S.—

- Recommended Dietary Allowances (RDAs) are the amount of vitamins and minerals needed to provide for adequate nutrition in most healthy persons. RDAs for a given nutrient may vary depending on a person's age, sex, and physical condition (e.g., pregnancy).
- Daily Values (DVs) are used on food and dietary supplement labels to indicate the percent of the recommended daily amount of each nutrient that a serving provides. DV replaces the previous designation of United States Recommended Daily Allowances (USRDAs).

For Canada—

- Recommended Nutrient Intakes (RNIs) are used to determine the amounts of vitamins, minerals, and protein needed to provide adequate nutrition and lessen the risk of chronic disease.

Vitamin E is available in various forms, including *d*- or *dl*-alpha tocopheryl acetate, *d*- or *dl*-alpha tocopherol, and *d*- or *dl*-alpha tocopheryl acid succinate. In the past, the RDA for vitamin E have been expressed in Units. This term has been replaced by alpha tocopherol equivalents (alpha-TE) or milligrams (mg) of *d*-alpha tocopherol. One Unit is equivalent to 1 mg of *dl*-alpha tocopherol acetate or 0.6 mg *d*-alpha tocopherol. Most products available in stores continue to be labeled in Units.

Normal daily recommended intakes in milligrams (mg) of alpha tocopherol equivalents (mg alpha-TE) and Units for vitamin E are generally defined as follows:

Persons	U.S.		Canada	
	mg alpha-TE	Units	mg alpha-TE	Units
Infants and children				
Birth to 3 years of age	3–6	5–10	3–4	5–6.7
4 to 6 years of age	7	11.7	5	8.3
7 to 10 years of age	7	11.7	6–8	10–13
Adolescent and adult males	10	16.7	6–10	10–16.7
Adolescent and adult females	8	13	5–7	8.3–11.7
Pregnant females	10	16.7	8–9	13–15
Breast-feeding females	11–12	18–20	9–10	15–16.7

Before Using This Dietary Supplement

If you are taking this dietary supplement without a prescription, carefully read and follow any precautions on the label. For vitamin E, the following should be considered:

Allergies—Tell your health care professional if you have ever had any unusual or allergic reaction to vitamin E. Also, tell your health care professional if you are allergic to any other substances, such as foods, preservatives, or dyes.

Pregnancy—It is especially important that you are receiving enough vitamins when you become pregnant and that you continue to receive the right amount of vitamins throughout your pregnancy. The healthy growth and development of the fetus depend on a steady supply of nutrients from the mother. However, taking large amounts of a dietary supplement during pregnancy may be harmful and should be avoided.

Breast-feeding—It is especially important that you receive the right amounts of vitamins so that your baby will also get the vitamins needed to grow properly. You should also check with your health care professional if you are giving your baby an unfortified formula. In that case, however, the baby must get the vitamins needed some other way. However, taking large amounts of a dietary supplement while breast-feeding may be harmful to the mother and/or baby and should be avoided.

Children—Problems in children have not been reported with intake of normal daily recommended amounts. You should check with your health care professional if you are giving your baby an unfortified formula. In that case, the baby must get the vitamins needed some other way. Some studies have shown that premature infants may have low levels of vitamin E. Your health care professional may recommend a vitamin E supplement.

Older adults—Problems in older adults have not been reported with intake of normal daily recommended amounts.

Medicines or other dietary supplements—Although certain medicines or dietary supplements should not be used together at all, in other cases they may be used together even if an interaction might occur. In these cases, your health care professional may want to change the dose, or other precautions may be necessary. Tell your health care professional if you are taking any other prescription or nonprescription (over-the-counter [OTC]) medicine.

Other medical problems—The presence of other medical problems may affect the use of vitamin E. Make sure you tell your health care professional if you have any other medical problems, especially:

- Bleeding problems—Vitamin E, when taken in doses greater than 800 Units a day for long periods of time, may make this condition worse

Proper Use of This Dietary Supplement

Dosing—The amount of vitamin E needed to meet normal daily recommended intakes will be different for different individuals. The following information includes only the average amounts of vitamin E.

- For *oral solution* dosage form:
  - —To prevent the following deficiencies in infants:
    - Infants receiving a formula high in polyunsaturated fatty acids—15 to 25 Units per day or 7 Units per 32 ounces of formula.
    - Infants with certain colon problems—15 to 25 Units per kilogram (kg) (6.8 to 11 Units per pound) of body weight per day. The water-soluble form of vitamin E must be used.
    - Infants of normal birthweight—5 Units per 32 ounces of formula.

- For *oral* dosage forms (capsules, tablets, oral solution):
  - —To prevent deficiency for individuals (other than infants), the amount taken by mouth is based on normal daily recommended intakes:

  For the U.S.
    - Adult and teenage males—10 milligrams (mg) of alpha tocopherol equivalents (mg alpha-TE) or 16.7 Units per day.
    - Adult and teenage females—8 mg alpha-TE or 13 Units per day.
    - Pregnant females—10 mg alpha-TE or 16.7 Units per day.
    - Breast-feeding females—11 to 12 mg alpha-TE or 18 to 20 Units per day.
    - Children 4 to 10 years of age—7 mg alpha-TE or 11.7 Units per day.
    - Children birth to 3 years of age—3 to 6 mg alpha-TE or 5 to 10 Units per day.

  For Canada
    - Adult and teenage males—6 to 10 mg alpha-TE or 10 to 16.7 Units per day.
    - Adult and teenage females—5 to 7 mg alpha-TE or 8.3 to 11.7 Units per day.
    - Pregnant females—8 to 9 mg alpha-TE or 13 to 15 Units per day.
    - Breast-feeding females—9 to 10 mg alpha-TE or 15 to 16.7 Units per day.
    - Children 7 to 10 years of age—6 to 8 mg alpha-TE or 10 to 13 Units per day.
    - Children 4 to 6 years of age—5 mg alpha-TE or 8.3 Units per day.
    - Children birth to 3 years of age—3 to 4 mg alpha-TE or 5 to 6.7 Units per day.
  - —To treat deficiency:
    - Adults, teenagers, and children—Treatment dose is determined by prescriber for each individual based on the severity of deficiency.

For individuals taking the *oral liquid form of this dietary supplement:*

- This preparation should be taken by mouth even though it comes in a dropper bottle.

- This dietary supplement may be dropped directly into the mouth or mixed with cereal, fruit juice, or other food.

Missed dose—If you miss taking a vitamin for one or more days there is no cause for concern, since it takes some time for your body to become seriously low in vitamins. However, if your health care professional has recommended that you take this vitamin, try to remember to take it as directed every day.

Storage—To store this dietary supplement:

- Keep out of the reach of children.
- Store away from heat and direct light.
- Do not store in the bathroom, near the kitchen sink, or in other damp places. Heat or moisture may cause the dietary supplement to break down.
- Keep the oral liquid form of this dietary supplement from freezing.
- Do not keep outdated dietary supplements or those no longer needed. Be sure that any discarded dietary supplement is out of the reach of children.

Side Effects of This Dietary Supplement

Along with its needed effects, a dietary supplement may cause some unwanted effects. When used for short periods of time at recommended doses, vitamin E usually does not cause any side effects. However, check with your health care professional as soon as possible if any of the following side effects occur:

With doses greater than 400 Units a day and long-term use

Blurred vision; diarrhea; dizziness; headache; nausea or stomach cramps; unusual tiredness or weakness

Other side effects not listed above may also occur in some individuals. If you notice any other effects, check with your health care professional.

Revised: 06/22/93
Interim revision: 07/20/94; 05/26/95

VITAMIN K   Systemic

Commonly used brand name(s):

In the U.S.—
AquaMEPHYTON[2]
Mephyton[2]

Note: For quick reference, the following medicines are numbered to match the corresponding brand names.

Other commonly used names are: phylloquinone[2], phytomenadione[2], vitamin K_1[2], and vitamin K_4[1].

This information applies to the following medicines:
1. Menadiol (men-a-DYE-ole) *†
2. Phytonadione (fye-toe-na-DYE-one) ‡§

*Not commercially available in the U.S.
†Not commercially available in Canada.
‡Generic name product may be available in the U.S.
§Generic name product may be available in Canada.

Description

Vitamins (VYE-ta-mins) are compounds that you *must* have for growth and health. They are needed in only small amounts and usually are available in the foods that you eat. Vitamin K is necessary for normal clotting of the blood.

Vitamin K is found in various foods including green leafy vegetables, meat, and dairy products. If you eat a balanced diet containing these foods, you should be getting all the vitamin K you need. Little vitamin K is lost from foods with ordinary cooking.

If you are taking anticoagulant medicine (blood thinners), the amount of vitamin K in your diet may affect how well these medicines work. Your doctor or health care professional may recommend changes in your diet to help these medicines work better.

Lack of vitamin K is rare but may lead to problems with blood clotting and increased bleeding. Your doctor may treat this by prescribing vitamin K for you.

Vitamin K is routinely given to newborn infants to prevent bleeding problems.

This medicine is available only with your doctor's prescription, in the following dosage forms:

Oral
Phytonadione
- Tablets (U.S.)

Parenteral
Phytonadione
- Injection (U.S. and Canada)

Before Using This Medicine

In deciding to use a medicine, the risks of taking the medicine must be weighed against the good it will do. This is a decision you and your doctor will make. For vitamin K, the following should be considered:

Allergies—Tell your doctor if you have ever had any unusual or allergic reaction to vitamin K. Also tell your health care professional if you are allergic to any other substances, such as foods, preservatives, or dyes.

Pregnancy—Vitamin K has not been reported to cause birth defects or other problems in humans. However, the use of vitamin K supplements during pregnancy is not recommended because it has been reported to cause jaundice and other problems in the baby.

Breast-feeding—Vitamin K taken by the mother has not been reported to cause problems in nursing babies. You should check with your doctor if you are giving your baby an unfortified formula. In that case, the baby must get the vitamins needed some other way.

Children—Children may be especially sensitive to the effects of vitamin K, especially menadiol or high doses of phytonadione. This may increase the chance of side effects during treatment. Newborns, especially premature babies, may be more sensitive to these effects than older children.

Older adults—Many medicines have not been tested in older people. Therefore, it may not be known whether they work exactly the same way they do in younger adults or if they cause different side effects or problems in older people. There is no specific information about the use of vitamin K in the elderly.

Other medicines—Although certain medicines should not be used together at all, in other cases two different medicines may be used together even if an interaction might occur. In these cases, your doctor may want to change the dose, or other precautions may be necessary. When you are taking vitamin K, it is especially important that your health care professional know if you are taking any of the following:

- Acetohydroxamic acid (e.g., Lithostat) or
- Antidiabetics, oral (diabetes medicine you take by mouth) or
- Dapsone or
- Furazolidone (e.g., Furoxone) or
- Methyldopa (e.g., Aldomet) or
- Nitrofurantoin (e.g., Furadantin) or
- Primaquine or
- Procainamide (e.g., Pronestyl) or
- Quinidine (e.g., Quinidex) or
- Quinine (e.g., Quinamm) or
- Sulfonamides (sulfa medicine) or
- Sulfoxone (e.g., Diasone)—The chance of a serious side effect may be increased, especially with menadiol

- Anticoagulants (blood thinners)—Vitamin K decreases the effects of these medicines and is sometimes used to treat bleeding caused by anticoagulants; however, patients receiving an anticoagulant should not take any supplement that contains vitamin K (alone or in combination with other vitamins or nutrients) unless it has been ordered by their doctor

Other medical problems—The presence of other medical problems may affect the use of vitamin K. Make sure you tell your doctor if you have any other medical problems, especially:

- Cystic fibrosis or other diseases affecting the pancreas or
- Diarrhea (prolonged) or
- Gallbladder disease or
- Intestinal problems—These conditions may interfere with absorption of vitamin K into the body when it is taken by mouth; higher doses may be needed, or the medicine may have to be injected

- Glucose-6-phosphate dehydrogenase (G6PD) deficiency—The chance of side effects may be increased, especially with menadiol
- Liver disease—The chance of unwanted effects may be increased

Proper Use of This Medicine

Take this medicine only as directed by your doctor. Do not take more or less of it, do not take it more often, and do not take it for a longer time than your doctor ordered. To do so may cause serious unwanted effects, such as blood clotting problems.

Dosing—The dose of these medicines will be different for different patients. *Follow your doctor's orders or the directions on the label.* The following information includes only the average doses of these medicines. *If your dose is different, do not change it* unless your doctor tells you to do so.

The number of tablets or injections that you take depends on the strength of the medicine. Also, *the number of doses you take each day, the time allowed between doses, and the length of time you take the medicine depend on the medical problem for which you are taking the medicine.*

For menadiol
- For *oral* dosage form (tablets):
  —For problems with blood clotting or increased bleeding, or for dietary supplementation:
  - Adults and children—The usual dose is 5 to 10 milligrams (mg) a day.

- For *injection* dosage form:
  —For problems with blood clotting or increased bleeding, or for dietary supplementation:
  - Adults and teenagers—The usual dose is 5 to 15 mg, injected into a muscle or under the skin, one or two times a day.
  - Children—The usual dose is 5 to 10 mg, injected into a muscle or under the skin, one or two times a day.

For phytonadione
- For *oral* dosage form (tablets):
  —For problems with blood clotting or increased bleeding:
  - Adults and teenagers—The usual dose is 2.5 to 25 milligrams (mg), rarely up to 50 mg. The dose may be repeated, if needed.
  - Children—Use is not recommended.

- For *injection* dosage form:
  —For problems with blood clotting or increased bleeding:
  - Adults and teenagers—The usual dose is 2 to 25 mg, rarely up to 50 mg, injected into a muscle or under the skin. The dose may be repeated, if needed.
  - Children—The usual dose is 2.5 to 10 mg injected into a muscle or under the skin. The dose may be repeated after six to eight hours, if needed.
  - Infants—The usual dose is 1 to 2 mg injected into a muscle or under the skin. The dose may be repeated after four to eight hours, if needed.
  —For dietary supplementation:
  - Adults and teenagers receiving total parenteral nutrition (TPN)—The usual dose is 5 to 10 mg, injected into a muscle, once a week.
  - Children receiving TPN—The usual dose is 2 to 5 mg, injected into a muscle, once a week.
  - Infants receiving unfortified milk substitutes or breast milk only—The dose is based on the amount of vitamin K in the infant's diet and must be determined by your doctor.
  —For prevention of bleeding in newborns:
  - The usual dose is 0.5 to 1 mg, injected into a muscle or under the skin, right after delivery. The dose may be repeated after six to eight hours, if needed.

Missed dose—If you miss a dose of this medicine, take it as soon as possible. However, if it is almost time for your next dose, skip the missed dose and go back to your regular dosing schedule. Do not double doses. *Tell your doctor about any doses you miss.*

Storage—To store this medicine:

- Keep out of the reach of children.
- Store away from heat and direct light.
- Do not store in the bathroom, near the kitchen sink, or in other damp places. Heat or moisture may cause the medicine to break down.
- Do not keep outdated medicine or medicine no longer needed. Be sure that any discarded medicine is out of the reach of children.

Precautions While Using This Medicine

Tell all medical doctors and dentists you go to that you are taking this medicine.

Always check with your health care professional before you start or stop taking any other medicine. This includes any nonprescription (over-the-counter [OTC]) medicine, even aspirin. Other medicines may change the way this medicine affects your body.

Your doctor should check your progress at regular visits. A blood test must be taken regularly to see how fast your blood is clotting. This will help your doctor decide how much medicine you need.

Side Effects of This Medicine

Along with its needed effects, a medicine may cause some unwanted effects. Although not all of these side effects may occur, if they do occur they may need medical attention.

Check with your doctor as soon as possible if any of the following side effects occur:

Less common—With menadiol or high doses of phytonadione in newborns

Decreased appetite; decreased movement or activity; difficulty in breathing; enlarged liver; general body swelling; irritability; muscle stiffness; paleness; yellow eyes or skin

Rare—With injection only

Difficulty in swallowing; fast or irregular breathing; lightheadedness or fainting; shortness of breath; skin rash, hives and/or itching; swelling of eyelids, face, or lips; tightness in chest; troubled breathing and/or wheezing

Rare

Blue color or flushing or redness of skin; dizziness; fast and/or weak heartbeat; increased sweating; low blood pressure (temporary)

Other side effects may occur that usually do not need medical attention. These side effects may go away during treatment as your body adjusts to the medicine. However, check with your doctor if any of the following side effects continue or are bothersome:

Less common

Flushing of face; redness, pain, or swelling at place of injection; skin lesions at place of injection (rare); unusual taste

Other side effects not listed above may also occur in some patients. If you notice any other effects, check with your doctor.

Revised: 05/28/99

VITAMINS AND FLUORIDE
Systemic

Commonly used brand name(s):

In the U.S.—

Adeflor[1]	Poly-Vi-Flor[1]
Cari-Tab[2]	Tri-Vi-Flor[2]
Mulvidren-F[1]	Vi-Daylin/F[1]

In Canada—
Adeflor[1]
Poly-Vi-Flor[1]
Tri-Vi-Flor[2]

Note: For quick reference, the following vitamins and fluoride combinations are numbered to match the corresponding brand names.

This information applies to the following medicines:
1. Multiple Vitamins and Fluoride
2. Vitamins A, D, and C and Fluoride

Description

This medicine is a combination of vitamins and fluoride. Vitamins are used when the daily diet does not include enough of the vitamins needed for good health.

Fluoride has been found to be helpful in reducing the number of cavities in the teeth. It is usually present naturally in drinking water. However, some areas of the country do not have a high enough level of fluoride in the water. To make up for this, extra fluorides may be added to the diet. Some children may require both dietary fluorides and fluoride treatments by the dentist. Use of a fluoride toothpaste or rinse may be helpful, as well.

Taking fluorides does not replace good dental habits. These include eating a good diet, brushing and flossing teeth frequently, and having regular dental checkups.

This medicine is available only with your medical doctor's or dentist's prescription, in the following dosage forms:

Oral
- Oral solution (U.S. and Canada)
- Chewable Tablets (U.S. and Canada)

Before Using This Dietary Supplement

In deciding to use a dietary supplement, the risks of taking the dietary supplement must be weighed against the good it will do. This is a decision you and your medical doctor or dentist will make. For multiple vitamins and fluoride, the following should be considered:

Allergies—Tell your medical doctor or dentist if you have ever had any unusual or allergic reactions to fluoride. Also, tell your medical doctor, dentist, and pharmacist if you are allergic to any other substances, such as foods, preservatives, or dyes.

Pregnancy—Fluoride occurs naturally in water and has not been shown to cause problems in infants of mothers who drank fluoridated water or took recommended doses of supplements.

Breast-feeding—Small amounts of fluoride pass into breast milk; however, problems have not been documented with normal intake.

© 2002 MICROMEDEX Thomson Healthcare

Children—Doses of fluoride that are too large or are taken for a long time may cause bone problems and teeth discoloration in children.

Older adults—This dietary supplement has not been shown to cause different side effects or problems in older people than it does in younger adults.

Medicines or other dietary supplements—Although certain medicines or dietary supplements should not be used together at all, in other cases they may be used together even if an interaction might occur. In these cases, your medical doctor or dentist may want to change the dose, or other precautions may be necessary. When you are taking multiple vitamins and fluoride it is especially important that your medical doctor or dentist, and pharmacist know if you are taking any of the following:

- Anticoagulants, coumarin- or indandione-derivative (blood thinners)—Use with vitamin K (in the multiple vitamins and fluoride preparations) may prevent the anticoagulant from working properly

- Iron supplements—Use with vitamin E (in the multiple vitamins and fluoride preparation) may prevent the iron supplement from working properly

- Vitamin D and related compounds—Use with vitamin D (in the multiple vitamins and fluoride preparations) may cause high blood levels of vitamin D, which may increase the chance of side effects

Other medical problems—The presence of other medical problems may affect the use of multiple vitamins and fluoride. Make sure you tell your medical doctor or dentist if you have any other medical problems, especially:

- Dental fluorosis (teeth discoloration)—Fluorides may make this condition worse

Proper Use of This Dietary Supplement

Take this dietary supplement only as directed by your medical doctor or dentist. Do not take more of it and do not take it more often than ordered. Taking too much fluoride and some vitamins (especially vitamins A and D) over a period of time may cause unwanted effects.

Do not take multiple vitamins and fluoride products at the same time as taking foods that contain calcium. It is best to space them 1 to 2 hours apart, to get the full benefit from the medicine.

For patients taking the *chewable tablet form* of this dietary supplement:

- Tablets should be chewed or crushed before they are swallowed.
- This dietary supplement works best if it is taken at bedtime, after the teeth have been thoroughly brushed.

For patients taking the *oral liquid form of* this dietary supplement:

- This dietary supplement is to be taken by mouth even though it comes in a dropper bottle. The amount to be taken is to be measured with the specially marked dropper.
- *Always store this dietary supplement in the original plastic container*. It has been designed to give you the correct dose. Also, fluoride will interact with glass and should not be stored in glass containers.

- This dietary supplement may be dropped directly into the mouth or mixed with cereal, fruit juice, or other food.

Missed dose—If you miss a dose of this dietary supplement, take it as soon as you remember. However, if it is almost time for the next dose, skip the missed dose and go back to your regular dosing schedule. Do not double doses.

Storage—To store this dietary supplement:

- Keep this dietary supplement out of the reach of children, since overdose is especially dangerous in children.
- Store away from heat and direct light.
- Do not store in the bathroom, near the kitchen sink, or in other damp places. Heat or moisture may cause the dietary supplement to break down.
- Protect the oral solution from freezing.
- Do not keep outdated dietary supplements or those no longer needed. Be sure that any discarded dietary supplement is out of the reach of children.

Precautions While Using This Dietary Supplement

The level of fluoride present in the water is different in different parts of the country. If you move to another area, check with a medical doctor or dentist in the new area as soon as possible to see if this medicine is still needed or if the dose needs to be changed. Also, check with your medical doctor or dentist if you change infant feeding habits (e.g., breast-feeding to infant formula), drinking water (e.g., city water to nonfluoridated bottled water), or filtering systems (e.g., tap water to filtered tap water).

Inform your medical doctor or dentist as soon as possible if you notice white, brown, or black spots on the teeth. These are signs of too much fluoride.

Side Effects of This Dietary Supplement

Along with its needed effects, a dietary supplement may cause some unwanted effects. Although not all of these side effects may occur, if they do occur they may need medical attention.

When the correct amount of this dietary supplement is used, side effects usually are rare. However, *taking an overdose of fluoride may cause serious problems.*

Stop taking this dietary supplement and check with your medical doctor immediately if any of the following side effects occur, as they may be signs of severe fluoride overdose:

Black, tarry stools; bloody vomit; diarrhea; drowsiness; faintness; increased watering of mouth; nausea or vomiting; shallow breathing; stomach cramps or pain; tremors; unusual excitement; watery eyes; weakness

Check with your medical doctor or dentist as soon as possible if the following side effects occur, as some may be early signs of possible chronic fluoride overdose:

Pain and aching of bones; skin rash; sores in the mouth and on the lips; stiffness; white, brown, or black discoloration of teeth

Other side effects not listed above may also occur in some patients. If you notice any other effects, check with your medical doctor or dentist.

Revised: 08/21/92

YOHIMBINE   Systemic

Commonly used brand name(s):

In the U.S.—

Actibine   Yocon
Aphrodyne   Yohimar
Baron-X   Yohimex
Dayto Himbin   Yoman
Prohim   Yovital
Thybine

Generic name product may be available.

In Canada—
PMS-Yohimbine
Yocon

Description

Yohimbine (yo-HIM-been) is used to increase peripheral blood flow. It is also used to dilate the pupil of the eye.

Yohimbine is available only with your doctor's prescription, in the following dosage form:

Oral
  • Tablets (U.S. and Canada)

Before Using This Medicine

In deciding to use a medicine, the risks of taking the medicine must be weighed against the good it will do. This is a decision you and your doctor will make. For yohimbine, the following should be considered:

Allergies—Tell your doctor if you have ever had any unusual or allergic reaction to yohimbine or any of the rauwolfia alkaloids, such as deserpidine (e.g, Harmonyl), rauwolfia serpentina (e.g., Raudixin), or reserpine (e.g., Serpalan). Also tell your health care professional if you are allergic to any other substances, such as foods, preservatives, or dyes.

Older adults—Many medicines have not been studied specifically in older people. Therefore, it may not be known whether they work exactly the same way they do in younger adults. Although there is no specific information comparing use of yohimbine in the elderly with use in other age groups, this medicine has been used in some elderly patients and has not been shown to cause different side effects or problems in older people than it does in younger adults.

Other medicines—Although certain medicines should not be used together at all, in other cases two different medicines may be used together even if an interaction might occur. In these cases, your doctor may want to change the dose, or other precautions may be necessary. Tell your health care professional if you are taking any other prescription or nonprescription (over-the-counter [OTC]) medicine.

Other medical problems—The presence of other medical problems may affect the use of yohimbine. Make sure you tell your doctor if you have any other medical problems, especially:
  • Angina pectoris or
  • Depression or
  • Other psychiatric illness or
  • Heart disease or
  • High blood pressure or
  • Kidney disease—Yohimbine may make these conditions worse
  • Liver disease—Effects of yohimbine may be increased because of slower removal from the body

Proper Use of This Medicine

Take this medicine only as directed by your doctor to help your condition as much as possible. Do not take more or less of it, and do not take it more or less often than your doctor ordered.

Missed dose—If you miss a dose of this medicine, take it as soon as possible. However, if it is almost time for your next dose, skip the missed dose and go back to your regular dosing schedule. Do not double doses.

Storage—To store this medicine:
  • Keep out of the reach of children.
  • Store away from heat and direct light.
  • Do not store in the bathroom, near the kitchen sink, or in other damp places. Heat or moisture may cause the medicine to break down.
  • Keep the medicine from freezing. Do not refrigerate.
  • Do not keep outdated medicine or medicine no longer needed. Be sure that any discarded medicine is out of the reach of children.

Precautions While Using This Medicine

It is important that your doctor check your progress at regular visits to make sure that this medicine is working properly.

Use yohimbine exactly as directed by your doctor. Do not use more of it and do not use it more often than ordered. If too much is used, the risk of side effects such as fast heartbeat and high blood pressure is increased.

Side Effects of This Medicine

Along with its needed effects, a medicine may cause some unwanted effects. Although not all of these side effects may occur, if they do occur they may need medical attention.

Check with your doctor as soon as possible if any of the following side effects occur:
  Less common
     Fast heartbeat; increased blood pressure

Other side effects may occur that usually do not need medical attention. These side effects may go away during treatment as your body adjusts to the medicine. However, check with your doctor if any of the following side effects continue or are bothersome:
  Less common
     Dizziness; headache; irritability; nervousness or restlessness
  Rare
     Nausea and vomiting; skin flushing; sweating; tremor

Other side effects not listed above may also occur in some patients. If you notice any other effects, check with your doctor.

Additional Information

Once a medicine has been approved for marketing for a certain use, experience may show that it is also useful for other medical problems. Yohimbine is used to treat men with the following medical condition:

  • Impotence (not able to have erections)

The way yohimbine works is not known for sure. It is thought, however, to work by increasing the body's production of certain chemicals that help produce erections. It does not work in all men who are impotent.

This medicine usually begins to work about 2 to 3 weeks after you begin to take it.

The dose of yohimbine will be different for different patients. *Follow your doctor's orders or the directions on the label.* The following information includes only the average doses of yohimbine. *If your dose is different, do not change it* unless your doctor tells you to do so.

The number of tablets that you take depends on the strength of the medicine.

- For *oral* dosage form (tablets):
  —For treating impotence:
  - Adults—5.4 to 6 milligrams (mg) three times a day.

Revised: 6/28/2000

ZAFIRLUKAST   Systemic†

Commonly used brand name(s):

In the U.S.—
    Accolate

---

†Not commercially available in Canada.

Description

Zafirlukast (za-FIR-loo-kast) is used by patients with mild-to-moderate asthma to decrease the symptoms of asthma and the number of acute asthma attacks. However, this medicine should not be used to relieve an asthma attack that has already started.

This medicine is available only with your doctor's prescription, in the following dosage form:

Oral
- Tablets (U.S.)

Before Using This Medicine

In deciding to use a medicine, the risks of taking the medicine must be weighed against the good it will do. This is a decision you and your doctor will make. For zafirlukast, the following should be considered:

Allergies—Tell your doctor if you have ever had any unusual or allergic reaction to zafirlukast.

Pregnancy—Zafirlukast has not been studied in pregnant women. Studies in animals have shown that this medicine causes problems only when given in doses many times higher than the usual human dose.

Breast-feeding—Zafirlukast passes into breast milk and may cause unwanted effects in nursing babies. Breast-feeding is not recommended while you are taking zafirlukast.

Children—Studies on this medicine have been done only in adult patients and there is no specific information comparing use of zafirlukast in children up to 7 years of age with use in other age groups.

Older adults—In studies, mild to moderate respiratory tract infections were more likely to occur in patients 55 years of age or older taking zafirlukast. It is not known whether these infections were caused by taking zafirlukast or by other factors.

Other medicines—Although certain medicines should not be used together at all, in other cases two different medicines may be used together even if an interaction might occur. In these cases, your doctor may want to change the dose, or other precautions may be necessary. When you are taking zafirlukast, it is especially important that your health care professional know if you are taking any of the following:

- Warfarin (e.g., Coumadin)—Zafirlukast may increase the effects of this medicine

Proper Use of This Medicine

Zafirlukast is used to prevent asthma attacks. It is not used to relieve an attack that has already started. For relief of an asthma attack that has already started, you should use another medicine. If you do not have another medicine to use for an attack or if you have any questions about this, check with your health care professional.

Food may change the amount of zafirlukast that is absorbed. For this reason, it should be taken on an empty stomach, 1 hour before or 2 hours after a meal.

Dosing—The dose of this medicine will be different for different patients. *Follow your doctor's orders or the directions on the label.* The following information includes only the average doses of zafirlukast. *If your dose is different, do not change it* unless your doctor tells you to do so.

- For *oral* dosage form (tablets):
  —For asthma:
  - Adults and children 12 years of age and older—20 milligrams (mg) two times a day, on an empty stomach, at least 1 hour before or 2 hours after meals.
  - Children between 7 and 11 years of age—10 milligrams two times a day, on an empty stomach, at least 1 hour before or 2 hours after meals.
  - Children up to 7 years of age—Use and dose must be determined by your doctor.

Missed dose—If you miss a dose of this medicine, take it as soon as possible. However, if it is almost time for your next dose, skip the missed dose and go back to your regular dosing schedule. Do not double doses.

Storage—To store this medicine:
- Keep out of the reach of children.
- Store away from heat and direct light.
- Do not store in the bathroom, near the kitchen sink, or in other damp places. Heat or moisture may cause the medicine to break down.
- Do not keep outdated medicine or medicine no longer needed. Be sure that any discarded medicine is out of the reach of children.

Precautions While Using This Medicine

To work properly, zafirlukast must be taken every day at regularly spaced times, even if your asthma seems better.

You may be taking other medicines for asthma along with zafirlukast. Do not stop taking or reduce the dose of the other medicines, even if your asthma seems better, unless you are told to do so by your doctor.

Side Effects of This Medicine

Along with its needed effects, a medicine may cause some unwanted effects. The following side effects may go away during treatment as your body adjusts to the medicine. However, check with your doctor if any of the following side effects continue or are bothersome:

Less common
 Headache; nausea

Developed: 7/18/97
Revised: 01/13/00

ZALCITABINE   Systemic

Commonly used brand name(s):

In the U.S.—
 HIVID

In Canada—
 HIVID

Another commonly used name is ddC.

Description

Zalcitabine (zal-SITE-a-been) (also known as ddC) is used in the treatment of the infection caused by the human immunodeficiency virus (HIV). HIV is the virus that causes acquired immune deficiency syndrome (AIDS).

Zalcitabine (ddC) will not cure or prevent HIV infection or AIDS; however, it helps keep HIV from reproducing and appears to slow down the destruction of the immune system. This may help delay the development of problems usually related to AIDS or HIV disease. Zalcitabine will not keep you from spreading HIV to other people. People who receive this medicine may continue to have other problems usually related to AIDS or HIV disease.

Zalcitabine may cause some serious side effects, including peripheral neuropathy (a problem involving the nerves). Symptoms of peripheral neuropathy include tingling, burning, numbness, or pain in the hands or feet. Zalcitabine may also cause pancreatitis (inflammation of the pancreas). Symptoms of pancreatitis include stomach pain, and nausea and vomiting. *Check with your doctor if any new health problems or symptoms occur while you are taking zalcitabine.*

Zalcitabine is available only with your doctor's prescription, in the following dosage form:

Oral
 • Tablets (U.S. and Canada)

Before Using This Medicine

In deciding to use a medicine, the risks of taking the medicine must be weighed against the good it will do. This is a decision you and your doctor will make. For zalcitabine, the following should be considered:

Allergies—Tell your doctor if you have ever had any unusual or allergic reaction to zalcitabine. Also tell your health care professional if you are allergic to any other substances, such as foods, preservatives, or dyes.

Pregnancy—Zalcitabine has not been studied in pregnant women. However, studies in animals have shown that zalcitabine causes birth defects when given in very high doses. Before taking this medicine, make sure your doctor knows if you are pregnant or if you may become pregnant.

Breast-feeding—It is not known whether zalcitabine passes into the breast milk. However, if your baby does not already have the AIDS virus, there is a chance that you could pass it to your baby by breast-feeding. Talk to your doctor first if you are thinking about breast-feeding your baby.

Children—Zalcitabine can cause serious side effects in any patient. Therefore, it is especially important that you discuss with your child's doctor the good that this medicine may do as well as the risks of using it. Your child must be seen frequently and your child's progress carefully followed by the doctor while the child is taking zalcitabine.

Older adults—Zalcitabine has not been studied specifically in older people. Therefore, it is not known whether it causes different side effects or problems in the elderly than it does in younger adults.

Other medicines—Although certain medicines should not be used together at all, in other cases two different medicines may be used together even if an interaction might occur. In these cases, your doctor may want to change the dose, or other precautions may be necessary. When you are taking zalcitabine, it is especially important that your health care professional know if you are taking any of the following:

• Alcohol or
• Asparaginase (e.g., Elspar) or
• Azathioprine (e.g., Imuran) or
• Estrogens (female hormones) or
• Furosemide (e.g., Lasix) or
• Methyldopa (e.g., Aldomet) or
• Pentamidine by injection (e.g., Pentam, Pentacarinat) or
• Sulfonamides (e.g., Bactrim, Septra) or
• Sulindac (e.g., Clinoril) or
• Tetracyclines or
• Thiazide diuretics (water pills) (e.g., Diuril, Hydrodiuril) or
• Valproic acid (e.g., Depakote)—Use of these medicines with zalcitabine may increase the chance of pancreatitis (inflammation of the pancreas)

• Aminoglycosides by injection (amikacin [e.g., Amikin], gentamicin [e.g., Garamycin], kanamycin [e.g., Kantrex], neomycin [e.g., Mycifradin], netilmicin [e.g., Netromycin], streptomycin, tobramycin [e.g., Nebcin]) or
• Amphotericin B (e.g., Fungizone) or
• Foscarnet (e.g., Foscavir)—Use of these medicines with zalcitabine may increase the chance of side effects

• Antacids, aluminum- and/or magnesium-containing (e.g., Maalox, Mylanta)—Use of antacids with zalcitabine may decrease the absorption of zalcitabine; antacids and zalcitabine should not be taken at the same time

• Chloramphenicol (e.g., Chloromycetin) or
• Cisplatin (e.g., Platinol) or
• Dapsone (e.g., Avlosulfon) or
• Didanosine (e.g., Videx, ddl) or
• Disulfiram (e.g., Antabuse) or
• Ethambutol (e.g., Myambutol) or
• Ethionamide (e.g., Trecator-SC) or
• Gold (arthritis medicine) or
• Hydralazine (e.g., Apresoline) or
• Isoniazid (e.g., Nydrazid) or
• Lithium (e.g., Eskalith, Lithobid) or
• Metronidazole (e.g., Flagyl) or
• Nitrous oxide or
• Phenytoin (e.g., Dilantin) or
• Ribavirin (e.g., Virazole) or

- Stavudine (e.g., Zerit, d4T) or
- Vincristine (e.g., Oncovin)—Use of these medicines with zalcitabine may increase the chance of peripheral neuropathy (tingling, burning, numbness, or pain in your hands or feet)

- Cimetidine (e.g., Tagamet) or
- Probenecid (e.g., Benemid)—Use of these medicines with zalcitabine may increase the chance of side effects of zalcitabine

- Nitrofurantoin (e.g., Furadantin, Macrodantin)—Use of nitrofurantoin with zalcitabine may increase the chance of side effects, including peripheral neuropathy (tingling, burning, numbness, or pain in your hands or feet) and pancreatitis (inflammation of the pancreas)

Other medical problems—The presence of other medical problems may affect the use of zalcitabine. Make sure you tell your doctor if you have any other medical problems, especially:

- Alcohol abuse or
- Increased blood triglycerides (or a history of) or
- Pancreatitis (or a history of)—Patients with these medical problems may be at increased risk of pancreatitis (inflammation of the pancreas)

- Alcohol abuse, history of, or
- Liver disease—Zalcitabine may make liver disease worse in patients with liver disease or a history of alcohol abuse

- Kidney disease—Patients with kidney disease may have an increased chance of side effects

- Peripheral neuropathy—Zalcitabine may make this condition worse

Proper Use of This Medicine

Take this medicine exactly as directed by your doctor. Do not take more of it, do not take it more often, and do not take it for a longer time than your doctor ordered. Also, do not stop taking this medicine without checking with your doctor first.

Keep taking zalcitabine for the full time of treatment, even if you begin to feel better.

This medicine works best when there is a constant amount in the blood. *To help keep the amount constant, do not miss any doses*. If you need help in planning the best times to take your medicine, check with your health care professional.

Only take medicine that your doctor has prescribed specifically for you. Do not share your medicine with others.

Dosing—The dose of zalcitabine will be different for different patients. *Follow your doctor's orders or the directions on the label*. The following information includes only the average doses of zalcitabine. Your dose may be different if you have kidney disease. *If your dose is different, do not change it* unless your doctor tells you to do so:

- For *oral* dosage form (tablets):
  —For treatment of HIV infection:
  - Adults and children 12 years of age and older— 0.75 milligrams (mg), together with other HIV infection medicine, every eight hours; or 0.75 mg alone every eight hours.
  - Children up to 12 years of age—Use and dose must be determined by your doctor.

Missed dose—If you miss a dose of this medicine, take it as soon as possible. However, if it is almost time for your next dose, skip the missed dose and go back to your regular dosing schedule. Do not double doses.

Storage—To store this medicine:
- Keep out of the reach of children.
- Store away from heat and direct light.
- Do not store in the bathroom, near the kitchen sink, or in other damp places. Heat or moisture may cause the medicine to break down.
- Do not keep outdated medicine or medicine no longer needed. Be sure that any discarded medicine is out of the reach of children.

Precautions While Using This Medicine

It is very important that your doctor check your progress at regular visits.

Do not take any other medicines without checking with your doctor first. To do so may increase the chance of side effects from zalcitabine.

HIV may be acquired from or spread to other people through infected body fluids, including blood, vaginal fluid, or semen. *If you are infected, it is best to avoid any sexual activity involving an exchange of body fluids with other people. If you do have sex, always wear (or have your partner wear) a condom ("rubber")*. Only use condoms made of latex, and *use them every time you have vaginal, anal, or oral sex*. The use of a spermicide (such as nonoxynol-9) may also help prevent transmission of HIV if it is not irritating to the vagina, rectum, or mouth. Spermicides have been shown to kill HIV in lab tests. Do not use oil-based jelly, cold cream, baby oil, or shortening as a lubricant—these products can cause the condom to break. Lubricants without oil, such as *K-Y Jelly*, are recommended. Women may wish to carry their own condoms. Birth control pills and diaphragms will help protect against pregnancy, but they will not prevent someone from giving or getting the AIDS virus. *If you inject drugs*, get help to stop. *Do not share needles or equipment with anyone*. In some cities, more than half of the drug users are infected, and sharing even 1 needle or syringe can spread the virus. If you have any questions about this, check with your health care professional.

Side Effects of This Medicine

Along with its needed effects, a medicine may cause some unwanted effects. Although not all of these side effects may occur, if they do occur they may need medical attention.

Check with your doctor immediately if any of the following side effects occur:
  More common
    Tingling, burning, numbness, or pain in the hands, arms, feet, or legs

  Less common
    Fever; joint pain; muscle pain; skin rash; ulcers in the mouth and throat

  Rare
    Fever and sore throat; nausea and vomiting; stomach pain (severe); yellow eyes or skin

Other side effects may occur that usually do not need medical attention. These side effects may go away during treatment as your body adjusts to the medicine. However, check with

your doctor if any of the following side effects continue or are bothersome:

Less common
 Diarrhea; headache; stomach pain (mild)

Other side effects not listed above may also occur in some patients. If you notice any other effects, check with your doctor.

Revised: 02/01/95
Interim revision: 04/17/98

ZALEPLON   Systemic†

Commonly used brand name(s):

In the U.S.—
 Sonata

†Not commercially available in Canada.

Description

Zaleplon (ZAL–e–plon) belongs to the group of medicines called central nervous system (CNS) depressants (medicines that make you drowsy or less alert). Zaleplon is used to treat insomnia (trouble sleeping). In general, when sleep medicines are used every night for a long time, they may lose their effectiveness. In most cases, sleep medicines should be used only for short periods of time, such as 1 or 2 days, and generally for no longer than 1 or 2 weeks.

This medicine is available only with your doctor's prescription, in the following dosage form:

Oral
 • Capsules (U.S.)

Before Using This Medicine

Sleep medicines may cause a special type of memory loss or "amnesia". When this occurs, a person does not remember what has happened during the several hours between use of the medicine and the time when its effects wear off. This is usually not a problem since most people fall asleep after taking the medicine. In most instances, memory problems can be avoided by taking zaleplon only when you are able to get at least 4 hours of sleep before you need to be active again. Be sure to talk to your doctor if you think you are having memory problems.

In deciding to use a medicine, the risks of taking the medicine must be weighed against the good it will do. This is a decision you and your doctor will make. For zaleplon, the following should be considered:

Allergies—Tell your doctor if you have ever had any unusual or allergic reaction to zaleplon. Also tell your health care professional if you are allergic to any other substances, such as foods, preservatives, or dyes.

Pregnancy—Zaleplon has not been studied in pregnant women. However, studies in pregnant animals have shown that zaleplon slows down the development of the offspring when given to the mother in doses many times the human dose. Before taking this medicine, make sure you doctor knows if you are pregnant or if you may become pregnant.

Breast-feeding—Zaleplon passes into breast milk, but the effect on nursing babies is unknown

Children—Studies on this medicine have been done only in adult patients, and there is no specific information comparing use of zaleplon in children younger than 18 years with adults.

Older adults—Elderly patients are usually more sensitive than younger adults to the effects of zaleplon.

Other medicines—Although certain medicines should not be used together at all, in other cases two different medicines may be used together even if an interaction might occur. In these cases, your doctor may want to change the dose, or other precautions may be necessary. When you are taking zaleplon, it is especially important that your health care professional know if you are taking any of the following:

• Alcohol (with chronic use) or
• Barbiturates, especially phenobarbital or
• Carbamazepine (e.g., Tegretol) or
• Glutethimide (e.g., Doriglute) or
• Phenylbutazone (e.g., Butazolidin) or
• Phenytoin (e.g., Dilantin) or
• Primidone (e.g., Mysoline) or
• Rifampin (e.g., Rifadin)—These medicines may decrease the effectiveness of zaleplon

• Cimetidine (e.g., Tagamet)—Cimetidine may interfere with the breakdown of zaleplon in the body, possibly leading to unwanted effects

• Other central nervous system (CNS) depressants (medicines that cause drowsiness) or
• Tricyclic antidepressants (medicine for depression)—The CNS depressant effects of either these medicines or zaleplon may be increased, possibly leading to unwanted effects

Other medical problems—The presence of other medical problems may affect the use of zaleplon. Make sure to tell your doctor if you have any other medical problems, especially

• Alcohol abuse (or history of) or
• Drug abuse or dependence (or history of)—Dependence on zaleplon may develop

• Breathing problems or
• Mental depression—Zaleplon may make the condition worse
• Liver disease—Higher blood levels of zaleplon may result, increasing the chance of side effects.

Proper Use of This Medicine

Take this medicine only as directed by your doctor. Do not take more of it, do not take it more often, and do not take it for a longer time than your doctor ordered. If too much is taken, it may become habit-forming (causing mental or physical dependence).

Take zaleplon just before going to bed, when you are ready to go to sleep. This medicine works very quickly to put you to sleep.

Do not take this medicine when your schedule does not permit you to get at least 4 hours of sleep. If you must wake up before this, you may continue to feel drowsy and may experience memory problems, because the effects of the medicine have not had time to wear off.

Zaleplon may be taken with or without food or on a full or empty stomach. However, taking this medicine with or immediately after a heavy or a high fat meal may make zaleplon not work as fast.

Dosing—The dose of zaleplon will be different for different patients. *Follow your doctor's orders or the directions on the label.* The following information includes only the average doses of zaleplon. *If your dose is different, do not change it* unless your doctor tells you to do so

The number of capsules that you take depends on the strength of the medicine.

- For *oral* dosage form (capsules):
  —For the treatment of insomnia (trouble in sleeping):
  - Adults—10 milligrams (mg) at bedtime
  - Older adults—5 mg at bedtime
  - Children up to 18 years of age—Use and dose must be determined by doctor

Missed dose—If you miss a dose of this medicine, skip the missed dose and go back to your regular dosing schedule. Do not double doses.

Storage—To store this medicine:

- Keep out of the reach of children.
- Store away from heat and direct light.
- Do not store in the bathroom, near the kitchen sink, or in other damp places. Heat or moisture may cause the medicine to break down.
- Do not keep outdated medicine or medicine no longer needed. Be sure that any discarded medicine is out of the reach of children.

Precautions While Using This Medicine

If you think you need to take zaleplon for more than 7 to 10 days, be sure to discuss it with your doctor. Insomnia that lasts longer than this may be a sign of another medical problem.

This medicine will add to the effects of alcohol and other central nervous system (CNS) depressants (medicines that cause drowsiness). Some examples of CNS depressants are antihistamines or medicine for hay fever, other allergies or colds; sedatives, tranquilizers, or sleeping medicines; prescription pain medicine or narcotics; barbiturates; medicine for seizures; muscle relaxants; or anesthetics, including some dental anesthetics. *Check with your doctor before taking any of the above while you are using this medicine.*

This medicine may cause some people, especially older persons, to become drowsy, dizzy, lightheaded, clumsy or unsteady, or less alert than they are normally. Even though zaleplon is taken at bedtime, it may cause some people to feel drowsy or less alert on arising. *Make sure you know how you react to zaleplon before you drive, use machines, or do anything else that could be dangerous if you are dizzy, unsteady, or are not alert or able to see well.*

If you develop any unusual and strange thoughts or behavior while taking zaleplon, be sure to discuss it with your doctor. Some changes that have occurred in people taking this medicine are like those seen in people who drink alcohol and then act in a manner that is not normal. Other changes may be more unusual and extreme, such as confusion, hallucinations (seeing, hearing, smelling, or feeling things that are not there), and unusual excitement, nervousness, or irritability.

If you will be taking zaleplon for a long time, do not stop taking it without first checking with your doctor. Your doctor may want you to reduce gradually the amount you are taking before stopping completely. Stopping this medicine suddenly may cause withdrawal side effects.

After taking zaleplon for insomnia, you may have difficulty sleeping (rebound insomnia) for the first few nights after you stop taking it.

If you think you or someone else may have taken an overdose of this medicine, get emergency help at once. Taking an overdose of zaleplon or taking alcohol or other CNS depressants with zaleplon may lead to breathing problems and unconsciousness. Some signs of an overdose are clumsiness or unsteadiness, confusion, severe drowsiness, low blood pressure, unusual dullness or feeling sluggish, and troubled breathing.

Side Effects of This Medicine

Along with its needed effects, a medicine may cause some unwanted effects. Although not all of these side effects may occur, if they do occur they may need medical attention.

Check with your doctor as soon as possible if any of the following side effects occur:

Less common
Anxiety; blurred or double vision; not feeling like oneself

Rare
Nosebleed; seeing, hearing, smelling, or feeling things that are not there

Symptoms of overdose
Confusion; clumsiness or unsteadiness, severe; dizziness or fainting; drowsiness, severe; weak muscle tone; troubled breathing; unusual dullness or feeling sluggish

Other side effects may occur that usually do not need medical attention. These side effects may go away during treatment as your body adjusts to the medicine. However, check with your doctor if any of the following side effects continue or are bothersome:

More common
Dizziness; headache; muscle pain; nausea

Less common
Abdominal pain; burning, prickling, or tingling sensation; constipation; cough; difficulty concentrating; drowsiness; dryness of mouth; excess muscle tone; eye pain; fever; heartburn, indigestion, or acid stomach; itching; itching or burning eyes; joint stiffness and/or pain; memory loss; menstrual pain; mental depression; nervousness; sensitive hearing; severe headache; shortness of breath; skin rash; tightness in chest; trembling or shaking; troubled breathing; unusual weakness or tiredness; wheezing

After you stop using this medicine, your body may need time to adjust. The length of time this takes depends on the amount of medicine you were using and how long you used it. during this period of time, check with your doctor if you notice any of the following side effects:

Abdominal and muscle cramps; convulsions (seizures); increased sweating; sadness; trembling or shaking; vomiting

Developed: 10/5/99

Zanamivir   Inhalation—Systemic

Commonly used brand name(s):

In the U.S.—
Relenza

In Canada—
Relenza

Description

Zanamivir (zan-AM-e-veer) is used in the treatment of the infection caused by the flu virus (influenza A and influenza B). Zanamivir may reduce flu symptoms (weakness, headache, fever, cough, and sore throat) by 1 to 1.5 days. Zanamivir does not prevent influenza infection.

This medicine must be started within 2 days of having flu symptoms (weakness, headache, fever, cough, and sore throat). Zanamivir will not keep you from spreading the flu virus to other people. Zanamivir may not work for everybody. Zanamivir may not be for you if you are severely sick or have a breathing problem (like asthma or chronic obstructive pulmonary disease). If you receive the flu vaccine every year, continue to do so.

Before Using This Medicine

Allergies—Tell your doctor if you have ever had any unusual or allergic reaction to zanamivir.

Pregnancy—Zanamivir has not been studied in pregnant women. However, zanamivir has not been shown to cause birth defects or other problems in animal studies.

Breast-feeding—It is not known whether zanamivir passes into breast milk. Although most medicines pass into breast milk in small amounts, many of them may be used safely while breast-feeding. Mothers who are using this medicine and who wish to breast-feed should discuss this with their doctor.

Children—This medicine is not recommended for use in children younger than 7 years of age

Note: This medicine is available in Canada. It is not recommended in children younger than 12 years of age.

Teenagers—This medicine has been tested in children 12 years and older and has not been shown to cause different side effects or problems in these children than it does in adults.

Older adults—This medicine has been tested in older adults and has not been shown to cause different side effects or problems in older adults than it does in younger adults.

Other medicines—Although certain medicines should not be used together at all, in other cases two different medicines may be used together even if an interaction might occur. In these cases, your doctor may want to change the dose, or other precautions may be necessary. Tell your health care professional if you are taking any other prescription or nonprescription (over the counter [OTC]) medicine before using zanamivir.

Other medical problems—The presence of other medical problems may affect the use of zanamivir. Make sure to tell your doctor if you have any other medical problems, especially:

- Lung Disease—Patients with lung disease (chronic obstructive pulmonary disease or asthma) may experience

trouble breathing with the use of zanamivir. Zanamivir may not work in patients with chronic lung disease.

- Heart Disease—Zanamivir may not work in patients with heart disease.

Proper Use of This Medicine

Talk to your doctor about the possibility of getting a flu shot if you have not had one yet. This medicine works best if taken as soon as possible after exposure to people who have the flu. If you already have the flu, *continue taking this medicine for the full time of treatment* even if you begin to feel better after a few days. This will help to clear up your infection completely. If you stop taking this medicine too soon, your symptoms may return. This medicine should be taken for 5 days.

Inhaled zanamivir is used with a special inhaler and usually comes with patient directions. Read the directions carefully before using this medicine. If you do not understand the directions or you are not sure how to use the inhaler, ask your health care professional to show you what to do.

To load the inhaler:

- Pull off the blue cover. Make sure the mouthpiece is clean and free of foreign objects.
- Pull the white mouthpiece until the tray is extended.
- Hold the corners of the white tray and pull out gently until you can see all the raised ridges on the sides of the tray.
- Put your finger and thumb on the ridges, squeeze inward, and gently pull the tray out of the body of the inhaler.
- Place a disk on the wheel and then slide the tray back into the inhaler
- To replace the empty disk with a full disk, follow the same steps you used to load the inhaler.

To use the inhaler:

- Hold the inhaler flat in your hand.
- A plastic needle will break the blister containing one inhalation of medicine. When the flap is raised as far as it will go, the blister will be pierced. Do not lift the flap if the cartridge is not in the inhaler. Doing this will break the needle and you will need a new inhaler.
- After the blister is broken open, close the lid. Keeping the inhaler flat and well away from your mouth, breathe out to the end of a normal breath.
- Raise the inhaler to your mouth, and place the mouthpiece in your mouth.
- Close your lips around the mouthpiece and tilt your head slightly back. Do not bite down on the mouthpiece. Do not block the mouthpiece with your teeth or tongue. Do not cover the air holes on the side of the mouthpiece.
- Breathe in through your mouth as steadily and as deeply as you can until you have taken a full deep breath.
- Hold your breath and remove the mouthpiece from your mouth. Continue holding your breath as long as you can up to 10 seconds before breathing out. This gives the medicine time to settle in your airways and lungs.
- Hold the inhaler well away from your mouth and breathe out to the end of a normal breath.
- Prepare the cartridge for your next inhalation. Pull the mouthpiece to extend the tray then push it in until it clicks. The disk will turn to the next dose. Do not pierce the blister until just before the inhalation.
- Take the second puff following exactly the same steps you used for the first puff.

- When you are finished, wipe off the mouthpiece and replace the cover to keep the mouthpiece clean and free of foreign objects.

Dosing—Follow your doctor's orders or the directions on the label.

—For treatment of flu (Influenza A and Influenza B)

- Adults and children 7 years and older—Two puffs twice daily (approximately 12 hours apart in the morning and evening) for 5 days. Two doses should be taken on the first day of treatment whenever possible provided there are at least 2 hours between doses. Zanamivir must be started within 48 hours after the onset of signs and symptoms of the flu.

—Canada: For treatment of flu (Influenza A and Influenza B)

- Adults and children 12 years and older—Two puffs twice daily (approximately 12 hours apart in the morning and evening) for 5 days. Two doses should be taken on the first day of treatment whenever possible provided there are at least 2 hours between doses. Zanamivir must be started within 48 hours after the onset of signs and symptoms of the flu.

Missed dose—This medicine works best when there is a constant amount in the lungs. To help keep the amount constant, do not miss any doses. If you miss a dose of this medicine, use it as soon as possible. If it is almost time for your next dose, skip the missed dose and go back to your regular dosing schedule. Do not double doses. It is best to take the doses at evenly spaced times day and night.

Storage—To store this medicine:

- Keep out of the reach of children.
- Store away from heat and direct light.
- Do not store in the bathroom, near the kitchen sink, or in other damp places. Heat or moisture may cause the medicine to break down.
- Keep the medicine from freezing. Do not refrigerate.
- Do not keep outdated medicine or medicine no longer needed. Be sure that any discarded medicine is out of the reach of children.

Precautions While Using This Medicine

Zanamivir will not keep you from spreading the flu virus to other people. This medicine may cause people with lung disease (chronic obstructive lung disease or asthma) to experience trouble breathing. If this should happen contact your doctor immediately. Zanamivir may not work in patients with lung disease, heart disease, or serious medical conditions.

Bronchospasm (wheezing) is a risk for patients with asthma or chronic respiratory disease. Always have a fast-acting inhaled bronchodilator available for your use.

Side Effects of This Medicine

Along with its needed effects, a medicine may cause some unwanted effects. Although not all of these side effects may occur, if they do occur they may need medical attention.

Stop using this medicine and get emergency help immediately if either of the following side effects occur:

  Rare

    Shortness of breath or troubled breathing

Other side effects may occur that usually do not need medical attention. These side effects may go away during treatment as your body adjusts to the medicine. However, check with your doctor if any of the following side effects continue or are bothersome:

  Less common

    Change in hearing; cough; cough producing mucus; diarrhea; dizziness; earache; ear drainage; ear, nose and throat infections; headache; nasal signs and symptoms; nausea; pain and pressure over cheeks; pain in ear; shortness of breath; tightness in chest; vomiting; wheezing

Other side effects not listed above may also occur in some patients. If you notice any other effects, check with your doctor.

Developed: 09/24/1999
Revised: 12/13/2000

ZIDOVUDINE   Systemic

Commonly used brand name(s):

In the U.S.—
  Retrovir

In Canada—
  Apo-Zidovudine
  Novo-AZT
  Retrovir

Another commonly used name is AZT.

Description

Zidovudine (zye-DOE-vue-deen) (also known as AZT) is used, alone or together with zalcitabine (ddC), in the treatment of the infection caused by the human immunodeficiency virus (HIV). HIV is the virus responsible for acquired immune deficiency syndrome (AIDS). Zidovudine is used to slow the progression of disease in patients infected with HIV who have advanced symptoms, early symptoms, or no symptoms at all. This medicine also is used to help prevent pregnant women who have HIV from passing the virus to their babies during pregnancy and at birth.

Zidovudine will not cure or prevent HIV infection or AIDS; however, it helps keep HIV from reproducing and appears to slow down the destruction of the immune system. This may help delay the development of problems usually related to AIDS or HIV disease. Zidovudine will not keep you from spreading HIV to other people. People who receive this medicine may continue to have the problems usually related to AIDS or HIV disease.

Zidovudine may cause some serious side effects, including bone marrow problems. Symptoms of bone marrow problems include fever, chills, or sore throat; pale skin; and unusual tiredness or weakness. These problems may require blood transfusions or temporarily stopping treatment with zidovudine. *Check with your doctor if any new health problems or symptoms occur while you are taking zidovudine.*

Zidovudine is available only with your doctor's prescription, in the following dosage forms:

  Oral

- Capsules (U.S. and Canada)
- Syrup (U.S. and Canada)
- Tablets (U.S. and Canada)

Parenteral
- Injection (U.S. and Canada)

Before Using This Medicine

In deciding to use a medicine, the risks of taking the medicine must be weighed against the good it will do. This is a decision you and your doctor will make. For zidovudine, the following should be considered:

Allergies—Tell your doctor if you have ever had any unusual or allergic reaction to zidovudine. Also tell your health care professional if you are allergic to any other substances, such as foods, preservatives, or dyes.

Pregnancy—Zidovudine crosses the placenta. Studies in pregnant women have shown that zidovudine decreases the chance of passing HIV to your baby during pregnancy and at birth. In these studies, zidovudine did not increase the occurrence of birth defects. In most studies in animals, zidovudine has not been shown to cause birth defects except at extremely high doses; however, it has been shown to decrease the number of successful pregnancies in rats and rabbits at doses many times higher than human doses.

Breast-feeding—Zidovudine passes into breast milk. Breast-feeding is usually not recommended in patients with HIV infection because of the risk of passing HIV to the infant.

Children—Zidovudine can cause serious side effects in any patient. Therefore, it is especially important that you discuss with your child's doctor the good that this medicine may do as well as the risks of using it. Your child must be carefully followed, and frequently seen, by the doctor while he or she is taking zidovudine.

Older adults—Zidovudine has not been studied specifically in older people. Therefore, it is not known whether it causes different side effects or problems in the elderly than it does in younger adults.

Other medicines—Although certain medicines should not be used together at all, in other cases two different medicines may be used together even if an interaction might occur. In these cases, your doctor may want to change the dose, or other precautions may be necessary. When you are taking zidovudine, it is especially important that your health care professional know if you are taking any of the following:

- Amphotericin B by injection (e.g., Fungizone) or
- Antineoplastics (cancer medicine) or
- Antithyroid agents (medicine for overactive thyroid) or
- Azathioprine (e.g., Imuran) or
- Chloramphenicol (e.g., Chloromycetin) or
- Colchicine or
- Cyclophosphamide (e.g., Cytoxan) or
- Flucytosine (e.g., Ancobon) or
- Ganciclovir (e.g., Cytovene) or
- Interferon (e.g., Intron A, Roferon-A) or
- Mercaptopurine (e.g., Purinethol) or
- Methotrexate (e.g., Mexate) or
- Plicamycin (e.g., Mithracin)—Caution should be used if these medicines and zidovudine are used together; taking zidovudine while you are using or receiving these medicines may make anemia and other blood problems worse

- Clarithromycin (e.g., Biaxin)—Clarithromycin may decrease the amount of zidovudine in the blood

- Probenecid (e.g., Benemid)—Probenecid may increase the amount of zidovudine in the blood, increasing the chance of side effects

- Ribavirin (e.g., Virazole)—Ribavirin may cause this medicine to be less effective

Other medical problems—The presence of other medical problems may affect the use of zidovudine. Make sure you tell your doctor if you have any other medical problems, especially:

- Anemia or other blood problems—Zidovudine may make these conditions worse

- Liver disease—Patients with liver disease may have an increase in side effects from zidovudine

- Low amounts of folic acid or vitamin B_{12} in the blood—Zidovudine may worsen anemia caused by a decrease of folic acid or vitamin B_{12}

Proper Use of This Medicine

Patient information sheets about zidovudine are available. Read this information carefully.

Take this medicine exactly as directed by your doctor. Do not take more of it, do not take it more often, and do not take it for a longer time than your doctor ordered. Also, do not stop taking this medicine without checking with your doctor first.

Keep taking zidovudine for the full time of treatment, even if you begin to feel better.

For patients using *zidovudine syrup:*

- Use a specially marked measuring spoon or other device to measure each dose accurately. The average household teaspoon may not hold the right amount of liquid.

This medicine works best when there is a constant amount in the blood. *To help keep the amount constant, do not miss any doses.* If you need help in planning the best times to take your medicine, check with your health care professional.

Dosing—The dose of zidovudine will be different for different patients. *Follow your doctor's orders or the directions on the label.* The following information includes only the average doses of zidovudine. *If your dose is different, do not change it* unless your doctor tells you to do so.

- For the treatment of HIV infection:
  - —For *oral* dosage forms (capsules, syrup, and tablets):
    - Adults and children 12 years of age and older—100 milligrams (mg) every four hours for a total of 500 mg a day; or a total of 600 mg a day in divided doses; or 200 mg of zidovudine together with other medicine to treat HIV infection every eight hours.
    - Children 3 months to 12 years of age—Dose is based on body size and must be determined by your doctor.
  - —For *injection* dosage form:
    - Adults and teenagers—Dose is based on body weight and must be determined by your doctor. The usual dose is 1 to 2 mg per kilogram (kg) (0.45 to 0.9 mg per pound) of body weight, injected slowly into a vein every four hours five to six times a day. The injection dosage form is given until you can take zidovudine by mouth.

- Children 3 months to 12 years of age—Dose is based on body size and must be determined by your doctor.
- To help prevent pregnant women from passing HIV to their babies during pregnancy and at birth:
  —For *capsule* dosage form:
  - Pregnant women (after 14 weeks of pregnancy, up to the start of labor)—100 milligrams (mg) five times a day until the start of labor.
  —For *syrup* dosage form:
  - Pregnant women (after 14 weeks of pregnancy, up to the start of labor)—100 milligrams (mg) five times a day until the start of labor.
  - Newborn infants—Dose is based on body weight and must be determined by your doctor. The usual dose of syrup is 2 mg per kilogram (kg) (0.9 mg per pound) of body weight every six hours starting within twelve hours of birth and continuing through six weeks of age.
  —For *injection* dosage form:
  - Pregnant women (during labor and delivery)— Dose is based on body weight and must be determined by your doctor. The usual dose is 2 milligrams (mg) per kilogram (kg) (0.9 mg per pound) of body weight infused into a vein over the first hour, followed by 1 mg per kg (0.45 mg per pound of body weight) infused into a vein each hour until the umbilical cord is clamped.
  - Newborn infants—If the infant is unable to receive zidovudine syrup, the injection form may be used instead. Dose is based on body weight and must be determined by your doctor. The usual dose is 1.5 mg per kilogram (kg) (0.7 mg per pound) of body weight every six hours.

Missed dose—If you do miss a dose of this medicine, take it as soon as possible. However, if it is almost time for your next dose, skip the missed dose and go back to your regular dosing schedule. Do not double doses.

Storage—To store this medicine:
- Keep out of the reach of children.
- Store away from heat and direct light.
- Do not store capsule in the bathroom, near the kitchen sink, or in other damp places. Heat or moisture may cause the medicine to break down.
- Do not keep outdated medicine or medicine no longer needed. Be sure that any discarded medicine is out of the reach of children.

Precautions While Using This Medicine

It is very important that your doctor check your progress at regular visits. This medicine may cause blood problems.

Do not take any other medicines without checking with your doctor first. To do so may increase the chance of side effects from zidovudine.

Zidovudine may cause blood problems. These problems may result in a greater chance of certain infections and slow healing. Therefore, you should be careful when using regular toothbrushes, dental floss, and toothpicks not to damage your gums. Check with your medical doctor or dentist if you have any questions about proper oral hygiene (mouth care) during treatment.

HIV may be acquired from or spread to other people through infected body fluids, including blood, vaginal fluid, or semen. *If you are infected, it is best to avoid any sexual activity involving an exchange of body fluids with other people. If you do have sex, always wear (or have your partner wear) a condom ("rubber").* Only use condoms made of latex, and *use them every time you have vaginal, anal, or oral sex.* The use of a spermicide (such as nonoxynol-9) may also help prevent the spread of HIV if it is not irritating to the vagina, rectum, or mouth. Spermicides have been shown to kill HIV in lab tests. Do not use oil-based jelly, cold cream, baby oil, or shortening as a lubricant—these products can cause the condom to break. Lubricants without oil, such as *K-Y Jelly*, are recommended. Women may wish to carry their own condoms. Birth control pills and diaphragms will help protect against pregnancy, but they will not prevent someone from giving or getting the AIDS virus. *If you inject drugs*, get help to stop. *Do not share needles with anyone.* In some cities, more than half of the drug users are infected, and sharing even one needle can spread the virus. If you have any questions about this, check with your health care professional.

Side Effects of This Medicine

Along with its needed effects, a medicine may cause some unwanted effects. Although not all of these side effects may occur, if they do occur they may need medical attention.

Check with your doctor immediately if any of the following side effects occur:
More common
   Fever, chills, or sore throat; pale skin; unusual tiredness or weakness
   Note: The above side effects may also occur up to weeks or months after you stop taking this medicine.

Rare
   Abdominal discomfort; confusion; convulsions (seizures); diarrhea; fast, shallow breathing; general feeling of discomfort; loss of appetite; mood or mental changes; muscle pain, tenderness, weakness, or cramping; nausea; shortness of breath; sleepiness

Other side effects may occur that usually do not need medical attention. These side effects may go away during treatment as your body adjusts to the medicine. However, check with your doctor if any of the following side effects continue or are bothersome:
More common
   Headache (severe); nausea; trouble in sleeping
Less common
   Bluish-brown colored bands on nails; changes in skin color

Other side effects not listed above may also occur in some patients. If you notice any other effects, check with your doctor.

Additional Information

Once a medicine has been approved for marketing for a certain use, experience may show that it is also useful for other medical problems. Although this use is not included in product labeling, zidovudine is used in certain patients with the following medical condition:

- Human immunodeficiency virus (HIV) infection due to occupational exposure (possible prevention of)

Other than the above information, there is no additional information relating to proper use, precautions, or side effects for this use.

Revised: 06/15/99

ZILEUTON   Systemic†

Commonly used brand name(s):

In the U.S.—
   Zyflo

---

†Not commercially available in Canada.

Description

Zileuton (zye-LOO-ton) is used by patients with mild to moderate chronic asthma to decrease the symptoms of asthma and the number of acute asthma attacks. However, this medicine should not be taken to relieve an asthma attack that has already started.

This medicine is available only with your doctor's prescription, in the following dosage form(s):

Oral
   - Tablets (U.S.)

Before Using This Medicine

In deciding to use a medicine, the risks of taking the medicine must be weighed against the good it will do. This is a decision you and your doctor will make. For zileuton, the following should be considered:

Allergies—Tell your doctor if you have ever had any unusual or allergic reaction to zileuton.

Pregnancy—Zileuton has not been studied in pregnant women. However, studies in rabbits have shown that this medicine causes problems when given in doses equal to the maximum human dose. Before taking this medicine, make sure your doctor knows if you are pregnant or if you may become pregnant.

Breast-feeding—Zileuton passes into breast milk and may cause unwanted effects in nursing babies. Taking zileuton is not recommended while you are breast-feeding.

Children—Studies on this medicine have been done only in adult patients and there is no specific information comparing use of zileuton in children up to 12 years of age with use in other age groups.

Older adults—This medicine has been tested and has not been shown to cause different side effects or problems in older people than it does in younger adults.

Other medicines—Although certain medicines should not be used together at all, in other cases two different medicines may be used together even if an interaction might occur. In these cases, your doctor may want to change the dose, or other precautions may be necessary. When you are

taking zileuton, it is especially important that your health care professional know if you are taking any of the following:

- Beta-adrenergic blocking agents (acebutolol [e.g., Sectral], atenolol [e.g., Tenormin], betaxolol [e.g., Betoptic, Kerlone], bisoprolol [e.g., Zebeta], carteolol [e.g., Cartrol], labetalol [e.g., Normodyne], levobunolol [e.g., Betagan], metipranolol [e.g., Optipranolol], metoprolol [e.g., Lopressor], nadolol [e.g., Corgard], oxprenolol [e.g., Trasicor], penbutolol [e.g., Levatol], pindolol [e.g., Visken], propranolol [e.g., Inderal], sotalol [e.g., Sotacor], timolol [e.g., Blocadren, Timoptic]) or
- Terfenadine (e.g., Seldane) or
- Theophylline (e.g., Theo Dur) or
- Warfarin (e.g., Coumadin)—Zileuton may increase the effects of these medicines

Other medical problems—The presence of other medical problems may affect the use of zileuton. Make sure you tell your doctor if you have any other medical problems, especially:

- Active alcoholism or
- Liver disease—The chance of serious side effects may be increased

Proper Use of This Medicine

Zileuton is used to prevent asthma attacks. It is not used to relieve an attack that has already started. For relief of an asthma attack that has already started, you should use another medicine. If you do not have another medicine to use for an attack or if you have any question about this, check with your health care professional.

Dosing—*Follow your doctor's orders or the directions on the label.* The following information includes only the average doses of zileuton. *If your dose is different, do not change it* unless your doctor tells you to do so.

- For *oral* dosage form (tablets):
   —For asthma:
      - Adults and children 12 years of age and older—600 milligrams (mg) four times a day.
      - Children up to 12 years of age—Use and dose must be determined by your doctor.

Missed dose—If you miss a dose of this medicine, take it as soon as possible. However, if it is almost time for your next dose, skip the missed dose and go back to your regular dosing schedule. Do not double doses.

Storage—To store this medicine:

- Keep out of the reach of children.
- Store away from heat and direct light.
- Do not store in the bathroom, near the kitchen sink, or in other damp places. Heat or moisture may cause the medicine to break down.
- Do not keep outdated medicine or medicine no longer needed. Be sure that any discarded medicine is out of the reach of children.

Precautions While Using This Medicine

To work properly, *zileuton must be taken every day at regularly spaced times, even if your asthma seems better.*

It is very important that your doctor check your progress at regular visits. *Your doctor will want to have certain tests done regularly to see if side effects may be occurring in your liver without your knowing it.*

Check with your health care professional if more inhalations (puffs) than usual of an inhaled, short-acting bronchodilator are needed to relieve an acute attack or if more than the maximum number of puffs of the bronchodilator prescribed for a 24-hour period are needed.

You may be taking other medicines for asthma along with zileuton. *Do not stop taking or reduce the dose of the other medicines, even if your asthma seems better, unless you are told to do so by your health care professional.*

Side Effects of This Medicine

Along with its needed effects, a medicine may cause some unwanted effects. Although not all of these side effects may occur, if they do occur they may need medical attention.

Check with your doctor as soon as possible if any of the following side effects occur:

Rare
 Flu-like symptoms; itching; right upper abdominal pain; unusual tiredness or weakness; yellow eyes or skin

Other side effects may occur that usually do not need medical attention. These side effects may go away during treatment as your body adjusts to the medicine. However, check with your doctor if any of the following side effects continue or are bothersome:

More common
 Nausea; upset stomach

Less common
 Abdominal pain; weakness

Other side effects not listed above may also occur in some patients. If you notice any other effects, check with your doctor.

Developed: 12/29/97
Interim revision: 03/22/99

ZINC SUPPLEMENTS   Systemic

Commonly used brand name(s):

In the U.S.—
Orazinc[3]
Verazinc[4]
Zinc-220[4]

Zinc 15[4]
Zinca-Pak[4]
Zincate[4]

In Canada—
PMS Egozinc[4]

Note: For quick reference, the following zinc supplements are numbered to match the corresponding brand names.

This information applies to the following:
1. Zinc Chloride (zink KLOR-ide) †‡
2. Zinc Gluconate (zink GLOO-coh-nate) ‡§
3. Zinc Gluconate and Zinc Sulfate (zink GLOO-coh-nate and zink SUL-fate)‡§
4. Zinc Sulfate (zink SUL-fate) †‡

†Not commercially available in Canada.
‡Generic name product may be available in the U.S.
§Generic name product may be available in Canada.

Description

Zinc supplements are used to prevent or treat zinc deficiency.

The body needs zinc for normal growth and health. For patients who are unable to get enough zinc in their regular diet or who have a need for more zinc, zinc supplements may be necessary. They are generally taken by mouth but some patients may have to receive them by injection.

Zinc supplements may be used for other conditions as determined by your health care professional.

Lack of zinc may lead to poor night vision and wound-healing, a decrease in sense of taste and smell, a reduced ability to fight infections, and poor development of reproductive organs.

Some conditions may increase your need for zinc. These include:
- Acrodermatitis enteropathica (a lack of absorption of zinc from the intestine)
- Alcoholism
- Burns
- Diabetes mellitus (sugar diabetes)
- Down's syndrome
- Eating disorders
- Intestine diseases
- Infections (continuing or chronic)
- Kidney disease
- Liver disease
- Pancreas disease
- Sickle cell disease
- Skin disorders
- Stomach removal
- Stress (continuing)
- Thalassemia
- Trauma (prolonged)

In addition, premature infants may need additional zinc.

Increased need for zinc should be determined by your health care professional.

Claims that zinc is effective in preventing vision loss in the elderly have not been proven. Zinc has not been proven effective in the treatment of porphyria.

Injectable zinc is given by or under the supervision of a health care professional. Other forms of zinc are available without a prescription.

Zinc supplements are available in the following dosage forms:

Oral
Zinc Gluconate
- Lozenges (U.S.)
- Tablets (U.S. and Canada)
Zinc Sulfate
- Capsules (U.S.)
- Tablets (U.S. and Canada)
- Extended-release tablets (U.S.)

Parenteral
Zinc Chloride
- Injection (U.S.)
Zinc Sulfate
- Injection (U.S.)

Importance of Diet

For good health, it is important that you eat a balanced and varied diet. Follow carefully any diet program your health care professional may recommend. For your specific dietary vitamin and/or mineral needs, ask your health care professional for a list of appropriate foods. If you think that you are not getting enough vitamins and/or minerals in your diet, you may choose to take a dietary supplement.

Zinc is found in various foods, including lean red meats, seafood (especially herring and oysters), peas, and beans. Zinc is also found in whole grains; however, large amounts of whole-grains have been found to decrease the amount of zinc that is absorbed. Additional zinc may be added to the diet through treated (galvanized) cookware. Foods stored in uncoated tin cans may cause less zinc to be available for absorption from food.

The daily amount of zinc needed is defined in several different ways.

For U.S.—
- Recommended Dietary Allowances (RDAs) are the amount of vitamins and minerals needed to provide for adequate nutrition in most healthy persons. RDAs for a given nutrient may vary depending on a person's age, sex, and physical condition (e.g., pregnancy).
- Daily Values (DVs) are used on food and dietary supplement labels to indicate the percent of the recommended daily amount of each nutrient that a serving provides. DV replaces the previous designation of United States Recommended Daily Allowances (USRDAs).

For Canada—
- Recommended Nutrient Intakes (RNIs) are used to determine the amounts of vitamins, minerals, and protein needed to provide adequate nutrition and lessen the risk of chronic disease.

Normal daily recommended intakes in milligrams (mg) for zinc are generally defined as follows:

Persons	U.S. (mg)	Canada (mg)
Infants and children		
Birth to 3 years of age	5–10	2–4
4 to 6 years of age	10	5
7 to 10 years of age	10	7–9
Adolescent and adult males	15	9–12
Adolescent and adult females	12	9
Pregnant females	15	15
Breast-feeding females	16–19	15

Before Using This Dietary Supplement

If you are taking this dietary supplement without a prescription, carefully read and follow any precautions on the label. For zinc supplements, the following should be considered:

Allergies—Tell your health care professional if you are allergic to any substances, such as foods, preservatives, or dyes.

Pregnancy—It is especially important that you are receiving enough vitamins and minerals when you become pregnant and that you continue to receive the right amount of vitamins and minerals throughout your pregnancy. The healthy growth and development of the fetus depend on a steady supply of nutrients from the mother. There is evidence that low blood levels of zinc may lead to problems in pregnancy or defects in the baby. However, taking large amounts of a dietary supplement in pregnancy may be harmful to the mother and/or fetus and should be avoided.

Breast-feeding—It is important that you receive the right amounts of vitamins and minerals so that your baby will also get the vitamins and minerals needed to grow properly. However, taking large amounts of a dietary supplement while breast-feeding may be harmful to the mother and/or baby and should be avoided.

Children—Problems in children have not been reported with intake of normal daily recommended amounts.

Older adults—Problems in older adults have not been reported with intake of normal daily recommended amounts. There is some evidence that the elderly may be at risk of becoming deficient in zinc due to poor food selection, decreased absorption of zinc by the body, or medicines that decrease absorption of zinc or increase loss of zinc from the body.

Medicines or other dietary supplements—Although certain medicines or dietary supplements should not be used together at all, in other cases they may be used together even if an interaction might occur. In these cases, your health care professional may want to change the dose, or other precautions may be necessary. When you are taking zinc supplements, it is especially important that your health care professional know if you are taking any of the following:

- Copper supplements or
- Tetracycline (medicine for infection)—Use with zinc supplements may cause these copper supplements or tetracycline to be less effective; zinc supplements should be given at least 2 hours after copper supplements, or tetracycline

Other medical problems—The presence of other medical problems may affect the use of zinc supplements. Make sure you tell your health care professional if you have any other medical problems, especially:

- Copper deficiency—Zinc supplements may make this condition worse

Proper Use of This Dietary Supplement

Dosing—The amount of zinc needed to meet normal daily recommended intakes will be different for different individuals. The following information includes only the average amounts of zinc.

- For *oral* dosage form (capsules, lozenges, tablets, extended-release tablets):
  - To prevent deficiency, the amount taken by mouth is based on normal daily recommended intakes (Note that the normal daily recommended intakes are expressed as an actual amount of zinc. The dosage form [e.g., zinc gluconate, zinc sulfate] has a different strength):

For the U.S.
- Adult and teenage males—15 milligrams (mg) per day.
- Adult and teenage females—12 mg per day.
- Pregnant females—15 mg per day.
- Breast-feeding females—16 to 19 mg per day.
- Children 4 to 10 years of age—10 mg per day.
- Children birth to 3 years of age—5 to 10 mg per day.

For Canada
- Adult and teenage males—9 to 12 mg per day.
- Adult and teenage females—9 mg per day.
- Pregnant females—15 mg per day.
- Breast-feeding females—15 mg per day.
- Children 7 to 10 years of age—7 to 9 mg per day.

- Children 4 to 6 years of age—5 mg per day.
- Children birth to 3 years of age—2 to 4 mg per day.
—To treat deficiency:
- Adults, teenagers, and children—Treatment dose is determined by prescriber for each individual based on severity of deficiency.

Zinc supplements are most effective if they are taken at least 1 hour before or 2 hours after meals. However, if zinc supplements cause stomach upset, they may be taken with a meal. You should tell your health care professional if you are taking your zinc supplement with meals.

Missed dose—If you miss taking zinc supplements for one or more days there is no cause for concern, since it takes some time for your body to become seriously low in zinc. However, if your health care professional has recommended that you take zinc, try to remember to take it as directed every day.

Storage—To store this dietary supplement:
- Keep out of the reach of children.
- Store away from heat and direct light.
- Do not store in the bathroom, near the kitchen sink, or in other damp places. Heat or moisture may cause the dietary supplement to break down.
- Keep the dietary supplement from freezing. Do not refrigerate.
- Do not keep outdated dietary supplements or those no longer needed. Be sure that any discarded dietary supplement is out of the reach of children.

Precautions While Using This Dietary Supplement

When zinc combines with certain foods it may not be absorbed into your body and it will do you no good. If you are taking zinc, the following foods should be avoided or taken 2 hours after you take zinc:
- Bran
- Fiber-containing foods
- Phosphorus-containing foods such as milk or poultry
- Whole-grain breads and cereals

Do not take zinc supplements and copper, iron, or phosphorus supplements at the same time. It is best to space doses of these products 2 hours apart, to get the full benefit from each dietary supplement.

Side Effects of This Dietary Supplement

Along with its needed effects, a dietary supplement may cause some unwanted effects. Although not all of these side effects may occur, if they do occur they may need medical attention.

Check with your health care professional as soon as possible if any of the following side effects occur:
Rare—With large doses
Chills; continuing ulcers or sores in mouth or throat; fever; heartburn; indigestion; nausea; sore throat; unusual tiredness or weakness
Symptoms of overdose
Chest pain; dizziness; fainting; shortness of breath; vomiting; yellow eyes or skin

Other side effects not listed above may also occur in some individuals. If you notice any other effects, check with your health care professional.

Additional Information

Once a medicine or dietary supplement has been approved for marketing for a certain use, experience may show that it is also useful for other medical problems. Although this use is not included in product labeling, zinc supplements are used in certain patients with the following medical condition:
- Wilson's disease (a disease of too much copper in the body)

Other than the above information, there is no additional information relating to proper use, precautions, or side effects for this use.

Revised: 9/8/2000

ZIPRASIDONE   Systemic— INTRODUCTORY VERSION

Commonly used brand name(s):

In the U.S.—
Geodon

Description

Ziprasidone (zi-PRAS-uh-done) is used to treat schizophrenia which is a mental disorder.

This medicine is available only with your doctor's prescription, in the following dosage forms:
Oral
- Capsules (U.S.)

Before Using This Medicine

In deciding to use a medicine, the risks of taking the medicine must be weighed against the good it will do. This is a decision you and your doctor will make. For ziprasidone, the following should be considered:

Allergies—Tell your doctor if you have ever had any unusual or allergic reaction to ziprasidone. Also tell your doctor and pharmacist if you are allergic to any other substances, such as foods, preservatives, or dyes.

Pregnancy—Ziprasidone has not been studied in pregnant women. However, studies in animals have shown that ziprasidone causes birth defects and other problems. Before taking this medicine, make sure your doctor knows if you are pregnant or if you may become pregnant.

Breast-feeding—It is not known whether ziprasidone passes into the breast milk. However, ziprasidone is not recommended during breast-feeding, because it may cause unwanted effects in nursing babies.

Children—Studies on this medicine have been done only in adult patients, and there is no specific information comparing use of ziprasidone in children with use in other age groups.

Older adults—Many medicines have not been studied specifically in older people. Therefore, it may not be known whether they work exactly the same way they do in younger adults or if they cause different side effects or problems in older people. There is no specific information comparing use of ziprasidone in the elderly with use in other age groups.

Other medicines—Although certain medicines should not be used together at all, in other cases two different medicines may be used together even if an interaction might occur. In these cases, your doctor may want to change the dose, or other precautions may be necessary. When you are taking ziprasidone, it is especially important that your doctor and pharmacist know if you are taking any of the following:

- Dofetilide (eg, Tikosyn) or
- Moxifloxacin (eg, Avelox) or
- Pimozide (eg, Orap) or
- Quinidine (eg, Quinidex, Quiniglute,) or
- Sotalol (eg, Betapace) or
- Sparfloxacin (eg, Zagam) or
- Thioridazine (eg, Mellaril)—May cause serious problems with your heart.

Other medical problems—The presence of other medical problems may affect the use of ziprasidone. Make sure you tell your doctor if you have any other medical problems, especially:

- Heart attack (recent) or
- Heart disease or
- Irregular heartbeat or
- Heart failure—Ziprasidone may make these conditions worse
- Low level of magnesium in your blood or
- Low level of potassium in your blood—This increases chance for heart problems
- Neuroleptic Malignant Syndrome (NMS) or
- Tardive Dyskinesia—May appear or worsen with ziprasidone therapy
- Seizures or
- Alzheimer's disease—Increased risk of seizures and aspiration pneumonia

Proper Use of This Medicine

Do not chew the capsules, swallow whole.

Dosing—The dose of ziprasdone will be different for different patients. *Follow your doctor's orders or the directions on the label.* The following information includes only the average doses of ziprasidone. *If your dose is different, do not change it* unless your doctor tells you to do so.

The number of capsules that you take depends on the strength of the medicine. Also, *the number of doses you take each day, the time allowed between doses, and the length of time you take the medicine depend on the medical problem for which you are taking ziprasidone.*

- For *oral* dosage form (capsules):
  —For treating schizophrenia:
    - Adults—To start, 20 milligrams (mg) twice a day with food. Your doctor may increase your dose if needed. However, the dose is usually not more than 80 mg twice a day.
    - Children—Use and dose must be determined by your doctor.

Missed dose—If you miss a dose of this medicine, take it as soon as possible. However, if it is almost time for your next dose, skip the missed dose and go back to your regular dosing schedule. Do not double doses.

Storage—To store this medicine:
- Keep out of the reach of children.
- Do not store in the bathroom, near the kitchen sink, or in other damp places. Heat or moisture may cause the medicine to break down.

- Do not keep outdated medicine or medicine no longer needed. Ask your health care professional how you should dispose of any medicine you do not use. Be sure that any discarded medicine is out of the reach of children.

Precautions While Using This Medicine

It is very important that your doctor check you at regular visits to make sure your medicine is working for you. Your doctor will check your blood to make sure your potassium is normal.

Check with doctor if fainting, dizziness, fast, racing, pounding, or irregular heartbeat, or other unusual symptoms occur

This medicine may cause some people to become drowsy, dizzy, or less alert than they are normally. *Make sure you know how you react to this medicine before you drive, use machines, or do anything else that could be dangerous if you are dizzy or are not alert. Avoid use of alcohol.*

Avoid activities involving high temperature or humidity. This medicine may reduce your body's ability to adjust to the heat.

Side Effects of This Medicine

Along with its needed effects, a medicine may cause some unwanted effects. Although not all of these side effects may occur, if they do occur they may need medical attention.

Less common
  Fast, pounding, or irregular heartbeat or pulse; palpitations

Rare
  Dizziness; fainting or feeling faint; persistent, painful erection; seizures

Symptoms of overdose

  Get emergency help immediately if any of the following symptoms of overdose occur
  Drowsiness; sleepiness; slurred speech

Other side effects may occur that usually do not need medical attention. These side effects may go away during treatment as your body adjusts to the medicine. However, check with your doctor if any of the following side effects continue or are bothersome.

More common
  Lack or loss of strength; weakness; uncontrollable movements of body parts; constipation; diarrhea; acid or sour stomach; belching; heartburn; indigestion; stomach discomfort, upset or pain; difficulty speaking; drooling; loss of balance control; muscle trembling; jerking or stiffness; restlessness; shuffling walk; stiffness of limbs; twisting movements of body; nausea; rash; weight gain

Less common
  Change in vision; loss of appetite; weight loss; dry mouth; inability to move eyes; increasing blinking or spasms of eyelid; sticking out of tongue; trouble in breathing, speaking or swallowing; unusual facial expressions; itching or reddening of skin; cracked, dry, scaly skin; swelling; muscle tightness; muscle ache; feeling faint upon standing; stuffy nose; runny nose; sneezing

Other side effects not listed above may also occur in some patients. If you notice any other effects, check with your doctor.

Developed: 05/30/2001

ZOLMITRIPTAN Systemic

Commonly used brand name(s):

In the U.S.—
Zomig

Description

Zolmitriptan (zohl-mi-TRIP-tan) is used to treat severe migraine headaches. Many people find that their headaches go away completely after they take zolmitriptan. Other people find that their headaches are much less painful, and that they are able to go back to their normal activities even though their headaches are not completely gone. Zolmitriptan often relieves symptoms that occur together with a migraine headache, such as nausea, vomiting, sensitivity to light, and sensitivity to sound.

Zolmitriptan is not an ordinary pain reliever. It should not be used to relieve any kind of pain other than migraine headaches.

Zolmitriptan may cause serious side effects in some people, especially people who have heart or blood vessel disease. Be sure that you discuss with your doctor the risks of using this medicine as well as the good that it can do.

Zolmitriptan is available only with your doctor's prescription, in the following dosage form:

Oral
- Tablets (U.S.)
- Oral disintegrating tablets (U.S.)

Before Using This Medicine

In deciding to use a medicine, the risks of taking the medicine must be weighed against the good it will do. This is a decision you and your doctor will make. For zolmitriptan, the following should be considered:

Allergies—Tell your doctor if you have ever had any unusual or allergic reaction to zolmitriptan. Also tell your health care professional if you are allergic to any other substances, such as foods, preservatives, or dyes.

Pregnancy—Zolmitriptan has not been studied in pregnant women. However, in some animal studies, zolmitriptan caused harmful effects to the fetus. These unwanted effects usually occurred when zolmitriptan was given in amounts that were large enough to cause harmful effects in the mother.

Breast-feeding—Although most medicines pass into breast milk in small amounts, many of them may be used safely while breast-feeding. Mothers who are taking this medicine and who wish to breast-feed should discuss this with their doctor.

Children—There is no specific information comparing use of zolmitriptan in children with use in other age groups.

Teenagers—There is no specific information comparing use of zolmitriptan in teenagers with use in other age groups.

Older adults—There is no specific information comparing use of zolmitriptan in patients older than 65 years of age with use in younger adults.

Other medicines—Although certain medicines should not be used together at all, in other cases two different medicines may be used together even if an interaction might occur. In these cases, your doctor may want to change the dose, or other precautions may be necessary. Tell your health care professional if you are taking any other prescription or nonprescription (over-the-counter [OTC]) medicine, especially other prescription medicine for migraine headaches, or if you smoke tobacco.

When you are taking zolmitriptan, it is especially important that your health care professional know if you are taking the following:

- Monoamine oxidase-A (MAO-A) inhibitors (isocarboxazid [e.g., Marplan], phenelzine [e.g., Nardil], procarbazine [e.g., Matulane], selegiline [e.g., Eldepryl])—Taking zolmitriptan while you are taking or within 2 weeks of taking MAO inhibitors may cause sudden high body temperature, extremely high blood pressure, and severe convulsions; at least 14 days should be allowed between stopping treatment with one medicine and starting treatment with the other.

Other medical problems—The presence of other medical problems may affect the use of zolmitriptan. Make sure you tell your doctor if you have any other medical problems, especially:

- Angina (chest pain) or
- Fast or irregular heartbeat or
- Heart or blood vessel disease or
- High blood pressure or
- Kidney disease or
- Liver disease or
- Stroke (history of)—The chance of side effects may be increased. Heart or blood vessel disease and high blood pressure sometimes do not cause any symptoms, so some people do not know that they have these problems. Before deciding whether you should use zolmitriptan, your doctor may need to do some tests to make sure that you do not have any of these conditions.

- Phenylketonuria (PKU)—The oral disintegrating tablets may contain aspartame, which can make your condition worse

Proper Use of This Medicine

Do not use zolmitriptan for a headache that is different from your usual migraines. Instead, check with your doctor.

To relieve your migraine as soon as possible, use zolmitriptan as soon as the headache pain begins. Even if you get warning signals of a coming migraine (an aura), you should wait until the headache pain starts before using zolmitriptan.

Lying down in a quiet, dark room for a while after you use this medicine may help relieve your migraine.

Ask your doctor ahead of time about other medicine you might take if zolmitriptan does not work. After you take the other medicine, check with your doctor as soon as possible. Headaches that are not relieved by zolmitriptan are sometimes caused by conditions that need other treatment.

If you feel much better after a dose of zolmitriptan, but your headache comes back or gets worse after a while, you may use more zolmitriptan. However, *use this medicine only as directed by your doctor. Do not use more of it, and do not use it more often, than directed.* Using too much zolmitriptan may increase the chance of side effects.

Your doctor may direct you to take another medicine to help prevent headaches. *It is important that you follow your doctor's directions, even if your headaches continue to occur.* Headache-preventing medicines may take several weeks to start working. Even after they do start working, your headaches may not go away completely. However, your headaches should occur less often, and they should be less severe and easier to relieve. This can reduce the amount of zolmitriptan or other pain medicines that you need. If you do not notice any improvement after several weeks of headache-preventing treatment, check with your doctor.

For patients using the *oral disintegrating tablet* form of this medicine:

- Make sure your hands are dry.
- Remove tablet from package, and immediately place the tablet on top of your tongue.
- The tablet will dissolve in seconds, and you may swallow it with your saliva. You do not need to drink water or other liquid to swallow the tablet.

Dosing—The dose of zolmitriptan will be different for different patients. *Follow your doctor's orders or the directions on the label.* The following information includes only the average doses of zolmitriptan. *If your dose is different, do not change it* unless your doctor tells you to do so.

- For *oral* dosage form (tablets):
  —For migraine headaches:
  - Adults—2.5 mg or lower (tablet may be broken in half) as a single dose. If the migraine comes back after being relieved, another dose may be taken two hours after the last dose. *Do not take more than 10 mg in any twenty-four-hour period* (one day).
  - Children—Use and dose must be determined by your doctor.
- For *oral* dosage form (oral disintegrating tablets):
  —For migraine headaches:
  - Adults—2.5 mg placed on top of your tongue. If the migraine comes back after being relieved, another dose may be taken two hours after the last dose. *Do not take more than 10 mg in any twenty-four-hour period* (one day).
  - Children—Use and dose must be determined by your doctor.

Storage—To store this medicine:

- Keep out of the reach of children since overdose is especially dangerous in children.
- Store away from heat and direct light.
- Do not store tablets in the bathroom, near the kitchen sink, or in other damp places. Heat or moisture may cause the medicine to break down.
- Do not keep outdated medicine or medicine no longer needed. Be sure that any discarded medicine is out of the reach of children.

Precautions While Using This Medicine

Drinking alcoholic beverages can make headaches worse or cause new headaches to occur. People who suffer from severe headaches should probably avoid alcoholic beverages, especially during a headache.

Some people feel drowsy or dizzy during or after a migraine, or after taking zolmitriptan to relieve a migraine. As long as

you are feeling drowsy or dizzy, *do not drive, use machines, or do anything else that could be dangerous if you are dizzy or are not alert.*

Side Effects of This Medicine

Along with its needed effects, a medicine may cause some unwanted effects. Although not all of these side effects may occur, if they do occur they may need medical attention.

Stop using this medicine and check with your doctor immediately if any of the following side effects occur:
  More common
    Chest pain (severe); heaviness, tightness, or pressure in chest and/or neck; sensation of burning, warmth, heat, numbness, tightness, or tingling

  Less common or rare
    Abdominal pain (severe); changes in facial skin color; cough or hoarseness; diarrhea; fast or irregular heartbeat; fever or chills; loss of appetite; lower back or side pain; nausea; painful or difficult urination; puffiness or swelling of the eyelids or around the eyes, face, or lips; shortness of breath, troubled breathing, tightness in chest, and/or wheezing; skin rash, hives, and/or itching; weakness

Other side effects may occur that usually do not need medical attention. Some of the following effects, such as nausea, vomiting, drowsiness, dizziness, and general feeling of illness or tiredness, often occur during or after a migraine, even when zolmitriptan has not been used. However, check with your doctor if any of the following side effects continue or are bothersome:
  More common
    Dizziness; nausea; sleepiness; unusual tiredness or muscle weakness

  Less common
    Agitation; anxiety; depression; discomfort in jaw, mouth, or throat; difficulty in swallowing; dry mouth; fainting; heartburn; itching of the skin; large non-elevated blue or purplish patches in the skin; muscle aches; pounding heartbeat; sudden large increase in frequency and quantity of urine; sweating; swelling of face, fingers, feet and/or lower legs

Other side effects not listed above may also occur in some patients. If you notice any other effects, check with your doctor.

Developed: 04/03/1998
Revised: 05/21/2001

ZOLPIDEM   Systemic†

Commonly used brand name(s):

In the U.S.—
  Ambien

†Not commercially available in Canada.

Description

Zolpidem (ZOLE-pi-dem) belongs to the group of medicines called central nervous system (CNS) depressants (medicines that slow down the nervous system). Zolpidem is used to treat insomnia (trouble in sleeping). Zolpidem helps you get to sleep faster and sleep through the night. In general, when sleep medicines are used every night for a long time, they may lose their effectiveness. In most cases, sleep medicines should be used only for short periods of time, such as 1 or 2 days, and generally for no longer than 1 or 2 weeks.

This medicine is available only with your doctor's prescription, in the following dosage form:

Oral
- Tablets (U.S.)

Before Using This Medicine

Sleep medicines may cause a special type of memory loss or "amnesia". When this occurs, a person does not remember what has happened during the several hours between use of the medicine and the time when its effects wear off. This is usually not a problem since most people fall asleep after taking the medicine. In most instances, memory problems can be avoided by taking zolpidem only when you are able to get a full night's sleep (7 to 8 hours) before you need to be active again. Be sure to talk to your doctor if you think you are having memory problems.

In deciding to use a medicine, the risks of taking the medicine must be weighed against the good it will do. This is a decision you and your doctor will make. For zolpidem, the following should be considered:

Allergies—Tell your doctor if you have ever had any unusual or allergic reaction to zolpidem. Also tell your health care professional if you are allergic to any other substances, such as foods, preservatives, or dyes.

Pregnancy—Zolpidem has not been studied in pregnant women. However, studies in pregnant animals have shown that zolpidem slows down the development of the offspring when given to the mother in doses many times the human dose. Before taking this medicine, make sure your doctor knows if you are pregnant or if you may become pregnant.

Breast-feeding—Although zolpidem passes into breast milk, it has not been reported to cause problems in nursing babies.

Children—Studies on this medicine have been done only in adult patients, and there is no specific information comparing use of zolpidem in children with use in other age groups.

Older adults—Confusion and falling are more likely to occur in the elderly, who are usually more sensitive than younger adults to the effects of zolpidem.

Other medicines—Although certain medicines should not be used together at all, in other cases two different medicines may be used together even if an interaction might occur. In these cases, your doctor may want to change the dose, or other precautions may be necessary. When you are taking zolpidem, it is especially important that your health care professional know if you are taking any of the following:

- Other central nervous system (CNS) depressants (medicines that cause drowsiness) or
- Tricyclic antidepressants (amitriptyline [e.g., Elavil], amoxapine [e.g., Asendin], clomipramine [e.g., Anafranil], desipramine [e.g., Pertofrane], doxepin [e.g., Sinequan], imipramine [e.g., Tofranil], nortriptyline [e.g., Aventyl], protriptyline [e.g., Vivactil], trimipramine [e.g., Surmontil])—The CNS depressant effects of either

these medicines or zolpidem may be increased, possibly leading to unwanted effects

Other medical problems—The presence of other medical problems may affect the use of zolpidem. Make sure you tell your doctor if you have any other medical problems, especially:

- Alcohol abuse (or history of) or
- Drug abuse or dependence (or history of)—Dependence on zolpidem may develop
- Emphysema, asthma, bronchitis, or other chronic lung disease or
- Mental depression or
- Sleep apnea (temporary stopping of breathing during sleep)—Zolpidem may make these conditions worse
- Kidney disease or
- Liver disease—Higher blood levels of zolpidem may result, increasing the chance of side effects

Proper Use of This Medicine

Take this medicine only as directed by your doctor. Do not take more of it, do not take it more often, and do not take it for a longer time than your doctor ordered. If too much is taken, it may become habit-forming (causing mental or physical dependence).

Take zolpidem just before going to bed, when you are ready to go to sleep. This medicine works very quickly to put you to sleep.

Do not take this medicine when your schedule does not permit you to get a full night's sleep (7 to 8 hours). If you must wake up before this, you may continue to feel drowsy and may experience memory problems, because the effects of the medicine have not had time to wear off.

Zolpidem may be taken with or without food or on a full or empty stomach. It may work faster if you take it on an empty stomach. However, if your doctor tells you to take the medicine a certain way, take it exactly as directed.

Dosing—The dose of zolpidem will be different for different patients. *Follow your doctor's orders or the directions on the label.* The following information includes only the average doses of zolpidem. *If your dose is different, do not change it* unless your doctor tells you to do so.

The number of tablets that you take depends on the strength of the medicine.

- For *oral* dosage form (tablets):
  —For the treatment of insomnia (trouble in sleeping):
    - Adults—10 milligrams (mg) at bedtime.
    - Older adults—5 mg at bedtime.
    - Children up to 18 years of age—Use and dose must be determined by the doctor.

Missed dose—If you miss a dose of this medicine, skip the missed dose and go back to your regular dosing schedule. Do not double doses.

Storage—To store this medicine:
- Keep out of the reach of children.
- Store away from heat and direct light.
- Do not store in the bathroom, near the kitchen sink, or in other damp places. Heat or moisture may cause the medicine to break down.
- Do not keep outdated medicine or medicine no longer needed. Be sure that any discarded medicine is out of the reach of children.

Precautions While Using This Medicine

If you think you need to take zolpidem for more than 7 to 10 days, be sure to discuss it with your doctor. Insomnia that lasts longer than this may be a sign of another medical problem.

This medicine will add to the effects of alcohol and other CNS depressants (medicines that slow down the nervous system, possibly causing drowsiness). Some examples of CNS depressants are antihistamines or medicine for hay fever, other allergies, or colds; sedatives, tranquilizers, or sleeping medicine; prescription pain medicine or narcotics; barbiturates; medicine for seizures; muscle relaxants; or anesthetics, including some dental anesthetics. *Check with your doctor before taking any of the above while you are using this medicine.*

This medicine may cause some people, especially older persons, to become drowsy, dizzy, lightheaded, clumsy or unsteady, or less alert than they are normally. Even though zolpidem is taken at bedtime, it may cause some people to feel drowsy or less alert on arising. Also, this medicine may cause double vision or other vision problems. *Make sure you know how you react to zolpidem before you drive, use machines, or do anything else that could be dangerous if you are dizzy, or are not alert or able to see well.*

If you develop any unusual and strange thoughts or behavior while you are taking zolpidem, be sure to discuss it with your doctor. Some changes that have occurred in people taking this medicine are like those seen in people who drink alcohol and then act in a manner that is not normal. Other changes may be more unusual and extreme, such as confusion, worsening of depression hallucinations (seeing, hearing, or feeling things that are not there), suicidal thoughts, and unusual excitement, nervousness, or irritability.

If you will be taking zolpidem for a long time, do not stop taking it without first checking with your doctor. Your doctor may want you to reduce gradually the amount you are taking before stopping completely. Stopping this medicine suddenly may cause withdrawal side effects.

After taking zolpidem for insomnia, you may have difficulty sleeping (rebound insomnia) for the first few nights after you stop taking it.

If you think you or someone else may have taken an overdose of this medicine, get emergency help at once. Taking an overdose of zolpidem or taking alcohol or other CNS depressants with zolpidem may lead to breathing problems and unconsciousness. Some signs of an overdose are severe drowsiness, severe nausea or vomiting, staggering, and troubled breathing.

Side Effects of This Medicine

Along with its needed effects, a medicine may cause some unwanted effects. Although not all of these side effects may occur, if they do occur they may need medical attention.

Check with your doctor as soon as possible if any of the following side effects occur:
Less common
    Clumsiness or unsteadiness; confusion—more common in older adults; mental depression
Rare
    Dizziness, lightheadedness, or fainting; falling—more common in older adults; fast heartbeat; hallucina-

tions (seeing, hearing, or feeling things that are not there); skin rash; swelling of face; trouble in sleeping; unusual excitement, nervousness, or irritability; wheezing or difficulty in breathing
Symptoms of overdose
    Clumsiness or unsteadiness (severe); dizziness (severe); double vision or other vision problems; drowsiness (severe); nausea (severe); troubled breathing; slow heartbeat; vomiting (severe)

Other side effects may occur that usually do not need medical attention. These side effects may go away during treatment as your body adjusts to the medicine. However, check with your doctor if any of the following side effects continue or are bothersome:
Less common
    Abdominal or stomach pain; daytime drowsiness; diarrhea; double vision or other vision problems; drugged feelings; dryness of mouth; general feeling of discomfort or illness; headache; memory problems; nausea; nightmares or unusual dreams; vomiting

After you stop using this medicine, your body may need time to adjust. The length of time this takes depends on the amount of medicine you were using and how long you used it. During this time check with your doctor if you notice any of the following side effects:
    Abdominal or stomach cramps or discomfort; agitation, nervousness, or feelings of panic; convulsions (seizures); flushing; lightheadedness; muscle cramps; nausea; sweating; tremors; uncontrolled crying; unusual tiredness or weakness; vomiting; worsening of mental or emotional problems

Other side effects not listed above may also occur in some patients. If you notice any other effects, check with your doctor.

Developed: 06/29/94
Revised: 01/20/00

ZONISAMIDE   Systemic†

Commonly used brand name(s):

In the U.S.—
Zonegran

†Not commercially available in Canada.

Description

Zonisamide (zoh-NIS-a-mide) is used to control some kinds of seizures in the treatment of epilepsy.

This medicine is available only with your doctor's prescription, in the following dosage form:
Oral
    • Capsules (U.S.)

Before Using This Medicine

In deciding to use a medicine, the risks of taking the medicine must be weighed against the good it will do. This is a decision

you and your doctor will make. For zonisamide, the following should be considered:

Allergies—Tell your doctor if you have ever had any unusual or allergic reaction to zonisamide, or to sulfonamide antibiotics (for example, Bactrim® or Septra®). Also tell your doctor and pharmacist if you are allergic to any other substances, such as foods, preservatives, or dyes.

Pregnancy—Zonisamide has not been studied in pregnant women. However, studies in animals have shown that zonisamide causes birth defects and other serious problems with the pregnancy. Before taking this medicine, make sure your doctor knows if you are pregnant or if you may become pregnant.

Breast-feeding—Zonisamide has been shown to pass into breast milk. However, it is not known whether this medicine causes problems in nursing babies. Mothers who are taking zonisamide and who wish to breast-feed should discuss this with their doctor.

Children—A decreased ability to sweat, occasionally accompanied by high fever during warm weather, may be especially likely to occur in children younger than 17 years of age. Safety and efficacy have not been established.

Older adults—Many medicines have not been studied specifically in older people. Therefore, it may not be known whether they work exactly the same way they do in younger adults. Although there is no specific information comparing use of zonisamide in the elderly with use in other age groups, this medicine is not expected to cause different side effects or problems in older people than it does in younger adults.

Other medicines—Although certain medicines should not be used together at all, in other cases two different medicines may be used together even if an interaction might occur. In these cases, your doctor may want to change the dose, or other precautions may be necessary. When you are taking zonisamide, it is especially important that your doctor and pharmacist know if you are taking any of the following:

- Alcohol or
- Carbamazepine [e.g. Tegretol]) or
- Phenobarbital [e.g. Barbita or Mysoline] or
- Phenytoin [e.g. Dilantin] or
- Valproate [e.g. Depakote]—Taking any of these medicines with zonisamide may decrease the amount of zonisamide in the blood, causing an decrease in effectiveness, and a possible increase in seizure frequency
- Central nervous system depressants (medicines that cause drowsiness)—Using these medicines or alcohol with zonisamide may cause increased drowsiness

Other medical problems—The presence of other medical problems may affect the use of zonisamide. Make sure you tell your doctor if you have any other medical problems, especially:

- Kidney disease or
- Liver disease

Proper Use of This Medicine

Take this medicine only as directed by your doctor to help your condition as much as possible. Do not take more or less of it, and do not take it more or less often than your doctor ordered.

Zonisamide may be taken with or without food, on a full or empty stomach. Swallow capsule whole. Do not break or crush.

Dosing—The dose of zonisamide will be different for different patients. *Follow your doctor's orders or the directions on the label.* The following information includes only the average doses of zonisamide. *If your dose is different, do not change it* unless your doctor tells you to do so.

The number of capsules that you take depends on the strength of the medicine. Also, *the number of doses you take each day, the time allowed between doses, and the length of time you take the medicine depend on the medical problem for which you are taking zonisamide*

- For *oral* dosage form (capsules):
    - For partial seizures (epilepsy)
        - Adults and teenagers 16 years of age and older— At first, 100 milligrams (mg) a day for two weeks. The dose may then be increased by 100 mg a day once every two weeks, as decided by your doctor. However, the dose is usually not more than 400 mg a day, taken one or two times a day.
        - Children up to 16 years of age—Use and dose must be determined by the doctor.

Missed dose— If you miss a dose of this medicine, take it as soon as possible. However, if it is almost time for your next dose, skip the missed dose and go back to your regular dosing schedule. Do not double doses.

Storage—To store this medicine:

- Keep out of the reach of children.
- Do not store in the bathroom, near the kitchen sink, or in other damp places. Heat or moisture may cause the medicine to break down.
- Do not keep outdated medicine or medicine no longer needed. Ask your health care professional how you should dispose of any medicine you do not use. Be sure that any discarded medicine is out of the reach of children.

Precautions While Using This Medicine

It is very important that your doctor check your progress at regular visits. This will allow your doctor to see if the medicine is working properly, and to check for unwanted effects.

If your condition does not improve within a few weeks or if it becomes worse, check with your doctor.

This medicine may cause some people to become drowsy, dizzy, or less alert than they are normally. *Make sure you know how you react to this medicine before you drive, use machines, or do anything else that could be dangerous if you are dizzy or are not alert.*

This medicine will add to the effects of alcohol and other CNS depressants (medicines that make you drowsy or less alert). Some examples of CNS depressants are antihistamines or medicine for hay fever, other allergies, or colds; prescription pain medicines, or sleep medicines. Do not take other medicines unless they have been discussed with your doctor. This especially includes nonprescription medicines for appetite control, asthma, colds, cough, hay fever, or sinus problems.

Contact your doctor immediately if you develop skin rash, experience fever, sore throat, oral ulcers, easy bruising, or worsening of seizures, or if a child taking zonisamide is not sweating as usual.

Use effective birth control methods to prevent pregnancy if you are sexually active and able to become pregnant.

Do not stop taking zonisamide without first checking with your doctor. Stopping the medicine suddenly may cause your seizures to return or to occur more often. Your doctor may want you to gradually reduce the amount you are taking before stopping completely.

It is important that you *drink plenty of fluids every day* during therapy with zonisamide to help prevent kidney stones from forming.

Side Effects of This Medicine

Along with its needed effects, a medicine may cause some unwanted effects. Although not all of these side effects may occur, if they do occur they may need medical attention.

Symptoms of overdose
Get emergency help immediately if any of the following symptoms of overdose occur
Confusion; difficult or labored breathing; faintness; loss of consciousness; slow or irregular heartbeat

Check with your doctor immediately if any of the following side effects occur:
Less common
Agitation; delusions; hallucinations; rash

Check with your doctor as soon as possible if any of the following side effects occur:
More common
Shakiness or unsteady walking

Less common
Bruising; large, flat, blue or purplish patches on the skin; mood or mental changes; rash

Other side effects may occur that usually do not need medical attention. These side effects may go away during treatment as your body adjusts to the medicine. However, check with your doctor if any of the following side effects continue or are bothersome.
More common
Anxiety; dizziness; loss of appetite; restlessness; sleepiness; unusual drowsiness

Less common
Aching muscles or joints; acid or sour stomach; bad, unusual, or unpleasant taste in mouth; belching; change in taste; chills; constipation; diarrhea; difficulty in speaking; difficulty in thinking; difficulty with memory; double vision; dry mouth; fever; general ill feeling; headache; heartburn; indigestion; mental slowness; nausea; nervousness; runny or stuffy nose; sleeplessness; sneezing; tingling, burning, or prickly feelings on skin; trouble in sleeping; uncontrolled, back and forth, or rolling eye movements; unusual tiredness or weakness; weight loss

Other side effects not listed above may also occur in some patients. If you notice any other effects, check with your doctor.

Developed: 06/13/2000

ZOPICLONE   Systemic

Commonly used brand name(s):

In Canada—
Imovane

Description

Zopiclone (ZOP-i-klone) belongs to the group of medicines called central nervous system (CNS) depressants (medicines that make you drowsy or less alert). This medicine is used to treat insomnia (trouble in sleeping). Zopiclone helps you get to sleep faster and sleep through the night. In general, when sleep medicines are used every night for a long time, they may lose their effectiveness. In most cases, sleep medicines should be used only for short periods of time, such as 1 or 2 days, and generally for no longer than 1 or 2 weeks.

This medicine is available only with your doctor's prescription, in the following dosage forms:

Oral
• Tablets (Canada)

Before Using This Medicine

Sleep medicines may cause a special type of memory loss or "amnesia". When this occurs, a person does not remember what has happened during the several hours between use of the medicine and the time when its effects wear off. This is usually not a problem since most people fall asleep after taking the medicine. In most instances, memory problems can be avoided by taking zopiclone only when you are able to get a full night's sleep (7 to 8 hours) before you need to be active again. Be sure to talk to your doctor if you think you are having memory problems.

In deciding to use a medicine, the risks of taking the medicine must be weighed against the good it will do. This is a decision you and your doctor will make. For zopiclone, the following should be considered:

Allergies—Tell your doctor if you have ever had any unusual or allergic reaction to zopiclone. Also tell your doctor and pharmacist if you are allergic to any other substances, such as foods, preservatives, or dyes.

Pregnancy—Zopiclone has not been studied in pregnant women. In studies of pregnant animals that received doses of zopiclone many times the human dose, fewer offspring survived. Before taking this medicine, make sure your doctor knows if you are pregnant or if you may become pregnant.

Breast-feeding—Zopiclone passes into breast milk and may cause unwanted effects in nursing babies. It may be necessary for you to take another medicine or to stop breast-feeding during treatment. Be sure you have discussed the risks and benefits of the medicine with your doctor.

Children—Studies on this medicine have been done only in adult patients, and there is no specific information comparing use of zopiclone in children with use in other age groups.

Older adults—Confusion, lack of coordination, and falling are more likely to occur in the elderly, who are usually more sensitive than younger adults to the effects of zopiclone.

Other medicines—Although certain medicines should not be used together at all, in other cases two different medicines may be used together even if an interaction might occur. In these cases, your doctor may want to change the

dose, or other precautions may be necessary. When you are taking zopiclone, it is especially important that your doctor and pharmacist know if you are taking any of the following:

- Other central nervous system (CNS) depressants (medicines that cause drowsiness) or
- Tricyclic antidepressants (medicines for depression)—The CNS depressant effects of either these medicines or zopiclone may be increased, possibly leading to unwanted effects

Other medical problems—The presence of other medical problems may affect the use of zopiclone. Make sure you tell your doctor if you have any other medical problems, especially:

- Alcohol abuse (or history of) or
- Drug abuse (or history of)—Dependence on zopiclone may develop
- Emphysema, asthma, bronchitis, or other chronic lung disease or
- Mental depression or
- Myasthenia gravis or
- Sleep apnea (temporary stopping of breathing during sleep)—Zopiclone may make these conditions worse
- Kidney disease or
- Liver disease (severe)—Higher blood levels of zopiclone may result, increasing the chance of side effects

Proper Use of This Medicine

Take this medicine only as directed by your doctor. Do not take more of it, do not take it more often, and do not take it for a longer time than your doctor ordered. If too much is taken, it may become habit-forming (causing mental or physical dependence).

Do not take this medicine when your schedule does not permit you to get a full night's sleep (7 to 8 hours). If you must wake up before this, you may continue to feel drowsy and may experience memory problems, because the effects of the medicine have not had time to wear off.

Dosing—The dose of zopiclone will be different for different patients. *Follow your doctor's orders or the directions on the label.* The following information includes only the average doses of zopiclone. *If your dose is different, do not change it* unless your doctor tells you to do so.

The number of tablets that you take depends on the strength of the medicine.

- For *oral* dosage form (tablets):
  —For the treatment of insomnia (trouble in sleeping)
  - Adults—5 to 7.5 milligrams (mg) at bedtime.
  - Older adults—3.75 mg at bedtime; dose may be increased to 5 to 7.5 mg as determined by your doctor.
  - Children up to 18 years of age—Use and dose must be determined by your doctor.

Missed dose—If you miss a dose of this medicine, skip the missed dose and go back to your regular dosing schedule. Do not double doses.

Storage—To store this medicine:

- Keep out of the reach of children.
- Store away from heat and direct light.
- Do not store in the bathroom, near the kitchen sink, or in other damp places. Heat or moisture may cause the medicine to break down.
- Do not keep outdated medicine or medicine no longer needed. Be sure that any discarded medicine is out of the reach of children.

Precautions While Using This Medicine

If you think you need to take zopiclone for more than 7 to 10 days, be sure to discuss it with your doctor. Insomnia that lasts longer than this may be a sign of another medical problem.

This medicine will add to the effects of alcohol and other CNS depressants (medicines that cause drowsiness). Some examples of CNS depressants are antihistamines or medicine for hay fever, other allergies, or colds; sedatives, tranquilizers, or sleeping medicine; prescription pain medicine or narcotics; barbiturates; medicine for seizures; muscle relaxants; or anesthetics, including some dental anesthetics. *Check with your doctor before taking any of the above while you are using this medicine.*

This medicine may cause some people, especially older persons, to become drowsy, dizzy, lightheaded, clumsy or unsteady, or less alert than they are normally. Even though zopiclone is taken at bedtime, it may cause some people to feel drowsy or less alert on arising. *Make sure you know how you react to zopiclone before you drive, use machines, or do anything else that could be dangerous if you are dizzy, or are not alert or able to see well.*

If you develop any unusual and strange thoughts or behavior while you are taking zopiclone, be sure to discuss it with your doctor. Some changes that have occurred in people taking this medicine are like those seen in people who drink alcohol and then act in a manner that is not normal. Other changes may be more unusual and extreme, such as confusion, worsening of depression, hallucinations (seeing, hearing, or feeling things that are not there), suicidal thoughts, and unusual excitement, nervousness, or irritability.

If you will be taking zopiclone for a long time, do not stop taking it without first checking with your doctor. Your doctor may want you to gradually reduce the amount you are taking before stopping completely. Stopping this medicine suddenly may cause withdrawal side effects.

After taking zopiclone for insomnia, you may have difficulty sleeping (rebound insomnia) for the first few nights after you stop taking it.

If you think you or someone else may have taken an overdose of this medicine, get emergency help at once. Taking an overdose of zopiclone or taking alcohol or other CNS depressants with zopiclone may lead to breathing problems and unconsciousness. Some signs of an overdose are clumsiness or unsteadiness, mental or mood changes, severe drowsiness, or unusual tiredness or weakness.

Side Effects of This Medicine

Along with its needed effects, a medicine may cause some unwanted effects. Although not all of these side effects may occur, if they do occur they may need medical attention.

Check with your doctor as soon as possible if any of the following side effects occur:
More common
confusion—more common in older adults; clumsiness or unsteadiness—more common in older adults; daytime anxiety and/or restlessness; difficulty with

coordination—more common in older adults; mood or mental changes

Less common

Drowsiness (severe); shortness of breath; difficult or labored breathing; tightness in chest; wheezing; skin rash; aggressiveness; behavior changes

Rare

Memory problems—more common in older patients; behavior or mental changes

Symptoms of overdose

Get emergency help immediately if any of the following symptoms of overdose occur

Clumsiness; unsteadiness; mental or mood changes; drowsiness (severe); unusual tiredness or weakness; sluggishness; reduced physical activity; unusual sleepiness; loss of consciousness

Other side effects may occur that usually do not need medical attention. These side effects may go away during treatment as your body adjusts to the medicine. However, check with your doctor if any of the following side effects continue or are bothersome.

More common

Dizziness; Dryness of mouth; heartburn; impaired vision; increased appetite; indigestion; loss of appetite—more common in older adults; stomach upset; difficulty speaking; constipation; decreased muscle tone; weight loss

Less common

Agitation—more common in older adults; chills; fast, irregular, or pounding heartbeat—more common in older adults; feeling of heaviness of arms and legs; increase in the amount of saliva—more common in older adults; increased sweating—more common in older adults; tingling, burning or prickly sensation; trembling and shaking of fingers, hands, arms, feet, or legs—more common in older adults; vomiting—more common in older adults

After you stop using this medicine, your body may need time to adjust. The length of time this takes depends on the amount of medicine you were using and how long you used it. During this time check with your doctor if you notice any of the following side effects:

Abdominal or stomach cramps or pain; nausea; vomiting; more difficulty in sleeping than before treatment; muscle cramps or discomfort; anxiety; nervousness; irritability; restlessness; increased sweating; tremors; seizures

Zopiclone may cause you to have a coated tongue, bad breath, or a bitter taste. These effects are to be expected when you are taking this medicine.

Other side effects not listed above may also occur in some patients. If you notice any other effects, check with your doctor.

Developed: 05/30/2000

Glossary

Abdomen—The body area between the chest and pelvis; the belly. It contains the stomach and intestines.

Abnormal—Not normal or usual.

Abortifacient—Agent that causes abortion.

Abrade—Scrape or rub away the outer cover or layer of a part.

Abrasion—Minor wound or injury caused by scraping, rubbing, or wearing.

Absorption—Passing of substances into or across tissues of the body, for example, digested food into the blood from the small intestine, or poisons through the skin.

Achlorhydria—Absence of acid that normally would be found in the stomach.

Acidic—1. Refers to sharp, sour taste. 2. Referring to an acid (a chemical characterized by the way it combines with certain other substances). Opposite of alkaline.

Acidifier, urinary—Medicine that makes the urine more acidic.

Acidosis—A condition in which certain body fluids and tissues become too acidic.

Acne—Condition caused by inflammation of certain glands and hair follicles of the face, neck, and upper back, marked by red raised areas, pimples, and cysts.

Acromegaly—Enlargement of the face, body, hands, and feet because of too much growth hormone.

Acute—Describes a condition that begins suddenly, often has severe symptoms, and usually lasts a short time.

Added fiber—In food labeling, at least 2.5 grams of more fiber per serving than reference food.

Addison's disease—Disease caused by not enough corticosteroid hormones being produced by the adrenal glands; causes brownish discoloration of the skin, weakness, salt loss, and low blood pressure.

ADHD (attention-deficit hyperactivity disorder)—Syndrome marked by short attention span, disruptive behavior, learning difficulties, and an excessive level of activity.

Adhesion—The joining together, by fibrous tissue, of body parts and tissues that are normally separate.

Adjunct—An additional or secondary treatment that is helpful but may not be necessary for treatment of a particular condition; not effective for that condition if used alone.

Adjuvant—1. A substance added to or used with another substance to assist its action. 2. Something that assists or enhances the effectiveness of medical treatment.

Adrenal cortex—Outer layer of tissue of the adrenal gland, which produces corticosteroid (cortisone-like) hormones.

Adrenal glands—Two organs located next to the kidneys. They produce the hormones epinephrine (adrenaline) and norepinephrine and corticosteroid (cortisone-like) hormones.

Adrenaline—*See* Epinephrine.

Adrenal medulla—Inner part of the adrenal gland, which produces epinephrine (adrenaline) and norepinephrine.

Adrenocorticoids—*See* Corticosteroids.

Adverse effect—Any unwanted effect produced by a drug or therapy that is harmful to the patient.

Aerosol—Suspension of very small liquid or solid particles in compressed gas. Drugs in aerosol form are dispensed in the form of a mist by releasing the gas.

African sleeping sickness—*See* Trypanosomiasis, African.

Agent—A force or substance able to cause a change.

Agoraphobia—Abnormal fear and avoidance of public places or open spaces.

Agranulocytosis—Disease marked by a severe decrease in the number of granulocytes (one type of white blood cell) normally present in the blood. Also called *granulocytopenia*.

AIDS (acquired immunodeficiency syndrome)—Disease caused by human immunodeficiency virus (HIV). The disease results in a breakdown of the body's immune system, which makes a person more likely to get some other infections and some forms of cancer.

Alcohol-abuse deterrent—Medicine used to help alcoholics avoid the use of alcohol.

Alkaline—Referring to an alkali (a chemical characterized by the way it combines with certain other substances). Opposite of acidic.

Alkalizer, urinary—Medicine that makes the urine more alkaline.

Alkalosis—A condition in which certain body fluids and tissues become too alkaline.

Allergen—Any substance that induces an allergic reaction.

Allergy—Abnormal, high sensitivity to particular substances that are ordinarily harmless; common reactions include hives, itching, sneezing, stuffy nose, and swelling of mucous membranes, such as the tissues lining the nose, mouth, and throat.

Alopecia—Loss or absence of hair from areas where it normally is present.

Altitude sickness agent—Medicine used to prevent or lessen some of the effects of high altitude on the body.

Alzheimer's disease—Disease of the brain, usually beginning in late middle age, that is marked by gradual and worsening loss of mental performance, changes in personality and/or behavior, and inability to perform daily tasks.

Amenorrhea—Abnormal absence of menstrual periods.

Amino acid—One of a large group of compounds that contain carbon and nitrogen. Amino acids are the building blocks of protein and also the end product of protein digestion.

Aminoglycosides—A class of chemically related antibiotics used to treat some serious types of bacterial infections.

Ampul—Small sealed glass or plastic container holding a sterile solution, usually for injection. Also, *ampule*.

Anabolic steroid—Any of a group of compounds resembling testosterone that aid in the building of body tissues.

Analgesic—Medicine that relieves pain.

Anaphylaxis—Sudden, life-threatening allergic reaction.

Androgen—Hormone, such as testosterone, that promotes male characteristics, such as a deep voice and beard growth.

Anemia—Reduction, to below normal, of hemoglobin (the oxygen-carrying substance found in red blood cells) in the blood.

Anesthesiologist—A physician who is qualified to give an anesthetic and other medicines to a patient before and during surgery.

Anesthetic—Medicine that causes a loss of feeling or sensation, especially of pain, sometimes through loss of consciousness.

Aneurysm—A balloon-like swelling that forms at a weak place in the wall of an artery, vein, or the heart.

Angina—Pain, tightness, or feeling of heaviness in the chest, due to a lack of oxygen supply for the heart muscle. The pain may be felt in the left shoulder, jaw, or arm instead of or in addition to the chest. Symptoms often occur during physical activity.

Angioedema—Condition marked by hives and continuing swelling of areas of the skin, usually in the head and neck area. Swelling of the tongue or the tissues lining the mouth and throat may also occur, causing breathing problems.

Anorexia—Loss of appetite for food.

Anoxia—Absence of oxygen. (The term is sometimes incorrectly used for hypoxia.)

Antacid—Medicine used to neutralize excess acid in the stomach.

Antagonist—Drug or other substance that blocks or works against the action of another.

Anthelmintic—Medicine used to destroy or expel intestinal worms.

Antiacne agent—Medicine used to treat acne.

Antianemic—Agent that prevents or corrects anemia.

Antianginal—Medicine used to prevent or treat angina attacks.

Antianxiety agent—Medicine used to treat excessive nervousness, tension, or anxiety.

Antiarrhythmic—Medicine used to prevent or correct irregular heartbeats.

Antiasthmatic—Medicine used to treat asthma.

Antibacterial—Agent that kills or slows the growth of bacteria.

Antibiotic—Medicine used to treat certain types of infections.

Antibody—Protein produced by the immune system that acts against a specific antigen. Antibodies help the body fight infection and are involved in allergic reactions. Also called *immunoglobulin*.

Antibulimic—Medicine used to treat bulimia.

Anticholelithic—Medicine used to dissolve gallstones.

Anticoagulant—Medicine used to decrease or slow the clotting of blood.

Anticonvulsant—Medicine used to prevent or treat convulsions (seizures).

Antidepressant—Medicine used to treat mental depression.

Antidiabetic agent—Medicine used to control blood sugar levels in patients with diabetes mellitus (sugar diabetes).

Antidiarrheal—Medicine used to treat diarrhea.

Antidiuretic—Medicine used to decrease urine output (for example, in patients with diabetes insipidus).

Antidiuretic hormone—*See* Vasopressin.

Antidote—Medicine used to prevent or treat harmful effects of another medicine or a poison.

Antidyskinetic—Medicine used to help treat the loss of muscle control caused by certain diseases or by some other medicines.

Antidysmenorrheal—Medicine used to treat menstrual cramps.

Antiemetic—Medicine used to prevent or relieve nausea and vomiting.

Antiendometriotic—Medicine used to treat endometriosis.

Antienuretic—Medicine used to help prevent bedwetting.

Antifibrotic—Medicine used to treat fibrosis.

Antiflatulent—Medicine used to help relieve excess gas in the stomach or intestines.

Antifungal—Medicine used to treat infections caused by a fungus.

Antigen—Any substance that causes an immune reaction.

Antiglaucoma agent—Medicine used to treat glaucoma.

Antigout agent—Medicine used to prevent or relieve gout attacks.

Antihemorrhagic—Medicine used to prevent or help stop serious bleeding.

Antihistamine—Medicine used to prevent or relieve the symptoms of allergic reactions, such as itching, rash, swelling, runny nose, and sneezing.

Antihypercalcemic—Medicine used to help lower the amount of calcium in the blood.

Antihyperlipidemic—Medicine used to help lower high levels of lipids (fatty substances) in the blood.

Antihyperphosphatemic—Medicine used to help lower the amount of phosphate in the blood.

Antihypertensive—Medicine used to help lower high blood pressure.

Antihyperuricemic—Medicine used to prevent or treat gout or other medical problems caused by too much uric acid in the blood.

Antihypocalcemic—Medicine used to increase calcium blood levels in patients with too little calcium.

Antihypoglycemic—Medicine used to increase blood sugar levels in patients with low blood sugar.

Antihypokalemic—Medicine used to increase potassium blood levels in patients with too little potassium.

Anti-infective—Medicine used to treat infection.

Anti-inflammatory—Medicine used to relieve pain, swelling, and other symptoms of inflammation.

Anti-inflammatory, nonsteroidal—An anti-inflammatory medicine that is not a cortisone-like medicine. Also called *NSAID*.

Anti-inflammatory, steroidal—A cortisone-like anti-inflammatory medicine.

Antimetabolite—Substance that interferes with the normal processes within cells, preventing their growth.

Antimuscarinic—Medicine used to block the effects of a certain chemical in the body; often used to reduce smooth muscle spasms, especially abdominal or stomach cramps or spasms.

Antimyasthenic—Medicine used to treat myasthenia gravis.

Antimyotonic—Medicine used to prevent or relieve night-time leg cramps or muscle spasms.

Antineoplastic—Medicine used to treat cancer.

Antineuralgic—Medicine used to treat nerve pain (neuralgia).

Antioxidant—Substance that protects tissues of the body against oxygen damage. Examples of antioxidants are vitamins A, C, and E, and betacarotene.

Antiprotozoal—Medicine used to treat infections caused by protozoa.

Antipruritic—Medicine used to prevent or relieve itching.

Antipsoriatic—Medicine used to treat psoriasis.

Antipsychotic—Medicine used to treat certain mental and emotional conditions, including psychosis.

Antipyretic—Medicine used to reduce fever.

Antirheumatic—Medicine used to treat arthritis (rheumatism).

Antirosacea—Medicine used to treat rosacea (a form of acne).

Antiseborrheic—Medicine used to treat dandruff and seborrhea.

Antiseptic—Medicine that stops the growth of germs. Antiseptics are used on the skin or mucous membranes to prevent or treat infections.

Antispasmodic—Medicine used to reduce smooth muscle spasms (for example, stomach, intestinal, or urinary tract spasms).

Antispastic—Medicine used to treat muscle spasms.

Antithyroid agent—Medicine used to treat an overactive thyroid gland.

Antitremor agent—Medicine used to treat tremors (trembling or shaking).

Antitubercular—Medicine used to treat tuberculosis (TB).

Antitussive—Medicine used to relieve cough.

Antiulcer agent—Medicine used to treat stomach and duodenal ulcers.

Antivertigo agent—Medicine used to prevent dizziness (vertigo).

Antiviral—Medicine used to treat infections caused by a virus.

Anus—The opening at the end of the digestive tract through which waste matter (feces) passes out of the body.

Anxiety—An emotional state with apprehension, worry, or tension in reaction to real or imagined danger or dread; accompanied by sweating, increased pulse, trembling, weakness, and fatigue.

Apnea—Temporary absence of breathing.

Apoplexy—*See* Stroke.

Appendicitis—Inflammation of the appendix.

Appetite—A desire for food.

Appetite stimulant—Medicine used to help increase the desire for food.

Appetite suppressant—Medicine used in weight control programs to help decrease the desire to eat.

Arrhythmia—Abnormal heart rhythm.

Arteritis, temporal—Inflammation of arteries in the area around the eyes; occurs in older people.

Artery—Blood vessel that carries blood away from the heart.

Arthralgia—Pain in a joint.

Arthritis, rheumatoid—Chronic disease, mainly of the joints, marked by inflammation (pain, redness, and swelling).

Ascites—Accumulation of fluid in the abdominal cavity.

Asthma—Disease marked by inflammation with constriction (narrowing) of the bronchial tubes (air passages). The constricted airways result in wheezing and difficult breathing. Attacks may be brought on by allergens, virus infection, cold air, or exercise.

Atherosclerosis—Common disease of the arteries in which artery walls thicken and harden.

Athlete's foot—Fungus infection or ringworm of the feet. Also called *tinea pedis*.

Atrophy—A wasting away or reduction in size and function of a cell, tissue, or part.

Avoid—To keep away from deliberately.

Backbone—*See* Spinal column.

Bacteremia—Presence of bacteria in the blood.

Bacteria—Any of a group of one-celled microorganisms found widely in nature. Many diseases and infections are caused by bacteria.

Bancroft's filariasis—Disease transmitted by mosquitoes in which an infection with the filarial worm occurs; affects the lymph system, producing inflammation.

Basophil—One type of white blood cell; plays a role in allergic reactions.

Beriberi—Disorder caused by too little vitamin B_1 (thiamine), marked by an accumulation of fluid in the body, extreme weight loss, inflammation of nerves, or paralysis.

Bile—Thick fluid produced by the liver and stored in the gallbladder; helps in the digestion of fats.

Bile duct—Tube which carries bile from the liver to the gallbladder, or from the gallbladder to the intestine.

Bilharziasis—*See* Schistosomiasis.

Biliary—Relating to bile, the bile duct, or the gallbladder.

Bilirubin—The bile pigment that is orange-colored or yellow; an excess in the blood may cause jaundice.

Biofeedback—Process that aims to help the patient gain some control over blood pressure, skin temperature, or other involuntary function.

Bipolar disorder—Severe mental illness marked by repeated episodes of depression and mania. Also called *manic-depressive illness*.

Bisexual—One who is sexually attracted to both sexes.

Black fever—*See* Leishmaniasis, visceral.

Blood cell—Any of the cells that are present in the blood. Major types are red blood cells (erythrocytes, which carry oxygen to the tissues), white blood cells (leukocytes, which help protect against infection), and platelets (thrombocytes, which are necessary for blood clotting).

Blood plasma—The liquid in which blood cells and other substances are carried through the arteries and veins.

Blood pressure—Pressure of the blood upon the walls of the arteries; usually measured by both the highest (systolic) and lowest (diastolic) pressures.

Bone marrow—Soft material filling the cavities of bones. Bone marrow is the main place in the body where blood cells and platelets are formed.

Bone marrow depression—Condition in which the production of red blood cells, white blood cells, or platelets by the bone marrow is decreased.

Bone resorption inhibitor—Medicine used to prevent or treat certain types of bone disorders; helps prevent bone loss.

Bowel—Intestine.

Bowel disease, inflammatory, suppressant—Medicine used to treat certain intestinal disorders, such as colitis and Crohn's disease.

Bradycardia—Slow heart rate, usually less than 60 beats per minute in adults.

Bronchitis—Inflammation of the bronchial tubes (air passages) of the lungs.

Bronchodilator—Medicine used to open up the bronchial tubes (air passages) of the lungs to increase the flow of air through them.

Bruise—Discoloration of the skin caused by an injury to the tissue beneath without a break in the skin. Most bruises slowly change in color from reddish purple to bluish to greenish yellow.

Buccal—Relating to the cheek. A buccal medicine is taken by placing it between the cheek and the gum and letting it slowly dissolve.

Bulimia—Eating disorder, mostly of females, marked by bouts of excessive eating followed by self-induced vomiting, hard exercise, or fasting.

Bulk—In nutrition, fiber that absorbs water while in the intestine; helps formation and movement of the stool. Also called *roughage*.

Bursa—Small fluid-filled sac that helps reduce friction; located between body parts that move over one another (such as in a joint).

Bursitis—Inflammation of a bursa.

Calorie—Unit of heat that measures the energy value of food.

Calorie free—In food labeling, fewer than 5 calories per serving.

Candidiasis of the mouth—Overgrowth of the yeast *Candida* in the mouth; marked by white patches on the tongue or inside the mouth. Also called *thrush* or *white mouth*.

Candidiasis of the vagina—Yeast infection of the vagina caused by the yeast *Candida;* associated with itching, burning, and a curd-like white discharge.

Canker sore—Acute, painful ulcer inside the mouth.

Carbohydrate—Any one of a large group of compounds from plants, including sugars and starches, that contain only carbon, hydrogen, and oxygen. Carbohydrates are a source of energy and fiber for animals and humans.

Carbon dioxide—A colorless, odorless gas. In the body, it is a final product in the breakdown of foods and is breathed out of the body through the lungs.

Cardiac—Relating to the heart.

Cardiac arrhythmia—*See* Arrhythmia.

Cardiac load–reducing agent—Medicine used to ease the workload of the heart by allowing the blood to flow through the blood vessels more easily.

Cardiotonic—Medicine used to improve the strength and efficiency of the heart.

Cardiovascular—Relating to the heart and blood vessels.

Caries, dental—Tooth decay, sometimes causing pain, leading to tooth damage. Also called *cavities*.

Cartilage—Type of connective tissue; it is elastic and softer than bone and makes up a part of the skeleton.

Cataract—A cloudiness in the lens of the eye that impairs vision or causes blindness.

Catheter—Tube inserted into various openings or blood vessels in the body so that fluids can be put in or taken out.

Caustic—1.Burning or corrosive. 2.Substance that is irritating and destructive to living tissue.

Cavity—1. Hollow space within the body. 2. Hole in a tooth caused by dental caries.

Cell—Basic unit that makes up the tissues of all living animals and plants. A cell usually consists of a nucleus, which contains the cell's genetic material, and various other structures outside of the nucleus that are enclosed within a cell membrane.

Central nervous system—The brain and spinal cord.

Cerebral—Relating to the brain.

Cerebral palsy—Permanent disorder of motor weakness and loss of coordination due to damage to the brain.

Cervix—Lower end or necklike opening of the uterus into the vagina.

Characterized by—Term used to describe properties that identify a particular condition (for example, measles is a disease characterized by a high fever, cough, and a blotchy rash).

Chemotherapy—Treatment of illness or disease by chemical agents. The term most commonly refers to the use of drugs to treat cancer.

Chickenpox—*See* Varicella.

Chlamydia—A family of microorganisms that cause a variety of diseases in humans. One form is commonly transmitted by sexual contact. Infection can be transmitted to a baby during the birth process.

Cholesterol—Fatlike substance made by the liver but also absorbed from the diet; found only in animal tissues. Too much blood cholesterol is associated with several potential health risks, especially atherosclerosis (hardening of the arteries) and heart disease.

Cholesterol free—In food labeling, less than 2 milligrams of cholesterol and 2 grams or less of saturated fat per serving.

Chromosome—The structure in the cell nucleus that contains the DNA and carries the genes. Most human cells normally contain 46 chromosomes.

Chronic—Describes a condition of long duration, which is often of gradual onset and may involve very slow changes.

Cirrhosis—Chronic liver disease marked by destruction of its cells and abnormal tissue growth, resulting in abnormal function.

Clitoris—Small, erectile organ that is part of the female external sex organs.

Clotting factor—Any of a group of substances in blood plasma that are involved in the process of blood clotting.

CNS—*See* Central nervous system.

Coagulation, blood (blood clotting)—Process that changes blood from a liquid to a solid, forming a clot.

Cold sores—*See* Herpes simplex.

Colic—Waves of sudden, severe abdominal pain, which are usually separated by relatively pain-free intervals. Often occurs in infants, causing crying and irritability.

Colitis—Inflammation of the colon (large bowel).

Collagen—A tough, strong protein found mostly in bone, skin, tendons, and ligaments.

Colon—Large intestine (bowel), from the end of the ileum to the rectum.

Colony stimulating factor—Protein that stimulates the production of one or more kinds of cells made in the bone marrow.

Colostomy—Operation in which part of the colon (large bowel) is brought through the abdominal wall to create an artificial opening (stoma). The contents of the intestine are passed out of the body through the opening.

Coma—Sleeplike state from which a person cannot be aroused.

Coma, hepatic—Disturbances in alertness and mental function caused by severe liver disease.

Compliance—The extent to which a patient follows medical advice.

Component—Any ingredient that helps make up a substance.

Compound—Substance made up of two or more units, elements, ingredients, or parts.

Condom, male—Thin sheath or cover, made of latex (rubber) or animal intestine, that is worn over the penis during sexual intercourse to prevent pregnancy. Condoms made of latex (rubber) are also used to prevent infection.

Congestion—Abnormal accumulation of fluid, especially of blood, within an organ or part of the body.

Congestive heart failure—Condition of inadequate blood flow caused by the inability of the heart to pump strongly enough; characterized by breathlessness and edema.

Conjugated estrogens—A mixture of naturally occurring estrogens (female hormones) that have been processed and made into a medicine.

Conjunctiva—Delicate mucous membrane covering the front of the eye and the inside of the eyelid.

Conjunctivitis—Inflammation of the conjunctiva.

Connective tissue—Material of the body that joins and supports other tissue and body parts; includes skin, bone, and tendons.

Constipation—A condition in which hard bowel movements are passed infrequently and/or with difficulty.

Constriction—Squeezing together and becoming narrower or smaller, such as constriction of blood vessels or eye pupils.

Contagious disease—Most often refers to disease that can be transmitted from one person to another. May also refer to disease that can be transmitted from an animal to a person.

Contamination—The introduction of germs or unclean material into or on normally sterile substances or objects.

Contraceptive—Medicine or device used to prevent pregnancy.

Contraction—A shortening or tightening, as in the normal function of muscles.

Convulsion—*See* Seizure.

Corrosive—Causing slow wearing away by a destructive agent.

Corticosteroids—Group of cortisone-like hormones that are secreted by the adrenal cortex and are critical to the body. The two major groups of corticosteroids are glucocorticoids, which affect fat and body metabolism, and mineralocorticoids, which regulate salt/water balance. Also called *adrenocorticoids*.

Cortisol—Natural cortisone-like hormone produced by the adrenal cortex, important for carbohydrate, protein, and fat metabolism and for the normal response to stress; synthetic cortisol (hydrocortisone) is used to treat inflammations, allergies, collagen diseases, rheumatic disorders, and adrenal failure.

Cot death—*See* Sudden infant death syndrome (SIDS).

Cowpox—*See* Vaccinia.

Creutzfeldt-Jakob disease—Rare disease, probably caused by a slow-acting virus that affects the brain and nervous system.

Crib death—*See* Sudden infant death syndrome (SIDS).

Criteria—Standards on which a judgment or decision is based.

Crohn's disease—A chronic inflammatory disease of the digestive tract, usually the lower portion of the small intestine (the ileum) or the large intestine.

Croup—Inflammation and blockage of the larynx (voice box) and air passages in young children. Symptoms of croup include harsh, difficult breathing and a barking cough.

Crystalluria—Crystals in the urine.

Cushing's syndrome—Condition caused by too much cortisone-like hormone, leading to weight gain, round face, osteoporosis (thinning of bones), diabetes mellitus (sugar diabetes), and high blood pressure.

Cycloplegia—Paralysis of certain eye muscles; can be caused by medication for certain eye tests.

Cycloplegic—Medicine used to induce cycloplegia.

Cyst—Abnormal sac or closed cavity filled with liquid or semisolid matter.

Cystic—Marked by cysts.

Cystic fibrosis—Hereditary disease of children and young adults which mainly affects the lungs. Exocrine glands do not function normally, and excess mucus is produced.

Cystine—An amino acid found in most proteins; it is released by the breakdown of the protein.

Cystitis, interstitial—Inflammation of the bladder that occurs mainly in women and is associated with pain, frequent urge to urinate, and burning urination.

Cytomegalovirus—One of a group of viruses. One form may be transmitted sexually or by infected blood and can cause death in patients with weakened immune systems.

Cytoplasm—The contents of a cell outside the nucleus.

Cytotoxic agent—Chemical that kills cells or stops cell division; used to treat cancer.

Daily Value (DV)—Value used on food and dietary supplement labels to indicate the percent of the recommended daily amount of each nutrient that a serving provides. DV takes the place of USRDA (United States Recommended Daily Allowance).

Dandruff—Scalp condition marked by the shedding of thin, dry flakes of dead skin.

Decongestant, nasal—Medicine used to help relieve nasal congestion (stuffy nose).

Decongestant, ophthalmic—Medicine used in the eye to relieve redness, burning, itching, or other eye irritation.

Decubitus ulcer—Bedsore; damage to the skin and underlying tissues caused by constant pressure.

Dehydration—Condition that results from an excessive loss or a deficiency of body water. Vomiting, diarrhea, sweating, or inadequate water intake may lead to dehydration.

Dental—Related to the teeth and gums.

Depression, mental—Condition marked by deep sadness; associated with lack of any pleasurable interest in life. Other symptoms include disturbances in sleep, appetite, and concentration, and difficulty in performing day-to-day tasks.

Dermatitis herpetiformis—Skin disease marked by sores that develop suddenly and by intense itching.

Dermatitis, seborrheic—Type of eczema found on the scalp and face.

Dermatomyositis—Inflammatory disorder, mainly of the skin and muscle fibers.

Deterioration—Process of growing worse in quality, ability, or state.

Diabetes insipidus—Disorder in which the patient produces large amounts of dilute urine and is constantly thirsty. This condition is caused by a lack of the hormone vasopressin, and is different from diabetes mellitus (sugar diabetes). Also called *water diabetes*.

Diabetes mellitus—Disorder in which the body does not produce enough insulin or else the body tissues are unable to use the insulin present. This leads to hyperglycemia (high blood sugar). Also called *sugar diabetes*.

Diagnose—Find out the cause or nature of a disorder. This often includes physical examination, laboratory tests, or other tests.

Diagnostic procedure—A process carried out to determine the cause or nature of a condition, disease, or disorder.

Dialysis, renal—Process using mechanical or other means to remove waste materials or poisons from the blood when the kidneys are not working well.

Diarrhea—Frequent passing of abnormally soft or liquid stools.

Dietary fiber—The part of food that cannot be broken down and digested; recommended as part of a balanced diet. Also called *bulk* or *roughage*.

Dietary supplement—Nutrient eaten or taken into the body in addition to the usual food.

Digestant—Agent that helps digestion.

Dilatation—Condition of being stretched or expanded beyond normal dimensions.

Diplopia—Awareness of two images of a single object at one time; double vision.

Discharge—1. Material that is released and flows away from an organ or body part. 2. Release of electrical energy by a nerve cell.

Disintegration—The process of breaking down into small pieces. In relation to medicines, a measure of how fast a tablet or capsule breaks into small pieces in stomach fluids.

Disorder—Abnormal physical or mental state.

Dissolution—1. The breaking down of a substance into its separate parts. 2. The act of being dissolved (completely merged with a liquid). In relation to medicines, a measure of how fast the contents of a tablet or capsule dissolve in body fluids.

Diuretic—Medicine used to increase the amount of urine produced by helping the kidneys get rid of water and salt.

Diverticulitis—Inflammation of a diverticulum (sac or pouch) in the intestinal tract.

Diverticulum—Sac or pouch formed at a weak place in the mucous membrane lining the wall of a canal or cavity, such as the intestine or bladder.

DNA—Deoxyribonucleic acid; the genetic material that controls heredity. DNA is found chiefly in the cell nucleus.

Down syndrome—Disorder associated with the presence of an extra chromosome 21. People with Down syndrome are mentally retarded and are marked physically by a round head, flat nose, slightly slanted eyes, and short stature. Formerly called *mongolism.*

Drug interaction—The action of one drug upon another when taken close together; depending on the drugs and the patient's medical condition, may be harmful to the patient.

Duct—Tube or channel, especially one that serves to carry secretions from a gland.

Dumdum fever—*See* Leishmaniasis, visceral.

Duodenal ulcer—Open sore in that part of the small intestine closest to the stomach.

Duodenum—First of the three parts of the small intestine.

Dyskinesia—Refers to abnormal, involuntary movement or having difficulty in performing voluntary movement.

Dysmenorrhea—Painful menstruation.

Dyspnea—Shortness of breath; difficult breathing.

Eczema—Inflammation of the skin, marked by itching, a red rash, and oozing sores that become crusted and scaly.

Edema—Swelling of body tissue due to accumulation of excess fluids.

Eighth-cranial-nerve disease—Disease of the eighth cranial nerve, which serves the inner ear; results in dizziness, loss of balance, impaired hearing, nausea, or vomiting.

Electrolyte—In medical use, chemicals (ions), such as bicarbonate, chloride, sodium, and potassium, in body fluids and tissues. Healthy functioning of the body depends on correct amounts and balances of electrolytes.

Element—In chemistry, a simple substance that cannot be broken down into simpler substances by chemical means; made up of atoms of only one kind.

Elimination—The act of expelling waste products (urine, feces) and other substances from the body.

Embolism—Sudden blocking of a blood vessel by a blood clot or other substances carried by the blood.

Embryo—In humans, a developing fertilized egg within the uterus (womb) from about two to eight weeks after fertilization.

Emergency—Extremely serious unexpected or sudden happening or situation that calls for immediate action.

Emetic—Substance that causes vomiting; used in some cases of drug overdose and poisonings.

Emollient—Substance that soothes and softens, such as an emollient lotion.

Emphysema—Lung condition in which the air spaces are enlarged and damaged, causing poor exchange of oxygen and carbon dioxide during the process of breathing in and out.

Encephalitis—Inflammation of the brain.

Encephalopathy—Any degenerative disease of the brain; caused by many different medical conditions.

Endemic—Refers to a disease that is normally present in a specific human community or geographic location.

Endocarditis—Inflammation of the lining of the heart; may lead to fever, heart murmurs, and heart failure.

Endocrine gland—A gland that has no duct, but releases its secretion directly into the blood or lymph.

Endometriosis—Condition in which material similar to the lining of the uterus (womb) appears at other sites, usually within the pelvic cavity, causing pain or bleeding.

Endoscope—An instrument inserted through an opening into the body, such as the mouth or anus, so that the doctor can see the inside of a body structure, such as the esophagus, stomach, or intestine.

Enema—Solution introduced into the rectum and colon to help empty the bowel, give nutrients or medicine, or help x-ray the lower intestines.

Enteric coating—Special coating on tablets or on the contents of capsules that allows them to pass through the stomach unchanged. The tablets or capsule contents are broken up in the intestine and absorbed.

Enteritis—Inflammation of the small intestine, usually causing diarrhea.

Enuresis—Urinating while asleep (bedwetting).

Enzyme—One type of protein produced by cells. Enzymes usually bring about or speed up normal chemical body reactions.

Eosinophil—One type of white blood cell; plays a role in allergic reactions and in fighting parasite infections.

Eosinophilia—Condition in which the number of eosinophils in the blood is abnormally high.

Epidemic—Refers to a disease that is present in a community only occasionally, but affects a large number of people when it is present.

Epidural space—Area in the spinal column into which medicines (usually for pain or local anesthesia) can be administered.

Epilepsy—Any of a group of brain disorders marked by sudden seizures or other symptoms that are brought on by abnormal electrical brain activity.

Epinephrine—Hormone produced by the adrenal gland. It stimulates the heart, constricts blood vessels, and relaxes some smooth muscles. Also called *adrenaline.*

EPO—*See* Erythropoietin.

Ergot alkaloids—A class of medicines that cause narrowing of blood vessels; some are used to treat migraine headaches, and others are used to reduce bleeding in childbirth.

Erythrocyte—Red blood cell. Erythrocytes contain hemoglobin and transport oxygen.

Erythropoietin—Hormone, secreted by the kidney, that controls the production of red blood cells by the bone marrow; also available as a synthetic drug (EPO). It is used to treat anemia in some patients with cancer, HIV, or kidney disease.

Esophagus—The part of the digestive tract that connects the pharynx (throat) to the stomach.

Estrogen—Principal female sex hormone necessary for the normal sexual development of the female. During the menstrual cycle, its actions help prepare for possible pregnancy.

Excessive—Describes an amount or degree that is more than what is proper, usual, or normal.

Excrete—To throw off or eliminate waste material from the body, blood, or organs.

Exocrine gland—Any gland that discharges its secretion through a duct directly onto or into a body part, but not into the blood.

Exophthalmic goiter—*See* Graves' disease.

Exophthalmos—Thrusting forward of the eyeballs in their sockets giving the appearance of the eyes sticking out too far; commonly associated with hyperthyroidism.

Expectorant—Medicine used to help the patient cough up and expel mucus from the air passages.

Expel—To force out.

Extrapyramidal symptoms—Movement disorders occurring with certain diseases or with use of certain drugs, including trembling and shaking of hands and fingers, twisting movements of the body, shuffling walk, and stiffness of arms or legs.

Facial—Relating to the face.

Factor—Substance that is necessary to produce a result in a specific process of the body.

Familial Mediterranean fever—Inherited condition involving inflammation of the lining of the chest, abdomen, and joints. Also called *recurrent polyserositis*.

Fasciculation—Small, repeated contraction of a few muscle fibers, which is visible through the skin; muscular twitching.

Fat—An energy-rich organic compound that occurs naturally in animals and plants. Fats are an essential nutrient for humans.

Fat free—In food labeling, less than 0.5 grams of fat per serving.

Fatty acid—One of the basic organic compounds that make up lipids.

Favism—Inherited condition resulting from sensitivity to broad (fava) beans; marked by fever, vomiting, diarrhea, and acute destruction of red blood cells.

Feces—Waste material remaining after food has been digested, which is passed out of the intestine through the anus. Also called *stool*.

Fertility—Ability to bring about the start of pregnancy or produce offspring.

Fertilization—Union of an ovum with a sperm.

Fetal—Relating to the fetus.

Fetus—In humans, a developing baby within the uterus (womb) from about the beginning of the third month of pregnancy.

Fewer calories—In food labeling, at least 25 percent fewer calories per serving than the reference food.

Fiber—1. In nutrition, the carbohydrate material of food that cannot be digested. Fiber adds bulk to the diet. 2. In medicine, a thin, threadlike structure that combines with others to form certain tissues, for example, muscles and nerves.

Fibrocystic—Describes a benign (noncancerous) tumor that consists of a cyst surrounded by fibrous tissue.

Fibroid tumor—A noncancerous tumor of the uterus formed of fibrous or fully developed connective tissue.

Fibrosis—Scarring and thickening of connective tissue causing it to tighten and become less flexible.

Fibrous—Made up of fibers or containing fibers.

Fistula—Abnormal tubelike passage connecting two internal organs or one that leads from an abscess or internal organ to the body surface.

Flatulence—Excessive amount of gas in the stomach or intestine.

Flu—*See* Influenza.

Flushing—Temporary redness of the face and/or neck.

Folic acid—A vitamin of the B complex. Lack of folic acid may lead to anemia.

Follicle—A sac or pouchlike cavity. For example, a hair follicle is a small cavity from which a hair grows.

Food Guide Pyramid—An eating plan developed by Health and Human Services and the Department of Agriculture that describes the basic food groups. It serves as a guide for having a proper diet.

Fungus—Any of a group of simple organisms, including molds and yeasts.

Fungus infection—Infection caused by a fungus. Some common fungus infections are tinea pedis (athlete's foot), tinea capitis (ringworm of the scalp), tinea cruris (ringworm of the groin or jock itch), and mouth or vaginal candidiasis (yeast infections).

Gait—Manner of walk.

Gallbladder—An organ that stores bile. It is attached to the liver.

Gamma globulin—A group of proteins in the blood that act as antibodies in fighting infection.

Gastric—Relating to the stomach.

Gastric acid secretion inhibitor—Medicine used to decrease the amount of acid produced by the stomach.

Gastritis—Inflammation of the stomach, especially of the stomach lining.

Gastroenteritis—Inflammation of the stomach and intestine.

Gastroesophageal reflux—Backward flow of stomach contents into the esophagus. The condition is often characterized by "heartburn."

Gene—A part of a DNA molecule that acts as a basic unit of genetic information, located on a chromosome. Genes transmit the traits that a parent passes on to its offspring.

Generic—General in nature; relating to an entire group or class. In relation to medicines, generic refers to a medicine's chemical name, which is not protected by a trademark and can therefore be used by all manufacturers or providers of the medicine.

Genetics—The study of genes and their passing on of a quality or trait from parent to offspring.

Genital—1. Relating to the organs concerned with reproduction; the sexual organs. 2. Relating to reproduction.

Genital warts—Small growths found on the genitals or around the anus; caused by a virus. The disease may be transmitted by sexual contact.

Geriatric—Relating to the care of elderly people and the treatment of disorders that commonly affect them.

Gilles de la Tourette syndrome—*See* Tourette's disorder.

Gingiva—Tissue that surrounds the teeth, or the gums.

Gingival hyperplasia—Excessive growth of the gums.

Gingivitis—Inflammation of the gums.

Gland—Group of cells or an organ specialized to produce one or more secretions.

Glandular fever—*See* Mononucleosis.

Glaucoma—Condition of abnormally high pressure in the eye; may lead to loss of vision if not treated.

Glomeruli—Clusters of capillaries (tiny blood vessels) in the kidney that act as filters of the blood.

Glomerulonephritis—Inflammation of the glomeruli of the kidney; not directly caused by infection.

Glucose—A simple sugar. In living organisms, it is formed by the breakdown of carbohydrates and is the chief source of energy.

Glucose-6-phosphate dehydrogenase (G6PD) deficiency—Lack of or reduced amounts of an enzyme (glucose-6-phosphate dehydrogenase) that helps the breakdown of certain sugar compounds in the body. People with this condition may be more likely to develop a form of anemia.

Gluten—Type of protein found primarily in wheat and rye.

Goiter—Enlargement of the thyroid gland that causes the neck to swell; usually results from a lack of iodine in the diet or overactivity of the thyroid gland.

Gonadotropin—Any hormone that stimulates the activities of the ovaries or testes.

Gonorrhea—An infectious disease, usually transmitted by sexual contact. It causes infection in the genital organs in both men and women, and may result in disease in other parts of the body.

Good source of fiber—In food labeling, 2.5 grams to 4.9 grams of fiber per serving.

Gout—Disorder caused by uric acid in the joints and kidneys, leading to painful inflammation of the joints and kidney stones.

Granulation—Small, fleshy outgrowths on the healing surface of a wound or ulcer; a normal stage in healing.

Granulocyte—One type of white blood cell.

Granulocytopenia—*See* Agranulocytosis.

Granuloma—A granular growth or mass produced in response to chronic infection, inflammation, a foreign body, or to unknown causes.

Graves' disease—Enlargement of the thyroid gland (goiter) and overproduction of thyroid hormones, causing fast heart beat, bulging eyes, tremor, sweating, and weight loss. Also called *exophthalmic goiter*.

Groin—The area where the abdomen meets the thigh.

Growth factor—Substance, usually a vitamin, hormone, or mineral, that promotes the process of growing.

Guillain-Barré syndrome—Nerve disease marked by sudden numbness and weakness in the limbs that may progress to paralysis; recovery usually follows.

Gynecomastia—Excessive development of the breast tissue in the male.

Haemophilus—Closely related group of bacteria. Some varieties are found normally in the upper respiratory tract (the nose and throat) but may sometimes cause infections, including infections of the respiratory tract, eyes, and the tissues covering the brain and spinal cord. Also *Hemophilus*.

Hair follicle—Sheath of tissue surrounding a hair root.

Hansen's disease—*See* Leprosy.

Hartnup disease—Hereditary defect in protein metabolism that leads to mental retardation, rough skin, and poor control of muscle movement.

Healthy—1. Food labeling term that may be used if the food is low in fat and saturated fat and a serving does not contain more than 480 milligrams of sodium or more than 95 milligrams of cholesterol. The food must also contain at least 10% of the daily value (DV) per serving of vitamin A, vitamin C, calcium, iron, protein, and fiber. 2. Being in a state of physical, mental, and social wellness.

Heart attack—*See* Myocardial infarction.

Heartburn—Warmth or burning felt behind the breastbone. Heartburn is usually caused by stomach contents rising toward the mouth.

Helicobacter pylori—Organism that has been associated with gastritis and certain ulcers.

Hematologic—Relating to the blood.

Hematuria—Presence of blood or red blood cells in the urine.

Heme—A blood pigment containing iron; a component of hemoglobin.

Hemoglobin—Iron-containing substance found in red blood cells that transports oxygen from the lungs to the tissues of the body.

Hemolytic anemia—Type of anemia resulting from breakdown of red blood cells.

Hemophilia—Hereditary disease marked by delayed blood clotting, leading to uncontrolled bleeding even after minor injuries. Generally, only males have the disease.

Hemorrhoids—Enlarged veins in the walls of the anus. Also called *piles*.

Hepatic—Relating to the liver.

Hepatitis—Inflammation of the liver; may be caused by virus infection.

Hereditary—Genetically passed on from parent to offspring.

Hernia, hiatal—Condition in which the stomach passes partly into the chest cavity through the opening for the esophagus in the diaphragm.

Herpes simplex—The virus that causes genital herpes infections and "cold sores," both of which are marked by the appearance of painful blisters that can be transmitted from one person to another. In genital herpes, the blisters appear on the genitals (sex organs) and are often transmitted by sexual contact. "Cold sores" may appear on the lips, in or around the mouth, or around the nose.

Herpes zoster—The virus that causes chickenpox and shingles. Shingles is an infectious disease usually marked by pain and blisters along one nerve, often on the face, chest, stomach, or back.

Heterosexual—One who is sexually attracted to persons of the opposite sex.

High blood pressure—*See* Hypertension.

High fiber—In food labeling, 5 grams or more of fiber per serving. (Foods making high-fiber claims must meet the definition for low fat, or the level of total fat must appear next to the high-fiber claim.)

Hirsutism—Excessive hair growth or the growth of hair in unusual places, especially in women.

Histamine—Chemical, found in all body tissues, that dilates capillaries (small blood vessels), contracts smooth muscle, and stimulates gastric (stomach) secretions. Histamine is released during allergic reactions, producing swelling and inflammation.

HIV (human immunodeficiency virus)—Virus that causes AIDS.

Hives—*See* Urticaria.

Hoarseness—Gruff, husky, quality of the voice.

Hodgkin's disease—Malignant condition marked by swelling of the lymph nodes, with weight loss and fever.

Homosexual—One who is sexually attracted to persons of the same sex.

Hormone—A chemical substance, produced in the body, that controls or regulates the activity of specific organs or cells.

The term hormone may also refer to manufactured substances that act like a hormone.

Hot flashes—Sensations of heat of the face, neck, and upper body, often accompanied by sweating and flushing; commonly associated with menopause.

Hydrocortisone—*See* Cortisol.

Hyperactivity—Abnormally increased activity and shortened attention span.

Hypercalcemia—Abnormally high amount of calcium in the blood.

Hypercalciuria—Abnormally high amount of calcium in the urine.

Hypercholesterolemia—Excessive amount of cholesterol in the blood.

Hyperglycemia—Abnormally high amount of glucose in the blood.

Hyperkalemia—Abnormally high amount of potassium in the blood.

Hyperkeratosis—Overgrowth or thickening of the outer layer of the skin.

Hyperlipidemia—General term for an abnormally high level of lipids (fats or fatlike substances) in the blood.

Hyperphosphatemia—Abnormally high amount of phosphate in the blood.

Hypersensitivity—An excessive response by the body to a foreign substance.

Hypertension—Blood pressure in the arteries (blood vessels) that is higher than normal for the patient's age group. Hypertension may lead to a number of serious health problems. Also called *high blood pressure.*

Hyperthermia—Abnormally high body temperature; fever.

Hyperthyroidism—Condition in which there is too much thyroid hormone in the body, leading to fast heart beat, trembling, sweating, bulging of the eyes, and weight loss.

Hypertrophy—Increase in bulk or size of a body part, brought about by excessive development rather than an increase in the number of cells.

Hypocalcemia—Abnormally low amount of calcium in the blood.

Hypoglycemia—Abnormally low amount of glucose in the blood.

Hypokalemia—Abnormally low amount of potassium in the blood.

Hypotension, orthostatic—Excessive fall in blood pressure that occurs when standing or upon standing up.

Hypothalamus—Area of the brain that controls many body functions, including body temperature, certain metabolic and endocrine processes, and some activities of the nervous system.

Hypothermia—Abnormally low body temperature.

Hypothyroidism—Condition caused by thyroid hormone deficiency, which results in a decrease in metabolism.

Hypoxia—Broad term meaning that not enough oxygen is being supplied to, or used by, body tissues.

Ileostomy—Operation in which the ileum is brought through the abdominal wall to create an artificial opening (stoma). The contents of the intestine are discharged through the opening.

Ileum—Last of the three portions of the small intestine, farthest from the mouth.

Immune—Having protection against infectious disease.

Immune deficiency condition—Lack of immune response to protect against infectious disease.

Immune system—Complex network of the body that defends against foreign substances or organisms that may harm the body.

Immunity—The body's ability to resist infection.

Immunizing agent, active—Agent that causes the body to produce its own antibodies for protection against certain infections or substances.

Immunocompromised—Decreased natural immunity caused by certain medicines, diseases, genetic disorders, or use of immunosuppressants.

Immunoglobulin—*See* Antibody.

Immunosuppressant—Medicine that reduces the body's natural immunity.

Impair—To decrease, weaken, or damage ability or function, usually because of injury or disease.

Impairment—Decrease in strength or ability, often because of illness or injury (for example, hearing impairment).

Impetigo—Contagious bacterial skin infection most common in babies and children. The infection starts as a red patch, which develops into blisters that break and form a thick crust.

Implant—1. Special form of medicine, often a small pellet or rod, that is inserted into the body or beneath the skin so that the medicine will be released continuously over a period of time. 2. To insert or graft material or an object into a body site. 3. Material or an object inserted into a body site, such as a lens implant or a breast implant. 4. Action of a fertilized ovum becoming attached or embedded in the uterus.

Impotence—Difficulty or inability of a male to have or maintain an erection of the penis.

Incontinence—Inability to control natural passage of urine or of bowel movements.

Induce—To cause or bring about.

Infection—Invasion and multiplication of a disease-causing microorganism in body tissue.

Infertility—Refers to the inability of a woman to become pregnant or of a man to cause pregnancy.

Inflammation—Pain, redness, swelling, and heat in a part of the body, usually in response to injury or illness.

Inflammatory bowel disease—Irritation of the intestinal tract; usually refers to a chronic condition, such as Crohn's disease or ulcerative colitis.

Influenza—Highly contagious respiratory virus infection, marked by coughing, headache, chills, fever, muscle pain, and general weakness. Also called *flu.*

Ingredient—One of the parts or substances that make up a mixture or compound.

Inhalation—1. Act of drawing in the breath or drawing air into the lungs. 2. Medicine that is breathed (inhaled) into the lungs. Some inhalations work locally in the lungs, while others produce their effects elsewhere in the body. Also called *inhalant.*

Inhalator—Device used to help the patient breathe in air, anesthetics, or other gases, or medicinal mists or vapors. Also called *inhaler.*

Inhibitor—Substance that prevents or slows a process or reaction.

Inner ear—The liquid-filled system of cavities and ducts deep inside the ear that make up the organs of hearing and balance.

Inorganic—Being made up of matter that is not living and has never lived.

Insomnia—Inability to sleep or remain asleep.

Insulin—Hormone that controls the way the body uses and stores sugar (glucose). Injections of insulin are used to treat diabetes mellitus (sugar diabetes) that cannot be controlled by diet, exercise, or other medicines.

Interferon—Substance produced by cells that stops the growth and the spread of viruses; may also have effects on cells fighting cancer.

Intestine—The part of the digestive tract that extends from the stomach to the anus.

Intra-amniotic—Within the sac that contains the fetus and amniotic fluid (fluid surrounding the fetus).

Intra-arterial—Within an artery.

Intracavernosal—Into the corpus cavernosa (cavities in the penis that, when filled with blood, produce an erection).

Intracavitary—Into a body cavity (for example, the chest cavity or bladder).

Intramuscular—Into a muscle.

Intrauterine device (IUD)—Small plastic or metal device placed in the uterus (womb) to prevent pregnancy.

Intravenous—Into a vein.

Involuntary—Not under conscious control (for example, digestion of food is an involuntary action).

Ion—Atom or group of atoms carrying an electric charge.

Irrigation—Washing of a body cavity or wound with a stream of sterile water or a solution of a medicine.

Ischemia—Condition caused by inadequate blood flow to a part of the body; usually caused by constriction or blocking of blood vessels that supply the part of the body affected.

Jaundice—Yellowing of the eyes and skin due to the presence of bilirubin, a substance that may be released into the blood and tissues of patients with certain medical problems, such as hepatitis (inflammation of the liver, often caused by a virus infection).

Jock itch—Ringworm of the groin or the area around the scrotum.

Kala-azar—See Leishmaniasis, visceral.

Kaposi's sarcoma—Malignant (cancerous) tumor that usually first appears as purple or brown patches on the skin of the feet. The tumors slowly grow in number and size, spreading toward the upper part of the body. One severe form occurs in immunocompromised patients, including transplant recipients and AIDS patients.

Keratin—Tough protein substance found in hair, nails, and the outer layer of the skin.

Keratolytic—Medicine used to soften thickened or hardened areas of the skin, such as warts.

Ketoacidosis—A condition in which acidosis and large amounts of ketones are present in the body tissues and fluids. This condition occurs when the body burns fat, instead of carbohydrates, for energy. It is especially likely to occur in patients with poorly controlled diabetes mellitus (sugar diabetes).

Kidney—Organ that removes waste products from the blood and excretes them in the form of urine. Also, controls the amounts of several ions, such as hydrogen, sodium, potassium, and phosphate, in body fluids.

Lactation—Secretion of breast milk.

Lactose—A sugar found in milk.

Larva—The immature form of life of some insects and other animal groups that hatch from eggs.

Larynx—Organ that serves as a passage for air from the pharynx (throat) to the lungs; it contains the vocal cords.

Laxative—Natural or synthetic substances used to stimulate passage of bowel movements.

Laxative, bulk-forming—Laxative that acts by absorbing liquid and swelling to form a soft, bulky stool. The bowel is then stimulated normally by the presence of the bulky mass.

Laxative, hyperosmotic—Laxative that acts by drawing water into the bowel from surrounding body tissues. This provides a soft stool mass and increased bowel action.

Laxative, lubricant—Laxative that acts by coating the bowel and the stool mass with a waterproof film. This keeps moisture in the stool. The stool remains soft and its passage is made easier.

Laxative, stimulant—Laxative that acts directly on the intestinal wall. The direct stimulation increases the muscle contractions that move the stool mass along. Also called *contact laxative.*

Laxative, stool softener—Laxative that acts by helping liquids mix into the stool and prevent dry, hard stool masses. The stool remains soft and its passage is made easier. Also called *emollient laxative.*

Lean—Food labeling term for seafood or game meat, meals, and main dishes. May be used if a serving contains less than 10 grams of total fat, 4.5 grams or less of saturated fat, and less than 95 milligrams of cholesterol. Seafood and game meat must meet these criteria per 100 grams of food. Meals and main dishes must meet these criteria per 100 grams of food and per labeled serving.

Legionnaires' disease—A severe bacterial infection in the lungs, which causes a high fever and pneumonia. It sometimes also affects other parts of the body.

Leishmaniasis, visceral—Tropical disease, transmitted by sandfly bites, which causes liver and spleen enlargement, anemia, weight loss, and fever. Also called *black fever, Dum-dum fever,* or *kala-azar.*

Lennox-Gastaut syndrome—Type of childhood epilepsy.

Leprosy—Chronic infectious disease marked by skin lesions. It is slowly progressive and leads to loss of feeling, tissue destruction, and deformity. Also called *Hansen's disease.*

Lesion—A defined area of diseased or injured tissue.

Less cholesterol—In food labeling, at least 25 percent less cholesterol and 2 grams or less of saturated fat per serving than the reference food.

Less fat—In food labeling, at least 25 percent less fat per serving than the reference food.

Less saturated fat—In food labeling, at least 25 percent less saturated fat per serving than the reference food.

Less sodium—In food labeling, at least 25 percent less sodium per serving than the reference food.

Less sugar—In food labeling, at least 25 percent less sugar per serving than the reference food.

Leukemia—Malignant disease of the blood and bone marrow in which too many white blood cells are produced; results in anemia, bleeding, and low resistance to infections.

Leukocyte—White blood cell. Leukocytes help protect the body against foreign substances and are active in antibody production.

Leukoderma—See Vitiligo.

Leukopenia—Abnormally low number of leukocytes in the blood.

Ligament—Tough, fibrous tissue that connects one bone to another or supports organs.

Lipid—Term applied generally to fat or fatlike substances not soluble in water.

Local effect—Affecting a limited area at or near the place to which the medicine is applied, rather than the whole body (for example, local anesthetics causing numbness only around the place of injection).

Long-acting—Refers to a medicine that is made up in a special way so that it is slowly released in the body; the medicine's effect lasts longer than usual.

Low calorie—In food labeling, 40 calories or less per serving. However, for small servings (30 grams or less or 2 table-spoons or less), low calorie is 40 calories or less per 50 grams of the food.

Low cholesterol—In food labeling, 20 milligrams or less of cho-lesterol and 2 grams or less of saturated fat per serving. How-ever, for small servings (30 grams or less or 2 tablespoons or less), low cholesterol is 20 milligrams or less of cholesterol per 50 grams of the food and 2 grams or less of saturated fat per serving.

Low fat—In food labeling, 3 grams or less of fat per serving. However, for small servings (30 grams or less or 2 table-spoons or less), low fat is 3 grams or less of fat per 50 grams of the food.

Low saturated fat—One gram or less of fat per serving and not more than 15 percent of calories from saturated fatty acids.

Low sodium—In food labeling, 140 milligrams or less of sodium per serving. However, for small servings (30 grams or less or 2 tablespoons or less), low sodium is 140 milligrams or less of sodium per 50 grams of the food.

Lozenge—A dry, medicated tablet or disk to be placed in the mouth and allowed to dissolve slowly. Also called *troche*.

Lugol's solution—Deep brown liquid containing iodine and po-tassium iodide.

Lupus—*See* Lupus erythematosus, systemic.

Lupus erythematosus, systemic—Chronic inflammatory dis-ease most often affecting the skin, joints, and various internal organs. Also called *lupus* or *SLE* (systemic lupus erythema-tosus).

Lyme disease—Acute disease transmitted by the bite of certain ticks. The disease is marked by a slowly spreading rash, and fever, headache, and flu-like symptoms. Left untreated, the disease may later cause heart or nerve disorders, arthritis, or joint pain.

Lymph—Fluid that bathes the tissues. It is formed in tissue spaces in all parts of the body and circulated by the lymphatic system.

Lymphatic system—Network of vessels that conveys lymph from the spaces between the cells of the body back to the bloodstream.

Lymph node—A small rounded body found at intervals along the lymphatic system. The nodes act as filters for the lymph by keeping bacteria and other foreign particles from entering the bloodstream. They also produce lymphocytes.

Lymphocyte—A type of white blood cell found in the blood, lymph, and lymphatic tissues. They are involved in immunity.

Lymphoma—Malignant tumors that arise in lymph nodes or the tissue where lymphocytes are formed.

Lyse—To cause breakdown. In cells, damage or rupture of the membrane results in destruction of the cell.

Macrobiotic—Vegetarian diet consisting mostly of whole grains.

Malaise—General feeling of discomfort, uneasiness, and being unwell.

Malaria—Tropical blood infection caused by protozoa (tiny, one-celled animals); symptoms include chills, fever, sweats, head-aches, and anemia. Malaria is spread to humans by the bite of an infected mosquito.

Malignant—Refers to a condition, usually a cancer, that can be-come life-threatening if untreated.

Malnutrition—Condition caused by a diet that is not balanced or one that does not provide the right amount of food for main-taining good health.

Mammogram—X-ray picture of the breast.

Mania—Mental state in which fast talking and excited feelings or actions are out of control.

Mast cells—Cells that release histamine and other chemicals that cause inflammation and signs of allergic reactions.

Mastocytosis—Accumulation of too many mast cells in tissues.

Mediate—To bring about or accomplish.

Medicinal—Refers to a substance that has the ability to cure, heal, or relieve.

Megavitamin therapy—Taking very large doses of vitamins to prevent or treat certain medical problems.

Melanoma—Highly malignant (cancerous) tumor, usually occur-ring on the skin.

Meniere's disease—Disease affecting the inner ear that is char-acterized by ringing in the ears, nausea, dizziness, and pro-gessive hearing loss.

Meningitis—Inflammation of the tissues that cover the brain and spinal cord; often caused by an infection.

Menopause—The time in a woman's life when the ovaries no longer produce an egg cell at regular times and menstruation stops.

Menstruation—Monthly flow of blood and small pieces of tissue from the uterus through the vagina. Normally, menstruation occurs from puberty to menopause, except during pregnancy.

Metabolism—Sum of all physical and chemical processes that occur in cells to maintain growth and function, including build-ing-up processes, breaking-down processes, and energy changes.

Methemoglobin—Substance formed when hemoglobin has been chemically changed; in this form, hemoglobin cannot act as an oxygen carrier.

Methemoglobinemia—Presence of excessive amounts of met-hemoglobin in the blood.

Microorganism—Any organism too small to be seen by the na-ked eye.

Middle ear—Chamber of the ear lying behind the eardrum; con-tains the three bones that transmit sound waves.

Migraine—Throbbing headache, usually affecting one side of the head; often accompanied by nausea, vomiting, and sen-sitivity to light.

Mineral—One of many elements needed in small amounts for many body functions, including blood clotting, muscle move-ment, and fluid balance.

Miotic—Medicine used in the eye that causes the pupil to con-strict (become smaller).

Mongolism—*See* Down syndrome.

Mono—*See* Mononucleosis.

Monoclonal—Derived from a single cell; related to production of certain drugs by genetic engineering, such as monoclonal an-tibodies.

Mononucleosis—Infectious viral disease occurring mostly in adolescents and young adults, marked by fever, sore throat, swelling of the lymph nodes in the neck and armpits, and by severe fatigue. Also called *mono* or *glandular fever*.

More fiber—*See* Added fiber.

Motility—Ability to move without outside aid, force, or cause.

Motor—Relating to structures that bring about movement, such as nerves and muscles.

MRI (magnetic resonance imaging)—Technique that produces an image of internal body tissue by computer. The technique uses radio waves and a strong magnetic field, but no x-rays.

Mucolytic—Medicine that breaks down or dissolves mucus.

Mucosal—Relating to mucous membrane.

Mucous membrane—Moist layer of tissue surrounding or lining many body structures and cavities, including the mouth, lips, inside of nose, throat, digestive tract (esophagus, stomach, intestines, and anus), and vagina.

Mucus—Thick fluid produced by the mucous membranes and glands.

Multiple sclerosis (MS)—Chronic, inflammatory nerve disease marked by weakness, unsteadiness, shakiness, and speech and vision problems.

Muscular dystrophy—Hereditary disease characterized by gradual wasting of muscles and increasing disability.

Myalgia—Tenderness or pain in a muscle or muscles.

Myasthenia gravis—Chronic disease marked by abnormal weakness, and sometimes paralysis, of certain muscles.

Mydriatic—Medicine used in the eye that causes the pupil to dilate (become larger).

Myelogram—X-ray picture of the spinal cord.

Myeloma, multiple—Cancerous bone marrow disease.

Myocardial infarction—Interruption of blood supply to the heart, leading to symptoms such as tightness or feeling of heaviness in the chest and/or pain in the chest, left shoulder, jaw, or arm, and damage to the heart muscle. Also called *heart attack*.

Myocardial reinfarction prophylactic—Medicine used to help prevent additional heart attacks in patients who have already had one attack.

Myotonia congenita—Hereditary muscle disorder marked by difficulty in relaxing a muscle or releasing a grip after any strong effort.

Narcolepsy—Condition in which the patient is unable to prevent himself or herself from repeatedly falling asleep, often at inappropriate times and places.

Nasal—Relating to the nose.

Nasogastric (NG) tube—Tube that is inserted through the nose, down the throat, and into the stomach. It may be used to remove fluid or gas from the stomach or to give medicine, fluid, or nutrients to the patient.

Nausea—Uncomfortable sensation in the stomach along with an urge to vomit.

Nebulizer—Instrument that changes a liquid into a fine spray.

Necrosis—Death of tissue, cells, or a part of a structure or organ, surrounded by healthy parts.

Neonate—A newborn baby less than four weeks old.

Neoplasm—New and abnormal growth of tissue in or on a part of the body, in which the multiplication of cells is uncontrolled and progressive. Also called *tumor*.

Nephron—Unit of the kidney that contributes to formation of urine by filtering the blood, adding substances to the fluid formed, and removing substances from it.

Nerve—Bundle of fibers that carries messages, in the form of electrical impulses, between the brain or spinal cord and other parts of the body.

Neuralgia—Severe stabbing or throbbing pain along the course of one or more nerves.

Neuralgia, trigeminal—Severe burning or stabbing pain along certain nerves in the face. Also called *tic douloureux*.

Neural tube—Hollow tube in the embryo that gives rise to the brain and spinal cord.

Neural tube defects—Severe, abnormal conditions resulting when the nerve tract in the fetus fails to close fully. *See* Spina bifida.

Neuritis, optic—Disease of the nerves in the eye.

Neuritis, peripheral—Inflammation of nerves or nerve endings located at or near the surface of the body, usually associated with pain, abnormal sensations (such as a burning or prickling feeling), muscle wasting, and loss of reflexes.

Neutropenia—Abnormally small number of neutrophils (a type of white blood cell) in the blood.

Neutrophil—The most common type of granulocyte (a type of white blood cell); important in the body's protection against infection.

Nit—Egg of a louse.

No added sugar—In food labeling, no sugars added to food during processing or packing. This includes ingredients that contain sugars, for example, fruit juices, applesauce, or dried fruit.

No sugar added—*See* No added sugar.

Nodule—Small, rounded mass, lump, or swelling.

Nonsuppurative—Not discharging pus.

NSAID (nonsteroidal anti-inflammatory drug)—*See* Anti-inflammatory, nonsteroidal.

Nucleus—The part of the cell that contains the chromosomes.

Nutrient—Food substance that provides a source of energy or aids in growth and repair. Nutrients include carbohydrates, fats, proteins, minerals, and vitamins.

Nutrition—1. Study of food and drink relating to the building of sound bodies and promoting health. 2. All the body processes that are part of taking in food and using it.

Nutrition Labeling and Education Act (NLEA) of 1990—The law that required the Food and Drug Administration to develop new labeling requirements for foods and dietary supplements.

Nystagmus—Rapid, rhythmic, involuntary movements of the eyeball; may be from side to side, up and down, or around.

Obesity—Excess accumulation of fat in the body along with an increase in body weight that exceeds the healthy range for the body's frame.

Obstetrics—Field of medicine concerned with the care of women during pregnancy and childbirth.

Obstruction—Something that blocks or closes up a passage or structure.

Occlusive dressing—Dressing (such as plastic kitchen wrap) that cuts off air to the skin.

Occult—In medicine, refers to an abnormality that cannot be seen by the human eye (for example, occult blood in the stools or feces can be detected only by microscope or chemical testing).

Offspring—Children or descendants of parents.

Ooze—To slowly give out or pass off moist material.

Ophthalmic—Relating to the eye.

Opioid—1. Any synthetic narcotic with opium-like actions; not derived from opium. 2. Natural chemicals that act at the same cell sites where opium exerts its actions.

Oral—Relating to the mouth.

Orchitis—Inflammation of the testis.

Organ—A body part that performs a particular function or functions.

Organic—1. In nutrition, a term used to describe plants that have been treated with animal or vegetable fertilizers instead of chemicals. 2. Refers to matter that is part of or produced by living organisms, including animals and plants.

Organism—Any individual living thing; may consist of a single cell or may be made up of many cells.

Osteitis deformans—*See* Paget's disease of bone.

Osteomalacia—Softening of the bones due to lack of vitamin D.

Osteoporosis—A condition in which thinning of bone tissue occurs, producing bones that are easily fractured (broken). Often occurs in elderly people because of a loss of calcium from bone tissue.

OTC (over the counter)—Refers to medicine or devices available without a prescription.

Otic—Relating to the ear.

Otitis media—Inflammation of the middle ear.

Ototoxicity—Having a harmful effect on the organs or nerves of the ear concerned with hearing and balance.

Ovary—Female sex organ that produces egg cells and sex hormones.

Overactive thyroid—*See* Hyperthyroidism.

Ovulation—Process by which an ovum (egg cell) is released from the ovary. In human menstruating females, this usually occurs once a month.

Ovum—Mature female sex cell or egg cell. If fertilization of an ovum occurs, a new individual begins to develop.

Oxidize—To lose electrons or to combine with oxygen.

Paget's disease of bone—A chronic, painful bone disease in which the bones gradually become thickened, deformed (abnormal in shape), and weak. Also called *osteitis deformans*.

Palpitation—Rapid, forceful, or throbbing heart beat.

Pancreas—Large gland that secretes digestive enzymes into the intestine and hormones, including insulin, into the bloodstream.

Pancreatitis—Inflammation of the pancreas.

Pancytopenia—Reduction in the number of red cells, all types of white cells, and platelets in the blood.

Pap test—Test that helps detect cancerous or precancerous conditions or certain infections of the female genital tract (vagina, cervix, and uterus). The test, in which cells from this area are examined under a microscope, can also help determine whether the cells are working normally. Also called *Papanicolaou test*.

Paralysis agitans—*See* Parkinson's disease.

Parathyroid glands—Four small bodies situated beside the thyroid gland; secrete parathyroid hormone that regulates calcium and phosphorus metabolism.

Parenteral—Most often refers to injecting a medicine directly into a body part (for example, into a vein or a muscle).

Parkinsonism—*See* Parkinson's disease.

Parkinson's disease—Brain disease marked by tremor (shaking), stiffness, and difficulty in moving. In addition to brain disease, symptoms similar to those of Parkinson's disease may be caused by certain medications, head injury, or other causes. Also called *Parkinsonism, paralysis agitans,* or *shaking palsy*.

Patent ductus arteriosus (PDA)—Condition in babies in which an important fetal blood vessel fails to close as it should, resulting in faulty circulation and serious health problems.

Pathogen—Any microorganism that causes a disease.

Pediculicide—Medicine that kills lice.

Pediculosis—Infestation of the body, most often of the pubis (genital region) or scalp, with lice.

Pellagra—Disease caused by too little niacin, which results in scaly skin, diarrhea, and mental depression.

Pelvis—Bony structure of the skeleton that includes the hip bones and the bottom part of the backbone. It is located at the lowest part of the trunk, just above the legs.

Pemphigus—Skin disease marked by successive outbreaks of blisters.

Peptic ulcer—Open sore in the esophagus, stomach, or duodenum.

Peritoneum—Membrane lining the abdominal wall and covering the liver, stomach, spleen, gallbladder, and intestines.

Peritonitis—Inflammation of the peritoneum.

Peyronie's disease—Dense, fiber-like growth in the penis, which can be felt as an irregular hard lump, and which usually causes bending and pain when the penis is erect.

Pharynx—Space just behind the mouth that serves as a passageway for food from the mouth to the esophagus and for air from the nose and mouth to the larynx; the throat.

Phenol—Substance used as a preservative for some injectable medicines. It is also used as an antiseptic and pain reliever in some mouth and throat products (mouthwashes, throat lozenges, etc.)

Pheochromocytoma—Tumor of the adrenal medulla.

Phlebitis—Inflammation of a vein; often caused by a blood clot.

Phlegm—Thick mucus produced in the respiratory passages.

Piles—*See* Hemorrhoids.

Pituitary gland—Pea-sized body located at the base of the brain. It produces a number of hormones that are essential to normal body growth and functioning.

Placebo—Medicine that, unknown to the patient, has no active medicinal substance; its use may relieve or improve a condition because the patient believes it will. In some studies it may be used as a "control" against which the medicine being studied can be compared. Also called *sugar pill*.

Plaque, dental—Mixture of saliva, bacteria, and carbohydrates that forms on the teeth, leading to caries (cavities) and gum disease.

Platelet—Small, disk-shaped body found in the blood. Platelets play an important role in blood clotting.

Platelet aggregation inhibitor—Medicine used to help prevent the platelets in the blood from clumping together. This effect reduces the chance of heart attack or stroke in certain patients.

Pledget—Small mass of gauze or cotton used to apply or absorb fluids, cover a wound, or act as a plug to keep out air.

Pleura—Membrane covering the lungs and lining the chest cavity.

PMS—*See* Premenstrual syndrome.

Pneumococcal—Relating to certain bacteria that cause pneumonia and certain other infections.

Pneumocystis carinii—Organism that causes pneumocystis carinii pneumonia.

Pneumocystis carinii pneumonia—A lung infection of infants and weakened persons, including those with AIDS or those receiving drugs that weaken the immune system.

Polymorphous light eruption—A skin problem in certain people, which results from exposure to sunlight.

Polymyalgia rheumatica—A rheumatic disease, most common in elderly patients, which causes aching and stiffness in the shoulders and hips.

Polyp—Tumor or mass of tissue attached with a stalk or broad base; found in cavities such as the nose, uterus, or rectum.

Porphyria—A group of uncommon, usually inherited diseases of defective porphyrin metabolism.

Porphyrin—One of a number of chemicals that can combine with certain metal ions. Porphyrins occur in living organisms throughout nature (for example, as constituents in heme, chlorophyll, vitamin B_{12} and certain enzymes).

Potency—The strength of a medicine, chemical, or vitamin that will bring about a certain effect.

Pregnancy—Condition during which a woman is carrying a developing embryo or fetus in the uterus.

Pregnant—Containing one or more developing young within the body.

Premenstrual syndrome—Condition of physical or mental changes, including anxiety, headache, depression, bloating, and fatigue, that occurs in some women during the two-week period before menstruation.

Prenatal—Refers to the stage or period before birth.

Preservative—Substance added to a product to destroy or prevent the growth of microorganisms.

Prevent—To stop or to keep from happening.

Priapism—Prolonged abnormal, painful erection of the penis.

Prickling—Stinging or tingling sensation.

Proctitis—Inflammation of the rectum.

Progesterone—Natural steroid hormone responsible for preparing the uterus for pregnancy. If fertilization occurs, progesterone's actions carry on or maintain the pregnancy.

Progestin—A natural or synthetic hormone that has progesterone-like actions.

Progressive—In medicine, refers to an illness or condition that continues to worsen or become more severe with time.

Prolactin—Hormone secreted by the pituitary gland that stimulates and maintains milk flow in women following childbirth.

Prolactinoma—A pituitary tumor; results in secretion of excess prolactin.

Prophylactic—1. Agent or medicine used to prevent the occurrence of a specific condition. 2. Condom.

Prostate—Gland surrounding the neck of the male urethra just below the base of the bladder. It secretes a fluid that helps make up semen.

Prostatitis—Inflammation of the prostate gland.

Prosthesis—Any artificial substitute for a missing body part.

Protein—One of a group of compounds that make up the greatest part of plant and animal tissues. Enzymes, immunoglobulins, and several body structures, including muscles, are proteins. They are responsible for or involved in many body functions and are an essential nutrient in the diet.

Protozoa—Tiny, one-celled animals; some cause diseases in humans.

Psoralen—Chemical found in plants and used in certain perfumes and medicines. Exposure to a psoralen and then to sunlight may increase the risk of severe burning.

Psoriasis—Chronic skin disease marked by itchy, scaly, red patches.

Psychosis—Severe mental illness marked by loss of contact with reality, often involving delusions, hallucinations, and disordered thinking.

Puberty—Period in life during which sexual organs mature, making reproduction possible.

Pulmonary—Relating to the lungs.

Puncture—Wound or opening made by piercing with a pointed object or instrument.

Purity—Describes a measure of freedom from contamination.

Purpura—Tiny, purple-colored spots that appear at areas where bleeding into the skin occurs; similar to, but much smaller than, a bruise. May be caused by defects in the capillaries or a decreased number of platelets.

Pus—Yellowish liquid matter formed in certain infections, made up of leukocytes, bacteria, and dead tissue.

PUVA (psoralen plus ultraviolet light A)—Treatment for psoriasis and other conditions by use of a psoralen, such as methoxsalen or trioxsalen, and long-wave ultraviolet light.

Rachischisis—*See* Spina bifida.

Radiation—General term for any form of energy moving in all directions from a common center, including radioactive elements and x-ray tubes.

Radiopaque agent—Substance that makes it easier to see an area of the body with x-rays. Radiopaque agents are used to help diagnose a variety of medical problems.

Radiopharmaceutical—Radioactive agent used to diagnose certain medical problems or treat certain diseases.

Raynaud's syndrome—Condition caused by poor blood circulation in the hands; marked by numbness, tingling, and color change (white, blue, then red) in the fingers when they are exposed to cold.

Receptor—Structure within the cell or on the cell surface that binds with a specific substance to bring about a response.

Recommended Dietary Allowances (RDAs)—In the U.S., the amount of vitamins and minerals needed to provide for adequate nutrition in most healthy persons. RDAs for a given nutrient may vary depending on a person's age, sex, and physical condition (for example, pregnancy).

Recommended Nutrient Intakes (RNIs)—In Canada, values used to determine the amounts of vitamins, minerals, and protein needed to provide adequate nutrition and lessen the risk of chronic disease.

Rectal—Relating to the rectum.

Reduced calories—*See* Fewer calories.

Reduced cholesterol—*See* Less cholesterol.

Reduced fat—*See* Less fat.

Reduced saturated fat—*See* Less saturated fat.

Reduced sodium—*See* Less sodium.

Reduced sugar—*See* Less sugar.

Reference food—A basic food item. In food labeling, reference food is compared against the same food that has had something added to it or taken away from it.

Relapse—To fall back into illness after recovery has begun or after a remission.

Remission—State of an illness or disease during which symptoms lessen or disappear.

Renal—Relating to the kidneys.

Reproduction—Process in animals and plants that gives rise to new individuals or offspring.

Respiratory tract—The structures that are associated with breathing, including the nose, larynx, trachea, bronchial tree, and lungs.

Reye's syndrome—Serious disease affecting the liver and brain that sometimes occurs after a virus infection, such as influenza or chickenpox. It occurs most often in young children and teenagers, especially those who have been treated with aspirin during the illness. The first sign of Reye's syndrome is usually severe, prolonged vomiting.

Rheumatic heart disease—Heart disease marked by scarring and chronic inflammation of the heart and its valves, occurring after rheumatic fever.

Rhinitis—Inflammation of the mucous membrane inside the nose; often caused by an infection (such as a cold) or an allergy. Symptoms include runny or stuffy nose and sneezing.

Rickets—Bone disease usually caused by too little vitamin D, resulting in soft and malformed bones.

Rigidity—Lacking the ability to bend or be bent; stiffness.

Ringworm—*See* Tinea.

Risk—The possibility of injury or of suffering harm.

River blindness—Tropical disease produced by infection with worms of the Onchocerca type. The condition usually causes severe itching and may cause blindness.

Rosacea—Skin disease of the face, usually in middle-aged and older persons. Also called *adult acne.*

Saliva—Liquid secreted into the mouth by salivary glands; breaks down starch and moistens food for easy swallowing.

Sarcoidosis—Chronic disorder marked by enlarged lymph nodes in many parts of the body and inflammation, often in the muscles, eye, lungs, liver, and spleen.

Saturated fat—In chemistry, a fat that has all of the possible hydrogen atoms present on the carbon atoms and no double or triple bonds between the carbon atoms.

Saturated fat free—In food labeling, less than 0.5 grams of fat and less than 0.5 grams trans fatty acid per serving.

Scabicide—Medicine used to treat scabies (itch mite) infection.

Scabies—Contagious dermatitis caused by a mite burrowing into the skin; marked by tiny skin eruptions and severe itching.

Schistosomiasis—Tropical infection in which worms enter the skin from infested water and settle in the bladder or intestines, causing inflammation and scarring. Also called *bilharziasis.*

Schizophrenia—Severe mental disorder. The patient loses contact with reality, expresses disturbed thinking and behavior, and may become agitated (anxious and restless) or withdrawn.

Scintigram—Image obtained by photographing emissions made by a radiopharmaceutical introduced into the body.

Scleroderma—Chronic disease first seen as hardening, thickening, and shrinking of the skin; later, certain organs also are affected.

Scotoma—Area of decreased vision or total loss of vision in a part of the visual field; a blind spot.

Scrotum—Sac that holds the testes (male sex glands).

Scurvy—Disease caused by a deficiency of vitamin C (ascorbic acid), marked by bleeding gums, bleeding beneath the skin, and body weakness.

Sebaceous gland—Skin gland that secretes sebum.

Seborrhea—Skin condition caused by the excess release of sebum from the sebaceous glands, accompanied by dandruff and oily skin.

Sebum—Fatty secretion produced by sebaceous (oil) glands of the skin.

Secretion—1. Process in which a gland in the body or on the surface of the body releases a substance for use. 2. The substance released by the gland.

Sedative-hypnotic—Medicine used to treat excessive nervousness, restlessness, or insomnia.

Sedation—A profoundly relaxed or calmed state.

Seizure—A sudden attack, usually referring to contractions of muscles as seen in some forms of epilepsy or other disorders.

Semen—Fluid released from the penis at sexual climax. It is made up of sperm suspended in secretions from the reproductive tract.

Sensory—Relating to the senses (smell, taste, hearing, sight, and touch).

Severe—Of a great degree (for example, severe pain or distress).

Sexually transmitted disease (STD)—Any disease that is spread by sexual contact. Formerly called *venereal disease.*

Shaking palsy—*See* Parkinson's disease.

Shingles—*See* Herpes zoster.

Shock—A condition in which blood supply to the tissues is dangerously low, often caused by severe bleeding, overwhelming infection, or heart problems. Signs of shock include very low blood pressure, fast heartbeat, and mental confusion.

Short-acting—Refers to a medicine that is effective for a short amount of time.

Shunt—A passage that transfers or channels blood or other fluid from one part of the body to another. Shunts may occur naturally or they may be created for a specific purpose by a surgical procedure.

SIADH (secretion of inappropriate antidiuretic hormone) syndrome—Disease caused by excess production of antidiuretic hormone; the body retains (keeps) more fluid than normal. A syndrome similar to SIADH may also be a side effect of some medicines.

Sickle cell anemia—Hereditary disorder of chronic anemia caused by abnormal hemoglobin. The name of the disorder comes from the sickle-shaped red blood cells that are formed in the blood of patients. The disorder mainly affects people of African or Arabian ancestry.

Sign—Possible evidence of a disease or other change in condition that can be seen or measured by someone other than the person experiencing it (for example, a skin rash or high blood pressure). *See also* Symptom.

Sinusitis—Inflammation of a sinus.

Sjögren's syndrome—Condition usually occurring in older women, marked by dry eyes, dry mouth, inflamed salivary glands, and other problems such as rheumatoid arthritis, systemic lupus erythematosus (SLE), or scleroderma.

Skeletal muscle relaxant—Medicine used to relax certain muscles and help relieve the pain and discomfort caused by strains, sprains, or other injury to the muscles.

Skeleton—The bony framework of the body that supports the soft tissues and organs.

SLE—*See* Lupus erythematosus, systemic.

Sloughing of skin—Peeling away of dead skin tissue (for example, after a sunburn).

Sodium fluoride—A chemical that makes teeth stronger and helps prevent cavities; in many communities, small amounts are added to the drinking water.

Sodium free—In food labeling, less than 5 milligrams of sodium per serving.

Soluble—Able to be dissolved in a fluid.

Soothe—To relieve or make less painful.

Spasticity—Increase in normal muscular tone, causing stiff, awkward movements.

Spastic paralysis—Paralysis marked by muscle rigidity or spasticity in the part of the body that is paralyzed.

Sperm—Mature male reproductive or sex cell. When a sperm fertilizes an ovum, a new organism begins developing.

Spermicide—Substance that kills sperm.

Spina bifida—Birth defect caused by failure of the neural tube of the fetus, a structure that develops into the backbone, to close normally. In many cases, part of the infant's spinal cord and its coverings are not completely surrounded by the spinal column (backbone). Also called *rachischisis*.

Spinal column—The column made up of vertebrae that extends from the base of the skull to the end of the trunk. Also called *spine* or *backbone*. It helps to support the body and protects the spinal cord, which passes through it.

Spine—*See* Spinal column.

STD—*See* Sexually transmitted disease.

Stenosis—Abnormal narrowing of a canal or duct of the body.

Sterility—1. Inability to produce offspring. 2. The state of being free of living microorganisms.

Stimulant, respiratory—Medicine used to stimulate breathing.

Stimulate—To promote greater activity of a body part or function.

Stomatitis—Inflammation of the mucous membrane of the mouth; causes ulcers or sores that may be painful.

Stool—*See* Feces.

Strength—1. In relation to medicines, a measure of the amount of active ingredient present. 2. In nutrition, the measure of a vitamin's health value.

Streptokinase—Enzyme that dissolves blood clots.

Stroke—Very serious event in which blood flow to the brain is stopped; an artery to the brain may become clogged by a blood clot or it may burst and cause hemorrhage. Stroke can affect speech, memory, and behavior, and may result in paralysis. Also called *apoplexy*.

Stye—Infection of one or more sebaceous glands of the eyelid, marked by swelling.

Subcutaneous—Under the skin.

Sublingual—Under the tongue. A sublingual medicine is taken by placing it under the tongue and letting it slowly dissolve.

Sudden infant death syndrome (SIDS)—Sudden death of an apparently well infant from an unknown cause; death usually occurs during sleep. Also called *crib death* or *cot death*.

Sugar diabetes—*See* Diabetes mellitus.

Sugar free—In food labeling, less than 0.5 grams of sugar per serving.

Sugar pill—*See* Placebo.

Sulfite—Type of preservative; causes allergic reactions, such as asthma, in sensitive people.

Sunscreen—Substance that blocks ultraviolet light and helps prevent sunburn when applied to the skin.

Suppository—Mass of medicated material shaped for insertion into a body cavity, such as the rectum or vagina. A suppository is solid at room temperature but melts at body temperature or dissolves in body fluids.

Suppressant—Medicine that slows or stops an action or condition.

Suspension—A form of medicine in which the drug particles are mixed with a liquid but not dissolved in it. When left standing, some suspensions may separate, with the particles settling at the bottom of the container and the liquid rising to the top. Most suspensions must be shaken before use.

Symptom—Possible evidence of a disease or other change in condition that is apparent only to the person experiencing it (for example, a headache). *See also* Sign.

Syncope—Sudden loss of consciousness due to inadequate blood flow to the brain; fainting.

Syndrome—Group of signs and symptoms that occur together and characterize a particular disorder.

Synthetic—A substance that is manufactured rather than occurring naturally.

Syphilis—An infectious disease, usually transmitted by sexual contact. The three stages of the disease may be separated by months or years.

Syringe—Medical device used to inject liquids into the body or remove material from a part of the body. Some types are used to help wash out a body cavity.

Systemic—Having general effects throughout the body; applies to most medicines when taken by mouth or given by injection into a blood vessel or a muscle.

Tachycardia—Abnormal rapid beating of the heart, usually at a rate over 100 beats per minute in adults.

Tardive dyskinesia—Slow, involuntary movements, often of the tongue, lips, or arms, usually brought on by certain drugs.

TB—*See* Tuberculosis.

Temporomandibular joint (TMJ)—Hinge that connects the lower jaw to the skull.

Tendinitis—Inflammation of a tendon.

Tendon—Band of tough tissue that attaches a muscle to bone.

Teratogenic—Causing abnormal development in an embryo or fetus, resulting in birth defects.

Testicle—Male sex organ that produces sperm and testosterone.

Testosterone—Principal male sex hormone.

Tetany—Condition marked by spasm and twitching of the muscles, particularly those of the hands, feet, and face; caused by a decrease in the calcium ion concentration in the blood.

Therapeutic—Relating to the treatment of a specific condition.

Thimerosal—Chemical used as a preservative in some medicines, and as an antiseptic and disinfectant; contains mercury.

Thorax—The part of the body between the neck and abdomen; the chest.

Thrombolytic agent—Substance that dissolves blood clots.

Thrombophlebitis—Inflammation of a vein accompanied by the formation of a blood clot.

Thrombus—Blood clot that obstructs a cavity of the heart or a blood vessel.

Thrush—*See* Candidiasis of the mouth.

Thyroid gland—Gland in the lower front of the neck. It releases thyroid hormones, which control body metabolism.

Thyrotoxicosis—Condition resulting from excessive amounts of thyroid hormones in the blood, causing increased metabolism, fast heartbeat, tremors, nervousness, bulging eyes, and increased sweating.

Tic—Repeated involuntary movement or spasm of a muscle.

Tic douloureux—*See* Neuralgia, trigeminal.

Tinea—Fungus infection of the surface of the skin, particularly the scalp, feet, and nails. Also called *ringworm.*

Tinnitus—Ringing in the ears.

Tone—In medicine, the normal amount of tension or resistance to stretching of a tissue, such as a muscle or the skin.

Topical—In medicine, refers to a medicine being applied to a particular surface area, usually the skin.

Tourette's disorder—Rare condition beginning in childhood, marked by tics and other unnecessary movements and barks, sniffs, or grunts (may be swearing). Also called *Gilles de la Tourette syndrome.*

Toxemia—Blood poisoning caused by bacterial production of toxins.

Toxemia of pregnancy—Condition occurring in pregnant women marked by hypertension, edema, excess protein in the urine, convulsions, and possibly coma.

Toxic—Poisonous; related to or caused by a toxin or poison.

Toxin—A substance that may cause damage to body tissues or disturb body functions, causing illness or even death; a poison.

Toxoplasmosis—Disease caused by a protozoa in the blood, usually transmitted to humans from cats or by eating raw meat; generally the symptoms are mild and self-limited.

Tracheostomy—A surgical opening through the throat into the trachea (windpipe) to bypass an obstruction to breathing.

Trait—In genetics, any characteristic that is inherited.

Tranquilizer—Medicine that produces a calming effect. It is used to relieve mental anxiety and tension.

Transdermal—A method of applying a medicine to the skin that produces a prolonged systemic effect rather than a local effect. The medicine is contained in a special patch, disk, or ointment, from which it slowly passes through the skin and is absorbed into the bloodstream, which carries it through the body.

Transmit—In medicine, to pass or spread infection or disease from one person to another.

Tremble—Shake or shiver.

Trichomoniasis—Infection of the vagina and the male genital tract resulting in inflammation of genital tissues; symptoms may include itching, burning (in men, burning while urinating), and discharge. The infection can be passed between sex partners.

Triglyceride—A molecular form in which fats are present in food and the body; triglycerides are stored in the body as fat.

Troche—*See* Lozenge.

Trypanosome fever—*See* Trypanosomiasis, African.

Trypanosomiasis, African—Tropical disease, transmitted by tsetse fly bites, which causes fever, headache, and chills, followed by enlarged lymph nodes and anemia. Months or even years later, the disease affects the central nervous system, causing drowsiness and lethargy, coma, and death. Also called *African sleeping sickness.*

Tuberculosis (TB)—Infectious disease that most commonly affects the lungs, producing symptoms that include cough, fever, night sweats, weight loss, and spitting up blood.

Tumor—Abnormal growth or enlargement in or on a part of the body.

Tyramine—Chemical present in many foods and beverages. Its structure and action in the body are similar to epinephrine.

Ulcer—Open sore or break in the skin or mucous membrane; often fails to heal and is accompanied by inflammation.

Ulcerative colitis—Chronic, recurrent inflammation and ulceration of the colon.

Ulceration—1. Formation or development of an ulcer. 2. Condition of an area marked with ulcers loosely associated with one another.

Ultraviolet rays—Invisible radiation having a wavelength shorter than that of visible light but longer than that of x-rays. These rays are responsible for sunburns, tanning, damage to skin cells, and skin cancers.

Underactive thyroid—*See* Hypothyroidism.

Ureter—Tube through which urine passes from the kidney to the bladder.

Urethra—Tube through which urine passes from the bladder to the outside of the body.

Uric acid—Product of protein metabolism, excreted in the urine. High levels of uric acid in the body can lead to gout and kidney stones.

Urination—Act of passing urine from the bladder.

Urine—Fluid containing waste products that is formed and excreted by the kidneys. It is then stored in the urinary bladder until the individual urinates.

Urticaria—An eruption of itching wheals on the skin. Also called *hives.*

USRDA—Labeling term formerly used to indicate how much of a nutrient a serving provided. This term is now stated as Daily Value (DV).

Uterus—Hollow organ in the female in which the fetus develops until birth.

Vaccine—Preparation, usually made from specially treated microorganisms or parts of microorganisms, that is given to stimulate production of antibodies that protect against the disease that the microorganisms cause.

Vaccinia—The skin and sometimes body reactions associated with smallpox vaccine. Also called *cowpox.*

Vagina—Passage in the female leading from the cervix of the uterus to the outside of the body.

Vaginal—Relating to the vagina.

Varicella—Very infectious virus disease marked by fever and itchy rash that develops into blisters and then scabs. Also called *chickenpox.*

Vasoconstrictor—Medicine or enzyme that causes smooth muscles of blood vessels to contract, raising blood pressure.

Vascular—Relating to the blood vessels.

Vasodilator—Medicine that dilates the blood vessels, permitting increased blood flow. Sometimes used to lower blood pressure.

Vasopressin—A hormone that prevents excessive water loss by its action on the kidney and raises blood pressure by constricting small blood vessels. Also called *antidiuretic hormone, ADH.*

Vein—Blood vessel that carries blood from various parts of the body toward the heart.

Venous—Relating to veins.

Ventricular fibrillation—Life-threatening condition of fine, quivering, irregular movements of many muscle fibers of certain heart muscle; replaces the normal heart beat and interrupts pumping function.

Ventricle—A small cavity, such as one of the two lower chambers of the heart or one of the several cavities of the brain.

Vertebra—Any of the thirty-three bones that make up the spinal column.

Vertigo—Sensation of motion, usually whirling, or dizziness, either of oneself or of one's surroundings.

Very low sodium—In food labeling, 35 milligrams or less of sodium per serving. However, for small servings (30 grams or less or 2 tablespoons or less), very low sodium is 35 milligrams or less of sodium per 50 grams of the food.

Veterinary—Relating to animals and their diseases and treatment.

Virus—Any of a group of simple microbes too small to be seen by a light microscope. They grow and reproduce only in living cells. Viruses cause many diseases in humans, including the common cold.

Visual—Relating to vision or sight.

Vitamin—Any of a group of substances, needed in small amounts only, for growth and health. Vitamins are usually found naturally in food, but may also be man-made.

Vitamin, natural—A vitamin that comes from natural sources such as plants.

Vitamin, synthetic—A vitamin that does not come from natural sources, but instead is man-made.

Vitamins, fat-soluble—Vitamins that can be dissolved in fat (vitamins A, D, E, K). They are stored in fat tissue.

Vitamins, water-soluble—Vitamins that can be dissolved in water (vitamin C and the B-complex vitamins). They are stored in small amounts by the body.

Vitiligo—Condition in which some areas of skin lose pigment and turn white. Also called *leukoderma*.

von Willebrand's disease—Hereditary blood disorder characterized by delayed blood clotting, which leads to excessive bleeding even after minor injuries.

Wart—Small, usually hard, benign growth on the skin, caused by a virus.

Wasting—Gradual loss of weight and strength.

Water diabetes—*See* Diabetes insipidus.

Water pill—*See* Diuretic.

Wheal—Temporary, small, raised area of the skin, usually accompanied by itching or burning; welt.

Wheezing—A whistling sound made when there is difficulty in breathing.

White mouth—*See* Candidiasis of the mouth.

Wilson's disease—Inborn defect in the body's ability to process copper. Too much copper may accumulate and lead to jaundice, cirrhosis, mental retardation, or symptoms like those of Parkinson's disease.

Without added sugar—*See* No added sugar.

Zollinger-Ellison syndrome—Disorder in which a tumor of the pancreas causes overproduction of stomach acid, leading to diarrhea and ulcers.

Appendix I

ADDITIONAL PRODUCTS AND USES

The following information is new information that could not be included in the text of this book. The information should be available to review in the respective monograph by accessing the *USP DI* Updates Online website (see the back cover of book for details on accessing the site). Refer to the Glossary for definitions of medical and technical terms.

GENERIC NAME (Brand name)	DOSAGE FORM(S)	USE	COMMENTS
Abacavir/Lamivudine/Zidovudine (*Trizivir* [U.S. and Canada])	Tablets	HIV antiviral	New drug
Alemtuzumab (*Campath-1H* [U.S.])	Injection	Transplantation; Lymphoid cancer	New drug
Almotriptan (*Axert* [U.S. and Canada])	Tablets	Migraine headache	New drug
Bimatoprost (*Lumigan* [U.S. and Canada])	Ophthalmic solution	Glaucoma	New drug
Capecitabine (*Xeloda* [U.S. and Canada])	Tablets	Antineoplastic	New FDA-approved use
Cerivastatin (*Baycol* [U.S. and Canada])	Tablets	Hypercholesterolemia	New dosing information
Dornase Alfa (*Pulmozyme* [U.S. and Canada])	Solution for Inhalation	Cystic fibrosis	New dosing and allergy information
Drospirenone/Ethinyl Estradiol (*Yasmin* [U.S. and Canada])	Tablets	Contraception; Premenstrual dysphoric disorder	New drug
Gemtuzumab (*Mylotarg* [U.S. and Canada])	Injection	Acute myeloid leukemia	New warning; contraindicated with gemfibrozil
Hyaluronidase (*Supartz* [U.S.])	Injection	Osteoarthritis of the knee	New drug
Hydroxyurea (*Hydrea* [U.S. and Canada])	Capsule	Antineoplastic	Additional dosage form
Ipratropium/Albuterol (*Duoneb* [U.S.])	Solution for Inhalation	Bronchospasm	Additional dosage form
Lamivudine (*Epivir* [U.S. and Canada])	Tablets Oral solution	HIV antiviral; Chronic hepatitis B	New warning and precautions: new dosage information
Levomethadyl (*Orlaam* [U.S.])	Oral solution	Opioid dependency	New black box warning; cardiac effects
Lopinavir/Ritonavir (*Kaletra* [U.S. and Canada])	Capsules Oral solution	HIV antiviral	New pediatric dosage recommendations
Mesalamine (*Canasa* [U.S.])	Suppository	Ulcerative proctitis	New FDA-approved use
Mesoridazine (*Serentil* [U.S. and Canada])	Tablets	Antipsychotic	New FDA-approved use
Midazolam (*Versed* [U.S. and Canada])	for Injection	Sedation; Anxiolysis	New dosage form

© 2002 MICROMEDEX Thomson Healthcare

Additional Products and Uses *(continued)*

GENERIC NAME (Brand name)	DOSAGE FORM(S)	USE	COMMENTS
Minocycline—(Dental) (*Arestin* [U.S.])	Dry Powder	Periodontitis	New dosage form
Nefazodone (*Serzone* [U.S.])	Tablets	Depression	New warning; visual disturbances noted
Pantoprazole (*Protonix* [U.S. and Canada])	Tablets	Gastroesophageal reflux disease; Gastric and duodenal ulcer	New FDA-approved use
Peginterferon Alfa-2b (*PEG-Intron* [U.S.])	Injection	Chronic hepatitis C	New drug
Saquinavir (*Fortovase*; *Invirase* [U.S.])	Capsules	HIV antiviral	New black box warning
Terbinafine (*Lamisil* [U.S.])	Tablets	Antifungal	New dosage form
Thiabendazole (*Mintezol* [U.S.])	Tablets Suspension	Anthelmintic	New FDA-approved use
Travoprost (*Travatan* [U.S.])	Ophthalmic solution	Glaucoma	New drug
Valganciclovir (*Valcyte* [U.S. and Canada])	Tablets	CMV retinitis	New drug
Zidovudine (*Retrovir* [U.S. and Canada])	Capsules Tablets Oral solution	HIV antiviral	New precautions: lactic acidosis and hepatomegaly with steatosis

Appendix II

POISON CONTROL CENTER LISTING

The following is a list of emergency telephone numbers for United States and Canadian poison control centers, as of June, 2000.

UNITED STATES

Center names in bold print are Certified Regional Poison Centers. Source: American Association of Poison Control Centers.

ALABAMA
Alabama Poison Center
2503 Phoenix Drive
Tuscaloosa, AL 35405
Emergency Phone: (800) 462-0800 (AL only);
(205) 345-0600

Regional Poison Control Center
Children's Hospital
1600 7th Avenue South
Birmingham, AL 35233
Emergency Phone: (800) 292-6678 (AL only);
(205) 933-4050

ALASKA
Anchorage Poison Control Center
3200 Providence Drive
P.O. Box 196604
Anchorage, AK 99519-6604
Emergency Phone: (800) 478-3193; (907) 261-3193

ARIZONA
Arizona Poison & Drug Info Center
Arizona Health Sciences Center
Room 1156
1501 North Campbell Avenue
Tucson, AZ 85724
Emergency Phone: (800) 362-0101 (AZ only);
(520) 626-6016

Samaritan Regional Poison Center
Good Samaritan Regional Medical Center
1111 E. McDowell--Ancillary 1
Phoenix, AZ 85006
Emergency Phone: (800) 362-0101 (AZ only);
(602) 253-3334

ARKANSAS
Arkansas Poison & Drug Information Center
College of Pharmacy
University of Arkansas for Medical Sciences
Mail Slot 522
4301 W. Markham
Little Rock, AR 72205
Emergency Phone: (800) 376-4766
TTY/TDD: (800) 641-3805

CALIFORNIA
California Poison Control System - Fresno/Madera Division
Valley Children's Hospital
9300 Valley Children's Place, MB15
Madera, CA 93638-8762
Emergency Phone: (800) 876-4766 (CA only)
TTY/TDD: (800) 972-3323

California Poison Control System - Sacramento Division
UC Davis Medical Center
2315 Stockton Boulevard
Sacramento, CA 95817
Emergency Phone: (800) 876-4766 (CA only)
TTY/TDD: (800) 972-3323

California Poison Control System - San Diego Division
University of California, San Diego, Medical Center
200 West Arbor Drive
San Diego, CA 92103-8925
Emergency Phone: (800) 876-4766 (CA only)
TTY/TDD: (800) 972-3323

California Poison Control System - San Francisco Division
UCSF Box 1369
1001 Potrero Avenue, Room 1E86
San Francisco, CA 94143-1369
Emergency Phone: (800) 876-4766 (CA only)
TTY/TDD: (800) 972-3323

COLORADO
Rocky Mountain Poison & Drug Center
1010 Yosemite Circle
Building 752
Denver, CO 80230-6800
Emergency Phone: (800) 332-3073 (CO only/outside metro area); (303) 739-1123 (Denver metro)

CONNECTICUT
Connecticut Poison Control Center
University of Connecticut Health Center
263 Farmington Avenue
Farmington, CT 06030-5365
Emergency Phone: (800) 343-2722 (CT only);
(860) 679-3456
TTY/TDD: (866) 218-5372 (toll-free)

DELAWARE
The Poison Control Center
3535 Market Street, Suite 985
Philadelphia, PA 19104-3309
Emergency Phone: (800) 722-7112;
(215) 386-2100
TTY/TDD: (215) 590-8789

DISTRICT OF COLUMBIA
National Capital Poison Center
3201 New Mexico Avenue, NW
Suite 310
Washington, DC 20016
Emergency Phone: (202) 625-3333
TTY/TDD: (202) 362-8563

FLORIDA
Florida Poison Information Center - Jacksonville
655 West Eighth Street
Jacksonville, FL 32209
Emergency Phone: (800) 282-3171 (FL only);
(904) 244-4480
TTY/TDD: (800) 282-3171 (FL only)

Florida Poison Information Center - Miami
University of Miami
Department of Pediatrics
Jackson Memorial Medical Center
P.O. Box 016960 (R-131)
Miami, FL 33101
Emergency Phone: (800) 282-3171 (FL only);
(305) 585-5253

Florida Poison Information Center - Tampa
Tampa General Hospital
P.O. Box 1289
Tampa, FL 33601
Emergency Phone: (800) 282-3171 (FL only);
(813) 844-4444

GEORGIA
Georgia Poison Center
Hughes Spalding Children's Hospital
Grady Health System
80 Butler Street, SE
P.O. Box 26066
Atlanta, GA 30335-3801
Emergency Phone: (800) 282-5846; (404) 616-9000
TTY/TDD: (404) 616-9287 (TDD)

HAWAII
Hawaii Poison Center
1319 Punahou Street
Honolulu, HI 96826
Emergency Phone: (808) 941-4411 (Oahu)
(800) 362-3585 (outer islands toll free)

IDAHO
Rocky Mountain Poison & Drug Center
1010 Yosemite Circle
Building 752
Denver, CO 80230-6800
Emergency Phone: (800) 860-0620 (ID only)

ILLINOIS
Illinois Poison Center
222 S. Riverside Plaza, Suite 1900
Chicago, IL 60606
Emergency Phone: (800) 942-5969 (IL only)
TTY/TDD: (312) 906-6185

INDIANA
Indiana Poison Center
Methodist Hospital
Clarian Health Partners
I-65 at 21st Street
Indianapolis, IN 46206-1367
Emergency Phone: (800) 382-9097 (IN only);
(317) 929-2323
TTY/TDD: (317) 929-2336 (TTY)

IOWA
Iowa Statewide Poison Control Center
St. Luke's Regional Medical Center
2720 Stone Park Boulevard
Sioux City, IA 51104
Emergency Phone: (800) 352-2222; (712)
277-2222

KANSAS
Mid-America Poison Control Center
University of Kansas Medical Center
3901 Rainbow Blvd., Room B-400
Kansas City, KS 66160-7231
Emergency Phone: (800) 332-6633 (KS
only);
(913) 588-6633
TTY/TDD: (913) 588-6639 (TDD)

KENTUCKY
Kentucky Regional Poison Center
Medical Towers South, Suite 572
234 East Gray Street
Louisville, KY 40202
Emergency Phone: (800) 722-5725; (502)
589-8222

LOUISIANA
**Louisiana Drug and Poison Information
   Center**
University of Louisiana at Monroe
College of Pharmacy
Sugar Hall
Monroe, LA 71209-6430
Emergency Phone: (800) 256-9822 (LA only)

MAINE
Maine Poison Center
Maine Medical Center
22 Bramhall Street
Portland, ME 04102
Emergency Phone: (800) 442-6305 (ME
only);
(207) 871-4720
TTY/TDD: (877) 299-4447 (ME only); (207)
871-2879

MARYLAND
Maryland Poison Center
University of MD at Baltimore
School of Pharmacy
20 North Pine Street, PH 772
Baltimore, MD 21201
Emergency Phone: (800) 492-2414 (MD
only);
(410) 706-7701
TTY/TDD: (410) 706-1858 (TDD)

National Capital Poison Center
3201 New Mexico Avenue, NW
Suite 310
Washington, DC 20016
Emergency Phone: (202) 625-3333
TTY/TDD: (202) 362-8563 (TTY)

MASSACHUSETTS
**Regional Center for Poison Control and
   Prevention Serving Massachusetts
   & Rhode Island**
300 Longwood Avenue
Boston, MA 02115
Emergency Phone: (800) 682-9211 (MA & RI
only); (617) 232-2120
TTY/TDD: (888) 244-5313

MICHIGAN
Children's Hospital of Michigan
Regional Poison Control Center
4160 John Harper Professional Office
Building
Suite 616
Detroit, MI 48201
Emergency Phone: (800) 764-7661 (MI
only);
(313) 745-5711
TTY/TDD: (800) 356-3232 (TDD)

**DeVos Children's Hospital Regional
   Poison Center**
1840 Wealthy S.E.
Grand Rapids, MI 49506-2968
Emergency Phone: (800) 764-7661 (MI only)
TTY/TDD: (800) 356-3232 (TTY)

MINNESOTA
Hennepin Regional Poison Center
Hennepin County Medical Center
701 Park Avenue
Minneapolis, MN 55415
Emergency Phone: (800) 222-1222 (MN)
(800) POISON1 (SD only)
TTY/TDD: (612) 904-4691 (TTY)

MISSISSIPPI
Mississippi Regional Poison Control Center
University of Mississippi Medical Center
2500 N. State Street
Jackson, MS 39216
Emergency Phone: (601) 354-7660

MISSOURI
**Cardinal Glennon Children's Hospital
   Regional Poison Center**
1465 S. Grand Blvd.
St. Louis, MO 63104
Emergency Phone: (800) 366-8888; (314)
772-5200

MONTANA
Rocky Mountain Poison & Drug Center
1010 Yosemite Circle
Building 752
Denver, CO 80230-6800
Emergency Phone: (800) 525-5042 (MT
only)

NEBRASKA
The Poison Center
Children's Hospital
8200 Dodge Street
Omaha, NE 68114
Emergency Phone: (800) 955-9119 (NE &
WY only); (402) 955-5555

NEVADA
Oregon Poison Center
Oregon Health Sciences University
3181 SW Sam Jackson Park Road
CB550
Portland, OR 97201
Emergency Phone: (503) 494-8968

Rocky Mountain Poison & Drug Center
1010 Yosemite Circle
Building 752
Denver, CO 80230-6800
Emergency Phone: (800) 446-6179 (NV
only)

NEW HAMPSHIRE
New Hampshire Poison Information Center
Dartmouth-Hitchcock Medical Center
One Medical Center Drive
Lebanon, NH 03756
Emergency Phone: (800) 562-8236 (NH
only);
(603) 650-8000

NEW JERSEY
**New Jersey Poison Information and
   Education System**
201 Lyons Avenue
Newark, NJ 07112
Emergency Phone: (800) POISON-1 (NJ
only)
TTY/TDD: (973) 926-8008

NEW MEXICO
**New Mexico Poison & Drug Information
   Center**
Health Science Center Library
Room 130
University of New Mexico
Albuquerque, NM 87131-1076
Emergency Phone: (800) 432-6866 (NM
only);
(505) 272-2222

NEW YORK
Central New York Poison Center
750 East Adams Street
Syracuse, NY 13210
Emergency Phone: (800) 252-5655 (NY
only);
(315) 476-4766

**Finger Lakes Regional Poison & Drug Info
   Center**
University of Rochester Medical Center
601 Elmwood Avenue
P.O. Box 321
Rochester, NY 14642
Emergency Phone: (800) 333-0542 (NY
only);
(716) 275-3232
TTY/TDD: (716) 273-3854 (TTY)

Hudson Valley Regional Poison Center
Phelps Memorial Hospital Center
701 North Broadway
Sleepy Hollow, NY 10591
Emergency Phone: (800) 336-6997 (NY
only);
(914) 366-3030

**Long Island Regional Poison & Drug
   Information Center**
Winthrop University Hospital
259 First Street
Mineola, NY 11501
Emergency Phone: (516) 542-2323; (516)
663-2650
TTY/TDD: (516) 924-8811 (TDD Suffolk);
(516) 747-3323 (TDD Nassau)

New York City Poison Ctrl Center
NYC Department of Labs
455 First Avenue
Room 123, Box 81
New York, NY 10016
Emergency Phone: (800) 210-3985; (212)
340-4494;
TTY/TDD: (212) 689-9014 (TDD)

**Western New York Regional Poison
Control Center**
Children's Hospital of Buffalo
219 Bryant Street
Buffalo, NY 14222
Emergency Phone: (800) 888-7655; (716)
878-7654

NORTH CAROLINA
Carolinas Poison Center
Carolinas Medical Center
5000 Airport Center Parkway, Suite B
Charlotte, NC 28208
Emergency Phone: (800) 848-6946; (704)
355-4000

NORTH DAKOTA
North Dakota Poison Information Center
Meritcare Medical Center
720 4th Street North
Fargo, ND 58122
Emergency Phone: (800) 732-2200 (ND,
MN, SD only);
(701) 234-5575

OHIO
Central Ohio Poison Center
700 Children's Drive, Room L032
Columbus, OH 43205
Emergency Phone: (800) 682-7625 (OH
only);
(800) 762-0727 (Dayton, OH only)
TTY/TDD: (614) 228-2272

**Cincinnati Drug & Poison Information
Center**
Regional Poison Control System
3333 Burnet Avenue
Vernon Place - 3rd Floor
Cincinnati, OH 45229
Emergency Phone: (800) 872-5111 (OH
only);
(513) 558-5111

Greater Cleveland Poison Control Center
11100 Euclid Avenue
Cleveland, OH 44106-6010
Emergency Phone: (888) 231-4455 (OH only);
(216) 231-4455

OKLAHOMA
Oklahoma Poison Control Center
Children's Hospital of Oklahoma
940 N.E. 13th Street
Oklahoma City, OK 73104
Emergency Phone: (800) 764-7661 (OK only);
(405) 271-5454
TTY/TDD: (405) 271-1122

OREGON
Oregon Poison Center
Oregon Health Sciences University
3181 SW Sam Jackson Park Road, CB550
Portland, OR 97201
Emergency Phone: (800) 452-7165 (OR
only);
(503) 494-8968

PENNSYLVANIA
Central Pennsylvania Poison Center
Pennsylvania State University
The Milton S. Hershey Medical Center
500 University Drive
MC H043 PO Box 850
Hershey, PA 17033-0850
Emergency Phone: (800) 521-6110; (717)
531-6111
TTY/TDD: (717) 531-8335

Pittsburgh Poison Center
Children's Hospital of Pittsburgh
3705 Fifth Avenue
Pittsburgh, PA 15213
Emergency Phone: (412) 681-6669

The Poison Control Center
3535 Market Street, Suite 985
Philadelphia, PA 19104-3309
Emergency Phone: (800) 722-7112; (215)
386-2100;
TTY/TDD: (215) 590-8789

PUERTO RICO
San Jorge Children's Hospital Poison Center
Calle San Jorge #252
Santurce, Puerto Rico 00912
Emergency Phone: (787) 726-5674

RHODE ISLAND
**Regional Center for Poison Control and
Prevention Serving Massachusetts &
Rhode Island**
300 Longwood Avenue
Boston, MA 02115
Emergency Phone: (800) 682-9211 (MA & RI
only); (617) 232-2120
TTY/TDD: (888) 244-5313

SOUTH CAROLINA
Palmetto Poison Center
College of Pharmacy
University of South Carolina
Columbia, SC 29208
Emergency Phone: (800) 922-1117 (SC
only);
(803) 777-1117

SOUTH DAKOTA
Hennepin Regional Poison Center
Hennepin County Medical Center
701 Park Avenue
Minneapolis, MN 55415
Emergency Phone: (800) POISON1 (SD
only);
TTY/TDD: (612) 904-4691 (TTY)

TENNESSEE
Middle Tennessee Poison Center
501 Oxford House
1161 21st Avenue South
Nashville, TN 37232-4632
Emergency Phone: (800) 288-9999 (TN
only);
(615) 936-2034 (Greater Nashville)
TTY/TDD: (615) 936-2047 (TDD)

Southern Poison Center
University of Tennessee
875 Monroe Avenue
Suite 104
Memphis, TN 38163
Emergency Phone: (800) 288-9999 (TN
only);
(901) 528-6048

TEXAS
Central Texas Poison Center
Scott and White Memorial Hospital
2401 South 31st Street
Temple, TX 76508
Emergency Phone: (800) POISON-1(TX
only);
(254) 724-7401

North Texas Poison Center
Texas Poison Center Network
Parkland Health & Hospital System
5201 Harry Hines Blvd.
P.O. Box 35926
Dallas, TX 75235
Emergency Phone: (800) 764-7661(TX only)

South Texas Poison Center
Univ of Texas Health Science Ctr - San
Antonio
Department of Surgery
Mail Code 7849
7703 Floyd Curl Drive
San Antonio, TX 78229-3900
Emergency Phone: (800) 764-7661 (TX only)
TTY/TDD: (800) 764-7661 (TX only)

Southeast Texas Poison Center
The University of Texas Medical Branch
3.112 Trauma Building
Galveston, TX 77555-1175
Emergency Phone: (800) 764-7661 (TX
only);
(409) 765-1420
TTY/TDD: (800) 764-7661 (TX only)

Texas Panhandle Poison Center
1501 S. Coulter
Amarillo, TX 79106
Emergency Phone: (800) 764-7661 (TX only)

West Texas Regional Poison Center
Thomason Hospital
4815 Alameda Avenue
El Paso, TX 79905
Emergency Phone: (800) 764-7661 (TX
only)

UTAH
Utah Poison Control Center
410 Chipeta Way, Suite 230
Salt Lake City, UT 84108
Emergency Phone: (800) 456-7707 (UT
only);
(801) 581-2151

VERMONT
Vermont Poison Center
Fletcher Allen Health Care
111 Colchester Avenue
Burlington, VT 05401
Emergency Phone: (877) 658-3456 (toll free);
(802) 658-3456

VIRGINIA
Blue Ridge Poison Center
University of Virginia Health System
PO Box 800774
Charlottesville, VA 22908-0774
Emergency Phone: (800) 451-1428 (VA only);
(804) 924-5543

National Capital Poison Center
3201 New Mexico Avenue, NW
Suite 310
Washington, DC 20016
Emergency Phone: (202) 625-3333
TTY/TDD: (202) 362-8563

© 2002 MICROMEDEX Thomson Healthcare

Virginia Poison Center
Medical College of Virginia Hospitals
Virginia Commonwealth University
P.O. Box 980522
Richmond, VA 23298-0522
Emergency Phone: (800) 552-6337; (804)
828-9123

WASHINGTON
Washington Poison Center
155 NE 100th Street, Suite 400
Seattle, WA 98125-8012
Emergency Phone: (800) 732-6985 (WA
only);
(206) 526-2121
TTY/TDD: (206) 517-2394 (TDD);
(800) 572-0638 (TDD WA only)

WEST VIRGINIA
West Virginia Poison Center
3110 MacCorkle Ave, S.E.
Charleston, WV 25304
Emergency Phone: (800) 642-3625 (WV
only)

WISCONSIN
Children's Hospital of Wisconsin Poison
Center
P.O. Box 1997, Mail Station 677A
Milwaukee, WI 53201-1997
Emergency Phone: (800) 815-8855 (WI
only);
(414) 266-2222
TTY/TDD: (414) 266-2542

University of Wisconsin Hospital & Clinics
Poison Control Center
600 Highland Avenue, F6/133
Madison, WI 53792
Emergency Phone: (800) 815-8855 (WI
only);
(608) 262-3702

WYOMING
The Poison Center
Children's Hospital
8200 Dodge Street
Omaha, NE 68114
Emergency Phone: (800) 955-9119 (NE &
WY only);
(402) 955-5555

ANIMAL POISON CENTER

ASPCA
Animal Poison Control Center
1717 South Philo Road
Suite 36
Urbana, IL 61802
Emergency Phone: (888) 426-4435

CANADA
Source: Canadian Poison Control Centres.

ALBERTA
P.A.D.I.S.
Foothills General Hospital
1403 29th Street N.W.
Calgary, AB T2N 2T9
1-800-332-1414 toll-free
(403) 670-1414 local
(403) 670-1472 fax

BRITISH COLUMBIA
British Columbia Drug and Poison
Information Centre
St. Paul's Hospital
1081 Burrard Street
Vancouver, B.C. V6Z 1Y6
1-800-567-8911 toll-free
(604) 682-5050 Greater Vancouver & lower
mainland
(604) 806-8262 fax

MANITOBA
Provincial Poison Information Centre,
Children's Hospital Health Sciences Centre,
840 Sherbrook St.,
Winnipeg, MB R3A 1S1
(204) 787-2591 local
(204) 787-4807 fax

NEW BRUNSWICK
Poison Information Centre
Clinidata
774 Main St. 6th floor
Moncton, NB
E1C 9Y3
(506) 857-5555
(506) 867-3259 fax

NEWFOUNDLAND
Poison Control Centre
Janeway Hospital
300 Prince Phillip Dr.
St John's, NF A1B 3V6
(709) 722-1110
(709)726-0830 fax

NORTHWEST TERRITORIES
Emergency Department
Stanton Regional Hospital
P.O.B. 10
Yellowknife NT X1A 2N1
(403) 669-4100
(403) 669-4171 fax

NOVA SCOTIA / PEI
Poison Control Centre
The IWK/Grace Health Care Centre
P.O. Box 3070
Halifax, NS B3J 3G9
1-800-565-8161
(902) 428-8161
(902) 428-3213 fax

ONTARIO
Ontario Regional Poison Information
Centre
Children's Hospital of Eastern Ontario
401 Smyth Road
Ottawa, ON K1H 8L1
1-800-267-1373 toll-free
(613) 737-1100 local
(613) 738-4862 fax

Ontario Regional Poison Information
Centre
The Hospital for Sick Children
555 University Avenue
Toronto, ON M5G 1X8
1-800-268-9017 toll-free
(416) 813-5900 local
(416) 813-7489 fax

QUEBEC
Centre anti-poison du Québec
aile L, 1st Floor
1050 Chemin Ste - Foy
Quebec, Qc G1S 4L8
1-800-463-5060 Toll-free
(418) 656-8090 local
(418) 654-2747 fax

SASKATCHEWAN
Regina
Emergency Department
Regina General Hospital
1440 14th Avenue
Regina, SK S4P 0W5
1-800-667-4545 toll-free Southern
Saskatchewan
(306) 766-4545 local
(306) 766-4357 fax

Saskatoon
Emergency Department
Royal University Hospital
Saskatoon, SK S7N 0X0
1-800-363-7474 toll-free
(306) 655-1010 local
(306) 655-1011 Fax

YUKON
Emergency Department
Whitehorse General Hospital
5 Hospital Road
Whitehorse YK Y1A 3H7
(867) 667-8726 local
(867) 667-8762 fax

Appendix III

USP PEOPLE 2000 – 2005

Peter R. Byron, Ph.D., Richmond, VA;
Ronald J. Callahan, Ph.D., Boston, MA;
Edward M. Cohen, Ph.D., Newtown, CT;
Mark G. Papich, DVM, Raleigh, NC;
David B. Roll, Ph.D., Salt Lake City, UT;
Stephen G. Schulman, Ph.D., Gainesville, FL;
James T. Stewart, Ph.D., Athens, GA;
Henry S. I. Tan, Ph.D., Cincinnati, OH;
Timothy J. Wozniak, Ph.D., Indianapolis, IN

Nomenclature and Labeling Expert Committee (2000 – 2005)

Herbert S. Carlin, D.Sc., *Chair*, Califon, NJ;
Loyd V. Allen, Jr., Ph.D., Edmond, OK;
Joseph M. Betz, Ph.D., Silver Spring, MD;

Dawn M. Boothe, DVM, College Station, TX;
Daniel L. Boring, Ph.D., Rockville, MD;
Edward M. Cohen, Ph.D., Newtown, CT;
Stephanie Y. Crawford, Ph.D., Chicago, IL;
Thomas S. Foster, Pharm.D., Lexington, KY;
Douglas D. Glover, M.D., Morgantown, WV;
Michael J. Groves, Ph.D., Deerfield, IL;
R. David Lauper, Pharm.D., San Ramon, CA;
Keith Marshall, Ph.D., Brick, NJ;
Jerry Phillips, BS, Rockville, MD;
Rosemary C. Polomano, Ph.D., Hershey, PA;
Thomas P. Reinders, Pharm.D., Richmond, VA;
Philip D. Walson, M.D., Cincinnati, OH

2000 – 2005 INFORMATION EXPERT COMMITTEES

Members who serve as Chairs are listed first.

The information presented in this text represents an ongoing review of the drugs contained herein and represents a consensus of various viewpoints expressed. The individuals listed below have served on the USP Expert Committees for the 2000-2005 revision period and have contributed to the development of the 2002 USP DI database. Such listing does not imply that these individuals have reviewed all of the material in this text or that they individually agree with all statements contained therein.

Anesthesiology

Carl E. Rosow, Ph.D., *Chair*, Boston, MA; Charles J. Cote, M.D., Chicago, IL; Peter Glass, M.D., Stoneybrook, NY; Michele E. Gold, Ph.D., Los Angeles, CA; Thomas K. Henthorn, M.D., Denver, CO; Michael B. Howie, Ph.D., Columbus, OH; Robert Hudson, M.D., Winnipeg, MB, Canada; Susan K. Palmer, M.D., Aurora, CO; Mark A. Schumacher, Ph.D., M.D., San Francisco, CA; Peter S. Sebel, Ph.D., Atlanta, GA; Theodore W. Striker, M.D., Cincinnati, OH; Mehernoor F. Watcha, M.D., Philadelphia, PA; Matthew B. Weinger, M.D., San Diego, CA; David H. Wong, M.D., Long Beach, CA

Cardiovascular and Renal Drugs

Alexander M. Shepherd, M.D., *Chair*, San Antonio, TX; Ellen D. Burgess, M.D., Calgary, Alberta, Canada; Moses S.S. Chow, Pharm.D., Shatin, Hong Kong; Ross D. Feldman, M.D., London, ON, Canada; Jean D. Gray, M.D., Halifax, NS, Canada; Brian B. Hoffman, M.D., Palo Alto, CA; Joseph Izzo, M.D., Buffalo, NY; Howard R. Knapp, M.D., Ph.D., Billings, MT; Peter Kowey, M.D., Wynnewood, PA; Barry Massie, M.D., San Francisco, CA; Jean M. Nappi, Pharm.D., Charleston, SC; Cynthia L. Raehl, Pharm.D., Amarillo, TX; Addison A. Taylor, M.D., Ph.D., Houston, TX; Gerald J. Wilson, MA, Bethesda, MD

Clinical Toxicology and Substance Abuse

Edward P. Krenzelok, Pharm.D., *Chair*, Pittsburgh, PA; Bruce D. Anderson, Pharm.D., Baltimore, M.D.; Donald G. Barceloux, M.D., Topanga, CA; Neal L. Benowitz, M.D., San Francisco, CA; Jeffrey Brent, M.D., Denver, CO; Gregory G. Gaar, Pharm.D., Tampa, FL; Robert S. Hoffman, M.D., New York, NY; Jude McNally, Tucson, AZ; Elizabeth Scharman, Pharm.D., Charleston, WV; Rose Ann G. Soloway, MS, Washington, DC; Christine M. Stork, Pharm.D., Syracuse, NY; Milton Tenenbein, M.D., Winnipeg, MB, Canada; J. Allister Vale, M.D., Birmingham, England; William A. Watson, Pharm.D., San Antonio, TX

Critical Care and Emergency Medicine

Daniel A. Notterman, M.D., *Chair*, Princeton, NJ; Michael Banner, Gainesville, FL; Philip Barie, M.D., New York, NY; Joseph Carcillo, M.D., Pittsburgh, PA; Eugene Y. Cheng, M.D., Milwaukee, WI; George Foltin, M.D., New York, NY; Louis J. Ling, M.D., Minneapolis, MN; Steven Lowry, M.D., New Brunswick, NJ; Catherine MacLeod, M.D., Waukegan, IL; Elena Mandez-Rico, Pharm.D., New York, NY; Gail McCarver, M.D., Milwaukee, WI; Mary McCready, RN, New York, NY; Lewis Nelson, M.D., New York, NY; Arthur Slutsky, M.D., Toronto, ON, Canada

Dentistry

Bridget E. Byrne, DDS, *Chair*, Richmond, VA; Gary C. Armitage, DDS, San Francisco, CA; Sebastian G. Ciancio, DDS, Buffalo, NY; Barbara Clark, Pharm.D., Kansas City, MO; Frederick A. Curro, DMD., Ph.D., Jersey City, NJ; Raymond A. Dionne, DDS, Bethesda, MD; Tommy W. Gage, Ph.D., Dallas, TX; Michael Glick, M.D., Philadelphia, PA; Daniel A. Haas, Ph.D., Toronto, ON, Canada; Arthur H. Jeske, Ph.D., Houston, TX; Christopher L. Maestrello, DDS, Richmond, VA; Joel M. Weaver, DDS, Columbus, OH; Clifford W. Whall, Ph.D., Chicago, IL; John A. Yagiela, DDS, Ph.D., Los Angeles, CA

Dermatology

Michael E. Bigby, M.D., *Chair*, Boston, MA; Robert B. Armstrong, M.D., Skillman, NJ; Mary-Margaret Chren, M.D., San Francisco, CA; Vincent Falanga, M.D., Providence, RI; Gordon L. Flynn, Ph.D., Ann Arbor, MI; Aditya K. Gupta, M.D., London, ON, Canada; Vincent Ho, M.D., Vancouver, BC, Canada; Sewon Kang, M.D., Ann Arbor, MI; David Margolis, M.D., Philadelphia, PA; Scott Norton, M.D., Chevy Chase, M.D.; Jean-Claude Roujeau, M.D., Creteil, France; Matthew Stiller, M.D., New York, NY; Dennis P. West, Ph.D., Chicago, IL

Diagnostic Agents – Nonradioactive

Sachiko T. Cochran, M.D., *Chair*, Los Angeles, CA; Max D. Adams, Ph.D., St. Charles, MO; Michael A. Bettmann, M.D., Lebanon, NH; Martin J.K. Blomley, MBBS, London, ON, Canada; Robert C. Brasch, M.D., San Francisco, CA; Henry Bryant, Ph.D., Bethesda, M.D.; William H. Bush, Jr., M.D., Seattle, WA; Richard W. Katzberg, M.D., Sacramento, CA; Elliott C. Lasser, M.D., La Jolla, CA; Jane Matsumoto, M.D., Rochester, MN; Maythem Saeed, DVM, San Francisco, CA; Udo P. Schmiedl, M.D., Seattle, WA; Jovitas Skucas, M.D., Rochester, NY; David B. Spring, M.D., Oakland, CA

Dietary Supplements

Tieraona Low Dog, M.D., *Chair*, Albuquerque, NM; Marilyn L. Barrett, Ph.D., San Carlos, CA; Werner R. Busse, Ph.D., Karlsruhe, Germany; Elaine Chiquette, Pharm.D., San Antonio, TX; Cynthia T. Culmo, RPh, Austin, TX; Adriane J. Fugh-Berman, M.D., Washington, DC; Kathryn L. Grant, Pharm.D., Tucson, AZ; Gail B. Mahady, Ph.D., Chicago, IL; Paolo Morazzoni, Ph.D., Milano, Italy; Harold H. Sandstead, M.D., Galveston, TX; Judith S. Stern, ScD, Lafayette, CA

Endocrinology

Lawrence A. Frohman, M.D., *Chair*, Chicago, IL; Stuart J. Brink, M.D., Waltham, MA; Karin Anton Calis, Pharm.D., Bethesda, M.D.; David S. Cooper, M.D., Towson, M.D.; Betty J. Dong, Pharm.D., San Francisco, CA; Selna L. Kaplan, M.D., San Francisco, CA; Michael Kleerekoper, M.D., Detriot, MI; James Liu, M.D., Cincinnati, OH; Shlomo Melmed, M.D., Los Angeles, CA; John E. Morley, M.D., St. Louis, MO; Paul Saenger, M.D., Bronx, NY; Arthur B. Schneider, M.D., Chicago, IL; Ronald Swerdloff, M.D., Torrance, CA

Gastroenterology

Karl E. Anderson, M.D., *Chair*, Galveston, TX; Jeffrey P. Baker, M.D., Toronto, ON, Canada; Paul Bass, Ph.D., Madison, WI; Gerald Friedman, M.D., New York, NY; Flavio M. Habal, M.D., Toronto, ON, Canada; Melvin B. Heyman, M.D., San Francisco, CA; Karen C. Hobdy-Henderson, Pharm.D., Augusta, GA; Alan F. Hofmann, M.D., La Jolla, CA; Paul E. Hyman, M.D., Orange, CA; Gordon L. Klein, M.D., Galveston, TX; William Snape, M.D., Long Beach, CA; Keith G. Tolman, M.D., Salt Lake City, UT

Gerontology

Darrell R. Abernethy, M.D., *Chair*, Baltimore, M.D.; Larry A. Bauer, Pharm.D., Seattle, WA; John C. Beck, M.D., Pacific Palisades, CA; James W. Cooper, Ph.D., Athens, GA; Barry J. Cusack, M.D., Boise, ID; Jerry Gurwitz, M.D., Worcester, MA; Joseph T. Hanlon, Pharm.D., Minneapolis, MN; Patricia D. Kroboth, Ph.D., Pittsburgh, PA; Shari M. Ling, M.D., Baltimore, M.D.; Paul A. Mitenko, M.D., Nanaimo, BC, Canada; Maureen J. Osis, RN, Calgary, Alberta, Canada; Bruce G. Pollock, M.D., Pittsburgh, PA; Janice B. Schwartz, M.D., San Francisco, CA; Joanne G. Schwartzberg, M.D., Chicago, IL; Brian L. Strom, M.D., Philadelphia, PA; Alastair J. Wood, M.D., Nashville, TN

Hematology, Blood and Blood Products

Patrick A. McKee, M.D., *Chair*, Oklahoma City, OK; Morris A. Blajchman, M.D., Hamilton, ON, Canada; Kenneth Bridges, M.D., Boston, MA; Ron Gilcher, M.D., Oklahoma City, OK; Margo Kruskall, M.D., Boston, MA; Naomi Luban, M.D., Washington, DC; Joe Moake, M.D., Houston, TX; Kevin Moore, M.D., Oklahoma City, OK; Peggy Pierce, Ph.D., Knoxville, TN; David S. Rosenthal, M.D., Cambridge, MA

Immunizing Agents

Cheston M. Berlin, M.D., *Chair*, Hershey, PA; Ron Dagan, M.D., Beer-sheva, Israel; John D. Grabenstein, Ph.D., Burke, VA; Jill Hackell, Pearl River, NY; Barbara J. Howe, M.D., Collegeville, PA; Karen Kaplan, M.D., Blue Bell, PA; Benjamin Levi, M.D., Hershey, PA; Carlton Meschievitz, Swiftwater, PA; Janak Patel, M.D., Galveston, TX; Richard J. Whitley, M.D., Birmingham, AL

Infectious Disease Therapy

John G. Bartlett, M.D., *Chair*, Baltimore, M.D.; Joan Chesney, M.D., Memphis, TN; Glenn Cobbs, M.D., Birmingham, AL; Courtney Fletcher, Pharm.D., Minneapolis, MN; Ron Jones, M.D., North Liberty, IA; Carol Kauffman, M.D., Ann Arbor, MI; Calvin M. Kunin, M.D., Columbus, OH; Steve Piscitelli, Pharm.D., Bethesda, M.D.; Douglas Richman, M.D., La Jolla, CA; Roy T. Steigbigel, M.D., Stoney Brook, NY; Tom Yoshikawa, M.D., Los Angeles, CA

Information Development and Dissemination

William G. Troutman, Pharm.D., *Chair*, Albuquerque, NM; William G. Felkey, MS, Auburn, AL; Reed Gardner, M.D., Salt Lake City, UT; Thomas M. Gesell, Pharm.D., Morris Plains, NJ; Akima R. Howard, Pharm.D., Hampton, VA; Edward J. Huth, M.D., Bryn Mawr, PA; Patrick M. Malone, Pharm.D., Omaha, NE; Dennis F. Thompson, Pharm.D., Oklahoma City, OK

Neurology

Thomas P. Bleck, M.D., *Chair*, Charlottesville, VA; Brian K. Alldredge, Pharm.D., San Francisco, CA; Mitchell Brin, M.D., New York, NY; Robyn R. Lim, Ph.D., Ottawa, ON, Canada; Judith Paice, Ph.D., Chicago, IL; Roger J. Porter, M.D., Radnor, PA; Neil Raskin, M.D., San Francisco, CA; Howard Weiner, M.D., Boston, MA

Nutrition and Electrolytes

Robert M. Russell, M.D., *Chair*, Boston, MA; Dennis M. Bier, M.D., Houston, TX; Leon Ellenbogen, Ph.D., New City, NY; Walter H. Glinsmann, M.D., Washington, DC; John Hathcock, Ph.D., Washington, DC; Lyn J. Howard, MA, Albany, NY; Bonnie F. Liebman, MS, Washington, DC; Robert D. Lindeman, M.D., Albuquerque, NM; Schrab Mobarhan, M.D., Maywood, IL; Edward Saltzman, M.D., Boston, MA; Michael D. Sitrin, M.D., Chicago, IL; Judith R. Turnlund, Ph.D., San Francisco, CA; Stanley Wallach, M.D., Clearwater, FL

Obstetrics and Gynecology

Marilynn C. Frederiksen, M.D., *Chair*, Chicago, IL; Rudi Ansbacher, M.D., Ann Arbor, MI; Gerald G. Briggs, Bpharm, Long Beach, CA; Florence Comite, M.D., New Haven, CT; Andre Leroux, M.D., Ottawa, ON, Canada; Jennifer R. Niebyl, M.D., Iowa City, IA; Robert Rebar, M.D., Birmingham, AL; Ronald J. Ruggiero, Pharm.D., San Francisco, CA; Kate Stika, M.D., Chicago, IL; Phillip Stubblefield, M.D., Boston, MA

Oncologic Disease

Raymond B. Weiss, M.D., *Chair*, Rockville, M.D.; James Atkins, M.D., Goldsboro, NC; Susan M. Blaney, M.D., Houston, TX; Lisa E. Davis, Pharm.D., Philadelphia, PA; Merrill Jon Egorin, M.D., Pittsburgh, PA; William D. Figg, Pharm.D., Bethesda, M.D.; Judith Kaur, M.D., Rochester, MN; Ellis G. Levine, M.D., Buffalo, NY; Fredric A. Lombardo, Pharm.D., Washington, DC; Herbert K. Lyerly, M.D., Washington, DC; Michael Mastrangelo, M.D., Philadelphia, PA; Mark J. Ratain, M.D., Chicago, IL; Robert H. Rudolph, M.D., Seattle, WA; F. Marc Stewart, M.D., Seattle, WA; Richard M. Stone, M.D., Boston, MA; Paul S. Wissel, M.D., Research Triangle Park, NC; John W. Yarbro, M.D., Columbia, MO

Ophthalmology

David A. Lee, M.D., *Chair*, Hershey, PA; Jules L. Baum, M.D., Chesnut Hill, MA; Neil M. Bressler, M.D., Baltimore, M.D.; Forrest D. Ellis, M.D., Indianapolis, IN; Frederick T. Fraunfelder, M.D., Portland, OR; Kelly A. Hutcheson, M.D., Baltimore, M.D.; Peter F. Kador, Ph.D., Bethesda, M.D.; Joel S. Mindel, M.D., New York, NY; Arthur H. Neufeld, Ph.D., St. Louis, MO; John R. Samples, M.D., Portland, OR; Kirk R. Wilhelmus, M.D., Houston, TX; Thom J. Zimmerman, M.D., Louisville, KY

Otorhinolaryngology

Randal A. Otto, M.D., *Chair*, San Antonio, TX; Robert A. Dobie, M.D., Bethesda, M.D.; Aina Julianna Gulya, M.D., Bethesda, M.D.; James A. Hadley, M.D., Rochester, NY; David B. Horn, M.D., Minneapolis, MN; Helen F. Krause, M.D., Pittsburgh, PA; Bradley F. Marple, M.D., Dallas, TX; Robert A. Mickel, M.D., San Francisco, CA; Monique Richer, Pharm.D., Ste-Foy, Quebec, Canada; William Shockley, M.D., Chapel Hill, NC; C. Blakely Simpson, M.D., San Antonio, TX

Parasitic and Tropical Disease

Brian G. Schuster, M.D., *Chair*, Washington, DC; Michele Barry, M.D., New Haven, CT; Ralf P. Brueckner, M.D., Silver Spring, M.D.; Jeffrey D. Chulay, M.D., Research Triangle Park, NC; Phillip Coyne, M.D., Silver Spring, M.D.; Lawrence L. Fleckenstein, Pharm.D., Iowa City, IA; Jay S. Keystone, M.D., Toronto, ON, Canada; Hans Lobel, M.D., Atlanta, GA; Douglas W. macPherson, M.D., Ottawa, ON, Canada; Will Milhous, M.D., Silver Spring, M.D.; Theresa A. Shapiro, M.D., Baltimore, M.D.; Terrie E. Taylor, BA, East Lansing, MI; David L. Wesche, M.D., Washington, DC; Martin S. Wolfe, M.D., Washington, DC

Pediatrics

Wayne R. Snodgrass, M.D., *Chair*, Houston, TX; Jeff Blumer, M.D., Cleveland, OH; Michelle Brill-Edwards, M.D., Ottawa, ON, Canada; Peter Gal, Pharm.D., Greensboro, NC; Ralph E. Kauffman, M.D., Kansas City, MO; Gregg Kearns, Pharm.D., Kansas City, MO; Joan M. Korth-Bradley, Ph.D., Philadelphia, PA; George Lambert, M.D., Belle Nead, NJ; Carolyn H. Lund, MS, Oakland, CA; David G. Oelberg, M.D., Norfolk, VA; Janice M. Ozias, Ph.D., Austin, TX; Michael Reed, Pharm.D., Cleveland, OH; George Rylance, M.D., Birmingham, UK; Stephen Spielberg, M.D., Titusville, NJ; Philip D. Walson, M.D., Cincinnati, OH; Robert M. Ward, M.D., Salt Lake City, UT

Psychiatry

William E. Fann, M.D., *Chair*, Houston, TX; Ross J. Baldessarini, M.D., Belmont, MA; Larry Ereshefsky, Pharm.D., San Antonio, TX; Paul Grof, M.D., Ottawa, ON, Canada; Dilip Jeste, M.D., San Diego, CA; Norman L. Keltner, RN, Birmingham, AL; Gary M. Levin, Pharm.D., Gainesville, FL; Constance Moore, M.D., Houston, TX; Bruce Perry, M.D., Houston, TX; Elliott Richelson, M.D., Jacksonville, FL; Gary C. Rosenfeld, Ph.D., Houston, TX; Colette F. Strnad, Ph.D., Ottawa, ON, Canada; Karen Theesen, Pharm.D., Overland Park, KS; Kareen D. Wagner, M.D., Galveston, TX; Julie M. Zito, Ph.D., Baltimore, M.D.

Pulmonary Disease/Allergy

I. Leonard Bernstein, M.D., *Chair*, Cincinnati, OH; David I. Bernstein, M.D., Cincinnati, OH; Leonard Bielory, M.D., Newark, NJ; Elliot Israel, M.D., Boston, MA; James P. Kemp, M.D., San Diego, CA; Dennis Ledford, M.D., Tampa, FL; Lionel D. Lewis, M.D., Lebanon, NH; Shirley Murphy, M.D., Research Triangle Park, NC; David Pearlman, M.D., Aurora, CO; Sheldon Spector, M.D., Los Angeles, CA; Karen J. Tietze, Pharm.D., Philadelphia, PA; John H. Toogood, M.D., London, ON, Canada

Radiopharmaceuticals

Barry A. Siegel, M.D., *Chair*, St. Louis, MO; Jorge R. Barrio, Ph.D., Los Angeles, CA; Edward Coleman, M.D., Durham, NC; David Gilday, M.D., Toronto, ON, Canada; Alvin J. Lorman, JD, Washington, DC; Don Lyster, Ph.D., Vancouver, BC, Canada; Carol S. Marcus, Ph.D., Los Angeles, CA; James A. Ponto, MS, Iowa City, IA; Laura L. Ponto, Ph.D., Iowa City, IA; Edward B. Silberstein, M.D., Cincinnati, OH; James B. Stubbs, Ph.D., Alpharetta, GA; Dennis P. Swanson, MS, Pittsburgh, PA; Mathew Thakur, Ph.D., Philadelphia, PA; Richard L. Wahl, M.D., Baltimore, M.D.

Rheumatology-Clinical Immunology

Evelyn V. Hess, M.D., *Chair*, Cincinnati, OH; Roy D. Altman, M.D., Miami, FL; John Baum, M.D., Rochester, NY; Laurence A. Bradley, Ph.D., Birmingham, AL; David H. Campen, M.D., Oakland, CA; Daniel Eric Furst, M.D., Seattle, WA; Jean G. Gispen, M.D., Oxford, MS; Esther Gonzales-Pares, M.D., San Juan, PR; Daniel J. Lovell, M.D., Cincinnati, OH; Walter Maksymowych, Edmonton, Alberta, Canada; Donald R. Miller, Pharm.D., Fargo, ND; Frank N. Pucino, Pharm.D., Bethesda, M.D.; Lee S. Simon, M.D., Boston, MA; George Spencer-Green, M.D., Seattle, WA

Therapeutic Decision Making

Elizabeth A. Chrischilles, Ph.D., *Chair*, Iowa City, IA; Edward Paul Armstrong, Pharm.D., Tucson, AZ; Lisa A. Bero, Ph.D., San Francisco, CA; Richard S. Blum, M.D., East Hills, NY; Robert P. Craig, Pharm.D., Scottsdale, AZ; Stanley Finklestein, M.D., Cambridge, MA; Starlin Haydon-Greattin, MS, Springfield, IL; Mark L. Horn, M.D., New York, NY; Ada G. Jacox, Ph.D., Ann Arbor, MI; Judith K. Jones, Ph.D., Arlington, VA; Duane M. Kirking, Ph.D., Ann Arbor, MI; Karen E. Koch, Pharm.D., Tupelo, MS; Paul C. Langley, Ph.D., St. Paul, MN; Michael D. Murray, Pharm.D., Indianapolis, IN; Nicholaas Otten, Pharm.D., Gloucester, ON, Canada; Michael Peterson, M.D., Iowa City, IA; Martha J. Radford, M.D., New Haven, CT; Betty L. Sleath, Ph.D., Chapel Hill, NC; Edward Westrick, M.D., Providence, RI

Transplant Immunology

Ali Naji, M.D., *Chair*, Philadelphia, PA; Gene Gibson, Pharm.D., Philadelphia, PA; Henry Lau, M.D., Baltimore, M.D.; Kevin Mange, M.D., Philadelphia, PA; Ilene Markmann, RN, Philadelphia, PA; Leslie Shaw, Ph.D., Philadelphia, PA

Urology

Culley C. Carson, III, M.D., *Chair*, Chapel Hill, NC; John A. Belis, M.D., Camp Hill, PA; Betty Jean Czarapata, BS, Fairfax, VA; Sam D. Graham, M.D., Richmond, VA; Mierille Gregoire, M.D., Montreal, Quebec, Canada; John Lavelle, M.D., Chapel Hill, NC; Marguerite Lippert, M.D., Charlottesville, VA; Michael G. Mawhinney, Ph.D., Morgantown, WV; William F. Tarry, M.D., Morgantown, WV; Chris M. Teigland, M.D., Charlotte, NC

INFORMATION DIVISION
ADDITIONAL CONTRIBUTORS

The information presented in the USP DI database represents ongoing review and the consensus of various viewpoints expressed. In addition to the individuals listed below, many schools, associations, pharmaceutical companies, and governmental agencies have provided comment or otherwise contributed to the development of the 2002 USP DI database. This listing does not imply that these individuals have reviewed all of the material in the database or that they individually agree with all statements contained herein.

Kishor Avasarala, M.D., Oakland, CA
Patsy Barnett, Pharm.D., Cynthiana, KY
Gregory P. Bergt, St. Paul, MN
Wayne Bradley, R.Ph., M.B.A., Duluth, GA
Michael Camilleri, M.D., Rochester, MN
Kenneth Castro, M.D., Atlanta, GA
James W. Cooper, Pharm.D., Athens, GA
Clinton N. Corder, Ph.D., M.D., Oklahoma City, OK
Thomas D. DeCillis, North Port, FL
Peyton Eggleston, M.D., Baltimore, MD
Phyllis Flomenseng, M.D., Philadelphia, PA
Jose P.B. Gallardo, R.Ph., M.S., Iowa City, IA
Wallace A. Gleason, M.D., Houston, TX
David Gregory, M.D., Albuquerque, NM
Christopher Hendel, M.S., Burlington, VT
Melvin B. Heyman, M.D., San Francisco, CA
M. E. Hoar, Springfield, MA
William Hopkins, Pharm.D., Atlanta, GA
Robert R. Jacobson, M.D., Carville, LA
Daryl E. Krepps, B.S.P., Ottawa, CN
Sandy Labahn, Sioux City, IA
Norman Levine, M.D., Tucson, AZ
Howard I. Maibach, M.D., San Francisco, CA
Linda Gore Martin, Pharm.D., Laramie, WY
Takashi Matsunaga, Ph.D., New York, NY

Bernard L. Mirkin, M.D., Chicago, IL
Susan Orenstein, M.D., Pittsburgh, PA
Gail Pauling, D.V.M., Guelph, Ontario, CN
Jerry D. Razook, M.D., Oklahoma City, OK
Lee B. Reichman, M.D., M.P.H., Newark, NJ
Alfred J. Remillard, Pharm.D., Saskatoon, Saskatchewan, CN
Wolfgang Rosch, M.D., Frankfurt, Germany
Jeff A. Ruell, Ph.D., Cambridge, MA
Evelyn Salerno, Pharm.D., Hialeah, FL
Larry A. Schafer, M.D., P.C., Wheat Ridge, CO
Gisela F. Schecter, M.D., M.Ph., San Francisco, CA
Alan Shalita, M.D., Brooklyn, NY
Allen F. Shaugnessy, Pharm.D., Harrisburg, PA
Patricia Simone, M.D., Atlanta, GA
Geralynn B. Smith, Detroit, MI
E. Richard Stiehm, M.D., Los Angeles, CA
John J. Stern, M.D., Philadelphia, PA
Michael R. Sullivan, Pharm.D., Oaklawn, IL
Michael Valentino, M.H.S.A., R.Ph., Hines, IL
Donald G. Vidt, M.D., Cleveland, OH
Tom Walsh, M.D., Bethesda, MD
David C. Warltier, M.D., Ph.D., Milwaukee, WI
William Warner, Ph.D., New York, NY
Michael Weintraub, M.D., Rockville, MD
Frederick J. Zucchero, Chesterfield, MO

MEMBERS OF THE UNITED STATES
PHARMACOPEIAL CONVENTION

as of June 18, 2001

Committee Members
Barbara A. Durand Ed.D., *Tempe, AZ*
John H. Block Ph.D., *Corvallis, OR*

Consumer Organizations and Individuals Representing Public Interests
National Consumers League, Washington, DC, Brett M. Kay M.P.P.
Citizens for Public Action on Blood Pressure and Cholesterol, Inc., Bethesda, MD, Gerald J. Wilson M.A., M.B.A.
Consumers Union, South Burlington, VT, Christopher J. Hendel

Domestic, Foreign, and International Manufacturers, Trade, and Affiliated Associations,
Council for Responsible Nutrition, Washington, DC, V. Annette Dickinson Ph.D.
National Association of Chain Drug Stores, Alexandria, VA, Robert A. Shapiro
The Cosmetic, Toiletry and Fragrance Association, Washington, DC, Gerald N. McEwen Ph.D., J.D.
Nonprescription Drug Manufacturers Association of Canada, Ottawa, ON CANADA, David S. Skinner

Healthcare Distribution Management Association (formerly NWDA), Reston, VA, Thomas M. Schafer M.B.A.
World Self-Medication Industry, London,UK, Jerome A. Reinstein Ph.D.
Pharmaceutical Care Management Association, Arlington, VA, Delbert D. Konnor
Pharmaceutical Research and Manufacturers of America Science and Regulatory Section, Washington, DC, Thomas X. White
Pharmaceutical Research and Manufacturers of America, Washington, DC, Gillian R. Woollett D.Phil., M.A.
Parenteral Drug Association, Bethesda, MD, Russell E. Madsen M.S.
American Hospital Association, Chicago, IL, Donald M. Nielsen M.D.

Governmental Bodies
Therapeutic Goods Administration of Australia, Canberra, ACT AUSTRALIA, R. Joseph Smith Ph.D.
FDA Center for Biologics Evaluation and Research, Rockville, MD, Jerome A. Donlon M.D., Ph.D.
Centers for Disease Control and Prevention, Atlanta, GA, John A. Becher
Department of Veterans Affairs Veterans Health Administration, Burke, VA, John E. Ogden

University of New Mexico College of Pharmacy, Albuquerque, NM, William M. Hadley Ph.D.

University of North Carolina School of Pharmacy, Chapel Hill, NC, Anthony J. Hickey Ph.D.

University of Oklahoma College of Pharmacy, Edmond, OK, Loyd V. Allen, Jr. PhD

University of Pittsburgh School of Pharmacy, Pittsburgh, PA, Dennis P Swanson MS

University of Puerto Rico, Medical Sciences Campus School of Pharmacy, San Juan, PR, Ilia I. Oquendo Ph.D.

University of Rhode Island College of Pharmacy, Kingston, RI, Hossein Zia Ph.D.

University of Southern California School of Pharmacy, Los Angeles, CA, Wei-Chiang Shen Ph.D.

University of Tennessee College of Pharmacy, Memphis, TN, Dick R. Gourley Pharm.D.

University of Texas at Austin College of Pharmacy, Austin, TX, Salomon Stavchansky Ph.D.

University of the Pacific School of Pharmacy, Stockton, CA, William Chan Ph.D.

University of Montana School of Pharmacy and Allied Health Sciences, Missoula, MT, David S. Forbes Ph.D.

University of Washington School of Pharmacy, Seattle, WA, Gary W. Elmer Ph.D.

University of Missouri-Kansas City School of Pharmacy, Kansas City, MO, Patrick J. Bryant Pharm D.

University of Wyoming School of Pharmacy, Laramie, WY, Kurt Dolence Ph.D.

Virginia Commonwealth University/Medical College of Virginia School of Pharmacy, Richmond, VA, Mary Ann Kirkpatrick Ph.D.

Washington State University College of Pharmacy, Spokane, WA, Danial E. Baker Pharm.D.

Wayne State University College of Pharmacy and Allied Health Professions, Detroit, MI, Craig K. Svensson Pharm.D., Ph.D.

West Virginia University School of Pharmacy, Morgantown, WV, Arthur I. Jacknowitz Pharm.D.

Xavier University of Louisiana College of Pharmacy, New Orleans, LA, Tarun K. Mandal Ph.D.

Howard University College of Pharmacy, Nursing & AHS, Washington, DC, Pedro J. Lecca Ph.D.

Western University of Health Sciences College of Pharmacy, Pomona, CA, Sunil Prabhu Ph.D.

Texas Tech University School of Pharmacy, Amarillo, TX, Arthur A. Nelson Ph.D.

University of Florida College of Pharmacy, Gainesville, FL, Michael W. McKenzie Ph.D.

University of Arkansas for Medical Sciences College of Pharmacy, Little Rock, AR, Jonathan J. Wolfe Ph.D.

Midwestern University College of Pharmacy - Glendale, Glendale, AZ, Edward Fisher Ph.D.

University of Utah College of Pharmacy, Salt Lake City, UT, David B. Roll Ph.D.

The University of Georgia College of Pharmacy, Athens, GA, James T Stewart PhD

Idaho State University College of Pharmacy, Pocatello, ID, Thomas R. LaHann Ph.D.

Massachusetts College of Pharmacy and Health Sciences, Boston, MA, David A. Williams Ph.D.

Mercer University Southern School of Pharmacy, Atlanta, GA, J. Grady Strom Ph.D.

Midwestern University Chicago College of Pharmacy, Downers Grove, IL, Thomas J. Reutzel Ph.D.

NOVA Southeastern University College of Pharmacy, Ft. Lauderdale, FL, William D. Hardigan Ph.D.

Ohio Northern University College of Pharmacy, Ada, OH, Kimberly Broedel-Zaugg Ph.D.

Oregon State University College of Pharmacy, Corvallis, OR, Wayne A. Kradjan Pharm.D.

Purdue University School of Pharmacy & Pharmacal Sciences, West Lafayette, IN, Stephen R. Byrn PhD

Samford University McWhorter School of Pharmacy, Birmingham, AL, H. Anthony McBride Ph.D.

Rutgers University College of Pharmacy, Piscataway, NJ, Thomas Medwick PhD

Southwestern Oklahoma State University School of Pharmacy, Weatherford, OK, Keith W. Reichmann Ph.D.

University of Nebraska College of Pharmacy, Omaha, NE , Clarence T. Ueda Pharm D., Ph.D.

Texas Southern University College of Pharmacy and Health Sciences, Houston, TX, Dong Liang Ph.D.

Ferris State University College of Pharmacy, Big Rapids, MI, Kim E. Hancock Ph.D.

The University of Arizona College of Pharmacy, Tucson, AZ, Michael Mayersohn PhD

University of California San Francisco School of Pharmacy, San Francisco, CA, Emil T. Lin Ph.D.

University of Cincinnati College of Pharmacy, Cincinnati, OH, Arthur R. Buckley Ph.D.

University of Colorado School of Pharmacy, Denver, CO, Louis Diamond Ph.D.

University of Connecticut School of Pharmacy, Storrs, CT, Michael C. Gerald Ph.D.

University of Houston College of Pharmacy, Houston, TX, Mustafa F. Lokhandwala Ph.D.

University of Illinois College of Pharmacy, Chicago, IL, John F. Fitzloff Ph.D.

The University of Iowa College of Pharmacy, Iowa City, IA, Dale E. Wurster Ph.D.

University of Kansas School of Pharmacy, Lawrence, KS, J. Howard Rytting Ph.D.

University of Maryland School of Pharmacy, Baltimore, MD, Larry L. Augsburger PhD

University of Michigan College of Pharmacy, Ann Arbor, MI, Duane M. Kirking PhD

University of Mississippi School of Pharmacy, University, MS, Christy M. Wyandt Ph.D.

University of the Sciences in Philadelphia, Philadelphia, PA, Daniel A. Hussar Ph.D.

DRUG INFORMATION ON-LINE!

Space constraints prevent us from printing information on every drug available on the market. But you can access this hard-to-find drug information right from our website, 24 hours a day, seven days a week. You can view information on the computer or download and print as needed.

If you have any questions, please call us at 1-800-525-9083 or e-mail us at uspdi@mdx.com.

To access the website, log on to the MICROMEDEX website at:

http://www.uspdi.micromedex.com/cdr

You will need to enter the following user name and password:

User name: **crcdr**
Password: **moredrugs**

Each drug listing is saved as a PDF file. To view the PDF files, you must install the LATEST version of Adobe Acrobat Reader. Adobe Acrobat can be downloaded from the following Internet site for free:

http://www.adobe.com/supportservice/custsupport/download.html

Scroll down to Acrobat Re⌐   th your computer (Macintosh, Windows, etc.)